AWARDS, HONORS & PRIZES

AWARDS, HONORS & PRIZES

An International Directory of Awards and Their Donors Recognizing Achievement In Advertising, Architecture, Arts and Humanities, Business and Finance, Communications, Computers, Consumer Affairs, Ecology, Education, Engineering, Fashion, Films, Journalism, Law, Librarianship, Literature, Medicine, Music, Performing Arts, Photography, Public Affairs, Publishing, Radio and Television, Religion, Science, Social Science, Sports, Technology, and Transportation

VOLUME 1
UNITED STATES AND CANADA
25th EDITION

TARA ATTERBERRY
CONTENT PROJECT MANAGER

THOMSON
GALE™

Detroit • New York • San Francisco • San Diego • New Haven, Conn. • Waterville, Maine • London • Munich

THOMSON
GALE

Awards, Honors and Prizes, 25th Edition
Volume 1: United States and Canada

Product Manager
Jennifer Bernardelli

Editorial
Tara Atterberry, Amanda Sams

Editorial Support Services
Charles Beaumont

Composition and Electronic Prepress
Evi Seoud

Manufacturing
Rita Wimberley

For more information, contact
Thomson Gale
27500 Drake Rd.
Farmington Hills, MI 48331-3535
Or you can visit our Internet site at
http://www.gale.com

ISBN 0-7876-7806-6 (Volume 1)
ISBN 0-7876-7807-4 (Volume 2)
ISBN 0-7876-7805-8 (Set)
ISSN 0196-6316

Printed in the United States of America
10 9 8 7 6 5 4 3 2 1

Contents

International awards are covered in Volume 2

Volume 1: United States and Canada

Highlights . . . vii

Introduction . . . ix

User's Guide . . . xi

Descriptive Listings . . . 1

Indexes

Subject Index of Awards . . . 1135

Organization Index . . . 1295

Award Index . . . 1383

Highlights

Volume 1 of *Awards, Honors & Prizes (AHP)* is the single most comprehensive source of information on awards offered by organizations in the United States and Canada. These awards recognize achievements in all fields of human endeavor, including:

- Advertising
- Agriculture
- Arts and Humanities
- Botany
- Business and Finance
- Communications
- Computers
- Conservation
- Ecology
- Education
- Engineering
- Environment
- Ethics
- Fashion
- Films
- Journalism
- Law
- Library Science
- Literature
- Management
- Medical Research
- Music
- Performing Arts
- Photography
- Public Affairs
- Publishing
- Radio and Television
- Religion
- Safety
- Science
- Social Science
- Sports
- Technology
- Transportation

Volume 1 provides contact information for more than 21,000 organizations and awards. (For information on awards given by organizations in more than 100 countries outside the United States and Canada, consult Volume 2 of *AHP*.)

Features of This Edition

AHP continues to track trends in award giving, which in turn reflect the current values and priorities of society. This edition features listings for new awards under organizations in such fields as art, literature, education, and science, and covering such contemporary issues as the environment, religion, AIDS, national security, and international relations. *AHP* also lists e-mail and website addresses for more than 7,400 organizations.

Many Uses for *AHP*

Awards, Honors & Prizes can be used:

- by organizations, associations, and individuals to locate information on awards in a particular field of interest or that are mentioned in the media;
- by organizations and individuals to determine their eligibility for particular awards;
- by organizations to provide guidance in establishing a new award or expanding an existing program; and
- by employers in evaluating the significance of the awards listed on a job applicant's resume.

Available in Electronic Formats

Licensing. *Awards, Honors and Prizes* is available for licensing. The complete database is provided in a fielded format and is deliverable on such media as disk or CD-ROM. For more information, contact Gale's Business Development Group at 1-800-877-GALE, or visit us on our web site at www.gale.com/bizdev.

The greatest of humankind's efforts have long provided occasion for recognition and celebration. From the ancient Greek Olympics to the new Lemelson-MIT Prize for Invention and Innovation, societies worldwide continue to acknowledge extraordinary accomplishment in all fields of human endeavor.

Awards, Honors & Prizes seeks to honor individuals and groups who foster intellectual growth, set records, stimulate creativity, demonstrate courage, and inspire and encourage humanitarian efforts and international understanding. Following is a representative sampling of established awards designed to confer such recognition.

Science and Technology

- The Lemelson-MIT Prize for Invention and Innovation seeks to raise the status and visibility of American inventors and innovators. The annual award carries a $500,000 award for U.S. citizens who have shown excellence in creativity, invention, and/or innovation in the fields of medicine and health care, energy and environment, telecommunications and computing, consumer products, and durable goods and industrial products.
- Excellence in the field of aerospace engineering is rewarded by a gold medal and $100,000 by the American Institute of Aeronautics and Astronautics' Walter J. and Angeline H. Crichlow Trust Prize.
- Important work in applied or industrial physics is honored by the Institut de France, which each year presents the Prix Mesucora.

Education

- The Thomas J. Brennan Award, given by the Astronomical Society of the Pacific, recognizes high school astronomy teachers for excellence in teaching.
- Students in the ninth and tenth grades are given monetary awards for excellence in analytical thinking and writing through the Anthem Essay Contest, which is sponsored by the Ayn Rand Institute.

International Relations

- A monetary prize of 5,000,000 Japanese yen is awarded annually by the Victor Company of Japan to the person, company, or group that best demonstrates the importance of international contribution and cooperation.
- The John D. and Catherine T. MacArthur Foundation awards grants of $10,000 to $15,000 to support intellectual and scientific efforts for research and policy analysis in the countries of the former Soviet Union to scholars, journalists, policy analysts and other citizens residing in the territory of the former Soviet Union.
- The Edouard Saouma Award includes a monetary prize of $25,000 for the regional institution that has managed a particularly efficient project funded by the Food and Agriculture Organization of the United Nations.

Journalism

- The Goldsmith Prize in Investigative Reporting honors journalists whose investigative reporting best promotes more effective and ethical conduct of government, public policy making, or political practice.
- The National Lesbian and Gay Journalists Association presents the annual Crossroads Market/NLGJA Prize for excellence in print journalism on issues concerning the gay and lesbian community.

Arts and Entertainment

- The Truman Capote Awards for Literary Criticism in memory of Newton Arvis honor lifetime achievement and the best book of general literary criticism. The lifetime achievement award, administered by Stanford University, is bestowed every four years and carries a $100,000 cash prize. The best book prize of $50,000 is awarded annually by the University of Iowa, Iowa Writer's Workshop.
- The Australia Council for the Arts honors artists who have made a great contribution to the recognition of aboriginal and Torres Strait Island art and culture in the wider community at both the national and international levels with its Red Ochre Award. This award, which includes a cash prize of $50,000, was established to mark the International Year for the World's Indigenous People.

Sports

- The ESPY Awards, established by ESPN Inc., honor excellence in 34 categories of sports performance.
- The United States Olympic Committee established the Robert J. Kane Award to recognize athletes who have distinguished themselves in Olympic Festival competition by exemplifying the spirit and ideals of the Olympic movement.

News reports, by their very nature, frequently convey information that is less than welcome to world audiences. War, civil unrest, political upheaval, crime, health and environmental concerns, and other issues and events claim a majority of media attention. Perhaps that is why news of awards and their recipients, often featured prominently in print and broadcast media reporting, comes as a welcome change.

Humankind has long celebrated achievement of all kinds and in every field, from art and literature to science and technology. Individuals of all ages and from all walks of life are recognized when they transcend the boundaries of the ordinary to provide encouragement and inspiration by establishing new records, exploring new frontiers, demonstrating extraordinary courage, challenging the intellect, establishing new standards of excellence, creating beauty, or improving the quality of everyday life.

Awards, Honors & Prizes (AHP), now in its 24th edition, continues to provide perspective on the variety, scale, significance, and number of awards given throughout the world to acknowledge distinguished achievement. Volume 1 of *AHP* is the single major source of descriptive information on awards bestowed in all subject areas by organizations, foundations, corporations, universities, and government bodies in the United States and Canada. Volume 2 covers international awards.

Content and Arrangement

Volume 1 of *Awards, Honors & Prizes* comprises descriptive listings for awards and their administering organizations, and three indexes.

Descriptive Listings are arranged alphabetically by administering organization; entries for the awards administered by each organization are listed alphabetically following organization entries.

Subject Index of Awards classifies awards by their principal areas of interest.

Organization Index provides an alphabetical listing of all organizations appearing in both volumes that administer or sponsor awards, including alternate and foreign names.

Award Index provides an alphabetical listing of all award names, including alternate, former, and popular names listed in both volumes.

Preparation of This Edition

The 25th edition of *Awards, Honors & Prizes* represents the revision and updating of the previous edition. Information was obtained via survey mailings and follow-up correspondence and electronic mail as well as through the websites of administering organizations.

Volume 2 Covers International Awards Scene

Information on awards given by organizations located in countries other than the United States and Canada is available in Volume 2 of *AHP*. It provides descriptive information on more than 9,200 awards and national and international organizations, foundations, universities, corporations, and government bodies located in more than 100 countries.

Acknowledgments

The editors are grateful to the large number of individuals in organizations throughout the world who generously responded to our requests for updated information. Without their cooperation, this book would not be possible.

Comments and Suggestions Welcome

If you are interested in additional information about *AHP* or are interested in information about other Gale business products, please contact **Jennifer Bernardelli**, Product Manager.

If your award is listed in *AHP* and you have a question pertaining to your profile, or if you would like your award listed, please contact **Project Editor, *Awards, Honors, and Prizes*.** Either can be reached at:

Thomson Gale
27500 Drake Rd.
Farmington Hills, MI 48331-3535
Phone: (248)699-GALE
Toll-free: 800-347-GALE
Fax: (248) 699-8075
E-mail: Tara.Atterberry@Thomson.com
Jennifer.Bernardelli@Thomson.com
URL: http://www.gale.com

Descriptive Listings

The descriptive listings are arranged alphabetically by administering organization; entries on the awards administered by each organization follow that organization's listing.

The organization and award entries shown below illustrate the kind of information that is or might be included in these entries. Each item of information is preceded by a number and is explained in the paragraph of the same number following the sample entry.

Sample Entry

1 ★4266★
2 Canadian Parks/Recreation Association
3 (Association Canadienne des Loirsirs/Parc)
4 333 River Rd.
Vanier City, ON, Canada K1L 8H9
5 Phone: (613)748-5651
6 Free: 800-748-5600
7 Fax: (613)748-5652
8 E-mail: par@rec.assn.can
9 Home Page: http://www.can.park.rec
10 Formerly: (1980) Canadian Parks Association
11 ★4267★ **12** Award of Merit **13** (Prix de Merite)
14 To give national recognition for meritorious achievements at the municipal, regional, or provincial levels that have made significant and distinct contributions to the furtherance of some aspect of local parks/recreation. Canadian individuals or organizations are eligible. The deadline for applications is February 15. **15** A wood plaque is **16** awarded annually. **17** Established in 1965. **18** Sponsored by the Canadian Park Service. **19** (Discontinued in 1985). **20** Formerly: (1982) Canadian Park Service Award.

Descriptions of Numbered Elements

1 Organization Entry Number: Entries for administering organizations are listed alphabetically, each followed by an alphabetical listing of its awards. All entries—organization and award—are numbered in a single sequence. These numbers are used as references in the indexes. Organization entry numbers are preceded by a horizontal rule across the column.

2 Organization Name: The name of the organization administering the awards that follow.

3 Organization Name in Alternate Language(s): The name of the organization is given in up to two additional languages, when provided by the organization.

4 Mailing Address: The organization's permanent mailing address for information on awards.

5 Telephone Number: The telephone number(s) for the administering organization.

6 Toll-free Number: The toll-free telephone number for the administering organization.

7 Fax Number: The facsimile number for the administering organization.

8 E-mail: When provided in source material, electronic mail numbers are listed.

9 Home Page: Whenever possible, the home page or URL (universal resource locator) for Internet access to organization sites is provided.

10 Former Name of Organization: The former name of the organization is provided if the name has changed, the organization merged, or the organization absorbed another organization. The year the name change occurred is also provided, when available.

11 Award Entry Number: Entries on awards are listed alphabetically following the entry for their administering organization. All entries—organization and award—are numbered in a single sequence. These numbers are used as references in the indexes.

12 Award Name: Name of the award, honor, or prize is listed in English whenever possible.

13 Award Name in Alternate Language(s): The award name is provided in up to two additional languages, when provided by the organization.

14 Purpose of Award and Eligibility Criteria: The description of the award indicates the purpose for which it is given, the criteria for eligibility, whether one can apply or must be nominated for the award, and the application or nomination deadline.

15 Character: Identifies the nature of the award, such as a medal, monetary award, certificate, inclusion in a hall of fame, or the presentation of a lecture.

16 Frequency: Information on the frequency of award presentation and the occasion on which it is presented.

17 Year Established: The year the award was established and in whose honor or memory it is presented.

18 Sponsor: The sponsor or co-sponsor of an award, if it is an organization other than the administering organization.

19 Status: If an award has been discontinued or is currently inactive, the year it was discontinued or last presented may be provided.

20 Former Name: The former name of an award and the year of the name change, if provided.

Indexes

Subject Index of Awards

The Subject Index of Awards classifies all awards described in this volume by their principal areas of interest. The index contains more than 400 subject headings. Identically named awards are followed by an indented alphabetical list of the organizations administering an award by that name. Each award is indexed under all relevant headings. The index also contains numerous cross-references to direct users to related topics. Awards are listed alphabetically under each subject heading, and the number following an award name identifies that award's entry in the descriptive listings portion of this volume.

Organization Index

The alphabetical Organization Index provides access to all sponsoring and administering organizations listed in both volumes, as well as to organization acronyms and alternate-language and former names. Index references include the volume in which the organization appears and book entry numbers in the descriptive listings section. In the case of sponsoring organizations, citations are to the specific awards they sponsor.

Award Index

The Award Index provides an alphabetical listing of all award names listed in both volumes, as well as alternate-language, former, and popular award names, such as the Oscars and Tonys. In the case of generic award names (e.g., Gold Medal, Achievement Award, Grand Prize), the award name is followed by an alphabetical listing of the organizations administering an award by that name.

References to the volume in which the award may be found followed by the award's entry number in the descriptive listings section follow each award citation.

Volume 1
United States and Canada

• 1 •
3-A Sanitary Standards Committees
Timothy R. Rugh CAE, Exec.Dir.
1451 Dolley Madison Blvd., Ste. 210
McLean, VA 22101-3850
Phone: (703)790-0295
Phone: (703)790-0295
Fax: (703)761-6284
E-mail: trugh@3-a.org
Home Page: http://www.3-A.org

• 2 • 3-A Bronze Plaque
Recognizes outstanding service to the committees' standards program. Awarded periodically.

• 3 •
6th Bomb Group Association
Harry H. George, Historian & Bd. Member
1170 Gulf Blvd. Apt. 703
Clearwater, FL 33767-2781
Phone: (727)517-2577
E-mail: famdad@aol.com
Home Page: http://www.armyairforces.com/dbassociations.asp?Grou

• 4 • Memorial Plaques
Recognizes installation at Air Force Bases and locations in the USA. Awarded periodically.

• 5 •
11th Armored Cavalry's Veterans of Vietnam and Cambodia
Ollie Pickral, Treas.
1602 Lorrie Dr.
Richardson, TX 75080-3409
Phone: (612)929-1472
Fax: (612)929-1472
E-mail: armor11acr@aol.com
Home Page: http://www.11thcavnam.com

• 6 • Blackhorse Scholarship
Awarded to the children of 11th ACR troopers killed, wounded, or disabled while serving with the Regiment.

• 7 • Jack Quilter Award
Recognizes a member. Awarded annually.

• 8 •
60 Plus Association
James L. Martin, Pres.
1600 Wilson Blvd., Ste. 960
Arlington, VA 22209
Phone: (703)807-2070
Fax: (703)807-2073
E-mail: info@60plus.org
Home Page: http://www.60plus.org

• 9 • Guardian of Seniors' Rights
Award of recognition. Lawmakers or parties judged to be "pro-senior" are eligible. Awarded annually.

• 10 •
70th Infantry Division Association
Paul Sumner, Pres.
5825 Horton St.
Mission, KS 66202
E-mail: inquiries70th@trailblazersww2.org
Home Page: http://www.trailblazersww2.org

• 11 • Outstanding Trailblazer Award
Recognizes outstanding service. Awarded biennially.

• 12 •
78th Division Veterans Association
Gabriel Augustine, Pres.
104 Oak Glen Rd.
Pittsburgh, PA 15237
Phone: (412)364-1609
Fax: (412)369-7829
E-mail: red78div@bellatlantic.net
Home Page: http://home.pon.net/gregf/78thdva/78thdiv.htm

• 13 • Jonah E. Kelley Award
For a graduating senior from Keyser High School, in Keyser, WV. A monetary prize is given annually.

• 14 •
84th Infantry Division, Railsplitter Society
Forrest T. Lothrop, Exec.Sec.-Treas.
PO Box 827
Sioux Falls, SD 57101-0827
Phone: (605)334-8787
E-mail: liladay@aol.com

• 15 • Bolling Cross
Annual award of recognition. Winner is chosen by the president.

• 16 • Order of the Eagle
Annual award of recognition. Winner is chosen by the president.

• 17 • Railsplitter of the Year
Annual award of recognition. Members vote in a secret ballot for the man they feel is most deserving.

• 18 •
The 92nd Street Y
Sol Adler, Exec.Dir.
1395 Lexington Ave.
New York, NY 10128
Phone: (212)415-5500
E-mail: unterberg@92y.org
Home Page: http://www.92y.org

• 19 • "Discovery"/*The Nation* Contest
To recognize poets who have not yet published a book of poems (chapbooks, self-published books included). Individual poems that have been or will be published elsewhere may be submitted. All poems must be original and in English (no translations). A monetary award of $300, a reading at The Unterberg Poetry Center of the 92nd Street Y, and publication in *The Nation* are awarded to each of four winners annually in the spring. Established in 1964. Formerly: "Discovery" Award.

• 20 •
106th Infantry Division Association
Richard Rigatti, Treas.
113 Woodshire Dr.
Pittsburgh, PA 15215
Phone: (412)781-8131
Fax: (770)928-1347
E-mail: cubeditor106th@mm.com
Home Page: http://www.mm.com/user/jpk

• 21 • Order of the Golden Lion
Recognizes members' outstanding services. Awarded periodically.

Awards are arranged in alphabetical order below their administering organizations

• 22 •
303rd Bomb Group (H) Association
William H. Cox, Treas.
441 Sandstone Dr.
Vacaville, CA 95688-4225
Phone: (707)448-0571
E-mail: membership@303rdbga.com
Home Page: http://www.303rdbga.com

• 23 • Distinguished Service Award
Recognizes service in the 303rd Bomb Group during World War II.

• 24 •
369th Veterans' Association
Nathaniel James, Pres.
369th Regiment Armory
1 369th Plz.
New York, NY 10037
Phone: (212)281-3308
Fax: (212)281-6308
E-mail: nativets@earthlink.net
Home Page: http://home.earthlink.net/~natlvets/

• 25 • 369th Veterans' Association Service Award
For recognition of inspiring leadership, untiring efforts, and dedicated service to the association. The Board of Directors makes the selection. A plaque is awarded annually at the convention. Established in 1971.

• 26 •
A. Philip Randolph Institute
Clayola Brown, Pres.
815-16th St., NW
Washington, DC 20006
Phone: (202)508-3710
Fax: (202)508-3711
E-mail: info@apri.org
Home Page: http://www.apri.org

• 27 • A. Philip Randolph Achievement Award
For recognition of a ranking black trade unionist who has achieved high excellence and has made a major contribution to the improvement of the lives of workers. Candidate must hold a high ranking responsible position in the American trade union movement. A medallion is presented annually. Established in 1968 by A. Philip Randolph.

• 28 • A. Philip Randolph/Bayard Rustin Freedom Award
For recognition of outstanding contributions to the advancement of human rights and civil rights nationally and internationally. A medallion of A. Philip Randolph and Bayard Rustin is presented annually. Established in 1968 by A. Philip Randolph. Renamed in 1988 in honor of A. Philip Randolph and Bayard Rustin. Formerly: (1988) A. Philip Randolph Freedom Award.

• 29 • Bayard Rustin Humanitarian Award
For recognition of achievement in the areas of human rights and social justice. Nomination is by the Executive Committee of the Institute and approval by the National Board. A specially designed trophy is awarded annually. Established in 1989 in honor of Bayard Rustin, civil rights leader and champion for human rights and dignity.

• 30 • Rosina Tucker Award
For recognition of the contribution to the strengthening of the Black-labor alliance in the spirit of A. Philip Randolph. Nomination is by the Executive Committee of the Institute and approval by the National Board. A plaque is awarded annually. Established in 1989 in honor of Rosina Tucker, former President of Ladies' Auxillary of the Brotherhood of Sleeping Car Porters.

• 31 •
AACC International
Steven C. Nelson, Exec.VP
3340 Pilot Knob Rd.
St. Paul, MN 55121-2097
Phone: (651)454-7250
Fax: (651)454-0766
E-mail: aacc@scisoc.org
Home Page: http://www.aaccnet.org/

Formerly: (2005) American Association of Cereal Chemists.

• 32 • Endowment Fund
For students majoring in disciplines related to cereal science.

• 33 • Excellence in Teaching Award
Recognizes contributions to the association through teaching in the broad field of Cereal Science and Technology. AACC members and current teachers are eligible. $1500 and a plaque are awarded.

• 34 •
AACE International
Philip D. Larson CCE, Pres.
209 Prairie Ave., Ste. 100
Morgantown, WV 26501
Phone: (304)296-8444
Toll-Free: 800-858-2678
Fax: (304)291-5728
E-mail: info@aacei.org
Home Page: http://www.aacei.org

Formerly: (1992) American Association of Cost Engineers.

• 35 • Award of Merit
This, the organization's highest award, is presented to an individual for contributions to cost engineering. Membership is not necessary for consideration. Awarded annually. Established in 1957.

• 36 • Fellow
To recognize those members who have advanced cost engineering by service within the organization and to organizations outside of AACE. Awarded annually upon recommendation. Established in 1976.

• 37 • Honorary Life Member
In recognition of outstanding service in AACE International. Awarded annually. Established in 1959.

• 38 • Industrial Appreciation Award
To recognize outstanding corporate support to AACE and the cost engineering profession. Awarded annually. Established in 1972.

• 39 • Charles V. Keane Distinguished Service Award
To recognize a member of an AACE section who has consistently endeavored to enhance the professional image of cost engineering over an extended period of time. Awarded annually. Established in 1982.

• 40 • Outstanding Section and Region Award
To recognize sections and regions that have demonstrated excellence in serving their membership and the association as a whole. Awarded annually. Established in 1976. Formerly: (1987) Publications Award.

• 41 • O. T. Zimmerman Founder's Award
To recognize noteworthy contributions to the association. Awarded annually. Established in 1972. Formerly: Award of Recognition.

• 42 •
AAFRC Trust for Philanthropy
C. Ray Clements, Chair
4700 W Lake Ave.
Glenview, IL 60025
Phone: (847)375-4709
Toll-Free: 800-462-2372
Fax: (732)578-6594
E-mail: info@aafrc.org
Home Page: http://www.aafrc.org

• 43 • John Grenzebach Awards
To recognize, encourage, and disseminate research in philanthropy education. Monetary awards are presented. Awarded annually. Established in 1987 in memory of John Grenzebach.

• 44 •
AARL Foundation
Jim Haynie, Pres.
225 Main St.
Newington, CT 06111
Phone: (860)594-0397
Fax: (860)594-0259
E-mail: foundation@arrl.org
Home Page: http://www.arrl.org/arrlf

• 45 • ARRL Herb S. Brier Instructor of the Year Award
For recognition of achievement in voluntarily instructing amateur radio licensing classes without being personally compensated for doing so. Nominations must be received by March 1. Individuals must be ARRL members and registered with ARRL as instructors to be nominated. A plaque is awarded annually. Established in 1978 in honor of Herb Brier, an amateur radio instructor from Indiana. Co-sponsored by ARRL and LaPorte Amateur Radio Club, LaPorte, Indiana. Formerly: Herb S. Brier Instructor of the Year Award.

• 46 • ARRL Professional Educator of the Year Award
For recognition of achievement by professional educators who teach amateur radio or use it as a motivational technique to teach other subjects. Nominations must be received by March 1. A plaque is awarded annually. Established in 1987. Formerly: Professional Teacher of the Year Award.

• 47 • Cover Plaque Award
To honor the authors of outstanding articles published in the League's magazine, *QST*. A plaque is awarded monthly. Established in 1961.

• 48 • International Humanitarian Award
To recognize individuals who, through amateur radio, are devoted to promoting the welfare of mankind. Individuals who have performed extraordinary service for the benefit of others during times of crisis or disaster may be nominated by December 31. A plaque and major article in *QST* magazine are awarded annually at the National Convention. Established in 1985.

• 49 • Hiram Percy Maxim Memorial Award
To recognize academic excellence and dedication to public service by youth. Licensed radio amateurs under the age of 21 are eligible. A monetary award of $1,500, an engraved plaque, and travel expenses to attend the ARRL Convention are awarded as merited. Established in 1936. Formerly: Hiram Percy Maxim Gold Medal.

• 50 • Philip J. McGan Silver Antenna Award
To recognize the amateur radio operator who best exemplifies the volunteer efforts of the late Philip J. McGan to promote amateur radio to the general public. The recipient must be a full-time member of the American Radio Relay League at the time of nomination, and must not be compensated for his or her public relations work on behalf of amateur radio. A plaque is awarded annually. Established in 1992.

• 51 • Professional Instructor of the Year Award
To recognize the achievements of an amateur radio operator who teaches licensing classes in community colleges or vocational education institutes. The instructor must be personally compensated and may not be a professional (state-licensed) schoolteacher. A plaque is awarded annually. Established in 1993.

• 52 • Technical Excellence Award
To honor the best *QST*, *NCJ* or *QEX* technical article of the year. All authors are eligible. An engraved pewter loving cup on pewter base is awarded annually. Established in 1975.

• 53 • You've Got a Friend in Pennsylvania Award
To recognize a member of the ARRL, preferably residing within the commonwealth of Pennsylvania. Individual must have at least a general license. The award is $1,000 and is awarded annually.

• 54 •
ABA Marketing Network
Barbara Oayne, Mgr.
1120 Conneticut Ave. NW
Washington, DC 20036
Phone: (202)663-5283
Toll-Free: 800-BAN-KERS
Fax: (202)828-4540
E-mail: marketingnetwork@aba.com
Home Page: http://www.aba.com/MarketingNetwork/default.htm

Formerly: (2003) Bank Marketing Association.

• 55 • Advertising Awards
To honor creative excellence in financial services advertising and marketing. The competition features the following categories; television, radio, and print and a panel of the most reputable judges in the financial services and advertising industry. Two awards are offered: (1)The Certificate of Excellence which honors entries deemed as outstanding in tv, radio, print, website, direct mail and multi-media campaigns; and (2) Best of the Best which is presented to those winners deemed as the cream-of-the-crop of all entries. Recipients of this highly coveted award are truly among the "Best of the Best" in the field of financial services advertising.

• 56 •
Abarth Register, U.S.A.
Gerald Rothman, Dir.
54 School St., Ste. 102
Westbury, NY 11590-4469
Phone: (516)876-8754

• 57 • Golden Scorpion Award for Outstanding Service
To recognize achievement in service. Awarded annually.

• 58 •
ABET
George D. Peterson, Exec.Dir.
111 Market Pl., Ste. 1050
Baltimore, MD 21202-4012
Phone: (410)347-7700
Fax: (410)625-2238
E-mail: info@abet.org
Home Page: http://www.abet.org

Formerly: Engineers' Council for Professional Development.

• 59 • ABET Honor Roll
To recognize companies, industrial firms, government organizations and educational institutions that have given sustained, quality service to engineering and engineering education through active participation in ABET, either directly or through their personnel. Nominees must have the support of one or more employees which have served ABET as program evaluators, accreditation commission members, or Board members for at least five years. A letter and plaque to the CEO, and listing in the Annual Report for four years are awarded. A maximum of 25 may be conferred annually. Established in 1987.

• 60 • Linton E. Grinter Distinguished Service Award
To recognize outstanding service/contribution to engineering education and the profession through ABET related activities. An ABET medallion encased in a lucite hexagon may be conferred annually. Established in 1972 in honor of Linton E. Grinter, whose involvement in engineering education and the profession spans more than 60 years.

• 61 •
Abraham Lincoln Association
Roger D. Bridges, Pres.
One Old State Capitol Plz.
Springfield, IL 62701-1507
Phone: (217)782-2118
Fax: (217)785-7937
E-mail: rdbridges@verizon.net
Home Page: http://www.alincolnassoc.com

• 62 • Annual Achievement Award
No further information was provided for this edition.

• 63 • Logan Hay Medal
To recognize individuals who have made noteworthy contributions to the purpose for which the organization exists: to observe each anniversary of the birth of Abraham Lincoln; to preserve and make more accessible the landmarks associated with his life; and to actively encourage, promote and aid the collection and dissemination of authentic information regarding all phases of his life and career. A bronze medal is awarded infrequently. Established in 1967 by the Association and Logan Hay descendants in honor of Logan Hay, who played an important part in the formative years of the Association.

• 64 • Lincoln the Lawyer Award
Awarded to a lawyer or jurist who best exemplifies the ideal of Abraham Lincoln in his/her legal career. Awarded when merited. Established in 1985.

• 65 •
Abrasive Engineering Society
Ted Giese, Bus.Mgr.
144 Moore Rd.
Butler, PA 16001
Phone: (724)282-6210
Fax: (724)282-6210
E-mail: aes@abrasiveengineering.com
Home Page: http://www.abrasiveengineering.com

• 66 • AES Awards of Excellence
This is an international program to recognize excellence in abrasive methodology. Selection criteria include the following: exceptional or unusual grinding methods; increased production and/or cost reduction; improved quality control in a finished part; and innovations and new approaches to grinding problems. Users of abrasives in the manufacturing or processing of any part or product, whether it be metal, plastic, wood, glass, rubber or any other material, are eligible. Awarded at the Society's international conference.

• 67 • AES Man of the Year Award
To recognize an outstanding individual in the abrasive industry. Selection is based on activities in one of the following areas: (1) advancements of a technical nature founded on scientific contributions in engineering research or creation of a new product; (2) advancements in plant operations, practical mechanical processes, or applications related to economy and/or efficiency; or (3) progress in a non-scientific activity, such as educational functions, that enhances the reputation of the abrasive industry. Awarded annually at the Society's international conference.

• 68 • Jim Bottorf Award
To recognize educational service to the abrasive industry coupled with the humanitarian aspect of interest in the growth and development of persons in the industry. Established in 1982 in memory of the dedicated service of Jim Bottorf.

• 69 •
ACA International
Mark Davitt, Pres.
ACA Center
4040 West 70th St.
PO Box 390106
Minneapolis, MN 55439-0106
Phone: (952)926-6547
Fax: (952)926-1624
E-mail: aca@collector.com
Home Page: http://www.acainternational.org

• 70 • Paul Bunyan Award
To recognize the individual who has done the most work in the industry and the Association during the preceding year. A plaque is awarded annually. Established in 1952.

• 71 • Continuous Service Award
To recognize an individual for service in leadership in ACA for 10 or more consecutive years. A plaque is awarded annually. Established in 1960.

• 72 • International Fellowship of Certified Collectors
To encourage individual, business and association improvement and to recognize those who have such programs, achieving certain levels of personal and business development and making contributions to their association, the collection business and other groups and individuals. Applications cover five general categories: (1) collection and other business experience; (2) education and training; (3) association achievements and leadership; (4) personal contributions to improvements of collection service operations; and (5) accomplishments in public relations, community involvement, and business ethics. A plaque and a pinette are awarded annually at the convention.

• 73 •
Acacia Fraternity
Greg Gifford, Pres.
2255 Vine St.
Lincoln, NE 68503
Phone: (402)436-6162
Phone: (402)436-6160

• 74 • Acacia Leadership Scholarship
For exemplary leadership, academics, and human service. Monetary award bestowed annually.

• 75 •
Academy for Educational Development
Stephen F. Moseley, Pres. & CEO
1825 Connecticut Ave. NW
Washington, DC 20009-5721
Phone: (202)884-8000
Fax: (202)884-8400
E-mail: web@aed.org
Home Page: http://www.aed.org

• 76 • Alvin C. Eurich Award
Recognizes innovation in solving or addressing educational problems. Awarded annually.

• 77 •
Academy of American Poets
Tree Swenson, Exec.Dir.
584 Broadway, Ste. 604
New York, NY 10012-5243
Phone: (212)274-0343
Fax: (212)274-9427
E-mail: tswenson@poets.org
Home Page: http://www.poets.org

• 78 • Walt Whitman Award
To encourage emerging poets by securing publication of the winner's first first book open to living citizens of the United States who have not had a book of poems published in a standard edition. A monetary prize of $5,000 to the winning poet and publication of the manuscript are awarded annually in the spring. The winner will also receive a one-month residency at the Vermont Studio Center. Established in 1975, the prize is now given in memory of Eric Mathieu King.

• 79 •
Academy of Canadian Cinema and Television
(Academie Canadienne du Cinema et de la Television)
Maria Topalovich, Pres. & CEO
172 King St. E
Toronto, ON, Canada M5A 1J3
Phone: (416)366-2227
Toll-Free: 800-644-5194
Fax: (416)366-8454
E-mail: info@academy.ca
Home Page: http://www.academy.ca/

• 80 • Academy & Achievement Awards
Recognizes outstanding or ongoing contributions to the Canadian television industry. Nominations are accepted year round from all branches of the Academy. Given when merited as part of the Gemini Special Awards. Name of nominee, summary of reason for nomination and nominees name, membership number and phone number must be mailed or faxed.

• 81 • Gemeaux Awards
(Prix Gemeaux)
To recognize excellence and achievement in French language television production. Awards are presented in 50 categories covering programs, performance, and crafts. Awarded annually in Montreal in the fall. Established in 1985. The first awards were presented in 1987.

• 82 • Geminis
Recognizes outstanding achievements in Canadian English Language Television. A trophy is awarded annually.

• 83 • Genies
Recognizes outstanding achievements in Canadian Cinema. A trophy is awarded annually.

• 84 • Prix Gemeaux
Recognizes outstanding achievement in Canadian French Language Television. A trophy is awarded annually.

• 85 •
Academy of Country Music
Bob Romero, Exec.Dir.
4100 W Alemeda, Ste. 208
Burbank, CA 91505
Phone: (818)842-8400
Fax: (818)842-8535
E-mail: info@acmcountry.com
Home Page: http://www.acmcountry.com

• 86 • **Academy of Country Music Awards**
To recognize outstanding achievement in the country music industry. Awards are presented in the following categories: Album, Album/Artist, Album/Producer, Album/Record Company, Bass, Club, Disc Jockey, Drums, Entertainer, Female Vocalist, Fiddle, Guitar, Keyboard, Male Vocalist, New Female Vocalist, New Male Vocalist, New Vocal Duet or Group, Pioneer Award, Radio Station, Single Record, Single/Artist, Single/Producer, Single/Record Company, Song, Song/Artist, Song/Publisher(s), Song/Composer, Specialty/Instrument, Steel Guitar, Video/Artist, Video/Director, Video/Producer, Vocal Duet, and Vocal Group. Awarded annually. Established in 1965.

• 87 •
Academy of Criminal Justice Sciences
Mittie D. Southerland, Exec.Dir.
PO Box 960
Greenbelt, MD 20768-0960
Phone: (301)446-6300
Toll-Free: 800-757-ACJS
Fax: (301)446-2819
E-mail: execdir@acjs.org
Home Page: http://www.acjs.org

• 88 • **Academy Fellow**
To recognize a distinguished teacher in criminal justice education. Evidence of teaching effectiveness must include a list of courses taught and evaluations. The individual must have a minimum of five years teaching experience in a criminal justice program. Criteria for selection include scholarly achievement in the faculty member's discipline and professional contribution to the academy. Nominations are accepted. Established in 1980.

• 89 • **Anderson Student Paper Award**
For recognition of outstanding students and their contributions to the discipline of criminal justice. Selection is based on the following criteria: relevance of a research program, quality of theoretical orientation, rigor of empirical and/or logical documentation, and quality of writing. The deadline for nominations is August. Awarded annually. Established in 1982.

• 90 • **Founder's Award**
For recognition of excellence in criminal justice education and active participation in the academy. Active members for at least five consecutive years who have been involved in criminal justice education and research for the preceding five years and who have made substantial contributions to criminal justice's emerging body of knowledge are eligible. The deadline for nominations is August. Established in 1976.

• 91 • **Outstanding Book Award**
For recognition of the best book published in the area of criminal justice. An extraordinary contribution to the field of criminal justice is the basis for selection. The deadline for nominations is August.

• 92 • **William L. Simon/Anderson Publishing Outstanding Paper Award**
For recognition of excellence in a paper presented at the ACJS Annual Conference. The following criteria are considered: conceptual and methodological rigor in the development of the thesis and its subsequent empirical or logical documentation, theoretical or pragmatic relevance of the thesis and its importance to the development of a body of knowledge for criminal justice, and quality of writing. The deadline for nominations is August. Awarded annually. Established in 1982.

• 93 • **Bruce Smith Sr. Award**
For recognition of excellence in the demonstration of leadership in criminal justice. Criteria considered are: leadership in the administration of criminal justice as an academic and/or professional discipline in a manner that reflects the highest standards of integrity and performance, and active involvement in criminal justice research or other endeavor that has made substantial contributions to the emerging body of knowledge in criminal justice. Membership is not required. The deadline for nominations is August 31. Awarded each year at the annual meeting. Established in 1976.

• 94 •
Academy of Dentistry International
Robert L. Ramus DDS, Exec.Dir.
3813 Gordon Creek Dr.
PO Box 307
Hicksville, OH 43526-0307
Phone: (419)542-0101
Phone: (419)542-6883
E-mail: rramus@bright.net
Home Page: http://www.adint.org

• 95 • **The Award of Distinction**
Recognizes individuals who have distinguished themselves in the field of Continuing Dental Education. Awarded periodically.

• 96 • **Distinguished Fellowship**
Recognizes notable service and extraordinary contributions, to the Academy, the Dental and Health Care Professions, and outstanding leadership in the enhancement and betterment of his community, nation and mankind. Active, Retired or Life Fellow of the Academy are eligible. Awarded annually.

• 97 • **The Hillenbrand Award**
Recognizes exceptional devotion to the affairs and aim of beneficial service to the profession and the society.

• 98 • **Honorary Fellowship**
Recognizes the advancement of the profession and human welfare through eminent service. Individuals are nominated by the Awards Committee and elected by the Board of Regents.

• 99 • **The Humanitarian Award**
Recognizes significant contribution to the enhancement of the quality of life and the human condition. Awarded annually.

• 100 • **International Dentist of the Year**
This award is presented to the dentist who best exemplifies international leadership. Awarded annually.

• 101 •
Academy of International Business
G. Thomas M. Hult, Exec.Dir.
The Eli Broad College of Business
Michigan State University
7 Eppley Center
East Lansing, MI 48824-1121
Phone: (517)432-1452
Fax: (517)432-1009
E-mail: aib@aib.msu.edu
Home Page: http://www.aibworld.net

• 102 • **Richard N. Farmer International Business Dissertation Award**
To recognize the student/author of the best doctoral dissertation written each year in the area of international business. A monetary award of $1,000 and a plaque are awarded annually. Established in 1969. Named after Richard N. Farmer, a professor of international business at Indiana University and former president of the Academy. Formerly: International Business Dissertation Award.

• 103 • **Haynes Prize for Best Paper**
The winning paper must have been accepted for presentation at the AIB conference through the double-blind-review process, and have been written by an author or authors under 40 years of age. A plaque and $2000 are award at the annual meeting.

• 104 •
Academy of Marketing Science
Harold W. Berkman, Exec.VP/Dir.
Univ. of Miami
School of Business Administration
PO Box 248012
Coral Gables, FL 33124-6536
Phone: (305)284-6673
Fax: (305)284-3762
E-mail: ams.sba@miami.edu
Home Page: http://www.ams-web.org

• 105 • **Best Doctoral Dissertation of the Year Award**
To recognize the Academy member with the best doctoral dissertation. A monetary award is given annually.

• 106 • Best Student Paper of the Year Award
To recognize the Academy member with the best student paper. A monetary award is given annually.

• 107 • Concrete Achiever of the Year
For recognition of the person doing the most to promote the use of concrete and the standards of excellence in its use. Established in 1982 by the Inland Branch.

• 108 • Fulton Awards (Fulton Toekenning)
This premier civil engineering award in Southern Africa, is presented for recognition of excellence in the use of concrete in two categories: civil engineering structures and building structure. A project that is made substantially of concrete and has been completed in the year prior to the award is eligible. Certificates are awarded annually. Established in 1979 in honor of Dr. Sandrock Fulton.

• 109 • Marketing Practitioner of the Year Award
Annual award of recognition for members.

• 110 •
Academy of Motion Picture Arts and Sciences
Bruce Davis, Exec.Dir.
8949 Wilshire Blvd.
Beverly Hills, CA 90211
Phone: (310)247-3000
Phone: (310)247-3090
Fax: (310)271-3395
E-mail: publicity@oscars.org
Home Page: http://www.oscars.org

• 111 • Academy Honorary Awards
To recognize superlative and distinguished service in the making of motion pictures or for outstanding service to the Academy. The Oscar statuette is awarded by a vote of the Board of Governors of the Academy.

• 112 • Jean Hersholt Humanitarian Award
To recognize an individual in the motion picture industry whose humanitarian efforts have brought credit to the industry. The Oscar statuette is awarded by a vote of the Board of Governors of the Academy. This award cannot be given posthumously.

• 113 • Special Achievement Awards
To recognize an achievement that makes an exceptional contribution to the motion picture for which it was created, but for which there is no annual award category. An Oscar statuette is awarded by a vote of the Board of Governors. Established in 1976.

• 114 •
Academy of Operative Dentistry
Dr. Gregory E. Smith DDSMSD, Sec.
PO Box 14996
Gainesville, FL 32604-2996
Phone: (909)558-4640
Phone: (909)862-5732
Fax: (909)558-0253
E-mail: gesaod@ufl.edu
Home Page: http://operativedentistry.com

• 115 • Award of Excellence
To recognize teaching and service to the academy. Awarded annually. Established in 1986.

• 116 • Buonocore Memorial Lecturer
Annual award of recognition. Established in 1982.

• 117 • Hollenback Memorial Prize
To recognize contributions to operative dentistry by a dentist and by a dental student. Awarded annually. Established in 1975.

• 118 •
Academy of Parish Clergy
Dr. Paul J. Binder FAPC, Admin.VP
2249 Florinda St.
Sarasota, FL 34231-4414
Phone: (941)922-8633
E-mail: office@apclergy.org
Home Page: http://www.apclergy.org

Formerly: (1996) Academy of Parish Clergy.

• 119 • Book of the Year Award
To recognize the author of the best book written in the area of parish ministry. A monetary award is presented annually at the Academy's annual meeting. Established 1982.

• 120 • Certificate of Achievement of Focused Studies
For recognition of studies designed to enhance an individual's knowledge in specific areas of ministry as a result of the use of the *Guide for Continuing Growth*. The program of study is designed by the candidate in consultation with the Dean of Focused Studies. Established in 1990.

• 121 • Parish Pastor of the Year
To recognize excellence and faithfulness in parish ministry. The recipient need not be a member of the Academy. A plaque, check, and a year's membership in the Academy are presented at the Academy's annual meeting. Established 1992.

• 122 •
Academy of Science Fiction, Fantasy, and Horror Films
Robert Holguin, Pres.
334 W 54th St.
Los Angeles, CA 90037-3806
Phone: (323)752-5811
Fax: (323)752-5811
E-mail: scifiacademy@comcast.net
Home Page: http://www.saturnawards.org

• 123 • Saturn Awards
For recognition of outstanding achievement in science fiction, fantasy, and horror films. Films must be genre films screened for a general membership in the California area. Selections are made by members of the Academy. The following awards are presented: best science fiction film, best fantasy film, best horror film, best actor, best actress, best supporting actor, best supporting actress, best director, best writing, best music, best costumes, best make-up, best special effects, Life Career Award, President's Award, George Pal Memorial Award, best juvenile performance, Academy Service Award, best genre home video release, best genre television presentation, and Special Lifetime Achievement Award. A Saturn gold trophy is presented annually. Established in 1972 by Dr. Donald A. Reed.

• 124 •
Academy of Security Educators and Trainers
Dr. Richard W. Kobetz, Pres.
PO Box 802
Berryville, VA 22611-0802
Phone: (540)554-2540
Phone: (540)554-2547
Fax: (540)554-2558
Home Page: http://www.asetcse.org

• 125 • Academy Fellow
For recognition of distinguished service and accomplishment in the field of security education or training. Members of the Academy may be nominated by the Standing Fellowship Committee of the Academy. A trophy is awarded each year at the annual conference. Established in 1986.

• 126 •
Academy of Television Arts and Sciences
Karalee Vint, Dir.
5220 Lankershim Blvd.
North Hollywood, CA 91601
Phone: (818)754-2813
Phone: (818)754-2810
Fax: (818)769-9034
E-mail: vint@emmys.org
Home Page: http://www.emmys.org

Formerly: (1977) Hollywood Chapter of the National Academy of Television Arts and Sciences.

• 127 • Emmy Awards for Primetime Programming
To recognize the advancement of the arts and sciences of television and achievements broad-

cast nationally during prime time. Awards are given in 91 categories.

• 128 • **TV Hall of Fame**
To recognize individuals who have contributed notably to the electronic medium. Individuals are inducted annually. Established in 1983.

• 129 •
Access Intelligence LLC
1201 Seven Locks Rd., Ste. 300
Potomac, MD 20854
Phone: (301)340-1520
Fax: (301)309-3847
Home Page: http://www.accessintel.com

Formerly: Phillips Publishing.

• 130 • **Gold Key Laureates**
To recognize the advancement of public relations professionals to top management posts during the previous year, as recorded in *PR News*. Gold key certificates are awarded annually. Established in 1962.

• 131 • **PR Professional of the Year**
This award, often referred to as Public Relations' Hall of Fame, is given to recognize outstanding public relations executives who have practiced at the highest levels of ethics and performance and have contributed significantly to the field. Entries are judged within five categories: agency, corporate, education system, financial/investor relations, and nonprofit/association. Each year, a plaque is awarded to the winner in each category. Established in 1962. Co-sponsored by *PR News*.

• 132 •
Accounting Aid Society
Marshall Hunt, Interim Pres.
18145 Mack Ave.
Detroit, MI 48224
Phone: (313)647-9628
Fax: (313)647-9628

• 133 • **Jeanne Vost Celebration of Leadership**
For leadership in nonprofit management. Recognition award bestowed annually.

• 134 •
Accreditation Association for Ambulatory Health Care
John E. Burke PhD, Exec.Dir./CEO
3201 Old Glenview Rd., Ste. 300
Wilmette, IL 60091
Phone: (847)853-6060
Fax: (847)853-9028
E-mail: info@aaahc.org
Home Page: http://www.aaahc.org

• 135 • **President's Award**
To recognize service to quality standards in health care. Awarded annually.

• 136 •
Acoustical Society of America
Charles E. Schmid, Exec.Dir.
2 Huntington Quadrangle, Ste. 1N01
Melville, NY 11747-4502
Phone: (516)576-2360
Fax: (516)576-2377
E-mail: asa@aip.org
Home Page: http://asa.aip.org

• 137 • **Distinguished Service Citation**
For recognition of outstanding service to the society by a present or former member, or fellow of the society. A certificate is awarded when merited. Established in 1972.

• 138 • **Gold Medal**
For recognition of outstanding contributions to acoustics. Members of the society, without age limitation, are eligible. Awarded biennially until 1980. It is now awarded annually in the spring. Established in 1954 on the occasion of the Society's Twenty-Fifth Anniversary Celebration.

• 139 • **Helmholtz-Rayleigh Interdisciplinary Silver Medal**
For recognition of contributions to the advancement of science, engineering, or human welfare through the application of acoustic principles or through research accomplishments in acoustics. Awarded intermittently. Established in 1994.

• 140 • **Honorary Fellow**
To recognize an individual who has attained eminence in acoustics or who has rendered outstanding service to acoustics. At the time of election an Honorary Fellow need not be a member of the Society. Awarded when merited. Established in 1929.

• 141 • **R. Bruce Lindsay Award**
For recognition of substantial contributions through published papers to the advancement of theoretical or applied acoustics or both and for actively participating in Acoustical Society affairs. Members of the society under 35 years of age are eligible. The annual award consists of a $3,000 prize, a citation, and a complete set of JASA. Awarded biennially until 1986. It is now awarded annually in the spring. Established in 1942. Formerly: (1986) Biennial Award.

• 142 • **Pioneers of Underwater Acoustics Medal**
For recognition of outstanding contributions to the science of underwater acoustics through publications of research in professional journals or by other accomplishments. Individuals, regardless of nationality, age, or society affiliation are eligible for the award. Awarded intermittently. Established in 1959 in honor of five pioneers in the field: H. J. W. Fay, R. A. Fessenden, H. C. Hayes, G. W. Pierce, and P. Langevin.

• 143 • **Wallace Clement Sabine Medal**
For recognition of outstanding contributions to the field of architectural acoustics as evidenced by contributions to professional journals and periodicals or by other accomplishments. Individuals, regardless of nationality, are eligible. Presented intermittently. Established in 1957.

• 144 • **Silver Medal**
For recognition of contributions to the advancement of science, engineering, or human welfare through the application of acoustic principles, or through research accomplishment in acoustics. Awards may be presented in the following areas: acoustical oceanography, architectural acoustics, bioresponse to vibration and to ultrasound, engineering acoustics, musical acoustics, noise, physical acoustics, psychological and physiological acoustics, speech communication, structural acoustics and vibration, and underwater acoustics. Individuals of any age are eligible. Silver medals are awarded up to four times each year. Established in 1974.

• 145 • **Trent - Crede Medal**
For recognition of outstanding contributions to the sciences of mechanical vibration and shock, as evidenced by publication of research results in professional journals, or by other accomplishments in the field. Individuals, irrespective of nationality, age, or society affiliation are eligible for the award. Awarded intermittently. Established in 1969.

• 146 • **von Bekesy Medal**
To recognize individuals who have made outstanding contributions to the area of psychological or physiological acoustics, as evidenced by publication of research results in professional journals or by other accomplishments in the field. Individuals irrespective of nationality, age, or society affiliation are eligible. A medal and a certificate are awarded intermittently. Established in 1984.

• 147 •
ACSM Health Promotion
Ralph Callao, Co-Chm.
60 Revere Dr., Ste. 500
Northbrook, IL 60062-1577
Phone: (847)247-1557
Fax: (847)480-9282
E-mail: rcolao@hcsus.jnj.com
Home Page: http://www.uwsp.edu/hphd/awhp

Formerly: (1983) American Association of Fitness Directors in Business and Industry; Association for Fitness in Business.

• 148 • **Business and Industry Awards**
To recognize outstanding contributions in the field of health and fitness to or by an industrial, educational, medical, or governmental organization or individuals. A plaque is awarded annually. Established in 1976.

• 149 • **Lifetime Achievement Award**
Recognizes individuals and corporations. Awarded annually.

• 150 • **Merit Award**
Recognizes individuals and corporations. Awarded annually.

• 151 • **Professional Preparation Award**
To recognize individuals and corporations making contributions to the industry. A plaque is awarded annually. Established in 1986.

• 152 • **Service Award**
Recognizes service by individuals and corporations. Awarded annually.

• 153 •
Acta Materialia, Inc.
Prof. Karl A. Gchneider Jr., Chm.
% Prof. Subhash Mahajan
Dept. of Chemical and Materials Engineering
Arizona State University
1711 S Rural Rd.
Tempe, AZ 85287-6006
Phone: (480)965-9710
Fax: (480)965-0037
E-mail: smahajan@asu.edu
Home Page: http://actamat.web.cmu.edu

• 154 • **Gold Medal**
To recognize ability and leadership in materials research worldwide. Nominations must be made by a sponsoring or cooperating society of ACTA Materialia, Inc., by November 30. A gold medal and a certificate are presented at a major meeting of the nominating society. Awarded annually. Established in 1974.

• 155 • **J. Herbert Hollomon Award**
To recognize contributions to understanding the interaction between materials and societal concerns, or a contribution to materials technology that has had great impact on society. Nominations must be submitted by a sponsoring or cooperating society of Acta Materialia, Inc. or by its Board of Governors by November 30. A monetary award, a piece of Steuben sculpture, and a certificate are awarded annually. Established in 1989 to honor the memory of J. Herbert Hollomon, eminent metallurgist and administrator, and principal instigator of Acta Metallurgica.

• 156 •
Action for Post-Soviet Jewry
Judith K. Patkin, Exec.Dir.
24 Crescent St., Ste. 306
Waltham, MA 02453
Phone: (781)893-2331
Fax: (781)647-9474
E-mail: actionpsj@aol.com
Home Page: http://www.actionpsj.org

• 157 • **Freedom Award**
Recognizes significant work on behalf of Jews in the former Soviet Union.

• 158 •
Acton Institute for the Study of Religion and Liberty
161 Ottawa Ave. NW, Ste. 301
Grand Rapids, MI 49503
Phone: (616)454-3080
Toll-Free: 800-345-2286
Fax: (616)454-9454
E-mail: info@acton.org
Home Page: http://www.acton.org

• 159 • **Calihan Fellowships**
For outstanding promise in integrating religious ideas with core principles of the classical liberal tradition by graduate students.

• 160 • **Novak Award**
For outstanding new research into the interrelation of religion and economic liberty.

• 161 •
Actors' Equity Association
Alan Eisenberg, Exec.Dir.
165 W 46th St.
New York, NY 10036
Phone: (212)869-8530
Fax: (212)719-9815
E-mail: info@actorsequity.org
Home Page: http://www.actorsequity.org

• 162 • **Rosetta LeNoire Award**
To recognize those theatres and producing organizations under an equity contract that are exemplary in the hiring of ethnic minority and female actors through affirmative action, multiracial and non- traditional casting. Nominations from a theatre producing organization are accepted by October 31. Established in 1989 by the Ethnic Minorities Committee.

• 163 • **Paul Robeson Award**
To recognize the individual or organization who has best exemplified and practiced the principles and ideals to which Mr. Robeson devoted his life: concern for and service to fellow humans, respect for the dignity of the individual, freedom of expression and of association, universal brotherhood, and responsibility to profession. A plaque is awarded annually. Established in 1974 in honor of Paul Robeson.

• 164 •
Actors' Equity Foundation
Alan Eisenberg, Exec.Dir.
165 W. 46th St.
New York, NY 10036
Phone: (212)869-8530
Fax: (212)719-9815
E-mail: info@actorsequity.org
Home Page: http://www.actorsequity.org

• 165 • **St. Clair Bayfield Award**
To honor an outstanding actor or actress appearing in a non-featured role in a Shakespearean production offered in metropolitan New York, Stratford, Connecticut, or their environs during the theatre season ending Labor Day. Selection is made by a panel of drama critics. Awarded annually. Established in 1972 in memory of St. Clair Bayfield, a Shakespearean actor, by his widow, Kathleen. Award is presented in January.

• 166 • **Joe A. Callaway Award**
To recognize the best performance by both a male and female actor in a professional presentation of a classic play in a theatre in the New York Metropolitan area. Established in 1989 by long-time member Joe A. Callaway to encourage participation in the classics and non-profit theatre. Selection by a panel of drama critic. Award is presented in January.

• 167 • **Clarence Derwent Award**
To recognize the most promising female and male actors on the New York Metropolitan scene. A monetary award of $2,000 and an engraved crystal memento are awarded to each person annually. Established in 1944 by Clarence Derwent, distinguished actor and former president of Actors' Equity Association.

• 168 • **Paul Robeson Citation Award**
Recognizes a person whose life has emulated the spirit of Paul Robeson. Chosen by a ballot of committees in Chicago, Los Angeles, and New York. Awarded annually in the fall.

• 169 •
Actors' Fund of America
Joseph P. Benincasa, Exec.Dir.
729 Seventh Ave., 10th Fl.
New York, NY 10019
Phone: (212)221-7300
Fax: (212)764-0238
E-mail: jbeninca@actorsfund.org
Home Page: http://www.actorsfund.org

• 170 • **Actors' Fund Medal**
To recognize outstanding services rendered to the entertainment industry by individuals and/or organizations by assisting The Actors' Fund of America in the achievement of its goals. A gilded bronze medal, with the Classic Greek masques of Tragedy and Comedy sculpted in bas-relief on the obverse, and the muses of Comedy, Tragedy and choral dance and song on the reverse, is awarded when merited. Established in 1910.

• 171 •
Actors Theatre of Louisville
Alexander Speer, Exec.Dir.
316 W Main St.
Louisville, KY 40202-4218
Phone: (502)584-1265
Fax: (502)561-3300
E-mail: dking@actorstheatre.org
Home Page: http://www.actorstheatre.org

• 172 • **National Ten-Minute Play Contest**
For recognition of an outstanding new ten-minute play by an unknown or established playwright. Original ten-minute plays (10 pages or less) that have not received an Equity production may be entered in the contest by December

1. A monetary prize (the Heideman Award) of $1,000 is awarded annually, and the play may be produced in the Humana Festival of New American Plays. Established in 1979 in honor of Ted Heideman to recognize one-act plays. Reestablished in 1990 as a ten-minute play contest for plays ten pages or less. Formerly: (1989) National One-Act Play Contest.

• 173 •
Acupuncture Foundation of Canada Institute
(Institute de la Fondation D'Acupuncture du Canada)
Cheryll Kwok, Exec.Dir.
2131 Lawarence Ave. E, Ste. 204
Scarborough, ON, Canada M1R 5G4
Phone: (416)752-3988
Fax: (416)752-4398
E-mail: info@afcinstitute.com
Home Page: http://www.afcinstitute.com

• 174 • **Clifford G. Woolfe Award**
Award of recognition. Nominations are made by the board.

• 175 •
A.D. Johnson Family Association
John S. Walker, Family Historian/Pres.
930 W. Long Ave.
Du Bois, PA 15801-1737
Phone: (814)371-5149
Fax: (814)371-5149
E-mail: adjohnsonfamily@adelphia.net

• 176 • **Awards**
To recognize poets, musicians, and stage and screen artists; and to foster appreciation of Brel and his works and to encourage study of his life and art. A Hall of Fame is also maintained.

• 177 • **Genealogical Research Award**
To recognize AD Johnson Family members. Awarded annually.

• 178 •
ADARA: Professionals Networking for Excellence in Service Delivery with Individuals who are Deaf or Hard of Hearing
Sherri Fleishell, Natl.Off.Coord.
PO Box 480
Myersville, MD 21773
Phone: (301)293-8969
Fax: (301)293-9698
E-mail: adaraorgn@aol.com
Home Page: http://www.adara.org
Formerly: (1976) Professional Rehabilitation Workers With the Adult Deaf.

• 179 • **Bellfasher Award**
To honor the outstanding contribution at each biennial conference. The award may go to an individual or group of individuals. A plaque is awarded biennially at the conference. Established in 1974.

• 180 • **Outstanding Article Award**
To honor the author(s) of the outstanding article appearing in the *JADARA* during the two years immediately preceding each conference. A plaque is awarded biennially at the conference. Established in 1980.

• 181 • **Frederick C. Schreiber Award**
To recognize an individual who has contributed in an outstanding way to ADARA. A plaque is awarded biennially at the conference. Formerly: ADARN of the Year.

• 182 • **Boyce R. Williams Award**
To recognize individuals for outstanding and enduring contributions to improvements in the rehabilitation of deaf people. Extensive participation in rehabilitation efforts and leadership in activities that have resulted in better rehabilitation service and employment opportunities for deaf people are considered for the award. A plaque is awarded biannually. Established in 1972 in honor of Boyce R. Williams, an outstanding professional in the field of vocational rehabilitation.

• 183 •
Adhesion Society
Lynn Penn, Pres.
2 Davidson Hall - 0212
Blacksburg, VA 24061
Phone: (540)231-7257
Fax: (540)231-3971
E-mail: adhesoc@vt.edu
Home Page: http://www.adhesionsociety.org

• 184 • **Adhesion Society Award for Excellence in Adhesion Science**
To recognize work that has had a significant impact upon adhesion science or technology. The award is granted without regard to age, nationality, or field of expertise. Candidates may be currently active in, but need not be limited to, the fields of chemistry, materials science, physics, engineering, or life sciences. The significant work must have been performed in the areas of synthesis, characterization, surface analysis, theoretical analysis, test procedures, or any other area with a direct bearing on adhesion science. A monetary prize, a plaque, and travel expenses are awarded annually when merited at the banquet of the Society or another suspicious occasion. Established in 1987. Sponsored by 3M Company, St. Paul, Minnesota.

• 185 •
The Adirondack Council
Brian Houseal, Exec.Dir.
103 Hand Ave., Ste. 3
Box D-2
Elizabethtown, NY 12932
Phone: (518)873-2240
Toll-Free: 877-873-2240
Fax: (518)873-6675
E-mail: info@adirondackcouncil.org
Home Page: http://www.adirondackcouncil.org

• 186 • **Adirondack Council Annual Awards**
To recognize for support and initiatives in working for lasting protection and preservation of the Adirondack Park. Awards given include Conservationist of the Year Award; Public Service Award; Park Communicator Award; Park Stewardship Award; Park Heritage Award; and Park Educator Award.

• 187 •
ADISQ (Association Quebecoise de L'Industrie du Disque, du Spectacle et de la Video)
Solange Drouin, Dir.Gen.
6420 rue St. Denis
Montreal, QC, Canada H2S 2R7
Phone: (514)842-5147
Fax: (514)842-7762
E-mail: info@adisq.com
Home Page: http://www.adisq.com

• 188 • **Felix Awards, Artistic**
For recognition of achievement in record production or show business. Awards are given in the following categories: Best Children's Album of the Year; Best Comedy Album of the Year; Best Rock Album of the Year; Best Pop-Rock Album of the Year; Best MOR Album of the Year; Best Country Album of the Year; Best Folk Album of the Year; Best Jazz Album of the Year; Best Instrumental Album of the Year; Best Classical Album of the Year orchestra and ensemble; Best Classical Album of the Year - soloist and chamber music; Best Selling Album; Best Male Artist of the Year; Best Female Artist of the Year; Best Quebecois Artist - World Beat of the Year; Best Group of the Year; Most Popular Song of the Year; Best Author and/or Composer of the Year; Quebecois Artist Most Illustrated in Another Language (other than French); Best Known Quebecois Artist Outside of Quebec; Best Known Artist from French-Speaking Communities; Best Few Promising Artist of the Year; Best Show - Comedy of the Year; Best Concert - Singer of the Year; Best Concert - Author-Composer-Singer of the Year; Best Video-Clip of the Year; Industrial; and Tribute. Records and shows produced between June 1 and May 31 in Quebec are eligible. A trophy is awarded annually, usually in November. Established in 1979 to honor Felix Leclerc.

• 189 • **Felix Awards, Industrial**
For recognition of achievement in record production or show business. Awards are given in the following categories: Best Artist Manager of the Year; Best Record Production Company of the Year; Best Recording Company of the Year; Best Album Design of the Year; Best Record Distributor of the Year; Best Music Publisher of the Year; Best Promotion Firm of the Year; Best Press Agent of the Year; Record Producer of the Year; Show Writer of the Year, Show Diffuser of the Year; Best Sound Engineer of the Year Record; Best Arranger of the Year; Best Concert Producer of the Year; Best Concert Agency of the Year; Lighting Designer of the Year; Best Sound Engineer of the Year - Concert; Best Director of the Year; Best Concert Hall of the Year; Best Video Production Firm of the Year;

Best Video-clip Producer of the Year; Best Television Show of the Year - comedy; and Best Television Production Firm of the Year. Records and Shows produced between June 1 and May 31 are eligible. A trophy is awarded annually in November. Established in 1979 to honor Felix Leclerc.

• 190 •
Adoption Council of Canada
(Conseil d'adoption du Canada)
Eugenie Dore, Exec.Dir.
Bronson Centre
Room 210-211 Bronson Ave.
Ottawa, ON, Canada K1R 6H5
Phone: (613)235-0344
Phone: (613)235-0344
Fax: (613)235-1728
E-mail: acc@adoption.ca
Home Page: http://www.adoption.ca

• 191 • **Helen Allen Award**
For exemplary promotion of adoption, and advocacy for children who wait for families here and abroad. Awarded annually.

• 192 • **Judith Grove Adoption Activist Award**
For significant positive impact on adoption and adoption related issues. Awarded annually.

• 193 • **David Kirk Award**
For excellence in research and teaching in adoption, and for an outstanding contribution to our understanding of adoption kinship.

• 194 • **Victoria Leach Award**
For lengthy and outstanding services to adoptive families and the adoption community. Awarded annually.

• 195 •
Adoptive Families Today
Kathy Casey, Advisor
PO Box 1726
Barrington, IL 60011-1726
Phone: (847)382-0858
Fax: (847)382-0831
E-mail: adopadvo@aol.com
Home Page: http://www.adoptivefamiliestoday.org

• 196 • **AFT Foster Scholarship**
For foster child graduating from high school or getting GED to further their education. Scholarship awarded annually.

• 197 •
Adult Friends for Youth
Sidney M. Rosen Ph.D., Chief Exec. Officer
2119 N. King St., Ste. 303
Honolulu, HI 96819
Phone: (808)848-1411
Fax: (808)848-6873

• 198 • **Youth of the Year**
For agency youth who excels, adult who has contributed significantly to agency's programs. Trophy awarded annually.

• 199 •
Adult Video Association
William Margold, Creative Consultant
270 N Canon Dr., Ste. 1370
Beverly Hills, CA 90210
Phone: (323)436-0060
Fax: (323)654-6850
E-mail: bmargold@aol.com

• 200 • **Lifetime Achievement**
To recognize lifetime contributions to the adult entertainment industry in the performing, directing, first amendment anti-censorship, and general support areas. To be offered to an actor, actress, director, and in "good guy" and "freedom isn't free" categories. Awarded annually with a plaque. Established in 1988.

• 201 •
Advertising Age
Crain Communications Inc.
David Klein, Ed.
711 3rd Ave.
New York, NY 10017-4036
Phone: (212)210-0100
Home Page: http://www.adage.com

• 202 • ***Advertising Age* Awards**
To recognize the best in advertising. The following awards are presented: Advertising Executive of the Year - to recognize excellence in the advertising industry, established in 1971; Agency of the Year established in 1973; Best TV Commercials - for recognition of achievement in television commercials. Awards are presented in 12 categories. One category winner is designated best of show. Established in 1982; Magazine of the Year and Magazine Editor of the Year - to recognize an editor for quality of writing and graphics, as well as circulation and advertising gains; International Ad Agency of the Year - established in 1984; Star Presenter of the Year - to recognize a celebrity/star for outstanding performance in advertisements, established in 1986; Best TV Commercial of the Year - to recognize creative excellence and production values, sales results are considered; Best Original Commercial Music; Best Adaptation of Music for Commercial Use; Best Magazine Ad of the Year - sales results are considered; Best Newspaper Ad of the Year - sales results are considered; Best Radio Commercial of Year - sales results are considered; and Best Outdoor Ad of the Year.

• 203 •
Advertising and Design Club of Canada
Scott Christie, Dir.
160 Pears Ave., Ste. 318
Toronto, ON, Canada M5R 3P8
Phone: (416)423-4113
Fax: (416)423-3362
E-mail: info@theadcc.ca
Home Page: http://www.theadcc.ca

Formerly: Art Directors Club of Toronto.

• 204 • **Advertising Design Club of Canada Awards**
To recognize the best of Canadian creativity in the communication arts industry. Advertising, editorial, and graphic design work produced during the preceding year must be submitted by May 8. Awards are presented in the following categories: Advertising Print, Advertising TV, Advertising Radio, Editorial, and Graphic Design. Gold, silver, and merit awards are presented annually. All work is presented in the ADCC Show Annual. Established in 1948. Formerly: Art Directors Club of Toronto Awards and Show Presentation.

• 205 •
Advertising Club of New York
Gina Grillo, Exec.Dir.
235 Park Ave. S
New York, NY 10003
Phone: (212)533-8080
Fax: (212)533-1929
E-mail: gina@theadvertisingclub.org
Home Page: http://www.theadvertisingclub.org

• 206 • **ANDY Awards**
To honor creativity in advertising throughout the world, recognize the contributions of individuals and companies who create the work and encourage raising the standards of craftsmanship in the industry. Awards are given in print, radio, television, out-of-home, direct mail, video/cinema, interactive, and other media. Winners also compete for the GRANDY Award, which includes a cash prize of $50,000. Awarded annually. Established in 1964.

• 207 •
Advertising Council
Peggy Conlon, Pres./CEO
261 Madison Ave., 11th fl.
New York, NY 10016-2303
Phone: (212)922-1500
Toll-Free: 800-933-7727
Fax: (212)922-1676
E-mail: info@adcouncil.org
Home Page: http://www.adcouncil.org

• 208 • **Advertising Council Award for Public Service**
To recognize an American business leader who has contributed notably in public service to the welfare of the United States and fellow citizens. A sterling silver, engraved Paul Revere punch bowl is awarded annually in November. Established in 1954.

• 209 •
Advertising Media Credit Executives Association
Kay Rice, Pres.
8840 Columbia 100 Pkwy.
Columbia, MD 21045-2158
Phone: (410)992-7609
Fax: (410)740-5574
E-mail: amcea@amcea.org
Home Page: http://www.amcea.org

• 210 • **Advertising Credit Executive of the Year**
To recognize an outstanding credit manager. An inscribed metal plaque on a wood base is awarded annually at the Association's meeting in October. Established in 1953.

• 211 •
Advertising Production Club of New York
Caroll Ann Moore, Pres.
276 Bowery
New York, NY 10012
Phone: (212)334-2018
Fax: (212)431-5786
E-mail: admin@apc-ny.org
Home Page: http://www.apc-ny.org

• 212 • **Thomas Cochrane Sr. Scholarship Award**
To provide financial assistance to full-time graphic arts management students at New York City Technical College/City University of New York. Awarded annually.

• 213 •
Advertising Women of New York
Liz Schroeder, Exec.Dir.
25 W 45th St.
New York, NY 10036
Phone: (212)221-7969
Fax: (212)221-8296
E-mail: liz@awny.org
Home Page: http://www.awny.org

• 214 • **Advertising Woman of the Year**
Honors a woman in the communications industry who has made a significant contribution to her industry, is currently an active participant and can be considered a role model for women. Established in 1965.

• 215 • **Crystal Prism Award**
Recognizes an individual who consistently made contributions to her Club. The recipient is decided by a Board of Directors vote. Awarded annually by each AAF member advertising club in the District Two division. Established in 1971.

• 216 • **President's Award**
Recognizes outstanding contribution to the Club during the current term. Any AWNY member is eligible. Selection is made solely at the discretion of the President. Established in 1968.

• 217 • **Silver Medal Award**
Recognizes men and women who have made outstanding contributions to advertising and who have been active in furthering the industry's standards, creative excellence and responsibility in areas of social concern. Established in 1959.

• 218 •
Advocates for Youth
Bill Barker, Press Sec.
2000 M St. NW, Ste. 750
Washington, DC 20036
Phone: (202)419-3420
Fax: (202)419-1448
E-mail: information@advocatesforyouth.org
Home Page: http://www.advocatesforyouth.org

• 219 • **Teen Health Leadership Award**
Recognizes policymakers who have worked to decrease adolescent pregnancy and sexually transmitted disease, or have worked to increase teens' access to confidential and school-based health care services. Four awards are given annually.

• 220 •
***ADWEEK*, East Edition**
VNU Business Publications, USA, Inc.
770 Broadway
New York, NY 10003
Phone: (646)654-5421
Toll-Free: 800-722-6658
Fax: (646)654-5365
E-mail: info@adweek.com
Home Page: http://www.adweek.com

• 221 • ***Mediaweek*'s Media All-Stars**
To honor outstanding achievement in the field of media planning and buying. Awarded annually. Established in 1985.

• 222 • ***Mediaweek*'s Media Plan of the Year**
To recognize media planning teams for the uniqueness and creativity in placing media. Each year, awards given in different spending categories as well as in various categories of media (i.e. broadcasting, TV, radio, magazines, new media.)

• 223 • **Technology Marketing ICON Awards**
To recognize creative marketing of high-tech products and services. Awarded annually. Formerly: Marketing Computers ICON Awards.

• 224 •
AeA
William T. Archey, Pres. and CEO
North Bldg., Ste. 600
601 Pennsylvania Ave. NW
Washington, DC 20004
Phone: (202)682-9110
Toll-Free: 800-284-4232
Fax: (202)682-9111
E-mail: csc@aeanet.org
Home Page: http://www.aeanet.org

Formerly: (1978) Western Electronic Manufacturers Association - American Electronics Association.

• 225 • **Legislator of the Year Award**
Annual award of recognition for a legislator in the electronics industry.

• 226 • **Medal of Achievement**
For recognition of an industry leader who has made significant contributions to the advancement of electronics. A medal is presented annually. Established in 1959.

• 227 •
Aerospace Education Foundation
Danny D. Marrs, Managing Dir.
1501 Lee Hwy.
Arlington, VA 22209-1198
Phone: (703)247-5839
Toll-Free: 800-291-8480
Fax: (703)247-5853
E-mail: aefstaff@aef.org
Home Page: http://www.aef.org

Formerly: (1995) Air Force Association - Aerospace Education Foundation.

• 228 • **Christa McAuliffe Memorial Award**
Recognizes classroom programs that further concepts of aerospace technologies. Public, private, or parochial teachers - kindergarten through twelfth grade - are eligible. A letter of endorsement from an AFA sponsor, resume, description of the instructional environment description of research/curricular activities must be submitted.

• 229 •
Aerospace Medical Association
Russell B. Rayman MD, Exec.Dir./Sec.-Treas.
320 S Henry St.
Alexandria, VA 22314-3579
Phone: (703)739-2240
Fax: (703)739-9652
E-mail: info@asma.org
Home Page: http://www.asma.org

• 230 • **Louis H. Bauer Founders Award**
For recognition of a significant contribution in space medicine. Members of the Association are eligible for the award. Established in 1961 in honor of Louis H. Bauer, M.D., founder of the Association.

• 231 • Boothby - Edwards Award
For recognition of outstanding research and/or clinical practice directed at the promotion of health and prevention of disease in professional airline pilots. Members of the association are eligible. Established in 1961 in memory of Walter M. Boothby, M.D., pioneer aviation medicine researcher, and Howard K. Edwards, M.D., clinical practitioner of aviation medicine. Sponsored by Harvey W. Watt & Co. Formerly: (1985) Walter M. Boothby Award; (1985) Howard K. Edwards Award.

• 232 • Kent K. Gillingham Award
To recognize significant contribution in the fields of spatial disorientation and situational awareness by a member of the Association. Awarded annually. Established in 1997 to honor the memory of Kent K. Gillingham, M.D., Ph.D. Sponsored by AMST Systemtechnick G.m.b.H.

• 233 • Won Chuel Kay Award
Sponsored by the Korean Aerospace Medical Association and established in honor of Dr. Won Chuel Kay, the award is presented annually for outstanding contributions to international aerospace medicine. Established in 2001.

• 234 • Mary T. Klinker Award
To recognize outstanding contributions to, and achievement in the field of aeromedical evacuation. Established in 1968 by the Flight Nurse Section in memory of Mary T. Klinker, who was killed in a C-5A crash while performing a humanitarian mission. Formerly: Flight Nurse of the Year Award.

• 235 • Sidney D. Leverett, Jr. Environmental Science Award
To recognize those who have made a significant contribution in the field of environmental medicine through a publication in *Aviation, Space and Environmental Medicine* or by activities conducted in support of aerospace systems operations. Established in 1977. Renamed in 1989 to honor Sidney D. Leverett, Jr., Ph.D. Sponsored by NationsBank of Texas, N.A., Military Banking—Ft. Sam Houston Banking Center. Formerly: Environmental Science Award.

• 236 • Eric Liljencrantz Award
To honor excellence as an educator in aerospace medicine, or basic research in the problems of acceleration, altitude, or weightlessness by a member of the Association. Established in 1957 in memory of Cdr. Eric Liljencrantz, MC, USN, whose career in aviation medicine was cut short by his death in an airplane accident in 1942. Sponsored by SmithKline Beecham Pharmaceuticals.

• 237 • Raymond F. Longacre Award
For recognition of outstanding accomplishments in the psychological and psychiatric aspects of aerospace medicine. Members of the Association are eligible. Established in 1947 in memory of Mayor Raymond F. Longacre, MC, U.S.A. Sponsored by the NationsBank of Texas, N.A., Military Banking—Ft. Sam Houston Banking Center.

• 238 • Theodore C. Lyster Award
For recognition of outstanding achievements in the general field of aerospace medicine by a member of the Association. Established in 1947 in memry of Brig. Gen. Theodore C. Lyster, the first Chief Surgeon, Aviation Section, U.S. Army Signal Corps. Sponsored by Lockheed Martin Science and Engineering Service.

• 239 • Harry G. Moseley Award
For recognition of the most outstanding contribution to flight safety by a membr of the Association. Established in 1961 in memory of Col. Harry G. Moseley, USAF, MC, who made material contributions to flight safety.

• 240 • John Paul Stapp Award
To recognize outstanding contributions in the field of aerospace biomechanics and to promote progress in protection from injury resulting from ejection, vibration, and impact. Members of Association are eligible. Awarded annually. Sponsored by Environmental Tectonics Corporation.

• 241 • John A. Tamisiea Award
For recognition of an aviation medical examiner or other individual contributing to the advancement of the art and science of aviation medicine in its application to the general aviation field. Members of the Association are eligible. Established in 1963 in memory of John A. Tamisiea, M.D. Sponsored by the Civil Aviation Medical Association.

• 242 • Arnold D. Tuttle Award
For recognition of the most significant original research by a member of the Association that contributed toward the solution of a challenging problem in aerospace medicine and that was published in *Aviation, Space, and Environmental Medicine.* Established in 1952 in memory of Col. Arnold D. Tuttle, USAF, MC. Sponsored by ZENECA Pharmaceuticals Group.

• 243 • Julian E. Ward Memorial Award
For recognition of superior performance and outstanding achievement in the art and science of aerospace medicine during residency training. A member of the Association who is a resident in aerospace medicine or who completed residency training in the past year is eligible. Established in 1963 in memory of Julian E. Ward, the first member of the Society of U.S. Air Force Flight Surgeons to lose his life in an aircraft accident. Sponsored by the Society of USAF Flight Surgeons of the Aerospace Medical Association.

• 244 •
Aesthetics International Association
Pat Strunk, Sec.
2611 N Belt Line Rd., Ste. 140
Sunnyvale, TX 75182
Phone: (972)203-8530
Toll-Free: 877-968-7539
Fax: (972)226-2339
E-mail: aiathekey@aol.com
Home Page: http://www.beautyworks.com/aia

Formerly: Aestheticians International Association Headquarters.

• 245 • Make-Up Competition
For recognition of outstanding performances and achievement by local aestheticians. Plaques are awarded at shows.

• 246 •
Affaire de Coeur Magazine
3976 Oak Hill Rd.
Oakland, CA 94605
Phone: (510)569-5675
Fax: (510)632-8868
E-mail: louise@affairedecoeur.com
Home Page: http://www.affairedecoeur.com

• 247 • Short Story Contest
To recognize an original romance short story. Short stories must not have been published previously, and must not exceed 1,500 words. The first-place winner receives a monetary prize of $100 and the publishing of their story in the August issue of *Affaire de Coeur.* Held annually.

• 248 •
Africa Travel Association
Patrick Kalifungwa MP, Pres.
347 5th Ave., Ste. 610
New York, NY 10016
Phone: (212)447-1926
Fax: (212)725-8253
E-mail: africatravelasso@aol.com
Home Page: http://www.africa-ata.org

• 249 • Outstanding Leadership Award
For recognition of outstanding leadership within the Association. Members must be nominated by the committee. A plaque is awarded each year at the annual ATA International Congress. Established in 1976.

• 250 • Outstanding Promotional Service Award
For recognition of outstanding promotional service provided to the Association. Members must be nominated by the committee. A plaque is awarded each year at the annual ATA International Congress. Established in 1985 by Murray Vidocler, founder and former Executive Director of the Africa Travel Association.

• 251 • Outstanding Service Award
For recognition of outstanding service provided to the travel industry as it pertains to Africa. Members must be nominated by the committee.

A plaque is awarded each year at the annual ATA International Congress. Established in 1976.

• 252 •
African-American Women's Clergy Association
Bishop Imagene B. Stewart, Presiding Dir.
214 P St. N.W.
Washington, DC 20001
Phone: (202)518-8488
Fax: (202)518-1273
E-mail: imageneshelter@aol.com

• 253 • Social Activist of the Year Award
Annual award of recognition.

• 254 •
African Environmental Research and Consulting Group
Dr. Peter A. Sam, Chm.
14912 Walmer St.
Overland Park, KS 66223-1161
Phone: (913)897-6132
Fax: (913)897-6132
E-mail: aercgc31@juno.com
Home Page: http://www.africaenviro.org

• 255 • Environmental Personality of the Year in Africa
Recignizes achievements in environmental management and community education. Awarded annually.

• 256 •
African Peoples' Christian Organization
Rev. Herbert Daughtry, Pres.
415 Atlantic Ave.
Brooklyn, NY 11217
Phone: (718)596-1991
Fax: (718)625-3410

• 257 • Man/Woman of the Year
To recognize community service contributions. Awarded annually.

• 258 •
African Studies Association
Dr. Carol L. Martin, Exec.Dir.
Rutgers the State Univ. of New Jersey
132 George St.- Douglass Campus
New Brunswick, NJ 08901-1400
Phone: (732)932-8173
Phone: (732)932-3394
Fax: (732)932-3394
E-mail: clmasa@rci.rutgers.edu
Home Page: http://www.africanstudies.org

• 259 • Claude Ake Memorial Award
Encourages young African scholars/activists to carry out research, reflection, and writhing about their ideas and/or activities. Applicants must be Africans who are engage in knowledgebased and reality-informed problem solving to address the continent's development challenges. A stipend of $5000 for research aimed at meeting challenges facing the continent of Africa is awarded annually. An application form must be submitted. Established in 1999.

• 260 • Annual Meeting International Visitors Award
Funds the annual meeting attendance of international scholars. Most awards are made to Africans, preference is given to women and junior scholars, and to individuals who have not recently visited North America. Nominations can be made by individuals, including selfnomination and institution sponsored. Institution sponsors must be members of the African Studies Association and be prepared to arrange and find financial support for the visitor's itinerary. A completed nomination form; a sponsor written detailed cover letter including the extent and nature of support available from institutional and other sources; a two to three page vita; an abstract of the paper the nominee proposes to present; and an itinerary detailing the venue, purpose of visit, and arrival and departure dates must be submitted. The entire packet can be nor more than six pages, including the application form. Application deadline is March 15.

• 261 • Children's Africana Book Awards
Encourages the publication and use of accurate balanced children's materials in Africa. Books must be published in the United States about Africa. Books should be expressly written for children ages 4-18; contain at least 50% content on Africa; be copyrighted by December of the year preceding the award ceremony; and be published or republished U.S. publisher. Nominations must be made by the actual book publisher. A publisher can nominate as many titles as desired.

• 262 • Conover-Porter Award
Recognizes outstanding contributions to African List bibliography or reference works. A monetary prize of $300 is awarded biennially in even-numbered years.

• 263 • Distinguished Africanist Award
Recognizes lifetime of notable contributions to African studies. Nominations are made by ASA members. A vita of the nominee; a detailed letter of nomination justifying the candidature in terms of the criteria for the award; and three similar letters from ASA members must be submitted. A plaque and lifetime membership to the Association are awarded annually. Established in the 1980.

• 264 • Paul Hair Prize
Recognizes the best critical edition or translation into English of primary source materials on Africa. A monetary prize of $300 is awarded biennially in odd-numbered years. Formerly: Text Prize.

• 265 • Herskovits Award
To recognize the author of a distinguished work on Africa published or distributed in the United States during the preceding year. The winning work must be an original scholarly publication. Edited collections, symposia, new editions of previously published books, bibliographies, and dictionaries are not eligible. A monetary prize is awarded annually.

• 266 •
African Wildlife Foundation
Patrick J. Bergin PhD, Pres./CEO
1400 16th St. NW, Ste. 120
Washington, DC 20036
Phone: (202)939-3333
Toll-Free: 888-494-5354
Fax: (202)939-3332
E-mail: africanwildlife@awf.org
Home Page: http://www.awf.org

• 267 • African Wildlife Leadership Award
Presented in recognition of positive example-setting and leadership in line with the aims and mission of the AWF.

• 268 •
Africare
Julius E. Coles, Pres.
440 R St. NW
Washington, DC 20001-1935
Phone: (202)462-3614
Fax: (202)387-1034
E-mail: development@africare.org
Home Page: http://www.africare.org

• 269 • Bishop John T. Walker Humanitarian Award
Annual award of recognition. Selection is made by Africare Board of Directors. AFSIUI666379 UW(WUI)

• 270 •
AFS Intercultural Programs
Leslie Bains, Pres.
71 W 23rd St., 17th Fl.
New York, NY 10010
Phone: (212)807-8686
Toll-Free: 800-AFS-INFO
Fax: (212)807-1001
E-mail: info@afs.org
Home Page: http://www.afs.org

• 271 • Galatti Award for Outstanding Volunteer Service
To recognize an AFS volunteer who, over a sustained period of time, has supported AFS. Individuals affiliated with AFS on a volunteer basis any where in the world who have not previously received this award are eligible. Established in 1983 to honor Stephen Galatti, founder of AFS Exchange Programs.

• 272 •
AGC Education and Research Foundation
333 John Carlyle, Ste. 200
Alexandria, VA 22314
Phone: (703)548-3118
Fax: (703)548-3119
E-mail: info@agc.org
Home Page: http://www.agc.org/index.ww

• 273 • **James L. Allhands Essay Competition**
Recognizes a paper written on construction and/or general contracting. Senior-level students are eligible. $1000 and a trip to the AGC Annual Convention are awarded annually.

• 274 • **William A. Klinger Memorial Award**
$25,000 to develop programs to benefit the construction education community, to promote university-level construction education, and/or for the improvement of the facilities, faculty, and curriculum in construction education

• 275 • **Outstanding Educator Award**
Recognizes permanent university teaching faculty members in construction education. $5000 and all expense paid trip to the AGC Annual Convention are awarded annually. 440041 AGENERGY

• 276 •
Agri-Energy Roundtable
Nicholas E. Hollis, Exec.Dir.
1312 18th St., NW, Ste. 300
Washington, DC 20036
Phone: (202)887-0528
Phone: (202)887-0238
Fax: (202)887-9178
E-mail: agenergy@aol.com
Home Page: http://www.agribusinesscouncil.org/aer.htm

• 277 • **World Food Policy Award**
For recognition of enlightened leadership and exemplary diplomacy in forging effective public and private sector dialogue on food and energy cooperation aimed toward international economic peacekeeping. Selection is by nomination. A plaque is awarded annually at the International Agriculture Forum in Geneva, Switzerland. Established in 1983.

• 278 •
Agricultural and Forestry Experiment Station
School of Natural Resources and Agricultural Sciences
University of Alaska
PO Box 757140
Fairbanks, AK 99775
Phone: (907)474-7083
Fax: (907)474-6567
E-mail: fyafes@uaf.edy
Home Page: http://www.uaf.edu/salrm/afes

• 279 • **Neiland Award**
For academic excellence in natural resources management.

• 280 •
Agricultural History Society
C. Fred Williams, Exec.Sec.-Treas.
PO Box 5075
Department of History
Fargo, ND 58105-5075
Phone: (701)231-5831
Fax: (701)231-5832
E-mail: claire.strom@ndsu.edu
Home Page: http://www.usi.edu/libarts/history/AHS

• 281 • **Vernon Carstensen Memorial Award**
To encourage publication of outstanding articles in *Agricultural History* by recognizing the best article published each year. A monetary prize of $200 is awarded annually. Established in 1980. Additional information is available from Claire Strom, Editor, Agricultural History, North Dakota State University, Fargo, ND 58105-5075.

• 282 • **Everett Eugene Edwards Memorial Award**
To encourage research in the field of agricultural history. Articles by students pursuing a degree and accepted for publication in the quarterly journal, *Agricultural History*, are eligible. A monetary prize of $200 is awarded annually. Established in 1953. Additional information is available from Claire Strom, Editor, Agricultural History, North Dakota State University, Fargo, ND 58105-5075.

• 283 • **Theodore Saloutos Memorial Book Award**
To recognize the author of the best book in the field of the agricultural history of the United States. Books nominated by publishers or others by February 1 of the year following copyright date are eligible. A monetary prize of $500 is presented annually. Established in 1982 by Florence Saloutos in memory of her husband, Theodore Saloutos, an agricultural historian and past president of the society. Additional information is available from Claire Strom, Editor, Agricultural History, North Dakota State University, Fargo, ND 58105-5075

• 284 •
Agricultural Institute of Canada
Tom Beach, Exec.Dir.
280 Albert St., Ste. 900
Ottawa, ON, Canada K1P 5G8
Phone: (613)232-9459
Toll-Free: 888-277-7980
Fax: (613)594-5190
E-mail: office@aic.ca
Home Page: http://www.aic.ca

• 285 • **Agricultural Institute of Canada Fellow**
Recognizes professional distinction. Selection is based on integrity with noteworthy accomplishments in various areas of Canadian agriculture. Members of AIC member organizations are eligible. Official nomination forms are available at the above web site. Nomination deadline is January 31. Established in 1920.

• 286 • **Agricultural Institute of Canada Honorary Member Award**
For recognition of distinction associated with outstanding and continuing accomplishment in, or contribution to any field of Canadian agriculture. Non-members are eligible. Guidelines and nomination form are available at the above web site. Established in 1921.

• 287 • **Grindley Medal**
Recognizes significant contribution to Canadian agriculture. Canadian citizens are eligible. Contribution must have been made in the preceding five years and have a wide reaching impact. Guidelines and nomination form available at the above web site. Established in 1968.

• 288 • **Institute Recognition Award**
For recognition of special service to the institute. Individuals who are not members of the institute are eligible. Guidelines and nomination form are available at the above web site. Established in 1966.

• 289 • **International Recognition Award**
To recognize outstanding contributions to the development of agriculture in the Third World. Members and non-members are eligible. Awarded annually. Established in 1992.

• 290 • **Outstanding Young Agrologist Award**
Recognizes outstanding achievements and service to Canadian agriculture. Members of AIC's member organizations under the age of 40 are eligible. Guidelines and nomination form are available at the above web site. Established in 1995.

• 291 •
Agricultural Relations Council
Amy Keith McDonald, Pres.
62768 N Star Dr.
Montrose, CO 81401
Phone: (970)249-1465
Phone: (254)445-4333
Fax: (970)249-4385
E-mail: jennyp@nama.org
Home Page: http://www.agrelationscouncil.org

• 292 • **Golden ARC Awards**
To recognize excellence in agricultural public relations for campaigns. Awarded annually with plaques for first place and merit. Established in 1989.

• 293 •
AIA New York State, Inc.
33 Elk St.
Albany, NY 12207
Phone: (518)449-3334
Fax: (518)426-8176
E-mail: aianys@aianys.org
Home Page: http://www.aianys.org

Awards are arranged in alphabetical order below their administering organizations

• 294 • AIANYS Educator Award
Established in 2005. Recognizes notable contributions to an architectural educator within New York state.

• 295 • AIANYS Student Award
Established in 2005. Recognizes notable contributions of a student member of AIA/NYS.

• 296 • Community Development Award
Established in 1985. Recognizes individuals who have had a substantial impact on the built environment within New York state. May be granted to any individual, organization, governmental agency, or private corporation whose efforts have resulted in an improvement to the built environment.

• 297 • Matthew W. Del Gaudio Award
To recognize outstanding and valuable service to the profession through promoting the profession of architecture. Members who have provided distinguished service and leadership to the Association and have demonstrated notable competence advancing the profession of architecture are eligible for nomination. Awarded annually.

• 298 • Honorary Member of AUA New York State Award
Established in 1989. Recognizes the outstanding accomplishments of a person outside of the profession of architecture.

• 299 • James William Kideney Gold Medal Award
Established in 1981 in the honor of James William Kideney, one of the founders of the AIA/NYS. Given for notable contributions to the profession of architecture and the professional society. This award also recognizes an active interest in the professional society at the local, state and national level.

• 300 • Legislator of the Year Award
Estalished in 1977. Recognizes outstanding contributions to the profession of architecture by a New York state legislator.

• 301 • President's Award
Established in 1984. Recognizes outstanding commitment to education, industry or government by an AIA/NYS member. The winner will also had to have demonstrated a leadership role in the professional society at the local, state or national level.

• 302 •
AIA Pennsylvania
Caroline Boyce, Exec.Dir.
1405 N. Front St
Harrisburg, PA 17102-2634
Phone: (717)236-4055
Fax: (717)236-5407
E-mail: info@aiapa.org
Home Page: http://www.aiapa.org

• 303 • Design Award
For excellence in design. Recognition award bestowed annually.

• 304 •
AIDS Action Council
Dr. Marsha Martin, Exec.Dir.
1906 Sunderland Pl. NW
Washington, DC 20036
Phone: (202)530-8030
Fax: (202)530-8031
E-mail: aidsaction@aidsaction.org
Home Page: http://www.aidsaction.org

• 305 • National Leadership Awards
Award of recognition. Bestowed in each of four categories: public policy, media, community service, and advocacy. Awarded annually.

• 306 •
AIIM - The Enterprise Content Management Association
A. J. Hyland, Chair
1100 Wayne Ave., Ste. 1100
Silver Spring, MD 20910-5603
Phone: (301)587-8202
Toll-Free: 800-477-2446
Fax: (301)587-2711
E-mail: aiim@aiim.org
Home Page: http://www.aiim.org
Formerly: National Micrographics Association.

• 307 • AIIM Company of Fellows
To recognize those in the Association who merit recognition and distinction for their outstanding contributions to the field of document management; to the organization, applications and administration of document management systems; to the invention, preparation or design of equipment or supplies; or to education. Enrollments are limited to no more four individuals each year. The award was established in 1963.

• 308 • Thomas P. Anderson Sr. Micrographics Awards
To recognize an individual's achievement in overall contributions to the micrographics industry, outstanding program development and innovations and leadership. The award is not necessarily awarded annually.

• 309 • Award of Merit
The Award of Merit is the highest award the association can bestow and recognizes continued, distinguished, and exceptional service to the document management industry. The award, established in 1954, is limited to members of the Company of Fellows and is not necessarily awarded annually.

• 310 • Distinguished Service Citation
To recognize individuals whose outstanding service benefited the advancement of the document management sciences through activities in AIIM chapters, through specific and singularly commendable accomplishments in national activities, or the standards programs. No more than ten individuals are recognized each year. The award was established in 1973.

• 311 • Electronic Imaging Management Award
To recognize individuals or corporations for achievement in electronic imaging. A plaque is awarded annually. Established in 1988.

• 312 • Carl E. Nelson Engineering Award
To recognize outstanding accomplishments in the field of engineering document management. The award is given to individuals who have made significant contributions to the advancement of the field. The award is not necessarily awarded annually.

• 313 • Pioneer Award
To recognize those whose ground-breaking activities in significant areas of the field of document management have subsequently led to the advancement of the field as a whole. The award is not necessarily awarded annually.

• 314 • Special Award
To recognize individuals or organizations of exceptional achievement that have been of outstanding value to the entire field of document management. The award is not necessarily awarded annually.

• 315 •
AIM Magazine
AIM Publication Association
PO Box 1174
Maywood, IL 60153
Phone: (708)344-4414
E-mail: apiladoone@aol.com
Home Page: http://www.aimmagazine.org

• 316 • *Aim Quarterly Magazine* Short Story Award
To encourage and recognize short fiction that embodies and promotes the theme of the brotherhood of man. Works that are a maximum length of 4,000 words and adhere to the theme may be submitted by September 1. A monetary prize of $100 and publication of the story in the fall issue of *Aim Quarterly Magazine* are awarded annually. Established in 1984.

• 317 •
Air and Waste Management Association
Dick Scherr, Exec.Dir.
1 Gateway Ctr., 3rd Fl.
420 Duquesne Blvd.
Pittsburgh, PA 15222
Phone: (412)232-3444
Toll-Free: 800-270-3444
Fax: (412)232-3450
E-mail: info@awma.org
Home Page: http://www.awma.org

• 318 • Frank A. Chambers Award
For recognition of outstanding achievement in the science and art of air pollution control. It

requires accomplishment of a technical nature on the part of the recipient that is considered to be a major contribution to the science and art of air pollution control, the merit of which has been widely recognized by persons in the field. The coverage is intentionally broad since it is expected to recognize achievement in any line of technical endeavor in air pollution control, from pure research to applied science. Both members and nonmembers of A&WMA are eligible. Awarded annually. Established in 1954 in memory of Frank A. Chambers (1885-1951), founder of the Smoke Prevention Association of America, forerunner of A&WMA.

• 319 • **Fellow Grade of Membership**
To recognize members for outstanding contributions to the Association. Candidates can be nominated by an individual member, fellow member or self-nominated. Nominees must have worked in a field related to the mission and objectives of the Association for at least 15 years and put in at least 10 continuous years as an individual member. Established in 1986.

• 320 • **S. Smith Griswold Award**
To recognize outstanding accomplishments in the prevention and control of air pollution. The award is intended to recognize achievement in many types of activities carried on within the governmental prevention and control programs. The recipient may be a governmental agency staff member, past or present. Both members and nonmembers of A&WMA are eligible. Awarded annually. Established in 1971 in memory of S. Smith Griswold (1909-1971), a past president (1962), who focused international attention on air pollution control officers' activities, problems, and achievements.

• 321 • **Honorary Member**
Honorary Memberships are conferred on persons of widely recognized eminence in some part of the field of air pollution control that the Association aims to cover, or who have rendered especially meritorious service to the Association. This may be conferred on members or nonmembers of A&WMA. Awarded when merited.

• 322 • **Richard Beatty Mellon Award**
To recognize an individual whose contributions of a civic nature, whether administrative, legislative, or judicial have aided substantially in the abatement of air pollution. Eligibility for the award requires the sincere and constant effort of an individual over a period of time to develop or increase interest in or acceptance of the cause of air pollution control and waste management for the betterment of man's environment. This individual should have attained wide prominence and be well known for his interest in air pollution control. Both members and nonmembers of A&WMA are eligible. Awarded annually. Established in 1954 in memory of Richard Beatty Mellon (1858-1933) who, in the desire to benefit mankind, with his brother, Andrew William Mellon, established the Mellon Institute of Industrial Research in 1913 and led in instituting and sustaining the first modern investigations looking to ways and means for controlling the pollution of the atmosphere.

• 323 • **George T. Minasian Award**
To recognize the Association's Sections having the most outstanding records of activity and accomplishments during the previous year. Established to honor George T. Minasian, for his many years of distinguished service in the cause of clean air, particularly his local Section activities.

• 324 • **Lyman A. Ripperton Award**
Award of recognition. For inspiring students to achieve excellence. Awarded annually. Established in 1980 in memory of Lyman A. Ripperton (1921-1978), a practitioner in education and research for the control of air pollution.

• 325 • **J. Deane Sensenbaugh Environmental Technology Award**
In recognition of an outstanding organizational achievement waste management. Material/waste engineering projects worthy of consideration include, but are not limited to, production process changes that minimize by-product formation, processes for recycling/reuse of by-products or wastes, applied novel techniques for destroying wastes, and overall improved systems for waste disposal. Recipients can be a company or individual whose contribution to state of the art technology has been recognized and accepted in commercial status within the 10-year period prior to the request for nominations. Nomination deadline is November 1. Awarded annually. Established in 1986.

• 326 • **Waste Management Award**
To recognize outstanding achievement in waste management, waste prevention, or as an educator in waste management. Awarded annually. Established in 1989.

• 327 •
Air Force Association
Donald L. Peterson, Exec.Dir.
1501 Lee Hwy.
Arlington, VA 22209-1198
Phone: (703)247-5800
Toll-Free: 800-727-3337
Fax: (703)247-5853
E-mail: polcom@afa.org
Home Page: http://www.afa.org

• 328 • **AF ROTC Cadet of the Year Award**
To recognize the top Air Force ROTC Cadet. The majority of the Association's awards are presented at the national conference in September. Established in 1984.

• 329 • **AFMC Junior Management Award**
For outstanding contributions to management while assigned to Air Force Materiel Command. The majority of the Association's awards are presented at the national conference in September. Formerly: (1993) Air Force Association AFLC Logistics Junior Management Awards; (1993) Air Force Association AFSC Junior Management Award.

• 330 • **AFMC Logistics Executive Management Award**
For outstanding contributions to management while assigned to Air Force Materiel Command. The majority of the Association's awards are presented at the national conference in September. Formerly: (1993) Air Force Association AFLC Logistics Executive Management Award; (1993) Air Force Association AFSC Distinguished Award for Management.

• 331 • **AFMC Middle Management Award**
For outstanding contributions to management while assigned to Air Force Materiel Command. The majority of the Association's awards are presented at the national conference in September. Formerly: (1993) Air Force Association AFLC Logistics Middle Management Award; (1993) Air Force Association AFSC Management Awards.

• 332 • **AFRES Outstanding Unit Award**
To recognize the Air Force Reserve Unit that displays superior performance and outstanding achievement during the year. The majority of the Association's awards are presented at the national conference in September. Established in 1955.

• 333 • **Air Force Test Team of the Year Award**
To recognize outstanding achievement by a U.S. Air Force test team engaged in the test and evaluation of a defense acquisition program. Established in 1995.

• 334 • **Air National Guard Outstanding Unit Award**
To recognize an Air National Guard Unit for outstanding airmanship. The majority of the Association's awards are presented at the national conference in September. Established in 1955.

• 335 • **John R. Alison Award**
To acknowledge leadership in the defense community that has led to a deeper appreciation of the unique contributions of industry to national security. Established in 1992.

• 336 • **H. H. Arnold Award**
This, the Association's highest honor, is given to recognize aerospace's Man or Woman of the Year for the most outstanding contributions in the military field of aerospace activity. Both individuals and groups are eligible. A metal plaque mounted in a velvet-lined shadow box is awarded. The majority of the Association's awards are presented at the national conference in September. Established in 1948.

• 337 • **CMSAF Thomas N. Barnes Award**
To recognize the best Crew Chief in the Air Force. Awarded annually. The majority of the Association's awards are presented at the na-

Awards are arranged in alphabetical order below their administering organizations

tional conference in September. Established in 1988. Formerly: Crew Chief of the Year Award.

• 338 • Best Space Operations Crew Award
To recognize the outstanding efforts of our space crews. The majority of the Association's awards are presented at the national conference in September. Established in 1989.

• 339 • Lt. General Claire Lee Chennault Award
For recognition of the Outstanding Aerial Warfare Tactician(s) of the Air Force. A metal plaque on a walnut base is displayed in the Pentagon. Small replicas are presented to the winners. The majority of the Association's awards are presented at the national conference in September. Established in 1982 in honor of Lt. General Chennault, the tactician commander of the Flying Tigers.

• 340 • Citation of Honor
For recognition of distinguished activity in various aspects of the field of aeronautics. Both individuals and groups are eligible. Bronze plaques are awarded. The majority of the Association's awards are presented at the national conference in September. Established in 1978.

• 341 • Civil Air Patrol Aerospace Education Cadet of the Year
To recognize the top CAP Cadet in the aerospace education area. The majority of the Association's awards are presented at the national conference in September. Established in 1970. Formerly: Civil Air Patrol Cadet of the Year.

• 342 • Civilian Awards
To recognize civilian employees. The following awards are given: Civilian Wage Employee of Year Award, Civilian Program Specialist of the Year Award, Civilian Program Manager of the Year Award, and Civilian Senior Manager of the Year Award. The majority of the Association's awards are presented at the national conference in September. Established in 1989.

• 343 • Department of Veteran's Affairs Employee of the Year Award
For distinguished service to veterans by an employee of the Department of Veterans Affairs. A metal plaque on a walnut base is awarded. The majority of the Association's awards are presented at the national conference in September. Established in 1948. Formerly: Veteran's Administration Employee of the Year Award.

• 344 • Thomas P. Gerrity Award
For recognition of significant contributions to national security in the field of systems and logistics. A metal plaque on a walnut base is awarded. The majority of the Association's awards are presented at the national conference in September. Established in 1968.

• 345 • General Curtis E. LeMay Bomber Aircrew Award
For recognition of the most outstanding bomber aircrew in the U.S. Air Force. A metal plaque on a walnut base is displayed in the Pentagon. Winners are given small replicas. The majority of the Association's awards are presented at the national conference in September. Established in 1982 in honor of General LeMay, who developed formation bombing techniques in World War II and built Strategic Air Command into an all-jet force. Formerly: General Curtis E. LeMay Strategic Aircrew Award.

• 346 • General Billy Mitchell Award for C4 Excellence
To honor the C4 professional who most enhanced the Air Force's war-fighting capability. Established in 1991. Formerly: Gen. Billy Mitchell Award.

• 347 • Paul W. Myers Award
For outstanding contribution to the continued good health of the men and women of the United States Air Force by a young physician. The majority of the Association's awards are presented at the national conference in September. Established in 1982.

• 348 • General Jerome F. O'Malley Award
For recognition of the best reconnaissance crew in the United States Air Force. The majority of the Association's awards are presented at the national conference in September. Established in 1985.

• 349 • Joan Orr Award
To recognize the outstanding Air Force spouse of the year. The majority of the Association's awards are presented at the national conference in September. Established in 1987.

• 350 • Verne Orr Award
For recognition of the best utilization of human resources in the USAF. The majority of the Association's awards are presented at the national conference in September. Named for the former Secretary of the Air Force, Verne Orr. Established in 1985.

• 351 • General Thomas S. Power Missile Crew Award
For recognition of the most outstanding Missile Combat crew in the Air Force. A metal plaque on a walnut base is displayed in the Pentagon. The majority of the Association's awards are presented at the national conference in September. Established in 1982 in honor of General Thomas S. Power, the father of SAC's intercontinental ballistic missile force, who planned and introduced the Atlas, Titan, and Minuteman ICBMs. Formerly: General Thomas S. Power Strategic Combat Missle Crew Award.

• 352 • Presidents' Award for the AFRES
For recognition of the outstanding Air Force Reserve flight crew of the year. The majority of the Association's awards are presented at the national conference in September. Established in 1962. Formerly: AFA Air Force Reserve Troop Carrier Wing Trophy.

• 353 • General Edwin W. Rawlings Award for Environmental Achievement (Manager and Technician)
For outstanding environmental achievements within the United States Air Force. A metal plaque on a walnut base is awarded to a manager and a technician. The majority of the Association's awards are presented at the national conference in September. Established in 1981. Formerly: (1993) General Edwin W. Rawlings Award for Energy Conservation (Manager and Technician).

• 354 • Chief Master Sergeant Dick Red Award for ANG Aerospace Maintenance
For recognition of exceptional technical expertise, leadership, contributions to training, and aircraft maintenance by an enlisted member of ANG. The majority of the Association's awards are presented at the national conference in September. Established in 1984.

• 355 • Juanita Redmond Award for Nursing
For outstanding and sustained professional excellence in all aspects of nursing duty. The majority of the Association's awards are presented at the national conference in September. Established in 1981.

• 356 • Stuart Reichart Award
For recognition of the outstanding achievements in the field of law within the United States Air Force. The majority of the Association's awards are presented at the national conference in September. Established in 1982.

• 357 • Earl T. Ricks Award
For recognition of outstanding airmanship and flying skill within the Air National Guard. The majority of the Association's awards are presented at the national conference in September. Established in 1954.

• 358 • David C. Shilling Award
For distinguished service in the field of flight. A metal plaque on a walnut base is awarded. The majority of the Association's awards are presented at the national conference in September. Established in 1948.

• 359 • W. Stuart Symington Award
To recognize the greatest civilian contribution in the field of national defense. A metal plaque mounted in a velvet-lined shadow box is awarded. The majority of the Association's awards are presented at the national conference in September. Established in 1986.

• 360 • Lt. General William H. Tunner Aircrew Award
To recognize the most outstanding Strategic Airlift crew in the Air Force. A metal plaque on a walnut base is displayed in the Pentagon. Established in 1982 in honor of Lt. General Tunner, commander of the Berlin Airlift and engineer of the "Hump" resupply mission over the Himalayas from India during World War II.

• 361 • United States Air Force Twelve Outstanding Airmen of the Year
For recognition of outstanding airmen each year. Nominations are made by the major commanders, separate operating agencies, Air Force Reserve, and Air National Guard. The following criteria are considered: superior general job performance; job knowledge and leadership qualities applied to a specific Air Force problem or situation; development of new techniques or procedures resulting in increased mission effectiveness; noteworthy self-improvement through on- or off-duty educational studies, participation in professional or cultural societies/associations, or development of creative abilities; participation in social, cultural, or religious activities in the military and/or civilian community that contribute directly or indirectly to community or group welfare, morale, or status; other significant achievements on- or off-duty that by their nature or results clearly distinguish the Airman from others of equal or higher grade; Air Force or civilian awards in recognition of personal service or contribution; and demonstrated ability as an articulate and positive Air Force spokesperson. The majority of the Association's awards are presented at the national conference in September. Established in 1956.

• 362 • USAF Personnel Manager of the Year
For recognition of outstanding performance as a personnel manager while serving in the USAF. The majority of the Association's awards are presented at the national conference in September. Established in 1970.

• 363 • Hoyt S. Vandenberg Award
For distinguished service to national security in the field of aerospace education. A metal plaque on a walnut base is awarded. The majority of the Association's awards are presented at the national conference in September. Established in 1948.

• 364 • Theodore von Karman Award
For distinguished service in the field of science and engineering. A metal plaque on a walnut base is awarded. The majority of the Association's awards are presented at the national conference in September. Established in 1948.

• 365 • Gill Robb Wilson Award
For distinguished service in the field of arts and letters. A metal plaque on a walnut base is awarded. The majority of the Association's awards are presented at the national conference in September. Established in 1948.

• 366 •
Air Force Association of Canada (L'Association des Forces aeriennes du Canada)
Bob Tracy, Exec.Dir.
PO Box 2460. Sta. D
PO Box 2460, Sta. D
Ottawa, ON, Canada K1P 5W6
Phone: (613)992-7482
Fax: (613)995-2196
E-mail: director@airforce.ca
Home Page: http://www.airforce.ca

• 367 • Aviation Awards
Recognizes excellence in aviation in five categories. Awarded annually. Inquire for list of categories and additional application information.

• 368 •
Air Force Historical Foundation
Gen.(Ret.) William Y. Smith USAF, Pres.
1535 Command Dr., Ste. A-122
Andrews AFB, MD 20762-7002
Phone: (301)736-1959
Phone: (301)981-2139
Fax: (301)981-3574
E-mail: afhf@earthlink.net
Home Page: http://www.afhistoricalfoundation.com

• 369 • Air Force Academy Award
Recognizes an outstanding article on the history of airpower. Nominees must be Air Force Academy seniors. Papers for competition are selected and judged by the history department staff at the academy. An engraved plaque and $500 are awarded when merited.

• 370 • Air Force Institute of Technology Award
Recognizes the thesis that provides the most significant contribution to an understanding of the historical factors affecting an Air Force or DOD problem, event or process. An engraved plaque and $500 is awarded annually. Formerly: (2006) General Bryce Pow II Award.

• 371 • Air Force ROTC Scholarship
Recognizes leadership, citizenship, and outstanding academic and military achievement and rewards individuals demonstrating potential for future contributions in the national interest and to the Air Force. Nominations are made by commanders from four regions (Northeast, Northwest, Southeast, and Southwest). Candidates names and records must be submitted. $1000 is awarded.

• 372 • Air War College Award for Research and Writing
Recognizes the best aerospace report of major historical interest to the United States Air Force during the year. Authors must be students at the Air War College. An engraved plaque, $500 and a letter from the AFHF's president are awarded.

• 373 • Fellowship in Aviation History
To support either dissertation or post-doctoral research in aviation history. Individuals who have passed all requirements for the Ph.D. at any accredited university, except the dissertation, or who have their doctorate and are U.S. residents are eligible. A monetary award of $1,000 is presented annually in January. Established in 1975.

• 374 • Logistics Lessons Learned Award
Recognizes the best article published in the *Air Force Journal of Logistics* which contains logistics lessons learned. Three articles are selected by the Editor-in-Chief and his staff. They are then judged by the foundation president and staff. A plaque, a one-year membership in the foundation, and recognition on *Air Power History* is awarded annually.

• 375 • School of Advanced Airpower Studies Thesis Award
Recognizes the best aerospace report of major historical interest to the United States Air Force during the year. Authors must be students of the School of Advanced Airpower Studies. The winner is selected by the head of the school.

• 376 • Two Air Forces Award USAF/RAF
Recognizes the best article written during the year that drew on the USAF/RAF heritage and history. Given jointly from the U.S. Air Force Academy and the Royal Air Force Historical Society. Papers are selected from junior officers in the service of both organizations. A plaque and a congratulatory letter from the President of the Air Force Historical Foundation or the Chairman of the Royal Air Force Historical Society are awarded annually.

• 377 • Joe and Josephine Warth Air Force Historical Foundation Award
Supports education in airpower history. 14 schools are awarded a year subscription to *Air Power History*, the quarterly journal of the Air Force Historical Foundation.

• 378 • Writing Awards
For recognition of the best articles published each calendar year in *Air Power History* in the following categories: autobiographical, popular, and scholarly. Members of the Editorial Advisory Board of *Air Power History* may nominate writers of articles which appeared during the previous year in the magazine. A monetary award and a certificate are awarded annually. Established in 1979.

• 379 •
Air Traffic Control Association
Paul B. Bollinger Jr., Pres.
1101 King St., Ste. 300
Alexandria, VA 22314
Phone: (703)299-2430
Fax: (703)299-2437
E-mail: info@atca.org
Home Page: http://www.atca.org

Awards are arranged in alphabetical order below their administering organizations

• 380 • ACTA Special Medallion Award
To recognize an individual for outstanding achievement in air traffic control.

• 381 • Air Traffic Control Specialist of the Year Award
To recognize an individual military or civilian air traffic control specialist acting in a non-supervisory capacity who has during the previous year performed in an exemplary manner in support of the air traffic control system. A medallion is awarded in each specialist discipline in enroute, terminal, and flight service facilities.

• 382 • Airway Transportation Systems Specialist of the Year
To recognize an individual military or civilian airway facilities technician acting in a non-supervisory capacity who has during the previous year performed in an exemplary or extraordinary manner in support of the air traffic control system. A medallion is awarded. Formerly: Airway Facilities Technician of the Year.

• 383 • ATCA Industrial Award
To recognize an industry or group of industries for an outstanding achievement or contribution which has added to the quality, safety, or efficiency of the air traffic control system. A medallion is awarded.

• 384 • ATCA Life Cycle Management Award
Recognizes outstanding achievement or contribution which has added to the quality, safety, or efficiency of ATC. Individuals or groups of military or civilian life cycle management specialists are eligible.

• 385 • Chairman's Citation of Merit Awards
To recognize an individual for outstanding achievement in air traffic control.

• 386 • Glen A. Gilbert Memorial Award
To honor the outstanding long-term achievements of an individual in the field of aviation. Anyone who has demonstrated a long-term commitment to excellence in aviation from government, industry, education, or the private sector is eligible. The award is open to foreign nationals, as well as citizens of the United States. A trophy is awarded annually when merited. Established in 1986 in honor of Glen A. Gilbert, known as one of the "Fathers of Air Traffic Control," whose life personified commitment to achievement, professionalism, and excellence.

• 387 • George W. Kriske Memorial Award
To recognize an individual for an outstanding career which has added to the quality, safety, or efficiency of the air traffic control system. A medallion is awarded.

• 388 • William A. Parenteau Memorial Award
To recognize an individual for an outstanding achievement or contribution during the previous year which has added to the quality, safety, or efficiency of the air traffic control system. A medallion is awarded.

• 389 • General E. R. Quesada Memorial Award
To recognize an individual for an outstanding achievement and contribution during the previous year as a manager in the air traffic control system. A medallion is awarded. Formerly: General E. R. Quesada Award.

• 390 • Small and Disadvantaged Business Award
To honor a small business concern for an outstanding achievement or contribution which has added to the quality, safety, or efficiency of the air traffic control system. A medallion is awarded.

• 391 • Technical Writing Awards
To recognize an outstanding paper on the air traffic control system. Presented to the first, second, and third place technical article contributed to the *Journal of Air Traffic Control.* A medallion is awarded for first prize.

• 392 • Charles E. Varnell Memorial Award for Small Business
Recognizes outstanding achievement or contribution which has added to the quality, safety, or efficiency of ATC. Formerly: (2006) ATCA Small Business Award.

• 393 • Earl F. Ward Memorial Award
To recognize a group for an outstanding achievement or contribution during the previous year which has added to the quality, safety, or efficiency of the air traffic control system. A medallion is awarded.

• 394 •
Air Transport World
J.A. Donoghue, Editorial Dir.
The Blair Bldg.
8380 Colesville Rd.
Suite 700
Silver Spring, MD 20910
Phone: (301)650-2420
Fax: (301)650-2433
E-mail: bfreeman@penton.com
Home Page: http://www.atwonline.com

• 395 • *Air Transport World* Awards
To recognize airlines, members of the manufacturing industry serving the airlines, and other members of the airline community for outstanding service and achievement. Anyone may be nominated. Self-nomination is accepted. Members of the editorial staff of *Air Transport World* also submit nominations. Major factors considered in the selection process include: overall company health, overall excellence in operations, consistent growth and performance over the preceding few years, good safety record, an industry leader in one or more fields, and a particular category. The following awards are presented when merited: Airline of the Year, Commuter/Regional Airline of the Year, Technology Achievement Award, Passenger Service Award, Industry/Public Service Award, Financial Management Award, and Labor Relations Award and Airline Media/Public Relations Award. Awarded annually. Established in 1973.

• 396 •
Aircraft Owners and Pilots Association
Phil Boyer, Pres.
421 Aviation Way
Frederick, MD 21701
Phone: (301)695-2000
Toll-Free: 800-USA-AOPA
Fax: (301)695-2375
E-mail: aopahq@aopa.org
Home Page: http://www.aopa.org

• 397 • Joseph B. Hartranft Award
To recognize outstanding individuals in government who have made significant contributions to general aviation. Nominations are not accepted.

• 398 • Max Karant Award for Excellence in Aviation Journalism
To recognize individuals in the general, non-trade media who have made significant contributions to aviation through insightful coverage of the issues involved. Awards are presented in four categories: print, radio, and TV/cable - news or short feature and TV/Cable - program length. Works published or broadcast during the previous calendar year must be submitted by April 15. A monetary award of $1,000 is presented in each category. Awarded annually. Established in 1990 to honor Max Karant, former newspaper reporter, first editor of *AOPA PILOT* magazine and long-time senior officer of the Association.

• 399 • Laurence P. Sharples Perpetual Award
To recognize an outstanding individual in the private sector who has made a significant contribution to the advancement of general aviation and to provide an incentive for others to do the same. Nominations are not accepted. Established in honor of Laurence P. Sharples, an AOPA founder, recognized by his unselfish contributions to general aviation.

• 400 •
Airports Council International - North America
Maryanne Merkesas, Receptionist
1775 K St. NW, Ste. 500
Washington, DC 20006
Phone: (202)293-8500
Toll-Free: 888-424-7767
Fax: (202)331-1362
E-mail: mmerkezas@aci-na.org
Home Page: http://www.aci-na.org

• 401 • Airport Commissioners Roundtable Congressional Leadership Award
To recognize a member of Congress for his or her strong support of the legislative goals and objectives of the airports of the United States. Established in 1989.

• 402 • William E. Downes Jr. Memorial Award
For recognition of achievement in airport development and aviation leadership. Individuals may be nominated. Established in 1978 in memory of William E. Downes, Jr.

• 403 • Peggy Hereford Excellence in Communications Award
To recognize excellence in airport marketing, public relations, communications, and advertising campaigns. Nominations must be submitted by ACI-NA member airports, and associates, although outside production is accepted. Awarded annually at the Council's Annual Conference in the fall. Established in 1990. Formerly: Peggy Hereford Airport Communication Excellence Award.

• 404 •
Alabama Library Association
Jane Garrett, Pres.
The Bailey Bldg., Ste. 395
400 S Union St.
Montgomery, AL 36104
Phone: (334)263-1272
Toll-Free: 877-563-5146
Fax: (334)265-1281
E-mail: mdginc@bellsouth.net
Home Page: http://allanet.org

• 405 • Alabama Authors Award
To encourage and recognize Alabama authors and promote interest in local authors' books. Works of fiction, nonfiction, and children's literature are considered. Authors must have been born in Alabama or have lived in Alabama for at least five years. Honorees must be living. A monetary award of $100, a plaque, and travel expenses to the state convention are awarded annually in each category when merited. Established in 1957.

• 406 •
Alabama Sheriffs Association
Robert D. Timmons, Exec.Dir.
514 Washington Ave.
Montgomery, AL 36104-4385
Phone: (334)264-7827
Toll-Free: 800-622-7827
Fax: (334)269-5588
E-mail: alsheriffs@aol.com
Home Page: http://www.alabamasheriffs.com

• 407 • Alabama Sheriffs Association Scholarship
For Alabama students. Scholarship awarded annually.

• 408 •
Alabama Textile Manufacturers Association
5950 Carmichael Pl., Ste. 210
Montgomery, AL 36117
Phone: (334)279-1250
Fax: (334)279-1225

• 409 • Safety Achievement
For safety records. Recognition award bestowed annually.

• 410 • Textile Citizen of the Year
For community service. Monetary award bestowed annually.

• 411 •
Alabama Writers' Forum
Tess Ware, Asst. Dir.
Alabama State Council on the Arts
201 Monroe St.
Montgomery, AL 36130-1800
Phone: (334)242-4076
Fax: (334)240-3269
E-mail: awf@arts.alabama.gov
Home Page: http://www.writersforum.org

• 412 • High School Literary Arts Award
For grades 9-12 in poetry, fiction, drama, creative nonfiction, and senior portfolio. Monetary award bestowed annually.

• 413 •
Alamogordo Music Theatre
Tamara Hansen, Pres.
PO Box 266
Alamogordo, NM 88311
E-mail: daviess@zianet.com
Home Page: http://www.zianet.com/amt

• 414 • Don Fox Memorial Scholarship
For graduating high school senior studying the arts. Scholarship awarded annually.

• 415 •
Albanian Catholic Institute
Raymond Frost, Exec.Dir.
Univ. of San Francisco
650 Parker Ave.
San Francisco, CA 94118
Phone: (415)422-6966
Phone: (415)422-2188
Fax: (415)387-1867
Home Page: http://www.albanian-catholic-institute.org

• 416 • Skanderbeg Medal
Recognizes contribution to Albanian people and culture. Awarded periodically.

• 417 •
Alberta Irrigation Projects Association
David Hill, Exec.Dir.
909 Lethbridge Centre Tower
400 4th Ave. S
Lethbridge, AB, Canada T1J 4E1
Phone: (403)328-3063
Fax: (403)327-1043
E-mail: info@aipa.org
Home Page: http://www.aipa.org

• 418 • Bronze Irrigation Award
For the most valuable contribution of the year. Nominations are accepted in one of the following categories: Water and Agriculture Financial and Value Added and Goverance.

• 419 • Gold Irrigation Award
For meritorious/distinguished lifetime achievement. Applicants must have over 20 years of consistent support to irrigation.

• 420 • Silver Irrigation Award
Recognizes substantial contribution to irrigation. Applicants must display 10 to 20 year consistent commitment to the improvement of irrigation or irrigation related activities.

• 421 •
Alberta Motion Picture Industries Association
Alan Brooks, Exec.Dir.
Jasper Centre
11456 Jasper Ave., Ste. 401
Edmonton, AB, Canada T5K 0M1
Phone: (780)944-0707
Toll-Free: 800-814-7779
Fax: (780)426-3057
E-mail: abrooks@ampia.org
Home Page: http://www.ampia.org

• 422 • Alberta Film and Television Awards
To recognize outstanding achievements by Alberta filmmakers. Sometimes called the Rosie Awards, they are presented in 24 Class (Best Program)categories, including Best Documentary, Best Drama Over 60 Minutes (Best Movie) and Best Musical/Variety Special, etc., plus30 Craft categories, including Best Director, Best Screenwriter and Best Cinematography, etc. Two special awards are also presented: the Friend of the Industry Award and the Distinguished Achievement Award. Awarded annually with trophies. Established in 1974.

• 423 •
Alberta Theatre Projects
Gie Roberts, Mng.Dir.
220 9th Ave. SE
Calgary, AB, Canada T2G 5C4
Phone: (403)294-7475
Fax: (403)294-7493
E-mail: askatp@atplive.com
Home Page: http://www.atplive.com

• 424 • **Harry and Martha Cohen Award**
For recognition of a sustained and significant contribution to theatre in Calgary. Any individual or group of individuals who has made an outstanding and long-term contribution to theatre in Calgary is eligible for nomination. A monetary prize of $1,400 and a plaque are awarded annually. Established in 1985 by Philip, Cheryl, Faye, and David Cohen on the occasion of the 40th wedding anniversary of their parents, Drs. Harry and Martha Cohen.

• 425 •
Alcoa Inc.
201 Isabella St.
Pittsburgh, PA 15212-5858
Phone: (412)553-4545
Fax: (412)553-4498
Home Page: http://www.alcoa.com

• 426 • **Chairman's Award**
For recognition of significant contributions to the development and implementation of advanced materials and processing technology. Employees are selected by the Chairman of Alcoa. A plaque is awarded. Established in 1986.

• 427 • **Arthur Vining Davis Award**
For recognition of outstanding group contributions in the area of Alcoa technology. Projects recently implemented are considered. Patentability, technical intensity, and functional and economical advantage are considered measures of a project's novelty. It must also demonstrate corporate fit - strategic importance, commercial benefit, and cost effective and manufacturing capability. A medallion is awarded. Established in 1984 in honor of Arthur Vining Davis, Alcoa's Chairman from 1914-1948 and, more than any other individual, responsible for Aluminum's first century of success.

• 428 • **Francis C. Frary Award**
To recognize the individual who consistently has made outstanding contributions to Alcoa's technological progress. Individuals with a minimum of five years active employment who have demonstrated high standards of originality, dedication, and integrity in their work; have shown encouragement to technical colleagues; and have enhanced Alcoa's reputation as a leader in technology are eligible. A bust of Francis C. Frary is awarded. Established in 1984 in honor of Francis C. Frary, a leading world figure in aluminum research for more than 40 years.

• 429 •
Alcuin Society
Anne Carscallen, Sec.
PO Box 3216
Vancouver, BC, Canada V6B 3X8
Phone: (604)937-3293
Fax: (604)888-9052
E-mail: info@alcuinsociety.com
Home Page: http://www.alcuinsociety.com

• 430 • **Alcuin Book Design Awards**
Recognizes the work of Canadian book designers. Books published in Canada during the previous year are eligible. Selection is based on the relation of the design concept to the content; use of color, type, and illustration; stock used in text block; binding; covering; and overall finish. Publishers may submit titles in the following categories-Prose:Fiction; Prose:Non-Fiction; Prose:Non-Fiction-Illustrated; Poetry; Pictorial; Children's; Reference; and Limited Editions. Only Limited Editions are returned to the publisher. A $15 entry fee and completed nomination form (available on-line) must be submitted for each title. Established in 1982. 1982.

• 431 •
Alexander Graham Bell Association for the Deaf and Hard of Hearing
K. Todd Houston PhD, Exec.Dir./CEO
3417 Volta Pl. NW
Washington, DC 20007
Phone: (202)337-5220
Phone: (202)337-5221
Toll-Free: (866)337-5220
Fax: (202)337-8314
E-mail: info@agbell.org
Home Page: http://www.agbell.org

• 432 • **Alexander Graham Bell Award**
To recognize meritorious service to the deaf. Individuals or organizations, which are not engaged professionally in the field of education of the deaf, are eligible. Contributions to the field may be local, national, or international, and must have been made during the five years preceding the bestowal of the award. Nominations may be made by members of the Association. A plaque is presented when merited. Established in 1963.

• 433 • **Alexander Graham Bell DHHS Youth Achievement Award (Deaf and Hard of Hearing Section)**
To recognize the achievements of hearing-impaired youths who use speech, speech reading, and residual hearing to communicate. Children of Bell Association members who attend elementary or secondary school; have a hearing impairment; and use speech, speech reading and listening skills to communicate; are eligible. A certificate is awarded annually. Established in 1983. Formerly: (1983) ODAS Youth Achievement Award.

• 434 • **Alexander Graham Bell Honors**
To honor noteworthy and significant service to the deaf. Individuals in the field of education of the deaf or other fields of direct benefit to the deaf are eligible. Nominations may be made by members of the Association. A plaque is presented when merited. Established in 1965.

• 435 • **Alexander Graham Bell Volta Award**
For recognition of contributions in the development of public awareness of the problems and potentials of people who are hearing impaired. Individuals, publications, or agencies making a significant contribution, both nationally and internationally, are eligible. A plaque is awarded annually when merited. Established in 1971.

• 436 • **Youth Achievement Awards**
To recognize leadership qualities in oral deaf children and youth. Award is a non-monetary certificate.

• 437 •
All-America Rose Selections
Charlie Anderson, Pres.
Ruder Finn/Switzer
388 Market St., Ste. 1400
San Francisco, CA 94111
Phone: (415)348-2731
Phone: (415)541-0750
Fax: (415)541-0720
E-mail: walshe@ruderfinnswitzer.com
Home Page: http://www.rose.org

• 438 • **All-America Rose Selections Award of Excellence**
To encourage the production of outstanding rose hybrids. Plaques are awarded, and the award winning roses are publicized throughout the United States. Awarded annually, provided rose candidates of high quality are available. Established in 1939.

• 439 • **All-America Rose Selections Certificate of Merit**
To recognize AARS-accredited public rose gardens which are maintained in excellent condition throughout the growing season. Certificates are presented to the people who maintain the public rose gardens, but seldom receive credit for their good work. Awarded annually. Established in 1982.

• 440 • **Public Rose Garden Achievement Award**
To give recognition to public rose garden maintenance people who provide the public with outstanding rose gardens. Eligible candidates must be associated with a public rose garden of highest quality, have fine maintenance, and an active educational program for the public with regard to the care and culture of roses. A bronze plaque is awarded annually. Established in 1972.

• 441 •
All-America Selections
1311 Butterfield Rd., Ste. 310
Downers Grove, IL 60515-5605

• 442 • **Medallion of Honor**
For recognition of achievement in flower and/or vegetable and seed breeding and distinguished service to horticulture. Individuals of any nation are nominated by the council of judges. A silver medallion and plaque are awarded as merited. Awardees are considered annually and the number of awards presented varies as merited. Established in 1932.

• 443 •
Allergy/Asthma Information Association (Allergie Asthme Association d'information)
Mary Allen, Exec.Dir.
PO Box 100
Toronto, ON, Canada M9W 5K9
Phone: (416)679-9521
Toll-Free: 800-611-7011
Fax: (416)679-9524
E-mail: national@aaia.ca
Home Page: http://www.aaia.ca

• 444 • **Riva Cohen Award**
Recognizes outstanding voluntary contributions to the health and social well-being of allergic Canadians. Awarded annually.

• 445 • **Distinguished Volunteer Service Award**
Recognizes noteworthy contributions. Applicants must be association members. Awarded annually.

• 446 •
Alliance for Children and Families
11700 W Lake Park Dr.
Milwaukee, WI 53224-3099
Phone: (414)359-1040
Fax: (414)359-1074
E-mail: info@alliance1.org
Home Page: http://www.alliance1.org
Formerly: (1984) Family Service Association of America.

• 447 • **Biennial Communications Award**
To recognize member agencies that have developed high quality brochures, annual reports, newsletters, photos, special publications, and audio/video productions for use in their communities. Awards of Excellence and Awards of Merit are also given.

• 448 • **H. Barksdale Brown Voluntarism Award**
To recognize an FSA member agency whose exemplary initiatives in volunteer involvement and community participation demonstrably increased its effectiveness and stature as a voluntary family service agency. Awarded biennially. Established in 1981 in memory of H. Barksdale Brown, FSA president from 1974-1978.

• 449 • **H. Barksdale Brown Volunteer/ Community Service Award**
To recognize an individual(s) who has improved the quality of life for children and families on a local, regional, and national level. The award will be presented to an individual(s) who through a specific program or volunteer initiative has made a profound impact on children, families, and/or the communities in which they live. Awarded semiannually.

• 450 • **Robert Rice Innovative Program Award**
To recognize member agencies with innovative programs that effectively support families under stress through creative solutions that are well evaluated, cost effective, and replicable. Identified programs will demonstrate positive outcomes on individual and family functioning at home, at school, or in the community. Awarded annually. Established in 1993.

• 451 • **Margaret Elden Rich Memorial Award**
To recognize a member agency for distinguished leadership in undertaking or promoting significant community or legislative action that benefits family life. Established in 1959 in memory of Margaret Elden Rich, a leader in the family service movement for 50 years. Special Citations are also awarded.

• 452 •
Alliance for Children and Television (L'Alliance pour l'Enfant et la Television)
Caroline Fortier, Exec.Dir.
60 St. Clair Ave. E, Ste. 1002
Toronto, ON, Canada M4T 1N5
Phone: (514)597-5417
Fax: (514)597-5205
E-mail: cfortier@act-aet.tv
Home Page: http://www.act-aet.tv/

• 453 • **Awards of Excellence**
For recognition of excellence in Canadian children and youth television programming and interactive multimedia CD-ROM's (not considered if developed for academic curriculm). Plaques are awarded annually. Established in 1977.

• 454 • **Children's Choice Award**
To recognize excellence in Canadian children's television. Selection is made by polling Canadian children. Established in 1996. Formerly: Annual Children's Choice Award.

• 455 • **Lifetime Achievement Award**
To recognize individuals who have devoted their careers to improving the standards and quality of children's television programs in Canada. Selection is by nomination. Plaques are awarded annually. Established in 1977.

• 456 • **Outstanding Achievement Award**
To recognize individuals and/or institutions for outstanding work in a specific area of children's television in Canada. Selection is by nomination. Plaques are awarded annually. Established in 1977.

• 457 •
Alliance for Community Media
Anthony Riddle, Exec.Dir.
666 11th St. NW, Ste. 740
Washington, DC 20001
Phone: (202)393-2650
Fax: (202)393-2653
E-mail: acm@alliancecm.org
Home Page: http://www.alliancecm.org
Formerly: National Federation of Local Cable Programmers.

• 458 • **Hometown Video Festival**
To recognize creative local productions that meet many of the fundamental goals of community programming: programs that transcend the conventional commercial television model, address community concerns, and develop diverse community participation in the production. Any videotape that was cablecast over a local cable channel during the year prior to the deadline date is eligible. Winners in Overall Excellence are selected, as are winners and honorable mentions in the categories of Professional Programming, Non-Pro Programming, and Youth Programming. Plaques are awarded annually. Established in 1977.

• 459 •
Alliance for Transportation Research Institute
University of New Mexico
Judith Espinosa, Dir.
Science & Technology Park
801 University SE, Ste. 302
Albuquerque, NM 87106
Phone: (505)246-6410
Fax: (505)246-6001
E-mail: atr@unm.edu
Home Page: http://www.unm.edu/~atr

• 460 • **Awards for Science and Ethics in Transportation Research**
Recognizes outstanding contributions to transportation while committing to safety and the environment. Awarded annually.

• 461 • **Business and Industry Award**
Presented to an individual representing a private sector organization.

• 462 • **International Award**
Presented to any individual whose contribution is significant across national borders.

• 463 • **National Award**
Presented to an individual whose contribution is significant within the U.S.

• 464 • **Public Service Award**
Presented to an individual representing a public sector organization

Awards are arranged in alphabetical order below their administering organizations

• 465 •
Alliance of Cardiovascular Professionals
Peggy McElgunn, Exec.Dir.
4356 Benney Rd., Ste. 2-103
Virginia Beach, VA 23452
Phone: (757)497-1225
Fax: (757)497-0010
E-mail: peggymcelgunn@comcast.net
Home Page: http://www.acp-online.org

• 466 • **Award of Recognition**
To recognize outstanding service and contributions to society. Awarded annually.

• 467 •
Alliance of Motion Picture and Television Producers
15503 Ventura Blvd.
Encino, CA 91436
Phone: (818)995-3600
E-mail: f-excellent@hotmail.com
Home Page: http://www.amptp.org

• 468 • **Philadelphia International Film Festival (Philafilm Awards)**
To recognize and honor outstanding professional and creative achievement in film and videomaking by independent and Developing World film and videomakers, producers, directors, and craftspersons. Philafilm Awards are given in the following categories: Best Feature Film, Best Film Documentary, Best Video Documentary, Best Short Film, Best Short Video, Best Animation, Best Experimental Film, Best Student Film, Best Cinematography, Best Super 8mm, Best Music video, Best Foreign Film, and Best TV Series. Open to all film and video makers. Deadline is April 1st. The Leigh Whipper Gold Awards, Silver Awards,and Honorable Mention certificates are presented in each category annually at the Film Festival. Established in 1978 in honor of Leigh Whipper, Black actor, pioneer, and activist on behalf of actors' union; and in honor of Gordon Parks, Sr., photographer, director, composer, and producer.

• 469 •
Alliance of the American Dental Association
Sheila Duda, Exec.Dir.
211 E Chicago Ave., Ste. 730
Chicago, IL 60611
Phone: (312)440-2865
Toll-Free: 800-621-8099
Fax: (312)440-2587
E-mail: allianceada@allianceada.org
Home Page: http://www.AllianceADA.org

• 470 • **Thelma J. Neff Distinguished Service Award**
To recognize individual Alliance members (who have been a member for at least ten years) for outstanding contributions to their communities. Awarded annually.

• 471 • **Beulah K. Spencer Award**
To recognize individual Alliance members (who have been a member for less then ten years) for outstanding contributions. Awarded annually.

• 472 •
Allied Artists of America
Gary Erve, Pres.
15 Gramercy Park S.
New York, NY 10003
Phone: (212)582-6411
Phone: (201)330-9838
Home Page: http://www.alliedartistsofamerica.org

• 473 • **Annual Exhibition**
To recognize outstanding American artists. American citizens over 18 years of age who submit entry cards and one slide are eligible. Awards are given in the following categories: oil painting, watermedia, pastel, graphics, and sculpture. The following awards are presented annually in each category: Gold Medal of Honor and $1000; Silver Medal of Honor and $600; and additional awards of $100 to $500. Established in 1914 (first presented in 1926).

• 474 •
Alpha Chi Sigma
Paul R. Jones, Sec.-Treas.
2141 N. Franklin Rd.
Indianapolis, IN 46219
Toll-Free: 800-ALC-HEMY
Home Page: http://alphachisigma.org

• 475 • **Alpha Chi Sigma Pure Chemistry Award**
To recognize and encourage fundamental research in pure chemistry carried out in North America by young men and women. A nominee must not be over 35 years old and must have accomplished research of unusual merit for an individual on the threshold of his or her career. Special consideration is given to independence of thought and the originality shown in the research, which must have been carried out in North America. The award consists of $5000 and a certificate setting forth the reasons for the award. by A.C. and Irving Langmuir through 1937. In 1938, James Kendall financed the prize. No award was made in 1939. In 1940, Alpha Chi Sigma Fraternity assumed the financial obligation and has continued its support.

• 476 • **Alpha Chi Sigma Scholarship Award**
To recognize the Alpha Chi Sigma Scholar selected by the scholarship committee. A nominee must have been a member of Alpha Chi Sigma for one year and be enrolled in an institution of higher learning at the time of nomination. If an undergraduate, the nominee must have completed the junior year at the time of nomination. Graduate students may be nominated based upon their undergraduate and graduate records upon completion of the first year of graduate study. Graduate students may also be nominated based upon their graduate records after admission to candidacy for the terminal degree in the field of graduate study. The deadline for nominations is January 15. The award consists of a Gold Key, a certificate, and a monetary prize of $1000.

• 477 • **Award for Chemical Engineering Research**
Recognizes chemical engineering research conducted in the previous ten years. Individuals of all ages are eligible. A stipend of $5000 is awarded. Also sponsored by the AICHE.

• 478 • **John R. Kuebler Award**
Recognizes outstanding contributions to the profession of chemistry or a related field and to the fraternity. Fraternity members are eligible. A scroll is awarded biennially. Established in 1961.

• 479 •
Alpha Kappa Delta
Marc Matre, Contact
Box U-1147
Mobile, AL 36688
Phone: (251)461-1700
Fax: (251)460-7925
E-mail: akd@jaguar1.usouthal.edu
Home Page: http://www.alpha-kappa-delta.org

• 480 • **Undergraduate Student Paper Competition**
To encourage professional development and recognize scholarly research among sociology undergraduate students. Members of AKD who are undergraduate students at the time the paper is written are eligible. A monetary prize is awarded annually. Established in 1983.

• 481 •
Alpha Omega Alpha Honor Medical Society
Edward D. Harris Jr., Exec.Sec.
525 Middlefield Rd., Ste. 130
Menlo Park, CA 94025
Phone: (650)329-0291
Fax: (650)329-1618
E-mail: eharris@alphaomegaalpha.org
Home Page: http://www.alphaomegaalpha.org

• 482 • **Alpha Omega Alpha Distinguished Teacher Awards**
To provide national recognition to faculty members who have distinguished themselves in medical student education. Each U.S. and Canadian medical school may make one nomination annually. Four monetary awards of $10,000 in clinical or basic sciences are presented annually.An additional $5,000 will go to each of the awardees' faculties. Established in 1988. Administered by the Association of American Medical Colleges.

• 483 • **Alpha Omega Alpha Student Essay Award**
To encourage medical students to address general topics in medicine and to enable the Society to recognize, in a tangible way, excellent and thoughtful presentations. Works submitted must

be written by students while they are in medical school; authors do not have to be members of Alpha Omega Alpha. The topic of the essay may be any nontechnical aspect of medicine. A $750 honorarium and an all-expense paid trip to a national meeting of his or her choice are awarded annually in late winter/early spring. Up to five additional honorable mention awards of $500 each are presented. Established in 1982-83.

• 484 • Alpha Omega Alpha Student Research Fellowships

To stimulate interest in research among medical students. Areas of research may include clinical investigation, basic research, epidemiology, social sciences, and health services research. First, second, and third year medical students at schools with Alpha Omega Alpha chapters are eligible. Up to forty awards of $3,500 ($3,000 for the student and $500 for the faculty supervisor) are awarded annually in the spring for support of student research. Established in 1982.

• 485 •
Alpha Omega International Dental Fraternity
Susan Branscum, Ch. Staff Off.
101 Clarksville Rd.
Princeton Junction, NJ 08550
Phone: (609)799-6000
Toll-Free: 800-677-8468
Fax: (609)799-7032
E-mail: headquarters@ao.org
Home Page: http://www.ao.org/

Formerly: Alpha Omega Dental Fraternity.

• 486 • Achievement Award

To recognize an individual for outstanding contributions to dentistry or the allied sciences. A plaque is awarded at the fraternity's annual convention. Established in 1936.

• 487 • Meritorious Service Award

For recognition of meritorious contribution by a member to the fraternity. May be awarded at the annual convention. Established in 1923.

• 488 •
Alpha Sigma Lambda, Pennsylvania State University-University Park
Dr. Charlene Harrison, Dir.
Center for Adult Learner Services
323 Boucke Bldg.
University Park, PA 16802
Phone: (814)863-3887
Fax: (814)865-3810

• 489 • Outstanding Mentor Award

For personal assistance, advocacy, and personal qualities. Recognition award bestowed annually.

• 490 •
Alpha Tau Delta
Aileen Waltner, Contact
11252 Carmillo St.
Toluca Lake, CA 91602
Phone: (818)842-2232
Phone: (310)391-1333
E-mail: info@atdnursing.org
Home Page: http://www.atdnursing.org

• 491 • Alumni PRN Grant

To enhance and further nursing service. Awarded to a selected alumni member or member-at-large in need of financial assistance who has been accepted into a graduate or doctoral program in a related course of study. Awarded annually.

• 492 • Miriam Fay Furlong Grant

Awarded to an undergraduate member in good standing. Recipient must be a junior or senior in the upcoming year and must show financial need. Awarded annually.

• 493 • National Advisor of the Year Award

Recipients are selected from nominees submitted by each collegiate chapter. Winners receive a plaque and automatic submission for the next year's Faculty Advisor of the Year Award. Awarded annually.

• 494 • National Member of the Year Award

To recognize a junior or senior undergraduate, graduate, or doctoral student who has made the most contributions to the chapter. Nominations are made by each chapter and must be submitted by April 15. Final selection is made by the Awards Committee. Individual chapters may present their winners with an Honors Pin. The final national winner receives a recognition plaque and $100.

• 495 •
Alpha Zeta Omega
Paul Holly, Pres.
2201 Tremont St.
Philadelphia, PA 19115
E-mail: prhrph@aol.com
Home Page: http://www.azo.org/

• 496 • AZO Achievement Medal

To promote the status of the profession of pharmacy by honoring those people who have given many years of long and distinguished service to the profession. A bronze plaque is awarded annually. Established in 1954.

• 497 • AZO Meritorious Award

To reward members of Alpha Zeta Omega for long and meritorious service to the Fraternity. A certificate is awarded annually. Established in 1950.

• 498 • AZO Undergraduate Award

To reward AZO undergraduate members for scholarship and meritorious service to the Fraternity. Selection is determined by the Supreme Awards Committee. A certificate is awarded annually. Established in 1954.

• 499 • Sidney R. Rome Memorial Award

To recognize the best in each of the three types of AZO chapters Undergraduate, Alumni and Mixed. Awarded when merited. Formerly: Newspaper Award.

• 500 •
Alpine Club of Canada
Bruce Keith, Exec.Dir.
Box 8040
Canmore, AB, Canada T1W 2T8
Phone: (403)678-3200
Fax: (403)678-3224
E-mail: info@alpineclubofcanada.ca
Home Page: http://www.alpineclubofcanada.ca

• 501 • Distinguished Service Award

For recognition of outstanding service to the Club in matters other than mountaineering. ACC members are eligible. Nominations must be made by members and approved by the board of directors. Selection is based on nominees success in furthering the clubs aims; being a member of a club committee or participating in a Club project; providing leadership of a large club undertaking; and showing strong interests in the activities of a club section. A wall plaque with Alpine Club of Canada crest in pewter is awarded annually. Nomination forms are available at the above web site. Established in 1970. Formerly: (1987) Service Badge.

• 502 • Honourary Membership

Recognizes contributions to Canadian mountaineering. Individuals are eligible. Selection is based on the strength of the commitment and how it effects the industry. A written letter of nomination must be submitted. See above web site for format. Established in 1906.

• 503 • Silver Rope Award for Leadership

For excellence in leadership and technical ability in mountaineering and ski mountaineering. Members of the Club are eligible. Nominations must be made by at least two previous recipients of the award and approved by the board of directors. A pin and a plaque are awarded. Established in 1933. A nomination form is available at the above web site.

• 504 • A. O. Wheeler Legacy Award

Recognizes long term commitment to the goals of the club. Club members who have served at the National level on multiple committees, projects, or activities over seven years and have also won the Distinguished Service Award are eligible.

Awards are arranged in alphabetical order below their administering organizations

• 505 •
ALS Association, West Michigan Chapter
Michael Van Lindley, Pres.
731 Front St. NW
Grand Rapids, MI 49504-5342
Phone: (616)459-1900
Toll-Free: 800-387-7121
Fax: (616)459-4522
E-mail: mail@alsa-westmichigan.org
Home Page: http://www.alsa-westmichigan.org

• 506 • **Caregiver Appreciation Certificate**
For an individual who demonstrates compassionate care of a family member with ALS. Recognition award bestowed annually.

• 507 •
ALTA Foundation
6849 Peachtree Dunwoody Rd.
Atlanta, GA 30328
Phone: (770)913-9545
Fax: (770)399-0597
E-mail: altafoundation@office-altatennis.org

• 508 • **Everest and Jennings Player of the Year**
For recognition of sportsmanship, dedication to the sport, and improvement of play in the field of wheelchair tennis. Members of the Wheelchair Tennis Players Association are eligible. A monetary prize and a trophy are awarded annually at the U.S. National Championships. Established in 1985. Sponsored by Everest and Jennings.

• 509 • **NFWT Service Award**
To recognize an individual for services to wheelchair tennis in their community on a volunteer basis. Nominations must be submitted by October 1. A trophy is awarded annually at the U.S. Open Wheelchair Tennis Championships. Established in 1988.

• 510 •
Alternative Energy Resources Organization
Jonda Crosby, Contact
432 N Last Chance Gulch St.
Helena, MT 59601-5014
Phone: (406)443-7272
Fax: (406)442-9120
E-mail: aero@aeromt.org
Home Page: http://www.aeromt.org

• 511 • **Northern Rockies Sustainable Agriculture Award**
(Association des Musees Canadiens - Americain Foundation de Affaire de Coeur Societe)
To recognize pioneers in the development and promotion of farming systems that reduce the use of synthetic chemicals in a viable manner, increase crop production and income potential of farms, and make better use of a farm's internal resources. Two categories awarded: one for a food producer, and one for a researcher, educator, food/crop processor, marketer, or policymaker who resides in Alberta, British Columbia, Saskatchewan, Montana, Idaho, Washington, or Wyoming. Awarded annually. Established in 1987. Formerly: (1975) American Association of Collegiate Registrars and Admissions Officers Division of Psychopharmacology and Substance Abuse.

• 512 •
Aluminum Association Inc.
Extruded Products Division
J. Stephen Larkin, Pres.
900 19th St. NW
Washington, DC 20006
Phone: (202)862-5100
Fax: (202)862-5164
Home Page: http://www.aluminum.org

• 513 • **International Aluminum Extrusion Design Competition**
To recognize designers or manufacturers for the best example of an extrusion design using aluminum. Entries may be submitted by March 1. The following awards are presented: (1) Professional Grand prize of $2,000; (2) Professional 2nd - 6th prizes; of $500 each and (3) Students first prize of $750 and Students second prize of $250. Awarded biennially. Established in 1977.

• 514 •
Alumni Association of the City College of New York
Donald K. Jordan, EVP
Shepard Hall, Rm. 162
Convent Ave. & 139th St.
PO Box 177
New York, NY 10027
Phone: (212)234-3000
Fax: (212)368-6576
E-mail: info@alumniassociationccny.org
Home Page: http://www.alumniassociationccny.org

• 515 • **Alumni Service Award**
To recognize loyal, devoted, and continuous service to the Alumni Association and to the city college. Former students are eligible. A medal is awarded annually. Established in 1933.

• 516 • **Centennial Medal**
To recognize extraordinary service by an alumnus to the City College or the City College students. A college seal is awarded when merited. Established in 1947.

• 517 • **Faculty Service Award**
To recognize a faculty member whose exemplary dedication to the students and the college goes above and beyond the call of duty.

• 518 • **John H. Finley Award**
To recognize a citizen of New York who has made a significant contribution to advancing the welfare of that city. A sculptured likeness of John H. Finley encased in a lucite pyramid is awarded annually. Established in 1947 by the Class of 1918.

• 519 • **Townsend Harris Medal**
To recognize a distinguished achievement in one's chosen field of endeavor. Graduates are eligible. Awarded annually to not more than seven alumni. Established in 1933 by the Class of 1906.

• 520 •
Amateur Astronomers Association
Michael O'Gara, Pres.
Gracie Station
PO Box 383
New York, NY 10028
Phone: (212)535-2922
E-mail: president@aaa.org
Home Page: http://www.aaa.org/

• 521 • **Amateur Astronomers Medal**
To recognize meritorious service to the science of astronomy. A silver medal and a certificate are awarded when merited. To date, 20 medals have been awarded. Established in 1943.

• 522 •
Amateur Athletic Foundation of Los Angeles
Anita L. DeFrantz, Pres.
2141 W Adams Blvd.
Los Angeles, CA 90018
Phone: (323)730-4600
Fax: (323)730-9637
E-mail: info@aafla.org
Home Page: http://www.aafla.org

• 523 • **High School Awards Program**
To honor Southern California high school athletes, both boys and girls, in football, volleyball, basketball, baseball, soccer, and softball. Awarded annually. Foundation high school all-star teams have been selected by prep sports journalists since 1937.

• 524 • **Rose Bowl Player in the Game**
To recognize outstanding performance during the annual Rose Bowl game on New Year's Day in Pasadena, California. A trophy is presented to the recipient in the locker room at the end of the game. Established in 1945. Formerly: (1991) Most Valuable Player in the Rose Bowl.

• 525 •
Amateur Athletic Union
Francine Komarnitzky, Award Coord.
1910 Hotel Plz. Blvd.
PO Box 22409
Lake Buena Vista, FL 32830
Phone: (407)934-7200
Fax: (407)934-7242
Home Page: http://aausports.org

• 526 • **AAU Association Communications Award**
To recognize the AAU association and editor that publish the most comprehensive, regularly distributed association communication. The intent of the award is to encourage good commu-

Awards are arranged in alphabetical order below their administering organizations

nication within each association through the printed media. First awarded in 1983.

• 527 • AAU James E. Sullivan Memorial Award

To honor the outstanding amateur athlete in the United States. Qualities of the nominees should include leadership, character, sportsmanship, and the ideals of amateurism. A trophy with an athlete holding a symbolic victory wreath is awarded annually. Established in 1930 to honor the founder and past president of the AAU, James E. Sullivan.

• 528 • AAU Media Award

To recognize the newsman or newswoman who does the most during the year to present more accurately the programs and objectives of the Union. Awarded annually. Established in 1976.

• 529 • AAU Outstanding Wrestling Official of the Year

To recognize the outstanding wrestling official of the year. Awarded annually. Established in 1976.

• 530 • AAU Promotions Award

To recognize an AAU volunteer for outstanding contributions in promoting the programs of the Union.

• 531 • AAU Volunteer Hall of Fame

To recognize volunteers who have dedicated years of service to the AAU and amateur sports. Established in 1988.

• 532 • AAU Wrestling Person of the Year

To recognize an individual for outstanding contributions to the advancement of wrestling. Awarded annually. Established in 1978.

• 533 • Aerobics Athlete of the Year

To recognize the outstanding AAU aerobics athlete of the year. Awarded annually.

• 534 • Aerobics Contributor of the Year

To recognize the individual who most significantly contributes to the overall program objectives of the AAU aerobics program. Established in 1993.

• 535 • Aerobics Man and Woman of the Year

To recognize individuals as the outstanding man and woman of the year in the area of aerobics. Awarded annually. Established in 1981.

• 536 • Aerobics Official of the Year

To recognize the outstanding aerobics official of the year. Awarded annually.

• 537 • Arnie Aizstrauts Team Sportsmanship

Established in 1985 in memory of Arnie Aizstrauts, former U.S. Olympic Basketball Committee member, regional AAU Chairman, AAU Basketball Committee member, and strong, dedicated, and inspirational figure long associated with AAU Basketball.

• 538 • All-American Association Award

To recognize those Associations showing outstanding increases in activities over the previous year. Banners are awarded annually.

• 539 • Association Silver Pin Awards

To recognize individuals who have rendered at least 25 years of continuous dedicated service to the advancement of amateur sports on at least an Association level through the AAU Association.

• 540 • Association Wrestling Award

To recognize an AAU Association member for exemplary service to AAU wrestling. Awarded annually. First awarded in 1982.

• 541 • Association Youth Sport Membership Award

To recognize the AAU Association that registered the greatest number of AAU youth members during the program year.

• 542 • Association Youth Sport Programming Award

To recognize the AAU Association that offered the broadest base of youth programs by conducting the greatest number of Association Championships and the greatest number of youth sports.

• 543 • Baseball Outstanding Volunteer Award

To recognize the volunteer performing the most outstanding service to the AAU Baseball program. Awarded annually since 1990.

• 544 • Baton Twirling Achievement

To recognize an individual for outstanding service to baton twirling. Established in 1973. Last awarded in 1978.

• 545 • Boys' Basketball Past Chair Recognition

To honor former chairmen of the AAU Boys' Basketball Committee who have demonstrated exemplary leadership in the performance of their duties. Established in 1989.

• 546 • Boys' Basketball Vision Award

To recognize the individual best exemplifying the goals, objectives, and visions for the future of the AAU Boys' Basketball Committee. Awarded annually. First awarded in 1989.

• 547 • Emil Breitkreutz Leadership Award - Volleyball

To recognize outstanding leadership in volleyball. Awarded annually. Established in 1970 by the National AAU Volleyball Committee to honor Emil Breitkreutz, an Olympian, an outstanding official, and a volleyball enthusiast.

• 548 • Centurion Award

To recognize individuals in the sport of Karate. Established in 1984.

• 549 • Chinese Martial Arts Leadership Award

To recognize the individual best exemplifying leadership within the AAU Chinese Martial Arts community. Presented annually. First awarded in 1991.

• 550 • Chinese Martial Arts Outstanding Service Award

To recognize the person valued as providing the most outstanding service to the AAU Chinese Martial Arts program. Awarded annually. Established in 1992.

• 551 • Bud Estes Memorial Pioneer Jujitsu Award

To perpetuate the memory of Prof. Bud Estes who was the first to receive the Pioneer Award in 1980 and who died in 1981 after serving American Jujitsu for over 50 years. Awarded annually. Established in 1980.

• 552 • Girls' Basketball National Volunteer of the Year

To honor the volunteer who best serves the AAU Girls' Basketball program. Awarded annually. First awarded in 1991.

• 553 • Willard Greim Award

To recognize distinguished service to AAU Basketball. Established in 1985 to honor Willard Greim, who served as president of the AAU from 1944-46 and was the only American ever to hold the president's office of FIBA (International Amateur Basketball Federation). He was elected to that post three times and served from 1948 until 1960.

• 554 • Gymnastics National Volunteer of the Year

In recognition of those designated as outstanding volunteers within the AAU gymnastics community. Awarded annually. First presented in 1991.

• 555 • Colonel Harry D. Henshel Award

To recognize the winning team in the Men's AAU National Basketball Championship. A trophy is awarded annually. Established in 1963 in memory of Colonel Harry D. Henshel, who was devoted to the sport of basketball.

• 556 • The Ira Hurley Association Officers Award for Outstanding Achievement
To recognize an AAU volunteer who has given outstanding service to the AAU and amateur sports in general. Awarded annually. Established in 1994 to honor the late Ira Hurley.

• 557 • Jujitsu Outstanding Competitor
To recognize outstanding Jujitsu competitors by the AAU Jujitsu Committee. Awarded annually. First awarded in 1989.

• 558 • Jack Milne Memorial Award
To recognize volunteers in the sport of track and field. A trophy is presented annually at the National AAU Convention. Established in 1990 in memory of Jack Milne, who for many years was known as "Mr. AAU Track and Field."

• 559 • Herbert Joseph Mols Award
To recognize the best defensive player in the AAU National Men's Championship. Awarded annually. Established in 1988 to recognize Herbert Joseph Mols for his many years of service and contributions to AAU Men's Basketball.

• 560 • National Gold Pin Awards
To recognize individuals who have rendered at least 35 years of continuous dedicated AAU-oriented service to the advancement of amateur sports on a National level.

• 561 • Outstanding Newsletter Award
To recognize the AAU Association and editor voted as having the most outstanding newsletter. Established in 1983.

• 562 • Outstanding Service Award - Karate
To recognize outstanding service to karate. Awarded annually. Established in 1976.

• 563 • Pace Award
In recognition of leadership of AAU Associations demonstrating leadership in promoting registrations and interest in the athletic community for the advancement of AAU sports programs. Established in 1990.

• 564 • Pioneer Man-of-the-Year Chinese Martial Arts Award
To recognize those who distinguish themselves through contribution to the AAU Chinese Martial Arts program. Presented annually. First awarded in 1984.

• 565 • President's National Leadership
To recognize individuals and/or AAU Associations showing leadership in the promotion of AAU and amateur sports activities. Established in 1987.

• 566 • Progress Award
To recognize the AAU Association showing the greatest increase in activities over the previous year. Awarded annually. Established in 1934.

• 567 • Public Recreation Department of the Year
In recognition of the Public Recreation Department best servicing the needs of the AAU amateur sports community in the area of public recreation. First awarded in 1987.

• 568 • Public Recreation Man and Woman of the Year
To honor outstanding male and female leaders in the field of public recreation. Awarded annually. Established in 1963.

• 569 • Public Recreation Volunteer of the Year Award
To honor an outstanding volunteer leader in the field of public recreation.

• 570 • Public Relations Award
To recognize outstanding public relations contributions on behalf of amateur athletics. Awarded annually by the Public Relations Committee of AAU. Established in 1966.

• 571 • Professor Regennitter AAU Jujitsu Service Award
To recognize a person who has best served the AAU Jujitsu Program at the national level. Awarded annually. Established in 1980.

• 572 • David G. Rivenes Award - Taekwondo
To recognize an individual for dedicated service to the National AAU Taekwondo movement. Awarded annually. Established in 1976.

• 573 • Rookie Newsletter Award
To recognize the AAU association and editor of a newly-instituted (or revitalized) AAU association newsletter that communicates most effectively the message and programs of the Association. Established in 1993.

• 574 • Jack Schatz Award
To recognize the man and woman exhibiting outstanding dedication and promotion of AAU volleyball. First awarded in 1993 in honor of Jack Schatz, AAU volleyball volunteer and leader.

• 575 • Soccer Outstanding Service Award
To recognize those who have provided outstanding service to the AAU soccer program. Awarded annually. Established in 1991.

• 576 • Spirit Award
To recognize AAU Associations most aggressively and productively reflecting a positive and progressive spirit for the advancement of AAU programs. Awarded annually. Established in 1992.

• 577 • Sustained Superior Performance Award
To recognize an individual for long and outstanding contribution to wrestling at the grassroots level. A Sustained Superior Performance Award and a plaque are awarded annually. Established in 1967. Sponsored by the U.S. Wrestling Foundation.

• 578 • Arthur Carling Toner, Jr. Memorial Award
For recognition of distinguished registration service to the Amateur Athletic Union of the United States. Awarded annually. Established in 1974.

• 579 • Trampoline and Tumbling National Leadership Award
To recognize individuals demonstrating superb leadership in trampoline and tumbling. Awarded annually. First presented in 1993.

• 580 • Willard T. (Billy) Vandiver Award
To recognize an individual who has served the National AAU Youth Wrestling Program a minimum of 10 years while being instrumental in the development of association activity. Awarded in memory of Billy Vandiver, lifelong AAU wrestling enthusiast and dedicated amateur sports volunteer.

• 581 • Veterans Award
To recognize any individual who has served the Amateur Athletic Union at the national level for 50 years and has attained the age of 80. Awarded when merited. Established in 1970.

• 582 • Louis G. Wilke Memorial Award
To recognize the most valuable player of the National AAU Tournament. A trophy is awarded annually. Established in 1954 in memory of a former AAU President and a long-time figure in amateur basketball in both the United States and in the world governing body, the International Amateur Basketball Federation.

• 583 • Youth Softball Volunteer of the Year
To recognize those who have provided outstanding volunteer service for the AAU Youth Softball program. Awarded annually. First awarded in 1989.

• 584 •
Amateur Softball Association of America
Bill Desardins, Commissioner
2801 NE 50th St.
Oklahoma City, OK 73111
Phone: (405)672-1601
Fax: (405)672-1601
E-mail: info@softball.org
Home Page: http://www.softball.org

• 585 • All-American Award
To recognize national tournament performance. Awarded annually.

• 586 • **ASA National Championships**
To recognize the winner of the final game in annual amateur softball tournaments. Awards are given in 63 categories. 63 nationals for children and adults are held each year. Sixteen Junior Olympic National Championships are held each year. Established in 1933.

• 587 • **Erv Lind Award**
To honor the top defensive player in the women's major fast pitch national tournament. The winner is determined by a vote of a selection committee at the tournament. A plaque is awarded annually. Established in 1966 by the Amateur Softball Association in honor of Erv Lind, former sponsor of women's fast pitch teams.

• 588 • **National Softball Hall of Fame**
To recognize outstanding American amateur softball players throughout the years. Sixty nationals for children and adults are held each year. 127 people have been enshrined in the National Softball Hall of Fame. Established in 1957.

• 589 • **Bertha Tickey Award**
To honor the outstanding pitcher in the ASA Women's Major Fast Pitch National Championship. The award is named in honor of former Raybestos Brakette, picther Bertha Tickey. Awarded annually. Established in 1967.

• 590 •
Ambulatory Pediatric Association
Marge Degnon, Exec.Dir.
6728 Old McLean Village Dr.
Mc Lean, VA 22101
Phone: (703)556-9222
Fax: (703)556-8729
E-mail: info@ambpeds.org
Home Page: http://www.ambpeds.org

• 591 • **APA Public Policy and Advocacy Award**
Recognizes the cumulative contributions of an individual, pediatric department, or program whose public policy advocacy efforts at the state, regional, or national, or international level have improved the health and well-being of infants, children, and/or adolescents.

• 592 • **APA Research Award**
To recognize an individual for a contribution in advancing pediatric knowledge through excellence in research. Selection is based on originality, creativity, and methodological soundness. The findings should contribute significantly to the general health of children in such areas as understanding mechanisms of health and disease, methods of education, and innovative ways of providing children's services. Awarded annually. Established in 1989.

• 593 • **APA Teaching Award**
Fosters interest in the teaching of ambulatory pediatrics by giving national recognition to an outstanding ambulatory pediatric program. Selection is based on excellence in educational teaching methods, acceptance by students and/or residents, acceptance by the community and the institution, innovations and adaptability, or outstanding quality of the individuals trained in the program. Awarded annually. Established in 1972.

• 594 • **Distinguished Career Award**
Recognizes the promotion of improved patient care, teaching, and research in ambulatory pediatrics. Members of the Association who have fostered the goals of the Association through their careers.

• 595 • **Health Care Delivery Award**
Recognizes a program providing health care in the context of a teaching setting. The program must include residents and/or medical students and may provide general pediatric care. Care to children with special needs, or a system of care.

• 596 • **Ray E. Helfer Award**
Recognizes creative, scholarly work in pediatric education that is described in a paper submitted for the Annual APA meeting. The Ray E. Helfer Foundation for Children and Families provides financial Support for this award.

• 597 • **Ludwig-Seidel Award**
Recognizes the abstract that represents the best research project in pediatric emergency medicine in which a PEM fellow is the lead author. Fellow in pediatric emergency are eligible.

• 598 •
America-Israel Cultural Foundation
Vicki Marantz Friedman, Dir. of Devel.
51 E 42nd St., Ste. 400
New York, NY 10017
Phone: (212)557-1600
Fax: (212)557-1611
E-mail: info@aicf.org
Home Page: http://www.aicf.org

• 599 • **King Solomon Award**
To recognize outstanding service in furthering Israel's cultural life. A segment of Jerusalem stone with a bronze medallion with inscription, "A wise and an understanding heart", is awarded annually. Established in 1966 and named for the biblical King Solomon.

• 600 •
America the Beautiful Fund
Nanine Bilski, Pres.
Department AG
725 15th St. NW, Ste. 605
Washington, DC 20005
Phone: (202)638-1649
Phone: (202)638-1687
Toll-Free: 800-522-3557
Fax: (202)638-2175
E-mail: info@america-the-beautiful.org
Home Page: http://www.america-the-beautiful.org

• 601 • **National Recognition Award**
Recognizes superior projects in the United States. Awarded annually. Formerly: (2003) American Stars Awards.

• 602 •
American Academy for Cerebral Palsy and Developmental Medicine
Sheril King, Exec.Dir.
6300 N. River Rd., Ste. 727
Rosemont, IL 60018
Phone: (847)698-1635
Phone: (847)823-4239
Fax: (847)823-0536
E-mail: king@aaos.org
Home Page: http://www.aacpdm.org

Formerly: American Academy for Cerebral Palsy.

• 603 • **Richmond Cerebral Palsy Center Award**
To recognize the author/researcher of an outstanding paper relative to cerebral palsy or developmental medicine. The winning paper is presented at the annual meeting of the academy and is considered for publication in *Developmental Medicine and Child Neurology*. Established in 1969 by the Richmond Cerebral Palsy Center.

• 604 •
American Academy in Rome
Carmela Vircillo Franklin, Dir.
7 E 60th St.
New York, NY 10022-1001
Phone: (212)751-7200
Fax: (212)751-7220
E-mail: info@aarome.org
Home Page: http://www.aarome.org

• 605 • **Rome Prize Fellowships**
To provide artists and scholars six months to two years in Rome at the Academy for independent work or research in the following fields: architecture; landscape architecture; musical composition; design arts; and visual arts; literature (awarded by the American Academy of Arts & Letters) ancient studies, medieval studies, renaissance and early modern studies, and modern Italian studies. U.S. citizens (or permanent residents if applying for the post-doctoral fellowships in the humanities) with a B.A. or equivalent degree in a field of fine arts, or a pre-doctoral or post-doctoral candidate in a field of the humanities, may apply by November 15 each year. Up to 30 fellowships providing travel, room, board, studio/study, and a stipend are awarded annually. Established in 1894 by Charles Follen McKim.

• 606 •
American Academy of Addiction Psychiatry
Becky Stein, Exec.Dir.
1010 Vermont Ave. Ste. 710
Washington, DC 20005
Phone: (202)393-4484
Fax: (202)393-4419
E-mail: info@aaap.org
Home Page: http://www.aaap.org

Formerly: American Academy of Psychiatrists in Alcoholism and Addiction.

• 607 • Janssen Research Award
Acknowledges residents and/or PGY-U and VI residents who have completed outstanding research in the area of addiction during their residency. The recipient of the award will be invited to attend the AAAP Annual Meeting and Symposium. Registration fees will be waived and airfare and hotel costs will be paid for the awardee.

• 608 • Medical Student and Resident Travel Stipend
Designed to encourage medical students and residents to pursue a career in addiction psychiatry. The recipient of the award will be invited to attend the AAAP Annual Meeting and Symposium. Registration fees will be waived and airfare and hotel costs will be paid for the awardee. Awarded annually.

• 609 •
American Academy of Advertising
Dennis Martin, Exec.Sec.
Brigham Young University
Dept. of Communications
Provo, UT 84602-6403
Phone: (801)422-6845
Fax: (801)422-0160
E-mail: dennis_martin@byu.edu
Home Page: http://www.americanacademyofadvertising.org

• 610 • Distinguished Service Award
To recognize individuals who have rendered distinguished service to the Academy and/or advertising education. Applicants do not need to be association members. The award is expected to be given infrequently and only for truly distinguished service.

• 611 • Doctoral Dissertation Competition
To promote doctoral research in advertising. Dissertations on any advertising related topic are considered. Applicants must be academy members enrolled in a graduate program at the time of submission. Winners are expected to grant the *Journal of Advertising* right of first refusal of any papers resulting from the dissertation. One or two awards are generally given of $1,000-$2,000. One half of the award is given at the time of selection; the other half is given when the dissertation has been defended successfully.

• 612 • Journal of Advertising Best Article Award
To honor the best article published each year in the *Journal of Advertising.* Nominations are made by reviewers and tabulated by the Publications Committee. Winners are awarded $500 and a plaque at the association's annual conference. Established in 1988.

• 613 • Outstanding Contribution to Research Award
To honor individual who have made sustained and systematic contributions to advertising research. Nominations and selection are made through the Research Committee. Winners receive $1,000 and a plaque at the association's annual conference.

• 614 •
American Academy of Allergy, Asthma and Immunology
Audrey Mudek, Membership Service Mgr.
555 E Wells St., Ste. 1100
Milwaukee, WI 53202-3823
Phone: (414)272-6071
Fax: (414)272-6070
E-mail: membership@aaaai.org
Home Page: http://www.aaaai.org

• 615 • Jaffe Family Foundation Food Allergy Research Award
To support promising investigators and to promote research in this area of food allergy, specifically in the characterization of food allergens and the immunopathogenic mechanisms associated with food allergic disorders. Applicant must be a fellow-in-training, resident, or post-doctoral scholar associated with an approved allergy or immunology or clinical and laboratory immunology training program approved by the ACGME. $25,000 is awarded annually. Sponsored by the Jaffe Family Foundation.

• 616 • Respiratory Diseases Research Award
To support promising investigators and promote research in the areas of respiratory disease. Applicant must be a fellow-in-training, resident, or post-doctoral scholar associated with an approved allergy and immunology or clinical and laboratory immunology training program approved by the ACGME. $25,000 is awarded annually. Sponsored by GlaxoWellcome.

• 617 •
American Academy of Arts and Sciences
Leslie C. Berlowitz, Exec.Off.
Norton's Woods
136 Irving St.
Cambridge, MA 02138
Phone: (617)576-5000
Fax: (617)576-5050
E-mail: aaas@amacad.org
Home Page: http://www.amacad.org

• 618 • American Academy Award for Humanistic Studies
To recognize superior humanistic scholarship. Nominations are made by committee. A monetary award is presented periodically. Established in 1975.

• 619 • Francis Amory Prize
For recognition of outstanding work in reproductive physiology. Nominations are made by committee. A monetary prize and a certificate are presented. Established in 1940 and awarded periodically.

• 620 • Fellow or Foreign Honorary Member
To recognize individuals for outstanding contributions to the arts and sciences. Individuals are elected annually.

• 621 • Talcott Parsons Prize for Social Science
To recognize contributions to the social sciences throughout a career. Nominations are made by committee. A monetary prize and a medallion are awarded periodically. Established in 1974. Formerly: (1976) Social Science Prize of the American Academy.

• 622 • Rumford Prize
This, the Academy's oldest and most prestigious award, and one of the nation's oldest scientific awards, is given to recognize important discoveries concerning heat or light. Nominations are made by committee. A monetary prize and medal are awarded periodically. Established in 1839.

• 623 • Emerson - Thoreau Medal
For recognition of distinguished achievement in the broad field of literature. It is awarded to a person for a body of work. Nominations are made by committee. A monetary prize and a bronze medal, designed by Rudolph Ruzicka, are awarded periodically. Established in 1958.

• 624 •
American Academy of Child and Adolescent Psychiatry
Richard Sarles MD, Pres.
3615 Wisconsin Ave. NW
Washington, DC 20016-3007
Phone: (202)966-7300
Toll-Free: 800-333-7636
Fax: (202)966-2891
E-mail: executive@aacap.org
Home Page: http://www.aacap.org

Formerly: (1986) American Academy of Child Psychiatry.

• 625 • James Comer Minority Research Fellowship for Medical Students
To help stimulate minorities to participate in research in child and adolescent psychiatry. Awards include 5 research fellowships of $2,500 each for work during the summer with a child and adolescent psychiatrist researcher-mentor

plus five days at the AACAP annual meeting. The deadline for applications is April 1. Awarded annually. Established in 1991 to honor James Comer, M.D., child and adolescent psychiatrist who developed an innovative school-based management approach used in economically disadvantaged areas of New Haven, CT. The success of "the School Development Program" has made it a model increasingly used throughout the United States. For more information, contact Marilyn Benoit, Program Director. Formerly: Comer Awards.

• 626 • Robinson/Cunningham Award
To recognize an outstanding scientific paper on some aspect of child psychiatry. The paper should be based on work finished within three years of the completion of training in child psychiatry. Manuscripts must be submitted by June 1. The award consists of an honorarium of $100, travel expenses to the annual meeting, and an award certificate. Presented at the annual meeting. Established in 1970 in memory of J. Franklin Robinson, M.D., seventh president of the Academy. Re-named in 1989 to additionally honor James M. Cunningham, M.D., the fifth president of the Academy. Formerly: (1988) J. Franklin Robinson Award.

• 627 • Leadership Award for Residents
To recognize outstanding residents in general psychiatry. PGYII general psychiatry residents may be nominated by their training director by June 1. A plaque and expenses to attend the annual meeting are awarded to 10 residents each October. Established in 1989. Sponsored by Charter Behavioral Health Systems.

• 628 • Pilot Research Award for Junior Faculty and Child Psychiatry Fellows
To support a research infrastructure in child and adolescent psychiatry. Candidates must be board eligible, certified in child and adolescent psychiatry, or enrolled in a child psychiatry residency or fellowships program. They must have a full-time faculty appointment in an accredited medical school or be in a fully accredited child and adolescent psychiatry clinical or research training program. At the time of application, candidates may not have had more than two years of experience following graduation from residency or fellowship training. Candidates must also not have any previous significant, individual research funding. AACAP bestows six awards of $9,000 each for pilot research and five days at the Academy's annual meeting. Winners will be matched with a child and adolescent psychiatric investigator to act as a consultant or mentor during the course of the award. Work must be completed within one year of receipt of the award. Travel monies will be disbursed upon submission of the pilot data for a presentation at the annual meeting. Sponsored by Eli Lilly & Co.

• 629 • Presidential Scholar Award
To foster specialized competence among child and adolescent fellows in research, public policy, and consultative service. A first-year fellow may apply for the award or may be nominated by his or her training director or other AACAP members by June 1. Application and letters of nomination must indicate a candidate's competence and plans for proposed field of study. A topic must be specified in one of the following areas: research, public policy, or innovative service systems. Each of three winners will receive a certificate presented during the AACAP Annual Meeting. The award will pay expenses up to $2,500 for travel and lodging for one week's tutorial/exchange in the specified area of study with a senior Academy leader, as well as participation in the Academy's Annual Meeting. Established in 1986. Sponsored by Bristol-Myers-Squibb.

• 630 •
American Academy of Clinical Psychiatrists
Richard Balon MD, Pres.
PO Box 458
Glastonbury, CT 06033
Phone: (860)633-5045
Phone: (203)281-4322
Fax: (860)633-6023
E-mail: info@aacp.com
Home Page: http://www.aacp.com

• 631 • AACP Clinical Research Award
To recognize the best published paper in the *Annals of Clinical Psychology.* The winner receives a monetary award of $500, a plaque, travel expenses to the annual meeting for the presentation, and possible inclusion of the paper in the *Annals of Clinical Psychiatry.* The runner-up receives a monetary award of $200, a plaque, and travel expenses to the meeting. Presented annually. Established in 1979. Sponsored by Mead Johnson and Company. Additional information is available from Alicia A. Munoz, Executive Director.

• 632 •
American Academy of Clinical Toxicology
Jan Reisinger, Interim Exec.Dir.
777 E Park Dr.
PO Box 8820
Harrisburg, PA 17105-8820
Phone: (717)558-7847
Toll-Free: 888-633-5784
Fax: (717)558-7845
E-mail: jreisinger@pamedsoc.org
Home Page: http://www.clintox.org

• 633 • AACT Research Award
Applicants must be AACT members. An award of $ 2500 is available. An additional $750 is available for travel expenses to the ceremony. 8 copies of a description of the proposed project, a bibliography, data gathering form, budget, curriculum vitae (1 copy) letter of support from support from sponsoring faculty, and letter of 501c-3 status determination must be submitted, (1 copy). Complete form and details are available at the above address.

• 634 • Lampe-Kunkle Memorial Award
Recognizes research on natural products of toxicology. Applicants must be doctoral student, post-doctoral students, MDS residents or fellows or senior investigators who are AACT members. Application deadline is June 1st. Senior investigators are AACT members. Complete application and details are available at the above web site.

• 635 •
American Academy of Dermatology
Thomas P. Conway, Exec.Dir.
PO Box 4014
Schaumburg, IL 60168-4014
Phone: (847)330-0230
Toll-Free: 888-462-DERM
Fax: (847)330-0050
E-mail: memsrv@aad.org
Home Page: http://www.aad.org

• 636 • Award for Young Investigators
To recognize outstanding research by dermatologists-in-training and the educational institutions that support their efforts. Candidates must be citizens of the United States or Canada. Two awards of $5,000 are presented annually.

• 637 • Everett C. Fox, M.D. Memorial Lectureship
The selected lecturer will receive a cash award of $10,000 and present a lecture of approximately 30 minutes at the summer meeting of the American Academy of Dermatology. The individual selected must be a dermatologist who is an acknowledged expert clinician. The emphasis must be in selecting a person who is a practicing clinical dermatologist, including dermatopathology and dermatologic surgery, regardless of their area of practice. There should be no emphasis on a particular age group. The recipient must have proven communication skills. The lectureship was formed through a bequest from the estate of Everett C. Fox, MD. Dr. Fox had been a practicing clinician in Texas and was vice president of the American Academy of Dermatology in 1946. Awarded annually.

• 638 • Lila Gruber Memorial Cancer Research Award and Lectureship
To recognize individuals for outstanding research in cancer, and to encourage such research. A monetary prize of $10,000 and the opportunity to make a presentation at the annual national meeting are awarded each year. Established in 1972 by Dr. Murray Gruber in memory of his wife.

• 639 • Clarence S. Livingood Lectureship
First presented at the 1993 Annual Meeting, this lectureship and education fund was endowed by Settlor and Doris Giddey in memory of George H. Giddey. The Giddey's were both patients and friends of Dr. Livingood. Awarded annually.

• 640 • Marion B. Sulzberger Memorial Award and Lectureship
To recognize an outstanding individual in the field of dermatology. The recipient delivers a lecture at the annual meeting. Established in December 1983 by Dr. Murray Gruber as a living memorial in honor of Dr. Sulzberger. Formerly: Lila Gruber Fund Award of the AAD.

• 641 •
American Academy of Dramatic Arts
120 Madison Ave.
New York, NY 10016
Toll-Free: 800-463-8990
Fax: (212)685-8093
Home Page: http://www.aada.org

• 642 • **Charles Jehlinger Award**
To recognize personal and artistic growth. Individuals who have completed a two year degree program are eligible for consideration. The medal, an engraved pendant, is bestowed annually in the spring at graduation. Established in the late 1950s in memory of Charles Jehlinger, Director of the Academy for many years.

• 643 • **Sargent Award**
To recognize an individual for achievement in the dramatic arts for a body of work. A crystal trophy is awarded at the discretion of the academy's board at a gala fund-raising event. Established in 1956 as the Alumni Achievement Award. Re-named in 1985 in memory of Franklin Haven Sargent, founder of the American Academy of Dramatic Arts, and now awarded to distinguished members of the theatrical professions who are not necessarily alumni. Formerly: (1983) AADA Alumni Achievement Award; Alumni Achievement Award.

• 644 •
American Academy of Environmental Engineers
David A. Asselin, Exec.Dir.
130 Holiday Ct., No. 100
Annapolis, MD 21401
Phone: (410)266-3311
Fax: (410)266-7653
E-mail: academy@aaee.net
Home Page: http://www.aaee.net

• 645 • **Edward J. Cleary Award**
To honor an outstanding performer in the management of environmental protection enterprises conducted either under public (local, state, regional, federal, international) or private auspices. A walnut plaque is awarded biennially. Established in 1972.

• 646 • **Excellence in Environmental Engineering**
To recognize excellence in environmental engineering practice. Awards are presented in six categories: Research, Planning, Design, Operations/Management, University Research, and Small Projects. Open to all projects completed within two years of the date the award is given. An acrylic sculpture is presented to Grand Prize winners in each category and a superior achievement award presented to the best overall project. Awarded annually in April. Established in 1988.

• 647 • **Gordon Maskew Fair Memorial Award**
To recognize outstanding contributions to the professional development of environmental engineering and leadership in the field of environmental engineering as demonstrated by the following activities: exemplary direction and management of major environmental programs, political leadership, outstanding teaching of environmental engineers, successful research and effective consultation, or outstanding professional association or industrial leadership. Members of the engineering profession are eligible. A walnut plaque is awarded annually. Established in 1971.

• 648 • **Honorary Member**
To recognize an individual for outstanding contributions to environmental engineering. Awarded when merited. Established in 1982.

• 649 • **Stanley E. Kappe Award**
To honor a Diplomate of the American Academy of Environmental Engineers who is judged to have performed extraordinary and outstanding service contributory to significant advancement of public awareness to the betterment of the total environment and other objectives of the academy. Awarded annually when merited. Only one recipient is chosen in any year and no recipient may receive the award more than once. Established in 1983 by the professional associates of Stanley E. Kappe in recognition of the dedicated leadership, strong devotion, and tireless efforts in advancing the organizational development, growth, and enhancement of the academy that he demonstrated while serving as Executive Director of the academy during the period 1971 through 1981.

• 650 •
American Academy of Environmental Medicine
Bobbie Hinshaw, Exec.Dir.
7701 E Kellogg Dr. Ste. 625
Wichita, KS 67207-1705
Phone: (316)684-5500
Fax: (313)684-5709
E-mail: centraloffice@aaem.com
Home Page: http://www.aaem.com
Formerly: (1985) Society of Clinical Ecology.

• 651 • **Jonathan Forman Award**
For recognition of an individual's contribution to clinical ecology. A plaque is awarded annually at the convention. Established in 1968.

• 652 • **Carlton Lee Award**
For recognition of contributions to environmental medicine by a lay person. A plaque is awarded annually at the convention. Established in 1987.

• 653 • **Herbert J. Rinkel Award**
To recognize excellence in teaching. A plaque is awarded annually at the convention. Established in 1980.

• 654 •
American Academy of Equine Art
Julie Buchanan, Dir.
Kentucky Horse Pk.
4089 Iron Works Pkwy.
Lexington, KY 40511
Phone: (859)281-6031
Phone: (859)281-6043
E-mail: julieb@aaea.net
Home Page: http://www.aaea.net

• 655 • **AAEA Founders Award for Painting**
Recognizes overall excellence. Two-dimensional works of all painting and drawing mediums are eligible. A cash prize, certificate, and plaque are awarded. There must be at least three qualifying works for an award to be distributed. If jurors determine that there is no deserving work, regardless of number of entries, the award may be withheld. No individual artist may receive more than one award.

• 656 • **AAEA Founders Award for Sculpture**
For overall excellence in a three-dimensional sculpture work. A cash prize, certificate, and plaque are awarded. There must be at least three qualifying works for an award to be distributed. If jurors determine that there is no deserving work, regardless of number of entries, the award may be withheld. No individual artist may receive more than one award.

• 657 • **AAEA Museum Directors Award**
Awarded to a work that best depicts the horse in sport. Selection criteria is based on how the artists understands the sport and how accurately the work reflects the horse's role. A cash prize, certificate, and plaque are awarded. There must be at least three qualifying works for an award to be distributed. If jurors determine that there is no deserving work, regardless of number of entries, the award may be withheld. No individual artist may receive more than one award.

• 658 • **AAEA Sporting Art Award**
Awarded to a work best depicting the horse in sport. Two- and three-dimensional works in all mediums are eligible. Selection is based on how the artist understands the sport and how accurately the work reflects the horse's role. A cash prize, certificate, and plaque are awarded. There must be at least three qualifying works for an award to be distributed. If jurors determine that there is no deserving work, regardless of number of entries, the award may be withheld. No individual artist may receive more than one award.

• 659 • **Jean Bowman Memorial Award for Painting**
Awarded to a work that reflects a traditional, academic treatment of equine art. Two-dimensional works in all painting and drawing mediums are eligible. A cash prize, certificate, and plaque are awarded. There must be at least three qualifying works for this award to be given.

If jurors determine that there is no deserving work, regardless of number of works submitted, the prize may be withheld. No individual artist may receive more than one award.

• 660 • Leonard J. Meiselman Memorial Award for Painting
Awarded to a work that reflects a realistic treatment of the subject. A cash prize, certificate, and plaque are awarded. Two-dimensional works of all painting and drawing mediums are eligible. There must be at least three qualifying works for an award to be distributed. If jurors determine that there is no deserving work, regardless of number of entries, the award may be withheld. No individual artist may receive more than one award.

• 661 • Leonard J. Meiselman Memorial Award for Sculpture
Awarded to a work that reflects a traditional, academic and realistic treatment of the subject. A cash prize, certificate, and plaque are awarded. Three-dimensional works of all sculpture mediums are eligible. There must be at least three qualifying works for an award to be distributed. If jurors determine that there is no deserving work, regardless of number of entries, the award may be withheld. No individual artist may receive more than one award.

• 662 • Kimbel E. Oelke Memorial Award for Painting
Awarded to a work that reflects proficiency in dealing with the landscape and background in relation to the equine subject. Two-dimensional works of all painting and drawing mediums are eligible. A cash prize, certificate, and plaque are awarded. There must be at least three qualifying works for an award to be distributed. If jurors determine that there is no deserving work, regardless of number of entries, the award may be withheld. No individual artist may receive more than one award.

• 663 • Popular Choice Award
Awarded to a work selected by the viewing public. Two- and three dimensional works of all mediums are eligible. A certificate and a plaque are awarded. There must be at least three qualifying works for an award to be distributed. If jurors determine that there is no deserving work, regardless of number of entries, the award may be withheld. No individual artist may receive more than one award.

• 664 • Else Tuckerman Memorial Award for Painting
Awarded for excellence in classical equine portaiture. Two-dimensional works of all painting and drawing mediums are eligible. A cash prize, certificate, and plaque are awarded. There must be at least three qualifying works for an award to be distributed. If jurors determine that there is no deserving work, regardless of number of entries, the award may be withheld. No individual artist may receive more than one award.

• 665 •
American Academy of Facial Plastic and Reconstructive Surgery
Stephen C. Duffy, Exec.VP
310 S Henry St.
Alexandria, VA 22314
Phone: (703)299-9291
Toll-Free: 800-332-FACE
Fax: (703)299-8898
E-mail: info@aafprs.org
Home Page: http://www.aafprs.org

• 666 • The Ben Shuster Memorial Award
Presented for the most outstanding research paper by a resident or fellow in training on any clinical work or research in facial plastic and reconstructive surgery. Each entrant must be the sole or senior author and an AAFPRS member. A certificate and $1000 are presented. Deadline is February 28.

• 667 • Bernstein Grant
To encourage original research which will advance facial plastic and reconstructive surgery. Academy Fellow members are eligible. The deadline for entries is January 15. A $25,000 research award may be presented annually. Established in 1989 by Leslie Bernstein, MD, DDS.

• 668 • Community Service Award
To recognize an Academy member who has distinguished himself or herself by providing and/or making possible free medical service to the poor in his or her community. The deadline for nominations is February 28. May be awarded annually.

• 669 • John Dickinson Teacher Award
For recognition of a senior Fellow or Member of the Academy for the effective sharing of knowledge about the specialty of facial plastic surgery with the use of audiovisuals. The deadline for nominations is February 28. May be awarded annually. Established in 1980.

• 670 • Resident Research Grants
To stimulate and support resident research in projects that are well-conceived and scientifically valid in facial plastic surgery. AAFPRS Resident members are eligible. The deadline for entries is December 15. Three $5,000 grants may be awarded annually. Established in 1986.

• 671 •
American Academy of Family Physicians
Debbie Miller MD, Sr. Prog. Coor.
11400 Tomahawk Creek Pkwy.
Leawood, KS 66211-2672
Phone: (913)906-6000
Toll-Free: 800-274-2237
Fax: (913)906-6077
E-mail: fp@aafp.org
Home Page: http://www.aafp.org

• 672 • AAFP Award of Merit
To commend exceptional, individual effort on a single, significant endeavor. Awarded as merited.

• 673 • Certificate of Commendation
To recognize outstanding contributions to family practice by communications professionals. Awarded as merited.

• 674 • Honorary Member
This, the highest honor the Academy can bestow, is given to recognize individuals of distinction who have rendered outstanding service to the AAFP or to the medical profession. Awarded as merited.

• 675 • Thomas W. Johnson Award
To recognize outstanding contributions to education for family practice in undergraduate, graduate, and continuing education spheres. Awarded annually if merited.

• 676 • John G. Walsh Award
To recognize long-term dedication and effective leadership in furthering the development of family practice. Awarded as merited.

• 677 •
American Academy of Fixed Prosthodontics
Dr. Robert S. Staffanou, Sec.
PO Box 1409
Bodega Bay, CA 94923-1409
Phone: (707)875-3040
Toll-Free: 800-860-5633
Fax: (707)875-2927
E-mail: secaafp@comcast.net
Home Page: http://www.fixedprosthodontics.org
Formerly: (1991) American Academy of Crown and Bridge Prosthodontics.

• 678 • Stanley D. Tylman Research Grant Program
To support student research in the field of fixed prosthodontics. Students in accredited graduate and postgraduate programs are eligible. Applications must be submitted by March 1. Up to four grants of $4,000 are awarded annually. The grant may be used to fund equipment, supplies, contractual costs, and other specifically approved aspects of student research projects. In addition, the student researcher who authored the most outstanding research report receives funding to attend the next annual meeting of the academy and to present the report to the membership. Established in 1979. Additional information is available from Dr. Peter S. Lund, 917 W. Dickens Ave., Chicago, Il 60614. 60614. Formerly: (1990) Stanley D. Tylman Student Essay Award.

• 679 •
American Academy of Gnathologic Orthopedics
John Rothchild D.D.S., Exec.Dir.
2651 Oak Grove Rd.
Walnut Creek, CA 94598
Phone: (925)947-5750
Toll-Free: 800-510-AAGO
Fax: (925)676-7678
E-mail: info@aago.com
Home Page: http://www.aago.com

• 680 • **Wiebrecht Award**
For recognition of an outstanding contribution to the field of orthodontics by a member of the academy. A plaque is awarded. Established in 1983 in honor of Dr. Albert Wiebrecht, a founder of the Academy.

• 681 •
American Academy of Kinesiology and Physical Education
James R. Morrow Jr., Pres.
PO Box 5076
Champaign, IL 61820-2200
Phone: (217)351-5076
Toll-Free: 800-747-4457
Fax: (217)351-2674
E-mail: humank@hkusa.com
Home Page: http://www.aakpe.org

• 682 • **Hetherington Award**
To provide recognition for an academy fellow's service to the American Academy of Kinesiology and Physical Education and for contributions specifically related to the purpose of the academy as an organized professional group of leaders in kinesiology and physical education. Academy fellows (active or emeritus) who have retired from professional positions are eligible. A citation and an award are made annually. Established in 1956 to honor Clark W. Hetherington.

• 683 •
American Academy of Medical Administrators
Renee S. Schleicher CAE, Pres./CEO
701 Lee St., Ste. 600
Des Plaines, IL 60016
Phone: (847)759-8601
Fax: (847)759-8602
E-mail: info@aameda.org
Home Page: http://www.aameda.org

• 684 • **Chairman's Award**
To recognize an Academy Affiliate chosen by the Chairman of the Board for special services rendered to the Academy.

• 685 • **Distinguished Service Award**
For recognition of outstanding service and dedication to the Academy. Academy fellows and members in good standing are eligible. The deadline is July 1. A plaque is awarded yearly at the Annual Conference and convocation. Established in 1982. In addition, an Outstanding Service Award may be presented.

• 686 • **Faculty Publication of the Year**
To recognize excellence and originality in health care administration research and writing.

• 687 • **Honorary Fellowships**
To recognize distinguished service in the field of health care administration. All health care executives in the United States and Canada are eligible. The deadline is July 1. A plaque is awarded yearly at the Annual Conference and Convocation. Established in 1959.

• 688 • **Marriott Corporation Health Care Services Charles U. Letourneau Student Research Paper of the Year Award**
To recognize a student of health care administration for excellence, quality, and originality in health care administration research and writing. A monetary award of $500, a plaque, publication in the Academy publication, and travel expenses to the Annual Conference and Convocation are awarded annually. Established in 1973 in honor of Charles U. Letourneau, M.D. Sponsored by the Marriott Corporation.

• 689 • **William Newcomer Health Care Executive of the Year Award**
To recognize an individual for outstanding contributions to the field of medical administration. Academy Fellows and Members in good standing are eligible. The deadline for nominations is July 1. Awarded yearly at the annual conference and convocation. Established in 1971 in honor of William Newcomer, M.D.

• 690 • **Regional Director of the Year Award**
To recognize devotion, loyalty and contributions to the growth and purpose of the academy.

• 691 • **State Director of the Year Award**
To recognize the AAMA State Director who has performed outstanding service to the academy affiliate as chosen by the chairman of the board for special services rendered to the academy.

• 692 • **Statesman of the Year**
To recognize a public figure for distinguished achievements throughout his/her career in America. Established in 1989.

• 693 •
American Academy of Neurological and Orthopaedic Surgeons
Dr. Kazem Fathie MD, Chair
10 Cascade Creek Ln.
Las Vegas, NV 89113
Phone: (702)388-7390
Fax: (702)388-7395
E-mail: aanos@aanos.org
Home Page: http://www.aanos.org

• 694 • **Dr. James W. Cruickshank Award**
For recognition of scientific achievement. Awarded at the annual convention.

• 695 •
American Academy of Neurology
Catherine M. Rydell, Exec.Dir.
1080 Montreal Ave.
St. Paul, MN 55116-2325
Phone: (651)695-2717
Toll-Free: 800-879-1960
Fax: (651)695-2791
E-mail: memberservices@aan.com
Home Page: http://www.aan.com

• 696 • **George Cotzias Lecture**
For recognition in the field of neurology. Selection of the lecturer is made by the Awards Subcommittee of the Scientific Issues Committee. An honorarium of $3,000 plus travel expenses for this annual award lecture is provided by Hoffmann-LaRoche Inc. Established in 1977 in memory of Dr. George Cotzias for his work on the treatment of Parkinson's Disease.

• 697 • **John Dystel Prize for Multiple Sclerosis Research**
To recognize outstanding contributions to research in the understanding, prevention, or treatment of multiple sclerosis. The deadline for application is November 1. A monetary prize of $15,000 and travel expenses to the Annual Meeting are awarded annually.

• 698 • **Shelia Essey Award**
To recognize an individual who has made significant contributions in research in the search for the cause, treatment, prevention, and cure for amyotropic lateral sclerosis (ALS). An honorarium of $25,000 is awarded annually.

• 699 • **Founder's Award**
To recognize a junior member who is a senior author of a research-based manuscript and to encourage clinical research in neuroscience by physicians in clinical neurology training programs. The deadline is November 1. A monetary award of $1,000, a plaque, and a poster presentation of the selected manuscript are awarded each year at the Scientific Program of the annual meeting of the AAN. Established in 1993.

• 700 • **International Affairs Committee Foreign Scholarship Award**
To recognize a young investigator in neurology selected from a country outside of the United States and Canada. Investigators under the age of 35 may submit applications by December 31. The award is based on an abstract submitted for the Scientific Program and accepted for presentation by the Scientific Issues Committee. A stipend for expenses to attend the annual meeting is awarded.

• 701 • **Lawrence C. McHenry Award**
To recognize an individual for a paper on the history of neurology. Manuscripts must be submitted by November 1. A subcommittee of the Scientific Issues Committee selects the winner. A certificate is awarded annually. Established in 1986.

• 702 • Medical Student Essay Awards
To recognize the best essay in clinical neurology, the history of neurology, experimental neurology and neuroscience research. Applicants must be currently enrolled and in good standing in an accredited medical school in North America. The deadline is November 1. The following four awards may be made: G. Milton Shy Award for clinical neurology $350; Saul R. Korey Award for experimental neurology - $350; Roland P. Mackay Award for stimulating interest in neurology - $350; and Extended Neuroscience Research Award - $1,000, a one-year complimentary subscription to the journal *Neurology*, travel expenses to the annual meeting, and a certificate.

• 703 • S. Weir Mitchell Award
To recognize the author of a manuscript submitted by a junior member of the Academy on neurology research and to encourage basic or clinical research in the neurosciences by physicians enrolled in training programs in clinical neurology. Selection is based on originality, scientific merit, neurological interest, and clarity of expression. The deadline is December 8. The award consists of a monetary award of $1,000, travel expenses, a medallion, and the presentation of the selected manuscript at the scientific program of the annual meeting of the Academy. Awarded annually if merited. Established in 1955.

• 704 • Potamkin Prize for Research in Pick's, Alzheimer's, and Related Diseases
To recognize an individual for major contributions to the understanding of the causes and the prevention, treatment, and ultimately the cure for Alzheimer's disease and related disorders. Candidates may be nominated on a world-wide basis from any of the biological disciplines including biochemistry, molecular biology, molecular genetics, pharmacology, immunology, physiology, or cell biology. The deadline for applications is November 1. A monetary prize of $100,000 is awarded at the annual meeting. Established in 1987. The Potamkin Prize is funded through the philanthropy of the Potamkin Foundation.

• 705 • Bruce S. Schoenberg International Award in Neuroepidemiology
To recognize a young investigator involved in significant epidemiologic research in neurologic diseases. The lecturer is selected from submitted abstracts. Residents of developing countries or Eastern Europe, under the age of 45, are eligible. Travel, lodging expenses, and admission to educational programs offered at the annual meeting are awarded each year. Established in 1989 to honor Bruce S. Schoenberg for his work training neurologists internationally in epidemiologic methods.

• 706 • Robert Wartenberg Lecture
To recognize an outstanding neurological scientist/educator selected by a subcommittee of the Scientific Issues Committee. An honorarium of $3,000 and complimentary accommodations during the annual meeting are provided to the recipient. Established in 1957 to honor Dr. Robert Wartenberg.

• 707 •
American Academy of Nursing
Piper L. Plummer CRNA, Dir. Operations
555 E Wells St., Ste. 1100
Milwaukee, WI 53202
Phone: (414)287-0289
Fax: (414)276-3349
E-mail: info@aannet.org
Home Page: http://www.aannet.org

• 708 • AAN Media Award
Recognizes media accomplishments that have increased public awareness of the impact of pubic policies on the health of individuals, communities or the general population; motivated action to improve healthcare for diverse groups; depicted specific examples of health-enhancing interactions, culturally sensitive health care, health promoting activities or healing actions. Individuals and organizations are eligible. Entries can be in the format newspaper articles, radio programs, motion pictures, public service announcements, books, feature films, television shows, magazine articles, novels, documentaries, popular literature, creative endeavors, and multimedia. Entries are encouraged that highlight the nursing profession. Six copies of all application material and a $ 50 registration fee must be submitted. Form is available at the above web site. Application deadline is July 15th. participants in the health policy process; and Category 3 extent of exposure and impact (number of people reached); centrality of the nursing profession in the portrayal or the extent to which nurses are shown in a professional role as opposed to a personal role, the prominence of the nurse character in the plot, etc.; and the quality of the technical production or the ability to gain and maintain audience attention. A plaque is awarded annually at the Academy's national conference. Established in 1981.

• 709 •
American Academy of Ophthalmology
H. Dunbar Hoskins Jr., M.D., Exec.VP
PO Box 7424
San Francisco, CA 94120-7424
Phone: (415)561-8500
Fax: (415)561-8533
E-mail: customer_service@aao.org
Home Page: http://www.aao.org

Formerly: (1979) American Academy of Ophthalmology and Otolaryngology.

• 710 • Achievement Award
Recognizes participation in the scientific programs at the Annual Meeting. Individual members are eligible as points are accumulated. See web site For list of categories. 10 points are required to be eligible for the Achievement Award, 30 for the Senior Achievement Award and 60 For the Lifetime Achievement Award. A certificate is awarded. Established in 1953.

• 711 • Guest of Honor
To recognize physicians, teachers and researchers for their contributions to ophthalmology and dedication to the public welfare. Recipients are appointed by the Academy's president at the annual meeting. Established in 1939.

• 712 • International Blindness Prevention Award
To recognize an individual for significant accomplishments in the prevention of blindness. Awarded annually. Established in 1992.

• 713 • Edward Jackson Memorial Lecture Award
To recognize an outstanding ophthalmologist. Awarded during the Academy's annual meeting. Established in 1944 by the Ophthalmic Publishing Company.

• 714 • Outstanding Humanitarian Service Award
To recognize up to five ophthalmologists who have provided outstanding humanitarian service above and beyond their usual role as a physician. Awarded annually.

• 715 •
American Academy of Optometry
Lois Schoenbrun, Exec.Dir.
6110 Executive Blvd., Ste. 506
Rockville, MD 20852
Phone: (301)984-1441
Fax: (301)984-4737
E-mail: aaoptom@aol.com
Home Page: http://www.aaopt.org

• 716 • Garland W. Clay Award
For recognition of the author of a significant paper on clinical optometry published in *Optometry and Vision Science* and selected by the editorial council. A plaque and expenses to attend the annual meeting are awarded annually. Established in 1978 by the Clay family in memory of Garland W. Clay, academy president 1975-76.

• 717 • Eminent Service Award
For recognition of a fellow who has made distinguished, exemplary, or unique contributions to the academy. Nominations may be made to the awards committee by any member of the academy. Established in 1960.

• 718 • William Feinbloom Award
To recognize an individual who has made a distinguished and significant contribution to clinical excellence and the direct clinical advancement of visual and optometric service, and thus the visual enhancement of the public. Individuals who have made a distinguished and significant contribution to the total spectrum of clinical achievements are considered. Nominations must be received by the Academy Awards Chairman by June 1. A metallic wall shield and expenses to attend the annual meeting are awarded when merited. Established in 1983 in

memory of William Feinbloom, a pioneer in low vision.

• 719 • Founder's Award

To recognize outstanding contributions to clinical aspects of contact lens fitting. Awarded annually.

• 720 • Glenn A. Fry Lecture Award

For recognition of an outstanding scientist or clinician who currently is engaged in research of high relevance to the profession of optometry. A monetary award, a plaque, and the presentation of a paper are presented annually. Established in 1970 to honor Glenn A. Fry, a noted teacher, administrator, and writer of optometry. Sponsored by the American Optometric Foundation.

• 721 • Honorary and Life Fellowships

Honorary Fellowships recognize individuals who are not academy fellows for distinguished contributions in the academy and/or the science and art of optometry. Life Fellowships recognize those fellows who through long-time memberships in the academy have rendered distinguished service to the science and art of optometry. Established about 1964.

• 722 • Carel C. Koch Memorial Medal Award

For recognition of outstanding contributions to the field of interprofessional relations between optometry and other professions. The deadline for nominations is May 1. A bronze medal and expenses to the awards ceremony are awarded annually. Established in 1974 in honor of Carel C. Koch, a leader in the academy.

• 723 • Julius F. Neumueller Award in Optics

For recognition of an outstanding paper of not more than 3,000 words on one of the following topics: geometrical optics, physical optics, opthalmic optics, or optics of the eye. Students enrolled in accredited schools of optometry may submit papers by May 15. A monetary prize of about $500 and a plaque are awarded annually when merited. Established in 1969 through a trust fund set up by Dr. Julius F. Neumueller.

• 724 • Charles F. Prentice Medal

To recognize a significant contribution to the advancement of knowledge through research in the visual sciences. Nominations by the membership and past recipients of the award are accepted. A bronze medal, presentation of a paper, and expenses to attend the annual meeting are awarded annually when merited. Established in 1958 in honor of Charles F. Prentice, the noted pioneer in optometry.

• 725 •

American Academy of Oral and Maxillofacial Pathology
Brad Neville, Pres.
214 H. Hale St.
Wheaton, IL 60187
Toll-Free: 888-552-2667
Fax: (630)369-2488
E-mail: aaomp@b-online.com
Home Page: http://www.aaomp.org

• 726 • Dental Student Award

Annually award of recognition. Nominees are determined by dental schools.

• 727 •

American Academy of Oral and Maxillofacial Radiology
Dr. Michael K. Shrout DMD, Associate Exec.Dir.
PO Box 1010
Evans, GA 30809-1010
Phone: (706)721-2607
Fax: (601)984-6086
E-mail: mshrout@mail.mcg.edu
Home Page: http://www.aaomr.org

• 728 • Charles R. Morris Student Research Award

To encourage new investigators, not yet professionally established, to participate in research to further knowledge in oral and maxillofacial radiology, to develop competency in research, and to gain insight into scientific investigation. Open to candidates from accredited dental and dental hygiene programs who, at the time the research was carried out, were full-time pre-doctoral or undergraduate students. A monetary award of $1,000 is given annually.

• 729 • Howard R. Raper Oral and Maxillofacial Radiology Award

To recognize academic achievement in graduate studies and potential for a career in academia. A monetary prize of $700 is given annually.

• 730 • Albert G. Richards Graduate Student Research Grant

To assist postgraduate students doing applied research in oral and maxillofacial radiology. It provides funds for supplies, equipment, and other costs such as computer time or shop work. Available to students enrolled in graduate programs with an oral and maxillofacial radiology track. A monetary award of $1,000 is given annually.

• 731 • William H. Rollins Graduate Student Research Grant

To recognize outstanding research projects that have been completed by postgraduate students in ADA accredited oral and maxillofacial radiology graduate programs. Available to students currently enrolled in ADA accredited graduate programs with an oral and maxillofacial radiology track. A monetary prize of $1,500 is given annually. Sponsored by Instrumentarium Imaging.

• 732 • Student Award

To recognize senior dental students for achievement in oral and maxillofacial radiology.

• 733 •

American Academy of Oral Medicine
Joyce Caplan, Exec.Sec.
2517 Eastlake Ave. E, Ste. 200
Seattle, WA 98102
Phone: (206)267-4790
E-mail: info@AAOM.com
Home Page: http://www.aaom.com

• 734 • Lester Burket Award

To recognize graduate research in oral medicine. A monetary prize of $2,500 and a certificate are awarded annually. Established in 1993.

• 735 • Herschfus Memorial Award

For recognition of services to the Academy and services in the field of oral medicine. Members of this Academy who are not eligible for the S. C. Miller Award are considered for this award. A plaque is awarded annually. Established in 1984 in honor of Chuna and Sara Herschfus.

• 736 • Honorary Fellow

To recognize members for outstanding service to the Academy. Established in 1947.

• 737 • Samuel Charles Miller Memorial Lecture Award

To recognize outstanding contributions to oral medicine and education. Members of the dental, medical, or related scientific disciplines are eligible. A medal is awarded annually. Established in 1960 in memory of Samuel Charles Miller, the founder and first president of the Academy.

• 738 • Abraham Reiner Diamond Pin Award

This, the highest honor bestowed on a member, is given to recognize continued years of outstanding and devoted service, beyond that required by office, to the aims and organization of the Academy. A diamond pin with the insignia of the Academy is awarded annually. Established in 1966.

• 739 •

American Academy of Osteopathy
Stephen J. Noone CAE, Exec.Dir.
3500 DePauw Blvd., Ste. 1080
Indianapolis, IN 46268
Phone: (317)879-1881
Fax: (317)879-0563
E-mail: snoone@academyofosteopathy.org
Home Page: http://www.academyofosteopathy.org

Formerly: (1970) Academy of Applied Osteopathy.

• 740 • The Academy Award

Recognizes contributions and support to the profession. Applicants must be from outside the

AAO family. Selection is based on the demonstration of commitment to osteopathic principles and the profession; exhibition of outstanding efforts and/or special contributions to promote osteopathy; continuous support of and collaboration with osteopathic organizations; and possession of a vision that is complimentary to the Academy's Mission.

• 741 • Thomas L. Northup Lecturer Award
To recognize the individual chosen to deliver the annual Thomas L. Northup Lecture on the occasion of the annual meeting of the Academy. The nomination for the award should reflect the stature of the lecturer in such fields as education, research, clinical practice, professional management, and allied categories of activity. An illuminated scroll certificate is awarded annually. Established in 1948 and changed in 1973 to the Thomas L. Northup Award. Formerly: (1973) Annual Academy Lecturer.

• 742 • Andrew Taylor Still Medallion of Honor
To recognize accomplishments in scientific or professional affairs and exceptional understanding and application of osteopathic principles. Members of the Academy are eligible. A bronze plaque on a hard wood base is awarded annually. Established in 1946.

• 743 • Yearbook Dedication Award
To recognize services rendered to the public, the profession, or the Academy at one of the levels of osteopathic service. Members of the Academy are eligible. A certificate is awarded annually. Established in 1945.

• 744 •
American Academy of Otolaryngology - Head and Neck Surgery
Jennifer Felsher MD, Commun.Mgr.
1 Prince St.
Alexandria, VA 22314-3357
Phone: (703)836-4444
Phone: (703)519-1585
Fax: (703)683-5100
E-mail: jfelsher@entnet.org
Home Page: http://www.entnet.org

• 745 • Board of Governors Service Award—Model State/Regional Society Program
To recognize societies exhibiting effective leadership, instituting Academy and Foundation programs, and furthering Academy goals through active participation in the Board of Governors.

• 746 • Continuing Education Achievement Awards
To recognize significant physician participation in continuing medical education (CME). A certificate is awarded based upon a minimum number of CME hours completed over a three year period.

• 747 • Distinguished Service Award
To recognize members for dedicated volunteer service to the Academy following receipt of an Honor Award. The award is granted on the basis of a point system. A certificate is awarded when merited. Established in 1986.

• 748 • Exhibit and Poster Award
To recognize outstanding exhibits and posters at the annual meeting. The first place winner receives the President's Award, and the second place winner receives the Academy's Award. The honorees are selected by the Program Advisory Committee.

• 749 • Jerome C. Goldstein Public Service Award
To recognize public service work by otolaryngologists. The award winner receives a $1,000 honorarium and is selected by the executive and finance committee.

• 750 • Honor Awards
To recognize members who have rendered distinguished service to the Academy without reward or remuneration. The award is granted on the basis of a point system. Certificates are awarded each year at the annual meeting. Established in 1934.

• 751 • Humanitarian Efforts Award
To recognize established and post-residency otolaryngologists for their domestic and international humanitarian work.

• 752 • Practitioner Excellence Award
To recognize a prototypical clinical otolaryngologist. Applicants must have practiced medicine for at least 10 years in an exemplary manner and have been sought out by other physicians. Applicants must also demonstrate one or more of the following attributes: civic leadership, charitable activity, support of the arts, leadership involvement with state or local organizations, and community education.

• 753 • Presidential Citation
To recognize outstanding contributions to otolaryngology. A medallion and certificate are awarded at the annual meeting. The recipients are selected by the president, at his/her perogative.

• 754 • Research Awards in Otolaryngology
To recognize outstanding investigative basic and clinical research by an otolaryngology resident-in-training. A certificate and a cash prize is awarded annually. Established in 1958.

• 755 •
American Academy of Pediatrics
Carden Johnston MD, Pres.
141 Northwest Point Blvd.
Elk Grove Village, IL 60007-1098
Phone: (847)434-4000
Fax: (847)434-8000
E-mail: kidsdocs@aap.org
Home Page: http://www.aap.org

• 756 • AAP Excellence in Public Service Award
For recognition of distinguished service on behalf of children and child health. National officials, elected or appointed, are eligible. A plaque is awarded annually. Established in 1974.

• 757 • AAP Nutrition Award
For recognition of an individual or project achievement in nutrition research related to infants and children. The research must have been completed and publicly reported and must have been conducted in the United States and Canada. Nominations of individuals of any age are accepted. A monetary award of $3,000 and plaque are awarded each year at the Annual Meeting. Established in 1944. Sponsored by the International Formula Council.

• 758 • C. Anderson Aldrich Award
For recognition of outstanding contributions in child development. A monetary award of $1,000 and a plaque are awarded annually by the Section on Developmental and Behavioral Pediatrics. Established in 1964. Sponsored by Ross Products Division, Abbott Laboratories.

• 759 • Virginia Apgar Award
For recognition of distinguished service to perinatal pediatrics. A monetary award of $1,000 and a plaque are awarded annually. Established in 1975. Sponsored by Ross Products Division, Abbott Laboratories.

• 760 • Leonard Apt Lecture
To recognize outstanding contributions to the field of pediatric ophthalmology. A plaque and monetary award are given annually by the Section on Ophthalmology. Established in 2000.

• 761 • Award for Outstanding Service to Maltreated Children
To recognize a pediatrician or pediatric subspecialist who has demonstrated outstanding clinical care of and service to abused and neglected children and their families. A monetary award of $500 and a plaque are presented at the AAP Annual Meeting during the Section on Child Abuse and Neglect business meeting. Awarded annually. Established in 1999.

• 762 • Henry L. Barnett Award
To recognize an individual for outstanding contributions to the field of pediatric nephrology. Awarded annually by the Section on Nephrology. Established in 1991, the recipient is honored with a monetary award and plaque.

• 763 • William G. Bartholome Award for Ethical Excellence
To recognize an individual or group significantly impacting public discussion of ethical issues in pediatric medicine. A monetary award of $500 and a plaque are given annually by the Section on Bioethics. Established in 2000.

• 764 • E. H. Christopherson Lectureship Award
To recognize an internationally renowned pediatrician who has substantially contributed to the welfare of children worldwide. The award is named in honor of E.H. Christopherson, M.D., who was the AAP executive director from 1951-67. The lectureship is supported by the Institute of Pediatric Service of the Johnson & Johnson Baby Products Company.

• 765 • Murray Davidson Award
To recognize outstanding contributions to the field of pediatric gastroenterology and nutrition. A monetary award of $1,000 and a plaque are awarded annually by the AAP Section on Gastroenterology and Nutrition. Established in 1993.

• 766 • Distinguished Career Award
For recognition of outstanding contributions and service to the field of pediatric critical care. A monetary prize of $1,000 and a plaque are awarded annually by the Section on Critical Care at the AAP Annual Meeting.

• 767 • Distinguished Service Award
For recognition of outstanding contributions and service to both the section on emergency medicine and the field of pediatric emergency medicine. A monetary award of $1,000 and a plaque is awarded annually by the Section on Emergency Medicine at the AAP Annual Meeting. Established in 1988.

• 768 • Distinguished Service Award
To honor a professional in the field of pediatric orthopaedics who has contributed to the AAP Mission of excellence in patient care, research, or teaching. A monetary prize and a plaque are awarded annually by AAP's Orthopaedic Section. The winner presents a lecture at the annual educational program.

• 769 • John J. Downes Resident Research Award
To recognize outstanding service in the field of pediatric anesthesiology. Monetary awards of $500, $300 and $200 are presented to a pediatric anesthesiology resident by the AAP Section on Anesthesiology and Pain Medicine. Awarded annually. Established in 1997.

• 770 • Founders Award
Established in 1988 for recognition of outstanding service in the field of pediatric cardiology. A monetary award of $400 and a plaque are awarded. The presentor also receives a $1,000 honorarium. Presented at the AAP Annual Meeting by the Section on Cardiology.

• 771 • Founders of Adolescent Health Award
To recognize exemplary achievement on behalf of adolescents on a local level. A plaque and monetary award of $500 are presented at the AAP Annual Meeting during the Section on Adolescent Health business meeting.

• 772 • Stephen L. Gans Distinguished Overseas Lectureship
To encourage sharing between Section on Surgery members and pediatric surgeons from other countries and to recognize achievements in the field of pediatric surgery in other countries. The winner presents a forty-five minute lecture at the annual education program. A monetary prize and a plaque are awarded annually.

• 773 • Jerome Glaser Distinguished Service Award
For recognition of outstanding academic, clinical, or public service in the field of pediatric allergy and immunology to members of at least ten years. A monetary award of $500 and a plaque are awarded in alternate years during the AAP Annual meeting by the Section on Allergy and Immunology. Established in 1985.

• 774 • Clifford G. Grulee Award
For recognition of extraordinary service to the Academy. A silver medal and a plaque are awarded annually. Established in 1951 in honor of Clifford G. Grulee, first secretary and founding member of the Academy.

• 775 • Ray E. Helfer Award
To recognize outstanding contributions to the field of child abuse and neglect prevention. A plaque is awarded annually at the National Alliance of Children's Trust and Prevention Funds annual meeting. The award is co-sponsored by the AAP Section on Child Abuse and Neglect.

• 776 • Adele Dellenbaugh Hofmann Award
To recognize distinguished contributions in the field of adolescent health. A monetary award of $1,000 is presented during the business meeting of the Section on Adolescent Health at the AAP Annual Meeting. Established in 1984. Sponsored by McNeil Consumer Products Company. Formerly: Adolescent Health Award.

• 777 • Abraham Jacobi Award
To honor pediatricians for notable contributions to pediatrics on a national level. Pediatricians must be members of both the AAP and the AMA, and must participate in and cooperate with organized medicine in the broadest sense. Pediatricians may be recognized for teaching, patient care, and/or clinical research in the Jacobi tradition, rather than accomplishments in basic sciences; and long-term contributions rather than a single brilliant achievement. Individuals who are in practice or full-time at a university are eligible. A monetary award of $1,000 is presented at the AAP Annual Meeting where the winner presents the Jacobi Address. Established in 1963. Sponsored jointly by the Academy and the American Medical Association.

• 778 • Alvin H. Jacobs Award
To recognize outstanding service in the field of pediatric dermatology. A plaque is awarded at the AAP Annual Meeting by the Section for Dermatology. Awarded annually. Established in 1988.

• 779 • William E. Ladd Award
For recognition of unique contributions to pediatric surgery. A medal is awarded irregularly by the AAP Section on Surgery. Established in 1954, this is the highest award the section bestows on a pediatric surgeon.

• 780 • Lay Education Project Award
Presented to acknowledge an individual or group of pediatricians involved in innovative projects to educate parents, teachers, children, and others involved in child health. Recipients are guests at the AAP Annual Meeting in October, where they are presented with a crystal award and honorarium. Awards are supported by an educational grant from Ross Products Division Abbott Laboratories, Inc.

• 781 • Medical Education Awards
To recognize outstanding accomplishments at the residency level, postgraduate level, and continuing medical education. Awards are presented in three categories: (1) Professional Education Award; (2) Lay Education Award; and (3) Lifetime Achievement Award. A monetary award of $3,000, an engraved crystal, and travel expenses are awarded annually. Established in 1985. Sponsored by Ross Products Division, a division of Abbott Laboratories. Formerly: (1991) Ross Education Awards.

• 782 • Medical Education Lifetime Achievement Awards
Two awards are presented to recognize lifetime achievements in pediatric medical education. Award winners are guests at the AAP Annual Meeting in October, where the crystal award and honorarium are presented. The oral history of each winner is documented for the Academy archives, and the award is supported by an educational grant from the Ross Products Division of Abbott Laboratories, Inc.

• 783 • Neonatal Education Award
For recognition of career contributions to education in neonatal and prenatal medicine. Awarded annually by the Section on Perinatal Pediatrics. Established in 1996.

• 784 • Byron B. Oberst Award
To recognize outstanding contributions to the field of medical informatics in pediatrics. A plaque is awarded annually by the AAP Section on Computers and Other Technologies.

• 785 • Outstanding Chapter Awards
For recognition of outstanding chapter accomplishments. Chapters of the Academy are eligible. Awards are given in three categories: (1) large chapters; (2) medium chapters; and (3) small chapters. Three monetary awards of $1,000 for the large chapter, $2,000 for the medium chapter, and $3,000 to the small chapter. Plaques are awarded annually. Established in 1963. Sponsored by Wyeth-Lederle Vaccines and Pediatrics. Formerly: (1991) Wyeth-Ayerst Outstanding Chapter Awards.

• 786 • Outstanding Service Award for Military Pediatrics
For recognition of outstanding contributions to military Pediatrics. A monetary award of $300 and a plaque are awarded annually by the AAP Section on Uniformed Services. Established in 1975.

• 787 • Pediatric Resident Research Award
To recognize an individual for research carried out during residency training. Selection is based on quality of experimental design, execution, and scientific and clinical significance of the research. Candidates must be in residency or in first year following residency year at the point of nomination for the award. Research of clinical and applied research, epidemiological and behavioral studies, health services research, and population-based studies. The deadline is January 31. A monetary award of $1,000 and travel expenses are awarded annually at the annual meeting. Established in 1989.

• 788 • Pediatric Urology Medal
To recognize outstanding contributions to the field of urology. The award consists of a bronze medal and is presented during the meeting of the Section on Pediatric Urology. Established in 1984.

• 789 • Practitioner Research Award
To recognize a pediatrician who has made an outstanding contribution in research, although he spends at least 80 percent of his time in patient care. Results of the recipient's research must have been published in peer reviewed publications. Recipients are selected by the Committee on Pediatric Research. Nominations may be submitted by January 31. A monetary award of $1,500 and a plaque are presented annually. Established in 1986.

• 790 • Professional Education Project Award
Presented to acknowledge an individual or group of pediatricians who are actively involved in innovative projects to educate pediatricians, medical students, residents, and nurses. Recipients are guests at the AAP Annual Meeting in October, where they will be presented with a crystal award and honorarium. Awards are supported with an educational grant from Ross Products Division Abbot Laboratories, Inc.

• 791 • Bret Ratner Award
For recognition of notable contributions to research in pediatric allergy and immunology. A monetary award of $1,000 and a plaque are awarded in alternate years by the Section on Allergy and Immunology at the AAP Annual Meeting. Established in 1959. Sponsored by Ros Division, Abbott Laboratories.

• 792 • Resident and Fellow Achievement Awards
To recognize outstanding service in the field of injury and poison prevention by residents and fellows. Monetary awards of $1,000 and plaques are presented to a pediatric resident and an AAP Fellow by the AAP Section on Injury and Poison Prevention. Established in 1992.

• 793 • Dale Richmond Lectureship
For recognition of achievements in the field of child development. A monetary prize of $500 and a plaque are awarded annually at the Section on Developmental and Behavioral Pediatrics at the AAP meeting. Established in 1973.

• 794 • Arnold M. Salzberg Mentorship Award
To recognize a Section on Surgery member who has become distinguished in the capacity of mentoring an aspiring pediatric surgeon. Awarded annually. Established in 1997.

• 795 • Milton J. E. Senn Lectureship and Award
To recognize outstanding contributions to the field of school health. A monetary prize of $100 and a plaque is awarded annually by the AAP Section on School Health.

• 796 • Thomas E. Shaffer Award
To recognize an individual who has made a lifelong contribution to the field of pediatric sports medicine. A plaque and monetary award of $500 are given annually at the AAP Annual Meeting by the Section on Sports Medicine and Fitness. Established in 2000.

• 797 • Job Lewis Smith Award
For recognition of outstanding service in community pediatrics. A monetary prize of $250 and a plaque are awarded annually by the AAP Section on Community Pediatrics. Established in 1977.

• 798 • Robert M. Smith Award
For recognition of outstanding service in the field of pediatric anesthesiology. A plaque and monetary award are presented irregularly by the AAP Section on Anesthesiology. Established in 1987.

• 799 • Martin C. Ushkow Community Service Award
To recognize outstanding contributions to the promotion of comprehensive school health or health professional education in school health. A plaque and monetary sum of $100 are awarded annually by the Section on School Health. Established in 1995.

• 800 •
American Academy of Periodontology
Alice DeForest, Exec.Dir.
737 N Michigan Ave., Ste. 800
Chicago, IL 60611-2615
Phone: (312)787-5518
Fax: (312)787-3670
E-mail: aapsite@perio.org
Home Page: http://www.perio.org

• 801 • American Academy of Periodontology Student Award
To honor senior dental students who have done outstanding work in the field of periodontics. A certificate and a year's subscription to the *Journal of Periodontology* are awarded annually. Established in 1964.

• 802 • Clinical Research Award in Periodontology
To recognize the author of the most outstanding published scientific paper having direct clinical relevance and application to the practice of periodontics. Papers that appear in the referenced scientific literature within the prior calendar year are eligible. A monetary prize of $3,000 and a certificate are awarded annually. Established in 1984.

• 803 • Fellow
To recognize an academy member for distinguished service to the academy. A monetary award of $1,000 and a certificate are presented annually.

• 804 • William J. Gies Foundation Award in Memory of Arthur Hastings Merritt
To recognize outstanding contributions to dental science, especially with reference to the periodontal literature. Candidates may be nominated by the academy, but the recipient is selected by the Gies Foundation. A monetary award of $200, a certificate, and a plaque are awarded annually. Established in 1964 by the William J. Gies Foundation. The award honors Dr. William John Gies, the noted biochemist, and Dr. Arthur Hastings Merritt, a famous periodontist.

• 805 • Gold Medal Award
This, the highest award bestowed by the academy, honors an academy member for significant contributions to the understanding of the etiology, prevention, and treatment of periodontal disease. A monetary award of $4,000 and a gold medal are awarded annually. Established in 1967.

• 806 • Honorary Member
To recognize an individual for outstanding contributions to the art and science of periodontology. The individual may or may not be a member of the academy at the time this honor is given. A certificate is awarded when merited.

• 807 • Master Clinician Award
To recognize an academy member who has practiced and demonstrated consistent excellence in periodontics, and has willingly and unselfishly shared clinical expertise with members of the profession. The awardee is held in the highest esteem and is recognized as a master clinician in periodontics. A monetary award of $2,500 is presented when merited. Established in 1987.

• 808 • Balint Orban Prize
To recognize a student paper in the area of periodontology. Students enrolled in graduate or postgraduate training, or who have completed such training within the past year, are eligible. A monetary prize of $500 is awarded.

• 809 • Presidential Award
To recognize an academy member for distinguished service over a period of years. A monetary award of $3,000 is presented annually. Established in 1987.

• 810 • R. Earl Robinson Periodontal Regeneration Award
To recognize the author(s) of peer-reviewed published paper that has best contributed to knowledge of periodontal regeneration in a given calendar year. The research may be either in the basic or clinical sciences. A monetary award of $2,000 is presented. Established in 1989 by Dr. R. Earl Robinson to encourage research on periodontal regeneration.

• 811 • Special Citations
To recognize individuals who have contributed to the work of the academy in a noteworthy manner. Awarded annually.

• 812 •
American Academy of Physician Assistants
Steve Crane, Exec.VP/CEO
950 N Washington St.
Alexandria, VA 22314-1552
Phone: (703)836-2272
Fax: (703)684-1924
E-mail: aapa@aapa.org
Home Page: http://www.aapa.org

• 813 • AAPA National and International Humanitarian Physician Assistant of the Year
To honor a physician assistant who has demonstrated an outstanding commitment to human rights with local, national, or international significance and who exemplifies the physician assistant profession's philosophy of providing accessible and quality health care. Current members of the Academy are eligible. A monetary award of $2,500 and a crystal PAragon are awarded annually at the Physician Assistant Conference. In addition, $2,500 is donated to the charity of the winner's choice. Established in 1986. Sponsored by National Professional Group. Formerly: (1997) AAPA Humanitarian Physician Assistant of the Year.

• 814 • AAPA Outstanding Physician Assistant of the Year Award
To honor a physician assistant for exemplary service to the profession and the community. Members in good standing for the past three years who do not currently serve the AAPA in a national leadership position are eligible. A monetary award of $2,500 and a crystal PAragon are presented to the recipient. In addition, $2,500 is donated to the Physician Assistant Foundation in the award winner's name. Awarded annually at the Physician Assistant Conference. Established in 1986. Sponsored by AAPA and Pfizer Inc.

• 815 • AAPA PA Awareness Achievement Award
To honor a physician assistant or non-physician assistant who, through some form of public education activity, has substantially increased public awareness about the PA profession. A monetary award of $2,500 and a crystal PAragon are presented to the recipient. In addition, a $2,500 matching contribution to the Physician Assistant Foundation of the American Academy of Physician Assistants is awarded. Presented annually at the Physician Assistant Conference. Established in 1987. Sponsored by AAPA and Zeneca Pharmaceuticals.

• 816 • AAPA Rural Physician Assistant of the Year
To honor a physician assistant who has provided accessible, quality health care in a rural community of the United States. Rural is defined as a community of fewer than 10,000 people. Current members of the Academy are eligible. A monetary award of $2,500 and a crystal PAragon are presented to the recipient. In addition, $2,500 is donated to the charity of the winner's choice. Presented annually at the Physician Assistant Conference. Established in 1987. Sponsored by the AAPA and Bristol-Myers Squibb.

• 817 • PA Service to the Underserved Award
To honor a physician assistant who has provided accessible, quality health care to the underserved in a rural community or an inner city setting of the U.S. Current members of the Academy are eligible. A monetary award of $2,500, a crystal Paragon, and a $2,500 donation to the charity of the winner's choice are presented each year at the annual Physician Assistant Conference. Established in 1993. Formerly: Inner City Physician Assistant of the Year.

• 818 • Physician Assistant Educator of the Year Award
To honor a PA educator who has contributed to the profession by excelling as an educator of PA students. Any physician assistant who is a current AAPA member in good standing and does not currently serve as a member of the judging committee may participate in the award competition by self-nomination or nomination by someone else. The recipient is given $2,500 and a crystal PAragon at the awards ceremony at the AAPA annual conference. A matching gift of $2,500 is donated to a charity of the recipient's choice. Nominations should be received by December 1. The award is sponsored by Searle.

• 819 •
American Academy of Professional Coders
Lan C. England, Exec.Dir.
309 West 700 South
Salt Lake City, UT 84101-2608
Toll-Free: 800-626-2633
Fax: (801)236-2258
E-mail: info@aapc.com
Home Page: http://www.aapc.com

• 820 • Coder of the Year Award
To recognize excellence in medical coding. A monetary award is awarded annually.

• 821 • Local Chapeter of the Year
To recognize group effort at networking on a local basis. A monetary award is given annually.

• 822 • Networker of the Year Award
To recognize efforts in connecting coders together for discussion leading to correct solutions of reimbursement. A monetary award is awarded annually.

• 823 •
American Academy of Psychiatry and the Law
Jacquelyn T. Coleman CAE, Exec.Dir.
One Regency Dr.
PO Box 30
Bloomfield, CT 06002-0030
Phone: (860)242-5450
Toll-Free: 800-331-1389
Fax: (860)286-0787
E-mail: office@aapl.org
Home Page: http://www.aapl.org

• 824 • AAPL Outstanding Service Award
To recognize individuals for service to the Academy. Members of the Academy who have contributed to the organization through service on committees, task forces, etc., are eligible. A wall plaque with a red apple attached is awarded annually in October. Established in 1985.

• 825 • Amicus Award
To recognize an individual for devoted service and numerous contributions over many years to the Academy. Non-members of the Academy are eligible. A certificate is awarded. Established in 1986.

• 826 • Golden Apple Award
To provide recognition to those members who have made significant contributions to the field of forensic psychiatry. Senior members who have achieved eminence in the field and contributed to the education of other forensic psychiatrists are generally considered for the award. A plaque with a gold apple is presented annually. Established in 1972 by Robert Sadoff, M.D.

• 827 • Seymour Pollack Distinguished Achievement Award
To recognize distinguished contributions to the field of forensic psychiatry. Non-members of the Academy are eligible. Certificates are awarded annually. Established in 1986 in memory of Seymour Pollack, M.D.

• 828 • Red Apple Award
Annual award of recognition.

• 829 •
American Academy of Religion
Barbara DeConcini, Exec.Dir.
825 Houston Mill Rd. NE, No. 300
Atlanta, GA 30329-4205
Phone: (404)727-3049
Fax: (404)727-7959
E-mail: aar@aarweb.org
Home Page: http://www.aarweb.org

• 830 • Award for Excellence in Teaching
Recognizes the importance of teaching in the field. Nominees must exhibit outstanding classroom performances; development of effective methods, courses, or materials; influence in interesting students in the field of religion and commitment to the profession. Nominees must have been teaching for at least three years. A 500 word letter of nomination, a curriculum vitae; and three letters o recommendation must be submitted. Submission deadline is October 15th. Formerly: Award for Excellence in Book Publication.

• 831 • Best First Book in the History of Religions
Recognizes an outstanding book on the history of religions. Nominated title must be the author's first book. Awarded annually.

• 832 • Ray L. Hart Service Award
To recognize a person whose dedication and service have made significant contributions to the AAR's mission of fostering excellence in the field of religion. A monetary award is given annually at the AAR Annual Meeting. Established in 1992.

• 833 • Martin E. Marty Public Understanding of Religion Award
To recognize works that appeal to the public as well as to the scholars. A monetary award is given at the AAR Annual Meeting. Established in 1996.

• 834 •
American Academy of Sanitarians
Gary Noonan, contact
720 S Colorado Blvd., Ste. 960-S
Denver, CO 80246
Phone: (678)584-9127
Fax: (678)584-9127
E-mail: gnoonan@charter.com
Home Page: http://Sanitarians.org

• 835 • Davis Calvin Wagner Sanitarian Award
To recognize an outstanding sanitarian for promoting the improvement of the public's health through the application of environmental health and public health practices. Diplomates of the academy who demonstrate professional, administrative, and technical skills, and who are involved in continuing education type programs, are eligible. The deadline for nominations is April 15. An honorarium of $500 and a plaque are awarded annually at the meeting of the National Environmental Health Association Education Conference. Established in 1981 by Assistant Surgeon General Carruth J. Wagner to honor the memory of his brother.

• 836 •
American Academy of Sleep Medicine
Jerome Barrett, Exec.Dir.
1 Westbrook Corporate Ctr., Ste. 920
Westchester, IL 60154
Phone: (708)492-0930
Fax: (708)492-0943
E-mail: asmf@aasmnet.org
Home Page: http://www.aasmnet.org
Formerly: (1987) Association of Sleep Disorders Centers.

• 837 • William C. Dement Academic Achievement Award
To recognize members of the sleep field who have displayed considerable initiative and progress in the areas of sleep education and academic research. The award represents a commitment to disseminating the truth about sleep and its disorders, and epitomizes the pursuit of knowledge and a never-ending commitment to helping others understand sleep disorders and the field of sleep medicine. An engraved award is presented annually to the recipient. Established in 1994 to honor William C. Dement, MD, PhD, one of the world's foremost authorities on the subject of sleep and sleep research.

• 838 • Mark O. Hatfield Public Policy Award
To recognize an individual who has achieved outstanding accomplishments on behalf of healthy sleep for all Americans. An engraved award will be presented annually to the recipient. Established in 1996 to honor a great man, Senior Senator Mark O. Hatfield from the state of Oregon, for his efforts and accomplishments in effecting change to deal with the ever-present societal problems of pervasive sleep deprivation and a pandemic of undiagnosed and untreated sleep disorders.

• 839 • Nathaniel Kleitman Distinguished Service Award
To honor service to the field of sleep research and sleep disorders medicine, especially generous and altruistic efforts in the areas of administration, public relations, and legislation. Established in 1981 to honor Dr. Nathaniel Kleitman, a scientist whose discoveries established the importance of the study of sleep physiology.

• 840 • Young Investigator's Award
Presented annually to students who have the potential to identify new technologic and scientific research methods, and the application of these methods to the field of sleep medicine. All abstracts that are submitted to the annual meeting with a student status designation are considered for the award (only students who are under 40 years of age as of the abstract submission deadline are eligible). One first-place winner and four runners-up are selected from these submissions. All award recipients receive a certificate and a monetary award; the first-place winner also receives a complimentary one-year student membership to the ASDA and is asked to serve on the Research Committee for one year.

• 841 •
American Academy of Somnology
Dr. David L. Hopper Ph.D., Founder & Pres.
PO Box 27077
Las Vegas, NV 89126
Phone: (702)222-6463
E-mail: somnology@aol.com

• 842 • Fellow
To recognize an individual for contributions to the field of somnology. Nominees must be Board certified (Diplomate) in somnology by the American Board of Somnology. A certificate is awarded biennially. Established in 1986.

• 843 •
American Academy of the History of Dentistry
Marc B. Ehrlich DMD, Sec.-Treas.
1371 Beacon St.
Brookline, MA 02446
Phone: (617)566-2734
E-mail: info@histden.org
Home Page: http://histden.org

• 844 • M. D. K. Bremner Awards
To encourage study and research in the history of dentistry and the dental profession. Dental students in American and Canadian Dental Colleges must submit original history-related essays through Dean of the college. A monetary award of $500, a certificate, and membership in the academy are awarded each year at the annual meeting. Established in 1960 and financed initially by the sale of M. D. K. Bremner's book *The Story of Dentistry*.

• 845 • Hayden-Harris Award
To recognize distinguished contributions to the history of dentistry. Eligibility is based on judgement of merit by the Committee of the Academy. A certificate is awarded when merited at the annual meeting of the Academy. Established in 1967 in memory of Horace H. Hayden, M.D., D.D.S., and Chapin A. Harris, M.D., D.D.S., founders of the Baltimore College of Dental Surgery, the world's first dental school, in 1840.

• 846 •
American Accordion Musicological Society
Stanley Darrow, Sec.
322 Haddon Ave.
Westmont, NJ 08108-0000
Phone: (856)854-6628
Phone: (856)854-6628

• 847 • **Biennial Composers Competition**
To add literature to the repertoire of the accordion. Serious composers are eligible for the award. Annual Accordion Symposium is always held the first week of March. Publication of the honored work is awarded biennially. Established in 1970.

• 848 •
American Accordionists' Association
Dr. Carmelo Pino, Pres.
580 Kearny Ave.
Kearny, NJ 07032
Phone: (201)991-2233
Fax: (201)991-1944
E-mail: aaa1938@aol.com
Home Page: http://www.ameraccord.com

• 849 • **American Accordionists' Association Contest and Festival**
To recognize outstanding accordionists. The competition is held for age divisions from 7 years through 18 and over. The deadline for entries is May 20. Awards are presented in the following categories: solos, duets, open band, open ensemble, pop combo, entertainment, standard ensemble, and standard band.

• 850 •
American Adoption Congress
Marilyn Waugh, Pres.
PO Box 42730
Washington, DC 20015
Phone: (202)483-3399
E-mail: ameradoptioncong@aol.com
Home Page: http://www.americanadoptioncongress.org/

• 851 • **Honorary Lifetime Membership**
To recognize individuals who have promoted openness and honesty in adoption and contributed their time and effort to the American Adoption Congress. Selection is by nomination and approval of the Board of Directors. A gold pin is awarded when merited. Established in 1979.

• 852 • **Emma May Vilardi Humanitarian Award**
To recognize lifelong contribution to adoption advocacy.

• 853 •
American Advertising Federation
Wally Snyder, Pres./CEO
1101 Vermont Ave. NW, Ste. 500
Washington, DC 20005-6306
Phone: (202)898-0089
Fax: (202)898-0159
E-mail: aaf@aaf.org
Home Page: http://www.aaf.org

• 854 • **AAF Best in the West Creative Competition**
To recognize outstanding, creative excellence in advertising. Awards are presented in the following categories: television, radio, consumer magazine, newspaper, business publications, outdoor, transit, direct mail, sales promotion, print, specialty advertising, public service, and complete campaign. Advertisers, agencies, production companies, and other organizations for advertising created in any of the 13 Western states or El Paso, Texas, are eligible. Trophies and certificates are awarded for First Prize, Second Prize, and Best of Division winners. Certificates are awarded to Merit Award winners. Awarded annually. Established in 1950 by the Advertising Association of the West.

• 855 • **Advertising Hall of Achievement**
To encourage and recognize those who have just begun to make a significant impact on, or contribution to, the advertising business. Men and women 40 years old or under who are employed in the advertising industry - agency, client, or media - anywhere in the United States or with an American company abroad are eligible. Nominees are evaluated by an industry Council of Judges on the following criteria: Primary - outstanding career achievements, with measurable results in the field of advertising, whether in publishing, marketing, sales or media. Secondary - Qualities that motivate others to excel, exhibited through mentoring, inspiring, training or volunteering in the business. Awarded annually to one or more recipients. Established in 1993.

• 856 • **Advertising Hall of Fame**
To recognize men and women who have completed their major work and careers, in advertising. Nominees are judged on the following criteria: Primary - The candidate's, accomplishments evidenced by creative, media research or marketing excellence; innovations to advertising education, the advertising process and structure or impact on brand and corporate success and leadership of his or her company. Secondary - The contributions the candidate have made to enhancing the reputation of the advertising industry through volunteer efforts outside of his or her company. The nominee's record of advertising and service must have been accomplished in the advertising industry in the United States or with an American company abroad. Both living and deceased persons are eligible. Nominations may be made by an advertising club or federation, an advertising association or group, members of the Council of Judges, or any firm or individual anywhere in the United States. Selection is made by an industry Council of Judges. Awarded annually. Established in 1948.

• 857 • **Aid to Advertising Education Award**
To recognize local advertising professionals, individually or as a group, for outstanding and crucial support provided to college chapters. Those who have served to further advertising education at their institutions are eligible. Awards are presented annually. Established in 1978.

• 858 • **The American Advertising Awards**
To honor excellent advertising campaigns and officially reward those who create advertising. Any advertiser or agency, individual writer, art director, producer or creative director, or medium supplier may enter. To be eligible for the national ADDY, an entry must first win in a local ADDY competition sponsored by one of the AAF's affiliated advertising clubs/federations. Most clubs begin accepting entries in January. Winners at the local level are then eligible to enter one of 15 district competitions. District winners may then progress to the nationals. Awarded annually in June. Established in 1968. Additional information is available from Gail Bozeman, Director, Club Services. Formerly: National ADDY Campaign Awards.

• 859 • **Distinguished Advertising Educator Award**
To recognize an educator who is or has been a full-time professor at an accredited college or university and who has made a significant impact upon advertising education during a career of distinguished teaching. Judges consider the following measures of distinction: Teaching excellence - must demonstrate an ability to affect student knowledge and to hold interest in the classroom; Scholarly research - must show ability to research and develop conclusions that stand the test of practical application; Writing - must express talent in the publication of books, articles, or monographs; Student advisement - must place value upon counseling/advising students and upon acting as a directed and caring role model for young people; Participation in regional or national professional advertising organizations - must demonstrate awareness of and involvement in current issues that impact the industry; Community service - must show an awareness of an obligation to the public through active participation in community projects, advertising federations, and other local organizations; Significant professional experience - must show an ability to mesh theory with reality. Teaching experience - must demonstrate dedication to advertising education through a minimum of 10 years of teaching experience. Nominations are accepted from individuals. Awarded annually. Established in 1987.

• 860 • **National Club Achievement Competition**
The AAF's National Club Achievement Competition is designed to recognize and honor the hard work of the many volunteers comprising the 218 AAF affiliated advertising clubs and federations. Clubs participating in the competition enter any combination of eight categories: Advertising Education, Club Management, Communications,

Diversity, Government Relations, Membership, Programs, and Public Service. To facilitate the fairest possible judging, clubs compete within their membership size divisions. Ad 2 clubs, for members under the age of 32, compete in their own division.

• 861 • National Student Advertising Competition (NSAC)

This competition provides undergraduate advertising students with a realistic advertising/marketing problem to be solved through team effort, knowledge, and creativity. It is intended to demonstrate the effectiveness of advertising education. Dues paid members who are full-time students may participate. Points awarded to each campaign are based on a combination of a Plans Book execution and a 20-minute presentation of creative material. Student teams from colleges in each of AAF's 15 districts compete locally. The winning team in each district goes on to present its proposal before a panel of national judges. Finals are held at AAF's National Advertising Conference. First, second, third, and fourth place teams receive plaques for their schools. All members of these teams receive individual prizes. All participating students and advisors receive certificates. Awarded annually. Established in 1973. Sponsors vary.

• 862 • Silver Medal Award

To recognize men and women who have made outstanding contributions to advertising and have been active in furthering the industry's standards, creative excellence, and responsibility in areas of social concern. Annually, each local advertising club is entitled to bestow this honor upon a deserving member of their community. Honorees are presented with a Silver Medal plaque or medallion. The award winners are chosen by the ad clubs and nominations are accepted.

• 863 •
American Agri-Women
Sandy Greiner, Pres.
1005 Hwy 92
Keota, IA 52248
E-mail: info@americanagriwomen.org
Home Page: http://www.americanagriwomen.org

• 864 • American Agri-Women Awards

For recognition of outstanding achievements in promoting agriculture for the benefit of the American people and the world. The following awards are given: (1) Agri-Women of the Year - established in 1976; (2) Communications Award - established in 1977; (3) President's Award established in 1978; and (4) Special Recognition - established in 1978. Plaques are awarded.

• 865 • Leaven Award

To recognize individuals who, to an outstanding degree, have acted as "leaven," a truly feminine concept since "lady" means "giver of bread." A plaque is awarded. Established in 1977.

• 866 • Veritas Award

To recognize individuals who have given public witness to "the pursuit of truth" in accordance with the principles enunciated in the AAW statement of philosophy, "The Call to Power." Of specific interest is responsible media coverage of issues, events or personalities of critical importance to the agricultural industry. Coverage may include reporting (news stories, features, documentaries), opinion (editorials, commentaries, surveys), and pictorial representation (photographs, and cartoons). A plaque is awarded. Established in 1981.

• 867 •
American Agricultural Economics Association
Donna F. Dunn, Exec.Dir.
415 S Duff Ave., Ste. C
Ames, IA 50010-6600
Phone: (515)233-3202
Fax: (515)233-3101
E-mail: info@aaea.org
Home Page: http://www.aaea.org

Formerly: (1968) American Farm Economics Association.

• 868 • Awards for Research and Outstanding Publications in Agricultural Economics

To recognize and encourage meritorious research and publication in agricultural economics. Selections are made from published research, textbooks, and extension publications. A maximum of five awards are offered each year: one or two awards are offered for outstanding research publications of the previous calendar year and are judged for the quality of their discovery; one or two awards are offered for outstanding publications of the previous calendar year and are judged for their quality of communication; and one is offered for an article published during the fifteen year period ending eleven years prior to the award and is judged for the enduring quality of its professional contribution. Awarded annually.

• 869 • Distinguished Extension Programs

To recognize achievement of excellence in extension economics teaching programs. Two awards are given: one for an individual, and one for a group. Awarded annually.

• 870 • Distinguished Policy Contribution

To recognize an outstanding contribution to policy decisions or to the advancement of public understanding and human welfare. They may related to either a national or international situation. Nominations may be submitted by individuals, groups, or institutions. A certificate is awarded annually.

• 871 • Distinguished Teaching Awards

To recognize and encourage meritorious performance in undergraduate and graduate teaching in agricultural economics. A maximum of three awards are made in the following categories: one for less than ten years' experience as a full-time professional; one for ten or more years undergraduate teaching as a full-time professional; and one for ten or more years graduate teaching as a full-time professional.

• 872 • Outstanding Article in *American Journal of Agricultural Economics* Award

To recognize the outstanding article in the *Journal*. The editor and associate editors of the *Journal*, with the editor as chairman, selects the article from the previous volume of the *Journal*. Awarded annually at the meeting of the Association.

• 873 • Outstanding Doctoral Thesis Award

To recognize the development of professional excellence by persons writing doctoral dissertations in agricultural, natural resource, or rural economics. A maximum of three awards of $250 each are presented annually.

• 874 • Outstanding Master's Thesis Award

To recognize the development of professional excellence by individuals writing master's theses in agricultural, natural resource, or rural economics. A maximum of three awards of $250 each are presented annually.

• 875 •
American Alliance for Health, Physical Education, Recreation and Dance
Michael G. Davis, CEO
1900 Association Dr.
Reston, VA 20191-1598
Phone: (703)476-3400
Toll-Free: 800-213-7193
Fax: (703)476-9527
Home Page: http://www.aahperd.org

• 876 • William G. Anderson Merit Award

To recognize persons who are not members of the Alliance, but who have contributed significantly to health education, physical education, sports, recreation, dance, and/or safety education through their efforts in allied or auxiliary fields such as medicine, public health, education, or government. Non-members of the Alliance who are 40 years of age or over are eligible. Not more than three certificates are awarded annually. Established in 1949.

• 877 • Luther Halsey Gulick Award

This, the highest award the Alliance bestows on its members, is given to recognize long and distinguished service to one of the professions represented in the Alliance. Individuals who have been active in the Alliance for at least 10 years are eligible. A medal is awarded annually if merited. Established in 1923.

• 878 • Charles D. Henry Award

For recognition of essential contributions of its members who, through distinguished service to the Alliance (or its component structures), increase involvement of ethnic minorities in AAHPERD, increase communication with greater numbers of ethnic minority members, and extend meaningful services to AAHPERD ethnic minorities. Members who have held such membership for at least five years and have served professionally in school (preschool, elementary, secondary), college, or community programs in AAHPERD for a period of at least five years may be nominated. A plaque is presented annually in a ceremony at the national convention. One award is given each year. Established in 1984.

• 879 • Honor Award
To recognize meritorious service on the part of members of the Alliance. Selection is based on evidence of successful experience in any five or more of the following categories: offices, leadership, committee work, writing, research, speaking, teaching, coaching, performing, supervising, or directing. Up to eight certificates are awarded annually as many as four to college/university personnel and four to non-college/university personnel. Established in 1931.

• 880 • Mabel Lee Award
To recognize younger members of the Alliance who have demonstrated outstanding potential for scholarship, teaching, and/or professional leadership. Active members of the Alliance who are 36 years of age or younger are eligible. Up to two awards presented annually. Established in 1976.

• 881 • R. Tait McKenzie Award
To recognize significant contributions of members made outside the framework of the Alliance, but which reflect prestige, honor, and dignity to the Alliance. These activites may include work in government, general education, public health, or international affairs. Up to two awards are presented annually. Established in 1968.

• 882 •
American Alliance for Theatre and Education
Janet E. Rubin, Pres.
7475 Wisconsin Ave., Ste. 300A
Bethesda, MD 20814
Phone: (301)951-7977
Fax: (301)968-0144
E-mail: info@aate.com
Home Page: http://www.aate.com

Formerly: Artists and Educators Serving Young People; American Association for Theatre in Secondary Education.

• 883 • AATE Distinguished Book Award
To recognize the outstanding book relating to any aspect of theater and education published during the past calendar year (January-December). An award is made both to the writer and to the publisher. Awarded annually. Established in 1989.

• 884 • AATE Research Award
To acknowledge exemplary research on drama/theater and education for young people of a historical, theoretical, critical, empirical, ethnographic, or other scholarly research. Open to any individual or collaborative team in any discipline engaged in drama/theater research. A monetary prize of $100 is awarded annually. Established in 1980.

• 885 • Alliance Award
To honor a member of the American Alliance for Theatre and Education for long-term and sustained service to the organization. Established in 1990.

• 886 • John C. Barner Teacher of the Year Award
To recognize an outstanding theater arts teacher. Awarded annually. Established in 1983 to honor John C. Barner, the first Director of SSTA and the only individual to also have served as President of SSTA. He was an active member of SSTA from its inception until his death in June, 1981.

• 887 • Campton Bell Lifetime Achievement Award
To recognize an individual for a lifetime of outstanding contributions to the field of child drama. Awarded annually. Established in 1983.

• 888 • Charlotte B. Chorpenning Playwright Award
To recognize an outstanding writer of plays for children. Playwrights of national recognition are considered. A silver cup is awarded annually when merited. Established in 1967.

• 889 • Creative Drama Award
To recognize a person or persons for outstanding achievement and service as a creative drama specialist. Only members of AATE may be nominated.

• 890 • Distinguished Play Awards
To recognize outstanding scripts in two categories: plays primarily for upper and secondary school age audiences, plays primarily for elementary and middle school age audiences. Awarded annually. Established in 1983.

• 891 • Ann Flagg Multicultural Award
To recognize an individual, organization, institution, or company making significant contributions to the field of theater/drama for youth or arts education dealing with multicultural issues and/or reaching diverse audiences and constituencies. Open to persons of any ethnic, racial, or cultural background and to nonmembers of AATE. Awarded annually. Established in 1993 in honor of Ann Flagg who worked as an elementary drama teacher in the Evanston, Illinois school district and as director and playwright at Karamu House in Cleveland, Ohio.

• 892 • Monte Meacham Award
To recognize a person or organization outside AATE for outstanding contributions to children's theater. Awarded annually. Established in 1959.

• 893 • Sara Spencer Artistic Achievement Award
To acknowledge a long established children's theater for meritorious achievement, or an individual for outstanding achievement in the field of theater for young audiences. The theater must have been in operation for a minimum of seven years. Awarded annually. Established in 1978.

• 894 • Winifred Ward & Award for Outstanding New Children's Theatre & Company
To recognize a graduate scholar of demonstrated intellectual and artistic ability in child drama/theater. Nominees are judged on the basis of scholarship, faculty recommendations, indication of strong professional interest and growth, successful performance in some aspect of children's theater of creative drama, and other criteria. Awarded annually by the Zeta Phi Eta A National Arts Fraternity Established in 1978.

• 895 • Zeta Phi Eta Winifred Ward Prize for Outstanding New Children's Theatre Company
To recognize a children's theater that has attained a high level of artistic production and sound management practices and has stimulated community interest in its endeavors. The organization must have been in operation for at least two full years, but not more than five years. Awarded annually. Established in 1957. Formerly: (1991) Zeta Phi Eta - Winifred Ward Prize.

• 896 • F. Loren Winship Secondary School Theatre Award
To recognize an individual or organization for outstanding contribution to the mission of secondary school theater. Awarded annually. Established in 1963 to honor those educators in high school theater who established the secondary school theater movement in the U.S. Formerly: Director's Award; Founder's Award.

• 897 • AATE Lin Wright Special Recognition Award
To recognize individuals and/or a group who have established special programs, made a distinctive educational contribution, developed special experimental work, or provided meritorious service for the betterment of child drama and the profession. Citations are awarded annually. Established in 1971.

• 898 • Youth Theatre Director of the Year Award
To recognize an individual for outstanding achievement as a director in a youth theater. The recipient should serve as a model of excellence and innovation as an artistic, educational, and/or management director in a theater in which some or all of the performers are young people. Awarded annually. Established in 1986.

• 899 •
American Amateur Press Association
Les Boyer, First VP
535 Kickerillo Dr.
Houston, TX 77079
Phone: (281)497-8493
E-mail: leswboyer@prodigy.net
Home Page: http://members.aol.com/aapa96/

• 900 • **Laureates**
Awards are given in the following categories: Journal of Overall Excellence; Letterpress Journal; Non-letterpress Journal; Fiction; Nonfiction, hobby-related; Nonfiction, general; Poetry; Art; Awards of Merit; and Special Recognition. Must be a member of the Association to Be eligible. Awarded annually.

• 901 •
American Animal Hospital Association
John W. Albers DVM, Exec.Dir.
12575 W Bayaud Ave.
Lakewood, CO 80228
Phone: (303)986-2800
Toll-Free: 800-252-2242
Fax: (303)986-1700
E-mail: info@aahanet.org
Home Page: http://www.aahanet.org

• 902 • **AAHA Award**
To recognize either an individual or organization who has made outstanding contributions, directly or indirectly, toward the betterment AAHA and the veterinary profession. Established in 1958.

• 903 • **Hill's Animal Welfare and Humane Ethics Award**
To recognize a veterinarian or non-veterinarian who has advanced animal welfare through extraordinary service or by furthering humane principles, education and understanding. A monetary award of $1,000, an engraved plaque, and paid travel expenses to the AAHA annual meeting accompany the award.

• 904 • **Innovative Veterinary Diets Award**
To recognize an individual who has made extensive contributions to the practice of veterinary medicine and surgery in general, and small animal veterinary medicine or surgery in particular. Established in 1947. Formerly: Gaines Award; (2004) Cycle Award.

• 905 • **Practitioner of the Year Award**
To recognize on the national level the year's most outstanding practicing veterinarian. The recipient must be a veterinarian, an AAHA member, involved in clinical private practice and have demonstrated commitment to AAHA, the profession the community, his or her patients and excellence in small animal medicine and surgery. A plaque is awarded annually at the convention. Established in 1975 in memory of Dr. Charles E. Bild.

• 906 • **Royal Canin Award**
To recognize an individual for outstanding public service activities that have resulted in the improvement of the well-being of companion animals in the veterinary world community. Established in 1988. Formerly: Kal Kan Award.

• 907 • **Student Achievement Award**
To recognize a senior student at college of veterinary medicine in the United States and Canada. The faculty of the individual college chooses the recipient with emphasis placed on accomplishments in small animal medicine and surgery. The award includes a plaque, a check for $200, and a complimentary registration to one AAHA regional and one AAHA annual meeting, and free membership in the AAHA for one year.

• 908 •
American Anthropological Association
Bill Davis, Exec.Dir.
2200 Wilson Blvd., Ste. 600
Arlington, VA 22201-3357
Phone: (703)528-1902
Fax: (703)528-3546
E-mail: members@aaanet.org
Home Page: http://www.aaanet.org

• 909 • **Anthropology in Media Award**
Recognizes successful communication of anthropology to the general public through the media. There are no eligibility restrictions. Awardee is recommended by the Awards Committee and chosen by the AAA Executive Board at its spring meeting. A certificate is awarded annually. Established in 1987.

• 910 • **Distinguished Lecture Award**
Recognizes intellectual contributions in anthropology. The honoree presents the lecture at the annual meeting of the association, which is then published in the *American Anthropologist.* A lecturer is selected biennially. Established in 1969.

• 911 • **Alfred Vincent Kidder Award for Eminence in the Field of American Archaeology**
Recognizes eminence in the field of American archaeology. A medal and citation are awarded every three years. Established in 1950.

• 912 • **Margaret Mead Award**
Recognizes a person clearly and integrally associated with research and/or practice in anthropology. Presented for a particular accomplishment, such as a book, film, monograph, service, or film, which interprets anthropological data and principles in ways that make them meaningful to the public. Nominees must have received a PhD degree within the past ten years. A monetary prize of $1000 and a plaque are awarded annually. Established in 1979 in memory of Margaret Mead, the noted anthropologist. Co-sponsored by the Society for Applied Anthropology.

• 913 •
American Antiquarian Society
Ellen S. Dunlap, Pres.
185 Salisbury St.
Worcester, MA 01609-1634
Phone: (508)755-5221
Fax: (508)753-3311
E-mail: library@mwa.org
Home Page: http://www.americanantiquarian.org

• 914 • **Fellowship for Creative and Performing Arts and Writers**
Projects relating to American history are eligible, but they are intended for the general public rather than academic or educational audiences. Fellowship projects may include, but are not limited to: historical novels, performances of historical music or dramas, poetry, documentary films, television programs, radio broadcasts, plays, libretti, screenplays, magazine or newspaper articles, costume designs, set designs, illustrations and other graphic arts, book designs, sculpture, paintings, other works of fine art and applied art, and nonfiction works of history designed for general audiences or children. Three fellowships will be awarded for residence of four weeks at the Society. A stipend of $1200 plus a travel allowance will be given as well.

• 915 • **Mellon Post-Dissertation Fellowship**
A minimum of twelve month fellowship for scholars no more than three years beyond receipt of their doctorate. Intended to provide the recipient with time and resources to extend research and revise the dissertation written for publication. Anything relevant to the society's library collections and programmatic scope of American history and culture through 1876 is eligible. Applicants must come from such fields as history, literature, American studies, political science, art history, music history, and others relating to America. The fellow is free to make his or her own arrangements for publication of a book that results from residence as a Mellon Post-Dissertation Fellow at the American Antiquarium Society. The twelve month stipend for this fellowship is $30,000.

• 916 • **Visiting Research Fellowships**
To recognize qualified scholars, in order to encourage imaginative and productive research in the Society's unparalleled library collections in early American history and culture. The following Visiting Research Fellowships are awarded: National Endowment for the Humanities Fellowships - at least two long-term fellowships generally tenable for six to twelve months, although new NEH guidelines permit the Society to arrange tenure of four to five months, with a maximum stipend of $40,000; Kate B. and Hall J. Peterson Fellowships - short-term fellowships of one to three months with monthly stipends of $1000. Open to individuals, including foreign nationals, and persons at work on doctoral dissertations, who are engaged in scholarly research and writing in any field of American history and culture through 1876; AAS - American Society for Eighteenth-Century Studies Fellowships - to promote research in any area of

American eighteenth-century studies for one to two months with a stipend of $1000 per month. Degree candidates are not eligible. The award is jointly funded by the American Society for Eighteenth-Century Studies and AAS; Stephen Botein Fellowships - to support research in the history of the book in American culture for one to two months with a stipend of $1000 per month funded by the income on an endowment established at AAS in memory of Stephen Botein. In all categories, the deadline is January 15. All fellowship awards are made not only on the basis of the applicant's scholarly qualifications and the general interest of the project, but also on the appropriateness of the inquiry to the Society's holdings.

• 917 •
American Arbitration Association
335 Madison Ave., Fl. 10
New York, NY 10017-4605
Phone: (212)716-5800
Toll-Free: 800-778-7879
Fax: (212)716-5905
E-mail: websitemail@adr.org
Home Page: http://www.adr.org

• 918 • Distinguished Service Award
To recognize outstanding service in the arbitration of labor-management disputes. A crystal owl is awarded annually. Established in 1979.

• 919 • Gavel Award
To recognize the retiring Chairman of the Board. A rosewood gavel is awarded at the discretion of the regional offices of the Association.

• 920 • Sylvan Gotshal World Trade Arbitration Medal
To recognize those who have contributed to the development and promotion of international arbitration. A bronze medal is awarded when merited. Established in 1967 by Sylvan Gotshal, a founding member of the firm of Weil, Gotshal and Manges.

• 921 • International Mediation Medal
To recognize an individual for mediation of international conflict. Awarded when merited. Established in 1979.

• 922 • Whitney North Seymour, Sr. Award
To recognize the contribution of a lawyer to the responsible use of arbitration. Lawyers who are active in arbitration are eligible. A bronze medal is awarded annually. Established in 1977 in honor of Whitney North Seymour, Sr., a former president of the American Arbitration Association and the American Bar Association.

• 923 •
American Armsport Association
Frank Bean, Exec.Dir.
176 Dean Rd.
Mooresburg, TN 37811
Fax: (432)272-6162
E-mail: armsport@usit.net
Home Page: http://www.armsport.com

Formerly: American Armwrestling Association.

• 924 • Armwrestler of the Year (Male and Female)
For recognition of achievement and a contribution to the sport of arm wrestling. Members of the Association are eligible. A plaque is awarded annually to a male and a female. Established in 1985.

• 925 • National Championship Awards
To determine the best male and female armwrestlers. Awards are presented in various categories annually.

• 926 •
American Art Therapy Association
Edward J. Stygar Jr., Exec.Dir.
1202 Allanson Rd.
Mundelein, IL 60060-3808
Phone: (847)949-6064
Toll-Free: 888-290-0878
Fax: (847)566-4580
E-mail: info@arttherapy.org
Home Page: http://www.arttherapy.org

• 927 • Gladys Agell Award for Excellence in Research
To recognize the most outstanding project completed within the past year by an art therapist. Project must use a statistical measure in the area of applied art therapy. A monetary prize of $100 is awarded annually.

• 928 • Honorary Life Member
For recognition of major contributions that have broad influence on the field of art therapy. Professional/credentialed members of AATA are eligible. The following criteria are considered: breadth of influence upon the entire field of art therapy, enduring effect upon the entire field of art therapy, and importance as evaluated from an interdisciplinary viewpoint. A plaque and life membership in the Association are awarded each year at the annual National Conference. Established in 1969.

• 929 •
American Artists Professional League
Sonja Weir, Pres.
47 5th Ave.
New York, NY 10003
Phone: (212)645-1345
Fax: (212)645-1345
E-mail: aaplinc@aol.com
Home Page: http://www.americanartistsprofessionalleague.org

• 930 • Grand National Exhibition
To recognize outstanding works in the annual exhibition. Awards are presented in the following categories: oil and polymer painting, watercolor painting, graphic and pastel, and sculpture. Monetary awards totaling over $10,000 and gold medals are presented annually. The Newington Prize of $1,000 is awarded for the best painting in any medium. Established in 1929.

• 931 •
American Assembly
Daniel A. Sharp, Pres./CEO
475 Riverside Dr., Rm. 456
New York, NY 10115-0456
Phone: (212)870-3500
Fax: (212)870-3555
E-mail: amassembly@columbia.edu
Home Page: http://www.americanassembly.org/index.php

• 932 • Service to Democracy Award
To honor two national leaders who have contributed significantly to the development of public policy. One is selected from the public sector; the other from the private sector. Nominations are made by the awards committee. the Eisenhower Medals are presented annually in the fall. Established in 1980 in memory of the late President of the United States, Dwight D. Eisenhower, who had the ability to bring together people of different persuasions with divergent views to develop a common interest in finding a consensus that will lead to changes for the national good. Sponsored by various corporations.

• 933 •
American Assembly for Men in Nursing
Russell G. Tranbarger RN, Pres.
11 Cornell Rd.
Latham, NY 12110-1499
Phone: (518)782-9400
Fax: (518)782-9530
E-mail: aamn@aamn.org
Home Page: http://aamn.org

Formerly: (1971) National Male Nurses Association.

• 934 • Luther Christman Award
To recognize a person or persons who have made an outstanding contribution to nursing that also reflects highly on men in nursing or significantly contributes to the purposes of AAMN. A wood plaque with gold is awarded annually, and winner becomes an honorary member of AAMN for life. Established in 1975 to honor Luther Christman, R.N., Ph.D.

• 935 •
American Association Family Consumer Sciences
Sharon Nikols, Pres.
400 N Columbus St., Ste. 202
Alexandria, VA 22314
Phone: (703)706-4600
Toll-Free: 800-424-8080
Fax: (703)706-4663
E-mail: info@aafcs.org
Home Page: http://www.aafcs.org

Formerly: American Home Economics Association Foundation.

• 936 • AAFCS Leaders Award
Recognizes significant contributions to the field through involvement with the AAFCS. Family and consumer sciences professionals are eligible.

• 937 • AAFCS New Achievers Awards
Recognizes the potential for making significant contributions in or through family and consumer sciences. Emerging professionals are eligible.

• 938 • Borden Award
Recognizes a researcher in the field of nutrition and/or experimental foods who employs fundamental principals of research. Selection is based on published research by a home economist with preference to AHEA members. The deadline is February 1. Presented annually. Established in 1937. Cosponsored by Borden Inc.

• 939 • Commemorative Lecture Award
Designed to stimulate critical thinking and the articulation of family and consumer sciences subject matter and its relationship to society as well as to recognize and honor the professional and intellectual stature of association members. Nominations/applications must be postmarked by January 15. Winners will be announced in April. The winning 30 minute lecture, on any one of the association's priority issues, will be presented at the association's annual meeting and reprinted in the *Journal of Family and Consumer Sciences*. The winner also receives a commemorative plaque and a $2500 honorarium.

• 940 • Excellence in Extension Award
To honor outstanding Extension System programming which enables people to improve their lives and communities through learning partnerships that put knowledge to work in family and consumer sciences programs. Programs considered for this award include: nutrition, health and environment; human development and family resiliency; and family and consumer resource management. Applicants must be current members of the association. Awards may be made to individuals or teams. Winners receive an honorarium of $1,000 and a commemorative plaque that will be presented during the association's annual meeting. Formerly: Extension 2000 Award.

• 941 • Massachusetts Avenue Building Assets Fund Grants Program
Provides funding for initiatives that enhance the well-being of families and which support the program of AAFCS.

• 942 • National Family and Consumer Sciences Teacher of the Year Award Home Economics Teacher of the Year Award
Identifies and recognizes outstanding educational programs, methods, techniques, and activities that provide the stimulus for and give visibility to family and consumer sciences elementary and secondary education. Each participating state selects its state Teacher of the Year. Teacher of the Year is selected from state entries. The deadline is in March of each year. The first place winner receives a monetary prize and a plaque. Presented annually at the annual meeting in June. Established in 1973. plaque displayed at AHEA headquarters. Presented annually at the annual meeting in June. Established in 1973. Co-sponsored by Glencoe/Macmillan/McGraw-Hill.

• 943 • Ruth O'Brien Project Grants
Recognizes research and development in family and consumer sciences. Individuals are eligible.

• 944 • Teacher of the Year Award
Identifies and recognizes outstanding educational programs, methods, techniques, and activities that provide the stimulus for and give visibility to family and consumer sciences elementary and secondary education. Candidates must have been association members for at least three years and full-time permanent teachers of family and consumer sciences in grades K-12. Recipients receive $1,000, a commemorative plaque, and up to $500 to attend the meeting. Awarded annually.

• 945 • Wiley-Berger Award for Volunteer Service
To recognize outstanding effort in a volunteer capacity to improve the public well-being. Nominees must demonstrate how family and consumer sciences can contribute to the community through either sustained volunteer service or over a period of years, or through the implementation of an exemplary volunteer service project. Self-nominations, nominations by affiliates, and nominations by local, state, or national community service organizations are accepted. One award of a commemorative plaque and $1,000 will be given at the association's annual meeting.

• 946 •
American Association for Adult and Continuing Education
Cle Anderson, Mgr.
10111 Martin Luther King, Jr. Hwy., Ste. 200C
Bowie, MD 20720
Phone: (301)459-6261
Fax: (301)459-6241
E-mail: aaace10@aol.com
Home Page: http://www.aaace.org

Formed by merger of: (1982) Adult Education of the U.S.A.; National Association for Public Continuing and Adult Education.

• 947 • Cyril O. Houle World Award for Literature in Adult Education
To recognize a scholarly work in English in the field of adult education. The publication may be by one or more authors. Printed publications in book form may be submitted. Only copyrighted publications, with the year of the copyright determining the year of consideration for the award, are eligible. The deadline for nominations is July 1. A monetary award is presented annually at the National Conference. Established in 1981 by the Adult Education Association of the USA to honor Cyril O. Houle, the respected scholar and longtime professor of adult education at the University of Chicago, whose work is exemplary, frequently cited, and influential. influential.

• 948 • Malcolm Knowles Award for Outstanding Adult Education Program Leadership
To recognize teams or individuals for outstanding leadership to programs, in accordance with andragogical processes, that demonstrate particular effectiveness, relevancy, creativity, immediacy, institutional cooperation or collaboration and legislative impact. Program must have been executed within two years of nomination. Awarded annually.

• 949 • Membership Award
To recognize the association member who recruits the most members in an association year. The AAACE national office staff tallies the recruiters' data from membership applications. Nominations are not accepted.

• 950 • Imogene Okes Award
To recognize outstanding research in adult education. Books, research articles, or public documents published or printed during the five years preceding the year of the award are eligible. The selection committee seeks a recipient whose work: (1) is based on a topic that is broad in scope and has significant implications for adult and continuing education; (2) builds on and expands the fund of knowledge on which adult education is based; (3) uses sound and appropriate research methodology or provides a comprehensive analysis of existing research, and; (4) embodies an excellence consistent with the best traditions of adult education research and comparable to the work of prior recipients. Winners must attend the conference at which the award is given to receive the award, and lead a session based on the methods or findings of the

work. A nominal monetary prize and a plaque are awarded annually. Established in 1976 by the late Imogene Okes.

• 951 • Outstanding Adult Learner
To recognize the learner who serves as an exemplar for adult education students throughout the nation. Awarded annually.

• 952 • Outstanding Service Medallion
To recognize a person who has an outstanding record of service to the profession of adult and continuing education at the state, national, or international level. The nominator and nominee must be AAACE members.

• 953 • President's Award for Exceptional and Innovative Leadership in Adult and Continuing Education
To recognize exceptional leadership to, or in support of, adult and continuing education. Nominees for this award should demonstrate and ability to envision a new reality and aid in its translation into concrete terms; currently be engaged in a leadership role; be exemplary and held in high esteem by their peers; be engaged beyond the boundaries of a single unit or institution when considering and shaping adult and continuing education. Nominees can be from the areas of education, government, industry, or other sectors.

• 954 •
American Association for Aerosol Research
Elizabeth McDannell, Exec.Dir.
17000 Commerce Pky., Ste. C
Mount Laurel, NJ 08054
Phone: (856)439-9080
Fax: (856)439-0525
E-mail: info@aaar.org
Home Page: http://www.aaar.org

• 955 • Sheldon K. Friedlander Award
To recognize an outstanding dissertation by an individual who has earned a doctoral degree in the past three years. The dissertation may be in any discipline in the physical, biomedical, or engineering sciences but must be in an aerosol science and technology related field. A monetary award and a certificate are awarded at the annual conference. Established in 1997 in honor of Sheldon Friedlander for his leadership as a researcher, teacher and pioneer in aerosol science.

• 956 • Thomas T. Mercer Joint Prize
To recognize excellence in the areas of pharmaceutical aerosols and inhalable materials by an aerosol scientist. The award is based strictly on achievement in the field of inhalable materials and medicinal aerosols. No other qualifications are required of the recipient. A monetary award and certificate are presented at the AAAR annual conference. Awarded jointly by the American Association for Aerosol Research (AAAR) and the International Society of Aerosols in Medicine. Established in 1995 in honor of Thomas T. Mercer, a researcher and author whose work encompassed aerosol physics and chemistry as well as inhalation toxicology, industrial hygiene, and health physics.

• 957 • David Sinclair Award
To recognize sustained excellence in aerosol science by established scientists still active in their careers. Any individual whose highest degree was conferred in 1987 or later is eligible. A monetary award and a certificate are awarded each year at the annual conference. Established in 1987 in honor of David Sinclair, a pioneer in aerosol science. Additional information is available from James W. Gentry, telephone: (301) 405-1915.

• 958 • Kenneth T. Whitby Award
To recognize outstanding technical contributions to aerosol science and technology by beginning scientists, and to support and encourage their continued work in the field. Any individual whose highest degree was conferred in 1987 or later is eligible. A monetary award and a certificate are awarded at the annual meeting. Established in 1984 in honor of Kenneth T. Whitby, an aerosol scientist known for his contributions to aerosol properties, behavior and measurement. Additional information is available from E. James Davis; telephone: (206) 543-3778.

• 959 •
American Association for Agricultural Education
Ed Osbourne, Pres.
Dept. of Agricultural Education and Communications
University of Florida
PO Box 110540
Gainesville, FL 32611-0540
Phone: (352)392-0502
E-mail: ewo@ufl.edu
Home Page: http://www.aaaeonline.org
Formerly: (1990) American Association of Teacher Educators in Agriculture.

• 960 • AAAE Outstanding Young Member Award
To recognize an outstanding young member who has made significant contributions to agricultural education. Nominee must have seven years or less service as a teacher educator. Criteria for selection are the same as that used for the Distinguished Service Award. A plaque is awarded annually. Established in 1984.

• 961 • Distinguished Service Award
To recognize superior contributions to the field of teacher education in agriculture. Members of the Association are eligible. Criteria for selection of recipients include: excellence in teaching undergraduate, graduate students or both; significant research in the field of agricultural education and general education; scholarly writing pertaining to the field of education; and service to agricultural education and the total field of education. A monetary award of $500, a certificate and a plaque are awarded annually. Established in 1962.

• 962 • Fellow Designation
To recognize superior and sustained contributions to the field of teacher education in agriculture. Members of the Association are eligible. A certificate is awarded to up to six individuals at the annual meeting. Established in 1992.

• 963 •
American Association for Cancer Research
Margaret Foti PhD, CEO
615 Chestnut St., 17th Fl.
Philadelphia, PA 19106
Phone: (215)440-9300
Fax: (215)440-9313
E-mail: membership@aacr.org
Home Page: http://www.aacr.org

• 964 • Bruce F. Cain Memorial Award
To recognize preclinical research leading to the improved care of cancer patients. Nominations are accepted from Association members for candidates who are members or nonmembers. An honorarium, plaque, and travel expenses are awarded each year at the annual meeting. Established in 1982 by Warner Lambert Company in honor of Bruce F. Cain, former AACR member.

• 965 • Career Development Awards
Provides important tranitional support to investigators moving from the ranks of postdoctoral studies to faculty. A two year grant of $50,000 per year is awarded biennially. Deadline is November 14.

• 966 • G. H. A Clowes Memorial Award
To recognize sustained outstanding accomplishments in basic cancer research. Nominations are accepted from Association members for candidates who are members or nonmembers. An honorarium, medallion, and travel expenses are awarded each year at the annual meeting. Established in 1961 by the Eli Lilly Co. for G. H. A. Clowes, a founding member of AACR and a research director at Eli Lilly.

• 967 • Gertrude Elion Cancer Research Award
Annual award of recognition.

• 968 • Fellowship for Cancer Research
Fellowships awarded research in cancer. Deadline: October 15.

• 969 • Travel Grants
To enhance the education and training of medical and graduate students by providing financial support for attendance at AACR Annual Meetings, Special Conferences, and other scientific meetings sponsored by the AACR worldwide. Several grants of various amounts are awarded annually. Established in 1986.

• 970 •
American Association for Clinical Chemistry
Richard Flaherty, Exec.VP
2101 L St. NW, Ste. 202
Washington, DC 20037-1558
Phone: (202)857-0717
Toll-Free: 800-892-1400
Fax: (202)887-5093
E-mail: info@aacc.org
Home Page: http://www.aacc.org

• 971 • **AACC International Travel Fellowship Award**
To enable a well-recognized clinical chemist with broad experience in the field to promote the profession of clinical chemistry abroad or to provide an opportunity for a scientist outside the U.S. to visit and study within the U.S. in order to raise the quality of clinical chemistry as it is practiced in the recipient's home country. Individual members, a group of members, or a local section may submit applications by December 31 and must include a specific description of countries and institutions that would be visited, a description of activities to be undertaken, and services to be rendered. If available, letters of invitation from institutions and host countries are requested. Established in 1979. Awarded annually.

• 972 • **AACC Lectureship Award**
To recognize an outstanding individual whose efforts have made significant impact on the field of clinical chemistry. The impact may have been achieved through excellence in basic or clinical research, preventive medicine, medical economics, or health administration. Any AACC member, group of members, or local section, may submit nominations by December 31 of the year preceding the year of the award. The award consists of a cash honorarium and a framed chirograph. Additionally, the awardee presents a lecture at the plenary session of the annual meeting of the Association on the day the award is received. Awarded annually. Established in 1965. Sponsored by Bayer Corporation Diagnostics Group, Tarrytown, New York. Formerly: (1983) General Diagnostics Lectureship in Clinical Chemistry.

• 973 • **AACC Past President's Award**
To honor the immediate past president and to express appreciation for leadership and dedication during the term of office. A Steuben glass piece is awarded annually. Established in 1964. Sponsored by Allegiance Healthcare Corporation.

• 974 • **Animal Clinical Chemistry**
For outstanding contributions to animal clinical chemistry. The nominee's accomplishments should be included in the letter of nomination. The award comes in the form of $2,000.

• 975 • **Herbert O. Carne Service Award**
Given every two years, the award recognizes service in behalf of the section to advance the profession in the educational, training, organizational, or legislative areas. The winner receives a plaque and $500.

• 976 • **Certificate of Honor**
Recognizes contributions to clinical chemistry. The plaque is given at the sole discretion of the New Jersey Executive Committee, without an application procedure.

• 977 • **Chaney Award**
Given to an individual who has closely emulated Dr. Chaney's contribution to research, education, and chemical technology. The award consists of a plaque and $1,000.

• 978 • **Max E. Chilcote Young Investigator Award**
The award recognizes the best paper by a person under the age of 35 at the spring meeting each year. The winner receives $250 and a letter of congratulations. Formerly: (2006) Lemuel J. Bowie Young Investigator.

• 979 • **Cooper Award**
Awarded to any lipids division member in good standing without formal nomination process for outstanding contributions to the area of lipids. The award is valued at $500.

• 980 • **Albert A. Dietz Service Award**
All winners of this award must be nominated by a Chicago section member for their cumulative years of service to the Chicago section. The winner will receive a plaque and some sort of permanent memento, such as a clock.

• 981 • **Distinguished Service Award**
For New Jersey section members who have contributed greatly to the that section, a plaque is awarded at the discretion of the Executive committee.

• 982 • **Education Award**
Awarded for outstanding high school science studies, the award values range from $50-200.

• 983 • **Garry/Labbe Award**
Awarded based on contributions to the field of laboratory assessment of nutritional status. The winner receives a plaque and $1,000.

• 984 • **Bernard J. Garulat Award**
Recognizes furthering public interest in clinical chemistry. The winner receives a plaque, and the award is given at the full discretion of the New Jersey Executive Committee. There is no application procedure.

• 985 • **Norman Kubasik Award**
To recognize long-term educational contributions in chemestry. The award consists of a plaque, a clock, and $500. The recipient is selected by the executive committee.

• 986 • **Richard Marshall Education Award**
Made for clinical chemistry students, including graduate students, from midwest states, the award is a $1000 travel grant to attend the Annual Meeting of the AACC. An abstract of completed works should be submitted.

• 987 • **Samuel Natelson Senior Investigation Award**
The award recognizes a significant body of work for the whole of a career that has scientific impact over the profession. Nominations must be made by a Chicago section member. The winner will receive an engraved plaque and $500. The award is sponsored by Instrumentation Laboratories.

• 988 • **Albert L. Nichols Innovation Award**
The award is intended to recognize a person, group, or organization for having implemented strategic innovation in the clinical laboratory field that have long term implications on improvements in patient diagnosis or treatment. The award is a plaque and $1,000. The winner must have been nominated by the nominating committee.

• 989 • **Outstanding Contributions for a Publication in the *Journal of Clinical Chemistry* Award**
Recognizes a paper published in *Clinical Chemistry* during the preceding calendar year. Papers that significantly advance clinical laboratory science and laboratory medicine are eligible. Reviews, editorials, and letters to the editor are not eligible. Presented to the corresponding author or his or her designee(s). Established in 2000.

• 990 • **Outstanding Contributions in Education**
To recognize meritorious contributions to education that enhance the practice and profession of clinical chemistry. Education is considered in its broadest sense to include training at all levels both in the form of didactic teaching and literary contributions. Any AACC member, group of members, or local section, may submit nominations by December 31. A cash honorarium and a plaque are awarded annually. Established in 1971.

• 991 • **Outstanding Contributions Through Service to the Profession of Clinical Chemistry**
To recognize outstanding contributions through service to clinical chemistry with special emphasis on advancing the professional status of clinical chemists and the professional objectives of the Association. Any AACC member, group of members, or local section, may submit nominations by December 31. A cash honorarium and a plaque are awarded annually. Established in 1966.

• 992 • Outstanding Contributions to Clinical Chemistry
This, AACC's highest award, is given to recognize outstanding contributions to clinical chemistry with special emphasis on scientific and educational achievements which in some way lead to an enhancement of the profession of clinical chemistry. Consideration for this award is based upon significant contributions in more than one area of clinical chemistry, including demonstrated meritorious accomplishment in research, education, leadership, or service to the profession. Membership in the AACC is not an essential requirement, but a candidate's activities that have an impact on the practice of clinical chemistry in the United States are an important aspect of the qualifications. Any AACC member, group of members, or local section, may submit nominations by December 31. A cash honorarium and a plaque are awarded annually. Established in 1952. Formerly: (1959) Ernst Bischoff Award.

• 993 • Outstanding Contributions to Clinical Chemistry in a Selected Area of Research
To recognize especially meritorious research contributions in a selected area of clinical chemistry. Membership in the AACC is not an essential requirement for this award, but research that has an impact on the practice of clinical chemistry in the United States is given highest consideration. Any AACC member, group of members, or local section, may submit nominations by December 31. A cash honorarium and a plaque are awarded annually. Established in 1973.

• 994 • Outstanding Contributions to Clinical Chemistry Through Science or Technology
To recognize meritorious contributions to clinical chemistry through scientific achievements.

• 995 • Outstanding Contributions to Education
Awarded to an individual who has shown outstanding contributions to education that enhance the practice and profession of clinical chemestry.

• 996 • Outstanding Scientific Achievements by a Young Investigator
To recognize and encourage the professional development of young investigators who have demonstrated exceptional scientific achievements early in their careers. Selection is based primarily on meritorious scientific research contributions by a principal investigator, rather than the collaboration of many individuals, in the area of clinical chemistry. Any AACC member, group of members, or local section, may submit nominations by December 31. The award is restricted to members who have not reached the age of 35 by January 1 in the year of the award. The nomination letter must include an evaluation of the originality of the candidate's contributions. Established in 1976. Established in 1976. Sponsored by Boehringer Mannheim Corporation, Indianapolis, Indiana.

• 997 • Pediatric Division Award for Outstanding Contributions to Pediatric Clinical Chemestry
For outstanding contributions to pediatric clinical chemistry, the award is $500 and a certificate. Nominations must be made through the nominating committee.

• 998 • Miriam Reiner Award
The award was created to recognize scientific contributions to the field of chemistry. The winner must give a lecture at the December section awards meeting and will receive $500.

• 999 • Roe Award
This award is open to AACC members in good standing, who have made significant contributions to the Capital section. The winner receives $300.

• 1000 • Seligson/Golden Award
Recognizes distinguished contributions through service to clinical chemistry. Information supporting the nomination must be submitted with the nomination. The winner will receive a plaque, certificate, and some sort of perminent momento.

• 1001 • Somogyi-Sendroy Award
To recognize contributions to clinical chemistry, the award of $250 and a certificate are given to an individual selected by the executive committee.

• 1002 • Student Research Awards
To recognize college students, college-level trainees, or post-doctoral fellows in clinical chemistry who are the authors of outstanding abstracts. First prize of $600, second prize of $300, and two honorable mentions of $100 are awarded in two categories: oral presentation and poster. Awarded annually.

• 1003 • Texas Service Award for Outstanding Contributions to Clinical Chemistry
The winner must be a section member showing outstanding contributions to clinical chemistry. The prize is a plaque and $1,000.

• 1004 • Travel Grant
Awarded to a qualified international applicant, preferably with an interest in lipids. The winner attends the annual meeting, on the $2,000 travel grant and is expected to submit a newsletter article.

• 1005 • Edwin F. Ullman Award
Recognizes individuals for contributions that advance the technology of clinical laboratory sciences. Awarded annually. Established in 1998.

• 1006 • Harold Van Remortel Service Award
For outstanding contributions through service to clinical chemistry. Information supporting the nomination should be sent with the nomination.

• 1007 • Van Slyke Award
Awarded for outstanding contributions to clinical chemistry the award is $750 and an engraved plaque. The winner is expected to give a lecture at an award dinner meeting.

• 1008 • Young Clinical Chemist Award
This award is open to Chicago section members only, who are under the age of 35 years, and must be nominated by another member of the Chicago section. The winner must have a publication about the work done, and will receive $250 and an engraved plaque. The award is sponsored in part by Dade Behring Inc.

• 1009 • Zak Award
To recognize outstanding contributions to scientific research in the areas of lipids. Eligibility is any lipids division member without the need for a formal nomination process. The winner receives $500.

• 1010 •
American Association for Employment in Education
B.J. Bryant, Exec.Dir.
3040 Riverside Dr., Ste. 125
Columbus, OH 43221-2550
Phone: (614)485-1111
Fax: (614)485-9609
E-mail: aaee@osu.edu
Home Page: http://www.aaee.org

• 1011 • Priscilla A. Scotlan Award for Distinguished Service
Annual award of recognition presented for professional growth and research and service to the association.

• 1012 •
American Association for Geodetic Surveying
Curt Smith, Dir.
6 Montgomery Village Ave., Ste. 403
Gaithersburg, MD 20879
Phone: (240)632-9716
Fax: (240)632-1321
E-mail: info@acsm.net
Home Page: http://www.acsm.net/aags

• 1013 • American Association for Geodetic Surveying Graduate Fellowship Award
To recognize outstanding graduate students committed to the pursuit of knowledge in geodetic surveying and by so doing to enhance the ability of the profession to better serve the needs of society. Nominations may be made by any member of ACSM or ASPRS. The criteria upon which the nominee is evaluated include: (1) enrollment in or acceptance by a graduate program with a significant focus upon geodetic surveying and/or geodesy; (2) academic record including scope of course work and level of achievement as indicated by grade point average; (3) letter(s) of recommendation with respect to academic qualification from not more than two faculty members familiar with the nomi-

nee's performance; (4) a letter of recommendation with respect to the ethical standards of the nominee; and (5) a personal statement of course of study and its relationship to career goals prepared by the nominee. A monetary award of $2,000 and an appropriate citation are presented annually at the annual meeting. Established in 1983.

• 1014 • Joseph F. Dracup Scholarship Award

To encourage outstanding undergraduates committed to a career in geodetic surveying. A monetary award of $2,000 and a citation are presented at the annual meeting. Established in 1988.

• 1015 •
American Association for Health Education
Becky J. Smith PhD, Exec.Dir.
1900 Association Dr.
Reston, VA 20191-1598
Phone: (703)476-3400
Toll-Free: 800-213-7193
Fax: (703)476-6638
E-mail: aahe@aahperd.org
Home Page: http://www.aahperd.org/aahe

Formerly: (1974) Health Education Division.

• 1016 • AAHE Distinguished Service Award

For recognition of an outstanding contribution to health education either by an individual or organization outside the health education profession. Individuals or organizations outside the health education profession who make a significant contribution to health education in any form (i.e., media development, legislation, creative arts, funding, or national impact) are eligible. A commercial organization may only be nominated for a unique contribution to a profession that is over and above their normal realm of activity. A plaque is awarded annually at the national convention. Established in 1975.

• 1017 • AAHE Scholar Award

To recognize an Association member who has had a scholarly record for a number of years as evidenced by publications and presentations. For consideration, an individual must currently be producing scholarly materials in health, must provide evidence of in-depth study, must be a member, and must be capable of communicating ideas or facts to groups with diverse memberships. A plaque is awarded annually at the national convention. Established in 1977.

• 1018 • Health Education Professional of the Year Awards

To recognize individuals who enrich the depth and scope of health-related activities by disseminating and/or articulating findings to the profession. Health education professionals in the following categories are eligible: School (K through 12), College/University, Agency/Public/Community, Clinical/Medical Care/Patient, and Business/Industry/Workplace. Nominations must be submitted by January 20. A plaque is awarded annually in each category. Established in 1989.

• 1019 • Horizon Award

To recognize an individual who demonstrates through his/her contributions to the field of health education outstanding potential to obtain prominence in the health education profession. To be considered an individual must be in the health education five years or less, be an active member (student or professional) of AAHE for at least five continuous years prior to receiving the Awards; be a contributor within the field of health education as demonstrated through some of the following: excellence in teaching, outstanding administrative achievement, significant contributions in research, active leadership in professional organizations, contributions to processional literature, and/or outstanding community service. A plaque is awarded annually at the national convention. Established in 1999.

• 1020 • Presidential Citation

To recognize outstanding contributions to health education. Awarded annually. Established in 1980.

• 1021 • Professional Service to Health Education Award

To recognize contributions to the profession and/or the association by members or professionals. To be considered, an individual must have a minimum of ten years in the profession; must be a member of AAHE; must have served the association as officer, committee member, or other; and must give evidence of service and leadership to the profession. A plaque is awarded annually at the national convention. Established in 1975.

• 1022 •
American Association for Laboratory Animal Science
Ann Tourigny Turner PhD, Exec.Dir.
9190 Crestwyn Hills Dr.
Memphis, TN 38125-8538
Phone: (901)754-8620
Fax: (901)753-0046
E-mail: info@aalas.org
Home Page: http://www.aalas.org

• 1023 • Pravin N. Bhatt Young Investigator Award

To recognize outstanding young scientists who have made significant contributions to the fields of laboratory animal science or comparative medicine. These individuals must have demonstrated a commitment to a career in science and displayed technical excellence (i.e. originality of thought and experimental design). Open to all scientists who are either 40 years of age or younger or who have been engaged in scientific research for less than five years. Nominees must be members of National AALAS. Winners receive a plaque and a $300 honorarium. Awarded annually. Established in 1994.

• 1024 • George R. Collins Award

For recognition of outstanding contributions in the field of laboratory animal technology. The deadline for nominations is May 1. A monetary award and a plaque are awarded annually. Established in 1961 and named after George R. Collins, a member of the first AALAS Animal Technician Certification Board and a pioneer in animal technical education and certification. Formerly: AALAS Animal Technician Award.

• 1025 • Joseph J. Garvey Award

For recognition of meritorious contribution or outstanding accomplishments in administration, education, or support programs relating to the care, quality, or humane treatment of animals used in biomedical research. Nominations of AALAS members may be made. A monetary award and a bronze plaque are awarded. Established in 1984 in honor of Joseph J. Garvey who retired after 22 years as AALAS Executive Secretary.

• 1026 • Charles A. Griffin Award

This, AALAS's oldest and most prestigious professional recognition, is given to an individual for outstanding accomplishments in the improvement of the care, quality, and environment of animals used in biologic and medical research. A monetary award and a bronze plaque are awarded annually. Established in 1957 in memory of Charles A. Griffin, D.V.M. of the Division of Laboratories and Research, New York State Department of Health, who was one of the active leaders of the Animal Care Panel in its early years.

• 1027 • Technician of the Year Award

To recognize the vital role of the laboratory animal technician as an integral member of the laboratory animal science research team. Individuals who have received the most recent Technician of the Year Award from each AALAS branch are qualified to compete for this national award. Qualified individuals who do not have the opportunity to receive such an award on a local level may be nominated for the national award by a trustee of AALAS. Nominees need not be members of the National AALAS. Criteria for selection include: a great interest in further education in the field of laboratory animal science, a dedication to the advancement of laboratory animal science through teaching and training junior technicians in appropriate techniques and practices, degree of respect received from supervisors and colleagues for dedication to common goals in laboratory animal science, and a display of interest to participate in AALAS on local and national levels. The award consists of a monetary award and a plaque. Formerly: Technician Recognition Award.

• 1028 • Technician Publication Award

For recognition of the most outstanding technical paper submitted during the previous year in *Laboratory Animal Science* and *Contemporary Topics in Laboratory Animal Science* by a technician who is a member of National AALAS and has been certified in one of the three levels of the AALAS Animal Technician Certification program. A cash honorarium and a plaque are awarded annually. Established in 1974. Formerly: AALAS Technical Notes Award.

• 1029 •
American Association for Leisure and Recreation
JoAnne D'Angelo, Program Coord.
1900 Association Dr.
Reston, VA 20191-1599
Phone: (703)476-3471
Phone: (703)476-3472
Toll-Free: 800-213-7193
Fax: (703)476-9527
E-mail: aalr@aahperd.org
Home Page: http://www.aahperd.org/aalr

• 1030 • **Friend of Recreation**
Recognizes the demonstration of meritorious contributions benefiting the Association or its programs. Applicants can be individuals, groups, or organizations. Awarded by the Professional Recreation Council when merited.

• 1031 • **Honor Award**
The highest recognition by the Association to one of its members who has contributed to recreation leadership through teaching, research, or administration. Awarded annually.

• 1032 • **Meritorious Service Award**
To recognize meritorious service at the state, district, or national level that contributes to the Association or its programs. Applicants must be association members. Awarded by the Professional Recreation Council when merited.

• 1033 • **Outstanding Council Award**
To recognize leadership in the areas of recreation, leisure, or other fields closely related to association programs. Applicants must be association members. Awarded annually by the Council.

• 1034 • **Tommy Wilson Award**
Recognizes contributions by members or nonmembers to recreation programming for individuals with disabilities. Awarded annually by the Adapted Physical Activity Council (APAC).

• 1035 •
American Association for Public Opinion Research
Michael Flanagan, Exec.Coord.
PO Box 14263
Lenexa, KS 66285-4263
Phone: (913)310-0118
Fax: (913)599-5340
E-mail: aapor-info@goamp.com
Home Page: http://www.aapor.org

• 1036 • **AAPOR Award**
To recognize exceptionally distinguished achievement in the field of public opinion research. A scroll is awarded annually. Established in 1949. Formerly: (1962) Julian Woodward Award.

• 1037 • **Student Paper Competition**
To stimulate students to do research and write papers related to methodological issues in the field of survey research, and/or to write papers which emphasize substantive findings of studies that advance the understanding of public opinion and social behavior. Undergraduate and graduate students in the United States are eligible. A monetary prize of $500 and travel expenses to the AAPOR National Conference to present the winning paper are awarded to the first place winner. Honorable mentions are presented as appropriate. Awarded annually. Established in 1967. Formerly: (1978) Helen S. Dinerman Memorial Prize.

• 1038 •
American Association for State and Local History
Harry Klinkhamer, Prog. Off.
1717 Church St.
Nashville, TN 37203-2921
Phone: (615)320-3203
Fax: (615)327-9013
E-mail: membership@aaslh.org
Home Page: http://www.aaslh.org

• 1039 • **Award of Distinction**
For recognition of long and distinguished service and contributions by individuals employed in the state, provincial, and local history profession who demonstrate leadership in that profession. Nominations are accepted by March 1. Awarded annually. Established in 1963.

• 1040 • **Award of Merit**
For excellence in programs or achievements in the field of state, provincial, and local history. Individuals, historical societies, and agencies or other organizations are eligible. Nominations are accepted by March 1. Certificates are awarded each year at the annual meeting. Established in 1947.

• 1041 • **Certificate of Commendation**
For recognition of an outstanding accomplishment or program in the field of state, provincial, and local history, judged in the light of local limiting conditions. Individuals, historical societies, and agencies or other organizations are eligible. Nominations are accepted by March 1. Certificates are awarded annually at the annual meeting. Established in 1962.

• 1042 • **Albert B. Corey Award**
Recognizes small local societies with a remarkable variety of programs and for excellence in local historical endeavor. Nominations are accepted by March 1. A monetary award and a certificate are awarded at the annual meeting. Established in 1965. Considered the Association's highest honor.

• 1043 •
American Association for the Advancement of Science
Monica Amarelo, Contact
1200 New York Ave., NW
Washington, DC 20005
Phone: (202)326-6400
E-mail: membership@aaas.org
Home Page: http://www.aaas.org

• 1044 • **AAAS Academy Research Grants**
To promote student research by providing funds to affiliated academies of science. Proposals describing projects to encourage secondary school students to conduct research. Monetary grants are awarded annually.

• 1045 • **AAAS Award for Public Understanding of Science and Technology**
For recognition of working scientists and engineers who make outstanding contributions to the popularization of science. A monetary prize 0f $5,000 and a plaque are awarded annually. Established in 1987. Formerly: (1995) AAAS Westinghouse Award for Public Understanding of Science and Technology.

• 1046 • **AAAS Mentor Award**
Recognizes leadership that increases participation of underrepresented groups in science and engineering. Nominees must be individuals who have mentored and guided students in a qualifying category. Mentor role must have been maintained for up to 25 years. A monetary prize of $2,500 and a plaque are awarded annually.

• 1047 • **AAAS Science Journalism Awards**
To encourage and recognize outstanding reporting of the natural sciences and their engineering and technological applications, excluding the field of medicine. The awards are for reporting in (1) newspapers of over 100,000 daily circulation, (2) newspapers of under 100,000 circulation, (3) general circulation magazines, on (4) children's science news, and on (5) television, (6) radio, (7) and online. The deadline is July 15. A monetary prize of $2,500 and a plaque are awarded annually in each category. Established in 1946. Formerly: (1995) AAAS Westinghouse Science Journalism Awards - Whitaker Science Journalism Awards.

• 1048 • **AAAS Scientific Freedom and Responsibility Award**
Recognizes scientists and engineers whose exemplary actions, often taken at significant personal cost, have served to foster scientific freedom and responsibility. Scientists and engineers who have acted to protect the public's health, safety, or welfare; or focused public attention on potentially serious impacts of science and technology on society by their responsible participation in public policy debates; or established important new precedents in carrying out the social responsibility or in defending the professional freedom of scientists and engineers may be nominated by July 31. A monetary award of $2,500 and a plaque are presented annually at the AAAS Annual Meeting. Established in 1981.

• 1049 • **AAAS Philip Hauge Abelson Prize**
To recognize a public servant for sustained exceptional contributions to advancing science, or a scientist whose career has been distinguished both for scientific achievement and for other notable services to the scientific community. AAAS members are invited to submit nomina-

tions by August 1. The winner will be selected by a seven-member panel appointed by the Board. A monetary award of $2,500 and a bronze medal are awarded annually. Established in 1985.

• 1050 • Lifetime Mentor Award
Recognizes leadership that increases participation of underrepresented groups in science and engineering. Nominees must be individuals who have mentored and guided students in a qualifying category. Mentor role must have been maintained for 25 or more years. A monetary prize of $5,000 and a plaque are awarded when merited.

• 1051 • John P. McGovern Award Lecture in the Behavioral Sciences
To recognize the work of prominent behavioral scientists from around the world. A monetary award of $3,00 to $5,000 and a medal are presented. Established in 1988 by the McGovern Fund for the Behavioral Sciences.

• 1052 • Newcomb Cleveland Prize
To recognize the author(s) of a noteworthy paper published in *Science* magazine which represents an outstanding contribution to science. An eligible paper is one which (a) includes original research data, theory, or synthesis; (b) is a fundamental contribution to basic knowledge or a technical achievement of far-reaching consequence; and (c) is a first-hand publication of the author's own work. A monetary award and a bronze medal are awarded annually. Established in 1923. Formerly: AAAS Thousand Dollar Prize.

• 1053 •
American Association for the Advancement of Slavic Studies
Carol Saivetz, Exec.Dir.
8 Story St., 3rd Fl.
Cambridge, MA 02138
Phone: (617)495-0677
Fax: (617)495-0680
E-mail: aaass@fas.harvard.edu
Home Page: http://www.fas.harvard.edu/~aaass

• 1054 • Distinguished Contributions to Slavic Studies Award
For recognition of distinguished contributions to Slavic studies. North Americans over the age of 65 who have made a significant contribution to some aspect of Slavic studies are eligible. No posthumous awards are made. The deadline for nominations is February 1. A scroll is presented annually at the national convention.

• 1055 • Ed A. Hewett Prize
To recognize an outstanding English-language publication on the political economy of the centrally planned economies of the former Soviet Union and East Central Europe and their transitional successors. Works originally published the previous year in English in the form of monographs, chapters in books, and substantial articles are eligible. Deadline for submissions is May 13. A cash award is announced at the AAASS National Convention. Prize winning books are publicized nationally and internationally. Sponsored by NCEEER.

• 1056 • Barbara Jelavich Prize
To recognize a distinguished monograph published in English in the United States during the previous calendar year on any aspect of Southeast European or Habsburg studies since 1600, or nineteenth-and twentieth-century Ottoman or Russian diplomatic history. Authors must be scholars who are citizens or permanent residents of North America to be eligible. The deadline for submissions is May 15. A cash award is announced annually at the AAASS National convention. Prize-winning books are publicized nationally and internationally by the AAASS. Sponsored by Charles Jelavich.

• 1057 • Orbis Books Prize for Polish Studies
To recognize the best book in any discipline on any aspect of Polish affairs. The book must be a monograph, preferably by a single author, or by no more than two authors, published the previous year in English, outside of Poland. Textbooks, translations, bibliographies, and reference works are ineligible. Preference will be given to works by younger scholars. Nominations must be received by May 15. A cash award is presented at the AAASS national convention each year. Co-sponsored by the owners of Orbis Books Ltd., London, England.

• 1058 • Marshall Shulman Book Prize
For recognition of the best English language book on Russian/Eurasian foreign policy. The book must be a monograph, preferably by a single author, or by no more than two authors. Authors must be American scholars or residents of the United States. Textbooks, collections, translations, bibliographies, and reference works are ineligible. Nominations must be received by May 15. A cash award is announced at the AAASS national convention. Prize-winning book are publicized nationally and internationally by the AAASS. Institute. Institute.

• 1059 • Wayne S. Vucinich Prize
For recognition of the best book in Russian, Eurasian, and East European studies published in English in the previous year, preferably by a single author, or by no more than two authors. Authors must be American scholars or residents of the U.S. It may deal with any topic pertaining to Russia, Eurasia, or Eastern Europe, except contemporary policy studies. Collections, textbooks, bibliographies, translations, and reference works are not eligible. Nominations must be received by May 15. A monetary prize is presented at the national convention. Prize-winning books are publicized nationally and internationally by the AAASS. Co-sponsored by the Stanford University Center for Russian and East European Studies.

• 1060 •
American Association for the History of Medicine
Todd Savitt, Sec.Treas.
Dept. of Medical Humanities
East Carolina University
School of Medicine
Greenville, NC 27858-4354
Phone: (252)744-2797
Fax: (252)744-2319
E-mail: savittt@mail.ecu.edu
Home Page: http://www.histmed.org

• 1061 • William Osler Medal
Recognizes an unpublished essay that either is the result of original research or shows an unusual appreciation and understanding of historical problems relating to medicine. Authors must be medical students in the United States or Canada. The deadline is February 1. A bronze medallion and expenses to attend the annual meeting where the award is presented are awarded annually. Established in 1941.

• 1062 • Richard H. Shryock Medal
Recognizes an unpublished essay that either is the result of original research or shows an unusual appreciation and understanding of historical problems relating to medicine. Authors must be graduate students in a program leading to a degree in the humanities or social sciences in the United States or Canada. The deadline is February 1. A bronze medallion and expenses to attend the annual meeting where the award is presented are awarded annually. Established in 1982.

• 1063 • William H. Welch Medal
To recognize notable contributions of outstanding scholarly merit in the field of medical history. Single-author works published during the preceding five years are eligible. A bronze medal and expenses to attend the annual meeting where the award is presented are awarded annually. Established in 1949.

• 1064 •
American Association for the History of Nursing
Janet L. Fickeissen, Exec.Sec.
PO Box 175
Lanoka Harbor, NJ 08734-0175
Phone: (609)693-7250
Fax: (609)693-1037
E-mail: aahn@aahn.org
Home Page: http://www.aahn.org

• 1065 • Teresa E. Christy Award
To recognize excellence of historical research and writing done while the researcher was in a doctoral student status. A trophy is annually.

• 1066 • Lavinia L. Dock Award
Presented for exemplary historical research and writing. A trophy is presented annually. Two awards are given: one for book length and one for article length. Established in 1989.

• 1067 •
American Association for Women in Community Colleges
Dr. Marsi Liddell, Pres.
Phoenix College
1202 West Thomas Rd.
Phoenix, AZ 85013
Phone: (602)285-7449
Fax: (602)285-7832
E-mail: aawcc@pcmail.maricopa.edu
Home Page: http://www.pc.maricopa.edu/aawcc

• 1068 • Mildred Bulpitt Woman of the Year Award
Recognizes a living woman who has an outstanding record of service to women in the two-year college setting. Awarded annually.

• 1069 • Carolyn Desjardins President of the Year Award
Recognizes an individual who has donated an exceptional amount of staff time to achieving the AAWCC goals and/or meeting organizational needs. Awarded annually.

• 1070 • Trustee of the Year Award
Recognizes an individual who has championed causes consistent with AAWCC missions in the action of the College's Board of Trustees of Which he/she is a member. Awarded annually. Deadline is March 1.

• 1071 •
American Association for Women Radiologists
Ewa Kuligowska, Pres.
4550 Post Oak Pl., Ste. 342
Houston, TX 77027
Phone: (713)965-0566
Fax: (713)960-0488
E-mail: admin@aawr.org
Home Page: http://www.aawr.org

• 1072 • Marie Curie Award
To recognize a radiologist, radiation oncologist, or other person who has been a mentor, role model, or leader in the field, or an individual who has contributed significantly to the advancement of women in radiology. A plaque is awarded annually. Established in 1986.

• 1073 • Eleanor Montague Distinguished Resident Award in Radiation Oncology
To recognize residents specializing in radiation oncology who have made outstanding contributions in the field through clinical cae, teaching, research, or public service. Nominees must be members of AAWR as of January 1 of the year the award is presented. Nominations are accepted by directors of residency programs. A monetary prize of $500 and expenses to attend the annual meeting to accept the award is presented.

• 1074 • Lucy Frank Squire Distinguished Resident Award in Diagnostic Radiology
To recognize radiologist residents specializing in diagnostic radiology for outstanding contributions in clinical care, teaching, research, or public service. Nominees must be members of AAWR as of January 1 of the year the award is presented. Nominations are accepted from directors of residency programs. A monetary prize of $500 and expenses to attend the annual meeting to accept the award are presented.

• 1075 •
American Association of Advertising Agencies
O. Burtch Drake, Pres. and CEO
405 Lexington Ave., 18th Fl.
New York, NY 10174-1801
Phone: (212)682-2500
Fax: (212)682-8391
E-mail: obd@aaaa.org
Home Page: http://www.aaaa.org

• 1076 • O'Toole Agency Award
Three trophies are awarded annually in three subdivisions: agencies with billings of more than $300 million, agencies with billings between $30-$300 million, and agencies with billings of less than $30 million. Open to AAAA member agencies only. Awarded annually.

• 1077 • O'Toole Multicultural Advertising Award
To recognize an agency that targets multicultural consumer groups. Open to AAAA member agencies only. A trophy is awarded annually.

• 1078 • O'Toole Public Service Award
To recognize creative excellence in public service announcements. Open to AAAA member agencies only. Awards are presented annually in Print and Broadcast categories.

• 1079 •
American Association of Airport Executives, Great Lakes Chapter
Kenneth R. Newstrom, Exec.Dir., Sec.-Treas.
PO Box 218300
Columbus, OH 43221-8300
Phone: (614)487-1061
Fax: (614)487-1062
E-mail: info@glcaaae.org
Home Page: http://www.glcaaae.org

• 1080 • Award of Valor
For aircraft rescue and fire fighting. Recognition award bestowed annually.

• 1081 •
American Association of Anatomists
Andrea Pendleton, Exec.Dir.
9650 Rockville Pike
Bethesda, MD 20814-3998
Phone: (301)634-7910
Fax: (301)634-7965
E-mail: exec@anatomy.org
Home Page: http://www.anatomy.org

• 1082 • Henry Gray Award
To recognize an outstanding anatomist. Awarded annually. Contact the above address for additional information.

• 1083 • C. Judson Herrick Award
To recognize an outstanding young investigator in neuroanatomy. Awarded annually. Contact the above address for additional information.

• 1084 •
American Association of Avian Pathologists
Dr. Charles L. Hofacre, Sec.-Treas.
953 College Station Rd.
Athens, GA 30602-4875
Phone: (706)542-5645
Fax: (706)542-0249
E-mail: aaap@uga.edu
Home Page: http://www.aaap.info/

• 1085 • Bayer-Snoeyenbos New Investigator Award
To honor an AAAP member or associate member whose career as an independent investigator in poultry medicine began within at least seven years and who, during this time, has made meritorious research contributions to the avian field. A monetary award of $1,000 and travel expenses to the American Veterinarian Medical Association's Annual Meeting are awarded annually. Nomination deadline is February 1. Established in 1991. Formerly: .

• 1086 • Lasher-Bottorff Award
To recognize an avian diagnostician/technical service veterinarian who has significantly contributed to the poultry health programs in North American in the past 10 years. The recipient must be a veterinarian and a member of the AAAP, and may be affiliated with a government agency, academia, or industry. A monetary award and travel expenses to the American Veterinarian Medical Association's Annual Meeting are awarded annually. Nomination deadline is February 1. Established in 1988.

• 1087 • P.P. Levine Award
To recognize the author of the most outstanding research paper published in the journal *Avian Diseases*. A monetary award of $1,000 and an embossed plaque are awarded annually at the National Meeting. Established in 1964.

• 1088 • Phibro Animal Health Excellence in Poultry Research Award
To recognize sustained research accomplishments as related to the activities of avian medi-

cine by an AAAP member during the preceding period of seven years. A monetary award and a plaque are awarded. Nomination deadline is February 1. Established in 1978.

• 1089 • Special Service Award
To recognize outstanding contributions to avian medicine over a sustained period of time. Members of the Association are eligible. A monetary award and travel expenses to the American Veterinary Medical Association's Annual Meeting are awarded annually. Established in 1975.

• 1090 •
American Association of Bioanalysts
906 Olive St., Ste. 1200
St. Louis, MO 63101-1434
Phone: (314)241-1445
Fax: (314)241-1449
E-mail: aab@aab.org
Home Page: http://www.aab.org

• 1091 • Addine Erskine Outstanding Achievement Award
To recognize a member or group who has made an outstanding contribution to the clinical laboratory sciences. The deadline for nominations is November 1. A plaque is awarded annually. Established in 1984 in honor of Addine Gradwohl Erskine, RMT, associated with Gradwohl School of Laboratory Technique for over 50 years as its associate director and president of its Board of Directors. She was an educator, consultant, and author.

• 1092 • Lucien Dean Hertert Memorial Award
For recognition of dedication, loyalty, and service to the profession of bioanalysis. A hexagonal Baccarat crystal is awarded annually. Established in 1981 in honor of Lucien Dean Hertert, a founding member of AAB who was the driving force in AAB's programs in performance evaluation and scientific seminars.

• 1093 • Stanley S. Reitman Memorial Award
To recognize a member or group who has promoted and fostered the principles and philosophies of the AAB Associate member section. The deadline for nominations is November 1. A plaque is awarded annually. Established in 1984 in memory of Stanley S. Reitman, M. D., a founder of the former International Society for Clinical Laboratory Technology (now the AAB Associate Member Section) and world-renowned scientist, educator, and counselor to medical technology students.

• 1094 •
American Association of Blacks in Energy
Robert L. Hill, Pres./CEO
927 15th St. NW, Ste. 200
Washington, DC 20005
Phone: (202)371-9530
Toll-Free: 800-466-0204
Fax: (202)371-9218
E-mail: aabe@aabe.org
Home Page: http://www.aabe.org

• 1095 • The Chairman's Cup
Recognizes exemplary contribution to the organizations growth. Awarded annually.

• 1096 • James E. Stewart Award
For outstanding leadership. Awarded annually.

• 1097 •
American Association of Blacks in Energy, Arkansas
Leticia Finley, Contact
Entergy
PO Box 551, A9LA2E
900 S Louisiana Ave.
Little Rock, AR 72206
Phone: (501)918-6518
Fax: 800-223-3017
E-mail: lfinley@entergy.com
Home Page: http://www.aabe.org

• 1098 • AABE Scholarship
For scholastic achievement, need, essay. Monetary award bestowed annually.

• 1099 •
American Association of Blood Banks
Jennifer Garfinkel, Public Relations Dir.
8101 Glenbrook Rd.
Bethesda, MD 20814-2749
Phone: (301)907-6977
Fax: (301)907-6895
E-mail: aabb@aabb.org
Home Page: http://www.aabb.org

• 1100 • AABB Scholarship Awards
. Individuals enrolled in or accepted in accredited AABB/CAHEA Specialist in Blood Bank Technology education programs are eligible. Students are invited to submit original essays for review by the AABB Scientific Section Coordinating Committee special Projects Work Group.

• 1101 • Awards of Merit
For recognition of outstanding contributions to public understanding of blood banking on a local level. A plaque is awarded annually. Established in 1967.

• 1102 • Emily Cooley Memorial Award
Recognizes scientific and teaching ability. Candidates must demonstrate teaching ability in the technical aspects of immunohematology and have made a major contribution to the field of blood transfusion medicine or immunohematology. The award commemorates Emily Cooley, the medical technologist whose work contributed to the increased understanding of hematology technology.

• 1103 • Emily Cooley Memorial Award
To recognize scientific and teaching ability. The recipient must have demonstrated teaching ability in technical aspects of immunohematology and need not be an AABB member. Formerly: (1981) Emily Cooley Memorial Lectureship.

• 1104 • Ivor Dunsford Memorial Award
For recognition of outstanding research in immunohematology. Members of the Association only are eligible. Established in 1968 to honor Ivor Dunsford, British scientist and teacher, who made valuable contributions to blood group serology and genetics.

• 1105 • John Elliott Memorial Award
For recognition of significant contributions to the field of blood banking or transfusion therapy, or for distinguished services rendered to the AABB. Members of the Association only are eligible. Established in 1956 to honor John Elliott, who devised the closed system for the collection of blood into evacuated bottles. The recipient must be an AABB member.

• 1106 • Bernard Fantus, M.D., Medal
To recognize the person who has contributed the most to blood banking over the past 50 years. The recipient is selected by a panel of esteemed scientists and blood bankers, appointed by the AABB Board of Directors. It is given as seldom as every 10 years, and only when the recipient's lifetime contributions to the profession are deemed truly significant to the improvement of medical care. Established in 1987.

• 1107 • Sally Frank Memorial Lecturer Award
Rewarded to a technologist who shares Sally Frank's enthusiasm for red cell serology and education. Established to preserve the memory of Sally Frank, a technologist whose dedication to red cell serology and education inspired her students and enriched the field of investigative immunohematology.

• 1108 • Chapman-Franzmeier Memorial Award
Recognizes an individual who has made significant contributions locally and nationally to enhance recruitment of blood donors. The recipient delivers a lecture at the Annual Meeting. Members of the Association only are eligible. Established in 1983 and renamed in 1991 in honor of Nancy Chapman and Ronald Franzmeier. Formerly: Outstanding Donor Recruiter Award.

• 1109 • Morten Grove-Rasmussen Memorial Award
For outstanding service to the broad field of blood banking, including research, education, and development of technics. An honorarium of $1,000 and a scroll are awarded. Established in 1975 in memory of Martin Grove-Rasmussen, the physician who led the development of the AABB Reference Laboratory Program and Rare Donor File. Sponsored by Medsep Corporation.

• 1110 • Hemphill-Jordan Leadership Award
To recognize individuals from the blood banking and transfusion medicine community for significant contributions in the areas of administration, quality programs, law and/or government affairs.

Awards are arranged in alphabetical order below their administering organizations

Awarded annually. The recipient need not be a member of AABB, but must agree to lecture at the AABB Annual Meeting. Established in 1991; renamed in 2005 in honor of Bernice Hemphill and W. Quinn Jordan. Formerly: (2005) W. Quinn Jordan Memorial Award - X.

• 1111 • Bernice Hemphill Memorial Award

To recognize individuals who have made significant contributions to enhance the effective administration of blood banks and/or centers. Nominees must be members of the AABB. Established in 1981; renamed in 1991 in honor of Bernice Hemphill for commitment and contribution in an administrative role to the AABB and the blood bank. Formerly: Outstanding Administrator Award.

• 1112 • Karl Landsteiner Memorial Award

For recognition of outstanding contributions in immunohematology. The recipient must agree to lecture at the Annual Meeting. A monetary award of $5,000 and a scroll are awarded annually. Established in 1954. This award memorializes Dr. Karl Landsteiner, whose lifetime research laid the foundation for modern blood transfusion therapy. Sponsored by Ortho Diagnostic Systems Inc. The recipient need not be a member of AABB, But must agree to lecture at the AABB Annual Meeting.

• 1113 • Outstanding Achievement Award

To recognize those organizations and individuals who promote and support voluntary blood donations. Any group or individual who has made significant contributions in the form of increased public awareness about the need for blood donations in three or more AABB districts is eligible. Formerly: (1996) Presidential Award.

• 1114 • Dale Smith Memorial Award

Honors individuals or institutions that excel at innovation and creativity in the application of technology for improving transfusion medicine. Established in 2003 to honor Dale A. Smith who served as a pioneer and innovator in blood-based technologies, as well as a leader in research and development activities throughout his career. The recipient need not be an AABB member.

• 1115 • Joel Solomon Memorial Award

Recognizes contributions by AABB individual or institutional members that develop, promote, and enhance exceptional quality programs in blood centers or transfusion services. Established in 2000 to honor Joel M. Solomon, PhD, for his leadership and vision in introducing the concept of total quality improvement programs in blood banking, transfusion practice and transplantation medicine to the AABB Board of Directors.

• 1116 • Specialists in Blood Banking Scholarship Awards

Offered to students enrolled in AABB accredited programs for the education of Specialists in Blood Banking. Established in 1968.

• 1117 • Tibor Greenwalt Scientific Lectureship

Recognizes individual scientific achievement and the ability to effectively and succinctly communicate advanced scientific material. The individual need not be a member of the AABB.

• 1118 • Transfusion Medicine Fellowship Awards

Awarded to those with an interest in research, development and continuing education in the field of transfusion medicine. The applicant should have and MD or DO degree and be a fellow in a transfusion medicine program or a training program that includes at least one continuous year in transfusion medicine training.

• 1119 •

American Association of Botanical Gardens and Arboreta
Pamela Allenstein, Prog.Dir.
100 W 10th St., Ste. 614
Wilmington, DE 19801-6604
Phone: (302)655-7100
Fax: (302)655-8100
E-mail: pallenstein@aabga.org
Home Page: http://www.aabga.org

• 1120 • Award of Merit

To recognize an individual or organization that has made a special contribution to the development of the objectives of the Association. A certificate and a plaque are awarded annually. No more than two are given at each annual meeting. Established in 1969.

• 1121 • Dorothy E. Hansell Publication Award

To recognize institutional or organizational members for outstanding publications. Plaques are awarded annually. Established in 1979.

• 1122 •

American Association of Bovine Practitioners
PO Box 3610
Auburn, AL 36831-3610
Phone: (334)821-0442
Fax: (334)821-9532
E-mail: aabphq@aabp.org
Home Page: http://www.aabp.org

• 1123 • Amstutz-Williams Award

To recognize an individual for outstanding service to the veterinary profession. A hand carved wooden bull is awarded annually. Established in 1986 and named for Harold E. Amstutz and Eric L. Williams.

• 1124 • Fort Dodge Animal Health - Bovine Practitioner of the Year Award

To recognize a veterinarian in bovine practice for outstanding accomplishments. A diamond ring and a commemorative plaque are awarded annually. Established in 1978 by Syntex Animal Health.

• 1125 • Hoffman LaRoche-American Association of Bovine Practitioners Award for Excellence

To recognize a veterinarian in bovine practice for outstanding contributions in teaching, research, industry, or government areas. A plaque and a ring are awarded annually. Established in 1989.

• 1126 • MSD AGVET AABP Award for Excellence in Preventive Veterinary Medicine Beef Cattle

To promote bovine practice with an emphasis on preventive medicine. Veterinarians in bovine practice are eligible. A scholarship of $1,500 in the name of the recipient to the veterinary college of his choice, and a bronze plaque are awarded annually. Established in 1982 by MSD AGVET. Sponsored by MSD AGVET Division of Merck and Company.

• 1127 • MSD AGVET AABP Award for Excellence in Preventive Veterinary Medicine Dairy Cattle

To promote bovine practice with an emphasis on preventive medicine. Veterinarians in bovine practice are eligible. A scholarship of $1,500 in the name of the recipient to the veterinary college of his choice, and a bronze plaque are awarded annually. Established in 1982 by MSD AGVET. Sponsored by MSD AGVET Division of Merck and Company.

• 1128 • Pfizer Animal Health-AABP Distinguished Service Award

To recognize individuals who, through long and continued service, have promoted the goals of the Association and whose accomplishments have served as a model for service to bovine agriculture through organized veterinary medicine. A plaque and a certificate are awarded annually. Established in 1989.

• 1129 •

American Association of Cat Enthusiasts
Rob Seliskar, Pres.
PO Box 213
Pine Brook, NJ 07058
Phone: (973)335-6717
Fax: (973)334-5834
E-mail: info@aaceinc.org
Home Page: http://www.aaceinc.org

• 1130 • American Association of Cat Enthusiasts Annual Awards

To recognize the highest scoring cats, kittens, alters, and household pets. Awards are given for best of breeds, colors in championship, altered, and kittens. Awarded annually.

• 1131 •
American Association of Certified Orthoptists
Judy Petrunak, Contact
5733 Toronto Dr.
Sterling Heights, MI 48314
Phone: (586)286-7227
Fax: (319)384-9831
E-mail: orthoptics@att.net
Home Page: http://www.orthoptics.org

• 1132 • **Honor Certificate**
To recognize distinguished achievements in orthoptics in the areas of research, teaching, and leadership. Members of the Association are eligible. A certificate is awarded annually. Established in 1956.

• 1133 • **Lancaster Award**
Recognizes meritorious contributions to the field of orthoptics during her or his career. Members of the Association are eligible. A medallion is awarded annually. Established in 1952.

• 1134 • **Scobee Lecturer**
For recognition of outstanding orthoptists and ophthalmologists. Individuals are selected to deliver the lecture annually. Established in honor of Dr. Richard Scobee.

• 1135 •
American Association of Children's Residential Centers
Tammy J. Eisenhart, Off.Coord.
2020 Pennsylvania Ave. NW, Ste. 745
Washington, DC 20006
Phone: (301)738-6460
Toll-Free: 877-332-2272
Fax: 877-362-2272
E-mail: lmcinnis@soastc.org
Home Page: http://www.aacrc-dc.org

• 1136 • **Albert E. Trieschman Award**
For recognition of contributions to child care residential centers. Child care workers with at least five years direct care experience in residential treatment are eligible. A plaque, registration for the annual meeting, and a one-year membership in the association are awarded annually. Established in 1985 in memory of Al Trieschman, past president of AACRC, Founder of the Walker Home and School, and author of *The Other 23 Hours*. Additional information is available at the above Address.

• 1137 •
American Association of Christian Schools
Dr. Charles Walker, Exec.Dir.
2000 Vance Ave.
Chattanooga, TN 37404
Phone: (423)629-4280
Fax: (423)622-7461
E-mail: mrector@aacs.org
Home Page: http://www.aacs.org

• 1138 • **Athletic Competition**
Athletic competitions are sponsored in many states and regions, covering various sports for boys and girls. Schools desiring to participate should contact the association for more information.

• 1139 • **National Competition**
To determine the most successful contestants on the subjects of the Bible, Music, Speech, Art, and Academics. Participants must have won on a state or regional level. Awards are presented to the top three contestants in numerous subcategories. Held biennially in odd-numbered years.

• 1140 •
American Association of Code Enforcement
Kathy Davis, Pres.
5310 E Main St., Ste. 104
Columbus, OH 43213
Phone: (614)552-2633
Fax: (614)868-1177
E-mail: aace@aace1.com
Home Page: http://www.aace1.com

• 1141 • **Enforcement Officer of the Year**
Annual award of recognition. Participants must be nominated by peers.

• 1142 •
American Association of Colleges for Teacher Education
David G. Imig, Pres./CEO
1307 New York Ave. NW, Ste. 300
Washington, DC 20005
Phone: (202)293-2450
Fax: (202)457-8095
E-mail: aacte@aacte.org
Home Page: http://www.aacte.org

• 1143 • **Advocates for Justice Award**
Honors individuals who support equity issues, contribute in a meaningful way to the equity agenda of teaching and teacher education, and provide an example for others. Established in 2001.

• 1144 • **Award for Comprehensive Services in Education**
Recognizes a teacher education program that advances HIV/AIDS prevention.

• 1145 • **Award for the Innovative Use of Technology**
Recognizes teacher education institutions that model the innovative use of technology for others in the profession.

• 1146 • **Best Practice Award for Gender Equality**
Recognizes extraordinary accomplishment in advancing issues, programs, and innovations related to leadership development and/or gender equity issues. Formerly: (2006) Women's Leadership Development and Gender Equity Award.

• 1147 • **Best Practice Award for Global and International Teacher Education**
To recognize exemplary practice in the intercultural, global, cross-cultural, and international arenas of teacher education. Awarded annually.

• 1148 • **David G. Imig Award for Distinguished Achievement in Teacher Education**
Recognizes distinguished achievement in the fields of policy or research in teacher education.

• 1149 • **Gender Equity Architects Award**
Individuals at member institutions who through their professional work and personal values have constructed a foundation for gender equity in teacher education. Candidates are nominated and selected by the AACTE Committee on Women's Issues. Established in 2000.

• 1150 • **Lifetime Achievement Award**
Recognizes life accomplishments that have made valuable and significant contributions to the profession of teacher education. Awarded periodically.

• 1151 • **Margaret B. Lindsey Award for Distinguished Research in Teacher Education**
To recognize an individual in mid-career whose research over the last decade has had a major impact on teacher education. Awarded annually.

• 1152 • **Outstanding Dissertation Award**
To recognize excellence in doctoral dissertation research on teacher education. The award carries a professional recognition, publication of an article in the Journal of Teacher Education based on dissertation and a cash award. Individuals receiving a doctorate in education may submit an entry for this award.

• 1153 • **Outstanding Writing Award**
To recognize the most outstanding published work during the current year addressing the education of educators. A plaque is awarded annually at the Annual Meeting. Established in 1981. Formerly: Award for Excellence in Professional Writing.

• 1154 • **Edward C. Pomeroy Award**
To recognize outstanding contributions to teacher education. A plaque is awarded annually at the Annual Meeting.

• 1155 • **Support of Diversity Award**
Recognizes SCDE programs that have infused diversity into teacher education.

• 1156 • **Support of Teacher Education Accreditation Award**
Recognizes efforts to assist AACTE in pursuit of the strategic goal to encourage all member institutions to pursue NCATE accreditation.

Awards are arranged in alphabetical order below their administering organizations

• 1157 •
American Association of Collegiate Registrars and Admissions Officers
Thomas A. Bilger, Pres.
1 Dupont Cir. NW, Ste. 520
Washington, DC 20036
Phone: (202)293-9161
Fax: (202)872-8857
E-mail: info@aacrao.org
Home Page: http://www.aacrao.org

• 1158 • **Achieving Professional Excellence in Education Administration**
Recognizes individuals for Achieving Professional Excellence in administration and outstanding achievement and influence of their field. SCT donates $5,000 to name his or her college or university scholarship fund. is not renewable. Formerly: Award of Recognition: AACRAO Internships.

• 1159 • **Award of Recognition: State/ Regional Professional Activity**
To recognize outstanding professional activities of the state and regional associations and to encourage the development and expansion of quality professional activities among the state and regional associations. The deadline is July 1. A maximum of three awards ($500 each) are presented. The AACRAO Annual Meeting registration fee will be waived for expert speakers. Award winners in category one prepare a one page written summary of their activities for district workshop for state/regional association officers at AACRAO's Annual meeting. The Category two award will be used to subsidize transportation and housing for the guest speaker's association will also receive $500.

• 1160 • **Award of Recognition: Workshop Grant**
To stimulate the enhancement and expanded delivery of an existing workshop or the development of new workshop programs that meet specific needs within the profession. Selected workshop proposals are available for presentation at state, regional, and national AACRAO-affiliated meetings and at other activities. The deadline for entries is July 1. A monetary award is presented.

• 1161 • **Distinguished Service Award**
To recognize an active or retired AACRAO member for contributions to the profession in a volunteer capacity at the national level.

• 1162 •
American Association of Community Theatre
Julie Angelo, Exec.Dir.
8402 Briar Wood Cir.
Lago Vista, TX 78645
Phone: (512)267-0711
Toll-Free: (866)687-2228
Fax: (512)267-0712
E-mail: info@aact.org
Home Page: http://www.aact.org
Formerly: (1986) American Community Theatre Association.

• 1163 • **AACT Corporate Award**
To recognize a business or corporation for significant financial support of community theater on a regional or national basis. Awarded annually when merited. Established in 1987.

• 1164 • **American Association of Community Theatre Festival Award**
To recognize the best production in the national festival competition. Community theaters must win state, regional, and national competitions. A bronze casting is awarded biennially in odd-numbered years in June. Established in 1969. Formerly: (1987) Festival of American Community Theatre.

• 1165 • **David C. Bryant Outstanding Service Award**
For recognition of significant and valuable, and lasting service given to community theatre. Members of AACT are eligible. A plaque is awarded annually in June when merited. Established in 1978 in memory of David C. Bryant, past president of the American Community Theatre Association.

• 1166 • **Art Cole Award**
Honors a lifetime of leadership in community theatre by members of AACT who have provided leadership at the national, in addition to local and/or regional levels. A plaque is awarded annually in June when merited. Established in 1987 to honor Art Cole, past president of ACTA, founder of AACT/FEST and Director-Emeritus of the Midland (TX) Community Theatre.

• 1167 • **Distinguished Merit Award**
To recognize significant and valuable contributions made to promote and develop the highest standards for community theatre. Individuals or organizations are eligible. A plaque is awarded annually in June when merited. Established in 1979.

• 1168 • **Fellows of the American Association of Community Theatre**
An honorable designation bestowed for life on those members of AACT who over a period of years have contributed significantly to the idea and ideal of community theatre. A medallion is awarded annually in June to one to four individuals. Established in 1978. Formerly: (1986) Patron of the American Community Theatre Association.

• 1169 • **Robert E. Gard Superior Volunteer Award**
To recognize an individual over 65 years of age who has faithfully served community theatre on a non-paid basis for over 25 years. A plaque is awarded in June when merited. Established in 1982 by Robert E. Gard, one of the founders of the American Community Theatre Association. Formerly: (1995) Robert E. Gard Superior Citizen Volunteer Award.

• 1170 •
American Association of Critical-Care Nurses
Connie Barden RN, Pres.
101 Columbia
Aliso Viejo, CA 92656-4109
Phone: (949)362-2000
Toll-Free: 800-899-AACN
Fax: (949)362-2020
E-mail: info@aacn.org
Home Page: http://www.aacn.org

• 1171 • **Community Service Award**
To recognize significant contributions by critical care nurses (individuals or groups). Awarded to one or more recipients annually.

• 1172 • **Dale Medical Products Excellent Clinical Nurse Specialist Award**
For critical care clinical nurse specialists who function as expert practitioners. Awarded to one or more recipients annually. Sponsored by Dale Medical Products.

• 1173 • **Datascope Excellence in Collaboration Award - Multidisciplinary Teams**
For a multidisciplinary team that clearly practices key principles of collaboration and multidisciplinary practice. Awarded to one or more recipients annually.

• 1174 • **Datascope Excellence in Collaboration Award - Nurse to Family**
For initiatives and programs that innovatively and collaboratively meet the needs of families of the acute and critically ill. Awarded to one or more recipients annually.

• 1175 • **Excellence in Caring Practices Award**
To recognize critical care nurses whose caring practices are paramount in making possible the empowerment of patients and/or their families. Awarded to one or more recipients annually.

• 1176 • **Excellence in Education Award**
To recognize critical care educators who facilitate the acquisition and advancement of knowledge and skills required for competent practice and positive patient outcomes. Awarded to one or more recipients annually.

• 1177 • **Excellent Nurse Manager Award**
For critical care managers who demonstrate excellence in coordination of available resources to efficiently and effectively care for critically ill patients. Awarded to one or more recipients annually.

• 1178 • **Media Award**
For print and broadcast media excellence in the portrayal of healthcare providers, especially critical care nurses, contributing to a healthcare system driven by the needs of patients and families. Awarded annually.

• 1179 • Mentoring Award
To recognize individuals or groups who develop and enhance another's intellectual and technical skills, acculturating them to the professional community and modeling a way of life and professional achievement. Awarded to one or more recipients annually.

• 1180 • Special Contributor Award
To recognize significant contributions that affect the profession of critical care nursing. Awarded annually.

• 1181 •
American Association of Dental Examiners
Molly Nadler, Exec.Dir.
211 E. Chicago Ave., Ste. 760
Chicago, IL 60611
Phone: (312)440-7464
Fax: (312)440-3525
E-mail: info@aadexam.org
Home Page: http://www.aadexam.org

• 1182 • Citizen of the Year
To give recognition to a member of the Association who has distinguished himself through outstanding or unusual contributions or service to the public good both through dentistry and other types of public service. Nominations may be made by members. The deadline is June 1. A plaque mounted on walnut board is awarded annually. Established in 1967. Formerly: (1985) Dentist Citizen of the Year.

• 1183 •
American Association of Diabetes Educators
Christopher Laxton, Exec.Dir.
100 W Monroe, Ste. 400
Chicago, IL 60603-1901
Phone: (312)424-2426
Toll-Free: 800-338-3633
Fax: (312)424-2427
E-mail: aade@aadenet.org
Home Page: http://www.aadenet.org

• 1184 • Diabetes Camp Educator Award
To provide funds for the professional development of diabetes camp educators or to support projects related to diabetes camp education programs. A monetary prize of $1,000 and a plaque are awarded annually. Sponsored by Home Diagnostics, Inc.

• 1185 • Diabetes Educator of the Year Award
Honors a diabetes educator who has made a special contribution to the field through dedication, innovation, and sensitivity in patient care. A plaque, monetary prize of $5,000, and a $10,000 travel grant are awarded annually. Sponsored by Lifespan, Inc.

• 1186 • Distinguished Service Award
Recognizes outstanding contributions and service to the association. A monetary prize of $500 and a plaque are awarded annually. Sponsored by Becton Dickinson Consumer Products.

• 1187 • Nutrition Education Award
To recognize diabetes educators who have developed an original, outstanding, and effective patient education tool in the area of nutrition. A monetary prize of $500 and a plaque are awarded annually. Sponsored by the Estee Corporation.

• 1188 • Outstanding Chapter of the Year Award
Recognizes chapters that have taken on leadership roles in diabetes education and have supported the national organization's goals. A monetary prize of $500 and a commemorative plaque are awarded to the winner in each category (large and small chapter). Sponsored by Becton Dickinson Consumer Products.

• 1189 • Allene Von Son Diabetes Educator Award
Recognizes diabetes educators who have developed original, outstanding, and effective patient education tools. A monetary prize of $500 and a plaque are awarded to winners in three categories each year. Sponsored by Bayer Corporation.

• 1190 •
American Association of Endodontists
James M. Drinan, Exec.Dir.
211 E. Chicago Ave., Ste. 1100
Chicago, IL 60611-2691
Phone: (312)266-7255
Toll-Free: 800-872-3636
Fax: (312)266-9867
E-mail: info@aae.org
Home Page: http://www.aae.org

• 1191 • Edgar D. Coolidge Award
For recognition of active participation in the AAE during the individual's professional lifetime. Living members (Active, Life, Disabled Active, or Life) of the AAE who have displayed leadership and exemplary dedication to dentistry and endodontics are eligible. A plaque is awarded annually at the Coolidge Memorial Luncheon. Established in 1969.

• 1192 • Louis I. Grossman Award
For recognition of a cumulative publication of significant research studies that have made an extraordinary contribution to endodontology. Members of the AAE (Active, Life, Disabled Active, Associate, or Retired) are eligible. A medallion and a certificate are awarded annually. Established in 1973.

• 1193 • Edward M. Osetek Educator Award
To recognize an outstanding educator in endodontics or an endondontically related field. Awarded to an Active AAE member, who holds a full-time appointment in an ADA-accredited endodontic program at a rank less than that of full professor and has less than six years teaching experience. Awarded annually.

• 1194 • Ralph F. Sommer Award
For recognition of the principal author(s) of a publication of specific significance to the science and art of endodontology. The award may be given for articles describing development advances in methodology and/or materials and devices and for constructive influence on clinical practice. The paper(s) may not necessarily be based on research, but could be philosophical, social, technological, etc., pertaining to endodontics. A plaque is awarded annually. Established in 1977.

• 1195 •
American Association of Engineering Societies
Dan Bateson, Dir., Engineering Workforce Commission
1828 L St. NW, Ste. 906
Washington, DC 20036
Phone: (202)296-2237
Toll-Free: 888-400-2237
Fax: (202)296-1151
E-mail: dbateson@aaes.org
Home Page: http://www.aaes.org

• 1196 • Chairman's Award
To recognize one or more prominent Americans who have demonstrated significant applications in engineering to the uses and needs of man. The recipient may be proposed by or solicited from any source. Nominations may be submitted by September 30. Selection is at the discretion of the Chairman of the Board of Governors with concurrence of the Chairman of the Awards Committee. An illuminated scroll suitably inscribed with the name of the recipient, or recipients, and the circumstances of the award is awarded annually. Established in 1980.

• 1197 • National Engineering Award
To recognize an engineer or a group of engineers who has made outstanding contributions to the benefit of mankind. Nominations are accepted from any source by September 30. An illuminated scroll and a donation of $5,000 in the award winner's name for the purpose of advancing engineering education are awarded annually. Established in 1979.

• 1198 • Palladium Medal
To recognize outstanding engineering achievements in environmental conservation. Nominations may be submitted by September 30. A medal and a scroll are awarded annually. Co-sponsored by the National Audubon Society.

• 1199 • Joan Hodges Queneau Palladium Medal
To honor outstanding engineering achievement in environmental conservation. Professional engineers (civil, mechanical, chemical, electrical, etc.) are eligible. The medal, cast in palladium, a bronze replica of the medal, and a citation are awarded when merited. Established in 1976 in honor of Joan Hodges Queneau, an environmental conservationist.

• 1200 • **Kenneth Andrew Roe Award**
To recognize that member of the engineering community who has, in the last year, been the most effective in promoting such cooperation, understanding and unity among the engineering societies of this country that visible progress has been made in furthering the good of the engineering community as a whole. Nominations may be accepted from any source by September 30. A monetary honorarium and an illuminated scroll are awarded annually if merited. Established in 1983 by the Board of Directors of Burns and Roe, Inc. in honor of Kenneth Andrew Roe.

• 1201 •
American Association of Feline Practitioners
Rick Alampi, Exec.Dir.
203 Towne Ctr. Dr.
Hillsborough, NJ 08844-4693
Phone: (908)359-9351
Toll-Free: 800-204-3514
Fax: (908)359-7619
E-mail: info@aafponline.org
Home Page: http://www.aafponline.org

• 1202 • **Research Grant**
Recognizes meaningful research in feline medicine and/or surgery. Applicants must submit name, address, and a synopsis of the work they are presently engaged in as well as projected research. A monetary award of $15,000 is presented to the researcher whose application shows the most clinical merit. Awarded annually.

• 1203 •
American Association of Genito-Urinary Surgeons
41 Mall Rd.
Burlington, MA 01805
Phone: (781)744-5796
Fax: (781)744-5767
E-mail: barbara.t.lamont@lahey.org
Home Page: http://www.aagus.org

• 1204 • **Barringer Medal**
To recognize outstanding research in urology. A bronze medal is awarded annually when merited. Established in 1953.

• 1205 • **Keyes Medal**
To recognize notable contributions to the progress of urology. A gold medal with a bronze replica is awarded annually when merited. Established in 1933.

• 1206 •
American Association of Gynecologic Laparoscopists
Linda Michels, Exec.Dir.
13021 E Florence Ave.
Santa Fe Springs, CA 90670-4505
Phone: (562)946-8774
Toll-Free: 800-554-2245
Fax: (562)946-0073
E-mail: generalmail@aagl.com
Home Page: http://www.aagl.org

• 1207 • **Golden Hysteroscope Award**
Annual award of recognition presented for the best paper submitted on hysteroscopy by a physician. First-place winner receives a working gold-plated hysteroscope and a plaque; second- and third-place each receive a plaque.

• 1208 • **Golden Laparoscope Award**
Annual award of recognition presented to the best surgical video/film on gynecologic endoscopy submitted by a physician. First-place winner receives a working gold-plated laparoscope and a plaque; second- and third-place each receive a plaque.

• 1209 • **Jerome J. Hoffman Award for the Best Postgraduate Paper**
To recognize the best paper on minimally invasive gynecology by a physician in training. A monetary award of $1,000 is presented annually.

• 1210 •
American Association of Handwriting Analysts
Ed Jackson, Pres.
1060 Grandview Blvd., No. 622
Huntsville, AL 35824
Phone: (256)772-5326
Fax: (248)262-4851
E-mail: aahaemail@aol.com
Home Page: http://www.handwriting.org/aaha/aahamain.html

• 1211 • **Honorary Membership**
Award of recognition for outstanding service to the association and the field of graphology. Awarded when merited.

• 1212 •
American Association of Healthcare Administrative Management
Sharon Rosenblatt Galler, Exec.Dir.
11240 Waples Mill Rd., Ste. 200
Fairfax, VA 22030
Phone: (703)281-4043
Fax: (703)359-7562
E-mail: debra@statmarketing.com
Home Page: http://www.aaham.org

• 1213 • **AGPAM National Recognition Award**
To recognize outstanding individual achievement as recommended by officers and members. Winners are selected by committee. A wood plaque with metal plate is awarded annually.

• 1214 • **Certification Excellence Award**
To recognize the national AGPAM members who received the highest scores during the first sittings of the CPAM and CCAM certification exams. Two monetary prizes of $250 and plaques are awarded annually.

• 1215 • **Chapter Excellence**
For recognition of outstanding chapter achievement. Each chapter can submit a completed application regarding its accomplishments. The winner is selected by committee. A wood plaque with metal plate is kept by the winner for one year. Awarded annually at the President's Banquet.

• 1216 • **Leslie A. Hampel Award**
To recognize the AGPAM chapter that had the most newly certified members during the preceding period of July 1 - June 30. A plaque is awarded annually.

• 1217 • **National Editors Award**
To recognize a member of the Guild who contributes meaningful articles and information on health care related issues. Monetary prizes of $500 for first place, $250 for second place, and $100 for third place, as well as certificates, are awarded annually.

• 1218 • **National Journal Award**
To recognize excellence in journalism and graphics design in journals and newsletters of AGPAM chapters. Awards are given in three categories based on size of National membership. Plaques and certificates are awarded annually.

• 1219 • **National President's Award**
To recognize an individual(s) who is selected by the current National President and recognized for his outstanding individual service and support. A wood plaque with metal plate is awarded annually.

• 1220 • **New Member Sponsor Award**
To recognize a member of the guild and his or her chapter for successfully recruiting the greatest number of new national members for the current membership year. Plaques are awarded annually.

• 1221 •
American Association of Homes and Services for the Aging
Gary Marshall, Sr. Info Specialist
2519 Connecticut Ave. NW
Washington, DC 20008-1520
Phone: (202)783-2242
Fax: (202)783-2255
E-mail: info@aahsa.org
Home Page: http://capwiz.com/aahsa/home/

• 1222 • **Award of Honor**
Recognizes a member who has made an outstanding contribution in service on a national level to the aging. A life membership in the organization, a plaque and complimentary registration at the annual meeting are presented annually.

• 1223 • **Chair's Citation**
To recognize a person or an organization that has rendered special service in the field of ag-

Awards are arranged in alphabetical order below their administering organizations

ing, or for recognition of significant events in the field. Awarded when merited. Formerly: President's Citation.

• 1224 • Community Service Award

To recognize the achievements of up to three organizations that are full members of the association, and to honor a commitment by volunteers, leadership, and staff to meeting community needs as part of the organization's overall mission and planning. Examples of community service programs eligible for recognition include, but are not limited to, intergenerational programs, community education efforts, donation of facility resources for community use, resident-led volunteer service projects, and any activities designed to address pressing local community needs. Recipients receive a plaque.

• 1225 • Distinguished Service Award

To recognize the achievements of members or nonmembers in the field of aging services. Nominees must have made an outstanding contribution toward the welfare of older persons which is of national importance, and which adds to better understanding, knowledge and service in the aging services field.

• 1226 • Distinguished Service in Aging Award

To recognize a public figure who has performed extraordinary service to the aging that has had or could have an impact on the total field of care and service to the aging.

• 1227 • Excellence in Media Award

Recognizes outstanding achievement in media coverage of aging services or related issues. Print media (newspaper, magazine), radio, television and electronic media organization or their representatives are eligible. Nominations are accepted for material that either (1) appeals to the general public, such as general-interest newspaper or magazine reports, or (2) holds special interest for aging-services professionals, such as industry publications. Up to two media organizations or individuals will be recognized. Criteria for inclusion: portrays aging services, or related issues, realistically and thoughtfully; fosters increased audience understanding and/or support for positive change; and contains informative, and not solely promotional, content. A complete copy of the nominated material (article(s), audio cassette, VHS tape) must accompany the nomination. Permissions are the responsibility of the nominator.

• 1228 • Excellence in Practice Award

To recognize standards of excellence through programs that address some of the most complex challenges in the field of housing, care and services for the aging. By honoring benchmark, best practices in AAHSA-member organizations, this award seeks to showcase programs that demonstrate superior achievement throughout the continuum of aging services. An organization's total program of services or an individual program may be nominated. Criteria for inclusion: demonstrates an overall level of excellence that far exceeds what would be considered a merely good or even commendable standard of care and service; emphasizes quality of life for the individuals served, including the demonstrated capacity for change in response to their needs and desires; provides tangible, quantifiable benefits to persons being served; and in operation at least two years and ongoing. Each receives a plaque.

• 1229 • Innovation of the Year Awards

To recognize creative problem solving within the AAHSA membership, to encourage professionals to document, display, and share their successes in the spirit of mutual helpfulness, and to motivate others to a higher level of development and professional practice. Three AAHSA members whose innovations in their own facilities have proven beneficial receive this award each year. An abstract of an innovation may be submitted in any of the following categories: care and services to residents or clients, management operations, and community or public relations. Recognition by AAHSA and peers at the annual meeting, publication of selected innovations, and presentation of selected papers at an education session during the annual meeting are awarded.

• 1230 • Hobart Jackson Social Responsibility Award

To recognize significant commitment to affirmative action goals. The nominees must show commitment to social justice and equal opportunity for minorities. Members, an agency of AAHSA, and/or individuals associated with an AAHSA agency are eligible.

• 1231 • Meritorious Service Award

To recognize significant contributions to the field of long-term care, services, and housing for the elderly. Awarded to individuals whose organizations are full members of the association, or organizations that are full members. The nominee's accomplishments must show excellence, must have provided recognizable leadership in the aging services field, and must demonstrate a commitment to the nonprofit philosophy. The nominee's contribution must be of national importance.

• 1232 • National Organization on Disability Award

To recognize the efforts of one individual or member organization on behalf of the disabled. The $1,000 cash award will be awarded to an AAHASA member, organization that has an innovative and concrete program in place for assisting the elderly or other individuals with disabilities in the community that could be replicated by other AAHASA members.

• 1233 • Trustee of the Year Award

To recognize the outstanding achievements that a volunteer trustee or director has made to an AAHA member facility during his or her tenure on the member organization's board. The nominee must demonstrate a significant contribution to the well-being of the elderly and others the organization serves, must have displayed a personal commitment to the life of the organization, must have provided outstanding leadership to the organization and the community at large, and must have fostered growth and change through understanding the environment and the need for a continuum of care for the elderly. Primary consideration is given to notable acts or unusual commitment to service. Each recipient will receive a plaque, one night's lodging to attend the annual meeting in New Orleans and complimentary registration to the annual meeting's Governance Assembly. Established in 1985.

• 1234 •

American Association of Hospital Dentists
Kristen Smith, Exec.Dir.
401 N Michigan Ave.
Chicago, IL 60611
Phone: (312)527-6764
Fax: (312)673-6663
E-mail: SCD@SCDOnline.org
Home Page: http://www.scdonline.org

Formerly: American Association of Hospital Dental Chiefs.

• 1235 • Award for Special Service to Hospital Dentistry

For recognition of special and unusual service to hospital dentistry. A plaque is presented when merited. Established in 1977.

• 1236 • Lawrence J. Chasko Award

For recognition of distinguished service to hospital dentistry and the association. A plaque is presented annually. Established in 1978 in memory of Lawrence J. Chasko, DDS, a long-time member and officer in the AAHD.

• 1237 • Roerig Fellow in Hospital Dental Practice

To provide funds for a resident to work for two months in the national office of AAHD and complete a research project, national in scope, that advances the understanding of some aspect of hospital dental practice. Second year general practice residents from accredited 2-year GDR programs are eligible. Programs may submit nominations. A stipend to cover transportation and expenses for two months is awarded annually. Established in 1991 by the Roerig Division of Pfizer Pharmaceuticals.

• 1238 • Scientific Award

Award of recognition for service to the field of hospital dentistry.

• 1239 •
American Association of Housing Educators
Dr. Jean Memkin PhD, Exec.Dir.
5060 FCS Department
Illinois State University
Normal, IL 61790-5060
Phone: (309)438-5802
Fax: (309)438-5307
E-mail: jmemkin@rs6000.cmp.ilstu.edu
Home Page: http://www.extension.iastate.edu/Pages/housing/aahe-links.html

• 1240 • **Tessie Agan Award**
To encourage professional development and to provide an opportunity to present a paper at the annual conference. Both graduate and undergraduate students enrolled in an academic institution may submit a research or position paper on some aspect or current issue in housing. A monetary prize of $500 and an opportunity to present the paper at the annual conference (award contingent upon conference attendance) are awarded to the graduate winner. A monetary prize of $200 and an opportunity to present the paper at the annual conference are awarded to the undergraduate winner. Entries must be received by June 1. Awarded annually at the conference. Established in 1976 in honor of Tessie Agan, first president of AAHE in 1966.

• 1241 •
American Association of Immunologists
M. Michele Hogan PhD, Exec.Dir.
9650 Rockville Pike
Bethesda, MD 20814-3994
Phone: (301)634-7178
Fax: (301)634-7887
E-mail: infoaai@aai.org
Home Page: http://www.aai.org

• 1242 • **BD Biosciences Investigator Award**
To honor a young investigator who has made an outstanding contribution to the field of immunology. The individual must be a trainee or active member of AAI, must have received their degree within the last 15 years, and be nominated by an active AAI member. A plaque and monetary award of $3,000 is presented at the annual meeting. Awarded annually. Established in 1993. Sponsored by BD Biosciences. Formerly: (1998) Pharmingen Investigator Award.

• 1243 •
American Association of Law Libraries
Susan E. Fox, Exec.Dir.
53 W Jackson Blvd., Ste. 940
Chicago, IL 60604
Phone: (312)939-4764
Fax: (312)431-1097
E-mail: aallhq@aall.org
Home Page: http://www.aallnet.org

• 1244 • **AALL Lexis Nexis Call for Papers Awards Program**
To promote scholarship among practicing law libraries and in areas of interest to the profession; provide an outlet for creativity for law libraries and a forum for their scholarly activities; and recognize the scholarly efforts of established members, new members, and potential members of AALL. Papers may be submitted on any subject relevant to law librarianship and are judged in two categories: the Open Division for papers submitted by current AALL members who have been members for five or more years; and the New Member Division for papers submitted by individuals who have been AALL members for less than five years.

• 1245 • **AALL Public Access to Government Information Award**
Recognizes significant contributions to protect and promote greater public access to government information. Individuals and organizations are eligible. Established in 1998.

• 1246 • **AALL Spectrum Article of the Year Award**
Honors outstanding achievements in writing an article that contributes to topics relating to librarianship, law labrarianship, and practical applications for library work or to an understanding of legal materials, legal systems, legal information, or to professional and staff training and development. $500 is awarded annually. Established in 2000

• 1247 • **AALL/West Excellence in Marketing Award**
To recognize outstanding achievement in public relations activities during the previous year in five categories: Best Brochure, Best Newsletter, Best Campaign, Best Public Relations Tool Kit, and Best Use of Technology. Awarded annually. Established in 1998.

• 1248 • **Joseph L. Andrews Bibliographic Award**
To recognize a significant contribution to legal bibliographical literature published in the past year. The nominations deadline is February 1. A certificate is awarded annually at the Annual Meeting. Established in 1967 in honor of Joseph L. Andrews, reference librarian for the Bar Association of the City of New York Library.

• 1249 • **Best New Product Award**
For new legal information products that enhance or improve existing law library services or procedures or innovative products which improve access to legal information, the legal research process, or procedures for technical processing of library materials. New products may include but are not limited to computer hardware and/or software, educational or bibliographic material, or other products or devices that aid or improve library workflow, research, or intellectual access.

• 1250 • **Renee D. Chapman Memorial Award for Outstanding Contributions to Technical Services Law Librarianship**
Recognizes extended and sustained distinguished service to technical services law librarianship and to AALL.

• 1251 • **Marian Gould Gallagher Distinguished Service Award**
To recognize extended and sustained service to law librarianship for exemplary service to the Association, or for contributions to the professional literature. Individuals must be members of the American Association of Law Libraries and nearing retirement or recently retired from an active professional career to be eligible. The deadline for nominations is January 1. A plaque is awarded annually at the National Meeting. Established in 1984. Renamed in 1990 to honor Marian Gould Gallagher.

• 1252 • **Frederick Charles Hicks Award for Outstanding Contributions to Academic Law Librarianship**
Recognizes distinguished service to academic law libraranship that has been extended and sustained. Named in honor of the first great American law librarian/scholar, who was also the first academic law librarian to serve as President of AALL. Established in 2000.

• 1253 • ***Law Library Journal* Article of the Year Award**
To recognize an individual for outstanding achievement in researching and writing an article as by published in *Law Library Journal* for the preceding volume year. Awarded annually. Established in 1989.

• 1254 • **Law Library Publications Award**
To honor achievement in creating in-house library materials that are outstanding in quality and significance. Creating in-house works may include, but is not limited to, writing, compiling, editing, or designing print or non-print materials. The nomination deadline is February 1. Certificates are awarded annually at the Annual Meeting. Established in 1984.

• 1255 • **Bethany J. Ochal Award for Distinguished Service to the Profession**
Recognizes significant contributions to law librarianship by a State, Court and County Law Libraries Special Interest Section member who is nearing the end of his or her library career or who has recently retired. Winners are judged by service to the profession, contributions to legal research, teaching and outreach efforts, and recognition by members of the legal or government community.

• 1256 •
American Association of Managing General Agents
Bernd G. Heinze Esq., Exec.Dir.
150 S Warner Rd., Ste. 156
King of Prussia, PA 19406
Phone: (610)225-1999
Fax: (610)225-1996
E-mail: bernie.heinze@aamga.org
Home Page: http://www.aamga.org

• 1257 • **Achievement Award**
To recognize outstanding current committee chairmen in state Independent Insurance Agents (IIA) and Professional Insurance Agents

(PIA) organizations. Certificates are awarded annually per state organization. Established in 1960.

• 1258 •
American Association of Meat Processors
Scott Cunningham, Pres.
PO Box 269
Elizabethtown, PA 17022
Phone: (717)367-1168
Fax: (717)367-9096
E-mail: aamp@aamp.com
Home Page: http://www.aamp.com

• 1259 • **Accomplishment Award**
To recognize younger AAMP members who have made important strides in the meat industry in a relatively short period of time. The award recognizes a person or group who, for example, achieved outstanding company growth, successfully developed a new product, invention or service, or launched a noteworthy marketing campaign. A committee, made up of past winners, accepts nominations from any source and selects the next recipient. A plaque is awarded annually. Established in 1993.

• 1260 • **Achievement Award**
For recognition of outstanding leadership and meritorious services to the Association and to the meat processing industry. AAMP members or those associated with the meat processing industry are eligible. A plaque is presented annually at the convention. Established in 1951.

• 1261 • **American Cured Meat Championships**
Annual awards of recognition. Inquire for additional details.

• 1262 • **Best Booth Award**
To encourage exhibitors to be creative in their booth design and to increase the interest and activity level of their presentations. It will be based on enthusiasm and creativity as judged by persons anonymously walking through the exhibit hall. Awarded annually. Established in 1995.

• 1263 • **Cured Meats Hall of Fame**
To recognize individuals that have shown longstanding excellence in the production of cured meats. All AAMP members are eligible for nomination; nominees may be either living or deceased at time of nomination. A plaque is presented annually at the convention. Established in 1991.

• 1264 • **Golden Cleaver Award**
Annual award of recognition. A dramatic threetiered butcher-block with a golden cleaver slashed into the top block, is given to the individual who recruits the highest number of new AAMP members in one year. The membership recruiting year runs from convention to convention. The award is made at the Closing Session. A copy of the award is kept at the office in Elizabethtown and the name of each year's winner is engraved on a brass plate. Established in 1989. Formerly: Cleaver Club Award.

• 1265 • **Clarence Knebel Best of Show Memorial Award**
Recognizes the manufacturer of the top product in the American Cured Meat Championships receives this award, which is an engraved silver plate. The award was named for an outstanding AAMP and industry leader, Clarence Knebel. The winners' names are placed in the AAMP office. Awarded annually. Established in 1994.

• 1266 • **Outstanding Service Award**
To recognize noteworthy state, regional, or provincial associations or remarkable leaders whose dedication and enthusiasm have elevated the association to an outstanding degree. Awarded annually. Established in 1995.

• 1267 • **Sharpest Knife in North America Award**
Annual award of recognition. Inquire for additional details

• 1268 • **F. W. Witt Supplier of the Year Award**
Recognizes a supplier who makes outstanding contributions to the Association, the meat industry and the national community. Awarded annually.

• 1269 •
American Association of Medical Assistants, Linn Chapter
Judy Frits, Contact
Kirkwood Community College
Kirkwood Blvd. SW
PO Box 2068
Cedar Rapids, IA 52404-2068
Phone: (319)398-5564
Toll-Free: 800-228-2262
Fax: (319)398-1293

• 1270 • **Linn Chapter Scholarship**
Given to a medical assistant student of an accredited school. Scholarship awarded biennially.

• 1271 •
American Association of Mental Health Professionals in Corrections
J.S. Zil MD, JD, National Pres.
PO Box 160208
Sacramento, CA 95816-0208
Fax: (916)649-1080
E-mail: corrmentalhealth@aol.com
Formerly: (1976) Medical Correctional Society.

• 1272 • **Presidential Award**
To recognize outstanding contributions to correctional mental health. Candidates must be nominated to the Board of Directors. A trophy and a write-up in the Journal are awarded intermittently at the national meeting. Established in 1940.

• 1273 •
American Association of Motor Vehicle Administrators
Linda Lewis, Pres. & CEO
4301 Wilson Blvd., Ste. 400
Arlington, VA 22203-1800
Phone: (703)522-4200
Fax: (703)522-1553
E-mail: llewis@aamva.org
Home Page: http://www.aamva.org

• 1274 • **Customer Service Excellence Award**
To recognize the jurisdictional teams, divisions, or agencies within each region that has implemented a unique project or program to enhance customer service, such as, innovative technology, teambuilding, quality initiatives, or creative and unique approaches to serving customers. Awarded annually.

• 1275 • **Distinguished Service Award**
To recognize the outstanding services, contributions, and accomplishments of individuals in the field of motor vehicle administration and traffic law enforcement. Members of the Association who are employed by a motor vehicle or public safety agency are eligible in either of two categories: Category I - those who are active members of the Association, but have never served on the Board of Directors; and Category II - those who have served on the Board of Directors and have contributed to the advancement of the Association through outstanding services and accomplishments. Nominees in both categories must have worked at a member agency between September of the year prior to the award and June of the year the award is given. A plaque is awarded in each category annually at the international conference held in the fall. A Lifetime Achievement Award is also presented to an individual who was supportive of and active with the Association and a leader in his or her field, but no longer holds a position at a member agency. A potential candidate need not to have been employeed by a member agency during the previous year to be nominated. Established in 1964.

• 1276 • **Public Affairs Competition**
To recognize outstanding public relations, public affairs, and consumer education efforts for motor vehicle agencies across the U.S. and Canada. Awards are given in categories for audio, video, and print media. Plaques are awarded at regional and international levels annually. Established in 1978.

• 1277 •
American Association of Museums
Edward H. Able, Pres. & CEO
1575 Eye St. NW, Ste. 400
Washington, DC 20005
Phone: (202)289-1818
Fax: (202)289-6578
E-mail: membership@aam-us.org
Home Page: http://www.aam-us.org

• 1278 • Distinguished Service Award
For recognition of unusual excellence and distinguished contributions to the museum profession. Individuals may be nominated. A bronze medal is awarded annually. Established in 1980.

• 1279 • Nancy Hanks Memorial Award for Professional Excellence
For recognition of an outstanding contribution by an individual, with no more than ten years museum experience, to his or her institution or the museum field. Individuals may be nominated. An honorarium of $1,000 and a plaque are awarded annually. Established in 1984 in memory of Nancy Hanks, a friend and champion of museums throughout the country and chairwoman of the National Endowment for the Arts for eight years.

• 1280 • Medal for Distinguished Philanthropy
To honor outstanding philanthropic support to museums by an individual, corporation, or grantmaking organization. Individuals or organizations that champion and foster innovation and entrepreneurship in museums, and are active advocates, volunteer leaders, and supporters of collections, exhibitions, and mission-related museum programs are considered. A sterling silver medal designed by Elizabeth Jones, former chief sculptor and engraver for the United States Mint is awarded. Established in 1993.

• 1281 •
American Association of Neuromuscular and Electrodiagnostic Medicine
Shirlyn A. Adkins J.D., Exec.Dir.
421 1st Ave., SW, Ste. 300 East
Rochester, MN 55902
Phone: (507)288-0100
Fax: (507)288-1225
E-mail: aanem@aanem.org
Home Page: http://www.aanem.net

Formerly: (1990) American Association of Electromyography and Electrodiagnosis.

• 1282 • Distinguished Physician Award
Recognizes an individual who has performed distinguished service for a number of years or has provided overall support of association activities. Association members and/or educators are eligible. Awarded annually.

• 1283 • Distinguished Researcher Award
Recognizes members who have made continuous significant contributions to clinical neurophysiology research. A plaque is awarded annually.

• 1284 • Golseth Young Investigator Award
Recognizes original research in clinical neurophysiology. Based on scientific merit and methodology. Medical students, residents or fellows in training, or electrodiagnostic medicine consultants within 3 years following completion of the educational training recommended by the Association for the practice of electrodiagnostic medicine (M.D., neurology or physical medicine residency or equivalent, and 6 months full-time training in EMG), are eligible. A monetary prize, round trip transportation and three days hotel accommodations to the AAEM Annual Scientific Meeting are awarded annually. Contact the AAEM office for deadline. Established in 1979. Scientific Meeting are awarded when merited, generally annually. Contact the AAEM office for abstract deadline. Established in 1979. Formerly: (1983) Student/Resident Award.

• 1285 • Honorary Member
Candidate must be medical or osteopathic doctor or scientific investigator who holds a doctoral, veterinary, or dental degree. Candidate should be active in clinical practice or research related to electromyography or electrodiagnosis. Individual selected must be of international stature and recognized as a major contributor to the field by virtue of teaching, research and scholarly publications. One candidate per year may be nominated.

• 1286 •
American Association of Neuropathologists
Dr. George Perry, Sec.-Treas.
Institute of Pathology
Case Western Reserve University
2095 Adelbert Rd.
Cleveland, OH 44106
Phone: (216)368-2488
Fax: (216)368-8964
E-mail: aanp@cwru.edu
Home Page: http://www.aanp-jnen.com

• 1287 • Moore Award
For recognition of the best paper on Clinicopathologic Correlation presented at the annual meeting. Members or guests are eligible. A monetary award and a certificate are presented annually. Established in 1971 in honor of Matthew Moore.

• 1288 • Rubinstein Award
To recognize the best paper on Neuro-Oncology presented at the annual meeting. Members or guests are eligible. A monetary award and a certificate are presented annually. Established in 1991 to honor Lucien J. Rubinstein, a longtime member of the Association and a world authority on tumors of the nervous system.

• 1289 • Weil Award
For recognition of the best paper on Experimental Neuropathology presented at the annual meeting. Members or guests are eligible. A monetary award and a certificate are presented annually. Established in 1959 in honor of Arthur Weil.

• 1290 •
American Association of Nurse Anesthetists
Jeffery M. Beutler, Exec. Dir.
222 S Prospect Ave.
Park Ridge, IL 60068
Phone: (847)692-7050
Fax: (847)692-6968
E-mail: info@aana.com
Home Page: http://www.aana.com

• 1291 • Awards of Appreciation
To recognize individuals or institutions for contributions to nurse anesthesia. Awarded when merited. Established in 1947.

• 1292 • Clinical Instructor of the Year Award
To recognize an individual for significant contributions to the teaching of nurse anesthesia students in the clinical field through individual commitment to the profession and the advancement of educational standards that further the art and science of anesthesiology. The nominee must have been active in clinical education of student nurse anesthetists in the last fiscal year, demonstrating knowledge, commitment, and excellence in clinical teaching. A plaque is awarded annually at the AANA Annual meeting. Established in 1991.

• 1293 • Didactic Instructor of the Year Award
To recognize an individual for significant contributions to the classroom education of student nurse anesthetists through individual commitment to the profession and advancement of educational standards that further the art and science of anesthesiology. The nominee must have been active in classroom education of student nurse anesthetists in the last fiscal year, demonstrating knowledge, commitment, and excellence in classroom education. A Crystal is awarded annually at the AANA Annual. Established in 1991.

• 1294 • Agatha Hodgins Award for Outstanding Accomplishment
To recognize individuals whose outstanding accomplishment has furthered the art and science of nurse anesthesia on a national level. A Crystal is awarded annually. Established in 1975.

• 1295 • Honorary Member
To recognize an individual for an outstanding contribution to nurse anesthesia. Awarded when merited. Established in 1960.

• 1296 • Helen Lamb Outstanding Educator Award
To recognize the Certified Registered Nurse Anesthetist educator who has made the most significant contribution to the education of nurse anesthetists. A plaque and a travel allowance to the National Meeting are presented annually. Established in 1980 in honor of Helen Lamb Frost, nurse anesthesia pioneer and educator.

• 1297 • Alice Magaw Outstanding Clinical Practitioner Award
For recognition of important contributions to the advancement of nurse anesthesia practice. Certified Registered Nurse Anesthetists who are involved in direct patient care are eligible. Nominations may be submitted by May 1 by any state or educational district. A Crystal is awarded each year at the AANA Annual Meeting. Established in 1986 by the Council for Public Interest.

• 1298 • Program Director of the Year Award
To recognize a Certified Registered Nurse Anesthetist who has made a significant contribution as a program director to the educational process of student nurse anesthetists. The nominee must be a CRNA who is or has been an active program director in the last fiscal year, recognized as a mentor and role model to CRNAs and students, and a leader in nurse anesthesia education. A plaque is awarded annually at the AANA Annual meeting. Established in 1991.

• 1299 • Public Relations Recognition Award
To honor the state association, group, or individual who has contributed the most positive image to the profession of nurse anesthesia during the year. Any state association, education district, hospital, clinic, educational institution, or individual Certified Registered Nurse Anesthetist who prepares and submits evidence of a positive response to publicity for the CRNA is eligible. A certificate is presented, and the recipient's name is inscribed on a permanent plaque in the AANA Executive Offices. Awarded each year at the AANA Annual Meeting. Established in 1981.

• 1300 • Research in Action Award
For recognition of scientific study in the clinical, educational, or administrative fields that furthers the science of anesthesia. Certified Registered Nurse Anesthetists who present original research in the Research in Action session of the AANA Annual Meeting are eligible. A contribution is made to the school of nurse anesthesia of the winner's choice. Awarded each year at the annual meeting. Established in 1983 by the AANA Program Committee. Sponsored by Critikon. Additional information is available from Glen Ramsborg, CRNA, Director of Programs and Meeting Services.

• 1301 •
American Association of Nurse Attorneys
Belinda E. Puetz RN,PhD, Exec.Dir.
7794 Grow Dr.
Pensacola, FL 32514
Phone: (850)474-3646
Toll-Free: 877-532-2262
Fax: (850)484-8762
E-mail: info@taana.org
Home Page: http://www.taana.org

• 1302 • Cynthia Northrop Distinguished Service Award
Annual award of recognition for a leadership role in and significant contributions to the association. Applicants must be association members.

• 1303 • Outstanding Advocate Award
To recognize an individual member's outstanding legal advocacy. Examples of such advocacy can include making an impact on legislation, authoring scholarly works such as law review articles, books, journal articles, as well as achieving significant rulings in appellate practice, trial practice, and administrative law practice (e.g., hearings before various state boards). Awarded annually. Established in 1986.

• 1304 •
American Association of Occupational Health Nurses
Ann Cox, Exec.Dir.
2920 Brandy Wine Rd., Ste. 100
Atlanta, GA 30341
Phone: (770)455-7757
Fax: (770)455-7271
E-mail: ann@aaohn.org
Home Page: http://www.aaohn.org

• 1305 • Mary Louise Brown Research Recognition Award
In recognition of a registered nurse conducting research or innovative projects contributing to occupational health. The deadline for entries is December 1. A monetary award of $2,500 is awarded annually. Formerly: (1997) Mary Louise Brown Research Award.

• 1306 • Business Recognition Award
To recognize small and large businesses that support and promote the occupational and environmental health nursing profession. Any business, corporation, or government agency engaged in legal commerce, trade, or service is eligible. A crystal statuette is awarded to one small and one large business annually. Formerly: .

• 1307 • Constituent Association Award
Recognizes research of education, newsletter, government affairs, leadership, and scholarship. Awarded annually. Formerly: .

• 1308 •
American Association of Oral and Maxillofacial Surgeons
Dr. Robert Rinaldi, Exec.Dir.
9700 W Bryn Mawr Ave.
Rosemont, IL 60018-5701
Phone: (847)678-6200
Toll-Free: 800-822-6637
Fax: (847)678-6286
E-mail: inquiries@aaoms.org
Home Page: http://www.aaoms.org

Formerly: (1977) American Society of Oral Surgeons.

• 1309 • Committee Man of the Year
To recognize a member of a standing or special committee who has provided outstanding service to the association. Nominees must meet the following criteria: (1) demonstrate effective participation in committee decision-making through identification, evaluation, and analysis of needs, development of programs to meet such needs, and effective utilization of committee's resources, members, and staff to implement programs; and (2) demonstrate a conscious sense of responsibility as a committee member in furthering the purposes of the AAOMS in those areas within which the committee has bylaw purview through a cooperative attitude in development and execution of committee programs and demonstrated leadership which enhances the effectiveness of the committee during and beyond his tenure on the committee. Nominees are selected by secret ballot and submitted to the board. An engraved plaque is awarded at the annual meeting. In additon, travel, housing, and two days' per diem in accordance with policy and waiver of the annual meeting registration fee are awarded.

• 1310 • Distinguished Service Award
To recognize major and current contributions to the specialty of oral and maxillofacial surgery. Only one individual may be named in any one year. Members of the Board of Trustees are not eligible for nomination for a period of five years after completion of their term. Any fellow/member or substructure of the AAOMS may make nominations. Nominations should be submitted by the last Friday of the year annually. An engraved Steuben glass plaque is presented at the annual meeting. In addition, travel, housing, and two days' per diem in accordance with policy and waiver of the annual meeting registration fee are awarded.

• 1311 • Foundation Clinical Surgery Fellowship
To provide the opportunity for young surgeons to develop specialized surgical skills and to broaden knowledge, experience, and judgment in several areas of oral and maxillofacial surgery practice. Those selected for a one-year fellowship make a commitment to spend two years on the staff of an oral and maxillofacial surgery residency-training program thus disseminating the information and skills they have acquired to the next generation of surgeons. Fellowships valued at $40,000 are awarded to one or more recipients annually.

• 1312 • Foundation Research Award
To provide financial support for both promising pre-doctoral students as well as fully trained oral and maxillofacial surgeons who have pursued a career involving scientific inquiry. Eligible candidates include experienced investigators, investigators in training, oral and maxillofacial surgeons in private practice, residents, and health-professions students. Financial awards are presented to one or more recipients annually at the midwinter conference.

• 1313 •
American Association of Oriental Medicine
Gene Bruno, Pres.
909 22nd St.
PO Box 162340
Sacramento, CA 95816
Phone: (916)451-6950
Toll-Free: (866)455-7999
Fax: (916)451-6952
E-mail: info@aaom.org
Home Page: http://www.aaom.org

• 1314 • **Acupuncture Patient of the Year**
Annual award of recognition.

• 1315 • **Acupuncturist of the Year**
Annual award of recognition.

• 1316 • **Legislator of the Year**
Annual award of recognition. Awarded to a member of the legislature.

• 1317 •
American Association of Orthodontists
Chris Vranas, Exec.Dir.
401 N Lindbergh Blvd.
St. Louis, MO 63141-7816
Phone: (314)993-1700
Toll-Free: 800-424-2841
Fax: (314)997-1745
E-mail: info@aaortho.org
Home Page: http://www.braces.org

• 1318 • **James E. Brophy AAO Distinguished Service Award**
For recognition of substantial scientific, technical, and non-scientific contributions to orthodontics in addition to other valuable and devoted services to the Association and to its membership. Members of the Association are eligible. Awarded annually. Established in 1963.

• 1319 • **Thomas M. Graber Award of Special Merit**
To recognize outstanding papers relating to orthodontics. Awarded annually. Established in 1978.

• 1320 • **Milo Hellman Research Award**
To honor the author of an outstanding paper of unusual merit relating to orthodontics, either published or unpublished during the preceding year. Awarded annually. Established in 1944.

• 1321 • **Louise Ada Jarabak Memorial International Teachers and Research Award**
To recognize a teacher who has made outstanding research contributions in the field of orthodontics. Awarded annually.

• 1322 • **Harry Sicher First Research Essay Award**
For recognition of the most meritorious research in orthodontics or related areas. Authors who have had no prior scientific papers published or accepted for publication are eligible. Awarded annually. Established in 1968.

• 1323 •
American Association of Owners and Breeders of Peruvian Paso Horses
Edith Gandy, Pres.
PO Box 476
Wilton, CA 95693
Phone: (916)687-6232
Fax: (916)687-6691
E-mail: mjbpaso@msn.com
Home Page: http://www.aaobpph.org

• 1324 • **Harry Bennett Award**
To recognize the high point horses in 10 different areas for the current year. The horse must be registered and in good standing and the owner must be a member in good standing. The award consists of a chain of the medallions which is hung around horse's neck at the presentation. Awarded annually. Established in 1975.

• 1325 •
American Association of Petroleum Geologists
Stephen A. Sonnenberg, Pres.
1444 S. Boulder
Tulsa, OK 74101-0979
Phone: (918)584-2555
Toll-Free: 800-364-2274
Fax: (918)560-2694
E-mail: postmaster@aapg.org
Home Page: http://www.aapg.org

• 1326 • **Best Paper Award**
To recognize the best student paper presented at the current annual convention. First, second, and third place winners receive $1,000, $500, and $250 respectively, and their universities receiving double those amounts, respectively. Awarded annually.

• 1327 • **Best Student Paper Award**
Recognizes the best student paper presented at the current annual convention. The recipient does not have to be a member of AAPG, but does have to be a student when the paper was presented. $1000 cash first place award, $500 second place award and $250 third place award are given annually. All student presenters receive a $25 Bookstore Gift Certificate.

• 1328 • **Best Student Poster Award**
Recognizes the best student poster presented at the current annual convention. Recipients are not required to be AAPG members, but must be students at the time the papers are presented. $1000 first place, $500 second place, and $250 third place prizes are awarded annually. Funded by an annual contribution from the Shell Foundation.

• 1329 • **Ziad Beydoun Memorial Award for Best International Poster**
Recognizes the best AAPG poster session paper presented at the previous year's International conference. The recipient is not required to be an AAPG member. A $500 cash prize and a walnut plaque bearing the name of the winner and the title of the paper are presented annually. Established in 1990. Formerly: (2001) International Poster Award.

• 1330 • **Jules Braunstein Memorial Award**
To recognize the best poster session paper presented the previous year at the Association's national convention. The recipient need not be an AAPG member. A monetary prize of $500 and a walnut plaque are awarded. Established in 1984 in honor of Jules Braunstein, who established the first poster sessions in 1976. The award is funded through a gift from an AAPG Section, the Gulf Coast Association of Geological Societies.

• 1331 • **Carlos Walter M. Campos Memorial Award for Best International Student Paper**
Recognizes the best AAPG international student paper presented at the international conventions. The recipient is not required to be a member. A $500 cash award and a plaque are awarded annually. Established in 2001.

• 1332 • **Certificates of Merit**
Annual award of recognition.

• 1333 • **Gabriel Dengo Memorial Award for Best International Paper**
Recognizes the best AAPG paper presented at the previous year's International conference. Recipients are not required to be AAPG members. An engraved plaque with a miniature replica of a silver trophy cup is awarded to the winner. The name of the winner is engraved on a sliver trophy cup is retained in the AAPG headquarters. Awarded annually. Established in 1990.

• 1334 • **Distinguished Founders Award**
Annual award of recognition.

• 1335 • **Distinguished Service Awards**
For recognition of distinguished long-term service to the Association. Members of the Association are eligible. A walnut plaque with the AAPG emblem in brass and a brass plate bearing the recipient's name, date, and citation is awarded annually. Established in 1971.

• 1336 • **Robert H. Dott, Sr., Memorial Award**
To honor the authors/editors of the best special publication dealing with geology published by the Association. All special publications published by the association within the calendar year are automatically considered for this award. A monetary prize of $500 and a certificate bearing the recipient's name and the title of the award-winning publication and cash prizes are awarded annually. Established in 1945. Renamed in 1988 to honor Robert H. Dott, Sr. Formerly: (1988) President's Award.

• 1337 • Foundation Grants-in-Aid
Awarded annually. No additional information is available at this time.

• 1338 • Michel T. Halbouty Human Needs Award
To recognize an individual for the most outstanding application of geology to the benefit of human needs and to recognize scientific excellence. Two sterling silver medals mounted on a plaque are awarded annually. Established in 1972. Renamed in 1988. Formerly: (1988) Human Needs Award.

• 1339 • Honorary Membership
Recognizes service and devotion to the science and profession of petroleum geology and to the Association. Nomination is restricted to Association members only. Candidates must show contributions to the science and profession of petroleum geology in particular areas or combinations of discovery, thinking, applications, exploration, leasership, research and related areas. A walnut chest, dispalying the AAPG emblem when opened, is awarded. Established in 1919.

• 1340 • Journalism Award
For recognition of notable journalistic achievement in communications by any medium that contributes to public understanding of geology, energy resources, or the technology of oil and gas exploration. The recipient need not be a member of the Association. A walnut plaque is awarded periodically. Established in 1972.

• 1341 • A. I. Levorsen Memorial Award
Recognizes the best paper presented at each AAPG Section meeting, with particular emphasis on creating thinking toward new ideas in exploration. The award is made at the Section meetings for papers presented at the previous year's meeting. Recipients do not need to be members. Each section establishes its own judging committee. A walnut plaque displaying the AAPG emblem and a brass plate inscribed with the recipient's name, the date and the Section meeting at which the paper was presented is awarded. Awarded annually by each section. Established in 1966.

• 1342 • Life Membership Award
Annual award of recognition.

• 1343 • George C. Matson Memorial Award
To recognize the speaker presenting the best paper at the annual meeting of the Association, based on both scientific quality of content and excellence in presentation. The recipient need not be a member of the Association. The name of the winner is engraved on a large silver cup provided by the Matson family. The winner receives a plaque with a miniature silver cup replica. Co-authors receive a certificate. Awarded annually. Established in 1957 by the family of George C. Matson.

• 1344 • Grover E. Murray Distinguished Educator Award
To recognize distinguished and outstanding contributions to geological education. Contributions leading to consideration for this award will most often involve the teaching and counseling of students at the university level, but contributions to the education of the public and management of educational programs may also be recognized. Candidates must be living at the time of selection and be willing to be present to receive the award at the time and place designated by the Executive Committee. Up to three awards of oak shadow box with a removable silver medallion may be presented in any calendar year. Established in 1993. Formerly: (2006) Distinguished Educator Award.

• 1345 • Outstanding Explorer Award
Recognizes distinguished and outstanding achievement in exploration for petroleum or mineral resources. Members who have shown a consistent pattern of exploratory success, and with an intended emphasis on recent discovery are eligible. A standing figure resembling a geologist on a base and a embossed certificate are awarded. Established in 2000, amended in 2002.

• 1346 • Past Presidents' Award
Annual award of recognition.

• 1347 • Pioneer Award
To recognize long-standing members who have made significant contributions to the Association but have been unrecognized. The candidate must have been a Junior or Active member for not less than 35 years. A plaque is awarded annually. Established in 1996.

• 1348 • Sidney Powers Memorial Award
For recognition of distinguished and outstanding contributions to, or achievements in, petroleum geology. Active members of the Association may be nominated. A gold plated medal and an embossed certificate are awarded annually. Established in 1943 to honor Sidney Powers, founding member and 14th President of the Association.

• 1349 • Wallace E. Pratt Memorial Award
To honor and reward the authors of the best articles published in the *AAPG Bulletin* each calendar year. A monetary award of $1500 and a certificate bearing the recipient's name, the title of the award-winning article, and the appropriate bibliographical reference are presented annually. Co-authors share equally. Established in 1982 in memory of Wallace E. Pratt, a distinguished geologist and founder of the Association. Formerly: (1980) President's Award.

• 1350 • Public Service Awards
To recognize contributions of members of the Association to public affairs and to encourage geologists to take a more active part in public affairs. Members in any class are eligible. Public service work must be above and beyone the person's normal job responsibility. An inscribed walnut plaque is awarded annually. Established in 1971.

• 1351 • Special Awards
To recognize individuals or organizations that, for a variety of reasons, do not qualify for one of the existing Association honors or awards. Recommendations for special awards should be transmitted with substantial supporting data to the Executive Director of the Association for referral to the Honors and Awards Committee.

• 1352 • J. C. "CAM" Sproule Memorial Award
For recognition of an outstanding paper on petroleum geology written by a member of the Association, 35 years of age or younger, and published by the Association or an affiliated society, division, or section. A monetary prize of $500 and a certificate are awarded annually. Established in 1970 in honor of "CAM" Sproule, the 47th President of AAPG (1963-64).

• 1353 • Ozan Sungurlu Memorial Award for Best International Student Poster
Recognizes the best student poster presented at the international convention. Recipient does not have to be a member. A $500 cash prize and a plaque are awarded annually. Established in 2001.

• 1354 •
American Association of Physical Anthropologists
Dr. Fred H. Smith, Sec./Treas.
Office of the Dean
College of Arts & Sciences
Loyola University of Chicago
6525 Sheridan Rd.
Chicago, IL 60626
Phone: (773)899-3703
Phone: (773)508-3500
Fax: (773)508-3514
E-mail: fsmith3@luc.edu
Home Page: http://www.physanth.org

• 1355 • Juan Comas Prize
Recognizes outstandding anthropology students. Created in honor of Juan Comas (1900-1979). Born in Alayor, Mallorca, one of the Spanish Balearic Islands, Professor Comas moved to Mexico and became a Mexican citizen in 1940.

• 1356 • Charles R. Darwin Lifetime Achievement Award
To recognize an Association member's outstanding contributions to the field of physical anthropology. A statue of Charles Darwin is presented annually. Established in 1992.

• 1357 • Ales Hrdlicka Prize
Regocnizes outstanding anthropology students. Created in honor of Ales Hrdlicka (1869-1943). Dr. Hrdlicka was born in Humpolec, Bohemia (now the Czech Republic).

• 1358 • President's Excellence in Presentation Award
Annual award of recognition.

• 1359 • Student Prize Paper Award
To recognize research papers prepared and presented by students. Awarded annually.

• 1360 • Mildred Trotter Prize
Recognizes outstanding anthropology students. Created in honor of Mildred Trotter (1899-1991).

• 1361 • Sherwood L. Washburn Award
To recognize one of the four best student papers presented at the Association's annual meeting. A monetary prize of $200 is awarded annually.

• 1362 •
American Association of Physician Specialists
William J. Carbone, Exec. Dir.
2296 Henderson Mill Rd., Ste. 206
Atlanta, GA 30345
Phone: (770)939-8555
Toll-Free: 800-447-9397
Fax: (770)939-8559
E-mail: wcarbone@aapsga.org
Home Page: http://www.aapsga.org

Formerly: (1984) American Academy of Osteopathic Surgeons.

• 1363 • E. O. Martin Medallion
To recognize continuing achievement over a long period of time to the Association specifically and medicine generally, irrespective of the individual's practice specialty. Members of at least ten years who have received the honorary Degree of Fellow, been certified in a specialty, and have served on an administrative board are eligible. A bronze medal with a relief of Dr. E.O. Martin on the face is awarded annually at the annual meeting. Established in 1987 in honor of Dr. E.O. Martin, founding physician.

• 1364 • Physician of the Year
To recognize outstanding contributions to the Academy, Association and medical profession. Awarded annually at the Association's June Annual Meeting by the Association affiliate academies. Established in 1983 by the founding Academy, The American Academy of Osteopathic Surgeons.

• 1365 •
American Association of Physicists in Medicine
Angela R. Keyser, Exec.Dir.
One Physics Ellipse
College Park, MD 20740-3846
Phone: (301)209-3350
Fax: (301)209-0862
E-mail: aapm@aapm.org
Home Page: http://www.aapm.org

• 1366 • John R. Cameron Young Investigator Award
Recognizes the best presentation by a young investigator for the calendar year.

• 1367 • William D. Coolidge Award
Recognizes distinguished contributions in medical physics professions. Awarded annually.

• 1368 • Farrington Daniels Award
Presented for the best article on radiation dosimetry published in *Medical Physics Journal* for the calendar year. Presented annually.

• 1369 • Sylvia Sorkin Greenfield Award
Presented for the best paper on a subject other than radiation dosimetry published in *Medical Physics Journal* for the calendar year. Awarded annually to one or more recipients.

• 1370 •
American Association of Physics Teachers
Dr. Bernard V. Khoury, Exec.Off.
1 Physics Ellipse
College Park, MD 20740-3845
Phone: (301)209-3300
Fax: (301)209-0845
E-mail: aapt-web@aapt.org
Home Page: http://www.aapt.org

• 1371 • Distinguished Service Citation
For recognition of exceptional contributions to the teaching of physics. Inscribed certificates and citations are awarded annually at the Association's Winter Meeting. Established in 1953.

• 1372 • Excellence in Pre-College Physics Teaching Award
To recognize the contributions to pre-college physics education by an Association member whose primary responsibility is teaching. A monetary sum of $3,000, a certificate, and travel expenses to lecture at the Association's Summer Meeting are awarded annually. Established in 1993. Formerly: Pre-College Award.

• 1373 • Excellence in Undergraduate Physics Teaching Award
To recognize contributions to undergraduate physics education by an AAPT member for whom teaching is a primary responsibility. The recipient is chosen to give a lecture at the AAPT Summer Meeting and receives a monetary award of $3,000, a certificate, and travel expenses to the meeting. Awarded annually. Established in 1993.

• 1374 • Innovative Teaching of Secondary School Physics Award
To encourage change in instructional practices used in teaching high school physics courses. Up to three awards totaling $1,000 may be presented. In addition, awardees receive a citation and a certificate. Awarded annually at the Association's Winter Meeting. Established in 1970.

• 1375 • Klopsteg Memorial Lecture
To choose a lecturer to give a major address at the AAPT Summer Meeting on a topic of current significance suitable for non-specialists. A monetary award of $7,500, travel expenses to the meeting, and a certificate are awarded annually. Established in 1990 in memory of Paul Klopsteg.

• 1376 • Robert A. Millikan Medal
To recognize a college or university teacher for creative work in the teaching of physics. A monetary award of $7,500, travel expenses to the summer meeting, an inscribed silver medal, and a certificate are awarded annually at the Association's Summer Meeting. Established in 1964. Co-sponsored by Prentice-Hall Publishing Company.

• 1377 • Oersted Medal
To recognize a college or university teacher for notable contributions to the teaching of physics. A monetary award of $10,000, an inscribed medal, and a certificate are awarded annually at the Association's Winter Meeting. Established in 1936.

• 1378 • Melba Newell Phillips Award
For recognition of exceptional contributions to physics education through creative leadership in the Association. A monetary award of $7,500, an inscribed medal, a certificate, and travel expenses to an AAPT national meeting are awarded when merited. Established in 1981 in honor of Dr. Phillips' unique life of creative leadership and dedicated service as Associate Editor of both the *American Journal of Physics* and *The Physics Teacher* and as elected member of the Executive Board.

• 1379 • Richtmyer Memorial Lecture
To choose a lecturer to give a major address at the AAPT Winter Meeting on a topic of current significance suitable for non-specialists. A monetary award of $7,500, travel expenses to the meeting, and a certificate are given. Awarded annually. Established in 1941 in memory of Floyd K. Richtmyer.

• 1380 •
American Association of Plastic Surgeons
R. Christie Wray Jr.,MD, Pres.
900 Cummings St., Ste. 221-U
Beverly, MA 01915
Phone: (978)927-8330
Toll-Free: 888-475-2784
Fax: (978)524-8890
E-mail: executivesecretary@aaps1921.org
Home Page: http://www.aaps1921.org

• 1381 • James Barrett Brown Award
To stimulate excellence in the field of plastic surgery as exemplified by research and writing, and to recognize the author or authors of the best article published in *Plastic and Reconstructive Surgery* during the preceding calendar year. Nominations are made by the James Barrett Brown Award Committee and balloting is by the membership of the Association. A monetary award of $2,000 and a plaque are awarded an-

nually. Established in 1973 by Mrs. James Barrett Brown in memory of James Barrett Brown, M.D., outstanding clinician and teacher in plastic and reconstruction surgery and a former president of the Association. Co-sponsored by the James Barrett Brown Foundation.

• 1382 •
American Association of Poison Control Centers
3201 New Mexico Ave. NW, Ste. 310
Washington, DC 20016
Phone: (202)362-7217
E-mail: aapcc@poison.org
Home Page: http://www.aapcc.org

• 1383 • Recognition Awards
To recognize significant contributions to poison control. Awarded annually.

• 1384 •
American Association of Political Consultants
Kevin O'Neill, Exec.Dir.
600 Pennsylvania Ave., SE, Ste. 330
Washington, DC 20003
Phone: (202)544-9815
Fax: (202)544-9816
E-mail: info@theaapc.org
Home Page: http://www.theaapc.org

• 1385 • Pollie Awards
To honor achievement and promote professional development in political and campaign consulting. Awards are presented in various media and print categories. Entries in all advertising categories must have been published, printed, mailed, or broadcast for the first time during the previous two-year period. A trophy is awarded annually. Established in 1984.

• 1386 •
American Association of Psychiatric Technicians
Keith Hearn, Exec.Dir.
2000 O St., Ste. 250
Sacramento, CA 95814-5286
Phone: (916)443-1701
Toll-Free: 800-391-7589
Fax: (916)329-9145
E-mail: hearn@psychtechs.org
Home Page: http://www.psychtechs.org

• 1387 • Faculty Psychiatric Technician of the Year
To recognize outstanding mental health workers. A certificate and free membership in AAPT are awarded annually and are announced in an AAPT press release. Nominations are accepted from peers or supervisors and should include the signature of the Director of Training or Director of Nursing or equivalent. Only one award is given per hospital or facility. Established in 1993 in honor of Mental Health Workers' Week.

• 1388 • National Psychiatric Technician of the Year
To recognize the most outstanding mental health worker in the United States. A certificate, free membership in AAPT, and announcement in a press release are awarded annually. Nominations are accepted from peers or supervisors and should include the signature of the Director of Training or Director of Nursing or equivalent. Established in 1993 in honor of Mental Health Workers' Week.

• 1389 • Regional Psychiatric Technician of the Year
To recognize the most outstanding mental health worker in a multi-state area. A certificate, free membership in AAPT, and announcement in a press release are awarded annually to one person in each of the ten multi-state regions. Nominations are accepted from peers or supervisors and should include the signature of the Director of Training or Director of Nursing or equivalent. Established in 1993 in honor of Mental Health Workers' Week.

• 1390 • State Psychiatric Technician of the Year
To recognize the most outstanding mental health worker and to choose the spokesperson for mental health workers in each state. A certificate, free membership in AAPT, announcement in a press release, and admission to the National Advisory Board are awarded annually to one mental health worker in each state and the District of Columbia. Nominations are accepted from peers or supervisors and should include the signature of the Director of Training or Director of Nursing or equivalent. Established in 1993 in honor of Mental Health Workers' Week.

• 1391 •
American Association of Public Health Dentistry
Pamela J. Tolson, Exec.Dir.
1224 Centre W, Ste. 400B
Springfield, IL 62704
Phone: (217)391-0218
Fax: (217)793-0041
E-mail: natoff@aaphd.org
Home Page: http://www.aaphd.org

• 1392 • Leverett Graduate Student Merit Award for Outstanding Achievement in Dental Public Health
To recognize outstanding achievement by dental students and dental hygiene students in the field of community dentistry. Full-time dental hygiene students or predoctoral dental students in an accredited dental or dental hygiene school in the United States are eligible. Awarded annually. Established in 1970.

• 1393 •
American Association of Public Health Physicians
Arvind K. Goyal MD, Pres.
1307 New York Ave. NW, Ste. 200
Washington, DC 20005
Phone: (202)466-2044
Fax: (202)466-2662
E-mail: info@acpm.org
Home Page: http://www.aaphp.org

• 1394 • Distinguished Service Award
To recognize service to the organization by members of the Association. Established in 1962. Awarded periodically.

• 1395 •
American Association of Retired Persons
Christine Donohoo, Assoc.Exec.Dir.
601 E St. NW
Washington, DC 20049
Toll-Free: 888-OUR-AARP
Fax: (202)434-2320
E-mail: member@aarp.org
Home Page: http://www.aarp.org/

• 1396 • Age Diversity in the Workplace Award
To recognize an individual whose work within a company exemplifies the principles and goals of AARP's Worker Equity Program which are to: eliminate age discrimination in employment; present a positive image of older workers; eliminate stereotypes; encourage and assist employers to create innovative job opportunities; and inspire and encourage employers to establish age-neutral hiring, promotion and training practices. The recipient's workplace must be an equal employment employer, complying with all requirements of the Age Discrimination in Employment Act. A framed certificate was presented at a suitable occasion. Established in 1987. Formerly: Worker Equity Business Partnerships Award.

• 1397 • Andrus Award
To honor nationally recognized individuals who personify either through their work or through continuing achievements in later years the following goals: to serve and not be served; to enhance the quality of life for 50 and older; to promote independence, purpose and dignity for 50 and older; and to improve the image of aging. A handcrafted sculpture is presented at AARP's biennial convention. The recipient is expected to be present to accept the Award during the celebration honoring Dr. Ethel Percy Andrus. Established in 1978 to honor Dr. Andrus.

• 1398 • Chapter or Unit Anniversary Awards
A chapter or unit may present a Certificate of Appreciation to individuals outside the Association or to other groups to recognize service to the local chapter or unit, or to older people in general.

• 1399 • National Community Service Awards
To recognize outstanding volunteer contributions within an area in keeping with the goals and objectives of AARP. Individuals and organizations outside AARP were eligible. Framed certificates or plaques were awarded when merited. Established in 1985. Formerly: Area Community Service Awards.

• 1400 • State Public Official Award for Significant Legislative Achievement
To recognize a public official, active or former, who has made a significant contribution, via legislative or administrative action, to the older citizens of the state and/or the field of aging. The award is based on the recipient's efforts on a specific issue. It is not given on a partisan basis or to imply, in any manner, AARP's endorsement of the candidacy of the recipients. The award is not issued during the election season. The award bears the logo of AARP and is presented by the State Legislative Committee.

• 1401 • Widowed Persons Service Award
To recognize Widowed Persons Service programs completing five years of successful operation. The Program Department presents a certificate.

• 1402 •
American Association of School Administrators
Paul D. Houston, Exec.Dir.
801 N Quincy St., Ste. 700
Arlington, VA 22203
Phone: (703)528-0700
Fax: (703)841-1543
E-mail: info@aasa.org
Home Page: http://www.aasa.org

• 1403 • American Education Award
To recognize an American citizen who has achieved a distinguished career in his or her profession by serving as a role model to others. Awarded at the annual convention. Established in 1928. Additional information is available from Darlene S. Pierce at (703) 875-0736.

• 1404 • Shirley Cooper Architecture Award
To recognize school architecture judged outstanding for its educational environment. Nominations may be submitted by architectural firms. Awarded annually at the AASA convention. Additional information is available from Sharon Cannon at (703) 875-0727.

• 1405 • Distinguished Service Award
To recognize retired members of AASA who have exhibited leadership ability, and who have enhanced school administration in America. Seven plaques are awarded annually. Established in 1958.

• 1406 • Leadership for Learning Award
To recognize outstanding administrative leadership leading to improved learning by students. Superintendents who have served in their present districts or institutions for at least three years are eligible. A Steuben glass creation is presented to the honoree; and a monetary award of $4,000 is presented to his/her school district. Awarded annually in three categories: rural, urban, and suburban. Established in 1984.

• 1407 • National Superintendent of the Year Award
To recognize a school superintendent in each state and one representative nationally for their contributions to education and society. A gold medallion is awarded. A $10,000 scholarship is awarded to a student in the high school from which the honoree graduated. Established in 1988.

• 1408 •
American Association of School Librarians
Julie A. Walker, Exec.Dir.
50 E Huron St.
Chicago, IL 60611-2795
Phone: (312)280-4386
Phone: (312)280-4382
Toll-Free: 800-545-2433
Fax: (312)664-5276
E-mail: aasl@ala.org
Home Page: http://www.ala.org/ala/aasl/aaslindex.htm

• 1409 • AASL ABC/CLIO Leadership Grant
To encourage AASL affiliates to plan and implement leadership development programs at the state, regional, or local level. Programs that involve newer members in activities, workshops, or seminars designed to develop specific leadership qualities are considered. Application deadline is February 1. A monetary grant of $1,750 is awarded annually. Established in 1987. Sponsored by ABC - CLIO.

• 1410 • AASL Collaborative School Library Media Award
Recognizes collaboration and partnerships between school library media specialists and teachers. Collaboration must be geared toward meeting educational goals outlined in *Information Power: Building Partnerships for Learning* through joint planning of a program, unit, or event in support of the curriculum and using media center resources. Applicants must be AASL personal members. Application deadline is March 1.

• 1411 • AASL/Highsmith Research Grant
Encourages research for measuring and evaluating the impact of school library media programs on learning and education. Applicants must be AASL personal members. $5000 is awarded. Application deadline is February 1.

• 1412 • AASL Information Plus Continuing Education Scholarship
Encourages continued education in the field of library science. Applicants must be library media specialists, supervisors, or educators. $500 is awarded.

• 1413 • Distinguished School Administrators Award
To recognize school administrators for developing an exemplary school library media program and for having made an outstanding and sustained contribution to advancing the role of the school library media center as an agency for the improvement of education. Nominations must be made by AASL personal members. A monetary award of $2,000 and a plaque are awarded annually. Established in 1968. Sponsored by Social Issues Resources Series, Inc. $3,000 and a plaque are awarded annually at the ALA conference. Established in 1968. Sponsored by Social Issues Resources Series. Formerly: School Administrators Distinguished Library Service Award.

• 1414 • Distinguished Service Award
To recognize individual members of the library profession who have made outstanding national or international contributions to school librarianship and school library development. A monetary award of $3,000 is presented annually. Established in 1977. Application deadline is February 1. Sponsored by Baker and Taylor Books. Formerly: AASL President's Award.

• 1415 • Frances Henne Award
To recognize school library media specialists who have demonstrated leadership qualities in working with students, teachers, and administrators. Applicants must be AASL/ALA members, have one to five years experience as library media specialists at the building level, and have no previous attendance at an annual ALA conference or a national AASL conference. A monetary grant of $1,250 is awarded to enable the recipient to attend the ALA Annual Conference. The award is made possible by an annual gift from the R. R. Bowker. Established in 1986.

• 1416 • Information Technology Pathfinder Award
To recognize and honor library media specialists who have demonstrated innovative approaches to information technology in the library media center. Applicants must be AASL personal members. Applications must be submitted by February 2. $1,000 is awarded to the school library media specialist and $500 for each of the following two categories: elementary (K-6) and secondary (7-12). Established in 1985. Sponsored by the Follett Software Company. Formerly: Microcomputer in the Media Center Award.

• 1417 • Intellectual Freedom Award
To recognize the upholding of the principles of intellectual freedom as set forth in *Policies and Procedures for Selection of Instructional Materials*. Applicants must be personal members of the AASL. The deadline for nominations is Feb-

ruary 2. A monetary award of $2,000 is awarded annually to the recipient. In addition, a monetary award of $1,000 is awarded to a media center designated by the recipient. Established in 1982. Sponsored by Social Issues Resources Series. Formerly: AASL/SIRS Intellectual Freedom Award.

• 1418 • National School Library Media Program of the Year Award
To recognize large and small school districts and a single school for exemplary school library media programs that are fully integrated into the school's curriculum. Awards of $10,000 each are given in three categories for a total of $ 30,000. Application deadline is January 5. Donated by Follett Library Resources. Established in 1963. Formerly: AASL/EB School Library Media Program of the Year Award - AASL National School Library Media Program of the Year Award.

• 1419 • School Librarian's Workshop Scholarshp
Encourages education in the field of library media specialist. Applicants must be full-time students preparing to become specialist in on of the following levels: preschool, elementary, or secondary and must pursue a graduate level education at an ALA-accredited library school program or in a program meeting the ALA requirements. A personal statement, official transcripts and three references must be submitted along with the formal application form. Application deadline is March 1.

• 1420 •
American Association of School Personnel Administrators
Dr. Jody Shelton EdD, Exec.Dir.
533-B N Mur-Len Rd.
Olathe, KS 66062
Phone: (913)829-2007
Fax: (913)829-2041
E-mail: aaspa@aaspa.org
Home Page: http://www.aaspa.org

• 1421 • Recognition Award
To recognizes exemplary personnel practices. Awarded annually.

• 1422 •
American Association of Sex Educators, Counselors and Therapists
Stephen Conley PhD, Exec.Dir.
PO Box 1960
Ashland, VA 23005-1960
Phone: (804)752-0026
Fax: (804)752-0056
E-mail: aasect@aasect.org
Home Page: http://www.aasect.org

• 1423 • AASECT Award
To recognize individuals who have made outstanding contributions to human sexuality, sex education, sex counseling, and sex therapy. The designation of distinguished affiliate members is awarded. Established in 1971.

• 1424 •
American Association of State Climatologists
Ken Crawford, Pres.
Oklahoma Climatological Survey
University of Oklahoma
Sarkey's Energy Ctr.
100 E Boyd, Ste. 1210
Norman, OK 73019-1012
Phone: (405)325-2541
Fax: (405)325-2550
E-mail: ocs@ou.edu
Home Page: http://lwf.ncdc.noaa.gov/oa/climate/aasc.html

• 1425 • Honorary Life Membership
For recognition of significant contributions in the science of climatology. The executive committee makes the nominations. A certificate is awarded when merited at the annual meeting. Established in 1978.

• 1426 • Helmut Landberg Award for Excellence in Applied Climatology
For recognition of outstanding public service in the field of applied climatology. Members of the Association are eligible. A monetary prize of $200 and a plaque are awarded when merited at the convention. Established in 1987 in honor of Helmut Landberg, the founder of the State Climatology Programs.

• 1427 •
American Association of State Colleges and Universities
Constantine W. Curris, Pres.
1307 New York Ave. NW, 5th Fl.
Washington, DC 20005-4701
Phone: (202)293-7070
Phone: (202)478-4647
Fax: (202)296-5819
E-mail: currisc@aascu.org
Home Page: http://www.aascu.org

• 1428 • AASCU Distinguished Alumnus Award
To recognize an individual known nationally or internationally, who has made a significant contribution to the public life of the nation or to the intellectual and/or cultural life of the nation. The person must have attended an AASCU institution, and preferably graduated from that institution. An engraved plaque is awarded to the recipient; a framed photo is presented to the recipient's alma mater. Awarded at the annual meeting. Established in 1972.

• 1429 • Showcase for Excellence Awards
To highlight the pivotal role state colleges and universities play in the preparation of teachers and to provide educators with program models for improving and enhancing the teaching profession. Nominations are invited for programs in ten categories: attracting more talented students as majors in the field of education; developing more innovative curricula in teacher preparation programs; strengthening relationships with local school districts; building and sustaining new strategies for involving the entire university in teacher preparation programs and enhancing the institutional climate for teaching and learning; creating new strategies for ensuring the quality of graduates in the field of education; initiating innovative applied research projects in education and disseminating the findings to schools and other campuses, as well as throughout the institution; discovering new ways of training teachers to work with disadvantaged youth; providing professional leadership to influence state policies affecting the field of teacher ecucation; discovering new ways of attracting minority youth to enter the teaching profession; and creating new strategies for attracting minority faculty members to schools and colleges of education. Awarded annually. Formerly: AASCU Showcase for Excellence Awards.

• 1430 •
American Association of State Highway and Transportation Officials
John Horsley, Exec.Dir.
444 N. Capitol St. NW, Ste. 249
Washington, DC 20001
Phone: (202)624-5800
Fax: (202)624-5806
E-mail: info@aashto.org
Home Page: http://www.aashto.org

• 1431 • George S. Bartlett Award
For recognition of outstanding contributions to highway progress. Eligibility is limited to employees of the state highway and transportation departments of the United States or Canadian provinces who are members of AASHTO. Individuals are selected jointly by the association, the American Road and Transportation Builders Association, and the Transportation Research Board of the National Research Council. A silver plaque on a walnut base is awarded annually. Established in 1931.

• 1432 • Alfred E. Johnson Achievement Award
For recognition of outstanding technical and administrative service in the field of engineering or management. Eligibility is limited to employees of the state highway and transportation departments of the United States or Canadian provinces who are members of AASHTO. Active employees who are in a middle management position and are not officers of the association are eligible. A brass plate with an inscription on walnut backing is awarded annually. Established in 1973.

• 1433 • Thomas H. MacDonald Memorial Award
For recognition of continuous outstanding service to the association and/or exceptional contributions to the art and science of highway engineering. Eligibility is limited to employees of the state highway and transportation departments of the United States or Canadian provinces who are members of AASHTO. Individuals employed at least five years by any department of the association are eligible. A silver plaque on a walnut base is awarded annually. Established in

1957 to honor Thomas MacDonald's 34 years of service with the Bureau of Public Roads.

• 1434 • President's Modal Awards

To recognize individuals who have performed exemplary service during the year furthering the transporation activities of their state highway or transportation department that has or could have a salutary impact on transportation either regionally or on a national basis. Eligibility is limited to employees of the state highway and transportation departments of the United States or Canadian provinces who are members of AASHTO. Awards are presented in the following categories: rail, water, highways, public transportation, air, highway traffic safety, and intermodal. A plaque is awarded annually. Established in 1979.

• 1435 • Special President's Award of Merit

To recognize an individual who has made outstanding and exemplary contributions to the work of the association. Awarded annually when merited. Established in 1979.

• 1436 •
American Association of Suicidology
Dr. Alan Berman, Exec.Dir.
5221 Wisconsin Ave. NW
Washington, DC 20015
Phone: (202)237-2280
Toll-Free: 800-273-TALK
Fax: (202)237-2282
E-mail: info@suicidology.org
Home Page: http://www.suicidology.org

• 1437 • Louis I. Dublin Award

To recognize an individual for outstanding achievement in and contributions to the field of suicidology. A plaque is awarded annually. Established in 1969.

• 1438 • Edwin Shneidman Award

To recognize outstanding work in suicidology by a researcher under 40 years of age. Membership in the Association is not required. The award is based on an article published or accepted in any scientific journal which is of a theoretical, experimental, or practical nature. A plaque is awarded annually. Formerly: Young Contributor's Award.

• 1439 •
American Association of Surgeon Assistants
PO Box 867
Bernardsville, NJ 07924
Toll-Free: 888-882-2772
Fax: (732)805-9582
E-mail: theaaspa@aol.com

• 1440 • John W. Kirklin M.D. Award for Professional Excellence

To recognize a surgical physician assistant for outstanding professional excellence. Physician assistants currently practicing surgery are eligible. A plaque is awarded annually. Established in 1986 in honor of Dr. John W. Kirklin, founder of the concept of the surgeon assistant.

• 1441 •
American Association of Surgical Physician Assistants
Linda Kotrba, Exec.Dir.
PMB 201, 4267 NW Federal Hwy.
Jensen Beach, FL 34957
Toll-Free: 888-882-2772
Fax: (772)388-3457
E-mail: theaaspa@aol.com
Home Page: http://www.aaspa.com

• 1442 • John W. Kirklin MD Award

To honor practicing surgical physician assistants, physician assistants, or other individuals who have helped promote the surgical physician assistant. It is considered the highest award a surgical physician assistant can receive.Awarded when merited. Established in 1986.

• 1443 •
American Association of Teachers of German
Helene Zimmer-Loew, Exec.Dir.
112 Haddontowne Ct., No. 104
Cherry Hill, NJ 08034-3668
Phone: (856)795-5553
Fax: (856)795-9398
E-mail: headquarters@aatg.org
Home Page: http://www.aatg.org

• 1444 • Certificate of Merit

To provide recognition for outstanding achievement in the teaching of German. Nominations are accepted. A certificate is presented at the annual meeting. Established in 1978. Co-sponsored by the Goethe Institute Inter Nationes.

• 1445 • German Summer Study Award

Awarded to high school students. Winners live with a German family and attend Gymnasium and cultural field trips. Presented annually.

• 1446 • National Testing and Awards Program for Secondary Students

Awarded to 44 outstanding secondary students from every part of the U.S. The award consists of a four-week, all expenses paid study trip to Germany. Additional awards are offered by local chapters.

• 1447 • Outstanding German Educator Award

To recognize German teachers for excellence in teaching as evidenced by ability to stimulate and challenge students intellectually; for recognized professional growth; and contribution to the academic environment outside the classroom. Three awards are presented, one each at the elementary, secondary, and college/university level. Established in 1989.

• 1448 • Outstanding High School Senior in German

Rewarded to High School Seniors who have maintained an A average in German, and have demonstrated exceptional commitment to the study of German by participation in extracurricular activities related to German. A certificate and medal are awarded.

• 1449 •
American Association of Teachers of Italian
Pier Raimondo Baldini, Pres.
Department of Languages and Literatures
Arizona State University
Tempe, AZ 85287-0202
Phone: (480)965-7783
Phone: (480)775-2670
Fax: (480)965-0135
E-mail: pbaldini@asu.edu
Home Page: http://www.aati-online.org

• 1450 • Distinguished Service Award

Biennial award of recognition. Only members are eligible.

• 1451 •
American Association of Teachers of Spanish and Portuguese
Dr. Carol E. Klein, Exec.Dir.
423 Exton Commons
Exton, PA 19341-2451
Phone: (610)363-7005
Fax: (610)363-7116
E-mail: corporate@aatsp.org
Home Page: http://www.aatsp.org

• 1452 • Distinguished Service Award

For recognition of outstanding service in the field of teaching Spanish or Portuguese. Also awarded is the Honorary Fellow Award, the highest honor in the Association, and international summer travel and study scholarships (five to Spain and three to Mexico).

• 1453 • Outstanding Teacher of the Year Awards

Recognizes outstanding teachers in the fields of Spanish and Portuguese education. One award is presented annually in each of four categories: Elementary (grades K-8), Secondary (grades 9-12), Two-year college, and College/University.

• 1454 •
American Association of Textile Chemists and Colorists
John Y. Daniels, Exec.Dir.
PO Box 12215
Research Triangle Park, NC 27709-2215
Phone: (919)549-8141
Fax: (919)549-8933
E-mail: pattyb@aatcc.org
Home Page: http://www.aatcc.org

• 1455 • Harold C. Chapin Award

To recognize outstanding service in enabling the association to attain its objectives. Senior members of the association with at least 20 years of service are eligible. Nominations may be made by senior members. An illuminated scroll is awarded annually at the AATCC International Conference and Exhibition. Established in 1958 and first awarded to Harold C. Chapin who served as secretary of AATCC for a quarter century.

• 1456 • Henry E. Millson Award for Invention

To recognize and encourage contributions to textile wet processing technology. Inventions recognized as an innovative contribution to textile wet processing are eligible. Not limited to members or U.S. citizens. A walnut plaque is awarded annually, when merited, at the AATCC International Conference and Exhibition. Established in 1979 in honor of Henry E. Millson, renowned scientist, researcher, and textile chemist.

• 1457 • Olney Medal

This, the association's highest award, is given to encourage and afford public recognition for achievements in and contributions to textile chemistry. Selection is based on work in the areas of textile chemistry, or in polymer or other fields of chemistry of major importance to textile science, including the development of chemical agents or chemical processes used in the manufacture of textiles or methods for their evaluation. Nominations may be made by any member of the association in the senior classification. United States citizens are eligible. A gold medal, a scroll, and an honorarium are awarded annually at the AATCC International Conference and Exhibition. Established in 1944 in memory of Dr. Louis Atwell Olney, founder of AATCC and in recognition of his lifetime of devotion and contributions to the field of textile chemistry.

• 1458 •
American Association of the Deaf-Blind
Harry Anderson, Pres.
8630 Fenton St., Ste. 121
Silver Spring, MD 20910-4500
Phone: (301)495-4403
Phone: (301)495-4403
Fax: (301)495-4404
E-mail: info@aadb.org
Home Page: http://www.aadb.org

• 1459 • Laura Bridgman Memorial Award

To recognize leadership and independence of association members. Awarded annually.

• 1460 •
American Association of University Administrators
Dan L. King, Gen.Sec.
Rhode Island Coll.
Roberts Hall 407
Providence, RI 02908-1991
Phone: (401)456-2808
Fax: (401)456-8287
E-mail: dking@aaua.org
Home Page: http://www.aaua.org

• 1461 • Distinguished Service Award

Recognize excellence in the administration of higher education. Association members are eligible. A plaque is awarded annually. Established in 1987.

• 1462 • Eileen M. Tosney AAUA Award for Excellence in the Practice of Higher Education Administration

Recognizes excellence administration of higher education. A plaque is awarded annually. Established in 1984.

• 1463 •
American Association of University Professors
Mary A. Burgan, Gen.Sec.
1012 14th St. NW, Ste. 500
Washington, DC 20005
Phone: (202)737-5900
Toll-Free: 800-424-2973
Fax: (202)737-5526
E-mail: aaup@aaup.org
Home Page: http://www.aaup.org

• 1464 • AAUP Award for Excellence in Coverage of Higher Education

To recognize and stimulate coverage of higher education nationally and to encourage thoughtful and comprehensive reporting of higher education issues. Single articles or a series published in newspapers, magazines, or journals during the preceding year may be submitted by March 31. Editorials or columns are not considered. A plaque and travel expenses to attend the annual meeting are awarded annually in June. Established in 1970. Formerly: (1989) Higher Education Writers Award.

• 1465 • Beatrice G. Konheim Award

To recognize a chapter of the association for distinctive achievement in advancing the objectives of AAUP in academic freedom, student rights and freedoms, the status of academic women, the elimination of discrimination against minorities, or the establishment of equal opportunity for members of college and university faculties. A monetary prize of $1,000 is awarded annually. Established in 1974.

• 1466 • Alexander Meiklejohn Award

In recognition of an outstanding contribution to academic freedom made by an American college or university administrator or trustee, or by a board of trustees as a group. A bronze plaque is usually awarded annually. Established in 1958. Sponsored in part by alumni of the Experimental College, University of Wisconsin.

• 1467 • Georgina Smith Award

To recognize a person who has provided exceptional leadership in a given year to the improvement of the status of academic women or the advancement of academic collective bargaining and, through that work, improvement of the profession in general.

• 1468 •
American Association of University Women Educational Foundation
Mary Ellen Smyth, Pres.
1111 16th St. NW
Washington, DC 20036
Phone: (202)728-7602
Toll-Free: 800-326-AAUW
Fax: (202)872-1425
E-mail: foundation@aauw.org
Home Page: http://www.aauw.org/ef/index.cfm

• 1469 • Achievement Award

To recognize a woman of outstanding achievement in an academic or professional field. Awards are typically given to women whose achievements have spanned ten years or more. A monetary honorarium of $5,000 accompanies the award, which is given biennially. Established in 1943.

• 1470 • Annie Jump Cannon Award in Astronomy

To recognize a young woman with achievement and potential for research in the field of astronomy. Applicants must be in the early stages of their careers and have the pursuit of research in astronomy as career goals. Preference is given to applicants who have held a Ph.D. in astronomy or a related field for at least one year. There are no restrictions on nationality or the location of the research. The deadline is in February. A monetary award of $5,000 is presented annually in the spring. Established in 1934 by the American Astronomical Society in honor of Annie Jump Cannon, a prominent early 20th century woman astronomer. Ms. Cannon established the classification of stars now used by astronomers. Additional information is available from Anna Fiets, Education Department.

• 1471 • Career Development Grants

For women who are in the early stages of graduate studies in order to re-enter the work force, change careers, or advance their current careers. Applicants must be U.S. citizens and have earned a bachelor's degree. They must pursue course work at a fully accredited school or approved by the Federal Veterans Administration. Applicants must also enroll in courses that are prerequisites for professional employment plans. Special consideration is given to qualified AAUW members, women of color, women pursuing their first terminal degree, and women pursuing degrees in nontraditional fields. Funds are available for tuition, books. supplies, local transportation, and dependent care. Grants range from $2,000 to $8,000.

• 1472 • Fellowship Program

To provide graduate fellowships and grants to women who have demonstrated scholarly excellence. Assistance is available through the following programs: American Fellowships - postdoctoral and dissertation fellowships for women who are citizens or permanent residents of the United States. There are no restrictions as to place of study or age; Project Career Development Grants - to women pursuing course work to prepare for reentry into the work force, career advancement or a career change. Applicants must be U.S. citizens or permanent residents, hold a baccalaureate degree, and have completed their most recent degree not more than 5 years ago; Selected Professions Fellowships - to women who are citizens or permanent residents of the United States in designated fields where female participation traditionally has been low; and International Fellowships to women of outstanding academic ability who are not citizens or permanent residents of the United States for full-time graduate or postgraduate study or research in the United States. Applicants must hold the equivalent of a U.S. bachelor's degree.

• 1473 • Recognition Award for Young Scholars

To recognize women for outstanding teaching and research. Awarded annually.

• 1474 • Eleanor Roosevelt Fund Award

To recognize an individual, project, organization, or institution for outstanding contributions to equity and education for women and girls. The award is given for a broad range of activities including classroom teaching, educational and research contributions, and legal and legislative work in equity for women and girls. While the award focuses on education, the recipient need not be an educator. An honorarium of $5,000 is awarded annually. Established in 1989.

• 1475 •
American Association of University Women Legal Advocacy Fund
Jacqueline E. Woods, Exec.Dir.
1111 16th St. NW
Washington, DC 20036
Toll-Free: 800-326-AAUW
Fax: (202)872-1425
E-mail: laf@aauw.org
Home Page: http://www.aauw.org/laf/index.cfm

• 1476 • Equity Award

Financial award to a college or university program making significant progress for women on campus.

• 1477 •
American Association of Veterinary Immunologists
Eileen L. Thacker, Sec.-Treas.
2118 Vet Med Bldg.
Veterinary Microbiology & Preventive Medicine
Iowa State University
PO Box 646630
Ames, IA 50011
Phone: (515)294-5097
Phone: (509)335-6003
Fax: (515)294-8500
E-mail: ethacker@iastate.edu
Home Page: http://www.cvm.missouri.edu/aavi

• 1478 • Student Awards

To recognize an immunology related oral and poster presentation in the annual competition, at the conference of Research workers in Animal diseases.

• 1479 •
American Association of Veterinary Laboratory Diagnosticians
Dr. Allison Reitz, Sec.
PO Box 1770
Davis, CA 95617
Phone: (530)754-9719
Fax: (530)752-5680
E-mail: areitz@cvdls.ucdavis.edu
Home Page: http://www.aavld.org

• 1480 • E. P. Pope Award

For recognition of a noteworthy contribution to the organization, implementation, and recognition of the specialty of veterinary diagnostic medicine. Nomination is by the E. P. Pope Award Committee of the American Association of Veterinary Laboratory Diagnosticians. A plaque and dedication of annual proceedings of the scientific meeting for that year are awarded annually when merited. Established in 1975 in honor of E. P. Pope.

• 1481 •
American Association of Women Dentists
Dr. Jean Furuyama DDS, Pres.
330 S Wells St., Ste. 1110
Chicago, IL 60606
Phone: (312)280-9296
Toll-Free: 800-920-2293
Fax: (312)461-0238
E-mail: info@aawd.org
Home Page: http://www.womendentists.org

• 1482 • Colgate-Palmolive Research Scholarship Award

To recognize dental students achieving academic excellence and research. Applicants must be juniors or seniors currently enrolled in dental school. A monetary prize of $4,000 is awarded annually.

• 1483 •
American Association of Women Emergency Physicians
Dean Wilkerson, Exec.Dir.
1125 Executive Cir.
Irving, TX 75038-2522
Phone: (972)550-0911
Toll-Free: 800-798-1822
Fax: (972)580-2816
E-mail: execdirector@acep.org

• 1484 • Trish Blair Leadership Services Awards

Award of recognition. Applicants must be women emergency physicians. Awarded annually.

• 1485 •
American Association of Zoo Keepers
Ed Hansen, Exec.Dir.
3601 SW 29th St., Ste. 133
Topeka, KS 66614-2054
Phone: (785)273-9149
Toll-Free: 800-242-4519
Fax: (785)273-1980
E-mail: aazkoffice@zk.kscoxmail.com
Home Page: http://www.aazk.org

• 1486 • Certificate of Excellence in Exhibit Renovation

To recognize institutions or organizations in the zoological community for the design and renovation of existing animal facilities which involved active animal keeper participation in the process. The deadline for nominations is June 1. A certificate, a letter to the institution's director, and national recognition by professional journals are awarded annually at the AAZK Conference. Established in 1990.

• 1487 • Certificate of Merit for Zookeeper Education

To recognize individuals, institutions, and organizations in the zoological community most actively promoting educational programs for zookeepers. North American zoological staff individuals, institutions, or organizations are eligible for programs which have been in existence for at least one year. The deadline for nominations is June 1. A certificate, a letter to the institution's director, and national recognition by professional journals are awarded annually at the AAZK Conference. Established in 1978 by Jeff Roberts.

• 1488 • Jean M. Hromadka Excellence in Zookeeping Award

To recognize an individual for achievement and determination in the zookeeping field, and to foster professionalism. Full-time zookeepers employed for at least two years in any North American zoo or aquarium may be nominated by June 1. A certificate, a letter to the institution's director, and national recognition by professional journals are awarded annually at the AAZK Conference. Established in 1974 to honor zoologist R. Marlin Perkins. Formerly: (1984) Marlin Perkins Award.

• 1489 • Lifetime Achievement Award

To recognize, at the end of a keeper's career, outstanding commitment to professionalism as a zoo keeper over a long period of time, and significant contributions to the community. The deadline for nominations is June 1. A plaque, a letter of notification to the institution's director, and national recognition in professional journals are awarded annually at the AAZK Conference. Established in 1993.

• 1490 • Meritorious Achievement Award

To recognize zookeepers involved with AAZPA Bean Award winning projects in the zoo field who have unselfishly dedicated extra time to other zoo related activities (conservation, wildlife education, and individual breeding projects outside of the zoo proper). Association members who are full-time employees of any North American zoo, park, or aquarium for one year may be nominated by June 1. A certificate, a letter to the institution's director, and national recognition by professional journals are awarded annually at the AAZK Conference. Established in 1982 by Mike Crocker.

• 1491 •
American Association of Zoo Keepers - San Antonio Chapter
Michael Pacheco, Pres.
3903 N St. Mary's St.
San Antonio, TX 78212-3199
Phone: (210)734-7184
Fax: (210)734-7291
E-mail: hughdolly@sazoo-ag.org
Home Page: http://www.sazoo-aq.org

• 1492 • **Raymond Figeroa Keeper Scholarship**
For member of one year standing or more who has been an animal keeper for at least a year. Monetary award bestowed annually.

• 1493 •
American Association on Mental Retardation
Ms. M. Doreen Croser, Exec.Dir.
444 N. Capitol St. NW, Ste. 846
Washington, DC 20001-1512
Phone: (202)387-1968
Toll-Free: 800-424-3688
Fax: (202)387-2193
E-mail: dcroser@aamr.org
Home Page: http://www.aamr.org

Formerly: (1987) American Association on Mental Deficiency.

• 1494 • **AAMR Awards**
To recognize individuals or groups who have made outstanding contributions that have influenced positive change in the field of mental retardation for an extended period of time. Awards for outstanding contributions or special achievement are given in the following categories: Education - for significant contributions to dissemination of knowledge for the field of mental retardation; AAMR DYBWAD Humanitarian - for promotion of human welfare and social reform; Leadership - for courage and dedication resulting in an outstanding contribution to the field of mental retardation; Research - for formulations and investigations that have contributed significantly to the body of scientific knowledge in the field of mental retardation; Service - for contributions to the improvement of services to the retarded individual; Special - for an unusual or significant contribution or achievement not covered by other award categories; Full Community Inclusion - for culturally responsive programs that have succeeded in full community inclusion and participation; and The Hervey B. Wilbur Award for Historic Preservation - for contributions to historic preservation of the archives of the field of mental retardation and/or the Association. Candidates may be nominated, and recipients receive an award in only one category. Activities of recipients must have a national and/or international impact. Nominations must be submitted by October 31. A plaque is awarded at the annual meeting. Established in 1971.

• 1495 • **Special Student Awards**
To recognize student contributions to the field of mental retardation. A student must be nominated by two faculty members. Areas in which student awards may be given are: Service for contributions to improve service to individuals with mental retardation; Leadership for performance that has guided or directed other in improving the quality of programs for people with mental retardation, and is found to be extraordinarily significant; and Scholarship for performance that reflects a systematic application of scientific inquiry techniques to a problem of significance in the field of mental retardation, and is found to be extraordinarily significant. Awarded annually.

• 1496 •
American Astronautical Society
James R. Kirkpatrick, Exec.Dir.
6352 Rolling Mill Pl., Ste. 102
Springfield, VA 22152-2354
Phone: (703)866-0020
Fax: (703)866-3526
E-mail: aas@astronautical.org
Home Page: http://www.astronautical.org

• 1497 • **AAS Flight Achievement Award**
To recognize outstanding achievements as a flight crew or flight crew member. Awarded annually. Established in 1958.

• 1498 • **AAS Space Flight Award**
This, the highest award of the Society, is given to recognize outstanding efforts and achievements to the person who has contributed the most to the advancement of space flight and space exploration. Awarded annually. Established in 1955.

• 1499 • **Lloyd V. Berkner Award**
To recognize a person who has made significant contributions to the commercial utilization of space technology. Awarded annually. Established in 1967.

• 1500 • **Melbourne W. Boynton Award**
To recognize a physician who has performed research contributing with distinction to the biomedical aspects of space flight. Awarded annually. Established in 1957.

• 1501 • **Eugene M. Emme Astronautical Literature Award**
For recognition of the outstanding book published each year that increases public understanding on the impact of astronautics upon society. Nominations of books may be made by AAS members by May 31 of each year. A certificate is awarded annually. Established in 1982. Formerly: Astronautics Literature Award.

• 1502 • **Industrial Leadership Award**
To recognize an individual for outstanding leadership and contributions to the development and acquisition of space systems. Awarded annually. Established in 1992.

• 1503 • **John F. Kennedy Astronautics Award**
To recognize an individual who has made an outstanding contribution to public service through the leadership and promotion of space programs for the exploration and utilization of outer space. Awarded annually at Established in 1974. Formerly: Olin E. Teague Space Award.

• 1504 • **W. Randolph Lovelace II Award**
To recognize an individual for significant contributions to space science and technology. Awarded when merited. Established in 1965.

• 1505 • **Military Astronautics Award**
To recognize outstanding leadership in the application of astronautics to the development of space systems for national defense. Awarded when merited. Established in 1982.

• 1506 • **Victor A. Prather Award**
To recognize researchers, engineers, and flight crew members in the field of extra-vehicular protection in space. Awarded annually. Established in 1962.

• 1507 •
American Astronomical Society
Dr. Robert W. Milkey, Exec. Officer
2000 Florida Ave. NW, Ste. 400
Washington, DC 20009-1231
Phone: (202)328-2010
Fax: (202)234-2560
E-mail: aas@aas.org
Home Page: http://www.aas.org

• 1508 • **George Van Biesbroeck Prize**
For recognition of extraordinary and unselfish service to astronomy, well in excess of the expectation of his or her paid position. A monetary prize is normally awarded annually. Transferred to the AAS in 1997 from a nonprofit corporation where the prize originated.

• 1509 • **Priscilla and Bart Bok Award**
Recognizes outstanding astronomical research projects. Awarded annually.

• 1510 • **Dirk Brouwer Award**
To recognize outstanding contributions in the field of dynamical astronomy, including celestial mechanics, astronomy, geophysics, stellar systems, galactic, and extragalactic dynamics. Candidates of any age, nationality, occupation, or specific field of interest are eligible. An honorarium and a Certificate of Citation are awarded annually. Established in 1978. Awarded by the Division on Dynamical Astronomy.

• 1511 • Annie Jump Cannon Award in Astronomy

To recognize a woman for distinguished contributions to astronomy or for similar contributions in related sciences that have immediate application to astronomy. Since 1974, the award has been offered as a research award, by the AAUW with advice from the Society's Annie J. Cannon Award Committee. Awarded annually. Established in 1934.

• 1512 • George Ellery Hale Prize

To recognize a scientist for outstanding contributions over an extended period of time to the field of solar astronomy. Any living scientist without consideration of race, sex, or nationality is eligible. An honorarium, a medal, and a citation are awarded biennially. Awarded by the Solar Physics Division. Established in 1978.

• 1513 • Gerard P. Kuiper Prize

To recognize and honor outstanding contributors to planetary science whose achievements have most advanced our understanding of the universe. Candidates may be of any age or nationality. Awarded annually. Established in 1984. Awarded by the Division for Planetary Sciences.

• 1514 • Harold Masursky Award for Meritorious Service

To recognize outstanding scientific, teaching, and public information contributions to planetary science. Awarded annually by the Division of Planetary Science. Established in 1991.

• 1515 • Newton Lacy Pierce Prize in Astronomy

To recognize outstanding achievement during the five years preceding the award in observational astronomical research based on measurements for radiation from an astronomical object. Residents of North America (including Hawaii and Puerto Rico) or members of a North American institution who are stationed abroad and are under 36 years of age are eligible. A monetary prize and certificate are awarded annually. Established in 1974.

• 1516 • Bruno Rossi Prize

For a significant contribution to high energy astrophysics, with particular emphasis on recent work. Awarded annually by the High Energy Astrophysics Division. Established in 1984.

• 1517 • Henry Norris Russell Lectureship

To recognize senior astronomers for lifetime eminence in astronomical research. A monetary prize is awarded annually. Established in 1946.

• 1518 • Beatrice M. Tinsley Prize

To recognize an outstanding research contribution to astronomy or astrophysics of an exceptionally creative or innovative character. No restrictions are placed on a candidate's citizenship or country of residency. Awarded biennially. Established in 1986.

• 1519 • Harold C. Urey Prize

To recognize outstanding achievement in planetary research by a young scientist. Candidates must be residents of North America and must be either under 36 years of age, or the holder of a recognized doctorate for no more than six years. Awarded annually by the Division for Planetary Sciences. Established in 1984.

• 1520 • Helen B. Warner Prize for Astronomy

To recognize significant contributions to astronomy during the five years preceding the award. Residents of North America (including Hawaii and Puerto Rico) or members of a North American institution who are stationed abroad and are under 36 years of age at the time of selection are eligible. A monetary prize is awarded annually. Established in 1954.

• 1521 •
American Auto Racing Writers and Broadcasters Association
Dusty Brandel, Pres.
922 N. Pass Ave.
Burbank, CA 91505
Phone: (818)842-7005
Fax: (818)842-7020
E-mail: aarwba@compuserve.com
Home Page: http://www.aarwba.org

• 1522 • AARWBA All-America Auto Racing Teams

To recognize outstanding achievement for a single season in the field of auto racing. Twelve race drivers are presented with awards in the following categories: open wheel, stock cars, road racing, drag racing, short track, and at-large. Selection is made by a vote of the members of the association. Bronze "Horsepower" trophies are awarded annually at the end of the racing season. Additionally, the driver who receives the most votes receives the Jerry Titus Memorial Trophy Award. The trophy is a typewriter mounted on a walnut base and topped with a replica of Titus' racing helmet. Established in memory of Jerry Titus, a well known journalist and race driver who was fatally injured while racing.

• 1523 • AARWBA Hall of Fame Award (Legends of Racing)

To recognize individuals who have been outstanding in the field of auto racing. Active drivers as well as retired or deceased participants are considered for the Legends of Racing Award. An inscribed certificate, printed on parchment and framed, is awarded annually. Established in 1970.

• 1524 •
American Ballet Competition
F. Randolph Swartz, Exec.Dir.
2000 Hamilton, Ste. C200
Philadelphia, PA 19130
Phone: (215)636-9000
Toll-Free: 800-523-0961
Fax: (215)564-4206
E-mail: randy@dancecelebration.org
Home Page: http://www.dancecelebration.org

• 1525 • American Ballet Competition

To select and financially support American dancers participating in international ballet competitions. The primary goals of the program are: to ensure that the best dancers, partners, and coaches represent the United States in international competitions; to discover and publicize these promising dancers through regional and national competitions; to provide artistic guidance and administrative support to the American team; to award financial grants-in-aid to competitors for travel, lodging expenses, coaches, partners, music, rehearsal space, costumes, and shoes; to develop skills necessary for success in international competitions through workshops and seminars involving world-class coaches, choreographers, and dancers; to solidify the cultural and educational exchange process by providing opportunities for United States artists to meet and share ideas with their foreign peers; and to provide grants to schools and companies who developed and fostered those talented dancers selected for competition. The American team of dancers is selected following regional and national auditions. An excess of $225,000 in stipends has been awarded to more than 33 dancers participating in 13 international competitions. Established in 1979.

• 1526 •
American Bandmasters Association
Dr. William J. Moody, Sec.-Treas.
4250 Shorebrook Dr.
Columbia, SC 29206
Phone: (803)787-6540
E-mail: wmoody@mozart.sc.edu
Home Page: http://www.americanbandmasters.org

• 1527 • ABA Ostwald Band Composition Award

For recognition of an outstanding original unpublished composition for band. Compositions that are conceived and constructed so as to be effectively performed by professional, university, and high school bands are eligible. The deadline for submission of compositions and tapes is December 31. A monetary prize of $8,000 commission are awarded to the composer. Established in 1956. Funded for 25 years by the Uniforms by Ostwald Company, Staten Island, New York. Currently funded by the ABA Foundation. Awarded every four years. Next competition will be in 2006.

• 1528 •
American Baptist Homes and Hospitals Association
Aundreia Alexander, Dir.
PO Box 851
Valley Forge, PA 19482-0851
Phone: (610)768-2411
Toll-Free: 800-ABC-3USA
Fax: (610)768-2453
E-mail: aundreia.alexander@abc-usa.org
Home Page: http://www.nationalministries.org/mission/abhha/

• 1529 • **Merit Award**
To recognize unusual contributions by board, staff and volunteers of member facilities. The following factors are considered: (1) effective service; (2) length of service; (3) imaginative leadership; (4) general health and welfare contribution; and (5) denominational contribution. The individual's service should exceed 10 years, and while the individual need not be an American Baptist, preference will be given to American Baptists. A plaque is awarded biennially during the Association's meetings. Established in 1958.

• 1530 •
American Bar Association
Alfred P. Carlton, Pres.
321 N. Clark St.
Chicago, IL 60610
Phone: (312)988-5000
Toll-Free: 800-285-2221
Fax: (312)988-5522
E-mail: service@abanet.org
Home Page: http://www.abanet.org

• 1531 • **American Bar Association Medal**
To recognize conspicuous service to the cause of American jurisprudence. A medal is awarded at the discretion of the Association. Established in 1929.

• 1532 • **Judge Edward R. Finch Law Day U.S.A. Speech Award**
To recognize the most outstanding and effective Law Day (May 1) speech and to foster a deeper appreciation and understanding of the place of law in American life. A monetary prize of $1000 for first place and certificates for second and third place are awarded annually. Established in 1968. Additional information is available from Marcia L. Kladder; telephone: (312) 988-6133.

• 1533 • **Gavel Awards**
To accord national recognition to the United States news and entertainment media for outstanding published articles, books, films, theatrical performances, and radio and television broadcasts. Publication or media events must foster greater public understanding of the inherent values of our American legal and judicial system; inform and educate citizens as to the roles of the law, the courts, and the legal profession in today's society; disclose practices and procedures in need of correction or improvement so as to encourage and promote local, state, and federal legislative efforts to update and modernize the nation's laws, courts, and law enforcement agencies; and aid the legal profession and judiciary in attaining the goals set by the Model Rules of Professional Conduct and the Code of Judicial Conduct. Material originally published, broadcast, or presented during the previous calendar year may be submitted by February 1. Awards are given in the following classifications: newspapers - dailies and non-daily newspapers, newspaper magazine supplements, magazines, books, wire services/news syndicates, films, theater, television, and radio. The radio and television categories are divided into the following subcategories: network, syndicated, local and/or independent productions (top 10 markets), local and/or independent productions (markets areas 11-50), local and/or independent productions (markets over 50), and local non-commercial. In addition, television has a cable - local subcategory. Silver Gavel Awards and Certificate of Merit Awards are presented annually. Established in 1958.

• 1534 • **Law Day U.S.A. Public Service Awards**
To recognize outstanding Law Day U.S.A. programs that foster greater public understanding of the values of our American system of law and the duties of citizenship; inform and educate citizens about the courts, law enforcement agencies, the justice system, and the legal profession; to call attention to the principles and practice of American government; and adhere to the stated objectives of Law Day U.S.A. Applications must be submitted by July 1. Certificates of Recognition may be presented to winners in each of the categories. The awards program is conducted by the ABA Standing Committee on Association Communications.

• 1535 • **Outstanding Government Service Award**
To recognize an individual for outstanding government service. Established in 1989.

• 1536 • **Pro Bono Publico Awards**
To identify and honor up to four attorneys and one law firm or corporate law department that have enhanced the human dignity of others by improving or delivering volunteer legal services to the poor. Individual attorneys or law firms who do not obtain their income by delivering legal services to the poor are eligible. A law firm or corporate law department whose members have collectively made an outstanding contribution fitting one of the award's criteria are also eligible. Nominations must be submitted by April 1. Awarded annually. Established in 1984. Administered by the Association's Standing Committee on Lawyers' Public Service Responsibility. Additional information is available from D. Jackson, telephone: (312) 988-5766; fax: (312) 988-5483.

• 1537 • **Harrison Tweed Award**
To recognize the extraordinary achievements of state and local bar associations that develop or significantly expand projects or programs to provide access to civil legal services to poor persons or criminal defense services to indigents. Awarded annually. Established in 1956.

• 1538 •
American Baseball Coaches Association
Dave Keilitz, Exec.Dir.
108 S University Ave., Ste. 3
Mount Pleasant, MI 48858-2327
Phone: (989)775-3300
Fax: (989)775-3600
E-mail: abca@abca.org
Home Page: http://www.abca.org

Formerly: (1984) American Association of College Baseball Coaches.

• 1539 • **ABCA Twenty-Five Year Awards**
To honor coaches who have spent 25 years coaching baseball. The coach must be a member of the Association for at least five years. A plaque is awarded annually. Established in 1955.

• 1540 • **Century Club Award**
To recognize high school or college coaches achieving a century mark win during a season (example: 100th, 200th, 300th, etc.). Established in 1988.

• 1541 • **Coach of the Year Award**
For recognition of the most outstanding college, university, and high school baseball coaches of the year. Plaques are awarded annually. Established in 1955.

• 1542 • **Field Maintenance Award**
To recognize an outstanding amateur baseball field and the maintenance of it. An award is bestowed to the winner in each of two divisions: high school and college. Awarded annually.

• 1543 • **Lefty Gomez Award**
For recognition of the greatest contribution to collegiate baseball in the past year. A trophy is awarded annually. Established in 1961 by the Wilson Sporting Goods Company.

• 1544 • **Hall of Fame**
To honor member coaches who have a long time record of achievement in baseball. Plaques are awarded annually. Established in 1946.

• 1545 • **Honor Awards**
To honor individuals who participated or were involved in baseball and who have achieved success in their professions and have contributed to society over a period of years. Plaques are awarded annually. Established in 1973.

• 1546 • **Meritorious Service Award**
To recognize individuals for outstanding contributions to amateur baseball. Awarded annually. Established in 1980.

• 1547 • **National Championship**
To recognize the collegiate national baseball champion and each conference champions in all collegiate divisions. A crystal bat and scholarship are awarded annually.

• 1548 •
American Bashkir Curly Registry
Sue Chilson, Sec.
PO Box 151029
Ely, NV 89315
Phone: (775)289-4999
Fax: (775)289-8579
E-mail: secretary@abcregistry.org
Home Page: http://www.abcregistry.org

• 1549 • **ABC Breed Promotion**
To recognize an individual with the best record of breed promotion during the year. Members of ABC Registry are eligible. A trophy is awarded annually. Established in 1973.

• 1550 • **ABC Champion Performance Horse**
To recognize an ABC Registered Horse earning the most points in the Horse Show Arena Performance. A trophy is awarded annually. Established in 1973.

• 1551 • **ABC Champion Trail Horse**
To recognize an ABC Registered Horse earning the most points in Endurance and Competitive Trail Riding. A trophy is awarded annually. Established in 1973.

• 1552 • **Peter L. Damele Memorial Award**
To recognize the High-Point ABC Registered Performance Horse at the annual National All-Curly Horse Show at Ely, Nevada. A trophy is awarded. Established in 1982 by Bernard Damele in memory of his father, Peter L. Damele, premier curly horse breeder.

• 1553 • **Youth Award**
To recognize a Youth ABC member earning the most points for the year riding a registered ABC horse. The youth must be a member of ABC Registry and the horse ridden must be registered with ABC. A trophy is awarded annually. Established in 1979.

• 1554 •
American Beefalo World Registry
Robin Ellis, Contact
30 Stevenson Rd., No. 5
Laramie, WY 82070
Phone: (307)745-3505
Fax: (307)745-3505
E-mail: beefalo@abwr.org
Home Page: http://www.abwr.org

Formed by merger of: (1983) International Beefalo Association; World Beefalo Association; American Beefalo Association.

• 1555 • **American Beefalo World Registry's National Beefalo Show & Sale**
This annual event is held in conjunction with the Mid South Fair in Memphis, TN. The following awards are presented: (1) Premiere Breeders Award - for recognition of a contribution to the field of Beefalo breeding. The individual who is the largest breeder of animals entered in the National Beefalo Show is selected; (2) Premiere Exhibitor Award - to recognize the individual who is the largest owner of animals entered in the National Beefalo Show; and (3) $8,000 in prize money is awarded to top winners of the National Beefalo Show. Trophies and plaques are also awarded annually to the top winners. Awarded annually. Established in 1983.

• 1556 • **American Beefalo World Registry's Regional Beefalo Shows**
The Southeast Regional Beefalo Show is held in conjunction with the Georgia National Fair in Perry, Georgia. The following awards are presented: (1) Premiere Breeders Award - for recognition of contribution to the field of Beefalo breeding. The person who is the owner of the largest breeder of animals entered in the national Beefalo Show is selected; (2) Premiere Exhibitors Award - to recognize the person who is the owner of the largest number of animals entered in the national Beefalo Show; and (3) $7,000 in prize money is awarded to the top winners of the National Beefalo Show. Trophies and plaques are also awarded to the top winners.

• 1557 • **Southwest Regional Beefalo Show**
The Southwest Regional Beefalo Show is held in conjunction with the Oklahoma State Fair in Oklahoma City, Oklahoma. The following awards are presented: (1) Premiere Breeders Award - for recognition of contribution to the field of Beefalo breeding. The person who is the largest breeder of animals entered in the National Beefalo Show is selected; (2) Premiere Exhibitors Award - to recognize the person who is the owner of the largest number of animals entered in the National Beefalo Show; and (3) $3,500 in prize money is awarded to the top winners of the National Beefalo Show. Trophies and plaques are also awarded to the top winners.

• 1558 •
American Begonia Society
Arlene Ingles, Membership Chm.
PO Box 471651
San Francisco, CA 94147-1651
Phone: (707)764-5407
Fax: (707)764-5407
E-mail: ingles@cox.net
Home Page: http://www.begonias.org

• 1559 • **Herbert P. Dyckman Award for Service**
To recognize a member who has rendered long-time or very outstanding service above and beyond that usually expected from a member or officer of ABS. Nominations are accepted. A plaque is awarded annually at the yearly meeting of the Society. Established in 1968 to honor Herbert P. Dyckman (1884-1958), founder and first president of the California Begonia Society, renamed American Begonia Society in July 1934. Additional information is available from Mary Sakamot, Awards Chair, 6847 E. Sycamore Glen Dr, Orange, CA 92669.

• 1560 • **Eva Kenworthy Gray Award**
To recognize a member for his or her contribution of original material or to promoting good will and harmony. A plaque is awarded annually at the yearly meeting. Established in 1955 to honor Eva Kenworthy Gray (1863-1951), an early member of the ABS who first grew begonias in 1920, operated a begonia nursery until 1945, and in 1931 wrote and published *The Begonia Book*. For further information, contact Mary Sakamoto, Awards Chair, 6847 E. Sycamore Glen Dr., Orange CA 92669.

• 1561 • **Alfred D. Robinson Memorial Medal for Begonia Hybrid**
To recognize the most outstanding ABS-registered begonia hybrid released to the public at least five years but not more than 15 years prior to nomination. Nominations may be made by any member of the society. The nominee is judged by all members of the awards committee and must receive a majority vote. An inscribed medal is presented at the annual meeting. Established in 1945 to honor Alfred D. Robinson (1866-1942), an early member of the ABS who owned and operated Rosecroft Begonia Garden on Point Loma, San Diego, California from 1902 until his death. He produced 50 named begonias and was founder of the San Diego Floral Association and first editor of its publication, *California Gardens*. For further information, contact Mary Sakamoto, Awards Chair, 6847 E. Sycamore Glen Dr, Orange, CA 92669.

• 1562 •
American Bible Society
Dr. Eugene B. Habecker, Pres.
1865 Broadway
New York, NY 10023-7505
Phone: (212)408-1200
Toll-Free: 800-32-BIBLE
Fax: (212)408-1360
E-mail: webmaster@americanbible.org
Home Page: http://www.americanbible.org

• 1563 • **American Bible Society Award**
Bestowed to an individual or individuals who contribute greatly to the goals of the ABS. Awarded annually.

• 1564 • **Scholarship Award**
Recognizes high achievement in the study of the Bible. Applicants must be seminary or college students. Awarded annually.

• 1565 •
American Birding Association
Paul Green, Pres./CEO
PO Box 6599
Colorado Springs, CO 80934-6599
Phone: (719)578-9703
Toll-Free: 800-850-2473
Fax: (719)578-1480
E-mail: member@aba.org
Home Page: http://www.americanbirding.org

• 1566 • Ludlow Griscom Award
For recognition of outstanding contributions to field birding. Nominations must be made by the ABA Board of Directors. A plaque and an expense-paid trip to ABA's biennial convention are awarded. Established in 1980 by ABA in memory of Ludlow Griscom, who pioneered the use of field birding techniques without a gun.

• 1567 •
American Blind Bowling Association
Judith A. Fitzpatrick, Sec.-Treas.
6317 Phillips Ave.
Pittsburgh, PA 15217-1807
Phone: (412)421-1861

• 1568 • Medal Awards
To recognize sighted, partially-sighted, and blind men and women for high scoring games bowled. ABBA members are eligible. Silver medals, bronze medals, chevron patches, and pins are awarded. Approximately 300 awards are given annually. The awards are given for each award game bowled. Established in 1951.

• 1569 •
American Board for Occupational Health Nurses, Inc.
201 E. Ogden, Ste. 114
Hinsdale, IL 60521
Phone: (630)789-5799
Fax: (630)789-8901
E-mail: mamann@abohn.org
Home Page: http://www.abohn.org

• 1570 • ABOHN Research Award
To facilitate research related to some aspect of certification that is in progress or has been completed within one year. Up to $5,000 is available yearly. Applicants must be: 1. a certified OHN; or 2. an RN working with a certified OHN.Awarded annually during the American Occupational Health Conference. Established in 1994.

• 1571 • Employer Recognition Award
To recognize a company that has provided support and recognition of the ABOHN certification program and values certification in occupational health nursing. Applications are available from the ABOHN office and the deadline for submission is December 1 of each year. Selection is made by ABOHN Board members based on meeting established criteria. The award is presented during the American Occupational Health Conference during the ABOHN reception. Established in 1995.

• 1572 • Margarite Ahern Graff Excellence Award
To recognize an individual who achieved the highest score on the previous year's Certified Occupational Health Nurse (COHN) examination. Awarded annually to one or more recipients. The award is presented at the American Occupational Health Conference during the ABOHN reception. Established in 1997 in honor of Margarite Ahern Graff, the first chair of ABOHN.

• 1573 • Ada Mayo Stewart Awards
Presented to the individual who achieved the highest score on the previous year's case management certification exam. Awarded annually. Established in 2000.

• 1574 • Mayrose Synder Excellence Award
To recognize an individual who achieved the highest score on the previous year's Certified Occupational Health Nurse Specialist (COHN-S) examination. Awarded annually to one or more recipients. The award is presented at the American Occupational Health Conference during the ABOHN reception. Established in 1989 in honor of Mayrose Snyder, the first Executive Director of ABOHN.

• 1575 •
American Board of Orthodontics
Christine L. Eisenmayer, Exec.Sec.
401 N Lindbergh Blvd., Ste. 308
St. Louis, MO 63141-7839
Phone: (314)432-6130
Fax: (314)432-8170
E-mail: info@americanboardortho.com
Home Page: http://www.americanboardortho.com

• 1576 • Albert H. Ketcham Memorial Award
To recognize individuals for notable contributions to the science and art of orthodontics. A certificate is awarded annually by the American Board of Orthodontics. Established in 1937 in memory of Dr. Albert H. Ketcham.

• 1577 •
American Board of Professional Psychology
Dr. Russell J. Bent, Exec. Officer
300 Drayton St., 3rd Fl.
Savannah, GA 31401
Phone: (912)234-5477
Toll-Free: 800-255-7792
Fax: (912)234-5120
E-mail: office@abpp.org
Home Page: http://www.abpp.org

• 1578 • Distinguished Professional Achievement in Psychology
To recognize an individual for distinguished contribution to the field of professional psychology. Membership in the American Board of Professional Psychology is required. A plaque is awarded annually at the convention of the American Psychological Association. Established in 1970.

• 1579 •
American Board of Psychological Hypnosis
Samuel M. Migdole Ed.D., Pres.
North Shore Counseling Cetner
23 Bradway
Beverly, MA 01915
Phone: (978)922-2280
Fax: (978)927-1758
E-mail: pres.abph@prodigy.net

• 1580 • Diplomate of the American Board of Psychological Hypnosis
To certify competence in clinical and/or experimental hypnosis. Individuals must meet the following criteria: be a member of the American Psychological Association, be a diplomate or diplomate-eligible of the American Board of Professional Psychology, have state licensure, and have five years of acceptable experience using hypnosis, including two years of supervised experience. A certificate is awarded when merited. An examination is required. Established in 1959.

• 1581 •
American Booksellers Association
Avin Mark Domnitz, CEO
200 White Plains Rd.
Tarrytown, NY 10591
Phone: (914)591-2665
Toll-Free: 800-637-0037
Fax: (914)591-2720
E-mail: info@bookweb.org
Home Page: http://www.bookweb.org/

• 1582 • Book Sense Book of the Year Award
To recognize the book that members of the association have most enjoyed hand-selling in the preceding year. Awards given in Fiction, Nonfiction, Paperback, Children's Literature, Illustrated and Rediscovery. Winners announced at ABA's Celebration of Bookselling held annually in conjunction with BookExpo America. Four honor books are also recognized. Established in 1991. Formerly: (2004) ABBY Award; (2004) Children's ABBY Award.

• 1583 • Charley Haslam International Scholarship
To recognize an American bookseller age 40 or under for expertise in bookselling. A travel grant to attend the International Congress of Young Booksellers and a $500 cash award is presented annually. Established in 1984. Additional information is available from Willard Dickerson, Jr.

• 1584 •
American Bowling Congress
Roger Dalkin, Exec.Dir.
5301 S 76th St.
Greendale, WI 53129-1127
Phone: (414)421-6400
Toll-Free: 800-514-2695
Fax: (414)421-1194
E-mail: bowlinfo@bowlinginc.com
Home Page: http://www.bowl.com

• 1585 • *Bowling* Magazine Writing Competition
To recognize outstanding writers and articles covering the sport of bowling. Awards are given in three categories: Editorial - any opinion expressed concerning bowling; Feature - a story concerning any individual, facility, equipment or organization related to bowling involvement; and News - a bowling-related story written under deadline with proof of following day publication. All stories published or broadcast during the preceding year, other than those printed in

Bowling magazine, are eligible for the competition, but writers may submit only three entries in each category. They also may be submitted by someone other than the writer. A sum of $300 is awarded for first place in each category. In addition awards from $50 to $250 and Honorable Mention certificates are presented in each category. Awarded annually.

• 1586 • Local Association Public Relations Contest

To honor the work local affiliates perform for members to pass the word along about the sport of bowling and the American Bowling Congress. Local associations directly involved with publicity are eligible. Plaques for first, second, and third place in each of three divisions are awarded annually at the convention. Established in 1986. Renamed in 1990. Formerly: (1990) Local Association Publications Contest.

• 1587 • Local Association Service Award

To recognize associations for their volunteer efforts on behalf of their bowlers. Awards are presented annually at the ABC Convention. Established in 1979.

• 1588 •

American Bridge Teachers' Association
Pat Harrington, Dir.
14840 Crystal Cove Ct.
Fort Myers, FL 33919-7417
Phone: (239)437-4106
E-mail: abta@juno.com
Home Page: http://www.abtahome.com

• 1589 • Bridge Book of the Year

To encourage and recognize excellence in bridge books published during the preceding year. A plaque is awarded annually in July. Established in 1980.

• 1590 • Honorary Member

To recognize individuals for outstanding work for the world of bridge. A plaque is awarded when merited at the discretion of the Board of Directors. Established in 1959 for the first member, Charles Goren.

• 1591 •

American Brittany Club, Heart of Illinois
529 E. 2200th St.
Liberty, IL 62347
Phone: (217)645-3749
Fax: (217)645-3739
E-mail: gsalmons@ksni.net

• 1592 • Dog of the Year

For adult field, juvenile field, show, obedience, agility. Recognition award bestowed annually.

• 1593 •

American Brittany Club, Missouri
Harold Green, Pres.
12012 W 150th Cir.
Olathe, KS 66062
Phone: (913)897-3822
E-mail: whitecrof@aol.com
Home Page: http://www.missouribrittanyclub.com/missouribrittanyclub_com/door/

• 1594 • La Reine Pittman Memorial Award

Recognizes persons who have contributed to improvement of the breed. Award bestowed annually.

• 1595 •

American Bugatti Club
Paul Simms, Sec.
600 Lakeview Ter.
Glen Ellyn, IL 60137
Phone: (630)469-4920
Phone: (773)380-5480
E-mail: quiltbug57@sbcglobal.net
Home Page: http://www.AmericanBugattiClub.org

• 1596 • Honorary Member

For recognition of the efforts of particular individuals to further the appreciation of the art of the Bugatti family of artists in the automotive and other art media. Individuals are elected when need arises at the annual meeting held in Los Angeles County. A membership card and the waiving of the annual dues are awarded when merited. Established in 1963.

• 1597 •

American Burn Association
Dr. Lynn D. Golem MD, Pres.
625 N Michigan Ave., Ste. 1530
Chicago, IL 60611
Phone: (312)642-9260
Toll-Free: 800-548-2876
Fax: (312)642-9130
E-mail: info@ameriburn.org
Home Page: http://www.ameriburn.org

• 1598 • Harvey Stuart Allen Distinguished Service Award

To recognize an outstanding U.S. scientist for his contribution in the burn field. An honorarium of $1,500, an engraved medal, all expenses to the annual meeting, and the option of honorary membership in the American Burn Association are awarded annually at the annual meeting. Established in 1969 by Marion Laboratories to honor Harvey Stuart Allen, M.D. Sponsored by Marion Laboratories.

• 1599 • Curtis P. Artz Distinguished Service Award

To recognize a non-physician member for his/her outstanding contributions in the burn field. An honorarium of $1,500, an engraved medal, all expenses to the annual meeting, and the option for honorary membership in the American Burn Association are awarded annually at the annual meeting. Established in 1977 to honor Curtis P. Artz, M.D., founding member of the American Burn Association. Sponsored by Support Systems International.

• 1600 • Burn Prevention Award

To recognize individuals for contributions in burn prevention. The award is given for contributions in at least one of four areas: prevention work of worldwide, nationwide, or statewide impact; prevention work on a local level (must be replicated in two or more local areas and serve as a model prevention effort); collection of epidemiological data and the reporting of the data that serves as the basis for state or national prevention efforts; and education - to an individual who has had a major influence on shaping the careers of other burn prevention workers. Nominations may be submitted. A monetary award of $1,500 is awarded annually at the annual meeting. Established in 1987.

• 1601 • Everett Idris Evans Memorial Lecture

To recognize an outstanding scientist in the burn field outside the United States. Presentation of a lecture, an honorarium of $1,500, an engraved medal, expenses for the awardee and a guest to the annual meeting, and an honorary membership in the American Burn Association are awarded annually at the annual meeting. Established in 1969 to honor Everett Idris Evans.

• 1602 • Robert A. Lindberg Award

To recognize the best scientific paper submitted by a non-physician at the annual meeting. An honorarium of $300 and a medal are awarded annually at the annual meeting. Formerly: (1987) At-Large Award.

• 1603 • Carl A. Moyer Resident Award

To recognize the best paper submitted by a medical doctor who has not yet completed his formal training. An honorarium of $300 and an engraved medal are awarded annually at the annual meeting. The award honors Carl A. Moyer, M.D.

• 1604 • President's Continuing Education Grant

To provide funds for continuing education to a non-physician member of the American Burn Association who has made significant contributions to the care of the burned patient. Applicants must be sponsored by an M.D. who submits a letter by January 1. A medal and financial support are awarded annually at the annual meeting. Sponsored by Marion Laboratories.

• 1605 • Traveling Fellowship Award

To recognize a physician or post-doctoral fellow who has given evidence of a continuing interest and productivity in the field of burn care, teaching and/or research. A candidate's work in the field should continue after the proposed travel and be advanced by the travel. Senior physicians and scientists are not ordinarily considered as candidates. Applications must be submitted by January 1. A maximum $5000 reimbursement is awarded annually at the annual meeting. Established by Charles Fox, M.D., Traveling Fellowship Fund.

• 1606 •
American Business Media
Gordon T. Hughes II, Pres. and CEO
675 3rd Ave.
New York, NY 10017
Phone: (212)661-6360
Fax: (212)370-0736
E-mail: info@abmmail.com
Home Page: http://www.americanbusinessmedia.com
Formerly: (1985) Association of Business Publishers.

• 1607 • American Business Media G. D. Crain Award
For recognition of outstanding editorial initiative, leadership, and integrity. Individuals with a proven career record of editorial accomplishment are eligible. A monetary prize of $1,000 and a crystal trophy are awarded annually. Established in 1967 in honor of G.D. Crain, the founder of *Advertising Age*.

• 1608 • Jesse H. Neal National Business Journalism Awards
For recognition of outstanding editorial achievement and excellence in audited, independent business publications. Members of an ABP member publication editorial staff are considered for the award. Awards are given in each of three classifications of gross advertising revenues: up to $2,000,000; $2,000,000 to $5,000,000; and more than $5,000,000. The following awards are given: best article or subject-related series, best in-depth analysis or subject-related series, best staff-written editorials, best regularly featured department or column, and best how-to article or subject-related series. A bronze medallion plaque, and certificate of merit are presented annually in each category. Established in 1955 for Jesse H. Neal, the association's first managing director.

• 1609 •
American Business Women's Association
Jeanne Banks, Natl.Pres.
9100 Ward Pkwy.
PO Box 8728
Kansas City, MO 64114-0728
Phone: (816)361-6621
Toll-Free: 800-228-0007
Fax: (816)361-4991
E-mail: abwa@abwa.org
Home Page: http://www.abwa.org

• 1610 • Top Ten Business Women of ABWA
To recognize ten members for outstanding career achievements, community involvement, professional development, and educational accomplishments. Awarded annually. Established in 1956.

• 1611 •
American Camellia Society
Ann Walton, Exec. Dir.
Massee Lane Gardens
100 Massee Ln.
Fort Valley, GA 31030
Phone: (478)967-2358
Phone: (478)967-2722
Fax: (478)967-2083
E-mail: ask@camellias-acs.com
Home Page: http://www.camellias-acs.org

• 1612 • Evelyn A. Abendroth Award
To honor the best bloom of Camellia Japonica 'Rachel Tarpy' exhibited at a show held in conjunction with the ACS Annual Meeting. The award consists of a permanent cup which remains at the American Camellia Society Headquarters. The exhibitor is awarded a bronze plaque. Established in 1986 by G.F. Abendroth, Shreveport, LA, to honor his wife.

• 1613 • Australian Camellia Research Society Trophy
To honor outstanding camellias of Australian origin grown in the United States and exhibited at a show held in conjunction with the American Camellia Society Annual Meeting. This trophy, which may be awarded annually, is a round silver salver with an Australian black opal embedded in the center and is retained at ACS Headquarters. The winner's name as well as the variety are engraved on a plaque at Headquarters. The individual winning the award receives a parchment certificate. Established in 1975.

• 1614 • Harold Cawood Award
To encourage and recognize the development of outstanding white Camellia Japonicas. A suitable plaque is awarded when merited at the ACS Annual Meeting. Established in 1983 by Mrs. Ralph Clanton, Americus, GA, to honor the late Harold Cawood.

• 1615 • Arminta Cawood Japonica Award
To honor the most outstanding Camellia Japonica in a show held in conjunction with the ACS Annual Meeting. The exhibitor is awarded a brass shield on a walnut base. Established in 1976 by Harold Cawood, Americus, GA, in memory of his wife.

• 1616 • Fellow
To honor an individual for substantial and new contributions to scientific knowledge in the culture, care, and knowledge of camellias or in the development of camellia cloves or hybrids or similar advances in camellia culture. A certificate and life membership in the Society are awarded to not more than two individuals in any five year period. Established in 1947.

• 1617 • Harris Hybrid Award
To encourage and recognize the development of outstanding camellia hybrids and hybridizers. A metal plaque is awarded as merited. Established in 1963 by Aubrey C. Harris, Shreveport, LA.

• 1618 • Illges Seedling Japonica Award
To recognize the developer of a worthy seedling camellia japonica. A bronze medal is awarded as merited, not more often than once a year. Established in 1947 by the late John P. Illges, Columbus, GA.

• 1619 • Charlotte C. Knox Reticulata Award
To encourage the development of and to recognize outstanding seedlings of Camellia Reticulata or hybrid with Camellia Reticulata parentage. The award consists of a permanent cup to remain at the American Camellia Society Headquarters. The originator of the winning variety shall receive a bronze medal. Awarded annually when merited. Established in 1986 by Thomas P. Knox, Jr., Columbia, SC, to honor his late wife.

• 1620 • National Camellia Hall of Fame
To recognize the Camellia Japonica and Interspecific Hybrid of the Genus Camellia that wins the greatest number of Best in Show and Court of Honor Awards in ACS Cooperative Shows during a camellia growing season. A master plaque is exhibited at ACS headquarters. Suitable plaques are awarded to originators or, if deceased, to their spouses. Awarded annually. Established in 1978 by Spencer C. Walden, Jr., Albany, GA.

• 1621 • Peer Sasanqua Award
To encourage the development of and to recognize outstanding seedlings of Camellia Sasanqua, Camellia Hiemalis, and Camellia Vernalis. A metal plaque is awarded as merited. Established in 1958 by Mr. Ralph Peer, Los Angeles, CA.

• 1622 • Sewell Mutant Award
To recognize and encourage the selection and introduction of outstanding mutations or sports of Camellia Japonica. A silver Revere bowl is awarded as merited. Established in 1962 by John N. Sewell, Jacksonville, FL.

• 1623 • John A. Tyler, Jr. Miniature Award
To encourage and recognize the development of outstanding miniature camellias. A suitable plaque may be awarded annually. Established in 1978 by Mrs. John A. Tyler, Jr. to honor her late husband.

• 1624 •
American Camping Association
Peg L. Smith, Exec.Dir.
5000 State Rd. 67 N.
Martinsville, IN 46151-7902
Phone: (765)349-3310
Phone: (765)342-8456
Fax: (765)349-0301
E-mail: psmith@acacamps.org
Home Page: http://www.acacamps.org

• 1625 • Hedley S. Dimock Award
For recognition of those who have made significant contributions to camping through related fields such as outdoor education, conservation, recreation, medicine, education, architecture, or the social sciences. Contributions may be in the form of administrative or legislative support, professional contributions, or specific participation in local, state, or national program development. Members and non-members are eligible. Awarded annually at the Association's national conference. Deadline is May 30.

• 1626 • Distinguished Service Award
This, the highest honor of the Association, is given for recognition of members for outstanding service, research, teaching, or administration and is generally awarded to those who have been members for more than ten years and who are over the age of 40. Awarded annually when merited at the Association's national conference. Deadline is May 30.

• 1627 • Eleanor P. Eells Award for Program Excellence
To recognize camp programs that: develop effective, creative responses to the needs of people and/or societal problems using the camp environment; encourage continued development of such ideas; stimulate the exchange of creative ideas; and present to the public examples of positive contributions camp has made on the well being of individuals and society. To qualify, camp programs must demonstrate one or more of the following: ability to understand and make use of intergrouping - combining groups that have differences (physical abilities, ethnic and cultural backgrounds, etc.); develop programs suited to the needs and interests of teenage campers; broaden the range of services to persons with disabilities; emphasize awareness of interpersonal relationships and development of interpersonal skills; conduct continuing innovative and effective staff-development programs; and offer support activities or leadership that significantly expands the opportunities for human growth and enrichment through camping (for non-camp organizations). To be eligible for nomination, a program must have been in operation for at least one year (planning and development time do not count). Membership in the Association is not required. Awards are presented at the Association's national conference. Awarded annually. Established in 1976.

• 1628 • Honor Award
To recognize members for leadership and meritorious service in at least five of the following areas: member of ACA national board of directors; president of an ACA section; chair of a national ACA committee; section or region committee work for at least three years; chairing a national or regional conference steering committee; employed staff of the association; significant addresses before educational or recreational groups, conferences, radio, and television presentations, and other meetings held in the interest and promotion of camp; systematic research; author or co-author of at least one book on camping; author of at least five published articles by a magazine of national scope or brought out in monograph form; and articles in handbooks, newspapers, or magazines not covered above. To qualify a candidate must: be a current member of the association or former member who has retired from active participation in the field; have served in camp programs for a period of at least 10 years; and have high moral character, personal integrity, and exemplify a spirit of devoted service to the field and, through leadership and industry, have made a noteworthy contribution to the advancement of camping. Deadline is May 30.

• 1629 • Service Award
For volunteer work in the field.

• 1630 • Special Recognition Award
For recognition of groups, organizations, or individuals for their efforts to promote camping. Awarded annually at the Association's national conference. Deadline is May 30.

• 1631 •
American Camping Association, Wisconsin Section
Katherine Mace, Exec.
3217 Sandwood Way
Madison, WI 53713
Phone: (608)663-0051
Fax: (608)288-0960
E-mail: acawisconsin@charter.net
Home Page: http://www.acawisconsin.org

• 1632 • Acorn Award
For member contributing to camping movement. Recognition award bestowed annually.

• 1633 •
American Cancer Society
John R. Seffrin Ph.D., CEO
2200 Century Pky., Ste. 950
Atlanta, GA 30345
Phone: (404)816-4994
Toll-Free: 800-ACS-2345
Fax: (404)315-9348
E-mail: encic@cancer.org
Home Page: http://www.cancer.org

• 1634 • ACS Medal of Honor
This, the Society's highest award, is given in recognition of outstanding contributions in the field of cancer control. Awards are given for cancer research, clinical oncology, and to a layman. Nominations may be submitted by March 1. A citation and gold medal are presented at the annual meeting of the Society in each category when merited. Established in 1949. Formerly: National Award.

• 1635 • Courage Award
To recognize an individual for courage in his or her personal battle against cancer, thereby serving as a source of hope and inspiration to others. A plaque is awarded at a White House ceremony.

• 1636 • Distinguished Service Award
This, the second highest award of the Society, is given in recognition of major achievements in the field of cancer. Nominations must be submitted by March 1. A citation is awarded annually.

• 1637 • Humanitarian Award
To recognize distinction and accomplishment in the field of human welfare and social reform pertaining to cancer. Nominations must be submitted by March 1. A citation is presented when merited at the annual meeting of the Society.

• 1638 • National Volunteer Leadership Award
To recognize volunteers who have served as officers, chairmen of major committees and others who have given long and valuable service to the Society at the national level. Nominations must be submitted by March 1. A certificate is awarded annually.

• 1639 • St. George National Award
To recognize outstanding volunteer service at the Division (state) level. A bronze medal and citation are awarded three times annually. Presented by the National Board of Directors.

• 1640 •
American Cancer Society, Capital Region Unit
Michele Holloway, Regional Mgr.
3211 N Front St., Ste. 100
Harrisburg, PA 17110
Phone: (717)231-5780
Fax: (717)231-5784
Home Page: http://www.cancer.org

• 1641 • Community Partnership Grant
For community organizations holding breast cancer programs and activities. Grant awarded quarterly.

• 1642 •
American Cancer Society, Porter County Unit
Judy Rooney-Davis, Exec.Dir.
410 E Lincolnway
Valparaiso, IN 46383
Phone: (219)464-2895
Toll-Free: 800-227-2345
Fax: (219)465-1044
Home Page: http://www.cancer.org

• 1643 • Great Lakes Division Foundation
For survivor of cancer under 18. Scholarship awarded annually.

• 1644 •
American Carbon Society
Nidia C. Gallego, Sec.-Treas.
Bldg. 4508, Mailstop 6087
PO Box 2088
Oak Ridge, TN 37831-6087
Phone: (865)241-9459
Fax: (865)576-8424
E-mail: gallegonc@ornl.gov
Home Page: http://www.americancarbonsociety.org

Formerly: American Carbon Committee.

• 1645 • **Graffin Lectureship Award**
To encourage professional development in the field of carbon materials through college lecture series. Selection is by nomination. A monetary award is presented annually. A plaque is awarded triennially at the Carbon Conference. Established in 1978 by Asbury Graphite Mills in memory of George Graffin.

• 1646 • **Stanislaw W. Mrozowski Award**
To recognize the best conference oral presentation by a student.

• 1647 • **Petinos Foundation Award**
For recognition of recent outstanding accomplishments by an individual in the science and/or technology of carbon materials. Selection is by nomination. A monetary award and a plaque are awarded triennially at the Carbon Conference. Established in 1969 by the Charles E. and Joy C. Pettinos Foundation.

• 1648 • **SGL Carbon Award**
For recognition of a contribution to the science and technology of carbon materials. Selection is by nomination. A monetary prize and a plaque are awarded biennially at the Carbon Conference. Established in 1969 by the Great Lakes Carbon Corporation in honor of George Skakel. Formerly: (2006) Great Lakes Skakel Award.

• 1649 • **Philip L. Walker Jr. Award**
To recognize the best conference poster presentation by a student.

• 1650 •
American Cat Fanciers Association
Connie Vandre, Exec.Dir.
PO Box 1949
Nixa, MO 65714-1949
Phone: (417)725-1530
Fax: (417)725-1533
E-mail: acfa@aol.com
Home Page: http://www.acfacat.com

• 1651 • **Inter-American Awards**
To recognize the top-scoring felines of the year. Following the completing of the show season (May 1 through April 30), the scores of each feline is calculated. A plaque and a rosette are awarded in the following categories: Best Cat, Best Kitten, Best Alter, and Best HHP (Household Pet). Awarded annually. Established in 1957.

• 1652 •
American Catholic Historical Association
263 S 4th
Philedelphia, PA 19106
Phone: (215)763-3645
E-mail: e_mcmerty@yahoo.com
Home Page: http://www.amchs.org

• 1653 • **John Tracy Ellis Dissertation Award**
For recognition of scholarship and to assist a graduate student working on some aspect of the history of the Catholic Church. A monetary prize of $1,200 is awarded annually for research purposes. Established in 1998 in memory of Monsignor John Tracy Ellis, former editor of the Catholic Historical Review.

• 1654 • **Peter Guilday Prize**
To stimulate interest in the field of church history among young scholars. This award recognizes the best article accepted by *The Catholic Historical Review* that deals with some aspect of the history of the Catholic Church broadly considered, and which is the author's first scholarly publication. A monetary prize of $100 is awarded annually. Established in 1971 in honor of Peter Guilday, the Association's principal founder and secretary of many years.

• 1655 • **Howard R. Marraro Prize**
To promote research and writing on Italian history and Italo-American history and relations, and to give recognition to authors of distinguished works in this area. The author must be a citizen or permanent resident of the United States or Canada, and the work must be of book or essay length, and already published. A monetary award of $750 is awarded for selected books, a lesser award is presented for honored articles. Awarded annually. Established in 1973 and funded through a bequest of the late distinguished professor of Columbia University, Howard R. Marraro.

• 1656 • **John Gilmary Shea Prize**
For recognition of outstanding contributions to historical knowledge, with emphasis on works that deal with the history of the Catholic Church. Citizens or permanent residents of the United States or Canada are eligible for works published during the preceding year. A monetary prize of $750 is awarded annually at the January meeting of the Association. Established in 1944 in memory of John Gilmary Shea, the lay founder of the historiography of American Catholicism.

• 1657 •
American Catholic Historical Society
Rev. Msgr. Louis N. Ferrero, Pres.
263 S 4th
Philadelphia, PA 19106
Phone: (215)763-3645
Fax: (215)204-1663
E-mail: louferrero@earthlink.net
Home Page: http://www.amchs.org

• 1658 • **Barry Award**
To recognize an American who has been distinguished by his or her character and contributions to church and community, and by professional accomplishments. The award is hand-lettered and brightened with illuminated type on parchment in the historic manner used by medieval scholars to recognize those honored. Each award is individually created so that no two will ever be exactly the same. Awarded annually. Named for Commodore John Barry, Father of the American Navy, because his activity, lifestyle, patriotism, and achievement properly established the ideal for which the award is presented. First presented in the 1940s as Distinguished Service Award. Established annually as the Barry Award in 1982. Additional information is available from Mary M. Fisher, Corresponding Secretary. Formerly: (1982) Distinguished Service Awards.

• 1659 •
American Catholic Philosophical Association
Dr. Michael Baur, Natl.Sec.
Fordham University
Administration Bldg.
Bronx, NY 10458
Phone: (718)817-4081
Phone: (718)817-3295
Fax: (718)817-5709
E-mail: mbaur@fordham.edu
Home Page: http://www.acpa-main.org

• 1660 • **ACPA Young Scholars Award**
To recognize the best paper by a younger scholar not over 35 years of age. A monetary prize of $250 is awarded annually at the annual national meeting of the association. Established in 1995 by the American Catholic Philosophical Association.

• 1661 • **Aquinas Medal**
To recognize an outstanding philosopher. Scholars of international standing are eligible. A gold plate medal is awarded annually at the association's annual meeting. Established in 1951 by Cardinal Spellman.

• 1662 •
American Center for Children's Television
% Central Educational Network
James A. Fellows, Pres.
1400 E Touhy Ave., Ste. 260
Des Plaines, IL 60018-3305
Phone: (847)390-8700
Fax: (847)390-9435
E-mail: ceninfo@mcs.net
Home Page: http://www.tcom.ohiou.edu/hetc/cen-acct.html

Formerly: American Children's Television Festival.

• 1663 • **American Center for Children's Television - Fran Allison Award**
To recognize an individual(s) whose career contributions to children's television brought special joy to young people's lives. Awarded at the biennial "Ollie Awards" ceremony. Established in

1989 to honor Fran Allison, Ollie's human friend, foil, and co-star on "Kukla, Fran and Ollie." Formerly: American Children's Television Festival - Fran Allison Award.

• 1664 • American Center for Children's Television - Ollie Awards

To promote excellence in television programming for America's children. Any television program or series produced or co-produced by U.S. organizations for initial broadcast or cable distribution in the United States during the preceding two years is considered. Only programs specifically intended for home use are eligible. Entries must be submitted by July 1. Eight plaques are awarded biennially in fall of odd-numbered years. Established in 1985 as the Alpha Awards by the Central Educational Network and WTTW/Chicago. Renamed in 1987 to honor Burr Tillstrom, creator of "Kukla, Fran and Ollie." Formerly: (1987) Alpha Awards.

• 1665 •
American Ceramic Society
Glenn Harvey, Exec.Dir.
PO Box 6136
Westerville, OH 43086-6136
Phone: (614)890-4700
Fax: (614)899-6109
E-mail: info@ceramics.org
Home Page: http://www.ceramics.org

• 1666 • Alfred W. Allen Award

To recognize and honor authors of superior published technical papers on refractories. A certificate is awarded. Sponsored by the Refractory Ceramics Division of ACerS.

• 1667 • Albert Victor Bleininger Award

To recognize distinguished achievement in the field of ceramics. A medal and citation are awarded annually. Established in 1947. Sponsored by the Pittsburgh Section of ACerS.

• 1668 • S. Brunauer Award

This award is intended to stimulate high quality presentations of papers and to encourage submission of high quality papers for publication by the Society. Awarded annually. Established in 1987. Sponsored by the Cements Division of ACerS. Formerly: (1997) Brunauer Best Paper Award.

• 1669 • Robert L. Coble Award for Young Scholars

To recognize an outstanding scientist under the age of 35 who is conducting research in the field of ceramics in academia, industry, or a government- funded laboratory. Awarded annually. Established in 1996.

• 1670 • Copeland Award

Given in recognition of Copeland's significant contributions to the understanding of the microstructure of hardened cement pastes and its influence upon past properties. A certificate is awarded. Sponsored by the Cements Division of ACerS. Formerly: Cements Award.

• 1671 • Corporate Environmental Achievement Award

To recognize a single environmental achievement by a corporate member in the field of ceramics, preferably representing either an improvement of an existing process/product or development/implementation of a new process/product that reduces undesirable effluent streams, expands recycling of materials, reduces the environmental impact of products, or provides other environmental benefits over previous processes. Awarded to one or more recipients annually. Established in 1997.

• 1672 • Corporate Technical Achievement Award

To recognize a single technical achievement by a Corporate member in the field of ceramics that has been commercialized within the preceding eight years. A certificate and a Steuben are awarded.

• 1673 • W. E. Cramer Award

To recognize outstanding contributions to the Society, the Section and the ceramic industry. Sponsored by the Central Ohio Section of ACerS.

• 1674 • Distinguished Ceramist Award

To recognize achievements and contributions to the advancement of ceramic science and technology. Sponsored by the New England Section of ACerS.

• 1675 • Distinguished Life Member

This, the highest honor awarded by the Society, is given to recognize achievements in the ceramic arts or sciences. Members of the Society are eligible. An illuminated certificate is awarded.

• 1676 • Distinguished Speaker Award

In recognition of outstanding achievements in the field of ceramics. Established in 1978. Sponsored by the North Ohio Section of ACerS.

• 1677 • Harry E. Ebright Service Award

To recognize outstanding service to the Southwest Section. Sponsored by the Southwest Section of ACerS.

• 1678 • Fellow

To recognize productive scholarship in ceramic science and notable contributions to the ceramic arts and industry. A certificate is awarded.

• 1679 • Friedberg Lecture

To honor Dr. Arthur L. Friedberg through the presentation of a Plenary session lecture at the Annual Meeting. A certificate is awarded annually. Sponsored by the National Institute of Ceramic Engineers.

• 1680 • Frontiers of Science and Society - Rustum Roy Lecture

To honor Professor Rustum Roy of Pennsylvania State University, a nationally recognized individual in the area of science is selected yearly to present a lecture at the ACerS annual meeting. Established in 1997.

• 1681 • Richard M. Fulrath Award

To recognize an individual under the age of 45 years, for demonstrating excellence in research and development of ceramic sciences and materials.

• 1682 • Samuel Geijsbeek Award

For recognition in the field of ceramics. Sponsored by the Pacific Coast Sections of ACerS.

• 1683 • Arthur Frederick Greaves-Walker Award

To recognize outstanding service to the ceramic engineering profession. Members of the National Institute of Ceramic Engineers of the American Ceramic Society who are over 41 years of age and registered professional engineers are eligible. A certificate and a Steuben are awarded annually. Established in 1961. Sponsored by the National Institute of Ceramic Engineers.

• 1684 • Edward C. Henry Award

To recognize excellence of a paper published in a Society publication during the previous decade on a subject related to electronic ceramics. A certificate is awarded. Sponsored by the Electronics Division of ACerS. Formerly: (2006) Electronics Division Award.

• 1685 • Honorary Member

To recognize a non-member of the Society for outstanding achievements in the ceramic arts and sciences. An illuminated certificate is awarded.

• 1686 • John Jeppson Medal

To recognize individuals for scientific, technical or engineering achievements within the realms of ceramics. A gold medal and citation are awarded annually. Established in 1958.

• 1687 • W. David Kingery Award

To recognize distinguished lifelong achievements involving multidisciplinary and global contributions to ceramic technology, science, education, and art. Awarded annually. Established in 1997.

• 1688 • Howard Lillie Memorial Award

To recognize the winner of the annual Student Speaking Contest finals. Sponsored by the Ceramic Education Council of ACerS.

• 1689 • John E. Marquis Memorial Award

To recognize the author(s) of the most valuable paper on research, engineering or plant practices relating to whitewares or whitewares materials published during the previous calendar year in a publication of the Society. Members of the Society are eligible. A certificate and a Lenox plate are awarded. Sponsored by the Materials

& Equipment and Whitewares Divisions of ACerS.

• 1690 • George W. Morey Award
To recognize an outstanding publication on glass published during the previous year. A certificate is awarded. Sponsored by the Glass Division of ACerS.

• 1691 • James I. Mueller Lecture Award
To honor Dr. James I. Mueller through the presentation of the Plenary session lecture at the Engineering Ceramics Division Conference on Composites. A certificate is awarded. Sponsored by the Engineering Ceramics Division.

• 1692 • F. H. Norton Distinguished Ceramist Award
To recognize achievements and contributions to the advancement of ceramic science and technology. Sponsored by the New England Section of ACerS.

• 1693 • Edward Orton, Jr., Memorial Lecturer
To recognize scholarly attainments in ceramics or related fields. The award consists of a certificate and the honoree is invited to present a lecture. Established in 1933.

• 1694 • Outstanding Educator Award
To recognize truly outstanding work and creativity in teaching, in directing student research, or in the general education process (lectures, publications, etc.) of ceramic educators. A certificate and a Steuben are awarded. Sponsored by the Ceramic Educational Council of ACerS.

• 1695 • Ross Coffin Purdy Award
To recognize the author of the most valuable contribution to ceramic technical literature during the calendar year prior to selection. A citation is awarded annually. Established in 1949.

• 1696 • St. Louis Refractories Award
To recognize distinguished achievement in the field of refractories. Sponsored by the St. Louis Section of ACerS.

• 1697 • Schwartzwalder - PACE Award
To recognize the nation's outstanding young ceramic engineer. Members of the National Institution of Ceramic Engineers and the American Ceramic Society between the ages of 21-40 years are eligible. A gold medal and a certificate are awarded annually. Established in 1959 by Karl Schwartzwalder, former president of the American Ceramic Society. Sponsored by the National Institute of Ceramic Engineers.

• 1698 • Roland B. Snow Award
Presented to the Best of Show winner of the Ceramographic Competition, an annual event promoting the use of micrographs and microanalysis as tools in the scientific investigation of ceramic materials. First prize of $75, second prize of $50, and third prize of $25 is awarded by the Basic Science Division.

• 1699 • Sosman Memorial Lecture Award
To recognize an individual by an invitation to deliver the Sosman Memorial Lecture. A certificate is presented annually. Sponsored by the Basic Science Division of ACerS.

• 1700 • Hewitt Wilson Memorial Award
To recognize the most outstanding contribution to the field of ceramics during the previous year. Members of the Southeastern Section of the Society are eligible. A scroll is awarded annually. Established in 1954.

• 1701 •
American Chamber of Commerce Executives
Mick Fleming, Pres.
4875 Eisenhower Ave., Ste. 250
Alexandria, VA 22304-4850
Phone: (703)998-0072
Fax: (703)212-9512
E-mail: mfleming@acce.org
Home Page: http://www.acce.org

• 1702 • Chairman's Leadership Award
For recognition of meritorious service to the organization. A plaque is awarded annually at the discretion of the chairman. Established in 1984.

• 1703 •
American Chemical Society
John K. Crum, Exec.Dir.
1155 16th St. NW
Washington, DC 20036
Phone: (202)872-4600
Toll-Free: 800-227-5558
Fax: (202)776-8258
E-mail: awards@acs.org
Home Page: http://acswebcontent.acs.org/home.html

• 1704 • ACS Award for Computers in Chemical and Pharmaceutical Research
To recognize and encourage the use of computers in the advancement of chemical science. Individuals are considered without regard to age or nationality for outstanding achievement in the use of computers in research, development, or education in chemical science. The deadline for nominations is February 1. A monetary prize of $5,000, a suitably inscribed certificate, and traveling expenses incidental to the award presentation, up to a maximum of $1,000, are awarded annually. Established in 1984.

• 1705 • ACS Award for Creative Invention
To recognize a single inventor for the successful applications of research in chemistry and/or chemical engineering that contribute to the material prosperity and happiness of people. The nominee must be a resident of the United States or Canada. A patent must have been granted for the work to be recognized and it must have been developed during the preceding 17 years. The deadline for nominations is February 1. A monetary award of $5,000, a gold medal, and an allowance of up to $1,000 for travel to the award ceremony are awarded annually. Established in 1966. Sponsored by the ACS Committee on Corporation Associates.

• 1706 • ACS Award for Creative Work in Fluorine Chemistry
To recognize outstanding contributions to the advancement of the chemistry of fluorine. The deadline for nominations is February 1. A monetary award of $5,000, an inscribed certificate, and a travel allowance of $1,000 to attend the presentation ceremony are awarded annually. Established in 1971. Sponsored by Lancaster Synthesis, Inc.

• 1707 • ACS Award for Creative Work in Synthetic Organic Chemistry
To recognize and encourage outstanding creative work in synthetic organic chemistry that has been published. Deadline for nomination is February 1. A monetary award of $5,000, a certificate, and an allowance of up to $1,000 for travel expenses incidental to the conferral of the award are awarded annually. Additionally, the recipient's award address is reprinted in *Aldrichimica Acta*. Established in 1955 by Synthetic Organic Chemical Manufacturers Association. Sponsored by Aldrich Chemical Company, Inc.

• 1708 • ACS Award for Distinguished Service in the Advancement of Inorganic Chemistry
To recognize persons who have advanced inorganic chemistry by significant service in addition to performance of outstanding research. The nominee must have demonstrated extensive contributions to the advancement of inorganic chemistry. Activities recognized by the award may include such fields as teaching, writing, research, and administration. The nominee must be a member of the American Chemical Society. The deadline for nominations is February 1. A monetary award of $5,000, a certificate, and an allowance of not more than $1,000 for travel expenses to the meeting where the award is presented are awarded annually. Established in 1963. Sponsored by Sterm Chemicals.

• 1709 • ACS Award for Outstanding Performance by Divisions
To recognize outstanding activities and performance by divisions of the American Chemical Society in the following areas: technical program, membership recruitment and service, administrative and fiscal responsibility, cooperation with local sections and regional meetings, and the furthering of chemical education. Selection is based on the Division's annual report, and is made by the Council Committee on Divisional Activities. An appropriate certificate is presented to the officers of the division annually. Established in 1983.

• 1710 • ACS Award for Outstanding Performance by Local Sections

To recognize outstanding activities and performance by local sections of the Society in the following areas: the welfare of its members and the chemical profession, including teachers and students; and the public's awareness of the importance of the chemical profession to the general welfare. Selection of the recipients is based on the annual report submitted by each section and is made by the Council Committee on Local Section Activities. The deadline for nominations is February 1. An appropriate certificate is presented at a section meeting annually. Established in 1967.

• 1711 • ACS Award for Research at an Undergraduate Institution

To recognize the importance of research with undergraduates, and to honor a chemistry faculty member whose research in an undergraduate setting has achieved wide recognition and contributed significantly to chemistry and to the professional development of undergraduate students. Nominees are drawn from the tenured faculty of non-Ph.D.-granting institutions. The award is given for significant work over a long period of time rather than for a specific, limited project. The deadline for nominations is February 1. A monetary award of $5,000, an inscribed certificate, and travel expenses incidental to conferment of the award are awarded annually. A grant of $5,000 is awarded to the recipient's institution. Established in 1984 by Research Corporation, a private foundation for the advancement of science and technology.

• 1712 • ACS Award in Analytical Chemistry

To recognize and encourage outstanding contributions to the science of analytical chemistry, pure or applied, carried out in the United States or Canada. The nominee must be a resident of the United States or Canada and must have made an outstanding contribution to analytical chemistry. Special consideration is given to the independence of thought and the originality shown, or to the importance of the work when applied to public welfare, economics, or the needs and desires of humanity. The deadline for nominations is February 1. A monetary prize of $5,000, an etching, and travel expenses incidental to the conferring of the award are awarded annually. Established in 1947. Sponsored by Fisher Scientific Company, Inc.

• 1713 • ACS Award in Applied Polymer Science

To recognize and encourage outstanding achievements in the science or technology of plastics, coatings, polymer composites, adhesives, and related fields during the last ten years. Preference is given to avoid repeating specific areas of technology whenever recognized by the grant of this award in the two preceding years. The deadline for nominations is February 1. The award consists of a monetary prize of $5,000 and a certificate. Travel expenses to the meeting where the award is presented are will be reimbursed. Established in 1966. Formerly: (1982) Award in the Chemistry of Plastics and Coatings.

• 1714 • ACS Award in Chromatography

To recognize an individual for outstanding contributions to the field of chromatography, with particular consideration given to developments of new methods. The deadline for nominations is February 1. A monetary award of $5,000 and a certificate are presented. Reasonable travel expenses to the meeting at which the award will be presented will be reimbursed. Established in 1959. Sponsored by SUPELCO, Inc.

• 1715 • ACS Award in Colloid and Surface Chemistry

To recognize and encourage a resident of the United States or Canada who has made an outstanding scientific contributions to colloid and/or surface chemistry in the United States or Canada. Special consideration is given to areas that have not been recognized recently. The deadline for nominations is February 1. A monetary prize of $5,000 and a certificate are awarded. Travel expenses to attend the meeting where the award is presented will be reimbursed. In even-numbered years awards are given for advances in colloid chemistry, and in odd-numbered years for advances in surface chemistry. Established in 1952. Sponsored by Procter & Gamble Company.

• 1716 • ACS Award in Industrial Chemistry

To recognize outstanding contributions to industrial chemistry resulting in the commercialization of an economically significant new product or process. Any field of chemical, chemical engineering, or biochemical research is appropriate if it is of general interest and reflects the concerns of modern society. Any chemical researcher, whether industrial, government, or academic is eligible, provided the work was done in North America and yielded significant commercial results for a period of more than one year. The deadline for nominations is February 1. A monetary award of $5,000 and a certificate are awarded. Travel expenses to the meeting where the award is presented will be reimbursed. Established in 1989.

• 1717 • ACS Award in Inorganic Chemistry

To recognize and encourage fundamental research in the field of inorganic chemistry. The nominee must have accomplished outstanding research in the preparation, properties, reactions, or structure of inorganic substances. Special consideration shall be given to the independence of thought and originality shown. The award is granted without regard to age, nationality, or sex. The deadline for nominations is February 1. A monetary award of $5,000 and a certificate are awarded. Travel expenses to attend the meeting where the award is presented will be reimbursed. Established in 1960 by Texas Instruments Incorporated. Sponsored by Aldrich Chemical Co., Inc.

• 1718 • ACS Award in Organometallic Chemistry

To recognize a recent advancement that is having major impact on research in organometallic chemistry. A nominee must have shown outstanding research in the preparation, reactions, properties, or structure of organometallic substances. Special consideration will be given to demonstrated creativity and independence of thought. Preference is given to U.S. citizens. The deadline for nominations is February 1. A monetary prize of $5,000 and a certificate are awarded. Travel expenses to attend the meeting where the award is presented will be reimbursed up to $1,000. Established in 1983 by the Dow Chemical Company Foundation.

• 1719 • ACS Award in Polymer Chemistry

To recognize outstanding contributions to polymer chemistry. The award is granted without regard to age, nationality, or sex. The deadline for nominations is February 1. A monetary prize of $5,000 and a certificate are awarded. Up to $1,000 for travel expenses to the meeting at which the award will be presented will be reimbursed. Established in 1962 by Witco Chemical Corporation Foundation. Sponsored by Mobil Chemical Company.

• 1720 • ACS Award in Pure Chemistry

To recognize and encourage fundamental research in pure chemistry carried out in North America by young men and women. The nominee must be born after April 30, 1970 and must have accomplished research of unusual merit for an individual on the threshold of his or her career. Special consideration is given to independence of thought and the originality shown in the research, which must have been carried out in North America. The nomination deadline is February 1. A monetary prize of $4,000 and a certificate are awarded. Up to $1,000 for travel expenses to the meeting at which the award will be presented will be reimbursed. Established in 1931 by A. C. Langmuir. Sponsored by Alpha Chi Sigma Fraternity.

• 1721 • ACS Award in Separations Science and Technology

To recognize outstanding accomplishments in fundamental or applied research directed to separations science and technology. The award is granted to an individual without regard to age, nationality, or sex. The scope of the award is to be as broad as possible covering all fields where separation science and technology are practiced including (but not limited to) biology, chemistry, engineering, geology and medicine. The deadline for nominations is February 1. A monetary award of $5,000 and a certificate are presented annually. The recipient delivers a lecture at the annual I&EC Division Separation Science and Technology Symposium. Established in 1982. Sponsored by IBC Advanced Technologies and Millipore Corporation.

• 1722 • ACS Award in the Chemistry of Materials

To recognize and encourage creative work in the chemistry of materials. The nominee must have made outstanding contributions to the chemistry of materials, with particular emphasis placed on research relating to materials of actual or potential technological importance, where fundamental understanding of chemistry associated with materials preparation, processing, or use is critical. The deadline for nominations is February 1. A monetary award of $5,000, a certificate, and reimbursed travel expenses to attend the presentation ceremony are awarded annually, beginning in 1990. Established in 1988 by E. I. duPont de Nemours and Co. to commemorate the fiftieth anniversary of the commercialization of nylon and of the discovery of Teflon.

• 1723 • ACS Award in Theoretical Chemistry

To recognize innovative research in theoretical chemistry that either advances theoretical methodology or contributes to new discoveries about chemical systems. Emphasis in the selection process is on work characterized by depth, originality, and scientific significance. Nominations of individuals of any age or nationality may be made by February 1. A monetary prize of $5,000, a certificate, and reimbursement of travel expenses are awarded annually. Established in 1991 by IBM Corporation.

• 1724 • Roger Adams Award in Organic Chemistry

To recognize and encourage outstanding contributions to research in organic chemistry defined in its broadest sense. The award is granted to an individual without regard to nationality. The deadline for nominations is February 1 of even-numbered years. A monetary prize of $25,000, a gold medal, and a sterling silver replica of the medal are awarded biennially in odd-numbered years. Additionally, the recipient delivers a lecture at the Biennial National Organic Chemistry Symposium of the American Chemical Society where the award is presented. The travel expenses to the Symposium are reimbursed. Established in 1959. Sponsored by Organic Reactions, Inc., and Organic Syntheses, Inc.

• 1725 • Arthur W. Adamson Award for Distinguished Service in the Advancement of Surface Chemistry

To recognize distinguished and extensive services in the advancement of surface chemistry. Activities recognized by the award may include such fields as teaching, writing, research, and administration. Nominations must be submitted by February 1. A monetary prize of $5,000, a medallion with a presentation box, and a certificated. Up to $1,000 for travel expenses to attend the ceremony at which the award will be presented will be The medallion will be presented during the awards address. reimbursed. Established in 1991 by the Occidental Petroleum Corporation in honor of Arthur W. Adamson. Sponsored by the Occidental Petroleum Corporation.

• 1726 • Award for Cooperative Research in Polymer Science and Engineering

To recognize and encourage sustained cooperative research between industrial and academic or industrial and national laboratory polymer scientists. The cooperative research must be of significant importance to polymer science and technology. The award may be an individual award or shared between an academic and industrial scientist or between a national laboratories' scientist and an industrial scientist. The award consists of $2,000, a plaque, and a travel allowance to attend the meeting where the award is presented by the Division of Polymeric Materials: Science and Engineering. The awardee gives a lecture at the meeting. Established in 1992 and supported by a gift from the Eastman Kodak Company.

• 1727 • Award for Creative Advances in Environmental Science and Technology

To encourage creativity in research and technology or methods of analysis to provide scientific basis for informed environmental control decision making processes, or to provide practical technologies that will reduce health risk factors. A monetary award of $5,000 and a certificate are awarded; travel expenses are also reimbursed. Awarded annually. Established in 1978. Sponsored by Air Products and Chemicals, Inc.

• 1728 • Award for Creative Work in Synthetic Organic Chemistry

To recognize and encourage creative work in synthetic organic chemistry. A monetary award of $5,000 and a certificate are presented annually. Travel expenses are also reimbursed. Sponsored by Adrich Chemical Company, Inc.

• 1729 • Award for Encouraging Disadvantaged Students into Careers in the Chemical Sciences

To recognize individuals who have significantly stimulated or fostered the interest of students, especially minority and/or economically disadvantaged students, in chemistry and thereby promoting their professional development as chemists or chemical engineers, and/or increasing their appreciation of chemistry as the central science. A monetary prize of $5,000 and a certificate are awarded annually. In addition, a grant of $10,000 will be made to an academic institution, designated by the recipient, and up to $1,500 for travel expenses to the award ceremony is also provided. Established in 1993. Sponsored by the Camille and Henry Dreyfus Foundation, Inc.

• 1730 • Award for Encouraging Women into Careers in the Chemical Sciences

To recognize individuals who have significantly stimulated or fostered the interest of women in chemistry, thereby promoting their professional development as chemists or chemical engineers, and/or increasing their appreciation of chemistry as the central science. A monetary award of $5,000 and a certificate are presented. Up to $1,500 in travel expenses are reimbursed. Established in 1993. Awarded annually. Sponsored by The Camille and Henry Dreyfus Foundation, Inc.

• 1731 • Award for Excellence in Teaching

To recognize a member of the Division of Analytical Chemistry for outstanding contributions to education in analytical chemistry. Individuals who are or have been regular, full-time faculty members of colleges or universities in the United States or Canada for at least five years at the time the award is made are eligible. Nominations must be submitted by September 1 of each year. A monetary award of $4,000 and a certificate are awarded. Travel expenses to attend the meeting at which the award is presented are reimbursed. Established in 1982. Co-sponsored by E. I. du Pont de Nemours and Company.

• 1732 • Award for Team Innovation

To highlight the value and importance of technical teams and teamwork to the chemical and allied industries by recognizing a multi-disciplinary team for successfully moving an innovative idea to a product now in commercial use. A monetary award of $3,000 for each team member, a gold medal, and a certificate are presented. Travel expenses will be reimbursed to each team member for travel to the meeting for the award presentation. Awarded annually. Established in 1994. Sponsored by The Corporation Associates.

• 1733 • Award in Chemical Instrumentation

To recognize a member of the Division of Analytical Chemistry for original and eminent contributions to chemical instrumentation. Nominations must be submitted by September 1 of each year. A monetary award of $4,000 and a plaque are awarded. Travel expenses to attend the meeting at which the award is presented will be reimbursed. Established in 1953. Sponsored by the Dow Chemical Company Foundation.

• 1734 • Award in Electrochemistry

To encourage conceptualization, development, and use of electrochemistry to further the science of chemical analysis. Members of the Division of Analytical Chemistry are eligible. Nominations must be submitted by September 1 of each year. A monetary award of $4,000 and a plaque are awarded. Travel expenses to attend the meeting at which the award is presented will be reimbursed. Established in 1987. Sponsored by the Electrochemical Instruments Division of EG&G Princeton Applied Research.

• 1735 • Award in Spectrochemical Analysis

To recognize outstanding contributions to the advancement of the field of spectrochemical analysis and optical spectrometry. Members of the Division of Analytical Chemistry are eligible. Nominations must be submitted by September 1 of each year. A monetary award of $4,000 and a plaque are awarded. Travel expenses to attend the meeting at which the award is presented will be reimbursed. Established in 1986. Sponsored by the Perkin-Elmer Corporation.

• 1736 • Alfred Bader Award in Bioinorganic or Bioorganic Chemistry

To recognize outstanding contributions to bioinorganic or biorganic chemistry. Special consideration is given to applications of the fundamental principles and experimental methodology of chemistry to areas of biological significance. The deadline for nominations is February 1. A monetary award of $5,000 and a certificate are awarded annually. Reasonable travel expenses to the meeting at which the award will be presented will be reimbursed. The recipient's award address is reprinted in *Aldrichimica Acta.* Established in 1986 and financed by a gift to the ACS by Alfred R. Bader.

• 1737 • Fernley H. Banbury Award

To recognize an inventor and/or developer of innovations in commercially accepted production equipment, instrumentation, and control systems widely used in manufacturing of rubber or rubber-like articles. A monetary award of $3,000, a plaque, and a $500 travel allowance to attend the spring meeting of the Rubber Division at which the award is presented are bestowed when merited. Established in 1986 by the Rubber Division. Sponsored by Farrel Corporation.

• 1738 • Earle B. Barnes Award for Leadership in Chemical Research Management

To recognize outstanding achievements in chemical research management. A nominee must be a citizen of the United States. Nominees should have demonstrated success in research management by exhibiting the proven ability to manage research projects and people. The deadline for nomination is February 1. A monetary prize of $5,000, a certificate, and travel expenses to attend the meeting where the award is presented are awarded annually. Established in 1982. Sponsored by The Dow Chemical Company.

• 1739 • Edward Bartow Award

For recognition of a paper, outstanding both in content and manner of presentation, on some phase of water, waste, sanitation, or sewage chemistry. Nominees must be members of the American Chemical Society. A scroll and travel allowance of up to $500 to attend the Division of Environmental Chemistry dinner are bestowed. Awarded when merited. Established in 1956 by the Division of Environmental Chemistry.

• 1740 • Board of Directors Distinguished Service Award for Senior ACS Administrators

To recognize distinguished service to the Society over a period of years. The award is given at irregular intervals at the discretion of the Board to recognize outstanding service to the Society by a senior staff member over a period of years. It may be given to the widow or widower or child(ren) (as appropriate) of the person recognized. The award consists of a cash prize to be determined by the Board. Travel expenses incidental to conferring the award are paid. Established in 1988 by the Board of Directors of the American Chemical Society.

• 1741 • Brasted Memorial Lecture

To recognize a significant contribution to the advancement of chemical education internationally. The nominee must not be a citizen or resident of the United States. Travel to the Biennial Conference on Chemical Education to present the Brasted Lecture, membership in the Division of Chemical Education, and a subscription to the *Journal of Chemical Education* are awarded biennially. Established in 1987 in honor of Robert C. Brasted.

• 1742 • Alfred Burger Award in Medicinal Chemistry

To recognize outstanding contributions to research in medicinal chemistry. The award is granted without regard to age, sex, or nationality. The deadline for nominations is February 1 in any odd-numbered year. A monetary prize of $3,000, a certificate, and travel expenses incidental to the conferring of the award are presented biennially in even-numbered years. Additionally, the recipient presents an award address at the spring meeting of the Division of Medicinal Chemistry. Established in 1978. Sponsored by SmithKline Beecham Corporation.

• 1743 • Chemical Health and Safety Award

To recognize and encourage outstanding contributions to the science, technology, education, or communication of chemical health and safety. Nominations must be submitted by January 15. A monetary award of $2,000, a certificate of recognition, and travel expenses of up to $700 to attend the ACS National Meeting are awarded annually. Established in 1983.

• 1744 • James Bryant Conant Award in High School Chemistry Teaching

To recognize, encourage, and stimulate outstanding teachers of high school chemistry in the United States, its possessions or territories, at both the regional and national levels. To be eligible, one must have received the Regional Award in High School Chemistry Teaching. The deadline for submissions is November 15. The nominators of each winner of an ACS Regional Award in High School Chemistry Teaching for the three years preceding the award year will be invited to submit a nomination which conforms to the requirement for all other ACS awards. One of the regional winners or candidates is selected by the national award committee as the recipient of the James Bryant Conant Award in High School Chemistry Teaching. The national award consists of a monetary prize of $5,000, and a certificate. Travel expenses to attend the meeting where the award are reimbursed. Established in 1965 by E. I. duPont de Nemours and Company Inc. Sponsored by Albemarle Corporation.

• 1745 • Arthur C. Cope Award

To recognize outstanding achievement in the field of organic chemistry, the significance of which has become apparent within the five years preceding the year in which the award will be considered. The award is granted to an individual without regard to age, sex, or nationality. The deadline for nominations is February 1. The award consists of $25,000, a medallion with a presentation box, and a certificate, awarded annually. An unrestricted grant-in-aid of $150,000 for research in organic chemistry, under the direction of the recipient, designated Arthur C. Cope Fund Grant, is made to any university or nonprofit institution selected by the recipient. A recipient may choose to assign the Arthur C. Cope Fund Grant to an institution for use by others than the recipient for research or education in organic chemistry. Established in 1972 under the terms of the will of Arthur C. Cope.

• 1746 • Arthur C. Cope Scholar Award

To recognize and encourage excellence in organic chemistry. Ten (10)Arthur C. Cope Scholars will be named annually: Four (4)between the ages of thirty-six and forty-nine, four (4) age fifty or older, and two (2)thirty-five and younger all inclusive before April 30, of the year in which the award is presented. The deadline for nominations is February 1. The award consists of $5000 and a certificate. A certificate and a $40,000 unrestricted research grant, to be assigned by the recipient to any university or nonprofit institution, are awarded. The recipient is required to deliver a lecture at the annual Arthur C. Cope Symposium. Established in 1984 under the terms of the will of Arthur C. Cope. No individual may receive a second Arthur C. Cope Scholar Award; Arthur C. Cope Medalists are ineligible to be named Cope Scholars. Formerly: Arthur C. Cope Travel Grant.

• 1747 • Peter Debye Award in Physical Chemistry

To encourage and reward outstanding research in physical chemistry. The nominee must have accomplished outstanding research of a theoretical or experimental nature in the field of physical chemistry. The award is granted without regard to age, sex, or nationality. The deadline for nominations is February 1. A monetary award of $5,000 and a certificate are awarded. Travel expenses to attend the meeting where the award is presented are reimbursed. Established in 1960 by Humble Oil and Refining Company. Sponsored by E.I. duPont deNemours and Co.

• 1748 • Dexter Award in the History of Chemistry

To recognize an individual for an outstanding accomplishment in the history of chemistry. Qualified individuals must be nominated or must submit applications by January 1. A monetary award of $2,000 and a plaque are presented annually at the fall national American Chemistry Society meeting. Established in 1956 by Dr. Sidney Edelstein of Dexter Chemical Corporation. Sponsored by Dexter Chemical Corporation.

• 1749 • Distinguished Service Award

To recognize sustained and distinguished contributions to the field of fuel chemistry. Nominees must be members of the division for at least ten years and must have made a significant and continuous impact on the advancement of fuel chemistry. A monetary award of $1,000, a plaque, and travel allowance up to $500 to attend the fall national ACS meeting are bestowed by the Division of Fuel Chemistry. Awarded when merited. Established in 1986.

• 1750 • DivCHAS College Health and Safety Award
To recognize the college or university demonstrating the most comprehensive program of chemical laboratory safety. Awards are presented in two categories: universities offering advanced degrees in chemistry and colleges offering undergraduate degrees only. A monetary award of $1,000 to the institution's chemistry department to be used to support its Laboratory Safety Program and a plaque are presented annually when merited. Established in 1990.

• 1751 • Arthur K. Doolitte Award
For recognition of an outstanding paper presented before the Division at the spring or fall American Chemical Society meetings. All papers appearing in the preprint book are evaluated on the basis of content with emphasis on originality and development of new concepts and on the quality of the presentation. Recipients are selected by an anonymous committee appointed by the Division secretary. A monetary award of $1,000 is awarded semiannually at the spring and fall American Chemical Society meetings. Established in 1953 by Union Carbide Corporation and financed by a gift of royalties from A. K. Doolitte's book, *Technology of Solvents and Plasticizers*. Sponsored by Union Carbide Corporation. Additional information is available from Mr. David A. Cocuzzi, AKZO Coatings Inc.

• 1752 • ExxonMobil Solid State Chemistry Faculty Fellowship
To recognize solid state chemistry as a discrete discipline and to encourage greater participation by Americans in this branch of chemistry. Faculty members at an American university, who hold a tenure-track position and completed their PhD degree no more than six years prior to the award, are eligible. A monetary award of $10,000 and a travel allowance up to $500 is bestowed annually. Established in 1979. Sponsored by the ExxonMobil Foundation. Administered by the Division of Inorganic Chemistry.

• 1753 • Frank H. Field and Joe L. Franklin Award for Outstanding Achievement in Mass Spectrometry
To recognize outstanding achievement in the development or application of mass spectrometry. The award is granted without regard to age, nationality, sex, or the date of the achievement recognized by the award. In odd-numbered years, the award is presented for advances in techniques or fundamental processes in mass spectrometry. Recognition is given in even-numbered years to development of the applications of mass spectrometry. The deadline for nominations is February 1. A monetary prize of $5,000, a certificate, and an allowance of up to $1,000 for travel expenses to attend the meeting where the award is presented are awarded. Established in 1983.

• 1754 • Paul J. Flory Polymer Education Award
To recognize, encourage, and stimulate outstanding achievements by an individual in promoting undergraduate and/or graduate polymer education. Nominees must be a member or affiliate of the Division of Polymer Chemistry at the time of nomination. A monetary award of $2,000, a plaque, and a travel allowance to attend the meeting at which the award is given are bestowed biennially, in even-numbered years. The recipient presents a lecture at the meeting. Established in 1981. Sponsored by E. I. du Pont de Nemours and Company.

• 1755 • Francis P. Garvan-John M. Olin Medal
To recognize distinguished service to chemistry by women chemists, citizens of the United States. A monetary award of $5,000, a gold medal, a bronze replica, and a certificate are presented; travel expenses to the awards presentation are reimbursed. Awarded annually. Established in 1936.

• 1756 • Charles Goodyear Medal
To honor individuals for outstanding invention, innovation, or development that has resulted in a significant change in, or contribution to, the rubber industry. Nominee must be the principal inventor or developer of the project(s). A monetary award of $6,000, a gold medal, a certificate, a lifetime affiliate membership in the Rubber Division, and a $500 travel allowance to attend the meeting at which the award is presented are bestowed annually at the spring Rubber Division's meeting. Established in 1939 by the Division.

• 1757 • James T. Grady - James H. Stack Award for Interpreting Chemistry for the Public
To recognize, encourage, and stimulate outstanding reporting directly to the public that materially increases the public's knowledge and understanding of chemistry, chemical engineering, and related fields. The nominee must have made noteworthy presentations through a medium of public communication to increase the American public's understanding of chemistry and chemical progress. This information may be disseminated through the press, radio, television, films, the lecture platform, or books or pamphlets for the lay public. The deadline for nominations is February 1. A The award consists of $3,000, a medallion with a presentation box, and a certificate. Travel expenses to attend the meeting where the award is presented will be reimbursed. Established in 1955. Formerly: James T. Grady Award for Interpreting Chemistry for the Public.

• 1758 • Ernest Guenther Award in the Chemistry of Natural Products
To recognize and encourage outstanding achievements in analysis, structure elucidation, and chemical synthesis of natural products. This award is granted without regard to age, sex, or nationality. The deadline for nominations is February 1. A monetary prize of $5,000, a medallion, and a certificate are awarded annually. Up to $2,500 for travel expenses to the meeting at which the award will be presented will be reimbursed. Established in 1948 by Fritzsche-Dodge and Olcott Inc. Sponsored by Givaudan-Roure. Formerly: Ernest Guenther Award in the Chemistry of Essential Oils and Related Products.

• 1759 • E. B. Hershberg Award for Important Discoveries in Medicinally Active Substances
To recognize and encourage outstanding discoveries in the chemistry of medicinally active substances made during the previous two decades. The deadline for nominations is February 1 of even-numbered years and presented biennially in odd-numbered years. A monetary award of $3,000 and a certificate are presented. A travel allowance of $1,000 to attend the presentation ceremony is reimbursed. Established in 1988 by Schering-Plough Corporation in honor of the contributions of Emanuel B. Hershberg to the pharmaceutical industry, especially the application of organic chemistry, for the discovery and development of novel drugs. Sponsored by Schering-Plough Corporation.

• 1760 • Joel Henry Hildebrand Award in the Theoretical and Experimental Chemistry of Liquids
To recognize distinguished contributions to the understanding of the chemistry and physics of liquids. The award is granted without regard to age, sex, or nationality. The deadline for nominations is February 1. A monetary prize of $5,000, a certificate, and an allowance of up to $1,000 for travel expenses incidental to conferral of the award are presented annually. Established in 1980 in recognition of the scientific contributions of ACS past president, Joel H. Hildebrand. The first award was presented to Dr. Hildebrand as part of the observances of his hundredth birthday in November, 1981. Sponsored by Exxon Research and Engineering Company and Exxon Chemical Company.

• 1761 • Ralph F. Hirschmann Award in Peptide Chemistry
To recognize and encourage outstanding achievements in the chemistry, biochemistry, and biophysics of peptides. The deadline for nominations is February 1. A monetary award of $5,000 and a certificate are awarded annually. Up to $1,000 in travel expenses to the meeting at which the award will be presented will be reimbursed. Established in 1980 by Merck Sharp & Dohme Research Laboratories to honor Ralph F. Hirschmann. Sponsored by Merck Research Laboratories.

• 1762 • Claude S. Hudson Award in Carbohydrate Chemistry
To recognize outstanding contributions to carbohydrate chemistry in education, research, or applications. A monetary award of $3,000 and a certificate are presented, and travel expenses to the awards presentation are reimbursed up to $1,000. The award is presented biennially in odd-numbered years. Sponsored by National Starch & Chemical Company.

• 1763 • Ipatieff Prize

To recognize outstanding chemical experimental work in the field of catalysis or high pressure, carried out by men or women of any nationality and not over forty years of age. Deadline for nomination is February 1. Income from a trust fund of approximately $5,000 and a certificate are presented, and travel expenses to the awards presentation are reimbursed. The award is presented every three years.

• 1764 • Fraser Johnstone Award

For recognition of a paper, outstanding both in content and presentation, on air pollution. A nominee must be a member of the ASC. A scroll and travel allowance of up to $500 to attend the Division of Environmental Chemistry dinner are awarded when merited. Established in 1966 by the Division of Environmental Chemistry.

• 1765 • Frederic Stanley Kipping Award in Silicon Chemistry

To recognize distinguished contributions to the field of silicon chemistry and, by such example, to stimulate the creativity of others. A nominee must have accomplished distinguished achievement in research in silicon chemistry during the preceding ten years. There are no limits on age or nationality. The deadline for nominations is February 1 in any odd-numbered year. A monetary award of $5,000, and a certificate are issued. An allowance to cover travel expenses incidental to conferment of the award are presented biennially in even-numbered years. Established in 1960 to commemorate the achievements of Prof. Frederic Stanley Kipping. Sponsored by Dow Corning Corporation.

• 1766 • Victor K. LaMer Award

To recognize outstanding graduate research in colloid and surface chemistry. The Ph.D. thesis must have been accepted by a U.S. or Canadian university during a three-year period prior to August 31 of the year in which the award is given. A monetary award of $2,500 is bestowed annually by the Division of Colloid and Surface Chemistry. Established in 1970.

• 1767 • Irving Langmuir Award in Chemical Physics

To recognize and encourage outstanding interdisciplinary research in chemistry and physics in the spirit of Irving Langmuir. Nominees must have made an outstanding contribution to chemical physics or physical chemistry within ten years preceding the year in which the award is made. The nominee must be a resident of the United States. The deadline for nominations is February 1 in any odd-numbered year. A monetary award of $10,000 and a certificate are awarded biennially in even-numbered years. Reasonable travel expenses to the meeting at which the award will be presented will be reimbursed. Selection of the recipient in odd-numbered years is conducted by the Division of Chemical Physics of the American Physical Society. Established in 1964. Sponsored by General Electric Foundation.

• 1768 • Eli Lilly Award in Biological Chemistry

To recognize an individual for outstanding research in biological chemistry, and unusual independence of thought and originality. Nominees under 36 years of age who are actively engaged in the line of research for which the award is made are eligible. This prize cannot be made to a person who received another award sponsored by Eli Lilly and Company for the same technical accomplishment. An honorarium and a bronze medal are awarded annually. Established in 1934.

• 1769 • Herman F. Mark Division of Polymer Chemistry Award

To recognize outstanding research and leadership in polymer science. Nominee must be a member or affiliate of the Division of Polymer Chemistry. Selection is based on accomplishments and contributions to the advancement of polymer science through teaching, technical leadership, and scientific writings. A monetary award of $2,000, a plaque, and a travel allowance to attend the Biennial Polymer Symposium are awarded biennially in even-numbered years. The recipient gives an address at the Symposium. Established in 1976. Sponsored by Dow Chemical Company.

• 1770 • Carl S. Marvel Creative Polymer Chemistry Award

To recognize and encourage accomplishments and/or innovations of unusual merit in the field of basic or applied polymer chemistry by younger scientists. Nominee must be a member or affiliate of the Division of Polymer Chemistry, must have accomplished work in basic or applied polymer chemistry, and must be under 45 years of age on January 1 of the year in which the award is given. A monetary award of $2,000, a plaque, and a travel allowance to attend the meeting at which the award is given is bestowed biennially in odd-numbered years. The recipient is expected to give a lecture at the meeting. Established in 1980. Sponsored by Dow Chemical Company.

• 1771 • Medicinal Chemistry Award

To recognize outstanding achievement in science areas that contribute to the field of medicinal chemistry. Nominations may be made for any scientist in the U.S. or abroad whose research accomplishments have had a significant effect on medicinal chemistry. Emphasis is placed on medicinal chemistry, recent contributions, and young scientists whose accomplishments have not already been adequately recognized by other honors. A monetary award of $3,000, a scroll, and a travel allowance to attend the Medicinal Chemistry Symposium are awarded biennially. Established in 1979 and sponsored by the Division of Medicinal Chemistry.

• 1772 • Melvin Mooney Distinguished Technology Award

To honor members and affiliate members of the Rubber Division who have exhibited exceptional technical competence by making significant and repeated contributions to rubber technology. A monetary award of $3,000, a plaque, lifetime affiliate membership in the Division, and a $500 travel allowance to attend the meeting at which the award is presented are awarded when merited. Established in 1983. Presented in memory of Melvin Mooney, the developer of the Mooney Viscometer and other testing equipment. Sponsored by Uniroyal Chemical Company. Formerly: Award for Technical Excellence.

• 1773 • E. V. Murphree Award in Industrial and Engineering Chemistry

To stimulate fundamental research in industrial and engineering chemistry, the development of chemical engineering principles, and their application to industrial processes. A nominee must have accomplished outstanding research of a theoretical or experimental nature in the fields of industrial chemistry or chemical engineering. The award is granted without regard to age, sex, or nationality. The deadline for nominations is February 1. A monetary award of $5,000, a certificate, and an allowance of not more than $1,000 for travel expenses to attend the meeting where the award is presented are awarded annually. Established in 1955. Sponsored by Exxon Research and Engineering Company and Exxon Chemical Company.

• 1774 • Nakanishi Prize

To recognize and encourage significant work that extends chemical and spectroscopic methods to the study of important biological phenomena. A monetary award of $3,000, a bronze medal, and a certificate are presented, and travel expenses to the awards presentation are reimbursed. Awarded annually. Established in 1995 by the colleagues of Koji Nakanishi.

• 1775 • Nobel Laureate Signature Award for Graduate Education in Chemistry

To recognize an outstanding graduate student and his or her preceptor(s) in the field of chemistry, as broadly defined. The graduate student nominee must have completed a Ph.D. dissertation in chemistry within the 12-month period before the deadline for receipt of nominations. The award recognizes only work done while the nominee was a graduate student. This award is granted without regard to age, sex, or nationality. The deadline for nominations is February 1. The graduate student receives a monetary prize of $3,000 and a plaque containing the signatures of Nobel Laureates. The student's preceptor(s) receives $3,000 and a plaque for permanent display in the institution's Chemistry Department. Travel expenses of recipients incidental to the conferring of the award are reimbursed. Awarded annually. Established in 1978. Sponsored by Mallinckrodt Baker Inc. Formerly: (1980) Nobel Laureate Signature Award for a Graduate Student in Chemistry.

• 1776 • James Flack Norris Award in Physical Organic Chemistry

To encourage and reward outstanding contributions to physical organic chemistry. The deadline for nominations is February 1. A monetary prize of $5,000 and a certificate are awarded. Reasonable travel expenses to the meeting at which the award will be presented will be reimbursed. Established in 1963 in commemoration of James Flack Norris. Sponsored by the Northeastern Section, ACS.

• 1777 • George A. Olah Award in Hydrocarbon or Petroleum Chemistry

To recognize, encourage, and stimulate outstanding research achievements in hydrocarbon or petroleum chemistry. The nominee must be a resident of the United States or Canada and have accomplished outstanding research in the chemistry of hydrocarbon or petroleum and its products. The deadline for nominations is February 1. A monetary prize of $5,000 and a certificate are awarded annually. Reasonable travel expenses to the meeting at which the award will be presented will be reimbursed. Established in 1948 by Precision Scientific Company. Formerly: (1997) ACS Award in Petroleum Chemistry.

• 1778 • Charles Lathrop Parsons Award

To recognize outstanding public service by a member of the American Chemical Society. The nominee must be a member of the American Chemical Society and a citizen of the United States and performed outstanding public service. The deadline for nominations is February 1 in even-numbered years. The award normally shall be given not more than once every two years. However the Board of Directors may, at its discretion, reduce the interval to one year for anominee of its choice, if in its judgment circumstances in a given year warrant such action. A monetary prize of $3,000 and a certificate are awarded. Travel expenses to attend the meeting where the award is presented will be reimbursed. Established in 1952 by the American Chemical Society.

• 1779 • Anselme Payen Award

To recognize and encourage outstanding professional contributions to the science and chemical technology of cellulose and its allied products. Individuals from any country, without regard to age, may be nominated by December 1. A monetary award of $2,000 and a bronze medal are awarded annually at the spring ACS meeting. Established in 1962 to honor Anselme Payen (1795-1871), the distinguished French scientist who discovered cellulose. Additional information is available from Dr. Howard Needles, Department of Textiles and Clothing, University of California at Davis, Davis, CA; telephone: (916)752-0840.

• 1780 • Pfizer Award in Enzyme Chemistry

To recognize an individual for outstanding work in enzyme chemistry where the presence of enzyme action is unequivocally demonstrated. Nominees engaged in non-commercial work and under 40 years of age are eligible. This prize cannot be made to a person who received another award sponsored by Pfizer, Inc. for the same technical accomplishment. An honorarium and gold medal are awarded annually. Established in 1945.

• 1781 • George C. Pimentel Award in Chemical Education

To recognize outstanding contributions to chemical education. The nominee must have made outstanding contributions to chemical education considered in its broadest meaning, including the training of professional chemists; the dissemination of reliable information about chemistry to prospective chemists, to members of the profession, to students in other fields, and to the general public; and the integration of chemistry into the education system. Preference is given to American citizens. The deadline for nominations is February 1. A monetary prize of $5,000, and a certificate are awarded. Travel expenses to attend the meeting presentation ceremony will be reimbursed. Established in 1950 as the ACS Award in Chemical Education by Scientific Apparatus Makers Association and financed by its Laboratory Apparatus and Optical Sections through 1976. Sponsored by Union Carbide Corporation. Formerly: (1991) ACS Award in Chemical Education.

• 1782 • Priestley Medal

To recognize distinguished services to chemistry. Members and nonmembers, representatives of any nation, without regard to sex are eligible. Each nominee remains a nominee for three successive years without renomination, unless selected as medalist. The deadline for nominations is February 1. A gold medal designed to commemorate the work of Joseph Priestley, and a bronze replica of the medal are awarded. The award may not be presented more than once to the same individual. The travel expenses incidental to the conferring of the medal are reimbursed. Additionally, the honoree may be invited to deliver an address at the general meeting of the ACS at its spring meeting. Awarded annually. Established in 1922 by the American Chemical Society.

• 1783 • Procter & Gamble Award in Physical Chemistry

To recognize up to three graduate students each year for being the major authors of outstanding scientific papers accepted for publication in the *Journal of Physical Chemistry* (published by the American Chemical Society). Any predoctoral student in chemistry, chemical engineering, materials science, etc., who is a major author of a manuscript accepted for publication by July 1 of the award year, is eligible. Students must be entering at least the third year of graduate study. A monetary prize of $2,500 and an invitation to present a paper at a Procter & Gamble Award Symposium held a year later at a national American Chemical Society meeting are awarded annually. Established in 1982. Sponsored by Procter & Gamble Company.

• 1784 • Repligen Corporation Award in Chemistry of Biological Processes

To recognize an individual for outstanding contributions to the understanding of the chemistry of biological processes, with particular emphasis on structure, function, and mechanism. There are no restrictions on age or membership affiliation. An honorarium and a silver medal are awarded annually. Established in 1985 as a gift of the Repligen Company.

• 1785 • Glenn T. Seaborg Award for Nuclear Chemistry

To recognize and encourage research in nuclear or radiochemistry or their applications. There are no limits on age or nationality. The deadline for nominations is February 1. A monetary award of $3,000, a certificate, and travel expenses incidental to conferment of the award are awarded annually. Established in 1953 by Nuclear-Chicago Corporation, a subsidiary of G.D. Searle and Company. Sponsored by Gordon and Breach Publishing Group. Formerly: ACS Award for Nuclear Applications in Chemistry; (2006) ACS Award for Nuclear Chemistry.

• 1786 • Sherwin-Williams Student Award in Applied Polymer Science

For recognition of the best paper by a graduate student in applied polymer science. Candidates must be currently enrolled in graduate school or not more than one calendar year beyond their degree. Papers must be submitted by March 1. A monetary prize of $500, a plaque, and travel expense up to $500 are awarded annually at the fall American Chemical Society meeting. Established in 1984 by the Sherwin-Williams Company. Additional information is available from Murrae J. Bowden, Chairman, Sherwin-Williams Award Committee, Bellcore, 331 Newman Springs Rd., Redbank, NJ 07701.

• 1787 • Herman Skolnik Award

For recognition of outstanding contributions to, and achievements in, the theory and practice of chemical information science. Nominations must be submitted by June 1. A monetary award of $2,000 and a plaque are awarded annually at the American Chemical Society National Meeting. Established in 1976 to honor Herman Skolnik. Additional information is available from W.V. Metanomski, Chemical Abstracts Service, PO Box 3012, Columbus, OH 43210.

• 1788 • Tillmanns-Skolnok Award

To recognize an individual for outstanding, long-term service to the Division of Chemical Health and Safety. Active members of the division for at least five years are eligible. A monetary award of $200 and a plaque are awarded annually at the fall American Chemical Society National Meeting. Established in 1984 in memory of Emma June Tillmanns-Skolnik.

• 1789 • Smissman-Bristol-Myers-Squibb Award

To recognize outstanding impact on the practice of medicinal chemistry by exposition of new conceptual frameworks, publication, or teaching. Nominee must be a living scientist late in his/her career whose research, teaching, or service has had a substantial impact on the intellectual and theoretical development of medicinal chemistry. A monetary award of $3,000, a scroll, and a travel allowance to attend the fall national ACS meeting at which the award is given are bestowed. Established in 1975. Administered by the Division of Medicinal Chemistry.

• 1790 • **Sparks-Thomas Award**
To recognize and encourage young scientists, technologists, and engineers for outstanding contributions and innovations in the field of elastomers. Nominees must have completed their baccalaureate degree no more than 24 years before the year in which the award is presented. A monetary award of $4,000, a bronze medal, a plaque, and a $500 travel allowance to attend the meeting at which the award is presented are bestowed when merited. Established in 1986 by the Rubber Division in memory of William J. Sparks and Robert M. Thomas, chemists, who developed butyl rubber. Sponsored by Exxon Chemical Company.

• 1791 • **Henry H. Storch Award in Fuel Chemistry**
To recognize distinguished contributions within the preceding five years to fundamental or engineering research on the chemistry and utilization of coal or related materials. The deadline for nominations is February 1. A monetary award of $5,000, a certificate, and an expense allowance of up to $1,500 for travel to the presentation ceremony are presented annually. Established in 1964 by the Division of Fuel Chemistry, ACS and administered by the Division until 1985.

• 1792 • **Roy W. Tess Award in Coatings**
For recognition of outstanding contributions in the area of coatings science, technology, and engineering. Nominations must be submitted by September 1. A monetary prize of $1,000, a plaque, a half- to full-day symposium in honor of the awardee, and a reception in honor of the awardee at the symposium are awarded annually. Established in 1984 by Dr. and Mrs. Roy Tess and named in honor of Dr. Roy W. Tess, a distinguished technical figure in the coatings industry. Additional information is available from George Pilcher, AKZO Coatings Inc.

• 1793 • **George Stafford Whitby Award for Distinguished Teaching and Research**
To honor outstanding international teachers of chemistry and polymer science and to recognize innovative academic research. A monetary award of $3,000, a plaque, and a $500 travel allowance to attend the spring meeting of the Rubber Division at which the award is presented are bestowed when merited. Established in 1986 by the ACS Rubber Division. Sponsored by Nova Petrochemicals, Inc.

• 1794 • **E. Bright Wilson Award in Spectroscopy**
To recognize outstanding accomplishments in fundamental or applied spectroscopy in chemistry. The deadline for nominations is February 1. A monetary prize of $5,000, and a plaque are awarded annually. Expense allowance of up to $1,500 for travel to the presentation ceremony will be reimbursed. Established in 1994. Sponsored by Rohm and Haas Company.

• 1795 •
American Chemical Society, Philadelphia Section
Dr. Melissa Betz Cichowicz, Chair
University of Pennsylvania
Department of Chemistry
Philadelphia, PA 19104-6323
Phone: (215)382-1589
E-mail: philaacs@aol.com

• 1796 • **Philadelphia Section Award**
For chemists. Recognition award bestowed annually.

• 1797 • **Philadelphia Section Awards for Excellence in Science Teaching**
For outstanding science K-8 and chemistry teacher 9-12. Recognition award bestowed annually.

• 1798 •
American Chesterton Society
Dale Ahlquist, Pres.
4117 Pebblebrook Cir.
Minneapolis, MN 55437
Phone: (952)831-3096
Fax: (952)831-0387
E-mail: info@chesterton.org
Home Page: http://www.chesterton.org

• 1799 • **Lifetime Achievement Award**
Annual award of recognition.

• 1800 • **Outline of Sanity Award**
Annual award of recognition.

• 1801 •
American Chiropractic Association
Garrett F. Cuneo HCD, Exec.VP
1701 Clarendon Blvd.
Arlington, VA 22209
Phone: (703)276-8800
Toll-Free: 800-986-4636
Fax: (703)243-2593
E-mail: memberinfo@amerchiro.org
Home Page: http://www.amerchiro.org

• 1802 • **Health Journalism Awards**
To recognize journalists whose constructive thoughts suggest solutions to basic health problems, motivate consumers to take care of their health, and contribute to fair and responsible health reporting. Journalists or teams of writers who are responsible for the creation of either a single work, or series primarily aimed at the public, that is published or produced during the calendar year are eligible. Awards are given in five categories: newspapers; consumer magazines; television; radio; and trade, professional, or special interest publications and audio-visuals. Nominations are accepted from colleagues of the journalist or the journalist himself by March 1. Winners of the Gold Award receive $200 and a recognition piece; and runners-up receive the Bronze Award. Awarded annually. Established in 1976.

• 1803 •
American Cinema Editors
Alan Heim ACE, Pres.
100 Universal City Plz., Bldg. 2352 B, Rm. 202
Universal City, CA 91608
Phone: (818)777-2900
Fax: (818)733-5023
E-mail: amercinema@earthlink.net
Home Page: http://www.ace-filmeditors.org

• 1804 • **ACE Eddie Award**
To recognize superior achievement in the fields of motion picture, television, documentary and student editing. Awards are presented in the following categories: (1) Features; (2) Miniseries Episode; (3) Documentary; (4) Television Special; (5) Television Series Episode; and (6) Student. Members may submit nominations. A trophy is awarded annually in March. Established in 1952.

• 1805 •
The American Civil Defense Association
11576 S State St., Ste. 502
Draper, UT 84020
Toll-Free: 800-425-5397
E-mail: info@tacda.org
Home Page: http://www.tacda.org

• 1806 • **American Preparedness Award**
For recognition of outstanding achievement in civil defense. A plaque or trophy is awarded annually at the convention. Established in 1980.

• 1807 • **Lorne Greene Homeland Defense Award**
To recognize an individual for support of disaster response initiatives and homeland defense measures for the United States in emergency situations where human life and the nation are in mortal jeopardy. A plaque is awarded annually. Established in 1988 to honor Lorne Greene, a movie actor who was active in homeland defense.

• 1808 •
American Civil Liberties Union
Anthony D. Romero, Exec.Dir.
125 Broad St. 18 Fl.
New York, NY 10004-2400
Phone: (212)549-2500
Toll-Free: 800-775-2258
Fax: (212)549-2646
E-mail: aclu@aclu.org
Home Page: http://www.aclu.org/

• 1809 • **Medal of Liberty**
For recognition of distinguished lifetime service to the cause of civil liberties or an exceptional specific contribution to civil liberties. The award is intended to represent the pinnacle of achievement for those dedicated to the Bill of Rights. Nominations or applications may be submitted by October 25. Individuals in the legal public interest, academic and arts communities, in government service, and from the media are eligible. Nominees are screened by a selection com-

mittee of distinguished people knowledgeable in the field of civil liberties. A monetary award of $25,000 and a plaque are awarded biennially at a special event. In alternate years, an award is given for work in international human rights, in cooperation with the Lawyers Committee for Human Rights. Established in 1983. Formerly: (1989) Medal of Liberty.

• 1810 •
American Civil Liberties Union of the National Capital Area
1400 20th St. NW, Ste. 119
Washington, DC 20036-5920
Phone: (202)457-0800
Home Page: http://www.aclu-nca.org

• 1811 • **Alan Barth Service Award**
For recognition of volunteer service to the American Civil Liberties Union of the National Capital Area. The candidate must be a member, must have contributed volunteer service to the ACLU Fund of the National Capital Area, and must have been nominated by the board of ACLU/NCA. A plaque is presented annually at an awards dinner. Established in 1980 in memory of Alan Barth, former editorial writer for the Washington Post, for recognition of a lifetime of service to civil liberties.

• 1812 • **Henry W. Edgerton Civil Liberties Award**
For recognition of outstanding contributions in support and in defense of civil rights and civil liberties. Candidates must be nominated by the board. A plaque is presented annually at an awards ceremony. Established in 1964. Renamed in 1971 to honor Henry W. Edgerton, former Chief Judge of the U.S. Court of Appeals for the District of Columbia. Formerly: (1971) Oliver Wendell Holmes Bill of Rights Award.

• 1813 •
American Civil Liberties Union of Vermont
Allen Gilbert, Exec.Dir.
137 Elm St.
Montpelier, VT 05602
Phone: (802)223-6304
Fax: (802)223-6304
E-mail: info@acluvt.org
Home Page: http://www.acluvt.org

• 1814 • **Civil Liberties Award**
For exceptional dedication and service. Recognition award bestowed annually.

• 1815 • **Cooperating Atty Award**
For exceptional dedication and service. Recognition award bestowed annually.

• 1816 • **Volunteer of the Year**
For exceptional dedication and service. Recognition award bestowed annually.

• 1817 •
American Civil Liberties Union, Ohio Affiliate
Christine Link, Exec.Dir.
4506 Chester Ave.
Cleveland, OH 44103
Phone: (216)472-2200
Fax: (216)472-2210
E-mail: contact@acluohio.org
Home Page: http://www.acluohio.org

• 1818 • **Civil Liberties Award**
For significant contribution in defending the Bill of Rights. Recognition award bestowed annually.

• 1819 •
American Cockatiel Society
11152 Blackwood Dr.
New Port Richie, FL 34654
Toll-Free: 888-221-1161
E-mail: acs130p@yahoo.com
Home Page: http://www.acstiels.com/

• 1820 • **L/M Award**
For recognition of the best cockatiel in America each year. Birds are judged by confirmation as outlined by the ACS Standard of Perfection. There are no eligibility requirements. A trophy is awarded annually. Established in 1977. Formerly: (1983) Kellogg Award; Fritz Award; Frite Award.

• 1821 •
American College Health Association
Col. Doyle E. Randol MS, Exec.Dir.
PO Box 28937
Baltimore, MD 21240-8937
Phone: (410)859-1500
Fax: (410)859-1510
E-mail: pcrone@acha.org
Home Page: http://www.acha.org

• 1822 • **Lewis Barbato Award**
To recognize students who have made a major contribution to consumer involvement in the work of the national, regional, or state affiliate associations. Awarded annually. Established in 1977 in honor of Lewis Barbato, M.D., a past president of the Association.

• 1823 • **Ruth E. Boynton Award**
To recognize distinguished service to the Association. A plaque is usually awarded annually. Established in 1967 in honor of Ruth Boynton, past president of the Association and director of the health service at the University of Minnesota.

• 1824 • **Miguel Garcia-Tunon Memorial Award in Human Dignity**
To recognize a member whose life, work, writing, research, or way of living has promoted the cause of human dignity and nurtured our appreciation of human differences. Awarded annually. Established in 1989 in memory of Mr. Garcia-Tunon, whose life and work were examples of dignity and integrity.

• 1825 • **Edward Hitchcock Award**
To recognize outstanding contributions to the field of college health. A plaque is usually awarded annually. Established in 1961 in memory of Edward Hitchcock, founder of the first college health service at Amherst College in 1861.

• 1826 • **E. Dean Lovett Memorial Award**
To recognize members who have directed a college health service or contributed significantly to the development of a college health service in an exemplary manner. Awarded annually. Established in 1990 by ACHA's Nurse Director Section in honor of E. Dean Lovett, M.D. who was an advocate of nurses.

• 1827 • **Ollie B. Moten Award**
To honor a member of the Association who has made a significant impact on the institution of higher education in which they work, whether or not that individual has been active beyond the institution in publishing or holding office in the national or affiliate associations. Awarded annually. Established in 1992.

• 1828 •
American College of Allergy, Asthma and Immunology
James R. Slawny, Exec.Dir.
85 W Algonquin Rd., Ste. 550
Arlington Heights, IL 60005-4425
Phone: (847)427-1200
Fax: (847)427-1294
E-mail: mail@acaai.org
Home Page: http://www.acaai.org

• 1829 • **National Media Awards**
To recognize journalists who have excelled in communicating information about allergic disease and asthma to the public. Entries must have been published or broadcast during the preceding year. Awards are given in the following categories: Newspaper - for a news or feature story, comprehensive coverage or series; Television - for a comprehensive news report or series of reports, discussion program, or documentary; General Interest Magazine - for an article or series of articles; and Radio - for a comprehensive news report or series of reports, discussion program, or documentary. A monetary award of $1,000 is presented to first place winners in each of the three categories. Each winner also receives an expense-paid trip to the College's annual meeting site for an awards ceremony. Awarded annually. Established in 1986.

• 1830 •
American College of Angiology
H. E. Shaftel MD, Meeting Chm.
2549 SW 23rd Cranbrook Pl.
Boynton Beach, FL 33436-5701
Phone: (516)466-4055
Fax: (516)466-4099
E-mail: aca@collegeofangiology.org
Home Page: http://www.collegeofangiology.org

• 1831 • **Young Investigators Award**
To foster young physicians and research fellows in the field of vascular medicine and surgery, and to promote continued interest in research and management of vascular diseases. New and junior investigators who are interns or residents, or who hold an academic rank no higher than assistant professor are eligible. Original, unpublished works are considered. A monetary award and a certificate are presented annually. Established in 1988.

• 1832 •
American College of Apothecaries
Dr. D.C. Huffman Jr., Exec.VP
2830 Summer Oaks Dr.
Bartlett, TN 38134-3811
Phone: (901)383-8119
Toll-Free: 800-828-5933
Fax: (901)383-8882
E-mail: aca@acainfo.org
Home Page: http://www.acainfo.org

• 1833 • **J. Leon Lascoff Memorial Award**
To recognize individuals for outstanding efforts to improve health care. Recipients are nominated and selected by past presidents of the college. A plaque is awarded annually at the convention. Established in 1944.

• 1834 • **Albert E. Rosica, Jr. Memorial Award**
To recognize individuals for outstanding contributions to pharmacy education. Nominations are requested from the deans of Colleges of Pharmacy. The recipient is selected by the executive committee of the American College of Apothecaries. A $1,000 contribution to the school of pharmacy of the recipient's choice and a plaque are awarded annually at the convention. Established in 1979 to honor Albert E. Rosica, Jr.

• 1835 •
American College of Cardiology
Christine W. McEntee, CEO
9111 Old Georgetown Rd.
Bethesda, MD 20814-1699
Phone: (301)897-5400
Toll-Free: 800-253-4636
Fax: (301)897-9745
E-mail: exec@acc.org
Home Page: http://www.acc.org

• 1836 • **Distinguished Fellow**
To recognize outstanding service in the interest of the College. Fellows of the College are eligible. All candidates must be nominated by members of American College of Cardiology. Awarded annually. Established in 1965. Former college presidents are not eligible for this award.

• 1837 • **Distinguished Scientist**
To recognize major contributions to the advancement of scientific knowledge in the field of cardiovascular disease. Fellows of the College are eligible. All candidates must be nominated by members of American College of Cardiology. Awarded annually. Established in 1981.

• 1838 • **Distinguished Service**
To recognize profound contributions to medicine and/or the delivery of health care. Scientists, physicians, or laymen are eligible. All candidates must be nominated by members of American College of Cardiology. Awarded annually. Established in 1967. Former college presidents are not eligible for this award.

• 1839 • **Gifted Teacher**
To recognize outstanding teachers in the field of cardiovascular disease. Fellows of the College are eligible. All candidates must be nominated by members of American College of Cardiology. Awarded annually. Established in 1965.

• 1840 • **Honorary Fellow**
To recognize outstanding professional performance by a distinguished physician or scientist. Non-members of the College are eligible. All candidates must be nominated by members of American College of Cardiology. Awarded annually. Established in 1955.

• 1841 • **Presidential Citation**
Awarded when merited. Established in 1968.

• 1842 •
American College of Chest Physicians
Alvin Lever, Exec.VP/CEO
3300 Dundee Rd.
Northbrook, IL 60062
Phone: (847)498-1400
Toll-Free: 800-343-ACCP
Fax: (847)498-5460
E-mail: accp@chestnet.org
Home Page: http://www.chestnet.org

• 1843 • **Alfred Soffer Research Awards**
To recognize outstanding research papers judged best in scientific quality. All abstracts submitted are eligible. A monetary prize of $1,500 is awarded to each of two winners, and $1,000 to each finalist. Awarded annually. Established in 1968.

• 1844 • **Cecile Lehman Mayer Research Award**
To recognize an outstanding research paper on cardiovascular and pulmonary diseases. Physicians of residency or fellowship status under the age of 35 are eligible. Established in 1968.

• 1845 • **Young Investigator Awards**
To recognize the best outstanding original scientific research by investigators who are in residency or fellowship programs or who have completed their fellowship program within the last five years. A monetary award of $1,000 is presented.

• 1846 •
American College of Clinical Pharmacology
Susan S. Ulrich, Exec.Dir.
3 Ellinwood Ct.
New Hartford, NY 13413-1105
Phone: (315)768-6117
Fax: (315)768-6119
E-mail: accp1ssu@aol.com
Home Page: http://www.accp1.org

• 1847 • **McKeen Cattell Memorial Award**
To provide recognition for the best article published in the *Journal of Clinical Pharmacology* during the academic year preceding the Award. A monetary award and a certificate are presented annually. Established in 1980 originally to honor McKeen Cattell, M.D., Ph.D., and later in his memory.

• 1848 • **Distinguished Investigator Award**
To recognize superior scientific expertise and accomplishments by a senior investigator, usually involving a distinct area of research in basic or clinical pharmacology for which the individual is internationally known. The recipient may be either a member or a non-member. Awarded annually at the annual meeting. Established in 1988.

• 1849 • **Honorary Fellowship Award**
The award recognizes overall contributions by a senior investigator or authority having a national or international reputation in the scientific, public service, legislative, governmental or other area of endeavor impacting on the field. Awarded annually at the annual meeting. Established in 1986.

• 1850 • **Nathaniel T. Kwit Distinguished Service Award**
To recognize an individual for accomplishments of a general nature which benefit the field of clinical pharmacology. These may be in the area of teaching, administration, service with ACCP, long-term and wide-ranging scientific studies having practical importance, and other service related functions. The recipient may be either a member or non-member. Awarded annually at the annual meeting. Established in 1987.

• 1851 • **Tanabe Young Investigator Award**
To recognize the scientific accomplishments of a young investigator, at a relatively early stage of his/her career, who has made unusual strides in research relating to clinical pharmacology. The individual's career should show promise of outstanding achievements. Members and non-members under 40 years of age are eligible. An honorarium and a plaque are awarded biennially. Established in 1990. Formerly: (1996) Young Investigator Award.

• 1852 •
American College of Dentists
Dr. Stephen A. Ralls, Exec.Dir.
839-J Quince Orchard Blvd.
Gaithersburg, MD 20878-1614
Phone: (301)977-3223
Fax: (301)977-3330
E-mail: info@facd.org
Home Page: http://www.facd.org

• 1853 • **Award of Merit**
For recognition of unusual contributions made toward the advancement of the profession of dentistry and its service to humanity by persons other than Fellows of the College. An engraved certificate is awarded when merited at the Convocation. Established in 1959.

• 1854 • **Distinguished Service Award**
To recognize those Fellows of the College who have served the profession of dentistry with distinction and in support of the goals of the College for a period of fifty years. This Award is presented during the annual meeting of the College. Established in 1986.

• 1855 • **William John Gies Award**
To recognize and encourage unusual services in dentistry and in the allied fields of education, research, literature, etc. Fellows of the College are eligible for the award. An engraved certificate is awarded annually during the Convocation. Established in 1940 in honor of William John Gies who contributed much to the advancement of dentistry.

• 1856 • **Honorary Fellowship**
To recognize persons who, though not holding a dental degree, have contributed to the advancement of dentistry and to its service to the public. These contributions may have been made in many areas - education, research, administration, public service, public health, medicine, and many others. The College confers Honorary Fellowships at the Annual Convention upon those selected, giving them all the privileges of Fellowship except the right to vote. Established in 1930.

• 1857 • **Section Achievement Award**
To recognize outstanding activities of Sections in areas related to the College's mission and strategic directions. The award encompasses three broad categories: professional education, public education, and community service. The award is presented during the annual meeting of the College when merited. Established in 1995.

• 1858 •
American College of Emergency Physicians
Dr. Dean Wilkerson Jr., Exec.Dir.
1125 Executive Cir.
Irving, TX 75038-2522
Phone: (972)550-0911
Toll-Free: 800-798-1822
Fax: (972)580-2816
E-mail: execdirector@acep.org
Home Page: http://www.acep.org

• 1859 • **Award for Outstanding Contributions in Research and Education**
To recognize a member who has made a significant contribution to either research in emergency medicine or to the educational aspects of the specialty. Any College member may nominate himself or another member for the award. A set of bookends featuring the recipient's name and the ACEP logo in brass is awarded annually at a convocation ceremony. Established in 1986.

• 1860 • **Council Meritorious Service Award**
To recognize a College member who has served as a councillor for three years and has made consistent contributions to the growth and maturation of the ACEP Council. A walnut plaque with the ACEP Council logo is awarded annually at the Council meeting. Established in 1986.

• 1861 • **James D. Mills Outstanding Contribution to Emergency Medicine**
To recognize a member, other than an officer of the Board of Directors, for significant contributions to emergency medicine. A walnut plaque with an etched portrait of the recipient is awarded annually when merited. Established in 1978. Formerly: Mills Award for Meritorious Service.

• 1862 • **John G. Wiegenstein Leadership Award**
To recognize outstanding contributions to the College by current or past national College leaders. A walnut plaque with an etched portrait of the recipient is awarded annually. Established in 1975. Formerly: Wiegenstein Award for Meritorious Service.

• 1863 •
American College of Forensic Examiners International
Robert L. O'Block PhD, Exec.Dir.
2750 E Sunshine
Springfield, MO 65804
Phone: (417)881-3818
Toll-Free: 800-423-9737
Fax: (417)881-4702
E-mail: cao@acfei.com
Home Page: http://www.acfei.com

• 1864 • **Eagle Award**
To recognize excellence in the field of forensic examination. Awarded annually with a trophy and plaque. Established in 1993.

• 1865 •
American College of Healthcare Executives
Thomas C. Dolan PhDCAE, Pres./CEO
1 N Franklin, Ste. 1700
Chicago, IL 60606-4425
Phone: (312)424-2800
Fax: (312)424-0023
E-mail: geninfo@ache.org
Home Page: http://www.ache.org

Formerly: (1986) American College of Hospital Administrators.

• 1866 • **Affiliated Group Award**
To recognize outstanding officially-designated health care executive groups and women's health care executive networks affiliated with the College. A monetary prize of $1,000 is awarded annually at the College's Congress on Healthcare Management. Established in 1992. Each group nominated by their Regent-at-Large receives a $500 award.

• 1867 • **Dean Conley Award**
To recognize writers who contributed to healthcare management literature and to encourage practitioners in the field to write. The best article is selected from those published during the qualifying period from one of the major magazines serving the health care management field. A plaque is awarded annually to publisher and recipient. Established in 1958. Formerly: (1966) ACHA Article Award.

• 1868 • **Gold Medal Award**
To recognize exceptional individuals who exemplify the highest standard and values of the health care profession and have demonstrated outstanding leadership and excellence in health care management. Practicing health care executives who are Fellows of the College are eligible. A medal, a plaque, and a citation are awarded annually at the Congress on Healthcare Management. Established in 1964.

• 1869 • **James A. Hamilton Award**
For recognition of an outstanding book on general management and/or healthcare management published during the qualifiying period. Nominations are accepted. A plaque is awarded annually. Established in 1958 and sponsored by the Alumni Association of the Graduate Program in Healthcare Administration at the University of Minnesota in honor of James A. Hamilton, its founder and director between 1946 and 1966. Formerly: James A. Hamilton Hospital Administrators' Book Award.

• 1870 • **Edgar C. Hayhow Award**
To recognize the author of an outstanding article published in the ACHE journal, *Journal of Healthcare Management*. A plaque is awarded annually at the time of the Congress on Healthcare Management. Established in 1960 in honor of Edgar C. Hayhow, the 14th chairman of the College and the first practicing administrator to earn a doctoral degree.

• 1871 • Health Management Research Award
To enhance managerial effectiveness and career opportunities in health services administration. College affiliates who are full-time faculty members of health administration programs are eligible. A monetary prize of $25,000 is awarded annually. Established in 1988 by monies from Foster G. McGaw, founder of the American Hospital Supply Corporation.

• 1872 • Honorary Fellowship
To recognize distinguished leaders who are not eligible to join the College but whose accomplishments have had a beneficial influence on some aspect of public health and/or the profession of health services administration. A citation and a pin are awarded each year during the convocation ceremony at the College's Congress on Healthcare Management.

• 1873 • Robert S. Hudgens Memorial Award - Young Healthcare Executive of the Year
To recognize an exceptional health care executive under 40 years of age and a Diplomate or Fellow of the College serving as a CEO or COO of a Health services organization. Nominations are accepted. A plaque is awarded annually. Established in 1969 by the Alumni Association of the Dept. Of Health Administration at Virginia Commonwealth University, in memory of Robert S. Hudgens, the College's first elected vice president. Formerly: Robert S. Hudgens Memorial Award - Young Hospital Administrator of the Year.

• 1874 • Management Innovation Poster Session Award
To recognize the poster that best illustrates excellence and innovation in the health care management field. Awards are presented annually at the Management Innovation Poster Session held during the Congress on Healthcare Management. Established in 1993.

• 1875 • Student Chapter Awards
To recognize student chapters of the College whose programs have, over the preceding convocation year, demonstrated the greatest advancement of graduating students in the College. Awards are presented to both undergraduate and graduate programs in the following areas when minimum advancement requirements are met: the student chapter with the greatest percentage of graduating students advancing in the College; the student chapter with the greatest percentage of graduating members, diplomates and fellow in the college; and the student chapter with the greatest number of members, diplomates, and fellows in the college. Plaques are awarded annually at the Congress on Healthcare Management. Established in 1994.

• 1876 • Student Essay Competition in Healthcare Management
To stimulate student thinking and writing about important issues and developments in the field of health care management. Student Associates enrolled in graduate and undergraduate health administration programs in the U.S. and Canada that sponsor student chapters of the College are eligible to submit essays. The following prizes are awarded to finalists in both graduate and undergraduate divisions: first place - $3,000 to the author, a plaque, publication of the author's essay in the College journal, and $1,000 to the author's program; second place - $2,000; and third place - $1,000. Awarded annually during the Congress on Healthcare Management. Established in 1989.

• 1877 •
American College of Legal Medicine
Theodore R. LeBlang, Pres.
1111 N Plaza Dr., Ste. 550
Schaumburg, IL 60173
Phone: (847)969-0283
Toll-Free: 800-433-9137
Fax: (847)517-7229
E-mail: info@aclm.org
Home Page: http://www.aclm.org

• 1878 • Hirsh Award
For recognition of outstanding student paper on legal medicine. Candidates must be currently enrolled in an accredited program in dentistry, podiatry, nursing, pharmacy, health science, or health care administration. A monetary award of $1,000 and the possible publication of the paper in the *Journal of Legal Medicine* is presented annually. Established in 1990 by Harold L. Hirsh and Jane Rose Hirsh.

• 1879 • Letourneau Award
For recognition of outstanding original student paper on legal medicine. Candidates must be currently enrolled in an accredited law school in the United States or Canada. A monetary award of $1,000 and the possible publication of the paper in the *Journal of Legal Medicine* is presented annually. Established in 1976 by the Board of Governors to honor Charles U. Letourneau.

• 1880 • Schwartz Award
For recognition of outstanding original student paper on legal medicine. Candidates must be currently enrolled in an accredited medical school in the United States or Canada. A monetary award of $1,000 and the possible publication of the paper in the *Journal of Legal Medicine* is presented annually. Established in 1976 to honor George Schwartz.

• 1881 •
American College of Medical Practice Executives
Sarah J. Holt PhD, Sec.-Treas.
104 Inverness Terr. E
Englewood, CO 80112-5306
Phone: (303)799-1111
Toll-Free: 877-275-6462
Fax: (303)643-4439
E-mail: acmpe@mgma.com
Home Page: http://www.mgma.com/acmpe

• 1882 • Administrator of the Year Award
To recognize a group practice administrator from an MGMA member group who has exhibited exceptional leadership and enhanced the effectiveness of health care delivery in his/her practice and community. This award is the administrator counterpart of the Physician Executive Award. A plaque is awarded when merited. Established in 1981. Formerly: Management Achievement Award.

• 1883 • Fred Graham Award for Innovation in Improving Community Health
Awarded to a medical group practice led by an ACMPE or MGMA member that has developed creative and innovative activities and solutions to advance the effectiveness of health care delivery and improved community health. The deadline is June 1.

• 1884 • Harry J. Harwick Lifetime Achievement Award
For recognition of a lifetime of achievement to medical practice management with particular emphasis on the advancement of medical group practice. Candidates must be health administration practitioners. Awarded annually. An award piece and public recognition is given When merited. Applications accepted until June 1. Established in 1976 to honor Harry J. Harwick, Mayo Clinic business manager and first group practice administrator.

• 1885 • Physician Executive Award
To recognize a physician executive in a medical group practice led by an ACMPE or MGMA member who has exhibited outstanding leadership through a recent noteworthy achievement. An award piece and public recognition is awarded when merited. Application deadline is June 1. Established in 1981. Formerly: Medical Executive Award.

• 1886 •
American College of Musicians
Gloria Castro, Chairperson
PO Box 1807
Austin, TX 78767
Phone: (512)478-5775
E-mail: ngpt@aol.com
Home Page: http://www.pianoguild.com

• 1887 • All Sonatina, All Sonata, All Bach Programs
To encourage serious piano students to play All Sonatina, All Sonata, and All Bach programs in the examinations which are held annually. There are five complete sonatina and sonata programs, while the Bach programs consist of 15 Bach compositions in the early Bach and/or advanced program. Students of a Guild teacher who enter the auditions are eligible. A certificate, pin, and plaque are awarded annually. Established in 1968.

• 1888 •
American College of Neuropsychiatrists
Louis E. Rentz, Exec.Dir.
28595 Orchard Lake Rd., Ste. 200
Farmington Hills, MI 48334
Phone: (248)553-0010
Fax: (248)553-0818
E-mail: acn-aconp@msn.com

• 1889 • Distinguished Fellow Award
Distinguished Fellows are those Fellows who have rendered singular, outstanding, and unique contributions of the highest order. Established in 1984.

• 1890 • Distinguished Service Award
This, the highest award bestowed by the Board of Governors of the College, recognizes members who have demonstrated, over time, outstanding accomplishments in service to the American College of Neuropsychiatrists. Established in 1984.

• 1891 • Honorary Distinguished Physicians Award
To recognize non-member physicians who have demonstrated singular, outstanding, and unique service in the promotion of the fields of neurology, psychiatry, or mental health. A plaque and travel expenses to attend the annual convention may be awarded annually. Established in 1984.

• 1892 • Honorary Distinguished Service Award
This, the highest non-member/non-physician award, recognizes non-member/non-physicians who have demonstrated outstanding, singular and unique service in the promotion of the fields of neurology, psychiatry, or mental health. Established in 1984.

• 1893 • Sydney M. Kanev Memorial Award
To recognize the resident physician writing the most outstanding paper in the fields of neurology or psychiatry. A $750 honorarium is awarded annually and flight and 1 night hotel expense paid to the annual convention at the annual meeting. Established in 1984. Sponsored by Bristol Myers.

• 1894 •
American College of Neuropsychopharmacology
545 Mainstream Dr., Ste. 110
Nashville, TN 37228
Phone: (615)324-2360
Fax: (615)324-2361
E-mail: acnp@acnp.org
Home Page: http://www.acnp.org

• 1895 • Daniel H. Efron Research Award
To recognize outstanding basic research contributions to neuropsychopharmacology. The contributions may be preclinical, or work which emphasizes the interface between basic and clinical research. The honoree must be a citizen of the United States, reside and work in the United States, and be under 45 years of age. A monetary award and a plaque are awarded annually. Established in 1974 by ACNP and the family of Daniel Efron.

• 1896 • Joel Elkes International Award
To recognize a young scientist under 45 years of age for an outstanding clinical contribution to psychopharmacology. The work may comprise clinical studies and may mark an empirical advance or a theoretical construct based on laboratory findings. The contribution may be based on a single discovery or a cumulative body of work. Of particular interest in selecting the awardee are contributions that further understanding of self-regulatory processes as they affect mental function and behavior in disease and well-being. Nominations are submitted by the international community of scientists. A monetary prize and a plaque are awarded annually at the ACNP Annual Meeting. Established in 1986.

• 1897 • Paul Hoch Distinguished Award
To recognize unusually significant contributions to ACNP by a member. A monetary award and a plaque are awarded when merited. Established in 1965 to honor Paul H. Hoch, M.D. (1902-1964), one of the founding members of the College.

• 1898 • Pfizer Minority Summer Fellowship Award
To promote and enhance the interest of minority graduate students and residents in careers in psychopharmacology and the neurosciences by providing the opportunity to work in the laboratory of the immediate past president of the ACNP for six to eight weeks. The deadline is April 1. Total value of the grant is $15,000. Awarded annually. Sponsored by Pfizer Inc.

• 1899 • Postdoctoral Fellowship Awards for Minorities
To encourage the development of young scientists who are ethnic and racial minorities and have demonstrated through their research, teaching, or clinical activities, professional and scientific interest in the field of neuropsychopharmacology. Five fellowships to attend the ACNP Annual Meeting, plus $100 for ground transportation expenses and $50 per day for meals, are awarded annually. Sponsored by the National Institute of Mental Health.

• 1900 • Young Investigator Memorial Travel Awards
To encourage the involvement and development of young teacher-scientists in neuropsychopharmacology through exposure to the members and scientific meetings of ACNP. Applicants must be nominated by their program director. Twenty stipends to attend the ACNP Annual Meeting, plus $100 for ground transportation expenses and $50 per day for meals, are awarded annually.

• 1901 •
American College of Nurse-Midwives
Deanne Williams, Exec. Dir.
8403 Colesville Rd., Ste. 1550
Silver Spring, MD 20910
Phone: (240)485-1800
Fax: (240)485-1818
E-mail: info@acnm.org
Home Page: http://www.midwife.org

• 1902 • Hattie Hemschemeyer Award
For recognition of achievement and contributions to the field of nurse-midwifery. The following criteria are considered: recent, innovative, creative endeavors in maternal-child health or nurse-midwifery clinical practice, education, administration, or research; continuous outstanding contributions or distinguished service to nurse-midwifery and/or MCH; and contributions of historical significance to the development and advancement of nurse-midwifery, the ACNM, or MCH. A "consistent symbol of the award" depicting maternal-child or family interaction is awarded annually at the convention. In addition, the recipient's name is entered on a permanent HHA plaque which is maintained at headquarters and the recipient receives travel expenses to the ACNM meeting. Established in 1976 in memory of Hattie Hemschemeyer, CNM, the first Board of Directors' president (1955-1957).

• 1903 •
American College of Occupational and Environmental Medicine
Barry S. Eisenberg, Exec.Dir.
1114 N Arlington Heights Rd.
Arlington Heights, IL 60004-4770
Phone: (847)818-1800
Fax: (847)818-9266
E-mail: acoeminfo@acoem.org
Home Page: http://www.acoem.org

Formed by merger of: American Occupational Medical Association; American Association of Industrial Physicians and Surgeons; American Academy of Occupational Medicine.

• 1904 • Corporate Health Achievement Award
To recognize an organization or individual for the excellence of an occupational health program, the imagination in its concept, its dynamic execution, and the active participation of management and the employees in the program. A citation is awarded annually. Established in 1948. Formerly: Corporate Health Achievement Award; (2003) Health Achievement in Occupational Medicine Award.

• 1905 • Adoph G. Kammer Merit in Authorship Award
To recognize the author(s) of a work published during the preceding year that is judged to be the most outstanding from the standpoint of originality, scientific merit, clarity, objectivity, and significant contribution to industrial medicine. An embossed scroll is awarded annually. Established in 1947.

• 1906 • Robert A. Kehoe Award of Merit
To recognize distinguished contributions to the development of the specialty of occupational medicine. A bronze plaque mounted on walnut is awarded annually in the fall. Established in 1956 and named for Robert A. Kehoe, M.D., a pioneer in the field of environmental medicine and a past president of the College from 1949-1950.

• 1907 • Knudsen Award
This, the highest honor in the field of occupational medicine, is given in recognition of a physician who has made an outstanding contribution to the field. Members of the Association who have attained distinction through one major contribution or through a continuing contribution in the field of research, administration, teaching, or practice are eligible. A bronze plaque is awarded annually. Established in 1939 by General William S. Knudsen, then president of General Motors Corporation.

• 1908 • Meritorious Service Award
To recognize an outstanding contribution to the Association by a member. An embossed scroll is awarded annually. Established in 1945.

• 1909 •
American College of Oral and Maxillofacial Surgeons
Daniel Lanka, Exec.Dir.
1710 Route 29
Galway, NY 12074
Phone: (518)882-6729
Toll-Free: 800-522-6676
Fax: (518)882-6730
E-mail: director@acoms.org
Home Page: http://www.acoms.org

• 1910 • Harry Archer Award
For recognition of contributions to the advancement of the profession of oral maxillofacial surgery. Nominations may be submitted to the ACOMS awards committee. A pyramidal trophy with an inscribed base is awarded when merited. Established in 1979 and first presented in 1982 in honor of W. Harry Archer, past professor of oral maxillofacial surgery at the University of Pittsburgh.

• 1911 • Humanitarian Award
To recognize humanitarian achievements. Recipients are nominated by members and then selected by a vote of the officers. A cast or etched bronze plaque mounted on a walnut panel is awarded when merited. Established in 1990.

• 1912 • Walter Lorenz Research Award
To recognize and encourage excellence in the medical and surgical research of the mouth, head, and neck. Residents of recognized oral/maxillofacial surgery, and otorhinolaryngology (ear, nose, and throat) training programs are eligible. Two or three monetary awards totaling $5,000 and a certificate are presented annually. Established in 1989 to honor Walter Lorenz. Additional information is available from Robert Green, Executive Director.

• 1913 • Scientific Poster Awards
To recognize and encourage excellence for research and innovation in head and neck surgery. Three cash awards are given for what are judged the three best posters addressing research and innovation relative to head and neck surgery. Posters are submitted from residents and displayed during the ACOMS' Annual Meeting.

• 1914 •
American College of Physicians
J. Fred Ralston Jr., Chm.
190 N Independence Mall W
Philadelphia, PA 19106
Phone: (215)351-2600
Toll-Free: 800-523-1546
Fax: (215)351-2759
E-mail: neilk@mail.acponline.org
Home Page: http://www.acponline.org

• 1915 • American College of Physicians Award
To recognize distinguished contributions in science as related to medicine. Scientists of any country and in any field, whether non-clinical or clinical, biochemical, biological, physical, or social are eligible. A honorarium of $250, a bronze medal, and a certificate are awarded at the annual convocation. Established in 1958.

• 1916 • American College of Physicians Distinguished Teacher Award
To recognize an individual who has demonstrated the ennobling qualities of a great teacher as judged by the acclaim and accomplishments of former students in the field of medical education. Candidates must be newly elected or previously elected Masters of the ACP. An honorarium of $250, a bronze medal, and a certificate are presented. Established in 1968.

• 1917 • James D. Bruce Memorial Award
To recognize distinguished contributions in preventive medicine. An honorarium of $250, a bronze medal, and a certificate are presented at the annual convocation. Awarded annually. Established in 1946.

• 1918 • Ralph O. Claypoole, Sr. Memorial Award
To recognize an outstanding practitioner of clinical internal medicine. An honorarium of $250, and a certificate are awarded when merited at the annual convocation. Established in 1979. Sponsored by a grant from Mr. Ralph O. Claypoole, Jr., in memory of his father.

• 1919 • Nicholas E. Davies Memorial Scholar Award for Scholarly Activities in Humanities and History of Medicine
To recognize outstanding contributions to humanism in medicine and for their scholarly activities in history, literature, philosophy, and ethics. A monetary prize of $5,000 and a certificate is awarded annually. Established in 1992.

• 1920 • Honorary Fellow
To recognize members of the medical profession in countries other than those in which the College has an established region or affiliate region. Individuals who, on account of personal character, positions of honor and influence, or eminence in internal medicine or an allied specialty, shall be recommended by the Awards. Committee to the Board of Regents. Honorary Fellows are elected by the Board of Regents. Recipients may use the letters F.A.C.P. (Hon.) after their names. A certificate for the recipient is awarded.

• 1921 • Joseph F. Boyle Award for Distinguished Public Service
Awarded to a current or former government official or a physician acting in an official capacity (state or federal, executive or legislative) who has provided outstanding public service toward improving the delivery of healthcare. Established in 1990. Deadline July 1.

• 1922 • Edward R. Loveland Memorial Award
To recognize distinguished contributions in the health field. Both lay person and lay organizations are eligible. A certificate is awarded. Established in 1961.

• 1923 • Masters
To recognize fellows who, because of personal character, positions of honor and influence, eminence in practice or in medical research, or other attainments in science or in the art of medicine, are recommended by the Awards. Committee to the Board of Regents. Masters may use the letters MACP in connection with scientific publications at professional and academic functions and in connection with their professional activities. A certificate is awarded.

• 1924 • William C. Menninger Memorial Award
To recognize distinguished contributions to the science of mental health. An honorarium of $250, a bronze medal, and a certificate are presented at the annual convocation. Established in 1967.

• 1925 • Outstanding Volunteer Clinical Teacher Award
To honor a Fellow of the American College of Physicians who has consistently volunteered his or her services to teach medical students and residents. This individual should have demonstrated outstanding teaching prowess, displayed exemplary characteristics of care and concern for individual patients at the bedside, and served as a role model and mentor. His or her qualities as a distinguished teacher should have been recognized previously, for example, by teaching awards or citations from the nominee's institution, medical students or residents, or the local Chapter of the American College of Physicians. Applicants must be volunteer teachers who have clinical faculty appointments at the rank of at least Clinical Associate Professor at medical schools. Applicants must also be gen-

eral internist or in a subspecialty of internal medicine. Established in 1997.

• 1926 • John Phillips Memorial Award
To recognize distinguished contributions in clinical medicine. An honorarium of $250, a bronze medal, and a certificate are presented during the annual convocation. Established in 1929.

• 1927 • Richard and Hinda Rosenthal Foundation Awards
Two awards are given by the Rosenthal Foundation: to recognize a young physician-scientist, clinician, or scientific group whose recent innovative work is making a notable contribution to improve clinical care in the field of internal medicine (oncology is not included); and to recognize a young individual or an organization whose recent original approach in the delivery of health care or in the design of facilities for its delivery will increase its clinical and/or economic effectiveness. The award in each category consists of $2,000 to cover all expenses incurred in attending the convocation where the awards are presented and an inscribed bronze plaque. Established in 1976. Sponsored by the Richard and Hinda Rosenthal Foundation.

• 1928 • Alfred Stengel Memorial Award
To recognize outstanding service to the College in an official capacity. The candidate must be a newly elected or previously elected Master of the ACP. An honorarium of $250, a bronze medal, and a certificate are presented. Established in 1947.

• 1929 •
American College of Preventive Medicine
Jordan Richland MPH, Exec.Dir.
1307 New York Ave. NW, No. 200
Washington, DC 20005
Phone: (202)466-2044
Fax: (202)466-2662
E-mail: info@acpm.org
Home Page: http://www.acpm.org

• 1930 • Distinguished Service Award
To recognize and honor a member or fellow of the American College of Preventive Medicine for outstanding service to the college. A plaque and travel expenses are awarded annually at the PREVENTION meeting. Established in 1971.

• 1931 • Resident Award
To acknowledge and honor outstanding achievement of a resident in some or all of the following areas; community service, scholarship, research, training and overall leadership. Evidence of strong potential for future contributions to the field of preventive medicine required. A monetary award of $500 is presented annually.

• 1932 • Rising Star Award
To acknowledge and honor outstanding achievement of an ACPM member within seven years of completion of residency in some or all of the following areas; community service, scholarship, research, training and overall leadership. Evidence of commitment to preventive medicine and the potential to make a substantial impact and significant contributions to the field of preventive medicine and its organizations required.

• 1933 • Special Recognition Award
To recognize and honor outstanding achievement in and contributions to the field of preventive medicine. Awardee must be a physician or other scientist who has made contributions to humanity in research, teaching, or service. A plaque and travel expenses are awarded annually at the PREVENTION meeting. Established in 1970. Formerly: Honorary Fellowship.

• 1934 •
The American College of Psychiatrists
Charles F. Reynolds III, Pres.
732 Addison St., Ste. C
Berkeley, CA 94710
Phone: (510)704-8020
Fax: (510)704-0113
E-mail: aliceacp@aol.com
Home Page: http://www.acpsych.org

• 1935 • The (ACP) American College of Psychiatrists Bowis Award
To recognize outstanding contributions to and leadership in the College. A gold medal and a certificate are awarded each year at the annual meeting of The College. Established in 1963. Nominations deadline June 30. Open only to members of the college.

• 1936 • The (ACP) American College of Psychiatrists Dean Award
For recognition of research in schizophrenia. A $5,000 grant and a commemorative certificate are awarded annually. Established in 1962. Nominations deadline November 1.

• 1937 • The American College of Psychiatrists Award for Creativity in Psychiatric Education
For recognition of a teaching program which demonstrates creativity in psychiatric education. A $5000 grant and commemorative certificate are awarded annually. Nomination deadline is April 1.

• 1938 • The American College of Psychiatrists Distinguished Service Award in Psychiatry
For recognition of outstanding achievement and leadership in the field of psychiatry. A gold medal and a certificate are awarded at the annual meeting of The College. Established in 1963. Nominations deadline June 30. Formerly: (1983) E.B. Bowis Award.

• 1939 •
American College of Radiology
Harvey L. Neiman MD, Exec.Dir.
1891 Preston White Dr.
Reston, VA 20191-4397
Phone: (703)648-8900
Toll-Free: 800-ACR-LINE
Fax: (703)295-6773
E-mail: info@acr.org
Home Page: http://www.acr.org

• 1940 • Certificates of Honor and Appreciation
To recognize assistance to the American College of Radiology, usually in its educational programs. Certificates are awarded intermittently.

• 1941 • Gold Medal
To recognize an individual for distinguished and extraordinary service to the American College of Radiology or to the discipline of radiology. Service to radiology can be in teaching, basic research, clinical investigation, or radiologic statesmanship, such as outstanding contributions in work with the ACR, other medical organizations, governmental agencies, and quasi-medical organizations. The deadline for nominations by members is July 1. Not more than three gold medals may be awarded each year at the Convocation at the annual meeting. Established in 1923.

• 1942 • Honorary Fellow
To recognize preeminent contributions to the science or practice of radiology by individuals who are ineligible for admission as members of the College. Nominations must be submitted by a fellow of the College. The deadline is July 1. No more than three awards may be made each year. A certificate is awarded.

• 1943 • Radiology News Awards Competition
To recognize outstanding stories about the use of imaging devices and radiation to diagnose or treat disease. Entries are judged on the basis of originality, objectivity, and clarity. Stories published or broadcast during the preceding year must be submitted by February 1. Broadcast journalists should include a script if possible. First place awards of $750, and second place awards of $250 are presented in the following categories: print media (including science and general publications) and broadcast media. Established in 1980. Sponsored by the American College of Radiology, the Radiological Society of North America, the American Roentgen Ray Society, and the American Society for Therapeutic Radiology and Oncology.

• 1944 •
American College of Surgeons
Thomas R. Russell MD, Exec.Dir.
633 N Saint Clair St.
Chicago, IL 60611-3211
Phone: (312)202-5000
Toll-Free: 800-621-4111
Fax: (312)202-5001
E-mail: postmaster@facs.org
Home Page: http://www.facs.org

• 1945 • **American College of Surgeons Faculty Fellowship**
Assists in the development of new independent research programs. Ten fellowships are awarded including the : Franklin H. Martin, MD, FACS, Faculty Research Fellowship of the American College of Surgeons, and the C. James Carrico Faculty Research fellowship for the study of trauma. The fellowship is restricted to surgeons who have: completed the chief residency year or accredited fellowship training within the preceding three years and received a full-time faculty appointment in a department of surgery or a surgical specialty at a medical school accredited by the Liasion Committee on Medical Education in the United States or by the Committee for Accreditation of Canadian Medical Schools in Canada. Must be Fellows or Associate Fellows of the college.

• 1946 • **Australia/New Zealand Chapter Traveling Fellowship**
Applicants must be fellows of the college who hold full-time academic appointments in Canada or the United States and be under the age of 45 on the date the application is filed. The award is for attending the Annual Scientific Congress of the Royal Australasian College of Surgeons and visiting at least two medical centers in Australia and New Zealand. Awarded annually.

• 1947 • **George H. A. Clowes, Jr., M.D., F.A.C.S. Memorial Research Career Development Award**
Provide support for promising a young surgical investigator. Surgeons who have completed their specialty training in a residency or an accredited fellowship in general surgery or a surgical specialty within the preceding five years and received a full-time faculty appointment at an accredited medical school are eligible. A detailed research plan; a proposed five-year budget; approximately 400 word cover letter detailing objective, how it will achieved, and research protocal must be submitted. Applications must be submitted by August 1. The award consists of a grant of $40,000 for each of the five years and is not renewable thereafter. Sponsored by the Clowes Fund.

• 1948 • **Faculty Career Development Award for Toncology of the Head and Neck**
Supports clinical, basic science, or traditional research in the study of neoplastic disease of the head and neck. Surgeons who are members in good standing of the college and the American Head and Neck Society; completed specialty training within the previous five years; and have received full time faculty appointment at a medical school accredited by the Liaison Committee on Medical Education in the United States or the Committee for Accreditation of Canadian Medical School in Canada. Proof of research must be submitted. Recipients of current major research grants are not eligible. $ 40,000 per year for two years is awarded. Not offered annually. Please contact college to ask about the next deadline.

• 1949 • **International Guest Scholarships**
Provides an opportunity to visit clinical, teaching and research activities in North America and to participate in educational offerings of the clinical Congress. Competent young surgeons demonstrating an interest in teaching and research are eligible. Scholarships of $8,000 are awarded for visiting clinical, teaching, and research facilities. Applicants must be surgeons between the ages of 30 and 42. Application deadline is July 1.

• 1950 • **Resident Research Scholarship**
Assists the development of a new and independent research program. Surgeons who have completed two postdoctoral years in an accredited surgical training program in the United States or Canada at the time the scholarship is awarded and will not have completed residency for the following two years are eligible. The $30,000 scholarship is awarded for two years, and acceptance of it requires commitment for the two year period. The total amount is to support the research of the recipient and is not to diminish or replace the usual or expected compensation or benefits of the recipient. Application deadline is September 1st.

• 1951 •
American Comparative Literature Association
Kevin Carney, Admin.Asst.
University of Texas at Austin
Program in Comparative Literature
1 University Station B5003
Austin, TX 78712-0196
Phone: (512)471-8020
Fax: (512)471-8878
E-mail: info@acla.org
Home Page: http://www.acla.org

• 1952 • **Harry Levin Prize**
For recognition of the most significant book or monograph in literary history or interpretation. The deadline for submission is December 1. A plaque is awarded biennially when merited. The prize is awarded alternately with the Rene Wellek Prize. Established in 1977.

• 1953 • **Rene Wellek Prize**
For recognition of the most significant book or monograph in literary theory or the history of criticism. The deadline for submission is December 1. A plaque is awarded biennially when merited. Established in 1977. The prize is awarded alternately with the Harry Levin Prize.

• 1954 •
American Composers Alliance
Jasna Radonjic, Exec.Dir.
648 Broadway, Rm. 803
New York, NY 10012
Phone: (212)362-8900
Phone: (212)925-0458
Fax: (212)925-6798
E-mail: info@composers.com
Home Page: http://www.composers.com

• 1955 • **Laurel Leaf Award**
To recognize individuals or organizations for distinguished achievement in fostering and encouraging American music. A parchment scroll is awarded annually. Established in 1951.

• 1956 •
American Concrete Institute
William R. Tolley, Exec.VP
PO Box 9094
Farmington Hills, MI 48333-9094
Phone: (248)848-3700
Fax: (248)848-3701
E-mail: bill.tolley@concrete.org
Home Page: http://www.aci-int.org

• 1957 • **ACI Commemorative Lecture Series**
To provide a guest lecturer for the Opening Session of the ACI Fall Convention. The lecture subjects are chosen by the speaker and can relate to the entire range of institute interest. The speaker is selected each year by a committee of the Board of Direction. A plaque is awarded annually. Established in 1972 to honor Raymond E. Davis, noted teacher and researcher in concrete technology, and a past president and Honorary Member of the Institute. Re-established in 1988 to honor Professor Phil M. Ferguson, noted teacher, author, and researcher in concrete, and a past president and Honorary Member of the Institute. Re-established in 1998 on a multi-year cycle named to commemorate prominent deceased members. Formerly: (1987) Raymond E. Davis Lecture Series.

• 1958 • **ACI Construction Award**
For recognition of a paper of outstanding merit on concrete construction practice published by the American Concrete Institute. The award is not restricted to members of the Institute. The award is presented as a plaque. It may be awarded annually, but not necessarily. Established in 1944.

• 1959 • **ACI Design Award**
For recognition of advanced concepts and techniques applied to a specific design practice or project. A certificate is given to the author(s) of the paper and to the engineer or engineering firm responsible for design. The award need not be presented each year. Established in 1981. Formerly: (1997) Maurice P. van Buren Structural Engineering Award.

• 1960 • ACI Fellows
At the time of nomination, a Fellow shall have been a Member of the Institute, or a representative of an Organizational or Sustaining Member of the Institute, for at least ten years, including three of the last five years. A Fellow shall have made outstanding contributions to the production or use of concrete materials, products, and structures in the areas of education, research, development, design, construction, or management. In addition, a Fellow shall have made significant contributions to ACI through committees and/or local chapters. A Fellow shall retain that membership rank as long as membership in the Institute is maintained or until elected an Honorary Member.

• 1961 • Arthur R. Anderson Award
For recognition of outstanding contributions to the advancement of knowledge of concrete as a construction material. Individuals, firms, corporations, or organizations are eligible for the award. The award is a silver medal. It may be awarded annually, but not necessarily. Established in 1972.

• 1962 • Delmar L. Bloem Distinguished Service Award
To recognize noteworthy work on ACI technical committees. The award is given to a current (or recent) chairman of a technical committee or, under special circumstances, to deserving individuals other than committee chairmen in recognition of outstanding performance. Awarded as merited, usually annually. Established in 1969.

• 1963 • Chapter Activities Award
To recognize outstanding service in the promotion and development of a chapter or chapters by a member of the American Concrete Institute. A plaque is awarded as merited. Established in 1975.

• 1964 • Chester Paul Siess Award for Excellence in Structural Research
To recognize the author(s) of a peer-reviewed paper published by the Institute in the period subsequent to the last award that describes a notable achievement in experimental or analytical research related to structural engineering and, most importantly, recommends how the research can be applied to design. The award need not be presented each year. Established in 1972. At least one of the authors must be an ACI member. Formerly: Raymond C. Reese Structural Research Award.

• 1965 • Roger H. Corbetta Concrete Constructor Award
To recognize an individual or an organization who, or which, as a constructor, has made significant contributions as a constructor to progress in methods of concrete construction. The award is a plaque. The award need not be presented each year. Established in 1972.

• 1966 • Honorary Member
To recognize individuals of eminence in the field, or those who perform extraordinary meritorious service to the Institute. Awarded annually. Established in 1926.

• 1967 • Joe W. Kelly Award
For recognition of outstanding contributions to education in the broad field of concrete. A plaque may be awarded annually. Established in 1974 in honor of Joe W. Kelly, a past president of the Institute.

• 1968 • Henry L. Kennedy Award
For recognition of outstanding technical or administrative service to the Institute. Members are eligible. A certificate is awarded annually. Established in 1958 to honor Henry L. Kennedy, an active member who was a past president and, at the time of his death, chairman of the Institute's Building Committee.

• 1969 • Alfred E. Lindau Award
For recognition of outstanding contributions to reinforced concrete design practice. A bronze plaque bearing a bas-relief portrait of Mr. Lindau may be awarded annually. Established in 1947 by the Concrete Reinforcing Steel Institute to honor Alfred E. Lindau, a past president of the Institute.

• 1970 • Henry C. Turner Medal
For recognition of notable achievements in, or service to, the concrete industry. The award is not restricted to members of the institute nor to the achievements of any particular period. The award is a certificate and medal and need not be presented each year. Established in 1927.

• 1971 • Wason Medal for Materials Research
The award is bestowed on a member or members of the Institute reporting, in a peer-reviewed paper published by the Institute, original research work on concrete materials and their use, or a discovery that advances the state of knowledge of materials used in the construction industry. The award is restricted to members of the Institute, although all authors are eligible if any author is an ACI member. The award is a bronze medal and may not be given annually. Established in 1917.

• 1972 • Wason Medal for the Most Meritorious Paper
For recognition of the author(s) of the most meritorious paper published by the American Concrete Institute. All original papers are eligible. The award is a bronze medal and is awarded annually. At least one author must be an ACI member. Established in 1917.

• 1973 • Charles S. Whitney Medal
For recognition of noteworthy engineering development work in concrete design or construction. Firms, agencies, and individuals are eligible. A bronze medal may be awarded annually. Established in 1961 by Ammann and Whitney, Construction Engineers.

• 1974 • Cedric Willson Award
The Award is given for outstanding contributions in the areas of innovative materials and design, especially in lightweight concrete, and lightweight concrete masonry. Individuals, firms, and organizations are eligible. The award is a plaque and need not be given annually. Established in 1976 by the Northeast Texas Chapter of the Institute.

• 1975 •
American Concrete Institute - New Jersey Chapter
Dianne Johnston, Exec.Dir.
25 Ireland Brook Dr.
RR No. 4
North Brunswick, NJ 08902
Phone: (732)940-1803
Fax: (732)940-1804
E-mail: djnjaci@aol.com
Home Page: http://www.njaci.com

• 1976 • NJACI Merit Award
For graduating senior with highest performance in the area of concrete structures and technology at Rutgers U., Princeton U, NJIT and Stevens Inst. of Tech. Monetary award bestowed annually.

• 1977 •
American Concrete Pipe Association
John J. Duffy, Pres.
222 W. Las Colinas Blvd., Ste. 641
Irving, TX 75039-5423
Phone: (972)506-7216
Fax: (972)506-7682
E-mail: info@concrete-pipe.org
Home Page: http://www.concrete-pipe.org

• 1978 • Award of Merit
For recognition and appreciation of distinguished and outstanding technical contributions in the advancement of precast concrete pipe standards, design, and performance. A plaque is awarded annually. Formerly: .

• 1979 • Booster Award
For recognition and encouragement of membership recruiting. Members are eligible. A plaque is awarded annually. Formerly: .

• 1980 • Richard C. Longfellow Award
For recognition of an article in *Concrete Pipe News* that contributes most effectively to a better understanding of the uses of concrete pipe. Members are eligible. A plaque and clock are awarded annually. Formerly: (1976) Reporter of the Year Award; (1997) Longfellow Award.

• 1981 • Outstanding Service Award
For recognition and appreciation of individuals who have made distinguished and outstanding contributions to the precast concrete pipe through the publication of technical information benefiting the entire industry. A plaque is awarded annually. Formerly: (1997) American Concrete Pipe Association Award of Excellence.

Awards are arranged in alphabetical order below their administering organizations

• 1982 •
American Congress of Rehabilitation Medicine
Ric Morgan MBA, Exec.Dir.
6801 Lake Plz. Dr., No. B-205
Indianapolis, IN 46220-4049
Phone: (317)915-2250
Fax: (317)915-2245
E-mail: acrm@acrm.org
Home Page: http://www.acrm.org

• 1983 • **Bernard M. Baruch Essay Award For Students**
For recognition of an outstanding essay by a student pertaining to the field of physical medicine and rehabilitation. Topics must reflect the interdisciplinary character of rehabilitation. Essays may not exceed 3,000 words. The deadline for submissions is March 1. The following prizes are awarded: first prize - $200 and the Baruch Medal; second prize - $100; and third prize - $50. Awarded annually.

• 1984 • **John Stanley Coulter Memorial Lecturer**
To recognize an author and inspiring leader in the field of physical medicine. Nominations must be postmarked no later than January 10. A monetary prize of $250, a plaque, and travel expenses to present a lecture at the annual session of the Congress are awarded annually. Deadline: May 1. Established in 1951.

• 1985 • **Distinguished Member Award**
To honor those who have contributed to the development and functioning of the organization; demonstrated evidence of leadership skills, organizational abilities, and/or public service; and shown a dedication to the objectives of ACRM. The recipient must be an ACRM member. Nominations must be postmarked no later than April 1. Awarded annually. Established in 1988.

• 1986 • **Essay Contest for Professionals in Rehabilitation**
For recognition of an outstanding review article on a subject related to physical medicine and rehabilitation with an interdisciplinary focus. Manuscripts may not exceed 5,000 words. The deadline for submissions is March 1. A monetary prize of $200 is awarded annually. Established in 1953.

• 1987 • **Gold Key Award**
To recognize and honor those members of the medical and allied professions who have rendered extraordinary service to the cause of rehabilitation medicine. Nominations must be postmarked by January 10. An inscribed gold medal with the seal of the Congress is awarded annually. Established in 1932.

• 1988 • **Annual Conrad Jobst Foundation Award**
To recognize a physician or member of the allied health professions who has written the best scientific paper pertaining to the field of peripheral vascular disease or circulation in the extremities. Work not previously published is eligible. Manuscripts may not exceed 5,000 words. The deadline for submissions is March 1. A monetary award of $250 and a plaque are awarded annually.

• 1989 • **Edward W. Lowman Award**
To recognize an individual whose career reflects an energetic promotion of the spirit of interdisciplinary rehabilitation. The recipient must be an ACRM member. Nominations must be postmarked no later than April 1. Established in 1987 to honor Edward W. Lowman, M.D., who recognized the importance of all members of the multidisciplinary rehabilitation team during his career.

• 1990 •
American Congress on Surveying and Mapping
Curtis W. Sumner, Exec.Dir.
6 Montgomery Village Ave., Ste .403
Gaithersburg, MD 20879
Phone: (240)632-9716
Fax: (240)632-1321
E-mail: curtis.sumner@acsm.net
Home Page: http://www.acsm.net/

• 1991 • **ACA Honors Award**
To recognize individuals for outstanding contributions to cartography. Awarded occasionally when merited. Established in 1979.

• 1992 • **ACA Outstanding Achievement Award**
To recognize outstanding achievement in the field of cartography. Members of ACA are eligible. A framed certificate is awarded. Established in 1982.

• 1993 • **ACSM Map Design Competition Awards**
The following awards are presented: (1) Awards for Outstanding Achievement in Cartographic Design - to promote concern for map design and to recognize significant advances in cartography. Certificates and Exhibition at ACSM Annual Convention and conventions of other professional organizations are awarded. Maps become part of the U.S. Library of Congress permanent collection; (2) R.R. Donnelley & Sons Co. Awards to recognize the best student entries in the ACSM Map Design Competition on the basis of overall design, impression, use of color, and achievement of stated design objectives. One award is given to a student from an academic program and one to a student from a technical program. Entries may be submitted by February 15. A monetary award of $100 and a certificate are awarded in each category; and (3) Rand McNally Awards - to recognize the best student entries. Sponsored by Rand McNally Company and R. R. Donnelley and Sons Company.

• 1994 • **American Cartographic Association Scholarship Award**
To recognize outstanding cartography and mapping sciences students and to encourage the completion of an undergraduate program and/or the pursuit of graduate education in cartography or other mapping sciences. Any person who is a full-time student of junior or senior standing enrolled in a cartography or other mapping sciences curriculum, in a 4-year degree granting institution, is eligible. Previous candidates can be renominated in succeeding years. Any ACSM member may nominate a qualified student with appropriate documentation. Students may nominate themselves by completing the standard ACSM-ASPRS Fellowship or Scholarship Awards Application. The ACA Awards Committee selects the Scholarship recipient from among those nominated. A monetary prize of $1,000 and an appropriate certificate are presented at the annual meeting. Established in 1986.

• 1995 • **Awards for Outstanding Achievements in Cartographic Design**
To recognize outstanding cartographic design. Awarded annually. Established in 1990.

• 1996 • **Berntsen Scholarship in Surveying**
To provide financial assistance to a full-time undergraduate student pursuing a four-year degree in surveying. Any person who is enrolled in a four-year degree program in surveying may apply for this scholarship by January 1. Selection is based on appraisal of the applicant's (1) justification of award; (2) educational plan; (3) academic performance and standing; (4) potential for development; and (5) financial need. A scholarship of $500 is awarded. Sponsored by Berntsen International, Inc. of Madison, Wisconsin.

• 1997 • **Earle J. Fennell Award**
To recognize outstanding contributions to surveying and mapping science education. Members of ACSM or ASP who have worked in any of the education fields, such as baccalaureate, technical, continuing education, or independent study are eligible. The recipient may or may not be a professional educator. The nominee should have a sustained record of performance in education extending over at least 10 years at the local, state, or national level. A plaque is awarded.

• 1998 • **Honorary Member**
To honor the leaders in surveying and mapping science. Any person who has attained outstanding national or international recognition by contributions to the surveying and mapping profession may be elected by the Board of Direction. A plaque is awarded.

• 1999 • **Leica Surveying Scholarships**
To provide financial assistance to undergraduate students studying surveying at schools with two-or four-year degree programs in surveying or a related field. Applications may be submitted by January 1. Two monetary awards of $1,000 each are presented. Formerly: Wild Heerbrugg Surveying Scholarships; Wild-Leitz Surveying Scholarships.

• 2000 • Andrew McNally Award
To recognize the author of the paper published by ACSM which does the most to promote the theory and practice of cartography. Papers published in any ACSM publication during the calendar year immediately preceding the ACSM Annual Convention may be submitted. A $200 honorarium is awarded annually. Established in 1970. Sponsored by Rand McNally & Company.

• 2001 • National Geographic Society Award
To recognize the best computer assisted map design or mapping project by a student. Awarded annually. Established in 1988.

• 2002 • Outstanding Paper in Surveying
To recognize the author of the paper published by ACSM which does the most to promote the theory and practice of surveying. Established in 1986. Sponsored by Thorpe Smith.

• 2003 • Presidential Citations for Exceptional Service
To recognize and honor exceptional service to ACSM. A certificate is awarded.

• 2004 • Schonstedt Scholarship in Surveying
To provide for undergraduate study in surveying. Students who have completed at least two years of a four-year curriculum leading to a degree in surveying may apply by January 1. A scholarship of $1,500 is awarded. Sponsored by Schonstedt Instrument Company of Reston, Virginia.

• 2005 • Sustaining Members Twenty-Year Awards
To honor long-term Sustaining Members who complete twenty years of membership in ACSM. A plaque is awarded.

• 2006 • *Time* Magazine Award for Outstanding Map Design on Current Events
To recognize outstanding map design on current events. Awarded annually. Established in 1980.

• 2007 • Wild Heerbrugg Geodetic Fellowship
To encourage qualified candidates to pursue graduate education in geodesy and to promote the development of geodetic science. Competition is open to any member of the Congress on Surveying and Mapping or the American Society for Photogrammetry and Remote Sensing or any regular student of an accredited school who is sponsored by a member of the American Congress on Surveying and Mapping or the American Society for Photogrammetry and Remote Sensing. Every applicant must have completed at least one undergraduate course in surveying or photogrammetry prior to the receipt of the fellowship. The applications are judged on the following criteria: (1) previous academic record; (2) applicant's statement of his or her study objectives; (3) applicability of previous courses to graduate work in geodesy; (4) recommendation of faculty member; and (5) financial need. The deadline for application is January 15. A $4,000 fellowship is awarded annually for graduate study at an accredited school of his or her choice. Sponsored by Wild Heerbrugg Instruments, Inc.

• 2008 •
American Consulting Engineers Council
David A. Raymond, Pres.
1015 15th St. NW, Ste. 802
Washington, DC 20005
Phone: (202)347-7474
Fax: (202)898-0068
E-mail: acec@acec.org
Home Page: http://www.acec.org

• 2009 • Engineering Excellence Awards
For recognition of engineering achievements demonstrating the highest degree of merit and ingenuity and providing a major contribution to technical, economic and social advancement. Any firm engaged in the private practice of consulting engineering is eligible to enter the contest whether or not the firm is an ACEC member. Both member and non-member entries must be submitted to the ACEC national competition through a member organization. Engineering achievements which have won awards in other state or national organizations' design awards programs may be entered. Projects entered in the competition may have been executed anywhere in the world. Research studies must have been publicly disclosed by the client. Construction of projects must have been substantially completed and in use. Entries in the national competition may deal with any one of the following categories: (1) Studies, Research, Consulting Engineering Services; (2) Building and Structures (3) Support Systems; (4) Energy Production/Conservation; (5) Environmental; (6) Water Resources; (7) Transportation; and (8) Special Projects. A Steuben glass piece is awarded for the Grand Conceptor Award that may come from any of the categories and is the top national winner. Honor Awards may be presented to other selected entries of superior quality. The top projects in the other categories may, upon the judges' discretion, be designated as Grand Awards, in lieu of Honor Awards. Awarded annually. Established in 1968.

• 2010 • Fellows Distinguished Award of Merit
For recognition of an outstanding contribution to engineering, pure or applied science, or engineering and scientific education. Established in 1952.

• 2011 •
American Contact Dermatitis Society
Kathryn A. Zug MD, Pres.
138 Palm Coast Pkwy. NE, No. 333
Palm Coast, FL 32137
Phone: (386)437-4405
Fax: (386)437-4427
E-mail: info@contactderm.org
Home Page: http://www.contactderm.org

• 2012 • ACDS Mentoring Award
Recognition is given to medical residents and fellows.

• 2013 • Alexander A. Fisher Resident Award
A monetary award for resident or medical student.

• 2014 • Howard Maibach Travel Award
Financial award for investigators outside U.S

• 2015 •
American Contract Bridge League
Mr. J. Baum, CEO
2990 Airways Blvd.
Memphis, TN 38116-3847
Phone: (901)332-5586
Toll-Free: 800-467-1623
Fax: (901)398-7754
E-mail: service@acbl.org
Home Page: http://www.acbl.org

• 2016 • $1000 King of Bridge Award
Bestowed to a graduating high school senior with the best record at bridge. One scholarship is awarded annuallly.

• 2017 • Homer Shoop $5000 Preteen 10-Year Maturity Bond Certificate
Recognizes the best achievement in bridge. ACBL members 12 or younger are eligible. One scholarship is awarded annually.

• 2018 • Youth Flight
Recognizes each member of pair with highest score in September ACBL-Wide I Instant Matchpoint Game. A $ 500 scholarship is awarded annually.

• 2019 •
American Coon Hunters Association
Opal Johnston, Sec.-Treas.
20217 N State Hwy. 21
Cadet, MO 63630
Phone: (573)438-3527
Fax: (573)438-3527

• 2020 • ACHA World Champion Coonhound
To promote coonhounds and coonhound competition hunting, and to preserve the raccoon and its habitat. Twenty trophies are awarded annually. Established in 1948.

• 2021 •
American Correctional Association
James A. Gondles, Exec.Dir.
4380 Forbes Blvd.
Lanham, MD 20706
Phone: (301)918-1800
Toll-Free: 800-222-5646
Fax: (301)918-1886
E-mail: jeffw@aca.org
Home Page: http://www.aca.org/

• 2022 • **E. R. Cass Correctional Achievement Award**

To recognize outstanding contributions in the field of corrections. Active members of the Association of five years' standing are eligible. Nominations are due December 1. A medallion and life membership are awarded annually at the ACA Congress of Correction. Established in 1963 to honor Edward R. Cass, a longtime general secretary of the Association.

• 2023 • **Community Service Award**

To recognize an ACA chapter or affiliate that has made significant contributions in community service. Nominations must name projects that have met the following criteria: targeted a community activity in need of assistance, enhancement, support, etc., or a population in need of substantial assistance; accomplished assistance or work through the direct involvement of the state association or by staff of the member agency. At least some portion of the agency's involvement must be on a purely voluntary basis. Nominations due June 1. Award presented at the Winter Conference. Established in 1996.

• 2024 • **Corrections Film Festival**

To recognize the producers of films on topics in the correctional field from three categories: in-house production, professional production, and special interest category, e.g., public special announcement. Plaques are presented annually at the ACA Congress of Correction. Established in 1977.

• 2025 • **Exemplary Offender Program Award**

To honor a deserving program serving adult or juvenile offenders, to broaden the knowledge of successful program interventions throughout ACA and to recognize annually an outstanding correctional program. The program should be successful in one or more of the following areas: reducing the offender rate of return; increasing offenders' educational levels; increasing the marketability for employment of released offenders; increasing the cognitive and life skills of offenders; and integrating family into treatment. Awarded annually. Established in 1996.

• 2026 • **Martin Luther King, Jr. Scholarship Award**

To assist a minority nominee who has demonstrated a need and willingness to participate in "self-help" programs in order to continue an educational mission toward a college education or graduate training. Nominations must be submitted by June 1. A scholarship of $1,000 is presented at the Association's winter conference. Established in 1989 to honor the late Dr. Martin Luther King, Jr., who fought for the freedom and upward mobility of all people.

• 2027 • **Peter P. Lejins Research Award**

To recognize an individual for research in the field of corrections. ACA members who have been active for more than three years are eligible. Nominations must be submitted by June 1. Awarded annually at the ACA Winter Conference. Established in 1989 in honor of Peter P. Lejins, a past president of ACA and professor emeritus at the University of Maryland, College Park, in recognition of his commitment and dedication to the ACA.

• 2028 • **Medal of Valor Award**

To recognize corrections professionals who have gone beyond the call of duty and exhibited extreme bravery and courage either on or off the job. Nominations must be submitted by June 1. Awarded annually at the ACA winter conference. Established in 1989.

• 2029 • **Outstanding Journalism Award**

To recognize the editor or news director of the media outlet viewed by ACA as having done the most in the past year to increase public knowledge about corrections issues. The award is open to professional journalists of all categories. Eligible pieces may encompass any area of corrections and entail ongoing coverage of correctional issues over a long period of time, a series of pieces, or a single piece. Submitted materials must have been released within three years of nomination. Award presented at Winter Conference.

• 2030 •
American Cotswold Record Association
Vicki Rigel, Sec.Treas.
PO Box 59
Plympton, MA 02367
Phone: (781)585-2026
Fax: (781)585-2026
E-mail: orionacres@aol.com

• 2031 • **Premier Breeder at the North American International Livestock Exposition**

To recognize contributions made by Cotswold breeders on behalf of the breed. A prize is awarded annually. Established in 1985.

• 2032 • **Top Ranking Cotswold Breeder's Young Flock at the Illinois State Fair**

To encourage purebred Cotswold breeders. Breeders must raise Cotswolds and show them at the Illinois State Fair to be eligible. A trophy is awarded annually. Established in 1981.

• 2033 •
American Council of Christian Churches
Dr. Ralph Colas Jr., Exec.Sec.
PO Box 5455
Bethlehem, PA 18015
Phone: (610)865-3009
Fax: (610)865-3033
E-mail: accc@juno.com

• 2034 • **College Awards**

To encourage professional development. Senior ministerial students are eligible. A monetary award and a plaque are awarded annually. Established in 1986.

• 2035 • **Contender's Award**

To honor those who have contributed to the furtherance of the gospel and the Fundamentalist Movement. A plaque is awarded annually. Established in 1975.

• 2036 •
American Council of Learned Societies
Barbara Martinez Henning, Exec. Asst.
633 3rd Ave.
New York, NY 10017-6795
Phone: (212)697-1505
Fax: (212)949-8058
E-mail: info@acls.org
Home Page: http://www.acls.org

• 2037 • **American Council of Learned Societies Fellowships**

To provide support for postdoctoral research in the humanities and related social sciences, post and predoctoral research on Eastern Europe and in China, and dissertation work in American art history.

• 2038 •
American Council of the Blind
Melanie Brunson, Exec.Dir.
1155 15th St. NW, Ste. 1004
Washington, DC 20005
Phone: (202)467-5081
Toll-Free: 800-424-8666
Fax: (202)467-5085
E-mail: info@acb.org
Home Page: http://www.acb.org

• 2039 • **Robert S. Bray Award**

To recognize outstanding achievement in extending library service, access to published materials, or the improvement of communication devices and techniques for the blind. Awarded occasionally. Established in 1975.

• 2040 • **George Card Award**

To honor an outstanding blind or visually impaired person who has made noteworthy contributions to the welfare of his fellow blind. A certificate is awarded occasionally. Established in 1968.

• 2041 • **Ned E. Freeman Writing Award**

To recognize the author of the best article written and published in either the *Braille Forum*, or in a chapter newsletter (nominated by the newsletter editor). A monetary prize and a certificate are awarded annually at the Council's national convention. Established in 1970.

• 2042 • **Vernon Henley Media Award**

To recognize an individual, either sighted or blind, who has created a radio, television, or print media product conveying positive and useful information concerning blind people in general and the American Council of the Blind in particular. Nominations must be submitted by May 1. A plaque is awarded periodically. Established in 1989 by the ACB Board of Publications to honor Vernon Henley.

• 2043 • Durward K. McDaniel Ambassador Award
To recognize a blind or visually impaired person who has performed distinguished service to the community or in the state where he or she resides. A certificate is awarded annually at the Council's national convention. Established in 1964. Formerly: (1987) Ambassador Award.

• 2044 •
American Council on Consumer Interests
Terri Haffner, Exec.Dir.
415 S Duff Ave., Ste. C
Ames, IA 50010-6600
Phone: (515)956-4666
Fax: (515)233-3101
E-mail: info@consumerinterests.org
Home Page: http:// www.consumerinterests.org

• 2045 • ACCI Thesis/Dissertation Award
To identify and recognize outstanding graduate student research that addresses issues relevant to the well-being of consumers. The thesis or dissertation must have been granted no earlier than January 1 two years prior to the granting of the award. Applications must be submitted by October 1. Two awards are presented: best M.S. thesis and best doctoral dissertation. Winners who choose to present their research at the conference receive a monetary award of $300 each. Established in 1985. Formerly: (1984) Research Award Competition.

• 2046 • Applied Consumer Economics Award
To encourage consumer professionals to address the practical and everyday problems that consumers face. A completed manuscript, not previously published by the council, must be submitted by November 1. Criteria used for selection of the winning paper are: it must address an important consumer problem, perhaps in an innovative and creative way; it must articulate practical solutions to the problem; and it must present information or ideas that have immediate usefulness for consumers directly or indirectly via consumer professionals and policy makers. A monetary award of $200 and an automatic slot on the annual conference program are awarded. The winner must attend the conference and present the paper in some form.

• 2047 • Distinguished Fellows Award
To honor individuals who have made significant contributions to ACCI over a long period of time and are widely recognized as leaders in the consumer field. Established in 1972.

• 2048 • Russell A. Dixon Award
To recognize the best applied paper published in *Advancing the Consumer Interest* each year. A monetary prize of $200 is awarded annually.

• 2049 • Friend of Consumers Award
To recognize individuals who have made specific, significant contributions to local, state, national, or international policy whose implementation promotes "the consumer interest," and to encourage policies and practices in different arenas that promote "the consumer interest." Activities may have occured over a long period of time or may be a single, outstanding contribution. Contributions to policy development may be in different arenas or contexts, including government (executive or legislative), marketplace practices (including journalism), and advocacy groups. Established in 1995.

• 2050 • Stewart M. Lee Consumer Education Award
To acknowledge and encourage other outstanding efforts in consumer education that exemplify the qualities of Stewart M. Lee and his work. Individuals who have made significant contributions to the field of consumer education are eligible. In most cases, the contributions are over a long period, but single, uniquely outstanding contributions of lasting impact may be recognized as well. Contributions include teaching, research, or service to consumer education. Any member of the Council may submit nominations. A monetary prize of $500 and a plaque are awarded. Organizations receive a plaque. Established in 1988 to recognize the outstanding, long-term contributions of Stewart M. Lee to consumer education.

• 2051 • Mid Career Award
To recognize achievement and service by an ACCI member with fifteen years or less of professional work. Selection will be made based on excellence in the field either in research, education, and/or policy combined with service defined as contributions that further consumer interests including service to ACCI as a professional organization, forging collaborations with other consumer interest organizations and groups, supporting policy making, etc. Established in 1995.

• 2052 •
American Council on Education
David Ward, Pres.
1 Dupont Cir. NW, Ste. 800
Washington, DC 20036
Phone: (202)939-9300
Fax: (202)833-4760
E-mail: web@ace.nche.edu
Home Page: http://www.acenet.edu

• 2053 • ACE Distinguished Service Award for Lifetime Achievement
To recognize an individual for outstanding lifetime contributions in the field of higher education. A Steuben glass "Galaxy" is awarded occasionally at the ACE Annual Meeting. Established in 1980.

• 2054 • ACE Fellows Program
To enable faculty and administrators with a minimum of five years of college le vel experience as faculty members and/or as administrators to participate in ac ademic administration and policy making. Candidates are encouraged to intern a t a host institution, but under special circumstances may intern at their home institutions. Fellows spend a full academic year in mentor/intern relationship s with college or university presidents and other senior administrators, attend seminars and national conferences, and visit other colleges and universities. Nominations must be submitted by November 1. Awarded annually. Established in 1957.

• 2055 •
American Council on the Teaching of Foreign Languages
Bret Lovejoy, Exec.Dir.
700 S Washington St., Ste. 210
Alexandria, VA 22314
Phone: (703)894-2900
Fax: (703)894-2905
E-mail: headquarters@actfl.org
Home Page: http://www.actfl.org

• 2056 • ACTFL Nelson Brooks Award for Excellence in the Teaching of Culture
To recognize a foreign language educator who has made a significant contribution to the teaching of culture in the foreign language classroom, and who has influenced large numbers of professionals over an extended period of time. The deadline is May 23. A monetary award of $500 is presented annually. Established in 1978. Sponsored by Harcourt Brace Jovanovich, Inc.

• 2057 • ACTFL Edwin Cudecki International Business Award
To recognize an individual for a significant contribution in promoting a closer relationship between international business and language education and/or international studies. The recipient must show evidence of leadership in bringing together language educators and international business communities, in enhancing the capacity of the United States to engage in international business, or in other ways demonstrating exceptional efforts to link the business world and foreign language education. The recipient may be in corporate, public, or professional service. Foreign language educators are not eligible. Member organizations of ACTFL must submit nominations by May 23. A monetary award of $500 is presented annually. Established in 1987 with the support of the Illinois Foreign Language Teachers Association, the International Business Council MidAmerica and the Illinois Ethnic Consultation.

• 2058 • ACTFL Anthony Papalia Award for Excellence in Teacher Education
To recognize a foreign language educator who has demonstrated excellence in the preparation and continuing education of teachers for the profession. Members of the Council who have a minimum of five years experience as teacher-educators at the undergraduate level, graduate level, or both are eligible. Nominations must be submitted by May 23. A monetary award of $500 is awarded annually. Established in 1987. Sponsored by the New York State Association of Foreign Language Teachers.

• 2059 • ACTFL - MLJ Paul Pimsleur Award for Research in Foreign Language Education
To recognize the author of an outstanding published contribution to research in foreign lan-

guage or second language education. The research may be language-specific or general and published during the two years preceding the award. Nominations are accepted. A monetary award of $500 is presented annually. Established in 1977 to honor Paul Pimsleur. Sponsored by *The Modern Language Journal*.

• 2060 • ACTFL Florence Steiner Award for Leadership in Foreign Language Education, K-12

To recognize outstanding leadership in foreign language education by a public or private school teacher or administrator/supervisor. Individuals who have been members of ACTFL for at least three years and have a minimum of five years teaching experience are eligible. A monetary award of $500 is presented annually. Established in 1982 to honor Florence Steiner. Nominations to chairperson must be submitted by May 23.

• 2061 • ACTFL Florence Steiner Award for Leadership in Foreign Language Education, Postsecondary

To recognize outstanding leadership in foreign language education by an individual in either post-secondary foreign language education or administration. Individuals who have been members of ACTFL for at least three years and have a minimum of five years teaching experience are eligible. Nominations to chairperson must be submitted by May 23. A monetary award of $500 is presented annually. Established in 1982 to honor Florence Steiner.

• 2062 • ACTFL - MLJ Emma Marie Steiner Award for Leadership in Foreign Language Research in Foreign Language Education

To recognize doctoral dissertation research in foreign language education that contributes significantly to the advancement of the profession. The deadline for nominations is May 23. A monetary award of $500 is presented annually. Established in 1980 by royalties from *Foreign Language Learning Today*, Pergamon Press, Limited, London, England. Sponsored by *The Modern Language Journal*.

• 2063 •

American Counseling Association
Richard Yep, Exec.Dir.
5999 Stevenson Ave.
Alexandria, VA 22304-3300
Phone: (703)823-9800
Toll-Free: 800-347-6647
Fax: (703)823-0252
E-mail: ryep@counseling.org
Home Page: http://www.counseling.org

Formerly: American Association for Counseling and Development.

• 2064 • ACA Extended Research Award

To honor researchers conducting high quality research over a period of time and to promote extended investigation by the awardee. Nominations dates change annually. The research can be systematic inquiry or investigation into a subject to discover facts or principles; involving an idea to be tested; examination of data through statistical design and techniques; and an initiative resulting in usable interpretation of findings and recommendations for the field. The research must be in areas of interest to one or more of the Divisions or Organizational Affiliates of ACA. A plaque and certificate are awarded annually. Established in 1987.

• 2065 • ACA Legislative Service Award

To recognize outstanding work of a public official or public agency staff member who has made a significant contribution to the counseling profession or recipients of the professions services by impacting public policy at the national level. Established in 1976.

• 2066 • ACA Professional Development Award

To recognize outstanding professional service and development of techniques and systems that have strengthened, expanded, enhanced, improved, and/or otherwise had demonstrable benefit to clients. Members who have a documented record of long continued contributions, relevance to the profession in general, a history of effort to create and improve opportunities for all to realize full potential, and efforts to strengthen, improve, and enhance the profession may be nominated. A monetary award is presented annually. Established in 1975. Formerly: Clarence W. Failor Award.

• 2067 • ACA Research Award

To honor and recognize high quality research in area(s) of interest to the counseling and human development profession and the divisions, or organizational affiliates of ACA. Research published in ACA journals and those in counseling psychology, measurement, and educational research journals between September 1, and August 31 are considered, along with unpublished research by ACA members. To qualify for this award, the research must include: empirical systematic inquiry or investigation, a clearly stated hypothesis, examination of data through statistical techniques, careful interpretation of results, and relevance to one or more ACA divisions. Established in 1956. divisions. Established in 1956.

• 2068 • Ralph F. Berdie Memorial Research Award

To encourage fruitful explorations in the area of college student personnel work or related phases of education, and to serve as the initial project which would then be funded from other sources for further exploration. A grant is awarded annually. Established in 1977.

• 2069 • Kitty Cole Human Rights Award

To honor a member who has made significant contributions in one or more areas of the broad spectrum of human rights. Human rights contributions include, but are not limited to, services to people with special needs or handicaps, abused and neglected children, minority groups, economically disadvantaged, or other underserved populations. Nominees should have contributed to the field of human rights either through a special project, direct services, or a life's work and role. Nominees should have contributed a significant amount of time and effort to the area or project for which they were nominated, thus demonstrating a long-term commitment to the field of human rights. Awarded annually. Established in honor of Kitty Cole, an active leader in the counseling profession.

• 2070 • Arthur A. Hitchcock Distinguished Professional Service Award

To honor and recognize a member for outstanding service at the local, state, or national level that reflects a significant contribution to the professional concerns of ACA and to stimulate future service for the well being of the profession. Nominees must be able to document outstanding service to promote the profession, widespread general effects of their work, a history of scientific and scholarly accomplishments which benefit the public in general, and service related to areas of interest of one or more ACA divisions. Awarded annually. The award was named for Arthur A. Hitchcock, who served as executive director of the American Personnel and Guidance Association from 1955-1966. Established in 1976. Formerly: AACD Distinguished Professional Service Award; Arthur A. Hitchcock Award for Distinguished Service.

• 2071 • Glen E. Hubele National Graduate Student Award

For recognition of outstanding scholarship by an ACA student member. Graduate degree candidates in the field of counseling, guidance, and human development are eligible. A monetary award is presented annually. Established by Mrs. Cicely D. Hubele in honor of her son, Glen E. Hubele, a former professor of Educational Psychology and Guidance at Eastern Illinois University, Charleston, IL.

• 2072 • Local, State Branch, and Regional Award

To recognize in an official local/state branch and regional counseling associations celebrating their 25th or 50th anniversaries. The association must be currently active as a unit ACA; possesses an official ACA charter; and shows evidence of continuous professional service to ACA members for 25 to 50 years. Awarded annually. Established in 1993.

• 2073 • Carl D. Perkins Government Relations Award

To recognize outstanding work at the national or state level that influences public policy and results in a significant contribution to the counseling profession or to recipients of the profession's services; and to stimulate future legislation for the well-being of the counseling profession or for recipients of the profession's services. Nominees must be current members of ACA. Award is named in memory of the late Kentucky congressman who chaired the House Committee on Education and Labor. Awarded annually. Established in 1993.

• 2074 • Gilbert and Kathleen Wrenn Award for a Humanitarian and Caring Person
To recognize a person who gives to others without fanfare or expectation of reward other than personal satisfaction in seeing other persons made happier or the social milieu given more integrity. Members who have demonstrated unselfish involvement over time; impact on the lives of others through caring in a personal way; caring through social action which improves the lot of others; and effectiveness in communicating caring are eligible. A monetary award of $1,000 is presented annually. Established in 1977 by Dr. and Mrs. C. Gilbert Wrenn.

• 2075 •
American Craft Council
Carmine Branagan, Exec.Dir.
72 Spring St.
New York, NY 10012-4019
Phone: (212)274-0630
Toll-Free: 800-724-0859
Fax: (212)274-0650
E-mail: council@craftcouncil.org
Home Page: http://www.craftcouncil.org

• 2076 • American Craft Council Fellows
To recognize excellence in craftsmanship and commitment to the American craft movement. Candidates are nominated by peers. Individuals who have worked 25 years as professionals demonstrating outstanding ability and/or contribution to the craft field are eligible. Practicing craftsmen are eligible to be fellows; individuals other than craftsmen are eligible to be Honorary Fellows. A Fellow Pin and certificate are awarded. Established in 1975. Formerly: American Craft Council Honorary Fellow.

• 2077 • Awards of Distinction
To recognize organizations, publications, and individuals for specific achievements. A certificate is awarded.

• 2078 • Gold Medal
To recognize consummate craftsmanship. A gold medal and a certificate are awarded.

• 2079 • Aileen Osborn Webb Award
To recognize dedication to and patronage of the crafts. A silver medal and a certificate are awarded. Formerly: Aileen Osborn Webb Service Award.

• 2080 •
American Crossword Puzzle Tournament
55 Great Oak Ln.
Pleasantville, NY 10570
Phone: (914)769-9128
E-mail: wshortz@aol.com
Home Page: http://www.crosswordtournament.com

• 2081 • American Crossword Puzzle Champion
To recognize the champion of the country's oldest crossword puzzle tournament which is based on a two day puzzle competition and scored on accuracy and speed. The tournament consists of 21 prize events. Contestants may compete in all events for which they are eligible: Division A - everyone; Division B - contestants who have not won a Division A or Division B prize during their last seven sanctioned tournaments. Division C - contestants who have not finished within the top 20 percent during their last three tournaments; Division D contestants who have not finished within the top 40 percent during the last three tournaments; Division E-contestants who have not finished within the top 65 percent during the last three tournaments; Juniors - solvers 25 years and under; Fifties - solvers 50-59 years; Sixties - solvers 60-69 years; Seniors - solvers 70 years and over; and top solvers in each of 11 geographical zones. The first prize winner in Division A receives a monetary award of $2,000. Additional monetary awards and trophies are presented. The Top Rookie is recognized. Each prizewinner receives a Merriam-Webster dictionary. Awarded annually at the Stamford Marriott Hotel in Stamford, CT. Established in 1978 by the Stamford Marriott Hotel and Will Shortz, crossword editor of *The New York Times*. Sponsored by Kappa Publishing Group, St. Martin's Press, and New York Times Digital.

• 2082 •
American Crystallographic Association
PO Box 96
Ellicott Sta.
Buffalo, NY 14205-0096
Phone: (716)856-9600
Fax: (716)852-4846
E-mail: aca@hwi.buffalo.edu
Home Page: http://www.hwi.buffalo.edu/aca/

• 2083 • ACA Public Service Award
To recognize a non-crystallographer for contibutions to science policy, science funding, or to communication of crystallography to the general public. Awarded on an irregular basis at the discretion of the ACA Council. Established in 1988.

• 2084 • Martin J. Buerger Award
To recognize mature scientists who have made contributions of exceptional distinction in areas of interest to the Association. There are no restrictions as to nationality, race, sex, religion, or membership in the ACA. A monetary prize of $1,500 and $1,500 travel expenses to accept the award is awarded triennially in memory of Martin J. Buerger, Institute Professor Emeritus of M.I.T. and University Professor Emeritus of the University of Connecticut, a mineralogist who made major contributions to many areas of crystallography. Established in 1980.

• 2085 • Charles E. Szper Memorial Fund
Supports crystallographic education and awareness. Established in 1992

• 2086 • Elizabeth A. Wood Science Writing Award
Annual award of recognition awarded to authors of books or articles that bring science to the attention of a wider audience.

• 2087 • Peggy Etter Student Travel Award Fund
A restricted endowment fund in memory of Margaret C. Etter. The award is granted to students for travel costs associated with attending the annual meeting.

• 2088 • Isidor Fankuchen Award
To recognize contributions to crystallographic research by one who is known to be an effective teacher of crystallography. There are no geographic or age restrictions. The honoree delivers a number of lectures at the Polytechnic Institute of New York, at several additional colleges, and to the Association. The award consists of $3,000 and up to $2,000 in travel expenses incurred in connection with the lectures. Awarded every three years. Established in 1971 in memory of Dr. I. Fankuchen, Professor of Physics at the Polytechnic Institute of Brooklyn from 1942 to 1964.

• 2089 • Kenneth N. Trueblood Awards
Recognizes exceptional achievement in computational or chemical crystallography. The award is given tri-annually. The award was established in 2001 in memory of Professor Kenneth N. Trueblood, who was a major force in the early use of computers and the development of crystallographic computer programs. An honorarium plus travel expenses to accept the award are presented.

• 2090 • Margaret C. Etter Early Career Award
Recognizes outstanding achievement and exceptional potential in crystallographic research demonstrated by a scientist at an early state of their independent career. An honorarium plus travel expenses to accept the award and present a lecture at the ACA meeting are awarded annually. Established in 2002.

• 2091 • A. Lindo Patterson Award
To recognize and encourage outstanding research in the structure of matter by diffraction methods, including significant contributions to the methodology of structure determination and/or innovative application of diffraction methods and/or elucidation of biological, chemical, geological, or physical phenomena using new structural information. The deadline for nominations is June 1. A monetary award of $1,500, travel expenses and a certificate are awarded every three years. Established in 1980.

• 2092 • Pauling Prize
To recognize the best student poster presentation at the Annual Meeting. Five monetary prizes of $200 each are awarded annually. Established in 1987.

• 2093 • Public Service Award
Recognizes a non-crystallographer for contributions to science policy, to science funding, or to communication of crystallography to the general public. Awarded on an irregular basis at the discretion of the ACA Council.

• 2094 • Service Awards
Honors the dedicated efforts of ACA members who voluntarily work behind the scenes on the business of the organization. A certificate and a small gift are awarded.

• 2095 • Bertram E. Warren Diffraction Physics Award
To recognize an important recent contribution to the physics of solids or liquids using X-ray, neutron, or electron diffraction techniques. Works published within a six-year period ending June 30 of the year preceding the Award year may be nominated. A monetary award of $1,500 and up to $1,500 in travel expenses are awarded every third year. Established in 1970 by students and friends of Professor B.E. Warren on the occasion of his retirement from the Massachusetts Institute of Technology.

• 2096 •
American Dairy Science Association
Brenda Carlson, Exec.Dir.
1111 N Dunlap Ave.
Savoy, IL 61874
Phone: (217)356-5146
Fax: (217)398-4119
E-mail: adsa@assochq.org
Home Page: http://www.adsa.org

• 2097 • American Feed Industry Association Award
To recognize outstanding research in the field of dairy cattle nutrition. Research work must have been performed at a public institution, hospital, or similar institution. Members of the Association who are residents of the United States, Canada, or Mexico are eligible. A monetary stipend and a plaque are awarded annually. Established in 1948 by the American Feed Manufacturers Association. An award and monetary stipend are presented at the annual meeting of the American Dairy Science Association. Formerly: American Feed Manufacturers Association Award.

• 2098 • Award of Honor
To recognize distinguished contribution to the Association. Individuals who have at least 25 years of membership in the Association are eligible. A plaque and monetary stipend of $1500 are awarded annually.

• 2099 • Cargill Animal Nutrition Young Scientist Award
To recognize an outstanding young scientist. Nominees must have demonstrated outstanding research in dairy cattle production areas; have published original research work within five calendar years immediately prior to year of award; be under 40 years of age; have reached his or her Ph.D., or latest degree, not more than 10 years before nomination; be and have been a member of ADSA for at least five successive years; and be a resident of the United States, Canada, or Mexico. $1,500 and a plaque are awarded at a presentation during the annual meeting of the American Dairy Science Association. Established in 1983 by Agway Inc., Syracuse, New York. Formerly: (2004) Agway Inc. Young Scientist Award.

• 2100 • DeLaval, Inc. Dairy Extension Award
To recognize outstanding achievements in the field of dairy extension in the broad areas of production, manufacturing, marketing, and youth work. Members resident in the United States, Canada, or Mexico with a minimum of ten years of dairy extension work in educational or public-type institutions are eligible. A monetary stipend and a plaque are awarded annually. Established in 1951. Sponsored by Alfa Laval Agri, Inc. Formerly: (2004) Alfa Laval Agri Dairy Extension Award; DeLaval Dairy Extension Award.

• 2101 • Distinguished Service Award
To recognize individuals who have contributed in an unusual outstanding manner to the welfare of the dairy industry, either directly or indirectly, in areas such as industrial leadership, science, engineering, public health, or education. Individuals need not be members of the Association. A plaque and monetary stipend of $1500 are awarded annually. Established in 1961.

• 2102 • National Milk Producers Federation - Richard M. Hoyt Award
To recognize research efforts that have direct application to the solution of problems facing the dairy industry. Graduate students at an American or Canadian college or university enrolled in a program leading to an advanced degree in a department of dairy production, dairy processing, food science, or a related department are eligible. A monetary stipend of $1000 and a plaque are awarded annually. Sponsored by the National Milk Producers Federation.

• 2103 • International Dairy Foods Association Research Award
To recognize individuals whose research findings have allowed dairy foods processors to develop new products or to make significant improvements in the quality, safety, or processing efficiency of dairy foods. Nominees must have conducted research at public and/or private institutions; have published the research during the ten calendar years prior to the award, except for the first three years of the award when the past fifteen years of research are considered; have been members of the American Dairy Science Association for at least the past five years; and must be resident citizens of the United States, Canada, or Mexico. Monetary award of $1,500 and plaque given annually. Established in 1993 by the International Dairy Foods Association.

• 2104 • International Dairy Production Award
To recognize an individual for a meritorious scientific contribution by way of teaching, research, or other service to dairy production in one or more of the developing and/or developed areas of the world over a period of five or more years. Particular attention is paid to the longtime effects of the contribution. It is not necessary that the nominee be a member of ADSA or a citizen of any country. A monetary award of $1,500 and plaque are given annually. Established in 1988 by Ralston Purina International, St. Louis, Missouri. Sponsored by Ralston Purina International.

• 2105 • Land O'Lakes, Inc.
To recognize a meritorious scientific contribution or discovery pertaining to dairy manufacturing or dairy production; or an invention of a plan, process, or device that is useful, valuable, or significant in the practice of dairy manufacturing or production. Members of the Association who are residents of the United States, Canada, or Mexico are eligible. A monetary award of $2,500 and a plaque are awarded annually. Established in 1937 by Borden. Formerly: (2004) Borden Award.

• 2106 • Land O'Lakes/Purina Teaching Award in Dairy Production
To recognize outstanding undergraduate teaching in dairy science. Active teachers with no less than ten years of active teaching at an accredited college or university who are members of the Association and residents of the United States, Canada, or Mexico are eligible. A monetary stipend of $1500 and a plaque are awarded annually. Established in 1973. Formerly: Ralston Purina Company Teaching Award in Dairy Science; (2004) Purina Mills, Inc. Teaching Award.

• 2107 • J. L. Lush Award
To recognize outstanding research in animal breeding. Research work published in the ten years immediately preceding the award year in any area of animal breeding and genetics that has or had the potential for improvement of dairy cattle is considered. Nominees must be members of ADSA for at least five years and be residents of the United States, Canada, or Mexico. A plaque and monetary stipend of $1500 are awarded annually. Established in 1982. Sponsored by the American Breeders Service.

• 2108 • Marschall Rhodia Award
To recognize outstanding accomplishments in research and development outside the United States and Canada in chemistry, biochemistry, microbiology, technology, and engineering pertaining to the dairy foods industries. The impact of these contributions on the marketplace may be a factor in the selection. $1,000 in cash and travel expenses (up to $2000) awarded and a plaque are awarded annually. Established in 1981 by Marschall Products-Rhone-Poulenc, Inc., Madison, Wisconsin. Formerly: Miles - Marschall International Award; (2004) Marschall

- Rhone - Poulenc International Dairy Science Award.

• 2109 • Milk Industry Foundation and Kraft General Foods Teaching Award in Dairy Science

To recognize demonstrated outstanding ability as an undergraduate teacher of dairy science. Active teachers at accredited colleges or universities with no less than ten years of active teaching, who are members of the Association and residents of the United States, Canada, or Mexico are eligible. A monetary award of $1500 and a plaque are awarded annually. Established in 1955. Sponsored by the Milk Industry Foundation and Kraft General Foods.

• 2110 • National Milk Producers Federation Graduate Student Paper Presentation Contest

To recognize outstanding research papers by graduate students. Awards are presented in two categories: dairy production and dairy foods research. A monetary award of $1500 and plaque are given annually. Travel and Hotel expense up to $1000.

• 2111 • Nutrition Professionals, Inc. Applied Dairy Nutrition Award

To stimulate and recognize outstanding achievement in research, teaching, extension, and/or industry in applied dairy nutrition. Nominees must: have made the contribution within ten years prior to the award year; have been a member of the American Dairy Science Association for at least five consecutive years; and be a resident of the United States, Canada, or Mexico. A plaque and monetary award of $2,000 are presented annually. Established in 1991 by Microbial Genetics, a Division of Pioneer Hi-Bred International Inc., West Des Moines, Iowa. Sponsored by Pioneer Hi-Bred International.

• 2112 • Pfizer Animal Health Physiology Award

To recognize an individual for research work relating to dairy cattle physiology. Work published during the five calendar years immediately prior to the award year is considered. Research may pertain to any area of dairy cattle physiology. Members of ADSA who are residents of the United States, Canada, Mexico are eligible. A monetary award and a plaque are presented annually. Established in 1981 by the Upjohn Company, Kalamazoo, MI.

• 2113 • Pioneer Hi-Bred Forage Award

To recognize outstanding research (basic and/or applied) and/or educational contributions in the area of forage production, processing, storage, or utilization. Nominees must have made the contribution within five years prior to the award year; have been a member of the Association for at least five consecutive years; and be residents of the United States, Canada, or Mexico. A monetary award of $ 2,000 and plaque are presented annually. Established in 1991 by Microbial Genetics, a Division of Pioneer Hi-Bred International, Inc., West Des Moines, Iowa. Sponsored by Pioneer Hi-Bred International.

• 2114 • West Agro, Inc. Award

To recognize an individual for meritorious scientific or technical contributions in research on mastitis; milking management and systems related to hygiene, udder health, and milk quality; milk yield, composition, flavor, and microbiological quality as related to feeding and management; and the detection or analysis of foreign substances in milk. Research work published during the five calendar years immediately prior to the award year is considered. Members of ADSA who are residents of the United States, Canada, or Mexico are eligible. A monetary award of $1500 and a plaque are presented annually. Established in 1979 by West Agro, Kansas City, Missouri.

• 2115 •
American Dance Festival
Charles L. Reinhart, Dir.
Box 90772
Lenox Hill Sta.
Durham, NC 27708-0772
Phone: (919)684-6402
Fax: (919)684-5459
E-mail: adf@americandancefestival.org
Home Page: http://americandancefestival.org

• 2116 • Balasaraswati/Joy Ann Dewey Beinecke Chair for Distinguished Teaching

To bring visibility and to pay tribute to those responsible for inspiring generations of excellent dancers. When possible the individual selected remains in residence at the American Dance Festival throughout its six week season. Established in 1991 through an endowment of $135,000 contributed by Luise Elcaness Scripps, Walter Beinecke, the daughters of Joy Ann Dewey Beinecke, and the American Dance Festival. It commemorates the memories of Balasaraswati and Joy Ann Dewey Beinecke. Ms. Balasaraswati was one of India's legendary dancers and teachers; Joy Ann Dewey Beinecke was a dancer and a member of the dance faculty at Williams College.

• 2117 • Samuel H. Scripps/American Dance Festival Award

To honor a choreographer who has made a significant lifetime contribution to modern dance. A monetary award of $35,000 and a plaque are given annually at the American Dance Festival in the summer. Established in 1981 by Samuel H. Scripps, a patron of the arts and member of the Scripps newspaper family.

• 2118 •
American Dance Guild
Marilynn Danitz, Pres.
PO Box 2006
Lenox Hill Sta.
New York, NY 10021
Phone: (212)932-2789
Fax: (212)222-7204
E-mail: americandanceguild@hotmail.com
Home Page: http://www.americandanceguild.org

• 2119 • ADG Award for Outstanding Achievement in Dance

To recognize meritorious and unique contributions to the field of dance. Individuals outstanding in the field of dance are eligible. A statuette is awarded annually. Established in 1970. Formerly: American Dance Guild Award.

• 2120 • Award of Artistry

No further information was available for this edition.

• 2121 •
American Darts Organization
Roger Bick, Pres.
230 N Crescent Way, Ste. K
Anaheim, CA 92801
Phone: (714)254-0212
Fax: (714)254-0214
E-mail: adooffice@aol.com
Home Page: http://www.adodarts.org/

• 2122 • ADO National Champions

To recognize the best male and female darts player in the United States each year. ADO members are eligible. Participation is limited to the Top ten men and Top five women with the highest points per dart averages in the annual ADO All Star Challenge, together with members (six men and three women) of the ADO National Team. A monetary prize and a plaque are awarded annually. Established in 1990.

• 2123 • ADO Points Champions

To recognize the best male and female tournament darts players in the United States based on an annual points system. Players earn points based on a top four finish in 200 ADO sanctioned tournament events. ADO members are eligible. A monetary prize, a plaque, and a certificate are awarded annually. Established in 1979.

• 2124 •
American Defense Institute
Eugene "Red" McDaniel, Pres.
1055 N. Fairfax St., 2nd Fl.
Alexandria, VA 22314
Phone: (703)519-7000
Fax: (703)519-8627
E-mail: rdt2@americandefinst.org
Home Page: http://www.ojc.org/adi/

• 2125 • Outstanding Leadership Award

Recognizes commitment to America's national defense. Individual citizens are eligible.

• 2126 •
American Dental Association
James Bramson, Exec.Dir.
211 E. Chicago Ave.
Chicago, IL 60611
Phone: (312)440-2500
Fax: (312)440-2800
E-mail: publicinfo@ada.org
Home Page: http://www.ada.org

• 2127 • Community Preventive Dentistry Award
To recognize achievements in community preventive dentistry. The award is open to any individual or organization responsible for creating and implementing a community preventive dentistry program. The first prize includes a monetary award of $2,000 and a plaque, and up to three meritorious awards of $300 and a plaque may also be awarded. The entry deadline is May 15. Awarded annually at the ADA annual session. Established in 1972, the award is administered through the ADA Health Foundation, with the support of JOHNSON & JOHNSON Professional Division, a division of JOHNSON & JOHNSON Consumer Products.

• 2128 • Geriatric Oral Health Care Award
To recognize and reward those individuals and organizations who have improved the oral health care of the elderly through innovative health care delivery projects. The award is open to any individual or organization responsible for developing research or projects that further the understanding of dental caries, periodontal disease, denture stomatitis, or other oral diseases in older Americans. The entry deadline is May 15. The first prize consists of a monetary award of $2,500 and a plaque. A meritorious award of $500 and a plaque may also be awarded. Awarded annually at the ADA annual session. The award is administered by the ADA, through the ADA Health Foundation, with the support of the Warner-Lambert Company Consumer Health Products Group. Established in 1984.

• 2129 •
American Dental Hygienists' Association
Isaac Carpenter, Exec.Dir.
444 N Michigan Ave., Ste. 3400
Chicago, IL 60611
Phone: (312)440-8911
Phone: (312)440-8900
Toll-Free: 800-243-ADHA
Fax: (312)467-1806
E-mail: mail@adha.net
Home Page: http://www.adha.org

• 2130 • Alfred C. Fones Award
For recognition of achievement in and contribution to the dental hygiene profession and to the association. To be eligible, an individual must be a current member of the association, have been a member for twenty-five continuous years, and must have practiced dental hygiene for over twenty-five years in a private setting. A plaque and one year's membership in the association are awarded annually in June. Established in 1976 in honor of Alfred C. Fones, who established the first school of dental hygiene in Connecticut.

• 2131 •
American Design Drafting Association
Terry Schultz, Exec.VP
105 E Main St.
Newbern, TN 38059
Phone: (731)627-0802
Fax: (731)627-9321
E-mail: corporate@adda.org
Home Page: http://www.adda.org

Formerly: (1989) American Institute for Design and Drafting.

• 2132 • Awards Program
To recognize and honor the professional achievements of councils, student chapters, and individual members, as well as the contributions of individuals outside of the association. The following awards are presented as merited: Outstanding Council, Outstanding Student Chapter (Division 1), Outstanding Student Chapter (Division 2), Life Membership, Honorary Membership, Achievement, and Merit. Awards are presented at the annual conference.

• 2133 •
American Diabetes Association
PO Box 363
Mt. Morris, IL
Toll-Free: 800-806-7801
E-mail: askada@diabetes.org
Home Page: http://www.diabetes.org

• 2134 • ADA Career Development Awards
To assist exceptionally promising young investigators who are establishing their independence in diabetes research. Members of university-affiliated institutions or equivalent within the United States who are U.S. citizens or have permanent resident status are eligible. Applicant must be an assistant professor at the time of the ward, and have cleared institutional commitment. Applications may be submitted by January 15 and July 15.. The award supports the researcher's salary and project for four years, not to exceed $150,000. Formerly: Research and Development Award.

• 2135 • Ada-EASD Trans-Atlantic Fellowship Award
Encourages research into basic or clinical questions in diabetes and fosters development of investigators who intend to devote their research careers to diabetes. Awards of $50,000 will be made to the host institution. Four fellowships are available each year. Application deadline is February 2.

• 2136 • ADA Research Awards
Provide grant support to new and established investigators. Applications will be considered in any area that is relevant to The etiology or pathophysiology of diabetes and its complications. Applicants must be U.S. citizens or have (or have applied for) permanent resident status and hold full-time faculty positions at U.S. university-affiliated institutions. Applications may be submitted by Jan. 15 and July 15. Grants provide up to $100,000 a year for three years. Awarded annually. Formerly: Feasibility Grants.

• 2137 • Clinical Research Grants
To support research that directly involves the study of humans. New and established diabetes investigators whose studies directly involve patients are considered. The application deadline is Jan. 15 and July 15. Applicants must be U.S. citizens or permanent residents who hold appointments at U.S. university-affiliated institutions. Award recipients must be members of the American Diabetes Association's Professional Section. Up to $100,000 a year for three years is awarded annually. Established in 1989.

• 2138 • Junior Faculty Award
To support new medical investigators. The applicant must hold any level of faculty appointment within his/her institution. Application deadlines are Jan. 15 and July 15. Funds up to $120,000 per year for three years. Applicants must be U.S. citizens, or hold permanent residence, and award recipients must be members of the American Diabetes Association's Professional Section.

• 2139 • Lions SightFirst Diabetic Retinopathy Research Program
To support clinical and applied research in diabetic retinopathy in the United States and abroad. Applications may be submitted by Jan. 15. Awards are given to support new treatment regimens, epidemiology, and translation research. Grants provide up to $100,000 a year for three years. Established in 1983. Award recipients must be members of the American Diabetes Association's Professional Section. Sponsored by the Lions Club International Foundation. Formerly: Lions Club International Clinical Research Program in Diabetic Eye Disease.

• 2140 • Medical Student Diabetes Research Fellowship Program
To promote medical student interest in careers of diabetes-related clinical investigation or basic research. Applications may be made by students who have qualified sponsors. The student must have completed at least two years of medical school. Award recipients must be members of the American Diabetes Association's Professional Section. The deadline is Jan. 15 . Provides one year of research support of $30,000.

• 2141 • Mentor-Based Minority Fellowship
Supports the training of minority scientists who are underrepresented in the field of diabetes research. A stipend of $35,000 per year of a minority postdoctoral fellow to work closely with the mentor. Application deadline is July 15.

• 2142 • Mentor-Based Postdoctoral Fellowships
To enable established diabetes investigators to support the training of postdoctoral fellows working in their laboratories. Mentors must be U.S. citizens or permanent residents, hold appoint-

ments at U.S. research institutions, and have demonstrated success in training postdoctoral fellows. Award recipients must be members of the American Diabetes Association's Professional Section. The fellow must have an M.D. or Ph.D. degree and not more than three years of postdoctoral research experience. The application deadline is October 1. Funds up to $30,000 per year are awarded for three years. Awarded annually. Established in 1987.

• 2143 • Physician Scientist Training Award

Produces new leaders in diabetes research. Three years of support at $30,000 per year for the doctoral portion of an MD/PhD degree. Application deadline is January 15. Awarded annually.

• 2144 •
American Dietetic Association Foundation
Rebecca S. Reeves, Pres.
120 S. Riverside Plaza, Ste. 2000
Chicago, IL 60606-6995
Phone: (312)899-0040
Toll-Free: 800-877-1600
Fax: (312)899-1739
E-mail: webmaster@eatright.org
Home Page: http://www.eatright.org

• 2145 • ADA Foundation Awards for Excellence

To recognize excellence in the practice of seven areas of dietetics. The deadline for nominations is March 1. A monetary award of $1,000 is awarded annually. Formerly: (1989) ADA Foundation Award for Excellence in the Practice of Clinical Nutrition.

• 2146 • ADA Foundation Scholarships

To provide scholarships for continuing study in the field of dietetics. The general qualifications are: Status as a dietetic intern technician or a junior or senior in a baccalaureate or coordinated program of a CAADE-accredited college or university (application for ADA membership must be received before scholarship is granted); planned or current enrollment in CAADE approved pre-professional practice program or admission to or present pursuit of a program of graduate study; intention to practice in the field of dietetics; and U.S. citizenship or permanent U.S. residency. The application deadline is February 15. Must be an ADA member to apply.

• 2147 • Lenna F. Cooper Memorial Lecturer

To recognize distinguished efforts in dietetics. The awardee has the responsibility of presenting a paper in the area of specific expertise. Awarded annually.

• 2148 •
American Donkey and Mule Society
Leah Patton, Off.Mgr.
PO Box 1210
Lewisville, TX 75067
Phone: (972)219-0781
Fax: (972)420-9980
E-mail: adms@juno.com
Home Page: http://www.lovelongears.com

• 2149 • Merit of Breeding Award

To recognize superior foundation breeding stock. A plaque in the shape of a donkey head is awarded when an appropriate number of points is earned. Established in 1970.

• 2150 • National Champion Donkey, National Champion Mule

To recognize the national show champion of each breed. Silver trophies or plaques are awarded annually to each breed. Established in 1968.

• 2151 • Riding Hours and Riding Miles Awards

To award animals who are used, and the riders who use them, in the fields of riding, packing, or driving. Patches and stickers for various degrees of mileage, and a mule head plaque for each 1,000 miles are awarded when points (mileage) are accumulated. Established in 1981.

• 2152 • Versatility Hall of Fame

To reward activity and appearances before the public that promote donkeys and mules, and their abilities. A plaque in the shape of a mule or donkey head is awarded when an appropriate number of points is earned. Established in 1980.

• 2153 •
American Economic Association
John J. Siegfried, Sec./Treas.
2014 Broadway, Ste. 305
Nashville, TN 37203-2418
Phone: (615)322-2595
Fax: (615)343-7590
E-mail: aeainfo@vanderbilt.edu
Home Page: http://www.vanderbilt.edu/AEA

• 2154 • John Bates Clark Medal

For recognition of a significant contribution to economic thought and knowledge. American economists under the age of 40 who are members of the association are eligible. Established in 1947.

• 2155 • Distinguished Fellow

For recognition of high distinction in the field of economics in the United States and Canada. Economists who are members of the association are eligible. Not more than three certificates are awarded annually. Established in 1965.

• 2156 • Richard T. Ely Lecture

To recognize an individual by the presentation of a lecture. Awarded annually. Established in 1962.

• 2157 • Foreign Honorary Member

To recognize contributions to economics by foreign economists. Established in 1950.

• 2158 •
American Educational Research Association
Marlyn Cochran-Smith, Pres.
1230 17th St. NW
Washington, DC 20036
Phone: (202)223-9485
Fax: (202)775-1824
E-mail: webmaster@aera.net
Home Page: http://www.aera.net

• 2159 • Raymond B. Cattell Early Career Award for Programmatic Research

To recognize scholars in any field of educational inquiry within the first decade following receipt of the doctoral degree. Nomination should be for a distinguished program of cumulative educational research. A monetary award and a plaque are presented annually. Established in 1984.

• 2160 • Distinguished Contributions to Education Research

To recognize individuals for outstanding contributions that help practitioners and lay-groups understand how educational research has improved educational practice. Awards are presented in two categories: (1) Interpretive Scholarship - for individuals who have published, in a nonresearch serial publication, an interpretive article or testimony relating research to practice; and (2) Professional Service - for individuals who have related research findings to practice through direct involvement with the educational community. Established in 1964. Formerly: AERA - PDK Award for Distinguished Contributions Relating Research to Practice.

• 2161 • Palmer O. Johnson Memorial Award

To recognize an outstanding article appearing in an AERA-sponsored publication. Established in 1967 by the former colleagues and students of Palmer O. Johnson, a dedicated educator and a pioneer in educational research and methodology.

• 2162 • E. F. Lindquist Award

To encourage sophisticated research on substantive issues of college student growth and development; to facilitate the impact of research on students; and to recognize research scholars who have made important contributions toward better understanding of college students. Outstanding completed research articles, books or projects by people in the Association are eligible. A monetary award of $1,500 and a certificate are awarded annually. Established in 1971. Formerly: AERA - American College Testing Program Award.

• 2163 • Outstanding Book Award

To recognize the best book-length publication in educational research and development. To be considered, a book must be concerned with the improvement of the educational process through research or scholarly inquiry, must have a research base, and must have a copyright date within the past two years. A book may be nominated by the author or by another scholar. The book may have been published anywhere in the world, but must be available in English. No edited volumes are considered. Awarded annually. Established in 1983.

• 2164 • Relating Research to Practice Awards
To stimulate and recognize outstanding contributions by individuals to increasing practitioner and lay group understanding of the contributions of educational research to the improvement of educational practice. There are two categories: (1) Interpretive Scholarship Award - for an individual who has published in a non-research publication, e.g., an interpretive article, essay, or testimony (not a book-length work) that relates research to practice; and (2) Professional Service Award - for an individual who has related research findings to practice through direct involvement with the educational community, e.g., work with a school district or state department of education that provides reliable information based on research studies that address promising solutions (or alternatives) to locally identified problems. Work and publications completed in the preceding year are considered. An honorarium and a scroll are awarded. Established in 1983.

• 2165 • Review of Research Award
To recognize an outstanding review of research article appearing in an AERA-sponsored publication. Established in 1978.

• 2166 •
American Electroplaters and Surface Finishers Society
Jon Bednerik, Exec.Dir.
3660 Maguire Blvd., Ste. 250
Orlando, FL 32803-3075
Phone: (407)281-6441
Fax: (407)281-6446
E-mail: aesf@aesf.org
Home Page: http://www.aesf.org

Formerly: (1985) American Electroplaters' Society.

• 2167 • AESF Charles Henry Proctor Leadership Award
To recognize a member who has demonstrated outstanding leadership qualities in furthering the objectives of the society or enhancing its dignity, prestige, or progress. A plaque is awarded annually. Established in 1960. Formerly: Charles Henry Proctor Memorial Leadership Award.

• 2168 • AESF Franklane Industrial Achievement Award
For recognition of outstanding industrial achievements. A plaque is awarded annually. Established in 1967. Formerly: Frank E. Lane Industrial Award.

• 2169 • AESF Gold Medal
To recognize the author of best paper published in the society's journal, *Plating and Surface Finishing.* A gold medal plaque and b$ 1,000 per paper are awarded annually.

• 2170 • AESF Kergan Wells Service Award
To recognize unselfish giving on the part of a member for the benefit of all the members. Any member of the society who has demonstrated outstanding service to a branch or regional group of the society over a period of years or during the past year, as a symbol of the very essence of the society, is eligible. Awarded annually. Established in 1977.

• 2171 • AESF Scientific Achievement Award
For recognition of persons whose outstanding scientific contributions have advanced the theory and practice of electroplating, metal finishing, and the allied arts; have raised the quality of processes and products; or have enhanced the dignity and status of the profession. A plaque is awarded annually. Established in 1958.

• 2172 • AESF Silver Medal
To recognize the authors of the four next best papers published in the society's journal, *Plating and Surface Finishing.* Silver medals, plaques and $ 100 per paper are awarded annually.

• 2173 •
American Endurance Ride Conference
Kathleen Henkel, Exec.Dir.
PO Box 6027
Auburn, CA 95604
Phone: (530)823-2260
Toll-Free: (866)271-AERC
Fax: (530)823-7805
E-mail: aerc@foothill.net
Home Page: http://www.aerc.org

• 2174 • 500 Mile Limited Distance Horse Program
Upon completion of 500 miles in Limited Distance sanctioned rides, the horse will be awarded a medallion at the annual convention.

• 2175 • 1000 Mile Horse Program
Horses will receive a medallion for each 1000 miles completed. The medallion is awarded at the annual convention.

• 2176 • AERC Hall of Fame
Honors lifetime achievements by recognizing outstanding performance or contributions. Nominations are made by ballots submitted by members. Prizes are awarded in both equine and member categories. Established in 1975.

• 2177 • Husband/Wife Team Award
Honors husband/wife teams with the most points accumulated on any number of horses. Should a spouse have less mileage, his/her total must be equal to one-third the mileage total completed by the partner. 10 plaques are awarded annually.

• 2178 • Jim Jones Award - Most Miles Stallion Award
Given to the stallion with the most miles, completed during the ride season, regardless of the number of riders. The top 10 stallions are awarded. Established in memory of Jim Jones who campaigned an Arabian stallion.

• 2179 • Junior Division Award
Recognizes three junior riders per region. A junior rider is under the age of 16 as of December 1. A junior rider must ride in the company of a sponsor who is 21 years of age or older. Juniors receive points per mile only and are not considered for overall placements. Each making the list at the year end will receive an award jacket.

• 2180 • Limited Distance Program
Recognizes riders who have completed 250 miles of Limited Distance Rides. A Limited Distance Rider Mileage patch and a 250 mile chevron are awarded. Riders achieving these plateaus are acknowledged in the *Endurance News.*

• 2181 • National 100 Mile Award
Recognizes rider team with the most points accumulated on one day rides of 100 miles or more. Junior and senior riders complete equally. Divisions are not acknowledged in this competition. The top ten senior horse/rider teams are honored.

• 2182 • National Best Condition Award
For the horse who has earned the most Best Condition points during the ride season. The horse may have had any number of riders. The top tem placements are awarded.

• 2183 • National Limited Distance Mileage Award
For one senior rider, one horse highest mileage ridden in one season. Sponsored by the Orange County Endurance Riders.

• 2184 • National Mileage Championship
Recognizes rider and horse teams with the most miles accrued during one season. Honors the top 10 senior and top 5 junior teams. This award is based solely on mileage.

• 2185 • National Series Championship
Recognizes the top 10 of each division plus 3 juniors. Based on National Series Championship rides, one per region. Rules and Qualifications, and type of award, varies annually. Refer to the Web site at *endurance or news* for more details.

• 2186 • Pard'ners Award
Recognizes the partnership between rider and horse. Looks for a spirit of friendship, enthusiasm and championship. Must also show competitiveness and sportsmanship. Recipients re-

ceive keepsake plaques and engraved on the perpetual trophy.

• 2187 • Perfect Ten (Equine Only) Award
Recognizes riders who have completed 10 years, 10,000 miles, 10 top ten finishes, and 10 best conditions. Established in 1997. Created and sponsored by Joe Long, past president, former SE director, and member of the Hall of Fame.

• 2188 • Pioneer Award
For most points on a multi-day event (3-5 days). Qualification is accumulative score horse and rider team. Three placements are awarded per division, including juniors.

• 2189 • Regional Best Conditions Award
Honors up to 5 horses winning Best Condition throughout the season. Ponts are awarded on a per mile basis, not vet scores.

• 2190 • Rider Mileage Championship
Recognizes 2 senior and 1 junior with the greatest mileage accrued in that season. A rider may ride up to 2 horses. This achievement is listed on their award jacket.

• 2191 • Rider Mileage Program
Awarded upon completion of 250 miles. A Rider Mileage patch and a 250 mile chevron are awarded.

• 2192 • Bill Stuckey Award
For recognition of the senior rider who has completed the most sanctioned miles in one year. Regardless of the number of horses used. Senior riders above the age of 65 are eligible for the award. One keepsake plaque is awarded and the winners name engraved onto the perpetual trophy annually. Established in memory of Bill Stuckey, a southwest region AERC member who rode actively until his death in 1982.

• 2193 • Bill Thornburgh Family Award
To recognize the family with the most miles in one year (father, mother, and child; father and child; or mother and child) and to encourage more families to ride together. Eligible rides are those where at least one parent and one child start a distance at an event. A keepsake plaque is awarded and the winners names are engraved onto the perpetual trophy annually. Established by Susan Gibson, editor of *Trail Blazer* magazine. Given in memory of Bill Thornburgh, a southwest region AERC rider who rode endurance with his entire family.

• 2194 •
American Enterprise Institute for Public Policy Research
Christopher C. DeMuth, Pres.
1150 17th St. NW
Washington, DC 20036
Phone: (202)862-5800
Fax: (202)862-7177
E-mail: info@aei.org
Home Page: http://www.aei.org

• 2195 • Irving Kristol Lecture on Public Policy
To recognize an individual who has developed notable insights on one or more aspects of the relationship between the nation's private and public sectors. Focusing on the public interest, the lecture demonstrates how new concepts may illuminate public policy issues and contribute to the dialogue by which the public interest is served. The person delivering the lecture need not be a professional scholar, a government official or a business leader. The principal considerations determining the selection are the quality and appositeness of the lecturer's thought, rather than his or her formal qualifications. A monetary award of $15,000 is awarded annually in Washington, DC. Formerly: (2003) Frances Boyer Lecture on Public Policy.

• 2196 •
American Epilepsy Society
M. Suzanne C. Berry CAE, Exec.Dir.
342 N Main St.
West Hartford, CT 06117-2507
Phone: (860)586-7505
Fax: (860)586-7550
E-mail: sberry@aesnet.org
Home Page: http://www.aesnet.org

• 2197 • Epilepsy Research Awards Program
To encourage and reward clinical and basic science investigators whose research contributes importantly to understanding and conquering epilepsy. Two awards of $10,000 each are presented to active scientists and clinicians annually.

• 2198 •
American Equilibration Society
Shel Marcus, Exec.Dir.
8726 N Ferris Ave.
Morton Grove, IL 60053
Phone: (847)965-2888
Fax: (847)965-4888
E-mail: aesdental@sprynet.com
Home Page: http://www.occlusion-tmj.org/

• 2199 • Achievement Award
To recognize outstanding performance in the science of occlusion and temporomandibular joint function during undergraduate dental education as selected by the dental schools. Engraved certificates are awarded annually. Established in 1978.

• 2200 • Scientific Investigation and Research Award
To encourage research in the field of occlusion and TMJ (Temporomandibular Joint Disorders). Monetary grants are awarded annually when merited. Established in 1982-83 by Dr. Peter A. Dawson.

• 2201 •
American Ethical Union
John Hartman, Exec.Dir.
2 W. 64th St.
New York, NY 10023
Phone: (212)873-6500
Fax: (212)362-0850
E-mail: aeucontact@aeu.org
Home Page: http://www.aeu.org

• 2202 • Elliott - Black Award
Recognizes two people who have made a significant ethical contribution to society at personal risk and hardship. A plaque is awarded to the winner and airfare and accommodations to attend the National Assembly. Established in 1971.

• 2203 •
American Evaluation Association
Susan Kistler, Mgr.
16 Sconticut Neck Rd., No. 290
Fairhaven, MA 02719
Phone: (508)748-3326
Toll-Free: 888-232-2275
Fax: (508)748-3326
E-mail: aea@eval.org
Home Page: http://www.Eval.org

Formed by merger of: Evaluation Network; Evaluation Research Society.

• 2204 • Marcia Guttentag Award
To recognize an individual in the first five years of their career whose accomplishments indicate outstanding promise for the future. This award combines two earlier categories of award: the Perloff President's Prize and the Marcia Guttentag Fellowship. Nominations must be submitted by May 30. A small stipend and a plaque are awarded annually. Established in 1987.

• 2205 • Robert Ingle Service Award
To recognize an individual for service to the Association. Nominations must be submitted by May 30. A plaque is awarded annually. Established in 1987.

• 2206 • Lazarsfeld Award for Evaluation Theory
For recognition of significant contributions to research and scholarship in evaluation research. Scholars, government employees, and private consultants are eligible. Nominations must be submitted by May 30. A plaque is awarded annually. Established in 1975. This award represents an earlier combination of the Myrdal Award for Science and the Lazarsfeld Award for Research.

• 2207 • **Myrdal Award for Government Service**
For recognition of distinguished and innovative leadership in using or providing evaluation research in government agencies. Federal, state, or local government employees and private consultants are eligible. Nominations must be submitted by May 30. A plaque is awarded annually. Established in 1977.

• 2208 • **Alva and Gunnar Myrdal Practice Award**
For recognition of outstanding contributions in human service delivery and evaluation. Federal, state, or local government employees, university staff, and private consultants are eligible. Nominations must be submitted by May 30. A plaque is awarded annually. Established in 1977. Formerly: (1986) Gunnar Myrdal Human Service Delivery Award.

• 2209 •
American Ex-Prisoners of War
Clydie Morgan MS, National Adjutant
3201 E Pioneer Pky., No. 40
Arlington, TX 76010
Phone: (817)649-2979
Fax: (817)649-0109
E-mail: hq@axpow.org
Home Page: http://www.axpow.org

Formerly: (1949) Bataan Relief Organization.

• 2210 • **Barbed Wire Award**
To recognize the member of Congress who has supported and helped former POWs with legislative actions. Current members of Congress are considered. A trophy is awarded annually at a reception in Washington, DC. Established in 1988.

• 2211 • **Dr. John Nardini Award**
For recognition for outstanding service in the medical fields of treatment, studies, and research for former Prisoners of War. Nominations must be received by April 1 of each year. A plaque is awarded annually at the National Convention. Established in 1987 by PNC Stanley G. Sommers, Chair, Medical Research Committee in honor of Dr. John Nardini, a former POW who helped with research to assist former POWs prove medical claims.

• 2212 •
American Ex-Prisoners of War, East Tennessee Chapter
Al Godin, Cmdr.
407 Pine Hill Rd.
Elizabethton, TN 37643
Phone: (423)928-6031
Phone: (423)543-2820
Fax: (423)543-0411

• 2213 • **P.O.W. of the Year**
For outstanding service and participation. Recognition award bestowed annually.

• 2214 •
American Family Therapy Academy
Barbro Miles, Admin.Dir.
1608 20th St. NW, 4th Fl.
Washington, DC 20009
Phone: (202)483-8001
Fax: (202)483-8002
E-mail: afta@afta.org
Home Page: http://www.afta.org

Formerly: American Family Therapy Association.

• 2215 • **American Family Therapy Academy Awards**
For recognition of achievement in family therapy. Awards are given for Distinguished Contribution to Family Therapy Theory and Practice, Distinguished Contribution to Family Therapy Research, and work on Cultural and Economic Diversity. Nominations may be submitted by academy members and the awards committee. Plaques are awarded annually at the June convention. Formerly: American Family Therapy Association Awards.

• 2216 • **Distinguished Contribution to Social Justice Award**
To recognize a professional who is directing, developing or deeply involved in a clinical service, training program or research project designed to advance the quality or availability of family therapy to people of diverse cultural backgrounds and/or economic circumstances. Awarded annually. Formerly: Cultural and Economic Diversity Award.

• 2217 •
American Fancy Rat and Mouse Association
Karen Robbins, Founder
9230 64th St.
Riverside, CA 92509-5924
Phone: (626)966-0350
Phone: (760)945-4259
Fax: (818)592-6590
E-mail: afrma@afrma.org
Home Page: http://www.afrma.org

• 2218 • **Challenge Trophies**
For recognition of rats and mice in their respective classes. Awards are given in about 15 categories for each. The owners of the rats or mice must be members of the Association. Trophies, plaques, silver plates, and cups are awarded annually at the annual show in January. Also, three perpetual trophies given by the National Fancy Rat Society in England for the Best English Rat, Best Standard English, and Best Rex English are given at each show.

• 2219 •
American Farm Bureau Federation
Bob Stallman, Pres.
600 Maryland Ave. SW, Ste. 800
Washington, DC 20024
Phone: (202)406-3600
Fax: (202)406-3604
Home Page: http://www.fb.org

• 2220 • **American Farm Bureau Federation's Award for Distinguished Service**
To recognize distinguished and meritorious service in the interest of American agriculture and an unselfish desire to advance the well-being of farm people. Nominations are accepted only from State Farm Bureau Federations or Associations. Selection is made by a panel of distinguished judges. Awarded annually. Established in 1928.

• 2221 •
American Federation for Aging Research
Hadley C. Ford, Chair
70 W 40th St., 11th Fl.
New York, NY 10018
Phone: (212)703-9977
Toll-Free: 888-582-2327
Fax: (212)997-0330
E-mail: info@afar.org
Home Page: http://www.afar.org

• 2222 • **Paul B. Beeson Career Development Awards in Aging Research**
Recognizes outstanding research in the field of aging. Aimed at bolstering the current and severe shortage of academic geriatricians. The John A. Hartford Foundation, The Commonwealth Fund, and the Alliance for Aging Research on behalf of donor friends, provide $450,000 for three years to allow junior faculty to devote their time to research and training activities related to aging and care of the elderly. Awarded annually. Established in 1995. Formerly: Paul Beeson Physician Faculty Scholar in Aging Research Award.

• 2223 • **Irving S. Wright Award of Distinction**
To recognize exceptional accomplishments and contributions to the field of aging research. Nominations are by invitation only. A monetary award of $500 and a plaque are awarded annually. Established in 1981 to honor Dr. Irving S. Wright, founder of AFAR. Formerly: (1987) AFAR Award of Distinction.

• 2224 •
American Federation of Aviculture
Jerry McCawley, Dir. of Membership
PO Box 7312
North Kansas City, MO 64116
Phone: (816)421-2473
Fax: (816)421-3214
E-mail: afaoffice@aol.com
Home Page: http://www.afabirds.org

• 2225 • **Avy Award**
Annual award of recognition for service to aviculture.

• 2226 •
American Federation of Labor - Congress of Industrial Organizations
John J. Sweeney, Pres.
Community Services Network
815 16th St. NW
Washington, DC 20006
Phone: (202)637-5191
Fax: (202)637-5012
E-mail: cmarston@aflcio.org
Home Page: http://www.aflcio.org

• 2227 • **Murray-Green-Meany-Kirkland Award for Community Service**
This, the AFL-CIO's highest honor, philanthropic is presented to recognize outstanding contributions made by individuals and organizations, in this country and abroad, that have improved the health and welfare of people everywhere and to stimulate and encourage leadership in the field of social welfare. Nominations are accepted from all AFL-CIO affiliates and their members. A $5,000 grant and an appropriately inscribed medallion are presented annually. Established in 1947 as the Philip Murray Award and changed to the Murray-Green award in 1955. Since 1980, the award has honored three American labor leaders, Phillip Murray, William Green, and George Meany who presided over the Congress of Industrial Organizations (1940-1952), the American Federation of Labor (1924-1952), and the AFL-CIO (1955-1979), respectively, as well as the traditions of service exemplified by their lives. The name of Lane Kirkland President of the AFL-CIO from 1979 - 1985, was added o the award in 1996. Formerly: (1979) Murray - Green Award.

• 2228 •
American Federation of Mineralogical Societies
Steve Weinberger, Central Office Administrator
2706 Lascassas Pk.
Murfreesboro, TN 37130-1541
Phone: (615)893-8270
E-mail: central_office@amfed.org
Home Page: http://www.amfed.org

• 2229 • **AFMS Scholarship Foundation Honorary Award**
To recognize individuals who have made outstanding contributions to the earth sciences field and to the hobby of mineralogy. Scholarships of $2,000 per student per year for two school years are awarded.

• 2230 •
American Federation of School Administrators
Baxter M. Atkinson, International Pres.
1729 21st St. NW
Washington, DC 20009-1101
Phone: (202)986-4209
Fax: (202)986-4211
E-mail: afsa@admin.org
Home Page: http://www.admin.org

• 2231 • **Administrator of the Year**
To recognize an outstanding school administrator. A plaque is awarded annually. Established in 1989.

• 2232 •
American Federation of Teachers, AFL-CIO
Edward J. McElroy, Pres.
555 New Jersey Ave. NW
Washington, DC 20001
Phone: (202)879-4400
Toll-Free: 800-238-1133
Fax: (202)879-4545
E-mail: online@aft.org
Home Page: http://www.aft.org

• 2233 • **Human Rights Award**
For recognition of achievement and contribution to public education and human and democratic rights of all people. Nominations are made by the Human Rights Committee of AFT. A monetary award and a plaque are presented biennially. Established in 1971 by Henry Bennett, Chairman, AFT Civil Rights Committee.

• 2234 •
American Fighter Aces Association
Donald Gordon, Pres.
9404 E Marginal Way S
Seattle, WA 98108-4907
Phone: (206)768-7155
Fax: (206)764-5707
E-mail: afaa@museumofflight.org

• 2235 • **AFAA Airmanship Award**
To recognize the USAF Academy cadet who demonstrates the most promise as a pilot. A plaque is awarded annually.

• 2236 • **AFAA Honorees**
For recognition of outstanding contributions to military aviation or AFAA. One to three plaques are awarded annually.

• 2237 • **Joseph J. Foss Award**
To recognize the Marine Corps lead-in fighter pilot trainee with the highest scores in air-air combat. A plaque is awarded annually.

• 2238 • **Francis S. Gabreski Award**
To recognize the USAF lead-in fighter pilot trainee with the highest scores in air-air combat. A plaque is awarded annually.

• 2239 • **David McCampbell Award**
To recognize the U.S. Navy lead-in fighter pilot trainee with the highest scores in air-air combat. A plaque is awarded annually.

• 2240 •
American Film Institute
Jean Firstenberg, Dir.
John F. Kennedy Center for the Performing Arts
Washington, DC 20566
Phone: (202)833-2348
Toll-Free: 800-774-4234
Fax: (202)659-1970
Home Page: http://www.afi.com

• 2241 • **Outstanding American Films of the Year Awards**
Identifies the 10 most outstanding American films of the year. The program also recognizes the creative ensembles that collaborate to create the year's outstanding movies and television programs, as well as singular achievements in several individual categories. Will also identify up to six AFI Moments of Significance events that occurred during the previous calendar year which reflect the impact of culture, politics, new technologies, or other influences on the moving image arts that will become a permanent part of AFI's ongoing almanac. Established in 2000.

• 2242 •
American Finance Association
David H. Pyle, Pres.
Univ. of California Berkeley
Haas School of Business
545 Student Services Bldg.
Berkeley, CA 94720-1900
Phone: (510)642-2397
E-mail: subscrip@blackwellpub.com
Home Page: http://www.afajof.org

• 2243 • **Brattle Prizes in Corporate Finance**
For outstanding papers on corporate finance. Papers are chosen by the Associate Editors of the *Journal of Finance* from the papers published in the journal in the prior year. Awarded annually. Sponsored by The Brattle Group, Inc.

• 2244 • **Smith Breeden Prizes**
To recognize outstanding papers published in the *Journal of Finance* and to promote excellence in research in financial economics. Papers published in the December, March, June and September issues of the Journal are eligible. Associate editors of the Journal select the winners. Awarded annually. Sponsored by Smith Breeden Associates.

• 2245 •
American First Day Cover Society
D. A. Kelsey, Exec.Dir.
PO Box 65960
Tucson, AZ 85728
Phone: (520)321-0880
Fax: (520)321-0879
E-mail: info@afdcs.org
Home Page: http://www.afdcs.org

• 2246 • AFDCS Distinguished Service Award

To recognize distinguished service to the Society. Members are eligible. A walnut plaque is awarded annually. Established in 1970.

• 2247 • Grand Award

To encourage exhibition of First Day Covers at the Annual Convention Exhibition. A silver plate tray is awarded annually. Established in 1957. Formerly: Norman H. Lee Grand Prize.

• 2248 • Philip H. Ward, Jr. Memorial Award

For recognition of excellence in First Day Cover literature. Authors of articles during the year are eligible. A plaque is awarded annually. Established in 1964 to honor Philip H. Ward, Jr., noted philatelic journalist during the first half of the 20th century.

• 2249 •
American Fisheries Society
Gus Rassam, Exec.Dir.
5410 Grosvenor Ln., Ste. 110
Bethesda, MD 20814
Phone: (301)897-8616
Fax: (301)897-8096
E-mail: main@fisheries.org
Home Page: http://www.fisheries.org

• 2250 • AFS Award for Excellence in Fisheries Education

Recognizes excellence in formal instruction and advising in the field of fisheries. AFS members engage in education with the past five years and with at least 10 years of industry experience are eligible. At least one nominator must be an AFS member. Nomination deadline is April 15th. Awarded annually. Contact Phillip Bettoli, Award chair, Tennessee Tech. University, Box 5114, Cookville, TN 38505, Phone: (615) 372-3086 or fax Number (615) 372-6257. Established in 1988.

• 2251 • AFS Award of Excellence

Recognizes outstanding contributions to the field of fisheries science and aquatic biology. Member and non-member scientists are eligible. A bronze medal and a certificate mounted on a walnut plaque are awarded at the banquet. Nomination deadline is May 4th. Contact Churchill Grimes, Award Chair, NMFS, Institute of Marine Science, University of California, Santa Cruz, CA 95064. Phone number: (415) 435-3149 or fax number (415) 435-3675.

• 2252 • AFS Distinguished Service Award

To recognize outstanding contributions of time and energy for special projects or activities by AFS members. The number of recipients may vary, Awarded at the annual banquet and the Society's annual business meeting. Nomination deadline is January 31st. Contact Kenneth Beal, Award Chair, NMFS, 1 Blackburn Dr., Gloucester, MA 01930. Phone: (978) 281-9267 or Fax number (978) 281-9117.

• 2253 • AFS Meritorious Service Award

To recognize an individual for leadership, dedication, and service to the Society and to the profession. A bronze plaque is awarded annually. Established in 1986. Nomination deadline is May 4th. Contact John Casselman, Award Chair, OMNR Glenora Fisheries Station, RR4, Picton, Ontario, Canada KOK 2TO, Phone number (613) 476-3287 or fax number (613) 476-7131.

• 2254 • Dr. J. Frances Allen Scholarship Award

To provide funds for a female fisheries science PhD student whose research emphasis is in an area of fisheries science. Applicant must be an AFS member. Established in 1986 at the annual meeting during a caucus of Women in Fisheries. The award honors Dr. Allen, who pioneered women's involvement in AFS. Application deadline is March 10th. Visit our web site for additional application information.

• 2255 • Honorary Membership

To recognize individuals who have achieved outstanding professional or other attainments or have given outstanding service to the Society. Must be nominated by at least 100 active members and elected by a 2/3 majority of active members.

• 2256 • President's Fishery Conservation Award

To recognize an individual or unit for a singular accomplishment that advances the aquatic resource conservation at the regional or national level. One or more awards annually when warranted in the following two categories; AFS individual or unit and non-AFS individual or entity. Awarded annually.

• 2257 • William E. Ricker Resource Conservation Award

To recognize any entity for accomplishment or activity in resource conservation that is significant at the national, continental, or international level. Awarded when merited, but not more than once a year.

• 2258 • Skinner Memorial Fund Award

Supports student participation in AFS annual meeting. Graduate students or select undergraduate students are eligible is made by the AFS Education section and is based on academic qualifications, professional services and promise, and reasons for wanting to attend the meeting. No more than $ 500 is awarded annually per person. Application deadline is May 15th. Contact Christopher Guy, Award Chair, Kansas Cooperative Fish and Wildlife Research Unit, Kansas State University, 205 Leasure Hall, Manhattan, KS 66506, Phone number (785) 532-6635 or fax number (785) 532-7159.

• 2259 • Student Writing Contest

To recognize students who do an excellent job of communicating the value of fisheries research to the general public. Three winners will be selected. Their articles will be published in the AFS magazine and they will be presented with a plaque. Awarded annually. Submission deadline is May 4th. Contact Laura Bird, Units Coordinator at the above address.

• 2260 • Carl R. Sullivan Fishery Conservation Award

To recognize an individual or organization, professional or nonprofessional, for outstanding contributions to the conservation of fishery resources. Accomplishments are not restricted and may include political, legal, educational, scientific, and managerial success. A trophy and travel to the annual meeting are awarded each year. Established in 1991 to commemorate Carl R. Sullivan. Nomination deadline is May 4th. Contact Kenneth L. Beal, Award Chair, NMFS, 1 Blackburn Dr., Gloucester, MA 01930. Phone: (978) 281-9267 or Fax number (978) 281-9117.

• 2261 • Carl R. Sullivan Memorial Membership Award

To support AFS membership for non-North American fisheries scientists from English-speaking countries. Awardees are chosen by a committee of the AFS International Fisheries Section. Established in 1991 by the late Carl R. Sullivan, former Executive Director.

• 2262 • C. W. Watson Award

To recognize an individual who has made a great contribution to wildlife or fish conservation during their previous year or years. Preference is given to nominees in the southeastern United States.

• 2263 •
American Folklore Society
Tim Lloyd, Exec.Dir.
Mershon Ctr.
Ohio State University
1501 Neil Ave.
Columbus, OH 43201-2602
Phone: (614)292-3375
Fax: (614)292-2407
E-mail: lloyd.100@osu.edu
Home Page: http://afsnet.org/

• 2264 • W. W. Newell Prize

To encourage and recognize scholarship in the area of children's folklore. Graduate or undergraduate students are considered for an article or project that was written/conducted within the preceding academic year. An honorarium of $400 is awarded each year at the annual meeting of the American Folklore Society. Established in 1983 in honor of W. W. Newell, a pioneer researcher in children's folklore.

• 2265 • Peter and Iona Opie Prize

To recognize an outstanding contribution to the scholarly understanding of the folklore and folklife of children. Edited volumes, collections of folklore, and authored studies published in English during the preceding year are eligible. A monetary prize of $200 is awarded annually. Established in 1988 in memory of Peter Opie, internationally recognized author of books on children's folklore.

• 2266 •
American Football Coaches Association
Grant Teaff, Exec.Dir.
100 Legends Ln.
Waco, TX 76706
Phone: (254)754-9900
Fax: (254)776-3744
E-mail: info@afca.org
Home Page: http://www.afca.com

• 2267 • AFCA Coach of the Year
To recognize five regional Coach of the Year winners in four divisions (I-A, I-AA, Division II and Division III) and one national Coach of the Year winner in the same four divisions. The regional winners are announced near the end of each college football season. The national winners are announced at the AFCA's annual banquet that concludes the AFCA Convention each year in early January. Winners of both the regional and national awards are selected based on voting by AFCA-member coaches. The AFCA is the host of the award presentation and banquet. National winners receive a plaque, regional winners receive a medallion. A coach can win both regional and national honors but does not have to win regional honors to be eligible for the national award. The AFCA has selected national Coach of the Year winners since 1935 and regional winners since 1960.

• 2268 • All American Team
Annual Award of Recognition

• 2269 • Coach of the Year
Annual Award of Recognition

• 2270 • Tuss McLaughry Award
To recognize a distinguished American for the highest distinction in service to others. A cast bronze plaque is usually awarded annually. Established in 1964 in honor of Tuss McLaughry, a former president of the Association who also served as its executive director for 26 years.

• 2271 • Amos Alonzo Stagg Award
To recognize the individual, group or institution whose services have been outstanding in the advancement of the best interest of football. The award is a replica of the plaque presented to Coach Stagg at the 1939 meeting of the American Football Coaches Association, commemorating his 50 years of service to football. Awarded annually when merited. Established in 1940.

• 2272 •
American Forage and Grassland Council
Dana Tucker, Exec.Sec.
PO Box 94
Georgetown, TX 78627
Phone: (512)868-9842
Toll-Free: 800-944-AFGC
Fax: (512)931-1166
E-mail: dtucker@io.com
Home Page: http://www.afgc.org

• 2273 • Distinguished Grasslander Award
To recognize individuals who have served the forage and grassland segment of agriculture with distinction during their careers. Nominees must have completed at least one career in the forage and grassland segment of agriculture and be 55 years of age or over at the time of nomination. The award carries a lifetime membership in AFGC. Awarded when merited.

• 2274 • Medallion Award
Given for recognition of outstanding contributions in behalf of forages and grasslands and the American Forage and Grassland Council that have earned national recognition for work in research, teaching, extension, or industrial development. Nominations are accepted. An engraved medallion and certificate are awarded annually at the Annual Meeting of AFGC or at another appropriate occasion as determined by the Board of Directors. Established in 1960.

• 2275 • Merit Award
To recognize individuals who have made outstanding contributions in some phase of forage and grassland agriculture. Up to ten certificates may be presented annually. Nominees must have earned recognition among their colleagues in public service or private industry for contributions in support of some phase of forage or grassland agriculture in research, teaching, extension, industrial development, production, or service. The Awards Committee selects the recipients from nominations. As many as three certificates may be presented to outstanding farmers or ranchers each year. Awards are presented each year during the Annual Meeting of AFGC or at an occasion as determined by the Board of Directors.

• 2276 • Outstanding Grassland Farmer or Rancher Award
To recognize farmers, farm managers or ranchers who have done an exceptional job of forage crop production or grassland or range management and utilization. The state or Provincial Forage Council is responsible for nominations and selecting the winners. As many as ten farmers or ranchers in each state or province having a Forage Council affiliated with AFGC are eligible. Awarded annually at suitable functions as established by the state or provincial council, where feasible.

• 2277 •
American Foreign Service Association
John Limbert, Pres.
2101 E St. NW
Washington, DC 20037
Phone: (202)338-4045
Phone: 800-704-AFSA
Fax: (202)338-6820
E-mail: limbert@afsa.org
Home Page: http://www.afsa.org
Formerly: (1924) American Consular Association.

• 2278 • Avis Bohlen Award
To recognize the accomplishments of a foreign service family member whose relations with the American and foreign communities at a Foreign Service Post, through the tradition of volunteer service, have done the most to advance the interests of the United States. Nominations for this award may be submitted by anyone at post with knowledge of the nominee's accomplishments. The nominator must state his/her relationship with the nominee. Self-nominations are not eligible. A monetary award and a certificate are awarded annually at the AFSA awards ceremony held at the end of June. Established in 1982 by Mrs. Pamela Harriman in honor of Avis Bohlen, the widow of the late Ambassador Charles E. Bohlen. Mrs. Bohlen was well known for charitable works directed at the local community,, as well as her concern for the American staff at Post.

• 2279 • Delavan Award
Established in 1991 by AFSA in memory of Nelson B. Delavan, and funded by the Delavan Foundation, to recognize the significant contributions of a Foreign Service office management specialist to post or office effectiveness, professionalism and morale beyond the framework of job responsibilities. Any office management specialist may be nominated by anyone with knowledge of the nominee's accomplishments. Self-nominations are not eligible. A monetary award and a certificate are awarded annually at the AFSA awards ceremony held at the end of June.

• 2280 • W. Averell Harriman Award
Established in 1968 by W. Averell Harriman to recognize and encourage constructive dissent by demonstrating intellectual courage, initiative and the integrity to challenge conventional wisdom, question the status quo and take a stand for one's beliefs, regardless of the consequences. Junior Foreign Service officers, (Grade Levels FS6-FS4), may be nominated by anyone with knowledge of the nominee's accomplishments. Self-nominations are not eligible. A monetary award and a certificate are awarded annually at the AFSA awards ceremony held at the end of June.

• 2281 • The Heather Laxdal Memorial Vocal Award/The Golan E. Hoole Memorial Shield
Awarded to the runner-up in the vocal competition of the Grand Awards Competition. $300 is awarded.

• 2282 • Christian A. Herter Award
Established in 1968 by Mrs. Christian Herter and her son, Christian Herter, Jr., in memory of Christian A. Herter, to recognize and encourage constructive dissent by demonstrating intellectual courage, initiative, and the integrity to challenge conventional wisdom, question the status quo, and take a stand for one's beliefs, regardless of the consequences. Senior Foreign Service officers (Grade Levels FE-OC-FE-CA) may be nominated by anyone with knowledge of the nominee's accomplishments. Self-nominations

are not eligible. A monetary award and a certificate are awarded annually at the AFSA awards ceremony held at the end of June.

• 2283 • William R. Rivkin Award
Established in 1968 by W. Averell Harriman to recognize and encourage constructive dissent by demonstrating intellectual courage, initiative and the integrity to challenge conventional wisdom, question the status quo and take a stand for one's beliefs, regardless of the consequences. Mid-level foreign service officers (Grade Levels FS3-FS1) may be nominated by anyone with knowledge of the nominee's accomplishments. Self-nominations are not eligible. A monetary award and a certificate are awarded annually at the AFSA awards ceremony held at the end of June.

• 2284 • Matilda W. Sinclaire Award
Established by a bequest from Ms. Sinclaire, a former Foreign Service officer, to AFSA in 1982 to promote and reward superior achievement by career and career conditional members of the Foreign Service who have distinguished themselves in the study of hard languages and their associated cultures. Hard languages are those that have proven relatively difficult for native English speakers to learn and that normally require eight months or more of intensive study. All candidates are nominated by language training supervisors at the school of language studies of the Foreign Service Institute, National Foreign Affairs Training Center at the Department of State. A monetary award and a certificate are awarded annually and announced in the Foreign Service Journal and other AFSA publications.

• 2285 •
American Forensic Association
James W. Pratt, Exec.Sec.
Box 256
River Falls, WI 54022
Phone: (715)425-3198
Toll-Free: 800-228-5424
Fax: (715)425-9533
E-mail: amforensicassoc@aol.com
Home Page: http://www.americanforensics.org/

• 2286 • Distinguished Service Award
To recognize individuals who have made outstanding long-term contributions to the field of speech advocacy. Awards are presented to members and non-members. Engraved plaques are awarded annually. Established in 1978.

• 2287 •
American Forest and Paper Association
John Mechem, Contact
1111 19th St. NW, Ste. 800
Washington, DC 20036
Phone: (202)463-2700
Toll-Free: 800-878-8878
Fax: (202)463-2471
E-mail: info@afandpa.org
Home Page: http://www.afandpa.org

• 2288 • Environment and Energy Achievement Awards Program
To recognize paper industry and forest products displaying significant innovations and accomplishments. Any company engaged in timber growing and harvest or in the manufacture of pulp, paper, and paperboard or solid wood products may enter. Entries are limited to U.S. based facilities. The deadline for entries is March. Awards are given in five major environmental and energy areas: Air Pollution Control, Water Pollution Control, Solid Waste Management, Forest Management and Energy Management and Innovation. Plaques are awarded annually when merited. Established in 1973. awarded annually when merited. Established in 1973.

• 2289 • George Olmsted Award
Recognizes original and outstanding paper industry-related research. Young scientists and engineers are eligible. A monetary award is given annually.

• 2290 •
American Forest and Paper Association
American Wood Council
John Mechem, Contact
1111 19th St. NW, Ste. 800
Washington, DC 20036
Phone: (202)463-2700
Toll-Free: 800-878-8878
Fax: (202)463-2471
E-mail: info@afandpa.org
Home Page: http://www.afandpa.org

Formerly: National Forest Products Assocation.

• 2291 • Environmental and Energy Achievement Award
Recognizes companies display significant innovation and accomplishments in five major environmental and energy areas: air pollution control, water pollution control, solid waste management, energy management and innovation, and forest management. Awarded annually.

• 2292 • Wood Design Award
For recognition of outstanding examples of wood construction exemplifying the practical environment benefits of wood as well as versatility. Structures must be completed within a specified date of the awards program, use wood systems and products, and have a dominant wood appearance. Award certificates are presented annually. In addition, local and national publicity in consumer trade publications is awarded. Established in 1981.

• 2293 •
American Forum for Jewish-Christian Cooperation
Dr. David Z. Ben-Ami, Chm. & Founder
1407 Montfort Dr.
Harrisburg, PA 17110
Phone: (717)236-0437
Phone: (301)675-3133
Fax: (717)541-5487
E-mail: display@localnet.com

• 2294 • American Statesman Award
Recognizes a U.S. or European Ambassador. Awarded annually.

• 2295 • Guardian of Liberty
Award of recognition.

• 2296 • Religious Freedom Award
Recognizes a Bishop or statesman. Awarded annually.

• 2297 •
American Foundation for Aging Research
Biochemistry Dept.
North Carolina State University
Campus Box 7622
Raleigh, NC 27695-7622
Phone: (919)515-5679
Fax: (919)515-2047
E-mail: afar_office@ncsu.edu
Home Page: http://www.ncsu.edu/project/afar

• 2298 • Cecille Gould Memorial Fund for Cancer Research
Given to applicants actively involved in a specific biomedical or biochemical research project. An annual monetary award given to a candidate for the purpose of cancer research. Applicants must be undergraduate, graduate or pre-doctoral students enrolled in degree programs at colleges or universities in the United States. Established in 1985.

• 2299 •
American Foundation for the Blind
Carl R. Augusto, Pres.
11 Penn Plz., Ste. 300
New York, NY 10001
Phone: (212)502-7600
Toll-Free: 800-232-5463
Fax: (212)502-7777
E-mail: afbinfo@afb.net
Home Page: http://www.afb.org

• 2300 • Access Awards
To honor individuals, corporations, and organizations that are eliminating or substantially reducing inequities faced by people who are blind or visually impaired by enhancing access to information, the environment, technology, education, or employment, including making mainstream products and services available.

• 2301 • William F. and Catherine T. Gallagher Award
Recognizes blind or visually impaired individuals who have demonstrated exemplary participation in the workplace and community, and have served as role models for other people who are blind or visually impaired.

• 2302 • Helen Keller Achievement Awards
Established to acknowledge her extraordinary efforts and promote notable achievement of individual and organizations that have improved the

quality of life for people who are blind or visually impaired.

• 2303 • Migel Medal for Outstanding Service to Blind Persons
To honor professionals and volunteers whose dedication and achievements have significantly improved the lives of people who are blind or visually impaired. Two medals are awarded annually: one to a professional; and one to a lay person.

• 2304 • Alexander Scourby Narrator of the Year Award
To recognize outstanding achievement in professional narration of Talking Books. Talking Book narrators are eligible. A plaque is awarded annually. Established in 1986 in memory of Alexander Scourby who, for 48 years, contributed much of his time, talent and energy to the recording of books for blind, visually impaired, and physically handicapped people. He recorded nearly 450 books, far more than any narrator in the history of Talking Books.

• 2305 •
American Friends of The Hebrew University
Ira Lee Sorkin, Pres.
1 Battery Park Plz., 25th Fl.
New York, NY 10004
Phone: (212)607-8500
Toll-Free: 800-567-AFHU
Fax: (212)809-4430
E-mail: info@afhu.org
Home Page: http://www.afhu.org

• 2306 • S. Y. Agnon Gold Medal
To recognize an individual for extensive investment in philanthropic, educational and cultural activities. A gold medal is awarded annually. Established in 1967 by the Society of the Founders of American Friends.

• 2307 • Solomon Bublick Hebrew University Awards
For recognition of the most significant contribution to the progress and development of Israel in the previous two years. An Israeli who must have been associated with the Hebrew University at some time and a non-Israeli are eligible alternately. A monetary award of $1,000 and a scroll are awarded annually. Established in 1949.

• 2308 • Judah L. Magnes Award
For recognition of concern with the future of Jewry and involvement in projects which insure its survival. An antique bronze Menorah Galvano and two gold-plated Judah L. Magnes bronze medals are awarded. Established in 1972 by the Society of the Founders.

• 2309 • Scopus Award
To recognize an individual for community leadership and generosity in philanthropy. A metal plaque is awarded. Established in 1961.

• 2310 • Torch of Learning Award
To recognize leaders of American Jewish communities who have influenced the course of higher learning in the United States and Israel. A bronze statuette signed by the artist, Chaim Gross, is awarded annually. Established in 1970.

• 2311 •
American Fuchsia Society
Rodney Bergquist, Pres.
6979 Clark Rd.
Paradise, CA 95969
Phone: (530)876-8517
E-mail: ejsalome@aol.com
Home Page: http://www.americanfuchsiasociety.org/

• 2312 • Achievement Award
Recognizes outstanding service performed in the field of service and/or fuchsia culture. Applicants must be association members.

• 2313 • Longevity Award
Recognizes accomplishments in photography, unregistered seedlings, and other industry related areas.

• 2314 •
American Galvanizers Association
Phil Rahrig, Exec. Marketing Dir.
6881 S Holy Cir., Ste. 108
Centennial, CO 80112
Phone: (720)554-0900
Toll-Free: 800-468-7732
Fax: (720)554-0909
E-mail: aga@galvanizeit.org
Home Page: http://www.galvanizeit.org

• 2315 • Excellence in Hot-Dip Galvanizing Awards
Recognizes projects that utilize hot-dip galvanized steel in an ideal creative, or monumental fashion. Awards are presented in the following categories: artistic; bridge and highway; building and architecture; civic contribution; duplex systems; electrical, utility, and communications; food and agriculture; industrial; international; original equipment manufacturing; recreation and entertainment; transportation; and water and marine. All applicants are also considered for the Most Distinguished Project Award. Each award recognizes the galvanizer, specified architect, and engineer. Winners receive a plaque and copies of the color award brochures.

• 2316 •
American Gear Manufacturer Association
Joe T. Franklin Jr., Pres.
500 Montgomery St., Ste. 350
Alexandria, VA 22314-1581
Phone: (703)684-0211
Fax: (703)684-0242
E-mail: webmaster@agma.org
Home Page: http://www.agma.org

• 2317 • Administrative Division Executive Committee Award
To recognize an individual for efforts to enhance the art of management in the gear industry. Individuals who have made noteworthy contributions to promote the welfare of company members of AGMA are eligible. A scroll is awarded annually. Established in 1966. Formerly: Product Division Executive Committee Award.

• 2318 • Board of Directors' Award
For recognition of meritorious service to the members of the Association and to the gear industry. Individuals, upon completion of a four-year term as a member of the board or for satisfactory performance of any other sustained effort of particular benefit to the officers, board or general membership of the Association, are eligible. Nominations are accepted. A scroll is awarded annually without restriction to number. Established in 1966.

• 2319 • Edward P. Connell Award
To recognize contributions to the Association or the gear industry above and beyond ordinary obligations to serve or improve the industry. Individuals who, preferably, have been active in the Association, and with specific attention to younger persons who are bringing important advancements in the industry, are eligible. Nominations are accepted. A scroll and a sterling silver medallion are awarded annually. Established in 1942 by the Falk Corporation.

• 2320 • Technical Division Executive Committee Award
To recognize an individual for outstanding contributions to the art of gear design and utilization. A scroll is awarded annually, without restriction to number. Established in 1966.

• 2321 •
American Gem Society
Ruth Batson, Exec.Dir./CEO
8881 W Sahara Ave.
Las Vegas, NV 89117
Phone: (702)255-6500
Fax: (702)255-7420
E-mail: info@ags.org
Home Page: http://www.ags.org

• 2322 • Robert M. Shipley Award
To recognize an individual for outstanding service to the Society, a significant contribution to the science of gemology, or for exemplifying the high purpose, objectives, and ideals of the Society in the member's own community. Any member, by nomination and subsequent selection, who meets these guidelines is eligible. A plaque is awarded annually at the National Conclave. Established in 1967 by the Board of Directors to honor Robert M. Shipley, founder of the Society.

Awards are arranged in alphabetical order below their administering organizations

• 2323 •
American Gem Trade Association
Douglas Hucker, Exec.Dir.
PO Box 420643
3030 LBJ Freeway, Ste. 840
Dallas, TX 75234
Phone: (214)742-4367
Toll-Free: 800-972-1162
Fax: (214)742-7334
E-mail: info@agta.org
Home Page: http://www.agta.org

• 2324 • **Cutting Edge Gemstone Competition**
To increase industry and consumer awareness of quality gemstones and excellent cutting. The competition is open to all gemstones of natural origin. The Showcase will yield an outstanding collection of fine quality, well-cut gemstones from a variety of sources. The competition honors creativity and excellence among North American lapidary artists. The Competition will yield a total of 18 winners from 6 categories, forming a spectacular collection of innovative gemstone designs and objects d'art fashioned by North American lapidaries. Established in 1991.

• 2325 • **Fashion Forward Awards**
Recognizes the outstanding use of colored gemstone and/or cultured pearls in artful, trend-setting jewelry.

• 2326 • **Spectrum Awards Design Competition**
To recognize the creative use of natural colored gemstones by North American and international jewelry designers. Original designs featuring natural colored gemstones in fine jewelry may be submitted by the entry deadline in late September. First, second, and third places are awarded in each of the eight categories. Awarded annually in February at the AGTA GemFair in Tucson, Arizona. Established in 1983.

• 2327 •
American Geographical Society
Mary Lynne Bird, Exec.Dir.
120 Wall St., No. 100
New York, NY 10005
Phone: (212)422-5456
Fax: (212)422-5480
E-mail: ags@amergeog.org
Home Page: http://www.amergeog.org

• 2328 • **Cullum Geographical Medal**
To recognize distinguished contributions to the advancement of geographical science or outstanding geographical discoveries. A gold medal is awarded when merited. Established in 1896 by a bequest from Major General W. Cullum of the U.S. Army, vice president of the society from 1877 to 1892.

• 2329 • **Charles P. Daly Medal**
To recognize valuable or distinguished geographical services. A gold medal is awarded when merited. Established in 1902 by a bequest of Judge Daly, president of the society from 1864 to 1899.

• 2330 • **George Davidson Medal**
To recognize exceptional achievement in research or exploration in the Pacific Ocean or the lands bordering thereon. A gold medal is awarded. Established in 1946 by a bequest of Ellinor Campbell Davidson in memory of her father, George Davidson, the great California scientist and geographer.

• 2331 • **David Livingstone Centenary Medal**
To recognize scientific achievement in the field of geography of the southern hemisphere. Gold, silver, or bronze medals are awarded when merited. Established in 1913 by the Hispanic Society of America in memory of David Livingstone, the African explorer, on the centenary of his birth.

• 2332 • **McColl Family Fellowship**
Provides travel money for field work leading to the writing of an article suitable for publication in *Focus* magazine. Awarded annually. Established in 1999.

• 2333 • **O. M. Miller Cartographic Medal**
To recognize outstanding contributions in the field of cartography or geodesy. A gold medal is awarded when merited. Established in 1968.

• 2334 • **Samuel Finley Breese Morse Medal**
To encourage geographical research. A gold medal is awarded when merited. Established in 1902 with funds bequeathed to the society by Professor Morse, discoverer of the recording telegraph. First awarded in 1928.

• 2335 • **Van Cleef Memorial Medal**
To recognize outstanding contributions in the field of applied urban geography. A gold medal is awarded intermittently. Established in 1970 by Dr. Eugene Van Cleef in memory of his wife, Frieda.

• 2336 • **Paul P. Vouras Medal**
To recognize outstanding scholarly contributions in regional geography. A gold medal is awarded. Established in 1988 by a bequest of Professor Paul P. Vouras.

• 2337 • **Wrigley-Fairchild Prize**
Recognizes the best article published in the *Geographical Review* by a younger or early-career scholar over a three-year period. A cash prize is awarded. Established in 1994; first awarded in 1998.

• 2338 •
American Geological Institute
Dr. Marcus E. Milling, Exec.Dir.
4220 King St.
Alexandria, VA 22302-1502
Phone: (703)379-2480
Fax: (703)379-7563
E-mail: agi@agiweb.org
Home Page: http://www.agiweb.org

• 2339 • **Award for Outstanding Contribution to Public Understanding of the Geosciences**
To recognize a contribution or contributions that lead to greater public appreciation and better understanding of the role of geology in the affairs of our society. Awarded annually and presented in the form of a plaque.

• 2340 • **Medal in Memory of Ian Campbell**
To recognize singular performance in and contribution to the profession of geology. Awarded annually with a medal.

• 2341 • **William B. Heroy, Jr. Award for Distinguished Service to AGI**
To recognize the exceptional and beneficial long-term service to AGI. Awarded annually with a plaque.

• 2342 •
American Geophysical Union
Fred Spilhaus, Exec.Dir.
2000 Florida Ave. NW
Washington, DC 20009-1277
Phone: (202)462-6900
Toll-Free: 800-966-AGU1
Fax: (202)328-0566
E-mail: service@agu.org
Home Page: http://www.agu.org

• 2343 • **N.L. Bowen Award**
To recognize a single outstanding contribution to volcanology, geochemistry, or petrology during the preceding five years. Given by the Volcanology, Geochemistry, and Petrology Section. Established 1981. Formerly: (1997) VGP Award.

• 2344 • **William Bowie Medal**
For recognition of outstanding contributions to fundamental geophysics and for unselfish cooperation in research. A medal is awarded annually. Established in 1939.

• 2345 • **Walter H. Bucher Medal**
For recognition of original contributions to the basic knowledge of the Earth's crust. A medal is awarded biennially in even-numbered years. Established in 1966.

• 2346 • **Maurice Ewing Medal**
For recognition of significant original contributions to understanding physical, geophysical, and geological processes in the ocean; significant original contributions to scientific ocean en-

gineering, technology, and instrumentation; and/or outstanding service to marine sciences. A medal is awarded annually. Established in 1974. Co-sponsored by the United States Navy.

• 2347 • Excellence in Geophysical Education Award
To recognize a sustained commitment to excellence in geophysical education by an individual, team, or group of individuals of exceptional merit. Awarded annually. Established in 1995.

• 2348 • Fellow
To recognize members of the Union who have distinguished themselves in geophysics.

• 2349 • John Adam Fleming Award
For original research and technical leadership in geomagnetism, atmospheric electricity, aeronomy, and related sciences. A medal is awarded annually. Established in 1960.

• 2350 • Edward A. Flinn III Award
To recognize those individuals who personify the Union's motto, "unselfish cooperation in research," through their facilitating, coordinating, and implementing activities. Established in 1990.

• 2351 • Harry H. Hess Medal
For recognition of outstanding achievements in research of the constitution and evolution of Earth and sister planets. A medal is awarded biennially in odd-numbered years. Established in 1984.

• 2352 • Robert E. Horton Medal
For outstanding contributions to the geophysical aspects of hydrology. A medal is awarded annually. Established in 1974.

• 2353 • Hydrology Section Award
To recognize outstanding contribution to the science of hydrology over a career, emphasizing the last five years. Given by the Hydrology Section. Established in 1956. Formerly: (2006) Robert E. Horton Award.

• 2354 • Inge Lehmann Medal
For recognition of outstanding contributions toward the understanding of the structure, composition and/or dynamics of the Earth's mantle and core. A medal is awarded biennially in odd-numbered years. Established in 1997.

• 2355 • James B. Macelwane Medal
For recognition of significant contributions to the geophysical sciences by a young scientist of outstanding ability. Individuals younger than 36 years of age are eligible. May be awarded to as many as five recipients. Established in 1961.

• 2356 • Ocean Sciences Award
To recognize outstanding and long-standing service to the ocean science. Up to three awards a year may be given by the Ocean Sciences Section.

• 2357 • Roger Revelle Medal
For recognition of outstanding accomplishments or contributions toward the understanding of the earth's atmospheric processes, including its dynamics, chemistry, and radiation, or the roles of atmosphere, atmosphere-ocean coupling, or atmosphere-land coupling in determining the climate, biogeochemical cycles, or other key elements of the integrated climate system. Established in 1991.

• 2358 • Waldo E. Smith Medal
For recognition of extraordinary service to geophysics. A medal is awarded biennially in even-numbered years. Established in 1982 in honor of Waldo E. Smith.

• 2359 • Charles A. Whitten Medal
For recognition of outstanding achievement in research on the form and dynamics of the Earth and planets. A medal is awarded biennially in odd-numbered years. Established in 1984.

• 2360 •
American Geriatrics Society
Linda Hiddemen Barondess, Exec.VP
350 5th Ave., Ste. 801
New York, NY 10118
Phone: (212)308-1414
Toll-Free: 800-247-4779
Fax: (212)832-8646
E-mail: info@americangeriatrics.org
Home Page: http://www.americangeriatrics.org

• 2361 • Edward Henderson Memorial Student Award
To recognize medical students who have demonstrated initiative and excellence in the area of clinical geriatrics, and who have a commitment to a career in that field. Students must be nominated by one faculty member with letters of recommendation from at least two other faculty members. An honorarium of $500 (which includes travel expenses to attend the Society's annual meeting) and a certificate are awarded annually. The deadline for nominations is in early December. Established in 1973 in memory of Dr. Edward Henderson, Executive Director of the Society, 1962-1973.

• 2362 • New Investigator Awards
To recognize individuals whose original work reflects new and relevant research in geriatrics and who have a commitment to a career in aging research. The awards are restricted to fellows-in-training and new and junior investigators holding an academic appointment not longer than five years post-fellowship. The work must not have been published. Awardees are chosen on the basis of originality, scientific merit, and relevance of research. Honorariums of $1,500 and waivers of the registration fee are awarded to ten individuals each year at the Society's annual scientific meeting. At least one award will be presented specifically for research in the neurosciences. The deadline for nominations is early December. Sponsored by Merck U.S. Human Health. Established in 1985.

• 2363 •
American Gloxinia and Gesneriad Society, Grow and Study Chapter
Al Striepens, Pres.
2225 Deepgrove Ave.
Rowland Heights, CA 91748-4208
Phone: (626)964-4462
E-mail: alstriepens@juno.com

• 2364 • Best Gesneriad
For best gesneriad in judged shows. Recognition award bestowed annually.

• 2365 •
American Group Psychotherapy Association
Marsha S. Block CAE, CEO
25 E 21st St., 6th Fl.
New York, NY 10010
Phone: (212)477-2677
Toll-Free: 877-668-2472
Fax: (212)979-6627
E-mail: info@agpa.org
Home Page: http://www.agpa.org

• 2366 • Fellowship in the Association
To recognize outstanding professional competence or leadership. Selection is based on leadership in at least two of the following five areas: (1) leadership in the Association and its affiliates; (2) clinical practice; (3) teaching and training; (4) research; and (5) publications. Certificates are awarded annually. Established in 1942.

• 2367 •
American Guild of Organists
Harold Calhoun, Competitions Man.
475 Riverside Dr., Ste. 1260
New York, NY 10115
Phone: (212)870-2310
Toll-Free: 800-AGO-5115
Fax: (212)870-2163
E-mail: info@agohq.org
Home Page: http://www.agohq.org

• 2368 • AGO/ECS Publishing Award in Choral Composition
To encourage composition of works done for chorus and organ in which the organ plays a distinctive and significant role. Composers of any age or nationality may apply. The deadline for entry varies in even years. There is a monetary prize of $2,000, plus publication and performance of the work at the biennial AGO National Convention. Additional information is available from Harold Calhoun, Competitions Manager. Formerly: (1995) Moller/AGO Award in Choral Competition.

• 2369 • AGO Examination Prize
For recognition of the individual attaining the highest average of all candidates taking the American Guild of Organists Examinations. A

monetary prize of $300 is awarded annually. Formerly: (1995) S. Lewis Elmer Award.

• 2370 • Holtkamp/AGO Award in Organ Composition

To encourage young composers to compose for the organ. Composers of any age or nationality may apply. The deadline for entry varies in odd numbered years. There is a monetary prize of $2,000, plus publication and performance of the work at the biennial AGO National Convention. Additional information is available from Harold Calhoun, Competitions Manager.

• 2371 • National Competition in Organ Improvisation

To further the art of improvisation by recognizing and rewarding superior performers in the field. Seeks to promote the skills necessary for this challenging art form. Open to all organists. Competition is three rounds. Awards for the final round are $2,000 for first place, $1,500 for second, and $750 for third place. Applications are collected in the fall of odd numbered years. Awarded biennially in even-numbered years.

• 2372 • National Young Artists Competition in Organ Performance

To recognize young organists between the ages of 22 and 32 years in a national competition. The competition has 3 rounds and begins with an initial preliminary recorded round. The final round takes place at the biennial National Convention. The following are awarded: first place Lillian Murtagh Memorial Prize, $2,000, and an offer of a career guidance program for young artists in consultation with Karen McFarlane; second place - $2,000; third place - $1,000; and an audience choice prize - $500. Established in 1950. Additional information is available from Harold Calhoun, Competitions Manager.

• 2373 • Quimby Regional Competitions for Young Organists

To recognize young organists in regional competitions. Organists under 23 years of age by August 1 may compete in the American Guild of Organists region of their school or home. Contestants need not belong to the AGO. Each region awards a $1,000 cash prize for first place and a $500 cash prize for second place. Awarded biennially in odd-numbered years.

• 2374 •
American Guild of Organists, Region II
David S. Macfarlane, Regional Councilor
70 W Grove St.
Bogota, NJ 07603
Phone: (315)695-6677
Phone: (315)652-1068
Fax: (315)622-4500
E-mail: tdhenry2@aol.com
Home Page: http://www.agohq.org

• 2375 • RYOC

For young organ contestant. Monetary award bestowed biennially.

• 2376 •
American Guild of Organists, Wyoming (606)
Beverly K. Reese CAGO, Contact
1020 S Lincoln St.
Casper, WY 82601-3331
Phone: (307)235-5709
Fax: (307)473-2833
E-mail: firstpc@trib.com

• 2377 • AGO Scholarship

For need and serious intent to continue as deemed worthy by members.

• 2378 •
American Gynecological and Obstetrical Society
Cassandra Larkins, Admin.Dir.
409 12th St. NW
Washington, DC 20024-2188
Phone: (202)863-1648
Fax: (202)554-0453
E-mail: clarkins@acog.org
Home Page: http://www.agosonline.org

Absorbed: American Gynecological Society.

• 2379 • Charles A. Hunter, Jr. Award Thesis

For recognition of outstanding investigative work in the field of obstetrics and gynecology. A monetary award is presented annually. Established in 1938. Formerly: (1980) Foundation Prize Awards.

• 2380 • Joseph Price Oration

For recognition of an individual distinguished in a field of special interest to the association from outside the United States. A monetary award is presented annually. Established in 1927.

• 2381 •
American Handwriting Analysis Foundation
Prof. Dorothy W. Hodos, Admin.Asst.
PO Box 6201
San Jose, CA 95150-6201
Phone: (408)377-6775
Toll-Free: 800-826-7774
E-mail: ahafeditor@aol.com
Home Page: http://www.morenofidof.org

• 2382 • Flandrin/Michon Life Achievement Award

To recognize an individual for exemplary contributions to graphology. A plaque is awarded when merited. Established in 1982. This award is named for both Abbe Louis Flandrin, a French monk who lived in the 1800s and dedicated his life to graphology, and his disciple, Abbe Jean Michon, who coined the term graphology.

• 2383 • President's Award

For recognition of excellence in and/or contributions to the field of graphology. AHAF members are eligible for the award. A gold nib pen and diploma certificate are presented annually at the convention banquet. Established in 1952. Additional information is available from Dorothy Hodos, 1211 El Solyo Ave., Campbell, CA 95008-3307. Formerly: Gold Nibs Award.

• 2384 • The Geri Stuparich "Heart of Gold" Award

To recognize an individual from one of the many handwriting organizations or from one of the chapters of AHAF. Awarded by the Northern California Chapter.

• 2385 •
American Hanoverian Society
Hush Bellis-Jones, Exec.Dir.
4067 Iron Works Pike, Ste. 1
Lexington, KY 40511-8483
Phone: (859)255-4141
Fax: (859)255-8467
E-mail: ahsoffice@aol.com
Home Page: http://www.hanoverian.org

• 2386 • Awards Program

Recognizes the best Hanoverian horses and riders in the following categories: Dressage, Eventing, Hunters and Jumpers, and Sport Horse Breed Shows. Additional awards include the Dr. Hartwig Prize, MPT Benchmark Award, Young Jumper Award, and Perpetual Trophies. Awarded annually.

• 2387 •
American Headache Society
Linda McGillicuddy, Exec.Dir.
19 Mantua Rd.
Mount Royal, NJ 08061
Phone: (856)423-0043
Fax: (856)423-0082
E-mail: ahshq@talley.com
Home Page: http://www.ahsnet.org

• 2388 • AHS/Merck US Human Health Migraine and Women's Health Research Award

This one-year $20,000 award is for the best research proposal for basic or clinical research on the relationship between women's health issues and migraine. For more information and a complete application, please visit the AHS website at http://www.ahsnet.org.

• 2389 • Kaplan Award for Chronic Daily Headache

$1,000 is awarded to the author of the best abstract on chronic daily headache submitted for the AHS Annual Meeting. Inquire for application details.

• 2390 • Resident/Fellow Travel Award Program - Annual Scientific Meeting

Up to five awards are available based on the quality of abstracts submitted for the AHS Annual Scientific Meeting, as well as a letter of recommendation from the applicant's training director or department chair. Recipients are invited to present their papers in a platform or poster presentation at the AHS Annual Scientific Meeting, and will receive complimentary meeting registration and expenses for travel, hotel accommodations and meals. Recipients also receive a one-year Trainee membership in AHS (if they are not already a member). Inquire for application details.

• 2391 • Harold G. Wolff Lecture Award
Awarded for the best paper on headache, head or face pain, or the nature of pain itself submitted in abstract for the AHS Annual Scientific Meeting. Recipient receives $10,000 plus complimentary meeting registration and expenses for travel, lodging, and meals during the meeting. Recipient is invited to present the paper at the AHS Annual Scientific Meeting. Inquire for application details.

• 2392 •
American Health Care Association
Dr. Charles H. Roadman II, CEO
1201 L St. NW
Washington, DC 20005
Phone: (202)842-4444
Fax: (202)842-3860
Home Page: http://www.ahca.org

• 2393 • Adult Volunteer of the Year
To recognize outstanding contributions in the field of nursing home volunteer work. Adults, 20 years of age or older, who have been nominated by the State Association are eligible. A plaque and travel to the convention are awarded annually. Formerly: Volunteer of the Year.

• 2394 • Better Life Award
To recognize individuals or organizations possessing the highest qualities of concern and accomplishment in the area of long-term health care. A plaque is awarded.

• 2395 • Group Volunteer of the Year Award
To recognize outstanding contributions by groups in the field of nursing home volunteer work. Church and civic organizations as well as other "groups" of individuals nominated by an AHCA state affiliate are eligible. Awarded annually.

• 2396 • Teen Volunteer of the Year
To recognize outstanding contributions in the field of nursing home volunteer work. Teenagers nominated by the State Association are eligible. Awarded annually.

• 2397 •
American Health Information Management - Wisconsin Chapter
Cassandra Bissen RHIA, Executive Director
2350 South Ave., Ste. 107
La Crosse, WI 54601
Phone: (608)787-0168
Phone: (608)787-6608
Fax: (608)787-0169
E-mail: sbissen@execpc.com
Home Page: http://www.whima.org

• 2398 • Health Information Management Scholarship
For student in accredited health information management or health information technology program enrollee. Scholarship awarded annually.

• 2399 •
American Healthcare Radiology Administrators
Edward J. Cronin Jr., Exec.Dir.
490-B Boston Post Rd., Ste. 101
Sudbury, MA 01776
Phone: (978)443-7591
Toll-Free: 800-334-2472
Fax: (978)443-8046
E-mail: info@ahraonline.org
Home Page: http://www.ahraonline.org

Formerly: (1987) American Hospital Radiology Administrators.

• 2400 • Gold Award
This, the highest honor of the organization, is given to an active member who has made significant contributions to the profession of radiology administration. Only active members of AHRA are considered for the award. Member Recognition team members may not be considered during their term.

• 2401 •
American Heart Association
M. Cass Wheeler, CEO
7272 Greenville Ave.
Dallas, TX 75231-4596
Phone: (301)223-2307
Toll-Free: 800-242-8721
E-mail: aharesume@heart.org
Home Page: http://www.americanheart.org

• 2402 • Award of Merit
For recognition of important service to the American Heart Association in the development of its national program. Awarded annually. Established in 1952.

• 2403 • Basic Research Prize
For recognition of outstanding contributions to the advancement of cardiovascular science. A $5,000 honorarium is presented at the opening session of the annual Scientific Sessions. Established in 1990.

• 2404 • Howard W. Blakeslee Awards
For recognition of significant contributions by any medium of mass communication to public understanding of progress in research and in the prevention, care, or treatment of heart and blood vessel diseases. Categories include: newspaper with more than 100,000 circulation, newspaper with less than 100,000 circulation, magazine, special medical and scientific publication, book, radio, local and regional TV, and network TV. Entries are judged on the basis of accuracy, significance, skill, and originality. The deadline is February 1. A monetary award of $1,000, a citation, and travel expenses to receive the award are presented annually. Established in 1952 in memory of Howard W. Blakeslee, Science Editor of the Associated Press, and a founder of the National Association of Science Writers.

• 2405 • Clinician - Scientist Award
To encourage promising physicians to undertake careers in investigation. Awardees are supported during an initial period of rigorous, full-time research training under a preceptor, and during a subsequent period when they are expected to initiate an independent investigative program in a clinical department in the sponsoring institution. Applicants must hold an MD, DO, or equivalent medical degree, have no more than one year of relevant postdoctoral research training after completion of residency, and be citizens or permanent residents of the United States. Applications must be submitted by June 1. A stipend of $40,000-$44,000 is awarded annually.

• 2406 • Established Investigator Award
To assist promising physicians and scientists to develop research careers in academic medicine and biology. Applicants must hold an MD, PhD, DO, or equivalent domestic or foreign degree and must be citizens or permanent residents of the United States. Applicants must show evidence of ability to conduct independent research, but not have reached a position of eminence in a chosen field. Applications must be submitted by June 1. A $45,000 stipend plus project support of $6,000 in the first year of the award, with incremental increases of $1,000 annually for five years is awarded.

• 2407 • Gold Heart Award
This, the highest award of the Association, is given for recognition of distinguished service by an individual to the Association and notable contribution to the national heart program. A certificate and a gold plaque are awarded annually. Established in 1950.

• 2408 • Heart of the Year Award
For recognition of personal achievement, faith, and courage in meeting the challenge of heart disease, thereby inspiring people with confidence in the objectives and programs of the Association. Distinguished Americans are eligible. A plaque is awarded periodically. Established in 1959.

• 2409 • James B. Herrick Award
To recognize physicians for outstanding achievements in clinical cardiology. A medallion and a citation are awarded annually by the Council on Clinical Cardiology. Established in 1968.

• 2410 • Martha N. Hill New Investigator Award
To encourage the professional growth of new investigators by recognizing their outstanding contribution to the understanding, prevention, and treatment of cardiovascular diseases. Both basic and clinical research is recognized. Candidates must have completed their doctoral de-

gree no more than seven years prior to application. They must also be members of the Council on Cardiovascular Nursing at the time of submission. Awards are designated on the basis of scientific merit, quality, and originality of the manuscript submitted. The application deadline is the last Friday in May. The first place winner receives a plaque and cash award of $1,500. Two semi-finalists receive a plaque and a cash award of $500 each. Sponsored by the Council on Cardiovascular Nursing.

• 2411 • Melvin Judkins Young Clinical Investigator Award

To recognize meritorious research and promotes careers in cardiovascular radiology. Candidates must be pursuing research in the basic biological or medical sciences or related fields. The first-prize winner will receive a plaque and$500; the other finalists will each receive a plaque and a$500 travel award. Awarded annually. Sponsored by the Council on Cardiovascular Radiology and Intervention.

• 2412 • Louis N. Katz Basic Science Research Prize for Young Investigators

To encourage investigation in basic science and related fields. Meritorious manuscripts based on an independent investigation pertinent to cardiovascular phenomena are considered. Candidates must also have a doctoral degree (completed after January 1, 1992) or equivalent experience and be pursuing research in the basic biological or medical sciences or related fields. If candidates are faculty members, they must have been appointed after January 1, 1992. The first prize winner receives a plaque and a cash award of $1,500. Four runners-up receive a plaque and $500. The application deadline is the first Friday in May. Established in 1969. Sponsored by the Council on Basic Science.

• 2413 • Katharine A. Lembright Award

To recognize and encourage excellence in cardiovascular research by established nurse scientists. A $2,000 monetary award and invitation to present a lecture are awarded at the Annual Scientific Sessions. Sponsored by the Council on Cardiovascular Nursing.

• 2414 • Samuel A. Levine Young Clinical Investigator Award

To recognize innovative research and promote careers in clinical cardiovascular investigation. Candidates must be within three years of completion of cardiovascular fellowship training and must be members, members-in-training, or fellows of the Council on Clinical Cardiology, or have a letter from a Council fellow. Finalists are selected for meritorious manuscripts based on clinical research involving patients or human subjects. Multicenter trials are not eligible. The application deadline is the last Friday in May. The winner receives a cash award of $1,500 and four runners-up receive $500. Each awardee also receives a plaque designating the award. Sponsored by the Council on Clinical Cardiology.

• 2415 • Melvin L. Marcus Young Investigator Awards in Cardiovascular Sciences

To encourage young investigators to continue research careers in cardiovascular or circulatory physiology. Candidates must have a doctoral degree or equivalent experience, have completed training after January 1, 1992 and rank no higher than Assistant Professor for three years. Manuscripts describing studies of integrated physiology, vascular biology, and molecular mechanisms relating directly to cardiovascular physiology will be considered. Finalists are selected for meritorious manuscripts based on independent investigations of cardiovascular integrated physiology and abstract submission. The application deadline is May 7. The first place winner receives a plaque and a cash award of $1,500. Four runners-up each receive a plaque and a cash award of $500. Awarded annually. Sponsored by the Council on Basic Cardiovascular Sciences.

• 2416 • Minority Scientist Development Award

To recognize promising minority scientists (black, Hispanic, Native American, or Pacific Islander) underrepresented in the field of cardiovascular research. Awardees are supported for a five-year period of full-time training and independent research. Applicants must be U.S. citizens or permanent residents and have two to five years of postdoctoral research experience. The deadline for applications is June 1. A $40,000 stipend with $1,000 incremental increases annually for five years and project support of $33,000 in the third or fourth year of the award is presented.

• 2417 • Irvine H. Page Award for Young Investigators

To encourage young investigators to continue careers in arteriosclerosis research and to recognize talented investigators at an early stage of their careers. Candidates must be working in any area of research that is concerned with aspects of arteriosclerosis, have sustained effort in the research area, and have at least one prior publication. Unpublished manuscripts are considered if the applicant is the sole or principal author. First prize winners receive a plaque and a $1,500 cash award. Four runners-up receive plaques. The application deadline is the last Friday in May. Established in 1977. Sponsored by the Council on Arteriosclerosis.

• 2418 • Research Achievement Award

To recognize an individual for distinguished scientific achievement in the field of cardiovascular research. A monetary award of $1,000 and a citation are awarded annually. Established in 1953. Formerly: (1961) Albert D. Lasker Award.

• 2419 • Louis B. Russell, Jr., Memorial Award

For recognition of leadership in promoting and enhancing the relationship between the American Heart Association and the minority or low-income community. Nominees must be active members or volunteers of the Association. Established in 1977 in memory of Louis B. Russell, Jr., who, as a volunteer, gave willingly and freely of himself to benefit others.

• 2420 • Cournand and Comroe Young Investigator Prize

To acknowledge the accomplishments of young investigators and to encourage investigators to continue their research in biomedical sciences. Candidates must be working in any area of research that is concerned with aspects of pulmonary and critical care biology. The application deadline is the last Friday in May. The first place winner receives a plaque and a cash award of $500. Two runners-up receive plaques and cash awards of $250. The remaining two finalists receive honorable mentions. Sponsored by the Council on Cardiopulmonary, Perioperative and Critical Care.

• 2421 • Young Investigator Prizes in Thrombosis

To encourage fundamental and applied research in thrombosis including the mechanism, detection, treatment, and prevention of thrombotic disorders. Candidates must have completed postdoctoral training at least two years before nomination. The first prize winner receives an engraved plaque and cash award of $1,000 plus a $500 travel stipend. Four runners-up receive plaques and a $500 travel stipend. Awarded annually. Sponsored by the Council on Arteriosclerosis, Thrombosis and Vascular Biology.

• 2422 •

American Heart Association, Talbot County Branch
Lyn von Spaeth, Chm.
PO Box 17025
Baltimore, MD 21297-0191
Phone: (410)685-7074
Fax: (410)539-5049
Home Page: http://www.americanheart.org

• 2423 • Research Awards

For cardiovascular disease research. Grant awarded annually.

• 2424 •

American Helicopter Society
Morris E. Rhett Flater, Exec.Dir.
217 N Washington St.
Alexandria, VA 22314-2530
Phone: (703)684-6777
Fax: (703)739-9279
E-mail: staff@vtol.org
Home Page: http://www.vtol.org

• 2425 • AHS Fellows

To recognize Society members whose work towards the interest of the industry constitutes an outstanding achievement. Awarded annually. A certificate is awarded. Under award guidelines, up to four Fellows maybe recognized an any single year.

• 2426 • Gruppo Augusta International Helicopter Fellowship Award
For recognition of significant contribution to international vertical flight cooperation by an individual or group. Awarded annually. The award consists of a trophy by the noted Italian sculptor Felice Ludovisi entitled "Pegasus" that is kept by the Society. A miniature of the trophy is given to the recipient. Established in 1989 in memory of Paolo Bellavita.

• 2427 • Francois Xavier Bagnoud Award
To recognize outstanding contributions to vertical flight technology by a member under the age of 30. Awarded annually. Established in 1992. Formerly: Director's Award.

• 2428 • Grover E. Bell Award
To foster and encourage research and experimentation in helicopter development in the U.S. Awarded annually to the person or persons who have made an outstanding contribution within the field during the preceding year. Established in 1957.

• 2429 • Frederick L. Feinberg Award
To recognize the helicopter pilot who accomplished the most outstanding achievement during the preceding year. Military or civilian pilots are eligible. A monetary award of $200 and a certificate are awarded annually. Established in 1961 by the Kaman Aerospace Corporation in memory of Frederick L. Feinberg, an outstanding helicopter test pilot.

• 2430 • Paul E. Haueter Award
To recognize an individual or company making significant contributions to the development of vertical take-off and landing aircraft other than helicopters. Awarded annually. Established in 1966.

• 2431 • Honorary Fellows
To recognize Society members whose work toward the interest of AHS has constituted an outstanding achievement. A certificate and life membership are awarded annually to two awardees. Established in 1944.

• 2432 • Howard Hughes Award
To recognize an outstanding improvement in fundamental helicopter technology brought to fruition during the preceding calendar year. Awarded annually. Established in 1977 to honor the memory of Howard Hughes and his accomplishments in aviation.

• 2433 • Harry T. Jensen Award
For recognition of an outstanding contribution to the improvement of helicopter reliability, maintainability, and safety through improved design brought to fruition during the preceding year. Awarded annually. A trophy, a certificate, and the engraving of the recipient's name on a permanent plaque are awarded. Established by Sikorsky Aircraft Division, UTC, in 1986, to honor Harry T. Jensen for his contributions to helicopter safety and structural reliability.

• 2434 • Dr. Alexander Klemin Award
For recognition of notable achievement in the advancement of rotary wing aeronautics. A certificate is awarded annually. Established in 1951 by Frank H. Piasecki in memory of Dr. Alexander Klemin, an aeronautical engineer and pioneer in rotary-wing aeronautics.

• 2435 • Captain William J. Kossler, USCG Award
For recognition of achievement in the practical application or operation of rotary wing aircraft, the value of which has been demonstrated by actual service during the preceding year. A certificate is awarded. Established in 1951 in memory of Captain William J. Kossler, U.S. Coast Guard airman, aeronautical engineer, and early advocate of helicopters in USCG operations. Awarded annually.

• 2436 • Robert L. Lichten Award
For recognition of the best technical paper presented at a regional meeting of the Society during the preceding calendar year. A monetary prize of $250 from a contribution by Bell Helicopter Textron to the Vertical Flight Foundation is awarded. Established in 1975 in memory of Robert L. Lichten, a rotary-wing aeronautical engineer and the Society's 22nd president.

• 2437 • Alexander A. Nikolsky Honorary Lectureship
For recognition of an individual who reflects the highest ideals, goals, and achievements in the field of helicopter and VTOL aircraft engineering and development. Nominations are made by AHS members based upon the individual's distinguished career, the significance and appropriateness of the subject matter, the ability to compose an archival lecture document, and a willingness to present the lecture to the various regions of the Society. A medallion and a certificate are awarded. The lecture, which is presented at the Annual Forum, is also published in the *Journal of the American Helicopter Society.* Established in 1981.

• 2438 • Robert L. Pinckney Award
In recognition of notable achievement in manufacturing research and development for rotorcraft or rotorcraft components brought to fruition in recent years. Awarded annually. Established in 1995.

• 2439 • Igor I. Sikorsky International Trophy
To recognize the company that is the designer and builder of a pure helicopter, establishing an official record during the preceding calendar year in the official Class E-1 Category for maximum speed, altitude, distance, or payload. A small replica of the trophy goes to the winner, and the flight crew receives certificates. Awarded annually by the United Technologies Corporation. Established in 1961.

• 2440 • Supplier Excellence Award
To recognize a supplier that, through the quality, innovation, and cost-effectiveness of its products, has made a notable contribution within the vertical flight industry. Awarded annually. Established in 1995.

• 2441 •
American Helvetia Philatelic Society
Richard Hall, Sec.
PO Box 15053
Asheville, NC 28813-0053
E-mail: secretary@swiss-stamps.org
Home Page: http://swiss-stamps.org

• 2442 • Honorary Life Member
For recognition of outstanding contributions to Swiss philately and the American Helvetia Philatelic Society. Nominations are accepted. The honoree is mentioned in the Society's Journal, *TELL*, and dues for succeeding years are waived. Awarded irregularly. Established in 1975.

• 2443 •
American Hemerocallis Society
Maurice Greene, Pres.
3717 Whitworth Dr.
Knoxville, TN 37938-4228
E-mail: president@daylilies.org
Home Page: http://www.daylilies.org

• 2444 • Bertrand Farr Medal
To recognize members who have attained outstanding results in the field of hybridizing. Selection is made by the Board of Directors on the basis of letters of recommendation sent in by the membership. Credits, not number of votes, are the deciding factor. A silver medal is awarded annually. Established in 1950.

• 2445 • Helen Field Fischer Medal
This, the society's highest honor, is given to members in recognition of distinguished and meritorious service to the society. Selection is made by the Board of Directors on the basis of letters of recommendation sent in by the membership. Credits, not number of votes, are the deciding factor. A gold medal is awarded annually if merited. Established in 1950.

• 2446 • Photography Awards
For recognition of outstanding photography of daylilies. The Mildred Schlumpf Award is given for recognition of the best photograph in the single bloom and landscape categories. Awarded annually. The A. D. Roquemore Memorial Award is given for recognition of the best color slide of a clump of daylilies. Awarded annually. The Sarah Sikes Sequence Award is given for recognition of the best color slides of a sequence of events involving daylilies. Awarded annually. The Lazarus Memorial Award is given for the best video recording of a presentation relating to daylilies. Awarded annually.

• 2447 • Tri-Color Trophy
To recognize the best tri-color arrangement by a society member in an accredited show as judged from photographs of national council judges. Awarded annually.

• 2448 • **Varietal Awards**
To recognize a hybridizer of daylilies. The following awards are presented: Stout Medal, given annually, is the society's highest varietal award; Donn Fischer Memorial Cup, given annually to recognize the outstanding miniature (under 3 inches); Annie T. Giles Award, given annually to recognize the outstanding small-flowered (3 to 4 1/2 inch) variety; Lenington All-American Award, given annually for recognition of the daylily which performs outstandingly in all parts of the country. Varieties must have been introduced for ten years; Ida Munson Award, given annually to recognize the best double flower variety; Don C. Stevens Memorial Award, given annually to recognize the best eyed banded daylily, Harris Olson Award, to recognize an outstanding spider or spider variant daylily, the Lambert/Webster Award to recognize the best daylily of unusual form; the R.W. Munson Jr. Award to recognize the best distinctly patterned daylily, and Eugene Foster Award, to recognize an outstanding late blooming daylily; David Hall Memorial Medal, awarded annually on a regional basis to recognize a hybridizer as determined by vote of the members in the popularity poll.

• 2449 •
American Hibiscus Society
Valerie Longson, Exec.Sec.
PO Box 1580
Venice, FL 34284-1580
Phone: (941)408-9309
Fax: (321)783-2576
E-mail:
exec.secretary@americanhibiscus.org
Home Page: http://
www.americanhibiscus.org

• 2450 • **Hibiscus of the Year Award**
Annual award of recognition.

• 2451 •
American Hiking Society
Mary Margaret Sloan, Pres.
1422 Fenwick Ln.
Silver Spring, MD 20910-3328
Phone: (301)565-6704
Fax: (301)565-6714
E-mail: info@americanhiking.org
Home Page: http://www.americanhiking.org

• 2452 • **AHS Business Partner Award**
To recognize a company which has supported trail development and improvement, nationally or locally. An engraved plaque is presented annually. Established in 1989. Formerly: (2006) American Hiking Society Award.

• 2453 • **Butch Henley Award**
Recognizes an outstanding career or achievement of a staff or board leader of a non-profit hiking organization. Awarded annually.

• 2454 • **Richard Douthit Public Service Award**
To recognize exemplary service by an employee of a trail managing agency in the field. Awarded annually.

• 2455 • **Jim Kern Award**
To recognize outstanding service and commitment to the American Hiking Society, including volunteer work in promotion, creation, or improvement of hiking trails. Established in 1984 to honor James A. Kern, one of the founders of the American Hiking Society.

• 2456 • **Public Service National Leadership Award**
Recognizes public officials at the national level who have demonstrated special interest in trails. Awarded annually.

• 2457 • **Glenn T. Seaborg Award**
To recognize a prominent citizen who has been an effective national advocate for the development and improvement of hiking trails. An engraved plaque is presented annually. Established in 1989.

• 2458 • **Trail Development Award**
Recognizes one or more trail clubs or organizations for their work to complete a trail project or for success in a trail protection initiative. Awarded annually.

• 2459 • **Bill Wilcox Award**
To recognize the contributions of a Society member under the age of 30, whose volunteer work resulted in the design or construction of a new trail, or has significantly improved hiking trails in his/her community. A monetary prize of $100 is presented at the annual meeting. Established in 1990.

• 2460 •
American Historic Inns
PO Box 669
Dana Point, CA 92629
Phone: (949)497-2232
Fax: (949)499-4022
E-mail: comments@iloveinns.com
Home Page: http://
www.iloveinns.safeshopper.com

• 2461 • **Outstanding Achievement Award**
To recognize innkeepers who have made significant contributions to the preservation of historic properties. A plaque is awarded annually. Established in 1989.

• 2462 •
American Historical Association
Heater Pensack, Exec.Asst.
400 A St. SE
Washington, DC 20003-3889
Phone: (202)544-2422
Fax: (202)544-8307
E-mail: aha@theaha.org
Home Page: http://www.historians.org

• 2463 • **Herbert Baxter Adams Prize**
To encourage scholars who have not yet obtained an established reputation in the field of European history. Awarded annually for an author's first substantial book dealing with European history. Chronological coverage follows 2 year rotation; even years-ancient through 1815; odd years-1815 through 20th century. The deadline is May 15. Established in 1901 in memory of Herbert Baxter Adams, first secretary of the Association.

• 2464 • **George Louis Beer Prize**
To recognize outstanding historical writing by a United States citizen or permanent resident in European international history since the year 1895. The deadline is May 15 annually for works published during the preceding year. Established in 1920. Sponsored by a bequest of George Louis Beer.

• 2465 • **Albert J. Beveridge Award**
To promote and honor outstanding historical writing in English on the history of the United States, Latin America, or Canada from 1492 to the present. The deadline is May 15 annually for works published during the preceding year. Established in 1927 in memory of Senator Beveridge.

• 2466 • **Paul Birdsall Prize in European Military and Strategic History**
To recognize the author of a major work in European military and strategic history since 1870. Preference is given to the international aspects of military history (military/diplomatic) but the impact of technological developments, strategic planning, and military events on society political, economic, social - also qualify. Purely technical studies divorced from historical context are not eligible. Preference is given to younger academics, but older scholars and nonacademic candidates are not excluded. Authors must be citizens of the United States or Canada. Books published during the preceding two years are eligible to be submitted by May 15, biennially. Established in 1986 by an anonymous donor to honor the late Paul Birdsall of Williams College.

• 2467 • **James Henry Breasted Prize**
To recognize the author of the best book in English in any field of history prior to 1000 A.D. Works of high scholarly and literary merit published during the preceding four years are eligible to be submitted by May 15, annually. Established in 1985 by Joseph O. Losos to honor James Henry Breasted, a pioneer in ancient Egyptian and Near Eastern history and president of the Association in 1928.

• 2468 • Albert B. Corey Prize in Canadian-American Relations
To honor the best book dealing with the history of Canadian-American relations or the history of both countries. The deadline is May 15, biennially, in even-numbered years. Established in 1963. Co-sponsored by the Canadian Historical Association, Public Archives of Canada, 395 Wellington St., Ottawa, Ontario K1A 0N3, Canada.

• 2469 • John H. Dunning Prize in United States History
To recognize young scholars for an outstanding monograph in either manuscript or print form on any subject relating to United States history. An author's first or second book, published or completed during the preceding two years, is eligible. The deadline is May 15, biennially. Established in 1927. Sponsored by a bequest of Miss Mathilde Dunning.

• 2470 • John K. Fairbank Prize in East Asian History
To recognize outstanding books on the history of China proper, Vietnam, Chinese Central Asia, Mongolia, Manchuria, Korea, or Japan since the year 1800 that are of high scholarly and literary merit. The deadline is May 15, annually.

• 2471 • Herbert Feis Award
To recognize distinguished research and publication by an independent scholar or public historian in the form of a book, article, or series of articles of seminal importance, or an in-house publication shown to have had a major impact on policy. Individuals outside academe for a minimum of three years prior to the award year are eligible. Works published during the preceding year must be submitted by May 15, annually. Established in 1984 in memory of Herbert Feis, public servant and historian of recent American foreign policy. Sponsored by the Rockefeller Foundation. Formerly: Herbert Feis Award for Nonacademically-Affiliated Historians.

• 2472 • Morris D. Forkosch Prize
To recognize the best book written in English in the field of British, British Imperial, or British Commonwealth history since 1485. The deadline for submissions is May 15, biennially in odd-numbered years. Established in 1993.

• 2473 • Leo Gershoy Award
To recognize outstanding historical writing in the fields of 17th and 18th century western European history. The deadline is May 15, annually. Established in 1975 by Mrs. Leo Gershoy in memory of her late husband.

• 2474 • Littleton - Griswold Prize in American Law and Society
To recognize the author of the best book in any subject on the history of American law and society. Only books of high scholarly and literary merit published during the preceding year are considered. The deadline for submissions is May 15, annually. Established in 1985.

• 2475 • Clarence H. Haring Prize
To recognize a Latin American who has published the most outstanding book on Latin American history during the preceding five years. There is no language limitation on works submitted. The deadline is May 15. Awarded every five years. Established in 1965.

• 2476 • J. Franklin Jameson Prize for Editorial Achievement
To honor outstanding achievement in the editing of historical sources. Books published between April 30, 1995 and May 1, 2000 are eligible. Review and journal editing are not eligible. A certificate is awarded every five years. Established in 1980.

• 2477 • Joan Kelly Memorial Prize
To recognize an outstanding work in any chronological period, geographical location, or in any area of feminist theory that incorporates a historical perspective. Books published during the preceding year are eligible to be submitted by May 15, annually. Established in 1984 by the Coordinating Committee on Women in the Historical Profession and the Conference Group on Women's History.

• 2478 • Waldo G. Leland Prize
To honor an outstanding reference tool in the field of history. An honorary award is presented every five years and will be awarded next in 2006. Established in 1981.

• 2479 • Howard R. Marraro Prizes in Italian History
To honor outstanding writings of Italian history in any epoch, Italian cultural history, or Italian-American relations. Entries must first have been published in English by a historian whose usual residence is North America. The deadline is May 15, annually. Awarded by the AHA, American Catholic Historical Society, and the Society for Italian Historical Studies, respectively. Established in 1973 in accordance with the bequest by Howard R. Marraro.

• 2480 • Premio del Rey Prize
To recognize a distinguished book in English in the field of early Spanish history, covering the period of 500-1516 A.D. and the medieval period. The deadline is May 15, biennially in even-numbered years. Established in 1990 by an endowment from Robert I. Burns, S.J., from his Llull and Catalonia prizes.

• 2481 • James Harvey Robinson Prize
To honor the teaching aid that has made the most outstanding contribution to the teaching of history in any field. The deadline is May 17, biennially. A one-year AHA membership is presented. Established in 1978.

• 2482 • Wesley-Logan Prize
To recognize an outstanding book on some aspect of the history of the dispersion, settlement, adjustment, and/or return of peoples originally from Africa. Eligible for consideration are books in any chronological period and any geographical location. Awarded annually. Established in 1992. Co-sponsored by the Association for the Study of African American Life and History.

• 2483 •
American Historical Association, Pacific Coast Branch
History Dept.
Claremont Graduate University
121 E 10th St.
Claremont, CA 91711
Phone: (909)621-8612
Fax: (909)607-1221
E-mail: janet.brodie@cgu.edu
Home Page: http://
arachnid.pepperdine.edu/amerhistassocp

• 2484 • The W. Turrentine Jackson Prize
To recognize a graduate student whose essay on a topic within the fields of concentration of the *Pacific Historical Review* is of outstanding quality. A monetary prize of $750, a plaque, and publication of the winning essay in PHR are awarded annually.

• 2485 •
American Historical Print Collectors Society
Nancy Braun, Mail Mgr.
PO Box 201
Fairfield, CT 06824
Phone: (203)255-1627
E-mail: webmaster@ahpcs.org
Home Page: http://www.ahpcs.org

• 2486 • Ewell L. Newman Award
For recognition of a publication that enhances understanding and appreciation of prints as part of the history and culture of the United States. To be considered, publications should relate a specialized branch of illustration to the broader history of American printmaking. Awarded annually. Established in 1989 in honor of Ewell L. Newman, one of the founders of AHPCS.

• 2487 •
American Hockey Coaches Association
Joe Bertagna, Exec.Dir.
7 Concord St.
Gloucester, MA 01930
Phone: (781)245-4177
Fax: (978)281-2081
E-mail: jbertagna@hockeyeastonline.com
Home Page: http://www.ahcahockey.com

• 2488 • Coach of the Year Award
Annual award of recognition. Inquire for additional information.

• 2489 • Jim Fullerton Award
Recognized an individual for enthusiasm of the sport of hockey. Applicants can be coaches, administrators, trainers, officials, journalists, or fans. Awarded annually. Established in 1992 to honor James Fullerton a former Brown University Coach and AHCA spiritual leader.

• 2490 • Edward Jeremiah Award/College Division Coach of the Year
To recognize the college division Hockey Coach of the Year. The winner is selected by a vote of the membership. A silver trophy is awarded annually. Established in 1970 in memory of Edward Jeremiah, a former hockey coach and Writer of instructional text.

• 2491 • Jofa All American Hockey Squad (East and West) for Colleges
To recognize the top college division hockey players. Awarded annually. Formerly: (2004) Titan All America Hockey Squad (East and West) for Colleges.

• 2492 • Jofan All-American Hockey Squad (East and West) for Universities
To recognize the top university division hockey players. Awarded annually. Formerly: (2004) Titan All-America Hockey Squad (East and West) for Universities.

• 2493 • John Snooks Kelly - Founder's Award
Recognizes contributions to the growth and development of ice hockey in the United States. All ice hockey coaching professionals are eligible. Awarded annually. Established in 1981. Formerly: Founders Award.

• 2494 • John MacInnes Award
Recognized contributions to amateur hockey and youth programs. Nominees' programs must have had high winning percentages, high graduation rates, and produced well rounded men. Awarded annually. Established in 1983 in honor of John Macinnis, a Michigan Tech Coach.

• 2495 • John Mariucci Award
To recognize a high school hockey coach. Candidates must show the spirit, dedication, and enthusiasm of John Mariucci, former Minnesota player and coach. A trophy is awarded annually. Established in 1986 in honor of John Mariucci.

• 2496 • Spencer Penrose Award/ University Division Coach of the Year
To recognize the University Division Hockey Coach of the Year. The winner is selected by a vote of the membership. A silver trophy is awarded annually. Named for the benefactor who built the Broadmoor Hotel in Colorado Springs which was the home of the first ten NCAA Championships. Established in 1951.

• 2497 •
American Hockey League
David Andrews, Pres. & CEO
1 Monarch Pl. No. 2400
Springfield, MA 01144-4019
Phone: (413)781-2030
Fax: (413)733-4767
E-mail: slam@canoe.com
Home Page: http://www.theahl.com

• 2498 • Aldege Baz Bastien Memorial Trophy (Outstanding Goaltender)
To recognize the goaltender judged by the American Hockey League Broadcasters and Writers Association to be the best at his position. Awarded annually. Established in the 1983-84 season to honor "Baz" Bastien, who for many years was associated with the American Hockey League. At the time of his death in 1983, "Baz" was the General Manager of the Pittsburgh Penguins and Alternate Governor of the Baltimore Skipjacks.

• 2499 • Jack A. Butterfield Trophy
To honor the player voted by the coaches as the Most Valuable Player in the Calder Cup Playoffs. Awarded annually. Established in 1983 to honor Jack A. Butterfield, the current Chairman of the Board of the AHL.

• 2500 • Calder Cup (Playoff Champion)
To recognize the AHL playoff champion. Awarded annually. Established to honor Frank Calder, the National Hockey League's first president. Mr. Calder was instrumental in helping establish the International, American-International, and American Hockey Leagues.

• 2501 • Canadian Chrysler Cup
To recognize the Canadian Division team that earns the most points during the regular season. Awarded annually. Established in the 1993-94 season in conjunction with Chrysler Canada. Formerly: (1997) Atlantic Chrysler Cup.

• 2502 • Richard F. Canning Trophy
To recognize the team that wins the Eastern Conference Championship in the Calder Cup Playoffs. Awarded annually. Established in the 1989-90 season to honor Richard F. Canning, best remembered as the "Father" of the league's Constitution, By-laws, and Regulations.

• 2503 • John Chick Trophy (Empire Division Champion)
To recognize the regular season championship team in the Empire Division of the AHL. Awarded annually. Established in 1962 to honor John D. Chick, former president of the American Hockey League.

• 2504 • Robert W. Clarke Trophy (Western Conference Trophy)
To recognize the team that wins the Western Conference Championship in the Calder Cup Playoffs. Established in the 1989-90 season to honor Robert W. Clarke, whose name has been synonymous with the League and the Rochester Americans franchise for over 35 years.

• 2505 • Les Cunningham Award (Most Valuable Player)
To recognize the most valuable player selected by the media and players of the League. Awarded annually. Established in 1947 to honor Les Cunningham, the first AHL player to score 200 points in regular season play.

• 2506 • James H. Ellery Memorial Award (Outstanding Media)
To recognize the individuals in the news media who have contributed most to the progress of the League. Awarded annually. Established in 1964 to honor Jim Ellery for 17 years service to the AHL. At his death he held both the position of the League Secretary and Publicity Director.

• 2507 • Dudley (Red) Garrett Memorial Award (Rookie of the Year)
To recognize the League's outstanding rookie. This award is voted by the media and players of the American Hockey League. Awarded annually. Established in 1947 to honor Dudley (Red) Garrett, a young player who gave his life during World War II while in the service of the Canadian Navy.

• 2508 • James C. Hendy Memorial Award (Outstanding Executive)
To recognize the executive who has made an outstanding contribution to the League. Awarded annually. Established in 1961 to honor Jim Hendy, General Manager of the Cleveland Barons when he died January 14, 1961.

• 2509 • Harry (Hap) Holmes Memorial Award (Outstanding Goaltender)
To recognize the team with the lowest goals-against average. The trophy is inscribed with the team's goaltender(s) name(s), providing each has played in 25 regular scheduled championship games. Awarded annually. Established in 1947 to honor Harry (Hap) Holmes, who was an early figure in professional hockey and one of the most outstanding goaltenders of his era.

• 2510 • Fred T. Hunt Memorial Award (Sportsmanship, Determination, and Dedication to Hockey)
To recognize the player who best exemplifies the qualities demonstrated by Fred Hunt: sportsmanship, determination, and dedication to hockey, as voted by the American Hockey League Broadcasters and Writers Association. The original trophy was donated by the Buffalo Sabres and is awarded annually. Established in the 1977-78 season to honor Mr. Hunt, who had served the League as a player, General Manager, and Governor in Buffalo.

• 2511 • Kilpatrick Trophy
To recognize the club finishing the regular season with the best overall record. Awarded annually. The award is named for the AHL's current Senior Vice President and long-time board member Macgregor Kilpatrick.

• 2512 • Frank Mathers Trophy
To recognize the Eastern Conference's regular season champion team. Awarded annually. Established in 1996 to honor Frank Mathers, a member of the Hockey Hall of Fame and long-time contributor to the AHL.

• 2513 • Ken McKenzie Award (Outstanding Executive - PR and Marketing)
To recognize the individual adjudged to have done the most in promoting his or her particular team in the AHL. Awarded annually. Established in the 1977-78 season to honor Ken McKenzie, the long-time owner and publisher of *The Hockey News.*

• 2514 • F. G. (Teddy) Oke Trophy (New England Division Champion)
To recognize the New England Division regular season champion. Awarded annually. First presented to the championship team of the old International League in 1927. In 1936, the birth date of the AHL, the Oke Trophy was given to the Western Division championship team. In the 1952-53 season, when the AHL began operating with only one division, the Oke Trophy was then awarded to the overall champion. The Frank Fontaine Trophy, awarded to the Eastern Division champion from 1926 to 1952, was retired. In 1961 the League went back to two divisions and the Oke Trophy and the Chick Trophy were adopted by the League's Board of Governors as the championship trophies for the Northern and Southern Divisions respectively. (The names of the Divisions were changed from East to North and West to South at the start of the 1973-74 season.)

• 2515 • Louis A. R. Pieri Memorial Award (Coach of the Year)
To recognize the outstanding coach in the American Hockey League as voted by the American Hockey League Broadcasters and Writers Association. Awarded annually. Established in 1967 to honor Louis A. R. Pieri, a long-time contributor to the League as owner of the Providence Reds.

• 2516 • Sam Pollock Trophy
To recognize the North Division's regular season champion team. Awarded annually. Named in honor of Sam Pollock, long-time General Manager of the Montreal Candadiens and member of the Hockey Hall of Fame.

• 2517 • Eddie Shore Plaque (Outstanding Defenseman)
To recognize the player voted by the media and players of the AHL judged to be the best defenseman in the League. Awarded annually. Established in 1958. Renamed in 1985 to honor Eddie Shore, owner of the AHL's Springfield franchise for 27 years, a member of the Hockey Hall of Fame, and recipient of the Lester Patrick Award. Shore is widely acknowledged as one of hockey's greatest defensemen.

• 2518 • John B. Sollenberger Trophy (Leading Scorer - Regular Season)
To recognize the individual who accumulated the most points over the course of the regular season. Awarded annually. Established in 1947. Renamed in 1955 to honor Mr. Sollenberger, longtime contributor to the AHL as Manager and President of the Hershey Bears, and former Chairman of the Board of Governors of the American Hockey League. Formerly: (1954) Wally Kilrea Trophy; Carl Liscombe Trophy.

• 2519 •
American Holsteiner Horse Association
Bruce Cottew, Exec.Dir.
222 E Main St., Ste. 1
Georgetown, KY 40324
Phone: (502)863-4239
Fax: (502)868-0722
E-mail: ahhambr@bellsouth.net
Home Page: http://www.holsteiner.com

• 2520 • Awards Program
Recognizes Holsteiner horses in the areas of Dressage; Sporthorse Breeding and Hunter Breeding; Jumpers and Hunters; and Eventing. Awarded annually.

• 2521 •
American Homebrewers Association
Charlie Papazian, Pres.
736 Pearl St.
Boulder, CO 80302
Phone: (303)447-0816
Toll-Free: 888-822-6273
Fax: (303)447-2825
E-mail: gary@aob.org
Home Page: http://www.beertown.org/homebrewing

• 2522 • AHA National Homebrew Competition Awards
To provide recognition in the field of home brewing. Prizes are awarded in the following categories: Homebrewer of the Year - awarded to Best of Show; Meadmaker of the Year; Ninkasi Award - awarded to the individual high point brewer; Cidermaker of the Year; Homebrew Club of the Year; and first, second, and third place awards are given in 29 additional categories. Established in 1978.

• 2523 •
American Horticultural Society
Katy Moss Warner, Pres./CEO
7931 E Boulevard Dr.
Alexandria, VA 22308-1300
Phone: (703)768-5700
Toll-Free: 800-777-7931
Fax: (703)768-8700
E-mail: sdick@ahs.org
Home Page: http://www.ahs.org

• 2524 • Liberty Hyde Bailey Medal
This, the highest honor the Society bestows upon an individual and considered the top award in horticulture, is given to recognize a pioneering spirit rather than for pure achievement. Residents of the North American continent who have made significant national contributions in at least three of the following areas of horticultural activity are eligible: teaching, research, writing, plant exploration, administration, art, business, and leadership. A bronze medal is awarded when merited at the annual meeting. Established in 1958 by the American Horticultural Council.

• 2525 • Luther Burbank Award
To recognize extraordinary achievement in the field of plant breeding. Awarded when merited. Established in 1993.

• 2526 • Paul Ecke Jr. Commercial Award
To recognize outstanding achievement in commercial horticulture. Prizes may be given in the following two categories: to an individual who, because of his or her commitment to the highest standards of excellence in the field of commercial horticulture, contributes to the betterment of gardening practices everywhere; and to a firm or company that has retained high standards and is making significant contributions to gardening. Medals are awarded at the annual meeting if merited. Established in 1974. Formerly: (2004) Commercial Award.

• 2527 • G. B. Gunlogson Medal
To recognize the creative use of new technology to make home gardening more productive and enjoyable and to benefit people-plant relationships. A medal is awarded when merited at the annual meeting. Established in 1974 by G. B. Gunlogson of Racine, Wisconsin.

• 2528 • Horticultural Communication Award
To recognize effective communication using media and research techniques for the purpose of expanding horticultural awareness. Awarded when merited. Established in 1987.

• 2529 • Horticultural Therapy Award
To recognize a significant contribution to the field of horticultural therapy. Awarded when merited. Established in 1985.

• 2530 • Horticultural Writing Citation
To recognize an individual, who through the body of his or her written work in the field, has made a significant contribution to horticulture. A medal is presented when merited at the annual meeting. Established in 1953.

• 2531 • Landscape Design Award
To recognize an individual whose work in landscape architecture or design contributes to a better awareness of the field of horticulture. A medal is presented when merited at the annual meeting. Established in 1974.

• 2532 • Local Horticulture Award
To recognize an individual or group who has contributed to the improvement or excellence of horticulture in the host city for the Society's annual meeting. A medal is presented, when merited, at the meeting. Established in 1982.

• 2533 • Meritorious Service Award
To publicly recognize a member or friend of the Society for outstanding and exemplary service in support of the Society's goals, services, or activities. A medal is presented when merited at the annual meeting. Established in 1974.

• 2534 • Frances Jones Poetker Award
To recognize a person who has made significant contributions to the appreciation of creative floral designs in publications, on the platform, and to the public. Awarded biennially.

• 2535 • Professional Award
To recognize an individual who makes his or her living as director of an arboretum or botanical garden and whose career achievements represent a significant contribution to horticulture. A medal is presented when merited at the annual meeting. Established in 1953.

• 2536 • Scientific Award
To recognize an individual who has enriched horticulture through outstanding and notable research. A medal is presented when merited at the annual meeting. Established in 1953.

• 2537 • Catherine H. Sweeney Award
To recognize extraordinary and dedicated efforts in the field of horticulture. Awarded at annual meeting when merited. Established in 1985 in honor of Catherine H. Sweeney who devoted her life to horticulture as evidenced by her preservation and expansion of The Kampong in Florida.

• 2538 • Teaching Award
To recognize an individual whose ability to share his or her knowledge of horticulture with others has contributed to a better public understanding of the plant world and its impact on humanity. A medal is presented when merited at the annual meeting. Established in 1953.

• 2539 • Urban Beautification Award
To recognize an individual and/or a company that has made significant contributions to urban horticulture. A medal is presented when merited at the annual meeting. Established in 1985.

• 2540 •
American Hospital Association
Richard J. Davidson Ph.D., Pres.
1 N. Franklin
Chicago, IL 60606-3421
Phone: (312)422-3000
Fax: (312)422-4796
Home Page: http://www.aha.org

• 2541 • AHA Hospital Awards for Volunteer Excellence
To help hospitals attract and retain volunteers by recognizing outstanding contributions by organized programs of volunteer service. Only one nomination per member institution may be submitted. Awards are given in one or more categories: (1) Community service programs; (2) Inservice hospital volunteer programs; (3) Fundraising programs; and (4) Community outreach and/or collaboration programs; To be eligible for an award, volunteer efforts must be: (1) affiliated with an AHA member institution; (2) capable of demonstrating a significant contribution to the hospital field; (3) accomplished by persons who have served without monetary remuneration; and (4) in effect throughout the preceding year. Awards are given when suitable recipients are identified, up to a total of four per year (one for each of the above categories); all four awards may not be presented every year. Each award winning program is given a plaque, and travel expenses to attend the meeting. Awarded annually. Established in 1983.

• 2542 • Award of Honor
For recognition of an outstanding contribution to the health and well-being of the people. Individuals need not have a primary occupation within the health care field to be eligible. Established in 1966.

• 2543 • Distinguished Service Award
This, the Association's highest award, is given for recognition of noteworthy service, contributions or achievements in hospital administration activities. Individuals who have made a career in the hospital or health field are eligible. In selecting the recipient, primary consideration is given to the following factors: welfare of hospital patients; improvements in administrative methods and practices; service in local, state or provincial, or national organizations in the health care field; furtherance of good public relations; assistance to and collaboration with other hospitals; promotion of social and other legislation relating to better patient care; and advancement of the art and science of health care administration. Established in 1934.

• 2544 • Federal Health Care Executive Special Achievement Award
To recognize the accomplishments of career government employees in health care.

• 2545 • Honorary Life Membership
For recognition of individuals for outstanding contributions to the health care field and the health care of the people. Individuals whose careers have not been in the field of health care administration are eligible. Awarded when merited. Established in 1901.

• 2546 • Justin Ford Kimball Award
To recognize an individual for significant contributions to innovative approaches to the financing of health and hospital care in the private, voluntary sector. The individual may have a primary occupation either within or outside the health field. Established in 1958.

• 2547 • Leadership Award
To recognize an individual or corporation that has made significant contributions to advance the state-of-the-art of materials management or has demonstrated an extraordinary level of leadership and professional competence in the field of materials management. Nominees need not be members of ASHMM. The following criteria are considered for the award: (1) a leadership role in enhancing the practice and role of materials management in hospitals; (2) specific contributions and noted advances in the state-of-the-art; and (3) personal and professional qualities. Awarded as merited during a special Leadership Award Presentation of the Annual Meeting of the Society. Established in 1966 in memory of George R. Gossett, the first president of the Society, who was killed in an automobile accident. Mr. Gosset made outstanding contributions to the field of hospital purchasing and materials management. Formerly: (1983) George R. Gosset Award.

• 2548 • Trustees Award
To recognize an individual for outstanding contributions to the programs and activities of the Association. The awardee may have a primary occupation either within or outside the health field. Established in 1959.

• 2549 •
American Hosta Society
Kevin P. Walek, Pres.
8702 Pinnacle Rock Ct.
Lorton, VA 22079-3029
Phone: (703)690-3021
Fax: (440)729-2836
E-mail:
ahsmembershipsecretary@earthlink.net
Home Page: http://www.hosta.org/

• 2550 • AHS Best Variegated Hosta in a Tour Garden Award
For recognition of the best, registered variegated hosta growing in a clump containing three or more divisions and displayed in an AHS National Convention tour garden, as voted by the attendees. A silver bowl and a certificate are awarded to the garden owner. Established in 1985. Sponsored by the Alabama Hosta Society (AlaHoSo).

• 2551 • Best Hosta in a Tour Garden Award
To recognize the best, registered small-leaved cultivar, smaller than *H. undulata,* growing in a garden on tour at the AHS National Convention. Attendees at the convention select the hosta by vote. A walnut plaque is awarded when merited to the hybridizer or introducer of the hosta for permanent retention. Established in 1976 to honor the second AHS Secretary-Treasurer, Mrs. Eldren W. Minks of Albert Lea, MN. Formerly: (2006) Nancy Minks Award.

• 2552 • Best Hosta Seedling or Sport in a Tour Garden Award
To recognize the best new seedling or sport in an AHS National Convention tour garden. The hosta is selected by vote of the convention attendees, and the award is given to the hybridizer or introducer. A shield-shaped walnut plaque with the name of the winner, is awarded when merited. Established in 1980, in honor of Robert W. Savory, Edina, MN, a hosta hybridizer and AHS Advisory Board member. Formerly: (2006) Savory Shield Award.

• 2553 • Big Bucks Award
Annual award of recognition. Inquire for additional information on this award.

• 2554 • Cut Leaf Show Awards
Annual award of recognition. Inquire for additional information on this award.

• 2555 • Eunice Fisher Award
To recognize the best, registered large-leaved cultivar growing in an AHS National Convention tour garden. The hosta is selected by a vote of the convention attendees. A walnut plaque with an engraving of a hosta on one of the metal plates is awarded when merited to the hybridizer or introducer of the hosta for permanent retention. Established in 1972 to honor the first AHS Secretary-Treasurer, the late Mrs. Glen Fisher of Oshkosh, WI.

• 2556 • Harshbarger Landscape Design Plaque
For recognition of the best landscape use of a hosta in a home garden on tour at the AHS National Convention. An inscribed certificate with a drawing of hostas is presented in honor of Gretchen Harshbarger of Iowa City, IA. Established in 1980.

• 2557 • Honorary Life Membership
To recognize individuals who have devoted their time, knowledge and ability to the advancement of interests of the Society. Award candidates are proposed by the AHS Awards and Honors Committee and approved by the AHS Board of Directors. A certificate is awarded when merited. Established in 1972.

• 2558 • Minnesota Blue Award
For recognition of the best blue-leaved hosta in the cut-leaf exhibit show at the AHS National Convention. A walnut plaque in the shape of the State of Minnesota with a blue-colored metallic leaf attached, is awarded to the exhibitor of the entry for permanent retention. Awarded when merited. Established in 1980.

• 2559 • Minnesota Gold Award
For recognition of the best gold or yellow-leaved hosta in the cut-leaf exhibit show at the AHS National Convention. A plaque in the shape of the State of Minnesota, with a gold-colored metal leaf, is awarded to the exhibitor of the entry for permanent retention. Awarded when merited. Established in 1980.

• 2560 • President's Exhibitor Trophy
To recognize the exhibitor of the overall champion in the cut-leaf exhibit show at the AHS National Convention. A clear plaque engraved with a drawing of a garden scene on the front and part on the back, giving a three-dimensional effect, on a black plastic stand is awarded when merited. Established in 1978.

• 2561 • Schutt Silver Cup
To recognize the exhibitor of the best artistic design arrangement in the exhibit show at the AHA National Convention. A silver cup mounted on a walnut base, engraved with the name of each year's winner, is awarded when merited. Established in 1980, in honor of Theresa A. Schutt of Woodstock, IA.

• 2562 • Lucille Simpers Award
To recognize the best large or giant leaved blue Hosta growing in an AHS National Convention Tour Garden. The Hosta is selected by vote of the convention attendees. A sundial is awarded to the garden owner for permanent retention and a certificate is awarded to the hybridizer. Established in 1989, in memory of Lucille Simpers of Salem, IN.

• 2563 • Alex J. Summers Distinguished Merit Award
To recognize a member of the Society for outstanding service to the development of the genus *Hosta,* the Society, or both. A certificate is awarded annually. Established in 1982 to honor the first President of The American Hosta Society, Alex J. Summers, Bridgeville, DE. Sponsored by the Mid-Atlantic Regional Hosta Society.

• 2564 •
American Hot Rod Association
Orville Moe, Exec.VP
N. 101 Hayford Rd.
Spokane, WA 99224
Phone: (509)244-2372
Phone: (509)244-3663
Fax: (509)244-2472
E-mail: srp@spokaneracewaypark.com
Home Page: http://www.spokaneracewaypark.com

• 2565 • Drivers World Champions
Annual award of recognition for the winner of the race.

• 2566 •
American Hotel and Lodging Association
Joseph A. McInerney, Contact
1201 New York Ave. NW, Ste. 600
Washington, DC 20005-3931
Phone: (202)289-3100
Fax: (202)289-3199
E-mail: info@ahla.com
Home Page: http://www.ahla.com
Formerly: (2001) American Hotel & Motel Association.

• 2567 • AH&MA Achievement Awards
To encourage and assist AH&MA members to initiate public relations activities and programs that will generate favorable publicity for the lodging industry. Entries may be submitted by AH&MA properties or those hotels, motels, and systems having a significant number of properties which are members of AH&MA, or their public relations agencies on their behalf. The entry deadline is January 5. Awards are given in the following categories: community service, enviromanagement, guest relations, and special events and promotions (one time only and ongoing programs/campaigns). Three awards are given in each category, one for the outstanding individual property program (large and small) and one for the outstanding chain program presented during the AH&MA annual convention. A plaque is awarded. Sponsored by Visa USA.

• 2568 • Outstanding General Manager
No further information was provided for this edition.

• 2569 • Outstanding Lodging Employee of the Year
To provide hotels and motels an opportunity to recognize exemplary professionalism and exceptional service by an employee in a management or non-management position. The nominees are judged on performance that goes above and beyond normal job responsibilities, including outstanding and unusual service to the hotel/motel, to the guests, and/or community. A nominee must have served in the lodging industry for a minimum of three years. Only one nominee may be entered per property. The deadline for nominations is January 5. The award winner is flown to the awards ceremony held during the annual convention, to receive a special award, and $1,500 cash. Awarded annually. Sponsored by Visa USA. Formerly: Bellman/Bellwoman of the Year.

• 2570 • Outstanding Lodging Manager
No further information was provided for this edition.

• 2571 •
American Humane Association
Timothy O'Brien, Pres.
63 Inverness Dr. E
Englewood, CO 80112-5117
Phone: (303)792-9900
Toll-Free: 800-227-4645
Fax: (303)792-5333
E-mail: info@americanhumane.org
Home Page: http://www.americanhumane.org

• 2572 • Waco F. Childers, Jr., Award
To recognize an individual for an outstanding contribution to animal welfare, the American Humane Association, and the humane movement.

• 2573 • Vincent De Francis Award
To recognize an outstanding individual or agency working in the child protective services field. A bronze statuette of children is awarded annually. Established in 1976.

• 2574 • Humane Award
To recognize significant contributions to the ideals of the Association through an outstanding humane act. Individuals, clubs, and business firms are eligible. A plaque is awarded as merited. Established in 1968. In addition, humans who have rescued animals and animals who have rescued humans are recognized annually. The Roberta Wright Reeves Award and Rosemary Ames Award are also presented.

• 2575 • Kal Kan Volunteer of the Year
To recognize an individual for an outstanding voluntary contribution to the humane movement.

• 2576 • Rutherford T. Phillips Award
To recognize a major contribution to animal protection on the part of an American legislator or journalist. A bronze statuette of Saint Francis of Assisi is awarded annually. Established in 1976.

• 2577 • President's Award
To recognize an outstanding contribution to the humane movement.

• 2578 • William O. Stillman Award
To recognize a humane act of rescuing animals at personal risk, or the rescue of human life by an animal by virtue of extreme intelligence in an emergency. Both individuals and animals are eligible. Gold, bronze, or silver medals, or plaques are awarded as merited. Established in 1900.

• 2579 •
American Humanics
Kala M. Stroup PhD, Pres./CEO
4601 Madison Ave.
Kansas City, MO 64112
Phone: (816)561-6415
Toll-Free: 800-343-6466
Fax: (816)531-3527
E-mail: kstroup@humanics.org
Home Page: http://www.humanics.org

• 2580 • Exemplar of Humanics Award
This award was created for special and very infrequent recognition for volunteer service of a highly distinctive nature.

• 2581 • Honorary Life Membership
A highly honorary designation created to give an honorable status to individuals who have given outstanding service to American Humanics.

• 2582 •
American Humanist Association
Tony Hileman, Exec.Dir.
1777 T St. NW
Washington, DC 20009-7125
Phone: (202)238-9088
Toll-Free: 800-837-3792
Fax: (202)238-9003
E-mail: aha@americanhumanist.org
Home Page: http://www.americanhumanist.org/

• 2583 • Chapter of the Year Award
To recognize a chapter which, in the previous fiscal year, has served both humanism and the AHA in an exceptional manner. There are certain criteria that must be met in order to be named Chapter of the Year. The chapter must have fulfilled all the requirements of a chartered chapter, be responsible for an increase in AHA membership, and be engaged in the promotion of humanism to the general public.

• 2584 • John Dewey Humanist Award
To honor a person(s) whose life work contributed significantly to the advancement and understanding of the philosophical system established by Dr. John Dewey. A John Dewey scholar who devoted a significant portion of his or her career to the study and advancement of the philosophy of John Dewey was eligible. Nominations are accepted from Association members. Selection is made by the Awards Committee with approval of the Board. A bronze plaque on hardwood accompanies the award. Awarded occasionally as suitable awardees become known. Established in 1972.

• 2585 • Humanist Arts Award
To recognize a person whose career in any field of the arts, including literature, has contributed significantly to the advancement of humanism and/or the improvement of the human condition. Nominations are accepted from Association members. Selection is made by the Awards Committee with approval of the Board. A bronze plaque on hardwood accompanies the awards. Awarded annually. Established in 1977.

• 2586 • Humanist Contributions to Science Award
To recognize a person or team of researchers whose scientific work has contributed significantly to the advancement of humanist values. Nominations are accepted from Association members. Selection is made by the Awards Committee with approval of the Board. A bronze plaque on hardwood accompanies the award. Awarded occasionally. Established in 1988.

• 2587 • Humanist Distinguished Service Award
To honor an individual who has made a major contribution to humanism and/or the improvement of the human condition. Nominations are accepted from Association members. Selection is made by the Awards Committee with approval of the Board. A bronze plaque on hardwood is awarded annually. Established in 1954. Formerly: (1978) Humanist Fellow Award.

• 2588 • Humanist Hero Award
Established in 1994.

• 2589 • Humanist Heroine Award
To recognize a woman who has made a significant contribution to humanism and feminism. Nominations are accepted from members of the AHA Feminist Caucus and Association members. Selection is made by the Awards Committee with approval of the Board. A bronze plaque on hardwood accompanies the award. Awarded annually. Established in 1988.

• 2590 • Humanist Media Award
No further information was provided for this edition.

• 2591 • Humanist of the Year Award
To recognize a person of national or international reputation who, through the application of humanist values, has made a significant contribution to the improvement of the human condition. Selection of the awardee is based on research derived from biographical data, writings, studies, and contributions to humanity. Nominations are accepted from Association members. Selection is made by the Awards Committee with approval of the Board. A bronze plate bearing an inscription is awarded annually at the Annual Conference. The awardee's acceptance speech is published in the *Humanist*. Established in 1953.

• 2592 • Humanist Pioneer Award
To recognize an individual whose career has been devoted to the advancement of humanism in or out of AHA circles. Nominations are accepted from Association members. Selection is made by the Awards Committee with approval of the Board. A bronze plaque on hardwood is awarded annually, often to more than one person. Established in 1954.

• 2593 •
American Hungarian Foundation
Dr. Zsolt Harsanyi, Chm.
300 Somerset St.
PO Box 1084
New Brunswick, NJ 08903
Phone: (732)846-5777
Fax: (732)249-7033
E-mail: info@ahfoundation.org
Home Page: http://www.ahfoundation.org

• 2594 • Abraham Lincoln Award
For persons who have aided Hungary or Hungarian people and for people of Hungarian descent who have achieved success in the U.S. Presented annually.

• 2595 •
American Indian Heritage Foundation
Dr. Wil Rose, Ch.Exec.Off.
PO Box 6301
Falls Church, VA 22040
Phone: (703)819-0979
Phone: (703)237-7500
Fax: (703)532-1921
E-mail: wilrose@indians.org
Home Page: http://www.indians.org

• 2596 • Friend of the American Indian
To recognize outstanding contributions on behalf of American Indians. Artists, writers, broadcasters, journalists, corporations, clubs, religious groups, civic groups, individuals, or organizations are eligible. Medals and certificates are awarded annually. Established in 1985 by Princess Pale Moon.

• 2597 • Outstanding American Indian Awards
To recognize outstanding achievements in the following categories: Youth, Man and Woman of the Year, Tribal Tribute, Corporate Cause-Related Marketing, and Celebrity Sponsorship. Monetary prizes, medals, trophies, and certificates are awarded annually during National

American Indian Heritage Month. Established in 1983.

• 2598 •
American Indian Horse Registry
Nanci Falley, Pres.
Rancho San Francisco
9028 State Park Rd.
Lockhart, TX 78644
Phone: (512)398-6642
E-mail: nanci@indianhorse.com
Home Page: http://www.indianhorse.com

• 2599 • **Counting Coup Award**
For recognition of achievement in many fields, including Counting Coup Shows, Counting Coup - Trail, Counting Coup - Lessons, or other fields. One hundred points in one field of endeavor must be earned to receive the award. Established in 1991.

• 2600 • **Horseback Hours Award**
To encourage owners of Indian Horses to saddle up and ride non-competitively for awards. Members of AIHR who own registered American Indian Horses or Ponies are eligible. The following awards are presented whenever hours are reached and recorded: certificates for 50, 100, 250, 500 and 1,000 hours of riding; patches for 500 hours; and buckles for 1,000 hours. In addition, since 1986 add-on-patches, an Indian shield with feathers added as miles/hours accumulate may be awarded. Established in 1980.

• 2601 • **Horseback Miles Award**
To encourage owners of Indian Horses to saddle up and ride non-competitively for awards. Members of AIHR who own registered American Indian Horses or Ponies are eligible. The following awards are presented whenever hours are reached and recorded: certificates for 100, 250, 500 and 1,000 miles; patches for 500 miles; and a buckle for 1,000 miles. Established in 1980.

• 2602 • **Indian Horse Hall of Fame Award**
For recognition of life-time achievement and versatility of American Indian Horses. AIHR members riding registered American Indian Horses or Ponies are eligible. A handmade shield, patterned after an American Indian design, is presented when the applicant has earned 200 versatility points. Established in 1982. In addition, the following awards are presented: Indian Horse Supreme Hall of Fame Award for 1,000 versatility points, Indian Horse Farm or Ranch Hall of Fame for 400 versatility points, and Indian Horse Youth Hall of Fame for 300 versatility points by youth age 18 and under.

• 2603 •
Native American Institute
Leland L. Conner, Chief
960 Walhonding Ave.
Logan, OH 43138
Phone: (614)385-7136
E-mail: lelandconner@webtv.net
Home Page: http://www.nativeaminstitute.org

Formerly: (2005) American Indian Lore Association.

• 2604 • **Catlin Peace Pipe Award**
To recognize Indian and/or non-Indian individuals who have made special contributions to Indian lore. A rustic wood plaque in the shape of an arrowhead with an engraved brass plaque is awarded annually at the Catlin Peace Pipe Awards dinner in December. Established in 1970 in honor of George Catlin.

• 2605 • **Hall of Fame**
To recognize those individual leaders whose fields of lifetime interests are related to the various facets of Indian lifeways, including arts and crafts, music, dances, history, and folklore. The inductee need not be an American Indian by birth. A rustic wood plaque with brass engraving is awarded annually. Established in 1967 by the Sun Lodge Society of the association.

• 2606 •
American Indian Science and Engineering Society
Teresa Gomez, Contact
PO Box 9828
Albuquerque, NM 87119-9828
Phone: (505)765-1052
Fax: (505)765-5608
E-mail: info@aises.org
Home Page: http://www.aises.org

• 2607 • **Ely ("Eli") S. Parker Award**
To recognize American Indians who have made significant contributions in the science, engineering, and technology fields and who have served the American Indian community in a significant manner. American Indians in the fields of science and/or engineering are eligible. A medal is awarded annually. Established in 1983 in honor of Eli S. Parker, the first American Indian engineer. Scholarships are also awarded to Indian high school graduates and college students who wish to study in the fields of science or engineering.

• 2608 •
American Industrial Hygiene Association
Steven Davis, Exec.Dir.
2700 Prosperity Ave., Ste. 250
Fairfax, VA 22031
Phone: (703)849-8888
Fax: (703)207-3561
E-mail: infonet@aiha.org
Home Page: http://www.aiha.org

• 2609 • **Edward J. Baier Technical Achievement Award**
Recognizes significant contribution to industrial hygiene in recent years. Individuals, groups of individuals, companies, academic institutions, organizations, and associations are eligible. A monetary award is given annually. Sponsored by Clayton Environmental. Established in 1984.

• 2610 • **John J. Bloomfield Award**
To recognize younger people for contributions to the profession of industrial hygiene. Industrial hygienists who pursue the problem of occupational health hazards, primarily doing field work, and who demonstrate a significant contribution are eligible. Awarded annually. Contact Seth J. Burmeister. Established in 1978.

• 2611 • **Donald E. Cummings Memorial Award**
Recognizes outstanding contributions to the knowledge and practice of the profession of industrial hygiene. The recipient presents the Cummings Memorial Lecture at the Environmental Health and Safety Conference & Expo. Established in 1943 as a tribute to Donald E. Cummings, AIHA's third president.

• 2612 • **Distinguished Service Award**
Recognizes distinguished service in the advancement of industrial hytiene and unique technical contributions to the aims and goals of the Association. Association members are eligible. Selection is based on accomplishments with excellence in any aspect of industrial hygiene. Awarded annually. Established in 1978.

• 2613 • **Alice Hamilton Award**
Recognizes an outstanding woman who has made a definitive, lasting achievement in the field of occupational and environmental hygiene through public and community services, social reform, technological innovation or advancements in the scientific approach to the recognition, evaluation, and control of workplace hazards. Awardees must have been engaged in occupational hygiene or a related discipline a minimum of 10 years and must be recognized by her peers to be competent in her chosen field, dedicated to scientific truth, and committed to positive change for worker health. Established in 1993. First awarded in 1995.

• 2614 • **Honorary Member**
Recognizes an individual distinguished in the general field of industrial hygiene or in a closely related field. Nominees must not be eligible for the fellow category. Established in 1955.

• 2615 • **Kusnetz Award**
Recognizes a certified hygienist who has not reached his or her fortieth birthday by May 1 of the year in which the award is presented; who is currently employed in the private sector and has been so employed for a majority of his or her professional career; who by exhibiting high ethical standards and technical abilities has provided for the highest standards of health and safety protection for employees for whom he or

she is responsible; and who show promise of leadership in the industrial hutiene profession. Established in 1987. Awarded annually at the annual conference. Named for its donors, Florence and Past President Howard Kusnetz.

• 2616 • Meritorious Achievement Award
To recognize a member for outstanding contributions to the progress of occupational health and industrial hygiene. Awarded at the annual American Industrial Hygiene Conference and Exposition. Contact William Burgess. Established in 1957.

• 2617 • Michigan Industrial Hygiene Society Award for Authorship
Recognizes outstanding publication in the *American Industrial Hytiene Association Journal*. Selection is made by the MIHS Award Committee, a committee appointed by the president of the Society each year specifically for this purpose and which is national in origin. Presentation of the award is made at the annual meeting of the Association. Established in 1957. First presented in 1958.

• 2618 • Poster Session Awards
To recognize excellence in poster presentations. Selection is based on technical content and visual communication. The first- and second-place winners receive certificates of recognition during a special hoto-op and acknowledgements in *The Synergist*. Awarded annually. Established in 1990.

• 2619 • William Steiger Award
To recognize an individual who has made a significant, long-term contribution to occupational safety and health. The award honors the late Congressman, William Steiger of Wisconsin, co-sponsor and defender of the Occupational Safety and Health Act of 1970. Awarded annually. Contact Phillip Landrigan. Established in 1979.

• 2620 • Herbert E. Stokinger Award
To recognize an individual who has made a significant contribution in the broad field of industrial and environmental toxicology. The Stokinger Award Lecture is presented annually by the award recipient at the American Industrial Hygiene Conference and Exposition. Contact George M. Rusch. Established in 1977.

• 2621 • William B. Yant Award
Recognizes outstanding contributions in industrial hygiene or allied fields. Individuals living outside the United States are eligible. A monetary prize, an engraved stainless steel award, and travel expenses are presented annually. Established in 1964 to commemorate the leadership and breadth of contributions to industrial hytiene of William P. Yant. Sc.D, the first president of the Association. Sponsored by Mine Safety Appliances Company.

• 2622 •
American Institute for Contemporary German Studies
Dr. Jackson Janes, Exec.Dir.
1755 Massachusetts Ave. NW, Ste. 700
Washington, DC 20036-2121
Phone: (202)332-9312
Fax: (202)265-9531
E-mail: info@aicgs.org
Home Page: http://www.aicgs.org

• 2623 • DAAD Prize for Distinguished Scholarship in German Studies
Annual award of recognition.

• 2624 • Global Leadership Award
Annual award of recognition.

• 2625 •
American Institute for Patristic and Byzantine Studies
Prof. Constantine N. Tsirpanlis PhDThD, Founder & Pres.
12 Minuet Ln.
Kingston, NY 12401
Phone: (845)336-8797
Fax: (845)331-1002

• 2626 • The Byzantine-Patristic Medal and Certificate
For professional excellence in the fields of humanities, Byzantine-Greek and Ecumenical scholarship, authorship, teaching, and church leadership. A medal is awarded annually.

• 2627 •
American Institute for Public Service
Sam Beard, Pres./CEO
100 W 10th St., Ste. 215
Wilmington, DE 19801
Phone: (302)622-9101
Fax: (302)622-9108
E-mail: info@aips.jeffersonawards.org
Home Page: http://www.aips.org/

• 2628 • Jefferson Awards
To recognize the finest ideals and contributions in the field of public service in the United States, to raise the consciousness of Americans to the vitality of our national purpose and to give a sense of unity through that common purpose. National awards are presented in the following categories: (1) to an appointed or elected official; (2) to a private citizen; (3) to an individual for service to the disadvantaged; (4) to an individual under the age of 35 who has contributed the most to public service; and (5) to an individual for service benefiting local communities. Nominations are submitted by the Board of Selectors, the Board of Nominators, and national institutions and organizations. The Board of Selectors votes to determine the winners. In addition, five Jacqueline Kennedy Onassis Awards of $1,000 each are presented to five private individuals who have performed extraordinary public services in their local communities. Individuals are not eligible for the local awards if they receive compensation for their public service efforts. Awarded annually at U.S. Supreme Court. Established in 1972 by Jacqueline Kennedy Onassis, Senator Taft, Jr., and Samuel S. Beard.

• 2629 •
American Institute of Aeronautics and Astronautics
Alan R. Mulally, Pres.
1801 Alexander Bell Dr., Ste. 500
Reston, VA 20191-4344
Phone: (703)264-7500
Toll-Free: 800-NEW-AIAA
Fax: (703)264-7551
E-mail: custserv@aiaa.org
Home Page: http://www.aiaa.org/

• 2630 • Aeroacoustics Award
To recognize an individual for an outstanding technical or scientific achievement in the field of aircraft community noise reduction. A certificate of citation, a rosette pin, and an engraved bronze medal are awarded annually at the Institute's Aeroacoustics Conference. Established in 1973. Deadline is October 1.

• 2631 • Aerodynamic Measurement Technology Award
To recognize continued contributions and achievements toward the advancement of advanced aerodynamics flowfield and surface measurement techniques for research in flight and ground test applications. The award is presented in even-numbered years at the AIAA Aerospace Ground Testing/Aerodynamic Measurement Conference. Established in 1995.

• 2632 • Aerodynamics Award
For meritorious achievement in the field of applied aerodynamics recognizing notable contributions through the development, application and evaluation of aerodynamic concepts and methods. A medal, certificate of citation, and a rosette pin are presented during the Applied Aerodynamics Conference. Established in 1983.

• 2633 • Aerospace Communications Award
To recognize a person who has outstanding contribution in the field of aerospace communications. A medal, a certificate of citation, and a rosette pin are awarded biennially AIAA International at the Communications Satellite Systems Conference and Exhibit. Established in 1967.

• 2634 • Aerospace Contribution to Society Award
To recognize a notable contribution to society through the application of aerospace technology to societal needs. A medal, certificate of citation, and a rosette pin are presented annually at the Aerospace Sciences Meeting and Exhibit. Established in 1977.

• 2635 • Aerospace Design Engineering Award
To recognize design engineers who have made outstanding technical, educational, or creative

achievements that exemplify the quality and elements of design engineering. A medal, certificate of citation, and a rosette pin are awarded at the Structures, Structural Dynamics and Materials Conference. Established in 1992.

• 2636 • Aerospace Maintenance Award

To recognize an individual who has made a major contribution to aerospace maintenance discipline, specifically in aviation, missiles, and space, resulting in a significant improvement in operational and cost effectiveness. A medal, certificate of citation, and a rosette pin are awarded at the AIAA Aircraft Technology, Integration and Operations Forum. Established in 1987.

• 2637 • Aerospace Power Systems Award

For recognition of a significant contribution in the broad field of aerospace power systems, specifically as related to the application of engineering sciences and systems engineering to the production, storage, distribution, and processing of aerospace power. The award consists of a medal, certificate of citation, and rosette pin and is generally presented annually at the Intersociety Energy Conversion Engineering Conference. Established in 1981.

• 2638 • AIAA Aerospace Software Engineering Award

To recognize an individual for outstanding technical and/or management contribution to aeronautical or astronautical software engineering. A medal, certificate of citation, and a rosette pin are awarded biennially in odd-numbered years at the Digital Avionics Conference. Established in 1989.

• 2639 • AIAA Air Breathing Propulsion Award

For meritorious accomplishment in the arts, sciences and technology of air breathing propulsion system. The award consists of a medal, a certificate of citation, and a rosette pin. The award is generally presented at the AIAA/ASME/SAE/ASEE Joint Propulsion Conference. Established in 1975.

• 2640 • AIAA Aircraft Design Award

To recognize a design engineer or team for the conception, definition, or development, of an original concept leading to a significant advancement in aircraft design or design technology. A medal, certificate, and a rosette pin are awarded annually at the AIAA Aircraft Technology, Integration, and Operations Forum. Established in 1968.

• 2641 • AIAA Career Enhancement Award

Recognizes section programs that are beneficial to career development, such as: Time Management Workshops, Career Transition Workshops, Career Benefits Workshops (health care reform, financial planning, pension portability, etc.), Technical v. Management Career Path Workshops, Resume Writing and related topics. Established in 1997.

• 2642 • AIAA Certificate of Merit Awards

To promote technical and scientific excellence, certificates of merit are given in connection with a nationally sponsored AIAA activity. Established in 1978.

• 2643 • AIAA Command, Control, Communication & Intelligence Award

For significant contribution to the overall effectiveness of C3I systems through the development of improved C3I Systems and System Technology. A medal, certificate of citation, and a rosette pin are awarded biennially in odd-numbered years at the AIAA Space Conference and Exhibition. The first award was presented in 1991.

• 2644 • AIAA Computer-Aided Engineering and Manufacturing Award

To recognize an individual who has conceived, defined, or developed an original concept leading to a significant advancement in the use of interactive computer graphics for conceptual design, computer imagery, or computer-aided design and computer-manufacturing. A medal, certificate of citation, and a rosette pin are awarded biennially in odd-numbered years at the AIAA Digital Avionics Conference. Established in 1988.

• 2645 • AIAA Digital Avionics Award

To recognize outstanding achievements in technical management and/or implementation of digital avionics in space or aeronautical systems, including system analysis, design, development, or application. A medal, a certificate of citation, and a rosette pin are presented at the AIAA Digital Avionics Conference and Technology Display biennially in odd-numbered years. Established in 1984.

• 2646 • AIAA Distinguished Service Award

To recognize distinguished service over a period of years to the Institute. Members of the AIAA are eligible. A certificate is awarded annually at the Honors Night Banquet. Established in 1968.

• 2647 • AIAA Energy Systems Award

To recognize significant contributions in the broad field of energy systems, specifically as related to the application of engineering sciences and systems engineering to the production, storage, distribution, and conservation of energy. A medal, a certificate of citation, and a rosette pin are awarded annually at the Intersociety Energy Conversion Engineering Conference. Established in 1981.

• 2648 • AIAA Engineer of the Year Award

To recognize an individual member of AIAA who has made a recent significant contribution that is worthy of national recognition. A medal and a certificate of citation are presented during the AIAA Aircraft Technology, Integration, and Operations Forum. Established in 1989.

• 2649 • AIAA Fluid Dynamics Award

To recognize an outstanding contribution to the understanding of the behavior of liquids and gases in motion as related to needs in aeronautics and astronautics. A medal and a citation are awarded annually at the Fluid Dynamics, Plasmadynamics, and Laser Conference. Established in 1975. Formerly: Fluid and Plasmadynamics Award.

• 2650 • AIAA Foundation National Student Conference Awards

To recognize the authors of the best papers presented in the graduate and undergraduate classifications during the AIAA National Student Conference. The award carries a $500 honorarium, a medal, and a certificate of citation for each category and is presented during the Aerospace Sciences Meeting and Exhibit. Established in 1948.

• 2651 • AIAA Ground Testing Award

To recognize outstanding achievement in the development or effective utilization of technology, procedures, facilities, or modeling techniques for flight simulation, space simulation, propulsion testing, aerodynamic testing, or other ground testing associated with aeronautics and astronautics. A medal, a certificate of citation, and a rosette pin are presented biennially at the AIAA/ASME/SAE/ASEE Joint Propulsion Conference and the Aerospace Ground Testing Conference. Established in 1975. Formerly: Simulation and Ground Testing Award.

• 2652 • AIAA Haley Space Flight Award

To recognize an outstanding contribution by an astronaut or flight test personnel to the advancement of the art, science, or technology of astronautics. A medal, certificate of citation, and a rosette pin are awarded biennially in odd-numbered years at the Aerospace Sciences Meeting and Exhibit. Established in 1954 in honor of Andrew G. Haley, one of the founders of the American Rocket Society. Formerly: (1966) Astronautics Award.

• 2653 • AIAA HAP Arnold Award for Excellence in Aeronautical Program Management

Presented to an individual for outstanding contributions in the management of a significant aeronautical or aeronautical related project. A medal, certificate, and a rosette pin are awarded at the AIAA Aircraft Technology, Integration, and Operations Forum. Established in 1997.

• 2654 • AIAA History Manuscript Award

To recognize the best historical manuscript dealing with the science, technology, and/or impact of aeronautics and astronautics on society. Authors of an original work are eligible. A medal, certificate, and a rosette pin are presented at the Aerospace Sciences Meeting annually. Established in 1967.

• 2655 • AIAA Information Systems Award

To recognize outstanding technical and/or management contributions in space and aeronautics computer and sensing aspects of information technology and science. A medal, certificate, and a rosette pin are awarded biennially in odd-numbered years at the AIAA Digital Avionics Conference. Established in 1975.

• 2656 • AIAA International Cooperation Award

To recognize an individual(s) who has made significant contributions to the initiation, organization, implementation and/or management of activities with significant US involvement that includes extensive international cooperative activities in space, aeronautics, or both. Awarded annually at the Honors Night Banquet, in conjunction with the Global Air and Space International Business Forum and Exhibition. Established in 1988.

• 2657 • AIAA Losey Atmospheric Science Award

To recognize outstanding contributions to the atmospheric sciences as applied to the advancement of aeronautics and astronautics. A medal and certificate are usually presented at the Aerospace Sciences Meeting and Exhibit. Established in 1940 in memory of Captain Robert M. Losey, a meteorological officer who was killed while serving as an observer for the U.S. Army, the first officer in the service of the United States to die in World War II. Formerly: (1975) Robert M. Losey Award.

• 2658 • AIAA Mechanics and Control of Flight Award

To recognize an outstanding recent technical or scientific contribution by an individual to the mechanics, guidance, or control of flight in space or the atmosphere. A medal, certificate, and a rosette pin are awarded annually at the Guidance, Navigation, and Control Conference. Established in 1967.

• 2659 • AIAA National Faculty Advisor Award

To recognize the faculty advisor of a chartered AIAA Student Branch who, in the opinion of student branch members and the AIAA Student Activities Committee, has made outstanding contributions as a faculty advisor, as evidenced by the record of his student branch in local, regional, and national AIAA Activities. A certificate of citation is awarded at the Aerospace Sciences Meeting. Established in 1984.

• 2660 • AIAA Outstanding Section Awards

Presented to a section judged for its outstanding overall achievement and contributions throughout the year. First place winners are honored at the AIAA Aerospace Sciences Meeting and Exhibit.

• 2661 • AIAA Pendray Aerospace Literature Award

To recognize an outstanding contribution(s) to aeronautical and astronautical literature in the recent past, preferably three years, with emphasis on the high quality or major influence of the piece rather than, for example, the importance of the underlying technological contributions. A medal, certificate, and a rosette pin are awarded annually at the Aerospace Sciences Meeting and Exhibit. Established in 1950 in honor of Dr. G. Edward Pendray, a founder and past president of the American Rocket Society. Formerly: (1975) G. Edward Pendray Award.

• 2662 • AIAA Piper General Aviation Award

Presented for outstanding contributions leading to the advancement of general aviation. A medal, certificate, and a rosette pin are presented at the Aircraft Technology, Integration, and Operations Forum. Established in 1979. Renamed in 1989 to honor William T. Piper, Sr., who made Piper the name synonymous with general aviation. Formerly: (1988) General Aviation Award.

• 2663 • AIAA Pre-College Outreach Award

Presneted to a Section that has developed and implemented an outstanding pre-college outreach program. The award omination should describe the section acrivities that have had an impact relative to the goals of the AIAA Precollege Outreach National Committee which are the following: 1. to provide quality educational resources for the Nation's K-12 teachers in the ares; and 2. to provide role models and mentors for their students. Established in 1996.

• 2664 • AIAA Propellants and Combustion Award

To recognize outstanding technical contributions to aeronautical or astronautical combustion engineering. A medal, certificate, and a rosette pin are presented at the annual Joint Propulsion Conference. Established in 1990.

• 2665 • AIAA Public Service Award

To recognize an individual outside the aerospace community who has shown consistent and visible support for national aviation and space goals. The award is presented at the Honors Night Banquet. Established in 1985.

• 2666 • AIAA Reed Aeronautics Award

This, one of the highest awards the Institute bestows, is given to honor the most notable achievement in the field of aeronautical science and engineering. A medal and certificate are awarded annually at the Honors Night Banquet. Established in 1933 in memory of Dr. Sylvanus A. Reed, aeronautical engineer, designer, and founding member of the Institute of Aeronautical Sciences. Formerly: (1975) Sylvanus Albert Reed Award.

• 2667 • AIAA Section Public Policy Award

For recognition of stimulating public awareness of the needs and benefits of aerospace research and development, particularly on the part of government representatives, and for educating its members in the value of public policy activities. The award is presented in five categories: up to 99, 100-249, 250-399, 400-999, and 1,000 and over. Judging is by the Public Policy Subcommittee. A certificate is presented to the public policy officer each year at the AIAA Aerospace Sciences Meeting and Exhibit. Established in 1980.

• 2668 • AIAA Space Processing Award

For recognition of significant contributions in space processing or in furthering the use of microgravity for space processing. Awarded biennially in even-numbered years at the Aerospace Sciences Meeting and Exhibit.

• 2669 • AIAA Space Science Award

Reestablished in 1998 and is now presented to an individual for demonstrated leadership of innovative scientific investigations associated with space missions. Originally established in 1961.

• 2670 • AIAA Space Systems Award

To recognize outstanding achievements in architecture, analysis, design, and implementation of space systems. A medal and certificate are awarded at the AIAA Space Meeting and Exhibition. Established in 1968. Formerly: (1984) Spacecraft Design Award.

• 2671 • AIAA Structures, Structural Dynamics, and Materials Award

To recognize an individual who has been responsible for outstanding recent technical or scientific contribution in aerospace structures, structural dynamics, or materials. A medal, certificate, and a rosette pin are awarded at the AIAA Structures, Structural Dynamics, and Materials Conference. Established in 1967.

• 2672 • AIAA Support Systems Award

To recognize significant contribution to the overall effectiveness of aeronautical or aerospace systems through the development of improved support systems technology. A medal, certificate, and a rosette pin are presented annually at the Space Logistics Symposium. Established in 1975.

• 2673 • AIAA System Effectiveness and Safety Award

To recognize outstanding contribution to the field of system effectiveness and safety or its related disciplines. A medal, certificate, and a rosette pin are presented at the annual International Reliability and Maintainability Symposium. Established in 1975.

• 2674 • AIAA Thermophysics Award

To recognize an outstanding singular or sustained technical or scientific contribution by an individual in thermophysics, specifically as related to the properties and mechanisms involved in thermal energy transfer and the study of environmental effects in such properties and mechanisms. A medal, certificate, and a rosette pin are awarded at the Thermophysics and Heat Transfer Conference. Established in 1975.

• 2675 • J. Leland Atwood Award
To recognize a recent outstanding educational achievement and to encourage innovative improvements in aerospace education. A certificate and $2,000 honorarium are presented at the Aerospace Sciences Meeting and Exhibit. Established in 1974.

• 2676 • Chanute Flight Award
To recognize an outstanding contribution by a pilot or test personnel to the advancement of the art, science, and technology of aeronautics. A medal, certificate of citation, and a rosette pin are awarded biennially at the AIAA Aircraft Technology, Integration, and Operations Forum. Established in 1939 to honor Octave Chanute, pioneer aeronautical investigator. Formerly: Octave Chanute Award.

• 2677 • Communications Award
To recognize AIAA sections that have developed and implemented an outstanding communication outreach program during the section year. Winning criteria includes the following: level of difficulty and complexity as well as timeliness, multiple methods of communications, frequency, format, and content of the communication outreach. Awarded to one or more recipients annually.

• 2678 • Walter J. and Angeline H. Crichlow Trust Prize
To recognize excellence in aerospace materials, structural design, analysis, or structural dynamics. A certificate, a gold medal, and an honorarium of $100,000 are presented every four years at the AIAA Structures, Structural Dynamics, and Materials Conference. Established in 1994.

• 2679 • De Florez Award for Flight Simulation
Presented for an outstanding individual achievement in the application of flight simulation to aerospace training, research, and development. A certificate of citation, a medal, and a rosette pin are awarded annually at the AIAA Modeling and Flight Technologies Conference. Established in 1965 to honor Admiral de Florez. Formerly: (1982) De Florez Award for Modeling and Simulation.

• 2680 • AIAA Dryden Lectureship in Research
To recognize outstanding research efforts in aeronautics and astronautics. By research scientists and engineers. The award consists of a medal, certificate, and a rosette pin. Awardees must deliver a lecture at the annual Aerospace Sciences Meeting and Exhibit. Awarded annually. Established in 1960. Renamed in 1967 in honor of Dr. Hugh L. Dryden, renowned leader in aerospace research programs. Formerly: Research Award.

• 2681 • Durand Lectureship for Public Service
For notable achievements by a scientific or technical leader whose contributions have led directly to the understanding and application of the science and technology of aeronautics and astronautics for the betterment of mankind. The award consists of a medal, a certificate of citation, and a rosette pin. Awarded biennially in even-numbered years. Established in 1983 in honor of William F. Durand.

• 2682 • Goddard Astronautics Award
This, one of the highest awards the Institute bestows, is given for the most notable achievement in the field of astronautics. A medal, certificate, and a rosette pin are awarded annually at the Honors Night Banquet. Established in 1963 to honor Robert H. Goddard, rocket visionary, pioneer, bold experimentalist, and superb engineer whose early liquid rocket engine launches opened up the world of astronautics. Formerly: (1975) Goddard Award.

• 2683 • Jeffries Aerospace Medicine and Life Sciences Research Award
To recognize the importance to aeronautics of science endeavors in the field of medicine. A medal, certificate, and a rosette pin are generally presented at the Aerospace Sciences Meeting. Established in 1940 in memory of John Jeffries, an American physician who made the earliest recorded scientific observations from the air. Formerly: John Jeffries Award.

• 2684 • Theodor W. Knacke Aerodynamic Decelerator Systems Award
To recognize significant contributions to the effectiveness and/or safety of aeronautical or aerospace systems through development or application of the art and science of aerodynamic decelerator technology. A medal, certificate of citation, and a rosette pin are awarded at the AIAA Aerodynamic Deceleration Conference. Established in 1976.

• 2685 • William Littlewood Memorial Lecture
To provide for a lecture in memory of William Littlewood, renowned for the many significant contributions he made to the design of, and operational requirements for, civil transport aircraft. The lecture is sponsored biennially in odd-numbered years.

• 2686 • AIAA George M. Low Space Transportation Award
To recognize timely outstanding contributions to the field of space transportation. Awarded biennially in even-numbered years at the AIAA Space Conference & Exhibit. Established in 1988 to honor the achievements in space transportation by Dr. George M. Low, who played a leading role in planning and executing all the Apollo missions, and originated the plans for the first manned lunar orbital flight, Apollo 8.

• 2687 • Membership Award
To recognize the membership chairperson for successfully increasing the section's membership by planning and implementing effective new member recruitment and retention campaigns. Categories, based on the number of section members, include: up to 99, 100-249, 250-399, 400-999, and 1,000 and over. The following prizes are awarded to each of the five member categories: first place - $400; second place - $200; and third place $100. First place winners are honored at the AIAA Aerospace Sciences Meeting and Exhibit. Awarded annually.

• 2688 • Missile Systems Award
To recognize an investigator or program leader who was instrumental through his or her technical efforts, system design skill, and/or system management skills in developing innovative design solutions and/or managing the system development and deployment of advanced tactical or strategic missile systems. A medal, certificate of citation, and a rosette pin are presented biennially at the Missile Sciences Conference. Established in 1981.

• 2689 • Multidisciplinary Design Optimization Award
To recognize outstanding contributions to the development and/or application of techniques of multidisciplinary design optimization in the context of aerospace engineering. Presented biennially in even-numbered years at the Symposium on Multi-disciplinary Analysis Optimization. Established in 1993.

• 2690 • AIAA F. E. Newbold V/STOL Award
To recognize outstanding creative contributions to the advancement and realization of powered lift flight in one or more of the following areas: initiation, definition, and/or management of key V/STOL programs; development of enabling technologies including critical methodology; program engineering and design; and other relevant related activities or combinations thereof that have advanced the science of powered lift flight. A medal, certificate, and a rosette pin are awarded biennially at the International Power Lift Conference.

• 2691 • Plasmadynamics and Lasers Award
To recognize outstanding contributions to the understanding of the physical properties and dynamic behavior of matter in the plasma state and lasers as related to need in aeronautics and astronautics. Awarded annually. Established in 1991.

• 2692 • Space Operations and Support Award
For recognition of outstanding efforts in overcoming space operations problems and assuring success, and to recognize the teams or individuals whose exceptional contributions were critical to an anomaly recovery, crew rescue, or space failure. Awarded biennially in odd-

numbered years at the AIAA Space Conference and Exhibition. Established in 1991.

• 2693 • AIAA Jay Hollingsworth Speas Airport Award
To recognize that person or persons judged to have contributed most outstandingly during the recent past towards achieving compatible relationships between airports and/or heliports and adjacent environments. The award consists of a certificate and a $10,000 honorarium to the recipient. Established in 1983.

• 2694 • Special Service Citation
To recognize voluntary contributions of time and effort that have substantially and uniquely benefited a branch, section, or region during the section year.

• 2695 • AIAA Lawrence Sperry Award
To recognize a notable contribution made by a young person to the advancement of aeronautics or astronautics. Individuals under the age of 35 are eligible. A medal, certificate, and a rosette pin are awarded annually at the Aerospace Sciences Conference. Established in 1936 to honor Lawrence B. Sperry, pioneer aviator and inventor, who died in 1923 in a forced landing while attempting a flight across the English Channel. Formerly: Lawrence Sperry Young Achievement Award.

• 2696 • Survivability Award
To recognize an individual or a team for outstanding achievement or contribution in design, analysis, implementation, and/or education of survivability in an aerospace system. Presented biennially in even-numbered years at the Structures, Structural Dynamics and Materials conference. Established in 1993.

• 2697 • von Braun Award for Excellence in Space Program Management
To give national recognition to an individual or group for outstanding contributions in the management of a significant space or space-related program or project. Awarded annually at the AIAA Space and Exhibit. Established in 1987.

• 2698 • von Karman Lectureship in Astronautics
To honor an individual who has performed notably and distinguished himself or herself technically in the field of astronautics. A medal and citation are awarded annually. The awardee is expected to present a lecture at the Aerospace Sciences Meeting. Established in 1962 in honor of Theodore von Karman, a fundamentalist in the aerospace sciences. Formerly: (1975) Von karman Lecture.

• 2699 • Otto C. Winzen Lifetime Achievement Award
To recognize outstanding contributions and achievements in the advancement of free flight balloon systems or related technologies. Awarded biennially in odd-numbered years. Established in 1993 in memory of Otto C. Winzen, a pioneer of modern day ballooning.

• 2700 • Wright Brothers Lectureship in Aeronautics
To emphasize significant advances in aeronautics by recognizing major leaders and contributors thereto. The award consists of a medal, a certificate, and the responsibility to present a lecture at the AIAA Aircraft Technology, Integration, and Operations Forum. Awarded annually. Established in 1937 to commemorate the first powered flights made by Orville and Wilbur Wright in 1903. Formerly: Wright Brothers Lecture.

• 2701 • Wyld Propulsion Award
To recognize outstanding achievement in the development or application of rocket propulsion systems. A medal, certificate, and a rosette pin are awarded annually at the AIAA/ASME/ASE/ASEE Joint Propulsion Conference. Established in 1964 in honor of James H. Wyld, the developer of the regeneratively-cooled rocket engine. Formerly: (1975) James H. Wyld Propulsion Award.

• 2702 • Young Professional Activity Award
To recognize sections of AIAA that demonstrate excellence in planning and executing successful events that encourage participation of young members in AIAA and to provide opportunities for leadership at the section, regional, and national levels. Categories, based on the number of section members, include: up to 99, 100-249, 250-399, 400-999, and 1,000 and over. The following prizes are awarded to each of the five member categories: first place - $400; second place - $200; and third place - $100. A certificate is also presented to the young member activity chairperson. First place winners are honored at the AIAA Aerospace Sciences Meeting and Exhibit. Awarded annually.

• 2703 • Abe M. Zarem Award for Distinguished Achievement
To recognize the work of students pursuing a higher degree in aeronautics and astronautics. Bronze medals, certificates, and travel stipends for students to present their work at the International Congress of the Aeronautical Sciences or the International Astronautical Federation Congress are awarded at the Aerospace Sciences Meeting and Exhibit. Established in 1990.

• 2704 •
American Institute of Aeronautics and Astronautics - Stanford University Branch
Howard Hamilton, Pres.
Stanford University
Department of Aero. & Astro.
MC 4035
Stanford, CA 94305-4035
Phone: (650)725-3296
Fax: (650)725-3377
E-mail: howardh@leland.stanford.edu
Home Page: http://www.stanford.edu/group/aiaa

• 2705 • Teaching Excellence Awards
For member of faculty and for teaching assistant; based on student evaluations. Recognition award bestowed annually.

• 2706 •
American Institute of Architects
Eugene C. Hopkins FAIA, Pres.
1735 New York Ave. NW
Washington, DC 20006-5292
Phone: (202)626-7300
Toll-Free: 800-AIA-3837
Fax: (202)626-7547
E-mail: infocentral@aia.org
Home Page: http://www.aia.org

• 2707 • AIA/ACSA Topaz Medallion for Excellence in Architectural Education
To recognize outstanding contribution to architectural education by an individual. Any colleague, student, or former student may nominate candidates by October 27. Candidates must have spent at least a decade primarily involved in architectural education and must be living at the time of nomination. The candidate's primary contribution to architectural education must have been on the North American continent. Awarded annually. Established in 1976. Co-sponsored by the Association of Collegiate Schools of Architecture. Formerly: (1985) AIA/ACSA Award for Architectural Education.

• 2708 • AIA/ALA Library Buildings Award
To honor design achievements in library building design. Open to libraries of all types with public access. Libraries are judged in six categories: academic, public, school, state, federal and international. Prizes are given in the following categories: new buildings; additions; renovations/restorations; conversion to library use; and interior redesign and refurnishing. Certificates are presented to the architects and the owners of all winning libraries during the ALA Annual Conference. Awarded biennially. Administered jointly by the American Institute of Architects and the American Library Association/Library Administration & Management Association.

• 2709 • Architecture Firm Award
The highest honor the Institute can bestow on an architecture firm that has consistently produced distinguished architecture for a period of at least 10 years. Members of the Board of Directors nominate eligible firms. The deadline for nominations is July 15. The Board of Directors selects the recipient and only one recipient is selected each year. Established in 1962.

• 2710 • College of Fellows Grants
To advance the understanding and awareness of architecture, both to the general public and the profession. The College of Fellows has supported a variety of endeavors, including research and subsequent publications, architectural education projects, exhibitions, conference, and lectures, tv and video production, and the preservation of architectural records. All applications are accepted for review.

The deadline for submission of applications is January. A monetary prize of $5,000 (on the average) and up to $10,000 is awarded annually in April. Established in 1963.

• 2711 • Fellowship

To elevate architects who have been members of the AIA for at least ten years and who have made a significant contribution to architecture and society and who have achieved a standard of excellence in the profession. The deadline is October 21.

• 2712 • Gold Medal

This, the highest honor the Institute can bestow on an individual, is given in recognition of a significant body of work of lasting influence on the theory & practice of Architecture. Individuals must be nominated by a AIA national Board member. Any natural person, living or dead and not necessarily an architect or an American, that the Board believes is qualified may receive the award. Nominations must be postmarked by July 15. One gold medal may be awarded annually. Established in 1907.

• 2713 • Honorary Fellowship

To recognize an architect of esteemed character and distinguished achievements who is not a citizen or resident of the United States, and who does not primarily practice architecture within the domain of the Institute. Submissions must be postmarked by November 18. Awarded annually.

• 2714 • Honorary Member

To recognize distinguished service to the profession of architecture or the allied arts and sciences. National and component staff members who have served on staff for a continuous period of at least ten years and individuals of esteemed character not eligible for membership in the Institute are eligible. Nominations must be postmarked by December 16.

• 2715 • Institute Honor Awards for Architecture

To recognize design excellence of any newly constructed or restoration project designed by an architect registered in the United States and built by a date specified in the Institute Honor Awards program. Selection is made by a jury of nine members: at least six architects, an allied professional, an associate member, and an architecture student. Entries may be submitted in the following categories: design resolution and design advancement. Societal advancement, technical advancement, environmental advancement, and preservation/restoration are also considered. Entry forms must be postmarked by August 5. Established in 1949.

• 2716 • Institute Honor Awards for Interiors

To recognize the quality of building interiors created by American architects and to draw attention to the broad diversity of completed interior architecture. Entries may be large or small in scope and may involve new construction, renovation or preservation/restoration. Entry forms must be postmarked by August 19. Established in 1991. Formerly: Interior Architecture Awards of Excellence.

• 2717 • Institute Honor Awards for Regional and Urban Design

To recognize the architectural profession's role in urban design city planning and community development, and to identify projects and programs that involve public participation and contribute to the quality of the urban environment. Entries may be submitted by owners, individual practitioners, private design firms, public agencies, civic organizations, and public interest groups. Entry forms must be postmarked by September 9. Awards are presented annually to elected officials, owners or sponsors, and representatives of the design teams. Formerly: (1991) Citation for Excellence in Community Architecture; Urban Design Awards for Excellence.

• 2718 • Institute Honors for Collaborative Achievements

To recognize and encourage distinguished achievements that constitute a beneficial influence on the architectural profession. Candidates for the awards are nominated by the AIA members, chapters, or committees and final decisions are made by a jury comprising four AIA members, two past recipients of the awards, an AIA Associate member. Individuals or organizations responsible for a body of work that relates to or influences architecture are eligible. The following are considered: the design, creation and execution of murals, graphics, paintings, bas-reliefs, mosaics, stained glass, sculptures, fountains, or furniture for architectural settings; recording and illustration that improves the promotion, interpretation, and understanding of architecture in various media, including film, television, delineation, and model making; and research and education, building product and equipment manufacture, furniture design and manufacture, lighting design, legislation, architectural criticism, and writing. Individuals or organizations responsible for a significant single achievement that relates to or influences architecture are also eligible. Nominations must be postmarked by October 6. Citations are awarded. Established in 1983. The Institute Honors were previously known as Fine Arts Medal, Craftsmanship Medal, Architectural Photography Medal, Allied Professions Medal, Industrial Arts Medal, Architectural Critics' Medal and Citation, and AIA Medal for Research.

• 2719 • Thomas Jefferson Awards for Public Architecture

To recognize achievements in the following three categories: private sector architects who have established a portfolio of accomplishment in the design of architecturally distinguished public facilities; public service architects who manage or produce quality design within their agencies; and public officials or other individuals who by their role of advocacy have furthered the public's awareness and/or appreciation of design excellence. Nominations must be postmarked by October 6. Established in 1991.

• 2720 • Edward C. Kemper Award

To recognize a member who has contributed significantly to the Institute and to the profession. Current members of the AIA national Board and past presidents of the Institute less than three years out of office are not eligible for this award. Selection is made by the Board of Directors and one selection is made each year. Nominations must be postmarked by October 6. Established in 1950 in honor of Edward C. Kemper, the first executive director of the Institute.

• 2721 • Twenty-Five Year Award

To recognize architecture that has best withstood the test of time. Any project designed by a registered architect in the United States that was completed between 25 and 35 years prior to submission is eligible. The deadline is September 1. Projects may be located in the United States or abroad. The Institute Honor Awards for Architecture jury selects one winner each year.

• 2722 • Young Architects Award

To recognize significant contributions made during the early stages of an architect's career that exemplify outstanding built work at any scale, as well as projects, initiatives, and brilliant beginnings that warrant national attention of the profession or the public. Members of the AIA who have been licensed to practice architecture less than 10 years are eligible for nomination by October 14. Awarded annually.

• 2723 • Whitney M. Young, Jr., Award

To recognize an architect or architecturally-oriented organization that has contributed significantly toward meeting the responsibilities of current social issues. Current issues include, for example, housing the homeless/affordable housing, increased participation by minorities or women in the profession, access for the disabled, and literary. Present members of the Board are not eligible. Selection is made by the Board of Directors. Nominations must be postmarked by October 14. A certificate is awarded annually. Established in 1971 to honor the late Whitney M. Young, Jr. who challenged the architectural profession to assume its professional responsibility to the social issues of today. responsibility to the social issues of today.

• 2724 •
American Institute of Architects
New York Chapter
Douglas L. Steidl FAIA, Pres.
1735 New York Ave. NW
Washington, DC 20006-5292
Phone: (202)626-7300
Toll-Free: 800-AIA-3837
Fax: (202)626-7547
E-mail: infocentral@aia.org
Home Page: http://www.aia.org

• 2725 • Allwork Grants

To recognize a high level of academic achievement and financial need among students enrolled in architectural program at schools in New York City and New York State. Nominations must be made by the Deans of architectural schools by February 12.

• 2726 • **Arnold W. Brunner Grant**
To encourage advanced study in any area of architectural investigation that effectively contributes to the knowledge, teaching, or practice of the art and science of architecture. Any U.S. citizen who is engaged in the profession of architecture, or those in related fields who have a background more advanced than is implied by five years of architectural training, is eligible. The proposed investigation is expected to result in a final written work, design project, research paper, or other form of presentation. Monetary awards of up to $15,000 are presented annually. Established in 1947 to honor Arnold W. Brunner.

• 2727 • **Haskell Awards**
To encourage excellence in writing on architecture and related design subjects. Available for students enrolled in a professional architecture or related program, such as history, interior design or urban studies. A minimum prize or prizes totaling $1,000 are awarded annually. Deadline is February 12.

• 2728 • **Travel Grants**
To provide stipends for full-time practitioners, registered or non-registered, for travel programs which will further their architectural education and professional development. Up to five grants totaling $15,000 will be awarded. Deadline is February 12. Funded from the consolidation of the Stewardson, Keefe and LeBrun bequests.

• 2729 •
American Institute of Architects, Arizona Chapter
Tina Gobbel, Exec.Dir.
30 N 3rd Ave. No. 200
Phoenix, AZ 85003
Phone: (602)252-4200
Phone: (602)257-1924
Toll-Free: 800-367-2781
Fax: (602)273-6814
E-mail: tina@aia-arizona.org
Home Page: http://www.aia-arizona.org

• 2730 • **Design Awards**
For designs by AIA architects. Recognition award bestowed annually.

• 2731 •
American Institute of Architects, Southern Arizona
Brent L. Davis, Exec. Dir.
4633 E. Broadway, Ste. 101
Tucson, AZ 85711
Phone: (520)323-2191
Fax: (520)323-3399
E-mail: brent@aia-arizona.org
Home Page: http://www.aia-arizona.org

• 2732 • **AIASAC Design Award**
For excellence in design. Recognition award bestowed annually.

• 2733 •
American Institute of Architects, Tampa Bay
Ms. Dawn Mayes, Exec.Dir.
200 N Tampa St., Ste. 100
Tampa, FL 33602
Phone: (813)229-3411
Fax: (813)229-1762
E-mail: aia.tampab@verizon.net
Home Page: http://www.aiatampabay.com

• 2734 • **Medal of Honor**
For overall service to profession. Medal awarded annually.

• 2735 • **Pullara Award**
For service to chapter. Recognition award bestowed annually.

• 2736 •
American Institute of Architects Vermont
Hanne N. Williams AIA/VT, Exec. Dir
1662 Mill Brook Rd.
Fayston, VT 05673
Phone: (802)496-3761
Fax: (802)496-3294
E-mail: aiavt@madriver.com
Home Page: http://www.aiavt.org

• 2737 • **Robert Brady Award**
For scholastic improvement. Monetary award bestowed annually.

• 2738 • **Ruth Freeman Award**
For scholastic excellence. Monetary award bestowed annually.

• 2739 •
American Institute of Biological Sciences
Dr. Richard T. O'Grady, Exec.Dir.
1444 I St. NW, Ste. 200
Washington, DC 20005-2210
Phone: (202)628-1500
Toll-Free: 800-992-2427
Fax: (202)628-1509
E-mail: rogrady@aibs.org
Home Page: http://www.aibs.org

• 2740 • **AIBS Distinguished Service Award**
To recognize contributions in the service of biology, especially in the advancement and integration of biological disciplines, the application of biological knowledge to the solution of humanity's problems, and the improvement of public policy and planning by the introduction of pertinent biological considerations. Nominations must be submitted by October 1 and include a statement of the individual's service to biological science as a profession. A plaque is bestowed at the annual meeting and the winner is recognized in *Bio Science*, the official AIBS journal. Established in 1972.

• 2741 • **Media Awards**
Recognizes outstanding reporting on biological research in both print and broadcast journalism; encourages the communication of biology to the general public; and aims to foster a better understanding of how biology research is relevant to society as a whole. Freelancer and staff writers are eligible. Awards are limited to nontechnical journalism. Applicants may submit a single contribution or a series focusing on a single topic. Stories must have been published or broadcast between December 1 and November 30 of the preceding year. The following will not be considered: submissions by scientists writing in their area of research; articles appearing in *BioScience*, AIBS's flagship journal; books and articles in technical journals. An application form accompanied by five copies of the submission (print copies, cassette tapes, video tapes, or excerpts of radio or television series not to exceed two hours) must be submitted. Entries will be judged on clarity, reporting and writing skills, originality, and appeal to the general public. $1000 and paid expenses to attend the awards ceremony will be awarded. Awarded annually. Established in 1995.

• 2742 •
American Institute of Building Design
Steven Mickley, Exec.Dir.
2505 Main St., Ste. 209B
Stratford, CT 06615
Phone: (203)378-3480
Toll-Free: 800-366-2423
Fax: (203)378-3568
E-mail: bobbi@aibd.org
Home Page: http://www.aibd.org

• 2743 • **AIBD Design Competition**
Recognizes the best examples of individual effort in building design and community betterment. Awards are presented in the following categories: Best of Show, Designer's Choice, Working Drawings, Residential - custom design, Residential - remodel and restore, Residential - builders model, working drawings, unbuilt design, published designs, and Commercial Projects. Crystal awards and plaques are awarded annually at the convention. Established in 1950 by the AIBD national office. Sponsored by HomeStyles Publishing and Marketing.

• 2744 •
American Institute of Certified Public Accountants
Barry C. Melancon, Pres./CEO
1211 Ave. of the Americas
New York, NY 10036-8775
Phone: (212)596-6200
Phone: (201)938-3750
Toll-Free: 888-777-7077
Fax: (212)596-6213
E-mail: bmelancon@aicpa.org
Home Page: http://www.aicpa.org

• 2745 • **AICPA Accredited in Business Valuation (ABV) Hall of Fame Award**
Recognizes individuals whose lifetime achievements and contributions have significantly advanced the valuation discipline, and that have enhanced the profession for CPAs. Awarded when merited at the Business Valuation Conference in November or December of each year.

More than one award may be given. Established in 1999.

• 2746 • AICPA Business and Industry Hall of Fame

Recognizes the achievements of individual CPAs employed in business and industry and designed to promote the CPA designation as the premier professional credential for financial managers. Judges place primary emphasis on the nominee's business achievements and secondary emphasis on the nominee's contribution to the growth and enhancement of the profession. Involvement in public service is an enhancement to the nominee's application, but not a condition for selection. The nominee must be a CPA but does not need to be a member of the AICPA or a state CPA society. The deadline for nominations to be considered is July. Presented annually at the AICPA National Industry Conference.

• 2747 • AICPA Distinguished Achievement in Accounting Education Award

Recognizes full-time college accounting educators distinguished for excellence in teaching and for national prominence in the accounting profession. The award has the dual function of extending profession-wide recognition to the recipient as well as promoting role models in academe. The nominee must be a current full-time or recently retired (within the past five years) accounting educator at a post-secondary educational institution; must be distinguished for excellence in classroom teaching; must be involved in curriculum development; must be contributing to the accounting profession; and must exemplify the philosophy of the CPA Vision. Educators who are noted for their teaching abilities but are now primarily involved in administration or research are eligible for the award. The nominee need not be a CPA or hold a doctoral degree. The award is presented at the AICPA Spring Meeting of Council. Individuals may not nominate themselves. Nominations must be submitted by February 1.

• 2748 • AICPA Gold Medal Award for Distinguished Service

For recognition of a person whose influence on the profession as a whole is distinguished when compared with other contemporary leaders. Nominations are sought from members of the Awards Committee, recent past chairs of the Institute's Board of Directors, past award winners, management staff of the AICPA, and other knowledgeable sources. Selection criteria include: quality and length of service; motivation; and influence and personal attributes. The Awards Committee meets prior to Spring AICPA Meeting of Council to review nominations. Winner is announced at the Fall AICPA Meeting of Council. Nominations are submitted each year by December 15. Established in 1944.

• 2749 • AICPA Medal of Honor

To recognize an individual who is not a CPA but whose work has had a significant impact on the profession. The Awards Committee meets prior to the Spring AICPA Meeting of Council to review nominations. Winner is announced at the Spring or Fall AICPA Meeting of Council. Nominations must be submitted by December 15. Established in 1980.

• 2750 • AICPA Outstanding CPA in Government Award

Recognizes the achievements of CPAs employed in government and promotes the CPA designation as the premier professional credential for accounting, auditing, and finance professionals in government. Nominees must be an AICPA or state CPA society member employed in the appropriate level of government for the current award year. Current government employees and former employees who have been retired for less than one year are eligible. Awarded annually at the AICPA National Governmental Accounting and Auditing Update Conference. Nomination deadline: April 1.

• 2751 • AICPA PFP Distinguished Service Award

Given in recognition of years of volunteer service to advance the efforts of CPAs in practicing personal financial planning, and to increase recognition of the Personal Financial Specialist accreditation. Nominees must be a member of the Personal Financial Planning Division of the AICPA and cannot have been chair of the PFP executive committee within the past five years. Winner is selected by the PFP team and executive committee. The award is presented annually at the AICPA PFP Technical Conference in January. There is no set deadline for nominations, but the winner must be chosen far enough in advance of the PFP Technical Conference to allow enough time for the certificate to be printed.

• 2752 • AICPA Public Service Award

Honors one candidate who has demonstrated outstanding public service activities from among a select field of candidates, each of whom have been nominated by AICPA members or state societies. The winner is recognized at the AICPA Spring Meeting of Council. Deadline: August.

• 2753 • AICPA Special Recognition Award

Given to a member who has performed or contributed to the success of a particular project or initiative and whose contributions are of an outstanding nature. Awarded when merited; more than one award may be given. Nominations must be submitted by December 15.

• 2754 • Joint AICPA/AAA Accounting Literature Award

Recognizes books and/or articles that make an outstanding contribution to the accounting literature. This award is co-sponsored by the American Accounting Association. A committee of representatives from both organizations selects the winner. $2,500 and a plaque is awarded annually at the AAA annual meeting in August. Nominated items must have been published within the past five years. Nominations are submitted in January to the chair of the AAA screening committee.

• 2755 •
American Institute of Chemical Engineers
Joe Cramer, Dir.
3 Park Avenue
New York, NY 10016-5991
Phone: (212)591-7338
Toll-Free: 800-242-4363
Fax: (212)591-8897
E-mail: xpress@aiche.org
Home Page: http://www.aiche.org

• 2756 • Award for Outstanding Scholastic Achievement

To recognize outstanding achievements by a chemical engineering student who serves as a role model for disadvantaged minority students. A plaque, a cash prize of $1,500, and a travel allowance to the awards presentation are given. Awarded when merited by the Minority Affairs Committee. Established in 1996.

• 2757 • Award for Service to Society

To recognize outstanding contributions by a chemical engineer to community service and the solution of socially oriented problems. Eligible members include those who have given in an outstanding manner of themselves in the identification and solution of problems of the community and of society at large and whose actions reflect their concern for the common good. A monetary award of $2,000 and a plaque are awarded not more than once a year. Established in 1972. Sponsored by the Fluor Daniel, Inc.

• 2758 • Award in Chemical Engineering Practice

To recognize outstanding contributions by a chemical engineer in the industrial practice of the profession. Institute members are eligible. A plaque is awarded annually. The monetary stipend associated with this award is dependent upon securing a new sponsor. Established in 1972.

• 2759 • Thomas Baron Award in Fluid-Particle Systems

To recognize outstanding scientific/technical accomplishments by an individual with significant impact on the field of fluid-particle systems or in a related field. Any chemical engineering professional is eligible for the award, regardless of Institute affiliation. The deadline for nominations is March 31. A monetary award of $1,000 and a plaque are presented annually by the Particle Technology Forum. Winners are invited to present a lecture at the annual meeting and are required to present a written manuscript. Sponsored by Shell Global Solutions Inc.

• 2760 • Richard E. Bellman Control Heritage Award

This, the highest recognition of professional achievement for U.S. control systems engineers and scientists, is given to honor distinguished career contributions to the theory or application of automatic control. Nomination deadline is December 1. A medal and a $1,000 honorarium are awarded annually by the American Automatic Control Council.

• 2761 • Lawrence K. Cecil Award

For recognition of outstanding chemical engineering contributions and achievements toward the preservation or improvement of the natural environment (air, water, or land). The deadline for nominations is February 15. A monetary award of $2,500 and a plaque are awarded annually if merited at the annual meeting, where the winner presents an address. Established in 1972 in honor of Lawrence K. Cecil. Sponsored by BP America, Inc.

• 2762 • Allan P. Colburn Award for Excellence in Publications by a Young Member of the Institute

To recognize a notable contribution to the publications of the Institute by a younger member. Individuals who have made significant contributions to chemical engineering through publications are eligible. The recipient must be under the age of 36 at the end of the calendar year. A plaque, a monetary award of $5,000 and a $500 travel allowance are awarded annually when merited at the annual meeting. Established in 1945. Sponsored by E. I. du Pont de Nemours and Company.

• 2763 • Community Outreach Award

For recognition of outstanding achievements in community relations and communication with the public that promote the positive aspects of chemical engineering and the industries it serves. Eligibility is limited to companies in industries served by chemical engineers. Public interaction and/or communication can be on issues of health, safety, environment/ecology, or other worthy causes. Nominations for the Award may be submitted to the Public Relations Committee or its officers at any time. The deadline for nominations is March 1. A plaque is presented at the AIChE Spring National Meeting.

• 2764 • Computing in Chemical Engineering Award

To recognize outstanding contributions in the application of computing and systems technology to chemical engineering. The nomination deadline is April 15. The award consists of a monetary award of $3,000, a plaque, and an address delivered by the honoree. Presented annually at the meeting of the Computing and Systems Technology Division of the Institute's annual meeting. Established in 1979. Sponsored by Dow Chemical Company and Mitsubishi Chemical Company.

• 2765 • Computing Practice Award

To recognize outstanding contributions in the practice or application of chemical engineering to computing and systems technology. Nominations should be made by April 15. The award consists of a monetary prize of $3,000 and a plaque. Awarded annually at a meeting of the CAST Division at the AIChE Annual Meeting. Established in 1987. Sponsored by Aspen Technology, Inc. and ExxonMobil Chemical Company.

• 2766 • Distinguished Service Award

To recognize a member for sustained service and outstanding achievements that advance the goals of the Minority Affairs Committee, including reducing the under-representation of minorities in the Institute, the chemical engineering profession, and engineering as a whole. Up to three awards may be presented annually. A plaque is awarded. Established in 1995.

• 2767 • William H. Doyle Award

To recognize the best paper presented at the previous year's Loss Prevention Symposium. A plaque was awarded. Established in 1988 in memory of Bill Doyle, who was one of the founders of the AIChE Loss Prevention Symposium series and who contributed greatly to the knowledge and understanding of loss prevention in the chemical industry for over 50 years.

• 2768 • Engineering and Construction Contracting Division Award

To recognize the outstanding contribution by an individual in the engineering and construction industry. This award recognizes excellence in the leadership, management, and/or technological areas of contracting and the more general field of project management in the engineering and construction industry. Deadline: January 1. The recipient need not be a member of the ECC Division or the Institute. A Plaque of Acknowledgement for an individual's outstanding contribution is awarded annually at the annual ECC Division Conference. Established in 1988.

• 2769 • Fluidized Processes Recognition Award

In recognition of significant contribution to the science and technology of fluidization or fluidized processes and for leadership service to the engineering community. Only members of the Particle Technology Forum are eligible. The deadline for nominations is March 31. A monetary award of $1,000 and a plaque are presented biennially in odd-numbered years. Sponsored by Dow Chemical Company Foundation.

• 2770 • Food, Pharmaceutical and Bioengineering Division Award in Chemical Engineering

To recognize an individual for outstanding chemical engineering contributions and achievements in those industries involved in food, pharmaceutical, and bioengineering activities. Contributions may have been made in industrial, governmental, academic, or other organizations. The recipient need not be a member of the Institute. The deadline for nominations is March 25 each year. A monetary award of $4,000 and a plaque are awarded annually. Established in 1970. Sponsored by E.I. du Pont de Nemours and Company.

• 2771 • Forest Products Division Award in Chemical Engineering

For recognition of outstanding chemical engineering contributions and achievements in the forest products and related industries. The award is based on: significant discoveries, research, or development that lead to successful implementation on a commercial scale; outstanding contribution of a chemical engineering nature in the field of design, operation of management of production, or related facilities leading to significant improvements of relevant technology; or distinguished service as an educator in the field of chemical engineering with emphasis on application of chemical engineering principles to the technologies of the forest products industries. Selection is based on the presentation of a paper at one of the division's symposia describing the engineer's original contribution in the application of chemical engineering in forest products. The deadline for nominations is September 2. A plaque and an honorarium are presented annually at the annual meeting. Established in 1976. Sponsored by the Forest Products Division of AIChE. For additional information, contact the Institute.

• 2772 • Founders Award for Outstanding Contributions to the Field of Chemical Engineering

To recognize a member for outstanding contributions to the chemical engineering field. A monetary award of $3,000, a gold medal, and a plaque are awarded. Awarded annually. Established in 1958.

• 2773 • Fuels and Petrochemical Division Award

To recognize individuals who have made substantial contributions to the technology and advancement of the fuels and petrochemical industries. Selection is based on a combination of technical achievement, management skills, business acumen, academic leadership, and general service to the profession. Deadline: September 30. The awardee addresses the Division Luncheon at the AIChE Spring National Meeting. Awarded annually. Established in 1969. Sponsored by the Fuels and Petrochemical Division of AIChE.

• 2774 • Clarence (Larry) G. Gerhold Award

To recognize outstanding contributions in research, development, or application in chemical separations technology. Individuals who have been members of the Institute for at least 15 years and who have an extensive record of service to the Separations Division of the Institute are eligible. The deadline for nominations is March 31. A monetary award of $3,000, a plaque, and travel allowance are awarded at the dinner meeting of the Separations Division during the annual AIChE meeting. Sponsored by Universal Oil Products.

• 2775 • William W. Grimes Award for Excellence in Chemical Engineering

To recognize a chemical engineer for outstanding achievements as a distinguished role model for minorities. A monetary award of $1,000, a plaque, and $500 travel allowance are presented when merited. Established in 1995 in honor of William W. Grimes, the first African-American Fellow of AIChE.

• 2776 • Heat Transfer & Energy Conversion Division Award
To recognize an individual's outstanding chemical engineering contribution and achievement in heat transfer or energy conversion. The deadline for nominations is February 15. A plaque and a $500 monetary honorarium are awarded.

• 2777 • John C. Heiman Impact Award for Excellence in Educational Support
To recognize a local section for outstanding educational initiatives. The deadline for nominations is April 1. An engraved crystal apple is awarded annually by the Committee on Public Awareness.

• 2778 • HTEC Division Award
To recognize outstanding chemical engineering contributions and achievements in heat transfer or energy conversion. The award is judged by one or more of the following criteria: distinguished service of a chemical engineering nature as a professional engineer, educator, or AIChE leader; outstanding contributions in design, construction, operation, or management; and/or research or development of new processes or equipment. Members are eligible. A plaque and an honorarium of $500 are awarded annually. The recipient is invited to address the audience at the award presentation. Established in 1989. For further information, contact the Institute.

• 2779 • Institute Award for Excellence in Industrial Gases Technology
To recognize sustained excellence in contribution to the advancement of technology for the production, distribution, and application of industrial gases. Any individual is eligible, regardless of Institute affiliation. A monetary award of $3,000, a $500 travel allowance, and a plaque are presented annually at a meeting of the Institute. Sponsored by Praxair, Inc.

• 2780 • Marx Isaacs Awards for Outstanding Newsletter
To recognize excellent newsletters published by the various AIChE activity groups. The five categories are: Best Division or Forum Newsletter, Best Student Chapter Newsletter, Best Large Local Section Newsletter, Best Mid-Size Local Section Newsletter, and Best Small Local Section Newsletter. The deadline for nominations is April 1. An engraved paperweight is awarded annually by the Committee on Public Awareness.

• 2781 • Donald Q. Kern Award
To recognize individuals who have demonstrated outstanding expertise in some field of heat transfer or energy conversion. Nominations may be submitted by June 1. Membership in AIChE is not required. The award consists of a monetary award of $1,500 and a plaque, and the honoree is invited to present a lecture at the National Heat Transfer Conference. Additionally, a written review is printed and distributed to division members. Awarded annually when merited at a meeting sponsored by the Institute. Established in 1973 in honor of Donald Q. Kern. Supported by Heat Transfer Research, Inc. For further information, contact the Institute.

• 2782 • Warren K. Lewis Award for Contributions in Chemical Engineering Education
For recognition of distinguished and continuing contributions to chemical engineering education. The following criteria are considered: success as a teacher, to be established as to both competence in subject matter and ability to inspire students and colleagues to high achievement; contributions of lasting educational influence such as superior textbooks, lectures, and laboratory techniques or models; impact upon the education of chemical engineering students as a result of creative ability evidenced by scholarly contributions to literature, by inventions, by contributions to developments in industry, through consulting or through government service; and the key leadership in administering a department or equivalent group that has made the outstanding contributions that this award aims to recognize. A monetary award of $5,000, up to $500 for travel expenses, and a plaque are awarded annually. Established in 1963. Sponsored by ExxonMobil Research and Engineering Company and Exxon Chemical Company.

• 2783 • Arthur Dehon Little Award for Chemical Engineering Innovation
To recognize outstanding chemical engineering contributions to a successful innovation of commercial or societal importance. Innovation means the creation of new technology - new process, product, or applications technology - and its successful commercialization. It shall be awarded for a single innovation of great importance; it is not to be awarded for contributions to a number of different innovations of lesser importance. The contribution may be in one or more of the various phases of the innovation process, such as conception, research, development, design, etc. The contribution may be made in the form of an individual contribution or in the form of leadership and integration, where the leadership involves technological leadership, not just administrative leadership. It shall be awarded to a member of the Institute or to a team of persons not to exceed three in number. When it is awarded to a team of two or three persons, at least two must be members of AIChE. The award consists of $12,000 (to be shared equally when there is more than one recipient), a plaque, and a $500 travel allowance for each award recipient. The award is presented at a meeting sponsored by AIChE every three years. Established in 1987. Sponsored by A. D. Little, Inc.

• 2784 • Management Division Award
To recognize an individual who has made a substantial contribution to the management of engineers involved in the Chemical Process Industries, or to management techniques and procedures utilized in those industries. The deadline for nominations is July 15. A plaque and a $1,000 monetary honorarium are awarded annually. Established in 1984.

• 2785 • North American Mixing Forum Award
To recognize an individual in the profession who has demonstrated excellence in engineering and scientific contributions to the theory and practice of mixing. A $1,000 honorarium and a plaque are presented annually.

• 2786 • Professional Progress Award for Outstanding Progress in Chemical Engineering
To recognize outstanding progress in the field of chemical engineering. Individuals under 45 years of age at the time of receipt of the award are eligible. Award is open to all chemical engineering professionals regardless of Institute affiliation. A monetary award of $4,000 plus $500 travel allowance and a plaque are presented, and the recipient is invited to deliver an address. Awarded not more than once every calendar year. Established in 1948. Sponsored by Air Products and Chemicals, Inc.

• 2787 • John R. Ragazzini Award
To recognize outstanding contributions to automatic control education in any form. Contributions can be made from any source and in any media. Nomination deadline is December 1. The award consists of a plaque and a $1,000 honorarium. Administered by the American Automatic Control Council. Formerly: Education Award.

• 2788 • Randall D. Sheeline Award for Excellence in Public Relations
To recognize the local section that has most effectively communicated or interacted with the general public, government, and/or news media on behalf of AIChE, the chemical engineering profession, and the industries chemical engineers serve. The deadline for nominations is March 1. An engraved paperweight with medallion is awarded annually.

• 2789 • Charles M. A. Stine Award in Materials Engineering and Science
To recognize outstanding contributions by members of AIChE to the scientific, technological, educational, or service areas of materials engineering and science, thus encouraging the continuation of such contributions and enhancing the visibility, recognition, and value of the Division within AIChE. Membership is required. The deadline for nominations is February 15. Selection is made by an Awards committee consisting of the Division's past chairman and the three most recent award recipients. The award consists of a monetary prize of $1,500, a plaque, and an invitation to deliver an address at the time of the presentation. Awarded annually at a Division event at the Annual Meeting. Established in 1978. Sponsored by the Materials Engineering and Sciences Division of AIChE. Sup-

ported by E. I. du Pont de Nemours and Company.

• 2790 • Student Awards

To recognize student contributors who are working in the field of chemical engineering. The following awards are presented: Environmental Division Undergraduate Student Paper Award; Environmental Division Graduate Student Paper Award; National Student Design Competition; Regional Student Paper Competition; National Student Paper Competition; Plastics Recycling Competition; Nuclear Engineering Division Student Award; Separations Division Student Paper Award; Graduate Research Award; AIChE Awards for Student Achievement; Ted Peterson Student Paper Award; Donald F. Othmer Sophomore Academic Excellence Award; Outstanding Student Chapter Award; and Student Contest Problem Awards. Plaques and monetary prizes are awarded. For further information, contact the Institute.

• 2791 • John A. Tallmadge Award for Contributions to Coating Technology

To recognize significant contributions to the understanding or improvement of the coating or continuous webs in all its aspects. A monetary award of $1,000, a plaque, and travel allowance are awarded annually at an International Coating Symposium.

• 2792 • F. J. & Dorothy Van Antwerpen Award for Service to the Institute

To recognize a member chemical engineer for outstanding contributions and service to the Institute. A monetary award of $5,000, a plaque, and a $500 travel allowance to the awards presentation are given. Awarded annually. Established in 1978. Sponsored by The Dow Chemical Company.

• 2793 • William H. Walker Award for Excellence in Contributions to Chemical Engineering Literature

To recognize an outstanding contribution to chemical engineering literature. The recipient must be the author or coauthor of an outstanding work in chemical engineering published in the preceding three years. Members of the Institute are eligible. A monetary award of $5,000, a plaque, and a $500 travel allowance are awarded at the annual meeting. Established in 1936.

• 2794 • Norton H. Walton/Russell L. Miller Award

For recognition of outstanding chemical engineering contributions and achievements in the loss prevention, safety, and health fields. Its objective is to encourage the continuation of such contributions and enhance the visibility, recognition, and value of the Safety and Health Division within AIChE. It shall be awarded to a member of the Institute. There is no age limit. Nominations are to be submitted by members of the Division to the Chairman of the Division by June 30th of each year. A plaque and a $500 travel allowance are presented at a Division event annually. Established in 1987.

• 2795 • R. H. Wilhelm Award in Chemical Reaction Engineering

To recognize significant and new contributions in chemical reaction engineering. Individuals who have advanced the frontiers of chemical reaction engineering with emphasis on originality, creativity, and novelty of concept and application are eligible. A monetary award of $3,000, a $500 travel allowance, and a plaque are awarded annually. Established in 1972. Sponsored by ExxonMobil Research & Engineering Company.

• 2796 • Robert E. Wilson Award in Nuclear Chemical Engineering

To recognize outstanding chemical engineering contributions and achievements in the nuclear industry by a member of AIChE, and to promote the objectives of the Nuclear Engineering Division of AIChE. The deadline for nominations is October 1 of each year. A plaque and $1,000 prize are awarded annually. Presented at a Division event at the Spring National Meeting. Established in 1967 in honor of Robert E. Wilson. Sponsored by the Nuclear Engineering Division of AIChE. For further information, contact the Institute.

• 2797 •
American Institute of Chemists
Mr. Sharon Dobson, Exec.Dir.
315 Chestnut St.
Philadelphia, PA 19106-2702
Phone: (215)873-8224
Fax: (215)925-1954
E-mail: info@theaic.org
Home Page: http://www.theaic.org

• 2798 • AIC Ethics Award

To recognize outstanding contributions to ethics in the chemical profession. Individuals who meet the following criteria are considered: perform duties dictated by ethical considerations, in the face of difficulties, for the benefit of the public and/or workers in chemistry and chemical engineering; display leadership in an organization's ethical relationships with the public and/or employees in the field; and/or perform effective advocacy of organizational and/or governmental policies relating to chemistry that encourage ethical treatment of individuals. Nominations must be submitted by February 28. A plaque and a $500 travel allowance are awarded annually at the convention. Established in 1991 by Mr. Joseph Hyman.

• 2799 • Emmitt B. Carmichael Members and Fellows Lecture Award

To recognize prominent chemists or chemical engineers by inviting them to present a lecture on a topic of current professional interest to the institute members. An engrossed scroll is awarded when merited. Established in 1967. Formerly: (1996) Members and Fellows Lecture Award.

• 2800 • Chemical Pioneer Awards

To recognize chemists, chemical engineers, or their associates who have made outstanding contributions that have had a major impact on advances in chemical sciences and industry and/or the chemical profession. Four engrossed scrolls and one year free membership are awarded annually. Established in 1966.

• 2801 • Gold Medal

This, the institute's highest honor, is presented to recognize a person who has stimulated activities of service to the science of chemistry, or the chemistry or chemical engineering professions in the United States. Life fellowship in the institute is awarded annually. Established in 1926.

• 2802 • Honorary Fellow Award

To recognize persons who, by reason of service to the chemical profession and the public and by professional accomplishment, have attained unusual distinction. Selection is made by the Board of Directors. An engrossed scroll and life membership are awarded. Established in 1928.

• 2803 •
American Institute of Fishery Research Biologists
Dr. Richard Schaefer, Pres.
6211 Madawaska Rd.
Bethesda, MD 20816
Phone: (301)320-5202
Fax: (858)546-5653
E-mail: dickschaef@aol.com
Home Page: http://www.aifrb.org

• 2804 • Outstanding Achievement Award-Group

To recognize organizations with outstanding records of scientific contribution to fishery science or fishery resource policy. A plaque is awarded periodically. Established in 1982.

• 2805 • Outstanding Achievement Award-Individual

To recognize individuals who have made significant contributions to the advancement of fishery science. A plaque is awarded periodically. Established in 1979.

• 2806 • W. F. Thompson Award

To recognize the best paper published by a student on any topic in the field of freshwater or marine fishery science. The paper must have been published within the last three years and must concern work done while the principal author was a student. Eligibility is not restricted to United States citizens. Anyone may nominate qualified papers for consideration. A monetary award of $500 and a certificate are awarded.

• 2807 •
American Institute of Graphic Arts
Richard Grefe, Exec.Dir.
164 5th Ave.
New York, NY 10010
Phone: (212)807-1990
Toll-Free: 800-548-1634
Fax: (212)807-1799
E-mail: comments@aiga.org
Home Page: http://www.aiga.org

• 2808 • 50 Books/50 Covers Competition
To recognize the best books published in the year with an emphasis on graphics and quality of manufacture. Certificates are presented annually to exhibitors. Established in 1923. Deadline is in May. Formerly: Fifty Books of the Year.

• 2809 • AIGA Medal
To recognize individuals for distinguished achievements, services, or other contributions within the field of the graphic arts. Selection is made by a committee. A gold plated bronze medal is awarded annually. Established in 1920.

• 2810 • Communications Graphics
To recognize the best examples of art and design in every media including promotional material, posters, brochures, annual reports, and stationery, interactive media, illustration, photography, video, film titles, etc. An AIGA Certificate of excellence is awarded to those who participated in the creation of accepted entries. Deadline is in April. Established in 1940.

• 2811 • Corporate Leadership Award
To recognize the role of the perceptive and forward-thinking client who has been instrumental in the advancement of design by application of the highest standards, as a matter of policy, to all its visual communications. Selection is made by a committee. A silver plated bronze medal is awarded each year at the annual meeting. Established in 1980. Formerly: (2006) AIGA Design Leadership Award.

• 2812 • Greening of Design
To recognize design excellence in all aspects of the graphic arts. Projects must be ecologically minded in regards to its materials, concept, or process. The deadline is November 1.

• 2813 • Information Graphics: Design of Understanding
To recognize work designed to advance educational, commercial, environmental, experiential, and emotional understanding. Categories are: Print - poster, chart, or illustration, fewer than four pages; Print System - catalogues or books, four pages or more; Electronic - video, infomercials, or TV; Electronic Interactive; and Exhibits, Exhibitions, 3D. All entries must have been originated or been published or produced in the Unites States, Mexico or Canada within the last year. Printed matter must have been produced in quantities in excess of 250 impressions. An AIGA Certificate of Excellence is awarded to those who participated in the creation of accepted entries. The deadline is in January.

• 2814 •
American Institute of Mining, Metallurgical, and Petroleum Engineers
J. Rick Rolater, Exec.Dir.
PO Box 270728
Littleton, CO 80127-4012
Phone: (303)948-4255
Fax: (303)948-4260
E-mail: aime@aimehq.org
Home Page: http://www.aimehq.org

• 2815 • AIME Distinguished Service Award
For recognition of extraordinary and dedicated service in furtherance of the goals, purposes and traditions of AIME. An engraved plaque is awarded annually at the Annual Meeting of the Institute. Established in 1989.

• 2816 • Frank F. Aplan Award
In recognition of engineering or scientific contributions that further the understanding of the technology of coal and/or mineral processing. Formerly: (2004) Douglas Rand McConnell Distinguished Service Award.

• 2817 • James Douglas Gold Medal
To recognize an individual for distinguished achievement in nonferrous metallurgy, including both the beneficiation of ores and the alloying and utilization of nonferrous metals. A gold medal is awarded annually. Established in 1922.

• 2818 • Environmental Conservation Distinguished Service Award
To recognize an individual for significant contributions to environmental conservation by: addition to knowledge; the design or invention of useful equipment or procedure; or outstanding service to governmental or private organizations devoted to any field of environmental conservation. A certificate is awarded annually. Established in 1972.

• 2819 • Benjamin F. Fairless Award
To recognize an individual for distinguished achievement in iron and steel production and ferrous metallurgy. A silver plaque is awarded annually. Established in 1954 by the US Steel Corporation in memory of its longtime Chairman of the Board.

• 2820 • Anthony F. Lucas Gold Medal
To recognize an individual for distinguished achievements in improving the technique and practice of finding or producing petroleum. A gold medal is awarded annually. Established in 1936.

• 2821 • Robert Earll McConnell Award
To recognize an individual or group of engineers for beneficial service to mankind through significant contributions which tend to advance the nation's standard of living or replenish its natural resource base. A bronze trophy is awarded annually. Established in 1968. Formerly: (1971) Engineering Achievement Award.

• 2822 • Mineral Economics Award
To recognize an individual for distinguished contributions to the advancement of mineral economics. A certificate mounted on walnut base is awarded annually. Established in 1966.

• 2823 • Mineral Industry Education Award
To recognize distinguished contributions to the advancement of mineral industry education. A silver medal is awarded annually. Established in 1956.

• 2824 • Erskine Ramsay Medal
To recognize an individual for distinguished achievement in coal mining including both bituminous coal and anthracite. A gold medal is awarded annually. Established in 1948.

• 2825 • Charles F. Rand Memorial Gold Medal
To recognize an individual for distinguished achievement in mining administration including metallurgy and petroleum. A gold medal is awarded annually. Established in 1932.

• 2826 • W. Raymond Award
To recognize the best paper published pertaining to mining, metallurgy, or petroleum technology. Applicants must be members of the Institute under 33 years of age. A monetary award of $300 and a certificate are awarded annually. Established in 1945.

• 2827 • Robert H. Richards Award
To recognize an individual for achievement in any form that unmistakably furthers the art of mineral beneficiation in many of its branches. An engraved silver plaque is awarded annually. Established in 1948.

• 2828 • William Lawrence Saunders Gold Medal
To recognize an individual for distinguished achievement in mining other than coal. A gold medal is awarded annually. Established in 1927.

• 2829 • Hal Williams Hardinge Award
Recognizes outstanding achievement which has benefited the field of industrial minerals. Established in 1958.

• 2830 •
American Institute of Physics
Dr. Marc H. Brodsky, Exec.Dir. & CEO
1 Physics Ellipse
College Park, MD 20740-3843
Phone: (301)209-3100
Fax: (301)209-0843
E-mail: brodsky@aip.org
Home Page: http://www.aip.org

• 2831 • AIP Science Writing Awards
To encourage excellence in science writing in physics and astronomy for the nonspecialist. Awards are presented to a journalist, a scientist, and a child writer. $3,000, a Windsor Chair, and a certificate for both the author and the publisher are awarded annually.

• 2832 • Karl Taylor Compton Award
For outstanding statesmanship in science. Distinguished United States physicists who have made outstanding contributions to physics are eligible. A monetary award of $10,000, a bronze

medal and a certificate are awarded quadrennially. Established in 1957.

• 2833 • Andrew Gemant Award
To recognize the accomplishments of a physicist who has made significant contributions to the cultural, artistic, or humanistic dimension of physics. A cash prize of $5,000, invitation to deliver a public lecture, and grant of $3,000 to the institution of the recipient's choice is awarded annually.

• 2834 • Dannie N. Heineman Prize for Astrophysics
To recognize outstanding work in the field of astrophysics. A monetary prize of $7,500 and a certificate are awarded each year at the Annual Meeting of the American Astronomical Society. Established in 1979 for a ten-year period. Sponsored by the Heineman Foundation for Research, Educational, Charitable, and Scientific Purposes, Inc., and administered jointly by The American Astronomical Society.

• 2835 • Dannie N. Heineman Prize for Mathematical Physics
To recognize outstanding publications in the field of mathematical physics. Selection is based solely on valuable contributions made in the field of mathematical physics with no restrictions placed on a candidate's citizenship or country of residence. Publication is defined as either a single paper, a series of papers, a book, or any other communication which can be considered a publication. The prize may be awarded to more than one person on a shared basis. The prize consists of a monetary award of $7,500 and a certificate citing contributions made by the recipient. Established in 1959. Administered jointly by the American Institute of Physics and The American Physical Society. Sponsored by the Heineman Foundation for Research, Educational, Charitable, and Scientific Purposes.

• 2836 • William F. and Edith R. Meggers Project Award
To recognize projects designed to improve high school physics and projects directed towards the advancement and diffusion of physics and its application to human welfare. A monetary award of $25,000 is presented in each category biennially.

• 2837 • Outstanding SPS Chapter Advisor Award
Awarded by the Society of Physics Students to recognize outstanding service by a faculty advisor. A citation and monetary prize of $5,000 are awarded annually.

• 2838 • Prize for Industrial Applications of Physics
To recognize outstanding contributions by an individual(s) to the industrial applications of physics. A monetary prize of $10,000 and a certificate are awarded every two years. Established in 1977.

• 2839 • Sigma Pi Sigma Undergraduate Research Award
To support research projects by Society of Physics Students chapters. Four awards of $2,000 are made each year. Formerly: (1997) Allied-Signal Awards.

• 2840 • John T. Tate International Award
To recognize foreign nationals for distinguished service to the profession of physics, particularly through efforts that further international understanding and exchange, rather than for research accomplishments. A monetary award of $10,000, a bronze medal and a certificate are awarded at intervals of three to five years. Established in 1959.

• 2841 • Marsh W. White Award
To support projects designed by Society of Physics Students chapters to promote interest in physics among K-12 students and the general public. Approximately six awards of $300 are presented each year. Sponsored by the Sigma Pi Sigma Trust Fund.

• 2842 •
American Institute of Professional Geologists
William Siok, Exec.Dir.
1400 W. 122nd. Ave., Ste. 250
Westminster, CO 80031
Phone: (303)412-6205
Fax: (303)253-9220
E-mail: aipg@aipg.org
Home Page: http://www.aipg.org

• 2843 • John T. Galey, Sr. Memorial Public Service Award
Recognizes service to the public. Applicants must be Institute members. In considering an individual for the Award, contributions are not limited to political activity. The application of geology to the needs of the general public may be in many different forms. Individuals nominated for this award should have outstanding records of public service well beyond their normal job responsibilities. Also, the contributions of nominated individuals need not be on the national level, but may be on the state or local level. A plaque is awarded annually at the annual meeting. Established in 1982. Formerly: Public Service Award.

• 2844 • Honorary Member
For recognition of distinguished service to the profession and to the institute. A certificate of Honorary Membership is awarded at the annual meeting when merited. Established in the Institute's Constitution in 1963 and first awarded in 1984.

• 2845 • Ben H. Parker Memorial Medal
Recognizes outstanding service to the profession of geology. Consideration of an individual for this medal should emphasize a continual record of contribution to the profession of geology. A wide variety of contributions can be considered, such as the education and training of geologists; professional development of geologists; service to the institute; leadership in the surveillance of laws, rules, and regulations affecting geology, geologists, and the public; and activity in local and regional affairs of geologists. Publication and scientific achievement are not a requisite for consideration. A bronze medal mounted on a marble base is awarded annually at the annual meeting. Established in 1969.

• 2846 • Martin C. Van Couvering Memorial Award
Recognizes outstanding service to the association. Applicants must be members of the Institute. A gold pin mounted on a plaque is awarded annually at the annual meeting. Established in 1979 in memory of Martin C. Van Couvering, first president of the Institute.

• 2847 •
American Institute of Steel Construction
Lou Gurthet, Pres.
1 E Wacker Dr., Ste. 3100
Chicago, IL 60601-2000
Phone: (312)670-2400
Fax: (312)670-5403
Home Page: http://www.aisc.org

• 2848 • Architectural Awards of Excellence
To recognize designers of steel framed buildings that are outstanding in their appearance and show imaginative creation. Buildings must be located in the United States and framed with steel produced and fabricated in the United States. A mounted bronze bas relief was presented to the architect, and a certificate is awarded to the structural engineer, fabricator, general contractor, steel erector and owner. Awarded biennially in alternate years with the Prize Bridge Award. Established in 1960.

• 2849 • T. R. Higgins Lectureship Award
Acknowledges the best paper on new steel developments. A monetary award and an engraved citation are awarded annually. Established in 1970.

• 2850 • Prize Bridge Award
To recognize the designers of steel bridges which have been selected as the most beautiful of those opened to traffic during the previous five years. Bridges must be framed in steel that was produced and fabricated in the United States and must be located in the United States. A mounted bronze bas relief plaque is presented to the designer, and a certificate is awarded to the fabricator, erector, general contractor and owner. Awarded biennially in alternate years with the Architectural Awards of Excellence. Established in 1928.

• 2851 • Special Citation Award
To recognize outstanding contributions to the fabricated structural steel industry. A framed certificate is awarded annually. Established in 1970.

• 2852 •
American Institute of Stress
Paul J. Rosch MD, Pres. & Chm.
124 Park Ave.
Yonkers, NY 10703
Phone: (914)963-1200
Fax: (914)965-6267
E-mail: stress125@optonline.net
Home Page: http://www.stress.org

• 2853 • **Hans Selye Award**
To recognize distinguished contributions to the field of stress research. Individuals are selected by nomination. A plaque is awarded at the International Congress. Established in 1988 to commemorate Hans Selye.

• 2854 •
American Institute of Timber Construction
R. Michael Caldwell, Exec.VP
7012 S Revere Pkwy. Ste. 140
Englewood, CO 80112
Phone: (303)792-9559
Fax: (303)792-0669
E-mail: info@aitc-glulam.org
Home Page: http://www.aitc-glulam.org

• 2855 • **Carl E. Darrow Student Wood Design Competition**
Open to members, invited guests, and advisors. No additional information available.

• 2856 •
American Institute of Ultrasound in Medicine
Carmine M. Valente PhDCAE, CEO
14750 Sweitzer Ln., Ste. 100
Laurel, MD 20707-5906
Phone: (301)498-4100
Toll-Free: 800-638-5352
Fax: (301)498-4450
E-mail: admin@aium.org
Home Page: http://www.aium.org

• 2857 • **William J. Fry Memorial Lecture**
To honor a current or retired AIUM who has significantly contributed, in his/her particular field, to the scientific progress of medical diagnostic ultrasound. A plaque is presented at the annual convention, along with travel expenses for the honoree to present a lecture. Established in 1969 by Joseph H. Holmes in memory of William J. Fry.

• 2858 • **Joseph H. Holmes Pioneer Award**
To recognize AIUM members who have, for many years, significantly contributed to the growth and development of diagnostic ultrasound. A plaque and travel expenses are awarded annual to two members at the annual convention. Established in 1977. Formerly: Pioneer Award.

• 2859 • **Honorary Fellow Award**
To recognize non-members of the Society who have significantly contributed to the field of ultrasound. Individuals are selected based on nine or more years in medical, scientific, or engineering work related to medical ultrasound, five or more publications in refereed journals, exemplary educational teaching accomplishments, and exemplary community, clinical, or organizational service. Nominees are typically, but not always, foreign and are involved with the activities of the AIUM. A plaque, and lifetime membership are bestowed annually at the annual convention.

• 2860 • **Memorial Hall of Fame Award**
To honor posthumously a physician, research scientist, or individual, who, during his/her lifetime, contributed to the field of ultrasound medicine. A plaque is presented to the family of the honoree at the annual convention. Awarded annually. Established in 1981.

• 2861 •
American Intellectual Property Law Association
Meghan Donohoe, Dep. Exec. Dir. for Oper.
2001 Jefferson Davis Highway, Ste. 203
Arlington, VA 22202
Phone: (703)415-0780
Fax: (703)415-0786
E-mail: aipla@aipla.org
Home Page: http://www.aipla.org

Formerly: (1984) American Patent Law Association.

• 2862 • **International Science and Engineering Fair**
To encourage young inventors to continue and learn about the patent system. 3 prizes of $500 and 3 of $250, as well as certificates, are awarded annually.

• 2863 • **Giles Sutherland Rich Moot Court Competition**
To stimulate law students' grasp of intellectual property law problems. An annual moot court competition is held at the regional and national levels for school teams. A monetary prize of $1,000 and a certificate are awarded for first place; the runners-up receive $600 and a certificate; and regional finalists receive a certificate. Regional finals are held in March each year with national finals in Washington, DC, in mid-April.

• 2864 • **Robert C. Watson Award**
To recognize the best article in the field of intellectual property law by a full-time day/night law student. A monetary prize of $2,000 and a certificate are awarded annually. Established in 1962 in honor of Robert C. Watson.

• 2865 •
American Iris Society
Jill Bonino, Sec.
3110 Kirkham Dr.
Glendale, CA 91206-1128
Phone: (818)790-3256
E-mail: aissecjill@earthlink.net
Home Page: http://www.irises.org

• 2866 • **American Iris Society Gold Medal**
To honor exceptional service to the American Iris Society by a member of the Society. The winner must be voted on unanimously by the AIS Board of Directors. A gold medal is awarded as merited. Only seven have been awarded in the last 59 years. Established in 1930.

• 2867 • **Distinguished Service Award**
Recognizes outstanding service to the Society. Applicants must be members. A bronze medal is awarded annually when merited. More than one may be given in a year. Established in 1940.

• 2868 • **Dykes Medal Award**
To honor the hybridizer of the Iris receiving the most votes each year by accredited judges of the American Iris Society. A medal is awarded annually. Established in 1927.

• 2869 • **Hybridizer's Medal**
To honor iris hybridizers for many years of outstanding work with iris. A bronze plaquette is awarded annually when merited. More than one may be awarded in any one year. Established in 1940.

• 2870 •
American Irish Historical Society
William D. Cobert, Exec.Dir.
991 5th Ave.
New York, NY 10028
Phone: (212)288-2263
Fax: (212)628-7927
E-mail: info@aihs.org
Home Page: http://www.aihs.org

• 2871 • **Gold Medal**
Recognizes an outstanding man or woman of Irish lineage in recognition of extraordinary contributions and selfless dedication to improving life in America. A medal is awarded annually.

• 2872 •
American Iron and Steel Institute
Andrew G. Sharkey III, Pres. and CEO
1140 Connecticut Ave. NW, Ste. 705
Washington, DC 20036
Phone: (202)452-7100
Fax: (202)463-6573
E-mail: webmaster@steel.org
Home Page: http://www.steel.org

• 2873 • **American Iron and Steel Institute Medal**
For the stimulation of improvement in the iron and steel industry through the presentation of a technical paper. A certificate and bronze medal are awarded annually at the May meeting. Established in 1927.

• 2874 • **Benjamin F. Fairless Memorial Award**
For recognition of distinguished service through business or public administration, business and government relationships, management and

labor relationships, and service toward preserving economic freedom and human liberty. A gold medal and certificate are awarded at the discretion of the Board of Directors at the May meeting. Established in 1962.

• 2875 • **Gary Medal**

For recognition of outstanding achievement in the iron and steel industry. A certificate and a gold medal are awarded at the discretion of the Board of Directors at the May meeting. Established in 1927.

• 2876 •
American-Israel Environmental Council
Jessica Muller, Dir. of Operations
25 W 45th St., Ste. 1405
New York, NY 10036
Phone: (212)840-1166
Fax: (212)840-1514

• 2877 • **CBI International Environmental Award**

For individuals who exhibit interest and help in environmental causes. Awarded annually.

• 2878 •
American-Israel Numismatic Association
Florence Schuman, Treas.
12555 Biscayne Blvd., No. 733
North Miami, FL 33181
Phone: (305)466-2833
Fax: (305)466-2834
E-mail: ainamel@aol.com
Home Page: http://amerisrael.com

• 2879 • **Annual Medal Design Award**

To recognize an outstanding design submitted for the annual membership medal. Eligible candidates must be members of the Association. A $100 prize is awarded annually. Established in 1985.

• 2880 • **Ben and Sylvia Odesser Judaic Literary Award**

To recognize the best Judaic numismatic articles during the previous year. A plaque is awarded at the Tokens and Medals Society Meeting during the American Numismatic Association Annual Conference. Established in 1980 by the Tokens and Medals Society.

• 2881 •
American Italian Historical Association
Dominic Candeloro, Exec.Dir.
169 Country Club Rd.
Chicago Heights, IL 60411
Phone: (708)756-7168
Fax: (708)756-7168
E-mail: d-candeloro@govst.edu
Home Page: http://www.aiha.fau.edu

• 2882 • **Memorial Fellowships**

Assists in the pursuing of Italian-American studies. Applicants must be graduate students. Two $ 500 fellowships are awarded. Three copies of a 2 - 3 page description of the work; a resume, and two letters of recommendation must be submitted.

• 2883 •
American Jewish Committee
David Harris, Exec.Dir.
PO Box 705
New York, NY 10150
Phone: (212)751-4000
Fax: (212)891-1492
E-mail: pr@ajc.org
Home Page: http://www.ajc.org

• 2884 • **American Liberties Medallion**

To recognize individuals for exceptional advancement of the principles of human liberty. An engraved silver medallion is awarded annually. Established in 1955.

• 2885 • **Judge Learned Hand Award**

To recognize an individual for outstanding achievement in the legal profession and service to the general community to benefit the Society. A plaque is awarded several times a year nationally. Established in 1964 to honor Judge Learned Hand, a distinguished occupant of the Federal bench, and a staunch advocate of the rights of the individual and the importance of democratic values in an orderly society.

• 2886 • **Herbert H. Lehman Human Relations Award**

To honor those individuals whose lives and works have been a distinguished contribution to human relations. An engraved silver medallion is awarded annually. Established in 1963.

• 2887 • **National Human Relations Award**

To recognize prominent support in community for human relations. Applicants can be corporate members of the business community as well as individuals. Awarded annually.

• 2888 • **National Mass Media Award**

To recognize leadership in advancing human understanding through the mass media. An engraved silver plaque is awarded annually. Established in 1960.

• 2889 •
American Jewish Congress
Jack Rosen, Ch.
15 E. 84th St.
New York, NY 10028
Phone: (212)879-4500
Fax: (212)249-3672
E-mail: chairman@ajcongress.org
Home Page: http://www.ajcongress.org/

• 2890 • **Accountants, Bankers and Factors Division Award**

For recognition of exemplary service to the business community. Outstanding persons in the field of finance who have given outstanding community service are eligible. A plaque is awarded annually. Established in 1964.

• 2891 • **Communications Award**

For recognition of distinguished imaginative leadership, vision and courage in the field of communications. Individuals who are active in the field of communications are eligible. A plaque is awarded when merited. Established in 1966.

• 2892 • **Community Relations Award (Labor)**

To recognize outstanding contributions to community relations in labor. Awarded when merited. Established in 1978.

• 2893 • **Cultural Achievement Award**

For recognition of a distinguished contribution to the world of music and theater. A plaque is awarded when merited. Established in 1982.

• 2894 • **Deborah Award**

To acknowledge the value of Jewish women's contributions to society. A plaque is awarded annually. Established in 1989 by the AJCongress' Commission on Women's Equality to honor the Biblical heroine Deborah.

• 2895 • **Justice Award/Fund for Religious Liberty Award**

For recognition of unswerving devotion to the twin concepts of religious freedom and separation of church and state. Outstanding attorneys in the field of civil rights are eligible. A plaque is awarded annually. Established in 1980.

• 2896 • **Horace M. Kallen Award**

For recognition of distinguished community service. Social activists or civil servants are eligible. A plaque is awarded annually. Established in 1975 in memory of Horace Meyer Kallen, an educator, philosopher, social idealist and activist.

• 2897 • **Louise Waterman Wise Award**

For recognition of tireless efforts, both here and abroad, on behalf of World Jewry. Any person who has enriched society in the areas of Israel and Jewish survival, democratic freedom, the welfare of children and the arts is eligible. A plaque is awarded annually. Established in 1963 in memory of Mrs. Louise Waterman Wise, a leader of the Congress.

• 2898 • **Stephen S. Wise Award**

To recognize outstanding service in the field of human rights, social justice, Jewish welfare, or the development of Israel. Nominations are accepted. A plaque is awarded annually. Established in 1949 in memory of Rabbi Stephen S. Wise, the founder of the American Jewish Congress and in recognition of 50 years of leadership in the American Jewish community.

• 2899 •
American Jewish Historical Society
Michael Feldberg PhD, Exec.Dir.
15 W 16th St.
New York, NY 10011
Phone: (212)294-6160
Fax: (212)294-6161
E-mail: ajhs@ajhs.org
Home Page: http://www.ajhs.org

• 2900 • **Administrative Committee Prize**
To promote research and writing in the field of local American Jewish history by recognizing the best article submitted to *American Jewish History*. A monetary prize of $100 is awarded annually. Established in 1980.

• 2901 • **Ruth B. Fein Prize**
To enable a graduate student to undertake research at the American Jewish Historical Society. The prize is a travel stipend of up to $1,000. Established to honor Ruth B. Fein, a past president of the Society.

• 2902 • **Lee Max Friedman Award Medal**
To recognize outstanding service to the field of American Jewish history. Any individual, group or association is eligible. Distinguished service includes special achievements in research, scientific or popular writing, teaching, encouragement and/or support of specific historical projects, or in the field of mass communication. A medal is awarded. Established in 1960 to honor Lee Max Friedman, a past president of the Society.

• 2903 • **Jewish Historical Society of New York Fellowships**
To facilitate research involving the collections of the American Jewish Historical Society. The subject matter must have a New York Jewish historical component. Graduate students are eligible. One fellowship of $2,500 is awarded. When research is completed, recipients may be invited to lecture at a meeting of the Jewish Historical Society of New York.

• 2904 • **Saul Viener Prize**
To recognize the best book published in the field of American Jewish history. One $1,000 prize is awarded every two years. Established in 1984 to honor Saul Viener, a past president of the Society. One $1,000 prize is awarded every two years.

• 2905 • **Leo Wasserman Foundation Prizes**
To promote scholarly research and writing in the field of American Jewish history. Two awards are presented annually: (1) $250 to the author of the best article published in *American Jewish History* during the preceding year; and (2) $100 for the best article submitted by a student. If accepted by the Editorial Board, the student article will be published in *American Jewish History*. Established in 1979.

• 2906 •
American Jewish Press Association
Toby Dershowitz, Exec.Dir.
1255 New Hampshire Ave. NW, No. 702
Washington, DC 20036
Phone: (202)250-6144
Fax: (202)250-6151
E-mail: info@ajpa.org
Home Page: http://www.ajpa.org

• 2907 • **Joseph Polakoff Award**
To recognize exemplary service to the field of Jewish journalism, integrity in Jewish journalism, and distinguished career service in the field of Jewish journalism. Nominations are solicited from the AJPA membership, and the winner is determined by a special committee. Established in 1981 in honor of Joseph Polakoff, former Washington Bureau Chief of the Jewish Telegraphic Agency, and a columnist for numerous publications in North America.

• 2908 • **Simon Rockower Awards for Excellence in Jewish Journalism**
To recognize and encourage excellence in the Jewish press in North America. Awards are presented in the following categories: Excellence in Editorial Writing, Excellence in Commentary, Excellence in Investigative Reporting, Excellence in Comprehensive Coverage, Excellence in Spot News Reporting, Excellence in Feature Writing, Excellence in Arts and Criticism News and Features, Excellence in Overall Graphic Design, Excellence in Special Sections or Supplements, Excellence in Special Projects Community Guidebooks, Excellence in Photography, and The Noah Bee Award for Excellence in Editorial Cartooning or Illustrating. Members of the American Jewish Press Association or employees of a newspaper that is a member of the Association are eligible. The deadline for applications is mid-December. First place, second place, and honorable mention winners are awarded in each category annually at the convention. Established in 1981 by I. Budd Rockower in memory of Simon Rockower, his father.

• 2909 • **Boris Smolar Award for Excellence in North American Jewish Journalism**
To recognize outstanding journalists in North America whose work appears in Jewish publications. Established in 1972 by the Council of Jewish Federations, in honor of the late Boris Smolar, a distinguished journalist, author, and longtime Editor-in-Chief Emeritus of the Jewish Telegraphic Agency.

• 2910 •
American Judicature Society
Beth Tigges, Asst. to the Exec.Dir.
Drake University
The Opperman Center at Drake University
2700 University Ave.
Des Moines, IA 50311
Phone: (515)271-2281
Fax: (515)279-3090
E-mail: asobel@ajs.org
Home Page: http://www.ajs.org

• 2911 • **Herbert Harley Award**
To give special recognition to those individuals who have made outstanding efforts and contributions that substantially improve the administration of justice in their states. The contribution must be a long-lasting, if not permanent effect on the justice system. A plaque-mounted citation is awarded. Established in 1972 and named for the founder of the society, Herbert Harley.

• 2912 • **Justice Award**
This, the society's most prestigious award, honors and recognizes one individual annually who has made significant contributions nationally to the cause of improving the administration of justice. A plaque-mounted citation is awarded. Established in 1965.

• 2913 • **Special Merit Citation**
For recognition of projects and efforts that benefit some aspect of the judicial system, including those that are narrowly focused or time specific. Individuals, publications, state or local courts, organizations, and educational institutions may be recognized. A plaque-mounted citation is awarded. Established in 1982.

• 2914 •
American Junior Shorthorn Association
Ron Bolze, Exec.Sec./Treas.
8288 Hascall St.
Omaha, NE 68124
Phone: (402)393-7200
Fax: (402)393-7203
E-mail: bolze@shorthorn.org
Home Page: http://www.shorthorn.org

• 2915 • **Outstanding Junior Shorthorn Breeder Award**
To recognize an individual for achievements with Shorthorn/Polled Shorthorn beef cattle. Members of the association are eligible. A plaque and an inscription of name on a permanent plaque are awarded annually. Established in 1972.

• 2916 •
American Kenpo Karate International
Mr. Paul Mills, Pres./Founder
PO Box 768
Evanston, WY 82931
Phone: (307)789-4124
E-mail: headquarters@akki.com
Home Page: http://www.akki.com

• 2917 • **KKI Black Belt Certification**
Award of recognition.

• 2918 •
American Kidney Fund
Karen M. Sendelback CFRE, Exec.Dir.
6110 Executive Blvd., Ste. 1010
Rockville, MD 20852
Phone: (301)881-3052
Toll-Free: 800-638-8299
Fax: (301)881-0898
E-mail: helpline@kidneyfund.org
Home Page: http://www.kidneyfund.org

• 2919 • **Clinical Scientist in Nephrology Fellowship Award**
To improve the quality of care provided to kidney patients by enhancing the training of nephrologists who desire to pursue an academic career and whose primary professional commitment is to scholarship in the provision of patient care. Established in 1988.

• 2920 • **National Torchbearer Award**
To recognize an individual, family, or group whose success in professional life is complemented by efforts dedicated to enhancing the health and welfare of others in the community. A trophy is awarded annually. Established in 1988.

• 2921 •
American Kitefliers Association
Mel Hickman, Exec.Dir.
PO Box 1614
Walla Walla, WA 99362
Toll-Free: 800-252-2550
Fax: 800-252-2550
E-mail: aka@aka.kite.org
Home Page: http://www.aka.kite.org

• 2922 • **Steven Edeiken Memorial Kiteflier of the Year Award**
To recognize the kiteflier of the year. Nominations are based on character and contributions to kiting. A trophy for one year and a permanent plaque are awarded annually when merited at the convention. Established in 1983 in memory of Steve Edeiken, killed in a kiting accident. Formerly: (2006) Edeiken Trophy.

• 2923 •
American Laryngological Association
Maxine Cunningham, Admin.
Vanderbilt University Medical Ctr.
Medical Center North
S-2100 MCN
Nashville, TN 37232-2559
Phone: (615)322-6326
Fax: (615)343-7604
E-mail: maxine@alahns.org
Home Page: http://www.alahns.org

• 2924 • **American Laryngological Association Award**
To recognize an individual for outstanding achievement, either in medicine or another discipline, that has contributed significantly to laryngology or rhinology. Awarded annually. Established in 1987.

• 2925 • **Casselberry Fund**
For recognition of an outstanding manuscript(s) or accomplishment(s) thesis or theses in laryngology and rhinology. Individuals whose abstracts are accepted for inclusion on the program of the Annual Scientific Meeting must submit their completed manuscript by December 1. A monetary award of $1,000, and a certificate or plaque are awarded annually when merited. Established in 1906 by a bequest from the estate of William B. Casselberry, who was President of the Association in 1898. Formerly: (2006) Casselberry Award.

• 2926 • **Seymour R. Cohen Award**
To promote outstanding research in their area of pediatric laryngolgy and/or pediatric neurolaryngology. The prospective candidate must perform basic science research in order to be eligible. The scope of the award is limited to citizens of the United States of America and Canada. Should multiple candidates collaborate in the research, all authors must comply with the citizenship requirements. The primary author must certify that he/she has done at least 70 percent of the work and must also attest to the fact that a majority of the material has been previously unpublished. Awarded bi-annually. Established in 1989 in honor of Seymour R. Cohen with the bequest of $100,000 from the Cohen family.

• 2927 • **deRoaldes Award**
To recognize an individual for outstanding accomplishments in the field of laryngology and rhinology. Residents of the Americas may be recommended on the basis of outstanding accomplishments in laryngology and rhinology. The award may be made anytime a candidate has been selected by action of the council or recommendation of the committee. Established in 1907 in honor of Dr. A. W. deRoaldes, President of the association in 1906.

• 2928 • **James E. Newcomb Award**
To recognize a fellow of the American Laryngological Association for service to the Association or for outstanding contributions to the literature of laryngology and rhinology. Fellows may suggest members of the Association to the secretary, but the council alone makes the selection. Awarded annually. Established in 1939 in memory of James E. Newcomb.

• 2929 • **Gabriel F. Tucker Award**
To recognize an individual for significant contributions, either to the field of pediatric laryngology and/or to the Association. Awarded annually when merited. Established in 1987.

• 2930 •
American Lawyers Auxiliary
Rene Acosta, Pres.
321 N Clark St.
Chicago, IL 60610-4714
Phone: (312)988-6387
Fax: (312)988-5494
E-mail: moisantj@staff.abanet.org
Home Page: http://www.abanet.org/publiced/ala/

Formerly: (1983) National Lawyers Wives.

• 2931 • **Advocacy for the Disabled Award**
Recognizes programs designed to enhance the full participation of persons with disabilities in all aspects of life. A monetary award is given.

• 2932 • **Auxiliary Excellence Award**
Recognizes outstanding service to the community. Affiliated auxiliaries are eligible. A monetary award is given. Deadline is November 10.

• 2933 • **Alice Carr Award**
To recognize educators who have demonstrated excellence in instruction, imaginative resources, and leadership in the area of law-related education. High school, middle school, and elementary school teachers are eligible for consideration. The deadline for nominations is April 10. Three monetary awards of $1,000 and a plaque are awarded annually. Established in 1985.

• 2934 • **Law Day U.S.A.**
Annual award recognition. Inquire for additional details.

• 2935 • **Law-Related Education Teacher of the Year Award**
To recognize elementary, middle, and high school teachers who have made outstanding contributions to law-related education. Three Alice Carr Scholarship awards of $1,000 each are presented annually.

• 2936 • **Outstanding Individual Volunteer Award**
To recognize an individual ALA member who most effectively increases member and public understanding of law and the American legal system. A lifetime membership to ALA is awarded annually.

• 2937 • **Volunteer Service Award**
To recognize affiliated groups of American Lawyers Auxiliary for excellence in volunteer service programs with an effort to raise money to support the goals of the ALA and to promote public understanding and the appreciation of the law and the American legal system. Categories include state affiliates with less than 50 members, state affiliates with 50 or more members, local affiliates with less than 50 members, and local affiliates with 50 of more members. The deadline for entries is May 20. A plaque and certificates are awarded annually. Established in 1967.

• 2938 •
American League of Professional Baseball Clubs
Bud Selig, Commissioner
245 Park Ave.
New York, NY 10167
Phone: (212)931-7600
Fax: (212)949-5405
Home Page: http://www.mlb.com

• 2939 • **Joe Cronin Award**
To recognize significant achievement in American League baseball. Active American League baseball players are eligible. A large golden cup on a walnut base topped by a figurine depicting the award winner is awarded annually at the end of the baseball season. Established in 1973.

• 2940 •
American Leather Chemists Association
Carol Adcock, Exec.Sec.
1314 50th St. Ste. 103
Lubbock, TX 79412
Phone: (806)744-1798
Fax: (806)744-1785
E-mail: alca@leatherchemists.org
Home Page: http://www.leatherchemists.org

• 2941 • **Alsop Award**
For recognition of outstanding work published in areas of interest to the Association. Awarded annually. Established in 1939.

• 2942 • **Dr. Robert M. Lollar Prize Paper Award**
Present to the best papers that show originality of research and contribute to the technical understanding of the leather making process, leather by-products, or the industry's impact on the environment. Awarded bi-annually. Established in 2002.

• 2943 • **Fred O'Flaherty Service Award**
For recognition of persons who have contributed their services and worked hard for the association over a period of years. Awarded annually. Established in 1974.

• 2944 • **John Arthur Wilson Memorial Lecture Award**
To recognize an outstanding authority in leather chemistry. The awardee has the responsibility of presenting a lecture in his area of expertise. Awarded annually. Established in 1960.

• 2945 •
American Legion
John A. Brieden III, Natl.Comdr.
PO Box 1055
Indianapolis, IN 46206
Phone: (317)630-1200
Toll-Free: 800-433-3318
Fax: (317)630-1223
E-mail: natlcmdr@legion.org
Home Page: http://www.legion.org

• 2946 • **American Legion Fourth Estate Award**
For outstanding achievement in the field of journalism by an individual, publication, or broadcast. The subject matter must deal with a topic or issue of national interest or concern. The activity or accomplishment must have been completed in the calendar year immediately preceding the date the award is given. The deadline for nominations is January 31. The awardee is required to attend the national convention in August or early September and is awarded a trophy and $2,000 to cover travel costs. Awarded annually at the convention. Established in 1958. Formerly: (1960) American Legion Mercury Award.

• 2947 • **Distinguished Service Medal**
To recognize an individual for outstanding service to the United States. A gold American Legion medallion is awarded annually. Established in 1929.

• 2948 • **National Commander's Public Relations Award**
To recognize an outstanding individual and/or organization for distinguished public service in the field of communications. A bronze plaque is awarded annually. Established in 1961.

• 2949 •
American Legion A.J. Jurek Post 1672
Tim Van Patten, Compliance Officer
655 New Rd.
PO Box 759
East Amherst, NY 14051-0759
Phone: (716)688-9011

• 2950 • **Americanism Award**
Given to three students who demonstrate Americanism, patriotism during school year. Monetary award bestowed annually.

• 2951 •
American Legion Auxiliary
Katherine Morris, Pres.
777 N Meridian St., 3rd Fl.
Indianapolis, IN 46204-1189
Phone: (317)955-3845
Fax: (317)955-3884
E-mail: alahq@legion-aux.org
Home Page: http://www.legion-aux.org

• 2952 • **Heart of America**
To recognize print and broadcast professionals who make positive contributions to American women, children, and families by informing the public on timely issues, providing valuable thought-provoking information, or promoting positive images of women and children in America. A first place and one honorable mention prize is awarded in the following categories: radio, television, electronic media, magazine, and newspaper. Nominations must be submitted by April 21. Submissions published or broadcast between March 31 of the previous year and April 1 of the current year are eligible. Trophies are awarded annually at the National Convention. The Golden Mike Awards were established in 1957 and the Golden Press Awards in 1968. The two awards were combined in 1989 as the Heart of America.

• 2953 •
American Legion, Sumner
John A. Scott, Adjutant
113 E. 1st St.
Sumner, IA 50674
Phone: (319)578-5721
Phone: (319)578-3438

• 2954 • **Boys State Scholarship**
For school and community leadership and service. Scholarship awarded annually.

• 2955 •
American Legion Virginia
Dale Chapman, Dept.Adj.
1708 Commonwealth Ave.
Richmond, VA 23230
Phone: (804)353-6606
Fax: (804)358-1940
E-mail: eeccleston@valegion.org
Home Page: http://www.valegion.org

• 2956 • **Americanism Award**
For work with and for veterans. Scholarship awarded annually.

• 2957 •
American Legislative Exchange Council
Duane Parde, Exec.Dir.
1129 20th St. NW Ste. 500
Washington, DC 20036
Phone: (202)466-3800
Fax: (202)466-3801
E-mail: info@alec.org
Home Page: http://www.alec.org

• 2958 • **Warren Brookes Award for Excellence in Journalism**
To recognize an individual who exemplifies excellence in writing on free market economic issues. Awarded annually. Established in 1992 in honor of the late columnist for the *Detroit News*.

• 2959 • **Thomas Jefferson Freedom Award**
To recognize an individual who, by personal example, best exemplifies the tenets of Jeffersonian Democracy - individual liberty, limited government, free markets, and the right to private property. Candidates must be nominated by the Council. A Thomas Jefferson bust is awarded at the Council's annual meeting. Established in 1989.

• 2960 • **Adam Smith Free Enterprise Award**
To recognize an individual who exemplifies the entrepreneurial nature of American free enterprise. A plaque with the only known three-dimensional representation of Adam Smith, the brilliant Scottish philosopher and economist who first articulated the fundamental principles of the

Awards are arranged in alphabetical order below their administering organizations

free-market system, is awarded at the Council's Annual Meeting. Established in 1993.

• 2961 •
American Library Association
Ethnic and Multicultural Information Exchange Round Table
Plummer Alston Jones Jr., Chm.
% Sarah Smith, Sec.
San Joaquin Valley Library System
2420 Mariposa St.
Fresno, CA 93721
Phone: (559)488-3260
Toll-Free: 800-545-2433
E-mail: sarah.smith@sjvls.org
Home Page: http://www.ala.org/ala/emiert/emiert.htm

• 2962 • **Gale/EMIERT Multicultural Award**
To recognize outstanding achievement and leadership in serving the multicultural/multiethnic community with significant collection building, public and outreach services to culturally diverse populations, and creative materials and programs. The deadline is December 1. A monetary award of $1,000 and a citation are presented annually. Sponsored by the Gale Group.

• 2963 •
American Library Association
Exhibits Round Table
Amy Rosenbaum, Chm.
50 E. Huron St.
Chicago, IL 60611
Phone: (312)280-3219
Toll-Free: 800-545-2433
Fax: (312)280-3224
E-mail: dross@ala.org
Home Page: http://www.ala.org/ala/ert/exhibitsround.htm

• 2964 • **Christopher J. Hoy/ERT Scholarship**
Encourages education in the fields of library and information studies. Individuals who will be attending an ALA-accredited program leading to a master's degree are eligible. $3000 is awarded. Donated by the family of Christopher Hoy.

• 2965 • **Kohlstedt Exhibit Award**
Recognizes the best single, multiple, and island booth at the Annual Conference. Companies or organizations are eligible. A citation is awarded. awarded annually. Established in 1954 to honor Donald W. Kohlstedt for his hard work for better library conference exhibits.

• 2966 •
American Library Association
Governance Office
50 E. Huron St.
Chicago, IL 60611
Phone: (312)280-3247
Toll-Free: 800-545-2433
Fax: (312)280-3297
E-mail: awards@ala.org
Home Page: http://www.ala.org/ala/governance/recognition/recognitionawards.htm

• 2967 • **ALA Equality Award**
To recognize outstanding contributions toward promoting equality between women and men in the library profession. The contribution may be either a sustained one or a single outstanding accomplishment. Applicants can be individuals or groups. The award may be given for an activist or scholarly contribution in such areas as pay equity, affirmative action, legislative work, and nonsexist education. The deadline for nominations is December 1. A monetary award of $500 and a gold-framed citation are awarded. Established in 1984. Sponsored by Scarecrow Press, Inc.

• 2968 • **ALA/Information Today Library of the Future Award**
To recognize a library, library consortium, group of librarians, or support organization for innovative planning for application or development of patron training programs about information technology in a library setting. The deadline is December 1. A monetary award of $1,500 and a gold framed citation are awarded annually. Sponsored by Information Today Inc. Formerly: (1996) ALA/Mecklermedia Library of the Future Award.

• 2969 • **Beta Phi Mu Award**
To recognize a distinguished contribution to education for librarianship. Individuals and library-school faculty members are eligible. A monetary award of $500 and a gold-framed citation are awarded annually. Established in 1954. Sponsored by Beta Phi Mu International Library Science Honorary Society. Application deadline is December 1.

• 2970 • **W.Y. Boyd Literary Award**
Recognizes the author of a military novel honoring the service of American veterans during a time of war, 1861-1865, 1914-1918, and 1939-1945. $5000 and a gold-framed citation are awarded. Donated by William Young Boyd. Application deadline is December 1.

• 2971 • **Marshall Cavendish Excellence in Library Programming Award**
Recognizess excellence in library programming. Applicants must be school or public libraries with program with community impact and response to community needs. Selection criteria is based on advocacy, partnerships, and creativity of the resources regardless of the size of the library. $5000 and a gold-framed citation are awarded. Application deadline is April 14. Donated by Marshall Cavendish Corp.

• 2972 • **Melvil Dewey Medal**
To recognize a recent creative professional achievement of high order, particularly in the fields of library management, library training, cataloging and classification, and the tools and techniques of librarianship. A medal and a gold-framed citation are awarded. Application deadline is December 1. Established in 1952. Sponsored by OCLC/Forest Press, Inc.

• 2973 • **Tom C. Drewes Scholarship**
Assists with education in the field of library science. Applicants must be library support staff persons pursuing a master's degree in library science at an ALA-accredited program and must be U.S. or Canadian citizens or permanent residents. $3000 is awarded.

• 2974 • **EBSCO ALA Conference Sponsorship**
To allow librarians to attend ALA's annual conferences. An essay of no more than 250 words must be submitted by December 1. Ten awards of up to $1,000 in reimbursed expenses for annual conferences are awarded each year. Sponsored by EBSCO Subscription Services.

• 2975 • **Elizabeth Futas Catalyst for Change Award**
Recognizes and honors positive change in the profession of librarianship. Librarians with invested time and talent are eligible. $1000 and a gold-framed citation are awarded. Application is December 1. Donated by the Elizabeth Futas Memorial Fund.

• 2976 • **Loleta D. Fvan Public Library Research Grant**
For the development and improvement of public libraries and the services they provide. Libraries, library schools, associations, units or chapters of ALA or individuals are eliglble. One or more grants of up to $10,000 are awarded.

• 2977 • **Gale Financial Development Award**
To recognize a library organization that exhibits meritorious achievement in carrying out a library financial development project to secure new funding resources for a public or academic library entity. The deadline for applications is December 1. A monetary award of $2,500 and a gold-framed citation are awarded annually. Established in 1983. Sponsored by Gale.

• 2978 • **Mary V. Gaver Scholarship**
To further education in the field of library youth services. Applicants must be library support staff, U.S. or Canadian citizens or permanent residents, and be pursuing a master's degree in library science.

• 2979 • Grolier Foundation Award
To recognize an unusual contribution to the stimulation and guidance of reading by children and young people. Librarians in a community or in a school are eligible. The deadline for applications is December 1. Selection is based on outstanding work with children and young people through high school age, for continuing service, or in recognition of one particular contribution of lasting value. A monetary award of $1,000 and a gold-framed citation are awarded annually. Established in 1953. Sponsored by Grolier Educational Corp.

• 2980 • Highsmith Library Literature Award
To recognize an individual for an outstanding contribution to library literature issued during the three years preceding the award. The deadline for applications is December 1. A monetary award of $500 and a citation are awarded. Established in 1985. Sponsored by G. K. Hall and Company. Formerly: Knowledge Industry Publications, Inc. Award for Library Literature; (2006) G. K. Hall Award for Library Literature.

• 2981 • Paul Howard Award for Courage
Recognizes unusual courage for the benefit of library programs or services. Applicants must be librarians, library boards, library groups, or individuals. $1000 and a gold-framed citation are awarded every two years. Application deadline is December 1. Donated by Paul Howard.

• 2982 • Joseph W. Lippincott Award
To recognize distinguished service to the profession of librarianship, including outstanding participation in the activities of professional library associations, notable published professional writing, or other significant activity on behalf of the profession and its aims. A monetary award of $1,000 and a citation are awarded annually. Deadline is December 1. Established in 1937. Sponsored by Joseph W. Lippincott, Jr.

• 2983 • H. W. Wilson Library Staff Development Grant
Recognizes the development goals and objectives of library staffs. Open to all libraries. A $3,500 grant and a gold-framed citation are awarded. Application deadline is December 1. Donated by The H.W. Wilson Co.

• 2984 • World Book - ALA Goal Grant
To recognize units of the American Library Association that encourage and advance the development of public, academic, and/or school library service and librarianship through recognition and support of programs that implement the goal and priorities of ALA. The deadline for all applications is March 1. One grant of up to $10,000 or two smaller grants totaling up to $10,000 are awarded. Established in 1962. Sponsored by World Book, Inc. Formerly: J. Morris Jones and Bailey K. Howard World Book Encylopedia - ALA Goal Awards.

• 2985 •
American Library Association
Intellectual Freedom Round Table
Nanette Perez, Proj. Coor.
50 E. Huron St.
Chicago, IL 60611
Phone: (312)280-4223
Toll-Free: 800-545-2433
Fax: (312)280-4227
E-mail: oif@ala.org
Home Page: http://www.ala.org/ala/ifrt/ifrtinaction/ifrtawards/awards.htm

• 2986 • John Phillip Immroth Memorial Award for Intellectual Freedom
To honor an intellectual freedom fighter in or outside the library profession who has made a notable contribution to intellectual freedom and demonstrated remarkable personal courage in defense of freedom of expression. Any person may nominate individuals or organizations by December 1. A monetary award of $500 and a citation are awarded annually at the Annual Conference. Established in 1976 to honor John Phillip Immroth, author, teacher, scholar, advocate and defender of First Amendment rights, and co-founder and first Chair of the Intellectual Freedom Round Table.

• 2987 • Intellectual Freedom Round Table State and Regional Achievement Award
To recognize the state or region that has implemented the most successful and creative intellectual freedom project. One-time, one year, or ongoing multi-year projects are eligible. Examples of appropriate award projects could be: exemplary PR program for promoting awareness of intellectual freedom; effective assistance in an intellectual freedom crisis; successful coalition-building projects/activities; innovative support structure for intellectual freedom. The deadline for nominations is December 1. A monetary award of $1,000 and a citation are awarded annually. Established in 1984. Sponsored by the Social Issues Resources Series (SIRS). Formerly: Intellectual Freedom Round Table State Program Award.

• 2988 • Eli M. Oboler Memorial Award
For recognition of the best published work in the area of intellectual freedom. The author or authors of an article (including a review article), a series of thematically connected articles, a book, or a manual, published on the local, state, or national level, in English or in English translation are eligible. The works to be considered must have as their central concern one or more issues, events, questions, or controversies in the area of intellectual freedom, including matters of ethical, political, or social concerns related to intellectual freedom. The work or works need not have appeared in the "library press," nor have been written by a librarian, but they must be relevant to the concerns and needs of members of the library community. The work must have been published within the two-year period ending the December prior to the ALA Annual Conference at which the award is given. A monetary award of $500 is awarded biennially. Established in 1986 to honor Eli M. Oboler, the prolific and eloquent author and "champion of intellectual freedom" who "demanded the dismantling of all barriers to freedom of expression." Sponsored by Providence Associates, Inc.

• 2989 •
American Library Association
International Relations Committee
Delin Guerra, Administrative Assistant
50 E. Huron St.
Chicago, IL 60611
Phone: (312)280-3201
Toll-Free: 800-545-2433
Fax: (312)280-4392
E-mail: intl@ala.org
Home Page: http://www.ala.org/ala/iro/awardsactivities/awardsgrants.htm

• 2990 • John Ames Humphrey/OCLC/Forest Press Award
To recognize an individual who has made a significant contribution to international librarianship. The contribution may include publication of professional literature, participation in library organizations, introduction of new technologies or theories, or outstanding teaching. Primary consideration is given to contributions in the field of classification and subject analysis, and to work in Third World countries, but the award is not limited to these areas. A monetary prize of $1,000 and a certificate are awarded annually. Established in 1987. Formerly: John Ames Humphry/Forest Press Award.

• 2991 • Bogle/Pratt International Library Travel Fund
To enable a member or members of the association to attend an international conference for the first time. Grants of $1000 each are presented annually. Established in 1982 by the Bogle Memorial Fund.

• 2992 •
American Library Association
Library History Round Table
Kathy Bork, Staff Liason
50 E. Huron St.
Chicago, IL 60611
Phone: (312)280-4273
Toll-Free: 800-545-2433
Fax: (312)280-4392
E-mail: kpotts@toto.csustan.edu
Home Page: http://www.ala.org/ala/lhrt/lhrthome.htm

• 2993 • Phyllis Dain Library History Dissertation Award
To recognize the author of a dissertation treating the history of books, libraries, librarianship, or information science. A monetary award of $500 and a certificate are awarded biennially in odd-numbered years.

• 2994 • Donald G. Davis Article Award
Recognizes an article in the field of United States and Canadian library history. Eligible articles must be written in English. A certificate is awarded biannually.

Awards are arranged in alphabetical order below their administering organizations

• 2995 • **Eliza Atkins Gleason Book Award**
Recognizes the best book in the field of library history. Eligible books must be written in English. A certificate is presented every three years.

• 2996 • **Justin Winsor Prize Essay**
To encourage excellence in research in library history. Essays not previously published or submitted for publication, not currently under consideration for publication, and that embody original historical research on a significant subject in library history are eligible. A monetary prize of $500 and an invitation for publication in *Libraries and Culture* are awarded annually.

• 2997 •
American Library Association
Office for Research and Statistics
Denise M. Davis, Dir.
50 E Huron St.
Chicago, IL 60611
Phone: (312)280-4273
Toll-Free: 800-545-2433
Fax: (312)280-4392
E-mail: ors@ala.org
Home Page: http://www.ala.org/ala/ors/researchstatistics.htm

• 2998 • **Carrol Preston Baber Research Grant**
For innovative research that may lead to an improvement in library services to any specified group or groups of people. The deadline is December 1. A monetary grant of up to $3,500 is awarded annually. Sponsored by Eric A. Baber.

• 2999 •
American Library Association
Public Information Office
Mark Gould, Dir.
50 E. Huron St.
Chicago, IL 60611
Phone: (312)280-4020
Toll-Free: 800-545-2433
Fax: (312)280-5274
E-mail: pio@ala.org
Home Page: http://www.ala.org/ala/pio/publicinformation.htm

• 3000 • **Grolier National Library Week Grant**
To recognize the best proposal from libraries or library associations of all types for a public awareness campaign supporting the goals of National Library Week in the year the grant is awarded. The deadline is October 15. A monetary award of $5,000 is presented annually. Established in 1975. Sponsored by the American Library Association and Grolier Educational Corporation.

• 3001 •
American Library Association
Social Responsibilities Round Table
Elaine Harger, Coordinator
50 E. Huron St.
Chicago, IL 60611
Phone: (312)944-6780
Fax: (312)440-9374
Home Page: http://www.libr.org/SRRT

• 3002 • **Jackie Eubanks Award**
Recognizes the promotion of acquisition and use of alternative media in libraries. $500 and a certificate are awarded. Donated by AIP Task Force.

• 3003 • **Gay/Lesbian Book Award**
Recognizes books of merit relating to the gay/lesbian experience. Titles can be fiction or nonfiction. A citation is awarded. Application deadline is November 1.

• 3004 • **Coretta Scott King Book Award**
To recognize African-American authors and illustrators for promoting understanding and appreciation of culture and contributions of all people. The noted book must be published in the calendar year preceding the year of award presentation. The deadline for nominations is December 31. The winners are announced during the ALA's midwinter meeting in January. The award consists of a plaque and $1,000 award. Certificates are awarded to those chosen for honorable mention. Encyclopedia Britannica and World Book donate sets of encyclopedias. Awarded annually. Established in 1969 to commemorate the life and works of Dr. Martin Luther King, Jr., and to honor Mrs. Coretta Scott King for her courage and determination in continuing work for peace and world brotherhood. Sponsored by Johnson Publishing Co., Encylcopedia Britannica, and World Book, Inc.

• 3005 • **New Talent Award**
Recognizes an outstanding book by a black writer or artist. Applicants must be at the beginning of his/her career as a published book creator.

• 3006 •
American Liszt Society
Justin Kolb, Exec.Sec.
1136 Hog Mountain Rd.
Fleischmanns, NY 12430
Phone: (845)586-4457
Phone: (845)586-3588
Fax: (301)384-9022
E-mail: mellon@catskill.net
Home Page: http://www.americanlisztsociety.org

• 3007 • **Liszt Medal**
For recognition of outstanding contributions in either performance or scholarship on behalf of Franz Liszt. Professionals may be considered for contributions such as books, record collections, or outstanding performances. Individuals may be nominated by the board. Medals are awarded annually. Established in 1984. Formerly: Award for Excellence.

• 3008 •
American Literary Translators Association
Jessie Dickey, Sec.
University of Texas at Dallas
PO Box 830688-JO51
Richardson, TX 75083-0688
Phone: (972)883-2093
Fax: (972)883-6303
E-mail: jdickey@utdallas.edu
Home Page: http://www.literarytranslators.org

• 3009 • **National Translation Award**
Recognizes outstanding translations. The award carries a $2,500 stipend. The award is presented in the followng categories: Fiction, Poetry, Non-fiction, and Literature of the Past (no criticism or philosophy). U.S. publishers are invited to nominate one book in each category. To be eligible, a work must be a full-length book or anthology translated from another language into English and published the previous year. Send four copies of the book. The deadline for nomination is March 31. One book is honored annually. Established in 1992. Formerly: (2004) ALTA Outstanding Translations of the Year.

• 3010 •
American Liver Foundation
Alan P. Brownstein, Pres./CEO
75 Maiden Ln., Ste. 603
New York, NY 10038
Phone: (212)668-1000
Phone: 800-4HEP-USA
Toll-Free: 800-GO-LIVER
Fax: (212)483-8179
E-mail: info@liverfoundation.org
Home Page: http://www.liverfoundation.org

• 3011 • **Distinguished Service Award**
To recognize the achievements and contributions to medicine. Established in 1987.

• 3012 •
American Lung Association
John L. Kirkwood, CEO
61 Broadway, 6th Fl.
New York, NY 10006
Phone: (212)315-8700
Toll-Free: 800-LUN-GUSA
Fax: (212)315-8872
E-mail: info@lungusa.org
Home Page: http://www.lungusa.org

• 3013 • **President's Award**
To recognize an individual, nonprofit, or commercial organization for an outstanding contribution in an area of importance to the goals of the Lung Association, but not as a result of a Board or regular volunteer involvement with Lung Association activities or programs. Awarded annually when merited. Established in 1983.

• 3014 • Will Ross Medal
For recognized and outstanding services as a volunteer which are creative and/or innovative in public health and/or community action aspects of the prevention and control of lung disease and the promotion of lung health on a local, state, national, or international level. A bronze medal is awarded annually. Established in 1952 to honor Will Ross, a distinguished president of the Association.

• 3015 • Trudeau Award
For meritorious contributions to the control, prevention, and treatment of pulmonary disease. A bronze medal is awarded annually. Established in 1926 to honor Edward Livingston Trudeau, the first president of the Association.

• 3016 •
American Lung Association of Eastern Missouri
Lori C. Pickens, CEO
1118 Hampton Ave.
St. Louis, MO 63139-3196
Phone: (314)645-5505
Toll-Free: 800-LUNG-USA
Fax: (314)645-7128
E-mail: lpickens@lungmo.org
Home Page: http://www.lungusa.org

• 3017 • Research Grants
For medical/scientific research which may lead to cure for lung disease. Grant awarded annually.

• 3018 •
American Lung Association of Massachusetts
Carlos Alvarez, Exec.Dir.
One Abbey Ln.
Middleboro, MA 02346-3230
Phone: (508)947-7204
Toll-Free: 800-586-4872
Fax: (508)947-7208
E-mail: alam@gis.net
Home Page: http://www.lungusa2.org/massachusetts/

• 3019 • Edward J. Welsh M.D. Memorial Research Fund
For lung disease research. Grant awarded annually.

• 3020 •
American Lung Association of Rhode Island
Margaret E. Kane, Exec.Dir.
298 W. Exchange St.
Providence, RI 02903-3700
Phone: (401)421-6487
Toll-Free: 800-LUNG-USA
Fax: (401)331-5266
E-mail: alari@lungri.org
Home Page: http://lungusa2.org/rhodeisland

• 3021 • Harry L. Gardner Award
For R.I. resident going on to medical school. Scholarship awarded annually.

• 3022 •
American Machinist
Robert S. Rosenbaum, Publisher
1300 E 9th St.
Cleveland, OH 44114-1503
Phone: (216)696-7000
Fax: (216)931-9524
E-mail: ameditor@penton.com
Home Page: http://www.americanmachinist.com

• 3023 • Excellence in Manufacturing Technology Achievement Awards
For recognition of the world leaders in manufacturing technology. Winners are determined by readers of *American Machinist*. Awarded annually. Formerly known as the American Machinist Award.

• 3024 •
American Marketing Association
Dennis Dunlap, CEO
311 S Wacker Dr., Ste. 5800
Chicago, IL 60606
Phone: (312)542-9000
Toll-Free: 800-262-1150
Fax: (312)542-9001
E-mail: info@ama.org
Home Page: http://www.marketingpower.com/

• 3025 • AMA/Irwin Distinguished Marketing Educator Award
To recognize and honor a living marketing educator for distinguished service and outstanding contributions in the field of marketing education. Marketing educators who have made sustained contributions to marketing over an extended period of time are eligible. Such contributions may take a variety of forms and are not limited to a single achievement. Nominations must be submitted by April 1. Established in 1985. Co-sponsored by the Richard D. Irwin Company, Homewood, Illinois.

• 3026 • George Hay Brown/AMA Marketing Scholar of the Year
To recognize a marketing scholar for exceptional academic achievement. Criteria for judging the award candidates include: grade point average, honors and awards, full-or part-time employment prior to receiving the graduate degree, extracurricular activities, Graduate Management Admission Test (GMAT) scores, and recommendation of a member of the marketing faculty at the school from which the student receives the graduate degree. A monetary award of $8,500, a plaque, and a one-year AMA professional membership are awarded. In addition, five runners-up receive monetary awards of $850. Established in 1986.

• 3027 • Chapter Excellence Awards and Chapter of the Year Award
To recognize those chapters of the association that achieve a level of excellence in the operation of chapter affairs and in service to their members and the marketing community. A permanent plaque is displayed in the association's international headquarters; individual awards are presented to the presidents of award-winning chapters and banners are presented to the chapters. Press releases are sent to the local media, and local governors and mayors are notified. Awarded annually. Established in 1973.

• 3028 • Edison Awards
To recognize the best new products of the year. There is no official entry form. The AMA membership is asked to submit nominees for this award, and a blue-ribbon panel of judges makes the final decision. There are 10 winners in no particular categories. Awarded annually.

• 3029 • The Philip Kotler Award for Excellence in Healthcare Marketing
To recognize an individual who is a leader, an innovator, and an entrepreneur. Nominees should demonstrate outstanding contributions to healthcare marketing, either through a lifetime of work or a single project or activity, the leadership abilities to initiate important strategies to advance the cause of the customer, noteworthy conduct as a healthcare marketer, and significant regional or national impact on healthcare marketing. The recipient is recognized at the Annual Symposium on Healthcare Marketing in Minneapolis.

• 3030 • Wayne A. Lemburg Award for Distinguished Service
To recognize members of AMA and the international headquarters staff. Awarded annually. Established in 1986.

• 3031 • Marketer of the Year
To recognize an outstanding company. A panel of judges chooses the winner based on several criteria. Awarded annually at the AMA's New Products conference.

• 3032 • Marketing Person of the Year and Marketing Firm of the Year
To recognize outstanding contributions to the discipline of marketing. Plaques are awarded annually. One or both of these awards are sponsored by various chapters of the association and each chapter establishes its own criteria.

• 3033 • Harold H. Maynard Award
To recognize an outstanding article appearing in the AMA's *Journal of Marketing.*

• 3034 • William O'Dell Award
To recognize an outstanding article appearing in the AMA's *Journal of Marketing Research.*

Awards are arranged in alphabetical order below their administering organizations

• 3035 • Parlin Award
To recognize significant contributions to the field of marketing. Business persons from the United States or Canada are eligible. A plaque is awarded annually. Established and administered by the Philadelphia chapter of the association. Established in 1945 in honor of Charles Coolidge Parlin.

• 3036 • H. Paul Root Award
To recognize the 'Journal of Marketing' article that the JM Editorial Review Board believes has made the most significant contribution to the advancement of the practice of marketing. The winner receives a cash prize and certificate for the Alpha Kappa Psi Foundation, and AMA provides a complimentary registration to the Summer Educators' Conference. Awarded annually. Formerly: (2006) Alpha Kappa Psi Award.

• 3037 •
American Mathematical Association of Two-Year Colleges
Cheryl Cleaves, Exec.Dir.
5983 Macon Cove
Memphis, TN 38134
Phone: (901)333-4643
Fax: (901)383-4651
E-mail: amatyc@amatyc.org
Home Page: http://www.amatyc.org

• 3038 • Mathematics Excellence Award
To recognize educators who have made outstanding contributions to mathematics or mathematics education at two-year colleges. A plaque and AMATYC Life Membership are awarded biennially at the national conference. Established in 1984.

• 3039 •
American Mathematical Society
Dr. John Ewing, Exec.Dir.
201 Charles St.
Providence, RI 02904-2294
Phone: (401)455-4000
Toll-Free: 800-321-4AMS
Fax: (401)331-3842
E-mail: ams@ams.org
Home Page: http://www.ams.org/

• 3040 • Award for Distinguished Public Service
To recognize a research mathematician who has made a distinguished contribution to the mathematics profession through public service during the preceding five years. Awarded biennially. Established in 1990.

• 3041 • George David Birkhoff Prize in Applied Mathematics
To recognize an outstanding contribution to applied mathematics in the highest and broadest sense. Members of the American Mathematical Society or the Society for Industrial and Applied Mathematics who are residents of the United States, Canada, or Mexico are eligible. Awarded every three years. Established in 1967. Cosponsored by the Society for Industrial and Applied Mathematics in honor of Professor George David Birkhoff.

• 3042 • Bocher Memorial Prize
For recognition of a notable research memoir in analysis that has appeared during the previous six years. The author must be a member of the Society or the memoir must be published in a recognized North American journal. A monetary prize is awarded every three years. Established in 1923 in memory of Professor Maxime Bocher.

• 3043 • Frank Nelson Cole Prizes in Algebra and Number Theory
To recognize notable research in algebra and number theory. Mathematical scientists who are members of the Society or whose papers were published in a recognized North American journal are eligible. Awards in algebra and number theory are presented every three years. Established in 1928 in honor of Professor Frank Nelson Cole, on the occasion of his retirement as secretary of the AMS and editor-in-chief of the *Bulletin*.

• 3044 •
American Meat Institute
J. Patrick Boyle, Pres. & CEO
1700 N. Monroe St., Ste. 1600
Arlington, VA 22209
Phone: (703)841-2400
Fax: (703)527-0938
Home Page: http://www.meatami.com

• 3045 • Industry Advancement Award
For recognition of outstanding contributions to the promotion of the meat industry. A plaque is awarded annually.

• 3046 • Edward C. Jones Community Service Award
For recognition of outstanding service to the Institute. A plaque is awarded annually.

• 3047 • Supplier of the Year Award
To recognize a supplier of equipment, ingredients, or services who has worked cooperatively with packers and processors to enhance the success and profitability of the meat and poultry industry. Awarded annually. Established in 1995.

• 3048 •
American Meat Science Association
Thomas Powell, Exec.Dir.
1111 N Dunlap Ave.
Savoy, IL 61874
Phone: (217)356-5368
Fax: (217)398-4119
E-mail: information@meatscience.org
Home Page: http://www.meatscience.org

• 3049 • Achievement Award
To recognize and foster development of young AMSA members who have demonstrated significant scientific skills in muscle foods research/technology that contributes to the animal products industry and the Association. Awarded with a wristwatch and an appropriate memento.

• 3050 • Distinguished Extension-Industry Service Award
To recognize outstanding achievement in the field of meat science extension and/or industry service. Awarded with an honorarium, a wristwatch, and an appropriate memento.

• 3051 • Distinguished Research Award
To recognize outstanding research in the meat industry. Awarded with an honorarium, a wristwatch, and an appropriate memento.

• 3052 • Distinguished Teaching Award
To recognize excellence in teaching of undergraduate and graduate meat science courses. Awarded with an honorarium, a wristwatch, and an appropriate memento.

• 3053 • Intercollegiate Meat Judging Meritorious Service Award
To recognize outstanding contributions within the various areas of the meat science field and contribute to advancements in the meat industry. Awarded annually with a plaque.

• 3054 • International Award
To honor an individual for internationally recognized contributions to the field of meat science and technology. Awarded with an honorarium, an appropriate memento, and travel expenses to the Reciprocal Meat Conference.

• 3055 • Meat Processing Award
To recognize outstanding achievement in meat processing. Awarded with an honorarium, a wristwatch, and an appropriate memento.

• 3056 • R. C. Pollock Award
To honor an AMSA member whose work, through teaching, extension, research or service, represents an extraordinary and lasting contribution to the meat industry. Awarded with an honorarium and appropriate citation.

• 3057 • Signal Service Award
To recognize members for devoted service and lasting contribution to the meat industry and the Association. Awarded with a wristwatch and an appropriate memento.

• 3058 • Special Recognition Award
To honor any individual for a truly significant service to the meat industry or the Association. Awarded with a citation.

• 3059 •
American Medical Athletic Association
Barbara Balwin, Contact
4405 E West Hwy., Ste. 405
Bethesda, MD 20814
Phone: (301)913-9517
Toll-Free: 800-776-2732
Fax: (301)913-9520
E-mail: bbaldwin@americanrunning.org
Home Page: http://www.amaasportsmed.org/

• 3060 • **Steven Royce, Jr. Award**
Recognizes a member who does the most to further the rewards of endurance exercise. Awarded annually.

• 3061 •
American Medical Technologists
Christopher A. Damon J.D., Exec.Dir.
710 Higgins Rd.
Park Ridge, IL 60068-5765
Phone: (847)823-5169
Toll-Free: 800-275-1268
Fax: (847)823-0458
E-mail: mail@amt1.com
Home Page: http://www.amt1.com

• 3062 • **The Becky Award**
For recognition of outstanding dedication and service as a District Councilor to the members and officers of State Societies. Granted for the first time in 1993 in memory of Rebecca J. Moretz, MT.

• 3063 • **Leona Lyons Carter Award**
For recognition of the state society that has demonstrated outstanding, continuous organizational achievement. Awarded annually.

• 3064 • **Distinguished Achievement Awards**
To recognize outstanding contributions to state societies and the professions of medical technology and allied health care. Approximately 15 awards are presented annually.

• 3065 • **Exceptional Merit Awards**
To recognize outstanding contributions in the professions of medical technology and allied health care at the state and national levels. Approximately five awards are granted annually.

• 3066 • **Medallion of Merit**
This, the most prestigious of the RMT awards, is given for recognition of accomplishment and dedication above and beyond exceptional meritorious achievement in the profession of medical assistant, and to recognize an individual who has contributed immeasurably at all levels over the years. Individuals are nominated and selected by special vote of the AMT Board of Directors. A gold medallion, plaque, and all-expense paid trip to the national convention where the award is presented are awarded annually. Established in 1987.

• 3067 • **Order of the Golden Microscope**
This, the highest national honor bestowed upon a medical technologist or a medical laboratory technologist by the organization, is presented for outstanding organizational and professional contributions in the field of medical technology on the state, district, and national levels. The Board of Directors selects the nominees. A gold microscope medallion is awarded annually at the national meeting. Established in 1950.

• 3068 • **Outstanding Student Award**
For recognition of students enrolled in Allied Health programs whose achievements are judged to be outstanding. Criteria include: academic record, extracurricular or profession-related activities, attendance, cooperation and conduct, initiative, and the ability to get along with people. Awards are presented in the following categories: medical laboratory technician, medical assistant, dental assistant, and phlebotomy technician. A monetary prize of $250 and a plaque are awarded annually. Formerly: AMT's Outstanding Medical Assistant Students.

• 3069 • **The Pillar Award**
For recognition of dedication and service at the state level.

• 3070 • **President's Award**
To honor the president of an AMT state society for exemplary service. A plaque is awarded annually. Established in 1981.

• 3071 • **RMA of the Year**
To recognize outstanding professional contributions to the field of medical assisting through occupational activities and participation in the organization during the previous year. A plaque and an all-expense paid trip to the national convention where the award is presented are awarded annually. Established in 1977.

• 3072 • **The Silver Service Award**
For recognition of dedication and service at the national level.

• 3073 • **State Society Publications Awards**
Three awards are granted in each of three categories for content and creative communication: journal, newsletter, and bulletin. Outstanding state editors receive individual awards.

• 3074 • **Technical and Feature Writing Awards**
For recognition of authors of the best technical and feature papers submitted for publication. Members of the organization are eligible. Monetary awards and plaques are presented annually.

• 3075 • **Technologist of the Year**
In recognition of continuous pursuit of scientific accomplishment in the profession of medical technology. Members of the organization are eligible. A plaque and an all-expense paid trip to the national convention where the awards are presented are awarded annually.

• 3076 •
American Medical Women's Association
Diane Helentjaris MD, Pres.
801 N Fairfax St., Ste. 400
Alexandria, VA 22314
Phone: (703)838-0500
Fax: (703)549-3864
E-mail: info@amwa-doc.org
Home Page: http://www.amwa-doc.org

• 3077 • **Carroll L. Birch Award**
For recognition of the best scientific research paper written by a woman medical student. Established in 1965. Sponsored by AMWA's Branch 2, Chicago.

• 3078 • **Janet M. Glasgow Achievement Award**
To recognize women medical students graduating first or in the top ten percent of their classes. Established in 1941.

• 3079 • **Glasgow-Rubin Student Achievement**
Recognizes a major contribution to medicine by a woman physician. A medal is awarded annually. Established in 1949. Formerly: Elizabeth Blackwell Medal.

• 3080 •
American Medical Writers Association
Donna Munari PhD, Exec.Dir.
40 West Gude Dr., No. 101
Rockville, MD 20850-1192
Phone: (301)294-5303
Fax: (301)294-9006
E-mail: info@amwa.org
Home Page: http://www.amwa.org

• 3081 • **Walter C. Alvarez Memorial Award**
For recognition of excellence in the following areas: the writing of scientific papers, articles, editorials, and other material; design, printing, and illustrations; and distinguished service to the medical profession. A plaque is awarded annually. Established in 1980 in memory of Walter C. Alvarez.

• 3082 • **AMWA Medical Book Awards**
For recognition of the best book on a medical subject in each of three categories: books for physicians, books for allied health professionals, and trade. Authors of books published during the previous year are eligible. Trophies for first place and certificates for honorable mention are awarded annually. Established in 1972.

• 3083 • **Eric W. Martin Memorial Award**
To recognize an outstanding article, brochure, or monograph written by an AMWA member on a subject related to the pharmaceutical sciences. The award honors the memory and contributions of Dr. Eric W. Martin, a former AMWA

President, and the author of AMWA's Code of Ethics.

• 3084 • **John P. McGovern Award**

To recognize an individual for a preeminent contribution to any of the various facets of medical communication. A medal is awarded. Established in 1984 by the John P. McGovern Foundation.

• 3085 • **Harold Swanberg Distinguished Service Award**

To recognize distinguished contributions to medical literature or unusual and distinguished services to the medical profession. Members of the Association are eligible. A plaque is awarded annually. Established in 1952.

• 3086 •
American Mental Health Counselors Association
W. Mark Hamilton PhD, Exec.Dir./CEO
801 N Fairfax, Ste. 304
Alexandria, VA 22314
Phone: (703)548-6002
Toll-Free: 800-326-2642
Fax: (703)548-5233
E-mail: mhamilton@amhca.org
Home Page: http://www.amhca.org

• 3087 • **Counselor Educator of the Year**

To recognize an individual for an outstanding contribution to the profession of mental health counseling. Counselors must spend at least 51 percent of their time in academic pursuits, including teaching, training, consulting, supervising, and research. A plaque is awarded annually at the convention.

• 3088 • **Counselor of the Year**

To recognize an individual for an outstanding contribution to the profession of mental health counseling. Counselors who spend at least 51 percent of their time in direct counseling with clients and relevant consultation activities are eligible. They may be private practitioners or employed in agencies or institutions, but their primary role must be that of direct service counseling providers. A plaque is awarded annually at the convention.

• 3089 • **Researcher of the Year**

To recognize an individual for outstanding contribution to the profession of mental health counseling. The work must be clearly related to the discipline of mental health counseling and must have been published in an Association or Division Journal, preferably in the *Journal of Mental Health Counseling.* A plaque is awarded annually at the convention.

• 3090 •
American Merchant Marine Library Association
Talmage E. Simpkins, Pres.
20 Exchange Pl., Ste. 2901
New York, NY 10005
Phone: (212)269-0711
Fax: (212)269-5721
E-mail: ussammla@ix.netcom.com
Home Page: http://www.uss-ammla.com

• 3091 • **Great Lakes Crew Award of Merit**

Recognizes donations to the ship's literary club. Awarded annually.

• 3092 • **Honorable Mention Award**

Annual award of recognition.

• 3093 • **Ocean Crew and Great Lakes Awards of Merit**

To recognize the top contributing American flag ships to the Association. Any member is eligible for consideration for these awards. Awarded each year in May at the Library's annual meeting in New York City. Established in 1921 by Alice S. Howard.

• 3094 • **Ocean Crew Award of Merit**

Recognizes donations to the ship's literary club. Awarded annually.

• 3095 •
American Meteorological Society
Ronald D. McPherson, Exec.Dir.
45 Beacon St.
Boston, MA 02108-3693
Phone: (617)227-2425
Fax: (617)742-8718
E-mail: amsinfo@ametsoc.org
Home Page: http://www.ametsoc.org/AMS

• 3096 • **Fellow**

To recognize individuals for outstanding contributions to meteorology. Awarded annually.

• 3097 • **Howard H. Hanks, Jr., Scholarship in Meteorology**

In recognition of academic excellence and achievement in meteorology by a college or university student entering his or her final undergraduate year. The student must be a major in a meteorology department or some aspect of the atmospheric sciences, and intend to make atmospheric science his or her career. A prize of $700 is awarded annually. The scholarship honors the late Howard H. Hanks, Jr., Vice President of Weather Corporation of America, who was engaged in applied and industrial meteorology at the time of his death in 1969. William J. Hartnett, Board Chairman of Weather Corporation of America, provided funds for the scholarship. Established in 1973.

• 3098 • **Industry/Government Graduate Fellowships**

To encourage young scientists to prepare for careers in the meteorological, oceanic, and hydrologic fields. Awards are based on the applicant's performance as an undergraduate student and his or her qualifications to pursue a career in the atmospheric and related oceanic and hydrologic sciences. A $15,000 stipend is awarded to students entering their first year of graduate study. Awarded annually.

• 3099 • **Industry Undergraduate Scholarships**

To encourage outstanding undergraduate students to pursue careers in the atmospheric and related oceanic and hydrologic sciences. The awards are based on merit and are given to students who have shown the potential for accomplishment in these fields. A monetary prize of $2,000 for a nine-month period and an additional $2,000 for a subsequent nine-month period in the senior year are awarded to students who will be juniors in the following academic year. Awarded annually.

• 3100 • **Father James B. Macelwane Annual Awards in Meteorology**

To recognize outstanding papers in the atmospheric sciences written by college and university students. The papers must be original and concerned with some phase of the atmospheric sciences. All registered undergraduate students of a college or university in the Americas are eligible for participation, but no more than two students from any one institution may enter papers in any one contest. The following prizes are awarded: first prize - $300. Established in 1960.

• 3101 • **Howard T. Orville Scholarship in Meteorology**

In recognition of academic excellence and achievement in meteorology by a college or university student entering his or her final undergraduate year. The student must be a major in a meteorology department or some aspect of the atmospheric sciences and intend to make atmospheric science his or her career. A cash prize of $2,000 is awarded annually. The Orville Scholarship honors the late Howard T. Orville, Head of the Naval Aerological Service, 1940-1950, when he retired as Captain, USN. Captain Orville was President of the American Meteorological Society 1948-1949. Established in 1965.

• 3102 •
American Meteorological Society - National Weather Association, Aloha Chapter
Robert Farrell, Pres.
92-6056 Kahemakapii St.
Makakilo, HI 96707
Phone: (808)672-0100
Phone: (808)973-5280
Fax: (808)973-5281
E-mail: aloha@makakilo.com

• 3103 • **Science Fair**

For best project in meteorology. Monetary award bestowed annually.

• 3104 •
American MGB Association
Frank J. Ochal, Pres.
PO Box 11401
Chicago, IL 60611
Phone: (773)878-5055
Toll-Free: 800-723-MGMG
Fax: (773)769-3240
E-mail: info@mgclub.org
Home Page: http://www.mgclub.org

• 3105 • **Most Popular Convention Award**
For recognition of the car that convention attendees like the best. MGB or MG Midget Cars are eligible. A trophy is awarded annually. Established in 1978.

• 3106 •
American MGC Register
Keith Sanders, Chm.
2809 Copter Rd.
Pensacola, FL 32514
Phone: (850)478-3171
Phone: (850)994-1354
Fax: (850)475-5335
E-mail: amgcr@juno.com
Home Page: http://www.mgcars.org.uk/amgcr/

• 3107 • **Best Cars**
For recognition of the best MGC and MGC-GT cars at the National Meet. The members vote for the best cars. Trophies are awarded annually. Established in 1981.

• 3108 •
American Military Retirees Association
Bernard Matt Dillon, Natl.Pres.
5436 Peru St., Ste. 1
Plattsburgh, NY 12901
Phone: (518)563-9479
Phone: (518)563-9479
Toll-Free: 800-424-2969
Fax: (518)324-5204
E-mail: info@amra1973.org
Home Page: http://www.amra1973.org

• 3109 • **Douglas R. Drum Memorial Scholarship Award**
To provide scholarship assistance for members, spouses, children, and grandchildren. Fifteen scholarships awarded annually: one at $2,000; two at $1,500; two at $1,000; and ten at $500. Established in 1990.

• 3110 •
American Milking Shorthorn Society
David J. Kendall, Exec.Sec.
800 Pleasant St.
Beloit, WI 53511-5456
Phone: (608)365-6644
Phone: (608)365-6644
E-mail: milkshorthorns@tds.net
Home Page: http://www.milkingshorthorn.com

• 3111 • **Sam Beadleston Memorial Award**
To recognize the top producing two-year-old cow for milk in the previous calendar year. Established in 1991.

• 3112 • **Donald H. Cande Memorial Trophy**
To recognize the highest milk producing four year old cow.

• 3113 • **Dairy Progressive Breeder Awards**
To recognize outstanding breeders. Awards are given on three levels of herd performance: (1) Gold awards to breeders having herd average 30% above breed; (2) Silver awards to breeders with herd average 20% above breed; and (3) Bronze awards to breeders with herd average 10% above breed average.

• 3114 • **Gain Program Awards**
To recognize the top-gaining bull, top-gaining heifer, and the top-gaining steer. Pearl, ruby, and silver awards are presented to cows with offspring gaining the greatest total weight.

• 3115 • **W. J. Hardy Awards**
To recognize a lifetime production of milk and fat. Gold, silver, and bronze awards are given for production to date of over 200,000 lbs. of milk and 7,000 lbs. of fat; 150,000 lbs. of milk and 6,000 lbs. of fat; and 100,000 lbs. of milk and 6,000 lbs. of fat, respectively.

• 3116 • **Irving Meyer Memorial Award**
To recognize the top producing three-year-old cow in milk for the previous calendar year. Established in 1991.

• 3117 • **Protein Awards**
To recognize the top cow and top herd with the highest actual pounds of protein. Individuals who are members of the Society and on DHIR are eligible. A trophy or plaque is presented annually at the National Meeting. Established in 1989.

• 3118 • **Lillian B. Wood Rowe & John O. Rowe Citizen of the Year Award**
To recognize outstanding service and contributions made by an individual for the Milking Shorthorn breed. Those involved in some way with the dairy industry are eligible. A plaque is awarded at the convention. Established in 1983 by Stuart and Lillian Rowe in memory of John O. Rowe, a California Milking Shorthorn breeder who possessed strong dairy skills. Additional information is available from J. Stuart Rowe, Rt. 1, Box 2800 Davis, CA 95616

• 3119 • **W. Arthur Simpson Memorial Award**
To recognize the highest producing cow in milk and butterfat.

• 3120 • **W. C. Wood Memorial Trophy**
To recognize the polled Milking Shorthorn cow scoring highest in both production and classification. Awarded annually.

• 3121 •
American Morgan Horse Association
Fred Braden, Exec.Dir.
122 Bostwick Rd.
PO Box 960
Shelburne, VT 05482
Phone: (802)985-4944
Fax: (802)985-8897
E-mail: fredb@morganhorse.com
Home Page: http://www.morganhorse.com

• 3122 • **AMHA Man of the Year Award/ AMHA Woman of the Year Award**
To recognize a man and a woman who have made particularly outstanding contributions to the improvement and promotion of the Morgan breed. Nomination must be by an AMHA member. A plaque is awarded annually at the AMHA Convention. Established in 1964 by Green Mountain Stock Farm.

• 3123 • **AMHA Medal Class Awards**
To recognize excellence in equitation. Individuals must be youth members of AMHA. Silver Medals are awarded at approved horse shows. Gold Medals are presented annually at the Grand National and World Champion Morgan Horse Show. Established in 1977.

• 3124 • **AMHA Open Competition Awards**
To recognize the Morgans that are successfully competing in All-Breed competitions. Registered Morgan horses are eligible if their owners and riders are members of the Association. Plaques and certificates are awarded annually. Established in 1977.

• 3125 • **AMHA Trail Ride Award**
To recognize the high scoring Morgan horses that compete in competitive and endurance trail rides. Registered Morgan Horses are eligible. A commemorative Morgan Award and certificate are awarded when earned. Established in 1985.

• 3126 • **AMHA Youth of the Year Award**
To identify an outstanding Morgan youth. Individuals must be 21 years of age or under and must compete in a four phase contest. A plaque, trophy, and month-long award trip to the country of their choice are awarded annually at the Grand National and World Championship Morgan Show. Established in 1978.

• 3127 • **AMHA Youth Person of the Year Award**
To recognize an adult who has made outstanding contributions to the Morgan Youth Program. Nomination must be by an AMHA Youth member. A plaque is awarded annually at the AMHA Convention. Established in 1979.

Awards are arranged in alphabetical order below their administering organizations

• 3128 • AMHAY Horsemastership Awards

To recognize young people that can demonstrate the horsemastership skills outlined in each of the five educational levels. Individuals must be 21 years of age or under and must be members of AMHA. Awards are presented whenever requirements are met. Established in 1976.

• 3129 • Cecil J. Brown Memorial Sportsmanship Award

To recognize an individual who exemplifies sportsmanship in and out of the ring during horse show competition. Awarded annually. Established in 1993.

• 3130 • Golden Reins Award

To recognize professional trainers and instructors who have been involved with the breed for at least 30 years. Active or retired trainers and instructors who have made a lasting impact on the breed on a daily basis through their dedication to working with horses and riders are eligible for nomination. Awarded annually. Established in 1995.

• 3131 • Hall of Fame

To recognize individuals for a lifetime of support to the breed through the activities of the Association. Typically, three or four individuals are inducted each year. Established in 1985.

• 3132 • Judges Award

To recognize those judges who have held a Morgan judges card for 25 or 30 years.

• 3133 • Therapy Horse of the Year Award

To honor the outstanding registered Morgan horse who has contributed above and beyond expectations as a therapy horse.

• 3134 •

American Mosquito Control Association
Martin S. Chomskey, Bus.Admin.
US Hwy. 1 South
North Brunswick, NJ 08902
Phone: (732)214-8899
Fax: (732)214-0110
E-mail: amca@mosquito.org
Home Page: http://www.mosquito.org

Formerly: (1944) Eastern Association of Mosquito Control Workers.

• 3135 • John N. Belkin Memorial Award

For meritorious contributions to the field of mosquito systematics and/or mosquito biology. Anyone judged by their peers to be worthy may be nominated. A plaque is awarded annually at the conference. Established in 1981 in honor of John N. Belkin.

• 3136 • Medal of Honor Award

This, the highest award of the AMCA, is given for recognition of exceptional contributions to mosquito control or related fields. Only members are eligible. One engraved plaque is awarded annually at the conference. Established in 1972.

• 3137 • Memorial Lecturer Award and Honoree(s)

To recognize an outstanding speaker with an invitation to be the Memorial Lecturer and present the annual lecture in honor of the Memorial Lecture Honoree(s). The Memorial Lecture Honoree(s) must have made exceptional contributions to the broad field of mosquito control during their lifetimes. A plaque is awarded annually at the conference. Established in 1979.

• 3138 • Meritorious Service Award

For recognition of outstanding service to the AMCA. Only AMCA members in good standing who are not past presidents of the association are eligible to be recommended by the AMCA Awards Committee and confirmed by the Board of Directors. A maximum of two Meritorious Service Award plaques are awarded annually at the conference. Established in 1972.

• 3139 • Presidential Citation

To recognize individuals not eligible to receive other AMCA awards, but who are eminently deserving of special recognition by the association. Nominees are selected by the AMCA Awards Committee and must be confirmed by the Board of Directors. A maximum of two Presidential Citation plaques are presented annually at the conference. Established in 1980.

• 3140 •

American Mothers, Inc.
Sue Hickenlooper, Pres.
15 DuPont Cir. NW
Washington, DC 20036
Phone: (202)234-7375
Toll-Free: 877-242-4AMI
Fax: (202)234-7390
E-mail: info@americanmothers.org
Home Page: http://www.americanmothers.org

Formerly: American Mothers Committee.

• 3141 • Alice Abel Cultural and Creative Arts Program

To encourage and honor all mothers in their artistically creative pursuits. The program's purpose is to strengthen moral and spiritual values in the family and in the home. The exhibit offers an expression of the beauty and meaning of art in the life of the mother and family today. Entries may be submitted in the following categories: Fine Arts, Literature, and Vocal, Piano, and Violin Music. Entries are limited to one in each category per state. The following monetary awards are presented annually: (1) Fine Arts: sculpture - $1,000; painting - $1,000; graphics $1,000; and crafts - $500; (2) Literature: poetry - $400 for first place and $100 for second place; short story - $400 for first place and $100 for second place; and essay or article - $400 for first place and $100 for second place; and (3) Vocal Music - $1,000, Violin - $1,000, Piano $1,000.

• 3142 • Phyllis B. Marriott President's Award

To recognize a state chapter for outstanding achievement in the field of record keeping of events within their state organization that year. Awarded annually.

• 3143 • Mother of the Year

To encourage the strengthening of moral and spiritual foundations of the home, and to give to the observance of Mother's Day a spiritual quality that highlights the standards of ideal motherhood in the home, community, nation, and the world. A citation and diamond pin are awarded annually. Established in 1935. Additional information is available from American Mothers, Inc. P.O. Box 400 Pound Ridge, NY 10576.

• 3144 • Ethel Parham Memorial Award

To recognize a young mother who has shown outstanding service to American Mothers, Inc. in the program for mothers of young children. The following factors are considered: leadership among mothers, organizing new chapters, increasing membership, and serving as an example of quality mothering to other young women. A medallion is awarded. Established about 1978.

• 3145 • Young Mother Representative

To encourage young mothers as they work to raise their children with moral strength, spiritual roots, and family bonds. To provide tools to make the job easier, the Young Mother Representative communicates throughout the year with all young mothers members and represents them at the National AMI Board. In thanks, a special sculpture and other gifts are given to the representative.

• 3146 •

American Motion Picture Society
Ned Cordery, Pres.
30 Kanan Rd.
Oak Park, CA 91377
Phone: (310)498-1634
E-mail: roger@ampsvideo.com
Home Page: http://www.ampsvideo.com

• 3147 • American International Film/Video Festival

To recognize and give exposure to the best motion picture work by today's non-professional motion picture film and video makers. The deadline for entries is August 1. Awards are presented in the following categories: first place - Class A; the Ten Best List; Honorable Mentions; Best Story Award; Best Documentary Award; Best Editing Award; Best Animation Award; Best Foreign Film Award; Best Nature Award; Best Entry Made by a Club; Best Cinematography Award; Class B (Student Entries) Awards; and Class C (Commercial) Awards. Monetary awards of $500, $300, and $200 are presented for first, second, and third place in Class A. Trophies are awarded in four categories and certificates are given to all winners in all categories. Established in 1930 by the Amateur Cinema League in New York City.

• 3148 • Ten Best of the West Film Festival

To recognize and give exposure to the best motion picture work being done by today's nonprofessional filmmakers. Candidates living in the Western United States (west of the Mississippi River) or in Western Canada are eligible. Films must be non-commercial. Certificates are awarded annually each fall, usually in October. Established in 1956 by George W. Cushman. Various film associations in the Western United States and Canada sponsor this festival each year.

• 3149 •
American Motorcyclist Association
Robert Rasor, Pres.
13515 Yarmouth Dr.
Pickerington, OH 43147
Phone: (614)856-1900
Toll-Free: 800-262-5646
Fax: (614)856-1920
E-mail: ama@ama-cycle.org
Home Page: http://www.ama-cycle.org

• 3150 • Daytona 200

This annual motorcycle race, which is 200 miles in length, is held each year in Daytona Beach, Florida at the Dayton International Speedway. The race draws contestants from all parts of the world. It has become known as the "Indianapolis of Motorcycle Racing", and was first held in 1937. Formerly: (1996) National Championship.

• 3151 • Dud Perkins Award

To recognize outstanding contributions to the sport of motorcycling. A plaque is awarded annually. Established in 1970.

• 3152 •
American Moving and Storage Association
Joe Harrison, Pres.
1611 Duke St.
Alexandria, VA 22314
Phone: (703)683-7410
Fax: (703)683-7527
E-mail: info@moving.org
Home Page: http://www.promover.org

• 3153 • Distinguished Service Award

To recognize individuals who have made industry-wide contributions through leadership, originality, technological development, sales innovation or revolutionary advancement of industry operations resulting in industry growth and development over the years. Individuals active in the industry may be nominated by another person from the industry. A plaque is awarded annually at the convention. Established in 1983.

• 3154 •
American Museum of Natural History
Ellen V. Futter, Pres.
Central Park W at 79th St.
New York, NY 10024-5192
Phone: (212)769-5100
Fax: (212)769-5427
E-mail: members@amnh.org
Home Page: http://www.amnh.org

• 3155 • Frank M. Chapman Memorial Fund Award

To provide grants-in-aid for ornithological research and postdoctoral fellowships. While there is no restriction on who may apply, the Committee particularly welcomes and favors applications from graduate students. Applications should be submitted by November 15. Applications by FAX are not accepted.

• 3156 • Lerner-Gray Fund for Marine Research Award

To provide funds for projects in marine zoology with emphasis on systematics, evolution, ecology, and field-oriented behavioral studies. The deadline is March 15. Applications by FAX are not accepted. Awards usually range from $200-$1,000.

• 3157 • Postdoctoral Fellowship Program

To provide appointments in residence at the museum to study systematics, evolutionary biology and museum-related disciplines. The deadline for entry is January 15. Applications by FAX are not accepted. Appointments can be up to 2 years.

• 3158 • Theodore Roosevelt Memorial Fund Award

To provide funds for research on North American fauna. The deadline is February 15. Applications by FAX are not accepted. Awards usually range from $200-$1,000.

• 3159 •
American Music Awards
649 W Jefferson Blvd.
Los Angeles, CA 90036-4727
Phone: (818)841-3003
Fax: (323)939-5799

• 3160 • American Music Awards

To recognize the American public's favorites in contemporary music. Winners are determined by votes cast by a cross-section of the American record-buying public. Awards are presented in eight main categories: Pop/Rock, Country, Hip Hop/R&B, Adult Contemporary, Latin Music, Contemporary Inspirational, Soundtrack and Alternative Music. Within each main category, awards are given for favorite artists and/or recordings. In addition, a special Award of Merit is presented to recognize outstanding contributions to the musical entertainment of the American public. Trophies are awarded annually in January or February on a television special. Established in 1974. television special. Established in 1974.

• 3161 •
American Music Center
Joanne Cossa, Exec.Dir.
30 W 26th St., Ste. 1001
New York, NY 10010-2011
Phone: (212)366-5260
Fax: (212)366-5265
E-mail: center@amc.net
Home Page: http://www.amc.net/index.html

• 3162 • Letter of Distinction

Recognizes distinction in the field of contemporary American music. Awarded annually. Formerly: (1986) Copying Assistance Program.

• 3163 •
American Music Festival Association
W. Harrison Wasinack, Exec.Dir.
PO Box 2987
Anaheim, CA 92814
Phone: (714)827-4562
Phone: (714)401-3934
Fax: (562)949-3850

• 3164 • Achievement and Hall of Fame Award

To recognize significant musical achievement. Awarded annually.

• 3165 •
American Music Scholarship Association
Gloria Ackerman, Exec.Dir.
441 Vine St., Ste. 1030
Cincinnati, OH 45202
Phone: (513)421-5342
Phone: (513)421-5346
Fax: (513)421-2672
E-mail: amsa@queencity.com
Home Page: http://www.amsa-wpc.org

Formerly: (1968) Cincinnati Scholarship Association.

• 3166 • World Piano Competition

To identify, develop, and expose young pianists to the formative influence of great musicians' performances, to provide standards for teaching technical mastery and artistic excellence, and to generate greater music appreciation among audiences through exposure to talented artists. Piano students who are between 5 and 30 years of age are eligible. The deadline for entry is February 28. The following monetary awards are presented in the Artist Division (ages 18-30): first prize - Alice Tully Hall debut valued at $35,000; second prize - $3,000; third prize - $2,000; fourth prize $1,000; fifth prize - $500; and sixth prize - $300. Monetary prizes are also presented in the pre-college Young Artist Division and Regional Awards. Awarded annually. Established in 1956 by Gloria Ackerman. Formerly: AMSA International Piano Competition.

• 3167 •
American Music Therapy Association
8455 Colesville Rd., Ste. 1000
Silver Spring, MD 20910
Phone: (301)589-3300
Fax: (301)589-5175
E-mail: info@musictherapy.org
Home Page: http://www.musictherapy.org

• 3168 • **Gaston Writing Award**
To encourage scholarship by recognizing outstanding written composition by music therapy students. Individuals enrolled in a music therapy degree program offered at an NAMT-recognized university are eligible. A monetary prize is awarded annually. Established in 1973.

• 3169 •
American Musical Instrument Society
Kathryn Shanks Libin, Pres.
389 Main St., Ste. 202
Malden, MA 02148
Phone: (781)397-8870
Fax: (781)397-8887
E-mail: amis@guildassoc.com
Home Page: http://www.amis.org/

• 3170 • **Nicolas Bessaraboff Prize**
To honor publications that best further the Society's goal to promote study of the history, design, and use of musical instruments in all cultures and from all periods. Book-length work in English must be submitted by October 31. A monetary prize of $500 and a certificate are awarded biennially in odd-numbered years. Established in 1986 in honor of Nicolas Bessaraboff, whose early publications reflected the goals of the AMIS and the modern systematic study of musical instruments.

• 3171 • **Frances Densmore Prize**
To honor publications that best further the Society's goal to promote study of the history, design, and use of musical instruments in all cultures and from all periods. Article-length publications in English are eligible for submission by October 31. A monetary prize of $500 and a certificate are awarded biennially in even-numbered years. Established in 1986 in honor of Frances Densmore, whose early publications reflected the goals of the AMIS and the modern systematic study of musical instruments.

• 3172 • **Curt Sachs Award**
To honor those who have made important contributions towards the Society's goal to promote the study of the history, design, and use of musical instruments in all cultural and formal periods. Members in good standing are eligible to submit nominations to the Board of Governors, which has final responsibility for selection. A certificate and an invitation to attend the Society's annual meeting to address the Society are awarded annually at the discretion of the Society's Board of Governors. Established in 1983 in memory of Curt Sachs, one of the founders of the modern systematic study of musical instruments.

• 3173 •
American Musicological Society
Robert Judd, Exec.Dir.
201 S 34th St.
Philadelphia, PA 19104-6313
Phone: (215)898-8698
Toll-Free: 888-611-4267
Fax: (215)573-3673
E-mail: ams@sas.upenn.edu
Home Page: http://www.ams-net.org

• 3174 • **Philip Brett Award**
To honor exceptional musicological work in the field of gay, lesbian, bisexual, transgender/transsexual studies completed during the previous two academic years (ending June 30), in any country and in any language. By "work" is meant a published article, book, edition, annotated translation, a paper read at a conference, teaching materials, and other scholarly work accepted by the award committee that best exemplifies the highest qualities of originality, interpretation, theory, and communication in this field. A monetary award of and a certificate are awarded annually.

• 3175 • **Einstein Award**
To honor a young scholar for an outstanding musicological article of exceptional merit published by a scholar in the early stages of his or her career who is a citizen or permanent resident of Canada or the United States.

• 3176 • **Noah Greenberg Award**
The award is intended to stimulate active cooperation between scholars and performers by recognizing and fostering outstanding contributions to historically-aware performance and to the study of historical performing practices. Both scholars and performers may apply.

• 3177 • **Alvin H. Johnson AMS 50 Dissertation Fellowships**
To encourage advancement of research in the various fields of music as a branch of learning and scholarship. Candidates must be registered for a doctorate at a North American university, in good standing, and have completed all formal degree requirements except the dissertation at the time of full application. Any submission for a doctoral degree in which the emphasis is on musical scholarship is eligible. Final application is due January 15. AMS Fellowships are awarded solely on the basis of academic merit. Winners receive a twelve-month stipend, currently set at $15,000. Fellows may elect to accept the award on an honorary or partly honorary basis, thus freeing scarce resources for others. The fellowships are intended for full-time study. Winners will be selected in the Spring, announced in the Summer issue of the Newsletter, and given formal recognition at the AMS Annual Meeting. Formerly: (2004) AMS 50 Fellowships.

• 3178 • **Otto Kinkeldey Award**
To honor the author of the most notable full-length work in any branch of the discipline of musicology published within the previous calendar year. American or Canadian authors are eligible. Selection is made by a specially appointed committee. A monetary prize of $400 and a certificate are awarded yearly at the annual meeting of the society. Established in 1967 in honor of Otto Kinkeldey, the scholar-librarian who was the society's first president (1934-1936), and named honorary president in 1960 in which capacity he served until his death in 1966.

• 3179 • **Paul A. Pisk Prize**
To honor a graduate student for a scholarly paper, to be read at the annual meeting of the society. 424296 ANSI UI

• 3180 •
American National Standards Institute
Dr. Mark W. Hurwitz, Pres. & CEO
1819 L St. NW, No. 6th Fl.
Washington, DC 20036
Phone: (202)293-8020
Fax: (202)293-9287
E-mail: info@ansi.org
Home Page: http://www.ansi.org

• 3181 • **Astin - Polk International Standards Medal**
To honor distinguished service in promoting trade and understanding among nations through personal participation in the advancement, development, or administration of international standardization, measurement, or certification. Citizens of any nation are eligible. Nominations must be submitted by July 11. Established in 1973 to honor Dr. Allen V. Astin and Dr. Louis F. Polk, Sr., outstanding advocates of international standardization and measurement.

• 3182 • **Howard Coonley Medal**
To recognize an executive who has rendered service in advancing the national economy through voluntary standardization and supported standardization as a management tool. Nominations must be submitted by July 11. A medal is awarded when appropriate. Established in 1950 to honor Howard Coonley, who served three terms as President of the Association and twenty-two years on its Board of Directors.

• 3183 • **Finegan Standards Medal**
To recognize an individual who has shown exceptional leadership in the development and application of voluntary national standards. Nominations must be submitted by July 11. A medal is awarded when appropriate. Established in 1951. Renamed in 1985 to honor Richard J. Finegan, Vice-President of Liberty Mutual Insurance Company, who for more than a decade provided leadership and strong support for ANSI and the voluntary standards system. Formerly: (1984) Standards Medal.

• 3184 • **Edward Lohse Information Technology Medal**
To recognize an individual who has contributed significantly to standardization by promoting the development of information technology standards both domestically and internationally and

by providing leadership in the promulgation of such standards. Nominations must be submitted by January 1. Established in 1991 to honor Edward Lohse, who for over 20 years played a leading role in both domestic and international standards development for information and telecommunications technologies.

• 3185 • Meritorious Service Award
To recognize an individual who has a record of significant contribution to voluntary standardization and has contributed outstanding service to the ANSI federation. Nominations must be submitted by January 1. This award recognizes active participation in national and/or international standards efforts that enables the American National Standards Institute to attain the goals for which it was founded.

• 3186 • George S. Wham Leadership Medal
To recognize outstanding contributions by an individual who has provided direction and long-range planning to the ANSI standards federation in commitment and support of the national and/or international standards system or in a specific area of voluntary standardization. Nominations must be submitted by January 1. Established to honor Dr. George S. Wham, Technical Director at *Goodhousekeeping Magazine*, who served as a past chairman of ANSI's Board of Directors.

• 3187 •
American Nature Study Society
Steven A. Melcher, Contact
RR 2, Box 1010
Dingmans Ferry, PA 18328
Phone: (570)828-9692
Phone: (716)425-1059
Fax: (570)828-9695
E-mail: anssonline@aol.com
Home Page: http://www.hometown.aol.com/anssonline

• 3188 • Eva L. Gordon Award
To recognize an author of children's science literature whose works exemplify high standards of accuracy, readability, sensitivity to inter-relationships, timeliness, and joyousness while at the same time, extending either directly or subtly, an invitation for the reader to become involved. A certificate is awarded annually at the conference or workshop. Established in 1964 in memory of Eva L. Gordon, author, reviewer, and professor of children's science literature at Cornell University. Formerly: Eva L. Gordon Award for Children's Science Literature.

• 3189 •
American Needlepoint Guild
Susan H. Davis, Contact-Pres.
7600 Terrace Ave., Ste. 203
Middleton, WI 53562
Phone: (608)836-1503
Fax: (608)831-5122
E-mail: membership@needlepoint.org
Home Page: http://www.needlepoint.org

• 3190 • American Needlepoint Guild Literary Award
For recognition of outstanding literary or publishing contributions to the field of needle work. A monetary award and a certificate are awarded annually when merited. Established in 1976. Formerly: (1986) American Needlepoint Guild Book Award.

• 3191 •
American Neuropsychiatric Association
Richard M. Restak, Pres.
700 Ackerman Rd., Ste. 625
Columbus, OH 43202
Phone: (614)447-2077
Fax: (614)263-4366
E-mail: anpa@osu.edu
Home Page: http://www.anpaonline.org

• 3192 • Central Neuropsychiatric Association Resident Award
To recognize basic research and clinical study made by resident doctors in the fields of psychiatry and neurology. Eligibility is limited to residents in the fields of neurology, psychiatry and neurosurgery. The essay or research study must be completed during the candidates' residency. The deadline is May 30. The winner receives a $300 honorarium and is expected to present his or her paper at the annual meeting in October. Two honorable mention awards of $50 each are also presented. Awarded annually. Established in 1966 to honor the late "Dr. Will" C. Menninger, an esteemed member of the Association. Formerly: (1977) William C. Menniger Award.

• 3193 •
American North Country Cheviot Sheep Association
8708 S. Co. Rd. 500 W.
Reelsville, IN 46171
Phone: (765)672-8205
Fax: (765)672-4275
E-mail: yuccafl@ccrtc.com

• 3194 • American North Country Cheviot Hall of Fame
Recognizes service to breed and sheep industry. Awarded biennially.

• 3195 • International Show and Sale
To recognize the champion ram and champion ewe at the International Show. Selection is by a judge. Trophies are awarded biennially. Established in 1979.

• 3196 •
American Numismatic Association
Christopher Cipoletti, Exec.Dir.
818 N. Cascade Ave.
Colorado Springs, CO 80903-3279
Phone: (719)632-2646
Fax: (719)634-4085
E-mail: ana@money.org
Home Page: http://www.money.org

• 3197 • ANA Numismatic Art Award for Excellence in Medallic Sculpture
This award, popularly known as the Outstanding Sculptor of the Year Award, is given to recognize outstanding medallic sculpture. An inscribed gold medal is awarded annually. Established in 1966.

• 3198 • Terry Armstrong Memorial Award for Outstanding Regional Coordinator
To recognize the most outstanding regional coordinator. A plaque is awarded annually. Established in 1994.

• 3199 • Award for Private Mint Issues
To recognize the top three exhibitors in private mint issues since 1960, that is, all non-denominated numismatic material issued by private mints of any country, including philatelic-numismatic covers. The following prizes are awarded annually: first place - plaque with gold-plated seal medal; second place - plaque with nickel silver seal medal; third place - plaque with bronze seal medal. Established in 1985. Formerly: Franklin Mint Exhibit Award.

• 3200 • Al Baber Member Booster Award
To recognize the dealer and member who procure the most new members in a year. Two plaques are awarded annually. Established in 1982.

• 3201 • George Bauer Memorial Exhibit Award
To recognize the top three exhibitors in military medals, decorations, orders, and badges. The following prizes are awarded annually: first place - plaque with gold-plated seal medal; second place - plaque with nickel silver seal medal; and third place - plaque with bronze seal medal. Established in 1980.

• 3202 • Best Radio Script for "Money Talks" Award
To recognize the best script aired during the previous year. A plaque is awarded annually.

• 3203 • James L. Betton Youth Exhibit Award
To recognize the top three youth exhibitors in foreign coins. The following prizes are awarded annually: first place - plaque with gold-plated seal medal; second place - plaque with nickel silver seal medal; and third place - plaque with bronze seal medal.

• 3204 • Ray Byrne Memorial Literary Award
To recognize the young numismatist who writes the best article displaying in-depth numismatic research. The article must have been published in *The Numismatist, First Strike,* or another recognized numismatic publication. A plaque is awarded annually for first place; certificates or framed acknowledgements for second and third place are awarded as merited.

• 3205 • Helen Carmody-Lebo Memorial Award for Outstanding District Delegate
To recognize the district delegate who most fully promotes coin collection, coin clubs, and the ANA. A plaque is awarded annually. Established in 1989.

• 3206 • Century Award
To recognize individuals who recruit 100 new members to the ANA. An engraved plaque is awarded annually. Established in 1980.

• 3207 • Menachem Chaim and Simcha Tova Mizel Memorial Exhibit Award
To recognize the top three exhibitors in issues of the government of Israel. The following prizes are awarded annually: first place - plaque with gold-plated seal medal; second place - plaque with nickel silver seal medal; and third place - plaque with bronze seal medal. Established in 1985.

• 3208 • Henry Christensen Memorial Exhibit Award
To recognize the top three exhibitors in Latin American numismatics. The following awards are presented annually: first place - plaque with gold-plated seal medal; second place - plaque with nickel silver seal medal; and third place - plaque with bronze seal medal. Established in 1985.

• 3209 • Fred Cihon Exhibit Award
To recognize the top three exhibitors in local interest numismatic material. The following prizes are awarded annually: first place - plaque with gold-plated seal medal; second place - plaque with nickel silver seal medal; and third place - plaque with bronze seal medal. Established in 1983.

• 3210 • Dr. Charles W. Crowe Memorial Exhibit Award
To recognize the top three exhibitors in coins issued prior to 1500 A.D. The following prizes are awarded annually: first place - plaque with gold-plated seal medal; second place - plaque with nickel silver seal medal; and third place - plaque with bronze seal medal. Established in 1982.

• 3211 • John S. Davenport Memorial Exhibit Award
To recognize the top three exhibitors in foreign coins issued since 1500 A.D. The following prizes are awarded annually: first place - plaque with gold-plated seal medal; second place - plaque with nickel silver seal medal; and third place - plaque with bronze seal medal. Established in 1982.

• 3212 • Dealer Booster Award
To recognize the dealer who procures the most new members in a year. A plaque is awarded annually.

• 3213 • Gaston DiBello Memorial Exhibit Award
To recognize the top three exhibitors in U.S. gold coins. The following prizes are awarded annually: first place - plaque with gold-plated seal medal; second place - plaque with nickel silver seal medal; and third place - plaque with bronze seal medal. Established in 1982.

• 3214 • William Donlan Memorial Exhibit Award
To recognize the top three exhibitors in obsolete paper money issued in the United States. The following prizes are awarded annually: first place - plaque with gold-plated seal medal; second place - plaque with nickel silver seal medal; and third place - plaque with bronze seal medal. Established in 1986.

• 3215 • R.R. Donnelley & Sons Co. Exhibit Award
To recognize the top three general or specialized exhibitors. The following awards are presented annually: first place - plaque with gold-plated seal medal; second place - plaque with nickel silver seal medal; and third place - plaque with bronze seal medal. Established in 1987.

• 3216 • Edgerton-Lenker Memorial Youth Exhibit Award
To recognize the top three youth exhibitors in U.S. coins. The following prizes are awarded annually: first place - plaque with gold-plated seal medal; second place - plaque with nickel silver seal medal; and third place - plaque with bronze seal medal. Formerly: Gordon Z. Greene Memorial United States Numismatics - YN Exhibit Award.

• 3217 • Exemplary Service Award
To recognize an individual or entity who has performed services on behalf of the Association that are "above and beyond the call." A certificate and citation are awarded annually. Established in 1991.

• 3218 • Aaron Feldman Memorial Exhibit Award
To recognize the top three exhibitors in numismatic literature. The following prizes are awarded annually: first place - plaque with gold-plated seal medal; second place - plaque with nickel silver seal medal; and third place - plaque with bronze seal medal. Established in 1992.

• 3219 • Fifty Year Club Member Certificate
To recognize club members who have been ANA members for fifty years. A certificate mounted on a plaque is awarded annually.

• 3220 • Fifty Year Membership Medal and Pin
To recognize individuals who have been ANA members for fifty years. An engraved gold medal and fifty year pin are awarded annually.

• 3221 • Forty Year Membership Pin
To recognize individuals who have been ANA members for forty years. A forty year pin is awarded annually.

• 3222 • Goodfellowship Award
To recognize the General Chairman of the convention. A silver medal with a ribbon and a plaque is awarded semi-annually. Established in 1986.

• 3223 • Gould Memorial Literary Award
To recognize the young numismatist who writes the best article displaying in-depth numismatic research. The article need not have been published. A plaque is awarded annually for first place; certificates or framed acknowledgements are awarded for second and third place as merited.

• 3224 • Heath Literary Award
To recognize the authors of outstanding original research articles published in the official journal of ANA, *The Numismatist*. Members of the Association are eligible. The following prizes are awarded: first prize - a silver medal and a monetary prize of $250; second prize - a bronze medal and $100; third prize - a bronze medal; honorable mention certificates of recognition; and non-member certificates of recognition. Awarded annually. Established in 1978.

• 3225 • Robert Hendershott Award
To recognize the top three exhibitors in primitive, odd, and curious money. The following prizes are awarded annually: first place - plaque with gold-plated seal medal; second place - plaque with nickel silver seal medal; and third place - plaque with bronze seal medal. Established in 1990.

• 3226 • William C. Henderson Memorial Exhibit Award
To recognize the top three exhibitors in Western Americana. The following prizes are awarded annually: first place - plaque with gold-plated seal medal; second place - plaque with nickel silver seal medal; and third place - plaque with bronze seal medal. Established in 1985.

• 3227 • Alan Herbert Youth Exhibit Award
To recognize the top youth exhibitors in errors and varieties. A plaque with a gold-plated seal medal is awarded annually.

• 3228 • Incoming President Award
To honor the incoming president. A gavel with a nameplate is awarded biennially in odd-numbered years.

• 3229 • Judges Appreciation Award
To show appreciation to each exhibit judge for their participation. A silver medal is awarded to the Chief Judge and bronze medals for all other judges are awarded semi-annually.

• 3230 • Kagin Family Paper Money Youth Exhibit Award
To recognize the top youth exhibitor in paper money. A plaque is awarded annually. Formerly: Kurt Krueger Paper Money - YN Exhibit Award.

• 3231 • Melvin and Leona Kohl Memorial Exhibit Award
To recognize the top three exhibitors in foreign gold coins. The following prizes are awarded annually: first place - plaque with gold-plated seal medal; second place - plaque with nickel silver seal medal; and third place - plaque with bronze seal medal. Established in 1980.

• 3232 • Abe Kosoff Memorial Literary Award
To recognize the young numismatist who writes the best article or gives the best talk on a basic numismatic subject. A plaque is awarded annually for first place; certificates and framed acknowledgements are awarded for second and third place as merited.

• 3233 • Robert J. Leuver Exhibit Award
To recognize the top three exhibitors in foreign paper money. The following prizes are awarded annually: first place - plaque with gold-plated seal medal; second place - plaque with nickel silver seal medal; and third place - plaque with bronze seal medal. Established in 1984.

• 3234 • Lifetime Achievement Award
To recognize an individual, family, firm, or juridical entry that has made outstanding contributions to organized numismatics. A certificate and citation are awarded annually. Established in 1992.

• 3235 • Charles "Cheech" Litman Memorial Youth Exhibit Award
To recognize the top youth exhibitor in medals and tokens. A plaque is awarded annually.

• 3236 • Local Committee Appreciation
To thank the local committee chairpersons for their participation. A plaque with the ANA logo and a convention medal are awarded semi-annually. Established in 1992.

• 3237 • Love Token Society Exhibit Award
To recognize the top three exhibitors in love tokens. The following prizes are awarded annually: first place - plaque with gold-plated seal medal; second place - plaque with nickel silver seal medal; and third place - plaque with bronze seal medal. Established in 1985.

• 3238 • Master of Ceremonies - ANA Banquet
To show appreciation for emceeing the banquet. An encased medal is awarded to the emcee at the Annual Convention and a certificate of appreciation is awarded to the emcee at the Midwinter Convention.

• 3239 • Medal of Merit
This, ANA's second highest award, is given to recognize individuals for outstanding contributions to the science of numismatics. A silver medal is awarded annually. Established in 1947.

• 3240 • Merit of Exhibits
To show appreciation to all exhibitors. A bronze medal is awarded semi-annually.

• 3241 • National Coin Week
To recognize the top three clubs and individuals. Plaques and certificates are awarded annually for first, second, and third place. Established in 1924.

• 3242 • Numismatic Error Collectors Exhibit Award
To recognize the top three exhibitors in numismatic errors and error varieties. The following prizes are awarded annually: first place - plaque with gold-plated seal medal; second place - plaque with nickel silver seal medal; and third place - plaque with bronze seal medal. Established in 1985.

• 3243 • Outgoing Governor Award
To show appreciation for a term of office. A clock and bronze medal are awarded biennially in odd-numbered years.

• 3244 • Outgoing President Award
To show appreciation for a term of office. A gold medal, half gavel, bronze medal, and a clock are awarded biennially in odd-numbered years.

• 3245 • Outstanding Adult Advisor Award
To recognize adult leaders as advisors who have donated time and effort to develop and assist beginning and advanced young numismatists. A plaque is awarded annually.

• 3246 • Outstanding Club Publication Award
To recognize local and regional ANA club publications (newsletters and journals). A framed certificate is awarded annually for both local and regional categories.

• 3247 • Outstanding Club Representative Award
To recognize those individuals who serve their coin club with exemplary enthusiasm and dedication. A plaque is awarded annually. Established in 1965.

• 3248 • Outstanding Government Service Award
To recognize an individual in public service, working for a governmental agency or international organization, or who has retired or been separated from such an organization during the 12 months preceding the granting of the award, who has helped advance the interests of all those who collect coins, tokens, medals, and paper money. A certificate and citation are awarded annually. Established in 1990.

• 3249 • Outstanding Young Numismatist of the Year
To recognize young numismatists who serve their coin club with exemplary enthusiasm and dedication. A plaque is awarded annually. Established in 1987.

• 3250 • People's Choice Award
To allow convention attenders to select their favorite exhibit. A 2-1/4 inch convention medal in a dark blue velvet shadow box with a silver medallion holder is awarded semi-annually. Established in 1987.

• 3251 • John Jay Pittman, Sr. Memorial Exhibit Award
To recognize the top three exhibitors in Canadian coins and currency. The following prizes are awarded annually: first place - plaque with gold-plated seal medal; second place - plaque with nickel silver seal medal; and third place - plaque with bronze seal medal. Established in 1986.

• 3252 • Wayte and Olga Raymond Literary Award
To recognize distinguished numismatic achievement in the field of U.S. numismatics. A monetary award of $400 is awarded annually. Established in 1977.

• 3253 • Lelan G. Rogers Memorial Exhibit Award
To recognize the top three exhibitors in U.S. coins. The following prizes are awarded annually: first place - plaque with gold-plated seal medal; second place - plaque with nickel silver seal medal; and third place - plaque with bronze seal medal. Established in 1981.

• 3254 • Burton Saxton Memorial Exhibit Award
To recognize the top three exhibitors in medals. The following prizes are awarded annually: first place - plaque with gold-plated seal medal; second place - plaque with nickel silver seal medal; and third place - plaque with bronze seal medal. Established in 1983.

• 3255 • Seventy-Five Year Club Member Certificate
To recognize clubs who have been ANA members for seventy-five years. A certificate mounted on a plaque is awarded annually.

• 3256 • Catherine Sheehan Award for U.S. Paper Money Studies
To recognize authors for the best articles about paper money and scrip published in the *The Numismatist.* A plaque and $100 are awarded for first place, and a framed certificate and $50 are awarded for second place. Awarded annually. Established in 1992.

• 3257 • M. Vernon Sheldon Audio-Visual Award
To recognize the best audio-visual program submitted to ANA during the previous calendar year. A plaque is awarded annually. Established in 1983.

• 3258 • Sixty Year Membership Medal
To recognize individuals who have been ANA members for sixty continuous years. An engraved, electrum medal is awarded annually.

• 3259 • Glenn Smedley Memorial Award
To recognize outstanding dedicated service to the hobby. A bronze medal, certificate, and citation are awarded annually. Established in 1990.

• 3260 • Sidney W. Smith Memorial Exhibit Award
To recognize the top three exhibitors in U.S. paper money. The following prizes are awarded annually: first place - plaque with gold-plated seal medal; second place - plaque with nickel silver seal medal; and third place - plaque with bronze seal medal. Established in 1981.

• 3261 • Twenty-Five Year Club Member Certificate
To recognize clubs who have been ANA members for twenty-five years. A certificate mounted on a plaque is awarded annually.

• 3262 • Twenty-Five Year Membership Medals
To recognize individuals who have been ANA members for twenty-five years. An engraved silver medal is awarded annually.

• 3263 • Melissa Van Grover Youth Exhibit Award
To recognize the top youth exhibitor in Israeli or Judaic numismatic material. A plaque is awarded annually.

• 3264 • Louis S. Werner Host Club Award
To show appreciation to the host club for their dedication, devotion, and assistance in putting together the ANA convention. A plaque with a medal is awarded semi-annually.

• 3265 • Charles H. Wolfe Sr. Youth Best of Show Exhibit Award
To recognize the youth Best-of-Show exhibit. A wooden plaque and a scholarship to the following year's ANA Summer Conference are awarded annually.

• 3266 • Charles H. Wolfe Sr. Youth Exhibit Award
To recognize the top youth exhibitor in medieval and ancient. A plaque is awarded annually.

• 3267 • Howland Wood Memorial Award for Best of Show Exhibit
To recognize the Best-of-Show exhibit. A special wood plaque with a rotating silver medal is awarded annually. Established in 1978.

• 3268 • B. P. Wright Memorial Exhibit Award
To recognize the top three exhibitors in tokens, stamps, and other items used unofficially as a medium for exchange of goods and services. The following awards are presented annually: first place - plaque with gold-plated seal medal; second place - plaque with nickel silver seal medal; and third place plaque with bronze seal medal. Established in 1984.

• 3269 • Farran Zerbe Award
This, ANA's highest award, is given for outstanding contributions to numismatics in general and the Association in particular. Members of the Association who are not officers are eligible. A gold medal is awarded annually at the Convention. Established in 1952.

• 3270 •
American Numismatic Society
Ute Wartenberg, Exec.Dir.
140 William St.
New York, NY 10038
Phone: (212)234-3130
Fax: (212)234-3381
E-mail: info@amnumsoc.org
Home Page: http://www.amnumsoc.org

• 3271 • American Numismatic Society Graduate Fellowship
To provide support for a doctoral dissertation that employs numismatic evidence. Applicants may be from the fields of classical studies, history, archaeology, art history, economic history, or related disciplines and must: have completed the general examinations (or the equivalent), be writing a dissertation during the year in which the use of numismatic evidence plays a significant part and have attended one of the American Numismatic Society's Graduate Seminars prior to the time of application. The society's council reserves the right to waive any of the listed requirements. Applications must be completed by March 1. A fellowship of $3,500 is awarded.

• 3272 • Donald Groves Fund
To promote publication in the field of early American numismatics involving material dating no later than 1800. Funding is available for travel and other expenses in association with research as well as for publication costs. Applications are reviewed periodically by a committee that makes its recommendations to the society's council. Please check our website for updated information.

• 3273 • Archer M. Huntington Medal Award
To recognize outstanding scholarly contributions in the field of numismatics. A silver medal is awarded annually at the meeting in January. Established in 1918 by Archer M. Huntington.

• 3274 • J. Sanford Saltus Medal Award
To recognize sculptors who have achieved merit in the field of medallic art. A medal is awarded at the annual meeting in January. Awarded irregularly since 1919 and annually since 1983. Established in 1919 by J. Sanford Saltus.

• 3275 •
American Nurses Association
Barbara A. Blakeney, Pres.
8515 Georgia Ave., Ste. 400
Silver Spring, MD 20910
Phone: (301)628-5000
Toll-Free: 800-274-4262
Fax: (301)628-5001
E-mail: memberinfo@ana.org
Home Page: http://www.nursingworld.org

• 3276 • CMA Affirmative Action Award
To recognize a constituent state nurses' association demonstrating outstanding development in implementation of affirmative action policy and programming that encourages the elimination of all barriers preventing the full participation of minorities in the total organizational programming. The deadline for nominations is August 31st. Awarded biennially. Established in 1988.

• 3277 • Distinguished Membership Award
To recognize outstanding leadership and participation in and contributions to the purposes of the Association by a member(s). Nominees must be members of the nursing profession and the association for at least 10 years; held an elective national office; and demonstrate leadership. The deadline for nominations is August 31st. Awarded biennially. Established in 1967. Formerly: (1966) Honorary Membership Award.

• 3278 • Honorary Human Rights Award
For recognition of an outstanding commitment to human rights and exemplifying the essence of nursing's philosophy about humanity. Current SNA members are eligible. The deadline for nominations is August 31st. Awarded biennially. Established in 1985.

• 3279 • Honorary Nursing Practice Award
To recognize a registered nurse whose practice is devoted to direct patient care. Registered nurses who through strength of character, commitment, and competence are recognized by peers as having contributed to outstanding nursing practice are eligible. Eligible nurses also should participate in community and organizational affairs, demonstrate an ability to work with others, and have an innovative outlook. The deadline for nominations is August 31st. The nominee must be a current member. Awarded biennially. Established in 1974. Formerly: Honorary Nurse Practitioner Award.

• 3280 • Honorary Recognition Award
To recognize persons who have rendered distinguished service or valuable assistance to the nursing profession and whose contributions and/or accomplishments are of national or inter-

national significance to nursing. United States citizens are eligible. If nominees are nurses, they must be a current SNA member for at least 10 consecutive years. The deadline for nominations is August 31st. Awarded biennially. Established in 1954.

• 3281 • **Mary Mahoney Award**
To honor an individual nurse or group of nurses for significant contributions to opening and advancing equal opportunities in nursing to members of minority groups and who have also made a significant contribution to nursing. The impact of the contribution toward the integration, retention, and advancement of minorities must be current and demonstrate that the outcome has had an effect on nursing and on the advancement of intergroup relations. The deadline for nominations is August 31st. Awarded biennially. Established in 1936 by the National Association of Colored Graduate Nurses in honor of Mary Eliza Mahoney, the first African-American nurse in the United States, and her efforts to raise the status of African-American nurses in professional life. Awarded by the ANA since 1952 following dissolution of the NACGN.

• 3282 • **Pearl McIver Public Health Nurse Award**
Recognizes contributions of a public health nurse. Nominees must be CMA members; have expertise in professional and technical performance; show leadership in the field; and participate in the Association. The deadline for nomination is August 31. Awarded biennially. Established in 1956 as a lasting tribute to Pearl McIver, a noted public health nurse for 35 years.

• 3283 • **Hildegard Peplau Award**
Recognizes a nurse who has made significant, lifetime contributions to nursing practice through scholarly activities, clinical practice, and policy development, specifically directed towards the psychosocial and psychiatric aspects of nursing care delivery. Current SNA members are eligible. A pin is awarded biennially. Established in 1990 to honor Hildegard Peplau, a major force within the profession and discipline of nursing for over three decades.

• 3284 • **Jessie M. Scott Award**
To recognize a registered nurse whose accomplishments in a field of practice, education, or research demonstrate the interdependence of these elements and their significance for the improvement of nursing and health care. Selection is based on the following criteria: nominees must be a registered nurse who has demonstrated the interdependent relationships among nursing practice, nursing education, and nursing research; must agree to present the Jessie M. Scott Lecture at the ANA convention; must be a current SNA member; and must be a citizen of the United States. The deadline for nominations is August 31st. Awarded biennially. Established in 1979 to honor Jessie M. Scott, former assistant surgeon general and director of the Division of Nursing, Health Resources Administration, Public Health Service, U.S. Department of Health, Education, and Welfare.

• 3285 • **Shirley Titus Award**
To recognize nurses for contributions to the Association's economic and general welfare program and for significant national contributions to the program. Nominees must also possess expertise in the professional and technical areas of economic and general welfare. Current SNA members are eligible. The deadline for nominations is August 31st. Awarded when merited. Established in 1976 in honor of Shirley Titus, who devoted her life to progress of nursing in its "tortuous evolution from the status of a craft to the status of a profession."

• 3286 •
American Nurses Foundation
Leo Schargorodski, Exec.Dir.
8515 Georgia Ave., Ste. 400W
Silver Spring, MD 20910
Phone: (202)651-7227
Toll-Free: 800-274-4ANA
Fax: (202)651-7354
E-mail: anf@ana.org
Home Page: http://www.nursingworld.org/anf

• 3287 • **Distinguished Contribution to Nursing Science Award**
To recognize significant contributions made by a registered nurse to the field of nursing research. U.S. registered nurses with a minimum of a master's degree who are members of a constituent state association of the American Nurses Association are eligible. A plaque is awarded biennially. Established in 1980.

• 3288 • **Distinguished Scholar Program**
To facilitate analysis of policy related to economics, delivery of nursing services, nursing practice, and nursing education. U.S. registered nurses are named by the ANF Board of Trustees. A grant to conduct a project is awarded when determined by the ANF Board of Trustees. Established in 1984.

• 3289 •
American Occupational Therapy Association
Frederick P. Somers JD, Exec.Dir.
4720 Montgomery Ln.
PO Box 31220
Bethesda, MD 20824-1220
Phone: (301)652-2682
Phone: (301)652-6611
Toll-Free: 800-377-8555
Fax: (301)652-7711
E-mail: aotapresident@aol.com
Home Page: http://www.aota.org

• 3290 • **Academy of Research Honorary Member**
To recognize excellence and sustained contributions to the development of occupational therapy theory and practice. Scholarly achievement through research and publication are the criteria considered for the award. Membership in an honorary Academy of Research, an inscribed plaque, and a lapel pin bearing the logo of the Academy are awarded. Established in 1983. The first ten recipients are named charter members.

• 3291 • **Award of Merit**
This, the highest honor of the Association, is given to recognize outstanding global contributions to the profession of occupational therapy. The nominee must be an occupational therapist, registered, and a member in good standing of the Association at the time of nomination and on January 15 of the year the award is presented. Nominees must have made an outstanding global contribution to the profession of occupational therapy that enhances the quality of life and must have served as leaders within the professional and the health care community, fostering growth and development of the profession and the Association. A certificate is awarded annually. Established in 1950.

• 3292 • **Lindy Boggs Award**
To recognize significant contributions by an OTR or a COTA in promoting occupational therapy in the political arena by increasing recognition of the field in federal or state legislations, regulations, and/or policies, or by increasing appreciation and understanding of occupational therapy by elected or appointed officials and to provide an incentive for others to take an active role in the legislation process, advocacy, and/or policy making that affects occupational therapy. Nominees must be members of the Association in good standing at the time of the nomination and on Jan. 15 of the year in which the award is presented, and must have demonstrated outstanding participation in one or more of the following categories: training and organizing therapists to take part in federal or state legislation, regulations, and/or policies; the education of legislators or other key government officials in the purpose and function of occupational therapy; response to requests for action from the Government and Legal Affairs Division of the Association; advocacy for consumers of health care and educational services; and state activities related to AOTA/PAC and/or state PACs. A certificate is awarded annually at the AOTA Conference. Established in 1983 in honor of Coreen C. (Lindy) Boggs, U.S. Congresswoman of Louisiana.

• 3293 • **Terry Brittell COTA/OTR Partnership Award**
To recognize a certified occupational therapy assistant and a registered occupational therapist who, through their collaborative efforts to promote the profession of occupational therapy, exemplify the professional partnership, and to provide an incentive for other COTA/OTR partnerships to contribute to the advancement of occupational therapy through a COTA/OTR partnership. The nominees must be a certified occupational therapy assistant and a registered occupational therapist, who are both members in good standing of the Association at the time of the nomination and on January 15 of the year that the award is presented. Two certificates designating the partnership as a recipient of the COTA/OTR Partnership Award are presented. Formerly: AOTA COTA/OTR Partnership Award.

• 3294 • Certificate of Appreciation
To recognize contributions to the profession of occupational therapy, including financial contributions, political support, pioneer work, or outstanding leadership role. Members whose services or contributions are clearly beyond those of normal professional duties and nonmembers whose services or contributions have markedly benefited occupational therapy are eligible. A certificate is awarded annually. Established in 1973.

• 3295 • COTA Award of Excellence
To recognize contribution(s) of the certified occupational therapy assistant to the advancement of occupational therapy, and to provide an incentive to contribute to the development and growth of the profession. Nominees must be certified occupational therapy assistants and members in good standing of the Association at the time of nomination and on January 15 of the year the award is presented. Areas where excellence has been demonstrated might include but are not limited to: clinical practice, administration, education, and/or communication. A certificate is awarded at the annual conference and the winner is named to the Roster of Honor of the Association. The Award of Excellence is the highest Association honor for a COTA.

• 3296 • Health Advocate Award
For recognition of extraordinary contributions of national significance that led to the advancement of health and health care. Nominees may be members in good standing at the time of nomination or nonmembers who have made significant contributions towards the advancement of health and health care. These contributions may include, but are not limited to: legislation, political support of health care, financial contributions, and leadership in improving health care. A certificate is awarded annually at the AOTA Conference. Established in 1983.

• 3297 • Cordelia Myers Writers Award
For recognition of an outstanding article written by a first-time contributor to the *American Journal of Occupational Therapy*. A certificate is presented each year at the AOTA Annual Conference. Established in 1983.

• 3298 • Roster of Fellows
To recognize members of the Association who, with their knowledge and expertise, have made significant contributions to the profession of occupational therapy through therapeutic practice, education, research and/or administration. Members of the Association in good standing who are registered occupational therapists are eligible. A certificate is awarded annually. Established in 1973.

• 3299 • Roster of Honor
To recognize members of the Association who, with their knowledge and expertise, have made a significant contribution to the continuing education and professional development of members of the Association. Nominees must be certified occupational therapy assistants, members in good standing of the Association, and contribute through therapeutic practice, education, administration/supervision, or research. Certified occupational therapy assistant recipients of the Eleanor Clarke Slagle Lectureship or COTA Award of Excellence are named to the Roster of Honor. A certificate is awarded. Established in 1982.

• 3300 • Service Award
To recognize individuals who have provided service to the Association and/or profession through time- ortask-limited activities. Nominees may be an individual or group of individuals who are not members of the association. They may also be registered occupational therapists or certified occupational therapy assistants, or students and members in good standing of the Association who have served in national offices. Chairs of standing and ad hoc committees of the executive board, officials of the Representative Assembly, or committee chairs of the Representative Assembly and Association senior officers are automatically given the award. A certificate is awarded.

• 3301 • Eleanor Clarke Slagle Lectureship
To honor a member of the Association who has creatively contributed to the development of the body of knowledge of the profession, through research, education and/or clinical practice. To acknowledge the development of theory, standards and improved methods that enhance service to consumers and promote public awareness and understanding of occupational therapy. Nominees shall be an OTR or COTA, and a member in good standing of the Association who have shared knowledge and inspired others through both written communications (publications) and oral presentations (workshops, lectures, seminars, conference presentations). Individual Association members or a group of members, such as a state association, who are in good standing at the time of the nomination and on January 15 of the year in which the award is presented, are eligible to submit nominations. A monetary prize and an inscribed plaque highlighting the awardee's contributions and the year selected are awarded annually when merited. Established in 1955 in memory of Eleanor Clarke Slagle, one of the outstanding pioneers in the profession of occupational therapy.

• 3302 •
American Occupational Therapy Foundation
Martha Kirkland, Exec.Dir.
4720 Montgomery Ln.
PO Box 31220
Bethesda, MD 20824-1220
Phone: (301)652-6611
Toll-Free: 800-729-2682
Fax: (301)656-3620
E-mail: aotf@aotf.org
Home Page: http://www.aotf.org

• 3303 • American Occupational Therapy Foundation Awards
To recognize individuals and organizations for outstanding contributions to the field of occupational therapy. The following awards are presented: Honorary Life Membership, A. Jean Ayers Award, Meritorious Service Award, and Certificate of Appreciation.

• 3304 •
American Oil Chemists' Society
Jean Wills, Exec.Dir.
2211 W Bradley Ave.
PO Box 3489
Champaign, IL 61821-1827
Phone: (217)359-2344
Fax: (217)351-8091
E-mail: general@aocs.org
Home Page: http://www.aocs.org

• 3305 • AOCS/Supelco Research Award
To recognize outstanding original research in lipid chemistry, the results of which have been presented through publications of high quality. Preference is given to those individuals actively involved in lipid research whose work has affected large segments of the lipid field. A monetary award of $8000 and an engraved plaque are awarded annually when merited. Established in 1964.

• 3306 • Award of Merit
For recognition of outstanding service to the society. Members of the society are eligible. An engraved plaque is awarded annually when merited to one or more individuals. Established in 1967.

• 3307 • Alton E. Bailey Award
To recognize outstanding research or outstanding service in the field of fats, oils, waxes, their constituents or allied and associated products. An engraved certificate is awarded annually. Established in 1959 by the North Central Section of the Society.

• 3308 • A. Richard Baldwin Distinguished Service Award
To recognize individuals for long-term, distinguished service to the American Oil Chemists' Society in positions of significant responsibility. An honorarium of $2,000 is awarded. Established in 1981. Sponsored by Cargill, Inc.

• 3309 • Stephen S. Chang Award
To recognize researchers who have made significant accomplishments in the utilization of basic research to solve problems which lead to the improvement or development of food products related to lipids. A honorarium award of approximately $6,000 and a jade horse symbolizing the award are awarded annually at the AOCS National Meeting. Established in 1990 by Stephen S. Chang and Lucy D. Chang.

• 3310 • Honored Student Award
To recognize outstanding students. Graduate students at any institution of higher learning, in

any area of science dealing with fats and lipids, who are doing research toward an advanced degree and who are interested in the areas of science and technology fostered by AOCS are eligible. Travel expenses to attend the AOCS annual meeting are awarded.

• 3311 • Ralph H. Potts Memorial Fellowship Award
To promote research in the field of fats and oils. Graduate students at any North American Institution working in the chemistry of fats and oils and their derivatives are eligible. An honorarium of $1,000, a plaque, and a travel allowance are awarded annually at the national meeting. Established in 1960 to honor Ralph H. Potts, a pioneer in industrial research and technology of fatty acids. Sponsored by Akzo Chemical America. Additional information is available from Gerald Szajer, Akzo Nobel, Inc. 1 Livingstone Ave., Dobbs Ferry, NY 10522.

• 3312 •
American Ophthalmological Society
Charles P. Wilkinson MD, Sec.Treas.
PO Box 193940
San Francisco, CA 94119-3940
Phone: (415)561-8578
Fax: (415)561-8531
E-mail: admin@aosonline.org
Home Page: http://www.aosonline.org

• 3313 • Howe Medal
For recognition of outstanding service by an ophthalmologist in the clinical area, administration, or research in the field of ophthalmology. A medal is awarded annually. Established in 1921 in memory of Lucien Howe, M.D.

• 3314 •
American Optometric Association
Michael D. Jones, Exec.Dir.
243 N Lindbergh Blvd.
St. Louis, MO 63141
Phone: (314)991-4100
Fax: (314)991-4101
Home Page: http://www.aoanet.org/

• 3315 • Apollo Award
Recognizes individuals organizations, educational institutions, or programs outside of optometry who have made, or are making significant contributions to the visual welfare of Americans. The nomination deadline is December 1. A bronze trophy of Phoebus Apollo is awarded annually at the national meeting in June. Established in 1961.

• 3316 • Distinguished Service Award
Recognizes an optometrist unusually significant contributions and outstanding achievements contributing to the advancement of the profession. Of optometry. A plaque is awarded annually. Established in 1980.

• 3317 • National Optometrist of the Year Award
Recognizes an optometrist for outstanding service on behalf of the profession and to the visual welfare of the public. Members of the Association are eligible for nomination by May 1. A plaque is awarded annually at the national meeting in June. Established in 1967.

• 3318 • Young Optometrist of the Year
Recognizes an optometrist who have been in practice less than 10 years and shows remarkable leadership skills when serving their patients, their profession, and their community. Nominations must be channeled through the appropriate state optometric association. The deadline for nominations is May 1. Awarded annually at the AOA national meeting in June. Established in 1995.

• 3319 •
American Orchid Society
Lee S. Cooke, Exec.Dir.
16700 AOS Ln.
Delray Beach, FL 33446-4351
Phone: (561)404-2000
Fax: (561)404-2100
E-mail: theaos@aos.org
Home Page: http://www.aos.org

• 3320 • AOS Show Trophy
To encourage the improvement of the standards of exhibits at any show staged by an affiliated society within or outside the United States that has conformed to the procedures for securing AOS sanction for the show, including the exclusive use of AOS judges for award judging. It is intended that this trophy encourage excellence by recognizing in competition the best collective material meritoriously displayed in public exhibition. The awarding of the trophy is not obligatory. The pooling of resources by groups or individuals is permitted. The following regulations apply: all certified judges present may participate in the decision whether or not to award the trophy; nominations may be made and the balloting based on these nominations; to qualify for the trophy, two-thirds of the judges must vote in favor of some exhibit, and the winning exhibit must receive a majority of the votes cast. In the event of a tie or where no majority is obtained, new ballots may be cast; and only those exhibits receiving the two highest vote totals will be considered. An exhibit must be scored by each judge and a favorable vote must consist of a score of at least 80 points. The factor of labeling is evaluated on completeness, correctness of names, neatness, and legibility to the viewing public.

• 3321 • Artistic Certificate (for Artistic Display of Orchids in Use)
For recognition of an outstanding exhibit that the judges consider to be exceptionally artistic. No restriction is applied to the class of exhibitor, whether an amateur, commercial, or professional florist. The award is given only upon the unanimous decision of the judging team assigned. Judges are expected to consider the exhibit with the point scale in mind. Although actual point scoring is optional, no award should be made to an exhibit that a judge believes could not score at least 90 points. Awarded when merited.

• 3322 • Award of Distinction
For recognition of a crossbreeding, exhibited individually or collectively, representing a worthy new direction in breeding. The award is granted unanimously without scoring by the judging team assigned. If the hybridizer and exhibitor are different, each receives a certificate. Awarded when merited.

• 3323 • Award of Merit
For recognition of an orchid species or hybrid of excellent quality that scores between 80 and 89 points inclusive on the point scales. A certificate is awarded when merited.

• 3324 • Award of Quality
For recognition of crossbreeding, exhibited by a single individual as a group of not less than 12 clones or the inflorescences thereof of a raised species or hybrid that may or may not have been made before when the result is a sufficient improvement over the former type. It is granted unanimously, without scoring by the judging team assigned. If the hybridizer and exhibitor are different, each receives a certificate. Awarded when merited.

• 3325 • Butterworth Prize
To recognize the grower of the orchid plant, either species or hybrid, which is regarded as the most outstanding example of orchid culture to have been awarded a Certificate of Cultural Merit or Certificate of Cultural Excellence during the preceding calendar year. A nomination is made by each regional committee and forwarded with the appropriate color transparencies to the Judging Committee Chair at least 60 days prior to the fall meeting of the Board of Trustees. A monetary prize is awarded annually. Established in 1966 through the gift to AOS from Mrs. Rachel Butterworth Dietz in memory of her parents, John and Nancy Butterworth, and of George Butterworth, past president of AOS.

• 3326 • Certificate of Botanical Recognition
For recognition of a species or natural hybrid deemed worthy of recognition for rarity, novelty, and educational value. The entire plant must be exhibited and not just the inflorescense. The plant need not have special horticultural desirability. No award of any kind may have previously been made to the species as a taxon. No point scale is used, but the award is granted only by the affirmative vote of at least two-thirds of the judging team assigned. Awarded provisionally and filed with the regional chairman pending the exhibitor supplying full taxonomic verification by a taxonomist acceptable to AOS. A species or natural hybrid shall not receive, at the same judging, a CBR and a CHM. Awarded when merited.

• 3327 • **Certificate of Cultural Merit**
To recognize the exhibitor of a specimen plant of robust health and appearance with an unusually large number of flowers. The plant must have been in the care of the exhibitor at least six months immediately prior to the award. The plant must score at least 80 points on the point scale. Awarded when merited.

• 3328 • **Certificate of Meritorious Arrangement**
For recognition of an outstanding exhibit in the flower arrangement class of a show in which orchid flowers are dominant. This certificate is available to AOS-sanctioned shows and may be awarded by nationally accredited decorative or flower arrangement judges. If judges without these qualifications are used to judge flower arrangements, they may recommend an award, but the recommendation must be concurred by a team of AOS certified judges assigned for the purpose. The following stipulations apply: there must not be a limitation on size, orchids must be dominant in the arrangement, and orchid flowers need not have been grown by the exhibitor. Corsages are considered arrangements for purposes of this award. The award is presented only once at any show. If nationally-accredited flower show judges present the award, this fact will be noted and authenticated by the chairman on the summary sheet. Photographic records are not required.

• 3329 • **Educational Exhibit**
For recognition of an educational exhibit of outstanding excellence that scores at least 80 points on the point scale. Awarded when merited.

• 3330 • **First Class Certificate**
For recognition of an orchid species or hybrid of outstanding excellence that scores 90 points or more on the point scales. A certificate is awarded when merited.

• 3331 • **Gold Certificate**
For recognition of groups, collections, or cut flower exhibits that score at least 90 points on the point scale. Awarded when merited.

• 3332 • **Gold Medal of Achievement**
To recognize an individual for distinguished work in orchid culture or in scientific research on orchids and for outstanding service to AOS. The Board of Trustees makes the selection. A gold medal is awarded when merited.

• 3333 • **Highly Commended Certificate**
For recognition of an orchid species or hybrid that scores between 75 and 79 points inclusive on the point scales. Awarded when merited.

• 3334 • **Ann and Phil Jessup Botanical Trophy**
To recognize the grower of the orchid species plant that is regarded as the most outstanding orchid species having received an award during the previous calendar year. A nomination is made by each regional committee and forwarded with appropriate color transparencies to the Judging Committee Chair at least 60 days prior to the fall meeting of the Board of Trustees. Formerly: (2004) Nax Trophy.

• 3335 • **Judges' Commendation**
For recognition of flowers or plants, individually or in groups, for a distinctive characteristic or aspect of historical or other importance, which in the opinion of the judges, are worthy of recognition. Judges' commendations must record the specific values for which the award is given. Granted unanimously, without scoring by at least 75% of the judging team assigned. Awarded when merited.

• 3336 • **Silver Medal of Merit**
To recognize an individual for outstanding service to AOS or some major contribution to the orchid world. The Board of Trustees makes the selection. Awarded when merited.

• 3337 • **W. W. Wilson Cypridedioideae Award**
To recognize the grower of an orchid plant, either species or hybrid, regarded as the most outstanding example of the cypripedium alliance to have been awarded during the preceding calendar year. Nominations may be made by regional judges and forwarded with the appropriate color transparencies and award descriptions to the Judging Committee Chair at least 60 days prior to the fall meeting of the Board of Trustees. A certificate is awarded annually. Established in 1990 in honor of Dr. William W. Wilson.

• 3338 •
American Ornithologists' Union
Ross Lein, Sec.
1313 Dolley Madison Blvd., Ste. 402
Mc Lean, VA 22101
Phone: (703)790-1745
Fax: (202)633-8084
E-mail: aou@aou.com
Home Page: http://www.aou.org

• 3339 • **William Brewster Memorial Award**
To encourage the study of Western Hemisphere birds and to recognize the author of the most important work relating in whole or in major part to the birds of the Western Hemisphere during the past ten years. Recipients are selected by a committee. A medal and an honorarium are awarded annually at a banquet during the annual meeting. Established in 1919 by the friends and co-workers of William Brewster.

• 3340 • **Elliott Coues Award**
For recognition of contributions that have had an important impact on the study of birds within the Western Hemisphere. Recipients are selected by a committee. A certificate is awarded annually at a banquet during the annual meeting. Established in 1971 in memory of Elliott Coues.

• 3341 •
American ORT
Jeffrey M. Reiff, Ch.
817 Broadway, 10th Fl.
New York, NY 10003-4756
Phone: (212)353-5800
Toll-Free: 800-364-9678
Fax: (212)353-5888
E-mail: info@aort.org
Home Page: http://www.aort.org

• 3342 • **American ORT Chapter of the Year**
Annual award of recognition.

• 3343 • **Paul Bennick New Leadership Award**
Annual award of recognition. Chapter supporter of the year awards, annual awards (12) of recognition.

• 3344 • **William Haber Prize**
Recognizes commitment and leadership in the organization. Awarded annually.

• 3345 • **Man of the Year Award**
Annual award of recognition.

• 3346 • **Yitzah Rabin Award**
Award of recognition.

• 3347 •
American Orthodontic Society
Tom Chapman, Exec.Dir.
11884 Greenville Ave., No. 112
Dallas, TX 75243-3537
Phone: (972)234-4000
Phone: (972)234-4067
Toll-Free: 800-448-1601
Fax: (972)234-4290
E-mail: tchapman@orthodontic.com
Home Page: http://www.orthodontics.com

• 3348 • **Dr. Richard L. Moore Distinguished Service Award**
Recognizes an outstanding contribution to organized dentistry in the field of orthodontics. Awarded annually.

• 3349 •
American Orthopaedic Society for Sports Medicine
Irvin E. Bomberger, Exec.Dir.
6300 N River Rd., Ste. 500
Rosemont, IL 60018
Phone: (847)292-4900
Toll-Free: 877-321-3500
Fax: (847)292-4905
E-mail: irv@aossm.org
Home Page: http://www.sportsmed.org

• 3350 • **Cabaud Memorial Award**
Recognizes the best overall paper that exemplifies clinically relevant hypotheses driven basic science research, including hard or soft tissue biology, in-vitro research, labortory or bench-

type research or in-vivo animal research. An honorarium of $500, a plaque, and an invitation to deliver the award lecture at the annual meeting are awarded annually. Consideration of publication in *The American Journal of Sports Medicine* is also given.

• 3351 • Excellence in Research Awards
To recognize the best overall paper submitted in any category by an original author under the age of 40. Only papers completed by the AOSSM's annual summer meeting are accepted. Papers are reviewed and evaluated with emphasis on scientific merit, quality of composition, and possible clinical impact relevant to sports medicine. The award consists of $1,000 to the principal investigator and $1,500 to the sponsoring institution, a plaque, an invitation to deliver the award lecture at the annual meeting, and consideration of publication in the *American Journal of Sports Medicine.*

• 3352 • O'Donoghue Sports Injury Research Award
To provide recognition for outstanding clinical or laboratory-based research efforts that are applicable to the understanding, care, or prevention of injuries in sports. An honorarium of $2,500, a certificate or plaque, an invitation to deliver the award lecture at the annual meeting, and consideration of publication of the manuscript in the *American Journal of Sports Medicine* are awarded annually prior to the annual meeting in July.

• 3353 •
American Osteopathic Academy of Orthopedics
Morton Morris DOJD, Exec.Dir.
PO Box 291690
Davie, FL 33329-1690
Phone: (954)262-1700
Toll-Free: 800-741-2626
Fax: (954)262-1748
E-mail: exec@aoao.org
Home Page: http://www.aoao.org

• 3354 • Award of Fellow
For professional recognition by peers in the field of orthopedics. Fellows of the Academy may nominate members of the Academy. A medal and a certificate are awarded annually at the convention. Established in 1975.

• 3355 • President's Appreciative Award
To recognize a member of the profession who has made an outstanding contribution, preferably related to orthopedics.

• 3356 •
American Osteopathic College of Pathologists
Jason Friske, Interim Exec.Dir.
142 E Ontario St.
Chicago, IL 60611-8224
Phone: (312)202-8197
Fax: (312)202-8224
Home Page: http://www.aocp-net.org

• 3357 • Fellow
To recognize outstanding contributions to the practice, teaching or administration of pathology. Members of the College are eligible. A certificate is awarded annually. Established in 1960.

• 3358 •
American Otological Society
Dr. Shirley Gossard, Admin.Off.
2720 Tartan Way
Springfield, IL 62711
Phone: (217)483-6966
Fax: (217)483-6966
E-mail: segossard@aol.com
Home Page: http://www.americanotologicalsociety.org

• 3359 • Award of Merit
For recognition of outstanding accomplishment and distinguished service in the field of otology. Members are eligible. An honorarium, a medal, and a certificate are awarded each year at the annual meeting. Established in 1948.

• 3360 • Honorary Member
To recognize individuals for outstanding service to the Society.

• 3361 •
American Park and Recreation Society
John A. Thorner CPRP, Exec.Dir.
22377 Belmont Ridge Rd.
Ashburn, VA 20148-4150
Phone: (703)858-0784
Fax: (703)858-0794
E-mail: info@nrpa.org
Home Page: http://www.nrpa.org/content/default.aspx?documentId=

• 3362 • Distinguished Fellow
This, the highest award of the Society, is given for outstanding service and leadership. The eligibility requirements are: (1) membership in APRS; (2) bachelor's degree or equivalent in study; (3) at least ten years experience in the general field of parks and/or recreation; (4) substantial contribution to the profession on a national level and/or to APRS; and (5) fine moral character.

• 3363 • Meritorious Service Award
For recognition of special achievement through a specific program, project, event, or contribution of exceptional merit which has extensively and directly benefited the public at large. Awards are given in the following categories: (1) Professional - open to members of the Society or any other member in the professional branches of the National Recreation and Park Association; (2) Young Professional - open to members of the Society who are 29 years of age or less as of November 1 in the nominating year; and (3) Citizen - open to any individual who is not a member of the Society or any other professional branch of the National Recreation and Park Association. Established in 1977.

• 3364 •
American Parkinson Disease Association
K.G. Whitford, Contact
1250 Hylan Blvd., Ste. 4B
Staten Island, NY 10305-1946
Phone: (718)981-8001
Toll-Free: 800-223-2732
Fax: (718)981-4399
E-mail: apda@apdaparkinson.org
Home Page: http://www.apdaparkinson.com

• 3365 • Fred Springer Award
To recognize an individual for research in Parkinson's disease. A monetary award of $10,000 is presented annually. Established in 1989 to honor Fred Springer, former president of the association.

• 3366 •
American Peanut Council
Patrick Archer, Pres.
1500 King St., Ste. 301
Alexandria, VA 22314
Phone: (703)838-9500
Fax: (703)838-9508
E-mail: info@peanutsusa.com
Home Page: http://www.peanutsusa.com

Formerly: National Peanut Council.

• 3367 • Peanut Hall of Fame
Recognizes life-time achievement.

• 3368 • Peanut Research and Education Award
To stimulate and encourage research and education, including extension service, among those persons engaged in projects dealing with peanuts or peanut products, and to recognize outstanding achievement in peanut research and education projects that benefit the entire peanut industry. Any person or team conducting peanut research and education in any segment of a state government, the federal government (including all USDA/University research groups), the private sector, or an employee(s) of the cooperative extension service is eligible. Entries may be submitted by any individual or a group engaged in or familiar with peanut research achievements in the areas of production, processing, storage, marketing, or manufacturing or by those familiar with extension field services as they relate to peanut production, processing, storage, marketing, or other meaningful work to the industry. A monetary award of $1,000, a gold finished bronze plaque mounted on hand-rubbed walnut, and an expense paid trip for two to the annual convention of the USA Peanut Congress are awarded annually. Established in 1960. Formerly: Golden Peanut Research and Education Award.

• 3369 •
American Pediatric Society
Kathy A. Cannon, Assoc.Exec.Dir.
3400 Research Forest Dr., Ste. B7
The Woodlands, TX 77381-4259
Phone: (281)419-0052
Fax: (281)419-0082
E-mail: info@aps-spr.org
Home Page: http://www.aps-spr.org

• 3370 • **John Howland Award**

To recognize outstanding contributions to pediatrics that have aided the advancement of the profession. A bronze medal is awarded annually. Established in 1952.

• 3371 •
American Pet Products Manufacturer Association
Robert Vetere, COO/Mktg. Dir.
255 Glenville Rd.
Greenwich, CT 06831
Phone: (203)532-0000
Toll-Free: 800-452-1225
Fax: (203)532-0551
E-mail: info@appma.org
Home Page: http://www.appma.org

• 3372 • **New Product Showcase Award**

Award of recognition for best new products exhibited at trade show. Awarded annually. 62771747

• 3373 •
American Petroleum Institute
Jim Craig, Dir.
1220 L St. NW
Washington, DC 20005-4070
Phone: (202)682-8000
Fax: (202)682-8029
Fax: (202)682-8029
E-mail: craigj@api.org
Home Page: http://www.api.org

• 3374 • **Gold Medal**

To recognize an individual for substantial contributions or advancements to the arts and sciences of the petroleum industry, its human relations, its business practices, and its organization, when such contributions have enabled the industry to serve the public welfare better. There are no limitations with respect to either nationality or membership in the American Petroleum Institute. The candidate must be living, and able and willing to present himself in person at the time of the award. Officers and employees of the API are ineligible during their term of office. Awarded annually. Established in 1946.

• 3375 •
American Pharmacists Association
John A. Gans, EVP and CEO
2215 Constitution Ave. NW
Washington, DC 20037-2985
Phone: (202)628-4410
Toll-Free: 800-237-APHA
Fax: (202)783-2351
E-mail: apha-appm@mail.phanet.org
Home Page: http://www.aphanet.org

• 3376 • **Academy of Pharmaceutical Research and Science Fellow**

To recognize members of the Academy of Pharmaceutical Research and Science who have demonstrated progressive, exemplary service and achievement in the pharmaceutical sciences and professional practice. Fellows also have rendered above average service to the profession through activities in APhA and its academies, and in other national, state and local professional organizations. Any APRS member may nominate a scientist for the honor. APRS Fellows receive framed certificates during the APhA Annual Meeting.

• 3377 • **Academy of Pharmacy Practice and Management Fellow**

To recognize members of the Academy of Pharmacy Practice and Management who have demonstrated progressive and exemplary experience and above average achievements in professional practice. Fellows also have rendered above average service to the profession through activities in APhA and its academies, and in other national, state and local professional organizations. Any APPM member may nominate a practitioner for the honor. APPM Fellows receive framed certificates during the APhA Annual Meeting.

• 3378 • **American Pharmacists Association Fellows**

Open to Academy members who have shown exemplary service and achievement in their specialized field. Awarded regardless of Academy affiliation, a board still makes the final decision on the winner.

• 3379 • **APHA - APPM Merit Awards**

To recognize individual pharmacy practitioners for singular, significant contributions to pharmacy practice. Awarded annually. Established in 1988.

• 3380 • **William H. Briner Nuclear Pharmacy Practice Award**

For a significant contribution or sustained contributions to the provision of pharmaceutical care within the practice of nuclear pharmacy.

• 3381 • **Distinguished Achievement Award in Clinical/Pharmacotherapeutic Practice**

Recognizes the achievements of individuals who have made significant contributions or sustained contributions to the provision of pharmaceutical care in clinical or pharmacotheraputic practice.

• 3382 • **Distinguished Achievement Award in Community and Ambulatory Practice**

Recognizes the achievements who have made significant contributions or sustained contributions to the provision of pharmaceutical care in community and ambulatory care.

• 3383 • **Distinguished Achievement Award in Hospital and Institutional Practice**

Recognizes the achievements of individuals who have made significant contributions or sustained contributions to the provision of pharmaceutical care in hospital and institutional practices.

• 3384 • **Distinguished Achievement Award in Specialized Pharmaceutical Services**

For significant contributions or continued contributions to the provision of special pharmaceutical services.

• 3385 • **H. A. B. Dunning Award**

Recognizes outstanding assistance to the field of Pharmacy. Applicants must be pharmaceutical manufacturing firm. Presented annually at the Annual Meeting. Nominations may be submitted by members by December 31. Established in 1984 in memory of the pharmacist Henry Armitt Brown Dunning (1877-1962), who as a long-standing APhA leader was instrumental in the funding and building of the APhA headquarters building in Washington, D.C.

• 3386 • **Ebert Prize**

This, the oldest pharmacy award in the United States, is given to recognize the author of the best report of original investigation of a medicinal substance published in the *Journal of Pharmaceutical Sciences* in the past year. A silver medal and certificate are awarded annually at the national meeting. Established in 1873 by Albert E. Ebert, then the residing President of APhA.

• 3387 • **Gloria Niemeyer Francke Leadership Mentor Award**

Recognizes individuals who have promoted and encouraged pharmacists to attain leadership roles in pharmacy through examples as role models and mentors. A monetary prize of $1,000, a crystal plaque, and travel expenses are awarded annually. Established in 1995.

• 3388 • **Good Government Pharmacist of the Year Award**

To recognize an individual pharmacist who actively contributes to the community through his or her involvement in the political process. Any APhA member may nominate individuals who are active members of APhA and a state pharmacy association. APhA and state association staff members, lobbyists, and state or federal officials are not eligible. The government affairs activity in which the nominee participated must have raised pharmacists' awareness of the political process, improved the pharmacy profession and the political process, as well as improved service and education to the patient. The activity may not necessarily have been issue-specific or resulted in passed legislation. Awarded annually. Established in 1992. Sponsored by Glaxo, Inc.

• 3389 • Takeru Higuchi Research Prize
To recognize a scientist who has demonstrated effective and persistent efforts in pioneering a new concept applicable to the pharmaceutical sciences. The prize consists of a bronze medal and an honorarium, and is bestowed no more frequently than every other year. Established in 1981 in honor of Takeru Higuchi, the first scientific academy President.

• 3390 • Honorary Member
To recognize individuals whose activities and achievements have had a significant impact upon the public health, the profession of pharmacy, and its practitioners. Traditionally, only one honorary member is selected annually.

• 3391 • Honorary President
For recognition of a lifetime of distinguished and dedicated public service and contributions to the profession. A plaque, travel expenses, and one-year term as president are awarded annually. Established in 1979.

• 3392 • Hubert H. Humphrey Award
To recognize APhA members who have made major contributions in government and/or legislative service at the local, state, or national level. A plaque and honorarium are awarded annually at the annual meeting. Established in 1978.

• 3393 • Kilmer Prize
To recognize meritorious work in pharmacognosy or natural products by an undergraduate or graduate pharmacy student. An inscribed gold key, an honorarium of $200, and up to $300 to allow the prize winner to attend the APhA Meeting at which the prize is presented are awarded annually at the national meeting. Co-sponsored by the American Society of Pharmacognosy. Established in 1935 by Dr. Frederick B. Kilmer.

• 3394 • Outstanding Chapter Advisor Award
To recognize advisors of APhA-ASP (Academy of Students of Pharmacy) chapters who have promoted with distinction the welfare of pharmacy students through various professional activities. Awarded annually. Established in 1988.

• 3395 • Postgraduate Best Paper Award
The award recognizes the author of the best contributed paper (podium or poster session) presented at each APhA Annual Meeting by a postgraduate student who must be an APhA member.

• 3396 • Remington Honor Medal
To recognize distinguished service on behalf of American pharmacy during the preceding years, culminating in the past year, or during a long period of outstanding activity or fruitful achievement. The jury consists of all living APhA past presidents. A gold medal is awarded annually at the annual meeting. Established in 1918 by the APhA New York Chapter.

• 3397 • Research Achievement Awards in the Pharmaceutical Services
To recognize individuals for their outstanding research contributions. The following awards are presented: Justin L. Powers Research Achievement Award in Pharmaceutical Analysis, Research Achievement Award in Economic, Social and Administrative Sciences, Sidney Riegelman Research Achievement Award in Pharmaceutics, Research Achievement Award in Pharmacodynamics, Research Achievement Award in Pharmaceutical and Medicinal Chemistry, Research Achievement Award in Natural Products, and Stimulation of Research Award. The award consists of an honorarium, an inscribed certificate and travel expenses to attend the Annual Meeting. Awarded biennially. Established in 1961.

• 3398 • Hugo H. Schaefer Award
To recognize an individual for outstanding voluntary service to APhA and to the profession of pharmacy. A medal is awarded annually at the yearly meeting. Established in 1964 in honor of Hugo Schaefer, for a lifetime of contributions to the profession of pharmacy and the APhA.

• 3399 • Daniel B. Smith Practice Excellence Award
To recognize outstanding professional performance by a pharmacist in any practice setting. A 14K diamond ring is awarded annually. Established in 1964 in honor of Daniel B. Smith, the first president of APhA who was a community pharmacist and president of the Philadelphia College of Pharmacy and Science. In 1995, the Daniel B. Smith Award merged with the Practice Excellence Award to form the current award. Formerly: (1995) Daniel B. Smith Award; (1995) Practice Excellence Award.

• 3400 • Student Leadership Awards
To recognize outstanding academic achievement and leadership ability of students entering their last year of pharmacy school. A plaque and a $500 scholarship are awarded to one or more recipients each year. Established in 1983. Endowed by Procter & Gamble Health Care.

• 3401 • Linwood F. Tice Friend of the APhA-ASP Award
To recognize an individual whose long-term services and contributions have benefited the APhA Academy of Students of Pharmacy, and thereby pharmacy students in general. A crystal statuette and travel expenses are awarded annually. Established in 1988.

• 3402 • Tyler Prize for Stimulation of Research
To recognize an individual for encouraging research by peers, students, fellows, residents, and others via publications or by directing research, serving as a preceptor, or mentoring in any discipline of the pharmaceutical sciences. An engraved plaque, monetary prize of $1,000, and travel expenses are awarded triennially. Established in 1962. Formerly: (2002) Stimulation of Research Award.

• 3403 •
American Philatelic Congress
Roos A. Towle, Contact
400 Clayton St.
San Francisco, CA 94117-1912
E-mail: rosstowle@yahoo.com
Home Page: http://www.americanphilateliccongress.org

• 3404 • Helen August Memorial Award
Recognizes the best article on U.S. postal history or best article on the first day covers in 20th Century. Authors may receive this award only once. Established in 1990 by Leo August, President of Washington Press, through a grant to the Congress, in honor of his late wife.

• 3405 • Jere. Hess Barr Award
Recognizes outstanding philatelic writing and oratory. Selection is based on the quality of presentation and the speaker's handling of the subsequent discussion, if any. Winners need not be Congress members. Established in 1959 in honor of Jere. Hess Barr, a late former President of the Congress and editor of several Congress books. Awarded annually.

• 3406 • Dorothy Colby Memorial Award
Recognizes philatelic writings in periodicals. Entries must have been published during the 18-month period (at least the final part, if serialized) preceding the convention of the Congress, and may be submitted by editors, authors, columnists, or others to the Secretary of the Congress, at least 90 days before the convention. Criteria for evaluation are depth of research and/or study, and quality of writing and illustrations, as concerns articles in the philatelic press; or popular appeal, through subject matter and treatment, in the lay press. Winners need not be Congress members. Established in 1973 in memory of Dorothy Colby, deceased wife of Sylvester Colby, a prominent dealer and Congress member. Awarded annually.

• 3407 • Erani P. Drossos Award
Recognizes excellence in philatelic writing. Selection is based on philatelic knowledge and/or research, thoroughness of treatment and usefulness, and benefit to philately generally. Winners need not be Congress members. Established in 1981 in memory of the late wife of Pandelis J. Drossos, a long-time member of the Congress, dealer, and philatelic author. Awarded annually.

• 3408 • James Waldo Fawcett Award
For recognition of meritorious service to the Congress. Established in 1959 in honor of James Waldo Fawcett, a philatelic journalist who was the first editor of the Congress Book.

• 3409 • Eugene Klein Award
For recognition of the best recent philatelic book written by a Congress member. Entries solicited by the Congress through notices in the U.S. philatelic press must have been published during the two years preceding the convention of the Congress. They may be submitted by editors, authors, or others to the Secretary of the Congress at least 90 days before the convention. Criteria for evaluation are evidence of author's original research in problem solving or problems of importance to philately, as well as verification of the new information. Importance of discoveries, depth of research, and clarity of presentation (text and illustrations) are considered. Established in 1960 in honor of the late founder and first President of the Congress, a dealer and student of philately, especially of ship mail on U.S. waterways. Awarded annually.

• 3410 • Walter R. McCoy Award
For recognition of the best article in the current Congress book, based on philatelic knowledge and/or research, thoroughness of treatment and usefulness and benefit to philately generally. Winners need not be Congress members. The President may appoint the editor as a non-voting advisory member of the jury. The editor and the editorial board, if any, are ineligible for consideration. Established in 1953 in honor of Walter R. McCoy, the late editor of several Congress books. Awarded annually.

• 3411 • Meritorious Service Award
Award of recognition. Inquire for additional information on this award.

• 3412 • C. Corwith Wagner Award
Recognizes philatelic writings on the 19th Century U.S. postal history. The criteria for evaluation are importance (breadth and depth) of contribution to American postal history, quality (originality and soundness) of research, and clarity (organization, simplicity of language) of writing. Winners need not be Congress members. A trophy is awarded annually. Established in 1981 in memory of Corwith Wagner, a student of early U.S. postal history, especially Western territories and expresses as well as inland waterways.

• 3413 •
American Philatelic Society
Robert E. Lamb, Exec.Dir.
100 Oakwood Ave.
PO Box 8000
State College, PA 16803-8000
Phone: (814)237-3803
Fax: (814)237-6128
E-mail: apsinfo@stamps.org
Home Page: http://www.stamps.org

Formerly: (1908) American Philatelic Association.

• 3414 • Champion of Champions
To recognize the winner of the APS World Series of Philately held annually at STAMPSHOW, the Society's convention/exhibition. The World Series of Philately is open to the Grand Award winners from APS certified national exhibitions. The award is the foremost national philatelic exhibition award given in the United States. Established in 1968.

• 3415 • Luff Awards
These most prestigious awards of the Society are awarded to living philatelists in each of the following categories: for distinguished philatelic research; for exceptional contributions to philately; for outstanding service to the American Philatelic Society. Nominations may be made to the Luff Awards Committee. Committee recommendations are submitted to the Board of Directors during the APS Winter Meeting. Presented annually during the APS Summer Convention. Recipients sign the coveted Luff Award Scroll and are presented with engraved rings and individually prepared mementos. Established in 1940 in honor of John N. Luff, philatelic author and APS president, 1907-1909. 1907-1909.

• 3416 • Philatelic Hall of Fame
To recognize outstanding contributions to philately. As many as three deceased philatelists are selected annually. Nominations may be made to the Hall of Fame Committee. Recommendations from the committee are submitted to the APS Board of Directors during the APS annual convention where honorees are announced. A permanent plaque is maintained in the American Philatelic Building. Established in 1941.

• 3417 •
American Philological Association
Adam D. Blistein PhD, Exec.Dir.
Univ. of Pennsylvania
292 Logan Hall
249 S 36th St.
Philadelphia, PA 19104-6304
Phone: (215)898-4975
Toll-Free: 800-548-1784
Fax: (215)573-7874
E-mail: apaclassics@sas.upenn.edu
Home Page: http://www.apaclassics.org

• 3418 • Awards for Excellence in Teaching of the Classics
To recognize and foster excellence in teaching classics at the undergraduate level. One to three monetary awards and certificates are awarded annually. Established in 1979.

• 3419 • Charles J. Goodwin Award of Merit
For recognition of an outstanding contribution to classical scholarship, which may be a book, monograph, or article by a member of the association published before the end of the calendar year preceding each annual meeting. A monetary award and a certificate are awarded annually at the association's annual meeting. Established in 1950 in honor of Charles J. Goodwin for his generous bequest of over $60,000 in 1935. Formerly: (1968) Award of Merit.

• 3420 •
American Philosophical Association
William Mann, Acting Exec.Dir.
University of Delaware
31 Amstel Ave.
Newark, DE 19716
Phone: (302)831-1112
Fax: (302)831-8690
E-mail: apaonline@udel.edu
Home Page: http://www.apa.udel.edu/apa

• 3421 • APA/PDC Prize for Excellence and Innovation in Philosophy Programs
To recognize departments, research centers, institutes, societies, publishers, or other organizations for creating programs that risk undertaking new initatives in philosophy, and do so with excellence and success. Awarded annually, the winner receives $1,000.

• 3422 • Article Prize
The winner of this award is selected by the committee appointed by the Chair of the Committee on Lectures, Publications, and Research, in consultation with LPR committe members. The $2,000 award is given every other year.

• 3423 • David Baumgardt Memorial Fellowship
To recognize an individual whose research has some bearing on the philosophical interests of the late David Baumgardt. Open to candidates of any nationality working in any country. The winning entry is selected by a committee appointed by the Chair of the APA's Committee on Lectures, Publications, and Research in consultation with LPR committee members. A monetary award of $5,000 is presented every five years. Established in 1975.

• 3424 • Fred Berger Memorial Prize
To recognize an outstanding published article in the philosophy of law. The winning entry is selected by the APA's Committee on Philosophy and Law. A monetary award of $500 is awarded biennially in odd-numbered years. Established in 1989.

• 3425 • Book Prize
The winners for this award are selected by a committee appointed by the chair of the Committe on Lectures, Pulications, and Research, in consultation with LPR committee members. The $4,000 prize is awarded every other year.

• 3426 • Carus Lectures
To recognize outstanding contributions to philosophy. The lecturer is selected by a committee appointed by the Chair of the APA's Committee on Lectures, Publications, and Research, in consultation with LPR committee members. A monetary prize of $5,000, plus $5,000 for publication of manuscript by Open Court Publishing Co. is awarded biennially in odd-numbered years. Established in 1925.

• 3427 • Rockefeller Prize

To recognize the best unpublished work in philosophy by a nonacademically affiliated philosopher. The winning entry is selected by a committee appointed by the Chair of the APA's Committee on Lectures, Publications, and Research, in consultation with LPR committee members. A monetary prize of $1,000 is awarded biennially in even-numbered years. Established in 1993. Sponsored by the Rockefeller Foundation.

• 3428 • Patrick Romanell Lecture

To provide a lecture on philosophical naturalism. The lecturer is selected by a committee appointed by the Chair of the APA's Committee on Lectures, Publications, and Research in consultation with LPR committee members. A monetary prize of $1,200, plus a maximum of $750 for travel costs, is awarded annually. The lecture is presented at a divisional meeting of the APA.

• 3429 • Royce Lectures in the Philosophy of the Mind

To provide a lecture on philosophy in accordance with, and in the spirit of, the bequest of Mable Lisle Ducasse and Curt John Ducasse to honor Josiah Royce. The lecturer is selected by a committee appointed by the Chair of the APA's Committee on Lectures, Publications, and Research in consultation with members of the Brown University Philosophy Department. A monetary prize of $4,000, plus $3,000 to be paid upon the submission of the manuscript to a publisher, is awarded every four years.

• 3430 • Schutz Lecture

To provide a lecture on a topic inspired by the work of the late Alfred Schutz, concerning the philosophy of history or the philosophy of the social sciences. The lecturer is selected by a committee appointed by the Chair of the APA's Committee on Lectures, Publications, and Research together with representatives of the Council for Advanced Research in Phenomenology and Society for Phenomenology and Existential Philosophy. The lecture is presented at the meeting of the Society for Phenomenology and the Human Sciences, and published in the *Human Studies Journal.* A monetary prize of $1,000, plus some travel and lodging expenses, is awarded annually. Established in 1968.

• 3431 • Frank Chapman Sharp Memorial Prize

To recognize the best unpublished essay or monograph on the philosophy of war and peace. The lecturer is selected by a committee appointed by the Chair of the APA's Committee on Lectures, Publications, and Research in consultation with LPR committee members. A monetary prize of $1,500 is awarded biennially in odd-numbered years. Established in 1991.

• 3432 •

American Philosophical Society
Frank H.T. Rhodes, Pres.
104 S 5th St.
Philadelphia, PA 19106-3387
Phone: (215)440-3400
Fax: (215)440-3436
Home Page: http://www.amphilsoc.org

• 3433 • Benjamin Franklin Medal for Distinguished Achievement in Science

To recognize distinguished scientists. The medal was designed by Louis and Augustus St. Gaudens. The United States authorized the commemorative medal, and a gold copy was presented, "under the direction of the President of the United States (Theodore Roosevelt, APS 1904)" to the Republic of France; 50 struck in bronze were given to the APS for its use. A hand-illuminated certificate accompanies the medal. Created in 1906 to mark the 200th anniversary of the birth of Benjamin Franklin.

• 3434 • Benjamin Franklin Medal for Distinguished Public Service

To honor individuals for exceptional contributions to general welfare. An engraved medal and hand-illuminated certificate is presented. Established in 1987.

• 3435 • Thomas Jefferson Medal for Distinguished Achievement in the Arts, Humanities, or Social Sciences

To recognize distinguished achievement in the arts, humanities, or social sciences. Created in 1992 to mark the 250th anniversary of the Society and the birth of Thomas Jefferson. A medal designed by James Ferrell of the U.S. Mint and a hand-illuminated certificate are awarded annually. Established in 1993.

• 3436 • Judson Daland Prize

Awards outstanding achievement in patient-oriented clinical investigation. A monetary award of $18,000 and a certificate are awarded. Established in 2001.

• 3437 • Karl Spencer Lashley Award

For recognition of useful and significant work in the field of neurobiology. A monetary prize of $18,000 and a hand-illuminated citation are awarded annually. Established in 1957.

• 3438 • John F. Lewis Award

To recognize the best APS publication in a given year. American citizens are eligible. A monetary award of $2,500 and a certificate are awarded annually. Established in 1935.

• 3439 • Magellanic Premium Award

To honor discoveries relating to navigation or astronomy. A monetary award of $18,000, a medal, and a hand-illuminated certificate are awarded every other year. Established in 1786 by John Hyacinth de Magellan of London. This award is the oldest scientific prize presented by an American institution.

• 3440 • Henry Allen Moe Prize in the Humanities

To recognize the author of a distinguished paper in the humanities read at a meeting of the Society. A monetary award of $2,500 and a certificate are awarded annually. Established in 1982 by Edith N. Moe to honor Henry Allen Moe, head of the Guggenheim Foundation and president of the APS from 1959 to 1970.

• 3441 • Henry M. Philips Prize in Jurisprudence

To recognize outstanding lifetime contributions to the field of jurisprudence and important publications with illustrate that accomplishment. A monetary award of $10,000 and a hand-illuminated certificate are awarded when merited. Established in 1888.

• 3442 •

American Photographic Historical Society
Larry Berke, Treas.
28 Marksman Ln.
Levittown, NY 11756-5110
Phone: (516)796-7280

Formerly: (1986) Photographic Historical Society of New York.

• 3443 • Special Citation in Honor of Rudy and Hertha Benjamin

To recognize an original work on the history of photography published in English during the preceding year. A monetary prize of $100 and a diploma are awarded annually. Established in 1975.

• 3444 •

American Physical Society
Judy R. Franz, Exec.Off.
1 Physics Ellipse
College Park, MD 20740-3844
Phone: (301)209-3200
Phone: (301)209-3269
Fax: (301)209-0865
E-mail: exoffice@aps.org
Home Page: http://www.aps.org

• 3445 • David Adler Lectureship Award in the Field of Materials Physics

To recognize an outstanding contributor to the field of materials physics who is noted for the quality of his/her research, review articles, and lecturing. Nominations are open to anyone doing research, writing, and lecturing in the field of materials physics. The lectureship consists of an award of no less than $1,000 and a certificate citing the contribution made by the recipient. Awarded annually. Established in 1988 by contributions from friends of David Adler. Deadline July 3.

• 3446 • Will Allis Prize for Study of Ionized Gases

To recognize and encourage outstanding research into the microscopic or macrosopic behavior of ionized gases. Nominations are open to scientists of all nationalities regardless of geographical location at which work was done. A monetary prize of $5,000 and a certificate are awarded in even-numbered years. Established in 1989 in recognition of the outstanding contributions of Will Allis to the study of ionized gases.

• 3447 • Leroy Apker Award

To recognize outstanding achievement in physics by an undergraduate student and to thereby provide encouragement to a young physicist who has demonstrated great potential for future accomplishments. Nominations are open to students at colleges or universities in the U.S. who were enrolled as undergraduates during at least part of the 12 month period preceding the June 15 deadline. Only one candidate may be nominated by a physics department. Selection is based on demonstrated exceptional potential by an original contribution to physics. The award consists of $5,000, an allowance for travel to the meeting of the Society at which the award is announced, and a certificate citing the work and school of the recipient. Finalists receive $500 and a certificate. Awarded annually. Established in 1978 as a memorial to LeRoy Apker through an endowment donated by Jean Dickey Apker. Deadline June 15.

• 3448 • Award for Excellence in Plasma Physics Research

To recognize a particular recent outstanding achievement in plasma physics research. Nominations are open to scientists of all nationalities, regardless of the geographical site at which the work was done. The award consists of a monetary prize of $5,000, to be divided equally in the case of multiple winners, and a certificate to each recipient. Presented at the Annual Meeting Banquet of the Division of Plasma Physics. Awarded annually if merited. Established in 1981. Deadline April 2.

• 3449 • Biological Physics Prize

To recognize and encourage outstanding achievement in biological physics research. Nominations are open to scientists of all nationalities regardless of the geographical site at which the work was done. The prize consists of a monetary award of $5,000, an allowance for travel to the meeting at which the prize is awarded, and a certificate citing the contributions made by the recipient or recipients. Established in 1981 by friends of the Biological Physics Division. Deadline July 1.

• 3450 • Tom Bonner Prize in Nuclear Physics

To recognize and encourage outstanding experimental research in nuclear physics, including the development of a method, technique, or device that significantly contributes in a general way to nuclear physics research. Nominations are open to physicists whose work in nuclear physics is primarily experimental, but a particularly outstanding piece of theoretical work will take precedence over experimental work. There are no time limitations on the work described. A monetary award of $7,500, and a certificate citing the contribution made by the recipient are awarded annually. Established in 1964 as a memorial to Tom W. Bonner by his friends, students, and associates. Deadline July 3.

• 3451 • Edward A. Bouchet Award

To promote the participation of under-represented minorities in physics by identifying and recognizing a distinguished minority physicist who has made significant contributions to physics research. The Lectureship consists of a stipend of $3,500 plus travel expenses to an APS meeting. Award is presented annually. Established in 1994.

• 3452 • Herbert P. Broida Prize

To recognize and enhance outstanding experimental advancements in the fields of atomic, molecular, or chemical physics. Emphasis will be given to work done within the five years prior to the award. Preference will be granted to an individual whose contributions have displayed a high degree of breadth, originality, and creativity. The prize consists of a $5,000 stipend and a certificate citing the contributions made by the recipient. Awarded biennially in odd-numbered years. Established in 1979 in memory of Herbert P. Broida, Professor of Physics at the University of California, Santa Barbara, by his friends and the Office of Naval Research. Deadline July 3.

• 3453 • Oliver E. Buckley Prize in Condensed Matter Physics

To recognize and encourage outstanding theoretical or experimental contributions to condensed-matter physics. The prize consists of $5,000 and a certificate citing the contributions made by the recipient(s). Established in 1952. Sponsored by the AT&T Bell Laboratories as a means of recognizing outstanding scientific work in America. Deadline July 3.

• 3454 • Davisson-Germer Prize in Atomic or Surface Physics

To recognize and encourage outstanding work in atomic physics or surface physics. The prize consists of a monetary award of $5,000 and a certificate citing the contributions made by the recipient(s). Awarded in alternate years for outstanding work in atomic physics, and for outstanding work in surface physics. Established in 1965. Sponsored by AT&T Bell Laboratories as a means of recognizing outstanding scientific work in America. Deadline July 3.

• 3455 • John H. Dillon Medal for Research in Polymer Physics

To recognize outstanding research accomplishments by a young polymer physicist. The award consists of $ 2,000 up to $10,000 allowance for travel and the John H. Dillon Medal and a certificate citing the contributions made by the recipient. Awarded annually. Established in 1983 by the American Physical Society Division of High Polymer Physics. Deadline July 3.

• 3456 • Dissertation in Nuclear Physics Award

To recognize a recent Ph.D. in nuclear physics. Nominations are open to any person who has received a Ph.D. degree in nuclear physics from a North American university within the two-year period preceding the deadline. The award consists of $2,000 and an allowance for travel to the annual meeting of the Division of Nuclear Physics of the American Physical Society at which the award is presented. Awarded biennially. Established in 1985 by members and friends of the Nuclear Physics Division. Deadline July 3.

• 3457 • Fluid Dynamics Prize

To recognize and encourage outstanding achievement in fluid dynamics research. The prize consists of a monetary award of $6,000, an allowance for travel to the meeting at which the prize is awarded, and a certificate citing the contributions made by the recipient. Established in 1979 with support from the Office of Naval Research as a means of recognizing outstanding scientific work and disseminating information in fluid dynamics and the physics of the fluid state. Deadline January 19.

• 3458 • Frank Isakson Prize for Optical Effects in Solids

To recognize and encourage outstanding contributions to the field of optical effects in solids. Nominations are open to scientists of all nations regardless of the geographical site at which the work was done. The prize consists of $5,000, an allowance for travel to the meeting of the Society at which the prize is awarded, and a certificate citing the contributions made by the recipient. Five prizes are awarded biennially in even-numbered years as a memorial to Frank Isakson. Sponsored by Solid State Communications published by Elsevier Ltd. Deadline July 2.

• 3459 • Joseph F. Keithley for Advances in Measuresment Sciences

Recognize the development of measurement techniques or equipment providing better measurements for the physics community. All physicists are eligible. $ 500.00, a certificate, and travel expenses are of the nomination form and supporting materials must be submitted. Nominations are active for three years. Endowed by Keithley Instruments, Inc. and the Instrument and Measurement Topical Group.

• 3460 • Irving Langmuir Prize in Chemical Physics

To recognize and encourage outstanding interdisciplinary research in chemistry and physics in the spirit of Irving Langmuir. The recipient must be a resident of the United States at the time of selection and the prize funds must be used in the United States or its possessions. The prize consists of $10,000 and a certificate citing the contributions made by the recipient. In even-numbered years, The American Chemical Society selects the prizewinner and presents the prize. In odd-numbered years, The American Physical Society selects the prizewinner and presents the prize. An allowance is provided for travel expenses of the recipient to the General Meeting of the Society at which the prize is bestowed. Established in 1964 by the General Electric Foundation as a memorial to and in recognition of the accomplishments of Irving Langmuir. Deadline July 3.

• 3461 • Langmuir Prize in Chemical Physics Langmuir Prize in Chemical Physics

To recognize an individual for a most outstanding contribution to physics. The prize consists of $10,000, a certificate citing the contributions made by the recipient, and expenses for three lectures by the recipient given at an APS general meeting, a research university, and a predominantly undergraduate institution. Awarded annually. Established in 1988 under the terms of a bequest of Beatrice Lilienfeld in memory of her husband, Julius Edgar Lilienfeld. Deadline July 3.

• 3462 • Otto Laporte Award for Research in Fluid Dynamics

To recognize outstanding accomplishments in research in fluid dynamics. The award consists of $5,000 and a certificate citing the contributions made by the recipient. The recipient is invited to present a plenary lecture at the Annual Meeting of the Division of Fluid Dynamics. Established as an APS Award in 1985, but existed as a Division Prize for twelve previous years to honor Otto Laporte. It is supported by the friends of Otto Laporte and the Division of Fluid Dynamics. January 19.

• 3463 • James Clerk Maxwell Prize for Plasma Physics

To recognize outstanding contributions to the field of plasma physics. United States residents whose work was done primarily in the United States are eligible. The prize consists of a monetary award of $5,000 and a certificate citing the contribution made by the recipient. Awarded annually. Established in 1975 by the Maxwell Laboratories, Inc., San Diego, CA. Deadline April 2.

• 3464 • James C. McGroddy Prize in New Materials

Recognizes and encourages achievement in the science and application of new materials. Sciences of all nationalities are eligible. $ 5000 a certificate, and a travel allowance are awarded annually. Endowed by IBM. 5 copies of the nomination material must be submitted. Application deadline is July 2. Nominations are active for 3 years. Forum on Physics and Society. Forum on Physics and Society.

• 3465 • Lars Onsager Prize

To recognize outstanding research in theoretical statistical physics including the quantum fluids. The research should be in the unique spirit of Lars Onsager. In the same spirit the prize is available to workers in statistical physics covering a wide range of physical phenomena. The prize is to be considered international in character, and only active scientists at the time of the award are qualified. The award consists of $15,000 to be bestowed annually, and was endowed by Russell and Marian Donnelly in 1993.

• 3466 • Outstanding Doctoral Thesis Research in Atomic, Molecular, or Optical Physics Award

Recognizes doctoral thesis research in atomic, molecular, or optical physics and encourages effective written and oral presentation of research results. Applicants must be doctoral students at any university in the United States or abroad who have passed their thesis defense for the PhD in the disciplines of atomic, molecular, or optical physics not more than 24 months before the nomination deadline, except for those whose thesis advisors serve on the current Selection Committee. A monetary award of $2,500, a certificate, and a travel stipend of $500 are awarded annually.

• 3467 • Outstanding Doctoral Thesis Research in Beam Physics Award

To recognize doctoral thesis research of outstanding quality and achievement in beam physics and engineering. The award consists of $2,500 and a certificate. Established in 1990. Supported by Universities Research Association.

• 3468 • George E. Pake Prize

To recognize and encourage outstanding work by physicists combining original research accomplishments with leadership in the management of research or development in industry. A monetary award of $5,000, an allowance for travel to the meeting at which the prize is awarded, and a plaque recognizing the contributions of the recipient are awarded annually. Established in 1983 in honor of the outstanding achievements of George E. Pake, a research physicist and a director of industrial research. Sponsored by the Xerox Corporation. Deadline July 3.

• 3469 • W. K. H. Panofsky Prize in Experimental Particle Physics

To recognize and encourage outstanding achievements in experimental particle physics. Nominations are open to scientists of all nations regardless of the geographical site at which the work was done. The prize is ordinarily awarded to one person but the prize may be shared among recipients when all recipients have contributed to the same accomplishment. The prize is normally awarded for contributions made at an early stage of the recipient's career. The prize consists of $5,000, an allowance for travel to the meeting at which the prize is awarded, and a certificate citing the contributions made by the recipient. Established in 1985 by the friends of W.K.H. Panofsky and the Division of Particles and Fields. Deadline July 3.

• 3470 • Earle K. Plyler Prize for Molecular Spectroscopy

To recognize and encourage notable contributions to molecular spectroscopy. Nominations are open to scientists in North America. The prize may be given for experimental or theoretical achievements for a single dramatic innovation, or for a series of research contributions which, when integrated, amounts to a major contribution to the field of molecular spectroscopy. The prize consists of $5,000, a certificate citing the contributions made by the recipient, and travel expenses to attend the award ceremony. Established in 1976 and sponsored by the George E. Crouch Foundation. Deadline July 3.

• 3471 • Polymer Physics Prize

To recognize outstanding accomplishments and excellence of contributions high polymer physics research. Nominations are open to scientists of all nations regardless of the geographical site at which the work was done. A monetary award of $10,000 and a certificate citing the contributions made by the recipients are awarded annually. Established in 1960 and sponsored by the Ford Motor Company. Deadline July 3.

• 3472 • Prize to a Faculty Member for Research in an Undergraduate Institution

To honor a physicist whose research in an undergraduate setting has achieved wide recognition and contributed significantly to physics and who has contributed substantially to the professional development of undergraduate physics students. Nominees must be from faculty of predominantly undergraduate institutions in the United States. The nominee's department may offer a program leading to a masters degree but shall not have a doctoral program in physics. The award consists of a $5,000 stipend to the awardee and a separate $4,000 unrestricted grant for the research of the recipient to the awardee's institution. An additional travel allowance to attend the APS meeting at which the award ceremony will take place, and a certificate citing the contribution by the recipient are presented. Established in 1984 by a grant from the Research Corporation, a private foundation for the advancement of science and technology. Sponsored by the Research Corporation.

• 3473 • I. I. Rabi Prize in Atomic, Molecular and Optical Physics

To recognize and encourage outstanding research in atomic, molecular, and optical physics. Research performed by investigators who have held a Ph.D. for not more than 10 years is considered. Nominations are open to scientists of all nationalities regardless of the geographical location at which the work was done. The prize consists of $7,500, a certificate citing the contributions made by the recipient, and travel expenses to attend the award ceremony. Awarded biennially in odd-numbered years. Established in 1989 by family, friends, and colleagues of I.I. Rabi. Deadline July 1.

• 3474 • Aneesur Rahman Prize for Computational Physics

To recognize and encourage outstanding achievement in computational physics research. A monetary prize of $5,000, a certificate, and travel expenses, as well as an invitation to present the Rahman Lecture, are awarded annually. Established in 1992.

• 3475 • J. J. Sakurai Prize for Theoretical Particle Physics

To recognize and encourage outstanding achievement in particle theory by a young physicist. Nominations are open to scientists of all nationalities regardless of the geographical site at which the work was done. The prize will normally be awarded for theoretical contributions made at an early stage of the recipient's research career. The prize consists of $5,000, an allowance for travel to the meeting of the Society at which the prize is awarded, and a certificate citing the contributions made by the recipient. Awarded annually. Established in 1984 in memory of J.J. Sakurai by his family and friends. Deadline July 3.

• 3476 • Arthur L. Schawlow Prize in Laser Science

To recognize outstanding contributions to basic research which uses lasers to advance our knowledge of the fundamental physical properties of materials and their interaction with light. Some examples of relevant areas of research are; nonlinear optics, ultrafast phenomena, laser spectroscopy, squeeze states, quantum optics, multiphoton physics, laser cooling and trapping, physics of lasers, particle acceleration by lasers and short wavelength laser. A monetary prize of $10,000, a certificate, and travel expenses are awarded annually. Established in 1991.

• 3477 • Shock Compression Science Award

To recognize contributions to understanding condensed matter and non-linear physics through shock compression. All members of the scientific community are eligible for nomination. A single award is normally given to no more than one individual and is presented at the biennial Topical Group Conference. A plaque citing the accomplishments of the recipient, an allowance for travel to the meeting at which it is given, and a cash award of $3,000 are awarded biennially. Established in 1987 by the Friends of the Topical Group on Shock Compression of Condensed Matter Physics.

• 3478 • Leo Szilard Lectureship Award

To recognize outstanding accomplishments by a physicist in promoting the use of physics for the benefit of society in such areas as the environment, arms control, and science policy. Any living physicist is eligible. The award consists of a medal, a certificate citing the contributions of the recipient, a sculpture to be held one year and passed on to the next winner, travel expenses to attend the award ceremony, and $ 1,000 plus $ 2,000 for travel expenses, awarded annually. Established in 1974 by the Forum on Physics and Society as a memorial to Leo Szilard in recognition of his concern for the social consequences of science. Deadline July 3.

• 3479 • George E. Valley Prize

Recognize scientific contribution to the knowledge of physics. Individuals under the age of 30 at the time of nomination are eligible. $ 20,000, a certificate, and expenses to receive the award presented biannually. Established in 2000. Five copies of the nomination and supporting material must be submitted.

• 3480 • John Wheatley Award

Honors and recognizes the dedication of physicists' contributions made to the development of physics in countries of the third world. Awarded to the physicist who, working in developing, country has made an outstanding contribution to the development of physics in that region by working with local physicists in physics research or teaching. Open to physicists of all nationalities but the award will not be given to a person for working in his or her own country. A stipend of $3,000 and a certificate citing the contributions made by the recipient are presented biennially in odd-numbered years.

• 3481 • Robert R. Wilson Prize for Achievement in the Physics of Particle Accelerators

To recognize and encourage outstanding achievement in the physics of particle accelerators. Nominations are open to scientists of all nations regardless of the geographical site at which the work was done. The prize shall ordinarily be awarded to one person but may be shared among recipients when all recipients have contributed to the same accomplishment. The prize will normally be awarded for contributions made at an early stage of the recipient's career. The prize consists of $5,000, an allowance for travel to the meeting at which the prize is awarded, and a certificate citing the contributions made by the recipient. Established in 1986 by the friends of Robert R. Wilson, the Division of Particles and Fields, and the Topical Group on Particle Beam Physics. Deadline July 3.

• 3482 •
American Physical Therapy Association
Ben F. Massey Jr., Pres.
1111 N Fairfax St.
Alexandria, VA 22314-1488
Phone: (703)684-2782
Phone: (703)683-6748
Toll-Free: 800-999-2782
Fax: (703)684-7343
E-mail: benmassey@apta.org
Home Page: http://www.apta.org

• 3483 • Dorothy E. Baethke - Eleanor J. Carlin Award for Excellence in Academic Teaching

To recognize teaching excellence in the field of physical therapy. The nominee must be a clinical or academic educator who is engaged in teaching physical therapists or physical therapist assistant students in formal educational programs for at least five years. The deadline for nominations is December 1. A certificate and an engraved plaque, located at APTA headquarters, are awarded annually. Established in 1981 in honor of both Dorothy E. Baethke and Eleanor J. Carlin, who displayed dedication and excellence in teaching physical therapy. Formerly: (1987) Dorothy E. Baethke - Eleanor J. Carlin Award for Teaching Excellence.

• 3484 • Lucy Blair Service Award

For recognition of exceptionally valuable contributions in any of the areas of concern to the Association, e.g., service rendered to chapters, districts, sections, task forces, etc., as well as at the national level. Nominations may be submitted by components of the Association and individual members. The deadline for nominations is December 1. A certificate and a pin are awarded annually. Established in 1969 in honor of Lucy Blair who served the national headquarters as Poliomyelitis Consultant, Associate Director, and Executive Director.

• 3485 • Dorothy Briggs Memorial Scientific Inquiry Award

To recognize a physical therapist member of the Association who as a student developed an experimental investigation that subsequently was published in *Physical Therapy*. One award may be granted for a study undertaken at each of three academic levels; (1) doctoral degree programs; (2) master's degree programs beyond entry level; (3) certificate, baccalaureate, and entry level master's degree programs. Established in 1969 in honor of Dorothy I. Briggs, Ph.D., former Chairman of the editorial board of *Physical Therapy.*

• 3486 • Signe Brunnstrom Award for Excellence in Clinical Teaching

To recognize individuals who have made significant contributions to physical therapy clinical education through excellence in clinical teaching. The nominee must be a physical therapist who is a member of the APTA and has been actively engaged in clinical teaching of physical therapist students (entry or advanced level) or physical therapist assistant students for at least five years. The nominee may be either a center coordinator of clinical education or a clinical instructor, and must be employed or self employed in a clinical setting. The individual who holds a full-time faculty appointment within an academic setting is not eligible for the award. The clinical teaching must occur in a clinical setting, under an arrangement or contract with one or more accredited physical therapist or physical therapist assistant education programs, or advanced level programs for physical therapists, and must occur with students earning an academic credential. Members of the Committee on Physical Therapy Education and the Board of Directors are not eligible for the award during terms of service. Nominations are evaluated on the following criteria: (1) The nominee's exceptional teaching effectiveness in the clinical setting; (2) The nominee's excellence as a role model in clinical teaching; and (3) The nominee's distinct expertise in at least one area of practice to which the clinical teaching has been directed. The deadline for nominations is December 1. A certificate is awarded. Established in 1987. Formerly: (1987) Award for Excellence in Clinical Teaching.

• 3487 • Chapter Award for Minority Enhancement

To recognize outstanding efforts of an APTA chapter in fostering minority representation and participation in physical therapy. The recipient must be a chapter organization of the APTA. The deadline for entry is December 1. Chapters must demonstrate exceptionally valuable contributions that enhance minorities in any area of the Profession, including but not limited to education, chapter activities, and Association activities. A plaque is awarded. Established in 1984.

• 3488 • Chattanooga Research Award

To encourage the publication of outstanding physical therapy clinical research reports and for recognition of the best article on clinical research in *Physical Therapy* during the preceding year. Members are eligible. A monetary prize of $1,000 is awarded annually. Established in 1980. Sponsored by the Chattanooga Corporation.

• 3489 • Golden Pen Award

To recognize individuals who have made significant contributions to the advancement of *Physical Therapy*. Individuals who have demonstrated superior writing skill in one or more articles published in *Physical Therapy* or who have collaborated with or encouraged others to make similar contributions or contributed outstanding leadership and effort in initiating activities to improve *Physical Therapy* are eligible. Established in 1964.

• 3490 • Helen J. Hislop Award for Outstanding Contributions to Professional Literature

To recognize physical therapists who have made significant contributions to the literature on physical therapy, or in other health care disciplines. Members are eligible. The nominee must have published in at least two different health care professional journals, or contributed to at least two books or monographs or proceedings from scientific meetings. Awarded annually. Established in 1991 to honor Helen J. Hislop.

• 3491 • Honorary Member

For recognition of individuals who have made contributions which are: (1) significant to the field of physical therapy; (2) national in recognition and scope; (3) beyond the scope of work done as part of paid employment; and (4) of a unique quality. The deadline for chapters to submit recommendations is December 1. At an appropriate occasion, chapter officers make the presentation to the recipient. Established in 1936.

• 3492 • Henry O. Kendall and Florence P. Kendall Award for Outstanding Achievement in Clinical Practice

To give public recognition to members of the Association who are outstanding clinicians as demonstrated by their dedication to their patients, their profession, and by their sharing of knowledge with others. Members may be nominated by individual members, chapters, districts, or sections of the APTA by December 1. A plaque and a monetary donation made to the charity of the honoree's choice are awarded. Presented annually in honor of Henry O. Kendall (deceased 1978) and Florence P. Kendall, who have been outstanding physical therapist clinicians in Maryland for over 50 years.

• 3493 • Mary McMillan Lecture Award

For recognition of distinguished contribution to the profession of physical therapy in one or more of the following categories: administration; education; patient care; or research. The deadline for nominations is December 1. The honoree presents a lecture and receives an honorarium of $250, a plaque and a medallion. Awarded as merited. Established in 1963 in honor of Mary McMillan, a pioneer in physical therapy and founding President of the Association.

• 3494 • Eugene Michels New Investigator Award

To recognize an outstanding new investigator who has demonstrated a commitment to a defined, research theme. The nominee must be a physical therapist who is a member of the APTA and has been engaged in independent research activities for not more than five years after completion of formal education. There must be a demonstrated relationship between the research theme and the field of physical therapy. Any member of the Association may nominate candidates for this award by December 1. A monetary prize of $1,000 is awarded when merited. Established in 1989 in honor of Eugene Michels who has been instrumental in developing a plan to foster research among physical therapists.

• 3495 • Minority Achievement Award

To recognize continuous achievement by an entry-level accredited physical therapy program in the recruitment, admission, retention, and graduation of minority students. The applicant must be accredited by the American Physical Therapy Association. The efforts for minority students must have been ongoing for at least three years. The deadline for entry is December 1. A certificate and monetary award of $1,000 are presented. Established in 1984.

• 3496 • Minority Initiatives Award

To recognize the efforts of a physical therapy education program in the initiation and/or improvement of recruitment, admission, retention, and graduation of minority students, and the provision of services for students from racial and ethnic minority groups. Eligible applicants are accredited education programs in physical therapy and physical therapy education programs which have been granted accreditation candidacy status. The deadline for entry is December 1. A monetary prize of $1,000 and a certificate are awarded. Established in 1984.

• 3497 • Margaret L. Moore Award for Outstanding New Academic Faculty Member

To recognize an outstanding new faculty member who is pursuing a career as an academician and has demonstrated excellence in research and teaching. The nominee must be a physical therapist who is a member of the APTA and has been actively engaged in teaching physical therapist (entry or advanced level) students for at least two, but not more than five years; must have a full-time faculty academic appointment, but may be of any rank; and must be employed in an academic setting within one or more accredited physical therapist education programs, or advanced level program for physical therapists, from which students earn an academic degree. Teaching solely as a component of continuing education does not constitute eligibility for this award. Any member of the APTA may nominate candidates for this award. A certificate is presented at the annual conference. Established in 1989.

• 3498 • Jack Walker Award

For recognition of the best article on clinical practice published in *Physical Therapy*. The article should be a noteworthy contribution to the improvement of patient care (e.g., therapeutic procedures, patient/family education, or delivery of health care) and should have been published in *Physical Therapy* during the preceding year. A monetary prize of $1,000 and a certificate are awarded. Established in 1978.

• 3499 • Marian Williams Award for Research in Physical Therapy

For recognition of research which has been conducted by a physical therapist in basic or clinical science or education. Criteria for nomination include evidence that research has been sustained and outstanding, that research results have been disseminated widely, and that the nominee has shown continuity of commitment to the profession. The Committee on Research recommends candidates by December 1. Established in 1963 to commemorate Marian Williams, Ph.D., whose professional life was dedicated to the promotion of physical therapy through teaching, writing, and research. A bronze medal is awarded as merited. Established in 1963.

• 3500 • Catherine Worthingham Fellows of APTA

To recognize those persons whose work has resulted in lasting and significant advances in the science, education, and practice of physical therapy. Criteria for nomination are that the individual should be an active member who has held active membership status for a minimum of 15 years; has demonstrated nationally prominent leadership in advancing at least one of the three areas of the science, education, or practice of physical therapy; has documented achievements in at least two of the three areas of the profession, or is known nationwide. The deadline for nominations is December 1. A pin and recognition as a fellow are awarded as merited. Established in 1980 in honor of Catherine Worthingham, a leader in physical therapy education, science, and practice for more than fifty years.

• 3501 •
American Physical Therapy Association, New Hampshire Chapter
James H. Bradley APR, Exec.Dir.
PO Box 978
Manchester, NH 03105
Phone: (603)497-8989
Fax: (603)497-8983
E-mail: office@nhapta.org
Home Page: http://www.nhapta.org

• 3502 • Mary Stanton Scholarships

For NH resident in last year of PT or PTA program; must agree to work one year in New Hampshire. Scholarship awarded annually.

Awards are arranged in alphabetical order below their administering organizations

• 3503 •
American Physicians Art Association
Lawrence Travis MD, Sec.-Treas.
2410 Patterson St., Ste. 202
Nashville, TN 37203
Phone: (615)327-4944
Fax: (615)327-4704
E-mail: lawrencewtravismd@comcast.net
Home Page: http://www.americanphysiciansartassociation.com

• 3504 • **Annual National Art Exhibition**
To recognize the artistic accomplishments of beginner, advanced, and master artists in the medical profession. Recipients must be members of the Association. Numerous medals, plaques, and ribbons are awarded annually, including Best in Show and People's Choice Award. Established in 1937.

• 3505 •
American Physiological Society
Martin Frank, Exec.Dir.
9650 Rockville Pike
Bethesda, MD 20814-3991
Phone: (301)634-7164
Fax: (301)634-7241
E-mail: mfrank@the-aps.org
Home Page: http://www.the-aps.org

• 3506 • **AAAS Mass Media Science and Engineering Fellowship**
To allow an individual to spend 10 weeks over the summer working for a newspaper, magazine, radio, or television newsroom; also includes expenses for traveling to sessions and the job site as well as a weekly stipend based on the local cost of living. Applicants must be currently enrolled as a graduate or postgraduate student of physiology or a related discipline. Fellows must attend a one-week orientation in Washington, DC, to help develop their ability to communicate complex scientific issues to nonscientists. Deadline January 15. Awarded annually. Sponsored by American Association for the Advancement of Sciences (AAAS).

• 3507 • **Abbott Laboratories Distinguished Research Award**
To recognize a senior physiologist. $500 is awarded.

• 3508 • **Bowditch Award Lecture**
For recognition of exceptional research accomplishments of a young physiologist. Members of the Society under 42 years of age are eligible. A monetary prize of $2500 is awarded annually at the spring meeting. A curriculum vitae and three letters covering the nominee's status, contributions, and potential must be submitted. Established in 1956 in honor of Henry P. Bowditch, the first president of the Society. Deadline October 1.

• 3509 • **Michael J. Brody Young Investigator Award**
To recognize a young investigator who has made a significant contribution through his/her research to our understanding of neural control and autonomic regulation. Applicants must be graduate students, postdoctoral fellows, or clinical fellows. A monetary prize of $500 and a certificate are awarded by the Neural Control and Autonomic Regulation Section annually. Co-sponsored by Merck & Co., Inc.

• 3510 • **Physiology in Perspective: Walter B. Cannon Lecture**
For recognition of exceptional scientific accomplishment in the physiological sciences. Scientists of any country designated by the APS Council are eligible. A monetary prize of $4000 a plaque and travel expenses to deliver the lecture are awarded annually at the spring meeting. A curriculum vita, three letters covering the nominee's status and contributions must be submitted. Established in 1983. Deadline October 1.

• 3511 • **Cardiovascular Section Young Investigator Award**
Encourages commitment to continued contributions to the field. Applicants must be members of the APS Cardiovascular Section with a Ph. D., M.D., DSC., D.V.M or D.D.S. Degree. A letter nomination, a second letter from someone Outside of the nominee's institution, and a CV of the candidate must be submitted. A cash prize of $1,000 is awarded annually.

• 3512 • **Caroline tum Suden/France Hellebrandt Professional Opportunity Awards**
To recognize up to 36 graduate students or postdoctoral fellows who present a contributed paper at the Experimental Biology meeting. Candidate must be first author of an abstract submitted to APS and either candidate or the abstract sponsor must be an APS member. Recipients are obligated to attend the experimental Biology meeting and present a paper. A cash award of $500, complimentary registration, and placement service fees are awarded during the APS Business Meeting.

• 3513 • **Central Nervous System Section Van Harrevold Memorial Award**
To recognize outstanding research in neuroscience by a graduate student or postdoctoral fellow. The recipient must be first author on an abstract presented at the Experimental Biology meeting. A monetary award of $300 is presented annually.

• 3514 • **Comparative Physiology Section Scholander Award**
To recognize an outstanding young investigator presenting a paper as first author in a comparative physiology slide session at the spring Experimental Biology meeting. A certificate and cash prize of $300 is awarded annually.

• 3515 • **Ray G. Daggs Award**
For recognition of distinguished service to the Society and to the science of physiology. Members of the Society are eligible. A monetary prize of $500 a certificate, and expenses to participate in the annual meeting are awarded annually. Established in 1973 in honor of Ray G. Daggs, first executive secretary-treasurer of the Society.

• 3516 • **Environmental and Exercise Physiology Section Gatorade Young Investigator Award**
Recognizes predoctoral investigation in environmental, exercise or thermal physiology. Applicants must be first authors on the submitted abstract. The winner is expected to present at the annual EEP Sectin banquet. Deadline is November 6. A plaque, $600, and reimbursement of the registration fee are awarded annually.

• 3517 • **Giles F. Filley Memorial Awards for Excellence in Respiratory Physiology and Medicine**
To recognize excellence in respiratory physiology and medicine. Applications are accepted from members of the APS working within the United States who have demonstrated outstanding promise based on their research program. Monetary awards of $20,000 are designated for use of the awardee in their research program, a plaque, and travel expenses to attend the APS Business Meeting where awards are presented are awarded annually.

• 3518 • **Arthur C. Guyton Awards for Excellence in Integrative Physiology**
To recognize promise based on research program in feedback control systems, quantitative modeling, and integrative physiology. Applicants must be members of the APS. The application deadline is November 1. A cash prize of $15,000 is awarded annually for use in the research project. Established in 1993.

• 3519 • **Liaison with Industry Committee Novel Disease Model Award**
For the best abstract to submitted to the Experimental Biology meeting that describes a novel disease model. Candidates must be graduates students or postdoctoral fellows. $500 is awarded to the graduate student winner and $800 is awarded to the postdoctoral fellow winner. Awarded annually.

• 3520 • **Lazaro J. Mandel Young Investigator Award**
Recognizes individuals demonstrating outstanding promise based on his/her research program in epithelial or renal physiology. Applicants must be APS members working in the US and holding an academic rank no higher than assistant professor. A monetary prize of $7,500 is awarded annually. Deadline November 1. Established in 1999.

• 3521 • **Mead Johnson Research Award in Endocrinology and Metabolism**
Recognizes the best abstract for research in the area of endocrinology and metabolism at the Experimental Biology meeting. Applicants must be graduate students, residents, or postdoctoral fellows, and first author on a submitted abstract and should enclose a completed student award certification form, and a letter from the sponsor of the abstract. A monetary prize of $500 is

awarded by the Endocrinology and Metabolism Section annually.

• 3522 • Minority Travel Fellowship Awards

To increase participation of the predoctoral and postdoctoral minority students in physiological sciences. Fellowships are open to advanced undergraduate, predoctoral, and postdoctoral scientists who have obtained their undergraduate education in Minority Biomedical Research Programs (MBRP) and MARC-eligible institutions, as well as students in the APS Porter Development Program. Funds awarded provide transportation, meals, and lodging to attend the annual spring Experimental Biology meeting. Awarded annually.

• 3523 • John F. Perkins, Jr. Memorial Award

To provide supplementary support to families of foreign scientists who have already arranged for fellowships or sabbatical leave to carry on scientific work in the United States. Preference is given to physiologists working in the fields of respiratory physiology, neurophysiology, and temperature regulation. Applications from scientists in developing countries are also given special attention. The deadlines are April 15 and October 15. Recipient receives funds not to exceed $5000. Awarded annually.

• 3524 • Porter Physiology Fellowships for Minorities

Provides predoctoral fellowships for African Americans, Hispanics, Native Americans, Native Alaskans, and Native Pacific Islanders. Primarily, applicants must be predoctoral students in physiology. Under special circumstances, the award may be granted to first-year postdoctoral students. Applicants must be U.S. citizens or permanent residents of the U.S. or its territories. A $20,772 stipend is awarded annually.

• 3525 • Postdoctoral Fellowship in Physiological Genomics

To promote careers in mammalian organ system physiology. Candidates must identify a laboratory and sponsor under whose supervision a project in mammalian organ system physiology and molecular biology/genomics can be combined. A $36,000 annual stipend and $3,500 trainee allowance ($38,000 second year stipend with $3,500 trainee allowance) is awarded. Each award lasts two years. Deadline is January 15.

• 3526 • Procter & Gamble Professional Opportunity Awards

To recognize predoctoral students who present a paper on physiology at the spring Experimental Biology meeting. Candidates must be the first author of an abstract submitted to the APS and within 12-18 months of completing his or her PhD; be a student member of the APS or have an a advisor or sponsor who is a member; and a U.S. citizen or have a permanent resident Visa. Monetary prizes of $500 and complementary registration for the meeting are awarded to at least 17 predoctoral students who present a contributed paper at the meeting.

• 3527 • Renal Section Pfizer Predoctoral Excellence in Renal Research Award

To promote and develop excellence in predoctoral research related to molecular, cellular, and organ mechanisms expressed by the kidneys. Applicants must be first authors on an abstract submitted to renal and electrolyte physiology for programming at the experimental biology meeting. A cash award is presented annually.

• 3528 • Orr E. Reynolds Award

To recognize the best historical article on some aspect of the history of physiology. Members of the Society are eligible. A monetary prize of $500 is awarded annually at the spring meeting. Established in 1986 to honor Orr E. Reynolds, Second Executive Secretary-Treasurer of the Society. Deadline December 1.

• 3529 • Teaching Career Enhancement Awards

To enhance the career potential of APS members. Monetary awards of up to $4,000 are presented annually.

• 3530 • Shih-Chun Wang Young Investigator Award

To recognize an individual demonstrating outstanding promise based on his/her research program in the physiological sciences. Applicants must be APS members working in the US and holding an academic rank no higher than assistant professor. A monetary prize of $7,000, travel expenses, and a plaque are awarded annually. Deadline November 1. Established in 1998.

• 3531 • Young Investigator Award in Regulatory and Integrative Physiology

To recognize important contributions to the understanding of the integrative aspects of cardiovascular, renal, and neuroendocrine physiology in health and/or disease. Applicants must be young investigators (less than 40 years old). Award consists of $500, a plaque, and free registration to the annual Experimental Biology meeting. The recipient will also be invited to present a short lecture on his/her research work during one of the scientific sessions of the Experimental Biology meeting. Application deadline is December 1.

• 3532 •

American Phytopathological Society
Steven C. Nelson, Exec.VP
3340 Pilot Knob Rd.
St. Paul, MN 55121-2097
Phone: (651)454-7250
Fax: (651)454-0766
E-mail: aps@scisoc.org
Home Page: http://www.apsnet.org

• 3533 • Ruth Allen Award

For recognition of an innovative research contribution that has changed or has the potential to change the direction of work in plant pathology. A monetary prize is awarded annually. Established in 1965.

• 3534 • APS Fellow

In recognition of distinguished contributions to plant pathology. Members of the society are eligible. Awarded annually. Established in 1965.

• 3535 • Award of Distinction

This, the highest award of the society, is presented for truly exceptional contributions to plant pathology. Awarded when merited. Established in 1967.

• 3536 • William Boright Hewitt and Maybelle E. Ball Hewitt Award

Recognizes a young scientist who has made an outstanding innovative contribution directed towards the control of plant diseases. Established in 2000.

• 3537 • Distinguished Service Award

To honor individuals who have provided sustained outstanding leadership to the society while also furthering the science of plant pathology.

• 3538 • Excellence in Extension Award

For recognition of excellence in extension plant pathology. Individuals involved in formal plant pathology extension with recognized superior contributions in development or implementation of leadership roles in local, regional, or national honor societies or professional organizations are eligible. Established in 1988.

• 3539 • Excellence in Teaching Award

For recognition of excellence in teaching plant pathology. Individuals with active responsibility for one or more courses in plant pathology and distinguished proficiency in teaching, as indicated by the development and effectiveness of courses taught, are eligible. Established in 1987.

• 3540 • Lee M. Hutchins Award

For recognition of the best published basic or applied research paper on virus or virus-like infectious diseases of perennial fruit plants. A monetary prize is awarded annually. Established in 1979.

• 3541 • Syngenta Award

To recognize significant recent contributions to teaching, research, or extension in plant pathology. Members of the society are eligible. A trophy and an expense-paid trip to Basel, Switzerland are awarded annually. Priority for this award is given to young members of APS, who are in the first decade of a career in plant pathology. Established in 1975. Sponsored by Syngenta Corporation.

• 3542 •
American Pianists Association
Helen Small, Pres./CEO
Clowes Memorial Hall
Butler Univ.
4600 Sunset Ave.
Indianapolis, IN 46208
Phone: (317)940-9945
Fax: (317)940-9010
E-mail: apainfo@americanpianists.org
Home Page: http://
www.americanpianists.org

• 3543 • American Pianists Association Classical Fellowship Awards
To support the careers of America's rising young pianists by providing a two-year fellowship/educational outreach program which, in turn, enhances the quality of life for audiences of all ages. Candidates are selected through a nomination process. The fellowships, awarded to two pianists equally in even numbered years, includes a cash grant of $15,000 each and includes promotional support, and national recital and concerto engagements. Awarded triennially. Established in 1981.

• 3544 •
American Planning Association
Paul Farmer, Exec.Dir.
122 S Michigan Ave., Ste. 1600
Chicago, IL 60603-6107
Phone: (312)431-9100
Fax: (312)431-9985
E-mail: research@planning.org
Home Page: http://www.planning.org

Formed by merger of: (1978) American Institute of Planners; American Society of Planning Officials.

• 3545 • AICP National Historic Planning Landmarks and Pioneers Program
For recognition of a project 25 or more years old which has contributed significantly to American communities; and for recognition of an individual having made innovations in American planning that significantly impact planning practice, education, theory or organization on a national scale, with long-term beneficial results. Awarded annually. Established in 1986. Sponsored by the American Institute of Certified Planners.

• 3546 • AICP Student Project and Outstanding Student Awards
To recognize works are judged for originality, quality, application to other projects, comprehensiveness, and implementation. Submissions are accepted. A certificate is awarded at the national conference. Awarded annually. Established in 1984. Sponsored by the American Institute of Certified Planners.

• 3547 • APA Journalism Awards
To honor newspapers for public service rendered in the advancement of city and regional planning through outstanding journalism. Eligible articles include those that support, improve, or initiate planning programs or those that help the public understand planning issues affecting their community or region. Articles may be submitted in the following categories: (1) Large Newspaper - circulation over 100,000; (2) Medium Newspaper - circulation between 35,000 and 100,000; and (3) Small Newspaper - circulation under 35,000. A monetary award of $150 is presented to the first place winner in each category. Awarded annually. Application deadline is January 14th. Established in 1960. Additional information is available from Sylvia Lewis Deadline January 1.

• 3548 • Daniel Burnham Award
In recognition of an individual who is not a member of the APA, or an organization whose efforts have contributed to the elevation of planning principles, greater awareness of the value of planning and an improved quality of life in one or more communities. Selection is based on industry support, effectiveness, and results. Open to nonmembers only. The award honors Daniel Burnham for his contributions to the planning profession and to a greater awareness of the benefits of planning for all communities.

• 3549 • Current Topic Award
To recognize an exemplary planning initiative that mediates between the conservation of local identity and the transformations associated with economic and social change. The types of projects that can be nominated for an award are plans that establish a well-considered strategy for managing the conservation and transformation of an area; policies or programs that implement specific plans, such as financing or resource management, or ongoing educative and interpretive initiatives; projects for structures, spaces, or districts that have played a critical or catalytic role in advancing a larger, comprehensive plan; and research that establishes a framework for the types of plans, policies, and projects described. Inquire for current topic. Members and non-members are eligible.

• 3550 • Paul Davidoff Award
To recognize projects or individuals reflecting a social commitment to advocacy planning in support of the needs of society's less fortunate members. Members and non-members are eligible. Selection is based upon advocacy and effectiveness. The award honors the late APA member for his contributions to the Association and the planning field.

• 3551 • Distinguished Contribution Award
Recognizes contribution to the Association's goals and objectives and to its organizational development. Nominees must be Associations members making contributions of a short period. Nominees will be judged based on their support of the APA, the extent to which their work has increased the understanding of planning principles and the planning process, and their effectiveness in implementing those plans and ideas. Open to APA members only. Any APA member other than the person nominated may submit the member's name for consideration.

• 3552 • Distinguished Leadership Award for a Citizen Planner
Recognizes an individual elected to a citizen planner for a significant contribution to planning. Awarded annually.

• 3553 • Distinguished Leadership Award for a Professional Planner
Recognizes an individual elected to public office for a significant contribution to planning. Awarded annually.

• 3554 • Distinguished Leadership Award for a Student Planner
Recognizes a student planner for a significant contribution to planning. Awarded annually.

• 3555 • Distinguished Leadership Award for an Elected Official
Recognizes an individual elected to public office for a significant contribution to planning. Awarded annually.

• 3556 • Divisions' Council Awards
Recognizes a special project, overall achievements, and individual contribution. All division chairs will receive applications in the fall. Three awards are given.

• 3557 • Diana Donald Award
To recognize contributions on planning issues related to women and family. The recipient should have demonstrated significant contributions to the profession, held a responsible management position in planning, and devoted substantial effort to community service particularly service involving the attainment of women's rights both in the planning profession and in the community at-large. Nominations of members and non-members may be made by any person or organization. Awarded annually. This award honors the late APA Board of Directors member for her contributions to the Association.

• 3558 • Outstanding Planning Awards
To recognize outstanding planning for group achievement in four categories: Plan, to recognize a significant advancement to the science and art of planning, emphasizes planning in one of its original and most basic forms, the written plan; Project/Program/Tool, to recognize a significant advancement to the cause of planning, emphasizes results and demonstrates how a project, program, or tool implemented a plan; Special Community Initiative, to recognize an initiative that illustrates how the community or jurisdiction utilized the planning process to address a need outside the normal sphere of planning initiatives; and Implementation, to recognize an effort that demonstrates a significant advancement for the jurisdiction resulting in real and documentable change, emphasizes long term, measurable results and demonstrates that sustained implementation makes a difference for the jurisdiction. Selection is based on originally, transferability, quality, comprehensiveness, public participation, role of planners, and effectiveness of results. One award and two

honorable mentions are presented in each category annually.

• 3559 • Secretary's Opportunity and Empowerment Award

Recognizes a plan, program, or project whose efforts show improved quality of life for low- and moderate income community residents. Selection is based on how creatively housing, economic development and other programs, and private investments were used in the plan. And how these plans overcame difficult community issues, such as low investment, crime, abandoned buildings, unemployment, low civic participation and disagreement. Documentation showing how the nominated programs addressed the need for increased economic, employment and housing choice and/or mobility among low- and moderate-income residents; improved the quality of life for the people served; provided examples for others; used innovative approaches to address the need for increased choice and community empowerment; related to existing plans and the role the planner(s) had in meeting the results; the planning process was important to subsequent implementation; all stakeholders in the community supported and contributed to results; is the effort cost-effective. For submissions with a physical aspect: does it demonstrate attention to detail and urban design including, materials, context, amenities, historic, and cultural features. Open to APA members and nonmembers. Held in conjunction with U.S. Department of Housing and Urban Development.

• 3560 • Student Planner Award

Recognizes outstanding achievement during the nominee's academic career in planning. Nominees must be individuals in the final year of an APA-accredited planning program at the undergraduate level or have graduated or will graduate from such a program during the year of the nomination. Individuals meeting the same criteria, but from a graduate level program are also eligible. Documentation showing the extent of the nominee's academic planning principles and the planning process participation; enthusiasm in advanced excellence produced by the nominees participation in the program; and possibility for potential success in the field must be presented at the time of nomination. Nominees do not have to be APA members. One nomination is accepted from each accredited graduate and undergraduate program.

• 3561 •

American Podiatric Medical Association
Glenn B. Gastwirth DPM, Exec.Dir.
9312 Old Georgetown Rd.
Bethesda, MD 20814-1621
Phone: (301)571-9200
Toll-Free: 800-FOOTCARE
Fax: (301)530-2752
E-mail: askapma@apma.org
Home Page: http://www.apma.org

Formerly: American Podiatry Association.

• 3562 • Journalism Award

To recognize outstanding achievement in print media covering foot care and podiatric medicine. A monetary award of $500 and a plaque are presented to one or more recipients annually. Established in 1991.

• 3563 • William J. Stickel Awards

To promote research in podiatric medicine and to provide members with the most current techniques and information in the field. A monetary prize of $1,500 and a gold award certificate, $800 and a silver award certificate, and $500 and a bronze award certificate are awarded annually. Established in 1955. Sponsored by the *Journal of the APMA* and PICA.

• 3564 •

American Police Hall of Fame
6350 Horizon Dr.
Titusville, FL 32780
Phone: (321)264-0911
Fax: (321)264-0033
E-mail: policeinfo@aphf.org
Home Page: http://www.aphf.org

Formerly: American Federation of Police.

• 3565 • Certificate of Appreciation

To recognize the assistance given by citizens in aiding local police through any act or service that would merit some form of thanks and encourage others to cooperate with police officials. Nominations of any person, any age, are accepted from another person or him or herself, anytime during the year. A certificate and full-size medal is awarded when warranted.

• 3566 • Criminal Investigation Award

To recognize the men and women who quietly work to solve cases through long hours of detective work and for recognition of their talents that lead to the closing of a difficult case. Nominations of any person, any age, are accepted from another person or him or herself, anytime during the year. A certificate and full-size medal is awarded when merited.

• 3567 • Distinguished Service Award

To recognize police officers and high ranking officials who distinguish themselves with honor in outstanding service to their state and community. Nominations of any person, any age, are accepted from another person or him or herself, anytime during the year. A certificate and full-size medal is awarded.

• 3568 • General Commendation

To recognize officers who have, through an act of service or by professional police work, earned a special commendation on an individual basis. Nominations of any person, any age, are accepted from another person or him or herself, anytime during the year. A certificate and full-size medal is awarded.

• 3569 • Good Samaritan Award

To recognize both law enforcement and civilians for an act of charity that aids those less fortunate, thus carrying on the biblical act of the Good Samaritan. Nominations of any person, any age, in spirit are accepted from another person or him or herself, anytime during the year. A certificate and full-size medal awarded when merited.

• 3570 • John Edgar Hoover Police Service Award

To honor police and citizens for service and valor nationwide. Any person, any age, is and can be nominated either by another person or by him or herself anytime during the year. Established in 1966 in honor of police officers and friends of police officers.

• 3571 • K-9 Dog Award

For recognition of police dogs of all breeds that have come to be special animals in that they help save lives and fight crime. Awarded when merited.

• 3572 • Knights of Justice Award

To recognize community service and valor by lawmen who are all "Blue Knights of Justice" and are considered to carry out the work of the world's first police officer, Michael the Archangel. Nominations of any person, any age, are accepted from another person or him or herself, anytime during the year. An honorary knighthood is awarded as merited.

• 3573 • Merit Award for Excellent Arrest

For recognition of the apprehension of a felon who was endangering the life and safety of the community. The arrest is considered by the department to be outstanding from the normal day-to-day arrests. Full-size medal and certificate are awarded when merited.

• 3574 • News Media Award for Community Service

For recognition of an individual or media firm that produces police stories, films, TV shots, or radio broadcasts that aid the community and police. A citation is awarded when merited.

• 3575 • Patriots Award

For recognition of organizations and individuals whose patriotic acts or service promote liberty and justice in the United States. Nominations of any person, any age, are accepted from another person or him or herself, anytime during the year. A certificate and full-size is awarded when merited.

• 3576 • Police Medal of Honor

For recognition of police officers injured in the line of duty. A full-size medal is awarded.

• 3577 • Police Officer of the Year

To recognize law enforcement officers who have served above and beyond the line of duty and survived. Any law enforcement officers in the

U.S.A. are eligible. A medal, a trophy, and expenses to attend the conference are awarded annually in May. In addition, posthumous awards of valor for officers killed in the line of duty may be presented. Established in 1960.

• 3578 • Police Posthumous Medal of Honor

To provide the family of any police officer killed in the line of duty with a tribute to his great sacrifice. A medal, flag, and citation are issued posthumously, and the name of the officer is placed in the American Police Hall of Fame. Awarded when warranted.

• 3579 • Silver Star for Bravery

To recognize an officer for an act of daring and valor in a life-threatening situation that is above and beyond the line of duty. Nominations by any person, any age, are accepted from another person or him or herself, anytime during the year. A Silver Star certificate and full-size medal is awarded as merited.

• 3580 •

American Political Science Association
Michael Brintnall, Exec.Dir.
1527 New Hampshire Ave. NW
Washington, DC 20036-1206
Phone: (202)483-2512
Fax: (202)483-2657
E-mail: apsa@apsanet.org
Home Page: http://www.apsanet.org

• 3581 • Richard F. Fenno, Jr. Book Prize

To honor the outstanding book published during the preceding year in legislative studies, including American, non-American, cross-national, and sub-national works. Authors and others interested are invited to nominate outstanding books in legislative studies by March 1. The prize is announced and conferred at the Awards Ceremony of the Legislative Studies Section held during and in conjunction with the annual meeting of the American Political Science Association.

• 3582 •

American Pomological Society
Essie Fallahi, Award Chair
103 Tyson Bldg.
University Park, PA 16802-4200
Phone: (814)863-6163
Fax: (814)863-6139
E-mail: aps@psu.edu
Home Page: http://americanpomological.org

• 3583 • U. P. Hedrick Awards

To encourage promising and gifted students to specialize in the field of pomology. Manuscripts by undergraduates, graduate students alone, or co-authored with an advisor having a special interest in horticulture and, particularly fruit, are eligible. Entries should be submitted to the Awards Committee no later than 60 days before the annual APS meeting. Society membership is not mandatory. The paper content should relate to cultivars of deciduous, tropical, or subtropical fruits as related to climate, soil, rootstocks, a specific experiment, a breeding project, history and performance of new or old cultivars, a library review pertinent to pomology, an MS or PhD thesis paper, or a personal experience with a particular fruit cultivar. The award consists of a monetary award of $300 first place and $100 second place with mounted certificates. Additionally, the first place honored work will be published in *Fruit Varieties Journal*. Presented annually at the APS meeting held in conjunction with the annual meeting of the American Society of Horticultural Science, usually in August. Established in 1983 in honor of Dr. U.P. Hedrick, renowned pomologist known for fruit variety improvement, who was Director of the New York State Agricultural Experiment Station, Geneva, New York. Additional information is available from The Secretary, 103 Tyson Building, University Park, PA 16802. Formerly: (1982) Bregger Essay Award.

• 3584 • Paul Shepard Award

To recognize an outstanding research paper published in *Fruit Varieties Journal*. A certificate is awarded annually. Established in 1960.

• 3585 • Wilder Medal

To recognize distinguished service and contributions to the field of horticulture. A silver medal is awarded annually. Established in 1873 in honor of Marshall Pinckney Wilder, a founder and the first president of the society for 35 years.

• 3586 •

American Power Boat Association
Gloria J. Urbin, Exec.Admin.
17640 Nine Mile Rd.
Eastpointe, MI 48021
Phone: (586)773-9700
Fax: (586)773-6490
E-mail: apbahq@apba-racing.com
Home Page: http://www.apba-racing.com/Home.html

• 3587 • APBA Gold Cup

To recognize the winner of the Association's annual APBA Gold Cup race for "unlimited hydroplanes." The gold loving cup resting on four tiers with gold medals representing 100 years of winners is awarded annually. Established in 1904.

• 3588 • APBA Honor Squadron

To recognize the outstanding individuals who have made distinguished contributions to the sport of power boat racing. Drivers, owners, designers, builders, engineers, organizers, and officials are eligible. Certificates are awarded each year at the Association's annual meeting in January. Established in 1953.

• 3589 • Colonel Green Round Hill Trophy

To recognize the owner, driving his own equipment, who earns the most points tabulated for all Professional Racing Outboard regattas sanctioned by the American Power Boat Association. A trophy is awarded annually in November. Established in 1986.

• 3590 • Hall of Champions

To recognize the Association's most outstanding drivers from each season. Awards are given in the following categories: Inboard, Inboard Endurance, J Class, Modified Outboard, Offshore, Outboard Performance Craft, Professional Racing Outboard, Stock Outboard, and Unlimited. Points and achievements in a class form the basis for selection. Plaques, patches, and decals are awarded annually at the Association's annual convention. Established in 1974.

• 3591 • Randy Tilton Memorial Award

For recognition of attitude, sportsmanship, and racing achievement by Outboard Performance Craft participants. Awarded annually. Established in 1977 in memory of Randy Tilton.

• 3592 •

American Primrose Society
Julia Haldorson, Treas.
PO Box 210913
Auke Bay, AK 99821
Phone: (907)789-5860
E-mail: julia.haldorson@ak.net

• 3593 • Dorothy Stredicke Dickson Memorial Award

To recognize outstanding service to the American Primrose Society. Society members are eligible to be selected by the Society's Board of Directors. A bronze medallion is awarded annually. Established in 1985 in memory of Dorothy Stredicke Dickson's outstanding example of service to the Society.

• 3594 •

American Printing History Association
Stephen Crook, Exec.Sec.
PO Box 4519, Grand Central Sta.
New York, NY 10163-4519
Phone: (212)930-9220
Fax: (212)930-0079
E-mail: sgcrook@printinghistory.org
Home Page: http://www.printinghistory.org

• 3595 • Individual Award

To recognize an individual for distinguished contributions to printing history. Awarded annually. Established in 1976.

• 3596 • Institutional Award

To recognize an institution for distinguished contributions to printing history. Awarded annually. Established in 1985.

• 3597 •
American Probation and Parole Association
Carl Wicklund, Exec.Dir.
2760 Research Pk. Dr.
Lexington, KY 40511-8410
Phone: (859)244-8203
Phone: (859)244-8207
Fax: (859)244-8001
E-mail: appa@csg.org
Home Page: http://www.appa-net.org

• 3598 • **APPA Awards for Excellence in Community Crime Prevention**
Recognizes the integration of community crime prevention initiatives into the traditional roles of supervision, intervention, and sacntioning of offenders. Community corrections agencies or community crime prevention programs coordinating with a community corrections agency are eligible to receive this award.

• 3599 • **APPA Community Awareness Through Media Award**
Recognizes a media broadcast, publication or film capable of reaching a national audience that broadens the public's awareness and understanding of issues in the American criminal justice system in an accurate, fair and balanced manner and also shares the vision of the APPA. Sponsored by the APPA Public Relations Committee.

• 3600 • **APPA Member of the Year Award**
Recognizes the work and energy of a worthy APPA member. Current APPA members who have been members for at least one year and have provided significant contributions to the organization through promotion of vision and mission of APPA are eligible. Any member may submit a nomination. A complimentary ten year membership is awarded. Elected members of the Board of Directors are not eligible.

• 3601 • **Walter Dunbar Memorial Award**
To recognize significant contributions by a practicing professional or a retired practitioner in the field of probation and/or parole. Nominations may be submitted from January through April. Awarded annually. Established in 1986 in memory of Walter Dunbar, who served as Director of the California Department of Corrections, Chairman of the U.S. Parole Commission, and Director of the New York State Division of Probation.

• 3602 • **Sam Houston State University Award**
To recognize an individual for a published article concerning probation, parole, or community corrections that provides new information and insight into the operation, effectiveness, or the future of the community corrections profession. Articles published in national or regional journals may be submitted from January through April. Awarded annually. Established in 1986.

• 3603 • **Joe Kegans Award for Victim Services in Probation and Parole**
Honors exemplary services to victims of crim. Individuals working in community corrections are eligible. Nominees may be living or deceased. Preference will be given to community correction professions or volunteers who have personallly experienced criminal victimization and have used that experience to help others. Estblished in honor of Judge Joe Kegans, a founding member of APPA's Victim Issues Committee, who devoted her career as a jurist to bettering the lives of all with whom she came into contact.

• 3604 • **Scotia Knouff Line Officer of the Year Award**
This, the most competitive and prestigious practitioner award, is given to recognize the probation, parole, or community corrections officer who has performed assigned duties in an outstanding manner and/or made significant contributions to the probation, parole, or community corrections profession at the local, regional, or national level and/or brought credit or honor to the profession through participation or involvement in community activities or programs. Nominations may be submitted from January through April. Awarded annually. Established in 1986.

• 3605 • **President's Award**
To recognize exemplary community correction programs that serve to advance the knowledge, effectiveness, and integrity of the system. Organizations that have exemplified the management and innovations necessary to lead community corrections toward the future are considered. Eligible candidates that meet all or a combination of the following criteria are eligible: changes or contributes to the broad field of community corrections and helps to move the field forward; a clear correlation exists between the candidate's goals and their effect; makes a difference that is supported by impact data; the elements of the project/program/agency can be repeated by others; and shows clear evidence of the supportive nature of the environment. The candidates are evaluated on the following characteristics: program implementation process, client assessment practices, characteristics that match the client's needs, therapeutic integrity, relapse prevention techniques, staff characteristics, and evaluation. Awarded annually.

• 3606 • **University of Cincinnati Award**
To recognize an individual for significant contributions to the probation and parole field or technology. (This is not a practitioner award.) Individuals from academic, research, or government agencies not engaged in providing probation and public services are eligible. Nominations may be submitted from January through April. Awarded annually. Established in 1986.

• 3607 •
American Professional Society on the Abuse of Children
Daphne Wright, Oper.Mgr.
PO Box 30669
PO Box 26901
Charleston, SC 29417
Phone: (843)764-2905
Toll-Free: 877-402-7722
Fax: (803)753-9823
E-mail: apsac@comcast.net
Home Page: http://www.APSAC.org

• 3608 • **Outstanding Media Coverage of Child Maltreatment Award**
Recognizes balanced, accurate, and in-depth reporting on any issue concerning child maltreatment. Deadline is April 1. Annually.

• 3609 •
American Psychiatric Association
Richard K. Harding, Pres.
1000 Wilson Blvd., Ste. 1825
Arlington, VA 22209-3901
Phone: (703)907-7300
Toll-Free: 888-357-7924
Fax: (703)907-7322
E-mail: apa@psych.org
Home Page: http://www.psych.org

• 3610 • **Administrative Psychiatry Award**
To honor a nationally recognized clinician executive whose effectiveness as an administrator of major mental health programs has expanded the body of knowledge concerning management of the mental health services delivery system, and whose effectiveness and interest in this important aspect of psychiatry has made it possible for him or her to function as a role model for other psychiatrists. Nominees must be APA members. $500 and a plaque are awarded. The winner may be asked to present a lecture at the annual meeting. Established in 1983. Funded by the American Association of Psychiatric Administators.

• 3611 • **APA Assembly Warren Williams Awards**
To recognize outstanding recent or current activity or contribution in the field of psychiatry and mental health in each area council. The area councils have discretion and flexibility in nominations for recipients. Selections by the area councils are ratified by the Assembly Executive Committee, and presentation of the individual awards is made at the area council meetings or at the Assembly meetings. A total of $1,000 in each area council is allocated annually. Established in 1984. Funded by McNeil Pharmaceuticals.

• 3612 • **APA Award for Research in Psychiatry**
To recognize outstanding a single research accomplishment in psychiatry and its basic sciences Intended to cover all aspects of psychiatric research. United States or Canadian citizens are eligible and must be nominated by a APA sponsor. Inquire for additional guidelines. A

monetary award and a plaque are awarded annually. Established in 1976 as the Hofheimer Prize. Formerly: Hofheimer Prize Award.

• 3613 • Award for Exemplary State/ University Collaboration

To recognize state mental health programs engaged and University departments of psychiatry in collaborative activities. Programs are judged on strength, research, education and/or recruitment, and retention efforts. Nominations are accepted from state programs, Universities, or others not involved in the nominated effort and should include eight copies of the nomination and supporting materials. A plaque is presented at the Institute on Psychiatric Services. Established in 1989. Funded by Pew Memorial Trust.

• 3614 • Award for Patient Advocacy

To recognize a public figure respected for personal accomplishments and beliefs, who has promoted the improvement of services for people coping with mental disorders and substance abuse, and who has fought stigma by speaking out about experiences with mental illness and psychiatric treatment. Selection is made by the Scientific Program Committee in consultation with the Joint Commission on Public Affairs. An honorarium of $2,000 and a plaque are awarded. A lecture is presented at the APA Annual Meeting. Established in 1987. Funded by Scientific Program Committee.

• 3615 • Simon Bolivar Award

Recognizes a prominent Hispanic statesman or spokesperson, and to sensitize the APA membership to the problems and goals of Hispanics. The lecturer is selected by the Committee on Hispanic Psychiatrists. An honorarium of $500 with travel expenses for nonmember winners is awarded. The winner presents a lecture at the APA Annual Meeting. Established in 1975.

• 3616 • Distinguished Service Awards

To honor individuals and/or organizations for exceptional service to American psychiatry. Two plaques may be awarded annually. One for contributions to the association and open only to members. One for contributions to the field and open to members and nonmembers. Established in 1964.

• 3617 • Marie H. Eldredge Award

For recognition of research work on the cause and treatment of neuroses of all age groups and retarded persons of all age groups. Members or residents under the age of 40 living and working in the states of Hawaii, Pennsylvania, or New Jersey are eligible. Applications must be submitted by December 15. A monetary prize of $1,000 and a plaque are awarded annually. Established in 1964. Funded by a bequest from Marie H. Eldredge.

• 3618 • Solomon Carter Fuller Award

To recognize an African American individual who has pioneered in an area that has significantly benefited the quality of life for African Americans. The winner is selected by the Committee of Black Psychiatrists. An honorarium of $500, a plaque, and travel expenses paid for nonmember winners are awarded. The winner presents a lecture at the APA Annual Meeting. Established in 1969 in honor of the first African American psychiatrist in the United States.

• 3619 • Manfred S. Guttmacher Award

For recognition of an outstanding contribution to the literature of forensic psychiatry in the form of a book, monograph, paper, or any other work, submitted to or presented at any professional meeting during the year. Applications must be submitted by May 15. A monetary award of $500, a plaque, and travel expenses (up to $500.00 for non-members) to present a lecture at the annual meeting of the American Academy of Psychiatry and the Law are awarded annually. Established in 1975. Sponsored by the American Academy of Psychiatry and the Law and funded by Professional Risk Management Services Inc.

• 3620 • Human Rights Award

To recognize an individual or organization exemplifying the capacity of human beings to protect others from damage at the hands of other human beings to help them recover from acts already committed. Individuals (psychiatrists or others such as public servants, authors, or members of the media) or organizations (predominantly humanitarian or professional) are eligible. A plaque is awarded. A letter describing the basis for the nomination and a curriculum vitae must be submitted. Application deadline is February 15. Established in 1990.

• 3621 • Blanche F. Ittleson Research in Child Psychiatry Award

To recognize an individual child psychiatrist or group of investigators for published research results on the mental health of children. The findings of such research will have led, or strongly promise to lead, to a significant improvement of the mental health of children. United States and Canadian citizens may submit work that was published within the last five Years or accepted for publication in the near future. Applications must be submitted by November 1st. A monetary prize of $2,000 and a plaque are awarded annually. Established in 1976 to honor Blanche F. Ittleson, a long-time friend to all of the mental health fields and a dedicated supporter of the well-being of children. Funded by a grant from the Ittleson Foundation.

• 3622 • Jacob K. Javits Public Service Award

To recognize contributions to the field of mental health by a public servant. The winner is chosen by the Joint Commission on Government Relations. An honorarium of $1,000 is presented at either the State Legislative Seminar or Federal Legislative Institute. Established in 1986.

• 3623 • APA/Kempf Fund Award for Research Development in Psychobiological Psychiatry

To recognize research on the causes and treatment of schizophrenia. Applicants must be senior researchers acting in both a research and Mentor role $ 1500 is awarded to the senior researcher and $20,000 is awarded for the development of a young researcher working as a mentor Trainee for the winning senior researcher. An original and five copies of all required material must be submitted. Application deadline Is October 14th. Inquire for guideline information.

• 3624 • Kun-Po Soo Award

To recognize significant contributions toward understanding the impact and import of Asian cultural heritages in areas relevant to psychiatry. The award also seeks to encourage scholarship and research in culture-specific mental health issues and treatment needs of Asian populations and to stimulate scientific exchange on transcultural issues. The winner may be asked to present a lecture at an APA Annual Meeting. Nominees need not be Asians, Americans, psychiatrists, or APA members. An honorarium of $1,000 is awarded. A letter of nomination and supporting documents must be submitted. Established in 1987. Formerly: (1997) Asian/Asian-American Award.

• 3625 • APA/Lilly Products Resident Research Award

To recognize three psychiatry residents for excellence in research undertaken during residency. Residents or fellows in an accredited psychiatry training program in the United States or Canada may submit scientific papers by January 20. A CV and a research paper describing research study or a scholarly case presentation must be submitted. An honorarium for the recipient and $1,000 to the resident's parent department are awarded. Established in 1984 as the APA/Pennwalt Resident Research Award. Renamed in 1988. Funded by Lily Products Co. Deadline January 20. Formerly: (1988) APA/ Pennwalt Resident Research Award.

• 3626 • APA/Lilly Psychiatric Research Fellowship

This one-year fellowship is awarded to a postgraduate medical trainee specifically to focus on research and personal scholarship. Applications are evaluated on the basis of the applicant's qualifications, preceptor's qualifications, quality of research training plan, and adequacy of institutional resources and facilities. Individuals must have earned either an M.D. or D.O. degree and have completed residency training in psychiatry or child psychiatry by the time the fellowship commences; and be members of APA. The deadline is October 14. A stipend of $45,000 is paid to the Institution for disbursement to the fellow. Established in 1988. Funded by Lily Research Labs.

• 3627 • Bruno Lima Award for Excellence in Disaster Psychiatry

Recognizes outstanding contributions of district branch members to the care and understanding of the victims of disasters. Contributions include designing disaster response plans, providing direct service delivery in time of disaster, or in disaster consultation, education, and/or research. Award certificate signed by APA president and president of awardee's district branch, to be presented at the district branch; names published in *Psychiatric News.* Awarded annually by the Committee on Psychiatric Dimensions of Disaster. Established in 1994.

• 3628 • Agnes Purcell McGavin Award
To honor a psychiatrist who has made significant contributions to the prevention of mental disorders in children. Contributions must be in the form of framing concepts, developing proofs, or creating applications. Nominations are to be submitted by November 30. A monetary award of $1,500 and a certificate are awarded annually when merited. Established in 1964.

• 3629 • Adolf Meyer Lectureship
To advance psychiatric research by enabling psychiatrists to hear from leading scientists and to exchange new research information with colleagues. Researchers in the U.S. and abroad are eligible. The lecturer is chosen by the Scientific Program Committee from among outstanding investigators in the U.S. and abroad. An honorarium of $3,000 is awarded. A lecture is given at the APA Annual Meeting. Established in 1957. Funded by Dista Products Co. a division of Eli Lily and Co.

• 3630 • Robert T. Morse Writer's Award
To recognize outstanding contributions to furthering the public understanding of psychiatry and mental illness. Writers outside the field of psychiatry are eligible. Applications must be submitted to the Joint Commission on Public Affairs by January 1st. A monetary award of $1,000 and a plaque are awarded annually. Established in 1964 in memory of Robert T. Morse, M.D.

• 3631 • Oskar Pfister Award
To honor an outstanding contributor in the field of psychiatry and religion. Selection is made by the Committee on Religion and Psychiatry in consultation with representatives of the American Mental Health Clergy. An honorarium of $1,000 and a plaque are presented at the APA Convocation. The winner may be asked to present a lecture at the annual meeting. Established in 1983. Supported by the Harding Foundation.

• 3632 • Presidential Commendations
To recognize individuals selected by the APA President. Plaques are presented at the APA Annual Meeting during the Convocation. Established in 1979.

• 3633 • Public Affairs Network Awards
To recognize outstanding achievements in the development of public affairs activities and programs by the District Branches. The competition is open to all district branches. Selections are made in the categories of Coalition building, Media relations; Mental Illness Awareness Week; Public Information Projects; and Overall Public Affairs Programs. The deadline is September 6. Plaques are presented biennially during the Public Affairs Network Institute. Established in 1989.

• 3634 • Isaac Ray Award in Memory of Margaret Sutermeister
For recognition of outstanding contributions to forensic psychiatry or to the psychiatric aspects of jurisprudence. Psychiatrists, attorneys, or professionals in the field of human behavior are eligible. An honorarium of $1,500 is awarded, and the winner is responsible for presenting a lecture or series of lectures on some aspect of forensic psychiatry or psychiatric jurisprudence, and preparing a manuscript for publication. Awarded biennially in even-numbered years. Established in 1951 in memory of Margaret Sutermeister by her mother, Bertha B. Sutermeister.

• 3635 • Robert L. Robinson Awards
To recognize productions that contribute significantly to a better public understanding of psychiatry and mental illness. An award may be given for both radio and television. Submissions must be made by January 1st. An honorarium of $1,000 and a plaque to either/or both winners are awarded. If two awards are given each winner receives $ 500. Established in 1983 in honor of "Robbie" Robinson, former APA Public Affairs Director.

• 3636 • Nancy C. A. Roeske Certificate of Recognition for Excellence in Medical Student Education
To recognize an APA member or fellow who has made a significant and sustained contribution to medical student education. Each school develops its own nomination procedure and can submit unlimited nominations. The deadline is September 1st. A certificate is awarded. Established in 1989.

• 3637 • Benjamin Rush Lectureship Award
To recognize an individual who has achieved renown for a contribution to the history of psychiatry from fields even other than psychiatry, such as medical history, anthropology, and sociology. An honorarium of $1,000 for member winners, $500 for non-member winners is presented, and the winner is responsible for presenting a lecture on a broad theme related to the history of psychiatry. Awarded annually. Established in 1967. Funded by Roche Laboratories a division of Hoffman LaRoche..

• 3638 • Assembly William Sorum Awards
To recognize a Member-in-Training and a District Branch in each area who has made the most notable progress in MIT activities, involvement, participation, or representation in the APA. Nomination letters must be submitted to the Area Council Award Board. The nominee must be a Member-in-Training and currently active in a District Branch. Established in 1991.

• 3639 • George Tarjan Award
Recognizes an individual who has made significant contributions to the enhancement of the integration of International Medical Graduates (IMGs) into American psychiatry. Nominations are accepted from groups, institutions or individuals. Self nominations are also accepted. A plaque and monetary prize of $500 are awarded annually by the Committee on International Medical Graduates. Established in 1992 in memory of George Tarjan MD.

• 3640 • Arnold L. van Ameringen Award in Psychiatric Rehabilitation
To recognize an individual, institution, or organization that has made an outstanding contribution to the field of psychiatric rehabilitation, in the areas of clinical service, research, education, advocacy, or a combination thereof. Nominations must be submitted by October 1. An honorarium of $5,000 and a plaque are awarded at the Institute on Psychiatric Services. If appropriate, the recipient may be invited to present a lecture at an APA meeting. Established in 1985.

• 3641 • Seymour D. Vestermark Award for Psychiatric Education
For recognition of outstanding contributions to undergraduate, graduate, and continuing medical education in psychiatry, and the education of behavioral scientists for research. Nominations must be submitted by March 15. A monetary award of $1,000 is awarded annually. Established in 1969 in memory of Seymour Vestermark, an international authority in the field of professional mental health training and education. Co-sponsored by the National Institute of Mental Health. Formerly: (1997) Seymour Vestermark Award.

• 3642 • Jack Weinberg Memorial Award for Geriatric Psychiatry
To honor a psychiatrist who has demonstrated special leadership or who has done outstanding work in clinical practice, training, or research into geriatric psychiatry anywhere in the world. Nominations must be submitted by December 1, and must be made by a member of the APA. An honorarium of $500 and a plaque are awarded annually. Established in 1983 in memory of Jack Weinberg.

• 3643 •
American Psychological Association
Adult Development and Aging Division (Division 20)
℅ Jane Berry, Sec.
Department of Psychology
University of Richmond
Richmond, VA 23173
Phone: (804)289-8130
Fax: (804)287-1905
E-mail: jberry@richmond.edu
Home Page: http://apadiv20.phhp.ufl.edu

• 3644 • M. Powell Lawton Distinguished Contribution Award for Applied Gerontology
To recognize distinguished contributions to the scientific study of the psychology of adult development and aging. Eligibility is based on scientific record. Deadline for nominations is May 15. An engraved plaque and monetary prize of $1,000 are awarded at the annual business meeting held at the APA annual convention.

• 3645 • Student Research Awards
To recognize excellent research by students in adult development and aging. Certificates and monetary prizes ranging from $250 to $500 are presented to the winner in two categories: Completed Research and Research Proposals. Awarded at the annual business meeting, held at the APA annual convention.

• 3646 •
American Psychological Association
American Psychology-Law Society (Division 41)
Edie Greene, Pres.
% Margaret B. Kovera
Department of Psychology
City University of New York
445 W 59th St.
New York, NY 10019
Phone: (305)348-0274
Fax: (305)348-3879
E-mail: mkovera@jjay.cuny.edu
Home Page: http://www.ap-ls.org

• 3647 • Dissertation Award
To recognize the best doctoral dissertation within a given year in psychology and law. The dissertation must take into regard the importance and design of the research. Deadline for submission is May 1. A monetary prize of $100 is presented at the Division's business meeting at the APA annual convention.

• 3648 • Distinguished Contribution to Psychology and Law
For recognition of outstanding and sustained contributions to the field of psychology and law. Self-nominations are not accepted, and nominees need not be psychologists nor members of the Division. Deadline for submission is February 15. A plaque is presented at the mid-year, biennial conference of the Division.

• 3649 •
American Psychological Association
Applied Experimental and Engineering Psychology Division (Division 21)
Ronald Gary Shapiro, Pres.
% Scott Shappell, Sec.-Treas.
Clemson University
Department of Industrial Engineering
121 Freeman Hall
Clemson, SC 29634-0929
Phone: (864)656-4662
Fax: (864)656-0795
E-mail: HFENG@clemson.edu
Home Page: http://www.apa.org/divisions/div21

• 3650 • Earl A. Alluisi Award
To recognize outstanding early career achievement. Restricted to scholars within the first ten years of their receipt of a Ph.D. Awarded annually.

• 3651 • George E. Briggs Dissertation Award
To recognize an outstanding dissertation on engineering psychology. Dissertations must have been approved in the previous year. Deadline for submissions is in March. A monetary prize of $200 and a plaque are awarded at the annual business meeting at the APA annual convention.

• 3652 • Franklin V. Taylor Award
For recognition of outstanding contributions in the field of applied experimental and engineering psychology. Awarded at the annual business meeting at the APA annual convention.

• 3653 •
American Psychological Association
Behavior Analysis Division (Division 25)
% Eric Jacobs
Department of Psychology
Southern Illinois University
Carbondale, IL 62901-6502
Phone: (618)453-3555
Fax: (618)453-8271
E-mail: eajacobs@siu.edu
Home Page: http://www.auburn.edu/~newlamc/apa_div25

• 3654 • Experimental Analysis of Behavior Dissertation Award
To recognize an outstanding doctoral dissertation in the field of basic behavioral processes. The award consists of a certificate, an invitation to present the dissertation at the next APA convention, and monetary support to help the recipient with convention travel expenses.

• 3655 • Don F. Hake Basic/Applied Research Award
For recognition of outstanding published work that bridges the basic/applied continuum of behavior analysis and best applies it to socially significant problems. A certificate is awarded along with an invitation to present an address at the APA annual convention.

• 3656 • Fred S. Keller Behavioral Education Award
To recognize a member of the behavioral community for distinguished contributions to education in behavior analysis. Research should have significantly affected educational policy, practice, conceptualization, and implementation of major education programs. A certificate is presented along with an invitation to speak at the annual APA convention.

• 3657 • B. F. Skinner New Researcher Award
To recognize innovative and important research in the field of behavior analysis within the first five years after receiving a doctorate. A certificate is presented along with an invitation to speak at the APA annual convention.

• 3658 •
American Psychological Association
Behavioral Neuroscience and Comparative Psychology Division (Division 6)
Chana Atkins, Sec.-Treas.
Dept. of Psychology
University of Kentucky
Lexington, KY 40506
Phone: (606)257-1103
E-mail: ckakin1@uky.edu.edu
Home Page: http://www.apa.org/divisions/div6

• 3659 • D. O. Hebb Distinguished Scientific Contribution Award
To recognize the best poster or platform presentation by a young investigator who is within five years of receiving a Ph.D. A monetary prize of $100 and a certificate are awarded at the business meeting at the APA annual convention.

• 3660 •
American Psychological Association
Counseling Psychology Division (Division 17)
750 1st St. NE
Washington, DC 20002-4242
Phone: (202)216-7602
Toll-Free: 800-374-2721
Fax: (202)218-3599
E-mail: div17@mchsi.com
Home Page: http://www.div17.org

• 3661 • John D. Black Award for Outstanding Achievement in the Practice of Counseling Psychology
To stimulate and reward outstanding achievement in the practice of counseling psychology. Awarded annually. A monetary prize of $1,000 is donated by Consulting Psychologists Press.

• 3662 • John Holland Award for Outstanding Achievement in Career or Personality Research
To honor notable research on career or personality topics by a psychologist who has received his or her doctoral degree in the last 8-18 years. A monetary prize of $1,000 is awarded annually. Established by Psychological Assessment Resources, Inc.

• 3663 • Barbara A. Kirk Award for Outstanding Graduate Student Research
To honor the best research (dissertation or other) produced by a graduate student conducting independent research while enrolled in a counseling psychology program. A monetary prize of $500 is awarded annually. Sponsored by the Consulting Psychologists Press.

• 3664 • Fritz and Linn Kuder Early Career Scientist/Practitioner Award
To honor early career achievement in the science and practice of counseling psychology. Candidates must have received the Ph.D. within the past ten years. A monetary prize of $500 is awarded annually.

• 3665 • Senior Recognition Award for Distinguished Contributors to the Division of Counseling Psychology

To recognize members of the division, 65 years of age or older, who have served as Fellows, ABPPs, or elected officers. Awarded to numerous recipients every five years.

• 3666 • Leona Tyler Award

To stimulate and reward exemplary research or professional achievement in counseling psychology. Deadline for nominations is in November. A monetary prize and a certificate are awarded annually. In addition, the recipient delivers an invited address at the APA Convention.

• 3667 •

American Psychological Association Developmental Psychology Division (Division 7)
Lynn Liben, Contact
% Catherine Haden
Department of Psychology
Loyola University of Chicago
6525 N Sheridan Rd.
Chicago, IL 60626
E-mail: chaden@luc.edu
Home Page: http://classweb.gmu.edu/awinsler/div7/homepage.shtml

• 3668 • Developmental Psychology Awards

To recognize outstanding contributions to developmental psychology. The following awards are presented: Boyd R. McCandless Award, G. Stanley Hall Award, Eleanor Maccoby Book Award, Urie Bronfenbrenner Award, Mentor Award in Developmental Psychology, and Dissertation Award in Developmental Psychology. Awarded at the APA annual convention.

• 3669 •

American Psychological Association Division of Family Psychology (Division 43)
Mark Stanton, Pres.
% Nancy Elman, Sec.
5F28 Posvar Hall
University of Pittsburgh
Pittsburgh, PA 15260
Phone: (412)682-8172
Phone: 800-374-2721
Fax: (412)624-7231
E-mail: elman@pitt.edu
Home Page: http://www.apa.org/divisions/div43

• 3670 • Certificate of Appreciation

To honor individual in two categories: to outgoing chairs of divisional committees, outgoing members of the Executive Board, and other members who have rendered outstanding service to the Division (Category I); and to persons who have made outstanding contributions to family psychology in the media, in the legislature, and/or in the public service arenas (Category II). Awarded when merited.

• 3671 • Family Psychologist of the Year

To recognize individuals for contributions to the family psychology discipline. Members of the Division may be nominated. A plaque is awarded each year at the APA annual convention. Established in 1986.

• 3672 • Fellows Awards

In recognition of division members' outstanding and unusual contributions to psychology, especially family psychology.

• 3673 • Student Research Award

For recognition of student research that reflects a coherent, theoretical perspective and represents excellence in content, methodology, and statistics. Papers must reflect empirical contributions and have an underlying philosophy that is family oriented. Division members are eligible. The award recipient must be a doctoral candidate when nominated, with his or her research completed. Deadline for nomination is December 1. A monetary award of $50 and a certificate are awarded at the APA annual convention.

• 3674 •

American Psychological Association Division of State, Provincial, and Territorial Psychological Association Affairs (Division 31)
Lina Grossman, Pres.
400 E Town St., Ste. G20
Columbus, OH 43215-1599
Phone: (614)224-0034
Fax: (614)224-2059
E-mail: mranney@ohpsych.org
Home Page: http://www.apa.org/divisions/div31

• 3675 • Outstanding Executive Director of a State, Provincial, and Territorial Association (SPTA) Award

For recognition of outstanding, longstanding, and continuous contributions to the development, enhancement, and growth of state or provincial psychological associations. All APA members are eligible. Nominations are due June 1. A plaque is presented at the Division's reception.

• 3676 • Outstanding Psychologist Award

For recognition of outstanding, longstanding, and continuous contributions to the development, enhancement, and growth of state or provincial psychological associations. All APA members are eligible. Nominations are due June 1. A plaque is presented at the Division's reception.

• 3677 •

American Psychological Association Educational Psychology Division (Division 15)
James G. Greeno, Pres.
750 1st St. NE
Washington, DC 20002
Phone: (202)216-7602
Fax: (202)218-3599
E-mail: kcooke@apa.org
Home Page: http://www.apa.org/divisions/div15

• 3678 • Paul R. Pintrich Outstanding Dissertation Award

To recognize a recent recipient of a doctorate in educational psychology who has completed an outstanding dissertation. Deadline for nominations is May 30. A $250 cash prize and a plaque are awarded at the APA annual convention.

• 3679 • Richard E. Snow Early Career Award in Educational Psychology

To recognize members who have obtained a doctorate within the preceding seven-year period and have made an impressive contribution to educational psychology. Deadline for nominations is January 15. A plaque is presented at the APA annual convention.

• 3680 • Edward L. Thorndike Award for Career Achievement in Educational Psychology

To recognize individuals, not necessarily members, who have made an outstanding contribution to educational psychology. A plaque and an honorarium are presented each year at the annual convention.

• 3681 •

American Psychological Association Exercise and Sport Psychology Division (Division 47)
Penny McCullagh, Pres
% Diane Finley, Sec.-Treas.
Department of Psychology
Prince George's Community College
301 Largo Rd.
Largo, MD 20774
Phone: (301)322-0869
E-mail: dfinley@pgcc.edu
Home Page: http://www.psyc.unt.edu/apadiv47

• 3682 • Outstanding Dissertation Award

For recognition of an outstanding dissertation on exercise and sport psychology. A 750-word abstract must be submitted by February 1. A plaque is awarded at the Division's business meeting at the APA annual convention.

• 3683 •
American Psychological Association
General Psychology Division (Division 1)
Bonnie R. Strickland, Contact
% Neil Lutsky, Sec.-Treas.
Department of Psychology
Carelton College
1 N College St.
Northfield, MN 55057
E-mail: nlutsky@carleton.edu
Home Page: http://www.apa.org/divisions/div1

• 3684 • **Ernest R. Hilgard Award for Distinguished Contributions to General Psychology**
To honor lifetime contributions to general psychology. The award includes a plaque or certificate and a prize of $500.

• 3685 • **William James Book Award**
To recognize a book, published within the past five years, that provides an integration of the diverse subfields of psychology. Deadline for submissions is May 1. A monetary prize of $1,000 is awarded annually.

• 3686 • **Gardner Lindzey Dissertation Award**
To recognize an outstanding recent doctoral dissertation in general psychology. The award includes a plaque or certificate and a prize of $500.

• 3687 • **George A. Miller Award**
To recognize an outstanding recent article in general psychology. The award includes a plaque of certificate and a prize of $500.

• 3688 •
American Psychological Association
Health Psychology Division (Division 38)
David S. Krantz, Pres.
% Mary Davis, Sec.
Box 871104
Arizona State University
Tempe, AZ 85287-1104
Phone: (480)965-2057
Toll-Free: 800-374-2721
Fax: (480)965-8544
E-mail: mary.davis@asu.edu
Home Page: http://www.health-psych.org

• 3689 • **Outstanding Contributions to Health Psychology**
To recognize outstanding contributions to health psychology. Two awards are presented: one to a senior member (someone who received his/her terminal degree at least 10 years ago) of the Division and one to a junior member (someone who has not earned his/her terminal degree within the past 10 years) of the Division. A citation and a plaque are presented to each winner at the APA annual convention. Established in 1980.

• 3690 •
American Psychological Association
Mental Retardation and Developmental Disabilities Division (Division 33)
Sara Sparrows, Pres.
% Sara Sparrow, Pres.
Yale University
333 Cedar St.
New Haven, CT 06510
E-mail: sara.sparrow@yale.edu
Home Page: http://www.apa.org/divisions/div33/homepage.html

• 3691 • **Edgar A. Doll Award**
To recognize the most outstanding contribution in research, service, and training in the field of mental retardation and developmental disabilities. A plaque is awarded at the APA annual convention.

• 3692 •
American Psychological Association
Population and Environmental Psychology Division (Division 34)
John R. Aiello, Pres.
% Susan Clayton, Sec.
College of Wooster
930 College Mall
Wooster, OH 44691
Phone: (330)263-2565
E-mail: sclayton@wooster.edu
Home Page: http://www.cas.ucf.edu/psychology/APA34/

• 3693 • **Graduate Student Research Competition in Population and Environmental Psychology**
To recognize the graduate student who wins the competition for research on population and environmental psychology. Monetary prizes are awarded for the winner - $300 and the runner-up - $100.

• 3694 •
American Psychological Association
Psychoanalysis Division (Division 39)
David Ramirez, Pres.
2615 Amesbury Rd.
Winston Salem, NC 27103
Phone: (336)768-1113
Fax: (336)768-4445
E-mail: div39@namgmt.com
Home Page: http://www.division39.org

• 3695 • **Psychoanalysis Doctoral Award**
To recognize a doctoral student for the best dissertation and/or paper on a psychoanalytical issue. A monetary prize of $250 is awarded.

• 3696 • **Psychoanalysis Post-Doctoral Award**
For recognition of an outstanding scholarly paper, theoretical or clinical, on a psychoanalytical issue. The author must be within ten years of receipt of the doctorate. A monetary prize of $350 is awarded.

• 3697 •
American Psychological Association
Psychologists in Public Service Division (Division 18)
5100 Cascabel Rd.
Atascadero, CA 93422-2345
Phone: (805)468-2480
Fax: (805)461-0674
E-mail: bsafarjan@tcsn.net
Home Page: http://www.apa.org/divisions/div18

• 3698 • **Harold M. Hildreth Award**
This, the Division's highest honor, is presented to an individual who has demonstrated exceptional dedication and achievement in public service. Presented each year at the APA annual convention. Established in 1966 in honor of Harold M. Hildreth.

• 3699 • **Special Achievement Awards**
To recognize individuals who have made unique or significant contributions to the field of public service psychology. Contributions may be in the area of public interest, science, practice, or education. Plaques are awarded at the annual convention. Formerly: Certificates of Recognition/Appreciation.

• 3700 •
American Psychological Association
Psychology of Religion (Division 36)
Mark McMinn, Pres.
% Dr. Ralph L. Piedmont
Department of Pastoral Counseling
Loyola College
8890 McGaw Rd., Ste. 380
Columbia, MD 21045
E-mail: rpiedmont@loyola.edu
Home Page: http://www.apa.org/divisions/div36

• 3701 • **William C. Bier Award**
To recognize outstanding contributions in the application of psychology to the service of religion through leadership, teaching, writing, service, or organizational activities. Nominations must be submitted January 3. A certificate is awarded at the APA annual convention. Established in 1982 in memory of Rev. Dr. William C. Bier, S.J., who established the Psychologists Interested in Religious Issues Division of the American Psychological Association.

• 3702 • **William James Award**
To recognize individuals who have made an outstanding contribution, through publication and professional activity, to basic research and theory in the psychology of religion and related areas. A certificate is awarded at the APA annual convention. Nominations must be submitted by January 3. Established in 1976 to commemorate William James' contribution to American psychology.

• 3703 •
American Psychological Association
Psychotherapy Division (Division 29)
Armand Cerbone, Sec.
3625 N Paulina
Chicago, IL 60613
Phone: (773)755-0833
Toll-Free: 800-374-2721
Fax: (773)755-0834
E-mail: arcerbone@aol.com
Home Page: http://www.divisionofpsychotherapy.org

• 3704 • **Distinguished Psychologist Award**
To honor the outstanding contributions to the field of psychology and psychotherapy from a member of the Division. Awarded annually.

• 3705 • **Graduate Student Awards**
For recognition of the best papers in the areas of psychotherapy practice, research, and education/training. Theoretical and research papers, single-case studies, and papers developed from dissertation proposals and masters theses are invited. A two-page abstract and a ten-page paper are due by December 10. Monetary prizes are awarded for first place ($350) and second place ($150).

• 3706 • **Jack D. Krasner Memorial Award**
To recognize a member or a fellow of the Division who, within approximately one decade following receipt of the doctorate, has made an outstanding contribution to psychotherapy research, theory, or practice. A monetary prize of $500 and a certificate are awarded at the APA annual convention.

• 3707 •
American Psychological Association
Rehabilitation Psychology Division (Division 22)
Stephen T. Wegener, Pres.
PO Box 133207
Atlanta, GA 30330
Phone: (404)870-9800
Toll-Free: 800-374-2721
E-mail: swegener@jhmi.edu
Home Page: http://www.apa.org/divisions/div22

• 3708 • **Roger Barker Distinguished Research Contribution Award**
For recognition of work in the field of rehabilitation psychology. Awarded at the APA annual convention.

• 3709 • **Outstanding Contribution to Rehabilitation Award**
For recognition of outstanding contribution in the field of rehabilitation. Awarded at the APA annual convention.

• 3710 •
American Psychological Association
School Psychology Division (Division 16)
Cecil R. Reynolds, Pres.
101 Reynolds Ct.
Bastrop, TX 78602
Phone: (512)656-5075
Fax: (512)321-4785
E-mail: crrh@earthlink.net
Home Page: http://http://www.indiana.edu/~div16/

• 3711 • **Outstanding School Psychological Services in Public Schools Award**
To recognize a field-based program delivering school psychological services. Awarded biennially in cooperation with the National Association of School Psychologists.

• 3712 • **Lightner Witmer Award**
To recognize young professional and academic school psychologists who have demonstrated scholarship that merits special recognition. Nominees must be under 35 years of age or must have received the doctorate within the past seven years. Nominations must be submitted by May 1. A plaque is presented at the business meeting at the annual convention.

• 3713 •
American Psychological Association
Society for Community Research and Action: Division of Community Psychology (Division 27)
Bldg. 4, Ste. 403
1800 Canyon Park Cir.
Edmond, OK 73013
Phone: (405)341-4960
Fax: (405)330-4150
E-mail: scra@telepath.com
Home Page: http://www.apa.org/divisions/div27

• 3714 • **Community Psychology Dissertation Award**
To honor the winner of the annual competition for the best dissertation, which follows the criteria of relevance to emerging directions in community psychology, excellence of scholarship, innovation in methodological or theoretical approaches, contributions of new knowledge, elegance of design, and clarity. Dissertations must be completed during the previous year. A monetary prize of $250 and a plaque are awarded at the APA annual convention.

• 3715 • **Distinguished Contribution to Child Advocacy Award**
To recognize a non-psychologist who has made a series of substantial contributions to child and family advocacy/public policy. Nominations are accepted from Division members. Deadline for submission is December 1. Awarded at the APA annual convention. Established in 1982.

• 3716 • **Distinguished Contribution to Practice in Community Psychology Award**
To recognize a psychologist whose career of high quality and innovative applications of psychological principles has resulted in contribution to the practice or application of the principles of community psychology. Society members are eligible. A plaque is presented each year at the APA annual convention.

• 3717 • **Distinguished Contribution to Theory and Research in Community Psychology Award**
To recognize a psychologist whose career of high quality and innovative research and scholarship has resulted in a contribution to the knowledge of community psychology. Society members are eligible. A plaque is awarded each year at the APA annual convention.

• 3718 • **Barbara Dohrenwend Lecture in Social and Community Epidemiology**
To recognize a lecturer in the field of social and community epidemiology. A plaque is awarded when merited. Established in honor of Barbara Dohrenwend.

• 3719 • **Nicholas Hobbs Award**
To recognize a psychologist for substantial contributions to child and family advocacy/public policy. Division members are eligible. Deadline for submission is December 1. Awarded at the APA annual convention. Established in 1983.

• 3720 • **Special Award**
For recognition of an individual who has made significant contributions to further the goals of community research and action. A plaque is awarded each year at the APA annual convention.

• 3721 •
American Psychological Association
Society for Military Psychology (Division 19)
Dana Born, Divisional Leader
% Michael Rumsey, Sec.
Selection and Assignments Research Unit
U.S. Army Research Institute
5001 Eisenhower Ave.
Alexandria, VA 22333
Phone: (703)617-8275
Toll-Free: 800-374-2721
Fax: (703)617-5461
E-mail: rumsey@ari.army.mil
Home Page: http://www.apa.org/divisions/div19

• 3722 • **Charles S. Gersoni Military Psychology Award**
For recognition of meritorious scientific and professional contributions to military psychology. Deadline for nominations is in March. A plaque and a citation are awarded at the APA annual convention.

• 3723 • Military Psychology Student Paper Award

To recognize the best paper by a graduate student on the application of scientific psychology to national security issues. The Deadline for nominations is in March. A monetary prize of $250 is presented. The recipient is invited to present the paper at the APA annual convention.

• 3724 • Robert M. Yerkes Award

To recognize non-psychologists for significant contributions to military psychology. Deadline for nominations is at the end of March. A plaque and a citation are awarded annually. Established in honor of Robert Yerkes, the father of military psychology.

• 3725 •

American Psychological Association Society for Personality and Social Psychology (Division 8)

Margaret Clark, Pres.
% Kristin Tolchin
Dept. of Psychology
Cornell University
Ithaca, NY 14853
Phone: (585)275-8724
Home Page: http://www.spsp.org

• 3726 • Donald T. Campbell Award for Distinguished Research in Social Psychology

To recognize a social psychologist for continuing contributions and current research that have made a major impact on the field. A monetary prize of $500 is presented biennially at the APA annual convention.

• 3727 • Henry A. Murray Award

To recognize individuals working in the demanding and difficult tradition of Henry A. Murray. A monetary prize of $1,000 is awarded at the APA annual convention.

• 3728 •

American Psychological Association Society for the History of Psychology (Division 26)

Benjamin Harris, Pres.
% Trey Buchanan, Sec.
Department of Psychology
Wheaton College
501 College Ave.
Wheaton, IL 60187
E-mail: Trey.Buchanan@wheaton.edu
Home Page: http://shp.yorku.ca

• 3729 • Best Paper Published in History of Psychology

To recognize the best student paper on history of psychology that is submitted to the Division's program. A monetary prize of $200 is awarded at the APA annual convention.

• 3730 •

American Psychological Association Society for the Psychology of Women (Division 35)

Cynthia de las Fuentes, Pres.
750 1st St. NE
Washington, DC 20002-4242
Phone: (202)336-6013
Fax: (202)318-3599
E-mail: div35@apa.org
Home Page: http://www.apa.org/divisions/div35

• 3731 • Geis Memorial Award

To fund doctoral students conducting dissertation research in feminist psychology. To qualify for funding, the research must be 1. feminist, 2. address a feminist/womanist issue, 3. use social psychology research methods, and 4. make a significant contribution to social psychology theory and research. Proposals will be judged on suitability, feasibility, merit of the research, and the potential of the student to have a career as a feminist researcher in social psychology. Funding need not be used solely to fund the research project. Awarded annually. Established in honor of Florence L. Geis.

• 3732 • Heritage Award

For recognition of contributions relating to advances for women. Nominees must have made distinguished and longstanding contributions that relate to women, gender, or related issues. Five awards are presented: Heritage APA Service Award, Heritage Practice Award, Heritage Public Policy Award, Heritage Publications Award - for contributions consisting of a body or authored or edited books and book chapters and Heritage Research Award - for recognition of the contribution of a body of original research published in professional journals. Awarded annually.

• 3733 • Hyde Graduate Student Research Award

To recognize outstanding psychological research on women and gender roles done by students. A $500 monetary prize is awarded annually.

• 3734 • Hyde Graduate Student Research Grant

To recognize outstanding psychological research by students on women and gender roles. A monetary prize of $150 is awarded annually.

• 3735 • Research Award on Psychotherapy with Women

For recognition of the best unpublished paper on psychotherapy with women presented during the year. Research papers are judged on originality, research design and analysis, writing style, and contributions to the field of psychotherapy and treatment with female clients. A monetary prize of $300 is awarded.

• 3736 • Section on the Psychology of Black Women Award

To recognize outstanding original graduate research on basic or applied work in social, clinical, development, experimental, or any other area of psychology that has particular relevance to the increased understanding of gender role influences on the behavior of Black women. A $100 monetary prize is awarded annually.

• 3737 • Carolyn Wood Sherif Award

To encourage further contributions to feminist psychology. Contributions include evidence of excellence in teaching, research, and other scholarly activity; and mentoring and professional leadership. Contributions to knowledge include empirical and theoretical work in feminist psychology on: gender and the sex/gender system; social values, attitudes, interaction processes, and social change; and the self esteem. An honorarium is presented at the APA national convention.

• 3738 • Barbara Strudler Wallston Award

To recognize the journal(s) that makes the greatest strides toward an appropriate representation of underrepresented groups in the publication process (women, gays, disabled, ethnic minorities, etc.).

• 3739 •

American Psychological Association Society for the Study of Peace, Conflict, and Violence (Division 48)

Linda M. Woolf, Pres.
Kathleen Dockett, Sec.
University of the District of Columbia
Washington, DC 20008
E-mail: kdockett@aol.com
Home Page: http://www.webster.edu/peacepsychology

• 3740 • Presidential Award for Outstanding Contribution to Peace Psychology

For recognition of outstanding contribution to peace psychology through research, education, advocacy, activism, or service to the Division. Executive Committee members of the Division are eligible. Deadline for submission is early June. A plaque is awarded at the Division's award ceremony at the APA annual convention.

• 3741 •

American Psychological Association Society for the Teaching of Psychology (Division 2)

% John Williams
Department of Psychology
University of Northern Iowa
Cedar Falls, IA 50614
Phone: (409)741-4356
Fax: (409)740-4962
E-mail: john.williams@uni.edu
Home Page: http://teachpsych.lemoyne.edu

• 3742 • Teaching Awards Program
To recognize outstanding teachers of psychology. Teachers are nominated in four categories: high school, two-year college, graduate student with teaching appointment, and four-year college or university. Selection is based on student involvement, development of effective teaching methods and/or materials, outstanding performance as a classroom teacher, and professional activity as a teacher of psychology. Deadline for nominations is January 5. A monetary prize of $250 and a plaque are presented at the APA annual convention.

• 3743 •
American Psychological Association Society of Clinical Psychology (Division 12)
Linda Carter Sobell, Pres.
PO Box 1082
Niwot, CO 80544
Phone: (303)652-3126
Fax: (303)652-2723
E-mail: div12apa@comcast.net
Home Page: http://www.apa.org/divisions/div12/homepage.html

• 3744 • Distinguished Awards for the Contributions to the Science and Professional of Clinical Psychology
To recognize individuals who have made outstanding professional contributions to clinical psychology. Recipients are invited to address the audience on topics of their special interests from prepared texts, which may be published in *The Clinical Psychologist.* Deadline for submission of nominations is September 1. A plaque is awarded at the APA annual convention. Established in 1958.

• 3745 • Distinguished Scientific Contribution Award
To recognize individuals who have made outstanding theoretical or empirical contributions to basic research in psychology. Recipients are invited to address the audience on topics of their special interests from prepared texts, which may be published in *The Clinical Psychologist.* Deadline for submission of nominations is September 1. A plaque is awarded at the APA annual convention.

• 3746 • Distinguished Scientist Award
To recognize active involvement in research over a period of years that has earned national recognition and influenced the work of others. Awarded at the APA annual convention.

• 3747 • Distinguished Service Award
To recognize outstanding service to the field of pediatric psychology and the Society. Deadline for nominations is December 1. A plaque and an invitation to present an address at the APA annual convention are awarded.

• 3748 • Florence Halpern Award for Distinguished Professional Contributions
To recognize outstanding professional contributions to clinical psychology. Selection criteria include the candidate's work history with children, creative or innovative concepts for programs that the candidate has developed for the solution of clinical child problems, research or other efforts to implement such concepts or programs for the benefit of children, and other significant accomplishments of special merit in work with children. Deadline for nominations is May 15. Awarded at the Section I annual meeting of the APA annual convention.

• 3749 • Outstanding Dissertation Award
To recognize a dissertation by a recent clinical psychologist who shows promise of advancing clinical psychology as an experimental-behavioral science. The dissertation must have been published in a major journal in the year prior to selection and/or nomination. Deadline for nominations is December 15.

• 3750 • Student Research Award for Clinical Child Psychology
To encourage and reward high quality research for issues related to clinical child psychology. All research work must have been completed while the candidate was a student, and the candidate must be within one year of completing the degree for which the research was conducted. Deadline for submissions is November 15. A monetary prize of $300 is presented at the APA annual convention.

• 3751 •
American Psychological Association Society of Consulting Psychology (Division 13)
Debra Robinson, Pres.
27400 Northwestern Hwy.
Southfield, MI 48034
Phone: (248)352-2500
E-mail: Debrar@umr.edu
Home Page: http://www.apa.org/divisions/div13

• 3752 • Harry and Miriam Levinson Award
To recognize an APA member who has demonstrated an exceptional ability to translate psychological theory into concepts understandable to laypeople who lead and manage others in organizations. Deadline is March 15. A monetary prize of $3,000 and a certificate are awarded at the APA annual convention.

• 3753 • RHR International Award for Excellence in Consultation
To recognize a psychologist whose career achievements reflect outstanding service to organizations, public or private, by helping them respond more effectively to human needs. Nominees must be APA members. Deadline for nominations is January 15. A monetary prize of $1,500 and a certificate are awarded at the APA annual convention. Sponsored by Rohrer, Hibler and Replogle. Formerly: (1996) Perry L. Rohrer Consulting Psychology Practice Award.

• 3754 •
American Psychological Association Society of Pediatric Psychology (Division 54)
Dennis Drotar PhD, Pres.
Dept. of Pediatrics
Rainbow Babies and Children's Hospital
11100 Euclid Ave.
Cleveland, OH 44106
E-mail: dxd3@po.cwru.edu
Home Page: http://www.apa.org/divisions/div/54/

• 3755 • Routh Student Research Grant
To recognize an outstanding research proposal by a student in the area of pediatric psychology. Deadline for submissions is June 30. A monetary grant of $750 is awarded at the APA annual convention.

• 3756 • Student Research Award Competition
To encourage and reward quality research on issues related to pediatric psychology and health care of children. All research work must have been completed while the candidate was a student, and the candidate must be within one year of completing the degree for which the research was conducted. Application deadline is April 1. The awardee receives $750 and the option of publishing the paper in the *Journal of Pediatric Psychology.* Awarded biennially in even-numbered years.

• 3757 • Logan Wright Distinguished Service Award
For recognition of excellence and significant contributions in establishing the scientific base of pediatric psychology. Deadline or submission of nominations is December 1. A plaque and an invitation to present an address at the APA annual convention are awarded biennially in odd-numbered years.

• 3758 •
American Psychological Association Society of Psychological Hypnosis (Division 30)
Frank De Piano, Pres.
Darlene Osowiec
2247 Blackberry Dr.
Geneva, IL 60134-1076
E-mail: fdepiano@aol.com
Home Page: http://www.apa.org/divisions/div30

• 3759 • Best Research Paper
For recognition of the best research paper on the topic of psychological hypnosis. A monetary prize of $100 is awarded at the APA annual convention.

• 3760 • Best Theoretical Paper Award
To recognize the best paper on clinical aspects of psychological hypnosis. A monetary prize of $100 and a certificate are awarded at the APA annual convention.

• 3761 • E. R. Hilgard Best Graduate Level Academic Thesis Award

For recognition of the best dissertation, completed during the past year, related to the field of psychological hypnosis. A 10-20 page abstract and the date of completion must be sent to the Chair of the Hilgard Dissertation Award Committee by May 1. A monetary prize of $200 is awarded at the APA annual convention.

• 3762 • Nicholas P. Spanos Best Graduate Student Paper Award

For recognition of the best original paper by a graduate student, based on the primary contribution made in carrying out the work and writing the presentation. A monetary prize of $100 is awarded at the APA annual convention.

• 3763 •

American Psychological Association (Division 28)
Anthony Liguori Ph.D., Awards Chair.
% Anthony Liguori, PhD
Dept. of Physiology and Pharmacology
Wake Forest University School of Medicine
Medical Center Blvd.
Winston Salem, NC 27157
Phone: (336)716-8543
Fax: (336)716-8501
E-mail: aliguori@wfubmc.edu
Home Page: http://www.apa.org/about/division/div28awards.html

• 3764 • Brady/Schuster Award

To recognize a mid-career or senior scientist who has made significant contributions to the advancement of research psychopharmacology/substance abuse. Nominations are accepted from members of the Division of Psychopharmacology and Substance Abuse of the American Psychological Association. Deadline for nomination is January 1. A monetary award, an engraved plaque, and reimbursement of travel to the annual meeting of the American Psychological Association are awarded. Established in 1999. Sponsored by MED Associates.

• 3765 • Outstanding Dissertation Award

To recognize a recent graduate for the best doctoral thesis in psychopharmacology or substance abuse. The dissertation must have been completed during the two previous calendar years. Nominations are accepted from members of the Division of Psychopharmacology and Substance Abuse of the American Psychological Association. Deadline for nomination is January 1. A monetary award of $250, an Engraved plaque, and reimbursement of travel to the annual meeting of the American Psychological Association are awarded. Sponsored by Friends Research Institute.

• 3766 • Wyeth Young Psychopharmacologist Award

To recognize a young scientist for original, meritorious work in psychopharmacology and to encourage excellence in research in the disciplines of psychology and pharmacology. Individuals must be nominated by a member or fellow of the Division of Psychopharmacology, and nominations must be based on work in psychopharmacology, behavioral pharmacology, neuropharmacology, or drug abuse. Nominees must not be more than five years past their doctoral degree. Deadline for nomination is January 1. A monetary award of $500, an engraved plaque, and reimbursement of expenses to attend the annual meeting of the American Psychological Association are awarded each year. Sponsored by Wyeth Research.

• 3767 •

American Psychological Association Division of Independent Practice
Division of Independent Practice
Jeffrey E. Barnett, Pres.
Div. 42, Central Office
919 W Marshall Ave.
Phoenix, AZ 85013
Phone: (602)246-6768
Toll-Free: 800-374-2721
Fax: (602)246-6577
E-mail: div42apa@cox.net
Home Page: http://www.apa.org/about/division/div42.html

• 3768 • Distinguished Psychologist of the Year

To recognize achievement in the field of psychology. Members of the Division who display distinguished, sustained service in the practice of psychology are eligible. The candidate must be licensed and devote a significant portion of time to the delivery of services. Deadline for nominations is March 1. A plaque and an opportunity to speak to the Division are awarded at the APA annual convention. Established in 1981.

• 3769 • Distinguished Public Service Award

To honor a government official or employee for outstanding contributions to the field of mental health. Deadline for nominations is March 1. A plaque is awarded at the APA annual convention.

• 3770 • Rosalee G. Weiss Award

To recognize outstanding leaders in arts or science whose contributions have significance for psychology, but whose careers are not directly in the spheres encompassed by psychology, and/or outstanding leaders in any of the special areas within the spheres of psychology. The recipient delivers an invited address at the Annual Convention and receives an honorarium and travel expenses to the convention. Established by Raymond Weiss to honor his wife.

• 3771 •

American Psychopathological Association
Linda Cottler PhD, Pres.
Dept. of Psychiatry
Washington University School of Medicine
40 N Kingshighway, Ste. 4
St. Louis, MO 63108
Phone: (314)286-2252
Fax: (314)284-2265
E-mail: cottler@jhsph.edu
Home Page: http://www.appassn.org

• 3772 • Samuel Hamilton Award

A monetary award is given annually. Inquire for additional details.

• 3773 • Joseph Zubin Award

To recognize an individual for a seminal contribution to the field in the area of the annual meeting. A monetary prize is awarded annually. Established to honor Joseph Zubin, Ph.D., for his service and contributions to the American Psychopathological Association for over 50 years.

• 3774 •

American Public Gas Association
Bert Kalisch, Pres.
11094-D Lee Hwy., Ste. 102
Fairfax, VA 22030-5014
Phone: (703)352-3890
Fax: (703)352-1271
E-mail: bkalisch@apga.org
Home Page: http://www.apga.org

• 3775 • Distinguished Service Award

To recognize outstanding contributions to public gas, outstanding public service, unusual devotion to duty, or contributions to the welfare of the community, the area, or the nation. Officials or executives of an APGA member system who have been active in the Association for at least five years are eligible. A framed certificate is awarded sparingly so as to retain its distinguished honor. Established in 1964.

• 3776 • Personal Service Award

To recognize a substantial contribution toward the attainment of the goals of APGA, or a substantial contribution toward enhancing the prestige of the APGA. Employees of an APGA member with at least three years of active participation are eligible. An engraved plaque is awarded annually. Established in 1964.

• 3777 •

American Public Health Association
Georges Benjamin MD, Exec.Dir.
800 I St. NW
Washington, DC 20001-3710
Phone: (202)777-2742
Fax: (202)777-2534
E-mail: comments@apha.org
Home Page: http://www.apha.org

• 3778 • APHA Award for Excellence
Recognizes individuals for outstanding contributions to the improvement of public health. One individual is chosen for contributions made nationally or internationally. A $2,500 honorarium, a tagliare crystal symbol, and travel expenses are awarded annually. Established in 1973.

• 3779 • Jay S. Drotman Memorial Award
To recognize a young health professional who demonstrates potential in the health field by challenging traditional public health policy or practice in a creative and positive manner. A monetary honorarium, a commemorative plaque, and round-trip airfare to APHA's Annual Meeting are awarded annually. Established in 1970. Sponsored by an endowment from Dr. Peter Drotman.

• 3780 • Sedgwick Memorial Medal
Recognizes those who have advanced public health knowledge and practices. Contributions in the fields of research, administration, education, technical service, and all specialties of public health practice receive equal consideration. A symbolic medallion and certificate and travel expenses to attend the presentation ceremony at the annual meeting are awarded annually. Established in 1929 in honor of Professor William Thompson Sedgwick, president of APHA in 1915.

• 3781 •
American Public Human Services Association
Jerry W. Friedman, Exec.Dir.
810 1st St. NE, Ste. 500
Washington, DC 20002
Phone: (202)682-0100
Fax: (202)289-6555
E-mail: pubs@aphsa.org
Home Page: http://www.aphsa.org

• 3782 • Leadership in Human Services Award
To recognize outstanding efforts by national and state policy- makers to assist poor Americans. Awarded annually.

• 3783 •
American Public Power Association
Jan Schori, Chair
2301 M St. NW
Washington, DC 20037-1484
Phone: (202)467-2900
Fax: (202)467-2910
Home Page: http://www.APPAnet.org

• 3784 • Annual Report Award
To honor member utilities for the production of outstanding annual reports, based on readability and conciseness of text, overall appearance, and attractiveness of art work, layout, and cover. A plaque is awarded annually at the association's Energy/Customer Services and Communications Workshop.

• 3785 • APPA Century Award
To recognize public power utilities that have continuously served their consumers and community for 100 years. A certificate is presented to a public power utility at the time of its 100-year anniversary. Established in 1987.

• 3786 • APPA Honor Roll
To recognize employees or officials of APPA member systems who have made significant local contributions to public power. Officials or employees of an APPA member system with at least 10 years of service in public power are eligible. Awarded periodically when merited. Established in 1978.

• 3787 • APPA Safety Contest Awards
For recognition in the electric utility industry of an outstanding safety record. Awards are given for the lowest overall incidence rate of injuries/illnesses per man-hours worked in several size categories determined by total number of man-hours of exposure annually. Plaques are awarded in the eight categories annually at the Engineering and Operations Workshop.

• 3788 • Community Service Award
To recognize good neighbor activities that demonstrate the commitment of the utility and its employees to enhancing the quality of life in the community. Any APPA member utility is eligible. Established in 1990.

• 3789 • James D. Donovan Individual Achievement Award
For recognition of an individual who has made a great contribution to the electric industry, to public power, and to the programs of the association. Employees of an APPA member system who have been active participants in APPA affairs for at least five years are eligible. Established in 1959 to honor James P. Donovan, one of the founders of APPA and its first president.

• 3790 • Energy Innovator Award
To honor local publicly-owned electric utilities that have made outstanding advances in the development or application of highly creative energy-efficient techniques or technologies. Participants in the APPA Demonstration of Energy-Efficient Developments program are eligible. Established in 1980. Formerly: Utility Design Awards.

• 3791 • Larry Hobart Seven Hats Award
To recognize utility managers who serve in the nation's smaller communities and whose management responsibilities extend well beyond those of a manager in a larger system with a larger staff. The Seven Hats refer to qualities and skills in the following areas: planning and design, administration, public relations, field supervision, accounting, personnel or employee direction, policies, etc, and community leadership. Superintendents or managers of a member utility of the association serving not more than 2,500 electric meters are eligible. Established in 1966; renamed in 1995 to honor Larry Hobart, who served as APPA executive director from 1986-1995.

• 3792 • Harold Kramer - John Preston Personal Service Award
For recognition of personal service that has made a substantial contribution toward the attainment of the goals of the association or toward enhancing the prestige of the association in the United States. Employees of an APPA member system who have actively participated in the association for at least five years are eligible. Established in 1959 to honor Harold Kramer who played a leading role in the formation of APPA and served as its first executive secretary and general manager, and John Preston who served as the first vice president of the association.

• 3793 • Public Service Award
To recognize exceptional leadership by public officials in the public power field. Publicly elected or appointed officials are eligible. Criteria considered are: substantial contributions to public power nationally, activities that have received national recognition, and contributions of the nominee must have had a lasting impact. Established in 1978.

• 3794 • Alex Radin Distinguished Service Award
This, the association's highest honor, is given to recognize exceptional leadership in and dedication to public power. Officials of an APPA member system who have been active in the association for at least ten years are eligible. Established in 1953. Renamed in 1986 to honor Alex Radin who served as APPA's executive director from 1951 to 1986. Formerly: (1986) Distinguished Service Award.

• 3795 • E. F. Scattergood System Achievement Award
For recognition of outstanding achievements in the operation of a public power system. The achievement must be recognized in the public power field, enhance the prestige of public power and the association in the nation, improve service to customer-owners, and represent an earnest coordinated effort on the part of the system. APPA member systems are eligible. Established in 1959 as a tribute to E.F. Scattergood of the Los Angeles Department of Water and Power, who played an important part in the formation of the association and served as its president in 1947.

• 3796 • Spence Vanderlinden Public Official Award
To recognize service to the association by an elected or appointed official of a member system. Those nominated may be elected or appointed members of a policy board or commission of APPA who have actively participated in APPA for at least five years. Criteria considered are: personal service to APPA that has made a substantial contribution toward the attainment of the goals of APPA, substantial contributions towards enhancing the prestige of the association in the nation generally, and contribu-

tions to the community. Established in 1984 to honor Spence Vanderlinden, who served as the first chairman of the APPA Policy Board's Advisory Council.

• 3797 •

American Public Works Association
Pete King, Exec.Dir.
2345 Grand Blvd., Ste. 500
Kansas City, MO 64108
Phone: (816)472-6100
Toll-Free: 800-595-APWA
Fax: (816)472-1610
E-mail: pking@apwa.net
Home Page: http://www.apwa.net/

• 3798 • **APWA Distinguished Service Award**
For recognition of outstanding service rendered to the people of the United States.

• 3799 • **Award of Merit**
To recognize the dedicated service of public works or related agency personnel at the operational level who perform their responsibilities in an exceptionally efficient and courteous manner. Any unit of government city, county, state, province, or federal agency - may nominate one or more individuals in accordance with a population schedule. A nominee need not be a member of APWA, but must have been employed by a public works related agency or agencies for a period of not less than five years. A certificate is awarded annually during National Public Works Week.

• 3800 • **Contractor of the Year Award**
To honor a contractor for outstanding achievement in the construction of a public works project. The project nominated must have been completed during the preceding calendar year and must qualify as a public works project. Nominations are made by public works agencies and must conform to an established set of criteria, including: (1) use of good construction management techniques and completion of the project on schedule; (2) safety performance as indicated by the number of lost time injuries to contractor personnel and evidence of an effective overall safety program during construction; (3) community relations as evidenced by the contractor's efforts to minimize public inconvenience due to construction, safety precautions to protect lives and property, provision of observation areas, guided tours, and other means of improving relations between the contractor and the public; (4) demonstrated awareness of the need to protect the environment during construction; (5) unusual accomplishments under difficult conditions such as adverse weather or other site conditions over which the contractor had no control; and (6) additional considerations of importance to the public works agency such as exceptional efforts of the contractor to maintain quality control or construction innovations evidenced by time and money-saving techniques. A special Contractor of the Year Award Committee selects the recipient, subject to the approval of the APWA's Board of Directors. The award consists of an etched metal plaque and a bronze monument for placement on the winning project. Established in 1974.

• 3801 • **Rodney R. Fleming Award**
To recognize high-quality presentations at the International Public Works Congress and Equipment Show and excellence in articles published in the *APWA Reporter*. A monetary award of $500 and an engraved plaque are presented during the annual Congress.

• 3802 • **Samuel A. Greeley Local Government Service Award**
To recognize public works officials who have honorably and efficiently served a single local public agency in an official capacity for 30 years or more and who have been members of APWA for at least 15 years. A single local public agency is interpreted as any city, village, borough, town, township, county, or special district, but not a state or the federal government. Persons entering their 15th year of membership in APWA are sent an eligibility questionnaire. A hand-lettered certificate is presented at the annual Congress or at some other time. Established in 1932 by Samuel A. Greeley of the consulting firm, Greeley and Hansen, Chicago, IL.

• 3803 • **Heritage Award**
To recognize the APWA Chapter which has conducted the most comprehensive historical program during the previous calendar year. The purpose of the award is to promote chapter members' awareness of their public works heritage and to demonstrate the importance of the past in understanding and solving some of today's problems facing public works engineer-administrators. Activities can range from chapter histories and historical calendars to photographic exhibits and community or school programs which document the heritage of public works. The winning chapter receives $1,000 to be used in support of the chapter's historical program for internships, publications, awards, exhibits, or other activities or as a scholarship for a young person wishing to enter the public works field. In addition, the chapter receives a statuette, the Aedile, named for the early Roman public works official, as well as an emblem for the chapter banner. Awarded annually. Established in 1974.

• 3804 • **Honorary Member**
This, the highest honor that the Association bestows is given to indicate to the greatest possible extent the Association's esteem, respect, and regard. Candidates for Honorary Membership should have been persons who are prominent in the field of public works, and/or have rendered service of enduring value and benefit to the membership of the Association, and have been members for the preceding five years. Election is made by the Board of Directors. One Honorary Member is selected each year. A plaque is presented at the annual APWA banquet held in conjunction with the International Public Works Congress and Equipment Show. Established in 1935.

• 3805 • **Meritorious Service Award**
To recognize outstanding achievement of an APWA member from the private sector and to acknowledge the important role of private enterprise in providing public works services. Selection is based on professional activities which have resulted in the enhancement of the quality, efficiency, or cost-effectiveness of services provided by public agencies. Candidates must be nominated by their Chapters. An engraved, mounted plaque is awarded annually at a Chapter function. Established in 1982.

• 3806 • **Charles Walter Nichols Award**
To recognize outstanding and meritorious achievement in the field of sanitation. Nominees must be active members of APWA employed by a political subdivision of a state or province on a full-time basis and, as such, should not be in a position to receive commercial return for the achievement. An honorarium of $500 and a mounted certificate describing the recipient's achievement are awarded during the annual Congress. Established in 1951 by Charles Walter Nichols, of Nichols Engineering and Research Corp., New York, NY.

• 3807 • **Donald C. Stone Award**
To recognize an individual for outstanding and meritorious achievement in the area of continuing graduate professional education for public works professionals. The field of education may include: (1) graduate or continuing public works education instruction, administration, and promotion; (2) authorship of public works texts/educational materials; (3) involvement in ensuring governmental support for continuing professional education; and (4) serving as an advocate for public works educational programs. Active members of the Association who have served the Association on behalf of the Education Foundation are eligible. An engraved pewter and walnut plaque is awarded during the annual Congress. Established in 1988 to honor Donald C. Stone, who helped pioneer the development of curriculum for graduate training of public works administrators.

• 3808 • **Harry S. Swearingen Award**
To recognize valuable and dedicated service as a member of APWA primarily at the chapter level. Nominations are accepted from individuals and/or chapters. An engraved mounted medallion is presented annually. Established in 1958 in memory of Harry Sellers Swearingen (1900-1957), who worked untiringly on behalf of the Association and its purposes.

• 3809 • **Top Ten Public Works Leaders of the Year**
To recognize outstanding performance by public works engineers and administrators. Nonelected full-time employees of a federal, state, provincial, county, or municipal government whose responsibilities are public works related are eligible. Nominations may be made by any individual or group, and neither the recipient nor the nominator need be an APWA member. Selection is made by a panel of judges representing educators, the media, APWA and some

of the eleven organizations co-sponsoring National Public Works Week. They select individuals whose work reflects the highest standards of conduct for public works professionals and whose achievements are noteworthy in relation to the personnel and financial resources available. Each recipient receives a plaque and Top Ten jewelry at appropriate ceremonies in the local community as close as possible to National Public Works Week, normally the third week of May. Established in 1960.

• 3810 • Abel Wolman Award

To encourage and provide recognition to historical publications on the development of public works structures, facilities, technologies, and services. Books on the history of water resources, transportation, solid waste, public works planning, engineering or administration, public buildings and grounds, or public works equipment are eligible. Individual authors or their publishers may submit books published during the preceding year. A monetary award of $1,000 is presented annually. Established in 1986 to honor Dr. Abel Wolman (1893-1989), a long-time professor at Johns Hopkins University, and a leading figure in the history of public works in the twentieth century.

• 3811 •
American Rabbit Breeders Association
Glen C. Carr, Sec.
PO Box 426
Bloomington, IL 61702
Phone: (309)664-7500
Fax: (309)664-0941
E-mail: arbapost@aol.com
Home Page: http://www.arba.net

Formerly: (1995) Champagne d'Argent Federation.

• 3812 • National Convention Awards Program

To recognize and award the breeders of winning rabbits. Awards are given in the following categories: the Best Senior Buck and Doe; the Best Intermediate (6/8) Buck and Doe; and the Best Junior Buck and Doe. From these, the Best of the Breed and the Best Opposite Sex of Breed are selected. Also awarded is Best Display at the show. Members of the American Rabbit Breeders Association are eligible. Trophies are awarded annually at the National Convention. Established in 1931.

• 3813 •
American Radium Society
James D. Cox MD, Pres.
53 W Jackson Blvd., Ste. 663
Chicago, IL 60604
Phone: (312)322-0730
Fax: (312)322-0732
E-mail: info@americanradiumsociety.org
Home Page: http://www.americanradiumsociety.org

• 3814 • Janeway Medal

To recognize scientific contributions in the field of ionizing radiation and in the treatment of neoplastic and allied diseases. A gold medal and an invitation to deliver a lecture are awarded annually. Established in 1933 in memory of Dr Henry H. Janeway (1873-1921), an American pioneer in the therapeutic use of radium.

• 3815 • Young Oncologist Essay Awards

To encourage participation of young oncologists in an annual meeting through participation of unpublished material representing research carried out during training. Awards are given in the following categories: radiation oncology, medical oncology, surgical oncology, and gynecological oncology. The paper must be submitted by an in-training, young oncologist working with or sponsored by a member of the American Radium Society; it must be read by the young oncologist at the annual meeting; papers may be submitted by those who are out of training up to one year, providing the work was carried out during the training; and the paper must be written by and represent primarily the work of the young oncologist, although co-authors may be listed. The work should be current but need not be confined entirely to the present year. Papers already presented elsewhere, submitted for publication or published are not eligible for consideration. The paper must deal with some phase of cancer research, including a clinical study, basic research, or a relevant theoretical dissertation in either of the four categories. The entry deadline is October 31. The award consists of a monetary award of $250, a Certificate of Award, and travel expenses for the winner and spouse of up to $1,250 to attend the Annual Meeting. Awarded annually if merited. Established in 1970. Formerly: (1984) Resident Essay Award.

• 3816 • Young Oncologist Travel Grants

To encourage attendance of young oncologists at the annual meeting of the American Radium Society. Grants are given in the following categories: radiation oncology, surgical oncology, medical oncology, and gynecological oncology. Candidates, in the final year of their training program or less than three years since completion of training, who are not yet eligible for membership, may apply. Recipients, who demonstrate academic intent, will be evaluated on the likelihood of meeting the ARS membership requirements. Applicants must be recommended by their training director or department chairman. The deadline for applications is October 31. Four monetary awards of $1,000 each for travel and meeting expenses are presented at the annual meeting. In each category, an award will be given only if there is a qualified applicant. The deadline for applications is September 30. Established in 1984.

• 3817 •
American Railway Development Association
E. Gilbert Tyckoson Jr., Exec.Dir.
PO Box 44369
Eden Prairie, MN 55344-4369
Phone: (952)828-9750
Fax: (952)828-9751
E-mail: tyck0001@aol.com

• 3818 • Distinguished Service Award

Recognizes service contributions to the railway industry. A plaque is awarded annually. Established in 1968.

• 3819 •
American Recorder Society
Brook Erickson, Exec.Dir.
1129 Ruth Dr.
St. Louis, MO 63122-1019
Phone: (314)966-4082
Phone: (303)347-1181
Toll-Free: 800-491-9588
Fax: (314)966-4649
E-mail: recorder@americanrecorder.org
Home Page: http://www.americanrecorder.org

• 3820 • ARS Distinguished Achievement Award

To recognize individuals for their contributions to the teaching, performance, research, or making of the recorder. Nominations must be submitted to the Board of Directors. Awarded periodically. Established in 1986.

• 3821 •
American Red Cross National Headquarters
Marsha J. Evans, Pres./CEO
2025 E St. NW
Washington, DC 20006
Phone: (202)303-4498
Phone: (202)303-4498
Toll-Free: 800-438-4636
Fax: (202)639-3267
E-mail: info@usa.redcross.org
Home Page: http://www.redcross.org

• 3822 • Certificate of Merit

To recognize an individual for the performance of an act utilizing skills learned in a Red Cross first aid, small craft, or water safety course of instruction that is judged meritorious in saving or sustaining a human life. About 600 awardees receive certificates and pins annually. Established in 1928.

• 3823 • Cultural Diversity Outreach Award

To recognize Red Cross unit excellence in achieving reciprocity with locally diverse groups through outreach efforts, programs, and services. The award is made in recognition of the chairman's and manager's teamwork that led the unit in pursuit of excellence. Established in 1987.

• 3824 • Jane A. Delano Award

To recognize a paid staff or active reserve status nurse of the American Red Cross who has made an outstanding contribution to strengthening or improving Red Cross programs and services and advancing the involvement of nurses throughout the organization. Established in honor of Jane A. Delano, founder of Red Cross Nursing and Health Services, who was responsible for creating the Nurse Enrollment program.

• 3825 • Charles R. Drew Award

For recognition of a volunteer or employee who has made an outstanding For recognition of a volunteer or employee who has made an outstanding contribution to strengthening or improving blood services. Established in 1981 in honor of Dr. Charles R. Drew, the noted surgeon and researcher.

• 3826 • George M. Elsey Award for Outstanding Involvement of Youth

To recognize a Red Cross unit whose success in the integration of youth involvement has resulted in exemplary service to members of its community and served as an inspiration for other units to involve youth in service. Any American Red Cross unit is eligible to be nominated. Established in honor of George M. Elsey, Red Cross President Emeritus, in recognition of his outstanding contributions to youth throughout his career and in gratitude for his continuing support of and dedication to a viable Red Cross youth program.

• 3827 • Samuel Gompers American Red Cross National Labor Award

4To recognize an active or retired labor union member or a labor union organization for exemplary volunteer service given through the American Red Cross. Established in 1989 in memory of Samuel Gompers, first president of the American Federation of Labor.

• 3828 • Good Neighbor Award

To recognize an individual and/or organization outside the American Red Cross for a significant humanitarian contribution to the local, national, or international community in support of the American Red Cross. Established in 1986.

• 3829 • Harriman Award for Distinguished Volunteer Service

This, the most prestigious volunteer award bestowed by the American Red Cross, recognizes a Red Cross volunteer for service of an especially distinguished nature. Extraordinary accomplishment rather than merely length of service are considered and must be merited under a strict application of criteria. Established in 1974, in honor of E. Roland and Gladys Harriman.

• 3830 • International Certificate of Appreciation

To recognize volunteers and employees for outstanding service as representatives of the American Red Cross on an international level. A certificate and a special International Services pin are awarded.

• 3831 • International Humanitarian Service Award

To recognize individual or group acts that exemplify or inspire practice of the Fundamental Principles of the International Red Cross and Red Crescent Movement and their humanitarian values of human dignity, respect, compassion, and the protection and assistance implicit in the principles.

• 3832 • Labor Participation Citation for Services

To recognize an individual union member, a local labor council, a local union, or a state or national union membership for participation in and support of Red Cross services. A certificate is awarded annually.

• 3833 • Ann Magnussen Award

For recognition of an outstanding Red Cross volunteer registered nurse who has made an outstanding contribution to strengthening and improving the American Red Cross programs and services. It is the highest honor of nursing achievement in the Red Cross. Established in 1968. The award honors Ann Magnussen, a former national director of American Red Cross Nursing and Health Services.

• 3834 • National Volunteer Disaster Services Award

To recognize an individual who has demonstrated exceptional leadership in coordinating, directing, motivating, and successfully completing specific Disaster Services activities. These activities must have resulted in strengthening or enhancing service delivery in preparedness, education, or disaster operations. Primary consideration is given to actions of merit undertaken during the current calendar year, but the total years of service and combined impact of disaster-related activities is taken into account.

• 3835 • Partnership Award

To promote cooperative partnership work between volunteers and employees including youth volunteers. This award honors outstanding job performance on a project, in a unit, or in a line of service. Partnership initiative is based on a written negotiated agreement describing the job to be performed and also on team members' roles in carrying out the agreement. This award is given at three levels: the local (first) level, the region/area (second) level, and the national (third) level. A partnership, for the purpose of this award nomination, is understood generally to consist of one salaried and one volunteer staff member. An all-volunteer unit, however, may nominate a partnership with two members who are volunteers. A bronze medal is awarded at the local level, a silver medal at the region/area level, and a gold medal at the national level.

• 3836 • Philos Award - Philanthropist of the Year

To recognize the individual, organization, corporation, or foundation that best exemplifies the spirit of charitable giving. The gift must contribute significantly to the programs and services of the American Red Cross and should have motivated other financial contributions. Established in 1987.

• 3837 • School & Community Award for Youth in Health & Safety

To recognize schools, individual youth, youth groups, and adult youth leaders who have, through the development and direction of specific activities, improved health and safety practices of the schools and the community. Formerly: Health and Safety Award.

• 3838 • Tiffany Awards for Employee Excellence

To recognize superior job performance demonstrated by paid full-time employees of the Red Cross. The award is given at three levels: the first (or local) level, the second (or region/area) level, and the third (or national) level. At each award level, a winner is selected in three employee categories: support service, professional or technical service, and management. Nominees must be full-time Red Cross employees, having performed at least two years of paid service. The awards derive their meaning from the three beautiful Tiffany windows that grace the Board of Governors Hall at national headquarters. The panels depict caring, truth, and fortitude - qualities embodied by the Red Cross.

• 3839 • Volunteer Fund Raiser of the Year

To recognize an individual for exceptional leadership in coordinating, motivating, and successfully completing fund-raising efforts involving volunteers, and/or personally soliciting major gifts of significant magnitude. Established in 1987.

• 3840 • Cynthia Wedel Award

To recognize distinguished volunteer service performed at the local unit or beyond the chapter by a person whose status and type of work are not covered by any other national award. Any Red Cross volunteer who has sustained superior and outstanding leadership service at the chapter, regional, national, or international level is eligible for nomination. The award(s) are presented at the annual American Red Cross National Convention. Established in honor of Cynthia Wedel, National Chairman of Volunteers and Deputy National Volunteer Consultant for Blood Services.

• 3841 • Woodrow Wilson Award

For recognition of a young person (under the age of 21) who has made exemplary and enduring contributions to the American Red Cross and to the community while serving as a Red Cross volunteer. It is the highest youth award of the Red Cross. A framed citation, signed by the Chairman of the Board of Governors, is presented annually at the national convention. Established in 1980. The award commemorates President Woodrow Wilson, who established the Junior Red Cross by proclamation in 1917.

• 3842 •

American Red Magen David for Israel - American Friends of Magen David
Daniel R. Allen, Exec.VP
888 7th Ave., Ste. 403
New York, NY 10106
Phone: (212)757-1627
Toll-Free: (866)632-2763
Fax: (212)757-4662
E-mail: info@armdi.org
Home Page: http://www.armdi.org

• 3843 • International Humanitarian Award

For recognition of achievement in humanitarian causes. Nominations must be submitted by January 30. A trophy is awarded annually at a testimonial luncheon in April. Established in 1978.

• 3844 •

American Revolution Round Table
David W. Jacobs, Chairman
6 Grovedale Rd.
Niantic, CT 06357
Phone: (860)739-6859
Phone: (860)786-8204
Fax: (860)786-8230
E-mail: djacobs0l@snet.net
Home Page: http://www.arrt-ny.org

• 3845 • American Revolution Round Table Book Award

For recognition of the author of the best book on the subject of the American Revolution published in the preceding calendar year. A plaque or a scroll is awarded annually. Established in 1958.

• 3846 • Award of Merit

For recognition of a man or woman who has made a significant lifetime contribution to the understanding of the American Revolution. A plaque is awarded. Established in 1972.

• 3847 •

American Rhinologic Society
Marvin P. Fried MD, Sec.
Montefiore Medical Center Dept. of Otolaryngology
3400 Bainbridge Ave.
3rd Fl. MAP
Bronx, NY 10467
Phone: (318)675-6262
Toll-Free: 888-520-9585
Fax: (318)675-6260
E-mail: info@american-rhinologic.org
Home Page: http://www.american-rhinologic.org

• 3848 • Dr. Maurice H. Cottle Honor Award

Recognizes original clinical investigation in Rhinology presented at the Fall scientific meeting of the American Rhinologic Society. Residents and practitioners of otorhinolaryngology, plastic surgery, or individuals in allied fields in Rhinology are eligible. The deadline for abstract submission is March 1. A monetary award and a certificate are awarded annually at the annual scientific meeting in the Fall. Established in 1977, sponsored by the American Rhinologic Society. Named after Maurice H. Cottle, M.D., founder of the American Rhinologic Society.

• 3849 • Resident Research Award

To recognize a resident for presenting solid research related to rhinology. Residents from any country are eligible. The deadline for abstract submission is November 1; the deadline for manuscript submission is March 1. A monetary award and a certificate are presented annually at the fall meeting of the Society. Established in 1989. Formerly: Resident Case of the Year Award.

• 3850 •

American Rhododendron Society
Laura Grant, Exec.Dir.
PO Box 525
Niagara Falls, NY 14304
Phone: (416)424-1942
Fax: (905)262-1999
E-mail: lauragrant@arsoffice.org
Home Page: http://www.rhododendron.org

• 3851 • Gold Medal

To recognize outstanding contributions to the Society and an active and continuing desire to broaden the knowledge of the genus rhododendron. Members of the Society are eligible. A gold medal may be awarded annually. Established in 1952.

• 3852 • Silver Medal

To recognize an individual for distinguished efforts to improve and broaden knowledge of the genus rhododendron and for notable activity in the Society. A silver medal is awarded. Established in 1965.

• 3853 •

American Risk and Insurance Association
Anthony Biacchi, Exec.Dir.
716 Providence Rd.
Malvern, PA 19355-3402
Phone: (610)640-1997
Fax: (610)725-1007
E-mail: aria@cpcuiia.org
Home Page: http://www.aria.org

• 3854 • Kulp Wright Award

For recognition of a publication that has made a contribution to the literature of risk management and insurance. A certificate is awarded annually. Formerly: (2004) Clarence Arthur Kulp Memorial Award.

• 3855 • Robert I Mehr Award

Recognizes outstanding articles from The Journal of Risk and Insurance that have stood the test of time in the field of risk management and insurance. A certificate is awarded annually.

• 3856 • Les B. Strickler Innovation in Instruction Award

A certificate is awarded annually.

• 3857 • Witt Award

Recognizes a best feature article in The Journal of Risk and Insurance. A certificate is awarded annually.

• 3858 •

American Road and Transportation Builders Association
Peter Ruane, Pres./CEO
The ARTBA Bldg.
1010 Massachusetts Ave. NW
Washington, DC 20001-5402
Phone: (202)289-4434
Fax: (202)289-4435
E-mail: artbadc@aol.com
Home Page: http://www.artba.org

Formerly: (1977) American Road Builders Association.

• 3859 • ARTBA Award

To recognize individuals who have made outstanding contributions toward advancing the broad objectives of the Association. A plaque is awarded annually at the convention. Established in 1960. (Each year since 1972, an award has been presented to one industry leader and one member in public service.)

• 3860 • Bartelsmeyer Award

To recognize a public official for dedication and service to ARTBA and the community. Individual must be a member or have been a member of ARTBA through the Transportation Officials Division, and must exhibit professional integrity, and dedication. A plaque is awarded annually at the TOD Conference on Local Transportation. Established in 1982 by ARTBA in cooperation with the Illinois Department of Transportation.

• 3861 • Golden Wheel Society Awards

To recognize members who have made a significant contribution to increasing membership in ARTBA. A plaque is awarded. Established in 1986.

• 3862 • Guy Kelsey Award

To recognize a Planning and Design Division member who has made an outstanding contribution to the division and ARTBA. A plaque is awarded annually at the ARTBA convention. Established in 1975 to honor Guy Kelsey, founder of the consulting engineering firm of Edwards & Kelsey.

• 3863 • John C. "Jake" Landen ARTBA Annual Highway Safety Award

To recognize an individual for an outstanding contribution to highway safety. Nominations may be submitted by members of ARTBA's Traffic Safety Industry Division, at least 60 days prior to the annual convention. A plaque is awarded annually at the convention. Established in 1989 in honor of John C. "Jake" Landen.

• 3864 • Life Membership Award

To recognize individuals who have made outstanding contributions toward advancing the broad objectives of the Association. A plaque is awarded annually at the convention.

• 3865 • **Paul F. Phelan Memorial Award**
To recognize members of the Materials and Services Division of the Association who have made an outstanding contribution to the Division and the Association by emulating the spirit and dedication of the late Paul F. Phelan. A plaque is awarded annually at the convention. Established in 1971 in memory of Paul F. Phelan.

• 3866 • **S. S. Steinberg Award**
To recognize an individual who has made an outstanding contribution to transportation education. An outstanding educator in the field of transportation (e.g., civil engineer, economist, planning, construction, public policy) is eligible. A monetary award of $500 and a plaque are awarded annually at the ARTBA convention. Established in memory of Professor S.S. Steinberg, the first president of the ARTBA Educational Division. Sponsored by CH2M Hill.

• 3867 • **Nello L. Teer, Jr. Award**
To recognize a member of the ARTBA Contractor's Division who has made outstanding contributions to the transportation construction industry and to the Division through participation in its activities and in pursuit of its goals. Members of ARTBA Contractor's Division who are active at the national and/or state level and have contributed to the development of the transportation construction industry are eligible. A plaque is awarded annually at the convention. Established in 1988 to honor Nello L. Teer, Jr.

• 3868 •
American Romanian Academy of Arts and Sciences
Prof. Dr. Nicolae H. Pavel, Pres.
Ohio University
Department of Mathematics
Athens, OH 45701
Phone: (740)593-1267
Fax: (740)593-9805
E-mail: npavel@bing.math.ohiou.edu
Home Page: http://www.meca.polymtl.ca/ion/ARA-AS/index.htm

• 3869 • **American Romanian Academy Awards**
To recognize distinguished contributions to science, the creative arts, economics, and social science. Special ARA Awards, ARA Awards for Contribution to the Cause of Freedom and Human Rights, and Special Book Awards are presented. Plaques are awarded annually at the convention. Established in 1983.

• 3870 • **ARA Annual Award**
Recognizes renowned scholars and artists contributing to the enhancement of Romanian culture and science. Awarded annually.

• 3871 •
American Rose Society
Benny Ellerbe, Exec.Dir.
PO Box 30000
8877 Jefferson Paige Rd.
Shreveport, LA 71119
Phone: (318)938-5402
Toll-Free: 800-637-6534
Fax: (318)938-5405
E-mail: ars@ars-hq.org
Home Page: http://www.ars.org

• 3872 • **Gold Honor Medal**
For recognition of outstanding service to and for the American Rose Society. Consideration for the award is given to members of the Society. A medal is usually awarded annually or biennially as merited. Established in 1933.

• 3873 •
American Rottweiler Club
Diane Garnett, Sec.
1463 Sailcrest Ct.
Fort Collins, CO 80526
E-mail: garnetts@att.net
Home Page: http://www.amrottclub.org/

• 3874 • **Friend of the Rottweiler**
To recognize individuals who have contributed to the betterment of the Rottweiler breed. Established in 1988.

• 3875 • **Good Sportsmanship Award**
To recognize individuals in the field of Rottweilers concerned with showing and obedience who work for the progress of the Club and the breed.

• 3876 • **Top Archite**
To recognize outstanding service by a member to the American Rottweiler Club. Members who are actively working for the progress of the Club are eligible. Nominations may be made by peers. A plaque is awarded annually at the Club's annual meeting. Established in 1973 by William C. Stahl.

• 3877 •
American-Scandinavian Foundation
Edward P. Gallagher, Pres.
58 Park Ave.
New York, NY 10016
Phone: (212)879-9779
Fax: (212)686-1157
E-mail: info@amscan.org
Home Page: http://www.amscan.org

• 3878 • **ASF Awards for Scandinavians**
To provide opportunities for Scandinavians to undertake study or research programs in the United States. Applicants must be citizens of Denmark, Finland, Iceland, Norway or Sweden. Candidates for awards are recommended to ASF by the following organizations in Scandinavia: Danmark-Amerika Fondet, Fiolstraede 24, 3.Sal, 1171 Copenhagen K, Denmark; Suomi-Amerikka Yhdistysten Liitto, Mechelininkatu 10A, SF-001 00 Helsinki 10, Finland; Islenzk-Amerika Felagid,Raudaraustigur 25, 150 Reykjavik, Iceland; Norge-Amerika Foreningen, Radhusgt. 23BC, 0158 Oslo, Norway; and Sverige-Amerika Stiftelsen, Box 5280, S-102 46 Stockholm, Sweden. The number of awards totaling approximately $500,000 varies each year.

• 3879 • **ASF Translation Prize**
To encourage translation of the best contemporary Scandinavian literature into English in order to bring the culture of the Nordic countries to a larger audience. Translations of poetry, fiction, drama, or literary prose written by Scandinavian authors born after 1800 are considered. An honorarium of $2,000, a bronze medal, and publication in the Foundation's journal, *Scandinavian Review,* are awarded annually. Established in 1980. The Inger Sjoberg Prize of $1000 will be awarded to the runner-up. Established in 1993.

• 3880 •
American Schleswing-Holstein Heritage Society
Doug Ratermann, Registrar
PO Box 506
Walcott, IA 52773-0506
Phone: (563)284-4184
Fax: (563)284-4184
E-mail: ashhs@ashhs.org
Home Page: http://www.ashhs.org

• 3881 • **Endowment Fund**
For the preservation of German heritage. Recognition award bestowed annually.

• 3882 •
American School and University
Susan Lustig, Exec.Dir.
Primedia Business Magazine & Media
9800 Metcalf Ave.
Overland Park, KS 66212
E-mail: slustig@primediabusiness.com
Home Page: http://asumag.com

• 3883 • ***American School and University* Annual Architectural Portfolio**
The November issue of *American School and University* is devoted to award-winning and other outstanding school, college, university, and specialized educational facilities design, for both new buildings and renovations/additions. Two main awards, a varying number of citations, and honorable mentions are presented each year by a jury of architects and educational administrators. Established in 1983.

• 3884 • **Educational Interiors Showcase**
The August issue of *American School and University* features award-winning and other outstanding facilities that were completed in the previous two years. Projects are selected in the following categories: administrative areas, auditoriums/music rooms, cafeterias, chapels, childcare centers, classrooms, common areas, exhibition space/galleries, interior renovation, laboratories, libraries/media centers, multipurpose rooms, physical education facilities, resi-

dence halls/lounges, student centers, and vocational/industrial arts. Two grand prize winners are awarded a $1,000 scholarship fund donation to the school or university program of their choice; citations and commemorative plaques are also awarded. Awarded annually. Established in 1990.

• 3885 • Management Effectiveness Awards
For recognition of innovative cost-cutting ideas in the areas of educational facilities, energy, and administration. Superintendents, chief business officers, purchasing officers, and facility directors of school districts are eligible for consideration. Monetary awards and plaques are awarded annually in December. Established in 1985.

• 3886 • National School Plant Manager of the Year Award
In recognition of physical plant managers, *American School & University* and the National School Plant Managers Association (NSPMA) honor outstanding achievement and service to the school plant profession. One main recipient and honorable mentions are selected. Winners are announced in the June issue of *American School & University.*

• 3887 •
American School Health Association
Susan F. Wooley PhD, Exec.Dir.
PO Box 708
7263 State Rte. 43
Kent, OH 44240
Phone: (330)678-1601
Toll-Free: 800-445-2742
Fax: (330)678-4526
E-mail: asha@ashaweb.org
Home Page: http://www.ashaweb.org

• 3888 • Distinguished Service Awards
To recognize outstanding contributions to the child health field through the association. Members of the Association are eligible. Awarded annually. Established in 1961.

• 3889 • William A. Howe Award
Recognizes distinguished service in school health. The award is not limited to members of the Association. Awarded annually. Established in 1941.

• 3890 • Outstanding School Health Educator Award
To recognize a professional health educator who has made significant contributions to the promotion of child health through the schools. The award is not limited to members of the association. Established in 1990.

• 3891 • Outstanding School Nurse of the Year Award
To recognize an outstanding professional school nurse, either active or retired. School nurses who are actively involved with a professional organization that emphasizes the importance of school nursing are eligible. The award is not limited to members of the Association. Awarded annually. Established in 1984.

• 3892 • Research Council Award
For recognition of an outstanding researcher in the field of school health. The award is not limited to members of the association.

• 3893 •
American Scientific Glassblowers Society
Amy Collins, Off.Mgr.
PO Box 778
Madison, NC 27025
Phone: (336)427-2406
Fax: (336)427-2496
E-mail: natl-office@asgs-glass.org
Home Page: http://www.asgs-glass.org

• 3894 • J. Allen Alexander Award
To recognize outstanding contributions in furthering the aims and ideals of the ASGS, based on long service with committee work and elected office. A plaque is awarded annually. Established to honor J. Allen Alexander, founder of the Society.

• 3895 • Helmet Drechsel Achievement Award
To recognize devotion to the Society based on time, knowledge and abilities, and service that is not necessarily associated with elected office. A plaque is awarded annually. Formerly: Achievement Award.

• 3896 •
American Shetland Pony Club/American Miniature Horse Registry
Larry Parnell, Pres.
81-B E Queenwood Rd.
Morton, IL 61550
Phone: (309)263-4044
Fax: (309)263-5113
E-mail: info@shetlandminiature.com
Home Page: http://www.shetlandminiature.com

• 3897 • Shetland People Hall of Fame
To give public recognition to individuals in the Shetland industry for outstanding contributions to the development of the Shetland Pony and the ASPC since 1888. The membership votes on nominees at the annual convention. Individual plaques are awarded annually. A large plaque for all those elected is displayed at the Club's office. Established in 1987.

• 3898 •
American-Slovenian Polka Foundation
Cecilia Dolgan, Pres.
605 E 222nd St.
Euclid, OH 44123
Phone: (216)261-3263
Toll-Free: (866)66P-OLKA
Fax: (216)261-4134
E-mail: polkashop@aol.com
Home Page: http://www.clevelandstyle.com

• 3899 • Annual Achievement Awards
Annual award of recognition. Given for the band of the year and other outstanding achievement. Recording of the Year, Cultural/Heritage, Best vocalist, musician of the year, Sideman of the Year, Button Accordion Player of the Year, Button Accordian Group, Support and Promotion, and Best New Young Band.

• 3900 • Lifetime Achievement Award
Annual award of recognition. Given for lifetime contributions and impact.

• 3901 • Trustees' Honor Roll
Annual award of recognition. Given for lifetime contribution.

• 3902 •
American Society for Adolescent Psychiatry
Frances M. Roton, Exec.Dir.
PO Box 570218
Dallas, TX 75357-0218
Phone: (972)686-6166
Fax: (972)613-5532
E-mail: info@adolpsych.org
Home Page: http://adolpsych.org

• 3903 • ASAP - Gralnick Foundation Research Award
To recognize a resident or fellow in adolescent psychiatry. The recipient delivers a research paper at the annual meeting. Established in 1979.

• 3904 • Distinguished Service Award
To recognize an outstanding contribution to the welfare of the American Society for Adolescent Psychiatry. A monetary award and a plaque are awarded as merited. Established in 1979.

• 3905 • Fellow
To recognize outstanding active members of the society. Fellows are elected on the basis of the following five criteria: board certification; community participation, particularly with reference to the psychiatric needs of youth; outstanding clinical and administrative contributions to mental health services, particularly those serving the needs of youth; outstanding academic contributions, including aspects of adolescent psychiatry; and contributions to psychiatric research and/or publications.

• 3906 • William A. Schonfeld Award (Honorary Members)
This, ASAP's highest honor, is given to recognize an outstanding contributor to the field of adolescent psychiatry. Adolescent psychiatrists or other individuals who have contributed to the goals of the society are eligible. A plaque and honorarium are awarded annually. The recipient delivers a clinical lecture at the annual meeting. Established in 1969 in memory of ASAP's founding president, William A. Schonfeld.

• 3907 •
American Society for Advancement of Anesthesia and Sedation in Dentistry
Dr. David Crystal DDS, Exec.Sec.
6 E Union Ave.
Bound Brook, NJ 08805
Phone: (732)469-9050
Fax: (732)271-1985
E-mail: info@sedation4dentists.com
Home Page: http://www.sedation4dentists.com

• 3908 • **Certificate of Honor**
To recognize an individual for meritorious work to the society. A scroll was presented only once in the history of the society in 1979. Established in 1950.

• 3909 • **Hillel Feldman Award**
For recognition of outstanding efforts to improve the delivery of dentistry and the elimination of pain. The award is based on the following criteria: 15 years in practice, literary scientific contributions, and active participation in seminars and educational activities related to dental anesthesia both nationally and internationally. Individuals without regard to age, sex, citizenship, or membership in the society may be nominated by the executive board. A fellowship is awarded annually. M. Hillel Feldman, the founder of the society.

• 3910 •
American Society for Aesthetic Plastic Surgery
Sue Dykema, Deputy Exec.Dir.
36 W 44th St., Ste. 630
New York, NY 10036
Phone: (212)921-0500
Toll-Free: 888-272-7711
Fax: (212)921-0011
E-mail: media@surgery.org
Home Page: http://www.surgery.org

• 3911 • **Journalism Achievement on Aesthetic Surgery Award**
Annual award of recognition.

• 3912 •
American Society for Aesthetics
Curtis L. Carter PhD, Sec.-Treas.
Marquette University
PO Box 1881
Milwaukee, WI 53201-1881
Phone: (414)288-7831
Phone: (414)228-7827
Fax: (414)228-5415
E-mail: asa@aesthetics-online.org
Home Page: http://www.aesthetics-online.org

• 3913 • **John Fisher Memorial Prize**
Awarded annually. A monetary prize is given to winners of the essay competition in various categories.

• 3914 •
American Society for Bariatric Surgery
Georgeann Mallory RD, Exec.Dir.
100 SW 75th St., Ste. 201
Gainesville, FL 32607
Phone: (352)331-4900
Fax: (352)331-4975
E-mail: info@asbs.org
Home Page: http://www.asbs.org

• 3915 • **Resident/Trainee Award**
Recognizes a resident or trainee in the field of bariatric surgery. A monetary award is given annually.

• 3916 •
American Society for Biochemistry and Molecular Biology
Barbara Gordon, Contact
9650 Rockville Pike
Bethesda, MD 20814
Phone: (301)530-7145
Fax: (301)571-1824
Home Page: http://www.faseb.org/asbmb

Formerly: (1987) American Society of Biological Chemists.

• 3917 • **ASBMB/Amgen Award**
For recognition of outstanding research in biochemistry and molecular biology by an individual who received a doctorate within the past 15 years. Research must be related to the understanding of disease. A monetary prize of $5,000, a plaque, and $20,000 for research and travel are awarded each year. Established in 1992.

• 3918 • **ASBMB/Avanti Award in Lipids**
To recognize an outstanding investigator who is currently carrying out seminal studies in lipid metabolism, lipid enzymology, or lipids in membranes. A plaque, a monetary prize of $3,000, and travel expenses are awarded annually. The recipient will deliver a lecture on his/her latest research results at the Annual Meeting. Established in 1994. Co-sponsored by the Biophysical Society.

• 3919 • **ASBMB - Merck Award**
For recognition of outstanding research in biochemistry and molecular biology. Nomination must be made by a member of the Society. A monetary prize of $5,000, a plaque, and travel to the annual meeting are awarded each year at the scientific meeting. Established in 1981. Sponsored by Merck and Company. Formerly: (1987) ASBC - Merck Award.

• 3920 • **ASBMB/Schering Plough Institute Award**
For recognition of outstanding research in biochemistry and molecular biology by an individual who received a doctorate within the past ten years. A monetary prize of $5,000, a plaque, and travel expenses of up to $1,000 to the annual meeting is awarded each year. Established in 1993.

• 3921 • **Fritz Lipmann Lectureship**
To recognize a speaker who has made outstanding contributions to biochemistry and molecular biology, designated by the planning committee from among the invited speakers at the annual meeting. Established in 1988 in honor of Nobel Laureate Fritz Lipmann and funded by contributions from his friends and students.

• 3922 • **William C. Rose Award**
For recognition of outstanding research in biochemistry and molecular biology and to promote an interest in training young scientists. A monetary prize and a plaque are awarded annually at the scientific meeting. Established in 1976 by a group of students of the late William C. Rose, a professor of Biochemistry at the University of Illinois, Urbana, on his 90th birthday.

• 3923 • **Herbert Sober Award**
For recognition of outstanding research in biochemistry and molecular biology with an emphasis on techniques and methods. A monetary prize and a plaque are awarded biennially in even-numbered years at the scientific meeting. Established in 1978 by friends of Dr. Sober.

• 3924 •
American Society for Bioethics and Humanities
Karen Nason, Exec.Dir.
4700 W Lake Ave.
Glenview, IL 60025-1485
Phone: (847)375-4745
Toll-Free: 877-734-9385
Fax: 877-734-9385
E-mail: info@asbh.org
Home Page: http://www.asbh.org

• 3925 • **Distinguished Service Award**
Recognizes outstanding and dedicated service to the ASBH. The award is presented to individuals or groups who have advanced the mission of the ASBH in a significant and lasting way.

• 3926 • **Lifetime Achievement Award**
Recognizes outstanding contributions and significant publications that have helped shape the direction of the field of bioethics and medical humanities. The awardee The recipient must agree to make a major presentation at the annual ASHA meeting. Applicants must be nominated by another member by the deadline.

• 3927 • **Student Paper Award**
Recognizes one student paper submitted and accepted for presentation by the ASBH Annual Meeting Program Committee. To be considered for the award, students must submit an abstract of their paper through the ASBH Call for Abstract Submission process and forward a hard copy of their full paper to the SBH staff. Recipients will present their papers at the annual ASBH meeting and receive $1,000.

• 3928 •
American Society for Bone and Mineral Research
Joan R. Goldberg, Exec.Dir.
2025 M St. NW, Ste. 800
Washington, DC 20036-3309
Phone: (202)367-1161
Fax: (202)367-2161
E-mail: asbmr@smithbucklin.com
Home Page: http://www.asbmr.org

• 3929 • **Fuller Albright Award**
For recognition of meritorious scientific accomplishment in the bone and mineral field. Members who have not reached 41 years of age before July 1 of the year in which the award is presented are eligible. A $2000 honorarium and a plaque are awarded annually. Nominations must be submitted to the ASBMR Director. Previous non-winning nominations must be updated and resubmitted. Established in 1980 in memory of Dr. Fuller Albright.

• 3930 • **Louis Avioli Founders Award**
Recognizes basic research by honoring a member for fundamental contributions. One award consisting of $2000 honorarium and a plaque is awarded annually. Nomination deadline is May 1. Established in 2000.

• 3931 • **Award for Outstanding Research in the Pathophysiology of Osteoporosis**
Recognizes the highest ranking abstract submitted to this category. Selection is based on scientific merit and scored using a blind-review system. Nominees are not accepted. A $1,500 honorarium and a plaque are awarded annually.

• 3932 • **Frederic C. Bartter Award**
To recognizes outstanding clinical investigation of disorders of bone and mineral metabolism. Members must be nominated by May 1. $ 2000 honorarium and a plaque are awarded annually. Previous non-winning nominations may be updated and resubmitted. Select issues of the *Journal of Bone and Mineral Research* contains nomination letter criteria from the ASBMR web site. Established in 1986 in memory of Dr. Frederic C. Bartter.

• 3933 • **Shirley Hohl Service Award**
To recognize an individual whose activities best represent the dedicated and unselfish devotion in service to the Society and to its goals that were exemplified by Shirley Hohl. A plaque and honorarium of $2,000 are awarded annually.

• 3934 • **Most Outstanding Abstract Award**
Recognizes the lead investigator of the highest scored abstract submitted for persentation at the annual meeting. Nominations are not accepted. Selection is based only on the scientific merit of the abstract. A $1000 honorarium and a plaque are awarded annually.

• 3935 • **William F. Neuman Award**
To recognizes outstanding and major scientific contributions to associates in the area of bone and mineral research and for contributions to associates and trainees in teaching, research and administration. Society members must be nominated by May 1. A $ 2000 honorarium and a plaque are awarded annually. Previous non-winning nominations may be updated and resubmitted. Established in 1981 in memory of Dr. William F. Neuman.

• 3936 • **President's Book Award**
To recognize the top ranking student abstract. Recipient receives $1000 honorarium and a special book presented and signed by the president. A $1,500 honorarium and a plaque are awarded annually.

• 3937 • **Gideon A. Rodan Excellence in Mentorship Award**
Recognizes outstanding support given by a person, a group of people or an institution that helps promote the independent careers of young investigators. One award is given in the area of basic research studies and one in clinical bone research annually. Formerly: (2006) Excellence in Mentorship Awards.

• 3938 • **Young Investigator Awards**
Recognizes young investigators for excellence in bone and mineral research. Individuals who are the first and presenting author of the highest ranking abstracts in each category; within five years of completion of a Ph.D. A plaque and honorarium of $2,000 are awarded annually.

• 3939 •
American Society for Cell Biology
Elizabeth Marincola, Exec.Dir.
8120 Woodmont Ave., Ste. 750
Bethesda, MD 20814-2762
Phone: (301)347-9300
Fax: (301)347-9310
E-mail: ascbinfo@ascb.org
Home Page: http://www.ascb.org

• 3940 • **ASCB/Bruce Alberts Award for Distinguished Contributions to Science Education**
For innovative and sustained activities in science education. Emphasis is placed on the local, regional and/or national impact of the nominee's activities. Winners are selected by the ASCB Education Committee.

• 3941 • **ASCB/Promega Early Career Life Scientist Award**
For an outstanding scientist. Applicants must have earned their doctorates no more than 12 years earlier and have served as an independent investigator for no more than seven years.

• 3942 • **E.E. Just Lecture Award**
Recognizes outstanding scientific achievements by a minority scientist. Awardee is selected by the ASCB Minorities Affairs Committee. Established to memorialize early 20th Century biologist E.E. Just.

• 3943 • **MAC Poster Awards**
Recognizes the best minorities posters presented at the ASCB Annual Meeting MAC Poster Session.

• 3944 • **MBC Paper of the Year Award**
Recognizes the first author of the paper judged to be the best of the year, from June to May. Chosen by *MBC* Associate Editors.

• 3945 • **The Merton Bernfield Memorial Award**
Award of merit. Nominations due August 1.

• 3946 • **Public Service Award**
Recognizes outstanding national leadership in support of biomedical research. Selected by the ASCB Public Policy Committee.

• 3947 • **E. B. Wilson Medal**
The ASCB's highest honor for Science, the E.B. Wilson Medal is presented at the Annual Meeting of the Society for significant and far-reaching contributions to cell biology over the course of a career. Nominations from the ASCB membership are welcome by March 31, 2004.

• 3948 • **Women in Cell Biology**
WICB Committee recognizes outstanding achievements in cell biology by presenting two Career Recognition Awards at the ASCB Annual Meeting. Junior Award is given to a women in early stage of her career (assistant professor or equivalent) who has made exceptional scientific contributions to cell biology and exhibits the potential for contributing to a high level of scientific endeavor while fostering the career development of young scientists. The Senior Award is given to a woman or man in a later career stage (full professor or equivalent) whose outstanding achievements are coupled with a long-standing record of support for women in science and by mentorship of both men and women in scientific careers.

• 3949 • **Young UK Cell Biologist of the Year Award**
Presented by the British Society for Cell Biology.

• 3950 •
American Society for Clinical Laboratory Science
Elissa Passiment EdM, Exec.VP
6701 Democracy Blvd., Ste. 300
Bethesda, MD 20817
Phone: (301)657-2768
Fax: (301)657-2909
E-mail: ascls@ascls.org
Home Page: http://www.ascls.org

• 3951 • **Baxter Healthcare, Scientific Products Division Graduate Scholarship**

To assist clinical laboratory practitioners and educators in pursuing graduate or advanced studies in the clinical laboratory or related sciences. Open to any clinical laboratory practitioner or educator who: (1) fulfills requirements for admission or is currently enrolled in a program leading to a Master's or doctoral degree in the clinical laboratory or related sciences; (2) is a citizen or permanent resident of the United States; and (3) has performed clinical laboratory functions for at least one year. A monetary award of $1,000 is presented. Established in 1989. Sponsored by Baxter Healthcare Corporation.Availability of the award is contingent on funding by Baxter Healthcare Corporation.

• 3952 • **Gloria F. "Mike" Gilbert Memorial Trustee Award**

To recognize professional excellence and to assist individuals within the profession of clinical laboratory science in their development or improvement of skills in laboratory administration through continuing education in structured or independent modes of study. A clinical laboratory practitioner who has been engaged in the practice of clinical laboratory science for at least three years, and has position responsibilities including supervision, administration or management, or has established goals consistent with professional development, is eligible. The deadline for applications is February 1. A monetary prize of up to $300 is awarded. Established in 1983 by Region III.

• 3953 • **Ruth I. Heinemann Memorial Trustee Award for Educational Development**

To assist individuals within the profession of clinical laboratory science in developing educational strategies, preparing educational media, or designing innovative methods of instruction. In addition to filing an application, the applicant should submit a proposal. Educational materials for publication are not required, but it is encouraged that an article describing and evaluating the educational experience be submitted. Educators in a structured program in medical technology or its specialties, or graduate students preparing to become educators, who are citizens or permanent residents of the United States and have been involved in an instructional role for at least one year, are eligible. The deadline for applications is February 1. A monetary prize of up to $500 is awarded. Established in 1978 by the Founders Group.

• 3954 • **Joseph J. Kleiner Memorial Awards**

To recognize authors of outstanding articles published in *Clinical Laboratory Science.* All unsolicited papers, except for those reporting research or study activities mandated and financed by ASMT, will automatically be considered for awards. Authors need not be members. For journal authors only. The deadline for applications is February 1. Two monetary prizes of $1,000 each are awarded to the senior or sole authors of two papers. Established in 1979 by the Joseph J. Kleiner Memorial Fund to honor J.J. Kleiner, the inventor of the Vacutainer.

• 3955 • **Robin H. Mendelson Memorial Awards**

To honor outstanding service and contributions to the Society, (for members only) the ASMT Education and Research Fund, Inc., or clinical laboratory science in general. All elected or appointed officers, committee chairs and members, and employees of ASMT or the ASMT Education and Research Fund, Inc., or other persons whose contributions have been particularly commendable and deserving of recognition for a particular service or position, are eligible. Nominations are accepted. The deadline is February 1. Up to four awards are presented annually, one of which is to the ASMT president. Established in 1971 in memory of Robert H. Mendelson, a courageous young man of 18 who struggled for five years to survive kidney dialysis and two transplants during the infancy of that technology.

• 3956 •
American Society for Clinical Nutrition
Sandra A. Schlicker PhD, Exec.Dir.
9650 Rockville Pike
Bethesda, MD 20814-3998
Phone: (301)634-7110
Fax: (301)634-7350
E-mail: sschlick@ascn.faseb.org
Home Page: http://www.ascn.org

• 3957 • **Dannon Institute Award for Excellence in Medical/Dental Nutrition Education**

To recognize an outstanding career in medical and/or dental education. Nominations must be submitted by October 7. A monetary prize of $1,000 and an inscribed plaque are awarded annually.

• 3958 • **Robert H. Herman Memorial Award**

To recognize outstanding research in clinical nutrition particularly the biochemical and metabolic aspects of human nutrition. Nominations must be submitted by November 15. A monetary award of $1,000 and a plaque are awarded annually. Established in 1982.

• 3959 • **Norman Kretchmer Memorial Award in Nutrition and Development**

To recognize a young investigator who is 45 years of age or younger for a substantial body of independent research in the field of nutrition and development with potential relevance to improving children's health. A cash prize and inscribed medal are awarded. Prizes are provided by the Ross Products Division, Abbott Laboratories. Established in 1997.

• 3960 • **The McCollum Award**

To recognize outstanding research in the field of clinical nutrition. Nominations must be submitted by November 15. A monetary award of $1,000 and a scroll are awarded annually. Established in 1965. Sponsored by the :Novartis Nutrition.

• 3961 • **Young Investigator Award Competition**

To promote interest in clinical nutrition and to encourage excellence in research papers presented by young investigators who are still training in graduate and medical schools. Fellows and students working toward an advanced degree are eligible to submit a single abstract. The applicant must be the senior author on the abstract and must have played a major role in the planning and conduct of the research being reported. The applicant must also be supported by a mentor who is a member of the ASCN. The mentor must write a letter and may sponsor no more than three applicants. Each finalist will receive a $750 travel award and plaque inscribed with his or her name and the meeting year. The winner of the competition will receive an additional $500 cash award. Sponsored by Nestle Nutrition Institute.

• 3962 •
American Society for Clinical Pathology
Dr. John R. Ball, Exec.VP
2100 W Harrison
Chicago, IL 60612
Phone: (312)738-1336
Toll-Free: 800-621-4142
Fax: (312)738-1619
E-mail: info@ascp.org
Home Page: http://www.ascp.org
Formerly: (2002) American Society of Clinical Pathologists.

• 3963 • **ASCP Associate Member Lifetime Achievement Award**

To recognize an associate member of the society who is actively engaged in one or more of the following: laboratory operations, research, management/supervision or education. The nominee must have demonstrated commitment to the profession through long-standing contributions to the advancement of the profession and Society activities over a lifetime. These contributions include participation in leadership roles and support of the ASCP-AMS mission. Formerly: (1987) Medical Technologist of the Year; (1996) Technologist of the Year.

• 3964 • **ASCP Associate Member Section Distinguished Service Award**

To recognize individuals who have made substantial contributions to the ASCP in the areas of teaching, publications, or service. Associate or clinical scientist members of the ASCP are eligible. A pewter plate is awarded annually at the National Meeting. Established in 1985. Formerly: (1987) Associated Member Distinguished Service Award.

• 3965 • **ASCP - CAP Joint Distinguished Service Award**

For recognition of outstanding contributions to American pathology and to the American Society of Clinical Pathologists and the College of American Pathologists. Members of ASCP or CAP are eligible. A plaque and gift are awarded annually. Established in 1965 by the American Society of Clinical Pathologists and the College of American Pathologists. Formerly: ASCP - CAP Joint Annual Award.

• 3966 • ASCP Medical Photography Competition

To recognize outstanding photography in the following categories: gross or macroscopic, microscopic, and electron microscopic. Judging is based on scientific merit, content, composition, quality of image, and originality. Entry must be composed and photographed by entrant and not have been submitted for publication elsewhere. Monetary awards for first, second, third place, and honorable mention are presented annually in the three categories. Established in 1979. Sponsored by Nikon, Inc..

• 3967 • ASCP Sheard - Sanford Medical Student Award

To recognize original student research in pathology and to stimulate interest in pathology among medical students. Fourth-year medical students who have conducted research in clinical pathology are eligible. The two awardees receive all-expense paid trips to the national meeting held in the fall, as well as certificates from ASCP, and a gift from Leica. Presented annually. Established in 1928 and made possible from the royalties of sales of the photelometer developed by Dr. Charles Sheard and Dr. Arthur H. Sanford. Co-sponsored by Leica.

• 3968 • ASCP Distinguished Service to Clinical Pathology Award Honoring Ward Burdick

For recognition of meritorious contributions to the science of clinical pathology. Members of the society are eligible. A certificate, and an all-expense paid trip for the awardee and spouse are awarded annually. Established in 1929 in memory of Ward Burdick, who played a major role in the organization of the society in 1922.

• 3969 • ASCP Outstanding Research Award Honoring Philip Levine

For recognition of outstanding work in immunohematology and transfusion. An honorarium, a medallion, a plaque and an all-expense paid trip for the awardee and spouse, are awarded annually. Established in 1969 in honor of Dr. Philip Levine, who described the etiology of Rh hemolytic disease of the newborn. Cosponsored by Ortho Diagnostic Systems, Inc.

• 3970 • ASCP Distinguished Pathology Educator Award Honoring H. P. Smith

To recognize a member for a distinguished scientific career with outstanding contributions in the study of human disease or continuing medical education. A certificate and an all-expense paid trip for the awardee and spouse are awarded annually. Established in 1974 to honor H. P. Smith, who was active in the society, and received the Ward Burdick Award in 1941 and the Joint ASCP-CAP Distinguished Service Award in 1965.

• 3971 •
American Society for Clinical Pharmacology and Therapeutics
Sharon J. Swan CAE, Exec.Dir.
528 N Washington St.
Alexandria, VA 22314-2314
Phone: (703)836-6981
Phone: (703)836-6982
Fax: (703)836-5223
E-mail: info@ascpt.org
Home Page: http://www.ascpt.org

• 3972 • William B. Abrams Award in Geriatric Clinical Pharmacology

To honor individual scientists for outstanding contributions to the general area of geriatric clinical pharmacology. A monetary award, a plaque, and travel expenses to attend the annual meeting are awarded annually. Established in 1996 to honor Dr. William B. Abrams, for his important contributions to geriatric clinical pharmacology.

• 3973 • Henry W. Elliott Distinguished Service Award

To recognize an individual for outstanding service to ASCPT. Such accomplishments include: establishment of effective programs, administrative work, effective advocacy of important solutions to major issues effecting clinical pharmacology, and development of important liaisons among appropriate groups. Members who contribute in the North American arena are eligible. A monetary award of $1,000, a medallion, and travel expenses to attend the annual meeting are awarded each year. Established in 1978. Deadline to submit nominations is September 30. Nominations may be submitted online.

• 3974 • Leon I. Goldberg Young Investigator Award of the ASCPT

To encourage and recognize young scientists active in the field in which they earned their doctoral degrees. Nominated candidates must not be more than 41 years of age by March 1 of the year of the award presentation. Nominations may be submitted by December 1. A monetary award, a plaque, and travel expenses to attend the annual meeting are awarded each year. The award recipient delivers a lecture during the ASCPT annual meeting. Established in 1985. Deadline to submit nominations is September 30. Nominations can be submitted online.

• 3975 • Oscar B. Hunter Memorial Award in Therapeutics of the ASCPT

This, the premier award of the Society, honors scientists for outstanding contributions to clinical pharmacology and therapeutics in the areas of drug research, patient care, and teaching. Members and non-members are eligible. A monetary award of $1,500, a bronze medal mounted on a plaque in the likeness of Dr. Hunter, and travel expenses to the annual meeting are awarded each year. The recipient delivers a lecture during the ASCPT annual meeting. Established in 1955 to honor Dr. Oscar Benwood Hunter, Sr., an outstanding Washington physician, who joined the ASCPT in 1928, held office as president and secretary, and was for many years the guiding spirit of the Society. Deadline to submit nominations is September 30. Nominations may be submitted online.

• 3976 • Rawls-Palmer Progress in Medicine Lecture and Award

To bring the efforts of modern research to the care of the patient. Nominations may be submitted by December 1. A monetary award of $1,000, a medallion, and travel expenses to attend the annual meeting where the winner presents a lecture are awarded each year. Established in 1978 to honor Mr. and Mrs. Gray M. Rawls and Mr. and Mrs. Nathaniel J. Palmer. Deadline to submit nominations is September 30. Nominations may be submitted online.

• 3977 •
American Society for Colposcopy and Cervical Pathology
Kathleen G. Poole, Exec.Dir.
20 W Washington St., Ste. 1
Hagerstown, MD 21740
Phone: (301)733-3640
Toll-Free: 800-787-7227
Fax: (301)733-5775
E-mail: kpoole@asccp.org
Home Page: http://www.asccp.org

• 3978 • Colposcopy Recognition Award

Annual award of recognition.

• 3979 • G. Trombetta Teaching Award

Recognizes the best paper written by a resident. Awarded biennially.

• 3980 •
American Society for Competitiveness
Abbas J. Ali, Exec.Dir.
PO Box 1658
Indiana, PA 15705
Phone: (724)357-5928
Phone: (724)357-7788
Fax: (724)357-7768
E-mail: aaali@iup.edu
Home Page: http://www.eberly.iup.edu/asc

• 3981 • Leadership Award

Annual medal for contribution to quality and competitiveness.

• 3982 • Philip Crosby Award

For contribution to quality and competitiveness. A medal is awarded annually.

• 3983 • Quality Award

For contribution to quality and competitiveness. A medal is awarded annually.

• 3984 •
American Society for Cybernetics
Robert Martin, Sec.
2115 G St. NW, Ste. 403
Washington, DC 20052
Phone: (202)994-1681
Fax: (202)994-3081
Home Page: http://www.asc-cybernetics.org

• 3985 • **ASC Recognition Award**
For recognition of contributions to the field of cybernetics of an organizational or administrative nature. A plaque is awarded irregularly. Established in 1986.

• 3986 • **Warren Sturgis McCulloch Award**
For recognition of intellectual and practical contributions to a specific subfield of cybernetics. A plaque is awarded irregularly. Established in 1970.

• 3987 • **Norbert Wiener Medal**
For recognition of sustained, lifelong intellectual contributions to the field of cybernetics. Originally an award for young scholars, it has been awarded since 1983 to prominent cyberneticians of all ages. A gold medal is awarded irregularly. Established in 1968.

• 3988 •
American Society for Dermatologic Surgery
Rhoda S. Narins MD, Pres.
5550 Meadowbrook Dr., No. 102
Rolling Meadows, IL 60008
Phone: (847)956-0900
Toll-Free: 800-441-2737
Fax: (847)956-0999
E-mail: info@asds.net
Home Page: http://www.asds.net

• 3989 • **Award for Distinguished Service**
Recognizes significant contribution toward furthering the goals of the society through education and/or research. Awarded annually.

• 3990 •
American Society for Eighteenth-Century Studies
Byron R. Wells, Exec.Dir.
Wake Forest University
PO Box 7867
Winston-Salem, NC 27109
Phone: (336)727-4694
Fax: (336)727-4697
E-mail: asecs@wfu.edu
Home Page: http://asecs.press.jhu.edu/

• 3991 • **James L. Clifford Prize**
To recognize an outstanding article on 18th-century studies published in a journal, festschrift, or other serial publication. The article should not be longer than 7500 words and must have been in print during the previous year. Members are eligible. The deadline for nominations is December 30. A monetary prize of $500 is awarded annually. Established in 1976 in honor of Professor James L. Clifford, past president of the society.

• 3992 • **Louis Gottschalk Prize**
To recognize an outstanding historical or critical study on a subject of eighteenth-century interest. A book by a member published during the previous year in the field of 18th-century studies, and submitted by a publisher not later than November 15, is eligible. Books that are primarily translations are not eligible. A monetary prize of $1,000 is awarded annually. Established in 1976 in memory of Professor Louis Gottschalk, the second president of the society.

• 3993 •
American Society for Engineering Education
Frank Huband, Exec.Dir.
1818 N St. NW, Ste. 600
Washington, DC 20036-2479
Phone: (202)331-3500
Fax: (202)265-8504
E-mail: aseeexec@asee.org
Home Page: http://www.asee.org

• 3994 • **Aglient Technologies Award for Excellence in Laboratory Instruction**
To recognize outstanding contributions in providing and promoting excellence in experimentation and laboratory instruction. One award is presented to an individual; the second is presented to either an individual or a group. The deadline for nominations is January 15. Two prizes of $1,000 and certificates are awarded at the discretion of the ASEE Divisions for Experimentation and Laboratory-Oriented Studies and Instrumentation. Established in 1981. Sponsored by The Fluke Corporation. Formerly: (2006) Fluke Corporation Award for Excellence in Laboratory Instruction.

• 3995 • **ASEE Minorities in Engineering Award**
For outstanding achievements by an engineering educator to increase participation by minority and/or women students in the engineering curricula. A monetary prize of $1,500, a certificate, and a grant of $500 for travel expenses to the ASEE Annual Conference are awarded. Established in 1979. Funded by Corning, Inc. Formerly: (1978) Vincent Bendix Award; (1995) Vincent Bendix Minorities in Education Award.

• 3996 • **ASEE Section Outstanding Teaching Award**
To recognize outstanding classroom performance. Candidates must be teachers of any subject included in an ABET/CEAB accredited engineering or engineering technology program. The deadline for nominations is January 15. Each Section of ASEE selects a recipient, who receives an honorarium and a certificate. Established in 1964. Formerly: (1984) Western Electric Fund Award; (1995) AT&T Foundation Awards.

• 3997 • **John Leland Atwood Award**
To recognize a recent outstanding educational achievement and to encourage original, innovative improvements in aerospace engineering. The deadline for nominations is January 15. A monetary prize of $2,000 and a certificate are awarded annually. In addition, the American Institute of Aeronautics and Astronautics (AIAA) provides a medal and a certificate at the annual Aerospace Sciences Meeting. Established in 1974 by the Aerospace Division. Renamed in 1985 to honor John Leland Atwood, who played a major role in the development of aviation and aerospace technologies for more than 50 years. Endowed by Rockwell International. Formerly: (1984) Aerospace Division/AIAA Educational Achievement Award.

• 3998 • **Ferdinand P. Beer and E. Russell Johnston Jr. Outstanding New Mechanics Educator Award**
To recognize individuals who have shown a strong commitment to mechanics education. Individuals who have no more than five years of academic experience past their first regular academic appointment are eligible. A monetary prize of $200, a plaque, and registration for the Conference are awarded to up to three individuals annually. Established in 1992 by the Mechanics Division.

• 3999 • **Frederick J. Berger Award**
To recognize and encourage both programmatic and individual excellence in engineering technology education. Individuals and engineering technology schools or departments that have exhibited outstanding leadership in presentation, documentation, innovation, and administration in engineering technology education are eligible. The deadline for nominations is January 15. A $500 honorarium and a bronze medallion are awarded to the educator and a $500 honorarium and a plaque are awarded to the academic department. Awarded annually when merited. Established in 1990. Formerly: Wiley Award for Excellence in Engineering Technology Education.

• 4000 • **Homer I. Bernhardt Distinguished Service Award**
To recognize work that contributes to the advancement and development of excellence in engineering libraries. The deadline for nominations is January 15. A plaque is awarded each year by the Engineering Libraries Division.

• 4001 • **Best Paper Award**
To recognize the author of the most significant paper published or presented in the Civil Engineering Division's activities during the previous year. Papers appearing in the Division's publications or presented at a Civil Engineering Division sponsored session at the ASEE Annual Conference and published in the conference proceedings are considered. The deadline for nominations is January 15. A plaque is presented during the awards ceremony of the ASEE Annual Conference.

• 4002 • Joseph M. Biedenbach Distinguished Service Award
To acknowledge outstanding leadership and service in the field of continuing professional development for engineers, as well as noteworthy service within the CPD division itself. Awarded annually. The deadline for nominations is January 15. Established in 1976 by the Continuing Professional Development Division of ASEE.

• 4003 • Alvah K. Borman Award
For significant and sustained contributions to the promotion of the philosophy and practice of cooperative education in engineering and engineering technology. Cooperative Education Division members, past or present, are eligible. The deadline for nominations is January 15. A monetary award of $500, a plaque, and a certificate are awarded annually. Established in 1979.

• 4004 • Chester F. Carlson Award for Innovation in Engineering Education
To recognize an individual innovator in engineering, or engineering technology education who, by motivation and ability to extend beyond accepted tradition, has made a significant contribution to the profession. The deadline for nominations is January 15. A monetary award of $1,000 and a plaque are awarded annually. Established in 1973 in memory of Chester F. Carlson who is noted for the invention of xerography. Sponsored by the Xerox Corporation.

• 4005 • Certificate of Merit
To recognize outstanding and noteworthy contributions to the Continuing Professional Development Division. The criteria considered for the award are: innovative leadership over a period of several years or a single unique contribution of major significance. Members are eligible. A Certificate of Merit is presented. Established in 1981 by the Continuing Professional Development Division.

• 4006 • Willard D. Cheek Exemplary Service Award
To recognize an individual who has served the Society with distinction over an extended period of time. The deadline for nominations is January 15. A monetary award of $1,000 to attend the College-Industry Education Conference meeting and a memento are awarded annually by the Relations with Industry Division. Established in 1986.

• 4007 • W. Leighton Collins Award
For recognition of highly significant contributions to education in engineering, engineering technology, and allied fields. The deadline for nominations is January 15. An inscribed medallion is awarded when merited. Established in 1971 to honor W. Leighton Collins, executive director of ASEE for 14 years.

• 4008 • William H. Corcoran Award
To recognize the author of the outstanding article published in *Chemical Engineering.* The deadline for nominations is January 15. A plaque is awarded by the Chemical Engineering Division.

• 4009 • John A. Curtis Lecture Award
For recognition of the best oral and written paper presented at the Computers in Education Division's session at the ASEE Annual Conference. The deadline for nominations is January 15. A monetary prize of $300, a plaque, and a certificate are awarded annually. Established in 1978 in honor of John A. Curtis founder of the Computers in Education Division.

• 4010 • Benjamin J. Dasher Best Paper Award
For recognition of the most outstanding paper presented at the Frontiers in Education Conference. The deadline for nominations is January 15. A plaque and a certificate are awarded. Established in 1980 by the Educational Research and Methods Division/IEEE.

• 4011 • Distinguished Educator and Service Award
To recognize distinguished contributions to the teaching of physics to engineering and engineering technology students and for service to the Division. A framed certificate is awarded annually to a member of the Physics Division.

• 4012 • Distinguished Service Award
To recognize individuals for their significant contributions toward furthering the goals of the Division for Experimentation and Laboratory Oriented Studies. Awarded annually.

• 4013 • Distinguished Service Citation
For recognition of long, continuous, and distinguished service to engineering and engineering technology education or related fields. The deadline for nominations is January 15. A certificate is awarded. Established in 1975.

• 4014 • Distinguished Teaching Award
To recognize an outstanding engineering or engineering technology teacher. Candidates must be members of the Middle Atlantic Section of ASEE who teach any subject included in an accredited engineering or engineering technology degree. The deadline for nominations is January 15. A $250 honorarium, a certificate, and registration to the meeting at which the award us presented is awarded annually.

• 4015 • Dow Outstanding New Faculty Award
To recognize young faculty for interest in the Society as evidenced by participation in local, section, or national activities; enthusiasm for engineering education; ability to communicate suggestions and comments of colleagues; and willingness to contribute to the improvement of the Society and to the teaching of engineering. Faculty members of ASEE member institutions under 36 years of age who are also members of the Society are eligible. One individual is selected from each of the 12 ASEE geography sections to attend the annual conference of the Society with all expenses paid. The deadline for nominations is January 15. Certificates and travel expenses are awarded annually. Established in 1969 by the Dow Chemical Company.

• 4016 • EAI Award
To recognize an outstanding *CoED Journal* paper on analog computers and computation. The deadline for nominations is January 15. A monetary prize $400 and a certificate are awarded annually by the Computers in Education Division. This award commemorates the contributions of Electronic Associates, Inc.

• 4017 • Woody Everett Award
To recognize the best paper/presentation/demonstration at the Computers in Education Division poster session of the ASEE Annual Conference. The deadline for nominations is January 15. A monetary prize of $300, a plaque, and a certificate are awarded annually.

• 4018 • Fellow Grade Membership
To recognize members who have been a member of any grade for at least 10 years for outstanding contributions to engineering or engineering technology education. The deadline for nominations is January 15. Awarded annually. Established in 1983.

• 4019 • Clement J. Freund Award
To recognize an individual in business, industry, government, or education who has made a significant impact on cooperative education programs in engineering and engineering technology. A $2,000 honorarium, a plaque, a certificate, and travel expenses to the ASEE Conference are awarded every odd year. Sponsored by Caterpillar Tractor Company, Danly Machine Corporation, Diamond Shamrock Corporation, Dow Chemical U.S.A., John Deere, Sundstrand Corporation, and Union Carbide Corporation.

• 4020 • General Electric Senior Research Award
To recognize and honor a member of the staff or faculty of a college of engineering who has made significant contributions to engineering research by pushing forward the frontiers of knowledge, perfecting and applying the latest scientific advances to engineering problems, or providing administrative leadership to important engineering research programs. The deadline for nominations is January 15. A gold medal, a certificate, and travel expenses to the annual conference are awarded each year. Established in 1969. Sponsored by the General Electric Company. Formerly: (1978) Vincent Bendix Award.

• 4021 • Eugene L. Grant Award
To honor the author of the best paper published in the *Engineering Economist*, the joint quarterly publication of the Engineering Economy Division and the Institute of Industrial Engineers. The deadline for nominations is January 15. An honorarium is awarded annually. Established in 1966 by the Engineering Economy Division.

• 4022 • Archie Higdon Distinguished Educator Award
For recognition of outstanding service to the Mechanics Division with particular emphasis on contributions to the teaching of engineering mechanics. The deadline for nominations is January 15. A plaque and a certificate are presented annually. Established in 1977.

• 4023 • Honorary Member
To members and non-members of ASEE for eminent and distinguished service to humanity in engineering and engineering technology education or allied fields. The deadline for nominations is January 15. The awardee is entitled to active lifetime membership in the Society without annual dues and receives a commemorative plaque. Established in 1953.

• 4024 • Benjamin Garver Lamme Award
This, the Society's most prestigious award, is given to a distinguished engineering educator for contributions to the art of teaching, research and technical literature, and for achievements that contribute to the advancement of the profession and engineering college administration. The deadline for nominations is January 15. A gold medal and certificate are awarded annually. Established in 1928 in memory of Benjamin Garver Lamme.

• 4025 • Donald E. Marlowe Award
To recognize distinguished education administration. Success as a teacher, long-lasting contributions to education, and scholarly contributions affecting engineering students are considered. The deadline for nominations is January 15. A plaque and travel expenses for the awardee and spouse to attend the ASEE Annual Conference to receive the award are awarded when merited. Established in 1981 in honor of Donald E. Marlowe.

• 4026 • J. J. Martin Award
To recognize the most outstanding paper of the Chemical Engineering Division presented at the ASEE Annual Conference. A plaque is awarded annually.

• 4027 • James H. McGraw Award
For recognition of outstanding service in engineering technology education. Teachers, authors, or administrators who are, or have been, affiliated with an institution that provides engineering technology education are eligible. The deadline for nominations is January 15. An honorarium of $1,000 and a certificate are awarded annually. Established in 1950 by the McGraw-Hill Book Company.

• 4028 • Curtis W. McGraw Research Award
To recognize outstanding early achievements by young engineering college research workers and to encourage the continuance of such productivity. The recipient must be under 40 years of age. The deadline for nominations is January 15. An honorarium of $1,000 and a certificate are awarded annually. Established in 1957. Sponsored by the Engineering Research Council with the assistance of the McGraw-Hill Book Company.

• 4029 • Fred Merryfield Design Award
To recognize an engineering educator for excellence in the teaching of engineering design and other contributions related to engineering design teaching. The deadline for nominations is January 15. A monetary prize of $2,500, a $500 stipend for travel to the ASEE Annual Conference, and a plaque are awarded annually. In addition, the awardee's institutional department receives a monetary award of $500. Established in 1981. Sponsored by CH2M Hill.

• 4030 • Merl K. Miller Award
To recognize an outstanding *CoED Journal* paper on teaching or instructional methods. The deadline for nominations is January 15. A monetary prize $400 and a certificate are awarded annually by the Computers in Education Division.

• 4031 • Glenn Murphy Award
To recognize a distinguished nuclear engineering educator for contributions to the teaching of undergraduate and/or graduate nuclear engineering students. Full-time members of a college faculty who are actively engaged in teaching in the United States or Canada are eligible. The deadline for nominations is January 15. An honorarium of $750 and a certificate are awarded annually. Established in 1976 by the Nuclear Engineering Division of the Society and endowed by former students and friends of the late Glenn Murphy, Edison Electric Institute, and Iowa State University.

• 4032 • Olmsted Liberal Education Award for Innovation
To honor those ASEE members who have applied their creative talents and made significant innovations in the teaching or administering of liberal education in engineering education. The deadline for nominations is January 15. The recipient is presented with a personal commemorative award plaque at the ASEE annual conference and his or her name is entered on a permanent plaque retained by the Division. The award honors Sterling P. Olmsted.

• 4033 • Oppenheimer Award
For recognition of the author of the best paper presented in the mid-year conference of the Engineering Design Graphics Division. The deadline for nominations is January 15. A $100 honorarium is awarded annually. Established in 1970 by Frank Oppenheimer of West Germany, a long time member of the Division.

• 4034 • Outstanding Community College Educator Award
To recognize excellence in the instruction of engineering and/or engineering technology and to serve as an incentive to the recipient and other faculty to make further significant contributions to engineering education. Any full-time faculty member at a two-year college in the Pacific Southwest Section who is a member of ASEE may be nominated by January 15. A $1,000 honorarium and a certificate are awarded annually by the Pacific Southwest Section.

• 4035 • Outstanding Educator Award
To recognize an individual for excellence in the instruction of engineering, engineering technology, or engineering science. Any individual within the St. Lawrence Section boundaries may be nominated. A certificate and travel expenses to attend the annual section meeting are awarded. Sponsored by Anaren Microwave, Inc.

• 4036 • Outstanding Paper Award
To recognize the author of the most significant paper presented at the College-Industry Education Conference held the previous year, based on the quality of both the oral and written presentations. The deadline for nominations is January 15. A certificate is awarded by the Continuing Professional Development Division. Established in 1981 by the Continuing Professional Development Division.

• 4037 • Outstanding Section Campus Representative Award
To recognize those ASEE Campus Representatives who have achieved excellence in their roles as the Society's representative on campus. The deadline for nominations is January 15. A certificate is awarded annually to the campus representative and the respective deans. Established in 1988 by the Campus Liaison Board of ASEE.

• 4038 • Outstanding Zone Campus Representative Award
To recognize the outstanding campus representative and the respective dean in each of the four geographic zones of the Society. The deadline for nominations is January 15. A plaque is awarded annually to the ASEE Campus Representative. Established in 1980. Formerly: (1982) Outstanding Zone Campus Activity Coordinator Award.

• 4039 • Theo C. Pilkington Outstanding Educator Award
To recognize an educator for significant contributions to the biomedical engineering and education professions as well as service to the Society and the Division. The deadline for nominations is January 15. A monetary award of $300 and a commemorative plaque are awarded annually. Established in 1981 by the Biomedical Engineering Division. Formerly: (1995) Biomedical Engineering Outstanding Educator Award.

• 4040 • Helen L. Plants Award for Special Events
For recognition of the presenter of the most outstanding non-traditional session workshop, seminar discussion, or demonstration offered at the Frontiers in Education Conference that precedes the most recent FIE Conference. The deadline for nominations is January 15. A plaque and a certificate are awarded. Estab-

lished in 1982 by the Educational Research and Methods Division.

• 4041 • Ralph Coats Roe Award

To recognize a mechanical engineer educator who is an outstanding teacher. Candidates may have contributed to the profession through the development of a significant technique or method of analysis, procedure, or synthesis; the involvement of students and colleagues with innovative aspects of design through problems which are relevant to real life situations; the conception of an idea of great importance to the advancement of the engineering profession or engineering education; teaching, directing, or conducting significant research; providing outstanding leadership; the creation of an important invention; or carrying out distinguished service and leadership to the college, the community, the nation, or humankind. Candidates must be a full-time member of a college faculty. A $10,000 honorarium, a plaque, and travel expenses to the conference are awarded annually by the Mechanical Engineering Division. Funded by Burns and Roe, Inc.

• 4042 • Ronald J. Schmitz Award for Outstanding Contributions to the Frontiers in Education Conference

To recognize an individual for an outstanding contribution to the Frontiers in Education Conference. The deadline for nominations is January 15. Co-sponsored by ASEE/ERM and IEEE.

• 4043 • Harden-Simons Prize

To recognize an outstanding *CoED Journal* paper on computational methods. The deadline for nominations is January 15. A monetary prize of $400 and a certificate are awarded annually by the Computers in Education Division.

• 4044 • Ray H. Speiss Award

To recognize an outstanding *CoED Journal* paper on hybrid/analog/digital computers and computation. The deadline for nominations is January 15. A monetary prize $400 and a certificate are awarded annually by the Computers in Education Division.

• 4045 • Frederick Emmons Terman Award

To recognize an outstanding young electrical engineering educator for his or her contributions to the profession as evidenced by authorship of an outstanding text in electrical engineering, and achievements in teaching, research, guidance of students and related activities. Authors under 45 years of age are eligible. The deadline for nominations is January 15. A monetary award of $4,000, a gold-plated medal, a bronze replica, a scroll, and travel expenses to the ASEE Frontiers in Education Conference are awarded each year. Established in 1969 by the Electrical Engineering Division of the Society. Sponsored by the Hewlett-Packard Company.

• 4046 • Union Carbide Lectureship Award

To recognize a distinguished engineering educator, and to recognize and encourage outstanding achievement in an important field of fundamental chemical engineering theory or practice. The deadline for nominations is January 15. A certificate is awarded annually. Established in 1963 by the Chemical Engineering Division of the Society.

• 4047 • George K. Wadlin Distinguished Service Award

To recognize sustained distinguished service to the Civil Engineering Division of ASEE and support of its activities and notable contributions to civil engineering education. The deadline for nominations is January 15. A plaque and a certificate are awarded at the Civil Engineering Division awards ceremony at the ASEE Annual Conference.

• 4048 • George Westinghouse Award

To recognize young educators for outstanding ability and distinguished contributions to the improvement of, and innovation in, teaching methods for engineering students. Teachers of any subject matter normally taken by engineering students are eligible, but candidates must be under the age of 45. The deadline for nominations is January 15. A monetary award of $5,000, a certificate, a $500 honorarium toward the individual's school or department, and $500 for travel expenses to attend the annual conference are awarded each year. Established in 1946 by the Westinghouse Educational Foundation.

• 4049 • Meriam/Wiley Distinguished Author Award

For recognition of a work that contributes to the advancement of technical and professional competence at undergraduate and graduate levels of engineering education. First edition books published within two years of the award deadline are eligible. The deadline for nominations is January 15. An honorarium of $2,000, a certificate, and travel expenses are awarded biennially when merited at the ASEE Annual Conference. Established in 1986 by John Wiley & Sons, Inc. in honor of James L. Meriam. Sponsored by John Wiley & Sons Publishing Company.

• 4050 •
American Society for Engineering Management
Kellie Davis, MSD Mgr.
PO Box 820
PO Box 820
Rolla, MO 65402-0820
Phone: (573)341-2101
Fax: (573)364-3500
E-mail: asemmsd@rollanet.org
Home Page: http://www.asem.com

• 4051 • Academic Excellence for Leadership of Engineering and Technical Management for Undergraduate Programs

Awarded to the University which is judged to have shown excellence in the operation of an academic program that results in the receipt of a BS degree in Engineering Management. A plaque is awarded annually.

• 4052 • ASEM Fellows

Awarded annually to individual members of ASEM and are based upon continuing distinguished service and contributions to the Society and the profession of Engineering Management. Candidates must have had unbroken membership in ASEM for 8 years. A plaque is awarded. Nominations are due by April 1.

• 4053 • Bernard R. Sarchet Award

Recognizes an ASEM Member who has contributed the most to ASEM both on a local and national basis. A plaque is awarded.

• 4054 • Engineering Manager of the Year Award

Recognizes individuals who have made the most significant contributions to the advancement of Engineering Management during the current year. Nominations must be received by April 1 accompanied with a photograph.

• 4055 • Founders Award

Recognizes the best student section based on total membership participation in activities and contributions to the discipline of engineering management. A plaque is awarded annually.

• 4056 • Franklin B.W. Woodbury Award for Special Achievement

Recognizes an individual who has demonstrated special achievement that resulted in special advancement of the purposes of the Society or of the profession of Engineering Management. Awarded occasionally.

• 4057 • Merl Baker Best Conference Paper Award

Presented to the individual who is judged to have submitted the best paper at the annual conference. A plaque and monetary prize are awarded annually.

• 4058 • Merrit Williamson Best Student Paper Award

Presented t the student who is judged to have submitted and presented the best paper at the annual conference. A plaque and monetary prize are awarded annually.

• 4059 • Presidental Award

Award of recognition awarded to the best local section based on total membership participation in activities and contributions to the discipline of engineering management.

• 4060 • **Ted Eschenbach Best EMJ Journal Paper Award**
Recognizes the individual whose paper in the Engineering Management Journal (EMJ) is judged to have been the best paper Published in the annual volume of EMJ. A plaque and monetary Prize are awarded annually.

• 4061 •
American Society for Enology and Viticulture
Lyndie M. Boulton, Exec.Dir.
PO Box 1855
Davis, CA 95617
Phone: (530)753-3142
Fax: (530)753-3318
E-mail: society@asev.org
Home Page: http://www.asev.org

Formerly: American Society of Enologists.

• 4062 • **Honorary Research Lecture**
To recognize a guest lecturer who has done research related to enology or viticulture. An honorarium of $500 and guest status at the annual meeting in June are awarded annually. Established in 1973.

• 4063 • **Merit Award**
For recognition of achievement in the advancement and improvement of the wine and grape industry or wine research and contributions to the society. An honorarium of $500, a plaque, and status as a full guest of the Society at the annual meeting in June are awarded annually. Established in 1955.

• 4064 •
American Society for Environmental History
Lisa Mighetto, Exec.Dir.
119 Pine St., Ste. 207
Seattle, WA 98101
Phone: (206)343-0226
Fax: (206)343-0249
E-mail: mighetto@hrassoc.com
Home Page: http://www.aseh.net

• 4065 • **Alice Hamilton Prize**
Recognizes the best article in a journal other than Environmental History. Awarded annually.

• 4066 • **George Perkins Marsh Prize**
Recognizes the best book in environmental history. Awarded annually.

• 4067 • **Leopold-Hidy Prize**
Recognizes the best article in the *Environmental History* journal. Awarded annually.

• 4068 • **Rachel Carson Prize**
Recognizes the best dissertation in environmental history. Awarded annually.

• 4069 •
American Society for Ethnohistory
Shepard Krech III, Pres.
PO Box 906660
Durham, NC 27708-0660
Phone: (919)687-3602
Toll-Free: 888-387-5687
Fax: (919)687-3602
Home Page: http://ethnohistory.org/eth3.html

Formerly: (1966) American Indian Ethnohistoric Conference.

• 4070 • **Robert F. Heizer Prize**
For recognition of the best article concerning ethnohistory. The awards committee of ASE reviews all books and journals relating to ethnohistory published during the previous year and makes the selection. A monetary prize and a certificate are awarded annually. Established in 1980 in honor of Dr. Robert F. Heizer, ethnohistorian and archaeologist noted for his research in California and Mesoamerica.

• 4071 •
American Society for Gastrointestinal Endoscopy
Patricia V. Blake, Exec.Dir.
1520 Kensington Rd., Ste. 202
Oak Brook, IL 60523
Phone: (630)573-0600
Toll-Free: (866)353-ASGE
Fax: (639)573-0691
E-mail: info@asge.org
Home Page: http://www.asge.org

• 4072 • **Distinguished Educator Award**
To recognize an individual for his or her longitudinal contributions to the teaching of endoscopy. These contributions may include the education of fellows, endoscopy seminars, participation in national postgraduate courses and published scholarly reviews or education materials, including videos. Awarded to one or more recipients when merited at the ASGE Annual Meeting.

• 4073 • **Distinguished Service Award**
In recognition of the unique contributions made by individuals to the Society and the field of gastrointestinal endoscopy. The deadline for nominations is October 15. Awarded when merited at the ASGE Annual Meeting.

• 4074 • **Master Endoscopist Award**
To recognize up to three individuals annually for their excellence in the practice of gastrointestinal endoscopy. These awards will be given to clinicians who spend the majority of their time in patient care and are recognized regionally or nationally for their expertise and longitudinal contributions to the practice of gastrointestinal endoscopy. Awarded when merited at the ASGE Annual Meeting.

• 4075 • **Schindler Award**
To recognize a gastrointestinal endoscopist who is a member of the Society for accomplishments in endoscopic research, teaching, and/or service to the Society and who best exemplifies the standards and traditions established by Dr. Rudolf Schindler. Nominations may be made by any member of the Society by October 15. Awarded when merited at the ASGE Annual Meeting. Established in 1954.

• 4076 •
American Society for Gravitational and Space Biology
Christopher S. Brown, Pres.
5712 Loyal Ave.
Durham, NC 27713
Phone: (919)806-3076
Fax: (919)806-3076
E-mail: asgsb@unc.edu
Home Page: http://www.asgsb.org

• 4077 • **ASGSB Founder's Award**
Recognition is given for outstanding contributions to field space and gravitational biology.

• 4078 • **ASGSB President's Award**
Recognition is given for outstanding service and contributions to society.

• 4079 • **Linda D. Barber Award**
Recognizes best research associate publication.

• 4080 • **Orr E. Reynolds Distinguished Service Award**
For distinguished service to society. Recognition is given.

• 4081 • **Special Distinguished & Outstanding Service Award**
Recognition is given.

• 4082 • **Thora W. Halstead Young Investigator's Award**
Recognition is given to young scientists

• 4083 •
American Society for Horticultural Science
Michael W. Neff, Exec.Dir.
113 S West St., Ste. 200
Alexandria, VA 22314-2851
Phone: (703)836-4606
Fax: (703)836-2024
E-mail: ashs@ashs.org
Home Page: http://www.ashs.org

• 4084 • **ASHS Hall of Fame**
Educates and increases the awareness of younger members of the profession and the general public by honoring persons who have made extraordinary contributions to horticulture. Persons involved in any aspect of horticulture are eligible. Nominees may be deceased or retired and may be from any country. Primary emphasis is given to nominees who are deceased. A plaque with the awardees name and likeness is kept at the ASHS Headquarters. Nomination deadline is February 4. Established in 1989.

• 4085 • Commercial Horticulture Distinguished Achievement Award

Recognizes extension activities in the broad area of commercial horticulture. Five copies of the nomination material (available on-line) must be submitted.

• 4086 • Consumer Horticulture Distinguished Achievement Award

Recognizes extension activities within the broad area of consumer horticulture. Five copies of the nomination material (available on-line) must be submitted.

• 4087 • Educational Materials Award

For educational pieces published or released during the previous year. Awards are given in the following categories: book of 100 or more pages; bulletin of 31-100 pages; fact sheet of 9-30 pages; leaflet of 1-8 pages; CD-ROM; video; website; newsletter; slide set/PowerPoint presentation; and mostly visual (calendar, poster, etc.). Entrants may only have one entry per category and must be ASHS members. Six copies of application material (available on-line) must be submitted.

• 4088 • Industry Division ASHS President's Corporate Council Award

Recognizes outstanding industry contributions to the field of horticulture. Nominees need not be members, but must be nominated by a member. Nominees must also be currently active in industry and/or should have spent most of his/her career in the private sector.Contributions eligible for nomination include those to the science and profession of horticulture through an original research project, method, invention, or other innovative application in the private sector. Contact Larry D. Knerr, Shamrock Seed Co., 3 Harris Place, Salinas, CA 93901 for additional details.

• 4089 • Outstanding Extension Educator Award

To recognize exceptional contributions to the science and profession of horticulture, the horticultural industry, and/or home and urban horticulture through innovative extension programs for a period of ten or more years. A plaque or a certificate is awarded annually. Established in 1970. A copy of the nominee's curriculum vita, a brief letter stating the reason for the nomination, and three letters of support, including at least one from another institution must be submitted. See web site or additional information and electronic submission guidelines. Formerly: Carl S. Bittner Extension Award in Horticulture; Nursery Extension Award for Distinguished Service to the Nursery Industry.

• 4090 • Outstanding Graduate Educator Award

To encourage and recognize excellence in graduate teaching of horticulture. Established in 1971 in memory of professor M. A. Blake, an outstanding pioneer teacher of horticulture at Rutgers University and president of the Society in 1961. Renamed in 1981 in honor of Norman F. Childers, upon his retirement from Rutgers University; and renamed again in 1986. A copy of the nominee's curriculum vita, a brief letter stating the reason for the nomination, and three letters of support, including at least one from another institution must be submitted. See web site or additional information and electronic submission guidelines. Formerly: Norman F. Childers Award for Distinguished Graduate Teaching; M. A. Blake Award for Distinguished Graduate Teaching.

• 4091 • Outstanding Industry Scientist Award

To recognize a horticultural crops scientist working in the private sector who has made outstanding and valuable contributions to horticultural science, the horticultural industry, and the horticultural profession for a period of 10 or more years. The nominee must be a member of ASHS actively working, i.e., a substantial portion of the nominee's current effort is involved in horticultural activity regardless of the nominee's employment. The nominee may not be a previous recipient of this award. An engraved plaque is presented during the Society's Annual Meeting. Established in 1991. A copy of the nominee's curriculum vita, a brief letter stating the reason for the nomination, and three letters of support, including at least one from another institution must be submitted. See web site or additional information and electronic submission guidelines.

• 4092 • Outstanding International Horticulturist ASHS Career Awards

Encourages excellence in horticultural teaching and research by recognizing contributions in horticultural science. Active ASHS members actively engaged in research, extension, or teaching for 10 or more years are eligible. Nominators must be active members of the association. A copy of the nominee's curriculum vitae; a brief letter containing the reason for the nomination; and three letters of support, including at least one from another institution must be submitted. Nomination deadline is February 4. Six career awards are presented annually.

• 4093 • Outstanding Researcher Award

To recognize a distinguished record of research on one or more horticultural crops (or plants) for a period of ten or more years and research which has made a significant contribution to scientific knowledge, basic or applied, dealing with or applicable to improvements in the breeding, selection, propagation, quality, harvesting, processing, marketing, or utilization of horticultural crops, plants, or products thereof. A plaque or a certificate is awarded annually. Established in 1985. A copy of the nominee's curriculum vita, a brief letter stating the reason for the nomination, and three letters of support, including at least one from another institution must be submitted. See web site or additional information and electronic submission guidelines.

• 4094 • Outstanding Undergraduate Educator Award

To recognize distinguished contributions to undergraduate education in horticultural science for a period of ten or more years. A plaque or a certificate is awarded annually. A copy of the nominee's curriculum vita, a brief letter stating the reason for the nomination, and three letters of support, including at least one from another institution must be submitted. See web site or additional information and electronic submission guidelines. Established in 1964. Formerly: (1986) L. M. Ware Award for Distinguished (Undergraduate) Teaching.

• 4095 • Undergraduate Student Awards for an Outstanding Horticulture Student

Recognizes exceptional undergraduate horticulture students in baccalaureate programs. Students enrolled in horticulture, including pomology, olericulture, floriculture, and landscape or ornamental horticulture or in a plant science/crop science department with an emphasis or major in horticulture are eligible. Selection is basis on academic achievements, leadership abilities, participation in campus/club activities, and service to their departments. One award is given per institution. Students' names and photographs will be published in the April issue of the ASHS Newsletter, and students also receive a certificate and a letter of congratulations from the ASHS president. Nominations may be submitted by mail; a letter from the department head or other designated individual, briefly summarizing the student's qualifications, along with a photograph, or the same information may be submitted electronically. Application deadline is February 11. Send nominations to: ASHS Outstanding Horticulture Student Award, 113 South West St. Suite 200, Alexandria, VA 22314-2851, e-mail: ashs@ashs.org.

• 4096 • Working Group Vegetable Breeding Working Group Award of Excellence

Recognizes breeding programs that have had a significant impact on the vegetable industry. The nominated contribution must have been made within the past 20 years and must have provided salient basic information and/or cultivar or germplasm releases. Nominees do not need to be ASHS members but must be nominated by a member. A description of the accomplishments and documentation listing publication and/or specific cultivar or germplasm releases; and an estimate of the effect on the industry must be submitted to Mikel Stevens, Brigham Young University, Dept. of Agronomy and Horticulture, 287 Widstoe Bldg., Box 25183, Provo, UT 84602-5183, email mikel_stevens@byu.edu by March 1. The award is given annually.

• 4097 • Working Groups Distinguished Achievement Award for Nursery Crops

Recognizes superior, productive, innovative, or noteworthy accomplishments in research, teaching, and/or extension in production, physiology, and/or use of woody landscape plants. ASHS members of at least three years are eligible. Previous recipients are not eligible. Individuals must be nominated by another ASHS member. Biographical informaiton, a curriculum vitae, and no more than five pages describing the accomplishments or programs being nominated must be submitted to Jeff Gillman, University of Minnesota, 305 Alderman Hall, 1970 Folwell Ave., St. Paul, MN 55108 by March 1.

• 4098 • Working Groups Outstanding Fruit Cultivar Award
Recognizes a a cultivar or germplasm release of a temperate or tropical fruit or nut crop species. The species must have been released withing the past 25 years and had a scientific or commercial impact on the fruit industry. Breeders, releasers, or institutions responsible for the cultivar or germplasm release are eligible. A 3 inch bronze medal depicting a figure of Adam and Eve and the cultivar name and names of those associated with its breeding, testing, and introduction is awarded annually at the buisness meeting of FRBR during the ASHS Annual International Conference. The medal is funded by royalties from Janick and Moore's books *Advances in Fruit Breeding* and *Methods in Fruit Breeding*. Contact Peter Cousins, P.O. Box 41, Geneva, NY 14456 for application material and guidelines. Application deadline is April 15.

• 4099 •
American Society for Information Science and Technology
Richard B. Hill, Exec.Dir.
1320 Fenwick Ln., No. 510
Silver Spring, MD 20910
Phone: (301)495-0900
Fax: (301)495-0810
E-mail: asis@asis.org
Home Page: http://www.asis.org

Formerly: (1968) American Documentation Institute.

• 4100 • ASIS Research Award
To recognize an individual or organization for outstanding research contributions in the field of information science and achievement of significant impact based on recent research or previous research whose contribution has been recently recognized. Awarded occasionally when merited. Established in 1984. Application deadline is June 15.

• 4101 • Award of Merit
This, the Society's highest honor, recognizes a member of the information science profession for a noteworthy contribution to the profession. Anyone in the information science profession is eligible. A certificate and silver bowl are awarded at the annual meeting. Established in 1964. Application deadline is July 1.

• 4102 • Best Chapter Event Award
To recognize the best event held by a Chapter (or jointly by two or more Chapters) during the previous year (July-June). Any type of Chapter event is eligible, including technical programs, seminars, panels, workshops, CE courses, product exhibitions, tutorials, fundraisers, or other events. Joint events held with other associations are also eligible. A certificate is awarded. Nominations are solicited by the Chapter Assembly Director and can be made by any member. Seven copies of a 250 word letter or nomination; name, address, phone number, and chapter of nominator; a maximum of two letters of support; a maximum of three supporting documents; and a 50 word citation must be submitted by July 1. Established in 1991.

• 4103 • Best Information Science Book Award
To recognize the book that has made the most outstanding contribution to the field of information science. Nominated books must be published in the previous year. A citation is awarded at the annual meeting. Established in 1969. Application deadline is June 15.

• 4104 • Best *JASIS* Paper Award
To recognize members of the Society for significant contributions to the field of information science that also act as a further stimulus to the preparation and submittal of high quality papers. Papers published in the *Journal of the American Society for Information Science* during the year prior to the annual meeting are considered, with the exception of "Perspective" articles. $ 1500 plus $ 500 travel reimbursement to attend the associations annual meeting are awarded. Established in 1969; has been sponsored by John Wiley and Sons Inc. since 1997.

• 4105 • Best SIG Publication Award
To recognize the best publication produced by a SIG (or jointly by two or more SIGs) during the previous year (July-June). Any type of SIG publication is eligible, including newsletters, transactions, directories, or other publications. A certificate is awarded. Established in 1991.

• 4106 • Chapter Member-of-The-Year Award
To recognize the service of an individual to a particular Chapter. It is given for significant contributions to the membership of the Chapter through participation in and support of its meetings and publications, fund-raising, recruitment, or other significant activities. It is intended that this award recognize contributions at the local level. All chapter members are eligible. Nominations are solicited by the Chapter Assembly Director and can be made by any member. Seven copies of a 250 word letter or nomination; name, address, phone number, and chapter of nominator; a maximum of two letters of support; a maximum of three supporting documents; and a 50 word citation must be submitted by July 1. A certificate is awarded annually. Established in 1991. Application deadline is July 1st.

• 4107 • Chapter of the Year Award
To recognize outstanding Chapters of the Society for their participation in and contributions to ASIS and the advancement of information science. Criteria for selection include membership and recruitment, member activities, continuing education programs, chapter activities, and communications. A certificate is awarded to each member at he winning chapter's governing body at the annual meeting. Established in 1975. Application deadline is August 15th.

• 4108 • Chapter Publication of the Year Award
To recognize the ASIS Chapter that has prepared the outstanding publication during the year prior (June - July). Publication can be created by an individual chapter or by two or more chapter jointly and can be include newsletters, meeting proceedings, or directories . All chapter publications from the designated time period are automatically eligible. Deadline is July 15. A personalized citation is awarded to the chapter chair and chapter members. Established in 1991.

• 4109 • James M. Cretsos Leadership Award
To recognize a new ASIS member who has demonstrated outstanding leadership qualities in professional ASIS activities. Any ASIS member who has been a member for no more than seven years is eligible. Application deadline is July 15th. A plaque is awarded. Established in 1992.

• 4110 • Watson Davis Award
To recognize a member active in the Society for a minimum of five years for continuous dedicated service to the Society through participation in and support of its programs, Chapters, Special Interest Groups (SIGs), committees, publications, or other Society activities. Prior Watson Davis Award winners and current members of the Membership Committee are not eligible. An engraved plaque is awarded at the annual meeting. Application deadline is July 15th. Established in 1975 to honor Watson Davis, the founder of the Society.

• 4111 • Outstanding Information Science Teacher Award
To recognize an individual for excellence in teaching information science in an academic or non-academic setting. $ 1000 plus $ 500 travel expenses for attending the annual meeting are awarded. In addition $ 250 for headquarters administrative fees is also awarded. Established in 1980. Sponsored by the Institute for Scientific Information. Application deadline is July 1. See the above web address or contact the above address for additional guidelines and eligibility information.

• 4112 • Pratt-Severn Best Student Research Paper Award
Recognizes students work in the field of information science while encouraging research and writing. Students enrolled in master degree-granting institutions are eligible. Doctoral theses are not accepted. Registration for the associations annual meeting and $ 500 in travel expenses are awarded. Established in 1972. Formerly: Best Student Paper Award.

• 4113 • SIG Member-of-The-Year Award
To recognize the service of an individual to the program of a particular SIG and for significant contributions to the membership of the SIG through participation in and support of its events at the annual and mid-year meetings, its publications, and its other activities. Any ASIS member who is currently a member of the nominating SIG is eligible to receive the award. Nomination deadline is August 15th. A certificate is awarded. Established in 1991.

• 4114 • SIG-of-the-Year Award
To recognize a Special Interest Group for professional accomplishments that reflect a major impact on the field of information science. The accomplishments may be in the form of outstanding publications, a public service, a program at the annual or mid-year meeting of ASIS, or special projects. Nomination deadline is August 15th. A certificate is awarded to each member of the governing body of he SIG at the annual meeting. Established in 1975.

• 4115 • Special Award
To recognize a public figure (a government or industry leader) for long-term contributions to the advancement of information science and technology that have resulted in increased public awareness of the field and its benefits to society. This award is designed to: recognize a public figure for supporting information science through development of policy, enactment of legislation, enhancement of public access to information, and/or discovery of mechanisms for improved transfer and utilization of knowledge; encourage other public figures to support research and development in information science and technology; and increase publicity for and visibility of the Society. Nominations must be submitted by April 15. An appropriate memento (bowl, plaque, certificate, etc.) is awarded periodically. Established in 1954.

• 4116 • Student Chapter of the Year Award
To recognize the outstanding ASIS Student Chapter for participation in and contribution to ASIS and the advancement of information science. Criteria for selection include membership, meetings, activities, continuing education programs and member communications. Nomination deadline is July 31st. A certificate is awarded annually. Established in 1986.

• 4117 •
American Society for Investigative Pathology
Mark E. Sobel MD,PhD, Exec.Off.
9650 Rockville Pke.
Bethesda, MD 20814-3993
Phone: (301)634-7130
Fax: (301)634-7990
E-mail: asip@asip.org
Home Page: http://www.asip.org

Absorbed: American Association of Pathologists and Bacteriologists; American Society for Experimental Pathology.

• 4118 • Amgen Outstanding Investigator Award
To recognize outstanding contributions to pathology. Members of the Society under 43 years of age are eligible. A monetary prize and a bronze medallion are awarded annually. Established in 1957 by the American Society of Experimental Pathology. Formerly: Parke-Davis Award; (2006) Pfizer Outstanding Investigator Award.

• 4119 • Chugai Award for Meritorious Mentoring and Scholarship
Presented to a member of the American Society for Investigative Pathology with a distinguished career that especially links Excellence in mentoring and education with outstanding research Achievements in experimental and investigative pathology. The awardee will present the keynote lecture. A $2,500 honorarium and plaque will be awarded.

• 4120 • Experimental Pathologist-in-Training Award
To recognize experimental pathologists who are still in training. The awardees are chosen on the basis of abstracts submitted. All abstract forms must be sponsored and signed by a member of FASEB. One monetary prize of $1,500 and two $750 prizes to post-doctoral and graduate student each and certificates are awarded annually. Established in 1983.

• 4121 • The Gold-Headed Cane Award
Recognizes long-term contributions to pathology, including meritorious research, outstanding teaching, and general excellence in the field. The awardee will receive a mahogony cane at the Annual Meeting.

• 4122 • Rous-Whipple Award
To recognize a member of the society, 50 years of age or older, with a distinguished career in research and continued productivity at the time of the award. A monetary prize and a commemorative plaque are awarded when merited. Established in 1972 by the American Society for Experimental Biology.

• 4123 • Trainee Travel Awards
Recognizes graduate students and postdoctoral fellows. Awardees are chosen on the basis of abstracts submitted. Twelve or more monetary prizes of $500 are awarded.

• 4124 •
American Society for Legal History
Prof. Walter F. Pratt Jr., Contact
Notre Dame Law School
PO Box R
Notre Dame, IN 46556
Fax: (574)631-3595
E-mail: walter.f.pratt.1@nd.edu
Home Page: http://www.h-net.org/~law/ASLH/aslh.htm

• 4125 • Erwin C. Surrency Prize
To encourage research and publication in the field of legal history. The award is given for the best article or review essay published the previous year in the society's journal *Law and History Review* (University of Illinois Press). A monetary award of $500 and a certificate are awarded annually. Established in 1982 to honor Erwin C. Surrency, Professor Emeritus, Temple University School of Law.

• 4126 • Donald M. Sutherland Prize
To encourage research and publication in the field of English legal history. Authors who have written articles making a significant contribution to English legal history published anywhere in the previous year are eligible. A monetary award of $500 and a certificate are awarded annually. Established in 1988 in memory of Donald M. Sutherland, Professor of History, University of Iowa.

• 4127 •
American Society for Microbiology
Michael I. Goldberg Ph.D., Exec.Dir.
1752 N St. NW
Washington, DC 20036
Phone: (202)737-3600
Fax: (202)942-8341
E-mail: oed@asmusa.org
Home Page: http://www.asm.org

• 4128 • Abbott Laboratories Award in Clinical and Diagnostic Immunology
To honor distinguished scientists in the field of clinical or diagnostic immunology. A monetary award of $2,000, a certificate, and travel expenses to receive the award at the ASM General Meeting are awarded annually. An award nomination cover letter (available on the society's web site); a nominating letter; a curriculum vitae; and two supporting letters must be submitted. Nominations will be considered for three years without updating. The deadline for nominations is October 1. Sponsored by the Diagnostics Division of Abbott Laboratories.

• 4129 • ASM Founders Distinguished Service Award
To recognize a member for outstanding professional contributions to ASM in a volunteer capacity at the national level. Candidates must have served in a volunteer capacity at the national level for a minimum of five years. The deadline for nominations is October 1. A commemorative plaque and travel expenses to attend the ASM General Meeting are awarded when merited.

• 4130 • Becton Dickinson and Company Award in Clinical Microbiology
To honor distinguished microbiologists identified with clinical microbiology. Selection is based on outstanding research accomplishments, clinical or non-clinical, leading to or forming the foundation for important applications in clinical microbiology. The deadline for applications is October 1. A monetary award of $2,000, a commemorative prize, and travel expenses to attend the ASM General Meeting are awarded annually. Established in 1975. Sponsored by Becton Dickinson and Company. Formerly: (1977) Wyeth Award in Clinical Microbiology.

• 4131 • bioMerieux Sonnenwirth Award for Leadership in Clinical Microbiology
To recognize a distinguished microbiologist who has exhibited exemplary leadership in clinical microbiology. Also recognizes promotion of innovation in clinical laboratory science and high

Awards are arranged in alphabetical order below their administering organizations

dedication and commitment to the ASM and to the advancement of clinical microbiology as a profession. Deadline is October 1. A $2,000 cash prize and a commemorative piece are awarded annually, as are travel expenses to receive award. Established in 1986 in honor of Alexander Sonnenwirth, PhD. Sponsored by bioMerieux Inc. Formerly: Sonnenwirth Memorial Award.

• 4132 • Biotechnology Research Award
To recognize outstanding contributions to biotechnology through fundamental research, developmental research, or reduction to practice. A single exceptionally significant achievement or the aggregate of a number of exemplary achievements are considered. The deadline is October 1. A monetary award of $5,000, a certificate, and travel expenses to receive the award are presented annually at the ASM general meeting where the recipient delivers the Biotechnology Research Award lecture. Established in 1987. Formerly: Cetus Corporation Biotechnology Research Award.

• 4133 • Carski Foundation Distinguished Teaching Award
To provide recognition to a mature individual for distinguished teaching of microbiology at the undergraduate level and to encourage subsequent achievement. Individuals who have taught for at least 10 years and who are actively teaching in a college or university in the United States or where there is an active branch of the Society are eligible to apply by October 1. A monetary award of $2,000, a commemorative piece, and travel expenses attend the ASM general meeting are awarded annually at the national meeting. An award nomination cover letter (available on the society's web site); a nominating letter; a curriculum vitae; and two supporting letters must be submitted. Nominations will be considered for three years without updating. Established in 1968.

• 4134 • Dade Behring MicroScan Young Investigator Award
For recognition of research excellence and further educational and research objectives of an outstanding young clinical scientist. Postdoctoral students of fellows and scientist who have completed postdoctoral training in the past three years in clinical microbiology, clinical immunology or infectious diseases are eligible. Nomination deadline is October 1. A monetary prize of $2,000, a certificate, and travel expenses to receive the award at the ASM general meeting are awarded annually. Established in 1992. Supported by Dade Behring Inc. MicroScan Microbiology Systems. Formerly: (1996) Baxter Diagnostics MicroScan Young Investigator Award.

• 4135 • Honorary Member
This, the highest recognition given by ASM, recognizes a person who has made outstanding contributions to microbiology or served the Society with eminence.

• 4136 • Eli Lilly and Company Research Award
To stimulate and recognize outstanding fundamental research in microbiology or immunology. Researchers in the United States or Canada who are under 40 years of age are eligible. The selection is made from nominees by an awards committee whose members come from ASM, the American Association of Immunologists, and the American Society of Clinical Pathologists. The deadline is October 1. A monetary award of $5,000, a certificate, and travel expenses to attend the ASM general meeting are awarded annually when merited. Established in 1936.

• 4137 • Merck ICAAC Young Investigator Awards
To recognize and reward young investigators for excellence in research in the broad areas of microbiology, infectious diseases and related fields. Postdoctoral students and fellows not more than 36 months beyond their training who are actively conducting research within North America. Research is limited to the study and understanding of infectious disease and any of the other sciences associated with the discovery and applications of hemotherapeutic agents. microbiology and infectious diseases are eligible. An award nomination cover letter (available on the society's web site); a nominating letter; a curriculum vitae; and two supporting letters must be submitted. Nominations will be considered for three years without updating. Up to two awards are made each year. The deadline for nominations is April 3. The awardees are selected by the award committee on the basis of research potential and quality. A monetary award of $2,500 for travel expenses to receive the award is given annually at the Interscience Conference on Antimicrobial Agents. Established in 1983. Sponsored by Merck U.S. Human Health Division of Merck and Co.

• 4138 • Procter & Gamble Award in Applied and Environmental Microbiology
To stimulate research and development in applied microbiology (excluding clinical fields) and environmental microbiology. Applicants must be actively engaged in research or development. The deadline for nominations is October 1. Selection is made by an awards committee. A monetary award of $2,000, travel expenses to receive the award at the ASM general meeting, and a certificate are awarded annually. An award nomination cover letter (available on the society's web site); a nominating letter; a curriculum vitae; and two supporting letters must be submitted. Nominations will be considered for three years without updating. Established in 1993. Formerly: Fisher Scientific Company Award for Applied and Environmental Microbiology; ASM Award in Applied and Environmental and Microbiology.

• 4139 • USFCC/J. Roger Porter Award
To recognize microbiologists for outstanding contributions to the objectives of the United States Federation for Culture Collections. Nominations deadline is October 1. A monetary award of $2,000, a commemorative piece, and travel expenses to receive the award at the ASM general meeting are awarded annually. Established in 1982 in honor of J. Roger Porter.

• 4140 •
American Society for Microbiology, Arizona Chapter
Edward A. Birge Ph.D., Sec.-Treas.
Dept. of Microbiology
Arizona State University
Tempe, AZ 85287-2701
Phone: (480)965-7292
Fax: (480)965-0098
Home Page: http://microvet.arizona.edu/asm/index.htm

• 4141 • Travel Grant
For best presentation by students at annual meeting. Monetary award bestowed annually.

• 4142 •
American Society for Nondestructive Testing
Wayne Holliday, Exec.Dir.
1711 Arlingate Ln.
PO Box 28518
Columbus, OH 43228-0518
Phone: (614)274-6003
Toll-Free: 800-222-2768
Fax: (614)274-6899
Home Page: http://www.asnt.org

Formerly: (1967) Society for Nondestructive Testing.

• 4143 • ASNT Fellows
Open to ASNT members only. To recognize a member of outstanding professional distinction who has made continued significant contributions to the advancement of nondestructive testing and evaluation in areas such as management, engineering, science, education, administration, or planning. Individuals with 15 years of professional experience and at least 10 years of consecutive membership in the Society are eligible. Up to fifteen awards are made each year. Established in 1973.

• 4144 • ASNT Fellowship Award
To provide a grant to an educational institution for specific research in NDT at the post-graduate level. Up to three awards of $15,000 each are presented in July.

• 4145 • Lou Di Valerio Technician of the Year Award
Open to ASNT members only. To recognize an individual who has distinguished himself or herself by showing exceptional merit as an NDT technician and/or through service to the Society. Level I and Level II technicians are eligible. Awarded annually at the fall conference. Established in 1984.

• 4146 • Philip D. Johnson Honorary Member Award
Open to ASNT members only. To recognize an individual of acknowledged eminence in the domain covered by the Society and/or one who has

been recognized as a benefactor to the Society through service. No more than one Honorary Member may be elected annually.

• 4147 • Lester Honor Lecture
To honor an individual with the presentation of a lecture on a subject with direct bearing on the use of NDT and its application to materials evaluation. Awarded biennially in alternate years with the Mehl Honor Lecture. Established in 1943 to honor Dr. H. H. Lester, who was senior physicist at the Watertown Arsenal in Watertown, MA, and an outstanding contributor to the field of nondestructive testing.

• 4148 • Robert C. McMaster Gold Medal
Open to ASNT members only. To recognize a member who has made an outstanding contribution to the field of nondestructive testing and its advancement, or who has rendered meritorious service to the Society. A medal is awarded annually at the national meeting. Established in 1965. Formerly: ASNT Gold Medal.

• 4149 • Mehl Honor Lecture
To recognize an outstanding person in the field of nondestructive testing. Awarded biennially in alternate years with the Lester Honor Lecture. Established in 1941 to honor Dr. Robert F. Mehl for his outstanding research in the field of gamma radiography and countless other contributions.

• 4150 • Outstanding Paper Awards
To recognize two papers that display a high degree of effort and technical, educational, or managerial achievement in nondestructive testing through publication in ASNT's journals. Awards are presented for research in materials evaluation and nondestructive evaluation. Selection is based on originality, usefulness and clarity, and the appropriateness and accuracy of its supporting data. Awarded annually when merited at the fall conference. Established in 1992.

• 4151 • President's Award
Open to ASNT sections only. To recognize a local section of the Society that exhibits the greatest degree of proficiency in management and operation during the current fiscal year. Awarded annually. Established in 1964. Formerly: President's Points Award.

• 4152 • Charles N. Sherlock Meritorious Service Award
To recognize member's outstanding voluntary service to the Society at the national level through single or aggregate activities. Activities performed as a function of an office or paid position are not considered. Nominations may be made by members of the Board of Directors, Councils, the Awards Committee or local sections, headquarters staff, or by an ASNT member. Awarded annually.

• 4153 • Tutorial Citation Award
To recognize outstanding contributors to the field of nondestructive testing education. A plaque is awarded annually. Established in 1971.

• 4154 • Young NDT Professional Award
To recognize young members whose initial career contributions exemplify high standards of excellence in the areas of professional achievement and meritorious service. Supervisors, educators, managers, researchers, consultants, developers, and other ASNT members with five to ten years of active involvement in the nondestructive testing (NDT) industry are eligible. Applicants must be sponsored by a local ASNT section, council, or national society committee. Awarded annually when merited.

• 4155 •
American Society for Nutritional Sciences
Richard G. Allison PhD, Exec.Off.
9650 Rockville Pke., Ste. 4500
Bethesda, MD 20814-3990
Phone: (301)634-7050
Fax: (301)634-7892
E-mail: sec@asns.org
Home Page: http://www.asns.org

• 4156 • Bio-Serv Award in Experimental Animal Nutrition
For recognition of meritorious research in nutrition performed within ten years of receipt of a doctoral degree. The research must have been done with experimental animals used as models. The deadline for nominations is October 1. A monetary prize of $1,000 and a plaque are awarded annually at the AIN Annual Meeting. Established in 1981. Sponsored by Bio-Serv Company, Frenchtown, New Jersey.

• 4157 • Conrad A. Elvehjem Award for Public Service in Nutrition
For recognition of specific and distinguished service to the public through the science of nutrition. Such service would be rendered primarily through distinctive activities in the public interest in governmental, industrial, private, or international institutions, but contributions of an investigative character would not be excluded. A monetary award of $1,500 and a plaque are awarded annually. Established in 1966. Sponsored by Nabisco Brands.

• 4158 • Fellow
To recognize scientists who have had distinguished careers in nutrition. Individuals who are at least 65 years of age are eligible for nomination by October 1. Membership in the Institute is not a requirement. Up to ten Fellows may be chosen each year.

• 4159 • Lederle Award in Human Nutrition
To recognize recent investigative contributions to the understanding of human nutrition. Preference is given to scientists in the Western Hemisphere. Nominations are accepted by October 1. A monetary prize of $1,500, an inscribed scroll, and a travel subsidy to the presentation ceremony are awarded each year at the annual meeting of AIN. Established in 1981. Sponsored by Lederle Laboratories.

• 4160 • E. V. McCollum International Lectureship in Nutrition
To encourage sound advancements in nutritional science and their application for improving the health and well-being of people worldwide, and to commemorate the life and contributions of E. V. McCollum. Nominations are accepted. An outstanding nutritionist is invited to lecture on a topic consistent with the purpose of the lectureship in a location that will assure a large and broad audience. Multiple presentations are encouraged. Established in 1991.

• 4161 • Mead Johnson Award
For recognition of a single, outstanding piece of nutrition research or a series of recent papers on the same subject accomplished within ten years of completing post graduate training. The deadline for nominations is October 1. A monetary award of $1,500 and an inscribed scroll are awarded annually. Established in 1939. Sponsored by Mead Johnson and Company.

• 4162 • Osborne and Mendel Award
For recognition of outstanding, recent, basic research accomplishments in nutrition. Preference is given to research workers in the United States and Canada. The deadline for nominations is October 1. A monetary award of $2,500 and an inscribed scroll are awarded annually. Established in 1949. Sponsored by ILSI-North America.

• 4163 • E.L.R. Stokstad Award
To recognize outstanding fundamental research in nutrition, with preference to scientists at relatively early stages in their careers. A $2,500 monetary prize and an engraved plaque are awarded annually.

• 4164 •
American Society for Parenteral and Enteral Nutrition
Robin Kriegel, Exec.Dir.
8630 Fenton Ste., No. 412
Silver Spring, MD 20910-3805
Phone: (301)587-6315
Fax: (301)587-2365
E-mail: aspen@nutr.org
Home Page: http://www.nutritioncare.org

• 4165 • Stanley J. Dudrick Research Scholar Award
To recognize young investigators for past research accomplishments and future research potential in the field of specialized nutrition support. Society members with advanced degrees who are currently in a training program or have completed formal training in nutrition research/support within the past six years are eligible. Individuals must demonstrate exceptional research productivity during and/or following formal training; and current academic appointments can rank no higher than Assistant Professor. A monetary award of $5,000 is awarded at the annual Clinical Congress. Estab-

lished in 1985 in honor of Dr. Stanley Dudrick for his research leadership leading to the dramatic discovery of total parenteral nutrition. Formerly: (1985) ASPEN Research Scholar Award.

• 4166 • Jonathan E. Rhoads Lecture

For recognition of major contributions to the field of specialized nutrition support and a commitment to the provision of optimum nutrition to all patients. A $1,000 honorarium, and an invitation to deliver a lecture at the plenary session of the annual Clinical Congress are awarded annually. Established in 1978 in honor of Dr. Jonathan Rhoads, who had a pivotal role in the field of specialized nutrition support.

• 4167 • Harry M. Vars Award

To recognize a young investigator for outstanding research work. Individuals must submit an acceptable research abstract and manuscript in specialized nutrition support to be considered. A monetary award of $1,000 and an invitation to present the paper at the plenary session at the Society's annual Clinical Congress are awarded. Established in 1982 in honor of Dr. Harry Vars, for his pioneering developments in total parenteral nutrition.

• 4168 •
American Society for Pharmacology and Experimental Therapeutics
Christine K. Carrico PhD, Exec. Officer
9650 Rockville Pike
Bethesda, MD 20814-3995
Phone: (301)634-7060
Fax: (301)634-7061
E-mail: info@aspet.org
Home Page: http://www.aspet.org

• 4169 • ASPET Award for Experimental Therapeutics

To recognize and stimulate outstanding research in pharmacology and experimental therapeutics. This includes basic laboratory or clinical research that has had, or potentially will have a major impact on the pharmacological treatment of disease. Nominations by members of ASPET must be submitted by September 15. A monetary award of $2,500, a bronze medal, and travel expenses are awarded annually. Established in 1969. Six copies of a summary describing the candidates work; six published articles or manuscripts accepted for publication; a brief biographical sketch of the candidate; and the candidates curriculum vitae must be submitted.

• 4170 • Bernard B. Brodie Award in Drug Metabolism

For recognition of outstanding original research accomplishment in the field of drug metabolism and disposition. Sponsors may nominate members by September 15. A monetary award of $2,000, a commemorative medal, and travel expenses are awarded biennially. Six copies of a summary describing the candidates work; six published articles or manuscripts accepted for publication; a brief biographical sketch of the candidate; and the candidates curriculum vitae must be submitted. Established in 1978.

• 4171 • Epilepsy Research Award for Outstanding Contributions to the Pharmacology of Antiepileptic Drugs

To recognize and stimulate outstanding research leading to better clinical control of epileptic seizures. This research may include the basic screening and testing of new therapeutic agents, studies on mechanisms of action, metabolic disposition, pharmacokinetics, and clinical pharmacology studies. Nominations must be submitted by September 15 by members of any recognized scientific association for work accomplished in the five-year period prior to each award. A monetary award of $2,000, a certificate, and travel expenses are awarded biennially. Six copies of a summary of nominee's achievements; six papers; list of nominee's publications' and curriculum vitae must be submitted. Established in 1978. Sponsored by Warner-Lambert/Parke-Davis, Morris Plains, New Jersey.

• 4172 • Goodman and Gilman Award in Drug Receptor Pharmacology

For recognition of research accomplishment in the field of drug receptor pharmacology. Members of the society must submit nominations by September 15. A monetary award of $2,500, a plaque, and travel expenses are awarded biennially. Established in 1980. Sponsored by the Smith Kline Corporation.

• 4173 • P.B. Dews Award

Recognizes outstanding lifetime achievements in research, teaching and professional service in the field of Behavioral pharmacology as a discipline. Awarded biennially. $750, a plaque, and travel expenses to the award ceremony at the ASPET annual meeting are awarded. Deadline is September 15.

• 4174 • Pharmacia-ASPET

For recognition of outstanding fundamental research in pharmacology and experimental therapeutics by young investigators. Individuals under the age of 39 as of April 30th of the nominating year must be nominated by September 15. A monetary award of $2,500, a bronze medal, and travel expenses are awarded annually. Six copies of a summary describing the candidates work; six published articles or manuscripts accepted for publication; a brief biographical sketch of the candidate; and the candidates curriculum vitae must be submitted. Established in 1947 by Eli Lilly and Company, Indianapolis, Indiana.

• 4175 • Torald Sollmann Award in Pharmacology

To recognize significant contributions over many years to the advancement and extension of knowledge in the field of pharmacology. The award is presented to an individual regardless of employment affiliation, age, sex, or nationality. A monetary award of $3,500, a bronze medal, and travel expenses are awarded biennially. Six copies of up to five written by nominators describing nominees eligibility and a curriculum vitae must be submitted. Established in 1961 by Wyeth Ayerst Research.

• 4176 •
American Society for Pharmacy Law
Pamela Tolson CAE, Exec.Dir.
1224 Centre W, Ste. 400B
Springfield, IL 62704
Phone: (217)391-0219
Fax: (217)793-0041
E-mail: member.services@aspl.org
Home Page: http://www.aspl.org

• 4177 • James Hartley Beal Award

Award of recognition for best industry-related manuscript.

• 4178 • President's Award

Award of recognition for outstanding contributions to the field of pharmacy law.

• 4179 •
American Society for Public Administration
Mary Hamilton, Exec.Dir.
1120 G St. NW, Ste. 700
Washington, DC 20005-3885
Phone: (202)393-7878
Fax: (202)638-4952
E-mail: info@aspanet.org
Home Page: http://www.aspanet.org

• 4180 • Louis Brownlow Award

To recognize the outstanding article in *Public Administration Review* by a practitioner or manager. Awarded at the ASPA National Conference.

• 4181 • Laverne Burchfield Award

For recognition of the best book review in *Public Administration Review*. Awarded at the ASPA National Conference.

• 4182 • Marshall E. Dimock Award

For recognition of the best lead article in *Public Administration Review* during a volume year. Awarded at the ASPA National Conference. Established in 1971.

• 4183 • Equal Opportunity/Affirmative Action Exemplary Practices Award

To recognize a person or organization making an outstanding contribution to a more equal society. The emphasis is on achievements and results, not simply effort. The following criteria are considered: complexity of the problems addressed and organizations directed; severity of the problems addressed, use of original/innovative/effective approaches, impact of contributions, including extent of long-term or lasting benefits of the nominee's accomplishments, and contributions to the attainment of the goals of ASPA's EO/AA national policy positions. Up to four awards are presented to individuals or organizations in the following categories: federal, state, or local government units, educational institutions, non-profit institutions, and private sector organizations. Presented at the ASPA National Conference. Formerly: National Equal Employment/Affirmative Action Exemplary Practices Award.

• 4184 • Charles E. Levine Memorial Award for Excellence in Public Service
&To recognize a faculty member for excellence in teaching, research, and service to the wider public administration community. The winner receives $1,000 worth of publications from Jossey-Bass Publishers. Awarded at the ASPA National Conference.

• 4185 • William E. Mosher and Frederick C. Mosher Award
For recognition of an outstanding article in *Public Administration Review* by an academician/researcher. Awarded at the ASPA National Conference.

• 4186 • NASPAA/ASPA Distinguished Research Award
For recognition of research by an individual whose published work has had a substantial impact on public administration.

• 4187 • Donald C. Stone Award
To recognize members of ASPA who make contributions to the achievement of ASPA goals, objectives, and program initiatives. Awarded at the ASPA National Conference.

• 4188 • Dwight Waldo Award
To recognize an individual who has made outstanding contributions to the professional literature of public administration over a career of more than ten years. Awarded at the ASPA National Conference.

• 4189 • James E. Webb Award
For recognition of the best National Training Conference paper. Awarded at the ASPA National Conference.

• 4190 •
American Society for Stereotactic and Functional Neurosurgery
Andres Lozano MDPhD, Contact
Department of Neurosurgery
New Jersey Medical School
90 Bergen St., Ste 8100
Newark, NJ 07103-2499
Phone: (973)972-2907
Fax: (973)972-2333
E-mail: lozano@uhnres.utoronto.ca
Home Page: http://www.assfn.org

• 4191 • Resident's Award
Recognizes an outstanding abstract on the topic of dermatology. Awarded annually.

• 4192 •
American Society for Technion-Israel Institute of Technology
Melvyn H. Bloom, Exec.VP
55 E 59th St., No. 124
New York, NY 10022-1112
Phone: (212)407-6300
Fax: (212)753-2925
E-mail: info@ats.org
Home Page: http://www.ats.org

• 4193 • Albert Einstein Award
Recognizes exemplary service to the organization.

• 4194 •
American Society for the Prevention of Cruelty to Animals
Dr. Ed Sayres, Pres.
424 E 92nd St.
New York, NY 10128
Phone: (212)876-7700
Fax: (212)876-9571
E-mail: information@aspca.org
Home Page: http://www.aspca.org

• 4195 • Henry Bergh Medal of Honor
To recognize public servants (firefighters and police officers) who have shown unusual compassion or bravery towards animals in performance of their duties. Established around 1970.

• 4196 • Founder's Award for Humane Excellence
To recognize an individual for an extraordinary humane commitment. Candidates must be nominated and approved by ASPCA's Board of Directors.

• 4197 •
American Society for Theatre Research
Nancy J. Erickson, Admin.
Erickson & Assoc. Counseling
6000 Ridgewood Cir.
Georgetown University
Downers Grove, IL 60516
Phone: (630)964-7241
Fax: (630)964-7141
E-mail: nericksn@aol.com
Home Page: http://www.astr.umd.edu

• 4198 • Dissertation Award
To assist PhD candidates with the expenses of travel to national and international collections to conduct research projects connected with their dissertations. Applicants must be PhD candidates who have passed their qualifying exams within the last 2 years and have begun working on their dissertations. Application deadline is March 1. A monetary prize of $600 is awarded annually.

• 4199 • Barnard Hewitt Award
Recognizes research in theatre history. A cash prize is awarded annually at the ASTR convention in November.

• 4200 • Errol Hill Award
Recognizes an outstanding book-length manuscript or scholarly essay in African American theatre, drama, and/or performance studies. The book or essay must have been published during the year current year. Books for nominations must be sent to Prof. Harry J. Elam Jr., Dept. of Drama, 551 Serra Mall, Stanford University, Stanford CA 94305-5010 by June 15.

• 4201 • Gerald Kahan Scholars Prize
For recognition of the best published article by a North American scholar, who is untenured, and is no more than seven years past the doctorate or by a student at the time the essay is published. Selection is by nomination. A $500 prize is awarded annually. Deadline March 15. Established in 1984. Contact David Savran dsavran@gc.cuny.edu for additional information.

• 4202 • Thomas F. Marshall Travel Fellowship
Encourages students to become active members of the Society and provides funding to attend the annual meeting. Higher education students majoring in theatre or drama are eligible. Up to three grants of $600 apiece are awarded each year. The completed application form, a curriculum vitae, a sponsoring letter from an ASTR member, and a supporting letter from someone outside of the society but familiar with the work must be submitted to Prof. Bob Vorlicky, Dept. of Drama, Tisch School of the Arts, New York University, 721 Broadway, 3rd Fl., New York NY 10003, (212)998-1570, Email: rhvl@nyu.edu by March 1.

• 4203 •
American Society for Training and Development
Kimo Kippen, Sec.
1640 King St.
PO Box Box 1443
Alexandria, VA 22313-2043
Phone: (703)683-8100
Toll-Free: 800-628-2783
Fax: (703)683-8103
Home Page: http://www.astd.org

• 4204 • Gordon M. Bliss Memorial Award
This, the highest for leadership a member can receive from ASTD, is given to recognize significant contributions in three areas: contribution to ASTD; contribution to the individual's employer/client; and contribution community. The entry deadline is September 15. Awarded annually at the ASTD International Conference. Established in 1969 to honor Gordon M. Bliss, ASTD's first Executive Director.

• 4205 • Dissertation Award
For recognition of the outstanding dissertation in workplace learning and performance during the previous academic year. The study must focus on an issue or relevance to the practice of workplace learning and performance, such as Training and Development, Organization Development, Learning, Performance Analysis, Work Design, Human Resources Planning, and Career Development. The candidate must be recommended and sponsored by his/her committee chair. The dissertation must report a study for which a degree was granted in the previous academic year. The deadline for submission of application is September 15. A plaque and $500 stipend are awarded annually.

• 4206 • Distinguished Contribution to Workplace Learning and Performance

To recognize an individual for an exceptional contribution of sustained impact to the field of workplace learning and performance. Individuals are eligible who demonstrate evidence of sustained impact on the field including: (1) the extent to which the contribution is based on original concepts and/or innovative practices recognized throughout the field; (2) Evidence of influence upon practitioners, organizations, thought leaders and research; and (3) the extent to which the contribution affirms that people are value-added contributors to organizational success. Individuals must be ASTD members or nominated by an ASTD member. The entry deadline is September 15. Awarded annually at the ASTD International Conference. Established in 1986.

• 4207 • Public Policy Award

To recognize outstanding public service in support of workplace learning and performance by an individual(s) while serving in the legislative or executive branches of the U.S. or State Government or in any other national or state policy-making role. Nominations for this award are named by ASTD's Public Policy Council. Awarded annually at the ASTD International Conference. Formerly: (1996) National Affairs Award.

• 4208 • Torch Award

To recognize a maximum of four members who have excelled in advancing ASTD's vision and goals. Selection is based on the magnitude of contribution and impact of results either during a targeted period or over a significant period of time. The entry deadline is September 15. Awarded annually at the ASTD International Conference.

• 4209 •
American Society of Abdominal Surgeons
Diane Pothier MD, Office Mgr
1 E. Emerson St.
Melrose, MA 02176
Phone: (781)665-6102
Fax: (781)665-4127
E-mail: office@abdominalsurg.org
Home Page: http://www.abdominalsurg.org

• 4210 • Distinguished Service Award

To recognize a surgeon who has made important contributions in teaching and research in the field of surgery. A monetary award of $500 and an illuminated certificate are awarded annually. Established in 1961.

• 4211 •
American Society of Agricultural and Biological Engineers
M. Melissa Moore, Exec.VP
2950 Niles Rd.
St. Joseph, MI 49085-9659
Phone: (269)429-0300
Phone: (269)428-6321
Toll-Free: 800-371-2723
Fax: (269)429-3852
E-mail: moore@asae.org
Home Page: http://www.asabe.org

• 4212 • AE 50 Company Recognition Program

To recognize exceptional new products and systems that are vital in transferring technology to the marketplace for application by a wide spectrum of users in food and agriculture. Outstanding innovations that help farmers, processors and equipment manufacturers to cut costs, enhance quality, boost nutrition and improve profitability are eligible. Winners are showcased in the September issue of *Resource*. Additional information is available from ASAE, 2950 Niles Rd., St. Joseph, MI 49009; phone: (616) 429-0300.

• 4213 • ASABE Fellows

For recognition of an engineer of unusual professional distinction, with outstanding and extraordinary qualifications and experience in the field of agricultural engineering. Individuals who have been members for 20 years, and who have 20 years of active practice in the profession of engineering or teaching of engineering are eligible. Fellows are elected to the distinction, they may not apply. The grade of Fellow has honorary status.

• 4214 • ASABE Paper Awards

To honor the authors of the papers with the highest merit ratings as reference literature, as published in *Resource and Transactions of the ASAE*, *Applied Engineering in Agriculture*, and *Journal of Agricultural Safety and Health*. A certificate is awarded annually. Formerly: Doerfer Engineering Concept of the Year Award.

• 4215 • ASAE Past Presidents Award

To acknowledge outstanding support of Society activities by companies, organizations, agencies, or groups. Chief officers of those organizations whose support of ASAE, its membership and its objectives has been outstanding are eligible. A plaque is presented annually.

• 4216 • ASAE Student Paper Awards

To encourage undergraduate students in the preparation of better papers on agricultural engineering subjects. The awards are divided into two competitions - one written and one oral. Authors of the three best written papers receive cash awards and an invitation to attend the Annual Meeting as guests of the Society and to participate in the oral competition for the K.K. Barnes Student Paper Award. Three cash prizes of $500, $300 and $200 for first, second and third place respectively and a plaque are awarded. The competitions are held annually. Established in 1949 for written papers. The K. K. Barnes Student Paper Award was established by family and friends in 1977 to honor ASAE President-elect and Fellow Barnes.

• 4217 • Award for the Advancement of Surface Irrigation

To recognize and publicize those efforts that enhance the acceptance and efficient use of surface irrigation methods. An engraved plaque and monetary prize of $500 is awarded. Established in 1999.

• 4218 • John Deere Medal

For recognition of distinguished achievement in the application of science and art to the soil. An inscribed gold medal is awarded annually. Established in 1937 in memory of John Deere, who forged a piece of saw blade into a plow form to create the world's first all-steel moldboard.

• 4219 • Educational Aids Competition Blue Ribbon Awards

For recognition of outstanding effort and achievement in the development of noteworthy educational aids. Exhibit classifications in (A) public service and (B) private industry categories are: models and instructive displays; slides, films, videotapes, satellite conferences and overhead transparencies; publications (fact sheets, circulars, bulletins or manuals, periodicals or newsletters, models or instructive displays, and web pages); extension methods; computer programs. The competition recognizes entries judged outstanding in originality and effectiveness as specific aids to education that can be copied, emulated, or otherwise used in the interest of agriculture far beyond the range of their original application. Blue ribbons are awarded annually. Established in 1949.

• 4220 • Engineering Achievement Awards Program

For recognition of outstanding contributions to the advancement of the profession and to stimulate professional achievement. Four separate awards to honor individuals pursuing different lines of endeavor are presented: Sunkist Young Designer Award, New Holland Young Researcher Award, Nolan Mitchell Young Extension Worker Award, and A.W. Farrall Young Educator Award. Members of the Society who are under 40 years of age are eligible. Plaques are awarded annually. Established in 1972.

• 4221 • A. W. Farrall Young Educator Award

To honor outstanding success motivating the application of engineering principles to the problems of agricultural engineering. Applicants must be individuals under the age of 40 at the time of selection. An engraved bronze medallion on a plaque is awarded.

• 4222 • Henry Giese Structures and Environment Award

To honor distinguished service in advancing the knowledge and science of agricultural structures and environment. An engraved plaque on a wooden base is awarded.

• 4223 • G. B. Gunlogson Countryside Engineering Award

To encourage and recognize outstanding engineering contributions that have resulted in significant progress for the development of the countryside. Members of the Society are eligible. A plaque is awarded annually. Established in 1975 by ASAE Life Fellow G.B. Gunlogson of the Countryside Development Foundation, Inc.

• 4224 • Hancor Soil and Water Engineering Award

For noteworthy contributions to the advancement of soil and water engineering in teaching, research, planning, design, construction, management, or methods and materials. Candidates must be sponsored by ASAE members. A plaque is awarded annually. Established in 1966 by Hancor, Inc., and the Society. Formerly: Hancock Brick and Tile Soil and Water Engineering Award.

• 4225 • IAFIS-FPEI Food Engineering Award

To honor those who have made original contributions in research, development, or design, or in the management of food processing equipment or techniques of significant economic value to the food industry and the consumer. An annual award alternation between recognition for a "distinguished" Food Engineer in odd-numbered years, and an "Emerging" Food Engineer (with less than ten years practice), in even numbered years. Evaluation criteria include: degree to which human performances and progress in the application of engineering and technology has been significantly advanced; development of machines, processes or methods for the food industry; leadership shown in the professional development of the food industry; and examples of the individual's activities in the food industry. A monetary award of $2,000, a gold medal, and a certificate are presented biennially at the annual conference of the Dairy and Food Industries Supply Association during odd-numbered years. The winner also is honored at an ASAE national meeting that same year. Co-sponsored by the Dairy and Food Industries Supply Association, Inc., 6245 Executive Blvd., Rockville, MD 20852.

• 4226 • Kishida International Award

To recognize outstanding contributions to engineering-mechanization-technology related programs of education, research, development, consultation, or technology transfer that have resulted in improved food production, living conditions, and/or education outside the United States. Living members of the Association are eligible. A monetary award of $1,000 and an engraved plaque are awarded annually at the ASAE summer meeting. The deadline for nominations is April 15. Established in 1978 in honor of Yoshikuni Kishida, founder of Shin-Norinsha Company Limited of Japan and pioneering agricultural mechanization leader in Japan and much of Asia. Sponsored by Shin-Norinsha Company Limited of Japan.

• 4227 • Massey-Ferguson Educational Award

To honor dedication to the spirit of learning and teaching in the field of agricultural engineering by which agricultural knowledge and practice has been advanced. A gold medal is awarded annually. Established in 1965 to honor Daniel Massey, a pioneer innovator and agricultural machinery manufacturer, and Harry Ferguson, inventor and ardent exponent of agricultural mechanization.

• 4228 • Mayfield Cotton Engineering Award

To encourage and to recognize outstanding engineering contributions to the cotton industry. Nominations may be submitted by any corporate member of ASAE by letter. The nominee must be a corporate member of the American Society of Agricultural Engineers; must have a good long-term job performance record with at least five years' experience in cotton; and should have made a specific recent engineering-related contribution to the cotton industry. The deadline for nominations is April 15. An inscribed plaque is presented at the Annual Meeting of the Society and acknowledged at the following Beltwide Cotton Conference. Established in 1985 by William Donald Mayfield, an extension agricultural engineer whose career has been devoted to the enhancement of cotton mechanization and ginning through the application of engineering fundamentals. Sponsored by John Deere & Co.

• 4229 • Cyrus Hall McCormick - Jerome Increase Case Medal

For recognition of exceptional and meritorious engineering achievements in agriculture. An inscribed gold medal is awarded annually. Established in 1931 by Mrs. Emmons Blaine, Cyrus H. McCormick, and Mrs. Harold F. McCormick in memory of their father, Cyrus H. McCormick, the inventor of the self-rake reaper. In 1986, the award name was changed to honor Jerome Increase Case, the developer of the reliable threshing machine. Co-sponsored by Case IH. Formerly: (1986) Cyrus Hall McCormick Medal.

• 4230 • Nolan Mitchell Young Extension Worker Award

To honor dedicated use of scientific methodology to seek out facts or principles significant to agricultural engineering. Applicants must be individuals under the age of 40 at the time of selection. An engraved bronze medallion on a plaque is awarded.

• 4231 • NAMIC Engineering Safety Award

To encourage and to recognize outstanding contributions to the advancement of agricultural safety engineering in research, design, education, or promotion. These contributions shall have been either in the form of published literature, notable performance, product innovation, and/or special actions that have served to advance agricultural safety. The nominee must be a member of the American Society of Agricultural Engineers. The deadline is April 15. An appropriately engraved desk pen set is presented annually at the annual meeting of the Society. Established in 1985. Co-sponsored by the Packer Engineering Associates, Inc. Formerly: (2006) Packer Engineering Safety Award.

• 4232 • National Food and Energy Council Electric Technology Award

To honor individual agricultural engineers for their personal and professional contributions to the progress made in the utilization of electrical energy in the production and processing of agricultural products. A plaque is awarded annually. Established in 1969. Formerly: (1987) George W. Kable Electrification Award.

• 4233 • National Student Design Competition

To encourage undergraduate students to participate in design of an engineering project for needed agricultural systems, components, or processes. The following awards are presented annually: first place - a monetary award of $1,250 and an individual engraved plaque; second place $1,000 and individual certificates; and third place - $750 and individual certificates. In addition, the university engineering department from which the winning entry originated also receives a $300-scholarship grant and a wall plaque which lists the names of the winning team members and of their faculty advisor. Established in 1977. Sponsored by AGCO. Formerly: Deutz-Allis National Student Design Competition.

• 4234 • New Holland Young Researcher Award

To honor dedicated use of scientific methodology to seek out facts or principles significant to agricultural engineering. Applicants must be individuals under the age of 40 at the time of selection. An engraved bronze medallion on a plaque is awarded.

• 4235 • Rain Bird Engineering Concept of the Year Award

To honor an engineer or an engineering team that makes a development or advancement of a new engineering concept. Description of the new concept must have been published in one of the Society's publications. A plaque is awarded annually. Established in 1974. Sponsored by Rain Bird, Inc. Formerly: Doerfer Engineering Concept of the Year Award.

• 4236 • Robert E. Stewart Engineering-Humanities Award

To recognize outstanding contributions to the advancement of the interaction of the profession and the humanities. Graduate and undergraduate student members of ASAE are eligible to be nominated. An engraved plaque is presented annually. Established in 1986 by Bonnie Stewart as a tribute to her husband, a past president and fellow of ASAE.

• 4237 • Sunkist Young Designer Award

To honor the development or creation of a technical plan that is materially influencing agricultural engineering progress, as evidenced by use in the field. Applicants must be individuals under the age of 40 at the time of selection. An engraved bronze medallion on a plaque is awarded.

• 4238 •
American Society of Agronomy
Ellen Bergfeld, Exec.VP
677 S. Segoe Rd.
Madison, WI 53711
Phone: (608)273-8080
Fax: (608)273-2021
E-mail: headquarters@agronomy.org
Home Page: http://www.agronomy.org

• 4239 • **Agronomic Extension Education Award**
For recognition of effective extension performance as evidenced by demonstrated ability to communicate ideas clearly, influence client attitudes, and motivate change in client or audience action. The focus is on educational contributions of extension agronomists, industrial agronomists, or others whose primary contributions are in teaching or education outside the university classroom. Contributions must have been made within the last ten years. Nominations are accepted from active members of the Society. The deadline is in March of each year. A certificate and $1000 honorarium are awarded annually. Established in 1978.

• 4240 • **Agronomic Industry Award**
To recognize outstanding performance by a private sector agronomics in the development, acceptance, and implementation of advanced agronomic programs, practices, or products. Nominees must be active within the private sector, and must be employed by any public agency. A cash prize of $1,000 is awarded annually.

• 4241 • **Agronomic Resident Education Award**
For recognition of effective resident teaching as evidenced by demonstrated ability to communicate ideas clearly, influence student attitudes, and motivate change in students. The focus is on educational contributions of classroom teachers. Contributions must have been made within the last ten years. Nominations are accepted from active members of the Society. The deadline is in March of each year in March of each year. A certificate and $1000 honorarium are awarded annually. Established in 1978.

• 4242 • **Agronomic Service Award**
For recognition of service to the field of agronomy. Consideration is given to the following criteria: development of an agronomic service program, practices, and products which are accepted by the public; effectiveness of public relations activities designed to promote the understanding and use of agronomic science and technology by the public, the government, and other organized groups; and advances in the science, practice, and status of the professional resulting from administrative skill and effort. The focus is an agronomic service with associated educational, public relations, and administrative contributions of industrial agronomists, governmental, industrial, or university administrators and others. Established in 1961.

• 4243 • **Environmental Quality Research Award**
To recognize contributions which have enhanced the basic understanding of the behavior and fate of pollutants in terrestrial and/or aquatic ecosystems and stability of an ecosystem in response to disturbances resulting from the use of land for food and energy production and society's needs to dispose of and/or utilize waste products. Principal criteria to be used in the selection process are creativity and originality of the research and significance of the research and its contribution to the field of environmental quality.

• 4244 • **Fellow of the American Society of Agronomy**
For recognition of outstanding work in agronomy. Ten-year members of the Society are eligible. Outstanding contributions in an agronomic area of specialization in research, teaching, extension, or administration, whether in public, commercial, or private service activities will be considered. Nominations may be made by any active member of the Society except members of the Fellows Committee and the ASA Executive Committee. A certificate is awarded annually. Established in 1924.

• 4245 • **Honorary Member**
To recognize sustained outstanding services to agronomy. Eligibility for election is limited to nonmembers of the Society. Members must make nominations by April 16. A nominee must receive a two-thirds affirmative vote of the Board of Directors to be awarded Honorary Membership.

• 4246 • **International Service in Agronomy Award**
For recognition of service to the field of agronomy through international activity, research, or education. The focus is on the creative character, relevance, and effectiveness of the nominee's international agronomic activities. Membership in the Society is not required. Nominations are accepted from active members of the Society. The deadline is April 16. A certificate and $1000 honorarium are awarded annually. Established in 1968.

• 4247 • **Werner L. Nelson Award for Diagnosis of Yield Limiting Factors**
To recognize leadership in development and implementation of diagnostic workshops; development of diagnostic check lists; development of new diagnostic techniques; and use of diagnostic techniques to identify yield limiting factors. Membership in the Administering Society is not a requirement for the nominee; nominators, however, must be active members of ASA. A $5000 honorarium and a certificate are awarded annually. Established in 1989 by the Potash Phosphate Institute in honor of Werner L. Nelson.

• 4248 • **Carl Sprengel Agronomic Research Award**
For recognition of major research accomplishments resulting from basic or applied research in agronomy involving the environment. The focus is on research accomplishments that have been adopted. The award may be made for discoveries, techniques, inventions, or materials that increase crop yields, improve crop quality, food products, land and water development, environmental quality, or conservation. Contributions must have been made within the past ten years. Nominations are accepted from active members of the Society. The deadline is in March of each year. A certificate and $1000 honorarium are awarded annually. Established in 1975.

• 4249 • **Syngenta Crop Protection Recognition Award**
In recognition of outstanding performance in teaching and/or service in agronomy. The focus is on young scientists and on educational and service activities of classroom teachers, extension agronomists, or industrial agronomists. In addition, candidates should show superior potential for development in their field of interest and usefulness of the award (a trip to Europe) in their current educational program and to the students or clientele with whom they work. The candidate must have a minimum of five years active and current experience in teaching in a college or university, in the Cooperative Extension Service, or in industrial education and service, and must be 37 years of age or under. A trophy is also awarded annually. Established in 1970.

• 4250 •
American Society of Animal Science
Dr. Jerry Baker, Exec.Dir.
1111 N Dunlap Ave.
Savoy, IL 61874-9604
Phone: (217)356-9050
Fax: (217)398-4119
E-mail: asas@assochq.org
Home Page: http://www.asas.org

• 4251 • **American Feed Industry Association Award**
For recognition of notable research in the feeding and nutrition of farm animals, based on articles published during the previous five years by a member of the society. A monetary award of $1,500 and a plaque are awarded annually. Established in 1948 by the American Feed Manufacturers Association.

• 4252 • **Animal Growth and Development Award**
To stimulate research in animal growth and development. Original basic or applied research in any phase of growth or development of animals published within ten years preceding the year of the award are eligible for consideration. A monetary award of $1,500 and a plaque are awarded. Sponsored by Roche Vitamins, Inc.

• 4253 • Animal Industry Service Award

To stimulate a high level of service to the animal industry and to recognize members of the Society who have distinguished themselves in service to the animal industry. A monetary award of $1,500 and memento are awarded annually. Established in 1974 and sponsored by the Pharmacia and Upjohn Co.

• 4254 • Animal Management Award

For recognition of research in biological or production management, or a significant contribution to production management. The awardee shall have conducted basic or applied research in animal behavior, environmental science, economics, or other biological or production management topics. A monetary prize of $1000 is awarded annually. Established in 1972. Sponsored by Merial Ltd.

• 4255 • Animal Physiology and Endocrinology Award

To recognize a member for outstanding basic or applied research in physiology and endocrinology with all classes of large and small animals. A monetary award of $1,500 and a plaque are awarded annually. Established in 1962. Sponsored by the Monsanto Co.

• 4256 • ASAS Extension Award

For recognition of outstanding and noteworthy contributions to the field of extension in animal husbandry. Members of the Society who are employed by a state, provincial, or federal extension service, and have been actively engaged as extension specialists for at least eight years are eligible. A monetary prize of $1,500 is awarded annually. Established in 1959. Sponsored by Charles Pfizer Inc.

• 4257 • ASAS Fellow

To recognize distinguished service to the livestock industry or the Society for at least 25 years. Awards are presented in the following categories: teaching, research, extension, administration, industry, and at-large. A plaque is awarded annually. Established in 1958.

• 4258 • Bouffault Memorial Award in International Animal Agriculture

To recognize and stimulate distinguished service to animal agriculture in the developing areas of the world. Members of the Society, who have made meritorious contributions over a period of at least five years in one or more developing countries, are eligible. $1,500 and memento are awarded annually. Established in 1975.

• 4259 • L. E. Casida Award

To recognize excellence in the education of graduate and/or postdoctoral students. Published research contributing to knowledge in reproductive physiology and endocrinology is considered. Emphasis is based on the quality rather than quantity of the work presented and upon its relationship to the philosophy of L. E. Casida as expressed in his paper in the "Journal of Animal Science" (25:1235-1239, 1966). A monetary award of $1,500, a medal mounted on a plaque, and presentation of a lecture are awarded at the Triennial Reproduction Symposium. Established in 1987.

• 4260 • Distinguished Teacher Award

For recognition of outstanding ability and distinguished achievement in the undergraduate teaching of animal science. Members of the Society who have been active teachers for the previous eight years are eligible. A monetary award of $1,500 and a plaque are awarded annually. Established in 1959. Sponsored by Purina Mills, Inc.

• 4261 • Meats Research Award

For recognition of notable basic or applied research by members of the Society in all phases of meat research, based on research published during the previous ten years. A monetary prize of $1,500 is awarded annually. Established in 1962. Sponsored by Elanco Animal Health.

• 4262 • Morrison Award

For recognition of a meritorious scientific discovery or contribution in the field of animal science pertaining to beef cattle, dairy cattle, horses, sheep, or swine. A monetary award of $3,500 and a watch are awarded annually. Established in 1946. Sponsored by the F. B. Morrison family.

• 4263 •

American Society of Artists
Nancy J. Fregin, Pres.
PO Box 1326
Palatine, IL 60078
Phone: (312)751-2500
E-mail: asoa@webtv.net
Home Page: http://www.americansocietyofartists.com

• 4264 • Certificate of Appreciation

To recognize those individuals who have provided outstanding and dedicated service to ASA over an extended period of time. A Certificate of Appreciation is presented as merited. Established in 1972 in memory of those members who were supportive of the arts and their fellow artists, specifically Rudi Considine, Betty Odmark, Reid Childers, and Hector Martinez.

• 4265 • Honorary Member

To recognize individuals and organizations for their support of the visual arts and to encourage the support of the visual arts by all individuals and organizations, not just by working artists. The support must be for an extended period of time, but need not be highly visible. Honorary Membership in the American Society of Artists and a certificate are presented when merited. Established in 1978.

• 4266 •

American Society of Association Executives
John H. Graham IV, Pres./CEO
1575 I St. NW
Washington, DC 20005-1103
Phone: (202)371-0940
Phone: (202)626-2803
Toll-Free: 888-950-2723
Fax: (202)371-8315
E-mail: pr@asaenet.org
Home Page: http://www.asaenet.org

• 4267 • ASAE Fellow

To recognize ASAE executive members who are proven leaders and promise future accomplishment within the field of association management. Nominees must be employed full-time by an association at the time of nomination and have made significant contributions to their current and previous employing associations. Awarded annually.

• 4268 • Key Award

This, the society's highest award, is given to recognize outstanding accomplishments of ASAE leaders and their contributions to voluntary organizations, ASAE and its affiliates, and participation in civic and community affairs. Full-time employment as chief staff executive of an association at the time of nomination, employment in present position for at least one year, and regular voting membership in ASAE for at least the past five years are required. Established in 1960.

• 4269 •

American Society of Business Publication Editors
Janet Svazas, Exec.Dir.
710 E Ogden Ave., Ste. 600
Naperville, IL 60563-8603
Phone: (630)579-3288
Fax: (630)369-2488
E-mail: info@asbpe.org
Home Page: http://www.asbpe.org

Formerly: (2002) American Society of Business Press Editors.

• 4270 • Editorial and Design Excellence Awards

To encourage and recognize editorial and design excellence in approximately 40 categories for business magazines, newsletters, e-newsletters, and websites. Editorial staff and/or design staff are eligible. Magazine entries must accept advertising and be listed in *SDRS Business Publication Advertising Source.* National and regional awards are given.

• 4271 • Magazine of the Year Award

Annual award of recognition to the business magazine that demonstrates highest and most consistent editorial and design quality.

• 4272 •
American Society of Cataract and Refractive Surgery
Priscilla P. Arnold MD, Pres.
4000 Legato Rd. No., 850
Fairfax, VA 22033
Phone: (703)591-2220
Fax: (703)591-0614
E-mail: ascrs@ascrs.org
Home Page: http://www.ascrs.org

Formerly: (1985) American Intraocular Implant Society.

• 4273 • Binkhorst Medal Lecture
To recognize member ophthalmologists who have contributed to the advancement and understanding of anterior segment ophthalmic surgery. A medal is awarded annually. Established in 1976 in honor of Prof. Dr. Cornelius D. Binkhorst, for his early achievements with cataract extraction and intraocular lens implantation procedures.

• 4274 • Charles D. Kelman Innovator's Lecture
To recognize the most innovative ophthalmologist. Members of the Society are eligible for selection by the award committee. A sculpted trophy is awarded when merited. Formerly: (2006) Innovator Award.

• 4275 •
American Society of Certified Engineering Technicians
Kurt H. Schuler, Gen.Mgr.
PO Box 1348
Flowery Branch, GA 30542-0023
Phone: (770)967-9173
Fax: (770)967-8049
E-mail: general_manager@ascet.org
Home Page: http://www.ascet.org

• 4276 • Chapter of the Year Award
To recognize a chapter for extraordinary contributions to the local members, the community, and the society. The selected chapter receives a plaque at the annual meeting and an article in the *Certified Engineering Technician* magazine. Established in 1978.

• 4277 • Employer of the Month Award
To recognize employers of engineering technicians for their recognition and support efforts. A certificate and a picture and article in the *Certified Engineering Technician* magazine are awarded. Established in 1981.

• 4278 • Employer of the Year Award
To recognize employers of engineering technicians for extraordinary support of the society at the local, regional, and national levels of participation. Honorees receive a plaque at the annual meeting and a picture and article in the *Certified Engineering Technician* magazine. Established in 1987.

• 4279 • Member of the Year Award
To recognize engineering technicians or technologists for extraordinary contributions to the society at local, regional, and national levels of participation. Honorees receive a plaque at the annual meeting and a picture and article in the annual meeting program and *Certified Engineering Technician* magazine. Established in 1981.

• 4280 • Student Chapter of the Year Award
To recognize a chapter for extraordinary contributions to the local members, their school, and the community. The selected chapter receives a plaque at the annual meeting and a article in the *Certified Engineering Technician* magazine. Established in 1977.

• 4281 • Technician of the Month Award
To recognize a certified engineering technician or technologists for outstanding achievement. Members are eligible. A picture and an article in *Certified Engineering Technician* magazine are awarded monthly. Established in 1966.

• 4282 • Technician/Technologist of the Year Award
To recognize engineering technicians or technologists for extraordinary technical achievements. Honorees receive a plaque at the annual meeting and a picture and article in the annual meeting program and *Certified Engineering Technician* magazine. Established in 1965.

• 4283 •
American Society of Church History
Henry W. Bowden, Exec.Sec.
409 Prospect St., Rm. S127
New Haven, CT 06511
Phone: (732)345-1787
Fax: (732)345-1788
E-mail: asch@yale.edu
Home Page: http://www.churchhistory.org

• 4284 • Frank S. and Elizabeth D. Brewer Prize
For recognition of a booklength manuscript on Church History. Prize ia limited to first books. Preference is given to topics relating to the history of Congregationalism. Manuscripts must be submitted by November 1. A monetary prize of $1,500 towards publication of the manuscript is presented annually when merited.

• 4285 • Jane Dempsey Douglass Prize
To recognize the author of the best published essay on some aspect of the role of women in the history of Christianity. Graduate students are eligible. Entries must be submitted by August 1. A monetary award of $250 and publication of the essay in *Church History* are awarded annually when merited at the annual meeting of the Society in December. Established in 1990.

• 4286 • Sidney E. Mead Prize
To recognize the author of the best unpublished essay in any field of church history written by a doctoral candidate or recent recipient whose manuscript stems directly from doctoral research. Entries may be submitted by July 1. A monetary award of $300 and publication of the manuscript in *Church History* are awarded annually.

• 4287 • Albert C. Outler Prize in Ecumenical Church History
To recognize the author of a book-length manuscript on ecumenical church history. The following categories are eligible: studies of ecumenical church history dealing with historical controversies and divisions, or with notable instances of reconciliation and consensus; analyses of church councils, dialogues, and debates; biographical studies of ecumenical leaders; critical editions (preferably annotated) of significant ecumenical documents; bibliographical reviews and evaluations in major areas of ecumenical church history; and pioneering studies that advance ecumenical understanding. Works of a partisan nature are excluded. A monetary award of $1,500 to the author and possibly a grant of up to $3,000 in subvention of publication (or in exceptional cases, for publication) are awarded annually. Nominations must be received by March 1 in even-numbered years.

• 4288 • Philip Schaff Prize
For recognition of the author of the best book originating in the North American scholarly community and presenting original research or interpretation in the history of Christianity or any period thereof. Any member of the Society may nominate titles published during the previous two-year period. The deadline for nominations is March 1 in odd-numbered years. A monetary award of $1,000 is awarded at the annual meeting of the Society in December. Established in 1981.

• 4289 •
American Society of Civil Engineers
Patrick J. Natale, Exec.Dir.
1801 Alexander Bell Dr.
Reston, VA 20191-4400
Phone: (703)295-6300
Toll-Free: 800-548-2723
Fax: (703)295-6222
Home Page: http://www.asce.org

Formerly: American Society of Civil Engineering.

• 4290 • O. H. Ammann Research Fellowship in Structural Engineering
To encourage the creation of new knowledge in the field of structural design and construction. Applicants must be members of the Society in any grade, or applicants for membership. A Fellowship of $5,000 is awarded annually. Established in 1963 by O. H. Ammann, Hon. M. ASCE.

• 4291 • Arid Lands Hydraulic Engineering Award
To recognize an individual for a paper or other original contribution in hydraulics, hydrology (including climatology), planning, irrigation and drainage, hydroelectric power development, or

navigation especially applicable to arid or semi-arid climates. Given without regard to Society membership. Nominations must be submitted by November 1. An honorarium and a plaque are awarded annually. Established in 1986 by the endowment of Ibrahim Mahmoud Elassiouti, an hydraulic engineer and M. ASCE, who devoted many years of concern and effort to development of the Nile River.

• 4292 • ASCE News Correspondent Award

To recognize correspondents who are selected for their special contributions. An inscribed desk/pen set is awarded annually at the Annual Meeting of ASCE. Established in 1976 by the Technical Activities Committee.

• 4293 • ASCE Presidents' Award

To recognize a member who has given distinguished service to his or her country. Individuals of any nationality are eligible. A bronze plaque bearing the likeness of George Washington and a monetary award are presented at the Annual Meeting of the Society. Established in 1976, America's Bicentennial Year, in honor of the nation's first President, who was a civil engineer and land surveyor.

• 4294 • ASCE Presidents' Medal

To recognize the accomplishments and contributions of eminent engineers to the profession, the Society or the public. A bronze medal and certificate are awarded annually. Established in 1986.

• 4295 • ASCE State-of-the-Art of Civil Engineering Award

To recognize an individual professional of a technical division for a review article or state of the art paper that enables engineers to cope with the information expansion. Each division may nominate a paper by November 1. A plaque and certificate are awarded annually. Established in 1966.

• 4296 • Award for Service To People

To recognize individuals who have performed outstanding service to people in their communities, and to further public understanding and recognition of the identification, "Civil Engineering: A People-Serving Profession." A certificate is awarded annually. Established in 1980.

• 4297 • Award of Excellence of the Pipeline Division

To recognize a Fellow, Member, or Associate Member of ASCE for outstanding continuous and conspicuous service to the Profession, ASCE, and the Pipeline Division. Nominations must be submitted by March 1. A plaque is awarded annually. Established in 1988 by the Pipeline Division.

• 4298 • Harland Bartholomew Award

To recognize outstanding professional accomplishments and the contributions of a member to the enhancement of the role of the civil engineer in urban planning and development. Fellows, members, and associate members are eligible. Nominations may be submitted by November 1. A wall plaque and a certificate are awarded annually. Established in 1968 by the Urban Planning and Development Division.

• 4299 • Stephen D. Bechtel, Jr. Energy Award

To recognize outstanding achievements in the energy field by a civil engineer. The award is made to an ASCE member who has made a definite contribution to the advancement of the energy field in research, planning, design, or construction. Nominations must be submitted by November 1. A plaque and a certificate are awarded annually.

• 4300 • Stephen D. Bechtel Pipeline Engineering Award

To recognize a member who has made a definite contribution to the advancement of pipeline engineering, either in research, planning, design, or construction. Nominations must be submitted by November 1. A plaque and a certificate are awarded annually. Established in 1970 in honor of the contributions made by Stephen D. Bechtel.

• 4301 • John O. Bickel Award

To recognize the author or authors of the best original article or paper published by the Society during the specified annual period and not previously published concerning the design and/or construction of a rail or vehicular tunnel. Special consideration may be given to articles or papers dealing with tunnels constructed by the immersed or sunken tube method. Articles or papers by members and non-members published in the twelve months ending with June of the year preceding the year of award are eligible for consideration. Nominations must be submitted by November 1. A monetary prize and a certificate are awarded annually. Established in 1986 by the Board of Direction and endowed by Parsons Brinckerhoff, Inc. in honor of John O. Bickel, a retired partner of the firm, an eminent engineer for rail and vehicular tunnels and for over fifty years an employee of Parsons Brinckerhoff.

• 4302 • Arthur J. Boase Award of the Reinforced Concrete Research Council

To recognize a person, persons, or organizations for outstanding activities and achievements in the reinforced concrete field. Nominations must be submitted by November 1. A certificate is awarded annually. Established in honor of Arthur J. Boase (1892-1949).

• 4303 • Can-AM Civil Engineering Amity Award

To recognize civil engineers who have made outstanding and unusual contributions toward the advancement of professional relationships between the civil engineers of the United States and Canada. Nominations must be submitted by November 1. A plaque and a certificate are awarded annually. Established in 1972.

• 4304 • Arthur Casagrande Professional Development Award

To recognize an individual for outstanding accomplishments as evidenced by completed works, reports, or papers in the field of geotechnical engineering. It is intended to further the professional development of an outstanding practitioner, researcher, or teacher of geotechnical engineering under the age of 35. Nominations must be submitted by November 1. An honorarium and a certificate are awarded annually. Established in 1989 by the Geotechnical Engineering Division of ASCE as a memorial to the outstanding contributions of Arthur Casagrande, Hon. M. ASCE, to the teaching, research, and practice of geotechnical engineering.

• 4305 • Ven Te Chow Award

To recognize lifetime achievement in the field of hydro logic engineering. The award is presented to an individual whose career in the field of hydro logic engineering has been distinguished by exceptional achievement and significant contributions to research, education, or practice. The award consists of a plaque, certificate and cash prize determined annually. Established in 1995. Cosponsored by Sinotech Engineering Consultants, Inc.

• 4306 • Civil Engineering History and Heritage Award

To recognize outstanding contributions toward a better knowledge of, or appreciation for, the history and heritage of civil engineering. Individuals need not necessarily be members of the Society to be eligible. Nominations must be submitted by November 1. A plaque and certificate are awarded annually. Established in 1966.

• 4307 • Civil Government Award

To recognize an individual who has contributed substantially to the status of the engineering profession by meritorious public service in elective or appointive positions in civil government that do not require the qualifications of an engineer. Members of the Society are eligible. Nominations must be submitted by April 1. A wall plaque and certificate are awarded annually. Established in 1963.

• 4308 • Collingwood Prize

To recognize an outstanding paper published by the Society, which describes an engineering work with which the author(s) have been directly connected; records investigations contributing to engineering knowledge to which the author(s) contributed some essential part; and contains a rational digest of results. Associate members of the Society less than 35 years of age are eligible. A wall plaque and a certificate are awarded annually. Established in 1894 by Francis Collingwood, Past Secretary and M. ASCE.

• 4309 • Construction Management Award

To recognize a member who has made contributions in the field of construction management in the application of the theoretical aspects of engineering economics, and related mathematically oriented disciplines to problems of construction management, estimating, cost accounting, planning, scheduling and financing. Members must be nominated by November 1. A plaque and a certificate are awarded annually. Established in 1973 by Marvin Gates and Amerigo Scarpa, Fellows of the Society.

• 4310 • J. James R. Croes Medal
To recognize a previously unpublished paper that makes an outstanding contribution to engineering science that is next in merit to the paper for which the Norman Medal is awarded. Members must be nominated by November 1. A gold-plated medal and a certificate are awarded annually. Established in 1912 in honor of the first recipient of the Norman Medal.

• 4311 • Charles Martin Duke Lifeline Earthquake Engineering Award
To recognize an outstanding contribution to earthquake engineering. Established in 1990 by the Technical Council on Lifeline Earthquake Engineering to honor Charles Martin Duke for his pioneering contributions in lifeline earthquake engineering.

• 4312 • Hans Albert Einstein Award
To recognize a member of the Society who has made a significant contribution to the engineering profession in the areas of erosion control, sedimentation and/or waterway development either in teaching, research, planning, design, or management. Contributions can be made either in the form of papers or through notable performances that have served to advance engineering in these areas. Nominations must be submitted by November 1. A plaque and an honorarium are awarded annually. Established in 1988 by the Waterway, Port, Coastal and Ocean Division and the Hydraulics Division to honor Hans Albert Einstein for his outstanding contributions to the engineering profession and his advancements in the areas of erosion control, sedimentation and alluvial waterways.

• 4313 • Freeman Fellowship
To aid and encourage young engineers, especially in research work. Grants are awarded biennially in odd-numbered years. In addition, traveling scholarships are available to members younger than 45 years of age. Established in 1924 by John R. Freeman, past President and Honorary Member, ASCE.

• 4314 • Simon W. Freese Environmental Engineering Award and Lecture
To invite a distinguished person to prepare for publication and deliver the Simon W. Freese Environmental Engineering Lecture. A certificate and an honorarium are awarded annually. Established in 1975 by the Environmental Engineering Division and endowed by the firm of Freese and Nichols in honor of their partner, Simon W. Freese.

• 4315 • Alfred M. Freudenthal Medal
To recognize an individual for distinguished achievement in safety and reliability studies applicable to any branch of civil engineering. Nominations must be submitted by November 1. A bronze medal is awarded every two years. Established in 1975 by the Engineering Mechanics Division.

• 4316 • Edmund Friedman Professional Recognition Award
To recognize professional attainment that advances, by example, the science and profession of engineering. Members of the Society are eligible. Nominations must be submitted by April 1. A wall plaque and a certificate are awarded annually. Established in 1960 by Edmund Friedman, past president, ASCE.

• 4317 • Edmund Friedman Young Engineer Award for Professional Achievement
To recognize members who are 35 years of age or less and who have attained significant professional achievement. Nominations must be submitted by Februrary 1. A certificate is presented at the National Convention. Established in 1972.

• 4318 • John Fritz Medal
To recognize notable scientific or industrial achievement. The award is international in scope with no restriction on nationality or sex. Awarded jointly by five national societies: American Society of Civil Engineers; American Institute of Mining, Metallurgical and Petroleum Engineers; The American Society of Mechanical Engineers; The American Institute of Chemical Engineers; and the Institute of Electrical and Electronics Engineers. A medal and a certificate are awarded annually. Established in 1902 in honor of the 80th birthday of John Fritz, Hon. M. ASCE, of Bethlehem, PA.

• 4319 • Government Civil Engineer of the Year Award
To recognize distinguished civil engineers employed in public service for significant contributions to Public Service Engineering. Engineers of recognized standing, preferably registered and citizens of the United States are eligible. Award nominees are judged on the following: sustained outstanding civil engineering performance in the public sector; evidence of high character and professional integrity; minimum of 15 years of public service as a civil engineer; and five of the fifteen years at the senior administrative level. Nominations must be submitted by October 1. Up to four recipients may be designated in any year, no more than one from each Zone. The award consists of a suitably inscribed certificate. Established by the Committee on Civil Engineers in Government.

• 4320 • Samuel Arnold Greeley Award
To recognize the author(s) of the paper that makes the most valuable contribution to the environmental engineering profession. Members of the Society or employees in the private practice of environmental engineering are eligible. Nominations must be submitted by November 1. A plaque and certificate are awarded. Established in 1968 by the Sanitary Engineering Division (now the Environmental Division) in honor of Samuel Greeley, Past Director.

• 4321 • Shortridge Hardesty Award
To recognize an individual(s) who has contributed substantially in applying fundamental results of research to solution of practical engineering problems in the field of structural stability. Members must be nominated by November 1. An honorarium and a certificate are awarded annually. Established in 1987 by the firm of Hardesty & Hanover to honor the contributions of Shortridge Hardesty as first chairman of the Column Research Council.

• 4322 • Rudolph Hering Medal
To recognize the author(s) of a paper published by the Society or presented to the Society, which contains the most valuable contribution to the increase of knowledge in, and to the advancement of, the environmental branch of the engineering profession. Nominations must be submitted by November 1. A bronze medal and a certificate are awarded annually. Established in 1924 by the Sanitary Engineering Division in honor of Rudolph Hering, past Vice President of the Society.

• 4323 • Karl Emil Hilgard Hydraulic Prize
To recognize the author(s) of a paper that contributes to the field of water resources development. Members holding any grade are eligible. A wall plaque and a certificate are awarded annually. Established in 1939.

• 4324 • Julian Hinds Award
To recognize the author(s) of a paper that contributes to the field of water resources development. Members holding any grade are eligible. Nominations must be submitted by November 1. An honorarium and a certificate are awarded annually. Established in 1974.

• 4325 • Phillip R. Hoffman Award
To recognize an engineer who has made a definite contribution to the field of hydroelectric generation-pumped storage. The contribution can be in the form of a published paper or performance in the field. Nominations must be submitted by November 1. A plaque and an inscribed certificate are awarded annually. Established in 1987 by Nevenka Hoffman, widow of Phillip R. Hoffman, to honor her husband's special interest in the design and development of hydroelectric generation-pumped storage.

• 4326 • Honorary Fellow
To recognize and honor individuals who have demonstrated achievement and contributed noteworthy services in any field of endeavor, who have adhered to high standards of conduct, and whose efforts have benefited their communities, the nation, and mankind. A certificate is awarded when merited. Established in 1986.

• 4327 • Honorary Member
To recognize an individual who has attained acknowledged eminence in some branch of engineering or in the arts and sciences related thereto, including the fields of engineering education and construction.

• 4328 • Hoover Medal
To recognize distinguished public service. Awarded jointly by five national societies: American Society of Civil Engineers; American Institute of Mining, Metallurgical, and Petroleum Engineers; The American Society of Mechanical Engineers; The American Institute of Chemical Engineers; and the Institute of Electrical and Electronics Engineers. Established in 1929 to commemorate the civic and humanitarian achievements of Herbert Hoover, Hon. M. ASCE.

• 4329 • Wesley W. Horner Award
To recognize the author(s) of the paper that makes the most valuable contribution to the environmental engineering profession. Selection is based on contributions by authors who are in the private practice of engineering. Nominations must be submitted by November 1. A plaque and certificate are awarded . Established in 1968 in honor of Wesley W. Horner, past president of the Society.

• 4330 • Robert Horonjeff Award of the Air Transport Division
To recognize and honor a person(s) or organizations for outstanding achievements in, and contributions to the advancement of the field of air transportation engineering. Nominations must be submitted by October 1. A plaque and certificate are awarded when merited. Established in 1979 in honor of Robert Horonjeff.

• 4331 • Ernest E. Howard Award
To recognize an individual who has made a definite contribution to the advancement of structural engineering in either research, planning, design or construction. Members of the Society are eligible. Nominations must be submitted by November 1. A monetary award, a gold-plated medal, and a certificate are awarded annually. Established in 1954 to honor Ernest E. Howard, past president, ASCE.

• 4332 • Walter L. Huber Civil Engineering Research Prizes
To recognize notable achievements in research related to civil engineering. Members of the Society, preferably under 40 years of age, are eligible. Nominations must be submitted by October 1. Up to five monetary awards and certificates are presented every year. Established in 1964 in honor of Walter L. Huber, past President.

• 4333 • Hydraulic Structures Medal
To recognize an individual(s) for significant contributions to the advancement of the art and science of hydraulic engineering as applied to hydraulic structures. The contribution may be in the form of a paper published in the Society's technical journals, innovative application of hydraulic principles, individual achievements, or distinguished or meritorious service. A contribution of fundamental principles or design criteria having general application to multiple structures and usefulness over wide geographical areas is given preferred consideration over a contribution specific to a single structure or limited area. The award is given without restrictions as to Society membership or nationality. Nominations must be submitted by November 1. A gold-plated medal and a certificate are awarded annually. Established in 1983 by Fred. W. Blaisdell, F. ASCE, to honor the contributions of Melvin M. Culp, M. ASCE, and William O. Ree, F. ASCE, for their conception and development of generalized procedures for the design and application of hydraulic structures, and for their exemplary ethical and professional standards.

• 4334 • Innovation in Civil Engineering Award
To recognize a member for creativity in the form of innovative concepts in structural framing members or arrangements, fabrication and erection procedures, construction techniques, and repair and maintenance measures implemented in the six-year period preceding the date of award. Selection is based on the degree of innovation exemplified in developing a concept or basic idea for creating an entity or performing a task as distinguished from the subsequently needed analysis and design, routine procedures of execution, or publication of a technical paper. Nominations must be submitted by November 1. An honorarium and a plaque are presented to the winner, and an Award of Merit to the runner-up. Awarded annually. Established in 1981.

• 4335 • International Coastal Engineering Award
To provide international recognition for outstanding leadership and development in the field of coastal engineering. There is no restriction to nationality or Society membership. Selection is based on contribution to the advancement of coastal engineering in the manner of engineering design, teaching, professional leadership, construction, research, planning, or a combination thereof. Nominations must be submitted by November 1. A specially designed plaque, a certificate, and an honorarium are awarded annually. In even-numbered years the award will, if possible, be presented at the International Coastal Engineering Conference. In odd-numbered years the award will be presented at an ASCE national or specialty conference as desired by the recipient. Established in 1977 in honor of Mauricio Porraz. Formerly: Mauricio Porraz International Coastal Engineering Award.

• 4336 • Martin S. Kapp Foundation Engineering Award
To recognize an individual on the basis of the best example of innovative or outstanding design or construction of foundations, earthworks, retaining structures, or underground construction. Membership is not required. Nominations must be submitted by November 1. A plaque and certificate are awarded annually. Established in 1973 in memory of Martin S. Kapp, F. ASCE.

• 4337 • James Laurie Prize
To recognize an individual who has made a definite contribution to the advancement of transportation engineering, either in research, planning, design, or construction. Members of the Society are eligible. Nominations must be submitted by November 1. A plaque and certificate are awarded annually. Established in 1912 in honor of James Laurie, the first president of the Society.

• 4338 • T. Y. Lin Award
To encourage the preparation of meaningful papers in the field of prestressed concrete. Nominations must be submitted by November 1. A monetary award, a plaque, and a certificate are awarded. Established in 1968 by T.Y. Lin, F. ASCE.

• 4339 • Frank M. Masters Transportation Engineering Award
To recognize a member for the best example of innovative or noteworthy planning, design, or construction of transportation facilities. Nominations may be submitted November 1. A medal and certificate are awarded annually. Established in 1975.

• 4340 • Daniel W. Mead Prizes
To recognize papers on professional ethics. The specific topics (if any) of the contests for the forthcoming year are selected by the Committee on Younger Members in the case of the Associate Member award, and by the Committee on Student Services for the Student award. The national winners receive certificates and wall plaques, and the papers are published in the *Issues in Engineering - Journal of Professional Activities* or in *Civil Engineering*. Established in 1939 by Daniel W. Mead, Past President and Honorary Member, ASCE. A Daniel W. Mead Prize for Younger Members and a Daniel W. Mead Prize for Students are also awarded annually.

• 4341 • Thomas A. Middlebrooks Award
To recognize the author(s) of an outstanding article which contributes to the fields of soil mechanics or foundation engineering. Young engineers whose papers were published by the Society during the previous year may be nominated by November 1. An honorarium is awarded annually when merited. Established in 1955 in honor of Thomas A. Middlebrooks.

• 4342 • John G. Moffat - Frank E. Nichol Harbor and Coastal Engineering Award
To recognize new ideas and concepts that can be efficiently implemented to expand the engineering or construction techniques available for harbor and coastal projects. Nominations must be submitted by November 1. An honorarium, a plaque, and a certificate are awarded annually. Established in 1977 by the firm of Moffat & Nichol to honor John G. Moffat and Frank E. Nichol.

• 4343 • Moisseiff Award
To recognize an important paper published by the Society that deals with the broad field of structural design. Nominations must be submitted by November 1. The author(s) of the article receives a monetary award, a bronze medal, and a certificate. Awarded when merited. Established in 1947 in memory of Leon S. Moisseiff, M. ASCE.

• 4344 • Nathan M. Newmark Medal
To recognize a member who has helped to strengthen the scientific base of structural engineering. Nominations must be submitted by November 1. A gold-plated medal and a certificate are awarded annually. Established in 1975 by the Engineering Mechanics and Structural Division in honor of Nathan M. Newmark, for his outstanding contributions in structural engineering and mechanics.

• 4345 • Alfred Noble Prize
For recognition of a technical paper of exceptional merit accepted by the Committee on Publications, or a committee of like standing, for publication in any of their technical publications, provided the author has not passed his/her 31st birthday at the time the paper is submitted to the society in practically its final form. Members of any grade of the American Society of Civil Engineers; American Institute of Mining, Metallurgical, and Petroleum Engineers, Inc.; The American Society of Mechanical Engineers; The Institute of Electrical and Electronics Engineers; or the Western Society of Engineers are eligible. Papers must be submitted by April 1. The prize consists of a cash award and a certificate. Established in 1929 in honor of Alfred Noble, past President of the American Society of Civil Engineers and the Western Society of Engineers.

• 4346 • Norman Medal
To recognize the author(s) of a paper judged worthy of special commendation for its merit as a contribution to engineering science. Members of the Society must be nominated by November 1. A gold-plated medal and a certificate are awarded. Established in 1872 by George H. Norman, M. ASCE.

• 4347 • Outstanding Civil Engineering Achievement
To recognize an engineering project that demonstrates the greatest engineering skills and represents the greatest contribution to engineering progress and mankind. A bronze plaque is presented to the owner of the project. In addition, Awards of Merit winners may be selected. Awarded annually. Established in 1960.

• 4348 • John I. Parcel - Leif J. Sverdrup Civil Engineering Management Award
To encourage effective leadership and management skills in the civil engineering profession. Members of the Society are eligible. Nominations must be submitted by March 1. A cash honorarium, a plaque, and a certificate are awarded. Established in 1976.

• 4349 • Peurifoy Construction Research Award
To recognize individuals who have made outstanding contributions to the advancement of construction engineering through research and development of new technology, principles or practices. Nominations must be submitted by November 1. A cash honorarium and a certificate are awarded annually. Established in 1986 by the friends, former students and associates of Dr. R.L. Peurifoy.

• 4350 • Harold R. Peyton Award for Cold Regions Engineering
To recognize a member of the Society who has made outstanding contributions to cold regions engineering or to a basic understanding of cold environments, including dissemination of knowledge of cold climate technology through publishing innovative technical or research papers. Nominations must be submitted by November 1. A plaque and framed certificate are awarded annually. Established in 1989 as a memorial to the outstanding professional accomplishments of Harold R. Peyton, F. ASCE, and to stimulate awareness and interest in the challenges of cold regions engineering.

• 4351 • Raymond C. Reese Research Prize
To recognize outstanding contributions to the application of structural engineering research. The authors of papers published in the previous twelve-month period must be nominated by November 1. A plaque and a certificate are awarded annually. Established in 1970.

• 4352 • Rickey Medal
To recognize the author(s) of a meritorious paper, published by the Society in the general field of hydroelectric engineering, including any of its branches. Both members and non-members must be nominated by November 1. A gold-plated medal and a certificate are awarded annually. Established in 1947 by Mrs. Rickey in honor of her husband, James W. Rickey, a leader in hydroelectric engineering progress.

• 4353 • Robert Ridgway Student Chapter Award
To recognize the most outstanding Student Chapter of the Society. A plaque, with copies for each member of the chapter, of the memoir of past President Ridgway is awarded annually at an appropriate meeting by a national officer of the Society. Established in 1965 by Isabel L. Ridgway in honor of her husband, Robert Ridgway.

• 4354 • Roebling Award
To recognize and honor an individual who has made an outstanding contribution toward the advancement of construction engineering. Nominations may be submitted by November 1. The recipient of the Award will deliver a Roebling Lecture at an appropriate meeting of the Society. An honorarium and a plaque are awarded annually when merited. Awarded without restrictions as to Society membership or nationality. Established in 1987 by the Construction Division of the Society in memory of three outstanding constructors, John A. Roebling, Washington Roebling and Emily Roebling.

• 4355 • Hunter Rouse Hydraulic Engineering Lecture
To select a distinguished person to deliver the Hunter Rouse Hydraulic Engineering Lecture at an appropriate meeting of the Society. Nominations must be submitted by November 1. An honorarium and a certificate are awarded annually. The lecture is published in the division's journal. Established in 1979.

• 4356 • Thomas Fitch Rowland Prize
To recognize a paper published by the Society that describes in detail accomplished works of construction, cost, and errors in design and execution. The author(s) of the paper need not be members of the Society to be eligible. Nominations must be submitted by November 1. A wall plaque and a certificate are awarded annually. Established in 1882. Endowed in 1884 by Thomas Fitch Rowland.

• 4357 • Wilbur S. Smith Award
To recognize an individual who, during the fiscal year preceding the year of the award, is judged worthy of special commendation for his contribution to the enhancement of the role of the civil engineer in highway engineering. The contribution may be made in the form of a paper published by the Society or may be his personal efforts and achievements toward that goal. The award is restricted to Fellows, Members and Associate Members of the Society. Nominations must be submitted by November 1. A plaque and a certificate are awarded annually. Established in 1984 by the Highway Division of the Society in recognition of the outstanding professional accomplishments of Wilbur S. Smith, Hon. M. ASCE.

• 4358 • J. Waldo Smith Hydraulic Fellowship
To assist that graduate student, preferably an Associate Member of the Society, who gives promise of best fulfilling the ideals of the fellowship. The fellowship is offered every third year. It runs for one full academic year and provides $4,000, plus up to $1,000 as may be required for physical equipment connected with the research. Such equipment becomes the property of the institution upon completion of the work. Established in 1938 and made possible by J. Waldo Smith, past Vice President and Hon. M. ASCE, who bequeathed funds to the Society.

• 4359 • J. C. Stevens Award
To recognize the author(s) of the best discussion of the field of hydraulics, including fluid mechanics and hydrology, that is published by the Society. Members of the Society are eligible. Nominations must be submitted by November 1. A collection of books (restrictions apply) of the winner's choice is awarded annually. Established in 1943 by John C. Stevens, past president, ASCE.

• 4360 • **Surveying and Mapping Award**
To recognize a member who has made a contribution during the year to the advancement of surveying and mapping in either teaching, writing, research, planning, design, construction, or management. Nominations must be submitted by November 1. A plaque and certificate are awarded annually. Established in 1969.

• 4361 • **Karl Terzaghi Lecture**
To recognize a distinguished engineer by an invitation to deliver the Terzaghi Lecture at an appropriate meeting of the Society. The lecturer receives an honorarium and a certificate. Established in 1960 by the Soil Mechanics and Foundation Division.

• 4362 • **Royce J. Tipton Award**
To recognize an individual who has made a definite contribution to the advancement of irrigation and drainage engineering in either teaching, research, planning, design, construction, or management. Members of the Society must be nominated by November 1. A plaque and a certificate are awarded annually. Established in 1964.

• 4363 • **Richard R. Torrens Award**
To honor volunteer Journal editors who make outstanding contributions to the ASCE publications program. The award will be made by the ASCE Board Committee on Publications to a Journal editor whose contributions are considered outstanding. No more than one award shall be made in a single year, and it shall not be required that an award be made every year. A certificate is awarded when merited. Established in 1984 in memory of Richard R. Torrens who served ASCE for 17 years in the Publications Department at Headquarters, and was Manager of Professional and Technical Publications.

• 4364 • **Francis C. Turner Lecture**
To recognize a distinguished professional for contributions to the advancement of the knowledge and practice of transportation engineering. The recipient need not be a member of the Society. The lecture is given at a national meeting of the Society. A plaque and an honorarium are awarded annually. Established in 1988 jointly by the Highway and Urban Transportation Divisions of the Society.

• 4365 • **Theodore von Karman Medal**
To recognize an individual for distinguished achievement in engineering mechanics applicable to any branch of civil engineering. Individuals regardless of age, nationality, and Society membership are eligible. A bronze medal is awarded annually. Established in 1960 by the Engineering Mechanics Division of the Society in honor of Theodore von Karman.

• 4366 • **Washington Award**
To recognize accomplishments that preeminently promote the happiness, comfort, and well-being of humanity. The award is not restricted by any society or locality requirement. Awarded jointly by the following National Societies: Western Society of Engineers; American Society of Civil Engineers; American Institute of Mining, Metallurgical and Petroleum Engineers; The American Society of Mechanical Engineers; The Institute of Electrical and Electronics Engineers; and The National Society of Professional Engineers. Nominations must be submitted by November 1. A bronze medal or other work of art is awarded annually. Established in 1916 by John W. Alvord, Hon. M. ASCE, and administered by the Western Society of Engineers.

• 4367 • **Arthur M. Wellington Prize**
To recognize an outstanding paper on transportation on land, on the water, in the air, or on foundations and closely related subjects, not including contributions in the form of reports and manuals. The award is not restricted to members of the Society. Nominations must be submitted by November 1. A wall plaque and a certificate are awarded annually. Established in 1921 by *The Engineering News-Record* to honor Arthur M. Wellington, former editor and author.

• 4368 • **George Winter Award**
To recognize outstanding achievements of an active structural engineering researcher, educator or practitioner. Established in 1990 to honor George Winter for his humanistic approach to the profession, i.e., an equal concern for matters technical and social, for art as well as science, for soul as well as intellect.

• 4369 • **William H. Wisely American Civil Engineer Award**
To recognize individuals or groups who have exhibited continuing efforts to better the history, tradition, developments and technical and professional activities of the Society. Members of ASCE are eligible. Nominations must be submitted by November 1. A plaque, a certificate, and an honorarium are awarded annually. Established in 1983 in memory of William H. Wisely, Honorary Member, ASCE, who for nearly two decades guided the activities of the Society as its chief staff officer.

• 4370 • **Young Government Civil Engineer of the Year Award**
To recognize distinguished civil engineers employed in public service for significant contributions to Public Service Engineering. Engineers of recognized standing, preferably registered and citizens of the United States are eligible. Award nominees are judged on the following: excellent performance that has demonstrated leadership potential in public sector civil engineering; evidence of high character and professional integrity; 35 years of age or less on December 31 in the year of the award; and between five and ten years in public service. Nominations may be submitted by October 1. The award consists of a suitably inscribed certificate. Established by the Committee on Civil Engineers in Government.

• 4371 • **Younger Member Group Award**
To promote excellence among the Younger Member groups of the Society. Younger member groups are defined as Associate Member Forums (AMF), Younger Member Forums (YMF), Younger Member Committees (YMC), etc. that operate at the Section and Branch level. It does not include younger member councils. Nominations must be submitted by March 1. A certificate is presented to the Younger Member Group at an appropriate meeting by a national officer of the Society. Established in 1985.

• 4372 •
American Society of Colon and Rectal Surgeons
Bruce G. Wolff MD, Pres.
85 W Alqonquin Rd., Ste. 550
Arlington Heights, IL 60005
Phone: (847)290-9184
Toll-Free: 800-791-0001
Fax: (847)290-9203
E-mail: ascrs@fascrs.org
Home Page: http://www.fascrs.org/

• 4373 • **National Media Awards**
Recognizes journalists who have excelled in communicating information about colon and rectal disease. Awards of $1,000, an engraved plaque, and an expense-paid trip to the association's annual meeting are given for the best work in three main categories: print, broadcast, and Internet. Awarded annually.

• 4374 •
American Society of Composers, Authors and Publishers
Marilyn Bergman, Pres.
1 Lincoln Plz.
New York, NY 10023
Phone: (212)621-6000
Fax: (212)724-9064
E-mail: info@ascap.com
Home Page: http://www.ascap.com

• 4375 • **ASCAP Chamber Music Awards**
To recognize chamber music ensembles and presenters who have demonstrated adventurous programming of music composed since 1970. Awards are presented in four categories: (1) Chamber ensembles that present contemporary music exclusively; (2) Chamber ensembles that perform mixed repertoire, including music composed after 1950; (3) Chamber music presenters or festivals who present 10 or more concerts per season; and (4) Chamber music presenters or festivals who present 9 or fewer concerts per season. Recipients must be voting members of Chamber Music America. Monetary prizes of $350 and $150 and plaques are awarded annually. Established in 1987. Additional information is available from Chamber Music America, 545 Eighth Avenue, New York, NY 10018, (212) 244-2772.

• 4376 • **ASCAP - Deems Taylor Awards**
To recognize the author of outstanding books and articles about music, musicians, or composers, published in the United States during the preceding calendar year. Plaques and monetary prizes of $500 are awarded for the best book and $250 for the best journal, newspaper, or

magazine article. Awarded annually. Established in 1967.

• 4377 • ASCAP - Richard Rodgers Award
To recognize outstanding contributions to the American musical theatre. A monetary award of $5,000 and an engraved scroll are awarded annually. Established in 1982.

• 4378 • ASCAP Triple Play Award
To recognize the composer having three hit musicals running simultaneously in both New York and London. Established in 1988.

• 4379 • Nathan Burkan Memorial Competition
To recognize law students for outstanding essays on copyright law. Established in 1938 in honor of Nathan Burkan, ASCAP's first general counsel.

• 4380 • Grants to Young Composers
To encourage composers under the age of 30, the ASCAP Foundation awards grants annually to members and nonmembers who are U.S. citizens or permanent residents.

• 4381 • Rudolf Nissim Award
To recognize the best concert work for a large ensemble requiring a conductor. Awarded annually. Established in 1980. Open to ASCAP members. Deadline November 15.

• 4382 • Pied Piper Award
To honor an individual for lifetime achievements in the musical industry. The award has been given nine times since it was established in 1962.

• 4383 •
American Society of Criminology
Chris W. Eskridge, Exec.Dir.
1314 Kinnear Rd., Ste. 212
Columbus, OH 43212-1156
Phone: (614)292-9207
Fax: (614)292-6767
E-mail: ceskridge@unl.edu
Home Page: http://www.asc41.com

• 4384 • Herbert Bloch Award
To recognize outstanding services to criminology and to the society. Awarded annually. Established in 1961.

• 4385 • Sellin - Glueck Award
To recognize persons outside the United States who have gained international recognition for their contributions in criminology. Awarded annually. Established in 1974.

• 4386 • Edwin H. Sutherland Award
To recognize outstanding contributions to theory or research in criminology on the etiology of criminal and deviant behavior, the criminal justice system, corrections, law, or justice system. Selection is based on contributions that may be a single outstanding book or work, a series of theoretical or research contributions, or the accumulated contributions of a senior criminologist. Awarded annually. Established in 1960.

• 4387 • August Vollmer Award
To recognize outstanding contributions to justice or to the control, treatment, or prevention of criminal and deviant behavior. Selection is based on a single major effort by a social activist or leading practitioner in the criminal justice system, or a series of contributions to control, treatment, prevention, or justice over a period of time. Awarded annually. Established in 1960.

• 4388 •
American Society of Cytopathology
Elizabeth A. Jenkins, Exec.Admin.
400 W 9th St., Ste. 201
Wilmington, DE 19801
Phone: (302)429-8802
Fax: (302)429-8807
E-mail: asc@cytopathology.org
Home Page: http://www.cytopathology.org

• 4389 • Cytotechnologist Award for Outstanding Achievement
For recognition of meritorious service or accomplishment in the field of cytology. Associate or cytotechnologist members of the Society are eligible. The deadline for nomination is February 10. A monetary award of $1500, a certificate, and travel expenses to attend the annual meeting are awarded each year. Established in 1969. Made possible by a contribution from Shandon Inc., Pittsburgh, Pennsylvania. Formerly: Cytotechnologist of the Year Award.

• 4390 • Cytotechnologist Scientific Presentation Award
To recognize the cytotechnologist or cytotechnology student who gives the best presentation of a scientific paper at a platform or poster session. The awardee must be a cytotechnologist, student member of the Society, or a cytotechnology student in a program that leads to eligibility to take the examination for CT(ASCP) or CT(IAC). The deadline for submissions is April 10. An honorarium of $500 and a certificate are awarded annually. Established in 1969. Formerly: Cytotechnologist Award of the American Society of Cytology.

• 4391 • Excellence in Education Award
Presented annually to a cytotechnologist or pathologist in recognition of meritorious service in the field of cytotechnology education. A $1,000 is awarded. Established in 1998.

• 4392 • Geno Saccamanno, M.D. New Frontiers in Cytology award
Presented to an ASC member in good standing when an original paper shows significant innovation, good study design and potential diagnostic utility. The paper should contribute to better understanding of cell biology or enhanced diagnosis. An honorarium of $500 is awarded. Established in 1993.

• 4393 • Geraldine Colby Zeiler Award
Awarded annually to five cytotechnology students based on their academic performance and diagnostic skills, leadership ability, initiative, acceptance of responsibility, dedication, and relationship with colleagues. A certificate and monetary award of $1,000 is awarded. Established in 1990.

• 4394 • Guest Lectureship Award on Basic Cell Research in Cytology
To honor a cytologist with the presentation of the Basic Cytology Lecture at the Meeting. An honorarium of $3,000, a certificate, and travel expenses to attend the annual meeting are awarded each year. Established in 1967. Made possible by a contribution from Quest Diagnostics, Inc.

• 4395 • Impact of Workload on Diagnostic Accuracy Award
Presented in recognition of the most meritorious research platform/ poster presentation addressing the relationship between workload and accuracy. An honorarium of $500 is awarded. Established in 2001

• 4396 • Warren R. Lang Resident Physician Award
To recognize the resident from an approved Residency Training Program presenting the best scientific paper in cytology at a platform or poster session. Selection is based on quality of the scientific content and presentation. The deadline for nominations is April 1. A monetary award of $500 and a certificate are presented annually. Established in 1978. Re-named in memory of Warren R. Lang, M.D. Formerly: Resident Physician's Prize Paper Award; Warren R. Lang Prize Paper Award; Warren R. Lang Prize Paper Award.

• 4397 • New Frontiers in Cytology Award
To recognize the scientific paper presented at either a platform or poster session that contributes to a better understanding of cell biology or enhanced diagnosis by describing new methods, or modifications of existing methods for characterizing or measuring cells or their components. The work must be original and any member of the Society in good standing is eligible. The deadline for submissions is April 1. A monetary prize of $500 and a certificate are awarded annually. Established in 1993 by the Committee on Current Concepts and Technology in Cytology.

• 4398 • Papanicolaou Award of the American Society of Cytology
To recognize an individual for meritorious contributions in the field of cytology. The deadline for nominations is February 18. A monetary award of $3000, a certificate, a bronze medal, and travel expenses to attend the annual meeting are awarded each year. Established in 1958. Sponsored by the late Harry and Helen C. Roth. Mr. Roth was Chairman of the Board, Clay-Adams Company, Division of Becton Dickenson Company, Parsippany, New Jersey. Formerly:

(1964) American Society of Cytology Award for Meritorious Achievement in Cytology.

• 4399 • **President's Award**
Presented annually to a member and is selected at the discretion of the ASC President. An honorarium of $500 is awarded. Established in 1992.

• 4400 •
American Society of Directors of Volunteer Services
Audrey Harris, Exec.Dir.
One N Franklin, 27th Fl.
Chicago, IL 60606
Phone: (312)422-3939
Fax: (312)422-4575
E-mail: asdvs@aha.org
Home Page: http://www.asdvs.org

• 4401 • **Volunteer Leader**
Recognizes a national leader/celebrity who has made major contributions to healthcare issues/volunteerism. Awarded annually.

• 4402 •
American Society of Electroneurodiagnostic Technologists
Sheila R. Navis CAE, Exec.Dir.
426 West 42nd St.
Kansas City, MO 64111
Phone: (816)931-1120
Fax: (816)931-1145
E-mail: info@aset.org
Home Page: http://www.aset.org

Formerly: (1987) American Society of Electroencephalographic Technologists.

• 4403 • **Maureen Berkeley Memorial Award**
For recognition of the author, either American or European, of the best paper published in the *American Journal of Electroneurodiagnostic Technology* during the previous year. The candidate must be an EEG technologist. An inscribed silver plate is awarded annually when merited. Established in 1965 to perpetuate the lifetime ideals of Maureen Berkeley, one of the eleven original Registered Electroencephalographic Technologists.

• 4404 •
American Society of Farm Managers and Rural Appraisers
Doug Slothower, Exec.VP
950 S Cherry St., Ste. 508
Denver, CO 80246-2664
Phone: (303)758-3513
Fax: (303)758-0190
E-mail: info@agri-associations.org
Home Page: http://www.asfmra.org

• 4405 • **Distinguished Service to Agriculture**
To recognize individuals who have made contributions to agriculture. Established in 1974.

• 4406 • **D. Howard Doane Award**
To recognize an individual who has made an outstanding contribution in the field of agriculture, with emphasis on farm management and rural appraisal. Preference is given to members of the society. Established in 1951 in honor of D. Howard Doane, first president of the society.

• 4407 • **Gold Quill Award**
To recognize the authors of the most outstanding article in the society's professional *Journal* during the previous year. A plaque is awarded annually. Established in 1975. Formerly: (1980) Silver Page Award.

• 4408 • **Meritorious Service in Communications Award**
To acknowledge an individual company or association involved in the area of communications that has promoted understanding and goodwill between producers and consumers of agricultural products.

• 4409 •
American Society of Furniture Designers
Christine Evans, Exec. Dir.
144 Woodland Dr.
New London, NC 28127
Phone: (910)576-1273
Fax: (910)576-1573
E-mail: info@asfd.com
Home Page: http://www.asfd.com

• 4410 • **ASFD Life-Time Achievement Award**
To recognize individuals for sustained achievement in the area of furniture design. A plaque, certificate, and honorary membership, when applicable, are awarded annually. Established in 1985.

• 4411 • **Distinguished Designer Award**
To recognize an individual for outstanding achievement in the area of furniture design. A plaque, certificate, and honorary membership, when applicable, are awarded annually. Established in 1985.

• 4412 • **Honorary Member**
To provide for honorary membership in the Society. Awarded when merited.

• 4413 • **Pinnacle Design Achievement Award**
To promote designers within the retail home furnishings industry, promote the ASFD as an organization devoted to the recognition of design and designers, and to promote increased quality of design in retail home furnishings. Winner receives glass Pinnacle statue, with the finalists receiving certificates. Awarded annually. Established in 1996.

• 4414 •
American Society of Genealogists
Roger D. Joslyn, Pres.
PO Box 1515
Derry, NH 03038-1515
Home Page: http://www.fasg.org

• 4415 • **Donald Lines Jacobus Award**
To honor the best genealogical work published within the preceding five-year period by individuals other than Fellows of the American Society of Genealogists. A monetary award of $100 and a certificate are awarded annually when merited. Established in 1972 to honor the memory of Donald Lines Jacobus, an early twentieth-century genealogist who laid the foundations of modern genealogical scholarship.

• 4416 •
American Society of Heating, Refrigerating and Air-Conditioning Engineers
Jeff Littleton, Sec.
1791 Tullie Cir. NE
Atlanta, GA 30329
Phone: (404)636-8400
Toll-Free: 800-5-ASHRAE
Fax: (404)321-5478
E-mail: ashrae@ashrae.org
Home Page: http://www.ashrae.org

• 4417 • **Homer Addams Award**
To recognize a graduate student working on an ASHRAE Research Project, and to advance his or her engineering education and knowledge gained through research in the arts and sciences of heating, ventilating, air conditioning, and refrigeration. A monetary prize of $1,500 and a certificate are presented annually. Established in 1956 in memory of Homer Addams, charter member and past president. Formerly: ASHRAE ASHAE - Homer Addams Award.

• 4418 • **F. Paul Anderson Award**
This, the Society's highest award, recognizes a member for notable scientific achievement, outstanding work, or service performed in the field of heating, refrigeration, ventilating, or air conditioning. A medal and a certificate are awarded annually. Established in 1930 in memory of F. Paul Anderson, past president of the Society.

• 4419 • **ASHRAE - Alco Medal for Distinguished Public Service**
To recognize a member of the Society for outstanding public service in his community. A medal and a certificate are given annually. Established in 1965. Sponsored by the Alco Control Company.

• 4420 • **ASHRAE Fellows**
To recognize individuals who have attained distinction in the fields of heating, refrigeration, air conditioning, ventilation, or the allied arts and sciences through teaching, research, invention, design, and/or supervision of projects of unusual or important scope. Individuals who have been members for a minimum of ten years are eligible. A certificate is awarded.

• 4421 • ***ASHRAE Journal* Paper Award**
To recognize excellence in technical information presented by the Society by recognizing the author of the best paper published in the *ASHRAE Journal* during the preceding calendar year. A monetary award of $500 and a certificate are awarded annually. Established in 1972.

• 4422 • **ASHRAE Symposium Paper Award**
To encourage excellence in technical information by the Society by recognizing an individual(s) responsible for the best papers presented at a symposium at Society meetings. A monetary award of $500 and a certificate are awarded for each paper. Established in 1972.

• 4423 • **ASHRAE Technical Paper Award**
To recognize the best technical papers presented at Society meetings. A monetary award of $500 and a certificate are awarded for each paper. Established in 1972.

• 4424 • **Andrew T. Boggs Service Award**
To recognize a past Distinguished Service Award recipient for continuing, unselfish, dedicated, and distinguished service to the Society. A medal and certificate are awarded annually. Established in 1986 in honor of A. T. Boggs, ASHRAE Executive Vice President Emeritus.

• 4425 • **Lincoln Bouillon Award**
To recognize the individual who performs the most outstanding work in increasing the membership of the Society. The award consists of a medal and a certificate and is given annually. Established in 1967 in memory of Presidential Member Lincoln Bouillon's outstanding effort in recruiting new members.

• 4426 • **E. K. Campbell Award of Merit**
To honor outstanding service and achievement in teaching. A certificate and a $2,000 cash award is presented by the Life Members Club annually. Established in 1958.

• 4427 • **ASHRAE - Willis H. Carrier Award**
For the best published paper of outstanding quality presented by a member of any grade who is 32 years of age or less at the time of presentation. A monetary award of $500 and a certificate are awarded annually. Established in 1958. Sponsored by the Carrier Corporation.

• 4428 • **William J. Collins, Jr. Research Promotion Award**
To honor the Chapter Research Promotion Chairman who excels in raising funds for ASHRAE research. A certificate, engraved medal, and transportation to the Society's annual meeting are awarded annually. Established in 1985.

• 4429 • **Distinguished 50-Year Member Award**
To recognize individuals who have been ASHRAE members for 50 years, were a past Society president, a fellow, a recipient of the Distinguished Service Award, or otherwise performed outstanding service for the Society. Certificates are awarded annually. Established in 1970.

• 4430 • **Distinguished Service Award**
To recognize individuals for serving faithfully with distinction and giving freely of their time and talent on behalf of the Society. Certificates are awarded annually. Established in 1962.

• 4431 • **Crosby Field Award**
For recognition of the best paper or article chosen from among the best technical, symposium, and Journal Papers. A monetary award of $750 and a certificate are awarded. Established in 1972.

• 4432 • **Milton W. Garland Refrigeration Award**
To recognize the chapter Refrigeration Committee Chairman who has done the most outstanding work in promoting the science of refrigeration at the chapter level. An engraved medal, certificate, and transportation expenses to the annual meeting are awarded annually. Established in 1990 to honor Milton W. Garland, a recognized leader in the refrigeration field.

• 4433 • **Government Affairs Award**
To recognize effective participation by ASHRAE Chapters for outstanding effort and achievement in state, provincial, and local government activities in connection with technical issues related to the purpose of the Society. A certificate is awarded annually. Established in 1990.

• 4434 • **Hall of Fame**
To recognize deceased members who have made milestone contributions to the growth of ASHRAE-related technology and/or the development of ASHRAE as a Society. Individuals inducted into the Hall of Fame must have been Society members (any grade) or a member of a predecessor Society and must have shown evidence of distinction in the Society, either technically of academically. Up to five inductees may be presented annually. A crystal award for the inductee's family and recognition in the form of a permanent display at the Society headquarters is awarded annually. Awarded when merited. Established in 1994.

• 4435 • **Louise and Bill Holladay Distinguished Fellow Award**
To recognize a fellow for continuing preeminence in engineering or research work. An inscribed medal and citation are awarded annually. Established in 1979.

• 4436 • **Honorary Member**
To recognize an individual of preeminent professional distinction without regard to whether the individual is, or has been, a member of ASHRAE. A certificate is awarded. Established in 1936.

• 4437 • **John F. James International Award**
To recognize a member of the Society who has done the most to enhance the Society's international presence. A certificate is awarded annually. Established in 1983. Formerly: (1996) International Activities Award.

• 4438 • **Ralph G. Nevins Physiology and Human Environment Award**
To recognize a promising investigator under 40 years of age for significant accomplishment in the general area of humanity's response to the environment. An honorarium of $300 and a certificate are awarded annually. Established in 1978.

• 4439 • **Standards Achievement Award**
To recognize an individual for significant and exceptional service in standards leadership and standards technical contribution. A certificate is awarded annually. Established in 1995.

• 4440 • **Student Design Project Competition**
To recognize undergraduate students who have completed research or design projects based on topics of current interest to the Society. A monetary award of $1,500 and expenses to attend the winter meeting are awarded for first place/ teams. Second place teams receive expenses to attend the Winter Meeting. Awarded annually. Established in 1988. Formerly: Student Award.

• 4441 • **Technology Award/Award of Engineering Excellence**
To recognize on an international scale successful applications of innovative design, which incorporate ASHRAE standards for effective energy management, indoor air quality, and mechanical design management technology. Up to three engraved plaques are presented annually in each of the seven categories. Formerly: (1989) ASHRAE Energy Awards.

• 4442 •
American Society of Hematology
Martha Liggett, Exec.Dir.
1900 M St., NW, Ste. 200
Washington, DC 20036
Phone: (202)776-0544
Fax: (202)776-0545
E-mail: ash@hematology.org
Home Page: http://www.hematology.org

• 4443 • **ASH Scholar Awards**
To encourage young hematologists to begin an academic career specifically in hematology by providing partial salary or other support during that critical period required for completion of training and achievement of status as an independent investigator. To be eligible for consideration for the Junior Faculty Scholar Award, applicants must be faculty members and not be more

than two years at the rank of assistant professor or equivalent at the time of application. The nominee must be sponsored by a member of the Society. Applicants are required to submit the original plus twenty copies of the Scholar Award application, which includes: the applicant's curriculum vitae and bibliography; letter of recommendation from the sponsor. Deadline September 1.

• 4444 • Dameshek Prize
To recognize an individual for an outstanding contribution during the preceding year in the field of hematology. A plaque is awarded at the annual meeting, and a $5,000 honorarium as well as reimbursement of air fare, lodging, and meal expenses incurred for the meeting. Established in 1970 in honor of Dr. William Dameshek, former president of the American Society of Hematology and the first editor of its journal *BLOOD*.

• 4445 • Ham-Wasserman Lecture
To recognize an individual who has made a major contribution to the understanding of an area relating to hematology. The Lectureship confers a $5,000 honorarium and a plaque at the annual meeting as well as air fare, lodging, and meal expenses incurred for the meeting. Established in honor of former Society presidents Dr. Thomas H. Ham and Dr. Louis R. Wasserman

• 4446 • Henry M. Stratton Medal
To recognize an individual whose contributions to hematology are well-recognized and have taken place over a number of years. A $5,000 honorarium and a latex-encased medal are presented at an annual meeting, in addition to reimbursement of air fare, lodging, and meal expenses incurred for the meeting. Established in 1974 by Dr. Henry Maurice Stratton, founder of the Grune & Statton medical publishing firm with L.H. Grunebaum. Formerly: (1992) Henry M Statton Lecture.

• 4447 • E. Donnall Thomas Lecture and Prize
To recognize pioneering research achievements in hematology. A $5,000 honorarium and a plaque are awarded at the annual meeting, as well as reimbursement for air fare, lodging, and meal expenses incurred for the meeting. Established in 1992 in honor of the Noble Prize laureate and former Society president E. Donnall Thomas.

• 4448 •
American Society of Human Genetics
Elaine Strass, Exec.Dir.
9650 Rockville Pke.
Bethesda, MD 20814-3998
Phone: (301)634-7300
Toll-Free: (866)HUM-GENE
Fax: (301)530-7079
E-mail: society@ashg.org
Home Page: http://www.ashg.org

• 4449 • William Allan Award
To recognize substantial and far-reaching scientific contributions to human genetics, carried out over a sustained period of scientific inquiry and productivity. A medal and $10,000 in cash is awarded annually. Additionally, the winner presents a 30-45 minute address to the ASHG meeting participants. Established in 1961.

• 4450 •
American Society of Ichthyologists and Herpetologists
Maureen A. Donnelly, Sec.
Department of Biological Sciences
College of Arts & Science
Florida International University
North Miami, FL 33181
Phone: (305)919-5651
Fax: (305)919-5964
E-mail: asih@fiu.edu
Home Page: http://www.asih.org

• 4451 • Gaige Fund Award
To provide support to young herpetologists for museum or laboratory study, travel, field work, or any other activity that effectively enhances their professional careers and their contributions to the science of herpetology. The deadline for applications is March 1. A monetary award is ranging from $400 to $1,000 is presented annually. Established in the honor of Frederick and Helen Gaige (1890-1976), who were a major influence on biology, herpetology in particular, in the United States.

• 4452 • Robert H. Gibbs, Jr. Memorial Award
To recognize an outstanding body of published work in systematic ichthyology by a citizen of a Western Hemisphere nation. Nominations must be submitted by March 1. A monetary award and a plaque are presented annually. Established to honor Robert H. Gibbs, Jr. distinguished fellow of the Society.

• 4453 • Raney Fund Award
To provide support for young ichthyologists for museum or laboratory study, travel, field work, or any other activity that effectively enhances their professional careers and their contributions to the science of ichthyology. Applicants must be members of ASIH and be enrolled for an advanced degree. The deadline for applications is March 15. A monetary award ranging from $400 to $1,000 is presented annually. Established in honor of Edward C. Raney (1909-1984), who was a member of the faculty of Cornell University and authored over 75 papers dealing with the systematics, behavior, and ecology of fishes.

• 4454 • Storer Award
To recognize student judged to have prepared the best paper/poster in ichthyology and herpetology. One award is made in each discipline. A monetary award and 10 years of back issues of the ASIH journal, *Copeia*, are awarded at the annual meeting. Established in 1988.

• 4455 • Stoye Awards
To recognize the best student paper (oral) in the following areas: general ichthyology; general herpetology; ecology and ethology; physiology and physiological ecology; and genetics, development, and morphology. Five monetary prizes, 10 years of back issues of the ASIH journal, *Copeia*, and of books from the University of Chicago Press are awarded each year at the annual meeting. Established in 1939.

• 4456 •
American Society of Indexers
Francine Butler, Exec.Dir.
10200 W 44th Ave., Ste. 304
Wheat Ridge, CO 80033
Phone: (303)463-2887
Fax: (303)422-8894
E-mail: info@asindexing.org
Home Page: http://www.asindexing.org

• 4457 • H. W. Wilson Company Indexing Award
For recognition of achievement in preparing an outstanding index to an English-language monograph in the United States during the previous calendar year. Society members are eligible. A monetary award of $1,000 to the indexer and citations to the indexer and publisher are awarded annually. Established in 1978 by the American Society of Indexers and the H. W. Wilson Company.

• 4458 •
American Society of Interior Designers
Michael Alin, Exec.Dir.
608 Massachusetts Ave., NE
Washington, DC 20002
Phone: (202)546-3480
E-mail: asid@asid.org
Home Page: http://www.asid.org

Formed by merger of: (1975) National Society of Interior Design; American Interior Designers.

• 4459 • ASID Designer of Distinction Award
To recognize an ASID interior designer who has made outstanding contributions toward achieving ASID's goal of design excellence. ASID Professional Members who have practiced for least 10 years are eligible. The national president and awards committee members during the year of incumbency are not eligible. Selection is based on published work, professional achievements, and creative and innovative concepts that serve as a pilot to the advancement of good design. The award is presented by the ASID president during the annual conference. Awarded annually when merited.

• 4460 • Design for Humanity Award
To recognize an individual or institution for a significant contribution to and concern for improving the quality of the human environment through design related activities. Individuals or design teams, institutions, associations, organizations, corporations, and cultural or civic bodies are eligible. The award includes, but is not

limited to, one of the following fields: health; handicapped or barrier-free; energy conservation; safety; fire prevention; communication; or transportation. The contribution must be oriented to the human environment, beneficial to the community at large, nonpartisan, and judged on its own merits regardless of size. Formerly: (1990) ASID Human Environment Award.

• 4461 •
American Society of International Law
Charlotte Ku, Exec.Dir. and Exec.VP
2223 Massachusetts Ave. NW
Washington, DC 20008-2864
Phone: (202)939-6000
Fax: (202)797-7133
E-mail: services@asil.org
Home Page: http://www.asil.org

• 4462 • **Goler T. Butcher Medal**
To recognize a distinguished person who has contributed to furthering human rights around the globe. A gold medal is awarded when merited to one or more recipients. Established in 1995 in memory of Goler T. Butcher.

• 4463 • **Certificate of Merit**
To recognize a work (book, monograph, or article) in international law for its preeminent contribution to creative scholarship or because it exhibits high technical craftsmanship and is of high utility to practicing lawyers and scholars. Open to all regardless of nationality or the language or place of publication of the work. The work must have been published within the 24-month period preceding February 1 of the year in which the award is made. Copies must be received by December 15. A certificate is awarded annually at the annual meeting. Established in 1962.

• 4464 • **Francis O. Deak Award**
To recognize a work of exceptional scholarship by a younger contributor to the *American Journal of International Law*. A monetary award of $350 is presented annually. Established in 1974 by Philip E. Cohen, president of the Institute for Continuing Education in Law and Librarianship. A second Frances O. Deak Award is presented by the International Law Students Association for the best article to appear in a student international law journal.

• 4465 • **Manley O. Hudson Medal**
For recognition of a distinguished person who has contributed to the scholarship and achievement of his or her time in international law. A gold medal and a certificate are awarded when merited. The winner is announced at the annual meeting. Established in 1956 by Ralph G. Albrecht in memory of Manley O. Hudson.

• 4466 •
American Society of Journalists and Authors
Brett Harvey, Exec.Dir.
1501 Broadway, Ste. 302
New York, NY 10036
Phone: (212)997-0947
Fax: (212)768-7414
E-mail: staff@asja.org
Home Page: http://www.asja.org
Formerly: (1975) Society of Magazine Writers.

• 4467 • **ASJA Outstanding Article Award**
To honor a Society member who has, during the preceding calendar year, published an article demonstrating excellence in nonfiction writing. The award is available only to members. Established in 1979. Formerly: Mort Weisinger Award.

• 4468 • **ASJA Outstanding Author Award**
To recognize a contemporary author who, through his or her nonfiction writing, has made a significant contribution to American culture and/or has exercised substantial influence over the way people think, feel, or behave. The recipient may have produced either a single book or a body of work (including writings produced during the preceding three years) that meets these criteria. The award is available only to members. Established in 1978. Formerly: Author of the Year Award.

• 4469 • **Conscience In Media Award**
To recognize individuals who have demonstrated outstanding commitment to the highest principles of journalism at notable personal cost or sacrifice. The award is available only to members. Nominations are made by the Professional Rights Committee. A medal is awarded at the discretion of the Society. Established in 1975.

• 4470 • **Open Book Awards**
To recognize those who have undertaken courageous personal actions to combat censorship of books. The award is available only to members. Nomination is made by the Professional Rights Committee of ASJA. A plaque is given at the discretion of the Committee. Established in 1983.

• 4471 •
American Society of Landscape Architects
Nancy C. Somerville, Exec.VP
636 Eye St. NW
Washington, DC 20001-3736
Phone: (202)898-2444
Toll-Free: 888-999-ASLA
Fax: (202)898-1185
E-mail: jlofton@asla.org
Home Page: http://www.asla.org/

• 4472 • **The ASLA Design Medal**
Recognizes an individual landscape architect who has produced a body of exceptional design work at a sustained level for a period of at least ten years. Landscape architects are eligible. A medal is awarded annually. Established in 2002.

• 4473 • **ASLA Medal**
Recognizes a landscape architect whose lifetime achievements and contributions to the profession have had a unique and lasting impact on the welfare of the public and the environment. All landscape architects are eligible. One medal is awarded annually. Established in 1971.

• 4474 • **ASLA President's Medal**
For recognition of unselfish and devoted service to ASLA at the national level over a period of five years. Members of the Society are eligible. A medal is awarded annually. Established in 1978.

• 4475 • **Community Service Award**
Recognizes pro bono public and community service over a sustained period of no less than five years. Individual landscape architects, landscape architecture firms, landscape architecture educational programs, or ASLA chapters are eligible. Selection is based on the impact on or relevance to landscape architecture, the public, and the environment, while demonstrating sound principles of landscape architecture. More than one awarded may be given annually. Established in 2002.

• 4476 • **Fellows Medal**
For recognition of outstanding contributions to the profession by excellence in works of landscape architecture, in administrative professional work in public agencies, in professional school instruction, in professional writing, or in direct service to the Society. Members of the Society for at least ten contiguous years are eligible. Medals are awarded annually.

• 4477 • **Honorary Member**
To recognize service to ASLA, significant contributions to the profession, or contributions to the environment either physically or through policy or education. Any non-landscape architect is eligible. Recipients are recognized at the annual meeting.

• 4478 • **Alfred B. LaGasse Medal**
Recognizes individuals who have made notable contributions to the management and conservancy of natural resources and/or public lands. Nominees in the Landscape Architect Category must be a landscape architect or hold a degree in landscape architecture and possess a minimum of ten years experience in the profession. Nominees in the Non-Landscape Architect Category must possess a minimum of five years in a position directly responsible for managing natural resources or public lands. No more than two medals are awarded annually; one toe a landscape architect and one to a non-landscape architect. Established in 1981 in honor of Alfred B. LaGasse, past executive director of the American Institute of Park Executives and executive vice president of the National Recreation and Parks Association.

• 4479 • **The Landmark Award**
Recognizes the significant contribution landscape architecture makes to the public realm, calls attention to the element of time in land-

scape architecture, and emphasizes the long-term benefits by the landscape architecture profession. Built projects that have been completed for not less than 15 years and not more than 50 years are eligible. Selection is based on the profound and enduring significance the project has held in its community; the substantial contribution it has made to the community's quality of life; and evidence that the project has remained consistent with or increased its level of importance since the project's completion. Awarded annually. Established in 1991.

• 4480 • The Landscape Architecture Film Award

Recognizes bodies of distinguished work influencing the professional practice of landscape architecture. Any firm or successor firms in which the continuing colleboration among individuals of the firm has been the principal force in consistently producing the distinguised landscape architecture for a period of at least 10 years are eligible. Members of the ASLA Executive Committee and their firms are not eligible. No more than one award is given annually. Established in 2002.

• 4481 • Landscape Architecture Medal of Excellence

Recognizes significant contributions to landscape architecture policy, research, education, project planning and design, or a combination of these items. The body of work must have been maintained at a consistent level of excellence for at least 10 years. Individuals, firms, programs, organizations, or agencies are eligible. One medal is awarded annually. Established in 1992.

• 4482 • National Student Competition

To recognize the best works of landscape architecture and research performed by students in three categories: Undergraduate, Graduate, and Graduate Research. Students in the last two years of study in landscape architecture at an accredited program are eligible. A written narrative must be provided as part of the submission providing background on the project that must submit as part of a traveling exhibit. Certificates, complimentary annual meeting registrations, and a display at the annual meeting are awarded annually.

• 4483 • Frederick Law Olmsted Medal

Recognizes environmental leadership, vision, and stewardship. Individuals, organizations, agencies, or programs outside the profession of landscape architecture are eligible. One medal is awarded annually. Established in 1990.

• 4484 • Professional Awards Program

The Design category recognizes specific works of landscape architecture, including urban design. Large incremental projects, with at least the first stage completed are eligible. Selection is based on the quality of design; functionality; context; environmental responsibility; and relevance to the profession, the public, and the environment. The Analysis and Planning category recognizes the wide variety of professional activities that lead to, guide, or evaluate landscape architecture design. The Research category recognizes projects that identify, examine, and address challenges and problems that are resolved using solutions of value to the profession. Selection is based on clarity and adequacy of execution of the needed five points, overall significance and relevance to the profession, and quality of the presentation. The Communications category recognizes achievements in communicating landscape architecture information, technology, theory, or practice to within or outside of the profession. Formerly: President's Award of Excellence, Honor and Merit.

• 4485 •

American Society of Law, Medicine and Ethics
Benjamin W. Moulton, Exec.Dir./Exec.VP
765 Commonwealth Ave., Ste. 1634
Boston, MA 02215
Phone: (617)262-4990
Phone: (617)437-7596
Fax: (617)437-7596
E-mail: info@aslme.org
Home Page: http://www.aslme.org

• 4486 • The Jay Healey Award

For recognition of outstanding contributions in the field of health law.

• 4487 • Presidents Award

For recognition of outstanding contributions to the fields of law and medicine.

• 4488 •

American Society of Limnology and Oceanography
Helen S. Lemay, Mgr.
5400 Bosque Blvd., Ste. 680
Waco, TX 76710-4446
Phone: (254)399-9635
Toll-Free: 800-929-ASLO
Fax: (254)776-3767
E-mail: business@aslo.org
Home Page: http://www.aslo.org

Formerly: Limnological Society of America.

• 4489 • G. Evelyn Hutchinson Award

To recognize continued excellence in research in any aspect of oceanography or limnology. ASLO members whose work was done in the preceding five years are considered for the award. A medal is presented annually at the June Meeting. Established in 1982 in honor of G. Evelyn Hutchinson.

• 4490 • R. Lindeman Award

To recognize excellence in an aquatic publication an outstanding paper by a scientist under the age of 36. Papers must deal with aquatic sciences, be written in English, and be published in a reviewed journal during the previous year. A medal is presented annually at the winter meeting. Established in 1986 in honor of R. Lindeman.

• 4491 •

American Society of Magazine Editors
Marlene Kahan, Exec. Dir.
810 7th Ave., 24th Fl.
New York, NY 10019
Phone: (212)872-3700
Fax: (212)906-0128
E-mail: asme@magazine.org
Home Page: http://asme.magazine.org

• 4492 • National Magazine Awards

For recognition of editorial excellence and to encourage editorial vitality, demonstrated by consistently superior performance in carrying out stated editorial objectives, innovative editorial techniques, journalistic enterprise, and compatibility and vigor in layout and design. Any magazine edited, published and sold in the United States may submit entries. To be considered a magazine, a publication must be issued at regular intervals at least four times per year and must be distributed or sold independently of other publications. Newspaper supplements, in-house company publications, newsletters, and foreign-language publications are not eligible. Awards are given in the following categories: General Excellence (in six circulation categories), Personal Service, Leisure Interests, Reporting, Feature Writing, Public Interest, Profile Writing, Columns and Commentary Design, Single-Topic Issue, Photography, Fiction, Essays, Reviews and Criticism, and General Excellence online. Any magazine published and sold in the United States may be considered for the award. The deadline for submission of entries is in January. A bronze plaque and a reproduction of Alexander Calder's stabile, "Elephant," are awarded annually in April. Established in 1966 by the American Society of Magazine Editors. Administered by Columbia University - Graduate School of Journalism.

• 4493 •

American Society of Mammalogists
Bruce D. Patterson, Contact
810 E 10th St.
PO Box 1897
Lawrence, KS 66044-1897
Phone: (785)843-1235
Toll-Free: 800-627-0629
Fax: (785)843-1274
E-mail: asm@allenpress.com
Home Page: http://www.mammalsociety.org/

• 4494 • American Society of Mammalogists Award

To recognize excellence in pre-doctoral research. Recipient must not have had the Ph.D. degree any earlier than the previous summer. A monetary prize of $500 is awarded annually.

• 4495 • B. Elizabeth Horner Award

To aid students in professional research. A monetary prize of $100 is awarded annually. Established in 1986.

• 4496 • Brazier Howell Award
To recognize excellence in pre-doctoral research. Recipient must not have had the Ph.D. degree any earlier than the previous summer. A monetary prize of $500 is awarded annually. Established in 1960.

• 4497 • Anna M. Jackson Award
To recognize excellence in pre-doctoral research. Recipient must not have had the Ph.D. degree any earlier than the previous summer. A monetary prize of $500 is awarded annually. Established in 1969.

• 4498 • Hartley H. T. Jackson Award
To honor members for long and outstanding service to the Society. A certificate is awarded annually. Established in 1977.

• 4499 • C. Hart Merriam Award
To honor recent contributions to mammalogy through research, teaching, and service. A bronze sculpture of a bison is awarded annually. Established in 1974.

• 4500 • Albert R. and Alma Shadle Fellowship
To promote a professional career in mammalogy by allowing the recipient greater freedom to pursue research. A monetary prize of $3,500 is awarded annually.

• 4501 •
American Society of Mechanical Engineers
Dr. William A. Weiblen, Pres.
3 Park Ave.
New York, NY 10016-5990
Phone: (973)882-1167
Phone: (212)591-7722
Toll-Free: 800-THE-ASME
Fax: (212)591-7674
E-mail: infocentral@asme.org
Home Page: http://www.asme.org

• 4502 • ASME Medal
For recognition of eminently distinguished engineering achievement. The nominations deadline is March 1. One ASME Medal may be awarded annually. A monetary award of $15,000, a gold medal, and a certificate are presented. Established in 1920.

• 4503 • Blackall Machine Tool and Gage Award
To recognize the author(s) of the best paper concerned with the design or application of machine tools, gages, or dimensional measuring instruments. The deadline is February 1. A monetary award of $1,000 (to be divided equally if there is more than one recipient) and a plaque are awarded annually. Established in 1954 by Frederick S. Blackall, Jr., Fellow and 72nd president of the Society.

• 4504 • Per Bruel Noise Control and Acoustics Medal
For recognition of eminent achievement and extraordinary merit in the field of noise control and acoustics. The achievement must include useful applications of the principles of Noise Control and Acoustics to the art and science of mechanical engineering. An honorarium of $1,000, a vermeil medal, a certificate, and travel expenses are awarded. Established in 1987.

• 4505 • Edwin F. Church Medal
To recognize the individual who has rendered eminent service in increasing the value, importance, and attractiveness of mechanical engineering education. Individuals of any age must be nominated by February 15. A monetary award of $2,500, a bronze medal embedded in Lucite, travel expenses, and a certificate are awarded annually. Established in 1972 from a bequest of Edwin F. Church, Jr.

• 4506 • John P. Davis Award
To recognize an individual for an outstanding gas turbine application paper. Papers published anywhere in the world are eligible. Authors are not restricted by nationality, age, profession, or membership in any engineering society or other organization. A monetary award and plaque are presented annually, when merited, at the annual conference. Established in 1985 to honor John P. Davis.

• 4507 • Dedicated Service Award
To honor unusual dedicated voluntary service to the Society marked by outstanding performance, demonstrated effective leadership, prolonged and committed service, devotion, enthusiasm, and faithfulness. Selected individuals who have a minimum of at least ten years service to the Society in one or more of the following areas are eligible: Sections/Regions/Member Affairs, Codes and Standards, Engineering, Public Affairs, Education, Committees reporting to the Board of Governors, and the ASME Auxiliary, Inc. Nominations must be submitted by December 1. A plaque, a lapel pen, and a certificate are awarded to no more than 54 individuals annually. Established in 1983.

• 4508 • William T. Ennor Manufacturing Technology Award
To recognize an individual or team of individuals for developing or contributing significantly to an innovative manufacturing technology, the implementation of which has resulted in substantial economic and/or societal benefits. Nominations must be submitted by February 1. A monetary award of $1,000, a vermeil medal, and a certificate are presented. Established in 1990 by the Production Engineering Division in conjunction with the Alcoa Company.

• 4509 • Fluids Engineering Award
To recognize outstanding contributions over a period of years to the engineering profession, and especially to the field of fluids engineering through research, practice, and/or teaching. Nominations must be submitted by September 30. A bronze medal, $1,000 honorarium, and a certificate are awarded. Established in 1968 by the Fluids Engineering Division.

• 4510 • Freeman Scholar Award
To recognize a person of wide experience in fluids engineering who will review a topic in his or her specialty (including a comprehensive statement of the state of the art) and suggest key future research needs. The recipient may be from industry, government, education, or private professional practice. The nominations deadline is February 1, in even-numbered years. An honorarium of $7,500, a certificate, and a travel allowance are awarded. Established in 1926.

• 4511 • Henry Laurence Gantt Medal
To recognize distinguished achievement in management as a service to the community. A medal is awarded annually. Established in 1929 to memorialize the accomplishments and service to the community by Henry Laurence Gantt, a distinguished management engineer, industrial leader, and humanitarian. Co-sponsored by The American Society of Mechanical Engineers.

• 4512 • Gas Turbine Award
To recognize the author(s) of the best paper concerned with the design of gas turbines and components, related problems, applications, and operations. The nominations deadline is January 1. An honorarium award of $1,000 (to be divided equally if there is more than one recipient) and a plaque are awarded annually. Established in 1963 by the Gas Turbine Division.

• 4513 • Melvin R. Green Codes and Standards Medal
To recognize meritorious contributions to the development of documents, objects, or devices used in any part of the national or international Society programs of technical codification, standardization, and certification. Individuals who have served on ASME Committees or American National Standards Committees or International Standards Technical Advisory Groups administered by ASME are considered. Nominations must be submitted by November 1. An honorarium prize of $1,000, a bronze medal, and certificate are awarded annually. Established in 1976. Formerly: (1997) Codes and Standards Medal.

• 4514 • Heat Transfer Memorial Award
To recognize an individual for outstanding contributions to the field of heat transfer through teaching, research, design, or publications. Selection is based on papers in an area of heat transfer or on a paper dealing with the science or art of heat transfer. Awards are made in the following categories: the science of heat transfer, the art of heat transfer, and the general subject of heat transfer. Nominations must be submitted by November 1. An honorarium of $500, a plaque, memorial booklet, and certificate are awarded annually. Established in 1959 as a Divisional award and elevated to a Society Award in 1974.

• 4515 • Mayo D. Hersey Award
To recognize an individual for outstanding and continued contributions to the field of lubrication science and engineering. The recipient need not a be member of ASME. Nominations may be submitted by February 1. A plaque and honorarium of $1,000 are awarded annually. Established in 1965 in honor of Mayo D. Hersey, a leader in lubrication science and engineering.

• 4516 • Henry Hess Award
To recognize the best original technical paper presented to or published by the Society during the year. Members of the Society under 31 years of age at the time of submission of the paper are eligible. The deadline is March 1. A monetary award of $1,000 and a certificate are awarded annually. Established in 1914. Formerly: (1964) Junior Award.

• 4517 • Holley Medal
To recognize an individual who, by some great and unique act(s) of an engineering nature, has accomplished a great and timely public benefit. Nominations must be submitted by March 1. An honorarium of $1,000, a vermeil medal, a lapel pin, and a certificate are awarded annually. Established in 1924 in honor of Alexander L. Holley, a charter member of the Society.

• 4518 • Soichiro Honda Medal
To recognize outstanding achievement or significant contributions in the field of personal transportation. The nomination deadline is February 1. A monetary award of $7,500, a gold medal, travel supplement, a certificate are awarded. Established in 1980 in honor of Honda's contribution to personal transportation. Sponsored by the Honda Motor Company.

• 4519 • Honorary Member
In recognition of distinguished service that contributes significantly to the attainment of the goals of the engineering profession. Honorary Membership has come to be regarded as recognition of a lifetime of service to engineering or related fields. The nomination deadline is March 1. Not more than five certificates, lapel pins, and badges are awarded annually. Established in 1880.

• 4520 • Hoover Medal
To honor engineers whose pre-eminent services have advanced the well-being of humanity and whose talents have been devoted to the development of a richer and more enduring civilization. Professional engineers are eligible. A gold medal and certificate are awarded annually when merited. Established in 1930. Jointly sponsored by the American Society of Mechanical Engineers, the American Institute of Mining, Metallurgical and Petroleum Engineers, and the Institute of Electrical and Electronics Engineers.

• 4521 • Internal Combustion Engine Award
To recognize eminent achievement or distinguished contributions in any phase of research or engineering of internal combustion engines. Citizens of the United States are eligible. The nomination deadline is February 1. An honorarium award of $1,000 (to be divided equally if there is more than one recipient) and a plaque are awarded annually. Established in 1966 by the Diesel and Gas Engine Power Division. Formerly: (1986) Diesel and Gas Engine Power Award.

• 4522 • International Gas Turbine Institute Scholar Award
To recognize an individual with a significant depth of knowledge in some aspect of gas turbine technology who will write a learned and comprehensive paper and present it as a lecture to an audience of his/her peers. The Scholar may be from industry, government, education or private professional practice and need not be a member of The American Society of Mechanical Engineers. Applications may be submitted by August 15. An honorarium of $7,500, a plaque and travel expenses are awarded annually. Established in 1989.

• 4523 • Max Jakob Memorial Award
To recognize eminent achievement or distinguished service in the area of heat transfer. A bronze plaque, certificate, and cash honorarium are presented. Established in 1961. In 1962 the award became a joint activity of the Society and the American Institute of Chemical Engineers.

• 4524 • James N. Landis Medal
To recognize personal performance related to designing, constructing, or managing the operation of major steam-powered electric stations using nuclear or fossil fuels, and for personal leadership in some humanitarian pursuit that may include committee activity, selection leadership, or the broad non-technical professional activity in the nominee's engineering society. Nominations must be submitted by February 1. A monetary award of $5,000, a bronze medal, a certificate, and a travel allowance are awarded annually. Established in 1977 in honor of James N. Landis, President of ASME in 1958.

• 4525 • Bernard F. Langer Nuclear Codes and Standards Award
To recognize an individual(s) who has contributed to the nuclear power plant industry through the development and promotion of ASME Nuclear Codes and Standards or the ASME Nuclear Certificate Program. The nomination deadline is February 1. An honorarium of $1,000, a crystal oracle, and a certificate are awarded annually. Established in 1977 in honor of Bernard F. Langer, who was instrumental in the development of the rules for nuclear vessels.

• 4526 • Gustus L. Larson Award
For recognition of outstanding achievement in mechanical engineering in over twenty years following graduation. Nominations are accepted by February 1. A monetary award of $1,000, a travel allowance, and a certificate are awarded annually. Established in 1974 in honor of Gustus L. Larson, ASME Fellow and founder of Pi Tau Sigma at Wisconsin.

• 4527 • H. R. Lissner Award
To recognize an individual for outstanding contributions in the area of bioengineering. Nominations may be submitted by November 1. An honorarium of $1,000, a certificate, and travel expenses are awarded. Established in 1988 to honor H. R. Lissner for his pioneering contributions in biomechanical research.

• 4528 • Machine Design Award
To recognize distinguished service or eminent achievement in the field of machine design. The deadline for nominations is February 1. An honorarium of $1,000, a plaque, and a certificate are awarded annually. Established in 1958.

• 4529 • Charles T. Main Awards
To recognize a student member whose leadership and service qualities have contributed over a period of more than one year to the program and operation of a Student Section of the Society. Nominations must be submitted by March 1. The following prizes are awarded: first place - a monetary award of $3,000 and a silver medal; and second place - $2,000 and a bronze medal. A certificate and travel expenses are awarded for both prizes. Established in 1919 and combined with the Arthur L. Williston Medal Contest in 1971. Given in honor of Charles T. Main, the 37th President of ASME.

• 4530 • Melville Medal
This, the highest ASME honor, is given for the best current original paper not previously published elsewhere. The paper must have been presented before ASME or approved for publication by ASME during the two calendar years preceding the year of the award. One of the authors must be a member of the Society. Nominations must be submitted by March 1. A monetary award of $2,000, a bronze medal, and a certificate are awarded annually. Travel expenses to the presentation ceremony are provided. Established in 1914 by the bequest of Admiral George W. Melville, Honorary Member and the 18th President of the Society; first awarded in 1927.

• 4531 • M. Eugene Merchant Manufacturing Medal
To recognize significant efforts in improving the productivity and efficiency of manufacturing operation(s). Established in 1986.

• 4532 • Nadai Medal
To recognize distinguished contributions to the field of engineering materials, particularly in the area of plasticity. The deadline is December 1. A monetary award of $1,000, a plaque, and a certificate are awarded annually. Established in 1975 to honor Arpard L. Nadai, a pioneer in the field of engineering materials who contributed to the field of plasticity.

• 4533 • Burt L. Newkirk Award
To recognize notable contributions to the field of tribology in research and development as established by a paper accepted for publication in the *ASME Journal on Lubrication*. Authors who

have not passed their 35th birthday on July 1 of the year in which the award is conferred are eligible. The deadline is February 1. A $1,000 monetary award, and a certificate are awarded annually. Established in 1975 in honor of Burt L. Newkirk, who made notable achievements in the theory and application of tribology.

• 4534 • Percy Nicholls Award

To recognize notable scientific or industrial achievement in the field of solid fuels. Established in 1942. Awarded jointly by the American Society of Mechanical Engineers and the American Institute of Mechanical Engineers.

• 4535 • Old Guard Prizes

To recognize the three best presentations of technical papers at the National Contest during the ASME Winter annual meeting. This National Contest is between the student members who won first prize at each Regional Student Conference. All contestants win an expense paid trip to the Winter Annual Meeting. The winners of the four best papers receive the following prizes: first prize - $2,000; second prize - $1,500; third prize - $1,000; and fourth prize - $500. Certificates and travel expenses are also presented. Established in 1956.

• 4536 • Rufus Oldenburger Medal

In recognition of an individual for significant contributions and outstanding achievements in the field of automatic control. The nominations deadline is February 1. A monetary award of $2,000, a bronze medal, and certificate are awarded annually. Established in 1968.

• 4537 • Performance Test Codes Medal

To recognize an individual(s) for outstanding contributions to the development and promotion of ASME Performance Test Codes, including the Supplements on Instruments and Apparatus, and to recognize the first voluntary codes and standards activity in the Society and in the United States. The nomination deadline is January 1. An honorarium of $1,000, a bronze medal, and a certificate are presented. Established in 1981.

• 4538 • Pi Tau Sigma Gold Medal

To recognize outstanding achievement in mechanical engineering in up to ten years following graduation. Nominations are accepted by February 1. A monetary award of $1,000, a gold medal, a certificate, and travel expenses are awarded annually. Established in 1938 by Pi Tau Sigma, Honorary Mechanical Engineering Fraternity.

• 4539 • James Harry Potter Gold Medal

To recognize eminent achievement or distinguished service in the appreciation of the science of thermodynamics in mechanical engineering. The basis of the award includes contributions involving the teaching, appreciation, or utilization of thermodynamic principles in research, development, and design in mechanical engineering. The nomination deadline is February 1. A monetary award of $1,500, a vermeil medal, and a certificate are awarded annually. Established in 1980.

• 4540 • Pressure Vessel and Piping Award

To recognize outstanding contributions in the field of pressure vessel and piping technology including, but not limited to, research, development, teaching, and significant advancements of the state of the art. The nomination deadline is July 15. A monetary award of $1,000, a bronze medal, and certificate are awarded annually. Established in 1980 by the Pressure Vessel and Piping Division.

• 4541 • Prime Movers Committee Award

To recognize the author(s) of the best published paper concerning thermal electric station practice or equipment. The nominations deadline is February 1. A $1,000 honorarium and a certificate are awarded annually. Established in 1954 by the Prime Movers Committee of Edison Electric Institute.

• 4542 • Charles Russ Richards Memorial Award

To recognize an individual for outstanding achievement in mechanical engineering twenty years or more following graduation. The nomination deadline is February 1. A monetary award of $1,000, a certificate, and travel expenses are awarded annually. Established in 1944 by Pi Tau Sigma in memory of Charles Russ Richards, the founder of Pi Tau Sigma at the University of Illinois, former head of mechanical engineering, and Dean of Engineering at the University of Illinois.

• 4543 • Ralph Coats Roe Medal

To recognize an individual who has contributed most effectively to a better understanding and appreciation of the engineer's worth to contemporary society. The deadline for nominations is December 1. A monetary prize of $10,000, a gold medal, a certificate, and travel expenses are awarded annually. Established in 1972 in honor of Ralph Coats Roe, a pioneer and innovator in the design and construction of highly efficient power plants and advanced desalting processes.

• 4544 • Safety Codes and Standards Medal

To recognize one or more individuals who have contributed to the enhancement of public safety through the development and promotion of ASME Codes and Standards or the ASME Safety Accreditation Activity. Nominations must be submitted by January 1. An honorarium of $1,000, a bronze medal, and a certificate are awarded. Established in 1986.

• 4545 • R. Tom Sawyer Award

To recognize distinguished contributions to the field of gas turbines and to the International Gas Turbine Institute over a substantial period of time. The nomination deadline is March 1. An honorarium of $1,000, a plaque, and certificate are awarded annually. Established in 1972 to honor R. Tom Sawyer who, for four decades, toiled zealously to advance gas turbine technology in all of its aspects.

• 4546 • Ben C. Sparks Medal

To recognize a mechanical engineering or mechanical engineering technology educator for eminent service to ASME and contributions to engineering education and/or engineering technology education. Nominations must be submitted by October 15. A monetary award of $1,000, a bronze medal, and a certificate are awarded annually. Established in 1990 to honor Ben C. Sparks, a devoted member of ASME, and a dedicated teacher of mechanical engineering technology and mechanical engineering.

• 4547 • Spirit of St. Louis Medal

To recognize an individual for meritorious service in the advancement of aeronautics and astronautics. The award is not limited to members of ASME. Nominations must be submitted by February 1. An honorarium of $1,000, a vermeil medal, and a certificate are awarded annually. Established in 1929 by Phillip D. Ball, ASME members, and citizens of St. Louis, Missouri.

• 4548 • Student Section Advisor Award

To recognize a current or former outstanding faculty advisor whose leadership and service qualities have contributed, for a period of at least three years, to the program and operations of a Student Section of the Society. Nominations must be submitted by February 1. A monetary award of $1,000, a silver medal, and a certificate are presented. Established in 1990.

• 4549 • J. Hall Taylor Medal

To recognize distinguished service or eminent achievement in the field of codes and standards pertaining to the broad fields of piping and pressure vessels. Preference is given to members of ASME. The nomination deadline is November 1. A monetary award of $1,000, a bronze medal in acrylic block, and a certificate are awarded annually. Established in 1965 by Taylor Forge and Pipe works to honor J. Hall Taylor, a pioneer in the field of standardization of industrial products and safety codes and their usage.

• 4550 • Timoshenko Medal

To recognize distinguished contributions to applied mechanics. The nomination deadline is November 1. An honorarium of $1,000, a bronze medal, and a certificate are awarded annually. Established in 1957 to honor Stephen Timoshenko, an author and teacher of applied mechanics.

• 4551 • Worcester Reed Warner Medal

To recognize an outstanding contribution to permanent engineering literature. The paper or book must be at least five years old to be eligible. Contributions may be single papers, treatises or books, or a series of papers. They must deal with progressive ideas relative to engineering, scientific, and industrial research associated with mechanical engineering; the design and operation of mechanical and associated equipment; industrial engineering or management, organization, operation, and the concomitants of each; or other subjects closely associated with the foregoing. The nomination deadline is March 1. A monetary award of $2,000, a gold medal, and a certificate are awarded annually. Established in 1930 by a bequest of Worcester Reed Warner, a charter member and 16th president of the Society.

• 4552 • George Westinghouse Medals

To recognize eminent achievement or distinguished service in the power field of mechanical engineering. Considering power in the broad sense, selection is based on contributions of utilization, application, design, development, research, and the organization of such activities in the power field. Candidates are not restricted by profession or by membership in any engineering society or organization. Nominations must be submitted by February 1. The following awards are presented annually: a monetary award of $1,500 and a vermeil medal; a monetary award of $1,000, a silver medal, and a certificate. The silver medal is bestowed upon one who is not yet 41 years old on June 30 of the year in which the medal is awarded. The vermeil medal was established in 1952, and the silver medal in 1971 by the Westinghouse Educational Foundation in honor of George Westinghouse, Honorary Member and 29th President of the Society.

• 4553 • Arthur L. Williston Medal

To recognize the best paper or thesis by an undergraduate or junior engineer fostering a spirit of civic service. Nominations must be submitted by March 1. The following prizes are awarded: first prize $1,000, a bronze medal, travel expenses, and a certificate; second prize $500 and a certificate; and third prize - $250 and a certificate. Established in 1954 by Arthur L. Williston, ASME Member.

• 4554 • Henry R. Worthington Medal

To recognize an individual for eminent achievement in the field of pumping machinery in the areas of research, development, design, innovation, management, education, or literature. The nomination deadline is February 1. A monetary award of $5000, a scholarship of $1000, a bronze medal, and a certificate are awarded annually. Established in 1980 by Worthington Pump, Inc.

• 4555 •

American Society of Mining & Reclamation
Margaret Dunn, Pres.
3134 Montavesta Rd.
Lexington, KY 40502
Phone: (859)335-6529
Fax: (859)335-6529
E-mail: asmr@insightbb.com
Home Page: http://ces.ca.uky.edu/asmr

• 4556 • William T. Plass Award

This, the most prestigious award of the Society, recognizes contributions in the areas of mining, teaching, research, and/or regulating authority as they relate to land reclamation. Individuals involved in reclamation for a minimum of 10 years are eligible, but it is not required that they be actively involved at the time of their nomination. Those nominated should be recognized nationally and internationally for their contributions in the field and should have contributed to this field for a significant portion of their career. A plaque is awarded when merited. Established in 1990 in honor of William T. Plass for his accomplishments in land reclamation and leadership in developing the national and international standing of the Society.

• 4557 • Reclamation Researcher of the Year

To recognize research scientists who have made substantive contributions to the advancement of reclamation science and/or technology, or contributed meaningful information relating to the economic, social, environmental, or ecological effects of surface mining. Nominees must be or have been active in some areas of reclamation at the time of their nomination. A plaque is awarded annually. Established in 1984.

• 4558 • Reclamationist of the Year

To recognize individuals demonstrating outstanding accomplishments in the application or evaluation of reclamation technology. Nominee must have been active in some area of reclamation at the time of nomination. A plaque is awarded annually. Established in 1984.

• 4559 •

American Society of Music Arrangers and Composers
Scherr Lillico, Dir.
PO Box 17840
Encino, CA 91416
Phone: (818)994-4661
Fax: (818)994-6181
E-mail: properimage2000@earthlink.net
Home Page: http://www.asmac.org

• 4560 • Golden Score Award

For recognition of continued excellence and achievement in the arts of music composing, arranging, and orchestrating. Nominations may be made by the Board of Directors based on the length of professional career and maintenance of high standards. A plaque is awarded annually. Established in 1982.

• 4561 •

American Society of Naturalists
Dr. Mary E. Power, Pres.
PO Box 37005
Chicago, IL 60637
Phone: (773)753-3347
Fax: (773)753-0811
E-mail: subscriptions@press.uchicago.edu
Home Page: http://www.amnat.org

• 4562 • President's Award

To recognize the best paper published in *The American Naturalist* during the previous year. An honorarium of $1,000 is awarded.

• 4563 • Sewall Wright Award

To recognize a senior-level active researcher for significant and continuous contributions to the objectives of the Society. A monetary prize of $1,000 is awarded at the annual banquet. Established in 1991.

• 4564 • Young Investigators' Prizes

To recognize outstanding and promising work by investigators who have received their doctorate in the preceding three years or who are in their final year of graduate school. Awarded at the Society's annual meeting.

• 4565 •

American Society of Naval Engineers
Capt. Dennis K. Kruse CAE, Exec.Dir.
1452 Duke St.
Alexandria, VA 22314
Phone: (703)836-6727
Fax: (703)836-7491
E-mail: asnehq@navalengineers.org
Home Page: http://www.navalengineers.org

• 4566 • Gold Medal Award

To recognize significant contribution to navel engineering through personal effort. Individuals are eligible. Contribution must have been made within the past five years. American citizens are eligible. A gold medal, citation, and life membership certificate are awarded annually. Established in 1958.

• 4567 • Jimmy Hamilton Award

To recognize the author(s) of the best original technical paper published during the year in the *Naval Engineers Journal*. A plaque and a citation are awarded annually. Established in 1967.

• 4568 • Claud A. Jones Fleet Engineer Award

Recognizes significant contribution to improving operational engineering or material readiness of our maritime forces. Field and fleet engineers are eligible. Contribution must have been made with the past three years of nomination. The award is limited to United States personnel directly involved in the total repair effort and/or engineering operations of ships or support facilities. An embedded medallion mounted on a stand and a citation are awarded annually at ASNE Day (annual convention). Established in 1987 to honor RADM Claude A. Jones, USN, who was awarded the Medal of Honor as Engineer Officer, USS Tennessee, when she was wrecked by a tidal wave on August 29, 1916.

• 4569 • Frank G. Law Award

To recognize an individual member of the society who has made outstanding and long term significant contributions through individual efforts or by the direction of others to the society resulting in betterment of the society operations, advancement of the objectives of the society, and of increase in the professional stature of the society. The nominee must have demonstrated leadership, selfless dedication, effective contribution and personal commitment in support of society interest, goals, and ideals over a number of years. A plaque and citation certificate are awarded annually. Established in 1980 to recognize the years of selfless dedication of Captain Frank G. Law, U.S. Navy (RET) in service to the society during his tenure as Secretary-Treasurer.

• 4570 • **Harold E. Saunders Award**
To recognize the individual whose reputation in naval engineering spans a long career of notable achievement and influence. American citizens are eligible. An embedded medallion mounted on a stand, a citation, and a life membership certificate are awarded annually. Established in 1977.

• 4571 • **Solberg Award**
To recognize the most significant contribution to naval engineering through personal research. American citizens are eligible. Research must have been conducted within the past three years. A plaque, citation, and a life membership certificate are awarded annually. Established in 1967.

• 4572 •
American Society of Neuroimaging
Rohit Bakshi MD, Pres.
5841 Cedar Lake Rd., No. 204
Minneapolis, MN 55416
Phone: (952)545-6291
Fax: (952)545-6073
E-mail: asn@llmsi.com
Home Page: http://www.asnweb.org

• 4573 • **William M. McKinney Award**
For recognition of outstanding clinical research in the area of neurosonology. The manuscript must be based on clinical research in these forms of imaging as applied to the practice of neurology or neurosurgery. Residents, medical students, or fellows in pediatrics, neurology, or neurosurgery must submit manuscripts by November 15. An honorarium of $500 and travel to the annual meeting are awarded each year. Established in 1987 in honor of William M. McKinney, M.D., for his outstanding work in the area of neurosonography.

• 4574 • **William H. Oldendorf Award**
For recognition of outstanding clinical research in the field of neuroimaging. Manuscripts may be submitted by medical students, residents, or fellows in pediatrics, neurology, or neurosurgery. The manuscript must be based on clinical research in computerized tomography, nuclear magnetic resonance, or PET scanning as applied to the practice of neurology or neurosurgery. A $500 honorarium and travel to the annual meeting are presented each year. Established in 1981 in honor of William H. Oldendorf, M.D., for his outstanding contributions to the field of neuroimaging.

• 4575 •
American Society of Newspaper Editors
Scott Bosley, Exec.Dir.
11690B Sunrise Valley Dr.
Reston, VA 20191-1409
Phone: (703)453-1122
Fax: (703)453-1133
E-mail: asne@asne.org
Home Page: http://www.asne.org

• 4576 • **Distinguished Writing Award in Commentary/Column Writing**
To recognize any writing that expresses a personal point of view: columns, criticism, and other forms of journalism opinion. A prize of $2,500 is awarded annually. Formerly: Commentary/Column Writing.

• 4577 • **Distinguished Writing Award in Editorial Writing**
To recognize editorials, signed or unsigned, written by one individual that speak for the newspaper. A prize of $2,500 is awarded annually.

• 4578 • **Distinguished Writing Award in Local Watchdog Reporting**
To recognize outstanding work done by newspapers that holds important local institutions accountable for their actions. The work must be anchored within the community—reports from overseas or national reporting does not qualify. A prize of $2,500 is awarded annually. Formerly: .

• 4579 • **Distinguished Writing Award in Non-Deadline Writing**
To recognize any writing not accomplished on deadline (except commentary), from any section of the newspaper. This category may include investigative and news-related material as well as any material under the general category of features: profiles, trend stories, lifestyle, and travel articles. A prize of $2,500 is awarded annually. Formerly: Non-Deadline Writing.

• 4580 • **Jesse Laventhol Prizes for Deadline News Reporting**
To recognize breaking news events covered under deadline pressure. Entries will be evaluated in terms of descriptive power and literary style, depth and breadth of reporting, timeliness, completeness, and perspective. One award for an individual and one award for a team ($10,000 each) are presented annually.

• 4581 •
American Society of Orthopedic Professionals
PO Box 7440
Seminole, FL 33775
Phone: (727)394-1700
E-mail: cbarocas@asop.org
Home Page: http://www.asop.org

• 4582 • **Orthopedic Allied Professional of the Year**
For lifetime achievement. Recognition is given annually.

• 4583 •
American Society of Pharmacognosy
Jim McAlpine, Pres.
PO Box 28665
Scottsdale, AZ 85255-0161
Phone: (623)572-3500
Fax: (480)513-2782
E-mail: mcalpine@ecopiabio.com
Home Page: http://www.phcog.org

• 4584 • **American Society of Pharmacognosy Awards and Grants**
To recognize individuals in pharmacognosy and to stimulate interest in all phases of natural products research. The following awards are presented: (1) Research Starter Grants - members of the Society who are within the first five years of assuming their first professional position are eligible for a grant of $2,000 to $5,000 to aid in their research; (2) Travel Grants for Active Members - members of the Society who are within the first five years of assuming their first professional position are eligible for a grant of $300 to $500 to enable them to present a paper at an annual meeting of the Society; (3) Travel Grants for Graduate Students - graduate students working under supervision of a Society member are eligible for a grant of $300 to $500 to enable them to present a paper at an annual meeting of the Society; and (4) Undergraduate Research Awards undergraduate students interested in investigating a career in natural products research are eligible for a research award to study under the direction of a Society Member on the faculty of an American college or university. Monetary awards of $2,000 to the student and $500 to the advisor are presented.

• 4585 •
American Society of Plant Biologists
Dr. Crispin Taylor, Exec.Dir.
15501 Monona Dr.
Rockville, MD 20855-2768
Phone: (301)251-0560
Fax: (301)279-2996
E-mail: info@aspb.org
Home Page: http://www.aspb.org

• 4586 • **Charles Reid Barnes Life Membership Award**
To recognize outstanding work in plant physiology. Life membership in the society is awarded annually. Established in 1925 to honor Dr. Charles Reid Barnes, the first professor of plant physiology at the University of Chicago.

• 4587 • **Adolph E. Gude, Jr. Award**
To recognize a scientist or lay person residing in North America for outstanding service to the science of plant physiology. Nominations may be made by any of the five sections of the society or by the executive committee. A certificate is awarded at least triennially at the annual meeting. Established in 1981 to honor the Gude family, who established the Gude Plant Science Center.

• 4588 • Stephen Hales Prize
To recognize a resident of North America who has served the science of plant physiology in some noteworthy manner. A monetary prize is awarded biennially in even-numbered years. Established in 1927 to honor Stephen Hales, who published *Vegetable Staticks* in 1727.

• 4589 • Dennis Robert Hoagland Award
To recognize distinguished research in the application of plant physiology to agricultural science. Awarded at the annual meeting of the society. Established in 1985 in honor of the noted plant physiologist, Dennis Robert Hoagland. Sponsored by Monsanto Agricultural Products Company.

• 4590 • Charles F. Kettering Award
To recognize an individual for an outstanding contribution to the field of photosynthesis. A monetary prize is awarded biennially in even-numbered years. Established in 1962 and funded by a grant from the Charles F. Kettering Foundation.

• 4591 • Charles Albert Shull Award
To recognize outstanding investigations in the field of plant physiology. Scientists residing in North America who are under 40 years of age or less than ten years from earning a doctoral degree are eligible. A monetary prize and a certificate are awarded biennially in odd-numbered years. Established in 1971 to honor Dr. Charles A. Shull, whose personal interest and support were largely responsible for the founding and early growth of the society.

• 4592 •
American Society of Plant Taxonomists
Linda Brown, Bus.Off.Man.
Department of Botany 3165
University of Wyoming
1000 E University Ave.
Laramie, WY 82071
Phone: (307)766-2556
Phone: (307)766-2380
Fax: (307)766-2851
E-mail: aspt@uwyo.edu
Home Page: http://www.sysbot.org

• 4593 • George R. Cooley Award
To recognize the best paper presented at the Society's annual meeting. A monetary prize of $500 is awarded annually. Established in 1956.

• 4594 • Graduate Student Research Grant
To support competitive research in systemic botany by graduate students. Several grants are awarded each year.

• 4595 • Asa Gray Award
To recognize outstanding service in the field of botanical systematics. A plaque is presented annually. The awardee need not be a member of the society. Established in 1983.

• 4596 • Peter Raven Award
Honors exceptional efforts at outreach to non-scientists. Plant systematists are eligible. A plaque is awarded annually.

• 4597 •
American Society of Psychoanalytic Physicians
Christine Cotter, Exec.Sec.
13528 Wisteria Dr.
Germantown, MD 20874
Phone: (301)540-3197
Fax: (301)540-3511
E-mail: cfcotter@yahoo.com
Home Page: http://pubweb.northwestern.edu/~chessick/aspp.htm

Formerly: (1985) American Society of Physician Analysts.

• 4598 • Sigmund Freud Award
To honor those people who have advanced psychoanalytical work. Individuals may be nominated by members of the society. A plaque is presented at the annual meeting dinner. Established in 1969.

• 4599 •
American Society of Psychopathology of Expression
Dr. Irene Jakab, Pres.
74 Lawton St.
Brookline, MA 02446
Phone: (617)738-9821
Fax: (617)975-0411

• 4600 • Ernst Kris Prize
For recognition of outstanding scholarly research and for innovative clinical and educational work in the field of psychopathology of expression. A medal is awarded every two to three years. Established in 1973 in honor of Ernst Kris, psychoanalyst and art historian.

• 4601 •
American Society of Safety Engineers
Fred Fortman, Exec.Dir.
1800 E. Oakton St.
Des Plaines, IL 60018
Phone: (847)699-2929
Fax: (847)768-3434
E-mail: customerservice@asse.org
Home Page: http://www.asse.org

• 4602 • American Society of Safety Engineers Fellow
This, the Society's highest honor, is bestowed on its professional members who demonstrate the highest levels of achievement and service to the Society and the safety profession. The selection is voted on by the Society Board of Directors upon recommendation of the Fellow Review Committee. A medal and plaque are awarded annually. Established in 1961.

• 4603 • Charles V. Culbertson Outstanding Volunteer Service Award
To recognize one or more national ASSE Board members, division administrators, committee/task group members, or chairmen for distinguished or superior service to the Society. An engraved clock is awarded annually. Established in 1981 in memory of Charles V. Culbertson, the late Vice President of Loss Prevention at the Marriott Corporation and Vice President of Communications on the Board of Directors of ASSE.

• 4604 • Honorary Member
To recognize prominent citizens for significant contributions to the Society and/or safety profession through legislation, research, scientific activities, or government service. A mounted or engraved certificate and publicity are awarded. Established in 1946.

• 4605 • Mine Safety Appliance Company Student Section Scholarship Award
To provide a scholarship to a college/university where the outstanding ASSE Student Section is located. Sections are judged for Society, campus and community involvement, professionalism, and service to members. Awarded annually. Established in 1982. Co-sponsored by Mine Safety Appliances Company. Formerly: Tenneco Student Section Scholarship Award.

• 4606 • *Professional Safety* Paper Awards
To recognize outstanding professional papers published in the Society's journal, *Professional Safety*, and to stimulate the acquisition of knowledge and its interchange among members of the safety profession. A joint VOS-ASSE five-member judging panel evaluates papers each six months. Authors must be members of the Society or of Veterans of Safety. The following prizes are awarded: first prize - $600; second prize - $500; and third prize - $400. Awarded annually. Established in 1965 and co-sponsored by the Veterans of Safety.

• 4607 • Edgar Monsanto Queeny Safety Professional of the Year Award
This, the Society's second highest honor, recognizes a Society member with significant accomplishments and contributions in the broad field of occupational safety and health within the past five years as selected by the Awards and Honors Review Committee. Criteria for selection include: demonstrated technical expertise in the field of safety; thorough knowledge of the operational aspects of safety employment; and professional contributions to advance the safety profession, such as fostering professional development, public or community services, instructor at educational institutions, involvement in codes and legislation, articles written, and work with allied groups. A $1,000 honorarium and a statuette are presented annually at the Society's annual Professional Development Conference. In addition, Regional Safety Professional of the Year and Divisions Safety Professional of the Year awards are presented. Established in 1979

Awards are arranged in alphabetical order below their administering organizations

by Edgar Monsanto Queeny. Sponsored by the Monsanto Company.

• 4608 •
American Society of Safety Engineers, Arkansas/Louisiana/Texas Chapter
Ray A. Tabor, Membership Chm.
7104 Williams Rd.
Keithville, LA 71047
Phone: (318)925-6207
Fax: (318)925-6208
E-mail: ratabor@aol.com

• 4609 • **Safety Professionals of the Year**
For nomination by peers-based on safety accomplishment. Recognition award bestowed annually.

• 4610 •
American Society of Sanitary Engineering
Shannon Corcoran, Exec.Dir.
901 Canterbury, Ste. A
Westlake, OH 44145
Phone: (440)835-3040
Fax: (440)835-3488
E-mail: info@asse-plumbing.org
Home Page: http://www.asse-plumbing.org/

• 4611 • **Henry B. Davis Award**
To recognize an individual who has contributed the most toward the advancement of sanitation in accord with the ideals of the Society. Members only are eligible. Awarded annually.

• 4612 • **Dewey R. Dedrick, Jr. Award**
To recognize the Society chapter that has the best performance for the year. Awarded annually.

• 4613 • **Fellow of the A.S.S.E.**
To recognize outstanding contributions by members who have served in an exemplary manner at both the local and national levels. A certificate is awarded annually. Established in 1980.

• 4614 •
American Society of Swedish Engineers
Ulf Hammarskjold, Pres.
780 3rd Ave.
King of Prussia, PA 19406-1410
Phone: (610)265-1939
Fax: (610)265-4608

• 4615 • **American Society of Swedish Engineers Award**
For recognition of outstanding scholastic achievement in the technical and scientific field. Graduating seniors at a technical college, university, or school in the United States and Sweden are eligible. A monetary award of $1,000, and a letter or certificate are awarded in the United States, and 5,000 kronor in Sweden are awarded annually, alternately in the United States and Sweden. Established in 1947.

• 4616 • **John Ericsson Medal Award**
For recognition of outstanding achievements in the technical and scientific fields. Nominations may be made by recognized scientific, industrial, or engineering organizations by September 1. Recommendation to the Board is made by a committee of eight, consisting of two groups of four members each; one group of members of the American Society of Swedish Engineers and the other of members of the Swedish Academy of Engineering Science. Swedish citizens or persons of Swedish extraction residing in the United States or Canada are eligible. A gold medal is awarded every two years alternately in Sweden and United States on February 11, the anniversary of the Society. Established in 1926 in memory of the Swedish born American inventor and engineer, Captain John Ericsson, who designed the Monitor for the U.S. Navy, its first iron-clad warship.

• 4617 • **Honorary Member**
To recognize individuals for outstanding accomplishments. Awarded occasionally when merited.

• 4618 •
American Society of Transportation and Logistics
Laurie P. Hein, Exec.Dir.
1700 N Moore St., Ste. 1900
Arlington, VA 22209
Phone: (703)524-5011
Fax: (703)524-5017
E-mail: astl@nitl.org
Home Page: http://www.astl.org

Formerly: (1983) American Society of Traffic and Transportation.

• 4619 • **Award for Best Exam**
To recognize the highest score on the Society's written examination series each year. A plaque is awarded annually. Established in 1976. Formerly: Award for Outstanding Candidate.

• 4620 • **Award for Outstanding Research Paper**
To recognize the best research paper written during the year. A plaque is awarded annually. Established in 1976.

• 4621 • **Outstanding Transportation & Logistics Executive in North America**
To recognize the executive and/or educator whose innovative contributions have had a profound impact on the industry.

• 4622 • **The Partnership Award**
To recognize two or more organizations that have worked together to improve service, production and logistics in a unique manner. The award is open to all types of partnerships. Cosponsored by *Distribution Magazine*.

• 4623 •
American Society of Travel Agents
William A. Maloney CTC, Exec.VP & COO
1101 King St., Ste. 200
Alexandria, VA 22314
Phone: (703)739-2782
Toll-Free: 800-440-2782
Fax: (703)684-8319
E-mail: askasta@astahq.com
Home Page: http://www.astanet.com

Formerly: (1931) American Steamship and Tourist Agents Association.

• 4624 • **Allied Member Award**
To recognize an Allied member who has made significant contributions to the advancement of the travel agency community and the industry it serves. A crystal trapezoid created by Tiffany & Company is presented annually at the World Travel Congress. Established in 1986.

• 4625 • **Melva C. Pederson, CTC Award**
To recognize an individual for extraordinary journalistic achievement in the field of travel. Established in 1988 and first presented at the 1988 ASTA World Travel Congress in Budapest, Hungary. The award was inspired by ASTA travel agent and journalist Melva C. Pederson, whose spirited writing articulated the travel agent point of view and the evolution of the travel agent profession.

• 4626 • **Travel Agent of the Year Award**
To recognize the travel agent who has made the greatest contribution to the travel industry, and whose outstanding influence and activity have advanced the professional status of the agency business. A crystal piece is presented annually at the World Travel Congress. Established in 1970 in memory of Joseph W. Rosenbluth, a dedicated member of ASTA. Formerly: Joseph W. Rosenbluth Memorial Travel Agent of the Year Award; Joseph W. Rosenbluth Memorial Award.

• 4627 • **Travel Hall of Fame**
To recognize those individuals whose careers have made a longstanding impact on the development and expansion of the travel and tourism industry. Individuals from any domestic or international segment of the travel industry who have contributed significantly to the travel or tourism industry are eligible. Current national or local officers may not be nominated.

• 4628 •
American Society of Tropical Medicine and Hygiene
Peter F. Weller, Pres.-Elect
60 Revere Dr., Ste. 500
Northbrook, IL 60062
Phone: (847)480-9592
Fax: (847)480-9282
E-mail: astmh@astmh.org
Home Page: http://www.astmh.org

• 4629 • Bailey K. Ashford Medal
For recognition of distinguished work in the field of tropical medicine. Customarily, the award is given to an individual who is not more than 45 years of age on the first day of the year in which the award is made. The selection committee is composed of the three immediate past presidents of the Society. A certificate and an inscribed medal are awarded every three years on a rotating basis with the other awards of the Society. Established in 1941 by Eli Lilly and Company.

• 4630 • Ben Kean Medal
To recognize a clinician or educator whose dedication to clinical tropical medicine and impact on the training of students, fellows and/or practitioners of tropical medicine is in keeping with the tradition. Established by Dr. Kean.

• 4631 • Joseph Augustin LePrince Medal
For recognition of outstanding work in the field of malariology. The selection committee is composed of the three immediate past presidents of the Society. A certificate and an inscribed medal are awarded every three years on a rotating basis with the other awards of the Society. Established in 1951 by the National Malaria Society.

• 4632 • Walter Reed Medal
For recognition of distinguished accomplishment in the field of tropical medicine. The selection committee is composed of the three immediate past presidents of the Society. A certificate and an inscribed medal are awarded every three years on a rotating basis with the other awards of the Society. Established in 1936.

• 4633 • Fred L. Soper Lecture
To provide for a lecture on environmental control and preventive medicine in the tropics. Nomination is made jointly by the Award Committee of the American Society of Tropical Medicine and Hygiene and the Chairman of the Board of Directors, Gorgas Memorial Institute. Travel expenses to the site of the annual meeting and an invitation to deliver the Soper Lecture are presented biennially. Established in 1978 in honor of Fred L. Soper, M.D., M.P.H., a leader in international health, distinguished investigator, research administrator, and spokesman for disease control and eradication. Co-sponsored by the Gorgas Memorial Institute and the American Society of Tropical Medicine and Hygiene.

• 4634 •
American Society on Aging
Gloria H. Cavanaugh, Pres.
833 Market St., Ste. 511
San Francisco, CA 94103-1824
Phone: (415)974-9600
Toll-Free: 800-537-9728
Fax: (415)974-0300
E-mail: info@asaging.org
Home Page: http://www.asaging.org

• 4635 • The ASA Award
To recognize an ASA member who has made outstanding contributions to aging-related research, administration, or advocacy. The deadline for submissions is November 1. A cash prize of $500 is awarded each year at the ASA annual meeting.

• 4636 • ASA-Metlife Foundation MindAlert Awards
Identifies and recognizes programs that provide valuable information and activities supporting enhances cognitive function in later life. Submission deadline is September 16. Sponsored by MetLife Foundation.

• 4637 • ASA Undergraduate Student Award
Recognizes exemplary original work related to the team of the Joint Conference of the National Council on the Aging and the American Society on Aging. Undergraduate students are eligible. Submission deadline is October 14.

• 4638 • Award for Best Practices in Human Resources and Aging
Presented to an organization or agency for significant contributions in the field of staff recruitment, training, and/or management. Application deadline is October 14. Awarded annually in collaboration with Brookdale Center on Aging of Hunter College.

• 4639 • Business and Aging Awards
To recognize exemplary business programs or services that meet the needs of older persons and their families. The deadline for submissions is September 17. Awards are presented to one company with more than 1,000 employees and one company with less than 1,000 employees each year at the ASA annual meeting. Complimentary one-year memberships in ASA and Business Forum on Aging are awarded.

• 4640 • The Gloria Cavanaugh Award for Excellence in Training and Education in Aging
Recognizes continued excellence in training and education in the field of aging. Only ASA members are eligible. Nomination deadline is October 31.

• 4641 • Graduate Student Research Award
To recognize graduate research projects in the field of aging. Entrants must currently be graduate students, or no more than one year out of school at time of submission. Applicants must be sponsored by a faculty member who is a member of the ASA, but applicants need not be members. Application deadline is October 20. A cash prize of $500, a certificate, a presentation at ASA's annual meeting, and complimentary membership in ASA for one year are awarded annually.

• 4642 • Hall of Fame Award
To recognize an elder member of ASA who has, through advocacy and community service, made important contributions toward improving the lives of older persons. The deadline for submissions is October 31. A cash prize of $1,000 is awarded to one or more recipients each year at the ASA annual meeting.

• 4643 • Healthcare and Aging Awards
Recognizes innovative programs that have demonstrated improved health outcomes for older adults. Nominations deadline: September 16. Sponsored by Pfizer.

• 4644 • Leadership Award
To recognize an ASA member who has made significant contributions to the growth and development of ASA and to the field of aging. The deadline for submissions is October 31. A cash prize of $500 is awarded each year at the ASA annual meeting.

• 4645 • Media Awards
To recognize a journalist or journalists whose work has had an exceptional impact on public awareness of aging issues at the local, regional, or national level. Two categories exist: national media and local/regional media. The deadline for submissions is September 16. Awarded each year at the ASA annual meeting.

• 4646 •
American Sociological Association
Sally T. Hillsman, Exec. Officer
1307 New York Ave. NW, Ste. 700
Washington, DC 20005
Phone: (202)383-9005
Phone: (202)872-0486
Fax: (202)638-0882
E-mail: executive.office@asanet.org
Home Page: http://www.asanet.org

• 4647 • Award for the Public Understanding of Sociology
To recognize a person or persons who have made exemplary contributions to advance the public understanding of sociology, sociological research, and scholarship among the general public. The award may recognize a contribution in the preceding year or for a longer career of such contributions. Nominations consisting of a one to two page statement of the candidate's accomplishments in the field are due June 15. Awarded annually.

• 4648 • Jessie Bernard Award
For recognition of a scholarly work that has enlarged the horizons of the discipline of sociology to encompass fully the role of women in society. The contribution may be in empirical research, theory, or methodology. The award may be given for an exceptional single work, several pieces of work, or for significant cumulative work done throughout a professional career. The award is open to work by women or men and is not restricted to works by sociologists. Candidates must be nominated with a one to two pages statement by June 15. Scholarly nomina-

Awards are arranged in alphabetical order below their administering organizations

tions must include a one or two page statement of the work. Career achievement nominations must include two copies of the vitae and examples of the material been nominated. A certificate is awarded annually.

• 4649 • Career of Distinguished Scholarship Award

To honor scholars who have shown outstanding commitment to the profession of sociology and whose cumulative work has contributed to the advancement of the discipline. The body of lifetime work may include theoretical and/or methodological contributions. A certificate and a lectureship are presented annually. Nominations are due by June 15 and must include the nominee's curriculum vitae and letters of support. Nominations remain under active consideration for five award cycles. Established in 1980. Formerly: (1977) Stouffer Award.

• 4650 • Dissertation Award

To honor the best Ph.D. dissertation from among those submitted by advisors and mentors in the discipline of sociology. Nominations must be received from the student's advisor or the scholar most familiar with the student's research. Nominations should explain the precise nature and merits of the work. Established in 1989. Deadline February 1.

• 4651 • Distinguished Career Award for the Practice of Sociology

To honor outstanding contributions to sociological practice. Award may recognize work that has facilitated or served as a model for the work of others, work that has significantly advanced one or more specialty areas in sociology and elevated the professional status of the field as a whole, or work that has been honored or recognized outside the discipline for its significant impacts, particularly in advancing human welfare. Nominations deadline is June 15. Awarded annually. Established in 1986.

• 4652 • Distinguished Contributions to Teaching Award

For recognition of outstanding contributions to the undergraduate and/or graduate teaching of sociology. A career contribution or a specific product such as a textbook, course, curricular innovation, or technique are considered for the award. Individuals, departments, schools, or other collective groups are eligible. Name of nominee, a one to two page statement on the nomination, a vitae, and a supporting materials must be submitted. Nominations are due June 15. A certificate is awarded annually. Established in 1980.

• 4653 • Distinguished Scholarly Publication Award

For recognition of an outstanding a single book or monograph, that has contributed to the profession of sociology within the three calendar years preceding the year of the award. Name of author, title of book, date of publication, publisher, and a brief explanation of its reason or nomination must be submitted. A certificate and a Sorokin Lectureship are presented annually. Established in 1968 as the Sorokin Award. Deadline June 15. Formerly: (1986) Distinguished Contribution to Scholarship Award.

• 4654 • DuBois-Johnson-Frazier Award

For recognition of outstanding contributions by sociologists in the tradition of W.E.B. DuBois, Charles S. Johnson, and E. Franklin Frazier. The award is given either to a sociologist for a lifetime of research, teaching, and service to the community or to an academic institution for its work in assisting the development of scholarly efforts in this tradition. A nomination should indicate career or achievements, teaching, or publications and the way in which these are consistent with the traditions of these outstanding African-American scholars and educators. Certificates are awarded annually. Deadline June 15. Established in 1971.

• 4655 •
American Solar Energy Society
Thomas Starrs, Ch.
2400 Central Ave., Ste. A
Boulder, CO 80301
Phone: (303)443-3130
Fax: (303)443-3212
E-mail: ases@ases.org
Home Page: http://www.ases.org

• 4656 • Charles Greeley Abbot Award

To recognize an individual who has provided exceptionally valuable service to the Society or has made exceptionally significant contributions to the solar energy field. To be considered, an individual need not be a member of the Society. A luncheon and a plaque are awarded annually. Established in honor of Charles Greeley Abbot, a prominent researcher in solar energy who developed a number of instruments for measuring insulation, and who was the founder of the Smithsonian Radiation Biology Lab.

• 4657 •
American Spaniel Club
Dorothy Mustard, Sec.
30 Cardinal Loop
Crossville, TN 38555-5899
Phone: (931)456-6690
Fax: (931)707-8504
E-mail: ascsecy@earthlink.net
Home Page: http://www.asc-cockerspaniel.org

• 4658 • Award of Merit

Awarded annually to members with breed-obedience-field work-dogs.

• 4659 •
The American Spectator
George Neumayr, Exec.Dir.
1611 N Kent St., Ste. 901
Arlington, VA 22209
Phone: (703)807-2011
Fax: (703)807-2013
E-mail: amspec@spectator.org
Home Page: http://www.spectator.org

• 4660 • J. Gordon Coogler Award

To recognize the worst book published by a major American publisher in the preceding calendar year. Recognition is given in a major article in the *American Spectator* magazine. Awarded annually within the first two months of the following year. Established in 1979 by R. Emmett Tyrrell, Jr. in memory of J. Gordon Coogler, minor American poet of the first half of the 20th century. Formerly: (1981) Harold Robbins Award.

• 4661 •
American Speech Language Hearing Association
Lawrence W. Higdon, Pres.
10801 Rockville Pike
Rockville, MD 20852
Toll-Free: 800-638-8255
Fax: (301)897-7355
E-mail: actioncenter@asha.org
Home Page: http://www.asha.org

Formerly: American Speech and Hearing Association.

• 4662 • ASHA Media Awards for Journalists

To recognize an outstanding contribution that increases public understanding and knowledge of speech-language pathology and audiology. Material published or broadcast during the previous 12-month period may be submitted by June 30. Awards are given in the following categories: newspaper, television, magazine, and radio. Work or ideas about speech language pathologists or audiologists must have been published or broadcast during the year. Materials produced for and readily available to the general public are eligible. The nomination deadline is June 30. A monetary prize of $1,000, a plaque, and expenses to the ASHA National Convention are awarded in each category. Awarded annually. Established in 1978.

• 4663 • Distinguished Service Awards

For recognition of significant contributions to the field of speech-language pathology and audiology by persons who are not members of the American Speech-Language-Hearing Association. A plaque is awarded annually. Established in 1960.

• 4664 • Fellows of the Association

To recognize a member for achievement. A fellow must have been active in the Association as evidenced by publications, appearance on the convention programs, or service on committees and must have a record of achievement, unquestionable and sustained, of one or more of the following types: original contributions to the advancement of knowledge; distinguished educational, professional, or administrative activity; and outstanding service to the Association. Awarded annually at the convention. Established in 1951.

• 4665 • Honors of the Association

For recognition of distinguished service to the profession. Individuals are recommended by the

Committee on Honors with the approval of the Council. Awarded annually at the convention. Established in 1944.

• 4666 •
American Spice Trade Association
Louis Sanna, Pres.
2025 M St. NW, No. 800
Washington, DC 20036
Phone: (202)367-1127
Fax: (202)367-2127
E-mail: info@astaspice.org
Home Page: http://www.astaspice.org

• 4667 • International Chili Cook-off
To recognize the spice creativity of contestants at the International Chili Cook-off. The Golden Chili Pepper Award, a medal, is awarded annually. Established in 1979.

• 4668 •
American Spinal Injury Association
Jack E. Zigler MD, Pres./Dir.
2020 Peachtree Rd. NW
Atlanta, GA 30309-1402
Phone: (404)355-9772
Fax: (404)355-1826
E-mail: mars@northwestern.edu
Home Page: http://www.asia-spinalinjury.org

• 4669 • Lifetime Achievement Award
To recognize significant achievements in spinal cord injury management. A crystal artwork on a lead base is awarded at the Annual Scientific Meeting of the Association. Awardees must be nominated by the Association's award committee. Awarded when merited. Established in 1987.

• 4670 •
American Sportfishing Association
Mike Nussman, Pres.
225 Reinekers Ln., No. 420
Alexandria, VA 22314
Phone: (703)519-9691
Fax: (703)519-1872
E-mail: info@asafishing.org
Home Page: http://www.asafishing.org

• 4671 • Andrew J. Boehm Graduate Fellowship in the Fisheries Sciences
To encourage graduate studies leading to professional careers in marine conservation and scientific management of recreational fisheries. Graduate students with a commitment to a professional career in fish conservation, having an academic average of B or better, or equivalent point standing, are eligible to be nominated. Supervising professors may submit research proposals by March 15. A monetary grant of 1,000 to $10,000 is awarded to one or more graduate students annually. Established in 1974 to honor Andrew J. Boehm.

• 4672 •
American Sports Medicine Institute
Lanier Johnson, Exec.Dir.
1313 13th St. S
Birmingham, AL 35205
Phone: (205)918-0000
Fax: (205)918-0800
Home Page: http://www.asmi.org

• 4673 • James R. Andrews Award for Excellence in Baseball Sports Medicine
For individual or group that made significant contribution to baseball sports medicine.

• 4674 •
American Sportscasters Association
Louis O. Schwartz, Exec.Dir. & Pres.Founder
225 Broadway, Ste. 2030
New York, NY 10007
Phone: (212)227-8080
Fax: (212)571-0556
E-mail: lschwa8918@aol.com
Home Page: http://www.americansportscasters.com

• 4675 • Hall of Fame Award
To recognize the outstanding contributions of past and present sports broadcasters. Sportscasters who, over the past 60 years, have distinguished themselves as champions of professionalism and fair play, and who have profoundly influenced sports coverage by the electronic media are eligible. Inductees are announced annually at the awards dinner. A trophy is awarded. Established in 1984 by Louis O. Schwartz.

• 4676 • Hero of the Year
To recognize an individual for outstanding courage in the war against drugs. Citizens who stand their ground and refuse to let drugs invade their lives are eligible. Established in 1991.

• 4677 • Humanitarian Award
For recognition of humanitarian contributions in the field of sports. Awarded when merited.

• 4678 • International Sportscasters of The Year
To honor sportscasters from other countries. A plaque is awarded annually. Established in 1987 by Louis O. Schwartz, founder of the American Sportscasters Association.

• 4679 • Graham McNamee Award
To recognize a former sportscaster who has gained prominence in another field or endeavor. Awarded annually. Established in 1985.

• 4680 • National Sportscaster of the Year/Play by Play/Studio Host/Color Analyst/Reporter Award
For recognition of professional excellence in sports broadcasting. Members of the Association vote for the nominee. Plaques are awarded annually for each section. Established in 1984 by Louis O. Schwartz. Formerly: (1997) National Sportscaster of the Year.

• 4681 • Mel Allen Service Award
Annual award of recognition. Inquire for additional details.

• 4682 • Sports Legend of the Year Award
Annual award of recognition.

• 4683 • Sports Personality of the Year Award
To recognize the contribution of a sports broadcasting pro whose charisma and personality have added quality, professionalism, and entertainment value to the sportscasting field. Any professional sports broadcaster, generally a "Color Commentator," is eligible. Selection is made by the Board of Directors. A trophy/plaque is awarded annually when merited. Established in 1985.

• 4684 •
American Staffing Association
Kathy B. Rogers, Ch.
277 S. Washington St., Ste. 200
Alexandria, VA 22314-3646
Phone: (703)253-2020
Fax: (703)253-2053
E-mail: asa@staffingtoday.net
Home Page: http://www.staffingtoday.net

Formerly: (1995) National Assoiation of Temporary Services.

• 4685 • Chapter Merit Awards
To recognize and honor outstanding achievement in six areas of chapter programming by organizations affiliated with the Association. Plaques are awarded annually at the Convention. Established in 1980.

• 4686 • Industry Leader Hall of Fame Award
To recognize outstanding individual contributions made through dedicated service to the Association and the industry. A handcrafted, imported lead crystal trophy is awarded annually at the Convention. Established in 1985.

• 4687 • National Temporary Employee of the Year Award
To recognize and honor the temporary employee who best represents the temporary help industry. Nominations come from member companies from across the nation. Through a random drawing at NATSS headquarters, a temporary employee of the year is chosen. The winner is named during National Temporary Help Week held annually in October.

• 4688 • Cedric A. Richner, Jr. Scholarship Award
To assist law students at the University of Michigan. A monetary award is presented annually at the Convention. Established in 1985 in memory of Cedric A. Richner, Jr., who defended and

protected the temporary help industry from adverse legislation and restrictive regulations for 15 years. The scholarship is created in Mr. Richner's name at the University of Michigan Law School, his alma mater.

• 4689 • Staffing Industry Communications Awards
To recognize and honor outstanding achievements of members in the fields of advertising and public relations. Entries are separated into two classifications - independent and national staffing firms - and are judged in 15 categories, including direct mail, radio/TV advertising, use of ASA logo, multimedia, and public service. Additional awards include the Crystal Award for the top entry overall, the Communications Award for the entry that best advances the overall image of the industry, and the Judges' Award. Certificates and plaques are awarded annually at the Convention. Established in 1978.

• 4690 • Touch of Knowledge Award
To recognize and honor the NATSS member who best fulfills the mission and creed of the Preparing Youth for Industry (PYI) business-education partnership program. The nominee for the award must show exceptional participation in and/or support of the PYI program during the previous year(s) and have instituted one or more of the eight points within the PYI creed. They must be a member, chapter or associate member in good standing with NATSS, or a client, student or teacher. Nominations can only be made by NATSS members or associate members in good standing. The award is presented at the annual convention.

• 4691 •
American Statistical Association
William B. Smith, Exec.Dir.
1429 Duke St.
Alexandria, VA 22314-3415
Phone: (703)684-1221
Toll-Free: 888-231-3473
Fax: (703)684-2037
E-mail: asainfo@amstat.org
Home Page: http://www.amstat.org

• 4692 • Fellows of the American Statistical Association
For recognition of individuals in the field of statistics. Individuals with activities in the following areas are eligible: consulting on statistical problems, statistical applications and data collection, administration of statistical activities, teaching and dissemination of statistical knowledge, list of major publications having statistical content, activities in the Association, and activities in related professional organizations. Awarded annually.

• 4693 • Founders Award
Recognizes members who have given distinguished service to the Association. Accomplishments must be in more than two capacities. Up to five awards may be given. However, the award does not have to be given every year. Nomination deadline is May 1st. A framed certificate is awarded to up to five recipients each year. Established in 1988.

• 4694 • Outstanding Statistical Application Awards
To recognize a paper which is an outstanding application of statistics in any field. The following criteria are considered: the impact of the statistical application in a substantive field of science and the ingenuity/novelty of the statistical treatment. Papers or monographs published during the preceding two years are eligible for nomination. Nomination deadline is May 1st. Established in 1986.

• 4695 • George W. Snedecor Award
Recognizes a notable publication in biometry produced in the three years prior to the award date. An individual with significant input is selected by a committee. Nomination deadline is March 1st. Established in 1974.

• 4696 • Statistics in Chemistry Award
Recognizes collaborative endeavors between statisticians and chemists. Selection is based on the innovative use of statistics to solve a chemistry problem and the impact it has. Applicants must be ASA members. Application deadline is April 1. A certificate and $2,000 is awarded annually. Established in 1993. Sponsored by Merck & Co. Inc.

• 4697 • Wilks Memorial Award
To recognize a statistician for contributions to statistical theory or practice, through publications or participation in programs of instruction on practical application that directly or indirectly have benefited the United States Government or the country generally. A medal, citation, and a cash honorarium are awarded annually. Nomination deadline is April 15th. Established in 1964.

• 4698 • W. J. Youden Award in Interlaboratory Testing
To recognize a publication that makes an outstanding statistical contribution to the design and/or analysis of interlaboratory tests or describes ingenious applications to the planning and evaluation of data from interlaboratory tests. Eligible publications must appear in professionally refereed journals or monograph series. Publications of the preceding two years are eligible. The deadline for nominations is March 5th. A certificate and $1000 and awarded. Established in 1985.

• 4699 •
American String Teachers Association
John Reed, Pres.
4153 Chain Bridge Rd.
Fairfax, VA 22030
Phone: (703)279-2113
Fax: (703)279-2114
E-mail: asta@astaweb.com
Home Page: http://www.astaweb.com

• 4700 • Artist-Teacher Award
For recognition of a string teacher who is also a performer. An award, specially designed for the recipient, is presented annually. Established in 1959.

• 4701 • Elizabeth A.H. Green School Educator Award
Annual award of recognition. Formerly: (2006) String Teacher of the Year Award.

• 4702 •
American String Teachers Association/ National School Orchestra Association
Donna Sizemore Hale, Exec.Dir.
4153 Chain Bridge Rd.
Fairfax, VA 22030
Phone: (703)279-2113
Fax: (703)279-2114
E-mail: asta@astaweb.com
Home Page: http://www.astaweb.com

• 4703 • Merle J. Isaac Composition Contest
To encourage the composition, publication, and performance of full and string orchestra music for the benefit of school orchestra programs. Original, unpublished compositions that are suitable for string orchestra at the middle/junior high school or high school level are accepted. Application deadline is April 1. A monetary prize of $1,500 for the winning selection is awarded annually. Established in 1958.

• 4704 •
American Studies Association
John F. Stephens, Exec.Dir.
1120-19th St., NW, Ste. 301
Washington, DC 20036
Phone: (202)467-4783
Fax: (202)467-4786
E-mail: asastaff@theasa.net
Home Page: http://www.georgetown.edu/ crossroads/asainfo.html

• 4705 • Annette K. Baxter Awards
Recognizes excellence conference papers. Applicants must be graduate students. A travel reimbursement of $200 is awarded annually.

• 4706 • Bode - Pearson Prize
For recognition of outstanding contributions to American Studies. Life membership is awarded. The prize is awarded to an individual for a lifetime of achievement and service within the field of American studies. Established in 1975.

• 4707 • Constance M. Rourke Prize
Awarded annually to the best article published in American quarterly. $100 is awarded. Established in 1987.

• 4708 • John Hope Franklin Publication Prize
To recognize the best published book in American Studies. Members of the Association are eligible. A monetary prize of $750 is awarded

annually. Established in 1987 to honor John Hope Franklin.

• 4709 • Ralph Henry Gabriel Dissertation Prize

For recognition of the best completed dissertation in American Studies. Members are eligible. A monetary prize of $500 is awarded annually at the Association convention. Application deadline is July 1. Established in 1987 in honor of Ralph Henry Gabriel, Professor Emeritus at Yale University and past president of the Association.

• 4710 • Lora Romero First Book Publication Prize

Awarded for the best-published first book in American Studies that highlights the intersections of race with gender, class, sexuality, and/or nation. The prize consists of a lifetime membership in the ASA, and is awarded annually. The deadline is March 1.

• 4711 • Mary C. Turpie Award

Given to the candidate who has demonstrated outstanding abilities and achievement in American Studies teaching, advising, and program development at the local or regional level. The award is named for the late Mary C. Turpie. The prize is awarded periodically at the annual meeting.

• 4712 • Gene Wise - Warren Susman Prize

For recognition of the best student paper presented at the annual conference. Members are eligible. A monetary prize is awarded. Established in 1987.

• 4713 • Yasuo Sakakibara Prize

Awarded to an individual with the best paper presented by an international scholar at the annual meeting. The winning paper may deal with any aspect of American History, culture, or society. Awarded annually. A certificate and $500 are awarded.

• 4714 •

American Subcontractors Association of Mississippi
John Sullivan, Contact
PO Box 84
Jackson, MS 39205
Phone: (601)352-9273
Fax: (601)352-7131
E-mail: jms@gpac.net
Home Page: http://www.asams.com

• 4715 • M. C. Vaughan Scholarship Fund

For high school graduating senior of a chapter member's family. Scholarship awarded annually.

• 4716 •

American Supplier Institute
Mr. Shin Taguchi, Pres.
38705 7 Mile Rd., Ste. 345
Livonia, MI 48152
Phone: (734)464-1395
Toll-Free: 800-462-4500
Fax: (734)464-1399
E-mail: asi@asiusa.com
Home Page: http://www.amsup.com

• 4717 • Taguchi Award

To recognize individuals or teams who have successfully overcome obstacles and have achieved substantive improvements in quality and reductions in cost through the use of quality engineering using Taguchi methods. Applicants are selected through an evaluation criterion. The deadline is July 31. A crystal award is presented to the "Best Case Study." Established in 1985.

• 4718 •

American Swimming Coaches Association
John A. Leonard, Exec.Dir.
2101 N Andrews Ave., Ste. 107
Fort Lauderdale, FL 33311
Phone: (954)563-4930
Toll-Free: 800-356-2722
Fax: (954)563-9813
E-mail: asca@swimmingcoach.org
Home Page: http://www.swimmingcoach.org

• 4719 • ASCA Awards of Excellence

To recognize coaches for contributions to the present success and future growth of the tradition of excellence in American swimming. Awards are presented in the following categories: NCAA Division I Women - coaches placed one or more swimmers in the top 8 places at the NCAA Division I Championships; NCAA Division I Men - coaches placed one or more swimmers in the top 8 places at the NCAA Division I Championships; NCAA Division II Women - coaches placed one or more swimmers in the top 4 places at the NCAA Division II Championships; NCAA Division II Men - coaches placed one or more swimmers in the top 4 places at the NCAA Division II Championships; NCAA Division III Women - coaches placed one or more swimmers in the top 2 places at the NCAA Division III Championships; NCAA Division III Men - coaches placed one or more swimmers in the top 2 places at the NCAA Division III Championships; NAIA Men - coaches placed swimmers in the top 2 places at the NAIA Championships; NAIA Women - coaches placed swimmers in the top 2 places at the NAIA Championships; YMCA Men - coaches placed 2 swimmers in the top 3 places of the YMCA Championships; YMCA Women - coaches placed 2 swimmers in the top 3 places at the YMCA Championships; and U.S. Swimming Men & Women - coaches placed at least one swimmer in the top 8 places at the USS Short or Long Course Championships. Special awards are presented to those coaches who have received the annual Award of Excellence for a period of twenty (Gold), fifteen (Silver), and ten years (Bronze).

• 4720 • ASCA Chapter Age Group Coaches of the Year

To recognize coaches working with athletes 14 years of age and under. Awarded annually to each ASCA Chapter throughout the country. Established in 1986.

• 4721 • ASCA Coaches Hall of Fame

To recognize outstanding ASCA coaches. Criteria for the Hall of Fame are as follows: Coached swimming at the high school, club, or college level for a period of twenty years or more; and must have demonstrated and achieved a degree of excellence in coaching by: placing a team in the top ten at the NCAA1/AIAW/IAAU or USS Senior Nationals, and having coached an individual national champion in one of the above, or having made a significant contribution to the sport of swimming, the community, and the profession of coaching.

• 4722 • Coach of the Year Award

To recognize the ASCA Coach of the Year. Awarded annually. Established in 1961.

• 4723 • Councilman Creative Coaching Awards

To recognize coaches for new ideas. Awards are presented in two categories: Best Contract, and Best Use of Equipment for Training. Monetary awards totaling $3,000 are presented annually. Formerly: (1989) Best Ideas Contest.

• 4724 • Robert Ousley Special Service Award

To recognize an individual for unusual and distinctive service to the Association. Awarded when merited. Established in 1983 to honor Robert Ousley, Executive Director of the Association from 1972-1983.

• 4725 • Schlueter Stroke Awards National Winners

To recognize outstanding stroke coaching of age group swimmers. Six coaches and six athletes from across the United States are selected annually.

• 4726 •

American-Swiss Foundation
Eugene Waering, Exec.Dir.
232 E. 66th St.
New York, NY 10021-6703
Phone: (212)754-0130
Fax: (212)754-4512
E-mail: amswfo@aol.com
Home Page: http://www.americanswiss.org/

• 4727 • Friendship Award

Bestowed to an individual who has made significant contribution in furthering friendship between America and Switzerland.

• 4728 •
American Symphony Orchestra League
Henry Fogel, CEO/Pres.
33 W 60th St., 5th Fl.
New York, NY 10023
Phone: (212)262-5161
Fax: (212)262-5198
E-mail: league@symphony.org
Home Page: http://www.symphony.org

• 4729 • **Audrey Baird Gold Ribbon Audience Development Awards**
To recognize the most innovative or creative season ticket campaigns, stand-alone concert, pre/post concert event, community events, or other events that help attract new audience members by member orchestra volunteer associations. Certificates of excellence are awarded annually. Established in 1980.

• 4730 • **Gold Baton Award**
To recognize an individual or organization for outstanding service to music and the arts. A plaque is awarded annually. Established in 1948.

• 4731 • **Sally Parker Education Gold Ribbon Awards**
To recognize the most innovative or creative education programs by member orchestra volunteer associations. Certificates of excellence are awarded annually.

• 4732 • **Helen M. Thompson Award**
To recognize an executive director and music director in alternate years. To be eligible for the award, a nominee must: hold the position of music director or executive director at one or more North American League member orchestra(s), have no more than five years total combined experience as a music director or executive director, be nominated by an orchestra board officer, musician, or another music director or executive director, and be present to accept the award at the national Conference of the American Symphony Orchestra League. The deadline for nominations is late March. A monetary award of $1,500 is presented annually. Established in 1982 to commemorate Helen M. Thompson who developed and promoted the cause of the local symphony orchestra in the United States.

• 4733 • **Volunteer Council Fundraising Gold Ribbon Awards**
To recognize the most creative or successful fund-raising projects by Symphony Orchestra Volunteer Associations. Certificates of excellence are awarded annually to one or more recipients.

• 4734 •
American Teleservices Association
Tim Searcy, Exec.Dir.
1666 K St. NW, Ste. 1200
Washington, DC 20006
Phone: (317)816-9336
Toll-Free: 877-779-3974
Fax: (202)463-8498
E-mail: contact@ataconnect.org
Home Page: http://www.ataconnect.org

• 4735 • **TELO Award**
To recognize companies for excellent design and/or implementation of an inbound or outbound telemarketing program. Trophies are awarded each year at the annual fall convention of the Association.

• 4736 •
American Theatre Organ Society
Michael W. Fellenzer, Exec.Sec.
PO Box 551081
Indianapolis, IN 46205-5581
Phone: (317)251-6441
Fax: (317)251-6443
E-mail: fellenzer@atos.org
Home Page: http://www.atos.org

• 4737 • **Hall of Fame**
To recognize individuals for service to the cause of the theatre pipe organ. Awarded annually. Established in 1959.

• 4738 • **Honorary Member**
To recognize a member of long standing and faithful service to the society. A plaque with engraved metal plate is awarded annually. Established in 1959.

• 4739 • **Theatre Organist of the Year**
To recognize an active theatre organist with long service and devotion to the cause of the theatre pipe organ. Awarded once a year. Established in 1970.

• 4740 •
American Theatre Wing
Howard Sherman, Exec.Dir.
570 Seventh Ave.
New York, NY 10018
Phone: (212)765-0606
Fax: (212)307-1910
E-mail: mailbox@americantheatrewing.org
Home Page: http://www.americantheatrewing.org

• 4741 • **American Theatre Wing's Henry Hewes Design Awards**
To recognize outstanding theatrical designers of Broadway, off-Broadway, and off-off Broadway plays and musicals for designs originating in the United States. Stage and costume designers are eligible. Four awards of $250 are presented in the following categories: scenic design, costume design, lighting, and unusual effects. Honoraria and citations are awarded annually at a luncheon. Established in 1965. Formerly: Maharam Theatrical Design Awards.

• 4742 •
American Therapeutic Recreation Association
1414 Prince St., Ste. 204
Alexandria, VA 22314
Phone: (703)683-9420
Fax: (703)683-9431
Home Page: http://www.atra-tr.org/atra.htm

• 4743 • **American Therapeutic Recreation Association Awards**
To recognize members for outstanding contributions to the association and to the field of therapeutic recreation. The following awards are presented: Distinguished Fellow Award, Outstanding Professional Award, Member of Year Award, Institution or Organization Award, Certificate of Recognition, Excellence in Education Award, and Scholarly Achievement Award. Plaques are awarded annually at the national conference. Established in 1986.

• 4744 •
American Thyroid Association
Barbara R. Smith, Exec.Dir.
6066 Leesburg Pike, Ste. 550
Falls Church, VA 22041
Phone: (703)998-8890
Toll-Free: 800-THY-ROID
Fax: (703)998-8893
E-mail: admin@thyroid.org
Home Page: http://www.thyroid.org

• 4745 • **Sidney H. Ingbar Distinguished Lectureship Award**
To recognize outstanding academic achievements in the field of thyroidology in keeping with the innovation and vision that epitomized Dr. Ingbar's brilliant investigative career. It is conferred upon an established investigator who has made major contribution in thyroid related research over many years. Nominations may be submitted by March 1. Established in 1990 in memory of Sidney H. Ingbar.

• 4746 • **Paul Starr Clinical Day Lectureship Prize**
To recognize an individual for distinguished contributions to clinical thyroidology. Nominations may be submitted by March 1. An honorarium of $2,000, and expenses of $1,000 are awarded annually. Established in 1981.

• 4747 •
American Topical Association
Ray Cartier, Exec.Dir.
PO Box 57
318 W Main St.
Arlington, TX 76004-0057
Phone: (817)274-1181
Fax: (817)274-1184
E-mail: americantopical@msn.com
Home Page: http://www.americantopicalassn.org

• 4748 • Best in Topical Awards
To recognize the best exhibit of topical stamps of an annual philatelic show. Exhibitors in philatelic shows at the local, regional, national, or international levels are eligible. The show must provide a separate classification for topicals and brochures on ATA and topical collecting must be distributed at the show. Topicals must be a collection of philatelic material selected and arranged by subject, design, or theme rather than by country of issuance or type of postal service rendered. Gold, Silver, and Bronze medals are awarded based on points given by judges. A Novice Award consisting of the book *Adventures in Topical Collecting* is offered to all first-time exhibitors. Most Popular Exhibit award is given to the exhibit receiving the most votes from attendees, and other awards are offered to specific topical collections by Study Units of the ATA.

• 4749 • Distinguished Topical Philatelist Award
To recognize one outstanding collector for activities to improve topical philately and the American Topical Association. A plaque, medal, ribbon, and signing of a scroll are awarded annually at the convention. Established in 1952 by Jerome D. Husak.

• 4750 •
American Translators Association
Walter W. Bacak Jr.CAE, Exec.Dir.
225 Reinekers Ln., Ste. 590
Alexandria, VA 22314
Phone: (703)683-6100
Fax: (703)683-6122
E-mail: ata@atanet.org
Home Page: http://www.atanet.org

• 4751 • Lewis Galantiere Literary Translation Prize
To recognize distinguished literary translations from any language, except German, into English. Works published in the United States within the previous two year period are eligible. The deadline is May 15 of even-numbered years. A monetary award of $500 and a certificate are presented biennially. See the above web site for additional application details.

• 4752 • German Translation Award
For recognition of an outstanding literary translation from German into English. Published works are eligible. The deadline is May 15 of odd-numbered years. A monetary award of $500 and a certificate are presented biennially. Formerly: (1996) Translators Association Unger Award.

• 4753 • Alexander Gode Medal
For recognition of distinguished service to the cause of translation. Individuals or organizations, regardless of nationality are eligible. The award is not limited to ATA members. Application deadline is May 1. A silver medal is awarded annually. Established in 1964 in honor of Alexander Gode, a founder and first president of the Association. See the above web site for additional application guidelines.

• 4754 • Student Translation Award
For recognition of a worthy student translation project. Applicants must be graduated or undergraduate's students enrolled in an accredited college or university in the United States. Preference is given to students enrolled in translation programs. Previously published translators are not eligible. Proposed work must have the potential for post-grant applicability. Dissertations and abstracts are not accepted. Translation must be in English. $ 500, a certificate of recognition, and ATA conference travel expenses are awarded. Application deadline is April 15th. Awarded annually.

• 4755 •
American Truck Historical Society
Bill Johnson, Mng.Dir.
PO Box 901611
Kansas City, MO 64190-1611
Phone: (816)891-9900
Fax: (816)891-9903
E-mail: info@ahts.org
Home Page: http://www.aths.org

• 4756 • Founder Award
To recognize men and women who were in the trucking industry prior to October 1, 1935 and who have spent most of their working lives in the trucking industry. The following individuals are eligible: owners or co-owners of a company owning or operating at least one commercial vehicle; a truck operated for commercial purposes; a company manufacturing trucks, truck parts, or equipment; or a company whose primary purpose is serving the trucking industry, such as suppliers, insurance, publications, associations; inventors or developers of trucks, truck parts, or equipment; or any person whose primary business purpose was to serve the trucking industry. A plaque is presented at any time at appropriate functions that are truck related. Established in 1975.

• 4757 • Harris Saunders Sr. Award
To recognize a member for outstanding achievements in furthering the goals of the American Truck Historical Society. Four such awards have been granted since 1987. Established in 1987 in memory of Harris Saunders Sr., founder, life member, president, chairman of the board, and leader in the growth of the Society.

• 4758 •
American Truck Historical Society, Arizona Chapter
William S. Myers, Contact
12120 S 43rd Ave.
Laveen, AZ 85355-9784
Phone: (602)237-2030
E-mail: aths@mindspring.com
Home Page: http://www.aths.org

• 4759 • Founders Award
For pioneer trucking achievement. Recognition award bestowed annually.

• 4760 •
American Truck Historical Society, Gateway Chapter
John Lamke, Exec. Officer
625 W Main St.
Union, MO 63084-1013
Phone: (636)583-3573
Home Page: http://www.aths.org

• 4761 • Founders Award of American Truck Historical Society
For 50 years in the trucking industry. Recognition award bestowed annually.

• 4762 •
American Truck Historical Society, Metro Jersey Chapter
Scott Baker, Treas.
143 Vreeland Ave.
Bloomingdale, NJ 07403
Phone: (973)838-5026
Home Page: http://www.aths.org

• 4763 • Founders Award
For individual involved in trucking prior to 1935. Recognition award bestowed periodically.

• 4764 •
American Trucking Associations
Bill Graves, Pres./CEO
2200 Mill Rd.
Alexandria, VA 22314-4677
Phone: (703)838-1700
Toll-Free: 800-ATA-LINE
Fax: (703)684-5720
E-mail: feedback@trucking.org
Home Page: http://www.truckline.com

• 4765 • Achievement Award
To recognize motor carriers who attain and maintain a good loss and damage prevention program and to inspire carriers to greater efforts in the field of loss and damage prevention. Members of the National Freight Claim and Security Council are eligible. Plaques and company name plates are awarded annually at the membership meeting. Established in 1953.

• 4766 • J. Frank Dickson Award
To recognize an outstanding council affiliated with the National Accounting and Finance Council. A monetary award and silver tray are presented annually at the membership meeting. Established in 1958 to honor J. Frank Dickson.

• 4767 • James E. Roelker Award
To recognize an outstanding NAFC member for long and active service to the Council. A crystal eagle is awarded annually at the management conference. Established in 1981 to honor James Roelker.

• 4768 •
American Trucking Associations
Safety Management Council
2200 Mill Rd.
Alexandria, VA 22314
Phone: (703)838-1700
Toll-Free: 888-333-1759
Fax: (703)683-9752
Home Page: http://www.trucking.org

• 4769 • **ATA National Truck Driving Championships**
To recognize National Champion Truck Drivers of eight basic types of trucks and combination units. Eligibility is based on one year of accident-free driving, plus one year of continuous employment with the entering driver. The following special awards are presented: Vehicle Condition Award, Sontheime Award, Team Trophy Award, Grand Champion, and Rookie of the Year. Monetary awards, trophies, and plaques are awarded annually. Established in 1937. Formerly: ATA National Truck Rodeo.

• 4770 • **Driver of the Year Award**
To recognize the best safety record among truck drivers of the United States and to encourage improved driving performance and a greater appreciation for highway safety. A Driver of the Year pin, trophy, and certificate are awarded annually. Established in 1947.

• 4771 • **Industrial Safety Contest**
To recognize those fleets with low employee injury rates. Plaques are awarded annually. Established in 1954.

• 4772 • **President's Trophy**
To recognize and promote overall safety within a trucking company. Only winners of the Fleet Safety Award are eligible. A trophy is awarded at the annual meeting of the ATA Safety Management Council. Established in 1938 by the Trailmobile Division of Pullman, Inc., Chicago, IL.

• 4773 • **Safe Worker Award**
To recognize those employees who successfully meet the challenge of working without injury, and to provide incentive to all employees to work in a safe manner. Local drivers, intercity drivers, dockmen, shop employees, working foremen in the above classifications, miscellaneous-custodial employees, watchmen, and spotters are eligible. The award consists of a distinctive pin showing the number of years worked without injury, and a wallet-size card attesting to this record, signed by the ATA Director of Safety.

• 4774 • **Safety Director of the Year Award**
To recognize an outstanding job done by a safety director of a trucking company. Individuals employed full-time directing the safety activities of a truck fleet are eligible. A monetary award of $1,500, a diamond ring, and a plaque are awarded annually by the ATA Safety Management Council. Established in 1960. Sponsored by Transport Insurance Company, Dallas, TX.

• 4775 • **Truck Safety Contest**
To recognize an outstanding record of highway fleet safety. A trophy and plaque are awarded annually. Established in 1936. Formerly: Fleet Safety Award.

• 4776 •
American Underground Construction Association
Susan R. Nelson, Exec.Dir.
3001 Hennepin Ave. S., Ste. D202
Minneapolis, MN 55408
Phone: (612)825-8933
Fax: (612)825-8944
Home Page: http://www.auca.org/
Formerly: American Underground Association.

• 4777 • **Award of Merit - Earth Shelter and Architecture**
To recognize achievement in earth shelter and architecture. A certificate is awarded biennially. Established in 1987.

• 4778 • **Award of Merit - Planning and Development**
To recognize achievement in the planning and development of underground space. A certificate is awarded biennially. Established in 1987.

• 4779 • **Award of Merit - Tunnels and Deep Space**
For recognition of achievement in the field of tunnels and deep space. A certificate is awarded biennially. Established in 1987.

• 4780 • **Kenneth S. Lane Award**
To recognize and encourage outstanding scholarship and publication in the field of underground space. Nominations are made by the Awards Committee based upon submitted papers. A monetary award of up to $500 (based upon investment earnings) and a certificate of recognition are presented biennially at a membership meeting. Established in 1983 in honor of Kenneth S. Lane, founding member and supporter of the Association.

• 4781 •
American University
National Center for Health Fitness
Nebraska Hall, Lower Level
4400 Massachusetts Ave. NW
Washington, DC 20016-8037
Phone: (202)885-6275
Fax: (202)885-6288
E-mail: nchfaa@american.edu
Home Page: http://www.american.edu/healthpromotion

• 4782 • **Dean Meyerson Award**
For leadership in health promotion. Annual award of recognition.

• 4783 •
American University
School of Public Affairs
William M. LeoGrande, Dean
Ward Circle Bldg., Rm. 104
4400 Massachusetts Ave. NW
Washington, DC 20016
Phone: (202)885-2940
Fax: (202)885-2353
E-mail: spa@american.edu
Home Page: http://spa.american.edu

• 4784 • **Roger W. Jones Award for Executive Leadership**
To recognize two career executives in the federal government who are committed to organizational and staff development for the effective continuity of government and who demonstrate superior leadership which results in outstanding organizational achievement and a strong commitment to the effective continuity of government by successfully bringing about the development of managers and executives. Presidential appointees and other administration appointees must submit nominations by December 1. A bronze plaque and citation are presented annually to two individuals at The American University in a special ceremony held on campus in the fall. Established in 1978 in honor of Roger W. Jones, a former senior career government official who, in both top career and presidential appointments, helped improve government operations through the education and training of managers and executives.

• 4785 •
American Urological Association
G. James Gallagher, Exec.Dir.
1000 Corporate Blvd.
Linthicum, MD 21090
Phone: (410)689-3700
Toll-Free: (866)746-4282
Fax: (410)689-3800
E-mail: aua@auanet.org
Home Page: http://www.auanet.org

• 4786 • **Certificate of Achievement**
Presented annually to recognize lifetime career achievements in urology. Indications for consideration include a successful residency program, success in research, successful coordination of other departments, successful productivity in the national AUA, seminars conducted, and international activities. A hand-lettered certificate is awarded annually. Established in 1991.

• 4787 • **William P. Didusch Award**
To recognize outstanding urological art including, but not limited to, illustrations, sculptures, still photography, movies, and television presentations. A hand-lettered, framed certificate is presented annually. Established in 1983 in memory of Mr. William P. Didusch.

• 4788 • **Distinguished Contribution Award**
To recognize an individual who has made outstanding contributions to the science and prac-

tice of urology. A hand-lettered, framed certificate is awarded annually. Established in 1989.

• 4789 • **Distinguished Service Award**
To recognize an individual who is deemed to have made outstanding contributions to the goals of the American Urological Association. A hand-lettered, framed certificate is awarded annually. Established in 1983.

• 4790 • **Eugene Fuller Triennial Prostate Award**
For recognition of an individual who has made an outstanding contribution to the study of the prostate gland and its associated diseases. A handlettered, framed certificate and an honorarium from a trust fund are established by the family of the late Dr. Eugene Fuller once every three years. Established in 1977.

• 4791 • **Gold Cane Award**
To recognize a senior urologist who has made outstanding contributions to the profession and to the American Urological Association, and has not been recognized in any other way. A certificate and lapel pin are awarded annually. Established in 1990.

• 4792 • **Gold Cystoscope Award**
For recognition of a urologist who has distinguished him or herself by outstanding contributions to the profession within ten years of completing residency training. A gold cystoscope, a hand-lettered framed certificate; and an honorarium are awarded annually. Provided by Circo Acmi. Established in 1977.

• 4793 • **Ramon Guiteras Award**
Recognizes an individual for outstanding contributions to the art and science of urology. A hand-lettered framed, certificate and an honorarium are awarded annually in memory of Dr. Ramon Guiteras, founder and first President of the AUA. Financed by C.R. Bard. Established in 1963.

• 4794 • **Health Science Award**
To recognize a company for its outstanding help in promoting the educational, scientific, and research goals of the AUA. A hand-lettered, framed certificate is awarded annually. Established in 1977.

• 4795 • **Presidential Citations**
To recognize one or more individuals who have significantly promoted urology's cause during a specific period of time. Citations may be given in conjunction with the American Foundation for Urologic Disease, or solely by the American Urological Association. A certificate is awarded annually.

• 4796 • **Special Certificate of Appreciation**
To recognize an individual who, as Local Arrangements Chairman, has provided extraordinary contributions leading to a successful and outstanding contribution. A hand-lettered, framed certificate is awarded annually. Established in 1989-1990.

• 4797 • **Hugh Hampton Young Award**
To recognize the outstanding contributions of an individual to the study of genitourinary tract disease. A hand-lettered framed certificate and an honorarium are awarded annually. Financed by Karl Stgorz. Established in 1969.

• 4798 •
American Urological Association Foundation
Dr. Rodney Cotten, Research Coor.
1000 Corporate Blvd.
Linthicum, MD 21090
Phone: (410)689-3750
Phone: 800-828-7866
Toll-Free: (866)746-4282
Fax: (410)689-3850
E-mail: research@auanet.org
Home Page: http://www.afud.org

• 4799 • **AFUD Ph.D. Research Scholar Program**
To assist post-doctoral basic scientists with a research interest in urologic or related diseases and dysfunctions. A commitment to dedicate two years in the AFUD/PhD. program as a full-time researcher is required. The deadline for applications is September 1. A stipend of $30,000 is awarded annually.

• 4800 • **AFUD Research Scholars**
To encourage urologists to choose an academic research career path. The program is not intended as a source of funding for junior clinical faculty. The application deadline is September 1. The total stipend is $60,000 annually; $30,000 from AFUD and $30,000 from the scholar's sponsor.

• 4801 • **Practicing Urologist Research Awards**
To aid and encourage practicing urologists with research ideas to undertake collaborative investigations at a urological research laboratory. The application deadline is September 15. A grant of $5,000 to be matched by the sponsoring institution is awarded.

• 4802 • **Summer Student Fellowships**
To attract the best medical students into urological research. A pre-approved study program and sponsor recommendation are required. The application deadline is February 1. Stipends of $2,000 are available for medical students to work in a urological research laboratory during their summer break.

• 4803 •
American Vaulting Association
Janet Brown, Office Mgr.
8205 Santa Monica Blvd.
West Hollywood, CA 90046
Phone: (323)654-0800
Fax: (323)654-4306
E-mail: americanvaulting@aol.com
Home Page: http://www.americanvaulting.org

• 4804 • **Competition and Achievement Awards**
For recognition of outstanding athletic performance at the Annual National Championship Vaulting Fest and for achievement of skill levels. Members who demonstrate excellence in competition or achievement of prescribed skill levels are eligible. The Competition Awards consist of ribbons, medals, and plaques, and the skill level awards consist of medals or pins. Competition Awards are presented at the Annual National Championship. Skill level awards are given when earned by taking the test. Service Awards are also presented at annual meetings. Established in 1968 by Elizabeth Friedlander Searle.

• 4805 •
American Veterinary Exhibitors Association
Karolyn Kiburz, Exec.Dir.
7375 E. 6th Ave. No.9
Scottsdale, AZ 85251
Phone: (480)990-1887
Toll-Free: 877-990-1836
Fax: (480)990-1889
E-mail: karolyn@mcsource.net

• 4806 • **Best Booth in Show**
For recognition of the best presentation of an exhibit booth at major veterinarian conventions. Awards are given for the best single, best double, and best multiple size booth in the show. Exhibits at major veterinarian conventions with the specific purpose of providing products or services to the professional services of the veterinary industry are eligible. A plaque (nonmember receives one-year membership) is awarded at major conventions. Established in 1936.

• 4807 •
American Veterinary Medical Association
Angela Whitsett, Sec.
1931 N Meacham Rd., Ste. 100
Schaumburg, IL 60173-4360
Phone: (847)925-8070
Toll-Free: 800-248-2862
Fax: (847)925-1329
E-mail: avmainfo@avma.org
Home Page: http://www.avma.org

• 4808 • **American Feed Industry Association Award (AFIA)**
To recognize outstanding research by a veterinarian on nutrition, physiology or disease affecting livestock or poultry production. Original work published during the ten calendar years preceding the year the award is to be given is eligible

Awards are arranged in alphabetical order below their administering organizations

for consideration. Private practitioners as well as institutional workers and others residing in the United States and Canada are eligible. Selection is made by the AVMA Council on Research. A monetary award of $1,500 and a plaque are awarded annually. Established in 1948 by the American Feed Industry Association. Application deadline is February. AVMA was invited to participate in 1969.

• 4809 • American Kennel Club Career Achievement Award in Canine Research

For recognition of long-term contributions to the field of canine research. The recipient of this award, selected by the AVMA Council on Research, will provide the keynote AKC Lecture at the Advances in Veterinary Medicine Symposium. A cash award of $5,000 and a Tiffany crystal sculpture are awarded annually. Established in 1994.

• 4810 • American Kennel Club Excellence in Research Awards

To recognize excellence in canine research. Travel expenses and a $500 cash prize are awarded to up to three individuals annually.

• 4811 • Animal Welfare Award

To recognize a member of the AVMA who has advanced animal well-being, shown exemplary dedication to animal care, and contributed to the community and society. The nominee's achievements can be through any or all of the following areas: leadership, public service, volunteer service, research findings, product development, public policy development, animal advocacy, and humane education. A 12-inch clear lucite pyramid is awarded annually. Established in 1989 by the AVMA Executive Board as part of Animal Welfare Week.

• 4812 • AVMA Award

To recognize a distinguished member of the Association who has contributed to the advancement of veterinary medicine in its organizational aspects. Veterinarians who have exerted outstanding leadership in the building of stronger local, state or regional associations, or who have contributed to the improvement of the national organization are eligible. Selection is made by the AVMA Executive Board. A monetary award of $500 and a Tiffany crystal sculpture are awarded. The award has been presented annually since 1946. Established in 1931, but first activated in 1943. Deadline February 1, 2001.

• 4813 • AVMA Humane Award

To recognize a nonveterinarian or nonveterinary organization that has demonstrated exceptional compassion for the welfare of animals. Nominations are accepted from AVMA members, constituent associations or the humane community. Selection is made by the AVMA Executive Board from the three finalists selected by the Council on Public Relations. A monetary award of $500, a Tiffany crystal sculpture, and travel expenses are awarded annually. Established in 1984. Deadline January 15.

• 4814 • Bustad Companion Animal Veterinarian Award

To recognize a distinguished member of the veterinary profession for pioneering work in the human/animal bond field. A monetary award of $10,000 is distributed as follows: $5,000 to the honored veterinarian, and $5,000 to the veterinary school or non-profit service program designated by the award recipient to further work in the human/animal bond. A plaque is also presented. Established in 1985. Co-sponsored by AVMA, Delta Society and Hill's Pet Nutrition, Inc. Deadline April 1.

• 4815 • Charles River Prize

To recognize distinguished contributions to the field of Laboratory Animal Medicine and science by a veterinarian who is a member of the AVMA and is currently engaged in laboratory animal science. Nominations should be submitted to the Charles River Foundation. Selection is made by the AVMA Executive Board. A monetary award of $2,500 and a plaque are awarded annually. Established in 1977 by the Charles River Foundation. Deadline February 1.

• 4816 • International Veterinary Congress Prize

To recognize outstanding service by members of the association who has contributed to the international understanding of veterinary medicine are eligible. Selection is made by the AVMA Executive Board. A monetary award of $500 and a Tiffany crystal sculpture are awarded annually. Established in 1936. Deadline February 1.

• 4817 • Practitioner Research Award

To encourage clinical research in veterinary science by veterinary practitioners. Members of the Association who are full-time private practitioners and who have carried out the major portion of an important phase of a research problem and published the results while engaged in practice are eligible. The recipient is selected by the AVMA Council on Research. A monetary award of $500 and a Tiffany crystal sculpture are awarded annually. Established in 1955.

• 4818 • President's Award

Honors and recognizes an achievement or activity that deserves more than a letter of commendation, but would not qualify for an existing AVMA award. Veterinarians, veterinary associations, and other individuals or companys are eligible. Up to three awards are given annually at the discretion of the AVMA president. A hand-inscribed mounted plaque is awarded. Application deadline is February 1. Established by the AVMA Executive Board.

• 4819 • Public Service Award

To recognize long terms of outstanding public service or unusual contributions to the practice or science of public health and regulatory veterinary medicine. Outstanding public service rendered by an AVMA member while an employee of a municipal, county, state, or federal agency in the field of regulatory activities associated with animal disease prevention or control, food hygiene, or public health is eligible. AVMA members who, while on the faculty of a college or department of veterinary medicine, have performed outstanding service in the education and training of veterinarians in these public service activities also are eligible. The recipient is selected by the AVMA Council on Public Health and Regulatory Veterinary Medicine. A monetary award of $500 and a Tiffany crystal sculpture are awarded annually. Established in 1968.

• 4820 • Royal Canin Award

To foster progress in the field of small animal medicine and surgery by encouraging and recognizing achievements that favor such progress. The recipient must be a veterinarian whose work within the preceding five years in either clinical research or the basic sciences is judged to have contributed significantly to the advancement of small animal medicine and surgery. Achievements made known through publication in a recognized veterinary periodical and/or through presentation at a professional meeting are considered. Nominations may be made by anyone. The recipient is selected by the AVMA Executive Board. A monetary award of $1,000 and a Fido statuette are awarded annually. Established in 1957. Deadline February 1.

• 4821 •

American Water Resources Association
Robert J. Moresi, Pres.
4 W Federal St.
PO Box 1626
Middleburg, VA 20118-1626
Phone: (540)687-8390
Fax: (540)687-8395
E-mail: info@awra.org
Home Page: http://www.awra.org

• 4822 • William C. Ackermann Medal for Excellence in Water Management

To recognize an individual who has achieved eminence in the design and/or implementation of exemplary water management practices at the state, regional, or local government levels. A medal is awarded annually or when merited. Established in 1988 to honor William C. Ackermann, an individual who achieved eminence and compiled a distinguished record in the design and implementation of exemplary water management practices at the state, regional, and local government levels.

• 4823 • AWRA Board of Directors Service Awards

To recognize individuals for outstanding service to the association.

• 4824 • AWRA Outstanding State Section Award

To recognize the State Section which has provided outstanding service in the furtherance of the objectives of AWRA. The contribution of the Section to an understanding of the state's water resources issues, the size of membership, meritorious activities, and the impact of the Section on the examination of State water resources issues through cooperation with other organizations concerned with water resources are considered as criteria. Awarded annually. Established in 1975.

• 4825 • William R. Boggess Award

For recognition of the author(s) of the best paper published in the *Water Resources Bulletin* during the preceding year that best describes, delineates, or analyzes a major problem or aspect of water resources from either a theoretical, applied, or philosophical standpoint. A plaque is awarded annually. Established in 1973 to honor William R. "Randy" Boggess, a charter member of the association, one of the first directors and a former president of the association, and editor of the *Water Resources Bulletin.*

• 4826 • Henry P. Caulfield, Jr. Medal for Exemplary Contributions to National Water Policy

To recognize an individual for achievements and contributions in setting, designing, and implementing water resources practices at the national level. A medal is awarded annually. Established in 1988.

• 4827 • Sandor C. Csallany Institutional Award for Exemplary Contributions to Water Resources Management

To recognize a water resources institution with an extraordinary record of achievements in setting, designing, influencing, and/or implementing water-related policies, practices, or programs at the national, state, or local government level. The institution nominated may have its roots in federal, state, or local government, private enterprise, or public interest. The nature of the institution's contribution to better water management may take many paths, but it must be substantial and uncommon. A medal is awarded annually.

• 4828 • Fellow Member

To recognize an individual for an eminent record in water resources science or technology and for outstanding service to the association. Members of the association for at least 10 consecutive years who have served as officers, directors, or on a committee for one year, and have an eminent record in a branch of water resources science or technology are eligible. A certificate is awarded annually. Established in 1974.

• 4829 • Richard A. Herbert Memorial Scholarships

For undergraduates enrolled in programs related to water resources and graduates enrolled in programs related to water resources. Awarded annually.

• 4830 • Honorary Member

For recognition of eminence in a branch of water resources science and technology. A certificate is awarded annually at the association's conference in the fall. Established in 1970.

• 4831 • Icko Iben Award

To recognize individuals who have made outstanding contributions to the promotion of communication among the various disciplines concerned with water resources problems. A plaque is awarded annually at the association's conference in the fall. Established in 1971 in memory of Dr. Icko Iben, a co-founder of the association who contributed extensively during his lifetime to the understanding and communication between those involved in the diverse disciplines related to water resources.

• 4832 • Mary H. Marsh Medal for Exemplary Contributions to the Protection and Wise Use of the Nation's Water Resources

To recognize an individual with an extraordinary record of achievements in setting, designing, influencing, and/or implementing water-related policies, practices, or programs at the national, state, or local government level. The individual nominated may have demonstrated these talents while associated with a governmental agency, a legislative body, a commission or committee, or a public-minded organization. The contribution to protecting and wisely using the nation's waters, rather than the field of expertise, is the deciding factor for the award. Awarded annually.

• 4833 • Outstanding Student Chapter Award

To recognize the student chapter that has provided outstanding service in the furtherance of the objectives of AWRA. This award is based upon the holding of regularly scheduled meetings to advance water resources knowledge, especially through presentations by invited speakers or by students on their research and special activities (during the academic year) that contribute to the student's educational program. Awarded annually. Established in 1983.

• 4834 • President's Award for Outstanding Service

To recognize those who have made significant contributions to AWRA. Nominations are not accepted. Awarded when merited at the discretion of the President of the association. Established in 1979.

• 4835 • Pyramid Award

Recognizes and encourages young professionals as the future leaders of water resources research, management, and education. Young professionals who demonstrate outstanding achievement, talents, and leadership potential through their professional activities realted to water resources are eligible. Awarded annually. Established in 2000. 45-0895 AWWA DVR

• 4836 •
American Water Works Association
Jack W. Hoffbuhr, Exec.Dir.
6666 W Quincy Ave.
Denver, CO 80235
Phone: (303)794-7711
Toll-Free: 800-926-7337
Fax: (303)347-0804
E-mail: rrenner@awwa.org
Home Page: http://www.awwa.org

• 4837 • Academic Achievement Award

To encourage academic excellence and to give recognition to those graduate students who have made outstanding contributions to the field of public water supply through their work at a university. Master theses and doctoral dissertations are eligible. For doctoral dissertations a $ 3000 one time first place award and a $ 1500 one-time second place awards are given. For masters thesis a $ 3000 one-time place award and a $ 1500 onetime second place award are given. Application deadline is October 1st annually.

• 4838 • Education Award

To recognize students, 19 years old or younger, at the elementary, junior high, high school, or technical school level who have created a water related project of superior quality. The award commemorates the exceptionally outstanding efforts of the late AWWA Past-President John H. Stacha to bring water education and water educational materials and information to the youth of the United States, Canada, and Mexico.

• 4839 •
American Watercolor Society
Janet Walsh, Pres.
47 5th Ave.
New York, NY 10003
E-mail: AWS@watercolor-online.com
Home Page: http://
www.americanwatercolorsociety.com/

• 4840 • Arjomaria/Arches/Rivers Award

To recognize an outstanding watercolor painting entered in the Society's annual exhibition. A monetary prize of $1,000 is awarded annually. Formerly: Arches Papers Award.

• 4841 • *The Artist's Magazine* Award

To recognize an outstanding watercolor painting entered in the Society's annual exhibition. A monetary award of $500 is presented.

• 4842 • AWS Bronze Medal of Honor

To recognize achievement in watercolor painting. Any artist entered in the Society's exhibition is eligible. A monetary award of $1,500 and a medal are awarded annually.

• 4843 • AWS Gold Medal of Honor

To recognize achievement in watercolor painting. Any artist entered in the Society's exhibition is eligible. A monetary award of $2,000 and a medal are awarded annually.

• 4844 • AWS Silver Medal of Honor

To recognize achievement in watercolor painting. Any artist entered in the Society's exhibition is eligible. A monetary award of $1,600 and a medal are awarded annually.

• 4845 • Harrison Cady Award

To recognize an outstanding watercolor painting entered in the Society's annual exhibition. A monetary prize of $200 is awarded in even-numbered years.

• 4846 • Elizabeth Callan Memorial Medal
To recognize an outstanding watercolor painting entered in the Society's annual exhibition. A monetary prize of $500 is awarded.

• 4847 • CFS Medal
To recognize an outstanding watercolor painting entered in the Society's annual exhibition. A monetary award of $1,000 is presented.

• 4848 • Mario Cooper Award
To recognize achievement in watercolor painting entered in the Society's annual exhibition. A monetary prize of $300 is awarded annually.

• 4849 • Dolphin Medal
To recognize an individual for outstanding long-term contributions to art, especially watercolor painting. A bronze medal designed by Mario Cooper is awarded when merited. Recipients become Honorary Members of the Dolphin Fellowship. Established in 1990.

• 4850 • Ann Williams Glushien Award
To recognize an outstanding watercolor painting entered in the Society's annual exhibition. A monetary award of $300 is presented.

• 4851 • Emily Goldsmith Award
To recognize achievement in watercolor painting entered in the Society's annual exhibition. A monetary prize of $300 is awarded annually.

• 4852 • Hardie Gramatky Memorial Award
To recognize an outstanding watercolor painting entered in the Society's annual exhibition. A monetary prize of $400 is awarded annually. Established in 1980 in memory of Hardy Gramatky.

• 4853 • Walser S. Greathouse Medal
To recognize achievement in watercolor painting entered in the Society's annual exhibition. A monetary prize of $1,200 and a medal are awarded annually. Established in 1977.

• 4854 • High Winds Medal
To recognize an outstanding watercolor painting entered in the Society's annual exhibition. Four monetary prizes of $1,200 and a medal each are awarded annually.

• 4855 • Honorary Member
To recognize individuals for outstanding contributions to the art of watercolor painting.

• 4856 • Samuel Leitman Memorial Award
To recognize achievement in watercolor painting entered in the Society's annual exhibition. A monetary award of $500 is presented.

• 4857 • Mary S. Litt Medal
To recognize achievement in watercolor painting entered in the Society's annual exhibition. Non-members of the Society are eligible. A monetary prize of $500 and a medal are awarded annually.

• 4858 • Emily Lowe Memorial Award
To recognize achievement in watercolor painting entered in the Society's annual exhibition. A monetary prize of $300 is awarded annually.

• 4859 • Marthe T. McKinnon Award
To recognize achievement in watercolor painting entered in the Society's annual exhibition. A monetary prize of $300 is awarded in even-numbered years.

• 4860 • Barse Miller Memorial Award
To recognize an artist for an outstanding watercolor painting entered in the Society's annual exhibition. A monetary prize of $500 is awarded annually.

• 4861 • Lucy B. Moore Memorial Award
To recognize an outstanding watercolor painting entered in the Society's annual exhibition. A monetary award of $300 is presented.

• 4862 • Lena Newcastle Award
For recognition of an achievement in watercolor painting. Artists entered in the Society's exhibition are eligible. A monetary prize of $650 is awarded annually.

• 4863 • Mary Pleissner Memorial Award
To recognize an artist for an outstanding watercolor painting entered in the Society's annual exhibition. A monetary prize of $500 is awarded annually.

• 4864 • Ogden Pleissner Memorial Award
To recognize an outstanding watercolor painting entered in the Society's exhibition. A monetary award of $500 is presented annually. Established in 1984 in memory of Ogden Pleissner.

• 4865 • Nicholas Reale Memorial Award
To recognize an outstanding watercolor painting entered in the Society's annual exhibition. A monetary prize of $500 is awarded.

• 4866 • Paul B. Remmey AWS Memorial Award
For recognition of an achievement in watercolor painting entered in the Society's annual exhibition. A monetary prize of $300 is awarded annually.

• 4867 • Paul Schwartz Memorial Award
To recognize an outstanding watercolor painting entered in the Society's annual exhibition. A monetary award of $300 is presented.

• 4868 • Clara Stroud Memorial Award
To recognize an outstanding watercolor painting entered in the Society's annual exhibition. A monetary award of $1,000 is presented.

• 4869 • Ida Wells Stroud Memorial Award
To recognize an outstanding watercolor painting entered in the Society's annual exhibition. A monetary award of $1,000 is presented.

• 4870 • Traveling Show Appreciation Award
To recognize achievement in watercolor painting entered in the Society's exhibition. A monetary award of $250 is presented annually. Established in 1983.

• 4871 • Edgar A. Whitney Award
To recognize the artist of an outstanding watercolor painting displayed at the Society's annual exhibition. A monetary prize of $1,000 is awarded.

• 4872 • Winsor and Newton Award
To recognize achievement in watercolor painting entered in the Society's exhibition. A monetary prize of $750 is awarded annually. Established in 1951.

• 4873 • John Young - Hunter Memorial Award
To recognize an outstanding watercolor painting entered in the Society's annual exhibition. A monetary prize of $300 is awarded annually.

• 4874 •
American Welding Society
Ray Shook, Exec.Dir.
550 NW Le Jeune Rd.
Miami, FL 33126
Phone: (305)443-9353
Toll-Free: 800-443-9353
Fax: (305)443-7559
E-mail: info@aws.org
Home Page: http://www.aws.org

• 4875 • Comfort A. Adams Lecture Award
To recognize a notable scientist or engineer for an outstanding lecture presenting some new and distinctive development in the field of welding. An honorarium and the Adams Lecture Certificate are awarded each year at the annual meeting of the Society. Established in 1943 in honor of Comfort A. Adams, founder and first President of the Society.

• 4876 • Adams Memorial Membership Award
To recognize educators whose teaching activities are considered to have advanced the knowledge of welding of the undergraduate or post-graduate students in their respective engineering institutions. Each year the Society's Committee on Awards selects up to five educators in accredited engineering institutions and

awards to each a four-year membership in the American Welding Society. Each awardee receives a certificate and all current volumes of the *Welding Handbook*. Established in 1960.

• 4877 • **Howard E. Adkins Memorial Instructor Membership Award**

To recognize high school, trade school, technical institute, or junior college instructors whose teaching activities are considered to have advanced the knowledge of welding to students in their respective schools. Each awardee receives a certificate and a two-year full membership in the American Welding Society. Awarded annually. Established in 1965. Sponsored by Howard E. Adkins.

• 4878 • **Arsham Amirikian Memorial Maritime Welding Award**

To recognize the best article published in the *Welding Journal* during the previous calendar year describing how maritime structures have been greatly improved through the substitution of new methods where welding plays an important part. An honorarium and a plaque are awarded.

• 4879 • **Robert J. Conkling Memorial Award**

To recognize the schools that trained the two first-place winners in the national VICA welding competition. A monetary award is presented. Established to honor Robert J. Conkling, who encouraged young people to study welding, and contributed generously of his time and talent to the development of the AWS Welding Exposition.

• 4880 • **A. F. Davis Silver Medal Award**

To honor the author of a paper demonstrating notable achievements in welded design published in the *Welding Journal* during the previous calendar year. Categories include: machine design, maintenance and surfacing, and structural design. A silver medal and a certificate are awarded annually. Established in 1957 by A. F. Davis, formerly Vice-President and Secretary of Lincoln Electric Company.

• 4881 • **Dalton E. Hamilton Memorial CWI of the Year Award**

To recognize AWS members participating in the CWI/CAWI Program whose inspection, Society, and civic activities are considered to have enhanced public awareness of both the Society and the CWI Program or otherwise have made an outstanding contribution to the science of welding inspection. Awarded annually. Formerly: CWI of the Year Award.

• 4882 • **McKay - Helm Award**

For recognition of the best contribution to the advancement of knowledge on low alloy steel, stainless, or surfacing weld metals involving the use, development, or testing of these materials as represented in articles published in the *Welding Journal* during a given calendar year. A $1,000 honorarium and a certificate are awarded annually. This award is sponsored by McKay Welding Products, a division of Illinois Tool Works Company to honor James C. McKay and Dr. David F. Helm, two pioneers of the welding industry.

• 4883 • **W. H. Hobart Memorial Medal Award**

To honor the author of the best paper published in the *Welding Journal* on the subject of pipe welding, the structural use of pipe or similar applications, excluding the manufacture of pipe. A medal and certificate are awarded annually. Established in 1965 by Hobart Brothers Company, Hobart Square, Troy, Ohio, in honor of William H. Hobart, Sr.

• 4884 • **Honorary Membership Award**

To recognize a person of acknowledged eminence in the welding profession, or who may be accredited with exceptional accomplishments in the development of the welding art. Honorary Members have full rights of membership. Not more than two Honorary Members are elected in any one fiscal year. Certificates are presented. Established in 1939.

• 4885 • **William Irrgang Memorial Award**

To recognize the individual who has done the most to enhance the American Welding Society's goal of advancing the science, technology, and application of welding over the last five years. The award consists of a certificate with an honorarium of $2,500. No recipient of this award will repeat within a five year period. Awarded annually. Established in 1986 to honor William Irrgang.

• 4886 • **Charles H. Jennings Memorial Award**

To recognize a student or faculty representative of a college or university for a valuable contribution to welding literature as presented in a paper published in the *Welding Journal* during the previous calendar year. A monetary award of $200 and a certificate are awarded annually. Established in 1973 in memory of Charles H. Jennings, AWS president from 1951-52.

• 4887 • **James F. Lincoln Gold Medal Award**

To honor the author of the best paper published in the *Welding Journal* during the previous calendar year that represents the greater original contribution to the advancement and use of welding. A gold medal and certificate are awarded annually. Established in 1936 by James F. Lincoln, former Chairman of the Board of the Lincoln Electric Company who sponsored and endowed the prize.

• 4888 • **Professor Koichi Masubuchi Award**

To recognize an individual who have made significant contributions to the advancement of the science and technology of materials joining through research and development. Individual must be under 40 years of age. The deadline for nominations is December 1. A plaque and a honorarium of $5,000 are awarded annually. Established in honor of Professor Koichi Masubuchi, who made significant contributions to the science of welding, especially welding fabrication of marine and space structures. Sponsored by the Massachusetts Institute of Technology, Center for Ocean Engineering.

• 4889 • **Samuel Wylie Miller Memorial Medal Award**

For recognition of meritorious achievement and conspicuous contributions to the advancement of the art of welding and cutting. A medal and a certificate are awarded annually. Established in 1927 by Samuel Wylie Miller, executive of Union Carbide and Carbon Company.

• 4890 • **National Meritorious Award**

For recognition of loyalty, counsel, and devotion to the affairs of the Society and assistance in promoting cordial relationships with industry and other organizations. Not more than two certificates are awarded annually. Established in 1956.

• 4891 • **Robert L. Peaslee Brazing Award**

To recognize the paper considered to be the best contribution to the science or technology of brazing published in the *Welding Journal* during the previous calendar year. An honorarium and a certificate are awarded. Sponsored by the Wall Colmonoy Corporation.

• 4892 • **Plummer Memorial Educational Lecture Award**

To recognize outstanding contributions to the National Education Lectures at the annual meeting of the Society. The lecturer is selected by the Educational Activities Committee of the American Welding Society and is given a bronze medal and a certificate. Established in 1957 as the Educational Lecture and renamed the Plummer Memorial Educational Lecture Award in honor of Fred L. Plummer, president of the Society from 1952-54, and Executive Director from 1957-69.

• 4893 • **Safety and Health Award**

To recognize individuals for promoting welding safety and health through research, educational activities, developing safe practices, or disseminating information through publications or other means, thereby fostering public safety awareness and welfare.

• 4894 • **Warren F Savage Memorial Award**

To recognize original and innovative research resulting in a better understanding of the metallurgical principles related to welding. Papers on this topic published during the previous calendar year in the *Research Supplement of the Welding Journal* are eligible. The award consists of a certificate and honorarium of $250. In the event the paper selected has more than one author, the stipend is divided equally among the authors and a certificate is given to each. Established in 1986 by friends and former students of Warren F. "Doc" Savage to recognize his lifetime accomplishments and dedication in the field of welding metallurgy.

• 4895 • Silver Quill Editorial Achievement Award

To recognize the editors and publishers of a magazine outside the welding field that publishes the best original editorial coverage on the subject of welding during the previous June 1 to May 31 period. A certificate is awarded annually.

• 4896 • William Spraragen Memorial Membership Award

To recognize the author of the best research paper printed in the research supplement of the *Welding Journal* during the twelve month period ending with the December issue. A monetary award of $250 and a certificate are awarded annually. Established in 1961 in honor of William Spraragen for his contributions to the art and science of welding.

• 4897 • R. D. Thomas Memorial Award

For recognition of notable contributions to the activities of the International Institute of Welding by a member of the American Council of the Institute or the American Welding Society. An honorarium of $250 and a certificate are awarded annually. Established in 1965 in honor of R. D. Thomas, a charter member of the Society. Sponsored by the Arcos Corporation.

• 4898 • Elihu Thomson Resistance Welding Award

To recognize a living individual who has made an outstanding contribution to the technology and application of resistance welding as evidenced by: invention or production of new resistance welding equipment innovations, a unique application of resistance welding in a production environment, a technical paper published in the *Welding Journal* or other similarly prestigious publication, or other contribution as the AWS National Awards Committee shall deem worthy of recognition. The deadline for nominations to AWS Headquarters is September 15. The award consists of an honorarium of $500 (which may be presented in cash or as a scholarship, at the recipient's option) and a certificate. Awarded annually. Established in 1985, during the RWMA's 50th Anniversary, for initial presentation in 1986 to celebrate the 100th Anniversary of the invention of resistance welding. Sponsored by the Resistance Welder Manufacturers' Association.

• 4899 • Prof. Dr. Rene D. Wasserman Memorial Award

To honor the author(s) of the best paper published in the *Welding Journal* that demonstrates application of welding, brazing, or thermal spraying for maintenance and repair. An honorarium of $1,000 and a certificate are awarded annually. Established in 1967 and sponsored by the Eutectic Castolin Corporation.

• 4900 • George E. Willis Award

To recognize an individual for promoting the advancement of welding internationally by fostering cooperative participation in areas such as technology transfer, standards rationalization, and the promotion of industrial goodwill. No recipient of this award will repeat within a five year period. A certificate and an honorarium of $2,500 are awarded annually. Established in honor of George E. Willis, Chairman of the Board and Chief Executive Officer. Sponsored by Lincoln Electric Company.

• 4901 •
American Whig-Cliosophic Society
3 Whig Hall
Princeton University
Princeton, NJ 08544
Phone: (609)258-2583
Fax: (609)258-3206
E-mail: mmacdona@princeton.edu

• 4902 • James Madison Award for Distinguished Public Service

To honor those who have distinguished themselves through a lifetime of outstanding public service. The award, like the Society, entails no political bias. The recipient is determined by a vote of the Governing Council from among those suggested by the general membership. An honorarium and a Society diploma, which confers honorary membership, are presented at the Society's Annual James Madison Banquet. Established in 1960 in honor of James Madison, founder of the Society and fourth president of the United States. The American Whig-Cliosophic Society at Princeton University is the oldest college political and debating society in the nation.

• 4903 •
American White American Creme Horse Registry
Carley Daugherty, Sec./Treas.
90000 Edwards Rd.
Naper, NE 68755
Phone: (402)832-5560
E-mail: carleyd@juno.com
Home Page: http://www.whitehorseranchnebraska.com

Formerly: (1998) International American Albino Association and White Horse Ranch National Foundation.

• 4904 • National and International High Points Competition

To recognize all pure white and cream white horses known as the American Albino. Points are awarded for professional or amateur, local and state shows, parades, trail rides, games, exhibitions, etc. Certificates are presented in the following categories: International Champion, U.S.A. Grand Champion, and IAAA Honor Awards. Established in 1989 by the International American Albino Association. Active.

• 4905 •
American Wine Society
Angel Nardone, Exec.Dir.
3006 Latta Rd.
Rochester, NY 14612-3298
Phone: (585)225-7613
Fax: (585)225-7613
E-mail: angel910@aol.com
Home Page: http://www.americanwinesociety.com

• 4906 • Award of Merit - Life Member

To recognize an individual for an outstanding contribution to the furthering of American wine. A plaque is awarded annually. Established in 1971.

• 4907 • Commercial Wine Competition Awards

To recognize outstanding commercial wine. Submitted wines are judged by a professional team. Gold, silver, and bronze medals are awarded annually. Outstanding wines are listed in the *AWS Journal.*

• 4908 • Honorary Life Members

To recognize an individual for an outstanding contribution to the Society over a period of years. Awarded occasionally when merited. Awards were presented in 1973, 1984, 1990, 1998, and 2002.

• 4909 • Journal Contributor Awards

To recognize individuals for contributions to *The American Wine Society Journal.* Established in 1985.

• 4910 • National Amateur Wine Competition Awards

To recognize outstanding wine making ability. Awards may be presented in the following categories: best of show, best hybrid, sparkling, fruit, native, hybrid red, hybrid white, rose, vinifera red, vinifera white, vidal blanc, Riesling, estate bottled, and dessert. Members of the society are eligible. The wine submitted is judged by peers first, and then by a panel of professional judges. Grand Awards and Special Mention Awards are presented each year at the annual meeting of the American Wine Society. Established in 1974.

• 4911 • Outstanding Member

To honor a member for significant contribution to the society. A plaque is awarded annually. Established in 1976.

• 4912 •
American Zoo and Aquarium Association
Syndey Butler, Exec.Dir.
8403 Colesville Rd., Ste. 710
Silver Spring, MD 20910-3314
Phone: (301)562-0777
Fax: (301)562-0888
E-mail: generalinquiry@aza.org
Home Page: http://www.aza.org

Formerly: (1995) American Association of Zoological Parks and Aquariums.

• 4913 • **Edward H. Bean Award**
To recognize efforts in the captive management and husbandry of various animal species during the year. The award acclaims the most significant birth or hatching of a species and/or subspecies, or a significant propagation or management program contributing to the reproductive success of one of more species and/or subspecies. A citation is awarded annually to one or more institutions. Established in 1957.

• 4914 • **Conservation Awards**
To recognize outstanding conservation programs for habitat preservation, species restoration, and support of biodiversity in the wild. Two awards are presented: North American Conservation Award and International Conservation Award. Members of the Association are eligible. Awarded annually. Established in 1993.

• 4915 • **Education Award**
To recognize outstanding achievement in public education programs. Members of the Association are eligible. Programs are judged on their ability to promote conservation knowledge, attitudes and behavior, show innovation and measure success. Awarded annually. Established in 1977.

• 4916 • **Exhibit Award**
To recognize accomplishments in exhibit design and animal display. Members of the Association are eligible. Awarded annually to one or more recipients. Established in 1974.

• 4917 • **Munson Aquatic Conservation Exhibitory Award**
Recognizes excellence in aquatic exhibits. Exhibits must have conservation education incorporated into the design and presentation. All AZA member institutions are eligible; institutions with representatives on the review board are not eligible. The exhibit must be less than three years old as of May 1, 2001. Older exhibits are eligible if they have undergone major renovations within the past three years. The exhibit must contain piscine species (freshwater or marine). Two $25,000 prizes, one to an institution with an operating budget of $4,000,000 or less and one to an institution with an operating budget of over $4,000,000 are given annually in the form of a grant to each winning institution's Education Department. Seven copies of each entry, including a copy of the institution's 501(c) IRS letter; a 4" x 6" color photograph of the exhibit mounted in a clear plastic sheet or printed digitally; a written description of the exhibit, 1000 words or fewer; copie of all text considered part of the exhibit; dates of the exhibit installation and opening; and supplemental materials, including video tapes must be submitted. Exhibits will be judged on the accuracy of information, relevance of information and effectiveness of exhibit. Intent to enter forms are due by March 31, entries are due by May 1.

• 4918 • **North American Conservation Award**
To recognize achievements in local conservation efforts by member organizations in habitat preservation, species restoration, and support of biodiversity in the wild. Members of the Association are eligible. Awarded annually. Established in 1997.

• 4919 • **R. Marlin Perkins Award for Professional Excellence**
Recognizes outstanding service. Candidates must be members of AZA in good-standing; have demonstrated impeccable character and have a distinguished record of honorable service to the association; be strongly committed to education, conservation, science, recreation, and the welfare of animals, and actively involved in furthering these causes within the zoo and aquarium profession. Nominations must be supported by at least two professional fellows, one of whom must be an AZA Board member.

• 4920 •
Americanism Educational League
Thomas A. Flattery, Sec.
PO Box 5986
Buena Park, CA 90622
Phone: (714)522-7671
Fax: (714)522-3597
E-mail: michael@californialaw.org
Home Page: http://www.americanism.org

• 4921 • **Essay Contest for College Students**
To encourage the study of private enterprise/free market economics on university and college campuses all over the United States. Any registered undergraduate college student may submit a 1,500 word essay on the assigned subject by March 2. Essays are judged not on the basis of agreement or disagreement with the views of the Americanism Educational League, nor on the length of their bibliographies, but on their internal logic, coherence, originality, thoughtfulness, and evidence of sound research. The following awards are presented: first prize - $5,000; second prize - $2,500; third prize - $1,500; fourth prize - $1,000; fifth prize $500; and sixth prize - $500. Awarded annually in April. Established in 1983. Formerly: Milton Friedman Essay Contest.

• 4922 •
America's Cup Global Information Service
PO Box 2320
Olympic Valley, CA 96146
Phone: (530)581-0514
E-mail: paulrivard@americascupnews.com
Home Page: http://
www.americascupnews.com

Formerly: (1988) Sail America.

• 4923 • **America's Cup**
For recognition of excellence in sailing. The sailing regatta consists of numerous races over a four month period. Challenging nations provide their own boat and crew. Challengers are submitted by foreign yacht clubs, although the boat is frequently a national effort. A trophy has been awarded approximately every three to four years since 1958. Established in 1851 by George Schuyler, last surviving owner of the yacht *America* for which the trophy is named.

• 4924 •
America's Foundation
Vince Thornton, Sec.
PO Box 2016
Learned, MS 39154
Phone: (601)885-2288
E-mail: spiritofamerica@hotmail.com
Home Page: http://www.angelfire.com/ms/
champsite

• 4925 • **The Spirit of America Award**
To honor outstanding high school "athletes, citizens, and leaders." Presented annually with medals and certificates. Established in 1970.

• 4926 •
America's Junior Miss Foundation
Barbara Taylor, Exec.Dir.
PO Box 2786
Mobile, AL 36652-2786
Phone: (251)438-3621
Toll-Free: 800-256-5435
Fax: (251)431-0063
E-mail: foundation@ajm.org
Home Page: http://www.ajm.org/a/
foundation/index.asp

Formerly: (1983) America's Young Woman of the Year.

• 4927 • **America's Junior Miss**
Provide outstanding, college bound high school girls with opportunities to win scholarships and to encourage personal development in all young people through the "Be Your Best Self" national outreach program. Candidates must be female, high school juniors or seniors; US citizens and legal residents of the county and state of competition. Each contestant is evaluated on scholastics (20%), interview (25%), talent (25%), fitness (15%) and poise (15%). More than $ 1.8 million in cash scholarships are presented at he local, state and national levels of competition annually. Deadline dates vary by state. Students should consult with their high school guidance counselors early in their sophomore or junior

year. Formerly: (1989) America's Young Woman of the Year.

• 4928 •
Americas Society
William R. Rhodes, Pres.
680 Park Ave.
New York, NY 10021
Phone: (212)249-8950
Fax: (212)249-5868
E-mail: inforequest@as-coa.org
Home Page: http://www.americas-society.org

Formed by merger of: (1991) Pan American Society of the United States.

• 4929 • **Pan American Gold Insigne of the Americas Society**
Democratically elected heads of State of the American Republics are eligible for the award. A medal is presented on the occasion of their visit to the United States. Established in 1932.

• 4930 • **Pan American Gold Medal of the Americas Society**
To recognize private citizens of the Americas who work to promote greater awareness of the cultural, social, and political realities of the Americas, and to promote greater understanding among the nations and people of the Americas. A gold medal is presented when an appropriate occasion arises. Established in 1981.

• 4931 •
Ames Research Center
Astrobiology Institute
MS 240-1
Moffett Field, CA 94035-1000
Phone: (650)604-0809
Fax: (650)604-4251
E-mail: kburton@mail.arc.nasa.gov
Home Page: http://www.nai.arc.nasa.gov/

• 4932 • **Astrobiology Award**
Recognizes websites combining excellence in information and education pertaining to astrobiology. Inquire for application details.

• 4933 •
AMIT USA
Jan Schecter, Pres.
817 Broadway
New York, NY 10003
Phone: (212)477-4720
Toll-Free: 800-989-AMIT
Fax: (212)353-2312
E-mail: info@amitchildren.org
Home Page: http://www.amitchildren.org

Formerly: (1983) American Mizrachi Women.

• 4934 • **America/Israel Friendship Award**
To recognize distinguished contributions toward the development and furtherance of America-Israel friendship. Distinguished Americans who are not of the Jewish faith are eligible. An inscribed plaque is awarded. Established in 1948.

• 4935 • **Distinguished Achievement Award**
To recognize lifetime achievement of benefit to the Jewish people.

• 4936 • **Distinguished Service Award**
To honor exceptional service to humanity.

• 4937 • **Humanitarian Award**
For recognition of outstanding humanitarian efforts.

• 4938 • **Lifetime Achievement Award**
To recognize lifetime achievement that has benefited the Jewish people.

• 4939 • **Silver Medallion Award**
To recognize Jewish women who have made distinguished contributions to the building of Israel and the development of Jewish life and culture through individual talent or organizations contributing toward those goals. An inscribed plaque is awarded. Established in 1963. Occasionally men are honored.

• 4940 •
Amnesty International - Canadian Section
Alex Neve, Sec.Gen.
312 Laurier Ave. E
Ottawa, ON, Canada K1N 1H9
Phone: (613)744-7667
Toll-Free: 800-266-3789
Fax: (613)746-2411
E-mail: info@amnesty.ca
Home Page: http://www.amnesty.ca

• 4941 • **Media Awards for Excellence**
Recognizes excellence in reporting of international human rights issues in Canadian media. Awarded annually.

• 4942 •
Amusement and Music Operators Association
Jack Kelleher, Exec.VP
33 W Higgins Rd., Ste. 830
South Barrington, IL 60010
Phone: (847)428-7699
Toll-Free: 800-937-2662
Fax: (847)428-7851
E-mail: amoa@amoa.com
Home Page: http://www.amoa.com

Formerly: (1976) Music Operators Association.

• 4943 • **AMOA Cigarette Vending Machine Promotion Award**
Selected by vote of the membership.

• 4944 • **AMOA Games Awards**
For recognition of the most popular pinball, video, and other amusement game. Awards are presented in the following categories: Most Played Videogame (Dedicated), Most Played Pinball Game, Most Played Conversion Kit, Most Innovative New Technology, Most Played Dart Game, Most Played Pool Table, Most Played Jukebox, Most Played Redemption Game, Most Popular Other Game, and New Equipment Award. The membership votes on the most popular machine. A plaque is awarded annually at the Annual Exposition Banquet. Established in 1982.

• 4945 • **AMOA Jukebox Awards**
For recognition of the most popular artist(s) based on revenue in the nation's jukeboxes. Awards are given in the following categories: Pop Single of the Year, Country Single of the Year, R&B Single of the Year, Pop CD of the Year, Country CD of the Year, R&B CD of the Year, Latin CD of the year, Rising Star Award (Male), Rising Star Award (Female), Rising Star Award (Group), Jukebox Legend (Living), and Jukebox Legend (Deceased). The membership votes on the popularity of artist(s) in specified categories. Plaques are presented annually at the AMOA Exposition Banquet. Established in 1948.

• 4946 •
AMVETS - American Veterans
John Sisler, Nat. Commander
4647 Forbes Blvd.
Lanham, MD 20706-4380
Phone: (301)459-9600
Toll-Free: 877-726-8387
Fax: (301)459-7924
E-mail: amvets@amvets.org
Home Page: http://www.amvets.org

• 4947 • **AMVETS National Awards Program**
To recognize local, community based posts and state departments for providing service and participating in worthwhile programs. The following awards are presented: Bob Gomulinski Community Service Award; Special Olympics Award; White Clover Award; Scouting Awards; Public Relations Award; ROTC Award; and Department of Veterans Affairs Leadership/Volunteer of the Year Award. Awarded at the annual national (veteran member) convention in August.

• 4948 • **AMVETS National Employer of the Year Award**
Recognizes employers who, as a standard practice, go out of their way to hire veterans and serve the community. Awards are presented to employers in three categories: 25-100 employees, 101-300 employees, and 301 or more employees. Awarded annually at the national convention in August.

• 4949 • **AMVETS Silver Helmet Awards**
This award, the most prestigious honor given by this congressionally chartered veterans' service organization, is presented to distinguished Americans who have made significant contributions to Congress or in the conduct of Americanism, civil service, peace, national defense, and rehabilitation. The Silver Helmet, a silver-plated replica of the World War II GI helmet, is awarded annually in conjunction with the Spring National Executive Committee Meeting and Silver Helmet Awards Banquet in Washington, DC.

• 4950 •
Amy Foundation
PO Box 16091
Lansing, MI 48901
Phone: (517)323-6233
E-mail: amyfoundtn@aol.com
Home Page: http://www.amyfound.org

• 4951 • **Amy Writing Awards**
To recognize creative, skillful writing that presents in a sensitive, thought-provoking manner the Biblical position on issues affecting the world today. Articles published in a secular, non-religious publication during the previous year may be submitted by January 31. Biblical quotations must be taken from an accepted and popular edition of the Bible, such as the New International Version, The Living Bible, The King James, or the Revised Standard Version. The article must present God's position on an issue as relevant, timely and deserving of thoughtful consideration. Examples of issues for consideration, but not limited to these, are family life, divorce, value trends, media and entertainment character, pornography, political morality, U.S. National interests, abortion, religion and addiction to drugs and alcohol. The Biblical impact on individual character and outlook are also appropriate issues. The following monetary awards are presented: (1) First Prize - $10,000; (2) Second Prize - $5,000; (3) Third Prize - $4,000; (4) Fourth Prize $3,000; (5) Fifth Prize - $2,000; and (6) ten prizes of $1,000 each. Established in 1984.

• 4952 •
Anchor Bay Chamber of Commerce
Lisa Edwards, Exec.Dir.
35054 23 Mile Rd., Ste. 110
New Baltimore, MI 48047
Phone: (586)725-5148
Fax: (586)725-5369
E-mail: info@anchorbaychamber.com
Home Page: http://www.anchorbaychamber.com

• 4953 • **Gold Medal Award**
For chamber member demonstrating commitment to the community. Recognition award bestowed annually.

• 4954 •
Ancient Mediterranean Research Association
PO Box 49421
Los Angeles, CA 90049
Phone: (760)356-6620
Fax: (760)354-6335
E-mail: info@atlantisresearch.com
Home Page: http://www.atlantisresearch.com

• 4955 • **Honorary Service Awards**
For contributions to multicultural education.

• 4956 •
Animal Behavior Society
Dr. Ken Yasukawa, Pres.
Indiana University
2611 E 10th. St.
Bloomington, IN 47408-2603
Phone: (812)856-5541
Fax: (812)856-5542
E-mail: aboffice@indiana.edu
Home Page: http://www.animalbehavior.org

• 4957 • **ABS Founders' Memorial Award**
To recognize the best poster paper at the annual meeting. All members of the society in good standing are eligible to enter the competition. A monetary award of $100 and a certificate of achievement are presented each year at the Annual Meeting. Established in 1986 in honor of the founders of ABS.

• 4958 • **Warder Clyde Allee Best Student Paper Award of the Animal Behavior Society**
For recognition of achievement in the presentation of the best student paper at the annual meeting of the Animal Behavior Society. Unpublished student research by a single author may be entered in the competition. An individual may enter the competition only once, and cannot have completed defense of the doctoral dissertation before the preceding ABS annual meeting. A monetary award of $250 and a certificate of achievement are presented each year at the annual meeting. Established in 1972 in honor of Warder Clyde Allee, a leader of the "Chicago School of Animal Behavior" whose research included investigations about the cooperative social organizations of animals. Formerly: (1973) Animal Behavior Society Best Student Paper Award.

• 4959 • **Animal Behavior Society Film Festival Awards**
To recognize the best films presented at the Animal Behavior Society annual meeting. Two awards are presented: Film Award - for the best commercial film. New and original films must be submitted. A certificate is awarded annually when merited. Established in 1983; and Jack Ward Memorial Film Award - for the best film by an amateur. New and original films must be submitted. A monetary award of $250 is presented when merited. Established in 1983 in memory of Jack Ward, who served as Chairperson of the Animal Behavior Society Film Committee until his death in 1982.

• 4960 •
Animal Transportation Association
Alistair Macnab, Dir. Admin.
111 East Loop N
Houston, TX 77029
Phone: (713)532-2177
Fax: (713)532-2166
E-mail: info@aata-animaltransport.org
Home Page: http://www.aata-animaltransport.org
Formerly: (1989) Animal Air Transportation Association.

• 4961 • **AATA Animal Welfare Award**
To recognize a person who has worked with the transport of animals and has exhibited an outstanding job in promoting animal welfare.

• 4962 • **Dr. Robert Campbell Memorial Award**
For recognition of outstanding service or achievements in the humane, economical movement of animals for the benefit of mankind. A plaque and travel expenses are awarded annually at the international conference. Established in 1979 in honor of Dr. Robert Campbell, DVM, long-time head of Miami Animal Export/Import Station, and APHIS/U.S. Department of Agriculture employee.

• 4963 • **International Award**
To recognize an individual who has made outstanding contributions to the welfare of animals in international commerce. A plaque is awarded annually at the international conference. Established in 1985.

• 4964 • **Public Service Award**
To recognize an individual in public service who has contributed significantly to the welfare of animals in transit. A plaque is awarded annually at the international conference. Established in 1986.

• 4965 •
Animal Welfare Institute
Cathy Liss, Pres.
PO Box 3650, Georgetown Sta.
Washington, DC 20007
Phone: (703)836-4300
Fax: (703)836-0400
E-mail: awi@awionline.org
Home Page: http://www.awionline.org

• 4966 • **Albert Schweitzer Medal**
To recognize an individual who has made an outstanding contribution to animal welfare. Individuals without regard to nationality are eligible. A bronze medal is awarded annually when merited. Established in 1954 when a gold replica of the medal was presented to Dr. Schweitzer at Oslo where he accepted the Nobel Peace Prize.

• 4967 •
Ann Arbor Film Festival
Christen McArdle, Exec.Dir.
203 E Ann
Ann Arbor, MI 48104
Phone: (734)995-5356
Fax: (734)995-5396
E-mail: info@aafilmfest.org
Home Page: http://www.aafilmfest.org

• 4968 • **Ann Arbor Film Co-op Award**
To recognize a film that is unique, challenging, original, brash, irreverent, subversive, or obscene.

• 4969 • **Between the Lines Award Best Gay/Lesbian Film**
To honor the film that best deals with gay/lesbian issues. A monetary award of $500 is awarded annually. Formerly: Liberty St. Video Award.

• 4970 • **Ken Burns Best of the Festival Award**
To recognize the filmmaker with the most outstanding entry. The award honors the film that best represents the artistic and creative standards of the festival. A monetary award of $3,000 is presented. It is sponsored by documentary filmmaker Ken Burns, who graduated from Ann Arbor's Pioneer High School in 1971. Awarded annually. Formerly: Mosaic Foundation Best of the Festival Award.

• 4971 • **Honorable Mentions**
To recognize films that didn't receive top awards in the festival. Awarded annually.

• 4972 • **Lawrence Kasdan Award Best Narrative Film**
To recognize the narrative film that best makes use of the film medium's unique ability to convey striking and original stories. A monetary award of $1,000 is presented annually. Formerly: Screener's Choice Award for Narrative Integrity.

• 4973 •
Annenberg School for Communication
Nancy Ruiz, Asst. to the Dir.
School of Journalism
USC Annenberg School for Communication
3502 Watt Way, Ste. 325
Los Angeles, CA 90089-0281
Phone: (213)740-3914
Fax: (213)740-8624
E-mail: nruiz@usc.edu
Home Page: http://www.annenberg.usc.edu

• 4974 • **Selden Ring Award for Investigative Reporting**
To recognize a journalist(s) whose ingenuity, courage, and tenacity resulted in publication of an article or articles that exposed a major wrong and yielded results. Freelance of full-time writers or reporters working for a United States newspaper, wire service, or magazine are eligible. Articles published during the previous calendar year may be nominated. Deadline for nominations is February 1. A cash award of $35,000 is awarded annually. Established in 1989 by the late Selden Ring, a Los Angeles Philanthropist.

• 4975 • **Tyler Prize for Environmental Achievement**
This highly prestigious environmental world prize is given to honor living individuals or institutions of any nation who have benefited humanity in environmental fields in their broadest context. Citizens of all nations are invited to nominate individuals or institutions of any nation by October 1. Nominees can be associated with any field of science. Nominated institutions can be universities, foundations, corporations, or other types of organizations. Prizes are awarded for any one of the following: (1) the protection, maintenance, improvement or understanding of ecological and environmental conditions anywhere in the world; or (2) the discovery, further development, improvement, or understanding of known and new sources of energy. Selection is made by a vote of the members of the Tyler Prize Executive Committee. Awarded annually in the spring. From one to three prizes are given with a total monetary value of $150,000 and a gold medallion. Established in 1973 by the late John C. Tyler, the founder of Farmers Insurance Group, and his wife, Alice C. Tyler. Following Mrs. Tyler's death in 1993, an endowment was established at the University of Southern California to fund The Tyler Prize in perpetuity. The Prize has been administered at USC for the past fifteen years. Formerly: Tyler Ecology Award.

• 4976 •
Anti-Communist International
Kathleen Shedaker, CEO
PO Box 1095, Grand Central Sta.
New York, NY 10163-1095
E-mail: kshedaker5154@monroecollege.edu

• 4977 • **ACI Founders Award**
For contributions to anti-Communism. Gold, Silver, Cold War, and Victory Medals are awarded biennially.

• 4978 •
Anti-Defamation League
Department DJ
823 United Nations Plz.
New York, NY 10017
Phone: (212)490-2525
Fax: (212)867-0779
E-mail: webmaster@adl.org
Home Page: http://www.adl.org

• 4979 • **America's Democratic Legacy Award**
For recognition of distinguished contributions to the enrichment of America's democratic legacy. A silver medallion engraved with a torch of liberty is awarded periodically. Established in 1948.

• 4980 • **Courage to Care Award**
To recognize heroic efforts made by Christians in behalf of Jews. An inscribed work containing in miniature the bronze plaques that are the centerpieces of ADL's Holocaust Wall is awarded. Organized by the League's Braun Center for Holocaust Studies and the Jewish Foundation for Christian Resevers/ADL.

• 4981 • **Hubert H. Humphrey First Amendment Freedoms Prize**
To recognize an institution or individual who, like Hubert Humphrey, has made significant and lasting contributions to the preservation and advancement of the cherished ideal embodied in the First Amendment to the Constitution. Applications may be submitted in behalf of any organization or individual without regard to race, creed, sex, age, or national origin. Only one standard governs: the significance of the contribution made to the interpretation, preservation, strengthening and advancement of the Constitutional guarantees of the First Amendment. Applications must be sent by December 15. A monetary award of $10,000 and a medallion are awarded annually. Established in 1977 by a grant from the Andreas Foundation.

• 4982 • **Joseph Prize for Human Rights**
For recognition of those individuals whose life's work has been the improvement of human relations and the preservation or growth of human rights. The Prize reflects the concern of the late I.S. and Anna K. Joseph for the development of democratic institutions and practices that will lead to the fullest flowering of the human spirit. A monetary award of $10,000 and a medallion are awarded annually. Established in 1974 by the Joseph Foundation.

• 4983 • **Janusz Korczak Literary Competition**
To honor children's books, written for children and adults, that best exemplify Janusz Kaczak's the principles of selflessness and human dignity. Writers from any country are eligible. A monetary prize of $1,000 is awarded in each of the following categories: the best published book of fiction or nonfiction for young readers, and the best published book about the welfare and nurturing of children, directed to parents, educators, and others in the helping professions. Honorable Mention Awards are also given in each category, and where applicable, a Special Citation is given for translations. Established in 1980 in commemoration of a Jewish Polish pediatrician (born Henryk Goldszmidt) who founded two Warsaw orphanages and refused to leave children he taught in the Warsaw ghetto, perishing with them in the Nazi gas chambers of Treblinka.

• 4984 • **Dore Schary Awards**
To recognize undergraduate or graduate students whose film or video productions best exemplify the professional excellence and concern for humanity that were the hallmarks of Dore Schary's life. Undergraduate or graduate students who have completed a film or video production since Jan. 1, 1992 may enter by May 31. The following monetary prizes are awarded in film and video: first prize narrative - $1,000 each, first prize documentary - $1,000. The student winner's school receives a plaque. Awarded annually. Established in 1982 in honor of Dore Schary.

• 4985 •
Antioch College
Glen Helen Ecology Institute
405 Corry St.
Yellow Springs, OH 45387
Phone: (937)767-7375
Fax: (937)767-6659
E-mail: rswhyte@antioch-college.edu
Home Page: http://www.glenhelen.org

• 4986 • **Glen Helen Ecology Institute Awards**
Awards academic credit through Antioch College. Awarded annually.

Awards are arranged in alphabetical order below their administering organizations

• 4987 •
Antique Automobile Club of America, Northwestern Michigan Region
Edward H. Litchfield, Contact
8970 Alden Meadows Dr.
Alden, MI 49612
Home Page: http://www.aaca.org

• 4988 • **Ed Grace Memorial Award**
For leadership activity. Recognition award bestowed annually.

• 4989 •
Anvil Press
Brian Kaufman, Publisher
278 E 1st Ave.
Vancouver, BC, Canada V5T 1A6
Phone: (604)876-8710
Fax: (604)879-2667
E-mail: info@anvilpress.com
Home Page: http://www.anvilpress.com

• 4990 • **Three-Day Novel Contest**
To recognize the author of the best novel written over the Labour Day weekend. Novels may be written in any location and may use any method during the prescribed three days. The winning novel is published by Anvil Press; the runner-up receives a monetary award of $500. Established in 1977 by Stephen Osborne of Pulp Press. Formerly: Pulp Press International Three-Day Novel Competition.

• 4991 •
AOAC International
Jim Bradford, Exec.Dir.
481 N Frederick Ave., No. 500
Gaithersburg, MD 20877-2417
Phone: (301)924-7077
Toll-Free: 800-379-2622
Fax: (301)924-7089
E-mail: aoac@aoac.org
Home Page: http://www.aoac.org

Formerly: (1991) Association of Official Analytical Chemists.

• 4992 • **Harvey W. Wiley Award**
For recognition of a scientist or group of scientists for outstanding contributions to the development and validation of methods of analysis for foods, vitamins, supplements, pesticides, drugs, cosmetics, plants, feeds, fertilizers, hazardous substances, air, water, or other commodities and analytical watrices of interest to AOAC. Its primary purpose is to emphasize the role of the scientist in protecting the consumer and the quality of the environment. Nominations are accepted. A monetary award of $5,000, a plaque, and expenses up to $1,000 to attend the meeting for the award presentation are awarded annually. Established in 1956 to honor Dr. Harvey W. Wiley, father of the pure food and drug laws, a founder of AOAC, its president in 1886, secretary from 1889-1912, and honorary president until his death in 1930.

• 4993 •
Apex Awards
John De Lellis, Ed.
% Communications Concepts Inc.
7481 Huntsman Blvd., Ste. 720
Springfield, VA 22153-1648
Phone: (703)643-2200
Fax: (703)643-2329
E-mail: concepts@writingthatworks.com
Home Page: http://www.apexawards.com

• 4994 • **APEX - Awards for Publication Excellence**
To recognize excellence in publications work by corporate, nonprofit, independent and agency communicators. Awards are based on excellence in graphic design, editorial content, and the ability to meet stated objectives. APEX Grand Awards honor the outstanding works in 105 award categories, including Newsletters, Magazines, Magapapers, Journals, Brochures, Booklets, Catalogs, Annual Reports, Manuals, Guides and Reports, Video and Multi-media Publications, Web and Intranet Sites, Electronic and Online Publications, Campaigns and Programs, Writing, Design and Illustration, Help Files, Custom-Published Magazines, Marketing Plans, and Investor and Customer Relations Materials, Health and Medical Publications, Government Publications, and Special Publications. The application deadline is March 15. Entry fees are $59 for subscribers and $79 for non-subscribers. Open to corporate, non-profit, freelance, and agency communicators. Established in 1988.

• 4995 •
Appalachian Center
Willis D. Weatherford, Pres.
Berea College
CPO 2166
Berea, KY 40404
Phone: (859)985-3000
Fax: (859)985-3903
E-mail: gordon_mckinney@berea.edu
Home Page: http://www.berea.edu/apcenter

• 4996 • **W. D. Weatherford Award Competition**
To recognize outstanding published writing about Appalachia. Works published in the United States that best illustrate the problems, personalities, and unique qualities of the Appalachian South are eligible. The winning work may be book length or shorter; fact, fiction, or poetry; and one individual piece or a series of pieces. It must have been first published during the year for which the award is made. The nomination deadline is December 31. A monetary award of $500 is awarded annually by the Appalachian Center and the Hutchins Library of Berea College. The sponsors of the award also authorize the judges to present a second award of $200 to an author who has made longstanding or special contributions to the well-being of the region. Established in 1970 in memory of Dr. W.D. Weatherford Sr., an educator, pioneer youth worker, innovator in race relations, and the "father of the Appalachian idea." The awards were donated by Alfred H. Perrin of Berea. Sponsored by the Appalachian Center and the Hutchins Library of Berea College.

• 4997 • **Carter G. Woodson Award**
For recognition of efforts to foster either the development of unity, culture, or research of African American communities or equality and understanding in interracial and multicultural education. Individuals from the United States with special emphasis on the southern Appalachian region and adjacent urban areas are eligible for consideration. A plaque is awarded annually in February (Black History Month). Established in 1983 in memory of Carter G. Woodson, Berea alumnus and founder of Black History Month. Additional information is available from Linda Thomas-Buchanan, Director of the Black Cultural Center, Berea College, CPO Box 134, Berea, KY 40404.

• 4998 •
Appalachian Peace and Justice Network
Mara Giglio, Training and Program Coor.
18 N College
Athens, OH 45701-2436
Phone: (740)592-2608
Fax: (740)592-4846
E-mail: apjn@frognet.net
Home Page: http://frognet.net/~apjn

• 4999 • **Appalachian Ohio Peace Prize**
Based on submission of essay, poem, or artwork on a theme, grades 6-12. Monetary award bestowed annually.

• 5000 •
Appalachian Studies Association
Mary Thomas, Off.Mgr.
ASA Office
Marshall University
One John Marshall Dr.
Huntington, WV 25755
Phone: (304)696-2904
Fax: (304)696-6221
E-mail: asa@marshall.edu
Home Page: http://www.appalachianstudies.org

• 5001 • **Carl A. Ross Student Paper Award**
Open to students in two categories: (1) middle and high school; and (2) undergraduate and graduate. Student papers must adhere to the same guidelines and subject matter as other scholarly research conference papers. The recipients are selected annually by a multi-disciplinary committee composed of Appalachian Studies scholars. A certificate and $100 is awarded during the Saturday business luncheon at the ASA Conference. Established in 1988.

• 5002 • **Cratis D. Williams/James S. Brown Service Award**
Given to an individual who has made exemplary contributions to Appalachia and/or the Appalachian Studies Association. In most cases, the recipient is likely to be a member of the Association. Awarded annually.

Awards are arranged in alphabetical order below their administering organizations

• 5003 •
Appeal of Conscience Foundation
Rabbi Arthur Schneier, Pres./Founder
119 W 57th St.
New York, NY 10019-2401
Phone: (212)535-5800
Fax: (212)628-2513
E-mail: appealofconscience@msn.com
Home Page: http://
www.appealofconscience.org

• 5004 • **Appeal of Conscience Award**
To recognize outstanding service in the fields of human rights, religious freedom, and international cooperation through civic, business, and philanthropic activities. The award consists of a Steuben glass with the inscription, "More things are wrought by prayer than man dreams of". Awarded at the foundation's annual awards dinner. Established in 1969.

• 5005 •
Appraisal Institute
John Ross, Exec.VP
550 W Van Buren St., Ste. 1000
Chicago, IL 60607
Phone: (312)335-4100
Fax: (312)335-4400
E-mail: info@appraisalinstitute.org
Home Page: http://
www.appraisalinstitute.org

Formed by merger of: (1991) American Institute of Real Estate Appraisers; Society of Real Estate Appraisers.

• 5006 • **Robert H. Armstrong Award**
For recognition of the author of the most outstanding original article published in *The Appraisal Journal* based on pertinent appraisal interest, provocative thought, logical analysis, perceptive reasoning, clarity of presentation, and overall contribution to the literature of valuation. A monetary prize of $1000 and a plaque are awarded when merited at the Spring meeting. Established in 1963 to honor Robert H. Armstrong, a past chairman of *The Appraisal Journal* editorial board.

• 5007 • **Robert L. Foreman Award**
To give recognition to dedication to the enforcement of ethics and standards. A monetary award of $1,000 and a plaque are awarded when merited at the Spring meeting. Established in 1995 in honor of Robert L. Foreman.

• 5008 • **Sanders A. Kahn Award**
To recognize the author of the best article in the *The Appraisal Journal.* A monetary award of $1,000 and a plaque is awarded when merited at the Spring meeting.

• 5009 • **S. Edwin Kazdin Memorial Fund Award**
This award is presented at the discretion of the Trust Fund for the Institute membership. A monetary award of $1,000 and a plaque are awarded when merited at the Spring meeting. Established in 1978 in honor of the past president, S. Edwin Kazdin.

• 5010 • **Dr. William Kinnard, Jr. Academic Award**
To recognize professionalism in education. The criteria for this award requires the recipient to be an academic instructor or administrator, an individual, or a program that contributed to the education, knowledge, professionalism, or development of the real estate appraisal field. A monetary award of $1,000 and a plaque are presented when merited at the Spring meeting.

• 5011 • **Louise and Y. T. Lum Award**
For recognition of one or more individuals who have made distinguished contributions to the appraisal profession. A monetary prize of $1,000 and a plaque are awarded when merited at the Spring meeting. Established in 1963 by Y. T. Lum as a memorial for his wife.

• 5012 • **Arthur A. May Award**
For recognition of a notable literary contribution or other service to the advancement of the real estate appraisal profession. A monetary award of $500 and a plaque are awarded when merited at the Spring meeting. Established in 1964 in honor of Arthur A. May, former chief of the appraisal staff of the United States Government Services Administration.

• 5013 • **Alfred E. Reinman, Jr. Award**
To recognize individuals who have made outstanding contributions to the growth and development of the appraisal profession. A monetary award of $1,000 and a plaque are awarded when merited at the spring meeting.

• 5014 • **George L. Schmutz Award**
For recognition of an outstanding technical manuscript or publication on real estate valuation regardless of the author's occupation, affiliation, or publisher. A monetary prize of $1,000 and a plaque are awarded when merited at the spring meeting. Established in 1959 to honor George L. Schmutz, president of the Institute in 1940.

• 5015 • **Charles B. Shattuck Award**
To recognize authors of published writings that advance education and knowledge of real estate valuation and related topics. A monetary prize of $500 and a plaque are awarded at the spring meeting. Established in 1964 in honor of Charles B. Shattuck, the 1948 president of the Appraisal Institute and the 1961 president of the American Society of Real Estate Counselors.

• 5016 • **H. Grady Stebbins, Jr. Distinguished Service Award**
To recognize outstanding contributions to the field of real estate appraisal education. A monetary award of $1,000 and a plaque are presented when merited at the spring meeting.

• 5017 • **Percy and Betty Wagner Award**
To foster the training of persons in the science of real estate appraising and related subjects; to encourage improvements of appraisal techniques; to provide for needed research in the field of real estate valuation; to award scholarships to deserving students interested in the study of real estate valuation and related subjects; to give recognition to authors of published articles, writings, papers, or the like that enhance or advance education and knowledge in appraising; and for any other purpose that the Trustees deem worthy to improve the image of the professional appraiser or would further the work of the Institute. A monetary award of $1,000 and a plaque are presented at the spring meeting. Established in 1972 in honor of Percy Wagner for his lifelong dedication to real estate and appraisal education, and for the support provided by his wife Betty.

• 5018 •
Arab American Institute
Dr. James Zogby, Pres./Founder
1600 K St. NW, Ste. 601
Washington, DC 20006
Phone: (202)429-9210
Fax: (202)429-9214
E-mail: izogby@aaiusa.org
Home Page: http://www.aaiusa.org

• 5019 • **Kahlil Gibran Spirit of Humanity Award**
Recognizes individuals, corporations, organizations, and communities whose work, commitment, and support make a difference in promoting co-existence and inclusion in all walks of life. Awarded annually.

• 5020 •
Arabian Sport Horse Association, Inc.
Pamela M. Turner, Pres.
6145 Whaleyville Blvd.
Suffolk, VA 23438
Phone: (757)986-4486
Home Page: http://www.ashai.org

• 5021 • **Year End Awards**
To recognize achievements and encourage promotion of the Arabian as a sporting horse and to recognize Horse of the Year trainers. Presented annually with medals, trophies, plaques, coolers, and ribbons. Established in 1986.

• 5022 •
Arango Design Foundation
Anthony Abbate, Pres.
7063 SW 53 Ln.
Miami, FL 33155
Phone: (305)662-9181
Fax: (305)662-2694
E-mail: arangofoundation@aol.com
Home Page: http://www.arango-design.com/adf

• 5023 • **Arango Design Award**
Recognizes emerging talent, defined as designers under 40 or those, including students, who

have had their professional offices for no more than five years. Nominations may be made by anyone. Designer name, address, e-mail, phone and fax; location of the work; and no more than three pages of slides, photographs and/or plans or sketches must be submitted. Considered works are restricted to those designed in South Florida (Miami-Dade, Broward and Monroe counties) in the last five years, whether or not built. All of the design professions are considered as one to emphasize that they embrace the entire manmade environment. One cash prize of $1000 is awarded annually.

• 5024 •
The Arc of the US
Sue Swenson, Exec.Dir.
1010 Wayne Ave., Ste. 650
Silver Spring, MD 20910
Phone: (301)565-3842
Fax: (301)565-5342
E-mail: info@thearc.org
Home Page: http://www.thearc.org

• 5025 • Fellow for Research in Esoteric Areas of Knowledge
For recognition of metaphysical research and erudition bordering on the metaphysical. Members submitting published research are eligible. A plaque is awarded twice a year. Established in 1957 by Dr. Dell Lebo.

• 5026 • Second Intellectual List of Leaders Yearbook
To recognize leaders in the area of cognition, motivation, and advancement. A certificate and listing in the yearbook are awarded annually. Established in 1959.

• 5027 •
Arc of Tucson
Lynne A. Oland, Pres.
PO Box 44324
Tucson, AZ 85733
Phone: (520)570-1295
Fax: (520)760-1570
E-mail: arctucson@aol.com
Home Page: http://www.arcoftucson.org

• 5028 • The Jackie Award
For individual who actively promotes the inclusion of persons with disabilities in community life. Recognition award bestowed annually.

• 5029 •
Archaeological Institute of America
Bonnie R. Clendenning, Exec.Dir.
656 Beacon St., 4th Fl.
Boston, MA 02215-2006
Phone: (617)353-9361
Fax: (617)353-6550
E-mail: aia@aia.bu.edu
Home Page: http://www.archaeological.org

• 5030 • Conservation and Heritage Management Award
Recognizes an individual's or institution's exceptional achievements in any of the following areas: Archaeological conservation, archaeological conservation science, archaeological heritage management, or education/ public awareness of archaeological conservation through teaching, lecturing, and exhibition, or a publication. Deadline March 15.

• 5031 • Excellence in Undergraduate Teaching Award
To recognize exceptional teachers of archaeology on the undergraduate level. An award of $1,000 is presented annually. Established 1996.

• 5032 • Gold Medal Award for Distinguished Archaeological Achievement
To recognize outstanding achievement in the field of archaeology as evidenced by distinguished field work, publication, teaching, or a combination of these achievements. A gold medal and citation are awarded annually. Established in 1965. Deadline for nomination is November 1.

• 5033 • Martha and Arlenis Joukowsky Distinguished Service Award
To recognize outstanding volunteer work for the AIA. A citation is awarded each year at the AIA annual meeting in December. Volunteers must be AIA members and be nominated by September 1. Established in 1989.

• 5034 • Outstanding Public Service Award
Recognizes exceptional contributions that promote public understanding of, interest in, and support for archaeology and the preservation of the archaeological record. Individuals, organizations, or corporations may be nominated. Nominations may be made by any AIA member or AIA committee. Nomination deadline is March 1.

• 5035 • Pomerance Award for Scientific Contributions to Archaeology
To recognize interdisciplinary assistance of scientists to the advancement of archaeological research. A bronze medal and citation are awarded annually. Established in 1980. Deadline for nomination is May 1.

• 5036 • James R. Wiseman Book Award
To recognize outstanding archaeological publications. Books must have been published within the last four years for consideration. Deadline is May 1. A citation is awarded each year at the AIA Annual Meeting. Established in 1989 in recognition of James R. Wiseman, past president of the AIA.

• 5037 •
Architectural League of New York
Rosalie Genevro, Exec.Dir.
457 Madison Ave.
New York, NY 10022
Phone: (212)753-1722
Fax: (212)486-9173
E-mail: info@archleague.org
Home Page: http://www.archleague.org

• 5038 • Young Architects Forum
One of the League's important and popular programs is the Young Architects Forum, an annual competition, exhibition, and lecture series. A committee of young architects selects the competition theme, and then judges entries along with a jury of distinguished professionals. Winners receive a monetary award of $1000. A poster of the winning entries is distributed nationally. The Young Architects Forum provides a platform for talented young designers to be seen and heard by peers, journalists, critics, and established architects. Established in 1981.

• 5039 •
Architectural Record
McGraw-Hill Publications Co.
2 Penn Plz.
New York, NY 10121
Phone: (212)904-2594
Toll-Free: 877-876-8093
Fax: (212)904-4256
E-mail: rivy@mcgraw-hill.com
Home Page: http://archrecord.construction.com

• 5040 • Record Houses of the Year
To recognize architect-designed houses which, in the opinion of the editors of *Architectural Record*, are the best of the year. The houses must be designed by registered architects. A certificate and publication in the *Architectural Record* are awarded annually. Established in 1956.

• 5041 • Record Interiors of the Year
To recognize interior designs by architects which, in the opinion of the editors of *Architectural Record*, are the best of the year. Interiors must be designed by a registered architect and may be new or remodeling work. A certificate and publication in the *Architectural Record* are awarded annually.

• 5042 •
Arden Terrace Neighborhood Association
Mary Watkins, Pres.
2515 E Pentagon Pkwy.
Dallas, TX 75241-1526
Phone: (214)376-8109
Phone: (214)450-7254
E-mail: marywat15@msn.com

• 5043 • Appreciation Award
For student carrying a B-average. Scholarship awarded monthly.

• 5044 •
Aril Society International
Lowell Baumunk, Pres.
1102 C.R. 192
Carbon, TX 76435
Phone: (303)791-0456
E-mail: lbaumunk@aol.com
Home Page: http://www.arilsociety.org

• 5045 • **William Mohr Medal**
For recognition of irises of one-quarter or more aril content that do not meet the more restrictive requirements of the Clarence G. White Memorial Award. To be voted and awarded per AIS ballots of AIS accredited judges 2 years after receiving the AM Award. Membership in the American Iris Society or the Aril Society by the hybridizer is usual but is not required. The iris must be registered with the AIS, have been introduced to commerce and must have received the Award of Merit after winning the "Honorable Mention" Award by the American Iris Society. Medals will be presented at the annual AIS convention.

• 5046 • **Clarence G. White Medal**
For recognition of an Arilbred iris of one-half or more Aril parentage, judged to be the best in commerce by annual ballot of American Iris Society accredited judges. Iris must have two or more recognized Aril characteristics, and no iris can win more than once. Membership in the American Iris Society or the Aril Society by the hybridizer is usual but is not required. Iris must be registered with the AIS, have been introduced to commerce, and must have received an award of merit as well as an Honorable Mention Award by the American Iris Society. Awarded annually at the national convention of AIS. Established in 1958 by the Aril Society International with the cooperation of the American Iris Society in honor of Clarence G. White, one of the first successful hybridizers in crossing oncocylus or regelia irises with other pogon irises.

• 5047 •
Arizona Authors' Association
3509 E. Shea Blvd., Ste. 117
PO Box 87857
Phoenix, AZ 85080-7857
Phone: (602)769-2066
Fax: (623)780-0468
E-mail: info@azauthors.com
Home Page: http://www.azauthors.com

• 5048 • **Arizona Authors' Association Annual National Literary Contest**
To encourage creative writing and give recognition to individuals who write well. Awards are given for short story, poetry, and essay. Writers may enter works in the literary competition. Monetary prizes of more than $1,000 and publication of winning entries in the association's literary magazine are awarded annually. Established in 1982. Requires entry fees.

• 5049 •
Arizona Geriatrics Society
Bonnie L. Howard, Exec.Dir.
5020 N 8th Pl., Ste. C
Phoenix, AZ 85014
Phone: (602)265-0211
Fax: (602)274-8086
E-mail: info@arizonageriatrics.org
Home Page: http://www.arizonageriatrics.org

• 5050 • **Geriatrician of the Year**
For geriatric practitioners. Recognition award bestowed annually.

• 5051 •
Arizona Library Association
Laura Thomas Sullivan, Pres.
2302 N. 3rd St.
Phoenix, AZ 85004
Phone: (602)712-9822
Fax: (602)252-5265
E-mail: azla.admin@gilstrapmottacole.com
Home Page: http://www.azla.org

• 5052 • **Arizona Author Award**
To recognize outstanding writers. Three awards are presented: The Children's Author/Illustrated Award, The Young Adult, A Author Award of an Adult Book. Writers who live in Arizona or have lived in the state or the immediately surrounding area are eligible. A silver memento is awarded annually. Established in 1983. The Children Author/Illustrator Award and the Young Adult Author Award are sponsored by Libraries Limited of Arizona.

• 5053 • **Arizona Highways Adult Nonfiction Book Award**
Recognizes and promotes adult literature that contributes to an understanding of Arizona. $500 and a plaque are awarded.

• 5054 • **Arizona Young Readers Award**
To encourage Arizona young readers to read quality new books and to recognize books and authors. Books must have been published within the previous five years. Children who have read or have had read to them at least five of the nominated book titles may vote for their favorite book by March 15. Awards are presented in the following categories: picture book, chapter book, and young adult. Winners are honored at the Arizona Library Association/Arizona Reading Association's annual conferences.

• 5055 • **AzLA/SIRS Intellectual Freedom Award**
Recognizes an individual or library for the promotion of intellectual freedom in Arizona. A cash award for the purchase of library materials is awarded annually.

• 5056 • **Follett School Librarian of the Year Award**
Awarded to an individual who serves as a model for implementing the American Association of School Librarians (AASI) National Standards. A plaque is provided. Nominees must be certified school library media Specialists in Arizona who demonstrate notable or outstanding performance in the areas of collaboration with classroom teachers, educational leadership, technology, and advocacy for school libraries.

• 5057 • **Judy Goddard/Libraries Limited Awards**
Awarded for two types of writing, one for children up to twelve years old, and the second for young adults twelve to nineteen.

• 5058 • **LATA Scholarship Award**
Provided for the purpose of providing continuing education to a student in any library technology program in an Arizona community college who is pursuing and A.A.S. degree. A monetary award of $300 is given.

• 5059 • **Library Leadership Award**
To recognize an individual who has made a significant contribution to the advancement of libraries and librarianship through professional activities. Services must have been performed within the past three years. Current members of AZLA with continuous membership for the past three years are eligible. Awarded annually. Established in 1958.

• 5060 • **Outreach Services Award**
To recognize the library, librarian or a related group that provides the most exemplary services to underserved or minority groups. A monetary prize is awarded annually. Established in 1980.

• 5061 • **Outstanding Decision Maker Award**
To recognize an Arizona decision maker exhibiting significant support for libraries. Administrators (city, county, academic, school board) are eligible. Demonstrated support may be for a critical issue or for continuous support over a period of time. Awarded annually. Established in 1986.

• 5062 • **Outstanding Library Board Award**
To recognize a library board or equivalent management group under whose guidance a library or group of libraries has been substantially improved. Selection is based upon the board's policy, its success in promoting library service to its constituency and its relationship to the community. Awarded annually. Established in 1958.

• 5063 • **Outstanding Library Service Award**
Presented to an individual currently working in libraries, with or without an MLS, who has professional responsibilities to the end user in such service areas as reference, programming, cataloging, bibliographic or database instruction, collection development, or a combination of these and other professional responsibilities.

• 5064 • **Rising Moon Outstanding Youth Services Librarian Award**
Awarded to an individual who serves as a model for the important role Youth Services plays in public libraries. A $400 monetary awarded is Provided to purchase books for the youth collection of the winner's Library.

• 5065 • Rosenzweig Distinguished Service Award

To recognize a lay person, librarian, or board member. Applicants must show outstanding service in promoting Arizona library interests. An inscribed silver bowl is awarded annually. Established in 1963.

• 5066 • The Sharon G. Womack Outstanding Library Technician Award

Recognizes an individual portraying the importance of library technicians. Nominees must have been members of the association for at least one year. Selection is based on the demonstration of on-the-job excellence. Recipient receives a one-year free membership. Awarded annually. Formerly: (1996) Paraprofessional of the Year Award.

• 5067 •

Arizona Twirling Athletes
Becky Hewitt, Dir.
PO Box 26220
Phoenix, AZ 85068-6220
Phone: (602)997-0522

• 5068 • Senior Scholarships

For 3.5 grade average. Scholarship awarded annually.

• 5069 •

Arkansas Arts Center
Dr. Ellen Plummer, Dir.
501 E 9th St.
PO Box 2137
Little Rock, AR 72203
Phone: (501)372-4000
Fax: (501)375-8053
E-mail: info@arkarts.com
Home Page: http://www.arkarts.com

Formed by merger of: Museum of Fine Arts; Fine Arts Club of Arkansas.

• 5070 • Delta Art Exhibition

An art exhibition open to painting and sculpture artists who were born or reside in the states of Arkansas, Louisiana, Mississippi, Missouri, Oklahoma, Tennessee, or Texas for work completed during the previous year. The work must not have been exhibited previously in the Arkansas Arts Center. One monetary award of $1,500, and two of $500 are given. Established in 1957.

• 5071 • Prints, Drawings and Photographs Exhibition

To recognize outstanding regional artists entered in the Exhibition. Prizes are given in the following areas: prints in all media; drawings in all media (except watercolors); and photographs in color and/or monochrome. Artists born or residing in Arkansas, Louisiana, Mississippi, Missouri, Tennessee, Oklahoma, and Texas are eligible. The awards consist of Juror's Awards - monetary prizes of $200; and Purchase Awards that are for the permanent collection of the Arkansas Arts Center Foundation. Awarded biennially in odd-numbered years. Established in 1967.

• 5072 •

Arkansas Elementary School Council
Arkansas Department of Education
T. Kenneth James, Commissioner
4 State Capitol Mall, Rm. 302-B
Little Rock, AR 72201-1071
Phone: (501)682-4475
Fax: (501)682-9026
E-mail: jriggs@arkedu.k12.ar.us
Home Page: http://arkedu.state.ar.us

• 5073 • Charlie May Simon Children's Book Award

To encourage reading quality literature in Arkansas elementary schools, and to honor an Arkansas author. Books published at least two years prior to the award year and recommended by three educational sources are placed on a master reading list of approximately 20 books. Arkansas school students in the fourth, fifth, and sixth grades choose their favorite book from the list. A medallion is awarded annually to the author of the winning book and the runner-up receives a plaque as Honor Book winner. Established in 1970 by the Arkansas Elementary School Council of the Arkansas Department of Education, with the assistance of twenty-two cooperating organizations, to honor Charlie May Simon, a noted biographer and author of children's literature.

• 5074 •

Arkansas Historical Association
Donna Ludlow, Bus. Man.
Dept. of History
Univ. of Arkansas
Old Main 416
Fayetteville, AR 72701
Phone: (479)575-5884
Fax: (501)575-2775
E-mail: dludlow@uark.edu
Home Page: http://www.uark.edu/depts/arkhist/home

• 5075 • J.H. Atkinson Award for Excellence in Arkansas Teaching

A monetary award of $300 is given periodically. Inquire for additional application information.

• 5076 • Violet B. Gingles Award

To encourage the research and writing of an article on any Arkansas subject. Anyone may enter by February 1. A monetary prize of $500 and a framed certificate are awarded each year at the annual meeting of the Association. Established in 1980 by David Demuth of Benton, Arkansas, to honor Violet B. Gingles of Benton, Arkansas.

• 5077 • Lucille Westbrook Local History Award

To encourage the research and writing of an article on a local Arkansas subject. The subject must deal with some phase of neighborhood, city, county, or regional Arkansas history. Edited documents and memoirs will be considered. Entries must not have been submitted elsewhere or published previously. Anyone may enter by February 1. A monetary prize of $500 and a framed certificate are awarded each year at the annual meeting of the Association. All articles will be considered for publication in the *Arkansas Historical Quarterly*. Established in 1980 by Parker Westbrook of Nashville, Arkansas, to honor Lucille Westbrook.

• 5078 •

Arkansas Nurserymen's Association
PO Box 21715
Little Rock, AR 72221-1715
Phone: (501)225-0029
Fax: (501)224-0988
E-mail: growark@aol.com

• 5079 • Sturdy Oaks Award

For service to the association. Recognition award bestowed annually.

• 5080 •

Arkansas Technology Transfer Society
Ann L. Kerksieck, Contact
100 S Main St., Ste. 401
Little Rock, AR 72201
Phone: (501)324-9047
Fax: (501)324-9287
E-mail: alkerksieck@ualr.edu
Home Page: http://asbdc.ualr.edu/atts

• 5081 • Technology Transfer Award

For outstanding achievement. Recognition award bestowed annually.

• 5082 •

Arkansas Women's History Institute
PO Box 7704
Little Rock, AR 72217
Phone: (501)569-3235
Home Page: http://www.ualr.edu/%7Eawhi/

• 5083 • Susy Pryor Award

To recognize the best unpublished essay or article in Arkansas women's history. Manuscripts are judged on the basis of contribution to the knowledge of women in Arkansas history, judicious use of primary and secondary materials, creative interpretation and originality, and stylistic excellence. A monetary award of $1,000 is presented annually. Established in 1986 to honor Susy Pryor, an inspiring and energetic woman whose activities touched on all aspects of women's experience in Arkansas.

• 5084 •

Arlington Chamber of Commerce
Wes Jurey, Pres./CEO
505 E Border St.
Arlington, TX 76010
Phone: (817)275-2613
Phone: (817)265-1911
Fax: (817)261-7535
E-mail: info@arlingtontx.com
Home Page: http://www.arlingtontx.com

• 5085 • Warren Green Free Enterprise Scholarship
For academic standing understanding of free enterprise. Scholarship awarded annually.

• 5086 •
ARMA International - The Association of Information Management Professionals
Peter Hermann CAE, Exec.Dir./CEO
13725 W 109th St. Ste. 101
Lenexa, KS 66215
Phone: (913)341-3808
Toll-Free: 800-422-2762
Fax: (913)341-3742
E-mail: phermann@arma.org
Home Page: http://www.arma.org

Formerly: (1995) Association of Records Managers and Administrators.

• 5087 • Britt Literary Award
To recognize the author of the best article published during the year in *Records Management Quarterly*, the Association's journal. A plaque and lapel pin are awarded annually. Established in 1967 in honor of John F. X. Britt, one of the founders and past international presidents of ARMA International.

• 5088 • Chapter Newsletter of the Year Award
To acknowledge the best chapter newsletter in its size category (small, medium, large). Plaques are awarded during the Annual Conference in October.

• 5089 • Chapter of the Year
To recognize the chapter that most effectively demonstrates support and promotion of ARMA objectives as reflected in its program and activities. Awards are presented in three categories: small, medium, and large. Selection is based on performance in programming, research, membership growth and attendance, and international involvement. A large trophy and replica are presented to the honorees. Established in 1975.

• 5090 • Company of Fellows
To honor members of ARMA International who have distinguished themselves through outstanding achievements and contributions in records and information management and through noteworthy accomplishments within the Association at all levels.

• 5091 • Industry Specific Group of the Year Award
To acknowledge the Industry Specific Group (ISG) that most effectively demonstrates its support and promotion of ARMA International as reflected in ISG program and activities. A plaque is awarded during the Annual Conference in October.

• 5092 • Christine Zanotti Award for Excellence in Non-Serial Publications
To recognize exceptional contributions to the literature of the Records and Information Management profession. Includes, but not limited to, book, video, CD-ROM, CD-I, CD-Multimedia, computer-assisted instruction software, etc. A plaque and $500 are awarded during the Annual Conference in October.

• 5093 •
Armenian Behavioral Science Association
Prof. Harold Takooshian PhD, Exec.Off.
113 W 60th St., Rm. 916
New York, NY 10023
Phone: (212)636-6393
Fax: (201)262-7141
E-mail: takoosh@aol.com

• 5094 • Outstanding Achievement Award
Recognizes outstanding contributions to behavioral sciences. Awarded semiannually.

• 5095 •
Armenian Numismatic Society
Y. T. Nercessian, Sec.
8511 Beverly Park Pl.
Pico Rivera, CA 90660-1920
Phone: (562)695-0380
E-mail: armnumsoc@aol.com

• 5096 • Armenian Numismatic Memorial Award
Award of recognition. For articles on Armenian Numismatics. Awarded annually.

• 5097 •
Armstrong Memorial Research Foundation
Kenneth G. Goldstein, Pres.
Columbia University
1312 SW Mudd Bldg.
500 W 120th St.
New York, NY 10027
Phone: (212)854-3121
E-mail: kkg1@columbia.edu
Home Page: http://www.armstrongfoundation.org

• 5098 • Armstrong Memorial Research Foundation Awards
Offers an annual award of $1000 through the IEEE Foundation for a lifetime of achievement for researchers; $1000 to several graduating seniors and advanced degree recipients at Columbia, that will be extended to other engineering schools in coming years; and are in the process of funding another annual award for significant advances in communication innovations, either broadcast or internet. presented in the following three categories: Technical Achievement in Broadcasting; Innovations in Station Programming; and Outstanding Service by an Individual on Behalf of The Television and Radio Industries. A fee of $25 must accompany college and university entries; $50 for all others. Established in 1964 in memory of Edwin H. Armstrong, professor at Columbia Engineering School, who invented Frequency Modulation (FM) and other electronic circuits that make modern communications and high fidelity possible.

• 5099 •
Arnold Air Society
Stan Miller, Exec. Commander
PO Box 2117
Beaufort, SC 29901
Phone: (843)521-4945
Fax: (843)521-4533
Home Page: http://www.arnold-air.org/AASindex.php

• 5100 • AAS Distinguished Service Medallions
To recognize outstanding service benefiting the Air Force officer recruiting and training program, and the Arnold Air Society. Gold medallions are awarded annually for national recognition and silver medallions are awarded for regional or local recognition, Established in 1967.

• 5101 • AAS Honorary National Commander
Designation as Honorary National Commander is the highest tribute the Arnold Air Society can extend to one who is not an active member of the Society. Selection is made by the Executive Board of Directors at its fall meeting. Candidates are evaluated on the basis of their past contributions and possible assistance rendered to AAS. The presentation and installation is made at the National Conclave Banquet by the National Commander. This award consists of an AAS Fourragers, an honorary membership certificate, and an Honorary Commander Commission. Awarded annually.

• 5102 • AAS Individual Awards
The following awards are presented annually: H. H. Arnold Sabre, ASU Commander's Cup, Colonel George E. Day Cup, Christopher D. Nichols Award, Outstanding Financial Manager, and Arnold Air Letter Trophy.

• 5103 • AAS National Commander Awards
To recognize outstanding service. Awarded annually.

• 5104 • AAS National Medal and Ribbon
To recognize outstanding service. Awarded annually.

• 5105 • AAS Outstanding Area Advisor
Nominations are accepted from area commanders. The deadline is four weeks prior to Conclave. A gold AAS Medallion is awarded annually.

• 5106 • AAS Outstanding Squadron Advisor
To recognize AAS Squadron Advisors for distinguished leadership in connection with Arnold Air Society activities. This award may be presented

only once to any individual. The AAS Medallion is presented at the Opening Ceremony of the National Conclave by the AFROTC Commandant and the AAS National Commander. The award consists of a silver medallion for each AAS Squadron Advisor (one per area). Selection of each area's outstanding squadron advisor is made by the area headquarters awards committee. Awarded annually.

• 5107 • **AAS Squadron Awards**
The following awards are presented: Maryland Cup, Hagan Trophy, Chennault Trophy, LBJ Cup, Eagle Trophy, Apollo Award, Lemay-Ohio Award, Samuel E. Anderson Trophy, Robert E. Femoyer Trophy, Captain "Willie" Mays Award, Outstanding Public Affairs Award, and George Robert Hall Freedom Cup. Awarded annually.

• 5108 • **Air Force Association Special Presidential Citations**
To recognize outstanding service. Awarded annually.

• 5109 • **Honorary Member**
Honorary Members of the Society are eligible to participate in all functions of the Society at the discretion of the commander immediately concerned, but are not eligible to vote. A certificate of honorary membership, and a fourragere, furnished by the unit awarding membership, are awarded annually to those who are military personnel.

• 5110 • **Lieutenant Theodore C. Marrs Plaques**
To recognize outstanding service to the Society. Plaques are awarded each year at the conclusion of the National Conclave. Established in 1968.

• 5111 • **National Chief of Protocol**
To recognize outstanding service. Awarded annually. Formerly: Little General.

• 5112 • **Silver Wings Individual Awards**
The following awards are presented: Outstanding Region Advisor, Outstanding Region Executive Officer Award, Monica Browning Award, Sheri Lynette Cavin Award, Colonel A. T. Reid Crimson Glory Award, Elise Morley Award, Diane O'Malley Award, LT GEN. Robert D. Springer Award, Brig Gen Edward N. Brya Award, Ann T. Hawkins Award, and Mary Anee Thompson Award. Awarded annually.

• 5113 • **Silver Wings Unit Award**
The following awards are presented: Outstanding Chapter Award, Ciccoli Joint Operations Award, Walter R. "Waddy" Young Award, Bonnie J. Springer Award, Dr. Bonnie J. Dunbar Award, Colonel Bill Morley Award, Mary Moore Alumni Award, and James A. McDonnell Award. Awarded annually.

• 5114 •
Art Directors Club
Myrna Davis, Exec.Dir.
106 W 29th St.
New York, NY 10001
Phone: (212)643-1440
Fax: (212)643-4266
E-mail: info@adcglobal.org
Home Page: http://www.adcglobal.org

• 5115 • **Annual Exhibitions**
To recognize outstanding advertising, graphic design and new media in print, television, packaging, posters, books, photography, illustration, and environmental and interface design. Items produced, broadcast, or published anywhere in the world during the preceding year may be submitted. 3 inch polished cubes embossed with the winners' names as well as certificates are presented at the awards dinner in June. Medalists and Distinctive Merit winners are included in the annual exhibition. All accepted entries are reproduced in full color in the annual book. Awarded annually. Established in 1920.

• 5116 • **Art Directors Awards**
Recognizes winners of the annual competition. Awarded annually.

• 5117 • **Art Directors Club Hall of Fame**
To recognize individuals in visual communications who have made outstanding lifetime contributions to the profession and the industry and have profoundly influenced the visual environment. Nominations are made by the committee. A stylized, three-dimensional "AD" in polished aluminum is awarded to new laureates annually in November at the Hall of Fame dinner. Established in 1971. A special educator's award also may be presented.

• 5118 • **Management Award**
To recognize individuals or companies who distinguish themselves through the integration of design with performance, thereby contributing to a climate of creative excellence in communication, education, social awareness, or industry. Nomination is made by committee. An embossed lucite cube containing the Manship medallion is awarded at the annual awards dinner. Established in 1954.

• 5119 • **Vision Award**
Annual award of recognition.

• 5120 •
Art Niche New York
498 Broome St.
New York, NY 10013
Phone: (212)941-0130
Fax: (212)941-0138
E-mail: reginas@anny.org
Home Page: http://www.anny.org

• 5121 • **Annual Open Exhibition**
To recognize outstanding women artists whose works exemplify the finest representations of contemporary traditional art. The entry deadline for slides is usually in July. Awards are given in the following categories: oil, acrylic, water media, pastel, graphics, and sculpture. Monetary awards totaling over $8,000 are presented. Some of the awards presented are: the Catharine Lorillard Wolfe Medal of Honor - a $500 award in each of the four categories; the Anna Hyatt Huntington Bronze Medals awarded in each of the four categories: the Leonard J. Meliselman Memorial Award $300 for an oil or acrylic painting; and the Harriet W. Frishmuth Memorial Award - $200 for a bronze sculpture. Awarded annually. Established in 1896 by a group of women at Grace Church in New York to help the struggling, young, women art students.

• 5122 •
Arthouse at the Jones Center
Sue Graze, Exec.Dir.
The Jones Center for Contemporary Art
700 Congress Ave.
Austin, TX 78701
Phone: (512)453-5312
Fax: (512)459-4830
E-mail: info@arthousetexas.org
Home Page: http://www.arthousetexas.org

• 5123 • **New American Talent Show**
To promote the growth, development, and appreciation of contemporary visual art and artists in Texas. All artists living in the United States are eligible. Entries must have been completed within the last two years and not previously exhibited in a TFAA show. Work in all media is eligible. Send SASE for prospectus. This annual multi-media national show is tentatively chosen from slides, then viewed by the juror for final selection and the awarding of honors. A fully-illustrated catalogue is published, and selections tour throughout Texas.

• 5124 •
Arthritis Foundation
Dr. John H. Klippel, CEO/Pres.
PO Box 7669
Atlanta, GA 30357-0669
Phone: (404)872-7100
Phone: (404)965-7888
Toll-Free: 800-568-4045
Fax: (404)872-0457
Home Page: http://www.arthritis.org

• 5125 • **Russell L. Cecil Arthritis Medical Journalism Awards**
To recognize and encourage the writing of news stories, articles, and radio and television scripts for general circulation newspapers, newsletters, magazines, and broadcast media on the subjects of arthritis and the Arthritis Foundation. Five national awards are offered in this major medical writing contest - one in each of the following media categories: newspaper, newsletter, magazine, radio, and television. Published stories and broadcasts of the previous year are eligible. Entries are judged on their accuracy, originality/creativity, journalistic merit, and potential for stimulating greater public knowledge and understanding about arthritis. Entries must be submitted by February 15. A gold medallion imbedded in a lucite cube is

awarded annually when merited to the national winners at the Foundation's Annual House of Delegates Meeting and a plaque is awarded to regional winners at special ceremonies at the winner's Foundation chapter. Established in 1956 in memory of Russell L. Cecil, MD, pioneering rheumatologist and first medical director of the Foundation. Formerly: Russell L. Cecil Writing Awards.

• 5126 • Lee C. Howley, Sr. Prize for Research in Arthritis
To recognize a researcher whose contributions during the previous five years have represented a significant advance in the understanding, treatment, or prevention of arthritis and rheumatic diseases. Awarded annually. Established in 1984 to honor Lee C. Howley, Sr., former chairman of Revco D.S., Inc., who was instrumental in the establishment of the Revco Arthritis Research Center at Case Western Reserve University in Cleveland, Ohio.

• 5127 • National Research Awards
To provide funds for education and research related to rheumatic diseases. Applications must be submitted by September 1. The following awards are presented annually: New Investigator Grant, Doctoral Dissertation Award, Clinical Science Grant, Arthritis Investigator Award, Postdoctoral Fellowship, Biomedical Science Grant, and Physician Scientist Development Award.

• 5128 •
Arthritis Foundation, Rocky Mountain Chapter
James H. Goddard, Pres.
2280 S Albion St.
Denver, CO 80222-4906
Phone: (303)756-8622
Toll-Free: 800-475-6447
Fax: (303)759-4349
E-mail: info.rm@arthritis.org
Home Page: http://www.arthritis.org

• 5129 • Bio-Medical Research
For peer reviewed medical research. Grant awarded annually.

• 5130 •
Arthroscopy Association of North America
Edward A. Goss, Exec.Dir.
6300 N. River Rd., Ste. 104
Rosemont, IL 60018
Phone: (847)292-2262
Fax: (847)292-2268
E-mail: moreinfo@aana.org
Home Page: http://www.aana.org

• 5131 • Arthroscopy Research Grants
To provide grants for clinical or basic science research in the field of arthroscopic surgery or disorders amenable to arthroscopic treatment. Manuscripts must be submitted by December 1. Grants of up to $20,000 are awarded. Established in 1989 by the Research Committee.

• 5132 • Richard O'Connor Essay Award
This is the organization's most prestigious award. To recognize the best study and manuscript on a subject related to diagnostic or surgical arthroscopy in clinical or basic science research. Papers must be submitted by December 1. An honorarium of $2,000, a certificate, presentation of paper, and submission of the paper for publication in *Arthroscopy* are awarded at the annual meeting.

• 5133 • Resident/Fellow Essay Award
To recognize an orthopedic resident or fellow in training for the best study and manuscript on a subject related to diagnostic or surgical arthroscopy, in the following categories: clinical, and basic science. Papers must be submitted by December 1. An honorarium of $1,000, a certificate, presentation of the paper at the annual meeting, and submission of the paper for publication in *Arthroscopy* are awarded annually in each category. Established in 1985 by the Research Committee.

• 5134 •
Artist-Blacksmith's Association of North America
LeeAnn Mitchell, Central Office Administrator
PO Box 816
Farmington, GA 30638-0816
Phone: (706)310-1030
Fax: (706)769-7147
E-mail: abana@abana.org
Home Page: http://www.abana.org

• 5135 • Bealer Award
Recognizes outstanding service to the field of blacksmithing. Awarded annually.

• 5136 • Joe Humble Award
Award of recognition. Awarded annually to an affiliate newsletter editor.

• 5137 •
Artists' Fellowship
Marc Mellon, Pres.
47 5th Ave.
New York, NY 10003
Phone: (646)230-9833
Fax: (646)230-9833
Home Page: http://www.artistsfellowship.com

• 5138 • Benjamin West Clinedinst Memorial Medal
To recognize the achievement of exceptional artistic merit. Nomination must be made by the Board. A medal is presented each spring at various art clubs. The award was established in 1947.

• 5139 • Gari Melchers Memorial Medal
To provide recognition to a person or organization who has materially furthered the interest of the profession of fine arts. Nominations must be made by the Board. A medal is presented each spring at various art clubs. The award was established in 1945.

• 5140 •
Artists Guild of the Santa Ynez Valley
PO Box 1008
Santa Ynez, CA 93460-1008

• 5141 • Art Scholarship
Based on art talent, academic record, community service, and desire to pursue a career in art. Scholarship awarded annually.

• 5142 •
Artists International Presentations, Inc.
521 5th Ave., Ste. 1700
New York, NY 10117
Phone: (212)292-4444
Fax: (212)573-6355

• 5143 • Artists International New York Debut Award Auditions
To discover and promote gifted young artists from all over the world who are beginning their careers and outstanding artists who have launched their careers and are not under management. The New York Debut Auditions are open to instrumentalists, chamber ensembles, and singers who have not given a New York recital debut. There is no age limit. Application must be submitted by February 20. Winners in the New York Debut Auditions are presented in a solo New York recital debut in Artists International's New York Debut Winner Series at Weill Recital Hall at Carnegie Hall or Merkin Concert Hall or Alice Tully Hall, Lincoln Center. Established in 1972 by Leo B. Ruiz, Founder-Director. Founder-Director. Formerly: Young Musicians and Distinguished Artists Award Auditions; Young Artists and Distinguished Artists Award Auditions.

• 5144 •
***The Artist's Magazine* Annual Art Competition**
F+W Publications Inc.
4700 E Galbraith Rd.
Cincinnati, OH 45236
Phone: (513)531-2690
Fax: (513)891-7153
E-mail: tamedit@fwpubs.com
Home Page: http://www.artistsmagazine.com

• 5145 • Art Competition
Recognizes artists in the categories of Portrait, Still Life, Landscape, Experimental, and Animal Art. 5 first prizes of $2,000 will be awarded. 5 second place awards of $1,000 will be presented. 5 third place awards of $500 will be presented, and 15 honorable mentions of $100 will be presented. Entry Deadline is May 1.

• 5146 • *The Artist's Magazine* Art Competition
To recognize outstanding artistic talent. The competition categories may change each year and can be found in the February through May

Awards are arranged in alphabetical order below their administering organizations

issues of *The Artist's Magazine.* Amateur, professional, and student artists are eligible. Entries in traditional and unusual media accepted. Work done in photography is not considered. Monetary prizes totaling more than $20,000 are awarded. In addition, top award winners are profiled in *The Artists Magazine* with feature articles exploring their ideas and techniques and full color reproductions of their work. Formerly: *The Artist's Magazine* Still Life Painting Competition; The *Artist's Magazine Annual Painting Competition.*

• 5147 • Writers Digest Annual Writing Competition

Recognizes new writers in the categories of Inspirational Writing, Memoirs, Personal essay, Magazine Feature Articles, and Short Stories. Winners will Receive: Grand Prize, $1,500 and a choice of a Trip to New York City or a trip to Maui. 1st place $750, $100 of Writer's Digest Books, and a manuscript Critique and marketing advice, 2nd place $350 and $100 of Readers Digest Books, 3rd place $250 and $100 Writers Digest Books. Awarded annually. Established in 1931.

• 5148 •
Arts & Science Center for Southeast Arkansas
701 Main St.
Pine Bluff, AR 71601-4903
Phone: (870)536-3375
Fax: (870)536-3380
E-mail: asc@seark.net
Home Page: http://www.artssciencecenter.org

• 5149 • Irene Rosenzweig Biennial Competition

To recognize outstanding art work, to encourage professional development of an artist, and to build the museum's permanent collection. The competition is open to all artists residing in the following states: Arkansas, Louisiana, Mississippi, Missouri, Oklahoma, Tennessee, and Texas. The Best of Show Award may be given to one artist or split between artists. Held biennially in odd-numbered years. Established in 1978. Formerly: Simmons First National Bank Grand Purchase Award.

• 5150 •
Arts Council of Northwest Florida
Heather Holloway, Interim Office Mgr./Administrator
17 S Palafox, Ste. 335
Pensacola, FL 32502
Phone: (850)432-9906
Phone: (850)438-8888
Fax: (850)469-0786
E-mail: hholloway@artsnwfl.org
Home Page: http://www.artsnwfl.org

• 5151 • Cultural Development Fund

For local cultural organizations. Grant awarded annually.

• 5152 •
The Arts Guild of Old Forge
Deborah Jones, Exec.Dir.
3260 State Rte. 28
PO Box 1144
Old Forge, NY 13420
Phone: (315)369-6411
Fax: (315)369-2431
E-mail: info@artscenteroldforge.org
Home Page: http://www.artscenteroldforge.org

• 5153 • Adirondacks National Exhibition of American Watercolors

To recognize outstanding American artists in an annual exhibition. Thirty monetary awards totaling over $12,000 plus four medals and special awards are awarded annually. Included among these are: Adirondack Wilderness Award of $2,000 with the Rouse Gold Medallion; Ruth Rosenau Silver Medallion and $1,000; the Old Forge Hardware Prize of $1,000; and Forest Runes Award of $500. The exhibition was established in 1982.

• 5154 •
Arts Management
Alvin H. Reiss, Ed.
110 Riverside Dr., No. 4E
New York, NY 10024
Phone: (212)579-2039
Fax: (212)579-2049
E-mail: aebmedia@colum.edu
Home Page: http://www.artsmanagementnews.com

• 5155 • *Arts Management* Award for Arts Administrator of the Year

To honor an outstanding arts administrator for specific accomplishments of note and to focus national attention on the entire profession. An individual professionally employed as administrator of a cultural program during the year by an organization whose primary activity is in the field of the performing or visual arts is eligible. An original work of art is awarded annually during the spring. Established in 1969.

• 5156 • *Arts Management* Award for Career Service

To honor an outstanding arts administrator for contributions to cultural development over the past decade. An individual professionally employed as an administrator of a cultural program for the previous ten years or longer by an organization whose primary activity is in the field of the performing or visual arts is eligible. An original work of art. Held during the spring. Established in 1969.

• 5157 • *Arts Management* Special Award

To recognize an individual for outstanding contributions to the arts. Awarded when merited. Held during the spring. Established in 1976.

• 5158 •
Arts Midwest
David J. Fraher, Exec.Dir.
2908 Hennepin Ave., Ste. 200
Minneapolis, MN 55408-1954
Phone: (612)341-0755
Fax: (612)341-0902
E-mail: general@artsmidwest.org
Home Page: http://www.artsmidwest.org

• 5159 • Heartland Arts Fund

For non-profit performing arts presenters applicants. Grant awarded annually.

• 5160 •
The ARTS of the Southern Finger Lakes
Jan Amann, Interim Exec.Dir.
32 W Market St.
Corning, NY 14830
Phone: (607)962-5871
Fax: (607)962-4128
E-mail: amannj@corning-cc.edu
Home Page: http://www.earts.org

• 5161 • Project Funding Program

For arts projects which support regional arts goals. Grant awarded annually.

• 5162 •
Ascutney Mountain Audubon Society
Wally Elton, Pres.
PO Box 191
Springfield, VT 05156
Phone: (802)885-3267
Phone: (802)885-3267
E-mail: eb@vermontel.com
Home Page: http://www.sover.net/~mwalsh

• 5163 • AMAS Scholarship

For graduating high school senior living in service area; based upon interview and essay contest. Scholarship awarded annually.

• 5164 •
Asian American Journalists Association
Mr. Rene Astudillo, Exec.Dir.
1182 Market St., Ste. 320
San Francisco, CA 94102
Phone: (415)346-2051
Fax: (415)346-6343
E-mail: national@aaja.org
Home Page: http://www.aaja.org

• 5165 • Asian American Journalists Association National Awards

To encourage and recognize excellence among Asian American journalists, and to recognize outstanding coverage of Asian American issues. Awards are presented for Unlimited Subject Matter (open to Asian American professional journalists and to members of the AAJA), and for Asian American Issues (open to all professional journalists) in four sub-categories: print, television, radio, and photojournalism. Entries must be English language work published or aired during the previous calendar year. Student work is not eligible. The deadline is varies (usually about two months before the annual convention). A plaque is awarded at the annual national convention. Established in 1989. convention. Established in 1989.

• 5166 • Lifetime Achievement Award
To recognize an Asian American who demonstrates courage and commitment to the principles of journalism over the course of a life's work. The nominee's achievements in the field of journalism and in the furtherance of AAJA's goals have stood the test of time. Awarded annually.

• 5167 • Special Recognition Award
To honor a person (Asian or non-Asian, journalist or non-journalist) who has helped to advance AAJA's goals to assist high school and college students pursuing journalism careers. Awarded annually.

• 5168 •
Asian American Writers' Workshop
Quang Bao, Exec.Dir.
16 W 32nd St., Ste. 10A
New York, NY 10001
Phone: (212)494-0061
Fax: (212)494-0062
E-mail: desk@aaww.org
Home Page: http://www.aaww.org

• 5169 • Asian American Literary Awards
Recognition is given annually to writers.

• 5170 •
Asian/Pacific American Librarians Association
Dr. Ling Hwey Jeng, Exec.Dir.
1807 N Elm St., Ste. 444
PMB 26
Denton, TX 76201
Phone: (940)898-2602
Fax: (859)257-4205
E-mail: webmaster@apalweb.org
Home Page: http://www.apalaweb.org

• 5171 • APALA Distinguished Service Award
To recognize an individual for contributions to the understanding of Asian/Pacific Americans in any field and/or to an Asian/Pacific American for distinguished service in any field of endeavor. Nominations are accepted by the president of APALA by May 31. A plaque is presented annually. Established in 1981. For further information, contact Wilfred Fong, Assistant Dean/Editor.

• 5172 •
ASM International
Dr. William W. Scott FASM, Assoc. Managing Dir.
9639 Kinsman Rd.
Materials Park, OH 44073-0002
Phone: (440)338-5151
Toll-Free: 800-336-5152
Fax: (440)338-4634
E-mail: cust-srv@asminternational.org
Home Page: http://www.asminternational.org

Formerly: (1986) American Society for Metals.

• 5173 • ASM International and The Minerals, Metals and Materials Society Distinguished Lectureship in Materials and Society
To clarify the role of materials science and engineering in technology and in society in its broadest sense, to present an evaluation of progress made in developing new technology for the ever changing needs of technology and society, and to define new frontiers for materials science and engineering. Awarded annually. Established in 1971. Formerly: ASM International and The Metallurgical Society Distinguished Lectureship in Materials and Society.

• 5174 • Edward DeMille Campbell Memorial Lecture
To recognize outstanding demonstrated ability in materials science and engineering. A monetary award of $3,000 and a certificate are presented. Established in 1926 in memory of Professor Campbell who was blind for all but two years of his professional life.

• 5175 • Distinguished Life Member
To recognize those leaders who have devoted their time, knowledge, and abilities to the advancement of the materials industries. Established in 1954.

• 5176 • William Hunt Eisenman Award
To recognize unusual achievements in industry in the practical application of materials science and engineering through production or engineering use. A plaque is awarded annually. Established in 1960 in memory of William Hunt Eisenman, a founding member of the Society and its first secretary for 40 years.

• 5177 • Engineering Materials Achievement Award
To recognize outstanding achievement in materials or materials systems relating to the application of knowledge of materials to an engineering structure or to design and manufacture of a product. Awarded annually. Established in 1969.

• 5178 • Fellow
To recognize members for distinguished contributions in the field of materials science and engineering and to develop a broadly based forum for technical and professional leaders to serve as advisors to the Society. Additional Fellows may be elected to this distinguished body annually. Established in 1969.

• 5179 • Gold Medal
To recognize outstanding knowledge and great versatility in the application of science to the field of materials science and engineering, as well as exceptional ability in the diagnosis and solution of diversified materials problems. A 2 inch 14K gold medal designed by Walter Sinz is presented annually. Established in 1943.

• 5180 • Marcus A. Grossmann Young Author Award
To honor the author(s) of the best paper published in *Metallurgical and Materials Transactions* for individuals under the age of 40 are eligible. A plaque is awarded annually. Established in 1960 in memory of Dr. Grossmann, a former president of the Society.

• 5181 • Historical Landmarks Designation
To recognize permanently the many sites and events that have played a prominent part in the discovery, development, and growth of metals and metalworking. Recommended sites, structures, or events should be at least 50 years old. Established in 1969.

• 5182 • Honorary Member
To recognize distinguished service to the materials science and engineering profession, the Society, and the progress of mankind. Nominees must be members of the Society. Established in 1919.

• 5183 • Henry Marion Howe Medal
This, the Society's oldest medal, honors the author(s) of the best paper published in *Metallurgical and Materials Transactions.* The Howe Medal is awarded annually. Established in 1923 in memory of Henry Howe, a distinguished teacher, writer, and metallurgist.

• 5184 • International Graduate Student Paper Contest
To recognize the best graduate student technical paper in the fields of materials science or engineering and to encourage student participation in Society affairs. Entrants must be ASM students or ASM-TSM joint student members in good standing, and enrolled as full-time graduate students of a school or university offering courses in the fields of materials science or engineering. A monetary award of $500 and a certificate are awarded to the student and a complete set of ASM Handbooks are given to the winner's school or university. Awarded annually. Established in 1985.

• 5185 • International Student Paper Contest
To recognize the best student technical paper in the fields of materials science or engineering and to encourage student participation in Society affairs. Entrants must be ASM students or ASM-TMS joint student members in good stand-

ing, and enrolled full-time as undergraduate students of a school or university offering courses in the fields of materials science or engineering. A monetary award of $500 and a certificate are awarded to the student, and a complete set of ASM Handbooks are given to the winner's school or university. Awarded annually. Established in 1979.

• 5186 • IMS and ASM Jacquet-Lucas Award for Excellence in Metallography
To recognize the best entry in the annual ASM metallographic competition. Awarded annually. Established in 1946 and co-sponsored by the International Metallographic Society; an affiliate society of ASM, since 1972. Endowed by Buehler Limited. Formerly: Pierre Jacquet Gold Medal and the Francis F. Lucas Award for Excellence in Metallography.

• 5187 • Medal for the Advancement of Research
To recognize and honor an executive in an organization, one of whose important activities is the production, fabrication or use of metals and other materials. The recipient, over a period of years, shall have consistently sponsored research or development and by foresight and actions shall have helped substantially to advance the arts and sciences relating to materials science and engineering. A 2-inch 14K Gold Medal is awarded annually. Established in 1943.

• 5188 • Merit Award
To recognize individuals whose ideas and/or work have benefited IAEM as an organization in some special way. The nominee must have made an outstanding contribution to the creation or continuance of an IAEM project, and/or created or significantly enhanced a new program or project at chapter level. Up to four awards, two to Exposition Management Members and two to Associate Members, may be presented annually at the Annual Meeting.

• 5189 • Allan Ray Putnam Service Award
To recognize the efforts of outstanding members of ASM on behalf of the Society in order to further the Society's objectives and goals and to recognize those individuals whose contributions have been especially noteworthy and to whom the Society owes a particularly great debt of appreciation. Awarded annually. Established in 1988 in honor of Allan Ray Putnam, the Managing Director of the Society between 1959 and 1983.

• 5190 • Albert Sauveur Achievement Award
To recognize pioneering materials science and engineering achievements that have stimulated organized work to such an extent that a marked basic advance has been made in the knowledge of materials science and engineering. A plaque is awarded. Established in 1934 in honor of Albert Sauveur, a distinguished teacher, metallographer, and metallurgist.

• 5191 • Bradley Stoughton Award for Young Teachers
To recognize outstanding teachers of materials science, materials engineering, design, and processing. Individuals 35 years or younger are eligible. A monetary award of $3,000 and a certificate are awarded annually. Established in 1952 in memory of Bradley Stoughton, a former president of the Society. Formerly: Bradley Stoughton Award for Young Teachers of Metallurgy.

• 5192 • Albert Easton White Distinguished Teacher Award
To recognize unusually long and devoted service (not less than 15 years) in the teaching of, as well as significant accomplishments in, materials science or engineering. A plaque is awarded annually. Established in 1960 in memory of Albert Easton White, an outstanding teacher and research engineer.

• 5193 •
Asociacion de Psicologia de Puerto Rico
Marta Angelis Rivera PhD, Exec.Dir.
PO Box 363435
San Juan, PR 00936-3435
Phone: (787)751-7100
Fax: (787)758-6467
E-mail: appr@coqui.net
Home Page: http://www.asppr.org

• 5194 • Psychology Association Award
For good standing as a professional. Scholarship awarded annually.

• 5195 •
Aspen Filmfest
Lauren Thielen, Exec.Dir.
110 E. Hallam, Ste. 102
Aspen, CO 81611
Phone: (970)925-6882
Fax: (970)925-1967
E-mail: filmfest@aspenfilm.org
Home Page: http://www.aspenfilm.org

• 5196 • Aspen Filmfest
To recognize U.S. and international independent filmmakers Considers films of all genres and styles, except educational and instructional. Encourages submissions whose approach to both the chosen subject matter and medium of film reflects artistic originality, integrity, and technical excellence. Eligible films must have been completed after September 1 the preceding year. Held annually in the autumn. Established in 1979 by Ellen Kohner Hunt.

• 5197 • Aspen Shortsfest
An international shorts competition that encourages submissions whose approach to both the chosen subject matter and medium of film reflects artistic originality, integrity and technical excellence. An International Competition jury of prestigious film industry figures will award more than $20,000 in cash plus other prizes in several categories including Animation, Comedy, Documentary, Drama, Other, Children/Family, and Student. Best of Category winners may also qualify for Academy Awardregional consideration.

• 5198 •
Aspen Institute
Walter Isaacson, Pres./CEO
One Dupont Circle NW, Ste. 700
Washington, DC 20036-1133
Phone: (202)736-5800
Fax: (202)467-0790
E-mail: info@aspeninst.org
Home Page: http://www.aspeninstitute.org

• 5199 • Aspen Institute Corporate Award for Excellence in Leadership
For recognition of individuals who exemplify the twin goals of The Aspen Institute, outstanding leadership and furtherance of democratic values. Awarded annually. Established in 1984.

• 5200 • Aspen Institute Public Service Award for Excellence in Leadership
For recognition of individuals who exemplify the twin goals of The Aspen Institute, outstanding leadership and furtherance of democratic values. Awarded annually. Established in 1984.

• 5201 •
Asphalt Emulsion Manufacturer Association
Michael R. Krissoff, Exec.Dir.
3 Church Cir., PMB 250
Annapolis, MD 21401
Phone: (410)267-0023
Fax: (410)267-7546
E-mail: krissoff@aema.org
Home Page: http://www.aema.org

• 5202 • Hall of Fame Award
To recognize a member of AEMA, active or retired, who has made an innovative, substantial contribution over the long term to the development of the association and the advancement of the emulsion industry. Established in 1980.

• 5203 • Recognition of Achievement Award
To recognize an individual, active or retired, who has made a significant contribution to the development of emulsion technology. Awarded annually. Established in 1980.

• 5204 •
Asphalt Recycling and Reclaiming Association
Michael R. Krissoff, Exec.Dir.
3 Church Cir., PMB 250
Annapolis, MD 21401
Phone: (410)267-0023
Fax: (410)267-7546
E-mail: memberservices@arra.org
Home Page: http://www.arra.org

• 5205 • President's Award
To recognize an individual for outstanding contributions to the industry. Presented periodically

at the discretion of the ARRA president. Established in 1985.

• 5206 • Special Recognition Award
To recognize public officials for their overall professional contribution to and their recognition and promotion of the asphalt recycling and reclaiming industry. Individuals may be nominated by members of the association by November 1. Awards are presented in the following categories: Cold In-Place Recycling, John A. Miller Award for Excellence in Cold Planning, Full-Depth Reclamation, Hot In-Place Recycling, Hot Recycling, and General. A plaque is awarded annually at the annual meeting. Established in 1985.

• 5207 •
ASPRS - The Imaging and Geospatial Information Society
Jesse Winch, Program Mgr.
5410 Grosvenor Ln., Ste. 210
Bethesda, MD 20814-2160
Phone: (301)493-0290
Fax: (301)493-0208
E-mail: asprs@asprs.org
Home Page: http://www.asprs.org

Formerly: (2004) American Society of Photogrammetry; Imaging Geospatial Information Society.

• 5208 • Talbert Abrams Award
To recognize the authorship and recording of current, historical, engineering, and scientific developments in photogrammetry. Honorary, regular, associate, and student members of the Society are eligible. The Talbert Abrams Grand Award consists of possession of the Grand Trophy for one year, a replica of the trophy the following year, and a monetary award. Plaques are awarded for honorable mention. Awarded annually. Established in 1945.

• 5209 • Ford Bartlett Award
To reward members for actively promoting membership in the Society. Members who sponsored ten or more new members for the previous calendar year are eligible. A certificate and a one-year membership in the Society are awarded annually. Established in 1981. Sponsored by Lockwood, Kessler, and Bartlett, Inc.

• 5210 • Boeing Award
To recognize an individual for an outstanding technical publication on photographic interpretation. A monetary award of $500 and a plaque are awarded annually. Established in 1965.

• 5211 • John I. Davidson ASPRS President's Award for Practical Papers
To encourage and commend the individual(s) who publish papers of practical or applied value in *Photogrammetric Engineering and Remote Sensing.* The following awards are presented: a first prize of $500, a tankard, and a certificate; a second prize of $300; and a third prize of $200. Established in 1979.

• 5212 • ESRI Award for Best Scientific Paper in Geographic Information Systems
To encourage and commend the individual(s) who publish papers of scientific merit in the advancement of our knowledge about GIS technology. Selection is made by the editors of the ASPRS Journal, *Photogrammetric Engineering & Remote Sensing*, from papers published during the calendar year. The following awards are presented: first prize - $500 and a certificate; second prize - $300 and a certificate; and third prize $200 and a certificate. Established in 1991. Sponsored by Environmental Systems Research Institute, Inc. (ESRI).

• 5213 • Fellow
To recognize individual(s) who have performed exceptional service in advancing the science and use of the mapping sciences, (e.g., photogrammetry, remote sensing, surveying, geographic information systems, and related disciplines.) Nominees must be active members of the Society at the time of their nomination and must have been active members for a total of at least 10 years.

• 5214 • Honor Award
To recognize individuals or organizations outside the Society for significant accomplishments compatible with or supportive of the mission of the Society. No more than one Honor Award is presented each year.

• 5215 • Honorary Member
To recognize an individual who has rendered distinguished service to the Society or who has attained distinction in the field of photogrammetry, photo interpretation, remote sensing, or related sciences. The total number of Honorary Members must not exceed 21 at any given time. Honorary Members are elected for life.

• 5216 • KODAK International Educational Literature Award
To improve the quantity and quality of literature in the recipients' libraries that deals with the mapping sciences (i.e., photogrammetry, remote sensing, GIS, and related disciplines) by providing ASPRS educational materials and publications. The following is awarded to the most deserving applicant: $350 worth of books, manuals, or other literature published by ASPRS; proceedings of the annual convention and Fall technical meetings for a period of five years; one free registration to the Society's annual convention at the time of receiving the award for a member of the institution to whom the award is being given; and a certificate. Established in 1990. Supported by Eastman Kodak Company Aerial Systems Division and with assistance of ASPRS.

• 5217 • LEICA Geosystems Award for Best Scientific Paper in Remote Sensing
To encourage and commend the individual(s) who publish papers of scientific merit in the advancement of our knowledge about remote sensing technology. Selection is made by the Editors of the ASPRS Journal *Photogrammetric Engineering & Remote Sensing* from papers published during the calendar year. The following awards are presented: first prize - $500 and a certificate; second prize - $300 and a certificate; and third prize - $200 and a certificate. Established in 1991. Sponsored by LEICA GEOSYSTEMS, Inc.

• 5218 • Leica Geosystems Internship
To encourage graduate education in photogrammetry and to promote the development of photogrammetric science. Competition is open to any active or student member of the Society. The deadline for application is December 1. One internship of $2,500 is awarded annually. Formerly: Wild Leitz Photogrammetric Fellowship Award.

• 5219 • Ta Liang Memorial Award
To facilitate research-related travel by outstanding graduate students in remote sensing. Such travel includes field investigations, agency visits, participation in conferences, or any travel which enhances or facilitates a graduate research program. Student members of the Society who are currently pursuing graduate level studies in a recognized college or university in the United States or elsewhere are eligible. A grant of at least $500 is awarded annually. Established in 1989 to honor Ta Liang, a skilled civil engineer, an excellent teacher, and one of the world's foremost airphoto interpreters. Sponsored by the International Geographic Information Foundation.

• 5220 • Outstanding Service Award
To recognize members for outstanding and unusual efforts in helping the society develop and carry out its program over a sustained period of time. Nominees must be members of the Society at the time of their nomination and must have been a member for a total of at least 10 years.

• 5221 • Photogrammetric (Fairchild) Award
To stimulate the development of the art of aerial photogrammetry in the United States. Members of the Society are eligible. A silver plaque, a bronze replica plaque, and a certificate are awarded annually. Established in 1944.

• 5222 • Presidential Citations for Meritorious Service
To recognize members for meritorious and outstanding administrative contributions to the Society. Citations are awarded annually.

• 5223 • Region Newsletter of the Year Award
To recognize excellence of the region in providing service to the members and to the profession at large through publication of a newsletter. A certificate is awarded annually. Established in 1980.

• 5224 • Region of the Year Award
To recognize excellence of the region in providing service to the members and to the profession at large. A certificate and possession of the

Region of the Year banner for one year are awarded annually. Established in 1968.

• 5225 • Space Imaging Award for Application of High Resolution Digital Satellite Imagery

To support remote sensing education and to stimulate the development of applications of high-resolution digital satellite remote sensing data through the granting of Space Imaging imagery for applied research by undergraduate or graduate students. The award consists of a grant of data valued at up to $2,000, and a certificate(supplied by Space Imaging) inscribed with the recipient's name and his/her institution. Established in 1991. Sponsored by Earth Observation Satellite Company.

• 5226 •
Assaulted Women's Helpline
Margaret Haynes, Chair
PO Box 369, Sta. B
PO Box 369, Station B
Toronto, ON, Canada M5T 2W2
Phone: (416)364-4144
Toll-Free: (866)863-0511
Fax: (416)364-0563
E-mail: bjordan@awhl.org
Home Page: http://www.awhl.org

• 5227 • Rosemary Brown Award

Recognizes excellence in fighting to end violence against women. Awarded annually.

• 5228 •
Assisted Living Federation of America
Thomas H. Grape, Ch.
11200 Waples Mill Rd., Ste. 150
Fairfax, VA 22030
Phone: (703)691-8100
Fax: (703)691-8106
E-mail: info@alfa.org
Home Page: http://www.alfa.org

• 5229 • Best of Home Architectural Design Award

Annual award of recognition. No additional information is available at this time.

• 5230 • Hero Awards

To recognize outstanding employees or volunteers of assisted living facilities. A monetary prize of $250 is awarded to up to four recipients annually.

• 5231 • Pioneer Award

Award of recognition. For outstanding innovative state regulator in the area of assisted living. Awarded annually.

• 5232 •
Associated Builders and Contractors
Kirk Pickerel, Pres./CEO
4250 N Fairfax Dr., 9th Fl.
Arlington, VA 22203-1607
Phone: (703)812-2000
Fax: (703)812-8201
E-mail: gotquestions@abc.org
Home Page: http://www.abc.org

• 5233 • ABC Excellence in Construction Awards

To recognize quality and innovation in merit (open) shop construction, and to honor all members of the construction team: contractor, owner, and architect. Awards are presented in the following categories: Industrial & Heavy, Commercial, Institutional, and Specialty. Two awards are presented in each category: Award of Excellence - an ivory alabaster American Eagle perched on an arch of black onyx and clear lucite; and Award of Merit - a fountainhead faux marble pyramid. Awarded annually at the convention. Established in 1990.

• 5234 • John Trimmer Merit Shop Teaching Award of Excellence

To recognize a faculty member of a four-year construction program who best combines teaching skills; a philosophy of performance and pride, economy, and efficiency; interaction with the construction industry; and knowledge of construction. Any faculty member of a four-year construction degree program is eligible. Applicants must submit at least four recommendations, including one from the school's department head or dean, and one from the local ABC Chapter. A monetary award of $3,500, a plaque, and travel expenses to the Associated Builders and Contractors Annual Convention to receive the award are presented annually. Established in 1984 in honor of John Trimmer, who coined the phrase "Merit Shop," and served ABC as its Executive Vice President for 24 years. Additional information is available from studentchapters@abc.org.

• 5235 •
Associated Builders and Contractors, Southeast Pennsylvania Chapter
Geoffrey N. Zeh, Exec.Dir.
430 W Germantown Pike
East Norriton, PA 19403
Phone: (610)279-6666
Fax: (610)279-7052
E-mail: info@abcsepa.org
Home Page: http://www.abcsepa.org

• 5236 • Merit Shop Award of Excellence in Construction

Selected on basis of site visits by panel of judges. Trophy awarded annually.

• 5237 •
Associated Church Press
Mary Lynn Hendrickson, Exec.Dir.
1410 Vernon St.
Stoughton, WI 53589-2248
Phone: (608)877-0011
Fax: (608)877-0062
E-mail: acpoffice@earthlink.net
Home Page: http://www.theacp.org

• 5238 • Award of Merit

To recognize and encourage the pursuit of journalistic excellence among religious publications in 43 categories, including: General Excellence Newspapers, General Excellence - Magazine, General Excellence Newsletter, Editorial, Feature Article, News story, Department, and Front Page. Member publications and individuals of the ACP are eligible. A certificate and citation are awarded annually. Established in 1945.

• 5239 • Citation of Honor

To recognize an individual for outstanding contributions to the Associated Church Press and/or in the field of religious journalism. Nominations are accepted. A citation and token award are awarded when merited. Established in 1979.

• 5240 • William B. Lipphard Award for Distinguished Service to Religious Journalism

This, the highest honor ACP can confer, is given to individuals who have made long-term, distinguished contributions in the field of religious journalism; have performed with unusual distinction, courage, or integrity; have contributed influence that has markedly changed or advanced ACP ideals; or possess exemplary personal qualities and talents. The recipient need not be a participant in ACP. A citation and token award are presented when merited. Established in 1966 in memory of Dr. William B. Lipphard (1887-1971), a long-time participant in ACP and its first executive secretary.

• 5241 • Writing and Design Award

Recognizes excellence in content, makeup, and typography. Awarded annually.

• 5242 •
Associated Colleges of the Midwest
Scott Lewis, Dir. Publications
205 W Wacker Dr., Ste. 1300
Chicago, IL 60606
Phone: (312)263-5000
Fax: (312)263-5879
E-mail: acm@acm.edu
Home Page: http://www.acm.edu

• 5243 • Nick Adams Short Story Contest

To recognize outstanding short stories written by undergraduate students enrolled at ACM member colleges. Stories of 10,000 words or less that have not been published off-campus are considered. A monetary prize of $1,000 is awarded annually. Established in 1973 by an anonymous donor. The prize is named for the young Midwestern protagonist of many of Ernest Hemingway's short stories.

• 5244 •
Associated General Contractors of Vermont
Thom Serrani, Exec.Dir.
148 State St.
PO Box 750
Montpelier, VT 05601-0750
Phone: (802)223-2374
Phone: (802)223-2375
Fax: (802)223-1809
E-mail: info@agcvt.org
Home Page: http://www.agcvt.org

• 5245 • **Best Builder Award**
For outstanding building project. Recognition award bestowed annually.

• 5246 • **Richard A. Snelling Economic Development Award**
For major player in Vermont's economic development. Recognition award bestowed annually.

• 5247 •
Associated Landscape Contractors of Colorado
5290 E Yale Cir., Ste. 100
Denver, CO 80222
Phone: (303)757-5611
Toll-Free: 800-339-2441
Fax: (303)757-5636
E-mail: ksirovatka@alcc.com
Home Page: http://www.alcc.com

• 5248 • **Excellence in Landscape**
For projects done in Colorado in 22 different categories. Recognition award bestowed annually.

• 5249 •
Associated Press Managing Editors
Managing Editors Association
Deanna Sands, Pres.
450 W 33rd St.
New York, NY 10001
Phone: (212)621-1838
Fax: (212)506-6102
E-mail: apme@ap.org
Home Page: http://www.apme.com

• 5250 • **John L. Dougherty Award**
To recognize outstanding work by a young Associated Press writer. A monetary award of $1,000 and a plaque are awarded annually. The award is named for John Dougherty, an APME officer who died in 1980 and who had an abiding interest in good writing and in teaching young writers.

• 5251 • **Freedom of Information Award**
To recognize outstanding contributions in maintaining freedom of information standards or for widening the scope of information available to the public. Journalists and newspapers are eligible. An engraved plaque is awarded annually. Established in 1971.

• 5252 • **Public Service Award**
To recognize outstanding service by a newspaper to its community, state, or the nation. Associated Press member newspapers in each of two circulation categories are eligible. Plaques are awarded annually. Established in 1971.

• 5253 • **Top Performance Awards**
To recognize outstanding work by Associated Press reporters for enterprise, feature, and deadline writing, and to Associated Press photographers for spot and features photos. A monetary award of $1,500 and a plaque are awarded annually. Established in 1964.

• 5254 •
Associated Subcontractors of Massachusetts
Monica Lawton, Exec.Dir.
1 Washington Mall, 5th Fl.
Boston, MA 02108
Phone: (617)742-3412
Fax: (617)742-2331
E-mail: mail@associatedsubs.com
Home Page: http://www.associatedsubs.com

• 5255 • **Joseph M. Corwin Award**
For outstanding career service to the construction subcontracting industry. Recognition award bestowed biennially.

• 5256 •
Associated Taxpayers of Idaho
Randy Nelson, Pres.
PO Box 1665
Boise, ID 83701
Phone: (208)344-5581
Fax: (208)344-5582
E-mail: holly_cawley@qwest.net
Home Page: http://www.users.qwest.net/~ati-taxinfo/

• 5257 • **Max Yost Distinguished Services Award**
For individual achievement toward improving tax laws and procedures for having sustained and significant services, along with leadership and experience in the tax field. Recognition award.

• 5258 •
Associated Writing Programs
David W. Fenza, Exec.Dir.
George Mason Univ.
Mail Stop 1E3
Fairfax, VA 22030-4444
Phone: (703)993-4301
Fax: (703)993-4302
E-mail: awp@awpwriter.org
Home Page: http://www.awpwriter.org

• 5259 • **AWP Award Series**
To discover new talent and to make contemporary novels, creative nonfiction, poetry, and short fiction available to a wider audience by publishing four book-length manuscripts in these four genres. Book-length is defined as follows: 48 pages of poetry, 150 to 300 manuscript pages of creative nonfiction or a collection of short stories, and approximately 250 to 450 pages for novels. Mixed genre manuscripts, criticism, and scholarly monographs are not eligible. Open to all authors writing in English regardless of nationality or residence. Manuscripts may be submitted only with postmarks in January and February. An entry fee of $10 for members and $20 for nonmembers is required. Publication of the award-winning works with an independent or university press, and a $2,000 honorarium are presented annually. Established in 1974. Entrants should send SASE to AWP for complete guidelines before submitting work.

• 5260 •
Associates of Brand Library and Art Center
Sally MacAller, Pres.
1601 W Mountain St.
Glendale, CA 91201
Phone: (818)548-2051
Fax: (818)548-5079
Home Page: http://www.brand-arts.org

• 5261 • **Brand Annual Art Competition**
For recognition of achievement in art (media varies annually). U.S. residents working in aquamedia are eligible. Over $4,000 in cash and purchase awards are presented annually. Established in 1970.

• 5262 •
Association des auteurs des Cantons de l'Est
420, rue Marquette, local 129
Sherbrooke, QC, Canada J1H 1M4
Phone: (819)821-2221
Fax: (819)563-0962

• 5263 • **Gaston-Gouin, Alfred-DesRochers et Alphonse-Desjardins**
To recognize the quality of manuscripts, fiction and essay. Awarded annually with a monetary prize. Established in 1978.

• 5264 •
Association for Advancement of Behavior Therapy
Mary Jane Eimer CAE, Exec.Dir.
305 7th Ave., 16th Fl.
New York, NY 10001-6008
Phone: (212)647-1890
Toll-Free: 800-685-AABT
Fax: (212)647-1865
E-mail: mjeimer@aabt.org
Home Page: http://www.aabt.org

• 5265 • **Career/Lifetime Achievement Award**
Award of recognition. Nominees are solicited from the members of AABT governance. Attempts are made to avoid duplication of other awards in a given year.

• 5266 • Distinguished Friend to Behavior Therapy
Award of recognition. Nominees are solicited from the members of ABT governance. Awarded annually.

• 5267 • Outstanding Contribution by an Individual for Educational/Training Activities
To recognize individuals who have provided significant contributions to the literature advancing knowledge of educational and/or training in behavior therapy. Candidates must be members of AABT in good standing. Awarded triennially.

• 5268 • Outstanding Training Programs
Recognizes a training program (not an individual) that has made a significant contribution to behavior therapy. Programs can include graduate, predoctoral, internship, and postdoctoral; institutes or continuing education initiatives. Awarded annually.

• 5269 • President's New Researcher's Award
For recognition of outstanding research by authors who are less than five years out of a Ph.D. or residency program. The field of research is announced by the current president by February 1 of each year. The deadline is September 1. A monetary prize and a certificate are awarded annually at the meeting of members. Established in 1979.

• 5270 • Elise Ramos Awards
For the best student poster submitted at the convention. Awarded annually.

• 5271 • Student Dissertation Award
Recognizes a student's dissertation. A monetary prize is given annually. Inquire for more details.

• 5272 •
Association for Asian Studies
Michael Paschal, Exec.Dir.
1021 E Huron Street
Ann Arbor, MI 48104
Phone: (734)665-2490
Fax: (734)665-3801
E-mail: jwilson@aasianst.org
Home Page: http://www.aasianst.org

• 5273 • Harry J. Benda Prize
To recognize outstanding younger scholars in the field of Southeast Asian Studies. Nominees may be from any field or country. An honorarium of $1,000 is awarded each year at the annual meeting. Established in 1977 in memory of Harry Benda, a pioneering scholar and teacher in the field of Asian studies. Additional information is available from AAS Secretariat.

• 5274 • Anada Kentish Coomaraswamy Book Prize
To honor the author of the best English-language work in South Asian studies. Eligible books must be original, scholarly, nonfiction works on South Asia (India, Pakistan, Nepal, Sri Lanka, and Bangladesh) and may concern any topic in any discipline, or may cross disciplinary lines; be the first publication of the text in English anywhere in the world; and have an innovative approach that defines or redefines scholarly understanding of whole subject areas. Reference works, exhibition catalogues, textbooks, essay collections, poetry, fiction, memoirs, and autobiographies are not eligible. Translations are eligible only if they include a substantial introduction, annotation, or critical apparatus. Nominations may be made by authors, publishers, or other interested members in the field. A monetary prize of $1,000 is awarded annually. Established in 1992. Co-sponsored by the South Asia Council.

• 5275 • Distinguished Contributions to Asian Studies
To recognize an individual(s) who has rendered distinguished service in Asian Studies. Senior persons in the field of Asian Studies are eligible. A certificate is awarded at the annual meeting. Established in 1983. Formerly: Distinguished Service Award.

• 5276 • John Whitney Hall Book Prize
To recognize an outstanding book on Japan or Korea. Eligible works may treat any historical period from ancient to modern, so long as the subject matter falls within the humanities and social sciences. Reference works, exhibition catalogues, textbooks, essay collections, poetry, fiction, memoirs, or autobiographies are not eligible. Translations are eligible if they include a substantial introduction, annotation, or critical apparatus. Nominations may be made by trading book publishers and university presses. A monetary prize of $1,000 is awarded annually. Winners are announced at the annual meeting. Established in 1994 in honor of the distinguished historian, John Whitney Hall. Sponsored by the Northeast Asia Council of the Association for Asian Studies.

• 5277 • Joseph Levenson Prizes in Chinese Studies
To recognize outstanding scholarly books that further broaden understanding of China. Awards are given in two categories: works focusing on China before 1900 and works on the 20th century. English-language books in all disciplines and in all periods of Chinese history published in North America (no anthologies, edited works, pamphlets) at least two years prior to the award year are eligible. Two monetary prizes of $1,500 each are awarded at the annual meeting. Established in 1986 in honor of Joseph R. Levenson, a distinguished China scholar whose achievements were recognized beyond the China field.

• 5278 •
Association for Baha'i Studies
(Association d'Etudes Baha'ies)
Mrs. Parvin Rowhani, Office Mgr.
34 Copernicus St.
Ottawa, ON, Canada K1N 7K4
Phone: (613)233-1903
Fax: (613)233-3644
E-mail: editor@bahai-studies.ca
Home Page: http://www.bahai-studies.ca

• 5279 • Excellence in Baha'i Studies
Given for outstanding publishing research on Baha'i studies. Awarded annually.

• 5280 •
Association for Canadian Studies in the United States
David Archibald, Exec.Dir.
1424 16th St. NW, Ste. 502
Washington, DC 20036
Phone: (202)332-1151
Fax: (202)462-2420
E-mail: info@acsus.org
Home Page: http://www.acsus.org

• 5281 • Distinguished Dissertation Award
To recognize outstanding doctoral research on Canada at American institutions. The awardee will be expected to make a 20 minute presentation on his or her work at the conference. Nominations are accepted from faculty members of dissertation committees. A monetary prize of $500, travel support, membership and a certificate are awarded biennially in conjunction with the Association's national conference.

• 5282 • Donner Medal in Canadian Studies
For recognition of outstanding achievement in the field of Canadian studies. Nominations are accepted. A bronze medal is awarded biennially. Nominees must have contributions in at least one of the following categories: teaching, scholarship, administration, and public affairs. Established in 1975. The award honors the William Donner Foundation which has done much to promote Canadian studies in the United States.

• 5283 • Rufus Z. Smith Prize
For recognition of the best article *The American Review of Canadian Studies* during the two years preceding the biennial conference of the Association for Canadian Studies in the United States (ACSUS). A monetary prize of $ 250 and a certificate are awarded.

• 5284 •
Association for Canadian Theatre Research (Association de la Recherche Theatrale au Canada)
Anne Nothof, Pres.
University of Lethbridge
Lethbridge, AB, Canada T1K 3M4
Phone: (403)329-2463
E-mail: s.scott@uleth.edu
Home Page: http://www.umoncton.ca/facarts/anglais/actr/artc.htm

• 5285 • Jean-Cleo Godin Award
Recognizes the best French-language scholarly article in theatrical studies. Awarded annually. Established in 1989.

• 5286 • Robert G. Lawrence Prize
Recognizes the best paper presented by a new scholar at the ACTR convention. Awarded annually. Established in 1995.

• 5287 • Heather McCallum Scholarship
Supports a theater-related research project. A monetary prize of up to $1,000 is awarded annually. Established in 1987.

• 5288 • Richard Plant Award
Recognizes the best English-language scholarly article in theatrical studies. Awarded annually. Established in 1989.

• 5289 • Ann Saddlemyer Award
Recognizes the best book in theatrical studies. Awarded annually. Established in 1989.

• 5290 •
Association for Communication Excellence in Agriculture, Natural Resources, and Life and Human Sciences
Christine Penko, Coor.
PO Box 110811
Gainesville, FL 32611
Phone: (352)392-9588
Fax: (352)392-7902
E-mail: ace@ifas.ufl.edu
Home Page: http://www.aceweb.org
Formerly: American Association of Agricultural College Editors.

• 5291 • Awards of Excellence
To recognize those individuals whose media careers have exhibited professional excellence in the areas of: press; television and radio; teaching and research; graphic design; visual aids; and publications. Awarded annually. Formerly: Media-Field Award.

• 5292 • Reuben Brigham Award
To recognize a nonmember who has made a significant career contribution to agricultural; natural resource and/or home economics communications. Awarded annually. Established in 1947.

• 5293 • Pioneer Award
To recognize an individual whose professional contributions demonstrate communications excellence and whose service has furthered ACE goals. Members who are in their first 10 years of the agricultural communications profession are eligible. Presented annually. Established in 1957. Formerly: (1959) Frank Jeter Award.

• 5294 • Professional Award
To recognize a member whose career exemplifies communications professionalism. Established in 1973.

• 5295 • Service Award
To recognize exceptional service to the Association. The individual need not be a member of the Association. A plaque is awarded annually.

• 5296 •
Association for Computing Machinery
Virginia Gold, Contact
1515 Broadway, 17th Fl.
New York, NY 10036-5701
Phone: (212)626-0500
Toll-Free: 800-342-6626
Fax: (212)944-1318
E-mail: acmhelp@acm.org
Home Page: http://www.acm.org

• 5297 • ACM Doctoral Dissertation Award
To recognize the doctoral thesis in computer science and engineering that is judged to be the all-around best of those submitted to ACM. The honoree receives a monetary award of $5,000 and publication of the winning dissertation by Springer-Verlag. Awarded annually. Established in 1982.

• 5298 • ACM Eugene Lawler Award for Humanitarian Contributions within Computer Science and Informatics
Recognizes individuals or a group for humanitarian contributions made through the use of computing technology. Nominees cab be from the general public who have made contributions in areas such as, but not limited to aid for the disabled, education in inner city schools, intellectual property issues, educational opportunities for women or the underrepresented, and problem solving in developing countries. The award consist of $5,000 and travel expenses to the Awards banquet. Given every two years if merited. Established in 1999.

• 5299 • ACM Fellows
To recognize and honor members for achievements in computer science and information technology and for significant contributions to the mission of the ACM. Fellows serve as distinguished colleagues providing for guidance and leadership as the world of information technology evolves. Established in 1993.

• 5300 • Grace Murray Hopper Award
To recognize an outstanding young computer professional of the year for a single recent major technical or service contribution. The recipient must have been 35 years of age or less at the time the contribution was made. A monetary prize of $5,000 is awarded annually. Established in 1971. Financial support is provided by the Unisys Corporation.

• 5301 • Paris Kanellakis Theory and Practice Award
To honor specific theoretical accomplishments having significant and demonstrable effects on the practice of computing. A monetary prize of $5,000 is awarded to one or more recipients annually. Established in 1996. Supported by an endowment by the Kanellakis family and contributions from Brooks/Cole and Thompson Learning as well several ACM special interests groups.

• 5302 • Karl V. Karlstrom Outstanding Educator Award
To recognize an outstanding educator. Nominees must be appointed to a recognized educational baccalaureate institution; recognized for advancing new teaching methodologies, or effecting new curriculum development or expansion in computer science and engineering; or making a significant contribution to the educational mission of the ACM. Individuals who have been teaching for ten years or less are given special consideration. Nominations must be submitted by August 1. A monetary award of $5,000 is presented annually. Financial support is supplied by Prentice-Hall Publishing Company.

• 5303 • Eckert - Mauchly Award
To recognize an individual for contributions to computer and digital systems architecture where the field of computer architecture is considered at present to encompass the combined hardware-software design and analysis of computing and of digital systems. Contributions may be a series of papers, a patent, or a prototype of a mass produced system. The deadline for nominations is March 1. A monetary award of $5,000 is awarded jointly by ACM and the IEEE Computer Society. Awarded annually. Established in 1979.

• 5304 • Allen Newell Award
To recognize an individual for career contributions that have breadth within computer science, or that bridge computer science and other disciplines. This endowed award is supported by the American Association for Artificial Intelligence and by individual contributions. Established in 1994.

• 5305 • Outstanding Contribution to ACM Award
To recognize and honor individuals who have contributed significant service to ACM. Up to three individuals may be selected each year. A certificate is awarded annually. Established in 1976.

• 5306 • SIGPLAN Distinguished Service Award
To recognize contributions to ACM SIGPLAN, its conferences, publications, or its local activities. The award includes a prize of $2,500. Awarded on the basis of value and degree of services to the Programming Languages Community.

• 5307 • Software System Award
To recognize a software system that has had a lasting influence, as reflected in contributions to concepts or in commercial practice or in both. Either institutions or individuals responsible for developing and introducing the software system are eligible. A monetary award of $10,000, engraved plaque, and a certificate are awarded. Established in 1983. Financial support is provided by IBM. Formerly: Programming Systems and Languages Paper Award.

• 5308 • A. M. Turing Award
This, ACM's most prestigious technical award, is given in recognition of an individual's contribution of a technical nature made to the computing community. Selection is based on contributions that are of lasting and major technical importance to the computing field. The deadline for nominations is August 1. The award consists of a monetary prize of $25,000. Awarded annually. Established in 1966.

• 5309 •
Association for Computing Machinery Special Interest Group for Design of Communications
Brad Mehlenbacher, Chm.
PO Box 11315
New York, NY 10286-1315
Phone: (212)626-0500
Fax: (212)944-1318
E-mail: acmhelp@acm.org
Home Page: http://www.sigdoc.org/

• 5310 • Diana Award
To recognize organization, institution, or business for long-term contribution to the field of communication design. Awarded annually. Established in 1992 in honor of Diana Patterson, former president of SIGDOC.

• 5311 • Joseph T. Rigo Award
To honor an individual for a lifetime of significant work in the design of communication. Awarded annually. Established in 1988.

• 5312 •
Association for Computing Machinery Special Interest Group for Management of Data
Raghu Ramakrishnan, Chm.
1515 Broadway
New York, NY 10036
Phone: (212)626-0500
Toll-Free: 800-342-6626
Fax: (212)944-1318
E-mail: acmhelp@acm.org
Home Page: http://www.sigmod.org/

• 5313 • Edgar F. Codd Innovations Award
Given to a (group) person(s) who made a significant contribution to the field of database systems through research during the past ten years that has been reduced to practice and is in wide use. The award includes a prize of $1,000. Established in 1992. Formerly: (2004) SIGMOD Innovations Award.

• 5314 • SIGMOD Contributions Award
Given to a (group) person(s) who made a significant contribution to the field of database systems through research funding, education, professional services, etc. The award includes a prize of $1,000.

• 5315 •
Association for Computing Machinery Special Interest Group on Algorithm and Computation Theory
Richard E. Ladner, Chm.
1515 Broadway
New York, NY 10036
Phone: (212)626-0500
Toll-Free: 800-342-6626
Fax: (212)944-1318
E-mail: acmhelp@acm.org
Home Page: http://sigact.acm.org

• 5316 • Godel Prize
To recognize an outstanding paper in the area of theoretical computer science. Any single paper or series of papers published in a recognized referred journal are eligible. A $5,000 prize is awarded annually. Co-sponsored by the European Association for Theoretical Computer Science.

• 5317 • Donald E. Knuth Prize
To acknowledge major research accomplishments and contributions to the foundations of computer science over an extended period of time. Awarded every 1.5 years, the prize includes a $5,000 award and a $1,000 travel stipend for travel to the awards ceremony. Established in 1996.

• 5318 • SIGACT Distinguished Service Prize
Recognizes service contributions to the Theoretical Computer Science community by individuals. Eligibility is open to anyone with the exception of the sitting SIGACT Chair and will be accepted for a single contribution or a series of contributions. Nominations are accepted from Theory of Computing community members. A 500 word explanation of the candidates eligibility including address, phone number, and email address of the nominator must be submitted. $1000 plus a $500 travel grant are awarded.

• 5319 •
Association for Computing Machinery Special Interest Group on Computer Science Education
Henry M. Walker, Chm.
1515 Broadway
New York, NY 10036
Phone: (212)626-0500
Toll-Free: 800-342-6626
Fax: (212)944-1318
E-mail: sigcse-board@acm.org
Home Page: http://www.sigcse.org/

• 5320 • Award for Lifetime Service
To honor a lifetime of service to computer science education. Nominations are accepted from association member for association members. The award includes a plaque and prize of $1,000. Awarded annually. Established in 1997.

• 5321 • SIGCSE Award
Given for outstanding contributions to computer science education. The award includes a plaque and prize of $1,000. Awarded annually. Established in 1981.

• 5322 •
Association for Computing Machinery Special Interest Group on Data Communications
% Tilman Wolf, Sec.
Department of Electrical and Computer Enginnering
University of Massachusetts
Zirkel 2
Amherst, MA 01103-9284
Phone: (413)545-0757
Fax: (413)545-1993
E-mail: wolf@ecs.umass.edu
Home Page: http://www.acm.org/sigs/sigcomm

• 5323 • SIGCOMM Award
To recognize a lifetime contribution in the field of computer communications. Nominations must be submitted by ACM SIGCOMM members only. Deadline for nominations is May 30. A $2,000 prize, a plaque, and travel expenses to attend the annual SIGCOMM conference are awarded annually at the conference. Established in 1989.

• 5324 •
Association for Computing Machinery Special Interest Group on Hypertext, Hypermedia and the Web
Peter Nurnberg, Chm.
1515 Broadway
New York, NY 10036
Phone: (212)626-0500
Toll-Free: 800-342-6626
Fax: (212)944-1318
E-mail: acmhelp@acm.org
Home Page: http://www.sigweb.org/

• 5325 • Douglas Engelbart Best Paper Award
Promotes excellence in hypertext/hypermedia research and in the reporting of research results. A monetary prize of $1,000 is presented annually at the ACM SIGWEB Hypertext Conference. Established in 1996.

• 5326 •
Association for Conservation Information
David Warren, Pres.
Dept. of Wildlife Conservation
1801 N. Lincoln Blvd.
Oklahoma City, OK 73105
Phone: (405)521-3855
Fax: (405)521-6898
E-mail: dwarren@odwc.state.ok.us
Home Page: http://www.aci-net.org
Formerly: American Association for Conservation Information.

• 5327 • ACI Annual Awards
To recognize work in the area of conservation communication. Categories include: Magazines, Magazine Article, News Releases (print and electronic), Special Publications, Radio Programs, Television Programs, Public Service Announcements, Internal Communications, Photography, Web Sites, and Educational Programs. Entries must represent work from the previous calendar year. First place winners receive a trophy, and certificates are awarded to second and third place winners in each category. Awarded annually.

• 5328 •
Association for Convention Operations Management
Maura Middleton, Exec. Dir.
PO Box 727
Princeton Junction, NJ 08550
Phone: (609)799-3712
Fax: (609)799-7032
E-mail: info@acomonline.org
Home Page: http://www.acomonline.org/

• 5329 • Meeting Planner of the Year
To recognize client meeting planners who have conducted themselves and their business in a professional, productive, pleasant exemplary manner. Actual hands-on experience is considered. A plaque is awarded at the annual convention in January. Established in 1989.

• 5330 •
Association for Corporate Growth
Carl A. Wangman CAE, Exec.Dir.
1926 Waukegan Rd., Ste. 1
Glenview, IL 60025-1770
Phone: (847)657-6730
Toll-Free: 800-699-1331
Fax: (847)657-6819
E-mail: acghq@tcag.com
Home Page: http://www.acg.org

• 5331 • Emerging Company Award
To recognize the company with annual sales of less than $500 million that has shown outstanding growth performance for the three years immediately preceding the award presentation. Awarded annually with a crystal trophy. Established in 1985.

• 5332 • Outstanding Corporate Growth Award
To recognize companies with sales of more than $500 million that have demonstrated outstanding growth over the five-year period prior to the award date. Awarded annually.

• 5333 •
Association for Counselors and Educators in Government
Miles Sakaguchi, Pres.
American Association for Counseling and Development
5999 Stevenson Ave.
Alexandria, VA 22304
Phone: (703)823-9800
Fax: (703)823-0252
Home Page: http://www.dantes.doded.mil/dantes_web/organizations/aceg/index-text.htm

• 5334 • Notable Achievements
To recognize individuals who have made a substantial and lasting contribution to MECA. A plaque is awarded annually. Established in 1987.

• 5335 • President's Award
To recognize individuals and/or institutions who have made a substantial contribution to military education. A plaque is awarded annually. Established in 1987.

• 5336 •
Association for Education and Rehabilitation of the Blind and Visually Impaired
Mark Richert, Exec.Dir.
1703 N Beauregard St., Ste. 440
Alexandria, VA 22311
Phone: (703)671-4500
Toll-Free: 877-492-2708
Fax: (703)671-6391
E-mail: markr@aerbvi.org
Home Page: http://www.aerbvi.org

• 5337 • Alfred Allen Award
To recognize individuals whose character and dedication epitomize the spirit and quality of direct service to blind persons. Nominations should be accompanied by biographical material. Awarded biennially.

• 5338 • Mary K. Bauman Award
To honor an individual who has made a significant contribution to the education of the visually handicapped. Nominations must be accompanied by biographical material. Awarded biennially.

• 5339 • C. Warren Bledsoe Award
For recognition of an outstanding book or article on blindness (for author or editorial work) during the past five years. Nominations are accepted. Awarded biennially.

• 5340 • Douglas MacFarland Award
To recognize a person who influences policy and/or legislation, positively affecting the lives of individuals who are visually impaired.

• 5341 • John H. McAulay Award
For recognition of outstanding achievement in the placement of blind persons. Nominations must be accompanied by biographical material. Awarded biennially.

• 5342 • Ambrose M. Shotwell Memorial Award
To recognize individuals whose leadership and service have exerted influence on a national and international scale. Nominations should be accompanied by biographical material. Awarded biennially.

• 5343 •
Association for Education in Journalism and Mass Communication
Jennifer H. McGill, Exec.Dir.
234 Outlet Pointe Blvd., Ste. A
Columbia, SC 29210-5667
Phone: (803)798-0271
Fax: (803)772-3509
E-mail: aejmc@aejmc.org
Home Page: http://www.aejmc.org/
Formerly: (1982) Association for Education in Journalism.

• 5344 • Carol Burnett/University of Hawaii/AEJMC Ethics Prize
To promote ethics in the journalism and mass communication field. Students, graduate or undergraduate, enrolled in a journalism or communication program, are eligible to present a paper for this award. Selection is based on the quality of the paper. Two monetary awards of $350 each are awarded annually at the AEJMC convention in August. Established in 1985 by Carol Burnett. Co-sponsored by the University of Hawaii and Carol Burnett.

• 5345 • Krieghbaum Under-40 Award
To honor AEJMC members under 40 years of age who have shown outstanding achievement and effort in three areas: teaching research and public service in Journalism and Mass Communication. Nominees must be under 40 at the time of the April 1 deadline. A monetary prize of $1,000 and a plaque are awarded annually at the Association's convention in August. Established in 1981 by Hillier Krieghbaum, former AEJMC president.

• 5346 •
Association for Educational Communications and Technology and the ECT Foundation
Dr. Phillip Harris, Exec.Dir.
1800 N Stonelake Dr., Ste. 2
Bloomington, IN 47404
Phone: (812)335-7675
Toll-Free: 877-677-AECT
Fax: (812)335-7678
E-mail: aect@aect.org
Home Page: http://www.aect.org

• 5347 • **AECT Annual Achievement Award**
Recognizes the individual who has done the most in the past year to advance the field. Awarded annually.

• 5348 • **AECT Distinguished Service Award**
Recognizes outstanding leadership in advancing the theory or practice of educatioinal communications and technology. Awarded annually.

• 5349 • **AECT Leadership Development Grants**
To recognize leadership development activities in educational technology. Open to all affiliates, divisions, and regional organizations within AECT. Cash grants are awarded annually. Funded by the ECT Foundation.

• 5350 • **AECT Memorial Scholarship Award**
To recognize AECT graduate student members enrolled in programs of study related to educational technology. Monetary awards are presented annually. Funded by the ECT Foundation.

• 5351 • **AECT National Convention Internship Program**
To select students as convention interns to participate in a coordinated program of activities. Selection is based on education, employment background, professional memberships, personal statements, and letters of support. Applicant must be fulltime students in a recognized graduate program in educational communications and technology, and must be members of the association. The application deadline is October 15. Students receive complimentary convention registration and housing and a $150 monetary award. Funded by the ECT Foundation. Formerly: AECT National Convention - Earl F. Shrobehn Internship Program.

• 5352 • **AECT/SIRS Intellectual Freedom Award**
Annual award of recognition.

• 5353 • **AECT Special Service Award**
Recognizes notable service to AECT as a whole or to one of its programs or divisions. Awarded annually.

• 5354 • **James W. Brown Publication Award**
To recognize an outstanding nonperiodic publication in the field of educational technology. A nonperiodic publication in any media format in the field of educational technology published during the previous year may be nominated by October 15. Doctoral, masters, and other types of dissertations prepared in fulfillment of degree program requirements are not eligible. Selection is based on the significance of the item's content for the field of media/instructional technology, the professional quality of the item, and the potential impact of the item's content on the field of media/instructional technology. A monetary award is presented annually at the AECT Annual Conference. Funded by the ECT Foundation.

• 5355 • **Robert de Kieffer International Fellowship Award**
To recognize a professional in educational communications and technology at any level from a foreign country who has demonstrated leadership in the field. AECT members who normally reside outside of the United States are eligible. A monetary award and a plaque are presented. In addition, 3M provides the winner's institution a selected visual presentation product.

• 5356 • ***ETR&D* Young Scholar Award**
To recognize the best paper discussing a theoretical construct that could guide research in educational technology. The paper must be an original unpublished work and not a report of a specific study. Anyone who does not hold a doctorate degree or who received a doctorate not more than five years prior to the award year is eligible. The deadline for entries is October 15. A monetary award is presented annually when merited at the AECT annual conference, and the paper is published in *ETR&D.* Funded by the ECT Foundation.

• 5357 • **Robert M. Gagne Instructional Development Research Award**
To recognize the most significant contribution to the body of knowledge which instructional development is based. The work must have been completed within the past three years while the award candidate was enrolled as a graduate student. A monetary award up to $500 is awarded annually. Funded by the ECT Foundation.

• 5358 • **Richard B. Lewis Memorial Award**
To recognize outstanding school district media utilization. Public and private school districts having media utilization programs in place are eligible. Selection is based on: strong media utilization as gathered from special utilization studies conducted by or for the school district and specific instances of good utilization as described in writing by school district or other personnel; and evidence of having provided in the school district budget means of implementing good utilization programs in its schools, and the degree to that AECT/ALA media standards are met for services, equipment, and personnel. The deadline is October 15. A monetary award is presented at the AECT Annual Conference. Funded by the ECT Foundation.

• 5359 • **Carl F. and Viola V. Mahnke Film Production Award**
To honor film and video products that demonstrate excellence in message design and production for educational purposes. Eligibility is limited to film and video products that are educational in nature and produced by undergraduate or graduate students who must be members of AECT. Film entries are limited to 16mm; video entries may be 3/4" U-matic or 1/2" VHS. Products must have been completed within the previous two-year period. The entry deadline is October 15. The winning entry receives a monetary award. Awarded annually when merited at the AECT Convention. Funded by the ECT Foundation.

• 5360 • **Dean and Sybil McClusky Research Award**
To recognize a doctoral candidate currently enrolled in educational technology for research that has been accepted by his or her university. A monetary award is awarded annually. Funded by the ECT Foundation.

• 5361 •
Association for Evolutionary Economics
Helen Sauer, Association Coor.
Bucknell University
Department of Economics
Coleman Hall 168
Lewisburg, PA 17837
Phone: (570)577-3648
Fax: (570)577-2372
E-mail: afee@bucknell.edu
Home Page: http://www.orgs.bucknell.edu/afee

• 5362 • **Institutionalist Prize**
To recognize the best essays on any aspect of theoretical or applied institutional economics. Graduate students and people who have received a graduate degree within the previous three years are eligible. Up to two monetary awards of $1,000 are awarded each year at the annual meeting in January. Established in 1986. Additional information is available from AFEE, Office of Secretary-Treasurer.

• 5363 • **Veblen - Commons Award**
To recognize individuals for exemplary standards of scholarship, teaching excellence, public service, and research in the broad spectrum of purposeful, social, and institutional economics. An inscribed plaque is awarded annually when merited at a special session of the Annual Meeting. Established in 1969 in honor of Thorstein Veblen, an American social theorist, and John R. Commons, an exponent of the institutional school of economics. Additional information is available from AFEE, Office of Secretary-Treasurer.

• 5364 •
Association for Facilities Engineering
Michael Ireland, Exec.Dir.
8160 Corporate Park Dr., Ste. 125
Cincinnati, OH 45242
Phone: (513)489-2473
Fax: (513)247-7422
E-mail: mail@afe.org
Home Page: http://www.afe.org
Formerly: (1998) American Institute of Plant Engineers.

• 5365 • **Chapter of the Year Award**
One outstanding chapter will be chosen to receive the Chapter of the Year Award for its exemplary achievements in recruitment, retention, and chapter programming.

• 5366 • **Facilities Management Excellence Awards (FAME Awards)**
To recognize innovative solutions to typical plant engineering/facilities management problems, and to promote increased recognition of the outstanding contributions plant engineers make to the success of their employers. Creative ideas in energy management, building design, employee productivity, maintenance management, construction management, and environmental protection are considered. Plant engineers and facilities managers in all types and sizes of facilities are eligible. AFE membership is not necessary to enter. One Award of Excellence and three or four Awards of Merit plaques are awarded. The number of winners is determined by the judges. Awarded annually at AFE's national conference. Sponsored since 1984 by the AFE Foundation. Formerly: (1984) Outstanding Plant Engineering Program Awards.

• 5367 •
Association for Gay, Lesbian, and Bisexual Issues in Counseling
Colleen Connolly, Pres.
Texas State University - San Marcos
Department of Educational Administration and Psychological Services
Pecos Bldg., 2nd Fl., No. 201
601 University Dr.
San Marcos, TX 78666
Phone: (512)245-8677
Fax: (512)245-9627
E-mail: cconnolly@txstate.edu
Home Page: http://www.aglbic.org

• 5368 • **AGLBIC Service Award**
Award of recognition. For outstanding service of an AGLBIC member to the association/division.

• 5369 • **Joseph Norton Award**
Award of recognition. For promotion of lesbian/gay/bisexual issues in the counseling profession. Awarded annually.

• 5370 •
Association for General and Liberal Studies
Paul Ranieri, Exec.Dir.
English Department, RB 2109
Ball State University
Muncie, IN 47306
Phone: (765)285-8406
Phone: (765)285-2385
Fax: (765)285-2384
E-mail: pranieri@bsu.edu
Home Page: http://www.bsu.edu/web/agls

• 5371 • **Joseph Katz Award**
To recognize an individual whose commitment and activity has contributed greatly to the improvement of the educational experiences of students on his or her campus and to the understanding of the theory and practice of general and liberal education at the national level. Awarded biennially in odd-numbered years.

• 5372 •
Association for Gerontology in Higher Education
Betsy M. Sprouse, Pres.
1030 15th St. NW, Ste. 240
Washington, DC 20005-1503
Phone: (202)289-9806
Fax: (202)289-9824
E-mail: info@aghe.org
Home Page: http://www.aghe.org

• 5373 • **Mildred M. Seltzer Distinguished Service Recognition**
For recognition and thanks to colleagues who are retired or near retirement and who have given significant service to the Association. A certificate of recognition and a lifetime subscription to the Association's newsletter, the *AGHExchange*, are awarded annually. Established in 1994, and renamed in 1995 to honor Mildred M. Seltzer, a nationally known gerontologist and senior faculty member at Miami's Scripps Gerontology Center.

• 5374 • **Clark Tibbitts Award**
For recognition of significant achievements to the advancement of gerontology as a field of study in institutions of higher learning. Selection is by nomination. A certificate is awarded each year at the annual meeting and the awardee presents a lecture at a plenary session. Established in 1980. Re-named in 1987 to honor Clark Tibbitts, a pioneer in the field of gerontological education who founded the U.S. Administration on Aging and authored over 100 publications. Formerly: (1986) AGHE Award.

• 5375 •
Association for Gravestone Studies
Andrea Carlin, Admin.
278 Main St., Ste. 207
Greenfield, MA 01301-3230
Phone: (413)772-0836
Fax: (413)772-0836
E-mail: info@gravestonestudies.org
Home Page: http://www.gravestonestudies.org

• 5376 • **Harriette Merrifield Forbes Award**
To recognize individuals or organizations for exceptional service in the field of gravestone studies. Outstanding contributions in the areas of scholarship, publications, conservation, education, and community service are considered for the award. The Board of Trustees selects the honoree in January of each year. A plaque is presented annually at the Conference in June. Established in 1977. Formerly: (1978) AGS Award for Outstanding Contributions to Gravestone Studies.

• 5377 • **Oakley Certificate of Merit**
Annual award of recognition. Presented to individuals and groups to honor those whose work in the field of gravestone studies is worthy of recognition. Award presented at any time.

• 5378 •
Association for Healthcare Philanthropy
Dr. William C. McGinly, Pres.,CEO
313 Park Ave., Ste. 400
Falls Church, VA 22046
Phone: (703)532-6243
Fax: (703)532-7170
E-mail: anp@ahp.org
Home Page: http://www.ahp.org
Formerly: National Association for Hospital Development.

• 5379 • **Seymour Award**
This, the AHP's highest honor, recognizes distinguished leadership in the association's affairs and for fostering and promoting exemplary standards of excellence for volunteerism and philanthropic support. Members of AHP are eligible. A plaque is awarded annually at the international conference. Established in 1970 in honor of Harold J. "Si" Seymour, a pioneer of modern philanthropy.

• 5380 •
Association for Holotropic Breathwork International
(Societe Canadienne des Sciences du Cerveau, du Comportement et de la Cognition)
Sarah Brudge, Coord.
PO Box 7169
McMaster University
1280 Main St. W
Santa Cruz, CA 95061-7169
Phone: (520)760-2335
Fax: (520)760-7446
E-mail: office@breathwork.com
Home Page: http://www.breathwork.com/

• 5381 • **Donald O. Hebb Distinguished Contribution**
Recognizes an individual who has made significant contribution to the study of brain, behaviour, and cognitive science. Awarded annually.

• 5382 •
Association for Indiana Media Educators
Carl A. Harvey II, Pres.
% Kimberly Carr, Sec.
Monroe Central Jr./Sr. High School
1878 N County Rd. 1000 W
Parker City, IN 47368
Phone: (765)468-7545
Fax: (765)468-8878
E-mail: kimc@monroec.k12.in.us
Home Page: http://www.ilfonline.org/AIME/index.htm

• 5383 • **Esther V. Burrin Award**
To recognize excellence in a school media program. Awarded annually. Established in 1979 to honor Esther V.Burrin, a national advocate for school libraries and a founder of the state association.

• 5384 • **Edgar Dale Award**
To recognize outstanding service to the Association for Educational Communications and Technology and the Association for Indian Media Educators. Awarded annually. Established in 1972. The award honors Edgar Dale, a nationally known author and media specialist. A joint award of AECT and AIME.

• 5385 • **Sena Kautz Merit Award**
To recognize an outstanding contribution to the media field. Individuals who are not employed in the media field are eligible. Established in 1966. The award honors Sena Kautz, a former president of the association and an outstanding media specialist in Indiana. Formerly: (1983) Merit Award.

• 5386 • **Peggy Leach Pfeiffer Service Award**
To recognize outstanding service to the association. Awarded annually. Established in 1963. The award honors Peggy Leach Pfeiffer, an outstanding media specialist in Indiana. Formerly: (1982) Service Award.

• 5387 • **Eliot Rosewater Indiana High School Book Award**
To stimulate recreational reading by high school students and to encourage cooperation among administrators, school media specialists, and teachers in broadening the reading program. Presented annually to the author of one selected book. The award, also known as the Rosie Award, is selected by students in grades 9-12 of participating schools. An appropriate award (to be decided by the committee) will be presented to the winning author or author's representative at the annual conference. Established in 1995 and named for a character in Kurt Vonnegut's *God Bless You, Mr. Rosewater.*

• 5388 • **Young Hoosier Book Award**
To encourage recreational reading by upper elementary (grades 4-6) and middle/junior high school (grades 6-8) age children. Twenty books including both fiction and nonfiction, written within the last five years by authors living in the United States are selected for each list from titles suggested by students, teachers, and librarians. The books are read and voted upon by the students, who select their favorite book. A plaque, engraved with a Young Hoosier Book Award seal, is presented annually at the Spring AIME Conference. Established during the 1974-75 school year.

• 5389 • **Young Hoosier Picture Book Award**
To provide children with visual experiences as well as to stimulate reading and reading motivation among K-3 children. Twenty titles are selected from suggestions received from teachers and media specialists. Participating schools must have at least twelve titles from the list. Students vote for the book with their favorite illustrations. A plaque is presented to the winning illustrator at the annual spring conference of the association. Established during the 1991-92 school year.

• 5390 •
Association for Investment Management and Research
Thomas A. Bowman CFA, Pres. & CEO
560 Ray C. Hunt Dr.
PO Box 3668
Charlottesville, VA 22903-0668
Phone: (434)951-5499
Toll-Free: 800-247-8132
Fax: (434)951-5262
E-mail: info@cfainstitute.org
Home Page: http://www.cfainstitute.org

Formed by merger of: Financial Analysts Federation; Institute of Chartered Financial Analysts.

• 5391 • **AIMR Distinguished Service Award**
To honor those members who have made an extraordinarily significant contribution to AIMR, or its predecessor organizations, through their leadership, exceptional stewardship, and outstanding service over a period of years. A medal is awarded annually. Established in 1969.

• 5392 • **AIMR Special Service Award**
To recognize outstanding individuals for exceptional and extensive service over many years to the Federation, and now Association. Awarded when merited. Established in 1974.

• 5393 • **Award for Excellence in Corporate Reporting**
To encourage and recognize excellence in corporation financial communications. Evaluations are made within about 25 industry categories of some 500 companies. A plaque is awarded when merited, based on an annual review. Established in 1965.

• 5394 • **Award for Professional Excellence**
This award is presented periodically to a member of the investment profession whose exemplary achievement, excellence of practice, and true leadership have inspired and reflected honor upon our profession to the highest degree.

• 5395 • **Daniel J. Forrestal III, Leadership Award for Professional Ethics and Standards of Investment Practice**
To recognize a member who has championed the pursuit of excellence in professional ethics and standards of practice and who has provided outstanding leadership in elevating the integrity and competence of the profession. Established to honor Daniel J. Forrestal III, an outstanding leader of AIMR and its predecessor organizations and tireless champion of professional competence and ethics, whose untimely death cut short his term as a Governor. Awarded periodically.

• 5396 • **Graham and Dodd Award**
For recognition of excellence in financial writing as demonstrated in an article in the *Financial Analysts Journal* during the previous year. A plaque is awarded annually. Established in 1960 to honor Benjamin Graham and David L. Dodd for their enduring contributions to the field of financial analysis.

• 5397 • **Thomas L. Hansberger Leadership in Global Investing Award**
Presented periodically to an individual who has made an outstanding contribution to the investment profession globally through activities which encompass one or more of the following: enhancing education to expand the Body of Knowledge and/or to further the sharing of investment knowledge and experiences on a global basis; harmonizing worldwide regulatory or professional conduct standards; fostering cooperation among worldwide professional investment organizations and their members; and promoting the integration and openness of capital markets worldwide.

• 5398 • **Nicholas Molodovsky Award**
This, award is given to recognize those individuals who have made contributions of such significance as to change the direction of the profession and to raise it to higher standards of accomplishment. A plaque is awarded periodically. First presented in 1968 to Nicholas Molodovsky, one of the profession's outstanding scholars.

• 5399 • **C. Stewart Sheppard Award**
This award is presented periodically to individual CFA charterholders in recognition of their outstanding contributions, through dedicated effort and inspiring leadership, in fostering the education of professional investors through advancement of the Body of Knowledge and development of programs and publications to encourage continuing education in our profession. It was established to honor C. Stewart Sheppard, the founding Executive Director of the Institute of Chartered Financial Analysts.

• 5400 • **James R. Vertin Award**
Presented periodically to recognize individuals who have produced a body of research notable

for its relevance and enduring value to investment professionals. It has been established to honor James R. Vertin for his outstanding leadership in promoting excellence and relevancy in research and education.

• 5401 •
Association for Iron and Steel Technology
Ronald E. Ashburn, Exec.Dir.
186 Thorn Hill Rd.
Warrendale, PA 15086
Phone: (724)776-6040
Fax: (724)776-1880
E-mail: info@aist.org
Home Page: http://www.aist.org

Formerly: Iron and Steel Society of the American Institute of Mining, Metallurgical and Petroleum Engineers.

• 5402 • **Joseph Becker Award**
To recognize distinguished achievement in coal carbonization. A wooden desk plaque medal and a certificate are awarded when merited. The recipient muts be over 40 years old. Established in 1961 to honor Joseph Becker, a pioneer in the design of coke ovens.

• 5403 • **Charles W. Briggs Award**
To recognize the author(s) of the best paper presented at the Annual Electric Furnace Conference and published in the Proceedings. The award consists of a monetary award, a silver tray, and a plaque. Established in 1961.

• 5404 • **John Chipman Award**
To recognize an author(s) for excellence and originality in a paper on process technology or the application thereof, as it relates to the production and processing of iron and steel. A medal and a certificate are awarded. Established in 1972 to perpetuate the inspiration of John Chipman's contributions to the science of iron and steelmaking.

• 5405 • **Distinguished Member Award**
To recognize outstanding contributions to iron and steel production or in fields embracing the activities of the steel industry and the Society. Candidates must be AIST members. A certificate is awarded. Established in 1975.

• 5406 • **Electric Furnace Honorable Mention**
This award is the runner-up to the Briggs Award. A plaque and a certificate are awarded.

• 5407 • **Charles W. Herty, Jr., Award**
To recognize the author(s) of the best paper presented at the Annual Steelmaking Conference and published in the Proceedings. A plaque is awarded annually. Established in 1960 in honor of Charles W. Herty, Jr., a distinguished physical chemist working in the field of iron and steel technology.

• 5408 • **Howe Memorial Lecture**
The lecturer shall be an individual recognized for outstanding attainment in the science and practice of iron and steel metallurgy or metallography. The lecturer receives a plaque. Established in 1923 in honor of Henry Marion Howe, Past President of the Institute.

• 5409 • **Robert W. Hunt Award**
To recognize the author(s) of the best original paper relevant to the technology (applied or fundamental) related to the iron and steel industry. A certificate and a medal are awarded annually. The award was established in 2004 as result of combining the Robert W. Hunt Award and the John F. Kelly Award established in 1920 and 1943 respectively.

• 5410 • **J. E. Johnson, Jr., Award**
To recognize creative work in the metallurgy or manufacture of pig iron. Individuals under the age of 40 are eligible. A monetary award and a certificate are awarded annually. Established in 1921 in memory of J.E. Johnson, Jr., a prominent engineer and author of two valuable volumes on iron blast furnace construction and practice.

• 5411 • **Thomas L. Joseph Award**
To recognize distinguished contributions to ironmaking operations by an individual who has significantly increased iron production or decreased the cost of doing so. The recipient must be over 40 years old. A clock and a certificate are awarded when merited. Established in 1965 to honor Thomas L. Joseph, a devoted teacher and scientist who contributed much in the fundamental studies of blast furnace reactions.

• 5412 • **Josef S. Kapitan Award**
To recognize the author(s) of the best paper presented at the Annual Ironmaking Conference of the Society and published in the Proceedings. A monetary award and a certificate are awarded annually. Established in 1953.

• 5413 • **Frank B. McKune Memorial Award**
To recognize the author(s) of the best paper on steelmaking (open hearth or basic practices). Individuals under the age of 40 are eligible. A monetary award and a certificate are awarded annually. Established in 1940 in memory of Frank B. McKune, a faithful and inspiring worker in the Open Hearth Conference from its initial meeting in 1925.

• 5414 • **MWSP Meritorious Award**
This award is the runner-up to the Tenenbaum Award. A certificate is awarded.

• 5415 • **Steelmaking Conference Award**
This award is the runner-up to the McKune Award. A monetary award and a certificate are awarded annually. Established in 1944.

• 5416 • **Michael Tenenbaum Award**
In recognition of the best paper presented at the MWSP Conference and published in the Proceedings. A monetary award and a plaque are awarded. Established in 1971.

• 5417 •
Association for Library and Information Science Education
Deborah York, Exec.Dir.
1009 Commerce Park Dr., Ste. 150
Oak Ridge, TN 37830
Phone: (865)425-0155
Fax: (865)481-0390
E-mail: contact@alise.org
Home Page: http://www.alise.org

Formerly: (1983) Association of American Library Schools.

• 5418 • **ALISE Award for Professional Contribution to Library and Information Science Education**
To recognize an individual for outstanding professional contributions to library and information science education. Criteria include: evidence of regular and sustained service that promotes and strengthens the broad areas of library/information science education through the holding of appropriate offices and positions within the profession; contributions that promote and enhance the status of library/information science education; and evidence of leadership and initiative in dealing with issues related to library/information science education. A letter of nomination and supporting documentation must be submitted. Inquires for additional nomination information and application deadline. Awarded annually when merited. Established in 1987.

• 5419 • **ALISE Service Award**
To recognize an individual for outstanding contributions to the Association. Current members of ALISE are eligible. Criteria may include: evidence of regular and sustained service to ALISE through the holding of various offices and positions within the organization or accomplishing specific responsibilities for the organization; participation in activities that have enhanced the stature, reputation, and overall strength of ALISE; and representation of ALISE to other appropriate organizations, institutions, or governmental agencies. A Nomination letter and supporting documentation must be submitted. Inquire for additional nomination information deadline. Awarded annually. Established in 1987.

• 5420 • **Award for Teaching Excellence in the Field of Library and Information Science Education**
To recognize regular and sustained excellence in teaching library and information science. Selection criteria include contributions to curriculum design that demonstrate subject expertise and the ability to integrate new developments in library and information science; evidence of mentoring students, alumni, and/or practicing professionals outside the classroom; and the use of effective and innovative teaching methods. Awarded annually. Established in 1993.

• 5421 •
Association for Library Collections and Technical Services
Charles Wilt, Exec.Dir.
50 E Huron St.
Chicago, IL 60611
Phone: (312)280-5037
Toll-Free: 800-545-2433
Fax: (312)280-5033
E-mail: alcts@ala.org
Home Page: http://www.ala.org/alcts

Formerly: (1988) American Library Association - Resources and Technical Services Division.

• 5422 • **Best of LRTS Award**
To recognize the author(s) of the best paper published each year in the official journal of the Association for Library Collections & Technical Services, *Library Resources & Technical Services*. Each paper is judged on the following points: the value of its content to technical services librarians, the adequacy of support for statements in the paper by accurate data and/or documentation, and the clarity and readability of the writing style. Nominations must be submitted by December 1. A citation is awarded annually. Established in 1987.

• 5423 • **Blackwell's Scholarship Award**
To the author(s) of an outstanding monograph, published article, or original paper on acquisitions, collection development, and related areas of resources development in libraries. Publications from the two years prior to the year of the award are eligible. Nominations must be submitted by December 1. A citation to the winner and a $2,000 scholarship donated by Blackwell to a U.S. or Canadian library school designated by the winner are awarded annually at the ALA Annual Conference. Sponsored by Blackwell. Established in 1976.

• 5424 • **Bowker/Ulrich's Serials Librarianship Award**
In recognition of distinguished contributions to serials librarianship within the previous three years as demonstrated through such activities as leadership in serials-related activities through participation in professional associations and/or library education programs, contributions to the body of serials literature, conduct of research in the area of serials, development of tools or methods to enhance access to or management of serials, or other advances leading to a better understanding of the field of serials. Nominations must be submitted by December 1. The award may be divided among two or more individuals who have participated in the achievement for which it is granted. A monetary award of $1,500 and a citation are presented annually at the American Library Association Conference. Established in 1985. The award is donated by R. R. Bowker.

• 5425 • **Leadership in Library Acquisitions Award**
To recognize significant contributions by and outstanding leadership of an individual in the field of library acquisitions. Nominees must demonstrate leadership resulting in improvements in the field; achievements in the field in one or more of the following areas: contributions to professional associations, contributions to literature, contributions to education in the field, and contributions to the advancement of the field. Two letters of reference, biographical information, and statement of work and/or professional experience must be submitted. The deadline for nominations is December 1. A citation and a monetary award of $1,500 donated by Harrassowitz Co. are presented annually at the American Library Association Annual Conference. Established in 1995.

• 5426 • **Margaret Mann Citation**
To recognize a librarian for significant professional achievement during the past five years in the fields of cataloging or classification for: a notable publication, such as an article, a pamphlet, or a book; an outstanding contribution to the activities of professional cataloging associations; an outstanding contribution to the technical improvement of cataloging or classification or to the development of new techniques of recognized importance; or an outstanding contribution in the area of teaching cataloging and classification. The honoree may be of any nationality and need not be a member of the Association. Nominations must be submitted by December 1. A plaque and a $2,000 scholarship donated by OCLC to a U.S. or Canadian library school designated by the winner are awarded annually at the ALA Annual Conference. Established in 1951 in honor of Margaret Mann.

• 5427 • **Esther J. Piercy Award**
To recognize the contribution to librarianship in the field of technical services by a librarian, with not more than 10 years of professional experience, who has shown outstanding promise for continuing contributions and leadership. Criteria for the award are: leadership in professional associations at the local, state, regional, or national level; contributions to the development, application, or utilization of new or improved methods, techniques, and routines; significant contributions to professional literature; or conduct of studies or research in the technical services. Nominations must be submitted by December 1. A citation and a monetary award of $1,500 donated by YBP, Inc. are presented each year at the ALA Annual Conference. Established in 1968 in honor of Esther J. Piercy.

• 5428 • **First Step Award - Wiley Professional Development Grant**
To provide librarians new to the serials field with the opportunity to broaden their perspectives and to encourage professional development in ALA Conferences and participation in Serials Section activities. All ALA members, with five or fewer years of professional experience in the serials field, who have not previously attended an ALA Annual Conference, are eligible. The deadline for nominations is December 1. A $1,500 grant, donated by John Wiley & Sons, is applicable toward round trip transportation, lodging, registration fees, etc. Eligible applicants may apply more than once. Presented by the Serials Section. Established in 1991. Formerly: First Step Award.

• 5429 •
Association for Library Service to Children
Malore I. Brown, Exec. Dir.
50 E. Huron St.
Chicago, IL 60611
Phone: (312)280-2163
Toll-Free: 800-545-2433
Fax: (312)944-7671
E-mail: alsc@ala.org
Home Page: http://www.ala.org/alsc

Formerly: (1977) American Library Association - Children's Services Division.

• 5430 • **ALSC/Book Wholesalers Summer Reading Program Grant**
To recognize an ALSC member for an outstanding public library summer reading program for children. Applicants must plan and present an outline for a theme-based summer reading program in a public library. A monetary prize of $3,000 is awarded. Sponsored by Book Wholesalers, Inc.

• 5431 • **ALSC/Sagebrush Education Resources Literature Grant**
To recognize an ALSC member for development and implementation of an outstanding library program for children involving reading and the use of literature. The purpose is to bring children and reading together and to develop life-long reading habits. A monetary prize of $1,000 to be used to attend the ALA is awarded. Application forms are available from above address or at the above web site. Sponsored by Sagebrush Education Resources. Formerly: (2004) ALSC/Econo-Clad Literature Program Award.

• 5432 • **Mildred L. Batchelder Award**
To recognize the United States publisher of the most outstanding English language children's book originally published in a foreign language, in a foreign country, and subsequently published in the United States. A citation is awarded annually. Established in 1966 to honor ALSC's first executive secretary, Mildred L. Batchelder.

• 5433 • **Louise Seaman Bechtel Fellowship**
To provide librarians the opportunity to read and study at the Baldwin Library of the George Smathers Libraries, University of Florida. Candidates must be ALSC members; have at least 8 years of professional experience in direct service to children; have a graduate degree form an ALA-accredited program; and be willing to write a report about the experience. A description of the topic of study and a demonstration of ongoing commitment to motivating children to read must be submitted. The deadline is December 1. A Stipend of $4000 is awarded annually. Sponsored by Bechtel Fund.

• 5434 • **Pura Belpre Award**
Two awards to recognize an outstanding children's book by a Latino/Latina author and an outstanding book by a Latino/Latina illustrator who affirms and celebrates the Latino/Latina cultural experience in a work of literature for children. Presented every two years. Estab-

Awards are arranged in alphabetical order below their administering organizations

lished 1996 as a joint award of ALSC and REFORMA.

• 5435 • Bound to Stay Bound Books Scholarship

To provide for study in the field of library service to children toward the MLS or beyond in an ALA-accredited program. Four scholarships of $6,000 each are awarded annually. Sponsored by Bound to Stay Bound Books, Inc. Candidates must not have started the program. The deadline is March 1.

• 5436 • Randolph Caldecott Medal

For recognition of the most distinguished American picture book for children. Illustrators who are United States citizens or residents are eligible for books published in the United States during the preceding year. A bronze medal is awarded annually at the Newbery/Caldecott Awards celebration during ALA's annual conference. Honor books may be selected. Established in 1937 by Frederic G. Melcher, the distinguished publisher who originated and first donated the bronze medals. The award is named in honor of Randolph Caldecott, the noted nineteenth century English illustrator.

• 5437 • Andrew Carnegie Medal

To recognize a U.S. producer of the most distinguished video for children released in the previous year. Established in 1991. Sponsored by Carnegie Corporation of New York.

• 5438 • Distinguished Service Award

To honor an ALSC member who has made significant contributions to, and an impact on, library service to children and/or ALSC. A monetary award of $1,000 and a service pin are awarded.

• 5439 • May Hill Arbuthnot Honor Lecture Award

Recognizes achievement in the area of children's literature. Authors, critics, librarians, historians, or teachers of children's literature of any country are eligible. Selection is based on having made a significant contribution to the field of children's literature. Established in 1969.

• 5440 • Frederic G. Melcher Scholarship

To assist students entering the field of library service to children for graduate work in ALA-accredited program. Two scholarships of $6,000 are awarded annually. Candidates must not have started the program. The deadline is March 1.

• 5441 • John Newbery Medal

For recognition of the author of the most distinguished contribution to American literature for children. Authors must be citizens or residents of the United States. A bronze medal is awarded annually at the Newbery/Caldecott Awards celebration during ALA's annual conference. Honor books may be selected. Established in 1921 by Frederic G. Melcher, the distinguished publisher who originated and first donated the bronze medals. The award is named for John Newbery, the eighteenth-century British bookseller.

• 5442 • Penguin Putnam Books for Young Readers Group Award

To provide funds for children's librarians in school or public libraries with ten or fewer years of experience to attend an ALA annual conference for the first time. Members of ALSC are eligible. Four awards of $600 each are presented. Sponsored by Penguin Putnam Young Readers Group. Formerly: Putnam Publishing Group Award; (2001) - Putnam & Grosset Group Award.

• 5443 • Robert F. Sibert Informational Book Award

Recognizes an author of the most distinguished an informational book published during the preceding year. Awarded annually. Established in 2001 in honor of Robert F. Sibert, the long-time president of Bound to Stay Bound Books Inc.

• 5444 • Laura Ingalls Wilder Award

To recognize an author or illustrator whose books are published in the United States and have, over a period of years, made a substantial and lasting contribution to literature for children. A bronze medal is awarded every two years. Established in 1954.

• 5445 •
Association for Library Trustees and Advocates
Kerry Ward, Exec.Dir.
American Library Association
50 E. Huron St.
Chicago, IL 60611
Phone: (312)280-2161
Toll-Free: 800-545-2433
Fax: (312)280-3257
E-mail: alta@ala.org
Home Page: http://www.ala.org/ala/alta/alta.htm

• 5446 • ALTA/Gale Outstanding Trustee Conference Grant

To recognize public library trustees who have exhibited support to the local library. Current ALTA members serving on a local public library board and have not attended an ALA annual conference are eligible. Two monetary awards of $750 each are presented annually. Application deadline is December 1. Established in 1989. Co-sponsored by The Gale Group.

• 5447 • ALTA Literacy Award

To promote service toward eliminating illiteracy and to recognize an individual who, in a volunteer capacity, has done an outstanding job in making contributions toward the elimination of illiteracy. Applicants must be ALTA members. A citation is awarded annually at the ALA Conference. Established in 1980.

• 5448 • ALTA Major Benefactor Honor Award

To recognize benefactors of public libraries. Nominations of benefactors may be made by any person(s), institution, agency, or organization other than the proposed nominee. Significance of the gift is to be measured by the recipient library. Benefits may be in the form of money, real or personal property, negotiable paper, or other tangible contributions. A plaque is presented annually at the local site. Application deadline is December 1. Established in 1976.

• 5449 • American Library Association Trustee Citation

To recognize distinguished service performed on the local, state, regional or national level, or at a combination of levels for library development. An ALA plaque is awarded annually by the American Library Trustee Association Division at the Opening General Session of the American Library Association Conference. Established in 1941.

• 5450 •
Association for Moral Education
James M. DuBois PhD, Contact
National-Louis Univ.
Psychology Dept.
122 S Michigan Ave.
Chicago, IL 60603
E-mail: nnordmann@nl.edu
Home Page: http://www.amenetwork.org

• 5451 • Kuhmerker Award

Recognizes individuals making outstanding contributions to AME and the field.

• 5452 •
Association for Preservation Technology International
Tim Seeden, Admin.Dir.
4513 Lincoln Ave., Ste. 213
Lisle, IL 60532-1290
Phone: (630)968-6400
Fax: 888-723-4242
E-mail: information@apti.org
Home Page: http://www.apti.org

• 5453 • Oliver Torry Fuller Award

To recognize the author of the best article in the Association's *Bulletin* published in the preceding year. The article must appear in the current year's *Bulletin,* must be well written and illustrated, and must demonstrate original research and new preservation technology. A certificate is awarded annually at the conference. Established in 1985 in honor of Oliver Torrey Fuller.

• 5454 • Harley J. McKee Award

For recognition of the most distinguished work in the field of preservation technology. Membership is not necessary. Students, preservation enthusiasts, professionals in the preservation field, historical or cultural organizations, and corporations and government agencies are eligible. A certificate is awarded annually at the conference. Established in 1985 in honor of Harley J. McKee, A1A.

• 5455 •
Association for Professionals in Infection Control and Epidemiology
Barbara M. Soule, Pres.
1275 K St. NW, Ste. 1000
Washington, DC 20005-4006
Phone: (202)789-1890
Fax: (202)789-1899
E-mail: apicinfo@apic.org
Home Page: http://www.apic.org

• 5456 • **APIC New Investigator Research Award**
To recognize outstanding research in infection control. Awarded annually at the Annual Education Conference. Sponsored by Johnson & Johnson Medical, Inc.

• 5457 • **Bard UTI Research Award**
To recognize outstanding research in urinary tract infection control. Awarded annually at the Annual Education Conference. Sponsored by Bard Urological Division.

• 5458 • **Chapter of the Year**
For recognition of outstanding achievement and innovative ideas in infection control. Active chapters of APIC are eligible. A monetary award of $500 is awarded annually at the National Educational Convention.

• 5459 •
Association for Recorded Sound Collections
Peter Shambarger, Exec.Dir.
PO Box 543
Annapolis, MD 21404-0543
Phone: (410)757-0488
Phone: (410)956-5600
Fax: (410)349-0175
E-mail: shambarger@sprynet.com
Home Page: http://www.arsc-audio.org

• 5460 • **Award for Distinguished Service to Historical Recordings**
To recognize and publicize the finest published research dealing with historical recordings and recording artists, or other aspects of sound recording. Eight to twelve certificates are awarded annually in specific fields of music, speech, and technology. One Lifetime Achievement Award is also presented. Categories include, but are not limited to classical music; rock, rhythm and blues, or soul; general popular music; country, folk, or ethnic music; jazz or blues; spoken word recordings; record labels or manufacturers; vintage phonographs; and preservation or reproduction of recordings. The deadline for nominations is January 31. Awards are presented at the annual ARSC Conference in the spring. Established in 1991.

• 5461 •
Association for Research in Otolaryngology, Inc.
19 Mantua Rd.
Mt. Royal, NJ 08061
Phone: (856)423-0041
Fax: (856)423-3420
E-mail: headquarters@aro.org
Home Page: http://www.aro.org

• 5462 • **Award of Merit**
Recognizes outstanding contributions on otolaryngology research.

• 5463 •
Association for Research in Vision and Ophthalmology
9650 Rockville Pike
Bethesda, MD 20814-3998
Phone: (301)571-1844
Fax: (301)571-8311
E-mail: admin@arvo.arvo.org
Home Page: http://www.arvo.org

Formerly: (1970) Association for Research in Ophthalmology.

• 5464 • **Cogan Award**
To recognize an individual who is 40 years of age or younger for substantial contributions to research in ophthalmology or visual science. Contributions must be directly related to disorders of the human eye Or visual system. Nominations must be submitted by March 3. A plaque is awarded and a presentation of a lecture by the awardee occurs at the Association's Annual Meeting. Established in 1988 to commemorate the outstanding leadership of David G. Cogan, M.D., in the study of the diseased human eye.

• 5465 • **Friedenwald Memorial Award**
To honor outstanding research in the basic or clinical sciences as applied to ophthalmology. Nominations must be senior scientists. Nominations must be submitted by March 3. A plaque is awarded and a presentation of a lecture by the awardee occurs at the Association's Annual Meeting. Established in 1986 in memory of Dr. Jonas S. Friedenwald, an exceptional scientist and the first recipient of the Association's Proctor Medal. Nominees for this award are also considered for the Proctor Medal. Formerly: Jonas S. Friedenwald Memorial Award.

• 5466 • **Kupfer Award**
Recognizes distinguished public service on behalf of eye and vision research. Awardees receive a plaque at the annual meeting. A $5,000 honorarium donated by Dr. Kupfer is also awarded. Established in 1993.

• 5467 • **Proctor Medal**
To honor outstanding research in the basic or clinical sciences as applied to ophthalmology. Nominees must be senior scientists. Nominations must be submitted by March 3. The recipient is awarded a medal and presents lecture on his/her research at the Association's Annual Meeting. Established in 1949 in memory of Francis I. Nominees for this award are also considered for the Friedenwald Award. Proctor, M.D. Formerly: Francis I. Proctor Research Medal Award.

• 5468 • **Special Recognition Award**
To honor outstanding service to ARVO and the vision research community. Also presented to the outgoing President and Vice President(s) ARVO for dedication and service. Recipients receive a plaque at the Annual Meeting.

• 5469 • **Mildred Weisenfeld Award for Excellence in Ophthalmology**
To recognize an individual for distinguished scholarly contributions to the clinical practice of ophthalmology. Nominations must be submitted by March 3. A plaque is awarded and the awardee presents a lecture at the Annual Meeting. Established in 1986 as a tribute to Mildred Weisenfeld's outstanding contributions to the field.

• 5470 •
Association for Social Anthropology in Oceania
Dr. Jocelyn Armstrong, Sec.
University of Illinois at Urbana-Champaign
ASAO, % Department of Community Health
1206 South Fourth St. MC-588
Champaign, IL 61820
E-mail: jocelyn@uiuc.edu
Home Page: http://www.soc.hawaii.edu/asao/pacific/hawaiki.html

• 5471 • **Honorary Fellow**
To acknowledge outstanding professional achievements in the anthropology of Oceania. Candidates are elected by a ballot of ASAO Fellows and voting members. A parchment certificate is presented. The Association can have only 25 Honorary Fellows at one time. Established in 1974.

• 5472 •
Association for Social Economics
Elba K. Brown-Collier, Sec.
Education Management Information Systems
7116 Wandering Oak Rd.
Austin, TX 78749
Phone: (512)288-5988
Fax: (318)257-4253
E-mail: email@edmis.com
Home Page: http://www.socialeconomics.org

• 5473 • **Thomas F. Divine Award**
To recognize the lifetime contributions of an outstanding social economist. A monetary award and a medal are awarded annually at the Association's meeting. Established in 1986 for the Reverend Thomas F. Divine, S.J., founder and first president of the Association.

• 5474 • **Ludwig Mai Service Award**
To recognize an individual for extraordinary service to the Association and its members, espe-

Awards are arranged in alphabetical order below their administering organizations

cially service that is not visible. Awarded annually. Established in 1983 to honor Ludwig Mai, a former member who was known for his support and promotion of the work of the members of the Association.

• 5475 • Helen Potter Award of Special Recognition

To encourage promising scholars in social economics to submit articles to the *Review of Social Economy*, and to recognize the best article appearing in the *Review*. Authors who are not full professors are eligible. A plaque and a letter to the employer of the winner are awarded annually. Established in 1975 by Professor Helen Potter.

• 5476 •

Association for the Advancement of Automotive Medicine
Irene Herzau, Admin.Dir.
PO Box 4176
Barrington, IL 60011-4176
Phone: (847)844-3880
Fax: (847)844-3884
E-mail: info@aaam.org
Home Page: http://www.carcrash.org

Formerly: American Association for Automotive Medicine.

• 5477 • Award of Merit

To recognize long term, significant contributions to further the goals of traffic injury control and highway safety. An engraved gold/wood wall plaque is awarded annually. Established in 1972.

• 5478 • A. J. Mirkin Service Award

To recognize long term service to the Association. Applicants must be Association Members. An engraved desk set is awarded as merited. Established in 1980. Renamed to honor Dr. A.J. Mirkin, a founding member and first president of the Association. Formerly: AAAM Service Award.

• 5479 • John D. States Award

To recognize the best scientific manuscript on traffic injury control or impact biomechanics by a student in a field related to traffic injury control or highway safety. A cash honorarium of $ 500 and a certificate are awarded annually when merited. Established in 1979 to honor Dr. John D. States, an orthopedic surgeon who has spent his professional career fostering an understanding between medicine and engineering through biomedical research to control crash related injury.

• 5480 •

Association for the Advancement of Baltic Studies
Anita Juberts, Admin.Exec.Dir.
14743 Braemar Crescent Way
Darnestown, MD 20878-3911
Phone: (301)977-8491
Fax: (301)977-8492
E-mail: aabs@starpower.net
Home Page: http://www.balticstudies-aabs.lanet.lv/

• 5481 • Vilis Vitols Award

For the best article written for the *Journal of Baltic Studies.* Awarded annually.

• 5482 •

Association for the Advancement of International Education
Elsa Lamb, Pres.
American Nicaraguan School
Nicabox No. 192
PO Box 52-7444
Miami, FL 33152-7444
Phone: (505)265-8925
Phone: (505)265-8279
E-mail: elamb@ans.edu.ni
Home Page: http://www.aaie.org

• 5483 • AAIE Hall of Fame

To recognize an individual for long-term contributions to the Association. An individual of any nationality, stateside or overseas, who has made significant contributions over a period of ten or more years to American/international overseas education and who has furthered the goals of AAIE is eligible. A plaque and an AAIE watch are awarded annually. Established in 1990.

• 5484 • International Superintendent of the Year

To recognize an individual for outstanding achievement as a superintendent in an American/international school. Individuals who exhibit leadership for learning, communication skills, professionalism, and community involvement are eligible. A certificate and an AAIE watch are awarded annually. Established in 1990.

• 5485 •

Association for the Advancement of Medical Instrumentation
Michael J. Miller, Pres.
1110 N Glebe Rd., No. 220
Arlington, VA 22201-4795
Phone: (703)525-4890
Toll-Free: 800-332-2264
Fax: (703)525-1424
Home Page: http://www.aami.org

• 5486 • AAMI Annual Meeting Manuscript Awards

For recognition of two outstanding manuscripts or papers contributing to the advancement of healthcare technology and presented during AAMI's annual meeting. Manuscripts must be postmarked by March 15. Manuscripts submitted for the award are considered for publication in *Biomedical Instrumentation & Technology*. The following awards are presented: Spacelabs/AAMI Annual Meeting Research-Manuscript Award - $1,000 and a commemorative plaque; and AAMI Annual Meeting Management & Technology Award - $1,000 and commemorative plaque. Awarded when merited. Established in 1979.

• 5487 • AAMI Foundation Laufman - Greatbatch Prize

For recognition of an individual or group that has made a significant contribution to the advancement of medical instrumentation. Candidates shall have provided an outstanding service and/or accomplishment that has had a significant impact on a specific medical device or on instrumentation in general. Nominations may be submitted by March 1. An endowment of $5,000 and a plaque are presented annually at the Meeting Awards Recognition Banquet.

• 5488 • AAMI/GE Healthcare BMET of the Year Award

To recognize biomedical equipment technicians for individual dedication, achievement, and excellence. Nominees must fit the following criteria: current employment in the biomedical field, demonstrated contributions to the profession, and eligibility for certification as a biomedical equipment technician. Special consideration is given to those having SBET membership. A monetary prize of $1,500 and an engraved plaque are awarded annually. Formerly: SBET/Replacement Parts Industries BMET of the Year Award.

• 5489 • *Biomedical Instrumentation & Technology* Outstanding Paper Awards

To recognize the best papers published in each annual volume of the AAMI publication, *Biomedical Instrumentation & Technology*. Papers are judged for excellence in communicating information on the evaluation, maintenance, and/or management of medical equipment, or contributing to the professional development of healthcare engineers or technicians. Two awards are presented: The *Biomedical Instrumentation & Technology* Research Award - for the best research paper; and The *Biomedical Instrumentation & Technology* Management and Technology Award - for the best management or technology paper. Monetary awards of $1,000 each and plaques are presented at the annual AAMI Annual Meeting.

• 5490 • Clinical/Biomedical Engineering Achievement Award

To encourage continued discipline by singling out an individual who has made a substantial contribution as a clinical/biomedical engineer. Clinical/biomedical engineers who have been employed for at least five years and have been involved in relevant activities, such as publications and presentations, may be nominated by March 1. A monetary award of $2,500 and a plaque are presented annually, alternating between a clinical engineer one year and a biomedical engineer the next year. Established in 1980.

• 5491 • Becton Dickinson Career Achievement Award
To encourage and support further contributions made by an individual in medical instrumentation. The award seeks to identify, recognize, and encourage outstanding achievement(s) by a promising healthcare professional in the development or improvement of medical devices, instruments, or systems. Eligible candidates must be currently and directly involved with the use of technology in the delivery of health care as physicians, nurses, administrators, engineers, or technicians, and should be under the age of 40. Candidates must have demonstrated intent to continue their careers in the health care field. Nominations may be submitted by March 1. A monetary award of $1,000 and a plaque are presented at the AAMI Annual Meeting. Established in 1977.

• 5492 • Young Investigator Award
No further information was available for this edition.

• 5493 •
Association for the Advancement of Medical Instrumentation (AAMI) Foundation
Michael J. Miller, Pres.
1110 N Glebe Rd., Ste. 220
Arlington, VA 22201-4795
Phone: (703)525-4890
Fax: (703)276-0793
E-mail: customerservice@aami.org
Home Page: http://www.aami.org

• 5494 • Becton Dickinson Career Achievement Award
To recognize a candidate under the age of 40 who is currently and directly involved with the use of technology in the delivery of health care as a physician, nurse, administrator, engineer, technical, etc. A monetary prize of $1,500 and an engraved plaque are awarded annually. Established in 1993.

• 5495 • AAMI Foundation/ACCE Robert L. Morris Humanitarian Award
To recognize individuals whose humanitarian efforts have applied health technology to improving global human conditions. A monetary prize of $1,000 and an engraved plaque are awarded annually. Established in 2001.

• 5496 •
Association for the Advancement of Policy, Research and Development in the Third World
Dr. Mekki Mtewa, Exec.Dir.
804 Geranium St. NW
Washington, DC 20012
Phone: (202)726-8702

• 5497 • International Service Award
Recognizes outstanding leadership, scholarship, professional service, and community work. Awarded annually.

• 5498 •
Association for the Education of Teachers in Science
Dr. Walter S. Smith, Exec.Sec.
Department of Biology
Ball State University
820 Van Vleet Oval ECH 114
Muncie, IN 47306-0440
Phone: (765)285-8840
Fax: (765)285-8840
E-mail: wsmith@bsu.edu
Home Page: http://aste.chem.pitt.edu

• 5499 • Honorary Emeritus Membership
To recognize a distinguished career in teaching, research, or service to and in the area of education of teachers in science. The deadline for nominations is January 5. Five individuals may receive this award per year. Awarded annually. Established in 1980. In addition, a special Emeritus Award is presented occasionally.

• 5500 • Implications of Research for Educational Practice
To stimulate the writing of creative papers that interpret theory and research for practice. A monetary prize of $500 and a plaque are awarded annually. Established in 1981. Sponsored by the Carolina Biological Supply Company.

• 5501 • Innovation in Teaching Science Teachers
To encourage the development and dissemination of new designs for courses and curricula, new instructional methods or approaches, and other types of innovations in the pre- or in-service education of teachers in science. Science teacher educators are invited to submit papers of no more than 15 pages describing innovative programs/activities for the pre- or in-service education of teachers in science at the elementary, middle, or secondary level. A monetary award of $1,000 and an engraved plaque are presented. In addition, the paper of each year's honoree is published in the AETS *Journal of Science Teacher Education.* Sponsored by Delta Education. The first award was presented in 1991.

• 5502 • Mentor Award
To recognize an individual for outstanding mentoring in the field of education of teachers in science. Established in 1991. Formerly: (1995) Recognition Award.

• 5503 • Outstanding Science Educator of the Year
To recognize the personal achievements and contributions of science educators in the ascendant period of their careers. A monetary prize of $1,000 and a plaque are awarded annually. Established in 1979. Sponsored by the Carolina Biological Supply Company.

• 5504 •
Association for the History of Chiropractic
Alana Callender, Exec.Dir.
1000 Brady St.
Davenport, IA 52803
Phone: (563)884-5245
Phone: (563)884-5404
Fax: (563)884-5616
E-mail: callender_a@palmer.edu
Home Page: http://chirohistory.com

• 5505 • Lee - Homewood Chiropractic Heritage Award
For recognition of lifetime achievements benefiting the social and scientific advancement of the chiropractic profession. A certificate is awarded annually at the conference. Established in 1981 and renamed in 1983 for its first two recipients. Formerly: (1983) Honorary Award.

• 5506 •
Association for the Preservation of Virginia Antiquities
Tara Olive, Contact
204 West Franklin St.
Richmond, VA 23220
Phone: (804)648-1889
Fax: (804)775-0802
E-mail: apva@apva.org
Home Page: http://www.apva.org

• 5507 • Mary Mason Anderson Williams Award
To recognize a business or organization, individual, or governmental agency for its ongoing and outstanding efforts in preservation. Awarded annually.

• 5508 •
Association for the Study of African American Life and History, Dayton Branch
Ms. Margaret E. Peters, Pres.
1312 Princeton Dr.
Dayton, OH 45406
Phone: (937)274-8362
Fax: (937)276-6267
E-mail: mrgrtpeters@aol.com

• 5509 • ASALH/DLAMC African American History Essay Contest
For all students K-12 and certificate. Monetary award bestowed annually.

• 5510 •
Association for the Study of Connecticut History
Allen Ward, Pres.
% David White, Corresponding Sec.
35 Laurel Ridge Rd.
Tolland, CT 06084
Phone: (860)376-5383
E-mail: dolcwhite@aol.com
Home Page: http://asch.ccsu.edu

Awards are arranged in alphabetical order below their administering organizations

• 5511 • Homer D. Babbidge, Jr. Award
To recognize the best work on a significant aspect of Connecticut history published during the previous year. Monographs, articles, edited works, exhibitions, and television programs, etc. are considered. Nominations by someone other than the author must be submitted before September 1. The award is presented annually when merited at the fall meeting of the association. Established in 1986 in memory of Homer D. Babbidge, Jr., the former president of the University of Connecticut, who had a vital interest in and love for Connecticut history. Formerly: (1994) Homer D. Babbidge, Jr. Award.

• 5512 • Betty M. Linsley Award
To recognize the best work on a significant aspect of Connecticut history published in the preceding year by, for, or on behalf of a Connecticut historical organization. Deadline for nominations is August 31. A work will be considered only if nominated by someone other than the author. Awarded annually. Established in 1994.

• 5513 •
Association for Theatre in Higher Education
Kurt Daw, Actg.Pres.
PO Box 69
Downers Grove, IL 60515
Phone: (630)964-1940
Toll-Free: 888-284-3737
Fax: (630)964-1941
E-mail: info@athe.org
Home Page: http://www.athe.org

• 5514 • Career Achievement Award - Professional Theatre
To recognize an individual with a distinguished career in professional theatre who has made an outstanding contribution to theatre in higher education. A plaque is awarded annually at the national conference. Established in 1987.

• 5515 • Career Achievement Award - Teacher in Higher Education
To recognize an individual with a distinguished career in the academic theatre who has made an outstanding contribution to theatre in higher education. A plaque is awarded annually at the national conference. Established in 1988.

• 5516 • Outstanding Teacher of Theatre in Higher Education Award
To recognize an innovative teacher of theatre in higher education who has empowered and changed the lives of students. A plaque is awarded annually at the national conference. Established in 1993.

• 5517 • Research Award for Outstanding Booklength Study
To recognize the individual who has written the booklength study deemed the best on theatre practice and pedagogy of the year. A plaque and honorarium are awarded annually at the national conference. Established in 1990.

• 5518 • Research Award for Outstanding Journal Article
To recognize the individual who has written the journal article deemed the best theatre scholarship of the year. A plaque and honorarium are awarded annually at the national conference. Established in 1990.

• 5519 •
Association for Women Geoscientists
Carol Dicks, Bus.Mgr.
PO Box 30645
Lincoln, NE 68503-0645
Fax: (402)489-8122
E-mail: office@awg.org
Home Page: http://www.awg.org

• 5520 • Outstanding Educator Award
Award of recognition. For excellent teacher, motivators, mentors of young women. Awarded annually. Established in 1988.

• 5521 •
Association for Women in Communications
Patricia H. Troy, Exec. Dir.
780 Ritchie Hwy., Ste. 28-S
Severna Park, MD 21146
Phone: (410)544-7442
Fax: (410)544-4640
E-mail: pat@womcom.org
Home Page: http://www.womcom.org
Formerly: (1972) Theta Sigma Phi.

• 5522 • Clarion Awards
To recognize excellence in all areas of communications. The deadline for entries is May 15. Awards are presented in the categories of: broadcast, print, public relations, newspapers, newsletters, brochures, audio-visual, magazines, special publications, photography, advertising and over 125 other categories. Materials published, broadcast, or implemented between January 1 and December 31 of the preceding year are eligible. Awards are presented at the annual international conference. Established in 1973. Formerly: National Awards Contest.

• 5523 • Headliner Award
This, the highest honor the Association can bestow on a member, is given to recognize distinguished recent achievements as well as continued excellence of women in the field of communications. Active members of the organization are eligible. The deadline for submission is August 16. Selection is made by the Association's Board of Directors. An award is presented at the annual international conference. Established in 1939.

• 5524 •
Association for Women in Computing
Suford Lewis, Pres.
41 Sutter St., Ste. 1006
San Francisco, CA 94104
Phone: (415)905-4663
Fax: (415)358-4664
E-mail: info@awc-hq.org
Home Page: http://www.awc-hq.org

• 5525 • Augusta Ada Lovelace Award
To recognize individuals who have excelled in either or both outstanding scientific and technical achievement and extraordinary service to the computing community through their accomplishments and contributions on behalf of women in computing. Any person who has rendered extraordinary service to the computing industry through contributions on behalf of women in computing, or whose technical and scientific accomplishments are outstanding, is eligible for nomination. A certificate is awarded annually when merited. Established in 1981 in memory of Augusta Ada, Countess of Lovelace, considered to be the first woman in computing for her work with Charles Babbage, inventor of the "analytical engine," the first computer. She programmed the machine and understood its implications for the future.

• 5526 •
Association for Women in Mathematics
Dawn V. Wheeler, Dir., Membership/Mtgs./ Mktg.
4114 Computer and Space Science Bldg.
University of Maryland
College Park, MD 20742-2461
Phone: (301)405-7892
Fax: (301)314-9074
E-mail: awm@math.umd.edu
Home Page: http://www.awm-math.org

• 5527 • Louise Hay Award
Award of recognition for contributions to mathematics education. Awarded annually.

• 5528 • Alice T. Schafer Prize
Award of recognition. For outstanding undergraduate female mathematics. Awarded annually. Established in 1990.

• 5529 •
Association for Women in Science
Susan Ganter, Exec.Dir.
1200 New York Ave. NW, Ste. 650
Washington, DC 20005
Phone: (202)326-8940
Toll-Free: 800-886-AWIS
Fax: (202)326-8960
E-mail: awis@awis.org
Home Page: http://www.awis.org

• 5530 • AWIS Educational Foundation Predoctoral Award
To recognize women of excellence who are pursuing their doctoral degrees, and to assist them in achieving their career goals. Applicants must be women who are pursuing pre-doctoral studies in any area of science, usually at dissertation level. The deadline is January 15. Four monetary awards of $500 each are given annually. The award money may be used for any need associated with the applicant's educational endeavors.

• 5531 • AWIS Educational Foundation Undergraduate Award
For students intent on majoring in the sciences. Applicants must be undergraduate women. Awarded annually.

• 5532 •
Association for Women Veterinarians
Dr. Heidi Hulon, Sec.
310 North Indian Hill Blvd., Box 337
Claremont, CA 91711-4611
E-mail: mama.la@verizon.net
Home Page: http://www.awv-women-veterinarians.org

Formerly: (1980) Women's Veterinary Medical Association.

• 5533 • Distinguished Service Award
To recognize an individual for contributing toward advancing the status of women veterinarians. Awarded annually when merited. Established in 1976.

• 5534 • Outstanding Woman Veterinarian Award
For recognition of a woman veterinarian who has made a significant contribution to the field of veterinary medicine. Nominations are accepted. A plaque is presented annually. Established in 1951 and awarded annually between 1951 and 1958. The award was reinstituted in 1972.

• 5535 •
Association Francophone pour le Savoir
Genevieve Tanguay, Pres.
425, rue de la Gauchetiere Est
Montreal, QC, Canada H2L 2M7
Phone: (514)849-0045
Fax: (514)849-5558
E-mail: prix@acfas.ca
Home Page: http://www.acfas.ca/prix

• 5536 • ACFAS/Caisse de Depot et Placement du Quebec Prize (in Finance)
To recognize significant achievement in Finance. French-speaking Canadian citizens are eligible. A monetary award of $2500 is awarded. Sponsored by Caisse de depot et placement du Quebec.

• 5537 • Urgel Archambault Prize in Physical Sciences and Mathematics
To recognize significant achievements in the physical sciences and mathematics, both basic and applied, i.e., physics, chemistry, mathematics, earth sciences and engineering. French-speaking Canadian citizens are eligible. A monetary award of $2,500 and a medal are awarded annually. Established in 1953 in honor of Urgel Archambault, the founding director of Ecole Polytechnique de Montreal. Sponsored by Alcan Ltee.

• 5538 • J. Armand Bombardier Prize in Technological Innovation
To recognize significant achievement in technological innovation. French-speaking Canadian citizens are eligible. A monetary award of $2,500 and a medal are awarded annually. Established in 1979 in honor of J. Armand Bombardier, the inventor of the snowmobile. Sponsored by the Joseph-Armand Bombardier Foundation.

• 5539 • Michel Jurdant Prize in Environmental Science
For recognition of an exceptional scientific contribution to the study of the environment in relation to human activities. French-speaking Canadian citizens only are eligible. A monetary award of $2,500 and a medal are awarded annually. Established in 1980 in honor of Jacques Rousseau, a botanist, ethnologist and former secretary general of the ACFAS.

• 5540 • Leo Parizeau Prize in Biology
To recognize significant achievement in the natural sciences, i.e., zoology, botany, agronomy, forestry and ecology. French-speaking Canadian citizens are eligible. A monetary award of $2,500 and a bronze medal are awarded annually. Established in 1944 in honor of Leo Parizeau, the first president of ACFAS. Sponsored by the National Bank of Canada.

• 5541 • Prize in Humanities
For recognition of a significant achievement in the humanities. French-speaking Canadian citizens only are eligible. A monetary prize of $2,500 and a medal are awarded. Established in 1985 in honor of Andre Laurendeau, an editor of the newspaper *Le Devoir.* Formerly: (1995) Andre Laurendeau Prize in Humanities.

• 5542 • Marcel Vincent Prize in Human Sciences
To recognize significant achievement in human sciences, i.e., the humanities, education, and the behavioral sciences. French-speaking Canadian citizens are eligible. A monetary award of $2,500 and a medal are awarded annually. Established in 1975 in honor of Marcel Vincent, the first francophone president of Bell Canada.

• 5543 •
Association of Administrative Law Judges
Joel Elliott, Sec.
1454 Mendavia Ave.
Coral Gables, FL 33146
Phone: (414)297-3141
Fax: (503)326-3062
E-mail: info@aalj.org
Home Page: http://www.aalj.org

• 5544 • James "Tick" Vickrey Award
To recognize an outstanding contribution to the development of the principles of administrative justice system. A plaque is awarded annually. Established in 1986 for the honorable James "Tick" Vickrey. Additional information is available from Ronald G. Bernoski, N76 W22260 Cherry Hill Rd., Sussex, WI 53089.

• 5545 •
Association of Air Medical Services
Dawn Mancuso CAE, Exec.Dir./CEO
526 King St., Ste. 415
Alexandria, VA 22314-3143
Phone: (703)836-8732
Fax: (703)836-8920
E-mail: information@aams.org
Home Page: http://www.aams.org
Formerly: ASHBEAMS.

• 5546 • Jim Charlson Award
To recognize an individual who has made significant contributions to the overall enhancement, development or promotion of aviation safety within the air medical transport industry. The recipient receives an all expense paid trip to attend the annual Air Medical Transport Conference. Awarded annually.

• 5547 • Fixed Wing Scholarship
To recognize an individual working in the fixed wing arm of the industry. Eligible candidates must be employeed in a clinical, aviation, communication, or management role within their program. Recipients are selected on the basis of professional commitment and leadership ability. The recipient receives an all expense paid trip to attend the annual Air Medical Transport Conference.

• 5548 • Barbara A. Hess Award
To recognize an individual who, through research and/or educational efforts, has significantly contributed to the enhancement, development or promotion of the air medical industry. A plaque and registration to attend the annual Air Medical Transport Conference to accept the award are presented annually.

• 5549 • Marriott-Carlson Award
To recognize an individual who has made significant contributions to the overall enhancement, development or promotion of the air medical industry. The recipient receives an all expense paid trip to attend the annual Air Medical Transport Conference. Awarded annually.

• 5550 • Medical Crew/Crew Member of the Year Award
To recognize an individual who has made significant contributions to enhance the development or promote the improvement of patient care in the air medical transport industry. The recipient receives an all-expense paid trip to attend the annual Air Medical Transport Conference. Awarded annually.

• 5551 •
Association of American Colleges and Universities
Carol G Schneider, Pres.
1818 R St. NW
Washington, DC 20009
Phone: (202)387-3760
Toll-Free: 800-297-3775
Fax: (202)265-9532
E-mail: info@aacu.org
Home Page: http://www.aacu.org

• 5552 • **Frederic W. Ness Book Award**
For recognition of a book published between January 1 and December 31 during the preceding year that has made the most significant contribution to studies in liberal education. Submissions may be made in August. The criteria for eligibility are: the principal theme of the book must deal either with liberal education in higher education as that term is commonly understood in American colleges and universities, the relation of liberal education to other programs of higher education, or the role of liberal education in society; a book by two or more authors in which the work throughout is genuinely the product of joint study and interpretation; normally, anthologies of essays are not eligible, but a collection of essays by a single author that has some self-evident coherence or that presents perspectives on a common theme will receive consideration; handbooks, reference books, and works whose chief purpose is to present the results of empirical research, institutional studies, and experiments with programs of study or methods of instruction are not eligible; and histories of individual colleges and universities are not normally eligible, but may qualify if they are more than an institutional history and contribute to an understanding of the value of liberal education. A monetary prize of $2,000 is awarded annually. Established in 1979 in honor of Frederic W. Ness, president emeritus of the association.

• 5553 •
Association of American Editorial Cartoonists
Wanda Nicholson, Gen.Mgr.
1221 Stoneferry Ln.
Raleigh, NC 27606
Phone: (919)859-5516
Fax: (919)859-3172
E-mail: wnicholson@nc.rr.com
Home Page: http://www.editorialcartoonists.com

• 5554 • **John Locher Memorial Award**
For recognition of top level college or amateur editorial cartoonists. Individuals 18 to 25 years of age are eligible. A bronze plaque and expenses to the association's convention are awarded at the annual convention. Established in 1987 by Dick Locher, Chicago Tribune cartoonist, in memory of his son, John, who died in his twenties at the beginning of his cartooning career.

• 5555 •
Association of American Geographers
Douglas Richardson, Exec.Dir.
1710 16th St. NW
Washington, DC 20009-3198
Phone: (202)234-1450
Fax: (202)234-2744
E-mail: gaia@aag.org
Home Page: http://www.aag.org

• 5556 • **John Brinckerhoff Jackson Prize**
For recognition of a popular book of scholarly and literary merit on the human geography of the United States, particularly one that interprets geographical scholarship in language that nonprofessional readers can appreciate and enjoy. American authors of books written by geographers are eligible. One copy of the published book must be submitted by the publisher. Submission deadline is January 15th. A monetary prize of $1,000 is awarded at the annual meeting of the Association. Established in 1984 by John Brinckerhoff Jackson, founder and editor of *Landscape* magazine from 1951-1968. One copy should be submitted to the four committee members. Inquire for current committee members contact information.

• 5557 • **J. Warren Nystrom Award**
To recognize outstanding doctoral dissertations in geography. Established in 1980 by Warren Nystrom, former executive director of AAG. Application deadline is September 1st.

• 5558 •
Association of American Medical Colleges
Jordan J. Cohen MD, Pres.
2450 N St. NW
Washington, DC 20037-1136
Phone: (202)828-0400
Fax: (202)828-1125
E-mail: amcas@aamc.org
Home Page: http://www.aamc.org

• 5559 • **Award for Distinguished Research in the Biomedical Sciences**
To recognize outstanding biomedical research related to health and disease and demonstrated to have contributed to the substance of medicine. Nominees must serve on the faculty of an AAMC-member medical school or teaching hospital or hold membership in an AAMC member academic society. Nominations may be submitted by anyone on the faculty or staff of a medical school or teaching hospital or any member of an academic society. A monetary award of $5,000 and an award plaque are awarded each year at the annual meeting. Established in 1947. Formerly: (1981) Borden Award.

• 5560 • **Abraham Flexner Award for Distinguished Service to Medical Education**
To recognize extraordinary individual contributions to medical schools and to the entire medical education community. Any individual who has made a significant contribution to academic medicine may be nominated. Nominations are accepted from any faculty or staff member of a medical school or teaching hospital or from any member of an academic society. The deadline for nominations is May 9. A monetary award of $10,000 and a bronze medal are awarded each year at the AAMC annual meeting. Established in 1958 in honor of Abraham Flexner.

• 5561 • **Outstanding Community Service Award**
To recognize a U.S. member institution or organization with a longstanding, major institutional commitment to addressing community needs, demonstrated through the development of exceptional programs that go well beyond the traditional role of academic medicine and reach communities whose needs are not being met by the health system. Nominations must be received by April 11. The award, a commemorative piece and citation honoring the institution's extraordinary social commitment, will be presented at the AAMC annual meeting.

• 5562 • **David E. Rogers Award**
To recognize a member of a medical school faculty who has made major contributions to improving the health and health care of the American people. Individuals who have spent the majority of their careers in academic medicine in the United States are eligible. Nominations must be received by May 9. Presentation of the award and a monetary prize of $10,000 will be made at the AAMC annual meeting. Sponsored by the Association of American Medical Colleges and the Robert Wood Johnson Foundation.

• 5563 •
Association of American Publishers
Pat Schroeder, Pres./CEO
71 5th Ave., 2nd Fl.
New York, NY 10003-3004
Phone: (212)255-0200
Fax: (212)255-7007
E-mail: amyg@publishers.org
Home Page: http://www.publishers.org

• 5564 • **Curtis G. Benjamin Award for Creative Publishing**
To recognize individuals for exceptional innovation and creativity in publishing. A plaque is awarded annually. Established in 1974 by the friends of Mr. Benjamin.

• 5565 • **School Division Education Research Award**
Annual award of recognition. Inquire for additional details/

• 5566 •
Association of American University Presses
Peter J. Givler, Exec.Dir.
71 W 23rd St.
New York, NY 10010-4102
Phone: (212)989-1010
Fax: (212)989-0275
E-mail: info@aaupnet.org
Home Page: http://www.aaupnet.org

• 5567 • **AAUP Design Show**
For recognition of outstanding book jacket and journal designs. Entries must be submitted by individual presses that are members of the Association of American University Presses. Winners are on display at the Association's annual meeting and are available for display purposes to universities and libraries.

• 5568 • **Hiromi Arisawa Awards**
To encourage publishing in the social sciences and humanities on Japan and translations from the Japanese. Up to four books may be submitted by one of 114 member presses. Monetary awards of $10,000 for the publishers of two winners and $5,000 for the finalists are presented biennially at the Association's annual meeting. Established in 1990. Sponsored by the Hiroma Arisawa Memorial Fund, Japanese industry associations, Japanese corporations, and branches of U.S. business firms in Japan.

• 5569 •
Association of America's Public Television Stations
Jeffrey Davis, Communications VP
666 Eleventh St., NW, Ste. 1100
University of Maryland
Washington, DC 20001
Phone: (202)654-4200
Fax: (202)654-4236
E-mail: jeffrey@apts.org
Home Page: http://www.apts.org

• 5570 • **Grassroots Award**
Award of recognition. For person at public television station. Awarded annually.

• 5571 •
Association of Area Business Publications
C. James Dowden, Exec.Dir.
4929 Wilshire Blvd., No. 428
Los Angeles, CA 90010
Phone: (323)937-5514
Fax: (323)937-0959
E-mail: jdowden@prodigy.net
Home Page: http://www.bizpubs.org

• 5572 • **Editorial and Design Awards**
To honor outstanding publications in the local and regional business publications field. Awards are given in the following categories for magazines and newspapers: (1) General Excellence; (2) Best Front Page or Cover; (3) Best Feature Layout; (4) Best Overall Design; (5) Best Use of Photography; (6) Infographics; (7) Best Original (byline) Column; (8) Best Regular Feature; (9) Best Investigative Reporting; (10) Best Editorial; (11) Best Coverage of Local Breaking News; (12) Best Scoop; (13) Best Profile of a Person; (14) Best Explanatory Journalism; (15) Best Local Spin of National Business or Economic Story; and (16) Most Improved Publication. Membership in AABP is necessary for consideration. A plaque is awarded annually at the AABP summer meeting. Established in 1981.

• 5573 •
Association of Asphalt Paving Technologists
Eugene L. Skok, Sec.-Treas.
4711 Clark Ave., Ste. G
White Bear Lake, MN 55110
Phone: (651)293-9188
Fax: (651)293-9193
E-mail: aapt@qwest.net
Home Page: http://www.asphalttechnology.org/

• 5574 • **Board of Directors Award of Recognition**
To honor members of the Association who have contributed to the group's publications and meeting and have not otherwise been honored. A plaque is awarded annually. Established in 1972.

• 5575 • **Emmons Award**
To recognize the best paper presented at the annual meeting and technical sessions. A silver imprinted dish is awarded annually. Established in 1949 in honor of W. J. Emmons.

• 5576 • **Honorary Member**
To honor individuals recognized by the membership as having outstanding eminence and long experience in the practice of some phase of asphalt paving technology. Awarded when merited. Established in 1927.

• 5577 •
Association of Baptists for World Evangelism
Dr. Michael Loftis, Pres.
PO Box 8585
Harrisburg, PA 17105-8585
Phone: (717)774-7000
Fax: (717)774-1919
E-mail: info@abwe.org
Home Page: http://www.abwe.org

• 5578 • **Bomm/Presidential Citation**
Recognizes years of services, meritorious service. Awarded annually.

• 5579 •
Association of Behavioral Healthcare Management
Linda Rosenberg PhD, Pres./CEO
12300 Twinbrook Pkwy, Ste. 320
Rockville, MD 20852
Phone: (301)984-6200
Fax: (301)881-7159
E-mail: lindar@nccbh.org
Home Page: http://www.nccbh.org/abhm/

• 5580 • **Harold C. Piepenbrink Award for Outstanding Service to the Field of Mental Health Administration**
To recognize an individual for outstanding achievement in the field of mental health administration, or the development and publication of significant research in mental health. Members are eligible. A plaque is awarded each year at the annual meeting. Established in 1977 to honor Harold C. Piepenbrink, former president of the Association.

• 5581 •
Association of Boards of Certification
Stephen Ballou, Exec.Dir.
208 5th St.
Ames, IA 50010-6259
Phone: (515)232-3623
Fax: (515)232-3778
E-mail: abc@abccert.org
Home Page: http://www.abccert.org

• 5582 • **Harris F. Seidel Award**
To recognize an individual for an outstanding contribution toward establishing and/or advancing certification programs for operating personnel. Contributions must be of regional or international scope, and of lasting value in improved performance by more highly qualified operating personnel. Nominations must be submitted by June 30. A plaque is awarded at the international conference. Established in 1977 and renamed in 1981 to honor Harris F. Seidel. Formerly: (1981) ABC Certification Award.

• 5583 •
Association of Bone and Joint Surgeons
Colette I. Hohimer, Exec.Dir.
6300 N River Rd., Ste. 727
Rosemont, IL 60018-4226
Phone: (847)698-1636
Fax: (847)823-4921
E-mail: abjs@aaos.org
Home Page: http://www.abjs.org

• 5584 • **Nicolas Andry Award**
To recognize current or past original contributions to orthopaedic knowledge, research, or philosophy. There are no age, discipline, or geographic restrictions. The deadline for submissions is November 1. One award may be granted each year. The award winning work is submitted to *Clinical Orthopaedics and Related Research* for publication and must be presented at the annual meeting of the Association of Bone and Joint Surgeons. An momentary honorarium plus some expenses for the winner and an additional person to attend the annual meeting are awarded annually. Established in 1949.

• 5585 •
Association of Bridal Consultants
Gerard J. Monaghan, Pres.
56 Danbury Rd., Ste. 11
New Milford, CT 06776
Phone: (860)355-0464
Fax: (860)354-1404
E-mail: office@bridalassn.com
Home Page: http://www.bridalassn.com

• 5586 • **"Miss Dorothy" Heart**
Recognizes passion for the industry. Awarded annually.

Awards are arranged in alphabetical order below their administering organizations

• 5587 • **Wedding Professional of the Year**
Annual award of recognition. Voted by membership (peers).

• 5588 •
Association of Canadian Advertisers (Association Canadienne Des Annonceurs)
175 Bloor St. E
South Tower, Ste. 307
Toronto, ON, Canada M4W 3R8
Phone: (416)964-3805
Toll-Free: 800-565-0109
Fax: (416)964-0771
E-mail: info@aca-online.com
Home Page: http://www.aca-online.com

• 5589 • **ACA Gold Medal Award**
To recognize outstanding services to advertising in Canada, from singular accomplishments to sustained contributions to the general advancement of the industry. Nominations of Canadians are accepted. A medal and citation are bestowed annually. Established in 1941.

• 5590 •
Association of Catholic Colleges and Universities
Monika K. Hellwig LLBPhD, Pres./CEO
1 Dupont Cir., Ste. 650
Washington, DC 20036
Phone: (202)457-0650
Fax: (202)728-0977
E-mail: accu@accunet.org
Home Page: http://www.accunet.org

• 5591 • **Rev. Theodore M. Hesburgh, C.S.C., Award**
For recognition of outstanding contributions to Catholic higher education. The criteria for the award countenance a variety of outstanding contributions to Catholic higher education, from teachers whose reputations rarely extend beyond their own campuses, but who are educators in the finest sense of the tradition, to scholars who have combined excellent teaching with important research and publication, to administrators whose greatest contributions have occurred outside the classroom, to bishops, trustees and others who have supported Catholic higher education in myriad ways. As a rule, nominees are persons who have devoted themselves to Catholic higher education over an extended period of time, but are not persons currently serving a presidency at a Catholic college or university (unless retirement from that position is anticipated during the year). Nominees are solicited from member presidents of ACCU only. A citation and a personalized gift are awarded at the discretion of the ACCU Board at the annual meeting. Established in 1982 in honor of Theodore M. Hesburgh, C.S.C.

• 5592 • **Presidents' Distinguished Service Award**
To honor an individual not professionally involved in Catholic higher education who, over a lifetime, has made a unique contribution to the cause of Catholic higher education in the United States.

• 5593 •
Association of Certified Fraud Examiners
Toby J. F. Bishop, Pres./CEO
The Gregor Bldg.
716 W Ave.
Austin, TX 78701-2727
Phone: (512)478-9000
Toll-Free: 800-245-3321
Fax: (512)478-9297
E-mail: info@cfenet.com
Home Page: http://www.cfenet.com
Formerly: Institute for Financial Crime Prevention.

• 5594 • **Donald R. Cressey Memorial Award**
To recognize an individual for a lifetime of achievement in the detection and deterrence of fraud. A unique stone trophy is awarded annually. Established in 1989 in memory of Donald R. Cressey, a founder of the Associated of Certified Fraud Examiners.

• 5595 • **Morris R. Walker Memorial Award**
To recognize superior performance by the candidate who receives the highest score on the Uniform CFE Examination. Awarded annually. Established in 1989 in memory of Morris R. Walker, who was a charter Certified Fraud Examiner and nationally renowned white-collar crime expert.

• 5596 •
Association of Chartered Accountants in the United States
Guy Langford, Pres.
341 Lafayette St., Ste. 4246
New York, NY 10012-2417
Phone: (212)334-2078
Fax: (212)431-5786
E-mail: administration@acaus.org
Home Page: http://www.acaus.org

• 5597 • **Chartered Accountants/Beta Alpha Psi Scholarships**
To encourage education and research on international accounting issues. One open award of $1,000 and one restricted award of $500 are awarded annually. Open to active U.S. resident graduate or undergraduate members of Beta Alpha Psi.

• 5598 • **International Chartered Accountants Education Award**
To promote study and greater understanding of the effects on U.S./International trade and investment of rule-making and practice in the areas of Accounting, Auditing and Professional Regulation. Awarded annually with a prize of $2,500. Open to U.S.-resident accounting professors. Established in 1986.

• 5599 •
Association of Children's Museums
Janet Rice Elman, Exec.Dir.
1300 L St. NW, Ste. 975
Washington, DC 20005
Phone: (202)898-1080
Fax: (202)898-1086
E-mail: acm@childrensmuseums.org
Home Page: http://www.childrensmuseums.org

• 5600 • **Great Friend to Kids Award**
To honor individuals and organizations who have made outstanding contributions toward enriching the lives of children. Awarded annually. Established in 1991.

• 5601 •
Association of College and Research Libraries
American Library Association
Awards Program Assistant
50 E. Huron St.
Chicago, IL 60611
Phone: (312)280-2514
Toll-Free: 800-545-2433
Fax: (312)280-2520
E-mail: acrl@ala.org
Home Page: http://www.ala.org/acrl.html

• 5602 • **Academic/Research Librarian of the Year Award**
To honor an individual member of the library profession who has made an outstanding national or international contribution to academic and research librarianship and library development. Selection is based on service to the profession through ACRL and related organizations; research on academic or library service; publication of a body of scholarly and/or theoretical writing contributing to development in the field; planning and implementing of a program that can serve as a model for others. The nominator must submit eight copies of a letter including his/her name, address and phone number plus the name, address, and phone number of the person being nominated; a letter supporting the nomination written by the nominator; a vita for the nominee; and an unlimited number of letters of support from other librarians. Self nominations are accepted. The nomination deadline is December 1. A monetary award of $3,000 and a plaque are awarded each year at the annual conference of the American Library Association. Established in 1978. Sponsored by Baker and Taylor Books.

• 5603 • **Hugh C. Atkinson Memorial Award**
To recognize achievements in the areas of library automation, library management, and/or library development and research. Nominees must be librarians employed in a university, college, or community college library in the year prior to application for the award and must have a minimum of five years of professional experience in an academic library. Selection is based on achievement contributing to improvements in the areas of library automation, library management, and/or library development or research.

Five copies of documentation of the name, address and phone number of the nominee and the nominator; supporting narrative; and a current vita must be submitted to the above address. The nomination deadline is December 1. A monetary award of $2,000 and a citation are presented annually. Established in 1988 to honor Hugh C. Atkinson, one of the major innovators in modern librarianship. For additional information contact Donald Riggs, Award Committee Chair, Nova Southeastern University Libraries, Einstein Library, 3301 College Ave., Ft. Lauderdale, FL 33314 or Stephanie Sherrod at the above address.

• 5604 • Community College Learning Resources Library Achievement Awards

To recognize significant achievement in the areas of program development and leadership or community service. Individuals or groups from two-year institutions, as well as the two-year institutions themselves, are eligible. Nominees for the program development awards must have demonstrated significant achievement in one of the following areas: development of a unique and innovative learning resources/library program that enhances use by faculty and students; integration and exploration of media and technology to enhance services; and exemplary collection development policy model. Nominees for the leadership or community service award must have made significant achievement in one or more of the following areas: advocacy of learning resources/libraries by individuals, groups, or programs not directly affiliated with the program; community services; cooperative programs with schools, libraries, and other organizations; legislative advocacy; and special assignments associated with the mission of the community colleges (such as literacy) across the curriculum programs. The nomination deadline is December 1. A citation and $500 is awarded. Established in 1989. Sponsored by the Community and Junior College Libraries Section and EBSCO Subscription Services. Additional information is available from Thersa S. Byrd, PO Box 828, Glen Allen, VA 23060-0828; (804) 371-3220; e-mail: srbyrdt@jsr.cc.va.us

• 5605 • Distinguished Education and Behavioral Sciences Librarian Award

To honor a distinguished academic librarian who has made an outstanding contribution as an education and/or behavioral sciences librarian through accomplishments and service to the profession. Nominees should have demonstrated achievements in one or more of the following areas: service to the profession through ACRL/EBSS and related organizations; significant academic library service in the areas of education and/or behavioral sciences; significant research and publication in areas of academic library services in education and/or behavioral sciences; and planning and implementation of academic library programs in education and/or the behavioral sciences disciplines of exemplary quality that they could serve as a model for others. A citation and monetary award of $1,000 are awarded annually.

• 5606 • Doctoral Dissertation Fellowship

Fosters research in academic librarianship. Applicants must be doctoral students conducting dissertation research; have completed all course work. Selected on the bases of potential significance of the research; validity of the methodology and proposed methods of analysis; originality and creativity; presentation; and evidence of continuing interest in scholarship. $1500 and a citation are awarded. Six copies of a brief proposal, including research description, schedule for completion, budget and budget justification, name of dissertation advisor and committee members, and letter of endorsement from the advisor must be submitted. Application deadline is December 1. Donated by the Institute for Scientific Information. Send completed nomination packet or question to Stephanie Sherrod at the above address.

• 5607 • Miriam Dudley Instruction Librarian Award

To recognize a librarian who has made an especially significant contribution to the advancement of library instruction in a college or research library. Nominees must have achieved distinction in the following areas: planning and implementation of an academic instruction program that has served as a model for other programs nationally or regionally; production of a body of research and publication that demonstrates impact on the concepts and methods of teaching and information-seeking strategies; sustained participation in organizations (regional or national) devoted to the promotion and enhancement of academic instruction in a library environment; promotion, development, and integration of education for instruction in ALA accredited library schools or professional continuing education programs that have served as models for other courses or programs. Nominees need not necessarily meet all the criteria. A letter with the nominees name, address, phone number and a narrative of supporting information, a vita for the nominee and nominators name, address and phone number must be submitted. Nominations must be submitted by December 1. A monetary award of $1,000 and a plaque are awarded annually. Established in 1983 in honor of Miriam Dudley, one of the founders of the Instruction Section. Sponsored by Elsevier/JAI Press. Formerly: (1997) Miriam Dudley Award for Bibliographic Instruction.

• 5608 • EBSCO Community College Learning Resources and Library Achievement Awards

These two awards recognize significant achievement in the areas of programs and leadership. Individuals or groups from two-year institutions, as well as the two-year institutions themselves, are eligible. Nominees for the program award should demonstrate significant achievement in development of a unique and innovative learning resources/library program. Nominees for the leadership award should demonstrate significant achievement in advocacy of learning resources/library programs or services of leadership in professional organizations that are associated with the mission of community, junior, or technical colleges. Each award winner will receive $500 cash and a citation donated by donated by EBSCO Subscription Services. Awards are given out annually.

• 5609 • Excellence in Academic Libraries Award

Recognizes librarian and other staff accomplishments as members of teams supporting the mission of their institution. Applicants must be from community college, college, or university libraries. A total of $12,000 plus $3000 for travel to the presentation ceremony is awarded annually. Sponsored by Blackwell's Book Services.

• 5610 • Instruction Publication of the Year Award

To recognize an outstanding publication related to instruction in a library environment published in the preceding two years. Selection is based on relevance to the field of instruction in academic or research libraries, originality, timeliness, and quality of writing. Journal articles, books, book chapters, and published proceedings are eligible. Submissions may be written by one or more individuals, a group, organization, or committee. Instruction Section publications are not eligible. The deadline is December 2. A citation is awarded annually. Established in 1993. Formerly: (1997) BIS Bibilographic Instruction Publication of the Year Award.

• 5611 • Instruction Section Innovation Award

To recognize and honor librarians who have developed and implemented innovative approaches to instruction at their institutions or in the community. The emphasis of this award is on creativity and innovation. Recipients must have implemented their ideas in an academic or research library environment within the past two years. There are no restrictions as to the size of the instructional effort, academic discipline, target audience, or techniques employed. A certificate and monetary prize of $3000 is awarded annually. Donated by Lexis-Nexis.

• 5612 • Marta Lange/CQ Press Award

To recognize an academic or law librarian for contributions to bibliography and information service in law or political science. Selection is based on the planning and implementation of a model bibliography/information services program in a law or political science library; history of contributions to the field through research, publications, and other activities; service to the profession through ACRL or related regional and national organizations; and promotion or development of an education program that has served as a model for others. Five copies of a letter of nomination, including the name, address, and phone number of the nominator and the nominee, a narrative supporting the nominations, and a current vita must be submitted. Self nominations are accepted. The nomination deadline is December 1. A monetary award of $1,000 and a plaque are presented annually. The award is administered by ACRL's Law and Political Science Section and sponsored by CQ Press.

• 5613 • Samuel Lazerow Fellowship for Research in Collections and Technical Services in Academic and Research Libraries

To foster advances in acquisitions or technical services by providing fellowships to librarians for traveling or writing in those fields. The proposals will be judged on the following: potential significance of the project to acquisitions or technical services; originality and creativity; clarity and completeness of the proposal; and evidence of an interest in scholarship. Research projects in collection development or the compilation of bibliographies will not be supported. Recipients are required to submit a report of results of research for possible publication in *C&RL News*. A monetary prize of $1,000 and a citation donated by the Thomson Scientific will be awarded annually.

• 5614 • Katharine Kyes Leab and Daniel J. Leab *American Book Prices Current* Exhibition Catalogue Awards

For recognition of the best exhibition catalog published by American or Canadian institutions in conjunction with exhibitions and electronic exhibition catalogs issued within the digital/ web environment. Catalogs published between September and August of the year prior to the award are eligible. The entries are divided into three budget categories: expensive, moderate, and inexpensive, based upon production costs of the catalogs. Catalogs may be of varying formats, styles, and scope; but each must represent, either comprehensively or selectively, an exhibition which has taken place. Criteria for selecting winners include the level of accuracy, visual impact, contribution to scholarship, and usefulness to the intended audience. Four copies of the catalog and entry form must be submitted to Award Committee Chair, Diane Shaw, Smithsonian Institution Libraries, NHB30, Washington, DC 20560-0154. The deadline for submission is September 30. A citation is awarded annually. Established in 1985. Renamed in 1988 when Katharine Kyes Leab and Daniel J. Leab endowed the awards program. Formerly: (1988) RBMS Exhibition Catalogue Awards.

• 5615 • WESS Coutts Nijhoff International West European Specialist Study Grant

To support research pertaining to Western European studies, librarianship or the book trade. The criteria are the significance and utility of the proposed project as a contribution to the study of the acquisition, organization or use of library materials from or relating to Western Europe. Current or historical subjects may be treated. The proposal will be reviewed according to the following: what will be accomplished; what is the need for and value of proposed research; the methodology for carrying out work; is the work accomplishable within the proposed time frame; and are the applicants qualified to carry out study. A maximum of 4,500 Euros (or the U.S. equivalent) is awarded annually.

• 5616 • Oberly Award for Bibliography in the Agricultural Sciences

To recognize an American citizen who compiles the best English-language bibliography in the field of agriculture or a related science in the two-year period preceding the year that the award is made. Bibliographies may be a monograph, a completed series viewed as a body of work, or an ongoing publication in any format. Selection is based on accuracy, scope, usefulness, format, and special features such as explanatory introductions, annotations, and indexes. Nominations must be submitted by December 1. A $350 cash award and a plaque are awarded in odd-numbered years. Send nominations in the form of a letter and a copy of the bibliography to: Jeannie Miller, Texas A&M University, Sterling C. Evans Library, 5000 TAMU, College Station, TX 77843. Established in 1923 to honor Eunice Rockwood Oberly, late librarian of the Bureau of Plant Industry, U.S. Department of Agriculture. Formerly: Eunice Rockwell Oberly Memorial Award.

• 5617 • *Rare Books and Manuscripts Librarianship* Award

To recognize articles of superior quality published in the ACRL journal, *Rare Books and Manuscripts*. A monetary award of $1,000 and a citation are awarded in odd-numbered years.

• 5618 • K. G. Saur Award for Best Article in *College and Research Libraries*

To recognize and reward the most outstanding article published in *College and Research Libraries* during the preceding volume year. A monetary award of $500 is presented each year at the annual conference. Selected on the basis of originality, timeliness, relevance to ACRL areas of interest and concern, and quality of writing. Established in 1987. Sponsored by K. G. Saur Publishing.

• 5619 • SFORZA Medal

Recognizes outstanding leadership in philanthropy, civil society, and voluntary service. Awarded periodically.

• 5620 • WSS Achievement in Women's Studies Librarianship Awards Career Achievement Award

Recognizes long-standing contributions in women's studies during a career. $1000 is awarded annually. Nominees should show achievements in one or more of the following areas: service within the profession through ACRL/WSS and/or related organizations; academic or research library service in the area of women's studies; research and publication; planning and implementation of academic or research library programs that can be adapted to use by others. A completed nomination form; a letter covering the area(s) or criteria and citing specific examples; and three letters of support must be submitted. Application deadline is December 1. Sponsored by Greenwood Publishing Group, Inc.. For additional information contact Stephanie Sherrod at the above address.

• 5621 •
Association of College and University Housing Officers International
Sallie Traxler, Exec.Dir.
941 Chatham Lane, Ste. 318
Columbus, OH 43221-2416
Phone: (614)292-0099
Fax: (614)292-3205
E-mail: web@acuho-i.org
Home Page: http://www.acuho-i.org

• 5622 • ACUHO-I Award

For recognition of service to the Association and for contributions to the field of college and university housing and food service. All ACUHO-I past presidents actively employed in higher education may nominate an ACUHO-I member who is retired from higher education. A plaque and an invitation to be a guest of the Association at the Conference are awarded annually. Established in 1964.

• 5623 • James C. Grimm Leadership and Service Award

To recognize members who have unselfishly served ACUHO-I and the housing profession with outstanding leadership and dedicated service. A nominee must have at least 10 years of service with ACUHO-I; must have served on at least three different committees or task forces; must have chaired one committee or task force, or must have been a member of the Executive Board; and his or her contributions to ACUHO-I must be judged to have been above and beyond the normal service expected from a person in a position of leadership in the housing field. A plaque is awarded annually at the convention. Established in 1986. Formerly: (2006) Leadership and Service Awards.

• 5624 • James A. Hurd Award

To recognize a person of color who has consistently demonstrated a sincere interest and participation in the mission, programs, and educational focus of ACUHO-I. A plaque and recognition are presented at the annual conference. Established in 1991 in honor of James A. Hurd, past president of the Association.

• 5625 • S. Earl Thompson Award

To recognize non-members for contributions to the Association and the profession of college and university housing and food service. A trophy or plaque and travel expenses to receive the award are presented annually. Established in 1987 in honor of Dr. S. Earl Thompson, founding father of ACUHO-I and first president of the Association.

• 5626 •
Association of College English Teachers of Alabama
Jim Jolly, Pres.
English Dept., Samford University
800 Lakeshore Dr.
Birmingham, AL 35229-2260
Phone: (205)726-2926
Phone: (205)726-1946
Fax: (205)726-2112
E-mail: jjolly@gadsdenst.cc.al.us
Home Page: http://www.samford.edu/groups/aceta/

• 5627 • **Calvert, Woodall, and McMillan Writing Awards**
For Alabama faculty or students. Monetary award bestowed annually.

• 5628 •
Association of College Unions International
Marsha Herman-Betzen, Exec.Dir.
One City Centre, Ste. 200
120 W 7th St.
Bloomington, IN 47404-3925
Phone: (812)855-8550
Phone: (812)855-8533
Fax: (812)855-0162
E-mail: acui@indiana.org
Home Page: http://www.acuiweb.org

• 5629 • **Chester A. Berry Scholar Award for Excellence in Writing**
To encourage scholarly participation in writing and professional development in the field of the student union/student activities profession. Student and staff co-authorship is encouraged. A monetary prize of $500 is presented upon the recommendation of a panel of judges and awarded annually at the ACU-I International Conference. Established in honor of Chester A. Berry, the first full time executive director of ACU-I. Additional information is available from Nancy T. Davis, ACU-I Central Office.

• 5630 • **Butts - Whiting Award**
To recognize and honor outstanding leaders of the Association who have made significant contributions to the college union movement. Individuals who have been administrators of a college union for at least ten years, with records of accomplishment on campus, in the community, and in the Association are eligible. A bronze cast plaque is awarded annually if merited. Established in 1967 in honor of Porter F. Butts and Edgar Archibald Whiting.

• 5631 •
Association of Collegiate Schools of Architecture
Michael J. Monti, Exec.Dir.
1735 New York Ave. NW, 3rd Fl.
Washington, DC 20006
Phone: (202)785-2324
Fax: (202)628-0448
E-mail: info@acsa-arch.org
Home Page: http://www.acsa-arch.org

• 5632 • **ACSA Honors and Awards Program**
To recognize outstanding faculty achievements in architecture. The following awards are presented: AIA/ACSA Topaz Medallion, ACSA Distinguished Professor Award, ACSA Creative Achievement Award, ACSA Faculty Design Award, ACSA Collaborative Practice Award, and AIAS/ACSA New Faculty Teaching Award. Awarded annually.

• 5633 •
Association of Community Cancer Centers
E. Strode Weaver FACHE, Pres.
11600 Nebel St., Ste. 201
Rockville, MD 20852
Phone: (301)984-9496
Fax: (301)770-1949
E-mail: info@accc-cancer.org
Home Page: http://www.accc-cancer.org

• 5634 • **Clinical Research Award**
Award of recognition. For contribution to the field of community cancer care. Awarded Annually.

• 5635 •
Association of Conservation Engineers
John Bruner, Sec.
WYDOC-State Parks & Historic Sites
Herschler Bldg.
122 W 25th St., 1st Fl. E
Cheyenne, WY 82002
Phone: (307)777-6325
Fax: (307)777-6472
E-mail: jbrune@state.wy.us
Home Page: http://conservationengineers.org

• 5636 • **Eugene Baker Memorial Award**
To recognize an engineer for outstanding contributions to conservation engineering. A bronze plaque is awarded as merited. Established in 1964.

• 5637 • **President's Award**
To recognize a member for significant and outstanding contributions in the development, operation, or promotion of the Association. Established in 1978.

• 5638 •
Association of Consulting Engineers of Canada
(Association des Ingenieurs-Conseils du Canada)
Claude Paul Boivin, Pres./Chief Operating Officer
130 Albert St., Ste. 616
Ottawa, ON, Canada K1P 5G4
Phone: (613)236-0569
Toll-Free: 800-565-0569
Fax: (613)236-6193
E-mail: info@acec.ca
Home Page: http://www.acec.ca

• 5639 • **Awards of Excellence**
Annual award of recognition. Awarded to one or more recipients each year.

• 5640 • **Beaubien Award**
To honor an individual for lifetime achievements and contribution to the engineering industry and to the association. Awarded annually.

• 5641 • **Merit Award**
Annual award of recognition. Applicants must be association members.

• 5642 • **Public Service Award**
Recognizes excellence and innovation in all engineering discipline. Applicants must be association members. Awards criteria and entry form are available on the Association's web site. Held in conjunction with *consilting Engineer Magazine*. Established in 1967.

• 5643 • **Schreyer Award**
To recognize the most outstanding technical project overall. Awarded annually.

• 5644 •
Association of Consulting Foresters of America
Lynn C. Wilson, Exec.Dir.
312 Montgomery St., Ste. 208
Alexandria, VA 22314
Phone: (703)548-0990
Toll-Free: 888-540-8733
Fax: (703)548-6395
E-mail: director@acf-foresters.com
Home Page: http://www.acf-foresters.com

• 5645 • **ACF Public Service Award**
To recognize achievement in and contributions to the general area of forestry, with emphasis on the practice of consulting forestry. Members may submit nominations. A plaque is awarded annually at the convention. Established in 1977. Formerly: (1978) CFM Award.

• 5646 •
Association of Contingency Planners-Capital of Texas Chapter
Melody Nunn CBCP, Pres.
The 401K Co.
98 San Jacinto Blvd., Ste. 1100
Austin, TX 78701
Phone: (512)344-3933
Fax: (512)305-9785
E-mail: president@acp-centraltexas.com
Home Page: http://www.acp-centraltexas.com

• 5647 • **MVP of Year**
For annual contributions to profession. Recognition award bestowed annually.

Awards are arranged in alphabetical order below their administering organizations

• 5648 •
Association of Cooperative Educators
% The Cooperative Foundation
PO Box 64047
St. Paul, MN 55164
Phone: (703)578-1820
Fax: (651)355-5073
E-mail: leslie.mead@verizon.net
Home Page: http://www.wisc.edu/uwcc/ace/ace.html

• 5649 • **ACE Education Program Award**
To recognize ongoing or special programs that significantly advance education within co-operatives and credit unions. Excellence is determined by the degree to which a specific program meets predetermined goals and objectives, the measurement tools used, and the educational concepts utilized. ACE members may submit nominations. Awarded each year when merited at the annual institute or annual meeting of ACE.

• 5650 • **Reginald J. Cressman ACE Award Recognizing Commitment to Staff Development**
To recognize and individual demonstrating outstanding commitment to staff development. Nominations are accepted. Awarded annually. Established in honor of Reginald J. Cressman, former director of ACE, for his ability to create successful teams.

• 5651 • **The William Hlushko Award to Young Co-operative Educators**
To recognize an educator's achievement within co-operatives or credit unions. Factors for recognition include creativity, innovativeness, understanding, and promotion of the co-operative approach (co-operation). Skills in communication, program development, implementation and evaluation, audio/visual techniques, and the use of up-to-date approaches in adult education are considered. ACE members 35 years of age or younger are eligible and all members may submit nominations. Awarded each year when merited at the annual institute or annual meeting of ACE. Established in 1978.

• 5652 • **Outstanding Contribution to ACE by an Organization**
To recognize any co-operative or credit union organization that has provided special support to ACE. Factors for recognition include undertaking printing endeavors for the association, providing special expertise to the association, providing donations, etc. ACE members may submit nominations. Awarded each year when merited at the annual institute or annual meeting of ACE. Established in 1981.

• 5653 • **Outstanding Contribution to Co-operative Education and Training**
For recognition of long-term or continuous contributions to cooperative education, such as those made by teachers, educators, the development of training materials, publications, and organization or participative leadership in the co-operative and credit union movement. Recipients need not be members of ACE. ACE members may submit nominations. Awarded each year when merited at the annual institute or annual meeting of ACE.

• 5654 • **Professional Contribution by an ACE Member**
For recognition of an outstanding contribution to ACE or a professional contribution by an ACE member in advancing the stature of co-operative education and training. ACE members may submit nominations. Awarded each year when merited at the annual institute or annual meeting of ACE.

• 5655 •
Association of Departments of English
David Laurence, Dir.
26 Broadway, 3rd Fl.
New York, NY 10004-1789
Phone: (646)576-5130
Fax: (646)834-4045
E-mail: dlaurence@mla.org
Home Page: http://www.ade.org

• 5656 • **ADE Francis Andrew March Award**
To recognize men and women for distinguished service to the profession of English at the post-secondary level. Nominees should be eminent scholar-teachers from institutions in any of the four categories represented by ADE members: programs whose highest degrees are B.A.s, M.A.s, or Ph.D.s and programs in two-year colleges offering A.A.s. The deadline for nomination is February. (Names placed in nomination come from members of the ADE Executive Committee or chairs of ADE-member departments and must be confidential.) A citation is awarded annually. Established in 1984 in memory of Francis Andrew March (1823-1911), professor at Lafayette College and the first professor of English in America.

• 5657 •
Association of Directory Publishers
R. Lawrence Angove, Pres. & CEO
116 Cass St.
PO Box 1929
Traverse City, MI 49685-1929
Toll-Free: 800-267-9002
Fax: (231)486-2182
E-mail: hq@adp.org
Home Page: http://www.adp.org

• 5658 • **Gold Book Awards**
To recognize the most outstanding directory products and marketing innovations in the Yellow Pages industry. The awards are contested in two sections, with the Directory Division at the Mid-Year Convention in the fall and the Marketing and Promotion Division at the Annual Convention in the spring. Awarded semiannually.

• 5659 •
Association of Earth Science Editors
Nancy Gilson, Sec.-Treas.
101 Fire Academy Rd.
Socorro, NM 87801
E-mail: nancy@gis.nmt.edu
Home Page: http://www.aese.org

• 5660 • **AESE Award for Outstanding Editorial or Publishing Contributions**
To recognize outstanding contributions and achievements in editing and publishing that stimulate new or greatly improved accomplishments in teaching, research, and applications in the field of earth science. The awards committee nominates individuals. Application deadline is May 15th. A certificate is awarded annually when merited. Established in 1972.

• 5661 • **Award for Outstanding Publication**
To recognize an earth science publication based on the quality of editing, design, illustration, writing, production cost, and overall effectiveness in achieving its publication goal. Awarded to one or more recipients annually. Established in 1993.

• 5662 •
Association of Educational Publishers
Charlene F. Gaynor, Exec.Dir.
510 Heron Dr., Ste. 201
Logan Township, NJ 08085
Phone: (856)241-7772
Fax: (856)241-0709
E-mail: mail@edpress.org
Home Page: http://www.edpress.org

• 5663 • **EdPress Distinguished Achievement Awards for Excellence in Educational Journalism**
To honor excellence among publications in or about education. Publications are entered in any of the following categories: Publications for Adults: Editorial-Feature Article, How-to Feature, Personality Profile, One-theme Issue, Series, Department, Interview, Editorial, News Story, Learned Article, and Fiction; Publications for Adults: Design-Cover Design, Artwork, Education Photograph, Picture Story, and Design Treatment-Contents Page, Whole Publication, and Article; Publications for Adults: Editorial and Design-Annual Report, Special Publication, Sponsored Publication, Video (Promotional or Service), and Viewbook; Publications for Children: Editorial-Feature Article, How-to Feature, Personality Profile, One-theme Issue, Series, Department, Interview, Editorial, News Story, Learned Article, and Fiction; Publications for Children: Design-Cover Design, Artwork, Education Photograph, Picture Story, and Design Treatment - Article, Contents Page, and Whole Publication; and Publications for Children: Editorial and Design-Annual Report, Special Publication, Sponsored Publication, Video (Promotional or Service), and Viewbook. There is no limit to the number of awards granted within most categories. While criteria differ according to category, the overriding goal of the judges is to recognize and reward distinguished journalistic

achievement in service to education. Presented during the annual conference of the Association.

• 5664 • EdPress Honor Awards - Best Newsletter

To recognize newsletters that combine timely, informative reporting in tight, colorful, and readable prose with attractive, functional, consistent typography and a pleasing graphic look. Members of the Association are eligible. Two issues must be submitted. Awarded annually.

• 5665 • EdPress Honor Awards - Golden Lamp Award

This, the highest award of the EPAA, is given for an achievement of towering significance in the field of educational journalism. The award is given to a publication and its staff for significant and excellent achievement. Members of the Association are eligible. Entrants must send three consecutive issues to demonstrate consistency. The Golden Lamp plaque is awarded annually. Established in 1967. Contact Doug Ferguson at dferguson@edpress.org.

• 5666 • EdPress Honor Awards - Golden Shoestring

To recognize a serial publication that consistently demonstrates excellence in educational journalism despite working from very limited resources. To accommodate the range of educational publications, the judging criteria are broad and include overall writing and design quality. Entrants must send three consecutive issues to demonstrate consistency and include both a statement of up to 200 words describing why the publication should win and a description of resources called for on the entry form.

• 5667 • EdPress Honor Awards - Most Improved Publication

To recognize the publication that demonstrates obvious and concerted progress in the standards and quality of its editorial and graphic treatment over time, with excellence a hallmark of the most recent issue. Members of the Association are eligible. Entrants must send two separate issues that span a maximum of two years, the first of which shows the baseline before improvement. In the Most Improved Publication category, judges evaluate all entries competitively and determine only one award recipient each year.

• 5668 • Laurence B. Johnson Award

To recognize superior editorial writing in a periodical in the field of educational publishing during the year. Members of the Association and non-members who pay a fee are eligible. The deadline is early February each year. A certificate is awarded annually. Established in 1971 in honor of Laurence B. Johnson, former president and secretary-treasurer of the Association.

• 5669 •

Association of Energy Engineers
Ruth Marie, Dir.Info.Svcs.
4025 Pleasantdale Rd., Ste. 420
Atlanta, GA 30340-4264
Phone: (770)447-5083
Fax: (770)446-3969
E-mail: webmaster@aeecenter.org
Home Page: http://www.aeecenter.org

• 5670 • International Awards

To recognize achievers who have national or international prominence in the field of energy engineering. Candidates for awards may be nominated by themselves, another individual, chapter, or by officers of the association as long as they are members in good standing. The entry deadline is March 1. Awards are presented in the following categories: Energy Engineer of the Year, Corporate Energy Manager of the Year, Energy Professional Development of the Year, Energy Manager of the Year, Energy Executive of the Year, Energy Project of the Year-National, Energy Project of the Year-International, Environmental Project of the Year.

• 5671 •

Association of Engineering Geologists
Becky Roland, Ch. Staff Exec.
PO Box 460518
Denver, CO 80246
Phone: (303)757-2926
Fax: (303)757-2969
E-mail: aeg@aegweb.org
Home Page: http://www.aegweb.org

• 5672 • AEG Publication Award

For recognition of the person presenting the most outstanding paper published in any AEG publication during the fiscal year. A framed certificate is presented annually at the banquet. Established in 1968.

• 5673 • Claire P. Holdredge Award

For recognition of an outstanding contribution by a member of the association to the literature of the past five years that has had a wide impact on the engineering geology profession or in activities related to engineering geology. A plaque is awarded annually at the banquet when merited. Established in 1962 to honor Claire P. Holdredge, a founding member and first president of the association.

• 5674 • Richard H. Jahns Distinguished Lecturer in Engineering Geology Award

To provide funding for a distinguished Engineering Geologist to present an annual series of lectures at academic institutions, in order to increase awareness of students about careers in Engineering Geology. The award consists of a framed certificate and an honorarium presented at the Annual Banquet preceding the award year. Established in 1988 in co-sponsorship with Geological Society of America.

• 5675 • Floyd T. Johnston Service Award

To honor a member for outstanding, long, and faithful service to the association. An engraved plaque is awarded annually when merited. Established in 1982 to honor Floyd T. Johnston, the first executive director of the association.

• 5676 • Outstanding Environmental and Engineering Geologic Project Award

To recognize a project that displays national or international significance, demonstrates the application of the principles of environmental and engineering geology to the solution of a problem affecting the public, shows recognition of and respect for the environment and society, and provides an opportunity for public education in environmental and engineering geology, environmental issues, and the culture and history of the area. A cast bronze plaque to be placed near the project and a metal photo reproduced plate on a walnut plaque are awarded at the Annual Meeting when merited. Established in 1993.

• 5677 • Douglas R. Piteau Outstanding Young Member Award

To recognize an individual for technical accomplishments, service to the association, and/or service to the engineering geology profession. Members who are 35 years of age or less are eligible. Established in 1985 to honor Doublas R. Piteau, who distinguished himself early in his career as an expert on landslides and rock slope stability.

• 5678 • Special Awards

To recognize an individual who has performed an outstanding contribution to AEG or to the profession of engineering geology in general. An award of appreciation is presented by the President at the annual business luncheon.

• 5679 • Student Professional Paper

To recognize student members of the association for papers judged to be of merit and prepared in the style of the *AEG/GSA Environmental & Engineering Geoscience Journal*. Awards are presented for graduates and undergraduates. A monetary award, a certificate, and publication of the paper in the winter issue of the *AEG/GSA Environmental & Engineering Geoscience Journal* are awarded annually. Established in 1980.

• 5680 •

Association of Field Ornithologists
Eugene S. Morton, Pres.
PO Box 1897
Laboratory of Ornithology
159 Sapsucker Woods Rd.
Lawrence, KS 66044-1897
Home Page: http://www.afonet.org

Formerly: (1986) Northeastern Bird-Banding Association.

• 5681 • Bergstrom Research Award

To promote field studies of birds by helping to support a specific research or analysis project.

In judging among proposals of equal quality, special consideration is given to those on avian life history that use data collected all or in part by amateurs, or that employ bird-banding or other marking techniques. Amateurs or students below the level of Ph.D. who are beginning their research careers or have limited or no access to major funding are eligible. Applications are particularly encouraged from Latin America. The application deadline is January 15. Several monetary awards of approximately $500 each are presented annually. Established to honor E. Alexander Bergstrom's contributions to ornithology.

• 5682 •
Association of Film Commissioners International
Bill Lindstrom, CEO
PO Box 1419
314 N Main St., 3rd Fl.
Helena, MT 59601
Phone: (406)495-8040
Fax: (406)495-8039
E-mail: info@afci.org
Home Page: http://www.afci.org

• 5683 • **Dutch Horton Award**
To recognize the person who has done the most to promote the film commission movement. Members and supporters are eligible. A Silver Bowl is awarded annually at the convention. Established in 1982 in memory of Dutch Horton, first location scout.

• 5684 • **Arthur Loew Jr. Crystal Vision Award**
To recognize an AFCI Film Commissioner or staff member for creating, developing and implementing a project, program, or activity which imparts a significant beneficial impact on the future of the AFCI.

• 5685 •
Association of Food Journalists
Carol DeMasters, Exec.Dir.
38309 Genesee Lake Rd.
Oconomowoc, WI 53066
Phone: (262)965-3251
E-mail: carolafj@execpc.com
Home Page: http://www.afjonline.com

• 5686 • **AFJ Awards Competition**
To recognize excellence in food writing and graphics. Awards are presented in 10 categories: Best Newspaper Food Section; Food News Reporting; Food Feature Reporting; Food Column Writing; Restaurant Criticism; Series, Special Sections & Special Projects; Best Food Feature in a Magazine; Best Food Coverage on the Internet; Best Studio Food Photography; and Best Non-Studio Food Photography. Prizes in 22 category subdivisions are certificates plus $300 for first place, $200 for second place, and $100 for third place. Entry deadline is March 1. Held annually. Established in 1987.

• 5687 •
Association of Former Agents of the U.S. Secret Service
PO Box 4317
P O Box 4317
Leesburg, VA 20177-8425
Phone: (410)975-0120
Toll-Free: 877-392-4368
Home Page: http://www.oldstar.org

• 5688 • **Explorer Award**
Award of recognition. Additional information not available.

• 5689 • **Law Enforcement Award**
Award of recognition. Inquire for additional information.

• 5690 •
Association of Fraternity Advisors
Sue Kraft-Fussell, Exec.Dir.
9640 N Augusta Dr., Ste. 433
Carmel, IN 46032
Phone: (317)876-1632
Fax: (317)876-3981
E-mail: info@fraternityadvisors.org
Home Page: http://www.fraternityadvisors.org

• 5691 • **AFA Perspectives Award**
To recognize outstanding original articles published in the official AFA publication, *Perspectives.* The deadline is September 1. A plaque is awarded when merited at the convention. Established in 1988. Formerly: AFA Newsletter Award.

• 5692 • **Jack L. Anson Award**
To recognize those professionals outside the field of higher education who have provided outstanding support of fraternity/sorority affairs. Nominations must be submitted by September 1. A plaque is awarded annually at the convention in December. Established in 1982 in honor of Jack L. Anson, Phi Kappa Tau, upon his retirement as Executive Director of the National Interfraternity Conference.

• 5693 • **Distinguished Service Award**
To recognize college student personnel professionals who have exhibited high professional standards and achievements in fraternity/sorority advising as well as outstanding achievement in one or more of the following areas: programming affecting the recipient's specific campus; programming reaching beyond the recipient's specific campus; research; and writing. Nominations must be submitted by September 1. Current Officers of AFA and Awards Committee Members are not eligible. A monetary award and a plaque are presented to each AFA region (maximum of four). Awarded annually at the convention in December. Established in 1985.

• 5694 • **Robert H. Shaffer Award**
To recognize college student personnel professionals who have provided outstanding support to fraternity/sorority affairs by their involvement, mentoring, and personal example. Nominations must be submitted by September 1. A plaque is awarded annually at the convention in December. Established in 1980 in honor of Robert H. Shaffer, Professor Emeritus, Indiana University.

• 5695 •
Association of Free Community Papers
Craig S. McMullin, Exec.Dir.
1634 Miner
PO Box 1989
Idaho Springs, CO 80452
Toll-Free: 877-203-2327
Fax: (781)459-7770
E-mail: afcp@afcp.org
Home Page: http://www.afcp.org

Formerly: (1987) National Association of Advertising Publishers.

• 5696 • **Distinguished Service Award**
To recognize an outstanding contribution to the Association and the free paper industry over a period of years. Association publisher members are eligible. A plaque is awarded annually at the annual convention.

• 5697 • **Publisher of the Year**
For recognition of an outstanding contribution to the Association and the industry throughout the year. Association members are eligible. A plaque is awarded annually at the annual meeting. Established in 1966.

• 5698 •
Association of Fundraising Professionals
Colette M. Murray JD, Chair
1101 King St., Ste. 700
Alexandria, VA 22314
Phone: (703)684-0410
Toll-Free: 800-666-FUND
Fax: (703)684-0540
E-mail: mnilsen@afpnet.org
Home Page: http://www.afpnet.org

• 5699 • **Campbell & Company Award for Excellence in Fundraising**
Recognizes not-for-profit organizations' development departments or fund-raising programs that have developed an innovative initiative, program or project design, or technique that has increased their donor base, increased the amount of fund raised, and improved their fundraising return on investment. Also promotes the sharing of ideas for improving fund-raising operations and return on investment among not-for-profit organizations. Awarded annually. Formerly: (2004) AFP Award for Excellence in Fund Raising.

• 5700 • **Community Counselling Service Award for Outstanding Fundraising Professional**
To recognize outstanding individual fundraising professionals who practice their profession in an ethical manner. Criteria considered are: length and tenure of fundraising background and experience; demonstrated quality of leadership that is persuasive, effective, creative, and stimulat-

ing, and that illustrates their best as a team member; practice of the Code of Ethics and Professional Practices for fundraising executives; display of a commitment to voluntarism and a desire for professional improvement, verified participation in conferences, publication of articles, and presentation of speeches concerning the advancement of philanthropy; and participation and collaboration with other nonprofit organizations. The deadline for nominations is September 15. A plaque is presented annually at the AFP International Conference on Fund Raising. Established in 1980. Sponsored by Community Counselling Service. Formerly: (2004) Outstanding Fund Raising Executive Award.

• 5701 • Founders' Award for Public Service
Recognizes AFP chapters for their outstanding public service endeavors. Presented annually at the AFP International Conference on Fund Raising. Established in 1992.

• 5702 • Abel Hanson Awards Program
To recognize AFP chapters that provide regular and effective communication with members, prospective members, foundations, and other nonprofit organizations, corporations, legislator, regulators, and other constituents involved in the philanthropic process, as well as the general public. For awards are given annually, one for each chapter size category. Application deadline is September 15. Established in 1984 in honor of Dr. Able Hanson, first president of the Society.

• 5703 • Ketchum Award for Outstanding Volunteer Fundraiser
To recognize an individual or family for exceptional skills in coordinating and motivating groups of volunteers for fundraising projects for the benefit of charitable institutions, and for demonstrating a commitment to the advancement of philanthropy. A plaque is presented annually at the AFP International Conference on Fund Raising. Established in 1980. Formerly: (2004) Outstanding Volunteer Fund Raiser Award.

• 5704 • Paschal Murray Award for Outstanding Philanthropist
For recognition of individuals or families whose exceptional generosity encourages other individuals, companies, or foundations to take philanthropic leadership roles on a community, national, and/or international level. A plaque is presented annually at the AFP International Conference on Fund Raising. Established in 1980. Formerly: (2004) Outstanding Philanthropist Award.

• 5705 • Outstanding Corporation Award
For recognition of a corporation or its corporate foundation that demonstrates outstanding commitment through financial support and through encouragement and motivation of others to take leadership roles toward philanthropy and community involvement. The deadline for nominations is September 15. Established in 1989.

• 5706 • Outstanding Foundation Award
For recognition of outstanding commitment by a foundation through financial support and through encouragement and motivation of others to take leadership roles toward philanthropy and/or community involvement. The deadline for nomination is September 15. Established in 1989.

• 5707 •
Association of Government Accountants
Relmond Van Daniker Jr., EXE.DRC.
2208 Mount Vernon Ave.
Alexandria, VA 22301-1314
Phone: (703)684-6931
Toll-Free: 800-AGA-7211
Fax: (703)548-9367
E-mail: cculkin@agacgfm.org
Home Page: http://www.agacgfm.org/

• 5708 • Achievement of the Year Award
To give national recognition for leadership or outstanding achievement in developing, implementing, and improving financial management in government service. Individuals in government service, who are not necessarily members of the Association, are eligible. Service must have provided with the last year. A plaque and formal citation are awarded annually. Additional information is available on the Association's web site.

• 5709 • Author's Award
To recognize the best written articles appearing in the *Government Accountants Journal* during the previous calendar year. Awarded annually. Winners are selected by the Journal Editorial Committee.

• 5710 • Andy Barr Award
To recognize financial executives in the private sector who exemplify and promote excellence in governmental financial management, outstanding leadership, high ethical standards, and innovative management techniques. The award recognizes the cumulative achievements of private sector professionals who, throughout their career, have served as a role model for others and have consistently exhibited the highest personal and professional standards. The individual nominated must have been employed in the private sector at the time the work was performed. Nominees do not have to be members of AGA. A crystal award is presented. Nominations are accepted by AGA chapters, individuals, or government units. One original and 12 copies of the following must be submitted: contact information; nominee's biographical sketch; award justification; and citation. Additional information is available on the Association's web site. Application deadline is November 9th.

• 5711 • Chapter Service Award
To recognize individuals who have made outstanding contributions to the development and enhancement of an AGA Chapter. All active chapter members are eligible. Plaques are awarded annually. Application criteria is available on the Association's web site.

• 5712 • Distinguished Local Government Leadership Award
To recognize state and local government officials who exemplify and promote excellence in government management and have demonstrated outstanding leadership in enhancing sound financial management legislation, regulations, practices, policies, and systems. Nominees need not be members of AGA but must have served in a local government position at the time of contribution. A maximum of two crystal awards are presented annually.

• 5713 • Education and Training Awards
To recognize individuals who have made significant contributions to the education and training of governmental financial managers. Nominees need not be members of the Association or government employees. Nominees must have developed and/or presented education and training sessions that clearly have had a significant impact on governmental financial management, or advanced the state-of-the-art of governmental financial management. A crystal award is presented annually at the Association's annual Professional Development Conference. Twelve collated copies of the following must be submitted: contact information, including nominee's name and designations, position and title, address and phone number, and nominee's education and biographical sketch of the nominee's description of accomplishments. Total page should not exceed five pages. Application deadline is March 8th.

• 5714 • Excellence in Government Leadership Award
To recognize state and local government professionals who exemplify and promote excellence in government, outstanding leadership, high ethical standards, and innovative management procedures. Nominees need not be members of AGA but must have been a government employee when recognized work was performed. Nominations are accepted by AGA chapters, individuals, or government units. A crystal award is presented annually.

• 5715 • Frank Greathouse Distinguished Leadership Award
To recognize individuals in government service (federal, state, and local) who have provided sustained outstanding leadership in financial management over a period of years, resulting in a notable contribution to financial management. The awardees need not be members of the Association. Application deadline is March 8th. See the Association's web site for additional information. Crystal award is awarded annually.

• 5716 • Robert W. King Memorial Award
Recognizes a member of the Association for distinguished service of such significance as to have enhanced the Association's national prestige and stature. Crystal cube is awarded annually. Nominations are accepted from chapter (one per chapter) or individuals. One original and 12 copies of the following must be submitted: Nominator's signature, address and phone number; nominee's name and designa-

tions, positions and title and address and phone number; a biographical sketch; description of accomplishments and results of achievement. Nomination packet should not exceed five pages. Application deadline is March 8th.

• 5717 • National President's Awards
To recognize individuals who have made extraordinary contributions to the success of the Association's programs during a president's term of office. Awarded when merited as selected by the National president.

• 5718 • Newsletter Awards
To recognize the best newsletter in each of the five chapter groups. Awarded annually. Award details, including judging criteria are distributed to each chapter annually.

• 5719 • Private Sector Financial Excellence Award
To recognize financial executives in the private sector who exemplify and promote excellence in state or local government, financial management, outstanding leadership, high ethical standards, and innovative management techniques. Nominees need not be members of AGA. A maximum of two plaques are awarded annually.

• 5720 • Research Achievement Awards
To recognize distinguished achievements in government financial management research. Applicants may be individuals or organizations whose contribution has been completed within two years of nomination. Recipients enhance the image and effectiveness of government accountants, auditors, and financial managers by their efforts. Awards were given for basic research applied research, and education. One crystal award is given annually. Nomination package including contract information: a biographical sketch of the hominec; a description of the accomplishments being nominated and a citation to use for the award must be submitted by March 8th. See the above web site for more information.

• 5721 • Special Achievement Award
To give national recognition to younger AGA members for notable contributions toward improving financial management. Members of AGA under the age of 35 are eligible. A Crystal award is presented annually. Nominations are accepted from AGA Chapters. One original and twelve copies of the following must be submitted: contact information; biographical sketch of the nominee; description of accomplishments; results of accomplishments; and a citation. Additional information on each required segment is available on the Associate's web site. Application deadline is March 8th.

• 5722 • Elmer Staats Award
To recognize federal professionals who exemplify and promote: excellence in government, outstanding leadership, high ethical standards, and innovative management procedures. The award recognizes the cumulative achievements of federal professionals who throughout their public career have served as a role model for others and consistently exhibited the highest personal and professional standards. The individual nominated must have been employed by the federal government at the time the work was performed. Nominees do not have to be members of AGA. A crystal award is presented. Nominations are accepted by AGA chapters, individuals, or government units. One original and 12 copies of the following must be submitted: contact information; nominee's biographical sketch; award justification; and citation. Additional information is available on the Association's web site. Application deadline is November 9th.

• 5723 •
Association of Home Office Underwriters
Roland Paradis, Pres.
% Roland Paradis, Pres.
Lincoln Financial Group
350 Church St.
MBR 1
Hartford, CT 06103
Phone: (860)466-1247
E-mail: rgparadis@lnc.com
Home Page: http://registeredusers.loma.org/AHOU/AHOUcontent/welcome.cfm

• 5724 • Emmett Russell, Jr. Award
To recognize the professionalism of life underwriters who have made significant contributions to the field of risk selection and/or to the life insurance industry. Individual life underwriters, past or present, who have made valuable and lasting contributions to the risk selection process or related fields are eligible. A sterling silver bowl is awarded annually at the convention. Established in 1986 to honor Emmett Russell, Jr. For further information, contact Maureen B. Moreau.

• 5725 •
Association of Indians in America
Susheem Mehta, Contact
2 Debra Ct.
Old Westbury, NY 11568
E-mail: info@aianewyork.org
Home Page: http://www.aianewyork.org/

• 5726 • Honor Award
For recognition of unique contributions to arts and letters and to greater understanding between the people of India and the United States, and for recognition of creative entrepreneurship and business leadership. Residents of the United States may be nominated. The nominations are reviewed by a Committee. A plaque is awarded annually at the National Honor Banquet in the spring. Established in 1973. Additional information is available from Professor S.K. Saxena, (312) 953-1916.

• 5727 •
Association of Industrial Metallizers, Coaters and Laminators
Craig S. Sheppard, Exec.Dir.
2166 Gold Hill Rd.
Fort Mill, SC 29708
Phone: (803)802-7820
Fax: (803)802-7821
E-mail: aimcal@aimcal.org
Home Page: http://www.aimcal.org

• 5728 • Metallized Package/Label of the Year
To recognize technical or marketing excellence in packages or labels which use metallized substrates. Awards given in snack foods, other foods, non foods, health care, cosmetics, and toiletries—but only one package/label award.

• 5729 • Technology of the Year
To recognize AIMCAL member organizations for outstanding practical technical developments. Awarded annually with a trophy (returned each year) and a plaque.

• 5730 •
Association of Information Technology Professionals
Ernie Stewart, Exec.Dir.
401 N Michigan Ave., Ste. 2400
PO Box 809189
Chicago, IL 60611-4267
Phone: (312)245-1070
Toll-Free: 800-224-9371
Fax: (312)527-6636
E-mail: aitp_hq@aitp.org
Home Page: http://www.aitp.org
Formerly: Data Processing Management Association.

• 5731 • Distinguished Information Sciences Award
To recognize an individual for outstanding contributions to the information processing industry. Nominations must be made by AITP members but the award is not limited to members. The final selection is made by the AITP Executive Council. A bronze etched plaque and an honorary lifetime membership in the Association are bestowed annually at the AITP Conference and Business Exposition. Established in 1969. Additional information is available from AITP. Formerly: (1979) Computer Sciences Man of the Year.

• 5732 • Information Processing Public Service Award
To recognize public officials who have taken a leadership role on issues impacting the information management field. Members of the legislative or executive branch of the federal or state government are eligible. A plaque is awarded annually. Established in 1986.

• 5733 •
Association of International Health Researchers
Dr. Roy E. Kadel, Pres.
2665 Pleasant Valley Rd.
Mobile, AL 36606
Phone: (251)473-3946
Fax: (251)478-0022

• 5734 • **William D. Godbey Award**
For recognition of superb achievement in health research. Nominations may be submitted and approved by the membership. A trophy is awarded annually. Established in 1985 in honor of Dr. William D. Godbey, a health care researcher.

• 5735 •
Association of Jesuit Colleges and Universities
Rev. Charles L. Currie SJ, Pres.
One Dupont Cir. NW, Ste. 405
Washington, DC 20036
Phone: (202)862-9893
Fax: (202)862-8523
E-mail: office@ajcunet.edu
Home Page: http://www.ajcunet.edu

• 5736 • **Alpha Sigma Nu National Jesuit Book Award**
To honor outstanding publishing achievement by faculty and staff, of the 28 Jesuit colleges and universities in the United States. Any non-fiction book of high academic standards is eligible. The deadline for entries is March 1. Four monetary awards of $1,000 each and plaques are presented annually. Winners are announced on October 1. Established in 1980. Sponsored by Alpha Sigma Nu, the National Jesuit Honor Society. Additional information is available from AJCU One Dupont Circle, Ste. 405, Washington, DC. 20036.

• 5737 •
Association of Jewish Center Professionals
Harvey Rosenzweig, Exec.Dir.
15 E 26th St.
New York, NY 10010-1579
Phone: (212)786-5154
Phone: (212)786-5155
Fax: (212)481-4174
E-mail: info@ajcp.org
Home Page: http://www.ajcp.org

• 5738 • **Professional of the Year Award**
To recognize outstanding practice in community center work and to promote community center work. Two awards are presented; one to an individual who has given 5-15 years continuous service, and the other to an individual serving more than 15 years. Membership in AJCP is required. A plaque and gift are presented at the biennial meeting. Established in 1982. Formerly: Professional of the Year.

• 5739 •
Association of Jewish Libraries
Ronda Rose, Pres.
15 E 26th St., Rm. 1034
New York, NY 10010-1579
Phone: (212)725-5359
E-mail: ajl@jewishbooks.org
Home Page: http://www.jewishlibraries.org

• 5740 • **The AJL Scholarship for Library School Students**
To help pay the library school tuition of library or Jewish studies students who promise to be Judaica librarians. Formerly: (1997) Dr. May K. Simon Memorial Scholarship.

• 5741 • **Association of Jewish Libraries Reference Book Award**
To acknowledge the best reference work in Judaic studies/librarianship. A monetary award of $500 and a plaque are awarded. Established in 1985. Formerly: Harold Mason Reference Award; Research and Special Libraries Award.

• 5742 • **Doris Orenstein Memorial Fund**
To enable a first-time attendee (member) who is unfunded, to attend the annual AJL convention. Monetary awards of $150 each for up to two winners are awarded annually. The award honors Doris Orenstein, a children's book vendor and informal consultant of Jewish children's books.

• 5743 • **Sydney Taylor Body of Work Award**
To recognize an author or illustrator for outstanding, cumulative contributions to the field of children's literature. Books with a Jewish content and high literary merit are considered. A monetary award of $1,000 and a plaque are awarded as merited. Established in 1978 in memory of Sydney Taylor, the author of the All-of-a-Kind Family books.

• 5744 • **Sydney Taylor Children's Book Awards**
To select the book or books, upper elementary and picture, deemed to have made the most outstanding contribution to young people during the year of publication. Awards are presented in two categories: Younger Children's Book Award and Older Children's Book Award. A monetary award of $1,000 each, a plaque and award seals are awarded annually. Established in 1968 in memory of Sydney Taylor, the author of the All-of-a-Kind Family books. Formerly: (1985) Children's Book Award.

• 5745 • **Sydney Taylor Manuscript Competition**
To recognize the author of an original fiction manuscript with Jewish content and universal appeal for children from eight to twelve years of age. Authors who have not previously published a book are eligible for manuscripts between 60-200 pages. A monetary award of $1,000 is presented annually when merited at the National Convention. Established in 1985 in memory of Sydney Taylor, the author of the All-of-a-Kind Family books.

• 5746 •
Association of Late-Deafened Adults
Lois Maroney, Pres.
1131 Lake St., No. 204
Oak Park, IL 60301
Toll-Free: 877-907-1738
Fax: 877-907-1738
E-mail: board@alda.org
Home Page: http://www.alda.org

• 5747 • **Able ALDA Award**
To recognize the ALDA member of the year. An individual who goes way beyond the call of duty in furthering the development of ALDA is eligible. A plaque is awarded annually at the convention. Established in 1991.

• 5748 • **ALDA Angel Award**
To recognize an individual or organization that provides needed support, services or funding to ALDA. A plaque is awarded annually at the convention. Established in 1990.

• 5749 • **Bob Hawley Fearless Leader Award**
To recognize an ALDA chapter or group leader who displays superior leadership in advancing, maintaining or establishing an ALDA chapter or group. A plaque is awarded annually at the convention. Established in 1990.

• 5750 •
Association of Lunar and Planetary Observers
Richard W. Schmude Jr., Exec.Dir.
PO Box 13456
Springfield, IL 62791-3456
E-mail: will008@attglobal.net
Home Page: http://www.lpl.arizona.edu/alpo

• 5751 • **Walter H. Haas Award**
For recognition of excellence in observational amateur astronomy and contributions to scientific knowledge. Selection is by nomination. A plaque is awarded annually at the convention. Established in 1984 and named for Walter H. Haas, founder, first director, and director emeritus of the Association. Additional information is available from Walter H. Haas, 2225 Thomas Drive, Las Cruces, NM 88001.

• 5752 •
Association of Management/International Association of Management
Karin Klenke PhD, Co-Founder/Chair/CEO
PO Box 64841
Virginia Beach, VA 23467-4841
Phone: (757)482-2273
Fax: (757)482-0325
E-mail: aomgt@inter-source.org
Home Page: http://www.aom-iaom.org

• 5753 • Outstanding Professional Service Award

Recognizes professional service contributions to the association. Awarded annually.

• 5754 • The Ram Award

Award of recognition for professional service contributions to the association. Awarded annually.

• 5755 •
Association of Medical Illustrators
Janet McAndless, Exec.Dir.
245 1st St., Ste. 1800
Cambridge, MA 02142
Phone: (617)395-8186
Fax: (719)599-3075
E-mail: hq@ami.org
Home Page: http://www.ami.org

• 5756 • AMI Salon Awards

For recognition of outstanding achievement in the field of medical illustration. Awards may be presented in the following categories: Member's Choice Award, Ralph Sweet Award (voted by active membership); Fine Arts, Muriel McLatchie Miller Award (voted by active membership) - established in 1985; Medical Continuous Tone, Max Broedel Award; Medical Line, Russell Drake Award; Medical Color, Will Shephard Award; Projection Media; 3-Dimensional, Charlotte Holt Award; Exhibit Design, Tom Jones Award; Editorial Illustration; Advertising Illustration; Medical-Legal Illustration; Medical Book; Student Best of Show, Orville Parks Award; Student Medical Tone; Student Medical Line; Student Medical Color; Student Editorial; Student Advertising; Student 3-Dimensional; Student Exhibit Design; and Student Projection Media. Members are eligible. Awards of excellence and certificates of merit are awarded annually. Established in 1978.

• 5757 • Lifetime Achievement Award

To honor an AMI member who has made outstanding contributions to the profession of medical illustration. Awarded annually.

• 5758 • Literary Award

To recognize the best written contribution to the *Journal of Biocommunication* by a member.

• 5759 • Outstanding Service Award

To recognize an active or associate member who has served the AMI in an official capacity and deserves special recognition. Recipients are chosen by secret ballot of the awards committee and the executive committee. No more than two awards are presented in any given year.

• 5760 •
Association of Military Colleges and Schools of the United States
Dr. Lewis Sorley, Exec.Dir.
9429 Garden Ct.
Potomac, MD 20854-3964
Phone: (301)765-0695
Fax: (301)983-0583
E-mail: sorleydog@earthlink.net
Home Page: http://www.amcsus.org

• 5761 • AMCSUS President's Medal

To recognize the outstanding cadet in each member college or school. Graduating seniors are eligible. Medals with an accompanying ribbon for wear on the uniform are awarded annually in the spring or at commencement at AMCSUS-member colleges and schools. Established in 1963. Available only to graduates of member colleges or schools.

• 5762 •
Association of Military Surgeons of the United States
RADM Ret. Frederic G. Sanford MC USN, Exec.Dir.
9320 Old Georgetown Rd.
Bethesda, MD 20814
Phone: (301)897-8800
Toll-Free: 800-761-9320
Fax: (301)530-5446
E-mail: amsus@amsus.org
Home Page: http://www.amsus.org

• 5763 • AMSUS Award for Excellence in Clinical Pharmacy Practice

To recognize the leadership role of federal pharmacists who are transforming the pharmacy practice by working in a safe, efficacious, and cost-effective manner to optimize pharmacotherapies. A plaque and an honorarium are awarded. Established in 1991.

• 5764 • AMSUS Medical Student Award

To honor a medical student at USUHS for exceptionally meritorious achievements. An honorarium and a plaque are awarded annually. Established in 1980.

• 5765 • Joel T. Boone Award

In recognition of outstanding service to the Association. Members are eligible. Nominations must be submitted by May 31. An honorarium and a bronze plaque are awarded annually. Established in 1969 to honor Vice Admiral Joel T. Boone, MC USN Ret., Chief Medical Director of the Veterans Administration, personal physician to three presidents of the United States, recipient of the Congressional Medal of Honor, and President of the Association in 1949.

• 5766 • Ray E. Brown Award

For recognition of outstanding accomplishments in federal health care management. An honorarium and a plaque are awarded annually. Established in 1975 to honor Ray E. Brown, who played a major role in health care administration training.

• 5767 • John D. Chase Award for Physician Executive Excellence

To recognize a physician who has exhibited sustained outstanding performance and leadership in an executive position. A plaque is awarded annually. Established in 1992.

• 5768 • Clinical Nursing Excellence Award

To recognize and honor accomplishments and work performance in clinical nursing, resulting in contributions of an outstanding nature by a nurse, which have had substantial impact on the mission of a federal health agency. An honorarium and a plaque are presented to the recipient during the annual AMSUS meeting. Established in 1989.

• 5769 • Andrew Craigie Award

In recognition of outstanding accomplishment in the advancement of professional pharmacy within the federal government. An honorarium and a silver plaque are awarded annually. Established in 1959 to honor Andrew Craigie, the first Apothecary General of the United States, who served under George Washington during the Revolutionary War.

• 5770 • Federal Nursing Service Award

To recognize a professional nurse from the Federal Nursing Services who has submitted an original paper on the results of a study or scholarly paper that would have an impact on nursing. An honorarium and a scroll are awarded annually.

• 5771 • Founder's Medal

In recognition of outstanding contributions to military medicine and meritorious service to the Association. Members are eligible. A scroll and a medal are awarded annually. Established in 1941 to commemorate the 50th Anniversary of the Association.

• 5772 • Gorgas Medal

In recognition of distinguished work in preventive medicine. An honorarium, a medal, and a scroll are awarded annually. Established in 1942 in memory of Mayor General William Crawford Gorgas, whose work in preventive medicine made possible the construction of the Panama Canal.

• 5773 • Philip Hench Award

In recognition of outstanding contributions in the field of rheumatology and arthritis. Physicians in the federal medical services are eligible. An honorarium and a plaque are awarded annually. Established in 1966 in memory of Doctor Philip S. Hench, who first used cortisone in the treatment of arthritis.

• 5774 • Richard A. Kern Lecture Award

To recognize an AMSUS member or a person eligible for membership. The Program Committee selects the lecturer and the subject. An honorarium and a scroll are awarded. Established in 1979 to honor Rear Admiral Richard A. Kern,

Professor of Medicine, Emeritus, Temple University School of Medicine.

• 5775 • James A. McCallam Award

To recognize a Doctor of Veterinary Medicine for outstanding accomplishments in the field of medicine and health. Nominations are encouraged. An honorarium and a plaque are presented. This award honors the late Brigadier General James A. McCallam, a former Chief, United States Army Veterinary Corps and the first Washington Representative of the American Veterinary Medical Association.

• 5776 • Walter P. McHugh Award

This award is to be presented to a Medical Service Corps Officer of the Army, Navy or Air Force, or equivalent employee of the Department of Veteran Affairs or U.S. Public Health Service holding the grade of 0-1 to 0-4 and having not yet reached the age of 40 by the submission deadline. All nominees must be AMSUS members or eligible for membership. A plaque is awarded annually. Established in 1994.

• 5777 • New York Chapter History of Military Medicine Essay Award

To recognize an outstanding essay on some aspect of the history and evolution of military medicine. The essay topic is not limited to United States armed forces military medicine. Open to all AMSUS members and to individuals eligible for membership. A plaque and an honorarium are awarded. Established in 1991. Sponsored by the New York Chapter of AMSUS.

• 5778 • Outstanding Federal Services Health Administrator Award

To recognize a Medical Service Corps officer of the Army, Navy, Air Force, or a health care specialist of the Public Health Service or Department of Veterans Affairs for a conspicuously outstanding contribution in the field of medical administration. Members are eligible. Nominations are encouraged. An honorarium and a plaque are presented. Established in 1983.

• 5779 • Outstanding Medical Information Management Executive Award

Award is presented to a Senior Healthcare Executive (O-5 and above or civilian equivalent) in the Army, Navy, Air Force, U.S. Public Health Service, or Department of Veterans Affairs who has made outstanding contributions to Federal HealthCare through demonstrated superior leadership and visionary management ability in the area of medical information management, data quality, decision support, knowledge management, and/or business reengineering to capitalize on the value of new applications and technology.

• 5780 • Physician Assistant Award

To recognize outstanding professional service, achievement, and accomplishments by a physician assistant in the federal health services. Individuals who are members of AMSUS or eligible for membership may be nominated. Individuals must be certified and must be actively employed as physician assistants. The award includes a plaque and an honorarium. Established in 1989.

• 5781 • William C. Porter Lecture Award

To honor an individual for an outstanding contribution to the field of psychiatry. An honorarium, a scroll, and the presentation of a lecture are awarded annually. Established in 1958 to honor Colonel William C. Porter, a pioneer in military psychiatry.

• 5782 • Carl A. Schlack Award

For recognition of outstanding service in dental research and education by a federal dentist of one of the five federal medical services. An honorarium and a plaque are awarded annually. Established in 1971 to honor Captain Carl A. Schlack, DC USN Ret., whose accomplishments initiated and firmly established dental research in the Navy.

• 5783 • Lewis L. Seaman Awards for Oustanding Operational Support

Award named for the late Major Lewis L. Seaman, a surgeon of the First U.S. Volunteers, Spanish American War. Awards are presented to Active Duty, Reserved or Guard enlisted professional of the Army, Navy, Air Force or Coast Guard who have exhibited outstanding accomplishments in advancing the healthcare mission of their service through demonstrated compassionate and quality patient care and service, clinical support or healthcare management.

• 5784 • Colonel Thomas L. Spruiell Medical Field Training Excersize Planner Award

Awards honors an officer of the Army, Navy, Air Force or equivalent employee of the Department of Veternas Affairs or U.S. Public Health Service for outstanding accomplishments in the area of Total Force medical field training excercise planning. Award offered to AMSUS members only. A plaque and monetary award are presented.

• 5785 • Edward Rhodes Stitt Lecture Award

To recognize a pathologist in the field of laboratory medicine for an outstanding accomplishment. Individuals who are eligible for AMSUS membership are considered. An honorarium and a plaque are awarded. Established in 1954 to honor Rear Admiral Edward Rhodes Stitt, who played a major role in the field of military pathology. Re-established in 1978. Formerly: Stitt Award.

• 5786 • W. David Sullins Award for Outstanding Service in Optometry

To recognize members of the Association who have contributed significantly to the advancement of optometry and have provided selfless dedication, leadership, and service. A plaque is awarded annually. Established in 1993. Formerly: (2006) Optometry Outstanding Service and Recognition Award.

• 5787 • Sustaining Membership Lecture Award

In recognition of an outstanding contribution in the field of medical research. An honorarium and a scroll are awarded annually. Established in 1958. From 1958 to 1971, the Sustaining Membership Award was also given.

• 5788 • Paul F. Truran, Jr., Medical Materiel and Logistics Management Award

To recognize outstanding accomplishments in the field of medical logistics and the advancement of medical materiel management in the Department of Defense. A plaque is awarded annually. Established in 1992.

• 5789 • Sir Henry Wellcome Medal and Prize

To recognize an individual who has written an essay or report on original research dealing with the military aspects of medicine. Entries must be submitted by May 31. An honorarium and a silver medal are awarded annually at the meeting of the Association of Military Surgeons of the USA. Established in 1916 by Sir Henry Wellcome. Sponsored by the Wellcome Trust. Additional information is available from Burroughs Wellcome Co., 3030 Cornwallis Road, Research Triangle Park, NC 27709.

• 5790 • Paul Dudley White Award

To recognize an individual or group of researchers for a significant advancement in the field of cardiology that eventually will result in better health care to the people of the world. Awardees must be eligible for membership in the Association. An honorarium and a scroll are awarded annually. Established in 1977 to honor Doctor Paul Dudley White, the founder of modern cardiology.

• 5791 • Young Federal Healthcare Administrator Award

To recognize contributions to federal health care management by an American College of Hospital Administrators-affiliated person eligible for AMSUS membership. Nominations may be made by members. The candidate must not have reached his or her 40th birthday by May 31 of the award year. An honorarium and a plaque are presented. Established in 1981.

• 5792 •

Association of Municipal Recycling Coordinators
Ben Bennett, Mgr.
127 Wyndham St. N, Ste. 100
Guelph, ON, Canada N1H 4E9
Phone: (519)823-1990
Phone: (519)823-1387
Fax: (519)823-0084
E-mail: amrc@amrc.net
Home Page: http://www.amrc.guelph.org

• 5793 • AMRC P&E Awards

Recognizes municipal waste divisions with outstanding communication programs. Awarded annually.

• 5794 •
Association of New Jersey Environmental Commissions
Sally Dudley, Exec.Dir.
PO Box 157
Mendham, NJ 07945
Phone: (973)539-7547
Fax: (973)539-7713
E-mail: info@anjec.org
Home Page: http://www.anjec.org

• 5795 • **Environmental Achievement Award**
For demonstrated accomplishment in environmental field. Recognition award bestowed annually.

• 5796 •
Association of North American Radio Clubs
Dr. Harold Cones, Chm.
2 Whit Ct.
Newport News, VA 23606
E-mail: hcones@cnu.edu
Home Page: http://www.anarc.org

• 5797 • **DXer of the Year**
To recognize the individual who has done the most in the radio listening hobby for his or her fellow hobbyists. The person must be a member of one or more of the ANARC affiliated clubs. A plaque is awarded annually at the Winter SWL Festival in Kulpsville, Pennsylvania. Established in 1966. Formerly: (1997) North American Shortwave Broadcast DXer of the Year.

• 5798 •
Association of Official Racing Chemists
% Association of Racing Commissioners International
2343 Alexandria Dr., Ste. 200
Lexington, KY 40504
Phone: (859)224-7070
Fax: (859)224-7071
E-mail: aorc.mclellan@sympatico.ca
Home Page: http://www.arci.com

• 5799 • **AORC Award**
For recognition of outstanding contributions to the Association, either in academic output or in furthering the objectives of the Association. Members of the Association and other professionals working in the field of racing chemistry may be nominated by members of the Association. A plaque is awarded when merited at a convention. Established in 1957.

• 5800 •
Association of Official Seed Analysts
Janice Osburn, Exec.Asst.
PMB 411
1763 E University Blvd., Ste. A
Las Cruces, NM 88001
Phone: (505)522-1437
Fax: (505)522-1437
E-mail: aosaoffice@earthlink.net
Home Page: http://www.aosaseed.com

• 5801 • **Merit Award**
To recognize members of AOSA who have made contributions via their career activities to further the AOSA activities. Both full and associate members of AOSA are eligible. A plaque and a certificate are awarded annually. Established in 1958.

• 5802 •
Association of Oncology Social Work
Katherine Walsh-Burke PhD, Pres.
100 N 20th St., 4th Fl.
Philadelphia, PA 19103
Phone: (215)599-6093
Fax: (215)545-8107
E-mail: info@aosw.org
Home Page: http://www.aosw.org

• 5803 • **Leadership in Oncology Social Work Award**
To recognize an exceptional member of AOSW who has significantly contributed to the field of oncology social work and demonstrated leadership through administration, education, clinical practice or research. Awarded annually. Sponsored by the American Cancer Society.

• 5804 • **Oncology Social Worker of the Year**
To recognize an exceptional member of AOSW who, in the day-to-day delivery of compassionate service, is a model for the profession. Awarded annually. Sponsored by the Leukemia & Lymphoma Society.

• 5805 •
Association of Orthodox Jewish Teachers
Ruth Stillman, Exec.Dir.
1577 Coney Island Ave.
Brooklyn, NY 11230
Phone: (718)258-3585
Fax: (718)258-3585
E-mail: aojt@juno.com

• 5806 • **Association of Orthodox Jewish Teachers Awards**
To recognize outstanding educators, community leaders, and AOJT members for substantial contributions towards the work, policies, and goals of AOJT and the educational community. The following awards may be presented: AOJT Award, Organization Award, Akiva Club Award, Superintendent of the Year Award, Legislative Award, Humanitarian of the Year Award, Educator of the Year Award, Community School Board Award, and Outstanding Labor Leader Award. Awarded annually. Established in 1968.

• 5807 •
Association of Paroling Authorities International
Gail Hughes, Exec.Sec.
PO Box 211
California, MO 65018
Phone: (573)796-2113
Fax: (573)796-2114
E-mail: ghdh@aol.com
Home Page: http://www.apaintl.org/

• 5808 • **Vincent O'Leary Award**
Recognizes outstanding contributions in parole administration. Awarded annually.

• 5809 •
Association of Performing Arts Presenters
Sandra Gibson, Pres./CEO
1112 16th St. NW, Ste. 400
Washington, DC 20036
Phone: (202)833-2787
Toll-Free: 888-820-2787
Fax: (202)833-1543
E-mail: info@artspresenters.org
Home Page: http://www.artspresenters.org

• 5810 • **Dawson Awards**
To recognize creative achievement in arts administration. In past years, winning projects have included an arts education series, an arts advocacy handbook, a commissioned-works series, support for local artists and a unique collaborative publicity effort. Active or business affiliate members of the Association may submit achievements completed between September 1 of the previous year and August 31 of the award year. The deadline is October 11. Established to honor William M. Dawson for the services he provided to the field of arts administration in his 14 years as director of ACUCAA.

• 5811 • **Fannie Taylor Distinguished Service Award**
To recognize outstanding performing arts administrators who have made significant contributions to the field of presenting. Individuals who have demonstrated imaginative and beneficial innovations in the administration of the performing arts, administered performing arts programs that show a record of high achievement and excellent taste, reflect in their work a dedication to the goals of the Association, have participated in the presentation of the performing arts for a minimum of ten years, and are active in the field at the time of their nomination are eligible. The deadline for nominations is May 1. Awarded annually.

• 5812 •
Association of Personal Computer User Groups
Susy Ball, Pres.
3155 E Patrick Ln., Ste. 1
Las Vegas, NV 89120-3481
Phone: (301)423-1618
Toll-Free: 800-558-6867
E-mail: office@apcug.org
Home Page: http://www.apcug.org

• 5813 • **REACH Award**
Award of recognition. For community service by a personal computer user group. Awarded annually.

• 5814 •
The Association of Pool and Spa Professionals
Bill Weber, Pres./CEO
2111 Eisenhower Ave.
Alexandria, VA 22314
Phone: (703)838-0083
Fax: (703)549-0493
E-mail: memberservices@theapsp.org
Home Page: http://www.theapsp.org

Formerly: National Swimming Pool Institute.

• 5815 • **International Awards of Excellence**
To recognize the pool/spa and hot tub industry's most beautiful installations, to provide the industry with showcase examples of installations, and to gain media recognition of the industry and its products. Only members of APSP are eligible to enter. Awards are given in 48 categories classified by type of construction, style, size of installation, and include residential, semi-public, and public installations. Gold, silver, or bronze medals and awards of merit may be presented in each category. Application deadline is August 12. Awarded annually during the International Pool and Spa Expo. Established in 1957.

• 5816 •
Association of Private Enterprise Education
J.R. Clark, Sec.-Treas.
The University of Tennessee at Chattanooga
313 Fletcher Hall, Dept. 6106
615 McCallie Ave.
Chattanooga, TN 37403-2598
Phone: (423)425-4118
Fax: (423)425-5218
E-mail: j-clark@utc.edu
Home Page: http://www.apee.org

• 5817 • **Herman Lay Memorial Award**
To recognize an individual who has made a significant contribution towards the establishment of a private enterprise/entrepreneurship/economics education program at a college or university. This is APEE's way of thanking those who have committed significant amounts of time and/or resources toward the development of Chairs and Centers Programs at a particular institution. A plaque is awarded annually. Established in 1985 by Calvin A. Kent, Ph.D., in honor of Herman Lay, originator of the Frito Company, Dallas, Texas.

• 5818 • **Adam Smith Award**
This, the Association's highest honor, is given to recognize contributions to the theory and practice of private enterprise. A plaque is awarded annually. Established in 1984 by Calvin A. Kent, Ph.D., to honor Adam Smith, the "father" of economics.

• 5819 •
Association of Professional Chaplains
Josephine Schrader, Exec.Dir.
1701 E Woodfield Rd., Ste. 760
Schaumburg, IL 60173
Phone: (847)240-1014
Fax: (847)240-1015
E-mail: info@professionalchaplains.org
Home Page: http://www.professionalchaplains.org

Formerly: (1991) College of Chaplains of the American Protestant Health Association.

• 5820 • **Anton Boisen Professional Service Award**
To recognize College members who are currently making contributions to pastoral care in some unique way in their own area. Nominees for this award must be members of the College of Chaplains who have demonstrated innovativeness, creativity and outstanding service in their contributions to pastoral care. A plaque is awarded annually. Established in 1984. Formerly: (1991) Recognition of Professional Service Award.

• 5821 • **Chaplain Emeritus Award**
To recognize a Chaplain for ongoing significant contributions to pastoral care within the College. Nominees must be listed in the "retired" category of College membership and must have been a Board Certified Chaplain or Member of the College for a significant period of time. The Membership Services Council with Executive Committee approval decides on recipients. The nomination deadline is December 1. Awarded annually. Established in 1987.

• 5822 • **Distinguished Service Award**
To acknowledge persons who have made a unique and innovative contribution to the field of pastoral care through teaching, worship, community outreach, and research. A plaque with an inscribed metal plate is awarded annually. The nomination deadline is December 1. Established in 1972.

• 5823 • **Outstanding Local Leadership Award**
To recognize the service that occurs in the local arena and to enhance leadership potential. Nominees must be Board Certified Chaplains or Members of the College in state leadership positions. They must demonstrate contributions to the College in the state position represented, and documentation must focus primarily on the area where they serve and secondarily on their position within their specialized setting. Awarded to one or more recipients annually. Established in 1993. Formerly: (1998) Outstanding State Leader Award.

• 5824 •
Association of Professional Communication Consultants
Lee Johns, Pres.
515 Glendale Cir.
Ann Arbor, MI 48103
Phone: (918)743-4793
Fax: (615)269-5442
E-mail: leecjohns@prodigy.net
Home Page: http://www.consultingsuccess.org

• 5825 • **Excellence in Training**
Award of recognition. For outstanding training program. For members only.

• 5826 • **Honor Roll of Excellence in Communication**
Award of recognition. For outstanding commitment to excellent communication in a client organization. Awarded annually.

• 5827 •
Association of Psychologists of Nova Scotia
Kevin Rice, Pres.
1657 Barrington St., Ste. 417
Halifax, NS, Canada B3J 2A1
Phone: (902)422-9183
Fax: (902)462-9801
E-mail: apns@apns.ca
Home Page: http://www.apns.ca

• 5828 • **President's Award**
To honor individuals or groups that have contributed to the field of psychology in Nova Scotia over a period of time. Membership of the Association is not necessary for nomination. The deadline for submission of nomination is April 1. A plaque is awarded at the APNS Annual General Meeting in Halifax.

• 5829 •
Association of Public Treasurers of the United States and Canada
Kelly Noone, Exec.Dir.
962 Wayne Ave., Ste. 910
Silver Spring, MD 20910
Phone: (301)495-5560
Fax: (301)495-5561
E-mail: info@aptusc.org
Home Page: http://www.aptusc.org/news/index.html

Formerly: (2003) Municipal Treasurers Association of the United States and Canada.

• 5830 • **Dr. Jackson R. E. Phillips Award**
To recognize outstanding professional leadership in and significant contribution to professional treasury management as a means of encouraging the development of innovative programs in public finance. Criteria include: practicality, originality, and cost efficiency of the innovation(s); value to the government, both present and future; value to the treasury management profession; and clarity of presentation. Applicants must be active members of the Association. A plaque is presented annually at the

Convention. Established in 1980 in memory of Dr. Jackson R.E. Phillips, former Executive Vice President of Moody's Investor Services, New York, for effectiveness as a financial leader, and for his counseling and support of MTA US&C endeavors.

• 5831 • Service Awards
To encourage and recognize outstanding voluntary participation and achievement of members in furthering the purposes of the Association. Awarded annually. Established in 1986.

• 5832 •
Association of Retail Marketing Services
Gerri Hopkins, Exec.Dir.
10 Drs. James Parker Blvd., Ste. 103
Red Bank, NJ 07701-1500
Phone: (732)842-5070
Fax: (732)219-1938
E-mail: info@goarms.com
Home Page: http://www.goarms.com
Formerly: (1990) Trading Stamp Institute of America.

• 5833 • Promotion Retailer of the Year Award
Recognizes individuals for a significant contribution in the effective use of supermarket promotions. A prism is awarded when merited.

• 5834 •
Association of Schools of Allied Health Professions
Dr. Thomas W. Elwood PhD, Exec.Dir.
1730 M St. NW, Ste. 500
Washington, DC 20036
Phone: (202)293-4848
Toll-Free: 800-497-8080
Fax: (202)293-4852
E-mail: asahp3@asahp.org
Home Page: http://www.asahp.org

• 5835 • Board Awards
To recognize those persons who are regarded as having made important contributions to the Association during the previous fiscal year. Members of the Association are eligible. Selection is based on involvement in Association affairs. The level of involvement is determined annually by the Board of Directors. A Certificate of Appreciation is conferred by the Board of Directors. Awarded when merited. Established in 1984.

• 5836 • Certificates of Merit for Excellence in Writing - *Journal of Allied Health*
To recognize individuals for outstanding articles in *Journal of Allied Health.* Awarded annually. Established in 1985.

• 5837 • Cultural Pluralism Award
To recognize an individual who has furthered the principle of cultural pluralism in the academic setting. Members of the Association who have demonstrated leadership in conducting programs to promote cultural pluralism and diversity are eligible. A plaque is awarded. Established in 1989.

• 5838 • Distinguished Service Award
To recognize an individual who is not a member of the Society yet speaks publicly and forcefully on behalf of Allied Health. Individuals must be involved in some aspect of health care, such as health policy development or insurance. An individual who is a vocal spokesman for Allied Health, a recognized expert, or who has a commitment to quality education is considered for the award. A plaque is presented annually. Additionally, the recipient is responsible to submit an article to the *Journal of Allied Health* within one year following receipt of the award. Established in 1980.

• 5839 • Editor's Award - *Journal of Allied Health*
To recognize individuals for outstanding articles in *Journal of Allied Health.* Awarded annually. Established in 1985.

• 5840 • Fellows Program Award
To provide meaningful recognition to those members who have contributed significantly to allied health as administrators, educators, clinicians or researchers. Members of the Association for five years who are actively involved in an Allied Health Program are eligible. Selection is based on demonstrated leadership, publication in professional journals, and professional creativity. No more than five Fellows may be named in any given year. A plaque is awarded and the Fellow agrees to present a paper on the Annual Meeting program in the following year; include his or her name and resume in the ASAHP Expertise Exchange; and participate as an expert witness in written and/or oral testimony presented by the Association as part of its public policy program. Established in 1981.

• 5841 • Outstanding Member Award
To recognize a member who has contributed significantly to the Association and who, by example, has inspired others. Individuals who have had continuous membership for five years and have not received the award previously are eligible. Selection is based on demonstrated leadership, history of active involvement in Association affairs, previous honors or awards, and publication. A plaque is awarded annually. Additionally, the recipient accepts appointment to the Membership Committee for the following year and lists his/her name and resume in the Expertise Exchange. Established in 1985.

• 5842 • J. Warren Perry Distinguished Authors Award
To recognize members for publication of articles of high merit in the *Journal of Allied Health* within the past year. Articles are judged on content, organization, significance and style. A plaque is awarded annually in November. Established in 1965. Formerly: *Journal of Allied Health* Award.

• 5843 • President's Award
This Award acts as a means for the Association president to express his/her gratitude to those who have dedicated themselves to helping maintain the qualities of excellence that characterize a truly professional society. Members of the Association are eligible. A Certificate of Appreciation is awarded as merited. Established in 1984.

• 5844 •
Association of Schools of Journalism and Mass Communication
Jennifer H. McGill, Exec.Dir.
234 Outlet Pointe Blvd.
Columbia, SC 29210-5667
Phone: (803)798-0271
Fax: (803)772-3509
E-mail: jennifer@aejmc.org
Home Page: http://www.asjmc.org
Formerly: American Society of Journalism School Administrators.

• 5845 • ASJMC Distinguished Service Award
To recognize outstanding performance of the mass media. Individuals are eligible. Awarded annually at the Convention of the Association. Established in 1946 by ASJSA and renamed in 1985. Formerly: ASJSA Citation of Merit Award.

• 5846 •
Association of Science Fiction and Fantasy Artists
Teresa Patterson, Sec./Publication Ed.
PO Box 15131
Arlington, TX 76015-7311
E-mail: ladypegasus@compuserve.com
Home Page: http://www.asfa-art.org/about.html

• 5847 • ASFA Web Awards
Recognition is given for outstanding Web site and creator.

• 5848 • Chesley Awards
Recognition is given for individual works and achievements.

• 5849 •
Association of Southern Baptist Campus Ministries
Steve Masters, VP
Box 25118
Baton Rouge, LA 70894-5118
Phone: (225)343-0408
Fax: (225)343-0424
E-mail: lsubcm@eatel.net

• 5850 • Outstanding Contribution to Campus Ministry Award
To recognize outstanding service to the campus ministry. A plaque is awarded each year at the annual meeting. Established in 1985.

• 5851 •
Association of Space Explorers - U.S.A.
Andy Turnage, Exec.Dir.
1150 Gemini Ave.
Houston, TX 77058
Phone: (281)280-8172
Fax: (281)280-8173
E-mail: aseusa@aol.com
Home Page: http://www.space-explorers.org

• 5852 • **Planetary Award/Crystal Helmet**
Recognizes significant contribution in the fields of manned space research, environmental awareness, or international cooperation. Awarded annually.

• 5853 •
Association of Specialized and Cooperative Library Agencies
Cathleen Bourdon, Exec.Dir.
50 E Huron St.
Chicago, IL 60611
Phone: (312)280-4395
Toll-Free: 800-545-2433
Fax: (312)944-8085
E-mail: ascla@ala.org
Home Page: http://www.ala.org/ascla

• 5854 • **ASCLA Exceptional Service Award**
Recognizes service to patients, the homebound, medical, nursing and other professionals staff hospitals, and inmates. Also recognizes leadership, effective interpretation of programs, pioneering activity, and significant research of experimental projects. Librarians and libraries are eligible. Selection is based on current or past accomplishments such as publications, program development, and leadership. A citation and possibly a cash award are given. The nomination deadline is December 15. Established in 1957. Formerly: HRLSD Exceptional Service Award.

• 5855 • **ASCLA Leadership Achievement Award**
To recognize leadership and achievement in the areas of consulting, multi-type library cooperation and state library development. The award recognizes sustained activity that has been characterized by professional growth and effectiveness. The nomination deadline is December 15. A citation is awarded yearly at a reception at the ALA Annual Conference. Established in 1981. Additional information is available from the ASCLA Executive Director.

• 5856 • **Francis Joseph Campbell Award**
To recognize a person who has made an outstanding contribution to the advancement of library service for the blind and physically handicapped. The nomination deadline is December 15. A medal and citation are awarded annually at a reception at the ALA Annual Conference. Established in 1966. Additional information is available from the ASCLA Executive Director.

• 5857 • **Century Scholarship**
Promotes the ALA's mission of improving local service by developing a representative workforce reflecting communities served by all libraries. $2500 is awarded annually. Funds are to be used for accommodations or services not provided by law or the university, to a student or students with a disabillity pursuing a degree in library and information science. Established in 2000. The deadline to apply is March 1.

• 5858 • **Professional Achievement Award**
To recognize professional achievement within the areas of consulting, networking, statewide services, and programs. One or more citations are awarded annually. Nominees must be ASCLA members. Selection criteria include: record of accomplishment in developing or promoting statewide library services and programs or services and programs of multi-type library organizations; contributions which improve and enhance the status of state library agencies or multi-type library organizations; evidence of initiative in dealing with issues and challenges facing state library agencies or multi-type library organizations. The deadline for nominations is December 15. Awarded annually. Established in 1993.

• 5859 • **Service Award**
To recognize an ASCLA personal member for outstanding service and sustained leadership to the division. Selection is based on the proof of the following: sustained leadership and exceptional service through participation in activities which have enhanced the stature, reputation, and overall strength of the organization; representation of ASCLA to other appropriate organization, institutions, or governmental agencies. The deadline for nominations is December 15. Awarded annually. Established in 1993.

• 5860 •
Association of State and Provincial Psychology Boards
Robert T. Van Hook MSPH, Interim Exec.Off.
PO Box 241245
7177 Halcyon Summit Dr.
Montgomery, AL 36124-1245
Phone: (334)832-4580
Toll-Free: 800-448-4069
Fax: (334)269-6379
E-mail: asppb@asppb.org
Home Page: http://www.asppb.org

• 5861 • **Ming Fisher Award**
For significant contributions as administrator or other employee of a psychology board. Awarded annually.

• 5862 • **Norma P. Simon Award**
Recognizes significant contributions to psychology credentialing on the national or international level. Awarded annually.

• 5863 • **Roger C. Smith Award**
Recognizes significant contributions to psychology licensing and/or certification efforts at the state or provincial level. Awarded annually.

• 5864 •
Association of State and Territorial Health Officials
George E. Hardy Jr. MD, Exec.Dir.
1275 K St., NW, Ste. 800
Washington, DC 20005-4006
Phone: (202)371-9090
Fax: (202)371-9797
E-mail: ghardy@astho.org
Home Page: http://www.astho.org

• 5865 • **McCormack Award**
For recognition of accomplishment, tenure, and integrity in the field of public health administration. Public health officers who have been in public health for 10 years and have been a chief state health official for 5 years are eligible. A plaque is awarded annually. Established in 1950 in honor of Dr. Arthur T. McCormack, chief state health officer in Kentucky for 31 years and one of the founders of the Association.

• 5866 • **Noble G. Swearingen Award**
To recognize individuals for excellence in administrative management. Candidates must have at least 10 years experience in a state health agency in a generalist/administrative role, at least five years of service with the Management Subcommittee of ASTHO or an equivalent group, and at least two achievements or contributions to health services administration. A plaque is awarded annually. Established in 1979.

• 5867 •
Association of Steel Distributors
Ron Pietrzak, Exec.Dir.
401 N Michigan Ave.
Chicago, IL 60611
Phone: (312)644-6610
Fax: (312)527-6705
E-mail: asd@smithbucklin.com
Home Page: http://www.steeldistributors.org/asd/

• 5868 • **Presidents Award of Merit**
To recognize an individual for contributions to the steel distribution industry.

• 5869 • **Steel Distributor of the Year Award**
To recognize integrity, economic statesmanship, and devotion to the interests of the steel distribution industry. The recipient must be an executive of a company member of the association. A large etched copper shield on a walnut plaque is awarded each year at the annual convention. Established in 1956.

Awards are arranged in alphabetical order below their administering organizations

• 5870 •
Association of Surfing Professionals
Meg Bernardo, Events and Projects Mgr.
PO Box 309
Huntington Beach, CA 92648
Phone: (714)848-8851
Fax: (714)848-8861
E-mail: info@surfingamerica.org
Home Page: http://www.aspworldtour.com

Formerly: (1982) International Professional Surfers.

• 5871 • **ASP World Title**

To recognize the best surfers on the pro tour. Awards are presented in the following categories: Men, Women, Longboard and masters, and International Professional. The surfers who gain the most points by the end of the circuit are crowned world champions. A trophy and title are awarded annually at the Association of Surfing Professionals banquet. Established in 1976.

• 5872 •
Association of Surgical Technologists
William J. Teutsch, CEO
7108-C S Alton Way
Centennial, CO 80112-2106
Phone: (303)694-9130
Fax: (303)694-9169
E-mail: bteutsch@ast.org
Home Page: http://www.ast.org

• 5873 • **Education Award**

To give recognition to an AST Member who has made a significant contribution to surgical technology education. The individual must have developed an educational program that has been instrumental in improving the quality of surgical technology care in a specific geographic area, or, consistently participated in the presentation of outstanding educational seminars or workshops in a specific geographic area, or written educational materials in the area of surgical technology. Any individual or group may nominate an AST member by March 15. Winners will be announced at the AST annual national conference and will receive an award and recognition in the official AST publications, and notification will be sent to their employer.

• 5874 • **Leadership Award**

To give recognition to an AST member who has performed a leadership role above and beyond the level of his or her peers. The individual must promote and support the purposes of AST; have held leadership roles at the local, state, regional, or national level; develop leadership potential within his or her own setting; and motivate others to assert themselves and accomplish tasks. Any individual or group may nominate an AST member by March 15. Winners will be announced at the AST annual national conference and will receive an award and recognition in the official AST publications, and notification will be sent to their employer.

• 5875 • **Legislation Award**

To give recognition to an AST member who has been instrumental in legislative activities regarding the surgical technologist, the operating room, or health care services in general. The individual must have worked at the local, state, or national level for the advancement of surgical technology or health care services in general that affect the surgical technologist and have been instrumental in the advancement of surgical technology practice or health care services in general. Any individual or group may nominate an AST member by March 15. Winners will be announced at the AST annual national conference and will receive an award and recognition in the official in the official AST publications, and notification will be sent to their employer.

• 5876 • **Public Relations Award**

To give recognition to an AST member who has made a significant contribution to promoting the recognition of the surgical technologist to the general public or other health care professional. The following criteria are considered: the individual, through specific activities or by example, must have increased the awareness of the general public or other health care professionals of the knowledge, experience, and importance of the surgical technologist as a member of the operating room team; have developed and/or distributed materials informing others of the role of the surgical technologist; and have participated in health fairs, written articles for local newspapers, or participated in TV/Radio programs representing surgical technology. Any individual or group may nominate an AST member by March 15. Winners will be announced at the AST annual national conference and will receive an award and recognition in the official AST publications, and notification will be sent to their employer.

• 5877 •
Association of Teacher Educators
Marilyn L. Nicholas, Interim Exec.Dir.
1900 Association Dr., Ste. ATE
Reston, VA 20191
Phone: (703)620-3110
Fax: (703)620-9530
E-mail: atel@aol.com
Home Page: http://www.ate1.org

• 5878 • **Distinguished Dissertation in Teacher Education**

To encourage, recognize, and promote exemplary doctoral level research which substantially contributes to the improvement of teacher education. Special recognition is also extended to the professor who directed the dissertation.

• 5879 • **Distinguished Programs in Teacher Education**

To recognize and honor outstanding teacher education programs which exemplify joint participation by local education agencies and higher education institutions in program development and administration. Awarded annually. Established in 1977.

• 5880 • **Distinguished Research in Teacher Education**

To encourage research in teacher education in institutions of higher learning, in local education and in local education agencies. Awarded annually. Established in 1973. Formerly: Research Award in Teacher Education.

• 5881 • **Kappa Delta Pi National Student Teacher/Intern of the Year Award**

To recognize a student teacher who has demonstrated an outstanding ability to plan instructional strategies that support the needs of all students, establish effective interpersonal relationships with students, parents, and staff, and reflect the teaching and learning process. Awarded annually.

• 5882 •
Association of the United States Army
Gen. Gordon R. Sullivan, Pres.
2425 Wilson Blvd.
Arlington, VA 22201
Phone: (703)841-4300
Toll-Free: 800-336-4570
Fax: (703)525-9039
E-mail: ausa-info@ausa.org
Home Page: http://www.ausa.org

• 5883 • **Association of the United States Army Awards**

The Association presents awards in the following order of merit: George Catlett Marshall Medal - the highest honor of the Association for recognition of selfless service to the United States of America. A gold medal is awarded annually. Established in 1960; General Creighton W. Abrams Medal - for recognition of outstanding service to the United States Army. A gold medal is awarded annually. Established in 1965; President's Medal - for outstanding service and support to the Association. Members are eligible. A gold medal is awarded annually. Established in 1959; John W. Dixon Medal - for recognition of outstanding contributions to national defense by a member of the industrial community. Established in 1989; Award for Distinguished Service - for recognition of distinguished service to the United States of America by officials holding national level elective or appointed offices. Usually more than one certificate is awarded annually. Established in 1973; Citation for Exceptional Service in Support of National Defense - to recognize and encourage efforts by the press, industry, local government, and similar organizations or individuals who have made significant contributions in support of the Association, the U.S. Army, or national defense. A framed citation is awarded. Established in 1967; Certificate of Achievement - for recognition of service of achievements in support of the United States Army or the Association. Members are eligible. A framed certificate is awarded; and Certificate of Appreciation - for recognition of service to the United States Army or the Association. Members are eligible. A framed certificate is awarded.

• 5884 •
Association of the Wall and Ceiling Industries - International
Ken Navratil, Pres.
803 W Broad St., Ste. 600
Falls Church, VA 22046-3108
Phone: (703)534-8300
Fax: (703)534-8307
E-mail: info@awci.org
Home Page: http://www.awci.org

Formerly: International Association of Wall and Ceiling Contractors.

• 5885 • **Distinguished Chapter Award**
To recognize the achievements of AWCI's chartered chapters in service to industry, membership growth and retention and continuous support of the Association. Established in 1990.

• 5886 • **J. D. McNulty Award**
To recognize an individual for advancement in research and development, education, and information dissemination for the construction industry. The winner is selected by the Foundation of the Wall and Ceiling Industry. Sponsored by the Foundation of the Wall and Ceiling Industry.

• 5887 • **Outstanding Association Executive Award**
To recognize the local, state, or national association executive who has made significant contributions to his or her own association and to AWCI. Exceptionally dedicated individuals who have provided superior service to the industry are eligible. Established in 1990.

• 5888 • **Outstanding Committee Chairman Award**
To recognize the committee chairman who has done the most outstanding job for his committee and for AWCI. Open to both contractor and supplier members. Established in 1990.

• 5889 • **Outstanding Regional Chairman Award**
To recognize the ACWI Regional Chairman (there are seven in all) who has done the best job in developing and implementing his regional conference program. Awarded when merited. Established in 1990.

• 5890 • **Pinnacle Award**
To recognize the individual who has made outstanding contributions to the wall and ceiling industry. Membership in the Association is not required for the award. A marble and bronze trophy is awarded annually when merited. Established in 1964. Formerly: (1982) E. F. Venzie Award.

• 5891 • **Supplier Member of the Year Award**
To recognize the supplier member who has contributed his/her time and talent to AWCI and the wall and ceiling industry through committee service, attendance and participation in meetings, sponsoring new members, exhibiting and/or sponsoring at conventions, etc. Individuals must have held membership for at least two years. Established in 1990.

• 5892 • **Unsung Hero Award**
To recognize the contractor or supplier member who has a record of strong loyal support and attendance and active participation in AWCI functions. Members for at least five years who have not served on the Board of Directors nor as committee or regional chairman within the past five years are eligible. Established in 1990.

• 5893 • **Winning Spirit Award**
To recognize an individual or an organization for major contributions to and achievement on behalf of the construction industry. The recipient does not have to be a member of the Association. Established in 1988.

• 5894 • **Young Member Achievement Award**
To recognize the contractor or supplier member under the age of 40 who holds an executive-level position in his or her company and has been an active participant in AWCI for at least two years in committee work, regional activities, conventions, etc. Established in 1990.

• 5895 •
Association of Third World Studies
Dr. Shu-hui Wu, Exec.Dir.
Mississippi State University
Department of History
Mississippi State, MS 39762
Phone: (662)325-4020
E-mail: shuwu@ra.msstate.edu
Home Page: http://itc.gsw.edu/atws/

• 5896 • **Award for Academic Excellence in Global Awareness**
To recognize the achievements of the student who contributes the most to promoting global awareness on campus. Nominee must be a student at Georgia Southwestern State University. A cash award of $25 and a certificate are presented every May at the University's Honors Convocation. Established in 1991.

• 5897 • **Award for Outstanding Performance in Third World Studies**
To recognize outstanding performances by students who participate in the Third World in Perspective Program Seminar Series held at Georgia Southwestern State University. Nominees must be students at Georgia Southwestern State University. From three to six certificates are awarded each May at the University's Honors Convocation. Established in 1991.

• 5898 • **Cecil B. Currey Book-Length Publications Award**
To recognize the best book published by an ATWS member during the preceding year. Awarded annually. Established in 1997.

• 5899 • **Presidential Award for Outstanding Contributions to the Promotion of Scholarship in the Third World**
To recognize significant contributions to the field of Third World studies. Nominees must be members of the Association of Third World Studies and must have served as an officer and/or on the Board of Editors of the *Journal of Third World Studies*. Plaques are presented at the ATWS annual meeting. Established in 1992.

• 5900 • **Dr. Lawrence Dunbar Reddick Memorial Scholarship Award**
To recognize the best article on Africa published in the *Journal of Third World Studies* (JTWS) during the preceding year. Awarded annually. Established in 1996 in honor of Dr. Lawrence Dunbar Reddick, an internationally-known scholar.

• 5901 •
Association of Travel Marketing Executives
Kristin Zern, Exec.Dir.
3331 W 57th St., Ste. 482
New York, NY 10019
Phone: (212)765-0625
Toll-Free: 800-526-0041
Fax: (212)765-0624
E-mail: admin@atme.org
Home Page: http://www.atme.org

• 5902 • **ATME Atlas Awards**
Recognizes an outstanding travel marketing executive. A plaque and a silver bowl are awarded at the annual conference. Established in 1990. Formerly: (2003) Atlas Travel Marketing Executive Award.

• 5903 • **ATME Awards**
Recognizes career achievement and innovation. Formerly: (2003) Atlas Travel Marketing Campaign Awards.

• 5904 •
Association of Universities and Colleges of Canada
(Association des universites et colleges du Canada)
Claire Morris, Pres./CEO
350 Albert St., Ste. 600
Ottawa, ON, Canada K1R 1B1
Phone: (613)563-1236
Phone: (613)563-3961
Fax: (613)563-9745
E-mail: info@aucc.ca
Home Page: http://www.aucc.ca

• 5905 • **C.D. Howe Memorial Foundation Engineering Awards Program**
Two awards (one for a male, one for a female) of $7,500 are awarded to candidates of Canadian citizenship or permanent residency who have completed the first year of an engineering program. Applications are by nomination by deans of engineering only. Deadline is July 2. Awarded annually.

• 5906 • National Access Awareness Week Student Awards Program
Open to disabled persons who are Canadian citizens or who have lived in Canada as permanent residents for at least two years, and who are entering or enrolled in an undergraduate, graduate or college program of study. Deadline is March 15.

• 5907 • Queen Elizabeth Silver Jubilee Endowment Fund for Study in a Second Official Language Award Program
Open to Canadian citizens or permanent residents who are enrolled in the second or third year of their first undergraduate university program. All disciplines, except translations, are eligible. A maximum of 6 monetary awards of $5,000 plus travel expenses, are awarded. Nonrenewable.

• 5908 •
Association of University Architects
Evie Asken, Contact
% Evie Asken
Western Michigan University
Kalamazoo, MI 49008
E-mail: aua@auaweb.net
Home Page: http://www.auaweb.net

• 5909 • Distinguished Service Award
For recognition of continuing outstanding service to the Association. An engraved silver tray and certificate are awarded when merited at the annual conference. Established in 1971.

• 5910 • Honor Awards
To recognize individuals for outstanding contributions to the physical development of academic institutions. Awarded occasionally when merited. Established in 1984.

• 5911 •
Association of University Programs in Health Administration
Lydia M. Reed MBA, Pres./CEO
2000 N 14th St., Ste. 780
Arlington, VA 22201
Phone: (703)894-0940
Fax: (703)894-0941
E-mail: aupha@aupha.org
Home Page: http://www.aupha.org

• 5912 • Baxter Allegiance Prize Health Services Research
For recognition of a significant contribution to the improved medical care of the public through innovative health services research worldwide. An individual's specific contribution or a career-long achievement may be recognized. The prize acknowledges national or international contributions of health services research, defined as a product of the application of analytic methods to the organization, financing, and/or delivery of health services. Nominees are considered based on: (1) contribution in the area of Health Services Management, (2) contribution in the area of Health Policy Development, and (3) contribution in the area of Health Care Delivery, and Health Care Management. Health services research addresses the entire range of health services, including health promotion and disease prevention, primary care, secondary and tertiary care, as well as long-term care. Deadline for applications is February 1. The prize consists of an individual award of $10,000. In addition, $15,000 is awarded to a not-for-profit institution designated by the recipient, to support his or her work. Awarded annually at the Association annual meeting in June. Established in 1986. Formerly: (1987) Baxter American Foundation Prize.

• 5913 •
Association of Women Surgeons
Judith Keel, Exec.VP
414 Plaza Dr., Ste. 209
Westmont, IL 60559
Phone: (630)655-0392
Fax: (630)655-0391
E-mail: info@womensurgeons.org
Home Page: http://
www.womensurgeons.org

• 5914 • Distinguished Member Award
Given to a member surgeon who exemplifies the ideals and mission of the association. Awarded annually. Established in 1990.

• 5915 • Honorary Member Award
Given to individuals supportive of the goals of the association. Awarded annually. Established in 1990.

• 5916 • Nina Starr Braun Wald Award
Given to a member or non-member surgeon in recognition of outstanding contributions to the advancement of women in surgery. Awarded annually.

• 5917 •
Association on Higher Education and Disability
Stephan J. Smith, Exec.Dir.
PO Box 540666
Waltham, MA 02454
Phone: (781)788-0003
Fax: (781)788-0033
E-mail: ahead@ahead.org
Home Page: http://www.ahead.org.

Formerly: Association on Handicapped Student Service Programs in Postsecondary Education.

• 5918 • Professional Recognition Award
Annual award of recognition.

• 5919 •
Association pour l'Avancement des Sciences et des Techniques de la Documentation
Louis Cabral, Dir.Gen.
3414, ave. du Parc
Bur. 202
Montreal, QC, Canada H2X 2H5
Phone: (514)281-5012
Fax: (514)281-8219
E-mail: info@asted.org
Home Page: http://www.asted.org

• 5920 • Prix Alvine-Belisle
To honor the author of the best children's book published in French in Canada. Works that appear during the preceding year are eligible. A monetary prize of $500 is awarded annually. Established in 1974.

• 5921 •
Association Quebecoise des Critiques de Cinema
PO Box 1134
Montreal, QC, Canada H2Y 3J6
Phone: (514)933-9473
Fax: (514)933-0162
E-mail: cast49@sympatico.ca

• 5922 • Prix de la Critique Internationale
For recognition of outstanding films of the world. Organized by the Association and given in the name of Federation internationale de la presse cinematographique (FIPRESCI) at international film festivals. Established in 1986.

• 5923 •
***Association Trends* Newsweekly**
Jill M. Cornish, Pres.
7910 Woodmont Ave., No. 1150
Bethesda, MD 20814-3062
Phone: (301)652-8666
Fax: (301)656-8654
E-mail:
associationtrends@associationtrends.com
Home Page: http://www.assntrends.com

• 5924 • Association Executive of the Year
For recognition of achievement in the field of association management. Selection is by previous award winners, based on career success and achievement of organization objectives. A major trophy, and an inscription on a permanent plaque on display in the Trends office, are awarded annually, usually in January in Washington, at the *Association Trends* Awards Luncheon. Established in 1980 by Frank Martineau, CAE. founding editor of *Association Trends*

• 5925 •
ASTM International
James Thomas, Pres.
100 Barr Harbor Dr.
West Conshohocken, PA 19428
Phone: (610)832-9585
Fax: (610)832-9555
E-mail: jthomas@astm.org
Home Page: http://www.astm.org

Formerly: (1982) American Society for Testing and Materials.

• 5926 • **Adhesives Award**
To recognize people in the adhesive and sealants industries who have made outstanding contributions to the two industries. Presented by Committee D-14 on Adhesives.

• 5927 • **Advanced Ceramic Award**
To recognize the continuous and outstanding contributions of an individual for the work of ASTM Committee C-28 (Advanced Ceramics), through its various subcommittees, sections and task groups.

• 5928 • **Harlan J. Anderson Award**
To recognize outstanding contributions toward the successful operation of Committee C-26 on the Nuclear Fuel Cycle. Both ASTM and C-26 members are eligible. A plaque is awarded annually. Established in 1978 in honor of Harlan J. Anderson, the first chairman of C-26.

• 5929 • **ASTM Award of Merit**
To recognize distinguished service by an individual to the Society and to the cause of voluntary standardization. An engraved plaque, a lapel pin and the honorary title of Fellow are awarded annually. Established in 1949. Highest award given by ASTM.

• 5930 • **P. H. Bates Memorial Award**
To recognize an excellent paper and its presentation on a subject relating to the manufacture, handling, testing, usage, or any other aspect of hydraulic cement that comes within the scope of Committee C-1 on Cement. A certificate is awarded biennially. Established in 1969.

• 5931 • **Kenneth J. Boedecker Jr. Distinguished Service Award**
To recognize exceptional service to Committee AO5 (Metallic-Coated Iron and Steel Products), one of its subcommittees, or one of its activities. Established in 1998.

• 5932 • **Frank C. Brautigam Award**
To recognize outstanding and effective work in developing a new ASTM standard as exemplified by Frank C. Brautigam, who was Chairman of the Task Groups. Awarded annually by the Committee G-2 on Wear and Erosion. Established in 1988.

• 5933 • **Charles W. Briggs Award**
To recognize continuous and outstanding contributions of an individual to the work of ASTM Committee E-7 on Nondestructive Testing, through its various Subcommittees, Sections and Task Groups. No more than two such awards are presented in any single year. Established in 1978.

• 5934 • **W. T. Cavanaugh Memorial Award**
To recognize an individual of eminence in the voluntary standards system. Members and nonmembers may be nominated by April 15. The title of Honorary Member is bestowed on recipients of the award. No more than two award recipients shall be named in a calendar year. Established in 1987 to honor W.T. Cavanaugh, who firmly established ASTM as the world leader in the development and dissemination of voluntary consensus standards during his service as Chief Executive Officer from 1970 until his death in 1985.

• 5935 • **H. V. Churchill Award**
To recognize meritorious service to Committee E-2. Both members or past members of Committee E-2 on Emission Spectroscopy are eligible. A certificate is awarded annually. Established in 1967 in honor of the first chairman of the Committee, H.V. Churchill.

• 5936 • **Committee D-2 Award**
To recognize outstanding achievement in the field of petroleum products and lubricants by a member of the Committee. Members of Committee D-2 are eligible. A scroll is awarded annually. Established in 1923.

• 5937 • **Committee D-12 Award**
To recognize distinguished achievement in the field of soap and detergent technology as reported in recognized publications or in lectures before scientific and technical societies. A certificate is awarded annually. Established in 1957.

• 5938 • **Committee D-20 Award of Excellence**
To recognize outstanding personal performance in the plastics field by a member of the Committee who has contributed the most toward the development and use of consensus standards or who has fostered competency and proficiency in the plastics field. Awarded annually. Established in 1985 by Committee D-20 on Plastics.

• 5939 • **Committee E-8 Fracture Mechanics Medal**
Presented for technical or other significant contributions to an individual or a group of individuals who, by their technical or other significant contributions, have exerted a profound, positive effect on the development of the scientific discipline of fracture mechanics.

• 5940 • **Committee E-8 on Fatigue and Fracture Best Student Paper Award**
To encourage students to develop, present and publish high quality research papers in the field of fracture and subcritical crack growth.

• 5941 • **Copper Club Award/Committee B-5 Award**
To recognize individuals who have done the most to advance the standardization of copper and copper alloy products. Established in 1979. Administered by an Awards Subcommittee under the jurisdiction of Committee B05 on Copper and Copper Alloys.

• 5942 • **Margaret Dana Award**
To recognize individuals who have made outstanding contributions to the advancement of voluntary standards for consumer products. A walnut and bronze shadow box plaque is awarded annually. Established in 1979.

• 5943 • **Anthony DeBellis Award**
Established in 1988 in memory of Anthony DeBellis, who was an active participating member and officer of Committee E-28, Subcommittee E28.06 on Indentation Hardness Testing, and USA representative to ISO/TC164/SC34 on Hardness.

• 5944 • **Harold F. Dodge Award**
To recognize an ASTM member who has performed outstanding work in the field of applied statistics. A walnut and bronze shadow box plaque is awarded not more than once a year. Established in 1978.

• 5945 • **Charles B. Dudley Medal**
To honor the author(s) of a paper or book of outstanding merit which constitutes an original contribution to research in engineering materials and has been published by the Society. An engraved plaque is awarded annually. Established in 1925.

• 5946 • **Wayne P. Ellis Award**
In recognition of meritorious contributions to the cause of voluntary standardization, specifically with respect to fire standards. Presented by the Committee E-5 for Fire Standards. In honor of the late Wayne P. Ellis, ASTM President and member of ASTM Committee E-5.

• 5947 • **Euverard Innovation Award**
Presented annually to a member of Committee D-1 (Paint and Related Coatings, Materials, and Applications) who has developed an innovative test apparatus or technique or demonstrated sustained technical competence in the development of standards.

• 5948 • **Fatigue Achievement Award**
Presented by the E-8 Committee (Fatigue and Fracture) to those individuals who have made outstanding contribution to the field of fatigue of materials. Established in 1986.

• 5949 • **The Forensic Sciences Award**
In recognition for continuous and outstanding contributions of an individual for the work of ASTM Committee E-30 (Forensic Sciences) through its various subcommittees, sections and task groups.

• 5950 • Henry A. Gardner Award
To recognize a committee member who has demonstrated sustained outstanding competence in managing a unit of ASTM Committee D-1 on paint and related coatings. A monetary prize and a certificate are awarded annually. Established in 1977.

• 5951 • R. A. Glenn Award
To recognize an individual who has made outstanding contributions in the development of ASTM standards relating to coal and coke. A certificate is awarded annually. Established in 1973.

• 5952 • Daniel H. Green Award
To recognize an ASTM committee member of D-15 on Engine Coolants who has performed outstanding work in the committee's activities. A certificate is awarded annually. Established in 1972.

• 5953 • John L. Hague Award
To recognize significant technical contributions to the initiation, preparation, or development of Committee E-16 standards for testing ores. Both E-16 members or former members are eligible. A plaque is awarded annually. Established in 1982 in honor of John L. Hague, the first chairman of E-16.

• 5954 • Max Hecht Award
To recognize a member of Committee D-19 on Water who has performed some outstanding work in the committee or in the field of water. A plaque is awarded annually. Established in 1954 in honor of Max Hecht.

• 5955 • C. A. Hogentogler Award
To honor the author(s) of a paper of outstanding merit on soils for engineering purposes which has been presented during a meeting or published by the Society. A certificate is awarded annually. Established in 1953.

• 5956 • Prevost Hubbard Award
To recognize a member or former member of ASTM Committee D-4 on Road and Paving Material who has performed outstanding work in the field of bituminous road and paving materials. A certificate is awarded annually. Established in 1972.

• 5957 • William F. Hulse Memorial Award
To recognize outstanding contributions to maintain and support the establishment of voluntary full-consensus standards to enhance the safety of organized and individual sport. The award is intended to recognize individuals or organizations that best exemplify the example demonstrated by the life and career of William F. Hulse. Presented by the F-8 Committee for Sports Equipment and Facilities. Established in 1996.

• 5958 • S. H. Ingberg Award
To recognize outstanding achievement in fire resistance research, fire loss prevention, and the development of fire test methods. A certificate is awarded annually. Established in 1969.

• 5959 • Charles H. Irvine Memorial Award
Established in Committee F-13 on Safety and Traction for Footwear and will be submitted to the ASTM Board of Directors. Dedicated to the memory of Charles H. Irvine, the first Chairman of Committee F-13 and a life-long leader in the development of standards to promote workplace safety, reduce incidence of pedestrian slip-and-fall accidents, further the science of floor slipperiness and shoe sole slipperiness, and to better design stairways. Established in 1996.

• 5960 • George R. Irwin Medal
To recognize an individual who has made a significant new contribution to the application of fracture mechanics concepts and methodology. Both members and non-members are eligible. A plaque is awarded annually. Established in 1978.

• 5961 • Charles A. Johnson Award
To recognize a committee member who best exemplifies Mr. Johnson's interest and dedication to ASTM Committee D-27 on Electrical Insulating Liquids and Gases. A certificate is awarded annually when merited. Established in 1977.

• 5962 • A. Ivan Johnson Outstanding Achievement Award
To recognize a member of the committee whose efforts have produced a particular outstanding result or significant contribution to the work of D-18 (Soil and Rock). Recipient's name will be inscribed on a plaque mounted at the Society's headquarters and he or she will be presented with a framed citation. Established in 1979.

• 5963 • Noah A. Kahn Award
To recognize a graduating student of Brooklyn Polytechnic Institute and Lehigh University who is outstanding in metallurgical engineering or its materials aspects. A certificate is awarded annually. Established in 1963.

• 5964 • Gary M. Kralik Distinguished Service Award
To recognize exceptional service to Committee B-2, one of its subcommittees, or one of its activities. Administered by the Awards Subcommittee of Committee B-2 on Nonferrous Metals and Alloys. Established in 1992.

• 5965 • Francis L. LaQue Memorial Award
In recognition of outstanding contributions to Committee G-1 (Corrosion of Metals) and to the field of corrosion testing and evaluation as exemplified by the distinguished accomplishment by Francis L. LaQue. Established in 1988.

• 5966 • Robert R. Litehiser Memorial Award
To recognize outstanding work in the field of concrete pipe by a member or former member of Committee C-13. A plaque is awarded annually. Established in 1981 in memory of Robert R. Litehiser, chairman of Committee C-13 from 1952-62.

• 5967 • Frederick A. Lowenheim Memorial Award
To recognize high professionalism in the members of Commitee B-8 on Metallic and Inorganic Coatings. A plaque is awarded annually. Established in 1982 in memory of Dr. Frederick A. Lowenheim, who exemplified high professionalism.

• 5968 • Lundell-Bright Memorial Award
To recognize outstanding work in the Committee E-3. Members of Committee E-3 on Chemical Analysis of Metals of at least three years standing are eligible. A certificate is awarded annually. Established in 1964.

• 5969 • B. Charles Malloy Leadership Award
In recognition of outstanding organizational leadership, symposia management, or task group leadership. The award is given in memory of Charles Malloy, founder and past Chairman of Committee D-34 (Waste Management). Established in 1990.

• 5970 • L. J. Markwardt Award
To recognize the author(s) of a technical paper of outstanding merit published by the Society, covering broadly the field of wood as an engineering material. A monetary prize and an engraved plaque are awarded annually. Established in 1968.

• 5971 • Katharine and Bryant Mather Award
To recognize a committee officer, executive subcommittee member or administrative or technical subcommittee officer who has performed the administrative and managerial duties of the position in an exceptional manner, so as to enhance the status of concrete technology as a discipline. Awarded not more than every three years by Committee C-9 (Concrete and Concrete Aggregates). Established in 1993.

• 5972 • John Nachtsheim
To encourage women college seniors or first-year graduate students to pursue the study of physical metallurgy or materials science, with emphasis on the relationship of microstructure and properties. Awarded annually. Established in 1975 and administered by Committee E04 on Metallography.

• 5973 • Mary R. Norton Memorial Scholarship Award for Women
To encourage women college seniors or first-year graduate students to pursue the study of physical metallurgy or materials science, with

emphasis on relationship of microstructure and properties. Established in 1975. Administered by Committee E-4 on Metallography.

• 5974 • H. R. "Russ" Ogden Award
To recognize outstanding accomplishments in the science and technology of reactive and refractory metals and alloys. A plaque is awarded annually. Established in 1983 by Committee B-10 on Reactive and Refractory metals and alloys. Given in honor of H.R. "Russ" Ogden, B-10's first chairman.

• 5975 • William T. Pearce Award
To recognize outstanding work and a technical paper of merit published within the preceding five years relating to the science of testing paints and paint materials. Members of the Committee are eligible. A medal and a certificate are awarded annually. Established in 1969.

• 5976 • David R. Peryam Award
To recognize outstanding professionals in the applied sensory science field. Established in 1995 by Committee E-18 on Sensory Evaluation of Materials and Products.

• 5977 • Cedric Powell Award
To recognize a member or participant in Committee E-42 on Surface Analysis for outstanding contributions to the national or international development of standards for surface analysis. Limited to no more than one recipient per year. It may be presented to an individual who, or involuntary reasons, is no longer active. All nominees should have long records of meritorious services.

• 5978 • Frank W. Reinhart and Henry "Butch" Kuhlmann Award
To recognize Committee F-17 (Plastic Piping Systems) members and others persons for distinguished and outstanding contributions on behalf of plastics piping standardization, and for meritorious technical achievement in the field of the Committee. Awarded at intervals of not less than one year. Established in 1993 in memory of Frank W. Reinhart and Henry W. Kuhlman who, by their leadership, dedication and contributions, exemplify the qualities honored by this award.

• 5979 • Frank W. Reinhart Award
To recognize an outstanding and unusual member for a contribution to ASTM in the area of terminology. A plaque is awarded annually. Established in 1981 by the ASTM Committee on Terminology in honor of Dr. Frank W. Reinhart.

• 5980 • Frank E. Richart Award
To recognize notable contributions in the work of the Society and concrete aggregates. Members or committee members of the Society are eligible. An engraved plaque is awarded triennially. Established in 1953 by Mrs. Frank E. Richart.

• 5981 • Lowrie B. Sargent, Jr. Award
To recognize a member, or former member of Committee D-2 on Petroleum Products and Lubricants who has exhibited outstanding leadership in the standards work of that committee. A plaque is awarded as merited. Established in 1982 in honor of Lowrie B. Sargent, Jr., chairman of D-2, 1966-75.

• 5982 • Arnold H. Scott Award
To recognize notable achievement in the field of electrical insulation technology. A plaque is awarded annually. Established in 1965.

• 5983 • B. F. Scribner Award
To recognize a particular accomplishment and outstanding service to ASTM Committee E-2 on Emission Spectroscopy. A certificate is awarded annually. Established in 1973.

• 5984 • Sealants Hall of Fame Award
To recognize an active member of Committee C-24 for distinguished service in the area of building seals and sealants and for their contribution to the stimulation of research, promotion of knowledge and exceptional service to the building seals and sealants industry and ASTM Committee C-24. Awarded annually. Established in 1972, retroactive to 1970.

• 5985 • SES - ASTM Robert J. Painter Memorial Award
To recognize service in the field of standards. A medal and a certificate are awarded annually. Established in 1956 by ASTM and the Standards Engineering Society.

• 5986 • Tilton E. Shelburne Award
To recognize an individual for outstanding work in the field of the committee's activity on skid resistance. Both current and past members of ASTM Committee E-17 on Skid Resistance are eligible. A certificate is awarded annually. Established in 1977.

• 5987 • Woodland G. Shockley Memorial Award
To recognize eminence in the work of Committee D-18 on Soil and Rock. Recipients receive the title Honorary Member of Committee D-18, and have their name inscribed on a special plaque mounted at Society headquarters. Established in 1992.

• 5988 • Howard DeWitt Smith Memorial Award
To recognize outstanding achievement in the field of textile fiber utilization. Citizens of the United States and Canada are eligible. An engraved plaque is awarded annually. Established in 1949 by Fabric Research Laboratories, Inc., and the Society.

• 5989 • Wayne W. Stinchcomb Memorial Lecture and Award
To honor an individual who has made outstanding contributions, with emphasis on mentorship in research, engineering, or teaching the technology of composite materials. Presented by Committee D-30 (Composite Materials). Established in 1995 in memory of the technical and humanitarian leadership of Wayne W. Stinchcomb.

• 5990 • Richard L. Templin Award
To honor the author(s) of an outstanding paper describing new and useful mechanical apparatus and testing techniques. An engraved plaque is awarded annually. Established in 1945 by Richard L. Templin.

• 5991 • Moyer D. Thomas Award
To recognize an outstanding achievement in the standardization of sampling and analysis of atmospheres. Both present and past members of ASTM Committee D-22 are eligible. A gold-filled engraved medal and certificate are awarded annually. Established in 1975.

• 5992 • Sanford E. Thompson Award
To honor the author(s) of a paper published by the Society that is of outstanding merit in the field of concrete and concrete aggregates. A plaque and certificate are awarded annually. Established in 1938.

• 5993 • Robert D. Thompson Memorial Award
To recognize an ASTM committee member who has performed outstanding work on ASTM Committee E-20 on Temperature Measurement. A certificate is awarded annually. Established in 1974.

• 5994 • Sam Tour Award
To honor the author(s) of a technical paper published by the Society that is of outstanding merit in the field of improvements and evaluation of corrosion testing methods and to encourage both research and the preparation of technical papers in this field. A plaque is awarded annually. Established in 1946 by Sam Tour.

• 5995 • Joseph R. Vilella Award
To honor the author(s) of a paper of outstanding merit in the field of metallography. A walnut and bronze plaque is awarded annually when merited. Established in 1974.

• 5996 • Walter C. Voss Award
To recognize notable contributions to knowledge in the field of building technology, with emphasis upon materials used which constitute significant advances or innovations. Both engineers and scientists are eligible. A plaque is awarded annually. Established in 1962.

• 5997 • Wallace Waterfall Award
To recognize an individual for outstanding contributions to the development, preparation, and acceptance of standards in acoustics. A plaque is awarded annually. Established in 1975.

• 5998 • L. L. Wyman Memorial Award
To recognize significant and meritorious contributions to standardization in the field of metallography through the work of ASTM Committee E-4 on Metallography. A certificate is awarded and the honoree's name is placed on a permanent display plaque. Awarded biennially in the even-numbered years. Established in 1977.

• 5999 • Alan H. Yorkdale Memorial Award
To recognize the author or authors of the best paper concerning clay, shale, concrete, or sand-lime masonry. Award is presented annually by Committee C-15 for Manufactured Masonry Units. Established in 1987 to honor Alan H. Yorkdale who was a leading proponent of the advancement of masonry engineering and research.

• 6000 •
Astronomical League
Jackie Beucher, Exec.Sec.
11305 King St.
Overland Park, KS 66210-3421
Phone: (913)469-0135
E-mail: m31@everestkc.net
Home Page: http://www.astroleague.org/

• 6001 • Astronomical League Award
To recognize an individual for outstanding service in amateur or scientific astronomy. A walnut plaque with an inscribed bronze overlay is awarded annually if merited. Established in 1951.

• 6002 • National Young Astronomer Award
To recognize outstanding U.S. resident high school students for outstanding achievement in astronomy-related research, public education, telescope design, astronomical imaging, organizational leadership, observational astronomy, and writing. Winners are selected by a national panel of professional judges. The top three winners receive large engraved plaques. The first place winner also receives a Meade LX200 10 inch Schmidt-Cassegrain telescope donated by the Meade Instrument Corporation and an expense-paid trip to the League's national convention. Awarded annually. Established in 1993.

• 6003 • Leslie C. Peltier Award
To recognize outstanding contributions to observational astronomy by an amateur astronomer. The nominations deadline is January 1 of the year in which the award is to be given. Nominations are kept on file for future consideration. A plaque is awarded annually at the national convention. Established in 1980 in honor of Leslie C. Peltier, the premier variable star observer in American history who also discovered twelve comets and several novae. Sponsored by Meade Instruments.

• 6004 • Bob Wright Al Service Award
To recognize an individual for service to the League.

• 6005 •
Astronomical Society of the Pacific
Michael A. Bennett, Exec.Dir.
390 Ashton Ave.
San Francisco, CA 94112
Phone: (415)337-1100
Fax: (415)337-5205
E-mail: mdelgado@astrosociety.org
Home Page: http://www.astrosociety.org

• 6006 • Amateur Achievement Award
In recognition of significant contributions by amateurs to the field of astronomy. Selection is made by the Board of Directors from nominations by members and others. A monetary award of $500 and a plaque are awarded annually at the Society's summer meeting. Established in 1978.

• 6007 • Thomas J. Brennan Award
To recognize excellence in teaching astronomy at the high school level. Selection is made by the Board of Directors from a nomination list compiled by national leaders in astronomy education. A monetary prize of $250 and a plaque are awarded annually. Established in 1993.

• 6008 • Catherine Wolfe Bruce Medal
This, one of the most prestigious awards in the field of astronomy, is given in recognition of lifetime research achievement in astronomy and astrophysics. Selection is made by the Board of Directors from nominees proposed by three American and three foreign observatories. A medal with the seal of the Society is awarded annually at the summer meeting. Established in 1897 by Miss Bruce.

• 6009 • Klumpke-Roberts Award
In recognition of outstanding efforts in fostering better public understanding and appreciation of astronomy. The recipient may be a professional or an amateur astronomer or layperson. The contribution may be in the form of one or more popular articles or books, lectures, TV or movie productions, or service to public education in astronomy of any other nature. Nominations are accepted from members. The awardee may be asked to write an article for *Mercury* magazine or give a public lecture at a meeting sponsored by the Society. A monetary prize of $500 and a plaque are awarded annually. Established in 1974.

• 6010 • La Cumbres Ameteur Outreach Award
Honors outstanding educational outreach by an amateur astronomer to K-12 children and the interested public. Nominations are made By the ASP Amateur Advisory Committee, plus other members of the Astronomical community. Established in 2000.

• 6011 • Maria and Eric Muhlmann Prize
To recognize significant recent astronomical research that makes use of innovations in instrumentation, software, or support infrastructure. A monetary award of $500 and a plaque are awarded annually. First established in 1983. Re-established in 1994.

• 6012 • Robert J. Trumpler Award
To recognize a recent recipient of a PhD degree whose thesis research is considered unusually important to astronomy, broadly conceived. Nominations are solicited from major observatories and astronomy departments worldwide. The thesis must have been written at a North American university and published at the time of the award, and the PhD must have been awarded within two years. Nominations may be made by chairpersons of all astronomy and physics departments in North America. The awardee receives $500 and a plaque, and presents a talk about his or her work at the ASP summer meeting. Awarded annually. Reactivated in 1973 in honor of the 20th century astronomer, Robert J. Trumpler, who made major contributions to the study of star clusters and the structure of our galaxy.

• 6013 •
Athenaeum of Philadelphia
Dr. Roger W. Moss, Exec.Dir.
219 S 6th St.
Philadelphia, PA 19106
Phone: (215)925-2688
Fax: (215)925-3755
E-mail: athena@philaathenaeum.org
Home Page: http://www.philaathenaeum.org

• 6014 • Athenaeum Literary Award
For recognition of outstanding literary achievement by Philadelphia authors. Authors nominated by January 1 for the previous year are eligible. A certificate is awarded annually in April. Established in 1949. For more detail and list of past winners, contact Athenaeum's homepage.

• 6015 • Fellow of The Athenaeum
To recognize outstanding contributions to nineteenth century studies. Nominations are to be made by current Fellows and a special committee of the Board of Directors by December 1. A certificate and life membership in The Athenaeum are bestowed annually. Established in 1977. For more detail and list of past winners, contact Athenaeum's homepage.

• 6016 • Charles E. Peterson Fellowships/Internships
Provides cash grants for advanced research in early American architectural history and building technology. Applications are accepted from January 1 to March 1. Grants ranging from $1,000 to $15,000 are awarded annually. Established in 1988 in honor of Charles E. Peterson, one of America's leading restoration architects and founder of the Historic American Buildings Survey. For more detail and list of past winners, contact Athenaeum's homepage. Formerly: Charles E. Peterson Fellows.

• 6017 • Charles Wharton Stork Fellow

To recognize outstanding literary achievement. Nominations are made by a special committee of the Board of Directors. The honoree delivers a special public lecture. Established in 1983 by the heirs of Charles Wharton Stork (1881-1971), author, poet, and editor. For more detail and list of past winners, contact Athenaeum's homepage.

• 6018 •
Athletes in Action
Lorri Phillips, Chief of Staff
651 Taylor Dr.
Xenia, OH 45385
Phone: (937)352-1000
Fax: (937)352-1001
E-mail: athletesinaction@aia.com
Home Page: http://www.aia.com

• 6019 • Bart Starr Award

For an NFL player exemplifying outstanding character and leadership. A trophy is awarded annually.

• 6020 •
Athletes United for Peace
Doug Harris, Exec.Dir.
712 Peralta Ave.
Berkeley, CA 94707
Phone: (510)273-9235
E-mail: dharris@athletesunitedforpeace.org
Home Page: http://www.athletesunitedforpeace.org

• 6021 • Athletes United for Peace Award

For recognition of a contribution to improve relations and foster a better understanding between people of the United States and the USSR and other countries, thereby helping to create a more peaceful world. Professional, and Olympic or international amateur athletes are eligible. A medal is awarded annually. Established in 1987.

• 6022 •
Atlanta Advertising Club
Sandra Morse, Exec.Dir.
PO Box 500846
Atlanta, GA 31150
Phone: (770)888-1400
Fax: (770)888-8697
E-mail: creativityatl@bellsouth.net
Home Page: http://www.atlantaadclub.org

• 6023 • American Advertising Awards

For creative excellence. Recognition award bestowed annually.

• 6024 •
Atlanta Film Festival
IMAGE Film and Video Center
535 Means St., Ste. C
Atlanta, GA 30318
Phone: (404)352-4225
Fax: (404)352-0173
E-mail: imageinfo@imagefv.org
Home Page: http://www.imagefv.org

Formerly: (1983) Atlanta Independent Film and Video Festival.

• 6025 • Atlanta Film and Video Festival

To recognize excellence in independent film and video achievement. Entries may be made to the following categories: animation, narrative, documentary, student, and experimental. All independent (non-commercial) media artists may apply to the Festival. The deadline is end of January, late deadline mid-February. Monetary awards totaling $5,000 and/or film and video production equipment are presented annually. Most cash awards are between $250-$500. Established in 1977.

• 6026 •
Atlanta Tipoff Club
Bret Kovacs, Contact
% Atlanta Sports Council
235 Andrew Young International Blvd.
Atlanta, GA 30303
Phone: (404)586-8584
E-mail: bkovacs@macoc.com
Home Page: http://www.naismithawards.com

• 6027 • Naismith College Coach of the Year

To recognize the outstanding male and female college basketball coach of the year. Established in 1987.

• 6028 • Naismith College Officials of the Year

To recognize the top men's and women's college officials as chosen by Division 1 Conference Supervisors. Established in 1987-88.

• 6029 • Naismith Collegiate Awards (Naismith Trophy)

To recognize the nation's top collegiate man and woman basketball player of the year (Naismith College Player of the Year.) A nationwide electorate of coaches, sportswriters, sportscasters, sports editors, and at-large voters selects the winner. A bronze trophy is bestowed annually. The trophy is permanently displayed in the Basketball Hall of Fame in Springfield, Massachusetts. Established in 1969 to honor Dr. James Naismith, the inventor of basketball. The women's trophy was established in 1983.

• 6030 • Naismith High School Awards

To recognize the nation's male and female prep player of the year (Naismith Prep Player of the Year) based on a nationwide poll of sportswriters, broadcasters, coaches, and administrators under the auspices of the Atlanta Tipoff Club. A bronze trophy is awarded. Established in 1987.

• 6031 • Naismith Outstanding Contribution to Basketball Award

To recognize an individual who has made an outstanding contribution to basketball. A trophy is awarded annually. Established in 1982.

• 6032 •
Atlantic Film Festival Association
Andrea Gosine, Operations Dir.
PO Box 36139
Halifax, NS, Canada B3J 3S9
Phone: (902)422-3456
Fax: (902)422-4006
E-mail: festival@atlanticfilm.com
Home Page: http://www.atlanticfilm.com

• 6033 • Atlantic Film Festival (Festival du Film de l'Atlantique)

To recognize achievement in the areas of film and video production. The following awards are presented: The People's Choice Award sponsored by TMN: The Move Network, an Astral Media Network. *Atlantic Canadian Awards*: Best Short Film $5000 cash prize. Sponsored by Telefilm Canada. Open to all Atlantic work under 60 minutes. Outstanding Writer's Award. A $3500 cash prize. Sponsored by Salter Street Films, Ltd. Rex Tasker Award for Best Documentary A $1500 cash prize. Sponsored by National Film Board of Canada. Open to all Atlantic documentary films and videos. Outstanding Performance by an Actor Award. A $1000 cash prize. Sponsored by ACTRA and the Linda Joy Most Promising New Director Award. A $1500 cash prize. Sponsored by Directors Guild of Canada. Cinematography Award. A $7500 prize of equipment and services. Sponsored by William F. White. Best First-time Direction Award. A prize of $5000 in services. Sponsored by Casablanca Sound & Picture. Excellence in Art Direction Award, Excellence in Editing Award, Excellence in Sound Design Award, and Excellence in Music Composition Award are also presented. *Canadian Awards:* Best Canadian Feature Award. A $3500 cash prize. Sponsored by Famous Players. Best Canadian Short Award. A $1500 cash prize. Sponsored by Famous Players. Established in 1981.

• 6034 •
Atlantic Journalism Awards
Bill Skerrett, exec.Dir.
% Canada Post
6175 Almon St.
Halifax, NS, Canada B3K 5N2
Phone: (902)425-2727
Fax: (902)462-1892
E-mail: office@ajas.ca
Home Page: http://www.ajas.ca

• 6035 • Atlantic Journalism Awards

To recognize excellence and achievements in Atlantic Canadian journalism. The categories are: Spot News Reporting (Print, Television and Radio); Spot News Photojournalism (Print and Television); Feature Writing (Print, Television and Radio); Feature Photojournalism (Print and Television); Continuing Coverage (Print, Television and Radio); Enterprise Reporting (Print, Television and Radio); (Sports Reporting); Arts & Entertainment Reporting; Atlantic Magazine Article; Atlantic Magazine Best Cover; Atlantic Magazine Best Profile Article; Video Journalist (Television); Commentary; and Editorial Cartooning. Additional awards include the Jim MacNeill New Journalist Award, Province of Nova Scotia Scholarship, Prix d'Excellence Aliant, Atlantic Lottery Corporation Achievement Award, Canada Post Corporation Journalism Prize, Emera Prize for Journalism Excellence, and the Student Prize of Excellence. Awarded annually with a framed certificate. Established in 1981.

• 6036 • Atlantic Lottery Corporation Achievement Award

Honoras a journalism student form Holland College, New Brunswick Community CollegeWoodstock, Nova Scotia Community College-Kingstec, or College of the North Atlantic-Bay St. George Campus. A monetary prize of $250 and a certificate are awarded annually. Established in 1997.

• 6037 • Imperial Oil Prize for Excellence

To honor a graduating journalism student from the University of King's College. Awarded annually with a monetary prize of $500 and a certificate. Established in 1981.

• 6038 • Journalistic Achievement Award

To recognize an outstanding contribution to journalism in Atlantic Canada. The recipient may be an individual journalist, a team of journalists, or a media organization. A framed certificate is awarded annually.

• 6039 • Le Prix D' Excellence Aliant

Honors a journalism student from the University of Moncton. A monetary prize of $500 and a certificate are awarded annually. Established in 1997.

• 6040 •
Atlantic Offshore Lobstermen's Association
114 Adams Rd.
Candia, NH 03034
Phone: (603)483-3030
Fax: (603)483-4862

• 6041 • Atlantic Offshore Fishermen's Association Annual Award

For recognition of a contribution to the commercial fishing industry of the Atlantic Coast. Nominations may be made by the AOFA Board of Directors. Award winners generally are not active commercial fishermen. A decorative hand-painted and inscribed swordfish sword is awarded annually at the Annual Meeting. Established in 1981.

• 6042 •
Atlantic Salmon Federation
Bill Taylor, Pres./CEO
PO Box 5200
St. Andrews, NB, Canada E5B 3S8
Phone: (506)529-1033
Fax: (506)529-4438
E-mail: asfweb@nbnet.nb.ca
Home Page: http://www.asf.ca

Formerly: (1982) International Atlantic Salmon Federation.

• 6043 • Olin Fellowships

To provide for improvement of knowledge or skills in advanced fields while looking for solutions to current problems in Atlantic salmon biology, management, or conservation. Applicants must be legal residents of the United States or Canada. The deadline is March 15. A monetary prize of $1,000 to $3,000 is awarded annually. Established in 1974. Application is available at the above web site.

• 6044 •
Atlantic Seed Association
Carrie E. Bohrer, Exec.Dir.
8204 Goodhurst Dr.
Gaithersburg, MD 20882
Phone: (240)631-6946
Fax: (240)631-6946
E-mail: carrieb@newsomseed.com
Home Page: http://www.atlanticseed.org

• 6045 • Seedsman of the Year, Honorary Member

For service to ASA and total industry. Recognition award bestowed annually.

• 6046 •
Atlas Economic Research Foundation
2000 North 14th. St, Ste. 500
Arlington, VA 22201
Phone: (703)934-6969
Fax: (703)352-7530
E-mail: atlas@atlasusa.org
Home Page: http://www.atlasusa.org

• 6047 • Sir Antony Fisher International Memorial Award

For recognition of the best published contribution to public understanding of the political economy of a free society. Publications must have been produced by independent public policy institutes. A monetary prize is awarded annually. Established in 1990 in memory of Sir Antony Fisher, founder of the sister Institute in England.

• 6048 •
Attorneys Bar Association of Florida
Harvey M. Alper, Contact
112 W. Citrus St.
Altamonte Springs, FL 32714-2502
Phone: (407)869-0900
Fax: (407)869-4905

• 6049 • James C. Adkins Award

For given to an individual who shows great courage in the advancement of independent legal practice. Recognition award bestowed annually.

• 6050 •
Audio Engineering Society
Roger Furness, Exec.Dir.
60 E 42nd St., Rm. 2520
New York, NY 10165-2520
Phone: (212)661-8528
Fax: (212)682-0477
E-mail: hq@aes.org
Home Page: http://www.aes.org

• 6051 • AES Publications Award

To recognize excellence in scientific work in the field of audio engineering and to reward those who publish their work on important and timely subjects in the field. Authors must be under 35 years of age. A monetary award and a certificate of recognition are awarded annually. Established in 1972.

• 6052 • Audio Engineering Society Medal Award

To recognize an individual for significant contributions to the advancement of the Society. Awarded annually. Established by an endowment of the late C. J. LeBel, one of the founders and the first President of the Society.

• 6053 • Board of Governors Award

To recognize members for special service rendered to the operation of the Society. Established in 1979.

• 6054 • Gold Medal Award

For recognition of outstanding achievements, sustained over a period of years, in the field of audio engineering. Awarded annually. Established in memory of John H. Potts by his widow in 1949. Formerly: (1971) John H. Potts Memorial Award.

• 6055 • Silver Medal Award

For recognition of a single outstanding development or achievement in the field of audio engineering. Awarded annually. Established by the Berliner family in 1953. The award now honors the audio pioneers Alexander Graham Bell, Emile Berliner, and Thomas A. Edison. Formerly: (1971) Emile Berliner Award.

• 6056 •
AudioVideo International
Dempa Publications Inc.
275 Madison Ave.
New York, NY 10016
Phone: (212)682-3755
Fax: (212)682-2730
E-mail: avi@dempa.com
Home Page: http://avi.dempa.net

• 6057 • Autosound Grand Prix Awards

To recognize outstanding auto sound equipment. Sound fidelity, design and engineering excellence, reliability, and the performance value of a specific product as it measures against the cost of that product are considered. Awards are presented in the following categories: (1) CD Tuners; (2) CD Receivers; (3) CD Changers; (4) Cassette Receiver/CD Controllers; (5) Cassette Tuner/CD Controllers; (6) Cassette Receivers; (7) Cassette Tuners; (8) Power Amplifiers; (9) DAT Players; (10) Equalizers; (11) Signal Processors; (12) Rear-Mount Speakers; (13) Flush-Mount Speakers; (14) Component Speaker Systems; (15) Speaker Separates; (16) Enclosed Speakers; (17) Security Systems; (18) Accessories; and (19) Technology Awards. Awarded annually. Established in 1983.

• 6058 • **Hi-Fi Grand Prix Awards**
To recognize outstanding Hi-Fi equipment. Products of the Year are selected in the following categories: (1) Receivers; (2) CD Players; (3) CD Changers; (4) Portable CD Players; (5) Floorstanding Speakers; (6) Bookshelf Speakers; (7) 3-Piece Speaker Systems; (8) In-Wall Speakers; (9) Tape Decks; (10) Turntables; (11) Tuners; (12) Integrated Amplifiers; (13) Power Amplifiers; (14) Preamplifiers; (15) Sound Processors; (16) Audio Tapes (Metal); (17) Audio Tapes (Standard/High Bias); (18) Headphones; (19) One-Brand Systems; (20) Tabletop Systems; (21) Turntables; and (22) Engineering Awards. Awarded annually. Established in 1979.

• 6059 • **Video Grand Prix Awards**
To recognize outstanding video equipment. Products are chosen by a committee consisting of *Audio Video*'s editorial staff and a panel of expert video critics. Equipment is evaluated on the following five criteria: (1) fidelity of video reproduction; (2) design and engineering excellence; (3) reliability; (4) craftsmanship and product integrity; and (5) price-performance relationship. Awards are presented in the following categories: (1) Color TVs (up to 21-inch); (2) Color TVs (25- to 27-inch); (3) Color TVs (29- to 31-inch); (4) Color TVs (32-inch and over); (5) Rear-Projection TVs (Under 50-inch); (6) Rear-Projection TVs (50-inch and over); (7) Two-Piece Projection TVs; (8) Laserdisc Players; (9) Monaural VCRs; (10) Hi-Fi VCRs; (11) High-Resolution VCRs; (12) Full-Size Camcorders; (13) Compact Camcorders; (14) Sub-Compact Camcorders; (15) High-Resolution Camcorders; (16) High-Grade Video Tape; (17) Super VHS Video Tape; (18) 8mm Video Tape; (19) VHS-C Video Tape; (20) Camcorder Accessories; (21) Editing Accessories; and (22) Other Accessories. Awarded annually. Established in 1988.

• 6060 •
Audubon Artists
Anthony Padovano, Pres.
47 5th Ave.
New York, NY 10003
Phone: (845)528-5743
Phone: (732)774-0707
E-mail: vinart@usamailbox.com
Home Page: http://www.audubonartists.org

• 6061 • **Annual Exhibition**
To recognize outstanding art displayed at the annual exhibition. Selection is based on works in oil, aquamedia, sculpture, and graphics. The following prizes are awarded annually: Medals of Honor and monetary awards; and silver medals. Established in 1942.

• 6062 •
Audubon Naturalist Society of the Central Atlantic States
Neal Fitzpatrick, Exec.Dir.
8940 Jones Mill Rd.
Chevy Chase, MD 20815
Phone: (301)652-9188
Fax: (301)951-7179
E-mail: contact@audubonnaturalist.org
Home Page: http://
www.audubonnaturalist.org

• 6063 • **Paul Bartsch Award**
To recognize individuals for outstanding contributions to the field of natural history and conservation. Preference is given to nominees who have had some connection with the Society. Nominations may be made at any time. A bronze medal and a certificate are awarded as merited. Established in 1962 in honor of Paul Bartsch, an outstanding naturalist who was active in the Society during the first half of this century and worked at the Smithsonian in the field of malacology (study of mollusks).

• 6064 • **Conservation Award - Private Citizen**
To recognize outstanding efforts to promote conservation in the region. Selection criteria based on advocacy, other activism, and achievement.

• 6065 • **Conservation Award - Public Official**
To recognize legislator or government official - country, state, or federal - whose dedication to environmental issues has been outstanding, resulting in significant governmental conservation actions.

• 6066 • **Corporate Award**
To recognize a company that has provided an outstanding example of corporate responsibility to the environment.

• 6067 • **Education Award**
To recognize advancements in the cause of environmental education in the region. Selection criteria include audience, curriculum, and results.

• 6068 • **Journalism Award**
To recognize a journalist whose writings have made an outstanding impact on the public by inspiring visible conservation actions.

• 6069 • **Natural History Award**
To recognize an individual who has contributed outstandingly to the knowledge or preservation of plant or animal life, especially in the mid-Atlantic region.

• 6070 • **Volunteer Award**
To recognize an individual whose volunteering has made outstanding contributions to the Society. Selection based on length of service, skills, and accomplishments. Presented at the fall meeting.

• 6071 •
Audubon of Florida
444 Brickell Ave., Ste. 850
Miami, FL 33131
Phone: (305)371-6399
Fax: (305)371-6398
Home Page: http://
www.audubonofflorida.org

• 6072 • **John Brooks' Memorial Award**
To recognize an official of local government whose achievements in protecting Florida's sensitive environmental habitats exemplifies the example set by John Brooks during his lifetime. Awarded annually. Established in 1988.

• 6073 • **Certificate of Recognition**
To recognize an individual who has given outstanding service to the cause of conservation in Florida. Local chapter members working on particular issues are considered. Awarded annually when merited. Established in 1980.

• 6074 • **Chapter of the Year**
To recognize an Audubon Chapter for valuable service. Awarded annually. Established in 1983.

• 6075 • **Conservationist of the Year**
To recognize a private individual and a government official - local, state, or federal - for dedication to environmental issues. Awards are presented in each category annually. Established in 1973.

• 6076 • **Corporate Award**
To recognize industry for significant contributions to environmental issues. Awarded when merited. Established in 1985.

• 6077 • **Allan D. Cruickshank Memorial Award**
To recognize an individual whose interest in conservation and wildlife most nearly exemplifies the concerns and ideals of Allan Cruickshank. Awarded annually. Established in 1975.

• 6078 • **Legislative Excellence Award**
To recognize legislators for outstanding service to the cause of conservation in Florida. Awarded annually when merited. Established in 1980.

• 6079 • **Outstanding Journalist Award**
To recognize a journalist for service to the cause of conservation. Awarded annually when merited. Established in 1984.

Awards are arranged in alphabetical order below their administering organizations

• 6080 • Polly Redford Memorial Award
To recognize an individual who shows personal dedication and moral courage in the cause of conservation. Awarded annually. Established in 1973 to honor Polly Redford, a dedicated and effective fighter against those who would despoil Florida. She was responsible in large measure for the establishment of the Biscayne National Monument and labored during the last days of her life to assure future generations that life would still be worth living long after her days.

• 6081 • Special Commendation Award
To recognize individuals and organizations for service to the cause of conservation. Awarded annually when merited. Established in 1980.

• 6082 •
Audubon Society of New Hampshire
Miranda Levin, Commn.Dir.
3 Silk Farm Rd.
Concord, NH 03301
Phone: (603)224-9909
Fax: (603)226-0902
E-mail: asnh@nhaudubon.org
Home Page: http://www.nhaudubon.org

• 6083 • Goodhue-Elkins Award
To recognize outstanding contributions to the study of New Hampshire birds. Named for Charles Goodhue and Kimball Elkins, two of the state's most well-known birders. Established in 1995.

• 6084 • Tudor Richards Award
To recognize the individual who best exemplifies Tudor Richard's love and knowledge of the outdoors, and who has worked tirelessly and effectively on behalf of conservation in New Hampshire. Individuals must be nominated by the Board of Trustees of the Society. An inscribed silver bowl is awarded annually. In addition, the recipient's name is inscribed on the silver bowl that resides at ASNH Headquarters. Established in 1982 to honor Tudor Richards, former president and executive director of ASNH, a naturalist, forester, and ornithologist.

• 6085 • Volunteer of the Year Award
To recognize outstanding service that strengthens the organization and inspires and motivates others. Established in 1997.

• 6086 •
Augusta National Golf Club
PO Box 2086
Augusta, GA 30913
Phone: (706)667-6000
Fax: (706)731-0611
Home Page: http://www.masters.org

• 6087 • Masters Golf Tournament
To recognize the winners of the annual Masters Tournament. The following awards are presented: the name of the winner is engraved on the permanent Masters Tournament trophy which remains at the club. A sterling silver replica of this trophy is awarded along with a gold medal, to the winner; the name of the runner-up is engraved on the permanent Masters Tournament trophy. A silver salver and a silver medal are awarded, to the runner-up; an engraved silver is awarded to the low amateur and a silver medal to the amateur runner-up. Crystal Awards - an engraved crystal vase is presented to the player who turns in the low score on each of the four days of the tournament, an engraved crystal bowl to each player who scores a hole-in-one, a pair of crystal goblets to each player who scores an eagle, and a large crystal bowl for a double eagle. In addition, cash prizes are awarded to professionals in the tournament. Established in 1934.

• 6088 •
Augustan Society
Dr. Robert Cleve, Ch.
PO Box 75
Daggett, CA 92327-0075
Phone: (760)254-9223
Fax: (760)254-1953
E-mail: rcleve@msn.com
Home Page: http://
www.augustansociety.org

• 6089 • Fellowship of the Augustan Society
To recognize outstanding contributions to the fields of history, heraldry, genealogy, chivalry, or related fields of study. The award is usually presented to a member of the Society, but occasionally it is given to non-members who have made significant contributions to the field of study of interest to the Society. A certificate is awarded annually. Established in 1965.

• 6090 •
Augustinians of the Assumption
Dennis Gallagher, Regional Superior
Assumptionist Center
330 Market St.
Brighton, MA 02135
Phone: (617)783-0400
Fax: (617)783-8030
E-mail: info@assumption.us
Home Page: http://www.assumption.us

• 6091 • Emmanuel d'Alzon Medal
To recognize values, qualities, and activities that exemplify the ideals of Father Emmanuel d'Alzon, founder of the Assumptionists, in his service to church or country. A bronze medal is awarded as merited. Established in 1954 by the Assumptionists Order, Rome, Italy.

• 6092 •
The Austin Chronicle
Louis Black, Ed.
PO Box 49066
Austin, TX 78765
Phone: (512)454-5766
Fax: (512)458-6910
E-mail: mail@austinchronicle.com
Home Page: http://
www.austinchronicle.com

• 6093 • *The Austin Chronicle* Best of Austin
To recognize some of the best aspects of life in Austin, Texas. Categories include architecture and lodging, arts and entertainment, food and drink, kidstuff, media, outdoors and recreation, politics and personalities, shopping, and services. There are over 200 readers' categories and over 200 critics' categories. Certificates are awarded annually in September. Established 1989.

• 6094 • *The Austin Chronicle* Hot Sauce Contest
To recognize the best hot sauce (salsa). Individuals, restaurants, and commercial bottlers from any country may enter in 10 categories. Trophies and certificates are awarded at the contest in August.

• 6095 • *The Austin Chronicle* Readers' Poll Music Awards
To recognize musicians and individuals in music-related businesses in Austin who are voted by the readers of *The Austin Chronicle.* The poll ballot is printed four times each year. Awards are presented in more than 50 categories. Plaques are awarded annually in March at the Austin Music Awards. Established in 1981.

• 6096 • *The Austin Chronicle* Readers' Restaurant Poll
For recognition of outstanding area restaurants. Ballots are run four times in September with over 100 categories. Results are printed and certificates mailed to winners annually in October. Critics' poll is also included. Established in 1986.

• 6097 •
Automated Imaging Association
Dana Whalls, Mkgt. & Pub.Rel.Mgr.
900 Victors Way
PO Box 3724
Ann Arbor, MI 48106
Phone: (734)994-6088
Fax: (734)994-3338
E-mail: aia@automated-imaging.org
Home Page: http://
www.machinevisiononline.org

Formerly: (1988) Automated Vision Association.

• 6098 • Automated Imaging Achievement Award
To recognize outstanding contributions to machine vision and imaging in four categories: technology, leadership, industrial application, and scientific application. Selection is by nomination. A trophy is awarded annually. Established in 1991.

Awards are arranged in alphabetical order below their administering organizations

• 6099 •
Automobile Journalists Association of Canada
(Association des Journalistes Automobile du Canada)
Beth Xenarios, Mgr.
PO Box 398, Main PO
Cobourg, ON, Canada K9A 4L1
Phone: (905)342-9061
Toll-Free: 800-361-1516
Fax: 800-439-0989
E-mail: beth@ajac.ca
Home Page: http://www.ajac.ca

• 6100 • **Art of the Automobile Competition**
Recognizes the best amateur artist or art student's work on an automobile theme. Awarded annually.

• 6101 • **Best New Design**
Annual award of recognition. Inquire for application details.

• 6102 • **Best New Technology**
Annual award of recognition. Inquire for application details.

• 6103 • **Car of the Year Awards**
Recognizes the best new vehicles. Annual awards are given in several categories.

• 6104 • **Car of the Year (COTY)**
Annual award of recognition. Inquire for application details.

• 6105 • **Journalist of the Year**
Annual award of recognition. Inquire for application details.

• 6106 • **Truck of the Year**
Annual award of recognition.

• 6107 •
Automotive Communications Council
Doug Ferguson, Pres.
4600 East-West Highway, Ste. 300
Bethesda, MD 20814
Phone: (240)333-1089
Fax: (301)654-3299
E-mail: acc@aftermarket.org
Home Page: http://www.acc-online.org/

• 6108 • **Promotional Achievement Awards**
Award of recognition. For automotive wholesalers. Awarded annually.

• 6109 •
Automotive Hall of Fame
Dr. David Cole, Exec.Dir.
21400 Oakwood Blvd.
Dearborn, MI 48124
Phone: (313)240-4000
Fax: (313)240-8641
Home Page: http://www.automotivehalloffame.org
Formerly: (1981) Automotive Organization Team.

• 6110 • **Induction into the Automotive Hall of Fame**
Bestowed on individuals who have dedicated their careers to the automotive industry. Induction is reserved for individuals who have made a dramatic impact on the development of the automobile or the automotive industry. Induction is reserved for those who are deceased or have retired from the industry. Established in 1967.

• 6111 • **Automotive Industry Leader of the Year**
For recognition of outstanding leadership in the automotive industry currently. Supporting members of the Hall of Fame are eligible to nominate candidates. Established in 1982.

• 6112 • **Award for Young Leadership and Excellence**
Celebrates the role of the individual in the motor vehicle industry. The membership makes nominations and electees are chosen by a special committee. Nomination deadline is November 2. Established in 1980.

• 6113 • **Distinguished Service Citation**
Recognizes men and women who have contributed to the motor vehicle industry in some significant manner, through either sustained superior performance or a specific important achievement. A recipient may be actively engaged in or retired from the industry when selected. Established in 1940 by Automobile Old Timers.

• 6114 •
Automotive Industry Action Group
Darlene Miller, Managing Dir.
26200 Lahser Rd., Ste. 200
Southfield, MI 48034
Phone: (248)358-3003
Phone: (248)358-3570
Fax: (248)799-7995
E-mail: memberinfo@aiag.org
Home Page: http://www.aiag.org

• 6115 • **Outstanding Achievement Award**
Award of recognition. For volunteers who benefit AIAG and the automotive industry. Awarded annually.

• 6116 •
Automotive Occupant Restraints Council
George Kirchoff, Pres.
1081 Dove Run Rd. Ste. 403
Lexington, KY 40502
Phone: (859)269-4240
Fax: (859)269-4241
E-mail: info@aorc.org
Home Page: http://www.aorc.org/

• 6117 • **Pathfinder Award**
Award of recognition. For vision and leadership in auto, occupant safety. Awarded annually.

• 6118 •
Automotive Oil Change Association
Stephen Christie, Exec.Dir.
12810 Hillcrest, Ste. 221
Dallas, TX 75230
Phone: (972)458-9468
Toll-Free: 800-331-0329
Fax: (972)458-9539
E-mail: info@aoca.org
Home Page: http://www.aoca.org

• 6119 • **Member of the Year**
Award of recognition. For outstanding contribution for the association's growth & enhanced programs and/or the oil change industry. Awarded annually.

• 6120 •
Automotive Training Managers Council
Ed M. Jones, Pres.
101 Blue Seal Dr. SE, No. 101
Leesburg, VA 20175-5646
Phone: (703)669-6634
Fax: (703)669-6126
E-mail: brodriguez@asecert.org
Home Page: http://www.atmc.org

• 6121 • **Automotive Training Awards**
To recognize employee or customer training programs in the areas of automotive technology, sales, and general management. Any automotive training program developer or automotive training provider is eligible. The following awards are presented: Grand Award, Award of Excellence, and Honorable Mention. A plaque and a news release in the trade press are awarded annually at the ASIA International Convention. Established in 1985.

• 6122 •
Automotive Warehouse Distributors Association
Fletcher Lord Jr., Chm.
7101 Wisconsin Ave., Ste. 1300
Bethesda, MD 20814
Phone: (301)654-6664
Fax: (301)654-3299
E-mail: info@awda.org
Home Page: http://www.awda.org

• 6123 • **Automotive Leader of the Year**
To recognize an individual for outstanding and significant contributions to the automotive after-

Awards are arranged in alphabetical order below their administering organizations

market. Individuals who are employed in the aftermarket and who have contributed to the aftermarket segment of the automotive industry in some unique way are eligible. The deadline for nominations is July 26. A trophy is awarded annually at the AWDA annual business conference. Established in 1959. Formerly: Automotive Man of the Year.

• 6124 •
Aviation Distributors and Manufacturer Association
Talbot H. Gee, Exec.Dir.
1900 Arch St.
Philadelphia, PA 19103-1498
Phone: (215)564-3484
Fax: (215)963-9784
E-mail: adma@fernley.com
Home Page: http://www.adma.org

• 6125 • Aviation Education Certificates of Merit
To recognize individuals for their positive contributions to aviation education. Certificates of Merit are presented annually.

• 6126 • Janice Marie Dyer Award
To recognize outstanding achievements in furthering aviation education. Any group, company, agency, or individual who has made significant efforts to promote and advance aviation education as an industry, hobby, vacation, or in the national interest is eligible. Companies engaged in the specific commercial production of educational materials and programs are not eligible. A full-color embossed scroll is awarded annually. Established in 1969 in memory of Stewart G. Potter, former Executive Vice President. Formerly: Stuart G. Potter Award.

• 6127 •
Aviation Hall of Fame and Museum of New Jersey
Teterboro Airport
400 Fred Wehran Dr.
Teterboro, NJ 07608
Phone: (201)288-6344
Fax: (201)288-5666
E-mail: info@njahof.org

• 6128 • Aviation Hall of Fame and Museum of New Jersey
To honor men and women from New Jersey who have played a significant role in the history of New Jersey aviation. New Jersey residents or persons who have brought national recognition to New Jersey by their activities in the state are eligible. A bronze plaque in relief of the inductee's likeness is awarded annually at the induction dinner. Established in 1972.

• 6129 • Distinguished Service Medals
To recognize individuals for outstanding contributions to aviation. Awarded annually.

• 6130 • Fred L. Wehran Aviation Achievement Award
To recognize outstanding contributions to aviation. Industry, airports, and airlines are eligible. Awarded annually. Established in 1979.

• 6131 •
Aviation Safety Institute
Charles Minshall, Dir.
6797 North High St.
Worthington, OH 43085
Phone: (614)885-4242
Fax: (614)793-1708
E-mail: 110364.3550@compuserve.com
Home Page: http://www.techexpo.com/tech_soc/asi.html

• 6132 • Airport Crash/Fire/Rescue/Medical Preparedness Award
To recognize airports and their communities for high levels of preparedness or efforts to elevate the level of preparedness for any airport-related disaster. A metal plaque is awarded annually when merited. Established in 1976.

• 6133 •
Aviation Technician Education Council
Dr. Richard Dumaresq, Contact
2090 Wexford Ct.
Harrisburg, PA 17112-1579
Phone: (717)540-7121
Fax: (717)540-7121
E-mail: info@atec-amt.org
Home Page: http://www.atec-amt.org/

• 6134 • Ivan D. Livi Outstanding Aviation Maintenance Technology Instructor
To recognize outstanding achievement by an aviation maintenance technology instructor. This achievement may be in the form of a single event or long-term outstanding performance but must have had direct impact on the aviation maintenance student. Active instructors of Airframe and/or Powerplant employed by an ATEC member institution are eligible. Nominations may be submitted in early December. A plaque, travel expenses, and scholarship money are awarded annually at the convention. Established in 1989. Additional information is available from Richard Dumaresq, Executive Director.

• 6135 •
Aviation Week & Space Technology
1200 G St., Suite 922
Washington DC, DC 20005
Phone: (202)383-2346
Fax: (202)383-2346
E-mail: p02cs@mcgraw-hill.com
Home Page: http://www.aviationnow.com

• 6136 • Laurels/Laureates Awards
To recognize individuals or teams for outstanding contributions in the field of aerospace during the previous year or throughout a lifetime of service. A trophy is awarded annually in each of six major categories: (1) Air Transport; (2) Space/Missiles; (3) Electronics; (4) Operations; (5) Government/Military; and (6) Aeronautics/Propulsion. Established in 1958.

• 6137 • Lifetime Achievement Award
No additional information available for this edition.

• 6138 • Special Achievement Award
No additional information available this edition.

• 6139 •
Avicultural Advancement Council of Canada
Mr. Mark Curtis, Exec.Dir.
PO Box 123
Chemainus, BC, Canada V0R 1K0
Phone: (250)246-4803
Fax: (250)246-4912
E-mail: exec@aacc.ca
Home Page: http://www.aacc.ca

• 6140 • First Breeding Award
For the first breeding of an avicultural subject in Canada. Awarded annually.

• 6141 •
Avon Books
HarperCollins Publishers Inc.
Flare Young Adult Novel Competition
10 E 53rd St.
New York, NY 10022
Phone: (212)207-7000
Fax: (212)207-7145
Home Page: http://www.harpercollins.com/imprints.asp?imprint=Avon

• 6142 • Distinguished Career Awards
No further information was available for this edition.

• 6143 • Special Awards
No further information was available for this edition.

• 6144 •
Avon Products, Inc.
Women of Enterprise Awards
1345 Avenue of the Americas
New York, NY 10105
Phone: (212)282-5000
Toll-Free: 800-FOR-AVON
Fax: (212)282-6049
Home Page: http://www.avon.com

• 6145 • Women of Enterprise Awards
Established in 1987 by Avon Products, Inc. in conjunction with the U.S. Small Business Administration, the award recognizes women business owners who have been profitably self-employed for at least of five years and who have overcome significant hardships to achieve success. Candidates may be nominated by women's and civic organizations or may apply directly. The deadline for applications is December 1. Five winners each receive a exclusively-

designed trophy award and a three-day trip to New York City. They will also have the opportunity to speak at self-employment seminars and conferences for women. A matching $1,000 grant is also awarded to organizations which nominate winning candidates. Avon's Women of Enterprise Awards is the first corporate-sponsored awards program for women entrepreneurs.

• 6146 •
AVS
David E. Aspnes, Pres.
120 Wall St., 32nd Fl.
New York, NY 10005
Phone: (212)248-0200
Fax: (212)248-0245
E-mail: avsnyc@.avs.org
Home Page: http://www.avs.org

• 6147 • **Fellow of the Society**
Recognizes members who have made sustained and outstanding technical contributions in areas of interest to AVS. Current AVS members who have mad sustained and outstanding scientific and technical contributions in research, engineering, technical advancement, academic education, or managerial leadership for at least ten years and have been members for at least five consecutive years are eligible. A certificate is awarded. A nomination packet, including the nomination form (available at the above web site) must be submitted electronically in MS Word format by March 31.

• 6148 • **Gaede-Langmuir Award**
To recognize and encourage outstanding discoveries and inventions in the sciences and technologies of interest to the Society. The contribution may be in the nature of a new invention, process or discovery; this shall include significant advances in theory, the discovery of a new effect, phenomenon or process or the invention of a novel device, instrument, technique or measurement. Selection is by nomination. The award may be bestowed to more than one person if several person shared in the invention or discovery. $10,000, a plaque, and honorary lectureship at a regular session of the International Symposium are awarded. Travel expenses of the awardee(s) to the meeting at which the award is presented is also reimbursed. Awarded biennially. A nomination letter, description of highlights, biographical materials, and supporting letters must be submitted by March 31. Established in 1977 by an endowing grant from Dr. Kenneth C. D. Hickman.

• 6149 • **Graduate Research Award**
To recognize and encourage excellence in graduate studies in the sciences and technologies of interest to the Society. Students must be registered graduate students in an accredited academic institution in North America to be eligible. The prize may be awarded to a given individual only once. Students working directly with a member of the Scholarships and Awards Committee are not eligible to apply. A monetary award of $1,000 a certificate and travel expenses to attend the International Symposium are awarded annually to approximately 10 students. Completed application and report on candidate forms (available at the above web site) must be submitted electronically by March 31. Established in 1984.

• 6150 • **George T. Hanyo Award**
Recognizes outstanding performance in technical support of research or development in areas of interst to the AVS. Persons outside normal professional circles are eligible. A nominee must have contributed unusual skills and creative scientific or technical ideas in support of at least one major research or development program. The work must have been provided oave a period of at least ten years. A $1500 cash prize, a certificate, and riembursement of travel expenses to the meeting at which the award is presented are awarded. A complete package, including a curriculum vitae; statement of objectives; list of publications mentioning the nominee in the acknowledgements section; list of publications authored or coauthored by the nominee; photgraphs, drawings or equicalent records showing examples of the nominee's work; letters attesting to the value of the work must be submitted electronically in a MS Word document to Angela Klink, AVS (212)248-0200, Fax: (212)248-0245, email: angela@avs.org by March 31. Established in 1996 by the Kurt J. Lesker Co. in memory of Geroge T. Hanyo, a highly skilled, long-time employee of the company.

• 6151 • **Dorothy M. and Earl S. Hoffman Award**
Recognizes and encourages excellence in graduate studies in the sciences and technologies of interest to the AVS. Nominees must be registered graduate students in an accredited academic institution at the time when the applications are due. A $1500 cash prize, a certificate, and reimbursement of travel support to attend the International Symposium are awarded. A completed application form and report on candidate form (available at the above web site) must be submitted electronically by March 31.

• 6152 • **Dorothy M. and Earl S. Hoffman Scholarship**
Recognizes and encourages excellence in continuing graduate studies in the sciences and technologies of interest to the AVS. Nominees must be registered graduate students in an accredited academic institution at the time when the applications are due. A $1000 cash prize, certificate, and reimbursement of travel support to attend the International Symposium are awarded. Completed application and report on candidate forms (available at the above web site) must be submitted electronically by March 31. Established in 2002. Funded by a bequest for Dorothy M. Hoffman who was president of AVS in 1974.

• 6153 • **Honorary Member**
To recognize an individual who has performed eminent service to the Society or who has made outstanding contributions in science, engineering, or allied fields of interest to the Society. Nominees may be proposed to the Board of Directors in writing by the Scholarships and Awards Committee or by at least ten members of whom no more than three shall be members of the Board of Directors. At least a three-fourths majority vote by the Board is necessary for election to Honorary Membership. Not more than two are awarded annually. Established in 1955.

• 6154 • **Peter Mark Memorial Award**
To recognize outstanding theoretical or experimental work by a young scientist or engineer. The nominee must be a young scientist or engineer, born in or after the year 1967, who has contributed outstanding theoretical or experimental work, at least part of which must have been published in the *Journal of Vacuum Science and Technology.* A monetary award of $6,500, travel expenses to the meeting at which the award is presented, honorary lectureship at a regular session of the International Symposium, and a certificate are awarded. A nomination letter, description of highlights, biographical materials, and supporting letters must be submitted by March 31. Established in 1979 in memory of Dr. Peter Mark, who served as Editor of the *Journal of Vacuum Science and Technology* from 1975 until his death in 1979.

• 6155 • **Albert Nerken Award**
To recognize outstanding contributions to the solution of technological problems in areas of interest to the Society. A nominee must be a recognized worker in his or her field with an outstanding record of sustained (five years or more) contributions to the solution of technological problems. A monetary prize of $5000 and a certificate are awarded annually. Travel expenses of the awardee to the meeting at which the award is presented shall be reimbursed. A nomination letter, description of highlights, biographical materials, and supporting letters must be submitted by March 31. Established in 1984 by Veeco Instruments, Inc., in recognition of its founder, Albert Nerken, for his role as a founding member of the Society, his early work in the field of high vacuum and leak detection, and his contributions to the commercial development of that instrumentation.

• 6156 • **John A. Thornton Memorial Award and Lecture**
To recognize outstanding research or technological innovation in the areas of interest to the AVS, with emphasis on the fields of thin films, plasma processing, and related topics. A monetary award of $10,000, a plaque and travel expenses to attend the National Symposium and present a lecture are awarded biennially. A nomination letter, description of highlights, biographical materials, and supporting letters must be submitted by March 31. Established in 1989 to honor Dr. John A. Thornton, whose devotion to science, singular contributions to the generation and study of thin films, effectiveness as an educator, and unfailing humility won him the uncommon esteem and affection of his colleagues.

• 6157 • **Russell and Sigurd Varian Fellowship**
To recognize and encourage excellence in graduate studies in vacuum science. The nominee

must be a full time graduate student in an accredited academic institution in North America. Selection is made on the basis of academic record, proven excellence in research, and, for finalists, an interview with the trustees. A one year fellowship of $1500, a certificate, and reimbursement of travel support to attend the International Symposium are awarded annually. Completed application and report on candidate forms (available at the above web site) must be submitted electronically by March 31. Established in 1982 to commemorate the pioneering work of Russell and Sigurd Varian in the field of vacuum science and technology. The award is supported by Varian Associates.

• 6158 • John L. Vossen Memorial Award
Recognizes and encourages the development of high school science demonstration experiments of interest to the AVS. Active high school or middle school science teachers in the United States, Canada, or Mexico are eligible. Current AVS Board of Directors and Scholarship Awards Committe and their families are not eligible. An equipment grant of up to $2000, a $1000 cash prize, and reimbursement of travel expenses to attend the AVS International Symposium are awarded annually. A 200-300 word abstract; two page maximum proposal; a letter of support from the school principal or director; a budget for equipment must be submitted electronically in a MS Word document to Angela Klink, AVS, (212)248-0200, FAX: (212)248-0245; Email: angela@avs.org must be submitted by February 28. Established in memory of John Vossen who served the AVS for more than 25 years.

• 6159 • Medard W. Welch Award in Vacuum Science
To recognize outstanding research in fields of interest to the Society. The nominee must have accomplished outstanding theoretical or experimental research within the ten years preceding the year in which the award is made. Special consideration is given to nominees currently engaged in an active career of research. A monetary award of $10,000, a gold medal, a certificate, and honorary lectureship at a regular session of the International Symposium are awarded. Travel expenses of the awardee to the meeting at which the award is presented shall be reimbursed. At least one award is given annually. A nomination letter, description of highlights, biographical materials, and supporting letters must be submitted by March 31. Established in 1969 in memory of M.W. Welch, founder of the Society.

• 6160 • Nellie Yeoh Whetten Award
To recognize and encourage excellence by women in graduate studies in the sciences and technologies of interest to the Society. The nominee must be a registered graduate student in an accredited academic institution in North America. A monetary award of $1,500, a certificate, and travel expenses to attend the National Symposium are awarded annually. An application form and report on candidate form (available at the above web site) must be submitted electronically by March 31. Established in 1989 to honor Nellie Yeoh Whetten.

• 6161 •
Awana Clubs International
Jim Jordan, Dir. Communications
1 E Bode Rd.
Streamwood, IL 60107-6658
Phone: (630)213-2000
Toll-Free: (866)292-6227
Fax: 877-292-6232
E-mail: customerservicehelp@awana.org
Home Page: http://www.awana.org

• 6162 • Citation Award
Annual award for achievement.

• 6163 • Meritorious Trophy
Annual award for achievement.

• 6164 • Timothy Trophy
Annual award for achievement.

• 6165 •
Awards and Recognition Association
Charles Miles PhD, Pres.
4700 W Lake Ave.
Glenview, IL 60025
Phone: (847)375-4800
Toll-Free: 800-344-2148
Fax: (732)460-7320
E-mail: info@ara.org
Home Page: http://www.ara.org

Formed by merger of: (1980) Trophy Dealers of America; American Award Manufacturers Association.

• 6166 • ARA Hall of Fame Award
To honor the creativity, foresight, and organization of men and women who have shaped the awards and engraving industry and laid the foundation for its present growth. Nominees must have made a significant and lasting contribution to the awards and engraving industry. They must be: originators of a new product or equipment for the industry or new designs for awards, or originators of a leading company that has had an impact on the industry; or leaders who help the whole industry through product development, sales or sales management, the local community, or the association. Established in 1977. Formerly: TDMA Hall of Fame.

• 6167 • Best Trade Show Product and Best Booth Display
For recognition of the best trade show product and the best booth display. An awards committee selects the best single and multiple booths at the International Winter Awards Market. Attendees select the best new products at the show. Established in 1984.

• 6168 • Branch Leadership Award
No further information was available for this edition. Formerly: (1997) Chapter and Regional Director of the Year.

• 6169 • The Founders Award
To honor the person(s) who has unselfishly worked for the success of the association. Nominations by members are accepted. The ARA Obelisk is presented annually at the International Winter Awards Market. Established in recognition of the contributions of the original 13 founders of the association. Formerly: John and Jessie Crittenden Memorial Award.

• 6170 • Retailer of the Year Awards
To recognize the best member retailers. Must be nominated by members suppliers. Awarded annually. Established in 1990. Formerly: (1997) Dealer Awards.

• 6171 • Supplier of the Year Award
To recognize the best member suppliers. Awarded annually. Formerly: (1997) Dealer and Supplier Volunteer of the Year Award.

• 6172 •
Ayn Rand Institute
Dr. Yaron Brook, Exec.Dir.
2121 Alton Pkwy., Ste. 250
Irvine, CA 92606
Phone: (949)222-6550
Fax: (949)222-6558
E-mail: mail@aynrand.org
Home Page: http://www.aynrand.org

• 6173 • *Anthem* Essay Contest
To encourage analytical thinking and writing excellence among 9th and 10th graders. Named for Ayn Rand's novelette, *Athem*. Essay deadline is March 30. A monetary award of $2,000 is bestowed for first place, $200 is bestowed to each of the 10 second place winners, and $100 is bestowed to each of the 20 third place winners. Winners are announced annually in June. Established in September 1992.

• 6174 • *The Fountainhead* Essay Contest
To encourage critical thinking and writing on significant philosophic and psychological issues. High school juniors and seniors (or the last two years of secondary school in Canada) may submit essays on predetermined topics relating to *The Fountainhead* by April 25. The following awards are presented: First prize - $10,000; five second prizes of $2,000 each; 10 third prizes of $1,000 each; 45 finalists receive $100 each; and 175 semifinalists receive $50 each. Awarded annually. Established in 1986.

• 6175 •
Ayrshire Breeders' Association
Becky Payne, Exec.Sec.
1224 Alton Creek Rd., Ste. B
Columbus, OH 43228
Phone: (614)335-0020
Fax: (614)335-0023
E-mail: info@usayrshire.com
Home Page: http://www.usayrshire.com

• 6176 • Distinguished Service Award
To recognize an outstanding contribution in service and dedication to the Association, and a contribution to the development of the breed. Individuals who are associated with the Ayrshire Breeders' Association and are employed by the Association or who breed purebred Ayrshires are eligible. A hand-lettered certificate is awarded at the annual meeting. Established in 1948.

• 6177 •
Babson College
Brian M. Barefoot, Pres.
231 Forest St.
Babson Park, MA 02457-0310
Phone: (781)235-1200
Fax: (617)239-4464
Home Page: http://www3.babson.edu

• 6178 • Academy of Distinguished Entrepreneurs
To honor outstanding achievement in entrepreneurship in the United States and throughout the world. There are no restrictions other than personal accomplishment. A plaque and a certificate are presented annually on Founder's Day in April.

• 6179 • Cruickshank Alumni Leadership Award
Recognizes the volunteer work of the alumni in a diversity of areas over an extended period of time.

• 6180 • Distinguished Recent Alumnus Award
Recognizes the volunteer work of recent Babson graduates.

• 6181 • Distinguished Service to College Award
Recognizes alumni volunteer work contributing to the college community.

• 6182 • The Douglass Foundation Graduate Business Plan Competition
Recognizes feasible business plans. Applicants must be individual graduate students or teams of graduate students. One award is given to the best plan and one to the first runner-up and the second runner-up. Plans can be in any one of the following areas: start-ups; acquisitions; company growth; real estate development; or entrepreneurship.

• 6183 • John H. Muller Jr. Undergraduate Business Plan Competition
Recognizes the best business plan for an entrepreneurial venture. Candidates must be individual graduate students or teams of undergraduate students.

• 6184 • Student Business Initiative Award
Recognizes a student business owner. Applicants must be Babson undergraduate students. Winners are selected by the Award Committee based on initiative, character, originality, persistence, and success in running one's own venture. $1000 and a lifetime invitation to the Founder's Day Ceremony are awarded.

• 6185 •
Babson College
Center for Information Management Studies
Babson Hall 323
Wellesley, MA 02457
Phone: (781)239-4531
Fax: (781)239-6416
E-mail: staff@babson.edu
Home Page: http://www.babson.edu/cims

• 6186 • Paul F. Greene Telecommunications Research Fund Award
For those interested in the telecommunications field.

• 6187 • Information Systems Award
for the student with the Recognizes the best MIS academic performance. Babson College students are eligible. Awarded annually.

• 6188 •
BACCHUS Network
Drew Hunter MPA, Pres./CEO
PO Box 100430
PO Box 100430
Denver, CO 80250-0430
Phone: (303)871-0901
Fax: (303)871-0907
E-mail: drew@bacchusgamma.org
Home Page: http://www.bacchusgamma.org

• 6189 • Advisor of the Year
Annual award of recognition. Entrants are selected by nomination.

• 6190 • Chapter of the Year
Award of recognition. For outstanding chapter of the year. Awarded annually.

• 6191 • Outstanding Program
Award of recognition. Awarded annually.

• 6192 •
Gina Bachauer International Piano Foundation
Paul Pollei, Artistic Dir.
138 W Broadway, Ste. 220
Salt Lake City, UT 84101
Phone: (801)297-4250
Fax: (801)521-9202
E-mail: info@bachauer.com
Home Page: http://www.bachauer.com

• 6193 • Gina Bachauer International Piano Competition
For recognition of excellence in piano performance. Pianists of any nationality age 19 through 32 are eligible. Finalists of previous Gina Bachauer competitions are not eligible. The six finalists are ranked by the International Jury, and first through sixth prizes are awarded. Additional special prizes are presented. The Gina Bachauer First Prize includes a commemorative gold medal; $ 3,000 a Utah symphony concert engagement, concert and recital engagements worldwide, a professional camera study, and a CD solo recording. Second Prize includes a commemorative silver medal, a monetary award of $15,000, a concert performance opportunities. Third prize winners receive a commemorative bronze medal, a monetary prize of $10,000, and concert and recital engagements. The Fourth prize and the Fifth Prize include monetary awards of $8,000 and $6,000 respectively. Sixth prize carries a monetary award of $4,000. Also awarded are an Audience Prize of $1,000 to the finalist receiving the most votes by members of the audience attending both evenings of the final round. Competitors receiving prizes are required to be present for all events of the competition. Awarded quadrennial. Established in 1976 by Paul C. Pollei, in honor of Gina Bachauer, for her contributions as a pianist to the musical life of Utah.

• 6194 •
Baker Street Irregulars
Steven Rothman, Ed.
PO Box 465
Hanover, PA 17331
Phone: (717)633-8911
E-mail: email@bakerstreetjournal.com
Home Page: http://www.bakerstreetjournal.com

• 6195 • Irregular Shillings
Award of recognition. For Sherlockians who have shown serious interest over a period of years. Awarded periodically and is the formal induction to the society.

• 6196 • Morley/Montgomery Award
Recognizes the best paper in the society's publication *The Baker Street Journal*. Awarded annually.

• 6197 •
Bakerstown Beagle Club
486 Browns Hill Rd
Valencia, PA 16059-2704

• 6198 • Beagle Brace Consistency Award
For performance in brace beagle trials. Trophy awarded annually.

Awards are arranged in alphabetical order below their administering organizations

• 6199 •
Bald-Headed Men of America
John T. Capps III, Founder
102 Bald Dr.
Morehead City, NC 28557
Phone: (252)726-1855
Fax: (252)726-6061
E-mail: jcapps4102@aol.com
Home Page: http://members.aol.com/BaldUSA/join.htm

• 6200 • **Bald is Beautiful**
To eliminate vanity associated with baldness and to instill pride and dignity in being bald headed. Criteria considered are: a bald head, chrome-dome or a haircut with a hole in it. Awards may be given in the following categories: Mr. Clean, Yul Brynner, Trapper John, Smallest Bald Spot, Winner Best All Round, Smoothest, Sexiest, Most Kissable, Solar Dome, and Bald Look-A-Likes, and Bald Hall of Fame. A plaque, a certificate, and media recognition are awarded annually in September. Established in 1973.

• 6201 •
Baldridge National Quality Program
National Institute of Standards and Technology
Thomas Schamberger, Exec.Dir.
100 Bureau Dr., Stop 1020
Gaithersburg, MD 20899
Phone: (301)975-2036
Fax: (301)948-3716
E-mail: nqp@nist.gov
Home Page: http://www.quality.nist.gov

Formerly: (1989) National Bureau of Standards.

• 6202 • **Malcolm Baldrige National Quality Award**
This, the highest level of national recognition a U.S. company can receive, is given to recognize business excellence and quality achievement and to promote greater quality awareness among U.S. businesses. Privately or publicly-owned businesses located in the United States may apply for the Award each April. Subsidiaries of companies may apply if they primarily serve either the public or businesses other than the parent company. Applications are examined against seven examination categories weighted according to importance. The award criteria categories and weights are: Leadership - the company's leadership system, values, expectations, and public responsibilities (9%); Information and Analysis the effectiveness of information collection and analysis to support customer-driven performance, excellence, and marketplace success (7.5%); Strategic Planning - the effectiveness of strategic and business planning and development of plans, with a strong focus on customer and operational performance requirements (5.5%); Human Resource Development and Management - the success of efforts to realize the full potential of the work force to create a high performance organization (14%); Process Management - the effectiveness of systems and process for assuring the quality of products or services (14%); Business Results - the company's performance and improvement in key business areas (product and service quality, productivity and operational effectiveness, supply quality, and financial performance indicators linked to these areas) (25%); and Customer Focus and Satisfaction - the effectiveness of systems to determine customer requirements and satisfaction and the demonstrated success in meeting customers' expectations (25%). Awards are made to qualifying companies in each of the following categories: Manufacturing Companies, Service Companies, and Small Businesses (independently-owned with less than 500 employees). A maximum of two awards per category can be given each year. A company receiving an award is ineligible to receive another award in the same category for five years. Award recipients may publicize and advertise receipt of the award, provided they agree to share information about their successful quality strategies with other U.S. organizations. A crystal medal is awarded. Managed by the National Institute of Standards and Technology and administered by the American Society for Quality Control. Established in 1987.

• 6203 •
Ball State University
Department of Journalism
Art and Journalism, Ste. 300
2000 W University Ave.
Muncie, IN 47306-0485
Phone: (765)285-8200
Fax: (765)285-7997
E-mail: bsujourn@bsu.edu
Home Page: http://www.bsu.edu/journalism

• 6204 • **Joseph Costa Courtroom Photography Award**
To recognize a print media photographer for work in courtroom photography. Established in 1984 in honor of Joseph Costa, leading advocate of courtroom photography. Deadline is January 15.

• 6205 • **John R. Emens Award for Support of a Free Student Press**
To recognize a college or university administrator who is a vigorous champion of a free student press and typifies the attitude toward the student press as practiced by President John R. Emens. Established in 1977.

• 6206 • **Indiana Journalism Award**
To recognize journalists in Indiana who have made outstanding contributions to the profession. Individual reporters, columnists, editors and publishers as well as foundations, newspapers, wire services, and professional organizations are eligible. Awarded annually. Established in 1965.

• 6207 • **Indiana Scholastic Journalism Award**
To recognize a person who has displayed leadership in the field of scholastic journalism. Established in 1961.

• 6208 • **Journalism Alumni Award**
To recognize graduates from Ball State University who made outstanding contributions to the field of journalism. Established in 1961.

• 6209 • **Journalism Hall of Fame**
To recognize outstanding journalists. Individuals are nominated by the Ball State Journalism Alumni Board. Awarded annually. Established in 1985.

• 6210 • **Anthony Majeri Jr. Award for Innovation and Leadership in Graphic Journalism**
Recognizes innovation and leadership in professions of Graphic Journalism. A plaque is awarded annually. Established in 1998.

• 6211 • **National Public Relations Achievement Award**
To recognize an outstanding individual in the field of public relations. Honorees are selected by the faculty. Established in 1977.

• 6212 • **Eugene S Pulliam National Journalism Writing Award**
To recognize an American newspaper or magazine writer. A monetary prize of $1,500 is awarded by a panel. Established in 1960. Renamed in 1999. Sponsored by the Pulliam Family. Formerly: (1984) National Journalism Award.

• 6213 • **Special Citation in Journalism**
For recognition in the field of journalism. Established in 1968.

• 6214 •
Balloon Federation of America
Sharon Ripperger, Office Mgr.
PO Box 400
Indianola, IA 50125
Phone: (515)961-8809
Fax: (515)961-3537
E-mail: bfaoffice@bfa.net
Home Page: http://www.bfa.net

• 6215 • **BFA President's Award**
For recognition of meritorious service to the BFA through noteworthy assistance to the President. The BFA President alone determines the winner or winners. Established in 1980.

• 6216 • **Chairman of the Board Awards**
To recognize significant merits to the Competition Division. Trophies are awarded.

• 6217 • **Championship Director Awards, Competition Division**
To recognize the director's staff for their contributions to the U.S. National Championships. Small awards are given.

• 6218 • **Albert Desmond Memorial Award, Competition Division**
To recognize a credible presence in the sport of ballooning who has contributed to the better-

Awards are arranged in alphabetical order below their administering organizations

ment of the sport. Competitors, officials, or organizers of BFA events are eligible. A framed certificate is awarded. Additional information is available from Award Committee Chairperson.

• 6219 • Farmer Appreciation Award
To recognize a farmer/landowner who exhibits exemplary hospitality and/or service to the BFA National Championships. Nominations are made by any pilot (competitive or non-competitive) at the championships. A plaque is presented at the annual awards banquet. Established in 1975.

• 6220 • Gas Balloon Championships
To recognize the top three competitors in gas ballooning. Trophies are awarded annually. Established in 1980.

• 6221 • National Point Leader Award, Competition Division
To recognize the competitor who places highest nationally in the BFA sanctioned tasks each year.

• 6222 • Annie Pryne Memorial Award, Competition Division
To recognize an observer who has a commitment to the sport of ballooning and the improvement of the observer corps. A framed certificate is awarded. Established in 1993 by the Northeast Ohio Balloon Pilots Association.

• 6223 • Regional Directors Award
For recognition of meritorious service to the BFA. The BFA directors determine the recipient at their discretion. A plaque is awarded. Additional information is available from Award Committee.

• 6224 • Rookie of the Year
To recognize the first time competitor who places highest nationally at the National Championships. A plaque is awarded annually. Established in 1980.

• 6225 • Shields-Trauger Award
This, the most prestigious award of the Association, is given to recognize a contribution in the areas of sport, science, or safety in Aerostation. Nominees are solicited from the general membership via *Pilot News* and voted upon by the Board of Directors. A scroll is presented at the National Championships Award Banquet. Established in 1970. Additional information is available from Awards Committee Chairperson.

• 6226 • U.S. National Hot Air Balloon Champion
To recognize the winner of the U.S. National Hot Air Balloon Championships competition. A trophy and medallion are awarded to the winner. Each year, medallions are given to second through tenth place finishers at the U.S. National Championships. Established in 1970.

• 6227 •
Baltic American Freedom League
Valdis Pavlovskis, Pres.
PO Box 65056
Los Angeles, CA 90065
Phone: (323)255-4215
Fax: (323)255-8730
E-mail: valdisp@aol.com
Home Page: http://www.bafl.com

• 6228 • Baltic Freedom Award
For recognition of contributions to strengthening democracy, economic development, security and sovereignty of Estonia, Latvia, and Lithuania. Nominations may be made by a member of the Executive Board. A plaque or scroll is presented as outstanding accomplishments are made. Established in 1985.

• 6229 •
Baltimore Film Forum
℅ Baltimore Museum of Art
10 Art Museum Dr.
Baltimore, MD 21218
Phone: (410)235-2777
Fax: (410)235-3111

• 6230 • Baltimore Independent Film/ Video Makers Competition
For recognition of achievement in independent film and video making and, especially, to encourage professional development. Applications are accepted. Monetary prizes for first, second, third place and honorable mention are awarded annually in the following film categories: animation, documentary, drama, and experimental. In addition, the Helen Cyr Gold Reel Award is presented for the Best of the Festival and the Stuart Rome Memorial Award is presented for the best work of a Maryland resident. Established in 1970 by Harvey Alexander. Sponsored by Enoch Pratt Free Library.

• 6231 •
Baltimore Opera Company
Michael Harrison, Gen.Dir.
Lyric Opera House, Ste. 306
110 W Mount Royal Ave.
Baltimore, MD 21201-5732
Phone: (410)625-1600
Fax: (410)625-6474
E-mail: rchewning@baltimoreopera.com
Home Page: http://www.baltimoreopera.com

• 6232 • The Canticum Dominum Vocal Competition
To encourage and support the study of sacred vocal music in general, and in particular, sacred music written by American composers during the years 1850-1950. American singers ages 20-35 are eligible. Deadline for applications is January 1. Auditions will be held in Baltimore in early February. A monetary prize of $750 and an appearance on the St. Cecilia Society Concert Series in Baltimore, Maryland, are awarded annually. Sponsored by the St. Cecilia Society of St. Mark's Lutheran Church, Baltimore, Maryland. For an application, contact James Harp, 1900 St. Paul St., Baltimore, MD 21218.

• 6233 •
The Banff Centre
Mary E. Hofstetter, Pres. and CEO
107 Tunnel Mountain Dr.
Box 1020
Banff, AB, Canada T1L 1H5
Phone: (403)762-6100
Toll-Free: 800-565-9989
Fax: (403)762-6444
E-mail: arts_info@banffcentre.ca
Home Page: http://www.banffcentre.ca

Formerly: (1988) Banff School of Fine Arts.

• 6234 • Banff International String Quartet Competition (Banff Concours International de Quatuor A Cordes)
To recognize young professional quartets of all nationalities. All quartet members must be under 35 years of age at the time of the competition. Tapes must be submitted by December 10. Competition is held every three years. The following prizes are awarded: First prize - $20,000 Canadian, a quartet of bows, and a recital; Second prize - $12,000; Third prize $8,000; and Fourth prize - $5,000. Additional information is available from Executive Director, Banff International String Quartet Competition, the Banff Centre.

• 6235 • Banff Mountain Book Festival
A celebration of mountain literature which awards prizes in the categories of: mountain image; mountain literature; adventure travel; mountain exposition; mountaineering history, as well as an overall grand prize and the Canadian Rockies Award. Monetary awards are presented annually on the first weekend of November.

• 6236 • Banff Mountain Film Festival
To recognize films that celebrate the spirit of mountain adventure. The following awards are presented: Grand Prize ($4,000); Best Film on Mountain Environment Award ($2,000); Alpine Club of Canada Award for Best Film on Climbing ($2,000); Best Film on Mountain Culture Award ($2,000); Best Film on Mountain Sports Award ($2,000); People's Choice Award ($2,000); Best Short Mountain Film Award ($2,000); Best Feature-Length Mountain Film Award ($2,000); and Bill Roberts Award for Young Filmmakers. Presented annually on the first weekend in November. Established in 1976 by the Banff Centre.

• 6237 • Banff Mountain Photography Competition
Categories for competition are: mountain adventure; mountain landscape; mountain culture; mountain environment; and mountain flora and fauna. Additional prizes include Grand Prize and the Y2Y Prize. Monetary prizes are awarded annually.

• 6238 •
Banff World Television Festival
Patricia Douey, COO
% Achilles Media Ltd.
100 Rundle Dr.
Canmore, AB, Canada T1W 2L9
Phone: (403)678-1216
Fax: (403)678-3357
E-mail: info@achillesmedia.com
Home Page: http://www.banfftvfest.com

Formerly: (1982) International Festival of Films for TV.

• 6239 • **Banff Television Festival**
For recognition of overall excellence in television program production worldwide. The competition is open to all television programs falling within the categories listed below and meeting the conditions of the Festival. Entries must have been made for television - films in theatrical release at any time prior to telecast are not eligible. Entries originally in English or French must have been shown on television for the first time anywhere in the world between February 24 and May 1. Entries produced in a language other than English or French must have been shown on television for the first time anywhere in the world within the past year. Made for tv movies and feature-length documentaries that have been prize-winners at any other festival in Canada are not eligible. The festival welcomes quality entries in the following categories: Made for tv Movies, Mini-Series, Continuing Series, Short Dramas, Comedies, Social and Political Documentaries, Popular Science Programs, Arts Documentaries, Performance Specials, Children's Programs, Information Programs, Animation Programs, and Sports Programs. Producers of programs judged best in each of the categories receive a Banff Rockie Award, a polished bronze sculpture created by Alberta artist Roy Leadbeater. A Grand Prize is awarded to the program judged *Best of the Festival*. The jury may also make two Special Awards for outstanding achievements deemed worthy of special recognition. Awarded annually. Established in 1979.

• 6240 •
Bank Street College of Education
Linda Greengrass, Award Dir.
610 W. 112th St.
New York, NY 10025
Phone: (212)875-4450
Fax: (212)875-4558
E-mail: lindag@bnkst.edu
Home Page: http://streetcat.bankstreet.edu/html/isb.html

• 6241 • **Irma S. and James H. Black Award for Excellence in Children's Literature**
To encourage excellence of text as well as excellence in graphics in books for young children. Books must emphasize the harmonious blend of text and illustration with the content relevant to children's experiences in terms of the world around them and to their emotional responses expressed in fresh vivid sensory language. The following prizes are awarded: scrolls to the author and the illustrator; and a seal designed by artist/writer Maurice Sendak, to the publisher for affixing to copies of the award winning book. Awarded annually in May. Only books published during the preceding year are eligible. Established in 1972. Formerly: Irma Simonton Black Award for Excellence in Children's Literature.

• 6242 •
Baptist History and Heritage Society
Charles W. Dewesee, Exec.Dir.
5001 Maryland Way
PO Box 728
Brentwood, TN 37024-0728
Phone: (615)371-7938
Toll-Free: 800-966-2278
Fax: (615)371-7939
E-mail: cdeweese@tnbaptist.org
Home Page: http://www.baptisthistory.org

Formerly: (2003) Southern Baptist Historical Society.

• 6243 • **Norman W. Cox Award**
To recognize the writer of the best article published by the Historical Society in the preceding calendar year. The candidate must have had an article published by the Historical Society, not dated. A monetary prize, a plaque, and travel expenses are awarded annually during the Historical Society meeting. Established in 1975 in honor of Norman W. Cox, first executive director of the Historical Commission of the Southern Baptist Convention (1951-59).

• 6244 • **Distinguished Service Award**
To recognize and pay tribute to individuals who have made outstanding contributions to the cause of Baptist history. Work in the areas of writing, teaching, denominational development, and library development is considered. The deadline for submissions is December 31. A plaque is awarded annually. Established in 1982.

• 6245 • **Davis C. Woolley Award**
To recognize Southern Baptist state history programs and directors for outstanding achievement in the preceding calendar year. Accomplishments in publications, library and archival services, and other creative programs and projects are considered. The application deadline is December 31. A monetary prize and a plaque are awarded annually in April during the Historical Society meeting. Established in 1990 in honor of Davis C. Woolley, second executive director of the Historial Commission of the Southern Baptist Convention (1959-1971).

• 6246 •
Baptist Mid-Missions
Dr. Gary L. Anderson, Pres.
7749 Webster Rd.
PO Box 308011
Cleveland, OH 44130-8011
Phone: (440)826-3930
Fax: (440)826-4457
E-mail: info@bmm.org
Home Page: http://www.bmm.org

• 6247 • **Service Pin Award**
Award of recognition. For years of service. Applicants must be members. Awarded every 5 years after first 20 years of service.

• 6248 •
Barlow Endowment for Music Composition
Thomas Durham, Exec.Dir.
Harris Fine Arts Ctr., Ste. A-501
Brigham Young University
Provo, UT 84602
Phone: (801)422-2818
Fax: (801)422-0253
E-mail: barlowendowment@byu.edu
Home Page: http://barlow.byu.edu

• 6249 • **Barlow Prize**
To discover and stimulate interest and production among talented composers throughout the world. The prize is open to any composer without regard to nationality, age, race, creed, sex, or political persuasion. Applications must be submitted by June 1. The Barlow Prize is designed to encompass several fields of music endeavor and thus changes its focus each year in a four-year cycle featuring and chamber music (2005). Established in 1985 by Milton and Gloria Barlow. Formerly: (2003) Barlow International Competition.

• 6250 •
Barnard-Seyfert Astronomical Society
Michael G. Benson, Contact
PO Box 198672
Nashville, TN 37219-8672
Phone: (615)883-6571
E-mail: ocentaurus@aol.com
Home Page: http://www.bsasnashville.com

• 6251 • **Astronomical League Observing Awards**
For documented observations. Recognition award bestowed periodically.

• 6252 • **BSAS Science Fair Prize**
For best astronomy exhibit at Middle Tennessee Science Fair. Monetary award bestowed annually.

• 6253 •
Barnes & Noble Inc.
Stephen Riggio, CEO
122 5th Ave.
New York, NY 10011
Phone: (212)633-3300
Fax: (212)352-3660
Home Page: http://www.barnesandnobleinc.com

• 6254 • **Discover Award**
To recognize works by debuting or underappreciated American authors. Authors whose publishers have paid fees to Barnes & Noble to have the author's work promoted in the "Discover Great New Writers" program are eligible. Nationwide display attention and monetary awards of $5,000 are bestowed each year to the winner

in the Fiction and Non-Fiction categories. Established in 1993.

• 6255 •
Baromedical Nurses Association
Claude Wreford-Brown, Pres.
PO Box 18994
Denver, CO 80218-0994
Phone: (303)918-9686
Fax: (303)282-7031
E-mail: hnrcew@vmmc.org
Home Page: http://www.hyperbaricnurses.org

• 6256 • **Diane Norkool Award**
Award of recognition. For excellence in baromedical nursing. Awarded annually.

• 6257 •
Baronial Order of Magna Charta and the Military Order of Crusades
James W. Marvin Jr., Marshal
109 Glenview Ave.
Wyncote, PA 19095
Phone: (215)887-8207
Fax: (215)884-2032
E-mail: marshal@magnacharta.com
Home Page: http://magnacharta.com

• 6258 • **Magna Charta Day Award**
To recognize individuals who, by their services to the U.S. and the countries of the world, further the principles established by the Magna Charta. One scroll is awarded annually in June in Philadelphia. Established in 1954, the first recipient was Sir Winston Churchill.

• 6259 •
Baruch Entertainment
1497 Chainbridge Rd., Ste. 105
McLean, VA 22101
Phone: (703)833-1777
Fax: (703)737-0725

• 6260 • **Rhythm and Blues Award Show**
To recognize outstanding black rhythm and blues and rap artists. Awards are presented in numerous categories, including: (1) Top Rap Artist; (2) Top Male Vocalist; (3) Top Single and Top Album; (4) Most Promising Male Vocal Group; (5) Most Promising Female Group; (6) Top New Female Group; (7) Most Promising New Male Vocalist; and (8) Top Female Rap Vocalist. Winnes are chosen by *Black Radio Exclusive Magazine*. Established in 1980. Additional information is available from WAQT Productions, % John Jackson, 200 E. 94th St., Ste. 910, New York, NY 10128, phone: (212) 722-4463.

• 6261 •
Baseball Canada
Jim Baba, Dir.Gen.
2212 Gladwin Cres., Ste. A7
Ottawa, ON, Canada K1B 5N1
Phone: (613)748-5606
Fax: (613)748-5767
E-mail: info@baseball.ca
Home Page: http://www.baseball.ca

• 6262 • **Coach of the Year**
Annual award of recognition. Nominations must be made by a provincial association or executive member.

• 6263 • **Jimmy Rattlesnake Award**
Recognizes an individual exhibiting exceptional ability and sportsmanship on the Canadian senior youth team. Awarded annually.

• 6264 • **Senior Team Canada Junior MVP**
Awarded annually to the most valuable player on the Canadian senior youth team.

• 6265 •
Baseball Writers Association of America
Jack O'Connell, Sec.-Treas.
PO Box 610611
Bayside, NY 11361
Phone: (718)767-2582
Phone: (631)236-2648
Fax: (718)767-2583
E-mail: bbwaa@aol.com
Home Page: http://baseballwriters.org

• 6266 • **Kenesaw M. Landis Award (Most Valuable Player)**
To recognize the most valuable player in each major league of baseball. Awarded annually. Established in 1931. This award is often cited as the American League Most Valuable Player and National League Most Valuable Player.

• 6267 • **Manager of the Year Award**
To recognize the outstanding manager in each major league. Awarded annually. Established in 1983.

• 6268 • **Cy Young Award**
For recognition of the best pitcher in each major baseball league. Awarded annually. Established in 1956 in honor of Denton (Cy) Young, who won more games (511) than any pitcher in history.

• 6269 •
BASICS in Milwaukee
Arn Quakkelaar, Pres./CEO
2224 W Kilbourn Ave., Ste. 206
Department 86
Milwaukee, WI 53233
Phone: (414)372-7200
Phone: (262)574-5910
Fax: (414)372-7294
E-mail: arn@quakkelaar.com
Home Page: http://www.basicsinmke.org

• 6270 • **Ministry Support Award**
For Christian nonprofit organizations serving impoverished people in the Milwaukee, WI area. Monetary award bestowed periodically.

• 6271 •
Bath County Historical Society
Margo Oxendine, Admin.
PO Box 212
Warm Springs, VA 24484
Phone: (540)839-2543
Fax: (540)839-2566
E-mail: bathcountyhistory@tds.net
Home Page: http://www.rootsweb.com/~vabath

• 6272 • **Bath County Historical Society Scholarship**
For essay contest winner. Scholarship awarded annually.

• 6273 •
Bay Area Independent Publishers Association
Margaret Speaker Yuan, Exec.Dir.
PO Box E
Corte Madera, CA 94976
Toll-Free: (866)622-1325
Fax: (866)622-1325
E-mail: info@baipa.net
Home Page: http://www.baipa.net

Formerly: (1989) Marin Self Publishers Association; Marin Small Publishers Association.

• 6274 • **Jack Mason Award**
To recognize a member for outstanding service to the organization and contribution to the field of self-publishing. Nominees are chosen by the Board of Directors from active members. An individual plaque is awarded annually at the March meeting, and a perpetual plaque hangs in the Jack Mason Museum/Library, Inverness, CA. Established in 1985 in memory of Jack Mason, historian of Marin and founding father of MSPA.

• 6275 •
Bay Area Video Coalition
Jennifer Gilomen, Communications Mgr.
2727 Mariposa St., 2nd Fl.
San Francisco, CA 94110
Phone: (415)861-3282
Fax: (415)861-4316
E-mail: bavc@bavc.org
Home Page: http://www.bavc.org

• 6276 • **Artist Equipment Access Awards**
For inkind equipment access. Recognition award bestowed annually.

Awards are arranged in alphabetical order below their administering organizations

• 6277 •
Bay Chamber Concerts
Thomas Wolf, Exec.Dir.
10 Summer St., Ste. 102
Rockport, ME 04856
Phone: (207)236-2823
Toll-Free: 888-707-2770
E-mail: ann@baychamberconcerts.org
Home Page: http://www.baychamberconcerts.org

• 6278 • **Andrew Wolf Chamber Music Award**
To recognize a pianist for commitment and contribution to the chamber music field. U.S. citizens under the age of 40 are eligible. A monetary award of $15,000 is presented every three years. Established in 1986 by the Bay Chamber Concerts.

• 6279 •
Bay Improvement Group
Steven Barrison, Pres.
30 Dooley St.
Brooklyn, NY 11235
Phone: (718)646-9206
Phone: (212)750-5560
Fax: (212)888-7306
E-mail: whwboat@aol.com
Home Page: http://members.aol.com/bayimpgrp

• 6280 • **Big Oscars**
For dedication and participation over time to the community. Recognition award bestowed annually.

• 6281 • **Lifetime Achievement**
For dedication and participation over time to the community. Recognition award.

• 6282 •
Baylor College of Medicine
Roy M. and Phyllis Gough Huffington Center on Aging
1 Baylor Plz., M320
Houston, TX 77030
Phone: (713)798-5804
Fax: (713)798-6688
E-mail: rsmith@bcm.tmc.edu
Home Page: http://www.hcoa.org

• 6283 • **Etta Nathan Award**
Award of recognition. Baylor College of Medicine fellows and faculty in geriatric medicine are eligible.

• 6284 •
Baytown Chamber of Commerce
Tracey S. Wheeler-Martinez, Pres. & CEO
4721 Garth Rd., Ste. C
PO Box 330
Baytown, TX 77522-0330
Phone: (281)422-8359
Fax: (281)428-1758
E-mail: info@baytownchamber.com
Home Page: http://www.baytownchamber.com

• 6285 • **Baytown Chamber of Commerce Scholarship**
For local high school graduates who plan to attend Lee College.

• 6286 • **Fire Fighter of the Quarter**
For area fire fighter. Recognition award bestowed quarterly.

• 6287 • **Public Safety Recognition**
For public safety personnel in the areas of fire fighter, police officer, and emergency medical technician. Recognition award bestowed annually.

• 6288 •
BC Innovation Council
David Dolphin, CEO
1188 W Georgia St., 9th Fl.
Vancouver, BC, Canada V6E 4A2
Phone: (604)438-2752
Toll-Free: 800-665-7222
Fax: (604)438-6564
E-mail: info@bcinnovationcouncil.com
Home Page: http://www.bcinnovationcouncil.com

• 6289 • **Chairman's Award for Career Achievement**
To recognize an individual who has made important and sustained contributions to innovative science or technology in British Columbia. A recipient may still be an active or retired scientist or engineer. Eligible candidates need not reside in British Columbia, but they must have conducted a portion of their work in a British Columbian institution. The deadline for nominations is April 1. A trophy is awarded when merited. Established in 1990.

• 6290 • **Gold Medal Awards**
To recognize an outstanding contribution to science and/or technology by a British Columbian individual or small team in Business/Education Partnership, Industrial Innovation, Solutions through Research, and New Frontiers in Research. The work must have been conducted in British Columbia or by a person normally a resident of British Columbia. The deadline for nominations is April 1. Up to six gold medals are awarded annually. (Awards in each category are not made every year). Winners are announced in the autumn. Established in 1980.

• 6291 • **Cecil Green Award for Technology Entrepreneurship**
To recognize an individual, small team, or company who has started or developed a knowledge-based company in British Columbia that has demonstrated an ability to make and sell nationally or internationally commercially viable, innovative world-class products over a sustained period of time. The deadline for nominations is April 1. Awarded when merited. Established in 1990 to honor Cecil Green, who cofounded Texas Instruments.

• 6292 • **Eve Savory Award for Science Communication**
To recognize an individual for exceptional achievement in describing or organizing activities that explain the potential innovation impact of science and technology to the general public. A single identifiable publication or article, exhibit, lecture series, program, or broadcast that is directly accessible to the people of British Columbia is eligible. Open to individuals or small project teams whose residence and work is in British Columbia. The deadline for nominations is April 1. A trophy is awarded when merited. Established in 1990 to honor Eve Savory, a native of Duncan, B.C., who is the national science reporter for CBC Television News.

• 6293 • **Volunteer of the Year**
To recognize that volunteers are the lifeblood of Science Council and other groups which help foster science and technology in British Columbia. This award honors an individual who has made an outstanding contribution to the success of an organization(s) or initiative(s).

• 6294 • **Young Innovator Award**
To recognize an individual under the age of 40 who has had a remarkable impact on British Columbia science and technology either in a business, academic or collaborative environment. This person will have played the main role in the development of a new innovation or research delivery. Awarded annually.

• 6295 •
BDA
Bonnie Barrio, Membership/Awards Coor.
9000 Sunset Blvd., No. 900
West Hollywood, CA 90069
Phone: (310)789-1509
Fax: (310)712-0039
E-mail: sean@promax.tv
Home Page: http://www.bda.tv

• 6296 • **BDA International Design Award**
Recognizes excellence in various categories of media design. Awarded annually.

• 6297 •
Beauty and Barber Supply Institute
Steve Sleeper, Exec.Dir.
15825 N 71st St., No. 100
Scottsdale, AZ 85254
Phone: (480)281-0424
Toll-Free: 800-468-2274
E-mail: info@bbsi.org
Home Page: http://www.bbsi.org/index2.html

• 6298 • **North American Hairstyling Awards**
To celebrate the artistry and skill of the professional salon industry. Only licensed cosmetologists from North America and Canada are eligible. Awards are given in twelve categories. Three finalists are chosen in each category; one trophy is awarded in each category. Awards ceremony includes introduction of all finalists and winners, including the North American Hairstylists of the Year, and presentation of Lifetime Achievement Award to a well-known contemporary hair designer and Hall of Leaders to a well known industry innovator/visionary. All winning entries are published in *Beauty Inc.*, *Modern Salon*, and other trade publications. Deadline is February 1st of each year.

• 6299 •
Beaver Lake Literacy Council
PO Box 372
Bentonville, AR 72712-0372
Phone: (479)273-3486
Fax: (479)273-7545
E-mail: read@specent.com

• 6300 • **Student/Tutor Recognition Certificates**
For progression and achievement. Recognition award bestowed annually.

• 6301 •
Before Columbus Foundation
Gundars Strads, Exec.Dir.
655-13th St., Ste. 300
Oakland, CA 94612
Phone: (510)268-9775

• 6302 • **American Book Awards**
To recognize outstanding contributions to contemporary American literature. Books published in the United States must be submitted for consideration by December 31. There are no categories. The winners are selected by a panel of authors, editors, and publishers representing the broad spectrum of the American multicultural literary tradition. The awards ceremonies are presented annually in May or June. All winners are accorded equal standing. In addition, a special Lifetime Achievement Award is given to recognize the life's work of a particular author without restriction to a recently published book. Established in 1978.

• 6303 •
Belgian American Educational Foundation
Emile L. Boulpaep, Pres.
195 Church St.
New Haven, CT 06510
Phone: (203)777-5765
Fax: (203)785-4951
E-mail: emile.boulpaep@yale.edu
Home Page: http://www.baef.be

• 6304 • **Belgian American Educational Foundation Fellowships**
To provide the opportunities for graduate studies or research in Belgium by U.S. students. American citizens, preferably under 30 years of age, with a speaking and reading knowledge of French, Dutch, or German, who have a Masters degree or are working towards a Ph.D. or equivalent degree must be nominated by a graduate school Dean. Fellowships for study in Belgium of $13,000 for ten months are awarded annually. Established in 1920 by Herbert Hoover to commemorate the relief work of the "Commission for Relief in Belgium" during World War I. The Foundation also offers awards for Belgian students to study in the United States.

• 6305 •
Bellarmine University
Joseph J. McGowan, Pres.
2001 Newburg Rd.
Louisville, KY 40205-0671
Phone: (502)452-8000
Toll-Free: 800-274-4723
Fax: (502)452-8033
E-mail: helpdesk@bellarmine.edu
Home Page: http://www.bellarmine.edu

• 6306 • **Bellarmine Medal**
To honor those persons who, on the national or international level, exemplify in a special manner the qualities of justice, charity, and temperateness in dealing with difficult and controversial problems. Selection is based on a high level of personal and professional integrity, sensitivity to contemporary problems, and significant contribution of self and personal talents to meet problems of fellow human beings. A sterling silver medal is awarded at a presentation dinner. Established in 1955 in honor of Saint Robert Bellarmine, patron of the college.

• 6307 •
Belleek Collectors' International Society
Angela H. Moore, Contact
PO Box 1498
Great Falls, VA 22066
Phone: (703)847-6207
Toll-Free: 800-BEL-LEEK
Fax: (703)272-6271
E-mail: info@belleek.com
Home Page: http://www.belleek.ie

• 6308 • **Belleek Hall of Fame Award**
Recognizes outstanding contributions to the BCIS. Candidates must be Society members. Awarded annually.

• 6309 •
Belted Galloway Society
Laura Glassmann, Sec.-Treas.
98 Eidson Creek Rd.
Staunton, VA 24401
Phone: (540)885-9887
Fax: (540)885-9897
E-mail: beltiecows@aol.com
Home Page: http://www.beltie.org

• 6310 • **Harry T. Burn Award**
To recognize members for significant and outstanding contributions to the society and/or the Belted Galloway breed of cattle through education, research, breed improvement, management, marketing, economics writing, or other forms of service that have markedly enhanced that industry. A plaque or memento is awarded occasionally. Established in 1984 to honor Harry T. Burn, one of the founders of the Society.

• 6311 •
Benevolent and Loyal Order of Pessimists
Jack Duvall, Pres.
PO Box 1945
Iowa City, IA 52244
Phone: (319)351-2973
Phone: (319)351-1201
Fax: (319)354-5657
E-mail: dleshtz@ia.net

• 6312 • **Pessimist of the Year**
To recognize and promote meritorious achievement in pessimism. Although it is futile, the organization tries to fight fatuous optimism and encourage a more realistic view of life. Any pessimist is eligible, regardless of race, creed, or social class. Attitude is the key factor in selection. A gold trophy in the shape of a horse's behind is awarded annually at the convention, traditionally held the Saturday closest to Income Tax Day. Established in 1977 by the original members from the 1976 convention.

• 6313 •
Bentley College
Center for Business Ethics
175 Forest St., AAC 108
Waltham, MA 02452-4705
Phone: (781)891-2981
Fax: (781)891-2988
E-mail: cbeinfo@bentley.edu
Home Page: http://ecampus.bentley.edu/dept/cbe/index.html

• 6314 • **Business Ethics Award**
Recognizes outstanding business ethics practices.

• 6315 • **Executive Scholar and Research Fellow Programs**
No additional information available.

Awards are arranged in alphabetical order below their administering organizations

• 6316 •
Bet Nahrain
Dr. Sargon Dadisho, Pres.
PO Box 4116
Modesto, CA 95352
Phone: (209)538-4130
Phone: (209)537-0933
Fax: (209)538-2795
E-mail: betnahrain@hotmail.com
Home Page: http://www.betnahrain.org

• 6317 • **Bet Nahrain National Awards**
Recognizes excellence in Assyrian education, arts, literature and other forms. Awarded annually.

• 6318 •
Beta Alpha Psi
Hadassah Baum, Exec.Dir.
1211 Ave. of the Americas, 6th Fl.
New York, NY 10036-8775
Phone: (212)596-6090
Fax: (212)596-6288
Home Page: http://www.bap.org

• 6319 • **Annual Manuscript Award**
For the best student graduate and undergraduate paper. A scholarship is awarded annually.

• 6320 • **Outstanding Accountant of the Year Award**
Annual award of recognition.

• 6321 • **Outstanding Faculty Development Award**
Annual award of recognition.

• 6322 •
Beta Beta Beta National Biological Honor Society
University of North Alabama
UNA Box 5079
Florence, AL 35632
E-mail: tribeta@una.edu
Home Page: http://www.tri-beta.org

• 6323 • **Lloyd M. Bertholf Award for Chapter Excellence**
To recognize the work of chapters that have best promoted the society's triple aims of scholarship, dissemination of scientific information and promotion of biological research in the preceding academic year. Applications from any Beta Beta Beta chapter received by November 1 of the following academic year are considered for the award. Both the winner and the two honorable mentions receive plaques. Outstanding chapters receive inscribed certificates. As many as 10 percent of the chapters may receive this designation. Presented annually. Established in 1961 in honor of Lloyd M. Bertholf, the third president of Beta Beta Beta. Formerly: (1969) Lloyd M. Bertholf Award for Chapter Efficiency.

• 6324 • **Frank G. Brooks Award for Excellence in Student Research**
To honor undergraduate achievement in biological research. A candidate must be an undergraduate TriBeta member. A plaque and inscribed certificate for first place winners and a monetary prize of $75 if the noted work is published in *BIOS*, the society's journal. The award is presented biennially at the national conventions and annually at the district conventions. Established in 1928. The award honors Frank G. Brooks, the founder of Beta Beta Beta. Formerly: (1963) F. G. Brooks Undergraduate Essay Competition.

• 6325 • **Chapter History Award**
For recognition of outstanding display of chapter activities in scrapbook format. Awarded biennially at national convention and annually at district conventions.

• 6326 • **Honorary Member**
To recognize individuals for outstanding contributions to biology and/or unusual service to TriBeta. Established in 1935.

• 6327 • **John C. Johnson Award**
For excellence in undergraduate research presented in a poster format at district or national meetings of the society. A plaque and inscribed certificate is awarded to first place winners with a monetary prize of $75 if the noted work is published in *BIOS,* the society's journal. Established in 1992 to honor both John C. Johnson, Sr. and John C. Johnson, Jr., presidents of Beta Beta Beta.

• 6328 • **McClung Award**
To honor the best undergraduate paper published in the society's journal, *BIOS*, during each publication year. All undergraduate papers by TriBeta members published in *BIOS* are automatically entered in the competition each year. A monetary award of $100 and an inscribed certificate are presented annually. Established in 1935 in honor of Dr. C.E. McClung, the second president of Beta Beta Beta.

• 6329 • **Research Scholarships**
To support undergraduate research by awarding cash scholarships annually to TriBeta member students conducting student research. Awarded annually. Established in 1990.

• 6330 •
Beta Gamma Sigma
James A. Viehland, Exec.Dir.
125 Weldon Pkwy.
Maryland Heights, MO 63043
Phone: (314)432-5650
Toll-Free: 800-337-HNRS
Fax: (314)432-7083
E-mail: bgshonors@betagammasigma.org
Home Page: http://www.betagammasigma.org

• 6331 • **International Honorees**
To recognize individuals who have furthered the ideals of the Society through outstanding business and managerial leadership and/or meritorious contributions to education for business and administration. Established in 1963.

• 6332 • **Medallion for Entrepreneurship**
To recognize individuals who combine innovative business achievement with service to humanity. Established in 1986.

• 6333 •
Beta Kappa Chi
Dr. Carmellia Moses Okpodu, Pres.
PO Box 10046
Florida A&M University
Baton Rouge, LA 70813
Phone: (225)771-4845
Phone: (850)599-3595
E-mail: mzdjames@aol.com
Home Page: http://betakappachi.org

• 6334 • **Undergraduate Research Paper Awards**
Recognizes high quality research, ability to present understanding of research. Students are eligible. Awarded annually.

• 6335 •
Bethesda Lutheran Homes and Services
David Geske PhD, Pres./CEO
600 Hoffman Dr.
Watertown, WI 53094
Phone: (920)261-3050
Toll-Free: 800-369-4636
Fax: (920)261-8441
E-mail: dgeske@blhs.org
Home Page: http://www.blhs.org

• 6336 • **Career Awareness Award**
Recognizes high school age Lutheran students. A monetary award is given annually.

• 6337 • **Developmental Disabilities Awareness Award**
Recognizes outstanding Lutheran Schools. Awarded annually.

• 6338 • **Developmental Disabilities Scholastic Achievement Scholarship**
For study in Human Services, Special Education or MR/DD Profession and volunteer work in DD. Lutheran College Juniors with a grade point average of 3.0 are eligible. A scholarship is given annually.

• 6339 •
Better Business Bureau
Scott Mecham, Pres.
11811 P St.
Omaha, NE 68137
Phone: (402)391-7612
Toll-Free: 800-649-6814
Fax: (402)391-7535

• 6340 • Better Business Bureau Integrity Award
For business practices and activities which exemplify BBB's mission and principles. Recognition award bestowed annually.

• 6341 •
Better Business Bureau of Western Michigan
Kenneth J. VanderMeeden, Pres.
354 Trust Bldg.
40 Pearl St. NW, Ste. 354
Grand Rapids, MI 49503
Phone: (616)774-8236
Toll-Free: 800-684-3222
Fax: (616)774-2014
E-mail: bbbinfo@iserv.net
Home Page: http://www.grandrapids.bbb.org

• 6342 • Best in Business Award
For integrity and involvement in advertising, customer service and community service. Recognition award bestowed annually.

• 6343 •
Better Business Bureau Serving Upstate South Carolina
Kathy W. Barrett, Pres.
408 N Church St., Ste. C
Greenville, SC 29601
Phone: (864)242-5052
Fax: (864)271-9802
E-mail: info@greenville.bbb.org
Home Page: http://www.greenville.bbb.org

• 6344 • Golden Torch Award
For BBB values: excellence, integrity, teamwork, trust, respect. Recognition award bestowed annually.

• 6345 •
Better Government Association
Jay E. Stewart, Exec.Dir.
11 E Adams St., Ste. 608
Chicago, IL 60603
Phone: (312)427-8330
Phone: (312)503-4774
Fax: (312)386-9203
E-mail: info@bettergov.org
Home Page: http://bettergov.org

• 6346 • BGA Tribute Award
Annual award of recognition.

• 6347 • Civic Achievement Award
Annual award of recognition.

• 6348 •
Beverly Hills Theatre Guild
2815 N Beachwood Dr.
PO Box 148
Beverly Hills, CA 90213
Phone: (213)465-2703
Home Page: http://www.beverlyhillstheatreguild.org

• 6349 • Beverly Hills Theatre Guild Play Competition for Children's Theatre
To encourage the creation of dramatic works of excellence for youth audiences: plays that not only entertain, but also foster an appreciation for and an interest in live theatre. Applicants must be U.S. citizens. Entries must be unpublished, unproduced dramatic works suitable for youth audiences seven through 14 years of age. Play length must be from 40 to 50 minutes playing time. Co-authorships are permissible. Entries may be original, or adaptations and/or translations. The Marilyn Hall Award of $1,000 will be divided: $750 to the winner and $250 to the runner-up. Submissions must be postmarked after January 15 and before the last day of February. Send business size SASE for submission procedures. Established in 1998.

• 6350 • Julie Harris Playwright Award Competition
To discover new dramatists and encourage established and aspiring playwrights to develop quality plays for the theatre. Authors who are U.S. citizens may submit full-length plays (90 minutes minimum playing time) that are unpublished, unproduced, and not currently under option. Authors may submit only one entry, whether under his or her own name, a pseudonym, or as a co-author. The following entries are not eligible: musicals, short one-act plays, adaptations, translations, plays for children, plays that have won other competitions, and plays that were entered in any prior year's Beverly Hills Theatre Guild Playwright Award Competition. Scripts may be submitted from August 1 through November 1. First prize winners receive a monetary award of $5,000. The June Moray Award. Second prize winners receive the Janet & Maxwell Salter Award, which includes a $2,000 cash award. Third prize winners receive the Dr. Henry and Lilian Nesburn Award, which includes a $1,000 cash award. All submissions must include an application form; guidelines and application available upon request with a business-size, self-addressed stamped envelope. Established in 1978. Formerly: (1985) Playwright Award Competition.

• 6351 •
Bevill Manufacturing Technology Center
401 Korner St.
Gadsden, AL 35903
Phone: (256)549-8160
Fax: (256)547-5790
E-mail: contact@gadsden.atn.org
Home Page: http://www.bevillcntr.org

• 6352 • Advanced Manufacturing Technology Engineering Certification
Awarded to engineering students.

• 6353 •
Biblenets
% National Bible Foundation
711 Lamar St., Ste. 135
Fort Worth, TX 76102
Phone: (212)408-1225
Fax: (212)408-1448
E-mail: biblenets@nationalbible.org
Home Page: http://www.biblenetusa.com

Formerly: (1987) Laymen's National Bible Committee.

• 6354 • Citation of Appreciation
To honor achievements which promote and/or facilitate increased reading and study of the Bible in the United States. Individuals or organizations in the United States are eligible. Hand-lettered citations or Bibles with hand-lettered inscriptions are presented annually. Established in 1940.

• 6355 • Isaacs Lifetime Achievement Award
To recognize an individual for his or her outstanding service to the Bible cause through a lifetime of activities that have honored the Bible's teachings and made the Bible known to others. Chosen by vote of the LNBA Board of Directors upon recommendation by the Recognition Committee. A hand-lettered Citation of Appreciation and a hand-inscribed Bible are awarded annually, or at the LNBA Board's discretion. Established in 1986 to honor Judge Julius Isaacs, attorney, New York City magistrate, author, lecturer, LNBA Director and Vice President. Formerly: (1989) LNBA Lifetime Achievement Award.

• 6356 • Kupferman Award
To recognize a member of the judiciary who best cites the Bible to illustrate and/or substantiate a decision or determination. Any member of the judiciary including arbitrators, administrative law judges, magistrates, etc., is eligible. An engraved plaque is awarded annually or at the discretion of LNBA's Board. Established in 1987 by Hon. Theodore R. Kupferman, Director and former Chairman of LNBA, former U.S. Congressman, and retired New York State Supreme Court Justice, Appellate Division.

• 6357 • Witherspoon Memorial Chaplain's Award
To honor chaplains in the United States military who have conducted effective or successful Bible ministries or programs in their ministry to military personnel and their dependents. Individuals who are on active duty as chaplains with the United States Army, Navy, or Air Force are eligible. An award is given to a chaplain of one branch of the service in the following annual rotation: Navy, Army, Air Force. Selection is made by the Chief of Chaplains of each branch. An inscribed Bible and travel expenses to attend the National Bible Week Inaugural Luncheon in New York are awarded annually. Established in 1980 in memory of Captain Maurice Witherspoon, an outstanding chaplain with the U.S. Navy in World Wars I and II, and a long-time Director and supporter of LNBA.

• 6358 •
Bibliographical Society of Canada
(Societe Bibliographique du Canada)
Anne McGaughey, Sec.
PO Box 575, Sta. P
Toronto, ON, Canada M5S 2T1
E-mail: mcgaughe@yorku.ca
Home Page: http://www.library.utoronto.ca/bsc

• 6359 • **Amtmann Fellowship**
Candidates must be scholars working in Canadian, book, collecting, bookselling, or bibliography. Awarded triennially.

• 6360 • **Tremaine Fellowship**
Assists with travel and research expenses. Applicants must be bibliographic researchers. Awarded annually.

• 6361 • **Marie Tremaine Medal**
Recognizes outstanding service to Canadian bibliography. Awarded annually.

• 6362 •
Bichon Frise Club of America
Mrs. Joanne Styles, Sec.
32 Oak St.
Centereach, NY 11720-3839
Phone: (631)588-2250
E-mail: membership@bichon.org
Home Page: http://www.bichon.org

• 6363 • **Breeder of Top Ten Winning Bichon Frises, Owner of Top Ten Winning Bichon Frises**
Recognizes the top 10 champions bred by members and the top 10 champions owned by members. Awarded annually.

• 6364 • **Register of Merit Award**
Recognizes the sire and dam of a recognized number of champions. Awarded annually.

• 6365 •
Big Brothers Big Sisters of America
Judy Vredenburgh, Pres./CEO
230 N 13th St.
Philadelphia, PA 19107
Phone: (215)567-7000
Fax: (215)567-0394
E-mail: lmbmlc@bbbsa.org
Home Page: http://www.bbbsa.org

Formed by merger of: Big Brothers of America; Big Sisters International.

• 6366 • **Big Brother of the Year**
For recognition of the most outstanding volunteer Big Brother selected from nominations of all Big Brothers Big Sisters of America Affiliated Agencies. A plaque is awarded annually. Established in 1971.

• 6367 • **Big Sister of the Year**
For recognition of the most outstanding volunteer Big Sister selected from nominations of all Big Brothers Big Sisters of America Affiliated Agencies. A plaque is awarded annually. Established in 1971.

• 6368 •
Big East Conference
Michael A. Tranghese, Commissioner
222 Richmond St., Ste. 110
Providence, RI 02903
Phone: (401)272-9108
Phone: (401)453-0660
Fax: (401)274-5967
Home Page: http://www.bigeast.org

• 6369 • **Big East Conference Academic Awards**
For recognition of academic and athletic achievement among athletes who compete in Big East Conference sports. Team members of a conference sport at one of the following 13 member institutions are eligible: Boston College, University of Connecticut, Georgetown University, University of Miami, University of Notre Dame, University of Pittsburgh, Providence College, Rutgers, the State University of New Jersey, St. John's University, Seton Hall University, Syracuse University, Villanova University, and West Virginia University. Awards are given in the following categories: Male Scholar-Athlete - scholarship and plaque; Female Scholar-Athlete - scholarship and plaque; Male Basketball Scholar-Athlete - scholarship and plaque; Female Basketball Scholar-Athlete - scholarship and plaque; Post Graduate Scholarship Team scholarships and plaques; and Academic All Star Teams in Basketball, Baseball, Field Hockey, Golf, Soccer, Men's and Women's Cross Country, Men's and Women's Track and Field, Softball, Men's and Women's Swimming, Tennis, and Volleyball. Certificates are presented. Established in 1985.

• 6370 • **Commissioner's Trophy Awards**
For recognition of the top all-around program based on conference championship and regular season results. The sports adhering to a full round robin conference schedule use final seasonal standings and those sports with a championship-only format use championship finish as the barometer. Points are awarded to parallel the number of teams which sponsor that specific sport.

• 6371 •
Big Muddy Film Festival
Department of Cinema and Photography
1100 Lincoln Dr., Rm. 1101
Southern Illinois University
Carbondale, IL 62901-6610
Phone: (618)453-1482
Fax: (618)453-2264
E-mail: bigmuddy@siu.edu
Home Page: http://www.bigmuddyfilm.com

• 6372 • **Big Muddy Film Festival Awards**
For recognition of outstanding achievement in independently produced films and videos that challenge the traditional boundaries of the visual media. Categories include Narrative, Documentary, Experimental, and Animation. Films and videos that have been completed no more than two years prior to the competition may be submitted by February 1. Various monetary awards are presented annually, including the Audience Choice Award and the John Michaels Memorial Film Award, presented to the work that best promotes human rights, peace and justice topics, or environmental issues. Established in 1979. Formerly: Entry Films Competition.

• 6373 •
Bilingual Foundation of the Arts
Carmen Zapata, Pres.
421 N Ave. 19
Los Angeles, CA 90031
Phone: (323)225-4044
Fax: (323)225-1250
E-mail: bfa99@earthlink.net
Home Page: http://www.bfatheatre.org

• 6374 • **El Angel Award - Distinguished Hispanic-American Artist**
To recognize an individual artist for a significant contribution to Hispanic arts, particularly the performing arts in the United States, by the demonstration of talent developed over a period of years or the encouragement of Hispanic Arts in America through the building of an arts institution or aiding in identification and development of Hispanic talent. Hispanic musicians, composers, dancers, choreographers, sculptors, painters, writers, fine artists, actors, and architects are eligible. The winner must be available to receive the award in person. An onyx and bronze statue of an angel is awarded annually at the awards dinner in May. Established in 1982.

• 6375 • **El Angel Award - For Corporate Contribution to the Development of Hispanic-American Arts**
To recognize corporations that have made outstanding contributions to the development of Hispanic Arts in America. Applications are by invitation only. An onyx and bronze statue of an angel is awarded annually at the awards dinner in May. Established in 1982.

• 6376 •
Billboard
VNU Business Publications USA
Barry A. Jeckell, Mng.Ed.
% Director of Conferences & Events
770 Broadway
New York, NY 10003
Phone: (646)654-5553
Toll-Free: 800-449-1402
E-mail: info@billboard.com
Home Page: http://www.billboard.com

• 6377 • ***Billboard* Music Awards**
To recognize chart-topping vocalists and musicians. Awards are given in a variety of music

categories, such as country, pop, hip hop, and dance, as well as Artist of the Year awards. An Artist Achievement Award and Century Award are also presented. Trophies are awarded annually.

• 6378 • *Billboard* Radio Awards

To recognize outstanding accomplishments in radio. The following awards are presented: (1) Radio Station of the Year; (2) Network or Syndicated Weekly National Music Program of the Year; (3) Radio Program Director/Operations Manager of the Year; (4) National Label Promotion Person of the Year; (5) Radio Music Director of the Year; (6) Radio Promotion Director of the Year; and (7) Radio Air Personality of the Year. Each award is presented in the following areas: Top 40, Adult, R & B, Country or Rock; and in market size (small, medium, or major) when appropriate. *Billboard* readers select the winners. Awarded annually. Established in the 1950s.

• 6379 •
Billiard and Bowling Institute of America
John Carzo, Pres.
PO Box 6363
West Palm Beach, FL 33405
Phone: (561)835-0077
Fax: (561)659-1824
E-mail: bbia@billiardandbowling.org
Home Page: http://www.billiardandbowling.org

• 6380 • Industry Service Award

To recognize a leading personality in the billiard or bowling industry for his or her contribution to the promotion of these sports. Members may nominate bowlers and billiard players, leaders of organizations, show business personalities, political leaders, and others who have made unique contributions to build the industry. A plaque is awarded annually at the convention in April. Established in 1954.

• 6381 •
Billiard Congress of America
Stephen D. Ducoff, Exec.Dir.
4345 Beverly St., Ste. D
Colorado Springs, CO 80918
Phone: (719)264-8300
Fax: (719)264-0900
E-mail: steve@bca-pool.com
Home Page: http://www.bca-pool.com

• 6382 • Hall of Fame

To honor an individual (man or woman) for a contribution to the billiard industry/sport that improves the image of the sport. Individuals are nominated by a committee from the board of directors and then voted on by the membership of the BCA. A plaque is awarded annually at a dinner with the winner as the guest of honor. Established in 1966.

• 6383 •
Billings Preservation Society
Ruth Towe, Exec.Dir.
914 Division St.
Billings, MT 59101-1921
Phone: (406)256-5100
Phone: (406)256-1402
Fax: (406)252-0091
E-mail: mail@mossmansion.com
Home Page: http://www.mossmansion.com

• 6384 • Historic Preservation Award

For outstanding preservation of local landmark. Recognition award.

• 6385 •
Worth Bingham Memorial Fund
Susan Talalay, Contact
1616 H St. NW, 3rd Fl.
Washington, DC 20006
Phone: (202)737-3700
Fax: (202)737-0530
E-mail: info@worthbinghamprize.org
Home Page: http://www.worthbinghamprize.org

• 6386 • Worth Bingham Prize

To honor newspaper or magazine reporting that investigates and analyzes situations of national significance where the public interest is being ill-served. There may be actual violations of the law, rule or code; lax or ineffective administration or enforcement; or activities which, while not specific violations of anything on the statute books, create conflicts of interest, entail excessive secrecy or otherwise raise questions of propriety. Judges are guided by such factors as the reporting enterprise, obstacles overcome in getting information, accuracy, clarity of analysis and writing style, magnitude of the situation, and impact on the public, including any reforms that may have resulted. Entries may include a single story, a related series of stories, or up to three unrelated stories. Columns and editorials are eligible. The entry deadline is February 15. A monetary award of $10,000 is presented at the White House Correspondents' Dinner in the spring. Awarded annually. Established in 1966 in memory of Robert Worth Bingham, a young journalist-editor who was killed in an accident at the age of 34.

• 6387 •
Biomedical Engineering Society
Patricia I. Horner, Exec.Dir.
8401 Corporate Dr., Ste. 225
Landover, MD 20785-2224
Phone: (301)459-1999
Fax: (301)459-2444
E-mail: info@bmes.org
Home Page: http://www.bmes.org

• 6388 • Distinguished Lecturer Award

To recognize an individual for outstanding achievements and leadership in the science and practice of biomedical engineering. Individuals who have received excellence by contributions within a university, industry, or government setting are eligible. A monetary award of $1,000, a plaque, and up to $1,000 for travel expenses is awarded annually. The awardee must deliver a lecture at the BMES Annual Fall Meeting and publish the text of the lecture in the *Annals of Biomedical Engineering*. An important purpose of the lecture is to critically review a field of biomedical engineering and offer a vision of its future. Formerly: Whitaker Distinguished Lectureship.

• 6389 • Graduate Student Awards

To recognize the best graduate student scientific abstract for presentation. Abstracts are judged on the basis of scientific merit, originality, and quality of presentation at the meeting. Certificates and five stipends of $600 each (plus travel expenses of $400) are awarded at the BMES Business Meeting. Awarded annually. Formerly: Whitaker Graduate Student Awards.

• 6390 • Rita Schaffer Young Investigator Award

To stimulate research careers, recognize originality and ingenuity of a published scientific work in biomedical engineering by a young investigator. Candidates must be within five years of receiving their highest degree. A monetary award of $1,000 and travel expenses of up to $1,000 is awarded each year at the annual fall meeting. The application deadline is July 1. Formerly: (1999) Whitaker Young Investigator Award.

• 6391 • Whitaker Senior Student Bioengineering Design Awards

To recognize bioengineering designs submitted by undergraduate students or student teams. Students must have senior standing at the time of submission. Both conceptual designs as well as prototypes may be submitted. Judging is based on originality, significance, thoroughness of design analysis, and performance evaluation. A certificate and five awards of $200 each are awarded. Submission deadline is June 2.

• 6392 •
Biotech Medical Management Association
Mark G. Fuller MD, Exec.Dir.
10592 Perry Hwy., No. 300
Wexford, PA 15090
Toll-Free: 888-990-2662
Fax: (866)706-8622
E-mail: general@bmma.org
Home Page: http://www.bmma.org

• 6393 • BMMA Awards

Recognizes contributions in the field. Health plans and manufacturers are eligible. Awarded annually.

• 6394 •
Biotechnology Industry Organization
James C. Greenwood, Pres./CEO
1225 Eye St. NW, Ste. 400
Washington, DC 20005
Phone: (202)962-9200
Toll-Free: 800-255-3304
Fax: (202)962-9201
E-mail: info@bio.org
Home Page: http://www.bio.org

• 6395 • Governor of the Year Award
Annual award of recognition.

• 6396 • High School Essay Contest
Award of recognition.

• 6397 • Legislator of the Year Award
Annual award of recognition.

• 6398 • Student Science Project Contest
Award of recognition.

• 6399 •
Birmingham Historical Society
Marjorie L. White, Dir.
One Sloss Quarters
Birmingham, AL 35222
Phone: (205)251-1880
Fax: (205)251-3260
E-mail: bhamhsoc@aol.com
Home Page: http://www.bhistorical.org

• 6400 • Preservation Award
For excellence in renovation of historic public and commercial buildings and sites. Recognition award bestowed annually.

• 6401 •
Birmingham-Southern College
Dr. David Pollick, Pres.
900 Arkadelphia Rd.
Birmingham, AL 35254
Phone: (205)226-4921
Toll-Free: 800-523-5793
Fax: (205)226-4931
E-mail: dcwilson@bsc.edu
Home Page: http://www.bsc.edu

• 6402 • Hackney Literary Awards
To encourage good writing. Awards are presented at Birmingham-Southern College's writers conference, Writing Today, in five categories: state short story, state poetry, national short story, national poetry, and novel. Original, unpublished manuscripts may be submitted by December 31 for poetry and short stories; and by September 30 for novels. Send SASE for guidelines for the Hackney Competition. Monetary awards totaling $5,000 are presented in each category annually for poems and short stories. Entries from Alabama are entered in the state competition unless specified for the national contest. An additional award was established for the novel in 1989 by Morris Hackney, son of Cecil Hackney who originally established the awards in 1969.

• 6403 •
Biscuit and Cracker Manufacturer Association
Kathy Kinter, Contact
8484 Georgia Ave., Ste. 700
Silver Spring, MD 20910
Phone: (301)608-1552
Fax: (301)608-1557
E-mail: kkinter@thebcma.org
Home Page: http://www.thebcma.org

• 6404 • Vender Heide Award
Recognizes the highest GPA graduate of course for the current year. Awarded annually.

• 6405 •
Black Archives of Mid-America
Pamela Ross, Exec.Dir.
2033 Vine St.
Kansas City, MO 64108
Phone: (816)483-1300
Fax: (816)483-1341
Home Page: http://www.blackarchives.org

• 6406 • Community Service Award
Annual award of recognition.

• 6407 • Personal or Academic Achievement Award
Annual award of recognition.

• 6408 •
Black Business and Professional Association
Hugh Graham, Pres.
675 King St. W, Ste. 210
Toronto, ON, Canada M5V 1M9
Phone: (416)504-4097
Fax: (416)504-7343
E-mail: bbpa@bellnet.ca
Home Page: http://www.bbpa.org

• 6409 • Harry Jerome Award
Recognizes individuals displaying excellence within the Black community. Awarded annually.

• 6410 • Harry Jerome Scholarship
Applicants must be outstanding post secondary students. Awarded annually.

• 6411 •
Black Caucus of the American Library Association
Andrew P. Jackson, Pres.
PO Box 5053
Hattiesburg, MS 39406-5053
Phone: (601)266-5111
Fax: (601)266-4410
E-mail:
andrew.p.jackson@queenslibrary.org
Home Page: http://www.bcala.org

• 6412 • Black Caucus Certificate of Appreciation
Recognizes excellence in the field of library science. A certificate is awarded annually.

• 6413 • Black Caucus of the American Library Association Literary Awards
To recognize outstanding work by African-American authors. Winners receive a monetary prize of $500 as well as a BCALA medallion. Certificates are given to the authors winning Honor Awards, Fiction Awards, Nonfiction Awards, First Novel Awards, and Outstanding Contribution to Publishing Awards. All awards are presented at the ALA Annual Conference.

• 6414 • Black Caucus of the American Library Association Trailblazer's Award
Recognizes outstanding accomplishments in the field of library science. Awarded every five years.

• 6415 • Black Caucus Special Recognition Plaques
Recognizes excellence in the field of library science. Plaques are awarded annually.

• 6416 • Coretta Scott King Award
Presented annually to African American authors and illustrators.

• 6417 • DEMCO/ALA Black Caucus Award for Excellence in Librarianship
Recognizes the promotion of African Americans in the library profession. $500 is awarded annually.

• 6418 • Distinguished Service Award
To honor significant contributions to the membership of the Black Caucus and the library profession. Awarded annually with a plaque. Established in 1977.

• 6419 • E. J. Josey Scholarship Award
Encourages African Americans to pursue careers in the library science field. Applicants must be currently enrolled in an ALA-accredited library science program. Awarded annually.

• 6420 •
Black Entertainment and Sports Lawyers Association
Ms. Phyllicia M. Hatton, Admin.Dir.
PO Box 441485
Fort Washington, MD 20749
Phone: (301)248-1818
Fax: (301)248-0700
E-mail: beslamailbox@aol.com
Home Page: http://www.besla.org

• 6421 • BESLA Award
Recognizes contribution to the Organization and to the community. Awarded annually.

• 6422 • Corporate Award
Recognizes contribution to the Organization and to the community. Awarded annually.

• 6423 • Legends Award
Recognizes contributions to the Organization and to the community. Awarded annually.

• 6424 •
Black Filmmakers Hall of Fame
Felix Curtis, Acting Exec.Dir.
13323 Campus Dr.
Oakland, CA 94619-3709
Phone: (510)562-5560
Phone: (510)562-5777
Fax: (510)639-7668
E-mail: bfhfinc@aol.com
Home Page: http://www.blackfilmmakersinc.com

• 6425 • **Sidney Poitier Fellowship**
Recognizes projects that are not commercially produced. African-American artists 18 or older are eligible. A monetary award is given semi-annually.

• 6426 •
Black, Indian, Hispanic, and Asian Women in Action
Alice O. Lynch, Exec.Dir.
1830 James Ave. N
Minneapolis, MN 55417
Phone: (612)521-2986
Fax: (612)529-6745
E-mail: info@biha.org
Home Page: http://www.biha.org

• 6427 • **Women of Color Recognition Award**
Recognizes volunteerism and community work. Women of color are eligible. Awarded annually.

• 6428 •
Black Lung Association
Bill Bailey, Exec. Officer
Box 872
Crab Orchard, WV 25827
Phone: (304)252-9654

• 6429 • **Black Lung Association Award**
To recognize those who make an effort to educate others about black lung disease, a condition especially prevalent in the coal mining industry. Local and national awards are presented. A dinner is awarded annually. Established in 1979. Sponsored by the National Black Lung Association.

• 6430 •
Black Mental Health Alliance
Tracee E. Bryant, Exec.Dir.
733 W 40th St., Ste. 10
Baltimore, MD 21211
Phone: (410)338-2642
Fax: (410)338-1771
E-mail: tbryant@blackmentalhealth.org
Home Page: http://www.blackmentalhealth.org/default1.htm

• 6431 • **Addison Pope, MD Award**
Recognizes Mental Health Clinicians. A trophy is awarded annually.

• 6432 • **Award of Special Recognition**
Recognizes outstanding contributions to the association. Awarded annually.

• 6433 • **Maxie T. Collier, MD Award**
Recognizes a family member or consumer of mental health services. Awarded annually.

• 6434 • **Volunteer of the Year**
Recognizes the provision of resources, spirit of helping and sharing to enhance the programs and services of the association. Awarded annually.

• 6435 •
Black Theatre Network
Gregory J. Horton, Pres.
7226 Virginia Ave.
St. Louis, MO 63111-3018
Phone: (314)352-1123
Fax: (314)352-1123
E-mail: btnoffice@sbcglobal.net
Home Page: http://www.blacktheatrenetwork.org

• 6436 • **S. Randolph Edmonds Young Scholars Competition**
To encourage research and scholarship in black theater. Applicants must submit a paper up to 10 pages in length on an aspect of black theatre in either the United States or throughout the world. Monetary awards of $250 for first place and $100 for second place are awarded each year in the undergraduate and graduate divisions at the Black Theatre Network annual convention. Established in 1987 in honor of Randolph Edmonds. Formerly: Young Scholars Competition.

• 6437 •
Blackhawk Standbys
Gladys Wheeler, Pres.
11555 Settlers Pond Way, Unit 2B
Orland Park, IL 60467
Phone: (708)479-7967
E-mail: hummelfriend@msn.com
Home Page: http://www.blackhawkstandbys.homestead.com

• 6438 • **Monthly Most Valuable Player Award**
Monthly award of recognition.

• 6439 • **Most Valuable Player Award**
Award of recognition.

• 6440 • **Player of the Year Award**
Annual award of recognition.

• 6441 •
Blacks in Law Enforcement
Tara Chester, Dir. of Administration
591 Vanderbilt Ave., Ste. 133
Brooklyn, NY 11238
Phone: (718)455-9059
Phone: (718)544-9002
Fax: (718)574-4236
E-mail: what2do100blacks@aol.com
Home Page: http://www.100blacks.org

Formerly: (1988) Top Blacks in Law Enforcement.

• 6442 • **Distinguished Officer of the Year**
To recognize officers who have gone above and beyond the call of duty and employment obligation with service to their department and concern for their community. Officers submitted by their department heads for entry in the BLE publication during the award year are eligible. Nominees may be submitted by past nominees and local, state and federal government officials. A plaque is awarded annually. Established in 1987 by Clyde R. Venson.

• 6443 •
***Blade* Magazine**
Krause Publications
700 E State St.
Iola, WI 54990-0001
Phone: (715)445-4612
Toll-Free: 800-258-0929
Fax: (715)445-4087
E-mail: blade@krause.com
Home Page: http://www.blademag.com

Formerly: American Blade Collectors Association and *The Blade Magazine*.

• 6444 • ***The Blade Magazine* Manufacturers Awards**
To recognize the very best in cutlery manufacturing. Candidates who are exhibitors at the annual convention and submit a representative sample of work at the show are considered for the award. A plaque and the right to use the award in advertising and other promotions are bestowed annually at the convention. Established in 1982.

• 6445 • **Cutlery Hall of Fame**
For recognition of outstanding contributions to the cutlery industry and knife collecting. A plaque is presented annually at the convention. Additionally, the honoree will be recognized in *The Blade Magazine*. Established in 1982 by Bruce Voyles and *The Blade Magazine*.

• 6446 •
Blair Society for Genealogical Research (Societe pour l'etude de l'architecture du Canada)
Bryce D. Blair, Pres.
726 Falling Oaks Dr.
Medina, OH 44256-2778
E-mail: brydblair1@juno.com
Home Page: http://www.blairsociety.org

• 6447 • Martin Eli Weil Prize
Recognizes the best paper on Canadian architecture. Papers submitted by university students are eligible. Awarded annually.

• 6448 •
Blazer Horse Association
Neil Hinck, Pres.
820 N Can-Ada Rd.
Star, ID 83669
Phone: (208)286-7267
Fax: (208)286-7267
E-mail: lorenzo@integrity.com
Home Page: http://www.integrity.com/homes/lorenzo/bha.htm

• 6449 • High Point Honors
Recognizes winners of timed events. Awarded annually.

• 6450 •
Blessed Kateri Tekakwitha League
Fr. John J. Paret, Vice Postulator
Office of the Vice Postulator
Auriesville, NY 12016
Phone: (518)853-3153
Fax: (518)853-3051
E-mail: paret@martyrshrine.org
Home Page: http://www.kateritekakwitha.org/kateri/

• 6451 • Tekakwitha Award
For recognition of promotion of the cause or devotion to the cause of Blessed Kateri Tekakwitha. Nomination is by the Board of Directors. A plaque is awarded annually. Established in 1972 in memory of Blessed Kateri Tekakwitha.

• 6452 •
Blind Service Association
Debbie Grossman, Exec.Dir.
22 W Monroe, 11th Fl.
Chicago, IL 60603
Phone: (312)236-0808
Fax: (312)236-8679
E-mail: blindsrvc@aol.com

• 6453 • Blind Service Association Scholarships
For blind college students.

• 6454 •
Blinded Veterans Association
Mr. Thomas H. Miller, Exec.Dir.
477 H St. NW
Washington, DC 20001
Phone: (202)371-8880
Toll-Free: 800-669-7079
Fax: (202)371-8258
E-mail: bva@bva.org
Home Page: http://www.bva.org

• 6455 • Certificate of Appreciation
To recognize an individual who has performed exemplary service to the Association. A scroll is awarded when merited.

• 6456 • Irving Diener Award
To recognize veterans for outstanding service to a regional group of the Association. Blinded veterans who are members or associate members are eligible for nomination. A scroll and a $50 stipend are awarded annually. Established in 1962 in honor of the late Irving Diener, a former member of the BVA National Advisory Committee.

• 6457 • Wilburn H. Long Employment Award
To recognize individuals, agencies, or employers who provide employment opportunities for blinded veterans. A certificate is awarded annually. Established in 1989 to honor the late Wilburn H. Long, former National Employment Director of the Blinded Veterans Association. Formerly: Employer of the Year Award.

• 6458 • Major General Melvin J. Maas Achievement Award
To recognize the achievement of outstanding service-connected blinded veterans in their adjustment to blindness, participation in community affairs, and employment. From the beginning, presentation of this award has contributed to the enhancement of a positive image of blind people and to the elimination of the concept of helplessness. A monetary award and a scroll are awarded annually. Established in 1945 and renamed in 1973 to honor General Maas, a former president of BVA, Congressman, and Chairman of the President's Committee on the Handicapped. Formerly: (1973) BVA Achievement Award.

• 6459 •
Blue Hill Peninsula Chamber of Commerce
Dr. Beverly J. Bartlett, Pres.
PO Box 520
Blue Hill, ME 04614-0520
Phone: (207)374-3242
Fax: (207)374-3242
E-mail: chamber@bluehillpeninsula.org
Home Page: http://www.bluehillpeninsula.org

• 6460 • Civic Scholarship
For civic-minded student from the Blue Hill Peninsula. Scholarship awarded annually.

• 6461 •
Blue Ridge English as a Second Language Council
Selene Mak, Exec.Dir.
214 Rugby Rd.
Charlottesville, VA 22903
Phone: (434)977-7988
Phone: (804)293-9893
Fax: (434)977-7988
E-mail: esltutors@hotmail.com
Home Page: http://avenue.org//bresl/

• 6462 • Virginia Literacy Foundation
For innovation in moving ESL to people. Monetary award bestowed annually.

• 6463 •
Blue Ridge Literacy Council
Diane Bowers, Exec.Dir.
PO Box 1728
Hendersonville, NC 28793-1728
Phone: (828)696-3811
Fax: (828)696-3887
E-mail: info@litcouncil.org
Home Page: http://www.litcouncil.org

• 6464 • Extra Mile Award
For service to the literacy council. Recognition award bestowed annually.

• 6465 • Lisa Morrill Volunteer Award
For service to literacy council. Recognition award bestowed annually.

• 6466 • G'anne Sparks Tutoring Award
For service to literacy council. Recognition award bestowed annually.

• 6467 •
Blue Star Mothers of America
Jean Burlingame, Natl.Pres.
PO Box 917
Flora Vista, NM 87415
Phone: (301)949-0114
E-mail: president@bluestarmothers.org
Home Page: http://www.bluestarmothers.org

• 6468 • Educational Assistance Award
A monetary award is given annually.

• 6469 •
Blues Alley Music Society
PO Box 3616
Washington, DC 20007
Phone: (202)544-3230
Fax: (202)337-7946
E-mail: executivedirector@bluesalley.org
Home Page: http://www.bluesalleymusicsociety.org

• 6470 • Felix Grant/Stan Getz Award
To recognize outstanding music students. Scholarships are awarded annually. Established in 1985.

• 6471 • Jazz Contribution Awards
For recognition of excellence in the field of music and in honor of contributions to the world of jazz. Selection is by nomination. A plaque is awarded annually. Established in 1981.

• 6472 •
The Blues Foundation
Jay Sieleman, Exec.Dir.
49 Union Ave.
Memphis, TN 38103
Phone: (901)527-2583
Toll-Free: 800-861-8795
Fax: (901)529-4030
E-mail: jay@blues.org
Home Page: http://www.blues.org

• 6473 • **Blues Hall of Fame**
To recognize individuals past and present who have made general contributions to the perpetuation of the Blues. The following categories are included in the Hall of Fame: Honor Roll - for outstanding performers throughout the entire history of the Blues; Classics of Blues Recording (Singles) - for outstanding examples of Blues performances on record 1920 to present; Classics of Blues Recording (Albums) - for outstanding Blues albums 1920 to present; and Classics of Blues Literature - for outstanding contributions to Blues knowledge. This category may include books, magazines, articles, booklets, liner notes, or foreign magazines. The special B. B. King Lucille Award is presented to the winners of the International Blues Talent Competition. New inductees to the Hall of Fame are honored annually during ceremonies in Los Angeles, CA. Established in 1980.

• 6474 • **Blues Music Awards (W. C. Handy Awards)**
To recognize the most outstanding performers of the Blues. Artists, record producers, and other contributors to the perpetuation of the Blues are elected through an international balloting system of members of the Blues Foundation and subscribers of certain blues magazines. The Handy Trophy is awarded annually. Established in 1980 in honor of W. C. Handy, the father of the Blues.

• 6475 • **Howlin' Wolf Award**
To recognize the Memphis-Chicago Blues connection. Presented annually to a Blues artist in honor of the late Blues pioneer Howlin' Wolf.

• 6476 • **Keeping the Blues Alive Awards**
To recognize individuals and organizations who have made significant contributions to the blues industry. Initial nominations are made by foundation-affiliated blues societies from around the country. These nominations are reviewed by a panel of blues promoters, musicians, and historians from the Blues Foundation Board of Directors. Awards are presented in the following categories: Blues Sponsor of the Year, Blues Organization of the Year, Blues Club Owner of the Year, Promoter of the Year, KBA in Education, KBA in Public Radio, KBA in Commercial Radio, KBA in Historical Preservation, KBA in Advertising, KBA in Film, KBA in Art, Special KBA, KBA in Journalism, and KBA in Print Media. Awards are presented at an annual banquet preceding the W. C. Handy Awards.

• 6477 • **Key to the Highway Award**
No further information was provided for this information.

• 6478 • **Lifetime Achievement Award**
Annually recognizes an individual for long-term contributions to the Blues. It is an opportunity for the Blues Foundation to recognize an individual for a lifetime of achievement in the world of music.

• 6479 •
BMW Riders Association International
Linda Gotcher, Administrator
PO Box 120430
West Melbourne, FL 32912-0430
Phone: (321)984-7800
Fax: (321)984-7800
E-mail: admin@bmwra.org
Home Page: http://www.bmwra.org

• 6480 • **Bill Harmer Award**
Recognizes outstanding service to the association. Awarded periodically.

• 6481 • **Walt Klein Award**
Awarded annually for signing up members.

• 6482 •
B'nai B'rith
Joel S. Kaplan, Intl.Pres.
2020 K St. NW, 7th Fl.
Washington, DC 20006
Phone: (202)857-6600
Toll-Free: 888-388-4224
Fax: (202)857-2780
E-mail: website@bnaibrith.org
Home Page: http://www.bnaibrith.org

• 6483 • **Chai Award**
To recognize an individual or group on a national level for outstanding contributions in the area of community service, citizenship, and humanitarianism. The awardee need not be Jewish or a member of B'nai B'rith. Awarded to those who honor life ("chai" is the Hebrew word for life) through their labors in the cause of humanity. A large inscribed family bible is awarded annually. Established in 1974.

• 6484 • **Sidney G. Kusworm Award**
To recognize one lodge, unit or chapter that is considered the best in the district or the region. A certificate is given annually for community service excellence. This award was created as a tribute to Sidney G. Kusworm, who served as head of the Community and Veterans Services Commission of the B'nai B'rith for more than forty years.

• 6485 • **Colonel Elliott A. Niles Award**
To recognize an individual for service to the community during the year. A certificate is awarded annually to a B'nai B'rith member. Established in memory of the late Colonel Elliott A. Niles, the founder of the Service Committee for Armed Forces and Veterans of the B'nai B'rith.

• 6486 •
B'nai Brith Canada
Dr. Frank Dimant, Exec.VP
15 Hove St.
Toronto, ON, Canada M3H 4Y8
Phone: (416)633-6224
Fax: (416)630-2159
E-mail: bnb@bnaibrith.ca
Home Page: http://www.bnaibrith.ca

• 6487 • **Award of Merit**
To recognize individuals for outstanding achievement in their chosen fields of endeavor as well as for leadership and involvement in communal activities that result in the betterment of life for all people. Nominations are made by a selection committee. Awards are presented annually in selected Canadian cities. Established in 1978.

• 6488 • **Humanitarian Award**
For exceptional leadership in communal activities realizing the betterment of life for all people as well as for outstanding achievement in chosen fields of endeavor. Nominations are made by the selection committee. Awarded when merited. Established in 1978.

• 6489 •
B'nai B'rith International
Joel S. Kaplan, Intl.Pres.
2020 K St. NW, 7th Fl.
Washington, DC 20006
Phone: (202)857-6600
Toll-Free: 888-388-4224
Fax: (202)857-2700
E-mail: webssite@bnaibrith.org
Home Page: http://bnaibrith.org/index.cfm

• 6490 • **Martin Luther King, Jr. - Abraham Joshua Heschel Award**
To recognize individuals for continuing commitment to the advancement of equality, human rights and a meaningful relationship between the Black and Jewish communities. A plaque is awarded periodically. Established in 1988 to honor Martin Luther King and Abraham Joshua Heschel, two distinguished clergymen from the Black and Jewish communities who struggled together in the American civil rights movement.

• 6491 •
Board of Directors of City Trusts acting for the City of Philadelphia
21 S 12th St.
Philadelphia, PA 19107
Phone: (215)568-0440
Fax: (215)568-0347

• 6492 • **John Scott Award**
To recognize the "most deserving" men and women whose inventions have contributed in some outstanding way to the "comfort, welfare and happiness" of mankind. Awarded to ingenious men or women who make useful inventions. Nominations are made by a committee of Philadelphians to the Board of Directors of City Trusts of the City of Philadelphia. A monetary

prize of up to $15,000, a copper medal and a certificate are awarded annually. Established in 1816 by John Scott, an Edinburgh druggist. First awarded in 1832.

• 6493 •
Boating Writers International
Greg Proteau, Exec.Dir.
108 9th St.
Wilmette, IL 60091
Phone: (847)736-4142
E-mail: info@bwi.org
Home Page: http://www.bwi.org

• 6494 • Boating Writers International Annual Writing Contest
14 contest categories are judged for "excellence in creating compelling stories about the boating lifestyle." Each category recognizes first($500), second($300) and third($200) place entries; winners also receive presentation plaques. All winning stories are entered into a "Phase II" Competition which culminates in a single selection honored with the West Marine Writer's Award and $5,000 cash prize at the Ft. Lauderdale Boat Show in October. BWI members are allowed four submissions to the contest at $35 for each submission ($35 is the same cost as an annual active membership in BWI). Deadline for entries is December 31 each year. Cash awards and plaques are presented to the winners at the Miami International Boat Show in mid-February. For more information about BMI and its award program, visit www.bmi.org and click on the "Writing Contest" tab.

• 6495 •
Boca Raton Historical Society
Mary Csar, Dir.
71 N. Federal Hwy.
Boca Raton, FL 33432
Phone: (561)395-6766
Fax: (561)395-4049
E-mail: info@bocahistory.org
Home Page: http://bocahistory.org

• 6496 • Myrtle Butts Fleming Award
For outstanding volunteer service. Recognition award bestowed annually.

• 6497 •
Boise Peace Quilt Project
Linda Mercer, Mgr.
PO Box 6469
Boise, ID 83707
Phone: (208)378-0293
Phone: (208)384-1155
Fax: (208)323-0848
E-mail: info@boisepeacequilt.org
Home Page: http://
www.boisepeacequilt.org

• 6498 • Peace Quilt Awards
To recognize achievement in peacemaking, to show friendship to people of other nations, and to raise consciousness about working for world peace. A handmade quilt designed for the recipient is awarded when merited. Established in 1982.

• 6499 •
Bonsai and Orchid Association
Le Roy Rench, Bd.Chm.
26 Pine St.
Dover, DE 19901
Phone: (302)736-6781
Toll-Free: 800-801-3791
Fax: (302)736-6763
E-mail: leroyrench@comcast.net

• 6500 • Bonsai and Orchid Association Award
To help promote the bonsai and orchid industry. First, second, and third place awards and Best Booth Display Award are presented for orchids, bonsai, or allied trades. Fifteen trophies are awarded each August at the annual convention and trade show. Established in 1989.

• 6501 •
Book Publishers Association of Alberta
10523 100th Ave.
Edmonton, AB, Canada T5J 0A8
Phone: (780)424-5060
Fax: (780)424-7943
E-mail: info@bookpublishers.ab.ca
Home Page: http://
www.bookpublishers.ab.ca

Formerly: Alberta Publishers Association.

• 6502 • Alberta Book Design Awards
Recognizes the publisher producing the best books in the following three categories: best overall design, best cover, and best illustratioins. Awarded annually as part of the Alberta Book Awards.

• 6503 • Alberta Children's Book of the Year
Recognizes an Alberts-based publisher producing the best children's or young adult book, including fiction, non-fiction, and picture books. Awarded annually as part of the Alberta Book Awards.

• 6504 • Alberta Educational Book of the Year
Recognizes an Alberta-based publisher producing the best book published specifically for the elementary or secondary school market. Awarded annually as part of the Alberta Book Awards.

• 6505 • Alberta Emerging Publisher of the Year
Honors an emerging publisher in Alberta who shows promise in book publishing. Awarded annually as part of the Alberta Book Awards. Established in 2000.

• 6506 • Alberta Publisher of the Year Award
Recognizes the Alberta publisher best exemplifies the spirit of Alberta and the book publishing industry. Selection is based on overall quality of books produced, innovation in all areas of the industry, service to clients, and activity in the community. Awarded annually as part of the Alberta Book Awards.

• 6507 • Alberta Scholarly Book of the Year
Recognizes an Alberts-based publisher producing the best book published primarily for the post-secondary post-graduate or other academic/scholarly market. Awarded annually as part of the Alberta Book Awards.

• 6508 • Trade Book of the Year
Recognizes an Alberta-based publisher producing the best book for the trade or bookstore market. Awarded annually as part of the Alberta Book Awards.

• 6509 •
Bookbuilders of Boston
Victor Curran, Pres.
44 Highland Cir.
Halifax, MA 02338
Phone: (781)293-8600
Fax: (866)820-0469
E-mail: office@bbboston.org
Home Page: http://www.bbboston.org

• 6510 • William A. Dwiggins Award
To recognize an individual who has contributed significantly to the creation of books, be it in the concept, design, manufacturing, or publishing of books, or to the community of bookmakers. Awarded annually in April. Established in 1957.

• 6511 • New England Book Show Juried Selection
To exhibit and honor the best of New England's book design and manufacturing. Awards are given in the following categories: (1) Book Categories - College; Professional-Illustrated; Professional-Unillustrated; El-Hi; Juvenile; General Trade-Illustrated; General Trade-Unillustrated; Pictorial; Multimedia; and (2) Jacket/Cover Categories - College; Professional; El-Hi; and General Trade. Entries may be submitted in July. A certificate is awarded annually. Established in 1957.

• 6512 •
Bookbuilders West
Elise Gochberg, Pres.
170 9th St.
PO Box 7046
San Francisco, CA 94120
Phone: (650)623-9741
Phone: (650)961-9393
E-mail: secretary@bookbuilders.org
Home Page: http://www.bookbuilders.org

• 6513 • Bookbuilders West Book Show
To recognize the finest achievements of the Western publishing community during the year. Awards are given in the following categories: college text; El-Hi; handmade/limited edition; scholarly; and trade. Books are selected by four distinguished judges.

• 6514 • Certificate of Merit
For recognition of achievement in the highest goals of book design and production. Books published in one of the 13 western states during the preceding year are eligible. A certificate is awarded annually at the Bookbuilders West Book Show.

• 6515 • Distinguished Service Award
Honors those individuals for their dedicated service and contributions to BBW and the industry. Canditates are selected by a committee. Awarded Annually.

• 6516 •
Boston Association for the Education of Young Children
Marcia L. Farris, Exec.Dir.
165 Brookside Ave. Ext.
Jamaica Plain, MA 02130
Phone: (617)522-0881
Fax: (617)782-0739
E-mail: office@baeyc.org
Home Page: http://www.baeyc.org

• 6517 • Abigail Eliot Award
For service to organization and contribution to early education field. Recognition award bestowed annually.

• 6518 •
Boston Athletic Association
Guy L. Morse, Exec.Dir.
40 Trinity Pl., 4th Fl.
Boston, MA 02116
Phone: (617)236-1652
Fax: (617)236-4505
E-mail: mile27@baa.org
Home Page: http://www.bostonmarathon.org

• 6519 • Boston Marathon
Boston is the world's oldest annual marathon. Except for minor changes at the start and finish, the 26.2-mile course has remained essentially the same throughout the history of the race. The Boston Marathon has been held annually on Patriots' Day (or the nearest Monday) since 1897. Only once, in 1918, was there an interruption in the traditional race format when a military relay race took its place because of World War I. The first official women's winner was recognized in 1972. Prizes are awarded in the following divisions: Open Division - men and women, Masters Division - men and women, Wheelchair Division - men and women, and Visually Impaired Division - men and women. Prize money is awarded to top finishers in the Open, Masters, and Wheelchair divisions. Boston was the world's first major marathon to offer equal prize money at all levels to men and women. Bonuses are awarded if a course and/or world record is set.

• 6520 •
Boston Book Review
331 Harvard St., Ste. 17
Cambridge, MA 02139
Phone: (617)497-0344
Fax: (617)497-0394
E-mail: bbr-info@bostonbookreview.org
Home Page: http://www.bookwire.com/bookwire/bbr/bbr-home.html

• 6521 • Literary Awards
Given for poetry, fiction, and non-fiction. Nominations and final choices are made by the judges. No submissions are necessary. These $1,000 prizes celebrate literary accomplishments: The Fisk Fiction Prize, given in memory of Lilla Fisk Rand; The Rea Non-Fiction Prize, given in memory of Anne Rea Jewell; and the Bingham Poetry Prize, given in memory of Belinda Bingham Pierce. Awarded annually. Established in 1994.

• 6522 •
Boston College
Center for Corporate Citizenship
55 Lee Rd.
Chestnut Hill, MA 02467
Phone: (617)552-4545
Fax: (617)552-8499
E-mail: ccc@bc.edu
Home Page: http://www.bc.edu/corporatecitizenship

• 6523 • Boston College Student Paper Competition
Recognizes a paper on corporate citizenship. Boston College students are eligible. $5000 is awarded.

• 6524 • Henry L. Shattuck Public Service Awards
Recognizes outstanding service to Boston. City and school employees are eligible.

• 6525 •
The Boston Globe
135 Morrisey Blvd.
PO Box 55819
Boston, MA 02205-5819
Phone: (617)929-2000
Fax: (617)929-3220
Home Page: http://www.hbook.com/awards/bghb/about.asp

• 6526 • *Boston Globe* - Horn Book Awards
To encourage and reward excellence in the writing and illustrating of children's books. Children's books initially published during the preceding year in the United States are eligible. Monetary prizes of $500 each are awarded to an author of fiction or poetry, to an author of nonfiction, and to an illustrator. Presented annually at the New England Library Association Conference. Established in 1967 by the Globe and Horn Book, Inc.

• 6527 •
Boston University
Anna Howard Shaw Center
School of Theology
745 Commonwealth Ave.
Boston, MA 02215
Phone: (617)353-3075
E-mail: shawctr@bu.edu
Home Page: http://www.bu.edu/sth/shaw/

• 6528 • Pioneer Woman Award
Recognizes women who embody those values expressed in the life of Anna Howard Shaw. Awarded biennially.

• 6529 •
Boston University
Department of Athletics
285 Babcock St.
Boston, MA 02215
Phone: (617)353-2872
Fax: (617)353-5286
E-mail: busid@bu.edu
Home Page: http://www.bu.edu/athletics

• 6530 • Murray Kramer
To recognize outstanding coverage of intercollegiate athletics. Sportswriters, sportscasters, sports columnists, and sports cartoonists are eligible. A plaque is awarded annually. Established in 1965 in honor of Murray Kramer, first sports information director at Boston University, who went on to enjoy an outstanding career as a sportswriter in Boston. Formerly: (2004) Murray Kramer Scarlet Quill Award.

• 6531 •
Boston University
Pike Institute on Law and Disability
765 Commonwealth Ave.
Boston, MA 02215
Phone: (617)353-2904
Fax: (617)353-2906
E-mail: pikeinst@bu.edu

• 6532 • Pike Prize for Service to People with Disabilities
To provide recognition to those whose accomplishments - by persons with disabilities or on behalf of promoting greater understanding of disability law - have been especially noteworthy. A trophy, citation, and monetary award are presented annually. Established in 1976. Formerly: Pike Prize for the Handicapped.

• 6533 •
**Boston University
School of Music
Walt Meissner, Dean
855 Commonwealth Ave.
Boston, MA 02215
Phone: (617)353-3350
Fax: (617)353-3340
E-mail: arts@bu.edu
Home Page: http://www.aleaiii.com/ALEACompetition.html**

• 6534 • **ALEA International Composition Prize**
To promote and encourage new music by composers of any nationality. Music of any style and esthetic direction that has never been performed is eligible. Eligible works may be for solo voice or instrument, or for chamber ensemble of up to fifteen performers, lasting from six to fifteen minutes. Instrumentation must be from the following: one flute (doubling piccolo or alto), one oboe (doubling English horn), one clarinet (doubling bass clarinet), bassoon, horn, trumpet, trombone, tuba, two percussion, harp, keyboard, guitar, strings (two violins, viola, cello, bass), tape, and one voice. Individuals under the age of 40 may submit one composition by March 15. Alea III, Performing Arts Ensemble in Residence at Boston University, performs the compositions of the 6 - 9 finalists. A monetary prize of $2,500 is awarded annually. Established in 1980 by Charles Politis, a Greek American industrialist. Re-established by an anonymous donor in 1984 to honor Melanya Kucyna, and renamed again in 1989 as the Alea III International Composition Prize. Formerly: (1989) Kucyna International Composition Prize; (1983) Politis Composition Prize.

• 6535 •
**Botanical Society of America
William Dahl, Exec.Dir.
4475 Castleman Ave.
St. Louis, MO 63166
Phone: (314)577-9566
Fax: (314)577-9519
E-mail: bsa-manager@botany.org
Home Page: http://www.botany.org**

• 6536 • **Ralph E. Alston Award**
For recognition of the best contributed paper presented at the annual meeting of the Phytochemical Section.

• 6537 • **Charles Edwin Bessey Award**
To recognize an individual for outstanding contributions to botanical instruction. Awarded annually by the Teaching Section of the BSA.

• 6538 • **BSA Merit Awards**
To recognize persons who have made outstanding contributions to botanical science. Awarded annually. Established in 1956.

• 6539 • **Michael Cichan Award**
To recognize a young scholar for a paper published during the previous year in the fields of evolutionary and/or structural botany. Awarded annually. Named in honor of the memory and work of Michael A. Cichan, who died in a plane crash in August 1987.

• 6540 • **Isabel C. Cookson Paleobotanical Award**
For recognition of the best contributed paper in paleobotany or palynology presented at the annual meeting.

• 6541 • **George R. Cooley Award**
For recognition of the best paper in plant systematics presented at the annual meeting. Awarded annually by the American Society of Plant Taxonomists.

• 6542 • **Corresponding Members**
To recognize distinguished senior scientists for outstanding contributions to plant biology. Only those scientists who live and work outside the United States are eligible. The number of such members is limited to fifty living persons.

• 6543 • **Darbaker Prize**
For recognition of meritorious work in the study of microscopical algae, judged primarily on papers published within the previous two years.

• 6544 • **Distinguished Paper in Phychology Award**
To recognize the most outstanding manuscript published in the *American Journal of Botany* in a given year dealing with any aspect of algal research. Established in 1991.

• 6545 • **Ecological Section Award**
To recognize the best student paper in ecology at the annual meeting. A certificate, monetary prize of $50, and opportunity to be a guest of the Ecological Section at the BSA banquet are awarded annually.

• 6546 • **Katherine Esau Award**
To recognize the outstanding graduate student paper in developmental and structural botany at the annual meeting. Awarded annually. Established in 1985.

• 6547 • **Henry Allan Gleason Award**
To recognize an outstanding recent publication in the fields of plant taxonomy, plant ecology, or plant geography. A monetary prize and certificate are awarded annually by the New York Botanical Garden.

• 6548 • **Jesse M. Greenman Award**
For recognition of the best paper in vascular plant or bryophyte systematics based on a doctoral dissertation published during the previous year. Awarded annually by the Alumni Association of the Missouri Botanical Garden.

• 6549 • **J. S. Karling Graduate Student Research Award**
To support and promote graduate student research in the botanical sciences. To be eligible, one must be a member of the Botanical Society of America, a registered full-time graduate student, have a faculty advisor who is also a member of BSA, and not have won the award previously. The application process includes: (1) a description of the research, (2) a budget detailing how the funds would be used, (3) a supporting letter from the advisor no longer than one page. Applications should be submitted to the chair of the section of the BSA that best matches the proposed research. A monetary award of $500 is presented annually.

• 6550 • **Margaret Menzel Award**
To recognize an outstanding paper presented during the contributed papers session of the annual meetings given by the Genetics Section.

• 6551 • **Jeanette Siron Pelton Award**
For recognition of sustained and imaginative productivity in the field of experimental plant morphology. A monetary prize of $1,000 is awarded not more frequently than annually. Sponsored by the Conservation and Research Foundation in memory of Jeanette Siron Pelton.

• 6552 • **Physiological Section Award**
To recognize the best presentation made by any student, regardless of subdiscipline, at the annual meeting. The Li-Cor prize is presented by the Physiological Section annually.

• 6553 • **Samuel Noel Postlethwait Award**
To recognize exceptional service on behalf of the Teaching Section of the BSA. Awarded annually. Established in 1990.

• 6554 • **A.J. Sharp Award**
For recognition of the best student paper presented in the American Bryological and Lichenological sessions.

• 6555 • **Edgar T. Wherry Award**
For recognition of the best paper presented during the contributed papers session of the Pteridological Section.

• 6556 •
**Bowling Proprietors' Association of America
John Berglund CAE, Exec.Dir.
PO Box 5802
615 Six Flags Dr.
Arlington, TX 76005
Phone: (817)649-5105
Toll-Free: 800-343-1329
Fax: (817)633-2940
E-mail: nate@bpaa.com
Home Page: http://www.bpaa.com**

• 6557 • **Victor Lerner Memorial Medal**
For recognition of a lifetime of selfless service to the bowling industry. Nominations submitted by

December 31 are judged each year by the Awards Committee. A plaque is awarded annually at the convention. Established in 1976 in honor of Victor Lerner.

• 6558 • President's Medal
For recognition of outstanding service to the Association during the past 18 months. Nominations submitted by December 31 are judged each year by the Awards Committee. A plaque is awarded annually at the convention. Established in 1976.

• 6559 • VA Wapensky Award
For recognition of outstanding service to the bowling industry during a specific or extended period. Proprietors (BPAA members) are not normally considered. Nominations submitted by December 31 are judged each year by the Awards Committee. A plaque is awarded annually at the convention. Established in 1985. Formerly: BPAA Special Award.

• 6560 •
Bowling Writers Association of America
Steve James, Exec.Dir.
8501 N Manor Ln.
Fox Point, WI 53217
Phone: (414)351-6085
E-mail: sjames2652@wi.rr.com
Home Page: http://www.bowlingwriters.com

• 6561 • Amateur Bowler of the Year
To recognize the outstanding male and female amateur bowlers of the year. Awarded annually. Established in 1991.

• 6562 • Bowler of the Month
To recognize an outstanding bowler each month of the year. Amateurs and professionals, men, women, and youth are eligible. An appropriate award is given to each recipient, one per year.

• 6563 • Bowler of the Year
To recognize the outstanding male and female bowler. Awarded annually. Established in 1942.

• 6564 • Collegiate Bowlers of the Year
To recognize the outstanding male and female collegiate bowlers of the year. Awarded annually. Established in 1990.

• 6565 • Mort Luby Senior Hall of Fame Award
BWAA Hall of Fame recognition for outstanding service to bowling through the medium of newspaper, radio, or television. Members of the association are eligible. An engraved ring is awarded annually. Established in 1952.

• 6566 • John O. Martino Award
For recognition of outstanding contributions to the sport of bowling over a number of years. Awarded annually. Established in 1976.

• 6567 • Senior Bowler of the Year
To recognize the outstanding senior bowlers of the year. Awarded to one male and one female bowler annually. Male category established in 1993; female in 2001.

• 6568 • Rip Van Winkle Award
To honor individuals for accomplishments in bowling that took place or began at least 20 years earlier and that might otherwise have gone unrecognized or unrewarded. A bronze plaque is awarded annually. Established in 1956.

• 6569 •
***Boxoffice* Magazine**
155 El Molino Ave., Ste. 100
Pasadena, CA 91101
Phone: (626)396-0250
Fax: (626)396-0248
E-mail: boxoffice@earthlink.net
Home Page: http://www.boxoffice.com

• 6570 • Barometer Star Poll
To recognize those performers who motion picture exhibitors feel had the most impact at the ticket window during the past year. The winners are announced in the annual "Barometer" issue of *Boxoffice* magazine, which is published in March. Established in 1936.

• 6571 • Blue Ribbon Awards
To recognize the most popular, the best, and the worst films of the fall/Christmas season, and the spring/summer season, as determined by the nation's theatre owners. The ten best spring/summer films, the ten most popular spring/summer films and the ten worst spring/summer films are announced in December; the ten best fall/Christmas films, the ten most popular fall/Christmas films and the ten worst fall/Christmas films are announced in July. Established in 1936.

• 6572 •
Boy Scouts of America
Roy Williams, Chief Scout Exec.
1325 W Walnut Hill Ln.
PO Box 152079
Irving, TX 75015-2079
Phone: (972)580-2000
Fax: (972)580-2502
Home Page: http://www.scouting.org

• 6573 • American Veterinary Medical Association Explorer Award
Recognizes individual Explorer Scouts who have made a significant contribution to the veterinary medicine field. A $500 cash award and a plaque are presented annually by the AVMA.

• 6574 • DEA Explorer Drug Abuse Prevention Service Award
Recognizes outstanding service displayed by law enforcement Explorer posts in community drug prevention programs. An engraved plaque is awarded by the Drug Enforcement Administration each year.

• 6575 • Distinguished Eagle Scout Award
This award is the only distinguished service recognition dependent on one's association with Scouting as a youth. The recipient must have attained the Eagle Scout rank a minimum of 25 years prior to his nomination, and must have rendered outstanding service to his fellow man over those years and attained a position of recognition, fame, or eminence. A Golden Eagle on ribbon and an engraved plaque are awarded through a local council by the National Court of Honor. Established in 1969 by Zenon C. R. Hansen.

• 6576 • District Award of Merit
To recognize an individual who has rendered noteworthy service to youth in general, and the Boy Scouts in particular. Registered Scouts are eligible. Presented by districts of the national organization when merited.

• 6577 • Eagle Scout
To earn the Eagle Scout rank, the highest advancement rank in Scouting, a Boy Scout must fulfill requirements in the areas of leadership, service, and outdoor skills. A number of specific skills are required to advance through the ranks - Tenderfoot, Second Class, First Class, Star, Life, and Eagle. To advance, a Boy Scout must pass specific tests which are organized by requirements and merit badges. All requirements must be completed prior to the Scout's 18th birthday. Established in 1912.

• 6578 • Explorer Leadership Award
To recognize deserving Exploring youth leaders. A certificate is awarded by the local council.

• 6579 • William T. Hornaday Bronze and Silver Medals
To recognize exceptional and distinguished service to conservation and environmental improvement by a Boy Scout, Varsity Scout, or Explorer. Boy Scout and Varsity Scout applicants must complete the application requirements by their 18th birthday and Explorer applicants before their 21st birthday. The medals are granted by the national office. The distinction between bronze and silver medals is based primarily on the quality of the projects and their impact on the local community. The silver medal is the most distinguished award in Scouting for exceptional conservation service. No more than eight silver medals can be awarded in a single year. Both awards include a medal (bronze or silver), a certificate, and an embroidered square knot. Established in 1914 by Dr. William T. Hornaday, an active and outspoken champion of natural resource conservation and a leader in saving the American bison from extinction.

• 6580 • William T. Hornaday Gold Certificate
To recognize an individual, corporation, or organization not affiliated with Scouting for an outstanding contribution to youth conservation education and commitment to the education of youth on a national or international level, reflecting the natural resource conservation and environmen-

tal awareness mission of the Boy Scouts of America. Candidates may be nominated by any recognized conservation/environmental organization. Up to six certificates may be awarded annually. Established in 1914 by Dr. William T. Hornaday, an active and outspoken champion of natural resource conservation and a leader in saving the American bison from extinction.

• 6581 • William T. Hornaday Gold Medal
To recognize an adult Scouter for unusual and distinguished service in natural resource conservation and environmental improvement at the council, state, national, or international level. Nominations are accepted from any recognized conservation/environmental protection organization. A gold medal is awarded to the recipient. Up to six medals may be granted annually. Established in 1914 by Dr. William T. Hornaday, an active and outspoken champion of natural resource conservation and a leader in saving the American bison from extinction.

• 6582 • William T. Hornaday Unit Award
To recognize a pack, troop, team, or post for planning and carrying out at least one local environmental/conservation project. At least 60 percent of the registered unit members must participate. These units may be nominated or they may apply to their local Boy Scouts of America council for recognition. A certificate is awarded. Established in 1914 by Dr. William T. Hornaday, an active and outspoken champion of natural resource conservation and a leader in saving the American bison from extinction.

• 6583 • ISCPP National Law Enforcement Explorer Community Crime Prevention Award
The International Society of Crime Prevention Practitioners presents a plaque and a certificate in recognition of outstanding local crime prevention programs developed by law enforcement Explorer posts. Awarded annually.

• 6584 • Law Enforcement Assistance Explorer Award
To recognize an Explorer who has performed an outstanding deed in law enforcement. A medal, a plaque, and a $1,000 scholarship are presented by the U.S. Secret Service each year.

• 6585 • Lifesaving and Meritorious Action Awards of the National Court of Honor
To recognize outstanding and unusual acts that demonstrate unusual heroism, skill, or bravery, and reflect Scouting ideals. The Court of Honor presents the following awards: Honor Medal with Crossed Palms for both unusual heroism and extraordinary skill or resourcefulness in saving, or attempting to save, a life at extreme risk of his own; Honor Medal - for unusual heroism and skill in saving, or attempting to save, a life at considerable risk of his own; Heroism Award - for heroism and skill in saving, or attempting to save, a life at minimum or no risk of his own; and Medal of Merit - for some outstanding act of service of an exceptional character putting into practice learned skills and/or demonstrating Scouting ideals. Such action does not involve risk of self. Nominations are accepted. Awarded when merited. Established in 1911.

• 6586 • Silver Antelope
To recognize outstanding service to youth within the territory of a Boy Scouts of America region. The recipient must be a registered adult member of the Boy Scouts of America. A silver medal and a certificate are awarded annually in connection with regional meetings, or at other public functions within the region. Established in 1942.

• 6587 • Silver Beaver
To recognize distinguished service to youth within a local Boy Scouts of America Council. Recipient must be a registered adult member of the Boy Scouts of America. A silver medal and a certificate are awarded annually at appropriate local functions. Established in 1931.

• 6588 • Silver Buffalo Award
This, scouting's highest recognition for volunteer service to young people, is given for noteworthy service to youth beyond the realm of the regular volunteer duties with the Boy Scouts of America. The service must be national in character and may be directly connected with the BSA or independent of the movement. A silver medal and a certificate are awarded biennially at meetings of the National Council. Established in 1925.

• 6589 • Silver World Award
To recognize world citizens for outstanding service to their nations' youth or to young people in other countries. Recipients must be citizens of countries whose Scout Associations are members of the World Scout Conference. United States citizens may receive the recognition only if they are not registered members of the Boy Scouts of America. Established in 1971.

• 6590 • William H. Spurgeon III Award
Recognizes outstanding contributions to the Exploring Division of the Boy Scouts of America on a council and a national basis. Individuals, churches, service organizations, businesses, trades, industries, and professions are eligible. A plaque and a lapel pin are presented. Recipients may wear a special square knot as described in the Scouting manual. William H. Spurgeon III, an Orange County, CA, business leader, is regarded as one of the principal founders of special-interest Exploring.

• 6591 • Volunteer Service Award for Law Enforcement Explorers
Recognizes Explorers who render outstanding service to law enforcement agencies. Recipients are presented with a U.S. savings bond and a plaque by the Federal Investigator's Association.

• 6592 • Young American Awards
To recognize exceptional young adults between the ages of 15 and 25 who have achieved excellence in the fields of science, religion, service, government, business, athletics, art, music, or literature. Recipients need not be members of Scouting. Both local and national awards are presented. Local awards are presented by the local council. National awards include five unrestricted grants of $5,000 which are presented to five outstanding young Americans during the annual National Council meeting in May.

• 6593 •
Boynton Beach Recreation & Park Department
100 E Boynton Beach Blvd.
PO Box 310
Boynton Beach, FL 33435-0310
Phone: (561)742-6000
Fax: (561)742-6090
E-mail: recdept@ci.boynton-beach.fl.us
Home Page: http://www.boynton-beach.org

• 6594 • Boynton's G.A.L.A. Artist Awards
For recognition of achievement in visual art. Three awards are presented in each of the following categories: 2-D Fine Art, 3-D Fine Art, Fine Craft, Crafts, and Wearable Arts. In addition, one award for Best Booth Display without regard to category is also presented. A monetary award and a ribbon are presented to each winner. Awarded annually. Established in 1982. Sponsored by the City of Boynton Beach. Formerly: .

• 6595 •
Boys and Girls Clubs of America
Roxanne Spillett, Pres.
1230 W Peachtree St. NW
Atlanta, GA 30309
Phone: (404)487-5700
Toll-Free: 800-854-CLUB
Fax: (404)487-5825
E-mail: info@bgca.org
Home Page: http://www.bgca.org

Formerly: (1990) Boys Clubs of America.

• 6596 • Boys & Girls Club Medallion
To recognize a volunteer or member of an organization within a Boys & Girls Club who has rendered extraordinary devoted service to the club over a considerable period of time. A medal embedded in a Lucite block is awarded. Established in 1991.

• 6597 • Gold Medallion
To recognize any individual for outstanding and extraordinary service to boys and girls of national significance. A gold medallion embedded in a Lucite block is awarded.

• 6598 • Golden Youth Awards
To recognize outstanding service to youth on a local Boys & Girls Club level. Local Boys Clubs members and volunteer laymen are eligible. A statuette is awarded irregularly.

• 6599 • Honor Awards for Program Excellence

To give national recognition to a Boys & Girls Club for outstanding programs reflecting creative, imaginative thought and planning. Illuminated scrolls are awarded in various categories annually. Established in 1965.

• 6600 • Herbert Hoover Humanitarian Award

To recognize an American citizen for outstanding service to the cause of youth. Laymen are eligible. A gold medallion is awarded annually. Established in 1964. Formerly: Herbert Hoover Memorial Award.

• 6601 • National Youth of the Year Award

To recognize a club member, age 12 to 18, for outstanding contribution to home, school, church, community, and the Boys and Girls Club. The awardee is chosen from Regional Youths of the Year who are finalists in the competition beginning with the local club's selection of State Youth of the Year. A bronze plaque and cash scholarship are awarded annually. Established in 1947. Sponsored by the Reader's Digest Foundation. Formerly: (1983) National Boy of the Year.

• 6602 • Service to Youth Award

To recognize individuals for long and devoted service to boys and girls. Board volunteers, professionals, or full-time secretarial and support staff who have served for 10 years or more are eligible. A medal embedded in a lucite block is awarded. Individuals may be honored again for each additional five years of service. Established in 1991.

• 6603 • Silver Medallion

To recognize a board volunteer for outstanding and extraordinary service to a Boys & Girls Club and the Boys & Girls Club Movement in an area or region. A silver medallion embedded in a Lucite block is awarded. Established in 1991.

• 6604 •

Brain Injury Association of America
Scott A. Peterson, Dir. of Operations
8201 Greensboro Dr., Ste. 611
McLean, VA 22102
Phone: (703)761-0750
Toll-Free: 800-444-6443
Fax: (703)761-0755
E-mail: familyhelpline@biausa.org
Home Page: http://www.biausa.org/Pages/splash.html

Formerly: (1995) National Head Injury Foundation.

• 6605 • William Fields Caveness, M.D. Memorial Award

To recognize an individual who has made outstanding contributions to the betterment of life for the survivors of head injury and their families. Individuals who work in the field of head injury are eligible. A monetary award of $1,000 and a plaque are presented annually. Established in 1981 in memory of William Fields Caveness, M.D., a pioneer in head injury research.

• 6606 • Founders Award

To recognize an individual who has made an outstanding volunteer service contribution to the National Head Injury Foundation or one of the state associations. A plaque is awarded annually. Established in 1985 in honor of the founders of the Foundation. Formerly: (1990) Martin Spivack Volunteer Service Award.

• 6607 •

Brain Injury Association of Utah
Ron S. Roskos, Exec.Dir.
1800 SW Temple, Ste. 203
Salt Lake City, UT 84115
Phone: (801)484-2240
Toll-Free: 800-281-8442
Fax: (801)484-5932
E-mail: biau@sisna.com
Home Page: http://www.biau.org/

• 6608 • Donette Rachelle White Memorial Award

For outstanding service in the field of brain injury. Recognition award bestowed annually.

• 6609 •

Brazilian-American Chamber of Commerce
Sueli C. Bonaparte, Exec.Dir.
509 Madison Ave., Ste. 304
New York, NY 10022
Phone: (212)751-4691
Fax: (212)751-7692
E-mail: info@brazilcham.com
Home Page: http://www.brazilcham.com

• 6610 • Person of the Year Award

To recognize and honor a Brazilian and an American for outstanding service to the cause of furthering Brazilian-American economic and business ties. Citizens of both countries are nominated by the Awards Committee of the sponsoring organization. Plaques are presented annually at a formal dinner. Established in 1970. Formerly: Man of the Year Award.

• 6611 •

Brazos Valley Council of Governments
Tom Wilkinson Jr., Exec.Dir.
PO Drawer 4128
Bryan, TX 77802
Phone: (979)595-2800
Fax: (409)775-3466
E-mail: info@bvcog.org
Home Page: http://www.bvcog.org

• 6612 • Glenn J. Cook Regional Services Award

For cooperation and development of strategies for regional economic or community development. Recognition award bestowed annually.

• 6613 •

Joseph L. Brechner Center for Freedom of Information
Sandra F. Chance, Exec.Dir.
College of Journalism & Communications
3208 Weimer Hall
PO Box 118400
University of Florida
Gainesville, FL 32611
Phone: (352)392-2273
Fax: (352)392-9173
E-mail: schance@jou.ufl.edu
Home Page: http://www.brechner.org

Formerly: (1988) Florida Freedom of Information Clearinghouse.

• 6614 • Joseph L. Brechner Freedom of Information Award

To recognize an outstanding feature-length magazine or newspaper article about freedom of information, access to government-held information, or the First Amendment. Articles of no less than 5,000 words, published in a magazine or newspaper during the preceding year, must be submitted by March 15. A monetary award of $3,000 and a plaque are presented annually. Established in 1985 by Joseph L. Brechner, a long-time broadcaster from Orlando.

• 6615 •

Brewster Society
Sherry Moser, Dir.
PO Box 95
Damascus, MD 20872
Phone: (706)348-6950
Fax: (706)348-6951
E-mail: admin@brewstersociety.com
Home Page: http://www.brewstersociety.com

• 6616 • Brewster Award for Creative Ingenuity

To recognize an innovative new break through in kaleidoscope design. Awarded when appropriate with glass trophy. Established in 1986.

• 6617 •

Bridge Publications Inc.
Don Arnow, Contact
4751 Fountain Ave.
Los Angeles, CA 90029
Phone: (323)953-3320
Toll-Free: 800-722-1733
Fax: (323)953-3328
E-mail: info@bridgepub.com
Home Page: http://www.bridgepub.com

• 6618 • L. Ron Hubbard's Writers of the Future Contest

To recognize new and amateur writers of short stories or novelets of science fiction or fantasy. All types of science fiction and fantasy are considered. Original works in English that have not been previously published in professional media may be submitted. Entries must be works of prose, either short stories (under 10,000 words) or novelets (under 17,000 words) in length. Poetry or works intended for children are not eligible. The contest is open only to those who have not professionally published a novel or short novel, more than three short stories, nor more than one novelet. Monetary awards are presented every three months: first prize $1,000, second prize - $750, and third prize - $500. In addition, a monetary award of $4,000 is presented to the grand prize winner selected from among the first prize winners for the period of October 1 through September 30. Winners also receive trophies or certificates. Established in 1984 by science-fiction writer L. Ron Hubbard.

• 6619 •
Bridge Syndicate
Shane Maki, Chair
PO Box 215
Duluth, MN 55801
Phone: (218)724-4184
Phone: (218)390-3715
E-mail: info@bridgesydnicate.org

• 6620 • **Bridge Awards**
For individual with commitment to improving the Twin Ports area. Recognition award bestowed annually.

• 6621 •
Brigantine Beach Chamber of Commerce
Rose Arnold, Office Mgr.
PO Box 484
Brigantine, NJ 08203
Phone: (609)266-3437
E-mail: info@brigantinechamber.com
Home Page: http://www.brigantinechamber.com

• 6622 • **Dolly Award**
For community service. Recognition award bestowed annually.

• 6623 •
Bristol-Myers Squibb Canada Co.
2365 Cote de Liesse
St. Laurent, QC, Canada H4N 2M7
Phone: (514)333-3200
Toll-Free: 800-267-1088
Home Page: http://www.bmscanada.ca

• 6624 • **Association of Faculties of Pharmacy of Canada Excellence in Teaching Award**
To recognize the development of major innovations in pharmacy education by members of the academic staff of faculties, colleges, or schools of Pharmacy in Canada. A monetary award and a sculpture are presented annually. Established in 1997.

• 6625 • **Bristol-Myers Squibb Award for Excellence in Medical Teaching**
To recognize one professor in each Canadian Faculty of Medicine, who in the opinion of the senior medical students has made the most outstanding contribution to their education. The following awards are presented: (1) Wilbrod Bonin Award - University of Montreal; (2) Osler Award McGill University; (3) School of Medicine Award - Memorial University of Newfoundland and Ottawa University School of Medicine; (4) Douglas Bocking Award - The University of Western Ontario; (5) Prix Galeano d'excellence Pedagogique - Universite de Sherbrooke; (6) W.F. Connell Award - Queen's University. A monetary award and a plaque are presented annually. Established in 1984.

• 6626 • **Bristol-Myers Squibb Award for Excellence in Pharmaceutical Teaching**
To recognize one professor in each Canadian Faculty of Pharmacy, who in the opinion of the senior pharmacy students, has made the most outstanding contribution to their education. The following awards are presented: (1) Bristol-Myers Squibb Award - University of Manitoba, University of Alberta and University of British Columbia; (2) Jessie T. MacKnight Award Dalhousie University; (3) Prix Albert-Emile Francoeur - Universite Laval; (4) Prix Alfred-Joseph Lawrence - Universite de Montreal; (5) Outstanding Teacher Award - University of Saskatchewan; and (6) Teacher of the Year Award - University of Toronto. A monetary award and an inscribed plaque are presented annually. Established in 1985.

• 6627 • **Canadian Cardiovascular Society Research Achievement Award**
This cardiovascular research award complements the K.M. Piafsky Young Investigator Award of the Canadian Society for Clinical Pharmacology, and recognizes an outstanding contribution in the field of investigative clinical pharmacology. Established investigators working in the area of cardiovascular research in Canada are eligible. There should be an identifiable theme in his or her research, and at least some of the work leading to the award should have been conducted in the previous five years. The recipient of the award may be a member of the Society or an individual well known to the Society. A monetary award, travel expenses, and a scroll are awarded at the Annual Meeting of the Society. Established in 1980. Additional information is available from the Canadian Cardiovascular Society.

• 6628 • **Past President's Award**
To recognize distinguished service rendered to pharmacy by the retiring presidents of each provincial pharmacy association in Canada. A brass sculpture with an engraved plate is awarded annually. Established in 1958. Formerly: Doctor Squibb Pan American Award.

• 6629 • **K.M. Piafsky Award of the Canadian Society for Clinical Pharmacology**
To recognize an achievement in investigative clinical pharmacology in Canada by a member of the Canadian Society for Clinical Pharmacology. Investigators who have not reached their 40th birthday are eligible. A $1000 monetary award and a diploma are awarded annually. Established in 1980 in memory of Dr. K.M. Piafsky who, despite a tragically short career, was recognized internationally as an outstanding investigator during his tenure at the University Hospital. Additional information is available from the Canadian Society for Clinical Pharmacology. Formerly: (1981) Young Investigator Award; (2006) K. M. Piafsky Young Investigator Award of the Canadian Society for Clinical Pharmacology.

• 6630 •
Brith Sholom
Jerry Verlin, Pres.
6410 N Broad St.
Philadelphia, PA 19120
Phone: (215)878-5696
Phone: (215)927-5800
Toll-Free: 800-622-6410
Fax: (215)878-5699
E-mail: jeromeverlin@brithsholom.org
Home Page: http://www.brithsholom.org

• 6631 • **Humanitarian Award**
To honor individuals and organizations for their outstanding contributions to the betterment of human lives and the advancement of civilization. Awarded annually with a plaque. Established in 1933.

• 6632 •
British Columbia Historical Federation
Ron Hyde, Sec.
PO Box 5254, Sta. B
PO Box 5254, Sta. B
Victoria, BC, Canada V8R 6N4
Phone: (604)277-2627
Fax: (604)277-2657
E-mail: rbhyde@shaw.ca
Home Page: http://www.bchistory.ca

• 6633 • **Best Article Award**
To recognize the writer of an article published in the *B.C. Historical News* magazine with the aim of encouraging amateur historians and/or students. Articles should be no more than 3,500 words, typed double-spaced, accompanied by photographs if available, and substantiated with footnotes if possible. Deadlines for quarterly issues are February 15, May 15, August 15, and November 15. Awarded annually.

• 6634 • **Lieutenant-Governor's Medal for Historical Writing**
To recognize the author of the most significant book on any facet of British Columbia history. Books must be received by December 31 in the year published. Entries are evaluated for content, presentation, illustrations, index, and readability. A monetary award, a medal and a certificate of merit are awarded annually. Additional awards may be presented at the judges' discretion to other outstanding entries. Established in 1983. Additional information is available from Shirley Cuthbertson, Chair, at the above address.

• 6635 •
British Columbia Psychological Association
1755 W Broadway, Suite 202
Vancouver, BC, Canada V6J 4S5
Phone: (604)730-0501
Toll-Free: 800-730-0522
Fax: (604)730-0502
E-mail: bcpa@telus.net
Home Page: http://www.psychologists.bc.ca

Formerly: (1995) College of Psychologists of British Columbia.

• 6636 • **Park O. Davidson Practice of the Profession Award**
To recognize an individual for a significant contribution to psychology in British Columbia. The contribution could include, but must not be limited to, research and publications, professional development, technical applications of practice, development of direct services to the public, and advocacy of psychology. The focus of the research should be on the development of psychology as practiced in British Columbia. Deadline for nomination submission is September. A certificate, registration at the annual general meeting, a banquet dinner, and $50 in travel expenses are awarded each year at the annual meeting in October.

• 6637 • **Donald K. Sampson Excellence in Teaching Award**
To recognize an outstanding teacher who is an innovator in the development of the teaching of psychology, or is especially effective at teaching psychology to those in other fields. The individual's work must be within settings in British Columbia. Members of the Association are eligible. Deadline for nomination submission is September. A certificate, registration at the annual general meeting, and $50 in travel expenses are awarded each year in October.

• 6638 •
British Schools and Universities Club of New York
Robert B.K. Dewar, Pres.
24 E. 39th St.
New York, NY 10016
Phone: (212)713-5713
E-mail: info@bsuc.org
Home Page: http://www.bsuc.org

• 6639 • **Pride of the 20th Century Award**
For achievement in field. Recognition award bestowed annually.

• 6640 •
Broadcast Cable Financial Management Association
Mary M. Collins, Pres./CEO
550 W Frontage Rd., Ste. 3600
Northfield, IL 60093
Phone: (847)716-7000
Fax: (847)716-7004
E-mail: info@bcfm.com
Home Page: http://www.bcfm.com

Formerly: (1991) Broadcast Financial Management Association.

• 6641 • **Avatar Award**
To recognize outstanding contributions to the financial aspects of the broadcast industry. Nominees must have made outstanding contributions to the communications industry in areas other than finance, including involvement in local community affairs. A plaque and monetary contribution of $1,000 to a charitable, educational, or other institution of the recipient's choice, subject to BCFM Board approval, is presented annually. Established in 1983. 12-7823

• 6642 •
Broadcast Music, Inc.
Del Bryant, Pres./CEO
320 W 57th St.
New York, NY 10019-3790
Phone: (212)586-2000
Fax: (212)956-2059
E-mail: newyork@bmi.com
Home Page: http://bmi.com

• 6643 • **BMI Student Composer Awards**
To honor the best original vocal or instrumental composition and to encourage the creation of classical music by student composers. Students actively engaged in the study of music who are under 26 years of age and are citizens of the Western Hemisphere are eligible. Monetary prizes totaling $20,000 and ranging from $500 to $5,000 are awarded annually at the discretion of the judges, permanently chaired by the American composer, Milton Babbitt. Established in 1951.

• 6644 •
Brock Center for Agricultural Communication
Dr. J. Scott Vernon, Dir.
California Polytechnic State University
San Luis Obispo, CA 93407
Phone: (805)756-2707
Phone: (805)756-6185
E-mail: svernon@calpoly.edu
Home Page: http://www.calpoly.edu/~brockctr

• 6645 • **Brock Awards**
To recognize distinguished writing about food and agriculture during the previous calendar year. Monetary awards totaling $3,300 are awarded in the categories of publications outside California with circulation above 100,000, publications outside California with circulation under 100,000, and publications in California.

• 6646 •
Samuel and Saidye Bronfman Family Foundation
Nancy Rosenfeld, Exec.Dir.
1170 Peel St., Ste. 800
Montreal, QC, Canada H3B 4P2
Phone: (514)878-5270
Fax: (514)878-5299
E-mail: info@bronfmanfoundation.org
Home Page: http://www.bronfmanfoundation.org

• 6647 • **Saidye Bronfman Award for Excellence in the Crafts**
Recognizes the work of an individual who has made a significant contribution to the development of the crafts in Canada. $25,000 is awarded annually. The jury process is administered on behalf of the Foundation by The Canda Council for the Arts. Funds are also provided to the Canadian Museum of Civilization for the purchase of works by each recipient for the museum's permanent collection. Established in 1977.

• 6648 •
Brookhaven Women in Science Scholarship Program
PO Box 183
Upton, NY 11973
E-mail: lsmart@bnl.gov

Formerly: Brookhaven Women in Science.

• 6649 • **Renate W. Chasman Scholarship for Women**
To encourage women to pursue a career in scientific research in the natural sciences, engineering, or mathematics. Candidates must have applied for, or be currently enrolled in (at least half-time), a degree-oriented program in a natural science, engineering or mathematics at an accredited institution. The program of study must be at the junior or senior undergraduate or graduate level, first year. Candidates must be resuming interrupted study, and must be citizens of the United States or permanent resident aliens and residents of Nassau or Suffolk Counties or Queens or Brooklyn, New York. Deadline is April 1. A one-time award of $2,000 is made directly to the recipient, to be applied towards expenses associated with an academic program. Established in 1986 to honor Renate W. Chasman, an accelerator physics theorist.

• 6650 •
Brooklyn Historical Society
Elaine R. Knowlton, Pres.
PO Box 90
Brooklyn, CT 06234-0090
Phone: (860)774-7728

• 6651 • **Brooklyn School Scholarship**
For excellence in social studies. Monetary award bestowed annually.

Awards are arranged in alphabetical order below their administering organizations

• 6652 •
Broome County Farm Bureau
Scott Whittaker, Pres.
840 Front St.
Binghamton, NY 13905
Phone: (607)535-3072
E-mail: whittfarm@aol.com

• 6653 • **Broome County Farm Bureau Scholarship**
For high school students interested in furthering their education in agricultural fields. Scholarship awarded annually.

• 6654 •
Bross Foundation
Dept. of Religion
Lake Forest College
555 N. Sheridan Rd.
Lake Forest, IL 60045
Phone: (847)735-5175
Fax: (847)735-6192
E-mail: rmiller@lfc.edu

• 6655 • **Bross Prize**
To recognize the authors of the best books on the relationship that exists between any discipline or topic of investigation and the Christian religion. Unpublished manuscripts may be submitted in the summer of the year the prize is to be awarded. The deadline is September 1. A monetary award is presented every ten years. In 2000, two first place awards of $15,000 each were presented. Established in 1879 by William Bross in memory of his son, Nathaniel.

• 6656 •
Brotherhood of the Knights of the Vine
Carol Bade, Exec.Dir.
2210 Northpoint Pkwy.
Santa Rosa, CA 95407
Phone: (707)579-3781
Fax: (707)579-3996
E-mail: carol.bade@kov.org
Home Page: http://www.kov.org

• 6657 • **Gold Vine Award**
To recognize individuals who have made the most significant contributions to advance the cause and awareness of wine in America. Nominations must be made by the wine industry or members of the Brotherhood. A gold vine trophy is awarded periodically. Established in 1977 by the Brotherhood. Additional information is available from Michael D. Doukas (916)972-8700.

• 6658 •
Brotherhood of Working Farriers Association
Mr. Ralph Casey, Pres./Dir.
14013 E Hwy. 136
Lafayette, GA 30728-5660
Phone: (706)397-8047
Fax: (706)397-8047
E-mail: farrierhdq@aol.com
Home Page: http://www.bwfa.net

• 6659 • **Hall of Fame**
For members who have displayed exceptional participation. Monetary award bestowed annually.

• 6660 •
Brown Alumni Association
Hanna B. Rodriguez-Farrar, Pres.
Maddock Alumni Ctr.
38 Brown St.
Brown University
Box 1859
Providence, RI 02912
Phone: (401)863-3307
Fax: (401)863-7070
E-mail: alumni@brown.edu
Home Page: http://alumni.brown.edu

• 6661 • **Brown Bear Award**
For recognition of outstanding personal service to Brown University over a period of years. Neither financial aid to the University nor achievement in the fields of business or a profession is considered for eligibility. Members of the award committee select a maximum of three honorees. A bronze Brown Bear and a citation are awarded at the annual Alumni Recognition Ceremony. Awarded when merited. Established in 1946.

• 6662 • **John Hope Award**
To recognize an alum who has made a significant impact in his/her community or society, and who demonstrates an unwavering commitment to public service either as a professional or a volunteer. Awarded annually. Established in 1994. Named in honor of John Hope, Brown Class of 1894.

• 6663 • **William Rogers Award**
To recognize an outstanding alumnus/a whose service to society in general is representative of the words of the Brown Charter: living a life "...of usefulness and reputation." A large silk-screened slate plaque is awarded annually at the Alumni Recognition Ceremony. Established in 1984 by Associated Alumni in honor of William Rogers, the first Brown University student.

• 6664 •
Brown University
Department of Biology
97 Waterman St., Rm. 124
Providence, RI 02912
Phone: (401)863-3133
Phone: (401)863-9624
Fax: (401)863-7411
E-mail: marjorie_thompson@brown.edu
Home Page: http://bms.brown.edu/bug

• 6665 • **Mac V. Edds Memorial Lecture in Developmental Biology**
To recognize an individual for distinguished achievement in developmental biology. A colloquium on the recipient's work and an honorarium are awarded annually in the spring. Established in 1976 in memory of Prof. Mac Vincent Edds, Jr.

• 6666 • **Charles A. Stuart Memorial Lectureship**
To select an individual to illustrate the many and varied aspects of microbiology and/or immunology. An honorarium is awarded annually. Established in 1963 in memory of Prof. C.A. Stuart, a Brown University biologist interested in microbiology, immunology, and medical science.

• 6667 •
Bruner Foundation
130 Prospect St.
Cambridge, MA 02139-1844
Phone: (617)492-8404
Fax: (617)876-4002
E-mail: info@brunerfoundation.org
Home Page: http://www.brunerfoundation.org

• 6668 • **Rudy Bruner Award for Urban Excellence**
To recognize urban places distinguished by quality design as well as by their social economic and contextual contributions to the urban environment. The award brings recognition to excellent urban places and encourages learning about their creation. An application may be submitted by any organization or person who has been involved in the planning, development, or operation of a project. The winning project receives $50,000 which it may use in any way it chooses to benefit the project. Up to four finalists receive a $10,000 honorarium. All finalists receive national media coverage. Awarded biennially.

• 6669 •
Buckeye Children's Book Award Council
Ada Kent, Pres.
% Ada Kent, Pres.
Ohio School for the Deaf
500 Morse Rd.
Columbus, OH 43214
Phone: (614)728-1414
E-mail: agkent@columbus.rr.com
Home Page: http://www.bcbookaward.info

• 6670 • **Buckeye Children's Book Award/Teen Buckeye**
To encourage children to read literature critically, to promote teacher and librarian involvement in children's literature programs, and to commend authors of such literature. Ohio children nominate and vote for their favorite books. Books must have been written by a citizen of the United States and originally copyrighted in the United States within the three years preceding the nomination year. Awards are presented in three reading levels: K-2, grades 3-5 and grades 6-8. A plaque is awarded biennially. Established in 1981 and named for the state tree of Ohio, the Buckeye. Sponsored by Ohio Council International Reading Association, Ohio Council of Teachers of English Language Arts, Ohio Educational Library Media Association, Ohio Library Council, and State Library of Ohio. The Teen Buckeye was established in 2003. It follows the same guidelines as the original BCBA, and has a nominations list of 12 titles called the Buckeye

Dozen, and is for grades 9-12. One winner is selected from 12 titles.

• 6671 •
Bucks County Historical Society
Douglas C. Dolan, Exec.Dir.
84 S Pine St.
Doylestown, PA 18901-4999
Phone: (215)345-0210
Fax: (215)230-0823
E-mail: info@mercermuseum.org
Home Page: http://www.mercermuseum.org

• 6672 • Henry Chapman Mercer Award
For individual who has made a contribution to the community in the spirit of Henry Mercer. Recognition award bestowed annually.

• 6673 •
Buffalo Audubon Society
Michael Petrinic, Pres.
1610 Welch Rd.
North Java, NY 14113
Phone: (585)457-3228
Toll-Free: 800-377-1520
Fax: (585)457-1378
E-mail: info@buffaloaudubon.org
Home Page: http://www.audubon.org

• 6674 • Summer Fellowship
Based upon the submission of experiment or research proposal. Grant awarded annually.

• 6675 •
Builder
Boyce Thompson, Ed.
Hanley-Wood, LLC
1 Thomas Circle NW, Ste. 600
Washington, DC 20005
Phone: (202)452-0800
Toll-Free: 800-829-9127
Fax: (202)785-1974
E-mail: bthomasso@hanley-wood.com
Home Page: http://www.builderonline.com

• 6676 • Builder's Choice Design and Planning Awards
To recognize excellence in design. Award categories recognize excellence in the design of new and remodeled housing, light commercial buildings, and overall community planning and design. Special Focus Awards honor the finest in kitchens and baths, exterior landscaping details, and other design details. Projects must not be older than two years. The deadline is late May/ early June. Project of the Year, Grand and Merit awards are presented annually. Winning projects are featured in the October issue of *Builder*. Established in 1980. Formerly: (1980) Builder's Choice Awards for Excellence in Design and Planning.

• 6677 •
Building Officials and Code Administrators International
Paul K. Heilstedt PE, CEO
4051 W Flossmoor Rd.
Country Club Hills, IL 60478
Phone: (708)799-2300
Toll-Free: 888-422-7233
Fax: 800-214-7167
E-mail: webmaster@iccsafe.org
Home Page: http://www.iccsafe.org

• 6678 • Albert H. Baum Award
For recognition of outstanding contributions to the building code enforcement profession. Nominations may be submitted by any member of a recognized building official, governmental, or industrial association. A walnut and brass plaque is awarded annually. Established in 1963 in memory of Albert H. Baum, Jr., former Building Commissioner of Saint Louis, Missouri, and a past president of the BOCA International.

• 6679 • Walker S. Lee Award
For recognition of an outstanding contribution to the Building Officials and Code Administrators International organization. Nominations may be submitted by any member of BOCA International. A brass and walnut plaque is awarded annually. Established in 1963 in memory of Walter S. Lee, former Superintendent of Buildings of Rochester, New York, and a past president of BOCA International.

• 6680 • Wilbur H. Lind Award
For recognition of exemplary integrity and professionalism. Nominations may be submitted by any member of the Council. A walnut and brass plaque is awarded annually. Established in 1993 in memory of Wilbur H. Lind, former Code Official for Hackensack, New Jersey, and a past president of BOCA International.

• 6681 •
Building Owners and Managers Association International
Henry Chamberlain, Pres./COO
1201 New York Ave. NW, Ste. 300
Washington, DC 20005
Phone: (202)408-2662
Fax: (202)371-0181
E-mail: info@boma.org
Home Page: http://www.boma.org

• 6682 • Earth Award
Member buildings, or buildings managed by members in good standing are eligible. Buildings must first win on the local level, then on the regional level. At least 50% of the space must be office space. See the above web site for application fees and submission details.

• 6683 • Government Affairs Award of Recognition
Recognition outstanding work of local BOMA Association volunteers in advocacy and education. Committees, programs or seminars from state and local associations are eligible. Awarded every two years. See web site for additional details.

• 6684 •
Building Owners and Managers Association International, San Antonio Federation
Lynn Forester, Exec.VP
PO Box 692088
San Antonio, TX 78269
Phone: (830)981-5223
Fax: (830)981-5188
E-mail: lynn@saboma.org
Home Page: http://www.saboma.org

• 6685 • The Office Building of the Year (TOBY)
For excellence in building operations and management in 10 categories. Recognition award bestowed annually.

• 6686 •
Building Stone Institute
Jeff Buczkiewicz, Exec.VP
300 Park Blvd., Ste. 335
Itasca, IL 60143
Phone: (630)775-9130
Toll-Free: (866)STO-NE13
Fax: (630)775-9134
E-mail: jeff@buildingstoneinstitute.org
Home Page: http://www.buildingstoneinstitute.org

• 6687 • Tucker Architectural Awards Competition
To recognize and honor those architectural firms whose excellence in concept and design have contributed significantly to architecture worldwide. Awards are given in the following categories: Category I - a non-residential structure completed within the last 5 years; Category II a stone structure completed at least 40 years ago and still in use today; Category III - a residential structure completed within the last five years; Category IV - landscape project in a residential or non-residential site development completed within the last five years; and Category V - a renovation or restoration project completed within the last five years. The program is open to all architects, designers, contractors and others who feel that their projects, or other projects with which they are familiar, have achieved the ideal of excellence and incorporate the use of natural stone. The entry deadline is March 1, 2001. Trophies are awarded annually at a special luncheon usually in April. Established in 1977 in memory of Beverley R. Tucker, Jr., a past president of the Institute.

• 6688 •
Bulgarian National Front
Alex Darvodelsky, Pres.
PO Box 46250
Chicago, IL 60646
Phone: (847)692-5460
Fax: (847)692-5460
E-mail: alexd906@aol.com

• 6689 • Struggle for Liberation of Bulgaria Award

For recognition of achievement and activity in the struggle for the liberation of Bulgaria from communist domination. Distinguished American and foreign personalities are eligible. Three classes of medals are awarded when merited, usually on March 3. Established in 1970.

• 6690 •
Bureau County Historical Society
Barbara Hansen, Dir.
109 Park Ave. W
Princeton, IL 61356
Phone: (815)875-2184

• 6691 • Maude C. Trimble History Award

For 8th grader with best essay on some aspect of county history. Monetary award bestowed annually.

• 6692 •
Burke County Chamber of Commerce
110 E. Meeting St.
Morganton, NC 28655-3549
Phone: (828)437-3021
Fax: (828)437-1613
E-mail: burkecoc@hci.net
Home Page: http://www.burkecounty.org

• 6693 • Safety award

For individual who has made safety contribution. Recognition award.

• 6694 •
Burlington Lions Club
Dennis Yanny, Pres.
PO Box 154
Burlington, WI 53105
Phone: (262)763-4484
Phone: (262)763-9322
Fax: (262)767-0190

• 6695 • Hefty Scholarship

For high school graduate attending a vocational school. Scholarship awarded annually.

• 6696 •
Burroughs Bibliophiles
George T. McWhorter, Dir.
University of Louisville
Rare Book Rm., Ekstrom Library
Louisville, KY 40292
Phone: (502)852-8729
Phone: (502)852-8729
Fax: (502)852-8734
E-mail: gtmcwh01@gwise.louisville.edu
Home Page: http://www.burroughsbibliophiles.com

• 6697 • ERB Life Achievement Award

To recognize an individual for outstanding achievement. An engraved bronze plaque mounted on wood with an inset photo of Edgar Rice Burroughs and lifetime honorary membership in the Burroughs Bibliophiles are awarded. Established in 1983 to honor the memory of Edgar Rice Burroughs.

• 6698 • Golden Lion Award

To express appreciation for contributions to the furtherance of fame or popularity of the works and/or the characters created by Edgar Rice Burroughs. A bronze plaque of Tarzan and the Golden Lion, adapted from the famous painting by J. Allen St. John (the best known illustrator of Burroughs' first editions), and lifetime honorary membership in the Burroughs Bibliophiles are awarded annually. Established in 1962.

• 6699 •
Bush Artist Fellows Program
Bush Foundation
Anita M. Pampusch, Pres.
332 Minnesota St., Ste. E-900
St. Paul, MN 55101
Phone: (651)227-0891
Toll-Free: 800-605-7315
Fax: (651)297-6485
E-mail: jdalgleish@bushfoundation.org
Home Page: http://www.bushfoundation.org/programs/ArtistFellowsProg.htm

• 6700 • Bush Artist Fellows Program

Bush Artists Fellowships provide artists with significant financial support that enables them to advance their work and further their contribution to their communities. Panelists consider the artist's past endeavors and future work, the impact a Bush Artist Fellowship may have on the applicant's life work and future directions, and the difference the artist may make in the region as a result of the Fellowship. Individuals must live in Minnesota, North Dakota, South Dakota, or western Wisconsin and be at least 25 years of age. Students are not eligible. Writers must be published. Awards are made in seven categories: Visual Arts, Two Dimensional; Visual Arts, Three Dimensional; Choreography/Multimedia/Performance Art; Literature; Music Composition; Scriptworks; and Film/Video. Each category rotates on a two-year cycle. 2004 BAF will consider Visual Arts, Two-Dimensional; Visual Arts, Three Dimensional; and Choreography/Multimedia/Performance Art. The 2005 BAF will consider Literature; Music composition; Scriptworks; and Film/Video. Deadlines are in October. Up to 15 stipends of $48,000 each are awarded annually. Established in 1976. Formerly: (1986) Bush Foundation Fellowships for Artists.

• 6701 •
Business Committee for the Arts
Judith A. Jedlicka, Pres.
29-27 Queens Plz. N, 4th Fl.
Long Island City, NY 11101
Phone: (718)482-9900
Fax: (718)482-9911
E-mail: info@bcainc.org
Home Page: http://www.bcainc.org

• 6702 • Business in the Arts Awards

To recognize businesses for their outstanding partnerships with the arts. Businesses headquartered in the United States and abroad that support the arts in the United States are eligible. Awards are given to small, mid-size, and large companies in three categories: commitment, innovation, and new initiative. Each winner receives a certificate and an original limited edition work of art created by an American artist. Awarded annually as merited. Established in 1966 by Arnold Gingrich, publisher of *Esquire Magazine* and is presently co-sponsored by *Forbes* magazine.

• 6703 • Founders Award

To recognize companies that have exhibited exceptional long-term leadership, vision, and commitment to developing alliances with the arts. A limited edition crystal presentation piece designed by Steuben artist Joel A. Smith is awarded annually when merited. Established in 1992 as part of BCA's 25th anniversary celebration.

• 6704 • Leadership Award

To recognize a business executive who has demonstrated exceptional leadership, vision, and commitment to encouraging and developing business-arts alliances. A certificate and a specially commissioned bronze sculpture by American artist Bob Haozous are awarded annually when merited. Established in 1993 by the Business Committee for the Arts, Inc. and *Forbes* magazine.

• 6705 •
Business Forms Management Association
Gary Parnham, Pres.
319 SW Washington, No. 710
Portland, OR 97204-2618
Phone: (503)227-3393
Fax: (503)274-7667
E-mail: tonya@bfma.org
Home Page: http://www.bfma.org

• 6706 • Award of Excellence

To recognize contributions to the Association by a member. Selection is made by the past president's council. A plaque is awarded annually when merited. Established in 1989.

• 6707 • Member of the Year - Regional

To recognize members for outstanding contributions to the Association. A plaque is awarded annually. Established in 1976.

• 6708 • Jo Warner Award

To recognize contributions to the forms profession and the Association. Selection is made by the past presidents council. A plaque is awarded annually when merited. Established in 1984.

• 6709 •
Business History Conference
Roger Horowitz, Sec.-Treas.
Hagley Museum & Library
PO Box 3630
Wilmington, DE 19807-0630
Phone: (302)658-2400
Fax: (302)655-3188
E-mail: rh@udel.edu
Home Page: http://www.h-net.org/~business/bhcweb

• 6710 • **Krooss Prize**
For recognition of the best dissertation in business history. Any thesis completed in the preceding two years and presented at the Business History Conference meetings may be considered. A monetary prize of $500 is awarded annually. Established by Daniel Hodas in memory of Herman E. Krooss.

• 6711 •
Business Marketing Association
Rick Kean CBC, Exec.Dir.
400 N Michigan Ave., 15th Fl.
Chicago, IL 60611
Phone: (312)822-0005
Toll-Free: 800-664-4262
Fax: (312)822-0054
E-mail: bma@marketing.org
Home Page: http://www.marketing.org
Formerly: Business/Professional Advertising Association.

• 6712 • **G. D. Crain Jr. Award**
To recognize outstanding career contributions to The Business Marketing Association and Business-to-Business Marketing Communications. Individuals who have been BMA members for at least five years are eligible. A monetary award of $1,000 and a certificate of election to the BMA Hall of Fame are awarded annually. Established in 1967. Co-sponsored by Crain Communications, Inc..

• 6713 • **International Pro-Comm Awards Competition**
To recognize outstanding business/industrial communications efforts in various communications media. Selection is based on effectiveness and originality of concept and execution, on efforts directed to industrial/business/professional markets. Awards are presented to first place winners in each category, and certificates are given to all winners. Awarded annually. Established in 1974.

• 6714 •
Business Volunteers for the Arts/Washington
Eileen Rappopat, Dir.
Cultural Alliance of Greater Washington
1436 U St., NW, Ste. 103
Washington, DC 20009-3997
Phone: (202)638-2406
Fax: (202)638-3388
Home Page: http://www.cultural-alliance.org

• 6715 • **Business Volunteers for the Arts Awards**
For outstanding volunteer service provided to arts organization. Recognition award bestowed annually.

• 6716 •
By Word of Mouth Storytelling Guild
Gladys Coggswell, Contact
PO Box 56
Frankford, MO 63441
Phone: (573)784-2589
Fax: (573)784-2364
E-mail: gladcogg@nemonet.com
Home Page: http://shorock.com/folk/bwom/8th/contact.html

• 6717 • **Langston Hughes Award**
Recognizes individuals involved in storytelling for at least five years. Awarded annually.

• 6718 • **Mark Twain Award**
Recognizes individuals involved in storytelling for at least five years. Awarded annually.

• 6719 • **StoryTeller of the Year Award**
Recognizes individuals involved in storytelling for at least five years. Awarded annually.

• 6720 •
Cabletelevision Advertising Bureau
Joe Ostrow, Pres. & CEO
830 Third Ave.
New York, NY 10022
Phone: (212)508-1200
Fax: (212)832-3268
Home Page: http://www.cabletvadbureau.com

• 6721 • **Award for Local Sales Achievement**
To recognize excellence in securing new businesses or upgrading an existing account to advertise on local cable through exemplary effort, strategies, and ideas. Outstanding presentations, promotions, and concepts that have resulted in sales success stories by CAB members are eligible.

• 6722 • **Creative Commercial Production Awards**
To recognize outstanding achievement in creative commercial production for locally-produced cable commercials. Local commercials designed for a client utilizing a theme or unique approach to fulfill a specific client need produced by CAB member companies are eligible. A trophy and a certificate are awarded annually in the spring at CAB's Local Cable Sales Management Conference. Established in 1982. Formerly known as Mission Accomplished Creative Commercial Production Awards.

• 6723 • **Network Affiliate Sales Achievement Award**
To recognize the sales achievements that have been made as a result of building strong partnerships between local cable ad sales organizations and network affiliate sales support staffs. Ad-supported cable networks that are members of CAB are eligible.

• 6724 •
Cajal Club
Dr. Henry J. Ralston MD, Contact
Department of Anatomy
University of California
513 Parnassus
San Francisco, CA 94143-0452
Phone: (415)476-1861
E-mail: hjr@phy.ucsf.edu

• 6725 • **Cajal Medal**
Recognizes outstanding research on the cerebral cortex. Awarded annually.

• 6726 • **Certificate of Recognition**
Recognizes outstanding research on the cerebral cortex. Awarded annually.

• 6727 • **Krieg Cortical Kudos**
Annual award of recognition.

• 6728 •
Calendar Marketing Association
Richard J. Mikes, Exec.Dir.
214 N Hale St.
Wheaton, IL 60187
Phone: (630)579-3264
Fax: (630)369-2488
E-mail: info@calendarassociation.org
Home Page: http://www.calendarassociation.org

• 6729 • **World and National Calendar Awards**
To recognize high quality calendar design and production, both nationally and internationally. Individuals or organizations that are involved in the production, distribution, and marketing of calendars are eligible. The World Calendar Awards are open to international calendars; the National Calendar Awards are open to U.S. calendars. Gold, Silver, and Bronze awards are made in each of twelve categories. Awarded annually.

• 6730 •
Califon Historical Society
Donald E. Philhower Freibergs, Pres.
25 Academy St.
PO Box 424
Califon, NJ 07830
Phone: (908)832-2266
Phone: (908)832-0878
Home Page: http://www.califonhistoricalsociety.org

• 6731 • **Student Achievement Award**
For written essay. Monetary award bestowed annually.

Awards are arranged in alphabetical order below their administering organizations

• 6732 •
California Academy of Sciences
875 Howard St.
San Francisco, CA 94103-3009
Phone: (415)321-8000
Fax: (415)750-7346
E-mail: info@calacademy.org
Home Page: http://www.calacademy.org

• 6733 • **Fellows' Medal**
To recognize exceptional scientific achievement and/or exceptional scientific support to the California Academy of Sciences. Fellows make the nominations. A bronze medal is awarded at the October annual Fellows' dinner and business meeting. Established in 1963.

• 6734 •
California Avocado Society
Derek Knobel, Pres.
PO Box 1317
Saticoy
Carpinteria, CA 93014
Phone: (805)562-8366
Phone: (805)684-2804
Fax: (805)644-1184
E-mail: administration@californiaavocadosociety.org
Home Page: http://www.californiaavocadosociety.org

• 6735 • **Award of Honor**
For recognition of outstanding meritorious service on behalf of the avocado industry. Election is by the Board of Directors. A gold and enamel replica of an avocado with hieroglyph, and a plaque are awarded annually. Established in 1938.

• 6736 •
California Canning Peach Association
Rich Hudgins, Pres./CEO
2300 River Plaza Dr., Ste. 110
Sacramento, CA 95833
Phone: (916)925-9131
Fax: (916)925-9030
E-mail: ccpa@calpeach.com
Home Page: http://www.calpeach.com

• 6737 • **Quality Award**
Recognizes the lowest offgrade. Awarded annually.

• 6738 •
California Engineering Foundation
Dr. Robert J. Kuntz, Pres.
2700 Zinfandel Dr.
Rancho Cordova, CA 95670-4827
Phone: (916)853-1914
Fax: (916)853-1921
E-mail: cef@innercite.com
Home Page: http://www.innercite.com/~cef

• 6739 • **Outstanding Service Award**
Recognizes outstanding service. Awarded periodically.

• 6740 •
California Federation of Mineralogical Societies
Pat LaRue, Exec. Sec.-Treas.
PO Box 1657
Rialto, CA 92377
Phone: (909)874-5664
E-mail: bplarue@earthlink.net
Home Page: http://www.cfmsinc.org

• 6741 • **CFMS Scholarship**
For an undergraduate with a 3.0 G.P.A. who is majoring in mineralogy and geology. Scholarship awarded annually.

• 6742 •
California Healthcare Institute
David Gollaher PhD, Pres./CEO
1020 Prospect St., Ste. 310
La Jolla, CA 92037
Phone: (858)551-6677
Fax: (858)551-6688
E-mail: chi@chi.org
Home Page: http://www.chi.org

• 6743 • **Visionary Award**
For thoughtful leadership in advancing biomedical science, biotechnology, pharmaceutical and medical device innovation in California. Recognition award bestowed annually.

• 6744 •
California Reading Association
3186 Airway Ave., Ste. D
Costa Mesa, CA 92626-4650
Phone: (714)435-1983

• 6745 • **California Young Reader Medal**
To honor the author of a book that California children have selected as their favorite and to encourage California children to become better acquainted with good literature. Original works of fiction in the English language written by a living author and published internationally within the previous five years are eligible. Titles are submitted for nomination by April 1 by young readers through their teachers and/or librarians. Awards are given in four categories: primary, intermediate, junior high, and high school. Bronze medals, with a relief map of California and a child reading, are presented annually at the annual meeting of CRA, CSLA and CATE. Established in 1975. Administered jointly by the California Reading Association, California School Library Association, California Library Assoc., and California Association of Teachers of English.

• 6746 •
California School Library Association
Steve Grant, Pres.
1001 26th St.
Sacramento, CA 95816
Phone: (916)447-2695
E-mail: csla@pacbell.net
Home Page: http://www.schoolibrary.org

• 6747 • **Innovation Award**
To recognize a library's achievement in planning and implementing an innovative or creative program or service which has had measurable impact on its users. A monetary award of $500 and a plaque are presented during the Annual Conference. Sponsored by Highsmith Inc.

• 6748 •
California Science Teachers Association
Christine Bertrand, Exec.Dir.
3800 Watt Ave., Ste. 100
Sacramento, CA 95821-2666
Phone: (916)979-7004
Fax: (916)979-7023
E-mail: csta@cascience.org
Home Page: http://www.cascience.org

• 6749 • **Distinguished Informal Science Educator Award**
Recognizes an outstanding science educator in an informal science organization, such as a museum; national, state, or local park; or community organization, who has demonstrated a commitment to science education through professional or volunteer work and involvement in professional and extra-curricular science education endeavors. Three letters of recommendation; a summary of science teaching background Conference and workshop attendance for the past two years; science fair Involvement and classroom involvement; group study summary; and views of a Current science education topic must be submitted.

• 6750 • **Future Science Teacher Awards**
To recognize high school and college students who demonstrate an interest in and commitment to science education through tutoring or teaching activities in a school setting, volunteer activities, courses taken in science, long-term career goals, and related activities, and who show promise to become outstanding science educators. No more than two Future Teachers Awards will be awarded in any year.

• 6751 • **Margaret Nicholson Distinguished Service Award**
To honor an individual who has made a significant contribution to science education in the state and who, through years of leadership and service, has truly made a positive impact on the quality of science teaching through a range of service, including professional involvement. Awarded annually. Established in 1981.

• 6752 •
California Sea Grant College Program
Russell A. Moll, Dir.
9500 Gilman Dr., Dept. 0232
University of California
La Jolla, CA 92093-0232
Phone: (858)534-4440
Fax: (858)534-2231
E-mail: caseagrant@ucsd.edu
Home Page: http://www-csgc.ucsd.edu

• 6753 • Isaacs Scholarship
California high school junior or senior. Inquire for application details.

• 6754 • Knauss National Marine Policy Fellowship
Graduate student in marine science/marine policy. Inquire for application details.

• 6755 • Sea Grant State Fellowship
Graduate student in marine science or technology with interest in marine policy are eligible. Inquire for application details.

• 6756 •
California Society of Anesthesiologists
Barbara Baldwin, Exec.Dir.
951 Mariner's Island Blvd., Ste. 270
San Mateo, CA 94404
Phone: (650)345-3020
Toll-Free: 800-345-3691
Fax: (650)345-3269
Home Page: http://www.csahq.org

• 6757 • Resident Research Award
For original research by residents in anesthesiology. Recognition award bestowed annually.

• 6758 •
California Society of Printmakers
Benny Alba, Pres.
PO Box 475422
San Francisco, CA 94147
E-mail: caprintmakers@yahoo.com
Home Page: http://www.caprintmakers.org

• 6759 • Distinguished Artist Award
Recognizes lifetime dedication to printmaking. Awarded annually.

• 6760 •
California Spa and Pool Industry Education Council
Donald C. Burns CAE, Pres./CEO
980 9th St., Ste. 430
Sacramento, CA 95814
Phone: (916)447-4113
Toll-Free: 800-991-SPEC
Fax: (916)444-7835
E-mail: spec@calspec.org
Home Page: http://www.calspec.org

• 6761 • Locksin Thompson Memorial Public Service Award
For outstanding public service. Recognition award bestowed annually.

• 6762 •
California State Beekeepers Association
Susan Bunch, Sec.
7220 E Grayson Rd.
Hughson, CA 95326
Phone: (209)667-4590
Phone: (530)633-4789
Fax: (209)667-4590
E-mail: contact@californiabeekeepers.com
Home Page: http://www.californiastatebeekeepers.com

• 6763 • Beekeeper of the Year
For member who demonstrates outstanding service to the industry. Recognition award bestowed annually.

• 6764 • Honorary Beekeeper of the Year
For member who demonstrates outstanding service to the industry. Recognition award bestowed annually.

• 6765 • Young Beekeeper of the Year
For member who demonstrates outstanding service to the industry. Recognition award bestowed annually.

• 6766 •
California State Polytechnic University, Pomona
John T. Lyle Center for Regenerative Studies
4105 W University Dr.
Pomona, CA 91768
Phone: (909)869-5155
Fax: (909)869-5188
E-mail: crs@supomona.edu
Home Page: http://www.csupomona.edu/~crs/

• 6767 • Nathaniel Dwings Award
California Fish and Game Grant. No additional information available.

• 6768 •
California Walnut Commission
Dennis A. Balint, CEO
1540 River Park Dr., Ste. 203
Sacramento, CA 95815-4609
Phone: (916)646-3807
Fax: (916)923-2548
E-mail: wmbcwc@walnuts.org
Home Page: http://www.walnuts.org

• 6769 • Distinguished Service Award
For someone who has provided great service to the industry. Recognition award bestowed periodically.

• 6770 •
Callerlab - International Association of Square Dance Callers
Jerry Reed, Exec.Dir.
467 Forrest Ave., Ste. 118
Cocoa, FL 32922
Phone: (321)639-0039
Fax: (321)639-0851
E-mail: info@callerlab.org
Home Page: http://www.callerlab.org

• 6771 • CALLERLAB Milestone Award
To honor outstanding contributions to square dancing and/or CALLERLAB. A Lucite pyramid set in a wooden base is awarded at the convention. Established in 1974.

• 6772 •
Cambridge Center for Behavioral Studies
336 Baker Ave.
Concord, MA 01742-2107
Phone: (978)369-2227
Fax: (978)369-8584
E-mail: center@behavior.org
Home Page: http://www.loebner.net/Prizef/loebner-prize.html

• 6773 • Loebner Prize Turing Test Award
To recognize the designer of the computer program that best emulates natural human behavior and satisfies the Turing Test. The annual contest pits people against machines, using procedures first proposed in 1950 by the late British mathematician, Alan M. Turing. Independent judges attempt to determine whether responses on a computer terminal are being produced by a computer or by a person. Designers of the computer program that best succeeds in fooling the judges receive a cash award and medal. An initial monetary award of $2000 is based on the interest generated from a fund established in 1990 by Dr. Hugh G. Loebner, a philanthropist and businessman from New York City. If at some point a program passes the test "in all its particulars," the entire fund - expected to be worth at least $100,000 - is paid to the program designer, and the prize will be abolished.

• 6774 •
Camp Fire USA
Stewart J. Smith, Natl. CEO
4601 Madison Ave.
Kansas City, MO 64112-1278
Phone: (816)756-1950
Fax: (816)756-0258
E-mail: info@campfireusa.org
Home Page: http://www.campfireusa.org

Formerly: (1989) Camp Fire.

• 6775 • On Behalf of Youth Award
To recognize contributions that have had a notable effect on improving conditions that affect youth in society. A lucite engraved block and a certificate are awarded biennially. Established in 1979.

• 6776 • Wohelo Order
To recognize a person for outstanding and continued service as a volunteer at the national level. A gold triangle pin and a certificate are awarded biennially. Established in 1924. Formerly: National Wohelo Order Award.

• 6777 •
Camp Fire USA El Dorado Council
415 Cordell St.
El Dorado, AR 71730
Phone: (870)862-3463
Fax: (870)862-0039
E-mail: campfire@arkansas.net

• 6778 • Leadership Award
For campfire member, senior, community service, leadership qualities. Monetary award bestowed annually.

• 6779 •
Camp Fire USA, Minnesota Council
Andrea Platt Dwyer, CEO
2610 University Ave. W
St. Paul, MN 55114-1090
Phone: (651)647-4407
Phone: (651)647-1090
Toll-Free: 888-335-8778
Fax: (651)647-5717
E-mail: info@campfireusa-mn.org
Home Page: http://www.minnesotacouncil.org

• 6780 • Youth Leadership Awards
For community leadership on youth issues. Recognition award bestowed annually.

• 6781 •
Campaign for United Nations Reform
418 7th St. SE, Ste. C
Washington, DC 20003
Phone: (202)546-3956
Toll-Free: 888-869-CUNR
Fax: (202)546-3749
E-mail: cunr@cunr.org

• 6782 • Global Statesman Award
To honor those members of the House and Senate who have a 100 percent voting record on issues concerning world order chosen by the Campaign for each Congress. A plaque and press coverage are awarded biennially after the end of each Congress. Established in 1978.

• 6783 •
Canada Council for the Arts
(Le Conseil des Arts du Canada)
Andree Bertrand, Info. Officer
350 Albert St.
PO Box 1047
Ottawa, ON, Canada K1P 5V8
Phone: (613)566-4414
Toll-Free: 800-263-5588
Fax: (613)566-4390
E-mail: info@canadacouncil.ca
Home Page: http://www.canadacouncil.ca

• 6784 • Jean-Marie Beaudet Award in Orchestra Conducting
To recognize a young Canadian orchestra conductor. The recipient is selected by a panel of the Music Section of the Canada Council from among the conductors-in-residence with the Canadian orchestras. A monetary award of $1,000 is presented annually.

• 6785 • Bell Canada Award in Video Art
To recognize an exceptional contribution to the advancement of video art in Canada and to the development of video languages and practices. Candidates are nominated by three professional curators and/or critics, specialists in Canadian video art, appointed annually by the Media Arts Section of the Canada Council. The winner is selected by the jury of professional video artists convened to assess applications in video art. A monetary award of $10,000 is presented annually. Established in 1991.

• 6786 • Canada - Australia Literary Prize
To honor an English-speaking Canadian or Australian writer on the basis of his/her complete works. Applications are not accepted. Administered in Canada by the Canada Council and in Australia by the Australia Council. Following the pre-selection by a jury in the writer's country, the Canadian winner is chosen by a jury set up by the Australian Council and vice versa. A monetary prize of $3,000 is awarded annually, alternately to a Canadian or Australian. Established in 1976. Co-sponsored by the Canadian Departments of External Affairs and International Trade Canada and the Australia Council.

• 6787 • Canada Council Molson Prizes
To recognize and encourage contributions to the cultural and intellectual heritage of Canada. This award is presented to two Canadians who have distinguished themselves in the arts and in the area of humanities or social sciences. Applications are not accepted. Two monetary prizes of $50,000 each are awarded annually. Established in 1963 by the Molson Family Foundation.

• 6788 • Canada - Japan Literary Awards
Recognizes excellence in writing about Japan, Japanese themes, or themes that promote mutual understanding between Japan and Canada. Canadian writers and translators of books from Japanese into English or French are eligible. Two to four awards of $5000 or $10,000 are awarded every two years.

• 6789 • CBC Literary Awards
To recognize writers in the English and French languages in the categories of Creative Nonfiction, Poetry, and Short Stories. First prize of $6,000 and second prize of $4,000 are awarded in each category annually. Established in 1979.

• 6790 • CBC Young Composers Competition
To recognize composers under the age of 30 in three specific categories: chamber music, electronic music, and works for orchestras. A grand prize of $5,000 is awarded biennially in even-numbered years.

• 6791 • Duke and Duchess of York Prize in Photography
Awarded to the best candidate in the competition for the Grants to Professional Artists in visual arts. This prize is given in addition to the arts grant. $8000 is awarded annually. Established in 1986 on the occasion of Prince Andrew's marriage.

• 6792 • Peter Dwyer Scholarships
To recognize the most promising students at the National Ballet School and the National Theatre School. Scholarships totaling $20,000 are awarded annually. Each school receives $10,000 and chooses the winners on behalf of the Canada Council.

• 6793 • Robert Fleming Prize
To encourage the careers of the most talented young Canadian composers of classical music. A monetary prize of $2,000 is awarded annually in memory of Robert Fleming. Established in 1991.

• 6794 • Sylva Gelber Foundation Award
To recognize the most talented Canadian artist under the age of 30 in the Council's grants competition for performers in classical music. A monetary award of $15,000 is bestowed annually. Established in 1981 in honor of Sylva Gelber. Sponsored by Sylva Gelber Foundation.

• 6795 • Glenn Gould Prize
Recognizes individuals who have made exceptional contributions to music. Awarded triennially.

• 6796 • Governor General's Awards in Visual and Media Arts
Recognizes excellence in visual and media arts. Six $15,00 prizes are awarded annually for career achievement. One $15,000 prize is awarded annually for contributions through voluntarism, philanthropy, board governance, or community outreach activities. Nominees must be Canadian citizens or permanent residents of Canada. Nominations must be made by specialists in the field. Self-nominations are not accepted. A peer assessment committee selects the winners.

• 6797 • Governor General's Literary Awards
For recognition of the best English-language and best French-language work in each of the following categories: children's literature (text) children's literature (illustration), drama, fiction, poetry, literary nonfiction, and translation. The juries review all books by Canadian authors, illustrators, and translators published in Canada or abroad during the previous year. In the case of translation, the original work also must be a Canadian-authored title. A formal application from the publisher is required. Monetary awards of $15,000 each are presented annually. Estab-

lished in 1936. Formerly: (1988) Governor General's Literary Awards for Children's Literature; (1988) Governor General's Literary Awards for Translation.

• 6798 • John Hirsch Prize
To recognize emerging Canadian theater directors who have demonstrated great potential for future excellence and exciting artistic potential. Candidates must be nominated by members of the professional theater community. A monetary prize of $6,000 is awarded annually, alternating each year between the anglophone and francophone communities. Established in 1995.

• 6799 • Jules Leger Prize for New Chamber Music
Encourages Canadian composers to write for chamber music groups and to foster the performance of Canadian chamber music by these groups. $7500 is awarded annually. Established in 1978.

• 6800 • Izaak Walton Killam Memorial Prizes
For recognition of distinguished career achievements by eminent Canadian scholars in the fields of the natural sciences, health sciences, or engineering. A candidate must be nominated by three experts in the particular field. Up to five prizes of $100,000 each are awarded annually. Established in 1980 by Mrs. Dorothy J. Killam. Izaak Walton Killam Research Fellowships are also awarded in the fields of humanities, social sciences, medicine, and engineering.

• 6801 • Jacqueline Lemieux Prize
Recognizes the most talented Canadian candidate in the Grants to Dance Professionals competition. $6000 is given in memory of Jacqueline Lemieux's contribution to the development of Canadian dance annually.

• 6802 • Victor Martyn Lynch-Staunton Awards
Designates several Canadian artists who have been awarded Canada Council grants in music and visual arts as holders. This designation is made to honour the memory of the benefactor whose bequest to the Canada Council enables it to increase the number of grants available to senior or established artists. These awards provide each recipient with $4000 in addition to the arts grant, which is also provided by the income from this bequest.

• 6803 • National Young Performers Competition
Every two years, two prizes of $15,000 are awarded to the winners of the arts and radio categories.

• 6804 • Virginia Parker Award
To encourage and assist a young Canadian classical musician, instrumentalist or conductor, into developing a professional career. The candidate must have received Canada Council grants from a Council juried program to qualify for the prize. Awarded on the recommendation of the Music Advisory Committee of the Canada Council's Music Section. A monetary prize of approximately $25,000 is awarded annually. Formerly known as the Virginia P. Moore Prize, the Virginia Parker Prize was established in 1982 by the late Virginia Parker. Formerly: Virginia P. Moore Award.

• 6805 • Petro-Canada Award in New Media
Recognizes an artist who has demonstrated outstanding and innovative use of new technology in the media arts. Candidates are nominated by a committee of three professional curators and/or critics who are specialists in new media and audio arts. The winner is selected by a committee of professional new media and audio artists. $10,000 is awarded approximately every three years. Established in 1987 to celebrate the centenary of engineering in Canada.

• 6806 • Prix de Rome in Architecture
Recognizes the work of Canadians actively engaged in the field of contemporary architecture. The recipient's career must be well under way and his/her personal work must show exceptional talent. The winner is chosen by a peer assessment committee convened by the Canada Council for the Arts. A monetary prize and the use of an apartment-studio on the Piazza Sant'Apollonia in the Trastevere quarter of Rome for one year is awarded annually. Established in 1987.

• 6807 • Ronald J. Thom Award for Early Design Achievement
Recognizes exceptional talent in architectural design. $10,000 is awarded every two years.

• 6808 • Saidye Bronfman Award
Recognizes excellence in fine crafts. $25,000 is awarded annually. Laureates are chosen by a peer assessment committee of distinguished craftspersons and experts in the fine crafts.

• 6809 • Joseph S. Stauffer Prizes
To recognize Canadian artists who have been awarded a grant in one of the fields of music, visual arts, and literature. The prizes are made to honor the memory of the benefactor whose bequest to the Canada Council enables it to encourage young Canadians of outstanding promise or potential. A prize of $5,000 is awarded in each category annually.

• 6810 • J. B. C. Watkins Award
To provide special grants for professional Canadian artists in any field who are graduates of any Canadian university postsecondary art institution or training school. Individuals who choose to carry out their postgraduate studies in Denmark, Norway, Sweden, or Iceland are especially considered. Applications must be submitted to the Canada Council. Established by the estate of John B.C. Watkins. Each award is $5000.

• 6811 • Healey Willan Prize
To recognize the amateur choir judged as having given the most convincing performance in terms of musicianship, technique, and program in the CBC National Radio Competition for Amateur Choirs. A monetary prize of $5,000 is awarded biennially.

• 6812 •
Canada Safety Council
(Conseil canadien de la securite)
Emile Therien, Pres.
1020 Thomas Spratt Pl.
Ottawa, ON, Canada K1G 5L5
Phone: (613)739-1535
Fax: (613)739-1566
E-mail: csc@safety-council.org
Home Page: http://www.safety-council.org

• 6813 • National Police Award for Traffic Safety
To recognize an individual or group of law enforcement officers for outstanding contributions in the areas of program management, personnel training, and/or implementation of public education and enforcement programs. Full-time Canadian federal, provincial, and municipal police officers, including military, railway, and Ports Canada police departments, both individuals and groups such as divisions, sections, or detachments are eligible. A trophy to be retained by the recipient for one year, a plaque, and travel expenses to attend the Annual Conference are awarded each year. Established in 1991.

• 6814 •
Canada - The Chancellery
Michaelle Jean, Gov.Gen.
Rideau Hall
1 Sussex Dr.
Ottawa, ON, Canada K1A 0A1
Phone: (613)993-8200
Toll-Free: 800-465-6890
Fax: (613)998-1664
E-mail: info@gg.ca
Home Page: http://www.gg.ca

• 6815 • Additional Honours
In addition to the following honours initiated in Canada, the Canadian family of honours includes the Order of Merit of the Police Forces, the Royal Victorian Order for personal services to the Sovereign and the Order of St. John of Jerusalem. Beyond these orders, the Canadian family also incorporates War Service Medals, United Nations Medals, International Commission for Supervision and Control Medals, as well as Commemorative Medals.

• 6816 • Canadian Coast Guard Exemplary Service Medal
To recognize long and meritorious service with the Canadian Coast Guard. Employees of the Department of Transport or the Department of Fisheries and Oceans, on or after October 25, 1990 who have completed 20 years of service with the Department, ten years of which must have been served with the Canadian Coast

Guard in the performance of duties involving potential risk, are eligible. A circular medal with the crest of the Canadian Coast Guard circumscribed with the words "Exemplary Service - Services distingues" on one side and Her Majesty's Cipher on the other, is awarded.

• 6817 • Canadian Forces Decoration

To recognize individuals for 12 years of service with good conduct in the Canadian Forces. Bars are awarded for each additional 10 years. Established in 1949.

• 6818 • Cross of Valour

To recognize acts of the most conspicuous courage in circumstances of extreme peril. The decoration may be awarded posthumously. Nominations are open to everyone. A gold cross with four equal limbs. Recipients are entitled to have the letters C. V. placed after their names, the highest decoration for bravery. Established in 1972. To date, 19 have been awarded.

• 6819 • Emergency Medical Services Exemplary Service Medal

To recognize professionals in the provision of pre-hospital emergency medical services who have performed their duties in an exemplary manner, characterized by good conduct, industry and efficiency. Applicants must have been employed with Canadian emergency medical services on or after October 31, 1991, and have completed 20 years of exemplary service, including 10 years in the performance of duties involving potential risk and may include, in the calculation of their 20 years of service, service completed in another profession, providing this service has not already been recognized by a good conduct, long service or exemplary service medal. Awarded annually. Established in 1994.

• 6820 • Insignia for Mention in Dispatches

To recognize members of the Canadian Forces on active service, in combat or near-combat conditions, and other individuals working with or in conjunction with the Canadian Forces, for valiant conduct, devotion to duty or other distinguished service, on or after November 1, 1990. A bronze oak leaf is awarded, worn horizontally on the designated ribbon with the stalk of the oak leaf farthest from the left shoulder.

• 6821 • Medal of Bravery

To recognize acts of bravery in hazardous circumstances. The decoration may be awarded posthumously. Nominations are open to everyone. A circular silver medal with a maple leaf surrounded by a laurel wreath. On the reverse appear the Royal Cipher and Crown and the words "Bravery Bravoure". Recipients are entitled to have the letters M.B. placed after their surnames. Established in 1972.

• 6822 • Medal of Military Valour

To honour an act of valour or devotion to duty in the presence of the enemy. Members of the Canadian Forces or of an allied armed force that is serving with or in conjunction with the Canadian Forces are eligible. The medal may be presented posthumously. A circular gold medal bearing a maple leaf surrounded by a wreath of laurel on one side and the Royal Cipher and Crown and the Latin inscription "Pro Valore" is awarded when merited. Recipients are entitled to have the letters M.M.V. placed after their surnames. Established in 1993.

• 6823 • Meritorious Service Cross - Civil Division

The Meritorious Service Cross (civil) was created in 1991. It recognizes a deed or activity performed in an outstandingly professional manner or of an uncommonly high standard that brings considerable benefit or great honour to Canada. The deed or activity must have occurred on or after June 11, 1984. The Meritorious Service Cross takes the form of a silver Greek cross, ends splayed and convexed, bearing the Royal Crown. On the obverse appears a maple leaf within a circle and a laurel wreath between the arms. Recipients of the Cross are entitled to use the letters "M.S.C." after their names.

• 6824 • Meritorious Service Cross - Military Division

The Meritorious Service Cross (military) was created in 1984. It recognizes a military deed or activity that has been performed in an outstandingly professional manner or of a rare high standard that brings considerable benefit or great honour to the Canadian Forces. The deed or activity must have occurred on or after June 11, 1984. The Meritorious Service Cross takes the form of a silver Greek cross, ends splayed and convexed, bearing the Royal Crown. On the obverse appears a maple leaf within a circle and a laurel wreath between the arms. Recipients of the Cross are entitled to use the letters "M.S.C." after their names.

• 6825 • Meritorious Service Medal - Civil Division

The Meritorious Service Medal (civil) was created in 1991. It recognizes a deed or activity performed in a highly professional manner or of a very high standard that brings benefit or honour to Canada. The deed of activity must have occurred on or after June 11, 1984. The Meritorious Service Medal consists of a circular medal of silver bearing the Royal Crown. On the obverse appears, centered, the design of the Cross. On the reverse appear the Royal Cipher and, within a double circle, the words "Meritorious Service Meritoire". Recipients are entitled to use the letters "M.S.M." after their names.

• 6826 • Meritorious Service Medal - Military Division

The Meritorious Service Medal (military) was created in 1991. It recognizes a military deed or activity that has been performed in a highly professional manner or of a very high standard that brings benefit or honour to the Canadian Forces. The deed or activity must have occurred on or after June 11, 1984. The Meritorious Service Medal consists of a circular medal of silver bearing the Royal Crown. On the obverse appears, centered, the design of the Cross. On the reverse appear the Royal Cipher and, within a double circle, the words "Meritorious Service Meritoire." Recipients are entitled to use the letters "M.S.M." after their names.

• 6827 • Order of Canada

This, Canada's highest distinction, is given in recognition of outstanding achievement and service in various fields of human endeavor. Canadian citizens are eligible. Individuals and organizations may make nominations. Awards are made on three levels of membership: Companion, Officer, and Member. Three investiture ceremonies are held annually. The badge of the Order is a stylized snowflake bearing the crown, a maple leaf, and a Latin motto "desiderantes meliorem patriam" - they desire a better country. Up to 15 appointments are made each year, and there can only be 165 living companions at any given time. Companions can use the letters C.C. after their name. Officers can use the letters O.C. after their name. Up to 64 appointments can be made each year. Members can use the letters C.M. after their name. Up to 136 appointments can be made each year.

• 6828 • Police Exemplary Service Medal

For recognition of long and meritorious service. The head of the police force may submit a nomination form outlining the dates of qualifying service and certifying that the candidate has had no serious disciplinary action taken against him or her. To be eligible, individuals must be serving police officers or were serving as of August 1, 1980 and have completed a minimum of twenty years of full-time service with one or more recognized Canadian police forces, including full-time police-cadet training, with a record of outstanding service.

• 6829 • Queen's Medal for Champion Shot

To recognize outstanding marksmanship. Two awards are presented annually: one to the member of the Canadian Forces (Regular) and one to the member of the Canadian Forces (Reserves) or Royal Canadian Mounted Police who obtains the highest aggregate score in stages one and two of the Queen's Medal Competition at Connaught Range. On August 28, 1991, Letters Patent were signed by Her Majesty to create the Queen's Medal for Champion Shot in Canada.

• 6830 • Royal Canadian Mounted Police Long Service Medal

To recognize Royal Canadian Mounted Police for 20 years of service and good conduct. A bar is also awarded for each additional five years of such good service. This component of the national system has been regularly awarded since its creation in 1934.

• 6831 • Star of Courage

To recognize acts of conspicuous courage in circumstances of great peril. A silver star of four points with a maple leaf in each of the four angles is awarded. Recipients are entitled to have the letters S.C. (E.C. in French) placed after their surnames. Established in 1972.

• 6832 • Star of Military Valour
To honour distinguished and valiant service in the presence of the enemy. Members of the Canadian Forces or of an allied armed force that is serving with or in conjunction with the Canadian Forces are eligible. The Star consists of a gold star with four points with a maple leaf in each angle, on the obverse of which a gold maple leaf is superimposed in the centre of a sanguine fidd surrounded by a silver wreath of laurel and on the reverse of which the Royal Cipher and Crown and the inscription "Pro Valore" appear. Recipients are entitled to have the letters S.M.V. placed after their names. Established in 1993.

• 6833 •
Canada's Aviation Hall of Fame
Victor Bennett, Chm.
Box 6360
Wetaskiwin, AB, Canada T9A 2G1
Phone: (780)361-1351
Toll-Free: 800-661-4726
Fax: (780)361-1239
E-mail: info@cahf.ca
Home Page: http://www.cahf.ca

• 6834 • Belt of Orion Award
Annual award of recognition.

• 6835 •
Canada's National History Society
E. James Arnett, Chair
No. 478-167 Lombard Ave.
Winnipeg, MB, Canada R3B 0T6
Phone: (204)988-9300
Toll-Free: 800-816-6777
Fax: (204)988-9309
E-mail: memberservices@historysociety.ca
Home Page: http://www.historysociety.ca

• 6836 • Pierre Berton Award
Recognizes distinguished achievement in popularizing Canadian history. Awarded periodically.

• 6837 • Governor General's Award
Recognizes excellence in teaching Canadian history. Awarded periodically.

• 6838 •
Canada's Research-Based Pharmaceutical Companies
Russell Williams, Pres.
55 Metcalfe St., Ste. 1220
Ottawa, ON, Canada K1P 6L5
Phone: (613)236-0455
Fax: (613)236-6756
E-mail: info@canadapharma.org
Home Page: http://www.canadapharma.org

• 6839 • Medal of Honour
To recognize outstanding and invaluable contributions to the advancement of science. The award is not restricted to Canadians, but research must have been performed in Canada. A solid gold medal that bears the likeness of the winged goddess of Samothrace, symbolizing man's conquest of disease and death, is awarded when merited. Established in 1945.

• 6840 • PMAC Health Research Foundation
Recognizes individuals engaged in pharmaceutical and toxicological research. Awarded periodically.

• 6841 •
Canada's Sports Hall of Fame
(Temple de la Renommee des Sports du Canada)
Sheryn Posen, COO
115 Princes' Blvd.
Exhibition Place
Toronto, ON, Canada M6K 3C3
Phone: (416)260-6789
Fax: (416)260-9347
E-mail: cshof@inforamp.net
Home Page: http://www.cshof.ca

• 6842 • Canada's Sports Hall of Fame
To recognize a Canadian citizen who has been distinguished as an athlete, an executive, or a coach. A cloth crest of Sports Hall, a blazer, and permanent recognition in an exhibit at the Hall of Fame are awarded annually. Established in 1955.

• 6843 •
Canadian Aberdeen Angus Association
Doug Fee, CEO
6715 8th St. NE, No. 142
Calgary, AB, Canada T2E 7H7
Phone: (403)571-3580
Toll-Free: 888-571-3580
Fax: (403)571-3599
E-mail: info@cdnangus.ca
Home Page: http://www.cdnangus.ca

• 6844 • Gold Show Award
For points collected for placing in designated Gold Shows.

• 6845 •
Canadian Academy of Recording Arts and Sciences
Ms. Meghan McCabe, Office Coor.
355 King St. W, Ste. 501
Toronto, ON, Canada M5V 1J6
Phone: (416)485-3135
Toll-Free: 888-440-JUNO
Fax: (416)485-4978
E-mail: info@carasonline.ca
Home Page: http://www.carasonline.ca

• 6846 • Juno Awards
To recognize outstanding achievements in recorded music. Awards are given in the following categories: International Album of the Year; Best Selling Album (foreign or domestic); Best Selling Francophone Album; Album of the Year; Single of the Year; Female Vocalist of the Year; Male Vocalist of the Year; Group of the Year; Instrumental Artist(s) of the Year; Northstar Rock Album of the Year; Best Rap Recording; Country Female Vocalist of the Year; Country Male Vocalist of the Year; Country Group or Duo of the Year; Best New Solo Artist; Best New Group (Sponsored by Factor); Songwriter of the Year (Sponsored by Socan) ; Best Children's Album; Best Classical Album - Solo or Chamber Ensemble; Best Classical Album - Large Ensemble or Soloist(s) with Large Ensemble Accompaniment; Best Classical Album - Vocal or Choral Performance; Best Classical Composition; Best Dance Recording; Best Contemporary Jazz Album; Best Mainstream Jazz Album; Best R&B/Soul Recording; Best Roots & Traditional Album - Solo; Best Roots & Traditional Album - Group; Best Global Album; Producer of the Year; Recording Engineer of the Year; Best Video; Best Album Design (sponsored by Ever-Reddy Packing Ltd.); Best Reggae Recording; Best Music of Aboriginal Canada Recording; Best Blues/Gospel Album; Best Alternative Album; Canadian Music Hall of Fame Award and Walt Grealis Special Achievement Award. Canadian citizens or landed immigrants are eligible for application and nomination. The deadline is November 22 for juried categories and January 2 for categories based on sales. A trophy, an acrylic stylized metronome, is awarded annually in each category. Formerly: (1970) Annual Gold Leaf Awards.

• 6847 •
Canadian Acoustical Association
Dave Quirt, Exec.Sec.
National Research Council of Canada
Institute for Research on Construction
Ottowa, ON, Canada K1A 0R6
Phone: (613)993-9746
Fax: (613)954-1495
E-mail: dave.quirt@nrc-cnrc.gc.ca
Home Page: http://www.caa-aca.ca

• 6848 • Best Use of Music or Sound
No further information available this edition.

• 6849 • Computer Animation
For the best animated film making use of computer animation technologies.

• 6850 • Directors' Awards
To honor authors of the best papers published in *Canadian Acoustics*. A $500 prize is awarded to the best paper by a student members and $500 to the best individual member. Awarded annually by CAA's Board of Directors.

• 6851 • Eckel Student Prize in Noise Control
To recognize excellent graduate research advancing the practice of noise control. Awarded annually with $500 prize money. Established in 1991.

• 6852 • Fessenden Student Prize in Underwater Acoustics
To support deserving graduate students in their research in underwater acoustics. Awarded annually with a monetary prize of $500. Established in 1990.

Awards are arranged in alphabetical order below their administering organizations

• 6853 • Edgar and Millicent Shaw Postdoctoral Prize in Acoustics
To provide a research stipend in support of one year of postdoctoral research in an established Canadian acoustics laboratory. Awarded annually with a monetary prize of $3,000. Established in 1988.

• 6854 • Student Presentation Award
To encourage participation of student members to present their research work and to provide exposure to the acoustical community. Three prizes of $500 are awarded annually.

• 6855 •
Canadian Actors' Equity Association (Association Canadienne des Artistes de la Scene)
Susan Wallace, Exec.Dir.
44 Victoria St., 12th Fl.
Toronto, ON, Canada M5C 3C4
Phone: (416)867-9165
Fax: (416)867-9246
E-mail: info@caea.com
Home Page: http://www.caea.com

• 6856 • Honorary Member
Annual award of recognition. Winners are chosen by a peer committee.

• 6857 • Life Member
Annual award of recognition. Winners are chosen by a peer committee.

• 6858 •
Canadian Adult Recreational Hockey Association
Mike Peski, Exec.Dir.
1420 Blair Pl., Ste. 610
Ottawa, ON, Canada K1J 9L8
Phone: (613)244-1989
Toll-Free: 800-267-1854
Fax: (613)244-0451
E-mail: hockey@carhahockey.ca
Home Page: http://www.carha.ca

• 6859 • Hockey Hall of Fame Builder Category
Recognizes work and dedication to build the association and its hockey programs. Awarded annually.

• 6860 • Hockey Hall of Fame International Friends
For the promotion of association's programs in other countries. Awarded annually.

• 6861 • Hockey Hall of Fame John Sergnese Category (Friends of CARHA)
For best service. Inquire for application details.

• 6862 • Hockey Hall of Fame Media Category
Recognizes an outstanding media person. Inquire for application details.

• 6863 • Hockey Hall of Fame Player Category
Recognizes individual commitment to the association's mission and goals. Awarded annually.

• 6864 • Hockey Hall of Fame Team Category
For team commitment to association's philosophy regarding the game. Awarded annually.

• 6865 •
Canadian Aeronautics and Space Institute (Institut Aeronautique et Spatial du Canada)
Mr. Geoffrey Languedoc, Exec.Dir.
1750 Courtwood Crescent, Ste. 105
Ottawa, ON, Canada K2C 2B5
Phone: (613)234-0191
Fax: (613)234-9039
E-mail: casi@casi.ca
Home Page: http://www.casi.ca

• 6866 • The Alouette Award
To recognize an outstanding contribution to advancement in Canadian space technology, application, science, or engineering. It may be awarded to an individual, group, organization, or group of organizations as appropriate to the nature of the contribution. The contribution must be recognized as a Canadian-led space endeavor or as a significant Canadian contribution to an international program. Preference shall be given to contributions which lead to new benefits for humankind. Established in 1995.

• 6867 • F. W. (Casey) Baldwin Award
To recognize the author of the best paper published in the *Canadian Aeronautics and Space Journal* during the preceding calendar year. Selection is based on originality of material, the significance in the field, and writing skills. A silver medal is awarded annually. Established in 1957.

• 6868 • C. D. Howe Award
For recognition of distinguished achievement in the fields of planning, policy making, and overall leadership in Canadian aeronautics and space activities and for outstanding personal performance in these fields for at least ten years. A silver plaque is awarded annually. Established in 1966.

• 6869 • McCurdy Award
For recognition of outstanding achievement in the art, science, and engineering of aeronautics and space research. Individuals residing in Canada when the contributions were made are eligible. A silver medal and trophy are awarded annually if merited. Established in 1954.

• 6870 • Trans-Canada (McKee) Trophy
This, the oldest aviation award in Canada, is given for recognition of outstanding achievement in the field of air operations. The achievement may be a single brilliant exploit or a sustained high level of performance. Pioneering of new areas of air operations and advancement of the use of aviation receive consideration over achievements serving no useful end. The recipient must have been a resident of Canada at the time of the achievement. A trophy and silver plaque are awarded annually if merited. Established in 1927.

• 6871 • W. Rupert Turnbull Award
For recognition of significant achievement in the scientific or engineering field of aeronautics of space research. Preference is given to Canadians or to individuals having some association with Canadian aerospace activities. The awardee must present a lecture in his or her specialty and receives a certificate and an honorarium. Awarded annually. Established in 1955.

• 6872 • Romeo Vachon Award
For recognition of an outstanding display of initiative, ingenuity, and practical skills in the solution of a particular physical problem in Canadian aeronautics and space activities. A bronze plaque is awarded annually if merited. Established in 1969.

• 6873 •
Canadian Aerophilatelic Society
R.K. Malott, Pres.
16 Harwick Crescent
Nepean, ON, Canada K2H 6R1
Phone: (613)829-0280
Fax: (613)829-7673
E-mail: rmalott@magma.ca

• 6874 • CAS Award for Accomplishment on Aerophilately
Recognizes individuals providing distinguished service to aerophilately. Awarded annually.

• 6875 •
Canadian Animal Health Institute
Ms. Jean Szkotnicki, Pres.
160 Research Ln., Ste. 102
Guelph, ON, Canada N1G 5B2
Phone: (519)763-7777
Fax: (519)763-7407
E-mail: cahi@cahi-icsa.ca
Home Page: http://www.cahi-icsa.ca

• 6876 • Industry Leadership Award
Recognizes leadership, accomplishments, innovative ability and commitment to animal health. Selection is based on a point system. Awarded annually.

• 6877 •
Canadian Architect
Ian Chodikoff, Ed.
12 Concorde Place, Suite 800
Toronto, ON, Canada M3C 4J2
Phone: (416)510-6807
Phone: (416)510-6845
Toll-Free: 800-268-7742
Fax: (416)510-5140
E-mail: editors@canadianarchitect.com
Home Page: http://www.cdnarchitect.com

• 6878 • Canadian Architect Magazine Art of CAD Competition
Acknowledges exemplary work and innovation in the area of computer-aided design. Open to all computer-aided design professionals. All typed of original computer-generated materials are eligible, including renderings, interactive models, 2D or 3D images and animation. Entries are judged on the inventiveness and quality of the work and on the extent to which digital technology has been explored and exploited. In addition to publication of the winners in *Canadian Architect Magazine*, selected entries are exhibited at the annual works festival of visual arts in Edmonton, Alberta, Canada. The competition and exhibition are sponsored by Southam, The Works Festival and Autodesk Canada. Prizes are awarded in four separate categories and consist of either software or cash awards. Established in 1995.

• 6879 • Canadian Architect Magazine Awards of Excellence
For recognition of architectural design projects by Canadian registered architects and architectural graduates. Projects in the design stage only are eligible. A separate award is given to projects by final year students in architecture programs in Canadian institutions. A plaque is awarded annually. Established in 1968. Formerly: Canadian Architect Yearbook.

• 6880 •
Canadian Association for Environmental Analytical Laboratories
(Association Canadienne des laboratories d'analyses environmentale)
Jaquie Vandenberg, Program Admin.
1565 Carling Ave., Ste. 310
Ottawa, ON, Canada K1Z 8R1
Phone: (613)233-5300
Fax: (613)233-5501
E-mail: rwilson@caeal.ca
Home Page: http://www.caeal.ca

• 6881 • CAEAL Appreciation Award
Recognizes providers of volunteer services to the CAEAL. Awarded annually.

• 6882 •
Canadian Association for Health, Physical Education, Recreation and Dance
Guy Tanguay, Exec.Dir.
403-2197 Riverside Dr.
Ottawa, ON, Canada K1H 7X3
Phone: (613)523-1348
Toll-Free: 800-663-8708
Fax: (613)523-1206
E-mail: info@cahperd.ca
Home Page: http://www.cahperd.ca

• 6883 • Physical Education School Recognition Award
The Physical Education School Award Program identifies, recognizes and encourages excellence in school physical education programs. These awards are presented to schools that meet the quality physical education standards established by CAHPERD. Schools that meet these standards earn the "QDPE School" or "QPE School" title for one year..

• 6884 • The R. Tait McKenzie Award of Honour
CAHPERD's most prestigious award. The Award epitomizes Dr. Tait McKenzie's professional ideals, service to humanity and dedication to the advancement of knowledge and understanding of physical and health education, recreation and dance. Awarded annually.

• 6885 • Student Award
To recognize undergraduate student leadership in the field of health, physical education, recreation or dance. One award presented to each Canadian university that offers a degree in PE or a related discipline.

• 6886 • Young Professional Award
This award is given to one individual per province who best epitomizes exemplary work on behalf of the profession. Must be a member of CAHPERD or a Liaison group and 35 years of age or younger.

• 6887 •
Canadian Association for Music Therapy
(Association de Musicotherapie du Canada)
Nicola Oddy MTA, Pres.
Wilfrid Laurier University
Waterloo, ON, Canada N2L 3C5
Phone: (519)884-1970
Phone: (519)886-9100
Toll-Free: 800-996-CAMT
Fax: (519)886-9351
E-mail: camt@musictherapy.ca
Home Page: http://www.musictherapy.ca

• 6888 • Norma Sharpe Award
Recognizes outstanding Canadian music therapists. Awarded annually.

• 6889 •
Canadian Association of Broadcasters
(Association Canadienne des Radiodiffuseurs)
Glenn O'Farrell, Pres./CEO
PO Box 627, Sta. B
Ottawa, ON, Canada K1P 5S2
Phone: (613)233-4035
Fax: (613)233-6961
E-mail: cab@cab-acr.ca
Home Page: http://www.cab-acr.ca

• 6890 • Broadcast Excellence Award
For recognition of outstanding service to Canadian private broadcasting at the local, regional, or national level. Awardee may be associated with an AM, FM, or television station, or group of stations or network that is a member in good standing of the Canadian Association of Broadcasters or individuals associated with private broadcasting. Priority is given to activities in the 12 months prior to the entry deadline of June 30. Selection is based on activities that include: exceptional human qualities, such as unselfish giving or skills, time and advice that go beyond the call of duty and enhance the image of Canadian private broadcasting; practical, innovative achievements that require imagination, dedication, and hard work and that benefit the industry and reflect a genuine concern for the highest broadcasting standards; and outstanding service that has made a significant contribution, in a single or continuing fashion, to the Canadian broadcasting system. CAB's Gold Ribbon is awarded at the gala Gold Ribbon dinner at the CAB annual meeting. Established in 1982. Formerly: Gold Ribbon for Distinguished Service.

• 6891 • Gold Ribbon for Community Service (Radio)
To honor the AM or FM member station and television member station, or group of member stations that has made the greatest single or continuing charitable or public service contribution within its community. Community service activities include assistance to listeners or viewers during emergencies (floods, fires, major storms, etc.), dealing with community issues; or contributions to charitable organizations. Priority is given to programs broadcast in the 12 months prior to the entry deadline. A Gold Ribbon is awarded to the winners and finalists are sent a certificate. Judging is based on impact to the community, station involvement, originality, documentation, community response, quality of production, and clarity of entry. Established in 1982.

• 6892 • Gold Ribbon for Community Service (Specialty/Pay/PPV)
Recognizes outstanding work in community service. Awards are given for programming-documentaries; programming-entertainment special/series; magazine programming; programming-new special/series; public affairs; programming-niche market; promotion-brand image; promotion-Canadian program/series. Awarded annually.

• 6893 • Gold Ribbon for Community Service (Television)
Recognizes outstanding production relating to community service. Awards are given for large, medium, and small markets; breaking news; special series; documentaries; public affairs; drama programming; magazine programming; entertainment programming; promotion-brand image; promotion Canadian program series. Awarded annually.

• 6894 • Gold Ribbon for Outstanding Community Service by an Individual Broadcaster
Recognizes outstanding work for community service. Awarded annually.

• 6895 • Gold Ribbon for Promotion of Canadian Talent (Radio)
To honor the AM or FM member station that has made the greatest single or continuing contribution to the creation, production, and presentation of Canadian talent through broadcast exposure in the entertainment/drama field. Priority is given to programs broadcast in the 12 months prior to the entry deadline. Judging is based on direct benefit to talent, station initiative, station involve-

ment, creative production techniques, national exposure for the artist, and clarity of entry. Established in 1982.

• 6896 •
Canadian Association of Career Educators and Employers
Jeremy O'Krafka, Natl.Mgr.
720 Spadina Ave., Ste. 202
Toronto, ON, Canada M5S 2T9
Phone: (416)929-5156
Toll-Free: (866)922-3303
Fax: (416)929-5256
E-mail: info@cacee.com
Home Page: http://www.cacee.com

• 6897 • **Award of Merit**
Recognizes exemplary contribution by members. Awarded annually.

• 6898 • **Life Membership Award**
Annual award of recognition.

• 6899 • **Outstanding Achievement Award**
Recognizes major, definable contribution to the field of career planning and/or recruitment. Awarded annually.

• 6900 • **Regional Recognition Award**
Recognizes volunteer contributions at the regional level. Awarded annually.

• 6901 • **Volunteer Recognition Award**
Recognizes outstanding volunteer contributions. Awarded annually.

• 6902 •
Canadian Association of Elizabeth Fry Societies
(Association Canadienne des Societes Elizabeth Fry)
Kim Pate, Exec.Dir.
151 Slater St., Ste. 701
Ottawa, ON, Canada K1P 5H3
Phone: (613)238-2422
Phone: (613)298-2422
Fax: (613)232-7130
E-mail: caefs@web.ca
Home Page: http://www.elizabethfry.ca

• 6903 • **Elizabeth Fry Memorial Award**
For women who have been in conflict with the law. Awarded annually.

• 6904 •
Canadian Association of Food Banks
(Association Canadienne des Banques Alimentaires)
Charles Seiden, Exec.Dir.
191 New Toronto St.
Toronto, ON, Canada M8V 2E7
Phone: (416)203-9241
Toll-Free: 877-535-0958
Fax: (416)203-9244
E-mail: info@cafb-acba.ca
Home Page: http://www.cafb-acba.ca/

• 6905 • **Outstanding Sponsor Award**
Recognizes outstanding CAFB support. Awarded annually.

• 6906 • **Personal Contribution Award**
Recognizes food bank advocacy work. Awarded annually.

• 6907 •
Canadian Association of Geographers
Valerie Shoffey, Exec.Sec.
Department of Geography
McGill University
805 Sherbrooke St. W, Rm. 425
Montreal, QC, Canada H3A 2K6
Phone: (514)398-4946
Fax: (514)398-7437
E-mail: cag@geog.mcgill.ca
Home Page: http://www.cag-acg.ca

• 6908 • **Award for Excellence in Teaching Geography**
In recognition of the primary importance of teaching in geographic education. Members of the CAG teaching in recognized universities, colleges, CEGEPS, and high schools are eligible. Nominees must at least be the member of the teaching staff, full or part-time, hired to teach a course in any one year, who has primary responsibility for organizing and presenting course material. Nominees are usually a member's of the teaching staff, who has distinguished themselves in courses with small and large enrollments, at different levels of instruction, over several years of teaching in the nominating institution. Awarded to one or more recipients annually. Established in 1997.

• 6909 • **Award for Geography in the Service of Government or Business**
In recognition of the primary importance of excellence in geography in the service of government or business. Members of the CAG who have carried out major work for or in the public or private sector are eligible. Nominees normally have distinguished themselves through the development or application of geographic techniques or tools used in the service of government or business, or have a record of achievement for geography in the service of government or business over a long period of time. Awarded annually. Established in 1997.

• 6910 • **CAG Award for Scholarly Distinction in Geography**
To recognize outstanding scholarly work in geography, either in the form of a single research contribution or as sustained contributions over a number of years. Nominations can include non-Canadians who have made a significant contribution to research of interest to Canadian geography. Nominations are also considered for group research and endeavors that merit recognition by the CAG. A framed certificate and expenses to attend the annual meeting for the presentation are awarded at the annual meeting of the association. Established in 1972.

• 6911 • **CAG Award for Service to the Profession of Geography**
To recognize exceptional service over a period of years in the university training of professional geographers, in administrative or similar activities in the public service, as an officer of a learned society, or in such other ways as have advanced the profession of geography. A framed certificate and expenses to attend the annual meeting for the presentation are awarded at the annual meeting of the Association. Established in 1972.

• 6912 • **Starkey Robinson Award**
Annual award of recognition to high quality graduate research that furthers understanding of the geography of Canada.

• 6913 •
Canadian Association of Home and Property Inspectors
(Association Canadienne des Inspecteurs de Biens Immobiliers)
Jennie Witteveen, Admin.
64 Reddick Rd.
PO Box 507
Brighton, ON, Canada K0K 1H0
Phone: (613)475-5699
Toll-Free: 888-748-2244
Fax: (613)475-1595
E-mail: info@cahi.ca
Home Page: http://www.cahi.ca

Formerly: (2002) Canadian Association of Home Inspectors.

• 6914 • **Stephen Greenford Award**
Award of recognition. Based on contribution to the industry. Awarded annually.

• 6915 • **President's Award**
Annual award of recognition.

• 6916 •
Canadian Association of Medical Radiation Technologists
(Association Canadienne des Technologues en Radiation Medicale)
Richard Lauzon Ph.D., Exec.Dir.
1095 Carling Ave., Ste. 500
Ottawa, ON, Canada K1Y 4P6
Phone: (613)234-0012
Toll-Free: 800-463-9729
Fax: (613)234-1097
E-mail: skamble@camrt.ca
Home Page: http://www.camrt.ca

• 6917 • **L. J. Cartwright Award**
To recognize the best educational essay. The subject matter should be a review or a new method to describe an established application or principle. Candidates must be student members in good standing. A monetary award of $500 and a trophy are awarded annually at the convention. Established in 1978 to honor Leslie J. Cartwright, who served the Association as editor of the *Focal Spot* for 26 years. Formerly: (1978) CSRT Essay Award.

• 6918 • **E. I. Hood Award**
To recognize the best non-technical essay related to the medical radiation health care system in the areas of departmental design or administration, economics, supply, or training systems. Candidates must be registered technologists and members in good standing of the Association. A monetary award of $500 and an trophy are awarded annually at the convention. Established in 1978 to honor Mrs. E. I. Hood, who served the Association for 17 years as executive secretary and registrar.

• 6919 • **Dr. M. Mallett Student Award**
To recognize the best scientific or technical exhibit prepared by a student, relating to a radiological technology, radiation therapy, or nuclear medicine. Student members of the Association are eligible. A monetary award of $500 and an engraved plaque are awarded annually at the convention. Established in 1986 to honor Dr. Marshall Mallet, who has demonstrated a keen interest in the training of students.

• 6920 • **PACS Technology Award**
To recognize innovative technical or educational essays on the outcomes of PACS technology utilization. The category is open to students and registered technologists in good standing. A monetary award of $500 and an etched-glass trophy are awarded for the best essay. Sponsored by AGFA Medical Systems.

• 6921 • **Dr. Petrie Memorial Award**
To recognize the most innovative technical or educational essay. The subject matter must contribute to an advanced level and promotion of medical radiation technology. The candidate must be a registered technologist or student member of the Association. A monetary award of $500 and trophy certificate are awarded annually at the convention. Established in 1972 in memory of Dr. Edward A. Petrie.

• 6922 • **Philips Rose Bowl**
To recognize the best teaching aid or basic principle exhibit displayed at the annual conference. Applicants must be registered technologists. A monetary award of $500 and a rose bowl are presented annually.

• 6923 • **George Reason Memorial Cup**
To recognize the most outstanding technical or scientific exhibit at an annual meeting. Exhibits must be related to radiological technology, radiation therapy, or nuclear medicine. Applicants must be registered technologists. A monetary prize of $500 and a trophy are awarded annually. Established in 1952 in honor of Felix George Reason, who was instrumental in forming the Association and became its first president.

• 6924 • **Sister Mary Arthur "Sharing the Light" Award**
To recognize the best non-technical essay on a health care topic related to the patient or the caregiver. Open to students and registered technologists in good standing. A monetary award of $500 and an etched-glass trophy are awarded. The award honors Sister Mary Arthur, RT, for her dedication to CAMRT, her patients and students, and her profession.

• 6925 •
Canadian Association of Oilwell Drilling Contractors
Don Herring, Pres.
540 5th Ave. SW, Ste. 800
Calgary, AB, Canada T2P 0M2
Phone: (403)264-4311
Fax: (403)263-3796
E-mail: info@caodc.ca
Home Page: http://www.caodc.ca

• 6926 • **Safety Awards**
Annual award of recognition for safety. Inquire for application details.

• 6927 •
Canadian Association of Pathologists
(Association Canadienne des Pathologistes)
Dr. Donald Cook, Pres.
774 Echo Dr.
Ottawa, ON, Canada K1S 5N8
Phone: (613)730-6230
Toll-Free: 800-668-3740
Fax: (613)730-1116
E-mail: cap@rcpsc.edu
Home Page: http://cap.medical.org

• 6928 • **William Boyd Lectureship**
To recognize a senior member of the Association. Established in 1981.

• 6929 • **Leica Canada Scientific Award**
To recognize meritorious scientific contributions to pathology. The scientific work may be submitted in the form of a paper(s) already published or accepted for publication or a thesis accepted by a faculty of medicine or graduate studies. The paper may be in English or French. The applicant should be under the age of 40. A monetary award of $750 and a plaque are presented at the annual meeting. Established in 1965. Sponsored by Leica Canada Inc. Formerly: (1991) Wild-Leitz Scientific Award; Leica Scientific Award.

• 6930 • **Donald W. Penner Prize**
To recognize the resident in pathology presenting the best paper and the best poster at the annual meeting. A monetary award of $300 is presented annually. Established in 1977 in honor of Dr. Donald W. Penner who served for 25 years on the Executive Board of the Association.

• 6931 •
Canadian Association of Physicists
(Association canadienne des physiciens et physiciennes)
F.M. Ford, Exec.Dir.
150 Louis Pasteur Private
University of Ottawa
Ste. 112, MacDonald Bldg.
Ottawa, ON, Canada K1N 6N5
Phone: (613)562-5614
Fax: (613)562-5615
E-mail: cap@physics.uottawa.ca
Home Page: http://www.cap.ca

• 6932 • **CAP Medal for Achievement in Physics**
(Medaille de l'ACP pour Contribution Exceptionnelle a la Physique)
For recognition of distinguished service to physics over an extended period of time and/or recent outstanding achievement. The award is not limited to members of the Association but to those who have spent a major part of their working careers in Canada. The deadline for nominations is December 16. An engraved medal is awarded annually. Established in 1956.

• 6933 • **Herzberg Medal**
To recognize outstanding achievement in any field of research by a physicist who, in the year of the award, is not more than 40 years of age. The deadline is December 16. Nominations are accepted from members. An engraved sterling medal is awarded annually. Established in 1970 in honor of Dr. Gerhard Herzberg of the National Research Council of Canada who was the Nobel Laureate in Chemistry in 1970. Deadline December 7.

• 6934 • **Peter Kirby Memorial Medal for Outstanding Service to Canadian Physics**
To recognize outstanding contribution to physics in Canada. The medal is intended to recognize service to the physics community. It is intended to provide a lasting memorial to Peter Kirby and recognize in others the qualities he is remembered best for: a vision of strong physics community, dedicated efforts to support that vision and, in all things, fairness and honesty. Candidates are required to be members of the CAP or the Canadian Organization of Medical Physicists (COMP). The award is a silver medal with the CAP and COMP logos on one side and the

name of the winner and the year awarded on the other side. An engraved medal is awarded biennially in even-numbered years. Established in 1996.

• 6935 • Medal for Excellence in Teaching
To recognize excellence in teaching physics at the undergraduate level at a Canadian institution. Honours faculty members who have a comprehensive knowledge and deep understanding of their subjects, and who possess an exceptional ability to communicate their knowledge and understanding in such a way as to lead their students to high academic achievement in physics. The award is not limited to CAP members, but the recipient must have spent the major part of his/her working career in Canada. Nominations must be received by December 8. Awarded annually. Established in 1995.

• 6936 • Medal for Outstanding Achievement in Industrial and Applied Physics
To recognize and promote the creativity of scientists working within Canada in the area of industrial and applied physics. The award particularly recognizes the successful application of physical principles to the creation of practical innovations. Open to all scientists and engineers, whether in industry, research institutes, universities, government, or elsewhere. An engraved medal is awarded biennially in odd-numbered years. Established in 1991. Formerly: Prize for Innovative Applied Physics of the Division of Industrial and Applied Physics.

• 6937 • Prize in Theoretical and Mathematical Physics
To recognize research excellence in the fields of theoretical and mathematical physics. The award is not limited to CAP members, but the candidates' research should have been done in Canada or in affiliation with a Canadian university or industry. An engraved medal and cash prize are awarded annually. Established in 1995. Co-sponsored by the Centre de Recherches Mathematiques.

• 6938 •
Canadian Association of Special Libraries and Information Services
Pat Routledge, Contact
965 North Dr.
Winnipeg, MB, Canada R3T 0A8
Phone: (204)475-1860
E-mail: parout@mts.net
Home Page: http://www.cla.ca/caslis

• 6939 • Award for Special Librarianship in Canada
To recognize an individual who has made an outstanding contribution to special librarianship in Canada. Awarded annually. For further information contact Brenda Shields, Membership Services, at CLA.

• 6940 • Library Research and Development Grants
To support theoretical and applied research in library and information science. One or more grants totaling $1,000 are awarded. Proposals are judged on: the originality or necessity of research, the appropriateness of the proposed project to the goals and objectives of the Canadian Library Association, cost-effectiveness of the research in terms of the expected influence and ramifications of the results, timeliness of the research, assurance of project management and control, appropriateness of the proposed research method and design, completeness of application, and availability to the researcher of other funding. Candidates must be CLA members. Application deadline is February 28. Awarded annually.

• 6941 •
Canadian Association of University Teachers
(Association canadienne des professeures et professeurs d'universite)
James L. Turk, Exec.Dir.
2675 Queensview Dr.
Ottawa, ON, Canada K2B 8K2
Phone: (613)820-2270
Fax: (613)820-7244
E-mail: acppu@caut.ca
Home Page: http://www.caut.ca

• 6942 • Academic Librarians' Distinguished Service Award
Biennial award of recognition.

• 6943 • J.H. Stewart Reid Memorial Fellowship
Annual fellowship. Awarded to doctoral students.

• 6944 • Sarah Shorten Award
Recognizes individuals promoting the advancement of women in Canadian universities. Awarded annually.

• 6945 •
Canadian Athletic Therapists Association
(Association Canadienne des Therapeutes du Sport)
Grant Slessor, Office Mgr.
1040 7th Ave. SW, Ste. 402
Calgary, AB, Canada T2P 3G9
Phone: (403)509-2282
Phone: (403)509-2283
Fax: (403)509-2280
E-mail: info@athletictherapy.org
Home Page: http://www.athletictherapy.org

• 6946 • Larry Ashley Award
For an outstanding athletic trainer in professional hockey. Awarded annually.

• 6947 • CATA Merit Award
Annual award of recognition.

• 6948 • CATA Writing Award
Annual award of recognition.

• 6949 • Distinguished Athletic Therapy Educator Award
Annual award of recognition.

• 6950 • Special Recognition Award
Annual award of recognition.

• 6951 •
Canadian Authors Association
Joan Eyolfson Cadham, Pres.
320 S Shores Rd.
PO Box 419
Campbellford, ON, Canada K0L 1L0
Phone: (705)653-0323
Toll-Free: (866)216-6222
Fax: (705)653-0593
E-mail: admin@canauthors.org
Home Page: http://www.canauthors.org

• 6952 • CAA Carol Bolt Award
For plays published or performed the year prior to the award. Applicants must be Canadian born, naturalized citizens, or landed immigrants. A completed entry form and $35 entry fee must be submitted by December 15. $1000 and a silver medal are awarded.

• 6953 • CAA Awards for Adult Literature
Awards are given in the categories of fiction, poetry, short stories, Canadian history, and Canadian biography. Applicants must be Canadian by birth, naturalized citizens, or landed immigrants. A completed entry form and $35 must be submitted by December 15. A monetary award of $2500 and a silver medal are given per category.

• 6954 • CAA Jubilee Award for Short Stories
For best collection of short stories by a single Canadian author. A monetary prize of $2500 and a Silver medal are awarded annually. Application deadline is December 15.

• 6955 • CAA Lela Common Award for Canadian History
For best historical non-fiction work by a Canadian. A prize of $2,500 and a Silver medal are given annually. Deadline December 15.

• 6956 • CAA MOSAID Technologies, Inc. Award for Fiction
For best full-length novel by a Canadian author. A monetary prize of $2500 plus a Silver medal are given annually. Deadline December 15. Formerly: (2004) Canadian Authors Association Award for Fiction.

• 6957 • CAA Jack Chalmers Award for Poetry
For best volume of poetry by a Canadian poet. A monetary prize of $1000 and a Silver medal are given annually. Deadline December 15. For-

merly: (2004) Canadian Authors Association Award for Poetry.

• 6958 • Allan Sangster Memorial Award
To honor a CAA member who follows Allan Sangster's example of long and distinguished service to the Association. Awarded annually at the CAA Conference in June. Established in 1983.

• 6959 •
Canadian Aviation Historical Society
Tony Soulis, Pres.
PO Box 705, Sta. P
Toronto, ON, Canada M5S 2Y4
Phone: (416)410-9774
Fax: (905)294-3525
E-mail: cahsnatsec@cahs.com
Home Page: http://www.cahs.com

• 6960 • Silver Dart Aviation History Award
To encourage research and writing in the field of Canadian aviation history. Students in universities, colleges, trade schools, aviation schools, or technical institutes may submit papers by March 15. A monetary award of $500 and a trophy are awarded annually at the society's annual convention. Runners-up also receive a prize. All winning papers are published in *The CAHS Journal*. Established in 1985 to commemorate the first heavier than air flight in Canada by the aeroplane, Silver Dart.

• 6961 •
Canadian Band Association
(Association Canadienne des Harmonies)
Jim Forde, Pres.
15 Pinecrest Bay
Winnipeg, MB, Canada R2G 1W2
Phone: (204)663-1226
Phone: (306)683-7620
Fax: (306)663-1226
E-mail: cbaband@shaw.ca
Home Page: http://cba.usask.ca

• 6962 • CBA National Music Award
Recognizes directors and composers who have contributed to the development of band music. Awarded periodically.

• 6963 •
Canadian Bar Association
(L'Association du Barreau Canadien)
Bill Johnson, Pres.
500-865 Carling Ave.
Ottawa, ON, Canada K1S 5S8
Phone: (613)237-2925
Phone: (613)237-1988
Toll-Free: 800-267-8860
Fax: (613)237-0185
E-mail: info@cba.org
Home Page: http://www.cba.org

• 6964 • Viscount Bennett Fellowship
To encourage a high standard of legal education, training, and ethics. Canadian citizens who have graduated or who, at the time of application, are pursuing final year studies as an undergraduate student at an approved law school are eligible. A monetary award of $25,000 (Canadian) is awarded annually from the trust established by the Right Honorable Viscount Bennett. The deadline for applications is November 15. Established in 1943 in honor of Viscount Bennett, a former Canadian Bar Association President who donated 200 shares of stock to the Association. Additional information is available from Stephen Hanson, Senior Director of Communications.

• 6965 • James H. Bocking Memorial Award
Recognizes the best scholarly paper or article related to Canadian competition law or policy.

• 6966 • CBA President's Award
Recognizes the significant contribution of a Canadian jurist to the legal profession, the CBA or the public life of Canada. Open to all Canadians except the current president, pastpresident within five years or members of the judiciary while on the bench. An engraved brass Scales of Justice is awarded annually. Nominations are made by the president. Nomination deadline is June 15th.

• 6967 • Department of Justice - CBA University Law School Essay Contest
Recgonizes an outstanding paper written by a law school student. Inquire for subject.

• 6968 • Ramon John Hnatyshyn Award for Law
To recognize outstanding contribution to law or legal scholarship in Canada. Open to Canadian citizens who have been nominated by individuals. Nominations must consist of a completed formal nomination form; three letters of support, stating reasons for the candidate's nomination; a concise curriculum vitae of the nominee; and all supporting documentation. The deadline is April 30. One award is presented annually.

• 6969 • Justica Awards
Awarded for excellence in journalism fostering public awareness and understanding of the Canadian Justice System, the awards are given for French or English stories in two categories: print and broadcast media. The award is a miniature bronze replica of the statue of Justica in front of the Supreme Court of Canada Building in Ottawa. Certificates of Merit may be presented for meritorious entries at the discretion of the judges.

• 6970 • Douglas Miller Award
In memory of Douglas Miller of Yellowknife, the award recognizes a Canadian Bar Association member who demonstrates outstanding dedication and team spirit in his or her ongoing involvement with the CBA. Each year the award, a sculpture entitled "Crane" carved from a musk ox horn by Northwest Territories artist Rex Goose, is presented to the winner in transfer from the previous winner. A photograph of the award and the commemorative plaque is presented to the winner when the award is transferred at year end.

• 6971 • Walter Owen Book Prize
Offered by the Foundation for Legal Research, the award is designed to recognize excellent legal writing and to reward new contributions to Canadian legal literature that enhances the quality of Canadian legal research. The award takes the form of a $5,000 Canadian cash prize funded by the Foundation For Legal Research.

• 6972 • PAJLO Award
Promotes the use of Canada's two official languages among law students' written works relating to common law or civil law. Authors must be Canadian citizens. Groups can be acknowledged as candidates. An essay relating either to common law, written in French; or civil law, written in English must be submitted. Two prizes of $800 each are presented annually.

• 6973 • Edward K. Rowan-Legg Award
Recognizes contribution to the CBA and participation in the Canadian Legal Conference. Student members are eligible.

• 6974 • Sexual Orientation and Gender Identity Conference Awards
Recognize those within the legal profession who advance the cause of gay, lesbian, bisexual, transgendered and two-spirited (GLBT) people. The awards will recognize the contribution of women and men, and will alternate each year between the genders. The (1) Sogic Ally is open to members not included in the (GLBT) community who have had a single significant action or several actions in a career. (2) Sogic Hero is for members of the (GLBT) community who have similarly contributed.

• 6975 • Louis St-Laurent Award of Excellence
Recognizes distinguished or exceptional service to the objectives and goals of the CBA. The award is a bronze statue made in the shape of the statue crafted by Ziggy Puchta, located in front of the Supreme Court of Canada Building in Ottawa.

• 6976 • John Tait Award of Excellence
Recognizes outstanding professional conduct and competence and contribution to social justice or community affairs. Public sector lawyers and law offices are eligible.

• 6977 • The Honourable Walter S. Tarnopolsky Human Rights Award
Named for a talented human rights advocate and scholar, the award recognizes a resident of Canada who has made an outstanding contribution to domestic or international human rights. The award is administered by the International Commission of Jurists (ICJ), Canadian Section, and is an inscribed bronze medallion and an honorarium of $1,000 Canadian. The award is presented at the annual meeting of the ICJ held

during the Canadian Bar Association Annual Meeting.

• 6978 • Touchstone Award
Recognizes significant national initiative to advance equality and/or contribution relating to race, disability, sexual orientation or other diversity issues in the community. Winners names are engraved on the soapstone sculpture which resides at the National Office in Ottawa. Candidates must be female Canadian citizens who are connected to the legal profession, the judiciary, or the legal community in Canada. Consideration will be given to candidates who have undertaken a national initiative to advance equality; worked on race, disability, sexual orientation or other diversity issues in their community; championed issues of equality within the institution of the legal profession, including the CBA, the Law Societies, the judiciary, or law schools; been involved in litigating important equality issues. A letter stating the reasons for the candidate's nomination; curriculum vitae; full name, address, telephone, fax, and email information of both the nominee and nominator must be submitted. Application deadline is May 1.

• 6979 • Young Lawyers' Pro Bono Award
Recognizes outstanding pro bono legal services to the community by a young Canadian Bar Association lawyer in Canada. The winner shall receive $750 Canadian from the sponsoring Canadian Bar Financial Corporation, and will be announced in a news release and tribute published in the Association magazine *National*.

• 6980 •
Canadian Booksellers Association
Susan Dayus, Exec.Dir.
789 Don Mills Rd., No. 700
Toronto, ON, Canada M3C 1T5
Phone: (416)467-7883
Toll-Free: (866)788-0790
Fax: (416)467-7886
E-mail: sdayus@cbabook.org
Home Page: http://www.cbabook.org

• 6981 • Author of the Year Award
To the Canadian author of an outstanding literary work that is a contribution to Canadian culture and that combines readability with strong sales. An author who has offered strong support to the bookselling industry.

• 6982 • Bookseller of the Year Award
To recognize an independent bookstore for excellence in book selling. Nominees must be members of the CBA. Selection criteria is based on the standard of store fitting; range of stock relative to store size; helpfulness and knowledge of staff; overall store atmosphere; customer service and new initiatives; and buying judgment. Awarded annually.

• 6983 • Campus Bookseller of the Year Award
Recognizes excellence in book retailing. Awarded to a university or college campus bookstore. Nominees must be members of the CBA. Selection criteria based on standard of store fitting; range of stock relative to store size; helpfulness and knowledge of staff; overall store atmosphere; customer service and new initiatives; and buying judgment. Awarded annually.

• 6984 • Chain Bookseller of the Year Award
Recognizes excellence in book retailing. Awarded to a chain (more than one store). Nominees must be members of the CBA. Selection criteria based on standard of store fitting; range of stock relative to store size; helpfulness and knowledge of staff; overall store atmosphere; customer service and new initiatives; and buying judgment. Deadline for nominations is March 31.

• 6985 • Children's Illustrator of the Year Award
Awarded to a Canadian illustrator who through their work on Children's literature has demonstrated artistic merit while complementing and enhancing the storyline.

• 6986 • Distributor of the Year Award
Recognizes outstanding support of the bookselling industry. Nominees must be members of the CBA. Selection criteria based on customer service; accuracy and speed of order fulfillment; correct invoicing; and efficient handling of returns and credits. Awarded annually.

• 6987 • Editor of the Year Award
Recognizes an in-house editor for excellence in the field. Selection criteria based on all-around skills; building of new authors; commitment to quality; commercial awareness; and originality. Awarded annually.

• 6988 • Fiction Book of the Year Award
For a Canadian work of fiction that had an outstanding impact on the Canadian bookselling industry, created wide media attention, brought people into bookstores, and had strong sales. Awarded annually.

• 6989 • First-Time Author of the Year Award
Recognizes an author for first-time achievement in the bookselling industry. Nominees must be Canadian authors whose first book is a contribution to Canadian culture and that combines readability with strong sales. Deadline for nominations is March 31.

• 6990 • Lifetime Achievement Award (Author)
Recognizes outstanding literary work that continues to contribute to Canadian culture and that combines readability with strong sales. Nominees must be Canadian authors with fifteen or more years experience. Deadline for nominations is March 31.

• 6991 • Non-Fiction Book of the Year Award
Awarded for a Canadian work of non-fiction that had an outstanding impact on the Canadian bookselling industry, created wide media attention, brought people into bookstores, and had strong sales. Awarded annually.

• 6992 • Publisher of the Year Award
Recognizes outstanding contribution to the Canadian bookselling industry. Nominees must be members of CBA. Selection criteria based on consistent high quality; editorial, production, and marketing skills; author loyalty; list building; and commercial success. Awarded annually.

• 6993 • Sales Representative of the Year Award
Recognizes excellence in customer service; product knowledge; selling skills; commitment to special promotions; market intelligence; and territory coverage. Nominees must be members of the CBA in the Prairie Provinces. Presented annually in memory of Gordon S. Garner.

• 6994 • Specialty Book of the Year
Awarded to a Canadian author of an outstanding work on a specialty area such as culinary, children's, performing arts, poetry, mystery, business, travel, etc.

• 6995 • Specialty Bookseller of the Year Award
Recognizes excellence in book retailing. Awarded to a specialty bookstore. Nominees must be members of the CBA. Selection criteria is based on the standard of store fitting; range of stock relative to store size; helpfulness and knowledge of staff; overall store atmosphere; customer service and new initiatives; and buying judgment. Awarded annually.

• 6996 •
Canadian Broadcasting Corp.
Robert Rabinovich, Pres.
Radio Communications
PO Box 500, Sta. A
Toronto, ON, Canada M5W 1E6
Phone: (416)205-3311
Toll-Free: (866)306-INFO
Fax: (416)205-6040
Home Page: http://www.cbc.ca

• 6997 • CBC Radio National Competition for Amateur Choirs
To offer opportunities for public exposure and to promote the development of Canadian amateur choirs. Prizes are awarded when merited in eight categories: Children's Choir, Youth Choirs, Adult Mixed Choirs, Adult Mixed Chamber Choirs, Adult Equal Voice Choirs, Large Choirs, Traditional and Ethnic Choirs, and Contemporary Choral Music. The following monetary prizes are awarded: a first prize of $3,000 in each of the eight categories; a second prize of $2,000 in each of the eight categories; two special monetary prizes of $1,000 for the best performance of a Canadian work by a children's or youth choir and by an adult choir; the $5,000

Canada Council Healey Willan Grand Prize for the choir that gives the most convincing performance in terms of musicianship, technique, and program; Awarded biennially. Established in 1976.

• 6998 • CBC Radio National Competition for Young Composers

To discover talent in music composition among young Canadians and to provide them with access to the airwaves. Canadian citizens or landed immigrants under the age of 30 are considered for the award. Up to $35,000 in prizes is offered for works in three categories: music for orchestra, electronic music (up to eight performers on electronic instruments or works combining acoustic and electronic instruments), and chamber music (up to 12 performers). The monetary prizes are awarded as follows: a grand prize of $5,000; a first prize of $5,000 in each of three categories; a second prize of $4,000 in each category; and a third prize of $1,000 in each category. Awarded biennially. Established in 1973.

• 6999 • CBC Radio National Competition for Young Performers

To offer young Canadian talent opportunities for exposure and to serve as a springboard for young Canadian performers. Categories alternate every two years: 1994-95 will feature piano and voice; 1996-97 will feature strings, woodwind, and brass. Canadian citizens or permanent residents between the ages of 15 and 30 (singers between 15 and 35) are considered for the award. The following prizes are awarded: a first prize of $8,000; a second prize of $5,000; and two special prizes of $2,000 each for the best performance of a Canadian work. Awarded biennially. Established in 1959. Formerly: CBC Radio Talent Competition.

• 7000 • Tilden Canadian Literary Awards

For recognition of original, unpublished works by Canadian writers in three categories: Short Story - 15-20 minutes long, or approximately 2500-3500 words; Poetry - 15-20 minutes long or approximately 2000-2500 words (may consist of a long poem, a sequence of poems, or a group of unconnected poems); and Personal Essay - 15-20 minutes long, or approximately 2500-3000 words. The deadline for submissions is December 31. A monetary prize of $10,000 is awarded in each category. The prize constitutes a license to perform the work twice on the CBC owned and affiliated stations of the English Language Networks and to publish the work in *Saturday Night* magazine. Awarded annually. Established in 1978. First sponsored by Tilden Interrent in 1994-5.

• 7001 •
Canadian Brown Swiss and Braunvieh Association
Jessie Weir, Sec.-Mgr.
RR No. 5, Hwy. 6
Guelph, ON, Canada N1H 6J2
Phone: (519)821-2811
Fax: (519)763-6582
E-mail: brownswiss@promark.ca
Home Page: http://www.clrc.on.ca/bswiss.html

• 7002 • Production Award

Recognizes farms with outstanding milk production. Awarded annually.

• 7003 • Show Award

Annual award of recognition.

• 7004 •
Canadian Bureau for International Education
Dr. Rob Turner, Chm.
220 Laurier Ave. W, Ste. 1550
Ottawa, ON, Canada K1P 5Z9
Phone: (613)237-4820
Fax: (613)237-1073
E-mail: info@cbie.ca
Home Page: http://www.cbie.ca

• 7005 • CIDA Awards for Canadians

To assist Canadians wishing to further develop their expertise in the field of international development. Applicants must be Canadian citizens (landed immigrants are not eligible), possess an undergraduate degree or diploma, and have a definite commitment and suitability for a career in the field of international development. Application deadline is March 31. Approximately 50 awards of up to $15,000 are awarded annually. Two categories of eligible applicants: 1. academic- for master level research or work, 2. professional- involved in International development through a volunteer project. Recipients develop research programs lasting up to 12 months in various sectors of international development assistance. Established in 1972.

• 7006 • CIDA Awards for Professionals

To assist mid-career Canadians working in the private and public sectors, who are interested in deepening their understanding of the cultural, political, historical, economic, and social forces that influence international development, and building long-term commercial relations with the developing world. Canadian citizens who possess a college or university degree, have at least seven years work experience (two of which have involved using the specific technical, managerial, or professional skills necessary to undertake the proposed project), and have a working knowledge of the language of the host country are eligible. Application deadline is May 31. Awards of up to $15,000 are given annually for projects of up to six months duration. Established in 1990.

• 7007 •
Canadian Burn Survivors Association
Donna Spence, Contact
Sunnybrook & Women's College Health Centre
247 Willow St.
Truro, NS, Canada B2N 5A3
Phone: (902)895-4895
Phone: (902)896-0005
E-mail: burnsurvivors@hotmail.com
Home Page: http://cburnsa.netfirms.com/welcome.htm

• 7008 • Achievement

Annual award of recognition for individual abilities. Inquire for application details.

• 7009 • Co-Sponsor Award

Annual award of recognition for individual abilities. Inquire for application details.

• 7010 • Volunteer of Year Award

Annual award of recognition for individual abilities. Inquire for application details.

• 7011 •
Canadian Business Press
Philip J. Boyd, Pres.
4195 Dundas St. W, Ste. 346
Toronto, ON, Canada M8X 1Y4
Phone: (416)239-1022
Fax: (416)239-1076
E-mail: admin@cbp.ca
Home Page: http://www.cbp.ca

• 7012 • Kenneth Wilson Awards

Recognizes individuals exhibiting excellence in graphic design and writing. Awarded annually.

• 7013 •
Canadian Camping Association
(Association des Camps du Canada)
Ramona Bortnowschi, Off.Admin.
PO Box 74030
Edmonton, AB, Canada T5K 2S7
Phone: (780)427-6605
Toll-Free: 877-427-6958
Fax: (780)427-6695
E-mail: info@ccamping.org
Home Page: http://www.ccamping.org

• 7014 • Achievement of Excellence

Recognizes individuals exhibiting outstanding commitment to the CCA over a prolonged period of time. Awarded annually.

• 7015 • Award of Honour

Recognizes individuals, camps, agencies, or corporations providing services to the CCA. Awarded annually.

• 7016 • Certificate of Appreciation

Recognizes individuals, camps, agencies, or corporations contributing to camping. Awarded periodically.

• 7017 • Letter from the CCA/ACC President
Recognizes individuals providing volunteer services to camps. Awarded periodically.

• 7018 • Volunteer Award
Recognizes individuals providing volunteer services to the CCA. Awarded annually.

• 7019 •
Canadian Catholic School Trustees Association
(Association Canadienne Des Commissaires D'Ecoles Catholiques)
Greg McNally, Exec.Dir.
Catholic Education Centre
570 W. Hunt Club Rd.
Nepean, ON, Canada K2G 3R4
Phone: (416)229-4455
Fax: (416)229-3187
E-mail: ccsta@tcdsb.org
Home Page: http://www.ccsta.ca

• 7020 • Justice J.A. Higgins Award
For exemplary service to Catholic education in Canada. Awarded annually.

• 7021 •
Canadian Celiac Association
(L'Association Canadienne de la Maladie Coeliaque)
Raji Sandhu, Exec.Asst.
5170 Dixie Rd., Ste. 204
Mississauga, ON, Canada L4W 1E3
Phone: (905)507-6208
Toll-Free: 800-363-7296
Fax: (905)507-4673
E-mail: customerservice@celiac.ca
Home Page: http://www.celiac.ca

• 7022 • JA Campbell Research Award
Annual award of recognition. Established gastroenterologists are eligible.

• 7023 • Young Investigators Award
Annual award of recognition. Medical students working on research for celiac disease or DH are eligible.

• 7024 •
Canadian Centre for Architecture
(Centre Canadien d'Architecture)
Dr. Phyllis Lambert, Chair
1920, rue Baile
Montreal, QC, Canada H3H 2S6
Phone: (514)939-7001
Fax: (514)939-7034
E-mail: ref@cca.qc.ca
Home Page: http://www.cca.qc.ca

• 7025 • CCA Competition
For the design of cities. $100,000 U.S. is awarded every three years.

• 7026 •
Canadian Centre for Ecumenism
(Centre Canadien d'Oecumenisme)
Dr. Janet Bigland-Pritchard, Dir.
2065 rue Sherbrooke W
Montreal, QC, Canada H3H 1G6
Phone: (514)937-9176
Fax: (514)937-4986
E-mail: ccocce@oecumenisme.ca
Home Page: http://www.oecumenisme.ca/cco/index_en.htm

• 7027 • Ecumenical Leadership Award
Recognizes outstanding ecumenical activities at local levels. Awarded annually.

• 7028 •
Canadian Club of New York
30 W 44th St.
New York, NY 10036
Phone: (212)403-6508
Fax: (206)279-4761
E-mail: membership@canadianassociationny.org

• 7029 • Arts and Letters Award
To recognize outstanding Canadians. Awarded annually. Established in 1982. Additional information is available from Ann Garneau, Cultural Affairs Office, Canadian Consulate, 1251 Avenue of the Americas, New York, NY 10020-1175, phone: (212) 596-1261.

• 7030 •
Canadian Co-Operative Wool Growers
Donna Zeman, Exec.Dir.
142 Franktown Rd.
Box 130
Carleton Place, ON, Canada K7C 3P3
Phone: (613)257-2714
Toll-Free: 800-488-2714
Fax: (613)257-8896
E-mail: ccwghq@wool.ca
Home Page: http://www.wool.ca

• 7031 • Certificate of Merit - Commercial Wool Production in Canada
To recognize those growers who best support the co-operative method of marketing wool through their knowledge and efforts of producing wool that goes far to promote Canadian wool to buyers. The selection is made by a panel of judges representing the shearing, warehousing, grading, selling, and buying aspects of wool. Consideration is given to volume, breeding, care of the fleece, proper preparation, and shipment to the Co-op. Factors such as geographic location are considered as well as allowances for unavoidable variations in things such as climate. Canadian wool producers are eligible for consideration by December 31. Plaques are awarded at the annual meeting. Established in 1980. meeting. Established in 1980.

• 7032 • Honorary Knights of the Golden Fleece
For recognition of achievement and contribution to the Canadian Co-operative Wool Growers Limited and to agriculture in Canada. Personnel and/or directors of the Co-operative are eligible. A plaque is awarded when merited at the annual meeting. Established in 1937.

• 7033 •
Canadian Community Newspapers Association
John Hinds, Exec.Dir.
8 Market St., Ste. 300
Toronto, ON, Canada M5E 1M6
Phone: (416)482-1090
Toll-Free: 877-305-2262
Fax: (416)482-1908
E-mail: info@ccna.ca
Home Page: http://www.communitynews.ca

Formerly: (1971) Canadian Weekly Newspapers Association.

• 7034 • Better Newspapers Competition
To recognize excellence in Canadian newspapers. Awards are presented in the following categories: General Excellence - awards are presented for Best All-Round, Best Front Page, and Best Editorial Page in six categories based on circulation size; Canadian Forces Base Papers; Premier Awards for Environmental Writing, National Newspaper Week coverage, Local Cartoon, Agricultural Edition, Outstanding Columnist, Community Service, Reporter Initiative, National Editorial, Local Editorial, News Story, and House Ad; and Special Competitions - three awards are presented in each of the following categories based on circulation size: Spot News Photo, Feature Photo, Sports Photo, Photo Essay, Christmas Edition, Sports Pages, Feature Story, Feature Series, Historical Story, Most Creative Ad, Newspaper Promotion, Car Care Pages, Car Care Section, and Special Section. Awards are presented at the annual convention. General Excellence winners receive the "Page" award, a statuette introduced in 1997. In addition, Blue Ribbons are awarded to all entrants in the General Excellence categories. Established in 1923.

• 7035 •
Canadian Conference of the Arts
(Conference Canadienne des arts)
Jean Malavoy, Natl.Dir.
804-130 Albert St.
Ottawa, ON, Canada K1P 5G4
Phone: (613)238-3561
Fax: (613)238-4849
E-mail: info@ccarts.ca
Home Page: http://www.ccarts.ca

• 7036 • Diplome d'honneur
For recognition of distinguished service to the arts in Canada over a prolonged period of time. Canadian citizens are eligible. Members of CCA may make nominations to the awards committee by December 30. A silver talisman, created by west coast craftsman Bill Reid, and a framed diploma are presented at the annual meeting and conference. Established in 1954.

Awards are arranged in alphabetical order below their administering organizations.

• 7037 • Keith Kelly Award for Cultural Leadership
Annual award of recognition.

• 7038 • Rogers Communications Inc. Media Award for Coverage of the Arts
To recognize and appreciate the consistent and/or innovative creation and production of arts programming in Canada. The producers eligible for this award must have created and/or produced a provincial or national broadcast, cable special, or a sustained series featuring the work of Canadian artists and drawing attention to the arts in Canada.

• 7039 •
Canadian Construction Association (Association Canadienne de la Construction)
Jeff Morrison, Dir. of Environment
75 Albert St., Ste. 400
Ottawa, ON, Canada K1P 5E7
Phone: (613)236-9455
Fax: (613)236-9526
E-mail: cca@cca-acc.com
Home Page: http://www.cca-acc.com

• 7040 • Ernest Dobbelsteyn Memorial Trophy
Periodic award of recognition.

• 7041 • Environmental Achievement Award
Periodic award of recognition.

• 7042 • Montgomery Memorial Award
Recognizes firms demonstrating innovation in construction practices. Awarded periodically.

• 7043 • Robert G. Saunders Memorial Award
Periodic award of recognition.

• 7044 • Robert Stollery Award
Recognizes a firm exhibiting leadership and excellence in construction. Awarded annually.

• 7045 • Jake Thygesen Membership Award
Periodic award of recognition.

• 7046 •
Canadian Council of Christians and Jews
Amanda L. Sherrington, Natl. Exec.Dir.
4211 Yonge St., Ste. 515
Toronto, ON, Canada M2P 2A9
Phone: (416)597-9693
Toll-Free: 800-663-1848
Fax: (416)597-9775
E-mail: info@cccj.ca
Home Page: http://www.cccj.ca

• 7047 • Good Servant Medal
To recognize individuals who have rendered extraordinary service to their community beyond the call of their normal duties. A scroll is awarded to one or more recipients each year. Established in 1973.

• 7048 •
Canadian Council of Land Surveyors
Sarah J. Cornett, Exec.Dir.
1390 Prom. Prince of Wales Dr., Ste. 400
Ottawa, ON, Canada K2C 3N6
Phone: (613)226-5110
Toll-Free: 800-241-7200
Fax: (613)224-9577
E-mail: admin@ccls-ccaq.ca
Home Page: http://www.ccls-ccag.ca

• 7049 • Champlain Award
To recognize achievements of those who had performed outstanding contributions in promoting and/or advancing the land surveying profession. Awarded annually. Established in 1986.

• 7050 •
Canadian Council of Professional Engineers (Conseil Canadien des Ingenieurs)
Marc Bourgeois, Dir., Comm. and Pub. Aff.
1100-80 Elgin St.
Ottawa, ON, Canada K2P 2K3
Phone: (613)232-2474
Fax: (613)230-5759
E-mail: awards@ccpe.ca
Home Page: http://www.ccpe.ca

Formerly: (1957) Dominion Council of Canada.

• 7051 • Canadian Engineers' Award-Gold Medal Award
For exceptional achievement and distinction in a field of engineering.

• 7052 • Canadian Engineers' Awards-Award for the Support of Women in the Engineering Profession
For outstanding support of women in the engineering profession and engineering excellence.

• 7053 • Canadian Engineers' Awards-Gold Medal Student Award
For outstanding leadership, contributions to society, and volunteerism by an undergraduate engineering student.

• 7054 • Canadian Engineers' Awards-Meritorious Service Award for Community Service
For exemplary voluntary contribution to a community organization or humanitarian endeavour.

• 7055 • Canadian Engineers' Awards-Meritorious Service Award for Professional Service
For outstanding contribution to a professional, consulting or technical engineering association or society in Canada.

• 7056 • Canadian Engineers' Awards-National Award for Engineering Achievement
For outstanding engineering projects or achievements by an engineering team in which Canadian engineers were involved.

• 7057 • Canadian Engineers' Awards-Young Engineer Achievement Award
For outstanding contribution in a field of engineering by an engineer 35 years of age or younger.

• 7058 • Medal for Distinction in Engineering Education
For exemplary contribution to engineering teaching at a Canadian university. Awarded annually as part of the Canadian Engineers' Awards program. Formerly: (1996) CCPE Faculty Teaching Award.

• 7059 •
Canadian Council of Snowmobile Organizations (Conseil Canadien des Organismes de la Motoneige)
David Campbell, Gen.Mgr.
29 Berkley Dr.
Riverview, NB, Canada E1B 2L4
Phone: (506)387-8960
Fax: (506)854-7211
E-mail: ccso@bconnex.net
Home Page: http://www.ccso-ccom.ca

• 7060 • Snowmobile Excellence Award
Recognizes contributions to organized snowmobiling. Awarded annually.

• 7061 •
Canadian Council of Technicians and Technologists (Conseil Canadien des Techniciens et Technologues)
Yaroslaw Zajac MBA, Exec.Dir.
285 McLeod St.
Ottawa, ON, Canada K2P 1A1
Phone: (613)238-8123
Fax: (613)238-8822
E-mail: ccttadm@cctt.ca
Home Page: http://www.cctt.ca

• 7062 • George Fletcher Award
Annual award of recognition.

• 7063 •
Canadian Country Music Association
Jan Cody, Pres.
626 King St. W, Ste. 203
Toronto, ON, Canada M5V 1M7
Phone: (416)947-1331
Fax: (416)947-5924
E-mail: country@ccma.org
Home Page: http://www.ccma.org

Formerly: (1986) Academy of Country Music Entertainment.

Awards are arranged in alphabetical order below their administering organizations

• 7064 • Canadian Country Music Association's Citation Awards
To recognize achievement in the Canadian country music industry. Awards are presented in the following categories: Back-up Band of the Year, Instrumentalist of the Year, Manager of the Year, Booking Agent of the Year, Country Club of the Year, On-Air Personality (major market), On-Air Personality (secondary market), Music Director (major market), Music Director (secondary market), Radio Station of the Year (major market), Radio Station of the Year (secondary market), Music Publishing Company of the Year, Record Producer of the Year, Major Record Company of the Year, Record Company Person of the Year, Retailer of the Year, Record Store of the Year, Country Music Person of the Year, Outstanding International Support, C.F. Martin Humanitarian Award, Independent Record Company of the Year, Video Director of the Year, Country Music Television Program or Special of the Year, Recording Studio of the Year, Talent Buyer or Promoter of the Year, and Album Graphics of the Year. Plaques are awarded annually at the convention. Established in 1982.

• 7065 •
Canadian Culinary Federation
(Federation Culinaire Canadienne)
Bruno Marti, Pres.
1281 W Georgia St., Ste. 700
Vancouver, BC, Canada V6E 3J7
Phone: (604)681-6087
Fax: (604)688-5749
E-mail: president@ccfcc.ca
Home Page: http://www.cfcc.ca
Formerly: (2003) Canadian Federation of Chefs and Cooks.

• 7066 • National Chef of the Year
Annual award of recognition.

• 7067 • President's Award
Annual award of recognition.

• 7068 • Sandy Sanderson Award
Annual award of recognition.

• 7069 •
Canadian Dam Association
(Association Canadienne Des Barrages)
R.D. Barnes, Pres.
PO Box 4490
S Edmonton Postal Sta.
Edmonton, AB, Canada T6E 4X7
Phone: (780)432-7236
Home Page: http://cda.ca

• 7070 • Inge Anderson Award
Recognizes significant contributions in the field of dam safety. Awarded biennially.

• 7071 • Student Award
Based on an essay competition. University students are eligible. A monetary award is given annually. Inquire for competition details.

• 7072 •
Canadian Dermatology Association
(Association canadienne de dermatologie)
Michelle Albagli, Exec.Dir.
1385 Bank St., Ste. 425
Ottawa, ON, Canada K1H 8N4
Phone: (613)730-6262
Toll-Free: 800-267-3376
Fax: (613)730-8262
E-mail: contact.cda@dermatology.ca
Home Page: http://www.dermatology.ca

• 7073 • Award of Merit
Awarded for excellence in leadership and contributions to the Canadian Dermatology Association over many years. Can be awarded locally, provincially, regionally, or nationally for any of the following: clinical and research activities; teaching; organizational and administrative ability; and community services.

• 7074 • President's Cup
Annual award of recognition.

• 7075 • Barney Usher Award
Recognizes the best manuscript submitted at the annual meeting. Manuscript must be in English or French, not previously published, , relevant to dermatology, and must relate to a study carried out or supervised by the applicant. Awarded annually.

• 7076 • Young Dermatologists' Volunteer Award
Recognizes outstanding volunteer medical and dermatological services to the community by young Canadian dermatologists in private practice. Awarded annually.

• 7077 •
Canadian Economics Association
(Association Canadienne d'Economique)
Frances Woolley, Sec.-Treas.
Dept. of Economics
Carleton Univ.
1125 Colonel By Dr.
Ottawa, ON, Canada K1S 5B6
Phone: (613)520-2600
Fax: (613)520-3906
E-mail: frances_woolley@carleton.ca
Home Page: http://economics.ca

• 7078 • Harry G. Johnson Prize
For recognition of the best paper published in the *Canadian Journal of Economics* the preceding year. Selection is made by a committee of three persons nominated by the Executive of the Association. A monetary award of $5,000 is presented annually. Established in 1977 in memory of Harry G. Johnson, a noted Canadian-born economist.

• 7079 •
Canadian Education Association
(Association Canadienne d'Education)
Penny Milton, Exec.Dir.
317 Adelaide St. W, Ste. 300
Toronto, ON, Canada M5V 1P9
Phone: (416)591-6300
Fax: (416)591-5345
E-mail: info@cea-ace.ca
Home Page: http://www.cea-ace.ca/

• 7080 • CEA Whitworth Award for Educational Research
To recognize individuals for contributions to educational research in Canada. Researchers or educational leaders must be nominated. A work of Canadian art is awarded annually at the Convention. Established in 1966 in honor of Dr. F.E. Whitworth, a former director of the Canadian Council for Research in Education.

• 7081 •
Canadian Environmental Network
(Reseau canadien de l'environment)
Brigitte Gagne, Exec.Dir.
300-945 Wellington St.
Ottawa, ON, Canada K1Y 2X5
Phone: (613)728-9810
Fax: (613)728-2963
E-mail: info@cen-rce.org
Home Page: http://www.cen-rce.org

• 7082 • CEN-IP
For strategic partnership on environmental issues in their international programming. Awarded annually.

• 7083 •
Canadian Federation for the Humanities and Social Sciences
Paul Ledwell, Exec.Dir.
151 Slater St., Ste. 415
Ottawa, ON, Canada K1P 5H3
Phone: (613)238-6112
Fax: (613)238-6114
E-mail: fedcan@fedcan.ca
Home Page: http://www.fedcan.ca

• 7084 • HSSFC Scholarly Book Prizes
For the best Canadian scholarly works written in English and French in the Social Sciences and Humanities.

• 7085 •
Canadian Federation of Amateur Baseball
Ray Carter, Pres.
2212 Gladwin Cres., Ste. A-7
Ottawa, ON, Canada K1B 5N1
Phone: (613)748-5606
Fax: (613)748-5767
E-mail: info@baseball.ca
Home Page: http://www.baseball.ca

• 7086 • Coach of the Year
Award of recognition. Must be nominated by a provincial association or executive member. Awarded annually.

• 7087 • Jimmy Rattlesnake Award
Award of recognition. For an individual exhibiting exceptional ability and sportsmanship on the Canadian senior youth team. Awarded annually.

• 7088 •
Canadian Federation of Biological Societies
(Federation canadienne des societes de biologie)
Wafaa H. Antonius PhD, Mgr, Admin & Planning
1750 Courtwood Crescent, Ste. 305
Ottawa, ON, Canada K2C 2B5
Phone: (613)225-8889
Fax: (613)225-9621
E-mail: wantonious@cfbs.org
Home Page: http://www.cfbs.org

• 7089 • Gordin Kaplan Award
Recognizes individuals exhibiting excellence in enhancing public awareness of science. Awarded annually.

• 7090 •
Canadian Federation of Humane Societies
(La Federation des Societes Canadiennes d'Assistance aux Animaux)
Robert Van Tongerloo, CEO
102-30 Concourse Gate
Ottawa, ON, Canada K2E 7V7
Phone: (613)224-8072
Toll-Free: 888-678-CFHS
Fax: (613)723-0252
E-mail: info@cfhs.ca
Home Page: http://www.cfhs.ca/index.html

• 7091 • Canadian Federation of Humane Societies Media Award
To recognize exceptional journalism promoting awareness and understanding of animal welfare issues. Awards are presented in two categories: newspaper/magazine and TV/radio/film. Entries must have been published or aired in Canada in the calendar year to which the award applies. The deadline for entries is April 1. Commemorative plaques are awarded each year at the annual general meeting. Established in 1987.

• 7092 •
Canadian Film and Television Production Association
(Association Canadienne de Production de Film et de Television)
Guy Mayson, Pres./CEO
151 Slater St., Ste. 605
Ottawa, ON, Canada K1P 5H3
Phone: (613)233-1444
Toll-Free: 800-656-7440
Fax: (613)233-0073
E-mail: ottawa@cftpa.ca
Home Page: http://www.cftpa.ca

Formerly: (1991) Canadian Film and Television Association.

• 7093 • Chetwynd Award for Entrepreneurial Excellence
To recognize an individual or partnership that has demonstrated private sector entrepreneurial achievement in the motion picture and/or television industry in Canada. Sponsored by Atlantis Films.

• 7094 • Jack Chisholm Award for Lifetime Achievement
To recognize an individual who has demonstrated over many years, noteworthy contributions to the success and progress of the motion picture and/or television industry in Canada. Sponsored by Kodak Canada.

• 7095 •
Canadian Film Centre
(Centre Canadien du Film)
Wayne Clarkson, Exec.Dir.
Windfields
2489 Bayview Ave.
Toronto, ON, Canada M2L 1A8
Phone: (416)445-1446
Fax: (416)445-9481
E-mail: info@cdnfilmcentre.com
Home Page: http://www.cdnfilmcentre.com

• 7096 • Lifetime Achievement Award
Recognizes career achievement and humanitarianism. Awarded biennially.

• 7097 •
Canadian Flag Association
(Association Canadienne de Vexillologie)
Kevin Harrington, Contact
50 Heathfield Dr.
Scarborough, ON, Canada M1M 3B1
Phone: (416)267-9618
Fax: (416)267-9618
E-mail: kevinhar@attcanada.ca
Home Page: http://flagspot.net/flags/vex-cfa.html

• 7098 • CFA Totem
To recognize the best lecture at FIAV congress. Awarded biennially.

• 7099 •
Canadian Football League
Tom Wright, Commissioner
50 Wellington St. E, 3rd Fl.
Toronto, ON, Canada M5E 1C8
Phone: (416)322-9650
Fax: (416)322-9651
E-mail: cflinfo@cfl.ca
Home Page: http://www.cfl.ca

Formerly: (1958) Canadian Football Council.

• 7100 • DeMarco - Becket Memorial Trophy
To recognize the most outstanding offensive lineman in the Western Division. Awarded annually. Established in 1957. Donated by the families of Mel Becket and Mario DeMarco, two prominent Saskatchewan players who were victims of the Mount Slesse aircraft disaster on December 9, 1956.

• 7101 • Canadian Football Hall of Fame and Museum
For recognition of individuals who have made contributions to the Canadian Football League as players or as supporters.

• 7102 • CFL Outstanding Player Awards
To recognize the most outstanding player in the Canadian Football League. Candidate must be an active player (not retired) in the CFL during the current season and voted upon by the members of the Football Reporters of Canada. A monetary prize is no longer given. Each player receives a ring plus additional prizes. Established in 1953. Formerly: (1989) Schenley Award - Most Outstanding Player.

• 7103 • Commissioner's Award
To recognize an individual (or individuals) who have demonstrated dedication and made a significant contribution to Canadian football. Individuals who work behind the scenes and have made an impact on the game are eligible. A plaque is awarded annually. Established in 1990 by Commissioner J. Donald Crump, CFL.

• 7104 • Leo Dandurand Trophy
To recognize the outstanding offensive lineman in the Eastern Division. Awarded annually. Established in 1975.

• 7105 • Dave Dryburgh Memorial Trophy
To recognize the player finishing first in scoring in the Western Division of the Canadian Football League. Awarded annually. Established in 1948 in honor of Dryburgh, a well-respected sports editor of the Regina Leader-Post who died in 1947.

• 7106 • Terry Evanshen Trophy
To recognize the Eastern Division Most Outstanding Player. Formerly known as the Jeff Russell Memorial Trophy. Established in 1994.

• 7107 • Norm Fieldgate Trophy
To recognize the outstanding defensive player in the Western Division. Established in 1974. Formerly: Western Conference Trophy.

• 7108 • Frank M. Gibson Trophy
To recognize the Outstanding Rookie in the Eastern Division. Established in 1975.

• 7109 • Grey Cup
For recognition of the winner of the championship game of the Canadian Football League. Awarded annually. Established in 1909 by Earl Grey, the Governor-General of Canada who donated a trophy for the Rugby Football Championship of Canada. The trophy, which subsequently became known as The Grey Cup, was originally open to competition only for teams which were registered with the Canada Rugby Union. Since 1954, only the teams of the Cana-

dian Football League have challenged for the Grey Cup.

• 7110 • Lew Hayman Trophy
Awarded annually to the outstanding Canadian player in the Eastern Division. Established in 1975.

• 7111 • Eddie James Memorial Trophy
To recognize the leading rusher in the Western Division of the Canadian Football League. Awarded annually. Established in 1950 in honor of Eddie James, the Saskatchewan all-time great running back who played for the Roughriders during the 1930's.

• 7112 • Dr. Beattie Martin Trophy
To recognize the outstanding Canadian player in the Western Division. Established in 1949 in honor of Dr. Martin, former President of the Saskatchewan Roughriders. Prior to 1971, this award recognized the outstanding Canadian rookie player in the Western Conference.

• 7113 • James P. McCaffrey Trophy
To recognize the outstanding defensive player in the Eastern Division. Established in 1975.

• 7114 • Jeff Nicklin Memorial Trophy
To recognize the player in the Western Division considered to be the most valuable to his team. Donated in 1946 by the first Canadian Paratroop Battalion in memory of its commanding officer, Lt.-Col. Jeff Nicklin, killed in action March 24, 1945. He had been an outstanding end with Winnipeg. Established in 1946.

• 7115 • Jackie Parker Trophy
To recognize the Western Division Rookie-of-the-Year. Awarded annually. Established in 1974.

• 7116 • Tom Pate Award
To recognize an outstanding player. This award is given at the CFL Outstanding Player Awards by the CFL Players Association.

• 7117 • Annis Stukus Trophy - Coach of the Year
To recognize the Coach of the Year as selected by members of the Football Reporters of Canada. Presented annually by the Edmonton Eskimo Alumni Association. Established in 1961.

• 7118 •
Canadian Forestry Association
(Association Forestiere Canadienne)
Dave Lemkay, General Mgr
185 Somerset St. W, Ste. 203
Ottawa, ON, Canada K2P 0J2
Phone: (613)232-1815
Fax: (613)232-4210
E-mail: cfa@canadianforestry.com
Home Page: http://www.canadianforestry.com

• 7119 • Forest Capital of Canada Award
To recognize communities for their commitment to and dependence on the forest, and the civic-minded recognition of the importance of the forests to the community. A community may be nominated by the Provincial Director of the Canadian Forestry Association. A certificate of recognition plus custody of a wooden trophy for one year are awarded annually, normally during National Forest Week. Established in 1979.

• 7120 • National Poster Challenge Award
To recognize the winner of the National Forest Poster Challenge. Winners of Provincial Forestry Association Poster Challenge are eligible for national judging. Established in 1960.

• 7121 •
Canadian Geotechnical Society
(Societe Canadienne de Geotechnique)
Dr. James Graham, Dir.Gen.
PO Box 937
Alliston, ON, Canada L9R 1W1
Phone: (705)434-0916
Toll-Free: 800-710-9867
Fax: (705)434-0917
E-mail: cgs@cgs.ca
Home Page: http://www.cgs.ca

• 7122 • Roger J. E. Brown Award
To recognize an individual (preferably Canadian) for publishing the best paper on permafrost science or engineering in the *Canadian Geotechnical Journal*, *Canadian Journal of Earth Sciences*, or *Proceedings of National or International Permafrost Conferences*; or to honor an individual for excellence in the field of permafrost. A certificate is awarded annually by the Chair of the CGS Cold Region Geotechnology Division. Established in 1986 to honor Roger J.E. Brown, the renowned Canadian scientist in permafrost.

• 7123 • Canadian Geotechnical Colloquium
To provide information of particular interest to the geotechnical community on topics of importance to Canadian geotechnique and to provide encouragement to a younger member of the Society in pursuing studies in its preparation. Candidates may be nominated by January 15. An honorarium of $2,500 and a framed certificate are awarded annually. The Colloquium is presented at the Annual Canadian Geotechnical Conference by the Chair of the Geotechnical Board and the Colloquium is submitted for consideration for publication in the *Canadian Geotechnical Journal.* Established in 1977.

• 7124 • John A. Franklin Award
To honor an individual who has made, during the three years previous to Award presentation, outstanding and significant contributions towards advancing rock engineering. Contributions can be either theoretical or practical. Candidates must be members in good standing of the Canadian Geotechnical Society, resident in Canada, and in the early or mid stages of their professional careers. Any member of CGS can nominate a candidate. Nominations must be received by June 1. A framed certificate is presented at the Awards Luncheon at the CGS Conference by the Chair of the Rock Mechanics Division. Established in 1993 to honor John A. Franklin, the past President of the International Society for Rock Mechanics (ISRM).

• 7125 • Graduate Student Paper Award
To encourage, recognize, and reward excellence in paper presentations by geotechnical graduate students. All graduate students at Civil, Geological, or Mining engineering departments of accredited Canadian Universities pursuing studies towards the M.Sc. or Ph.D. degrees are eligible. Student entrants must be principal authors and must have authored or co-authored their papers within the twelve month period preceding June 1 of the year the submission is made, while they were full time graduate students in residence within a three year period from first registration in their current graduate program. The following awards are announced annually at the Society's Awards Luncheon during the conference: First place - a $600 honorarium, a certificate, and a one year membership in the Society; Second place - a $400 honorarium, a certificate, and a one year membership in the Society. The Award is presented by the Vice President-Technical. Established in 1988.

• 7126 • R.M. Hardy Keynote Address
To recognize a prominent senior member of the Society at the Annual Conference by selecting the member to give the Keynote Address at the Canadian Geotechnical Conference. The Keynote Address is to be prepared in a form suitable for review for publication in the *Canadian Geotechnical Journal*. The speaker is selected by the Chairman of the Organizing Committee for the Annual CGS Conference and the CGS Vice President-Technical. A framed certificate is awarded and presented by the Chair of the Conference organizing committee. Established in 1987 in memory of the late Robert (Bob) M. Hardy, the prominent Canadian geotechnical engineer and lecturer.

• 7127 • R.F. Legget Award
This, the most senior and prestigious award of the Society, is given to recognize an individual who has made the most significant personal contributions in one of the following areas: the development of an understanding in Canada of the interrelationship of civil engineering and engineering geology through publications, research, or professional society activities; the development of theoretical and applied techniques to problems of national concern in the geotechnical field in Canada; the supervision of geotechnical or civil engineering projects of importance to the Canadian economy; the stimulation of geotechnical activities in Canada through the encouragement of co-workers, associates, and students; or any other achievements of permanent significance to the field of geotechnical engineering in Canada. Nominations by Society members may be submitted by May 15. An engraved framed certificate is awarded at the Soci-

ety's annual conference by the Society's President. Established in 1970.

• 7128 • Geofrey G. Meyerhof Award

To recognize an individual for outstanding and significant contributions to the art and science of foundation engineering. Contributions may be either theoretical or practical; concern the development of new theories or innovative applications of existing theories; novel construction methods, practices, and equipment; or contributions that have significantly advanced the art and science of foundation engineering. A framed engraved certificate is presented to the winner at the annual Society conference by the Chair of the Soil Mechanics and Foundations Division.

• 7129 • R.M. Quigley Award

To recognize an individual(s) whose paper was judged to be the best paper published during the preceding year in the *Canadian Geotechnical Journal.* A certificate is awarded annually. Established in 1973. Formerly: CGS Prize.

• 7130 • Thomas Roy Award

To recognize the author(s) of the best paper on the practice of engineering geology or geotechnical engineering in which the role of geology is emphasized. Papers published in Canada or by authors residing in Canada at the time of publication are eligible. Publication must have been within the three calendar years preceding the year in which the Award is made. Nominations may be submitted by June 1. A framed engraved certificate is presented by the Chair of the Engineering Geology at the annual general meeting. Established in 1982 to honor Thomas Roy, who is believed to have been the first North American engineering geologist.

• 7131 • Undergraduate Student Thesis and Report Awards

To recognize and award excellence in the preparation of a geotechnical thesis by an undergraduate student. Theses and reports eligible for the competition must be written by full time undergraduate geotechnical engineering students at Civil, Geological, or Mining Engineering departments of accredited Canadian Universities. There are two categories: the Thesis Award, prepared by one student, and the Report Award, prepared by one or more students. Each category has two awards: First place - a $600 honorarium, a certificate, and a one year free membership in the Society; and Second place - a $400 honorarium, a certificate, and a one year free membership in the Society. The Awards are presented by the Vice President-Technical. Winners are announced at the Society's Awards luncheon at the annual conference. Established in 1987.

• 7132 •
Canadian Gospel Music Association
Gary Dix, Pres.
50 Gervais Dr., Ste. 507
℅ Gary Dix
542 Paris Rd.
Toronto, ON, Canada M3C 1Z3
E-mail: info@cgmaonline.com
Home Page: http://www.cgmaonline.com

• 7133 • Covenant Awards

To recognize contributions to Christian music in Canada. The following Category Awards are presented: Favorite Soprano, Favorite Alto, Favorite Tenor, Favorite Baritone/Bass, Favorite Instrumentalist, Favorite Traditional Due/Group, Favorite Contemporary Duo/Group, and the CGMA Achievement Award to person(s) honored for their contributions to the overall Canadian Gospel Music Ministry/Industry. CGMA members are eligible. Winners are selected by balloting of artists and fans. A trophy is awarded annually in each category. In addition, four selected awards are given: Traditional Album of the Year, Traditional Song of the Year, Contemporary Album of the Year, and Contemporary Song of the Year. CGMA members are eligible. Winners are selected by a committee. A trophy is awarded annually in each category. Established in 1976.

• 7134 •
Canadian Hardware and Housewares Manufacturers Association
(Association Canadienne des Fabricants de Produits de Quincaillerie et d'Articles Menagers)
Vaughn Crofford, Pres.
1335 Morningside Ave., Ste. 101
Scarborough, ON, Canada M1B 5M4
Phone: (416)282-0022
Fax: (416)282-0027
E-mail: chhma@chhma.ca
Home Page: http://www.chhma.ca

• 7135 • Hall of Fame

Recognizes industry-related innovation and pioneering. Nominees must be Canadian citizens who are no longer in the industry but have at least 15 years industry experience and have built a successful business. Selection is based on outside activities benefiting the industry and personal characteristics such as ethics and integrity. Awarded annually to one or more recipients. Established in 1984.

• 7136 •
Canadian Health Libraries Association
(Association des Bibliotheques de la Sante du Canada)
3324 Yonge St.
PO Box 94038
Toronto, ON, Canada M4N 3R1
Phone: (416)485-0377
Fax: (416)485-6877
E-mail: chla@inforamp.net

• 7137 • Award of Outstanding Achievement

Candidates must have made a significant contribution to the field of health science librarianship in Canada. Periodic award of recognition. The candidate must also be currently registered as a member of the association, employed as a health sciences librarian, have been a health sciences librarian for part of a currently active career, or currently teach formally in health sciences librarianship or have contributed to the development of the teaching curricula.

• 7138 • BMC Research Paper Prize

Submissions are judged by a panel for: originality and timeliness of research; relationship of the research to the mission, strategic plant and goals of the CHLA/ABSC; appropriateness of the research method and design; and style and readability. A monetary prize is given annually.

• 7139 • Canadian Hospital Librarian of the Year Award

Recognizes the contribution of an individual hospital librarian to the advancement of healthcare and health librarianship in Canada. Awarded annually.

• 7140 • Donald Hawryliuk Rural and Remote Opportunities Grant

Supports continuing education for members in remote or northern communities. In particular with telecommunications and travel expenses involved in offering continuing education programs in urban areas. Formerly: (2006) Donald Hawryliuk Memorial Fund.

• 7141 • Honorary Life Membership

Recipients must have played an active role in the affairs of the Association, be at or near the end of an active career in health sciences librarianship, and hold a regular membership at the time of nomination.

• 7142 • Tenth Anniversary Commemorative Award

Recognizes chapter activities which have made a significant contribution to furthering the CHLA/ABSC mission. Awarded annually in the amount of $500.

• 7143 • Twentieth Anniversary Professional Development Award

Annual monetary award established in 1996, to enhance access to professional development opportunities for individual CHLA/ABSC members. The award is valued at a maximum of $200 for each winner, of which there may be more than one per year.

• 7144 •
Canadian Healthcare Association
Mary-Lou Rossiter, Dir. of Commun.
17 York St.
Ottawa, ON, Canada K1N 9J6
Phone: (613)241-8005
Fax: (613)241-5055
E-mail: info@cha.ca
Home Page: http://www.cha.ca/

Formerly: (1996) Canadian Hospital Association.

• 7145 • **Canadian Healthcare Association Award for Distinguished Service**

To recognize noteworthy service in the realm of health care leadership. Selection is based on consistent service and leadership over the years rather than for a single contribution or achievement. Personal efforts to advance the efficiency and welfare of Canadian health care institutions, to improve administrative methods, to develop national or provincial organizations, to provide assistance to other health care institutions, to foster better public relations for the furtherance of social and other legislation relating to health care, and for efforts to advance administrative policies in general are considered. A framed citation and a gift are awarded annually when merited at the annual conference. Established in 1949 in memory of Dr. George Findlay Stephens. Formerly: (1991) George Findlay Stephens Memorial Award.

• 7146 •
Canadian Heritage
Jeanne Le-Ber, Mon.
Heritage Award
25 Eddy St.
Gatineau, QC, Canada K1A 0M5
Phone: (819)997-0055
Toll-Free: (866)811-0055
Home Page: http://www.canadianheritage.gc.ca

Formerly: Environment Canada.

• 7147 • **Heritage Award**

To recognize achievement in natural and cultural heritage conservation. Individuals or groups, other than federal government employees, who have made an exceptional and significant contribution to the advancement of the heritage movement are eligible. The deadline for nominations is September 15. Awarded annually on Heritage Day, the third Monday in February. Established in 1978.

• 7148 •
Canadian Historical Association
(Societe historique du Canada)
Joanne Mineault-Dean, Contact
395 Wellington St.
Ottawa, ON, Canada K1A 0N3
Phone: (613)233-7885
Fax: (613)567-3110
E-mail: cha-shc@archives.ca
Home Page: http://www.cha-shc.ca/

• 7149 • **John Bullen Prize**

To recognize the best doctoral dissertation in Canadian history or in a field of history other than Canadian. An award is presented in each category in alternate years. Dissertations accepted for the doctoral degree during the period October 1 to September 30 of the year preceding the award year must be submitted by November 30. A monetary award of $500 is presented at the CHA annual meeting in June.

• 7150 • **Certificates of Merit Awards - Regional History**

To recognize individuals and organizations for meritorious publications or exceptional contributions to regional history. Nominations must be submitted December 1. Awards are presented in the following regions: Atlantic Canada, Quebec, Ontario, the Prairies and Northwest Territories, and British Columbia and the Yukon. Awarded annually.

• 7151 • **Albert B. Corey Prize in Canadian-American Relations**

To recognize the best book dealing with the history of Canadian-American relations or the history of both countries. Books bearing an imprint of the previous two-year period must be submitted by February 1. A monetary award of $1,000 Canadian is presented biennially in even-numbered years at the CHA annual meeting in June. Established in 1963. Co-sponsored by the American Historical Association.

• 7152 • **Wallace K. Ferguson Prize**

To recognize a Canadian citizen or Canadian immigrant who has published an outstanding scholarly book in a field of history other than Canadian history during the past year. Entries must be submitted by December 15. A monetary award of $1,000 is presented at the CHA annual meeting in June.

• 7153 • **Francois-Xavier Garneau Medal**

For recognition of a book of history of exceptional merit. A monetary award of $2,000, and a medal are awarded every five years at the annual meeting.

• 7154 • **Sir John A. Macdonald Prize (Le Prix Sir John Macdonald)**

For recognition of the best nonfiction work on Canadian history judged to have made the most significant contribution to an understanding of the Canadian past. Diaries, textbooks, edited collections of essays, translations, or books of documents are not eligible. Entries must be submitted by December 15. A monetary prize of $1,000 is awarded at the annual meeting. Established in 1978.

• 7155 • **Hilda Neatby Prize (Le Prix Hilda Neatby en Histoire des Femmes)**

To recognize outstanding articles on Canadian history. Any academic article published in Canada during the previous year and deemed to make an original and scholarly contribution to the field of women's history is eligible for nomination. The deadline for nominations is February 1. Two prizes are awarded: one for the best article in English and the other for the best article in French. Established in 1983 by the Canadian Committee on Women's History.

• 7156 •
Canadian HIV/AIDS Legal Network
(Reseau juridique canadien VIH/SIDA)
Ralf Jurgens, Exec.Dir.
417 Saint-Pierre St., Ste. 408
Montreal, QC, Canada H2Y 2M4
Phone: (514)397-6828
Fax: (514)397-8570
E-mail: info@aidslaw.ca
Home Page: http://www.aidslaw.ca

• 7157 • **Awards for Action on HIV/AIDS and Human Rights**

Recognizes outstanding contribution and long-term commitment to the field. Awarded annually.

• 7158 •
Canadian Image Processing and Pattern Recognition Society
(Association Canadienne de Traitement d'Images et de Reconnaissance des Formes)
Prof. Denis Laurendeau, Chair
Universite Laval
Ste.-Foy, QC, Canada G1K 7P4
Phone: (418)656-2984
Fax: (418)656-3159
E-mail: gel@gel.ulaval.ca
Home Page: http://www.gel.ulaval.ca

• 7159 • **CIPPS Distinguished Service Awards**

Recognizes research excellence and student training. Awarded annually.

• 7160 •
Canadian Industrial Transportation Association
(Association Canadienne de Transport Industriel)
J.E. Sisco, Contact
68 Robertson Rd., Ste. 105
Ottawa, ON, Canada K2H 5Y8
Phone: (613)726-1577
Fax: (613)726-7139
E-mail: info@cita-acti.ca
Home Page: http://www.cita-acti.ca

• 7161 • **Distribution Executive of the Year**

Recognizes an individual displaying innovation in the practice of industrial transportation and physical distribution management. Awarded annually.

• 7162 •
Canadian Information Processing Society (Association canadienne de l'informatique)
Ms. Mary Jean Kucerak, Exec.Dir.
2800 Skymark Ave., Ste. 402
Mississauga, ON, Canada L4W 5A6
Phone: (905)602-1370
Toll-Free: 877-275-2477
Fax: (905)602-7884
E-mail: info@cips.ca
Home Page: http://www.cips.ca

• 7163 • Canadian Information Technology Innovation Award
To recognize individuals or organizations who have demonstrated innovation in information technology. Both commercial and non-commercial innovations are eligible. Awarded annually with a plaque and gift. Established in 1988.

• 7164 • Canadian Software Systems Award
Recognizes a software system, originating in Canada, that has had a significant effect as evidenced by new concepts, market acceptance, increased competitiveness or influence on later software developments. This award may be given for a product or project, and may be given to an organization or group. Awarded annually with a plaque and gift. Established in 1988.

• 7165 • Customer Service Award
Recognizes an individual within the IT Sector who has consistently demonstrated a sincere, caring attitude towards their customers by identifying customer needs, taking ownership of customer problems, demonstrating the highest levels of integrity, demonstrating care and commitment in customer service, and providing innovative and creative solutions to stated problems. Awarded annually.

• 7166 • GALA (Got a Lot Accomplished) Award
Recognizes CIPS members who have made national, qualitative contributions resulting in specific advancement for the Society. Awarded annually with a plaque and gift. Established in 1988.

• 7167 • C. C. Gotlieb Contribution Award
To recognize members for outstanding contributions to CIPS, through years of substantial efforts for the Society. Awarded annually with a plaque and gift. Established in 1988.

• 7168 • Gary Hadford Professional Achievement Award
Recognizes CIPS members who are selected by their peers for their integrity and expertise, for their outstanding achievements in fields related to information processing, and for their high degree of competence. Awarded annually.

• 7169 •
Canadian Institute for the Administration of Justice
(Institut Canadien d Administration de la Justice)
Christine Huglo Robertson, Exec.Dir.
University of Montreal
Faculty of Law, Rm. 3421
PO Box 6128, Sta. Ctre. Ville
Montreal, QC, Canada H3C 3J7
Phone: (514)343-6157
Fax: (514)343-6296
E-mail: ciaj@ciaj-icaj.ca
Home Page: http://www.ciaj-icaj.ca

• 7170 • Justice Award
Mark of distinction and exceptional achievement to a person who has shown distinctive leadership in the administration of justice, or who, by his or her writings or other endeavors; has made a significant contribution to the administration of justice in Canada. Awarded biennially.

• 7171 •
Canadian Institute of Forestry
(Institut Forestier du Canada)
Roxanne Comeau RPF, Exec.Dir.
151 Slater St., Ste. 606
Ottawa, ON, Canada K1P 5H3
Phone: (613)234-2242
Fax: (613)234-6181
E-mail: cif@cif-ifc.org
Home Page: http://www.cif-ifc.org

• 7172 • Canadian Forestry Achievement Award
Recognition of unique and outstanding achievement in forestry in Canada. Objective is to encourage excellence in the forestry profession. A plaque and citation are awarded. Nominations must be received by May 1. Established in 1967.

• 7173 • Canadian Forestry Group Achievement Award
For outstanding achievement by teams and groups of natural resource managers, researchers and NGO groups in the complex, multidisciplinary field of forest resource related activities in Canada. Encourages excellence in group contribution to Canadian forest management. Nominations must be received by May. Established in 1998.

• 7174 • Canadian Forestry Scientific Achievement Award
For recognition of unique and outstanding achievement in forestry research in Canada. Objective is to encourage excellence in the field. A plaque and a citation are awarded annually as merited. Nominations must be received by May 1. Established in 1980.

• 7175 • Gold Medal
Awarded to students at each forestry baccalaureate school and each forestry diploma school in Canada, recognizing outstanding scholarship, sportsmanship and citizenship throughout the years of the program. Awarded annually.

• 7176 • International Forestry Achievement Award
To recognize outstanding achievement in international forestry. Encourages excellence in the field. A plaque and citation are awarded. Nominations must be received by May 1. Established in 1988.

• 7177 • James M. Kitz Award
To recognize the contributions of novice forest practitioners. Objective is to encourage excellence in the profession. Nominations must be received by May 1. Established in 1995.

• 7178 • Silver Ring
CIF/IFC provides this award as a welcome to the profession. It is a symbol of achievement in having completed a CIF/IFC recognized forestry program. Silver Ring signifies evidence of the national bond among Canadian forestry graduates - a bond that overrides differences in levels of responsibility, differences in employment status, differences in province of residence, and differences in language. Formerly: (2004) Foresters' Ring.

• 7179 • Tree of Life Award
Recognizes individuals who have made superior, dedicated or particularly effective contributions to sustainable forest resource management, forest renewal or sustained yield integrated management of the forest and its intrinsic resources. Awarded annually by CIF/IFC Sections.

• 7180 •
Canadian Institute of Mining, Metallurgy, and Petroleum
(Institut canadien des mines, Metallurgie et Petrole)
Jean Vavrek, Exec.Dir.
Ste. 1210
3400 de Maisonneuve Blvd. W
Montreal, QC, Canada H3Z 3B8
Phone: (514)939-2710
Fax: (514)939-2714
E-mail: cim@cim.org
Home Page: http://www.cim.org

• 7181 • Barlow Memorial Award
Established in 1916 as a memorial to Alfred Ernest Barlow, President of the Institute for the term 1912-14 and distinguished for his contributions to our knowledge of Precambrian geology. The prize is given for the best paper on economic geology published by the Institute during the preceding year.

• 7182 • Mel W. Bartley Award
The Mel Bartley Award is presented by the CIM Thunder Bay Branch to a CIM Branch which has demonstrated the most progress reaching the aims and objectives of the Institute.

• 7183 • Selwyn G. Blaylock Medal
Recognizes distinguished service to Canada through exceptional achievement in the field of mining, metallurgy, or geology. Applicants must

Awards are arranged in alphabetical order below their administering organizations

be CIM National Association members. Awarded annually.

• 7184 • Julian Boldy Memorial Award
The Julian Boldy Memorial Award commemorates the exceptional contributions made to the Geological Society of CIM.

• 7185 • CANMET Technology Transfer Award
CIM Council approved the CANMET Technology Transfer Awards in 1991. The award carries with it a $1,000 prize. CANMET, the Canada Centre for Mineral and Technology, sponsored the award to stimulate and recognize successful technology transfer leading to commercial exploitation. The award is usually presented each year for contributions to the Canadian minerals industry.

• 7186 • CIM Distinguished Lecturers
They are chosen on the basis of their accomplishments in scientific, technical, management or educational activities related to the minerals industry, and speak to CIM Branch meetings across the country.

• 7187 • CIM Fellowship
The CIM Fellowship recognizes members who have distinguished themselves through outstanding contributions to the mining, metallurgical and petroleum industries. A CIM Fellow can place FCIM after his or her name when deemed appropriate.

• 7188 • CIM/NRCan Journalism Awards
These awards are presented annually to journalists in Canada for technically accurate and balanced writing and broadcasting which enhance understanding of the minerals industry.

• 7189 • CIM Student Essay Competition
Each year, the Institute recognizes the accomplishments of the younger generation. The student essay competition recognizes undergraduate and graduate students who have submitted essays to CIM.

• 7190 • Coal Award
Established to honour CIM Members who have made outstanding contributions to the coal industry of Canada and who have also been longstanding, active participants in the Coal Division of CIM.

• 7191 • District Distinguished Service Awards
Recognizing an Institute member who has contributed much to the development of the industry and the Institute at their local or Branch level.

• 7192 • District Proficiency Medals
Recognizing a significant professional contribution to the mineral industry in each of the Institute Districts.

• 7193 • A.O. Dufresne Award
Recognizes exceptional achievements or distinguished contributions to mining exploration in Canada. Awarded annually.

• 7194 • Robert Elver Mineral Economics Award
The Robert Elver Mineral Economics Award was created in 1981, at the request of the Mineral Economics Committee. It is awarded to a Member of the Institute in good standing who has made a significant contribution in the mineral economics field in Canada.

• 7195 • Fifty Year Club
To mark the Institute's Diamond Jubilee in 1958, the CIM Council inaugurated the Fifty Year Club to which members could be elected as a mark of distinction for their continuous 50 years of long service.

• 7196 • INCO Medal
Recognizes an individual who has made a meritorious and practical contribution of outstanding importance to the mining and metallurgical industry of Canada. Awarded annually.

• 7197 • Institute Medal for Distinguished Service
Recognizes exceptional service to the Institute and the industry, not necessarily technical or scientific. Awarded annually, it was founded in 1957.

• 7198 • McParland Memorial Award
The Donald J. McParland Memorial Medal is awarded for outstanding performance in civil engineering design, general plant design, project engineering, and/or management of mine plants, and may also recognize innovations in mine plant installations or in operating and maintenance methods, as well as major improvements in equipment used in the mining or equipment manufacturing industry.

• 7199 • Members Award
Coopers and Lybrand Consulting Group sponsors this award, which is presented to one of the "Unsung Heroes" of the mining industry.

• 7200 • Metal Mining Division Award
The Metal Mining Division Award was established in 1983 to recognize outstanding achievement or contributions in the field of Mining Engineering.

• 7201 • Order of Sancta Barbara
This medal was designed by Madame Fran goise Drolet, who along with her husband Dr. Jean-Paul Drolet, President, CIM, 1978-79, donated and maintained this award "to recognize the important role played by women in the progressive development of Canadian mining communities."

• 7202 • Past Presidents' Memorial Medal
Presented to a member not more than forty-five years of age, who, by his or her accomplishments, has set an outstanding example to young members of the Institute and to young men and women contemplating a career in the minerals industry.

• 7203 • John T. Ryan Trophies
The John T. Ryan trophies are awarded by Mine Safety Appliances Canada Limited as a memorial to the founder of the company. The Canada trophies are awarded by the Institute to the metalliferous mine, the select mine and the coal mine which in the previous year experienced the lowest number of compensable accidents per million employee hours in all of Canada.

• 7204 • J.C. Sproule Memorial Plaque
Recognizes eminent achievement or distinguished contributions to the exploration and development of Canada's mineral resources in the northern region. Awarded annually.

• 7205 •
Canadian International Annual Film/Video Festival
Box 60554, Mountain Plaza Mail Outlet
Hamilton, ON, Canada L9C 7N7
Phone: (905)388-5840
Fax: (905)388-5840
E-mail: ciaff@canada.com
Home Page: http://ciaff.org

Formerly: Canadian International Amateur Film Festival.

• 7206 • Canadian International Annual Film/Video Festival
To recognize outstanding films and videos by amateurs, independent filmmakers, and pre-professional students of film. Super-8 and 16mm films and videos may be submitted by June 15. (If videos are chosen for public showing, the film version, will be requested. Submissions for pre-judging are preferred in VHS format). Awards are presented in the following categories: Best Amateur Film/Video in Festival, Best Documentary Film/Video, Best Scenario Film/Video, Best Animation Film/Video, Best Film/Video Promoting Canada, Best Humorous Film/Video, Best Experimental Film/Video, Best Use of Sound, Best Cinematography, Best Editing, Best Travel Film/Video, Best Youth Film/Video (Age Below 20), and Best Film/Video by an Independent Filmmaker, and Best Film/Video by Pre-Professional Students of Film. Trophies are awarded for first place in each category; second and third place winners receive certificates. Established in 1970. Formerly: Canadian International Amateur Film Festival.

• 7207 •
Canadian Interuniversity Sport
(Sport Interuniversitaire Canadien)
Marg McGregor, CEO
801 King Edward Ave., Ste. N205
Ottawa, ON, Canada K1N 6N5
Phone: (613)562-5670
Fax: (613)562-5669
E-mail: feedback@atsuniversitysport.ca
Home Page: http://www.universitysport.ca

• 7208 • **Stuart W. Aberdeen Memorial Trophy**
To honor the Men's Basketball Coach of the Year. Awarded annually, the trophy was dedicated in memory of the former head coach of the Acadia University Axemen. Established in 1972.

• 7209 • **Gladys Bean Memorial Trophy**
To recognize the women's Soccer Champions. Dedicated in honor of a pioneer for women in sport in Canada. Awarded annually. Established in 1987.

• 7210 • **BLG Awards**
To recognize Canadian university Athletes of the Year, and to encourage them to continue postgraduate studies in a Canadian University. The awards are based on athletic accomplishment, outstanding sportsmanship, and leadership ability. Eligible athletes must have participated in a CIS sport for a period of two years and be in their graduating year. Awarded annually to one female athlete and one male athlete. Sponsored by Borden Ladner Gervais LLP (BLG). Established in 1993. Formerly: (2003) Howard Mackie Awards.

• 7211 • **The Bronze Baby**
To honor the Women's Basketball Champions. Awarded annually, the trophy was donated in 1922 by the Students' Council of McGill University.

• 7212 • **Nan Copp Award**
To honor the outstanding women's basketball player of the year. Selection is made by the Women's Basketball Coaches. The trophy was dedicated in honor of the late official and organizer of the women's game. Presentation is made at the National Championship. Established in 1979.

• 7213 • **Hec Crighton Trophy**
To recognize the outstanding university football player in Canada. A trophy is awarded annually. Established in 1967 in memory of Hec Crighton, teacher, coach, referee, and author of the *Official Football Rule Book* and the *CIAU Rule Book*.

• 7214 • **Sam Davidson Memorial Trophy**
To honor the CIS men's Soccer Champions. Given annually, the award was dedicated in honor of a past president of the Canadian Soccer Association. Established in 1972.

• 7215 • **Peter Ennis Award**
To honor the Women's Basketball Coach of the Year. Selected by the CIS Coaches Association, this award is presented each year at the National Championship. Established in 1977.

• 7216 • **Peter Gorman Trophy**
To recognize the outstanding freshman football player at a CIS member institution. Selected by two coaches from each of the four regional conferences. Presented during Vanier Cup Week. Awarded annually. Dedicated in honor of the father of the Canadian College Bowl.

• 7217 • **Dr. Randy Gregg Award**
To reward excellence by a male student-athlete in three areas: hockey, academics, and community involvement. Awarded annually by The Sports Network. Established in 1990.

• 7218 • **Nelson C. Hart Trophy**
To recognize the university accumulating the highest point score in the men's competition of the CIS National Swimming Championship. Awarded annually. Established in 1964.

• 7219 • **Joe Johnson Memorial Trophy**
To recognize the outstanding men's soccer Player of the Year. Presented at the CIS Soccer Championship each year. Established in 1991.

• 7220 • **Fr. George Kehoe Memorial Award**
To recognize the men's hockey Coach of the Year. Selected by the CIS Coaches Association. Presentation is made at the National Championship each year. Established in 1970.

• 7221 • **Don Loney Trophy**
To recognize the most valuable player of the Mitchell Bowl game. Awarded annually by the Chairman of the Bowl Committee. Dedicated in honor of the coach with the most wins in Canadian college football.

• 7222 • **Austin-Matthews Award**
To recognize an individual who has made an outstanding contribution to interuniversity sport as demonstrated by his/her long term commitment and leadership as a coach, director, chairperson, and/or executive committee member at the local, provincial, and/or national levels of Canadian interuniversity sport. Presented in honor of Dr. Patricia Austin and Dr. Arnold Whitney Matthews in recognition of their significant role in the development of the CWIAU and CIS, respectively.

• 7223 • **McCrae Cup**
To honor the Women's Field Hockey Champions. Presented annually, the trophy was donated by the Atlantic Universities Athletic Association and awarded for the first time in 1977.

• 7224 • **W. P. McGee Trophy**
In recognition of the outstanding contribution in education and athletics made by W. P. McGee, teacher and coach at Assumption College throughout the 1920's and 1930's. Awarded annually to the winning team in the Men's Basketball Champions. The trophy was donated in 1963 by the University of Windsor Alumni Association.

• 7225 • **Marina Van Der Merwe Award**
To honor the Women's Field Hockey Coach of the Year. Selected by the CIS Coaches Association, this award is presented at the National Championship each year. Established in 1984.

• 7226 • **J. P. Metras Trophy**
To recognize the Outstanding Lineman in Canadian University Football. A trophy is awarded annually. Established in 1974, the centennial year of Canadian university football in honor of John Pius Metras who, for 30 years as head coach of the University of Western Ontario Mustangs, established a lifetime record of 106 victories, 76 losses, and 11 ties, including 9 league championships.

• 7227 • **Ted Morris Memorial Trophy**
To recognize the most valuable player of the Vanier Cup game. Selected by the media at the Vanier Cup and coordinated by a member of the National Office staff. Dedicated in 1965 in honor of the late Toronto Argonaut coach and player.

• 7228 • **Mike Moser Memorial Trophy**
To honor the outstanding male basketball player at a member institution. Presented annually at the National Championship, the trophy was donated in memory of the late University of Waterloo basketball player. Established in 1974.

• 7229 • **L. B. "Mike" Pearson Award**
To recognize a distinguished Canadian of outstanding achievement who has participated in interuniversity athletics and who exemplifies the ideals and purposes of interuniversity athletics and amateur sport. The award is presented by CIS when merited.

• 7230 • **President's Trophy (Football)**
To recognize the Outstanding Defensive Player (except for Down Linemen) at a CIAU Member Institution. A trophy is awarded annually. Established in 1980 by Ed Zemrau, CIAU Past President, and Robert Doty, Past President of the College Bowl.

• 7231 • **Fred Sgambati Award**
To recognize a member of the news media who has made a major contribution to the development and growth of Canadian Interuniversity Sport. Presented annually at the CIS Annual General Meeting.

• 7232 • **Soccer Coach of the Year**
Presented at the National Championship each year, the recipient is selected by members of the CIS Coaches Association. Established in 1981.

• 7233 • Robert L. Stanfield Trophy
To honor the winners of the Mitchell Bowl Football Game, a semi-final between the winners of the Ontario and Canada West divisions. Awarded annually, the trophy was donated in 1959 by the Premier of Nova Scotia Robert L. Stanfield, former Leader of the Opposition in the Federal Parliament.

• 7234 • Senator Joseph A. Sullivan Trophy
To recognize the men's hockey Player of the Year at a CIS member institution. Selected by the CIS Coaches Association. Awarded annually. Dedicated in honor of the goaltender of the 1928 Canadian gold medalist hockey team.

• 7235 • Swimming Coach of the Year
Selected annually at the CIS Championship by the coaches present at the Championship. Awards are presented annually in both the men's and women's coaching categories. Established in 1971 for men's coaches; 1977 for women's coaches.

• 7236 • Tantramar Trophy
To recognize the CIS men's Volleyball Champions. Awarded annually. The trophy was donated in 1967 by Mount Allison University and is named after the famous Tantramar Marshes near the Sackville, New Brunswick campus.

• 7237 • Frank Tindall Trophy
To recognize the CIAU Football Coach of the Year. The Selection Committee is composed of members of the Carleton University Old Crow Society. A trophy is awarded annually during Vanier Cup Week. Established in 1969 in honor of Frank Tindall, the former head coach of the Queen's Golden Gaels.

• 7238 • University Cup
To honor the CIS Men's Hockey Champions. Awarded annually. The trophy was presented by Queen's University of Kingston and the Royal Military College of Canada. Established in 1962.

• 7239 • Uteck Bowl
For annual presentation to the winner of the semi-final football game between the Quebec and Atlantic division champions. Established in 1956. Formerly: (2003) Churchill Bowl.

• 7240 • M. L. Van Vliet Trophy
To recognize the most valuable player of the Uteck Bowl game. Dedicated in honor of the former coach of the University of British Columbia Thunderbirds, the University of Alberta Golden Bears, and a past president of the CIS.

• 7241 • Vanier Cup Trophy
To honor the Football Champions. Awarded annually, the trophy was donated by the Canadian Save the Children Fund in 1965.

• 7242 • Volleyball Coach of the Year
Selected by the coaches present at the National Volleyball Championship. Awards are presented annually for both the men's and the women's categories. Established in 1977.

• 7243 • Wrestling Coach of the Year
Chosen annually by coaches present at the CIS wrestling championships. Awards are presented annually for both the men's and the women's categories. Established in 1974 for men's coaches; 1998 for women's.

• 7244 •
Canadian Journalists for Free Expression
Rod Macdonell, Exec.Dir.
489 Coll. St., Ste. 403
Toronto, ON, Canada M6G 1A5
Phone: (416)515-9622
Fax: (416)515-7879
E-mail: cjfe@cjfe.org
Home Page: http://www.cjfe.org

• 7245 • International Press Freedom Award
Awarded annually to journalists in Canada and abroad who have overcome censorship, harassment, imprisonment, and other threats to their work.

• 7246 • Journalists in Distress
Awarded periodically to media professionals or their families who are injured or in difficulty due to the hazards of their work.

• 7247 •
Canadian Library Association
Vicki Whitmell, Exec.Dir.
328 Frank St.
Ottawa, ON, Canada K2P 0X8
Phone: (613)232-9625
Fax: (613)563-9895
E-mail: info@cla.ca
Home Page: http://www.cla.ca

• 7248 • Award for Achievement in Technical Services
For recognition of achievement in technical services. The award goes to technical services units of libraries that have demonstrated achievement through: planning and implementing of an ongoing program, service, or special project; developing or utilizing new or improved methods, techniques, or routines; or implementing an innovative approach to solving a problem in any aspect of technical services. Any technical services unit whose library has an institutional membership in CLA may apply. Applications must be submitted by February 28. Awarded annually. Co-sponsored by 3M Canada.

• 7249 • CLA/Information Today Award for Innovative Technology
To honor CLA members for innovative use and application of technology in a Canadian library setting. Candidates are evaluated on the following criteria: innovation/use of technology to clients served, benefit of innovation/use of technology to the information community, impact of innovation/use on library operations, marketability of innovation/use, and impact of innovation/use on perception on the library or librarian in the work setting and to the specialized or general public. Winners are announced at the CLA Annual Conference, where they are presented with a $500 honorarium and an engraved plaque. Nominees must be members in good standing of CLA. Nomination deadline is February 28. Awarded annually. Sponsored by Information Today Inc. Formerly: (1996) CLA/Meckler Award for Innovative Technology.

• 7250 • Outstanding Service to Librarianship Award
To recognize outstanding service to Canadian public librarianship. The highest honor granted by CLA, a scroll and bronze plaque are awarded annually. The contribution made by the recipient should represent an achievement that is outstanding in its own field, and of lasting significance in the development of Canadian library service. Established in 1979. Letters of nomination should be sent to Chair, Special Awards Committee, % CLA. Nomination deadline is January 31.

• 7251 • Student Article Contest
To honor outstanding articles that discuss, analyze, or evaluate timely issues pertaining to librarianship or information science. The contest is open to all students registered in or recently graduated from a Canadian library school, library techniques program, or faculty of education library program. Registered students may be full- or part-time; graduate students must have completed their studies within one year of the competition's closing date. Articles must have been written while the student was enrolled in a program of study or within one year of graduation. Contestants must submit a faculty member's statement attesting to the fact that the article was written in accordance with the above requirements. Manuscript length should be between 2,500 and 5,000 words and may be in English or French. Judges look for originality, value and relevance of the information presented, consistency and accuracy, style and readability, and suitability for publication. The deadline for submissions is March 31. The first-prize winner receives $150 and free registration, accommodation, and transportation to CLA's Annual Conference; the winning article is published in *Feliciter*. Runners-up receive $75 worth of CLA publications as well as a monetary prize. All winners receive a copy of Micromedia's *Directory of Libraries in Canada*. Held annually.

• 7252 • Young Adult Canadian Book Award
To recognize the author of an outstanding English-language Canadian book that appeals to young adults between the ages of 13 and 18. To be eligible for consideration, the book must be a work of fiction (novel or collection of short stories). The book may be published in Canada in hardcover or paperback and the author must be a Canadian citizen or a landed immigrant. Entry deadline is December 31. A leather-bound copy

with the title, author, and award seal embossed on the cover in gold is awarded annually by the Young Adult Services Interest Group. Established in 1980.

• 7253 •
Canadian Library Association
Canadian Association of Children's Librarians
Don Butcher, Exec.Dir.
328 Frank St.
Ottawa, ON, Canada K2P 0X8
Phone: (613)232-9625
Fax: (613)563-9895
E-mail: info@cla.ca
Home Page: http://www.cla.ca

• 7254 • Canadian Library Association Book of the Year for Children Award
To recognize the author of a children's book published in Canada during the previous calendar year. The book must be written by a Canadian citizen or permanent resident. Any piece of creative writing is eligible. A silver gilt medal is awarded annually. Established in 1947. Application deadline is January 1st. Nominations should be sent to Melody Wood Moosejaw Public Library 461 Crescent, Moosejaw, SK Canada S6H 0X6, Phone (306) 6922787, email: mwood@pallister.libsk.ca Formerly: Book of the Year for Children Medal.

• 7255 •
Canadian Library Association
Canadian Association of Public Libraries
Vicki Whitmell, Exec.Dir.
328 Frank St.
200 Elgin St., Ste. 602
Ottawa, ON, Canada K2P 0X8
Phone: (613)232-9625
Fax: (613)563-9895
E-mail: info@cla.ca
Home Page: http://www.cla.ca

• 7256 • CAPL Public Library Services Award
To recognize a CAPL member who has made an outstanding contribution to public libraries at the local, provincial, or national level. Awarded annually. Nominations should be sent to Chair, CAPL Public Library Services Award Committee. Nomination deadline is January 31.

• 7257 • Rowe Marketing Award
To recognize public libraries with an award-winning public relations program, project, or campaign. The award includes airfare for one library representative to travel to the CLA Conference and a recognition award for display in the winning library. Application deadline is February 1.

• 7258 •
Canadian Library Association
Canadian School Library Association
Vicki Whitmell, Exec.Dir.
328 Frank St.
Ottawa, ON, Canada K2P 0X8
Phone: (613)232-9625
Fax: (613)563-9895
E-mail: info@cla.ca
Home Page: http://www.cla.ca

• 7259 • Book of the Year for Children Award
To merit consideration for the Medal, a book must have been published in Canada during the award year and the author must be a Canadian citizen or a permanent resident of Canada. Any work that is an act of creative writing, including fiction, poetry, and retelling of traditional literature is eligible. Nominations should be sent by January 1 to the Chair, Book of the Year Award Committee. Awarded annually.

• 7260 • Amelia Frances Howard-Gibbon Illustrator's Award
To recognize an outstanding illustrator of a children's book published in Canada during the award year. Eligible illustrators must be Canadian citizens or permanent residents of Canada and the text of the book must be worthy of the illustrations. Nominations should be sent by January 1 to Chair, Amelia Frances Howard-Gibbon Illustrator's Award Committee. Awarded annually.

• 7261 • National Book Service Teacher-Librarian of the Year Award
To recognize school-based teacher-librarians who have made outstanding contributions to school librarianship in Canada through planning and implementing school library programs, based on a collaborative model that integrates library and classroom programs. Deadline February 28. Awarded annually. Sponsored by National Book Service.

• 7262 • Margaret B. Scott Award of Merit
The Margaret B. Scott Award of Merit is given annually to honour an individual who has made an outstanding contribution to Canadian school librarianship at the national level. Formerly: Canadian School Library Association Merit Award.

• 7263 •
Canadian Library Trustees' Association
Brenda Shields, Exec.Dir.
% Canadian Library Association
328 Frank St.
Ottawa, ON, Canada K2P 0X8
Phone: (613)232-9625
Fax: (613)563-9895
E-mail: bshields@cla.ca
Home Page: http://www.cla.ca/divisions/clta/clta.htm

• 7264 • CLTA Achievement in Literacy Award
The CLTA Achievement in Literacy Award is presented annually to a public library board that has initiated an innovative program that is contributing significantly to the advancement of literacy in its community. Criteria: (1) Any public library board in Canada is eligible for the award. (2) Members or employees of the public library board are eligible to nominate their own board. (3) Each nomination must be sponsored by at least two individuals. (4) Nominations must be submitted on an official nomination form, available from the CLA Office or any member of the CLTA executive, and accompanied by required documentation. (5) The award will be presented at the time of the annual Canadian Library Association Conference. (6) If, in any year, no appropriate recipient is identified by the CLTA Achievement in Literacy Award Committee, no award will be made. For further information and an official CLTA Achievement in Literacy Award nomination form, contact Brenda Shields, Member Services, CLA Office, (613) 232-9625, Ext. 318; Fax: (613) 563-9895. Send nominations to Chair, CLTA Achievement in Literacy Award, % Brenda Shields, Canadian Library Association, 200 Elgin St., Suite 602, Ottawa, ON K2P 1L5. All nominations must be received by March 1.

• 7265 • CLTA Merit Award
The CLTA Merit Award is presented annually to a library trustee who has demonstrated outstanding leadership in the advancement of trusteeship and public library service in Canada. Criteria: (1) Nominee must be a current or past member of CLTA, who has provided distinguished service as a trustee at the local/regional, provincial or national levels, (any two levels of outstanding service). (2) Each nomination must be sponsored by at least two members of the Canadian Library Trustees Association. (3) Nominations must be submitted on an official nomination form, available from the CLA Office or any member of the CLTA executive, and accompanied by required documentation. (4) The award will be presented at the time of the annual Canadian Library Association conference. (5) If, in any year, no appropriate recipient is identified by the CLTA Merit Award Committee, no award will be made. For more information and an official CLTA Merit Award nomination form, contact Brenda Shields, Member Services, CLA Office, (613) 232-9625, Ext. 318; Fax: (613) 563-9895. Send nominations to CLTA Merit Award Committee, % Brenda Shields, Canadian Library Association, 200 Elgin St., Suite 602, Ottawa, ON K2P 1L5. All nominations must be received by March 1.

• 7266 •
Canadian Mental Health Association (Association Canadienne pour la Sante Mentale)
Penelope Marrett, Gen.Dir.
8 King St. E, Ste. 810
Toronto, ON, Canada M5C 1B5
Phone: (416)484-7750
Fax: (416)484-4617
E-mail: info@cmha.ca
Home Page: http://www.cmha.ca

• 7267 • Consumer Involvement Award
To recognize individuals or groups who have promoted consumer participation within CMHA. Nominations are accepted from any group or individual within CMHA. Established in 1988. Formerly: (2006) Consumer Participation Award.

• 7268 • C. M. Hincks Award
To recognize an outstanding individual or organization whose spirit, social commitment, and persistent endeavors have contributed significantly to the advancement of mental health in Canada. Individuals or organizations from the private, public, and voluntary sector are eligible for nomination. The deadline for nominations is July 1. Awarded annually. Established in 1986 to honor the founder of the Association.

• 7269 • Marjorie Hiscott Keyes Award
To recognize a psychiatric nurse who, in the course of duties, has demonstrated interest, understanding, and warmth of personality in daily contact with troubled people. Individuals who reside in Canada are eligible. A medal is awarded annually. Established in 1961 to honor Marjorie Hiscott Keyes, the first psychiatric social worker in Canada's first psychiatric clinic.

• 7270 • Mental Health in the Workplace Award
To recognize an organization that has demonstrated the promotion of mental health in the workplace and cooperation between employers, employees, and community agencies within the workplace. Any organization from the private, public, and voluntary sector, unions or employee associations, or a combination of an employer and union/employee association working together is considered eligible for nomination. The deadline for nominations is July 1. Established in 1988 as part of CMHA's five-year Mental Health in the Workplace Project.

• 7271 • National Distinguished Service Awards
To recognize the efforts of volunteers in every region across Canada who have advanced CMHA's cause in some singular manner. Awarded by the National President at the National Conference and/or at the Divisional Annual General Meeting. Established in 1982.

• 7272 • National Media Award
To honor representatives in the media who have made outstanding contributions to the coverage of mental health issues. Any form of broadcast or print material that has universal appeal, issue-orientation, technical and creative excellence, impact and positive stereotyping is eligible. Consideration is given to continuous mental health coverage, one article/segment focusing on a single mental health topic, a series of mental health articles/segments, or programs or the production of a public service announcement. The deadline is July 1. Established in 1991.

• 7273 • Special Recognition Award
To recognize individuals or groups who, through their work or volunteer activities, advocate for persons with mental disabilities. Any residents of Canada not working directly as mental health professionals or as CMHA volunteers are eligible. Nominations may be submitted by July 1. A parchment certificate is awarded when merited. Established in 1966.

• 7274 •
Canadian Meteorological and Oceanographic Society
(Societe Canadienne de Meteorologie et d'Oceanographique)
Dorothy Neale, Exec. Sec.
200 Kent St.
Sta. D
Ottawa, ON, Canada K1A 0E6
Phone: (613)990-0300
Phone: (613)991-4494
Fax: (613)990-1617
E-mail: info@cmos.ca
Home Page: http://www.cmos.ca

• 7275 • Citation for Outstanding Radio and Television Weather Presentation
Recognizes the best Canadian weather program.

• 7276 • Environmental Citation
Award of recognition.

• 7277 • Postgraduate Scholarship
Fosters the pursuit of advanced studies and research in atmospheric or oceanographic studies. Applicants must be Canadian citizens or have landed immigrant status. One award is given annually.

• 7278 • President's Prize
Annual award of recognition.

• 7279 • Prize in Applied Oceanography
Annual award of recognition.

• 7280 • Rube Hornstein Prize in Operational Meteorology
Annual award of recognition.

• 7281 • Tertia M.C. Hughes Memorial Prize
Graduate student prize for contribution of special merit.

• 7282 • Dr. Andrew Thomson Prize in Applied Meteorology
Annual award of recognition.

• 7283 • J.P. Tully Medal in Oceanography
Annual award of recognition.

• 7284 • Undergraduate Scholarships
Promotes studies in meteorological or oceanographic studies. Applicants must be in their final university year and be Canadian citizens or have landed immigrant status. Two awards are given annually.

• 7285 •
Canadian Mineral Analysts
Mr. John Gregorchuk, Managing Sec.
444 Harold Ave. W
Winnipeg, MB, Canada R2C 2E2
Phone: (204)224-1443
E-mail: jgregorchuk@shaw.ca
Home Page: http://www.canadianmineralanalysts.com

• 7286 • Canadian Mineral Analysts Scholarships
Provides scholarships of $500 to students in chemical and environmental sciences across Canada.

• 7287 •
Canadian Motorcycle Association
(L'Association Motocycliste Canadienne)
Marilyn Bastedo, Gen.Mgr.
PO Box 448
Hamilton, ON, Canada L8L 1J4
Phone: (905)522-5705
Fax: (905)522-5716
E-mail: registration@canmocycle.ca
Home Page: http://canmocycle.ca

• 7288 • Ambassadors Award
Annual award of recognition.

• 7289 • Award of Merit
Periodic award presented in recognition of long standing exceptional effort or achievement which reflects favorably on the CMA or furthers the aims and works of CMA.

• 7290 • Fulvio Callimaci Memorial Supporters Award
Award of recognition. For an individual or organization providing exceptional support or promotion to motorcycling. Awarded annually.

• 7291 • Bert Irwin Memorial Cup
Award of recognition. For the leading Canadian rider at the Team Enduro World Championships. Awarded annually.

• 7292 • Billy Matthews Memorial Fair Play Award
Award of recognition. For a dirt track or speedway driver exhibiting good sportsmanship. Awarded annually.

• 7293 • Media Award
Award of recognition. For electronic or print media providing favorable coverage of motorcycling. Awarded annually.

• 7294 • Schoolboy Motorcross Award
Annual award of recognition. For the best junior Motorcross cyclist.

• 7295 • White Trophy
Annual award of recognition for the best overall performer in CMA competitions.

• 7296 •
Canadian Museums Association
(Association des Musees Canadiens)
John G. McAvity, Exec.Dir.
280 Metcalfe St., Ste. 400
Ottawa, ON, Canada K2P 1R7
Phone: (613)567-0099
Fax: (613)233-5438
E-mail: info@museums.ca
Home Page: http://www.museums.ca

• 7297 • CMA Awards for Outstanding Achievement
To identify, recognize, publicize, and encourage outstanding achievement in museum practice. Open to any individual(s) involved in the museum field in any capacity. To be eligible for an award, the achievement must exceed the current standard of museum practice; set a useful example for museum practice; be nationally significant; have been completed within the past year; have been accomplished by a Canadian or be a Canadian project; demonstrate innovation, creativity, and leadership; and reflect an effective use of available resources. The deadline is February 5. One award may be given in each of the following categories: museum management, collection management, research, presentation, and publications. Awards are presented during the annual conference.

• 7298 •
Canadian Music Competition
(Concours de musique du Canada)
Louis Dallaire, Gen.Dir.
1450 City Councillors St., Ste. 220
Montreal, QC, Canada H3A 2E6
Phone: (514)284-5398
Fax: (514)284-6828
E-mail: mus@cmcnational.com
Home Page: http://www.cmcnational.com

• 7299 • Canadian Music Competitions (Concours de musique du Canada)
To encourage young Canadian musicians and to provide opportunities for them to perform before audiences beyond the reach of non-professionals. More than $1,000,000 in general categories scholarships and in International Stepping-Stone Scholarships have awarded since it was established in 1958.

• 7300 •
Canadian National Institute for the Blind
(L'Institut National Canadien pour les Aveugles)
Marilyn Rewak, Natl.Dir.
1929 Bayview Ave.
Toronto, ON, Canada M4G 3E8
Phone: (416)486-2500
Toll-Free: 800-513-7813
Fax: (416)480-7677
E-mail: marilyn.rewak@cnib.ca
Home Page: http://www.cnib.ca

• 7301 • E.A. Baker Foundation for the Prevention of Blindness Fellowships
Assists with advanced post-graduate training in ophthalmic sub-specialties and innovative research. An academic posting in Canada on completion of training is a requirement. The amount of Fellowships is determined annually.

• 7302 • Winston Gordon Award
To recognize technological advancements in the field of blindness and visual impairment internationally. Technology developed during the past 10 years worldwide is considered. A monetary prize of $15,000 (Canadian) and a gold medal are awarded annually in September. Established in 1988 in memory of Winston Gordon.

• 7303 • Wayne and Walter Gretzky Scholarship Foundation
Assists eligible blind and visually impaired students who are planning to study at the post-secondary level. Established in 1996.

• 7304 • Arthur Napier Magill Distinguished Service Award
To recognize long and distinguished service to blind people. Nominations are accepted. Award is presented annually. Established in 1975 in honor of Arthur N. Magill, a former managing director.

• 7305 • Ross C. Purse Doctoral Fellowship
To provide for further study to develop the knowledge and understanding of blindness. Doctoral candidates whose work is directly related to the field of blindness other than prevention may be nominated. A monetary prize is awarded annually. Established in 1980 in honor of Ross Purse, who served the Institute for 33 years.

• 7306 • Torgi Talking Book of the Year
To recognize a talking book for literary merit, excellence in narration, and technical merit. Awarded annually. Established in 1989. Renamed in 1990 to honor Morley Torgov, the first winner, for his own narration of his novel, *The Outside Chance of Maximilian Glick*. Formerly: (1990) Talking Book of the Year.

• 7307 • Grace Worts Staff Service Award
To recognize an employee or former employee who has made an effective direct contribution to work for blind persons and prevention of blindness services. An award is presented annually. Established in 1983 to honor Grace Worts, a long time employee, now retired, who made an effective contribution to work for blind people.

• 7308 •
Canadian Newspaper Association
(Association Canadienne des Journaux)
Bryan Cantley, VP Member Services
890 Yonge St., Ste. 200
Toronto, ON, Canada M4W 3P4
Phone: (416)923-3567
Fax: (416)923-7206
E-mail: bcantley@cna-acj.ca
Home Page: http://www.cna-acj.ca
Formerly: (1990) Canadian Daily Newspaper Publishers Association.

• 7309 • National Newspaper Awards (Concours Canadien de Journalisme)
To recognize excellence in newspaper work in Canada. Awards are given in the following categories: (1) Politics, (2) Beat Reporting, (3) Explanatory, (4) Short Features(under 1,200 words), (5) Long Features, (6) Sports, (7) Business, (8) Arts and Entertainment, (9) International, (10) Editorial Cartooning, (11) Presentation, (12) Special Project, (13) Editorial Writing, (14) Columns, (15) Investigations, (16) Breaking News, (17) News Photo, (18) Sports Photo, (19) Feature Photo, (20) Local Reporting(under 30,000 circulation). Competition is open to all whose work has appeared in a daily newspaper in Canada in a calendar year. Monetary awards of $2,000 and certificates are awarded annually. Established in 1949 by the Toronto Men's Press Club which administered the awards until 1987. Formerly: Toronto Press Club National Newspaper Awards.

• 7310 •
Canadian Nurses Foundation
(Fondation des Infirmieres et Infirmiers du Canada)
Linda Piazza, Exec.Dir.
50 Driveway
Ottawa, ON, Canada K2P 1E2
Phone: (613)237-2159
Fax: (613)237-3520
E-mail: info@cnursesfdn.ca
Home Page: http://www.canadiannursesfoundation.com

• 7311 • Jeanne Manco Award
Annual award of recognition.

• 7312 • Media Award
Annual award of recognition.

• 7313 • Royal Canadian Legion Fellowships in Gerontological Nursing
To assist nurses who are undertaking advanced studies in gerontology. Members of the Foundation and the Canadian Nurses Association who are Canadian citizens or landed immigrants and who have unconditional university acceptance into the proposed program of study were eligi-

Awards are arranged in alphabetical order below their administering organizations

ble. Awarded annually. Established in 1984. Sponsored by the Royal Canadian Legion.

• 7314 • Study Awards Program

To facilitate a course of study for Canadian registered nurses to further their training. Applicants must already have been accepted into the program for which the award is intended. The deadline for application is April 15. Monetary awards are for $1,500-$2,000 (for those pursuing a baccalaureate degree), $3,000-$5,000 (master's degree), and $4,500-$6,000 (doctorate).

• 7315 •
Canadian Ornamental Plant Foundation
Peggy Walsh Craig, Managing Dir.
Box 21083 RPO Algonquin
North Bay, ON, Canada P1B 9N8
Phone: (705)495-2563
Toll-Free: 800-265-1629
Fax: (705)495-1449
E-mail: info@copf.org
Home Page: http://www.copf.org

• 7316 • Keith Laver Award

Recognizes an outstanding contributor to industry-government relations. Awarded annually.

• 7317 •
Canadian Paediatric Society
(Societe Canadienne de Pediatrie)
Elizabeth Moreau, Dir. of Commun.
100-2204 Walkley Rd.
Ottawa, ON, Canada K1G 4G8
Phone: (613)526-9397
Fax: (613)526-3332
E-mail: info@cps.ca
Home Page: http://www.cps.ca

• 7318 • Canadian Pediatric Society Research Award

Recognizes outstanding clinical, epidemiological, or basic research. Awarded annually.

• 7319 • Ross Award

Annual award of recognition.

• 7320 •
Canadian Paper Money Society
Dick Dunn, Sec.-Treas.
PO Box 562
Pickering, ON, Canada L1V 2R7
Phone: (905)509-1146
E-mail: cpms@idirect.com
Home Page: http://www.nunetcan.net/cpms.htm

• 7321 • Literary Award

Award of recognition. For best Canadian paper money display at the annual Canadian Numismatic Association convention. Awarded annually.

• 7322 •
Canadian Parks and Recreation Association
(Association Canadienne des Parcs et Loisirs)
Kathleen Luten, Contact
2197 Riverside Dr., Ste. 404
Ottawa, ON, Canada K1H 7X3
Phone: (613)523-5315
Fax: (613)523-1182
E-mail: cpra@cpra.ca
Home Page: http://www.cpra.ca

• 7323 • Award of Merit
(Prix de Merite)

To give national recognition for meritorious achievements at the municipal, regional, or provincial levels that have made significant and distinct contributions to the furtherance of some aspect of local parks/recreation. Canadian individuals or organizations are eligible. A completed nomination form, description of achievement, proof of benefit, proof of years in service (individuals ten or more, organizations twenty or more), identification and letters of support must be submitted. The deadline for application is April 1. A wood plaque is awarded annually. Established in 1965.

• 7324 • Harry Boothman Bursary
(Bourse Harry Boothman)

To provide financial assistance to association members in their pursuit of an approved professional development program in parks, recreation, or leisure. A nomination form (available on the web site) and a 5 page proposal must be submitted. Applications must be submitted by April 1. Awarded annually. Established in 1977. The award honors Harry Boothman, Director of CP/RA for ten years, including two as President.

• 7325 • Citation of Outstanding Achievement
(Citations pour Service Eminent)

For recognition of an outstanding achievement in parks/recreation in a national level. Achievements by Canadian citizens or organizations that have enhanced the public image, or further developed the body of knowledge in parks/recreation to the benefit of all citizens of Canada are eligible. The deadline for application is April 1. Nomination form and additional nomination criteria are available at he above web site. A wood plaque is awarded annually. Established in 1958.

• 7326 • Excellence for Innovation Award

To recognize Canadian municipalities and organizations that have demonstrated innovative leadership in Canada in the provision of parks and recreation services in the areas of facilities, culture, programs, parks, operations and maintenance. The municipalities or organizations must demonstrate evidence of public involvement and support for the innovations, as well as a lasting improvement to the quality of life for its residents. The municipality or organization will have explored partnerships with the private sector and other agencies in the community and the innovation will be on the leading edge of development in comparison to other similar communities in Canada. The innovations must set a standard that other communities can follow.

• 7327 • Honorary Life Member
(Membres Honoraires a Vie)

For recognition of individuals or organizations who have contributed outstanding services towards the aims and purposes of the Association. Individual nominees must have at least ten years of service. Organization nominees must have at least 20 years of service. Nomination form and additional application details re available on the above web site. Awarded as merited.

• 7328 • Young Professional Award

Annual award of recognition. Inquire for additional application information.

• 7329 •
Canadian Parks and Wilderness Society
Timothy Feher, Exec.Dir.
250 City Centre Ave., Ste. 506
Ottawa, ON, Canada K1R 6K7
Phone: (613)569-7226
Toll-Free: 800-333-WILD
Fax: (613)569-7098
E-mail: info@cpaws.org
Home Page: http://www.cpaws.org

Formerly: (1986) National and Provincial Parks Association of Canada.

• 7330 • J. B. Harkin Conservation Award

To recognize individuals who have served with distinction in the parks and associated conservation areas of Canada. Selection is by nomination. To be eligible for consideration, an individual must have demonstrated a significant contribution through word and deed to the conservation of Canada's national and provincial parks and associated conservation areas. This contribution may have resulted from either an individual's activities through his or her occupation or professional responsibilities or it may have emanated from the individual's activities as a citizen or member of a citizens' group. A medal and citation are awarded on an irregular basis, upon various special occasions. Established in 1972 in memory of J.B. Harkin, first Commissioner of Canada's National Parks from 1911 to 1936. Additional information is available from R. Peart, 11166 Willow Road, Sidney, B.C., Canada, V8L 5K6. Formerly: J. B. Harkin Medal.

• 7331 •
Canadian Payroll Association
(Association canadienne de la paie)
Wendy McLean, Mgr., Mktg. & Commun.
250 Bloor St. E, 16th Fl.
Toronto, ON, Canada M4W 1E5
Phone: (416)487-3380
Toll-Free: 800-387-4693
Fax: (416)487-3384
E-mail: membership@payroll.ca
Home Page: http://www.payroll.ca

• 7332 • Volunteer Awards
Recognizes individuals making significant contributions to the Association. Awarded annually.

• 7333 •
Canadian Pharmacists Association
(Association des Pharmaciens du Canada)
Jeff Poston, Exec.Dir.
1785 Alta Vista Dr.
Ottawa, ON, Canada K1G 3Y6
Phone: (613)523-7877
Toll-Free: 800-917-9489
Fax: (613)523-0445
E-mail: info@pharmacists.ca
Home Page: http://www.pharmacists.ca

• 7334 • CPhA Centennial Award
For recognition of student achievement specifically related to student activity, involvement, and leadership coupled with academic achievement. Pharmacy students who have completed the third year of a four-year program from each school of pharmacy in Canada are eligible for consideration. A monetary prize of $300 and travel and registration for CPhA's Annual Conference are awarded annually. Established in 1967 on the occasion of Canada's Centennial. Sponsored by Apotex/PACE, Pharmasave and CPhA.

• 7335 •
Canadian Phytopathological Society
(Societe Canadienne de Phytopathologie)
Gayle Jesperson, Membership Sec.
200-1690 Powick Rd.
Kelowna, BC, Canada V1X 7O5
Phone: (250)861-7228
Fax: (250)861-7490
E-mail: gayle.jesperson@gems1.gov.bc.ca
Home Page: http://www.cps-scp.ca

• 7336 • Glenn Anderson Lectureship on World Food Security
To recognize an outstanding, internationally recognized plant scientist toward the security of world food supply. Selection is by the organizing committee of joint CPS/APS meetings (or one of its subcommittees), or of the International Congress of Plant Pathology. Individuals are invited to deliver lectures either at joint meetings of the two societies, at meetings of the International Congress of Plant Pathology, or to support lecture tours to third world countries, as circumstances permit. Established in 1986 in memory of Dr. Glenn Anderson, an outstanding contributor to the stability of third world food supplies through his work in developing high yielding, adapted cereal cultivars for these areas. Cosponsored by the American Phytopathological Society.

• 7337 • Award for Outstanding Research
To recognize outstanding contributions in research in plant pathology. Members of the Canadian Phytopathological Society may be nominated by the deadline which is usually three months before the annual meeting. A medal is awarded when merited at the annual meeting of the society. A registration fee waiver, waiver of page changes for publication of an invited review article for *Canadian Journal of Plant Pathology.* Additional travel expenses at the discretion of the Board. Established in 1977 as a gift from Dr. C. E. Yarwood, a charter member of the society and major input in 1991 from the Plant Pathology Society of Alberta in memory of the late Dr. A.W. Henry. Henry.

• 7338 • Best Student Presentation Award
To recognize the best student paper on the topic of Phytopathology. In each category of presentation chosen by the Awards Committee, the Society awards engraved plaques, one-year memberships in the Society, and cash awards, the amount of which shall be determined by the Board. More than one award in each category can be made in each year. The Candidates must be either enrolled at a university or have completed a program for a degree at a university not more than six months before the annual meeting. Candidates do not have to be members of the Canadian Phytopathological Society. The presentations for which the students received the awards must not have been made previously in competition before another professional society.

• 7339 • Fellow
To recognize regular members of the society who have rendered outstanding service to the society and to the profession of plant pathology. The number of Fellow awards is limited to a maximum of three and should not exceed five percent of the total membership of the society.

• 7340 • Gordon J. Green Outstanding Young Scientist Award
To recognize excellence among young scientists, particularly research accomplishments and other meritorious contributions to plant pathology. Scientists under 45 years of age throughout the calendar year in which the award is both announced and made, may be nominated by the deadline which is usually three months before the annual meeting. A medal is awarded annually at the meeting of the society as well as a registration fee waiver for the annual meeting. Additional travel expenses are at the discretion of the Board. Established in 1983 as a gift from the widow of Gordon J. Green, an eminent cereal rust pathologist at the Winnipeg Research Station, Agriculture Canada Research Branch (1953-1982).

• 7341 • Honorary Member
To recognize an individual not normally a member of the society who has rendered eminent service to plant pathology. Awarded when merited.

• 7342 •
Canadian Professional Sales Association
(L'association Canadienne des Professionnels de la Vente)
Terry J. Ruffell, Pres.
145 Wellington St. W, Ste. 610
Toronto, ON, Canada M5J 1H8
Phone: (416)408-2685
Toll-Free: 888-267-CPSA
Fax: (416)408-2684
Home Page: http://www.cpsa.com

• 7343 • C.H. Barnes Award
Recognizes outstanding volunteer services. Awarded annually.

• 7344 •
Canadian Psychological Association
(Societe Canadienne de Psychologie)
John C. Service PhD, Exec.Dir.
141 Laurier Ave. W, Ste.702
Ottawa, ON, Canada K1P 5J3
Phone: (613)237-2144
Toll-Free: 888-472-0657
Fax: (613)237-1674
E-mail: cpa@cpa.ca
Home Page: http://www.cpa.ca

• 7345 • Award for Distinguished Contributions in the Application of Psychology
Presented to individuals who have made distinguished theoretical or empirical advances in psychology leading to the understanding or amelioration of important practical problems. The award will be made to a Canadian citizen or landed immigrant.

• 7346 • Award for Distinguished Contributions to Education and Training in Psychology
To recognize an individual who has made a significant contribution to the education and training of psychology in Canada through excellence and/or leadership as a teacher, or work as a teacher, researcher, supervisor, and/or administrator that has influenced the methods and settings utilized in education or training. The winner may also have enhanced the knowledge base in these areas through personal scholarship, or had produced work that brought about changes in education or training practices. The award is open to Canadians or landed immigrants. Awarded annually. Established in 1994.

• 7347 • Award for Distinguished Contributions to Psychology as a Profession
Awarded to individuals who have made a significant contribution to Canadian Psychology as a profession. The recipient should be someone who: (1) has influenced the method, setting or persons involved in applied practice, in ways to benefit the profession and its clients, (2) has enhanced the knowledge base of professional psychology through empirical research, (3) has exerted influence as a teacher, clinician, theorist, or spokesperson in public or professional arenas, or (4) has had the effect of bringing

about changes in practice or training performed by others, or redirection of efforts in applied work. Canadians and landed immigrants are eligible. Awarded annually. Established in 1980.

• 7348 • Award for Distinguished Contributions to Public or Community Service
Awarded to individuals who have made significant contributions, through their knowledge and practical skills, to special populations such as those who have disabilities, are disadvantaged or underprivileged, or are members of a minority group. Psychologists active in legislative, legal, political, organizational and other areas that are directed toward providing benefits to the public or community, are also considered. Canadian citizens and landed immigrants are eligible.

• 7349 • Award for Distinguished Contributions to the International Advancement of Psychology
The award shall be made to individuals who have made significant contributions to the international advancement of psychology. The recipient of the award should be an individual who has made a distinguished and enduring contribution to international cooperation and advancement of knowledge in psychology. Candidates may be from any country.

• 7350 • Gold Medal Award for Distinguished Lifetime Contributions to Canadian Psychology
To recognize an individual who has made a significant contribution to Canadian psychology as a profession. Eligibility is limited to members or Fellows 65 years of age or older in good standing of CPA. The members of the Committee on Fellows and Awards and the members of the Board of Directors of the CPA shall be ineligible. Awarded annually.

• 7351 • Donald O. Hebb Award for Distinguished Contributions to Psychology as a Science
To recognize an individual who has made a significant contribution to Canadian psychology as a scientific discipline. The individual's research must enhance the knowledge base of psychology; his or her influence must be exerted through leadership as a teacher, as a theorist, as a spokesperson for the discipline, and/or as a director of public policy regarding the science of psychology; or his or her work must substantially influence the development of psychology. Members and fellows of the Canadian Psychological Association are eligible, as well as non-members of any nationality. Awarded annually. Established in 1980.

• 7352 • Humanitarian Award
To recognize a Canadian individual or organization whose contribution to psychology is shown to have made a significant impact on the psychological health and well-being of the Canadian community at any level. Canadians and people of resident status are eligible, and the organization must be registered as such with the Government of Canada. Any endeavors that show signs of intentions for self-advancement will be removed from consideration. Awarded when merited.

• 7353 • President's New Researcher Awards
To recognize exceptional quality of new researchers to psychological knowledge in Canada. A maximum of three awards will be conferred annually in diverse areas of psychology. Eligible papers must be authored by an individual who is a CPA member with five years or less of post-graduate training expertise, and currently be in-press or been published in the previous two years. The winners will receive a certificate and $500 Canadian cash award that will be presented during the CPA Annual General Meeting. The winner will also receive a year's free membership and a free registration to attend the following CPA Convention. Awarded to three or four recipients each year. Established in 1997.

• 7354 •
Canadian Public Health Association
(Association Canadienne De Sante Publique)
Elinor Wilson, CEO
Ste. 400
1565 Carling Ave.
Ottawa, ON, Canada K1Z 8R1
Phone: (613)725-3769
Fax: (613)725-9826
E-mail: info@cpha.ca
Home Page: http://www.cpha.ca

• 7355 • Certificate of Merit
To recognize individuals, groups, or associations who have given especially noteworthy services to public health and whose contribution furthers CPHA in achieving its objectives. Nominees do not have to be CPHA members. A 300 word maximum overview, a 250 word maximum biography/profile three letters of recommendation, and a resume must be submitted. Nomination deadline is May 31st. Awarded annually.

• 7356 • R. D. Defries Award
To recognize members who have made outstanding contributions in the broad field of public health. Preference is given to Canadian contributions and individuals who have substantially supported the objectives of the Association. A medal and a citation are awarded annually. A 300 word maximum overview, a 250 word maximum biography/profile three letters of recomendation, and a resume must be submitted. Nomination deadline is May 31st. Established in 1965 in honor of Dr. R. D. Defries, who devoted a lifetime to interests in public health.

• 7357 • Honorary Life Member
To recognize individuals for exceptional excellence as an educator, researcher, or practitioner in the field of public health, as demonstrated by achievements, valuable and outstanding research, or distinguished service in the advancement of public health knowledge and practice. A 300 word maximum overview, a 250 word maximum biography/profile three letters of recommendation, and a resume must be submitted. Nomination deadline is May 31st.

• 7358 • Janssen-Ortho Award
To recognize the candidate who has significantly advanced the cause and legitimized and stressed the responsibility and state of the art of public health. Candidates do not have to be CPHA members. A 300 word maximum overview, a 250 word maximum biography/profile three letters of recommendation, and a resume must be submitted. Nomination deadline is May 31st. Established in 1973.

• 7359 •
Canadian Public Relations Society
(Societe Canadienne des Relations Publiques)
Ms. Karen Dalton, Exec.Dir.
4195 Dundas St. W, Ste. 346
Toronto, ON, Canada M8X 1Y4
Phone: (416)239-7034
Fax: (416)239-1076
E-mail: kdalton@cprs.ca
Home Page: http://www.cprs.ca

• 7360 • CPRS Awards of Excellence Program
To recognize outstanding achievement in a comprehensive PR project or program. The program must be of such magnitude as to be identifiable as a complete entity, consisting of most of the elements of normal public relations practice. Open only to members in good standing. Awards are presented in the following categories: External Communications - for external public relation programs to improve relationships with the community, to influence public attitude and behavior, to generate greater public understanding of the organization and/or to increase corporate or organization identity with various audiences; Internal Communications for internal public relations programs to improve employee-management relations, increase employee and/or management morale, motivation, organization awareness, or explain new policies or plans; and Special Events - for an external and/or internal public relations program for openings, anniversaries, and other ceremonies commemorating a one-time or series of special events and occasions.

• 7361 • CPRS Major Awards Program
This program is Canada's most coveted public relations honor for individuals and member societies. Awards are presented to recognize involvement with the profession beyond the normal call of duty. Both the nominee and the nominator must be CPRS members in good standing. Awards are presented in the following categories: CPRS Lamp of Service - for distinguished and dedicated service to the society. Awarded to a CPRS member whose personal activities and/or leadership and devotion to the society's affairs resulted in a striking illustration of the society's principles, a notable advance in society prestige, or a consolidation of the society's sound establishment; CPRS Award of Attainment - for outstanding achievement and service to public relations. Presented to a society

member whose personal activities and/or leadership, beyond the call of duty or responsibility to employer or client, made a pronounced contribution to the status and acceptance of the public relations function; CPRS Shield of Public Service - for distinguished and dedicated service in the public interest. Awarded to a member of the society whose personal effort on behalf of a public service endeavor, apart entirely from the contribution required by client or employer, was outstanding in unselfish and persistent devotion to the cause or movement; CPRS Lectern - awarded annually to the member society that has demonstrated the greatest advancement in purposes and goals through growth in membership, achievement in attendance at its meetings, development of educational programs sponsored by the member society, initiation of PR for PR activities and growth in accreditation; Membership Achievement Award - presented annually as a society award and an individual award. It is made on the basis of the most new members inducted during the fiscal year (transfers excluded); and CPRS Societal Award - for recognition of a singular but major contribution made by a society member, that has resulted in the betterment of the society through enhancement of its image in the eyes of other Canadians or the world at large.

• 7362 • Philip A. Novikoff Memorial Award
For recognition of superior and outstanding service over time as a public relations professional. Awarded to an accredited member of the Society who, in the opinion of the judging panel, has furthered the standing of the public relations profession in Canada through professional and personal contribution to: the advancement of the Canadian public relations practice, the enhancement of the Society and the betterment of the community. Nomination must be made by a current accredited CPRS member and endorsed by three additional current accredited members of the Society. Established in 1989.

• 7363 • Don Rennie Memorial Award for Excellence in Government Public Relations
Established to recognize outstanding team achievement in developing and executing a strategic approach to government communications in addressing an issue. Submissions must reflect the Don Rennie vision of excellence in strategic communications, appropriate to the complexities of a government environment. Awards program is open to teams of government communications professionals in federal, provincial, or municipal jurisdictions. At least one member of the team should be a CPRS member. A scroll and a cash prize are awarded annually.

• 7364 •
Canadian Quaternary Association
(Association Canadienne pour l'Etude du Quarternaire)
Martin Batterson, Sec.-Treas.
Newfoundland Department of Mines and Energy
PO Box 8700
St. John's, NL, Canada A1B 4J6
Phone: (709)729-3419
Fax: (709)729-4270
E-mail: mjb@zeppo.geosurv.gov.nf.ca
Home Page: http://www.mun.ca/canqua

• 7365 • Johnson Medal
Recognizes a lifetime contributor to quaternary research. Generally awarded biennially.

• 7366 •
Canadian Railroad Historical Association
(Association Canadienne D'Histoire Ferroviaire)
Maurice Gervais, Sec.
110 rue St. Pierre
St. Constant, QC, Canada J5A 1G7
Phone: (450)638-1522
Phone: (450)632-2410
Fax: (450)638-1563
E-mail: mfcd@exporail.org
Home Page: http://www.exporail.org

• 7367 • Article Award
Recognizes the best industry-related published article. Awarded annually.

• 7368 • Book Award
Recognizes the best industry-related published book. Awarded annually.

• 7369 • Lifetime Achievement
Recognizes a person for significant contribution over a period of years. Awarded annually.

• 7370 • Preservation Award
Recognizes outstanding preservation or restoration activity. Individuals and groups are eligible. Awarded annually.

• 7371 •
Canadian Rehabilitation Council for the Disabled
65 Brunswick St.
Fredericton, NB, Canada E3B 1G5
Phone: (506)458-8739
Fax: (506)457-2863
Home Page: http://nzsa.rsnz.org/index.shtml/

• 7372 • Ability Fund/ March of Dimes Canada
To celebrate and recognize outstanding leadership and dedication by a volunteer through involvement with Ability Fund/ March of Dimes. A plaque is awarded when merited at the annual general meeting. Established in 1968.

• 7373 • CRCD Award (Prix CCRH)
To recognize and celebrate exceptional leadership and personal achievement by a person with a disability. Established in 1969.

• 7374 • Easter Seals Canada Award (Prix des Timbres de Paques)
To celebrate and recognize outstanding leadership and dedication by a volunteer to children with disabilities through involvement with Easter Seals. A citation is awarded as merited at the annual general meeting. Established in 1959.

• 7375 •
Canadian Research Institute for the Advancement of Women
151 Slater St., Ste. 408
Ottawa, ON, Canada K1P 5H3
Phone: (613)563-0681
Fax: (613)563-0682
E-mail: info@criaw-icref.ca
Home Page: http://www.criaw-icref.ca/

• 7376 • Robertine Barry Prize
Honors feminist journalism. Annual award of recognition. Inquire for application details.

• 7377 • Muriel Duckworth Award
Recognizes significant contribution to the advancement of Canadian women. Feminist are eligible.

• 7378 • Honorary memberships
Annual award of recognition. Inquire for application details.

• 7379 • Laura Jamieson Prize
Recognizes the best nonfiction feminist book. Canadian authors are eligible. Awarded annually.

• 7380 • Marion Porter Prize
Recognizes the best feminist article. Awarded annually.

• 7381 •
Canadian Science Writers' Association
(Association canadienne des redacteurs scientifiques)
Andy F. Viser-deVries, Admin.Dir.
PO Box 75, Sta. A
Toronto, ON, Canada M5W 1A2
Phone: (613)548-8500
Toll-Free: 800-796-8595
Fax: (613)548-8577
E-mail: office@sciencewriters.ca
Home Page: http://www.sciencewriters.ca

• 7382 • Herb Lampert Student Writing Award
To recognize and honor any student science writer who has a science article published in a student or other newspaper or magazine or aired on a radio or TV station in Canada. Competitors must be Canadian citizens or residents

of Canada. The award is presented for original material disseminated — in French or English print or broadcasting — during the calendar year. A monetary prize $750 is awarded annually at the Association annual conference.

• 7383 • **Science in Society Book Awards**
To recognize outstanding contributions to science writing intended for and available to the general public, including children. Competitors must be Canadian citizens or residents of Canada. Entries must be in either French or English and have been published in Canada during the calendar year. All entries must be submitted by December 15. Three monetary prizes of $1,000 are given annually in the categories of children's book, youth book, and general audience.

• 7384 • **Science in Society Journalism Awards**
(Prix de Journalisme Science et Societe)
To honor outstanding contributions to journalism in Canadian media during the calendar year. Each award offers $1,000. Awards are presented for original material disseminated, in French or English print or broadcasting, during the immediately preceding calendar year. Awards are given for print, radio, television and books. Deadline is January 31. Competitors must be Canadian citizens or residents of Canada. Established in 1973.

• 7385 •
Canadian Security Association
(L'Association Canadienne de la Securite)
Tracy Cannata, Exec.Dir.
610 Alden Rd., Ste. 100
Markham, ON, Canada L3R 9Z1
Phone: (905)513-0622
Toll-Free: 800-538-9919
Fax: (905)513-0624
E-mail: tcannata@canasa.org
Home Page: http://www.canasa.org

Formerly: Canadian Alarm and Security Association.

• 7386 • **R.A. Henderson Award**
Recognizes corporation making significant contributions to the industry. Awarded annually.

• 7387 •
Canadian Seed Growers' Association
(Association Canadienne des Producteurs de Semences)
Dale Adolphe, Exec.Dir.
PO Box 8455
Ottawa, ON, Canada K1G 3T1
Phone: (613)236-0497
Fax: (613)563-7855
E-mail: seeds@seedgrowers.ca
Home Page: http://www.seedgrowers.ca

• 7388 • **Honorary Life Member**
To recognize an individual for distinguished service to the Association and contribution to the betterment of Canadian agriculture. A certificate is awarded annually. Established in 1959.

• 7389 • **Clark - Newman Award**
To recognize an individual for an exceptional contribution to pedigreed seed production in Canada and to Canadian agriculture through research, plant breeding or administration. A grant to a university of $2,500 for a graduate student involved in seed research is awarded when merited. Established in 1991 to honor George Clark, who was instrumental in the formation of CSGA, and Leonard Newman, second Secretary Treasurer of the Association.

• 7390 • **Robertson Associate**
To recognize seed growers for high standards in producing seed over a number of years. Individuals who have grown seed for a number of years and who have served the community are eligible. A lapel pin and certificate are awarded annually. Established about 1906 in honor of the founder of the Association.

• 7391 •
Canadian Ski Council
(Conseil canadien du ski)
Colin S. Chedore, Pres.
5045 Orbitor Dr., Bldg. 7, Ste. 100
Mississauga, ON, Canada L4W 4Y4
Phone: (905)212-9040
Fax: (905)212-9041
E-mail: info@skicanada.org
Home Page: http://www.skicanada.org

• 7392 • **Judith Kilbourne Award**
Recognizes an individual leaving a legacy to the sports of skiing or snowboarding. Awarded annually.

• 7393 • **National Ski and Snowboard Week Best Event**
Recognizes ski areas with most successful National Ski Week promotions and activities. Awarded annually.

• 7394 • **National Ski Safety Award**
Recognizes an individual or a group promoting skiing safety in an exemplary fashion. Awarded annually.

• 7395 • **National Snow Industries Association Recognition Award**
Recognizes the most innovative and successful implementation of the Discovering Skiing/Snowboarding Program. Groups, associations, and organizations are eligible. Awarded annually.

• 7396 • **Skier/Snowboarding Development Recognition Award**
Recognizes outstanding contributions to skier development. Individuals and organizations are eligible. Awarded annually.

• 7397 •
Canadian Society for Bioengineering
James M. Townsend, Sec.Mgr.
PO Box 23101
RPO McGillivray
Winnipeg, MB, Canada R3T 5S3
Phone: (204)233-1881
Fax: (204)231-8282
E-mail: bioeng@shaw.ca
Home Page: http://www.bioeng.ca

• 7398 • **Jim Beamish Award**
To recognize a member for outstanding work in teaching, research, extension, or industry in the area of soil and water. A plaque is awarded annually. Established in 1989 to honor Jim Beamish, the first president of CSAE and a long-time worker in soil and water management. Sponsored by the Alumni Committee of P.F.R.A.

• 7399 • **John Clark Award**
To recognize a member for outstanding work in teaching, research, extension, or industry in one or more of the fields of electrical power and processing, energy, and food engineering. A plaque is awarded annually. Established in 1986 in memory of John Clark.

• 7400 • **CSAE Fellow**
To recognize a member of outstanding and extraordinary qualifications and experience in the field of agricultural, food, and/or biological engineering. Members of the Society for ten years who have twenty years of active practice in the profession may be nominated by ten members. Awarded when merited. Established in 1973.

• 7401 • **CSAE Maple Leaf Award**
This, the highest award given by the Society for leadership, recognizes members who have distinguished themselves as leaders in the profession. Personal qualities, society activities, and professional abilities are considered. Individuals who have been members of the Society for at least ten years are eligible. A plaque is awarded annually. Established in 1977.

• 7402 • **Glenn Downing Award**
To recognize a member for outstanding work in teaching, research, extension, or industry in the area of power and machinery. A plaque is awarded annually. Established in 1987.

• 7403 • **John Turnbull Award**
To recognize a CSAE/SCGR member for outstanding work in the structural field in teaching, research, extension, or industry. A plaque is awarded annually. Established in 1971. Formerly: CSAE/CSSBI Award.

• 7404 • **Young Agricultural Engineer of the Year Award**
To recognize and encourage outstanding work by younger members of the Society. Members under 40 years of age are eligible. Awarded for contributions to Canadian agricultural, food, and/or biological engineering through design and development, extension, and management,

or research and teaching. A plaque is awarded annually. Established in 1977. Formerly: Canadian Agricultural Engineering of the Year Award..

• 7405 •
Canadian Society for Chemical Engineering
(Societe canadienne de genie chimique)
Roland Andersson, Exec.Dir.
130 Slater St., Ste. 550
Ottawa, ON, Canada K1P 6E2
Phone: (613)232-6252
Toll-Free: 888-542-2242
Fax: (613)232-5862
E-mail: info@cheminst.ca
Home Page: http://www.chemeng.ca

• 7406 • **Award in Industrial Practice**
Recognizes distinguished contributions in the application of chemical engineering or industrial chemistry to the industrial sphere. Applicants must be Canadian residents, citizens, or groups. Awarded annually.

• 7407 • **R.S. Jane Memorial Lecture Award**
Recognizes exceptional achievement in the field of chemical engineering or industry chemistry. Applicants must reside in Canada. Awarded annually.

• 7408 • **Syncrude Canada Innovation Award**
Recognizes outstanding contributions to the field of chemical engineering. Applicants must be under the age of 40 and working in Canada. Awarded annually.

• 7409 •
Canadian Society for Civil Engineering
(Societe Canadienne de Genie Civil)
Michael Langelier, Exec.Dir.
4920 de Maisonneuve Blvd. W, Ste. 201
Montreal, QC, Canada H3Z 1N1
Phone: (514)933-2634
Fax: (514)933-3504
E-mail: info@csce.ca
Home Page: http://www.csce.ca

• 7410 • **Albert E. Berry Medal**
To recognize a civil engineer who has contributed significantly to the field of environmental engineering in Canada. Established in 1987 in honor of Dr. Albert E. Berry, an outstanding Canadian Environmental Engineer.

• 7411 • **CAN-AM Amity Award**
For recognition of civil engineers who have made outstanding and unusual contributions toward the advancement of professional relationships between the civil engineers of the United States and Canada. Established by the ASCE in 1972 by the initiative and endowment of James A. Vance.

• 7412 • **Camille A. Dagenais Award**
To give recognition to those civil engineers who have made outstanding contributions to the development and practice of hydrotechnical engineering in Canada. Established in 1981 to honor Camille A. Dagenais, Chairman of the Board of the SNC Group Inc. and one of the most renowned hydrotechnical engineers in the country.

• 7413 • **Fellow**
To recognize individuals for outstanding contributions to civil engineering and to the Society. Established in 1981.

• 7414 • **Gzowski Medal**
To recognize the best paper presented on a civil engineering subject in the areas of surveying, structural engineering, and heavy construction. Awarded annually. Established by the late Colonel Sir Casimir Gzowski, past president of the Engineering Institute of Canada.

• 7415 • **Donald Jamieson Fellowship**
To provide a scholarship to candidates with engineering-related experience for full-time graduate studies in structural engineering at a Canadian university. Established in 1987 in honor of Donald Jamieson, a prominent and talented structural engineer from Vancouver, B.C.

• 7416 • **Keefer Medal**
To recognize the best paper on a civil engineering subject. Established in 1942 to honor T.C. Keefer, the first President of the Canadian Society of Civil Engineering which, in 1918, became the Engineering Institute of Canada.

• 7417 • **Leipholz Medal**
To recognize the best paper in the field of engineering mechanics. Awarded annually. Established in 1990 to honor the late Professor Horst Leipholz, a most distinguished engineer.

• 7418 • **P. L. Pratley Award**
For recognition of the best paper in the field of bridge engineering. Awarded annually. Established in 1987 to honor P.L. Pratley, a distinguished bridge engineer.

• 7419 • **A. B. Sanderson Award**
To recognize outstanding contributions to the development and practice of structural engineering in Canada. Established in 1977 in honor of A.B. Sanderson, a distinguished engineer from British Columbia.

• 7420 • **James A. Vance Award**
To recognize a civil engineer whose dedicated service has furthered the advancement of the Society. Awarded annually. Established in 1977 in honor of James A. Vance, a former President of the EIC.

• 7421 • **E. Whitman Wright Award**
To recognize a civil engineer who has contributed significantly to the development of computer applications in civil engineering. Awarded annually. Established in 1985 in honor of Dr. E. Whitman Wright, founding Chairman of the CSCE Computer Applications Division.

• 7422 •
Canadian Society for International Health
(Societe Canadienne de Sante Internationale)
Ms. Janet Hatcher Roberts, Exec.Dir.
1 Nicholas St., Ste. 1105
Ottawa, ON, Canada K1N 7B7
Phone: (613)241-5785
Fax: (613)241-3845
E-mail: csih@csih.org
Home Page: http://www.csih.org

• 7423 • **CSIH Lifetime Achievement Award for International Health**
Annual award of recognition. Only members are eligible.

• 7424 •
Canadian Society for Mechanical Engineering
(Societe Canadienne de Genie Mecanique)
Dr. M.A. Rosen, Pres.
PO Box 23027
Westgate Postal Outlet
Cambridge, ON, Canada N1S 4Z6
Phone: (519)622-8168
Fax: (519)622-8323
E-mail: csme@rogers.com
Home Page: http://www.csme-scgm.ca

• 7425 • **Robert W. Angus Medal**
To recognize the best paper on a mechanical engineering subject. Awarded annually when merited. Established in 1957 to honor the late Robert W. Angus, who was for many years Professor of Mechanical Engineering at the University of Toronto.

• 7426 • **The Atomic Energy of Canada Ltd. Award**
Recognizes the first place winner of the CSME Student Design Competition. Awarded annually.

• 7427 • **Certificate of Service**
May be awarded to CSME members in recognition of outstanding service to the Society in a particular capacity.

• 7428 • **C. N. Downing Award**
To recognize a member of the Society for distinguished service to the Society over many years. Awarded annually. Established in 1993 to honor the 1968-1970 Chairman of the EIC Steering Committee for Mechanical Engineering.

• 7429 • **G. H. Duggan Medal**
To recognize the best paper dealing with the use of metals for structural or mechanical purposes. Awarded annually. Established in 1935 to honor Dr. G. H. Duggan, who was president of the EIC in 1916.

• 7430 • **Fellow of the CSME**
May be awarded to members who have attained excellence in mechanical engineering and who have contributed actively to the progress of their profession and society.

• 7431 • **National Research Council Canada, Division of Mechanical Engineering Award**
Recognizes the second place winner of the CSME Student Design Competition. Awarded annually.

• 7432 • **I. W. Smith Award**
To recognize an individual for outstanding achievement in creative mechanical engineering within 10 years after graduation. Awarded annually. Established in 1977 to honor Prof. I. Smith, who devoted a lifetime to teaching mechanical engineering at the University of Toronto.

• 7433 • **Jules Stachiewicz Medal**
To recognize an individual for outstanding contributions to heat transfer in Canada. Awarded biennially by the Canadian Society for Chemical Engineering and CSME in rotation. Sponsored by the Canadian Society for Chemical Engineering. Established in 1983 to honor Jules Stachiewicz, who was for many years Professor of Mechanical Engineering at McGill University.

• 7434 •
Canadian Society for Nutritional Sciences (Societe Canadienne des Sciences de la Nutrition)
Mary L'Abbe, Pres.
Nutrition Research Div., Bur. of Nutritional Sciences
Food Directorate, Health Products and Food Br.
P.L. 2203C
Health Canada
Ottawa, ON, Canada K1A 0L2
Phone: (514)398-7547
Phone: (514)235-5889
Fax: (514)398-7739
E-mail: mary_l'abbe@hc-sc.gc.ca
Home Page: http:// www.nutritionalsciences.ca

• 7435 • **Borden Award in Nutrition**
To recognize a member of the Society who has made an outstanding contribution to research in nutrition within the preceding five years. Members must be under 45 years of age to be eligible. A monetary prize of $2,000 and an inscribed scroll are awarded annually. Established in 1960. Sponsored by the Borden Foundation.

• 7436 •
Canadian Society for Traditional Music (Societe Canadienne pour les Traditions Musicales)
John Leeder, Sec.
PO Box 4232, Sta. C
Calgary, AB, Canada T2T 5N1
Phone: (403)230-0340
E-mail: hsparlin@yorku.ca
Home Page: http://www.yorku.ca/cstm

Formerly: Canadian Folk Music Society.

• 7437 • **Honorary Life Member**
To recognize individuals who have made an extraordinary contribution to the Society in the area of folk music. The honorees are designated by an annual general meeting of the Society. Honorary life membership is presented when merited. Four individuals may hold this honorarium at any time. Established in 1984.

• 7438 •
Canadian Society of Animal Science Agricultural Institute of Canada (Societe Canadienne de Zootechnie)
Karen Beauchemin, Pres.
PO Box 90
Lennoxville, QC, Canada J1M 1Z3
Phone: (819)565-4171
Fax: (819)564-5507
E-mail: info@csas.net
Home Page: http://www.csas.net

• 7439 • **Award for Technical Innovation in Enhancing Production of Safe Affordable Food**
Recognizes excellence in techical innovation and teaching with particular emphasis in the fields of biotechnology, genetics, physiology, and animal behavior. The award requires a demonstration that the recipient had contributed to the production of safe and affordable food. CSAS and AIC fellowship recipients are ineligible. The award is sponsored by Elanco. A plaque is awarded.

• 7440 • **Book Prize**
In recognition of superior academic achievement during the first three years of study within each of the Faculties of Agriculture at each Canadian University. Undergraduate students who have demonstrated superior academic performance during the first three years of related studies and who are enrolled in the fourth year in animal/poultry science may be nominated. A $100 gift certificate and a certificate are awarded annually to one student at each of the following universities: U.B.C., U. of A., U. of S., U. of M., U. of G., Macdonald College and U. of Laval, plus NSAC in 1984. Established in 1971. Sponsored by the Oxford Press.

• 7441 • **CSAS Fellowship Award**
This, the Society's highest honor, is given to recognize an individual for outstanding contributions in any field of animal agriculture. Members are eligible for nomination by March 31. A monetary prize of $1,000, a plaque, and annual dues are awarded annually.

• 7442 • **Graduate Student Paper Competition Awards**
In recognition of the top three presentations during the Graduate Student Competition at the annual meeting. Members enrolled in a master's or Ph.D. program, who register for the annual meeting and are senior authors and presenters of a paper, based on their own research, are eligible. Three monetary awards of $250, $150, and $100 each for the top three presentations are presented annually. Established in 1978. Sponsored by Pfizer

• 7443 • **Honorary Life Membership**
In recognition of active members, recently retired, who have demonstrated support of the CSAS aims and objectives. Members who have been active for the period of not less than ten years immediately preceding retirement from active employment may be nominated by March 31. A framed certificate and annual dues are awarded annually. Established in 1963.

• 7444 • **Past-President's Certificate**
In recognition of service to the Society during the term as President. Current presidents of the Society are eligible. A framed certificate is awarded at the conclusion of the president's term. Established in 1977.

• 7445 • **Shurgain Award for Excellence in Nutrition and MeatScience**
To recognize and encourage excellence in teaching, research, or extension in the area of animal nutrition or meat science. Members involved at provincial, federal, or international levels are eligible for nomination by March 31. A monetary prize of $1,000 and a plaque are awarded annually. Established in 1980. Sponsored by Shurgain Ltd. Formerly: Canada Packers' Medal.

• 7446 • **Young Scientist's Award**
To recognize the achievements of new members of the research community. Members who, within a period of no greater than seven years from obtaining Ph.D., have demonstrated excellence in any area of animal and/or poultry science may be nominated by March 31. Holders of AIC Fellowships or the CSAS Certificate of Merit are not eligible. A monetary prize of $800 and a plaque are awarded annually. Established in 1982. Sponsored by Pfizer. Formerly: Co-op Feeds Young Scientist's Award.

• 7447 •
Canadian Society of Association Executives (Societe Canadienne des Directeurs d'Association)
Michael Anderson CAE, Pres. & CEO
10 King St. E, Ste. 1100
Toronto, ON, Canada M5C 1C3
Phone: (416)363-3555
Toll-Free: 800-461-3608
Fax: (416)363-3630
E-mail: csae@csae.com
Home Page: http://www.csae.com

• 7448 • Award for Excellence in Association Leadership
Award of recognition. Individuals best representing new generation of leaders in association community are eligible. Awarded annually.

• 7449 • John Griner Award
Recognizes outstanding industry related contributions. Business member association management professionals are eligible. Awarded annually.

• 7450 • Pinnacle Award
Recognizes outstanding leadership to CSAE, their own association, and community. Awarded annually.

• 7451 •
Canadian Society of Biochemistry, Molecular and Cellular Biology
% Dr. Albert Clark
Dept. of Biochemistry and Pathology
Queen's University
Kingston, ON, Canada K7L 3N6
Phone: (613)533-2900
E-mail: clarkaf@post.queensu.ca
Home Page: http://www.csbmcb.ca

• 7452 • Boehringer Mannheim Award
For recognition of outstanding research in biochemistry and/or molecular biology undertaken in Canada by a Canadian scientist. Canadian citizens or landed immigrants may be nominated by a member of the Society by January 15. A monetary award of $1,000 and a plaque are awarded biennially. Established in 1981. Sponsored by Boehringer-Mannheim Canada. In addition, the Society offers the Merck Frosst-CSBMCB Travel Awards, the Jeanne Mannery Fisher Memorial Lectureship, the Boehringer Mannheim Student Poster Awards, and the CSBMCB Merck Frosst Prize.

• 7453 •
Canadian Society of Diagnostic Medical Sonographers
Rodney MacDonald, Pres.
PO Box 1220
Kemptville, ON, Canada K0G 1J0
Phone: (613)258-0855
Toll-Free: 888-273-6746
Fax: (613)258-0899
E-mail: csdms@bellnet.ca
Home Page: http://www.csdms.com

• 7454 • Certificate of Merit
Recognizes significant contribution to the continuing education of sonographers. Awarded annually.

• 7455 • Excellence in Ultrasound
For individuals who strive for excellence and are progressive in the education of fellow sonographers. A monetary prize is awarded annually.

• 7456 •
Canadian Society of Hospital Pharmacists (Societe Canadienne des pharmaciens d'Hopitaux)
Myrella Roy, Exec.Dir.
1145 Hunt Club Rd., Ste. 350
Ottawa, ON, Canada K1V 0Y3
Phone: (613)736-9733
Fax: (613)736-5660
E-mail: mroy@cshp.ca
Home Page: http://www.cshp.ca

• 7457 • Abbott Award
To recognize original scholarly papers and publications, significant innovations and developments, or original research in pharmaceutical technology in a hospital. Applications require the endorsement of the hospital. A monetary prize of $1,000 is presented as merited. Established in 1969.

• 7458 • AMGEN Award
For research on biopharmaceuticals. A monetary award is given annually.

• 7459 • Apotex Award
In recognition of an original scholarly paper by a member of the Society. The research must deal with management issues in pharmaceutical care. The best paper will make a significant contribution or innovation to improve patient quality care/quality of life while demonstrating the impact of pharmaceutical care on pharmacy management. Application deadline is September 1. Hospital endorsement is required. A monetary award of $1,500 is presented annually.

• 7460 • Baxter Award
To recognize an individual for original scholarly papers, significant innovations, or original research in IV therapy in health care settings. A monetary award of $1,000 is presented.

• 7461 • Bristol-Myers Squibb Award
To recognize original scholarly papers and publications, significant innovations and developments, and original research in clinical pharmacy programs. Applications require the endorsement of the hospital. A monetary award of $1,000 is presented annually. Established in 1969. Formerly: (1991) Bristol Award.

• 7462 • Distinguished Service Award by Ortho-McNeil
For outstanding achievement in hospital pharmacy practice. A monetary award is given annually.

• 7463 • Glaxco Award
For research in the pharmaceutical care area. A monetary award is given.

• 7464 • Horner Travel Award
Grant for pharmacist dong research on non-Canadian health care institutions. Awarded biennially.

• 7465 • Janssen Award
For research into infectious disease. A monetary award is given.

• 7466 • Merck Frosst Award
To recognize an original scholarly paper or publication that promotes rational drug use. Papers that demonstrate significant innovations, developments, and original research contributing to the more rational use of drugs are eligible. A monetary prize of $1,000 is presented annually as merited. Established in 1985.

• 7467 • NovoPharm Award
For new programs in patient counseling - papers or audio-visual. A monetary award is given.

• 7468 • Organon Award
Given to hospital pharmacy resident projects. A monetary award is given.

• 7469 • Parke-Davis Award
For research in long-term health care. A monetary award is given.

• 7470 • Roche Award
For research being performed in different specialty areas of pharmacy practice. A monetary award is given.

• 7471 • Sabex Award
Given for research n palliative care. A monetary award is given.

• 7472 • Sandoz Award
To recognize an individual for original scholarly papers in pharmacoeconomic research. A monetary award of $1,500 is presented. Established in 1991.

• 7473 • Schering Award
To recognize original scholarly papers and publications based on original research or significant innovations and developments involving the use of pharmacokinetic principles. Where actual information from an institution is used, the endorsement of the institution is required. A monetary award of $1,000 is presented as merited. Established in 1982.

• 7474 • Shering Award
Given for research in pharmacokinetic hospital or pharmacy-industry relations. A monetary award is given.

• 7475 •
Canadian Society of Landscape Architects (L'Association des architects paysagistes du Canada)
Fran Pauze, Exec.Dir.
PO Box 13594
Ottawa, ON, Canada K2K 1X6
Phone: (613)622-5520
Fax: (613)622-5870
E-mail: info@csla.ca
Home Page: http://www.csla.ca

• 7476 • **CSLA Awards of Excellence**
Recognizes outstanding landscape architecture students. Awarded annually.

• 7477 •
Canadian Society of Microbiologists
(Societe Canadienne des Microbiologistes)
Dr. Betty Worobec, Sec.-Treas.
570 W 7th Ave., Ste. 402
Vancouver, BC, Canada V5Z 1B3
Phone: (604)484-5698
Fax: (604)874-4378
E-mail: info@csm-scm.org
Home Page: http://csm-scm.org

• 7478 • **Canadian Society of Microbiologists Award**
To recognize residents of Canada who have done outstanding work in microbiology. Citizens or permanent residents may be nominated by November 1. A monetary award and a plaque are awarded annually at the general meeting. Established in 1963.

• 7479 • **Student Award**
To encourage excellence in oral presentations by students at the annual general meeting of the society. Students must be sponsored by a member of the society. An extended abstract (1000 words) of presentation plus a 50 word summary, relevant tables, and figures must be submitted in advance to determine scientific merit, and a 10 minute oral presentation must be given for grading by a jury of three. A monetary prize and a plaque are awarded annually at the general meeting. Established in 1979. Formerly: Graduate Student Award.

• 7480 •
Canadian Society of Petroleum Geologists
Tim Howard, Business Mgr.
No. 160, 540 5th Ave. SW
Calgary, AB, Canada T2P 0M2
Phone: (403)264-5610
Fax: (403)264-5898
E-mail: tim.howard@cspg.org
Home Page: http://www.cspg.org

• 7481 • **Andrew D. Baillie Award**
To recognize the excellence of orally presented technical papers at the annual convention of the Society. A monetary prize of $1,000 and a trophy are awarded annually. Established in 1991.

• 7482 • **CSPG Graduate Students Thesis Awards**
For recognition of the best M.Sc. and Ph.D. theses on Canadian sedimentary geology. Graduate theses submitted to any recognized university for credit leading to a degree at the fall convocation of the preceding year or the spring convocation of the current year are eligible. A certificate and $300 worth of CSPG publications are awarded annually in February. Established in 1958.

• 7483 • **R. J. W. Douglas Memorial Medal**
For recognition of contributions to regional tectonics and petroleum and structural geology, and to the general understanding of sedimentary rocks in Canada. All geologists are eligible. An engraved silver medal designed by the Canadian artist, Dora Hunt, is awarded annually in February. Established in 1980 in memory of R.J.W. Douglas, who made contributions to Canadian geology.

• 7484 • **Honorary Member**
For recognition of distinguished service to petroleum geology. Individuals who have made outstanding contributions to petroleum geology on an international or national basis are eligible. An engraved book and scroll and lifetime membership in the Society are awarded annually. Established in 1953.

• 7485 • **Link Award**
For recognition of the best oral presentation by a member to a CSPG technical luncheon meeting in Calgary. An engraved pewter mug is awarded annually in February. Established in 1958 by T.A. Link.

• 7486 • **Medal of Merit**
To recognize the best paper published each year on the petroleum geology of Canada and to bring an awareness of this scientific work to the public. Manuscripts must be published in a recognized scientific publication within the eligible year. An engraved silver medal is awarded annually in February. Established in 1952.

• 7487 • **President's Award**
For recognition of outstanding service to the Society. Awarded annually in February. Established in 1978.

• 7488 • **Regional Graduate Scholarships**
To promote graduate studies in the fields of geology and marine geoscience that have application to the petroleum industry. Three regional scholarships are awarded annually. Established in 1983. In addition, the Norcen/CSPG Undergraduate Scholarship is given each year to a second to fourth year geological student enrolled in a western Canadian university.

• 7489 • **Service Awards**
To recognize members or friends of the CSPG who have contributed to the welfare of the Society through committee or other volunteer work. Established in 1985.

• 7490 • **Stanley Slipper Gold Medal**
To recognize an explorationist who has made a significant contribution to petroleum exploration in Canada. Established in 1989.

• 7491 • **Tracks Award**
For recognition of outstanding contributions (which have made "tracks") to the Society by exceptional service. Members of the Society or other persons acting as friends of the Society are eligible. A handmade earthenware plaque and engraved plate are awarded quarterly when merited. Established in 1978.

• 7492 • **Volunteer Awards**
To recognize members or friends who have demonstrated significant service to the Society.

• 7493 •
Canadian Society of Sugar Artistry
Rebecca Wang, Mem.Chair
35 19th St.
Etobicoke, ON, Canada M8V 3L4
Phone: (416)251-7731
Phone: (416)251-7731

• 7494 • **Cake Show Competition Plaques**
Recognizes excellence in cake decorations and sugar artistry. Awarded annually. Inquire for application details.

• 7495 •
Canadian Society of Zoologists
(Societe Canadienne de Zoologie)
Dept. Biological Sciences, CW-405
Biological Sciences Bldg.
University of Alberta
Edmonton, AB, Canada T6G 2E9
Phone: (780)492-1293
Fax: (780)492-9234
E-mail: al.shostak@ualberta.ca
Home Page: http://www3.uqar.uquebec.ca/jpellerin/csz

• 7496 • **Helen I. Battle Award**
To recognize the best poster presentation by a student at the annual General Meeting of the Society. A monetary award of $100 is awarded annually. Established in 1987.

• 7497 • **T. W. N. Cameron Award**
To recognize an outstanding doctoral thesis in zoology in Canada. The winner presents the Cameron Lecture at the annual General Meeting of the CSZ. Awarded annually. Established in 1978.

• 7498 • **Fry Medal**
To recognize a Canadian zoologist for an outstanding contribution to knowledge and understanding in an area of zoology. Awarded annually. The winner presents the Fry Medal lecture at the annual conference.

• 7499 • **Hoar Award**
To encourage and acknowledge excellence in scientific research and communication by students. All candidates must be students. A monetary award of $300 is presented at the annual general meeting of the Society. Established in 1976 to honor Dr. William S. Hoar for his distinguished contributions to biology through research, teaching, writing, editorial guidance, and administration.

• 7500 • R. A. Wardle Award
For recognition of contributions to parasitology. Awarded by the Parasitology Section of the Society. A medallion is awarded.

• 7501 •
Canadian Sociology and Anthropology Association
(Societe Canadienne de Sociologie et d'Anthropologie)
Gilles LaFlamme, Dir.
Concordia University SB-323
1455 boulevard de Maisonneuse W
Montreal, QC, Canada H3G 1M8
Phone: (514)848-8780
Fax: (514)848-8780
E-mail: info@csaa.ca
Home Page: http://www.csaa.ca

• 7502 • Outstanding Contribution Award
To recognize outstanding contribution to sociology or anthropology in Canada.

• 7503 • Outstanding Service Award
To recognize outstanding dedication to the objectives of the association.

• 7504 • John Porter Tradition of Excellence Book Award
To recognize outstanding published scholarly contributions within the 'John Porter Tradition' to the advancement of sociological and/or anthropological knowledge in Canada. Awarded annually. Established in 1980. Formerly: John Porter Memorial Book Prize.

• 7505 •
Canadian Sport Massage Therapists Association
(Association Canadienne des Massotherapeutes du Sport)
Aurel Hamran, Pres.
1849 Yonge St., Ste. 814
Toronto, ON, Canada M4S 1Y2
Phone: (416)488-4414
Fax: (416)488-3079
E-mail: natoffice@csmta.ca
Home Page: http://www.csmta.ca

• 7506 • Award of Excellence
Recognizes members who volunteer time and expertise to further the association's goals. Awarded annually.

• 7507 •
Canadian Sport Parachuting Association
Judy Donnelly, Office Mgr.
300 Forced Rd.
Russell, ON, Canada K4R 1A1
Phone: (613)445-1881
Fax: (613)445-2698
E-mail: office@cspa.ca
Home Page: http://www.cspa.ca

• 7508 • CSPA Service Award
For recognition of longstanding service and contributions to the sport of parachuting. Nominations may be made by any member of the Association. A plaque is awarded annually when merited.

• 7509 • Glenn R. Masterson Memorial Trophy
To recognize a heroic action or other special contributions to the advancement of Canadian sport parachuting. Nominees who have made continuous efforts are considered. Individuals and groups need not be Canadian. A large trophy with marble base topped with a carved wing is awarded annually. Established in 1976 in honor of Mr. Masterson, a pioneer in the sport of parachuting and a founding member of the group.

• 7510 • National Championships
To recognize individuals and teams who participate in the National Championships. The events of the Championships are as follows: Individual Accuracy, male and female; Individual Style, male and female; Individual Overall Standing, male and female; Four-way Relative Work: the Airborne Regiment Trophy; Eight-way Relative Work; Junior Accuracy; Junior Style; Junior Four-way TRAC: the Terry Lafferty Memorial Trophy; and Four-way TRAC/Team Accuracy. Perpetual trophies are inscribed with the name(s) of the champion for the event; these trophies are displayed at the CSPA offices.

• 7511 •
Canadian Sporting Goods Association
Bill Patrick, Exec.Dir.
425 Viger Ave. W, Ste. 416
Montreal, QC, Canada H2Z 1X2
Phone: (514)393-1132
Toll-Free: 888-393-3002
Fax: (514)393-9513
E-mail: csga@csga.ca
Home Page: http://www.csga.ca

• 7512 • Jack Cooper Lifetime Achievement Award
Recognizes involvement in the Canadian sporting goods industry. Awarded annually.

• 7513 •
Canadian Theatre Critics Association
(Association des critiques de theatre du Canada)
Alvina Ruprecht, Co-Pres.
240 Dundas St., No. 700
Toronto, ON, Canada M5T 2Z5
Phone: (416)782-0966
E-mail: aruprech@ccs.carleton.ca
Home Page: http://www.canadiantheatrecritics.ca

• 7514 • Nathan Cohen Award
To recognize high critical standards and to give encouragement to those working professionally in the field of theatre criticism. Individuals working professionally on a continuing basis in the field of theatre criticism and theatre journalism in Canada are eligible. Entry categories in the English language division are: (1) Reviews of up to 750 words; and (2) Reviews, profiles and other theatrical features of 750 words to a maximum of 3,000 words. Up to three items may be submitted in either or both of the categories. Entries published during the period from January 1 of the previous year to December 31 of the award year may be submitted by March 15. A monetary award of $500 and a certificate are awarded in each category annually at the conference and general meeting. Established in 1982 by Drama Bench, Toronto, to honor Nathan Cohen, distinguished theatre critic of the *Toronto Star*.

• 7515 •
Canadian Toy Testing Council
Leigh A. Poirier, Exec.Dir.
1973 Baseline Rd.
Ottawa, ON, Canada K2C 0C7
Phone: (613)228-3155
Fax: (613)228-3242
E-mail: cttc@cyberus.ca
Home Page: http://www.toy-testing.org

• 7516 • Award of Excellence
Annual award of recognition.

• 7517 • Best Bet Awards
Annual awards of recognition.

• 7518 • Children's Choice Award
Annual awards of recognition.

• 7519 •
Canadian Trakehner Horse Society
Ingrid von Hausen, Contact
PO Box 6009
New Hamburg, ON, Canada N3A 2K6
Phone: (519)662-3209
Phone: (519)662-6466
Fax: (519)662-3209
E-mail: cantrakhsivh@golden.net
Home Page: http://www.cantrak.on.ca

• 7520 • CTHS Annual Award
For performance in any related discipline. A plaque is given annually.

• 7521 • Eleonora Hydar Memorial Award
Annual award of recognition. A monetary prize is given.

• 7522 • Elke Otremba Memorial Award
Annual award of recognition. A plaque is awarded.

• 7523 • Hanna Schmocker Memorial Award
Annual award of recognition. A plaque is awarded.

• 7524 • Hans Wulff Memorial Award
Annual award of recognition.

• 7525 • Young Competitor Award
Annual award of recognition.

• 7526 •
Canadian Trapshooting Association
Ron Todd, Pres.
3118 7th Ave. E
Regina, SK, Canada S4H 5G1
Phone: (306)761-2570
Phone: (306)787-2897
Fax: (306)787-7000

• 7527 • **Canadian Championship Trophies**
Recognizes winners of the championship events. Awarded annually.

• 7528 •
Canadian University Music Society (Societe de Musique des Universites Canadiennes)
Edward Jurkowski, Pres.
PO Box 507, Station Q
Toronto, ON, Canada M4T 2M5
Phone: (416)483-7282
Fax: (416)489-1713
E-mail: membership@cums-smuc.ca
Home Page: http://www.cums-smuc.ca

• 7529 • **George Proctor Prize**
To recognize the best paper presented at the annual conference of the Society by a graduate student. Canadian graduate students (Master's or Doctoral) who are members of the Society and do not hold full-time teaching positions are eligible. An abstract of the proposed paper must be submitted by December 1. A monetary award of $500 plus partial reimbursement of travel expenses to the Conference and consideration for publication in the *Canadian University Music Review* are awarded annually. Established in 1988 to honor Dr. George Proctor, noted Canadian scholar and a long-time member of the Society. Further details are available from the society.

• 7530 •
Canadian Veterinary Medical Association (Association Canadienne des Medecins Veterinaires)
Claude Paul Boivin, Exec.Dir.
339 Booth St.
Ottawa, ON, Canada K1R 7K1
Phone: (613)236-1162
Fax: (613)236-9681
E-mail: info@canadianveterinarians.net
Home Page: http://www.cvma-acmv.org

• 7531 • **CVMA Humane Award**
A monetary award is given annually.

• 7532 • **CVMA Plaque**
Recognizes students graduating in veterinary medicine. Awarded annually.

• 7533 • **President's Award**
Annual award of recognition.

• 7534 • **RVL Walker Award**
For veterinary students. A monetary award is given annually.

• 7535 • **Schering Veterinary Award**
For clinical veterinarians. A monetary award is given annually.

• 7536 • **Small Animal Practitioner Award**
To recognize a veterinarian whose work in small animal practice, clinical research, or basic science is judged to have contributed significantly to the advancement of small animal medicine, surgery, or the management of a small animal practice, including the advancement of the public's knowledge of the responsibilities of pet ownership. A monetary award of and a plaque are presented. Established in 1987.

• 7537 •
Canadian Wildlife Federation (Federation Canadienne de la Faune)
Colin Maxwell, Exec.VP
350 Michael Cowpland Dr.
Kanata, ON, Canada K2M 2W1
Phone: (613)599-9594
Toll-Free: 800-563-9453
Fax: (613)599-4428
E-mail: info@cwf-fcf.org
Home Page: http://www.cwf-fcf.org

• 7538 • **Canadian Conservation Achievement Award**
For furthering conservation in Canada. Awarded annually.

• 7539 • **Doug Clarke Conservation Award**
For recognition of the most outstanding conservation project completed by an affiliate, its clubs or its members. A trophy of a peregrine falcon, sculpted by Dennis Webster, and a framed certificate are presented at the annual general meeting. Established in 1982 in memory of Dr. C.H.D. (Doug) Clarke, a Canadian conservationist and Director of the Canadian Wildlife Federation who died in 1981.

• 7540 • **Stan Hodgkiss Canadian Outdoorsman Award**
To recognize an outstanding individual in the field of conservation. Canadians who have been active in conservation work in Canada are eligible for nomination. Established in 1975. Sponsored by Nature's Window Art Gallery. Formerly: (1995) Canadian Outdoorsman of the Year Award.

• 7541 • **Roland Michener Conservation Award**
To recognize an individual for commitment to conservation through active involvement in the promotion, enhancement, and the furtherance of the conservation of Canada's natural resources. A trophy of two Canadian geese, sculpted by Robert Kerr, is presented at the annual general meeting. Established in 1978. The award honors The Right Honorable Roland Michener, former Governor General of Canada, a prominent outdoorsman and past Honorary President of the CWF.

• 7542 • **National Wildlife Week Awards**
For furthering conservation in Canada. Awarded annually.

• 7543 • **Past Presidents' Canadian Legislator Award**
To recognize a provincial, territorial, or federal elected legislator who has made a significant contribution to the conservation of wildlife in Canada. Awarded annually. Established in 1988.

• 7544 •
Canadian Wood Council
Mrs. Pauline Rochefort, Pres.
400-99 Bank St.
Ottawa, ON, Canada K1P 6B9
Phone: (613)747-5544
Toll-Free: 800-463-5091
Fax: (613)747-6264
E-mail: ilazea@cwc.ca
Home Page: http://www.cwc.ca

• 7545 • **Wood Design Awards**
Recognizes excellence in the design of wooden buildings. Awarded annually.

• 7546 •
CANARIE
Andrew K. Bjerring, Pres.
110 O'Connor St., 4th Fl.
Ottawa, ON, Canada K1P 5M9
Phone: (613)943-5454
Fax: (613)943-5443
E-mail: info@canarie.ca
Home Page: http://www.canarie.ca

• 7547 • **National Iway Awards**
For Canadian information technology innovation. Awarded annually.

• 7548 •
Cancer Care Ontario
Terrence Sullivan, Pres. and CEO
620 University Ave.
Toronto, ON, Canada M5G 2L7
Phone: (416)971-9800
Fax: (416)971-6888
E-mail: publicaffairs@cancercare.on.ca
Home Page: http://www.cancercare.on.ca

• 7549 • **Clinician Scientist Awards**
Provides support for graduate students, post-doctoral fellows and clinical fellows.

• 7550 •
Cancer Control Society
Norman Fritz, Pres.
2043 N Berendo St.
Los Angeles, CA 90027
Phone: (323)663-7801
Fax: (323)663-7757
E-mail: cancercontrol@cox.net
Home Page: http://www.cancercontrolsociety.com

• 7551 • **Cancer Control Society Awards**
To recognize contributions to the nutritional and alternative approach to cancer and other diseases. Awarded annually at the annual convention. Established in 1973.

• 7552 •
Cancer Hope Network
Wanda Diak, Mng.Dir./COO
2 North Rd., Ste. A
Chester, NJ 07930
Phone: (908)879-4039
Toll-Free: 877-HOP-ENET
Fax: (908)879-6518
E-mail: info@cancerhopenetwork.org
Home Page: http://www.cancerhopenetwork.org

• 7553 • **Flame of Courage Award**
Annual recognition of an individual making significant difference in cancer patient's life or has shown courage in face of own cancer.

• 7554 •
Cancer Research & Prevention Foundation
Carolyn Aldige, Pres.
1600 Duke St., Ste. 500
Alexandria, VA 22314
Phone: (703)836-4412
Toll-Free: 800-227-2732
Fax: (703)836-4413
E-mail: info@preventcancer.org
Home Page: http://www.preventcancer.org

• 7555 • **CRFA Fellowship Grants**
To enable young researchers to participate in cancer prevention research. Awarded twice annually. Deadlines are March 1 and September 1. Established in 1987.

• 7556 •
Cancer Research Foundation
135 S LaSalle St., Ste. 2020
PO Box 0493
Chicago, IL 60690-0493
Phone: (312)630-0055
Fax: (312)630-0075
E-mail: crf@cancerresearchfnd.org

• 7557 • **Fletcher Scholar Awards**
To support a distinctive and timely laboratory research project by a Chicago senior cancer researcher. A $100,000 award is made annually or biennially. Established in 1989.

• 7558 • **Young Investigator Awards**
To recognize outstanding cancer researchers at Chicago medical schools and to encourage young scientists in the exploration of independent hypotheses with the help and guidance of mentors. Eligible candidates are researchers at the beginning of their careers who have not yet qualified for research support outside of their medical centers and do not have an established record as a medical researcher. Candidates must be nominated through the office of the deans at Chicago medical schools. Four to seven monetary prizes of $50,000 are awarded annually. Awards are presented in October. Established in 1947 by Maurice Goldblatt, founder of the Cancer Research Foundation.

• 7559 •
Cancer Research Institute, Inc.
681 5th Ave.
New York, NY 10022
Phone: (212)688-7515
Toll-Free: 800-992-2623
Fax: (212)832-9376
E-mail: info@cancerresearch.org
Home Page: http://www.cancerresearch.org

• 7560 • **Clinical Investigator Awards**
Inquire for application details.

• 7561 • **William B. Coley Award**
For distinguished research in basic and clinical Immunology.

• 7562 • **Oliver R. Grace Award**
For distinguished service in advancing cancer research.

• 7563 •
Canola Council of Canada
(Conseil de Canola du Canada)
Barbara Isman, Pres.
167 Lombard Ave., Ste. 400
Winnipeg, MB, Canada R3B 0T6
Phone: (204)982-2100
Fax: (204)942-1841
E-mail: wilkinsd@canola-council.org
Home Page: http://www.canola-council.org

• 7564 • **James McAnsh Award**
For recognition of an outstanding contribution to the canola industry by any person or group. Awarded when merited. Named in honor of James McAnsh.

• 7565 •
Canon Law Society of America
Rev. Arthur J. Espelage O.F.M., Exec.Coor.
108 N Payne St., Ste. C
Alexandria, VA 22314-2906
Phone: (703)739-2560
Fax: (703)739-2562
E-mail: coordinator@clsa.org
Home Page: http://www.clsa.org

• 7566 • **Role of Law Award**
To honor an outstanding canon lawyer who has contributed to the role of law in the Catholic Church. A bronze plaque is awarded annually. Established in 1973.

• 7567 •
Cantors Assembly
Steve Stoehr, Pres.
3080 Broadway, Ste. 613
New York, NY 10027
Phone: (212)678-8834
Fax: (212)662-8989
E-mail: caoffice@aol.com
Home Page: http://www.cantors.org

• 7568 • **Kavod Award**
Recognizes service to Judaism and the Jewish people and the Contorate. Awarded annually.

• 7569 • **Yuval Award**
Recognizes service to the organization. Awarded annually.

• 7570 •
Cape Cod Art Association
Richard Muccini, Pres.
3480 Rte. 6A
PO Box 85
Barnstable, MA 02630
Phone: (508)362-2909
E-mail: curator@capecodartassoc.org
Home Page: http://www.capecodartassoc.org

• 7571 • **Cape Cod Art Association Awards**
For recognition of the best work in an open competition in five categories: oil/acrylic, water media, pastel painting, graphics/drawing/mixed media and sculpture. Monetary prizes and medals are awarded at the winter open-juried exhibit, spring open-juried exhibit, the autumn open-juried exhibit and the New England Exhibit. Open to New England artists only.

• 7572 •
Cape Cod Museum of Natural History
869 Rte. 6A
Brewster, MA 02631
Phone: (508)896-3867
Fax: (508)896-8844
E-mail: info@ccmnh.org
Home Page: http://www.ccmnh.org

• 7573 • **Thoreau Award**
To recognize a individual's contribution to the museum in the areas of education, conservation, or natural history research on Cape Cod. A certificate & plaque are awarded annually. Nominations must be submitted to the Thoreau Committee at the Museum. Established in 1987.

• 7574 •
Capezio Ballet Makers Dance Foundation
1 Campus Rd.
Totowa, NJ 07512
Phone: (973)595-9000
Fax: (973)595-9120
E-mail: dfiorenzi@balletmakers.com
Home Page: http://www.capeziodance.com/about/foundation/index.jsp

Formerly: (1986) Ballet Makers Dance Foundation.

• 7575 • **Capezio Dance Award**
To recognize an individual, a company, or an organization for significant achievements in the field of dance in the United States. The winner is selected by the trustees who are advised by a small group of independent advisors. A monetary award of $10,000, and an engraved crystal piece are awarded annually. Established in 1951 by the Capezio Foundation.

• 7576 •
Capitol Association of Diabetes Educators
Kathy Gold RN,MSN, Pres.
2020 Pennsylvania Ave. NW, Ste. 848
Washington, DC 20006
Toll-Free: 800-941-4635

• 7577 • **Camps For Kids**
For child with type 1 diabetes. Scholarship.

• 7578 •
Capranica Foundation
Robert R. Capranica, Exec. Dir.
The Tompkins County Trust Co.
Trust Dept.
PO Box 460
Ithaca, NY 14851-9984
Phone: (607)273-3210
Fax: (607)273-0024
E-mail: decibel@aol.com

• 7579 • **Capranica Foundation Award in Neuroethology**
To recognize outstanding achievement or future promise in the field of Neuroethology (neural basis of natural animal behavior) by young scientists early in their careers. Papers in Neuroethology, published (or in press) in the award year, must be submitted by November 15. A monetary award of at least $1,000 is presented annually. Established in 1986.

• 7580 •
Car and Driver
2002 Hogback Rd.
Ann Arbor, MI 48105
Phone: (734)971-3600
Fax: (734)971-9188
E-mail: editors@caranddriver.com
Home Page: http://www.caranddriver.com

• 7581 • **10Best Cars**
To recognize the ten best cars selected by the editors of *Car and Driver* magazine. Cars with a base price over $54,000 are excluded (this amount usually changes from one year to the next). Approximately 50-60 cars are nominated, road-tested, and evaluated. Cars are selected annually and announced in the January issue of *Car and Driver*. Established in 1983.

• 7582 •
Career College Association
Jim Tolbert, Sec.
10 G St. NE, Ste. 750
Washington, DC 20002-4213
Phone: (202)336-6700
Fax: (202)336-6828
E-mail: cca@career.org
Home Page: http://www.career.org

Formerly: National Association of Trade and Technical Schools.

• 7583 • **NATTS Hall of Fame**
To recognize graduates of CCA schools who have had unusually successful and outstanding careers. Graduates of CCA member schools with at least seven years of job experience related to their training are eligible. A plaque is awarded every two years at the convention to the winner and the winner's school. Established in 1987.

• 7584 •
Career Communications Group
Tyrone D. Taborn, CEO
729 E Pratt St., 5th Fl.
Baltimore, MD 21202
Phone: (410)244-7101
Fax: (410)752-1837
E-mail: ppettit@ccgmag.com
Home Page: http://www.ccgmedia.com

• 7585 • **Black Engineer of the Year Awards**
To recognize black engineers who have excelled in their field. Awards are given in the following categories: (1) Black Engineer of the Year; (2) Technical Contribution; (3) Outstanding Achievement in Government; (4) President's Award; (5) Lifetime Achievement; (6) Entrepreneur; (7) Promotion of Engineering Education; (8) Affirmative Action; (9) Most Promising Engineer; (10) Higher Education; (11) Student Leadership; (12) Community Service; (13) Professional Achievement; and (14) Honorable Mention. Trophies are awarded in each category annually at the Award Conference. Established in 1987. Co-sponsored by Mobil Oil Corporation, *US Black Engineer* magazine, and the Council of Engineering Deans of the Historically Black Colleges and Universities.

• 7586 • **Hispanic Engineer National Achievement Awards**
To recognize Hispanic engineers who have excelled in their field. Awards are given in the following categories: (1) Hispanic Engineer of the Year; (2) Chairman's Award; (3) Education - High School Level; (4) Education College Level; (5) Student Leadership; (6) Most Promising Engineer in Government; (7) Entrepreneur; (8) Community Service; (9) Affirmative Action; (10) Most Promising Engineer in Industry; (11) Outstanding Technical Contribution; (12) Professional Achievement; (13) Professional Achievement in Government; and (14) Honorable Mention. Trophies are awarded annually in each category at the Award Conference. Co-sponsored by *Hispanic Engineer* magazine, the University of Houston, and Ford Motor Company. The event is produced by Mellado Communications. Established in 1989. Formerly known as the Hispanic Engineer of the Year Awards.

• 7587 •
Career Planning and Adult Development Network
Richard L. Knowdell, Exec.Dir./Founding Ed.
PO Box 1484
Pacifica, CA 94044
Phone: (650)359-6911
Toll-Free: 877-716-1794
Fax: (650)359-3089
E-mail: admin@careernetwork.org
Home Page: http://www.careernetwork.org

• 7588 • **Career Development Resource Award**
To recognize the achievements of a career development professional who serves as a "resource" for his or her fellow colleagues. A plaque is awarded each year at the Annual Career Conference in November. Established in 1989.

• 7589 •
Caribbean Conservation Corporation and Sea Turtle Survival League
David Godfrey, Exec.Dir.
4424 NW 13th St., Ste. A-1
Gainesville, FL 32609
Phone: (352)373-6441
Toll-Free: 800-678-7853
Fax: (352)375-2449
E-mail: ccc@cccturtle.org
Home Page: http://www.cccturtle.org

• 7590 • **Archie Carr Lifetime Achievement Award**
Recognizes accomplishments in conservation.

• 7591 •
Caribbean Hotel Association
Alec Sanguinetti, Dir.Gen./CEO
1000 Ponce De Leon Ave., 5th Fl.
San Juan, PR 00907-3668
Phone: (787)725-9139
Phone: (787)725-1839
Fax: (787)725-9108
E-mail: asanguinetti@chahotels.com
Home Page: http://www.caribbeanhotels.org

Formerly: (1962) Caribbean Hotel Council of the Caribbean Travel Association.

• 7592 • **Caribbean Hotel Association Awards**
To recognize hotels and hotel associations throughout the Caribbean region and to promote the improvement and expansion of the Carib-

bean tourism industry. The Association bestows the following awards at the Caribbean Hotel Industry Conference in June: Caribbean Hotelier of the Year, Employee of the Year, Supervisor of the Year, the Green Hotel of the Year, and Hotel Association Executive of the Year. Also, the Chef of the Year prize is awarded by the Caribbean Culinary Federation, a subsidiary of the CHA.

• 7593 •
Caribbean Studies Association
Dr. Emilio Pantojas Garcia, Pres.
PO Box 21606
Interamerican University of Puerto Rico
Call Box 5100
San Juan, PR 00931
Phone: (787)264-1912
Fax: (787)892-6350
E-mail: csapres@rrpac.upr.clu.edu
Home Page: http://csa2005.fiu.edu

• 7594 • **Annual Caribbean Review Award**
For an individual who has made an outstanding contribution to Caribbean studies. Awarded annually in collaboration with *CaribbeanReview*.

• 7595 • **Gordon K. Lewis Book Award**
To recognize the best book about the Caribbean published over the previous three years. The book must be written in one of the four leading Caribbean languages (Spanish, English, French, or Dutch). Preference will be given to those books approaching their subjects from a region-wide, interdisciplinary perspective. Awarded annually.

• 7596 •
The Caring Institute
320A St. NE
Washington, DC 20002
Phone: (202)547-4273
Fax: (202)547-6137
E-mail: info@carinfmuseum.org
Home Page: http://www.caring-institute.org

• 7597 • **Caring Award**
To recognize caring, compassionate individuals at work in society today. Anyone may submit nominations. Awarded annually. Established in 1985.

• 7598 •
Caritas of Austin
Brian DeRoeck, Pres.
PO Box 1947
Austin, TX 78767-1947
Phone: (512)479-4610
Phone: (512)472-4135
Fax: (512)472-4164
E-mail: info@caritasofaustin.org
Home Page: http://www.caritasofaustin.org

• 7599 • **Harvey Penick Award for Excellence in the Game of Life**
For emulation of the life of golf legend Harvey Penick. Recognition award bestowed annually.

• 7600 •
Carmel Music Society
Gina Gordon, Dir. Operations
Competition Committee
PO Box 1144
Carmel, CA 93921
Phone: (831)625-9938
Fax: (831)625-6823
E-mail: carmelmusic@sbcglobal.net
Home Page: http://www.carmelmusic.org

• 7601 • **Grand Prize**
To encourage professional development in music. To be eligible, an individual must be a resident or full-time student in California with no professional management, and be 18-30 years of age for non-singers and 18-32 years for singers. A monetary award of $4,000 and contract to perform in the next regular season are awarded annually, usually in April. The competition rotates its focus annually.

• 7602 •
Carnegie Hero Fund Commission
Walter F. Rutkowski, Sec.
425 6th Ave., Ste. 1640
Pittsburgh, PA 15219-1823
Phone: (412)281-1302
Toll-Free: 800-447-8900
Fax: (412)281-5751
E-mail: carnegiehero@carnegiehero.org
Home Page: http://www.carnegiehero.org

• 7603 • **Carnegie Medal**
To recognize persons who risk or lose their lives saving or attempting to save the lives of others. The heroic act must have been performed in the United States, Canada, or the waters thereof and must be brought to the attention of the Commission within two years of the date of the act. Individuals whose regular vocations do not require them to perform such acts are eligible. Medals and monetary grants are awarded as merited. Grants are given to heroes or to their surviving financial dependents for continuing support, education, or other worthy purposes. The Fund was established in 1904 by Andrew Carnegie.

• 7604 •
Carnegie Mellon University
Software Engineering Institute
4500 5th Ave.
Pittsburgh, PA 15213-3890
Phone: (412)268-5800
Fax: (412)268-6257
E-mail: customer-relations@sei.cmu.edu
Home Page: http://www.sei.cmu.edu

• 7605 • **IEEE Process Improvement Award**
Co-sponsored with IEEE. Inquire for application details.

• 7606 •
Carnegie Museum of Art
4400 Forbes Ave.
Pittsburgh, PA 15213
Phone: (412)622-3131
Phone: (412)622-3298
Fax: (412)622-3112
E-mail: st.telent@carnegiemuseums.org
Home Page: http://www.cmoa.org

• 7607 • **Carnegie Prize**
For recognition of the outstanding work(s) of art in the Carnegie International Exhibition of contemporary art. Art works selected to be included in the Carnegie International Exhibition are eligible. A monetary prize of $10,000 and a striking of the bronze medal first given in 1896 on the occasion of the inaugural Carnegie International Exhibition in Pittsburgh are awarded. The Exhibition awarded various combinations of first, second, and third place prizes, honorable mentions, and chronological medals from 1896 through 1939; after 1950 first through fifth prizes and honorable mentions were awarded; and in 1964 and 1967 six equal prizes were awarded. The first Carnegie Prize was awarded in 1985.

• 7608 •
Carolina's Citizens Freedom Foundation
Obie Oakley, Chairman
156 Huntley Pl.
Charlotte, NC 28207
Phone: (704)333-0377
Fax: (704)333-8179
E-mail: obieoakley@aol.com

• 7609 • **Freedom Award**
For involvement/influence in government, education, military, community. Recognition award bestowed annually.

• 7610 •
Carolinas Roofing and Sheet Metal Contractors Association
Dorothy S. Nagle, Exec.Dir.
710 Imperial Dr.
Charlotte, NC 28273
Phone: (704)556-1435
Toll-Free: 800-766-8176
Fax: (704)557-1736
E-mail: info@crsmca.com
Home Page: http://www.crsmca.com

• 7611 • **Gordon M. Waters Distinguished Service Award**
For service to industry. Recognition award bestowed annually.

• 7612 •
Carroll Center for the Blind
Rachel Ethier Rosenbaum, Pres.
770 Centre St.
Newton, MA 02458
Phone: (617)969-6200
Toll-Free: 800-852-3131
Fax: (617)969-6204
E-mail: dinarosen@carroll.org
Home Page: http://www.carroll.org

• 7613 • The Carroll Society
To recognize a blind or visually impaired employee in Massachusetts who has made a significant contribution to their organization through outstanding ability and job performance by admitting them into this select Society. Awarded to one or more recipients annually.

• 7614 •
Cartoonists Northwest
Maureen Gibbs, Founder
PO Box 31122
Seattle, WA 98103
Phone: (425)226-7623
Phone: (206)369-2123
Fax: (425)227-0511
E-mail: cartoonistsnw@aol.com
Home Page: http://www.cartoonists.net

• 7615 • Golden Toonie Award
To recognize outstanding talent in humorous illustration or cartooning fields. Awarded annually with a plaque. Established in 1991.

• 7616 •
Case Western Reserve University
Edward M. Hundert, Pres.
Adelbert Hall
10900 Euclid Ave.
Cleveland, OH 44106-7001
Phone: (216)368-2000
Fax: (216)368-4325
Home Page: http://www.cwru.edu

• 7617 • University Medal
This, Case Western Reserve University's highest honor, is awarded in recognition of leadership, dedication, and service to the University, to higher education, and to society. A committee of University faculty, trustees, and the president select the recipient. A sterling silver medal bearing the University seal on one side and the recipient's name and the date the medal is presented, on the other. The medal is awarded periodically. Established in 1971.

• 7618 •
Case Western Reserve University
Michelson Morley Award Committee
Physics Dept.
10900 Euclid Ave.
Cleveland, OH 44106
Phone: (216)368-4000
Fax: (216)368-5861
E-mail: pab6@cwru.edu
Home Page: http://www.phys.cwru.edu/events/mmal.php

• 7619 • Michelson - Morley Award
To honor a scientist or an engineer for significant contributions to knowledge and the well-being of mankind; to perpetuate the tradition of scholarly inquiry exemplified by the work of Albert A. Michelson and Edward W. Morley and, thereby, call to the attention of the public at large the continuing importance of the contributions of the scientist and engineer to the general welfare. Nominations are accepted. A monetary award of $5,000 and a plaque are awarded annually. Established in 1963 by Case Institute of Technology in honor of Albert A. Michelson and Edward W. Morley for their great contributions to research, including experiments related to the velocity of light which prepared the way for the work of Albert Einstein. Formerly: (1967) Albert A. Michelson Award.

• 7620 •
Casualty Actuarial Society
Cynthia R. Ziegler, Exec.Dir.
1100 N Glebe Rd., Ste. 600
Arlington, VA 22201
Phone: (703)276-3100
Fax: (703)276-3108
E-mail: office@casact.org
Home Page: http://www.casact.org

• 7621 • Dorweiler Prize
To stimulate original thinking and research in the solution of advanced insurance problems by recognizing outstanding papers by an Associate or Fellow of the Society who has attained his designation more than five years ago. A monetary prize of $2,000 is awarded annually if merited. Established in 1970 in honor of Paul Dorweiler.

• 7622 • Woodward - Fondiller Prize
To stimulate original thinking and research in the solution of advanced insurance problems by recognizing outstanding papers by an Associate or Fellow of the Society who has attained his designation within the last five years. A monetary award of $2,000 is awarded annually if merited. Established in 1963 in memory of Joseph H. Woodward and Richard Fondiller.

• 7623 • Charles A. Hachemeister Prize
To recognize the author of papers published in the ASTIN *Bulletin* or presented at an ASTIN colloquium judged to have practical casualty applications and be of the most interest to U.S. members. A monetary prize of $1,000 is awarded annually. Established in 1993 in memory of Charles A. Hachemeister's many contributions to Actuarial Studies in Non-Life Insurance (ASTIN) and his efforts to establish a closer relationship between the CAS and ASTIN.

• 7624 • Michelbacher Prize
To recognize the author of the best paper submitted in response to a call for discussion papers whenever the program is conducted by the Casualty Actuarial Society. Selection is based on originality, research, readability, and completeness of papers. Recipients need not be members of the CAS. A monetary prize of $1,500 is awarded annually. Established in 1979 in memory of Gustav F. Michelbacher.

• 7625 • Matthew Rodermund Service Award
To recognize CAS members who have made significant volunteer contributions to the actuarial profession. Volunteer contributions include, but are not limited to: committee involvement; participation in Society meetings and seminars; volunteer efforts for regional affiliates or special interest sections; and involvement with non-CAS actuarial professional organizations. A monetary prize of $1,000 is awarded annually if merited. Established in 1990 in honor of Matt Rodermund for his years of volunteer service to the Society.

• 7626 •
Catalyst
Ilene H. Lang, Pres.
120 Wall St., 5th Fl.
New York, NY 10005-3904
Phone: (212)514-7600
Fax: (212)514-8470
E-mail: info@catalystwomen.org
Home Page: http://www.catalystwomen.org

• 7627 • Corporate and Professional Firm Leadership Award
To celebrate corporate and professional firms' initiatives to promote women's leadership. Awarded annually in March. Established in 1976.

• 7628 •
Catboat Association
John Greene, Membership Sec.
PO Box 246
Cataumet, MA 02534-0246
Phone: (508)947-5093
Fax: (508)947-2013
E-mail: john.greene@catboats.org
Home Page: http://www.catboats.org

• 7629 • Broad Axe Award
To recognize significant achievement in catboat construction. Applicants must be association members. Construction is intended to be broadly construed to include restoration of an old cat and finishing a prefab catboat hull as well as building a new car. The award consists of a broad axe, suitably mounted, that belonged to catboat builders Charles C. Hanley (1886-1936) and Merton E. Long (1936-1976). Awarded annually. Established in 1977.

• 7630 • Dolphin Award
For recognition of exceptional service to the Catboat Association. Applicants must be association members. Selection of the recipient is made by members of the Awards Committee. Established in 1975 and named in honor of the last catboat owned by the late John Killam Murphy. Established in 1975.

• 7631 • John Killam Murphy Award
For recognition of contributions that preserve the tradition of sail in catboats or advance the use of catboats in some new form, or in some novel or unusual way, or to recognize an event such as an outstanding cruise in a catboat or the use of a catboat under hazardous conditions for rescue purposes. Members of the Association may nominate candidates for the award. The award consists of a half-hull model of Tabby, Murphy's fourth cat, designed by Fenwick C. Williams in 1948 and built by Seth Persson. The

model was made by Don Rosencrantz of Essex, Connecticut. Awarded annually.

• 7632 •
Catholic Academy for Communication Arts Professionals
Jeanean Merkel, Pres.
901 Irving Ave.
Dayton, OH 45409-2316
Phone: (937)229-2303
Phone: (301)603-7769
Fax: (937)229-2300
E-mail: admin@catholicacademy.org
Home Page: http://www.CatholicAcademy.org

Formerly: (2002) Catholic Broadcasting Association; Unda-USA, the National Catholic Association of Broadcasters and Communicators.

• 7633 • **Gabriel Award**
To honor works of excellence in broadcasting programs, features, spots and stations that serve viewers and listeners through positive, creative treatment of concerns to humankind. The single most important criterion of a Gabriel winning program is its ability to uplift and nourish the human spirit. A Gabriel-worthy program affirms the dignity of human beings; it recognizes and upholds universally-recognized values such a community, creativity, tolerance, compassion and the dedication to excellence. The award, while presented by a Catholic association of broadcasters, is not limited to any sectarian religious creed. All radio and television stations in the United States and Canada are eligible. Awards are presented in the following television program categories: entertainment, informational, religious, children's, arts, news story, community awareness campaign, public service announcements, and short features. Awards are presented in the following radio program categories: arts and entertainment, news/informational, religious, news, community awareness campaign, public service announcement, and short features. The Gabriel, a nine-inch silver figure mounted on wood, is awarded annually at the Unda-USA General Assembly. In addition, Certificates of Merit, the Gabriel Award for Personal Achievement to recognize outstanding leadership in the broadcasting community, the Television Station of the Year, and the Radio Station of the Year are awarded. Established in 1965. The award is named for Gabriel, the angel in the Gospel of Luke, who proclaimed the Good News.

• 7634 •
Catholic Book Club
106 W 56th St.
New York, NY 10019
Phone: (212)515-0112
Phone: (212)581-4640
Fax: (212)399-3596
E-mail: cbc@americamagazine.org
Home Page: http://www.americamagazine.org/CatholicBookClub.cfm

• 7635 • **Saint Edmund Campion Award**
For recognition of long-standing service and eminence in the field of Christian letters. Selection is made periodically by the editorial board of the Catholic Book Club. Established in 1955 in memory of the Jesuit Saint Edmund Campion (canonized in 1970), author of the essay, *The Brag.*

• 7636 •
Catholic Campus Ministry Association
Edmund L. Franchi, Exec.Dir.
1118 Pendleton St., Ste. 300
Cincinnati, OH 45202-8805
Phone: (513)842-0167
Toll-Free: 888-714-6631
Fax: (513)842-0171
E-mail: info@ccmanet.org
Home Page: http://www.ccmanet.org

• 7637 • **Charles Forsyth Award**
For recognition of a contribution to campus ministry on the local, regional, and national level and significant research or experimentation in areas related to campus ministry in such a way as to enlarge the scope and function of ministry. Members who have been campus ministers for at least five years are eligible. A plaque is awarded annually. Established in 1974 in honor of Rev. Charles Forsyth, O.S.B.

• 7638 • **Archbishop Paul Hallinan Award**
To recognize persons who are not members but who have given service to campus ministry. Established in 1976.

• 7639 •
Catholic Church Extension Society of the U.S.A.
Judith L. Gerth, VP of Development
150 S Wacker Dr., 20th Fl.
Chicago, IL 60606-4200
Phone: (312)236-7240
Toll-Free: 888-473-2484
Fax: (312)236-5276
E-mail: gerthj@catholic-extension.org
Home Page: http://www.catholic-extension.org

• 7640 • **Lumen Christi Award**
To honor a person who has done outstanding missionary work in the United States or its territories. Nomination must be made by a Roman Catholic bishop from the United States. Annually, monetary award of $10,000 is given to the recipient and $25,000 to the nominating bishop's diocese. Established in 1978.

• 7641 •
Catholic Health Association of Canada (Association catholique canadienne de la sante)
Dr. Beverly Rachwalski, Pres.
1247 Kilborn Pl.
Ottawa, ON, Canada K1H 6K9
Phone: (613)731-7148
Fax: (613)731-7797
E-mail: chac@on.aibn.com
Home Page: http://www.chac.ca

Formerly: (1976) Catholic Hospital Association of Canada.

• 7642 • **Performance Citation Award**
To recognize individuals or groups who make unique contributions to health care through leadership and dedication to others, particularly in a Christian context. A framed certificate is awarded annually. Established in 1981.

• 7643 •
Catholic Kolping Society of America
Patricia Farkas, Natl. Administrator
9 E 8th St.
PO Box 4907
Clifton, NJ 07011-1101
Phone: (201)712-9550
Toll-Free: 877-659-7237
Fax: (201)712-9552
E-mail: patfarkas@aol.com
Home Page: http://kolping.org/main.htm

• 7644 • **Distinguished Service Award**
To recognize extraordinary services to the society by individuals who have been members of the society for at least 10 years. Nominations are by the local branch, and are submitted a year prior to the convention. A plaque and pin are awarded biennially at the convention. Established in 1966.

• 7645 • **Kolping Award**
To recognize achievements and contribution to the community from persons other than Kolping members. Nominations are accepted from a Kolping branch. A plaque is presented biennially at the National Convention. Established in 1960.

• 7646 •
Catholic League for Religious and Civil Rights
William A. Donohue PhD, Pres.
450 Seventh Ave.
New York, NY 10123
Phone: (212)371-3191
Fax: (212)371-3394
E-mail: cl@catholicleague.org
Home Page: http://www.catholicleague.org

• 7647 • **John Paul II Religious Freedom Award**
To recognize individuals who have distinguished themselves in safeguarding Catholic beliefs, values, and practices and/or defending the religious freedom rights of Catholics and other religious believers. A plaque is awarded irregularly at fundraising dinners. Established in 1983 by

The Late Rev. Virgil C. Blum, S.J., founder and first president of the league in honor of Pope John Paul II.

• 7648 • St. Michael Religious Freedom Award
For recognition of outstanding journalistic efforts to safeguard the religious freedom rights of all citizens, especially members of the Catholic community, and to address the problem of anti-Catholic prejudice in society. Membership in the Catholic Press Association is necessary for consideration. A plaque is awarded annually. Established in 1984.

• 7649 •
Catholic Library Association
Jean R. Bostley SSJ, Exec.Dir.
100 North St., Ste. 224
Pittsfield, MA 01201-5109
Phone: (413)443-2252
Fax: (413)442-2252
E-mail: cla@cathla.org
Home Page: http://www.cathla.org

• 7650 • Aggiornamento Award
To recognize an individual who has made an outstanding contribution to the goals of the Section and to the growth of parish librarianship. Awarded annually.

• 7651 • Rev. Andrew L. Bouwhuis Memorial Scholarship
To provide funds for graduate study toward a master's degree in library science. A scholarship of $1,500 is awarded annually. Established in 1988 to honor the Reverend Andrew L. Bouwhuis, a great librarian and loyal member of CLA.

• 7652 • John Brubaker Memorial Award
To recognize an outstanding work of literary merit published in *Catholic Library World*, the official journal of the Association. Established in 1978 to honor John Brubaker, who served the Catholic Library Association as advertising representative for the Association's journal, *Catholic Library World*, for over twenty years until his death in April 1977.

• 7653 • Jerome Award
Recognizes outstanding contribution and commitment to excellence in scholarship embodying the association's ideals. Awarded annually by the association's Academic Libraries Section.

• 7654 • Regina Medal
To recognize an individual for continued distinguished contributions to children's literature in the spirit of Walter de la Mare's words, "Only the rarest kind of best in anything can be good enough for the very young." Authors of any religion or nationality are eligible. A silver medal is awarded annually at the National Convention. Established in 1959.

• 7655 • St. Katharine Drexel Award
To recognize an individual for an outstanding contribution to the growth of high school librarianship. Awarded annually by the High School Libraries Section.

• 7656 • World Book Award
For members of the Association to gain for expertise in school or children's librarianship. A monetary award of $1,500, which may be divided among three recipients, is awarded annually. Established in 1973. Sponsored by World Book Inc., Chicago, Illinois.

• 7657 •
Catholic Press Association
Owen McGovern, Exec.Dir.
3555 Veterans Memorial Hwy., Unit 0
Ronkonkoma, NY 11779
Phone: (631)471-4730
Fax: (631)471-4804
E-mail: rosep@catholicpress.org
Home Page: http://www.catholicpress.org

• 7658 • Catholic Book Awards
To recognize the best Catholic books published during the preceding year. Members and non members of the association are eligible. Certificates are awarded annually at the convention in the following categories: popular presentation of the faith, spirituality, theology, scripture, liturgy, pastoral ministry, professional books, educational, design and production, children's books, first-time authors, family life, history/biography, gender issues and Hispanic books. Established in 1970 by the Catholic Press Association and then sponsored by Religious Book Review for a few years, but returned to Catholic Press Association control in 1983.

• 7659 • Journalism Award
To recognize outstanding work by publishers. Awards are given in two main categories: newspapers and magazines for writing, photography, and advertising campaigns. Spanish language awards are also given. Publishers who are members of the association are eligible. Certificates are awarded annually at the convention. Established about 1930.

• 7660 • St. Francis de Sales Award
To recognize outstanding contributions to Catholic journalism. A journalist or editor on the staff of, or a contributor to a periodical or publisher that is a member of the Catholic Press Association, who has performed the work of Catholic journalism with overall excellence, and has contributed to raising the measure of performance of Catholic journalists or the development of new and more effective practices is considered. The work may have been done during the preceding year or throughout the individual's journalism career. The honoree is selected by vote of CPA members. A cast in bronze of the statue of St. Francis de Sales, designed by the sculptor Reverend Thomas P. McGlynn, O.P. is presented each year at the annual convention. Established in 1959.

• 7661 •
Catholic Theological Society of America
Dr. Dolores Christie PhD, Exec.Sec.
John Carroll Univ.
20700 N Park Blvd.
University Heights, OH 44118
Phone: (216)397-1631
Fax: (216)397-1804
E-mail: dlchristie@aol.com
Home Page: http://www.jcu.edu/ctsa

• 7662 • John Courtney Murray Award
For recognition of distinguished achievement in theology through publication, lectures, teaching, participation in research projects and committees, and evidence of leadership and influence in the search for understanding of the Catholic faith. Members of the society who are North American are eligible. A monetary award of $500, a silver medal, and a certificate are awarded annually. Established in 1972. Formerly: Cardinal Spellman Award.

• 7663 •
Catholic University of America Alumni Association
404 McMahon Hall
620 Michigan Ave. NE
Catholic University of America
Washington, DC 20064
Phone: (202)319-5608
Toll-Free: 800-288-ALUM
Fax: (202)319-4483
E-mail: cua-alumni@cua.edu
Home Page: http://alumni.cua.edu

• 7664 • Alumni Achievement Awards
For recognition of outstanding achievement and distinction in an individual's life work. Members of the Alumni of The Catholic University of America are eligible. Approximately ten engraved plaques are awarded annually. Established in 1958.

• 7665 • Cardinal Gibbons Medal
To recognize distinguished and meritorious services to the Roman Catholic Church, the United States of America, or The Catholic University of America. Selection is made by the Executive Committee of the Alumni Board of Governors. A gold medal is awarded annually at the annual Homecoming Banquet. Established in 1947 in memory of His Eminence, James Cardinal Gibbons, who was Bishop of Richmond, 1872-1877, Archbishop of Baltimore, 1877-1921, and first Chancellor of The Catholic University.

• 7666 • Hall of Fame Award
To recognize varsity letter alumni and past coaches for outstanding achievements in athletics. Awarded biennially by the Board of Governors of the Alumni Association. Established in 1976-1977.

• 7667 • Frank A. Kuntz '07 Award
To honor individuals for service to the University which might otherwise go unrecognized. Selection is made by the Executive Committee of the

Alumni Board of Governors. A maximum of three awards are presented annually. Established in 1977 in honor of Frank A. Kuntz '07, the first lay person to receive an undergraduate degree from CUA (1907).

• 7668 • George J. Quinn, Class of '50 Distinguished Service Award
To recognize conspicuous and meritorious service to the Alumni Association of The Catholic University of America. The following services are considered: carrying out Association objectives; faithful and continued effort in developing or maintaining Association organizations; active participation in Association affairs; making and securing donations; or assisting the expansion of the usefulness, influence, and prestige of the Association. Candidates must be alumni of The Catholic University of America. A maximum of five engraved certificates are awarded at the annual Homecoming Banquet. Established in 1964.

• 7669 • Young Alumni Merit Award
To recognize a recent graduate who is a leader, exhibits high levels of achievement, and is committed to serving others. Alumnus/ae of CUA for less than 15 years are eligible. An engraved plaque is awarded annually at homecoming and reunion banquets. Established in 1989.

• 7670 •
Catholic War Veterans of the United States of America
Leo J. Krichten, Exec.Dir.
441 N Lee St.
Alexandria, VA 22314
Phone: (703)549-3622
Fax: (703)684-5196
E-mail: cwvlmt@aol.com
Home Page: http://www.cwv.org

• 7671 • Americanism News Media Award
To recognize a newspaper, radio or TV station, or an individual for outstanding promotion of loyalty to our nation via the media. Awarded annually when merited. Established in 1970.

• 7672 • Celtic Cross Award
To recognize outstanding achievement in promoting zeal and devotion for God, country, and home. Awarded when merited. Established in 1959.

• 7673 • Father Washington Award
To recognize a Catholic person for the performance of an act of heroism, the performance of exemplary devotion to the welfare and ideals of CWV, or the performance of outstanding civic endeavors in the community in the promotion of good citizenry (a non-political affiliation required). Established in 1966.

• 7674 • *Honor et Veritas* Award
To recognize an outstanding American. A bronze upon wood plaque is awarded annually when merited. Established in 1959.

• 7675 • Most Outstanding Catholic War Veteran
To recognize the individual who, in the opinion of the national Department, has contributed most to the betterment of CWV. Established in 1969.

• 7676 • Most Outstanding Post of the Year Award
To recognize the post that has the best overall program participation in national programs. Established in 1969.

• 7677 •
Catholic Youth Organization of the Archdiocese of New York
David Denis, Dir.
34 W 124th St.
New York, NY 10037
Phone: (212)862-6401
Fax: (212)862-6421
E-mail: jpp@myrealbox.com

• 7678 • Club of Champions Award
To recognize outstanding leadership, inspiration and example given to American youth. National leaders are eligible. A gold medal is awarded annually. Established in 1936.

• 7679 • John V. Mara Memorial CYO Sportsman of the Year Award
To recognize the attainment of high caliber proficiency in the area of athletics and for the promotion or sponsorship of athletic programs. A plaque is awarded annually. Established in 1965.

• 7680 • Parish Volunteer Award
To recognize contributions made to parish youth programs. Volunteer leaders over 18 years of age who have contributed two years' service to a parish CYO program are eligible. A plaque is awarded annually. Established in 1951.

• 7681 • Teenage Youth Award
To recognize outstanding teenage leadership qualities and commendable acceptance of responsibility. Members of the CYO who are 14 to 18 years of age and have been active in programs for two years are eligible. A plaque is awarded annually. Established in 1960.

• 7682 •
Caucus for Television Producers, Writers and Directors
Vin Di Bona, Chm.
PO Box 11236
Burbank, CA 91510-1236
Phone: (818)843-7572
Fax: (818)846-2159
E-mail: info@caucus.org
Home Page: http://www.caucus.org

• 7683 • Distinguished Service Award
To recognize an individual for dedication to the work of the Caucus. Members are eligible. A trophy is awarded annually. Established in 1983.

• 7684 • Executive of the Year
To honor an executive for outstanding performance of duties and influence on television. Members of the television industry and related areas of communication are eligible. A trophy is awarded annually. Established in 1989.

• 7685 • Member of the Year
To recognize a member for a distinguished body of work in television. Members of the Caucus are eligible. A trophy is awarded annually. Established in 1983.

• 7686 •
CDS International
Robert Fenstermacher, Exec.Dir.
871 United Nations Plz., 15th Fl.
New York, NY 10017-1814
Phone: (212)497-3500
Fax: (212)497-3535
E-mail: info@cdsintl.org
Home Page: http://www.cdsintl.org

• 7687 • Robert Bosch Foundation Fellowship Program
To maintain ties of friendship and understanding between the U.S. and Germany by sponsoring young American professionals in full-time work internships in Germany. During the nine-month program (September-May), Fellows have the opportunity to live in Germany while worgking in the branches of the Federal Government as well as in high-level internships relating to their professional experience. The internships are accompanied by varous seminars in order to gain insight into the political, economic, and cultural environment of Europe with a particular emphasis on Germany. Applicants must be U.S. citizens who have outstanding credentials, including advanced degrees or equivalent work experience in the fields of journalism, public affairs, mass communications, law, economics, political science, business. DEM 3500/month is awarded. If necessary, Fellows can take a language course in Germany up to 3 months prior to the beginning of the program in Germany.

• 7688 •
Ceilings and Interior Systems Construction Association
Bonny Luck, Exec.Dir.
1500 Lincoln Hwy., No. 202
St. Charles, IL 60174
Phone: (630)584-1919
Toll-Free: 800-524-7228
Fax: (630)584-2003
E-mail: info@cisca.org
Home Page: http://www.cisca.org

Formerly: (1985) Ceilings and Interior Systems Contractors Association.

• 7689 • Construction Excellence Award
No information given for this edition.

• 7690 • Degelleke Award
For recognition of the most outstanding achievement, service, or contribution to the ceiling systems, acoustical, or interior systems industry as

a whole for the past year or for any past period. Contractors, manufacturers, consultants, or any other persons or groups connected with the industry are eligible. A hand-lettered and painted scroll is awarded annually. Established in 1960.

• 7691 • Superintendent of the Year Award

No further information given for this edition.

• 7692 •
Centennial Education Foundation
Robert Schrader, Exec.Dir.
433 Centennial Rd.
Warminster, PA 18974-5455
Phone: (215)441-6000
Fax: (215)441-0330
E-mail: schrro@centennialsd.org
Home Page: http://www.centennialef.org

• 7693 • Teacher Educational Mini-Grant

For teacher in the Centennial School District. Grant awarded annually.

• 7694 •
Center for Adult Reading and Enrichment
110 Irby St.
Jackson, TN 38301
Phone: (731)422-6175
E-mail: cdouglas1001@hotmail.com

• 7695 • Beverly Buntin Volunteer of the Year

For volunteer service. Recognition award bestowed annually.

• 7696 •
Center for Advanced Study in the Behavioral Sciences
Claude Steele, CEO
75 Alta Rd.
Stanford, CA 94305-8090
Phone: (650)321-2052
Fax: (650)321-1192
E-mail: info@casbs.org
Home Page: http://www.casbs.org

• 7697 • Fellow

To enable scientists and scholars who hold the PhD in the social sciences, biomedicine, and the humanities of any age, sex, race, or nationality to spend approximately 9 to 12 months in the company of stimulating colleagues in a relaxed environment pursuing their scientific and scholarly purpose and to recognize those who show exceptional promise or accomplishment as productive workers in their respective fields. Nominations may be made by academic officers or established scholars. Approximately 45 to 50 fellowships are awarded annually. Established in 1954 by a grant from the Ford Foundation.

• 7698 •
Center for Afroamerican and African Studies
The University of Michigan
505 S State St.
4700 Haven
Ann Arbor, MI 48109-1092
Phone: (734)764-5513
Fax: (734)763-0543
Home Page: http://www.umich.edu/~iinet/caas/

• 7699 • Du Bois-Mandela-Rodney Fellowship

This is a residential fellowship for post-doctoral researchers working on African or the African diaspora in, but not limited to, the humanities, social sciences, physical sciences and professional schools. Scholars who study the Gullah speaking Sea islands, Cape Verde islands, the Anglophone Caribbean, the Canary Islands, and Madagascar, or some other less studied area are especially encouraged to apply. The fellowship provides $42,000 as a stipend, $1,000 for research, and up to $2,000 for travel. Successful candidates can expect to maintain affiliation with CAAS as well as departments and research institutes that relate to their projects. Fellows wil be expected to conduct a CAAS work-in-progress seminar on their research during one of the semesters in residence.

• 7700 •
The Center for American and International Law
J. David Ellwanger, Pres.
5201 Democracy Dr.
Plano, TX 75024-3561
Phone: (972)244-3400
Fax: (972)244-3401
E-mail: cail@cailaw.org
Home Page: http://www.cailaw.org

• 7701 • John Rogers Award

To honor an individual associated with the petroleum industry in recognition of extraordinary professional and civic achievement. Awarded annually by the Center's Institute for Energy Law. Established in 1969.

• 7702 • Robert G. Storey International Award

For leadership in international law and personal qualities. Awarded annually. Established in 1990.

• 7703 •
Center for Aviation Research and Education
Henry Ogrodvinski, Pres./CEO
1010 Wayne Ave., Ste. 930
Silver Spring, MD 20910
Phone: (301)495-2848
Fax: (301)585-1803
E-mail: henryo@nasao.org
Home Page: http://www.nasao.org

• 7704 • Aviation Education Award

Recognizes an outstanding state program. Judged by aviation association professionals. Awarded annually.

• 7705 •
Center for Bioenvironmental Research
Health and Environmental Research Bldg.
1430 Tulane Ave., SL-3
New Orleans, LA 70112-2699
Phone: (504)585-6910
Fax: (504)585-6428
E-mail: cbr@tulane.edu

• 7706 • Aaron Allan Awards

Recognizes excellence in environmental studies. Inquire for application details.

• 7707 • CBR Scholar Awards

Inquire for application details.

• 7708 • SPRITE undergraduate summer research

Inquire for application details.

• 7709 •
Center for Book Arts
Alexander Campos, Exec.Dir.
28 W 27th St., 3rd Fl.
New York, NY 10001-6906
Phone: (212)481-0295
Fax: (212)481-9853
E-mail: info@centerforbookarts.org
Home Page: http://www.centerforbookarts.org

• 7710 • Poetry Chapbook Competition, Artist Residency Program

A monetary award is given annually.

• 7711 •
Center for Christian/Jewish Understanding of Sacred Heart University
Rabbi Joseph H. Ehrenkranz, Exec.Dir.
5151 Park Ave.
Fairfield, CT 06825
Phone: (203)365-7592
Fax: (203)365-4815
E-mail: daleg@sacredheart.edu
Home Page: http://www.ccju.org

• 7712 • Nostra Aetate Award

Recognizes service to humanity. Awarded annually.

• 7713 •
Center for Communication
Catherine Williams, Exec.Dir.
561 Broadway, Ste. 12-B
New York, NY 10016-1001
Phone: (212)686-5005
Fax: (212)504-2632
E-mail: info@cencom.org
Home Page: http://www.cencom.org

• 7714 • **Communication Award**
Recognizes an outstanding contributor within the field of communications. Awarded annually.

• 7715 •
Center for Contemporary Opera
Richard Marshall, Gen.Dir.
PO Box 258
New York, NY 10044-0205
Phone: (212)785-2757
Fax: (212)758-0389
E-mail: mail@conopera.org
Home Page: http://conopera.org

• 7716 • **International Opera Singers Competition**
To encourage singers to become acquainted with contemporary operatic literature written in English and to assist the most talented with their careers. All singers who have not yet achieved operatic careers in major opera houses are eligible. Monetary prizes and certificates are awarded annually for first place, second place, and third place. The first and second place winners are presented in a joint recital at Weill Recital Hall at Carnegie Hall. Applications, which are available from the Center, must be returned postmarked by May 15. Established in 1983.

• 7717 •
Center for Creative Leadership
Peter L. Richardson, Chm.
PO Box 26300
One Leadership Pl.
Greensboro, NC 27438-6300
Phone: (336)545-2810
Fax: (336)282-3284
E-mail: info@leaders.ccl.org
Home Page: http://www.ccl.org

• 7718 • **Kenneth E. Clark Research Award**
To recognize outstanding unpublished papers on leadership by undergraduate and graduate students. Eligible papers must address issues and trends that are significant to the study of leadership, show consideration of the relevant theoretical and empirical literature, develop implications for research into the dynamics and content of leadership, make a conceptual or empirical contribution to the issue of leadership, and apply the research to leadership identification and development. The winners of these awards will receive a prize of $1,500 and a trip to the Center to present the papers in the colloquium. Established in 1992 in honor of Kenneth E. Clark, former president of the Center.

• 7719 • **Walter F. Ulmer, Jr. Applied Research Award**
To stimulate outstanding field research and its creative application to the practice of leadership. First prize includes $1,500 and a trip to the Center to present research in a colloquium. Awarded annually. Established in honor of Walter F. Ulmer Jr., retired President and CEO of the Center.

• 7720 •
Center for Design of Analog-Digital Integrated Circuits
Washington State University
College of Engineering & Architecture
Pullman, WA 99164-2780
Phone: (509)335-5595
Fax: (509)335-9608
E-mail: ringo@wsu.edu
Home Page: http://www.eecs.wsu.edu/cdadic

• 7721 • **Awards**
Awards are give for Best Faculty Project and Best Student Poster. Awarded annually.

• 7722 •
Center for Ecoliteracy
Zenobia Barlow, Exec.Dir.
2522 San Pablo Ave.
Berkeley, CA 94702
Phone: (510)845-4595
Fax: (510)845-1439
E-mail: info@ecoliteracy.org
Home Page: http://www.ecoliteracy.org/

• 7723 • **BBC Environment Award**
Award of recognition.

• 7724 •
Center for Health Law and Policy at Southern Illinois University School of Law
Southern Illinois School of Law
1150 Douglas Dr.
Mailcode 6804
Carbondale, IL 62901
Phone: (618)453-8686
Toll-Free: (618)453-3317
E-mail: chlp@siu.edu
Home Page: http://www.law.siu.edu/healthlawmootcourt

• 7725 • **National Health Law Moot Court Competition**
To recognize the nation's best law school teams in health law. Each school may enter one or two teams up two or three members. Held over two days annually at the Southern Illinois University School of Law. The following awards are presented: $1,000 for first place; $750 for second place; $500 for third place, Best Brief, and Best Overall Oralist; and $250 for runner-up Best Brief and Best Preliminary Round Oralist. Cosponsored by the Department of Medical Humanities at the Southern Illinois University School of Medicine, the American College of Legal Medicine, and the American College of Legal Medicine Foundation.

• 7726 •
Center for Human-Computer Communication
OGI School of Science and Engineering
Dr. Phil Cohen, Co-Dir.
Department of Computer Science & Engineering
Oregon Health and Science University
20000 NW Walker Rd.
Beaverton, OR 97006
Phone: (503)748-1248
Fax: (503)748-1875
E-mail: pcohen@cse.ogi.edu
Home Page: http://www.cse.ogi.edu/CHCC

• 7727 • **NSF-Funded Paid Internships**
For HCI research studies. Inquire for application details.

• 7728 •
Center for Immigration Studies
1522 K St. NW, Ste. 820
Washington, DC 20005-1202
Phone: (202)466-8185
Fax: (202)466-8076
E-mail: center@cis.org
Home Page: http://www.cis.org

• 7729 • **Katz Award for Excellence in the Coverage of Immigration**
Annual award for journalist best challenging the norm of immigration reporting.

• 7730 •
Center for International Studies
University of Missouri-St. Louis
366 Social Sciences & Business Bldg.
8001 Natural Bridge Rd.
St. Louis, MO 63121-4499
Phone: (314)516-5753
Fax: (314)516-6757
E-mail: jglassman@umsl.edu
Home Page: http://www.umsl.edu/services/cis/cisworld/

• 7731 • **Global Citizen Award**
To honor an individual whose life and work are a powerful demonstration of the values of global citizenship. Awarded annually with a monetary prize and medal. Established in 1994.

• 7732 •
Center for Latin America and Caribbean Studies
Pearse Hall 168
2513 E Hartford Ave.
University of Wisconsin-Milwaukee
Milwaukee, WI 53201
Phone: (414)229-4401
Fax: (414)229-2879
E-mail: clacs@uwm.edu
Home Page: http://www.uwm.edu/Dept/CLACS/

• 7733 • **Americas Book Award for Children's and Young Adult Literature**
To recognize U.S. works (picture, books, poetry, fiction, folklore) published in the previous year in English or Spanish that authentically and engagingly present the experience of individuals in Latin America or the Caribbean or of Latinos in the United States. By combining both and linking the Americas, the award reaches beyond geographic borders. The award and the other commended books were selected for their quality of story, cultural authenticity/sensitivity, integration of text, illustration and design, and potential for classroom use. Awarded annually. Established in 1993.

• 7734 •
Center for Meteorite Studies
Arizona State University
PO Box 872504
Tempe, AZ 85287-2504
Phone: (602)965-3576
Fax: (602)965-2747
Home Page: http://meteorites.asu.edu

• 7735 • **Nininger Meteorite Award**
To generate interest in meteoritics and the ability to logically and objectively interpret experimental methods, data, and hypotheses and to learn by writing. Awarded annually with a monetary prize of $1,000. Established in 1961.

• 7736 •
Center for National Policy
Maureen S. Steinbruner, VP/Senior Policy Advisor
1 Massachusetts Ave. NW, Ste. 333
Washington, DC 20001
Phone: (202)682-1800
Fax: (202)682-1818
E-mail: thecenter@cnponline.org
Home Page: http://www.cnponline.org

Formerly: (1982) Center for Democratic Policy.

• 7737 • **Edmund S. Muskie Distinguished Public Service Award**
To recognize persons whose integrity and performance in public service exemplify the Center's purposes and ideals. Nominations are made by the Board of Directors. A plaque is awarded annually. Established in 1982. Formerly: Distinguished Public Service Award.

• 7738 •
Center for Nonprofit Management
1666 K St. NW, Ste. 440
Washington, DC 20006
Phone: (202)457-0540
Fax: (202)457-0549
E-mail: info@nonprofitadvancement.org
Home Page: http://www.nonprofitadvancement.org

• 7739 • **The Washington Post Award for Excellence in Nonprofit Management**
To recognize, promote, and teach good nonprofit management practices within the Washington DC metropolitan area. A monetary prize of $5,000 is awarded to the winner, and each of four honorable mentions receives $2,5000. Awarded annually. Established in 1994. Formerly: The WCA Award for Excellence in Non-Profit Management.

• 7740 •
Center for Philosophy, Law, Citizenship
Prof. James P. Friel, Pres./Dir.
SUNY
Knapp Hall 15
Farmingdale, NY 11735
Phone: (631)420-2047

• 7741 • **Citizen of the Year**
To encourage citizenship and to honor an individual who practices citizenship. U.S. citizens (generally) are eligible. A monetary prize and a plaque are awarded annually. Established in 1980.

• 7742 •
Center for Photography at Woodstock
Ariel Shanberg, Exec.Dir.
% Photographers Fund
59 Tinker St.
Woodstock, NY 12498
Phone: (845)679-9957
Fax: (845)679-6337
E-mail: info@cpw.org
Home Page: http://www.cpw.org

Formerly: (1988) Catskill Center for Photography.

• 7743 • **Photographers Fellowship Fund**
To support working artists using photographic media in a twenty county region. Residents of Albany, Columbia, Delaware, Dutchess, Essex, Fulton, Greene, Hamilton, Herkimer, Montgomery, Orange, Otsego, Rensselaer, Saratoga, Schenectady, Schoharie, Sullivan, Ulster, Warren, and Washington counties are eligible. A portfolio of ten slides of original work must be submitted. Deadline is in July. Contact the center for additional information. Two monetary fellowship awards of $1,000 each are presented annually. Established in 1980.

• 7744 •
Center for Science in the Public Interest
Michael F. Jacobson PhD, Sec.
1875 Connecticut Ave. NW, Ste. 300
Washington, DC 20009-5728
Phone: (202)332-9110
Fax: (202)265-4954
E-mail: cspi@cspinet.org
Home Page: http://www.cspinet.org

• 7745 • **Harlan Page Hubbard Lemon Award**
To recognize advertisements that have excelled in their ability to dupe the American public. Irresponsible, unfair, and misleading ads are considered. Winners are entitled to a Hubbard Lemon Trophy a bronze-colored victory figure grasping a lemon. Awarded annually. Established in 1985 and named for Harlan Page Hubbard, a 19th century advertising pioneer who promoted patent medicines as cures for virtually all ills. Unfortunately, most of his ads were notoriously false and misleading.

• 7746 •
Center for the Study of Aging, Inc.
706 Madison Ave.
Albany, NY 12208-3604
Phone: (518)465-6927
Fax: (518)462-1339
E-mail: csa@centerforthestudyofaging.org
Home Page: http://www.centerforthestudyofaging.org

• 7747 • **Outstanding Leadership and Research in Physical Activity and Aging Award**
Presented at International Conference. Inquire for application details.

• 7748 •
Center for the Study of Canada
Christopher Kirkey, Dir.
Plattsburgh State University of New York
133 Court St.
Suny Plattsburgh
Plattsburgh, NY 12901
Phone: (518)564-2086
Phone: (518)564-2394
Fax: (518)564-2112
E-mail: christopher.kirkey@plattsburgh.edu
Home Page: http://web.plattsburgh.edu/offices/academic/cesca

• 7749 • **Green Mountain Power**
Awarded biennially for the best article in Quebec studies.

• 7750 • **Prix du Quebec**
Recognizes outstanding contribution to field of Canadian studies. A monetary prize is given biennially.

• 7751 •
Center for the Study of Science Fiction
James Gunn, Dir.
Department of English
3114 Wescoe Hall
University of Kansas
Lawrence, KS 66045-2115
Phone: (785)864-3380
Fax: (785)864-1159
E-mail: jgunn@ku.edu
Home Page: http://www.ku.edu/~sfcenter/

• 7752 • **John W. Campbell Memorial Award**
To honor the best science-fiction novel of the year. Science-fiction novels published during the calendar year are considered. A trophy is inscribed annually. Established in 1972 by Harry Harrison and Brian W. Aldiss in memory of John W. Campbell, the long-time editor of *Astounding Science Fiction,* now named *Analog.*

• 7753 • Theodore Sturgeon Memorial Award

For recognition of the best short science fiction of the year. Short works of fiction published during the calendar year are considered. A trophy is inscribed annually. Established in 1987 by Jayne Sturgeon and James Gunn in memory of Theodore Sturgeon, the pre-eminent short-story writer of the science-fiction field.

• 7754 •
Center for the Study of Sport in Society
Northeastern Univ.
360 Huntington Ave., Ste 161 CP
Boston, MA 02115
Phone: (617)373-4025
Fax: (617)373-4566
Home Page: http://www.sportinsociety.org

• 7755 • Excellence in Sports Journalism Award

To encourage excellence in all phases of sports journalism. Awards have been presented in various categories: Film & Book, Print Journalism and Broadcast Journalism. Professional journalists are eligible. A plaque and travel expenses are awarded annually. In addition, a Special Award of Excellence in Sports Journalism may be awarded posthumously. Nominations should be submitted by April 1. Established in 1985.

• 7756 • Sport in Society Hall of Fame

To honor people from the world of sports who make especially significant contributions to society, those that extend far beyond the game itself. Awarded annually. Established in 1999.

• 7757 •
Center for the Study of the Presidency
David M. Abshire, Pres./CEO
1020 19th NW, Ste. 250
Washington, DC 20036
Phone: (202)872-9800
Fax: (202)872-9811
E-mail: center@thepresidency.org
Home Page: http://www.thepresidency.org

• 7758 • Moses Leo Gitelson Memorial Essay Awards

For recognition of outstanding essays on public policy issues, particularly as related to the American presidency. Undergraduate students in colleges and universities are eligible. Monetary awards, certificates, and books are awarded annually at the student symposium. Established in 1980 by Susan Aurelia Gitelson in memory of her father, Moses Leo Gitelson, American business and philanthropic leader.

• 7759 •
Center of the American Experiment
Dr. Mark S. Larson, Sec.
1024 Plymouth Bldg.
12 S 6th St.
Minneapolis, MN 55402
Phone: (612)338-3605
Fax: (612)338-3621
E-mail: amexp@amexp.org
Home Page: http://www.amexp.org

• 7760 • American Experiment Award

To honor the values of people which animate America's great experiment in freedom. Awarded annually with a plaque. Established in 1994.

• 7761 •
Centracare Health Foundation
Mark Larkin, Exec.Dir.
PO Box 2206
St. Cloud, MN 56302
Phone: (320)240-2810

• 7762 • Spirit of Caring Award

For collaborative effort to improve health in service area. Monetary award bestowed annually.

• 7763 •
Central Association of Obstetricians and Gynecologists
Rochelle Hickel, Contact
PO Box 3010
Minot, ND 58702-3010
Phone: (701)838-8323
Fax: (701)852-8733
E-mail: rhickel@caog.org
Home Page: http://www.caog.org

• 7764 • Annual Central Prize Award, President's Certificate of Merit Award, and Central Poster Award

For recognition of outstanding investigative or clinical work in the field of obstetrics and gynecology. Accredited physicians, teachers, research workers, and medical students whose research was done within the geographic area of the Association (Alabama, Arizona, Arkansas, Colorado, Idaho, Illinois, Indiana, Iowa, Kansas, Kentucky, Louisiana, Michigan, Minnesota, Mississippi, Missouri, Montana, Nebraska, New Mexico, North Dakota, Ohio, Oklahoma, South Dakota, Tennessee, Texas, Utah, West Virginia, Wisconsin, and Wyoming) are eligible. At least one of the authors of the manuscript submitted must be a member of the Association, and the manuscript must not have been previously presented, submitted, accepted, or published. The Annual Central Prize Award of $2,000 is presented for the best paper; the President's Certificate of Merit Award of $1,000 is given to the runner-up; and the Central Poster Award of $500 is given for to the best poster presentation. Awarded annually. Established in 1930. For further information, write to Paul G. Tomich, M.D., Bldg. 103, Rm. 1012, 2160 S. First Ave., Maywood, IL 60153. Formerly: Annual Central Prize Award and Certificate of Merit Award.

• 7765 • Community Hospital Award

To recognize an author(s) for clinical study or research in the field of obstetrics and gynecology by members located in community hospitals who are not full-time faculty in medical schools. Preference for this award is given to papers concerning gynecologic endoscopy or any other diagnostic or therapeutic procedures which enhance the quality of care of gynecologic or obstetric patients. At least one of the authors of the manuscript submitted must be a member of the Association, and manuscripts must not have been previously presented, submitted, accepted, or published . A monetary prize of $1,000 is awarded at the Annual Meeting of the Association.

• 7766 •
Central Connecticut Regional Planning Agency
Carl J. Stephani, Exec.Dir.
225 N. Main St., Ste. 304
Bristol, CT 06010-4993
Phone: (860)589-7820
Phone: (860)224-9888
Fax: (860)589-6950
E-mail: ccrpa@ccrpa.org
Home Page: http://www.ccrpa.org

• 7767 • Melvin J. Schneidermeyer Regional Leadership Award

For 5 areas of leadership impact, benefit, service, volunteer, and diversity. Recognition award bestowed annually.

• 7768 •
Central Louisiana Partners in Literacy
Darlene Dorsey, Exec. Dir.
204 Chester St.
Alexandria, LA 71301
Phone: (318)448-9070
Phone: (318)448-9685
Fax: (318)448-9685

• 7769 • Member of the United Way

For adult literacy. Grant awarded annually.

• 7770 •
Central Missouri State University
Art Center Gallery
Art Center 120
Warrensburg, MO 64093
Phone: (660)543-4481
Fax: (816)543-8006
E-mail: nwood@cmsu1.cmsu.edu
Home Page: http://www.cmsu.edu/art

• 7771 • Greater Midwest International Exhibition

To bring together quality artworks in all media that represent an international perspective on contemporary visual arts. Individuals 21 years of age and older may submit 35mm slides of artwork completed in the previous three-year period. The deadline for entries is October 15. Four monetary awards totaling $1,600 and exhibition contracts are awarded annually. For a prospectus and entry form, send a SASE. Established in

1984. Co-sponsored by the Missouri Arts Council.

• 7772 •
Central Pennsylvania Festival of the Arts
Rick Bryant, Exec.Dir.
403 S Allen St., Ste. 205A
PO Box 1023
State College, PA 16804-1023
Phone: (814)237-3682
Fax: (814)237-0708
E-mail: office@arts-festival.com
Home Page: http://www.arts-festival.com

• 7773 • **Banner Competition**
To exhibit and recognize outstanding banners. Groups and individuals are encouraged to submit entries. The deadline for submissions is June. Selected banners are hung during the Festival of the Arts along the Festival's streets. Four monetary prizes are awarded annually: first prize - $300; and second prize - $200. Established in 1966.

• 7774 • **Crafts National Exhibition**
To recognize and exhibit crafts that examine and make reference to the history of world art as well as to contemporary sculptural ideas. The deadline is in March. Monetary prizes totaling $3,000 are awarded at the judge's discretion. Established in 1966. Formerly: (1997) Juried Crafts Exhibition.

• 7775 • **Images Competition**
To recognize the best work in this juried exhibition. Open to all artists residing in Pennsylvania and the Mid-Atlantic region. Two-dimensional and three-dimensional work in any medium executed in the previous two years may be submitted by April 1. The following monetary awards totaling $2,000 are presented: a $1,000 Best of Show Award; and five $200 Merit Awards. Established in 1989.

• 7776 • **Sidewalk Sale and Exhibition**
To recognize outstanding quality of an individual exhibitor in this juried exhibition. A minimum of $15,000 is presented in various categories. The deadline is in mid-February. Established in 1987.

• 7777 •
Central Pennsylvania Paralegal Association
Cathleen Kohr, Pres.
PO Box 11814
Harrisburg, PA 17108
Phone: (717)234-4121
Fax: (717)232-6802
E-mail:
centralpennsylvania@paralegals.org

• 7778 • **Outstanding Paralegal Award**
For a paralegal who exemplifies the profession and who is an asset to both the job and the community. Monetary award bestowed annually.

• 7779 •
Cercles des Jeunes Naturalistes
Richard Cartier, Pres.
Jardin Botanique de Montreal
4101 rue Sherbrooke Est, bureau 262
Montreal, QC, Canada H1X 2B2
Phone: (514)252-3023
Fax: (514)254-8744
E-mail: cjn@cam.org
Home Page: http://www.cjn.cam.org

• 7780 • **Coupes Merites Aux Individus**
To recognize individuals for outstanding service to the Association. Established about 1987. For more information contact Gertrude Dechamplain at the above address.

• 7781 • **Naturalistes de l'Annee**
To recognize the exceptional achievement of one male and one female naturalist during their leisure time. Associate members of the Association who are under 17 years of age may be selected. A monetary prize, a medal, and a certificate are awarded annually. Established in 1931. For more information, contact Valerie Whear Pepin at the above address.

• 7782 • **Trophee Environment**
For recognition of youth groups that have done exceptional work to protect their local or regional environment. Groups affiliated with Les Cercles are eligible. Trophies are awarded annually. Established in 1975 by Victor Goldbloom, Minister of Environment of Quebec. Sponsored by the Ministry of Environment of Quebec. For more information, contact Cercle Bernadelle du Gave at the above address.

• 7783 • **Trophees Desjardins**
For recognition of youth groups that have worked markedly in their community to promote the young naturalists movement. Groups affiliated with Les Cercles are eligible. A monetary prize and a trophy are awarded annually. Established in 1960. Sponsored by Caisses Populaires Desjardins. For more information contact Jacques Eric Mercier at the above address.

• 7784 •
Cerebral Palsy of Louisiana
John P. Gustin, Exec.Dir.
2380 Barataria Blvd., Ste. 5
Marrero, LA 70072
Phone: (318)387-4560
Phone: (504)341-0676
Toll-Free: 800-375-8275
Fax: (504)341-0700
E-mail: cpla@bellsouth.net

• 7785 • **Ada Gruber Grant**
For a student studying physical therapy or speech therapy. Grant awarded annually.

• 7786 • **Johnny Roland Grant**
For a student studying biomedical engineering. Grant awarded annually.

• 7787 •
Cetacean Society International
William W. Rossiter, Pres.
PO Box 953
Georgetown, CT 06829
Phone: (203)770-8615
Fax: (860)561-0187
E-mail: rossiter@csiwhalesalive.org
Home Page: http://www.csiwhalesalive.org

• 7788 • **Cetacean Citation**
Recognizes exceptional work in wildlife conservation. Inquire for application details.

• 7789 •
Chain Link Fence Manufacturer Institute
Mark Levin CAE, Exec.VP
10015 Old Columbia Rd., Ste. B-215
Columbia, MD 21046
Phone: (301)596-2583
Fax: (301)596-2594
E-mail: clfmihq@aol.com
Home Page: http://www.chainlinkinfo.org

• 7790 • **Chainlink Fence Design Award**
To provide recognition for unique usage of chainlink fence materials and/or accessories. Licensed architects and fencing contractors are eligible. The deadline is November 1. A trophy or plaque is awarded annually. Established in 1985.

• 7791 •
Chamber Music America
Margaret M. Lioi, CEO
305 7th Ave., 5th Fl.
New York, NY 10001-6008
Phone: (212)242-2022
Fax: (212)242-7955
E-mail: info@chamber-music.org
Home Page: http://www.chamber-music.org

• 7792 • **Richard J. Bogomolny National Service Award**
For recognition of outstanding contributions to the field of chamber music. A certificate and a gift are awarded annually at the Annual Conference. Established in 1980. Formerly: National Service Award.

• 7793 • **Castleman Award for Excellence in Chamber Music Teaching**
To encourage professional development and recognize outstanding elementary or secondary school level chamber music education programs. Elementary or secondary school level teachers may apply by December 1. A monetary prize of $1,000 and publicity. Awarded annually. Established in 1987. Formerly: Gruber Award and Heidi Castleman Award for Excellence in Chamber Music.

• 7794 • **Chamber Music America Commissioning Program**
To enrich the chamber music repertoire as well as to foster creative partnerships among ensembles, composers and presenters. Awards are

made on the basis of artistic excellence and demonstrated commitment to the performance of contemporary music. Voting members of Chamber Music America who are either presenters or ensembles are eligible. Composers must be American citizens or permanent residents. The deadline for entry in early April . Grants are awarded. Awarded annually.

• 7795 • **CMA/ASCAP Awards for Adventuresome Programming**

To acknowledge and encourage programming of music composed after 1950. Chamber Music America members may apply by September 1. Awards are given in the following categories: (1) chamber music ensembles that present contemporary music exclusively; (2) chamber music ensembles that perform mixed repertoire, including music composed after 1950; (3) chamber music presenters who present 10 or more concerts per season; and (4) chamber music presenters who present nine or fewer concerts per season. Monetary awards of $350 and engraved plaques are awarded annually in each category at the National Conference. Established in 1987.

• 7796 •

Chamber Music Monterey Bay
Mark Huber, Exec.Dir.
PO Box 221458
Carmel, CA 93922
Phone: (831)625-2212
Fax: (831)625-2212
E-mail: cmmb@chambermusicmontereybay.org
Home Page: http://www.chambermusicmontereybay.org

• 7797 • **Carmel Chamber Music Competition**

For recognition of outstanding chamber music performances. Non-professional ensembles of from three to eight players under the direction of a qualified coach are eligible. Ensembles that develop a substantial portion of their time performing for fees are not eligible. The average (mean) age of the players in each ensemble must be under 26 on the day of the competition for which they are playing. Competition is held on the first Saturday in May. The following monetary awards are presented: AT&T National Pro-Am Youth Award - $3000, for strings; Billwiller Award - $3000, for woodwinds/brass; and Angie Machado Award - $2000. Formerly: Chamber Music Society of the Monterey Peninsula Competition.

• 7798 •

Chamber Music Society of Lincoln Center
Norma Hurlburt, Exec.Dir.
70 Lincoln Center Plz.
New York, NY 10023-6582
Phone: (212)875-5775
Fax: (212)875-5799
E-mail: info@chambermusicsociety.org
Home Page: http://www.chambermusicsociety.org

• 7799 • **Elise L. Stoeger Prize**

To recognize chamber music composers not already at the forefront of their field . The prize is awarded for achievement in chamber music composition, demonstrated by a body of work rather than by a specific piece. The winner must be currently involved in creating new chamber music works, and must have composed at least one chamber music work within the last five years. Composers are nominated to compete for this prize by committee, an may not apply directly. Monetary award is presented to one composer every two years. Established in 1988 by Milan Stoeger in memory of his wife, Elise L. Stoeger. Restructured in 1992 And 2001. Formerly: (1992) Elise L. Stoeger Composer's Chair.

• 7800 •

Chamber Music Yellow Springs
PO Box 448
Yellow Springs, OH 45387-0448
Phone: (937)767-2912
Fax: (937)767-7699
E-mail: info@cmys.org
Home Page: http://www.cmys.org

• 7801 • **Chamber Music Yellow Springs Competition**

To encourage deserving young performers of chamber music and to foster the enjoyment and appreciation of live chamber music. Balanced ensembles (not soloists with accompaniment) of three to six players, whose average age does not exceed 30 years are eligible. Not more than one member of the ensemble may have performed previously at a CMYS-sponsored concert. Applications and tapes must be submitted by January 15. Monetary prizes of $2,500 for the first place ensemble and $1,500 for the second place ensemble are awarded annually in April at a concert performed by the finalists. Established in 1985.

• 7802 •

Chamber of Commerce of Harrison County
Darrell R. Voelker, Exec.Dir.
310 N Elm St.
Corydon, IN 47112
Phone: (812)738-2137
Toll-Free: 888-738-2137
Fax: (812)738-6438
E-mail: dvoelker@harrisonchamber.org
Home Page: http://www.harrisonchamber.org

• 7803 • **Chamber of Commerce Scholarship Award**

For graduating senior in Harrison County. Scholarship awarded annually.

• 7804 •

Charcot-Marie-Tooth Association
Patrick Torchia, Chm./Pres.
2700 Chestnut St.
Chester, PA 19013-4867
Phone: (610)499-9264
Phone: (610)499-9265
Toll-Free: 800-606-CMTA
Fax: (610)499-9267
E-mail: info@charcot-marie-tooth.org
Home Page: http://www.charcot-marie-tooth.org

Formerly: (1990) National Foundation for Peroneal Muscular Atrophy.

• 7805 • **Research Award**

To facilitate scientific research in the field of the Charcot-Marie-Tooth (CMT) neurological disorder. The number and value of grants vary each year.

• 7806 • **Rebecca Sand Volunteer of the Year Award**

To recognize service to the CMTA. A plaque is awarded annually. Established in 1990 to commemorate Rebecca Sand.

• 7807 •

Charles A. and Anne Morrow Lindbergh Foundation
Marlene K. White, Pres./COO
2150 3rd Ave. N., Ste. 310
Anoka, MN 55303-2200
Phone: (763)576-1596
Fax: (763)576-1664
E-mail: info@lindberghfoundation.org
Home Page: http://www.lindberghfoundation.org

Formerly: (1995) Charles A. Lindbergh Fund.

• 7808 • **Lindbergh Grants**

To promote projects that support Charles and Anne Morrow Lindbergh's vision of balance between technological advancement and preservation of the human/natural environment. Applications are evaluated on the basis of technical merit and the ability to contribute to Lindbergh's vision. Grants are awarded to individuals only, and are given in the following categories: agriculture; aviation/aerospace; conservation of natural resources; education; exploration; health; and waste minimization and management. Approximately ten cash awards in amounts of up to $10,580 (the cost of the Spirit of St. Louis, Lindbergh's airplane, in 1927) are presented each June 1st. The deadline is in early June. Established in 1977 in an effort led by General James H. Doolittle and astronaut Neil Armstrong.

• 7809 •
Charles S. Peirce Society
Mark Migotti, Sec.-Treas.
Department of Philosophy
135 Park Hall
State University of New York at Buffalo
Buffalo, NY 14260-4150
E-mail: migotti@ucalgary.ca
Home Page: http://wings.buffalo.edu/research/peirce/index.html

• 7810 • **C. S. Peirce Essay Contest Award**
To recognize the best essay on any topic on or related to the work of C.S. Peirce. The purpose of the award is to advance Peirce scholarship and to provide younger scholars with the opportunity to contribute. Individuals of any nationality who are graduate students, or persons who have held the Ph.D or its equivalent for no more than seven years, may submit essays by September 15. A monetary award of $500, presentation of the essay at the Peirce Society meeting (in conjunction with the meeting of the American Philosophy Association, Eastern Div.), and possible publication in the Society's *Transactions* are awarded annually at the December meeting. Established in 1984.

• 7811 •
Charlotte Repertory Theatre
2424 N Davidson St., Ste. 113
Charlotte, NC 28205
Phone: (704)333-8587
Fax: (704)333-0224
E-mail: info@charlotterep.org

• 7812 • **Charlotte Festival/New Plays in America**
To introduce new works into the mainstream of American theatre through Equity-staged readings. The focus is on the text and the actors' contributions to the development of new characters, illuminating paths for additional exploration for the playwright. All scripts submitted must be full length, non-musical plays with no professional production history. The playwright is required to participate in the festival process.

• 7813 •
Chartered Institute of Logistics and Transport in North America
(Institut agree de la logistique et des transports Amerique du Nord)
Donald McKnight, Exec.Dir.
275 Slater St., Ste. 900
Ottawa, ON, Canada K1P 5H9
Phone: (613)688-1438
Fax: (613)688-0966
E-mail: ghonima@ciltna.com
Home Page: http://www.citna.com

• 7814 • **CSL Gold Medal**
Recognizes the best student paper on transportation. Awarded annually.

• 7815 •
Chattahoochee Valley Art Museum
Aimee Bowles, Interim Exec.Dir.
112 Lafayette Pky.
LaGrange, GA 30240
Phone: (706)882-3267
Fax: (706)882-2878
E-mail: info@cvam-online.org
Home Page: http://www.cvam-online.org

• 7816 • **Kaleidoscope - A Fair of the Arts**
To recognize excellence in arts and crafts, and to encourage professional development. Art work selected for exhibition at the annual festival is eligible for Best Booth and purchase awards totaling $2,000. In addition, an artist may be invited to exhibit works in a one-person show at CVAA. Awarded annually. Established in 1962. Formerly: (1995) Affair on the Square Art Festival.

• 7817 • **LaGrange National**
For recognition of outstanding paintings, prints, and drawings. All living artists residing in the United States are eligible to submit a total of five entries. Eligible categories are paintings, prints, drawings, sculpture, photography, and decorative arts. Up to $7,500 in Purchase Awards may be made. Purchases will be made for the permanent collections of the Chattahoochee Valley Art Association and LaGrange College. Merit Awards may also be made. Awarded biennially. Established in 1975. Co-sponsored by the Lamar Dodd Art Center, LaGrange College, LaGrange, GA.

• 7818 •
Chautauqua Center for the Visual Arts
Chautauqua Institution
Thomas Becker, Pres.
Wythe Ave.
Box 999
Chautauqua, NY 14722
Phone: (716)357-2771
E-mail: ccva@mainalley.com
Home Page: http://www.chautauqua-inst.org/CCVA

• 7819 • **Annual Chautauqua National Exhibition of American Art**
For recognition of achievement in the visual arts. The Exhibition is open to living adult artists, 18 years of age or older, residing within the United States and Canada. The Exhibition consists of works in: (1) Painting (oil, all watermedia, casine, egg tempra, etc.); (2) Watercolor (on paper); (3) Drawing (in any media); (4) Prints (hand pulled only); (5) Photography (black/white, color, handcolored, etc.); (6) 3 Dimensional (sculpture, ceramics, constructions, Assemblages jewelry, glass, etc.); (7) Fibers (2D or 3D, handmade paper, textiles, etc.); (8) Electronically generated images. Formerly: (1995) Chautauqua International Exhibition of American Art.

• 7820 •
Chelsea
Richard Foerster, Ed.
% Chelsea Associates
PO Box 773
Cooper Sta.
New York, NY 10276-0773
Home Page: http://www.poems.com/chelssmi.htm

• 7821 • **Chelsea Award**
For recognition of achievement in poetry and short fiction. Individuals may apply by December 15 for short fiction, and June 15 for poetry. A monetary award of $500 and publication in *Chelsea* magazine are presented twice annually. Established in 1989.

• 7822 •
Chemical Engineering
Chemical Week Publishing
McGraw-Hill, Inc.
110 William St., 11th Fl.
New York, NY 10038
Phone: (212)621-4900
Fax: (212)621-4949
Home Page: http://www.che.com

• 7823 • **Kirkpatrick Chemical Engineering Achievement Award**
To recognize and honor outstanding group accomplishments employing chemical process technology commercialized during the two-year period preceding the award year. Companies, divisions of a company, or groups of companies are eligible. A sculptured piece and a write up in *Chemical Engineering* are awarded biennially. Established in 1933 and named to honor the former editorial director of *Chemical Engineering*.

• 7824 • **Personal Achievement in Chemical Engineering Awards**
To give the recipient due professional recognition to act as a stimulant to other engineers in industry, and to help bolster the stature of chemical engineering in the eyes of the general public. Selection is based on outstanding personal achievement in chemical engineering in one of the following four fields: research and development, design, production, and unusual achievements that do not readily fall into the previous categories. An inscribed plaque and recognition in *Chemical Engineering* are awarded to as many as four individuals biennially. Established in 1968.

• 7825 •
The Chemical Institute of Canada
(Institut de Chimie du Canada)
Roland Andersson, Exec.Dir.
130 Slater St., Ste. 550
Ottawa, ON, Canada K1P 6E2
Phone: (613)232-6252
Toll-Free: 888-542-2242
Fax: (613)232-5862
E-mail: info@cheminst.ca
Home Page: http://www.cheminst.ca

• 7826 • Alcan Lecture Award
To recognize a scientist residing in Canada who has made a distinguished contribution in the fields of inorganic chemistry or electrochemistry while working in Canada. Nominations must be submitted by July 1. A monetary prize of $2,000 and a scroll are awarded annually. Established in 1979. Sponsored by Alcan Canada Limited.

• 7827 • Award for Pure or Applied Inorganic Chemistry
Recognizes outstanding contribution to industrial or academic inorganic chemistry within the past 5 years while working in Canada. Applicants must be Canadian citizens or landed immigrants. Awarded annually.

• 7828 • Alfred Bader Award in Organic Chemistry
To recognize a scientist for excellence in research in organic chemistry carried out in Canada. Scientists under the age of 60 must be nominated by July 1. A monetary prize of $3,000, a scroll, and up to $500 towards travel expenses to attend the annual conference are awarded each year. Established in 1986 by Alfred Bader, research chemist. First awarded in 1988.

• 7829 • Fred Beamish Award
To recognize distinguished contributions in the field of analytical chemistry. Scientists residing in Canada are eligible. A monetary award of $1,000, a scroll, and travel expenses to attend the annual conference are presented each year. Established in 1968. Sponsored by the Eli Lilly Formerly: (2004) Fisher Scientific Lecture Award.

• 7830 • Bernard Belleau Award
To recognize a distinguished contribution to the field of medicinal chemistry through research involving biochemical or organic chemical mechanism. The awardee is awarded a monetary prize of $1,000 and an inscribed certificate. Awarded annually at the Canadian Society for Chemistry Conference where the recipient presents a lecture. Established in 1982. Formerly: (1988) Syntex Award in Physical Organic Chemistry; (2004) Hoffman-LaRoche Ltd. Award.

• 7831 • Clara Benson Award
Recognizes distinguished contribution to chemistry. Applicants must be women working in Canada. Awarded periodically.

• 7832 • Best Paper Published in the *Canadian Journal of Chemical Engineering*
To recognize the author(s) of the best paper published during the year in the *Canadian Journal of Chemical Engineering*. An engraved tankard and certificate are awarded annually.

• 7833 • Boehringer Ingelheim Award for Organic or Bioorganic Chemistry
For a PhD thesis in the field of organic or bioorganic chemistry formally accepted by a Canadian university in the 12-month period preceding July 1. Applicants must be Canadian residents or landed immigrants. Awarded annually. Formerly: (2004) Bio-Mega/Boehringer Ingelheim Award for Organic or Bioorganic Chemistry.

• 7834 • Norman and Marion Bright Memorial Award
To recognize an individual who has made an outstanding contribution in Canada to the furtherance of chemical technology. The winner may be either a chemical sciences technologist or person from outside the field who has made a significant and noteworthy contribution to its advancement. The award is presented annually, and the deadline for submissions is December 1.

• 7835 • Canadian Society for Chemical Engineering Award in Industrial Practice
To recognize a resident of Canada, a Canadian citizen, or a Canadian group that has made a distinguished contribution in the application of chemical engineering or industrial chemistry to the industrial sphere. Open to all chemical engineers and industrial chemists or those practicing these disciplines; it is not restricted to those whose normal employment is in the industrial sphere. The contribution must relate to the practice of chemical engineering and/or industrial chemistry in research and development, design, construction, production, or some combination of these. Preference is given to activities specific to Canadian industry. The contribution should contain some element of innovation and/or leadership that leads to innovation; it may be via a well-known, long-standing reputation for translating chemical engineering principles into industrial practice and, through this, contribute to the profession as a whole. The nomination deadline is December 1. A monetary award of $1,500 and a plaque are awarded each year when merited at the Society's annual meeting. Established in 1975. Sponsored by Polysar Rubber Corporation.

• 7836 • Chemical Institute of Canada Medal
This, the Institute's most prestigious award, is given to recognize distinguished and notable contributions to the science of chemistry or chemical engineering in Canada. A palladium medal is awarded annually. Established in 1951 by INCO Limited (International Nickel Company of Canada).

• 7837 • CIC Fellowship
To recognize outstanding merit by those who have made, or are in the course of making, a sustained and major contribution to the science or the profession of chemistry or of chemical engineering. Consideration is given to the following criteria: degrees and honors; membership in professional organizations; experience and status; publications, patents, and copyrights; and statements of sponsors. Nominations must be submitted by October 1. Awarded as merited.

• 7838 • Honorary Fellow
To honor persons to whom the Institute wishes to grant special recognition. This distinction is awarded by a vote of at least 90 percent of Council members. There are not, at any time, more than 25 living Honorary Fellows. Awarded as merited. In addition, the Society recognizes 25 living Honorary Members.

• 7839 • R. S. Jane Memorial Lecture Award
To recognize exceptional achievements in the field of chemical engineering or industrial engineering attained while in residence in Canada. A monetary award of $2,000 and a scroll are awarded annually. Established in 1960 to honor Dr. Robert Stephen Jane.

• 7840 • Laidler Award
To recognize distinguished accomplishments in the field of physical chemistry. Scientists under 40 years of age who reside in Canada are eligible. A monetary award of $1,000, a scroll, and some travel expenses to attend the annual conference are awarded annually. Established in 1963. Formerly: (2004) Noranda Lecture Award.

• 7841 • Lanxess Inc. Award for High School Chemistry Teachers
To recognize excellence in the teaching of chemistry in Canada at the secondary level. Two monetary prizes of $500 each are awarded annually. Established in 1970. Sponsored by Bayer Inc.. Formerly: Domtar Awards of the Chemical Institute of Canada for High School Chemistry Teachers; (2004) Chemical Institute of Canada Awards for High School Chemistry Teachers; (2006) Bayer Inc. Awards for High School Chemistry Teachers.

• 7842 • R. U. Lemieux Award for Organic Chemistry
To recognize an organic chemist who has made a distinguished contribution to any area of organic chemistry while working in Canada. There is no age limit on the award. Nominations must be submitted by July 1 of the year preceding the award year. A monetary award of $1,000 and travel expenses, if required, are awarded each year at the Canadian Society for Chemistry Conference where the recipient presents a lecture. Established in 1992.

• 7843 • Macromolecular Science and Engineering Lecture Award
To recognize a scientist who, while residing in Canada, has made a distinguished contribution to macromolecular science or engineering. Nominations must be submitted by July 1. An honorarium of $1,500, a scroll, and travel expenses to attend a conference or symposium are awarded annually. Established in 1971 by the Dunlop Research Centre. Sponsored by NOVA Chemicals Corp. Formerly: (1989) Dunlap Lecture Award.

• 7844 • W. A. E. McBryde Medal
To recognize a young scientist who has made a distinguished contribution in the field of pure or

applied analytical chemistry. Scientists working in Canada must be nominated by July 1. A monetary prize of $1,000 and a medal are awarded annually at the Canadian Society for Chemistry Conference. Established in 1985.

• 7845 • Merck Frosst Centre for Therapeutic Research Lecture Award
To recognize distinguished contributions in the fields of organic chemistry or biochemistry. Scientists under 40 years of age who reside in Canada are eligible. A monetary award of $2,000 and a scroll are awarded annually. Established in 1955 by the Merck Frosst Centre for Therapeutic Research. Formerly: Merck Sharp & Dohme Lecture Award.

• 7846 • Montreal Medal
To recognize outstanding contributions to the profession of chemistry or chemical engineering in Canada. Residents of Canada are eligible. A medal is awarded annually. Established in 1956. Sponsored by the Montreal Section of the Chemical Institute of Canada.

• 7847 • John C. Polanyi Lecture Award
To recognize a scientist for excellence in research in physical and theoretical chemistry or chemical physics carried out in Canada. The scientist must not have reached the age of 65 years by January 1 of the nomination year. A monetary prize of $3,000, a scroll, and travel expenses to a maximum of $500 are awarded each year at the Canadian Society for Chemistry Conference. The recipient is required to present an award address at the conference. Established in 1992.

• 7848 • SNC-Lavalin Plant Design Competition
To recognize outstanding achievements in plant design by undergraduate students in Canadian chemical engineering programs. Awarded annually at the Canadian Society for Chemical Engineering Conference.

• 7849 • Jules Stachiewicz Medal
To recognize distinguished contributions in heat transfer, including design, research, manufacturing, and teaching. Contributions must have been made in Canada and preference is given to Canadians presently active in Canada. The deadline for nominations is December 1. A monetary prize of $500, a medal, and a certificate are awarded each year at the CSChE annual conference. Established jointly in 1982 with the Canadian Society for Mechanical Engineering.

• 7850 • Union Carbide Award for Chemical Education
To recognize outstanding contributions in Canada to education at any level in the field of chemistry or chemical engineering. A monetary award of $1,000, a framed scroll, and travel expenses of up to $400 to attend the Canadian Society for Chemistry Conference are awarded annually. Established in 1961.

• 7851 •
Cherokee National Historical Society
Mac R. Harris, Exec.Dir.
PO Box 515
Tahlequah, OK 74464-0515
Phone: (918)456-6007
Toll-Free: 888-999-6007
Fax: (918)456-6165
E-mail: info@cherokeeheritage.org
Home Page: http://www.powersource.com/heritage

• 7852 • Cherokee National Hall of Fame
To honor persons of Cherokee descent who have made outstanding contributions. A bust or other suitable monument on a native stone plaza forming the approach to the Cherokee National Museum is awarded irregularly. Established in 1970.

• 7853 •
Chesapeake and Ohio Historical Society
Margaret T. Whittington, Exec.Dir.
PO Box 79
Clifton Forge, VA 24422
Phone: (540)862-2210
Toll-Free: 800-453-2647
Fax: (540)863-9159
E-mail: cohs@cohs.org
Home Page: http://www.cohs.org

• 7854 • Certificate of Achievement
To recognize one-time achievements by members for such things as authorship of articles, work on a designated special project, or committee work. A certificate is awarded when merited. Established in 1977.

• 7855 • Certificate of Appreciation
To recognize persons for assisting the Society in furthering its goals of historical preservation or for some other service to the Society. A certificate is awarded annually. Established in 1977.

• 7856 • Honorary Member
To recognize non-members who have contributed to furthering the goals of the Society. A plaque and life-time free membership are awarded as merited. Established in 1975.

• 7857 • President's Awards
To recognize members of the Society who have contributed significantly to the operations of the organization through volunteer work on special projects or in regular offices over an extended period of time. Plaques are awarded annually. Established in 1975.

• 7858 •
Chesapeake Bay Foundation
William C. Baker, Pres.
Philip Merrill Environmental Ctr.
6 Herndon Ave.
Annapolis, MD 21403
Phone: (410)268-8816
Phone: (410)269-0481
Toll-Free: 800-445-5572
E-mail: ebuckman@savethebay.cbf.org
Home Page: http://www.cbf.org

• 7859 • Conservationist of the Year
Recognizes superlative service and commitment to the restoration and protection of the Chespeake Bay. Any individual, non-profit institution, or business is eligible. A mounted bronze bust is awarded annually. Established in 1980.

• 7860 • Environmental Educator of the Year
Recognizes an individual in the field of education who has contributed significantly to the understanding of the Bay ecosystem through an academic program. The winner receives a mounted bronze bust. Awarded annually. Established in 1997.

• 7861 •
Chess Journalists of America
Daniel Lucas, Pres.
1369 Field Creek Terr.
Lawrenceville, GA 30043-5334
Phone: (770)338-5803
E-mail: president@chessjournalism.org
Home Page: http://chessjournalism.org

• 7862 • Chess Journalism Merit Awards Competition
To recognize the top chess journalists, editors, and cartoonists, and to promote a higher level of excellence in chess journalism. Members of CJA and their publications/cartoonists, and to promote a higher level of excellence in chess journalism. Members of CJA and their publications/columns are eligible. A certificate is awarded annually. Established in 1975.

• 7863 •
ChevronTexaco Conservation Awards Program
6001 Bollinger Canyon Rd.
San Ramon, CA 94583
Phone: (925)842-2691
Phone: (925)842-1000
Fax: (925)842-3530
E-mail: conservn@chevron.com
Home Page: http://www.chevron.com/conservationawards

Formerly: Chevron USA.

• 7864 • ChevronTexaco Conservation Awards Program
This, the oldest privately-sponsored program of its kind in the United States, honors individuals and organizations for outstanding contributions to the conservation of natural resources. The program seeks to encourage those who have

received little or no national recognition as well as renowned conservationists. Anyone may nominate an individual or organization based on significant results of a conservation project that protects or enhances an area's natural resources. Nomination guidelines and application form are available at he above website. An independent committee of distinguished judges representing a variety of conservation activities evaluates the nominees. Awards are presented annually. Honorees each receive $10,000 and round trip airfare and lodging for two for the awards presentation. Established in 1954 by Ed Zern, a prominent outdoor writer, conservationist and columnist for *Field and Stream.*. Formerly: Chevron - Times Mirror Magazines Conservation Awards Program.

• 7865 •
Chian Federation of America
Alexandros Doulis, Pres.
44-01 Broadway
Astoria, NY 11103
Phone: (718)204-2550
Fax: (718)278-6199
E-mail: chianfed@chianfed.org
Home Page: http://www.chianfed.org

• 7866 • **Homeric Award**
To recognize friends and supporters of human rights, freedom of humankind and persons that have helped in the betterment of Greek-American relations. A plaque is awarded annually. Established in 1978 as part of the festivities celebrating the independence of the Greek island of Chios on November 11, 1912.

• 7867 •
Chicago Anti-Hunger Federation
Beverly Decker, Exec.Dir.
4345 W Division St
Chicago, IL 60651-1714
Phone: (773)252-3663
Fax: (773)252-9913

• 7868 • **Pearl Soil Hunger Fighter of the Year**
For excellent work in hunger issues. Monetary award bestowed annually.

• 7869 •
Chicago Asthma Consortium
Jura S. Scharf, Exec.Dir.
4541 N Ravenswood Ave., Ste. 303
Chicago, IL 60640
Phone: (773)769-6060
Fax: (773)769-6505
Home Page: http://www.chicagoasthma.org

• 7870 • **Mitch Trubitt Community Asthma Champion Award**
For community resident who has made a difference or improved the situation for persons with asthma in their community. Grant awarded annually.

• 7871 •
The Chicago Athenaeum: Museum of Architecture and Design
Christian K. Narkiewicz-Laine, Dir.
122 S Bench St.
Galena, IL 61036
Phone: (815)777-4444
Fax: (815)777-2471
Home Page: http://www.chi-athenaeum.org

• 7872 • **American Architecture Awards**
Recognizes excellence in architecture in the United States. All submissions must be the work of American Architects and architectural firms either working nationally or internationally for projects both in the US and abroad. Awarded for any commercial, corporate, institutional or residential building type built or designed since January 1, 2001. Deadline is February 15.

• 7873 • **GOOD DESIGN Competition and Exhibition**
To recognize products, industrial and graphic designers, and manufacturers for their contributions to contemporary design. Submissions are judged in 20 categories on criteria of the highest aesthetic in terms of innovation, form, materials, construction, concept, function, and utility. Deadline for entries is June 1. Winning submissions are awarded the museum's GOOD DESIGN Award and are exhibited at The Chicago Athenaeum. Awarded annually. Established in 1950 and remains the oldest competition of its kind nationally and internationally.

• 7874 • **Most Beautiful House in America Competition**
A national competition to find designs for "The Most Beautiful House in America." The competition is open to registered architects and engineers. Deadline for entries is November 15. For additional information, call (312) 251-0175. Formerly known as the Most Beautiful House in the World Competition.

• 7875 •
Chicago Book Clinic
Tammy Levy, Pres.
5443 N. Broadway, Ste. 101
Chicago, IL 60640
Phone: (773)561-4150
Fax: (773)561-1343
E-mail: chgobookclinic@aol.com
Home Page: http://www.chicagobookclinic.org

• 7876 • **Mary Alexander Award**
To recognize individuals for outstanding service to the Chicago Book Clinic. Established in 1987. Formerly: Outstanding Service Award.

• 7877 • **Distinguished Service Award**
To recognize distinguished contributions to the book publishing industry to one individual selected by the Board of Directors (not open for nomination). A plaque is awarded annually. Established in 1974.

• 7878 • **Honorary Member**
To recognize contributions to the Chicago Book Clinic. Awarded occasionally when merited.

• 7879 • **Top Honor Books, Chicago Book Clinic Annual Exhibit**
To commend and encourage excellent work in the planning, supervision, and execution of the physical and visual aspects of books. Books published, manufactured, or designed in Illinois, Michigan, Ohio, Indiana, Kentucky, Tennessee, Arkansas, Missouri, Oklahoma, Kansas, Nebraska, Iowa, South Dakota, Minnesota, or Wisconsin are eligible. Certificates are awarded annually to between 20 and 50 books following a juried competition. Established in 1950.

• 7880 •
Chicago Bulk Mail Center Area Local, American Postal Workers Union, AFL-CIO, LU 7033
James Wheeler, Contact
7500 W. Roosevelt
Forest Park, IL 60130
Phone: (708)583-4370
Phone: (708)848-2262
E-mail: cbmclocal@aol.com

• 7881 • **Scholarship Fund CBMC Area Local**
For union member, high school senior with average grades. Scholarship awarded annually.

• 7882 •
The Chicago Community Trust
Terry Mazany, Pres. and CEO
111 E Wacker Dr., Ste. 1400
Chicago, IL 60601
Phone: (312)616-8000
Fax: (312)616-7955
E-mail: info@cct.org
Home Page: http://www.cct.org

• 7883 • **James Brown IV Annual Award of Excellence for Outstanding Community Service**
For recognition of an outstanding not-for-profit agency in the community which has made whose services benefit the residents of metropolitan Chicago An unrestricted grant of $50,000 is awarded annually in the Spring. Established in 1974 in honor of James Brown IV, whose vision and leadership benefited the trust during his twenty-four years as an executive director.

• 7884 • **Community Service Fellowship**
To provide individuals employed in the not-for-profit or public sectors in Cook County, IL, with the opportunity to significantly enhance their skills and abilities in the area of community service. Fellows receive a monetary award equal to their current salary and related expenses. Awarded annually. Details regarding the application procedures will be available on www.cct.org.

• 7885 •
Chicago Film Critics Awards
Chicago Film Critics Association
155 E Algonquin Rd.
PO Box 280
Arlington Heights, IL 60006
Phone: (773)509-8155
Fax: (312)266-1287
E-mail: contact@chicagofilmcritics.org
Home Page: http://www.chicagofilmcritics.org

• 7886 • **Chicago Film Critics Awards - Chicago Flame**
To recognize outstanding national and international feature films and performances. Fourteen categories are recognized: Best Picture, Best Foreign Language Film, Best Director, Best Actor, Best Actress, Best Supporting Actor, Best Supporting Actress, Most Promising Actor, Most Promising Actress, Best Screenplay, Best Cinematography, Best Original Score, Big Shoulders, and Commitment to Chicago. Chicago critics vote for winners with the exception of the Commitment to Chicago Award and Big Shoulders, which are selected by the Board of Directors. Feature films screened or released by the Friday preceding Christmas are eligible. Winners are announced at an awards ceremony held in March. A glass-etched sculpture called the Chicago Flame is awarded annually. Established in 1989.

• 7887 •
Chicago International Children's Film Festival
David Edelberg, Pres.
% Facets Multi-Media, Inc.
1517 W Fullerton Ave.
Chicago, IL 60614
Phone: (773)281-9075
Toll-Free: 800-331-6197
Fax: (773)929-0266
E-mail: kidsfest@facets.org
Home Page: http://www.cicff.org

Formerly: (1991) Chicago International Festival of Children's Films.

• 7888 • **Chicago International Children's Film Festival**
To recognize excellence in filmmaking for children; and to encourage filmmakers to create high-quality media for children, both in aesthetics and content. Films must be entered by May 30 of each year for the Festival the following October. Awards are presented in the following categories: Adult Jury Awards for Live-Action Feature Films or Videos, Adult Jury Awards for Animated Feature Films or Videos, Adult Jury Awards for Short Live-Action Films or Videos, Adult Jury Awards for Short Animated Films or Videos, Adult Jury Awards for the Best Child-Produced Film or Video, Children's Jury Award for Live Action Feature Film or Videos, Children's Jury Award for Animated Feature Films or Videos, Children's Short Live-Action Feature Films or Videos, Children's Jury Award for the Best Child-Produced Film or Video, Most Popular Film of the Festival (selected by audience), The Kenneth F. and Harle G. Montgomery Award (cash prize, $2,500), and Liv Ullmann Peace Prize. A certificate and publicity are awarded annually on the last day of the Festival. Established in 1984. Presented by Facets Multi-Media, Inc., a not-for-profit film and video organization. Formerly: (1991) Chicago International Festival of Children's Films.

• 7889 •
Chicago Midwest Bead Society
Ayla Phillips, Exec. Officer
1511 Sherman Ave.
Evanston, IL 60201
Phone: (847)328-4040
Fax: (847)733-0086
E-mail: ayla@aylasoriginals.com
Home Page: http://www.aylasoriginals.com

• 7890 • **Beck Scholarship Fund**
For bead research. Scholarship awarded periodically.

• 7891 •
Chicago Tribune
Nelson Algren Awards
Literary Awards
435 N Michigan Ave., 2nd Fl.
Chicago, IL 60611-4041
Phone: (847)755-7571
E-mail: apindel@tribune.com
Home Page: http://www.chicagotribune.com

• 7892 • **Nelson Algren Awards for Short Fiction**
To recognize excellence in the writing of short fiction. Manuscripts to be considered are accepted from November 1 to February 28. The story must be unpublished and from 2,500 to 10,000 words in length, and the writer must be an American. A monetary first prize of $5,000 and three runners-up prizes at $1,500 each and publication are awarded annually in the fall. Established in 1981. Sponsored since 1985 by the *Chicago Tribune*.

• 7893 • **Heartland Prizes**
To recognize a novel and a book of nonfiction embodying the spirit of the nation's heartland. Books published between August 1 and July 31 of the next year are considered. Two monetary awards of $5,000 each are presented annually in the fall.

• 7894 •
Chihuahuan Desert Research Institute
Dr. Andrew Price PhD, Sec.-Treas.
PO Box 905
Fort Davis, TX 79734
Phone: (432)364-2499
Fax: (432)364-2686
E-mail: manager@cdri.org
Home Page: http://www.cdri.org

• 7895 • **W. Frank Blair Memorial Award**
To recognize an individual for excellence in the written presentation of scientific data. Graduate students enrolled at accredited colleges or universities may submit published or unpublished manuscripts pertaining to the natural sciences and the Chihuahuan Desert Region. A monetary award of $500 is presented annually. Established in 1986 in memory of W. Frank Blair, First Chairman, CDRI Board of Scientists.

• 7896 •
Children as the Peacemakers
Patricia Montandon, Founder/Pres.
1243 Lago Vista Dr.
Beverly Hills, CA 90210
Phone: (310)274-9801
Fax: (310)859-1325
E-mail: info@peace-kids.org
Home Page: http://www.peace-kids.org

Formerly: (1985) Children as Teachers of Peace.

• 7897 • **International Children's Peace Prize**
To recognize children's contributions to peace in the form of creative artwork or civic projects. Children from over fifty countries respond annually to an established theme related to peace at the invitation of the Foundation. Children between the ages of 6 and 11 are eligible. A glass sculpture is awarded to each child during ceremonies hosted by Disneyland of California. Awarded annually. Established in 1982 to promote peace.

• 7898 •
Children's AIDS Fund
Anita M. Smith, Pres.
PO Box 16433
Washington, DC 20041
Phone: (703)433-1560
Toll-Free: (866)829-1560
Fax: 800-577-8529
E-mail: info@childrensaidsfund.org
Home Page: http://www.childrensaidsfund.org

• 7899 • **Thomas Parran Award**
Recognizes significant contributions to limiting the spread of HIV/AIDS. Awarded annually. Inquire for application details.

• 7900 •
Children's Book Committee
Alice Belgray, Chair.
Bank Street College
610 W. 112th St.
New York, NY 10025
Phone: (212)875-4540
Fax: (212)875-4759
E-mail: bookcom@bankstreet.edu
Home Page: http://www.bankstreet.edu/bookcom

• 7901 • **Josette Frank Award**
To honor a book for children or young people that deals realistically and in a positive way with problems in their world. Any published book submitted for review becomes eligible. A monetary prize of $500 and a scroll are awarded annually. Established in 1943 by the Children's Book

Awards are arranged in alphabetical order below their administering organizations

Committee in memory of Florence N. Miller, a former member of the committee. Formerly: (1997) Children's Book Award.

• 7902 • Flora Stieglitz Straus Award
This award honors a distinguished work of nonfiction that fulfills Flora Straus's ideals and serves as an inspiration to young people. Flora Straus stood for the values of courage, hard work, truth and beauty; she championed diverse opinions; and she supported humanitarian efforts. A monetary prize of $500 and a scroll are awarded to one or more recipients annually. Established in 1994.

• 7903 •
Children's Book Council
Lori Benton, Chair
12 W 37th St., 2nd Fl.
New York, NY 10018-7480
Phone: (212)966-1990
Toll-Free: 800-807-9355
Fax: (212)966-2073
E-mail: info@cbcbooks.org
Home Page: http://www.cbcbooks.org

• 7904 • CBC Honors Program
To recognize persons whose work in books and other areas of communicating with children, sustained over a period of time, warrants special admiration. Awarded irregularly. Established in 1985. Formerly: Everychild Conference Honors Program.

• 7905 •
Children's Librarians of New Hampshire
Rachel Stolworthy, Sec.
Franklin Public Library
310 Central St.
Franklin, NH 03235
Phone: (603)934-2911
Fax: (603)271-6826
E-mail: rachel.stolworthy@franklin.lib.nh.us
Home Page: http://www.chilisnh.org

• 7906 • Great Stone Face Book Award
To encourage children to value the importance of recreational reading and to promote a life-long love of reading. Book appropriate for grades 4-6 that were published within three years of the current school year are eligible. The library committee prepares a list of 25 finalists based on child appeal and quality of writing. The winner is the book receiving the most votes by library patrons. A plaque or certificate is awarded annually. Established in 1980.

• 7907 •
Children's Literature Association
Kathryn Kiessling, Admin.
PO Box 138
Battle Creek, MI 49016-0138
Phone: (269)965-8180
Fax: (269)965-3568
E-mail: kkiessling@childlitassn.org
Home Page: http://www.childlitassn.org

• 7908 • Children's Literature Association Article Award
Recognizes outstanding published criticism of children's literature. A monetary award and a certificate are awarded annually. Established in 1978.

• 7909 • Children's Literature Association Book Award
Recognizes outstanding published criticism of children's literature. A monetary award and a certificate are presented annually. Established in 1987.

• 7910 • Children's Literature Association Research Fellowship
Recognizes innovative research in the field. Applicants must be members. Awarded annually.

• 7911 • Phoenix Award
To recognize the author, or the estate of the author, of a book published twenty years earlier that did not receive a major award at the time of its publication but which, from the perspective of time, is deemed worthy of special recognition for its literary quality. Books originally published in the English language are eligible to be nominated by ChLA members and others interested in promoting high critical standards in literature for children. A brass statue is awarded annually at the conference. Established in 1985.

• 7912 •
Children's Literature Council of Southern California
Melinda Steep, Pres.
PO Box 573462
Tarzana, CA 91357
Phone: (626)744-4389
E-mail: membership@childrensliteraturecouncil.org
Home Page: http://www.childrensliteraturecouncil.org

• 7913 • Book Awards
To encourage excellence in the field of literature for children and young people by honoring Southern California authors and illustrators of books. Residents of Southern California are eligible. The awards presented differ from year to year, both in the categories honored and the number of awards presented. However, two awards are presented regularly: the Dorothy C. McKenzie Award, which honors an individual for significant endeavors and/or outstanding service on behalf of children and literature; and the Myra Cohn Livingston Award for Poetry, in honor of the distinguished poet, Myra Cohn Livingston. Plaques are awarded annually at the Awards Banquet in the fall. Established in 1961 by Dorothy C. McKenzie, under the auspices of the California State College at Los Angeles.

• 7914 •
Children's Rights Council
John L. Bauserman Jr., Pres.
6200 Editors Park Dr., Ste. 103
Hyattsville, MD 20782
Phone: (301)559-3120
Phone: (202)547-6227
Toll-Free: 800-787-KIDS
Fax: (301)559-3124
E-mail: crcdc@erols.com
Home Page: http://www.gocrc.com

Formerly: (1991) National Council for Children's Rights.

• 7915 • Best in Media Awards
To recognize the best treatment of children of separation and divorce in the media or advertising. Possible contenders are: best treatment showing need of children for two parents in the news media (including newspapers, magazine, TV, and radio coverage); best media coverage of a county agency helping children of divorce with programs for both of their parents; and best TV series on abuse and false abuse charges. Awarded each year at the annual conference. Established in 1986.

• 7916 • Chief Justice Warren E. Burger Healer Awards
To recognize lawyers, judges, and others who promote healing in the domestic relations area. A healer might be a judge who takes the lead in promoting joint custody (shared parenting), a pre-court trial service that fosters mediation, or an attorney with a professional track record of promoting a child's access to two parents and others who have bonded with the child. Awarded each year at the annual conference. Established in 1986 to honor Warren E. Burger, who, as Chief Justice of the United States, urged lawyers to be healers, not just litigators.

• 7917 • Parenting Awards
To recognize efforts to improve parenting by fathers and mothers especially for children of separation and divorce. Programs that help with family formation and family preservation and programs that help parents in the event of a divorce are eligible. Awarded at the annual conference each year. Established in 1992.

• 7918 •
Children's Watch International
Vanessa von Struensee, Contact
2918 Yarling Ct.
Falls Church, VA 22042
E-mail: vvonstruen@hotmail.com
Home Page: http://www.webspawner.com/users/ChildrensWatch

• 7919 • Child Advocate of the Year
Awarded annually for outstanding children's advocate worldwide.

Awards are arranged in alphabetical order below their administering organizations

• 7920 •
Jane Coffin Childs Memorial Fund for Medical Research
Kim E. Roberts, Admin.Dir.
333 Cedar St.
LW300-SHM
New Haven, CT 06510
Phone: (203)785-4612
Fax: (203)785-3301
E-mail: info@jccfund.org
Home Page: http://www.jccfund.org

• 7921 • **Fellowship Awards of the Jane Coffin Childs Memorial Fund for Medical Research**
To provide fellowships for full-time postdoctoral studies in the medical and related sciences bearing on cancer. Applicants must hold either an M.D. or Ph.D. in the field they propose to study or furnish evidence of equivalent training and experience. Applicants may be citizens of any country but, for foreign nationals, awards are made only for study in the United States. American citizens may hold a fellowship either in the United States or in a foreign country. The deadline for applications is February 1. A basic stipend of $33,500 for the first year, $35,000 for the second year, and $37,000 for the third year, with an additional $750 for each dependent child is awarded; a travel allowance is provided to the Fellow and family and an allowance of $1,500 a year toward the cost of the research is made to the laboratory sponsoring the Fellow.

• 7922 •
China Stamp Society
Paul H. Gault, Sec.
PO Box 20711
Columbus, OH 43220
Phone: (614)451-8034
E-mail: pgault@columbus.rr.com
Home Page: http://www.chinastampsociety.org

• 7923 • **Philip W. Ireland Special Award**
To recognize a first-time collector of stamps of China and related areas.

• 7924 •
Gilbert Chinard Prize Committee
% Sylvia Neely, Chair
108 Weaver Hall
Department of History
Pennsylvania State University
University Park, PA 16802
E-mail: sxn13@psu.edu

• 7925 • **The Gilbert Chinard Prize**
To honor distinguished scholarly books on the history of themes shared by France and North, Central, and South America published by Canadian or American authors. Awarded annually with a monetary prize of $1,000 for a book or manuscript in page-proof. Funded by The Institut Francais de Washington; a committee of the Society for French Historical Studies determines the winners. Winners are announced at the annual meeting of the Society for French Historical Studies in the spring.

• 7926 •
Chinese American Librarians Association
Sally C. Tseng, Exec.Dir.
10980 Barranca Dr.
Southern Illinois University-Carbondale
650 Agriculture Dr., Mail Code 6632
Cupertino, CA 95014
Fax: (949)857-1988
E-mail: sctseng888@yahoo.com
Home Page: http://www.cala-web.org

• 7927 • **Chinese-American Librarians Association Distinguished Service Award**
To recognize individuals who have consistently demonstrated outstanding leadership and achievement in library and information services at the national and/or international level. A plaque and recognition are awarded annually at the annual meeting held in June or July.

• 7928 •
Chinese American Medical Society
Dr. Tak Kwan MD, Pres.
281 Edgewood Ave.
Teaneck, NJ 07666
Phone: (201)833-1506
Fax: (201)833-8252
E-mail: hw5@columbia.edu
Home Page: http://www.camsociety.org

Formerly: (1986) American Chinese Medical Society.

• 7929 • **Chinese American Medical Society Scientific Achievement Award**
For recognition of achievement in medicine or medical research. Physicians or medical scientists of Chinese descent must be nominated by the Nomination Committee of the society. A plaque is awarded annually at the Annual Scientific Meeting of the society. Established in 1973. Formerly: (1986) ACMS Scientific Achievement Award.

• 7930 •
Chinese Economists Society
Prof. Gordon Guoen Liu, Pres.
733 15th St. NW, Ste. 910
Washington, DC 20005
Phone: (202)347-8588
Fax: (202)347-8510
E-mail: ces@vmintl.net
Home Page: http://www.china-ces.org

• 7931 • **Fellow Membership**
Recognizes members who have made original contributions to economics, management sciences, Chinese economic studies, and have a good publication record in academic journals.

• 7932 •
Choate, Hall & Stewart LLP
2 International Pl.
53 State St.
Boston, MA 02110
Phone: (617)248-5000
Fax: (617)248-4000
E-mail: info@choate.com
Home Page: http://www.choate.com

• 7933 • **Amy Lowell Poetry Traveling Scholarship**
To advance the art of poetry by permitting poets to travel outside the continent of North America. U.S. citizens of good standing or able promise who agree to spend one year outside of the continent of North America are eligible for consideration. The application deadline is October 15. A monetary prize of approximately $37,000 is awarded annually. Established in 1953 by a bequest of Amy Lowell.

• 7934 •
Choice
American Library Association
Irving E. Rockwood, Ed.
100 Riverview Ctr.
Middletown, CT 06457
Phone: (860)347-6933
Fax: (860)704-0465
E-mail: choicemag@ala-choice.org
Home Page: http://www.ala.org/ala/acrl/acrlpubs/choice/home.htm

• 7935 • ***Choice* Outstanding Academic Books and Nonprint Materials**
For recognition of scholarship and quality scholarly publishing in all disciplines. The selection criteria include: the importance of the work compared with other literature in the field, whether the material is the first of its kind published in book form or otherwise unique or definitive, whether the work is of value to undergraduate students, and whether it is essential in building library collections. Titles are considered in the following categories: Reference; General; Humanities; Art; Photography; Communication Arts; Classical Studies; Language and Literature (English and American, Germanic, Romance, Slavic and other); Performing Arts (Dance, Music, Film, and Theater); Philosophy; Religion; Science and Technology; History of Science and Technology; Astronautics and Astronomy; Biology (Botany and Zoology); Chemistry; Earth Science; Engineering; Health Sciences; Information and Computer Science; Mathematics; Physics; Sports and Physical Education; Social and Behavioral Sciences; Anthropology; Business, Management, and Labor; Economics; Education; History, Geography, and Area Studies (Africa, Asia and Oceania, Europe, Latin America and the Caribbean, Middle East and North Africa, and North America); Political Science (Law); Psychology; Sociology; and Nonprint Reviews. Titles (book or nonprint work) reviewed in *Choice* magazine during the preceding twelve months are eligible. Approximately 600 titles are selected annually for a published list. The list is a tribute to quality in scholarly publishing in the United States today. Established in 1966 by the editors of *Choice*. Sponsored by the Association

of College and Research Libraries and *Choice*. Formerly: (1981) *Choice*'s Outstanding Academic Books.

• 7936 •
Chopin Foundation of the United States
Jadwiga Gewert, Exec.Dir.
1440 79th St. Causeway, Ste. 117
Miami, FL 33141
Phone: (305)868-0624
Fax: (305)868-5150
E-mail: info@chopin.org
Home Page: http://www.chopin.org

• 7937 • **American National Chopin Piano Competition**
To offer performance opportunity and financial support for young American pianists at career-level entry and to allow top prize-winners to represent the United States at the International Chopin Piano Competition in Warsaw, Poland at five-year intervals. Open to pianists holding U.S. citizenship (born or naturalized) between the ages of 17 and 28. The following awards are presented: first prize - a monetary award of $18,000, and concert engagements nationally and internationally; second prize - a monetary award of $12,000; third Prize a monetary award of $8,000; fourth prize - a monetary award of $ 5,000. The top four prize winners are sent to the Preliminary round for the International Competition in Warsaw with all expenses paid including air-fare and special prizes - $1,000 for Best Performance of a Mazurka; $1,000 for Best Performance of a Polonaise; and $1,000 for Best Performance of a Concerto. The U.S. Competition is held once every five years. The next competition will be held in March 2005. Established in 1977 by Blanka Rosenstiel.

• 7938 •
Choral Arts New England
Katherine Isaacs, Admin.
PO Box 608
Newton, MA 02456-0608
Phone: (781)721-7464

• 7939 • **Alfred Nash Patterson Grants**
For choruses and choral organizations in New England. Grant awarded annually.

• 7940 •
Chorus America
Ann Meier Baker, Pres./CEO
1156 15th St. NW, Ste. 310
Washington, DC 20005
Phone: (202)331-7577
Fax: (202)331-7599
E-mail: service@chorusamerica.org
Home Page: http://www.chorusamerica.org

• 7941 • **Chorus America/ASCAP Awards for Adventurous Programming**
To recognize choruses that demonstrate adventurous programming through performances in the United States of choral music written since 1970. The deadline is April 15. Awards are presented in three categories at the annual conference in June. Co-sponsored by the American Society of Composers, Authors and Publishers.

• 7942 • **Margaret Hillis Achievement Award for Choral Excellence**
To honor professional choruses, choruses with a core of professional singers, and volunteer choruses. The deadline is March 1. A monetary award of $5,000 is given annually in a repeating three-year cycle. Presented at the awards dinner during the annual conference of Chorus America. Established in honor of Miss Hillis for her more than 40 years of professional achievement, outstanding dedication, and contributions to the choral art.

• 7943 • **The Michael Korn Founder's Award**
To recognize an individual who has contributed significantly to the growth and development of the professional choral art. Nominees are selected by the Board of Directors. A plaque is awarded annually at the conference. Established in 1978.

• 7944 •
Chow Chow Club, Inc.
Bonnie Young, Pres.
8132 Eastern Ave. NW
Washington, DC 20012-1312
Phone: (202)726-9155
E-mail: secretary@chowclub.org
Home Page: http://www.chowclub.org

• 7945 • **Chow Chow Club Annual Awards**
To encourage the betterment of the Chow Chow breed by recognition of the accomplishments of the top Chow Chows in American Kennel Club Show Competition. The following awards are presented: Top Ten Chows, Supreme Chow of the Year, Chow Chow Defeating the Greatest Number of Chow Chows, Chow Chow Bitch Defeating the Greatest Number of Chow Chows, Junior Handler Award, Breeder of the Year, Stud Dog of the Year, Brood Bitch of the Year, and Obedience Awards. Membership is required. Trophies and certificates are awarded annually at the awards banquet in conjunction with the National Specialty Show.

• 7946 •
The Chris Awards
Susan B. Halpern, Exec.Dir.
1430 S High St., Rm. 322
Columbus, OH 43207
Phone: (614)444-7460
Fax: (614)444-7460
E-mail: info@chrisawards.org
Home Page: http://www.chrisawards.org

• 7947 • **Christopher Columbus Award**
For recognition of the film or video that shows the most originality and creativity at the Columbus International Film and Video Festival. Candidates are nominated from each division. A silver representation of Christopher Columbus is awarded.

• 7948 • **Columbus International Film and Video Festival**
For recognition of the best documentary films and videos at the Festival in the following categories: arts, humanities, business and industry, education and information, health and medicine for the general public, health and medicine for the professional, media of print, social issues, science, technology, travel, religion, screenwriting, and television and advertising. Firms or individuals responsible for the film or video are eligible. The entry deadline is July 1. The major award of the Festival, the Chris Statuette, an original bronze sculptured interpretation of the Christopher Columbus statue which stands in front of Columbus' City Hall, is awarded annually to the winning film in each category. In addition, Bronze Plaque Awards are presented to runners-up in each subject area of the categories, and Certificates of Honorable Mention are awarded. The Festival was established in 1950.

• 7949 • **Edgar Dale Award**
To recognize excellence in informational screenwriting with distinguished visual and literary qualities. Columbus International Film and Video Festival entries are eligible. Established in 1986 to honor Edgar Dale, a founder of the Council.

• 7950 • **Ben Franklin Award**
For recognition of the most creative and distinguished work from the Media of Print division at the Columbus International Film and Video Festival. Film art in the area of posters, and other promotional literature, such as prose written for a film review for newspapers and magazines, is considered. Related productions must be entered in regular catagories. A miniature bust of Ben Franklin mounted on a marble pedestal is awarded. Established in 1984.

• 7951 • **OSU Photography and Cinema Alumni Society Award**
To recognize the best student production in the areas of the documentary, the narrative film, and animation or experimentation shown at the Columbus International Film and Video Festival. A plaque is awarded annually by the Alumni Society of the Department of Photography and Cinema at Ohio State University. Established in 1993.

• 7952 • **President's Award**
To recognize the producer of the film or videotape that excels in photographic and technical excellence and excellence in use of communication skills, and is judged Best of the Festival at the Columbus International Film and Video Festival. Chris statuette winners are eligible. Established in 1972. Formerly: President's Chris Award.

• 7953 • **Robert W. Wagner Narrative Screenwriting Award**
To recognize the writer whose screenplay demonstrates excellence and creativity in writing in the dramatic form at the Columbus International Film and Video Festival. A plaque is awarded. Established in 1991. The award is similar to the

Edgar Dale Award in appearance. Formerly: Narrative Screenwriting Award.

• 7954 •
Christian Educators Association International
Finn Laursen, Exec.Dir.
PO Box 41300
Pasadena, CA 91114-8300
Phone: (626)798-1124
Phone: (626)720-8123
Toll-Free: 888-798-1124
Fax: (626)798-2346
E-mail: info@ceai.org
Home Page: http://www.ceai.org

• 7955 • **South California Educator of the Year Award**
Recognizes excellence in education, including inspiration of students and fellow staff. Applicants must be members of CEAI. Awarded annually.

• 7956 •
Christian Foundation for Children and Aging
Robert K. Hentzen, Pres.
1 Elmwood Ave.
Kansas City, KS 66103
Phone: (913)384-6500
Toll-Free: 800-875-6564
Fax: (913)384-2211
E-mail: mail@cfcausa.org
Home Page: http://www.cfcausa.org

• 7957 • **Individual and Organizational**
Recognizes mission dedication, support for children & aging in need. Awarded annually.

• 7958 •
Christian Holiness Partnership
Dr. Marlin Hotle, Exec.Dir.
263 Buffalo Rd.
Clinton, TN 37716-6821
Phone: (423)457-5978
Fax: (865)463-7280
Home Page: http://www.faithandvalues.com/fg_profiles/christian_holiness.asp

• 7959 • **Distinguished Service Award**
To recognize distinguished service. Individuals whose lifestyles exemplify holiness and who have contributed outstanding Christian services through the church in a social ministry to humanitarian needs as an expression of practical holiness are eligible. Selection is made by the Executive Committee. A plaque is awarded annually at the convention in April. Established in 1984.

• 7960 • **Holiness Exponent of the Year**
Recognized outstanding published work or leadership contributions. A plaque is awarded annually. Established in 1979.

• 7961 •
Christian Home Educators Association of California
Philip Troutt, Exec.Dir.
PO Box 2009
Norwalk, CA 90651-2009
Phone: (562)864-2432
Toll-Free: 800-564-CHEA
Fax: (562)864-3747
E-mail: cheaofca@aol.com
Home Page: http://www.cheaofca.org

• 7962 • **Teen Scholarship**
For a home-schooled senior student to attend the college or vocational school of their choice. Applicant must be CHEA member and member of CHEA support network group. Scholarship awarded annually.

• 7963 •
Christian Management Association
John Pearson, CEO
PO Box 4090
San Clemente, CA 92674
Phone: (949)487-0900
Toll-Free: 800-727-4CMA
Fax: (949)487-0927
E-mail: cma@cmaonline.org
Home Page: http://www.christianity.com/cma

Formerly: (1990) Christian Ministries Management Association.

• 7964 • **Chapter President of the Year Award**
Recognizes the chapter leader showing exemplary skills leading their chapter. Nominations must be made by a regional chapter director or CMA staff person by September 15. A plaque is awarded annually. Established in 1992.

• 7965 • **Christian Management Award**
To recognize an individual for outstanding Christian leadership. Nominations must be submitted by September 15. A plaque is awarded each year at the annual convention in February. Established in 1981.

• 7966 •
Christian Pharmacists Fellowship International
Allen Sharp P.D., Admin.Dir.
221 Franklin Dr.
PO Box 449
Blountville, TN 37617-0449
Phone: (423)323-1328
Toll-Free: 888-253-6885
Fax: (423)323-7215
E-mail: info@cpfi.org
Home Page: http://www.cpfi.org

• 7967 • **Warren Weaver Service Award**
To recognize outstanding service provided to the Fellowship by a member. A plaque is awarded each year at the annual meeting. Established in 1990.

• 7968 •
Christians Concerned for Racial Equality
Wesley H. Wakefield, Chm.
PO Box 223, Sta. A
Vancouver, BC, Canada V6C 2M3
Phone: (250)492-3376
Phone: (778)772-8014

• 7969 • **Special Recognition Award**
Periodic award of recognition.

• 7970 •
The Christophers
Dennis W. Heaney, Pres.
12 E 48th St.
New York, NY 10017
Phone: (212)759-4050
Toll-Free: 888-298-4050
Fax: (212)838-5073
E-mail: mail@christophers.org
Home Page: http://www.christophers.org

• 7971 • **Christopher Awards**
To recognize the creative writers, illustrators, producers, and directors who have achieved artistic excellence in films, books, TV and cable programming that affirms the highest values of the human spirit. Awards are given in the following categories: TV/Cable, Feature Films, Books for Adults and Books for Young People. There are also individual Special Christopher Awards. Including the Life Achievement Award and the James Keller Award, the latter for individuals who have contributed in a meaningful way to the well-being of young people.

• 7972 •
Chrysler 300 Club International
Eleanor Riehl, Exec.Sec.
4900 Jonesville Rd.
Jonesville, MI 49250
Phone: (517)849-2783
Fax: (517)849-7445
E-mail: crossram@optonline.net
Home Page: http://www.chrysler300club.com

• 7973 • **Concours**
For recognition of cars entered in the Concours attaining the highest overall points. Awards are presented in the following classes: Class I 1955 and 1956; Class II - 1957 to 1959; Class III - 1960 to 1962; Class IV - 1963 to 1965; Hurst Class - 1970 300 Hurst; and Seniors Class - for previous winner attaining first place in class and over 900 points, 1955 to 1965 300's are eligible for Seniors. An inscribed silver bowl - a traveling trophy - is presented annually at the fall meet to the Best of Show. In addition, first, second, and third place winners are chosen in each category. Established in 1977 by the Chrysler Corporation. Formerly: (1981) Seniors Division - Highest Point Car over 900 Points.

• 7974 •
Church and Synagogue Library Association
Judith Janzen, Administrator
PO Box 19357
Portland, OR 97280
Phone: (503)244-6919
Toll-Free: 800-LIB-CSLA
Fax: (503)977-3734
E-mail: csla@worldaccessnet.com
Home Page: http://www.worldaccessnet.com/~csla

• 7975 • **Honorary Life Member**
To recognize individuals for outstanding contributions to congregational libraries. Awarded when merited. Established in 1968.

• 7976 • **Helen Keating Ott Award for Outstanding Contribution to Children's Literature**
For recognition of a person or organization that has made a significant contribution to promoting high moral and ethical values through children's literature. Nominations of libraries, educators, clergy, authors, illustrators, editors, or publishers of children's books are accepted. Awardee is chosen by the Executive Board. A certificate is awarded annually. Established in 1980 to honor Helen Keating Ott, formerly a children's librarian and subsequently president of the board of trustees of the Mansfield (OH) Public Library. She held several offices in the Church and Synagogue Library Association and was the compiler of the CSLA bibliography, *Helping Children Through Books.*

• 7977 • **Outstanding Congregational Librarian**
To honor and encourage high-quality congregational librarianship through the recognition of a church or synagogue librarian who has given distinguished service to the congregation and/or community through devotion to the congregational library. Nominations are accepted. Awardee is chosen by the executive board. Volunteers or professional church or synagogue librarians are eligible. A certificate of appreciation from the association is awarded annually at the national conference. Established in 1976.

• 7978 • **Outstanding Congregational Library**
To honor and encourage high-quality congregational librarianship through the recognition of a church or synagogue library that has responded in a creative and innovative way to the library's mission of reaching and serving members of the congregation and/or the wider community. Nominations are accepted. Awardee is chosen by the executive board. A certificate of appreciation from the association is awarded annually at the national conference. Established in 1975.

• 7979 • **Outstanding Contribution to Congregational Libraries**
To honor and encourage high-quality congregational libraries through the recognition of a person or institution that has provided inspiration, guidance, leadership, or resources to enrich the field of church or synagogue libraries. Nominations are accepted. Awardee is chosen by the executive board. A certificate of appreciation from the association is awarded annually at the national conference. Established in 1968.

• 7980 • **Pat Tabler Memorial Award**
To recognize a new, or starting anew, congregational librarian who has creatively and systematically established a congregational library during the past year. Nominations are accepted. The awardee is chosen by the executive board. A certificate is awarded annually at the national conference. Established in 1987.

• 7981 •
Churches' Center for Theology and Public Policy
Rev. Barbara G. Green, Exec.Dir.
4500 Massachusetts Ave. NW
Washington, DC 20016
Phone: (202)885-8648
Toll-Free: 800-882-4987
Fax: (202)885-8559
E-mail: cctpp@wesleysem.edu
Home Page: http://www.cctpp.org

• 7982 • **James K. Mathews Service Award**
Annual award of recognition.

• 7983 •
Churchill Center
Daniel Myers, Exec.Dir.
1150 17th St. NW, Ste. 307
Washington, DC 20036
Phone: (202)223-5511
Toll-Free: 888-WSC-1874
Fax: (202)223-4944
E-mail: dmyers@winstonchurchill.org
Home Page: http://www.winstonchurchill.org

Formerly: (1971) Churchill Study Unit.

• 7984 • **Blenheim Award**
To recognize those individuals who have notably contributed to the International Churchill Society through service as an officer or director, by speaking at Society international events, or by contributing significantly to modern understanding of Churchill's life and thought. Established in 1974.

• 7985 • **Farrow Award**
To recognize outstanding work in the Churchill field by an academic. Awarded annually. Established in 1995.

• 7986 • **Honorary Member**
For recognition of outstanding contributions toward preserving the memory and legacy of Sir Winston Churchill, or for outstanding associates of Sir Winston Churchill during his lifetime. Nominations may be submitted by members, and the nominees require the unanimous approval of the Board of Directors. A certificate and lifetime membership in the Society are awarded when merited. Established in 1968.

• 7987 • **Emery Reves Award**
To recognize authors who notably demonstrate the relevance of Churchill's political thought to modern events and especially international relations. A Churchill bust by Oscar Nemon, with an appropriate brass plaque, is awarded when merited. Established in 1987 to honor Emery Reves, Churchill's postwar literary collaborator.

• 7988 •
Churchill Downs Inc.
Steve Sexton, Pres.
700 Central Ave.
Louisville, KY 40208
Phone: (502)636-4400
Fax: (502)636-4439
Home Page: http://www.churchilldowns.com

• 7989 • **Kentucky Derby**
A mile-and-one-quarter race for three-year-old Thoroughbred horses is held annually on the first Saturday in May. The maximum number of starters is twenty. The winner race is valued at $1 million minimum gross purse. The winner shall receive $700,000, second place receives $170,000 third place receives $85,000 and fourth place receives $45,000. This race is the first part of the Triple Crown. Any horse that sweeps the Kentucky Derby, Preakness Stakes and Belmont Stakes becomes a Triple Crown Champion, and earns a guaranteed five million dollars in purses and bonuses. Established in 1875. Sponsored since 1996 by Visa USA.

• 7990 • **Kentucky Oaks**
An annual Grade I Thoroughbred horse race for three-year-old fillies. Along with the Black-Eyed Susan Stakes (Pimlico Race Course) and the Acorn Stakes (Belmont Park), it is one of the three races that make up the Triple Crown. Established in 1875.

• 7991 •
CID Agents Association
Charlene Oestman-Thibeau, Membership/ Publicity Chm.
1896 Carlisle Rd.
Traverse City, MI 49686-9156
Phone: (231)932-2388
E-mail: cidaa@coslink.net
Home Page: http://www.onin.com/cidaa/

• 7992 • **CID Hall of Fame**
Recognizes outstanding CID member. A monetary award is given annually.

• 7993 • **CID Soldier of the Year**
Annually monetary prize is awarded annually.

Awards are arranged in alphabetical order below their administering organizations

• 7994 •
CIIT Centers for Health Research
Dr. Rusty J. Bramlage, HR Dir.
PO Box 12137
6 Davis Dr.
Research Triangle Park, NC 27709-2137
Phone: (919)558-1200
Fax: (919)558-1300
E-mail: ciitinfo@ciit.org
Home Page: http://www.ciit.org

Formerly: (2003) Chemical Industry Institute of Toxicology.

• 7995 • **Founders' Award**
To recognize contributions to advancements in the field of toxicology. A monetary prize of $2,000, a commemorative plaque, and a travel allowance for the awardee and spouse for the presentation are conferred at the annual meeting. Established in 1977 by CIIT in recognition of its founding members.

• 7996 •
CILQ-FM (Q107 Radio)
Blair Bartrem, Prog.Dir.
1 Dundas St. W., Ste. 1600
Toronto, ON, Canada M5G 1Z3
Phone: (416)221-0107
Toll-Free: 800-668-7625
Fax: (416)847-3300
Home Page: http://www.q107.com

• 7997 • **Q107 Homegrown Contest**
To foster and develop local Canadian music talent. Canadian musicians residing in the southern Ontario region who do not have a recording contract are eligible. A monetary award, the recording of a CD, and other music related products and services are awarded annually in June. Established in 1977.

• 7998 •
Cincinnati Opera Association
Julie Maslov, Dir. of PR
1243 Elm St.
Cincinnati, OH 45202
Phone: (513)241-2742
Phone: (513)768-5500
Toll-Free: 888-533-7149
Fax: (513)768-5552
E-mail: info@cincinnatiopera.com
Home Page: http://www.cincinnatiopera.org/index.jsp

• 7999 • **Cincinnati Opera Education Program**
To select an outstanding ensemble for a residency program from January through May. The Resident Company performs the education, outreach, and touring functions of the Cincinnati Opera, including a wide variety of entertainment and educational programs and productions performed for schools, colleges, communities, clubs, and organizations. Auditions are held in New York City and Cincinnati by invitation only. Round-trip airfare and a salary are paid during the residency program. Formerly: Ensemble Company of Cincinnati Opera (ECCO).

• 8000 •
Cinema/Chicago
Sophia Wong Boccio, Mng.Dir.
30 E Admas St., Ste. 800
Chicago, IL 60603
Phone: (312)683-0121
Fax: (312)683-0122
E-mail: info@chicagofilmfestival.com
Home Page: http://www.chicagofilmfestival.com

• 8001 • **Chicago International Film Festival**
To recognize outstanding international and American films and from experimental short subjects to features produced during the preceding year. Films may be entered by the filmmaker, producer, or distributor. The entry deadline is July 25. Separate jury heads and jury members are chosen for each major competitive category. Awards are given in the following categories: feature film, animation, documentary, short subject, student production, and television commercial. The following prizes are awarded: the Gold Hugo, the Silver Hugo, gold and silver plaques, certificates of merit, Best First or Second Feature, and The Chicago Award for the best production by a Chicago or Illinois artist. Awarded annually.

• 8002 • **The Hugos: The Chicago International Television Awards**
Honors and highlights television commercials and programming. Gold Hugo, Silver Hugo, Silver Plaque, and Certificate of Merit are awarded to the work that has the ability To move audiences and push the boundaries of this commanding medium. Deadline for entry is January. Awards are given annually. Established in 1964.

• 8003 • **INTERCOM: International Communication Film and Video Festival**
To honor the best corporate, business, educational and interactive productions made during the preceding year. Productions may be entered in any of the following categories: sales, public relations, training, human relations, politics, educational personal counseling, interactive digital multimedia sciences, and many more. The deadline is May 25. The following awards are presented: The Gold Hugo, Silver Hugo, gold and silver plaques, and certificates of merit. Awards are given annually.

• 8004 •
Circulation Council of DMA
Nicole Brown, Chair
1120 Avenue of the Americas
New York, NY 10036-6700
Phone: (212)768-7277
Fax: (212)302-6714
E-mail: nicole@nicolebowman.com
Home Page: http://www.the-dma.org

• 8005 • **Circulation Hall of Fame**
Awarded annually.

• 8006 •
Circumnavigators Club
Alfred Morasso Jr., Pres.
24 E 39th St.
New York, NY 10016-2555
Phone: (201)612-9100
Fax: (201)612-9595
E-mail: info@circumnavigatorsclub.org
Home Page: http://www.circumnavigatorsclub.org/index.php

• 8007 • **Order of Magellan**
To recognize individuals who are dedicated to advancing peace and understanding in all parts of the world and who have circumnavigated the globe. Only 28 individuals have received this award.

• 8008 •
Circus Fans Association of America
Cheryl Deptula, Exec.Sec.-Treas.
2704 Marshall Ave.
Lorain, OH 44052
Phone: (440)960-2811
Fax: (440)960-5932
E-mail: deptulascircus@centurytel.net
Home Page: http://circusfans.org

• 8009 • **Circus Fans Association of American Award**
Award of recognition.

• 8010 •
Citizens Budget Commission
Diana Fortuna, Pres.
1 Penn Plz., Ste. 640
New York, NY 10019
Phone: (212)279-2605
Fax: (212)868-4745
E-mail: info@cbcny.org
Home Page: http://www.cbcny.org

• 8011 • **CBC Medal**
For recognition of distinguished civic service to the city or state of New York. A bronze medal, designed by Wheeler Williams, is awarded annually. Established in 1951.

• 8012 •
Citizens Committee for New York City
Tamara Love, Dir., Neighborhood Resources Dept.
305 7th Ave.
15th Fl.
New York, NY 10001-6008
Phone: (212)989-0909
Fax: (212)989-0983
E-mail: info@citizensnyc.org
Home Page: http://www.citizensnyc.org

• 8013 • **New Yorker for New York Awards**
To recognize New Yorkers whose contributions have made the city a better place to live. Statuettes are awarded annually. Mayiyham Award for Public Service, Elizabeth Chapin Award for Volunteers in the Arts and Brooke Russell Astor

Awards are arranged in alphabetical order below their administering organizations

Award for Philanthropy also may be presented. Established in 1976.

• 8014 •
Citizens for Alternatives to Chemical Contamination
John Witocki, Contact
8735 Maple Grove Rd.
Lake, MI 48632-9511
Phone: (989)544-3318
Phone: (989)892-6174
Fax: (989)544-3318

• 8015 • **Citizens for Alternatives to Chemical Contamination Award**
Recognizes outstanding work for environmental equity and social justice, especially from grassroots. Awarded annually.

• 8016 • **Jefferson Award**
Annual award of recognition.

• 8017 •
Citizens League of Greater Cleveland/ Citizens League Research Institute
1331 Eucid Ave.
Cleveland, OH 44115
Phone: (216)241-5340
Fax: (216)736-7626
E-mail: staff@citizensleague.org

• 8018 • **Civic Service Award**
To recognize individual who have exhibited dedication to improving the quality of life in the community through their leadership in civic affairs. Awarded annually with a plaque. Established in 1985.

• 8019 •
Citizens Research Council of Michigan
Earl M. Ryan, Pres.
38777 W Six Mile Rd., Ste. 208
Livonia, MI 48152-2660
Phone: (734)542-8001
Phone: (517)485-9444
Fax: (734)542-8004
E-mail: crcmich@crcmich.org
Home Page: http://www.crcmich.org

• 8020 • **The Lent D. Upson-Loren B. Miller Fellowship**
For individuals pursuing a masters degree in public administration or a similar field. Scholarship awarded annually.

• 8021 •
Citizens Union of the City of New York
Dick Dadey, Exec.Dir.
299 Broadway, Ste. 700
New York, NY 10007-1976
Phone: (212)227-0342
Fax: (212)227-0345
E-mail: citizens@citizensunion.org
Home Page: http://www.citizensunion.org

• 8022 • **Civic Leadership Award**
To honor outstanding New Yorkers who have made meaningful contributions to the welfare of New York City and its people. A plaque or engraved crystal award is given each year at the annual dinner. Established in 1973. Formerly: Distinguished Service Award.

• 8023 •
City and Regional Magazine Association
C. James Dowden, Exec.Dir.
4929 Wilshire Blvd., Ste. 428
Los Angeles, CA 90010
Phone: (323)937-5514
Fax: (323)937-0959
E-mail: jdowden@prodigy.net
Home Page: http://www.citymag.org

• 8024 • **National, City and Regional Magazine Editorial and Design Awards**
To recognize outstanding city and regional magazines. Awards are presented in several categories. In the editorial category, awards are given for commentary, criticism, criticism on food or dining, investigative writing, works about home, local issues reporting, service to readers, special sections, General Excellence below 30,000 circulation, and General Excellence above 30,000 and up to 60,000 circulation. Design categories include color feature design, black and white feature design, spread design, color spread design, black and white spread design, typography, and cover design - photos & illustrations. The Medals for Excellence in Writing and Design; General Excellence Awards; gold, silver, and bronze medals; and Honorable Mention Awards are presented annually at the CRMA Conference. Established in 1984. Additional information is available from CRMA Awards, School of Journalism, Magazine Office, University of Missouri, 320 Lee Hills Hall, Columbia, MO 65211 Phone: (573)882-5722. Formerly: (1996) White Awards.

• 8025 •
City Club of New York
PO Box 897
New York, NY 10156
Phone: (212)684-6186
Fax: (212)699-0010
E-mail: cityclubofny@nycmail.com
Home Page: http://www.cityclub-ny.org

• 8026 • **Bard Awards for Excellence in Architecture and Urban Design**
To give public recognition to the best of the city's architecture and urban design, thereby encouraging architects and their clients to reach for higher standards of achievement. Projects must have been completed within the previous two years within the five boroughs of New York. A framed certificate is awarded annually. Established in 1962 in memory of Albert S. Bard, a former trustee of the Club (the oldest civic association in the city), who crusaded for 60 years to improve the quality of civic design and urban living.

• 8027 •
City College of New York
138th St. & Convent Ave.
New York, NY 10031
Phone: (212)650-7000
Fax: (212)794-5590
E-mail: support@ccny.cuny.edu
Home Page: http://www2.ccny.cuny.edu

• 8028 • **125th Anniversary Medals**
To recognize alumni and faculty of the City College of New York or community leaders who: through acts of advocacy offered keen support of the principle of free higher education; through their services advanced the welfare of the City College of New York and strengthened its role as a catalytic educational force in society; or through noble deeds demonstrated the inherent values that accrue within an urban society from those individuals who have been the beneficiaries of free public higher education at the City College of New York. A total of 125 gold medals may be awarded with no more than 20 medals to individuals who are not alumni or current or past faculty members of The City College of New York. Established in 1972.

• 8029 • **Chancellor's Medal**
To honor individuals who have distinguished themselves through service that merits recognition by, or reflects credit upon the City University of New York. A medal and citation are awarded at the discretion of the Chancellor in consultation with senior members of the board of trustees. Established in 1966.

• 8030 • **Forty Year Plaque**
To honor an individual on the faculty or staff of the College for 40 years of continuous service. A plaque is awarded annually. Established in 1960.

• 8031 • **James K. Hackett Award**
To recognize alumni and students for outstanding achievement in oratory or drama. A medal is awarded annually. Established in 1966.

• 8032 • **Robert J. Kibbee Award for Public Service and Achievement**
To recognize individuals who have contributed memorably and substantially to: the artistic, cultural, economic, or public life of New York City or to the public safety; the cause of higher education consistent with the mission of CUNY; the standards of academic excellence within the City University of New York; or the cause of intergroup harmony and understanding. Elected officials or others who are or may be candidates for public office are not eligible for this award. An honorarium not to exceed $5,000 and a medal are awarded annually. Established in 1981 in honor of Robert J. Kibbee, chancellor of the University from 1971 until his death in 1982.

• 8033 • **Martin Luther King, Jr. Medal**
To recognize an individual for lifelong dedication to humanitarian ideals. A medal is awarded as merited. Established in 1969.

• 8034 •
City of Beverly Hills
Recreation & Parks Dept.
455 N Rexford Dr.
Beverly Hills, CA 90210
Phone: (310)285-2536
Fax: (310)858-9238
E-mail: lgates@ci.beverly-hills.ca.us
Home Page: http://www.ci.beverly-hills.ca.us

• 8035 • **Affaire in the Gardens**
To recognize the best fine art and crafts at the outdoor exhibit. Awards are presented in the following categories: painting, mixed media/soft, drawings/prints/graphics, ceramics, sculpture, watercolor, mixed media/hard, photography, and jewelry. Presentation and technical ability are considered. Monetary awards and ribbons are presented. Best of Show recipients are selected. The exhibit is held biannually. Established in 1973 by the Recreation and Parks Department.

• 8036 •
City of Independence, Missouri
Office of the Mayor
111 E Maple Ave.
Independence, MO 64050
Phone: (816)325-7000
Fax: (816)325-7012
Home Page: http://www.ci.independence.mo.us

• 8037 • **Harry S. Truman Public Service Award**
For recognition of an American who best typifies the distinguishing qualities of President Harry Truman. Nominations of outstanding public servants are considered. A walking bronze statuette of Harry Truman, a replica of the statue on historic Independence Square, Independence, Missouri, is awarded annually on May 8, the birthdate of Harry Truman. Established in 1974 in memory of Harry S. Truman, the 33rd president of the United States.

• 8038 •
City of New York Department of Cultural Affairs
Kate D. Levin, Commissioner
330 W 42nd St.
New York, NY 10036
Phone: (212)643-7770
Home Page: http://www.nyc.gov/html/dcla

• 8039 • **Mayor's Awards for Excellence in Science and Technology**
Candidates must live or work in New York City. Awards are given in the areas of biological and medical sciences; mathematical, physical, and engineering sciences; technology; young investigators; and public understanding of science and technology. Judging varies for each award category.

• 8040 •
City of Ottawa
Ottawa City Hall
110 Laurier Ave. W
Ottawa, ON, Canada K1P 1J1
Phone: (613)580-2400
Toll-Free: (866)261-9799
Fax: (613)580-2495
E-mail: info@ottawa.ca
Home Page: http://www.ottawa.ca

• 8041 • **City of Ottawa Heritage Day Prize**
To recognize original research essays or studies on Ottawa's built heritage. An opportunity to present the winning paper to a public meeting of a local heritage organization and $2,000 is awarded. Students officially registered full-time or part-time in a degree or diploma program at the University of Ottawa, Carleton University, Algonquin College of Applied Arts and Technology, la Cite Collegiale, or Saint Paul University are eligible. Entries, which may be submitted in English or French, will examine the built environment within Ottawa city limits, and may range in scope from detailed architectural analyses of particular buildings to broader explorations of the built environment as reflection of cultural, social, political, or industrial history. Prize will be awarded on Heritage Day in February, at which time the winner will make a brief presentation on the submission.

• 8042 • **Ottawa Architectural Conservation Awards**
To recognize excellence in the preservation of Ottawa's built environment. Bronze plaques are awarded in three categories: Restoration, Adaptive Use, and Infill (addition or new construction within a historical context). Awarded annually.

• 8043 •
City of Toronto
Deptartment of the City Clerk
City Hall
100 Queen St. W
Toronto, ON, Canada M5H 2N2
Phone: (416)338-0338
Fax: (416)338-0685
E-mail: acesstoronto@toronto.ca
Home Page: http://www.city.toronto.on.ca

• 8044 • **Access Award**
To recognize an individual, group, or organization for a significant contribution towards improving the quality of life for the City's disabled residents. Established in 1982.

• 8045 • **Award of Merit**
To recognize persons who have attained high distinction and renown in various fields of endeavor and for outstanding achievements of significant benefit to the community. Nominees are selected by a non-political committee. Presented annually on Civic Honours Day. Established in 1956 by the Toronto City Council.

• 8046 • **City of Toronto Apprenticeship Screen Award**
To recognize excellence in Canadian film by a student from one of the local educational institutes, and to assist in the growth and promotion of Toronto's film and television industry by helping students develop their talents and business skills. Graduating students in film and television programs at local educational institutes are eligible. A monetary award is presented annually at the time of the Genie Awards. Established in 1984 by the Academy of Canadian Cinema and Television. Additional information is available from the Planning and Development Department, phone: (416) 392-7571.

• 8047 • **City of Toronto Awards for Excellence in Fashion Design**
To recognize outstanding achievement in the fashion industry. Awards are presented in five categories: (1) Designer of the Year - to recognize designers with at least five years experience who have brought distinction and prestige to the industry; (2) Most Promising New Designer - to recognize new designers who have produced between two and four collections; (3) Industry Achievement Award - to recognize a long-term contribution to Toronto's fashion business; (4) Most Promising Fashion Graduate Award - open to all current graduates of the five Toronto area fashion colleges; and (5) Courtier Award - to recognize another aspect of Toronto's fashion industry - Haute Couture. A framed citation is awarded annually. Established in 1984 by The Fashion Industry Liaison Committee to provide the vehicle through which the City supports the Fashion Industry and assists its growth and promotion by helping new designers to develop their talents and business skills. Additional information is available from the Department of Planning and Development, and The Fashion Industry Liaison Committee.

• 8048 • **City of Toronto Book Awards**
For recognition of books evocative of Toronto published in the previous year. Those books that center on the city itself, or describe important events, persons, or institutions in Toronto's history are considered for the award. Books must also have literary merit and be of general interest to Toronto citizens. Monetary awards totaling $15,000 are presented annually; $1,000 is given to the authors that make the short list, the remainder is given to the winning author. Established in 1973.

• 8049 • **Constance E. Hamilton Award**
For recognition of persons whose actions have been significant in helping secure equitable treatment for Toronto women in various aspects of economic, social, and cultural activities. Selected by nomination. A scroll is presented. Established in 1980. The award commemorates Constance E. Hamilton, the first woman member of the Toronto City Council.

• 8050 • **William P. Hubbard Race Relations Award**
To recognize individuals who have contributed significantly on a voluntary basis to the better-

ment of race relations within our community, but who have not been previously so honored nor have achieved a high profile for their efforts. Scrolls are awarded to up to three individuals annually on Civic Honours Day, a day honoring outstanding citizens of Toronto. Established in 1990 by Toronto Mayor's Committee on Community and Race Relations to honor William P. Hubbard, Toronto's first visible minority Alderman and Acting Mayor. He was elected to the City Council in 1894, and spearheaded the fight for the right of voters to directly elect Board of Control members. In 1904 he was chair of the Board of Control and Acting Mayor. Additional information is available from Janice Dembo, phone: (416) 392-7837.

• 8051 • Recognition of Service

For recognition of citizens appointed by the Toronto City Council who have served gratuitously on boards or commissions for five years or more. A medal is awarded annually on Civic Honours Day. Established in 1971.

• 8052 • Michael Sansone Award

To recognize two youths participating in the Department of Parks and Recreation athletic programs who display athletic ability and good sportsmanship, and contribute to the City's recreation program. Awarded annually. Established in 1985 by the bequest of Michael Sansone, a former playground leader with the City's Department of Parks and Recreation.

• 8053 •
City University of New York Graduate Center
Doctoral Theater Students Association
Theatre Program
365 Fifth Avenue
New York, NY 10016
Phone: (212)817-8870
Fax: (212)817-1538
E-mail: theatre@gc.cuny.edu

• 8054 • Edwin Booth Award

For recognition of significant contributions to theater in New York City by those individuals and organizations who represent the interdependence of the academic and professional theatrical communities. Nominations may be submitted by current department graduate students. A plaque is presented annually at an awards ceremony at the Graduate Center. Established in 1983 by the students of the Ph.D. Program in Theater. The award is named after Edwin Booth, the 19th century American actor/scholar.

• 8055 •
Civil War Society
Keith Poulter, Publisher
33756 Black Mountain Rd.
Tollhouse, CA 93667
Phone: (559)855-8637
Toll-Free: 800-546-6707
Fax: (559)855-8639
E-mail: tjohnston@northandsouthmagazine.com
Home Page: http://www.northandsouthmagazine.com

• 8056 • Anne D. Snyder Award

To recognize an individual who makes the greatest contribution to civil war historic preservation. Nominations must be made by members of the Society by May 1. A plaque is awarded annually and announced in *Civil War* Magazine. Established in 1989.

• 8057 •
Civil War Token Society
Dale Cade, Sec.
26548 Mazur Dr.
Rancho Palos Verdes, CA 90275
Phone: (310)378-4182
E-mail: cwts@worldnet.att.net
Home Page: http://home.att.net/~cwts/cwts.htm

• 8058 • The Jack Detwiler Memorial Service Award

To recognize the individual who has done the most to serve the CWTS each year. Members of CWTS are eligible. A plaque is awarded annually at the convention in August. Established in 1976.

• 8059 • Literary Awards Program

To recognize members of CWTS who have contributed an article(s) that was published in the quarterly publication, *The Civil War Journal*, and was judged worthy of an award. First, second, and third place plaques are awarded, and occasionally an honorable mention award. Established in 1976.

• 8060 •
Civitan International
W. John Rynearson CAE, Exec.VP
PO Box 130744
Birmingham, AL 35213-0744
Phone: (205)591-8910
Toll-Free: 800-CIV-ITAN
Fax: (205)592-6307
E-mail: civitan@civitan.org
Home Page: http://www.civitan.org

• 8061 • Civitan International Honor Keys

This, the highest individual award, is given to recognize service to Civitan International through work for a district or group of clubs in the formation of new clubs, the material increase in membership, the stimulation of greater service to the community in a group of clubs, or in unusual service to Civitan International. Individuals who have shown continued interest and service over a period are eligible. The entry deadline is May 1. Not more than five Gold Honor Keys are awarded annually.

• 8062 • District Bulletin Award

To recognize the best bulletin issued at least quarterly and produced by a Civitan district organization. Bulletins are judged on the basis of newsworthy content, format, attractiveness, readability, contribution to local district and international programs, and timelines. A plaque is awarded annually.

• 8063 • Founder's Award

To recognize the best overall club. Selection is based on total excellence and dedication on the part of every club member to the ideals of Civitan. Clubs are encouraged to submit as many programs, projects, and activities as deemed appropriate for this award. A plaque and a banner are presented annually.

• 8064 • Honor Club of Distinction

Recognition for these awards is based on achievements in the areas of knowledge, service, fellowship, and club management. The awards period for Honor Club is the Civitan administrative year, October 1 to September 30. The entry deadline is November 15. Each winning club receives a suitable emblem for the club banner. A club is also eligible to receive the Honor Club of Distinction Award by sponsoring a new club during the administrative year.

• 8065 • Outstanding Civitan Awareness Project

To recognize the club whose service project or promotion activity generates favorable publicity for the club or for the Civitan name. The entry deadline is December 1.

• 8066 • Outstanding Club Bulletin

To recognize the most attractive and informative club bulletin. Selection is based on newsworthy content, format, attractiveness, readability, contribution to programs, and timeliness. The entry deadline is December 1. First, second, and third place awards are presented. Awarded annually.

• 8067 • Outstanding Community Service Project

To recognize the club which provides the most outstanding service to the community through a single project. Any category of service is acceptable. Consideration is given to the project's overall benefit to the community and the club membership involved in the completion of the project. The entry deadline is December 1. A plaque is awarded annually.

• 8068 • Outstanding Service to the Mentally and/or Physically Handicapped

To recognize the club which has given the most outstanding service in any area of work with the mentally and/or physically handicapped, through a single project.

• 8069 • Outstanding Total Service to the Mentally and/or Physically Handicapped
To recognize the club which has given the most outstanding service in any one area of work with the mentally and/or physically handicapped. This award is based on a number of projects in the area of working with the physically and/or mentally handicapped. The entry deadline is December 1. First, second, and third place awards are presented. A plaque is awarded annually.

• 8070 • Outstanding Total Youth
To recognize the club which provides the most outstanding service in any area of youth work. This award is based on a total program, rather than on a single project. The entry deadline is December 1. First, second, and third place awards are presented. A plaque is awarded annually.

• 8071 • Outstanding Youth Project
To recognize the club which provides the most outstanding service in any area of youth work. This award is based on a single service project. The entry deadline is December 1. First, second, and third place awards are presented. A plaque is awarded annually.

• 8072 •
Clan Munro Association of Canada
Ian Angus Munro, Pres.
78-24 Fundy Bay Blvd.
100 City Centre Dr.
Toronto, ON, Canada M1W 3A4
Phone: (905)607-1439
Fax: (905)607-1439
E-mail: president@clanmunroassociation.ca
Home Page: http://www.clanmunroassociation.ca

• 8073 • Frank Munro Memorial Trophy
Recognizes the first place finisher in the piping competition. Awarded annually.

• 8074 •
Clark County Literacy Coalition
Mrs. Priscilla Marshall, Exec.Dir.
137 E High St.
Springfield, OH 45502-1215
Phone: (937)323-8617
Fax: (937)328-6911
E-mail: priscilla.marshall@clarkcountyliteracy.org
Home Page: http://www.clarkcountyliteracy.org

• 8075 • Edith Stager Memorial Award
Nominated by tutors and/or students based on commitment to improve reading skills or tutoring. Recognition award bestowed annually.

• 8076 •
Clarke College
Catherine Dunn, Pres.
1550 Clarke Dr.
Dubuque, IA 52001-3198
Phone: (563)588-6300
Toll-Free: 800-383-2345
E-mail: clarke-info@clarke.edu
Home Page: http://www.clarke.edu

• 8077 • Meneve Dunham Award for Excellence in Teaching
To recognize a faculty member for excellence in teaching. Nominees are judged for: (1) significant intellectual stimulation among a broad range of students; (2) creativity in assignments and teaching process; (3) effective evaluation of student performance; (4) course expectations that challenge a broad spectrum of students; and (5) relationship to the world beyond the classroom. Full time faculty members who have completed three years of service are eligible to be nominated by colleagues. A monetary award of $1,500 and a plaque are given annually in the spring. Established in 1985 by Meneve Dunham, a former president of Clarke College.

• 8078 •
Classic Car Club of America
Chuck Conrad, Pres.
1645 Des Plaines River Rd., Ste. 7A
Des Plaines, IL 60018-2206
Phone: (847)390-0443
Fax: (847)390-7118
E-mail: classiccarclub@aol.com
Home Page: http://www.classiccarclub.org

• 8079 • Bigelow Trophy
To recognize the Regional Club with the most distinguished record of overall activity for the year. A rotating trophy, which is held for one year, and a certificate as permanent evidence of superior achievement are awarded annually. Established in 1956.

• 8080 • Citation for Distinguished Service
To recognize Club members who have distinguished themselves through exceptional leadership, imagination and organizational ability, inspiring their associates in a concerted effort toward the fulfillment of worthwile Club goals. The Citation is not necessarily awarded annually. Established in 1972.

• 8081 • Coons Achievement Award
To recognize the most significant improvement in regional performance during the year. A silver bowl is awarded annually. Established in 1965.

• 8082 • Deutsch Memorial Trophy
To recognize the person who gave the most help on CARavan. A plaque is awarded annually. Established in 1977.

• 8083 • Dietrich Trophy
To recognize the region with the best participation in the national Club's annual meeting during the previous year. A rotating trophy and a certificate are awarded. Established in 1964.

• 8084 • Jack Gehrt Memorial Award
To recognize a Club member(s) who has contributed the most to the success of the last CARavan. A medal is awarded annually. Established in 1966.

• 8085 • Steiner Trophy
To recognize the region with the most notable record of participation in the Grand Classics event of the Club. A rotating trophy and certificate are awarded annually. Established in 1960 im memory of James B. Steiner, Director of the Buckeye Region.

• 8086 • Tarnopol Trophy
To recognize the region with the most notable participation in the CARavan of the previous summer. A rotating trophy and certificate are awarded. Established in 1956.

• 8087 • Turnquist Trophy
To encourage and recognize superior performance in communications through the medium of regional publications. A traveling trophy and a certificate are awarded. Established in 1959.

• 8088 •
Clay Minerals Society
Leslie Shivers, Mgr.
PO Box 460130
Aurora, CO 80046-0130
Phone: (303)680-9002
Fax: (303)680-9003
E-mail: cms@clays.org
Home Page: http://www.clays.org

• 8089 • Marilyn and Sturges W. Bailey Distinguished Member Award
To recognize outstanding scientific/professional contributions to clay mineralogy and related fields. Awarded periodically. Established in 1968.

• 8090 • George W. Brindley Lecture
To recognize a clay scientist who is both a dynamic speaker and involved in innovative research. An honorarium of $750 and travel expenses of $500 are awarded annually. Established in 1984.

• 8091 • Marion L. and Chrystie M. Jackson Mid-Career Clay Scientist Award
To recognize mid-career clay scientists (between ages 39 and 60) for excellence in the contribution of new knowledge to clay minerals science through original and scholarly research. Awarded annually. Established in 1992.

• 8092 • Pioneer in Clay Science Lecture
To recognize research contributions that have led to important new directions in clay minerals science and technology. An honorarium of $750

and travel expenses of $500 are awarded annually. Established in 1987.

• 8093 •
Cleft Palate Foundation
Nancy C. Smythe, Exec.Dir.
1504 E Franklin St., Ste. 102
Chapel Hill, NC 27514-2820
Phone: (919)933-9044
Toll-Free: 800-242-5338
Fax: (919)933-9604
E-mail: info@cleftline.org
Home Page: http://www.cleftline.org

Formerly: (1986) American Cleft Palate Education Foundation.

• 8094 • **Parent-Patient Leadership Award**
To recognize an individual for exceptional leadership and achievement in influencing the nature or availability of services for persons with congenital conditions. The parent of a child with craniofacial anomaly, a patient with a craniofacial anomaly, or an organization serving such individuals is eligible. A plaque and $500 for travel funds to the annual meeting are awarded annually. Established in 1989. Additional information is available from Mary Ellen Alexander, Executive Director.

• 8095 • **Donna Pruzansky Memorial Fund for Maternal and Child Health Nursing**
To encourage knowledge of and activity in the field of nursing care for patients with cleft palate and craniofacial anomalies. Nurses working in the field of cleft palate/craniofacial anomalies are eligible. Travel funds to meetings are awarded annually during the convention. Established in 1979 in memory of Donna Pruzansky.

• 8096 •
The Cleveland Foundation
Ronald B. Richard, Pres. and CEO
1422 Euclid Ave., Ste. 1300
Cleveland, OH 44115-2001
Phone: (216)861-3810
Fax: (216)861-1729
Home Page: http://www.clevelandfoundation.org

• 8097 • **Anisfield-Wolf Book Awards**
To recognize books published during the previous year that have made outstanding contributions to the appreciation of the richness or achievements of diverse human cultures or to the understanding of the mechanisms and injustices of racism. Books in English or English translation may be submitted by January 31. Plays and screenplays are not eligible. Stipends totaling $20,000 are usually divided between two works: one of a scholarly nature, the other of creative literature (fiction, poetry, biography). Awarded annually in April or May. Established in 1935, by Edith Anisfield Wolf, a Cleveland philanthropist, in memory of her husband Eugene E. Wolf and father, John Anisfield. For more information, contact Dr. Henry Louis Gates, Jr., Harvard University, 1430 Massachusetts Ave, Cambridge, MA 02138 (617)496-5468. Formerly: (1991) Anisfield-Wolf Book Award in Race Relations.

• 8098 •
Cleveland Institute of Music
David Cerone, Pres.
11021 East Blvd.
Cleveland, OH 44106
Phone: (216)791-5000
Fax: (216)791-3063
E-mail: cimmktg@cwru.edu
Home Page: http://www.cim.edu

• 8099 • **Art Song Festival**
To select 10 singer/pianist teams to participate in master classes with four great artists and to perform in recital at the festival. Interested singers and pianists must audition and be prepared to participate in the festival as a team. The application deadline for interested teams is February 1. Awarded biennially in even-numbered years.

• 8100 • **Cleveland International Piano Competition**
To encourage pianists to attain the finest elements of pianistic excellence, clarity of expression, and the fullest possible commitment to the highest level of musicianship while, at the same time, urging the reach into the great repertory not so generally regarded as standard. Pianists between the ages of 17 and 32 are eligible. The following awards are presented: First Prize - $15,000, a New York debut recital and two years of career development services; Second Prize $10,000; Third Prize $7,500; Fourth Prize - $5,000; and special prizes ranging from $500 to $2,000. Awarded biennially in odd-numbered years. Established in 1975. 1975. Formerly: (1995) Robert Casadesus International Piano Competition.

• 8101 •
Cleveland Police Historical Society and Museum
David C. Holcombe, Exec.Dir.
1300 Ontario St.
Cleveland, OH 44113
Phone: (216)623-5055
Fax: (216)623-5145
E-mail: museum@stratos.net
Home Page: http://www.clevelandpolicemuseum.org

• 8102 • **Hall of Fame**
For individuals who have made significant contributions to the safety and protection of Cleveland citizens. Recognition award bestowed annually.

• 8103 •
Cleveland State University Poetry Center
Rita Grabowski, Contact
2121 Euclid Ave.
Cleveland, OH 44115-2440
Phone: (216)687-3986
Toll-Free: 888-278-6473
Fax: (216)687-6943
E-mail: poetrycenter@csuohio.edu
Home Page: http://www.csuohio.edu/poetrycenter

• 8104 • **Cleveland State University Poetry Center Prize**
To encourage the writing of poetry of high quality. Submissions for the CSU Poetry Series must contain material for a book of 40 pages of poetry. A reading fee of $20 is required. Submissions are accepted only from November 1 to February 1; winners notified in June, results announced in July. A monetary prize of $1,000 and publication in the CSU Poetry Series are awarded annually. Awarded in two categories for unpublished and previously published poets. Established in 1987. Manuscripts are not returned. Send SASE for complete Guidelines or visit the website.

• 8105 •
Cleveland West Lutherans for Life
B. Hirsimaki, Contact
27993 Detroit Rd.
Westlake, OH 44145-2199
Phone: (440)835-3050

• 8106 • **Celebrate Life Essay and Poster Contest**
For winning essays and posters. Monetary award bestowed annually.

• 8107 •
Van Cliburn Foundation
Maria Guralnik, Gen.Mgr.
2525 Ridgmar Blvd., Ste. 307
Fort Worth, TX 76116-4593
Phone: (817)738-6536
Fax: (817)738-6534
E-mail: clistaff@cliburn.org
Home Page: http://www.cliburn.org

• 8108 • **Van Cliburn International Piano Competition**
Identifies and helps build careers for outstanding young pianists of all nationalities. Pianists between the ages of 18 and 30 who have prepared for a professional concert career are eligible. The following awards are presented: first prize (with a value totaling more than $250,000) - a monetary award of $20,000 the Nancy Lee and Perry R. Bass Gold Medal, orchestral and recital appearances, in the United States and abroad; second prize - a monetary award of $20,000 awarded by the Fuller Foundation and Marcia and Bobby French Van Cliburn Competition Silver Medal and orchestral and recital engagements in the United States and abroad; third prize - a monetary award of $20,000 awarded by the Mary Potishman Lard Trust, a Van Cliburn Competition Bronze Medal, and en-

gagements in the United States and abroad (all six finalists receive career management for up to three years); three finalists receive $10,000 each and six semifinalists receive $2,500 each. Awarded quadrennially. Established in 1962 in honor of the Texas pianist, Van Cliburn, and his victory in the Tchaikovsky International Piano Competition in Moscow in 1958. Established by Dr. Irl Allison, founder and president of the National Guild of Piano Teachers and Dr. Grace Ward Lankford, president of the Fort Worth Piano Teachers Forum. Other prizes and awards include Best Performance of a Chamber Work ($1000 cash); Best Performance of a New Work ($5000 cash); Jury Discretionary Awards (up to 4 cash prizes of $4000 each).

• 8109 •
Clinical Immunology Society
George C. Tsokos, Pres.
555 E Wells St., Ste. 1100
Milwaukee, WI 53202-3823
Phone: (414)224-8095
Fax: (414)272-6070
E-mail: info@clinimmsoc.org
Home Page: http://www.clinimmsoc.org

• 8110 • **Science Recognition Award for New Investigators**
To recognize students of clinical immunology. Travel expenses and a certificate are awarded annually to young investigators in the field who are no more than five years from the completion of their Ph.D. Between 5 and 15 awards are presented at the Annual Conference on Clinical Immunology. Established in 1987.

• 8111 •
Clio Awards Inc.
Ami Brophy, Exec.Dir.
770 Broadway, 6th Fl.
New York, NY 10003
Phone: (212)683-4300
Fax: (212)683-4796
E-mail: abrophy@clioawards.com
Home Page: http://www.clioawards.com

Formerly: (1959) American TV Commercials Festival.

• 8112 • **Clio Awards**
To recognize creative excellence in advertising worldwide. Open to television, print, radio, poster and outdoor advertising introduced during the previous year. The entry deadline is January 17 entries and international entries are judged separately, but finalists are judged to ascertain winners in approximately 150 categories, including technique and Classic Television Hall of Fame. Entries are judged against a scale of criteria, which includes concept, execution, music, illustration, direction, etc. Clio statuettes are awarded to top winners in each category at the annual awards show. Established in 1959 by Wallace Ross as the American TV Commercials Festival. Re-structured in 1991 by Clio Awards, Inc.

• 8113 •
Closter Historical Society
Patricia Garbe Morillo, Contact
68 Taylor Dr.
Closter, NJ 07624-2807
Phone: (201)767-7974
Phone: (201)768-1034
Fax: (201)767-5801

• 8114 • **Historic Preservation Awards**
For quality architectural restoration projects. Recognition award bestowed annually.

• 8115 •
CMP Educational Foundation of the Cincinnati Master Plumbers' Association
Joyce Frank, Exec.Mgr.
11020 Southland Rd.
Cincinnati, OH 45240
Phone: (513)742-CMPA
Fax: (513)742-8477
E-mail: info@cmpa-phcc.org
Home Page: http://www.cmpa-phcc.org

• 8116 • **Al Padur Scholarship Fund**
For plumbing apprentice. Scholarship awarded annually.

• 8117 •
Coalition for the Advancement of Jewish Education
Eliot G. Spack, Exec.Dir.
261 W 35th St., 12A Fl.
New York, NY 10001
Phone: (212)268-4210
Fax: (212)268-4214
E-mail: cajeny@caje.org
Home Page: http://www.caje.org

Formerly: (1987) Coalition for Alternatives in Jewish Education.

• 8118 • **David Dornstein Memorial Creative Writing Contest for Young Adult Writers**
To recognize authors of the three best stories based on a Jewish theme or topic, and to encourage professional and creative development of young writers. Any applicant between 18 and 35 years of age may submit an unpublished original short story of no more than 5,000 words. A monetary award of $700 for 1st place, $200 for 2nd, and $100 for 3rd place and publication in *The Jewish Education News* (JEN) publication are awarded annually in August. To verify submission requirements, a copy of a driver's license of another document confirming the author's age must be submitted, along with a signed statement attesting that the story has not been published. CAJE membership is welcome but not required for participation. All entries must be postmarked no later than December 31. Established in 1989 in memory of David Dornstein.

• 8119 •
Coalition to Protect Maryland Burial Sites
Edward W. Taylor, Pres.
PO Box 1533
Ellicott City, MD 21041-1533
Phone: (301)722-4624
Phone: (410)730-8278
E-mail: pres@cpmbs.org
Home Page: http://www.cpmbs.org

• 8120 • **Periwinkle Award**
For outstanding effort in preserving or protecting burial sites. Recognition award bestowed annually.

• 8121 •
Cocker Spaniel Club of Western Pennsylvania
Jeffrey M. Hanlin, Sec.
17 Concord Dr.
Irwin, PA 15642
Phone: (724)744-2706
Phone: (724)478-1195
E-mail: jmhanlin@aol.com
Home Page: http://cscwp.homestead.com

• 8122 • **Year-End Achievement Award**
Based upon titles won during the year. Recognition award bestowed annually.

• 8123 •
Cohasset Historical Society
David Wadsworth, Curator
14 Summer St.
Cohasset, MA 02025
Phone: (781)383-1434

• 8124 • **Burtram J. Pratt Memorial Award**
For high school student chosen by the school staff. Recognition award bestowed annually.

• 8125 •
Colby College
Stephen B. Collins, Sec., Lovejoy Selection Committee
4180 Mayflower Hill
Waterville, ME 04901-8841
Phone: (207)872-3276
Phone: (207)872-3000
Toll-Free: 800-723-3227
Fax: (207)872-3227
E-mail: lovejoy@colby.edu
Home Page: http://www.colby.edu/lovejoy

• 8126 • **Elijah Parish Lovejoy Award**
To recognize outstanding courageous actions in the fields of newspaper reporting, editing, and interpretive writing, and to promote a sense of mutual responsibility and cooperation between a journalistic world devoted to freedom of the press and a liberal arts college devoted to academic freedom. Editors, reporters, and publishers who show integrity, craftsmanship, character, intelligence, and courage, are eligible. A medal and an honorary degree are awarded annually when merited in the Fall at a speaking

forum convocation. Established in 1952 in memory of Elijah Parish Lovejoy, America's first martyr to freedom of the press.

• 8127 •
Coldwater Community Theater
14 S Hanchett
Coldwater, MI 49036
Phone: (517)278-3344
Fax: (517)279-8095

• 8128 • Robert J. Pickering Award for Playwriting Excellence
To recognize a playwright. Full length, unproduced manuscripts may be submitted by December 31. The following awards are presented: First Place - a monetary award of $200, full production of the manuscript, and housing to view the production; Second Place - $100; and Third Place - $50. Established in 1984 to honor Robert J. Pickering, whose contributions to area theater included the reactivation of Coldwater Community Theatre with his original play, *A Slight Exaggeration*, and production of two other original manuscripts, as well as countless hours of acting, producing, directing, and adding to the quality of area theater productions through CCT and Tibbits Summer Stock productions.

• 8129 •
Coleman Chamber Music Association
Kathy Freedland, Exec.Dir.
202 S Lake Ave., Ste. 201
Pasadena, CA 91101
Phone: (818)793-4191
Fax: (818)787-1294
E-mail: krfccma@aol.com

• 8130 • Coleman Chamber Ensemble Competition
Annual to recognize instrumental ensembles and to encourage young artists in their professional careers. The competition is open to nonprofessional instrumental ensembles from three to six players, prepared under the direction of a fully qualified professional coach. No member of the ensemble may function as a coach. Any ensemble which devotes a substantial portion of its time performing for a fee is not eligible to compete. The average age of the players must be under 26 years of age as of April 24 2004 the repertory must be two complete works of contrasting Characters from two different musical periods. Application forms and CD recordings of complete proposed repertory must be submitted by February 20. The following awards are presented: Coleman - Barstow Award for Strings $4,000 available only to String Ensembles with or without a keyboard or with or without one woodwind; Coleman Award for Woodwinds or Brass $4,000 available only to woodwind or brass groups or other non-string ensembles; Saunderson Award - $3,000 unrestricted; and Russell Award - $2,000 unrestricted. All winners are presented in public concert in Ramo Auditorium, California Institute of Technology, Pasadena, CA. Awarded annually. Established in 1945.

• 8131 •
Coleopterists' Society
Floyd Shockley, Treas.
Department of Entomology
413 Bio Sciences
University of Georgia
Athens, GA 30602-2603
Phone: (706)542-6187
Fax: (706)542-2279
E-mail: treasurer@coleopsoc.org
Home Page: http://www.coleopsoc.org

• 8132 • Coleopterists Society Youth Award
To stimulate interest in the study of beetles by junior high and high school students. Monetary awards of $125 and a one-year membership (with a subscription to *Coleopterists Bulletin*) are awarded annually. Established in 1989.

• 8133 •
Collectors Club
Wade E. Saadi, Pres.
22 E 35th St.
New York, NY 10016-3806
Phone: (212)683-0559
Phone: (212)683-0558
Fax: (212)481-1269
E-mail: collectorsclub@nac.net
Home Page: http://www.collectorsclub.org

• 8134 • Annual Competition - Grand Award (One-Frame Competition)
For recognition of the best exhibit displaying philatelic knowledge and research, philatelic importance and rarity, condition, completions presentation and balance. Honoree must be a Collectors Club member and display an exhibit of not more than sixteen pages. The Award varies annually. The second place winner is also recognized. Established in 1947. Formerly: (1997) Annual Competition - Grand Award.

• 8135 • Collectors Club Medal for Best Program Presented to the Collectors Club
For recognition of the presentation of the best lecture at the Collectors Club during the year. The Collectors Club Medal is presented to the best program, and the second best is given a certificate. Awarded annually. Established in 1948.

• 8136 • Collectors Club Medal for Outstanding Article in *The Collectors Club Philatelist*
To recognize contributions to *The Collectors Club Philatelist* representing an original research study. Presented at the annual awards dinner in May. Established in 1948.

• 8137 • Alfred F. Lichtenstein Medal
For recognition of distinguished philatelic service, regardless of race, nationality, economic status, club affiliations, or philatelic interest. Candidates are recommended by former recipients to the Board of Governors. A three = inch bronze medal with a high = relief bust of Alfred F. Lichtenstein is presented annually. Established in 1952 in honor of Alfred F. Lichtenstein, a philatelist of international reputation, who was a patron and champion of The Collectors Club.

• 8138 • President's Medal for Merit
To recognize members for outstanding and meritorious service to The Collectors Club. The Collectors Club Medal is presented irregularly. Established in 1959. Formerly: (1958) Collectors Club Medal for Devoted Service.

• 8139 •
Collectors of Religion on Stamps
Verna Shackleton, Sec.
425 N Linwood Ave., No. 110
Appleton, WI 54914-3476
Phone: (920)734-2417
Phone: (920)734-6711
E-mail: corosec@sbcglobal.net
Home Page: http://my.vbe.com/~cmfourl/coros1.htm

• 8140 • COROS Ribbon
To promote religious exhibiting. Religious stamp exhibits are eligible. Membership is not required. A Ribbon is awarded when merited. Religious exhibit must be 100% religious. Two exhibits in competition required award is a Best religious exhibit ribbon. Established in the late 1960s.

• 8141 •
College Art Association
Susan Ball, Exec.Dir.
275 7th Ave.
New York, NY 10001
Phone: (212)691-1051
Fax: (212)627-2381
E-mail: nyoffice@collegeart.org
Home Page: http://www.collegeart.org

• 8142 • Artist Award for a Distinguished Body of Work, Exhibition, Presentation or Performance
To recognize an individual for a distinguished body of work, exhibition, presentation, or performance mounted in the academic year preceding the award. Living artists who are citizens or permanent residents of the United States or its territones, Canada, or Mexico are eligible. A citation is awarded annually at the annual meeting. Established in 1987.

• 8143 • Alfred H. Barr, Jr. Award
For recognition of exemplary contributions to knowledge made by the author(s) of museum catalogs published in the penultimate year preceding the award. Citizens or permanent residents of the United States, Canada, or Mexico are eligible. Selection is made by a committee. A citation is awarded annually. Established in 1980.

• 8144 • College Art Association/National Institute for Conservation Award
For recognition of an outstanding contribution by one or more persons who, individual or jointly, have enhanced understanding of art through the application of knowledge and experience in con-

Awards are arranged in alphabetical order below their administering organizations

servation, art history, and art. Awarded annually. This joint award for distinction in scholarship and conservation was established in 1991.

• 8145 • Distinguished Artist Award for Lifetime Achievement
To recognize the lifetime achievement of a living artist who has demonstrated particular commitment to his or her work throughout a long career and has had an important impact nationally and internationally. Citizens or permanent residents of the United States or its territories, Canada, or Mexico are eligible. A citation is awarded annually at the annual meeting. Established in 1987.

• 8146 • Distinguished Teaching of Art Award
To recognize a distinguished artist who has made a significant contribution to the teaching of art. Citizens or permanent residents of the United States or its territories, Canada, or Mexico are eligible. Nominations may be submitted by November 1. A citation is awarded annually. Established in 1972.

• 8147 • Distinguished Teaching of Art History Award
To recognize a distinguished art historian who has made a significant contribution to the teaching of art history. Citizens or permanent residents of the U.S., its territories, Canada, or Mexico are eligible. Nominations must be submitted by November 1. A citation is awarded annually. Established in 1977.

• 8148 • Frank Jewett Mather Award
For recognition of distinction in art journalism. Citizens or permanent residents of the U.S., its territories, Canada, or Mexico are elibigle. Critics are eligible for published art criticism that has appeared in whole or in part during the preceding year. Selection is made by a committee. A citation is awarded annually. Established in 1963.

• 8149 • Charles Rufus Morey Book Award
For recognition of an especially distinguished book in the history of art, published in any language in the penultimate calendar year, by a citizen or permanent resident of the United States, its territories, Canada, or Mexico. Preference is given in the award of the prize to books, including *catalogues raisonnes* by a single author, but major publications in the form of articles or group studies may be considered. Publication of documents or inventories, unless specifically in the context of an exhibition, are also eligible. A citation is awarded annually. Established in 1953.

• 8150 • Arthur Kingsley Porter Prize
To recognize the best article published in *The Art Bulletin* by a scholar at the beginning of his or her career. The author must be under 35 years of age or have received a Ph.D within the last ten years by the time the article is accepted. Selection is made by committees that do not accept entries. A citation is awarded annually. Established in 1957.

• 8151 •
College English Association
Prof. Charles Ernst PhD, Exec.Dir.
Hilbert College
Arts and Sciences Dept.
5200 S Park Ave.
Hamburg, NY 14075
Phone: (716)649-7900
Fax: (716)649-0702
E-mail: cernst@hilbert.edu
Home Page: http://www.as.ysu.edu/~english/cea/ceaindex.htm

• 8152 • CEA Honorary Life Membership
To recognize an individual for extraordinary and sustained service to the Association and the profession. A plaque and remission of annual dues for life are awarded annually at the convention. Established in 1982.

• 8153 • CEA Professional Achievement Award
To recognize an Association member who has significantly contributed to teaching and scholarship at the college level. A plaque is awarded annually at the convention. Established in 1986.

• 8154 • Robert Hacke Scholar-Teacher Award
To help support a CEA junior teacher who is involved in a scholarly or pedagogic project relating to English studies. Those who are adjuncts or who hold the rank of instructor or assistant professor in a post-secondary institution (including community colleges), and who are members of the CEA are eligible. The deadline for applications is November 15. A cash award of $500 is announced each year at the annual College English Association conference. Established in 1992 in memory of Robert E. Lee Hacke, Executive Secretary of the CEA from 1977 to 1981.

• 8155 • Robert A. Miller Memorial Prize
To recognize the author of the best essay appearing in a CEA publication during the preceding year. Essays published in the *CEA Critic* or the *CEA Forum* are eligible. A monetary award of $100 is awarded annually at the annual convention. Established in 1978.

• 8156 • Joe D. Thomas CEA Distinguished Service Award
To recognize individuals for outstanding contributions and service to CEA. A plaque is awarded annually at the convention. Established in 1945. Since 1982, the award has been presented on a regular basis.

• 8157 •
College Gymnastics Association
Dr. Richard Aronson, Exec.Dir.
52 Evelyn Rd.
Needham, MA 02494
Phone: (617)444-3893
Fax: (402)472-9449
E-mail: fallen@huskers.unl.edu
Home Page: http://tigger.uic.edu/~cjgym
Formerly: (1997) National Association of College Gymnastics Coaches.

• 8158 • Coach of the Year
To honor outstanding active college and university gymnastics coaches. Four regional awards and two National Coach of the Year awards are presented. The coaches of the winning teams of the National Championship are named National Coach of the Year. Selection is made by a ballot of the membership of the Association. Plaques are awarded annually. Established in 1961.

• 8159 • First Interstate Athletic Foundation Gymnastics Hall of Fame Award
To recognize coaches and gymnasts. Induction ceremonies are held annually at the spring banquet meeting. Established in 1959 as the Helms Athletic Foundation Gymnastics Hall of Fame. Formerly: Citizens Savings Athletic Foundation Gymnastics Hall of Fame.

• 8160 • Honor Coach Award
To recognize a member-coach of 25 years or more who has gained the admiration of his coaching associates. Selection is made by the Honor Coach Award Committee through secret ballot. Awarded annually at the spring banquet meeting. Established in 1954.

• 8161 • Honor Coach Certificate
This award is made posthumously to a member of the coaching profession who was either too young to quality for the Honor Coach Award, or had not been nominated prior to his death for that award. Awarded when merited. Established in 1965.

• 8162 • Nissen-Emery Award
To recognize the country's outstanding senior collegiate gymnast. The award is presented not only for a gymnast's accomplishments in the sport itself, but also for his scholastic excellence and character. Nominees must have the following qualifications: be a college senior graduating at the end of the present school year; must have maintained a high standard of scholarship throughout his college career; be an example of good sportsmanship and fair play; and have had an outstanding record of gymnastics accomplishment during his college career. The winner is selected by collegiate gymnastics coaches and judges in secret ballot. An inscribed trophy is awarded annually at the NCAA Gymnastics Championships. Established in 1966. Formerly: Nissen Award.

• 8163 • Research Award
To recognize outstanding research in gymnastics. Applicants submit papers to the Research chairman for evaluation by the Research Committee. Papers must be submitted in a form suitable for publication in the research section of the *International Gymnast* magazine. A monetary award of $500 is provided by five sponsors: AMF, Gym Master, Nissen, Porter and Zwickel, each providing $100. Presentation of the award is made annually when merited by the chairman at the spring banquet. The name of the award alternates each year in a four-year cycle and honors one of the following individuals: Carl Patterson, Hartley Price, Lyle Welser, and Leopold Zwarg.

• 8164 • Special Service Award
To recognize individuals who have given unselfishly to the sport of gymnastics and to the Association. Nominations are accepted. A certificate is awarded annually at the spring meeting. Established in 1967.

• 8165 •
College Language Association
James J. Davis, Treas.
12138 Central Ave., Ste. 576
Modern Languages & Literatures Department
Mitchellville, MD 20721-1932
Phone: (202)806-6758
Phone: (202)806-6762
Fax: (202)806-4514
E-mail: jdavis@howard.edu
Home Page: http://www.clascholars.org

• 8166 • CLA Award Scholarship
Recognizes a scholarly publication. An article published in the *CLA Journal* or elsewhere, or a book that has been published, not just privately printed and copyrighted, is eligible. A plaque is awarded when merited. Established in 1940.

• 8167 •
College Media Advisers
Ronald E. Spielberger, Exec.Dir.
University of Memphis
MJ-300
Memphis, TN 38152-6661
Phone: (901)678-2403
Phone: (901)754-8112
Fax: (901)678-4798
E-mail: rsplbrgr@memphis.edu
Home Page: http://www.collegemedia.org

Formerly: National Council of College Publications Advisers.

• 8168 • Best of Collegiate Design
An annual publication which showcases the best work produced by student media designers. Respected professionals select the best entries for publication. Captions written by the judges explain the outstanding aspects of each entry.

• 8169 • John A. Boyd Hall of Fame Award
In recognition of long-time members whose dedication, commitment, and sacrifices have contributed to the betterment and value of student media programs both on their campus and nationally. It also honors the contributions of CMA members who have actively contributed to the organization through extensive and varied service on committees, the board of directors, and other leadership roles and have presented insightful, relevant, and well-prepared programs and sessions at meetings. Nominees must have contributed to college journalism education for 20 years or more while an active member of CMA. Any member of CMA may submit or sponsor nominations. Nominations from supervisors, colleagues, and students are also accepted. Equal consideration is given to the contributions of a nominee in the categories of service to collegiate journalism education and service to CMA. The deadline for nomination submission is February 15. Winners receive an engraved trophy or similar symbol at the fall National College Media Convention. The Hall of Fame is located at CMA's Headquarters Office at Memphis State University.

• 8170 • Business/Economic Writing Award
To recognize business and economic reporting by students whose advisers are CMA members. Entries must be submitted on behalf of a college student medium, must be the work of a student at that college, and must have appeared in or have been broadcast on the campus medium of that institution since October 1. A committee of professionals in the field judges the contest. Established in 1983. Formerly: Business and Economic Reporting Contest.

• 8171 • Distinguished Adviser Award
To honor outstanding advisers. Awards are given in 10 categories: Distinguished Four-Year College Newspaper Advisers, Distinguished Four-Year Magazine Advisers, Distinguished Four-Year Yearbook Advisers, Distinguished Four-Year Business Advisers, Distinguished Two-Year College Newspaper Advisers, Distinguished Two-Year College Magazine Advisers, Distinguished Two-Year College Yearbook Advisers, Distinguished Two-Year Broadcast Advisers, and Distinguished Multi-Media Advisors. An adviser may not receive an award more than once in a single category. Nominations are accepted. CMA members who have been college or university publications advisers and/or broadcast advisers for at least five years and are advisers at the time of nomination are eligible. A plaque and a certificate are awarded annually. Established in 1960.

• 8172 • Editorial and Cartoon Strip Contest
For recognition of the most outstanding cartoon in two categories: Editorial Cartoon and Cartoon Strip. The entry must be submitted on behalf of a college student publication, must be the work of a student at that college, and must have appeared in the campus publication of that institution since July 1. The deadline for entry is May 15. First, second, and third places are named in both categories, with possible honorable mentions. Winners are announced at the national convention. Established in 1974.

• 8173 • Honor Roll Adviser Award
To recognize CMA members with less than five years experience in student media advising. Nominations are accepted. Established in 1982.

• 8174 • Louis E. Inglehart First Amendment Award
To recognize a professional journalist, institution, or adviser who has made extraordinary, long-term contributions in support of the First Amendment. Non-CMA members may make nominations. Awarded when merited. Established in 1980. The award honors Louis E. Inglehart, Ball State University journalism professor who had dedicated much of his academic life to studying, writing about, and teaching the applications of the First Amendment to the U.S. Constitution.

• 8175 • Reid H. Montgomery Distinguished Service Award
To recognize an individual or institution that has made an outstanding contribution to the collegiate media or media advising. A student, faculty member, corporation, or non-academic individual or institution may be nominated. The award is not limited to CMA members. A plaque and certificate are awarded when merited. Established in 1962. The award honors Dr. Reid H. Montgomery, president of the National Council of College Publications Advisers and past treasurer and newsletter editor.

• 8176 • Noel Ross Strader Memorial Award
To honor the outstanding leadership and courage of an adviser who continues to maintain high principles and conduct, usually under trying circumstances. Eligible nominees include full-time teachers/advisers in campus journalism, not necessarily a member of CMA, who have exercised the principle of freedom of the press at some risk to personal or professional welfare or who have made a major contribution to the physical progress of a campus publication. Awarded when merited. Established in 1976 in memory of Noel Ross Strader, a long-time teacher/administrator in college journalism.

• 8177 • Yearbook Marketing Award
Recognizes a yearbook staff that has developed and implemented an outstanding comprehensive marketing campaign for the school's yearbook. A portfolio containing all elements of the campaign must be submitted and must be student produced.

• 8178 •
College of Mount Saint Joseph
Carolmarie Stock, Director, Alumni Relations and Special Events
Office of Alumni Relations
5701 Delhi Pike
Cincinnati, OH 45233
Phone: (513)244-4200
Toll-Free: 800-654-9314
Fax: (513)244-4222
E-mail: carolmarie_stock@mail.msj.edu
Home Page: http://www.msj.edu

Formerly: (1985) College of Mount Saint Joseph on the Ohio.

• 8179 • **Alumni Career Achievement Award**
To honor Mount graduates for outstanding achievement in career/vocational fields. All Mount graduates except present Alumni Board members are eligible. The nominee's accomplishments should clearly reflect significant service to humanity and be in keeping with the mission and goals of the College.

• 8180 • **Alumni Volunteer Leadership Award**
To honor an alum who supports alumni activities through volunteerism and is an advocate for the College. Candidates are nominated by The Alumni Board and/or College staff, with final confirmation by the College president. Awarded annually. Established in 1989.

• 8181 • **Sister Mary Lea Mueller Human Services Award**
To recognize Mount alumni who have devoted their lives to serving others, affirming the fullness and value of human existence. Service, either through career or volunteer activities, can be to educational, cultural, social, civic, or religious institutions. All Mount alumni are eligible. The award was established in 1994 as a tribute to Sister Mary Lea Mueller and her service to the college on the occasion of her 90th birthday.

• 8182 • **Loretta Richards Distinguished Alumni Award**
To recognize an alumnus distinguished for achievement in vocation, dedication to community service, and loyalty to the College of Mount Saint Joseph. The award is the highest honor bestowed. Members are eligible for nomination and final confirmation by the College president. A plaque is awarded annually at Reunion Weekend. Established in 1979 in honor of Loretta Richards, first alumnae president.

• 8183 •
College of Optometrists in Vision Development
Stephen C. Miller O.D., Exec.Dir.
243 N Lindbergh Blvd., Ste. 310
St. Louis, MO 63141
Phone: (314)991-4007
Toll-Free: 888-268-3770
Fax: (314)991-1167
E-mail: info@covd.org
Home Page: http://www.covd.org

• 8184 • **G. N. Getman Award**
For recognition of outstanding contributions in the field of vision development by an optometrist with clinical expertise. A plaque is awarded annually. Established in 1970.

• 8185 • **A. M. Skeffington Award**
For recognition of outstanding contributions by a Fellow of the Collegeto optometric literature. A plaque is awarded annually. Established in 1970.

• 8186 •
College of Physicians of Philadelphia Section on Dermatology
19 S 22nd St.
Philadelphia, PA 19103
Phone: (215)563-3737
Fax: (215)561-6477
E-mail: parish2@jeflin.tju.edu
Home Page: http://www.collphyphil.org

• 8187 • **Mohamed Amer Award**
To recognize the best resident papers in dermatology. Papers must be submitted by August in the award year. Two awards are presented: the Blue Award for an American resident and the White Award for an Egyptian resident. A plaque and travel expenses to receive the award are presented biennially. Established in 1982 to honor Mohamed Amer, M.D., Professor of Dermatology, Zagazig University, Zagazig, Egypt.

• 8188 •
College Sports Information Directors of America
Jeff Hodges, Sec.
University of North Alabama
PO Box 5038
Florence, AL 35632
Phone: (256)765-4595
Fax: (256)765-4659
E-mail: sportsinformation@una.edu
Home Page: http://www.cosida.com

• 8189 • **CoSIDA Backbone Award**
To recognize an individual who displays sound judgment and unusual courage in taking a stand on intercollegiate athletics which is contrary to prevailing opinion and public sentiment. A plaque with a gold shield is awarded when merited. Established in 1957.

• 8190 • **GTE Academic All-America Hall of Fame**
To recognize outstanding scholar-athletes.

• 8191 • **GTE Academic All-American of the Year**
To recognize an athlete who is most outstanding in both the academic and athletic areas. College men and women are eligible.

• 8192 • **Jake Wade Memorial Award and Honorary Membership**
To recognize an individual or an organization which has made an outstanding contribution in the communications media to the field of collegiate athletics. A plaque with a gold shield is awarded annually. Established in 1957.

• 8193 • **Arch Ward Memorial Award**
To recognize a member of the organization who has made an outstanding contribution in the field of college sports information or who, by his activities outside the field, has brought dignity and prestige to the profession. A plaque with gold shield is awarded annually. Established in 1957.

• 8194 •
College Swimming Coaches Association of America
Joel Shinofield, Sec.
PO Box 63285
Colorado Springs, CO 80962
Phone: (719)266-0064
Fax: (719)266-6844
E-mail: swimco@aol.com
Home Page: http://www.cscaa.org

• 8195 • **Charles McCaffree Award**
To recognizes outstanding contribution to swimming. Winners are selected by nomination and vote. A plaque is presented annually at the convention. Established in 1975 to honor Michigan State University swim coach, Charles McCaffree.

• 8196 • **National Collegiate and Scholastic Swimming Trophy**
To recognize an individual or organization for having an outstanding contribution to swimming as a competitive sport and healthful recreation activity in schools and colleges. Nominations are accepted. A sculpture, representing a swimming coach counseling one of his students, by the Princeton University Professor, Joseph Brown, is awarded annually at formal ceremonies. Established in 1957.

• 8197 • **Richard Steadman Award**
Recognizes outstanding contribution to swimming. Applicants can be individuals involved in the sport in any form.

• 8198 •
Collegium Internationale Neuro-Psychopharmacologicum
Oakley Ray PhD, Exec.Sec.
1608 17th Ave. S
Nashville, TN 37203
Phone: (615)297-3144
Fax: (615)385-3174
E-mail: cinp@cinp.org
Home Page: http://www.cinp.org

• 8199 • **Max Hamilton Memorial Prize**
To recognize a young scientist for outstanding contributions to psychopharmacology. Contributions may be in clinical evaluation or services, preclinical or clinical research, or any combination of these. Nominees need not be members of CINP, but must be under 41 years of age in the year the prize is awarded. A monetary prize of $10,000 and an engraved plaque are awarded

annually. Established in honor of Max Hamilton for his assessment of depressive illness through psychometrics.

• 8200 • Dr. Paul Janssen Schizophrenia Research Award
To recognize a young investigator who has performed outstanding research in the area of Clinical Neuroscience of Schizophrenia at a University institute or any other acknowledged scientific institution that is independent of the Pharmaceutical Industry. Investigators under 45 years of age on January 1 of the year of the award are eligible. A plaque and monetary prize of $15,000 are awarded. Supported by an educational grant for Janssen Research Council.

• 8201 • Rafaelsen Fellowship Award
To support the attendance of young scientists at the CINP Congresses. Researchers or clinicians under 36 years of age who are committed to the field of neuropsychopharmacology are eligible. Nominations must be made by CINP members. Ten awards consisting of a $500 stipend and a plaque are awarded annually. Established in 1986 by Ole Rafaelson and William Bunney and named for Dr. Rafaelson posthumously in 1987.

• 8202 •
Collier Building Industry Association
David Ellis, Exec.VP
4779 Enterprise Ave.
Naples, FL 34104
Phone: (239)436-6100
Fax: (239)436-3878
E-mail: info@cbia.net
Home Page: http://www.cbia.net

• 8203 • Sand Dollar
For new homes. Recognition award bestowed annually.

• 8204 •
Colonial Players, Inc.
Ed Wintermute, Pres.
Promising Playwright Contest
108 East St. Box Office
Annapolis, MD 21401
Phone: (410)268-7373
Home Page: http://www.cplayers.com

• 8205 • Promising Playwright Award
To encourage aspiring playwrights residing in any of the states descendant from the original 13 Colonies, which are Connecticut, Georgia, Massachusetts, New Hampshire, New Jersey, New York, South Carolina, Rhode Island, South Carolina, Maryland, Washington D.C., Virginia, Delaware, and Pennsylvania, West Virginia and Washington D.C.. Scripts must be postmarked between September 1 and December 31 of the year preceding the award. Only full-length plays suitable for arena production, with up to two settings and running not less than 1 to 2 hours, excluding intermission, are considered. Maximum cast size is 10 actors. Musicals and adaptations in copyright and plays that have been previously produced professionally are not considered. A monetary prize of $1,000 and a main stage production of the play by Colonial Players is awarded. In the event that no entry is deemed suitable for production in the theater, no prize is awarded. Awarded biennially.

• 8206 •
Colonial Society of Massachusetts
John W. Tyler, Editor
87 Mt. Vernon St.
Boston, MA 02108
Phone: (617)227-2782
Home Page: http://www.colonialsociety.org

• 8207 • Walter Muir Whitehill Prize
For best essay in a topic related to early New England history. A monetary prize of $2,500 is awarded annually.

• 8208 •
Colorado Business Committee for the Arts
Deborah Jordy, Exec.Dir.
200 Grant St., Ste. B-5
Denver, CO 80203
Phone: (303)282-5135
Fax: (303)282-5174
E-mail: main@cbca.org
Home Page: http://www.cbca.org

• 8209 • Business in the Arts
For outstanding business, art partnership. Recognition award bestowed annually.

• 8210 •
Colorado Congress of Foreign Language Teachers
Elizabeth Berwanger, Exec.Sec.
PO Box 621
Englewood, CO 80151-0621
Phone: (970)484-6168
E-mail: pdtunnel@msn.com
Home Page: http://ccflt.org

• 8211 • Spring Conference Scholarships
For personal statement with plan for sharing outcomes and letter of support from administrator. Scholarship awarded annually.

• 8212 • Ronald W. Walker Memorial Grant
For innovative, language-oriented student activities and trips, materials development and projects whose creativity may impact students directly.

• 8213 •
Colorado Language Arts Society
Jackie Swensson, Exec.Sec./Treas.
8105 S Shawnee St.
Aurora, CO 80016
E-mail: swenssoj@mscd.edu
Home Page: http://www.clas.us

• 8214 • Teacher Award
For excellence in teaching and service to the profession. Recognition award bestowed annually.

• 8215 •
Colorado Ranger Horse Association
Barbara Summerson, Contact
1510 Greenhouse Rd.
Wampum, PA 16157
Phone: (724)535-4841
Fax: (724)535-4841
E-mail: crha@adelphia.net
Home Page: http://www.coloradoranger.com

• 8216 • Jane Miller Memoriam
Given to the first place winner in UA English Pleasure. Established in 2000 in honor of Jane Miller, a zone director, member and supporter.

• 8217 • Most Versatile Horse Award
To recognize the horse with the most points in Halter and specified performance/pleasure classes at the National Show. Awarded annually in honor of John Morris, ex-secretary of the Association.

• 8218 • Mike Ruby Honorarium
To recognize members of the Association who have donated funds or promoted the Rangerhorse and its breeding. Adult members in good standing may be nominated by any other member or a Board member. Marble paperweights are awarded. Established in 1988 in memory of Mike Ruby, founder of the Association.

• 8219 • Herbert N. Swecker Award
To honor the first place winner in Youth Trail at the National Show. Presented by the Pennwoods Rangerbred Regional at the National Show in memory of Herbert N. Swecker, past president of the Association who passed away in 1986.

• 8220 •
Colorado River Watch Network
Steven Hubbell, Dir.
PO Box 220
Austin, TX 78767
Phone: (512)473-3200
Phone: (512)473-3333
Toll-Free: 800-776-5272
Fax: (512)473-4066
E-mail: info@lcra.org
Home Page: http://www.lcra.org

• 8221 • Outstanding Service Award
For consistency, longevity, exemplary stewardship. Recognition award bestowed annually.

• 8222 •
Colorado Society of Association Executives
2170 S Parker Rd., Ste. 265
Denver, CO 80231
Phone: (303)368-9090
Fax: (303)368-4222
E-mail: joant@csaenet.org
Home Page: http://www.csaenet.org

• 8223 • **Award of Excellence**
For service to industry and community. Recognition award bestowed annually.

• 8224 •
***Columbia*: A Journal of Literature and Art**
Lytton Smith, Editor-in-Chief
415 Dodge hall
2960 Broadway
New York, NY 10027
Phone: (212)854-7704
E-mail: columbiajournal@columbia.edu
Home Page: http://arts.columbia.edu/journal/

Formerly: (1996) *Columbia*: A Magazine of Poetry and Art.

• 8225 • **Poetry, Fiction and Nonfiction Contest**
To recognize outstanding works of fiction and poetry. Send no more than five poems at a time, or one short story/nonfiction entry not exceeding twenty double-spaced pages. All entries must be accompanied by a $12 reading fee. Fee includes copy of the issue in which winners are announced (a $12 value). The deadline for entry is December 31 1st. Winners in each category receive $500, plus publication in "COLUMBIA: A Journal of Literature and Art." Entries should be addressed to "Annual Contest." Formerly: (1986) Carlos Fuentes Fiction Award; (1986) Stanley Kunitz Poetry Award.

• 8226 •
Columbia College Chicago
Theater/Music Center
℅ Chuck Smith
72 E. 11 St.
Chicago, IL 60605
Phone: (312)344-6136
Fax: (312)344-8077
E-mail: chigochuck@aol.com

• 8227 • **Theodore Ward Prize for Playwriting**
To uncover and identify new African American plays that are promising and producible, to encourage and aid playwrights in the development of promising scripts, and to offer an opportunity for emerging and established playwrights to be exposed to Chicago's professional theater community through staged reading and/or fully mounted productions. All entrants must be of African American descent and residing within the United States. Only full length plays are considered. One acts and musicals are not accepted (with the exception of a play-with-music). Adaptations and translations are not eligible unless from works in the public domain. All rights for music or biographies must be secured by the entrant prior to submission. One completed script per playwright is accepted. Scripts that have received professional productions are not eligible. "Professional" includes Equity Showcase and Waiver productions, but does not include amateur and college productions where admission has not been charged. Scripts are accepted from April 1 to July 1 The following prizes are awarded: first prize - $2,000, a fully mounted production in the studio season, transportation (within the continental United States only), and housing for a portion of rehearsal period and performances; and second prize - $500 a staged reading in the studio theater directed by a faculty director. The playwright receives an audio tape of the reading. Established in 1986.

• 8228 •
Columbia Engineering School Alumni Association
K. Daniel Libby, Pres.
500 W 120th St., Rm. 540
New York, NY 10027
Phone: (212)854-4472
Fax: (212)932-9420
E-mail: kdl26@columbia.edu
Home Page: http://www.cesaa.org

• 8229 • **Egleston Medal**
This, the highest award of the association, is given to recognize a graduate of the Columbia University School of Engineering and Applied Science for distinguished engineering achievement. Notable application of engineering principles; the development of processes or techniques, materials, or an industry involving them; or the furtherance of a specific branch of the profession are considered. A medal is awarded annually. Established in 1939 in memory of Thomas Egleston, Jr., founder in 1864 of the Columbia College School of Mines, from which developed the Columbia University School of Engineering and Applied Science.

• 8230 • **Pupin Medal**
For recognition of distinguished service to the nation in engineering, science, or technology. Living engineers or scientists who were affiliated with Columbia University for at least one year either as an enrolled student, a faculty member, or a university administrator are eligible. A medal is awarded as merited. Established in 1958 to commemorate the centennial of the birth of Michael I. Pupin.

• 8231 •
Columbia Scholastic Press Association
Edmund J. Sullivan, Dir.
Mail Code 5711
Columbia University
New York, NY 10027-6902
Phone: (212)854-9400
Fax: (212)854-9401
E-mail: cspa@columbia.edu
Home Page: http://www.columbia.edu/cu/cspa

• 8232 • **Crown Awards**
Recognizes excellence in student media. Newspapers, magazines, and yearbooks are eligible. Editing, design, and photography are evaluated. Members of CSPA are eligible. Gold Crown Awards are presented for the highest level of achievement in each category; Silver Crown Awards recognize the second highest level of achievement. Publications must be submitted by the media staff. A $ 18.50 processing fee must also be submitted. Application deadline is October 15. A certificate mounted on a plaque is awarded annually in March in New York City. Established in 1982.

• 8233 • **Gold Circle Awards**
To recognize outstanding student journalism. Entries are accepted from newspapers, magazines, yearbooks or video and should be student-produced journalistic materials published or broadcast in the past year. Categories covered include writing, cartooning, design and layout. Applicants can be associate and regular members. Awarded annually.

• 8234 • **Gold Key Award**
To focus public and school attention on the continuous, unselfish, and unrewarded work of the large group of members of the teaching profession who give of their time and energy year after year to the betterment, encouragement, and advancement of school publication work. Faculty advisers to student publications and journalism professionals are eligible. A gold key surmounted by a crown, which is the symbol of Columbia University is awarded. Five to fifteen awards are presented annually at the Association's convention in March. Established in 1929 by Joseph M. Murphy, founder of CSPA.

• 8235 • **James Frederick Paschal Award**
To recognize an individual for meritorious service to a state scholastic press associations. Established in memory of James R. Paschaal, past editor of The CSPAA Bulletin and executive director of the Oklahoma Interscholastic Press Association at the University of Oklahoma.

• 8236 •
Columbia University
Lee C. Bollinger, Pres.
Office of the Pres.
202 Low Memorial Library
535 W 116th St.
Mail Code 4309
New York, NY 10027
Phone: (212)854-9970
Fax: (212)854-9973
Home Page: http://www.columbia.edu/cu/president

• 8237 • **Award for Distinguished Achievement**
For recognition of outstanding alumni of the University. Established in 1990.

• 8238 • **Bancroft Prizes**
To recognize the author of the best works in each of the categories of American history (including biography) and American diplomacy. Open to all persons whether connected with Columbia University or not. The deadline for submission is November 1. A monetary award of $4,000 and a certificate are awarded to each of two authors and a citation is presented to each publisher. Awarded annually for books published in the preceding year. Established in 1948.

• 8239 • Joseph H. Bearns Prizes in Music
For recognition of outstanding musical composition by U.S. citizens between the ages of 18 and 25. The following prizes are awarded: a monetary prize of $1,200 for a composition in one of the large media; and $900 for a composition in one of the smaller media. The winners are chosen by the Music Department of Columbia University. Awarded annually. Established in 1927.

• 8240 • Butler Medal
To recognize the most distinguished contribution made during the previous five years anywhere in the world to philosophy, or to educational theory, practice, or administration. Alumni are eligible. A gold medal and a certificate are awarded every five years, and a silver medal is awarded annually when merited. Established in 1914.

• 8241 • Columbia Journalism Award
To honor individuals not usually recognized in other major journalistic prizes for distinguished service in the public interest. A silver plaque is awarded as deemed appropriate by the faculty of journalism. Established in 1958.

• 8242 • Alice M. Ditson Conductor's Award
To recognize significant contributions to the advancement of contemporary American music. A monetary award of $1,000 and a citation are awarded annually by the Music Department and the Advisory Committee of the Alice M. Ditson Fund. Established in 1945.

• 8243 • Louisa Gross Horwitz Prize
To recognize an individual for outstanding basic research in biology or biochemistry. A monetary prize of $25,000 is awarded annually. Established in 1967 to honor Louisa Gross Horwitz, the daughter of Dr. Samuel David Gross (1805-1889), a prominent surgeon of Philadelphia, author of "Systems of Surgery" and a president of the American Medical Association.

• 8244 • Ambrose Monell Medal and the Ambrose Monell Prize for Distinguished Service in Mineral Technology
To recognize an individual who has made an outstanding contribution to the art, technology, science or business of mining, beneficiation, refining, or combination of metals. A monetary award and a gold medal are awarded every three years. Administered by the Henry Krumb School of Mines of Columbia University. Established in 1954.

• 8245 • University Medal for Excellence
To recognize Columbia University alumni/alumnae who have performed useful or exceptional service in public or professional life. Tradition dictates that the following criteria be followed in the selection of the medal recipient: an alumnus or alumna of any division of the University under 45 years of age whose record in scholarship, public service, and/or professional life is outstanding. Established in 1928 by the Trustees of Columbia University.

• 8246 • Vetlesen Prize
To recognize outstanding scientific achievement resulting in a clearer understanding of the earth, its history, or its relation to the universe. A monetary prize of $25,000 and a gold medal are awarded when merited. Established in 1959 by the G. Unger Vetlesen Foundation.

• 8247 •
Columbia University
Graduate School of Journalism
% Jane Folpe, Asst. Director, Programs and Prizes
2950 Broadway, Rm. 603
New York, NY 10027
Phone: (212)854-5974
Fax: (212)854-3800
E-mail: jf680@columbia.edu
Home Page: http://www.jrn.columbia.edu

• 8248 • Meyer Berger Award
To honor in-depth and enterprising reporting on individuals in the tradition of late Meyer "Mike" Berger. All newspaper reporters whose beat is the Metropolitan New York region(New York State, New Jersey, and Connecticut) are eligible-whether they report for dailies, weeklies or monthlies.The deadline is March 1. Established in 1961 by Louis Schweitzer to honor Meyer "Mike" Berger, the Pulitzer Prize-winning reporter for *The New York Times.* For further information, contact Lisa Redd, Program Coordinator, Graduate School of Journalism at 212-854-6468 or email lsr21@columbia.edu.

• 8249 • Maria Moors Cabot Prizes
To recognize sustained and distinguished journalistic contributions to inter-American understanding. The deadline is February 15. A medal, a $5,000 honorarium, and travel expenses to attend the ceremony at Columbia University are awarded. Established in 1939 by Dr. Godfrey Lowell Cabot of Boston as a memorial to his wife.

• 8250 • Knight-Bagehot Fellowships
To enable mid-career journalists to study economics, finance, and business at Columbia for one academic year. Open to journalists with at least four years' professional experience whose work regularly appears in the U.S. or Canada. The Fellowship is named for the John S. and James L. Knight Foundation and Walter Bagehot. The deadline is March 1. Fellows receive a stipend and tuition. For further information and applications, contact Terri Thompson, Director, Graduate School of Journalism; telephone: (212)854-6840.

• 8251 •
Columbia University
School of Law
Jerome L. Greene Hall
435 W 116 St.
New York, NY 10027
Phone: (212)854-2640
Fax: (212)678-0825
Home Page: http://www.law.columbia.edu

• 8252 • Lawrence A. Wien Prize for Social Responsibility
To honor individual attorneys who, like Mr. Wien, put their resources and legal skills to work for the public good. Recipients serve as positive role models for both law students and the law profession. The prize is bestowed annually with the participation of the Wien family. Since 1996, the award has been conferred by the Law School and is presented in conjunction with the School's Profession of Law course, which teaches legal ethics to all third-year law students at Columbia. Established in 1982 by both the Law and Business Schools.

• 8253 •
Columbia University
School of the Arts
Bruce W. Ferguson, Dean
305 Dodge Hall, Mail Code 1808
2960 Broadway
New York, NY 10027
Phone: (212)854-2875
Fax: (212)854-1309
E-mail: admissions-arts@columbia.edu
Home Page: http://arts.columbia.edu

• 8254 • William Schuman Award
To recognize the lifetime achievement of an American composer whose works have been widely performed and generally acknowledged to be of lasting significance. The Dean of the School of the Arts and composers choose the winner of the prize. A monetary prize of $50,000 is awarded biennially or when $50,000 has accumulated. Established in 1981 by the James Warburg family in honor of the American composer, William Schuman. The Bydale Foundation (a Warburg family foundation) established the award through a grant of $250,000 to the School of the Arts. Applications not accepted.

• 8255 •
Columbia University
Southern Asian Institute
420 W 118th St., 11th Fl.
Mail Code 3325
New York, NY 10027
Phone: (212)854-3616
Fax: (212)854-6987
E-mail: southasia@columbia.edu
Home Page: http://sipa.columbia.edu/REGIONAL/SAI/

• 8256 • Foreign Language and Area Studies Awards
For graduate students in the Department of Education. Inquire for application details.

• 8257 •
Columbian Squires
Robert A. Goossens, Dir., Fraternal Srvcs.
1 Columbus Plz.
New Haven, CT 06510
Phone: (203)752-4402
Fax: (203)752-4108
E-mail: bob.goossens@kofc-supreme.com
Home Page: http://www.kofc.org

• 8258 • **Corps d'Elite Award**
For recognition of outstanding local units (circles) of the Columbian Squires that meet specific standards of operation and effectiveness. Applications are due by the end of the program year (June 30). Plaques are awarded annually to qualifying circles.

• 8259 •
Columbus Blues Alliance
Herb Sollars, Pres.
1350 W Fifth Ave., Ste. 10-D
Columbus, OH 43212
Phone: (614)486-4575
Fax: (614)486-4575
E-mail: info@columbusblues.com
Home Page: http://
www.colsbluesalliance.org

• 8260 • **Lifetime Achievement Awards**
For blues musicians. Recognition award bestowed periodically.

• 8261 •
Combined Organizations of Numismatic Error Collectors of America
Mike Ellis, Pres.
PO Box 706
Eureka Springs, AR 72632
Phone: (479)253-5055
E-mail: gmmmike@arkansas.net
Home Page: http://www.conecaonline.org

• 8262 • **Dr. Lyndon King Award**
To recognize the member who exhibits exceptional activity in promoting numismatic error collecting and education. Individuals are selected by approval and recommendation of the Board of Directors. A plaque is awarded annually. Established in 1986 by J.T. Stanton in honor of Dr. Lyndon King, an unselfish advocate of the hobby.

• 8263 •
Combustion Institute
Sue Steiner Terpack, Exec. Administrator
5001 Baum Blvd., Ste. 635
Pittsburgh, PA 15213-1851
Phone: (412)687-1366
Fax: (412)687-0340
E-mail: office@combustioninstitute.org
Home Page: http://
www.combustioninstitute.org

• 8264 • **Sir Alfred Egerton Medal**
For distinguished, continuing, and encouraging contributions to the field of combustion. An inscribed gold medal and illuminated parchment certificate are awarded biennially. Established in 1958. The deadline for nominations is January 6th.

• 8265 • **Bernard Lewis Medal**
For brilliant research in the field of combustion. An illuminated parchment certificate and an inscribed gold medal are awarded biennially. Established in 1958. The deadline for nominations is January 6th.

• 8266 • **Silver Combustion Medal**
For recognition of the author of an outstanding paper presented at the international combustion symposium. A silver medal and a parchment certificate are awarded biennially. Established in 1958. The deadline for nominations is January 6th.

• 8267 • **Ya B. Zeldovich Gold Medal**
To recognize outstanding contributions to the theory of combustion or detonation. An inscribed gold medal and iluminated parchment certificate are awarded biennially. Established in 1990. The deadline for nominations is January 6th.

• 8268 •
Commemorative Air Force
Robert R. Rice, Exec.Dir.
PO Box 62000
Midland, TX 79711-2000
Phone: (432)563-1000
Fax: (432)563-8046
E-mail: publicrelations@cafhq.org
Home Page: http://
www.commemorativeairforce.org

Formerly: (2003) Confederate Air Force.

• 8269 • **Airman's Award**
To honor a CAF member for heroism involving voluntary risk of life. Awarded with a Citation and Plaque.

• 8270 • **Award of the Order of the Brass Jackass**
To recognize the CAF Officer who has demonstrated the single most ridiculous or irresponsible act of judgment or skill while serving in any capacity with the CAF. The Officer's name shall be inscribed on the award.

• 8271 • **CAF Unit Letter of Commendation**
To honor the CAF Unit who has displayed outstanding achievement in a single area of service to the CAF. Awarded with a letter.

• 8272 • **Distinguished Flying Medal**
To honor CAF aircraft crew members. Awarded with a Citation and Plaque.

• 8273 • **Distinguished Maintenance Award**
To honor CAF maintenance personnel. Awarded with a Citation and Plaque.

• 8274 • **Distinguished Service Medal**
To honor the extraordinary, meritorious, and exceptional services to the CAF. Highest award given in form of Citation and Plaque.

• 8275 • **Distinguished Unit Citation**
To honor the CAF Unit that has consistently demonstrated extraordinary, meritorious and exceptional service to the CAF. Awarded with a Citation and Plaque.

• 8276 • **Distinguished Unit Maintenance Award**
To honor the CAF Unit who has shown outstanding achievement in the maintenance or restoration of a CAF aircraft. Awarded with a Citation and Plaque.

• 8277 • **Individual Maintenance Award**
To recognize the meritorious achievement while conducting the maintenance or the restoration of a CAF aircraft. Awarded with a Citation and Plaque.

• 8278 • **Letter of Commendation**
To recognize the meritorious achievement while participating in any capacity with the CAF. Awarded with a letter.

• 8279 • **Letter of Commendation (Non-CAF Member)**
To recognize a non-member individual who has displayed outstanding achievement in a single area of service to the CAF. Awarded with a letter.

• 8280 • **Mission Award**
To honor CAF members who have participated in 25, 50, and 100 CAF sanctioned missions.

• 8281 • **Service Award (Non-CAF Member)**
To recognize a non-member individual who has consistently shown outstanding or exceptional service to the CAF. Awarded with a Plaque.

• 8282 • **Silver Magnolia Blossom Award**
To honor a CAF officer who has consistently displayed outstanding skill or achievement in any activity or service for the CAF. Awarded with a Citation and Plaque.

• 8283 • **Richard E. Szepski Award**
To honor the CAF Officer who displayed exceptional enthusiasm and dedication to the objectives of the CAF. Awarded with a Citation and Plaque.

• 8284 • Dolly Vinsant Flight Nurse of the Year Award
To honor the top USAF flight nurse of the year and to encourage professionalism. U.S. Military Flight Nurses on active duty who have performed service beyond the call of duty may be nominated. A monetary award, a plaque, and travel expenses to attend CAF "Airsho" are awarded annually. Established in 1986 to honor Lieutenant Dolly Vinsant, a WWII USAAF Flight Nurse killed in action in Eto.

• 8285 •
Commercial Development and Marketing Association
Vaughn E. Wurst, Assoc.Dir.
100 N 20th St.
Philadelphia, PA 19103
Phone: (215)564-3484
Fax: (215)963-9784
E-mail: info@cdmaonline.org
Home Page: http://www.cdmaonline.org
Formerly: Chemical Marketing Research Association.

• 8286 • Award for Executive Excellence
To recognize distinguished accomplishments involving marketing, management, business development, planning, business intelligence, and business/marketing research in the chemical or allied process industries. The award honors indebtedness to deceased member whose unselfish efforts have contributed to the growth and success of the Association. Candidates must be nominated by a Regular, Honorary, or Life member of the Association. A scroll and a monetary award of $4,000 are awarded annually.

• 8287 • Best Paper of the Year Award
To recognize the most outstanding paper presented at the National Meetings during the previous calendar year. A plaque is awarded annually. Established in 1976.

• 8288 • Distinguished Service Award
To recognize outstanding service to the marketing research profession and to the Association. Both regular and life members of the Association are eligible. As many as three plaques are awarded annually. Established in 1973.

• 8289 •
Commercial Finance Association
Bruce H. Jones, Exec.Dir.
225 W 34th St., Ste. 1815
New York, NY 10122
Phone: (212)594-3490
Fax: (212)564-6053
E-mail: info@cfa.com
Home Page: http://www.cfa.com
Formerly: (1990) National Commercial Finance Association.

• 8290 • Award for Achievement in Business Growth
To demonstrate to the general public the positive aspects of the asset-based financial services industry in helping companies with potential to grow and prosper and to recognize projects financed by a CFA member. A plaque is awarded annually. Established in 1955.

• 8291 •
Committee of Presidents of Statistical Societies
Steve Fineburg, Chm.
Department of Statistics
Stanford University
Stanford, CA 94305-4065
Fax: (415)725-8977
Home Page: http://www.e-stat.org/

• 8292 • R. A. Fisher Award
To recognize outstanding statisticians in the world. Individuals are nominated by statistical societies in the United States and Canada. A monetary prize and a plaque are awarded annually at the joint statistical meeting. Established in 1963 to commemorate Sir Ronald A. Fisher.

• 8293 • Presidents' Award
To recognize an outstanding statistician under the age of 40. Candidates must be a member of one of participating societies: Institute of Mathematical Statistics, Statistical Society of Canada, and the Biometric Society. A monetary prize and a plaque are awarded annually at the joint statistical meetings. Established in 1977 in honor of the presidents of the five statistical societies in the United States and Canada.

• 8294 • Elizabeth L. Scott Award
To recognize individuals who have helped foster opportunities in statistics for women by developing programs that encourage women to seek careers in statistics, by consistently and successfully mentoring female students or new researchers, by working to identify gender-based inequities in employment, or by serving in a variety of capacities as a role model. A plaque and cash award are given biennially in even-numbered years in recognition of Elizabeth L. Scott's lifelong efforts in the furtherance of the careers of women.

• 8295 • George W. Snedecor Award
To honor an individual who was instrumental in the development of statistical theory in biometry. The award is for a noteworthy publication in biometry within three years of the date of the award. A plaque and cash award are awarded biennially in odd-numbered years. Established in 1976. 910 2504794

• 8296 •
Committee to Protect Journalists
Ann K. Cooper, Exec.Dir.
330 7th Ave., 11th Fl.
New York, NY 10001
Phone: (212)465-1004
Phone: (212)465-9344
Fax: (212)465-9568
E-mail: info@cpj.org
Home Page: http://www.cpj.org

• 8297 • Burton Benjamin Memorial Award
To honor individuals who have demonstrated lifetime achievement in promotion press freedom. Awarded annually with a plaque. Established in 1991.

• 8298 • International Press Freedom Awards
To honor journalists who have courageously provided independent news coverage and viewpoints under difficult circumstances. Awarded annually with a plaque. Established in 1991.

• 8299 •
Common Cause
Chellie Pingree, Pres./CEO
1250 Connecticut Ave. NW, Ste. 600
Washington, DC 20036
Phone: (202)833-1200
Toll-Free: 800-926-1064
Fax: (202)659-3716
E-mail: grassroots@commoncause.org
Home Page: http://www.commoncause.org

• 8300 • Public Service Achievement Awards
To honor public servants, citizen activists, or other citizens who, by force of imagination, initiative and perseverance, have made an outstanding contribution in the areas of government performance and integrity. Nominations by Common Cause members, public officials, other organizations, and the general public are accepted. The deadline for nominations is December 15. A certificate and travel to Washington, DC are awarded annually at a special luncheon during the spring meeting of the National Governing Board. Established in 1981.

• 8301 •
Common Cause/Tennessee
Dick Williams, State Chair
PO Box 150781
Nashville, TN 37215
Phone: (615)321-9072
Phone: (615)356-2381
Toll-Free: 800-600-0482
Fax: (615)320-8897
E-mail: commoncause-tn@msn.com
Home Page: http://commoncause.org

• 8302 • Bird Dog Award
For outstanding service toward common cause priorities. Recognition award bestowed annually.

• 8303 •
Commonwealth Association for Public Administration and Management
Ms. Gillian Mason, Exec.Dir.
1075 Bay St.
Ste. 402
Toronto, ON, Canada M5S 2B1
Phone: (416)920-3337
Fax: (416)920-6574
E-mail: capam@capam.ca
Home Page: http://www.capam.org

• 8304 • **CAPAM International Innovations Award**
Recognizes effectiveness, innovation, relevance, significance, appropriateness to context. Awarded biennially.

• 8305 •
Commonwealth Club of California
Nicole Grant, Contact
595 Market St., 2nd Fl.
San Francisco, CA 94105
Phone: (415)597-6700
Fax: (415)597-6729
E-mail: club@commonwealthclub.org
Home Page: http://www.commonwealthclub.org

• 8306 • **Commonwealth Club of California Book Awards**
To recognize outstanding literary works produced by California residents. Gold and silver medals are presented as follows: one gold medal is awarded in both fiction, nonfiction and poetry. Silver medals area awarded to fiction, nonfiction, first work of fiction, "Californian", Young Adult (ages 0-10) and Juvenile Literature (ages 11-16). Winning authors must have been legal residents of California at the time the manuscripts were delivered to the publisher. Awarded annually at an awards program. The deadline for entry is January 31. Established in 1931.

• 8307 •
Communication Arts
110 Constitution Dr.
Menlo Park, CA 94025
Phone: (650)326-6040
Toll-Free: 800-258-9111
Fax: (650)326-1648
E-mail: ca@commarts.com
Home Page: http://www.commarts.com

• 8308 • **CA Advertising Annual**
For recognition of excellence in the field of advertising. Consumer magazine ads, consumer newspaper ads, trade ads, outdoor posters, point of purchase posters, television advertising, and radio advertising may be submitted by June. Winning entries are reproduced in the December issue of Communication Arts. Award of Excellence certificates are awarded. Established in 1959.

• 8309 • **CA Design Annual**
For recognition of excellence in the design of posters, brochures, packaging, trademarks, corporate identity, annual reports, catalogs, letterheads and signanfe. Entries may be submitted by June. All winning entries are reproduced in the November issue of Communication Arts. Award of Excellence certificates are awarded. Established in 1959.

• 8310 • **Illustration Annual**
For recognition of outstanding illustrations entered in the annual competition. Drawing, painting, collage, three-dimensional, or any form of media art that was commissioned for publication during the year is eligible. Entries are judged on the quality, originality and appropriateness of the solution for only the illustration. A distinguished, national representative jury of designers and art directors makes the selection. The deadline for entries is June 15. All of the winning entries are reproduced and everything originally produced in color is shown in color in the Annual, the July issue of Communication Arts. Award of Excellence certificates are given to the illustrator, client and art director of each accepted illustration.

• 8311 • **Photography Annual**
For recognition of outstanding photography entered in the annual competition. Photography that was commissioned for advertising, design, editorial or any other area of communication arts is eligible to be selected for the Photography Annual. A distinguished, nationally representative jury of designers and art directors makes the selection. The deadline for entries is June 15. All of the winning entries are reproduced and everything originally produced in color is shown in color in the Annual, the August issue of Communication Arts. Award of Excellence certificates are given to the photographer, client and art director of each accepted photograph. photograph.

• 8312 •
Community Associations Institute - Greater Houston Chapter
Lou Ann Lee, Exec.Dir.
2055 S. Gessner, Ste. 250
Houston, TX 77063
Phone: (713)784-5462
Fax: (713)977-2562
E-mail: caistaff@caihouston.org
Home Page: http://www.caihouston.org

• 8313 • **Community of the Year**
For a member community of CAI. Recognition award bestowed annually.

• 8314 •
Community Associations Institute - Orange County Regional Chapter
Stanley R. Kyker CAE, Exec. Dir.
23166 Los Alisos Blvd., No. 244
Mission Viejo, CA 92691
Phone: (949)380-7360
Fax: (949)380-4312
E-mail: office@caioc.com
Home Page: http://www.caioc.com

• 8315 • **Community Association Board Member of the Year**
Based upon submittal and selection. Recognition award bestowed annually.

• 8316 •
Community College Humanities Association
Prof. David Berry, Exec.Dir.
Essex County College
303 University Ave.
Newark, NJ 07102
Phone: (973)877-3577
Fax: (973)877-3578
E-mail: berry@essex.edu
Home Page: http://www.ccha-assoc.org

• 8317 • **Distinguished Humanities Educator**
To recognize achievement in strengthening the humanities in the nation's two-year colleges. A plaque and recognition in CCHA publications are awarded biennially at the national convention. Established in 1986.

• 8318 •
Community Colleges for International Development
John Halder Jr., Pres./Exec.Dir
PO Box 2068
East Campus Bldg. 12
Cedar Rapids, IA 52406-2068
Phone: (319)398-1257
Phone: (319)398-5653
Fax: (319)398-7113
E-mail: ccid@kirkwood.edu
Home Page: http://ccid.kirkwood.cc.ia.us

• 8319 • **CCID Faculty Fellowship Award**
For a project proposal. Selected by a peer review. A grant is awarded annually.

• 8320 • **CCID Presidents' Award**
Recognizes for sustained excellence in support for CCID programs chosen by CCID.

• 8321 •
The Compassionate Friends
Patricia Loder, Exec.Dir.
PO Box 3696
Oak Brook, IL 60522-3696
Phone: (630)990-0010
Toll-Free: 877-969-0010
Fax: (630)990-0246
E-mail: nationaloffice@compassionatefriends.org
Home Page: http://www.compassionatefriends.org

• 8322 • **The Compassionate Friends Award**
To recognize individuals and/or groups whose contributions have furthered and fostered the philosophy and goals of TCF on the national level. Any non-TCF affiliated individual/group whose contribution(s) have evidenced a commitment to bereaved parents and/or the national TCF organization is eligible. An engraved plaque and a letter of appreciation, or a lithograph mounted with an engraved presentation plate are awarded. 297742 SME UR

• 8323 •
Composites Manufacturing Association of the Society of Manufacturing Engineers
Barbara Johnson, Asst. Administrator
1 SME Dr.
Dearborn, MI 48121-0930
Phone: (313)271-2867
Phone: (313)271-1500
Toll-Free: 800-733-4763
Fax: (313)425-3400
E-mail: service@sme.org
Home Page: http://www.sme.org/cma

• 8324 • **J.H. Hall Composites Manufacturing Award**
Recognizes contributions to composites manufacturing in terms of achievements, patents, articles, courses, presentations, and job projects/activities. Awarded annually. 297742 SME UR

• 8325 •
Computer and Automated Systems Association of Society of Manufacturing Engineers
Nancy S. Berg, Exec.Dir.
One SME Dr.
PO Box 930
Dearborn, MI 48121-0930
Phone: (313)271-1500
Toll-Free: 800-733-4763
Fax: (313)271-2861
Home Page: http://www.sme.org/casa

• 8326 • **CASA/SME Industry and University LEAD Awards**
For leadership and excellence in application and development of enterprise wide integrated manufacturing. Awarded annually.

• 8327 •
Computer Measurement Group
Barbara Hazard, Office Mgr.
PO Box 1124
Turnersville, NJ 08012
Phone: (856)401-1700
Toll-Free: 800-436-7264
Fax: (856)401-1708
E-mail: cmghq@cmg.org
Home Page: http://www.cmg.org

• 8328 • **A.A. Michelson Award**
Recognizes an individual who is outstanding in the field. Awarded annually.

• 8329 • **Student Fellowship Award**
Recognizes a graduate student in computer science. One fellowship is awarded annually.

• 8330 •
Computer Professionals for Social Responsibility
Susan Evoy, Managing Dir.
PO Box 717
Palo Alto, CA 94302
Phone: (650)322-3778
Fax: (650)322-4748
E-mail: cpsr@cpsr.org
Home Page: http://www.cpsr.org

• 8331 • **Norbert Wiener Award for Social and Professional Responsibility**
To honor a distinguished computer professional who has, through personal example, demonstrated a deep commitment to the socially responsible use of computing technology. Awarded annually. Established in 1987.

• 8332 •
Computing Research Association
Daniel A. Reed, Chm.
1100 Seventeenth St. NW, Ste. 507
Washington, DC 20036-4632
Phone: (202)234-2111
Fax: (202)667-1066
E-mail: info@cra.org
Home Page: http://www.cra.org

• 8333 • **CRA Distinguished Service**
Recognizes contribution to the computing research community.

• 8334 • **Nico Haberman**
Recognizes contribution to members of underrepresented groups.

• 8335 •
Computing Technology Industry Association
John Venator, Pres./CEO
1815 S Meyers Rd., Ste. 300
Oak Brook Terrace, IL 60181-5228
Phone: (630)678-8300
Fax: (630)268-1384
E-mail: info@comptia.org
Home Page: http://www.comptia.org

• 8336 • **Golden Screen Award**
Recognizes advertising excellence. Awarded annually.

• 8337 •
Concord Coalition
Robert Bixby, Exec.Dir.
1011 Arlington Blvd., Ste. 300
Arlington, VA 22209
Phone: (703)894-6222
Toll-Free: 888-333-4248
Fax: (703)894-6231
E-mail: concordcoalition@concordcoalition.org
Home Page: http://www.concordcoalition.org

• 8338 • **Paul E. Tsongas Economic Patriot Award**
Recognizes outstanding leadership and commitment to Concord's goals of fiscal and generational responsibility. Awarded annually.

• 8339 •
Concordia Historical Institute
Rev.Dr. Martin R. Noland, Dir.
804 Seminary Pl.
St. Louis, MO 63105-3014
Phone: (314)505-7900
Fax: (314)505-7901
E-mail: chi@chi.lcms.org
Home Page: http://chi.lcms.org

• 8340 • **Award of Commendation**
To recognize outstanding and exemplary contributions to the fields of Lutheran history and archives during the previous calendar year in congregational history, family history, audio-visual media, books, articles, etc. Nomination forms are available upon request. At least two copies of the nominated material must be submitted to the awards committee before April 1 of the following calendar year. An institute medallion and an individually inscribed certificate are presented annually at the banquet in November. Established in 1972.

• 8341 • **Distinguished Service Award**
To recognize outstanding, exemplary, laudable contributions and service to the cause of American Lutheran history and archives. Nominations are made by the awards committee. The award consists of the Koch/Luther medal, a replica of the unique medal commemorating the death of Martin Luther in 1546, and an inscribed certificate. Not more than two are awarded annually when merited. Established in 1972.

• 8342 •
Concrete Foundations Association
Ed Sauter, Exec.Dir.
PO Box 204
Mount Vernon, IA 52314
Phone: (319)895-6940
Toll-Free: (866)232-9255
Fax: (319)895-8830
E-mail: esauter@cfawalls.org
Home Page: http://www.cfawalls.org

• 8343 • Bob Sawyer Award
Recognizes contribution to industry. Awarded annually.

• 8344 • Contractor of the Year Award
Recognizes contribution to industry. Awarded annually.

• 8345 •
Concrete Reinforcing Steel Institute
John J. Healy, Pres./CEO
933 N Plum Grove Rd.
Schaumburg, IL 60173
Phone: (847)517-1200
Toll-Free: 800-328-6306
Fax: (847)517-1206
E-mail: info@crsi.org
Home Page: http://www.crsi.org

• 8346 • CRSI Design Awards Program
To recognize creative design achievement utilizing site-cast, conventionally reinforced concrete in buildings, bridges, and other structures. Entries are judged by an independent panel of judges and are evaluated for architectural design, engineering achievement, innovative design, functional excellence, and economy of construction. The panel also weighs each structure's relationship to its environment and its efficient use of material. Co-sponsored by the American Institute of Architects and monitored by an AIA representative. Open to all registered architects and engineers (entrants may be individuals or teams). Eligible structures must be located in the United States or its Territories. Engraved commemorative plaques are awarded to the building owner, architect, structural engineer, and general contractor. A winner's brochure is prepared with national publicity. Awarded biennially. Established in 1974.

• 8347 •
Conductors Guild
R. Kevin Paul, Exec.Dir.
5300 Glenside Dr., Ste. 2207
Richmond, VA 23228
Phone: (804)553-1378
Fax: (804)553-1876
E-mail: guild@conductorsguild.net
Home Page: http://www.conductorsguild.org

• 8348 • Thelma A. Robinson Scholarship/Award in Conducting
To recognize the most outstanding participant in the Conductors Guild's conducting workshops in the two years preceding the award. American citizens under 35 years of age who attend at least one workshop and are members in good standing of the Guild are eligible. A monetary award of $1,000 to be used for any career-related purpose such as purchase of scores or books, travel to workshops and conferences, or tuition/lesson/coaching fees is awarded biennially in the spring after the last workshop of the season. Established in 1989 by the National Federation of Music Clubs to honor Thelma A. Robinson, a past president. Sponsored by the National Federation of Music Clubs and the Ohio Federation of Music Clubs.

• 8349 • Theodore Thomas Award
To recognize a conductor who has contributed significantly to the musical development of the United States, especially one whose work has been characterized by teaching as well as performing. A citation and a plaque are awarded at the annual conference. Established in 1988 to honor Theodore Thomas, a pioneer conductor, who traveled widely in the United States, and founded the Chicago Symphony and the Cincinnati May Festival. The Award is presented biennially.

• 8350 •
Confederate Memorial Literary Society
J.E.B. Stuart IV, Chm.
The Museum of the Confederacy
1201 E Clay St.
Richmond, VA 23219
Phone: (804)649-1861
Fax: (804)644-7150
E-mail: info@moc.org
Home Page: http://www.moc.org

• 8351 • Jefferson Davis Award
To recognize excellence in research and writing of a book length narrative history on the period of the Confederate States of America and the American Civil War. Authors of narrative histories published during the previous calendar year are eligible, either through nomination or application by February 1 of the following calendar year. A printed citation bearing a red wax impression of the Great Seal of the Confederacy is awarded annually. Established in 1970.

• 8352 • Founders Award
To recognize excellence in editing primary source material on the period of the Confederate States of America and the American Civil War. Editors of works published during the two previous calendar years are eligible, either through nomination or application by February 1. A printed citation bearing a red wax impression of the Great Seal of the Confederacy is awarded biennially. Established in 1970.

• 8353 • Virginius Dabney Award
Recognizes contribution to popular understanding of the American Civil War. Awarded periodically.

• 8354 •
Confederate Stamp Alliance
Kevin Baker, Sec.
3015 Fieldview Dr.
Murfreesboro, TN 37128
E-mail: kr.baker@comcast.net
Home Page: http://www.csalliance.org

• 8355 • CP Writers Award
Awarded Annually to recognize the best article in Confederate Philatelist. Established in 1988.

• 8356 • CSA Trophy
To recognize the member exhibiting the best and most comprehensive collection of Confederate stamps and/or covers at the annual exhibition. No member may receive the award more than once in five years. Established in 1945.

• 8357 • Dealer and Exhibit Awards
To recognize outstanding dealers and exhibits at the annual exhibition. The following awards are presented annually: Jack Molesworth Award established in 1954; Robt. Siegel Award - established in 1959; Wm. G. Bogg Memorial Award - established in 1963; Earl Weatherly Award - established in 1983; John H. Reagan Award - established in 1979; Richard Krieger Award - established in 1991; John W. Kaufmann Award established in 1968; Brian and Maria Green Award - established 1996.

• 8358 • August Dietz Award
To recognize distinguished service to Confederate philately in the field of research and writing by a member during the past year. A trophy is awarded annually at the convention. Established in 1962.

• 8359 • Honorary Life Member
For recogition in the field of Confederate philately. Established in 1950.

• 8360 • Haydn Myer Award
To recognize distinguished service to the alliance by a member during the past year. A member is not eligible for this award while he or she is holding office as a trustee. Awarded annually at the convention. Established in 1952.

• 8361 • President's Trophy
To recognize the best exhibit of Confederate stamps and/or covers, in any classification, exhibited by a member who has never previously been awarded any trophy at a Confederate Stamp Alliance Exhibition. Established in 1962.

• 8362 • Trustees Trophy
To recognize the best single frame exhibit of Confederate stamps and/or covers, in any classification, exhibited by a member who does not have another Confederate exhibit in competition at the same annual meeting. Established in 1983.

• 8363 •
Conference of California Historical Societies
Richard Proctor, Pres.
University of the Pacific
Stockton, CA 95211
Phone: (209)946-2169
Fax: (209)946-2578
E-mail: mnoyola@pacific.edu
Home Page: http://www.californiahistorian.com

• 8364 • Award of Merit - Commercial
To recognize significant collections of historical records, cooperation with organized historical groups, use of historical material in advertising, or financing of historical activities. Awarded annually.

• 8365 • Award of Merit - Governmental
To recognize outstanding accomplishments of a California political entity or official for significant historical assistance. Awarded annually with a certificate.

• 8366 • Award of Merit - Individual
To recognize outstanding accomplishments of historical activities by an individual. Awarded annually with a certificate.

• 8367 • Award of Merit - Preservation
To recognize outstanding accomplishments of organizations or individuals for completed acts of restoration or preservation. Awarded annually with a certificate.

• 8368 • Award of Merit - Scholastic/ Authorship
To recognize outstanding accomplishments of a school, student, or individual for a significant historical project or research in California history. Awarded annually with a certificate.

• 8369 • California History Day Award
To recognize an individual who has completed a significant History Day Project on some aspect of California history. Awards are based on historical accuracy, originality, significance, quality, and scholastic merit of project. Awards to be designated by the Education Committee of the Conference, and are presented annually at the California History Day judging in Sacramento.

• 8370 • Rockwell D. Hunt Young Historian Award
To recognize outstanding accomplishments by an individual or group of junior high or high school aged student. A certificate is awarded annually as part of the Award of Merit program.

• 8371 • Waddingham/Doctor Award
To recognize 25 years or more of consistent and outstanding service to a local historical organization. Awarded annually as part of the Award of Merit program. Established in honor of Gladys Waddingham and Joseph Doctor.

• 8372 •
Conference on Christianity and Literature
Prof. Paul Contino, Ed.
Pepperdine University
24255 Pacific Coast Hwy.
Humanities Div.
24255 Pacific Coast Highway
Malibu, CA 90263
Phone: (310)506-7232
Fax: (310)506-4206
E-mail: paul.contino@pepperdine.edu
Home Page: http://www.acu.edu/sponsored/ccl.html

• 8373 • CCL Book of the Year Award
To recognize the work that has contributed most to the dialogue between literature and the Christian faith. Books that are published within the final three months of one year and the first nine months of the year in which the award is made are eligible. A certificate is awarded and the winner is recognized at the annual meeting of CCL which is held in conjunction with the annual meeting of the Modern Language Association in December. Established in 1966.

• 8374 •
Conference on College Composition and Communication
Doug Hesse, Chm.
1111 W Kenyon Rd.
Urbana, IL 61801-1096
Phone: (217)328-3870
Toll-Free: 877-369-6283
Fax: (217)328-9645
E-mail: public_info@ncte.org
Home Page: http://www.ncte.org/groups/cccc

• 8375 • Richard Braddock Award
To recognize the author of an outstanding article on writing or the teaching of writing in the Conference journal, *College Composition and Communication.* Articles must have been published during the calendar year. A plaque is presented annually at the Convention in the spring. Established in 1974 in memory of Richard Braddock of the University of Iowa. Sponsored by National Council of Teachers of English.

• 8376 • CCCC Exemplar Award
To recognize an individual who has served or serves as an exemplar for the organization, representing the highest ideals of scholarship, teaching, and service to the entire profession. A plaque and a one-year comprehensive membership in NCTE/CCCC is presented when merited at the CCCC annual convention in the spring. Established in 1991.

• 8377 • CCCC James Berlin Memorial Outstanding Dissertation Award
To recognize a graduate whose dissertation improves the educational process in composition studies or contributes to the field's body of knowledge through research or scholarly inquiry. Presented each year at the CCCC annual convention in the spring. Established in 1992. Formerly: (1997) CCCC Outstanding Dissertation Award.

• 8378 • CCCC Outstanding Book Award
To recognize a book making an outstanding contribution to composition and communication studies. The book must have been published during the preceding calendar year. A plaque and a one-year comprehensive membership in NCTE/CCCC are awarded each year at the CCCC annual convention in the spring. Established in 1991.

• 8379 •
Conference on Latin American History
Dr. Thomas Holloway, Secretariat
University of California - Davis
One Shields Ave.
Davis, CA 95616
Phone: (530)752-3046
Fax: (530)752-5655
E-mail: clah@ucdavis.edu
Home Page: http://www.h-net.org/~clah

• 8380 • Herbert Eugene Bolton Memorial Prize
To recognize the author of an outstanding book in English on any significant aspect of Latin American history published during the previous year. Sound scholarship, grace of style, and importance of the scholarly contribution are among the criteria for the award. Normally not considered for the award are translations, anthologies of selections by several authors, reprints or reeditions of works published previously, and works not primarily historiographical in aim or content. A monetary prize of $500 is awarded annually. Established in 1956.

• 8381 • Howard Francis Cline Memorial Prize
To recognize the best article or book in English, German, or a Romance language on Latin American ethnohistory published during the two years preceding that of the award. A monetary prize of $500 and Honorable Mention are awarded biennially. Established in 1976.

• 8382 • Conference on Latin American History Prize
To recognize outstanding articles on any significant aspect of Latin American history published in a journal in the United States or Puerto Rico other than the *Hispanic American Historical Review.* A monetary prize of $500 is awarded annually. Established in 1961.

• 8383 • Distinguished Service Award
To recognize single contributions to the advancement of the study of Latin American history in the United States. Individuals in teaching, publishing, librarianship, institutional development, or other fields are eligible. A monetary prize of $500 and an inscribed plaque are awarded at the discretion of the Committee. Established in 1969.

• 8384 • James Alexander Robertson Memorial Prize
To recognize the author of an outstanding article about Latin American history appearing in the *Hispanic American Historical Review*. A monetary prize of $500 and Honorable Mention are awarded annually. Established in 1953.

• 8385 • James R. Scobie Memorial Award for Preliminary Ph.D. Research
To permit a short, exploratory research trip abroad to determine the feasibility of a Ph.D. dissertation topic dealing with some facet of Latin American history. Applications may be submitted by April 1. One or more travel grants of approximately $1,000 are awarded annually.

• 8386 •
Congregational Christian Historical Society
Dr. Margaret Bendroth, Exec.Sec.
14 Beacon St.
Boston, MA 02108
Phone: (617)523-0470
Fax: (617)523-0491
E-mail: mbendroth@14beacon.org
Home Page: http://www.cchsonline.org

• 8387 • Fagley Awards Competition
To recognize achievements in church anniversary programs and the writing of local church histories. The competition is held in the following categories: local church histories and anniversary programs for churches of more than 350 members and for churches with less than 350 members; and outstanding and unusual publications in the field of Congregational/Christian church history. Certificates are awarded annually. Established in 1965 in honor of the Reverend Dr. Frederick L. Fagley, a denominational official and historian of the old Congregational Christian churches, and first Executive Secretary of the society.

• 8388 •
Congress of Neurological Surgeons
P. David Adelson Jr., Sec.
10 N Martingale Rd., Ste. 190
Schaumburg, IL 60173
Phone: (847)240-2500
Toll-Free: 877-517-1267
Fax: (847)240-0804
E-mail: info@1cns.org
Home Page: http://www.neurosurgeon.org

• 8389 • Distinguished Service Award
To recognize a member of the Congress for many years of dedicated service. A certificate is awarded when merited. Established in 1951.

• 8390 • Galbraith Award
To encourage resident participation in clinical and laboratory research related to cerebrovascular surgery. The award is presented to the resident applicant submitting the best manuscript in clinical and laboratory research related to cerebrovascular surgery. A monetary prize, expenses to attend the annual meeting of the CNS, and a certificate are awarded. Established by the Joint Section of Cerebrovascular Surgery of the American Association of Neurological Surgeons and the Congress of Neurological Surgeons in recognition of the pioneering efforts in cerebrovascular surgery of Dr. Galbraith.

• 8391 • Mayfield Award
To recognize the resident applicant who presented the best manuscript relating to clinical or laboratory research regarding an issue pertinent to the diseases and injuries of the spinal column and/or spinal cord and its nerve roots. Two awards are available, one for clinical research and one for basic science research. Each recipient will receive a $1000 cash award and an honorarium up to $2000 to cover annual meeting Joint Spine Section meeting expenses.

• 8392 • Resident Award
To recognize a resident who has made a significant contribution in the field of neurosurgery. The individual must be a resident in an approved neurosurgery program. A certificate and reimbursement of all costs to attend the annual meeting are awarded each year. Established in 1974.

• 8393 •
Congress of Racial Equality
Roy Innis, Natl.Chm.
817 Broadway
New York, NY 10003
Phone: (212)598-4000
Fax: (212)598-4141
E-mail: core@core-online.org
Home Page: http://www.core-online.org

• 8394 • Martin Luther King, Jr. Achievement Award
For recognition of individuals who have accomplished within their chosen field and maintained a commitment to civil and human rights. A sculpture bust of Martin Luther King, Jr. is awarded annually at the King Holiday Dinner. Established in 1985 to commemorate Dr. Martin Luther King, Jr.

• 8395 •
The Congressional Award Foundation
Erica Wheelan Heyse, Natl.Dir.
379 Ford House Office Building
PO Box 77440
Washington, DC 20013
Phone: (202)226-0130
Fax: (202)226-0131
E-mail: information@congressionalaward.org
Home Page: http://www.congressionalaward.org

• 8396 • The Congressional Award
To recognize American youth for their voluntary public service; personal development; physical fitness; and expedition/exploration. The minimum age to register is 14. Goals must be achieved by age 24. The following are awarded: Bronze Certificate for 30 hours of volunteer public service; 15 hours of personal development; 15 hours of physical fitness; and one-day expedition/exploration activity. Silver Certificate for 60 hours of volunteer public service; 30 hours of personal development; 30 hours of physical fitness; and two-day expedition/exploration activity. Gold Certificate for 90 hours of volunteer public service; 45 hours of personal development; 45 hours of physical fitness; and three-day expedition/exploration activity. Bronze Medal for 100 hours of volunteer public service 100 hours of volunteer public service; 50 hours of personal development; 50 ours of physical fitness, and expedition/exploration activity - including a minimum of one overnight. Silver Medal for 200 hours of volunteer public service; 100 hours of personal development; 100 hours of physical fitness, and expedition/exploration activity - including a minimum of two overnights. Gold Medal for 400 hours of volunteer public service; 200 hours of personal development; 200 hours of physical fitness; and expedition/exploration activity - including a minimum of four overnights. All applicants must select an adult advisor who will help set challenging but achievable goals and plan activities to reach those goals. Hours dedicated to earning an award at one level are carried over to the next level.

• 8397 •
Congressional Hispanic Caucus Institute
Esther Aguilera, Pres. and CEO
911 2nd St.
Washington, DC 20002
Phone: (202)543-1771
Toll-Free: 800-EXCEL-DC
Fax: (202)546-2143
E-mail: chci@chci.org
Home Page: http://www.chci.org

• 8398 • Medallion of Excellence for Distinguished Service
To recognize an individual who has made a lasting contribution to improving the quality of life or promoting the interests of Hispanic Americans. This award, along with the Role Model Award, comprises the Medallions of Excellence. Formerly: (1995) Distinguished Service Award.

• 8399 • Medallion of Excellence for Role Model
To recognize an individual who serves as an exemplary national role model. This award, along with the Distinguished Service Award, comprises the Medallions of Excellence. Formerly: (1995) Role Model Award.

• 8400 •
Congressional Medal of Honor Society
Victoria Leslie, Dir.
40 Patriots Point Rd.
Mount Pleasant, SC 29464
Phone: (843)884-8862
Fax: (843)884-1471
E-mail: medalhq@earthlink.net
Home Page: http://www.cmohs.org

• 8401 • Distinguished Citizen Award
To recognize in a special way those distinguished Americans who have contributed of themselves in service to others and to our coun-

try in a spirit of self-sacrifice and patriotism which sets them apart from others. Established in 1968. In addition, a large plaque (with CMHS seal and emblem of each military service) is awarded to those who directly contribute in a truly unique and outstanding manner toward attainment of Society objectives. The standard plaque is awarded to those who provide assistance or support to a Region or to members in their local area in a truly unique and meaningful way.

• 8402 • Patriot Award

The Congressional Medal of Honor Society consists of recipients of the Congressional Medal of Honor. The Patriot Award, the Society's highest award, recognizes in a very special way distinguished Americans who exemplify the highest ideals of patriotism, service to others and to their nation. A gold plated medallion is awarded. The award was first presented in 1968. Formerly: American Dance Guild Award.

• 8403 •
Congressional Quarterly
Bob Merry, Pres. and Publisher
1255 22nd St. NW
Washington, DC 20037-1003
Phone: (202)419-8500
Toll-Free: 800-432-2250
Fax: (202)728-1863
E-mail: kwhite@cq.com
Home Page: http://www.cq.com

• 8404 • CQ Press Award

To honor the best paper by a graduate student in the field of law and courts. A monetary award of $200 is presented annually at the American Political Science Association's annual meeting. Established in 1985. Sponsored by the American Political Science Association.

• 8405 •
Connected International Meeting Professionals Association
Andrea Sigler Ph.D., Pres.
9200 Bayard Pl.
Fairfax, VA 22032
Phone: (703)286-2142
Fax: (703)291-2292
E-mail: info@meetingprofessionals.org
Home Page: http://www.cimpa.org

• 8406 • Tech-Savvy Hotels Award

Recognizes hotels that have the most up to date technology. Awarded annually.

• 8407 •
Connecticut Alliance for Music
61 Unquowa Rd.
Fairfield, CT 06824
Phone: (203)319-8271
Fax: (203)319-8273
E-mail: alliance.for.music@snet.net
Home Page: http://www.camusic.org

Formerly: (1997) Performers of Connecticut.

• 8408 • Heida Hermanns International Competition

To provide outstanding young classical musicians, vocalists, and instrumentalists with the challenge of a professional competition and to ease their career entry. Contestants from around the world between the ages of 19 and 30 (for voice, age 19-35) may apply. Categories rotate among woodwinds, voice, strings, and piano every four years. First, second, third, and honorable mentions receive $3,500, $2,000, $1,250, and $500, respectively. Presented annually in November. Established in 1972. Formerly: (1995) Young Artists Competition.

• 8409 •
Connecticut Association of Assessing Officers
Marsha L. Standish, Pres.
127 Norwich Ave.
Colchester, CT 06415
Phone: (860)537-7205
Fax: (860)537-1147
E-mail: webmaster@caao.com
Home Page: http://www.caao.com

• 8410 • CAAO Scholarship

Given to assessment personnel for whom municipality won't pay for assessment, appraisal courses. Scholarship.

• 8411 •
Connecticut Audubon Center at Glastonbury
Judy Harper, Dir.
1361 Main St.
Glastonbury, CT 06033-3105
Phone: (860)633-8402
Fax: (860)659-9467
E-mail: glastonbury@ctaudubon.org
Home Page: http://www.ctaudubon.org

• 8412 • Environmental Excellence Award

For business or individual who has shown good environmental project. Recognition award bestowed annually.

• 8413 •
Connecticut Bar Association
PO Box 350
New Britain, CT 06050-0350
Phone: (860)223-4400
Fax: (860)223-4488
E-mail: thazen@ctbar.org
Home Page: http://www.ctbar.org

• 8414 • Recognition for Legal Achievement

For public service. Recognition award bestowed periodically.

• 8415 •
Connecticut Forest and Park Association
16 Meriden Rd.
Rockfall, CT 06481-2961
Phone: (860)346-2372
Fax: (860)347-7463
E-mail: conn.forest.assoc@snet.net
Home Page: http://www.ctwoodlands.org

• 8416 • James L. Goodwin Memorial Scholarship

For Connecticut resident majoring in forestry. Scholarship awarded annually.

• 8417 •
Connecticut League for Nursing
Marcia B. Proto, Exec.Dir.
PO Box 365
Wallingford, CT 06492
Phone: (203)265-4248
Fax: (203)265-5311
E-mail: education@ctleaguefornursing.org
Home Page: http://www.ctleaguefornursing.org

• 8418 • Nursing Scholarship

For senior nursing students; school an agency member of CLN. Scholarship awarded annually.

• 8419 •
Connecticut River Watershed Council
Tom Miner, Co.Exec.Dir.
15 Bank Row
Greenfield, MA 01301
Phone: (413)772-2020
Fax: (413)772-2090
E-mail: crwc@crocker.com
Home Page: http://www.ctriver.org

• 8420 • Connecticut River Watershed Council Conservation Award

To recognize outstanding and dedicated conservation service for the benefit of the Connecticut River Valley. Established in 1955.

• 8421 •
Conseil de la Vie Francaise en Amerique
5350 boulevard Henri-Bourassa, Ste. 201
Quebec, QC, Canada G1H 5Y8
Phone: (418)626-5665
Fax: (418)626-5663
E-mail: cvfa@cvfa.ca
Home Page: http://www.cvfa.ca

• 8422 • Ordre du Conseil de la Vie Francaise en Amerique

To recognize an individual(s) who in some way contributed to or maintained French culture in North America. A medal and a certificate are awarded. Established in 1947.

• 8423 • Prix Champlain

For recognition of an outstanding literary or scholarly work by a Franco-American or French Canadian resident. The author must be living outside the province of Quebec, but in North

America. If living in Quebec, he or she must write on themes of interest to French speaking persons who are living in a situation where they are a minority in North America. The work must not have been published more than three years previous to the award year. A monetary prize of $1,500 and a certificate are awarded annually, alternately for a work of fiction and a scholarly essay. Established in 1957.

• 8424 •
Conservation Southeast Inc.
Mark Bailey, Sr. Biologist
2040 Old Federal Rd.
Shorter, AL 36075
Phone: (334)727-2040
Fax: (334)722-1005
E-mail: mail@conservationsoutheast.com
Home Page: http://www.conservationsoutheast.com

Formed by merger of: (1974) Apalachee Poetry Center.

• 8425 • **Anhinga Poetry Prize**
For recognition of achievement in writing poetry and to encourage poets to develop their talents. Outstanding book-length manuscripts of poetry in English are considered. Poets who have published no more than one full length book of poetry and those who have not yet published a book of poetry are eligible. Manuscripts may be submitted only from January 1 to March 15 each year. The winner is selected from among the finalists by a distinguished American poet. A monetary prize of $2,000 and publication of the winning manuscript are awarded annually. Fee: $20.00. Send SASE for details. Established in 1983.

• 8426 •
Construction Innovation Forum
Roger W. Lane, Chm.
7001 Haggerty Rd.
Canton, MI 48187
Phone: (734)455-0600
Fax: (734)455-3131
E-mail: info@cif.org
Home Page: http://www.cif.org

• 8427 • **NOVA Award**
Recognition is given.

• 8428 •
Construction Specifications Canada
Nick Franjic CAE, Exec.Dir.
120 Carlton St., Ste. 312
Toronto, ON, Canada M5A 4K2
Phone: (416)777-2198
Fax: (416)777-2197
E-mail: info@csc-dcc.ca
Home Page: http://www.csc-dcc.ca

• 8429 • **Lloyb Bobby Chapter of the Year Award**
Recognizes an outstanding local chapter. Awarded annually.

• 8430 • **National Award of Merit**
Annual award of recognition.

• 8431 • **Program Directors' Award**
Annual award of recognition.

• 8432 •
Construction Specifications Institute
Edith S. Washington, Pres.
99 Canal Center Plaza, Ste. 300
Alexandria, VA 22314
Phone: (703)684-0300
Toll-Free: 800-689-2900
Fax: (703)684-8436
E-mail: csi@csinet.org
Home Page: http://www.csinet.org/honorsandawards

• 8433 • **Robert P. Brosseau Memorial Award**
To recognize an industry or associate member who has rendered outstanding service in furthering the mission and programs of the Institute. Nominations and letters of endorsement must be received no later than December 1. A framed certificate is awarded.

• 8434 • **Continuing Publication Commendation**
To recognize an individual, team, firm, organization, chapter, or region for a continuing publication of interest to or related to CSI. Nominations must be received no later than December 1. A framed certificate is awarded to one or more recipients each year.

• 8435 • **Distinguished Service Award**
To recognize an individual (Honorary, Emeritus, Retired, Professional, Industry, or Associate member of CSI) who has rendered distinguished service to the Institute in the advancement of its mission or in its administration. Nominations and letters of endorsement must be received no later than December 1. A framed certificate is awarded. Formerly: Certificate of Appreciation.

• 8436 • **Electronic Innovation Commendation**
To recognize an individual team, firm, chapter, or organization for an outstanding innovative use of electronic technology in the advancement of the construction industry. Nominations and letters of endorsement must be received no later than February 1. A framed certificate is awarded when merited.

• 8437 • **Fellowship**
Fellowship is one of the two highest honors awarded by the Institute. Fellows, chosen by their peers, must have been members for at least five years; be in good standing; have provided distinguished service to the Institute; and notably contributed to the advancement of construction technology, the improvement of construction specifications, or education. Nominations and letters of endorsement must be received no later than November 1. A silver medal, framed citation, and gold lapel button are awarded.

• 8438 • **Honorary Membership**
This, the most prestigious award of the Institute, is conferred on individuals who have given distinguished service or made outstanding contributions to the construction industry in fields of activity related to the purposes of the Institute. Membership is not a requirement. Nominations and letters of endorsement must be received no later than January 2. A gold medal, framed citation, and silver lapel button are awarded.

• 8439 • **J. Norman Hunter Memorial Award**
To recognize an individual, team, or chapter for attaining special advancement in the field of education or the establishment of educational facilities in specification writing. Nominations and letters of endorsement must be received no later than December 1. A framed certificate is awarded.

• 8440 • **Dale C. Moll Memorial Quality Management Award**
To recognize an individual, firm, or organization whose continued commitment to the implementation, promotion, or enhancement of the quality management process has led to improvement in the construction industry. Nominations and letters of endorsement must be received no later than December 1. A framed certificate is awarded annually.

• 8441 • **Organizational Certificate of Appreciation**
To recognize a firm, organization or association for exceptional accomplishments that promote the mission of the Institute. The Award is the highest honor the Institute can bestow on a firm or an organization. Nominations and letters of endorsement must be received no later than December 1. A framed certificate is awarded.

• 8442 • **President's Plaques**
To recognize an individual for outstanding and exceptional work performed on behalf of the Institute. Up to five plaques are awarded.

• 8443 • **Ben John Small Memorial Award**
To recognize a professional member of the Institute who has attained special proficiency and outstanding stature as a practicing specification writer. Nominations and letters of endorsement must be received no later than December 1. A framed certificate is awarded.

• 8444 • **Student Liaison Award**
To recognize an individual, team, chapter, or region for preparing students of construction-related curricula to make a difference in the construction community. Nominee shall be a member of CSI. In the case of a team, a majority number of members of team shall be CSI members. Nominations and letters of endorsement must be received no later than December 1. A

framed certificate is awarded to one or more recipients each year.

• 8445 •
Construction Writers Association
Sheila Wertz, Exec.Dir.
PO Box 5586
Buffalo Grove, IL 60089-5586
Phone: (847)398-7756
Fax: (847)590-5241
E-mail: office@constructionwriters.org
Home Page: http://www.constructionwriters.org

• 8446 • **Robert F. Boger Award**
To recognize editorial excellence. Members of the Association who have written a single article, a series of articles on a single topic, or an editorial for a magazine/journal within the past year are eligible. The articles are judged on editorial impact, content, and presentation. A panel of judges selects the most outstanding contributions. Plaques are awarded annually at the meeting/banquet, usually in May. Established in 1971 in memory of Robert F. Boger, publisher of *Engineering News Record,* Vice President of McGraw Hill Publishing Company, and an initial sponsor of the organization.

• 8447 • **Kneeland Godfrey Award**
Recognizes and individual writer's versatility, intelligence and superior writing in construction journalism. Members submit samples of their work from the prior year. A plaque is awarded annually, usually in May. Established in 1999 to honor the late Kneeland "Ned" Godfrey, a former editor of *Civil Engineering* magazine and a past president of CWA. Mr. Godfrey also authored many newsletters and books.

• 8448 • **Marketing Communications Award**
Recognizes excellence in construction-related marketing communications in at least three categories: Corporate Communications, Advertising, and Public Relations. Organizations may submit their best work from the prior year. Awarded annually in the Fall. Established in 2001.

• 8449 • **T. Randolph Russell Award**
Recognizes an outstanding newsletter. Members of the Association who have written newsletters within the past year are eligible. Newsletters are judged on editorial impact, content, and presentation by a panel of judges. A plaque is awarded annually, usually in May. Established in 1993 in memory of T. Randolph Russell, Editor, American Road and Transportation Builder Association.

• 8450 • **Silver Hardhat Award**
To recognize a member or a non-member for outstanding contributions toward meeting the information needs of the construction industry or the association. A plaque is awarded annually at the discretion of the CWA Board of Directors at the meeting/banquet, usually in May. Established in 1959.

• 8451 • **Website Award**
Recognizes excellence in website design and information delivery. Websites may be informational or promotional in nature and are judged by a non-partisan committee. Awarded annually in the Fall. Established in 1998.

• 8452 •
Consulting Engineers Council of Metropolitan Washington
James Johnson, Exec.Dir.
8201 Greensboro Dr., Ste. 300
McLean, VA 22102-3814
Phone: (703)610-9019
Fax: (703)610-9005
E-mail: jjohnson@acecmw.org
Home Page: http://www.acecmw.org

• 8453 • **Engineering Excellence Award**
For innovative, on-time, under-budget engineering studies or designs. Recognition award bestowed annually.

• 8454 •
Consumer Credit Insurance Association
William F. Burfeind, Exec.VP
542 S. Dearborn, No. 400
Chicago, IL 60605
Phone: (312)939-2242
Fax: (312)939-8287
E-mail: ccia@cciaonline.com
Home Page: http://www.cciaonline.com

• 8455 • **CCIA Gavel Award**
Presented annually as a token of appreciation for the time and effort the Chairman of the board has given the CCIA during his term of office. A plaque is awarded annually. Established in 1969.

• 8456 • **Arthur J. Morris Award**
Recognizes outstanding contributions to the consumer credit insurance industry. The Executive Committee of the CCIA votes on this award once a year. All nominations must be received by January for consideration for an award given in the spring of the same year. A plaque is awarded when merited. Established in 1969 in honor of Arthur J. Morris, the founder of credit insurance.

• 8457 •
Consumer Electronics Association
Gary Shapiro, Pres./CEO
2500 Wilson Blvd.
Arlington, VA 22201-3834
Phone: (703)907-7600
Toll-Free: (866)858-1555
Fax: (703)907-7675
E-mail: cea@ce.org
Home Page: http://www.ce.org

• 8458 • **Hall of Fame Awards**
To recognize people who have chosen electronics for their vocation in life, who have made outstanding contributions to the industry, and who have served as inspiring examples for others to follow. Nominees may include inventors, engineers, business leaders, retailers, and journalists. A plaque is awarded annually at the Hall of Fame dinner. Established in 2000.

• 8459 •
Consumer Federation of America
Stephen J. Brobeck, Exec.Dir.
1424 16th St. NW, Ste. 604
Washington, DC 20036
Phone: (202)387-6121
Fax: (202)265-7989
E-mail: cfa@essential.org
Home Page: http://www.consumerfed.org

• 8460 • **Betty Furness Consumer Media Service Award**
For recognition of consumer reporting in the media that both inform the public and lead to corrective actions. A plaque is awarded annually. Established in 1970. Formerly known as the Outstanding Consumer Media Service Award and renamed in 1994 in memory of Betty Furness.

• 8461 • **Philip Hart Public Service Award**
To recognize public service in the interest of consumers. Senators, congressmen, or individuals in the regulatory arena are eligible. A plaque is awarded annually. Established in 1970 in memory of Senator Philip Hart.

• 8462 • **Esther Peterson Consumer Service Award**
To recognize commitment to consumers that has resulted in consumer legislation and regulations. A plaque is awarded annually. Formerly known as the Philip Hart Distinguished Consumer Service Award and renamed in memory of consumer advocate Esther Peterson. Formerly: CFA Distinguished Service Award.

• 8463 •
Consumer Specialty Products Association
Chris Cathcart, Pres./COO
900 17th St. NW, Ste. 300
Washington, DC 20006
Phone: (202)872-8110
Fax: (202)872-8114
E-mail: info@cspa.org
Home Page: http://www.cspa.org

Formerly: (2003) Chemical Specialties Manufacturers Association.

• 8464 • **Aerosol Package Design Award**
To stimulate interest and recognize excellence in the package design of aerosols. Member companies of CSMA, Inc., are eligible. A plaque is awarded to category winners and to the grand prize winner. Awarded biennially. Established in 1950.

• 8465 • **Charles Allderdice Award**
To recognize a member for outstanding service to the Association. Awarded annually.

• 8466 •
Consumers for World Trade
Robin Lanier, Exec.Dir.
1001 Connecticut Ave., NW, Ste. 1110
Washington, DC 20036
Phone: (202)293-2944
Fax: (202)293-0495
E-mail: cwt@cwt.org
Home Page: http://www.cwt.org

• 8467 • **CWT Award**
Recognizes distinguished service on behalf of open trade. Awarded annually.

• 8468 • **Distinguished Service in the Cause of Open and Competitive World Trade Award**
For recognition of achievement by formulators of U.S. trade policy in Congress, the Administration, the private sector or by a foreign trade dignitary. Those who have made a continued effort in achieving a more open world trading system are considered for the award. A trophy is presented annually. Established in 1981.

• 8469 •
Contact Lens Manufacturer Association
Pam Witham, Contact
PO Box 29398
Lincoln, NE 68529
Phone: (402)465-4122
Fax: (402)465-4187
E-mail: clmassociation@aol.com
Home Page: http://www.clma.net

• 8470 • **Joseph Dallos Award**
To recognize pioneering contributions to the contact lens industry and service to humanity. An engraved plaque is awarded annually. Established in 1970.

• 8471 •
Containerization and Intermodal Institute
Barbara Yeninas, Exec.Dir.
960 Holmdel Rd., Bdlg. 2, No. 201
West Caldwell, NJ 07006
Phone: (732)817-9131
Fax: (732)817-9133
E-mail: CII@bsya.com

• 8472 • **Connie Award**
To recognize an individual who has contributed to the progress of the containerization and intermodal industry. Individuals working in the transportation field are eligible. A plaque is awarded at a luncheon annually. Established in 1972.

• 8473 •
Contemporary A Cappella Society of America
Paul Prochaska, Off.Mgr.
2525 Van Ness Ave., Ste. 205
San Francisco, CA 94109
Phone: (415)563-5224
E-mail: casa@casa.org
Home Page: http://www.casa.org

• 8474 • **Contemporary A Cappella Recording Awards ("CARAs")**
To recognize excellence in recorded A Cappella in the categories of professional and academic recordings. Awarded biennially in odd-numbered years.

• 8475 •
Contemporary Record Society
724 Winchester Rd.
Broomall, PA 19008
Phone: (610)544-5920
Fax: (610)544-5921
E-mail: crsnews@erols.com

• 8476 • **Competition for Performing Artists**
To provide national recognition for a distinguished CRS performance/recording. Selection is by a Society committee. Audio and video tapes may be submitted for audition. The application fee is $50 for each tape submitted. The deadline for applications is October 19. The following prizes are awarded: first prize - a commercially distributed new compact disc recording grant featuring the performance of several composers' works and public exposure of the winner though feature articles; second and third prize - honorable mention toward future recordings with CRS and honorary life membership in the Society. Established in 1986. Send applicant requests with a S.A.S.E.

• 8477 • **National Competition for Composers Recording**
For recognition of an outstanding composer. Each composer may submit any number of works that does not exceed nine performers. The application fee is $50 for each work submitted. Society members and nonmembers are eligible for selection by a Society committee. The deadline for applications is October 19. A commercially distributed new compact disc recording grant featuring one composition along with other distinguished composers and performing artists is awarded annually at the CRS Auditions. Second and third place winners receive honorable mention toward future recordings with CRS and honorary life membership in the Soiety. The winner is eligible for CRS representation/commissions/lectures, additional CRS grants, and Honorary Life Membership. Established in 1985. Send applicants requests with a S.A.S.E.

• 8478 •
Continental Basketball Association
1412 W Idaho St., Ste. 235
Boise, ID 83702
Phone: (208)429-0101
Fax: (208)429-0303
E-mail: info@cbahoopsonline.com
Home Page: http://www.cbahoopsonline.com

• 8479 • **All-Star Game Most Valuable Player**
To recognize the most valuable player in the All Star Games in the professional minor basketball league. Candidates selected are voted upon by members of the media. Winners are announced through press releases, the *CBA News*, the newsletter of the Association, and the *CBA Official Guide and Register*. Awarded annually. Established in 1979.

• 8480 • **Coach of the Year**
For recognition of the outstanding coach in the professional minor basketball league. Candidates selected are voted upon by the general managers in the league. Winners are announced through press releases, the *CBA News*, the newsletter of the Association, and the *CBA Official Guide and Register*. Awarded annually. Established in 1978.

• 8481 • **Defensive Player of the Year**
To recognize the best defensive player. Voted by coaches.

• 8482 • **Most Valuable Player**
To recognize the most valuable player in the professional minor basketball league. Candidates selected are voted upon by the coaches in the league. Winners are announced through press releases, the *CBA News*, the newsletter of the Association, and the *CBA Official Guide and Register*. Awarded annually. Established in 1978.

• 8483 • **Newcomer of the Year**
For recognition of the player with Pro experience, but in his first year in the CBA. Candidates selected are voted upon by the coaches in the league. Winners are announced through press releases, the *CBA News*, the newsletter of the Association, and the *CBA Official Guide and Register*. Awarded annually. Established in 1979.

• 8484 • **Playoff Most Valuable Player**
To recognize the most valuable player in the Playoffs in the professional minor basketball league. Candidates selected are voted upon by the media. Winners are announced through press releases, the *CBA News*, the newsletter of the Association and the *CBA Official Guide and Register*. Awarded annually. Established in 1978.

• 8485 • **Rookie of the Year**
To recognize the outstanding rookie in the professional minor basketball league. Candidates selected are voted upon by the coaches in the league. Winners are announced through press releases, the *CBA News*, the newsletter of the Association, and the *CBA Official Guide and Register*. Awarded annually. Established in 1978.

• 8486 •
Continental Confederation of Adopted Indians
Leland L. Conner, Chief
960 Walhonding Ave.
Logan, OH 43138
Phone: (740)385-7136
E-mail: lelandconner@webtv.net

• 8487 • **Catlin Peace Pipe Award**
To recognize the outstanding achievements of those who strive to tear down negative stereotypes through Indian lore. Candidates must be nominated. Up to 10 plaques are presented annually. Established in 1970.

• 8488 •
Cooper Ornithological Society
Bonnie Bowen, Pres.
124 Science Hall II
Iowa State University
Ames, IA 50011
Phone: (515)294-6391
Fax: (515)294-7874
E-mail: bsbowen@iastate.edu
Home Page: http://www.cooper.org/

• 8489 • **Board of Directors Student Paper Awards**
To recognize students who present worthy papers at the annual meeting. Candidates must be the sole or senior author of the paper and not hold doctoral degrees in biology. Two monetary prizes of at least $50 and membership in the Society are awarded annually.

• 8490 • **A. Brazier Howell Award**
To recognize the student/author of the best paper presented at the annual meeting of the Society. Candidates must be an amateur student, or must have received his/her degree since the last annual meeting, and must be the sole author of the paper and must be members of the Society. A monetary prize of at least $150 is awarded annually.

• 8491 • **Loye and Alden Miller Research Award**
To recognize individuals with an extensive record of original research in any field of ornithology who have made significant advancements and major breakthroughs in the understanding of the biology of birds that have stood the test of time. A medallion is awarded each year at the annual meeting of the Society. Established in 1993 in honor of Loye H. and Alden H. Miller for their lifetime contributions to the study of ornithology.

• 8492 • **Mewaldt-King Student Research Award**
To support student research in any area of ornithology that relates to the conservation of birds. A monetary prize of $1,000 is awarded annually.

• 8493 • **Harry R. Painton Award**
To recognize the paper of greatest merit and significance published in the Society's publication, *The Condor,* in the preceding four years. A monetary award of at least $1000 is awarded biennially, when merited, in odd-numbered years.

• 8494 • **Frances Roberts Award**
To recognize the student author of the second best paper presented at the annual meeting of the Society. Candidates must be an an amateur student, or must have received his/her degree since the last Annual Meeting, and must be the sole author of the paper. A monetary prize of at least $100 and a 5 year subscription to the Condor is awarded annually.

• 8495 •
Cooper Union for the Advancement of Science and Art
George Campbell Jr., Pres.
Cooper Sq.
New York, NY 10003-7120
Phone: (212)353-4100
Fax: (212)353-4327
E-mail: alumni@cooper.edu
Home Page: http://www.cooper.edu

• 8496 • **Alumnus of the Year**
For recognition of service to the alma mater. Individual committees decide each award on the basis of candidates' past achievements. A medal is presented annually. Established in 1952. In 1991, an Alumnus-of-the-Decade Award was presented to celebrate Peter Cooper's 200th birthday.

• 8497 • **Gano Dunn Award**
To recognize professional achievement in science and engineering. A committee evaluates past achievements of the candidates for the award. A medal is presented annually. Established in 1955.

• 8498 • **Augustus St. Gaudens Medal**
To recognize professional achievement in art and architecture. A committee evaluates past achievements of the candidates for the award. A medal is presented annually. Established in 1962 and named after one of America's leading sculptors, Augustus St. Gaudens.

• 8499 •
Cooperative Council for Oklahoma School Administration
2901 N. Lincoln Blvd.
Oklahoma City, OK 73105
Phone: (405)524-1191
Fax: (405)524-1196

• 8500 • **Administrator of the Year**
For leadership, job performance, ethics. Scholarship awarded annually.

• 8501 •
Cooperative Education and Internship Association
Peggy Harrier, Pres.
16 Santa Ana Pl.
Walnut Creek, CA 94598
Phone: (925)947-5581
Toll-Free: 800-824-0449
Fax: (925)906-0922
E-mail: info@ceiainc.org
Home Page: http://www.ceiainc.org

• 8502 • **Co-Op Student of the Year Award**
To recognize an outstanding cooperative education student. Nominations must be submitted by CEA members. A plaque and $1,000 scholarship are awarded annually (alternating presentation at Cooperative Education Association and CED/ASEE conferences).

• 8503 • **Charles F. Kettering Award**
To recognize an employer in business, industry, or government for outstanding contributions to the advancement of the philosophy and practice of cooperative education. Nominations must be submitted by CEA members. A plaque is awarded annually. Established in 1978 and named after Charles F. Kettering. Kettering was a trustee and benefactor of Antioch College and Research Director of the General Motors Corporation.

• 8504 • **Dean Herman Schneider Achievement Award**
To recognize an individual for an outstanding contribution, or series of contributions, to the advancement of cooperative education. Nominations must be submitted by CEA members. A plaque is awarded annually. Established in 1966 and named for Herman Schneider who was Dean of the College of Engineering at the University of Cincinnati (1906-28) and President of the University (l929-32).

• 8505 • **Dr. Ralph W. Tyler Research Award**
To recognize educators for an outstanding contribution or series of contributions in the field of research that directly affects the advancement of cooperative education. Nominations must be submitted by CEA members. A plaque is awarded annually. Established in 1982 and named after Ralph W. Tyler who was the Director of the Center for Advanced Studies in The Behavioral Sciences in Stanford, California.

• 8506 •
Cooperstown Art Association
Janet G. Erway, Gallery Dir.
22 Main St.
Cooperstown, NY 13326
Phone: (607)547-9777
Fax: (607)547-1187
E-mail: coopart@telenet.net
Home Page: http://www.cooperstownart.com

Awards are arranged in alphabetical order below their administering organizations

• 8507 • Scholarship Award
For promising high school seniors residing in Otsego County. Awarded annually.

• 8508 •
Coos County Historical Society Museum
Steven Greif, Pres.
1220 Sherman Ave.
North Bend, OR 97459
Phone: (541)756-6320
Fax: (541)756-6320
E-mail: museum@uci.net
Home Page: http://www.cooshistory.org

• 8509 • Outstanding Citizen Award
For service to Coos County. Recognition award bestowed annually.

• 8510 •
Copper Country Audubon Club
PO Box 124
Houghton, MI 49931-0124
Phone: (906)487-2149
Phone: (906)482-3361
Fax: (906)487-2915
E-mail: dlrichte@mtu.edu

• 8511 • Best Bird of the Christmas Count
For person who has sighted most unique or rare bird. Recognition award bestowed annually.

• 8512 •
CoreNet Global Inc.
Peggy Binzel, Pres. and CEO
260 Peachtree St., Ste. 1500
Atlanta, GA 30303
Phone: (404)589-3200
Toll-Free: 800-726-8111
Fax: (404)589-3201
E-mail: pbinzel@corenetglobal.org
Home Page: http://www2.corenetglobal.org

• 8513 • Awards for Distinguished Service in Environmental Planning
To recognize business leaders who have demonstrated, in exemplary economic development projects, their commitment to environmental quality. A plaque is presented annually at IDRC Fall World Congress. Established in 1972 by IDRC and Conway Data, Inc., Atlanta, GA.

• 8514 • Awards for Outstanding Area Research
To recognize and reward those groups contributing works of significance to the expansion planning profession, to encourage additional area economic development research, and to enhance professionalism in the preparation of material designed to point out locational advantages. The deadline for nominations is March 1. A plaque is awarded annually at IDRC Spring World Congress. Established in 1980 by IDRC and Conway Data, Inc., Atlanta, GA.

• 8515 •
Corinthian Vintage Auto Racing Corporation
Arthur F. Summerville, Pres.
3818 Eugene Ct. S
Irving, TX 75062
Phone: (972)258-6934
Fax: (972)258-1987
E-mail: cvarrace@comcast.net
Home Page: http://www.corinthianvintagerace.com

• 8516 • Bob McLaughlin Vintage Spirit Award
For top finishers in car classes. Recognition award bestowed annually.

• 8517 •
Cornell Laboratory of Ornithology
Allison Wells, Dir. of Commun. & Mktg.
PO Box 11
159 Sapsucker Woods Rd.
Ithaca, NY 14851
Phone: (607)254-2425
Toll-Free: 800-843-2473
Fax: (607)254-2435
E-mail: cornellbirds@cornell.edu
Home Page: http://www.birds.cornell.edu

• 8518 • Arthur A. Allen Award
To honor persons who have made outstanding contributions to ornithology. Contributions of the awardee should reflect Dr. Allen's emphasis on widening the interest in ornithology through such media as lecturing, writing, or photography. A bronze medal is awarded whenever the selection committee chooses a candidate, usually annually. Established in 1967 in honor of Arthur A. Allen.

• 8519 •
Corona Norco United Way
Allen A. Villalobos, Exec.Dir.
PO Box 1809
Corona, CA 92878-1809
Phone: (909)736-0620
Phone: (909)793-2800
Fax: (909)736-0304
E-mail: allen@cnunitedway.org
Home Page: http://www.cnunitedway.org

• 8520 • Coordinator Award
For involvement in community. Recognition award bestowed annually.

• 8521 • Leadership Award
For involvement in community. Recognition award bestowed annually.

• 8522 •
Corporation for Public Broadcasting
Patricia De Stacy Harrison, Pres./CEO
401 9th St. NW
Washington, DC 20004-2129
Phone: (202)879-9600
Toll-Free: 800-272-2190
Fax: (202)879-9700
E-mail: comments@cpb.org
Home Page: http://www.cpb.org

• 8523 • CPB Public Radio Program Awards
To recognize outstanding programming in public radio broadcast during the previous year. Gold Awards (plaques) and Silver Awards (certificates) are awarded to stations and producers in nine categories including Performance, Public Affairs, Children's, and Special Achievement. Awarded annually. Established in 1971.

• 8524 • CPB Public Television Local Program Awards
To recognize outstanding local programming in public television broadcast during the previous year. Gold Awards (plaques) and Silver Awards (certificates) are awarded to stations and producers in nine categories including News, Performance, Community Service/Outreach, Independent Productions, and Special Achievement. Awarded annually. Established in 1971.

• 8525 • Ralph Lowell Award
This, public television's highest recognition of merit, is given to recognize an individual for outstanding contributions to public television. Candidates may be nominated by anyone and are not limited to public television professionals. The following criteria are considered: extraordinary efforts in public television programming, legislation for public broadcasting, leadership at the national level, and educational and professional development. A medal is awarded annually. Established in 1970 by the Lowell family in honor of the 80th birthday of Ralph Lowell, the Boston philanthropist and banker who was a pioneer in public broadcasting.

• 8526 • Edward R. Murrow Award
To recognize an individual for outstanding contributions to public radio. The contribution or achievement may have occurred over many years or during a short period of time. The individual need not be a professional in public radio, but should be active in fostering this unique informational and cultural resource. A plaque is awarded annually. Established in 1977 in honor of Edward R. Murrow, who was a spokesman for responsible, courageous, and imaginative use of the electronic media.

• 8527 •
Corporation of Professional Librarians of Quebec
Regine Horinstein, Dir.Gen.
353 rue St-Nicolas, bureau 103
Montreal, QC, Canada H2Y 2P1
Phone: (514)845-3327
Fax: (514)845-1618
E-mail: info@cbpq.qc.ca
Home Page: http://cbpq.qc.ca

• 8528 • **Annual Merit (Professional Librarian)**
To recognize exceptional accomplishments and contribution to the promotion of the goals of the corporation by a professional librarian. Awarded every year with a gold pin. Established in 1989.

• 8529 • **Public Person**
To recognize the contribution of the development of libraries in Quebec. Award is a sterling silver pin. Established in 1994.

• 8530 •
Correctional Education Association - Region III
Joanna Leftwich, Dir.
PO Box 740
London, OH 43140-0740
Phone: (740)852-9777
Home Page: http://cea.com

• 8531 • **Teacher of the Year**
For outstanding teacher. Grant awarded annually.

• 8532 •
Council for Agricultural Science and Technology
Teresa A. Gruber PhD, Exec.VP
4420 West Lincoln Way
Ames, IA 50014-3447
Phone: (515)292-2125
Fax: (515)292-4512
E-mail: cast@cast-science.org
Home Page: http://www.cast-science.org

• 8533 • **Charles A. Black Award**
Recognizes contributions to public understanding of food and agricultural science. Awarded annually.

• 8534 •
Council for Art Education
Deborah M. Fanning CAE, Exec.VP
PO Box 479
Hanson, MA 02341-0479
Phone: (781)293-4100
Fax: (781)294-0808
E-mail: sarahs@acminet.org
Home Page: http://www.acminet.org/cfae.htm

• 8535 • **Youth Art Month State Report Awards**
For recognition of highly successful leadership in promoting art education throughout one's state during the March Youth Art Month observance. Youth Art Month state chairpersons may submit a report of the state observances to the Council according to guidelines provided by the Council. A monetary award, to be equally divided between the chairperson and his or her state art education association, and a plaque are awarded annually at the National Art Education Association Convention. Established in 1961. Renamed in 1982 to honor Clare Flanagan, public relations director from 1961 to her death in 1981. Formerly: (2003) Clare Flanagan Youth Art Month Grand Award.

• 8536 •
Council for Business and Arts in Canada
Eileen Love, Exec.Sec.
165 University Ave., Ste. 903
Toronto, ON, Canada M5H 3B8
Phone: (416)869-3016
Fax: (416)869-0435
E-mail: info@businessforarts.org
Home Page: http://www.businessforarts.org

• 8537 • ***Financial Post* Annual Report Awards**
To promote good disclosure and interpretation of financial information and to improve the quality and relevance of the information provided by Canadian corporations in their annual reports. Candidates are selected from over 200 companies listed on the TSE 300. Established in 1951.

• 8538 • ***Financial Post* Design Effectiveness Awards**
To promote a clearer understanding of the vital role of design as a strategic corporate tool, to demonstrate that spending on design is an investment and not simply a cost, and to show that effective design achieves benefits for business. These are the first Canadian awards to judge the work of designers on the basis of commercial effectiveness. Entries may be submitted in September. Established in 1992 with the cooperation of the Group for Design in Business.

• 8539 • ***Financial Post* Environment Awards for Business**
To identify, encourage, and promote technology, design, and management initiatives that have helped to protect and/or improve the environment. The awards program recognizes individuals and companies who, by their example, are proving that taking care of the environment and taking care of business are mutually dependent objectives. Entries may be submitted in May/June. Established in 1991 by the *Financial Post*.

• 8540 • ***Financial Post* Outstanding CEO of the Year Award**
To honor the Chief Executive Officer of a private or public Canadian corporation who has, by his or her peers' assessment, made an outstanding contribution to Canada's global competitiveness. Established in 1990 by the Caldwell AMROP Partners International and the *Financial Post* to salute the efforts of those CEO's who lead their organizations and Canada to the forefront of global competition.

• 8541 • ***National Post* Awards for Business in the Arts**
To encourage the corporate sector's involvement with the visual and performing arts in Canada and to recognize those companies whose involvement in this area is an example to their peers. Awards are presented to one or more recipients in three categories: Best Arts/Entrepreneur Partnership; Most Innovative Marketing Sponsorship; and Most Effective Corporate Program. Statuettes are awarded annually. Established in 1979. Co-sponsored by the *National Post*. Formerly: *Financial Post* Awards for Business in the Arts.

• 8542 •
Council for Business and the Arts in Canada
Eileen Love, Exec.Sec.
165 University Ave., Ste. 903
Toronto, ON, Canada M5H 3B8
Phone: (416)869-3016
Fax: (416)869-0435
E-mail: info@businessforarts.org
Home Page: http://www.businessforarts.org

• 8543 • **Edmund C. Bovey Award**
To recognize outstanding support of the arts by a business person. A work of art for the winner and a monetary award for the recipient's favorite arts organization are awarded. Established in 1990 in memory of the council founder and former Telefilm Canada Chairman.

• 8544 • **John P. Fisher Award for Media Support of the Arts**
To recognize the important role that daily newspapers play in support of the arts in Canadian communities. The award aims to recognize an individual newspaper's corporate support of the arts, as well as honoring the quality of the arts journalism contained within its pages. Daily Canadian newspapers are eligible. The award is an original work of art specially commissioned for this purpose.

• 8545 •
Council for Exceptional Children
Dr. Jim McCormick, Pres.
1110 N Glebe Rd., Ste. 300
Arlington, VA 22201-5704
Phone: (703)620-3660
Toll-Free: 888-CEC-SPED
Fax: (703)264-9494
E-mail: service@cec.sped.org
Home Page: http://www.cec.sped.org

• 8546 • **Business Award**
To honor a business or corporation that has promoted and provided for the enhancement, awareness, and employment of individuals with disabilities or who are gifted and talented in order to promote and support their full participa-

Awards are arranged in alphabetical order below their administering organizations

tion in the community. A plaque with a citation is presented annually at the CEC convention in April. Established in 1992.

• 8547 • CEC Leadership Award

To recognize CEC members who have made a contribution to CEC at the local, state or provincial, national, and/or international levels over an extended period of time. A plaque with a citation is presented annually at the CEC Convention in April. Established in 1988. Formerly: (2004) CEC Outstanding Contributor Award.

• 8548 • CEC Research Award

To recognize individuals, groups of individuals, or institutions and agencies whose research has contributed to the body of knowledge about the education of exceptional children and youth. A plaque with a citation is presented annually at the CEC convention in April. Established in 1989.

• 8549 • Susan Phillips Gorin Award

To honor a regular member of The Council for Exceptional Children who has demonstrated exemplary personal and professional qualities while making outstanding contributions to the Student Council for Exceptional Children and to exceptional children. A plaque with a resolution is presented annually at the CEC Convention in April. Established in 1982 by the Student CEC Board of Governors in recognition of the contributions of Susan Gorin. Sponsored by the Student Council for Exceptional Children.

• 8550 • Graduation Awards

To recognize graduating student CEC members who have made outstanding contributions to persons with exceptionalities and the Student Council for Exceptional Children. Each year, one undergraduate and one graduate student are honored. Established in 1994 by the Student CEC Board of Governors. Sponsored by the Student Council for Exceptional Children.

• 8551 • Clarissa Hug Teacher of the Year Award

To honor a CEC member who is an outstanding teacher of children with disabilities and/or children who are gifted and talented. A plaque with a citation is presented annually at the CEC Convention in April. Established in 1984 in honor of Clarissa Hug, a member who taught children with disabilities for many years. The recipient receives a $500 cash award and a $500 gift certificate.

• 8552 • Outstanding Graduate Student Member of the Year Award

To recognize a current graduate student member of CEC who has contributed a great deal of time, energy, and support to the Student Council for Exceptional Children and to exceptional children. A plaque with a resolution is presented annually at the CEC Convention in April. Established in 1982 by the Student CEC Board of Governors. Sponsored by the Student Council for Exceptional Children.

• 8553 • Outstanding Public Service Award

To honor persons from the United States or Canada whose actions in the governmental and political arena have been of national significance for individuals who are disabled and/or gifted. A plaque with a citation is presented to the recipient(s) at an appropriate time. Established in 1963.

• 8554 • Outstanding Student CEC Undergraduate Member of the Year Award

To recognize a current undergraduate student member of CEC who has contributed a great deal of time, energy, and support to the Student Council for Exceptional Children and to exceptional children. A plaque with a resolution is presented annually at the CEC Convention in the spring. Established in 1982 by the Student CEC Board of Governors. Sponsored by the Student Council for Exceptional Children.

• 8555 • J. E. Wallace Wallin Lifetime Achievement Award

To honor a professional who has made significant contributions to the education of children with disabilities. A plaque with a citation is presented annually at the CEC Convention in April. Established in 1963 with an initial contribution by Dr. Wallin, a pioneer in the development of clinical psychology and special education. Formerly: (2004) J. E. Wallace Wallin Education of Handicapped Children Award.

• 8556 •

Council for Health and Human Services Ministries, United Church of Christ
Bryan W. Sickbert, Exec.Dir.
700 Prospect Ave.
Cleveland, OH 44115
Phone: (216)736-2253
Fax: (216)736-2251
E-mail: sickbert@chhsm.org
Home Page: http://www.chhsm.org

• 8557 • Hall of Fame

For recognition of dedication to the ideas of Diakonia, for compassionate services to persons in need, for a particular awareness of the future role of health and healing in the ministry of the church, and for faithfulness in responding to the love of Jesus. A person or organization recognized as having made outstanding contributions to the work of health and human service ministries is eligible. Candidates are not limited to members of the Council for Health and Human Service Ministries. A plaque is awarded annually at the council's annual meeting. Established in 1963. Additional awards are presented by the council to recognize trustees, directors, executives, and innovative programs of member agencies.

• 8558 •

Council for Learning Disabilities
Andrea Falzarano, Exec.Dir.
PO Box 4014
Leesburg, VA 20177-8187
Phone: (571)258-1010
Fax: (571)258-1011
E-mail: afalzarano@mcs-amc.com
Home Page: http://www.cldinternational.org

• 8559 • Floyd G. Hudson Service Award

Recognizes outstanding performance and commitment to individuals with learning disabilities. Professionals who are not necessarily special education classroom teachers are eligible. One award is given in each of the seven CLD regions annually. A complimentary one year membership in the Council for Learning Disabilities is awarded.

• 8560 • Outstanding Researcher Award

For recognition of outstanding manuscript-length papers on learning disabilities based on doctoral dissertations or master's studies completed in the last five years. A certificate and cash award are presented annually. In addition, papers will be considered for publication in the *Learning Disability Quarterly*.

• 8561 • Outstanding Teacher Award

To encourage and recognize quality instruction in the area of learning disabilities. Nominees are selected from state and local CLD chapters, which develop their own criteria for selection of an outstanding teacher from their area. Certificates are awarded annually to one or more recipients.

• 8562 •

Council for the Advancement of Science Writing
Diane McGurgan, Contact
PO Box 910
Hedgesville, WV 25427
Phone: (304)754-5077
Fax: (304)754-5076
E-mail: diane@nasw.org
Home Page: http://www.casw.org

• 8563 • Rennie Taylor/Alton Blakeslee Fellowship in Science Writing

To provide for both journalists and journalism students of proven ability. Journalists with two years of experience who wish to learn science writing receive priority in selection. Such applicants should be employed by daily newspapers, wire services, news magazines, radio stations, or television stations or networks. Students must have undergraduate degrees in science or journalism, and prove to the satisfaction of a selection committee that they have the ability to pursue a career in science writing. Fellows may attend school full-time or part-time. From FOUR fellows receive up to $2,000 each. Awarded annually. The fellowships honor the late Rennie Taylor, a science writer for Associated Press, and Alton Blakeslee, former science editor of Associated Press. Formerly: (1996) Nate

Haseltine Memorial Fellowship in Science Writing.

• 8564 •
Council for Wisconsin Writers
Michael Bowen, Pres.
PO Box 55222
Madison, WI 53705
Phone: (414)351-1707
E-mail: mbowen@foleylaw.com
Home Page: http://www.wisconsinwriters.org

• 8565 • Annual Awards Competition
To recognize outstanding Wisconsin writing of literary merit. Residents for six months or more of the State of Wisconsin are eligible. The entries must have been published during the preceding year. Monetary prizes of $500 to $1000 are awarded in the following categories: (1) Poetry Collection; (2) Juvenile Fiction Book; (3) Children's Picture Book; (4) Outdoor Writing; (5) Scholarly Work; (6) Short Nonfiction; (7) Drama; (8) Book Length Fiction; (9) Short Fiction; (10) Book Length Nonfiction; and (11) Juvenile Nonfiction Book. Awarded annually. Established in 1964.

• 8566 •
Council of Administrators of Special Education
Dr. Luann L. Purcell, Exec.Dir.
1005 State University Dr.
Fort Valley, GA 31030
Phone: (478)825-7667
Toll-Free: 800-585-1753
Fax: (478)825-7811
E-mail: lpurcell@bellsouth.net
Home Page: http://www.casecec.org

• 8567 • CASE Outstanding Administrator Award
To recognize individuals who demonstrate outstanding leadership in the field of special education administration. Persons from the United States or Canada who administer programs at any level for handicapped and/or gifted students are eligible. A plaque is awarded annually at the convention. Established in 1986.

• 8568 • Harrie M. Selenick - CASE Distinguished Service Award
To recognize outstanding career leaders in the administration of programs for handicapped and/or gifted students. Persons from the United States or Canada who are or have been special education administrators are eligible. A monetary award and a plaque are awarded annually at the annual convention. Established in 1984 in honor of Dr. Harrie M. Selznick, distinguished career leader in special education administration.

• 8569 •
Council of Chief State School Officers
G. Thomas Houlihan, Exec.Dir.
One Massachusetts Ave. NW, Ste. 700
Washington, DC 20001-1431
Phone: (202)336-7000
Fax: (202)408-8072
E-mail: info@ccsso.org
Home Page: http://www.ccsso.org

• 8570 • Distinguished Service Award
To recognize an outstanding and nationally recognized individual for outstanding leadership in the cause of education. An original artwork is awarded annually. Established in 1955.

• 8571 • National Teacher of the Year
To reward excellence in teaching. Selection is made from among this country's more than one million teachers. The search begins with the State Teacher of the Year program. Each school in the nation, elementary through high school, nominates one of its teachers for the State Teacher of the Year award. Selection is based on a candidate who has a sound professional education, successful teaching experience, a love of children and other qualities essential to good teaching. A committee chooses from four finalists. The national winner is honored at a White House ceremony at which a Crystal Apple, the symbol of excellence, is awarded. Established in 1952. Sponsored by ING Foundation.

• 8572 •
Council of Educational Facility Planners, International
Thomas A. Kube, Exec.Dir./CEO
9180 E Desert Cove Dr., Ste. 104
Scottsdale, AZ 85260-6231
Phone: (480)391-0840
Fax: (480)391-0940
E-mail: contact@cefpi.org
Home Page: http://www.cefpi.org

Formerly: National Council on Schoolhouse Construction.

• 8573 • Planner of the Year
This is the highest and most distinguished honor conferred by the council. Members in all categories who are in good standing are eligible. The activities upon which the nomination is based shall have produced a positive and significant regional, national, or international impact on educational planning during the preceding five years. Individuals who have previously received the Planner of the Year Award are not eligible. A trophy/plaque is awarded during the annual international conference. Established in 1967.

• 8574 •
Council of Fashion Designers of America
Stan Herman, Pres.
1412 Broadway, Ste. 2006
New York, NY 10018
Phone: (212)302-1821
Fax: (212)768-0515
Home Page: http://www.cfda.com

• 8575 • CFDA Fashion Awards
To recognize outstanding contributions made to American fashion by individuals from all areas of the arts and industry. Awards are given in such varied fields as publishing, retailing, photography, jewelry, and television. The Eugenia Sheppard Award is presented for fashion journalism. The Perry Ellis Award recognizes new talent. Awards are presented annually. Established in 1982.

• 8576 • Lifetime Achievement Award
To recognize an individual who has made an outstanding contribution to American fashion over his or her lifetime. Awarded annually.

• 8577 •
Council of Graduate Schools
Debra W. Stewart, Pres.
1 Dupont Cir. NW, Ste. 430
Washington, DC 20036-1173
Phone: (202)223-3791
Fax: (202)331-7157
E-mail: cflagg@cgs.nche.edu
Home Page: http://www.cgsnet.org

Formerly: (1987) Council of Graduate Schools in the United States.

• 8578 • Gustave O. Arlt Award in the Humanities
To recognize a young scholar-teacher in the humanities. The recipient must be teaching in a North American university, must have earned a doctorate within seven years of the award date, and must have written a book of scholarly importance. Nominations of members must be made by members of the Council of Graduate Schools. A stipend of $1,000 and a certificate are awarded annually. Established in 1972 to honor Gustave O. Arlt, CGS' first president.

• 8579 •
Council of Logistics Management
Mark Richards, Pres.
2805 Butterfield Rd., No. 200
Oak Brook, IL 60523
Phone: (630)574-0985
Fax: (630)574-0989
E-mail: clmadmin@clm1.org
Home Page: http://www.clm1.org/

Formerly: (1985) National Council of Physical Distribution Management.

• 8580 • Distinguished Service Award
To recognize an individual who has made a significant contribution to the art and science of logistics management. All individuals whose responsibilities involve them in logistics are eligible. This includes industrial personnel with responsibilities in a functional area of logistics or distribution, warehouse personnel, carrier personnel, educators, editors, or anyone who has made a significant contribution to the advancement of logistics. A person need not be a member of the Council to be nominated. Individuals not eligible for consideration for the current year's award include employees of the Council of Logistics Management, members of the Exec-

utive Committee of the Council of Logistics Management while serving in that capacity, the annual conference program chairperson while serving in that capacity, and individuals employed by firms under contract to the Council of Logistics Management in the year that the award is given. Nominations must be received by March 31. A plaque and an honorary life membership are awarded annually at the conference. Established in 1965 in memory of John Drury Sheahan, one of the founding partners of the New York consulting firm of Drake Sheahan/Stewart Dougall. Formerly: (1981) John Drury Sheahan Award.

• 8581 • Doctoral Dissertation Award

To provide recognition for an outstanding completed doctoral dissertation in logistics, inventory management, transportation management, materials management, and related fields. It is intended that the award will encourage research leading to advancement of the theory and practice of logistics management. Candidates must apply by March 31. A grant of $5,000 is awarded annually at the Council's conference. Established in 1973.

• 8582 •

Council of Residential Specialists
430 N Michigan Ave., 3rd Fl.
Chicago, IL 60611-4092
Toll-Free: 800-462-8841
Fax: (312)329-8551
E-mail: crshelp@crs.com
Home Page: http://www.crs.com

Formerly: National Institute of Real Estate Brokers.

• 8583 • Certified Residential Specialist Designation

For recognition of excellence in the field of residential sales. It is the highest professional designation awarded to realtors in the residential sales field. Member of the Council must maintain active Realtor or Realtor Associate membership in their local board/state association to be eligible. To qualify, certain production, education, and elective requirement must be met. A plaque, a pin and national exposure are awarded when merited.

• 8584 • Medallion Award

To recognize individuals for length of membership and outstanding service to the Council. Applicants must have 15 years of continuous Council membership, 10 years of continuous membership in their state CRS Chapter, and accumulate elective points for activities such as writing articles for *The Residential Specialist,* serving as a committee member or chair, serving as a chapter officer, etc. Awarded annually at the Annual Conference and Expo.

• 8585 •

Council of Scientific Society Presidents
Martin A. Apple Ph.D., Pres.
1155 16th St. NW
Washington, DC 20036
Phone: (202)872-6230
Phone: (202)872-4452
Fax: (202)872-4079
E-mail: cssp@acs.org
Home Page: http://www.cssp.us

• 8586 • CSSP Educational Research Award

To recognize individuals for outstanding achievement in original educational research that has measurably improved the learning and understanding of students.

• 8587 • Leadership Citation

To recognize individuals for exceptional leadership in the past year that benefited science. Award is presented semiannually. Formerly: (1996) Chair's Citation.

• 8588 • Sagan Award for Public Understanding of Science

To recognize individuals who have combined research and education to increase the public understanding and appreciation of science. Award is presented annually. Established in 1993 after Carl Sagan, astronomer.

• 8589 • Support of Science Award

To recognize an individual for dedicated support of U.S. science, including support of science and mathematics education, free scientific communication, and basic research. Awarded annually. Established in 1983.

• 8590 •

Council on Economic Priorities
30 Irving Pl.
New York, NY 10003
Phone: (212)420-1133
Toll-Free: 800-729-4237
Fax: (212)420-0988
E-mail: tknowlton@cepnyc.org

• 8591 • Corporate Conscience Award

To honor exemplary corporate social and environmental performance and to acknowledge those companies—both in the U.S. and internationally—that encourage others by their example. All corporations may nominate themselves and will be accepted as nominees according to standards developed in CEP's *Shopping for a Better World Series.* The final vote is by an independent judges' panel. Awards may be presented in the following categories: Community Partnership, Employee Empowerment, Environmental Stewardship, Most Improved, and Social Mission. Established in 1987.

• 8592 • Human Rights Award

No information was available at time of publication.

• 8593 • Pioneer Award

To recognize ground-breaking initiatives.

• 8594 •

Council on Foreign Relations
Elise Carlson Lewis, VP/Dir.
58 E 68th St.
New York, NY 10021
Phone: (212)434-9400
Phone: (212)434-9888
Fax: (212)434-9800
E-mail: communications@cfr.org
Home Page: http://www.cfr.org

• 8595 • International Affairs Fellowship Program

To offer young men and women an opportunity to broaden their expertise in the field of international affairs. The distinctive character of the International Affairs Fellowships lies in the provision of contrasting experiences for young professionals working at the nexus of policy research and policy action. Thus, academics, corporate executives, and other professionals from the private sector are enabled to apply their disciplines in a policy-oriented environment, and government officials are encouraged to consider problems in a scholarly atmosphere free from the pressures of decision-making. The program is open to all men and women holding American citizenship and between the ages of 27 and 35 (inclusive) in the calendar year of their application. The program does not fund pre-or postdoctoral scholarly research, work toward a degree, nor the completion of projects on which substantial progress has been made prior to the fellowship period. The competition is multidisciplinary; past recipients include scholars and practitioners representing the fields of political science, economics, history, anthropology, sociology, psychology, philosophy, law, journalism, business, and government. A fellowship for one year is awarded annually. Established in 1967. Sponsored by Hitachi, Ltd.,.

• 8596 •

Council on Foundations
Dorothy Ridings, Pres./CEO
1828 L St. NW, Ste. 300
Washington, DC 20036
Phone: (202)466-6512
Fax: (202)785-3926
E-mail: webmaster@cof.org
Home Page: http://www.cof.org

• 8597 • Distinguished Grant Maker Award

To recognize an individual for career achievement in philanthropy. The winner is the cover story of the March/April edition of Foundation News and Commentary. A sculpture is awarded each year at the annual conference. Established in 1984.

• 8598 • Henry Hampton Award for Excellence in Film and Digital Media

Annual award named after Henry Hampton, best known for his work which celebrated the resilience and nobility of the human spirit in the face of adversity and appealed to audiences throughout the world. Established in 2002.

• 8599 • Paul Ylvisaker Award for Public Policy Engagement
Recognizes a foundation that has demonstrated excellence in affecting public policy by using creative and effective strategies. A sculpture is awarded annually. Established in 2002 named after Paul Ylvisaker.

• 8600 • Wilmer Shields Rich Awards for Excellence in Communications
To encourage foundations to publish communications vehicles to highlight the importance of foundation accountability and communications and to provide models of excellence. The awards program is open only to members of the Council on Foundations. Awards are presented in the following categories: newsletters, magazines, public information campaigns, guidelines and special reports. Awarded each year at the annual conference. Established in 1983 in honor of Wilmer Shields Rich, the first executive director of the Council on Foundations, for her recognition of the need for public accountability by foundations.

• 8601 • Robert W. Scrivner Award for Creative Grantmaking
For recognition of creativity by an individual grantmaker in the philanthropic field. Individuals (not institutions) from private, community, or corporate foundations that are members of the council may be nominated. A monetary prize of $10,000, used for the recipient's professional enrichment and development, and a sculpture are awarded each year at the annual conference. Established in 1984 as a memorial to Robert W. Scrivner, executive director of the Rockefeller Family Fund.

• 8602 •
Council on Governmental Ethics Laws
Tony Kramer, Exec.Dir.
PO Box 417
Locust Grove, VA 22508
Phone: (540)972-3662
Fax: (540)972-3693
E-mail: info@cogel.org
Home Page: http://www.cogel.org

• 8603 • COGEL Award
To recognize distinguished service in the promotion of ethical conduct among public officials and candidates for office. Nominations may be submitted by May 30. There are no eligibility criteria. A plaque is awarded at the annual conference. Established in 1983.

• 8604 • Outstanding Service Award
To recognize outstanding service to the Council by a COGEL member, based on service to COGEL beyond expected service to the organization. Nominations must be submitted by May 30. Only members or employees of member agencies of COGEL are eligible. A plaque is awarded at the Annual Conference.

• 8605 •
Council on Hemispheric Affairs
Laurence R. Birns, Dir.
1250 Connecticut Ave. NW, Ste. 1C
Washington, DC 20036
Phone: (202)223-4975
Toll-Free: 888-922-9261
Fax: (202)223-4979
E-mail: coha@coha.org
Home Page: http://www.coha.org

• 8606 • Bernt Carlesson Memorial Award
Recognizes distinguished service to Latin America. Inquire for application details.

• 8607 •
Council on International Nontheatrical Events
1112 16th St. NW Ste. 510
Washington, DC 20036
Phone: (202)785-1136
Fax: (202)785-4114
E-mail: info@cine.org
Home Page: http://www.cine.org

• 8608 • CINE Eagle Award
To recognize excellence in the production of amateur and pre-professional films and videos through recognition and education. Amateur student and youth-made films are eligible. CINE Eagle Competitions are held twice annually. Winners are published in the CINE Annual Yearbook of Film and Video Festivals and Events. Established in 1957.

• 8609 • CINE Golden Eagle Award
To recognize excellence in the field of film and video production. Producers, sponsors, and filmmakers may submit films. The entry deadlines are in the Spring by February 1 or 15 and in the Fall by August 1 or 15. Judging is a peer review process performed in two stages by volunteer professionals in film and video production. A Golden Eagle Certificate is awarded to each selected professional title. Awarded twice annually. Established in 1957.

• 8610 • CINE Master's Series Award
Presented once a year, the Master's Series Awards are selected from all Golden Eagle or Eagle winners for the year. Awards are presented in three categories - Broadcast, Non-Broadcast, and Amateur/Pre-Professional. The highest level Cine winner, Master]s Series Award will be announced at the annual Cine Golden Eagle Awards event. A trophy and other gifts will be presented.

• 8611 •
Council on Technology Teacher Education
Dr. Michael DeMiranda, Pres.
1914 Association Dr.
Reston, VA 20191
Phone: (703)860-2100
Fax: (757)683-5227
E-mail: mdemira@cahs.colostate.edu
Home Page: http://www.teched.vt.edu/ctte
Formerly: (1986) American Council on Industrial Arts Teacher Education.

• 8612 • Technology Teacher Educator of the Year
To recognize an outstanding technology teacher educator. A plaque is awarded annually. Established in 1955. Formerly: (1986) Industrial Arts Teacher Educator of the Year.

• 8613 •
Count Dracula Society
Dr. Donald A. Reed, Pres.
334 W 54th St.
Los Angeles, CA 90037

• 8614 • Mrs. Inez M. Fauria Award
For recognition of outstanding services to the Society. A Count Dracula statuette is awarded annually. Established in 1974.

• 8615 • Mrs. Ann Radcliffe Awards
For outstanding achievements in television, cinema, and literature in the areas of fantasy, horror, terror, and science fiction. Awards are given in the following categories: Most Outrageous Fright Film of the Year, Fright Film of the Year, Career Achievement - Literary, Career Achievement - Film Performance, Vampire of the Year Award, Book of the Year, Career Achievement in Directing and Producing, and Career Achievement Filmmaker. A scroll is awarded annually. Established in 1962.

• 8616 • President Dr. Donald A. Reed Award
For recognition of unselfish service to the Society. A Count Dracula statuette is awarded. Established in 1962.

• 8617 • Rev. Dr. Montague Summers Memorial Award
To recognize an individual for outstanding achievements in the areas of horror films and gothic literature. A gold trophy is awarded annually. Established in 1962 by Dr. Reed.

• 8618 • Horace Walpole Gold Medal
To recognize an individual for achievements in fantasy, horror, terror, and science fiction literature and films in any medium. A gold medal and a Count Dracula statuette are awarded annually. Established in 1962 by the Noble Order of Count Dracula.

• 8619 •
Country Music Association
Edwin Benson, Pres.
1 Music Cir. S
Nashville, TN 37203-4312
Phone: (615)244-2840
Fax: (615)726-0314
E-mail: info@cmaworld.com
Home Page: http://www.cmaworld.com/

• 8620 • **Country Music Association Awards**
For recognition in the field of country music. Awards are given in the following categories: Entertainer of the Year - the highest award to a performer displaying competence in all aspects of the entertainment field, Single of the Year, Album of the Year, Song of the Year, Female Vocalist of the Year, Male Vocalist of the Year, Vocal Group of the Year, Vocal Duo of the Year, Vocal Event of the Year, Musician of the Year, Music Video of the Year, and Horizon Award. Crystal awards are presented to the performers annually. Established in 1967.

• 8621 • **Country Music Hall of Fame**
To recognize an individual for outstanding contributions to the advancement of country music, for definitive leadership in a field of country music activity, for an inspirational effect on others, and for the indelibility of the impact of his or her contributions. A bronze plaque is awarded and a portrait and tribute are made in the Hall of Fame in Nashville. Awarded annually. Established in 1961.

• 8622 •
Country Music Showcase International
Harold L. Luick, CEO
PO Box 368
Carlisle, IA 50047
Phone: (515)989-3748
Fax: (515)989-0235
E-mail: haroldl@cmshowcase.org
Home Page: http://www.cmshowcase.org

• 8623 • **Hall of Fame**
To recognize CMSI members for their contributions of time, talent, and volunteer participation to make the fund raisers, achievement of others, and professional development projects a success. Individuals may be nominated by the Board of Directors, President, Vice President and/or officers. Established in 1984 in memory of Lee Mace.

• 8624 • **Life-Time Membership Award**
To recognize a CMSI songwriter or entertainer for having demonstrated an unlimited amount of energy, talent, devotion, and dedication; for sharing of time and knowledge; and for providing help, information, guidance, and encouragement to other songwriters and entertainers through the years. Nominations may be submitted by any officer or member of the Showcase. A certificate is awarded annually. Established in 1984. Additional information is available from Barbara A. Lancaster.

• 8625 •
CPR Institute for Dispute Resolution
Joseph T. McLaughlin, Chm.
366 Madison Ave.
New York, NY 10017
Phone: (212)949-6490
Fax: (212)949-8859
E-mail: info@cpradr.org
Home Page: http://www.cpradr.org

Formerly: (1995) Center for Public Resources - CPR Legal Program.

• 8626 • **CPR Institute for Dispute Resolution Awards for Excellence and Innovation in Alternative Dispute Resolution**
To honor outstanding application of alternative dispute resolution, dispute prevention, and litigation management techniques and to recognize outstanding scholarship in the field of alternative dispute resolution. The focus is on innovative methods that address the resolution, prevention, or creative management of major disputes involving public or business institutions. Lawyers, judges, law teachers, and students are eligible. The deadline is November 15. The following awards are presented: for professional articles, first prize - $4,000 and second prize - $2,000; for student articles, first prize - $2,000 and second prize - $1,000; Book Prize - $4,000; and Practical Achievement Honors - for outstanding practical achievements by companies, law firms, court systems, other organizations, and individuals in the use of innovative methods and systems. Awarded annually at the winter meeting in New York City. Established in 1983. Sponsored by CIGNA Corporation.

• 8627 •
***CQ*, The Radio Amateur's Journal**
Dick Ross, Ed.
25 Newbridge Rd.
Hicksville, NY 11801
Phone: (516)681-2922
Toll-Free: 800-853-9797
Fax: (516)681-2926
E-mail: cq@cq-amateur-radio.com
Home Page: http://www.cq-amateur-radio.com

• 8628 • **5 Band WAZ Award**
In recognition of achievement for those who can prove contact with the 40 zones of the world on the 80, 40, 20, 15, and 10 meter bands. Applicants must be a holder of any 40-zone WAZ. The award is offered to for any combination of CW, SSB, RTTY, or for other mode contact, Mixed Mode only. Awarded annually.

• 8629 • ***CQ* DX Awards**
To promote multi-band usage and special operating skills, special endorsements are available. The *CQ* CW DX Award and *CQ* DX SSB Award are issued to any amateur station submitting proof of contact with 100 or more countries. Country endorsements for 150, 200, 250, 275, 300, 310, and 320 countries are issued. For more information, contact Award Manager Billy Williams, PO Box 9673, Jacksonville, FL 32208.

• 8630 • ***CQ* DX Honor Roll**
To recognize all stations with a total of 275 countries or more. For more information, contact Award Manager Billy Williams, PO Box 9673, Jacksonville, FL 32208.

• 8631 • **DX Hall of Fame**
To recognize members who have made major contributions to the hobby. Nominations are made through the *CQ* DX Awards Advisory Committee and require the positive vote of 75 percent of the Committee for acceptance. DX clubs or individuals may suggest names to the DX editor or any member of the Committee for consideration. Established in 1967.

• 8632 • **USA-CA Award**
To recognize confirmed two-way radio contacts with specified numbers of U.S. counties. The USA-CA is issued in seven different classes: each a separate achievement as endorsed on the basic certificate by use of special seals for higher class. Available to all licensed amateurs everywhere in the world. In addition, a special United States of America Counties Award is available to SWL's on a heard basis.

• 8633 • **Worked All Zones Award**
To recognize any licensed amateur station presenting proof of contact with the 40 zones of the world. Operators must prove that they have QSL cards from all 40 worldwide zones established by *CQ* magazine. Awards are given in the following categories: All Single Side Band (Mixed Frequencies); C.W. and Single Side Band (Mixed Frequencies); All C.W. (Mixed Frequencies); All Phone (Single Side Band and AM) Mixed Frequencies; Single Band - All Phone (80 Meters, 40 Meters, 20 Meters, 15 Meters, 10 Meters), Single Band, and all C.W. (80 Meters, 40 Meters, 20 Meters, 15 Meters, and 10 Meters); WARC Bands; RTTY; 160 Meters; Satellite; and 5 Band Worked All Zones. A certificate for achievement in any one category is awarded to an individual one time only. Additional information is available from the Award Manager, Jim Dionne, K1MEM, 31 De Marco Rd., Sudbury, MA 01776.

• 8634 • **WPX Award**
To recognize the accomplishments of confirmed QSO's with the many prefixes used by amateurs throughout the world. Separate distinctively marked certificates are available for two-way SSB, CW and mixed modes, the VPX Award is available for shortwave listeners, and the WPNX Award for novices. Certificates are issued for the following modes and number of prefixes: mixed (C.W. and SSB/phone only), 400 prefixes confirmed; C.W., 300 prefixes confirmed; and two-way S.S.B., 300 prefixes confirmed. Separate applications are required for each mode. Prefix endorsements are issued for each 50 additional prefixes submitted. For more information, contact Award Manager Norm Koch, K6ZDL, PO Box 593, Clovis, NM 88101.

• 8635 • **WPX Award of Excellence**
This is the ultimate award for the prefix DXer. The requirements are 1,000 prefixes mixed

mode, 600 prefixes s.s.b., 600 prefixes c.w., all 6 continental endorsements, and the 5 band endorsements 80-10 meters. For more information, contact Award Manager Norm Koch, K6ZDL, PO Box 593, Clovis, NM 88101.

• 8636 • **WPX Honor Roll**
To recognize operators and stations that maintain a high standing in confirmed, current prefixes. A minimum of 600 prefixes is required to be eligible for the Honor Roll. For more information, contact Program Manager Norm Koch, K6ZDL, PO Box 593, Clovis, NM 88101.

• 8637 •
Cranial Academy
Sidney N. Dunn, Exec.Dir.
8202 Clearvista Pkwy., No. 9-D
Indianapolis, IN 46256
Phone: (317)594-0411
Fax: (317)594-9299
E-mail: cranacad@aol.com
Home Page: http://
www.cranialacademy.com

• 8638 • **Exceptional Service Award**
To recognize an outstanding contribution in research, teaching, or practice. A plaque is awarded. Established in 1989. Formerly: Distinguished Service Award.

• 8639 • **Fellow of The Cranial Academy Award**
To recognize outstanding physicians and to honor members of the Cranial Academy who have distinguished themselves by providing exemplary leadership, dedication to teaching, and advocating and advancing osteopathy, specifically Cranial Osteopathy. Established in 1995.

• 8640 • **Honorary Life Member**
To recognize devoted service to the academy and/or to the science of osteopathy. A certificate is awarded when merited. Formerly: Meritorious Service Award.

• 8641 • **Sutherland Memorial Lecture**
To honor an outstanding member of the academy. The awardee is invited to present a lecture at the Cranial Academy Conference and receives a plaque of a sculpture of cranial bones and sacral bones balanced on a scale mounted on dark walnut. Awarded annually. Established in 1957.

• 8642 •
Creative Glass Center of America
Beth Lipman, Artist Program Mgr.
1501 Glasstown Rd.
Millville, NJ 08332-1566
Phone: (856)825-6800
Toll-Free: 800-998-4552
Fax: (856)825-2410
E-mail: mail@wheatonvillage.org
Home Page: http://
www.creativeglasscenter.com

• 8643 • **Fellowship**
To provide the time, facilities, and resources to allow gifted artists the freedom to explore and create their ideas in glass. Applicants must be at least 21 years of age and have basic hot glass working skills. Preference is given to artists who have several years of experience outside the educational environment. Recipients are given 24 hour access to glassmaking facilities, free housing, and a monthly stipend Twelve fellowships are given per year. Applications accepted annually in the fall, call for guidelines. Established in 1983.

• 8644 •
Creative Studies Alumni Foundation
Gary Gorski, Contact
% Creative Connections Network
Chase Hall, Rm. 244
Buffalo State College
1300 Elmwood Ave.
Buffalo, NY 14222-1095
Phone: (716)878-6223
Fax: (716)878-4040
E-mail: gmgorski@aol.com

• 8645 • **Achievement Award**
To recognize service to a program which has been influential in the lives of its students and instructors. Any active student in the master's program who has completed at least one full semester and all graduates of the program are eligible for the award. The award itself has three components: (1) recognition on the plaque listing all recipients of the award; (2) an engraved plaque presented to the recipients; and (3) a check for $300. Awarded annually. Established in 1984.

• 8646 •
Creative Writing Program
Ryan Jacobs, Admin. Associate
Dept. of English
Stanford University
Stanford, CA 94305-2087
Phone: (650)725-1208
Fax: (415)723-3679
E-mail: vfhess@stanford.edu
Home Page: http://www.stanford.edu/dept/english/cw

• 8647 • **Wallace E. Stegner Fellowships in Creative Writing**
To recognize promising writers who may benefit by a two years' residence at the University and by the instruction and criticism of the staff of the writing program. Writers may apply between September 1 and December 1. A annual stipend of $22,000 and the required tuition of about $6,000 are awarded. Established in 1947 by Wallace Stegner. Each year there are five fellowships in fiction and five in poetry awarded.

• 8648 •
Crime Writers of Canada
Cheryl Freedman, Sec.
3007 Kingston Rd., Box 113
Toronto, ON, Canada M1M 1P1
Phone: (416)597-9938
E-mail: info@crimewriterscanada.com
Home Page: http://
www.crimewriterscanada.com

• 8649 • **Arthur Ellis Award**
To recognize the best crime-related book published by a writer who resides in Canada or a Canadian living abroad in the preceding year regardless of language, setting, or place of publication. Awards are given for Best Crime Novel by a previously published author, Best Crime First Novel by a previously unpublished writer, Best non-fiction (formerly Best True Crime), Best Genre Criticism or Reference, Best Crime Short-Story published during the year, Best Play, Best Juvenile Crime book, Best Crime book published (Fiction, True Crime or Related Subjects, Publication in French). Contact the secretary about the deadline for submissions (for the previous year). Awards for the best in each category are presented at the Crime Writers of Canada annual awards dinner in Toronto in June. A trophy is given annually for each category. Established in 1984.

• 8650 •
Croatian Philatelic Society
Eckrem Spahich, Exec.Dir.
PO Box 696
Fritch, TX 79036-0696
Phone: (806)857-0129
E-mail: eck.spahich@croatianstamps.com
Home Page: http://
www.croatianstamps.com

• 8651 • **Best Written and Researched Article**
To encourage original research in Croatian and Balkan philately and numismatics. Members may submit articles by October 15. A monetary award is presented annually. Established in 1987.

• 8652 •
Crohn's and Colitis Foundation of Canada
Michael J. Howorth, Natl. Exec.Dir.
600-60 St. Clair Ave. E.
Toronto, ON, Canada M4T 1N5
Phone: (416)920-5035
Toll-Free: 800-387-1479
Fax: (416)929-0364
E-mail: ccfc@ccfc.ca
Home Page: http://www.ccfc.ca

Formerly: Canadian Foundation for Ileitis and Colitis.

• 8653 • **CCFC Book Prize**
For recognition of achievement in undergraduate study in the field of gastroenterology. Undergraduate medical students of a recognized Canadian University in the Faculty of Medicine are eligible. A book or books in gastroenterology

up to the amount of $125 are awarded annually at the close of the academic year. Formerly: CFIC Book Prize.

• 8654 • CCFC/CAG Student Research Award

For recognition of achievement in undergraduate research in the field of gastroenterology. Undergraduate students of a recognized Canadian University are eligible. Additional information is available from CCFC or Canadian Association of Gastroenterologists. Formerly: CFIC/CAG Student Research Award.

• 8655 • Finkelstein Award

To recognize a Canadian who has made an outstanding contribution to the field of inflammatory bowel disease. The award is intended to congratulate an individual whose work reflects excellence, either through a particular accomplishment or through continuous efforts over time. The award winner has a student scholarship named in their honor, and a special token is awarded in recognition of their contribution. Awarded annually. Established in 1997.

• 8656 •
Walter Cronkite Endowment for Journalism and Telecommunication
Walter Cronkite School of Journalism and Mass Communication
Arizona State University
Tempe, AZ 85287-1305
Phone: (480)965-5011
Phone: (480)965-0798
Fax: (480)965-7041
E-mail: jtschool@asu.edu

Formerly: (2003) Walter Cronkite Endowment for Journalism and Telecommunication.

• 8657 • Walter Cronkite Award for Excellence in Journalism and Mass Communication

For recognition of outstanding contributions to the media fields. Individuals who have evidenced excellence during the years that they have been associated with the media may be nominated. The endowment selection committee reviews the nominations and makes the selection. A plaque is awarded annually in the fall. Established in 1983. Formerly: (2003) Walter Cronkite Award for Excellence in Journalism and Telecommunication.

• 8658 •
Crop Science Society of America
Luther Smith, Exec.Dir.
677 S. Segoe Rd.
Madison, WI 53711
Phone: (608)273-8080
Fax: (608)273-2021
E-mail: lsmith@agronomy.org
Home Page: http://www.crops.org

• 8659 • Crop Science Award

To recognize outstanding work in crop science. Awarded annually. Established in 1957, and administered by the Crop Science Society since 1975.

• 8660 • Crop Science International Activity Award

For recognition of creativity and innovation in bringing about specific changes in practices, products, and/or programs in the crops area at the international level. Nominees must be active members of the Crop Science Society of America, and the recipient must be nominated by another active member of the Society. An honorarium and a certificate are awarded annually. Established in 1990.

• 8661 • Crop Science Teaching Award

Focuses on traits that characterize excellence in resident classroom teaching of crop science at the undergraduate and graduate levels. A certificate and honorarium of $1,000 are awarded annually.

• 8662 • Fellow of the Crop Science Society of America

For recognition of outstanding work in crop science. Active members of the Society for a total of at least 10 years are eligible. Awarded annually. Established in 1985.

• 8663 • Fred V. Grau Turfgrass Science Award

Recognizes significant career contributions in turf grass science during the most recent 15 years. A certificate and honorarium of $1,000 are awarded annually.

• 8664 • Honorary Member

Recognizes outstanding service to soil science by persons who are not members of the society.

• 8665 • Frank N. Meyer Memorial Medal

To recognize an individual for outstanding service of at least ten years to the national plant germplasm program. The individual selected shall have met the following principal criteria: been an effective proponent of national or international programs for collecting, maintaining, and utilizing plant germplasm; led or participated in major plant explorations; demonstrated superior ability to evaluate new plant introductions; developed techniques for preservation, evaluation, and utilization of plant germplasm; and developed concepts for assessing ecogeographic distribution of genetic diversity. An engraved bronze medal is awarded irregularly. Established in 1920.

• 8666 • Monsanto Crop Science Distinguished Career Award

To recognize a distinguished career in crop science. Awarded annually. Established in 1977.

• 8667 • Gerald O. Mott Scholarship

To provide a scholarship for a meritorious graduate student in crop science. The following criteria are considered: academic achievement and research/teaching contributions, personal qualities, and demonstrated leadership qualities. Nominees must have completed at least one year of graduate work leading to an M.S. or Ph.D. degree in a field of emphasis within crop science, and have a B.S. in crop science or related area. Also, the graduate student must be at a U.S. institution of higher learning and be studying in the United States when the scholarship is given. Membership (student or regular) in the Society or American Society of Agronomy is required. Awarded annually. Established in 1986.

• 8668 • NCCPB Genetics and Plant Breeding Award for Industry

To recognize scientists who have made significant contributions in genetics and plant breeding during their careers in the private sector. Active members of the Society or individuals affilated with companies that are members of the National Council of Commercial Plant Breeders are eligible. Awarded annually. Established in 1986. Sponsored by the Council of Commercial Plant Breeders.

• 8669 • Seed Science Award

Recognizes distinctive service to the development and utilization of quality seeds in agriculture. A certificate and honorarium of $1,000 are awarded annually.

• 8670 • Young Crop Scientist Award

To recognize a young crop scientist who has made an outstanding contribution in any area of crop science. Members of the Society who are 37 years of age or less on December 31 of the year that the award is presented are eligible. Awarded annually. Established in 1985.

• 8671 •
Crossroad Publishing Co.
481 8th Ave., Ste. 1550
New York, NY 10001-1020
Phone: (212)868-1801
Toll-Free: 800-707-0670
Fax: (212)868-2171
E-mail: ask@crossroadpublishing.com
Home Page: http://www.crossroadpublishing.com

Awards discontinued.

• 8672 • Continuum Women's Studies Award

To encourage and reward outstanding scholarship and other writing in women's studies, which Crossroad/Continuum recognizes as vitally important to literature, the arts, psychology, or social thought. Any book in women studies, widely defined, to be published under the Continuum or Frederick Ungar imprint as a scholarly monograph or a general trade book for serious readers is eligible. Manuscripts may be submitted by March 31. A $5,000 advance and publication are awarded annually in the fall. Established in 1988.

• 8673 •
The Crustacean Society
Mary Belk, Treas.
PO Box 7065
Lawrence, KS 66044-7065
Phone: (785)843-1221
Fax: (785)843-1274
E-mail: jeff@vims.edu
Home Page: http://www.vims.edu/tcs

• 8674 • **Best Student Paper/Poster Award**
To recognize outstanding presentations by student members at the annual meeting. A certificate, $50, and a one year subscription to the society's journal are presented at annual and regional meetings. Established in 1981.

• 8675 • **Excellence in Research**
For recognition of achievement in research on Crustacea. Nominations are accepted. A plaque is presented infrequently at the annual meeting. Established in 1981.

• 8676 •
Cryogenic Engineering Conference
Dr. Jay C. Theilacker, Contact
PO Box 500
Fermi National Lab
Kirk & Wilson Rds.
Batavia, IL 60510-0500
Phone: (630)840-3238
Fax: (630)840-4989
E-mail: tnicol@fnal.gov
Home Page: http://tdserver1.fnal.gov/nicol/cec

• 8677 • **Samuel C. Collins Award**
To recognize outstanding contributions to cryogenic technology. Individuals must be nominated by the awards committee and elected by the board of directors. A plaque is awarded when merited. Established in 1965 to honor Samuel C. Collins, the inventor of the practical helium liquefier.

• 8678 •
Cryogenic Society of America
Laurie Huget, Exec.Dir.
Huget Advertising
1033 South Blvd.
Oak Park, IL 60302
Phone: (708)383-6220
Fax: (708)383-9337
E-mail: laurie@cryogenicsociety.org
Home Page: http://www.cryogenicsociety.org

• 8679 • **Roger W. Boom Award**
To recognize young professionals who show promise for making significant contributions to the fields of cryogenic engineering and applied superconductivity. A plaque, $500, and a one-year membership are awarded periodically at a society function.

• 8680 • **Robert W. Vance Award**
To recognize outstanding service to the Cryogenic Society of America. Eligible candidates should be dedicated to a long-term commitment of time and energy to the advancement of the Society. A plaque and $500 cash award are given periodically at a society function. Established in 1996.

• 8681 •
CT NARAL, the Connecticut Affiliate of NARAL Pro-Choice America
Lynn Frederick Hawley, Exec.Dir.
135 Broad St.
Hartford, CT 06105
Phone: (860)524-1086
Fax: (860)524-1092
E-mail: info@pro-choicect.org
Home Page: http://www.pro-choicect.org

• 8682 • **Catherine Roraback Award**
For significant contribution towards the organization's mission. Recognition award bestowed annually.

• 8683 •
CTAM - Cable and Telecommunications Association for Marketing
Char Beales, Pres./CEO
201 N Union, Ste. 440
Alexandria, VA 22314
Phone: (703)549-4200
Fax: (703)684-1167
E-mail: info@ctam.com
Home Page: http://www.ctam.com

• 8684 • **Awards for Excellence in Cable Marketing and Advertising**
For recognition of excellence in cable marketing and advertising. The contest is divided into four divisions: Division I- Domestic Distributors (US and Canada) MSOS, Cable Systems and other video distribution systems; Division II- Domestic Programmers/Suppliers (US and Canada); Division International Distributors; Division IV- International Programmers; Awards are presented in the following categories: Program Promotion/Tune-in; Special Markets/Objectives; Retention; Best Adapted Work; Public and Community Relations; Marketing Using New Media; Internal Marketing; Trade Communications; Wild Card; Affiliate Communication; Customer Service Awareness; Subscriber Upgrade; Employee Communications; Non-Subscriber Acquisition; Image/Awareness; Pay Per View/Ancillary Revenue; and Consumer Contests/Sweepstakes. Within each of these categories, there are separate competitions for print, direct mail, television, radio, collateral interactive and campaigns using more than one medium. Entries may be submitted by February 28. A two-dimensional triangular lucite award is presented annually. Established in 1982. Sponsored by *CableVision* magazine.

• 8685 •
Cultural Arts Council of Estes Park
Ms. Lynda S. Vogel, Exec.Dir.
PO Box 4135
Estes Park, CO 80517
Phone: (970)586-9203
Fax: (970)586-9254
E-mail: cacep@earthlink.net
Home Page: http://www.estesarts.com

• 8686 • **Regifting Grants Program**
For resident of Park R-3 School District; funds used for furtherment of the arts. Grant awarded annually.

• 8687 •
CURE Childhood Cancer Association
Marynell Noonan, Exec.Dir.
200 Westfall Rd.
Rochester, NY 14620
Phone: (585)473-0180
Fax: (585)473-0201
E-mail: curemn@rochester.rr.com
Home Page: http://www.curekidscancer.com/

• 8688 • **Agnes K. Mackey Assistance Fund**
For individuals in need of assistance. Monetary award bestowed periodic ally.

• 8689 •
Cushman Foundation for Foraminiferal Research
Jennifer Jett, Sec.-Treas.
Smithsonian Inst.
Washington, DC 20013-7012
Phone: (202)633-1333
Fax: (202)786-2832
E-mail: jettje@si.edu
Home Page: http://www.cushmanfoundation.org

• 8690 • **Joseph A. Cushman Award**
For recognition of achievement and excellence in Foraminiferal research which is the study of marine rhizopods, typically having a calcereous shell perforated by small holes or pores. Any living individual carrying out research on the Foraminiferida is eligible. A plaque is awarded annually. Established in 1980.

• 8691 •
Cymbidium Society of America
Kenneth Jacobsen, Membership Sec.
195 Exeter Ave.
San Carlos, CA 94070
Phone: (909)483-5590
Fax: (909)483-5590
E-mail: cymsociety@prodigy.net
Home Page: http://cymbidium.org

• 8692 • **Gold, Silver, and Bronze Medals**
Recognizes flower quality. Each award is given annually.

• 8693 •
Cypress Creek Foundation for the Arts and Community Enrichment
Nanci Decker, Exec.Dir.
6823 Cypresswood Dr.
Spring, TX 77379
Phone: (281)379-3946
Phone: (281)379-3947

• 8694 • **Focus on Education**
For excellence in performing or visual arts, community involvement, academic standing. Scholarship awarded annually.

• 8695 •
Cystic Fibrosis Foundation
Robert J. Beall PhD, Pres./CEO
6931 Arlington Rd.
Bethesda, MD 20814
Phone: (301)951-4422
Toll-Free: 800-344-4823
Fax: (301)951-6378
E-mail: info@cff.org
Home Page: http://www.cff.org

• 8696 • **CFF/NIH Funding Award**
To support excellent CF-related research projects that have been submitted to and approved by the National Institutes of Health but cannot be supported by available NIH funds. Applications must fall within the upper 40th percentile with a priority score of 200 or better. CFF support ranges from $75,000 to $125,000 per year for up to two years. Applications are accepted on an ongoing basis.

• 8697 • **Cystic Fibrosis Foundation Special Research Awards**
To direct research efforts toward specific areas of CF-related research. The amount and duration will be determined by the CFF at the time of announcement.

• 8698 • **Pilot and Feasibility Awards**
To develop and support new hypotheses and/or methods and to support promising new investigators as they establish themselves in research areas relevant to CF. Proposed work must be hypothesis driven and must reflect innovative approaches to clinical questions in CF research. Up to $40,000 per year for two years may be requested. Application deadline is September 1.

• 8699 •
Czechoslovak Society of Arts and Sciences
Miloslav Rechcigl Jr., Pres.
5529 Whitley Pk. Ter.
Bethesda, MD 20814
Phone: (301)564-9081
Fax: (301)564-9069
E-mail: ojsafertal@aol.com
Home Page: http://www.svu2000.org/

• 8700 • **Student Awards**
Recognizes the best undergraduate or graduate paper dealing with some aspect of Czech or Slovak culture. Awarded annually.

• 8701 •
D. H. Lawrence Society of North America
Virginia Hyde, Pres.
Seidlin Hall
Division of English
1 Saxon Dr.
Alfred University
Alfred, NY 14802
Phone: (607)871-2292
Phone: (607)871-2256
Fax: (607)871-2831
E-mail: greiff@alfred.edu
Home Page: http://www.wsu.edu/~hydev/dhlsna.htm

• 8702 • **Harry T. Moore Award**
Recognizes outstanding lifetime contribution to Lawrence studies. Awarded biennially.

• 8703 • **New Scholar Award**
For excellence of research and promise of future scholarship. A monetary prize is awarded biennially.

• 8704 •
Dachshund Club of the Great Lakes
Mary Anne Fowler, Sec.
PO Box 901
Lake Forest, IL 60045-0901
Phone: (847)570-7024
Phone: (847)295-2707
E-mail: maryannefowler@earthlink.net

• 8705 • **Trial and Show Trophies**
For competition placement; based on scores. Recognition award bestowed annually.

• 8706 •
Daedalian Foundation
Maj. John M. Beebe, Sec.
PO Box 249
Randolph AFB, TX 78148-0249
Phone: (210)945-2113
Phone: (210)945-2111
Fax: (210)945-2112
E-mail: icarus@daedalians.org
Home Page: http://www.daedalians.org

• 8707 • **Daedalian Foundation Award of Recognition**
Recognizes distinguished performance in military activities and promotion of safety in flight. Awarded annually.

• 8708 •
The Dairy Barn: Southeastern Ohio Arts Center
Andrea Lewis, Exec.Dir.
8000 Dairy Ln.
PO Box 747
Athens, OH 45701-0747
Phone: (740)592-4981
Fax: (740)592-5090
E-mail: artsinfo@dairybarn.org
Home Page: http://www.dairybarn.org

• 8709 • **Quilt National Awards**
For recognition of outstanding contemporary quilts accepted for exhibition in this international exhibition. The work must possess the most basic structural characteristics of a quilt. It must be predominantly fiber (to which other materials may be added). The whole or, in the case of a sectioned work, the individual units must be composed of at least two distinct layers bound together by hand or machine-made stitches that are distributed throughout the surface of the work. All works must be original designs of the entrants. The following monetary prizes are awarded: Best of Show - $1,500; Award of Excellence - $1,200; Most Innovative Use of the Medium - $850; Domini McCarthy Award for Exceptional Craftsmanship - $250; The Rookie Award for a first time exhibition - $250; People's Choice Award - $100; Quilts Japan Prize - a trip to Japan. Send a self-addressed, stamped envelope for entry forms. Established in 1979.

• 8710 •
Dallas Area Paralegal Association
Kari L. Rabe, Exec.Dir.
PO Box 12533
Dallas, TX 75225
Phone: (972)991-0853
E-mail: director@dallasparalegals.org
Home Page: http://www.dallasparalegals.org

• 8711 • **Paralegal of the Year**
For service to the profession. Recognition award bestowed annually.

• 8712 •
Dallas Metropolitan Young Men's Christian Association
J. Ben Casey Jr., Contact
601 N Akard St.
Dallas, TX 75201
Phone: (214)880-9622
Fax: (214)871-3014
E-mail: recruiter@mycadallas.org
Home Page: http://www.ymcadallas.org

• 8713 • **Beasley Award**
For service. Recognition award bestowed annually.

• 8714 • **Father of the Year Award**
For displaying to children the character qualities: responsibility, trustworthiness, caring, respect, citizenship, fairness. Recognition award bestowed annually.

• 8715 •
Dallas Museum of Art
Dr. John R. Lane, Dir.
1717 N Harwood
Dallas, TX 75201
Phone: (214)922-1200
Fax: (214)954-0174
E-mail: mbleiberg@dallasmuseumofart.org
Home Page: http://www.dallasmuseumofart.org

• 8716 • Clare Hart DeGolyer Memorial Fund Award
To recognize exceptional talent and promise in young visual artists between 15 and 25 years of age who currently reside in and have maintained their principle residence for the past four years in the southwestern part of the United States (Texas, Oklahoma, New Mexico, Arizona, and Colorado). Applicants must demonstrate reasonable promise through consideration of their abilities, intelligence, talents, convictions, and industriousness of continuing their endeavors as artists. Applications must be submitted by March 1. A monetary prize, generally not to exceed $1,500, is awarded annually. Established in 1980.

• 8717 • Otis and Velma Davis Dozier Travel Grant
To enable an artist to travel, thus enriching his or her works. To be eligible, artists must be practicing professionals, be thirty years of age or older, have lived in Texas for the past three years, and be currently living in Texas. Applications must be submitted by March 1. There may be more than one grant recipient in a year. The total amount dispersed should not exceed $6,000.

• 8718 • Arch and Anne Giles Kimbrough Fund Award
To recognize exceptional talent and promise in visual artists under 30 years of age who have resided in Texas for the past three years and are currently living in Texas. Applications must be submitted by March 1. A monetary award, generally not to exceed $3,500, is presented annually. Established in 1980. Formerly: (1987) Anne Giles Kimbrough Fund Award.

• 8719 •
Dallas Songwriters Association
Barbara McMillen, Founder
℅ Sammons Center For The Arts
3630 Harry Hines Blvd. Box 20
Dallas, TX 75219
Phone: (214)750-0916
Phone: (214)691-5318
Fax: (214)692-1392
E-mail: info@dallassongwriters.org
Home Page: http://www.dallassongwriters.org

• 8720 • Songwriter of the Year
Awarded from monthly song entries of the monthly meeting critiques. Songwriter that has most songs wins for the year.

• 8721 •
Dalmatian Club of America
Mary Widder, Membership Chm.
864 Ettin Ave.
Simi Valley, CA 93065
Phone: (805)583-5914
Fax: (281)342-8407
E-mail: widderm@sbcglobal.net
Home Page: http://www.thedca.org

• 8722 • Best of Breed
To recognize the best Dalmatian in the United States. A silver medallion, trophies, and plaques are awarded annually to the owners and breeders. Established in 1905.

• 8723 •
Damfinos: The International Buster Keaton Society
Patrice Eliot Tobias, Pres.
161 W 75th St., No. 14-f
New York, NY 10023
Phone: (212)799-4949
Fax: (212)580-8698
E-mail: melbunting@aol.com
Home Page: http://www.busterkeaton.com

• 8724 • The Buster
Annual award of recognition.

• 8725 •
Damien-Dutton Society for Leprosy Aid
Howard E. Crouch, Pres.
616 Bedford Ave.
Bellmore, NY 11710
Phone: (516)221-5829
Phone: (516)221-9588
Fax: (516)221-5909
E-mail: info@damienleprosysociety.org
Home Page: http://www.damienleprosysociety.org

• 8726 • Damien - Dutton Award
For recognition of a person or organization that has made a significant contribution in research, medical care, rehabilitation, public education, or philanthropy toward the conquest of leprosy. A bronze medallion and medal are awarded annually. Established in 1953 in honor of Father Damien and Brother Joseph Dutton.

• 8727 •
Damon Runyon Cancer Research Foundation
Lorraine W. Egan, Exec.Dir.
675 3rd Ave., 25 Fl.
New York, NY 10017
Phone: (212)455-0500
Toll-Free: 800-445-2494
Fax: (212)455-0509
E-mail: info@drcrf.org
Home Page: http://www.cancerresearchfund.org
Formerly: (1987) Damon Runyon - Walter Winchell Cancer Fund.

• 8728 • Fellowship Award
To encourage all theoretical and experimental research that is relevant to the study of cancer and the search for cancer causes, mechanisms, therapies, and prevention. Applicants must have completed at least one of the following degrees or its equivalent: M.D., Ph.D., D.D.S., D.V.M. For Level 1 funding, basic and clinical science applicants must have received their degrees within the year prior to the SAC meeting at which their applications are to be considered. For Level II funding, applicants must have an M.D., or M.D./Ph.D, and have completed their residencies or clinical fellowship training within three years prior to the Scientific Advisory Committee meeting at which their applications are to be considered. The first year of the fellowship provides $41,000 for Level I and $55,000 for Level II; the second year provides $43,000 for Level I and $56,000 for Level II; the third year provides $44,000 for Level I and $57,000 for Level II; and an expense stipend of $2,000 is provided each year for both Level I and Level II. Awarded annually. Formerly: Damon Runyon - Walter Winchell Cancer Fund Fellowships.

• 8729 •
Charles A. Dana Foundation
Edward F. Rover, Chm.
745 5th Ave., Ste. 900
New York, NY 10151
Phone: (212)223-4040
E-mail: danainfo@dana.org
Home Page: http://www.dana.org

• 8730 • Charles A. Dana Awards for Pioneering Achievements in Higher Education
To recognize recent discoveries and innovations with demonstrated potential for promoting human health and for strengthening education. The Awards in Health focus on advances in fundamental or clinical neuroscience that have led or will lead to innovations in diagnosis, treatment, or prevention of human disease. The Awards in Education honor individuals whose innovations have demonstrated potential for improving the quality of K-12 education in this country. An award of $50,000 and a medallion are given annually. Guidelines available in October for awards in the following year.

• 8731 •
Dance Educators of America
Vickie Sheer, Exec.Dir.
PO Box 607
Pelham, NY 10803-0607
Phone: (914)636-3200
Toll-Free: 800-229-3868
Fax: (914)636-5895
E-mail: dea@deadance.com
Home Page: http://www.deadance.com

• 8732 • DEA Award
To recognize distinguished contributions to the American musical theatre. Current or recent past performances by performers on the Broadway stage, motion pictures, television, ballet or the concert stage are eligible. A cast dance figure on a four-inch base is awarded annually. Established in 1975.

• 8733 •
Dance Films Association
Deirdre Towers, Exec.Dir.
48 W 21st St., No. 907
New York, NY 10010
Phone: (212)727-0764
Fax: (212)727-0764
E-mail: dfa5@earthlink.net
Home Page: http://www.dancefilmsassn.org

• 8734 • **Jury Prize for the Dance on Camera Festival**
Annual, internationally touring festival to encourage and honor a synergy of dance and film, cosponsored by the Film Society of Lincoln Center. Producers and distributors of films and videotapes (features, documentaries, animation, and narrative shorts) completed in the last 2 years are eligible to submit. Winners are shown at the Walter Reade Theatre, Lincoln Center Plaza, in New York City, in January. Deadline for entries is September 25. Check website for entry form.

• 8735 •
Dance Magazine
Karla Johnson, Publisher
333 Seventh Ave., 11th Floor
New York, NY 10001
Phone: (212)979-4803
Fax: (646)674-0102
E-mail: kjohnson@dancemagazine.com
Home Page: http://www.dancemagazine.com

• 8736 • ***Dance Magazine* Annual Awards**
For recognition of outstanding contributions to the field of dance. Performers, choreographers, designers, musicians, administrators, and teachers are eligible. Sterling silver bowls are awarded annually. Established in 1954. Seventy-five year old *Dance Magazine* also continues to award scholarships to encourage young dancers and choreographers through established teaching organizations.

• 8737 •
Dance Masters of America
Robert Mann, Exec.Sec.
214-10 41st Ave.
PO Box 610533
Bayside, NY 11361-0533
Phone: (718)225-3696
Toll-Free: (866)9-JOINDMA
Fax: (718)225-4293
E-mail: dmamann@aol.com
Home Page: http://dma-national.org

• 8738 • **DMA Annual Award**
To recognize an individual for significant contributions to the dance profession. Individuals are nominated by the Board of Directors. Plaques are presented annually in August. Established in 1963.

• 8739 • **DMA President's Award**
Established in 1994. No additional information is available for this editon.

• 8740 • **Member of the Year Award**
To recognize a member for outstanding contributions to the Association. A plaque is presented annually. Established in 1980.

• 8741 •
Dance Notation Bureau
Ilene Fox, Exec.Dir.
151 W 30th St., Ste. 202
New York, NY 10001-4007
Phone: (212)564-0985
Fax: (212)216-9027
E-mail: dnbinfo@dancenotation.org
Home Page: http://www.dancenotation.org

• 8742 • **Distinguished Service Award**
To recognize outstanding leaders in the dance/notation field. An award is presented awarded annually at a gala. Established in 1983.

• 8743 • **Ben Sommers Award**
For recognition of special achievement of students in the field of dance notation. Notation trainees are considered. A scholarship award of $500 is presented. Established in 1983 to honor Ben Sommers, the founder of Capezio and the Capezio Foundation.

• 8744 •
Dance Theater Workshop
Marion Koltun Dienstag, Exec.Dir.
219 W 19th St.
New York, NY 10011
Phone: (212)691-6500
Fax: (212)633-1974
E-mail: dtw@dtw.org
Home Page: http://www.dtw.org

• 8745 • **New York Dance and Performance Awards (Bessie Awards)**
To honor outstanding creative achievements by innovative artists working in the fields of contemporary dance and related performance. Any performing artist presenting new work in New York City during the course of a particular performance season is eligible. Nomination is by a committee of producers, critics and artists. Awards are presented to choreographers, performers, designers and composers. Awarded annually in September. Established in 1984 by the Dance Theater Workshop with special funding from Morgan Guaranty Trust Company in honor of Bessie Schonberg, a renowned teacher of dance composition and mentor to many choreographers.

• 8746 •
Dance/U.S.A.
Andrea Snyder, Exec.Dir.
1156 15th St., NW, Ste. 820
Washington, DC 20005-1726
Phone: (202)833-1717
Fax: (202)833-2686
E-mail: asnyder@danceusa.org
Home Page: http://www.danceusa.org

• 8747 • **Dance/USA National Honors**
To recognize individuals and/or organizations that have made important contributions to the dance art form and field. The Board of Trustees makes the selection. A framed citation, and a piece of artwork are awarded biennially. Established in 1986.

• 8748 •
Dante Society of America
Todd Boli, Sec.-Treas.
PO Box 711
Framingham, MA 01701-0711
E-mail: dsa@dantesociety.org
Home Page: http://www.dantesociety.org

• 8749 • **Dante Prize**
To recognize the best undergraduate student essay in competition on a subject related to the life or works of Dante. A $250 monetary prize is awarded annually.

• 8750 • **Charles Hall Grandgent Award**
To recognize the best essay submitted by an American or Canadian student enrolled in any graduate program. A $500 monetary prize is awarded annually.

• 8751 •
Darien Chamber of Commerce
Carol Wilder Tamme, Exec.Dir.
17 Old Kings Hwy. S
Darien, CT 06820
Phone: (203)655-3600
Fax: (203)655-2074
E-mail: darienchamber@optonline.net
Home Page: http://dcc.darien.org/

• 8752 • **Citizen of the Year**
For involvement in the community. Recognition award.

• 8753 •
DateAble, Inc.
Dr. Robert Watson MSW, Exec.Dir.
15520 Bald Eagle School Rd.
Brandywine, MD 20613
Phone: (301)888-1177
Phone: (301)657-3283
Fax: (301)657-4327
E-mail: robert@dateable.org
Home Page: http://www.dateable.org

• 8754 • **Date Able Image Award**
Recognizes positive contribution to the image of people with disabilities. Awarded annually.

• 8755 •
Daughters of Union Veterans of the Civil War, 1861-1865
Ms. Cynthia VanAntwerp, Registrar
503 S Walnut
Springfield, IL 62704-1932
Phone: (217)544-0616
E-mail: duvcw@sbcglobal.net
Home Page: http://www.duvcw.org

• 8756 • **Daughters of Union Veterans of the Civil War, 1861-1865 Award**
Recognizes one cadet at each of four military academies. Awarded annually.

• 8757 •
Davison Area Chamber of Commerce
Phil Becker, Exec.Dir.
105 E 2nd St., Ste. 7
Davison, MI 48423
Phone: (810)653-6266
Fax: (810)653-0669
E-mail: dcofcomm@yahoo.com

• 8758 • Davison Chamber of Commerce Service Scholarship
For volunteer service in community. Scholarship awarded annually.

• 8759 •
Davy Devotees - The Official Fan Club for Davy Jones
Abby Alterio, Pres./Ed.
10930 Stratford Way
Fishers, IN 46038
E-mail: davydvotee@aol.com
Home Page: http://www.geocities.com/davydevotee/dd2.html

• 8760 • Crave the Dave Award
Recognizes outstanding web pages.

• 8761 •
The Dayton Playhouse
Adam Leigh, Exec.Dir.
1301 E Siebenthaler Ave.
Dayton, OH 45415
Phone: (937)333-SHOW
Fax: (937)333-2827
E-mail: adam@daytonplayhouse.com
Home Page: http://www.daytonplayhouse.com

Formerly: (1984) Dayton Repertory Theatre.

• 8762 • Dayton Playhouse Future Fest
To encourage professional development and recognize an outstanding play. The script must be an original, full-length work, not previously produced or published and a minimum of 75 minutes running time. Entries must be submitted between August 1 and September 30. A monetary prize of $1,000 with more prize money pending and possible production of the winning script are awarded annually in mid July. Established in 1983. For official rules, please send a SASE to above address, attention: FutureFest. Formerly: (1991) Dayton Playhouse National Playwriting Competition.

• 8763 •
Daytona International Speedway
Robin Braig, Pres.
1801 W International Speedway Blvd.
Daytona Beach, FL 32114
Phone: (386)254-2700
Fax: (386)257-0281
E-mail: daytonaspeedway@daytonainternationalspeedway.com
Home Page: http://www.daytonainternationalspeedway.com

• 8764 • "Cannonball" Baker Award
To recognize the crew chief of the Daytona 500 winning car.

• 8765 • Daytona Gatorade Victory Lane Award
To recognize the winner of the Daytona 500 NASCAR Winston Cup Series Stock Car Race. Established in 1996, this is a tradition unique in all of motorsport. The winning car from the Daytona 500 is placed in Daytona USA the day following its victory for period of one year.

• 8766 • Harley J. Earl Trophy (Daytona 500)
To recognize the winner of the Daytona 500 NASCAR Winston Cup Series Stock Car Race. This is the richest and most prestigious event in NASCAR's Winston Cup Series. Race car drivers licensed by NASCAR (National Association for Stock Car Auto Racing) are eligible. The winner receives one million dollars from stock car racing's biggest purse. The name of the winner is inscribed on a perpetual trophy housed at DAYTONA USA, the speedway's interactive motorsports attraction. Awarded annually in February. Established in 1959 in honor of Harley J. Earl, an automotive pioneer and designer.

• 8767 • Pepsi 400 Trophy
To recognize the winner of the Pepsi 400 NASCAR Winston Cup Stock Car Race. Race car drivers licensed by NASCAR are eligible. The award consists of a monetary prize and presentation of a trophy unique in motorsport: an internally illuminated glass sculpture of Daytona International Speedway on a square black base.

• 8768 • Rolex Trophy
To recognize the overall winners of the Rolex 24 at the Daytona sports car race. Race car drivers licensed by the Grand American Road Racing Association are eligible for the award. The winners' names are inscribed on a perpetual trophy housed at DAYTONA USA. Presented annually in late January or early February, this race is one of the only two 24-hour tests for the world's best sports cars and teams. This sports car race began as a three-hour event in 1962 and became a 24-hour event in 1966. The overall winner is the car which completes the most miles over the 24 hour period. Four classes of cars compete for individual class honors as well, from exotic Can-Am Prototypes to powerful production based coupes.

• 8769 • Winston Cup (Winston Cup Series)
To recognize the national champion of the NASCAR Winston Cup Championship. Race car drivers licensed by NASCAR are eligible. The champion is determined by the highest accumulated point total over a 36 race season. Presented in December, the champion receives a multi-million dollar award from the R.J. Reynolds Co. and his name inscribed on a perpetual trophy housed at DAYTONA USA. Formerly: (1971) NASCAR Grand National Championship.

• 8770 •
D.C. Commission on the Arts and Humanities
Tony Gittens, Exec.Dir.
Stables Art Center
410 8th St. NW, 5th Fl.
Washington, DC 20004
Phone: (202)724-5613
Fax: (202)727-4135
E-mail: cah@dc.gov
Home Page: http://www.dcarts.dc.gov

• 8771 • Mayor's Arts Awards
To recognize significant artistic contribution to Washington, D.C., through either service to the arts or excellence in artistic achievement. Residents and organizations in Washington, D.C., for at least one year are eligible. A lucite sculpture is awarded annually. Established in 1980.

• 8772 •
Deadline Club
David Joachim, Pres.
15 Gramercy Park S
New York, NY 10003
Phone: (212)353-9598
E-mail: deadline@spj.org
Home Page: http://www.spj.org/deadline

• 8773 • Deadline Club Awards
To honor the finest journalism by journalists based in the New York metropolitan area in print, radio, and television. The deadline for entries is February 16. Awards are given for the best spot news reporting, best series/investigative reporting, and best feature reporting in the following categories: Newspapers/News Agencies (circulation greater than 100,000) - reporters and reporting teams working for large-circulation newspapers and wire services may enter; Newspapers/News Agencies (circulation under 100,000) - reporters and reporting teams working for small-circulation newspapers and wire services may enter; Non-daily Newspapers - reporters & teams working for non-daily newspapers may enter; Magazines - writers and teams working for magazines, including trade magazines with general circulations, magazine sections of newspapers, and Sunday supplements may enter; Best Editorial; Best Personal Column; Radio - reporters, anchors, or reporting teams working for radio networks and local stations may enter; and Television - reporters, anchors, or reporting teams working for broadcast or cable television networks and local stations may enter. In Photography, photojournalists working either on staff or free-lance may enter the following categories: Still Photography - Best Spot News Photo; and Still Photography - Best Feature Photo. Business and financial journalists may enter categories for Best Business Story - Print; and Best Business Story - Broadcast. Entries in all media are eligible for the following two awards: Minority Issues Award - for the reporter or reporting team that best covers an issue of special interest or significance to a minority community; and the James Wright Brown Public Service Award - for the news organizations that render a public service to the communities they serve through extensive coverage of controversial issues facing those

communities. A $1,000 stipend, provided by *Editor & Publisher* is awarded. The Deadline Club Awards were established in 1982 in honor of James Wright Brown, Founder of *Editor & Publisher* magazine. A statuette is awarded to each winner. Sponsored by the New York City Chapter of the Society of Professional Journalists.

• 8774 •
Deaf and Hard of Hearing Entrepreneurs Council
Louis J. Schwarz CFP, Pres.
4405 East West Hwy., Ste. 502
Bethesda, MD 20814-4536
Phone: (301)587-8596
Fax: (301)587-5997

• 8775 • Deaf/Hard of Hearing Entrepreneur of the Year
For recognition of excellence in: being an entrepreneur in a deaf/hard of hearing community; helping in deaf/hard of hearing worthy causes; and providing good mentorship to others. Qualified deaf/hard of hearing entrepreneurs with at least five years in business are eligible. A plaque is awarded each year at the Annual Gala/Auction (late winter/early spring, usually in Metro Washington, DC). Established in 1992.

• 8776 •
Deafness Research Foundation
Armand D'Amato, Chm.
8201 Greensboro Dr., Ste. 300
McLean, VA 22102
Phone: (703)610-9025
Toll-Free: 800-829-5934
Fax: (202)293-1805
E-mail: info@drf.org
Home Page: http://www.drf.org

• 8777 • Award of Merit
To recognize an individual who has contributed exceptionally to advance the understanding or treatment of deafness, or who has inspired the deaf and hard of hearing as a person sharing that handicap in a life of exceptional merit. A medal is awarded as merited. Established in 1959. Formerly: Achievement Award.

• 8778 • Deafness Research Foundation Otological Research Fellowship for Medical Students
To provide for a fellowship in a Department of Otolaryngology conducting otological research, or in a related discipline. The fellowship is scheduled as a one-year block of time at the end of the third year of medical school, thus requiring a one-year leave of absence from the medical school curriculum. Applications must be received by March 15. A fellowship of $10,000 and up to $3,500 for animals and consumable supplies are awarded.

• 8779 • Grants for Otologic and Related Science Research Projects
To provide grants for research directed to any aspect of the ear; that is, investigation of function, physiology, biochemistry, genetics, anatomy, or pathology. The current policy favors the awarding of grants in support of projects directed by new investigators, so-called "seed money" support for studies in generally unexplored areas of research. It does not exclude grant support for new research by established investigators. The application deadline is June 1. The maximum award is $15,000. Awarded annually for a project period covering the subsequent calendar year beginning January 1.

• 8780 •
Death Penalty Information Center
Rion Dennis, Info.Spec.
1101 Vermont Ave., NW Ste. 701
Washington, DC 20005
Phone: (202)289-2275
Phone: (202)293-6971
Fax: (202)822-4787
E-mail: rdennis@deathpenaltyinfo.org
Home Page: http://www.deathpenaltyinfo.org

• 8781 • Thurgood Marshall Journalism Award
Recognizes the best print or electronic media stories about capital punishment. A monetary award is given annually.

• 8782 •
Decalogue Society of Lawyers
Carol Straus, Admin.Dir./Managing Ed.
39 S LaSalle St., Ste. 410
Chicago, IL 60603
Phone: (312)263-6493
Fax: (312)263-6512
E-mail: decaloguesociety@aol.com
Home Page: http://decaloguesociety.com

• 8783 • Intra-Society Merit Award
For recognition of distinguished, meritorious, loyal and sustained service to the Society and dedication to the furtherance of its aims and purposes. Members in good standing of the Society are eligible. A lettered scroll is awarded each year at the annual meeting of the Society. Established in 1942.

• 8784 • Merit Award
To recognize an outstanding citizen of the world for distinguished service to humanity or contributions to the arts, sciences, or culture. A lettered scroll is awarded annually. Established in 1941.

• 8785 •
Decision Sciences Institute
Carol J. Latta, Exec.Dir.
35 Broad St.
Georgia State University
Atlanta, GA 30303
Phone: (404)651-4005
Fax: (404)651-2804
E-mail: dsi@gsu.edu
Home Page: http://www.decisionsciences.org
Formerly: (1986) American Institute for Decision Sciences.

• 8786 • Instructional Innovation Award
To recognize outstanding contributions that advance instructional approaches within the decision sciences and to honor excellence in instruction. The description of the innovative instructional technique that has been developed must be submitted by April 16. A monetary prize of $1,500 to the winner and $250 each to the finalists are awarded annually. Established in 1979.

• 8787 •
Dedicated Wooden Money Collectors
Larry White, Treas.
2084 N Brook Cir.
York, PA 17403
Phone: (717)845-4295
Phone: (717)854-0223
Fax: (717)854-0223

• 8788 • Design Award
Recognizes the best design of wooden money. Awarded annually.

• 8789 • Harold Butner Award
Recognizes outstanding service to the DWMC. Awarded annually.

• 8790 • Literary Award
Recognizes the best article in the newsletter. Awarded annually.

• 8791 •
Deep Foundations Institute
Geordie Compton, Exec.Dir.
326 Lafayette Ave.
Hawthorne, NJ 07506
Phone: (973)423-4030
Fax: (973)423-4031
E-mail: dfihq@dfi.org
Home Page: http://www.dfi.org

• 8792 • Distinguished Service Award
Recognizes career achievement. Awarded annually.

• 8793 • Outstanding Project Award
Recognizes ingenuity in design/constructing of deep foundation projects. Awarded annually.

• 8794 •
Defense Credit Union Council
Roland A. Arteaga, Pres./CEO
601 Pennsylvania Ave. NW, Ste. 600
Washington, DC 20004-2601
Phone: (202)638-3950
Toll-Free: 800-356-9655
Fax: (202)638-3410
E-mail: dcuc1@cuna.com
Home Page: http://www.dcuc.org

• 8795 • Distinguished Service Award
Recognizes individuals outside the council for service to defense credit unions. Awarded annually.

• 8796 •
Defense Logistics Agency
United States Air Force
8725 John J. Kingman Rd., Ste. 2545
Fort Belvoir, VA 22060-6221
Phone: (703)767-6200
Fax: (703)767-6187
Home Page: http://www.dla.mil

• 8797 • **Achievement Medal: Air Force**
To recognize outstanding achievement or meritorious service.

• 8798 • **Achievement Medal: Army**
To recognize meritorious service or achievement of a lesser degree than required for award of the Army Commendation Medal. Members of the Armed Forces or members of the Armed Forces of a friendly foreign nation who served in any capacity with the Army in a noncombat area on or after August 1, 1981 are eligible.

• 8799 • **Achievement Medal: Coast Guard**
To recognize military personnel whose professional achievements exceed normal expectancy. The operational distinguishing device may be authorized.

• 8800 • **Achievement Medal: Navy - Marine Corps**
To recognize junior officers and enlisted men whose professional achievements exceed normal expectancy.

• 8801 • **Aerial Achievement Medal**
For recognition of sustained meritorious achievement while participating in aerial flight. Established in 1988.

• 8802 • **Air Reserve Forces Meritorious Service Medal - Air Force**
For recognition of exemplary behavior, efficiency, and fidelity during a four-year period while serving in an enlisted status in the Air Force Reserve Forces.

• 8803 • **Antarctica Service Medal**
For recognition of participating in an expedition, operation or support of a U.S. operation in Antarctica after Jan. 1, 1946. Established in 1960.

• 8804 • **Armed Forces Expeditionary Medal**
For recognition of participating in designated operations after July 1, 1958.

• 8805 • **Armed Forces Reserve Medal**
For recognition of 10 years of honorable service in Reserve components of the armed forces. Established in 1950.

• 8806 • **Army of Occupation Medal - Army-Air Force**
For recognition of 30 consecutive days service after World War II at a normal post of duty while assigned to an army of occupation.

• 8807 • **Army Reserve Components Achievement Medal**
For recognition of exemplary behavior, efficiency and fidelity while serving as a member of an Army National Guard or Reserve Troop Program Unit.

• 8808 • **China Service Medal - Navy, Marine Corps, Coast Guard**
For recognition of service in China, July 7, 1937, to Sept. 7, 1939, (Navy-Marine Corps) and Sept. 2, 1945, to April 1, 1957 (Navy- Marine Corps-Coast Guard). Established in 1940.

• 8809 • **Coast Guard Arctic Service Medal**
For recognition of participating in an expedition, operation or support of an operation in excess of 21 consecutive days in the Arctic.

• 8810 • **Coast Guard Reserve Good Conduct Medal**
For recognition of conduct for three-year periods of continuous Reserve service. Replaces the Coast Guard Reserve Meritorious Service Ribbon.

• 8811 • **Combat Readiness Medal**
For recognition of completion of an aggregate of two years of sustained individual combat or mission readiness or preparedness for direct weapon system deployment. Awarded by the Air Force.

• 8812 • **Commendation Medal: Navy**
Stipulations and decoration are similar to those of the Army Commendation Medal, except that the Navy Medal is awarded to members of the Navy, Marine Corps, or Coast Guard in time of war. Established in 1944.

• 8813 • **Defense Distinguished Service Medal**
To recognize a military service officer who, while assigned to joint staffs and other joint activities of the Department of Defense, distinguishes himself by exceptionally meritorious service to the Government in a position of unique and great responsibility. Awarded by the Secretary of Defense.

• 8814 • **Defense Meritorious Service Medal**
To recognize an active member of the Armed Forces of the United States who distinguishes himself by noncombat meritorious achievement or service while assigned to joint activity. Awarded in the name of the Secretary of Defense. Established in 1977.

• 8815 • **Defense Superior Service Medal**
To recognize a member of the Armed Forces of the United States who, while assigned to joint staffs and other joint activities of the Department of Defense, has rendered superior meritorious service in a position of significant responsibility. Awarded by the Secretary of Defense.

• 8816 • **Gold Lifesaving Medal**
To recognize heroic deeds in saving life from perils of the sea. The medal is presented by the Coast Guard. Established in 1949.

• 8817 • **Good Conduct Medal**
For recognition of exemplary behavior, efficiency, and fidelity in active Federal military service. It is awarded on a selective basis to each soldier who distinguishes himself from among his fellow soldiers by his exemplary conduct, efficiency, and fidelity throughout a specified period of continuous enlisted active Federal military service. There is no right or entitlement to the medal until the immediate commander has approved the award and the award has been announced in permanent orders. Good Conduct medals are given by the following: (1) Army, for exemplary behavior, efficiency and fidelity while on active duty; (2) Navy, for conduct for four years of continuous active service; (3) Marine Corps, for three years of continuous active service; (4) Air Force, for exemplary behavior, efficiency and fidelity during a three year period of service; and (5) Coast Guard, for three year periods of continuous active service. Established in 1941.

• 8818 • **Humanitarian Service Medal**
To recognize meritorious participation in a significant military act or operation of a humanitarian nature, performed after April 1, 1975. Service members must be on active duty at the time of direct participation in a DOD approved humanitarian act or operation. "Active duty" means full-time duty in the active military service of the United States. It includes duty on the active list, full-time training duty, annual training duty and attendance, while in the active military service, at a school designated as a Service school by law or by the Secretary of the Military Department concerned. This includes service as a cadet at the US Military Academy. Members of the National Guard are eligible provided that the use of active forces has been authorized in the act or operation. Service members must have directly participated in the humanitarian act or operation with a designated geographical area of operation and within specified time limits. Established by Executive Order in 1977.

• 8819 • **Joint Service Achievement Medal**
To recognize a member of the Armed Forces of the United States, below the grade of 0-6, who distinguishes himself by meritorious achievement or service while serving in any joint activity after 3 August 1983. Members on temporary duty for at least 60 days to joint activities are also eligible. The required achievement or service, while of lesser degree than that required for award of the Joint Service Commendation

Medal, must have been accomplished with distinction. Recommendations will be restricted to the recognition of outstanding performance of duty and meritorious achievement that is incontestably exceptional and of a magnitude that clearly places an individual above his peers.

• 8820 • Joint Service Commendation Medal
To recognize an active member of the Armed Forces of the United States who distinguishes himself by meritorious achievement or service while serving in any assignment after January 1, 1963. Individuals on temporary duty for at least 60 days are also eligible for this award. The required achievement or service, while of lesser degree than that required for award of the Meritorious Service Medal must nevertheless have been accomplished with distinction. Recommendations will be restricted to the recognition of outstanding performance of duty and meritorious achievement that are incontestably exceptional and of a magnitude that clearly places an individual above his peers. Awards made for acts or services involving direct participation in combat operations during the period 25 June 1963 to 31 March 1976 may include the "V" device. Effective 1 April 1976, the "V" device is authorized if the citation is approved for valor (heroism) in a designated combat area.

• 8821 • Korean Service Medal
For recognition of participation in operations in the Korean area between June 27, 1950, and July 27, 1954.

• 8822 • Legion of Merit
To recognize individuals who shall have distinguished themselves by exceptionally meritorious conduct in the performance of outstanding services. U.S. Armed Forces personnel or of a friendly foreign nation are considered. Awards are given in the following degrees: Chief Commander to the chief of state or head of government of another country; Commander - to the equal in another country of a chief of staff, in the United States, or to a leader of comparable degree; Officer - to foreign military attaches, and to foreign generals or flag rank personnel below the rating of chief of staff; and Legionnaire - to all others awarded the Legion of Merit. The decoration consists, to the degree of Chief Commander, of a large breast plate, white, purplish-red, and a gold five pointed star, centered by a blue field with white stars, surrounded by a ring of gold, with the whole medal superimposed on a green enamel laurel wreath. The decoration for each succeeding degree is similar, but succeedingly smaller as the degree decreases. Established in 1942 by an Act of the U.S. Congress for services rendered since September 1939.

• 8823 • Marine Corps Expeditionary Medal
For recognition of opposed landing on foreign territory or operations deserving special recognition for which service no other campaign medal has been awarded.

• 8824 • Meritorious Service Medal
To recognize a member of the Armed Forces of the United States or member of the Armed Forces of a friendly foreign nation who, while serving in a noncombat area after 16 January 1969 distinguishes himself by outstanding meritorious achievement or service.

• 8825 • Multinational Force and Observers Medal
For recognition of service with the Multinational Force and Observers Organization for at least 90 consecutive days.

• 8826 • National Defense Service Medal
For recognition of active federal service in the armed forces, including the Coast Guard, between June 27, 1950, and July 27, 1954, from Jan. 1, 1961, to Aug. 14, 1974, and from August 2, 1990 (when Iraq invaded Kuwait). Established in 1953.

• 8827 • Naval Reserve Medal
For recognition of 10 years of honorable service in the Naval Reserve (prior to Sept. 12, 1958). Established in 1938.

• 8828 • Navy Expeditionary Medal
For recognition of opposed landing on foreign territory or operations deserving special recognition for which service no other campaign medal has been awarded. Established in 1936.

• 8829 • Navy Occupation Service Medal - Navy-Marine Corps-Coast Guard
For recognition of occupation service during and after World War II.

• 8830 • Orders of the U.S. Air Force
The Medal of Honor is the highest military decoration that the nation can bestow upon a service member. Lesser degrees of recognition are acknowledged by other decorations in descending order of precedence. The following order of precedence is for wearing individual decorations and awards most likely to be worn today: Medal of Honor; Air Force Cross; Defense Distinguished Service Medal; Distinguished Service Medal - Air Force; Silver Star; Defense Superior Service Medal; Legion of Merit; Distinguished Flying Cross; Airman's Medal; Bronze Star Medal; Purple Heart; Defense Meritorious Service Medal; Meritorious Service Medal; Air Medal; Aerial Achievement Medal; Joint Service Commendation Medal; Air Force Commendation Medal; Joint Service Achievement Medal; Air Force Achievement Medal; Presidential Unit Citation; Joint Meritorious Unit Award; Air Force Outstanding Unit Award; Air Force Organizational Excellence Award; POW Medal; Combat Readiness Medal; Air Force Good Conduct Medal; Good Conduct Medal; Air Reserve Forces Meritorious Service Medal; Outstanding Airman of the Year; Air Force Recognition Ribbon; Army of Occupation Medal; National Defense Service Medal; Korean Service Medal; Antarctica Service Medal; Armed Forces Expeditionary Medal; Vietnam Service Medal; Humanitarian Service Medal; Air Force Overseas RibbonShort; Air Force Overseas Ribbon-Long; Air Force Longevity Service Award Ribbon; Armed Forces Reserve Medal; Air Force NCO Professional Military Education Graduate Ribbon; Basic Military Training Honor Graduate; Small Arms Expert Marksmanship Ribbon; Air Force Training Ribbon; Philippine Residential Unit Citation; Republic of Korea Presidential Unit Citation; Republic of Vietnam Gallantry Cross with Palm; United Nations Service Medal; United Nations Medal; and Republic of Vietnam Campaign Medal.

• 8831 • Orders of the U.S. Army
The Medal of Honor is the highest military decoration that the nation can bestow upon a service member. Lesser degrees of recognition are acknowledged by other decorations in descending order of precedence. The following order of precedence is for wearing individual decorations and awards most likely to be worn today: LEFT SIDE - Medal of Honor; Distinguished Service Cross; Defense Distinguished Service Medal; Distinguished Service Medal; Silver Star; Defense Superior Service Medal; Legion of Merit; Distinguished Flying Cross; Soldier's Medal; Bronze Star Medal; Purple Heart; Defense Meritorious Service Medal; Meritorious Service Medal; Air Medal; Joint Service Commendation Medal; Army Commendation Medal; Joint Service Achievement Medal; Army Achievement Medal; POW Medal; Good Conduct Medal; Army Reserve Components Achievement Medal; Army of Occupation Medal; National Defense Service Medal; Korean Service Medal; Antarctica Service Medal; Armed Forces Expeditionary Medal; Vietnam Service Medal; Humanitarian Service Medal; Armed Forces Reserve Medal; NCO Professional Development Ribbon; Army Service Ribbon; Overseas Service Ribbon; Army Reserve Components Overseas Training Ribbon; United Nations Service Medal; Inter-American Defense Board Medal; United Nations Medal; Multinational Force and Observers Medal; and Republic of Vietnam Campaign Medal. RIGHT SIDE: Presidential Unit Citation; Joint Meritorious Unit Award; Valorous Unit Award; Meritorious Unit Commendation; Army Superior Unit Award; Philippine Republic Presidential Unit Citation; Republic of Korea Presidential Unit Citation; Vietnam Presidential Unit Citation; Republic of Vietnam Gallantry Cross Unit Citation; and Republic of Vietnam Civil Actions Unit Citation.

• 8832 • Orders of the U.S. Coast Guard
The Medal of Honor is the highest military decoration that the nation can bestow upon a service member. Lesser degrees of recognition are acknowledged by other decorations in descending order of precedence. The following order of precedence is for wearing individual decorations and awards most likely to be worn today: Medal of Honor; Navy Cross; Defense Distinguished Service Medal; Distinguished Service Medal; Silver Star; Department of Transportation Gold Medal; Defense Superior Service Medal; Legion of Merit; Distinguished Flying Cross; Coast Guard Medal; Gold Lifesaving Medal; Bronze Star Medal; Purple Heart; Defense Meritorious Service Medal; Meritorious Service Medal; Air Medal; Silver Lifesaving

Medal; Department of Transportation Silver Medal; Joint Service Commendation Medal; Coast Guard Commendation Medal; Department of Transportation Bronze Medal; Joint Service Achievement Medal; Coast Guard Achievement Medal; Commandant's Letter of Commendation; Combat Action Ribbon; Presidential Unit Citation; Joint Meritorious Unit Award; Coast Guard Unit Commendation; Coast Guard Meritorious Unit Commendation; Navy "E" Ribbon; POW Medal; Good Conduct Medal; Coast Guard Reserve Good Conduct Medal; Naval Reserve Meritorious Service Medal; Navy Expeditionary Medal; China Service Medal; Navy Occupation Service Medal; National Defense Service Medal; Korean Service Medal; Antarctica Service Medal; Coast Guard Arctic Service Medal; Armed Forces Expeditionary Medal; Vietnam Service Medal; Humanitarian Service Medal; Coast Guard Special Operations Service; Coast Guard Sea Service; Coast Guard Restricted Duty; Coast Guard Basic Training Honor Graduate; Armed Forces Reserve Medal; Naval Reserve Medal; Philippine Presidential Unit Citation; Republic of Korea Presidential Unit Citation; Republic of Vietnam Presidential Unit Citation; Republic of Vietnam Gallantry Cross Unit Citation; Republic of Vietnam Civil Actions Unit Citation; United Nations Service Medal; United Nations Medal; Multinational Force and Observers Medal; Inter-American Defense Board Medal; and Republic of Vietnam Campaign Medal.

• 8833 • Orders of the U.S. Marine Corps

The Medal of Honor is the highest military decoration that the nation can bestow upon a service member. Lesser degrees of recognition are acknowledged by other decorations in descending order of precedence. The following order of precedence is for wearing individual decorations and awards most likely to be worn today: Medal of Honor; Navy Cross; Defense Distinguished Service Medal; Distinguished Service Medal; Silver Star; Defense Superior Service Medal; Legion of Merit; Distinguished Flying Cross; Navy and Marine Corps Medal; Bronze Star Medal; Purple Heart; Defense Meritorious Service Medal; Meritorious Service Medal; Air Medal; Joint Service Commendation Medal; Navy Commendation Medal; Joint Service Achievement Medal; Navy Achievement Medal; Combat Action Ribbon; Presidential Unit Citation; Joint Meritorious Unit Award; Navy Unit Commendation; Meritorious Unit Commendation; Navy "E" Ribbon; POW Medal; Good Conduct Medal; Selected Marine Corps Reserve Medal; Marine Corps Expeditionary Medal; China Service Medal; Navy Occupation Service Medal; National Defense Service Medal; Korean Service Medal; Antarctica Service Medal; Armed Forces Expeditionary Medal; Vietnam Service Medal; Humanitarian Service Medal; Sea Service Deployment Ribbon; Navy Arctic Service Ribbon; Navy and Marine Corps Overseas Service Ribbon; Armed Forces Reserve Medal; Marine Corps Reserve Ribbon; Philippine Presidential Unit Citation; Republic of Korea Presidential Unit Citation; Republic of Vietnam Presidential Unit Citation; Republic of Vietnam Gallantry Cross Unit Citation; Republic of Vietnam Civil Actions Unit Citation; United Nations Service Medal; Inter-American Defense Board Medal; United Nations Medal; Multinational Force and Observers Medal; and Republic of Vietnam Campaign Medal.

• 8834 • Orders of the U.S. Navy

The Medal of Honor is the highest military decoration that the nation can bestow upon a service member. Lesser degrees of recognition are acknowledged by other decorations in descending order of precedence. The following order of precedence is for wearing individual decorations and awards most likely to be worn today: Medal of Honor; Navy Cross; Defense Distinguished Service Medal; Distinguished Service Medal; Silver Star; Defense Superior Service Medal; Legion of Merit; Distinguished Flying Cross; Navy and Marine Corps Medal; Bronze Star; Purple Heart; Defense Meritorious Service Medal; Meritorious Service Medal; Air Medal; Joint Service Commendation Medal; Navy Commendation Medal; Joint Service Achievement Medal; Navy Achievement Medal; Combat Action Ribbon; Presidential Unit Citation; Joint Meritorious Unit Award; Navy Unit Commendation; Meritorious Unit Commendation; Navy "E" Ribbon; POW Medal; Good Conduct Medal; Naval Reserve Meritorious Service Medal; Fleet Marine Force Ribbon; Navy Expeditionary Medal; China Service Medal; Navy Occupation Service Medal; National Defense Service Medal; Korean Service Medal; Antarctica Service Medal; Armed Forces Expeditionary Medal; Vietnam Service Medal; Humanitarian Service Medal; Sea Service Deployment Ribbon; Navy Arctic Service Ribbon; Naval Reserve Sea Service Ribbon; Navy and Marine Corps Overseas Service Ribbon; Armed Forces Reserve Medal; Naval Reserve Medal; Philippine Presidential Unit Citation; Republic of Korea Presidential Unit Citation; Republic of Vietnam Presidential Unit Citation; Republic of Vietnam Gallantry Cross Unit Citation; Republic of Vietnam Civil Actions Unit Citation; United Nations Service Medal; United Nations Medal; Multinational Force and Observers Medal; Inter-American Defense Board Medal; Republic of Vietnam Campaign Medal; Expert Rifleman Medal; and Expert Pistol Shot Medal.

• 8835 • Prisoner of War Medal

To recognize individuals who have been taken prisoner during an armed conflict, i.e., World War I, World War II, Korea and Vietnam and who must have rendered honorable service during the period of captivity. The medal may be awarded posthumously to the legal next of kin. However, the next of kin of those who are listed as missing in action, but for whom there is no evidence of captivity as a POW, are not eligible. The law creating the medal indicates it may be awarded to anyone who ". . . was taken prisoner and held captive while engaged in an action against an enemy of the United States, while engaged in military operations involving conflict with an opposing foreign force, or while serving with friendly forces engaged in an armed conflict against an opposing armed force in which the United States is not a belligerent party." The front of the circular medal features a golden eagle standing with its wings outspread against a lighter gold background, ringed by barbed wire and bayonet points. Although symbolically imprisoned, the American eagle is alert to regain freedom, the hope that upholds the prisoner's spirit. Established in 1986; first awarded in 1988.

• 8836 • Republic of Vietnam Campaign Medal

For recognition of six months direct combat support or service in South Vietnam between March 1, 1961, and March 28, 1973. Also for those wounded, captured or killed in action or in the line of duty during the same period.

• 8837 • Selected Marine Corps Reserve Medal

For recognition of four consecutive years service in Selected Marine Corps Reserve. Established in 1939.

• 8838 • Silver Lifesaving Medal

To recognize deeds, lesser in degree than that of the Gold Lifesaving Medal, in saving life from perils of the sea. The medal is presented by the Coast Guard. Established by Act of Congress in 1874.

• 8839 • Silver Star: Navy

To recognize Navy or Marine Corps personnel for conspicuous gallantry and intrepidity in action. The decoration is the same as that for the Army. Established in 1942 by an Act of the U.S. Congress.

• 8840 • Southwest Asia Service Medal

To recognize individuals who served in the gulf during Operations Desert Shield and Desert Storm. A sand-colored ribbon with red, white, blue, green and black stripes incorporating the colors of the U.S. and the Gulf area supports a medal that shows military forces deployed on the desert and sea and the reverse side of the medal shows "an upraised sword entwined with a palm frond symbolizing military might and preparedness in defense of peace." Established in 1991.

• 8841 • United Nations Medal

For recognition of not less than six months service with one of the following United Nations' units: UN Observers Group in Lebanon, UN Truce Supervisory Organization in Palestine, UN Military Observers Group in India and Pakistan and UN Security Forces, Hollandia.

• 8842 • United Nations Service Medal (Korea)

For recognition of service in the Korean area in support of UN action from June 27, 1950, to July 27, 1954; and those who are also eligible for the Korean Service Medal.

• 8843 • Vietnam Service Medal

For recognition of service in Southeast Asia and contiguous waters or air space there over from July 4, 1965, through March 28, 1973.

• 8844 •
Delacorte Press
Department of Books for Young Readers
1745 Broadway, 9th Fl.
New York, NY 10019
Phone: (212)782-9062
Fax: (212)782-9452

• 8845 • **Marguerite de Angeli Prize**
To encourage the writing of middle grade fiction. The contest is open to U.S. and Canadian writers who have not previously published a novel for middle-grade readers. Submissions should consist of a contemporary or historical fiction manuscript set in North America, suitable for readers 7 to 10 years of age. Manuscript's length: between 40 and 144 pages. Foreign-language manuscripts and translations are not eligible. The award consists of a $1,500 cash prize and a $3,500 advance against royalties. Authors may not submit more than two manuscripts in the competition. Manuscripts must be postmarked between April 1 and June 30.

• 8846 • **Delacorte Press Prize for a First Young Adult Novel**
To encourage the writing of contemporary young adult fiction. The author must be American or Canadian, and may not have published a young adult novel. Foreign language manuscripts or translations are not eligible. The subject should be suitable for 12- to 18-year-olds. Submissions should consist of a book-length manuscript between 100 and 224 pages and a detailed plot summary. Include SASE for return of manuscript. The prize consists of a Delacorte hardcover and Dell paperback contract, a monetary award of $1,500, and a $6,000 advance towards royalties. All promotional costs for the winning book will be paid by the publishers. Awarded annually. Manuscripts must be postmarked between October 1 and December 31. Established in 1983.

• 8847 •
Delaware Association of School Administrators
Paul G. Carlson, Exec.Dir.
860 Silver Lake Blvd., Ste. 150
Dover, DE 19904
Phone: (302)674-0630
Fax: (302)674-8305
E-mail: pcarlson@edasa.org
Home Page: http://www.edasa.org

• 8848 • **DASA Scholarship**
For seniors going to college to major in education. Scholarship awarded annually.

• 8849 •
Delaware Contractors Association
John J. McMahon Jr., Exec.VP
527 Stanton-Christiana Rd.
Newark, DE 19713
Phone: (302)994-7442
Fax: (302)994-8185
E-mail: jmcmahon@e-dca.org
Home Page: http://www.e-dca.org

• 8850 • **DCA Scholarship**
For academics and need. Scholarship awarded annually.

• 8851 •
Delaware County Historical Society
Trudy B. Carroll, Library Adm.
85 N. Malin Rd.
Broomall, PA 19008-1928
Phone: (610)359-1148
Fax: (610)359-4155

• 8852 • **A. Lewis Smith Award**
For preservation and promotion of local history. Recognition award bestowed annually.

• 8853 •
Delaware Restaurant Association
Carrie Leishman, Pres./CEO
PO Box 8004
Newark, DE 19714
Phone: (410)838-0803
Toll-Free: (866)372-2545
Fax: (410)838-4885
E-mail: delrest@aol.com
Home Page: http://www.dineoutdelaware.com

• 8854 • **Restaurateur of the Year**
For outstanding professional restaurateur. Recognition award bestowed annually.

• 8855 •
Deloitte Touche Tohmatsu
1633 Broadway
New York, NY 10019-6754
Phone: (212)489-1600
Fax: (212)489-1687
Home Page: http://www.deloitte.com

• 8856 • **Doctoral Fellowship**
Each year the program offers up to ten grants of $20,000 to help outstanding graduate students complete their doctorate in accounting. Applications are reviewed by an idnependant selection comittee, composed of three eminent accounting educators. Those selected are designated as Deloitte & Touche Fellows. Each receives $5,000 durring the final year of course work and $15,000 during the subsequent year of writing a dissertation.

• 8857 • **Wildman Medal**
Awarded to an author or authors whose work is judged likely to make a highly significant contribution to the practice of public accounting. The award is accompanied by a $5,000 honorarium.

• 8858 •
Delphi International Program of World Learning
Peter Simpson PhD, Program Dir.
1015 18th St. NW, Ste. 1000
Washington, DC 20036-5272
Phone: (202)898-0950
Toll-Free: 800-826-0196
Fax: (202)842-0885
E-mail: delphi@worldlearning.org
Home Page: http://www.worldlearning.org/delphi

• 8859 • **International Cooperation Awards**
Recognizes significant contribution to work on behalf of the U.S. State Department's International Visitor LeadershipProgram. Awarded annually.

• 8860 •
Delray Beach Lions Club
Mrs. Donna Klemm, Pres.
PO Box 7117
Delray Beach, FL 33482-7117
Phone: (561)735-4558
Phone: (561)742-0852
Fax: (561)735-3171
E-mail: liondoc3@juno.com
Home Page: http://DelrayBeachFL.lionwap.org

• 8861 • **Atlantic High School Scholarship**
For high school senior with outstanding service to the community. Scholarship awarded annually.

• 8862 •
Delta Dental Plans Association
Kim Volk, Pres./CEO
801 Ogden Ave.
Lisle, IL 60532
Phone: (630)964-2400
Toll-Free: 800-323-1743
Fax: (630)964-2494
E-mail: csl@deltadentalil.com
Home Page: http://www.deltadental.com

• 8863 • **F. Gene Dixon, DDS Leadership Award**
To recognize an individual who has demonstrated extraordinary leadership and achievement in the field of dental care prepayment. A plaque is awarded annually. Established in 1977 in honor of F. Gene Dixon, DDS, in recognition of many years of dedicated service and leadership in the field of dental prepayment.

• 8864 •
Delta Kappa Epsilon Fraternity
David K. Easlick Jr., Exec.Dir.
2008 Libbie, Ste. 101
PO Box 17310
Richmond, VA 23226
Phone: (804)288-3592
Toll-Free: 800-560-DEKE
E-mail: dekehq@hotmail.com
Home Page: http://www.dke.org

• 8865 • **William M. Henderson Alumni Award**
This, the Fraternity's top alumni award, recognizes outstanding service by an alumnus to a chapter of Delta Kappa Epsilon. A silver julep cup is awarded annually. Established in 1975 to honor William M. Henderson, past Executive Director and Honorary President of DKE.

• 8866 • **Lion Trophy**
To honor outstanding achievement by an individual chapter of Delta Kappa Epsilon in the areas of scholarship, alumni relations, comunity service, and chapter improvement. A silver trophy and engrossed scroll are awarded annually. A trophy was originally presented to the last surviving founder of the Fraternity, William Boyd Jacobs, Yale 1846, in 1894. Re-established in 1955.

• 8867 •
Delta Nu Alpha Transportation Fraternity
Carol Hackett, Contact
1451 Elm Hill Pike, Ste. 255
Nashville, TN 37210
Phone: (615)360-6863
Toll-Free: (866)453-3662
Fax: (615)360-1891
E-mail: carolh24@msn.com
Home Page: http://deltanualpha.org

• 8868 • **Transportation Man of the Year**
To recognize contributions to the field of transportation. A plaque is awarded annually. Established in 1952.

• 8869 •
Delta Omega National Honorary Society, Pi Chapter
Allison Foster, Exec.Sec.
1101 15th St. NW, Suite 910
Washington, DC 20005
E-mail: afoster@asph.org
Home Page: http://www.deltaomega.org

• 8870 • **National Essay Contest on "The Role of Public Health in Healthcare Reform"**
To recognize the best student essay on the named subject. The essay may be based on empirical research, literature review and interpretation, or on any other thoughtful approach to the subject. Any student currently enrolled in an accredited School of Public Health in the United States may submit an essay with a maximum of 15 pages of text. Announcements about the contest are distributed in accredited Schools of Public Health in the fall of each year. Refer to a current announcement for deadline for receipt of essays (deadlines have varied from January 15 to April 15.) The following monetary awards are presented: first prize - $1,000; second prize - $500; and third prize - $250. In addition, each winner receives a certificate and an invitation to present the paper at the annual meeting of the American Public Health Association. Established in 1989. Formerly: National Essay Contest on Public Health as Social Justice.

• 8871 •
Delta Omicron
Julie Hensley, Exec.Sec.
718 E Ellis St., Ste. 3
Jefferson City, TN 37760
Phone: (865)471-6155
Fax: (865)475-9716
E-mail: doexecsec@aol.com
Home Page: http://www.delta-omicron.org

• 8872 • **Triennial Composition Competition**
To recognize and to encourage excellence in composition and the public performance of works. Composers of college age or over may submit works. A monetary award of $500 and a public premiere performance at the Triennial Conference are awarded triennially. Established in 1951. Additional information is available from Judith Eidson, 12297 West Tennessee Place, Lakewood, CO 80228.

• 8873 •
Delta Pi Epsilon
Dr. Robert B. Mitchell, Exec.Dir.
PO Box 4340
Little Rock, AR 72214
Phone: (501)219-1866
Fax: (501)219-1876
E-mail: dpe@ipa.net
Home Page: http://www.dpe.org

• 8874 • **Delta Pi Epsilon Research Award**
To encourage and recognize graduate research in business education. Outstanding doctoral research studies and master's theses in business education, completed during a particular calendar year in regionally accredited colleges or universities, are eligible. An abstract of the award-winning study is published in the *Delta Pi Epsilon Journal*. Bound studies must be submitted by March 1 following the calendar year of completion to, Dept of Workforce Education and Development, Southern Illinois University, Carbondale, IL 62901-4605. Two awards, one for the outstanding master's thesis and one for the outstanding doctoral dissertation, are awarded annually. Established in 1939.

• 8875 • **Independent Research Award**
To encourage and recognize independent research in the broad area of business education. Research associated with a graduate degree or chapter research activities is not eligible for consideration for this award. However, research funded by the Delta Pi Epsilon Research Foundation is eligible. The award may be presented biennially, with the presentation being made at the DPE National Research Conference held biennially in even-numbered years. The recipient will receive a plaque. These studies must be submitted to the Awards Committee Chairperson by March 1. Entry information, including an entry form, may be obtained from the DPE National Office near the time of submission. submission.

• 8876 •
Demello School Parent Teacher Organization
Maria C. Carreiro, Pres.
654 Dartmouth St.
Dartmouth, MA 02748-3005
Phone: (508)996-6759
Fax: (508)990-2519
E-mail: demellopto@yahoo.com
Home Page: http://us.geocities.com/demellopto/index.html

• 8877 • **DeMello School Scholarships**
For DeMello school alumni, parental involvement with PTO. Scholarship awarded annually.

• 8878 •
Democratic Socialists of America, Pittsburgh
Rob Shepherd, Contact
5848 Alderton St., No. 1
Pittsburgh, PA 15217-2431
Phone: (412)421-8503
E-mail: roboshep@aol.com

• 8879 • **Bread and Roses Award**
For outstanding women of the democratic socialist movement. Recognition award bestowed annually.

• 8880 •
Denver Film Society
Scott Rowitz, Exec.Dir.
1725 Blake St.
Denver, CO 80202
Phone: (303)595-3456
Fax: (303)595-0956
E-mail: dfs@denverfilm.org
Home Page: http://www.denverfilm.org

• 8881 • **Stan Brakhage Award for Best Short Subject**
Recognizes the best short fiction or documentary film. Presented annually as part of the Starz Denver International Film Festival. Nominations must be made online. See the above web site for complete nomination details.

• 8882 • **John Cassavetes Award**
To recognize outstanding achievement in independent filmmaking. American director/actors are eligible. A sculpture is awarded annually at the Starz Denver International Film Festival in October. Established in 1989 in memory of John Cassavetes and awarded to an individual who exemplifies his dedication to and talent for independent filmmaking. Nominations must be made

online. See the above web site for complete nomination details.

• 8883 • Krzysztof Kieslowski Award for Best Foreign Feature
Recognizes the best European film nominated at the Starz Denver International Film Festival. Films must be submitted online. Awarded annually. Established in 1997.

• 8884 • Mayor's Lifetime Achievement Award
Recognizes contributions to world cinema. Film artists are eligible. Awarded annually as part of the Starz Denver International Film Festival. Nominations must be made online. See the above web site for complete nomination information.

• 8885 • Starz People's Choice Award
Recognizes the most popular feature-length fiction filme and feature-length documentary. Selection is made by the audience. Awarded annually as part of the Starz Denver International Film Festival. Nominations must be made online. See the above web site for complete nomination details.

• 8886 •
Denver Public Library
Western History/Genealogy Department
Cynthia Rand, Bancroft Prize Coordinator
10 West 14th Ave. Pkwy.
Denver, CO 80204
Phone: (720)865-1906
Fax: (720)865-1880
E-mail: trand@denver.lib.co.us
Home Page: http://www.denver.lib.co.us

• 8887 • Caroline Bancroft History Prize
To recognize a notable non-fiction book on Colorado or Western American history. Entries must be published non-fiction books submitted by the publisher dealing with the history of the trans-Mississippi West, copyrighted the previous year and a minimum of 100 pages in length. Reprints without significant new material do not qualify. Books must be written in English or translated into English. The deadline is April 15. A $1,000 minimum prize is awarded annually. Established in 1988 by the estate of Caroline Bancroft to commemorate Ms. Bancroft, a noted chronicler of Colorado and benefactor of the Library.

• 8888 •
Department of World Arts and Culture
University of California, Los Angeles
David Gere, Chm.
Kaufman Hall, Ste. 150
120 Westwood Plz.
Box 951608
Los Angeles, CA 90095-1608
Phone: (310)825-3951
Phone: (310)206-1342
Fax: (310)825-2606
E-mail: wacinfo@arts.ucla.edu
Home Page: http://www.wac.ucla.edu

Formerly: (1995) Center for the Study of Comparative Folklore and Mythology.

• 8889 • Wayland D. Hand Award for Academic Achievement in Folklore and Mythology Studies
For recognition of professional promise and achievement in folklore and mythology studies. Students enrolled in the Folklore and Mythology Program at UCLA or in a related department are eligible. An honorarium and a certificate are awarded annually. Established in 1987 in memory of Wayland D. Hand, Professor of Germanic Languages and Folklore at UCLA, who helped establish the curriculum and research center in folklore and mythology.

• 8890 •
Dermatology Foundation
Sandra Rahn Benz, Exec.Dir.
1560 Sherman Ave., Ste. 870
Evanston, IL 60201-4808
Phone: (847)328-2256
Fax: (847)328-0509
E-mail: dfgen@dermatologyfoundation.org
Home Page: http://www.dermfnd.org

• 8891 • Career Development Award in Skin Research
To assist in the transition from Fellowship to established investigator. Applications will be accepted from Junior Investigators in the early stages of their academic career. The applicant has to be a faculty member in a Department or Division of Dermatology, demonstrate strong commitment to skin research, and have already had appropriate initial training (a 2-3 year research fellowship or equivalent experience) in biomedical research. A stipend of $55,000 per year is provided, which can be supplemented from other sources. Established in 1989.

• 8892 • Fellowship and Grant Award Program
To foster basic research in cancer and other diseases of the skin, hair, and nails so that their diagnosis, treatment, and methods of prevention will be improved; and to influence the commitment of young researchers to academic dermatology. Fellowship applicants must hold an M.D. or Ph.D. degree or equivalent and be no more than four years beyond the completion of their training are eligible. Fellowship recipients must limit clinical duties to no more than one half day per week. Research must be conducted in the United States. The applicant must designate a preceptor who has an academic appointment in a division or department of dermatology and has the appropriate credentials to supervise the proposed research. Monetary awards are presented annually. Established in 1964.

• 8893 •
Des Moines Education Association
John Vint, Exec.Dir.
206 Center St.
Des Moines, IA 50309-1629
Phone: (515)244-6040

• 8894 • Fischer Scholarship
For high school senior. Monetary award bestowed annually.

• 8895 • Galvin Scholarship
For 90 hours of course study in an educational program. Scholarship awarded annually.

• 8896 •
Desert Fishes Council
E.P. Pister, Exec.Sec.
PO Box 337
Bishop, CA 93515
Phone: (760)872-8751
Fax: (760)872-8751
E-mail: phil@desertfishes.org
Home Page: http://www.desertfishes.org

• 8897 • Carl L. Hubbs Award
Recognizes the best industry related student paper. Awarded annually.

• 8898 • Frances Hubbs Miller Award
Recognizes the best paper presented by a Mexican student. Awarded annually.

• 8899 •
Developing Countries Farm Radio Network (Reseau de radios rurales des pays en developpement)
Nancy Bennett, Exec.Dir.
1404 Scott St.
Ottawa, ON, Canada K1Y 4M8
Phone: (613)761-3650
Toll-Free: 888-773-7717
Fax: (613)798-0990
E-mail: info@farmradio.org
Home Page: http://www.farmradio.org

• 8900 • George Atkins Communications Award
Annual award of recognition for Network members.

• 8901 •
Dialogue: A Journal of Mormon Thought
Levi S. Peterson, Ed.
PO Box 58423
Salt Lake City, UT 84158
Phone: (801)274-8210
Toll-Free: 888-874-8210
E-mail: dialoguejournal@msn.com
Home Page: http://www.dialoguejournal.com

• 8902 • **Dialogue Writing Awards**
To encourage new writing in Mormon and religious studies, and to recognize excellence in literature. Submissions to Dialogue: A Journal of Mormon Thought during the calendar year are eligible, provided they have not been previously submitted or published elsewhere. Awards are given in the following categories: Essays and Articles, Fiction, Poetry, and Art. Cash prizes are awarded annually. $100-$500. Formerly: (1985) Dialogue-Silver Foundation Awards.

• 8903 •
Diamond Council of America
Terry Chandler, Pres./CEO
3212 W End Ave., Ste. 202
Nashville, TN 37203-5835
Phone: (615)385-5301
Toll-Free: 877-283-5669
Fax: (615)385-4955
Home Page: http://www.diamondcouncil.org

• 8904 • **Alpha Beta Kappa Award**
To recognize ten graduates with the highest course averages. Ten students are inducted annually in the Honor Society.

• 8905 • **Myer Barr Award**
To recognize the graduate with the highest average in the study of diamontology and gemology. Awarded annually.

• 8906 • **Melvin B. Foer Memorial Award**
To recognize individuals whose contributions to jewelry retailing and the jewelry industry have distinguished them among their peers. The award is not given on an annual basis, but when the DCA Board of Directors determines that there is a deserving individual(s). The presentation is made at the next annual DCA gathering.

• 8907 • **Barnett Helzberg Scholarship**
Awarded annually to the Diamontology graduate with the highest grade on a proctored exam. The scholarship entitles the honoree to a full GIA Diamond Course.

• 8908 • **Paul Storm Award**
To recognize the DCA jeweler with the greatest number of graduates. Awards are given in two categories: six stores or less and seven or more stores. Awarded annually.

• 8909 • **Lode Van Bercken Award**
To honor the outgoing president of the council for his leadership. An engraved plaque is awarded biennually. Established in 1974. Orginated in 1952 by the Diamond Dealers Association, Antwerp, Belgium.

• 8910 •
Dickinson College
PO Box 1773
Carlisle, PA 17013-2896
Phone: (717)243-5121
Fax: (717)245-1941
E-mail: nicholss@dickinson.edu
Home Page: http://www.dickinson.edu

• 8911 • **Dickinson College Arts Award**
To honor an individual or group for distinguished achievement in the arts, letters, or humanities. An honorarium and a medallion are awarded annually or, on occasion, biannually. Established in 1959.

• 8912 • **Joseph Priestley Award**
To honor an outstanding physicist, chemist, biochemist, or other scientist for research, a discovery, or production that benefits humankind. A monetary award and a medallion are awarded annually. Established in 1952 in memory of Joseph Priestley (1733-1804), the discoverer of oxygen, some of whose laboratory equipment was acquired by Dickinson in 1811 and is on exhibit in the College's Boyd Lee Spahr Library.

• 8913 • **Benjamin Rush Award**
To recognize a business leader who has demonstrated through his or her actions in the corporate world a personal commitment to the values of the liberal arts. Established in 1985 in memory of Benjamin Rush (1745-1813), colonial physician and Revolutionary War patriot, who was instrumental in the chartering of Dickinson as a college in 1783. The recipient is awarded a bronze medal bearing Rush/s likeness.

• 8914 •
Dighton Historical Society
1217 Williams
Dighton, MA 02715
Phone: (508)669-5514

• 8915 • **Celia Carr Flower Arranging Award**
To honor a Dighton student attending Bristol County Agricultural High School nominated by faculty. An award of $50.00 is awarded annually in the spring.

• 8916 • **Celia Carr Music Award**
To honor a Dighton student at Dighton Rehoboth Regional High School selected by his or her music teacher. No application is necessary. An award of $50.00 is awarded annually.

• 8917 • **Charlotte Crawford Art Award**
In the memory of Charlotte Crawford, this award is presented to a student at Dighton Rehoboth Regional High School who has been selected by his or her art teacher. A prize of $50.00 is awarded annually in June.

• 8918 • **Charles Harris Award**
To honor academic achievement by a student from Dighton attending Bristol County Agricultural High School. Awarded annually in June.

• 8919 • **Helen H. Lane History Award**
To honor a student at Dighton Middle School selected for achievement in History. An award of $25.00 is awarded yearly in June.

• 8920 • **Music Arts and Flowers History Award**
Award of recognition. Applicants must be Dighton students. Awarded three times per year.

• 8921 •
Dillmans Creative Arts Foundation
Dennis Robertson, Pres.
PO Box 98
Lac Du Flambeau, WI 54538-0098
Phone: (715)588-3143
Phone: (715)588-7322
Fax: (715)588-3110
E-mail: frontdesk@dillmans.com
Home Page: http://www.dillmans.com

• 8922 • **Dillman's Creative Arts Scholarship Award**
Based on need and interests. Scholarship awarded annually.

• 8923 •
Direct Marketing Association
John A. Greco Jr., Pres./CEO
1120 Avenue of the Americas
New York, NY 10036-6700
Phone: (212)768-7277
Fax: (212)302-6714
E-mail: president@the-dma.org
Home Page: http://www.the-dma.org

• 8924 • **Direct Marketing International ECHO Awards**
To honor and recognize the most successful direct response marketing campaigns each year. Companies, agencies, and individuals who have conceived, produced, or used programs that have been exceptionally successful in achieving sales, marketing, fundraising, or promotional goals - including those efforts that advance the state of the art are eligible. Gold, silver, and bronze trophies and a varying number of Direct Marketing Leader Plaques are awarded each year. The Diamond ECHO Award is given to recognize the best of show. In addition, the Gold Mailbox Award is given for the most innovative use of direct mail. Established in 1930. Additional information is available through the ECHO Department of the Association, at the above web site or send an email to echo@the-dma.org. Formerly: (1979) Worldwide Awards Competition.

• 8925 • **DMA Hall of Fame**
To recognize outstanding impact on the industry an honor achievements, accomplishments, and leadership. Four awards are given annually. Candidates do not necessarily have to be members of DMA. Any member of the Association may recommend a candidate for the Hall of Fame. Awarded annually when merited. Established in 1978.

• 8926 •
Direct Marketing Association of Detroit
Ann Dixon, Pres.
32425 Grand River Ave.
Farmington, MI 48336
Phone: (248)478-4888
Fax: (248)478-6437
Home Page: http://www.dmad.org

• 8927 • **Target Award**
For individual or company developing best direct mail or direct response program during preceding calendar year. Recognition award bestowed annually.

• 8928 •
Direct Marketing Club of New York
Stuart Boysen, Exec. Dir.
224 7th St.
Garden City, NY 11530
Phone: (516)746-6700
Fax: (516)294-8141
E-mail: info@dmcny.org
Home Page: http://www.dmcny.org

• 8929 • **Silver Apple**
In recognition of service and contribution to direct marketing for a period of 25 years or more. Recognition award bestowed annually. Awarded by vote of the past presidents of DMCNY.

• 8930 •
Direct Marketing Educational Foundation
H. Robert Wientzen, Pres./CEO
1120 Avenue of the Americas
New York, NY 10036-6700
Phone: (212)768-7277
Fax: (212)790-1561
E-mail: dmef@the-dma.org
Home Page: http://www.the-dma.org/dmef

Formerly: Direct Mail/Marketing Educational Foundation.

• 8931 • **Robert B. Clarke Outstanding Educator Award**
To recognize an academician for significant achievements in direct marketing and interactive marketing education, based on teaching, writing, research and speaking. Nominations must be submitted by July 1. A monetary award of $1,000 is presented annually at DMEF's Educators' conference in the fall. Established in 1989 to honor Robert B. Clarke, DMEF Trustee and former Chairman of Grolier, Inc.

• 8932 • **Edward N. Mayer Award for Educational Leadership**
To recognize individuals (non-academics) who have made outstanding contributions to direct marketing education at the college and university level. A committee of the DMEF's Board of Trustees makes the final selection on the basis of leadership in expanding and improving direct marketing education at the university level. A plaque is awarded annually. Established in 1977 in honor of Edward N. Mayer, Jr., who influenced, inspired and taught many of today's leading direct marketers. For more information contact David Chancey at the Direct Marketing Educational Foundation or email dchancey@the-dma.org.

• 8933 •
Direct Selling Association
Mr. Neil H. Offen, Pres.
1275 Pennsylvania Ave. NW, Ste. 800
Washington, DC 20004
Phone: (202)347-8866
Fax: (202)347-0055
E-mail: info@dsa.org
Home Page: http://www.dsa.org

• 8934 • **Hall of Fame Award**
To recognize an individual's lifetime achievements and contributions to direct selling. Recipients must be living, must have devoted significant years to direct selling, and must have attained stature and respect in the business community. A trophy is awarded when merited. Established in 1963.

• 8935 • **Industry Innovation Award**
To recognize member companies that have demonstrated innovative approaches to direct selling and have shared their expertise with others. Activities begun within the past five years must be submitted by member firms by February 28. A trophy is awarded annually at the convention. Established in 1990. Formerly: Innovation Award.

• 8936 • **Partnership Award**
To recognize supplier companies that provide a good or service that has had a measurable impact on growth or development of an active member company or that has increased the profitability of a member. Awarded annually.

• 8937 • **Vision for Tomorrow Award**
To recognize member companies that have substantially improved the quality of life in their communities through community service activities. DSA member firms must submit applications by February 28 for an activity begun within the past five years. A trophy is awarded annually at the convention.

• 8938 •
Directors Guild of America
Jay Roth, Exec.Dir.
7920 Sunset Blvd.
Los Angeles, CA 90046
Phone: (310)289-2000
Toll-Free: 800-420-4173
Fax: (310)289-2029
E-mail: darrellh@dga.org
Home Page: http://www.dga.org

• 8939 • **Robert B. Aldrich Service Award**
For recognition of outstanding service to the Directors Guild of America. Members are eligible. A trophy, a mounted replica of the DGA Seal, is awarded when merited. Established in 1984 in honor of Robert Aldrich, past president of the DGA.

• 8940 • **Frank Capra Achievement Award**
For recognition of a unit production manager or assistant director for a history of service to the guild and to the industry. A plaque is awarded when merited. Established in 1980.

• 8941 • **Commercial Director Award**
To recognize outstanding direction of television commercials. A gold medallion is awarded annually. Established in 1980.

• 8942 • **D. W. Griffith Award**
To recognize an individual for distinguished achievement in motion picture direction over an entire career. An etched-glass emblem medallion is awarded as merited. Established in 1953.

• 8943 • **Honorary Life Member**
To recognize and individual for outstanding creative achievement or contribution to the Guild or to the profession of directing. An etched glass emblem medallion is awarded when merited. Established in 1938.

• 8944 • **Lifetime Achievement Award**
To recognize outstanding accomplishment in motion pictures. Presented annually at the Awards Dinner in January. Established in 1953, it was renamed in 1980 to honor David Wark Griffith, the noted pioneer director. Formerly: (1980) David Wark Griffith Awards.

• 8945 • **Lifetime Achievement Award in News Direction**
To recognize career achievements in news direction. Awarded when merited. Established in 1995.

• 8946 • **Lifetime Achievement Award in Sports Direction**
To recognize career achievement in sports film direction. Awarded when merited. Established in 1991.

• 8947 • Outstanding Directorial Achievement Award for Feature Films

For recognition of outstanding directorial achievement in a feature film. Directors of feature films released in the New York and Los Angeles areas during the year are eligible. A gold medallion is awarded annually. Established in 1948.

• 8948 • Outstanding Directorial Achievement Award for Television

For recognition of outstanding directorial achievement in the following categories in television: Comedy Series, Dramatic Series - Night, Musical/Variety, Documentary/Actuality, and Daytime Serials, Children's Programming, and Dramatic Specials. Directors of television programs presented during the year are eligible. A gold medallion is awarded annually. Established in 1953.

• 8949 • Franklin J. Schaffner Achievement Award

To recognize an associate director or stage manager for service to the industry or the Guild. Established in 1991.

• 8950 •
Dirksen Congressional Center
2185 Broadway
Pekin, IL 61554-4219
Phone: (309)347-7113
Fax: (309)347-6432
E-mail: fmackaman@dirksencenter.org
Home Page: http://www.dirksencongressionalcenter.org

• 8951 • Congressional Research Grant Program

To provide funds for research on congressional leadership and the U.S. Congress. Anyone with a serious interest in studying Congress is eligible. The center seeks applications specifically from political scientists, historians, biographers, scholars of public administration or American studies, or journalists. Graduate students are encouraged to apply. The deadline is February 1. Grant funds totaling approximately $45,000 are awarded annually for travel to conduct research, duplication of research materials, costs of clerical or research assistance, or other qualified research expenses. Established in 1975.

• 8952 •
Disability Awareness Council of West Michigan
Maggie Carlson, Exec.Dir.
1041 E Broadway Ave.
Muskegon, MI 49444-2331
Phone: (231)830-0099
Fax: (231)830-0066

• 8953 • Cal Haworth Leadership Award

For disabled person. Scholarship awarded annually.

• 8954 •
Disabled American Veterans
Arthur H. Wilson, Natl.Adj.
PO Box 14301
Cincinnati, OH 45250-0301
Phone: (859)441-7300
Fax: (859)441-1416
E-mail: feedback@davmail.org
Home Page: http://www.dav.org

• 8955 • Outstanding Disabled Veteran of the Year

To recognize an outstanding wartime veteran with a service-connected disability/disabilities; and to call public attention, particularly that of business and industry, to the fact that the abilities of the physically handicapped often exceed those of their so-called normal counterparts. Consideration is given to the nature and severity of the nominee's disability and the persistence in surmounting his or her handicaps. Economic and employment achievements will also be considered. Nominations are accepted. A large wood and bronze plaque and an all-expense paid trip to the DAV national convention are awarded annually. Established in 1962.

• 8956 • Outstanding Disabled Veteran Outreach Coordinator

To recognize the significant contributions with regard to outreach, counseling, job development, training, placement, and employer contact on behalf of disabled veterans. Nominations are accepted. A large wood and bronze plaque and an all-expense paid trip to the DAV national convention are awarded annually. Established in 1977.

• 8957 • Outstanding Large and Small Employer Award

To accord public recognition to employers such as companies, firms, associations, government agencies, or individuals who demonstrate by their employment policies and hiring practices that disabled veterans may obtain suitable employment in their organizations. Two awards are presented in this category - one to an employer with 200 or more employees, and another to an employer of less than 200 employees. Nominations are accepted. A large wood and bronze plaque is presented at the DAV national convention. Established in 1962.

• 8958 • Outstanding Local Veterans' Employment Representative

To recognize significant contributions made by local veterans' employment representatives to enhance employment and training opportunities for disabled veterans. Nominations are accepted. A large wood and bronze plaque and an all-expense paid trip to the DAV national convention are awarded annually. Established in 1973.

• 8959 • George H. Seal Memorial Trophy Award

To recognize the extraordinary volunteer dedication to the needs of hospitalized veterans through the Department of Veterans Affairs (VA) Volunteer Service program. Nominations are accepted from all VA medical centers. A recipient from the Disabled American Veterans (DAV) and one from the DAV Auxiliary are chosen. Each receives a trophy replica and their names are engraved on the George H. Seal Memorial trophy permanently displayed at DAV National Headquarters at Cold Spring, Kentucky. In addition, the recipients receive travel expenses to attend the DAV national convention. The VA medical facility represented by each winner is awarded a large wood and bronze plaque. All nominees receive Honorable Mention Certificates.

• 8960 •
Disciples Peace Fellowship
Rev. Bruce Patton, Office Coor.
PO Box 1986
130 E Washington St.
Indianapolis, IN 46206
Phone: (317)713-2679
Phone: (317)713-2636
Toll-Free: 888-346-2631
Fax: (317)635-4426
E-mail: mail@dhm.disciples.org
Home Page: http://www.homelandministries.org/DPF

• 8961 • Will Wittkamper Peace Award

To recognize and honor a member of the Christian Church (Disciples of Christ) whose life and work have made significant contributions to the cause of peace. Ministers or laypersons dedicated to the ideas and deeds that make for peace among peoples and nations are eligible. The winner's name is inscribed on a permanent award trophy, and a small facsimile trophy is awarded to the recipient. Awarded biennially at the General Assembly of the Church. Established in 1980 in memory of Will Wittkamper (1892-1980), minister and pacifist peace activist.

• 8962 •
District of Columbia Library Association
Betty Landesman, Pres.
PO Box 14177
Benjamin Franklin Sta.
Washington, DC 20044
Phone: (202)872-1112
Home Page: http://www.dcla.org

• 8963 • Student Loan

For local students pursuing master's degrees in library sciences and demonstrating financial need; awarded competitively. Monetary award bestowed annually.

• 8964 •
District of Columbia Public Library
901 G St. NW
Washington, DC 20001
Phone: (202)727-0321
Fax: (202)727-1129
Home Page: http://www.dclibrary.org

• 8965 • **Martin Luther King, Jr. Leadership Awards**
To recognize and honor individuals in the District of Columbia who have made significant, sustained contributions to public library development, expansion, support, and use. By their actions, the honorees have exemplified King's courage, his commitment to education and reading, and his love for humanity. A bronze medallion is awarded. Established in 1988.

• 8966 •
Diving Equipment and Marketing Association
Tom Ingram, Exec.Dir.
3750 Convoy St., Ste. 310
San Diego, CA 92111-3741
Phone: (858)616-6408
Toll-Free: 800-862-3483
Fax: (858)616-6495
E-mail: info@dema.org
Home Page: http://www.dema.org

• 8967 • **Reaching Out Award - Diving Hall of Fame**
Recognizes contributions to the sport of diving. Awarded annually.

• 8968 •
Doberman Pinscher Club of America
Leslie Reeves-Hunt, Membership Sec.
PO Box 8195
Roseville, MI 48066
Phone: (810)326-3792
E-mail: dpcamembersecy@aol.com
Home Page: http://www.dpca.org

• 8969 • **Doberman Pinscher Club of America Awards Program**
For recognition of outstanding Doberman Pinschers. Awards are given in the following categories: (1) Conformation Awards; (2) Championship Awards; (3) Obedience Awards; and (4) Junior Showmanship Awards. A Doberman nominated for the awards program must have been owned by a Club member during the period of competition being considered.

• 8970 •
Dr. James Naismith Basketball Foundation (Fondation du Basket-Ball Dr. James Naismith)
John Gosset, Exec.Dir.
14 Bridge St.
PO Box 1991
Almonte, ON, Canada K0A 1A0
Phone: (613)256-0492
Fax: (613)256-0492
E-mail: info@naismithmuseum.com
Home Page: http:// www.naismithmuseum.com

• 8971 • **Canadian Basketball Hall of Fame**
Recognizes contributions to the sport of basketball. Awarded annually.

• 8972 •
Doctors to the World
Dr. Seiden, Contact
PO Box 37167
Denver, CO 80237
Phone: (303)758-5405
Fax: (303)758-4124
E-mail: dttw@juno.com
Home Page: http://www.dttw.org

• 8973 • **Humanitarian Award**
To recognize humanitarian efforts by individuals, corporations or organizations. Awarded annually with a plaque.

• 8974 •
Document Management Industries Association
Peter L. Colaianni, EVP
433 E Monroe Ave.
Alexandria, VA 22301
Phone: (703)836-6232
Fax: (703)836-2241
E-mail: dmia@dmia.org
Home Page: http://www.dmia.org

• 8975 • **Manufacturer Member of the Year**
To recognize the manufacturer member whose service has contributed most to the growth and progress of the association. Awarded annually. Formerly: Associate Member of the Year.

• 8976 • **Member of the Year**
To recognize the member or member company who has made the most outstanding contribution to the advancement of the Association. Awarded annually.

• 8977 • **President's Award**
To recognize the individual who have made a significant contribution to the business printing industry and to the Independent concept during the preceding year. Awarded annually.

• 8978 •
Dog Writers Association of America
Ranny Green, Pres.
173 Union Rd.
Coatesville, PA 19320
Phone: (610)384-2436
Fax: (610)384-2471
E-mail: dwaa@dwaa.org
Home Page: http://www.dwaa.org

• 8979 • **Annual Writing Competition**
To promote and recognize excellence in writing about dogs, their care and training, all aspects of dog ownership, and the sport of dogs. Awards are given in the following categories: newspapers; magazines and canine newspapers (privately published); club publications; books; graphic arts, poetry, short fiction, and pamphlets; and video tapes. Certificates are awarded annually. Established in 1935. Additional information is available from Janine Adams 703 Greenwood, Brooklyn, NY 11218, telephone: (718)4354047.

• 8980 •
Doll Artisan Guild
Karin Goulian, Exec.Dir.
118 Commerce Rd.
PO Box 1113
Oneonta, NY 13820-5113
Phone: (607)432-4977
Fax: (607)432-2042
E-mail: info@dollartisanguild.org
Home Page: http://dollartisanguild.org

• 8981 • **Aurora Award**
To recognize achievement in reproduction of small dolls. Members of DAG, except instructors and judges, are eligible. A trophy, the Aurora, is awarded for the best small doll in the show. Awarded at several worldwide competitions each year. Established in 1995.

• 8982 • **Rolf Ericson's Award for Outstanding Doll Sculpture**
For recognition of achievement in sculpting an original doll. Members of DAG, except instructors and judges, are eligible. A plaque is awarded for the best in the show. Awarded three times a year, at two competitions within the United States and also at the DAG Puppenmacher Festival in Germany. Established in 1983 by Rolf Ericson, Executive Director.

• 8983 • **Eva's Choice Award**
For recognition of achievement in porcelain dollmaking. Members of the DAG, except instructors and judges, are eligible. A large rosette is awarded annually at two competitions within the United States and at some DAG competitions abroad. Established in 1987 by Eva Oscarsson, former editor of *The Doll Artisan* magazine and a senior judge for the Guild.

• 8984 • **Magge Award**
To recognize achievement in reproduction of modern porcelain dolls. Members of DAG, except instructors and judges, are eligible. A trophy, the "Magge," is awarded at least three worldwide competitions each year for the best in the show. Two awards are presented at each event, one for professional and one for non-professional. Established in 1993 and named for Magge Head Kane, contemporary doll artist and pioneer.

• 8985 • **Millie Award**
For recognition of achievement in reproduction of antique porcelain dolls. Members of DAG, except instructors and judges, are eligible. A trophy, the "Millie," is awarded for the best in the show. Awarded at at least four different worldwide competitions each year. Established in 1979 and named for Mildred Seeley, founder of the organization.

• 8986 •
Dominican University
Donna M. Carroll, Pres.
7900 W Division St.
River Forest, IL 60305
Phone: (708)366-2490
Fax: (708)524-5990
E-mail: webmaster@dom.edu
Home Page: http://www.dom.edu

Formerly: (1997) Rosary College.

• 8987 • **Bravo Award**
To recognize an individual or organization whose exceptional contributions to the performance arts have enhanced the Chicagoland community's opportunities to appreciate and enjoy the best in music, opera, theatre, and the humanities. A crystal paper weight is awarded annually. Established in 1982.

• 8988 • **Excellence in Teaching Award**
To recognize an undergraduate faculty member for teaching excellence and leadership inside and outside the classroom. Faculty members are both nominated and selected by former award winners. Award is given biennially. Award winner receives $1,000 at Honors Convocation Ceremony.

• 8989 • **Follett Library Resources & Software Companies Excellence in Teaching Award (Graduate School of Library and Information Science)**
To recognize a faculty member in the Graduate School of Library and Information Science for teaching excellence. Awarded every third year. Faculty members are nominated and selected by students. Award winner receives $1,000 at May Commencement exercises. First award was given in May 1996. Endowed by Follett Library Resources Company and Follett Software Company.

• 8990 • **Midwest Bank Excellence in Teaching Award (School of Education)**
To recognize a faculty member in the School of Education for teaching excellence. Awarded every third year. Faculty members are nominated and selected by students. Award winner receives $1,000 at May Commencement exercises. Endowed by Midwest Bank.

• 8991 • **Mother Evelyn Murphy Excellence in Teaching Award**
To recognize a faculty member for excellence in teaching. Faculty members who have demonstrated excellence in teaching must be elected by the students. A monetary award of $1,000 is awarded biennially in odd-numbered years. Established in 1967 to honor Mother Evelyn Murphy, former Mother General of the Congregation of the Most Holy Rosary.

• 8992 • **St. Paul Federal Bank for Savings Excellence in Teaching Award (Graduate School of Business)**
To recognize a faculty member in the Graduate School of Business for teaching excellence. Awarded annually. Faculty members are nominated and selected by students. Award winner receives $1,000. First award was given in May 1995. Endowed by St. Paul Federal Bank for Savings.

• 8993 •
Donors Forum of Wisconsin
Deborah Fugenschuh, Exec.Dir.
759 N. Milwaukee St., Ste. 515
759 N. Milwaukee St., Ste. 408
Milwaukee, WI 53202
Phone: (414)270-1978
Toll-Free: 877-783-6786
Fax: (414)270-1979
E-mail: admin@dfwonline.org
Home Page: http://dfwonline.org

• 8994 • **Good Grant Award**
For creative partnership between a funder and a grantee. Recognition award bestowed annually.

• 8995 •
Door and Hardware Institute
Jerry Heppes CAE, Exec.Dir.
14150 Newbrook Dr., Ste. 200
Chantilly, VA 20151
Phone: (703)222-2010
Fax: (703)222-2410
E-mail: info@dhi.org
Home Page: http://www.dhi.org

• 8996 • **Award of Merit**
To recognize individuals who, although not members of the Institute, have rendered outstanding contributions to the advancement of the aims and objectives of the Institute and of the architectural openings industry. Nominations are based on contributions on a specific project or series of projects. The nominations deadline is May 1.

• 8997 • **Chapter Achievement Award**
To recognize chapters that perform in an outstanding manner in the area of programming, reporting of meetings, meeting attendance, and other projects. Awards are based on yearly performance for the period beginning June 1 and ending May 31.

• 8998 • **Founders' Memorial Award**
This, the Institute's highest award, is conferred on an individual who has demonstrated significant contributions and outstanding service to the Institute or to the architectural openings industry over an extended period of time. Only national or international level service, which is consistent with the Institute's aims and objectives, is considered. The nominations deadline is May 1. Awarded annually. Established in 1965.

• 8999 • **Outstanding Regional Director**
To recognize the regional or area director of the Institute who has made the greatest contribution of service in promoting and fostering the purposes and objectives of the Institute on both a chapter and national level. The nominations deadline is May 1.

• 9000 • **Recognition of Service and Involvement**
To recognize instructors, examination graders, and others for outstanding service and contributions of time to the Institute. The nominations deadline is May 1.

• 9001 • **Robert G. Ryan Memorial Award**
To recognize the author of the best article in *Doors and Hardware* in two categories: technical, and business-related. All feature articles written by industry personnel and published from May 1 through March 31 are nominated automatically. The articles are judged on content and execution. The judges are members of the DHI Publicity and Public Relations Committee. Awarded annually.

• 9002 •
Door County Environmental Council
Jerome M. Viste, Exec.Dir.
PO Box 114
Fish Creek, WI 54212
Phone: (920)743-6003
Phone: (920)743-5397
Fax: (920)743-6727
E-mail: jerrymv@itol.com
Home Page: http://tourpages.com

• 9003 • **Annual Essay Contest Award**
For grades 5-12; top six essays. Monetary award bestowed annually.

• 9004 • **Rosner/Johnson Memorial Scholarships**
For Door County high school students with environmental interests. Scholarship awarded annually.

• 9005 •
Doubleday
% Random House, Inc.
1745 Broadway
New York, NY 10019
Phone: (212)782-9000
Home Page: http://www.randomhouse.com/doubleday

• 9006 • **O'Henry Awards**
To recognize the author of the year's best short stories published by American or Canadian authors in American or Canadian magazines. Short stories may not be submitted. Monetary prizes are awarded annually. Established in 1919.

• 9007 •
Dow Jones Newspaper Fund
Richard S. Holden, Exec.Dir.
PO Box 300
Princeton, NJ 08543-0300
Phone: (609)452-2820
Fax: (609)520-5804
E-mail: newsfund@wsj.dowjones.com
Home Page: http://djnewspaperfund.dowjones.com

Formerly: Newspaper Fund.

• 9008 • National High School Journalism Teacher of the Year

For recognition of outstanding performance in the classroom, in student publications, in professional journalism, and in encouraging students towards news careers. Applications must be submitted by July 1. A $1,000 scholarship is awarded, in the name of the teacher selected as Journalism Teacher of the Year, to a student attending the teacher's school. The teacher receives a plaque, and will address the Adviser's Luncheon at the Journalism Education Association, the American Society of Newspaper Editors and the Dow Jones Newspaper Fund's board of directors. Travel expenses are paid by DJNF. Additionally, four $500 scholarships are awarded in the names of four journalism teachers named as Distinguished Advisers and given to students in the teachers' respective schools. Special recognition plaques are also given to outstanding journalism advisers. Awarded annually. Established in 1960.

• 9009 •
Downeast Association of Physician Assistants
Linda Roberts, Admin
PO Box 2027
Augusta, ME 04338-2027
Phone: (207)629-9417
Fax: (207)629-9243
E-mail: lindaroberts@bigplanet.com
Home Page: http://www.deapa.com

• 9010 • Robert Lapham Outstanding Service Award

For service to DEAPA and PA profession. Recognition award bestowed annually.

• 9011 • Outstanding Rural PA Award

For PA profession and community contributions. Recognition award bestowed annually.

• 9012 • Susan Vincent Memorial Scholarship

For acceptance to PA school, Maine resident with desire to practice in Maine and in need. Scholarship awarded annually.

• 9013 •
Downtown Jaycees of Washington, D.C.
1612 K St. NW, Ste. 202
PO Box 4985
Washington, DC 20008
Phone: (202)728-1135
Fax: (202)833-1835
E-mail: dcjaycees@aol.com

• 9014 • Downtown Jaycees Teachers Grant Awards

To recognize public school teachers from the District of Columbia for innovation and creativity in the field of education. Awarded annually.

• 9015 •
Dozenal Society of America
Jay Schiffman, Pres.
Nassau Community College
Math Department
Garden City, NY 11530
Phone: (631)669-0273
Phone: (215)923-6167
E-mail: contact@dozens.org
Home Page: http://www.dozens.org

Formerly: (1978) Duodecimal Society of America.

• 9016 • Ralph H. Beard Memorial Award

For recognition of outstanding work in promoting the duodecimal system of counting and measuring. Applications and nominations are accepted. A plaque is presented annually. Established in 1944. The society also honors certain individuals as honorary members, and some members as fellows. Renamed in 1988 in honor of Ralph H. Beard, a founder of the society and *The Duodecimal Bulletin*. Additional information is available from Prof. Gene Zirkel at the above address. Formerly: Annual Award of the Dozenal Society of America.

• 9017 •
Drama Desk
Lester Schecter, Contact
244 W 54th St., 9th Fl.
New York, NY 10019
Phone: (212)586-2600
Phone: (313)354-5124
E-mail: Lester.Schecter@verizon.net
Home Page: http://www.dramadesk.com

• 9018 • Drama Desk Awards

To honor outstanding achievement in the theatre season both on Broadway and off Broadway. (This is the only major professional organization to present awards in multiple categories, without regard as to whether productions originate on or off Broadway.) Recipients are chosen by vote of impartial theater media, e.g., critics, reporters, and editors. Awards are given in the following categories: Outstanding New Play; Outstanding Musical; Director/Play; Director/Musical; Actor/Play; Actor/Musical; Actress/Play; Actress/Musical; Featured Actor/Play; Featured Actor/Musical; Featured Actress/Play; Featured Actress/Musical; Music; Lyrics; Book of a Musical; Orchestration; Revival; Choreography; Set Design; Lighting Design; Outstanding Ensemble Acting; Costume Design; Sound Design/Music in a Play; Solo Performance/One Person Show; Musical Revue/Entertainment; Unique Theatrical Experience; and Special Awards. Drama Desk Award plaques are awarded annually. Established in 1955 and originally named for Vernon Rice, the first major theater critic to give Off Broadway serious coverage, and a past president of the Drama Desk. Formerly: Vernon Rice - Drama Desk Awards.

• 9019 •
The Drama League
Roger T. Danforth, Interim Exec.Dir.
520 8th Ave., 3rd Fl., Ste. 320
New York, NY 10018
Phone: (212)244-9494
Toll-Free: 877-NYC-PLAY
Fax: (212)244-9191
E-mail: info@dramaleague.org
Home Page: http://www.dramaleague.org

• 9020 • Drama League's Distinguished Performance Award

To recognize an actor or actress for the most distinguished performance on the Broadway stage for that season. The performance considered must have been performed in a Broadway theater between May 1 of one year and May 1 of the succeeding year. The award may be won only once. A medal is awarded annually at the Drama League's May Awards Lunch. Established in 1935. Formerly: (1980) Drama League's Delia Austrian Medal for Distinguished Performance.

• 9021 • Drama League's Musical Achievement Award

For recognition of unique accomplishment in musical theater. Established in 1985.

• 9022 • Drama League's Unique Contribution to the Theatre Award

For recognition of unique contributions to the theater. Awarded annually. Established in 1981.

• 9023 •
Dramatists Guild of America
Ralph Sevush, Associate Dir.
1501 Broadway, Ste. 701
New York, NY 10036
Phone: (212)398-9366
Fax: (212)944-0420
E-mail: director@dramatistsguild.com
Home Page: http://www.dramatistsguild.com

• 9024 • Elizabeth Hull - Kate Warriner Award

To recognize a playwright whose work deals with controversial subjects involving the field of politics, religion or social mores of the time. Plays produced in New York City may be nominated by The Dramatists Guild Council only. Dramatists cannot apply for the award. A monetary award of about $7,500 and a scroll are awarded annually. Established in 1970 by a bequest of Elizabeth Van Vechten Schaefer Hull.

• 9025 •
Driving School Association of the Americas
Charles Chauncy, Admin.VP
3090 E Gause Blvd., Ste. 425
Slidell, LA 70461
Toll-Free: 800-270-DSAA
Fax: (985)649-9877
E-mail: dsaa@charter.net
Home Page: http://www.thedsaa.org

• 9026 • **Catherine "Cathy" Hensel Award**
For recognition of contributions to the field of traffic safety during the past year over and above what is normally asked for. Female members of the industry are eligible. A monetary prize of $500 and a plaque are awarded annually in November. Established in 1987 by Catherine P. Hensel Trust in memory of Cathy Hensel, co-founder of the California Driving School, Inc., one of the largest in the nation, and the first woman mayor of the city of Montebello, CA.

• 9027 • **H. B. Vinson Award**
To recognize individuals within the industry who have contributed to the field of traffic safety during the past year. Members of the National Association must be selected by the awards committee. A trophy or plaque is awarded annually at the national convention in November. Established around 1960 in honor of H.B. Vinson, a past president, and other national leaders. Formerly: National Leader's Award - Moe Dollinger Award.

• 9028 •
Drug Strategies
Dr. Robert B. Millman, Chm.
1755 Massachusetts Ave. NW, Ste. 821
Washington, DC 20036
Phone: (202)289-9070
Fax: (202)414-6199
E-mail: dspolicy@aol.com
Home Page: http://www.drugstrategies.org

• 9029 • **Journalism Award**
Recognizes outstanding broadcast journalists.

• 9030 •
Dubuque County Fine Arts Society
Julie Steffen, Pres.
434 Loras Blvd.
Dubuque, IA 52001-4656
Phone: (563)557-9384
Phone: (319)588-9751
E-mail: stefiron@mwci.net

• 9031 • **Elisha Darlin Arts Award**
For contributors to the cultural life of Dubuque. Recognition award bestowed annually.

• 9032 •
Dubuque County-Key City Genealogical Society
Deanna Asleson, Pres.
PO Box 13
Dubuque, IA 52004-0013
Home Page: http://www.rootsweb.com/~iadckcgs

• 9033 • **Pioneer Certificate**
For someone who provides documentation of history before 1850 in IA. Recognition award bestowed periodically.

• 9034 •
Dubuque Fine Arts Players
1686 Lawndale
Dubuque, IA 52001
E-mail: gary.arms@clarke.edu
Home Page: http://groups.yahoo.com/group/Dbq-FAP

• 9035 • **DFAP National One-Act Playwriting Contest**
To recognize and encourage new playwrights. Two copies of original one-act plays of no more than 35 pages or 40 minutes running time must be submitted with a $10 entry fee and completed application by January 31. Children's plays, musicals, and previously produced or published works are not eligible. Three monetary prizes are awarded: first place - $600; second place - $300; and third place - $200. The winning plays are staged in full productions by Dubuque Fine Arts Players, if they can be produced in Dubuque. Awarded annually. Established in 1977 by the Dubuque Fine Arts Society. Send for guidelines and application to Gary Arms at the above address.

• 9036 •
Ductile Iron Society
Pete Guidi, Pres.
28938 Lorain Rd., Ste. 202
North Olmsted, OH 44070
Phone: (440)734-8040
Fax: (440)734-8182
E-mail: jhall@ductile.org
Home Page: http://www.ductile.org

• 9037 • **Ductile Iron Society Annual Award**
To recognize outstanding leadership and technical accomplishment in the use of ductile iron. A certificate is awarded annually. Established in 1963.

• 9038 •
Dudley Observatory
Janie Schwab, Exec.Dir.
107 Nott Terr., Ste. 201
Schenectady, NY 12308
Phone: (518)382-7583
Fax: (518)382-7584
E-mail: info@dudleyobservatory.org
Home Page: http://www.dudleyobservatory.org

• 9039 • **Ernest F. Fullum Award**
To provide encouragement and support for innovative research projects in astronomy or astrophysics. Each June, a faculty member, research associate, or post-doctoral student affiliated with a North American college observatory or university is chosen to receive a monetary award of up to $10,000. Established in 1993.

• 9040 • **Herbert C. Pollock Award**
To provide encouragement and support for innovative projects in the history of astronomy or astrophysics. Each January, one or more faculty members, research associates, or post-doctoral students associated with a North American college, university, or nonprofit research institution or observatory are chosen to receive a monetary award of up to $5,000. Established in 1996.

• 9041 •
Duke University
Donna Elliott, Contact
Physics Bldg., Science Dr.
Department of Physics
Box 90305
Durham, NC 27708-0305
Phone: (919)660-2500
Fax: (919)660-2525
E-mail: webmaster@phy.duke.edu
Home Page: http://www.phy.duke.edu

• 9042 • **Fritz London Memorial Award**
For recognition of achievement in the field of low temperature physics. Election is by a committee approximately six months before each international meeting of low temperature physics. A monetary prize and a certificate are awarded triennially at the international meeting. Monetary prize enhanced in 1994 through additional endowment made up of remaining funds from the 1993 international meeting and from a gift by Horst Meyer. Established in 1957 through the generosity of John Bardeen, who gave the money of his second Nobel prize to Duke for the purpose of honoring Fritz London, one of the great theorists of the first half of the twentieth century in condensed matter physics.

• 9043 •
Duke University
Center for Documentary Studies
Box 90802
Durham, NC 27708-0802
Phone: (919)660-3663
Fax: (919)681-7600
E-mail: docstudies@duke.edu
Home Page: http://cds.aas.duke.edu

• 9044 • **The CDS/Honickmand First Book Prize in Photography**
A biennial prize of $3,000 in grant money, inclusion in a traveling exhibition, and the publication of a book of photography will be given by the Duke University Press. Deadline is September 15.

Awards are arranged in alphabetical order below their administering organizations

• 9045 • **Dorothea Lange - Paul Taylor Prize**
To promote collaborative work between a writer and a photographer. A monetary award of $20,000 is given annually. Entries must be submitted before January 31. Awarded annually. Established in 1990 in honor of photographer Dorothea Lange and writer Paul Taylor.

• 9046 •
Duluth Art Institute
Samantha Gibb Roff, Exec.Dir.
506 W Michigan St.
Duluth, MN 55802
Phone: (218)733-7560
Fax: (218)733-7506
E-mail: getart@duluthartinstitute.org
Home Page: http://www.duluthartinstitute.org

• 9047 • **Arrowhead Biennial Exhibition**
For recognition of artistic achievement. This regional competition is open to artists over 18 years of age from Minnesota, Wisconsin, North and South Dakota, Iowa, and Michigan. Original drawings, paintings, prints, photographs, sculpture, or any combination of these mediums completed in the last two years may be submitted. Monetary awards totaling $2,000 are awarded at the biennial exhibition reception. Established in 1919.

• 9048 •
Dumbarton Oaks
Edward L. Keenan, Dir.
1703 32nd St. NW
Washington, DC 20007
Phone: (202)339-6401
Fax: (202)339-6419
E-mail: dumbartonoaks@doaks.org
Home Page: http://www.doaks.org

• 9049 • **Bliss Prize Fellowship in Byzantine Studies**
To provide encouragement, assistance, and training to outstanding college seniors who plan to enter the field of Byzantine Studies. Fellowship candidates must be in their last year of undergraduate education or have a B.A., they must have completed at least one year of ancient or medieval Greek by the end of the senior year, and they must be applicants to graduate school in any field or area of Byzantine Studies. Students currently enrolled or recent graduates in U.S. or Canadian universities or colleges, or American or Canadian citizens who are Enrolled at non-North American universities or colleges are eligible. Students must be nominated by their advisors by October 15 in a letter sent directly to Dumbarton Oaks. The deadline for applications is November 1. Graduate school tuition and living expenses, (as estimated by the graduate school in which the successful candiate enrolls) for two years are awarded. In addition, the Fellowship includes travel during the intervening summer (up to a maximum of $5,000) to areas that are important for an understanding of Byzantine civilization and culture. Students who have successfully completed two years as Bliss Fellows, have fulfilled all preliminary requirements for a higher degree, and are working on a dissertation, are offered a Junior Fellowship at Dumbarton Oaks, the year being determined by Dumbarton Oaks, in consultation with the student and academic advisor.

• 9050 • **Dumbarton Oaks Fellowships**
To enable scholars to pursue research in Byzantine studies, Pre-Columbian studies, and studies in landscape architecture at Dumbarton Oaks. The following criteria are considered: scholarly ability and preparation of candidate, interest and value of the project, and relevance of project to resources of Dumbarton Oaks. The deadline for submissions is November 1. The following resident fellowships are awarded: regular fellowships - for scholars who hold a doctorate (or appropriate final degree) or have established themselves in their field and wish to pursue their own research; junior fellowships - for students who have fulfilled all preliminary requirements for a Ph.D.or appropriate degree and are working on a dissertation or final project; and summer fellowships - to scholars on any level of advancement beyond the first year of graduate (postgraduate study). Project awards are generally made for appropriate field work. Fellowship amounts range from $17,600 and $37,700 depending on fellow's marital status. Awarded annually.

• 9051 •
Dungannon Foundation
Rea Award for the Short Story
53 W Church Hill Rd.
Washington, CT 06794
Home Page: http://www.reaaward.org

• 9052 • **Rea Award for the Short Story**
The $30,000 Rea Award for the Short Story form is given annually to a "a writer who has made a significant contribution to the short story." The Rea Award was established in 1986 by Michael M. Era and is sponsored annually by the Dungannon Foundation. Recipients are nominated and Selected by a jury. Individuals can neither apply nor nominate themselves for the award.

• 9053 •
Dystrophic Epidermolysis Bullosa Research Association of America
Faith Daniels, Pres.
5 W 36th St., Ste. 404
New York, NY 10018
Phone: (212)868-1573
Toll-Free: (866)332-7276
Fax: (212)868-9296
E-mail: staff@debra.org
Home Page: http://www.debra.org

• 9054 • **Debra Research Grants**
Supports scientific research in Epidermolysis Bullosa. A monetary award is given annually.

• 9055 •
Eagle Forum
Phyllis Schlafly, Pres.
PO Box 618
Alton, IL 62002
Phone: (618)462-5415
Fax: (618)462-8909
E-mail: eagle@eagleforum.org
Home Page: http://www.eagleforum.org

• 9056 • **Eagle Awards for Volunteer Service**
To recognize volunteer service.

• 9057 •
Early Music America
Maria Coldwell, Exec.Dir.
2366 Eastlake Ave. E, No. 429
Seattle, WA 98102
Phone: (206)720-6270
Toll-Free: 888-SAC-KBUT
Fax: (206)720-6290
E-mail: info@earlymusic.org
Home Page: http://www.earlymusic.org

• 9058 • **Thomas Binkley Award**
Recognizes outstanding educational accomplishments. Awarded annually.

• 9059 • **Howard Mayer Brown Award**
Recognizes lifetime achievement in early music. Awarded annually.

• 9060 • **Early Music Brings History Alive Award**
Recognizes outstanding educational accomplishments. A monetary award is presented annually.

• 9061 •
Earth Society Foundation
Stan Cohen, Pres.
41 Park Ave., Ste. 17-C
New York, NY 10016
Phone: (212)686-8200
Toll-Free: 800-3-EARTHDAY
Fax: (212)686-4900
E-mail: info@earthsocietyfoundation.org
Home Page: http://www.earth-society.org

• 9062 • **Earth Day Award**
Recognizes an individual who has served in the interest of harmony between man and nature. Awarded annually.

• 9063 •
Earthwatch Institute
3 Clock Tower Pl., Ste. 100
PO Box 75
Maynard, MA 01754
Phone: (978)461-0081
Toll-Free: 800-776-0188
Fax: (978)461-2332
E-mail: info@earthwatch.org
Home Page: http://www.earthwatch.org

Awards are arranged in alphabetical order below their administering organizations

• 9064 • Earthwatch Education Awards
Offers K-12 educators and administrators partial to full funding to join conservation research across the globe. Over 300 awards are made outstanding applicants each year. Applications are being accepted on a rolling basis. Fellowships range from $500-$3,000.

• 9065 • *EARTHWATCH* Film Awards
To recognize outstanding documentary films. A trophy, and travel expenses to attend the awards ceremony at the National Geographic Society in Washington, DC, are presented annually. Established in 1986. Additional information is available from Flo Stone, 1228 1/2 31ST St. N.W., Washington, DC 20007, phone: (202) 342-2564.

• 9066 •
East & West Artists
310 Riverside Dr., Ste. 313
New York, NY 10025-4116
Phone: (212)222-2433
E-mail: ewartists@hotmail.com
Home Page: http://www.geocities.com/eastandwestartists

• 9067 • East & West Artists International Auditions
To recognize and promote exceptionally gifted performers from all over the world. Classical music instrumentalists, singers, and ensembles with up to five members of any nationality who are at least age 16 with no upper age limit. Two-piano ensembles are not eligible. The deadline for applications and CD or cassettes is June 12. Auditions are in October. A fully subsidized recital at Weill Recital Hall at Carnegie Hall is awarded annually. Established in 1971 by Ms. Adolovni P. Acosta, Executive Director.

• 9068 •
East Baton Rouge Parish Medical Society
Laney Comoletti, Exec.Dir.
8224 Summa Ave., Ste. A
Baton Rouge, LA 70809
Phone: (225)757-9094
Fax: (225)757-9497
E-mail: laney@ebrpms.org

• 9069 • East Baton Rouge Parish Medical Society Premedical Scholarship Award
For pre-med LSU student. Monetary award bestowed annually.

• 9070 •
East Carolina University
Office of Research and Scholarship
Rivers Bldg., Rm. 215
School of Nursing
Greenville, NC 27858-4353
Phone: (252)328-4325
Fax: (252)328-2168
E-mail: engelkem@mail.ecu.edu
Home Page: http://www.ecu.edu

• 9071 • Collaborative Research Award
Hel in conjuction with medical center nursing administration. Inquire for application details.

• 9072 • Faculty Research Award
Inquire for application details.

• 9073 • Professional Organization Awards
Inquire for application details.

• 9074 • Seed and Pilot Programs
Inquire for application details.

• 9075 •
East Mount Airy Neighbors
Jane R. Cosby, Admin.
6817 Germantown Ave.
Philadelphia, PA 19119
Phone: (215)848-4163
Toll-Free: 800-347-4253
Fax: (215)848-4031
E-mail: eman@libertynet.org

• 9076 • Community Service Award
For academic standing and community service. Scholarship awarded annually.

• 9077 •
East Polk County Committee of 100
Ron Morrow, Exec.Dir.
PO Box 1420
Winter Haven, FL 33882-1420
Phone: (863)294-9454
Fax: (863)297-5818
E-mail: contact@epc100.org
Home Page: http://www.epc100.org

• 9078 • Gold Cup of Industry Award
For community involvement, leadership, growth, and capital investment. Recognition award bestowed annually.

• 9079 •
East Tennessee Environmental Business Association
Jenny Freeman, Exec.Dir.
PO Box 5483
Oak Ridge, TN 37831
Phone: (865)483-9979
Fax: (865)947-4788
E-mail: info@eteba.org
Home Page: http://www.eteba.org

• 9080 • ETEBA Scholarship
For students in environmental studies in East Tennessee. Scholarship awarded annually.

• 9081 •
East Texas Historical Association
Archie P. McDonald, Exec.Dir.
PO Box 6223, SFA Sta.
Nacogdoches, TX 75962
Phone: (936)468-2407
Fax: (936)468-2190
E-mail: amcdonald@sfasu.edu
Home Page: http://easttexashistorical.org

• 9082 • Ottis Lock Award
For recognition of excellence in teaching history in East Texas, and for the best book on East Texas History; to provide scholarships for history majors at a college or university located in East Texas; and to provide grants to scholars working on historical research involving the East Texas area. Individuals in the field of history, especially East Texas history, are eligible. The following prizes are awarded: Excellence in Teaching and Best Book Awards - $250 and a plaque; and Grants monetary awards based on need. Awarded annually. Established in 1984 to honor Ottis Lock, a distinguished leader in education, business, and government. association presents the Lucille Terry Preservation Awards, established in 1986; the C. K. Chamberlain Award, established in 1977; the Ralph W. Steen Award, established in 1978; and the Fellows Award, established in 1982. Nominating materials should be submitted before May 1.

• 9083 •
Easter Seals
James E. Williams, Pres.
230 W Monroe St., Ste. 1800
Chicago, IL 60606
Phone: (312)726-6200
Toll-Free: 800-221-6827
Fax: (312)726-1494
E-mail: nfo@easterseals.com
Home Page: http://www.easterseals.com

• 9084 • Award for Outstanding Achievement
To recognize individuals, teams of individuals, or organizations for substantial and sustained or single contributions to the advancement of Easter Seal services at any level of the Society. Easter Seals officers and volunteer leaders, campaign chairmen, medical and rehabilitation specialists, community organizations, leading citizens, media representatives, and celebrities are eligible. A certificate is awarded annually. Established in 1982.

• 9085 • Award for Outstanding Service
For recognition of individuals, teams of individuals, or organizations for sustained and substantial contributions to the advancement of Easter Seal services at any level of the Society. Easter Seal officers, Easter Seal campaign chairmen, medical and rehabilitation specialists, volunteer workers or organizations upon completion of a major project, leading community citizens or media representatives who have provided especially outstanding services, and celebrities are eligible. A certificate is awarded annually. Established in 1958 and expanded in 1976. This award includes the two former awards, the Cita-

tion for Distinguished Leadership and the Award for Sustained Service.

• 9086 • **Distinguished Service Award**
To recognize an individual for sustained efforts that have had a significant nationwide impact on the quality of life for persons with disabilities. Awarded annually.

• 9087 • **EDI Award for Corporate Leadership**
To honor corporations and businesses for exceeding the provisions of the American Disabilities Act to capture the spirit of the law, and to recognize corporations for promoting accessible work environments, providing disability awareness training, and developing marketing and advertising programs that target and include people with disabilities.

• 9088 • **EDI Awards (Equality/Dignity/Independence)**
To recognize and honor media efforts that further public understanding of disability issues and encourage equality, dignity, and independence for people with disabilities. Awards are presented in six categories: print journalism, broadcast journalism, photojournalism, advertising, television programming, and feature films/motion pictures. Awards are presented in the fall at a ceremony in New York City. Established in 1986. Formerly: (1990) NESS Communications Award.

• 9089 • **Outstanding Advocate Award**
To honor a municipal, state, or national legislator whose work has significantly improved the quality of life for persons with disabilities. One or more recipients are awarded annually. Established in 1991.

• 9090 • **Johanna Cooke Plaut Community Leadership Award**
To recognize persons with disabilities who have distinguished themselves as elected or appointed officials or as community leaders, and whose accomplishments have made their communities better places to live. Recipients must have a record of community leadership, and have chosen to advance the equality, dignity, and independence of people with disabilities. Awarded annually.

• 9091 • **Volunteer of the Year Award**
To honor an outstanding Easter Seal volunteer. Awarded annually at the national convention. Established in 1983. For further information, contact Sharon Kujawa, Administrative Assistant.

• 9092 •
Easter Seals of Connecticut
John R. Quinn, Pres.
85 Jones St.
PO Box 100
Hebron, CT 06248-0100
Phone: (860)228-9438
Toll-Free: 800-874-7687
Fax: (860)228-9670
E-mail: johnq@eastersealsofct.org
Home Page: http://ct.easterseals.com/site/PageServer?pagename=CTDR_homepage

• 9093 • **Camp Hemlocks Camperships**
For Connecticut residents in financial need. Monetary award bestowed periodically.

• 9094 •
Eastern Apicultural Society of North America
Loretta Surprenant, Sec.
Box 300
Box 300A
Essex, NY 12936
Phone: (518)963-7593
E-mail: secretary@easternapiculture.org
Home Page: http://www.easternapiculture.org

• 9095 • **DiVelbiss Award**
Annual award of recognition.

• 9096 • **FFA Award**
Annual award of recognition.

• 9097 • **Graduate Student Award**
Annual award of recognition.

• 9098 • **J. I. Hambleton Award**
Annual award of recognition.

• 9099 • **Roger A. Morse Teaching/Extension/Regulatory Award**
Annual award of recognition.

• 9100 •
Eastern Association of Rowing Colleges
Gary Caldwell, Contact
1311 Craigville Beach Rd.
PO Box 3
Centerville, MA 02632
Phone: (508)771-5060
Fax: (508)771-9481
E-mail: gcaldwell@ecac.org

• 9101 • **Russell S. Callow Memorial Award**
To recognize a crew (rowing) which overcomes great obstacles to achieve competitive services. The crew must be a college crew. A trophy is awarded annually. Established in 1970 by the EARC Coaches Association to honor Russell Callow, a former crew coach at the Naval Academy and the University of Pennsylvania.

• 9102 •
Eastern Bird Banding Association
Robert Pantle, Ed.
2366 Springtown Hill Rd.
Hellertown, PA 18055
Phone: (609)466-1871
Phone: (610)346-7754
E-mail: measede@enter.net
Home Page: http://www.frontiernet.net/~bpbird/

• 9103 • **Memorial Grants**
To provide financial assistance for research using banding techniques or bird banding data. Applicants should submit a resume of their banding and ornithological background, the project plan including the significance of the study site, and a budget. One or two grants of up to $500 in aid are awarded annually.

• 9104 •
Eastern Coast Breweriana Association
Larry Handy, Sec.
PO Box 64
Chapel Hill, NC 27514-0064
E-mail: ohhugo1@aol.com
Home Page: http://www.eastcoastbrew.com

• 9105 • **Golden Pen**
For recognition of original written articles in the field of collecting beer and brewing advertising items. A gold pen is awarded annually at the convention.

• 9106 • **Hall of Foam**
For recognition of achievement in the field of collecting beer and brewery advertising items. Membership is necessary for consideration. A plaque is awarded annually at the convention.

• 9107 •
Eastern College Athletic Conference
Phil Buttafuoco, Commissioner
1311 Craigville Beach Rd.
PO Box 3
Centerville, MA 02632
Phone: (508)771-5060
Fax: (508)771-9481
E-mail: pbuttafuoco@ecac.org
Home Page: http://www.ecac.org

• 9108 • **ECAC Distinguished Achievement Award**
This, the highest honor bestowed by ECAC, is given to recognize outstanding career success and an unusual contribution in the interest of intercollegiate athletics. Eastern collegiate athletic administrators are eligible and the award is given periodically. Revere bowls are awarded annually at the annual ECAC Awards Dinner. Established in 1957 in memory of James Lynah, the former Cornell Athletic Director. Formerly: James Lynah Memorial Award.

• 9109 • **ECAC Merit Medal**
To honor an athlete who is a member of a varsity team governed by ECAC rules of eligibility.

While the exact criteria for the awarding of the medal is left to the discretion of the individual college or university making the award, it is generally bestowed upon an athlete who has combined excellence on the fields of competition with excellence in the classroom, or outstanding service to the institution. A medal is awarded annually.

• 9110 • ECAC - SIDA Media Award
To recognize an individual either in print or electronic media for outstanding coverage of eastern intercollegiate athletics. A plaque is awarded annually at the ECAC-SIDA Workshop. Established in 1955. Sponsored by the Eastern College Athletic Conference Sports Information Directors Association.

• 9111 • George L. Shiebler Award
To recognize dedication as an avocational activity to amateur sport, in the capacity of an official. A Revere bowl is awarded annually at the Conference's Annual Awards Dinner. Established in 1962 and named after George L. Shiebler, former ECAC commissioner. Formerly: James P. Lyon Memorial Award.

• 9112 •
Eastern Music Festival
Tom Philion, Pres. and CEO
200 N Davis St.
PO Box 22026
Greensboro, NC 27420
Phone: (910)333-7450
Toll-Free: 877-833-6753
Fax: (910)333-7454
E-mail: info@easternmusicfestival.org
Home Page: http://www.easternmusicfestival.com

• 9113 • Joseph M. Bryan, Jr. Scholarships
To provide scholarships to string players to attend the Eastern Music Festival, an international summer program for the study and performance of classical music, featuring symphony orchestra, chamber music, private lessons, and master classes. U.S. string players currently enrolled in a college or university who are U.S. citizens and under age 21 are eligible. Four full scholarships are awarded annually. Established in 1986 by Joseph M. Bryan, Jr.

• 9114 • International Scholarship Program
To provide scholarships to string students living outside the United States. String students between the ages of 15 and 20 who are not United States citizens are eligible. Two or more scholarships are awarded annually. Eastern Music Festival is an international summer program for the study and performance of classical music, featuring symphony orchestra, chamber music, private lessons, and master classes.

• 9115 • Wynton Marsalis Scholarship
To provide funds for an outstanding trumpet student to attend the Eastern Music Festival, an international summer program for the study and performance of classical music, featuring symphony orchestra, chamber music, private lessons, and master classes. United States citizens between the ages of 14 and 20 are eligible, and preference is given to students of color. One full scholarship is awarded annually. Established in 1986 by Wynton Marsalis.

• 9116 •
Eastern Packard Club
John Harley, Pres.
PO Box 1259
Stratford, CT 06615
Phone: (201)307-4959
Home Page: http://clubs.hemmings.com/easternpackard/

• 9117 • Crawford Award
For best restoration of a Packard automobile. Recognition award bestowed annually.

• 9118 •
Eastern Surfing Association
Kathlyn B. Phillips, Exec.Dir.
PO Box 582
Ocean City, MD 21843
Phone: (410)213-0515
Toll-Free: (866)SURF-ESA
Fax: (410)213-2397
E-mail: info@surfesa.org
Home Page: http://www.surfesa.org

• 9119 • Dr. Colin J. Couture Award for Outstanding Volunteer Service to Eastern Surfing
To honor volunteers for dedication, commitment, and service to the Association and to East Coast surfing as a whole. Awarded annually.

• 9120 •
Eastman Kodak Company
Consumer Imaging
343 State St.
Rochester, NY 14650-0138
Phone: (585)724-4000
Toll-Free: 800-242-2424
Fax: (585)724-1089
Home Page: http://www.kodak.com

• 9121 • Kodak International Newspaper Snapshot Awards
To promote amateur photography. Black and white and color photos are accepted. Local participating newspapers forward up to eight finalists for international judging. Two hundred fifty-seven prizes totaling $52,500 are awarded annually. Winning photos are on display in Kodak's pavilion at EPCOT Center, Florida.

• 9122 •
Eastport Area Chamber of Commerce
Roland Lavelle, Pres.
23 A Water St.
PO Box 254
Eastport, ME 04631
Phone: (207)853-4644
E-mail: chamber@eastport.net
Home Page: http://www.eastport.net

• 9123 • Harry Mattin Award
For promoting community development. Trophy awarded annually.

• 9124 •
Eaton Literary Associates
Richard Lawrence, Vice Pres.
Eaton Literary Agency
PO Box 49795
Sarasota, FL 34230-6795
Phone: (941)366-6589
Fax: (941)365-4679
E-mail: info@eatonliterary.com
Home Page: http://www.eatonliterary.com

• 9125 • Eaton Literary Awards Program
To encourage professional development and for recognition of novels, books, short stories, and articles suitable for publication. Unpublished manuscripts over 10,000 words may be submitted by August 31 for the book-length program. Short stories or nonfiction works less than 10,000 words may be submitted by March 31 for the short story and article program. A monetary prize of $2,500 is awarded annually in September for the book-length program; $500 is awarded annually in April for the short story and article program. Established in 1984 by Ralph A. Eaton.

• 9126 •
Eau Claire Regional Arts Council
Peter Provost, Contact
316 Eau Claire St.
Eau Claire, WI 54702
Phone: (715)832-2787
Fax: (715)832-0828
E-mail: info@eauclairearts.com
Home Page: http://www.eauclairearts.com

• 9127 • Tributary Awards
Based on nomination; selected by jury. Recognition award bestowed annually.

• 9128 •
Eckhardt Gramatte National Music Competition
Nancy Nehring, Admin.Off.
QE II Music Bldg.
Brandon University
270 - 18th St.
Brandon, MB, Canada R7A 6A9
Phone: (204)728-8212
Fax: (204)728-6839
E-mail: eckhardt@brandonu.ca
Home Page: http://www.brandonu.ca/egre

Formerly: Brandon University.

• 9129 • Eckhardt-Gramatte National Competition for the Performance of Canadian Music
To encourage young musicians to perform pieces composed by contemporary (especially but not exclusively Canadian) composers. Each year, a newly written piece of music by a Canadian composer in the area of voice, piano, or strings is featured. The competition alternates annually among those three performance areas. Canadian citizens or Canadian residents may submit applications by mid-October. Individuals under 30 years of age for piano and strings and under 35 years of age for voice are eligible. The following monetary awards are presented annually: first prize: cash award of $5,000 and a national tour (recitals fees ca. $5,000); second prize:

• 9130 •
Ecological Society of America
Nancy B. Grimm, Pres.
1707 H St. NW, Ste. 400
Washington, DC 20006
Phone: (202)833-8773
Fax: (202)833-8775
E-mail: esahq@esa.org
Home Page: http://www.esa.org

• 9131 • E. Lucy Braun Award
To recognize the outstanding student poster presentation presented as a part of the annual program sponsored by the Ecological Society of America. The award is named after W. Lucy Braun, an eminent plant ecologist and first woman president of the Ecological Society of America.

• 9132 • Murray F. Buell Award
To recognize and reward an outstanding student paper presented at the annual meeting. A monetary prize and a certificate are awarded annually. Established in 1973.

• 9133 • W. S. Cooper Award
To honor one of the Society's outstanding contributors to the fields of geobotany and physiographic ecology. The award recognizes a recent, outstanding contribution in one of the fields in which Cooper worked.

• 9134 • Corporate Award
To recognize a corporation, company, non-profit entity, or program or individual of a company for its accomplishments in incorporating sound ecological concepts, knowledge, and practices into its planning and operating procedures. Established in 1988.

• 9135 • Distinguished Service Citation
For recognition of long and distinguished service to the Ecological Society of America and scientific community. Nominations of senior members may be made. The citation is awarded annually. Established in 1975.

• 9136 • Eminent Ecologist
To recognize an ecologist who has made an outstanding contribution to the science of ecology. A certificate and life membership are awarded annually. Established in 1973.

• 9137 • Honorary Member
To recognize any ecologist who has made exceptional scientific contributions and whose principal residence and site of ecological research are outside the United States, Canada and Mexico.

• 9138 • Robert H. MacArthur Award
To recognize an active, well-established ecologist. Nominations of mid-career ecologists are accepted. A monetary award, a certificate, and an invited lecture are awarded biennially at the convention. Established in 1983 in honor of Robert MacArthur, distinguished theoretical ecologist at Princeton University.

• 9139 • George Mercer Award
For recognition of an outstanding paper published in English by a researcher under the age of 40 in the field of ecology. A monetary prize and a certificate are awarded annually. Established in 1948.

• 9140 •
Econometric Society
Prof. Julie P. Gordon, Sec.
Northwestern University
Department of Economics
2003 Sheridan Rd.
Evanston, IL 60208-2600
Phone: (847)491-3615
Fax: (847)491-5427
E-mail: jpg@northwestern.edu
Home Page: http://www.econometricsociety.org

• 9141 • Frisch Medal Award
To encourage the creation of good applied work in the field of economic theory and its relation to statistics and mathematics. Applied articles (empirical or theoretical) published in *Econometrica* during the past five years are eligible. Awarded biennially. Established in 1978.

• 9142 •
Economic History Association
Alexander Field, Exec.Dir.
Dept. of Economics
500 El Camino Real
Santa Clara Univ.
Santa Clara, CA 95053-0385
Phone: (785)864-2847
Fax: (408)554-2331
E-mail: afield@scu.edu
Home Page: http://eh.net/EHA

• 9143 • Arthur H. Cole Grants-in-Aid
To support research in economic history of any time period or geographic area. Preference is given to recent Ph.D. recipients. The award is typically around $1,500 although in exceptional circumstances it may be higher.

• 9144 • Arthur H. Cole Prize
To recognize the author of the best article in the *Journal of Economic History* during the previous year.

• 9145 • Alexander Gerschenkron Prize
To recognize the best dissertation in non-American or Canadian economic history. A monetary prize of and potential publication of the Ph.D. dissertation by the Princeton University Press is presented annually at the convention in September. Established in 1984 by Donald N. McCloskey in honor of Alexander Gerschenkron, longtime professor of economics at Harvard, doyen of European economic history, literature, and quantitative historian. Send submitted dissertations to Prof. Carol Shiue at shiue@colorado.edu.

• 9146 • Alice Hanson Jones Prize
For recognition of an outstanding book on North American economic history (including the Caribbean). A monetary prize of $1,200 is awarded biennially in even-numbered years.

• 9147 • Allan Nevins Prize
Recognizes the best doctoral dissertation on American economic history. Awarded annually.

• 9148 • Ranki Prize in Economic History
For recognition of an outstanding book on European economic history. A monetary prize of $1,200 is awarded biennially in odd-numbered years. 510-660-8023

• 9149 •
ECRI
Jeffrey C. Lerner PhD, Pres./CEO
5200 Butler Pke.
Plymouth Meeting, PA 19462-1298
Phone: (610)825-6000
Fax: (610)834-1275
E-mail: info@ecri.org
Home Page: http://www.ecri.org

• 9150 • ECRI Medical Technology Media Awards Program
For recognition of the best English-language print and broadcast communications in the United States or Canada on medical technology intended for the general public. Submissions should be made at the same time that articles appear in public print or television shows are aired. The deadline is January 4. A first and second prize are awarded in each of the following categories: (1) Newspaper - article or series of articles; (2) Magazine - article or series of articles; and (3) Television - show or series of shows. Monetary prizes and plaques are awarded annually. Established in 1991.

• 9151 •
Ecumenical Council of San Diego County
Rev. Glenn S. Allison, Exec.Dir.
PO Box 3628
San Diego, CA 92163
Phone: (619)238-0649

• 9152 • Christian Unity Award
For ecumenical service to the San Diego community. Recognition award bestowed annually.

• 9153 • Julia Hull Schilling Award
For ecumenical service to the San Diego community. Recognition award bestowed annually.

• 9154 •
Edgar County Genealogical Society
A. Joyce Brown, Past Pres.
PO Box 304
Paris, IL 61944-0304
Phone: (217)463-4209
E-mail: ecgl@tigerpaw.com
Home Page: http://www.comwares.net/ecgl/

• 9155 • Edythe Stevens Family History Award
For service to the society and/or the library. Recognition award bestowed annually.

• 9156 •
Edgefield County Historical Society
Carrie Clark, Pres.
PO Box 174
Edgefield, SC 29824
Phone: (803)637-5304
Fax: (803)637-6066

• 9157 • Joanne T. Rainsford Memorial Scholarship
For Edgefield County senior. Scholarship awarded annually.

• 9158 •
Edison Electric Institute
Brian Farrell, Dir. of Member Relations
701 Pennsylvania Ave., NW
Washington, DC 20004-2696
Phone: (202)508-5000
Phone: (202)508-5649
Toll-Free: 800-334-4688
Fax: (202)508-5360
E-mail: bfarrell@eei.org
Home Page: http://www.eei.org

• 9159 • Edison Award
Recognizes distinguished leadership, innovation, and contribution to the advancement of the electric industry for the benefit of all. Awarded annually.

• 9160 •
Edison Media Arts Consortium
New Jersey City University
Media Arts Dept.
2039 Kennedy Blvd.
Jersey City, NJ 07305
Phone: (201)200-2043
Fax: (201)200-3490
E-mail: blackmariafest@aol.com
Home Page: http://www.njcu.edu/NETWORK/cn051404.html

• 9161 • Thomas A. Edison Black Maria Film and Video Festival
For recognition of outstanding films and videos. Anyone may enter. The deadline is in November. The following prizes are awarded: Jurors' Choice - a share of $2,500 or more; Jurors' Citations - a share of $2,000 or more; and Director's Choice - a share of $1,000 or more. In addition, exhibited works from all three categories receive a share of $5,000 or more Rental Honoraria, depending on length of film or video and screening frequency at the 60 or more host organizations and venues participating in the annual national tour. Awarded annually. Established in 1980 by John Columbus. Sponsored by the Geraldine R. Dodge Foundation, National Endowment for the Arts, New Jersey State Council on the Arts, New Jersey City University, Edison National Historic Site, Eastman Kodak Company, Johnson Family Foundation, and the Puffin Foundation.

• 9162 •
Editor & Publisher
Sid Holt, Editor-in-Chief
770 Broadway
New York, NY 10003-9595
Phone: (212)675-4380
Toll-Free: 800-336-4380
Fax: (646)654-5370
E-mail: edpub@editorandpublisher.com
Home Page: http://www.editorandpublisher.com

• 9163 • *Editor & Publisher*/INMA Marketing Awards
To recognize outstanding newspaper marketing efforts. Awards are given in the following categories: (1) In-Paper Promotion/Circulation; (2) In-Paper Promotion/Advertising; (3) In-Paper Promotion/Public Relations; (4) In-Paper Promotion/Editorial; (5) Printed Materials/Circulation; (6) Printed Materials/Advertising; (7) Printed Materials/Public Relations; (8) Radio Promotion; (9) Television Promotion; (10) Outdoor/Point-of-Purchase/Displays; (11) Multi-Media Promotion; (12) Newspaper Research/Data Books; (13) Public Relations Programs & Events; (14) Community Service; (15) Internal Communications; (16) Newspapers in Education; (17) Interactive Media; and (18) Premiums/Incentives. A first and second prize are awarded annually in each category in four circulation groupings. Established in 1931. Co-sponsored by the International Newspaper Marketing Association, (214) 991-5900, and *Editor & Publisher* magazine.

• 9164 • International Best Newspaper Online Services Award
To recognize organizations whose online services take full advantage of the new medium. Ten awards are offered: first and second place for each of three print circulation groups (1) Best Overall Newspaper Online Service; (2) Best Editorial Content in a Newspaper Online Service; (3) Best Use of Advertising in a Newspaper Online Service; and first and second place for the Best Online News Service by a Non-Newspaper Company. Awarded annually. Established in 1995.

• 9165 •
Editors' Association of Canada (Association canadienne des reviseurs)
Lynne Massey, Exec.Dir.
502-27 Carlton St.
Toronto, ON, Canada M5B 1L2
Phone: (416)975-1379
Toll-Free: (866)226-3348
Fax: (416)975-1637
E-mail: info@editors.ca
Home Page: http://www.editors.ca

• 9166 • Tom Fairley Award for Editorial Excellence
To recognize an individual providing outstanding freelance editorial contribution to a work published in Canada. A monetary prize of $2,000 is awarded annually. Established in 1983.

• 9167 •
Education Commission of the States
Piedad F. Robertsons, Pres.
700 Broadway, Ste. 1200
Denver, CO 80203-3460
Phone: (303)299-3600
Fax: (303)296-8332
E-mail: ecs@ecs.org
Home Page: http://www.ecs.org

• 9168 • James Bryant Conant Award
To recognize a person who has made an outstanding contribution with national impact on education in the United States and who has already attained a measure of recognition for such a contribution. A crystal obelisk is awarded annually. Established in 1977 in honor of James Bryant Conant, an internationally known scholar, scientist, statesman, author and co-founder of ECS.

• 9169 •
Education Writers Association
Lisa J. Walker, Exec.Dir.
2122 P St. NW, No. 201
Washington, DC 20037
Phone: (202)452-9830
Fax: (202)452-9837
E-mail: ewa@ewa.org
Home Page: http://www.ewa.org

• 9170 • National Awards for Education Reporting
Recognizes individuals in the field of education writing. Awarded annually.

• 9171 •
Educational Exhibitors Association
Lydia E. Walsh, Exec.Dir.
805 Airway Dr.
Allegan, MI 49010-8516
Phone: (269)673-2200
Fax: (269)673-9509

• 9172 • Person of the Year in Education
Award of recognition. Given through three educational associations, also scholarships to teachers in vocational education.

Awards are arranged in alphabetical order below their administering organizations

• 9173 • **SHIP Citation**
Award of recognition. Given three times per year.

• 9174 •
Educational Paperback Association
Marilyn Abel, Exec.Sec.
PO Box 1399
East Hampton, NY 11937
Phone: (631)329-3315
E-mail: edupaperback@aol.com
Home Page: http://www.edupaperback.org

• 9175 • **Jeremiah Ludington Memorial Award**
To honor an individual who has made a significant contribution to the use of paperbacks in education. Members of the academic community, librarians, publishers, and wholesalers of paperback books are eligible. Selection is made by the Board of Directors. Nominations are not accepted. A plaque is awarded annually and a $1,000 contribution is made to the charity of the recipients choice. Established in 1979.

• 9176 •
Educational Testing Service
Kurt Landgraf, Pres.
Rosedale Rd.
Princeton, NJ 08541
Phone: (609)921-9000
Fax: (609)734-5410
E-mail: etsinfo@ets.org
Home Page: http://www.ets.org

• 9177 • **ETS Award for Distinguished Service to Measurement**
To recognize an individual whose work has had significant impact on developments in educational and psychological measurement. Nominations are not accepted. A monetary award of $1,000 and a certificate are awarded annually. Established in 1970.

• 9178 • **Jacqueline A. Ross Dissertation Award**
To award doctoral dissertation research that makes a significant and original contribution to knowledge about and/or use and development of second/foreign language tests and testing. Awarded annually with a monetary prize of $2,500. Formerly: TOEFL Award.

• 9179 •
Educational Theatre Association
Michael J. Peitz, Exec.Dir.
2343 Auburn Ave.
PO Box 632347
Cincinnati, OH 45219
Phone: (513)421-3900
Fax: (513)421-7077
E-mail: info@edta.org
Home Page: http://www.edta.org
Formerly: (1969) National Thespian Society.

• 9180 • **Administrators' Award**
To recognize secondary school administrators who have strongly supported the educational theatre arts programs in their schools. Any school administration or school principal, providing the school is currently affiliated with the International Thespian Society, is eligible. A plaque is awarded annually at the Society's Thespian Festival. Established in 1983 by Robert Johnson, International Director. Deadline for application is February 28.

• 9181 • **Founders' Award**
To recognize individuals who have contributed to the advancement of secondary school theatre and the Society. The officers of the Society make the selection. A plaque is awarded annually when merited at the Society's Thespian Festival. Established in 1970 in honor of the three founders of the Society, Paul Opp, Earl Blank, and Harry Leeper.

• 9182 • **Innovative Educational Theatre Award**
To recognize teachers and/or directors for their contributions to the development and improvement of educational theater. The deadline for applications is March 31. The following awards are presented: First place - $300 and a plaque; and up to three Honorable Mentions - $100 and a plaque. Awarded annually.

• 9183 • **Outstanding School Award**
To recognize high schools whose theater programs exemplify and promote high standards of quality in educational theater. The deadline for applications is March 31. A maximum of twelve awards, consisting of a plaque and a $100 coupon toward the cost of attending the Thespian Festival, are awarded annually.

• 9184 • **Outstanding Theatre Education**
Recognizes association members. Selection is based on peer recommendation. Awarded annually.

• 9185 • **President's Award**
To recognize individuals who have made outstanding contributions to the Society. The Director of the Society makes the selection. A plaque is awarded annually at the Society's Thespian Festival. Established in 1978 by Robert Geuder, International Director. Formerly: International Director's Award.

• 9186 •
Educators for Social Responsibility, Grand Rapids Chapter
Michael Franz, Pres.
1850 Whirlaway Ct. SE
Grand Rapids, MI 49546
Phone: (616)956-0521
Phone: (616)234-4386
Fax: (616)234-4052
E-mail: mfranz@grcc.cc.mi.us

• 9187 • **Dr. Phillip Sigal Peace and Justice Scholarship**
For community involvement in peace and justice areas. Scholarship awarded annually.

• 9188 •
EIFS Industry Members Association
Steve Klamke, Exec.Dir.
3000 Corporate Center Dr., Ste. 270
Morrow, GA 30260
Phone: (770)968-7945
Toll-Free: 800-294-3462
Fax: (770)968-5818
E-mail: lwidzowski@eima.com
Home Page: http://www.eima.com

• 9189 • **Excellence in EIFS Construction**
Recognizes new construction and renovation construction in the current year. Awarded annually.

• 9190 •
Eire Philatelic Association
David J. Brennan, Sec.
PO Box 704
Bernardsville, NJ 07924-0704
Phone: (908)766-2728
Fax: (908)766-7783
E-mail: brennan704@aol.com
Home Page: http://home.att.net/~aranman/epa1.html

• 9191 • **Clark Award**
For recognition of outstanding services toward Irish philately. The deadline for nominations is August. A plaque is presented annually in the fall at a stamp exhibit near the honoree's home. Established in 1981 in honor of John C. Clark, an early member, secretary, and Irish stamp dealer.

• 9192 •
Eisenhower Fellowships
John S. Wolf, Pres.
256 S 16th St.
Philadelphia, PA 19102
Phone: (215)546-1738
Fax: (215)546-4567
E-mail: ike@eisenhowerfellowships.org
Home Page: http://eisenhowerfellowships.org

• 9193 • **Dr. Eisenhower Medal**
Annual award of recognition.

• 9194 •
El Paso Association for the Performing Arts
David D. Mills, Mng.Dir.
PO Box 31340
El Paso, TX 79931-0340
Phone: (915)565-6900
Toll-Free: 800-915-8482
Fax: (915)565-6999

• 9195 • **Image Award**
For outstanding lifetime contributions to the performing arts in El Paso. Trophy awarded annually.

• 9196 •
El Toro International Yacht Racing Association
Steve Lowry, Sec.
1014 Hopper Ave., No. 419
Santa Rosa, CA 95403-1613
Phone: (707)526-6621
Fax: (707)526-3838
E-mail: steve@swiftsail.net
Home Page: http://www.eltoroyra.org

• 9197 • **Junior, Intermediate, and Senior Championship Awards**
Recognizes winners of championship races. Trophies are awarded annually in each category.

• 9198 •
Electrical Apparatus Service Association
Linda J. Raynes, Pres./CEO
1331 Baur Blvd.
St. Louis, MO 63132
Phone: (314)993-2220
Fax: (314)993-1269
E-mail: easainfo@easa.com
Home Page: http://www.easa.com

• 9199 • **EASA Exceptional Achievement and Service Award**
Recognizes contributions to field industry. EASA members are eligible. Awarded annually.

• 9200 •
Electrical Equipment Representatives Association
John Commons CAE, Sec.
638 W 39th St.
Kansas City, MO 64111
Phone: (816)561-5323
Fax: (816)561-1249
E-mail: info2005@eera.org
Home Page: http://www.eera.org

• 9201 • **EERA Scholarships**
Awarded to sons, daughters, grandsons, and granddaughters of members and employees. Awarded annually.

• 9202 •
Electrical Generating Systems Association
Jalane L. Kellough, Exec.Dir.
1650 S. Dixie Hwy., Ste. 500
Boca Raton, FL 33432-7462
Phone: (561)750-5575
Fax: (561)395-8557
Home Page: http://www.egsa.org

• 9203 • **Leroy H. Carpenter Award**
To recognize long meritorious service to the Association. Members are eligible. A plaque is awarded annually. Established in 1971 to honor Leroy H. Carpenter.

• 9204 •
Electronic Document Systems Foundation
Jeanne Mowlds, Exec.Dir.
24238 Hawthorne Blvd.
Torrance, CA 90505-6505
Phone: (310)541-1481
Fax: (310)541-4803
E-mail: info@edsf.org
Home Page: http://www.edsf.org

• 9205 • **Excellence in Education Awards**
Annual award of recognition.

• 9206 • **Innovation in Higher Education**
Annual award recognizing a college/university for innovative academic programs relating to the document communications industry.

• 9207 •
Electronic Funds Transfer Association
H. Kurt Helwig, Exec.Dir.
950 Herndon Pkwy., Ste. 390
Herndon, VA 20170
Phone: (703)435-9800
Fax: (703)435-7157
E-mail: kurthelwig@efta.org
Home Page: http://www.efta.org

• 9208 • **Robert A. Mooney Distinguished Service Award**
Recognizes outstanding service to advance EFT over a career. Awarded annually.

• 9209 •
Electronic Industries Alliance
Dave McCurdy, Pres. and CEO
2500 Wilson Blvd.
Arlington, VA 22201
Phone: (703)907-7500
Fax: (703)907-7501
E-mail: dmccurdy@eia.org
Home Page: http://www.eia.org

• 9210 • **Clinton S. Lee Market Services and Engineering Award of Excellence**
To honor an individual who has served the industry and the Association with distinction in marketing or engineering. A medallion mounted on a plaque is awarded annually. Established in 1973.

• 9211 • **Design and Engineering Exhibition Award**
For recognition of creative excellence in the consumer electronics field. Consumer electronics related products that are available to the public in the year of the award are eligible for consideration. Plaques are awarded annually at the convention. Established in 1976. Additional information is available from Dennis S. Corcoran, Vice President, Consumer Electronics Group; telephone: (202) 457-4919.

• 9212 • **Distinguished Service Award**
To recognize and honor a member of the association who has performed services with distinction for the association on behalf of the industry. A freestanding block with upright medallion is awarded annually. Established in 1973.

• 9213 • **Engineering Award of Excellence**
To honor a member of the industry who has served with distinction in the Association's engineering program. A medallion mounted on a plaque is awarded annually. Established in 1973.

• 9214 • **Environmental Issues Council Corporate Award**
Presented annually in the spring. A medallion of logo mounted on a brass and walnut plaque is awarded.

• 9215 • **Individual Award**
Presented annually in the spring. A medallion of logo mounted on a brass/ walnut plaque is awarded.

• 9216 • **Medal of Honor**
For recognition of distinctive contributions to the advancement of the electronic industries, to the management associated with electronics manufacturing, or to a government or educational institution concerned with electronics. A gold medal is awarded annually. Established in 1952.

• 9217 •
Electronic Retailing Association
Ms. Barbara Tulipane CAE, Pres./CEO
2000 N 14th St., Ste. 300
Arlington, VA 22201
Phone: (703)841-1751
Toll-Free: 800-987-6462
Fax: (703)841-1860
E-mail: contact@retailing.org
Home Page: http://www.retailing.org

• 9218 • **ERA Awards**
Recognizes programs and personalities. Awarded annually.

• 9219 •
Electronics Technicians Association, International
Richard L. Glass, Pres.
5 Depot St.
Greencastle, IN 46135
Phone: (765)653-8262
Phone: (765)653-4301
Toll-Free: 800-288-3824
Fax: (765)653-4287
E-mail: eta@eta-i.org
Home Page: http://www.eta-sda.com

• 9220 • **Pat Porter Memorial Award - "Friend of the Satellite Dealer" Award**
To recognize an individual or company allied with the satellite industry who has contributed to the improvement of technology, distribution, re-

tailing, or servicing of satellites in an outstanding manner and who best personifies the enthusiasm, dedication, and leadership exhibited by Pat Porter, a respected contributor to the satellite industry. The deadline for nominations is July 1. Awarded annually.

• 9221 • Technician of the Year
To honor a practicing electronics technician as an incentive for all other technicians to achieve higher goals. A plaque is awarded annually. Established in 1979 in memory of Norris R. Browne, CET, Houston, Texas.

• 9222 •
Elkader Development Corp.
Edward W. Olson, Exec.Dir.
PO Box 323
Elkader, IA 52043
Phone: (319)245-1849
Fax: (319)245-1033

• 9223 • Ambassador of the Month
For outstanding community service. Recognition award bestowed monthly.

• 9224 •
Eller Family Association
Paula Eller, Pres.
PO Box 873509
Wasilla, AK 99687
E-mail: paula@yukontel.com
Home Page: http://www.eller.org

• 9225 • J. W. Hook Memorial Award
Recognizes notable research and service. Awarded biennially.

• 9226 •
Embassy of Spain in the United States Cultural Office
2375 Pennsylvania Ave. NW
Washington, DC 20037
Phone: (202)728-2334
Fax: (202)496-0328
E-mail: ocultura.spainemb@attglobal.net
Home Page: http://www.spainemb.org

• 9227 • Choreography and Flamenco Dance Competition
To recognize traditional forms of Spanish dance, especially the flamenco. The deadline for entry is June 13. The following awards are presented: choreography - first prize is 700,000 pesetas, second prize is 400,000 pesetas, and third prize is 150,000 pesetas; Outstanding Dancer - 300,000; and Original Music Composition for Spanish Dance and/or the Flamenco - 300,000 pesetas.

• 9228 • Contemporary Music Award
To honor the best performer of the compulsory. Awarded with 300,000 pesetas.

• 9229 • Cultural Cooperation Award
To encourage understanding and cooperation between Spain's Ministry of Culture and United States universities. The deadline for applications is April 30 and December 1. Grants are available for the following areas: publications, research, dissemination of Spanish Culture, symposia and seminars, visiting professors, curriculum development, subsidies for professional associations, and dissemination and study of Spanish Cinema in the United States. Up to a total of $6,000 in subsidies, based on matching funds, is awarded.

• 9230 • Edition International Film Festival
To recognize outstanding films. Awards are presented in the following categories: Official International Category for Videocreation, Electronic Graphics and Infographics. Open to any young video-maker born after January 1, 1964. The Official National Category for Short Fictions produced on video - open to any young video-maker born after January 1, 1968. Entries must have been produced after January 1993 and should not have taken part in previous editions of the Festival. The deadline for registration is April 29. The following prizes are awarded: International Official Category for Videocreation, Electronic Graphics and Infographics - Canal 9 Tvv Award, the Best International Videocreation is 700,000 pesetas, the Cinema Jove Award to the Best Creative Use of the Technological media is 300,000 pesetas, the Official National Category for Short Fictions produced on video - Cinema Jove Award to the Best Short Fiction in Video will receive 200,000 pesetas. Organized by the Institut Valencia de la Juventut.

• 9231 • International Piano Competition Prize
To honor pianists of any nationality with the exception of past winners. Three prizes awarded with money.

• 9232 •
Embassy Players
John Nicol, Chm.
5502 Beech Ave.
Bethesda, MD 20814-1702
E-mail: chairman@embassyplayers.org
Home Page: http://www.rubygriffith.org

• 9233 • Ruby Griffith Award
For recognition of all-around amateur theater production excellence by a group. The group must be a bona fide amateur theater group established for two or more years in the Washington, DC, metropolitan area. School and college groups are not eligible. A silver trophy and an inscribed certificate are awarded annually. Established during the 1968-69 theatre season in honor of Ruby Griffith, the British Embassy Players' first producer, director and artistic advisor.

• 9234 •
Emergency Medicine Residents' Association
Liz McDonald, Exec.Dir.
1125 Executive Cir.
Irving, TX 75038-2522
Phone: (972)550-0920
Toll-Free: 800-798-1822
Fax: (972)580-2829
E-mail: lmcdonald@emra.org
Home Page: http://www.emra.org

• 9235 • Dedication Award
To recognize an EMRA member who has demonstrated significant dedication in promoting the goals and objectives of EMRA at local, state, and national levels. In addition, the recipient must have a record of creativity, enthusiasm, and accomplishment in addressing issues pertaining to emergency medicine. The recipient is chosen by the Representative Council Nominating Committee and receives a $1,000 stipend. Awarded annually. Established in 1997. Sponsored by Weatherby Health Care.

• 9236 • Augustine D'Orta Award
To honor a physician who demonstrates outstanding community-minded, grass-roots oriented political involvement for community and emergency medicine issues. The winner receives $1,000. Awarded annually. Established in 1992. Sponsored by International Medical Consultants.

• 9237 • EMRA Academic Excellence Award
To recognize an EMRA member who has done outstanding work in research or other academic pursuits. A monetary award of $500 is presented at the annual meeting. Co-sponsored by Em-Care, Inc.

• 9238 • EMRA Award for Excellence in Teaching
To recognize an outstanding faculty member who has served as a unique role model for residents. A $1,000 contribution is given to the Emergency Medicine Foundation in the recipient's name. Awarded at the ACEP Scientific Assembly. Co-sponsored by Spectrum Emergency Care.

• 9239 • EMRA Clinical Excellence Award
To recognize a resident who has done outstanding work in the clinical aspect of emergency medicine. A monetary award of $1,000 is presented at the ACEP Scientific Assembly. Co-sponsored by Weatherby Health Care.

• 9240 • EMRA Leadership Award
To recognize a resident who has demonstrated outstanding leadership ability. A monetary award of $500 is presented at the ACEP Scientific Assembly. Co-sponsored by EMSA Limited Partnership Inphynet Management, Inc.

• 9241 • Jean Hollister Award
To recognize a resident who has made valuable contributions to prehospital care and emergency medical services. A monetary award of $1,000 is presented at the annual meeting. Sponsored by Coastal Emergency Services.

• 9242 • Joseph F. Waeckerle Founder's Award
To honor a physician who has made an extraordinary, lasting contribution to the success of EMRA. A plaque is awarded annually. Established in 1992.

• 9243 •
Emergency Nurses Association
Donna Nowakowski, Exec.Dir.
915 Lee St.
Des Plaines, IL 60016
Phone: 800-900-9659
Toll-Free: 800-243-8362
Fax: (847)460-4001
E-mail: execoffice@ena.org
Home Page: http://www.ena.org

Formerly: (1985) Emergency Department Nurses Association.

• 9244 • ENA Micromedex Best Original Research Award
To recognize the researcher who submits the best research abstract for presentation at the ENA Annual Meeting. A monetary prize of $1000 is awarded. Deadline is April 1. Formerly: Micromedex/ENA Emergency Nursing Research Award.

• 9245 • Ethics Award
To recognize an ENA member who demonstrates an outstanding commitment to ethical issues relating to the practice of emergency nursing. Awards are presented at the Association's General Assembly. Deadline is May 27.

• 9246 • Judith C. Kelleher Award
To recognize a member of the Association for excellence in emergency nursing and significant contributions to the profession. Candidates must have: consistently demonstrated outstanding knowledge and expertise in emergency nursing practice, education, research and professionalism; made contributions that have affected the profession within the community, region, or country; influenced emergency nursing in a professional role nationally (speaker, lecturer, writer); and served as a role model for emergency nurses. Awards are presented at a special luncheon and ceremony during the Association's General Assembly.

• 9247 • Media Award
To recognize a media presentation in television, radio, or print that portrayed emergency nursing in a positive, accurate, and professional manner. The presentation should be appropriate for possible use by ENA as a vehicle for educating the consumer about emergency nursing or emergency care issues. Award presented at the Association's General Assembly. Deadline is May 27.

• 9248 • Nurse Manager Award
To recognize an ENA member who has consistently demonstrated excellence in the profession of emergency nursing and who has made significant contributions to the profession through emergency nursing management. "Manager" is defined as a person who is responsible for hiring, firing, corrective action, personnel evaluation, staffing, and program development. Awarded annually.

• 9249 • Nursing Education Award
To recognize an ENA member who has made significant contributions to the education of colleagues, nursing students, EMS personnel, patients or families, through teaching formally or informally, publications of articles in nursing journals or textbooks, or the development of a specific emergency nursing curriculum. Award presented at the Association's General Assembly. Deadline May 27.

• 9250 • Nursing Practice Award
To recognize an ENA member who exemplifies outstanding nursing practice as demonstrated through clinical skills, caring, and compassion. This nurse consistently performs above and beyond the requirements of the job description in delivering quality care to his or her patient. Award presented at the Association's General Assembly. Deadline is May 27.

• 9251 • Nursing Professionalism Award
To recognize an ENA member who consistently demonstrates high professional behavior and commitment to professional values and is active within the profession. Awarded at the Association's General Assembly. Deadline is May 27.

• 9252 • Nursing Research Award
To honor a member of ENA who consistently recognizes and supports research as a means of affecting emergency care and has made contributions to the profession through conducting, disseminating, or utilizing research. Awards are presented at the Association's General Assembly. Deadline is May 27.

• 9253 • Special Board Recognition Award
To recognize either an individual or organization for significant contributions to the Association or emergency nursing.

• 9254 •
Employment Management Association
1800 Duke St.
Alexandria, VA 22314
Phone: (703)548-3440
Fax: (703)535-6490
E-mail: shrm@shrm.org
Home Page: http://www.shrm.org/ema

• 9255 • EMA Creative Excellence Awards
To encourage and honor excellence in recruitment advertising. All entries are judged on the basis of effectiveness of communication, visual impact, and creativity. Consideration is also given to the purpose of advertisement and the publication environment for which it was prepared. Any company or advertising agency involved in recruitment advertising may submit its own material, or have it submitted through its advertising agency. All work must have been published for the first time during the preceding year. The deadline for entry is mmid-January. Awards are presented in various categories divided into 3 broad areas: Newspaper, Tradepaper/Magazine, and Miscellaneous. The corporate client and its advertising agency each receives a lucite rectangular column for Best of Category and Best of Show. Client and agency winners of Certificate of Merit awards receive an appropriate certificate. A Best of Category and up to two Certificates of Merit are awarded in each category. Established in 1985.

• 9256 • EMA Foundation School/ Business Partnership Award
To recognize school and corporate collaborations in developing and implementing programs which address critical employment needs, including college preparatory, technical, and vocational field applications of accounting, allied health, computer sciences, mathematics, and chemical, biological, and physical sciences. Award is open to all private and public elementary and secondary schools and business that institute innovative programs. Winning schools will receive a monetary prize, an award, and recognition in *The Wall Street Journal*. $5000 and a plaque are awarded to the school and the business. Nominations must be received by late November. Established in 1993. Sponsored by *The Wall Street Journal*.

• 9257 •
Endocrine Society
Scott Hunt, Exec.Dir.
8401 Connecticut Ave., Ste. 900
Chevy Chase, MD 20815-5817
Phone: (301)941-0200
Fax: (301)941-0259
E-mail: endostaff@endo-society.org
Home Page: http://www.endo-society.org

• 9258 • Edwin B. Astwood Lecture Award
For recognition of outstanding research in endocrinology. A monetary prize of $2,000 and the honor of presenting a plenary lecture at the Society's annual meeting are awarded annually. Established in 1977.

• 9259 • Gerald D. Aurbach Lecture Award
To recognize outstanding contributions to research in endocrinology. A $1,000 honorarium is awarded and the winner delivers a plenary lecture at the Society's annual meeting based upon his/her research. Established in 1993 in memory

of Gerald D. Aurbach, past president of the Society.

• 9260 • Clinical Investigator Lecture Award

To recognize a nationally and internationally recognized clinical scientist/investigator who has made major contributions to patient-oriented research as it relates to the pathogenesis, pathophysiology and therapy of endocrine disease. The awardee receives an honorarium of $3,500 and delivers a plenary lecture at the Society's annual meeting based upon his/her work. Established in 1988. Formerly: (1997) Rhone Poulenc Rorer Clinical Investigator Lecture Award.

• 9261 • Sidney H. Ingbar Distinguished Service Award

For recognition of distinguished service in the field of endocrinology. A monetary prize of $2,000 is awarded. Established in 1992.

• 9262 • Fred Conrad Koch Award

For recognition of exceptional contributions to endocrinology. A monetary prize of $25,000 and a medal are awarded annually. Established in 1960 in memory of F.C. Koch, pioneer in the isolation of androgens. Formerly: (1957) Medal of the Endocrine Society.

• 9263 • Ernst Oppenheimer Memorial Award

For recognition of meritorious accomplishments in basic or clinical endocrinology. Young investigators under 45 years of age, are eligible for the award. An honorarium of $3,000 is presented. Established in 1942.

• 9264 • Richard E. Weitzman Award

For recognition of an exceptionally promising young investigator in the field of endocrinology and metabolism. Individuals under 40 years of age are eligible for the award. A monetary prize of $1,000 is awarded annually. Established in 1982 in memory of Richard E. Weitzman.

• 9265 • Robert H. Williams Distinguished Leadership Award

For recognition of outstanding leadership in fundamental or clinical endocrinology as exemplified by the recipient's contributions and those of his trainees and associates to teaching, research, and administration. A monetary prize of $5,000 and travel expenses to the annual meeting are awarded annually. Established in 1971 by Dr. Robert H. Williams.

• 9266 •

Engineering College Magazines Associated
Paul Sorenson, Co-Chair
Univ. of Minnesota Inst. of Technology
105 Walter Library
117 Pleasant St. SE
Minneapolis, MN 55414
Phone: (612)626-7959
Phone: (612)626-7959
Fax: (801)365-6396
E-mail: ecma@itdean.umn.edu
Home Page: http://www.ecmaweb.org

• 9267 • ECMA Awards

To recognize and to stimulate excellence in the publication of engineering college magazines. Awards are given in the following categories: Best All-Around Magazine - all issues; Best Single Cover; Best Covers - all issues; Best Single Editorial; Best Editorial - all issues; Best Single Issue; Best Art/Photography - single issue; Best Art/Photography - all issues; Best Layout - single issue; Best Layout - all issues; Best Non-Technical Article; Best Pure Technical Article for technology background; Best Article for general science background; Most Entertaining Feature; and Most Improved Magazine. Generally, an article is judged in the category in which it is submitted by the nominating magazine. The judges of each category determine suitability of categories chosen by the magazines when evaluating the nominations. All articles submitted for awards nominations must be written by full or part-time undergraduate or full-time graduate students during the time they hold such classification. Judging of a given magazine is based on a 12-month period set by that magazine to end not later than January 15 prior to the convention. Judging for "all issue" awards must include all issues of the preceding 12-month period. Wall plaques are awarded to the first place winner and certificates to second, third, and honorable mention winners. Awarded annually at the convention each spring.

• 9268 •

Engineering Institute of Canada
(Institut Canadien des Ingenieurs)
B. John Plant, Exec.Dir.
1295 Hwy. 2E
Kingston, ON, Canada K7L 4V1
Phone: (613)547-5989
Fax: (613)547-0195
E-mail: jplant1@cogeco.ca
Home Page: http://www.eic-ici.ca/

• 9269 • Canadian Pacific Railway Medal

Recognizes leadership and service to the Institute and its member societies at the regional and local levels. Awarded annually. Established in 1988.

• 9270 • Fellow

To recognize excellence in engineering practice and exceptional contributions to the well-being of the profession and the good of society. Corporate members in one of the member societies of the Engineering Institute of Canada, at least 45 years of age, with ten years responsible charge of important engineering works are eligible. A certificate is awarded annually. Established in 1963.

• 9271 • Honorary Member

To honor Canadians who are not engineers but who have achieved distinction through service to the profession of engineering in Canada. Nonmembers of the Institute, and non-engineers are eligible. A certificate is awarded annually. Established in 1950 to honor engineers and members of the Institute. Since 1975, Honorary Members were elected from non-members of the Institute.

• 9272 • Sir John Kennedy Medal

Recognizes outstanding service to the engineering industry. Awarded annually. Established in 1927.

• 9273 • K.Y. Lo Medal

Recognizes significant engineering contributions at the international level. Awarded annually. Established in 1997.

• 9274 • Julian C. Smith Medal

To recognize achievement in the development of Canada. Corporate members in one of the Member Societies of the Engineering Institute of Canada are eligible. A medal and a certificate are awarded annually. Established in 1939 by a group of senior members of the Institute to honor Julian C. Smith, a past president of the Institute.

• 9275 • John B. Stirling Medal

Recognizes leadership and service to the Institute and its member societies at the national level. Awarded annually. Established in 1988.

• 9276 •

English-Speaking Union of the United States
Alice Boyne, Exec.Dir./Pres.
144 E 39th St.
New York, NY 10016
Phone: (212)818-1200
Fax: (212)867-4177
E-mail: info@esuus.org
Home Page: http://www.english-speakingunion.org

• 9277 • Ambassador Book Awards

For recognition of American books, fiction or non-fiction, that are of outstanding merit in interpreting American life and culture to other English-speaking people. Only new, currently published works are eligible. Monetary awards of $1,000 and certificates are presented annually. Established in 1980. Formerly: (1982) Ambassador of Honor Book Awards.

• 9278 •
ENR: Engineering News-Record
The McGraw-Hill Cos., Inc.
Janice L. Tuchman, Editor-in-Chief
2 Penn Plz., 9th Fl.
New York, NY 10121
Phone: (212)512-2500
Toll-Free: 800-525-5003
Fax: (212)512-6630
E-mail: stussman@mcgraw-hill.com
Home Page: http://www.enr.com
Formerly: *Engineering News-Record.*

• 9279 • **Award of Excellence**
For recognition of contributions to the construction industry, and that industry's associated contribution to society. Individuals who have demonstrated a connection with the construction industry are eligible. A large bronze plaque is awarded annually. Established in 1966. Formerly: Constuction's Man of the Year.

• 9280 •
Entomological Foundation
April Gower, Contact
9332 Annapolis Rd., Ste. 201
Lanham, MD 20706
Phone: (301)459-9082
Fax: (301)459-9084
E-mail: april@entfdn.org
Home Page: http://www.entfd.org

• 9281 • **Award for Excellence in Integrated Pest Management**
Recognizes and encourages outstanding contributions to integrated pest management in North America. Award includes a plaque and a monetary award that varies from year to year.

• 9282 • **Jeffery P. LaFage Graduate Student Research Award**
Recognizes graduate research in the field of biology and control of termites or other pests in the urban environment. Established as a tribute to Prof. Jeffery LaFage, a professor who specialized in the study of the biology and control of termites. Sponsored by the Entomological Foundation. Award presented at the Entomological Society of America's annual meeting.

• 9283 • **President's Prizes for Outstanding Achievement in Primary and Secondary Education**
To recognize educators who have gone beyond the traditional teaching methods by using insects as educational tools. One winner will be chosen from among primary teachers (kindergarten through sixth grade) and one from among secondary teachers (grades seven through twelve). Nominations must be submitted electronically by July 1. Recipients are awarded all expense paid trips to the ESA Annual Meeting, a plaque, and $400 to the educators' institutions also to be used for educational materials. Awarded annually. Established in 1992.

• 9284 • **Henry and Sylvia Richardson Research Grant**
Provides research funds to postdoctoral members of the Entomological Society of America. The award is sponsored by the Entomological Foundation and presented at the Entomological Society of America's annual meeting.

• 9285 • **Snodgrass Memorial Research Award**
Recognizes outstanding research by graduate students in selected areas of entomology. Sponsored by the Entomological Foundation and presented at the Entomological Society of America's annual meeting.

• 9286 •
Entomological Society of America
Paula G. Lettice, Exec.Dir.
9301 Annapolis Rd., No. 300
Lanham, MD 20706-3115
Phone: (301)731-4535
Fax: (301)731-4538
E-mail: esa@entsoc.org
Home Page: http://www.entsoc.org

• 9287 • **ESA Distinguished Achievement Award in Extension**
To recognize the member of the Society deemed to be the most outstanding extension entomologist of the year. Nominations must be submitted electronically by July 1. This award, consisting of $500 and a plaque, is presented annually at the plenary session of ESA's annual meeting.

• 9288 • **ESA Distinguished Achievement Award in Regulatory Entomology**
To honor regulatory entomologists for their very valuable contribution to American horticulture. The nominee must have demonstrated excellent performance through innovations in insect detection techniques, pest control operations, regulatory activities, and regulatory entomology training efforts. Only society members may be considered. Previous recipients of this award are not eligible for future nomination. Nominations must be submitted electronically by July 1. A monetary prize of $500 and a plaque are awarded annually at the national conference. Sponsored by the American Nursery and Landscape Association.

• 9289 • **ESA Distinguished Achievement Award in Teaching**
To recognize the member of the Society deemed to be the most outstanding teacher. Nominations must be submitted electronically by July 1. This award, consisting of $500 and a plaque, is presented each year at the plenary session of ESA's annual meeting.

• 9290 • **ESA Founder's Memorial Award**
To recognize North American entomologists. Selection of the recipient is made one year in advance by a standing committee of the society on the basis of high and scholarly standards from the point of view of dedication and professional caliber. A monetary prize of $1,000 and a plaque are awarded annually at the plenary session of the Society's annual meeting, where the recipient must be invited to present the Founder's Memorial Lecture. Nominations must be submitted electronically by October 1 of the year prior to the year that the award is to be presented. Established in 1958.

• 9291 • **Fellow of ESA**
To recognize individuals who have made outstanding contributions to entomology. Individuals need not be members of the Society. Up to 10 designations many be made annually. Nominees must have made outstanding contributions in one or more of the following areas of entomology: research, teaching, extension, or administration. Nominations must be made electronically by March 15.

• 9292 •
Entomological Society of Canada
A. Devine, Office Mgr.
393 Winston Ave.
Ottawa, ON, Canada K2A 1Y8
Phone: (613)725-2619
Fax: (613)725-9349
E-mail: entsoc.can@bellnet.ca
Home Page: http://esc-sec.org

• 9293 • **Entomological Society of Canada Gold Medal Award**
For recognition of an outstanding achievement in Canadian entomology and/or service to the Society. Individuals may be nominated by members before February 28. A gold medal is awarded annually. Established in 1962.

• 9294 • **C. Gordon Hewitt Award**
For recognition of an outstanding achievement in Canadian entomology. Individuals who are under 40 years of age may be nominated by members by February 28. A silver medal and plaque is awarded annually to a qualifying candidate. Established in 1975.

• 9295 •
Environmental and Conservation Organization
Mary Jo Padgett, Exec.Dir.
121 3rd Ave. W, Ste. 4
Hendersonville, NC 28792-4912
Phone: (828)692-0385
Fax: (828)693-0942
E-mail: eco@main.nc.us
Home Page: http://eco-wnc.org

• 9296 • **Founders Award**
For person, business or organization that promotes conservation/preservation activities in Henderson County, NC. Recognition award bestowed annually.

• 9297 •
Environmental Business Council of New England
Daniel K. Moon, Pres.
333 Trapelo Rd.
Belmont, MA 02478-1856
Phone: (617)489-8555
Fax: (617)484-3192
E-mail: info@ebcne.org
Home Page: http://www.ebcne.org

• 9298 • **EBEE Award**
For outstanding individuals, companies, or organizations from the New England area that help promote environmental business. Recognition award bestowed annually.

• 9299 •
Environmental Design Research Association
Janet Singer, Exec.Dir.
PO Box 7146
Edmond, OK 73083-7146
Phone: (405)330-4863
Fax: (405)330-4150
E-mail: edra@telepath.com
Home Page: http://www.edra.org

• 9300 • **EDRA Career Award**
To recognize the individual, educational program, private organization or group of practicing architects that has made a sustained contribution to the field of environmental design research, environment/behavior research, or the application or implementation of research to design and to EDRA as an organization. Nominations may be made by members of the Association or by the Committee on the EDRA Award by September 15. Individually prepared citations are awarded annually at the Banquet. Established in 1977.

• 9301 • **EDRA Student Award**
To recognize the best student paper presented at the Annual Conference. Entries may be submitted by October 1. The following monetary awards are given: first prize - $500; and second prize t conference registration dee paid. Awarded annually.

• 9302 • **EDRA Student Design Competition**
To recognize the demonstration or application of environmental design research concepts in design projects. Proposals may be submitted by October 10. Monetary awards of $500 for first prize and $350 for second prize are presented annually.

• 9303 •
Environmental Mutagen Society
Leona Samson, Pres.
1821 Michael Faraday Dr., Ste. 300
Reston, VA 20190
Phone: (703)438-8220
Fax: (703)438-3113
E-mail: emshq@ems-us.com
Home Page: http://www.ems-us.org

• 9304 • **EMS Award**
For recognition of outstanding basic research contributions in the area of environmental mutagenesis. Nominations may be made to the awards committee by April 12. A monetary prize and a plaque are awarded annually at the annual meeting. Established in 1972.

• 9305 • **Alexander Hollaender Award**
To recognize an outstanding individual for applied work in the field of environmental mutagenesis and contributions to the Society The deadline for nominations is April 12. A monetary prize of $500 and a citation are awarded.

• 9306 • **Student and New Investigator Travel Awards**
Annual awards of recognition presented to graduate students and young investigators who are EMS members.

• 9307 •
Epilepsy Foundation
Eric R. Hargis, Pres./CEO
4351 Garden City Dr.
Landover, MD 20785-2223
Phone: (301)459-3700
Phone: (301)918-3772
Toll-Free: 800-332-1000
Fax: (301)577-4941
E-mail: postmaster@efa.org
Home Page: http://www.epilepsyfoundation.org

• 9308 • **Epilepsy Foundation of America Awards**
To recognize outstanding achievement in one of the following categories: (1) Advocacy; (2) Affiliate of the Year; (3) Golden Circle Fundraising Award; (4) Program Excellence; (5) Affliate Executive of the Year; (6) Volunteer of the Year; (7) Special Recognition; (8) Public Awareness. The deadline for nominations is July 1. An award is given annually at the national leadership conference.

• 9309 •
Episcopal Communicators
Laurie Wozniak, Pres.
RR1, Box 104M
Washington Island, WI 54246
Toll-Free: 800-318-4452
E-mail: lauriewozniak@episcopalwny.org
Home Page: http://www.episcopalcommunicators.org

• 9310 • **Polly Bond Award**
For recognition of achievement in, or contribution to Episcopal Church communications. Categories include several for electronic media, as well as all aspects of print communication. The competition is restricted to members of Episcopal Communicators. Certificates are presented annually at the meeting of Episcopal Communicators. Established in 1979 in honor of Polly Bond, Director of Communications for the Diocese of Ohio for more than 20 years.

• 9311 • **Janette Pierce Award**
To recognize an individual for achievement in, or contribution to Episcopal Church communications. Awarded occasionally at the discretion of the Board of Directors. Established in 1988 to honor Janette Pierce, one of the Episcopal Church's outstanding journalists.

• 9312 •
Epsilon Pi Tau
Jerry Streichler, Exec.Dir.
Technology Bldg.
Bowling Green State University
Bowling Green, OH 43403-0305
Phone: (419)372-2425
Fax: (419)372-9502
E-mail: jots@bgnet.bgsu.edu
Home Page: http://www.epsilonpitau.org

• 9313 • **Paul T. Hiser Exemplary Publication Award**
To recognize the author of authors of articles judged to be the best of those published each year in *The Journal of Technology Studies*. A monetary prize of $300 is awarded annually.

• 9314 • **William E. Warner Awards Program**
To stimulate and recognize excellence in local chapter operations, in research, and in writing. Awards are given in the following classifications: undergraduate student essay award; graduate or undergraduate student research award; regional chapter award; minilectureship award; and professional practice award. Applications are accepted. Monetary awards and certificates are presented annually with 40 awards totaling $18,000. Awarded in honor of William Everett Warner, the founder of Epsilon Pi Tau and an international leader who gave a lifetime of service and inspiration to young men and women while expressing the ideals of the honorary through the medium of education in technology.

• 9315 •
Epsilon Sigma Phi
Linda D. Cook, Exec.Dir.
PO Box 357340
Gainesville, FL 32635
Phone: (352)378-6665
Fax: (352)375-0722
E-mail: espoffice@espnational.org
Home Page: http://espnational.org

• 9316 • **International Service Award**
To recognize members who have contributed significantly to extension development in other countries throughout stateside and/or overseas work. Chapter nominations are due in the office of the National Executive Secretary by March 1. A certificate is awarded at the National Council Meeting Banquet annually.

• 9317 • **National Distinguished Service Ruby Award**
To recognize a member who has contributed to extension on a multi-state or national basis. Chapter nominations are due in the office of the

National Executive Secretary by March 1. A pin with ruby inset and a certificate are awarded annually at the National Council Meeting Banquet. Established in 1927.

• 9318 • National Friend of Extension Award

To recognize individuals who have rendered outstanding public service and support of the extension service and its programs on a multistate or national basis. Any chapter may nominate one individual for the award. Nominations may also be made by national board members. Nominations are due in the office of the National Executive Secretary by March 1. A certificate is awarded at the National Council Meeting Banquet annually.

• 9319 • Regional Distinguished Service Award

To recognize one member per region (Northeast, Southern, North Central, and Western) who has contributed significantly to extension on a state or regional basis. National Distinguished Service and Ruby Award recipients are not eligible. Chapter nominations are due in the office of the National Executive Secretary office by March 1. A certificate is awarded annually at the National Council Meeting Banquet.

• 9320 • Regional Mid-Career Award

To recognize one member per region (Northeast, Southern, North Central, and Western) who has shown outstanding competence in extension program planning, delivery, and/or administration on a state and regional level over a career of 10 to 20 years. Chapter nominations are due in the office of the National Executive Secretary by March 1. A certificate is awarded annually at the National Council Meeting Banquet.

• 9321 • Regional Team Award

To recognize one team per region (Northeast, Southern, North Central and Western) who have demonstrated outstanding efforts by an extension staff team in responding to and incorporating into a specific educational program one or more of the national initiatives identified by the cooperative extension system. Chapter nominations are due in the office of the National Executive Secretary by March 1. A certificate is awarded annually at the National Council Meeting Banquet.

• 9322 •
Equine Guelph
50 McGilvray St.
Guelph, ON, Canada N1G 2W1
Phone: (519)824-4120
Fax: (519)767-1081
E-mail: info@erc.on.ca

Formerly: (2004) Equine Research Centre.

• 9323 • Award of Excellence

Recognizes contribution to equine research in Canada.

• 9324 •
Erie Art Museum
John Vanco, Dir.
411 State St.
Erie, PA 16501
Phone: (814)459-5477
Fax: (814)452-1744
E-mail: publicist@erieartmuseum.org
Home Page: http://www.erieartmuseum.org

• 9325 • Annual Spring Show Award

For recognition of achievement in any medium in contemporary art. Works never exhibited before in the Erie area are selected by a juror for the show. Artists must reside within a 250-mile radius of Erie. Monetary prizes totaling $2,000 are awarded to the Juror's Award winners. Awarded annually. Established in 1923.

• 9326 •
Erie County Historical Society
Annita Andrick, Dir. of Library and Archives
419 State St.
Erie, PA 16501
Phone: (814)454-1813
Fax: (814)452-1744
E-mail: echs@eriecountyhistory.org
Home Page: http://www.eriecountyhistory.org

• 9327 • Local History Award

For outstanding contribution to local history. Recognition award bestowed annually.

• 9328 •
Ernest C. Manning Awards Foundation
Donald A. Park, Exec.Dir.
The Manning Innovation Awards
421-7 Ave. SW
Calgary, AB, Canada T2P 4K9
Phone: (403)645-8277
Fax: (403)645-8320
E-mail: manning@encana.com
Home Page: http://www.manningawards.ca

• 9329 • Manning Awards

To recognize individuals who have shown outstanding talent in conceiving and developing new concepts, procedures, processes, or products of potential widespread benefit to Canada and to society at large. Only Canadian citizens are eligible. A monetary prize of $100,000 for the Principal Award, one $25,000 Award of Distinction, and two $10,000 Innovation Awards are presented. Plaques are also awarded annually in the Fall. Established in 1982 and named after the late Ernest C. Manning, a longtime Premier of Alberta and a Canadian Senator. Beginning in 1992, 8 new cash prizes totaling $20,000 will be awarded to innovative young Canadians. These will be presented in conjunction with the Youth Science Foundation's Canada-wide Science Fair Program.

• 9330 •
Ernst & Young
5 Times Sq.
New York, NY 10036
Phone: (212)773-3000
Fax: (212)773-6350
E-mail: eyi.webmaster@uk.ey.com
Home Page: http://www.ey.com

• 9331 • Entrepreneur of the Year

To recognize those individuals and companies whose ingenuity, hard work, and innovation have created successful and growing business ventures. Nominees must be individuals primarily responsible for the recent performance of privately held companies that are at least two years old and founders of public companies, provided the founder is still active in top management. Anyone who has made an outstanding contribution to the entrepreneurial spirit or helped an entrepreneur(s) become successful is also eligible. Regional award recipients are selected for several award categories by independent judging panels. The regional award recipients are honored at local awards banquets and are inducted into the Entrepreneur Of The Year Institute at the institute's international conference. After the regional award recipients are selected, the National Entrepreneur of the Year is chosen by a national judging panel. A trophy, press recognition, complimentary registration at the international conference, and induction into the Entrepreneur of the Year Institute are awarded annually. Established in 1986 by Ernst & Young, and sponsored nationally by The Center for Entrepreneurial Leadership at The Kauffman Foundation, The Nasdaq Stock Market and USA Today.

• 9332 •
Errors, Freaks and Oddities Collector's Club
Stan Raugh, Sec.
955 S Grove Blvd.
Camden Point 65
Kingsland, GA 31548-5263
Phone: (912)729-1573
Fax: (912)729-1585
E-mail: cwouscgr@gate.net
Home Page: http://www.efoers.org

Formerly: (1995) Errors, Freaks, Oddities Collectors Association.

• 9333 • Robert E. Manning Award

To recognize an outstanding original article relating to freaks, errors, etc. Members are eligible. A plaque and free annual dues are awarded annually. Established in 1986 for Robert E. Manning, founder of the EFOCC.

• 9334 •
Escambia Amateur Astronomer's Association
Dr. J. Wayne Wooten, Prof. Of Astronomy, PJC
Physical Sciences Department
Pensacola Junior College
1000 College Blvd.
Pensacola, FL 32504
Phone: (850)484-1152
Fax: (850)484-1822
E-mail: wwooten@pjc.edu
Home Page: http://www.eaaa.net

• 9335 • **Education Awards**
For completing levels (5) of education program. Monetary award bestowed monthly.

• 9336 •
ESPN Inc.
ESPN Plz.
935 Middle St.
Bristol, CT 06010
Phone: (860)766-2000
Fax: (860)766-2213
Home Page: http://espn.go.com

• 9337 • **ESPY Awards**
To recognize excellence in sports performance. Awards are presented in 34 categories described below. Performer-of-the-Year awards comprise 17 awards bestowed in the areas of pro and college basketball, pro and college football, golf, tennis, track and field, baseball, boxing, hockey, horse racing, bowling, and motorsports. Performer-of-the Year award winners are selected by the performers' peers. Fans Choice Awards include eight awards bestowed for "Play-of-the-Year" in the areas of college basketball and football, Major League Baseball, NBA, NFL, NHL; Showstopper; Most Outrageous Play; and an athlete's performance in entertainment and "Game of the Year". The video awards are selected by ESPN viewers. "Cross-cutter" Awards comprise seven awards bestowed in the areas of Breakthrough, Comeback, Female and Male Athlete-of-the-Year, Coach/Manager-of-the-Year, Outstanding Performance Under Pressure, and Outstanding Team-of-the-Year from any sport. The "Cross-cutter" award winners are selected by ESPY Select Nominating Committee and select members of the media. Also awarded is the Arthur Ashe Award for Courage. Held annually.

• 9338 •
Essex Community Heritage Organization
Robert J. Hammerslag, Exec.Dir.
Rte. 22
PO Box 250
Essex, NY 12936
Phone: (518)963-7088
Fax: (518)963-4615
E-mail: echo@essexny.org
Home Page: http://www.essexny.org

• 9339 • **Community Service Award**
For local high school junior active in community service. Monetary award bestowed annually.

• 9340 • **Preservation Awards**
For home preservation/restoration. Monetary award bestowed annually.

• 9341 •
Eta Kappa Nu
Dr. Ronald A. Spanke, Exec.Sec.
PO Box 3535
Lisle, IL 60532
Toll-Free: 800-406-2590
Fax: 800-864-2051
E-mail: spanke@hkn.org
Home Page: http://www.hkn.org/

• 9342 • **Outstanding Chapter Award**
To recognize the chapter that has been most active in school and community activities. A certificate is awarded annually. Established in 1932.

• 9343 • **Outstanding Electrical Engineering Junior Award**
To recognize an outstanding electrical engineering junior for classwork, leadership, activities, and community service. Students must be a U.S. citizen and nominated by an Eta Kappa Nu chapter. A monetary prize and a certificate are awarded annually. Established in 1987 by Mr. and Mrs. Norman R. Carson.

• 9344 • **Outstanding Electrical Engineering Student Award**
To recognize an outstanding electrical engineering student for classwork and extra-curricular activities. Students must be a U.S. citizen and nominated by one of the chapters of Eta Kappa Nu. A monetary prize and a certificate are awarded annually. Established in 1965 in memory of Alton Zerby and Carl T. Koerner.

• 9345 • **Outstanding Teacher Award**
Award of recognition. Awarded annually.

• 9346 • **Outstanding Young Electrical Engineer Award**
For recognition of distinguished achievement in the field of electrical engineering and community work by a young electrical engineer in the United States. Engineers under 35 years of age who have graduated not more than ten years are eligible. An honorarium and certificate are awarded annually. Established in 1935 by R.I. Wilkinson. Formerly: Roger I. Wilkinson Outstanding Young Electrical Engineer Award.

• 9347 •
Ethical Culture Fieldston School
Joseph P. Healey, Hd.
33 Central Park W
New York, NY 10023-6001
Phone: (212)712-6220
Fax: (212)712-8444
E-mail: kcarter@ecfs.org
Home Page: http://www.ecfs.org

• 9348 • **Ethical Culture School Book Award**
To recognize the author of the best book in a specific category originally published in the United States in the preceding year. A scroll is awarded annually in May. At the ceremony, a short skit based upon the winning book is also performed. Established in 1975.

• 9349 •
Eugene V. Debs Foundation
Michael J. Sullivan, Pres.
PO Box 843
Terre Haute, IN 47808
Phone: (812)237-3443
Phone: (812)232-2163
Fax: (812)237-8072
E-mail: soking@isugw.indstate.edu
Home Page: http://www.eugenevdebs.com

• 9350 • **Eugene V. Debs Award**
To recognize an individual for excellence in the fields of industrial unionism, social justice or world peace. A bronze plaque and citation are awarded annually at a fall banquet in Terre Haute. Established in 1965.

• 9351 •
European Travel Commission
Robert K. Franklin, Exec.Dir.
50 W 23rd St., 11th Fl.
New York, NY 10010
Phone: (212)218-1200
Fax: (212)218-1205
E-mail: etc@spring-obrien.com
Home Page: http://www.VisitEurope.com

• 9352 • **Europa Award**
Recognizes contribution to marketing Europe in the US. Awarded annually.

• 9353 •
Evangelical Christian Publishers Association
Mark W. Kuyper, Pres./CEO
4816 South Ash Ave., Ste. 101
Tempe, AZ 85282
Phone: (480)966-3998
Fax: (480)966-1944
E-mail: info@ecpa.org
Home Page: http://www.ecpa.org

• 9354 • **Gold Medallion Book Awards**
To recognize excellence in Evangelical Christian literature. Publishers may submit titles published during the year. Awards are given in the following 20 categories: Bibles; Reference Commentaries; Fiction; Biography/Autobiography; Theology/Doctrine; Inspirational; Devotional; Christian Living; Christianity and Society; Missions/Evangelism; Christian Ministry; Christian Education; Children's Books - Pre-School; Children's Books - Elementary; Youth Books; Marriage, Family, and Parenting; Gift Books/Poetry; Bible Study; and Spanish. Selection is made by a panel of 220 experts including book sellers and book reviewers from leading Christian mag-

azines. A plaque and certificate are awarded annually. Established in 1978.

• 9355 • Jordan Christian Book of the Year Award

To recognize a book chosen not by the publishers, but by Christian book stores around the country. A plaque is awarded annually. Established in 1991.

• 9356 •
Everett Salty Sea Days Association
Marion A. Pope, Exec.Dir.
2520 Colby Ave., Ste. 101
Everett, WA 98201
Phone: (425)339-1113
Phone: (425)303-3317
Fax: (425)259-0131
E-mail: saltysea@aol.com

• 9357 • Awards for School Bands Youth Groups

For participants in parade. Monetary award bestowed annually.

• 9358 •
Evergreen Area Chamber of Commerce
Gary Matson, Pres.
28055 Hwy. 74, Ste. 201
PO Box 97
Evergreen, CO 80437-0097
Phone: (303)674-3412
Fax: (303)674-8463
E-mail: info@evergreenchamber.org
Home Page: http://www.evergreenchamber.org

• 9359 • Business of the Year

For community and business contributions. Recognition award bestowed annually.

• 9360 •
Evidence Photographers International Council
Robert F. Jennings, Exec.Dir.
600 Main St.
Honesdale, PA 18431
Phone: (570)253-5450
Phone: (570)253-1520
Toll-Free: 800-356-3742
Fax: (570)253-5011
E-mail: headquarters@epic-photo.org
Home Page: http://www.epic-photo.org

• 9361 • R. C. Hakanson Award

To recognize outstanding contributions to the field of evidence photography and to the council. Nominations are made by the board of managers. A plaque is presented at the annual meeting. Established in 1983 in honor of R.C. Hakanson, founder and secretary general of EPIC.

• 9362 •
Executive Office of the President
Executive Clerk's Office
The White House
1600 Pennsylvania Ave. NW
Washington, DC 20500
Phone: (202)456-1414
Fax: (202)456-2461
E-mail: president@whitehouse.gov
Home Page: http://www.whitehouse.gov

• 9363 • Presidential Citizens Medal

To recognize citizens of the United States who have performed exemplary deeds of service for their country or their fellow citizens. The Award may be bestowed by the President upon any citizen of the United States. A medal and citation are awarded by the President. Established in 1969.

• 9364 • Presidential Medal of Freedom

This, the highest civil award of the United States government, is awarded to persons who have made especially meritorious contributions to the security or national interests of the United States, world peace, or cultural or other significant public or private endeavors. A medal and citation are awarded by the President. The first group of candidates was selected by President John F. Kennedy, but received their awards after his death from President Johnson. To date more than 250 persons have received the medal. Established in 1963, replacing the Medal of Freedom initiated by President Truman in 1945 to reward meritorious, war-connected acts or services.

• 9365 • President's Environment and Conservation Challenge Awards

To recognize exemplary accomplishments by American citizens and organizations, and encourage innovative solutions to environmental challenges. Awards are given in the following categories: Partnership for fostering cooperative approaches to environmental needs at the local, regional or national level; Environmental Quality Management - for demonstration that environmental values can be integrated into sound management decisions and practices; Innovation - for developing creative technologies, programs, or services that are environmentally sensitive and economically sensible; and Education and Communications - for developing informational programs that inspire respect for the environment and raise the public's environmental awareness. Up to three awards may be presented in each category. The competition is open to all U.S. residents, businesses, nonprofit organizations, professional and trade associations, communities, and state and local governments. The deadline for entry is July 19. In addition to the Award winners, Presidential Citations are presented to finalists who demonstrate notable environmental achievements. Established by Executive Order in May, 1991. Administered by the Council on Environmental Quality, in a partnership with the National Geographic Society, the Hearst Corporation, the Business Roundtable and the World Wildlife Fund. A decision to continue this program under the Clinton administration is pending.

• 9366 • Special Awards Established by the President

Awards in this category are issued by the President on an individual basis. There are no laws or Executive Orders regulating their issuance. They are used to grant Presidential recognition to individuals and organizations for many worthwhile endeavors. Generally, they are presented to persons or organizations whose service to the nation or fellow citizens is of an unusual nature, such as extraordinary achievement, sustained and outstanding public service, etc., and particularly to persons for whom other categories of Presidential awards are not appropriate, such as the Presidential Medal of Freedom and the Presidential Citizens Medal. A Special Award for Exceptional Service, a Presidential Public Safety Communication Award, and a Presidential Commendation are examples of the Special Awards.

• 9367 •
Executive Search Roundtable
Victoria Clarke, Pres.
PO Box 3565
Grand Central Sta.
New York, NY 10163-3565
Phone: (212)439-4630
Phone: (914)526-6187
Fax: (914)526-8812
E-mail: info@esroundtable.org
Home Page: http://www.esroundtable.org

• 9368 • ESRA Award

Recognizes excellence in the field of executive search. Awarded annually.

• 9369 •
Exhibit Designers and Producers Association
Pete Dicks, Exec.Dir.
5775 G Peachtree-Dunwoody Rd., Ste. 500
Atlanta, GA 30342-0187
Phone: (404)303-7310
Fax: (404)252-0774
E-mail: edpa@edpa.com
Home Page: http://www.edpa.com

• 9370 • E-Cubed Awards

Recognizes innovative approaches to exhibit design. Categories are: Physical Environments; Presentation; Marketing; and Technical. First and second places awarded if qualified entries are received. Established in 1996 in conjunction with the Exhibit Designer World Symposium.

• 9371 • Hazel Hays Award

To recognize an individual for distinguished contribution to the exhibit industry. The EDPA Award Committee reviews all nominations and selects three finalists. These finalists are presented by mail ballot to the entire EDPA membership. A bronze plaque is awarded annually at the Association's convention. Established in 1976 to honor Hazel Hays for her service to the Association.

• 9372 •
Exotic Dancers League of America
Dixie Evans, Pres.
29053 Wild Rd.
Helendale, CA 92342
Phone: (760)243-5261
Fax: (760)955-8067
Home Page: http://www.exoticworldusa.com

• 9373 • **Fanny Award**
To recognize excellence in the art of striptease in the United States and to recognize a member or celebrity who has done the most for exotic dance or burlesque. U.S. citizens are eligible. A trophy in the shape of a female derriere is awarded annually. Established in 1956 by Jennie Lee. Sponsored by the Exotic Dancers Burlesque Historical Society. In addition, the Miss Exotic World Contest is also held the first Saturday in June at 2:00 pm annually.

• 9374 •
The Explorers Club
Nicole Young, Exec.Dir.
46 E 70th St.
New York, NY 10021
Phone: (212)628-8383
Fax: (212)288-4449
E-mail: executive@explorers.org
Home Page: http://www.explorers.org

• 9375 • **Explorers Medal**
To recognize extraordinary contributions directly in the field of exploration, scientific research, or the welfare of humanity. Individuals need not be members of the Club. Awarded when merited. Established in 1914.

• 9376 • **Edward C. Sweeney Medal**
For recognition of outstanding achievements in and contributions to the field of exploration and science. Members of the Club only are eligible. The recipient must have exhibited by word and action a profound interest in the welfare and principles of the Explorers Club as well as having rendered distinguished services in scientific work and in exploration. Awarded when merited. Established in 1968 the award is named after former club President Edward C. Sweeney.

• 9377 •
ExxonMobil Corporation
Downstream Operations
5959 Las Colinas Blvd.
Irving, TX 75039-2298
Phone: (972)444-1000
Fax: (972)444-1350
Home Page: http://www.exxon.mobil.com

Formerly: (1995) Mobil Oil Corporation.

• 9378 • **Mobil Five-Star Award**
For recognition of lodging (hotels, motels, resorts, guest ranches), restaurants, and spas that have achieved excellence in overall operations. The five-star award rating denotes one of the best in the continental U.S., Hawaii, Alaska, and Canada. Establishments listed in the *Mobil Travel Guide* are considered. A plaque is awarded annually. Established in 1966.

• 9379 • **Pegasus Prize for Literature**
To provide international recognition for distinguished works from countries whose literature is rarely translated into English. The awardee must be a citizen of the individual country where the prize is to be awarded, and the novel (or other specified genre) must have been written in the past 10 years. In each country chosen to award the prize, the selection is made by a panel of the country's most distinguished literary figures. The award, including a prize of $2,000 to $3,000, a bronze medal depicting Pegasus, the translation and publication of the work in English, and a trip to the United States to publicize the winning book are awarded annually. Established in 1977 in honor of the 50th anniversary of Mobil in Egypt.

• 9380 •
Eye Bank Association of America
Patricia Aiken-O'Neill, Pres./CEO
1015 18th St. NW., Ste. 1010
Washington, DC 20036
Phone: (202)775-4999
Fax: (202)429-6036
E-mail: info@restoresight.org
Home Page: http://www.restoresight.org

• 9381 • **Gift of Sight Award**
To recognize health professionals who have made outstanding contributions of humanitarianism in eye banking and sight restoration. Established in 1986.

• 9382 • **Heise Award**
To recognize lay people for their outstanding devotion to the EBAA's development, and for exemplifying the precepts of Leonard Heise, a major contributor to the fight against blindness and one of the EBAA's original founders. Awarded annually. Established in 1975.

• 9383 • **Paton Award**
To recognize ophthalmologists for their outstanding devotion to the EBAA's development, and for exemplifying the precepts of R. Townley Paton, M. D., a major contributor to the fight against blindness, the father of modern eye banking, and the founder of the first American eye bank. Established in 1982.

• 9384 •
Eye-Bank for Sight Restoration
Patricia Dahl, Exec.Dir./CEO
120 Wall St., 3rd Fl.
New York, NY 10005-3902
Phone: (212)742-9000
Fax: (212)269-3139
E-mail: info@ebsr.org
Home Page: http://www.eyedonation.org

• 9385 • **Man/Woman of Vision**
For recognition of outstanding contributions to the private sector on the part of corporate leaders, to draw public attention to the need for eye donations, and to elicit corporate support for The Eye-Bank for Sight Restoration, Inc. Awarded annually at a luncheon in the fall. Established in 1982.

• 9386 •
Fairbanks Education Association
Tom Richards, Pres.
2118 S Cushman St.
Fairbanks, AK 99701
Phone: (907)456-4435
Phone: (907)452-2297
Toll-Free: 888-456-4435
Fax: (907)456-2159
E-mail: fea@alaska.net
Home Page: http://www.ak.nea.org

• 9387 • **Friend of Education Award**
For those nominated by peers/parents. Recognition award bestowed annually.

• 9388 • **Teacher of the Year Award**
For teacher nominated by peers/parents. Recognition award bestowed annually.

• 9389 •
Fairbanks Symphony Association
Laura Bergh, Exec.Dir.
PO Box 82104
Fairbanks, AK 99708
Phone: (907)474-5733
Fax: (907)474-5147
E-mail: symphony@fairbankssymphony.org
Home Page: http://www.fairbankssymphony.org

• 9390 • **University Women's Association-Schaible-Strohmaier**
For full time student and orchestral musician. Scholarship awarded annually.

• 9391 •
Fairfield County Medical Association
Mark S. Thompson, Exec.Dir.
12 Cambridge Dr.
Trumbull, CT 06611-4764
Phone: (203)372-4543
Fax: (203)372-5293
E-mail: info@fcma.org
Home Page: http://www.fcma.org

• 9392 • **Magida Award**
For a physician and member of FCMA, under 40 years of age. Monetary award bestowed annually.

• 9393 •
Fairfield Historical Society
Steven K. Young, Dir.
636 Old Post Rd.
Fairfield, CT 06824
Phone: (203)259-1598
Fax: (203)255-2716
E-mail: info@fairfieldhs.org
Home Page: http://www.fairfieldhs.org

• 9394 • Historic Preservation Award
For appropriate restoration, renovation, or adaptive re-use of an historic structure in Fairfield. Recognition award bestowed annually.

• 9395 •
Families with Children from China - New England
Shanti Fry, Pres.
8 Berkeley St.
Cambridge, MA 02138
Phone: (617)876-3042
Fax: (617)441-5449
E-mail: shantifry@aol.com
Home Page: http://www.fwcc.org

• 9396 • Outstanding Contribution to the Adoption Community
For service to the community of adoption. Recognition award bestowed annually.

• 9397 •
Family, Career and Community Leaders of America
Debra Debates Jr., Chair
1910 Assn. Dr.
Reston, VA 20191-1584
Phone: (703)476-4900
Fax: (703)860-2713
E-mail: natlhdqtrs@fcclainc.org
Home Page: http://www.fcclainc.org

• 9398 • Distinguished Service Award
Recognizes distinguished service.

• 9399 • STAR Events - Students Taking Action with Recognition
Recognizes high challenge, low threat competitions.

• 9400 •
Family, Career, and Community Leaders of America, Arkansas Chapter
Rose Marie Willis, Exec. Officer
3 Capitol Mall
Luther Hardin Bldg.
Little Rock, AR 72201
Phone: (501)682-1489
Fax: (501)682-9440
E-mail: rose.willis@atsarkansas.gov
Home Page: http://dwe.arkansas.gov

• 9401 • STAR Awards
For proficiency and achievement in organization programs. Recognition award bestowed annually.

• 9402 •
Family Firm Institute
Judy L. Green PhD, Exec.Dir.
200 Lincoln St., Ste. 201
Boston, MA 02111
Phone: (617)482-3045
Fax: (617)482-3049
E-mail: ffi@ffi.org
Home Page: http://www.ffi.org

• 9403 • Barbara Hollander Award
Annual award of recognition.

• 9404 • Best Doctoral Dissertation
A monetary award is given annually.

• 9405 • Best Unpublished Research Paper
A monetary award is given annually.

• 9406 • Interdisciplinary Award
Annual award of recognition.

• 9407 • International Award
Annual award of recognition.

• 9408 • Richard Beckhard Practice Award
Annual award of recognition.

• 9409 •
Family Mediation Canada
Ned Courtney, Exec.Dir.
528 Victoria St. N
Kitchener, ON, Canada N2H 5G1
Phone: (519)585-3118
Toll-Free: 877-FMC-2005
Fax: (519)585-3121
E-mail: fmc@fmc.ca
Home Page: http://www.fmc.ca

• 9410 • Awards of Recognition
For individuals providing service to the field of family mediation. Awarded annually.

• 9411 •
Family Research Council
Tony Perkins, Pres.
801 G St. NW
Washington, DC 20001
Phone: (202)393-2100
Toll-Free: 800-225-4008
Fax: (202)393-2134
E-mail: corrdept@frc.org
Home Page: http://www.frc.org

• 9412 • Family Faith & Freedom
Recognizes significant contribution and outstanding leadership in promoting family values. Awarded periodically.

• 9413 •
Fargo-Moorhead Community Theatre
Charlene Hudgins, Artistic Dir.
333 4th St. S
Fargo, ND 58103
Phone: (701)235-1901
Toll-Free: 877-687-7469
Fax: (701)235-2685
E-mail: fmct@pol.org
Home Page: http://www.fmct.org

• 9414 • FMCT Playwrights Competition
To encourage and nurture new playwrights; to encourage production of original plays in geographic areas other than the east or west coasts; and to heighten interest in the North Dakota area for new plays and playwrights. Previously unproduced and unpublished one-act plays may be submitted May 1 through July 1 in odd-numbered years. Plays less than one hour playing time are considered. Nontraditional plays dealing with some aspect of the Midwest are preferred. A monetary award of $1,000; or if produced, $500 plus travel and housing expenses are awarded biennially in the spring of even-numbered years. Established in 1981.

• 9415 •
FARM (Farm Animal Reform Movement)
Alex Hershaft PhD, Pres.
10101 Ashburton Ln.
Bethesda, MD 20817
Phone: (301)530-1737
Toll-Free: 888-ASK-FARM
Fax: (301)530-5747
E-mail: info@farmusa.org
Home Page: http://www.farmusa.org

• 9416 • Bill Rosenberg Award
Recognizes significant contributions to end farm animal abuse. Youth activists are eligible. Awarded annually.

• 9417 • Sabina Fund
Recognizes grassroots organizations. Grants are awarded annually.

• 9418 •
Fashion Group Foundation of Houston
Gloria Pearson, Pres.
7615 Pagewood Ln.
Houston, TX 77063-6215
Phone: (713)782-4953
Fax: (713)782-4953

• 9419 • FGF Awards
Based upon recommendation by school faculty member. Scholarship awarded annually.

• 9420 •
Father's Day/Mother's Day Council
National Father's Day Committee
Stuart M. Goldblatt, Pres.
47 W 34th St., Ste. 534
New York, NY 10001
Phone: (212)594-5977
Fax: (212)594-9349
E-mail: fdcmdc@att.net
Home Page: http://www.momanddadday.com

• 9421 • Father of the Year
To provide recognition for the role-model father in conjunction with his contributions to contemporary lifestyle. Individuals who are biological, foster or adoptive fathers are eligible. Criteria include a close association with one's own children as well as involvement in community activi-

ties related to young people. A statue is awarded annually at the Father of the Year Awards Luncheon. Established in 1942.

• 9422 •
Faulkner County Literacy Council
Amy Hitchcock, Exec.Dir.
3200 W Tyler, Ste. B
Conway, AR 72034
Phone: (501)329-7323
Toll-Free: 877-329-7323
Fax: (501)329-7323
E-mail: fclc@conwaycorp.net

• 9423 • General Laubach Award
For accomplishments in literacy. Recognition award bestowed periodically.

• 9424 •
Federal Aviation Administration
Marion C. Blakey, Administrator
Office of Public Affairs
800 Independence Ave. SW
Washington, DC 20591
Phone: (202)366-4000
Fax: (202)267-5446
Home Page: http://www.faa.gov

• 9425 • Annual Aviation Mechanic Safety Award
To recognize aviation mechanics who make outstanding contributions to air safety through maintenance practices. This award is a joint FAA/industry award program.

• 9426 • Aviation Environment Award
To recognize efforts by airport operators, airport users, local units of government, citizens, manufacturers, planners, architects, designers, or others for outstanding design, notable restorations, preservations or efforts to enhance the environment affected by, or related to, aviation. Persons or organizations are eligible who have developed or implemented a program for enhancing environmental quality in the following areas: (1) aircraft noise reduction, control or abatement activities; (2) airport land use compatibility plans or controls; (3) protection of environmentally critical resources, e.g., public parks, recreation areas, wildlife refuges, wetlands, historic and archaeological sites; (4) promotion of public participation in efforts to enhance environmental quality; (5) aircraft or airport emissions reduction, control or abatement activities; and (6) architecture, landscape architecture, the use of graphic arts and other design considerations to improve the airport and its environs.

• 9427 • Award for Distinguished Service
This, the agency's second highest award, is given to recognize individuals not employed by the FAA who have made aviation safer, more economical, and/or more efficient. Individuals not employed by the FAA are eligible and must have accomplished one or more of the following: (1) displayed unusual courage in advancing aviation in the public interest; (2) rendered distinguished service in the public interest on behalf of aviation, with emphasis on flight safety; and (3) achieved outstanding results in efficiency and/or economy of unique benefit to the national aviation system or international aviation. A silver medal, lapel ribbon, and a certificate with the two-color embossed DOT seal signed by the Administrator are awarded.

• 9428 • Award for Extraordinary Service
To provide recognition and incentives for voluntary achievements, acts, and services contributing to increased air safety, efficiency, and economy. This, the agency's highest award, is given to recognize individuals not employed by the FAA who have made aviation safer, more economical, and/or more efficient. To be eligible, the nominee must have accomplished one or more of the following: (1) displayed extraordinary heroism in advancing aviation in the public interest; (2) exhibited remarkable ingenuity in developing or applying scientific, technological or engineering procedures that directly and tangibly improve aviation; (3) provided extraordinary leadership in advancing administrative matters on behalf of this country's national aviation missions and objectives; and (4) negotiated exceptional coordination and/or cooperation in matters pertaining to foreign air affairs or international aviation. A gold medal, lapel ribbon, and a certificate with the two-color embossed DOT seal signed by the Administrator are awarded.

• 9429 • Certificate of Appreciation
This, the fourth highest agency award, is given to recognize individuals not employed by the FAA who have made aviation safer, more economical, and/or more efficient and whose achievements are local or regional in scope. A certificate with the two-color embossed DOT seal and appropriate citation signed by the regional or center director are awarded.

• 9430 • Certificate of Commendation
This, the agency's third highest award, is given to recognize individuals not employed by the FAA who have made aviation safer, more economical, and/or more efficient. Individuals not employed by the FAA are eligible, and must have rendered a special act or service contributing to overall national aviation in a variety of areas such as aviation education, research, technical procedures, management improvements, aircraft design, noise abatement or legislative developments. A certificate with the two-color embossed DOT seal and appropriate citation signed by the Administrator or by the regional director are awarded.

• 9431 • Department of Transportation Award for Heroism
To recognize individual acts of heroism, which result in the avoidance of a disaster and/or the saving of life, by persons not employed by the Department. To be eligible for the award, a person must: (1) be employed in or directly associated with a transportation-related industry or activity and perform an act of heroism that endangers his own life, including but not limited to an attempt to save the life of another. The heroic act must be one that would not be expected in the performance of regular duties; and (2) perform an act of heroism that endangered his own life which was an attempt to prevent a wreck, disaster, or grave accident in any mode of transportation. Under this critierion, the nominee need not be employed by a transportation-related industry.

• 9432 • Flight Instructor of the Year Award Program
To recognize flight instructors who make outstanding contributions to air safety through flight instruction practices. This award is a joint FAA/industry award program.

• 9433 •
Federal Bar Association
Robyn J. Spalter, Pres.
2215 M St. NW
Washington, DC 20037-1416
Phone: (202)785-1614
Fax: (202)785-1568
E-mail: fba@fedbar.org
Home Page: http://www.fedbar.org

• 9434 • Chapter Activity Award Contest
To recognize the diligent work and accomplishment that outstanding FBA Chapters have made throughout the year. Chapters must submit applications detailing their activities. There are four award categories, based on the size of the Chapter. The winning entries are acknowledged during the FBA's annual meeting, as well as in the *News & Journal*.

• 9435 • Justice Tom C. Clark Award
To give public recognition to career lawyers who have performed outstanding work for the United States Government in the District of Columbia, or the Government of the District of Columbia. The following criteria are considered by the judging panel in selecting nominees: General accomplishments - a nominee may be qualified by outstanding legal ability, scholarship, and performance over a sustained period, even though the specific accomplishments are not related; or Specific accomplishments - a nominee may be qualified by virtue of a specific accomplishment which results in significant benefit to the government or to the legal profession and which constitutes a contribution to the development of public law. The accomplishment of the nominee should be reasonably related in time to the year preceding the nomination. A plaque is awarded annually. Established in 1959 in honor of Justice Tom C. Clark, former National President of the Association, a distinguished government attorney, Attorney General of the United States, Supreme Court Justice, and first Director of the Federal Judicial Center.

• 9436 • Elaine R. "Boots" Fisher Award
To stimulate, encourage, and recognize exemplary community, public, and charitable service by members of the Association. Any member of the Federal Bar Association who has been in good standing for at least two years at the time of nomination is eligible. The following criteria are considered: continuous general or specific contributions to community, charitable, or public service; specific accomplishment(s) for which the nominee is primarily responsible that serve

to enhance, promote, and encourage community, charitable, and/or public service; and specific personal achievements of the nominee that serve to provide inspiration and hope to others. Established in 1991 in memory of Elaine R. "Boots" Fisher.

• 9437 • Earl Kintner Award for Distinguished Service
To recognize an FBA member who has displayed outstanding achievement, distinguished leadership, and participation in the activities of the Association's Chapters and Committees throughout the nation. The award is named in honor of former National President Earl W. Kintner, whose own high level of dedicated service will always serve as a goal of excellence.

• 9438 • Publications Board's Newsletter Competition
To recognize the best newsletters published by FBA Chapters in each of the four Chapter groups and by FBA Sections and Committees during the fiscal year. Any FBA Chapter, Section, or Committee which has published at least two newsletters since October 1 of the preceding year is eligible to enter the competition. Judging of the newsletters focuses on overall sustained quality of the publication and emphasizes service to the members through the newsletter and considers content, creativity, and layout/design. The deadline for entry is August 16. Winners are announced at the Annual Publications Board Reception sometime in the early fall, as well as at the annual meeting and convention. Winners are also publicized in a subsequent issue of the *News & Journal*. Additional information is available from Margaret Simon, FBA Managing Newsletter Editor, telephone: (202) 638-0252.

• 9439 • Younger Federal Lawyer Award
To encourage younger federal lawyers throughout the nation and overseas to attain high standards of professional achievement and to accord public recognition for outstanding performance. Any civilian or military attorney under 36 years of age who is employed by the United States Government is eligible. A nominee may be qualified by outstanding legal ability and performance over a sustained period, or because of a specific accomplishment for which he or she is primarily responsible. A nominee may also be qualified because of a significant contribution to the legal profession and/or community not necessarily required by the nominee's government position.

• 9440 •
Federal Bar Council
Jeanette Redmond, Exec.Dir.
370 Lexington Ave., Ste. 1012
New York, NY 10017-6503
Phone: (212)883-1777
Fax: (212)692-4658
E-mail: federalbar@federalbarcouncil.com
Home Page: http://www.federalbarcouncil.org

• 9441 • Emory Buckner Medal
To recognize an individual for outstanding public service. A gold medal, suitably engraved and embossed, is awarded annually on the day before Thanksgiving. Established in 1961 in memory of Emory R. Buckner, United States Attorney for the Southern District of New York from 1925-1927.

• 9442 • Learned Hand Medal
To recognize excellence in Federal jurisprudence. A gold medal, suitably engraved and embossed, is awarded annually at the Law Day Dinner in May. Established in 1961 in memory of Learned Hand, the distinguished jurist.

• 9443 • Whitney North Seymour Award
To recognize outstanding public service performed by a member of the bar engaged in private practice. A barrister's wig box suitably inscribed is awarded annually. Established in 1987 and named in honor of the late Whitney North Seymour who served as president of the American Bar Association.

• 9444 •
Federal City Club
Lisa-Joy Zgorski, Exec.Dir.
1150 Connecticut Ave. NW, 9th Fl.
Washington, DC 20036
Phone: (202)234-3426
Fax: (202)828-4130
E-mail: lisajoy@ksg.harvard.edu
Home Page: http://www.federalcityclub.com

• 9445 • Distinguished Diplomatic Award
For recognition of outstanding international diplomatic service. Established in 1989.

• 9446 • Distinguished Journalism Award
To recognize individuals for outstanding work in journalism. Awarded annually. Established in 1996.

• 9447 • Federal City Club Award for Very Distinguished Public Service
To recognize individuals for outstanding national public service Awarded annually. Established in 1967.

• 9448 •
Federal Executive Institute Alumni Association
Awards Committee
PO Box 1001
Great Falls, VA 22066-9001
Phone: (703)406-0573
Toll-Free: (866)440-4919
Fax: (703)406-9724
E-mail: office@feiaa.org
Home Page: http://www.feiaa.org

• 9449 • Executive of the Year
To recognize extraordinary achievement in executive management and personal leadership at federal, state and local government levels. Executive leadership which produced substantial innovative achievements resulting in high quality public service, through great personal initiative, commitment, effort, and competence is considered. Nominations may be submitted by November 1. A plaque is awarded annually at a banquet ceremony held in conjunction with the animal conference, the Executive Forum. Established in 1981.

• 9450 •
Federal Globe: Gay, Lesbian, Bisexual and Transgender Federal Employees
Len Hirsch, Pres.
PO Box 23922
Washington, DC 20026-3922
E-mail: len@fedglobe.org
Home Page: http://www.fedglobe.org

• 9451 • Kameny Award
For significant contribution to the advancement of interests of GLBT employees in the federal government. Recognition award bestowed annually.

• 9452 •
Federally Employed Women
Patricia Wolfe, Pres.
1666 K St. NW, Ste. 440
Washington, DC 20006
Phone: (202)898-0994
Fax: (202)898-1535
E-mail: few@few.org
Home Page: http://www.few.org

• 9453 • FEW Distinguished Service Award
To recognize an individual who most notably has shown courage and leadership in furthering the cause of federally employed women. Nominations may be submitted by a FEW chapter or a member-at-large. A framed hand-lettered certificate is awarded annually at the National Training Program in July. Established in 1971.

• 9454 •
Federally Employed Women Legal & Education Fund
Patricia Wolfe, Pres.
1666 K St. NW, Ste. 440
Washington, DC 20006
Phone: (202)898-0994
Fax: (202)898-1535
E-mail: few@few.org
Home Page: http://www.few.org

• 9455 • Mary D. Pinkard Leader in Federal Equity Award
To recognize Federal employees who have advanced the cause of equity in the Federal government at personal and professional risk to themselves and who provide a positive role model for other employees. Any individual, organization, agency, or agency component may nominate any Federal employee or immediate past employee. The award may be given to more than one person each year. Nominations must be submitted by April 30. Awarded annually. Established to honor Mary D. Pinkard

(1916-1980), who, over three decades of public service, championed the disadvantaged in their struggle for decent housing and for freedom of choice in housing.

• 9456 •
Federation of Alberta Naturalists
Goulden Award Committee
11759 Groat Rd.
Edmonton, AB, Canada T5M 3K6
Phone: (780)427-8124
Fax: (780)422-2663
E-mail: info@fanweb.ca
Home Page: http://www.fanweb.ca

• 9457 • Loran L. Goulden Memorial Award
To recognize an individual for outstanding contributions to natural history in Alberta. The award recognizes both specific and long-term aggregate contributions to any field of natural history in Alberta. Nominations must be for work conducted in the province, but nominees need not live there. Nominations in writing are accepted at any time, but must be received by December 1 for consideration for the following year. A monetary award and a certificate are presented annually in January.

• 9458 •
Federation of American Hospitals
Charles N. Kahn III, Pres.
801 Pennsylvania Ave. NW, Ste. 245
Washington, DC 20004-2604
Phone: (202)624-1500
Home Page: http://www.fahs.com

Formerly: (1985) Federation of American Hospitals.

• 9459 • Individual of the Year Award
To recognize a nationally prominent individual with an interest in the health care field who has distinguished him or herself in an extraordinary manner. A plaque is awarded as merited at the Annual Convention. Established in 1972.

• 9460 • President's Achievement Award
To recognize a member or an associate member, whose contribution to the investor-owned hospital industry is above and beyond that normally expected. Nominations are accepted from members. A plaque is awarded annually when merited. Presented at the Annual Convention. Established in 1972.

• 9461 •
Federation of American Societies for Experimental Biology
Sidney Golub PhD, Exec.Dir.
9650 Rockville Pike
Bethesda, MD 20814
Phone: (301)634-7000
Fax: (301)634-7651
E-mail: admin@faseb.org
Home Page: http://www.faseb.org

• 9462 • FASEB Excellence in Science Award
To recognize outstanding achievement by women in biological sciences. All women who are members of one or more of the societies of the Federation are eligible. Nominees should be women whose excellent research has contributed significantly to the understanding of a particular discipline. A $10,000 unrestricted research grant, travel expenses to a scientific meeting, complimentary registration at the meeting, and a plaque are awarded annually. The awardee must agree to present an Excellence in Science Award lecture at the meeting. Established in 1988. Sponsored by Eli Lilly and Company.

• 9463 •
Federation of Analytical Chemistry and Spectroscopy Societies
Cindi Lilly, Exec.Asst.
PO Box 24379
Santa Fe, NM 87505
Phone: (505)820-1648
Fax: (505)989-1073
E-mail: facss@facss.org
Home Page: http://www.facss.org

• 9464 • FACSS Student Award
To recognize outstanding achievement in analytical chemistry or a related field by a graduate student. A scroll and expenses to the FACSS meeting are awarded annually. Established in 1975.

• 9465 • Hirschfeld Scholar Award
To recognize up to four graduate students with preference for diverse research specialties among the students. A scroll and expenses to the FACSS meeting are awarded annually. Established in 1987.

• 9466 •
Federation of BC Writers
Merrill Featon, Exec.Dir.
PO Box 3887, Sta. Terminal
Vancouver, BC, Canada V6B 2Z3
Phone: (604)683-2057
Fax: (604)608-5522
E-mail: fedoffice@bcwriters.com
Home Page: http://www.bcwriters.com

• 9467 • Literary Writers Competition
To recognize works of poetry, short fiction, or creative nonfiction. Theme of competition varies annually. A monetary prize, publication of the work, and a public reading are awarded annually.

• 9468 •
Federation of Defense and Corporate Counsel
Lewis F. Collins Jr., Pres.
11812-A N 56th St.
Tampa, FL 33617
Phone: (813)983-0022
Fax: (813)988-5837
E-mail: mstreeper@thefederation.org
Home Page: http://www.thefederation.org

Formerly: (2004) Federation of Insurance Counsel; Federation of Insurance and Corporate Counsel.

• 9469 • Federation of Insurance and Corporate Counsel Annual Award
To honor a person who has rendered distinguished service to the insurance and corporate industry and to his or her community, and who is recognized for dedication to the American ideal of free enterprise. A plaque is presented annually at the annual meeting of the federation. Established in 1952 in memory of George Henry Tyne, President of the Federation from 1948 to 1950. Formerly: (1985) Federation of Insurance Counsel Award.

• 9470 •
Federation of Fly Fishers
R.P Van Gytenbeek, CEO/Pres.
215 E Lewis
Livingston, MT 59047
Phone: (406)222-9369
Fax: (406)222-5823
E-mail: van@fedflyfisher.org
Home Page: http://www.fedflyfishers.org

• 9471 • Ambassador Award
To recognize a fly fisher who meets high standards of sportsmanship, fishing skill, and streamside etiquette in taking and conserving game fish internationally. A framed print is awarded annually. Established by the Bud Lilly Family.

• 9472 • Charles E. Brooks Memorial Award
To recognize an individual who demonstrates a deep affection for the outdoors; is an innovative fly tier; has written books, magazine articles, or pamphlets; is a member of the FFF and has a history of serving at banquets, seminars, or regional conclaves; and has a unique character. Awarded annually. Established in 1987 in memory of Charles E. Brooks, who wrote books, invented new fly patterns, and was a true student of nature.

• 9473 • Buz Buszek Memorial Award
To recognize a person who has made a significant contribution to the art of fly tying. Eligibility requires FFF membership. A plaque is awarded annually.

• 9474 • Council Award of Excellence
To recognize individuals who have made outstanding contributions to the Federation of Fly

Fishers at the regional or local level. Awarded annually.

• 9475 • FFF Conservation Award
To recognize an individual, group, or organization that has made an extraordinary contribution to the conservation of our fisheries resources. Individuals, groups, or organizations cannot have previously won the award. Awarded when merited.

• 9476 • Arnold Gingrich Memorial Award
To recognize an individual who has displayed outstanding achievement in areas related to the sport and science of fly fishing. Areas include angling writing, original fly-fishing theory, conservation and environmental protection, entomology, education in the sport, and innovation in fly fishing techniques. Life membership in the Federation is awarded.

• 9477 • Roderick Haig-Brown Award
To recognize an author of a book, books, or a combination of articles and books that embody the philosophy and spirit of Roderick Haig-Brown. Works must demonstrate respect for the ethics and tradition of fly fishing; an understanding of rivers, the inhabitants, and their environments; and concern for the philosophical side of fishing. Awarded annually. Established in 1991.

• 9478 • Don Harger Memorial Award
To recognize an individual (or, in his or her memory, to a family member) who is or has been actively engaged or closely related to some aspect of fly fishing as a vocation or avocation, and has made some noteworthy contribution as an educator, writer, environmental conservationist, photographer, fly tier, or proponent of fishing rights. A life membership in the Federation is awarded annually. Established in 1978 to honor Don Harger, a noted author, photographer, and flytier from Salem, Oregon.

• 9479 • Dr. James Henshall Award
To recognize an individual, club, group, or organization for extraordinary achievement in conservation of warm-water fisheries. Achievements include published articles and books related to the warm-water fisheries. Individuals and clubs must be members of the Federation and be in good standing, and the individual nominee must have initiated and directed a warm-water fisheries and conservation project. Groups or organizations need not be Federation affiliated. Awarded annually. Established in 1986 in memory of Dr. James A. Henshall.

• 9480 • Lew Jewett Memorial Award
To recognize an individual who has made a significant contribution to the field of fly fishing by: promoting the sport and/or enhancing the knowledge and ability of the fly fisher; devoting energy to youth education activities in the sport; being a proven fly fishing innovator in the equipment used or techniques developed; being a proven teacher or instructor in the sport; or making a contribution to the preservation and enhancement of resources utilized in fly fishing. A life membership in the Federation is awarded annually.

• 9481 • Stanley Lloyd Conservation Award
To recognize an FFF club project that deals with fishery-related conservation enhancement and preservation. Nominees must be active FFF affiliated clubs that have provided matching funds for the project of at least 50 percent of the total value of the project. More than one award is limited annually to the amount of interest earned on the fund. Established in 1992.

• 9482 • Man of the Year
To recognize the officer, senior advisor, or director who has demonstrated unusual devotion to the organization and has benefited the Federation as a national or international organization. Eligibility requires five years membership with the FFF. The individual must not have previously won the award and must have provided continuing service to the FFF. Awarded annually.

• 9483 • McKenzie Cup
To recognize the club that has made the most outstanding contribution in behalf of the Federation of Fly Fishers. Candidates must be an FFF group with a minimum of three years of continuous affiliation. Awarded annually. Formerly: McKenzie Plaque.

• 9484 • Memorial Life Membership Awards
To recognize an individual for significant contributions to fly fishing. Four awards are presented annually: Don Harger Memorial Award, Arnold Gingrich Literary Memorial Award, Lew Jewett Memorial Award, and Charles E. Brooks Memorial Award.

• 9485 • Dick Nelson Fly Tying Teaching Award
To recognize an individual who excels in teaching the art of fly tying to tiers at all skill levels. Awarded annually. Established in 2000.

• 9486 • Order of the Lapis Lazuli
To recognize the individual who has distinguished him or herself through remarkable and extraordinary contribution to the organization over a long period of time. Individuals must be nominated directly to any member of the Executive Board, must not have won the award previously, and must have eight years of voluntary service to the Federation. A ring is awarded.

• 9487 • President's Pin Award
To recognize service to the Federation and the president.

• 9488 • Warmwater Management Award
To recognize an individual or organization for an outstanding fishery management plan for a pond, stream, lake, or reservoir that makes a significant contribution to the protection, restoration, or enhancement of a warm water fishery. Awarded when merited. Established in 1985.

• 9489 • Woman of the Year
To recognize a woman who has demonstrated unusual devotion to the FFF and, through outstanding contributions, has benefited the Federation as a national or international organization. A minimum of five years membership and voluntary service to the Federation is required. The individual should not have previously won the award. Awarded annually.

• 9490 • Lee Wulff Award
To recognize the business side of fly fishing. To be eligible, a business must show, through their products, outstanding innovation in the fly fishing industry, outstanding stewardship for water and fisheries resources, or a combination of both. Awarded annually. Established in 1990.

• 9491 •
Federation of Gay Games
Kathleen Webster, Co-Pres.
584 Castro St., PMB 343
San Francisco, CA 94114
Phone: (415)695-0222
Fax: 800-887-1373
E-mail: info@gaygames.org
Home Page: http://www.gaygames.org

• 9492 • Tom Waddell Award
Recognizes volunteer contribution in time and affect on world-wide movement of the Gay Games. Awarded quadrennially.

• 9493 •
Federation of Genealogical Societies
Wendy Bebout Elliott PhD, Pres.
PO Box 200940
Austin, TX 78720-0940
Phone: (512)336-2731
Phone: (512)336-2731
Toll-Free: 888-FGS-1500
Fax: (512)336-2732
E-mail: fgs-office@fgs.org
Home Page: http://www.fgs.org

• 9494 • Award of Merit
To recognize an individual or an organization, not necessarily a member society for meritorious service or distinguished work in genealogy and family history. Several awards may be given each year. Established in 1983.

• 9495 • Certificate of Appreciation
A certificate presented to an individual or organization expressing thanks for duty performed in an exemplary and outstanding manner. Established in 1983.

• 9496 • Delegate Award
To recognize a current delegate of a member society in recognition of exemplary service to FGS as a member of and FGS standing committee or an active participant in an FGS project. A

certificate is presented annually. Established in 1993.

• 9497 • Director's Award

A plaque presented to an individual or an organization, generally not a member organization, in recognition of exceptional contribution to the field of genealogy and family history, and extra-mile effort to promote good will and improve services. Established in 1984.

• 9498 • Distinguished Service Award

A certificate presented to an individual or an organization for outstanding service to FGS or to a member society. The organization must be a member organization of FGS; individuals must be affiliated with a member organization. More than one such award may be given each year. Certificates are awarded annually. Established in 1983.

• 9499 • President's Citation

A certificate present to an individual or organization whose contributions or service to FGS or the genealogical community are singled out for recognition by the FGS president. A certificate is presented annually. Established in 1993.

• 9500 • Rabbi Malcolm H. Stern Humanitarian Award

A plaque presented to recognize the lifetime contributions of a rare individual whose positive personal influence and example have fostered unity in the genealogical community, provided leadership to its individual members, and helped to make family history a vital force in the community at large. Established in 1994.

• 9501 • David S. Vogels, Jr. Award

A plaque, presented to an individual in recognition of outstanding career contributions to FGS. Established in 1990.

• 9502 • George E. Williams Award

A plaque, presented to an individual for outstanding contributions in a single year to either FGS, a member organization or both. A plaque is awarded annually when merited. Established in 1981.

• 9503 •
Federation of Historical Bottle Collectors
June Lowry, Business Mgr.
401 Johnston Ct.
Raymore, MO 64083
Phone: (816)318-0160
E-mail: osubuckeyes71@aol.com
Home Page: http://www.fohbc.com

Formerly: (1991) Federation of Historical Bottle Clubs.

• 9504 • Elmer Lester Award

For recognition of the most improved operation of an antique bottle collecting club and to recognize the club with the best operation. The Contest is open to all clubs belonging to the Federation of Historical Bottle Clubs. A plaque is awarded annually at the convention. Established in 1974 in memory of Elmer Lester, first Chairman of the Federation of Historical Bottle Clubs. Additional information is available from Norm Barnett, P.O. Box 38, Flat Rock, IN 47234.

• 9505 • Newsletter Contest

To improve the quality of newsletters published by antique bottle collecting clubs and to recognize the best publications and their editors. The Contest is open to all clubs belonging to the Federation of Historical Bottle Clubs. Certificates and pens are awarded annually at the convention.

• 9506 • Show Flyer/Poster Contest

To encourage better quality poster/flyers regarding antique bottle shows. Posters or flyers used for advertising the bottle show of a member club are eligible. Certificates are awarded annually at the convention. Additional information is available from Howard and Lillian Dean, PO Box 115, Westernville, NY 13486.

• 9507 • Writers Contest

To honor the best writers of stories and research articles. Members of a member club or members at large of the Federation of Historical Bottle Clubs are eligible. Certificates and pens are awarded annually at the convention. Additional information is available from Steve Ketcham, Box 24114, Edina, MN 55424.

• 9508 •
Federation of Jewish Men's Clubs
Rabbi Charles E. Simon, Exec.Dir.
475 Riverside Dr., Ste. 832
New York, NY 10115-0022
Phone: (212)749-8100
Toll-Free: 800-288-3562
Fax: (212)316-4271
E-mail: international@fjmc.org
Home Page: http://fjmc.org

Formerly: National Federation of Jewish Men's Clubs.

• 9509 • Distinguished Service Award

For recognition of outstanding contributions and service which have furthered the cause of Judaism around the world. A scroll is awarded biennially. Established in 1928.

• 9510 • Presidential Award

Awarded only on very special occasions, this award has only been presented three times since its establishment in 1949.

• 9511 • Torch Award

For recognition of an outstanding program or activity conducted by an individual Men's Club, based on competitive entries. Awarded biennially at the Convention.

• 9512 • Youth Medallion

For recognition of outstanding services to the Youth Activity Program. Members of a Congregational Youth Program are eligible. A silver medallion and a scroll are awarded annually. Established in 1928.

• 9513 •
Federation of Materials Societies
Betsy Houston, Exec.Dir.
910 17th St. NW, Ste. 800
Washington, DC 20006
Phone: (202)296-9282
Fax: (202)833-3014
E-mail: betsyhou@ix.netcom.com
Home Page: http://www.materialsocieties.org

• 9514 • National Materials Advancement Award

To recognize individuals who have demonstrated outstanding capabilities in advancing the effective and economic use of materials and the multi-disciplinary field of materials science and engineering generally, and for contributing significantly to the application of the materials profession to national problems and policy. Nominations may be submitted by a Trustee, Officer, member of the Advisory Board, Educational Affiliate or Corporate Affiliate by September 1. A plaque is awarded annually. Established in 1985.

• 9515 •
Federation of Nova Scotian Heritage
Susan Charles, Exec.Dir.
1113 Marginal Rd.
Halifax, NS, Canada B3H 4P7
Phone: (902)423-4677
Toll-Free: 800-355-6873
Fax: (902)422-0881
E-mail: fnsh@hfx.andara.com
Home Page: http://www.fnsh.ns.ca

Formerly: (1981) Federation of Nova Scotia Historical and Heritage Societies; Federation of Museums, Heritage & Historical Societies of Nova Scotia.

• 9516 • Dr. Phyllis R. Blakeley Lifetime Achievement Award

Presented to any person who, for a period of not less than thirty (30) years, has been outstanding in the promotion, development and preservation of Nova Scotian Heritage.

• 9517 • Outstanding Exhibit Award

To honor individuals or organizations who have made significant contributions in the field of heritage promotion, interpretation and preservation. A silver bowl is presented for an exhibit created during the last calendar year which interprets local history.

• 9518 • Outstanding Promotion Award

To honor a federation member, group or organization for their outstanding accomplishments in self-marketing and promotion. A silver bowl and a certificate is awarded for recognition of winner's work in Nova Scotian heritage.

• 9519 • President's Awards
Presented to any individual who has given invaluable service by performing duties which have resulted in the success of projects and the efficient functioning of a member organization.

• 9520 •
Federation of Women Contractors
Beth Doria, Exec.Dir.
5650 S Archer
Chicago, IL 60638
Phone: (312)360-1122
Fax: (312)360-0239
E-mail: fwcchicago@aol.com
Home Page: http://www.fwcchicago.com

• 9521 • Women's Advocate Award
For contribution to women business owners in construction. Trophy awarded annually.

• 9522 •
Federation Petanque U.S.A.
John Rolland, Pres.
% Frank Pipal, Sec.
PO Box 180
Kenwood, CA 95452
Phone: (707)833-2020
E-mail: fpusasecretary@comcast.net
Home Page: http://www.usapetanque.org

Formerly: (1987) American Petanque Association U.S.A..

• 9523 • Annual Championship Prizes
To encourage national competition in the sport of petanque (an outdoor bowling game). Four national tournaments are held, two on the East Coast and two on the West Coast. Individuals who win first, second or third place in national petanque championships are eligible for champion shirts, medals, trophies and/or monetary prizes. Established in 1976.

• 9524 •
Fellows of the American Bar Foundation
Laura M. Curley, Dir.
750 N Lake Shore Dr.
Chicago, IL 60611-4403
Phone: (312)988-6596
Phone: (312)988-6596
Toll-Free: 800-292-5065
Fax: (312)988-6611
E-mail: lcurley@abfn.org
Home Page: http://fellows.abfn.org

• 9525 • Fifty-Year Award
To recognize a lawyer who has been in the active practice of law for more than fifty years, during which time he/she manifested adherence to the highest principles and traditions of the legal profession, and service to the community in which the attorney lived. Individuals may be nominated. A plaque is awarded annually. Established in 1957.

• 9526 • Research Award
To recognize an individual in law or government for outstanding research. Individuals may be nominated by members of the Fellows. A plaque is awarded annually. Established in 1957.

• 9527 •
Fellowship of Reconciliation - USA
Patricia Clark, Exec.Dir.
521 N Broadway
Nyack, NY 10960
Phone: (845)358-4601
Fax: (845)358-4924
E-mail: for@forusa.org
Home Page: http://www.forusa.org

• 9528 • Martin Luther King, Jr. Award
To recognize a person or group working quietly but effectively for peace and social justice in the revolutionary tradition of Martin Luther King, Jr. Nominations are accepted. The winners are selected by a panel of six judges which includes past Martin Luther King, Jr. Award winners. A monetary award of $2,500 and a scroll are presented annually. Established in 1979.

• 9529 • Pfeffer Peace Prize
To honor a person or group's outstanding work for peace and justice through nonviolent means. Open to nominees from anywhere in the world. Nominees are reviewed by an international panel of judges representing a variety of perspectives and backgrounds. A monetary award of $2,500 and a scroll are presented annually. Established in 1989 by Leo and Linda Pfeffer. Nominations welcome.

• 9530 •
The Feminist Press at the City University of New York
Lakes Volger, Contact
365 5th Ave., Ste. 5406
5th Fl.
New York, NY 10016
Phone: (212)817-7925
Fax: (212)817-1593
E-mail: lvolger@gc.cuny.edu
Home Page: http://www.feministpress.org

• 9531 • The Femmy Awards
For outstanding service to the Feminist Press. Recognition award bestowed annually.

• 9532 •
Feminists on the March
(Feministas en Marcha)
Ana I. Rivera-Lassen, Coord.
Apartado 21939, Estacion UPR
Rio Piedras, PR 00931-1939
Phone: (787)753-6430
Fax: (787)753-6430
E-mail: anarlfem@igc.apc.org

• 9533 • Golden Pig Award
Anti-award presented to individuals who have degraded the image of women in the media. Awarded annually.

• 9534 •
Ferret Fanciers Club
Mary Field, Exec.Dir.
2916 Perrysville Ave.
Pittsburgh, PA 15214
Phone: (412)322-1161

• 9535 • FFC Award of Recognition
To focus attention on an individual or group providing special services to ferrets or ferret owners. Nominations may be submitted by November 15. A certificate is awarded annually. Established in 1987.

• 9536 •
Festival International de Jazz de Montreal
822 Sherbrooke St. E
Montreal, QC, Canada H2L 1K4
Phone: (514)871-1881
Toll-Free: 888-515-0515
Fax: (514)525-8033
E-mail: media_jazz@equipespectra.ca
Home Page: http://www.montrealjazzfest.com

• 9537 • Jazz Prize
(Grand Prix de Jazz General Motors)
To recognize young jazz bands in Canada. Canadian groups of two to six musicians aged 35 years or under who have performed in Canada during the year preceding the entry period at recognized venues are eligible to perform at the Festival International de Jazz de Montreal. Selection of a winner is by a jury of five well-known personalities from the Canadian jazz scene. The prize winner receives a $5,000 grant plus an invitation to the next Festival, all expenses paid. The winner is also invited to play during the first half of the current Festival's closing concert given at the Salle Wilfrid-Pelletier by one of the world's leading jazz artists. Established in 1987 by ALCAN. For more information Caroline Johnson (514)525-7732. Formerly: Alcan Jazz Prize.

• 9538 •
Fiber Society
Dr. Subhash Batra, Sec.
Coll. of Textiles
North Carolina State Univ.
Raleigh, NC 27695-8301
Phone: (919)513-0143
Phone: (919)515-6555
Fax: (919)515-3057
E-mail: subhash_batra@ncsu.edu
Home Page: http://fs.tx.ncsu.edu

• 9539 • Distinguished Achievement in Basic or Applied Fiber Science
To recognize scientific achievement in basic or applied fiber science by an individual who is under 40 years of age. A monetary award of $1,500 and a scroll are awarded. Established in 1961.

Awards are arranged in alphabetical order below their administering organizations

• 9540 •
Film Advisory Board
Elayne Blythe, Founder & Pres.
7045 Hawthorn Ave., No. 305
Hollywood, CA 90028
Phone: (323)461-6541
Fax: (323)469-8541
E-mail: info@filmadvisoryboard.org
Home Page: http://www.filmadvisoryboard.org

• 9541 • **Award of Excellence**
Three awards are presented in the following categories: to recognize motion pictures, television programs, and videos as excellent family/children entertainment; to recognize the "Most Promising Young Newcomer" in the areas of film and television, and audio tapes, books, CD-ROMs, and inventions pertaining to the entertainment industry; and to recognize celebrities for their contributions to entertainment. Products may be submitted all-year-round at any time. Plaques are awarded monthly. Established in 1975. Film Advisory Board's "Award Winner" logo is known worldwide and is now featured in Spanish and Italian.

• 9542 •
Film Music Society
Christopher Young, Pres.
15125 Ventura Blvd., Ste. 201
Sherman Oaks, CA 91403
Phone: (818)789-6404
Fax: (818)789-6414
E-mail: info@filmmusicsociety.org
Home Page: http://www.filmmusicsociety.org

• 9543 • **Career Achievement Award**
To recognize an individual for outstanding achievements in the art of scoring for motion pictures. Living film composers are eligible. A plaque is awarded annually. Established in 1984.

• 9544 •
FilmLinc: Film Society of Lincoln Center
Claudia Bonn, Exec.Dir.
70 Lincoln Center Plz.
New York, NY 10023-6595
Phone: (212)875-5600
Fax: (212)875-5636
E-mail: wmccord@filmlinc.com
Home Page: http://www.filmlinc.com

• 9545 • **Tribute of the Film Society of Lincoln Center**
To recognize a distinguished film artist who has made a lasting contribution to the art of the motion picture. Tribute is paid to an honoree annually in the spring at a gala benefit. Established in 1972.

• 9546 •
Filson Historical Society
Mark Wetherington Ph.D., Exec.Dir.
1310 S 3rd St.
Louisville, KY 40208
Phone: (502)635-5083
Fax: (502)635-5086
E-mail: filson@filsonhistorical.org
Home Page: http://www.filsonhistorical.org

• 9547 • **Otto A. Rothert Award**
For best article in Filson Club History Quarterly each year. Recognition award bestowed annually.

• 9548 •
Financial Management Association International
Jennifer Conrad, Pres.
College of Business Administration
University of South Florida
4202 E Fowler Ave., BSN 3331
Tampa, FL 33620-5500
Phone: (813)974-2084
Fax: (813)974-3318
E-mail: fma@coba.usf.edu
Home Page: http://www.fma.org

• 9549 • **Competitive Papers Award**
To reward excellence in research in numerous specialties in the field of finance from among papers accepted for presentation at the upcoming FMA Annual Meeting. A monetary award is presented in each field annually at the FMA Annual Meeting.

• 9550 •
Financial Planning Association
5775 Glenridge Dr. NE, Ste. B-300
Atlanta, GA 30328-5364
Phone: (404)845-0011
Toll-Free: 800-322-4237
Fax: (404)845-3660
E-mail: membership@fpanet.org
Home Page: http://www.fpanet.org

• 9551 • **P. Kemp Fain, Jr. Award**
Recognizes an individual who has made an outstanding contribution to the financial planning profession in the areas of service to clients, society, academia, and/or government. Named after P. Kemp Fain, Jr. who formed the first International Association for Financial Planning (IAFP) chapter in the nation in 1971 and served as its first president. Formerly: Distinguished Service Award.

• 9552 •
Fine Arts Work Center in Provincetown
Hunter O'Hanian, Exec.Dir.
24 Pearl St.
Provincetown, MA 02657
Phone: (508)487-9960
Fax: (508)487-8873
E-mail: general@fawc.org
Home Page: http://www.fawc.org

• 9553 • **Fine Arts Work Center Fellowships**
To recognize visual artists and writers. Individuals who have completed their formal training. Deadline for writers is December 1 and February 1 for artists. Writers may apply in the categories of fiction and poetry. In the visual arts, painters, sculptors, installation artists, printmakers, and photographers are considered. Application forms are available by sending SASE (please indicate field of interest) or download from the above web site. A $600 monthly stipend and studio/living space for the October to May session are awarded annually to 10 visual artists and 9 writers. Established in 1968. Receives support from the National Endowment for the Arts and the Massachusetts Cultural Council and many others.

• 9554 •
Fire & Aviation Management
United States Forest Service
3833 S Development Ave.
Boise, ID 83705
Phone: (208)387-5092
Home Page: http://www.fs.fed.us/fire

• 9555 • **Director's Franklin Award**
Recognizes the best overall effort to assist underserved citizens in fire protection, using any or all of the three cooperative programs of the US Forest Service.

• 9556 • **Fire Management Award**
For recognition of outstanding achievement by persons involved in the protection of rural lands in the United States who have made notable contributions in fire management or have demonstrated exceptional valor or performance. Nominations are accepted. Plaques are awarded annually. Established in 1966. Formerly: Outstanding Service in Fire Management Award.

• 9557 • **Franklin Award for Federal Excess Personal Property**
To assist state and local fire services obtain equipment that might otherwise be unaffordable. Awarded to the State that demonstrates the best outreach to help underserved communities equip themselves to improve the fire protection they offer to their people.

• 9558 • **Franklin Award for State Fire Assistance**
To provide financial assistance, technical training, and equipment to ensure federal, state, and local fire agencies can deliver a coordinated response to wildfire. Awarded to the State that demonstrates the best use of these grants in this context that will help underserved people.

• 9559 • **Franklin Award for Volunteer Fire Assistance**
To assist smaller communities to improve (or begin) fire protection. Awarded to the state that demonstrates the best use of the grant in outreach to help underserved communities improve the fire protection they offer to their people.

• 9560 • National Smokey Bear Awards
To recognize organizations or individuals that have provided sustained outstanding public service to forest fire prevention over at least a two-year period. Nominations are accepted in the following awards: Golden Statuette - established in 1957 to recognize national service (no more than three are awarded annually); Silver Statuette - established in 1967 for regional (multi-state) service (no more than five are awarded annually); and Bronze Statuette - established in 1962 for statewide service (no more than 10 are awarded annually). Sponsored by The USDA Forest Service, The National Association of State Foresters, and the Advertising Council. Established in 1962.

• 9561 •
First Special Service Force Association
William Story CAE, Exec.Dir.
262 Pine Knob Cir.
Moneta, VA 24121-2609
Phone: (540)297-8304
Fax: (540)297-1136
E-mail: storfssf@infionline.net

• 9562 • Frederick Award for Outstanding Soldier
Major General Robert F. Frederick Award
To honor the outstanding soldier of the U.S. Army Special Forces. Soldier must be selected by his individual command. A plaque is issued to each winner and a plate is mounted on the Master Award at the headquarters of the winners. Awarded annually at the reunions. Established in 1980 in honor of MG Robert T. Frederick, former commander of the First Special Service Force of World War II.

• 9563 •
John Fischetti Editorial Cartoon Competition
Columbia College Chicago
600 S Michigan Ave.
Chicago, IL 60605-1996
Phone: (312)344-7630
Fax: (312)344-8059
E-mail: fischetti@colum.edu
Home Page: http://johnfischetti.org

• 9564 • John Fischetti Editorial Cartoon Competition
To encourage greater recognition of the unique journalistic endeavor of political cartoonists. Any salaried, staff, syndicated, or regularly published cartoonist may submit one entry (single cartoon or as many as three) on current social and political subjects published during the preceding calendar year. The deadline for submissions is January 31. Monetary prizes of $5,000 for the Grand Prize and two honorable mention awards are awarded annually at the John Fischetti Scholarship event in April or May. Established in 1981 to honor John Fischetti, Pulitzer Prize-winning editorial cartoonist.

• 9565 •
Fischoff National Chamber Music Association
Ann Divine, Exec.Dir.
University of Notre Dame
303 Brownson Hall
PO Box 1303
Notre Dame, IN 46556
Phone: (574)631-0984
Phone: (574)631-0599
Fax: (574)631-2903
E-mail: info@fischoff.org
Home Page: http://fischoff.org

Formerly: (1985) Century Productions.

• 9566 • Fischoff National Chamber Music Competition
To recognize the ensemble that gives the best performance at the Competition and to encourage its musical and career development. Any chamber music instrumental ensemble of three to six members whose average age does not exceed 30 at the time of the competition may apply. The following monetary prizes are awarded in both the string and wind categories: First prize - $3,000; Second prize - $1,200; and Third prize $500. In addition, the grand prize winner receives an additional $2,000 and a concert tour. In the Junior division (ages 18 and younger), monetary prizes of $1,200, $800, and $400 are awarded. Awarded annually. Established in 1973 by Joseph Fischoff and the South Bend Chamber Music Society. An alternate contact address is: AD. Bldg 239, Indiana University South Bend, 1700 Mishawaka Ave., South Bend, IN 46615.

• 9567 •
Fisheries and Oceans Canada
Communications Branch
200 Kent St., 13th Fl.
Sta. 13228
Ottawa, ON, Canada K1A 0E6
Phone: (613)993-0999
Fax: (613)990-1866
E-mail: info@dfo-mpo.gc.ca
Home Page: http://www.dfo-mpo.gc.ca

• 9568 • National Recreational Fisheries Awards
To recognize recipients for their significant and continued commitment to conversation, protection, and increasing public awareness of the importance of Canada's recreational fisheries resources. Awarded annually. Established in 1989.

• 9569 •
Fleischner Society
Christian J. Herold, Pres.
4550 Post Oak Pl., Ste. 342
Houston, TX 77027
Phone: (713)965-0566
Fax: (713)960-0488
E-mail: jboylan@meetingmanagers.com
Home Page: http://www.fleischner.org

• 9570 • Fleischner Society Memorial Award
For recognition of achievement in research in radiology or other imaging of the respiratory system. Individuals under 40 years of age are eligible. A monetary prize or an expense paid trip to the Fleischner Society meeting is awarded annually when merited. Established in 1979 in honor of George Simon, a British radiologist. Additional information is available from Victor Chernick, MD, C5514 Children's Hospital, 840 Sherbrook St., Winnipeg, MB, Canada R3A 1S1. Formerly: (1991) George Simon Award.

• 9571 •
Flexible Packaging Association
Marla Donahue, Pres.
971 Corporate Blvd., Ste. 403
Linthicum, MD 21090-2211
Phone: (410)694-0800
Fax: (410)694-0900
E-mail: fpa@flexpack.org
Home Page: http://www.flexpack.org

Formerly: (1979) National Flexible Packaging Association.

• 9572 • Award for Environmental Achievement
To recognize the flexible package that represents the most outstanding environmental achievement. Criteria include the amount of source reduction the package achieves, the use of recycled-content materials, new technology that achieves greater environmental advances, and the reduction of solvents, emissions, energy, or resources expended. A crystal globe trophy on a walnut stand with an inscribed plaque is awarded at the annual meeting. Established in 1993. Formerly: Green Globe Award for Environmental Achievement.

• 9573 • President's Award
This, the top award in the flexible packaging industry, is given to recognize the most outstanding achievement in flexible packaging. Winners of the Top Packaging Awards are eligible for consideration. The winner is determined by flexible packaging manufacturers at the Association's annual meeting.

• 9574 • Top Packaging Awards
To recognize advances, innovation, and excellence in flexible packaging and to promote the value of flexible packaging to customers and consumers alike. Flexible packaging is defined as any package that takes the shape of a bag, pouch, label, or wrap. Open to the manufacturers (or "converters") of flexible packaging. Winners receive plaques and publicity from trade and consumer presses. Awarded annually. Established in 1956.

• 9575 •
Flight Safety Foundation
Stuart Matthews, CEO & Pres.
601 Madison St., Ste. 300
Alexandria, VA 22314-1756
Phone: (703)739-6700
Fax: (703)739-6708
E-mail: wahdan@flightsafety.org
Home Page: http://www.flightsafety.org

• 9576 • **Airport Safety Award**
To recognize outstanding or significant improvement in the ramp safety environment through innovation and implementation of a ramp safety program including methods, practices, or policies. A framed certificate, honorarium and expense paid trip for recipient and guest to the Flight Safety Foundation's annual International Air Safety Seminar are awarded annually. Established in 1996. Formerly: Ramp Safety Award.

• 9577 • ***Aviation Week & Space Technology* Distinguished Service Award**
To recognize distinguished service in achieving safer utilization of aircraft. Nominations are accepted from national and international aviation organizations. The deadline for submissions is June. A framed citation and plaque are awarded annually at FSF's International Aviation Safety Seminar in the fall. Established in 1949. Sponsored by *Aviation Week & Space Technology* magazine, the award was created by Jerry Lederer, the founder of Flight Safety Foundation.

• 9578 • **Laura Taber Barbour Award**
To recognize outstanding achievement in both civil and military aviation safety. Nominations may be submitted by national and international aviation organizations by March. A gold medallion, and a certificate are awarded annually at the Foundation's International Aviation Safety Seminar in the fall. Established in 1956 by Dr. Clifford E. Barbour and his son Clifford Barbour, Jr. in memory of Mrs. Laura Taber Barbour, who lost her life in an airplane accident in 1945.

• 9579 • **Cecil Brownlow Publications Award**
To recognize outstanding service to safety in the publishing field. Selections are made from those publications that the Foundation receives during each calendar year. A framed citation is awarded annually at the Foundation's International Aviation Safety Seminar in the fall and the recipient receives $1,000. Established in 1968; renamed in 1988 in memory of Cecil Brownlow, for his service to the Foundation as Editor. Formerly: (1988) Publications Award.

• 9580 • **Business Aviation Meritorious Award**
To recognize distinguished service and dedication in the corporate aviation field. A framed citation is awarded annually at the Flight Safety Foundation's Corporate Aviation Safety Seminar in the spring. Established in 1975.

• 9581 • **Joe M. Chase Award**
To recognize distinguished contributions to safety in the aviation mechanics' field and its importance in aircraft safety and reliability. Selection is made by the Professional Aviation Maintenance Association. The award comprises a framed certificate and plaque presented by PAMA. Awarded annually at the Professional Aviation Maintenance Association meeting in the spring. Established in 1973.

• 9582 • **Admiral Luis de Florez Flight Safety Award**
To recognize outstanding individual contributions to aviation through basic design, device, or practice that have resulted in significant improvements in safety. Nominations from aviation organizations may be submitted by the end of June. An honorarium of $1,000 a plaque, and citation are awarded annually at the Flight Safety Foundation's International Aviation Safety Seminar in the fall. Established in 1966 as a result of a Trust instituted by the late Admiral Luis de Florez, former president of FSF, in his will.

• 9583 • **Heroism Award**
To recognize outstanding performance above and beyond the call of duty that results in the saving of aircraft and/or personnel by crew members on an air carrier or corporate aircraft. National and international aviation organizations may submit nominations by the end of July. A framed citation presented by the Flight Safety Foundation, and a miniature replica of a 15th Century two-handed battle sword manufactured by Wilkinson Sword Ltd., a sister company of Graviner, Ltd., England, are awarded annually at the Flight Safety Foundation's International Aviation Safety Seminar in the fall. Additionally there is a $1,000 cash award. Established in 1968. Sponsored by Kidde-Graviner, Ltd., the safety protection division of Wilkinson Match, Ltd., in England.

• 9584 •
Florida Alliance of Information and Referral Services
Mr. Tim Sylvia, Pres.
PO Box 10950
Tallahassee, FL 32302-2950
Phone: (850)681-9131
Fax: (850)561-3443
E-mail: rsnicklaus@211bigbend.org
Home Page: http://www.flairs.org

• 9585 • **George McKinney Award**
For leadership in I&R/hotline services, especially in area of youth. Scholarship awarded annually.

• 9586 •
Florida Arts Council
Brian R. Clark, Contact
Division of Cultural Affairs
Dept. of State
The Capitol
1001 Desoto Park Dr.
Tallahassee, FL 32301
Phone: (850)245-6470
Fax: (850)245-6497
E-mail: florida-arts-info@dos.state.fl.us
Home Page: http://www.florida-arts.org

• 9587 • **Florida Artists Hall of Fame**
To recognize and honor individuals who have made lasting and significant contributions to the arts in Florida. Nominees must have been born in Florida or have adopted Florida as their home state and base of operation. Established in 1986 by the Florida legislature.

• 9588 • **Florida Arts Recognition Awards**
To recognize excellence in the arts or in the promotion of the arts in Florida. Individuals, businesses, legislators, and institutions that have demonstrated notable contributions to the arts in Florida during the preceding year are eligible. Any individual or person representing an organization may submit nominations. Awards are presented in four major categories: Individual - arts administrators, arts educators, arts patrons, and individual artists; Business - corporations and corporation executives; Government - state and local level representatives; Other media, local governments, and not-for-profit institutions (e.g., United Way, Girl Scouts) that support the arts. Awards are not necessarily issued in every category every year. There is no set number of awards annually. Awards are announced by the Secretary of State and the Florida Arts Council. Established in 1973. Formerly: Governor's Awards for the Arts.

• 9589 • **State of Florida Fellowship**
To recognize individual artists for the quality of their work and their potential for additional development as an artist at the state and national level. Categories include dance, folklife/traditional arts, literature, media arts, music, theatre, visual arts, and interdisciplinary. Monetary awards of $5,000 each are presented to allow artists time to pursue a particular area of interest in their art form.

• 9590 •
Florida Association of Colleges and Universities
Dr. Daniel B. Crowder, Exec.Dir.
12106 Bruce Hunt Rd.
Clermont, FL 34711-6824
Phone: (352)242-2633
Fax: (352)242-6170
E-mail: exdirfacu@aol.com

• 9591 • **Distinguished Service Award**
For extraordinary service to all three sectors of Florida higher education. Recognition award bestowed annually.

• 9592 •
Florida Association of Nonprofit Organizations
Marina Pavlov, Pres.
7480 Fairway Dr., No. 206
Miami Lakes, FL 33014
Phone: (305)557-1764
Toll-Free: 800-362-3266
Fax: (305)821-5228
E-mail: fanoinfo@fano.org
Home Page: http://www.fano.org

• 9593 • **Lawton S. Heart Award**
For dedication in the improvement of the nonprofit community from a humanitarian position. Recognition award bestowed annually.

• 9594 •
Florida Automotive Industry Association
George Ehrhard ASE, Exec.VP
15619 Premiere Dr., Ste. 101
PO Box 533009
Tampa, FL 33624
Phone: (813)962-4445
Toll-Free: 800-989-1992
Fax: (813)962-4741
E-mail: office@faia.org
Home Page: http://www.faia.org

• 9595 • **Al Hines Award**
For past service commitment to industry. Recognition award bestowed annually.

• 9596 •
Florida Craftsmen
Lisa-Marie Confessore, Exec.Dir.
501 Central Ave.
St. Petersburg, FL 33701-3703
Phone: (727)821-7391
Fax: (727)822-4294
E-mail: info@floridacraftsmen.net
Home Page: http://www.floridacraftsmen.net

• 9597 • **Best of Show**
To distinguish an individual artist for accomplished work in the field of fine contemporary crafts, and to encourage continued professional development. A member who is 18 years of age or older, living and working in the state of Florida is eligible. A monetary prize and a ribbon are awarded at the annual conference and Exhibition. Awards of Excellence and Purchase Awards are also presented. Established in 1952.

• 9598 •
Florida Education Fund
201 E Kennedy Blvd., Ste. 1525
Tampa, FL 33602
Phone: (813)272-2772
Fax: (813)272-2784
E-mail: office@fl-educ-fd.org
Formerly: (1987) McKnight Programs in Higher Education.

• 9599 • **McKnight Doctoral Fellowship Program in Arts and Sciences, Mathematics, Business and Engineering**
To provide up to $5,000 in tuition and fees plus an annual tax-free stipend of $11,000 to 25 African-American citizens to pursue Ph.D. degrees at participating Florida universities. Applicants must hold or be receiving a bachelor's degree from a regionally-accredited college or university. The deadline for applications is January 15. Contingent upon successful academic progress, the maximum length of awards is five years. The Florida Education Fund provides for the first three years and the student's university continues funding at the same level of support, if required, for a fourth and fifth year. Established in 1984. Formerly: McKnight Black Doctoral Fellowship Program.

• 9600 •
Florida Federation of Music Clubs
Connie Tuttle-Hill, Pres.
PO Drawer G
White Springs, FL 32096
Phone: (904)397-2733
Fax: (904)397-4262
E-mail: fc52@aol.com
Home Page: http://www.ffmc-music.org

• 9601 • **"Jeanie" Musical Scholarship Winner**
To recognize an outstanding female vocalist between a senior in high school and 23 years of age who is capable of giving a creditable concert, radio, or TV appearance and to promote this talent. Florida women sponsored by a Florida federated music club who have never been married are eligible. A scholarship of $1,500 to a university, college, or school of music is awarded annually. In addition, four runners-up receive $750 scholarships. Established in 1951. Co-sponsored by Florida Federation of Music Clubs, and Florida Park Service.

• 9602 •
Florida Film Festival
Kat Quast, Gen.Mgr.
℅ Enzian Theater
1300 S Orlando Ave.
Maitland, FL 32751
Phone: (407)644-6579
Fax: (407)629-6870
E-mail: kquast@enzian.org
Home Page: http://www.floridafilmfestival.com

• 9603 • **Audience Awards**
To honor the best American independent films in the categories of Narrative Feature, Documentary Feature, Short Film, International Feature, and International Short. Awarded annually.

• 9604 • **Grand Jury Awards**
To honor the best American independent films in the categories of Documentary Feature, Narrative Feature, Documentary Short, Narrative Short, and Animated Short. Awarded annually.

• 9605 •
Florida Institute of Oceanography
830 1st St. S
St. Petersburg, FL 33701
Phone: (727)553-1100
Fax: (727)553-1109
E-mail: jogden@seas.marine.usf.edu
Home Page: http://www.marine.usf.edu/FIO/

• 9606 • **Behrens Award**
For best research paper by an undergraduate or graduate student. Awarded annually.

• 9607 •
Florida Irrigation Society
Jennifer Amarosa, Office Admin.
9340 56th St. N, Ste. 105
Temple Terrace, FL 33617
Phone: (954)974-4849
Toll-Free: 800-441-5341
Fax: (813)985-9820
E-mail: administration@fisstate.org
Home Page: http://www.fisstate.org

• 9608 • **Dalton S. Harrison/Florida Irrigation Society Scholarship**
For a student in University of Florida's Agricultural Biological Engineering Department. Scholarship awarded annually.

• 9609 •
Florida Nurserymen and Growers Association
Ben Bolusky, Exec.VP
1533 Park Center Dr.
Orlando, FL 32835-5705
Phone: (407)295-7994
Toll-Free: 800-375-3642
Fax: (407)295-1619
E-mail: info@fngla.org
Home Page: http://www.fnga.org

• 9610 • **Association and Industry Awards**
To recognize outstanding members of FNGA chapters. The following awards are given: Association Awards - Outstanding Chapter President, Outstanding Chapter Secretary, Outstanding Allied Person, Outstanding Committee Chairperson, and the Wendell E. Butler Award/Most Outstanding Nursery Professional; and Industry Awards - Outstanding Industry Person, Outstanding Horticulture Writer, and Outstanding Educator. Nominations may be made by chapter members, and should be accompanied by the individual's resume of accomplishments relative to the award. For more information contact Jessica Schaaf at jschaaf@fngla.org.

• 9611 • **Foliage Hall of Fame**
To provide a memorial to those in the industry that have given unselfishly of their time and effort in the development of the foliage industry. Any person who has given a minimum of 15 years of personal dedication to the development, growth and improvement of the foliage industry is eligible for nomination. A suitably-inscribed plaque is awarded annually at the

TPIE (Foliage Trade Show) ceremony. Established in 1977 the nomination deadline is March 1 annually. The Florida Nurserymen and Growers Association took over the development and distribution of the award from the Florida Foliage Association.

• 9612 • Foliage Writer of the Year Contest

To recognize outstanding garden writers for their support of the foliage industry and to encourage writers to continue creating unique and informative articles that inspire consumers to purchase foliage material. The submitted article must be published in one year between October 1 and October 1, and received by the second Friday in October. The winner receives a trip for two to Florida, including admission to the Tropical Plant Industry Seminar in Ft. Lauderdale and a backstage tour of Walt Disney World's EPCOT Center in Orlando.

• 9613 • Landscape Awards

For recognition of excellence in landscaping. Any industrial or commercial business, institution, municipality, or home grounds featuring 50 percent Florida-grown plant material is eligible. The deadline for entering is June 30. Categories include renovations, residential single family, residential multifamily, commercial, institutional/government, interiors, special projects, maintenance, mitigated site, and irrigation design and retrofit. Awards to be presented include the Roy S. Rood Award for the most outstanding entry, the Grower of the Year Award for the grower who has provided the highest quality of plant material and service, the Floriculture Award for the most effective use of bedding plants to create color and texture in the landscape, and the S. J. Blakely Award, for the FNGA nursery or garden center that has done the most to promote landscaping outside the place of business. Awards are presented at the Florida Nursery and Allied Trades Show.

• 9614 •
Florida Propane Gas Association
214 S. Monroe St.
PO Box 11026
Tallahassee, FL 32302-3026
Phone: (850)681-0496
Fax: (850)222-7892
E-mail: info@flgasassc.com

• 9615 • FPGA Scholarship Program

For children of member company employees. Scholarship awarded annually.

• 9616 •
Florida Sea Grant College Program
James C. Cato, Dir.
Bldg. 803, McCarty Dr.
University of Florida
PO Box 110400
Gainesville, FL 32611-0400
Phone: (352)392-5870
Fax: (352)392-5113
E-mail: jcato@ifas.ufl.edu
Home Page: http://www.flseagrant.org

• 9617 • Aylesworth Foundation Advancement Award

Recognizes excellence in Marine Science Scholarship.

• 9618 • Dean John A. Knauss Marine Policy Fellowship

Inquire for application details.

• 9619 •
Florida Society of Registered Nurses Retired
Christina K. Sharp, Pres.
2735 Mystic Cove Dr.
Orlando, FL 32812-5344
Phone: (407)382-0607
E-mail: rnrflorida@aol.com

• 9620 • RNR Chapter Community Service Award

For volunteer within RNR and community. Recognition award bestowed annually.

• 9621 •
Florida Space Grant Consortium
Dr. Jaydeep Mukherjee, Dir.
Bldg. M6-306, Rm. 7010
Center for Space Education
Mail Stop FSGC
Kennedy Space Center, FL 32899
Phone: (321)452-4301
Fax: (321)449-0739
E-mail: fsgc@mail.ucf.edu
Home Page: http://fsgc.engr.ucf.edu

• 9622 • Space Grant Fellowship Program

For full-time doctoral to graduate students. Inquire for application details.

• 9623 •
Florida Sports Foundation
Larry Pendleton, Pres.
2930 Kerry Forest Pkwy.
Tallahassee, FL 32309
Phone: (850)488-8347
Fax: (850)922-0482
E-mail: lpendleton@flasports.com
Home Page: http://www.flasports.com

• 9624 • Regional and Major Sports Grants

For approved application. Grant awarded quarterly.

• 9625 •
Florida State Archives
R.A. Gray Bldg.
500 S Bronough St.
Tallahassee, FL 32399-0250
Phone: (850)245-6700
Home Page: http://dlis.dos.state.fl.us/barm/fsa.html

• 9626 • Florida Folk Heritage Awards

To honor Floridians whose lifelong devotion to and whose skills and accomplishments in the folk arts and crafts are distinguished affirmations of the rich cultural legacy which the citizens of Florida wish to acknowledge, celebrate, and conserve. Nominations are made by letter to the Florida Folklife Council in care of the Bureau of Florida Folklife Programs and should describe the accomplishments and background of the nominee. The deadline is October 1. A certificate is awarded annually. Established in 1985.

• 9627 •
Florida State Golf Association
Jim Demick, Exec.Dir.
8875 Hidden River Pkwy., Ste. 110
Tampa, FL 33637
Phone: (813)632-FSGA
Toll-Free: (813)632-3742
Fax: (813)910-2129
E-mail: jdemick@fsga.org
Home Page: http://www.fsga.org

• 9628 • Clarence Camp Award

For college-bound members. Scholarship awarded annually.

• 9629 • Junior Golf Grant

For non-profit organization teaching underprivileged the game of golf. Grant awarded periodically.

• 9630 •
Florida State Grange
Gerry Watson, State Sec.
PO Box 205
Winter Beach, FL 32971-0205
Phone: (772)569-1168
Phone: (561)569-1168
Fax: (772)569-9175
E-mail: rfgwat@yahoo.com
Home Page: http://nationalgrange.org

• 9631 • Community Service Award

For participation, man-hours, donations, etc. Recognition award bestowed annually.

• 9632 •
Florida State University
Center for Performance Technology
4600-C University Center
Tallahassee, FL 32306-1636
Phone: (850)644-2570
Fax: (850)644-4952
E-mail: rbranson@cpt.fsu.edu
Home Page: http://www.cpt.fsu.edu

• 9633 • Teachers Quest Awards

Sponsored through the Leon County Department of Education. Inquire for application details.

• 9634 •
Florida TaxWatch
Dominic M. Calabro, Pres. & CEO
PO Box 10209
Tallahassee, FL 32302
Phone: (850)222-5052
Fax: (850)222-7476
E-mail: lwashington@floridataxwatch.org
Home Page: http://www.floridataxwatch.org

• 9635 • **Davis Productivity Awards Program**
Recognizes highly productive Florida government workers. Cash awards are given.

• 9636 •
Florida Trail Association
Deborah Stewart-Kent, Exec.Dir.
5415 SW 13th St.
Gainesville, FL 32608
Phone: (352)378-8823
Toll-Free: 877-HIKE-FLA
Fax: (352)378-4550
E-mail: fta@florida-trail.org
Home Page: http://www.florida-trail.org

• 9637 • **Champion of the Trail Award**
For elected officials who support the trail. Recognition award bestowed periodically.

• 9638 • **Friend of the Florida Trail Award**
For land owners and agencies that support and promote the trail. Recognition award bestowed annually.

• 9639 •
Flying Physicians Association
Frank Browning MD, Pres.
PO Box 677427
Orlando, FL 32867
Phone: (407)359-1423
Fax: (407)359-1167
E-mail: fpahq@aol.com
Home Page: http://www.fpadrs.org

• 9640 • **Airman of the Year**
For recognition of an airman physician. Awarded annually. Established in 1960.

• 9641 • **Distinguished Service Award**
For recognition of an airman physician. Members are eligible. Awarded annually when merited. Established in 1971.

• 9642 • **Honorary Member**
To recognize an airman physician. Honorary membership is awarded annually when merited. Established in 1955.

• 9643 •
FOCUS Greater Syracuse
Charlotte Holstein, Exec.Dir.
201 E Washington St.
Syracuse, NY 13202-1427
Phone: (315)448-8732
Fax: (315)448-8733
E-mail: focus@ci.syracuse.ny.us
Home Page: http://www.focussyracuse.org

• 9644 • **Rhea Eckle Clark Citizenship Award**
For person or organization exemplifying positive community change in Central New York. Recognition award bestowed annually.

• 9645 •
Folger Shakespeare Library
Dr. Kathleen Lynch, Exec.Dir.
201 E. Capitol St. SE
Washington, DC 20003
Phone: (202)544-4600
Fax: (202)544-4623
E-mail: webmaster@folger.edu
Home Page: http://www.folger.edu

• 9646 • **Folger Shakespeare Library Fellowships and National Endowment for the Humanities Senior Fellowships**
To assist senior scholars who have made substantial contributions in their field of research and who are pursuing research projects appropriate to the collections of the Folger. Applicants for the NEH Fellowships must be U.S. citizens. The deadline for applications is November 1. Fellowships are for a period of six to nine months and carry stipends of up to $18,000 and $30,000 and travel expenses, respectively. Two to three awards are presented annually.

• 9647 • **O. B. Hardison Jr. Poetry Prize**
To recognize a poet whose art and teaching demonstrate a spirit of inquiry, imagination, and scholarship. A monetary award of $10,000 is presented. Established in 1991 to honor O. B. Hardison, the library's former director and founder of the Folger Poetry Series.

• 9648 •
Food and Commercial Workers AFL-CIO, LU 513 T
Ronnie Davis, Pres.
PO Box 3394
Sherman, TX 75091-3394
Phone: (903)891-6211
Fax: (903)813-3711
E-mail: rdavis3@medus.jnj.com

• 9649 • **Billy Mayo/Rubin Jones Scholarship**
For GPA and other related areas of education. Scholarship awarded annually.

• 9650 •
Food and Drug Law Institute
Jerome A. Halperin, Pres.
1000 Vermont Ave. NW, Ste. 200
Washington, DC 20005-4903
Phone: (202)371-1420
Toll-Free: 800-956-6293
Fax: (202)371-0649
E-mail: comments@fdli.org
Home Page: http://www.fdli.org

• 9651 • **H. Thomas Austern Memorial Writing Competition**
To encourage students interested in the areas of law that affect foods, drugs, cosmetics, and devices. AJ.D. or L.L.B. candidates currently enrolled at any of the nation's law schools are eligible. Papers are judged on: legal analysis of the topic; thoroughness and currency of the research, including form and quality of citations; Evaluation of judicial precedents, statutes, and regulations; originality and timeliness of the topic; comformity with rules of competition, and writing style. Papers must be submitted by May 14. The following awards are presented: First prize - $1,500 and second prize $1,000. Winning papers are considered for publication in the *Food and Drug Law Journal*. The award honors H. Thomas Austern, who served on the Editorial Advisory Board of the *Food and Drug Law Journal* from its inception, and was a strong supporter of the Institute since its 1949 beginning.

• 9652 •
Food Distribution Research Society
Dr. Kellie Curry Raper, Membership VP
211C Agriculture Hall
Department of Agricultural Economics
Michigan State University
East Lansing, MI 48824-1039
Phone: (517)353-7226
Fax: (517)432-1800
E-mail: raperk@msu.edu
Home Page: http://fdrs.ag.utk.edu

• 9653 • **William Applebaum Award**
To recognize an outstanding college student with an interest in a career in the food industry. Ph.D. and M.S. students are considered. Six monetary awards of $1,000 and $500 are presented annually. Additional monetary awards may be presented to runners-up. Established in 1977 in honor of Dr. William Applebaum, Harvard University professor of Economics in Food Distribution.

• 9654 • **Presidential Award**
For excellence in research and communication.

• 9655 •
Food for the Poor
Robin G. Mahfood, Pres./CEO
550 SW 12th Ave., Dept. 9662
Deerfield Beach, FL 33442
Phone: (954)427-2222
Toll-Free: 800-427-9104
E-mail: contactffp@foodforthepoor.org
Home Page: http://www.foodforthepoor.com

Awards are arranged in alphabetical order below their administering organizations

• 9656 • **Chalice Award**
Recognizes consistent donors. 15-30 awards are given annually.

• 9657 •
Food Industry Association Executives
Barbara McConnell, Pres.
PO Box 2510
Flemington, NJ 08822
Phone: (908)782-7833
Fax: (908)782-6907
E-mail: bmcconnell@fiae.net
Home Page: http://www.fiae.net

• 9658 • **Communications Program Awards**
To inspire excellence in the food trade press. Awards are given in the following categories: general excellence magazines, tabloids, and newsletters; best convention issue; best overall design; best special issue or annual; best overall editorial content; best cover; best feature story; best editorial; most improved; and total communications program. The general excellence awardees receive monetary prizes and ribbons, which are sponsored by the Ralston Purina Company. Established in 1981.

• 9659 •
Food Marketing Institute
Timothy M. Hammonds, Pres.
655 15th St. NW
Washington, DC 20005
Phone: (202)452-8444
Fax: (202)429-4519
E-mail: fmi@fmi.org
Home Page: http://www.fmi.org

• 9660 • **William H. Albers Award**
For recognition of achievements that improve relations between food suppliers and food retailers/wholesalers. Food supplier executives are eligible. The winner is elected by the Institute Board of Directors. A medallion and plaque are awarded annually. Established in 1955 by Super Market Institute, a predecessor organization, in memory of William H. Albers, first President of Super Market Institute.

• 9661 • **FMI - *Woman's Day* Advertising Merit Awards**
To recognize excellence in supermarket advertising and to encourage improvements in advertising messages to the consumer. Company members of the Food Marketing Institute are eligible. Trophies and Certificates of Merit are awarded annually at the Food Marketing Institute's Convention. Established in 1966. Cosponsored by *Woman's Day*.

• 9662 • **Esther Peterson Consumer Service Award**
For recognition of outstanding contributions in helping grocery retailers serve their customers. Individuals in leadership positions in industry, government, education, consumer organizations and other community groups, the media and other fields are eligible. Selection is by the Institute Officers. A trophy and a plaque are awarded annually. Established in 1987 in honor of Esther Peterson, whose career exemplifies consumer service.

• 9663 • **Sidney R. Rabb Award**
For recognition of community service and industry statesmanship. A food retailer or wholesaler who has made outstanding contributions over his lifetime to the improvement of his community and his industry is eligible. Selection is by the FMI Awards Committee. A trophy and a plaque are awarded annually. Established in 1977 in honor of Mr. Sidney R. Rabb, whose career exemplified industry statesmanship and community service. Mr. Rabb died in 1985.

• 9664 •
Foodservice and Packaging Institute
John R. Burke, Pres.
150 S Washington St., Ste. 204
Falls Church, VA 22046
Phone: (703)538-2800
Fax: (703)538-2187
E-mail: fpi@fpi.org
Home Page: http://www.fpi.org
Formerly: (1987) Single Service Institute.

• 9665 • **Samuel J. Crumbine Consumer Protection Award**
For recognition of outstanding achievement in a comprehensive program of food and beverage sanitation at the local level. Achievement is measured by: program improvement or sustained excellence in quality; innovative and effective use of evaluation methods; effectiveness of planning and management; and information and education activities. Eligibility is limited to local units of government (county, district, city, town, township, etc.) that are legally and directly responsible for protecting the health of the consumer by assuring that public eating and drinking establishments meet required sanitation standards and observe proper sanitation procedures. A plaque is awarded annually at major public health association meetings. Established in 1954 in memory of Dr. Samuel J. Crumbine, M.D. pioneer health officer, Kansas. Additional information is available from Foodservice & Packaging Institute (see above for details).

• 9666 •
Foodservice Consultants Society International
David Drain, Exec.VP
304 W Liberty St., Ste. 201
Louisville, KY 40202-3068
Phone: (502)583-3783
Fax: (502)589-3602
E-mail: fcsi@fcsi.org
Home Page: http://www.fcsi.org

• 9667 • **Green Award**
Recognizes an individual for positive environmental impact. Awarded annually.

• 9668 • **Service Award**
Annual award of recognition. Inquire for application details.

• 9669 • **Trendsetter Award**
Annual award of recognition. Inquire for application details.

• 9670 •
Football Writers Association of America
Steve Richardson, Exec.Dir.
18652 Vista Del Sol
Dallas, TX 75287
Phone: (972)713-6198
Fax: (972)713-6198
E-mail: tigerfwaa@aol.com
Home Page: http://www.sportswriters.net/fwaa

• 9671 • **All America Team**
To recognize each player on the 24-man All America team chosen by the Football Association of America. Citations are awarded annually. Established in 1944.

• 9672 • **Citations of Merit**
To recognize coaches in both the university and college divisions for long and distinguished service to college football. Plaques are awarded annually. Established in 1960.

• 9673 • **Bronko Nagurski Award**
To recognize the best college football defensive player during the year. A trophy is awarded annually by the Charlotte Touchdown Club. Established in 1993. Formerly: (1996) College Football Defensive Player of the Year Trophy.

• 9674 • **Outland Trophy**
To recognize the outstanding interior lineman in major college or university football during the year. A trophy is awarded annually. Established in 1946 in honor of Dr. John Outland, All-American at Kansas and Pennsylvania in the 1890s.

• 9675 • **Grantland Rice National Championship Trophy**
To honor and recognize the national collegiate football championship team. A five-man committee appointed by the current FWAA President makes the selection. The Grantland Rice Trophy is awarded annually. Established in 1954.

• 9676 • **Eddie Robinson Coach of the Year**
For recognition of an outstanding coaching effort during the year. Football coaches at major schools are eligible. A plaque is awarded annually. Established in 1957. Formerly: Coach of the Year Award.

• 9677 •
Foothills Art Center
Jennifer Cook, Exec.Dir.
809 15th St.
Golden, CO 80401
Phone: (303)279-3922
Fax: (303)279-9470
E-mail: fac@foothillsartcenter.org
Home Page: http://www.foothillsartcenter.org

• 9678 • **North American Sculpture Exhibition Awards**
For recognition of excellence in sculpture. Artists residing in North America may submit only sturdy sculpture in various medium. The deadline for submissions varies. Awards totaling about $15,000 are given biennially. Established in 1979. Contact Center for entry form.

• 9679 • **Rocky Mountain National Watermedia Exhibition Awards**
For recognition of excellence in the arts. Paintings in watermedia on paper products are eligible. The deadline for submissions is May. Awards totaling over $15,000 are given annually. The top winner is featured in an article in *The Artist's Magazine*. Established in 1974. Contact Center for entry form.

• 9680 •
Gerald R. Ford Library
Elaine Didier, Dir.
1000 Beal Ave.
Ann Arbor, MI 48109
Phone: (734)205-0555
Fax: (734)205-0571
E-mail: ford.library@nara.gov
Home Page: http://www.ford.utexas.edu

• 9681 • **Gerald R. Ford Prize for Distinguished Reporting on National Defense**
To encourage the highest standards of accuracy, insight, and analysis in reporting on national defense, and to recognize reportorial excellence. Entries are judged on the basis of their value in fostering better understanding of national defense issues and policy. Competition is restricted to print journalism. Free-lance as well as staff journalists are eligible. Entries may be submitted by March 2. A monetary award of $5,000 and a plaque are presented annually. Established in 1988. Since 1988, the award has been based on reporting done in the previous calendar year.

• 9682 • **Gerald R. Ford Prize for Distinguished Reporting on the Presidency**
To encourage the highest possible standards of accuracy, insight, and analysis in reporting on the presidency; to foster a better public understanding of the presidency, and to recognize reportorial excellence. Entries are judged on the basis of their value in fostering better understanding of the nature and operations of the presidency. Competition is restricted to print journalism. Free-lance as well as staff journalists are eligible. Entries may be submitted by March 2. A monetary award of $5,000 and a plaque are presented annually. Established in 1988. Since 1988, the award has been based on reporting done in the previous calendar year.

• 9683 •
Fordham University
School of Law
William Treanor, Dean
140 W 62nd St.
New York, NY 10023
Phone: (212)636-6807
Fax: (212)636-6958
Home Page: http://law.fordham.edu

• 9684 • **Fordham - Stein Prize**
To recognize a member of the legal profession whose work exemplifies outstanding standards of professional conduct, promotes the advancement of justice, and brings credit to the profession by emphasizing in the public mind the contributions of lawyers to our society and to our democratic system of government. A stipend and a commemorative crystal sculpture designed by Tiffany & Company are awarded annually. Established in 1976 by Louis Stein, retired Chairman of the Board of Food Fair Stores, Inc.

• 9685 •
Foreign Affairs Canada
Enquiries Service
125 Sussex Dr.
Ottawa, ON, Canada K1A 0G2
Phone: (613)944-4000
Toll-Free: 800-267-8376
Fax: (613)996-9709
E-mail: enqserv@dfait-maeci.gc.ca
Home Page: http://www.fac-aec.gc.ca

• 9686 • **Canada Export Award (Ministere des Affaires etrangeres et du Commerce international)**
For recognition of demonstrated superior performance in the export marketplace. Open to all firms or divisions of firms resident in Canada that have been exporting goods or services for three or more years. The achievements of such companies and organizations, as well as of those facilitating exports, including those in the area of banking, transport, market research, packaging and promotion, are eligible for consideration. The Selection Committee looks for concrete evidence of significant achievement in export markets in terms of the sale of goods or services. It also considers particular merit in activities conducted in relation to the promotion, financing, or facilitation of export sales by Canadian firms. The committee is guided by, but not limited to, the following criteria: the extent to which the firm (over its latest three fiscal years) has shown significant increases in its export sales; success in breaking into new markets; and success in introducing new export products into world markets. A plaque bearing the Canada Export Award logo and a brief citation of the firm's accomplishments is awarded annually. Established in 1983.

• 9687 • **Minister for International Trade Challenge Cup**
To recognize the top Canadian team in the Dalhousie International Case competition. Awarded annually.

• 9688 • **Minister's Award for Consular Excellence**
To recognize outstanding counselor service to Canadians at home and abroad. Awarded annually to up to three recipients.

• 9689 • **Minister's Award for Foreign Policy Excellence**
To recognize outstanding individuals for collective contributions to Canada, Canadians, and Canadian foreign policy excellence. Up to three recipients may be honored annually.

• 9690 •
Foreign Language Association of North Dakota
Anne Olafson, Contact
1100 11th Ave. SW
Minot, ND 58701
Phone: (701)857-4525
Fax: (701)857-4521
E-mail: anne.olafson@sendit.nodak.edu
Home Page: http://www.jc.edu/users/faculty/stevenso/fland.html

• 9691 • **Pro Lingua Award**
For outstanding recognition from outside the foreign language profession. Recognition award bestowed annually.

• 9692 • **Graciela Wilborn Foreign Language Teacher of the Year in North Dakota**
For outstanding foreign language teacher of ND. Recognition award bestowed annually.

• 9693 •
Forest History Society
Steve Anderson, Pres./CEO
701 WM Vickers Ave.
Durham, NC 27701-3162
Phone: (919)682-9319
Fax: (919)682-2349
E-mail: stevena@duke.edu
Home Page: http://www.foresthistory.org

• 9694 • **Alfred D. Bell, Jr. Visiting Scholars Program**
To enable researchers to make use of the society's library and archives. Several travel grants of up to $950 are awarded annually. Established in 1990.

• 9695 • **Theodore C. Blegen Award**
For the best article on forest and conservation history published in a journal other than *Environmental History.* Editor's of scholarly journals are invited to submit nominations. Authors may encourage journals to submit articles. Submission deadline is February 25. Recognition and $500 are awarded. Established in 1973.

• 9696 • Collier Award
To recognize outstanding interest and reporting in forest history or conservation history. The award is a fellowship to an Institutes for Journalism in Natural Resources expedition and an expenses paid visit to the Forest History Society Library and Archives in Durham, NC. Open to any newspaper or general circulation magazine professional or freelance journalist in North America. Apply for an expedition and you are automatically considered for the Award. Awarded annually. Established in 1986. Application available at www.ijnr.org.

• 9697 • Charles A. Weyerhaeuser Award
For the best book in the field of forest and conservation history. Publishers' are invited to submit copies to a panel of judges. Authors encouraged to ensure that two copies of the beook are sent to the Forest History Society for review when published. Includes recognition and $500 for the author. Awarded biennially in odd numbered years. Established in 1977.

• 9698 •
Forest Landowners Association
Harry L. Haney, Pres.
PO Box 450209
Atlanta, GA 31145
Phone: (404)325-2954
Toll-Free: 800-325-2954
Fax: (404)325-2955
E-mail: info@forestlandowners.com
Home Page: http://www.forestlandowners.com

• 9699 • Forest Landowner Award
For outstanding service to southern forestry. Recognition award bestowed annually.

• 9700 •
Fort Collins Symphony Association
Donna Visocky, Exec.Dir.
PO Box 1963
214 S College Ave.
Fort Collins, CO 80522
Phone: (970)482-4823
Fax: (970)482-4858
E-mail: note@fcsymphony.org
Home Page: http://www.fcsymphony.org

• 9701 • Young Artist Competition
To recognize talented young artists in the annual competition. The deadline is January 20. Awards are presented in two divisions: Junior Division - for artists aged 12 to 18 in two categories, piano, and orchestral instruments (Monetary awards of $250 for first prize and $100 for second prizes are awarded in each category); and Senior Division - for musicians 25 years of age and younger. The Adeline Rosenberg Memorial Award is presented for the senior division: first prize is $3,000; second prize is $2,000; and third prize is $1,000. The three finalists compete with the Fort Collins Symphony in the senior division; piano in even years, instrumental in odd years. The Young Artist Competition was established in 1955. In 1985, Harry Rosenberg established a memorial award in memory of Adeline Rosenberg.

• 9702 •
Fort Scott Community College
James R. Miesner, Pres.
2108 S Horton
Ft. Scott, KS 66701
Phone: (316)223-2700
Toll-Free: 800-874-3722
Fax: (316)223-4927
E-mail: cindyp@fortscott.edu
Home Page: http://www.fortscott.edu

• 9703 • Gordon Parks Commemorative Photography Competition
To recognize photographers whose work follows the photojournalistic and documentary traditions of Gordon Parks - upholding family values, addressing social injustice, and preventing the suffering of others. Competition is open to both professionals and amateurs. Monetary awards of $1,000 for First prize, $500 for Second prize, and $250 for Third prize are awarded annually. Established in 1989. Sponsored by the Lucile James Fine Arts Committee, and Fort Scott Community College, Fort Scott Kansas.

• 9704 •
Foster Care Association of Oklahoma
Ronda Gray, Pres.
Rte. 1, Box 188
Wellston, OK 74881
Phone: (405)773-9495
Phone: (405)356-2824
Fax: (405)356-2876
E-mail: info@fostercareok.com
Home Page: http://www.fostercareok.com

• 9705 • Champions for Children
For outstanding service to foster children. Trophy awarded annually.

• 9706 •
Foundation for Digestive Health and Nutrition
James W. Freston MD, Chair
4930 Del Ray Ave.
Bethesda, MD 20814-3015
Phone: (301)222-4002
Toll-Free: (866)337-3346
Fax: (301)222-4010
E-mail: info@fdhn.org
Home Page: http://www.fdhn.org

Formerly: (1994) American Gastroenterological Association Foundation.

• 9707 • Distinguished Achievement Award
For recognition of a distinguished series of investigations in a segment of gastroenterology. Members of the American Gastroenterological Association are eligible. A monetary award of $1,000 and a certificate are awarded annually. Established in 1967. Sponsored by AGA.

• 9708 • Elsevier Research Initiative Award
To provide funds to investigators starting their research careers to help them establish their independence; and to support pilot projects that represent new research directions for established investigators. Investigators, M.D.s, or Ph.D.s who hold faculty positions at accredited North American institutions are eligible. Women and minorities are strongly encouraged to apply. Applications must be submitted by January 5. A monetary award of $25,000 per year is presented annually. Established through a gift from the Elsevier Scientific Publishing Company. Additional information is available from the ADHF.

• 9709 • Miles and Shirley Fiterman Foundation Basic Research Awards
To facilitate the career development of junior faculty members involved in basic research in any area of gastrointestinal or liver function or related diseases or to honor those who have already advanced these fields. Applicant must hold full-time faculty positions at a North American university or professional institute and either an M.D., Ph.D., or a combined degree. Deadline for application is January 10. Monetary awards of $35,000 are presented annually. Funded by the Miles and Shirley Fiterman Foundation.

• 9710 • International Travel Fellowship Awards
To enable non-North American investigators younger than 40 years old who are working in gastroenterology-related fields and who do not have travel funds to attend the ADHF annual meeting at Digestive Disease Week and present their abstracts. Applicants must have both performed the research for the abstract in an institution and currently reside outside of North America. Up to three fellowships with a maximum of $1,500 to $2,500 per fellowship are awarded annually. The application deadline is January 10, however, abstracts must be submitted in time for presentation at the annual meeting (generally in November). Additional information is available from the ADHF. ADHF. ADHF.

• 9711 • Miles and Shirley Fisherman Foundation Awards for Clinical Research
To recognize and help support investigative efforts in the area of clinical research. Two awards are presented: H.R. Butt Award in Hepatology or Nutrition and J.B. Kirsner Award in Gastroenterology. This award cannot be obtained by application. Nominations of appropriate individuals must be submitted by January 10. Each award, given annually, consists of $25,000 provided to the awardee's institution in support of the awardee's research program. Established in 1990 to honor Drs. Hugh R. Butt and Joseph B. Kirsner. Sponsored by the Miles and Shirley Fiterman Foundation. Additional information is available from the ADHF.

• 9712 • Research Scholar Award
To support young investigators working in any area of gastrointestinal or liver function and their related diseases. The overall objective is to enable young investigators to develop indepen-

dent productive research careers in gastroenterology-related fields. The applicant must hold a full-time faculty position at a North American university or professional institute. The award is not intended for fellows, but for young faculty who have demonstrated unusual promise and have some record of accomplishment in research. Non-physician candidates with a Ph.D. will also be considered. Candidates must devote at least 70 percent of their effort to research related to the gastrointestinal tract or liver. Established investigators are not appropriate candidates. Applications must be submitted by September 10. A monetary award of $65,000 per year for three years is awarded. Additional information is available from the ADHF. Formerly: (2006) Industry Research Scholar Awards.

• 9713 • **Student Research Fellowships**
To stimulate interest in research careers in digestive diseases by providing salary support for students engaged in research projects. High school, undergraduate, medical or graduate students (not yet engaged in thesis research) in accredited North American institutions are eligible. The award is for one year, and the work may take place at any time during the year. Applications must be submitted by March 5. Up to 20 awards of $2,000 to $3,000 each are available for research. Additional information is available from the ADHF. Formerly: AGA Student Summer Research Fellowships.

• 9714 •
Foundation of American Women in Radio and Television
Maria E. Brennan, Exec.Dir.
8405 Greensboro Dr., Ste. 800
McLean, VA 22102
Phone: (703)506-3290
Fax: (703)506-3266
E-mail: info@awrt.org
Home Page: http://www.awrt.org/foundation/index.html

• 9715 • **Achievement Award**
For recognition of a member who has earned the respect of peers, strengthened the role of women in the industry, and contributed to the betterment of the community. Awarded annually.

• 9716 • **The Gracie Allen Awards**
To honor excellence in programming for women, by women and about women. Entries in both the local and network radio and television categories are accepted. The local market and National winners will be honored at a ceremony in New York City. Established in 1976.

• 9717 • **Silver Satellite Award**
To recognize an individual who has made outstanding contributions to the field of broadcast communication. A silver sculpture is awarded at the annual convention. Established in 1967.

• 9718 •
Fragrance Foundation
Mary Ellen Lapsansky, Exec.Dir.
145 E 32nd St.
New York, NY 10016
Phone: (212)725-2755
Fax: (212)779-9058
E-mail: info@fragrance.org
Home Page: http://www.fragrance.org

Formerly: Fragrance Foundation and Fragrance Research Fund.

• 9719 • **Fifth Sense Commendation**
To recognize contributions to the Sense of Smell Institute to support educational programs that increase public awareness about the sense of smell and fragrance, including exhibits in museums and science centers. Steel sculpture awards are presented at the Institute's "Night of Honors" dinner in the fall. Established in 1993.

• 9720 • **Fragrance Foundation Recognition Awards (FIFI Awards)**
To recognize companies and individuals who have contributed significantly to creating greater interest in fragrance. Awards are presented in the following categories: Best Feature by a Magazine - judged by a special panel of judges; Certified Fragrance Sales Specialist of the Year selected by the Fragrance Foundation; National Advertising Campaign of the Year - men's and women's - judged by members of the advertising community; Fragrance Packaging Introductions of the Year - men's and women's voted on by a panel of judges; Fragrance Foundation Hall of Fame selected by the Board of Directors; The Fragrance Hall of Fame Award (Men's and Women's) voted on by membership and retailers; Innovation of the Year - judged by panel of technical experts. Also awarded are European Men's Fragrance of the Year; European Women's Fragrance Star of the Year; U.S. Men's Fragrance Star of the Year Private Label Stores; U.S. Men's Fragrance Star of the Year - Non-Store Venues; U.S. Men's Fragrance Star of the Year - Chain Stores; U.S. Men's Fragrance Star of the Year Specialty/Department Stores; U.S. Women's Fragrance Star of the Year Private Label Stores; U.S. Women's Fragrance Star of the Year - Non-Store Venues; U.S. Women's Fragrance Star of the Year - Chain Stores; U.S. Women's Fragrance Star of the Year Specialty/Department Stores; and U.S. Women's Fragrance Star of the Year Specialty/Department Stores. All are nominated by the Membership and Retailers. The awards comprise two 12-inch abstract crystal columns embracing a droplet, that symbolizes fragrance. Awarded annually. Established in 1972.

• 9721 • **Medal of Honor**
To recognize outstanding contributors who pledge support to the Sense of Smell Institute. Tiffany Medallions are presented at the Institute's "Night of Honors" dinner in the fall. Established in 1993.

• 9722 • **Olfactory Research Fund Sense of Smell Award**
To recognize a scientist for his/her study of the sense of smell, and a member of the business community who has played a major role in giving the public-at-large an opportunity to understand and appreciate the role of fragrance and the sense of smell in their lives. A trophy is awarded annually and is presented at the Fund's "Night of Honors" dinner in the fall. Established in 1984.

• 9723 •
Frameworks Alliance
Jason Neff, Exec.Dir.
2420 E Jefferson St.
Orlando, FL 32803
Phone: (407)898-7111
Home Page: http://www.cffvf.org

• 9724 • **Central Florida Film and Video Awards**
For quality of film. Monetary award bestowed annually.

• 9725 •
France and Colonies Philatelic Society
Walter E. Parshall, Sec.
103 Spruce St.
Bloomfield, NJ 07003-3514
Phone: (973)748-9442
Home Page: http://www.fcps.org.uk

• 9726 • **Gerard Gilbert Memorial Award**
For best English publication related to French philately. Awarded annually.

• 9727 •
Franciscan Retreats
16385 St. Francis Ln.
Prior Lake, MN 55372-2220
Phone: (952)447-2182
Fax: (952)447-2170
E-mail: director@franciscanretreats.net
Home Page: http://www.franciscanretreats.net

• 9728 • **Franciscan International Award**
Each year the Franciscan Order (Order of Friars Minor Conventual) presents an award to an individual or to an organization which is committed to serving the ideals of Christ, especially as they were proclaimed by St. Francis of Assisi. This Franciscan International Award is presented yearly through the Conventual Franciscans on behalf of Franciscan Retreats, Prior Lake, Minnesota. The award consists of a walnut plaque and shield bearing the Franciscan Coat of Arms, with the proper information about the recipient of the Award.

• 9729 •
Franciscan University of Steubenville
1235 University Blvd.
Steubenville, OH 43952
Phone: (740)283-3771
Toll-Free: 800-783-6220
Fax: (614)283-6472
Home Page: http://www.franciscan.edu/home2/Content/main.aspx

• 9730 • Poverello Medal
This, the highest non-academic award presented by the University, is given to recognize an individual or an organization for notable actions exemplifying the spirit of charity of the life of Saint Francis of Assisi. A medal cast of non-precious metals, symbolizing the ideals of Franciscan poverty that St. Francis gave to the world, is awarded annually. Established in 1949 by the College of Steubenville.

• 9731 • University Founders Award
For recognition of achievement. A plaque is awarded annually. Established in 1978.

• 9732 •
Frank Huntington Beebe Fund
Carol P. Woodworth, Sec.
290 Huntington Ave.
Boston, MA 02115
Phone: (617)585-1267
Fax: (617)585-1270
Home Page: http://www.beebefund.org

• 9733 • Frank Huntington Beebe Award
To provide several fellowships for young gifted musicians, generally performers and composers in classical disciplines, who wish to pursue advanced music study and performance abroad, usually in Europe. Fellowships are awarded to musicians at the outset of their professional lives, for whom this would be the first extended period of study abroad. Applicants must demonstrate a solid base of accomplishment in order to be considered. The applicant must develop a strong, well-planned project that will enhance his/her life work in music. Enrollment in a school or university is not required unless such study is an essential part of the project. Applications may be obtained starting October 1 of the preceding year. The deadline for submitting applications is mid- December. The Fund provides support - round-trip transportation, room and board, and other expenses approximately $16,000. Awarded annually. Established in 1932 by Frank Huntington Beebe.

• 9734 •
Frankfort-Elberta National Soaring Hall of Fame
PO Box 801
1219 Elm St.
Frankfort, MI 49635
Phone: (616)352-7694
E-mail: lockhartfield@hotmail.com

• 9735 • National Soaring Hall of Fame
To honor individuals who have committed their life's work to the sport of soaring and have helped promote the sport worldwide. Selection is by nomination. A picture of the inductee is placed in the Hall of Fame and the inductee receives a plaque. Awarded annually. Established in 1973. In 1991, awards were given to individuals who have promoted soaring in the midwest, particularly the Frankfort-Elberta (Michigan) area.

• 9736 •
Franklin and Eleanor Roosevelt Institute
David B. Woolner, Exec.Dir.
4079 Albany Post Rd.
Hyde Park, NY 12538
Phone: (845)486-1150
Fax: (845)486-1151
E-mail: info@feri.org
Home Page: http://www.feri.org

Formerly: (1987) Four Freedoms Foundation.

• 9737 • Franklin D. Roosevelt Four Freedoms Awards
To recognize individuals or organizations whose achievements have demonstrated a commitment to the Four Freedoms enumerated by the late President Franklin D. Roosevelt in his speech of January 6, 1941. An award is made for each of the freedoms: Freedom of Speech, Freedom from Want, Freedom of Worship, and Freedom from Fear. A fifth award, the Four Freedoms Medal, honors a lifetime of service in the cause of the Four Freedoms. Awarded internationally in Middelburg, the Netherlands, in even-numbered years; nationally in Hyde Park in odd-numbered years. Established as a single, annual award in 1945, and expanded to five awards in 1982.

• 9738 •
Franklin Institute
Dennis M. Wint, Pres. and CEO
222 N 20th St.
Philadelphia, PA 19103
Phone: (215)448-1200
Phone: (215)448-1181
Fax: (215)448-1364
E-mail: awards@fi.edu
Home Page: http://www.fi.edu

• 9739 • Stuart Ballantine Medal
To recognize outstanding achievement in the fields of communication and reconnaissance which employ electromagnetic radiation. Awards a gold medal. Established in 1946.

• 9740 • The Benjamin Franklin Medals
For outstanding achievement in sciences and technology. The competition is international. Nominations are accepted in the fields of physics, chemistry, life, earth, and computer and cognitive sciences, and engineering. Candidates must be living and the winner is expected to participate in the ceremony and other awards week events. The subject must be an invention, discovery, technological development or a body of work reflecting extraordinary insight, skills, or creativity. The work must have scientific value and/or proven utility. It must have provided significant direction for future research, solved an important problem, or provided great benefit to the public. There must be sufficient documentation to support further investigation. Nominations may be submitted by an individual or institution. Nominations must be submitted in English using the nomination form or a copy of that form. Reference letters are considered confidential and must be request by the nominator. Letters should be mailed directly from the reference to the Franklin Institute. There is no deadline for submissions. Nominations will be acknowledged promptly, but the case method review process requires a minimum of two years to complete. Nominations may be submitted by fax or email. Original supporting materials must be sent by mail or private courier service.

• 9741 • Bower Award and Prize for Achievement in Science
To recognize outstanding achievement in the life or physical sciences; to support innovation in the sciences and the training of scientists; and to encourage excellence in the applied sciences. Individuals, in any nation, whose work in the biological (life) or physical sciences, results in a brilliant discovery in the sciences, or whose developmental work or innovations in a field of science and/or a body of such work contributes to major advances in that field are eligible. Current general fields are physics, astronomical science, mathematical science, materials science, chemistry, industrial science and technology, geoscience, earth science, ocean science, polar science, engineering, biological systems, behavioral and neural science, cellular bioscience, molecular bioscience, and scientific instrumentation. Nominations are accepted in English, through the mail or electronically, from individuals, boards of advisors, and institutions of any nation. A monetary award of at least $250,000 and a gold medal are presented annually. Established in 1990 by the Benjamin Franklin National Memorial of the Franklin Institute through a generous bequest from the late Henry Bower (1896-1988), a Philadelphia chemical manufacturer and admirer of Benjamin Franklin.

• 9742 • Bower Award for Business Leadership
To recognize outstanding leadership in American business or industry; to promote the advancement of sound economic practice; to promote adherence to the highest ethical standards; and to inspire present and future leaders of business and industry. Any leader in an American business or industry who in his or her life and work personifies outstanding qualities and attainments in leadership, the advancement of sound economic practices, and adherence to high ethical standards is eligible. Nominees will not be disregarded in the award process solely because the business or industry with which they are associated is relatively small in size or importance. Special consideration is given to achievements in business leadership that reflect the practical, useful, entrepreneurial, humanitarian, and philanthropic spirit of Benjamin Franklin. Fields of business eligible for the award include finance, management, marketing,

statistics, accounting, legal studies, health care, insurance, public policy management, and decision sciences (including information systems and operations). Nominations are accepted from any individual, organization, or institution. Awarded annually. Established in 1990 by the Benjamin Franklin National Memorial of the Franklin Institute, through a generous bequest from the late Henry Bower (1896-1988), a Philadelphia chemical manufacturer and admirer of Benjamin Franklin.

• 9743 •
Fraternal Order of Eagles, Havre No. 166
202-1st St.
Havre, MT 59501
Phone: (406)265-9981

• 9744 • Research Awards
For research on cancer, diabetes, Alzheimer's, heart. Recognition award bestowed periodically.

• 9745 •
Fraternal Order of Eagles, Lisbon No. 2968
6540 Hwy. 32
Lisbon, ND 58054
Phone: (701)683-4786

• 9746 • Golden Eagle Grant
For senior citizens. Grant awarded annually.

• 9747 •
Fraternal Order of Eagles, Marshfield No. 624
1104 S Oak St.
Marshfield, WI 54449-4109
Phone: (715)384-3000
Fax: (715)384-5670

• 9748 • Fraternal Order of Eagles Education Scholarship
For high school senior or other individual related to a member seeking to continue education. Scholarship awarded periodically.

• 9749 •
Fraternal Order of Eagles, Stevenson No. 1744
148-150 1st St.
Stevenson, WA 98648
Phone: (509)427-5255

• 9750 • Eagle Scholarship
For Stevenson High School graduate. Scholarship.

• 9751 •
Fraternal Order of Police Lodge 86
Vince Huber, Pres.
1427 E Washington St.
Indianapolis, IN 46201
Phone: (317)637-1195
Phone: (317)636-1285
Fax: (317)267-0114
E-mail: lodge@fop86.org
Home Page: http://fop86.org

• 9752 • FOP86 Scholarship Fund
For children and grandchildren of active, retired, or deceased members of Lodge 86. Scholarship awarded annually.

• 9753 •
Fredericksburg Sister City Association
Phyllis C. Whitley, Contact
10225 Gordon Rd.
Spotsylvania, VA 22553-3723
Phone: (540)786-7010
Phone: (540)775-7545
Fax: (540)786-7006
Home Page: http://fsca.communitypoint.org

• 9754 • Alec Vitarius Memorial Scholarship
For an outstanding French language student who demonstrates financial need. Scholarship awarded semiannually.

• 9755 •
Freedom Forum
Peter S. Prichard, Pres.
1101 Wilson Blvd.
Arlington, VA 22209
Phone: (703)528-0800
Fax: (703)284-3770
E-mail: news@freedomforum.org
Home Page: http://www.freedomforum.org

• 9756 • A.l Neuharth Free Spirit of the Year Award
To recognize extraordinary achievement to an individual in the news who has stirred the public's hearts and souls by demonstrating the capacity to dream, dare and do. The award, along with an honorarium, is given to honor the winner's "free spirit" and provide the opportunity to perpetuate that ideal. Established in 1999 by the Freedom Forum, in honor of Al Neuharth, the founder of the Freedom Forum. Free Spirit of the Year is selected by a diverse committee of national and international members, presented at a ceremony in Washington D.C. Formerly: (2006) Free Spirit Award.

• 9757 •
Freedom Forum
Media Studies Center
Charles L. Overby, Chm., Pres. and CEO
1101 Wilson Blvd.
Arlington, VA 22209
Phone: (703)528-0800
Fax: (703)284-3770
E-mail: news@freedomforum.org
Home Page: http://www.freedomforum.org

Formerly: (1991) Columbia University - Gannett Center for Media Studies.

• 9758 • Residential Fellowships
To encourage media professionals, scholars, and others to examine major issues and problems facing the mass media and society, with special attention to media economics, the relationship between the media and other institutions, the role of minorities and women, media coverage of such topics as education, the environment, and the arts, and the advancement of journalism education. Applicants should be media professionals from print and broadcast organizations, journalism and mass communication educators, or scholars from other fields with a primary interest in media studies. The deadline is February 1. Awards are given to persons at three levels of attainment: senior fellowships - for mature individuals with substantial national reputations, fellowships - for accomplished persons at mid-career, and research fellowships - for those with five to eight years of experience. A stipend based on salary needs or matching sabbatical support, a housing allowance, and other benefits, as well as office space and secretarial and research assistance are awarded annually in April to 12 - 15 individuals. Established in 1985.

• 9759 •
Freedom House
Jennifer Windsor, Exec.Dir.
1319 18th St. NW
Washington, DC 20036
Phone: (202)296-5101
Fax: (202)296-5078
E-mail: fh@freedomhouse.org
Home Page: http://www.freedomhouse.org

• 9760 • Freedom Award
To recognize an individual or group for courageous, persistent work for freedom and commitment to social justice and human rights. Selection is made by the executive director and board members. A Baccarat crystal, called "menhir," is awarded occasionally. Established in 1943 by Freedom House, Inc. to commemorate the eternal struggle for freedom in the world. Additional information is available from Barbara Futterman, assistant to the executive director.

• 9761 •
Freedom to Read Foundation
Judith F. Krug, Sec./Exec.Dir.
50 E Huron St.
Chicago, IL 60611
Phone: (312)280-4226
Toll-Free: 800-545-2433
Fax: (312)280-4227
E-mail: ftrf@ala.org
Home Page: http://www.ftrf.org

• 9762 • Freedom to Read Roll of Honor
To recognize and honor those who have played an active role in the Freedom to Read Foundation in support of intellectual freedom through their commitment to and defense of the First Amendment, and to widen visibility of and underscore the importance of the freedom to read. Current and past foundation members, major donors, and participants in litigation are eligible. A plaque is awarded annually (at the discretion of the award committee) at the annual conference of the American Library Association. Established in 1987.

Awards are arranged in alphabetical order below their administering organizations

• 9763 •
Freedoms Foundation at Valley Forge
Aaron Siegel, Pres./CEO
1601 Valley Forge Rd.
Valley Forge, PA 19482-0706
Phone: (610)933-8825
Toll-Free: 800-896-5488
Fax: (610)935-0522
E-mail: ffvf@ffvf.org
Home Page: http://www.ffvf.org

• 9764 • **Distinguished Awards**
To recognize exceptionally meritorious endeavors reflecting the high ideals of human dignity and the fundamental principles of a free society. Nominations may be submitted by May 1. The following special awards may be granted by the National Awards Jury: National Service Medal (established in 1966); American Statesman Medal (established in 1959); Private Enterprise Exemplar Medal (established in 1978); American Exemplar Medal; National Recognition Medal; American Patriots Medal; Freedom Leadership Medal; and American Friendship Medal for other than U.S. nationals. Awards are presented during special ceremonies throughout the year. Formerly: (1996) Pamplin Distinguished Awards.

• 9765 • **Leavey Awards for Excellence in Private Enterprise Education**
A special awards program for any U.S. citizen or permanent resident teaching grades K-12, or a faculty member with full-time affiliation at an American accredited college or university who conceives and implements an innovative course or project that develops, principally among students, a better understanding and appreciation of the American private enterprise economic system. The deadline is October 1. Up to 20 monetary awards of $7,500 each may be awarded each year. The jury may also recommend a special award of $15,000 for an unusually meritorious project. Established in 1977.

• 9766 • **National Awards Program**
To recognize constructive words and deeds by individuals, organizations, and corporations that support the United States' social, political, and economic system, suggest solutions to basic problems, contribute to responsible citizenship, and strengthen an understanding of freedom and the fundamentals of a free society. Awards are given in the Youth, Adult and Military Essay Categories. Citizens and permanent residents of the United States are eligible. Nominations may be submitted by May 1. The following awards are presented annually: $100 savings bonds to principal recipients in the youth and military essay category; $50 savings bonds and medals in the Military Essay category; a framed George Washington Honor Medal to the principal awardee in each category; and bronze medals to meritorious awardees. Established in 1949.

• 9767 •
French-American Chamber of Commerce
Serge Bellanger, Pres.
122 E 42nd St., Ste. 2015
New York, NY 10168
Phone: (212)867-0123
Fax: (212)867-9050
E-mail: info@faccnyc.org
Home Page: http://www.faccnyc.org

• 9768 • **French-American Chamber of Commerce Person of the Year Award**
For recognition of achievement in the French-American business community. Individuals with a strong presence and an outstanding character who are active in both French and American societies, and have received national or international attention or recognition are eligible for nomination. A Baccarat crystal obelisk trophy is awarded annually. Established in 1984.

• 9769 •
French-Canadian Genealogical Society (Societe Genealogique Canadienne-Francaise)
Marcel Fournier, Pres.
3440 rue Davidson
Montreal, QC, Canada H1W 2Z5
Phone: (514)527-1010
Fax: (514)527-0265
E-mail: info@sgcf.com
Home Page: http://www.sgcf.com

• 9770 • **Prix Archange-Godbout**
Recognizes individuals making a career contribution to genealogy or family history. Awarded periodically.

• 9771 • **Prix Percy-W.-Foy**
Recognizes the best writers in various categories. Awarded annually. Inquire for categories and additional application details.

• 9772 •
Fresno-Madera Medical Society
Mr. Merwyn Scholten, Exec.Dir.
PO Box 28337
Fresno, CA 93729-8337
Phone: (559)224-4224
Fax: (559)224-0276
E-mail: info@fmms.org
Home Page: http://www.fmms.org

• 9773 • **Fresno-Madera Medical Society Scholarship**
For individual from Fresno or Madera County accepted to an accredited medical school. Scholarship awarded annually.

• 9774 •
The Friday Morning Music Club, Inc.
Juanita Wallace Jackson, Pres.
2233 Wisconsin Ave. NW. Ste. 326
Washington, DC 20007
Phone: (202)333-2075
E-mail: fmmc@fmmc.org
Home Page: http://www.fmmc.org

• 9775 • **Washington International Competition**
To assist young artists who are ready to launch professional careers. (The competition does not provide financial aid for individuals beginning conservatory or university studies.) The competition is offered alternately for pianists, string instrument players (violin, viola, and cello), and singers. Pianists and string instrument players must be between 18 and 28 years of age and singers must be between 20 and 32 years of age. Applicants must not be under professional contract management. Quarterfinalists are chosen from tape recordings of the repertory and must agree to audition in person on a given date. The following monetary prizes are awarded: First Prize - $7,000; Second Prize - $4,000; Third Prize $2,000; Judges Discretionary Awards - $500 each; and Audience Award $500. Additionally, the first prize winner appears in a solo recital at the Phillips Collection in Washington, D.C. Established in 1950. Sponsored by the Friday Morning Music Club Foundation.

• 9776 •
Friends in Residential Emergency Fire
W. Andrews, Sec.
501 N 9th St., Rm. 134
Richmond, VA 23219-1544
Phone: (804)646-0621
Phone: (804)646-6640
Fax: (804)646-7465

• 9777 • **Poster Contest**
For best poster about fire safety created by student. Monetary award bestowed annually.

• 9778 •
Friends of Alexandria Archaeology
Laura Heaton, Pres.
PO Box 21475
Alexandria, VA 22320-2475
Phone: (703)838-4399
Fax: (703)838-6491
E-mail: archaeology@ci.alexandria.va.us
Home Page: http://www.alexandriaarchaeology.org

• 9779 • **John Glaser Award**
For summer camp scholarship for needy students. Scholarship awarded annually.

• 9780 •
Friends of Algonquin Park
PO Box 248
Whitney, ON, Canada K0J 2M0
Phone: (613)637-2828
Fax: (613)637-2138
Home Page: http://www.algonquinpark.on.ca/friends.html

• 9781 • **Directors Award of The Friends of Algonquin Park**
To recognize individuals who have made a significant contribution toward the appreciation of Algonquin Park. Selection is made by the Directors of The Friends of Algonquin Park. A plaque

and a gift are presented annually at a special luncheon. Established in 1985.

• 9782 •
Friends of American Writers
Mrs. Vivian Mortensen, Chm.
506 Rose Ave.
Des Plaines, IL 60016
Phone: (847)827-8339
E-mail: vmortens@parkridge.lib.il.us

• 9783 • **Juvenile Awards**
To recognize those literary works that reflect the ideals of the Society, which are to encourage high standards and to promote literary ideals among writers. To be considered, the book must have been published during the calendar year; the author must live or have lived for approximately five years in the states of Arkansas, Illinois, Indiana, Iowa, Kansas, Michigan, Minnesota, Missouri, North Dakota, Nebraska, Ohio, South Dakota, or Wisconsin, or the locale of the book must be in the above mentioned region; the author should not have published more than three books and only prose writing that is not in manuscript form will be accepted. The entry deadline is December 1. Certificates to the publishers of the award winning books are awarded. Copies of the award winning book are also presented to the Chicago Public Library and to the Chicago Historical Society. Awarded annually at the Annual Awards Luncheon in April.

• 9784 • **Literary Awards**
To recognize those literary works that reflect the ideals of the Society, which are to encourage high standards and to promote literary ideals among writers. To be considered the book must have been published during the calendar year; the author must live or have lived for approximately five years in the states of Arkansas, Illinois, Indiana, Iowa, Kansas, Michigan, Minnesota, Missouri, North Dakota, Nebraska, Ohio, South Dakota, or Wisconsin, or the locale of the book must be in the above mentioned region; the author should not have published more than three books and only prose writing that is not in manuscript form will be accepted. The entry deadline is December 1. The following prizes are awarded: Literary Award - $1,600 for first place, and $1,000 for distinguished recognition; Young People's Literature Awards - $800 for first place, and $400 for distinguished recognition; and Publishers' Award - certificates to the publishers of the award winning books. Copies of award winning books are also presented to the Chicago Public Library and to the Chicago Historical Society. Awarded annually at the Annual Awards Luncheon in April. Established in 1928.

• 9785 • **Publishers Award**
To recognize those literary works that reflect the ideals of the Society, which are to encourage high standards and to promote literary ideals among writers. To be considered, the book must have been published during the calendar year; the author must live or have lived for approximately five years in the states of Arkansas, Illinois, Indiana, Iowa, Kansas, Michigan, Minnesota, Missouri, North Dakota, Nebraska, Ohio, South Dakota, or Wisconsin, or the locale of the book must be in the above mentioned region; the author should not have published more than three books and only prose writing that is not in manuscript form will be accepted. The entry deadline is December 1. Certificates to the publishers of the award winning books are awarded. Copies of the award winning book are also presented to the Chicago Public Library and to the Chicago Historical Society. Awarded annually at the Annual Awards Luncheon in April.

• 9786 • **Young People's Literature Awards**
To recognize those literary works that reflect the ideals of the Society, which are to encourage high standards and to promote literary ideals among writers. To be considered, the book must have been published during the calendar year; the author must live or have lived for approximately five years in the states of Arkansas, Illinois, Indiana, Iowa, Kansas, Michigan, Minnesota, Missouri, North Dakota, Nebraska, Ohio, South Dakota, or Wisconsin, or the locale of the book must be in the above mentioned region; the author should not have published more than three books and only prose writing that is not in manuscript form will be accepted. The entry deadline is December 1. First place prize of $800, distinguished recognition prize of $400, and certificates to the publishers of the award winning books are awarded. Copies of the award winning book are also presented to the Chicago Public Library and to the Chicago Historical Society. Awarded annually at the Annual Awards Luncheon in April.

• 9787 •
Friends of Casco Bay
Joseph E. Payne, Exec.Dir./Bay Keeper
2 Ft. Rd.
South Portland, ME 04106
Phone: (207)799-8574
Fax: (207)799-7224
E-mail: keeper@cascobay.org
Home Page: http://www.cascobay.org

• 9788 • **Friend of Casco Bay Award**
For individual or organization responsible for substantial contributions to the health of Casco Bay. Monetary award bestowed annually.

• 9789 •
Friends of Freedom Society
Cathy Nelson, Pres.
586 E Town St.
Columbus, OH 43215-4802
Phone: (614)868-1246
Fax: (614)365-5027
Home Page: http://www.ohioundergroundrailroad.org/

• 9790 • **Conductor of the Year**
For outstanding contributions toward the preservation and education of the Underground Railroad history. Recognition award bestowed annually.

• 9791 •
Friends of Libraries U.S.A.
Sally G. Reed, Exec.Dir.
1420 Walnut St., Ste. 450
Philadelphia, PA 19102
Phone: (215)790-1674
Toll-Free: 800-936-5872
Fax: (215)545-3821
E-mail: folusa@folusa.org
Home Page: http://www.folusa.org

• 9792 • **FOLUSA/Baker & Taylor Books Award**
To encourage the support of libraries by Friends groups. Awards are given in the following categories of Friends of Libraries groups: state Friends group, large public library Friends group, medium public library Friends group , small public library Friends group, academic library Friends group , and school library Friends group . The candidate must be a member of FOLUSA. A monetary award of $1,000 and a certificate are awarded annually in each category at FOLUSA Meetings at the ALA Convention. Established in 1982. Sponsored by the Baker and Taylor Company. Formerly: Friends of Libraries U.S.A. Award.

• 9793 • **Friend of Libraries U.S.A. Award (Friend of the Year)**
To recognize an individual for work done to benefit libraries. Public figures who have brought attention to libraries in a positive way are eligible. A plaque is awarded when merited. Established in 1981.

• 9794 • **Friends of Libraries U.S.A. Public Service Award**
To recognize public servants for outstanding contributions to libraries. Awarded annually. Established in 1989.

• 9795 • **Barbara Kingsolver Award**
To recognize a public library Friends group for outstanding community and volunteer involvement. Friends groups of small (annual operating budget of less than $1,000,000) public libraries are eligible to enter. The award is $10,000 to be used for the purchase of books and is presented at the FOLUSA author program at the ALA Annual Conference. Established in 1995. Sponsored by HarperCollins Publishers.

• 9796 •
Friends of Old-Time Radio
Jay Hickerson, Pres.
PO Box 4321
Hamden, CT 06514
Phone: (203)248-2887
Fax: (203)281-1322
E-mail: jayhick@aol.com

• 9797 • **Friends of Old-Time Radio Award**
For recognition of achievement in radio in its golden years, 1920-1960. Radio personalities who attend the annual convention are eligible. A trophy is awarded annually. Established in 1970.

• 9798 •
Friends of Patrick Henry
Bernadine Smith, Dir.
PO Box 1776
Hanford, CA 93232
Phone: (559)582-8534
Phone: (559)584-5209
Fax: (559)584-4084
E-mail: liberty89@libertygunrights.com
Home Page: http://www.libertygunrights.com

• 9799 • **Friends of Patrick Henry Awards**
To recognize individuals who have performed exemplary service in a meritorious effort, seeking to restore and protect the liberty and freedom of the individual, preserve national sovereignty and national independence, the restoration of the rights of the states and the people, and the re-institution of government under the Constitution of 1789. Awarded annually on May 29.

• 9800 •
Friends of Radio for Peace International
Debra L. Latham, CEO
Box 3165
Newberg, OR 97132
E-mail: info@rfpi.org
Home Page: http://www.rfpi.org

• 9801 • **Distinguished World Citizen**
To recognize communications and international understanding efforts. Awarded annually with a plaque. Established in 1992.

• 9802 • **World Citizen Humanitarian**
To recognize extraordinary efforts to serve humanity on an international level. Awarded annually with a plaque. Established in 1989.

• 9803 •
Friends of the Atlanta-Fulton Public Library System
John F. Szabo, Dir.
1 Margaret Mitchell Sq.
Atlanta, GA 30303
Phone: (404)730-1700
Fax: (404)730-1990
Home Page: http://www.af.public.lib.ga.us/friends_of_library.html

• 9804 • **Milner Award**
To recognize the favorite author of childrens' books as selected by the votes of Atlanta's school children, especially grades K - 8. Children vote during Children's Book Week each November. Authors must be American, living, and willing to come to Atlanta to receive the award, and must not have won the award before. An honorarium of $1,000, travel expenses, and a Hans Frabel glass sculpture are awarded annually in November. Established in 1983 in memory of Vera Milner, teacher and Friends member who left money in her will for the award.

• 9805 •
Friends of the Chicago Public Library
Harold Washington Library Center
400 S. State St., 105-7
Chicago, IL 60605
Phone: (312)747-4999

• 9806 • **Carl Sandburg Literary Arts Award**
To recognize outstanding Chicago authors. Residents of the six-county metropolitan areas and native-born Chicagoans may submit works by August 1. Books published during the preceding year, June 1 to May 31, are eligible. The following categories are considered: fiction, nonfiction, poetry, and children's literature. A commemorative medal and a monetary award are presented annually. Established in 1979 in memory of Carl Sandburg, an American poet.

• 9807 •
Friends of the Historical Museum
Marie Macklin, Pres.
610 North Julia Davis Dr.
Boise, ID 83702
Phone: (208)334-2120
Fax: (208)334-4059

• 9808 • **Friends of Historical Museum Awards**
For outstanding entry in an Idaho Historical subject-Idaho History Day competition. Monetary award bestowed annually.

• 9809 •
Friends of the Morrill Memorial Library
Maureen Susi, Pres.
33 Walpole St.
PO Box 220
Norwood, MA 02062-0220
Phone: (781)769-0200
E-mail: msusi10837@aol.com

• 9810 • **Norwood Cultural Council**
For artistic/live theatre for all patrons. Grant awarded annually.

• 9811 •
Friends of the Pendleton District
Donna Roper, Asst.Dir.
PO Box 565
Pendleton, SC 29670
Phone: (864)646-3782
Toll-Free: 800-862-1795
Fax: (864)646-2506
E-mail: pendletontourism@bellsouth.net
Home Page: http://www.pendleton-district.org

• 9812 • **Chairman's Award**
For one who serves in the field of history or tourism. Recognition award bestowed annually.

• 9813 •
Friends of the Princeton University Library
Dept. of Rare Books and Special Collections
1 Washington Rd.
Princeton, NJ 08544
Phone: (609)258-3184
Fax: (609)258-2324
E-mail: libraryf@princeton.edu
Home Page: http://www.fpul.org

• 9814 • **Elmer Adler Prize**
To honor best essays on book collecting by Princeton University undergraduates. Established in 1920 Named for Elmer Adler in 1964.

• 9815 • **Donald F. Hyde Award**
To recognize distinction in book collecting and service to the community of scholars. Collectors who have sought and preserved records that otherwise might have been lost, and made them available to scholars are eligible. A citation, hand bound in leather, is awarded when merited. Established in 1967 to honor Donald F. Hyde (1909-1966), book collector.

• 9816 •
Friends of the River
Steve Evans, Co-Dir.
915 20th St.
Sacramento, CA 95814-2207
Phone: (916)442-3155
Fax: (916)442-3396
E-mail: info@friendsoftheriver.org
Home Page: http://www.friendsoftheriver.org

• 9817 • **Mark Dubois Award**
For outstanding river conservation efforts in California. Awarded to one or more recipients annually.

• 9818 •
Friends of the Waterfront
Marlene Grissom, Contact
129 E River Rd.
Louisville, KY 40202-1335
Phone: (502)574-3768
Fax: (502)574-4111

• 9819 • **Silver Anchor Award**
For recipients who have provided exceptional assistance to the waterfront and its related programs. Recognition award bestowed annually.

• 9820 •
Front Range Young Farmers Chapter of the Colorado Young Farmer Educational Association
Nicole Jerger, Advisor/Coor.
530 Reynolds St.
Fort Lupton, CO 80621
Phone: (303)857-7100
Phone: (303)659-5596
Fax: (303)857-7179
Home Page: http://www.coloradoyoungfarmer.com

• 9821 • **Front Range Young Farmers Scholarship**
For agriculture-related major. Scholarship awarded annually.

• 9822 •
F.U.G.I.T.I.V.E.S.
Texas Bob Reinhardt, Founder
222 Softwind No. 1
Canyon Lake, TX 78133-9701
Phone: (830)935-4618

• 9823 • **"Kimble" - Fugitive of the Year**
Recognizes the promotion of members who best represent our clubs philosophy. Trophy is awarded annually. Established in 1994.

• 9824 •
Fulton Chapter, Ohio Genealogical Society
Brenda Wolfinger Woodling, Pres.
PO Box 337
Swanton, OH 43558
Phone: (419)335-0898
E-mail: kinfolks@bnnorth.net
Home Page: http://www.rootsweb.com/~ohfulton

• 9825 • **First Families Award**
For individuals with heritage dating back to 1860 in the Fulton County area. Recognition award bestowed annually.

• 9826 •
Fulton County Historical Society
Glenn Cordell, Admin.
PO Box 115
McConnellsburg, PA 17233
E-mail: fchs@fultonhistory.org
Home Page: http://www.fultonhistory.org

• 9827 • **Historian of the Year**
For significant contribution to preservation of local history. Recognition award bestowed annually.

• 9828 •
The Fund for American Studies
Roger R. Ream, Pres.
1706 New Hampshire Ave. NW
Washington, DC 20009
Phone: (202)986-0384
Toll-Free: 800-741-6964
Fax: (202)986-0390
E-mail: info@tfas.org
Home Page: http://www.dcinternships.org

• 9829 • **Clark Mollenhoff Award for Excellence in Investigative Reporting**
To recognize and outstanding university professor of journalism. The award was initiated in 1996 and is sponsored by the Institute on Political Journalism (IPJ), a cooperative educational program between the Fund For American Studies and Georgetown University. The guidelines are as follows: (1) story or series of stories — between 10 and 20 — in normal, eight-and-a-half-by-ten notebook style; (2) a letter outlining the nature of the reporting, obstacles overcome and results obtained; and, (3) in a separate section, any additional stories or back-up material considered pertinent. Named for Clark Mollenhoff, the late Pulitzer-Prize winning reporter and Washington and Lee University professor of journalism. The annual award carries a cash prize of $5,000 and is presented to a newspaper reporter, team of reporters, or an individual newspaper showing initiative similar to Mollenhoff's.

• 9830 •
Fund for Modern Courts
Ken Jockers, Exec.Dir.
351 W 54th St.
New York, NY 10019
Phone: (212)541-6741
Fax: (212)541-7301
E-mail: justice@moderncourts.org
Home Page: http://www.moderncourts.org

• 9831 • **Samuel J. Duboff Award**
To recognize laypersons (non-lawyers) or organizations of laypersons for outstanding contributions to improving the New York State court system. Any layperson is eligible. A plaque is awarded annually in December. Established in 1985 to honor Samuel J. Duboff of Scarsdale, NY.

• 9832 • **John J. McCloy Memorial Award**
To recognize lawyers for outstanding contributions to the causes of merit selection of judges and court reform. A plaque is awarded annually in December. Established in 1992 in honor of John J. McCloy, first chairman of Modern Courts.

• 9833 •
Fund for the City of New York
Mary McCormick, Pres.
121 Avenue of the Americas, 6th Fl.
New York, NY 10013-1590
Phone: (212)925-6675
Fax: (212)925-5675
E-mail: info@fcny.org
Home Page: http://www.fcny.org

• 9834 • **Sloan Public Service Awards of the Fund for the City of New York**
To focus attention on the excellence that exists in New York City's municipal workforce. The idea is to bring to the public's attention the importance of public service, to recognize individuals whose work performance and commitment to the public are extraordinary, and to encourage talented people to consider careers in city service. All employees of mayoral agencies, the Transit and Housing Authorities, the Health and Hospitals Corporation, the Department of Education and Board of Higher Education, District Attorney Office, and the Libraries of New York City are eligible. The emphasis is on people who have made a career of public service. Nominations are submitted from the widest possible variety of public and private sources, including citizens and neighborhood groups. The names of city employees who emerge from the nominating inquiry with the strongest favorable recommendations are submitted to the Selection Panel, an independent group of citizens picked on the basis of their standing in the community and their knowledge of government. A $7,500 grant is presented to each of six awardees annually. Established in 1973. Renamed in 1990 to recognize the Alfred P. Sloan Foundation's continued support of the program. Formerly: (1989) Public Service Awards.

• 9835 •
Fund for UFO Research
Don Berliner, Chm.
PO Box 277
Mount Rainier, MD 20712
Phone: (703)684-6032
Phone: (703)250-0709
Fax: (703)684-6032
E-mail: fufor@fufor.com
Home Page: http://www.fufor.com

• 9836 • **Donald E. Keyhoe Journalism Award**
To recognize and support serious journalism in the study of Unidentified Flying Objects. Any journalist working for a newspaper, magazine, radio or television station, whose story on UFOs was published or broadcast during the previous calendar year, is eligible. The deadline is February 1. A monetary award of $1,000 is presented annually. Established in 1989 to commemorate Donald E. Keyhoe.

• 9837 •
Fur Commission U.S.A.
Teresa Platt, Exec.Dir.
826 Orange Ave., PMB 506
Coronado, CA 92118-2698
Phone: (619)575-0139
Fax: (619)575-5578
E-mail: furfarmers@aol.com
Home Page: http://www.furcommission.com

• 9838 • **Merit Award**
Recognizes excellence in animal husbandry skills. Veterinary inspection is required.

• 9839 •
Fusion Power Associates
Stephen O. Dean, Pres.
2 Professional Dr., Ste. 249
Gaithersburg, MD 20879
Phone: (301)258-0545
Fax: (301)975-9869
E-mail: fpa@compuserve.com
Home Page: http://ourworld.compuserve.com/homepages/fpa

• 9840 • **Award for Excellence in Fusion Engineering**
To recognize and encourage fusion engineering professionals in the early part of their careers. Nominations, which may come from any source, are reviewed by an awards committee. Nominations are judged on the basis of thesis, published

Awards are arranged in alphabetical order below their administering organizations

materials, professional activities and letters of recommendation. A monetary award and certificate are awarded annually. Established in 1987 in memory of Prof. David J. Rose of MIT, who dedicated most of his career to getting young people interested in fusion and fusion engineering.

• 9841 • **Leadership Awards**
To recognize individuals who have shown outstanding leadership qualities in accelerating the development of fusion. Election is by the Fusion Power Associates Board of Directors. A certificate is awarded annually. Established in 1980.

• 9842 •
Future Business Leaders of America - Phi Beta Lambda
Ms. Jean M. Buckley, Pres./CEO
1912 Association Dr.
Reston, VA 20191-1591
Phone: (703)860-3334
Toll-Free: 800-325-2946
Fax: (703)758-0749
E-mail: general@fbla.org
Home Page: http://www.fbla-pbl.org

• 9843 • **Future Business Executive**
To recognize outstanding Phi Beta Lambda members who demonstrate executive potential, leadership qualities, and evidence of knowledge and skills essential for successful careers in business. Only active Phi Beta Lambda members are eligible. Plaques are presented annually. Established in 1969.

• 9844 • **Future Business Leaders**
For recognition of outstanding FBLA members who have demonstrated qualities of leadership, participation, and interest in FBLA, plus evidence of knowledge and skills essential for successful careers in business. Only active FBLA members are eligible. Plaque are presented annually. Established in 1969.

• 9845 • **Future Business Teacher**
To recognize outstanding Phi Beta Lambda members who demonstrate teaching potential, leadership qualities, and evidence of knowledge and skills essential for successful careers in teaching. Only active PBL members are eligible. Plaques are presented annually. Established in 1969.

• 9846 •
Future Problem Solving Program of New Jersey
Dr. Jeanne Carlson, Exec.Dir.
Box 474
Somers Point, NJ 08244
Phone: (609)927-3455
Phone: (609)927-3455
Toll-Free: 800-256-1499
Fax: (609)927-4410
E-mail: info@njfps.org
Home Page: http://www.njfps.org

• 9847 • **Adam Hirschfeld Creativity Scholarship**
For senior member of FPS team recommended by coach. Scholarship awarded annually.

• 9848 •
Gage County Convention and Visitors Bureau
Shellyn Sands, Tourism Dir.
226 S 6th St.
Beatrice, NE 68310
Phone: (402)223-3175
Toll-Free: 800-755-7745
Fax: (402)223-2339
E-mail: ssands@visitbeatrice.com

• 9849 • **Friend of Tourism**
For non-tourism employed person. Recognition award bestowed annually.

• 9850 •
Gairdner Foundation
Dr. John Dirks, Pres.
44 Charles St. W, Ste. 4706
Toronto, ON, Canada M4Y 1R8
Phone: (416)596-9996
Fax: (416)596-9992
E-mail: thegairdner@on.aibn.com
Home Page: http://www.gairdner.org

• 9851 • **Wightman Special Achievement Award**
To recognize a Canadian who, in the opinion of the Foundation, has demonstrated outstanding leadership in medicine and medical science consistent with the purpose of the Foundation. A monetary award of $40,000, a framed award, and a sculpture are awarded from time to time. Established in 1976 in honor of the late Dr. Keith J.R. Wightman, the award's first recipient in 1976.

• 9852 •
Galaxy International Pageants
944 Field St. NW
Canton, OH 44709
Phone: (216)373-6572
Fax: (330)493-0558
E-mail: galaxy@coronationinc.com
Home Page: http://
www.galaxypageants.com

• 9853 • **Miss Galaxy**
To develop a greater degree of self-awareness among all youth. Contestants must be an unmarried (single, divorced, widowed) "naturally born, genetic female" who are at least 19-29 years old as of September 1st following the international finals. Areas of competition include photogenic appeal and personality, interview, swimsuit, fashion, and evening gown, with an on-state question and answer segment for finalists. Deadline for entry is May 1st of year year. Established in 1974.

• 9854 •
Galesburg Civic Art Center
114 E Main St.
Galesburg, IL 61401
Phone: (309)342-7415
Fax: (309)343-2650
E-mail: info@galesburgarts.org
Home Page: http://www.galesburgarts.org

• 9855 • **Art in the Park Awards**
To recognize the worthiest entries at the juried outdoor art fair. The following cash awards are presented: Best of Show - $200, First Place 2-D - $100, First Place 3-D - $100, First Place Fine Craft - $100, and Juror's Choice Awards - $250. Held annually on the third Saturday of July. Established in 1987.

• 9856 •
Gallaudet University Alumni Association
Sam Sonnenstrahl, Exec.Dir.
Peikoff Alumni House
800 Florida Ave. NE
Washington, DC 20002-3695
Phone: (202)651-5060
Fax: (202)651-5062
E-mail:
samuel.sonnenstrahl@gallaudet.edu
Home Page: http://alumni.gallaudet.edu

• 9857 • **Outstanding Young Alumnus**
Recognizes the accomplishment of notable achievement. Alumnus or alumna who have graduated within the past 15 years are eligible. Awarded annually.

• 9858 • **Service to Others**
Recognizes individuals within the deaf community who have contributed significantly to the community, especially as volunteers. Awarded annually.

• 9859 •
Galt District Chamber of Commerce
Barbara Clare, Exec.Dir./CEO
PO Box 1446
PO Box 1446
Galt, CA 95632
Phone: (209)745-2529
Fax: (209)745-0840
E-mail: info@galtchamber.com
Home Page: http://www.galtchamber.com

• 9860 • **Business of the Year**
For community service. Recognition award bestowed annually.

• 9861 • **President of Chamber Award**
For community service. Recognition award bestowed annually.

• 9862 •
Galva Arts Council
Marge Dickinson, Exec.Dir.
PO Box 29
Galva, IL 61434
Phone: (309)932-2880
Fax: (309)932-8207
E-mail: mdart@inw.net

• 9863 • **Galva Arts Council Scholarship**
For Galva High school graduating senior majoring in one of the arts in college. Scholarship awarded annually.

• 9864 •
Galveston Historical Foundation
Marsh Davis, Exec.Dir.
502 20th St.
Galveston, TX 77550-2014
Phone: (409)765-7834
Fax: (409)765-7851
E-mail: foundation@galvestonhistory.org
Home Page: http://www.galvestonhistory.org/

• 9865 • **Steel Oleander Award**
For living female community activist in Galveston, Texas. Recognition award bestowed annually.

• 9866 •
Gamma Sigma Delta
Steven A. Henning, Pres.
Agricultural Economics and Agribusiness
101 Ag. Admin. Bldg.
Louisiana State Univ.
Baton Rouge, LA 70803-5604
Phone: (225)578-2718
Fax: (225)578-2716
E-mail: shenning@agctr.lsu.edu
Home Page: http://www.gammasigmadelta.org

• 9867 • **Distinguished Achievement in Agriculture Award**
For recognition of outstanding achievements in agriculture during the previous five years in the form of teaching, research, extension, or other distinguished service. Members of the Society are eligible. A monetary award of $1,000 and an embossed plaque are awarded annually. Established in 1951.

• 9868 •
Gangs Out of Downey
Stan Hanstad, Asst.Supt.
PO Box 13
Downey, CA 90241
Phone: (562)469-6541
Phone: (562)469-6542
Fax: (562)469-6555
E-mail: shanstad@dusd.net

• 9869 • **G.O.O.D. for You Award**
Honors citizens who take an active role in reporting gang activity. Recognition award bestowed annually.

• 9870 • **G.O.O.D. Friendship Award**
For a boy/girl in 11th grade who connects people and bridges the gap of misunderstanding. Monetary award bestowed annually.

• 9871 •
Gar Wood Society
Anthony S. Mollica Jr., Pres.
750 Mary St.
Clayton, NY 13624
Phone: (315)686-4104
Phone: (315)686-4104
Fax: (315)686-2775
E-mail: asmollica@aol.com
Home Page: http://www.garwood.com

• 9872 • **Gar Wood of the Year Award**
Recognizes accuracy and quality of boat restoration. Awarded annually.

• 9873 •
Garden Centers of America
Steve Echter, Pres.
PO Box 2945
La Grange, GA 30241
Phone: (202)789-2900
Toll-Free: 888-648-6463
Fax: (866)826-4857
E-mail: info@gardencentersofamerica.org
Home Page: http://www.gardencentersofamerica.org

• 9874 • **Jack F. Schneider Award**
To recognize significant contributions by an individual to the betterment of the retail nursery industry. Established in 1982. Formerly: Retail Nurseryman Award - Jack F. Schneider Award.

• 9875 •
Garden Club of America
Sheila Ratner, Exec. Administrator
14 E 60th St., 3rd Fl.
New York, NY 10022-7147
Phone: (212)753-8287
Fax: (212)753-0134
E-mail: info@gcamerica.org
Home Page: http://www.gcamerica.org

• 9876 • **Garden Club of America Medals and Awards**
To recognize individuals for outstanding contributions to horticulture. The following awards are presented: the Elizabeth Platt Corning Medal - to recognize a GCA member in a competitive horticulture class in a major flower show for an entry that is notable for both rarity and cultural difficulty, and that is presented with distinction and originality; the Bulkley Medal - to recognize GCA members, member clubs, non-members, or other organizations at major shows for a horticultural or conservation exhibit of exceptional merit that increases the knowledge and awareness of the viewing public; the Fenwick Medal - to recognize GCA members in competitive classes at a major flower show for creative work of outstanding beauty in the use and arrangement of growing or cut plant material, fruits, or vegetables; the Annie Burr Jennings Medal - to recognize the GCA Club accumulating the greatest number of points in all sections of a major flower show; Certificate of Excellence - to recognize members, member clubs, other clubs, organizations, societies or individuals for an exhibit of great distinction in a competitive class in a major flower show; the Catherine Beattie Medal - to recognize a member for horticultural excellence in a small flower show; the Harriet Dewaele Puckett Creativity Award - to recognize GCA members and non-members for a creative work of outstanding beauty in a small flower show; the Barbara Spaulding Cramer Zone Flower Arrangement Award - to recognize a member for outstanding achievement in flower arrangement and flower arrangement education; and the Garden Club of America Small Flower Show Award - to recognize a garden club or clubs that sponsor(s) an imaginative, well-executed, and exceptional small flower show.

• 9877 •
Garden Writers Association
Robert LaGasse, Exec.Dir.
10210 Leatherleaf Ct.
Manassas, VA 20111
Phone: (703)257-1032
Fax: (703)257-0213
E-mail: info@gwaa.org
Home Page: http://www.gwaa.org

• 9878 • **Fellow**
To recognize individuals for achievement and contributions to the advancement of the purposes and goals of the Association. Members of the Association are eligible. A plaque is awarded annually at the convention. Established in 1976.

• 9879 • **GWAA Hall of Fame**
To recognize individuals for achievement and contributions to the advancement of the purposes and goals of the Association. Members of the Association are eligible. A plaque is awarded annually at the convention. Established in 1976.

• 9880 • **GWAA Honorary Member**
For recognition of contributions to communications in the field of horticulture. Leaders in horticultural areas, both members and non-members, are eligible. A plaque is awarded as merited at the annual meeting. First presented in 1981.

• 9881 •
The Gardeners of America/Men's Garden Clubs of America
William J. Carney, Pres.
5560 Merle Hay Rd.
PO Box 241
Johnston, IA 50131-6245
Phone: (515)278-0295
Fax: (515)278-6245
E-mail: tgoasecy@dwx.com
Home Page: http://www.tgoa-mgca.org

• 9882 • **Johnny Appleseed Award**
To recognize an individual for outstanding work in horticulture in a spirit of service away from his vocation and at a definite cost or sacrifice by

Awards are arranged in alphabetical order below their administering organizations

overcoming resistance and even antagonism. Individuals need not be members of the organization. Awarded annually. Established in 1939.

• 9883 • Certificate of Appreciation
To recognize individuals, organizations, firms, companies, clubs, or city, county, state, and national governmental bodies and divisions thereof for services, gifts, or other courtesies rendered the Men's Garden Clubs of America. A certificate is awarded when merited. Established in 1973.

• 9884 • Certificate of Recognition
To recognize outstanding service and/or achievement of a local club.

• 9885 • Gardeners of America/Men's Garden Clubs of America Scholarship
Applicants must be students enrolled in an accredited community college, university, or college offering a major in horticulture or floriculture. Five $1000 scholarships are awarded annually. Applications may be obtained from scholarship or grants office on campus or a local club.

• 9886 • Gardening From the Heart Award
To recognize affiliated clubs activity in the Gardening From the Heart Programs of MGCA. Clubs may nominate a local program involving efforts with a group of children, youth, or adults that are physically, mentally, or emotionally disabled. Awarded annually. Established in 1984.

• 9887 • Gold Medal
To recognize a man for an outstanding achievement in the field of horticulture. Awarded annually. Established in 1949.

• 9888 • MGCA Beautification Certificate
To recognize communities, businesses, organizations, and individuals who are members of the Men's Garden Clubs of America for their efforts in contributing to the quality of the national beauty and environment. Nominations should include a black/white or color photograph, along with story of the project or business, and reasons it should be recognized as a contribution to the quality of national beauty and the environment. Awarded as merited.

• 9889 • MGCA Golden Quill Award
To recognize the contribution of any person whose continuing original journalistic contributions, on more than a community level, have encouraged gardening as a valuable and worthwhile activity, particularly if those writings have advanced the art and hobby of gardening as a national vocation. A plaque is awarded annually. Established in 1978.

• 9890 • Silver Medal
To recognize a member who has rendered outstanding service to the national organization. Awarded annually. Established in 1953.

• 9891 • Youth Gardening Award
To recognize an outstanding youth gardening program as developed by an affiliated club of the Men's Garden Clubs of America. A plaque is awarded annually at the convention. Established in 1989.

• 9892 •
Gas Processors Association
Rob Martinovich, Pres.
6526 E 60th St.
Tulsa, OK 74145
Phone: (918)493-3872
Fax: (918)493-3875
E-mail: gpa@gasprocessors.com
Home Page: http://gasprocessors.com

• 9893 • GPA Citation for Service
To provide recognition for outstanding service and contributions to the gas processing industry and the Association. An illuminated scroll summarising the individual/s contributions to the industry is awarded annually. Established in 1962.

• 9894 • GPA Recognition Award
To recognize long and honorable service to the welfare of the gas and/or gas processing industry in general. A walnut display box is awarded annually. Established in 1950.

• 9895 • Hanlon Award
To recognize outstanding achievement and effort which has significantly contributed to the advancement of technology of the gas and/or gas processing industry. A plaque is awarded annually. Established in 1937, the award was initiated by E. I. Hanlon, a pioneer in the early gas processing industry.

• 9896 • Donald L. Katz Award
To recognize outstanding research accomplishments in gas engineering, and excellence in engineering. An wall plaque is awarded when appropriate. Established in 1985 in honor of Dr. Donald L. Katz, Professor Emeritus of Chemical Engineering, The University of Michigan.

• 9897 •
Gateway Greening
Gwenne Hayes-Stewart, Contact
PO Box 299
St. Louis, MO 63166
Phone: (314)577-9484
Fax: (314)577-9435
E-mail: gwenne.hayes-stewart@mobot.org
Home Page: http://www.gatewaygreening.org

• 9898 • Neighborhood Greening Project
For commitment of group and need on projects related to building gardens and improving the greening of St. Louis. Recognition award bestowed annually.

• 9899 •
Gathering of Nations
Derek Mathews, Dir.
3301 Coors Blvd. NW, Ste. R300
Albuquerque, NM 87120-1229
Phone: (505)836-2810
Fax: (505)839-0475
E-mail: website@gatheringofnations.com
Home Page: http://www.gatheringofnations.com

• 9900 • Miss Indian World
To crown a young Indian (Native American) woman to reign as Miss Indian World. She must be an ambassador of goodwill and represent the Gathering of Nations and Native American people in the United States, Canada, and throughout the Americas (North, South, and Central). Candidates must be at least one-quarter Indian, and be 17 to 24 years of age. A traveling crown (beaded) to wear throughout the year, a banner, $1,200 cash and $1,800 travel expenses are awarded annually. Established in 1984 by Gathering of Nations Ltd.

• 9901 •
Gay and Lesbian Association of Choruses
Barbara McCullough-Jones, Exec.Dir.
PO Box 65084
Washington, DC 20035
Phone: (202)467-5830
Fax: (202)467-5831
E-mail: info@galachoruses.org
Home Page: http://www.galachoruses.org

• 9902 • Commission Matching Grants
Awarded to choruses engaging in the commissioning process for the first time. One grant is awarded annually.

• 9903 • Legacy Award
Recognizes leadership in the gay and lesbian choral movement. Awarded quadrennially.

• 9904 •
Geary 18 International Yacht Racing Association
Debra Eckrote, Contact
PO Box 4763
Federal Way, WA 98063
Phone: (253)946-2619
E-mail: stephethom@netscape.net
Home Page: http://www.geary18.org

• 9905 • Geary 18 International Yacht Racing Association Championship Regatta
To recognize the best sailor in the Championship Regatta. Members of the Association are eligible. A trophy and the inscription of the name of the winner on the perpetual trophy are awarded annually at the Championship Regatta. Established in 1935 by Ted Geary. Formerly: (1965) Flattie International Yacht Racing Association Championship.

• 9906 •
Gemini Theater Company
Denny Martin, Managing Dir.
7501 Penn Ave.
Pittsburgh, PA 15208-2559
Phone: (412)243-6464
Phone: (412)243-1092

• 9907 • **Outstanding Playwright for Year**
For produced production feedback. Monetary award bestowed annually.

• 9908 •
Genealogical Association of Nova Scotia
PO Box 641, Sta. Central
Halifax, NS, Canada B3J 2J3
Phone: (902)454-0322
E-mail: gans@chebucto.ns.ca
Home Page: http://www.chebucto.ns.ca/Recreation/GANS

Formerly: (1982) Royal N.S. Historical Society - Genealogical Committee.

• 9909 • **Life Membership**
To recognize outstanding leadership and achievement in the field of genealogy. Members of the association may be nominated by an ad hoc committee. A scroll is awarded at the annual meeting. Established in 1985.

• 9910 •
General Aviation Manufacturer Association
Peter J. Bunce, Pres./CEO
1400 K St. NW, Ste. 801
Washington, DC 20005
Phone: (202)393-1500
Fax: (202)842-4063
E-mail: pbunce@gama.aero
Home Page: http://www.gama.aero

• 9911 • **GAMA Excellence in Aviation Education Award**
To recognize educators who bring a better understanding of general aviation to students. Any teacher, grades K-12, who demonstrates a creative, original, and innovative use of aviation and has the ability to motivate students in the subject of aviation is eligible. Deadline for applications is January 31. A free "Discovery Flight" and a certificate are awarded annually. Established in 1989. Formerly: (1995) GAMA Learn to Fly Award for Excellence in Aviation Education.

• 9912 •
General Commission on Archives and History of the United Methodist Church
Dr. Charles Yrigoyen Jr., Gen.Sec.
PO Box 127
36 Madison Ave.
Madison, NJ 07940
Phone: (973)408-3189
Fax: (973)408-3909
E-mail: research@gcah.org
Home Page: http://www.gcah.org

• 9913 • **Jesse Lee Prize**
To recognize the best book-length manuscript dealing with some phase of the history of American Methodism. The Commission underwrites the publication of the winning manuscript by providing up to $2,000 towards the publication. Awarded every four years. Wstablished in 1966 by the Association of Methodist Historical Societies.

• 9914 • **John Harrison Ness Memorial Seminary Award**
To encourage historical study among United Methodist seminarians. Students of United Methodist and other seminaries accredited by the Association of Theological Schools who submit 5,000-10,000 word papers by February 1 on United Methodist history are eligible. A first prize of $200; and second prize of $100 are presented annually. Established in 1968. Renamed in 1980 by John H. Ness, Jr., in memory of his father, John H. Ness. Formerly: (1980) Seminary Award.

• 9915 •
General Federation of Women's Clubs
Gabrielle Smith, Exec.Dir.
1734 N St. NW
Washington, DC 20036-2990
Phone: (202)347-3168
Toll-Free: 800-443-GFWC
Fax: (202)835-0246
E-mail: gfwc@gfwc.org
Home Page: http://www.gfwc.org

• 9916 • **Jane Cunningham Croly/GFWC Print Journalism Award**
To honor the print journalist whose writing demonstrates a concern for women's rights, awareness of women's strengths and/or an attempt to counter sexism. Members are not eligible. A monetary award of $1,000 plus travel and expenses to the annual convention are presented.

• 9917 •
General Mills, Inc.
General Mills, Inc.
1 General Mills Blvd.
PO Box 9452
Minneapolis, MN 55440
Phone: (612)330-8889
Toll-Free: 800-767-4466
Fax: (612)330-7384
Home Page: http://www.pillsbury.com/bakeoff

• 9918 • **Pillsbury Bake-Off (R) Contest**
To recognize cooking skills and creativity in developing a recipe using designated Pillsbury products. There are six recipe categories: Dinner Made Easy; Wake Up to Breakfast; Simple Snacks; Weekends Made Special; Cooking for Two; and Brand New You. One hundred finalists are selected and receive an expense-paid trip to the contest site, where they prepare their recipes for final judging. Prizes include a $1,000,000 grand prize plus additional cash prizes. Awarded biennially. Established in 1949.

• 9919 •
General Motors Cancer Research Foundation
Connie Hogan, Contact
300 Renaissance Ctr.
Detroit, MI 48265-3000
Phone: (313)556-6028
Phone: (313)556-5000
Fax: (313)974-4451
E-mail: mary.ruemker@duke.edu
Home Page: http://www.gm.com/company/gmability/philanthropy/cancer_research

• 9920 • **Charles F. Kettering Medal**
For recognition of the most outstanding recent contribution to the diagnosis or treatment of cancer. The prize is given for a discovery or major contribution and with rare exception, is awarded in its entirety to one individual. However, in exceptional cases where research by two individuals, whether or not they worked together, interacted in important ways to create the prizeworthy work, the two persons can be selected to share a prize equally. The work must have been published in a recognized scientific or medical journal. Recipients must be living at the time of the official public announcement of the prizewinners. Recency of the contribution is defined as within the past 15 years. Earlier discoveries may be honored if their significance has been recognized only recently. Prizewinners are selected from nominations of the current prize year and, when available, from exceptionally well qualified candidates of the prior two years. Selections are made by an Awards Assembly composed of internationally prominent basic and clinical scientists. The deadline for nominations is September 30. A monetary prize of $100,000 and a gold medal are awarded annually. Established in 1978 in memory of Charles F. "Boss" Kettering, a gifted inventor, a General Motors Director, and a pioneer in establishing the General Motors Research Laboratories.

• 9921 • **Charles S. Mott Medal**
For recognition of the most outstanding recent contribution related to the causes or ultimate prevention of human cancer. The prize is given for a discovery or major contribution and with rare exception, is awarded in its entirety to one individual. However, in exceptional cases where research by two individuals, whether or not they worked together, interacted in important ways to create the prizeworthy work, the two persons can be selected to share a prize equally. The work must have been published in a recognized scientific or medical journal. Recipients must be living at the time of the official public announcement of the prizewinners. Recency of the contribution is defined as within the past 15 years. Earlier discoveries may be honored if their significance has been recognized only recently. Prizewinners are selected from nominations of the current prize year and, when available, from exceptionally well qualified candidates of the prior two years. The selections are made by an Awards Assembly composed of internationally prominent basic and clinical scientists. The deadline for nominations is September 30. A monetary prize of $100,000 and a gold medal are awarded annually. Established in 1978 in memory of Charles S. Mott, dean of the General

Motors Directors, a noted philanthropist and public benefactor.

• 9922 • **Alfred P. Sloan, Jr. Medal**

For recognition of the most outstanding recent basic science contribution to cancer research. The prize is given for a discovery or major contribution and with rare exception, is awarded in its entirety to one individual. However, in exceptional cases where research by two individuals, whether or not they worked together, interacted in important ways to create the prizeworthy work, the two persons can be selected to share a prize equally. The work must have been published in a recognized scientific or medical journal. Recipients must be living at the time of the official public announcement of the prizewinners. Recency of the contribution is defined as within the past 15 years. Earlier discoveries may be honored if their significance has been recognized only recently. Prizewinners are selected from nominations of the current prize year and, when available, from exceptionally well qualified candidates of the prior two years. The selections are made by an Awards Assembly composed of internationally prominent basic and clinical scientists. The deadline for nominations is September 30. A monetary prize of $100,000 and a gold medal are awarded annually. Established in 1978 in memory of Alfred P. Sloan, Jr., who is credited with building General Motors into one of the world's largest corporations and had a strong personal commitment to finding a cure for cancer.

• 9923 •
Genesis Academy
Karen Callahan, Dir.
City Colleges Center
640 N 1st Ave.
Phoenix, AZ 85003
Phone: (602)223-4200
Fax: (602)223-4210
E-mail: lbleuze@yahoo.com
Home Page: http://www.genesisacademy.com

• 9924 • **Honorary Fellow of the Genesis Academy**

To recognize the distinguished service and accomplishment in the fields of education, peace, and international brotherhood. Established in 1989.

• 9925 • **Honorary Fellow of the Photographic Society**

To recognize individuals for excellence in photography and for individuals with 20 or more years of experience who have made significant contributions to the field of photographic service. Established in 1990.

• 9926 • **Mandayam Chakravarthi Krishnan Award for Educational Excellence**

To recognize the female Indian postgraduate student with the best undergraduate marks on her course work. Applicants should have completed their first degree at an Indian University and be registered or be intending to register for a higher degree in the field of education. Awarded in February.

• 9927 • **The Rose of Sharon Award**

To recognize the female Eastern Indian postgraduate student with the best undergraduate marks on her course work. Applicants may have completed their first degree at a university and be registered or be intending to register for a higher degree in the United States. Winner receives $100.

• 9928 •
Genetic Alliance
Sharon Terry MSW, Pres./CEO
4301 Connecticut Ave. NW, Ste. 404
Washington, DC 20008
Phone: (202)966-5557
Toll-Free: 800-336-4363
Fax: (202)966-8553
E-mail: info@geneticalliance.org
Home Page: http://www.geneticalliance.org

• 9929 • **Art of Listening Award**

To recognize professionals who demonstrate exceptional care and concern by listening to those affected by genetic disorders. Professionals including physicians, nurses, social workers, or genetic counselors are eligible. The winner receives a framed rendering of a conch shell. Travel and lodging expenses of the winner and the nominator are also covered by the award. Awarded annually. Established in 1990.

• 9930 • **Art of Reporting Award**

In recognition of the contributions of science writers and broadcast journalists to advancing an understanding of consumer perspectives and social issues in reports relating to genetics. Nominations must be received by June of each year prior to the Annual Meeting of the Alliance of Genetic Support Groups. Awarded annually when merited. Established in 1993.

• 9931 •
Genetics Society of America
Elaine Strass, Exec.Dir.
9650 Rockville Pike
Bethesda, MD 20814-3998
Phone: (301)634-7300
Toll-Free: (866)486-4363
Fax: (301)530-7079
E-mail: estrass@genetics-gsa.org
Home Page: http://www.genetics-gsa.org

• 9932 • **Genetics Society of America Medal**

For recognition of a particularly outstanding contribution to genetics in the last 15 years. Members of the Society may be nominated. Established in 1981.

• 9933 • **Thomas Hunt Morgan Medal**

For recognition of a lifetime contribution to genetics. Members of the Society may be nominated. Established in 1981.

• 9934 •
Genetics Society of Canada
Rama Singh, Pres.
141 Laurier Ave. W., Ste. 112
53 Slalom Gate Rd.
Ottawa, ON, Canada K1P 5J3
Phone: (613)232-9459
Fax: (613)594-5190
E-mail: ellas@on.aibn.com
Home Page: http://life.biology.mcmaster.ca/GSC

• 9935 • **Award of Excellence**

To recognize distinguished contributions of a Canadian or foreign professional geneticist to genetic research and/or teaching and to encourage superior genetic studies in Canada. A plaque is awarded annually. Established in 1976.

• 9936 • **Presidential Citation**

To recognize an individual who has made outstanding contributions in genetics. Awarded annually.

• 9937 • **Young Scientist Award**

To recognize a notable paper or series of related papers based on original research in genetics or allied fields completed and published by the candidate in a refereed journal during the 15 years period immediately following the completion of a first degree. Established in 1987.

• 9938 •
Geochemical Society
Mr. Seth Davis, Business Mgr.
Washington University
EPSC
One Brookings Dr., CB 1169
St. Louis, MO 63130-4899
Phone: (314)935-4131
Fax: (314)935-4121
E-mail: gsoffice@gs.wustl.edu
Home Page: http://gs.wustl.edu

• 9939 • **V. M. Goldschmidt Medal**

To recognize major achievements in geochemistry or cosmochemistry, consisting of either a single outstanding contribution, or a series of publications that have had great influence on the field. A medal and an honorarium endowed by the late Lester W. Strock are awarded annually. Established in 1984.

• 9940 •
Geographical Society of Philadelphia
PO Box 67
Haverford, PA 19041
Phone: (610)649-5220
Fax: (610)645-9460
E-mail: geosocphil@aol.com
Home Page: http://www.geographicalsociety.org

• 9941 • Henry Grier Bryant Gold Medal
To recognize an individual for distinguished service to geography. A gold medal is awarded irregularly. Established in 1933.

• 9942 • Angelo Heilprin Literary Award Medal
To recognize distinguished writing about the world and its people. Authors of books with geographical background are eligible. A gold medal is awarded irregularly. Established in 1955.

• 9943 • Elisha Kent Kane Medal
To recognize an individual for eminent geographical research. A gold medal is awarded irregularly. Established in 1900.

• 9944 •
Geological Society of America
John W. Hess, Exec.Dir.
3300 Penrose Pl.
PO Box 9140
Boulder, CO 80301-1806
Phone: (303)447-2020
Phone: (303)357-1000
Toll-Free: 888-443-4472
Fax: (303)357-1070
E-mail: gsa@geosociety.org
Home Page: http://www.geosociety.org

• 9945 • Kirk Bryan Award
To honor the author of a published paper of distinction advancing the science of geomorphology or some related field such as Pleistocene geology. Papers published during the preceding five years must be nominated by February 1. A monetary award of $500 and a certificate are awarded annually. Established in 1951. Sponsored by the Quaternary Geology and Geomorphology Division.

• 9946 • E. B. Burwell, Jr., Award
To honor the author or authors of a published paper of distinction that advances the knowledge concerning principles or practice of engineering geology, or of related fields of applied soil, or rock mechanics where the role of geology is emphasized. The deadline for receipt of nominations is February 1. An embossed certificate is awarded annually when merited. Established in 1968. Sponsored by the Engineering Geology Division.

• 9947 • Gilbert H. Cady Award
To honor contributions that advance the field of coal geology in North America. Contributions by workers outside North America deemed to advance coal geology in North America may also be considered. The deadline for receipt of nominations is February 1. A silver tray and a certificate are awarded annually when merited. Established in 1971. Sponsored by the Coal Geology Division.

• 9948 • Arthur L. Day Medal
To recognize outstanding distinction in contributions to geological knowledge through the application of physics and chemistry and to inspire further efforts in the field. The deadline for receipt of nominations is February 1. A gold medal, a bronze replica, and the remission of society dues for life are awarded annually when merited. Established in 1948.

• 9949 • G. K. Gilbert Award
To recognize an individual who has contributed in an outstanding manner to the solution of fundamental problems of planetary geology in its broadest sense, including planetary geology, geochemistry, mineralogy, petrology, and geophysics, and the field of meteoritics. Such contributions may consist either of a single publication or a series of publications that have had great influence on the field. Normally the award will not be shared, except in highly unusual cases such as independent discoveries or joint work where the contributions of the co-workers are essentially equal. The recipient may be a citizen of any country and need not be a member of the society. The award may not be given posthumously unless the decision to give the award was made prior to the death of the awardee. The deadline for receipt of nominations is February 1. An engrossed certificate and an engraved plaque are awarded annually when merited. Established in 1983. Sponsored by the Planetary Geology Division.

• 9950 • GSA Distinguished Service Award
To recognize individuals for their exceptional service to the Society. Members, fellows, student associates, or, in exceptional circumstances, employees, may be nominated for consideration. The deadline for receipt of nominations is February 1. An engraved, free-standing plaque is awarded annually, or less frequently, at the discretion of the Council. Established in 1988.

• 9951 • History of Geology Award
To recognize an individual for contributions of fundamental importance to the understanding of the history of the geological sciences. The deadline for nominations is February 1. An engrossed certificate and a pewter Revere bowl are awarded annually when merited. Established in 1981. Sponsored by the History of Geology Division.

• 9952 • Honorary Fellow
To recognize internationally outstanding geologists who have distinguished themselves in geological investigations or in notable service to the society. Except in unusual circumstances, the candidates are normally non-North Americans who live and work outside of North America. Normally, three are named annually. The deadline for receipt of nominations is February 1. An engrossed certificate and life membership in the society are awarded annually when merited. The award was originally established in 1889 as the Correspondents category of membership.

• 9953 • O. E. Meinzer Award
To recognize the author(s) of a published paper or body of papers of distinction advancing the science of hydrogeology or some related field such as ground-water hydraulics or geochemistry. The deadline for receipt of nominations is February 1. A certificate, an engraved rotating silver Revere-style bowl, and a miniature silver replica are awarded annually when merited. Established in 1963. Sponsored by the Hydrogeology Division.

• 9954 • Penrose Medal Award
To recognize eminent research in pure geology and outstanding original contributions or achievements which mark a decided advance in the science of geology. The deadline for receipt of nominations is February 1. A gold medal, a bronze replica, and the remission of Society dues for life are awarded annually when merited. Established in 1927.

• 9955 • Rip Rapp Archaeological Geology Award
To recognize an individual who has contributed in an outstanding manner to the interdisciplinary field of archaeological geology. The recipient of the award need not be a member of the Geological Society of America nor a citizen of the United States. The deadline for receipt of nominations is February 15. An engrossed certificate and a small pewter Revere bowl are awarded annually when merited. Renamed in 1993. Established in 1982. Sponsored by the Archaeological Geology Division. Formerly: (1993) Archaeological Geology Division Award.

• 9956 • Structural Geology and Tectonics Division Career Contribution Award
To recognize an individual for career achievements that have led to major advances in the discipline of structural geology or tectonics. The recipient of the award may be a citizen of any country and need not be a member of the Society. The deadline for receipt of nominations is February 1. An engraved plaque and a certificate are awarded annually when merited. Established in 1984. Sponsored by the Structural Geology and Tectonics Division. Formerly: Best Paper Award.

• 9957 • George P. Woollard Award
To recognize an individual who has contributed in an outstanding manner to geology through the application of the principles and techniques of geophysics. The recipient of the award may be a citizen of any country and need not be a member of the Geological Society of America. The deadline for receipt of nominations is February 1. An engrossed certificate is presented annually when merited. Established in 1981. Sponsored by the Geophysics Division.

• 9958 • Young Scientist Award (Donath Medal)
To recognize a young scientist for outstanding achievement in contributing to geologic knowledge through original research that marks a major advance in the earth sciences. Individuals who are 35 years of age or younger during the year the award is presented are eligible. The deadline for receipt of nominations is February 1. A monetary award of $20,000, a gold medal,

called the Donath Medal, and a bronze replica are awarded annually when merited. Established in 1988 by Dr. and Mrs. Fred A. Donath.

• 9959 •
Georgetown University
Institute for the Study of Diplomacy
School of Foreign Service
1316 36th St. NW
Washington, DC 20007
Phone: (202)965-5735
Fax: (202)965-5811
E-mail: ejc28@georgetown.edu
Home Page: http://www12.georgetown.edu/sfs/isd/

• 9960 • **Edward Weintal Prize for Diplomatic Reporting**
To honor journalists for distinguished reporting on American foreign policy and diplomacy. One award is given to a member of the print media, and one to a member of the television and radio industries. The deadline for submissions is January. Nominations may be made on the basis of a specific story or series or on the basis of a journalist's overall news coverage. Monetary prizes totaling $10,000 and certificates are awarded annually. Established in 1974 in memory of Edward Weintal (1901-1973), a diplomatic correspondent for *Newsweek* magazine.

• 9961 •
Georgia Agricultural Commodity Commission for Peanuts
PO Box 967
Tifton, GA 31794
Phone: (229)386-3470
Fax: (229)386-3501
Formerly: Georgia Peanut Commission.

• 9962 • **Distinguished Service Award**
To honor an individual who contributed the most to the growth and development of the Georgia peanut industry. A plaque is awarded annually. Established in 1966.

• 9963 • **Georgia Media Award**
To recognize a company or individual involved in the dissemination of peanut information and general publicity of peanuts through radio, television, newspapers, or other media. A recommendation to the Executive Committee is made by the staff of the Commission working on a daily basis with the media. Awarded each year at the annual meeting. Established in 1985.

• 9964 • **Georgia Peanut Export Award**
To recognize a company or individual who has made significant contributions to the Commission in the area of exports, export market development and, in general, helping to expand world-wide use of Georgia peanuts. Awarded by the committee when appropriate. Established in 1984.

• 9965 • **Georgia Peanut Research and Education Award**
To recognize and honor the work of individuals engaged in research and the implementation of this research in the field through education (Extension Service activities), and to stimulate peanut research and education. Awarded each year at the annual meeting. The award generally rotates between honorees in the areas of research and education. Established in 1985.

• 9966 • **Peanut Hall of Fame**
This, the highest award from the Georgia Peanut Commission, is given to an individual or company who has provided leadership and stimulated industry growth, development, research, and education. The honoree's portrait is placed in the Board Room of the Commission. Presentations are made when appropriate. Established in 1982.

• 9967 • **Special Awards**
To recognize outstanding contributions to the Georgia peanut industry. Awarded annually. Established in 1987. In addition, a Special Memorial Award may be presented.

• 9968 •
Georgia Public Policy Foundation
Rogers Wade, Pres. and CEO
6100 Lake Forrest Dr., Ste. 110
Atlanta, GA 30328
Phone: (404)256-4050
Toll-Free: 800-423-8867
Fax: (404)256-9909
E-mail: gppf@gppf.org
Home Page: http://www.gppf.org

• 9969 • **Freedom Award**
Recognizes advancement of the principles of free enterprise, limited government, and individual responsibility. All Gerogians are eligible. Awarded annually.

• 9970 • **Georgia No Excuses Awards**
For high-poverty, high-achieving schools

• 9971 •
Georgia Writers Association and Young Georgia Writers
Geri Taran, Exec.Dir.
1071 Steeple Run
Lawrenceville, GA 30043
Phone: (678)407-0703
Fax: (678)407-9917
E-mail: director@georgiawriters.org
Home Page: http://www.georgiawriters.org

Formerly: (1988) Dixie Council of Authors and Journalists.

• 9972 • **Georgia Author of the Year Awards**
For annual recognition of contributions to literature in the following awards categories: Creative Non Fiction, Fiction, Short Stories, First Novel, Children's and Young Adult Literature, and Poetry. Eligible books are published in the calendar year preceding the award and are written by authors living and working in Georgia. A Lifetime Achievement Award is presented to an individual, not necessarily a writer, i.e., editor, publisher. A trophy is awarded in each category, annually. Established in 1964.

• 9973 •
German Marshall Fund of the United States
Craig Kennedy, Pres.
1744 R St. NW
Washington, DC 20009
Phone: (202)745-3950
Fax: (202)265-1662
E-mail: info@gmfus.org
Home Page: http://www.gmfus.org

• 9974 • **German Marshall Fund of the United States Fellowships and Awards**
To support and carry out activities that: (1) promote a more informed understanding of issues that arise between Western Europe and the United States; and (2) permit policymakers to learn how their counterparts on the other side of the Atlantic deal with certain domestic problems common to industrial societies. The Fund makes grants in these four program areas: (1) Economic Cooperation and Competition: (a) Challenges to the U.S. and Europe: and (b) Competitiveness and Human Resources: (2) Supporting Reform in Central and Eastern Europe: (a) Political Development Program; (b) Environmental Reform Program; (3) The Environment: International and Cooperation and Innovation and (4) Policy and Opinion Leaders: (a) Leadership Networks; (b) Journalists; (c) Scholars and Teachers. The Fund's four program areas include a number of fellowships. Some fellowship programs invite applications; in other programs, fellows are selected by independent boards or program officers. The German Marshall Fund of the United States is an independent American organization established in 1972 by a gift (renewed in 1985) from the Federal Republic of Germany as a memorial to the Marshall Plan, the American program which helped Europe rebuild after the destruction of World War II.

• 9975 •
German Shorthaired Pointer Club of Orange County
Karen Detterich, Pres.
1603 Sunup Circle
Riverside, CA 92501-1717
Phone: (909)682-6982
Fax: (909)682-6981

• 9976 • **Recognition of achievement**
For AKC titles completed during the year (previous). Recognition award bestowed annually.

• 9977 •
German Society of Pennsylvania
Mindy Ehrhart, Administrator
611 Spring Garden St.
Philadelphia, PA 19123
Phone: (215)627-2332
Fax: (215)627-5297
E-mail: contact@germansociety.org
Home Page: http://www.germansociety.org

• 9978 • **Language Proficiency Award**
Bestowed to high school students for proficiency in German and to high school teachers for excellence in teaching German. Awarded annually.

• 9979 •
German Texan Heritage Society
Van D. Massirer, Pres.
507 E 10th St.
PO Box 684171
Austin, TX 78768-4171
Phone: (512)482-0927
Toll-Free: (866)482-4847
Fax: (512)482-0636
E-mail: info@germantexans.org
Home Page: http://www.gths.net

• 9980 • **Ehrenstein Award**
Recognizes outstanding volunteerism. Awarded annually.

• 9981 •
Germans From Russia Heritage Society
Rachel Schmidt, Officer Mgr.
1125 W Turnpike Ave.
Bismarck, ND 58501-8115
Phone: (701)223-6167
Fax: (701)223-4421
E-mail: rachel@grhs.org
Home Page: http://www.grhs.com

• 9982 • **Literary Awards**
For recognition of articles written for the Society's publication, the *Heritage Review,* on the subject of ethnic heritage. Nominees are judged by a committee. A plaque is awarded each year at the annual convention. Established in 1979 in memory of Dr. Joseph S. Height.

• 9983 •
Germany Philatelic Society
Mike Peter, Sec.-Treas.
PO Box 6547
Chesterfield, MO 63006-6547
Fax: (410)757-6857
E-mail: chris@gps.nu
Home Page: http://www.gps.nu

• 9984 • **George A. Blizil Memorial Literature Award**
For recognition of the best article submitted for publication in the *German Postal Specialist.* Members may submit articles for selection by the editor and president. A monetary prize is awarded annually. Established in 1985 in memory of George A. Blizil, former editor of the *German Postal Specialist.*

• 9985 • **Herman L. Halle Research Award**
For recognition of the exhibit by a member of the Society showing the best original research. An engraved tray is awarded annually at the national convention. Established in 1988 in honor of Herman L. Halle.

• 9986 •
Gerontological Society of America
Carol A. Schutz, Exec.Dir.
1030 15th St. NW, Ste. 250
Washington, DC 20005
Phone: (202)842-1275
Fax: (202)842-1150
E-mail: geron@geron.org
Home Page: http://www.geron.org

• 9987 • **BSS Student Research Award**
To recognize student research at the pre-dissertation and dissertation level. The winner receives a copy of the *Handbook on Aging* (Social Sciences and Psychology editions) and a one-year membership in the Society. Membership in the Behavioral and Social Sciences Section is required.

• 9988 • **Clinical Medicine Person-in-Training Award**
To recognize a student of the Clinical Medicine section for the best student 1,500-word paper and presentation of the work at the society's annual scientific meeting. A monetary prize of $500 is awarded annually.

• 9989 • **Clinical Medicine Research Award**
To recognize an outstanding research paper by an individual engaged in a post doctoral fellowship. Abstracts must be submitted by April 2 for the annual meeting. A monetary award of $1,000 and a certificate are presented annually. Established in 1987 and administered by the Clinical Medicine Section.

• 9990 • **Distinguished Creative Contribution to Gerontology Award**
To honor theoretical papers, original and/or elegant research designs, or papers which address with unusual creativity a problem in applied gerontology. Papers published during the five previous calendar years must be submitted by July 1. A plaque is presented during the annual meeting. In addition, the recipient is announced in *Gerontology News.* Established in 1987 by The Behavioral and Social Sciences Section.

• 9991 • **Distinguished Mentorship in Gerontology Award**
To recognize individuals who have fostered excellence and who have had a major impact on the field of gerontology by virtue of their mentoring, and whose inspiration is sought by students and colleagues. Membership in the Behavioral and Social Sciences Section is required.

• 9992 • **Joseph T. Freeman Award**
To recognize a physician prominent in the field of aging - both in research and practice. Members of the GSA's Clinical Medicine Section must be nominated by July 1. The lecture is delivered during the annual meeting. A monetary award of $250 and a certificate are presented annually. Established in 1977 through a bequest from a patient's estate as a tribute to Dr. Joseph T. Freeman, one of the Clinical Medicine Section's distinguished members. Formerly: (1995) Freeman Lectureship in Geriatrics.

• 9993 • **Geron Corporation - Samuel Goldstein Distinguished Publication Award**
To recognize the best paper published in the Society's *Journal of Gerontology: Biological Sciences* for the period of May of the previous year to March of the current year. A monetary award of $1,500 and reimbursement of travel expenses up to $1,000 are awarded at the annual scientific meeting's Biological Sciences Scientific Program, where the winner will present his/her paper. Established in 1994.

• 9994 • **Richard Kalish Innovative Publication Award**
To recognize insightful and innovative publications on aging and life course development in the behavioral and social sciences. Publications published in the past three years and written in English are eligible. A monetary prize of $500 is awarded annually at the annual meeting. Established in honor of Dr. Richard Kalish. Sponsored by Baywood Publishing Company.

• 9995 • **Donald P. Kent Award**
To recognize a member who exemplifies the highest standard of professional leadership through teaching, service, and the interpretation of gerontology to the larger society. Nominees must be fellows of the Society. The deadline for nominations is May 5. The award requires a lecture at the time of the annual scientific meeting. Established in 1973 to honor Donald P. Kent, a pioneer in the field of gerontology.

• 9996 • **Robert W. Kleemeier Award**
To recognize a member for outstanding research in the field of gerontology. Nominees must be fellows of the Society. The deadline for nominations is May 5. The award requires a lecture at the time of the annual scientific meeting. Established in 1965 in memory of Robert W. Kleemeier, the Society's twenty-first president. Formerly: Searle Award.

• 9997 • **George Sacher Student Award**
To recognize the best student presentation by a GSA member at the Society's annual scientific meeting. A $500 monetary prize is awarded annually.

• 9998 • **Nathan Shock New Investigator Award**
To recognize outstanding original research in the field of gerontology through basic biological research. The deadline is May 5. A monetary award of $1,500 and a certificate are presented

Awards are arranged in alphabetical order below their administering organizations

at the Biological Sciences Section annual business meeting at the Society's annual meeting. Established in 1986 to honot Dr. Nathan Shock, a pioneer in gerontologiocal research.

• 9999 • Social Research, Policy & Practice Student Research Award
To recognize the best member student paper on the SRPP Annual Scientific Meeting program. A monetary prize of $500 is awarded by the Social Research, Policy & Practice Section. Formerly: (1997) Student Research Award.

• 10000 •
Get Involved for Mental Health
Michael Sitton, Pres.
647 Camino de los Mares, No. 108-251
San Clemente, CA 92673
Phone: (949)493-5898
Fax: (949)496-4694
E-mail: getinvolved4mh@cox.net
Home Page: http://www.getinvolved4mh.org

• 10001 • Silver Ribbon Award to Outstanding Volunteer
For child living with a mentally ill sibling or parent. Scholarship awarded annually.

• 10002 •
Getty Grant Program
Deborah Marrow, Dir.
1200 Getty Ctr. Dr., Ste. 800
Los Angeles, CA 90049-1679
Phone: (310)440-7300
Phone: (310)440-7320
Fax: (310)440-7703
E-mail: communications@getty.edu
Home Page: http://www.getty.edu/grants

• 10003 • Conservation Guest Scholars
To support professionals and scholars in conservation and allied fields to pursue independent research while in residence at the Getty Center. Designed to encourage innovative ideas and perspectives on heritage conservation, the program welcomes proposals that address the theoretical underpinnings of conservation and explore issues and applications related to conservation in the visual arts (including sites, buildings, and objects). Grants range from three to nine months in duration. Grantees will receive a stipend, and office at the Getty Center, and offsite housing.

• 10004 • Curatorial Research Fellowships
To support the professional scholarly development of curators by providing them with time off from regular museum duties to undertake shortterm research or study projects. Applicants must be full-time curators and employed at museums with art collections. Fellowships provide stipends for research periods of one to three months.

• 10005 • J. Paul Getty Postdoctoral Fellowships in the History of Art and the Humanities
To provide twelve-month periods of support for scholars whose doctoral degrees have been conferred within the past six years, to pursue interpretive research projects to make a substantial and original contribution to the understanding of art and its history. The fellowships provide a stipend of $35,000 for a research period of twelve months and the deadline is November 1. Established 1985.

• 10006 • Getty Scholars
Nine-month fellowships for senior scholars pursuing research related to the Institute's current specific theme. As part of the scholar community at the Getty Center, grantees will receive a stipend, an office at the Research Institute, and off-site housing.

• 10007 • Library Research Grants
To provide short-term support to scholars at all levels to pursue independent projects that will benefit from research in the collections housed in the Getty library. Projects need not relate to the theme of the scholar year. As part of the scholar community at the Getty Center, Grantees will receive partial support for costs related to research, travel, and living expenses for periods ranging from several days to a maximum of three months.

• 10008 • Senior Collaborative Research Grants
To provide opportunities for teams of scholars to collaborate on interpretive research projects that offer new explanations of art and its history. Teams may consist of two or more art historians, or of an art historian and one or more scholars from other disciplines. Funding is also available for the research and planning of scholarly exhibitions. Teams for these projects should include scholars from both museums and universities. Grant periods and stipends vary according to the needs of individual projects, but generally support research periods of 1-2 years. The deadline is November 1. Established in 1988.

• 10009 • Visiting Scholars
One to three months for senior scholars pursuing research related to the Getty Research Institute's current theme. As part of the scholar community at the Getty Center, grantees will receive a stipend, an office at the Research Institute, and off-site housing.

• 10010 •
Geyer - McAllister Publications
Gordon T. Hughes II, Pres. and CEO
% American Business Media
675 3rd Ave.
New York, NY 10017
Phone: (212)661-6360
Fax: (212)370-0736
E-mail: info@abmmail.com
Home Page: http://www.americanbusinessmedia.com

• 10011 • *Gifts and Decorative Accessories* Merchandising Achievement Awards
For recognition of excellence in store design, store promotion and display, and community service. Retailers of gifts, china and glass, home accessories, as well as greeting cards and social stationery are eligible. Gold and Silver Crystal awards are presented in each of the three categories. Established in 1951.

• 10012 • McAllister Editorial Fellowship Award
Promotes the study of writing for business-to-business publications. A crystal bowl and an honorarium are awarded. Established in 1995 in honor of Donald McAllister, Sr., Chairman of the Geyer-McAllister Co.

• 10013 • *Playthings* Merchandising Achievement Awards
For recognition of excellence in store design and store promotion. Retailers of toys, hobbies, crafts, dolls, and wheel goods are eligible. Awards are presented in the form of First Awards, Awards of Merit, Commendation Awards and a Special Achievement Award. Large gold plaques are awarded in each of the four categories. Silver plaques are also presented. Established in 1970.

• 10014 •
GI Joe Collectors Club
James DeSimone, Contact
PMB 9204
150 S Glenoaks Blvd.
Burbank, CA 91510
E-mail: gijoe@gijoeinformation.com
Home Page: http://www.gijoeinformation.com

• 10015 • GI Joe Fan Award
Award of recognition. Given by Hasbro.

• 10016 •
Giant Schnauzer Club of America
Cindy Kennard, Pres.
2376 Woodhouse Mine Rd.
West Point, CA 95255
Phone: (209)293-2339
E-mail: knokknok@castles.com
Home Page: http://www.giantschnauzerclubofamerica.com

• 10017 • Giant of the Year (The Gaines Award)
To recognize the member who, in the opinion of the members, has done the most to further the breed and/or the club during the preceding year.

• 10018 • Giant Schnauzer of the Year, Dog
To recognize the Giant Schnauzer dog that accumulates the greatest total number of points according to the point system. In addition, the following prizes are awarded: Giant Schnauzer of the Year, Bitch - to the Giant Schnauzer bitch that accumulates the greatest total number of

points according to the point system; Giant Schnauzer of the Year, Owner-Handled Dog - to the owner-handled dog receiving the most points; Giant Schnauzer of the Year, Owner-Handled Bitch - to the owner-handled bitch receiving the most points; Giant Schnauzer Obedience Dog of the Year - to the Giant Schnauzer dog that earns the greatest number of points as outlined in the point system; Giant Schnauzer Obedience Bitch of the Year - to the Giant Schnauzer bitch that earns the greatest number of points as outlined in the point system; Giant Schnauzer Stud Dog of the Year - to the Giant Schnauzer dog having the most offspring finishing championships during the calendar year; Giant Schnauzer Brood Bitch of the Year - to the Giant Schnauzer dog having the most offspring finishing championships during the calendar year; Champion/Companion Dog Excellent Award - both titles must be obtained in the same country, and limited to GSCA members; and Best in Show Award. Awarded annually.

• 10019 • **Outstanding Giant Schnauzer Award**

To recognize Giant Schnauzers that, through their outstanding conformation and intelligence, have accomplished a feat that is a first for their breed, or an outstanding achievement that has brought recognition and honor to the breed.

• 10020 • **Prinz Wilhelm Obedience Award (The Willie Award)**

To recognize the member who, in the opinion of the Board, has done the most to further the principles of obedience training and sportsmanship.

• 10021 •
Gift from the Heart Foundation
Krystyna B. Pasek, Pres.
2653 N Narragansett Ave.
Chicago, IL 60639
Phone: (773)237-4800
Phone: (773)237-1213
Fax: (773)237-1221
E-mail: giftheart@sbcglobal.net
Home Page: http://www.giftfromtheheart.org

• 10022 • **Merit Award**

Recognizes outstanding voluntary service.

• 10023 •
Gilbert and Sullivan Society of Austin
Libby Weed, Pres.
2026 Guadalupe, Ste. 309
Austin, TX 78705
Phone: (512)472-4772

• 10024 • **Young Musician Scholarship**

For financial need/interest in pursuing musical studies. Scholarship awarded periodically.

• 10025 •
Gilmanton Historical Society
Richard P. Arms, VP
PO Box 236
Gilmanton, NH 03237
Phone: (603)364-7405
E-mail: rparms@worldpath.net
Home Page: http://www.museumsusa.org/default.aspx?p=200476&ListingID=1163512

• 10026 • **Gilmanton Historic Essay Competition**

For eighth grade student at Gilmanton School. Recognition award bestowed annually.

• 10027 •
Gilpin County Arts Association
PO Box 98
Central City, CO 80427
Phone: (303)642-0649
E-mail: ulemorgan@att.net

• 10028 • **Gilpin County Arts Association Annual Exhibition**

For recognition of outstanding art in the fields of painting, sculpture, crafts, and photography. Works selected by the juror for exhibition are eligible for awards. Monetary awards totalling $2,000 are awarded annually. Established in 1947.

• 10029 •
Girl Scouts of the Pioneer Council
Janice Booth, Chief Exec. Officer
250 S New Hope Rd.
Gastonia, NC 28054-4805
Phone: (704)864-3245
Toll-Free: 800-627-6031
Fax: (704)864-9020
E-mail: council@girlscoutspc.org
Home Page: http://www.girlscoutspc.org

• 10030 • **Sylvia Holmes Scholarship**

For graduating senior in the jurisdiction that has been accepted to an accredited school or university. Scholarship awarded annually.

• 10031 •
Glass Art Society
Pamela Figenshow Koss, Exec.Dir.
3131 Western Ave., Ste. 414
Seattle, WA 98121
Phone: (206)382-1305
Fax: (206)382-2630
E-mail: info@glassart.org
Home Page: http://www.glassart.org

• 10032 • **Honorary Lifetime Membership Award**

Annual award of recognition.

• 10033 • **Lifetime Achievement Award**

Annual award of recognition. Artists are eligible.

• 10034 •
The Glaucoma Foundation
Scott R. Christensen, Pres./CEO
80 Maiden Ln., Ste. 1206
New York, NY 10038
Phone: (212)285-0080
Phone: (212)651-1900
Fax: (212)651-1888
E-mail: info@glaucomafoundation.org
Home Page: http://www.glaucomafoundation.org

• 10035 • **Kitty Carlisle Hart Award of Merit for Lifetime Achievement**

To honor an individual whose life has been profoundly affected by glaucoma and who has responded to the challenge with courage and distinction.

• 10036 •
Gleeson Library Associates
Bill O'Brien, Pres.
University of San Francisco
2130 Fulton St.
San Francisco, CA 94117-1080
Phone: (415)422-2036
Fax: (415)422-2233
E-mail: calhouns@usfca.edu
Home Page: http://www.usfca.edu/library/rarebook/gla

• 10037 • **Sir Thomas More Medal for Book Collecting**

To recognize outstanding private book collectors of national and international rank. Winners are selected exclusively by the Board of Directors of GLA. A round bronze medal with a portrait of Sir Thomas More and the inscription "Private Book Collecting: A Public Benefit" is awarded annually. The medal was established in 1968 by Fr. William J. Monihan to honor the spirit of book collecting.

• 10038 •
Gleitsman Foundation
Alan L. Gleitsman, Contact
PO Box 6888
Malibu, CA 90264
Phone: (310)457-6199
Fax: (310)457-8324
E-mail: gleits@ix.netcom.com
Home Page: http://www.gleitsman.org

• 10039 • **Citizen Activist Award**

Recognizes the exceptional achievement of people who have initiated positive social change in the United States. The amount of $100,000 is given in association with these awards.

• 10040 • **International Activist Award**

Honors individuals who have inspired social activism in the international community excluding the United States. $100,000 is given in association with the awards.

• 10041 •
Glencoe/McGraw Hill
The McGraw Hill Companies
1221 Avenue of the Americas
New York, NY 10020
Phone: (614)890-1111
Toll-Free: 800-848-1567
Fax: (614)899-4414
E-mail: customer.service@mcgraw-hill.com
Home Page: http://www.glencoe.com

• 10042 • **John Robert Gregg Award in Business Education**
To stimulate, encourage and reward outstanding contributions by an individual to the advancement of business education. The contribution may be a single achievement, or it may embrace a composite or group of achievements which are directly related to each other and lead to the contribution for which the recipient is recognized. Contributions may be made in the following areas: (1) teaching - theory, method, and/or classroom practice; (2) business and industry, with definite implications and significance for education; (3) teaching methodology; (4) professional literature; (5) research (through original research or the direction of research); (6) organizations (committees, associations, fraternities, etc.); and (7) the administration of business education programs in high schools, colleges, or business schools. The deadline for nominations is October 31. A monetary award of $1,500 and a citation are awarded annually. Established in 1953.

• 10043 •
Global Education Associates
Dr. Patricia Mische, Pres.
475 Riverside Dr., Ste. 1626B
New York, NY 10115
Phone: (212)870-3290
Fax: (212)870-2729
E-mail: gea475@aol.com
Home Page: http://globaleduc.org

• 10044 • **Jerry Mische Global Service Award**
Recognizes service to global community. Awarded annually.

• 10045 •
Global Health Council
Dr. Nils Daulaire, Pres./CEO
1111 19th St. NW, Ste. 1120
Washington, DC 20006
Phone: (202)833-5900
Fax: (202)833-0075
E-mail: ghc@globalhealth.org
Home Page: http://www.globalhealth.org

• 10046 • **International Health Advocacy Award**
To recognize individuals who have demonstrated outstanding leadership and made a major contribution by advocating international health. Nominations must be received by February 10. Awarded annually. Established in 1986.

• 10047 • **International Health Service Award for Individuals**
To recognize individuals who make an outstanding contribution to international health, usually those in the field who have not received adequate recognition. Nominations must be received by March 15. Awarded annually. Formerly: Mickey Leland Award for International Health Service.

• 10048 • **International Health Service Award for Organizations**
To recognize organizations and countries that make an outstanding contribution to international health. Nominations must be received by March 15. Awarded annually.

• 10049 • **Jonathatn Mann Award for Global Health and Human Rights**
Association Francois-Xavier Bagnoud, Doctors of the World, and The Global Health Council jointly award the cash prize to allow the recipient, either an individual or an organization, to freely pursue their work in health and human rights.

• 10050 •
Global Rights
Gay J. McDougall, Exec.Dir.
1200 18th St. NW, Ste. 602
Washington, DC 20036
Phone: (202)822-4600
Fax: (202)822-4606
E-mail: media@globalrights.org
Home Page: http://www.hrlawgroup.org

• 10051 • **Goler T. Butcher Award for Lifetime Achievement**
To recognize a lifetime of service and work in human rights, international development and world peace. Given annually at the awards dinner. Established in 1994.

• 10052 • **International Human Rights Law Award**
For recognition of outstanding and significant work of someone of international stature to the cause of human rights. Given annually at the awards dinner. Established in 1986.

• 10053 • **International Human Rights Partners Award**
To recognize an organization who works in the field with the International Human Rights Law Group. Given annually at the awards dinner. Established in 1994.

• 10054 •
Global Warming International Center
Dr. Sinyan Shen, Dir.
22W381, 75th St.
Naperville, IL 60565-9245
Phone: (630)910-1551
Fax: (630)910-1561
E-mail: gw14@globalwarming.net
Home Page: http://www.globalwarming.net

• 10055 • **The GWIC Award**
Recognizes contributions to global warming science and policy worldwide in his or her area of specialty.

• 10056 •
Godzilla Society of North America
Mr. J.D. Lees, Founder
Daikaiju Enterprises Ltd.
Box 3468
Steinbach, MB, Canada R0A 2A0
Phone: (204)326-7754
Fax: (204)326-7754
E-mail: submissions@g-fan.com
Home Page: http://www.g-fan.com

• 10057 • **Mangled Skyscraper Award**
Recognizes utstanding promotion of the Japanese monster genre. Awarded annually.

• 10058 •
Golden Gate Audubon Society
Elizabeth Murdock, Exec.Dir.
2530 San Pablo Ave., Ste. G
Berkeley, CA 94702-2047
Phone: (510)843-2222
Fax: (510)843-5351
E-mail: ggas@goldengateaudubon.org
Home Page: http://www.goldengateaudubon.org

• 10059 • **GGAS Service Awards**
To recognize individuals for significant contribution to GGAS and to its board of directors.

• 10060 • **Elsie Roemer Conservation Awards**
To recognize one member of GGAS and one member of the public for outstanding contributions in the preservation of the environment. Awarded annually.

• 10061 •
Golden Key International Honour Society
Alexander D. Perwich II, CEO
621 North Ave. NE, Ste. C-100
Atlanta, GA 30308
Phone: (404)377-2400
Toll-Free: 800-377-2401
Fax: (678)420-6757
E-mail: memberservices@goldenkey.org
Home Page: http://www.goldenkey.org

Formerly: (2001) Golden Key National Honor Society.

• 10062 • **Golden Key Scholar Awards**
To reward undergraduate students who demonstrate scholastic excellence, leadership, and community service. The winners will receive monetary awards of $10,000.

Awards are arranged in alphabetical order below their administering organizations

• 10063 •
Goldman Environmental Foundation
Amy Lyons, Exec.Dir.
211 Lincoln Blvd.
PO Box 29924
San Francisco, CA 94119
Phone: (415)345-6330
Fax: (415)345-9686
E-mail: info@goldmanprize.org
Home Page: http://www.goldmanprize.org

• 10064 • **Goldman Environmental Prize**
Represents the world's largest prize program honoring grassroots environmentalists. Six environmental heroes - one from each of the six continental regions (North America, South/Central America, Europe, Asia, Africa, and Island Nations)- are chosen annually to receive a $125,000 monetary award. Prize nominations are accepted from only two sources: a network of 21 internationally known environmental organizations; and a confidential panel of environmental experts from over 30 nations, including citizen activists and prominent policy makers. Recipients are chosen for their sustained and important efforts to protect or enhance the environment. The Prize does not grant awards for scientific, academic, or governmental activities. Examples of previous recipients' achievements include: coordinating a movement to establish the international protection of Antarctica; initiating a woman-based grassroots tree-planting effort to curtail deforestation and decertification in Kenya; leading an effort to evacuate 800 families from the toxic waste affected areas of Love Canal; organizing efforts to halt development of a dam in India that is threatening to displace thousands of tribal people and submerge vast stretches of forest. The Prize seeks to offer these environmental heroes with the recognition, visibility, and credibility their efforts deserve, in addition to financial assistance that enables them the freedom to pursue their visions for a better world. Established in 1989 by Richard and Rhoda Goldman.

• 10065 •
Golf Course Superintendents Association of America
Stephen F. Mona CAE, CEO
1421 Research Park Dr.
Lawrence, KS 66049-3859
Phone: (785)841-2240
Phone: (785)832-4430
Toll-Free: 800-472-7878
Fax: (785)832-4488
E-mail: infobox@gcsaa.org
Home Page: http://www.gcsaa.org

• 10066 • **Distinguished Service Award**
For recognition of individuals who have demonstrated dedication and outstanding service to golf course superintendents and the profession. Nominations are accepted but the nominee must not have been a recipient of this award in the preceding ten years. A plaque is presented annually. Established in 1932.

• 10067 • **Leo Feser Award**
To recognize a GCSAA member superintendent's literary talent and his contribution to higher levels of professionalism and the welfare of fellow superintendents. Candidate must be a member of GCSAA and a golf course superintendent, class A or B, and must have published an article in *Golf Course Management.* A plaque is presented annually. Established in 1956, and re-established in 1977. Given in honor of Leo Feser, a long-time editor of GCSAA's official magazine known today as *Golf Course Management.*

• 10068 • **Old Tom Morris Award**
To recognize an individual who, through a continuing, lifetime, selfless commitment to the game of golf, has helped to further the welfare of the game in a manner and style exemplified by Old Tom Morris. Nominations are accepted. An oil portrait, sculpture and honorary GCSAA membership are presented annually. Established in 1983 in honor of Old Tom Morris, the first "superstar" of golf, who was a greenkeeper, golf professional, club and ball maker, and a golf course architect who won the British Open four times between 1861 and 1867.

• 10069 • **President's Award for Environmental Stewardship**
To recognize individuals and organizations for exceptional environmental contributions to the game of golf that exemplify the golf course superintendent's image as steward of the land. Awarded to one or more recipients annually. Established in 1991.

• 10070 •
Golf Digest
20 Westport Rd.
PO Box 850
Wilton, CT 06897
Phone: (203)761-5100
Toll-Free: 800-962-5513
E-mail: editor@golfdigest.com
Home Page: http://www.golfdigest.com

• 10071 • **Most Improved Golfer Men/ Women Pros**
To recognize a male and female professional golfer who has greatly improved his and her game over the past year. Full-time tour players are eligible. Silver medals are awarded annually. Announced in the January issue of the *Golf Digest.* Established in 1953 for men; 1954 for women.

• 10072 • **Byron Nelson Award**
To recognize the male player who has won the most events during the previous year on the PGA Tour. A silver medal is awarded annually. Established in 1955.

• 10073 • **Rolex Rookie of the Year Men/ Women Pros**
To recognize the best male and female first-year professional golfers. Silver medals are awarded annually. Established in 1957 for men; 1962 for women.

• 10074 • **World Player of the Year**
To recognize a male or female player who has had an exceptional year. Professional golfers are eligible. A gold-filled medal is awarded annually. Established in 1985.

• 10075 • **Mickey Wright Award**
To recognize the female golfer who has won the most events during the previous year. Players on the PGA Tour are eligible. A silver medal is awarded annually. Established in 1955.

• 10076 •
Golf Writers Association of America
Melanie Hauser, Sec.-Treas.
10210 Greentree Rd.
Houston, TX 77042-1232
Phone: (713)782-6664
Fax: (713)781-2575
E-mail: golfwritersinc@aol.com
Home Page: http://www.gwaa.com

• 10077 • **Charlie Bartlett Award**
To recognize unselfish contributions to the betterment of society outside the immediate sphere of golf. Individuals playing professional golf are eligible. Awarded as merited. Established in 1970.

• 10078 • **Ben Hogan Award**
To recognize an individual who has continued to be active in golf despite a physical handicap. A stauette of Ben Hogan is awarded annually. Established in 1954.

• 10079 • **William D. Richardson Award**
To recognize the individual who has made consistently outstanding contributions to golf. A plaque is presented annually. Established in 1947.

• 10080 •
Goodwill Industries International
George W. Kessinger, Pres./CEO
15810 Indianola Dr.
Rockville, MD 20855
Phone: (301)530-6500
Toll-Free: 800-741-0186
Fax: (301)530-1516
E-mail: contactus@goodwill.org
Home Page: http://www.goodwill.org

• 10081 • **Achiever of the Year**
To recognize a person with disabilities who has shown the greatest progress and accomplishments in overcoming barriers to employment, while still benefitting from the Goodwill Industries work environment. A plaque and a certificate are presented at the Awards Banquet. Established in 1980. Formerly: National Goodwill Worker of the Year.

• 10082 • **Chairman's Award**
To recognize outstanding service to Goodwill Industries in a voluntary capacity. Established in 1964.

Awards are arranged in alphabetical order below their administering organizations

• 10083 • Gerald R. Clore International Award
To recognize the efforts of a North American Goodwill Industries executive in furthering the international mission of Goodwill Industries. A traditional green tartan fabric is symbolic of the award. The pattern is the official tartan pattern of the Province of Alberta in Canada and is registered with the Tartan Guild of Scotland. The fabric was created and, in the early years, handwoven by Goodwill Rehabilitation Services of Edmonton. Awarded annually. Established in 1973 by the International Council of Goodwill Industries in honor of Gerald R. Clore for his service to the international program.

• 10084 • Communications Awards
To recognize outstanding communications projects, programs, publications, and audio-visual efforts to promote Goodwill Industries. Awards are given in the following categories: Corporate Communications, Media Communications, Web site Marketing, Marketing and Communications Campaign, And Resource Development.

• 10085 • Employers of the Year
To recognize employers who have demonstrated outstanding concern and affirmative action in the training and employment of people with disabilities or disadvantages. Awards are given in the following categories: small employer - fewer than 200 employees; and large employer 200 or more employees. Established in 1980.

• 10086 • Goodwill Industries Volunteer Services (GIVS) Volunteer Group of the Year
To recognize an outstanding group of GIVS members working in support of a Local Goodwill Industries organization.

• 10087 • Goodwill Industries Volunteer Services (GIVS) Volunteer of the Year
To recognize an outstanding volunteer within the Goodwill Industries organization.

• 10088 • Graduate of the Year
This, Goodwill Industries of America's most prestigious award for clients, honors an outstanding person with disabilities or disadvantages who has graduated from a Goodwill Industries Career services program and competitive employment. A trophy, a certificate, and an expense-paid trip to Washington, D.C., are presented at the Awards Banquet. Established in 1980.

• 10089 • Edgar J. Helms Award for Staff and Graduate Staff
To recognize one's exemplification of Goodwill's mission through unselfish service to persons with disabilities or disadvantages. A plaque is awarded annually. Established in 1956 in honor of Edgar J. Helms, an ordained minister and founder of Goodwill Industries.

• 10090 • Kenneth K. King Management Award
To recognize outstanding management abilities and accomplishments of Goodwill Industries executives. A monetary award of $2,500, a diamond pin, and a plaque are awarded annually. Established in 1972 in honor of long-time volunteer board member and Denver financier, the late Kenneth K. King.

• 10091 • Operations-Services Awards
To recognize outstanding achievement, improvement over previous conditions, and excellence of operation or innovation in programming that serve as guides or examples for the entire Goodwill Industries network. Awards are given in the following categories: retail operations, career services, job placement services, contract services.

• 10092 • Outstanding International Service Award
To recognize outstanding service to an international associate member of Goodwill Industries. Awarded annually.

• 10093 • P. J. Trevethan Award
To recognize a Goodwill Industries executive for outstanding contribution to the training of Goodwill Industries personnel. A monetary award and a plaque are awarded by the Conference of Executives annually. The award is named for P.J. Trevethan, the late executive vice president of Goodwill Industries International, who established a fund for this purpose at the time of his retirement in 1966. Established in 1969.

• 10094 •
Goshen College
John D. Yordy, Interim Pres.
1700 S. Main
Goshen, IN 46526
Phone: (574)535-7393
Toll-Free: 800-348-7422
Fax: (574)535-7660
E-mail: douglc@goshen.edu
Home Page: http://www.goshen.edu

• 10095 • Peace Play Contest
For recognition of a one-act original play on a peace theme. A first place award of $500 and second place award of $100 are given biennially. Established in 1982. Deadline is December 31 of odd-numbered years.

• 10096 •
Goshen County Chamber of Commerce
Dick Fullmer, Exec.Dir.
350 W 21st Ave.
Torrington, WY 82240
Phone: (307)532-3879
Toll-Free: 800-577-3555
Fax: (307)534-2360
E-mail: goshenco@communicomm.com
Home Page: http://www.wyomingchambers.com/local_chambers.html

• 10097 • Big Chief Award
For volunteer services in the community. Recognition award bestowed annually.

• 10098 •
Goshen Historical Society
Earlene Nofziger, Pres.
Box 701
Goshen, IN 46526
Phone: (219)533-1053
E-mail: rnofziger@aol.com
Home Page: http://www.goshenhistoricalsociety.org

• 10099 • Historian of the Year
For contribution to the community throughout history. Trophy awarded annually.

• 10100 •
Gospel Music Association
John Styll, Pres.
1205 Division St.
Nashville, TN 37203
Phone: (615)242-0303
Fax: (615)254-9755
E-mail: info@gospelmusic.org
Home Page: http://www.gospelmusic.org

• 10101 • Dove Awards
For recognition of excellence and/or significant accomplishments in the quality and means of spreading the true word through gospel music. Awards are presented in the following categories: (1) Song of the Year, (2) Songwriter of the Year, (3) Male Vocalist of the Year, (4) Female Vocalist of the Year, (5) Group of the Year, (6) Artist of the Year, (7) New Artist of the Year, (8) Producer of the Year, (9) Rap/Hip Hop Recorded Song (of the Year), (10) Alternative/Modern Rock Recorded Song, (11) Metal/Hard Rock Recorded Song, (12) Rock Recorded Song, (13) Pop/Contemporary Recorded Song, (14) Inspirational Recorded Song, (15) Southern Gospel Recorded Song, (16) Country Recorded Song, (17) Urban Recorded Song, (18) Traditional Gospel Recorded Song, (19) Contemporary Gospel Recorded Song, (20) Rap/Hip Hop Album, (21) Alternative/Modern Rock Album, (22) Metal/Hard Rock Album, (23) Rock Album, (24) Pop/Contemporary Album, (25) Inspirational Album, (26) Southern Gospel Album, (27) Country Album, (28) Urban Album, (29) Traditional Gospel Album, (30) Contemporary Gospel Album, (31) Instrumental Album, (32) Praise & Woship Album, (33) Children's Music Album, (34) Special Event Album of the Year, (35) Musical of the Year, (36) Youth/Children's Musical of the Year, (37) Choral Collection, (38) Recorded Music Packaging, (39) Short Form Video, and (40) Long Form Video. Bronze sculptures of a dove perched on a harp are presented annually. Established in 1969.

• 10102 • Gospel Music Hall of Fame
To recognize and honor noteworthy individuals for outstanding contributions in the promotion and promulgation of gospel music. Both living and deceased individuals are eligible. Inductees are chosen by a panel of 150 electors. Awarded

annually. Established in 1967. Contact the International Gospel Music Hall of Fame, Research Library and Museum, 1205 Division St., Nashville, TN 37203.

• 10103 •
Government Computer News
Thomas R. Temin, Ed. and SVP
10 G St. NE, Ste. 500
Washington, DC 20002
Phone: (202)772-2500
Fax: (202)772-2516
E-mail: ttemin@postnewsweektech.com
Home Page: http://www.gcn.com

• 10104 • ***Government Computer News* Awards Program**
To recognize the government information technology community for furthering the development of cost effective information systems - systems that are vital to the continuing responsiveness of government to the national and international challenges that lie ahead. The following awards are presented annually: (1) GCN Government Executive of the Year; (2) GCN Agency Awards; (3) Information Technology Hall of Fame; (4) GCN Industry Executive of the Year; and (5) Industry Information Technology Awards. Established in 1984.

• 10105 •
Government Employees AFGE AFL-CIO, USDA, LU 3523
Josue Griego, Contact
1206 Sycamore St.
Amarillo, TX 79107
Phone: (806)383-0496
Phone: (806)358-0534
E-mail: espinoza@nts-online.net

• 10106 • **AFGE Local 3523 Education Award**
For highest GPA of graduating seniors. Monetary award bestowed annually.

• 10107 •
Government Executive
National Journal Group
600 New Hampshire Av. NW
Washington, DC 20037
Phone: (202)739-8501
Fax: (202)739-8511
E-mail: webmaster@govexec.com
Home Page: http://www.govexec.com

• 10108 • ***Government Technology* Leadership Award**
To recognize an individual for leadership during a career in the federal service. Criteria for the Award include: leadership in achieving public policy goals; leadership in breaking down barriers between political appointees and civil service executives, and between the executive and legislative branches; and improving the public's regard for government. Nominations may be submitted by March 9. Established in 1991. The award is presented in cooperation with the National Capital Area Chapter of the American Society for Public Administration. Formerly: *Government Executive* Leadership Award.

• 10109 •
Government Finance Officers Association of United States and Canada
Jeffrey L. Esser, Exec.Dir.
203 N LaSalle St., Ste. 2700
Chicago, IL 60601-1210
Phone: (312)977-9700
Fax: (312)977-4806
E-mail: inquiry@gfoa.org
Home Page: http://www.gfoa.org

Formerly: Municipal Finance Officers and Association of the United States and Canada.

• 10110 • **Awards for Excellence**
To recognize outstanding contributions and innovations in the field of government finance. All members of the Association, as well as students and non-members sponsored by an active GFOA member, are eligible. Entries may be submitted for consideration in any of the following categories: accounting, auditing, and financial reporting; budgeting and financial planning; cash management and investing; capital financing and debt administration; pensions and benefits; and financial management. The financial management award winners also may be nominated for the Louisville Award for Innovation in Financial Management. Recipients of this award must introduce a new concept or technique with enduring value to the government finance profession. The award is presented only in recognition of an exceptional accomplishment and is not necessarily awarded every year. Applications are available in early October of every year and must be submitted by the end of November. Awarded annually. Established in 1941.

• 10111 • **Canadian Award for Financial Reporting**
To encourage municipal governments in Canada to publish high quality financial reports and to provide peer recognition and technical guidance for officials preparing these reports. Awards are valid for one year and may be granted in successive years to qualified governments. Established in 1990.

• 10112 • **Certificate of Achievement for Excellence in Financial Reporting**
To encourage government units to publish high quality comprehensive annual financial reports and to provide peer recognition and educational assistance to the officials preparing them. Units choosing to participate in the program submit copies of their reports for review by an impartial Special Review Committee of qualified judges. Reports meeting program standards are awarded Certificates of Achievement. Awards are valid for one year and may be granted in successive years to qualified governments. Established in 1945.

• 10113 • **Distinguished Budget Presentation Award**
To recognize excellence in governmental budgeting. State, provincial and local governments in the United States and Canada are eligible for consideration. Awards are valid for one year and may be granted successively to qualified organizations. Established in 1984.

• 10114 • **Popular Annual Financial Reporting Award Program**
To encourage government units to prepare popular annual financial reports specifically designed to meet the needs of interested parties who may be unable or unwilling to use traditional financial reports. The goal of the program is not to replace financial reports prepared in conformity with generally accepted accounting principles, but to supplement such reports so as to make the information they contain more readily accessible to a broader audience than that served by traditional financial reporting. Those wishing to participate in the program must be successful participants in either the Certificate of Achievement for Excellence in Financial Reporting or the Canadian Award for Financial Reporting programs. Awards are valid for one year and may be granted in successive years to qualified governments. Established in 1991.

• 10115 •
Government Innovators Network
John F. Kennedy School of Government
Harvard University
79 John F. Kennedy St.
Cambridge, MA 02138
Phone: (617)495-0557
Fax: (617)496-4602
E-mail: info@innovations.harvard.edu
Home Page: http://www.innovations.harvard.edu

Formerly: (1995) Ford Foundation and Harvard University - Innovations Program.

• 10116 • **Innovations in American Government Awards Program**
To identify, reward, and promote outstanding examples of innovative approaches to public problem solving in American government. Applications are accepted from state, local, tribal governments, and federal government agencies across the United States. The deadline is in early January. The program provides grants of $100,000 to each of ten national award winners annually. Fifteen $20,000 grants are also awarded. Award winning innovations are promoted through the print press, electronic media, promotional films, conferences, and other venues. Established in 1986. Sponsored by the Ford Foundation and administered by the John F. Kennedy School of Government at Harvard University.

• 10117 •
Government Management Information Sciences
Joe M. Turner, Pres.
PO Box 365
Bayville, NJ 08721
Phone: (973)632-0470
Toll-Free: 800-460-7454
Fax: (732)606-9026
E-mail: headquarters@gmis.org
Home Page: http://www.gmis.org

• 10118 • Management Information Systems Annual Professional Award (MISAPA)

For recognition of the outstanding contributions of an Information Systems Professional to his/her organization. Only computer professionals from GMIS member agencies may be nominated. The award is not intended to recognize management personnel. Any person whose sole responsibility is that of manager of any computer center is ineligible. This does not, however, preclude persons who work in small centers and have both management and technical/professional duties. The winner will receive an expense-paid trip to the national conference in June, a special plaque, and be honored at the conference. Established in 1985.

• 10119 •
Government of Manitoba
Sustainable Development Coordination Unit
305-155 Carlton St.
Winnipeg, MB, Canada R3C 3H8
Phone: (204)945-1124
Fax: (204)945-0090
E-mail: fkoch@susdev.gov.mb.ca

• 10120 • Sustainable Development Award of Excellence

The program was established by the Manitoba Round Table on Environment and Economy to recognize Manitobans who embrace the spirit and principles of sustainable development. The awards place priority on ideas that best translate the principles and guidelines of sustainable development into concrete and lasting achievements. The nine categories: research and development, large business, education, non government organizations, small business, public sector, household neighborhoods, youth and international.

• 10121 •
Governmental Research Association
John R. Kennedy, Pres.
402 Samford Hall
Birmingham, AL 35229
Phone: (205)870-2482
Fax: (205)726-2900
E-mail: james.williams@samford.edu
Home Page: http://www.graonline.org

• 10122 • GRA Annual Awards

To recognize outstanding written material on governmental problems and issues. Awards are given in the following categories: distinguished research, policy achievement, effective education, and original presentation. Within each category, awards are given for local and state research efforts. Members of the Association are eligible. Plaques are presented in each category. Awarded annually.

• 10123 •
Governor Baxter School for the Deaf
Larry S. Taub, Supt.
Mackworth Island
Falmouth, ME 04105
Phone: (207)781-3165
Fax: (207)781-6296
E-mail: gbsd.com@gbsd.org
Home Page: http://www.gbsd.org

• 10124 • Certificate of Merit

To recognize teachers who have completed or are currently completing 20 years or more of active involvement in the provision of educational services to the hearing impaired, or upon retirement with at least 15 years of service. Membership is not required. A certificate is awarded annually as merited.

• 10125 •
Graham Foundation
Daniel Wheeler, Pres.
4 W Burton Pl.
Chicago, IL 60610-1416
Phone: (312)787-4071
E-mail: info@grahamfoundation.org
Home Page: http://www.grahamfoundation.org

• 10126 • Graham Foundation Grant

To provide funds in educational areas directly concerned with architecture - primarily at an advanced level - and with other arts that are immediately contributive to architecture. The Foundation supports a variety of endeavors including fellowship grants to individuals for independent study, normally with some end objective such as a book or monograph; grants to architectural schools for special projects, enrichment programs, new curricula; grants to museums, schools, and libraries for exhibitions, catalogues, and, in some cases, for acquisitions; and support for publications, usually to help make an important publication better or more affordable to students and teachers. The Foundation has sponsored fellowships at the American Academy in Rome and architectural internships at various museums. It has also sponsored competitions and assisted student publications, seminars and conferences on architectural subjects. Applications are considered twice a year. The deadlines are January 15 and July 15, and the awards are made approximately four months thereafter. Grants to individuals normally do not exceed $10,000. Grants to institutions may exceed $10,000. Established in 1956 by a bequest from Ernest R. Graham (1866-1936), a prominent Chicago architect. The Foundation provides no direct scholarship aid.

• 10127 •
Grand Haven-Spring Lake Convention and Visitors Bureau
Marci Cisneros, Exec.Dir.
1 S. Harbor Dr.
Grand Haven, MI 49417
Phone: (616)842-4910
Toll-Free: 800-303-4096
Fax: (616)842-0379
E-mail: mcisneros@grandhavenchamber.org
Home Page: http://www.visitgrandhaven.com

• 10128 • Tourism Employee Excellence Award

For excellent customer service. Recognition award bestowed monthly.

• 10129 •
Grandview Rotary Club
Barbara Olmstead, Sec.
PO Box 602
Grandview, WA 98930
Phone: (509)882-5355
Phone: (509)882-4337
Fax: (509)882-5900
E-mail: olmstead@quicktel.com
Home Page: http://www.quicktel.com/users/rotary/index.html

• 10130 • Rotary Scholarship

For the top male and female graduates of Grandview High School. Scholarship awarded annually.

• 10131 •
Graphic Arts Technical Foundation
George H. Ryan, Exec.VP
200 Deer Run Rd.
Sewickley, PA 15143-2600
Phone: (412)741-6860
Toll-Free: 800-910-GATF
Fax: (412)741-2311
E-mail: info@piagatf.org
Home Page: http://www.gain.net

• 10132 • Naomi Berber Memorial Award

To recognize women who have made a major contribution to the development of the graphic communications industries. Women who have worked in the graphic arts industry for at least 10 years, are actively working in the industry, and have an outstanding record of accomplishments and leadership are eligible. A hand engraved ivory pendant watch is awarded annually. Established in 1975 in memory of Naomi Berber, former administrative director, and the first woman to be elected to the Society of Fellows. Contact: Teresa Natalia Rees.

• 10133 • GATF Awards of Excellence in Education for an Individual in Industry and in Education

To recognize individuals who have strived to achieve a standard of excellence in their dedication to graphic arts education. Recipients are recognized for their distinguished service to graphic arts education in the schools and in the industry, improvement of the public image and economic well-being of the industry through an emphasis on education, contribution to greater understanding of employment and educational needs, display of leadership of the graphic arts industry, and effective participation in professional organizations at the national, state, and local levels. The Awards of Excellence and are awarded annually. Established in 1984. Contact: Teresa Natalia Rees. Formerly: Education Council/GATF Individual Award.

• 10134 • InterTech Technology Awards
To promote awareness and understanding of new technologies that are predicted to have a major impact on graphic arts within the next five years and to recognize the companies or individuals that have developed them. Selection is made by a panel of industry representatives. Special hand-crafted awards are awarded annually at the GATF/NSTF Annual Conference. Established in 1978. Contact: John Lind.

• 10135 • Frederick D. Kagy Education Award of Excellence
To honor a distinguished educator who was professor emeritus at the College of Applied Science and Technology in the Department of Industrial Technology at Illinois State University. Nominations due June 2. Textbooks valued at $1,000 are awarded annually. Established in 1991.

• 10136 • Robert F. Reed Technology Medal
To recognize an individual who has made a major contribution to the technical and scientific development of the graphic communications industries. The awardee must have worked in the graphic communications industry for ten years or more. The recipient will be presented with an engraved and die struck bronze medal. Established in 1974 in memory of Robert F. Reed, the dean of lithography. Contact: Teresa Natalia Rees.

• 10137 • William D. Schaeffer Environmental Award
To honor significant contributions toward optimizing environmentally sound operations within the graphic arts industry. A graphic arts industry advocate who significantly increases the knowledge of the effects of materials and processes used in printing on the environment is eligible. Established in 1990 by the GATF Research Steering Committee in honor of William Dwight Schaeffer, retired GATF Director of Research who was well known for his environmental concerns. Additional information is available from Teresa Natalia Rees.

• 10138 •
Graphic Design USA
Gordon D. Kaye, Ed.
79 Madison Ave., Ste. 1202
New York, NY 10016
Phone: (212)696-4380
Fax: (212)696-4564
E-mail: gkaye@gdusa.com
Home Page: http://www.gdusa.com

• 10139 • American Graphic Design Awards
To recognize the best of graphic design in Print, TV, Exhibit/Display, Packaging, Publishing and other pertinent media. All work created within the previous year may be submitted by April 30. A Certificate of Excellence is awarded annually. By *Graphic Design: USA* magazine. Formerly: (1995) DESI Awards.

• 10140 •
Great Lakes Colleges Association
Richard Detweiler, Pres.
535 W William, Ste. 301
Ann Arbor, MI 48103
Phone: (734)761-4833
Fax: (734)761-3939
E-mail: detweiler@glca.org
Home Page: http://www.glca.org

• 10141 • New Writers Awards
To recognize and encourage writers and to introduce them to the students and faculty of the twelve colleges of the Association. Awards are given in the following categories: the best first published volume of poetry and the best first published volume of fiction. Honorees are invited to tour the colleges in the Association; each college gives an honorarium. Awarded annually. Established in 1969. Additional information is available from Mark Clark, Director, GLCA, New Writers Awards, GLCA Philadelphia Center, 121 S. Broad Street, North American Bldg. Ste. 700, Philadelphia, PA 19107.

• 10142 •
Great Lakes Commission
Dr. Michael J. Donahue PhD, Pres./CEO
2805 S Industrial Hwy., Ste. 100
Ann Arbor, MI 48104-6791
Phone: (734)971-9135
Fax: (734)971-9150
E-mail: glc@glc.org
Home Page: http://www.glc.org

• 10143 • Outstanding Service Award
To recognize members and partners of the Great Lakes Commission for their continuous efforts to advance the goals of economic development and environmental quality in the Great Lakes region, commending their dedication, capability and wise counsel. An engraved plaque is awarded periodically, typically on an annual basis. Established in 1965.

• 10144 •
Greater Detroit Frozen Food Association
Joe Yurasek Jr., Chm.
Crossmark Sales & Marketing
PO Box 8032
Plymouth, MI 48170-8032
Phone: (734)207-7900
Phone: (734)207-9454
Fax: (734)207-0443
E-mail: joe.yurasek@crossmark.com

• 10145 • Golden & Silver Penguin Awards
For sales and merchandising excellence. Recognition award bestowed annually.

• 10146 •
Greater Haverhill Arts Association
Box 547
Haverhill, MA 01831
Phone: (978)372-6100
Phone: (978)374-1563

• 10147 • Greater Haverhill Arts Association Annual Exhibition
To recognize outstanding artwork at the annual exhibition. Professional and amateur artists may enter oil paintings or works in other media. The following awards are presented: Gertrude Dole Award - Best in Show; Ruth E. Hunkins Award - Best Amateur Entry; Presidential Citation; Founder's Award; Sophie Schlafman Award - for originality; Martin V. Beekler Award - for theme; and Haverhill Library Award; and Grumbacher Gold Medallion Award. Awarded annually.

• 10148 •
Greater Lynn Photographic Association
564 Boston St.
PO Box 9
Lynn, MA 01905
Phone: (781)592-9922
Fax: (978)664-2620
E-mail: glpa.info@comcast.net
Home Page: http://www.greaterlynnphoto.org

• 10149 • Greater Lynn International Color Slide Salon
To recognize excellence in color slide photography. The exhibition is open to everyone. There is no restriction on subject matter. The following awards are presented: PSA Medal - for the best slide of the show; PSA Contemporary Medal - for the best contemporary slide of the show; NECCC Medal - donated by the New England Camera Club Council for the best slide from a New England entrant; PSA Yankee Medal - presented to a highest scoring slide by a Photographic Society of America member that had not won another medal; FIAP Medals - donated by Federation Internationale de l'Art Photographique; and Greater Lynn Gold Medals. Established in 1977.

• 10150 •
Greater Mount Airy Chamber of Commerce
David Bradley, Pres.
200 N Main St.
PO Box 913
Mount Airy, NC 27030-0913
Phone: (336)786-6116
Toll-Free: 800-948-0949
Fax: (336)786-1488
E-mail: president@mtairyncchamber.org
Home Page: http://www.mtairyncchamber.org

• 10151 • **Citizen of the Year**
For community involvement. Recognition award bestowed annually.

• 10152 •
Greater Muskegon Music Teachers Association
Julie Browand, Pres.
509 Muskegon Ave.
Whitehall, MI 49461
Phone: (231)693-0433
E-mail: jkbrowand@juno.com

• 10153 • **Joseph/Wilson Study Grant**
For competitive recital. Scholarship awarded annually.

• 10154 •
Greater Omaha Sports Committee
Robert P. Mancuso, Pres.
7015 Spring St.
Omaha, NE 68106-3518
Phone: (402)346-8003
Fax: (402)346-5412

• 10155 • **First Data Corp. Outland Trophy Dinner Award**
For outstanding interior lineman (college tackle). Recognition award bestowed annually.

• 10156 •
Greater Philadelphia Chamber of Commerce
200 S Broad St., Ste. 700
Philadelphia, PA 19102
Phone: (212)545-1234
Fax: (215)575-2222
E-mail: programs@philachamber.com

Formerly: City of Philadelphia - Greater Philadelphia First Corporation.

• 10157 • **Philadelphia Liberty Medal**
To honor a man, woman, or organization from anywhere in the world who has made an outstanding contribution to the cause of human liberty. Recipients are chosen by an international commission of leaders in politics, world affairs, business, industry, education, and the arts. Emphasis in selection is on those with leadership and vision in the pursuit of liberty of conscience or freedom from oppression, ignorance, or deprivation. A one-page nomination may be submitted to the Liberty Medal Selection Commission, % Greater Philadelphia First at the above address. A monetary prize of $100,000 and a Liberty Medal are awarded annually on July 4 to mark the nation's birthday celebration. Established in 1988.

• 10158 •
Greater Quitman Area Chamber of Commerce
Mrs. Kimberly Connor, Administrator
101 E. Goode
PO Box 426
Quitman, TX 75783-0426
Phone: (903)763-4411
Toll-Free: (866)302-3884
Fax: (903)763-4913
E-mail: qtmncoc@peoplescom.net
Home Page: http://www.quitman.com

• 10159 • **Citizen of the Year**
For civic and community involvement. Recognition award bestowed annually.

• 10160 •
Greater St. Louis Amateur Baseball Hall of Fame
11920 Westline Industrial Dr.
St. Louis, MO 63146-3204

• 10161 • **Amateur Baseball Hall of Fame**
To recognize individuals for contributions to the amateur baseball program in the St. Louis area. Individuals over 50 years of age who are players of outstanding ability and contributors to amateur baseball or umpires of outstanding ability are eligible. A sterling silver ring, a certificate and a laminated membership card are awarded annually in the spring. Each year, 15 players, five contributors, and one umpire are inducted. The event is held at the Airport Marriott Hotel in March or April. Established in 1973. Additional information is available from Bob Broeg, *St. Louis Post Dispatch*, St. Louis, Missouri.

• 10162 • **Tom Gorman Memorial Award**
For recognition of contributions to amateur baseball. Awarded annually. Established in 1987.

• 10163 •
Greater Seattle Business Association
Louise Chernin, Exec.Dir.
2150 N 107th St., Ste 205
Seattle, WA 98133-9009
Phone: (206)363-9188
Fax: (206)367-8777
E-mail: office@thegsba.org
Home Page: http://www.thegsba.org

• 10164 • **GSBA Scholarships**
For persons committed to Lesbian, Gay, Bisexual and Transgender communities. Scholarship awarded annually.

• 10165 •
Greater Vancouver Professional Theatre Alliance
Susan Stevenson, Exec.Dir.
1405 Anderson St., 3rd Fl.
Vancouver, BC, Canada V6H 3R5
Phone: (604)608-6799
Fax: (604)608-6923
E-mail: info@gvpta.coa
Home Page: http://www.theatre.ubc.ca/gvpta

• 10166 • **Jessie Richardson Theatre Awards (Jessies)**
To honor and recognize excellence in Vancouver's professional theatre community. Actors, directors, designers, and playwrights are eligible for productions staged in Vancouver during the past year by a Vancouver Professional Theatre Alliance member company or a duly registered Equity Co-op. Awards are presented in the following suggested categories: Outstanding performance by an actor in a lead role; Outstanding performance by an actress in a lead role; Outstanding performance by an actor in a supporting role; Outstanding performance by an actress in a supporting role; Outstanding lighting design of a play or musical; Outstanding set design of a play or musical; Outstanding costume design of a play or musical; Outstanding sound design or original composition; Outstanding performance in a musical; Outstanding achievement in a musical - musical direction; Outstanding choreography of a play or musical; Outstanding direction of a play or musical; Outstanding production of a play or musical; and Outstanding original play or musical. These categories may be changed or deleted, and others may be added at the discretion of the nominimating committee. In addition, there may be nominations for significant outstanding achievement in such areas as body of work, ensemble performances, masks, puppets, or other achievements not covered in the listed categories. These nominations are voted on by members and a maximum of six are awarded in addition to the listed categories. Other awards include the Patron of the Arts Award, the Vancouver Professional Theatre Alliance Career Achievement Award, the Mary Phillips Award, the Ray Michal Award for Outstanding Emerging Director, the John Moffat Larry Lillo Award, and the Theatre for Young Audiences Juried Awards. Trophies are awarded annually. Established in 1983 to honor Jessie Richardson, a pioneer of theatre in Vancouver.

• 10167 •
Greater Waterbury Chamber of Commerce
Stephen R. Sasala II, Pres./CEO
83 Bank St.
PO Box 1469
Waterbury, CT 06721
Phone: (203)757-0701
Fax: (203)756-3507
E-mail: info@waterburychamber.com
Home Page: http://www.waterburychamber.org

• 10168 • Malcolm Baldrige Community Award
For area business leaders for outstanding community service. Recognition award bestowed annually.

• 10169 •
The Greensboro Review
Jim Clark, Ed.
Dept. of English
University of North Carolina
PO Box 26170
Greensboro, NC 27402-6170
Phone: (336)334-5459
Fax: (336)334-3281
E-mail: jlclark@uncg.edu
Home Page: http://www.uncg.edu/eng/mfa/gr

• 10170 • *The Greensboro Review* Literary Awards
For recognition of achievement in poetry and fiction. No previously published works, works accepted for publication, or dual submissions are eligible. Poetry may be any length; the maximum length for fiction is 7,500 words. Manuscripts may be submitted by September 15. A monetary prize of $500 is awarded for both poetry and fiction annually. Winning manuscripts appear in the winter issue of *The Greensboro Review*. Established in 1984.

• 10171 •
Greenwich Village Society for Historic Preservation
Vicki Weiner, Exec.Dir.
232 E 11th St.
New York, NY 10003
Phone: (212)475-9585
Fax: (212)475-9582
E-mail: gvshp@gvshp.org
Home Page: http://www.gvshp.org

• 10172 • Village Award
For people, places, and organizations that contribute significantly to the quality of life in Greenwich Village. Recognition award bestowed annually.

• 10173 •
Greeting Card Association
Marianne McDermott, Exec.VP
1156 15th St. NW, Ste. 900
Washington, DC 20005
Phone: (202)393-1778
Fax: (202)331-2714
Home Page: http://www.greetingcard.org

Formerly: National Association of Greeting Card Publishers.

• 10174 • International Greeting Card Awards (Louie Awards)
To recognize creative excellence among greeting card publishers. An applicant must be a greeting card publisher with a production run of 2,500 or more cards, sold and marketed in the United States during a given calendar year, and not previously submitted as an entry for the International Greeting Card Awards competition. All entries must be in finished production form. The deadline is December 1. A tinted crystal award featuring a star emerging from an envelope is awarded annually in approximately 70 plus categories based on cost along with Cards of the Year. Established in 1988 to commemorate Louis Prang, known as the Father of the American Christmas card. Additional information is available from the Greeting Card Association, (202)393-1778.

• 10175 •
Griffin Trust for Excellence in Poetry
Ms. Ruth Smith, Mgr.
6610 Edwards Blvd.
Mississauga, ON, Canada L5T 2V6
Phone: (905)565-5993
E-mail: info@griffinpoetryprize.com
Home Page: http://www.griffinpoetryprize.com

• 10176 • Griffin Poetry Prize
Awarded in June each year, the prize is awarded to an international poet as well as a Canadian poet. Canadians are also eligible for the international award. Each receives $40,000 in Canadian funds for their collection of poetry published in English or translated into English in the previous year. In the event that the translator and poet are different people sixty percent of the prize will go to the translator and forty percent will go to the poet. The application must originate directly from a publisher who may enter a maximum any number of entries. To be eligible for the International Prize a book of poetry must be a first-edition poetry collection of at least 48 pages with no less than five hundred copies published in the calendar year of submission. To be eligible for the Canadian Prize a book must be a first-edition written or translated by a Canadian citizen or permanent resident with a print run of no less than five hundred copies published in the calendar year of submission. Books must be published in English at any time in the calendar year preceding the year of the award. Winners are eligible to continue winning the award. Posthumous awards are not given, all books must have an ISBN, and no self-published books are eligible. Books must be the work of one poet, and a book will be defined as having at least forty pages. The final deadline for a publisher to submit an entry is the 31 of December in the previous year. Receipt will be acknowledged in writing, and four copies of each entry should be sent to the trust at the above address.

• 10177 •
The Grolier Poetry Book Shop
Louisa Solano, Pres.
6 Plympton St.
Cambridge, MA 02138
Phone: (617)547-4648
Phone: 800-234-POEM
Toll-Free: 800-234-POEM
Fax: (617)547-4230
E-mail: grolierpoetrybookshop@compuserve.com
Home Page: http://www.grolierpoetrybookshop.com

• 10178 • Grolier Poetry Prize
To encourage and recognize developing writers. Open to all poets who have not published either a vanity, small press, trade, or chapbook of poetry. Entries may be submitted between January 1 and May 1. Two first prizes of $200 and publication of up to four poems in the Grolier Poetry Prize *Annual* are awarded annually. In addition, four runner-up winners are also published in the *Annual*. Send a SASE for rules. Established in 1974. Co-sponsored by the Grolier Poetry Book Shop, Inc. and the Ellen La Forge Memorial Poetry Foundation.

• 10179 •
Groundwater Foundation
Susan Seacrest, Pres.
PO Box 22558
Lincoln, NE 68542-2558
Phone: (402)434-2740
Toll-Free: 800-858-4844
Fax: (402)434-2742
E-mail: info@groundwater.org
Home Page: http://www.groundwater.org

• 10180 • E. Benjamin Nelson Government Service Award
Recognizes and hors an elected or appointed public official who has significantly advanced environmental and groundwater stewardship. Any government official on the local, state, or federal level Is eligible to receive the award. Nomination deadline is July 14.

• 10181 • Edith Stevens Groundwater Hero Award
Recognizes groundwater educators who understand the importance of groundwater, motivates others to protect groundwater, and leads by personal example. Anyone who is actively involved with the implementation and delivery of groundwater education programs is eligible for this award. Nomination deadline is July 14.

• 10182 • Vern Haverstick Groundwater Hero Award
Recognizes groundwater protection activities by the efforts of community residents. Any member of the public is eligible for the award. Nomination deadline is July 14.

• 10183 •
Group for the Use of Psychology in History
Charles B. Strozier, Exec. Officer
John Jay Coll., CUNY
555 W 57th St., Ste. 601
New York, NY 10019
Phone: (212)237-8432
E-mail: strozier2@aol.com
Home Page: http://www.theaha.org/affiliates/group_use_psychology_his.htm

• 10184 • William L. Langer Award
For recognition of an article published on psychohistory appearing in *The Psychohistory Review*, the quarterly publication of GUPH. A monetary prize is awarded periodically. Established in 1982-83 in honor of William L. Langer.

Awards are arranged in alphabetical order below their administering organizations

• 10185 •
Gruppo Esponenti Italiani
Lucio Caputo, Pres.
PO Box 789
60 E 42nd St.
New York, NY 10150
Phone: (212)867-2772
Fax: (212)867-4114
E-mail: geinewyork@aol.com
Home Page: http://www.gei-ny.com/About%20GEI.htm

• 10186 • **GEI Award**
Recognizes significant contributions toward greater understanding between Italy and the U.S. Notable Italians and Americans are eligible. Awarded annually.

• 10187 •
Guadalupe Cultural Arts Center
R. Bret Ruiz, Pres.
1300 Guadalupe St.
San Antonio, TX 78207
Phone: (210)271-3151
Fax: (210)271-3480
E-mail: info@guadalupeculturalarts.org
Home Page: http://www.guadalupeculturalarts.org

• 10188 • **San Antonio Cine Festival**
For recognition of achievement in Latin film and video. All films and videos must be relevant to the Latino community, i.e. produced, directed, written, or performed by Latinos, or concerned with the Latino Experience. Awards are presented in the following categories: (1) Fiction (short/feature made for TV); (2) Documentary; (3) Animation/Experimental; (4) Home Video; (5) First film/video; and (6) Special Jury Award. The San Antonio Cine Festival has been held annually since 1975. The Premio Mesquite has been awarded since 1986, when the festival was first juried. A trophy of mesquite, a type of wood native to South Texas, sculpted by the artist, Jose Rivera is awarded.

• 10189 •
Guelph Spring Festival
John Booth, Gen. Man.
100 Crimea St., Unit 2B
Guelph, ON, Canada N1H 2Y6
Phone: (519)821-3210
Fax: (519)821-4403
E-mail: information@guelphspringfestival.org
Home Page: http://www.guelphspringfestival.org

• 10190 • **Guelph Spring Festival Music Competition**
To recognize gifted young musicians of the Guelph Region. Musicians between the ages of 18 and 25 are eligible to apply by April 1. Awards are presented in the following categories: strings, piano, and vocal. The following awards are given in each category: first prize - $1500; second prize - $1000; and third prize - $500. In addition, a Grand Prize of $2,500 is awarded to one of the first prize winners. Awarded annually in May at the Guelph Spring Festival. Established in 1970. Formerly: (1984) Edward Johnson Annual Scholarship Winners.

• 10191 •
John Simon Guggenheim Memorial Foundation
Edward Hirsch, Pres.
90 Park Ave.
New York, NY 10016
Phone: (212)687-4470
Fax: (212)697-3248
E-mail: fellowships@gf.org
Home Page: http://www.gf.org

• 10192 • **John Simon Guggenheim Memorial Foundation Fellowships**
To recognize men and women who have demonstrated an exceptional capacity for productive scholarship or exceptional creative ability in the arts. Fellowships are awarded through two annual competitions: one open to citizens and permanent residents of the United States and Canada, and the other open to citizens and permanent residents of Latin America and the Caribbean. The Fellowships are awarded by the Trustees upon nominations made by a Committee of Selection. The Foundation consults with distinguished scholars and artists regarding the accomplishments and promise of the applicants in relation to the plans that they propose. Appointments are ordinarily made for one year, but in no instance for less than six consecutive months. The amount of each grant is adjusted to the needs of the Fellows, considering their other resources and the purpose and scope of their plans. Established by U. S. Senator Simon Guggenheim and Mrs. Guggenheim as a memorial to their son who died April 26, 1922.

• 10193 •
Guide Dogs of America
Jay A. Bormann, Pres./Dir.
13445 Glenoaks Blvd.
Sylmar, CA 91342
Phone: (818)362-5834
Toll-Free: 800-459-4843
Fax: (818)362-6870
E-mail: mail@guidedogsofamerica.org
Home Page: http://www.guidedogsofamerica.org

• 10194 • **Gift of Sight Award**
Recognizes outstanding support of the association. Awarded annually.

• 10195 •
Guild Hall
158 Main St.
East Hampton, NY 11937
Phone: (631)324-0806
Fax: (631)324-2722
E-mail: info@guildhall.org
Home Page: http://www.guildhall.org

• 10196 • **Lifetime Achievement Awards**
To recognize outstanding achievement in the fields of the literary, visual, and performing arts. Residents of the area are eligible. A medal is awarded annually at a banquet in New York City. Established in 1985.

• 10197 •
Guild of Carillonneurs in North America
Dennis Curry, Pres.
PO Box 221
Gladwyne, PA 19035-0221
E-mail: aja3@hub.ofthe.net
Home Page: http://www.gcna.org

• 10198 • **Honorary Member**
For recognition of those who have made a significant contribution to the carillon. A certificate is usually awarded annually. Established in 1962.

• 10199 •
Guild of Catholic Lawyers
Gregory de Sousa, Pres. Emeritus & Exec.Dir.
6 MacDonald Pl.
Scarsdale, NY 10583
Phone: (914)723-3211
Fax: (914)725-4394

• 10200 • **Charles Carroll Award**
Annual award of recognition.

• 10201 •
Guild of Italian American Actors
Guy Palumbo, Pres.
Canal St. Sta.
PO Box 123
New York, NY 10013-0123
Phone: (212)420-6590
E-mail: info@giaa.us
Home Page: http://www.giaa.us

• 10202 • **GIAA Entertainment Achievement Awards**
Recognizes accomplishment in film, television and/or stage. Awarded annually.

• 10203 •
Guitar Foundation of America
Gunnar Eisel, Exec.Dir.
PO Box 1240
Claremont, CA 91711
Phone: (909)624-7730
Toll-Free: 877-570-3409
Fax: (909)624-1151
E-mail: info@guitarfoundation.org
Home Page: http://www.guitarfoundation.org

• 10204 • **Guitar Foundation of America Solo Guitar Competition**
To recognize achievement and to encourage professional development in guitar music. A monetary award of $5,000 and a concert tour are awarded annually.

• 10205 •
Guitar Player Magazine
Michael Molenda, Ed.
2800 Campus Dr.
San Mateo, CA 94403
Phone: (650)513-4300
Fax: (650)513-4616
E-mail: guitplyr@musicplayer.com
Home Page: http://www.guitarplayer.com

• 10206 • **Leo Award for Technical Innovation**
To recognize those designers and builders who have labored hard, sometimes in relative obscurity, to refine or revolutionize guitar gear and have succeeded in profoundly benefiting the worldwide guitar community. The recipient will be selected by the staff out of the nominations received. Established in 1993.

• 10207 •
Gungywamp Society
Paulette Buchanan, Corresponding Sec./ Researcher
PO Box 592
Colchester, CT 06415-0592
Phone: (860)537-2811
E-mail: gungywamp@ctol.net
Home Page: http://www.gungywamp.com

• 10208 • **Gungywamp Society Scholarship**
Awarded annually.

• 10209 • **H. W. Nelson Award**
Recognizes excellence in writing, drama, history. Awarded annually.

• 10210 • **Presidents Citation**
Annual award of recognition.

• 10211 • **Trustees Award**
Annual award of recognition.

• 10212 •
Hadassah Magazine
June Walker, Natl. Pres.
The Women's Zionist Organization of America
50 W 58th St.
New York, NY 10019
Phone: (212)688-0227
Toll-Free: 800-664-5646
Fax: (212)446-9521
E-mail: webmaster@hadassah.org
Home Page: http://www.hadassah.org

• 10213 • **Harold U. Ribalow Prize**
To recognize an outstanding English-language work of fiction on a Jewish theme. Novels and short stories published between January 1 and December 31 are eligible for that year's award. The award for a given year is made the following year. A monetary award of $2,000 is presented at a reception at Hadassah House, usually in November. In addition to the formal announcement, *Hadassah Magazine* will announce the winner in its editorial pages and print an excerpt from or major review of the winning book. Established in 1983 in memory of Harold U. Ribalow, noted writer, editor, and anthologist of American-Jewish fiction.

• 10214 •
Hadassah, The Women's Zionist Organization of America
June Walker, Pres.
50 W 58th St.
New York, NY 10019
Phone: (212)303-8061
Toll-Free: 800-664-5646
Fax: (212)303-4524
E-mail: webmaster@hadassah.org
Home Page: http://www.hadassah.org

• 10215 • **Henrietta Szold Award**
To recognize individuals for humanitarian and distinguished service in the fields of medicine, education, government, science, philanthropy, child welfare and youth, and communal work. A gift and a citation are awarded periodically, and only when the awardee can accept the award personally at the Awards Ceremony during the national annual convention. Established in 1949 in memory of Henrietta Szold, founder of Hadassah, who left a distinguished and enduring record of communal and Jewish service.

• 10216 •
Haddonfield Symphony
41 S Haddon Ave., Ste. 7
Haddonfield, NJ 08033
Phone: (856)429-1880
Fax: (856)428-5634
E-mail: symphony@haddonfield-symphony.org
Home Page: http://www.haddonfield-symphony.org

• 10217 • **Haddonfield Symphony Solo Competition for Young Instrumentalists**
To recognize talented young performers from the area served by the Symphony. String players in odd years and pianists in even years. Applicants must be between 16 and 25 years of age and reside in the northeastern United States or Washington, DC. The deadline is on or about December 1. A monetary award of $2,000 and a performance with the Haddonfield Symphony are awarded annually for First Prize. The runner-up receives $500. Established in 1954. Formerly: (1984) Haddonfield Symphony Solo Competition.

• 10218 •
Haiku Society of America
Ms. Carmen Sterba, Sec.
6116 Lakewood Dr. W, No. 8
University Place, WA 98467
Phone: (781)736-2145
E-mail: carmensterba@yahoo.com
Home Page: http://www.hsa-haiku.org/

• 10219 • **Gerald Brady Memorial Awards**
To recognize the best unpublished senryu. Up to 10 entries may be submitted. The deadline for entries is June 15. The following awards are presented: first prize - $100; second prize - $75; and third prize - $50. Winning senryu will be published in *Frogpond*.

• 10220 • **Bernard Lionel Einbond Renku Competition**
To recognize the best unpublished renku. A renku must consist of 12, 20, or 36 stanzas written by two or more persons, each of whom contributes a substantial number of individually-authored stanzas. A monetary prize of up to $150 and publication in *Frogpond* are awarded.

• 10221 • **Harold G. Henderson Memorial Award**
To recognize the best unpublished haiku. Up to 10 previously unpublished haiku may be submitted by July 31. The following awards are presented: first prize - $150; second prize - $100; and third prize - $50. All winning haiku will be published in the journal *Frogpond*. Awarded annually. An entry fee of $1.00 per haiku must also be submitted. The awards were established by Mrs. Harold G. Henderson in memory of Harold G. Henderson, who helped found The Haiku Society of America.

• 10222 • **Merit Book Awards**
To recognize excellence in published haiku, translation, and criticism. Work published during the preceding year is eligible. Monetary prizes are awarded annually. The list of awards will be published in *Frogpond*. The deadline for entries is May 31. An entry fee of $10 per submission must also be submitted. Any number of titles may be submitted.

• 10223 • **Museum of Haiku Literature Awards**
To recognize the Best of Issue haiku in each quarterly issue. Award-winning haiku are chosen by the HSA Executive Committee from those published in each issue of *Frogpond* and are announced in the following issue. A monetary award of $50 is presented annually.

• 10224 • **Nicholas A. Virgilio Memorial Haiku Competition**
To recognize outstanding haiku by high school students. Any student in grades 7-12 is eligible. All haiku entered must be previously unpublished, original work, and not entered in any other contest. The deadline for submissions is March 25. A monetary prize of $50 and publication in *Frogpond* are awarded annually. Established in memory of Nicholas A. Virgilio, a charter member of the Society.

• 10225 •
Halle Theatre
Jewish Community Center of Cleveland
3505 Mayfield Rd.
Cleveland, OH 44118
Phone: (216)382-4000
Fax: (216)382-5401
Home Page: http://www.clevejcc.org

Formerly: (1998) Jewish Community Center of Cleveland.

• 10226 • **Dorothy Silver Playwriting Competition**

To encourage the writing of new plays that provide fresh, significant perspectives on the range of Jewish experience. All entries must be original works not previously produced at the time of submission, suitable for a full-length presentation, and directly concerned with the Jewish experience. The deadline for submission is April 15. A monetary award of $1,000 and a staged reading of the winning play at the JCC Theater in Cleveland is awarded annually. Established in 1980 and renamed in 1989 to honor Dorothy Silver, former director of the Visual and Performing Arts Department. Formerly: (1989) Jewish Community Center Theater of Cleveland Playwriting Competition.

• 10227 •
Handweavers Guild of America
Sandra Bowles, Exec.Dir./Ed.-in-Chief
1255 Buford Hwy., Ste. 211
Suwanee, GA 30024
Phone: (678)730-0010
Fax: (678)730-0836
E-mail: hga@weavespindye.org
Home Page: http://www.weavespindye.org

• 10228 • **Certificates of Excellence**

Recognizes outstanding handspinning and handweaving. Awarded biennially.

• 10229 • **HGA Award**

Award of recognition.

• 10230 •
Hannibal Arts Council
Michael Gaines, Exec.Dir.
PO Box 120
Hannibal, MO 63401
Phone: (573)221-6545
E-mail: arts@nemonet.com
Home Page: http://www.visithannibal.com/arts/

• 10231 • **Past President Scholarship**

For arts related major. Scholarship awarded annually.

• 10232 •
Hanover Chamber of Commerce
Kathy Bruna, Pres.
PO Box 283
Hanover, KS 66945
Phone: (785)337-2215

• 10233 • **Chamber Scholarship Award**

For salutatorian, a business student. Scholarship awarded annually.

• 10234 •
Harcourt, Inc.
6277 Sea Harbor Dr.
Orlando, FL 32887
Phone: (407)345-2000
Fax: (407)345-9354
Home Page: http://www.harcourt.com

Formerly: Harcourt Brace Jovanovich.

• 10235 • **Walter J. Johnson Annual Prize**

To encourage postdoctoral research in the life sciences. The recipients are selected on a rotating basis by the editors of the *Archives of Biochemistry and Biophysics, Experimental Cell Research,* and the *Journal of Molecular Biology.* Individuals who have recently completed doctoral studies in the life sciences are eligible. A monetary prize of $10,000 is awarded annually. Established in 1987 in honor of Walter J. Johnson, founder of Academic Press and the publisher of the three journals.

• 10236 •
Hardin County Historical Museums
Shirley Ray, Dir.-Curator
215 N Detroit St.
Kenton, OH 43326
Phone: (419)673-7147
Phone: (419)673-0275
Fax: (419)675-3547
E-mail: hchm@dbscorp.net

• 10237 • **Jonathan Carter Award**

For excellence in teaching local history. Monetary award bestowed annually.

• 10238 •
Harkness Fellowships of the Commonwealth Fund
Karen Davis, Pres.
1 E 75th St.
New York, NY 10021
Phone: (212)606-3800
Fax: (212)606-3500
E-mail: info@cmwf.org
Home Page: http://www.cmwf.org

• 10239 • **Harkness Fellowships**

To promote international understanding by enabling individuals to study, travel, and gain practical experience in the continental United States. The Fellowships are open to married or single men and women who are citizens of the United Kingdom (up to 12 awards annually); citizens of Australia (4 awards annually); and New Zealand citizens (2 awards annually). There are no formal age limits. In the United Kingdom, preference is given to those between their late 20s and early 40s; in Australia to those between 21 and 36; and in New Zealand to those between 25 and 35. For the United Kingdom awards, study is restricted to the fields of Promoting Good Health, Human Resources in the 21st Century, and People in Cities. In Australia and New Zealand, there are no restrictions on field of study, but candidates must have a degree or equivalent professional qualification, or an outstanding record of achievement in the creative arts, journalism, or other comparable career. MBA candidates, in addition, must have had substantial full-time postgraduate administrative experience. Candidacy is not open to anyone who is already in the United States or holding another award. The deadline for applications is variable but normally in October of the year preceding award in the United Kingdom, and early August for Australia and New Zealand. Between 7 to 12 months' study is offered to United Kingdom candidates and between 12 and 21 months to those from Australia and New Zealand. Financial support includes travel to and from the United States. Established in 1925 by Anna M. Harkness and Mr. and Mrs. Edward S. Harkness. For more information, write to the appropriate email address in the country of award. Australia: Jane Hall at jane.hall@chere.uts.edu.au. New Zealand: Karen Poutasi at karen_poutasi@moh.govt.nz United Kingdom: Robin Osborn at ro@cmwf.org. Formerly: (1959) Commonwealth Fund Fellowships.

• 10240 •
Bryce Harlow Foundation
Linda Dooley, Pres.
1701 Pennsylvania Ave. NW, Ste. 400
Washington, DC 20006
Phone: (202)654-7812
Fax: (202)638-5178
E-mail: info@bryceharlow.org
Home Page: http://www.bryceharlow.org

• 10241 • **Bryce Harlow Business-Government Relations Award**

To recognize an individual who has made an outstanding contribution to the field of business-government relations. A specific single, but lasting, contribution to the field of business-government relations, or a series of activities which by advancing understanding, trust, respect, and cooperation between the business and government sectors has benefitted the country as a whole are considered. The awardee should embody qualities of integrity, dedication and performance in his/her field. Any present or recent past member of the business, government, journalism, or academic communities is eligible. Nominations may be submitted by January 15. A Steuben glass eagle and a monetary award to the educational institution of the recipients' choice are awarded annually. Established in 1982.

• 10242 •
Harmony, Inc.
Trinda Ernst, Intl. Pres.
684 Chelsea Cir.
Winfield, IL 60190
Toll-Free: 888-871-7762
Fax: (630)682-0487
E-mail: exsecretary@harmonyinc.org
Home Page: http://www.harmonyinc.org

• 10243 • **Accord Award**
To recognize the quartette showing the greatest improvement in consecutive international contests, as indicated by placement, and computed by the greatest advancement in rank from the previous year to the current one. A plaque is awarded annually at the convention. Established in 1988 by Four in Accord, the 1986-87 Harmony Queens.

• 10244 • **Bulletin Contest**
To recognize the winners of the Chapter Bulletin Contest. A plaque is presented annually. Established in 1967.

• 10245 • **Jerry Dunlop Memorial Award**
To recognize the novice director whose chorus places highest in the chorus contest. A novice director is defined as a director who has directed on the Harmony, Inc. international contest stage no more than three times, including the current contest. Established in 1991 by the Dunlop family in memory of Jerry Dunlop, former director of the Capital Chordettes, Ottawa, ON.

• 10246 • **Findlay Plaque**
For recognition of the best Novice Quartette rating the highest number of points in the international contest. This quartette may contain no more than one member who has previously competed in a registered quartette. A plaque is awarded annually. Established in 1970 by Ilene and Harry Findlay.

• 10247 • **G. Ruth Geils Memorial Award**
To recognize the highest scoring chorus with the least number of appearances on Harmony, Inc.'s international contest stage. Established in 1991 by the Geils family in memory of G. Ruth Geils, author of the Harmony, Inc. Creed.

• 10248 • **Harmony Queens**
For recognition of the outstanding quartette in the international contest. The quartette must have competed previously at an area level contest and contest singers must be Harmony, Inc. members. Permanent crowns and gold medallions on blue velvet ribbons are presented annually in November. Established in 1960.

• 10249 • **History Book Contest**
To recognize the winner of the History Book Contest. A plaque is awarded annually. Established in 1967.

• 10250 • **International Championship Chorus**
For recognition of the outstanding chorus in the Annual Contest. The chorus must qualify by point scores in local area spring competitions. All members must be Chapter and Harmony, Inc. members. A trophy and individual ribbons are presented annually in November to the first place chorus. Established in 1960.

• 10251 • **LABBS Trophy**
To recognize the highest scoring, non-medalist, chorus which did not compete in the previous international contest, excluding the immediate past championship chorus. This trophy was presented to Harmony, Inc. by the Ladies Association of British Barbershop Singers. An engraved silver tray is awarded annually. Established in 1984 by the Ladies Association of British Barbershop Singers.

• 10252 • **MacIntosh Award**
To recognize the small chorus (membership of 25 or less; but any number between 12 and 25 may appear on stage) attaining the highest non-medalist mark in contest. An engraved plaque is awarded annually. Established in 1976 by Bill and Barbara-Ann MacIntosh.

• 10253 • **Chris Scott Quartette Service Award**
To recognize the years of service to Harmony, Inc., the Chapter, and the community by one of Harmony's registered quartettes. A traveling trophy is presented. In addition, individual awards are presented to each member of the quartette. Established in 1981 by Stephen Scott in memory of Chris Scott, his wife, to be presented to the Canadian Quartette rating the highest number of points at the International Contest. Redesignated as a Harmony Quartette service award in 1984.

• 10254 • **Tait Trophy**
To recognize the chorus showing the greatest improvement in consecutive contests, as indicated by placement, and computed by the greatest advancement in rank from the previous year to the current one. A trophy is awarded annually. Established in 1970 by Marg Tait.

• 10255 • **Robert Turcotte Memorial Award**
To recognize the director of the first place chorus in international contests. This award is presented by the Harmonettes Chapter, North Attleboro, MA. A plaque is awarded annually. Established in 1982 by the Harmonettes Chapter, North Attleboro, MA.

• 10256 • **Sandi White Membership Award**
To recognize the chapter showing the greatest percentage increase in membership from one fiscal year to the next. Awarded annually. Established in 1993 by the Women of Note Chapter, Hudson, MA in memory of Sandi White.

• 10257 •
Harness Tracks of America
Stanley F. Bergstein, Exec.VP
4640 E Sunrise, Ste. 200
Tucson, AZ 85718
Phone: (520)529-2525
Fax: (520)529-3235
E-mail: info@harnesstracks.com
Home Page: http://www.harnesstracks.com

• 10258 • **Harness Track of America's Art Competition/Auction**
To recognize outstanding achievement in art relating to the subject of harness racing. Awards are given for paintings, bronze, woodcarving and other media. Monetary awards totaling $2,000 and ribbons are presented annually to the winners. Artists also retain a share of the proceeds of the auction sale of their work. Established in 1976.

• 10259 • **HTA/Hanover Show Farms Caretaker of the Year Award**
To recognize the outstanding caretaker of a standardbred racehorse during a given year. The deadline for nominations is January 1. Established in 1982 by the Harness Tracks of America and Delvin and Mary Lib Miller. The first 50 nominees receive a windbreaker jacke, certificate of recognition, and the Caretaker of the Yearl also receives an original oil portrait of their horse and caretaker.

• 10260 • **Nova Awards**
To honor the owners of the outstanding harness racehorses in each of ten divisions as voted by the racing secretaries of all member tracks. Trophies are presented annually. Established in 1982.

• 10261 •
Harriet Beecher Stowe Center
Katherine Kane, Exec.Dir.
77 Forest St.
Hartford, CT 06105
Phone: (860)522-9258
Fax: (860)522-9259
E-mail: kane@stowecenter.org
Home Page: http://www.HarrietBeecherStowe.org

• 10262 • **CT History Day Awards**
Recognizes the best women's history projects. A monetary award is given annually.

• 10263 •
Harrisburg Hunters' and Anglers' Association
Wm. Tyson, Pres.
6611 Hunters Run Rd.
Harrisburg, PA 17111
Phone: (717)545-6834
Fax: (717)545-5080
Home Page: http://www.harrisburghunters.org

• 10264 • **NRA Club Achievement Award**
For improvements to club. Recognition award bestowed annually.

Awards are arranged in alphabetical order below their administering organizations

• 10265 •
Harry S. Truman Library Institute for National and International Affairs
Michael J. Devine, Pres.
500 W U.S. Hwy. 24
Independence, MO 64050
Phone: (816)268-8200
Toll-Free: 800-833-1225
Fax: (816)268-8295
E-mail: truman.library@nara.gov
Home Page: http://www.trumanlibrary.org

• 10266 • **Harry S Truman Book Award**
For recognition of the best book dealing primarily and substantially with some aspect of the political, economic, and social development of the United States, principally between April 12, 1945 and January 20, 1953, or with the public career of Harry S Truman. Books written during the previous two years may be submitted by January 20. A monetary prize of $1,000 and a certificate are awarded biennially in even-numbered years. Established in 1963. Formerly: (1980) David D. Lloyd Prize.

• 10267 •
Harry Stephen Keeler Society
Richard Polt, Ed.
4745 Winton Rd.
Cincinnati, OH 45232
Phone: (513)591-1226
Phone: (513)745-3274
E-mail: polt@xavier.xu.edu
Home Page: http://keelersociety.mondoplex.com

• 10268 • **Imitate Keeler Contest**
Recognizes skill and wit in imitating Keeler's style. Awarded annually.

• 10269 •
Harvard Alumni Association
Yuki Moore Laurenti, Pres.
University Pl.
124 Mt. Auburn St., 6th Fl.
Cambridge, MA 02138
Phone: (617)495-5731
Fax: (617)495-0434
Home Page: http://www.haa.harvard.edu

• 10270 • **Harvard Alumni Association Award**
To recognize outstanding service to Harvard University through alumni activities, and to encourage continued commitment to Harvard in the future. Alumni of Harvard and Radcliffe Colleges, the graduate schools and the extension school are eligible for the award. A piece of Steuben glass with the statue of John Harvard etched on it is awarded annually at the fall Association meeting. Established in 1990.

• 10271 • **Harvard Medal**
To recognize extraordinary service to Harvard University in areas of teaching, fundraising, administration, management, generosity, leadership, and innovation. The candidate for the award is nominated by an alumnus, or, sometimes, by a current or former member of the faculty or staff. Alumni/ae, staff, and others who have given service to Harvard are eligible. A bronze medallion and a certificate are awarded at the Annual Meeting in June. Established in 1981.

• 10272 •
Harvard Business Review
David Wan, Pres. and CEO
300 N Beacon St.
Watertown, MA 02472
Phone: (617)783-7500
Toll-Free: 800-988-0886
Fax: (617)783-7555
E-mail: hbursubs@neodata.com
Home Page: http://www.hbsp.harvard.edu

• 10273 • **McKinsey Awards**
To recognize the two best articles published each year in the Harvard Business Review. These awards are presented for outstanding works that are likely to have a major influence on the actions of business managers worldwide. The winners receive cash awards and certificates, and are announced in the January-February issue. Established in 1959. Sponsored by the McKinsey Foundation for Management Research.

• 10274 •
Harvard Lampoon
44 Bow St.
Cambridge, MA 02138
Phone: (617)495-7801
E-mail: circulation@harvardlampoon.com
Home Page: http://www.harvardlampoon.com

• 10275 • **Elmer Award**
To honor an individual for a lifetime of achievement in comedy. Established in 1983.

• 10276 • **Movie Worsts Awards**
A tongue-in-cheek series of humorous awards in the following categories: (1) Ten Worst Movies of the Year; (2) Kirk Douglas Award for the Worst Actor of the Year; (3) Worst Supporting Actor of the Year; (4) Natalie Wood Award for Worst Actress of the Year; (5) Worst Supporting Actress of the Year; (6) The Arrested Development Oblation; (7) Best Use of Abe Vigoda; and (7) Ronald A. Weiner Award for best use of the British. A small blunt object is awarded annually. The awards are described in an issue of the *Harvard Lampoon.* Established in 1939.

• 10277 • **Andrew E. Robin Memorial Award**
To recognize an American novelist every year in a private ceremony at the Lampoon Castle. Winners names are never publicized. Interested writers should send their names in for consideration; the winner is notified in January. Awarded secretly. Established in 1989.

• 10278 • **The Elsa Shaine Memorial Award**
To recognize the performer who best exemplifies the spirit of the Lampoon's Spring Carnival. The only qualification is attendance at the Carnival, held every year in early April.

• 10279 • **Tall Man Water Freezer Award**
To honor that public figure or statesman for service above, beyond, and far between the call of duty. A public figure over six feet tall, or a statesman over five foot ten is eligible. A presentation of exotic woods is made. Awarded annually in May. Established in 1950 by Simon Rhee, Secretary, *Harvard Lampoon.* Formerly: (1985) Water Widget Medal.

• 10280 •
Harvard University
Graduate School of Design
420 Gund Hall
48 Quincy St.
Cambridge, MA 02138
Phone: (617)495-4731
Phone: (617)495-9345
Fax: (617)495-8949
E-mail: loeb_fellowship@gsd.harvard.edu
Home Page: http://www.gsd.harvard.edu

• 10281 • **Loeb Fellowship**
To provide for independent study at Harvard in the field of advanced environmental studies. The Loeb Fellowship is open to accomplished midcareer professionals in design, environmental, and related fields. In the past, Loeb Fellows have come from both the private and public sectors and have included architects, landscape architects, planners, housing specialists, architectural critics, urban affairs writers, and community advocates. The program has traditionally been limited to residents of the United States. Although there are no specific background requirements, applicants must have worked professionally for a minimum of five years. The program seeks applicants who can create independent study programs that make the most effective use of Harvard's resources and who will use the fellowship to benefit their own careers and society at large. Roundtrip airfare, a small fixed allowance, and housing are provided. Ten fellowships are awarded annually. Established in 1970 by the late John L. Loeb (Harvard College '24). Sponsored by Harvard Graduate School of Design.

• 10282 •
Harvard University Press
79 Garden St.
Cambridge, MA 02138
Phone: (401)531-2800
Toll-Free: 800-405-1619
Fax: (401)531-2801
E-mail: contact_hup@harvard.edu
Home Page: http://www.hup.harvard.edu

• 10283 • **Robert Troup Paine Prize**
To recognize the author of an unpublished manuscript of book length that is judged to be the best work on a specified subject accepted by the

Harvard University Press during the preceding four years. A monetary prize of $3,000 over and above the usual publication royalties is awarded every four years. Not open to the public. Established in 1962.

• 10284 • Thomas J. Wilson Award

For recognition of a young author's first published work. A monetary prize of $1,000 is awarded annually to a beginning author whose manuscript was accepted for publication in the previous calendar year. Established in 1970 to honor Thomas J. Wilson, the Director of the Press from 1947 to 1967. Not open to the public.

• 10285 •
The Hastings Center
Thomas H. Murray, Pres.
21 Malcolm Gordon Rd.
Garrison, NY 10524-5555
Phone: (845)424-4040
Fax: (845)424-4545
E-mail: mail@thehastingscenter.org
Home Page: http://www.thehastingscenter.org

• 10286 • Henry Knowles Beecher Award

Recognizes lifetime contributions to ethics and the life sciences. Awarded triennially.

• 10287 •
Hastings Literacy Program
Cindy McGrath, Contact
123 Marian Rd.
Hastings, NE 68901
Phone: (402)463-7323
Fax: (402)462-4568

• 10288 • Maynard Jensen Award

For length of service, other activities, etc. Monetary award bestowed annually.

• 10289 •
Hatebusters Incorporated
Ed Chasteen, Contact
Box 442
Liberty, MO 64069
Phone: (816)803-8371
E-mail: hatebuster@aol.com
Home Page: http://www.hatebusters.com

• 10290 • HateBuster Hero Award

For leading the fight against race violence. Recognition award bestowed annually.

• 10291 •
Hawaii Association of School Librarians
Tennye Kohatsu, Pres.
563 Kamoku St.
PO Box 235019
Honolulu, HI 96823
Phone: (808)943-2217
Fax: (808)943-2297
E-mail: ichoo@12.hi.us
Home Page: http://www.k12.hi.us/~hasl/

• 10292 • Nene Award

To honor an author whose book has been enjoyed by the children of Hawaii, based on votes cast by Hawaiian school children in grades four through six, and to help the children of Hawaii become acquainted with the best contemporary writers of fiction for children. The book must be fiction, suitable for children in grades four through six, copyrighted within the past six years, and the author must still be living. A Hawaiian wood carved plaque representing a Nene Goose, Hawaii's state bird, is awarded annually. The award is usually announced during National Library Week. Established in 1959 and bcame state-wide in 1964.

• 10293 •
Hawaii State Foundation on Culture and the Arts
Ronald K. Yamakawa, exec.Dir.
% Awards Committee
250 S Hotel St., 2nd Fl.
Honolulu, HI 96813
Phone: (808)586-0300
Toll-Free: 800-586-0740
Fax: (808)586-0308
E-mail: ken.hamilton@hawaii.gov
Home Page: http://www.state.hi.us/sfca

• 10294 • Governor's Award for Distinguished Achievement in the Arts

To recognize and celebrate outstanding long-term achievements in culture, the arts, and humanities. Contributions must be of great impact and significance on a long-term basis to the people of Hawaii. Awarded biennially at a reception. Established in 1969. Contact June Anami at june.anami@hawaii.gov, or call 808586-0302. Formerly: (1981) State of Hawaii Order of Distinction for Cultural Leadership; (1997) Governor's Award for Distinguished Achievement in Culture the Arts and Humanities.

• 10295 • Hawaii Award for Literature

To recognize and honor distinguished writers who have made significant contributions to the literature of Hawaii. A monetary award and a certificate are awarded annually. Established in 1974. Co-sponsored by the Hawaii Literary Arts Council.

• 10296 • Hawaiian Architectural Arts Award

To recognize a building architect and a building patron for their efforts in producing a building design that corresponds uniquely in form and function to the climate and culture of Hawaii. Any architecturally sound and outstanding building in Hawaii completed between five and twenty-five years prior and designed by a living architect who is registered in the state of Hawaii is eligible. Restoration projects are not eligible. A monetary award and a certificate are awarded annually. Established in 1984. Co-sponsored by the Hawaii Society - American Institute of Architects. Contact June Anami at june.anami@hawaii.gov, or call 808586-0302.

• 10297 • Individual Artists Fellowships

To recognize outstanding professional artists of Hawaii (must be Hawaii residents) who have demonstrated exemplary work, artistic excellence, and commitment in the arts. Awards are given in visual arts, dance, theatre, and music. Established in 1993. Formerly: (1997) Individual Artists Fellowship and Merit Awards.

• 10298 •
Hawk Migration Association of North America
Mark Blauer, Membership Sec.
18 W Hollow Rd.
Nescopeck, PA 18635
Phone: (570)379-3201
E-mail: mblauer@evenlink.com
Home Page: http://www.hmana.org

• 10299 • Maurice Broun Award

For recognition of outstanding contributions to raptor migration research, conservation, or education. HMANA members are eligible. A plaque is awarded at the direction of the Board of Directors, usually at the convention. Established in 1983 to honor Maurice Broun, first and long-time curator of the Hawk Mountain Sanctuary, Kempton, Pennsylvania.

• 10300 • Hawk Migration Association of North America Research Award

Recognizes innovative research on raptor migration. A monetary award is given annually.

• 10301 •
Hawk Mountain Sanctuary
Sam Magee, Sec.
1700 Hawk Mountain Rd.
Kempton, PA 19529
Phone: (610)756-6961
Phone: (610)756-6000
Fax: (610)756-4468
E-mail: info@hawkmountain.org
Home Page: http://www.hawkmountain.org

• 10302 • Hawk Mountain - Student Research Award

To provide funds for studies in raptor biology and science-based raptor conservation. Undergraduate and graduate students in degree-granting institutions are eligible to apply. The award is granted on the basis of a project's potential to improve understanding of raptor biology and its relevance to conservation. A monetary award of up to $2,000 is presented annually. Established in 1978.

• 10303 •
Hawk Mountain Sanctuary Association
Acopian Center for Conservation Learning
1700 Hawk Mountain Rd.
Kempton, PA 19529
Phone: (570)943-3411
Fax: (610)756-4468
E-mail: bildstein@hawkmtn.org
Home Page: http://www.hawkmountain.org

• 10304 • Hawk Mountain Sanctuary Award

For research on predatory birds. Awarded annually.

• 10305 •
Hazleton Art League
Kay Fritz, Co-Exec.Dir
225 E. Broad St.
Hazleton, PA 18201-6614
Phone: (570)454-0092

• 10306 • Jean Mantz Best of Show Student Award

For individuals pursuing art at an accredited college. Scholarship awarded annually.

• 10307 •
Headliners Foundation
Sue Meller, Mng.Dir.
221 W 6th St., Ste. 2100
PO Box 97
Austin, TX 78767-0097
Phone: (512)479-8080
Fax: (512)479-6409
E-mail: sue@headlinersclub.com
Home Page: http://www.headlinersclub.com

Formerly: (1983) Headliners Club.

• 10308 • Charles E. Green Journalism Awards

To encourage and recognize journalistic excellence by individuals rather than by groups. For newspapers and television stations, entries may be submitted only for staff members and entries must be made by the news organization, not by individual staff members. Entries in the Newspaper and Television categories must be made by Texas daily newspapers or broadcast stations; entries also are accepted from a Texas-based news service or from a Texas bureau of a national news service. Awards are given in the following categories: (1) Newspaper Master Awards - (a) Headliners Star Reporter of the Year; (b) Investigative Report of the Year; and (c) Spot News Story of the Year; (2) Weekly Newspaper Award (a) Outstanding Community Journalism; (b) Feature Writing; (c) Profile; (d) Governmental Affairs; (e) Sports Reporting; (f) Editorial Writing; (g) Headline Writing; (h) Column Writing; (i) Spot News Photography; (j) Feature Photography; (k) Sports Photography; (l) Photography; (m) Specialty Reporting; and (n) Business Reporting; (3) Broadcast Achievement Awards - (a) Television News; (b) Television Feature; (c) Television Investigative Reporting; and (d) Television Specialty Reporting; and (4) Magazine Achievement Award. Monetary prizes, a certificate and a medallion are awarded annually. Established in 1954 by Charles E. Green, founder of the Headliners Club and former publisher of *Austin American Statesmen*.

• 10309 •
Healing the Children, Northeast Chapter
Dr. Angeles Glick Ph.D., Exec.Dir.
PO Box 129
New Milford, CT 06776
Phone: (860)355-1828
Toll-Free: 877-HTC-NECT
Fax: (860)350-6634
E-mail: htcne@htcne.org
Home Page: http://www.htcne.org

• 10310 • HTCNE Service Award

For application submission - health needs a must. Monetary award bestowed annually.

• 10311 •
Health Industry Distributors Association
Matthew J. Rowan, Pres./CEO
310 Montgomery St.
Alexandria, VA 22314-1516
Phone: (703)549-4432
Toll-Free: 800-549-4432
Fax: (703)549-6495
E-mail: rowan@hida.org
Home Page: http://www.hida.org

• 10312 • Industry Award of Distinction

To recognize an individual for contributions to the healthcare industry. A plaque is awarded annually. Established in 1978.

• 10313 • Frank M. Rhatigan Award

To recognize the contribution made by manufacturers in the health industry to aid in the distribution of their products. Outstanding examples of catalogs, price lists, selling sheets, cartons, barcoding, and marketing data sheets are considered. First Place and Honorable Mention are awarded in each category annually. Established in 1964 in honor of Frank M. Rhatigan, executive secretary of the American Surgical Trade Association, HIDA's predecessor organization from 1953-1966.

• 10314 •
Health Information Resource Center
Patricia Henze, Exec.Dir.
1850 W Winchester Rd., Ste. 213
Libertyville, IL 60048
Phone: (847)816-8660
Toll-Free: 800-828-8225
Fax: (847)816-8662
E-mail: info@healthawards.com
Home Page: http://www.healthawards.com

• 10315 • National Health Information Awards

To recognize the best consumer health information programs and materials in the United States. All materials and/or programs developed for use by consumers during the preceding year are eligible. Gold, Silver, Bronze, and Merit prizes are awarded in several categories. Awarded annually.

• 10316 •
Health Physics Society
Richard J. Burk Jr., Exec.Sec.
1313 Dolley Madison Blvd., Ste. 402
McLean, VA 22101-3926
Phone: (703)790-1745
Fax: (703)790-2672
E-mail: hps@burkinc.com
Home Page: http://www.hps.org

• 10317 • Elda E. Anderson Award

For recognition of outstanding work in the field of health physics. Individuals under the age of 40 are eligible. A monetary award of $1,000 and a certificate are awarded annually. Established in 1962.

• 10318 • Distinguished Scientific Achievement Award

To acknowledge outstanding contributions to the science and technology of radiation protection. The recipient of the award is recognized for accomplishments of fundamental importance to the practice, acceptance, and advancement of the profession of health physics. Any individual except present members of the Society's board and awards committee is eligible. In addition, other individuals who contributed in an outstanding way to the development of scientific knowledge for the protection of humankind and the environment can be permanently memorialized by the presentation of the award in their names. A plaque and lifetime membership are awarded annually.

• 10319 • Fellow Awards

To honor senior members of the Society who have made significant administrative, educational, and/or scientific contributions to the profession of health physics. Members of the Society who will be 50 years or older by March 1 of the year the person is to be selected for the fellow class are eligible. Except under unusual circumstances, the individual must have been a member of the Society during the preceding five years. Awarded to one or more recipients annually.

• 10320 • Founders Award

To recognize exceptional service to the Health Physics Society or the health physics profession. In addition, others who were instrumental in the formation or development of the Health Physics Society can be permanently memorialized by the presentation of the award in their names. A plaque and lifetime membership are awarded annually.

• 10321 • Student Awards

Designed to stimulate interest in health physics and to encourage student participation in the student session of the annual meeting. Any undergraduate or graduate student, or recent graduate, who is presenting work performed while a student is eligible. Each student may present only one paper in the student session.

• 10322 •
Health Science Communications Association
Ronald Sokolowski, Exec.Dir.
39 Wedgewood Dr., Ste. A
Jewett City, CT 06351
Phone: (860)376-5915
Fax: (860)376-6621
E-mail: hesca@hesca.org
Home Page: http://www.hesca.org

• 10323 • **Achievement Awards**
To recognize individuals for significant accomplishments and contributions to the field of health sciences communications. The following awards are given: (1) Special Achievement Award - to recognize individuals who have accomplished a significant goal or established a landmark in the field of health sciences communications; and (2) Distinguished Achievement Award to recognize individuals who have accomplished significant goals over a period of time, and whose cumulative achievements are notable.

• 10324 • **Distinguished Service Award**
Recognizes outstanding service in a variety of association related areas over a long period of time. Association members are eligible.

• 10325 • **Golden Raster Award**
This, the most prestigious honor given by the Association, recognizes those members who have provided stability and inspiration to the HeSCA organization through imaginative leadership and unswerving service in the field of health science education and instructional technology. Members who meet the following criteria are eligible: (1) five years' consecutive membership in HeSCA; (2) active participation in the programs and activities of the Association; (3) notable service in positions such as: functional section officer, committee chair, board member, association officer, or the equivalent; (4) demonstrated leadership in the development and implementation of Association programs and activities; (5) demonstrated knowledge and skills at a level which identifies the individual as a leader in the field health sciences communications; (6) significant and varied accomplishments which have resulted in notable contributions to the field; and (7) documentation and dissemination of accomplishments through publication, presentation or distribution at a national level. Awarded periodically. Established in 1967 by the Council on Medical Television. Formerly: Raster Award.

• 10326 • **HeSCA Film Festival**
To recognize excellence in the production of health sciences films. Members and non-members of HeSCA are eligible. Plaques and certificates are awarded annually. Established in 1977. Formerly: (1996) HeSCA/Gilbert Altschul Film Festival.

• 10327 • **HeSCA Interactive Materials Festival**
To recognize excellence in the production of health science materials. Members and non-members are eligible. Awards are presented in the following categories: (1) Interactive Software; and (2) Computer-Based. Plaques and certificates are awarded. Established in 1987.

• 10328 • **HeSCA JBC Literary Award**
To recognize an outstanding contribution to *Journal of Biocommunication* which presents new information or point of view on a topic which adds significantly to the body of professional knowledge.

• 10329 • **HeSCA Print Media Festival**
To recognize excellence in the production of health sciences books, brochures, and newsletters. Awards are presented in the following categories: (1) Book/Monograph Division; (2) Logo/Masthead Division; (3) Poster Division; (4) Campaigns Division; (5) Brochure/Flyer Division; and (6) Periodical Division. Members and non-members of HeSCA are eligible. Plaques and certificates are awarded annually. Established in 1977. Formerly: HeSCA/Marion Laboratories Print Media Festival.

• 10330 • **HeSCA Video Festivals**
To recognize excellence in the production of health sciences videotapes. Awards are presented in the following categories: (1) Continuing Education Division; (2) Curriculum Based Education Division; (3) Patient Education Division; (4) General Information Division; and (5) Public Service Announcements Division. Members and non-members of HeSCA are eligible. Plaques and certificates are awarded annually. Established in 1974. Sponsored by the Network for Continuing Medical Education. Formerly: HeSCA/NCME Award.

• 10331 • **Service Awards**
To recognize members who have committed significant time and effort in furthering the goals and objectives of the Association. The following awards are given: (1) Certificate of Appreciation - for notable service or a valuable contribution to the Association; (2) Special Service Award for a significant and lasting contribution to the Association by virtue of a singular, outstanding accomplishment; and (3) Distinguished Service Award - for an outstanding level of service in a variety of areas over a long period of time.

• 10332 • **Special Achievement Award**
Recognizes significant goals or landmarks in the field of biocommunications. Industryrelated individuals are eligible.

• 10333 • **Special Awards**
The following special awards are presented: (1) Elmer Friman Best in Show; (2) Holly Harrington-Lux Creative Design Award - to recognize an individual for creative design of a piece or sequence of artwork determined to be the best in the festivals; and (3) HeSCA/Milton E. Adsjt in Veterinary Medicine Award. Nominations are made by festival coordinators.

• 10334 •
Healthcare Convention and Exhibitors Association
Eric Allen, Exec.VP
5775 Peachtree-Dunwoody Rd., Ste. 500, Bldg. G
Atlanta, GA 30342
Phone: (404)252-3663
Fax: (404)252-0774
E-mail: hcea@kellencompany.com
Home Page: http://www.hcea.org

Formerly: Health Care Exhibitors Association.

• 10335 • **Distinguished Service Award**
To recognize individuals who have made significant contributions to HCEA and the healthcare convention and exhibition industry over the course of at least ten years. Awarded when merited.

• 10336 •
Healthcare Financial Management Association
Richard L. Clarke, Pres./CEO
2 Westbrook Corporate Ctr., Ste. 700
Westchester, IL 60154-5700
Phone: (708)531-9600
Toll-Free: 800-252-HFMA
Fax: (708)531-0032
E-mail: jclarke@hfma.org
Home Page: http://www.hfma.org

Formerly: (1982) Hospital Financial Management Association.

• 10337 • **Board of Directors' Award**
To honor those persons who have contributed measurably to the healthcare financial management field. Individuals need not be members of the Association to be eligible. A plaque is awarded annually at the National Convention. Established in 1964.

• 10338 • **Graham L. Davis Awards of Excellence**
To recognize one chapter in each of the four leagues. All chapters that have qualified for Chapter Achievement Awards are eligible. A trophy is awarded annually in June at the national convention. Established in 1953 to honor Graham L. Davis, one of the founders of the HFMA.

• 10339 • **Frederick C. Morgan Award**
To recognize significant contributions to the field of healthcare financial management. Individuals need not be members of the Association to be eligible. A bronze plaque is awarded annually at the national meeting. Established in 1959 to honor Frederick C. Morgan. Formerly: Frederick C. Morgan Individual Achievement Award.

• 10340 • **Robert M. Shelton Award**
To recognize a Chapter for exemplary service to members over the past five-year period. Any

Chapter of HFMA that has a consistent record of exemplary service, programs and activities for its membership is eligible. Five trophies are presented, one to each of the chapter presidents who served during the five years. Awarded annually in June at the convention. Established in 1979 to honor Robert M. Shelton.

• 10341 •
Healthcare Information and Management Systems Society
H. Stephen Lieber CAE, Pres./CEO
230 E Ohio St., Ste. 500
Chicago, IL 60611-3270
Phone: (312)664-4467
Fax: (312)664-6143
E-mail: himss@himss.org
Home Page: http://www.himss.org

Formerly: (1987) Hospital Management Systems Society.

• 10342 • **Affiliated Chapter Awards**
To recognize affiliated chapters of the Society for outstanding achievements as official HIMSS organizations. Award categories include Membership, Programs, Financial Management, Community Service, Publications, and Member Satisfaction.

• 10343 • **Clinical Systems Award**
To recognize achievement in clinical systems by a HIMSS member.

• 10344 • **HIMSS John E. Gall Jr./CIO Award**
To recognize a HIMSS member for significant professional achievement as a chief information officer in the field of health care information and management systems. Established in 1990 in honor of John E. Gall who pioneered healthcare information systems at El Camino Hospital in the 1960s.

• 10345 • **Information Systems Award**
To recognize achievement in information systems by a HIMSS member.

• 10346 • **Management Engineering Award**
To recognize achievement in management engineering by a HIMSS member.

• 10347 • **John A. Page Outstanding Service Award**
To recognize an individual for significant, commendable, and long-standing contributions to HIMSS. Awarded annually. Established in 1990.

• 10348 • **Publications Awards**
To recognize outstanding publications in the health care information and management systems. Two awards are presented annually: Article of the Year and Book of the Year.

• 10349 • **Quality Management Award**
To recognize achievement in quality management by a HIMSS member.

• 10350 • **Telecommunications Award**
To recognize achievement in telecommunications by a HIMSS member.

• 10351 •
HEAR Center
Josephine F. Wilson MA, Exec.Dir.
301 E Del Mar Blvd.
Pasadena, CA 91101
Phone: (626)796-2016
Fax: (626)796-2320
E-mail: auditory@hearcenter.org
Home Page: http://www.hearcenter.org

Formerly: (1954) HEAR Foundation.

• 10352 • **Glen Bollinger Humanitarian Award**
To honor civic and service minded individuals for their efforts in behalf of hearing and speech impaired individuals, and for their loyalty and support of the HEAR Center. A plaque and/or trophy are awarded periodically. Established in 1979 for Glen H. Bollinger, co-founder of HEAR (and founder of Sparkletts Drinking Water Corporation, Los Angeles) in memory of his generous contributions to the welfare of others.

• 10353 •
William Randolph Hearst Foundation
George R. Hearst Jr., Pres.
Journalism Awards Program
90 Montgomery St., Ste. 1212
San Francisco, CA 94105
Phone: (415)543-6033
Toll-Free: 800-841-7048
Fax: (415)348-0887
E-mail: journalism@hearstfdn.org
Home Page: http://www.hearstfdn.org

• 10354 • **Journalism Awards Program**
To encourage excellence in journalism education by conducting monthly contests in writing, photojournalism, and broadcast news for undergraduate students majoring in journalism at accredited schools of journalism. Annual scholarships, grants, and stipends totaling $400,000 are awarded to students and schools. Established in 1960. In addition, the Foundation Board of Directors presents cash prizes to colleges and universities whose students accumulate the most points in the intercollegiate competitions in writing, photography, and broadcast, totalling $52,500.

• 10355 •
Hearst Newspapers
George B. Irish, Pres.
959 8th Ave.
New York, NY 10019
Phone: (212)649-2000
Fax: (212)765-3528
E-mail: hearstnewspapers@hearst.com
Home Page: http://www.hearstcorp.com/newspapers

• 10356 • **Hearst Newspapers Writing and Photography Contests**
To recognize papers for outstanding work in writing and photography. Awards are presented to the Hearst Newspapers in two categories: Community Group and Metro Group. The following awards are presented in the Community Group: (1) First prize - for best writing by an individual paper; (2) First prize - for photographic excellence by an individual paper; (3) Community Service Awards - for outstanding community service and accomplishment (exceptional nominations receive or share a $500 award); and (4) Individual Capital Prize Winners - for: (a) spot news, (b) features, (c) heads/captions, (d) enterprise, (e) sports, and (f) photos. The following awards are presented in the Metro Group: (1) The Chief Plaque - for the best written metro Hearst paper; (2) John Randolph Hearst Memorial Trophy - for photographic excellence; (3) The William Randolph Hearst, Jr. Prize to the winner of the Enterprise competition; (4) Community Service Awards - for outstanding community service and accomplishment (exceptional nominations receive or share a $1,000 award); and (5) Individual Capital Prize winners - for: (a) spot news, (b) features, (c) heads/captions, (d) enterprise, (e) sports, (f) business/finance, (g) art/graphics, (h) news photos, (i) feature photo, and (j) sports photos. Awarded annually. The Metro Group Awards were established in 1956; the Community Group Awards were established in 1981.

• 10357 •
Heart of Denver Romance Writers
Kathy Elbinger, Pres.
PO Box 3811
Englewood, CO 80155
Phone: (303)730-7849
E-mail: zbeewmn@aol.com
Home Page: http://www.hodrw.com

• 10358 • **Aspen Gold Award**
For excellence in published and unpublished writing. Recognition award bestowed annually.

• 10359 • **Molly Award**
For excellence in published and unpublished writing. Recognition award bestowed annually.

• 10360 •
Heart of New England Chihuahua Club
35 Anderson Rd.
Gilmanton Iron Works, NH 03837-9705

• 10361 • **Show Awards**
For competition event winners. Recognition award bestowed periodically.

• 10362 •
Heart of Tyler-Main Street
Kathy Comer, Exec.Dir.
PO Box 158
Tyler, TX 75710
Phone: (903)593-6905

Awards are arranged in alphabetical order below their administering organizations

• 10363 • Bruck Award
For service to the downtown area. Recognition award bestowed annually.

• 10364 •
Heart Rhythm Association
Anne Curtis, CEO
1400 K St. NW, Ste. 500
Washington, DC 20005
Phone: (202)464-3400
Fax: (202)464-3401
E-mail: jedwards@hrsonline.org
Home Page: http://hrsonline.org

• 10365 • Distinguished Scientist Award
To recognize individuals who have made major contributions to the advancement of scientific knowledge in the fields of cardiac pacing and/or cardiac electrophysiology. Eligible nominees must be members of the Society. Nomination deadline is September 15. A plaque is awarded annually. Established in 1982.

• 10366 • Distinguished Service Award
To recognize outstanding service to the field of cardiac pacing and electrophysiology. Nominations may be made. A plaque is awarded annually.

• 10367 • Distinguished Teacher Award
Recognizes an outstanding teacher in the field of cardiac pacing and electrophysiology. Nominations may be made. A plaque is awarded annually.

• 10368 • Pioneer Award
To recognize an individual who has been active in cardiac pacing and/or cardiac electrophysiology for many years, and has made significant contributions to the field. A certificate is awarded annually.

• 10369 • Young Investigators Awards
Recognizes original clinical investigation or basic research in the area of cardiac and/or cardiac electrophysiology. Any physician or scientist who is in a residency or fellowship program or who has been in one within the past three years in North America is eligible. A monetary award and a plaque are presented for first and second place winners annually. Runners-up receive monetary awards. Established in 1981.

• 10370 •
Hebrew Immigrant Aid Society
Neil Greenbaum, Pres./CEO
333 7th Ave., 16th Fl.
New York, NY 10001
Phone: (212)967-4100
Toll-Free: 800-HIA-S714
Fax: (212)967-4483
E-mail: info@hias.org
Home Page: http://www.hias.org

Formerly: (1954) United HIAS Service.

• 10371 • Harold Friedman Memorial Award
To recognize a former refugee who has made an important contribution to U.S. society. Established in 1992 in memory of HIAS President Emeritus, Harold Friedman.

• 10372 • Liberty Award
To recognize an individual for a substantial contribution to the furtherance of peace and freedom. Candidates are chosen by the HIAS Awards Dinner Committee. A metal casting of the Statue of Liberty mounted on hardwood with a brass plate inscribed with a quote from Emma Lazarus is awarded at the discretion of the Board of Directors annually at the HIAS Awards Dinner. Established in 1966.

• 10373 • Zvi Hirsch Masliansky Award
To recognize significant humanitarian services on behalf of refugees, migrants, and others forced by political or religious considerations to seek new countries of residence. Established in 1972 by Dr. Harold M. Weinberg in memory of his father-in-law, Reverend Zvi Hirsch Masliansky, an immigrant and a founder of the Society.

• 10374 •
Hebrew Union College - Jewish Institute of Religion
Rabbi David Ellenson, Pres.
Brookdale Center
1 W 4th St.
New York, NY 10012-1186
Phone: (212)674-5300
Fax: (212)388-1720
Home Page: http://www.huc.edu

• 10375 • The Dr. Bernard Heller Prize
To recognize an organization or individual whose work, writings or research reflects significant contributions in these areas, and carries an award of $10,000. Along with a citation, the prize is conferred annually at the Commencement Exercises of the Hebrew Union College-Jewish Institute of Religion in Cincinnati, Ohio.

• 10376 • Roger E. Joseph Prize
To honor an individual or organization whose conduct or work enhances or encourages the values or ideals which derive from religious teaching. A monetary prize of $10,000 is awarded annually. Established in 1978 by Burton M. Joseph and Mrs. Betty Greenberg to honor their brother, Roger Joseph, a man of high principle and moral determination. Sponsored by the Joseph Foundation, Minneapolis, Minnesota. Additional information is available from Dr. Alfred Gottschalk, President, 3101 Clifton Avenue, Cincinnati, OH 45220, phone: (513) 221-1875.

• 10377 •
The Heinz Family Foundation
Jeffrey R. Lewis, Pres.
3200 Dominion Tower
625 Liberty Ave.
Pittsburgh, PA 15222
E-mail: kodell@heinz.org
Home Page: http://www.heinzawards.net

• 10378 • Heinz Award in Public Policy
To recognize and honor individuals who have a positive impact on the process of public policy. Eligible recipients include individuals who have significantly influenced the administrative, legislative, or regulatory process. Specifically, this includes those who have identified, designed, and implemented changes to an area of public policy or individuals whose impact on laws, regulations, and policies has resulted in the advancement of liberty and the betterment of society. An unrestricted monetary prize of $250,000 and a medallion are awarded annually. Established in 1993.

• 10379 • Heinz Award in Technology, the Economy and Employment
To honor individuals who have created and implemented innovative programs to advance regional or national economic growth through job creation, technology advancement, competitiveness, and fair trade *t* all in a sustainable and environmentally safe manner. An unrestricted monetary prize of $250,000 and a medallion are awarded annually. Established in 1993.

• 10380 • Heinz Award in the Arts and Humanities
To recognize the individual creator, as well as those who best preserve, teach, interpret, and advance this spirit of curiosity and faith in the power of the human mind. An unrestricted monetary prize of $250,000 and a medallion are awarded annually. Established in 1993.

• 10381 • Heinz Award in the Environment
To recognize individuals who, like John Heinz, have confronted environmental concerns with a spirit of innovation and who demonstrate the same blend of action and creativity in approaching the protection of our environment. An unrestricted monetary prize of $250,000 and a medallion are awarded annually. Established in 1993.

• 10382 • Heinz Award in the Human Condition
To recognize individuals who have developed and implemented significant new programs to improve the human condition. It seeks to recognize outstanding efforts to empower and protect all individuals, based on a fundamental belief that the degradation or victimization of any of us ultimately impoverishes us all. An unrestricted monetary prize of $250,000 and a medallion are awarded annually. Established in 1993.

• 10383 •
Heiser Program for Research in Leprosy and Tuberculosis
450 E 63rd St.
New York, NY 10021-7999
Phone: (212)751-6233
Fax: (212)688-6794

• 10384 • **Heiser Program for Research in Leprosy and Tuberculosis**
To provide funds for research in leprosy and tuberculosis. Postdoctoral Research Fellowships are intended to support young biomedical scientists in beginning postdoctoral training for research in leprosy and/or tuberculosis. Applicants should have an M.D., Ph.D., or equivalent degree. While there is no age limit, candidates should be at an early stage of postdoctoral research training. There are no citizenship requirements. Initial awards are for one year, and are renewable for a second year. Stipend levels range from $22,000 to $28,000. Research Grants provide limited support to laboratories involved in leprosy research training or to fund the initiation of new research projects. Applicants must be senior investigators experienced in leprosy and associated with a laboratory that provides training opportunities in this field. Grants are limited in duration to one year, and do not exceed $20,000. The deadline for both programs is February 1. The awards honor Dr. Victor George Heiser, who devoted his life to the study and treatment of tropical diseases, leprosy in particular. Established in 1974. Sponsored by the New York Community Trust.

• 10385 •
Heisman Trophy Trust
National Sports Museum
New York, NY
E-mail: info@heisman.com
Home Page: http://www.heisman.com

• 10386 • **Heisman Memorial Trophy**
To recognize the Outstanding College Football Player in the United States. He is voted in by Heisman Electors, which includes 870 Press and Media (TV and Radio) and all past Heisman winners for a total of 919 Electors. A bronze trophy depicting a football player is presented annually in December. Established in 1935. The trophy was renamed the Heisman Memorial Trophy in honor of John W. Heisman, Director of Athletics for the Downtown Athletic Club at the time of his death in 1936. Heisman was a gifted and winning football coach and historian of the game. Formerly: (1936) DAC Trophy.

• 10387 •
Helen Keller International
Ms. Nan Dale, Pres./CEO
352 Park Ave. S, Ste. 1200
New York, NY 10010
Phone: (212)532-0544
Toll-Free: 877-535-5374
Fax: (212)532-6014
E-mail: info@hkworld.org
Home Page: http://www.hki.org
Formerly: (2000) Helen Keller Worldwide.

• 10388 • **Spirit of Helen Keller Award**
For the display of humanitarian qualities. Awarded when merit is determined.

• 10389 •
Helicopter Association International
Roy D. Resavage, Pres.
1635 Prince St.
Alexandria, VA 22314-2818
Phone: (703)683-4646
Fax: (703)683-4745
E-mail: questions@rotor.com
Home Page: http://www.ROTOR.com
Formerly: (1983) Helicopter Association of America.

• 10390 • **American Eurocopter Golden Hour Award**
To recognize an emergency medical services (EMS) helicopter pilot who has most distinguished himself by performing above and beyond the already high EMS standards, and who has made an outstanding contribution to a specific emergency, thereby advancing the helicopter in lifesaving operations. Awarded annually. Established in 1982.

• 10391 • **Lawrence D. Bell Memorial Award**
To recognize long and significant contributions to the civil helicopter industry. Nominees need not be licensed pilots. Employees of a member in good standing of the Association are eligible. A silver trophy inscribed with recipient's name and achievement is awarded annually. Established in 1971 and sponsored by Bell Helicopter Textron.

• 10392 • **Community Service Award**
To recognize an individual or organization for outstanding service to the community in, but not restricted to, the following areas: the establishment of public-use heliports; advancement of the use of helicopters in urban area operations; and the advancement of Fly Neighborly concepts. First awarded in 1967 as the Max Schumacher Memorial Award. Three awards were combined in 1989 to form the Community Service Award. Formerly: (1988) Fly Neighborly Award; (1988) Raise Your Sites Award; (1988) Max Schumacher Memorial Award.

• 10393 • **Crew of the Year Award**
For recognition of the support and team work of the specialized helicopter crew in performing the various missions of the civil helicopter. Nominees could have worked together on a particular mission, or in a consistently outstanding manner for a period of time. An engraved plaque is awarded annually. Established in 1980 this award was renamed the Igor Sikorsky Award for Humanitarian Service and is sponsored by Sikorsky Aircraft.

• 10394 • **Excellence in Communications Award**
To recognize the media journalist achieving the most creative and distinct dissemination of information about the helicopter. Individuals of the communication media are eligible. A monetary award of $500 and a plaque are awarded annually. Established in 1975.

• 10395 • **Helicopter Airframe Technician Award**
To recognize an individual for outstanding and innovative hands-on workmanship in the field of helicopter airframe maintenance and/or structural repair. Established in 1992.

• 10396 • **Helicopter Avionics Technician Award**
To recognize avionics systems and/or equipment troubleshooting, maintenance, overhaul, and/or repair. Established in 1992.

• 10397 • **Helicopter Electrical/ Electronics Technician Award**
To recognize an individual in maintenance, repair, and troubleshooting of helicopter electrical systems or the maintenance, overhaul, and repair of helicopter electronics equipment. Established in 1992.

• 10398 • **Helicopter Maintenance Award**
To recognize a distinguished contribution to aviation safety through good practice in the field of helicopter maintenance or through significant innovation. Individuals employed by a regular or associate class C member in good standing of the Association are eligible. An engraved plaque commemorating the individual's achievement is awarded annually. Established in 1973.

• 10399 • **Helicopter Powerplant Technician Award**
To recognize an individual for overhaul, troubleshooting, or repair capabilities in the field of helicopter powerplant maintenance. Established in 1992.

• 10400 • **Joe Mashman Safety Award**
To recognize an individual or organization who, through outstanding and dedicated service to others, has contributed significantly to the promotion of aviation safety and safety awareness in the civil helicopter industry. Members of the civil helicopter industry are eligible. A trophy is awarded annually. Established in 1987.

• 10401 • **McDonnell Douglas Law Enforcement Award**
To recognize a worthy contribution to the advancement of the crime-suppression concept of helicopter patrol service. The award is limited to anti-crime patrol service and related activities such as surveillance and pursuit, but not limited to pilots or necessarily restricted to law enforcement personnel. Individuals employed by members in good standing of the Association are eligible. An engraved plaque is awarded annually. Established in 1972 by Hughes Helicopter of Culver City, California. Formerly: Hughes Law Enforcement Award.

• 10402 • Outstanding Certified Flight Instructor Award
To recognize superlative contributions by a helicopter flight instructor in upholding the high standards of excellence for helicopter pilots. Established in 1985.

• 10403 • Pilot of the Year Award
To recognize an outstanding single feat performed by a helicopter pilot during the year, or extraordinary professionalism over a period of time. Nominees must be active civilian pilots. An engraved plaque is awarded annually. Established in 1960 by Stanley Hiller Jr., then president of Hiller Aircraft Corporation.

• 10404 • Pilot Safety Award
To recognize helicopter pilots worldwide who have made accident and violation-free civilian flight a priority. Qualified pilots will receive bronze, silver, or gold-colored certificates for 5,000, 10,000, 15,000, or 20,000 accident and violation-free civilian flight hours. Established in 1988.

• 10405 • Igor I. Sikorsky Award for Humanitarian Service
To recognize the individual(s) who best demonstrates the value of civil rotorcraft to society and their operators through the saving of life, protection of property, and amelioration of distress. Established in 1989 to honor Igor I. Sikorsky, founder of Sikorsky Aircraft.

• 10406 • Robert E. Trimble Memorial Award
To recognize an outstanding commercial helicopter pilot who has distinguished himself/herself in mountain flying, by displaying exceptional ability and good judgement in high-altitude mountain flying. Pilots employed by members in good standing of the Association are eligible. An engraved plaque is awarded annually. Established in 1961.

• 10407 •
Hemophilia Foundation of Michigan
Colleen Joiner MSW, Contact
1921 W Michigan Ave.
Ypsilanti, MI 48197
Phone: (734)544-0015
Toll-Free: 800-482-3041
Fax: (734)544-0095
E-mail: hfm@hfmich.org
Home Page: http://www.hfmich.org

• 10408 • Academic Scholarships
For Michigan residents affected by bleeding disorders. Awarded annually.

• 10409 •
Herb Society of America
Michelle Milks, Office Administrator
9019 Kirtland-Chardon Rd.
Kirtland, OH 44094
Phone: (440)256-0514
Fax: (440)256-0541
E-mail: herbs@herbsociety.org
Home Page: http://www.herbsociety.org

• 10410 • Certificate of Achievement
To recognize individuals, other than those who have received the Medal of Honor, who have made significant contributions in various ways to the Society or to the study of herbs. Nominations are not restricted to members of the Society. Awarded annually. Established in 1976.

• 10411 • Certificate of Appreciation
To recognize an individual, living or dead, for exceptional contributions to the Society or horticulture. Established in 1982.

• 10412 • Helen de Conway Little Medal of Honor
For recognition of outstanding contributions to the Society or in horticulture. Active members of the Society with at least five years active participation may make nominations by January 1. A medal is awarded annually. Established in 1955 and named The Helen de Conway Little Medal of Honor in 1966. Formerly: (1965) Medal of Honor.

• 10413 • Herb Society of America Grant
To further the knowledge and use of herbs and to contribute the results of the study and research to the records of horticulture, science, literature, history, art, or economics. Persons with a proposed program of scientific or academic investigation of herbal plants are eligible. A grant of up to $5,000 for a period of study not to exceed one year is awarded annually. Established in 1964, applications must be received on or before January 31.

• 10414 • Nancy Putnam Howard Award for Horticulture
For recognition of horticultural excellence in the field of herbs. Nominations are not restricted to members of the Society. Awarded annually. Established in 1985.

• 10415 •
Herbert Hoover Presidential Library Association
Patricia Forsythe CFRE, Exec.Dir.
PO Box 696
West Branch, IA 52358
Phone: (319)643-5327
Toll-Free: 800-828-0475
Fax: (319)643-2391
E-mail: info@hooverassociation.org
Home Page: http://www.hooverassociation.org

• 10416 • Herbert Hoover Book Award
To recognize the best scholarly book published during the calendar year on any aspect of American history during President Herbert Hoover's public life, from 1914 to 1964. Collections of essays are not eligible. Authors or publishers must submit seven copies of the book no later than December 31. A monetary prize and a bronze medallion are awarded in May at the annual member banquet. Established in 1992.

• 10417 •
Heritage Association of San Marcos
Frances Stovall, Coor.
PO Box 1806
San Marcos, TX 78667-1806
Phone: (512)392-9997
Phone: (512)392-5580
Fax: (512)393-3735
E-mail: frances76@centuryinter.net

• 10418 • Landmarks
For historic restoration and preservation. Recognition award bestowed annually.

• 10419 •
Heritage Canada Foundation
Brian Anthony, Exec.Dir.
5 Blackburn Ave.
Ottawa, ON, Canada K1N 8A2
Phone: (613)237-1066
Fax: (613)237-5987
E-mail: heritagecanada@heritagecanada.org
Home Page: http://www.heritagecanada.org

• 10420 • Heritage Canada Achievement Awards (Prix d'Excellence d'Heritage)
To recognize the exemplary accomplishments of individuals or groups in the preservation of heritage within their respective provinces or territories. The project or work must be concerned with the conservation of the built heritage and cultural landscapes within the candidate's province or territory. There must be evidence of a high level of performance in the candidate's project or work. Presented jointly by Heritage Canada and established provincial territorial umbrella groups or associations that are members of Heritage Canada and have juried award programs and award ceremonies. Each group or association, called a partner, is fully responsible for choosing its candidate within prescribed criteria and eligibility rules. In this way, Heritage Canada also recognizes these partners for their dedication and commitment to excellence in heritage preservation. A medal is presented jointly by Heritage Canada and the partner. Established in 1989.

• 10421 • Gabrielle Leger Medal (Medaille Gabrielle Leger)
To recognize an individual who has contributed a lifetime of service to heritage preservation on a national basis. Applications must be sponsored by an organized heritage group and/or elected officials at any level of government. A medal and a certificate are awarded annually. Established

Awards are arranged in alphabetical order below their administering organizations

in 1978 by Gabrielle Leger, widow of Governor General, the late Right Honorable Jules Leger. Nominations must be submitted by no later than March 31 each year.

• 10422 • Lieutenant-Governor's Medal (Medaille du Lieutenant-Gouverneur)
To recognize outstanding work in architectural conservation on a provincial level by an individual or group. The applicant must have demonstrated continuous efforts in the field of heritage preservation benefiting the province where the Foundation's Annual Meeting is being held. Applications must be sponsored by an organized heritage group and/or elected officials at any level of government. Entries must be submitted no later than March 31 of each year. A medal and a certificate are awarded annually. Established in 1979.

• 10423 •
Heritage Center
Peter Strong, Dir.
Red Cloud Indian School
100 Mission Dr.
Pine Ridge, SD 57770-2100
Phone: (605)867-5491
Fax: (605)867-1291
E-mail: redcloudpr@redcloudschool.org
Home Page: http://www.redcloudschool.org/museum/museum.htm

• 10424 • Red Cloud Indian Art Show
For recognition of excellent Native American art. Any tribal member of the native peoples of North America over 18 years of age is eligible. The deadline for applications is May 22. Monetary awards of $300 are presented in the following divisions: paintings - oils, tempera, casein, encaustic polymer, and acrylic; paintings - watercolors; graphics - pencil, pen and ink, craypas, crayon, wash, and charcoal; mixed media; and three dimensional works - sculpture and carvings, in any media other than pottery. Native Americans who enter the Art Show are eligible. In addition to merit awards in each division, the following awards are presented: Tony Begay Memorial Award of $50 in memory of Navajo artist Tony Begay by Tom Woodard of Gallup, New Mexico, to the artist whose works depict the most explicit development of an Indian theme; M. L. Woodard Award of $50 for the painting, drawing, or sketch depicting the most explicit development of an Indian theme; Bill and Sue Hensler Award of $50 for traditional representation in sculpture; Aplan Award of $100 for the outstanding young Indian artist, by Mr. and Mrs. Jim Aplan; Powers Award of $100 for the best representation of Indian women, by William K. and Marla Powers; Bonnie Erickson Award for the best representation of children; Allan and Joyce Niederman Award of $100 for the most traditional painting; Nicolaus Rostkowski Award of $100 for the best abstract painting; Gillihan Award of $100 for the most realistic rendering of an American Indian on horseback; Diederich Award of $250 to a young artist whose work shows the greatest improvement; Diederich Award of $250 for the best representation of a traditional Sioux Indian; Diederich Landscape Award of $250 for the best depiction of the Black Hills/Badlands; Diederich Landscape Award of $250 for the best depiction of Lakes, Mountains, or Prairies; Iron Cloud Family Award for best sense of humor; historic-cultural setting; Bennett County Booster Award of $100 to the most innovative artist; Oscar Howe Memorial Award, of $100 for the best cubist painting; and $1,500 Purchase Awards. Awarded annually. Established in 1969.

• 10425 •
Heritage Toronto
James M. Clemens, Treas
Historic St. Lawrence Hall, 3rd Fl.
157 King St. E
Toronto, ON, Canada M5C 1G9
Phone: (416)338-0684
Fax: (416)392-1772
E-mail: email@heritagetoronto.org
Home Page: http://www.heritagetoronto.org

• 10426 • Heritage Toronto Awards of Merit
To recognize individuals, groups, organizations, and publications for outstanding contributions to the preservation of the history or heritage of the city of Toronto. Nominations are accepted. A framed certificate is awarded annually. Certificates of Commendation are also awarded. Established in 1974.

• 10427 •
Herpetologists' League
Dr. Lora Smith, Treas.
PO Box 519
Emporia State University
Bainbridge, GA 39818
Phone: (229)246-7374
Fax: (229)734-6650
E-mail: hleague@bellsouth.net
Home Page: http://www.inhs.uiuc.edu/cbd/HL

• 10428 • Herpetologists' League Award for Graduate Research
To recognize a student for an outstanding professional paper presented orally and submitted with an extended abstract. A monetary award of $500, 10 volumes of back issues of the journal *Herpetologica* and an invitation to submit a manuscript to *Herpetologica*/*Herpetological* Monographs are presented annually when merited. Finalists for this award receive travel grants of $ 200. Established in 1963. Formerly: (1991) Herpetologists' League Student Prize.

• 10429 •
High Point Convention and Visitors Bureau
Charlotte M. Young, Pres./CEO
PO Box 2273
High Point, NC 27261
Phone: (336)884-5255
Toll-Free: 800-720-5255
Fax: (336)884-5256
E-mail: info@highpoint.org
Home Page: http://www.highpoint.org

• 10430 • Arts and Tourism Grants Program
For promoting travel and tourism in High Point. Monetary award bestowed annually.

• 10431 •
Hillel
Charles & Lynn Schusterman Intl. Ctr.
Arthur & Rochelle Belfer Bldg.
800 8th St. NW
Washington, DC 20001-3724
Phone: (202)449-6500
Fax: (202)857-6693
E-mail: info@hillel.org
Home Page: http://www.hillel.org

Formerly: (1995) B'nai B'rith Hillel Foundations.

• 10432 • William Haber Award
To recognize highly original programming and innovative projects that have strengthened the quality of Jewish life in the campus setting. Open to all communal agencies and organizations that provide significant service to the Jewish campus community. Nominations must be made by June 1. A plaque is presented annually. Established in 1976 by B'nai B'rith Hillel Commission. The award honors the late Dean William Haber of the University of Michigan.

• 10433 • Elie Wiesel Award for Jewish Art and Culture
To recognize original, innovative campus-generated projects and programs that enhance the quality of Jewish artistic life on the campus and in the general community. Open to all organizations and agencies that serve the Jewish university community. Established in 1989 to honor Professor Elie Wiesel, whose Nobel Prize for Peace testifies to the universal power of the artist's medium. Annual deadline: June 1.

• 10434 •
The Sidney Hillman Foundation, Inc.
Jo-Ann Mort, Exec.Dir.
% Unite Here
275 7th Ave.
New York, NY 10001
Phone: (212)265-7000
Fax: (212)582-3175
E-mail: info@hillmanfoundation.org
Home Page: http://www.hillmanfoundation.org

• 10435 • The Sidney Hillman Foundation Prize Awards
To recognize outstanding contributions dealing with social or economic themes and the advancement of social welfare. Contributions may be in the form of published daily or periodical journalism, nonfiction, radio, and television. All entries must have been published or produced during the award year. Material may be submitted by the author, publisher, or by anyone connected with it. The deadline for submissions is January 17. A monetary award of $2,000 and a plaque are awarded annually. Established in 1950 in honor of Sidney Hillman, the first presi-

dent of Amalgamated Clothing Workers of America.

• 10436 •
Hillsdale College
Center for Constructive Alternatives/The Shavano Institute
33 E College St.
Hillsdale, MI 49242
Phone: (517)437-7341
Toll-Free: 800-437-2268
Fax: (517)437-3923
E-mail: cca@hillsdale.edu
Home Page: http://www.hillsdale.edu/shavano

• 10437 • **Salvatori Teaching Award**
Recognizes outstanding high school teachers. $25,000 is awarded annually.

• 10438 •
Hillside Historical Society
Alan D. Zimmerman, Pres.
111 Conant St.
Hillside, NJ 07205
Phone: (908)353-8828
Phone: (908)352-9270

• 10439 • **U.S. History Award**
For the highest ranking senior at Hillside High School. Recognition award bestowed annually.

• 10440 •
The Hip Society
Karen V. Andersen, Exec.Dir.
951 Old County Rd., No. 182
Belmont, CA 94002
Phone: (650)596-6190
Fax: (650)508-2040
Home Page: http://www.hipsoc.org

• 10441 • **John Charnley Award**
Annual monetary award.

• 10442 • **Otto Aufranc Award**
Annual monetary award.

• 10443 •
Hispanic Council of St. Clair County
Jesus Castillo, Chairperson
3110 Goulden St.
Port Huron, MI 48060
Phone: (810)985-4589

• 10444 • **Hispanic Council Scholarship**
For Hispanic high school graduates in financial need. Scholarship awarded annually.

• 10445 •
Histochemical Society
William Stahl, Exec.Dir.
University Sta.
PO Box 85630
Seattle, WA 98145-1630
Phone: (206)616-5278
Fax: (206)616-5842
E-mail: mail@histochemicalsociety.org
Home Page: http://www.histochemicalsociety.org

• 10446 • **Ralph D. Lillie Award**
To recognize the most outstanding student presentation (poster or platform) for inclusion at the annual meeting of the Society. Candidates must be either doctoral students or in the first year of a postdoctoral program at the time of the meeting; and they must be the senior author of the paper. Membership of The Histochemical Society is required.A monetary award of $200, a certificate and a travel award is presented annually. Established to honor Ralph D. Lillie.

• 10447 •
Historic Albany Foundation
Elizabeth P. Griffin, Exec.Dir.
89 Lexington Ave.
Albany, NY 12206
Phone: (518)465-0876
Phone: (518)465-2987
Fax: (518)465-0876
Home Page: http://www.historic-albany.org

• 10448 • **Preservation Merit Awards**
For outstanding preservation effort. Recognition award bestowed annually.

• 10449 •
Historic Augusta
Erick D. Montgomery, Exec.Dir.
PO Box 37
PO Box 37
Augusta, GA 30903-0037
Phone: (706)724-0436
Fax: (706)724-3083
E-mail: info@historicaugusta.org
Home Page: http://www.HistoricAugusta.org

• 10450 • **Historic Preservation Award**
For exemplary restoration, rehabilitation or preservation activity in Augusta. Recognition award bestowed annually.

• 10451 •
Historic Chattahoochee Commission
Douglas Clare Purcell, Exec.Dir.
PO Box 33
Eufaula, AL 36072-0033
Phone: (334)687-9755
Phone: (334)687-6631
Toll-Free: 877-POO-CHIE
Fax: (334)687-6631
E-mail: hcc3@earthlink.net
Home Page: http://www.hcc-al-ga.org

• 10452 • **Achievement Award**
For heritage-tourism activities. Medal awarded annually.

• 10453 •
Historic Harmony
Kathy Luek, Admin.
218 Mercer St.
PO Box 524
Harmony, PA 16037
Phone: (724)452-7341
Toll-Free: 888-821-4822
E-mail: info@harmonymuseum.com
Home Page: http://harmonymuseum.org

• 10454 • **Historic Harmony Heritage Award**
For preservation, restoration, encouraging history education and appreciation. Recognition award bestowed annually.

• 10455 •
Historic Landmarks Foundation of Indiana
J. Reid Williamson Jr., Pres.
340 West Michigan St.
Indianapolis, IN 46202
Phone: (317)639-4534
Toll-Free: 800-450-4534
Fax: (317)639-6734
E-mail: info@historiclandmarks.org
Home Page: http://www.historiclandmarks.org

• 10456 • **Servaas Award**
For outstanding contributions to historic preservation in Indiana. Monetary award bestowed annually.

• 10457 •
Historic Mobile Preservation Society
Marilyn Culpepper, Exec.Dir.
300 Oakleigh Pl.
Mobile, AL 36604
Phone: (251)432-6161
E-mail: hmps@bellsouth.net
Home Page: http://www.historicmobile.org

• 10458 • **Architectural Awards**
For restoring houses and buildings. Recognition award bestowed annually.

• 10459 •
Historic New Orleans Collection
Williams Prize Committee
533 Royal St.
New Orleans, LA 70130-2179
Phone: (504)523-4662
Fax: (504)598-7108
E-mail: info@hnoc.org
Home Page: http://www.hnoc.org

• 10460 • **Kemper and Leila Williams Prize in Louisiana History**
To recognize excellence in the writing of Louisiana history. Entries must be submitted by January 15 and are eligible only in the year following

publication. A monetary award of $1,500 and a plaque are awarded to the best published work. Awarded annually at the Louisiana Historical Association's annual banquet. Established in 1974 by the Historic New Orleans Collection in cooperation with the Louisiana Historical Association in memory of General L. Kemper Williams and Leila Moore Williams, co-founders of the Kemper and Leila Williams Foundation, which operates as the Historic New Orleans Collection. Entrise must be submitted by January 15. Formerly: (1997) General L. Kemper Williams Prizes in Louisiana History.

• 10461 •
Historical Society of Frederick County
Mark S. Hudson, Exec.Dir.
24 E. Church St.
Frederick, MD 21701
Phone: (301)663-1188
Fax: (301)663-0526
E-mail: director@fwp.net

• 10462 • **Preservation Award**
For outstanding contribution by an individual to the field of preservation. Recognition award bestowed annually.

• 10463 •
Historical Society of Michigan
Larry J. Wagenaar, Exec.Dir.
1305 Abbott Rd.
East Lansing, MI 48823
Phone: (517)324-1828
Toll-Free: 800-692-1828
Fax: (517)324-4370
E-mail: hsm@hsmichigan.org
Home Page: http://www.hsmichigan.org

• 10464 • **Awards of Merit**
For historic preservation, Michigan history publications (university and commercial press, private printing, juvenile) media, special programs/ events, distinguished service, institutions, educational programs, educators, local societies, business. Recognition awards bestowed each Fall at the State History Conference.

• 10465 •
Historical Society of Palm Beach County
Debra Murray, Dir./Res.&Archv.
139 N County Rd., Ste. 25
Palm Beach, FL 33480
Phone: (561)832-4164
Fax: (561)832-7965
E-mail: historicalsocietypbc@yahoo.com
Home Page: http://gopbi.com/community/ groups/pbchistory/index

• 10466 • **Judge R. Knott Award**
For significant contribution to the history of Palm Beach County. Recognition award bestowed annually.

• 10467 •
Historical Society of Pennsylvania
David Moltke-Hansen, Pres. and CEO
1300 Locust St.
Philadelphia, PA 19107
Phone: (215)732-6200
Fax: (215)732-2680
E-mail: library@hsp.org
Home Page: http://www.hsp.org

• 10468 • **Jan Ilavsky Memorial Scholarship**
To encourage graduate students to select a topic in Slovak history or culture (broadly defined) for their Ph.D. dissertations. Applicants must be enrolled in a doctoral program of an accredited North American university. A scholarship of $2,000 is awarded annually in September. Established in 1985 in memory of Dr. Jan Ilavsky.

• 10469 •
Historical Society of Princeton
Maureen Smyth, Asst.Dir./Curator
Bainbridge House
158 Nassau St.
Princeton, NJ 08542
Phone: (609)921-6748
Phone: (609)921-6817
Fax: (609)921-6939
E-mail: maureen@princetonhistory.org
Home Page: http:// www.princetonhistory.org

• 10470 • **Preservation Awards**
For outstanding contributions to historic preservation in Princeton. Recognition award bestowed annually.

• 10471 •
Historical Society of Washington, DC
Shireen Dodson, Pres./CEO
801 K St., NW
Washington, DC 20001
Phone: (202)383-1800
Fax: (202)383-1870
E-mail: info@hswdc.org
Home Page: http://www.citymuseumdc.org/

• 10472 • **Renchard Prize**
For outstanding historic preservation projects. Recognition award bestowed annually.

• 10473 •
History of Dermatology Society
Lawrence C. Parish MD, Pres.
1760 Market St., No. 301
Philadelphia, PA 19103-4106
Phone: (215)563-8333
Fax: (215)563-3044
E-mail: larryderm@yahoo.com
Home Page: http://www.dermato.med.br/ hds

• 10474 • **Samuel J. Zakon Lectureship**
To recognize an individual who gives a lecture on the history of dermatology. A plaque is awarded annually at the December meeting. Established in 1972 to honor Samuel J. Zakon, the first historian of the American Academy of Dermatology.

• 10475 • **Samuel J. Zakon Prize**
To recognize the best paper(s) on the history of dermatology. A plaque is awarded annually at the December meeting. Established in 1980 to honor Samuel J. Zakon, the first historian of the American Academy of Dermatology.

• 10476 •
History of Economics Society
D. Wade Hands, Pres.
History of Economics Society
University of New Hampshire
McConnell Hall
15 College Rd.
Durham, NH 03824
Phone: (603)862-3336
E-mail: hes@orbit.unh.edu
Home Page: http://www.eh.net/HE/ HisEcSoc

• 10477 • **Distinguished Fellow Award**
For recognition of scholarly achievement in the area of the history of economic thought. Outstanding scholarly writing is considered for the award. A plaque is presented annually at the May meeting of the Association. Established in 1980.

• 10478 • **Service Award**
Recognize outstanding contributions to the IEEE Computer Society and its related activities.

• 10479 • **Seymour Cray Computer Science and Engineering Award**
Recognizes innovative contributions to high performance computing systems that best exemplify the creative spirit demonstrated by Seymour Cray. A crystal momento, an illuminated certificate and a $10,000 honorarium are awarded.

• 10480 •
History of Education Society
Linda Eisenmann, Pres.
Slippery Rock University
220 McKay Education Bldg.
Slippery Rock, PA 16057

• 10481 • **Henry Barnard Prize**
For recognition of the finest historical essay in educational research over the past two years written by a graduate student. Nominations are made by an HES Committee. A monetary prize of $500, and the publication of the winning essay in *History of Education Quarterly* are awarded biennially. Established in 1975 in memory of the first U.S. Commissioner of Education, Henry Barnard, the most distinguished educational historian of the 19th century.

• 10482 • History of Education Society Award

For recognition of the finest research article in educational history published during the preceding two years. Articles published in the requisite two year period and submitted to the nominating committee are considered for the award. A monetary award of $500 is presented biennially. A list of awardees is published in *History of Education Quarterly*. Established in 1976.

• 10483 • Outstanding Book Award

For recognition of the best book in the field of educational history. A monetary award of $500 is presented biennially.

• 10484 •
History of Science Society
Robert J. Malone, Exec.Dir.
University of Florida
PO Box 117360
Gainesville, FL 32611-7360
Phone: (352)392-1677
Fax: (352)392-2795
E-mail: info@hssonline.org
Home Page: http://www.hssonline.org

• 10485 • Watson Davis and Helen Miles Davis Prize

To recognize the author of an outstanding book published in the three preceding years. The work should be especially useful in teaching or promoting public understanding of the history of science. A monetary award of $1,000 is presented annually at the society's annual meeting. Established in 1985 in honor of Watson Davis, who devoted his career to the public understanding of science.

• 10486 • Derek Price-Rod Webster Award

To recognize the author of an outstanding article appearing in *Isis*, the society's quarterly journal, during the preceding three years. A monetary prize of $1,000 and a certificate are awarded annually. Established in 1979 by Jacob Zeitlin, a long-time friend of the society, it was renamed in 1988 to honor Derek Price, a long-time Professor of History of Science at Yale, and then changed to its current name to honor Roderick Webster, a generous supporter of the History of Science. Formerly: Zeitlin-Ver Brugge Prize.

• 10487 • Joseph H. Hazen Education Prize

Recognizes outstanding contributions to the teaching of History of Science. Education activities recognized by the award are to be construed to the broadest sense and should include but not limited to the following: classroom teaching (K-12, undergraduate, graduate, or extended education), mentoring of young scholars, museum work, journalism, organization, and administration of educational programs, influential writing, educational research, innovation in the methodology of instruction, preparation of pedagogical materials, or public outreach through non-profit media.

• 10488 • Margaret W. Rossiter History of Women in Science Prize

To encourage the development of the growing specialty of women in science within the history of science and to recognize those scholars who are pioneering and developing this field. A monetary prize of $1,000 is awarded annually, alternating each years between an award for an outstanding book and an outstanding article published in the previous four years. Established in 1987.

• 10489 • Pfizer Award

This most prestigious award is given to recognize the author of an outstanding book in the history of science published in English, either in its original edition or in translation, during the previous three years. A monetary award of $2,500 and a medal, designed by the sculptor Harold Tovish, are awarded annually. Established in 1958 by Pfizer, Inc.

• 10490 • Sarton Medal

This, the highest honor of the society, is given for recognition of an outstanding historian of science. The candidate is selected from the international scholarly community and is recognized for a career devoted to the field and for exceptional scholarship. A medal, designed by Bern Dibner, a longtime friend of the society, may be awarded annually. The award was established in 1955 and named for the founder of *Isis*, the society's quarterly journal.

• 10491 • Henry and Ida Schuman Prize

This prize was established to recognize an original essay in the history of science and its cultural influences by undergraduate and graduate students. Submissions must be in English or accompanied by an English translation, must be unpublished, and must not exceed 8,000 words in length. The deadline is April 1. It is hoped that the prize-winning essay will be published in *Isis*. The winner receives a monetary prize of $500 and up to $500 for expenses to attend the society's annual meeting. The prize was established in 1956 by Henry and Ida Schuman and was renamed The Nathan Reingold Prize in 2004.

• 10492 •
Hobey Baker Memorial Award
1321 E 78th St.
Minneapolis, MN 55401
E-mail: mfruth@stellusconsulting.com
Home Page: http://www.hobeybaker.com

• 10493 • Hobey Baker Memorial Award

To recognize the outstanding college hockey player in the United States. Candidates must comply with NCAA rules and be full-time students at an NCAA college or university. A trophy depicting a hockey player in action is awarded annually at the end of the collegiate hockey season at a formal ceremony at the Decathlon Athletic Club. Established in 1981 in memory of Hobey Baker, an outstanding sportsman and athlete of the 1910 era.

• 10494 •
Hockey Hall of Fame
William C. Hay, Chmn. and CEO
BCE Place
30 Yonge St.
Toronto, ON, Canada M5E 1X8
Phone: (416)360-7735
Phone: (416)360-7765
Fax: (416)360-1501
E-mail: info@hhof.com
Home Page: http://www.hhof.com
Formerly: (1983) Hockey Hall of Fame.

• 10495 • Elmer Ferguson Memorial Award

To recognize distinguished members of the newspaper profession whose words have brought honor to journalism and to hockey. Awarded annually. Selected by the Professional Hockey Writers' Association.

• 10496 • Foster Hewitt Memorial Award

To recognize members of the radio and television industry who made outstanding contributions to their profession and the game during their career in hockey broadcasting. Awarded annually. Selected by the NHL Broadcasters' Association.

• 10497 • Hockey Hall of Fame and Museum Honored Member

To honor the greats of hockey by recognizing playing ability, integrity, character, and contribution to their team and the game of hockey in general. There are three classes of membership - Players, Builders, and Referees. Nominations are accepted by the Selection Committee. Established in 1945.

• 10498 •
Houston Symphony Ima Hogg Young Artist Competition
Matthew VanBesien, Exec.Dir.
615 Louisiana St.
Houston, TX 77002
Phone: (713)224-4240
Fax: (713)224-0453
E-mail: e&o@houstonsymphony.org
Home Page: http://www.houstonsymphony.org
Formerly: Ima Hogg National Young Artist Audition.

• 10499 • Houston Symphony Ima Hogg Young Artist Competition

To provide the opportunity for qualified young musicians of standard orchestral instruments preparing for a professional career to perform with the Houston Symphony. Applicants must be between the ages of 19-29 inclusive; citizens of the United States, Canada, or Mexico, or foreign students currently enrolled in a U.S. institution. The awards consist of: first prize $5,000 and performance with the Houston Symphony; second prize - $2,500 and performance with the Houston Symphony; and third prize $1,000. Awarded annually. Established in 1976 in memory of Ima Hogg, distinguished benefactress of the city of Houston and founder of the Houston Symphony. Please call or write for detailed requirements.

• 10500 • Houston Symphony League Concerto Competition

Encourages musical talent and inspires student musicians to further their instrumental studies. Any student of a public, private, or home school living within a 75-mile radius of Houston, who is 18 years old or younger as of the competition date, who has not yet graduated from high school, who is compliance with the no pass no play mandate for Texas schools, who is not enrolled as a full-time student in a college, university, or conservatory, and who is capable of performing a full concerto on a standard orchestral instrument or piano from memory with an orchestra may apply. A gold medal, $1000 and a performance with the Houston Symphony; a silver medal and $500; and a bronze medal and $100 are awarded annually. Established in 1948. Formerly: (1979) Houston Symphony Student Auditions; (1996) Josie Tomforde Competition.

• 10501 •
Holistic Arts Fair Association
Eric A. Meece, Contact
3914 Leigh Ave.
San Jose, CA 95124-2910
Phone: (408)448-6726
E-mail: eameece@california.com
Home Page: http://www.california.com/~eameece/hafa.htm

• 10502 • Visionary Art Show Awards

For top paintings and graphics as determined by jury of art teachers. Recognition award bestowed annually.

• 10503 •
Holland Historical Trust
Paula Dunlap, Contact
31 W 10th St.
Holland, MI 49423
Phone: (616)394-1362
Toll-Free: 888-200-9123
Fax: (616)394-4756
E-mail: hollandmuseum@hollandmuseum.org
Home Page: http://www.hollandmuseum.org

• 10504 • Friend of History

Award of recognition. For preservation or communication of community's heritage fostering understanding and pride in all its people. Awarded annually.

• 10505 •
Holland Society of New York
Rev. Louis O. Springsteen, Sec.
122 E 58th St.
New York, NY 10022
Phone: (212)758-1675
Fax: (212)758-2232
E-mail: hollsoc@aol.com
Home Page: http://www.hollandsociety.org

• 10506 • Gold Medal for Distinguished Achievement

To recognize distinguished achievement by citizens of the United States and the Netherlands who are not members of the Society. Individuals must hold United States or Netherlands citizenship and must have made some distinguished contribution of benefit to society as a whole. A gold medal is generally awarded in the fall. Established in 1922.

• 10507 •
Holly Society of America
Rondalyn Reeser, Sec.
309 Buck St.
PO Box 803
Millville, NJ 08332-3819
Phone: (856)825-4300
E-mail: secretary@hollysocam.org
Home Page: http://www.hollysocam.org

• 10508 • William F. Kosar Award

To recognize outstanding contributions to the hybridization, evaluation, selection or introduction of hollies. Awarded as merited. Established in 1987 in honor of W.F. Kosar, an outstanding hybridizer formerly with the U.S. National Arboretum.

• 10509 • Shiu-Ying Hu Award

To honor Dr. Shiu-ying Hu of Harvard University for her lifetime of studies of the genus Ilex and her recognized position as an authority on the hollies of China. The award is presented to one or more individuals that have been found by the Committee to have achieved a record of distinguished performance.

• 10510 • Wolf-Fenton Award

To recognize outstanding contributions to the greater appreciation and scientific knowledge of holly. A certificate is awarded as merited. Established in 1982 to honor HAS founder Clarence R. Wolf. Formerly: (1989) Certificate of Honor - HSA; (1928) C. R. Wolf Award.

• 10511 •
Hollywood Foreign Press Association
Chantal Dinnage, Managing Dir.
646 N Robertson Blvd.
West Hollywood, CA 90069-5022
Phone: (310)657-1731
Fax: (310)657-5576
E-mail: info@hfpa.org
Home Page: http://www.hfpa.org

• 10512 • Cecil B. De Mille Award

For special recognition of outstanding contributions to the entertainment field. The winner is selected by a vote of the Board of Directors of the Association. A Golden Globe statuette is awarded annually. Established in 1952.

• 10513 • Golden Globe Awards

This, the highest award of the organization, is given for recognition of outstanding efforts in the entertainment field. Awards are given for motion pictures and television in the following categories: best motion picture - drama; best motion picture - musical/comedy; best foreign language film; best performance by an actress in a motion picture - drama; best performance by an actor in a motion picture - drama; best performance by an actress in a motion picture - comedy/musical; best performance by an actor in a motion picture - comedy/musical; best performance by an actress in a supporting role in a motion picture; best performance by an actor in a supporting role in a motion picture; best director - motion picture; best screenplay - motion picture; best original score - motion picture; best original song - motion picture; best television series - drama; best television series - comedy/musical; best mini-series or motion picture made for television; best performance by an actress in a television series - drama; best performance by an actor in a television series - drama; best performance by an actress in a television series musical/comedy; best performance by an actor in a television series - musical/comedy; best performance by an actress in a mini-series. or motion picture made for television; best performance by an actor in a mini-series, or motion picture made for television; best performance by an actress in a supporting role in a series, mini-series, or motion picture made for television; and best performance by an actor in a supporting role in a series, mini-series, or motion picture made for television. Golden Globe statuettes are awarded annually. Established in 1944.

• 10514 •
Hollywood Radio and Television Society
Dave Ferrara, Exec.Dir.
13701 Riverside Dr., Ste. 205
Sherman Oaks, CA 91423
Phone: (818)789-1182
Fax: (818)789-1210
E-mail: info@hrts.org
Home Page: http://www.hrts.org

• 10515 • Advertising Executive of the Year

To recognize outstanding efforts in international communications. A trophy is awarded annually. Established in 1960. Formerly: Man or Woman of the Year.

• 10516 • International Broadcasting Awards

To promote and improve radio and television advertising, honor men and women who create and produce it, and increase international cooperation in this field. Finalists are selected in 17 television and 12 radio categories. In May, an international board of final judges chooses one trophy winner in each category, and in June, chooses overall sweepstakes winners for both television and radio. The competition is open on an equal basis to television and radio commercials transmitted anywhere in the world during the year. The deadline for entries is in January. "Ollie" trophies are awarded for the best commercial in each category, certificates are awarded to all finalists, and plaques are awarded to sweepstakes winners. Awarded annually at the IBA Presentation Show. Established in 1960.

• 10517 •
Home Baking Association
Tom Payne, Pres.
2931 SW Gainsboro Rd.
Topeka, KS 66614-4413
Phone: (785)478-3283
Fax: (785)478-3024
E-mail: hbapatton@aol.com
Home Page: http://www.homebaking.org

• 10518 • Home Baking Association Educator Award
Annual award for home baking educators in two categories. One dor a Family and Consumer Science Educator and a second category for an educator with a Community-Based Baking Program.

• 10519 •
Home Builders Association of Western Massachusetts
Bradford L. Campbell, Exec.Dir.
240 Cadwell Dr.
Springfield, MA 01104
Phone: (413)733-3126
Toll-Free: 800-523-8320
Fax: (413)781-8416
E-mail: info@hbawm.com
Home Page: http://www.hbawm.com

• 10520 • Lifetime Achievement
For service to the industry, community and personal development throughout a lifetime. Recognition award bestowed annually.

• 10521 •
Home Wine and Beer Trade Association
Dee Roberson, Exec.Dir.
PO Box 1373
Valrico, FL 33595
Phone: (813)685-4261
Fax: (813)681-5625
E-mail: dee@hwbta.org
Home Page: http://www.hwbta.org

• 10522 • HWBTA Service Award
Recognizes an individual who has contributed outstanding service to the industry. Awarded annually.

• 10523 •
Esther Honens Calgary International Piano Competition
Stephen McHolm, Exec.Dir.
888 Tenth St. SW
Calgary, AB, Canada T2P 2X1
Phone: (403)299-0130
Toll-Free: 800-249-7574
Fax: (403)299-0137
E-mail: info@honens.com
Home Page: http://www.honens.com

• 10524 • Esther Honens International Piano Competition
To identify young performers gifted with outstanding musicianship, bring them to the attention of the music world, and assist in launching their professional careers. Pianists between the ages of 20 and 30 years are eligible. Monetary prizes totaling $92,500 are awarded. Top three Laureates are also offered a career development program which may include concert engagements, recordings, and marketing. The competition occurs every four years.

• 10525 •
Honeywell International Foundation
101 Columbia Rd.
PO Box 2245
Morristown, NJ 07962-2245
Phone: (973)455-2000
Toll-Free: 800-601-3099
Fax: (973)455-4807

• 10526 • Allied Signal Award for Research on Aging
To support promising biomedical research projects in the field of aging at leading research centers. A $200,000 grant, payable over two years. Established in 1992. Administered by the Alliance for Aging Research 2021 K Street, NW, Ste. 305, Washington, D.C. 20006-1003, telephone:(202) 293-2856; fax: (202) 785-8574. Formerly: (1995) Outstanding Project Award for Biomedical Research in Aging.

• 10527 •
Honolulu Board of Realtors
Judy Sobin, CEO
1136 12th Ave., Ste. 200
Honolulu, HI 96816
Phone: (808)732-3000
Fax: (808)732-8732
E-mail: hbradmin@hicentral.com
Home Page: http://www.hicentral.com

• 10528 • Aloha Aina Award
For realtor who has performed outstanding community service, contribution to profession, and exceptional service and follow-up to clients. Recognition award bestowed annually.

• 10529 • Realtor of the Year (ROTY)
For realtor with outstanding service to the Board, industry. Recognition award bestowed annually.

• 10530 •
Honolulu Publishing Co. Ltd.
N.C. Tinebra, CEO
707 Richards St., No. 525
Honolulu, HI 96813-4623
Phone: (808)524-7400
Toll-Free: 800-272-5245
E-mail: jmyers@honpub.com
Home Page: http://www.honolulupublishing.com

• 10531 • *HONOLULU* Magazine/Borders Books and Music Fiction Contest
For recognition of the short story voted the best by a panel of judges. Original stories with a Hawaiian theme, setting, and/or characters must be submitted by December. A monetary prize of $500 plus a $500 gift certificate to Borders Books and Music is awarded annually. Established in 1983. Co-sponsored by Borders Books and Music.

• 10532 •
Honor Society of Phi Kappa Phi
Perry Snyder, Exec.Dir.
PO Box 16000
Louisiana State Univ.
Baton Rouge, LA 70893-6000
Phone: (225)388-4917
Toll-Free: 800-804-9880
Fax: (225)388-4900
E-mail: awards@phikappaphi.org
Home Page: http://www.phikappaphi.org

• 10533 • Graduate Fellowships
To recognize and encourage superior scholarship among students of all disciplines for first-year graduate or professional study. Normally, 52 fellowships of $8,000 each and 30 Awards of Excellence of $1,500 each are awarded each year. For this national competition, each local chapter may nominate one student who must be an active member of the Society or have accepted membership. Established in 1932.

• 10534 •
Hop Barley and the Alers
Bob Kauffman, Past Pres.
PO Box 17935
Boulder, CO 80308-0935
Phone: (303)828-1237
E-mail: acmebrew@juno.com
Home Page: http://hopbarley.org

• 10535 • Brewer of the Year
For the most points earned from local, regional, and national beer competitions. Recognition award bestowed annually.

• 10536 •
Horace Mann League of the U.S.A.
Dr. Jack McKay, Exec.Dir.
61D N Chandler Ct.
KH 414
Port Ludlow, WA 98365
Phone: (360)437-1186
Phone: (402)554-2721
Fax: (360)437-0641
E-mail: jmckay@mail.unomaha.edu
Home Page: http://www.hmleague.org

• 10537 • **Leadership Award**
For recognition of an outstanding contribution to the development and preservation of the system of free public education and for unusual dedication and service to the public schools of the United States. Members of the League may make nominations. A plaque is awarded when merited. Established in 1981. Formerly: Horace Mann Guardian Award.

• 10538 •
Horatio Alger Association of Distinguished Americans
Terrence J. Giroux, Exec.Dir.
99 Canal Center Plz.
Alexandria, VA 22314
Phone: (703)684-9444
Fax: (703)548-3822
E-mail: association@horatioalger.com
Home Page: http://www.horatioalger.com

• 10539 • **Horatio Alger Awards**
To recognize modern-day individuals whose initiative and efforts led to significant success. These individuals are also dedicated community leaders. Awardees' lives typify Horatio Alger's concept of early life struggles, professional achievement, strong community involvement, and love of country. Each recipient becomes a lifetime member of the Association. Established in 1947.

• 10540 •
Horatio Alger Society
Robert E. Kasper, Sec.
PO Box 70361
Richmond, VA 23255
E-mail: has@ihot.com
Home Page: http://www.ihot.com/~has

• 10541 • **Luck and Pluck Award**
To recognize valued services to the Society. Members are eligible. A plaque is awarded annually. Established in 1966.

• 10542 • **Newsboy Award**
To recognize efforts that add to Horatio Alger's image. Individuals, who need not be members, or organizations that have done the most to add to our hero's image, are eligible. A plaque is awarded annually. Established in 1964.

• 10543 • **President's Awards**
Awarded annually. Established in 1977.

• 10544 • **Richard Seddon Award**
To recognize the member who best emulates the qualities and comradeship of Richard (Dick) Seddon. Awarded annually. Established in 1980.

• 10545 • **Strive and Succeed Award**
To honor a boy or girl who lives up to the standards described by Horatio Alger. Males or females under the age of 18 who live in the city where the annual convention is being held are eligible. The convention Chairperson and members and/or nonmembers appointed by him/her determine the winner. A monetary award of $300 is presented annually when merited. Established in 1970.

• 10546 •
Horizons Theatre
Leslie Jacobson, Artistic Dir.
3700 S Four Mile Run
Arlington, VA 22206-2304
Phone: (703)578-1100
Fax: (703)243-4561
E-mail: horizons@horizonstheatre.org
Home Page: http://www.horizonstheatre.org

Formerly: (1983) Pro Femina Theatre.

• 10547 • **Bravo Award**
To recognize an individual who has been outstanding in nurturing and supporting the arts in Washington. Individuals who have helped to make the arts in general and theater in particular flourish in the Washington area are eligible. A gift with a plaque is awarded annually. Established in 1984.

• 10548 •
Horror Writers Association
Nancy Etchemendy, Admin.Dir.
PO Box 50577
Palo Alto, CA 94303
Phone: (650)322-4610
E-mail: hwa@horror.org
Home Page: http://www.horror.org

• 10549 • **Bram Stoker Awards**
To recognize superior achievement and outstanding writing in the fields of dark fantasy, horror, and occult. Works of fiction or non-fiction of any length dealing with dark fantasy, horror, and occult are eligible. Work must be published in English. Six or more trophies are awarded annually in June. Established in 1987 by the HWA in honor of Bram Stoker, author of *Dracula*.

• 10550 •
Hospitality Sales and Marketing Association International
Robert A. Gilbert CHME, Pres./CEO
8201 Greensboro Dr., Ste. 300
McLean, VA 22102
Phone: (703)610-9024
Fax: (703)610-9005
E-mail: bgilbert@hsmai.org
Home Page: http://www.hsmai.org

Formerly: Hotel Sales Management Association.

• 10551 • **Al Bard Award**
To recognize members of the HSMAI awards committee who have made contributions to the annual HSMAI Adrian advertising and public relations competition. Awarded annually. Established in 1986 in honor of Albert Bard, an active member of the committee from 1959 until 1995.

• 10552 • **Frank W. Berkman Chapter of the Year Award**
To honor outstanding chapters based on their involvement with HSMA International, including the promotion of the CHSE Certification Program, local educational programming, and community relations. Established in 1979.

• 10553 • **Winthrop W. Grice Award**
To recognize individuals who have made significant contributions to public relations in the hospitality/travel industries. Awarded annually. Established in 1989 in honor of Winthrop W. "Bud" Grice, first senior vice-president of marketing of Marriott International.

• 10554 • **HSMAI Adrian Advertising Awards**
To increase recognition of the role of advertising in marketing, hospitality, and travel and to provide a showcase of the quality of advertising and promotional material created by hotels, resorts, inns, airlines, cruise lines, car rental, motorcoach, railroads, convention bureau/tourist boards, travel services/credit cards, area attractions/theme parks, and travel services. Entries may be submitted in the following categories: Single Entry Advertising - newspapers, magazine/consumer, trade media, radio, TV, direct mail, brochures, and in-house/on-board; Advertising Series; Complete Campaign; Special Category; and Franchise Sales. Entry deadline is September 12th. Platinum award plaques and gold, silver, and bronze certificates are awarded at a black-tie awards dinner held annually in New York. In addition, the H. Victor Grohmann Award is given for the best in show. Established in 1957. Formerly: (1990) HSMA Advertising Awards.

• 10555 • **HSMAI Golden Bell Public Relations Awards**
To recognize excellence in the application of public relations practices to the hospitality and travel industries. Awards are given in the following categories: Feature Placement Print/Trade Publication; Feature Placement Print/Consumer Newspaper; Feature Placement Print/Con-

Awards are arranged in alphabetical order below their administering organizations

sumer Magazine; Feature Placement Broadcast/Radio; Feature Placement Broadcast/Television; Magazine; Newsletter; Press Kit/Media Kit; Publicity Photo with Caption; Community Service; Crisis Communication; Employee Program; New Opening; New Ship Launching; Hotel Name Change; Internal Customer Promotions; Marketing Program - Trade; Marketing Program Consumer; Special Events; and Public Affairs. The Competition is open to hotels, resorts, inns, airlines, cruise lines, car rental, motorcoach, railroads, convention bureaus, tourist boards, travel services, credit cards, area attractions, theme parks, and travel agencies. Entry deadline is September 12th. Platinum award plaques and gold, silver, and bronze certificates are awarded at a black-tie awards dinner held annually in New York. In addition, the Edward L. Bernays Award is given for best in show. Established in 1987. Formerly: HSMAI Public Relations Competition.

• 10556 • HSMAI Hall of Fame
To honor outstanding achievements and contributions in the field of hospitality/travel sales and marketing. Hospitality industry executives who demonstrate pioneering activities and active involvement in sales and marketing education, training and industry advancement are eligible. No more than two persons may be selected in any one year. Established in 1968.

• 10557 • Albert E. Koehl Award
To recognize individuals who have made significant contributions to advertising in the hospitality/travel industries. Established in 1975 in honor of Albert E. Koehl, founder of Koehl, Landis & Landan, a New York-based advertising agency specializing in the international field of hotels, resorts, and travel.

• 10558 •
Hostelling International-American Youth Hostels
Russell Hedge, Exec.Dir./CEO
8401 Colesville Rd., Ste. 600
Silver Spring, MD 20910
Phone: (301)495-1240
Fax: (301)495-6697
E-mail: hostels@hiusa.org
Home Page: http://www.hiayh.org

• 10559 • AYH Pioneer Leader Award
To recognize an individual for breaking new ground for AYH, dedication to the principals of AYH, and embodying the spirit of hostelling. Established in 1991.

• 10560 • Golden Triangle Award
To recognize an individual(s) or organization for service to the American way of life as represented by AYH's founding principals, i.e., conservation, international peace, and educational travel. A plaque is awarded annually. Established in 1985.

• 10561 • Houseparents Length of Service Awards
To recognize houseparents for service at one, five, ten, and twenty-five years. Awarded annually. Established in 1986.

• 10562 • Interpret America Award
To introduce and improve the quality of interpretive programming through hostelling; for excellence in programs that incorporate international exchange; and/or to provide a unique and quality educational, historical, or recreational experience. Individuals, AYH entities, and outside organizations are eligible. Nominations must be submitted by October 1. An engraved U.S. plaque is awarded annually at the National Council Meeting in November. Established in 1987.

• 10563 • Robert B. Johnson Award
To recognize an individual for outstanding leadership in an AYH council, trip, or other program. Individuals under the age of 27 who embody the spirit of hostelling are eligible. Established in 1991.

• 10564 • Dick Leary Award
To recognize the best overall council newsletter for design, writing, and special feature. A plaque with a journalism medallion is awarded annually. Established in 1981.

• 10565 • Ruth and Bill Nelson Award
To recognize active hostel managers for: outstanding warmth, enthusiasm, and friendship in welcoming hostellers; combining personality with efficient operation of a clean, safe, hostel; and striving to attain the ideal concept of a hostel (complete facilities, full range of membership services, and adhering to hostel customs). A silver platter is awarded annually. Established in 1983.

• 10566 • Open Door Award
To recognize an individual or organization for significant achievement in the establishment of new hostels and/or for noteworthy assistance in promoting hostels as an important aspect of AYH's program. A plaque is awarded annually. Established in 1983.

• 10567 • Isabel and Monroe Smith Award
This, AYH's highest honor, is given to recognize an individual(s) for exemplifying the spirit of hostelling as embodied by AYH's founders, providing leadership that inspires others to make a commitment to AYH, and for extended service to the association. A medallion is presented when merited. Established in 1983.

• 10568 •
Houston Grand Opera
510 Preston St.
Houston, TX 77002
Phone: (713)546-0200
Toll-Free: 800-626-7372
Fax: (713)236-1533
E-mail: jmcbeth@hgo.com

• 10569 • Houston Opera Studio Member
To recognize and support young artists. Nine to twelve selected artists receive nine-month contracts with both training and performance opportunities. A $16,000 residency program, as well as monetary awards totalling $10,000, are presented at the final auditions for the program. Awarded annually. Established in 1977. Sponsored by the Houston Grand Opera.

• 10570 •
George A. and Eliza Gardner Howard Foundation
Prof. Henry F. Majewski, Admin.Dir.
Horace Mann Bldg., 4th Fl.
47 George St.
Brown University
PO Box 1867
Providence, RI 02912
Phone: (401)863-2640
Fax: (401)863-7341
E-mail: howard_foundation@brown.edu
Home Page: http://www.brown.edu/Divisions/Graduate_School/howard

• 10571 • Howard Fellows
To provide individuals in the middle stages of their careers with funds for independent projects in the fields that are selected within the following categories on a rotational basis each year: History, Anthropology, and Political Science; Archaeological Studies, History of Science, and Philosophy; Art History and Fine Arts (including painting, sculpture, musicology, and music composition); and Creative Writing and Literary and Film Criticism. Candidates must be professionally based in the United States either by affiliation with an institution or by residence. No fellowships are awarded for work leading to any academic degree or for coursework or training of any other sort. Nominations are accepted between September 1 and October 15. Stipends for the one-year period are $20,000. Established in 1952 by Nicea Howard in memory of her grandparents.

• 10572 •
Hoyt Institute of Fine Arts
124 E Leasure Ave.
New Castle, PA 16101
Phone: (724)652-2882
Fax: (724)657-8786
E-mail: hoyt@hoytartcenter.org
Home Page: http://www.hoytartcenter.org

• 10573 • Hoyt Mid Atlantic Art Show
For recognition of artwork of the highest quality and greatest diversity. Open to residents of Pennsylvania, Ohio, New York, New Jersey, Maryland, Delaware, and Washington, DC. 18

Awards are arranged in alphabetical order below their administering organizations

years of age or older, working in any fine arts medium. Two and three-dimensional size limits must not exceed 48 inches in any direction. Up to three works may be entered. Juror selection is by 35mm slides. The deadline for entry is June 15. Monetary prizes are awarded - usually exceeding $3,000. Established in 1982. Send self-addressed stamped-envelope for entry form and prospectus to: the above address. Formerly: Hoyt National Drawing and Painting Show.

• 10574 •
Hudson Valley Arabian Horse Association
Arlene Westerlund, Pres.
430 Rte. 82
Hopewell Junction, NY 12533
Phone: (845)221-2923
Fax: (845)221-2923
E-mail: hvaha1@aol.com

• 10575 • **Year End High Score Awards**
For horse and/or rider accumulating the most points through competition throughout the year. Trophy awarded annually.

• 10576 •
Human Factors and Ergonomics Society
Lynn Strother, Exec.Dir.
PO Box 1369
Santa Monica, CA 90406-1369
Phone: (310)394-1811
Fax: (310)394-2410
E-mail: info@hfes.org
Home Page: http://www.hfes.org

Formerly: Human and Ergonomics Factors Society.

• 10577 • **Alphonse Chapanis Best Student Paper Award**
To recognize the student/author of an outstanding paper presented at the Society's annual meeting. A certificate is awarded. Established in 1969.

• 10578 • **Distinguished International Colleague Award**
To recognize an outstanding individual working in human factors engineering outside the United States. Awarded annually.

• 10579 • **Jerome H. Ely *Human Factors* Article Award**
To recognize the author of the most outstanding paper published in each volume of *Human Factors*. Awarded annually.

• 10580 • **Paul M. Fitts Education Award**
To recognize an outstanding contribution to the education and training of human factors specialists. Awarded when merited.

• 10581 • **Jack A. Kraft Innovator Award**
To recognize significant efforts to diversify or extend the application of human factors considerations to new or unique areas of endeavor. Awarded when merited.

• 10582 • **A. R. Lauer Safety Award**
To recognize outstanding contributions to the understanding of human behavior in advancing safety. Awarded when merited.

• 10583 • **Alexander C. Williams, Jr., Design Award**
To recognize outstanding human factors contributions to the design of any product, service, or system. Awarded when merited.

• 10584 •
Human Growth Foundation
Patricia D. Costa, Exec.Dir.
997 Glen Cove Ave., Ste. 5
Glen Head, NY 11545
Phone: (516)671-4041
Toll-Free: 800-451-6434
Fax: (516)671-4055
E-mail: hgf1@hgfound.org
Home Page: http://www.hgfound.org/

• 10585 • **Small Research Grants Program**
For post-doctoral research in growth and growth-related disorders. Grant awarded annually.

• 10586 •
Human Rights and Race Relations Centre
Hasanai Ahmad Syed, Pres.
141 Adelaide St. W, Ste. 1506
Toronto, ON, Canada M5H 3L5
Phone: (416)481-7793
Toll-Free: 888-667-5877

• 10587 • **Employment Equity Gold Medals**
Recognizes excellence in race relations. Awarded annually.

• 10588 • **Race Relations Gold Medal**
Annual award of recognition. Inquire for application details.

• 10589 • **Race Relations Trophy**
Annual award of recognition. Inquire for application details.

• 10590 •
Human Rights Campaign
Elizabeth Birch, Exec.Dir.
1640 Rhode Island Ave. NW
Washington, DC 20036-3278
Phone: (202)628-4160
Toll-Free: 800-777-4723
Fax: (202)347-5323
E-mail: hrc@hrc.org
Home Page: http://www.hrc.org

• 10591 • **Human Rights Award**
For recognition of contributions to the advancement of gay and lesbian civil rights and responsible AIDS policy and service. Selection is by the local committee. A trophy, plaque or other gift is awarded annually in six different cities. Established in 1981.

• 10592 • **Diego Lopez Community Service Award in New York**
For outstanding service to the gay and lesbian and AIDS community. Selected by the local committee. A trophy, plaque or other gift is awarded annually. Established in 1985 in honor of Diego Lopez, outstanding leader of the HRCF, responsible for the creation of the "Buddy AIDS care system."

• 10593 • **Carroll Sledz - Lou Wener Community Service Award in Washington, DC**
For outstanding service to the gay and lesbian and AIDS community. Selected by the local committee. A trophy, plaque or other gift is awarded annually. Established in 1986 in honor of two who dedicated themselves to the gay and lesbian community of the nation's capitol. 9102401007FFEXPRSNNY

• 10594 •
Human Rights Watch
Kenneth Roth, Exec.Dir.
350 5th Ave., 34th Fl.
New York, NY 10118-3299
Phone: (212)290-4700
Fax: (212)736-1300
Fax: (212)736-1300
E-mail: hrwnyc@hrw.org
Home Page: http://www.hrw.org

• 10595 • **Hellman-Hammet Award**
Awarded to writers who had been victims of political persecution and are in financial need. In addition to providing much needed assistance the grants focus attention on repression of free speech and censorship by publicizing the persecution endured by the grant recipient. Grants total $150,000 to $200,000.

• 10596 •
Humane Society of the United States
Wayne Pavelle, CEO
2100 L St. NW
Washington, DC 20037
Phone: (202)452-1100
Fax: (202)778-6132
E-mail: membership@hsus.org
Home Page: http://www.hsus.org

• 10597 • **James Herriot Award**
To recognize an outstanding individual or agency who, through communication with the public, has helped to promote and inspire an appreciation of and concern for the animals of this world. A porcelain award depicting the animals of James Herriot's Yorkshire in a group setting is presented annually. Established in 1987 in honor of veterinarian, author, and storyteller James Herriot.

• 10598 • **Joseph Wood Krutch Medal**
To recognize an individual who has made a significant contribution toward the improvement

of life and the environment. A medal is awarded annually. Established in 1971 in memory of Dr. Joseph Wood Krutch, journalist and naturalist.

• 10599 • Russell and Burch Award

To recognize a scientist who has made an outstanding contribution toward the advancement of alternative methods in the areas of biomedical research, testing, or higher education. Alternative methods are those that can replace or reduce the use of animals in specific procedures, or refine procedures so animals experience less pain and suffering. A cash award of $5,000 is presented triennially.

• 10600 •
Humane Society of the United States, New England Regional Office
Joanne Bourbeau, Dir.
PO Box 619
Jacksonville, VT 05342
Phone: (802)368-2790
Fax: (802)368-2756
E-mail: nero@hsus.org
Home Page: http://www.hsus.org

• 10601 • Shaw-Worth Memorial Scholarship

For high school seniors from New England who have made a significant contribution to animal welfare/animal protection. Scholarship awarded annually.

• 10602 •
Humanist Association of Los Angeles
Lois Lyons, Pres.
PO Box 691
Malibu, CA 90265
Phone: (310)456-6642
Fax: (310)456-6642
E-mail: halanews@aol.com
Home Page: http://www.hala.org

• 10603 • Hala-Negri Award

For humanitarian work or writing. Recognition award bestowed annually.

• 10604 • Ashley Montagu Human Nurturance Award

For humanitarian work or writing. Recognition award bestowed annually.

• 10605 •
Humanist Association of Salem
Lloyd Kumley, Pres.
PO Box 4153
Salem, OR 97302
Phone: (503)371-1255
E-mail: lloydk@open.com
Home Page: http://css.peak.org/has/

• 10606 • Humanist of the Year

For member doing most to promote humanism and chapter. Recognition award bestowed annually.

• 10607 •
The Humanitas Prize
Chris Donahue, Exec.Dir.
17575 Pacific Coast Hwy.
PO Box 861
Pacific Palisades, CA 90272
Phone: (310)454-8769
Fax: (310)459-6549
E-mail: humanitasmail@aol.com
Home Page: http://www.humanitasprize.org

• 10608 • Humanitas Prize

To encourage, stimulate, and sustain the nation's entertainment writers in their humanizing task, and to give them the recognition they deserve. Writers of nationally broadcast teleplays or feature film screenplays are eligible. For the television prizes, scripts must have been written originally for television and telecast on a national commercial network, PBS, cable systems located in markets representing at least 50 percent of U.S. television homes, or syndicated to over 80 percent of the country within a four week period. For the feature film prize (established in 1994), a screenplay for an English language-feature film becomes eligible in the year in which the film is screened in at least 50 U.S. markets. The deadline for submitting scripts is April 15. The following awards are presented: Feature Film Screenplay - $25,000; Prime-time Network or Syndicated Cable Teleplay $25,000 (90 minutes or longer), $15,000 (60 minutes), and $10,000 (30 minutes); and Children's - $10,000 (live action) $10,000 (animated); Sundance Feature Film Screenplay - $10,000; Angell Comedy Fellowship $1,000. The money is awarded to the writers. Humanitas trophies are given to the producers, directors, story editors, production companies, and networks of these entertainment programs. Awards are presented annually. Established in 1974 and endowed by a coalition of media groups and individuals.

• 10609 •
Humboldt International Short Film Festival
Department of Theatre, Film and Dance
Humbodlt State University
1 Harpst st.
Arcata, CA 95521
Phone: (707)826-4113
Fax: (707)826-4112
E-mail: filmfest@humboldt.edu
Home Page: http://www.humboldt.edu/~filmfest

• 10610 • Humboldt International Film Festival

This, the oldest student-run film festival in the United States, seeks to provide a forum for the presentation of personal expression through the use of film, focusing on student and independent filmmakers. Categories include experimental, animation, documentary and narrative films. Entries (Super 8 and 16mm only) of under 60 minutes and completed within the past three years are accepted. Awards vary from year to year and include many cash prizes.

• 10611 •
Humboldt State University
Office for Research and Graduate Studies
1 Harpst St.
Arcata, CA 95521
Phone: (707)826-3949
Fax: (707)826-3939
E-mail: schafer@humboldt.edu
Home Page: http://www.humboldt.edu/~gradst

• 10612 • Creativity Awards

Recognizes outstanding faculty research.

• 10613 •
The Hunger Project
Joan Holmes, Pres.
15 E 26th St., No. 1401
New York, NY 10010
Phone: (212)251-9100
Toll-Free: 800-228-6691
Fax: (212)532-9785
E-mail: info@thp.org
Home Page: http://www.thp.org

• 10614 • Africa Prize for Leadership for the Sustainable End of Hunger

To honor a distinguished African man or woman who has exhibited exceptional leadership in bringing about the sustainable end of hunger at the national, regional, or continent-wide level. The prize is intended to acknowledge and honor the recipient's outstanding contribution to the general well-being of the people of Africa. In addition, the prize seeks to generate heightened awareness within the world community of the many African leaders who are making the difficult decisions and taking the necessary actions to resolve the pressing agricultural, economic, political, and social issues facing the continent. Individuals working in areas such as public policy, science, agriculture, education, and health whose leadership and policies reflect courage, initiative, creativity, boldness and, in some cases, personal sacrifice are eligible. Nominations must be submitted by May 15 each year. A monetary award of $100,000 and a sculpture designed by the international award-winning designer and sculptor, Takenobu Igarashi, are awarded annually. Established in 1987.

• 10615 •
Hunt Institute for Botanical Documentation
Carnegie Mellon Uniceristy
5000 Forbes Ave.
Pittsburgh, PA 15213-3890
Phone: (412)268-2434
Fax: (412)268-5677
E-mail: huntinst@andrew.cmu.edu
Home Page: http://huntbot.andrew.cmu.edu/HIBD

• 10616 • Lawrence Memorial Award

To support travel expenses of a doctoral candidate for research in systematic botany, horticulture, or the history of the plant sciences. A monetary prize of $2,000 is awarded annually. Established in 1979 to commemorate the life and achievements of Dr. George H. M. Lawrence.

• 10617 •
Hunterdon Museum of Art
7 Lower Center St.
Clinton, NJ 08809
Phone: (908)735-8415
Fax: (908)735-8416
E-mail: info@hunterdonmuseumofart.org
Home Page: http://www.hunterdonartmuseum.org

• 10618 • **Hunterdon Museum of Art National Print Exhibition Purchase Awards**
To add outstanding works of art to the museum's collection of prints. Artists may submit work in the area of graphics to be selected by a jury. Monetary prizes are presented annually. The following awards are given: Lynd Ward Prize; James R. Marsh Memorial Prize; Hunterdon Museum or Art and Johnson & Johnson Purchase Prizes. Established in 1952 by Ann Marsh.

• 10619 •
Huntington County Visitor and Convention Bureau
Rose Meldrum, Exec.Dir.
407 N Jefferson St.
PO Box 212
Huntington, IN 46750
Phone: (260)359-8687
Phone: 800-848-4282
Toll-Free: 800-848-4282
Fax: (219)359-9754
E-mail: info@visithuntington.org
Home Page: http://www.visithuntington.org

• 10620 • **Tourism Promotion Grant**
For increased promotions for attractions that have a draw for visitors from outside the county. Grant awarded semiannually.

• 10621 •
Huntington Society of Canada
Isla Horvath, Exec.Dir./CEO
151 Frederick St., Ste. 400
Kitchener, ON, Canada N2H 2M2
Phone: (519)749-7063
Toll-Free: 800-998-7398
Fax: (519)749-8965
E-mail: info@hsc-ca.org
Home Page: http://www.huntingtonsociety.org

• 10622 • **Certificate of Appreciation**
Annual award of recognition.

• 10623 • **Certificate of Merit**
Annual award of recognition.

• 10624 •
Hymn Society in the United States and Canada
Carl P. Daw Jr., Exec.Dir.
Boston University School of Theology
745 Commonwealth Ave.
Boston, MA 02215-1401
Phone: (617)353-6493
Toll-Free: 800-THE-HYMN
Fax: (617)353-7322
E-mail: hymnsoc@bu.edu
Home Page: http://www.thehymnsociety.org

Formerly: (1991) Hymn Society of America.

• 10625 • **Fellow**
For recognition of outstanding contributions in the field of hymnology. The winner is selected by the executive committee of the Society. A plaque is awarded annually. Established in 1942.

• 10626 •
Ibsen Society of America
Joan Templeton, Pres.
Dept. of English
Long Island University
1 Univ. Plz.
Brooklyn, NY 11201
Phone: (718)488-1050
Phone: (212)877-2124
Fax: (718)246-6302
E-mail: joan.templeton@liu.edu
Home Page: http://www.ibsensociety.liu.edu

• 10627 • **Honorary Member**
For recognition of meritorious service toward a fuller understanding of the works of Henrik Ibsen. Established in 1979 in memory of Henrik Ibsen, foremost Western dramatist between Shakespeare's time and the present.

• 10628 •
ICD - International Center for the Disabled
Les Halpert, Pres. and CEO
340 E 24th St.
New York, NY 10010-4019
Phone: (212)585-6000
Fax: (212)585-6161
E-mail: info@icdrehab.org
Home Page: http://www.icdrehab.org

• 10629 • **Freedom of the Human Spirit Award**
To recognize exemplary personal contributions for policies, programs, and awareness that improve the employment, social, and personal lives of persons with disabilities. A statue is awarded to one individual and one corporation annually at ICD's Award Dinner. Established in 1972.

• 10630 •
Ice Skating Institute
Patti Feeney, Managing Dir.
17120 N Dallas Pkwy., Ste. 140
Dallas, TX 75248
Phone: (972)735-8800
Fax: (972)735-8815
E-mail: isi@skateisi.org
Home Page: http://www.skateisi.org

• 10631 • **Ice Skating Hall of Fame**
To honor those who have made outstanding contributions to the ice skating world and ice rink industry. Skaters, teachers, producers of ice shows, builders or suppliers to the ice industry are eligible. Nominees must have made an outstanding and lasting contribution to the sport and recreation of ice skating not later than three years before the year the award is given in the areas of participation, advancement of skating interest, or facility development. An engraved plaque is awarded annually at the Annual Conference. Established in 1963.

• 10632 • **Ice Skating Man and Woman of the Year**
To recognize outstanding public service in the field of ice skating during the current year. An engraved plaque is awarded annually. Established in 1971. In addition, the following awards are also given: Special Recognition, Lifetime Achievement Award, Special Appreciation, Great Skate; Top 26 Rinks; and Top 26 Instructors.

• 10633 •
Icelandic Horse Trekkers
Dolores Hamelin, Pres.
PO Box 986
Kearney, MO 64060-0986

Formerly: (1989) Icelandic Pony Trekkers.

• 10634 • **Distance Award and Best-Conditioned & Trail Class Award**
To recognize and promote the sport of pony trekking and the stamina, smooth gaits, and excellent disposition of the Icelandic horse. Club members who own purebred Icelandic horses are eligible. A trophy is awarded annually. Established in 1990.

• 10635 •
I.D., The International Design Magazine
F+ Publications Inc.
David Sokol, Mng.Dir.
Editorial Offices
38 E 29th St., Fl. 3
New York, NY 10016
Phone: (212)447-1400
Fax: (212)447-5231
E-mail: idedit@fwpubs.com
Home Page: http://www.idonline.com

• 10636 • **ID Annual Design Review**
To recognize outstanding design. Any product or project introduced to or intended for the international market in the previous calendar year is eligible. The deadline for entries is December 1.

Awards are presented in seven categories: (1) Concepts; (2) Consumer Products; (3) Environments; (4) Equipment; (5) Furniture; (6) Graphics; and (7) Interactive Media. Panels of distinguished designers choose three levels of awards for each of the seven categories: Best of Category, Design Distinctions and Honorable Mentions. Winning entries are published in the special July/August double issue of the magazine and on www.idonline.com. Awarded annually. Established in 1954.

• 10637 •
Idaho Quality Award, Inc.
Idaho Department of Commerce
700 W State St.
Boise, ID 83720-0093
Phone: (202)334-2470
Toll-Free: 800-842-5858
Fax: (202)334-2631
E-mail: info@idoc.state.us

• 10638 • **Idaho Quality Award**
Promotes statewide organizationl excellence. The following awards are presented annually: Commitment Recognition Award for organizations showing commitment to the use of total quality principles; Idaho Quality Award Recognition for efforts in becoming role models for business and organizations; Gem State Award Recognition for businesses and organizations that have shown a systematic approach toward meeting the award criteria. Complete application details and forms are availabe at the above web site.

• 10639 •
Idaho Retailers Association
Pam Eaton, Pres.
1109 Main St., Mezzanine B
Boise, ID 83702
Phone: (208)342-0010
Fax: (208)342-0060
E-mail: idahoretailersas@qwest.net
Home Page: http://www.idahoretailers.org

• 10640 • **Retailer of the Year**
For Idaho retailer. Recognition award bestowed annually.

• 10641 •
IDEA Health and Fitness Association
Kathie Davis, Exec.Dir.
10455 Pacific Center Ct.
San Diego, CA 92121-3773
Phone: (858)535-8979
Toll-Free: 800-999-IDEA
Fax: (858)535-8234
E-mail: contact@ideafit.com
Home Page: http://www.ideafit.com

• 10642 • **IDEA Fitness Inspiration Award**
Annual award of recognition.

• 10643 • **IDEA Fitness Instructor of the Year**
Annual award of recognition.

• 10644 • **IDEA Personal Trainer of the Year Award**
Annual award of recognition.

• 10645 • **IDEA Program Director of the Year**
Annual award of recognition.

• 10646 •
Idea Innovative Directions an Educational Alliance
Patricia A. Hennessy, Contact
PO Box 222
Bronx, NY 10464-0216
Phone: (718)885-3781
E-mail: idea222@aol.com

• 10647 • **Maritime Heritage Award**
For contribution to the maritime industry. Recognition award bestowed annually.

• 10648 •
Iditarod Trail Committee
Stan Hooley, Exec.Dir.
PO Box 870800
Wasilla, AK 99687
Phone: (907)376-5155
Fax: (907)373-6998
E-mail: iditarod@iditarod.com
Home Page: http://www.iditarod.com

• 10649 • **Iditarod Trail International Sled Dog Race**
This, the longest sled dog race in the world, is an open class race for all dog mushers. Now known worldwide as "Iditarod, The Last Great Race on Earth" it is the ultimate test of mushers and dogs against the Alaskan wilderness. The trail is 1049 miles from Anchorage to Nome. Recognizing the varying degrees of experience, monetary support, and residence locations of a musher, the Trail Committee encourages and maintains the philosophy that the race be constructed to permit all who wish to enter and complete the race to do so. The object of the race is to determine which musher and dogs can cover the race in the shortest time under their own power and without the aid of others. Mushers must be 18 years of age as of the starting date for the race. Rookie mushers must submit with their application written proof of the completion of an accumulated five hundred miles in two ITC - santioned races during the two years preceding their Iditarod race. Mushers must begin the race with a minimum of 12 and a maximum of 16 dogs, and must finish with at least five dogs. Applications and fees must be submitted by December 1. Held annually on the first Saturday of March. Established in 1973.

• 10650 •
IEEE Dielectrics and Electrical Insulation Society
R.E. Hebner, Pres.
445 Hoes Ln.
PO Box 459
Piscataway, NJ 08855
Phone: (732)981-0060
Toll-Free: 800-678-4333
Fax: (732)981-0225
E-mail: jberberi@sju.edu
Home Page: http://tdei.sju.edu/deis

• 10651 • **Dakin Award**
Recognizes distinguished achievement or services. Awarded semiannually.

• 10652 • **Forster Award**
Recognizes distinguished achievement or service. Awarded semiannually.

• 10653 •
IEEE Education Society
Daniel Litynski Jr., Pres.
3 Park Ave., 17th Fl.
New York, NY 10016-5997
Phone: (212)419-7900
Fax: (212)752-4929
E-mail: dan.litynski@wmich.edu
Home Page: http://www.ewh.ieee.org/soc/es

• 10654 • **Best Transaction Paper**
Award of recognition.

• 10655 •
IEEE Industrial Electronics Society
Dr. John Y. Hung, Treas.
Electrical Engineering Department
Auburn University
Auburn, AL 36849-5201
Phone: (334)844-1813
Fax: (334)844-1809
E-mail: j.y.hung@ieee.org
Home Page: http://ieee-ies.org

• 10656 • **Mittlemann Achievement Award**
A monetary award is given annually.

• 10657 •
IEEE Lasers and Electro-Optics Society
Paul W. Shumate, Exec.Dir.
445 Hoes Ln.
PO Box 1331
Piscataway, NJ 08854-1331
Phone: (732)562-3891
Phone: (732)562-3892
Fax: (732)562-8434
E-mail: p.shumate@ieee.org
Home Page: http://www.i-leos.org

• 10658 • **John Tyndall Award**
Annual award of recognition.

• 10659 • LEOS Distinguished Service Award
Annual award of recognition.

• 10660 • LEOS Engineering Achievement Award
Annual award of recognition.

• 10661 • LEOS William Streifer Award
Annual award of recognition.

• 10662 • Quantum Electronics Award
Annual award of recognition.

• 10663 •
IEEE Professional Communication Society
Mr. W. Cleon Anderson, Pres./CEO
3 Park Ave., 17th Fl.
New York, NY 10016-5997
Phone: (212)419-7900
Fax: (212)752-4929
E-mail: president@ieee.org
Home Page: http://www.ieeepcs.org

• 10664 • Alfred N. Goldsmith Award
Recognizes service to improve engineering communication. Awarded annually.

• 10665 •
IES, Institute for the International Education of Students
Mary M. Dwyer PhD, Pres.
33 N LaSalle St., 15th Fl.
Chicago, IL 60602
Phone: (312)944-1750
Toll-Free: 800-995-2300
Fax: (312)944-1448
E-mail: info@iesabroad.org
Home Page: http://www.IESabroad.org

• 10666 • Lifetime Achievement Award
A monetary is awarded annually.

• 10667 • Professional Development Award
A monetary prize is given annually.

• 10668 •
Illinois Association of Meat Processors
Jeri Nieman, Exec.Sec.
1177 S Springfield Rd.
Freeport, IL 61032
Phone: (815)232-1006
Fax: (815)233-6299
E-mail: iamp@mwci.net
Home Page: http://www.illinoismeatprocessors.com

• 10669 • Cured Meat Awards
Based upon judging at product competition. Recognition award bestowed annually in a variety of categories.

• 10670 •
Illinois Conference of Churches
Rev.
2211 Wabash Ave.
Springfield, IL 62704
Phone: (217)698-3440
Fax: (217)698-3445

• 10671 • Local Ecumenical Award for Christian Unity and Mission
For initiatives that nurture growing relationships among Christian churches and/or generate ecumenical witness and mission. Recognition award bestowed triennially.

• 10672 •
Illinois Library Association
Robert P. Doyle, Exec.Dir.
33 W Grand Ave., Ste. 301
Chicago, IL 60610-4306
Phone: (312)644-1896
Fax: (312)644-1899
E-mail: ila@ila.org
Home Page: http://www.ila.org

• 10673 • Hugh C. Atkinson Memorial Award
To recognize sustained activity and contributions having a lasting impact in areas relating to multitype library cooperation and/or resource-sharing. Individuals need not be librarians or members of ILA, nor must groups be associated with ILA or with any specific library organization. Programs may have originated in any award-winning organization, such as a library, a library system or consortium, or a non-library organization. A monetary award of $500 and a citation are presented annually. The award honors Hugh C. Atkinson (1933-1986), whose contributions to librarianship reach far beyond the University of Illinois to enhance and enrich library service in all types of settings and situations. Sponsored by DEMCO, Inc.

• 10674 • Crosman Memorial Award
To recognize outstanding achievements of Illinois library workers who have been in the library field for ten years or less. Members of ILA are eligible. A plaque and a monetary award of $75 are awarded annually.

• 10675 • Davis Cup Award
To recognize an individual who has made an outstanding contribution to library service for young people. Members of ILA are eligible. An A monetary award of $250 and an engraved Revere bowl are awarded annually.

• 10676 • Highsmith Library Innovative Award
Recognizes a library's achievement in planning and implementing an innovative or creative program or service which has had measurable impact on its users. A plaque and $1,000 financial award is presented.

• 10677 • Illinois Academic Librarian of the Year Award
To recognize an Illinois librarian who has made an outstanding contribution to academic or research librarianship and to library development. Members of ILA are eligible. The recipient will receive a citation and a financial award totaling $500 and have name and date added to the plaque at the Illinois State Library. Awarded annually.

• 10678 • Intellectual Freedom Award
To recognize an individual for outstanding service in the interest of intellectual freedom. The recipient will be presented with a citation and a $500 financial award. The award was established in the early 1980s.

• 10679 • IREAD Awards
To recognize libraries that demonstrate outstanding summer reading program ideas for youth. The recipient will receive a $35 gift certificate for the next years IREAD products. Awarded annually.

• 10680 • Librarian of the Year
To recognize a librarian for distinguished service and leadership in the libraries of Illinois. Generally, the librarian so honored will have made an impact locally, statewide, and nationally. Any staff member of a library in Illinois working in a professional capacity is eligible. The recipient must meet at least two of the following criteria: (1) Active membership in ILA, as evidenced by attendance at conferences and workshops, participation on committees or on units of ILA, other support of the Association; (2) Leadership role in ILA; (3) Positive contributions to the library field, such as research, publications, innovative program development, etc.; and (4) Outstanding work on a particular aspect of library service in the home library of the nominee, e.g., grant award, successful referendum for tax increase or bonds for library construction, outstanding public relations program, etc. Established in 1985, the recipient receives a specially designated memento. is awarded annually.

• 10681 • Robert R. McClarren Legislative Development Award
To recognize an individual, group, or institution that has contributed significantly to library legislative development in Illinois. A citation is awarded annually, and the recipient;s name will be added to the permanent plaque at the Illinois State Library.

• 10682 • Oberman and Rich Award
In honor of Tobi Oberman and Tom Rich, who were instrumental in developing the Reaching Forward Conference for library support staff. Awarded annually. Established in 1995.

• 10683 • Jane O'Brien Award
To recognize an individual library support staff person who has made an outstanding contribution to the library community. A plaque is awarded annually.

Awards are arranged in alphabetical order below their administering organizations

• 10684 • **Reference Services Award**
To recognize an individual, group, department, or library for outstanding reference services. The recipient will receive a certificate and a financial award of $250. Awarded annually.

• 10685 • **Alexander J. Skrzypek Award**
To recognize a person who has made an outstanding contribution to the advancement of library services for the blind or physically disabled in Illinois. A plaque is awarded annually, and the recipient/s name will be added and a permanent plaque at the Illinois State Library.

• 10686 • **TBS, INC. Technical Services Award**
Awarded to an individual who has made a substantial contribution in the area of library technical services. The recipient will be presented with a plaque and a $350 financial award.

• 10687 • **Trustee Citation**
To recognize an Illinois public library trustee for achievement, leadership, and service to libraries. ILA members and ILA/Trustee Forum members are eligible. A plaque is awarded annually.

• 10688 • **Volunteerism Award**
To recognize and showcase the work, dedication, and creativity shown by volunteers and volunteer coordinators. A plaque is awarded. Sponsored by the Volunteer Coordinators Forum.

• 10689 •
Illinois Society for Microbiology
Michael Costello, Pres.
2148 Walnut Ct.
Glenview, IL 60025
Phone: (847)570-2732
Fax: (847)733-5314
E-mail: rgottschall@enh.org
Home Page: http://www.asm.org/branch/bril/page1.htm

Formerly: (1965) Society of Illinois Bacteriologists.

• 10690 • **Pasteur Award**
For public recognition of outstanding contributions to the science of microbiology. Members and non-members of the society mounted on a crystal arch may be nominated. An honorarium and a silver medallion are awarded annually at the autumn meeting and Pasteur Award Dinner. Established in 1948 to honor Louis Pasteur, the famous French microbiologist.

• 10691 •
Illuminating Engineering Society of North America
William Hanley, Exec.VP
120 Wall St., 17th Fl.
New York, NY 10005-4001
Phone: (212)248-5000
Fax: (212)248-5017
E-mail: iesna@iesna.org
Home Page: http://www.iesna.org

• 10692 • **Distinguished Service Award**
To recognize outstanding service to the Society, principally of a non-technical nature, which has conspicuously furthered the purposes of the Society. Members of the Society and, occasionally, non-members are eligible. A certificate and pin are awarded annually. Established in 1967.

• 10693 • **Fellow Designation**
To recognize individuals for valuable contributions to the technical activities of the Society, to the art or science of illumination, or to the related scientific or engineering fields. Individuals who have been members of the IESNA for at least five years are eligible. A certificate and gold pin are awarded each year at the annual conference. Established in 1945.

• 10694 • **IES Medal**
To recognize meritorious achievement that has conspicuously furthered the profession, art, or knowledge of illuminating engineering. A medal and certificate are awarded. Established in 1943. Formerly: IES Gold Medal.

• 10695 • **International Illumination Design Awards Program**
To recognize professionalism, ingenuity, and originality of lighting design based upon the individual merit of each entry judged against specific criteria. Judges are selected from a broad professional spectrum that represents knowledge of lighting and design excellence. Open to any entrant without limitation of professional affiliation. The following awards are presented: Edwin F. Guth Memorial Award for Interior Lighting Design, Paul Waterbury Award for Outdoor Lighting, Aileen Page Cutler Award for Residential Lighting, and Energy amd Environmental Design Award. Section Awards acknowledge commendable achievement in lighting design at the local level in the form of a certificate. If the project is deemed worthy for further consideration, it is forwarded to the regional level. Awards of Merit are given in recognition of good lighting design at the regional level (certificate); Awards of Excellence are given for an outstanding design contribution to the art and science of lighting (one crystal sculpture per project is presented to the design team and the owner receives a certificate); the Award of Distinction honors the exceptional lighting design submitted (one crystal sculpture per project is presented to the design team and the owner receives a plaque); and the Special Citation consists of two certificates, one for the designer and one for the owner. Awarded annually at the IES National Conference. Established in 1952 at the local level by Fred and Edwin Guth, Jr., in memory of their father.

• 10696 • **Lumen Award Program**
To encourage and recognize professionalism, ingenuity, and originality in lighting design. All projects considered must be completed in the 24 months prior to March 31. Established in 1966. Sponsored by the New York Section of the Illuminating Engineering Society.

• 10697 • **Louis B. Marks Award**
To recognize a member of the Society for exceptional service of a non-technical nature. Candidates must be members of IESNA. A certificate and crystal flame are awarded annually. Established in 1985 in honor of Louis B. Marks, the first president of the Illuminating Engineering Society.

• 10698 •
Image Industry Council International/ Institute for Image Management
Marily Mondejar, Exec.Dir.
PO Box 190007
San Francisco, CA 94119
Phone: (415)863-2573
Fax: (415)840-0655
E-mail: inquiry@image360.com
Home Page: http://www.image360.com

• 10699 • **Award of Excellence**
Recognizes significant contribution to the image industry. Awarded annually.

• 10700 • **Image Consultant of the Year**
Recognizes significant contribution to the image industry. Awarded annually.

• 10701 •
Imagine Canada
Georgina Steinsky-Schwartz, Pres. and CEO
425 University Ave., Ste. 900
Toronto, ON, Canada M5G 1T6
Phone: (416)597-2293
Toll-Free: 800-263-1178
Fax: (416)597-2294
E-mail: info@imaginecanada.ca
Home Page: http://www.imaginecanada.ca

• 10702 • **Imagine Mutual Fund Industry Corporate Citizenship Award**
Recognizes a Canadian mutual fund company that has made an outstanding contribution through its community investment program and support for employee giving and volunteering.

• 10703 • ***New Spirit of Community* Partnership Awards Program**
To recognize the alliance of Canadian businesses and charities that are making a difference in the community. The winners and runners-up are chosen by a panel of senior leaders from the private and voluntary sectors. Each year the applicants, across the country, demonstrating outstanding creativity and motivation in their corporate and voluntary sectors, work to make improvements to the communities in which they reside. Awarded annually to one or more recipients. Established in 1996.

• 10704 •
Immigration and Ethnic History Society
Betty A. Berglund, Sec.
California State University
Department of History
San Bernardino, CA 92407-2397
Phone: (909)880-5525
E-mail: betty.a.berglund@uwrf.edu
Home Page: http://www.iehs.org/

• 10705 • **George E. Pozzetta Dissertation Research Award**
For dissertation research. A monetary award is given annually. See website for details.

• 10706 • **Carlton C. Qualey Article Award**
For articles published in Journal of American Ethnic History. Monetary award is given bi-annually. See website for details.

• 10707 • **Theodore Saloutos Memorial Book Award in Immigration History**
Annual monetary award. See website for details.

• 10708 •
Incentive Manufacturer and Representatives Alliance
Thomas F. Renk CAECMP, Exec.Dir.
1801 N Mill St., Ste. R
Naperville, IL 60563
Phone: (630)369-7786
Fax: (630)369-3773
E-mail: info@imra1.org
Home Page: http://www.imra1.org

• 10709 • **Gold Key Award**
For recognition of outstanding incentive programs, and to honor and recognize the creativity and professionalism of the representatives, buyers, and manufacturers responsible for those outstanding programs. Programs must be submitted by an IMRA representative or manufacturer member to be considered. A plaque is awarded annually at the annual conference. Established in 1975.

• 10710 •
Independent Accountants Association of Illinois
Cathy Olson, Admin.Asst.
PO Box 1506
Galesburg, IL 61402-1506
Phone: (309)342-5400
Toll-Free: 888-222-2270
Fax: (309)342-2557
E-mail: iaai@grics.net
Home Page: http://www.illinoisaccountants.com/

• 10711 • **Independent Accountants Scholarship Award**
For college students pursuing a career in accounting and maintaining a B average. Scholarship awarded annually.

• 10712 •
Independent Bakers Association
Nicholas A. Pyle, Pres.
PO Box 3731
Washington, DC 20007
Phone: (202)333-8190
Phone: (202)333-8191
Fax: (202)337-3809
E-mail: independentbaker@yahoo.com
Home Page: http://www.mindspring.com/~independentbaker

• 10713 • **Horst G. Denk Congressional Award**
For recognition of outstanding service given to IBA members to members by members of the U.S. Congress whose actions have contributed positively to the baking industry. Members of the U.S. Congress are eligible. The award alternates every other year between two members of the House and two members of the Senate. However, in any given year, the two members chosen represent one Democrat and one Republican representative or senator. A plaque is awarded annually at the convention in June. Established in 1977. Formerly: Independent Bakers Association Congressional Award.

• 10714 •
Independent Colleges and Universities of Florida
111 S Monroe St., Ste. 2000-A
Tallahassee, FL 32301
Phone: (850)681-3188
Fax: (850)681-0057
E-mail: emoore@icuf.org
Home Page: http://www.icuf.org

• 10715 • **Champions of Higher Independent Education in Florida (C.H.I.E.F.) Awards**
For recognition of outstanding contributions of resources, time, or talent to the support of independent higher education in Florida. An ICUF president may submit a nomination for election by the 6 member presidents. Plaques are awarded to approximately 13 individuals annually. Established in 1972.

• 10716 • **Liberty Bell Award**
To recognize a public servant for outstanding work on behalf of the independent higher education in Florida. The nominee is selected by the President's Council of I.C.U.F. Awarded annually to one or more recipients. Established in 1980.

• 10717 •
Independent Curators International
Judith Olch Richards, Exec.Dir.
799 Broadway, Ste. 205
New York, NY 10003
Phone: (212)254-8200
Fax: (212)477-4781
E-mail: info@ici-exhibitions.org
Home Page: http://www.ici-exhibitions.org

• 10718 • **Leo Award**
Recognizes outstanding contributions to the contemporary art world. Awarded biennially.

• 10719 •
Independent Feature Project
Elizabeth Donius, Exec.Dir.
1104 S Wabash, Ste. 403
1104 S. Wabash, Ste. 403
Chicago, IL 60605
Phone: (312)235-0161
Fax: (312)235-0162
E-mail: edonius@ifp.org
Home Page: http://www.ifp.org

• 10720 • **Breakthrough Director Award**
To recognize an emerging filmmaker who went through exceptional means to make their first film. Awarded annually as part of the Gotham Awards. A sculpture and approximately $20,000 worth of services and equipment for film production are presented. Established in 1990. Formerly: Open Palm Award.

• 10721 • **Gotham Awards**
To honor outstanding talent in the film/entertainment industry. A jury of peers decides the winning selections in each of six categories. Awarded annually with a sculpture. Established in 1990.

• 10722 •
Independent Free Papers of America
Gary Rudy, Exec.Dir.
107 Hemlock Dr.
Rio Grande, NJ 08242
Phone: (609)408-8000
Toll-Free: 800-441-4372
Fax: (609)889-8359
E-mail: gary@ifpa.com
Home Page: http://www.ifpa.com

• 10723 • **Distinguished Service Award**
For recognition of outstanding service in furthering the principles and spirit of IFPA. Members of IFPA who are nominated are eligible. A plaque is presented annually at the convention. Established in 1983.

• 10724 • **Vic Jose Award for General Excellence**
For recognition of best all-around publication. Voted and selected by the membership present at the annual fall conference each year. First, second and third places awarded.

• 10725 • **Joe Skelnar Award**
For recognition of best editorial on a subject of local community interest which best personifies the strong hometown allegiance and fearless expression of opinion for which Joe is remembered.

• 10726 •
Independent Insurance Agents and Brokers of America
Thomas B. Ahart, Pres.
127 S Peyton St.
Alexandria, VA 22314
Phone: (703)683-4422
Toll-Free: 800-221-7917
Fax: (703)683-7556
E-mail: info@iiaba.org
Home Page: http://www.independentagent.com

• 10727 • **Walter H. Bennett Memorial Award**
To recognize the local board which has demonstrated outstanding achievements in one or more of the following areas: membership, promotion, legislation, civic contribution and education. Established in 1957 by the New Orleans Insurance Board, in honor of Walter H. Bennett.

• 10728 • **Harold S. Bowen Public Relations Award**
To recognize the state association, excluding Ohio, which has contributed the most to improving the public understanding of the American Agency System and the insurance industry generally. Judging of entries is based on results accomplished in the following main categories: (1) informing the public about insurance; (2) participation with the public in civic affairs; (3) teaching the public about insurance; and (4) activities and accomplishments in communicating state association positions via penetration in the insurance trade press and other trade media. Entries may be submitted by July 31. Established in 1951 by the Ohio Association to honor Harold S. Bowen, a past president.

• 10729 • **Bernard J. Burns Award**
To recognize the individual who has made the greatest overall contribution to InsurPac in the past year. Sponsored by the Connecticut Association in honor of Bernard J. Burns, InsurPac founder.

• 10730 • **Connecticut Association Membership Award**
To recognize the state association which, during the past fiscal year, has made the most outstanding performance in the following two categories, each of which will be given equal weight: membership growth; and the implementation of an effective membership development program. Entries may be submitted by July 31. Established in 1943 and sponsored by the Connecticut Association.

• 10731 • **Dach InVEST Award**
To recognize the independent agent who, through hard work and dedication, contributed substantially to the InVEST program and whose efforts resulted in the growth, improvement and increased awareness of InVEST. Established in 1990 in honor of Stephen R. Dach, "The Father of InVEST," who founded the InVEST program in California in 1970.

• 10732 • **Maurice G. Herndon National Legislative Award**
To recognize the state association whose national legislative efforts on behalf of the Independent Insurance Agents of America have been deemed most outstanding. Entries may be submitted by July 31. Presented by the Independent Insurance Agents of Illinois, Inc. The honor is named after the former head of IIABA's government affairs operation. For additional information contact Paul Equale, Senior Vice President Government Affairs, IIAA, 412 First St., SE, Ste. 300, Washington, D.C. 20003.

• 10733 • **IIAA Publications Award**
To recognize the state association or local board that has the most outstanding periodical, magazine or newspaper.

• 10734 • **InVEST Award**
To recognize the state or local association whose efforts to promote and enrich the InVEST program has been deemed most outstanding.

• 10735 • **L. P. McCord Education Award**
To recognize the state association which has provided its members with the best opportunity to broaden their knowledge in the insurance profession. Entries may be submitted by July 31. Established in 1911 by the Florida Association of Insurance Agents. Given in honor of L.P. McCord, of Jacksonville, FLorida, who served as chairman of the Association Education Committee for 15 years. For more information contact Bill Anderson, V. Pres., Education and Technical Affairs, IIAA, 127 S. Peyton St., Alexandria, VA 22314.

• 10736 • **Membership Service Award**
To recognize the state and/or local association that has introduced the most innovative membership service(s) resulting in the greatest positive improvement in a membership's competitive position or business operations. Entries may be submitted by July 31. Established in 1984.

• 10737 • **Outstanding Young Agents Committee Award**
To recognize the state young agents committee that contributes the most to its state association's efforts to foster an understanding of the insurance industry and to the improvement of the Independent Agency System.

• 10738 • **Sidney O. Smith National Award**
To recognize an individual for outstanding service to the Independent Insurance Agents of America in the field of government relations. Entries may be submitted by July 31. The award is named in honor of Sidney O. Smith, named in honor of an IIABA past president and Georgia agent. Additional information is available from Paul Equale, Vice President, Government Affairs, IIAA, 412 First St., SE, Ste. 300, Washington, DC 20003.

• 10739 • **Ezra M Sparlin Award**
To recognize the state association which, during the past year, has rendered the most comprehensive service to the American Agency System in all of the following major activities: membership and local board development; public relations; education; legislation; and fire safety and accident prevention. Established by Ezra M. Sparlin of Rochester, New York. Sponsored by the New York Association.

• 10740 • **Tennessee Big "I" Advertising Award**
To recognize the state association, exclusive of Tennessee, or the local board association which makes the best contribution to the IIAA national advertising program. Selection is based on the following: (1) financial support of the national advertising program; (2) tie-in programs; and (3) participation in the Big "I" Insurance Youth Golf Classic. Entries may be submitted by July 31. Established in 1962.

• 10741 • **Woodworth Memorial Award**
This, the Association's highest award for an individual, is given to recognize the member who has performed the most outstanding service for insurance. Awarded only when merited. Established in 1925 in memory of C.H. Woodworth of Buffalo, NY, second NAIA President (1898-1899).

• 10742 •
Independent Mystery Booksellers Association
℅ Chris Acevedo
Clues Unlimited
123 S Eastbourne
Tucson, AZ 85716
Phone: (520)326-8533
Fax: (520)326-9001
E-mail: info@cluesunlimited.com
Home Page: http://www.mysterybooksellers.com

• 10743 • **The Dilys Award**
To recognize the mystery of crime fiction title deemed "the most fun to sell." Awarded annually with a glass paperweight. Established in 1992.

• 10744 •
Independent Organic Inspectors Association
Margaret Scoles, Exec.Dir.
PO Box 6
Broadus, MT 59317-0006
Phone: (406)436-2031
Fax: (406)436-2031
E-mail: ioia@ioia.net
Home Page: http://www.ioia.net

• 10745 • **Andrew Rutherford Scholarship**
For individual going to a 101A inspector training facility. Scholarship awarded annually.

• 10746 •
Independent Sector
Diana Aviv, Pres.
1200 18th St. NW, Ste. 200
Washington, DC 20036
Phone: (202)467-6100
Toll-Free: 888-860-8118
Fax: (202)467-6101
E-mail: info@independentsector.org
Home Page: http://www.independentsector.org

• 10747 • **John W. Gardner Leadership Award**
To recognize living Americans, individuals working in or with the voluntary sector, who build, mobilize and unify people, institutions or causes. As a result of their efforts, society is better able to address its problems and reach towards its highest aspirations. Award recipients are builders - people who, quite apart from noteworthy personal feats, have raised the capacity of others to improve society. Their leadership has had national or international impact; if their work has been at the regional or local level, it has attracted wider recognition and imitation. Recipients may be of any age, though generally, because they have a long history of effective and innovative work in or for the sector, recipients tend to hold senior leadership positions. Gardner Award recipients may be the creators of needed institutions. They may concentrate on education and/or advocacy to change public opinion. Whatever the means, the result is that their work has transformed their chosen field and thereby contributed to the greater good. A monetary award of $10,000 and a replica of an original relief bust of John Gardner by the prominent Washington, DC, sculptor, Frederick Hart, are awarded annually. Established in 1985 to honor the leadership and the ideals of John W. Gardner. Sponsored by the GE Fund.

• 10748 •
India Study Circle for Philately
Gerald Sattin, Pres.
PO Box 7326
Washington, DC 20044
Phone: (202)564-6876
Fax: (202)565-2441
E-mail: info@indiastudycircle.org
Home Page: http://www.indiastudycircle.org

• 10749 • **India Study Circle Award**
For recognition of excellence in philately relating to India. Any medal winner in the American Philatelic Society's World Series of Philately exhibitions showing a facet of Indian sub-continent philately is eligible. A medal and/or certificate is awarded annually. Established in 1986.

• 10750 •
Indian and Northern Affairs Canada
Andy Scott, Min.
Terrasses de la Chaudiere
10 Wellington, North Tower
Ottawa, ON, Canada K1A 0H4
Phone: (819)997-0660
Toll-Free: 800-567-9604
Fax: (866)817-3977
E-mail: infopubs@ainc-inac.gc.ca
Home Page: http://www.inac.gc.ca

• 10751 • **Northern Science Award**
Recognizes contributions of indigenous knowledge to the scientific understanding of the North. Nominees can be individuals who have made distinguished contributions or indigenous groups who posses and share indigenous knowledge for the benefit of all. Nominations can be made by anyone and should include a letter of nomination; the candidates' basic personal data; evidence of achievement; information on other contributions or experience; and three letters of reference. Selection is based on quality of the work; productivity in field(s) of activity; contribution to Northern knowledge; relevance; and training or participation of northerners in the work. Each candidate is considered for three years after nomination. A monetary prize of $4,500 and the Centenary Medal are awarded annually, to either an individual or a group contributions or indigenous groups who posses and share indigenous knowledge for the benefit of all. Nominations can be made by anyone. Established in 1983 by the Department of Indian Affairs and Northern Development to mark the 100th Anniversary of the International Polar Year of 1882-83, when numerous countries came to the Arctic to carry out a fully coordinated research program.

• 10752 •
Indian Arts and Crafts Association
Loreen Floyd, Off.Mgr.
4010 Carlisle NE, Ste. C
Albuquerque, NM 87107
Phone: (505)265-9149
Fax: (505)265-8251
E-mail: info@iaca.com
Home Page: http://www.iaca.com

• 10753 • **Artist of the Year**
To identify and encourage native American Indian artists. IACA member artists who are enrolled members of state or federally recognized Indian tribes are eligible. A monetary award of $1,500 free booths at two markets, and a lifetime membership in the Association are awarded annually. Established in 1981.

• 10754 •
Indiana Arts Commission
Dorothy L. Ilgen, Exec.Dir.
150 W Market St., Ste. 618
Indianapolis, IN 46204
Phone: (317)232-1268
Fax: (317)232-5595
E-mail: indianaartscommission@iac.in.gov
Home Page: http://www.ai.org/iac/

• 10755 • **Indiana Governor's Arts Awards**
Given in various categories including individual, group, business, and community. Presented for significant contributions to further development of the arts in Indiana. Recognition award bestowed biennially.

• 10756 •
Indiana Black Expo
Alpha Garrett, Dir./Commun.
3145 N Meridian St.
Indianapolis, IN 46208-4776
Phone: (317)925-2702
Toll-Free: 800-897-2702
Fax: (317)925-6624
E-mail: agarrett@ibeonline.com
Home Page: http://www.indianablackexpo.com

• 10757 • **Founders Award**
To recognize an African-American citizen of Indiana for outstanding achievement.

• 10758 • **Freedom Award**
To recognize the individual whom Indiana Black Expo, Inc. feels has contributed the most effective service in promoting goodwill to all mankind through performance, accomplishments and contributions to our world. Awarded annually. Established in 1981.

• 10759 • **Indiana State Senator Carolyn Mosby Above and Beyond Award**
To recognize an African-American public figure for outstanding contributions and achievements. Awarded annually. Established in 1970.

• 10760 •
Indiana Holstein Association
Myron Moyer, Exec. Officer
11594 Ted Davis Rd.
Greens Fork, IN 47345
Phone: (765)478-4509
Fax: (765)478-5294
E-mail: sjmoyer@infocom.com

• 10761 • **Scholarship Award**
For college applicant. Scholarship awarded annually.

• 10762 •
Indiana Library Federation
Linda D. Kolb, Exec.Dir.
941 E 86th St., Ste. 260
Indianapolis, IN 46240
Phone: (317)257-2040
Fax: (317)257-1393
E-mail: lkolb@ilfonline.org
Home Page: http://www.ilfonline.org

• 10763 • **Citizen's Award**
To honor an individual, corporate entity, or group who has rendered outstanding service to Indiana libraries, such as aid to the physical building or the library collection, voluntary service efforts,

or endowment gifts. Awarded annually. Established in 1978.

• 10764 • Federation Leadership Award
To recognize any person in an Indiana Library Federation role or a Federation member who has performed far beyond the scope of his or her position. Awarded annually.

• 10765 • Danny Gunnells Intellectual Freedom Award
Honors an individual or group for promoting, supporting, or encouraging intellectual freedom in Indiana. Must be an Indiana Library Federation member. Awarded biennially in even-numbered years.

• 10766 • Hoosier Intellectual Freedom Award
Honors an individual or group for promoting, supporting, or encouraging intellectual freedom in Indiana. Recommendations made by the ILF Intellectual Freedom Committee. Awarded biennially in even-numbered years. Established in 1998.

• 10767 • Legislator Award
Honors a state or federal legislator or an individual who has promoted and supported legislative efforts which promote Indiana libraries and librarianship. Awarded biennially in even-numbered years. Established in 1986.

• 10768 • Outstanding Librarian Award
To recognize excellence and innovative leadership in the development of library service, and for remarkable service to the profession. Awarded annually. Established in 1978.

• 10769 • Outstanding Library Award
To recognize outstanding library service that consistently exceeds the expectations of the patrons and serves as an exemplary model for other libraries. Awarded annually. Established in 1978.

• 10770 • Outstanding New Librarian Award
Honors a recent master's level graduate who is making important contributions to his or her employing library and librarianship at large in areas such as special projects, communication skills, and contributions to the community. Awarded annually. Established in 1992.

• 10771 • Outstanding Support Staff Award
To recognize a support or paraprofessional staff person who has contributed to his or her employing library and librarianship in Indiana. Awarded when merited. Established in 1981.

• 10772 • Outstanding Trustee Award
To honor an individual member of the Board of Trustees who has introduced sound library policies and effective service, served as a liaison between the library and the community, and worked to advance library service on a community, regional, or state level. Awarded annually. Established in 1978.

• 10773 • Partnership Award
To recognize a corporation, organization, or group that has made significant contributions toward the goals of the ILF and helped develop Indiana libraries and services. Awarded when merited. Established in 1990.

• 10774 •
Indiana Opera Theatre
7515 E. 30th St.
PO Box 1941
Indianapolis, IN 46206
Phone: (317)202-0634
Fax: (317)253-2008
E-mail: opera@iquest.net
Home Page: http://indianaoperatheatre.com

• 10775 • MacAllister Awards for Opera Singers
To encourage the professional development of individuals pursuing a career in opera. The competition is held in three divisions: Professional Division - singers, age 36 and under, must be actively pursuing career objectives and have performed a stage role; College Division - singers, age 25 and under, must be enrolled in an accredited college or university; and Youth Competition - Indiana high school students, sophomore through senior level, are eligible. All contestants must be citizens of the United States. Auditions are held throughout the year at various locations across the United States. The following monetary awards are presented for professionals: first prize - $10,000; second prize - $5,000; third prize $3,000; fourth prize - $1,500; fifth through tenth prize - $1,000; and sixth through 20th prize - $500 each. The following college prizes are presented: first prize - $2,500; second prize - $1,000; and third prize $500. The following monetary awards are presented for youths: first prize - $1,000; second prize - $500; and third prize - $250. Finals for the Youth Competition are held annually in June. Other divisions are awarded annually in August. Established in 1980 by P. E. MacAllister, an Indianapolis industrialist and philanthropist.

• 10776 •
Indiana Repertory Theatre
Janet Allen, Artistic Dir.
Bonderman National Youth Theatre Playwriting Competition
140 W Washington St.
Indianapolis, IN 46204
Phone: (317)635-5277
Fax: (317)236-0767
E-mail: dwebb@iupui.edu
Home Page: http://www.indianarep.com

• 10777 • Waldo M. and Grace C. Bonderman IUPUI Youth Theatre Playwriting Competition and Workshop
To encourage playwrights to write artistic scripts for young audiences. Plays should be a minimum performance length of 45 minutes and must not have had a professional (equity) performance and not be committed to publication. The deadline for submission is August 31, 2006. Send a self-addressed, stamped envelope to receive contest and submission guidelines. Awards are presented to the top ten finalists. Three to five awards of $1,000 plus a week-long development residency are awarded to the top playwrights whose plays are showcased in professionally rehearsed readings. The rest receive certificates. Awarded biennially at the Children's Theatre Symposium. Established in 1984. Formerly: (1991) IUPUI National Children's Theatre Playwriting Competition.

• 10778 •
Indianapolis Motor Speedway
4790 W 16th St.
Indianapolis, IN 46222
Phone: (317)481-8500
Fax: (317)484-6759
E-mail: imspr@brickyard.com
Home Page: http://www.brickyard.com

• 10779 • Indianapolis 500 Mile Race
To recognize the winner of the Indianapolis 500 Mile Race, held annually on Sunday of the Memorial Day weekend. The race is run on a two-and-a-half mile rectangular course, built originally in 1909 as a proving ground for the rapidly growing automotive industry. The race is held annually on Sunday of Memorial Day weekend, and was first run in 1911.

• 10780 • Indianapolis Motor Speedway Hall of Fame
To recognize outstanding personalities in racing and the development of the automobile industry. Established in 1952 and designated as a National Historic Landmark in 1987. Also known as the Hall of Fame Museum.

• 10781 •
Industrial Designers Society of America
Kristina Goodrich, Exec.Dir.
45195 Business Ct., Ste. 250
Dulles, VA 20166-6717
Phone: (703)707-6000
Fax: (703)787-8501
E-mail: kristinag@idsa.org
Home Page: http://www.idsa.org

• 10782 • Industrial Design Excellence Awards (IDEA)
To foster and promote industrial design excellence, recognize the role industrial design plays in stimulating economic competitiveness, and meet the changing needs of consumers. Awards are given in the following categories: business and industrial products; computer equipment; consumer products; design explorations; design strategy; digital media and interfaces; environments; furniture; medical and scientific equipment; packaging and graphics research; student designs and transportation. All designers who are U.S. citizens or permanent residents may submit any design, regardless of where the designs are manufactured or distributed. All other designers may only enter designs distributed in

North America. All entries must be placed in distribution within two years of the February deadline for entry. Three levels of awards are given: Gold, Silver, and Bronze. Trophies are presented at the annual conference. Established in 1980. Sponsored by *Business Week*.

• 10783 •
Industrial Fabrics Association International
Stephen M. Warner CAE, Pres.
1801 County Rd. B W
Roseville, MN 55113-4061
Phone: (651)222-2508
Toll-Free: 800-225-4324
Fax: (651)631-9334
E-mail: generalinfo@ifai.com
Home Page: http://www.ifai.com

• 10784 • **International Achievement Awards Competition**
To recognize outstanding and innovative work that presents the latest accomplishments in design and manufacture incorporating industrial/technical fabric. The twenty category competition is an excellent opportunity for IFAI members and nonmembers to display work, gain professional recognition, and be distinguished on an international level. The competition has been sponsored by IFAI each year since 1947; entries are exhibited and winners announced at the Industrial Fabric & Equipment Exposition and other conferences, and are published in IFAI magazines. For more information contact Rita Chuk-Petroskas, Awards & Certification Manager.

• 10785 •
Industrial Research Institute
F.M. Ross Armbrecht Jr., Pres.
2200 Clarendon Blvd., Ste. 1102
Arlington, VA 22201
Phone: (703)647-2580
Fax: (703)647-2581
E-mail: gore@iriinc.org
Home Page: http://www.iriinc.org

• 10786 • **Maurice Holland Award**
To recognize and honor the author(s) of the best original paper on research management appearing in *Research-Technology Management* each calendar year. Criteria for the award-winning paper include: pertinence to the field of research management, significance of the contribution to the field of research management, and originality of new management concepts or of the research on which the paper is based. Awarded annually. A bronze sculpture depicting the pioneering spirit of Maurice Holland, founder of the Industrial Research Institute, is awarded. Established in 1982.

• 10787 • **Industrial Research Institute Achievement Award**
To recognize and honor outstanding accomplishments in individual innovation and creativity that contribute broadly to industry and the public welfare. An original work of art and certificate are awarded annually. Established in 1973.

• 10788 • **Industrial Research Institute Medal**
For recognition of leaders of technology for their outstanding accomplishments in technological innovation which have contributed to the development of industry and to the benefit of society. A medal and a certificate are awarded annually. Established in 1946.

• 10789 •
Infectious Diseases Society of America
Mark A. Leasure, Exec.Dir.
66 Canal Center Plz., Ste. 600
Alexandria, VA 22314
Phone: (703)299-0200
Fax: (703)299-0204
E-mail: info@idsociety.org
Home Page: http://www.idsociety.org

• 10790 • **Oswald Avery Award**
To recognize outstanding achievement in an area of infectious diseases by an individual fellow or member of IDSA who is 45 years of age or younger (during the calendar year in which the award is given). The award is based upon overall achievement, not a single study. A monetary award of $2,500 plus travel expenses is awarded each year at the IDSA Annual Meeting. Formerly: Squibb Award.

• 10791 • **Alexander Fleming Award**
To recognize a career reflecting major accomplishments and contributions to the acquisition of knowledge and its dissemination through teaching in an area of infectious diseases. A monetary award of $3,000 plus travel expenses is awarded each year at the IDSA Annual Meeting. Formerly: Bristol Award.

• 10792 • **Ortho Pharmaceutical Corporation and McNeil Pharmaceutical Young Investigator Award in Infectious Diseases**
To provide financial support to an outstanding young investigator in pursuit of academic research in the broad area of clinical investigation of infectious diseases. A monetary award of $30,000 is given annually for two years, for a total of $60,000.

• 10793 • **Society Citation**
To recognize an exemplary contribution to IDSA, an outstanding discovery in the field of infectious diseases, or a lifetime of outstanding achievement in research or clinical investigation. The award is granted periodically. Nominations must be received by May 30.

• 10794 • **Wyeth Young Investigator Award in Vaccine Development**
To provide funding for outstanding clinical research in vaccine development. A monetary award of $30,000 is given annually for two years, for a total of $60,000. Sponsored by Wyeth Vaccines Research.

• 10795 •
Information Technology Association of Canada
(Association canadienne de la technologie de l'information)
Caren Adno, Contact
2800 Skymark Ave., Ste. 402
Mississauga, ON, Canada L4W 5A6
Phone: (905)602-8345
Fax: (905)602-8346
E-mail: info@itac.ca
Home Page: http://www.itac.ca

• 10796 • **Canadian Information Productivity Awards**
Annual award of recognition. Individuals contributing to the industry and outstanding information technology students are eligible. Inquire for application details.

• 10797 •
Information Today, Inc.
Thomas H. Hogan, Pres.
143 Old Marlton Pke.
Medford, NJ 08055-8750
Phone: (609)654-6266
Toll-Free: 800-248-8466
Fax: (609)654-4309
E-mail: custserv@infotoday.com
Home Page: http://www.onlineinc.com

• 10798 • **Annual Award for Excellence in Writing on an Information Topic**
To recognize a published paper about the online industry appearing in *DATABASE*, *ONLINE* or *EMedia Professional* magazines, and to honor the best column about the online industry. The award is designed to encourage the highest level of professionalism among information managers and users of databases who want to share their experiences with their colleagues through journal articles. Articles published during the preceding year are considered. A monetary prize of $1,500 and an engraved plaque are awarded for the paper. Awarded annually. Established in 1980. Sponsored by Information Access Company. Formerly: UMI/Data Courier Award.

• 10799 • **Annual Award to Regular Columnists**
To recognize excellence in writing a regular column published in *ONLINE*, *DATABASE* or *EMedia Professional* during the preceding year. This award is based on excellence in research, clarity, originality, timeliness, and impact on the database industry. A monetary award of $500 and an engraved plaque are presented annually. Established in 1988. Sponsored by Information Access Company.

• 10800 •
Infusion Nurses Society
Mary Alexander, CEO
220 Norwood Park S
Norwood, MA 02062
Phone: (781)440-9408
Toll-Free: 800-694-0298
Fax: (781)440-9409
E-mail: linda.spada@ins1.org
Home Page: http://www.ins1.org

Formerly: National Intravenous Therapy Association.

• 10801 • **Chapter Presidents Trophy Award**
For recognition in the areas of Chapter management, presidential accomplishments and service to the Society and Chapter. Awarded annually at the annual banquet by the President of the Society. Established in 1984.

• 10802 • **Member of the Year Award**
For recognition of achievements in intravenous nursing and participation in the Association. Registered nurses who are members of the Association are eligible. A plaque is awarded annually at the convention. Established in 1983.

• 10803 • **Outstanding Performance Award**
For recognition of outstanding performance and contributions to intravenous nursing and the Association. Registered nurses who are members are eligible. A plaque is awarded when merited. Established in 1983.

• 10804 •
Inland Bird Banding Association
Mark Shieldcastle, Contact
13229 West State Rte. 2
Oak Harbor, OH 43449
E-mail: mark.shieldcastle@dnr.state.oh.us
Home Page: http://www.aves.net/inlandBBA/ibbamain.htm

• 10805 • **Willetta Lueshen Harris' Sparrow Endowment**
To foster research on the Harris' Sparrow. Individuals may apply. A monetary award is presented annually at the convention. Established in 1986 by Norman Sloan in honor of Willetta Lueshen, faithful servant of the IBBA.

• 10806 • **Willetta Lueshen Student Membership Award**
To recognize students who have demonstrated a sincere interest in bird banding and who show potential for making contributions to the knowledge of North American birds through the use of bird banding. High school, undergraduate, and graduate students may apply for the award. One year memberships in the Association are presented annually at the Conference. Established in 1978 in honor of Willetta Lueshen, who maintained continuing enthusiasm and recruited new members.

• 10807 • **Paul Stewart Endowment**
To provide for studying bird movements relative to the evolution of bird migration. Individuals may apply. A monetary prize is awarded annually at the convention. Established in 1986 by Paul A. Stewart.

• 10808 •
Inland Empire Reading Council
Cristie McCabe, Pres.
PO Box 5841
Riverside, CA 92517

• 10809 • **Celebrate Literacy**
For outstanding teacher or non-certified staff involved with literacy. Recognition award bestowed annually.

• 10810 •
Inland Press Association
Ray Carlsen, Exec.Dir.
701 Lee St., Ste. 925
Des Plaines, IL 60016
Phone: (847)795-0380
Fax: (847)795-0385
E-mail: inland@inlandpress.org
Home Page: http://www.inlandpress.org

• 10811 • **Ralph D. Casey Minnesota Award**
To honor a publisher, editor or senior newspaper staff who has performed distinguished service to his or her community, state, and nation through journalism over a long period of time. A plaque is awarded annually at the Association's convention by Inland Press Association and the School of Journalism of the University of Minnesota. Established in 1948. The award honors Professor Ralph D. Casey who identified the mutually supportive roles of journalism schools and the media. Sponsored by the University of Minnesota School of Journalism. Additional information is available from Linda Wilson, Assistant to the Daniel B. Wackman, Director, School of Journalism and Mass Communication, 111 Murphy Hall, 206 Church St., S.E., University of Minnesota, Minneapolis, MN 55455.

• 10812 • **Community Leadership Award**
For recognition of creative leadership in community projects over a period of years. Newspaper members of the Association are eligible. One award is given award in each of four circulation categories: less than 10,000; 10,000-25,000; 25,001 to 75,000 and more than 75,000. Established in 1949. Co-sponsored by the University of Missouri School of Journalism. Formerly: Distinguished Achievement Award for Community Service; (2003) Community Service Award.

• 10813 • **Editorial Excellence Award**
For recognition of excellence in editorial writing. Newspaper members of the Association are eligible. A plaque and certificate are awarded annually in the spring. Established in 1972. Sponsored by the William Allen White Foundation, School of Journalism, University of Kansas.

• 10814 • **Front Page Award**
For recognition of quality, completeness, and appeal in front pages. Open to all Inland-member, daily and non-daily newspapers. Sponsored by Medill School of Journalism, Northwestern University Formerly: Makeup and Design Award.

• 10815 • **Local News Writing Awards**
For recognition of excellence in the coverage of local government news. Any news story or feature, or series of news stories or features involving local government, written by a staff member of an Inland member newspaper is eligible. Awards are given in three categories according to circulation classes. First and second place certificates are awarded annually in October. Established in 1947. Sponsored by the University of Kentucky School of Journalism and Telecommunications. Formerly: (2003) Distinguished Achievement Awards for Local Public Affairs.

• 10816 • **News Picture Contest**
For recognition of excellence in newspaper photography in two competition classes: photography - open to staff photographers and those with photo duties on Inland member papers; and picture use - to recognize outstanding use by editors of photographs in Inland member publications. Newspaper members of the Association are eligible. A plaque is awarded annually. Established in 1940. Co-sponsored by Indiana University School of Journalism.

• 10817 •
Institut d'Histoire de l'Amerique Francaise
Lise McNicoll, Admin.Sec.
261, Ave. Bloomfield
Montreal, QC, Canada H2V 3R6
Phone: (514)278-2232
Fax: (514)271-6369
E-mail: ihaf@ihaf.qc.ca
Home Page: http://www.cam.org/~ihaf

• 10818 • **Prix Guy-Fregault**
For recognition of the best article published in a volume of the *Revue d'histoire de l'Amerique francaise.* All articles published in RHAF are considered. A monetary prize of $1,000 (Canadian) is awarded annually at the Congres de l'IHAF in October. Established in 1979 by IHAF and funded by the son of Quebec historian Guy Fregault, in his honor.

• 10819 • **Prix Lionel-Groulx-Foundation Yves-Saint-Germain**
For recognition of the best book length study concerning the history of the French experience in America published in a given year. Books published in the calendar year preceding the award are considered. A monetary award of $5,000 (Canadian) is awarded annually at the Congres de l'IHAF in October. Established in 1979 by IHAF, in memory of Lionel Groulx, a Quebec historian and founder of the IHAF. Sponsored by La Foundation Yves-Saint-Germain. Formerly: Prix Lionel - Groulx - les Cooperants.

• 10820 • Prix Maxime-Raymond

For recognition of the best French-Canadian biography published in french during the preceding three years and to encourage the publication of biographies of individuals who are important to Canadian history. A monetary prize of $1,500 is awarded every three years. Established in 1986 by the Fondation Lionel-Groulx.

• 10821 • Prix Michel-Brunet

For recognition of the work of young Quebec historians. Work may be in the form of a book, article, film, or recording provided that it is of a scientific nature, concerns any field of history, and is written in the French language. Quebec citizens under 35 years of age are eligible. A monetary prize of $1,000 (Canadian) is awarded annually. Established in 1984 by Michel Brunet, a noted Quebec historian.

• 10822 •
Institute for Communications Law Studies
David Irwin, Dir.
Columbus School of Law
Catholic University of America
Washington, DC 20064
Phone: (202)319-5140
Fax: (202)319-4459
E-mail: irwind@law.edu
Home Page: http://law.cua.edu/academic/institutes/institutes_a.cfm

• 10823 • First Amendment Defender Award

To recognize long-term service in the defense of free expression in the United States. Nominations by journalists, communications lawyers and academics are accepted for consideration by June. An honorarium and a plaque are awarded when merited in December. Established in 1984.

• 10824 •
Institute for Mediation and Conflict Resolution
Stephen E. Slate, Exec.Dir.
384 E 149th St., Ste. 330
Bronx, NY 10455
Phone: (718)585-1190
Fax: (718)585-1962
E-mail: info@imcr.org
Home Page: http://www.imcr.org

• 10825 • Theodore W. Kheel Award of the Institute for Mediation and Conflict Resolution

To recognize an individual for an outstanding contribution to the field of peacemaking, conflict resolution, or intergroup relations. Members who have been active with the Institute for at least ten years and have contributed to mediation services in all aspects are eligible. A scroll and a Roshemberg painting are awarded. The Award is named for the founder and Chairman Emeritus of the Institute, Theodore W. Kheel, an outstanding labor attorney of the Institute who served as a visionary and pioneer in applying negotiation and mediation to other than labor disputes.

• 10826 •
Institute for Mesoamerican Studies
Social Science, 263
University at Albany/Arts & Sciences 233
1400 Washington Ave.
Albany, NY 12222
Phone: (518)442-4722
Fax: (518)442-5710
E-mail: ims@albany.edu
Home Page: http://www.albany.edu/ims/

• 10827 • First Encounters Award

Recognizes outstanding field research in mesoamerica.

• 10828 • Graduate and Undergraduate Essay Awards

Inquire for application details.

• 10829 •
Institute for Policy Studies
Dorian Lipscombe, Dir. of Admin.
733 15th St. NW, Ste. 1020
Washington, DC 20005
Phone: (202)234-9382
Fax: (202)387-7915
E-mail: dorian@igc.org
Home Page: http://www.ips-dc.org

• 10830 • Letelier - Moffitt Memorial Human Rights Awards

To recognize those individuals and groups most dedicated to the struggle for human rights. Two awards are given each year: (1) a United States award; and (2) a Western Hemisphere award. A specially designed medallion, sculptured by Barry Johnston, which has faces of Orlando Letelier and Ronni Karpen Moffitt, and the words, "Peace, Justice, Dignity" inscribed, and travel expenses to the award ceremony are presented annually. Established in 1977 in memory of Orlando Letelier and Ronni Moffitt, who were murdered September 21, 1976.

• 10831 •
Institute for Public Relations
Frank Ovaitt, Pres./CEO
PO Box 118400
University of Florida
Gainesville, FL 32611-8400
Phone: (352)392-0280
Fax: (352)846-1122
E-mail: iprre@grove.ufl.edu
Home Page: http://www.instituteforpr.com

• 10832 • Master's Thesis Award

To recognize the Master's Thesis that contributes most to the public relations body of knowledge. The deadline for entries is August 31. A plaque and a monetary prize of $2,000 are awarded at the Institute's annual lecture in New York in late fall.

• 10833 • Pathfinder Award

To recognize a recent program of original scholarly research that has made a significant contribution to the body of knowledge and practice of public relations. Special consideration will be given to work for which a major article, chapter or book has been published within the past two years that integrates this program of research or articulates its importance to research and practice. Deadline for submissions is August 31. A plaque and a monetary prize of $2,000 are awarded at the Institute's annual lecture in New York in late fall.

• 10834 •
Institute for Research in Hypnosis and Psychotherapy
Dr. Milton V. Kline, Dir.
1991 Broadway, Ste. 18B
New York, NY 10023
Phone: (212)874-5290
Phone: (212)799-2727
Fax: (212)874-5290
E-mail: info@hypnosis-institute.org

• 10835 • Dr. Marco Marchesan Award

For recognition of contributions to hypnotherapy and the teaching of hypnotherapy. A plaque and a certificate are awarded.

• 10836 • Morton Prince, M.D. Award

In recognition of significant clinical research in the application of hypnotherapy. A plaque and certificate is awarded. Established in 1960 in honor of Morton Prince, M.D.

• 10837 •
Institute for Southern Studies
Chris Kromm, Exec.Dir.
PO Box 531
Durham, NC 27707
Phone: (919)419-8311
Fax: (919)419-8315
E-mail: info@southernstudies.org
Home Page: http://www.southernstudies.org

• 10838 • Southern Journalism Award

To recognize outstanding reporting by a daily journalist for a Southern newspaper in specific categories and divisions. Individual must be a reporter with a daily newspaper in a Southern city and have written an article or series published the previous year. The deadline is December 1. Awards may be presented for investigative reporting, feature reporting, reporting on money and politics, and on working people in the region. A monetary award of $300 for first prize, and certificates to first, second, and third prize winners are awarded annually. Excerpts from a selection of the winning entries are published in *Southern Exposure* magazine. Established in 1987.

• 10839 •
Institute for Supply Management
Paul Novak, CEO
PO Box 22160
PO Box 22160
Tempe, AZ 85285-2160
Phone: (480)752-6276
Toll-Free: 800-888-6276
Fax: (480)752-7890
Home Page: http://www.ism.ws

Formerly: (2003) National Association of Purchasing Management.

• 10840 • **J. Shipman Gold Medal Award**
This, the highest award accorded to purchasing executives, is given for sincere, modest, unselfish, and persistent efforts for the advancement of the supply management field. The award is not limited to members of the Association. A gold medal is awarded annually. Nomination deadline is January 31. Established in 1931 by the New York Association of Purchasing Management in honor of Johnson Shipman.

• 10841 •
Institute for the Study of American Cultures
Carole C. Sides, Sec.
PO Box 2707
Columbus, GA 31902
Home Page: http://www.j4fclub.org/isacnet

• 10842 • **Samuel W. Brown, Jr. Root Cutter Award**
To recognize achievements of individuals who have contributed to a more accurate and complete understanding of the history and culture of the peoples who inhabited the Americas before they were discovered by Christopher Columbus. Anyone is eligible for the award without restriction. A gold medallion is presented to no more than five individuals in a ceremony at the annual research conference. Established in 1989 in memory of Samuel W. Brown, Jr. (1874-1957), hereditary chief of the Yuchi Indian Tribe. Sponsored by the Yuchi Tribal Organization, Sapulpa, Oklahoma.

• 10843 •
Institute for the Study of Earth and Man
Louis L. Jacobs, Contact
Southern Methodist University
N.L. Heroy Science Hall
P.O. Box. 0724
Dallas, TX 75275-0274
Phone: (214)768-2425
E-mail: isem@mail.smu.edu
Home Page: http://www.smu.edu/isem/

• 10844 • **Claude C. Albritton, Jr. Award**
Recognizes significant accomplishment in research and continuing research promise on the part of a graduate student in Geology or Anthropology. Students are nominated for this award by their major professor. First consideration will be given to students whose research is interdisciplinary in nature. It is normally awarded at the beginning of the final year of residence and should assist in the writing of the dissertation. The award is endowed by gifts in memory in honor of Claude C. Albritton, Jr. (founding Vice President of ISEM Hamilton Professor of Geology, longtime Dean of Arts and Sciences and, later, Dean of Graduate Studies of SMU)

• 10845 • **Champlin Research Award**
For students who have completed, with distinction, at least one year of graduate study, and expressed the intention of entering the energy industry as a career and whose thesis research is broadly related to the search for energy resources. A student is nominated for this award by their major professor. The award was endowed by Champlin Refining and Chemicals, Inc., then a Subsidiary of Petroleos de Venezuela, SA.

• 10846 • **Hollis D. Hedberg Award in Energy**
Given annually to individuals who have made exceptional contributions to the understanding of the earth and its resources. Supported by Petroleos de Venezuela, S.A., the national oil company of Venezuela, where Dr. Hedberg devoted many years of his professional life to the discovery of significant oil reserves.

• 10847 • **ISEM Seed Grants**
Awarded to graduate students in the SMU Departments of Anthropology and Geological Sciences. These awards are intended to support dissertation -related research with the intention that additional funding be sought from other sources. In many cases, these awards help the students get into the field for preliminary research.

• 10848 •
Institute of Advanced Philosophic Research
Walter L. Koenig, CEO
PO Box 805
Moultonborough, NH 03254
Phone: (603)253-3311
Fax: (603)253-3311
E-mail: realia@cyberportal.net
Home Page: http://
www.contemporaryphilosophy.com

• 10849 • **Realia Honors**
For recognition of the best annual contemporary philosophy in a problem-solution paper during the preceding year. Professional papers on the definition of contemporary philosophy are considered. A plaque, commendations, and honors are awarded annually at a ceremony. Established in 1984.

• 10850 •
Institute of Certified Records Managers
Linda Cusimano CRM, Pres.
318 Oak St.
Syracuse, NY 13203
Phone: (315)234-1904
Toll-Free: 877-244-3128
Fax: (315)474-1784
E-mail: admin@icrm.org
Home Page: http://www.icrm.org

• 10851 • **Emmett Leahy Award**
For recognition of outstanding contributions to the field of information and records management. Any professional in the information and records management field may be nominated. The following criteria are considered: (1) Overall contribution to the information/records management profession; (2) Nominee's own program, methods used to make it outstanding, special projects developed and implemented, and results achieved in savings, new services, improved management capabilities, decreased time requirements, etc.; (3) Innovative concepts and techniques for improving practices and procedures; (4) Technological innovations; (5) Systems development; (6) Leadership in professional groups; (7) Courses, lectures, or seminars conducted; and (8) Articles and books authored. A plaque is awarded annually at the annual meeting of ICRM in October. Established in 1967 by Leahy Archives and Information and Records Management Magazine in memory of Emmett J. Leahy, who pioneered establishment of records management programs in federal government and private business. Sponsored by Iron Mountain. Additional information is available from the Institute.

• 10852 •
The Institute of Classical Architecture and Classical America
Henrika Taylor, Mng.Dir.
20 W 44th St.
New York, NY 10036
Phone: (212)730-9646
Fax: (212)730-9649
E-mail: institute@classicist.org
Home Page: http://www.classicist.org

• 10853 • **Arthur Ross Awards**
For recognition of contemporary contributions to the classical tradition in the arts. Painters, sculptors, architects, craftsmen, landscape architects, architectural renderers, gardeners, and patrons who are citizens of the United States are eligible. Mature work that exhibits a continued excellence and integrity in its application of classical ideals and canons is considered. The awards are chosen by a selection committee made up of members of the ICA & CA Board of Directors Advisory Council, Fellows, and distinguished members of related professions, and Are drawn from nominations received by the committee during the course of the year. Certificates are awarded annually at the National Academy of Design. Established in 1982 in honor of Arthur Ross.

• 10854 •
Institute of Electrical and Electronics Engineers
W. Cleon Anderson, Pres.
445 Hoes Ln.
Piscataway, NJ 08854
Phone: (732)981-0060
Toll-Free: 800-678-4333
Fax: (732)981-1721
E-mail: corporate-communications@ieee.org
Home Page: http://www.ieee.org

• 10855 • **W. R. G. Baker Prize Award**
To recognize the most outstanding paper reporting original work in the transactions, journals, proceedings, and magazines of the IEEE. Nominations must be received by July 1 and may include only papers in publications which have been issued between January 1 and December 31 of the preceding year. A monetary prize of $1,000 and a certificate are awarded annually. Established in 1956.

• 10856 • **Cledo Brunetti Award**
To recognize outstanding contributions of an individual or a team of not more than three members in the field of miniaturization in the electronic arts. The deadline for nominations is January 31. A monetary award of $1,000 and a certificate are presented. Established in 1975 through a bequest made by the late Cledo Brunetti, an executive of the FMC Corporation.

• 10857 • **Control Systems Award**
To recognize an individual for meritorious achievement in contributions to theory, design, or techniques, as evidenced by publications or patents in the area of control systems engineering, science, and technology. A monetary award of $3,000, a bronze medal, and a certificate are awarded annually. The deadline for nominations is January 31. Established in 1980. Sponsored by IEEE Control Systems Society.

• 10858 • **Edison Medal**
To recognize a career of meritorious achievements in electrical science, electrical engineering, or electrical arts and to serve as an honorable incentive to scientists, engineers, and artisans to maintain by their works the high standard of accomplishment which had been set by Edison. Members of IEEE may be nominated. Nominations with two supporting letters must be received by July 1. The award consists of a monetary prize of $10,000, a gold medal, a small gold replica, and a certificate. Awarded annually. Established in 1904 by an organization of associates and friends of Thomas A. Edison.

• 10859 • **Richard M. Emberson Award**
To recognize distinguished service to the development, viability, advancement, and pursuit of the technical objectives of the IEEE. Members may be nominated by July 1. A monetary award of $1,000, travel expenses to attend the award ceremony, a bronze medal, and an illuminated certificate are awarded annually. Established in 1986. Sponsored by the Technical Activities Board.

• 10860 • **Donald G. Fink Prize Award**
To recognize the outstanding survey, review, or tutorial paper in any of the IEEE transactions, journals, magazines, or proceedings of the IEEE. Nominations must be received by July 1 and may include only papers in publications which have been issued between January 1 and December 31 of the preceding year. A monetary award of $1,000 and a certificate are awarded annually. Established in 1979 in honor of Donald G. Fink, distinguished editor and author, who was a Past President of the IRE, and the first General Manager and Executive Director of the IEEE.

• 10861 • **Charles LeGeyt Fortescue Fellowship**
A one-year fellowship for full-time graduate work in electrical engineering at a recognized school in /the United States or Canada. A stipend of $24,000 is awarded annually. Established in 1939 as a memorial to Charles LeGeyt in recognition of his valuable contributions to the field of electrical engineering. Sponsored by Charles LeGeyt Fortescue Graduate Scholarship Fund.

• 10862 • **Founders Medal**
To recognize major contributions in the leadership, planning, or administration of affairs of great value to the electrical and electronics engineering profession. Members of IEEE may be nominated. Nominations and two supporting letters must be received by July 1. The award consists of a monetary award of $10,000, a gold medal, a bronze replica, and a certificate. Awarded annually. Established in 1952 by the Institute of Radio Engineers in 1952.

• 10863 • **Herman Halperin Electric Transmission and Distribution Award**
To recognize an individual for outstanding contributions to the field of electric transmission and distribution. The deadline for nominations is January 31. A monetary award of $2,000 and a certificate are awarded annually. Established in 1986 and supported by a fund from Herman and Edna Halperin.

• 10864 • **Richard W. Hamming Medal**
To recognize exceptional contributions to information sciences, systems and technology. Preference is given to an individual, but may be conferred on a team of not more than three. A monetary award of $10,000, a gold medal, a bronze replica, and a certificate are awarded annually. Established in 1986. Sponsored by AT&T Labs.

• 10865 • **Heinrich Hertz Medal**
To recognize an individual for outstanding achievements in Hertzian (radio) waves. The work may be theoretical or experimental in nature and achieved in any year preceding the year in which the award is made. The deadline date for nominations is July 1. A monetary prize of $10,000, a gold medal, a bronze replica, and a certificate are awarded annually. Established in 1987. Sponsored by Industry in Region 8.

• 10866 • **Masaru Ibuka Consumer Electronics Award**
To recognize outstanding contributions to the field of consumer electronics technology. Preference is given to an individual or team of up to three for achievement first recognized in the 10 years preceding the year in which the award is made. The deadline for nominations is January 31. A monetary prize of $2,000, a bronze medal, and a certificate are awarded annually. Established in 1987 in honor of Dr. Masaru Ibuka, Honorary Chairman and Co-Founder of Sony Corporation. Sponsored by Sony Corporation of America.

• 10867 • **IEEE Award in International Communication**
To recognize outstanding contributions to the field of international communication. Preference is given to achievement by a single individual, but may be conferred on a team of not more than three individuals. The deadline for nominations is January 31. The award consists of $2,000, a plaque, and a certificate. Established in 1966 through agreement with the International Telephone and Telegraph Corporation. The award honors Hernand and Sosthenes Behn.

• 10868 • **IEEE Corporate Innovation Recogniton Award**
To recognize a corporation for outstanding technical innovation. Awarded annually the award consists of a certificate and crystal sculpture. Established in 1985.

• 10869 • **IEEE Education Medal**
To recognize outstanding contributions to education for excellence in teaching and ability to inspire students; leadership in electrical engineering education through publication of textbooks and writings on engineering education; innovations in curricula and teaching methodology; and contributions to the teaching and engineering profession through research, engineering achievements, technical papers, and participation in the education activities of professional societies. Members of IEEE may be nominated. Nominations and two supporting letters must be received by July 1. The award consists of a monetary award of $10,000, a gold medal, a bronze replica, and a certificate. Established in 1956. Sponsored by Mathworks Inc., National Instruments Foundation, Pearson Prentice Hall and Xilinx Inc.

• 10870 • **IEEE Engineering Leadership Recognition**
To recognize an individual for outstanding leadership and management skills in the field of engineering. Awarded annually the award consists of a certificate and a crystal sculpture. Established in 1986, the award was renamed IEEE Ernst Weber Engineering Leadership Recognition to honor of Ernst Weber, first President of the IEEE.

• 10871 • IEEE Medal of Honor
This, the highest award offered by the Institute, is awarded for a particular contribution which forms a clearly exceptional addition to the science and technology of concern to the Institute. The award is normally made within a few years after recognition of the exceptional nature of such a contribution. The recipient need not be a member of the IEEE. The nomination deadline is July 1. The award consists of a monetary prize of $20,000, an inscribed gold Medal of Honor, a bronze replica, and a certificate. Established in 1917.

• 10872 • Richard Harold Kaufmann Award
To recognize an outstanding achievement in the field of industrial systems engineering. Preference is given to an individual, but may be conferred on a team of not more than three. Nominations may be submitted by January 31. A monetary award of $2,000, a bronze medal, and an certificate are awarded annually. Established in 1987 in honor of Richard Harold Kaufmann in memory of his many important contributions to industrial systems engineering and his dedicated service to the IEEE Industry Applications Society.. Sponsored by the IEEE Industry Applications Society.

• 10873 • Koji Kobayashi Computers and Communications Award
To recognize outstanding technical contributions in the field of computers and communications. Preference is given to an achievement by a single individual, but may be conferred on a team of not more than three. Nominations may be submitted by January 31. A monetary award of $2,000, a bronze medal, and a certificate are awarded annually. Established in 1987 in honor of Dr. Koji Kobayashi, who has been a leading force in advancing the integrated use of computers and communications. Sponsored by NEC Corporation.

• 10874 • Morris E. Leeds Award
To recognize an individual, or group of individuals not larger than three, making an outstanding contribution to the field of electrical measurement. Special consideration is given to the value of contributions made before the candidate's 36th birthday. The deadline for nominations is January 31. The award consists of $1,000 and an illuminated certificate. Established in 1958. Sponsored by the Leeds and Northrup Foundation.

• 10875 • Frederik Philips Award
To recognize outstanding accomplishments in the management of research and development resulting in effective innovation in the electrical and electronics industry. Preference is given for achievement by a single individual, but may be conferred on a team of not more than three individuals. The deadline for nominations is January 31. A monetary prize award of $2,000, a bronze medal, and a certificate are awarded annually. Established in 1971 by Philips Electronics N.V..

• 10876 • Emanuel R. Piore Award
To recognize outstanding achievement in the field of information processing, in relation to computer science, deemed to have contributed significantly to the advancement of science and to the betterment of society. Preference is given for achievement by a single individual, but may be conferred on a team of two individuals. The deadline for nominations is January 31. A monetary prize of $5,000, a gold-plated bronze medal, and a certificate are awarded annually. Established in 1976. Sponsored by Piore Award Fund.

• 10877 • Haraden Pratt Award
To recognize individuals who have conferred outstanding service to the institute. Nominees must be senior members or fellows of the IEEE. The deadline for nominations is July 1. A monetary award of $1,000, a bronze medal, an illuminated certificate, and travel expenses to attend the award ceremony are awarded annually. Established in 1971 in honor of Haraden Pratt, who served as an IEEE Officer, Director and Director Emeritus.

• 10878 • Simon Ramo Medal
To recognize significant achievement in systems engineering and systems science as evidenced by some major engineering contribution or for technical leadership in a major innovative engineering project within the scope of the IEEE. Members of IEEE may be nominated. Nominations and two supporting letters must be received by July 1. If the candidate has not previously published an IEEE paper on the subject of the award, the recipient may be requested to present a Simon Ramo lecture on an appropriate subject at a designated IEEE meeting. A monetary prize of $10,000, a gold medal, and a certificate are awarded annually. Established in 1982 in recognition of the distinguished engineering contributions of Dr. Simon Ramo, Vice Chairman of the Board and Chairman of the Excecutive Committee for TRW, Inc.

• 10879 • Judith A. Resnik Award
To recognize an electrical engineer for contributions to space engineering. Preference is given to an individual who has made the contribution prior to the 37th birthday and who holds membership in IEEE. Nominations may be submitted by January 31. A monetary award of $2,000, a bronze medal, a certificate, and up to $1,000 for travel expenses for the recipient and a companion to attend the award ceremony are awarded annually. Established in 1987 in memory of the Challenger astronaut, Judith A. Resnik. Sponsored by IEEE Aerospace and Electronic Systems Society, IEEE Control Systems Society, and IEEE Engineering in Medicine and Biology Society.

• 10880 • David Sarnoff Award
To recognize an outstanding contribution to the field of electronics. Preference is given to a single individual for achievement recognized during the five years preceding the year in which the award is made, but may be conferred on a team of not more than three individuals. The deadline for nominations is January 31. A monetary award of $2,000, a bronze medal, and a certificate are awarded annually. Established in 1959. Sponsored by the Sarnoff Corporation.

• 10881 • Solid-State Circuits Award
To recognize outstanding contributions in the field of solid-state circuits. Preference is given to an individual or team of up to three, for achievement first recognized in the 10 years preceding the year in which the award is made. The deadline for nominations is January 31. A monetary prize award of $2,000, a bronze medal, and a certificate are awarded annually. Established in 1987. Sponsored by IEEE Solid-State Circuits Council.

• 10882 • Charles Proteus Steinmetz Award
To recognize an individual for major contributions to the development of standards in the field of electrical and electronics engineering. The deadline for nominations is January 31. A monetary award of $5,000, a bronze medal, and a certificate are awarded annually. Established in 1979. Sponsored by the IEEE Standards Board.

• 10883 • Nikola Tesla Award
To recognize an individual or group of no more than three individuals for outstanding contributions in the field of generation and utilization of electric power. The deadline for nominations is January 31. A monetary prize of $2,000 and a plaque are awarded annually. Established in 1975. Sponsored by the The Grainger Foundation and the IEEE Power Engineering Society.

• 10884 •
Institute of Electrical and Electronics Engineers
Computer Society
Arthur W. Winston, Pres.
445 Hoes Lane
1730 Massachusetts Ave. NW
Piscataway, NJ 08854
Phone: (732)981-0060
Toll-Free: 800-678-4333
Fax: (732)981-1721
E-mail: corporate-communications@ieee.org
Home Page: http://www.ieee.org

• 10885 • Gordon Bell Prize
To recognize superior efforts in practical parallel-processing. Entries may be submitted by May 1. Awards are presented in three categories: (1) raw performance; (2) price/performance; and (3) compiler speed-up. A monetary award of $1,000 is presented annually in each category. Honorable Mention Awards are also given. Established in 1987. Sponsored by Gordon Bell, Vice President of Engineering at Ardent Computers in Sunnyvale, California.

• 10886 • Taylor Booth Award
To recognize an individual for an outstanding record in computer science and engineering education. Nominees must meet two or more of the following criteria: achieve recognition as a renown teacher in a relevant and applicable

Awards are arranged in alphabetical order below their administering organizations

course; write an influential text in computer science and engineering; lead, inspire, or provide significant educational content during the creation of a curriculum in the field; and/or inspire others to a career in computer science and engineering education. An honorarium of $5,000, a certificate, and a bronze medal are presented annually at a major IEEE Computer Society conference. Established in 1987 to honor the memory of the late Professor Booth, who had served the society for 16 years in various educational activities, and whose career exemplified an outstanding record in computer science and engineering education.

• 10887 • Computer Entrepreneur Award
To recognize managers responsible for the leadership that resulted in the growth of some segment of the computer industry, or technical managers whose entrepreneurial leadership built the computer industry. The efforts must have taken place over 15 years earlier, and the industry effects must be generally and openly visible. A museum quality sterling silver chalice is awarded. Established in 1989.

• 10888 • Computer Pioneer Award
To recognize and honor the vision of those people whose efforts resulted in the creation and continued vitality of the electronic computer industry. Individuals whose main contribution to the concepts and development of the computer field was made at least 15 years earlier are considered. A bronze medal is awarded annually. Established in 1981.

• 10889 • Computer Science and Engineering Undergraduate Teaching Award
Recognizes outstanding contributions to undergraduate education through both teaching and service and for helping to maintain interest, increase the visibility of the society and make a statement about the importance with which we view undergraduate education. A plaque, certificate, and a $2,000 are awarded.

• 10890 • Conference Contribution Award
Recognizes the most outstanding contribution to the state of the art within the scope of a Computer Society sponsored or cosponsored conference. A monetary prize is awarded annually.

• 10891 • Eckert - Mauchly Award
To recognize outstanding contributions to the field of computer architecture. A monetary award of $5,000 and a certificate are presented annually at the Computer Architecture Symposium. Administered jointly by the IEEE Computer Society and the Association for Computing Machinery.

• 10892 • Sidney Fernbach Memorial Award
To recognize outstanding contributions in the application of high performance computers using innovative approaches. The awardee will be invited to present a paper at the IEEE Computer Society Supercomputing or Compcon conference. A monetary award of $2,000 and a certificate are awarded annually. Established in 1992.

• 10893 • Harry M. Good Memorial Award
For recognition and encouragement of outstanding contributions to the information processing field. Recipients are selected on the basis of achievements that are either a single contribution of theory, design, or technique of outstanding significance, or the accumulation of important contributions on theory or practice over an extended period of time. A monetary award of $2,000, a bronze medal, and a certificate are awarded annually.

• 10894 • Harlan D. Mills Award
Recognizes researchers and practitioners who have demonstrated long-standing contributions to the theory and practice of the information sciences, focusing on contributions to the practice of software engineering through the application of sound theory. $3,000 is awarded annually. Established in 1999.

• 10895 • Harry Hayman Award for Distinguished Staff Service
For recognition of long and distinguished service of an exemplary nature in the performance of duties beyond those called for as a regular employee of the Society. A plaque and a $5,000 honorarium is awarded to each recipient. Established in 1985 to honor the retirement of its first executive secretary whose career exemplified the highest ideals of staff service to the Society.

• 10896 • Tsutomu Kanai Award
Presented in recognition of major contributions to the state-of-the-art distributed computing systems and their applications. A certificate, trophy, travel expenses, and $10,000 honorarium are presented annually at a major conference. This award was established by the Hitachi Corporation in 1995.

• 10897 • Hans Karlsson Award for Leadership and Achievement through Collaboration
Presented in recognition of outstanding skills and dedication to diplomacy, team facilitation and joint achievement, in areas of the computer industry where individual aspirations, corporate competition, and organizational rivalry could otherwise be counter to the common good. Nominations will be specifically solicited from the Computer Society Standards Activities Board committees. A plaque and monetary award of $2,000 are presented annually by the President of the Computer Society at a major conference or Standards meeting. This award was established in 1992 in memory of Hans Karlsson, considered the Father and Chairman of the IEEE 1301 group of standards.

• 10898 • W. Wallace McDowell Award
To recognize an individual whose professional work has been outstanding in concepts, technology, programming, education, or management in the computer field. A monetary prize of $2,000 and a certificate are presented annually. Established in 1966 by the International Business Machines Corporation. The award honors W. Wallace McDowell, a retired Vice President of International Business Machines Corporation.

• 10899 • Richard E. Merwin Award for Distinguished Service
For recognition of outstanding service to the Society, to the IEEE and other organizations, or to the computer profession. An honorarium of $5,000, a certificate, and a bronze medal are presented annually. Established in 1981 in memory of Richard Merwin, distinguished member and 1981 president whose career exemplified the highest ideals of service to the Society, to the Institute of Electrical and Electronics Engineers, and to the computer profession.

• 10900 • Software Process Achievement Award
To recognize outstanding achievement in improving the software process. Software professionals who participate in software development, support, or management, and are employed by and participate in the software work of an organization that produces, supports, enhances, or otherwise provides software-intensive products or services are eligible. The awardee is invited to produce a technical report describing the process improvement and results and to present a paper at the annual SEI Software Engineering Symposium. A plaque and monetary award of $1,500 is bestowed annually.

• 10901 • Technical Achievement Award
To recognize an individual for outstanding and innovative contributions to the fields of computer science or computer technology. Work done within the past ten, and not more than 15 years that has significantly promoted technical progress in the general computer field is considered. A certificate and memento are awarded at a major conference. Up to two awards may be made annually.

• 10902 •
Institute of Electrical and Electronics Engineers
Power Engineering Society
Arthur W. Winston, Pres.
445 Hoes Lane
Piscataway, NJ 08854
Phone: (732)981-0060
Toll-Free: 800-678-4333
Fax: (732)981-1721
E-mail: corporate-communications@ieee.org
Home Page: http://www.ieee.org

• 10903 • Award for Excellence in Power Distribution Engineering
To recognize engineering contributions that have enhanced the quality and economy of electric power distribution. Candidates must have a bachelor's degree in engineering from an accredited institution, a minimum of 15 years experience in industry and/or academia, and have been a member of IEEE/PES for at least 10 years. The recipient designates a college or university to receive a $4,000 scholarship for elec-

trical engineering students or for students attending schools where the curriculum is related to the power field. A plaque and a certificate are presented annually. Established in 1989.

• 10904 • Chapters Council Award
To recognize contributions made by Council members of a PES Chapter to the success of Council operations. A plaque is presented annually at the Summer Power Meeting. Established in 1980.

• 10905 • Walter Fee Outstanding Young Engineer Award
To recognize individuals for their leadership contributions in technical activities who are involved in local and/or transnational PES and other societies, or in community and humanitarian work. Candidates must be under 35 years of age as of January 1 of the presentation year and must have been members of PES for at least one year. The recipient designates a college or university to receive a $5,000 scholarship fund for electrical engineering. A plaque and a travel subsidy to attend the awards ceremony are bestowed annually at the Summer Power Meeting. Established in 1988.

• 10906 • T. Burke Hayes Student Prize Paper Award
To encourage advancement in science and practice of electric power engineering. Individuals or teams of up to three members working in the U.S., its territories, or in a geographic area where the Institute has an affiliate are eligible. A monetary prize of $1,500, a plaque, and a travel subsidy of up to $1,000 is awarded annually at the Winter Power Meeting. Established in honor of T. Burke Hayes, founder of CH2M Hill.

• 10907 • Meritorious Service Award
To recognize PES members who have made outstanding contributions to leadership and technical and educational activities of the Society. A plaque and a travel subsidy of up to $1,000 for the recipient to attend a presentation ceremony are awarded when merited. Established in 1972.

• 10908 • Outstanding Chapter Awards
For recognition of outstanding performance by a chapter of PES in technical programs, educational activities, fellow nominations, and membership growth. Two awards are presented: the Outstanding Small Chapter Award and the Outstanding Large Chapter Award. A banner is awarded to the chapter and certificates are bestowed to the chapter officers. Presented annually at the PES Conference. Established in 1973.

• 10909 • Outstanding Engineer Award
To recognize outstanding technical, professional, and Society contributions on behalf of the power engineering profession. A plaque or certificate is awarded annually by each chapter. Established in 1993.

• 10910 • Outstanding Power Engineering Educator Award
To recognize outstanding contributions and leadership in power engineering education. Teaching method and course development, promotion of student, and local, transitional, and technical activities are evaluated. Nominees must offer classroom instruction in electrical engineering at a college or university with an accredited electrical engineering program or the equivalent, and must have been a member of the PES for at least one year. Criteria include performance in classroom teaching, course development, student guidance, publication of technical papers or books, education administration, and research and development. A monetary award of $1,000, a plaque, and a travel subsidy for the recipient to attend the award ceremony are presented annually at the Summer Power Meeting. Established in 1989 the deadline for application is January 15. Additional information is available from Chanan Singh at singh@ee.tamu.edu.

• 10911 • Power-Life Award
To recognize outstanding contributions to the power engineering profession and to the improvement of quality of life by the harmonious development of electrical technology and the earth's environment. Accomplishments are evaluated based on publications and other recognized documentation. A monetary award of $2,000, a certificate, a replica of the sculpture "Heartbeat" , and a travel subsidy are awarded annually at a Power Engineering Society Conference. The name of the recipient and a citation are inscribed on a nameplate of the original "Heartbeat" sculpture located at IEEE Headquarters. Awarded annually. Established 1970.

• 10912 • Prize Paper Award
For recognition of two outstanding papers from those nominated by each Technical Committee. Papers must have been published within the previous three years. A monetary award of $200 to a single author, $100 to each author for a work by multiple authors, and a mounted certificate are awarded annually at the PES Summer Meeting. Established in 1966.

• 10913 • Technical Committee Prize Paper Awards
To recognize an outstanding paper published within the scope of each Technical Committee. Papers must have been published within the previous three years. Awards are presented to one or more recipients in each of 17 categories. A plaque is presented annually at the PES Summer Meeting.

• 10914 • Technical Council Distinguished Individual Service Award
In recognition of individuals whose efforts over many years have contributed to the advancement of committee technology. One or more individuals are honored in each of 19 categories. A plaque is awarded at the Winter Power Meeting.

• 10915 • Uno Lamm High Voltage Direct Current Award
To recognize individuals in the electric power engineering international community who have made outstanding contributions to high voltage/direct current technology. A monetary award of $1,000, a bronze medallion, a certificate, and travel expenses of up to $1,000 are awarded annually at the Summer Power Meeting. Established 1981.

• 10916 • Working Group Recognition Award
To recognize achievements and contributions in electric power by constituted PES Working Groups. Awards are given for technical reports and standards/guides. A plaque is awarded to the chairman of each group, and a certificate is presented to each group member. Bestowed annually at the Power Engineering Society Conference. Established in 1979.

• 10917 •
Institute of Environmental Sciences and Technology
Julie Kendrick, Exec.Dir.
5005 Newport Dr., Ste. 506
Rolling Meadows, IL 60008-3841
Phone: (847)255-1561
Fax: (847)255-1699
E-mail: iest@iest.org
Home Page: http://www.iest.org
Formerly: (1999) Institute of Environmental Sciences.

• 10918 • Climatics Award
For recognition for substantial contributions to the advancement of climatics technology through published papers, studies and reports. Established in 1986.

• 10919 • Park W. Espenschade Award
To recognize a student(s) interested in or involved with the environmental sciences. Established in 1976 to honor Park Espenschade's commitment to working with young people in the area of science education. A cash prize of $500 is awarded annually.

• 10920 • Fellow
To recognize individuals for outstanding contributions to the environmental sciences, the industry or the Institute. Members of the Institute are considered for the award which consists of election to the membership grade of Fellow of the Institute must have at least 15 years] professional experience. Awarded annually at the Annual Technical Meeting Awards Banquet.

• 10921 • Fred Hermann Memorial Award
To recognize members for outstanding service in chapter and regional activities. Established in 1989 to honor Fred Hermann who devoted countless hours to the IES. Deadline for application is January 15.

• 10922 • Honorary Fellow
To recognize individuals for outstanding contributions to the advancement of environmental sciences through their efforts in their professional field of endeavor. Non-members are eligible. The award consists of election to the membership classification of Honorary Fellow of the Institute. Awarded when merited at the Annual Technical Meeting Awards Banquet.

• 10923 • John Martin Outstanding Younger Member Award
To recognize outstanding younger members of the IES Chapters throughout the United States for their enthusisastic contributions to the respective chapters. Candidates must be 36 years old or younger. Awarded annually. Established in 1988.

• 10924 • James R. Mildon Award
To recognize individuals for contributions in the field of contamination control and/or to the awareness and effectiveness of contamination control activity in professional societies. Awarded at the Annual Technical Meeting Awards Banquet. Established in 1982 in honor of James R. Mildon, one of the original organizers of the American Association for Contamination Control which was absorbed by IES in 1973.

• 10925 • Newsletter Award
To recognize a chapter for excellence in newsletters. Awarded annually. Established in 1983.

• 10926 • President's Award
To recognize contributions to the Institute of Environmental Sciences. Presentations are made at the Annual Awards Banquet. Established in 1974.

• 10927 • Reliability Test and Evaluation Award
To recognize outstanding contributions to the field of reliability test and evaluation. Presentations are made at the Annual Awards Banquet. Established in 1978.

• 10928 • Monroe Seligman Award
To recognize members for significant contributions to the Institute. A plaque is awarded annually if merited. Established in 1972.

• 10929 • Maurice Simpson Technical Editor's Award
To recognize editors for contributions that advance technical publications. Presentations are made at the Annual Awards Banquet. Established in 1977.

• 10930 • Space Simulation Award
To recognize significant contributions to the development of successful space hardware through outstanding work in the measurement, analysis, and/or simulation of space environments. Awarded annually. Established in 1971.

• 10931 • Dr. Irwin Vigness Memorial Award
To recognize an individual for outstanding contributions to the field of acoustics, shock and vibration through published papers, studies, and reports. A plaque is awarded annually if merited. Established in 1967 in memory of Dr. Irwin Vigness, who carried out pioneering research in the field of mechanical shock and vibration.

• 10932 • Willis J. Whitfield Award
To recognize an individual(s) for the best presentation, either oral or printed, in the field of contamination control. Awarded at the Annual Awards Banquet. Established in 1980.

• 10933 •
Institute of Food Technologists
Herbert Stone CAE, Pres.
525 W Van Buren, Ste. 1000
Chicago, IL 60607
Phone: (312)782-8424
Toll-Free: 800-438-3663
Fax: (312)782-8348
E-mail: info@ift.org
Home Page: http://www.ift.org

• 10934 • Nicholas Appert Award
To honor an individual for preeminence in and contributions to the field of food technology. Nominations may be made by IFT members and non-members. Nomination deadline is December 1. An honorarium of $5,000 from IFT and a bronze medal from the Chicago Section are awarded annually when merited. Established in 1942.

• 10935 • Babcock-Hart Award
To recognize an IFT member for distinguished contributions to food technology which have resulted in improved public health through some aspect of nutrition or more nutritious food. The deadline is December 1. An honorarium of $3,000 and a plaque are awarded annually when merited. Established in 1947. Co-sponsored by the International Life Sciences Institute - North America.

• 10936 • Stephen S. Chang Award for Lipid or Flavor Science
To recognize an IFT-member food scientist or technologist who has made significant contributions to lipid or flavor science. Contributions must have had some impact on commercial operations. A $3,000 honorarium and a Steuben crystal sculpture are awarded annually.

• 10937 • William V. Cruess Award
For recognition of excellence in university teaching in the field of food science and technology. Members of the Institute who, by July 1 of the year of presentation, are (a)younger than 36 years of age, or (b)have received his or her highest degree within the previous 10 years, and have at least five years experience in university teaching are eligible. The deadline is December 1. An honorarium of $3,000 and a bronze medal from the Northern California Section are awarded annually when merited. Established in 1970.

• 10938 • Carl R. Fellers Award
To recognize a member of IFT and Phi Tau Sigma who has brought honor and recognition to the profession of food science and technology through a distinguished career in that profession displaying exemplary leadership, service and communication skills that enhance the effectiveness of all food scientists in serving society. Nominee must have been a Professional Member of IFT for at least fifteen years before the nomination deadline of December 1. Nominees who are not members of IFT of Phi Tau Sigma shall be simultaneously elected to Phi Tau Sigma membership by that organization upon selection as recipient of the Carl R. Fellers Award. The recipient receives a $3,000 honorarium from Phi Tau Sigma and a plaque from IFT. Awarded annually. Established in 1984. Co-sponsored by Phi Tau Sigma and IFT.

• 10939 • Food Technology Industrial Achievement Award
To honor a company or organization developing an outstanding new food process and/or product that represents a significant advance in the application of food science and technology to food production. The process or product must have been in commercial use for at least six months but no more than seven years prior to December 1 of the year the nomination is submitted. A bronze plaque for the winning company or institution is awarded annually when merited. Established in 1959.

• 10940 • IFT Food Science Journalism Awards
To honor the top newspaper, consumer magazine, and television news stories that offer balanced coverage of complex or controversial food science issues during the previous year. Stories must present the scientific perspective on food-related issues of compelling public interest in a clear, accurate, and objective manner. Television entries must be submitted on 3/4-inch videotape with one script and must have run on commercial or public television. A panel of distinguished food scientists, journalists, and public relations specialists select one story in each category to receive $1,000 and a plaque. The deadline for entries is March 1 for stories that ran during the previous calendar year.

• 10941 • IFT International Award
To honor an IFT member or institution whose outstanding efforts result in one or more of the following: international exchange of ideas in the field of food technology, better international understanding of the field of food technology, practical and successful transfer of food technology to an economically depressed area in a developing nation, and/or practical successful transfer of food technology to an economically depressed area in a developed nation. The deadline is December 1. An honorarium of $3,000 and a plaque are awarded annually when merited. Established in 1956.

• 10942 • **Industrial Scientist Award**
To recognize an IFT-member industrial scientist who has made a major technical contribution to the advancement of the food industry. Nominees must have made one or more major technical contributions to the advancement of the food industry while a member of an industrial food organization. The deadline is December 1. A $3,000 honorarium and a plaque are awarded annually.

• 10943 • **Marcel Loncin Research Prize**
To honor and provide research funding for an IFT-member or nonmember scientist or engineer conducting basic chemistry/physic/engineering research applied to food processing and improvement of food quality. Prize money is to be used in directing and carrying out a proposed research project, and to allow a successful scientist to help a young scientist(s) to also become successful. Application is not be a joint research proposal or a laboratory-manager proposal, although cooperative research is encouraged. Deadline is January. A $50,000 prize, awarded in two annual installments, and a plaque are awarded annually. Established in 1994.

• 10944 • **Samuel Cate Prescott Award**
To recognize an IFT member who has shown outstanding ability in research in some area of food science and technology, The nominee must, by July 1 of the year of the presentation, (a) be younger than 36 years of age, or (b) have received his or her highest degree within the previous 10 years. Special attention is given to contributions in methodology, competence shown, and effects of the research on advances in food science. An honorarium of $3,000 and a plaque are awarded annually when merited. Established in 1965.

• 10945 • **Research and Development Award**
To recognize an IFT member who has made a recent significant research and development contribution to the understanding of food science, food technology or nutrition. The nominee must be primarily responsible for an achievement within the past five years, in a research and development program. The achievement must significantly advance the discipline of food science, food technology or nutrition. The contribution may be basic or applied in nature, and must advance science or improve the human condition. The nominee may have worked in any field. Deadline is December 1. An honorarium of $3,000 and a plaque are awarded annually when merited. Established in 1997.

• 10946 • **Elizabeth Fleming Stier Award**
To honor an IFT member for pursuit of humanitarian ideals and unselfish dedication that have resulted in significant contributions to the well-being of the food industry, academia, students or the general public. Nominees must have been IFT members for the past 10 years and active in IFT at both the Section and National Levels. A $3,000 honorarium and a plaque are awarded.

• 10947 • **Calvert L. Willey Distinguished Service Award**
To honor an individual who has demonstrated meritorious and imaginative service to IFT. The Calvert L. Willey Distinguished Service Award, presented to Calvert L. Willey in 1987 and initiated on the 50th Anniversary of IFT in 1989. The nominee must have been a Professional Members of IFT for 15 years or more, or a Members of IFT for 25 years or more, or on the IFT staff for 25 years or more. Nomination deadline date is December 1. An honorarium of $3,000 and a plaque are awarded annually when merited. Established in 1989.

• 10948 •
Institute of Industrial Engineers
Don Greene, Exec.Dir.
3577 Parkway Ln., Ste. 200
Norcross, GA 30092
Phone: (770)449-0460
Phone: (770)449-0460
Toll-Free: 800-494-0460
Fax: (770)441-3295
E-mail: dgreene@iienet.org
Home Page: http://www.iienet.org

Formerly: American Institute of Industrial Engineers.

• 10949 • **Award for Outstanding Achievement in Management**
For recognition of significant contributions to the industrial engineering profession by the creation of a climate within an organization that permits industrial engineering techniques to be perfected and used with outstanding results. Individuals who are similarly high level executives of an industrial, governmental, or educational enterprise are eligible. Members and non-members are eligible. A plaque and citation are awarded annually when merited. Established in 1964.

• 10950 • **Award for Technical Innovation in Industrial Engineering**
To recognize significant innovative technical contributions to the industrial engineering profession as evidenced by: significantly expanding the body of knowledge in an Industrial Engineering function; meaningfully establishing yet another functional area of the profession; or providing exceptional technical leadership in a major interdisciplinary project. Members and non-members are eligible. Awarded annually. Established in 1984.

• 10951 • **Dr. David F. Baker Distinguished Research Award**
For recognition of outstanding research in the areas of industrial engineering activity that has significantly contributed to the advancement and progress of the profession. Members of the Institute are eligible. A plaque and citation are awarded annually when merited. Established in 1966 in memory of David Baker, former chairman of the Department of Industrial Engineering at The Ohio State University, whose interest in industrial engineering stimulated others to follow his lead.

• 10952 • **Fred C. Crane Distinguished Service Award**
To recognize members who have rendered long, arduous service to the Institute. A plaque and citation are awarded annually when merited. Established in 1956 in honor of Fred C. Crane, who served the Institute as the conference coordinator.

• 10953 • **Fellow Award**
To recognize outstanding leaders of the profession among members of the Institute of Industrial Engineers who have made significant, nationally recognized contributions to industrial engineering. Candidates must be at least 40 years old and have been senior members for ten years. Awarded annually when merited. Established in 1950.

• 10954 • **Frank and Lillian Gilbreth Industrial Engineering Award**
This, the most esteemed honor presented by the Institute, is given for recognition of distinguished accomplishments and outstanding contributions to the welfare of mankind in the field of industrial engineering. A plaque is awarded annually when merited. Established in 1962 in honor of Frank and Lillian Gilbreth, who were pioneers in the field of industrial engineering. The award is open to both members and non-members.

• 10955 • **Graduate Research Award**
To recognize excellence in thesis research at the Masters level. Three awards may be presented annually.

• 10956 • **Albert G. Holzman Distinguished Educator Award**
To recognize outstanding educators who have contributed significantly to the industrial engineering profession through teaching, research and publication, extension, teaching/learning innovation, and/or administration in an academic environment. Members who are associate or full professors are eligible. Awarded annually. Established in 1984, the award is sponsored by H.B. Maynard Co., Inc. Formerly: IIE Distinguished Educator Award.

• 10957 • **Honorary Member Award**
To acknowledge professional eminence by a non-member of IIE in any field where contributions have increased the effectiveness of human endeavor. The individual need not be an engineer, but the individual's professional achievement must be nationally or internationally recognized. One or two awards are presented annually when merited. Established in 1960.

• 10958 • **IIE Award for Excellence in Productivity Improvement**
To recognize companies or organizations that, through diligent and innovative means, have accomplished significant, measurable, and extensive achievements that increased productivity, eliminated human drudgery, or improved the quality of working life. All units within the companies and organizations are eligible. Awarded annually when merited. Established in 1980. For-

merly: AIIE Award for Excellence in Productivity Improvement.

• 10959 • IIE Excellence Award for Minority Advancement
To recognize organizations or individuals who, through innovative means, have developed programs/projects directed to the advancement of women, minorities, or the disabled within the field of industrial engineering. Sponsored by UPS.

• 10960 • IIE - Joint Publishers Book of the Year Award
To honor the author(s) of the outstanding book of the year on industrial engineering. Awarded annually when merited. Established in 1967 by H.B. Maynard Company. Formerly: (1976) H. B. Maynard Book of the Year Award.

• 10961 • *IIE Transactions* Award
To promote excellence in industrial engineering research and applications by recognizing the best paper published in the "Features Applications" department of *IIE Transactions.* The winning paper will be submitted for inclusion in the Outstanding IIE Publications Award selection process for that same year. Awarded annually.

• 10962 • Outstanding IIE Publication Award
This, the highest IIE honor for publications, recognizes the outstanding current original publication that has appeared in any IIE sponsored or co-sponsored medium. The award is made to the author(s) of that published work that is judged to be a meritorious contribution to the profession of industrial engineering. At least one author must be an IIE member at the time of publication and receipt of award. Awarded annually. Established in 1978. Formerly: (1985) *IIE Transactions* Development and Applications Paper Award.

• 10963 • Outstanding Young Industrial Engineer Award
To recognize individuals in academia and business who have demonstrated outstanding characteristics of leadership, professionalism, and potential in the field of industrial engineering. Open to individuals not over 35 years of age who have been members of a senior chapter for a minimum of five years. Awarded annually when merited. Established in 1983.

• 10964 • Pritsker Doctoral Dissertation Award
To recognize outstanding graduate research in the field of industrial engineering, thus promoting better industrial engineering research. Members and nonmembers are eligible. Awarded annually when merited the winner will receive a $1,000 cash prize. Sponsored by the Pritsker Corp. Established in 1986. Formerly: (1996) IIE Doctoral Dissertation Award.

• 10965 • Student Award for Excellence
To recognize distinguished excellence in scholarship and campus leadership. Awarded annually.

• 10966 • Systems Modeling Student Competition - Student
To provide an opportunity for teams of undergraduate students to compete in a simulation project. The students are given a case study to solve using Systems Modeling's simulation software package, "ARENA."

• 10967 • Undergraduate Student Paper Competition
To recognize excellence in technical writing at the undergraduate level. Awarded annually. Sponsored by Norfolk Southern.

• 10968 •
Institute of Internal Auditors
Dave A. Richards, Pres.
247 Maitland Ave.
Altamonte Springs, FL 32701
Phone: (407)937-1100
Fax: (407)937-1101
E-mail: iia@theiia.org
Home Page: http://www.theiia.org

• 10969 • Victor Z. Brink Award for Distinguished Service
To recognize individuals who have given unusual and outstanding service to the internal auditing profession through participation in the activities of the IIA. Awarded annually. Established in the original bylaws of the Institute in 1943. Renamed in 1993 in honor of one of the founders of the Institute and a prominent researcher, educator, and author.

• 10970 • Bradford Cadmus Memorial Award
For recognition of outstanding contributions in the field of internal auditing to research, education, or literature. This is the highest honor or tribute bestowed by the Institute. A calligraphic scroll and all expenses to the Institute's International Conferences for the winner and spouse are awarded annually. Established in 1966 in honor of the first managing director of the Institute, Bradford Cadmus.

• 10971 • Chapter Publications Contest
To recognize outstanding chapter newsletters and directories and to encourage high quality in writing and design. A plaque is awarded annually at the Institute's International Conference. Established in 1972.

• 10972 • Chapter Research Award
To honor the chapters that have done the most original research during the year. A plaque is presented annually at the Institute's International Conference.

• 10973 • Outstanding Contributor Awards
To recognize the authors of the five best articles published in the *Internal Auditor* each year. A certificate is awarded annually. Established in 1951.

• 10974 • Leon R. Radde - Educator of the Year Award
To recognize the individual who has made outstanding contributions to internal auditing in the area of education. Selection criteria covers: research studies, articles on internal audit education, education research, chapter programs, curriculum/course development, teaching, or other educational contributions. Established in 1986. Deadline for application is March 31.

• 10975 • Round Table Award
To recognize the chapter responsible for the best round table article submitted to the *Internal Auditor.* A plaque is awarded annually at the Institute's International Conference. Established in 1958.

• 10976 • John B. Thurston Award
To recognize the author of the most outstanding feature article in *Internal Auditor* during the previous calendar year. A bound copy of the journal and travel expenses to the International Conference are awarded annually. Established in 1951 as a tribute to the first president of the Institute, John B. Thurston.

• 10977 •
Institute of International Container Lessors
Henry F. White Jr., Pres.
555 Pleasantville Rd., Ste. 140 S
Briarcliff Manor, NY 10510
Phone: (914)747-9100
Fax: (914)747-4600
E-mail: info@iicl.org
Home Page: http://www.iicl.org

• 10978 • Chassis Inspectors Award
Recognizes the individual scoring the highest on the chassis inspector's certification examination. Awarded annually.

• 10979 • Container Inspectors Award
Recognizes the individual scoring the highest on the container inspector's certification examinations. Awarded annually.

• 10980 •
Institute of International Education
Dr. Allan E. Goodman, Pres./CEO
809 United Nations Plz., 7th Fl.
New York, NY 10017
Phone: (212)883-8200
Phone: (212)984-5453
Fax: (212)984-5452
E-mail: membership@iie.org
Home Page: http://www.iie.org

• 10981 • Cintas Foundation Fellowships
To foster and encourage the progressional development and recognition of talented creative artists of Cuban citizenship or direct lineage in the fields of architecture, visual arts and photography, music composition, and literature. Artists of Cuban citizenship or lineage (i.e. at least one parent or grandparent a Cuban), and who have completed their academic and technical training may apply. Fellowships of $10,000 each are awarded annually. Not all of the above fields are awarded each year - please write to the above address for guidelines and deadline. Established in 1964 in memory of Oscar B. Cintas, former Cuban Ambassador to the United States. Sponsored by the Cintas Foundation, Inc.

• 10982 •
Institute of Jazz Studies
John Cotton Dana Library
Rutgers University
185 University Ave.
Newark, NJ 07102
Phone: (973)353-5595
Fax: (973)353-5944
Home Page: http://www.libraries.rutgers.edu/rul/libs/jazz/jazz.shtml

• 10983 • American Jazz Hall of Fame
For recognition of outstanding contributions to jazz, past and present. The award is intended primarily for instrumentalists and singers, but non-performers (critics, scholars, producers) are also eligible. A plaque and permanent representation in the Hall of Fame are awarded posthumously as well as to the living. Awarded annually. Established in 1983 by Rutgers University and the New Jersey Jazz Society.

• 10984 •
Institute of Management Accountants
Paul Sharman, Pres./CEO
10 Paragon Dr.
Montvale, NJ 07645
Phone: (201)573-9000
Toll-Free: 800-638-4427
Fax: (201)474-1600
E-mail: ima@imanet.org
Home Page: http://www.imanet.org

Formerly: National Association of Accountants.

• 10985 • Robert Beyer Award
To recognize an individual for superior achievement at each CMA examination. A candidate must take all five parts at one time and pass them on the first attempt to be eligible for the awards. Gold, silver, and bronze medals are awarded to the candidates who achieve the top three scores. Awarded in honor of Robert Beyer, a former managing partner of the firm and a past national president of IMA. Sponsored by Touche, Ross and Company for the Institute of Certified Management Accountants.

• 10986 • Rawn Brinkley Award
To recognize the chapter with the highest overall performance for the previous five years. A trophy is awarded annually. Established in 1980 in honor of Rawn Brinkley, former executive director of IMA.

• 10987 • Carter Trophy
To recognize the chapter making the most improvement in its standings for the Stevenson Trophy during the current competition year as compared to the three previous competition years. A trophy and ten certificates of merit are awarded annually. Established in 1932.

• 10988 • Chapter Competition
To encourage the chapters to promote the objectives of the Institute and to provide a broad spectrum of activities and services to members. Chapters of the Institute are eligible. Trophies, banners, and other awards are presented for excellence in planning, performance, and reporting of chapter activities. Awarded at the annual meeting and annual dinner of the Institute in June and at chapter meetings in September, October, and November. Established in 1924.

• 10989 • Arthur B. Gunnarson Award
To recognize the affiliate with the highest final standing in the international competition. Only those international affiliates in existence at the beginning of the Chapter Competition year, June 1, are eligible. A trophy is awarded annually. Established in 1972.

• 10990 • Keller Trophy
To recognize the chapter making the most improvement in the Warner Trophy standings during the competition year, as determined by its standings in the Chapter Competition for the Warner Trophy at the end of the three previous competition years. A trophy and ten certificates of merit are awarded annually. Established in 1970.

• 10991 • Lybrand Medals
To recognize the authors of outstanding contributions to management accounting literature through manuscripts submitted in the chapter competition. The following prizes are awarded: the Lybrand Gold Medal - first place; Lybrand Silver Medal - second place; and Lybrand Bronze Medal - third place. Certificates of merit are also presented. Awarded annually at the annual conference. Established in 1949 by the partners of Lybrand, Ross Brothers and Montgomery in honor of William M. Lybrand's long service to the Institute.

• 10992 • Stuart Cameron McLeod Society Trophy
To recognize the chapter with the third-highest final standing in the competition for the Stevenson Trophy. A trophy is awarded annually. Established in 1972.

• 10993 • Newsletter Competition
For recognition of the top three chapters competing for the Stevenson Trophy and the Warner Trophy, and the person responsible for the newsletter. The newsletters are judged on overall visual appearance, quality and variety of content, and on other criteria developed by the national staff. A plaque, awarded to each chapter, is presented at the annual business meeting. Established in 1980.

• 10994 • J. Lee Nicholson Award
To recognize the chapter with the second highest final standing in the Chapter Competition for the Warner Trophy. A trophy is awarded annually. Established in 1972.

• 10995 • S. Alden Pendleton Award
To recognize the chapter with the greatest achievement in Community Responsibility Programs. Chapters are eligible based on the programs, results achieved, and evidence of publicity during the year. A medal is awarded annually to the winner and certificates to nine runners-up. Established in 1978.

• 10996 • Presidents' Award
To recognize the chapter that has shown the highest consistent good performance in the Chapter Competition for the last five years. All chapters that have completed five years in the Stevenson and Warner Divisions of the Chapter Competition for Trophies and Awards are eligible. A trophy is awarded annually. Established in 1975.

• 10997 • Public Relations Competition
For recognition of the greatest achievement in public relations activities. Chapters are judged in the following categories: public relations plan, utilization of the plan, publicity achieved during four quarterly periods, initiative in creating "on-the-spot" coverage, and special projects. Five plaques are presented annually. Established in 1962.

• 10998 • Remington Rand Trophy
To recognize the chapter that is runner-up in competition for the Stevenson Trophy. A trophy is awarded annually. Established in 1927.

• 10999 • Special Innovation Award
To recognize a chapter for achievement in performing an innovative community service project. This award is designed to reward the chapter that may not have an extensive community service program, but does have a high quality innovative project. The screening and selection processes for this award is performed by the same committee at the same time as the S. Alden Pendleton Award selection. This committee determines whether or not this award is to be given in any specific year.

• 11000 • Stevenson Trophy
To recognize the chapter with the highest final standing in the Stevenson Division. Chapters with a membership of 125 or more on June 1 of the year of the award are eligible. A trophy is awarded annually to the winner, with banners awarded to the 25 runners-up. Established in 1925.

• 11001 • **Vice Presidents' Award**
To recognize the regional council having the highest average chapter competition points. Established in 1989.

• 11002 • **Warner Trophy**
To recognize the chapter with the highest final standing in the Warner Divison. Chapters with a membership of 25 to 124 members on June 1 of the year of the award are eligible. A trophy is awarded annually to the winner, with banners awarded to the 20 runners-up. Established in 1966.

• 11003 •
Institute of Management Accountants, Rochester
Christopher F. Liucci, Pres.
PO Box 41152
Rochester, NY 14604
Phone: (585)251-5194
E-mail: sschiano@unimailcorp.com
Home Page: http://www.imarochester.org

• 11004 • **Financial Executive of the Year**
For success in financial accounting career. Recognition award bestowed annually.

• 11005 •
Institute of Mathematical Statistics
Elyse Gustafson, Exec.Dir.
PO Box 22718
Beachwood, OH 44122
Phone: (216)295-2340
Fax: (216)295-5661
E-mail: ims@imstat.org
Home Page: http://www.imstat.org

• 11006 • **Fisher Memorial Lecture**
To honor a statistician and to stimulate contribution to the field. The honoree presents a lecture annually. Established in 1964.

• 11007 • **Neyman Lecture**
To emphasize the interactions between statistical theory and scientific research. Awarded every third year, alternating with the Rietz and LeCam Lectures. Established in 1981.

• 11008 • **Rietz Lecture**
The lecture serves to clarify the relationship of statistical methodology and anaylsis to other fields. Selection is made by the Committee on Special Papers. The lecture is presented at an annual meeting of the institute biennially. Established in 1945 in honor of the institute's first president, Professor Henry L. Rietz.

• 11009 • **Wald Memorial Lecture**
To give a specialist sufficient time to develop material in the field of mathematical statistics, and make it accessible to persons not particularly conversant in that specialty. The Wald Lecturer need not be a member of the institute. A sequence of two to four lectures is presented at the annual meeting. Established in 1956 in honor of Professor Abraham Wald.

• 11010 •
Institute of Navigation
Lisa Beaty, Dir. of Operations
3975 University Dr., Ste. 390
Fairfax, VA 22030
Phone: (703)383-9688
Fax: (703)383-9689
E-mail: membership@ion.org
Home Page: http://www.ion.org

• 11011 • **Burka Award**
For recognition of outstanding papers that contribute to the advancement of navigation and space guidance. Authors of papers on navigation or space guidance published in the Institute's journal, *Navigation*, are eligible. A monetary award of $500 and a certificate are awarded annually. The deadline for nominations is February 15. Established in 1959 in memory of Dr. Samuel M. Burka, a dedicated public servant who devoted a long and distinguished career to research and development of air navigation equipment.

• 11012 • **Hays Award**
For recognition of encouragement, inspiration, and support that contribute to the advancement of navigation. Individuals engaged in management of the military services, civil government, or industry may be nominated. The deadline is February 15. A wall plaque is awarded annually. Established in 1965 by Rockwell International Corporation in memory of Norman P. Hays, an outstanding navigator, able engineer, and competent manager.

• 11013 • **ION Navigation Award (California Maritime Academy)**
To recognize outstanding scholarship in navigation at the California Maritime Academy. Cadets of the graduating class at the Academy, selected by the Academy, are eligible. The deadline is February 15. A wall plaque is awarded annually. Established in 1976.

• 11014 • **ION Navigation Award (U.S. Air Force Academy)**
To recognize outstanding scholarship in navigation at the United States Air Force Academy. Cadets of the graduating class at the Academy, selected by the Academy, are eligible. The deadline is February 15. A miniature sculpture of Eagle and Fledglings is awarded annually. Established in 1968.

• 11015 • **Superior Achievement Award**
For recognition of outstanding contributions to the advancement of navigation. Individuals who have given outstanding performances as practicing navigators are eligible. The deadline for nominations is February 15. A wall plaque is awarded annually. Established in 1964.

• 11016 • **Thurlow Award**
For recognition of contributions to the development of the science of navigation. Individuals who invent or design new equipment that applies to the science of navigation, develop a new method for use in navigation, or perform outstanding research or study along navigation lines are eligible. The deadline for nominations is February 15. A wall plaque is awarded annually. Established in 1945 in memory of Colonel Thomas L. Thurlow, U.S. Army Air Corps, an engineer, pilot, and officer who contributed significantly to the development and testing of navigation equipment and the training of navigators and pilots. Founded by Sherman Mills Fairchild.

• 11017 • **Weems Award**
To recognize continuing contributions to the art and science of navigation. Individuals making continuing contributions to the advancement of navigation over a period of years are eligible. The deadline for nominations is February 15. A plaque-mounted medallion is awarded annually. Established in 1981. Sponsored by The Institute of Navigation.

• 11018 •
Institute of Nuclear Materials Management
Cathy Key, Pres.
60 Revere Dr., Ste. 500
Northbrook, IL 60062
Phone: (847)480-9573
Fax: (847)480-9282
E-mail: inmm@inmm.org
Home Page: http://www.inmm.org

• 11019 • **Distinguished Service Award**
To recognize exceptional contributions to the field of nuclear materials management. A stainless steel plaque mounted on walnut is awarded annually. Established in 1978.

• 11020 • **Industry Award**
No further information was provided for this edition.

• 11021 • **Meritorious Service Award**
To recognize exceptional service to the INMM. A stainless steel plaque mounted on walnut is awarded as merited. Established in 1958.

• 11022 •
Institute of Packaging Professionals
Edwin Landon, Exec.Dir.
1601 N Bond St., Ste. 101
Naperville, IL 60563
Phone: (630)544-5050
Fax: (630)544-5055
E-mail: info@iopp.org
Home Page: http://www.iopp.org
Formerly: (1987) Society of Packaging and Handling Engineers.

• 11023 • **AmeriStar Package Awards**
To recognize outstanding innovative packaging designs. Entries are evaluated on product protection, innovation, economics and package performance. A Best of Show AmeriStar Award is awarded to the overall winner and engraved awards are presented to the Gold Star, Silver Star and Bronze Star winners in each category as appropriate. In addition, an Environmental Award and a People's Choice Award are pre-

sented. The Competition is held annually. Established in 1947. Formerly: SPHE Packaging Competition; SPHE International Packaging and Handling Design Competition.

• 11024 • Fellow Member
To recognize outstanding service to the IOPP. Nominee must be at least 35 years of age and a member in good standing of IOPP for a minimum of ten years.

• 11025 • Honorary Member
To recognize members who have contributed to the Institute over a long period of time, and who continue to be comitted to IOPP's objectives and purposes. Nominee must be at least 60 years of age and a member of IOPP for at least fifteen years.

• 11026 • Member of the Year
To recognize a member for outstanding service to the Institute and to the packaging profession during the previous year. Awarded annually.

• 11027 •
Institute of Public Administration of Canada
(L'Institut d'administration publique du Canada)
Jacques Galimberti, Exec.Dir.
1075 Bay St., Ste. 401
Toronto, ON, Canada M5S 2B1
Phone: (416)924-8787
Fax: (416)924-4992
E-mail: ntl@ipaciapc.ca
Home Page: http://www.ipaciapc.ca

• 11028 • Award for Innovative Management
To promote and reward excellence in public administration and organizational achievement. Gold, silver, and bronze medals are awarded annually. Established in 1990. Sponsored by IBM and KPMG.

• 11029 • Vanier Medal
To recognize those who have shown distinctive leadership or who, by writings or other endeavors, have made a distinctive contribution in the field of public administration in Canada. Awarded annually.

• 11030 •
Institute of Real Estate Management
Anthony W. Smith, Pres.
430 N Michigan Ave.
Chicago, IL 60611-4090
Phone: (312)329-6000
Toll-Free: 800-837-0706
Fax: 800-338-4736
E-mail: custserv@irem.org
Home Page: http://www.irem.org

• 11031 • Academy of Authors
To honor IREM members who have made significant contributions to disseminating real estate management knowledge in written form. Awarded annually in June at the Institute's awards ceremony.

• 11032 • ARM of the Year
To recognize the outstanding contributions made by Accredited Residential Manager (ARM) participants. Competition is based on the efforts of an individual ARM for the calendar year, including: participation in the local ARM committee and on a national level; submission of articles for *ARM News* and committee and chapter newsletters; speaking engagements; sponsorship of new members; and sharing ideas and information to further the professionalism of residential managers. Awarded at the institute's annual awards ceremony.

• 11033 • George M. Brooker Collegiate Scholarship for Minorities
To assist minority students who are committed to careers in real estate management upon graduation. The award is granted to those who emphasize a curriculum including property management, asset management, or related real estate subjects. The deadline for applications is March 31. Up to three awards are granted each June: a graduate level award of $2,500 and two undergraduate level awards of $1,000.

• 11034 • Certified Property Manager (CPM) of the Year Award
To recognize a deserving CPM who has provided outstanding service to the real estate management profession and community throughout the year. Awarded annually by local IREM chapters.

• 11035 • Communication and Marketing Awards
To recognize excellence in the creation of promotional and employee communications materials to support the profession of real estate management. CERTIFIED PROPERTY MANAGER (CPM) members of IREM, CPM candidates, ACCREDITED RESIDENTIAL MANAGER (ARM) program participants, and ARM applicants are eligible. Entries must be submitted by February 1. Awards are given in the following categories: residential project marketing brochures; nonresidential project marketing brochures; resident/tenant informational handbooks/manuals; resident/tenant disaster preparedness plans and emergency procedures manuals; resident/tenant retention programs; management company promotions to clients; logos, letterhead, business cards - company or property; management company employee education programs; videos; complete marketing campaigns company or property; newsletters; and wild card. Selection is made by the Public Relations Committee of the Institute. Awarded annually at the Institute's June mid-year business meeting. Formerly: (1992) Forms and Brochures Contest Awards.

• 11036 • Lloyd D. Hanford Sr. Distinguished Faculty Award
To recognize a member of the IREM faculty who best exemplifies extraordinary dedication to the educational process and advancement of knowledge within the real estate management profession. Awarded by the periodically when merited by the IREM Foundation. Established in memory of Lloyd D. Hanford Sr., CPM, a past national president and IREM faculty member.

• 11037 • *Journal of Property Management* Article of the Year Awards
To recognize the authors of the most outstanding articles in the fields of real estate management and asset management published in IREM's *Journal of Property Management* during the previous year. Open to members and nonmembers. Awarded annually in June.

• 11038 • Louise L. and Y. T. Lum Award
To recognize an individual actively engaged in real estate management who, whether a member of the Institute or not, has made a distinguished contribution to the real estate management profession. Awarded annually in November when merited. Sponsored by the IREM Foundation.

• 11039 • J. Wallace Paletou Award
To recognize an individual within or outside IREM for a significant and noteworthy contribution to the real estate management field. Awarded annually in November when merited by the IREM Foundation. Established in 1971 to honor J. Wallace Paletou, CPM, IREM's President in 1957.

• 11040 • Professional Achievement Award
To recognize CPM members who have distinguished themselves professionally. Applicants must have completed IREM's Courses 701 and 702, and must have met three of the following electives: taught any approved institute course or IREM chapter seminar for a minimum of 100 hours; written or contributed to a full-length book published by the institute; authored a cassette program published by the institute; published at least three articles in either the *Journal of Property Management, AMO Perspectives*, or *ARM News*; held a local chapter office as president, vice-president or the equivalent, secretary, or treasurer for at least three years; or held a national IREM position as president, president-elect, secretary/treasurer, senior vice-president, or vice division director.

• 11041 • Paul H. Rittle, Sr. Memorial Scholarship Award
To provide individuals who are financially incapable the opportunity to attend courses offered by IREM. Applicants must be currently employed in the real estate field. The deadlines for applications are May 1 and October 1. Scholarships are awarded biennially at the Mid-Year Meeting and the Annual Convention.

• 11042 •
Institute of Store Planners
Russell Sway FISP, Pres.
25 N Broadway
Tarrytown, NY 10591
Phone: (914)332-1806
Toll-Free: 800-379-9912
Fax: (914)332-1541
E-mail: adminisp@ispo.org
Home Page: http://www.ispo.org

• 11043 • **ISP Student Competition**
To recognize students for outstanding store interior design. Additional information is available from Dr. Asher Derman, (212)268-4944.

• 11044 • **ISP/*VM & SD* International Design Competition**
To promote recognition of the value of good design in store interiors and the contribution of ISP members to that end. The Store of the Year is selected and trophies and certificates are presented in the ten other categories. Awarded annually. Established in 1983. Sponsored by *VM & SD* magazine. Formerly: International Store Interior Design Competition.

• 11045 •
Institute of the Americas
10111 N Torrey Pines Rd.
La Jolla, CA 92037
Phone: (858)453-5560
Fax: (858)453-2165
E-mail: development@iamericas.org
Home Page: http://www.iamericas.org

• 11046 • **Leadership in the Americas Award**
Given to outstanding Latin Americans. Inquire for application details.

• 11047 •
Institute of Transportation Engineers
Steven D. Hofener, Intl.Dir.
1099 14th St. NW, Ste. 300 W
Washington, DC 20005-3438
Phone: (202)289-0222
Toll-Free: 800-982-4683
Fax: (202)289-7722
E-mail: ite_staff@ite.org
Home Page: http://www.ite.org

• 11048 • **District/Section Newsletter Award**
To recognize the district or section that, during a specific period of time, produces the best series of newsletters, to foster interest in improving the current district and section newsletters, and to encourage others to consider publishing a newsletter. Established in 1983. Since 1986, the awards have been presented in three categories, based on size of circulation.

• 11049 • **Innovative Intermodal Solutions for Urban Transportation Award**
To encourage reporting and publicity of activities and programs that effectively address urban transportation needs. Awarded annually. Established in 1992 in memory of Daniel W. Hoyt.

• 11050 • **Burton W. Marsh Distinguished Service Award**
To recognize a person who has made outstanding contributions to the advancement of ITE over a period of several years. Established in 1970.

• 11051 • **Burton W. Marsh Graduate Fellowship**
To encourage outstanding civil engineering students to pursue a career in traffic and transportation engineering. Established in 1989.

• 11052 • **Theodore M. Matson Memorial Award**
To recognize an individual who has made outstanding contributions in the field of traffic engineering, including practical application of traffic engineering techniques or principles, valuable contributions through research, successful adaptation of research findings to a practical traffic situation, or the advancement of the professsion through training or administration. Awarded annually. Established in 1957.

• 11053 • **Past Presidents' Award for Merit in Transportation**
To recognize young engineers in the transportation and traffic engineering field and to encourage the conduct and reporting of independent and original research. Nonstudent members of the Institute under the age of 35 may submit papers. Established in 1951.

• 11054 • **Section Activities Award**
To recognize outstanding technical activity at the ITE section level and to encourage active and timely participation by local section members in section technical projects by conducting and reporting study, research, and investigation of traffic and transportation subjects to provide a means for the Institute to recognize outstanding accomplishment in such activities. The winner receives $1,000 towards travel expenses and a plaque. Established in 1981. Formerly: (1995) Section Technical Award.

• 11055 • **Wilbur S. Smith Distinguished Transportation Educator Award**
To recognize an individual who has made an outstanding contribution to the transportation profession by relating academic studies to the actual practice of transportation. Awarded annually.

• 11056 • **Student Chapter Award**
To encourage the Institute's Student Chapters to achieve the objectives set forth by the Student Chapter charter: "to promote the advancement of transportation and traffic engineering by fostering the close association of students with the transportation and traffic engineering profession and the Institute; to acquaint Chapter members with topics of interest on transportation and traffic engineering, and with Chapter-sponsored trips; to foster the development of professional spirit; to promote common interests among Chapter members; to encourage the expansion of facilities for transportation and traffic engineering study," and to provide a means for the Institute to recognize outstanding accomplishments in such activities. Established in 1985.

• 11057 • **Student Paper Award**
To encourage student members of the Institute to conduct and report on independent and original research and investigation of traffic or transportation subjects and to recognize outstanding accomplishments in this area. Established in 1976, the award is nemed in honor of Daniel B. Fambro, professor at Texas A & M University and Associate Research Engineer at the Texas Transportation Institute.

• 11058 • **Transportation Achievement Award**
To recognize significant and outstanding transportation achievements by other entities concerned with transportation, such as governmental agencies, legislative bodies, consulting firms, industry, or other private sector organizations. Awards are presented to outstanding transportation achievements in the categories of operations and facilities. The award consists of a plaque. Established in 1984.

• 11059 • **Urban Traffic Engineering Achievement Awards**
To recognize urban traffic engineers and agencies for outstanding contributions to and/or excellence in urban traffic engineering. Established in 1988.

• 11060 • **Young Consultants Award**
To recognize achievement in transportation consulting by younger employees of the Institute's Consultants Council member firms. Established in 1985.

• 11061 •
Institute of Turkish Studies
Sabri Sayari, Exec.Dir.
Interculture Center, Georgetown University
Box 571033
Washington, DC 20057
Phone: (202)687-0295
Fax: (202)687-3780
E-mail: institute_turkishstudies@yahoo.com
Home Page: http://www.turkishstudies.org

• 11062 • **Academic Year Grant Program**
To serve as a support organization for the academic community of United States specialists in the field of Turkish Studies. Applications must be submitted by March 15. The following opportunities are available to individual scholars: Matching Conference Travel Grants for post-doctoral scholars; Summer Travel/Research in Turkey Grants for post-doctoral scholars; subventions towards the publication costs of manuscripts already accepted for publication of texts, documents, and translations of works directly related to the field of Turkish studies; and of periodicals in the field of Turkish Studies published in the

United States; Dissertation Writing Grants for Ph.D. candidates in the U.S.; and Teaching Aids Grants for the preparation of materials relating to Turkish studies. The following opportunities are available to institutions: Graduate Fellowships; Matching Seed-Money Grants for the establishment of new university positions in the field of Turkish studies; Matching Conference and Lecture Series Grants; and Grants for Workshops on Turkish studies sponsored by universities or other educational organizations.

• 11063 •
Institute on Religion and Democracy
Alan Wisdom, VP
1110 Vermont Ave. NW, Ste. 1180
Washington, DC 20005
Phone: (202)969-8430
Fax: (202)969-8429
E-mail: mail@ird-renew.org
Home Page: http://www.ird-renew.org

• 11064 • Religious Liberty Award
To recognize an individual who has made significant contributions to religious liberty in his own country or around the world. Selection is by the staff and board of directors of the institute. A plaque is awarded when merited. Established in 1982.

• 11065 •
Institutes for the Achievement of Human Potential
Janet Doman, Dir.
8801 Stenton Ave.
Chestnut Hill
Wyndmoor, PA 19038
Phone: (215)233-2050
Fax: (215)233-9312
E-mail: institutes@iahp.org
Home Page: http://www.iahp.org

• 11066 • The Leonardo da Vinci Award
For recognition of unconventional thinkers who have used brilliant insight and meaningful action to solve difficult human problems. Each May, a gold medal is awarded at the Annual Award Ceremonies of the World Organization for Human Potential. Established in 1982.

• 11067 •
Institution for Operations Research and the Management Sciences
Mark G. Doherty, Exec.Dir.
7240 Parkway Dr., Ste. 310
Hanover, MD 21076
Phone: (443)757-3500
Toll-Free: 800-4-INFORMS
Fax: (443)757-3515
E-mail: informs@mail.informs.org
Home Page: http://www.informs.org
Formerly: (1995) Operations Research Society of America; Institute of Management Sciences.

• 11068 • Bonder Scholarship for Applied Operations Research in Military Applications
Scholarship given to promote the development and application of process modeling and operations research analyses to military issues. The scholarship of $5,000 is given annually. Established 2002.

• 11069 • Bonder Scholarship in Health Care
Scholarship given to promote the development and application of process modeling and operations research analyses to military issues. The scholarship of $5,000 is given annually. Established 2002.

• 11070 • George B. Dantzig Dissertation Award
This award is given annually for the best dissertation that is innovative and relevant to practice in any area of operations research and the management sciences. The award is presented in the Fall.

• 11071 • Franz Edelman Award for Achievement in Management Science and Operations Research
This, the leading prize in the field of management science, is given to recognize outstanding examples of management science and operations research in practice. The prize is awarded for implemented work. The client organization that placed a winning project's results in use receives a prize citation; authors of the winning competition entry receive the cash award. Monetary awards totaling $15,000, with a first prize of $10,000, are presented annually. Established in 1972 by TIMS College on the Practice of Management Science. In 1982, the sponsorship shifted to the Institute of Management Sciences.

• 11072 • Expository Writing Award
To honor an operations researcher or management scientist whose publications demonstrate a consistently high standard of expository writing. Awarded annually at the fall national meeting.

• 11073 • INFORMS Fellow Award
Reserved for distinguished individuals who have demonstrated understanding and exceptional accomplishments and experience in operations research/ management science. A nominee must have been a full Member or retired member of INFORMS for at least 10 consecutive years. A plaque is awarded annually. Established in 2002.

• 11074 • INFORMS Prize
This prize is awarded each year for effective integration of operations research and management sciences (OR/MS) in an organization. The award is given primarily on the basis of the impact that OR/MS has had on the success of the firm. It is presented in the fall at the INFORMS nation meeting. Established in 1991. Formerly: (1994) ORSA Prize.

• 11075 • George E. Kimball Medal
To recognize individuals for distinguished service to the Institute and to the profession of operations research and the management sciences. Applications are not accepted; candidates are identified by a committee of the Institute. A medal and certificate are awarded annually. Established in 1974.

• 11076 • Frederick W. Lanchester Prize
To recognize the published work that best contributes to operations research and the management sciences. Eligible works must be: a paper, book, or group of books; written in English; published in the preceding three years; and be on an operations research/management science subject. Submission deadline is July 1. A monetary award of $5,000, an engraved medal, and a certificate are awarded annually. Established in 1954 in honor of Frederick W. Lanchester, an automotive engineer who co-invented the field of operations research.

• 11077 • Philip McCord Morse Lectureship Award
For recognition of contributions to the Institute, research accomplishments, and a clear view on the future of operations research and the management sciences. Members are eligible. A monetary prize of $2,000, a certificate, a $3,000 travel allowance, and a copy of Morse's autobiography are awarded biennially in odd-numbered years. Established in 1988 in honor of Philip M. Morse.

• 11078 • George Nicholson Student Paper Competition
To honor outstanding papers in the field of operations research and the management sciences written by a student. The following prizes are awarded: first place - $600; second place - $300; and up to four $100 honorable mentions. The top six recipients also receive certificates. Awarded annually. Established in 1976.

• 11079 • President's Award
To recognize and encourage important contributions to the welfare of society by members of INFORMS at the local, national, or global level. Achievements may be in technical or scientific education or in paid or voluntary consulting or management. Presented annually at INFORMS fall national meeting.

• 11080 • Prize for the Teaching of OR/MS Practice
To recognize a university or college teacher who has succeeded in helping his or her students to acquire the knowledge and skills necessary to be effective practitioners of operations research or the management sciences. Awarded annually at INFORMS fall national meeting.

• 11081 • John von Neumann Theory Prize
To recognize the scholar who has made fundamental, sustained contributions to theory in operations research and the management sciences. Criteria include significance, innovation,

depth, scientific excellence, and longevity of contributions. A monetary award of $5,000, an engraved medal, and a certificate are awarded annually at the fall national meeting. Established in 1974.

• 11082 •
Instituto de Cultura Puertorriquena
Dr. Jose Luis Vega, Exec.Dir.
Apt. 9024184
San Juan, PR 00902-4184
Phone: (787)724-0700
Fax: (787)724-8393
E-mail: www@icp.gobierno.pr
Home Page: http://www.icp.gobierno.pr

Awards discontinued.

• 11083 • **Artistic Capacity-Building Program**
Awarded to artists and non profit organizations. A total of $50,000 is awarded annually.

• 11084 • **Artists in Residence Program**
Awarded to elementary schools in Puerto Rico. $75,000 is awarded annually.

• 11085 • **Basic Subvention to the Arts and Cultural Work**
Awarded to artists and non profit organizations. $3000 is awarded to artists and $10,000 to organizations.

• 11086 • **Cultural Medal**
Recognizes a person or institution whose involvement with the development, enhancement, and enjoyment by the people of arts and cultural development of the People of Puerto Richo has been identified as outstanding. Awarded every five years.

• 11087 • **Fondo Puertorriqueno para el Financiamiento del Quehacer Cultural**
Awarded to artists, humanists, and non profit organizations. Not less than 50% of the total cost of the project or $5000 is awarded.

• 11088 • **Travel to Artists Grant**
Awarded to artists and non profit organization to represent Puerto Rico on international events or in order to attend to receive a prize. A total of $75,000 is awarded annually and is granted on a quarterly basis.

• 11089 •
Instructional Technology Council
Christine Mullins, Exec.Dir.
1 Dupont Cir. NW, Ste. 360
Washington, DC 20036-1143
Phone: (202)293-3110
Phone: (202)293-3132
Fax: (202)822-5014
E-mail: cmullins@itcnetwork.org
Home Page: http://www.itcnetwork.org

Formerly: (2002) Instructional Telecommunications Council.

• 11090 • **Awards for Excellence in Distance Learning**
To recognize individuals and organizations that have contributed to the field of distance learning and instructional telecommunications. Each fall, six awards are presented at the Telelearning Conference. Established in 1990.

• 11091 •
Insurance and Financial Communicators Association
Virginia Butler-Alderman, Pres.
PO Box 387
East Rutherford, NJ 07073
Phone: (201)939-4739
Fax: (201)584-0254
E-mail: cmorgan22@comcast.net
Home Page: http://www.ifcaonline.org

Formerly: (1984) Life Insurance Advertisers Association.

• 11092 • **Financial Security Nest Egg Award**
To give recognition to persons outside the life insurance industry bringing focus to the importance of life insurance as a fundamental cornerstone of financial security to the American public. A crystal sculptured egg on a walnut base is awarded annually. Established in 1978.

• 11093 • **The F.L. "Gus" Cooper Award for Meritorous Service**
To recognize an individual in the field of communications who has over a period of time evidenced a commendatory way of life in a business career. Since 1977, this award has been limited to members or former members of LCA. A framed certificate is awarded annually. Established in 1961.

• 11094 •
Insurance Marketing Communications Association
September J. Seibert, Exec.Dir.
PO Box 473054
Charlotte, NC 28247-3054
Phone: (704)543-1776
Fax: (704)543-6345
E-mail: tseibert@imcanet.com
Home Page: http://www.imcanet.com

• 11095 • **Golden Torch Award**
To recognize the individual or organization that has made the greatest contribution to insurance communications over his or her lifetime. Presented annually. Established in 1991.

• 11096 •
Intellectual Property Owners Association
Jessica L. Landacre, Chief Operating Exec.
1255 23rd St. NW, Ste. 200
Washington, DC 20037
Phone: (202)466-2396
Fax: (202)466-2893
E-mail: info@ipo.org
Home Page: http://www.ipo.org

Formerly: (2000) Intellectual Property Owners.

• 11097 • **National Inventor of the Year**
To recognize outstanding achievement by inventors and to increase public awareness of current inventors and how they benefit the nation's economy and quality of life. The invention must have been either patented or first commercially available during the previous 4 years and it must have been invented in the United States. A call for nominations is issued in December or January. A monetary award of $5,000 and a plaque are presented annually. Runners-up receive Distinguished Inventor Awards. Established in 1974.

• 11098 •
Inter-American Association of Sanitary and Environmental Engineering
Phillip Braswell, Pres.
PO Box 7737
McLean, VA 22106-7737
Phone: (703)247-8730
Fax: (703)243-9004
E-mail: turnerje@cdm.com
Home Page: http://www.aidis-usa.org

• 11099 • **AIDIS Prize**
To recognize official or private entities which have distinguished themselves in the field of sanitary engineering, either because of their scientific contribution or because of their effective support on behalf of the objectives of the Association. Members of the Association are eligible. An inscribed wooden plaque is awarded biennially. Presented by the U.S. Section of AIDIS.

• 11100 • **Biennial AIDIS Prize**
To recognize the national section of the Association that has displayed the greatest activity on behalf of AIDIS. A plaque is awarded biennially. Presented by the U.S. Section of AIDIS.

• 11101 • **Hemisphere Award**
For recognition of contributions to resolving the hemispheric water supply problem. Presented by the International Section of AIDIS.

• 11102 • **Abel Wolman Award**
To recognize the best research work prepared by two or more persons that is presented at the AIDIS Congress. A gold medal is awarded biennially. Presented by the International Section of AIDIS.

• 11103 •
Inter-American Organization for Higher Education
(Organisation Universitaire Interamericaine)
Marcel Hamelin, Exec.Dir.
Edifice Vieux-Seminaire, bureau 1244
1, Cote de La Fabrique
Quebec, QC, Canada G1R 3V6
Phone: (418)650-1515
Fax: (418)650-1519
E-mail: secretariat@oui-iohe.qc.ca
Home Page: http://www.oui-iohe.qc.ca

• 11104 • Interamerica Prize
To recognize individuals who have distinguished themselves either by supporting cooperation or by helping to establish close cultural ties among the countries in the Americas, and who have distinguished themselves by their academic work. The award also recognizes efforts to improve the welfare and the living conditions of the American peoples. Individuals are selected by nomination from North, Central, and South America. A plaque is awarded annually. Established in 1985.

• 11105 •
Inter American Press Association
(Sociedad Interamericana de Prensa)
Julio E. Munoz, Exec.Dir.
1801 SW 3rd Ave.
Jules Dubois Bldg.
Miami, FL 33129
Phone: (305)634-2465
Toll-Free: 877-747-4272
Fax: (305)635-2272
E-mail: info@sipiapa.org
Home Page: http://www.sipiapa.com

• 11106 • Cartoon Award
Recognizes cartoons with news and/or news and humor content. Open to one or more persons in the Americas. Direct members of the Association are not eligible. A monetary prize of $2,000 and a diploma are awarded annually.

• 11107 • Pedro Joaquin Chamorro Inter-American Relations Award
For news reports or series designed to highlight, improve, or resolve issues or problems in relations among the countries of the Americas. $2000 and a plaque are awarded. Open to one or more persons in the Americas for outstanding work in defense of freedom of the press. Direct members of the Association are not eligible. A monetary prize of $2,000 and a diploma are awarded annually.

• 11108 • Features Award
For special reports that are well written, accurate, and have impact and are not produced under deadline pressure. Open to one or more persons in the Americas. Direct members of the Association are not eligible. A monetary prize of $2,000 and a diploma are awarded annually.

• 11109 • IAPA-Pedro Joaquin Chamorro Inter-American Relations Award
For news reports or series designed to highlight, improve, or resolve issues or problems in relations among the countries of the Americas. $2000 and a plaque are awarded. Deadline: February 1. Must be a work published during the previous calendar year. Sponsored by LaPrensa, Managua, Nicaragua.

• 11110 • In-Depth Reporting Award
Recognizes major investigative reporting or campaigns that have required extensive investigative work. The work may have been published as a special section. Open to one or more persons in the Americas. Direct members of the Association are not eligible. A monetary prize of $2,000 and a diploma are awarded annually.

• 11111 • Infographics Award
For the most creative infographics, reflecting the capabilities of this specialty. Open to one or more persons in the Americas. Direct members of the Association are not eligible. A monetary prize of $2,000 and a diploma are awarded annually.

• 11112 • News Coverage Award
For any kind of news reporting. Open to one or more persons in the Americas. Direct members of the Association are not eligible. A monetary prize of $2,000 and a diploma are awarded annually.

• 11113 • Newspaper in Education Award
Recognizes the program with the best content and educational value. Open to one or more persons in the Americas. Direct members of the Association are not eligible. A monetary prize of $2,000 and a diploma are awarded annually.

• 11114 • Opinion Award
Recognizes reasoned opinion pieces (not series) including, where possible, recommendations. Open to one or more persons in the Americas. Direct members of the Association are not eligible. A monetary prize of $2,000 and a diploma are awarded annually.

• 11115 • Photography Award
For one or more news photos. Open to one or more persons in the Americas. Direct members of the Association are not eligible. A monetary prize of $2,000 and a diploma are awarded annually.

• 11116 •
Inter-American Safety Council
(Consejo Interamericano de Seguridad)
Glen F. Mickey, Pres. & Gen.Mgr.
936 Broad St.
Newark, NJ 07102-2614
Phone: (973)237-1766
Fax: (973)237-1755
E-mail: info@cias-iasc.org

• 11117 • Annual Contest
(Concurso Anual)
To recognize the efforts of employees of member companies in accident prevention. The following prizes are awarded: Contest Award (Premio del Concurso) - to member companies having the lowest accident frequency rate for the contest year in each division and Merit Award (Premio al Merito) to participants who reduce their disabling injury frequency rate 25 percent below the average of the previous two years. Awarded annually.

• 11118 • Extraordinary Plaque
(Placa Extraordinaria)
To recognize notable achievements in the reduction of disabling injuries or for not sustaining disabling injuries during a determined number of man-hours. A bronze medallion is awarded when merited. Established in 1961.

• 11119 • Gold Medal
(Medalla de Oro)
To recognize the effort of an employee of a member company who has saved a human life through the application of artificial respiration, cardiac massage, first aid, or some other lifesaving act. A gold medal and a certificate are awarded when merited.

• 11120 • Letter of Recognition
(Carta de Reconocimiento)
To recognize notable achievements in the prevention of disabling injuries. Selection is based on completion of 20,000 man-hours without incurring a disabling injury during a period of one year. A letter signed by the President of the Inter-American Safety Council is awarded when merited. Established in 1961.

• 11121 • Special Certificate
(Certificado Especial)
To recognize notable achievements in the prevention of disabling injuries. Selection is based on completion of 1,000,000 man-hours without incurring a disabling injury for a period of no less than 30 days. A certificate is awarded when merited. Established in 1961.

• 11122 •
Inter-Collegiate Sailing Association of North America
Mike Segerblom, Contact
Yocum Sailing Center
United States of America Merchant Marine Academy
Kings Point, NY 11024-1699
Phone: (516)773-5232
Fax: (516)773-5344
E-mail: mikesego@collegesailing.edu
Home Page: http://www.collegesailing.org

Formerly: (2000) Inter-Collegiate Yacht Racing Association of North America.

• 11123 • All American Inter-Collegiate Sailor
To recognize outstanding performance in an intercollegiate sailing competition during the past year. A certificate is awarded annually. Established in 1967.

• 11124 • Inter-Collegiate Sailing Hall of Fame
To recognize individuals who have made a significant contribution to the sport of inter-collegiate sailing either through competition, administration, or as benefactors. Selection is made by a committee after review of an individual's credentials. A certificate and permanent plaque are awarded annually or less frequently. Established in 1969.

• 11125 • Inter-Collegiate Sailor of the Year

To recognize the individual who is judged to have been the best inter-collegiate sailor during the past year, July 1 through June 30. Selection is made by a committee. A trophy and replica plaque are awarded annually. Established in 1968. Sponsored by United States Naval Academy.

• 11126 •
Inter-Society Color Council
Dr. Joanne C. Zwinkels, Pres.
11491 Sunset Hills Rd., Ste. 301
5 Princess Rd.
Reston, VA 20190
Phone: (703)318-0263
Fax: (703)318-0514
E-mail: iscoffice@iscc.org
Home Page: http://www.iscc.org

• 11127 • Godlove Award

To recognize a member or a former member of the Council for original contributions to the field of color. The contribution may be direct, it may be in the active practical stimulation of the application of color, or it may be an outstanding dissemination of knowledge of color by writing or lecturing, based on original contributions by the nominee. The candidates must have had at least five years experience in their particular field of interest in color. The nomination deadline is June for the following year. A trophy is awarded biennially in odd-numbered years. Established in 1957 by Margaret N. Godlove in memory of her husband, Dr. I. H. Godlove.

• 11128 • Macbeth Award

To recognize one or more recent outstanding members of the Council. The contribution to color may be direct, it may be in the active practical stimulation of the application of color, or it may be an outstanding dissemination of knowledge of color by writing or lecturing. The nomination deadline is June for the following year. A medal is awarded biennially in even-numbered years. Established in 1972 by Norman Macbeth, Jr., in memory of his father, Norman Macbeth.

• 11129 • Dorothy Nickerson-ISCC Award

To recognize outstanding long term contributions toward the advancement of the Council and its aims and purposes. The contribution may be in the form of organizational, clerical, technical, or other services that benefit the Council and its members. The candidates must be members of the Council and must have been active in the affairs of the Council. The nomination deadline is in January. Awarded annually when merited. Established in 1980. Formerly: ISCC Service Award.

• 11130 •
Interamerican Accounting Association (Asociacion Interamericana de Contabilidad)
Victor Manuel Abreu Paez, Exec.Dir.
275 Fountainebleau Blvd., Ste. 245
Miami, FL 33172
Phone: (305)225-1991
Fax: (305)225-2011
E-mail: oficina@contadoresaic.org
Home Page: http://www.contadoresaic.org

• 11131 • Meritorious Accountant of the Americas

To recognize an individual who represents high technical and ethical standards for the accounting profession in the Americas.

• 11132 •
Intercollegiate Men's Chorus, An International Association of Male Choruses
Gerald Polich, Exec.Sec.
Department of Music
McCain Auditorium
Kansas State University
Manhattan, KS 66506-4706
Phone: (785)532-3824
Fax: (785)532-5709
E-mail: polich@ksu.edu
Home Page: http://www.cco.caltech.edu/~dgc/imc.html

Formerly: (1987) Intercollegiate Musical Council.

• 11133 • Marshall Bartholomew Award

To honor outstanding service to the Council and male chorus singing. The awardee is chosen by a committee of IMC and is given at the annual seminar of the Council. A plaque and honorary life membership in IMC are awarded. Established in 1980 in honor of Marshall Bartholomew, long director of the Yale University Glee Club, for his publications of music for male chorus.

• 11134 •
Intercollegiate Rowing Association
Gary Caldwell, Dir.
1311 Craigville Beach Rd.
Centerville, MA 02632-4129
Phone: (508)771-5060
Fax: (508)771-9486
E-mail: gary.caldwell@tufts.edu
Home Page: http://rowing.ecac.org/index.html

• 11135 • National Championship Regatta

To recognize the winners of the rowing contests for men and women held each year on Cooper River in Camden, N.J. Collegiate rowing teams compete on a course of 2,000 meters in length. The Jim Ten Eyck Memorial Trophy is presented to the School with the best men's overall record. The Camden Freeholders Award is presented to the school with the best women's overall record. The contest was first run in 1895 on a four mile course in Poughkeepsie, New York.

• 11136 •
Intercollegiate Tennis Association
David A. Benjamin, Exec.Dir.
174 Tamarack Cir.
Skillman, NJ 08558-2021
Phone: (609)497-6920
Fax: (609)497-9766
E-mail: itatennis2@aol.com
Home Page: http://www.itatennis.com

• 11137 • Tennis Magazine/Arthur Ashe Collegiate Awards for Leadership and Sportsmanship

To recognize tennis playing accomplishments, scholastic and extracurricular achievements, sportmanship, character, humanitarian concern and accomplishments. Juniors or seniors from NCAA Divisions I, II, III and the NAIA are nominated by their tennis coaches. One man and one woman are recognized annually except Division I Men who received the Osuna Sportsmanship Award. A trophy is awarded annually. Established in 1982 to honor Arthur Ashe. Formerly: (1995) Head Arthur Ashe Sportsmanship Award.

• 11138 • Assistant Coach of the Year Award

To honor an assistant coach from NCAA Division I Men's and Women's tennis teams for their performance, contribution to college coaching, teaching, sportsmanship and community service. Must be a collegiate assistant coach for a minimum of two years. Winners receive a certificate and are recognized at the ITA Coaches Convention.

• 11139 • Ted Farnsworth Senior Player of the Year Award

To recognize a graduating male senior from NCAA Division I who has contributed the most to his team in leadership, sportsmanship, tennis performance and tennis improvement during his collegiate career. Winner receives a trophy and has his name added to the permanent trophy housed in the ITA Men's Collegiate Hall of Fame. Established in 1995 to honor Ted Farnsworth.

• 11140 • ITA All America Team

To recognize individuals and doubles teams who have achieved certain criteria during the tennis season: (A) for Singles: (1) Top 16 seed in NCAA Championship; (2) Reach round of 16 at NCAA Championship; (3) Finish in Top 20 of final Rolex Collegiate Rankings; and (B) for Doubles: (1) Top eight seed in NCAA Championship; or (2) Reach quarterfinals at NCAA Championship; or (3) Finish in Top 10 of final Rolex Collegiate Rankings. Selection is based on the final Rolex Collegiate Rankings and results from the NCAA Div. I, II, III, NAIA and Junior and Community College Championships. A certificate is awarded annually. Established in 1957 for Men and in 1982 for Women. Formerly: (1995) Volvo Tennis/All-America.

• 11141 • ITA/Osuna Sportsmanship Award
To recognize a junior or senior Division I man for tennis accomplishments, scholastic and extra curricular achievements, sportsmanship, character, humanitarian concern and accomplishments. A trophy is awarded annually. Established in 1969 to honor Rafael Osuna. Formerly: (1995) Osuna Sportsmanship Award.

• 11142 • ITA Rookie Player of the Year
To recognize a college freshman who has had the most outstanding first year of college tennis, been ranked in the top 50 for his/her respective division, and contributed to the team in the areas of leadership, sportsmanship and performance. First year competitors (college freshman) in NCAA Divisions I, II, III, the NAIA, and jc/cc are eligible. Certificates are awarded to four men and four women annually. Established in 1984. Formerly: (1995) Volvo Tennis/Rookie Player of the Year.

• 11143 • ITA Scholar-Athlete All-American
To recognize academic achievement. Junior and Senior Varsity tennis letter winners at NCAA/NAIA schools with a grade point average of 3.5 or above (on a 4.0 scale) or in the top ten percent of their class may be nominated. A certificate is awarded annually at the end of the school year. Established in 1982. Formerly: (1995) Volvo Tennis Scholar Athletes.

• 11144 • ITA Senior Player of the Year
To recognize a player who has contributed the most to his or her team throughout their tennis career and is ranked among the top 50 collegiate tennis players in each division of the NCAA and in the NAIA. Graduating seniors from men's and women's NCAA Divisions I, II, III and the NAIA are eligible. Certificates are awarded to four men and four women annually. Established in 1981. Formerly: (1995) Volvo Tennis/Senior Player of the Year.

• 11145 • Cissie Leary Sportsmanship Award
To recognize a Division I woman player who has demonstrated an inspiring commitment and dedication to her team with exceptional hard work, courage, sportsmanship and a positive cooperative spirit that enhances her team's performance and exemplifies the spirit of college tennis. The winner receives a plaque and has her name added to a permanent trophy housed in the ITA Women's Collegiate Hall of Fame. Established in 1997 to honor Cissie Leary.

• 11146 • Penn/ITA Player to Watch
To recognize an up and coming collegiate tennis player who has had an outstanding collegiate year, but has not yet won a Grand Slam. Open to the top 10 returning players in NCAA Division I, II, III, NAIA, NJCAA, and California community colleges. A certificate is awarded annually. Established in 1985. Formerly: (1995) Rolex Player to Watch.

• 11147 • Rolex Collegiate All-Star Team
To recognize top players from NCAA Divisions I, II, III, NAIA and Junior and Community College Schools. A trophy is awarded annually at a special outing and luncheon in New York City prior to the U.S. Open Tennis Championships. Established in 1984 by *Tennis Magazine*. Sponsored by Rolex Watch U.S.A., *Tennis* and ITA. Formerly: (1989) Intercollegiate All-Star Team.

• 11148 • Rolex/Tennis Magazine College Player of the Year
To recognize the individual who has had the most outstanding year in both individual and team competition, as determined by the ITA's National Awards Committee and with emphasis on the final Rolex Collegiate rankings. Division I men and women are eligible. A trophy is awarded annually at a special awards outing and luncheon hosted by *Tennis* in New York at the start of the U.S. Open. Established in 1980 for men, and in 1984 for women. Formerly: (1995) Volvo Tennis/Tennis College Player of the Year.

• 11149 • Tennis Magazine Collegiate Journalism Award
This award is open to all students at NCAA, NAM, NJCAA or California community colleges where the men's and/or women's varsity tennis program is a member of the ITA, who plan a career in sports journalism, specifically covering tennis. The winner is selected by Tennis Magazine editors and will be offered a summer internship at the magazine's office in Trumbull, CT. Established 1994.

• 11150 • Tennis Magazine/ITA Player of the Year
No further information was available for this award.

• 11151 • John Van Nostrand Memorial Award
To honor a graduating senior who currently attends an NCAA or NAIA school, who demonstrates financial need and will pursue a professional tennis career. Open to men only, by nomination of a special committee. A stipend is awarded annually at the NCAA Division I Championships. Established in 1985 by King Van Nostrand, to honor his son, John Van Nostrand, a former player at Pepperdine University who died in a car accident in 1984.

• 11152 • Wilson Coach of the Year Award
To honor coaches of men's and women's tennis teams from NCAA Divisions I, II and III, the NAIA and Junior Colleges for superior performance in tennis coaching, teaching achievements and contributions to college tennis and sportsmanship. ITA members who have coached at an NCAA, NAIA or junior college for at least three years are eligible. A plaque is awarded annually. All winners are recognized at the ITA Coaches Convention. Sponsored by Wilson Sporting Goods Company.

• 11153 •
InterFuture
David L. Robbins, Pres.
PO Box 282, State House Sta.
Boston, MA 02133
Phone: (617)573-8267
Fax: (617)573-8513
E-mail: drobbins@acad.suffolk.edu
Home Page: http://www.cas.suffolk.edu/interfuture/index.htm

• 11154 • Paul W. Conner Memorial Scholarship
To further diversify each year's class of InterFuture students and to encourage comparative study projects in third world countries and representation of minority groups whose heritage and interests lie outside Western Europe. Students who fulfill all the requirements of an InterFuture scholar are eligible. A monetary award applicable toward payment of the InterFuture fee is presented annually. Established in 1984 in memory of Paul W. Conner, founder and past president. Additional information is available from Prof. David Robbins, President, InterFuture, PO Box 282, State House Station, Boston, MA 02133.

• 11155 • Hugh H. and Mable M. Smythe International Service Citation
To honor individuals and agencies for distinguished contributions to international understanding. Recipients must have a record of devoted service to the ideal of a world community and exhibit a special interest in helping students and young people prepare for international leadership. Anyone may nominate persons of any nationality by December 1. Established in 1982 in honor of the Smythes, a husband-wife pair of scholar-diplomats who both served as United States ambassadors and who, as college professors, were an inspiration to hundreds of students.

• 11156 •
International 210 Association
Charles Henry, Pres.
5 Pratt Cir.
Duxbury, MA 02332
Phone: (781)910-5886
E-mail: vangon@210class.com
Home Page: http://www.210class.com

• 11157 • F. Gregg Bemis President's Trophy
To recognize the skipper who scores the best sailing average in three out of five of the following regattas: Mid-West Championship, New England Championship, Graves Plaque, Wells Bowl, and the National Championship. A trophy is awarded. Established in 1968. Formerly: (1991) President's Trophy.

• 11158 • Vice-President's Trophy
To recognize a skipper selected by the Vice-President. Criterion for the award is outstanding contribution to the Class and Local Fleet. A trophy is awarded. Established in 1976.

Awards are arranged in alphabetical order below their administering organizations

• 11159 •
International Academy for Child Brain Development
Janet Doman Ph.D., Dir.
8801 Stenton Ave.
Wyndmoor, PA 19038
Phone: (215)233-2050
Fax: (215)233-9312
E-mail: institutes@iahp.org
Home Page: http://www.iahp.org

• 11160 • The Statuette with Pedestal
To honor contributions to the growing storehouse of knowledge about human potential and to deepen the understanding of this all-important phenomenon. Two miniature statues of a young child atop a small pedestal are awarded annually during the award ceremonies of the World Organization for Human Potential on campus of the Institutes for the Achievement of Human Potential. Established in 1956.

• 11161 •
International Academy of Aviation and Space Medicine
(Academie Internationale de Medecine Aeronautique et Spatiale)
Dr. Claude Thibeault, Sec.Gen.
502-8500 Pl.
St. Charles
Brossard, QC, Canada J4X 2Z8
Phone: (450)923-6826
Fax: (450)923-1236
E-mail: ctebo@videotron.ca
Home Page: http://www.iaasm.org

• 11162 • Gold Medal
Award of recognition. Presented to individuals exhibiting an exceptional interest in aviation and its medical applications. Awarded periodically.

• 11163 •
International Academy of Olympic Chiropractic Officers
Dr. Stephen J. Press, Chm.
546 Broad Ave.
Englewood, NJ 07631
Phone: (201)569-1444
E-mail: admin@iaoco.org
Home Page: http://www.iaoco.org

• 11164 • Gold Member
Recognizes Olympic team doctor invited by National Olympic Committee.

• 11165 • Silver Member Medal
Award of recognition. Inquire for application details.

• 11166 •
International Academy of Trial Lawyers
Thomas V. Girardi Jr., Pres.
5841 Cedar Rd., Ste. 204
Minneapolis, MN 55416
Phone: (952)546-2364
Toll-Free: (866)823-2443
Fax: (952)545-6073
E-mail: iatl@llmsi.com
Home Page: http://www.iatl.net

• 11167 • Student Advocacy Award
To encourage law students to achieve the highest standards possible. Graduating students in law school, who have high standards, moral and ethical, are eligible. Illuminated scrolls are awarded annually to a graduating student at each of the 37 schools participating in the program. Established in 1960.

• 11168 •
International Administration of Administrative Professionals Razorback Chapter
Bonnie Swayze, Pres.
Bell Engineering, Rm. 4207
1 University of Arkansas
Fayetteville, AR 72701
Phone: (479)575-6029
Phone: (501)751-8824
Fax: (479)575-8431
E-mail: bss@engr.uark.edu
Home Page: http://www.razorbackiaap.org/

• 11169 • Secretary of the Year, Executive of the Year
For years of service and professional qualifications. Recognition award bestowed annually.

• 11170 •
International Advertising Association
Nubia Martinez, Exec.Asst.
521 5th Ave., Ste. 1807
New York, NY 10175
Phone: (212)557-1133
Fax: (212)983-0455
E-mail: iaa@iaaglobal.org
Home Page: http://www.iaaglobal.org

• 11171 • Cresta International Advertising Awards
To establish creative standards for excellence in consumer and business communications worldwide; and help agencies, studios, and production houses develop their reputations internationally. Awards are presented in five categories: Press, Poster, Ambient Media, TV/Cinema, and Interactive. The annual Cresta Awards were so named for "creative standards" and are cosponsored by Creative Standards International. Established in 1993.

• 11172 • Harrison Awards
Honors excellence in classroom performance, writing, and the drive to succeed in the marketing communications industry. Outstanding students and faculty at IAA accredited institutes are eligible.

• 11173 • InterAd
A global student advertising competition recognized worldwide. Works as a team-based project for an in-vivo client developing solutions to real issues. These are presented in a Plans Book and CD-ROM with media plans, creative implementations, and websites. Each year, thousands of students compete for the title.

• 11174 •
International Al Jolson Society
Jan Herstat, Pres.
246 Chance Dr.
Oceanside, NY 11572
Phone: (516)678-3524
Toll-Free: 888-4JO-LSON
E-mail: jolsonvp@optonline.net
Home Page: http://www.jolson.org

• 11175 • Irvin Warwick Memorial Award
Award of recognition. Recipient must show exceptional service to society.

• 11176 •
The International Alliance for Women
Hannah Sorscher, Pres.
8405 Greensboro Dr., Ste. 800
McLean, VA 22102-5120
Phone: (703)506-3284
Toll-Free: (866)533-8429
Fax: (703)506-3266
E-mail: info@tiaw.org
Home Page: http://www.tiaw.org

Formerly: (2003) The International Alliance, An Association of Executive and Profession - al Women.

• 11177 • Mandy Goetze 21st Century Award
For recognition of women who have distinguished themselves as national or international leaders or role models or mentors in their professions and communities. Each October, trophies are presented at the association's annual conference. Established in 1990.

• 11178 •
International Alliance for Women in Music
Anna Rubin, Pres.
1000 Holt Ave.
Rollins College
Box 2731
Winter Park, FL 32789-4499
Phone: (407)646-2400
Fax: (407)646-2533
E-mail: slackman@rollins.edu
Home Page: http://www.iawm.org

Formerly: (1996) International League of Women Composers.

• 11179 • Search for New Music
To encourage women composers of music in any style or medium. Full-time student women composers of any age are eligible. The award consists of a first prize of $250, and a second prize of $150, and honorable mentions. Awarded annually. Established in 1978. In addi-

tion, the Ellen Zwilich Award is given to recognize younger women composers (21 years of age or younger). A monetary award of $150 is presented annually. Established in 1989 to honor Ellen Zwilich, who received the Pulitzer Prize for Music in 1983 - the first woman to achieve this distinction. Additional information is available from Mary Lou Newmark at mln@greenangelmusic.com.

• 11180 • Van de Vate Prize for Orchestral Music

To honor persons in the area of orchestral music in the memory of ILWC founder Nancy Van de Vate.

• 11181 •
International Amateur-Professional Photoelectric Photometry
Douglas S. Hall, Pres.
A. J. Dyer Observatory
1000 Oman Dr.
Brentwood, TN 37027
Phone: (615)373-4897
Phone: (615)383-4630
Fax: (615)371-3904
E-mail: douglas.s.hall@vanderbilt.edu
Home Page: http://www.iapp.org

• 11182 • Richard D. Lines Award in Astronomy

To recognize outstanding student research in astronomy. Awarded to a student entering an exhibit at the I.S.E.F. A monetary prize of $5,000, a plaque, and a one-year subscription to *Communications* are awarded annually. Established in 1991.

• 11183 •
International ANDY Awards
235 Park Ave. S, 6th Fl.
New York, NY 10003
Phone: (212)533-8080
Fax: (212)533-1929
E-mail: info@andyawards.com
Home Page: http://www.andyawards.com

• 11184 • International ANDY Awards

An international advertising excellence award created to recognize the most outstanding, original, and creative work done by persons in the international advertising industry, and to encourage improved standards in the industry. Awards are given in the following categories: Direct Response, Magazine, Newspaper, Out of Home, Printed Materials, Radio, Promotional Materials, Television, and Video/Camera. Advertisements published, displayed, or broadcast in the world during the previous calendar year are eligible. The ANDY statuette, an engraved pewter head, and/or a certificate are awarded annually in May. Established in 1964.

• 11185 •
International Animated Film Society, ASIFA - Hollywood
(Association Internationale du Film d'Animation)
Antran Manoogian, Pres.
721 S Victory Blvd.
Burbank, CA 91502
Phone: (818)842-8330
Fax: (818)842-5645
E-mail: asifaalert-subscribe@yahoogroups.com
Home Page: http://www.asifa-hollywood.org

• 11186 • Annie Award for Best Animated Feature

To recognize creative excellence in the art of animation. Nominations are made by the membership of ASIFA-Hollywood. Only works completed during the year prior to the Annie Awards ceremony with a running time of 60 minutes or longer are eligible. A trophy is given during the annual Annie Awards ceremony and accepted by the producer of the feature on behalf of the winning production. Established in 1972.

• 11187 • Annie Award for Best Animated Television Commercial

To recognize creative excellence in the art of animation. Any animated television commercial to debut on television during the year prior to the Annie Awards Ceremony is eligible. A nominating committee selects between three and nine candidates based on entries submitted for consideration. A trophy will be awarded each year during the annual Annie Awards ceremony. Established in 1972.

• 11188 • Annie Award for Best Animated Television Production

To recognize creative excellence in the art of animation. Nominations are made by the membership of ASIFA-Hollywood. Only works completed during the year prior to the Annie Awards ceremony and under 60 minutes in length are eligible. Animated productions originally released on videocassette are also eligible. One trophy will be given each year during the annual Annie Awards ceremony. Established in 1972.

• 11189 • Annie Award for Outstanding Individual Achievement in the Field of Animation

To recognize achievements of excellence in the art and field of animation. Individual achievement nominees must be recommended by a member of ASIFA-Hollywood. A member may recommend a non-member, himself, or herself. Nominations may include animators, background artists, camera operators, color stylists, designers, directors, editors, layout artists, lyricists, music composers, producers, special effects animators, storyboard artists, voice artists, or writers. Only works completed during the year prior to the Annie Award ceremonies are eligible. Each year four trophies are awarded during the annual Annie Awards ceremony. Established in 1972.

• 11190 • Certificate of Merit

To recognize an individual or organization for service to the art, craft, and industry of animation. Nominations and selection of the recipients are made and approved by the Board of Directors of ASIFA-Hollywood. A certificate is awarded each year during the annual Annie Awards ceremony. Established in 1972.

• 11191 • June Foray Award

Given to an individual whose involvement in animation has made a positive and significant impact on the industry and the art form. The Board of Directors of ASIFA-Hollywood, shall either select a nominee based in nominations submitted by the membership of ASIFA-Hollywood, choose another recipient, or may elect not to give the award.

• 11192 • Windsor McCay Award

To recognize lifetime contributions to the art of animation in producing, directing, animating, design, writing, voice acting, sound and sound effects, technical work, music, professional teaching, or for other endeavors that exhibit outstanding contributions to excellence in animation. A committee selects recipients based on recommendation forms of members of ASIFA-Hollywood and from their own discretion. A maximum of three trophies are awarded each year during the annual Annie Awards ceremony. Established in 1972.

• 11193 •
International Association Auto Theft Investigators
John V. Abounader, Exec.Dir.
PO Box 223
Clinton, NY 13323-0223
Phone: (315)853-1913
Fax: (315)793-0048
E-mail: jvabounader@iaati.org
Home Page: http://www.iaati.org

• 11194 • 3M Vehicle Theft Investigators Award

Recognizes any person who has distinguished him or herself in the vehicle theft investigations where a VIN label played a significant part in the success of the investigation. Awarded annually.

• 11195 • AGC/IAATI Award

Recognizes distinction in the field of off road (farm construction) equipment investigation/recovery. Filed investigators and firs-line supervisors are eliglble.

• 11196 • Raymond H. Dreher Memorial Award

Recognizes distinguished service to the association or for other outstanding acts in the vehicle theft field. Only open to association members.

• 11197 • IAATI Award of Merit

Recognizes outstanding contribution in the area of vehicle theft investigation or prevention. Individuals, groups, departments and companies are eligible. Awarded annually.

• 11198 • **IAATI Lo-Jack Award**
Recognizes efforts, in conjunction with the use of an electronic tracking device, make the most significant impact on the recovery of stolen vehicles. Law enforcement officers are eligible. Awarded annually.

• 11199 • **A.T. Phillips Award**
Recognizes outstanding efforts resulting in the apprehension and/or detection of those individuals responsible for auto related criminal acts against the insurance industry. Individuals or units of any insurance carrier are eligible.

• 11200 •
International Association for Computer Information Systems
Dr. Robert P. Behling, Exec.Dir.
Oklahoma State University
College of Business Administration
Stillwater, OK 74078
Phone: (405)744-8632
Fax: (405)744-5180
E-mail: dnord@okstate.edu
Home Page: http://www.iacis.org

Formerly: (1991) Association for Computer Educators.

• 11201 • **Computer Educator of the Year**
To recognize an educator for significant contributions to computer and information systems education. Selection criteria include scholarly research and publication, curriculum development and innovation, the application of educational technology, and the preparation of computer and information systems instructors. An engraved plaque is awarded during the annual meeting of the International Association for Computer Information Systems, and the recipient is recognized in the *Journal of Computer Information Systems*. Established in 1966. Additional information is available from Dr. Robert Behling, Bryant College, Smithfield, RI 02917.

• 11202 •
International Association for Dental Research
Christopher H. Fox DDS, Exec.Dir.
1619 Duke St.
Alexandria, VA 22314-3406
Phone: (703)548-0066
Fax: (703)548-1883
E-mail: research@iadr.org
Home Page: http://www.iadr.com

• 11203 • **Award in Geriatric Oral Research**
To stimulate, encourage, and recognize outstanding research accomplishments in the field of geriatric oral research. The recipient must have conducted original and important investigations in any of the basic, clinical or epidemiological science (including health services research and behavioral science) associated with geriatric oral research. The award will be based upon the recipient's contributions to the scientific community, the impact of the research, publications in refereed journals, and other scholarly activities. There are no age restrictions. This award, consisting of a cash prize and a plaque, will be presented annually, provided a worthy recipient is nominated.

• 11204 • **Behavioral Science and Health Service Research Award**
In recognition of meritorious research in behavioral science and health services research related to oral health. The award was previously combined with the H. Trendly Dean Award. Awarded annually.

• 11205 • **Biological Mineralization Research Award**
To stimulate, encourage, and recognize basic research in the field of biological mineralization. In order to be considered, evidence of original thought and accomplishment in the field of calcification must be presented. This should include work done by an individual on the mechanism of the mineralization in biologic systems, including teeth, bone, ectopic deposits, or model systems is eligible. A monetary award and a plaque are awarded annually when merited. Established in 1964. Sponsored by Unilever Research.

• 11206 • **Craniofacial Biology Research Award**
To recognize individuals who have contributed to the body of knowledge in craniofacial biology over a significant period of time. It further recognizes these research contributions to be accepted by the scientific community. Criteria are based on: contributions to the scientific community throughout the applicant's career; the impact of the research on the particular discipline of craniofacial biology in which the research is done, the profession of dentistry, and health services as a whole; publications in referred journals; funded research through the peer-review mechanism; and other activities considered to be of a scholarly nature. The award consists of a monetary prize and plaque to be presented annually when merited. Established in 1986. Sponsored by Oral-B Laboratories. Formerly: Craniofacial Biology Group Distinguished Scientist Award.

• 11207 • **H. Trendley Dean Memorial Award**
To recognize meritorious research in epidemiology, and public health. A monetary award and a plaque are awarded annually if merited. Established in 1964 by Dr. Frank J. McClure in memory of Dr. Dean. Now supported by Colgate-Palmolive and the Frank J. McClure Estate.

• 11208 • **Edward H. Hatton Awards Competition for Junior Investigators**
To recognize young investigators for the presentation of meritorious papers on original research at the Association's annual meeting. Abstracts must be submitted to the Committee Chairman by September 1. Awards are given in the following categories: Pre-doctoral and Post-doctoral. A monetary first prize of $500 and a plaque, and a second prize of $250 and a plaque may be awarded in each category annually. The sponsor of each winner also receives a plaque. Sponsored by the Warner-Lambert Company.

• 11209 • **Pulp Biology Research Award**
To recognize, encourage, and stimulate outstanding research contributions in the field of pulp biology. The nominee must have contributed significantly to knowledge in the field of pulp biology through basic or clinical research. There are no age restrictions. The award consists of a cash prize and a plaque. Awarded annually when merited. Established in 1986. Sponsored by L.D. Caulk Division of Dentsply International.

• 11210 • **Research in Dental Caries Award**
To stimulate and recognize an individual for outstanding and innovative achievements contributing to the basic understanding of caries etiology and/or to the prevention of dental caries. At the time of nomination, the nominee must be actively engaged in the area of research for which the award is presented. Work considered for the award should be fully tested and accepted by the scientific community and must have been published not less than 10 years prior to the time of the nomination. A monetary prize and a plaque are awarded annually when merited. Established in 1977. Sponsored by Warner-Lambert Company.

• 11211 • **Research in Oral Biology Award**
To recognize outstanding research in any field of oral biology. Significant research achievements can have been accomplished either in basic sciences or applied clinical sciences. The award is intended to cover those fields not included in other IADR Science Awards. The recipient should not be a recipient of a previous IADR Award other than Edward H. Hatton or Young Investigator. A monetary award and a plaque are presented. Established in 1991. Sponsored by Church & Dwight Company.

• 11212 • **Research in Periodontal Disease Award**
To recognize, encourage, and stimulate outstanding research achievements by an individual in basic research in periodontal disease. There is no restriction on age, however, at the time of nomination the nominee must be actively engaged in the area of research for which the award is made. A monetary award and a plaque are awarded. Established in 1965. Sponsored by the Colgate-Palmolive Company.

• 11213 • **Research in Prosthodontics and Implants Award**
To encourage and give recognition to an individual for outstanding research accomplishments in the field of prosthodontics and implantology. The nominee must have contributed significantly to the basic knowledge related to prosthodontics and implantology. A monetary prize and a plaque are awarded annually when merited in memory of Dr. W.J. Tarbet. Established in 1967. Sponsored by Proctor and Gamble Denture Care. Formerly: (1990) Research in Prosthodontics Award.

• 11214 • Salivary Research Award
To stimulate and recognize outstanding and innovative achievements that have contributed to the basic understanding of salivary gland structure, secretion and function, or salivary composition and function. The recipient should not be a recipient of a previous IADR Science Award other than Edward H. Hatton or Young Investigator. A monetary award and a plaque are presented. Established in 1991. Sponsored by the William Wrigley, Jr. Company.

• 11215 • Bernard G. Sarnat Award in Craniofacial Biology
In recognition of best student contribution in craniofacial biology presented at the annual general meeting of the International Association for Dental Research. A plaque and monetary award are presented. Established in 1947. Sponsored by Dr. Bernard G. Sarnat and the Craniofacial Biology Group.

• 11216 • David B. Scott Student Research Fellowship
To recognize one or more dental students in one of the IADR Divisions. The award rotates alphabetically among the divisions. Awarded annually. Established in 1987 by Mrs. Nancy M. Scott to honor her husband, David B. Scott, past president of the Association. The award is for $2,500.

• 11217 • Wilmer Souder Award
To recognize an individual for outstanding achievements in the science of dental materials research. Awarded annually when merited. Established in 1955 in honor of Wilmer Souder, the motivating force in establishing the Dental Section at the National Bureau of Standards and the father of modern dental materials research. Sponsored by the William T. Sweeney Memorial Fund and the IADR Dental Materials Group.

• 11218 • Young Investigators Award
To stimulate basic research in all dental disciplines. The nominee must be under 36 years of age at the time of the award. A monetary prize and a plaque are awarded annually when merited. Established in 1963. Sponsored by the Procter & Gamble Company. Formerly: Oral Science Research Award.

• 11219 •
International Association for Dental Research Craniofacial Biology Group
University of Illinois at Chicago
Dept. of Orthodontics
801 S Paulina St., M/C 841
Chicago, IL 60612-7211
Phone: (312)996-7138
Fax: (312)996-0873
E-mail: caevans@uic.edu
Home Page: http://www.craniofacialbiology.com

• 11220 • Bernard G. Sarnat Prize
For best student presentation. Awarded annually.

• 11221 •
International Association for Energy Economics
David L. Williams, Exec.Dir.
28790 Chagrin Blvd., Ste. 350
Cleveland, OH 44122-4630
Phone: (216)464-5365
Fax: (216)464-2737
E-mail: iaee@iaee.org
Home Page: http://www.iaee.org
Formerly: (1988) International Association of Energy Economists.

• 11222 • Award for Outstanding Paper *The Energy Journal*
To recognize the best papers published in *The Energy Journal* during the previous year. A monetary award of $1,000 and a plaque are presented at the annual conference. Awarded annually. Established in 1988.

• 11223 • IAEE Journalism Award
For recognition of excellence in written journalism on topics relating to international energy economics. Work by an individual writer, or joint authors, that is published in an internationally recognized newspaper, non-academic magazine, or newsletter anywhere in the world during the previous year is eligible. A monetary prize of $1,500 and a citation are awarded at the annual conference. Established in 1983 in honor of the late John K. Evans, international entrepreneur and businessman, who was an advisory director to Pacific Resources, Inc., of Honolulu. Formerly: John K. Evans Award.

• 11224 • Outstanding Contributions to the IAEE
To recognize an individual for outstanding contributions to the Association. Awarded when merited. Established in 1984.

• 11225 • Outstanding Contributions to the Profession Award
To recognize an individual for outstanding contributions to the field of energy economics and its literature. Awarded annually. Established in 1981.

• 11226 •
International Association for Food Protection
David W. Tharp CAE, Exec.Dir.
6200 Aurora Ave., Ste. 200W
Des Moines, IA 50322-2864
Phone: (515)276-3344
Toll-Free: 800-369-6337
Fax: (515)276-8655
E-mail: info@foodprotection.org
Home Page: http://www.foodprotection.org

• 11227 • Harold Barnum Industry Award
To recognize outstanding service to public health by a member of the Association employed in industry. The individual must be a member for at least 5 years and be nominated by a member. A monetary award of $1,000 and a plaque are awarded annually. Established in 1982. Sponsored by Nasco International, Inc. Formerly: (1982) Educator-Industry Award.

• 11228 • Citation Award
To recognize an IAMFES member for outstanding service to the Association. A bronze plaque is awarded annually. Established in 1951.

• 11229 • Samuel J. Crumbine Consumer Protection Award
For recognition of excellence in a comprehensive program of food and beverage sanitation at the local level. The award is named in honor of Dr. Samuel J. Crumbine, a sanitarian-physician and public health pioneer. Awarded annually, the award consists of a bronze medal.

• 11230 • Developing Scientist Awards
To encourage graduate students to present their original research at the IAMFES Annual Meeting and to foster professionalism in graduate students through contact with peers and professional members of IAMFES. Graduate students enrolled in M.S. or Ph.D. programs at accredited universities or colleges whose research deals with problems related to environmental, food and/or dairy sanitation, protection and safety, are eligible. Candidates cannot have graduated more than one year prior to the deadline for submitting abstracts. The following awards are presented: 1st place, $500 and a plaque; 2nd place, $200 and a certificate; 3rd place, $100 and a certificate; 4th place, $50 and a certificate; and 5th place, $50 and a certificate. Awarded annually. Established in 1986 by the Foundation Fund of IAMFES.

• 11231 • Educator Award
To recognize outstanding service to public health sanitation by an educator. Individuals who have been members of the Association for five years or more are eligible. A monetary award of $1,000 and a plaque are awarded annually. Established in 1973 by the National Milking Machine Council and sponsored by Nelson-Jameson, Inc. Formerly: (1982) Educator-Industry Award.

• 11232 • Honorary Life Membership Award
To honor members of long standing who have contributed greatly to the Association. Retired members are eligible. A bronze plaque is awarded annually. Established in 1957.

• 11233 • International Leadership Award
Annual award of recognition. Inquire for application details.

• 11234 • Sanitarian's Award
To recognize outstanding service to the public's health on the community, state, and national level. Individuals who have been members of the Association for at least five years are eligible. A monetary award of $1,000 and a bronze plaque are awarded annually. Established in 1952. Sponsored by sponsored by Ecolab, Inc., Food and Beverage Division.

• 11235 • **Shogren Award**
To recognize an Affiliate of IAMFES for service to their members in the past year. A monetary award of $100 and a certificate are awarded.

• 11236 •
International Association for Great Lakes Research
Wendy L. Foster, Business Mgr.
2205 Commonwealth Blvd.
Ann Arbor, MI 48105
Phone: (734)665-5303
Fax: (734)741-2055
E-mail: office@iaglr.org
Home Page: http://www.iaglr.org

• 11237 • **Editor's Award**
In recognition of continuing service, dedication, and creative achievement that has contributed to the success of the *Journal of Great Lakes Research*. Awarded annually.

• 11238 • **Anderson - Everett Award**
To recognize an individual for outstanding contributions to the Association. The award honors the efforts of David Anderson and Margaret Everett for their significant early contributions to the association and the Great Lakes.

• 11239 • **Hydrolab/IAGLR Best Student Paper and Poster Competition**
To recognize the best student paper and poster presented at IAGLR's annual Conference on Great Lakes Research. A $250 monetary prize with a one-year student memebership to IAGLR is included. Awarded annually. Jointly sponsored by sponsored by IAGLR and Hydrolab/ Hach Corp.

• 11240 • **IAGLR Scholarship**
To recognize a promising Ph.D. student whose dissertation research is likely to make a significant contribution to the understanding of large lakes. Students engaged in doctoral study whose research topic is relevant to large lakes research are eligible. Two $2,000 scholarships and a one-year membership to IAGLR are awarded annually. Deadline is December 31.

• 11241 • **Chandler - Misener Award**
To acknowledge excellence in the fields of natural or social science or environmental engineering directly related to a Great Lake or other large lakes of the world based on an article published in the *Journal of Great Lakes Research*. Established in 1974, the award honors D.C. Chandler and A.D. Misener, IAGLR's first presidents. A certificate is awarded annually. Established in 1970.

• 11242 •
International Association for Housing Science
Dr. Oktay Ural, Pres.
PO Box 340254
Coral Gables, FL 33134
Phone: (305)446-9462
Fax: (305)461-0921
E-mail: uraloktay@aol.com
Home Page: http:// www.housingscience.org

• 11243 • **Annual Distinction Award**
Recognizes contributions to the field of housing. Awarded annually.

• 11244 •
International Association for Human Resource Information Management
Lynne Mealy, Pres./CEO
PO Box 1086
Burlington, MA 01803-1086
Phone: (512)453-6363
Toll-Free: 800-846-6363
Fax: (781)998-8011
E-mail: moreinfo@ihrim.org
Home Page: http://www.ihrim.org

• 11245 • **The Summit Award**
For contribution to organizations goals and objectives in its strategic plan. Awarded annually.

• 11246 •
International Association for Impact Assessment
Rita Hamm, CEO
1330 23rd St. S, Ste. C
Fargo, ND 58103
Phone: (701)297-7908
Phone: (701)297-7912
Fax: (701)297-7917
E-mail: info@iaia.org
Home Page: http://www.iaia.org

• 11247 • **IAIA - Rose Hulman Award**
For recognition of achievement in the field of impact assessment. A plaque is awarded annually. Established in 1985.

• 11248 •
International Association for Jazz Education
William F. McFarlin, Exec.Dir.
Box 724
Manhattan, KS 66505
Phone: (785)776-8744
Fax: (785)776-6190
E-mail: info@iaje.org
Home Page: http://www.iaje.org

Formerly: (2002) National Association of Jazz Educators; International Association of Jazz Educators.

• 11249 • **IAJE Hall of Fame**
To recognize those individuals whose musical contributions and dedication to jazz education over the past 25 years have created new directions and curricular innovations for music education worldwide. Individuals may be nominated by November 1. A trophy is awarded annually at a conference. Established in 1978.

• 11250 •
International Association for Oxygen Therapy
Nicole S. Sacks, Contact
PO Box 502
Nordman, ID 83848
Phone: (208)443-4319
Phone: (208)443-6633
Fax: (775)227-9353
E-mail: oxytherapies@yahoo.com

• 11251 • **International Oxidative Therapists Award**
To recognize advancements in Oxidative Technologies. Awarded annually with a monetary prize and plaque. Established in 1967.

• 11252 •
International Association for Professional Art Advisors
Kimberly Maier, Exec.Dir.
433 Third St., Ste. 3
Preston Hill Rd.
Brooklyn, NY 11215
Phone: (718)788-1425
E-mail: info@iapaa.org
Home Page: http://www.iapaa.org

• 11253 • **Australian Geography Competition**
Annual award of recognition for students under the age of 16 years who demonstrate proficiency in geography written and oral exams.

• 11254 •
International Association for Research in Income and Wealth
Jane Forman, Exec.Sec.
Department of Economics, Rm. 700
269 Mercer St.
New York, NY 10003
Phone: (212)924-4386
Fax: (212)366-5067
E-mail: iariw@nyu.edu
Home Page: http://www.iariw.org

• 11255 • **Nancy Ruggles Travel Awards**
To recognize an individual for a paper on a topic of interest to the Association, and to support travel to the general conference. Individuals under 35 years of age may submit previously unpublished papers. Travel funds are awarded biennially. Established in 1989 to honor Nancy Ruggles.

• 11256 •
International Association for Structural Mechanics in Reactor Technology
Dr. Vernon C. Matzen, Contact
Center for Nuclear Power Plants SEP
Campus Box 7908
North Carolina State University
Raleigh, NC 27695-7908
Phone: (919)515-7336
Fax: (919)515-5301
E-mail: matzen@eos.ncsu.edu
Home Page: http://www.iasmirt.org

• 11257 • **Thomas A. Jaeger Prize**
To encourage and stimulate basic research by young researchers in structural mechanics applied to reactor technology. The competition is open to those who are 40 years of age or younger. The work presented must be wholly original, related to the topics of the SMiRT Conference and not have been published elsewhere. The prize consists of a certificate, a cash stipend of $2,000 (to be divided equally among multiple authors), and the formal presentation of the paper during the SMiRT Conference. Awarded biennially in odd-numbered years. Established in 1981.

• 11258 •
International Association for the Fantastic in the Arts
Michael M. Levy, Pres.
ICFA Registrar
PO Box 4249
Salem, OR 97302-8249
E-mail: katy.hatfield@gmail.com
Home Page: http://www.iafa.org

• 11259 • **William L. Crawford Fantasy Award**
To recognize the best new/first fantasy novel. Awarded annually. Established in 1985.

• 11260 • **Graduate Student Awards**
To recognize the best graduate student essay presentations at the annual conference. A monetary prize of $250 is awarded annually.

• 11261 •
International Association for the Study of Pain
Louisa E. Jones, Exec. Officer
909 NE 43rd St., Ste. 306
Seattle, WA 98105-6020
Phone: (206)547-6409
Fax: (206)547-1703
E-mail: iaspdesk@iasp-pain.org
Home Page: http://www.iasp-pain.org

• 11262 • **Ronald Dubner Research Prize**
To recognize outstanding research by a trainee in the basic or clinical sciences related to pain. Candidates must be no older than 35. Every three years, a plaque, $2,500, and travel expenses are awarded at the IASP triennial World Congress on Pain. Established in 1993.

• 11263 • **Patrick D. Wall Young Investigator Award**
To recognize outstanding research in the field of pain by a person who has been in the field of pain less than ten years. Candidates must be 40 years of age or younger. Every three years, a plaque, $1,000, and travel expenses are awarded at the IASP triennial World Congress on Pain. Established in 1987.

• 11264 •
International Association for Women of Color Day
Suzanne Brooks, CEO/Pres.
3325 Northrop Ave.
Sacramento, CA 95864
Phone: (916)483-9804
Fax: (916)483-9805
E-mail: iawocday@aol.com
Home Page: http://www.womenofcolorday.com

Formerly: (2003) National Institute for Women of Color.

• 11265 • **Outstanding Women of Color**
To recognize individuals for achievement in an area of service and contributions to a community or a field of activity, and to encourage professional development. Women of color may be nominated by the board of directors of the Institute, may apply, or may be referred. A plaque is awarded every two years at the National Conference. Established in 1982.

• 11266 •
International Association of Assessing Officers
Lisa J. Daniels PRS, Dir.
130 E Randolph St., Ste. 850
Chicago, IL 60601
Phone: (312)819-6100
Fax: (312)819-6149
E-mail: daniels@iaao.org
Home Page: http://www.iaao.org

Formerly: (1959) National Association of Assessing Officers.

• 11267 • **Bernard L. Barnard Award**
To honor the author of an outstanding article published in the *Journal of Property Tax Assessment & Administration* and *Fair & Equitable* which has contributed the most to the improvement of assessment administration. Articles published during the past year are eligible. A monetary prize of $150 and a certificate are awarded each year at the annual conference. Multiple awards may be presented. Established in 1967 in honor of Bernard L. Barnard, a former research director of IAAO.

• 11268 • **Distinguished Assessment Jurisdiction Award**
To recognize the achievements of assessing jurisdictions that have instituted programs/procedures generally recognized as component(s) of a model assessment system. The new program must have been implemented within two years prior to submission. Public information programs are not eligible. A certificate is awarded each year at the annual conference. Established in 1983.

• 11269 • **Distinguished Research and Development Award**
To honor a nonprofit organization or individual for original research in property assessment and taxation and/or mass appraisal techniques/methods. Any individual or organization with a program or record of publications that has: furthered the understanding of property taxation or represents the dissemination of information on new techniques of mass appraisal/valuation, sponsored a program of continuing education for assessors over a period of years, or developed computer applications is eligible. A certificate is awarded. Established in 1983.

• 11270 • **Donehoo Essay Award**
To honor the author of the best non-technical essay on assessment and/or property tax administration. Selection is based on the following criteria: the author must be an IAAO member; the essay must be suitable for publication in either *Journal of Property Tax Assessment & Administration* or *Fair & Equitable*, both published by IAAO; and the essay may be an original, unpublished work or published in a non-IAAO publication in the two years prior to submission. A monetary prize of $150, a certificate, and publication of the essay in either the *Journal of Property Tax Assessment & Administration* or *Fair & Equitable* are awarded annually at the annual conference. Established in 1953 in honor of John C. Donehoo, the first IAAO President.

• 11271 • **Harry Galkin Award**
To honor the most active and valuable associate members of IAAO (associate members are usually appraisers in the private sector or tax representatives in businesses). Individuals active in promoting IAAO by recruiting new members, fund raising, and distinguished professional contributions as evidenced by publications or speaking are eligible. A certificate is awarded each year at the annual conference. Established in 1968 in honor of Harry Galkin, a long-time associate member of IAAO.

• 11272 • **IAAO Global Award**
To recognize a member who has contributed significantly to the establishment of a worldwide community of assessment professionals, as evidenced by one or more of the following: demonstrating a commitment to improving standards of assessment practice in countries other than his or her own; developing educational programs that contribute to worldwide understanding of property tax policy and assessment administration; promoting equity in the distribution of the property tax in countries other than his or her own; conducting research that contributes to worldwide improvement of assessment administration and to enlightened property tax policies; and promoting professionalism and an optimum environment for property assessment and taxation in countries other than his or her own. A plaque and free registration at the IAAO annual conference in the year following the award are presented. (Uncertain)

• 11273 • **IAAO Journalism Citation**
To recognize individuals or organizations in a news medium who have produced an original work that contributes to a better understanding of assessment administration. All works must have appeared or been broadcast within the calendar year prior to submission. Nominations may be made at any time. Citations are awarded throughout the year when merited.

• 11274 • **International Award**
To recognize an IAAO member who has contributed significantly to establishing a worldwide community of assessment professionals. Nominees must be IAAO members. Current committee chairs, executive board members, and previous Global Award winners are not eligible. A mounted bronze medallion and free registration at the next IAAO annual conference are awarded.

• 11275 • **International Property Tax Achievement Award**
To recognize a public official or agency, not formally connected with property tax administration, that has made an outstanding contribution to the improvement of property tax administration through an executive, legislative, or judicial action. The action must represent an affirmation of the goals and objectives of IAAO and must have taken place no more than two years prior to July of any year. A certificate is awarded each year at the annual conference. Established in 1983.

• 11276 • **Journalism Citation**
To recognize quality coverage of assessment and property tax issues in the media. Any original work for use in a news medium of general circulation published or broadcast within the calendar year prior to submission is eligible. Certificates are awarded throughout the year by local assessors. Established in 1979. (Uncertain)

• 11277 • **McCarren Award**
To honor the IAAO Representative who has done the most to promote IAAO in the year of service. Only currently serving IAAO Representatives are eligible. Points are awarded for specific activities. The award consists of a certificate and free registration at any course, workshop, or meeting solely sponsored by IAAO the year following presentation of the award. Presented each year at the annual conference. Established in 1958 in honor of Kenneth J. McCarren, the second IAAO President. Award criteria were restructured in 1990.

• 11278 • **Member of the Year Award**
To recognize the contributions of a new member to the Association who has made, in the previous callendar year, significant contributions to the association through active participation. The winner will have been a member for more than one but less than ten consecutive years. A certificate and free registration at any course, workshop, or meeting solely sponsored by IAAO in the year following presentation of the award are presented each year at the annual conference. Established in 1983.

• 11279 • **Most Valuable Member Award**
To honor a long-term member of the association who has made a significant contribution through participation in IAAO activities to the realization of IAAO's goals, i.e., the promotion of professionalism among assessors and equity in property taxation. Selection of members is based on the following criteria: must have been an IAAO member for at least ten years; must have served as an elected officer, committee chair, or instructor/speaker at IAAO programs/workshops, etc.; must have recruited new members; must have written distinguished professional publications; or served in other public service activities/associations. A certificate and free registration at any course, workshop, or meeting solely sponsored by IAAO in the year following presentation of the award are presented each year at the annual conference. Established in 1952.

• 11280 • **Outstanding Chapter Award**
To recognize the IAAO chapter that has made an outstanding contribution to the realization of the goals and objectives of IAAO. More than one award per year may be given.

• 11281 • **Verne W. Potorff Professional Designee of the Year Award**
To honor the IAAO professional designee who has contributed above and beyond assigned obligations in most effectively promoting the IAAO Professional Designation Program. Members holding an IAAO professional designation are eligible. A medallion is awarded each year at the annual conference. Established in 1969 in memory of Verne W. Potorff, an IAAO member who was an outstanding supporter of the Professional Designation Program. Formerly: (1980) Outstanding Professional Designee.

• 11282 • **Public Information Program Award**
To recognize assessment jurisdictions that have implemented an effective program for the dissemination of information to taxpayers concerning the assessment process. Any assessing jurisdiction implementing a public relations program in the two years prior to submission is eligible. A certificate is awarded each year at the annual conference. Established in 1983.

• 11283 • **Zangerle Award**
To honor the outstanding periodical publication of an assessors' association, IAAO chapter, or other similar organization. One award for a periodical with advertising and one for a periodical without advertising (the latter was instituted in 1983) are presented. Any periodical publication devoted wholly to the concerns of assessors is eligible. A certificate is awarded each year at the annual conference. Established in 1958 in honor of John A. Zangerle, the third IAAO President.

• 11284 •
International Association of Astacology
Bill Daniels, Pres.
Auburn University
Department of Fisheries and Allied Aquaculture
Rm. 123, Swingle Hall
Auburn University, AL 36849-5419
Phone: (334)844-9123
Fax: (334)844-9208
E-mail: daniewh@auburn.edu
Home Page: http://147.72.68.29/crayfish/IAA

• 11285 • **Honorary Life Membership**
Given for service to society and the development of crayfish services. Awarded periodically.

• 11286 •
International Association of Audio Visual Communicators
Phillip N. Shuey, Exec.Dir.
57 W. Palo Verde Ave.
PO Box 250
Ocotillo, CA 92259-0250
Phone: (760)358-7000
Fax: (760)358-7569
E-mail: sheemonw@cindys.com
Home Page: http://www.cindys.com

• 11287 • **International Competition Cinema in Industry (CINDY)**
Bestowed for films, videotapes, slide films, audio, and online and offline interactive multimedia productions. Awarded semiannually.

• 11288 • **Visual Communicators Department of the Year Awards**
Annual awards of recognition. Inquire for application details.

• 11289 •
International Association of Bryologists
Janice M. Glime, Contact
Department of Biological Sciences
Michigan Technical University
Southern Illinois University
Houghton, MI 49931
E-mail: jmglime@mtu.edu
Home Page: http://www.bryology.org

• 11290 • **Stanley Greene Award in Bryology**
To recognize a member of the Association for research in bryology. Applications must be submitted to the Secretary. Awarded biennially.

• 11291 • **S. Hattori Prize**
To recognize the best paper on bryology written by a member of the Association. A monetary prize of C$400 is awarded biennially. First award given in 1995.

• 11292 • **Hedwig Medal**
To recognize members of the Association for outstanding contributions to the development of bryology. A medal is awarded at the Interna-

tional Botanical Congress held at six-year intervals. Established in 1983.

• 11293 • Richard Spruce Award

To recognize an outstanding young bryologist for significant contributions to bryology. Recipient receives a plaque and an invitation to present the opening talk at the next IAB meeting. Awarded twice in a six-year period. First award given in 1995.

• 11294 •
International Association of Business Communicators
Heidi P.T. Upton, Public Relations Mgr.
1 Hallidie Plz., Ste. 600
San Francisco, CA 94102-2818
Phone: (415)544-4700
Toll-Free: 800-776-4222
Fax: (415)544-4747
E-mail: service_centre@iabc.com
Home Page: http://www.iabc.com

• 11295 • Excellence in Communication Leadership (EXCEL)

To recognize contributions to organizational communication by an individual who is not a member of IABC. Selection is based on achievements in initiating, directing, supporting, or sustaining outstanding organizational communication programs. The recipient cannot be an IABC member, but must be nominated by a IABC member. Established in 1961. Formerly: (1982) Achievement in Communication; (1975) Communicator of the Year Award.

• 11296 • IABC Chairman's Award

To recognize association members who have, over the years, given of their time and talents and diligently worked behind the scenes for IABC at the international level. Nominees must be members who have served on committees, participated as seminar speakers or coordinators, carried out conference assignments, worked with students, published articles in professional journals, or have otherwise demonstrated initiative, leadership, and willing contributions to the association and profession. A framed certificate is presented annually. Established in 1981-82. Formerly: President's Award.

• 11297 • IABC Fellow

This, the highest award IABC bestows upon one of its members, is given to recognize those who have continually made outstanding contributions to the communication profession through exemplary achievement within their own organization and through unselfish service to IABC and its members. Fellows are selected by a five-member committee. Only IABC members in good standing are eligible. Present office holders and persons having served as chairpersons during the past three years are not eligible. Established in 1970. The deadline for application is January 13, 2006.

• 11298 •
International Association of Campus Law Enforcement Administrators
Peter J. Berry CAE, Chief Staff Officer
342 N Main St.
West Hartford, CT 06117-2507
Phone: (860)586-7517
Fax: (860)586-7550
E-mail: info@iaclea.org
Home Page: http://www.iaclea.org

• 11299 • Recognition Award

To recognize individuals who have contributed to or performed outstanding services to make colleges and universities safer places in which to work and study. Any individual who is part of a campus community is eligible. An inscribed plaque or certificate is awarded annually. Established in 1960.

• 11300 •
International Association of Cancer Victors and Friends
C. McKenna, Coor.
5336 Harwood Rd.
San Jose, CA 95124-5711
Phone: (408)448-4094
Toll-Free: 888-613-6733
Fax: (408)264-9659

Formerly: (1985) International Association of Cancer Victims and Friends.

• 11301 • Distinguished Service Award

To honor the person who, in any one year, has given the most important service voluntarily to the Association. An engraved plaque is awarded annually. Established in 1968. The Association also offers a Special Service Award and a Student Award.

• 11302 • Hippocratic Oath Award

To honor a practicing physician in any country who has stood on the frontiers of medicine, especially as regards the use of non-toxic cancer therapies in the treatment of his patients. An engraved plate is awarded annually at the Association's convention. Established in 1975.

• 11303 • Cecile Pollack Hoffman Memorial Award

To honor that person whose life best exemplifies the ideas of the founder of the Association, Cecile Pollack Hoffman. A ceramic dove in flight, which is mounted and engraved, is awarded annually. Established in 1975.

• 11304 • Humanitarian Award

For recognition of distinguished contributions in science, medicine or the humanities, especially in regard to non-toxic cancer therapies. A plaque is awarded as merited. Established in 1968.

• 11305 • Leadership Award

To honor an individual who has the most service in a leadership position. An engraved plaque is awarded. Established in 1985.

• 11306 •
International Association of Chiefs of Police
Daniel N. Rosenblatt, Exec.Dir.
515 N Washington St.
Alexandria, VA 22314-2357
Phone: (703)836-6767
Toll-Free: 800-THE-IACP
Fax: (703)836-4543
E-mail: information@theiacp.org
Home Page: http://www.theiacp.org

• 11307 • Annual National Chief's Challenge

To recognize law enforcement agencies for new, continued, or expanded safety belt law enforcement efforts. Agencies compete with their peers by size and type of agency, whether state, county, or local. Sponsored by the IACP in cooperation with the National Highway Traffic Safety Administration (NHTSA), and the National Sheriffs' Association (NSA).

• 11308 • J. Stannard Baker Award for Highway Safety

To recognize individual law enforcement officers and others who have made outstanding lifetime contributions to highway safety. Awards are given in three categories: members of state law enforcement agencies, municipal law enforcement agencies, and private or public sector individuals such as traffic engineers, educators, judges, prosecutors, or motor vehicle examiners. Recipients and their spouses are invited expense-free to the IACP's Annual Conference. Awarded annually. Co-sponsored by the National Highway Traffic Safety Administration and the Center for Public Safety at Northwestern University.

• 11309 • National Law Enforcement Saved by the Belt/Air Bag Awards Program

To recognize those individuals in the law enforcement community whose lives were saved or injuries significantly reduced because they were wearing a safety belt or protected by an air bag and a safety belt at the time of a crash. Recipients receive an official letter of induction along with a Safety Belt Survivors' Club Plaque. Recipients also receive an IACP Safety Belt Survivors Club Pin and a one-year subscription to *Police Chief* magazine. Officers who have met the requirements to receive this award are also listed every month in the *Police Chief* magazine.

• 11310 • Police Officer of the Year Award

To recognize exemplary performance in police work. Nominations may be made for exceptional achievement in any police endeavour, including but not limited to, extraordinary valor, crime prevention, investigative work, community relations, traffic safety, drug control and prevention, juvenile programs, and training efforts. All sworn, full-time local, county, state, or federal officers below the rank of chief are eligible. Recipients are recognized in *PARADE* magazine and at an awards luncheon at the Annual Conference. Sponsored jointly by the IACP and

PARADE magazine. Formerly: *Parade* - IACP Police Service Award.

• 11311 • Webber Seavey Quality in Law Enforcement Award Program
To recognize the achievements of law enforcement agencies in the areas of: imaginative approaches that dramatically improve the quality and excellence of local law enforcement practice and contribute to the profession's body of knowledge; enhancement of services; strengthened police relations and the development of avenues for increased community interaction and involvement in the local law enforcement process; improved use and productivity of available department resources; and development of innovative ways to facilitate intra- and inter-agency communication. Awarded annually. Created jointly by IACP and Motorola and named for IACP's first president, chief of police in Omaha, Nebraska.

• 11312 • Survivors' Club
To recognize those deserving individuals who, as a result of wearing personal body armor, have survived a life-threatening incident. Life-threatening incidents include firearm assaults and attacks with knives, clubs, chains, and other weapons. Officers who meet the criteria are eligible to join the Survivors' Club. Co-sponsored by IACP and Du Pont KEVLAR.

• 11313 •
International Association of Clothing Designers and Executives
David M. Schmida, Exec.Dir.
124 W 93rd St., Ste. 3E
New York, NY 10025
Phone: (212)222-2082
Fax: (212)865-2445
E-mail: newyorkiacde@nyc.rr.com
Home Page: http://www.iacde.com

• 11314 • International Designer Awards
For recognition of outstanding design of garments for men and women in tailored clothing, separates, tailored outerwear, casual outerwear, and evening wear. Originality, sales potential and directional influence are considered. Designer members are eligible. The IDA Prizes are awarded at the Semi-Annual IACOE Convention in April or May.

• 11315 •
International Association of Conference Center Administrators
Janet Begley, Exec.Dir.
1270 N Wickham Rd., Ste. 16-111
Melbourne, FL 32935
Phone: (772)562-4017
Fax: (772)562-4017
E-mail: info@iacca.org
Home Page: http://www.iacca.org

• 11316 • Frank M. Washburn Award
Recognizes outstanding service to field of conference center administration. Awarded annually.

• 11317 •
International Association of Correctional Officers
Cece Hill, Contact
PO Box 15037
Lansing, MI 48901
Phone: (402)420-0602
Fax: (402)420-0604
E-mail: cecehill@cega.com

• 11318 • Correctional Officer of the Year
For recognition of meritorious and heroic line-of-duty performance by correctional officers in the United States and Canada. Full-time correction officers in federal, state, or local correction and/or detention facilities are eligible. A plaque and travel arrangements for the officer and family to visit the National Law Enforcement Memorial in Washington D.C. are awarded annually. Established in 1979.

• 11319 •
International Association of Counselors and Therapists
Jillian R. LaVelle, Pres./CEO
10915 Bonita Beach Rd., Ste. 1101
Bonita Springs, FL 34135
Phone: (239)498-9710
Fax: (239)498-1215
E-mail: iactnow@aol.com
Home Page: http://www.iact.org

• 11320 • Therapist of the Year
Annual award of recognition. Nominated and voted on by local chapters.

• 11321 •
International Association of Crime Writers - North American Branch
Mary Frisque, Exec. Dir.
PO Box 8674
New York, NY 10116-8674
E-mail: info@crimewritersna.org
Home Page: http://www.crimewritersna.org

• 11322 • Hammett Prize
To recognize the best work of literary excellence in crime fiction or nonfiction published in English by a US or Canadian author or permanent resident during the previous year. Established in 1988.

• 11323 •
International Association of Culinary Professionals
William K. Wallace, Pres.
304 W Liberty St., Ste. 201
Louisville, KY 40202
Phone: (502)581-9786
Toll-Free: 800-928-4227
Fax: (502)589-3602
E-mail: iacp@hqtrs.com
Home Page: http://www.iacp.com
Formerly: (1990) International Association of Cooking Professionals.

• 11324 • Caterer Award
Award of recognition.

• 11325 • Chef Award
Award of recognition.

• 11326 • Julia Child Cookbook Awards
To honor the best food and beverage books published during the previous calendar year. The awards program is intended to encourage and promote quality and creativity in writing and publishing and to expand the public awareness of culinary literature. Any new original book on food or beverage published in the English language and copywrited during the previous calendar year is eligible. Awards are presented in the following categories: Bread, Other Baking, and Sweets; International; Food Reference/Technical; General; Health and Diet; Illustrated/Photography; Literary Food Writing; Single Subject; Wine, Beer, or Spirits; First Book: the Julia Child Award; and American. A crystal obelisk is awarded annually. Established in 1966. In 1990, the program split. The James Beard Foundation also presents Food & Beverage Book Awards (see separate listing); sponsored by Joseph E. Seagram & Sons. Formerly: (1990) IACP Cookbook Awards.

• 11327 • Culinary Educator Award
To honor a vocational, avocational, or traveling teacher who effectively communicates an exceptional knowledge of culinary studies and techniques. Awarded annually. Formerly: Cooking Teacher of the Year Award.

• 11328 • Electronic Media Award
Recognizes the best in each category. Awarded biennially.

• 11329 • Entrepreneur Award
To recognize the founder, CEO, or key employee of an IACP small business member company who has played a key role in the development and marketing of the company and who has demonstrated high standards of business ethics and integrity. Awarded annually.

• 11330 • Bert Greene Memorial Awards
To recognize excellence in food journalism. Awards are presented annually in four categories: magazines, essays, newspapers, and Internet.

• 11331 • Marketing Publicist Award
Award of recognition.

• 11332 •
International Association of Defense Counsel
Robert A. Zupkus, Sec.-Treas.
1 N Franklin St., Ste. 1205
Chicago, IL 60606
Phone: (312)368-1494
Fax: (312)368-1854
E-mail: info@iadclaw.org
Home Page: http://www.iadclaw.org

Formerly: (1986) International Association of Insurance Counsel.

• 11333 • Legal Writing Contest
To recognize outstanding writing by students in law schools accredited by the American Bar Association. Articles generally are due by the first week of April. The topics must relate to the fields of tort law, insurance law, civil procedure, evidence or other areas of the law of practical concern to lawyers engaged in the defense or management of the defense of civil litigation. A monetary award of $2,000 for first prize, $1,000 for second prize, and $500 for third prize are presented annually.

• 11334 • Yancey Memorial Award
To recognize the author of the most outstanding article published in the Association's journal during the year. A bronze plaque is awarded annually in July. Established in 1934.

• 11335 •
International Association of Diecutting and Diemaking
Cindy C. Crouse CAE, CEO
651 W Terra Cotta Ave., Ste. 132
Crystal Lake, IL 60014
Phone: (815)455-7519
Toll-Free: 800-828-4233
Fax: (815)455-7510
E-mail: cccrouse@iadd.org
Home Page: http://www.iadd.org

• 11336 • Lifetime Achievement Award
Honors exceptional, long-term, and consistent contributions to the industry and the association. Awarded periodically.

• 11337 • S. Ray Miller International Award
Honors members instrumental in advancing diecutting or diemaking on an international basis. Awarded periodically.

• 11338 • Package Printing and Converting's Diecutter/Diemaker of the Year Award
Honors members who have demonstrated a significant contribution to the diecutting and diemaking process. Awarded annually.

• 11339 • Presidential Award
Honors exceptional leadership, active support of association programs and activities, significant contributions to the association, and achievement in the industry. Awarded annually.

• 11340 • Safety Award
Recognizes companies with the lowest incidence rates of accidents per hours worked. Awarded annually. 9102405482

• 11341 •
International Association of Educators for World Peace - USA
(Association Internationale des Educateurs pour la paix)
Dr. Charles Mercieca PhD, Pres.
Office of the President
2013 Orba Dr. NE
Huntsville, AL 35811-2414
Phone: (256)534-5501
Fax: (256)536-1018
E-mail: info@iaewp.org
Home Page: http://www.earthportals.com/Portal_Messenger/mercieca.html

• 11342 • Dharmaraja - King of Dharma
To recognize outstanding dedicated service to the promotion of international understanding and world peace while demonstrating a personal life characterized by virtue and self-sacrifice. Established in 1991.

• 11343 • Fountain of Universal Peace Award
To recognize those who by their example gave plenty of inspiration to others to lead a better and more productive life. Established 1990.

• 11344 • IAEWP Diploma of Honour
To recognize those who demonstrated hard work in an effort to promote international understanding and world peace, environmental protection and/or human rights.

• 11345 • IAEWP Membership in Good Standing
To recognize outstanding contributions made by IAEWP members in any of the following three areas: promotion of international understanding, protection of the environment, and/or implementation of the UN Universal Declaration of Human Rights. Established in 1970. More than 100 IAEWP members (mostly officers) have been given this award.

• 11346 • World Peace Academy Diploma
To recognize those who resolve to solve problems through negotiation and arbitration while doing everything possible to avert conflicts and wars. Established in 1974.

• 11347 •
International Association of Emergency Managers
Elizabeth B. Armstrong, Exec.Dir.
201 Park Washington Ct.
Falls Church, VA 22046-4513
Phone: (703)538-1795
Fax: (703)241-5603
E-mail: info@iaem.com
Home Page: http://www.iaem.com/

Formerly: (1983) United States Civil Defense Council; National Coordinating Council on Emergency Management.

• 11348 • Honorary Citations
To recognize individuals from any profession who have visibly and actively supported the Association in its efforts to improve the level of international preparedness. Awarded when merited.

• 11349 • Media Awards
To recognize outstanding publications and other communications in the field of emergency preparedness. Members may submit up to two entries in each of the five categories: newsletters, special publications, individual media items, audio visual, and computer products. Within each category, entries will be judged in various subcategories and in three divisions: 1. local; 2. state/regional/international/non-profit; and 3. commercial/for-profit. Entries must be submitted by September 2. Certificates are awarded for first, second, and third place winners, with the winning entries are displayed at the annual conference.

• 11350 • Presidential Citation
To recognize an outstanding contributor and representative of the principles and practices for which the Association stands. Awarded when merited.

• 11351 •
International Association of Fire Chiefs
Garry L. Briese, Exec.Dir.
4025 Fair Ridge Dr.
Fairfax, VA 22033-2868
Phone: (703)273-0911
Toll-Free: 800-661-3336
Fax: (703)273-9363
E-mail: membership@iafc.org
Home Page: http://www.iafc.org

• 11352 • Fire Explorer Post Award
To recognize outstanding achievement among fire fighting explorers (a division of Boy Scouts of America). A plaque is awarded annually. Established in 1986.

• 11353 • International Benjamin Franklin Fire Service Award
To provide worldwide recognition to fire fighters for a life-saving effort involving courage and the demonstration of expert training, professional service and dedication to duty. An active fire fighter of any country may be nominated by his Chief for an incident in which he saved a human

Awards are arranged in alphabetical order below their administering organizations

life. A plaque and medallion are awarded to the individual, and a plaque and a U.S. Savings Bond are awarded to the department. Awarded when merited. Established in 1948 and named for one of the first fire chiefs in the United States, Benjamin Franklin. Co-sponsored by the Motorola Corporation.

• 11354 •
International Association of Fire Fighters
Harold Schaitberger, Gen.Pres.
1750 New York Ave. NW, 3rd Fl.
Washington, DC 20006
Phone: (202)737-8484
Fax: (202)737-8418
E-mail: pr@iaff.org
Home Page: http://www.iaff.org

• 11355 • **IAFF Media Awards Contest**
To recognize outstanding stories, editorial comment, and photographs in U.S. and Canadian newspapers, or radio and television depicting the professionalism and hazardous nature of fire fighting. Entries must be published, broadcast, or telecast in the year under consideration and must be sponsored by a local, state, or provincial affiliate of the Association. The following monetary prizes are awarded in each category: $500 and a plaque for first prize; $250 and a certificate for a second prize; and a certificate for Honorable Mention. Awarded annually. Established in 1965. Formerly: (1995) IAFF International Media Awards.

• 11356 •
International Association of Fish and Wildlife Agencies
John Baughman, Exec.VP
444 N Capitol St. NW, Ste. 725
Washington, DC 20001
Phone: (202)624-7890
Fax: (202)624-7891
E-mail: info@iafwa.org
Home Page: http://www.iafwa.org

• 11357 • **Boone and Crockett Award**
To recognize outstanding achievement in promoting and encouraging programs in outdoor ethics. Two awards are presented: one to an agency and one to the individual who has been the prime mover of outdoor ethics in the agency. Established in 1987. Sponsored by the Boone and Crockett Club.

• 11358 • **Seth Gordon Award**
To recognize outstanding contributions of professional wildlife agency administrators. Members of the Association who have demonstrated unusual administrative ability are eligible. A Steuben crystal effigy of an owl mounted on a lacquered walnut base with brass plate is awarded as merited. Established in 1970.

• 11359 • **Outstanding Law Enforcement Achievement Award**
To recognize outstanding law enforcement efforts in support of wildlife. Individuals and agencies are eligible. Awarded annually. Established in 1982.

• 11360 • **Ernest Thompson Seton Award**
To recognize the state, provincial, or federal agency that has most effectively promoted a public awareness of the need for support of wildlife management policies and practices, and the individual most responsible for having done the work in the federal agency. A plaque and citation are presented annually. Established in 1977. Sponsored by Woodstream Corporation.

• 11361 •
International Association of Food Industry Suppliers
Stephen C. Schlegel, Pres.
1451 Dolley Madison Blvd.
McLean, VA 22101-3850
Phone: (703)761-2600
Fax: (703)761-4334
E-mail: info@iafis.org
Home Page: http://www.iafis.org

Formerly: (1997) Dairy and Food Industries Supply Association.

• 11362 • **DFISA-ASAE Food Engineering Award**
To recognize an individual for original contributions in research, development or design, or in the management of food processing equipment or techniques of significant economic value to the food industry and the consumer. A monetary award of $2,000, a gold medal, and a certificate are presented each odd-numbered year at the DFISA-Annual Meeting. The winner is also honored that same year at a national meeting of the American Society of Agricultural Engineers. Additional information is available from American Society of Agricultural Engineers, 2950 Niles Road, St. Joseph, MI 49085-9659.

• 11363 •
International Association of Human-Animal Interaction Organizations
Larry Norvell, Contact
580 Naches Ave. SW
Renton, WA 98055-2297
Phone: (425)430-2363
Fax: (425)235-1076
E-mail: info@deltasociety.org
Home Page: http://www.iahaio.org

• 11364 • **Distinguished Scholar Award**
Recognizes outstanding published research. Awarded every three years.

• 11365 • **Pets in Cities Award**
Recognizes an outstanding program instituted in urban area. Awarded every three years.

• 11366 •
International Association of Industrial Accident Boards and Commissions
Gregory Krohm, Exec.Dir.
5610 Medical Cir., Ste. 24
Madison, WI 53719
Phone: (608)663-6355
Fax: (608)663-1546
E-mail: fhowe@iaiabc.org
Home Page: http://www.iaiabc.org

• 11367 • **President's Award**
To encourage workers compensation boards and commissions from around the world to improve statutes, rules, and procedures in workers compensation. A plaque is awarded annually. Established in 1964. Formerly: Administrator of the Year.

• 11368 •
International Association of Lighting Designers
Marsha L. Turner CAE, Exec.VP
Merchandise Mart, Ste. 9-104
200 World Trade Ctr.
Chicago, IL 60654
Phone: (312)527-3677
Fax: (312)527-3680
E-mail: marsha@iald.org
Home Page: http://www.iald.org

• 11369 • **IALD International Lighting Design Awards**
To increase awareness of quality lighting design by recognizing quality lighting installations that display high aesthetic achievement, backed by technical expertise and exemplifying a synthesis of the architectural and lighting design process. As a collection of work, projects illustrate the diversity of techniques used to create outstanding lighting design. Submission may be a permanent interior or exterior architectural lighting design solution. Lighting products, lighting equipment, and lighting design for theatrical performances are not eligible. The deadline for submisions is February 3. Awards are presented at the IALD Awards Dinner and Presentation in conjunction with the trade show LIGHTFAIR International. Winning projects are published in leading architectural and design publications and included in the IALD slide library. Established in 1983.

• 11370 •
International Association of Official Human Rights Agencies
James Stowe, Pres.
444 N Capitol St., Ste. 536
Washington, DC 20001
Phone: (202)624-5410
Fax: (202)624-8185
E-mail: iaohra@sso.org
Home Page: http://www.sso.org/iaohra

• 11371 • **Human Rights Award**
To recognize an individual for a contribution to further human rights as it relates to enforcement. Awarded annually at the annual conference.

• 11372 •
International Association of Orthodontics
Detlef B. Moore, Exec.Dir.
750 N Lincoln Memorial Dr., Ste. 422
Milwaukee, WI 53202-4020
Phone: (414)272-2757
Toll-Free: 800-447-8770
Fax: (414)272-2754
E-mail: worldheadquarters@iaortho.org
Home Page: http://www.iaortho.org

• 11373 • Leon J. Pinsker Merit Award
To honor individuals who have made outstanding contributions to the organization. Members of the Association are eligible. A bronze plaque is awarded when merited at the annual meeting, usually in April. Established in 1975 in honor of Leon J. Pinsker, the founder of the Association.

• 11374 •
International Association of Pet Cemeteries
Stephen Drown, Exec.Dir.
PO Box 163
5055 Rte. 11
Ellenburg Depot, NY 12935-0163
Phone: (518)594-3000
Fax: (518)594-8801
E-mail: info@iaopc.com
Home Page: http://www.iaopc.com

Formerly: National Association of Pet Cemeteries.

• 11375 • Director of the Year
To recognize outstanding achievement. A bronze plaque mounted on maple is awarded annually at the Association's convention. Established in 1972.

• 11376 • President's Award
To recognize a "job well done." A bronze plaque mounted on maple is awarded annually at the Association's convention. Established in 1972.

• 11377 •
International Association of Physicians and Health Care Professionals
R.S. Rhinehart, Pres./CEO
PO Box 13089
Tallahassee, FL 32317
Phone: (850)878-3134
Fax: (850)878-1291
E-mail: broekhuysep@bigpond.com
Home Page: http://www.auschess.org.au

• 11378 • Koshnitsky Award
Annual award of recognition for chess administration. Inquire for application details.

• 11379 • Purdy Award
Annual award of recognition for chess journalism.

• 11380 • Steiner Award
Annual award of recognition for the player of the year.

• 11381 •
International Association of Physicians in AIDS Care
Jose M. Zuniga, Pres./CEO
33 N LaSalle St., Ste. 1700
Chicago, IL 60602-3527
Phone: (312)795-4930
Fax: (312)795-4938
E-mail: iapac@iapac.org
Home Page: http://www.iapac.org

• 11382 • Dag Hammarksjold Award
Recognizes world leaders instituting bold approaches to various aspects of the AIDS pandemic. Awarded periodically.

• 11383 • IAPAC Hero In Medicine
Periodic award of recognition. Inquire for application details.

• 11384 • Jonathan Mann Health & Human Rights Award
Periodic award of recognition. Inquire for application details.

• 11385 •
International Association of Pipe Smokers Clubs
Dave Edel, Pres.
647 S. Saginaw
Flint, MI 48502
Phone: (810)235-0581
Fax: (810)235-1300
E-mail: chairman@iapsc.net
Home Page: http://www.iapsc.net

• 11386 • Pipe Smoker of the Year
Recognizes a pipe smoker or collector. Awarded annually. Inquire for application details.

• 11387 •
International Association of Professional Bureaucrats
Dr. James H. Boren, Pres./Founder
2400 Jolinda Ln.
Whitesboro, TX 76273
Phone: (903)564-9290
Fax: (903)564-9430
E-mail: jim.boren@cox-internet.com
Home Page: http://www.jimboren.com/index.shtml

• 11388 • INATAPROBU Rejection Scroll
To recognize the correction of a bureaucratic wrong by an individual within the establishment. Awarded when the wrong, if not corrected, would have led to an Order of the Bird Award. An embossed scroll is awarded when merited. Established in 1971.

• 11389 • INATAPROBU Spirometric Citation
To give special recognition to dedicated bureaucrats of the governmental, academic, clerical, or corporate world who contribute to orbital dialogues, buzzistic communications, and the creative use of language. An embossed scroll and ribboned medallion are awarded when merited. Established in 1971.

• 11390 • Order of the Bird
To recognize particular contributions to the state of the bureaucratic art. Governmental, corporate, clerical, and academic bureaucrats throughout the world are eligible. A Boren metal sculpture of a bird, prepared for each individual winner based on his personality or contribution, is presented. Six awards are presented annually. Established in 1968.

• 11391 • Order of the Egg
To recognize individuals or organizations who do not quite earn the Order of the Bird but who may be approaching it. Nominations are made by the public. An original Jim Boren sculpture of a bird's foot with a leg topped by a nest containing an inscribed egg is awarded.

• 11392 •
International Association of Radiopharmacology
Dr. Steve McQuarrie, Exec.Sec.
Faculty of Pharmacy
University of Alberta
Edmonton, AB, Canada T6G 2N8
Phone: (403)492-2905
Fax: (403)492-1217
E-mail: smcquarrie@pharmacy.ualberta.ca
Home Page: http://www.pharmacy.ualberta.ca/iar

• 11393 • Research Presentation Award
Presented for notable speeches at biennial symposium.

• 11394 •
International Association of Registered Financial Consultants
Judith Losz, Exec.Dir.
PO Box 42506
2507 N Verity Pkwy.
Middletown, OH 45042-0506
Phone: (513)424-6395
Toll-Free: 800-532-9060
Fax: (513)424-5752
E-mail: director@iarfc.org
Home Page: http://www.iarfc.org

• 11395 • Loren Dunton Memorial Award
Recognizes significant contribution to financial services profession. Awarded annually.

• 11396 • President's Award
Recognizes contributions to the organization. Only members are eligible. Awarded annually.

• 11397 •
International Association of School Librarianship
Dr. Penny Moore, Exec.Dir.
PMB 292
1903 W 8th St.
Erie, PA 16505
Phone: (604)925-0266
Fax: (604)925-0566
E-mail: iasl@kb.com.au
Home Page: http://www.iasl-slo.org

• 11398 • IASL/SIRS International Commendation Award
To recognize outstanding and innovative programs, projects, and plans which serve as models for replication by other school libraries. Candidates must be nominated by a school li-

brary association which is a member of IASL. The deadline is April 1. A monetary prize and a plaque are awarded annually at the convention by the Social Issues Resources Series. Established in 1989 by IASL.

• 11399 • Jean Lowrie Leadership Development Grant
To recognize leaders in developing nations are invited to apply for assistance of $1,000 and registration to attend their first IASL annual conference. This grant assists leaders to share their needs and aspirations, to learn from other conference participants, to develop contacts to further their work and to identify strategies that can be used. A monetary award of $1,000 is awarded annually. Established in 1995 in honor of Dr. Jean E. Lowrie, the first president and first executive secretary of the IASL.

• 11400 • Takeshi Murofushi Research Award
To recognize a research project the criteria includes : (1) a clear description of the research project and methodology, (2) a proposed timeline and budget, (3) a personal resume of the researcher(s), demonstrating ability to undertake and successfully complete the project. A monetary of $500 is awarded annually. Established in 1997.

• 11401 •
International Association of Special Investigation Units
(Ffederasiwn Cerddoriaeth Amatur Cymru)
Daniel Fitzgerald, Pres.
8015 Corporate Dr., Ste. A
Bute Pl.
Baltimore, MD 21236
Phone: (410)931-3332
Fax: (410)931-2060
E-mail: iasiu@managementalliance.com
Home Page: http://www.iasiu.org

• 11402 • W.S. Gwynn Williams Award
Recognizes amateur music promoting societies. Monetary prizes are given annually.

• 11403 •
International Association of Sports Museums and Halls of Fame
Ms. Karen Bednarski, Exec.Dir.
PO Box 3093
Ponte Vedra Beach, FL 32004
Phone: (904)955-0126
Fax: (904)810-5305
E-mail: info@sportshalls.com
Home Page: http://www.sportshalls.com

Formerly: (1989) Association of Sports Museums and Halls of Fame.

• 11404 • Bill Schroeder Distinguished Service Award
To recognize an individual for distinguished service within the IASMHF, either to the parent group, a member organization, or both. A plaque is awarded annually at the convention. Established in 1985 to honor Willrich R. "Bill" Schroeder, a pioneer in the Hall of Fame movement.

• 11405 •
International Association of Theoretical and Applied Limnology
(Societas Internationalis Limnologiae)
Prof.Dr. Gene Likens, Pres.
Institute of Ecosystem Studies
Box AB
Millbrook, NY 12545
Phone: (919)843-4916
Fax: (919)843-4072
E-mail: likensg@ecostudies.org
Home Page: http://www.limnology.org

• 11406 • Einar Naumann - August Thienemann Medal
To recognize outstanding fundamental contributions to limnology. A bronze medal is awarded. Established in 1959.

• 11407 •
International Association of Wildland Fire
Dick Mangan, Pres.
PO Box 261
Hot Springs, SD 57747-0261
Phone: (605)890-2348
Fax: (206)600-5113
E-mail: iawf@iawfonline.org
Home Page: http://www.iawfonline.org

• 11408 • Safety Award
Annual award of recognition for safety.

• 11409 •
International Association of Women Police
Terrie S. Swann, Pres.
PO Box 2710
Phoenix, AZ 85002-2710
Phone: (602)382-8781
Fax: (602)382-8780
E-mail: terrieswann@aol.com
Home Page: http://www.iawp.org

• 11410 • International Recognition and Scholarship Award
To recognize the accomplishments of an officer from outside North America. The candidate must have the qualifications required for active membership in IAWP, and must be able to communicate in English or to provide an interpreter. The recipient attends the annual conference, where she is expected to give a short presentation on the role of women officers in her country. The award will pay up to $3,000 towards travel expenses.

• 11411 • Officer of the Year Awards
To recognize outstanding women of the law enforcement profession by a professional network of peer officers. In addition, the award has the following objectives: (1) to provide the members with the benefit of learning about achievements of sister officers; (2) to increase understanding and awareness of women in law enforcement and the International Association of Women Police; (3) to encourage police administrators to support the organization with their own membership as well as that of officers in their agencies; (4) to promote the annual training conference; and (5) to promote membership by all women law enforcement officers in IAWP. Women who are sworn law enforcement officers with the power of arrest, and who are currently employed may be nominated with the approval of the highest ranking official of the agency where the woman is employed. Nominations may be made when a woman officer has demonstrated meritorious police service, i.e., has at imminent risk of life performed deeds of valor or has rendered invaluable police service and is dedicated to her daily tasks. Travel and expenses to attend the annual conference are awarded annually in September or October. Established in 1977.

• 11412 •
International Association of Workforce Professionals
Mary Riddell, Mgr.
1801 Louisville Rd.
Frankfort, KY 40601
Phone: (502)223-4459
Phone: (502)223-4459
Toll-Free: 888-898-9960
Fax: (502)223-4127
E-mail: iapes@iapes.org
Home Page: http://www.iapes.org

Formerly: (1954) International Association of Personnel in Employment Services.

• 11413 • Award of Merit
To recognize an individual and a group for outstanding service to the employment security profession, the Association, and the community. A chapter's nominee must be a current and have been a member during the year of activity. The deadline for nominations is March. A monetary award, a plaque, a desk plate, and travel expenses to the Convention are awarded to first place winners annually. Established in 1944.

• 11414 • Citation of Merit
To recognize outstanding contributions to the field of employment security by someone other than employment security personnel. Chapters may nominate individuals. A plaque and travel expenses to receive the award (when necessary) are awarded annually at the convention. Established in 1948.

• 11415 •
International Banana Club
L. Ken Bannister, Pres. & Top Banana
14012 Siesta Dr.
Apple Valley, CA 92307-5968
Phone: (760)242-6724
E-mail: tb@bananaclub.com
Home Page: http://www.bananaclub.com

• 11416 • Banana Club (R) Man/Woman of the Year
To recognize the man or woman each year who has been actively involved in the club and for outstanding contributions through time and/or money to further the cause of the club: "To induce more laughter and good health in our life-

time." Members of the organization are eligible. A trophy, trip, and international recognition are awarded annually. Established in 1972 by L. Ken Bannister (Top Banana). (Also known as the Bananister Award)

• 11417 • Doctorate of Bananistry Medal
To reward knowledge of bananas. A medal and neck ribbon are awarded when merited.

• 11418 • Master of Bananistry Medal
To reward knowledge of bananas. A medal and neck ribbon are awarded when merited.

• 11419 •
International Black Writers and Artists
Wayne French, Pres.
PO Box 43576
Los Angeles, CA 90043
Phone: (323)964-3721
E-mail: info@ibwala.org
Home Page: http://members.tripod.com/~ibwa/home.htm

• 11420 • Alice C. Browning Award
To recognize excellence in writing. Published writers who are 18 years or older and members of the organization are eligible. A plaque and a certificate are presented annually. Established in 1986 by Mable Terrell in honor of Alice C. Browning, founder of the International Black Writers Conference.

• 11421 • Voice of the Dispora, Founders Achievement Award, UCLA Extension Scholarships
Recognizes individuals who show promise and/or achievement. Awarded annually.

• 11422 •
International Bluegrass Music Association
Dan Hays, Exec.Dir.
2 Music Cir. S, Ste. 100
Nashville, TN 37203
Phone: (615)256-3222
Toll-Free: 888-438-4262
Fax: (615)256-0450
E-mail: info@ibma.org
Home Page: http://www.ibma.org

• 11423 • IBMA Award of Merit
To recognize lifetime contributions to the bluegrass music industry, especially by those in non-performing roles. Selection is by the IBMA Award of Merit Committee. Nominations should be made in writing by May 30. A certificate and citation are awarded annually at the IBMA World of Bluegrass in Louisville, Kentucky. Established in 1986.

• 11424 • International Bluegrass Music Awards
To honor people who are known as, and have achieved fame as, bluegrass music performers. Categories include: Entertainer of the Year; Female Vocalist of the Year; Male Vocalist of the Year; Song of the Year; Album of the Year; Instrumental Group of the Year; Vocal Group of the Year; Gospel Recorded Performance of the Year; Instrumental Album of the Year; Instrumental Performers of the Year; Recorded Event of the Year; Emerging Artist of the Year; Best Graphic Design - Recorded Project; Best Liner Notes - Recorded Project; Broadcast Personality of the Year; Print Media Personality of the Year. Awarded annually. Established in 1990.

• 11425 •
International Board of Environmental Medicine
Dr. Kalpana Patel, Pres.
65 Wehrle Dr.
Cheektowaga, NY 14225
Phone: (716)837-1320
Phone: (716)833-2214
Fax: (716)833-2244

• 11426 • President's Award
Recognizes exceptional abilities in the field of environmental medicine. Awarded annually.

• 11427 •
International Book Project
William L. Hixson, Exec.Dir.
Van Meter Bldg.
1440 Delaware Ave.
Lexington, KY 40505
Phone: (859)254-6771
Toll-Free: 888-999-BOOK
Fax: (859)253-2293
E-mail: director@intlbookproject.org
Home Page: http://www.intlbookproject.org/

• 11428 • Harriet VanMeter Humanitarian Award for International Relations
Fosters international relations and global friendships through humanitarian aid or outreach. Awarded annually.

• 11429 •
International Bottled Water Association
Joseph K. Doss, Pres./CEO
1700 Diagonal Rd., Ste. 650
Alexandria, VA 22314
Phone: (703)683-5213
Toll-Free: 800-WAT-ER11
Fax: (703)683-4074
E-mail: ibwainfo@bottledwater.org
Home Page: http://www.bottledwater.org

Formed by merger of: (1982) American Bottled Water Association; Council of Natural Waters.

• 11430 • Aqua Awards
For recognition of achievement in advertising and public relations in the bottled water industry. Current members of the Association are eligible. Awards are given in the following areas: Television, Radio, Print Outdoor, and Vehicle Advertising, Labels and Package Design, Point-of-Purchase Materials, Direct Mail and Literature, Public Relations, Yellow Pages, Websites, and Special Promotions. Awards are presented in three company size categories: small, medium, and large. Awards also recognize international and supplier members. Plaques are awarded annually.

• 11431 •
International Bowling Museum and Hall of Fame
111 Stadium Plz.
St. Louis, MO 63102
Phone: (314)231-6340
Fax: (314)231-4054
E-mail: hofm@bowlingmuseum.com
Home Page: http://www.bowlingmuseum.com

• 11432 • Bowling Hall of Fame and Museum
To recognize outstanding bowlers. The Bowling Hall of Fame and Museum is the showcase facility for the halls of fame of the American Bowling Congress, Bowling Proprietors' Association of America, Professional Women's Bowling Association, Professional Bowlers Association, Women's International Bowling Congress, and the World Bowling Writers. Formerly: National Bowling Hall of Fame and Museum.

• 11433 •
International Bridge, Tunnel and Turnpike Association
Patrick D. Jones, Exec.Dir.
1146 19th St. NW, No. 800
Washington, DC 20036
Phone: (202)659-4620
Fax: (202)659-0500
E-mail: info@ibtta.org
Home Page: http://www.IBTTA.org

• 11434 • Toll Innovation Awards
Recognizes advances in management of toll facilities. Awarded annually.

• 11435 •
International Buckskin Horse Association
Arthur T. Handel, Pres.
PO Box 268
Shelby, IN 46377
Phone: (219)552-1013
Fax: (219)552-1013
E-mail: ibha@netnitco.net
Home Page: http://www.ibha.net

• 11436 • Honor Roll
For recognition of outstanding horsemanship. Awards are given in 32 categories. The Annual Honor Roll winner in each category is based on the greatest number of points earned in that category. Youth are given Honor Roll recognition in 17 categories. Amateurs are given honor roll awards in five categories. In addition, a World Champion is recognized in one multi-judged competition based on averaging the scores of each judge at the IBHA World Championship Show. Open World Champion awards are given in 32 categories of competition for registered horses. Youth Activity World Champion awards are given in 17 categories of youth competition. Amateur World Champion awardees are given in seven categories. Horses, youth contestants,

and amateurs are awarded Register of Merit awards upon earning 15 points in competition as defined in the IBHA rule book. Horse, youth, and amateur IBHA Champion titles are awarded after 30 points in competition have been earned as defined in the IBHA rule book. Supreme Champion awards are given to horse, youth, and amateur contestants upon earning 90 points as defined in the IBHA rule book. Awards are presented at the Annual Convention.

• 11437 •
International Builders Exchange Executives
Brenda L. Romano, Exec.VP
4047 Naco Perrin, Ste. 201A
San Antonio, TX 78217
Phone: (210)653-3900
Toll-Free: 877-MYB-XNET
Fax: (210)653-3912
E-mail: info@bxnetwork.org
Home Page: http://www.bxnetwork.org

• 11438 • Dan Patrick Award
To recognize Association managers for their leadership in management and excellence in performance. Members of the Exchange are eligible. A brass bell engraved with a walnut gavel is awarded annually. Established in 1956.

• 11439 •
International Bulb Society
Robert M. Turley, Pres.
PO Box 336
Sanger, CA 93657-0336
Phone: (337)475-8812
Fax: (337)475-8815
E-mail: membership@bulbsociety.org
Home Page: http://www.bulbsociety.org
Formerly: (1990) American Plant Life Society.

• 11440 • Herbert Medal
To recognize an individual for outstanding achievement in plant breeding or any phase of work with plants that have bulbs, corms, rhizomes and tubers. Researchers, botanists, taxonomists, amateurs, professional growers and plant breeders and members of the Society are eligible. E-mail is for Society members only. A medal is awarded annually. Established in 1937 in honor of Rev. William Herbert, an early authority on the *Amaryllidaceae*.

• 11441 •
International Burn Foundation
PO Box 24386
Denver, CO 80224
Phone: (303)985-4065
Fax: (303)985-3119
E-mail: intlburnfndn@yahoo.com

• 11442 • Tanner-Vandeput-Boswick Prize for Burn Research
To recognize an individual for a substantial contribution to any aspect of burn care during their lifetime and to motivate individual investigators to do research, study, and undertake patient care, treatment, and other aspects of the problem of burn injuries. Deadline for application varies. A monetary award and a gold and diamond lapel pin are awarded every four years at the Quadrennial Congress on Burn Injuries of the International Society for Burn Injuries. The recipient does not have to be a member of the ISBI or a physician. Established in 1984 by Dr. J.C. Tanner, co-inventor with Dr. Jacques Vandeput of the Tanner-Vandeput Mesh Dermatome. Formerly: Tanner-Vandeput Prize for Burn Research.

• 11443 •
International Camaro Club
D.M. Crispino, VP
2001 Pittston Ave. Dept. HOL
Scranton, PA 18505
Phone: (570)585-4082
E-mail: vfitom@aol.com
Home Page: http://clubs.hemmings.com/icccamaroregistry

• 11444 • Best Indy 500 Camaro Award
To recognize Camaros at the Camaro Street Nationals East. All Camaro Pacers for 1967, 1969, and 1982, the 1969 Z10 Coupes, and the 1993 Indy Camaro pace cars are eligible. The winning car will be the photo cover for ICC's May/June *Keeping Pace Special Edition* of the club's publication, *In the Fast Lane*. Established in 1991.

• 11445 • Best Stock Z28 Award
To recognize a 1967-1977 1/2 Z28 Camaro at the Camaro Street Nationals East. Stock original or restored Z28 Camaros entered in the show by members or non-members are eligible. Awarded annually. Established in 1986.

• 11446 • Member of the Year Award
To recognize a member who helped the International Camaro Club grow during the preceding year. A large plaque is awarded at the annual Camaro Street Nationals East. Established in 1985.

• 11447 • Presidential Award
This, the highest honor any member of the ICC can receive, is given to recognize an individual for devoted service and dedication beyond the expectations of the club. Awarded when merited.

• 11448 • Don Yenko Memorial Award
To recognize the best high performance Camaro at the Camaro Street Nationals East. Awarded annually. Established in 1987.

• 11449 •
International Card Manufacturers Association
Jeffrey E. Barnhart, Co-Founder/Exec.Dir.
PO Box 727
Princeton Junction, NJ 08550
Phone: (609)799-4900
Fax: (609)799-7032
E-mail: info@icma.com
Home Page: http://www.icma.com

• 11450 • Elan Awards
Award of recognition for card manufacturing excellence and community service. Presented annually.

• 11451 • Spiritus Awards
Award of recognition for card manufacturing excellence and community service. Presented annually.

• 11452 •
The International Cat Association
Larry Paul, Pres.
PO Box 2684
Harlingen, TX 78551
Phone: (956)428-8046
Fax: (956)428-8047
E-mail: membership@ticaeo.com
Home Page: http://www.tica.org

• 11453 • Judge of the Year
For recognition of contributions to the association in terms of time, effort, and hard work. An individual must be a TICA judge in good standing to be voted on by the membership. A plaque is awarded annually at the convention held on Labor Day weekend. Established in 1980.

• 11454 •
International Catholic Stewardship Council
Matthew R. Paratore, Sec.Gen.
1275 K St. NW, Ste. 980
Washington, DC 20005-4006
Phone: (202)289-1093
Fax: (202)682-9018
E-mail: icsc@catholicstewardship.org
Home Page: http://www.catholicstewardship.org

• 11455 • Christian Stewardship Award
To recognize an individual who has given outstanding service on behalf of stewardship. A wooden plaque with bronze plate and a statue of St. Paul with an inscription are awarded annually. Established in 1975 in honor of Father Paul Kaletta, founder of the Council. Formerly: (1986) Father Paul Kaletta Award.

• 11456 • Bishop William G. Connare Award for Distinguished Service
To recognize a Catholic diocesan development director who has a long and outstanding service record. The annual award was established in 1992 in honor of Bishop William G. Connare, former Episcopal moderator known for his theological concepts of stewardship and resource development.

• 11457 •
International Center for Comparative Criminology
(Centre International de Criminologie Comparee)
Serge Brochu, Dir.
Universite de Montreal
Case Postale 6128, Succursale Centre-ville
Montreal, QC, Canada H3C 3J7
Phone: (514)343-7065
Fax: (514)343-2269
E-mail: cicc@umontreal.ca
Home Page: http://www.cicc.umontreal.ca

• 11458 • **Herman Mannheim Award**
For recognition of an outstanding contribution to comparative criminological and criminal justice research and policy. Selection is by nomination. A trophy is awarded quannually. Established in 1970 in honor of Herman Mannheim, professor of comparative criminology at the London School of Economics.

• 11459 •
International Center in New York
Carlton S. Mitchell, Exec.Dir.
50 W 23rd St., 7th Fl.
New York, NY 10010-5205
Phone: (212)255-9555
Fax: (212)255-0177
E-mail: icny@intlcenter.org
Home Page: http://www.intlcenter.org

• 11460 • **Distinguished Individual of Foreign Birth Award**
Annually, for recognition of distinguished achievement by foreign-born individuals in the fields of the arts, humanities, science, and business. Recipients, who must reside in the United States, are honored for their extraordinary accomplishments within American life of positive international effect. Funds are used to help support immigrants in their acclimation to New York and learning English. Established in 1981.

• 11461 •
International Center of Photography
Willis Hartshorn, Dir.
1113 Avenue of the Americas, 43rd St.
New York, NY 10036
Phone: (212)857-0000
Fax: (212)857-0090
E-mail: info@icp.org
Home Page: http://www.icp.org

• 11462 • **Infinity Awards**
To acknowledge excellence in the field of photography. Awards are presented in the following categories: Young Photographer - to a photographer, 30 years or younger; Writing - for writing on photography; Applied Photography - for photography in illustration or advertising during the previous year; Publication - for a photographic book published during the previous year; Art - for use of photography in mixed media by a visual artist; Photo Journalism - for photographic reportage in the previous year; Lifetime Achievement - for contributions in advancement of the photographic medium; and the Corsell Capa Award for distinguished work in photography. A trophy and travel expenses to New York, if appropriate, are awarded annually. No applications accepted. Winners are selected by an international nominating and selection committee. Established in 1984. No applications accepted. Winners are selected by an international nominating committee and selection committee.

• 11463 •
International Centre for Human Rights and Democratic Development
Jean-Louis Roy, Pres.
1001 de Maisonneuve Blvd. E, Ste. 1100
Montreal, QC, Canada H2L 4P9
Phone: (514)283-6073
Fax: (514)283-3792
E-mail: dd-rd@dd-rd.ca
Home Page: http://www.dd-rd.ca

• 11464 • **John Humphrey Freedom Award**
Awarded to a non-governmental organization or individual for exceptional contributions to promote and defend human rights and democracy. Preference is given to those who are working under difficult circumstances in reference to political and legal institutions. The person or organization must not be affiliated with any political party. A sum of $25,000 is associated with these awards.

• 11465 •
International Chiropractors Association
Ronald Hendrickson, Exec.Dir.
1110 N Glebe Rd., Ste. 650
Arlington, VA 22201
Phone: (703)528-5000
Toll-Free: 800-423-4690
Fax: (703)528-5023
E-mail: chiro@chiropractic.org
Home Page: http://www.chiropractic.org

• 11466 • **Chiropractor of the Year**
To recognize outstanding achievement within the chiropractic profession. Members of the Association are eligible. A plaque is awarded annually. Established in 1926.

• 11467 • **Scientific Researcher of the Year**
To recognize an individual for significant contributions in research to advance the practice of Chiropractic. Established in 1986.

• 11468 •
International Christian Studies Association
Dr. Oskar Gruenwald, Pres.
1065 Pine Bluff Dr.
Pasadena, CA 91107-1751
Phone: (626)351-0419
E-mail: og@jis3.org
Home Page: http://www.JIS3.org

• 11469 • **David Morsey Award**
Recognizes the best biblical exegesis in JIS. Awarded annually.

• 11470 • **Oleg Zinam Award**
Awarded annually for the best essay in JIS.

• 11471 •
International City/County Management Association
Robert O'Neill Jr., Exec.Dir.
777 N Capitol St. NE, Ste. 500
Washington, DC 20002-4201
Phone: (202)289-4262
Phone: (202)962-3680
Toll-Free: 800-745-8780
Fax: (202)962-3500
E-mail: roneill@icma.org
Home Page: http://icma.org

• 11472 • **Award for Local Government Education**
To recognize an individual who has enhanced the understanding of local government for primary and secondary students. Entries must be submitted by April 15.

• 11473 • **Award for Skill in Intergovernmental Relations**
To recognize a member who has demonstrated significant success in representing his or her local government's policies at the state and/or federal level in such a way that regulatory or mandate relief is granted or legislative change affected that enables the local jurisdiction to better serve its citizens. Entries must be submitted by April 15.

• 11474 • **Award for Career Development in Memory of L.P. Cookingham**
To recognize an administrator for a significant and measurable contribution to the development of new talent in professional local government management. Members of the Association are eligible. Entries must be submitted by April 15. A plaque is awarded annually. Established in 1969 in honor of L.P. Cookingham, who trained his staff, especially young interns. Formerly: Award for Career Development in Honor of L.P. Cookingham.

• 11475 • **Award for Excellence in Honor of Mark E. Keane**
To recognize a professional local government administrator who has enhanced the effectiveness of local elected officials and consistently initiated creative and successful programs in local government. Members of the ICMA are eligible for nomination or self-nomination. Entries must be submitted by April 15. Awarded annually. Established in 1984 to honor years of service to the profession by Mark E. Keane. The Outstanding Management Innovator Award, established in 1972, merged with the Mark E. Keane Award for Excellence in 1987. Formerly: (1986) Outstanding Management Innovator Award; (1986) Mark E. Keane Award for Excellence.

• 11476 • **International Award in Honor of Orin F. Nolting**
To recognize a local government and its chief administrator who have furthered the cause of

Awards are arranged in alphabetical order below their administering organizations

international understanding and cooperation by either successfully adopting a program from another country, becoming actively involved in exchanges, sister cities' activities, or educational/cultural activities with another country, or establishing a relationship with a local government from another country that has resulted in innovative, concrete management improvements. Any local government whose chief administrator is an ICMA Corporate Member is eligible. The local government from which the idea was transferred will also be recognized. Entries must be submitted by April 15. Established in 1982 in honor of Orin Nolting, who has made a lasting and continuing contribution in fostering the exchange of innovative ideas among local government administrators around the world.

• 11477 • Program Excellence Awards
To recognize local governments and chief administrators in recognition of their creative and successful programs. Two award categories are presented for communities whose population is greater than 20,000 or less than 20,000. The following Program Excellence Awards are presented: Award for Programs for the Disadvantaged recognizes a local government that has enhanced the quality of life for the disadvantaged, including the homeless and people with AIDS. Established in memory of Carolyn Keane; Public Safety Program Excellence Award recognizes a creative local government public safety program, including programs that emphasize police/community relations. Established in memory of William H. Hanseii, Sr.; Citizensip Education Program Excellence Award recognizes innovative programs designed to inform citizens about local government services and ways in which they can access those services. The award highlights programs created primarily to disseminate information to citizens rather than those developed to attract or retain business or provide information to the media; Citizen Involvement Program Excellence Award recognizes successful strategies designed to encourage or enhance citizen participation in local government. The award will concentrate on such areas as community consensus building and adult (nonstudent) citizenship education; and Program Excellence Award for Innovations in Local Government Management recognizes the local government that has successfully applied the concepts of reinventing, reengineering, TQM, customization, or another cutting-edge organizational tool. Applications may include, but are not limited to, programs involving intergovernmental relations. Any local government whose chief administrator is an ICMA Corporate Member is eligible. Local governments are limited to one Program Excellence Award nomination per year. Entries must be submitted by April 15. Awarded annually. Formerly: (1986) Management Innovation Award; Awards for Program Excellence.

• 11478 • In-Service Training Award in Memory of Clarence E. Ridley
To recognize a professional local government administrator who has developed and implemented a highly effective in-service training program for local government employees. Members of the Association are eligible for nomination or self-nomination. Entries must be submitted by April 15. A plaque is awarded annually. Established in 1969, the award was established in memory of Clarence E. Ridley, a pioneer in the field of local government management.

• 11479 • Academic Award in Memory of Stephen B. Sweeney
To recognize an academic leader of a college or university who has made a significant contribution to the education of students pursuing careers in local government, or who has consistently worked with successful university/college public management programs. Entries must be submitted by April 15. Awarded annually. Established in 1976 jointly with the Fels Alumni Association to honor the contributions of Stephen B. Sweeney, Dean Emeritus of the Fels Institute of State and Local Government, University of Pennsylvania.

• 11480 • Assistant Excellence in Leadership Award in Memory of Buford M. Watson, Jr.
To recognize the contributions of local government professionals who serve as assistants to chief local government administrators and department heads and who have made significant contributions towards excellence in leadership. ICMA members who are full-time assistants reporting to chief local government administrators or department heads with at least one year in current position (not including internships in conjunction with an academic program) are eligible for nomination or self-nomination. Entries must be submitted by April 15. The award was established to honor former ICMA president Buford M. Watson, Jr.

• 11481 • Workplace Diversity Professional Development Award
To recognize an administrator who has designed outstanding career development programs, policies, and/or practices specifically to assist minorities and women in local government. ICMA Corporate Members are eligible for nomination or self-nomination. Entries must be submitted by April 15. Established in 1990.

• 11482 •
International Civil Aviation Organization (Organisation de l'Aviation Civile Internationale)
Assad Kotaite, Pres.
999 Univ. St.
999 University St.
Montreal, QC, Canada H3C 5H7
Phone: (514)954-8219
Fax: (514)954-6077
E-mail: icaohq@icao.int
Home Page: http://www.icao.int

• 11483 • Edward Warner Award
This, the highest honor the international civil aviation community bestows, is given to recognize an individual or institution for outstanding contributions to the safe and orderly development of international civil aviation. Institutions of a non-commercial nature and individuals not connected with ICAO at the time of their candidacy are eligible. A special committee of the Organization's council selects the honoree from nominations made by any government, institution, or individual. A gold medal and a diploma are awarded annually. Established in 1958 in honor of Dr. Edward P. Warner, the first president of the International Civil Aviation Organizational Council, an American, an aviation pioneer, and an educator in aeronautical engineering.

• 11484 •
International Clarinet Association
Rose U. Sperrazza, Exec.Dir.
PO Box 5039
Wheaton, IL 60189-5039
Phone: (630)665-3602
Fax: (630)665-3848
E-mail: membership@clarinet.org
Home Page: http://www.clarinet.org

Formed by merger of: International Clarinet Society; Clarinet International.

• 11485 • High School Solo Competition
To encourage and reward young clarinetists. Musicians under the age of 19 may audition. The following prizes are awarded: first prize - a monetary prize of $1,000; second prize - a monetary prize of $750; and third prize a monetary prize of $500. Awarded annually at the convention.

• 11486 • Young Artists Competition
To encourage and reward young clarinetists. Musicians under the age of 27 may audition. The following prizes are awarded: first prize - a monetary prize of $2,000 and a new artist clarinet; second prize - a monetary award of $1,500; and third prize - a monetary award of $1,000. Awarded annually at the convention. Established around 1973.

• 11487 •
International College of Angiology
Denise M. Rossignol, Exec.Dir.
5 Daremy Ct.
Nesconset, NY 11767-1547
Phone: (631)366-1429
Fax: (631)366-3609
E-mail: denisemrossignol@cs.com
Home Page: http://www.intlcollegeofangiology.org

• 11488 • Young Investigator Award
Fosters young physicians and research fellows in the field of vascular medicine and surgery.

• 11489 •
International Commission of Jurists - Canadian Section (Commission Internationale de Juristes - Section Canadienne)
Patricia Whiting, Exec.Dir.
865 Carling Ave., Ste. 500
Ottawa, ON, Canada K1S 5S8
Phone: (613)237-2925
Fax: (613)237-0185
E-mail: patw@cba.org
Home Page: http://www.icjcanada.org

• 11490 • Hon. Walter S. Tarnopolsky Medal

For outstanding contribution in the field of human rights. A medal and honorarium are awarded annually.

• 11491 •
International Commission on Radiation Units and Measurements
Thomas Hobbs, Exec.Sec.
7910 Woodmont Ave., Ste. 400
Bethesda, MD 20814-3095
Phone: (301)657-2652
Fax: (301)907-8768
E-mail: icru@icru.org
Home Page: http://www.icru.org

• 11492 • ICRU - Gray Medal

For recognition of an outstanding contribution in one of the fields of science which is of special interest to the Commission. Nominations may be made by any person or organization by July 1. A silver medal is awarded once every two years. Established in 1967 in memory of Louis Harold Gray, former member and Vice-Chairman of the Commission.

• 11493 •
International Committee of Sports for the Deaf/DEAFLYMPICS
(Comite International des Sports des Sourds)
Dr. Donalda K. Ammons, Interim Pres./Sec.Gen.
7310 Grove Rd., Ste. 106
Frederick, MD 21704
Fax: (301)620-2990
E-mail: info@deaflympics.com
Home Page: http://www.deaflympics.com

• 11494 • CISS Medallions of Honor

For recognition of meritorious services to those who distinguished themselves in working for the International Committee of Sports for the Deaf. Gold, silver, and bronze medals are given during the congress held in connection with the Summer Games every four years. Established in 1949.

• 11495 • Rubens-Alcais Challenge

To recognize countries that have promoted exceptionally well sports for the deaf. Member countries of the CISS are eligible. Awarded biennially. Established in 1967.

• 11496 • Sportsman/Sportswoman of the Year

To recognize the best athletes and their phenomenal performances.

• 11497 •
International Communications Industries Association
Kevin Madden, VP
11242 Waples Mill Rd., Ste. 200
Fairfax, VA 22030-6079
Phone: (703)273-7200
Toll-Free: 800-659-7469
Fax: (703)278-8082
E-mail: membership@infocomm.org
Home Page: http://www.infocomm.org

Formerly: National Audio-Visual Association.

• 11498 • ICIA Distinguished Achievement Award

To recognize individuals and organizations for significant contributions to the communications industry. production or special project; Dealership of the Year - presented to a dealership that has developed and implemented a highly innovative, effective marketing program for professional communications products and services; Multimedia Innovator of the Year presented to an individual or organization that has demonstrated an innovative multimedia or interactive adaptation and whose work exemplifies an exceptional or unusual achievement in state-of-the-art presentation and communications methods or who has advanced the multimedia technology in a special way; Systems and Facilities Design - presented to a communications professional or company for designing academic setting; PETC (Professional Education & Training Committee) - presented to a person whose continued participation in education and training within the communications industries promotes the newest technologies and methods, provides methods to sucessfully compete in the global market, fosters professionalism within our trade and promotes the industry as an exciting career opportunity. second, and third prizes may be awarded in each category. Awards are presented during the Association's annual convention and trade show. Formerly: (2004) ICIA Excellence in the Communications Industry Achievement Awards.

• 11499 •
International Community Corrections Association
Peter Kinziger, Exec.Dir.
PO Box 1987
La Crosse, WI 54602-1987
Phone: (608)785-0200
Fax: (608)784-5335
E-mail: icca@execpc.com
Home Page: http://www.iccaweb.org

• 11500 • Margaret Mead Award

Recognizes contributions to field of community corrections. Awarded annually.

• 11501 •
International Conference of Building Officials
James Lee Witt, CEO
5360 Workman Mill Rd.
Whittier, CA 90601-2298
Phone: (562)699-0541
Phone: (562)699-0543
Toll-Free: 888-422-7233
Fax: (562)692-3853
E-mail: jwitt@iccsafe.org
Home Page: http://www.iccsafe.org

• 11502 • John Fies Award

To honor members of the building industry whose contributions exemplify the ideals and purposes of the ICBO. Nominations may be submitted. A plaque is awarded annually at the meeting in September. Established in 1977 in honor of John Fies, recognized throughout the building industry for his continued diligent efforts and dedication both in building code work and as a conscientious construction industry representative.

• 11503 • A. J. (Jack) Lund Award

For recognition of achievement, leadership, and contributions in educational services. Nominations may be submitted. A plaque is awarded when merited at the annual meeting in September. Established in 1984 in honor of A.J. (Jack) Lund who laid the foundation for ICBO's educational services.

• 11504 • Phil Roberts Award

To recognize outstanding building officials and to honor contributions by building officials to the code enforcement field. Nominations may be submitted. A plaque is presented annually at the meeting in September. Established in 1974 in memory of Phil Roberts, former president of ICBO and building official of Boise, Idaho.

• 11505 •
International Conference of Funeral Service Examining Boards
John D. Runsvold, Pres.
1885 Shelby Ln.
Fayetteville, AR 72704
Phone: (479)442-7076
Fax: (479)442-7090
E-mail: cfseb@cfseb.org
Home Page: http://www.cfseb.org

• 11506 • Award of Recognition

To recognize those individuals who have contributed to the continued efforts of funeral service education. Institution directors, state board representatives, funeral service organizations and funeral service educators are eligible. A plaque is awarded annually during the convention. Established in 1952.

• 11507 •
International Consortium of Investigative Journalists
Wendell Rawals, Dir.
% Center for Public Integrity
910 17th St. NW, Ste. 700
Washington, DC 20006
Phone: (202)466-1300
Home Page: http://www.publicintegrity.org/icij

• 11508 • **Award for Outstanding International Investigative Reporting**
Recognizes excellence in investigative journalism. Six copies of the entry, a submission letter, curriculum vitae and application form must be submitted. Published and broadcast reports are eligible. A $20,000 first prize and up to five $1000 prizes are awarded annually. Complete application details and forms are available at the above web site.

• 11509 •
International Council for Canadian Studies (Conseil International d Etudes Canadiennes)
Catherine Bastedo-Boileau, Exec.Dir.
75 Albert, Ste. 908
Ottawa, ON, Canada K1P 5E7
Phone: (613)789-7834
Phone: (613)789-7828
Fax: (613)789-7830
E-mail: c.bastedo@iccs-ciec.ca
Home Page: http://www.iccs-ciec.ca

• 11510 • **Governor General's International Award in International Studies**
Recognizes a scholar making an outstanding contribution to the field. Awarded annually.

• 11511 • **ICCS Certificate of Merit**
Recognizes individuals making exceptional contributions to the field. Awarded annually.

• 11512 •
International Council for Small Business
Susan G. Duffy, Exec. Administrator
The George Washington University
School of Business and Public Mgt.
2115 G St. NW, Ste. 403
Washington, DC 20052
Phone: (202)994-0704
Fax: (202)994-4930
E-mail: icsb@gwu.edu
Home Page: http://www.icsb.org

Formerly: National Council for Small Business Management Development.

• 11513 • **Wilford L. White Fellow**
To recognize a person for meritorious contributions to small business. A plaque is awarded annually. Established in 1977 in honor of Dr. Wilford L. White, founder of the Council. 128285

• 11514 •
International Council of Shopping Centers
Michael P. Kercheval, Pres./CEO
1221 Avenue of the Americas, 41st Fl.
New York, NY 10020-1099
Phone: (646)728-3800
Fax: (732)694-1755
E-mail: icsc@icsc.org
Home Page: http://www.icsc.org

• 11515 • **European Awards Program**
To recognize significant accomplishments among ICSC's European members for innovation in shopping center projects. Awardees are announced at the European Convention. Established in 1977.

• 11516 • **ICSC International Design and Development Awards**
For dissemination of information on outstanding shopping center projects so that others may benefit from the experiences of their colleagues. Awards are given to ICSC developer members in the following categories: renovation or expansion of existing project and innovative design and construction. Applications are accepted. Judging is limited to the material presented and is based on the creativity and justification of the approaches taken, as well as the final results. A trophy is presented to each of the winners annually at the May Convention. Established in 1977. Formerly: ICSC Annual Awards.

• 11517 • **MAXI Awards Program**
To recognize and honor the shopping industry's outstanding examples of shopping center marketing excellence. Any shopping center may submit marketing efforts implemented during the previous year by July 6. MAXI and Merit Awards are presented in the following categories: community relations/service, sales promotion/merchandising event, consumer advertising, customer service, grand opening, expansion and renovation, retailer motivation/development, corporate marketing, single-property development, and overall marketing campaign. A trophy is awarded annually at the fall convention. Established in 1972. Additional information is available from JoAnn Laut.

• 11518 •
International Council of the National Academy of Television Arts and Sciences
George Leclere, Exec.Dir.
888 7th St., 5th Fl.
New York, NY 10019
Phone: (212)489-6969
Fax: (212)489-6557
E-mail: info@iemmys.tv
Home Page: http://www.iemmys.tv

• 11519 • **International Emmy Award**
To recognize broadcast or producing organizations outside the United States for excellence in programs telecast during the previous year. Awards are presented in six categories: Drama, Documentary, Arts Documentary, Performing Arts, Popular Arts, and Children and Young People. A Golden Emmy statuette is awarded annually. In addition, two special awards are presented when merited: Directorate Award - to an organization, or individual in management, administration, engineering, news, programming, and/or international relations for outstanding contributions, over a period of time, to the arts and sciences of international television; and Founders Award - to celebrate the accomplishments of an individual whose work is recognized throughout the world as embodying the vision of the founders of the International Council, crossing cultural boundaries to touch our common humanity. This "Emmy" is primarily an award for creative achievement. Established in 1963.

• 11520 •
International Council on Education for Teaching
Dr. Darrell Bloom, Exec.Dir.
1000 Capitol Dr.
Wheeling, IL 60090-7201
Phone: (847)465-0191
Toll-Free: 800-443-5522
Fax: (847)465-5617
E-mail: icet@nl.edu
Home Page: http://myclass.nl.edu/icet

• 11521 • **Distinguished Fellow Award**
To recognize outstanding leadership in international education. The title of Distinguished Fellow of the International Council on Education for Teaching, honoris causa, is conferred upon individuals who have made significant achievements in their national arenas and substantial contributions to international education which have been emulated or adopted by the education community worldwide. The award ceremony takes place during the annual World Assembly and award recipients receive a certificate. Established in 1982 by the ICET Board of Directors.

• 11522 •
International Council on Hotel, Restaurant and Institutional Education
Kathy McCarty, EVP and CEO
2810 N Parham Rd., Ste. 230
Richmond, VA 23294
Phone: (804)346-4800
Fax: (804)346-5009
E-mail: webmaster@chrie.org
Home Page: http://www.chrie.org

• 11523 • **Chef Herman Breithaupt Award**
To recognize outstanding achievement and contributions to foodservice education. Members who are chef-educators directly involved in food service education or administration may be nominated. Awarded annually. Established in 1980 to honor Chef Herman Breithaupt, a pioneer chef-educator.

• 11524 • **CHRIE Industry Recognition Award**
To recognize members of the hospitality and tourism industry for their ongoing commitment and efforts toward the advancement of hospitality and tourism education as a discipline. Individual industry executives, companies, and related

organizations are eligible. Nominations must be submitted by February 14.

• 11525 • John Wiley & Sons Award for Innovation in Teaching

To recognize a member of the Council for the implementation of innovative, creative, and effective teaching techniques. Examples of innovative teaching include course structure, teaching methods and delivery, eliciting student involvement, and methods for achieving learning outcomes. Nomination deadline is February 14. A monetary award of $1,500 and a plaque are awarded annually. Formerly: Van Nostrand Reinhold Award for Innovation in Teaching.

• 11526 • Howard B. Meek Award

To recognize significant and innovative lifetime achievement by an individual in hospitality industry education. This, the highest honor awarded to members, is presented to an individual actively engaged in teaching or administering educational programs that prepare students for careers in the hotel, restaurant, and institutional industry. The deadline for nominations is February 14. A trophy is awarded annually. Established in 1971 to honor Howard B. Meek, a pioneer in American hospitality education.

• 11527 • Outstanding Paper Awards

For recognition of outstanding papers selected for presentation at the conference.

• 11528 • Van Nostrand Reinhold Research Award

To recognize superior original published research in the hospitality industry. Members of CHRIE are eligible. A monetary award of $2,000 is presented annually. Established in 1989.

• 11529 • Stevenson Fletcher Achievement Award

To recognize individual educators for current contributions of ideas, methods, or programs that are advancing teaching, learning, or practice in the field of hospitality and tourism education. Formerly called the International CHRIE Achievement Award it was renamed in 1994 to honor Stevenson W. Fletcher, former program head of Hotel, Restaurant and Travel Administration at the University of Massachusetts-Amherst. Recipients must demonstrate exceptional professional ability and commitment through service to CHRIE and the industry. Members of CHRIE are eligible. A monetary award of $5,000 is presented. The award recipient receives $2,500, and the recipient's academic institution is also presented $2,500 to be used for special projects within the institution's hospitality and tourism education program. Established in 1981. Sponsored by Marriott.

• 11530 • John Wiley & Sons Award

To recognize an individual for lifetime contributions to outstanding scholarship and research in hospitality and tourism. The recipient must also have shown leadership in a specialized field of study. A monetary award of $1,500 and a plaque are presented annually. Sponsored by John Wiley & Sons.

• 11531 •
International Cryogenic Materials Conference
Don Gubser, Chm.
901 Front St., Ste. 130
Louisville, CO 80027
Phone: (303)499-2299
Fax: (303)499-2599
E-mail: cecicmc05@centennialconferences.com
Home Page: http://www.cec-icmc.org

• 11532 • Best Paper Award

To recognize outstanding papers on superconductors and structural materials. Authors must write and present papers at the conference held every other year in the United States. One award is given in each category. A separate award is given for the best paper by a student on any conference topic. A plaque is awarded biennially. Established in 1974.

• 11533 •
International Customer Service Association
Kimberly Mims, Pres.
401 N Michigan Ave.
Chicago, IL 60611
Phone: (312)321-6800
Toll-Free: 800-360-ICSA
Fax: (312)245-1084
E-mail: icsa@smithbucklin.com
Home Page: http://www.icsa.com

• 11534 • ICSA Award of Excellence

To recognize excellence in customer service. Awards honoring two outstanding companies that display consistent customer service excellence through all levels of their companies are presented annually in two categories: manufacturing and non-manufacturing. Established in 1983.

• 11535 •
International Dairy Foods Association
Cindy Cavallo, Membership Mgr.
1250 H St. NW, Ste. 900
Washington, DC 20005
Phone: (202)737-4332
Fax: (202)331-7820
E-mail: membership@idfa.org
Home Page: http://www.idfa.org

• 11536 • Achieving Excellence Award

For recognition of creative achievement in advertising and promotion of dairy foods in two categories: product-type (cheese, milk, ice cream, etc.) and media type (television, radio, FSI, etc.). Ads or promotions produced and presented during the previous two-year period may be submitted by September 7. A crystal trophy is awarded biennially at the International Dairy Show. Established in 1985.

• 11537 •
International Desalination Association
Patricia A. Burke, Sec.Gen.
PO Box 387
Topsfield, MA 01983
Phone: (978)887-0410
Fax: (978)887-0411
E-mail: info@idadesal.org
Home Page: http://www.idadesal.org

• 11538 • Dr. Robert O. Vernon Memorial Lecture Award

To recognize a member of a water supply agency for a significant contribution to water supply improvement. The honoree is invited to present a paper at the Association's annual conference and receives travel expenses. Established in 1964.

• 11539 • Water Quality Improvement Man of the Year Award

To honor an individual for outstanding contribution to the improvement of water supplies through desalting, wastewater reclamation or other water sciences. A certificate is presented during the Association's annual conference, usually in July. Established in 1974.

• 11540 •
International Documentary Association
Sandra J. Ruch, Exec.Dir.
1201 W 5th St., Ste. M320
Los Angeles, CA 90017
Phone: (213)534-3600
Fax: (213)534-3610
E-mail: admin@documentary.org
Home Page: http://www.documentary.org

• 11541 • International Documentary Association Achievement Awards

To recognize distinguished achievement in nonfiction film and videos. Any nonfiction work completed, or having primary release or telecast between January 1 and April 30 of the previous year is eligible for the Distinguished Documentary Achievement Awards categories (Features, Short, Limited Series, or Strand Program) as well as consideration for the ABCNews VideoSource Award for The Best Use of News Footage in a Documentary (Prize: $2,000 honorarium and $2,000 worth of research time at the ABCNews VideoSource facility in New York) and/or the Pare Lorentz Award (Prize: $2,500 honorarium). Winners are honored at the 13th Annual IDA Awards Gala on October 31. Deadline if June 16. Sponsored by the Eastman Kodak Company.

• 11542 • David L. Wolper Student Documentary Achievement Award

To recognize exceptional achievement in nonfiction film and video at the university level. Films and videos must be produced by registered students and completed between January 1 and April 30. A monetary award of $1,000 honorarium presented annually. In addition, Eastman Kodak contributes a certificate worth $1,000 toward the purchase of Kodak film.

• 11543 •
International Double Reed Society
Norma R. Hooks, Exec.Sec.-Treas.
2423 Lawndale Rd.
Finksburg, MD 21048-1401
Phone: (410)871-0658
Fax: (410)871-0659
E-mail: norma4idrs@verizon.net
Home Page: http://www.idrs.org

• 11544 • **Fernand Gillet Performance Competition**
To recognize outstanding performers of double reed instruments. Individuals who have not reached their 31st birthday before the date of the final round of the competition are eligible to enter. Previous winners of the first prize are not eligible. The competition alternates annually between oboists and bassoonists. Monetary awards of $8,000 for first place and $3,000 for second place are presented. Established in 1981 to honor Fernand Gillet, the late master oboist and honorary member of IDRS. Formerly: Fernand Gillet Young Artist Performance Competition.

• 11545 • **Honorary Life Member**
To provide recognition for outstanding contributions to the Double Reeds area. Nominations are accepted; nominees must be retired. Free membership and an honorary award are presented at the convention. Established in 1977.

• 11546 •
International Downtown Association
Dave Feehan, Pres.
1250 H St. NW, 10th Fl.
Washington, DC 20005
Phone: (202)393-6801
Fax: (202)393-6869
E-mail: question@ida-downtown.org
Home Page: http://www.ida-downtown.org

Formerly: International Downtown Executive Association.

• 11547 • **IDA Downtown Achievement Awards**
To recognize exemplary projects, strategies, and events in and for downtown revitalization, especially those with wide transferability. The awards provide a forum to highlight local downtown efforts and accomplishments within the broader context of the downtown revitalization movement. Awards are presented in the following categories: business recruitment and retention; downtown leadership and management; economic development; individual achievement; marketing and communications; organization communications; planning; public space; social issues; special events and promotions; sustainable development and transportation. tries should illustrate projects that have used innovations in transportation, access or parking to enhance downtown and increase user friendliness or economic viability. Projects may involve design improvements, facilities, management or marketing, or other activities that improve access. Members of IDA and other interested organizations and individuals are eligible. The deadline for submission of entries and projects that have been fully implemented during the previous year is July 15. A plaque, considerable publicity, and a possible feature in IDA's monthly publication are awarded annually. In addition, a merit award and a jury citation may also be presented. Established in 1978.

• 11548 •
International Dyslexia Association
Megan Cohen, Exec.Dir.
Chester Bldg., Ste. 382
8600 LaSalle Rd.
Baltimore, MD 21286-2044
Phone: (410)296-0232
Toll-Free: 800-ABC-D123
Fax: (410)321-5069
E-mail: member@interdys.org
Home Page: http://www.interdys.org

• 11549 • **Samuel T. Orton Award**
Given in recognition of an individual for outstanding contributions to the study, treatment, and prevention of developmental dyslexia. Recipients must: have made a vital contribution to our scientific understanding of dyslexia; significantly enhanced and advanced our capacity to successfully intervene and assist people with dyslexia; expanded national and international awareness of dyslexia, or demonstrated unusual competence and dedication in service for people with dyslexia. A finely printed parchment is awarded at the annual conference, usually in November. Awarded to one or more recipients each year. Established in 1966.

• 11550 •
The International Economy
Angela Wilkes, Mng. Ed.
888 16th St., Ste. 740
Washington, DC 20006
Phone: (202)861-0791
Fax: (202)861-0790
E-mail: internationaleconomy@att.net
Home Page: http://www.international-economy.com

• 11551 • **Policymaker of the Year**
For recognition of an outstanding policymaker in international trade or finance. The selection is made by a survey among international financial leaders. A plaque is awarded annually at the IMF/World Bank Meeting. Established in 1988.

• 11552 •
International Electrical Testing Association
Dr. Mary R. Jordan, Exec.Dir.
PO Box 687
106 Stone St.
Morrison, CO 80465-0687
Phone: (303)697-8441
Toll-Free: 888-300-NETA
Fax: (303)697-8431
E-mail: neta@netaworld.net
Home Page: http://www.netaworld.org

Formerly: (1985) National Electrical Testing Association.

• 11553 • **Man of the Year**
To recognize an individual for outstanding contributions to the electrical testing industry and the Association. A plaque and recognition in the technical journal are awarded annually at the technical conference. Established in 1980.

• 11554 •
International Embryo Transfer Society
Matthew Wheeler PhD, Pres.
1111 N Dunlap Ave.
Savoy, IL 61874
Phone: (217)356-3182
Phone: (217)398-4697
Fax: (217)398-4119
E-mail: iets@assochq.org
Home Page: http://www.iets.org

• 11555 • **Pioneer Award for Milestones**
To recognize milestones in embryo transfer research or application. Pioneering achievements, as determined by the awards committee through a search of the literature, are eligible. A medal, designed by Lois Etherington Betteridge, and lifetime honorary membership in IETS are awarded annually at the Conference. Established in 1982. Additional information is available from Sarah Seidel, 3101 Arrowhead Road, LaPork, CO 80535, phone: (303) 482-1088.

• 11556 • **Student Competition**
For recognition of the best abstract, oral and poster presentation of research at the Annual Conference. Awarded annually at the Convention. Established in 1982.

• 11557 •
International Executive Service Corps
Spencer King, Pres./CEO
901 15th St. NW, Ste. 1010
Washington, DC 20005
Phone: (202)326-0280
Toll-Free: 800-243-4372
Fax: (202)326-0289
E-mail: iesc@iesc.org
Home Page: http://www.iesc.org

• 11558 • **Frank Pace Award**
Recognizes an Outstanding Project of the Year. Awarded annually.

• 11559 •
International Facility Management Association
Joseph M. Dawson, Chm.
1 E Greenway Plz., Ste. 1100
Houston, TX 77046-0194
Phone: (713)623-4362
Fax: (713)623-6124
E-mail: ifma@ifma.org
Home Page: http://www.ifma.org

• 11560 • **Affiliate Corporation Award**
To recognize the firm of the Affiliate member of IFMA for its voluntary contribution of monetary or nonmonetary resources given for the purpose of advancing the science of facilities manage-

ment at the international or at the chapter level. Contributions may be in the form of providing space or audiovisual aids, making a presentation on professional services, sponsoring educational, research or social programs and providing technical assistance to member groups. Winners are featured in the *FMA News.*

• 11561 • Allied Corporation Award
To recognize the firm of the Allied member of IFMA for its voluntary contribution of monetary or nonmonetary resources given for the purpose of advancing the science of facilities management at either the international or local chapter level. Contributions may be in the form of providing space or audiovisual aids, making a presentation on equipment or funishings, sponsoring educational, research or social programs and providing technical assistance to member groups. Winners are featured in the *FMA News.*

• 11562 • Chapter Award for Excellence in Educational Programming
No further information was provided for this edition.

• 11563 • Chapter Award for Excellence in Membership Marketing
To recognize chapters for membership marketing. Awarded annually.

• 11564 • Chapter Award for Excellence in Newsletter Publishing
To recognize chapters for outstanding newsletters. Awarded annually.

• 11565 • Chapter of the Year Award
To recognize the most outstanding chapter overall. Awarded annually.

• 11566 • Council of the Year Award
To provide recognition to the IFMA council that has excelled in newsletter publishing, membership marketing and educational programming. Award is given to the council that has best provided networking opportunities and contributed to the education and information exchange of its members. The council will be reviewed on fiscal responsibility and the ability to communicate industry specific information to the membership. The council must be in good standing with IFMA. Award will be given to one council annually.

• 11567 • Distinguished Author Award
To recognize an individual for an outstanding paper, book or research report on a topic specifically directed to the science of facilities management. Current work relating to authorship of a paper, book, research or abstract is also recognized. Facility management professionals, educators, researchers or professionals in other disciplines who have been associated in the field of facilities and their management for at least five years are eligible. Winners are featured in the *FMA News.*

• 11568 • Distinguished Member Award
This, the highest recognition that IFMA gives its members, is given to recognize facility management executives for outstanding contributions to IFMA and the professionalism of facility management. Respected leaders, men and women who ably contribute to IFMA and its affiliated chapters, are considered. Full-time facility management executives employed in their present position for at least one year, and who are professional or associate members of IFMA for at least the past three years are eligible. Nominations may be submitted. Awards are presented at the annual conference in October. Winners are also profiled in *FMA News.* Established in 1983.

• 11569 • Educator Award
To recognize an individual(s) who has been engaged in the process of teaching subjects related to facilities management in an accredited college, university or institute. Specific academic institutions or full-time faculty members of academic institutions are eligible. Winners are featured in the *FMA News.*

• 11570 • Facility Management Achievement Award
To encourage professional development in the field of facility management. This award enables one to share their organization's most successful facility management ideas and programs with one's peers. Any management or technically oriented project is eligible, and is judged based on the merit of the idea or project and its value to the organization. Entries are divided according to staff size and facility size. All professional and associate members of IFMA may take part in the Facility Management Achievement Award program. Awards are presented at the annual conference in October. Winners are also profiled in *FMA News.* Established in 1985.

• 11571 • Golden Circles Award
To recognize a company for outstanding accomplishments in creating and managing humane and effective work environments that integrate the needs of managment with the needs of people in the workplace. Nominees may be corporations, government, health care or educational institutions whose in-house facility management executive is a Professional member in good standing of IFMA. Entries will be judged on the basis of the company's integrated approach to its facility management strategy, structure, policies, programs, objectives, values and behavior. Winners are featured in the *FMA News.*

• 11572 • Student Chapter of the Year Award
To recognize the most outstanding student chapter overall. Awarded annually.

• 11573 •
International Family Recreation Association
K. W. Stephens, Exec. Officer
PO Box 520
Gonzalez, FL 32560-0520
Phone: (850)937-8354
Toll-Free: 800-281-9186
Fax: (850)937-8356
E-mail: rltresource@spydee.net

• 11574 • Member of the Year Award
To recognize an individual member or commercial member who has made the greatest contribution of time or talent to the field of recreation. Members may make nominations but the nominee is not required to be a member of the association. A plaque is awarded annually at the convention. Established in 1982.

• 11575 •
International Fan Club Organization
Kay Johnson, Pres.
PO Box 40328
Nashville, TN 37204-0328
Phone: (615)371-9596
Fax: (615)371-9597
E-mail: 4info@ifco.org
Home Page: http://www.ifco.org

• 11576 • IFCO Tex Ritter Award
The legendary singer and actor, Tex Ritter was a friend, supporter and long-time member of IFCO. Following his death (January 2, 1974), we collaborated with his widow, Dorothy to establish the "IFCO Tex Ritter Award." We determined that recipients would be recognized for their contributions to country music, the music community,and fans everywhere. A plaque of dark stained wood with an engraved gold plate is awarded to each honoree.

• 11577 •
International Federation of Air Traffic Controllers' Associations
(Federation Internationale des Associations de Controleurs du Trafic Aerien)
Ms. Tatiana Iavorskaia, Off.Mgr.
1255 University St., Ste. 408
Montreal, QC, Canada H3B 3B6
Phone: (514)866-7040
Fax: (514)866-7612
E-mail: office@ifatca.org
Home Page: http://www.ifatca.org

• 11578 • IFATCA Award of Merit
Annual award of recognition. Open only to Association members.

• 11579 •
International Federation of Biomedical Laboratory Science
(Association Internationale des Technologistes de Laboratoire Medical)
Phyllis McColl, Off.Mgr.
PO Box 2830, LCD 1
Hamilton, ON, Canada L8N 3N8
Phone: (905)528-8642
Fax: (905)528-4968
E-mail: office@ifbls.org
Home Page: http://www.ifbls.org

• 11580 • **bioMerieux Award**
To encourage work in research and experimentation in all areas of clinical diagnosis: microbiology, clinical chemistry, coagulation, immunology, or radioimmunology. Members of a constituent member society of IAMLT are eligible. A monetary award of 10,000 French francs is awarded. The deadline for applications is November 1.

• 11581 • **Dade International Award**
To recognize outstanding services to medical laboratory technology.

• 11582 • **Evergreen Latex Award**
To stimulate and encourage medical laboratory science work. Applicants must have evidence of active membership of a constituent member society of IAMLT. Deadline is December 1. Prize consists of $1,000 U.S. dollars and may be divided.

• 11583 • **Good Poster Award**
To stimulate and encourage work in poster presentation. Candidates must have evidence of active membership of a constituent member society of IAMLT. The prize consists of a certificate signed by the IAMLT president and the Chairperson of the Organizing Committee of the Congress.

• 11584 • **IAMLT Award for Outstanding Services to Medical Laboratory Technology**
To recognize outstanding services to medical laboratory technology. Candidates must be a member of one the national associations for at least five years, be occupied full-time in the medical laboratory science field, have proper professional qualifications, and be active in a professional organization.

• 11585 • **IAMLT General Award**
To stimulate and encourage work in research and experimentation in hematology and to develop the communication of new methods and the presentation of articles. Applicant must have evidence of active membership of a constituent member society of IAMLT. Deadline is December 1. A 400,000 Y prize is awarded and may be divided.

• 11586 • **IAMLT Scholarship**
To further the education/training of qualified technologists who are active members of IAMLT.

• 11587 • **Nordic Award**
To enable an official representative from a constituent society of IAMLT with economical difficulties to attend the General Assembly of Delegates. Applicant must be officially appointed by his or her society to be the chief delegate at the Assembly. The deadline for applications is in November. A monetary prize of 20,000 Swedish crowns is awarded annually.

• 11588 • **Past President's Award**
To recognize outstanding services to international cooperation between medical laboratory technologists within IAMLT. An inscribed silver bowl and a diploma are awarded.

• 11589 • **Sysmex Award**
To encourage work in research and experimentation in hematology and to develop the communication of new methods and the presentation of articles covering this area of study.

• 11590 •
International Federation of Bodybuilders
(Federation Internationale des Culturistes)
Ben Weider, Pres.
2875 Bates Rd.
Montreal, QC, Canada H3S 1B7
Phone: (514)731-3783
Fax: (514)731-7082
E-mail: info@ifbb.com
Home Page: http://www.ifbb.com

• 11591 • **Special Medals for Fitness Achievement**
Award of recognition. For fitness and physical development. Awarded periodically.

• 11592 •
International Federation of Festival Organizations
(F.I.D.O.F. - Federation Internationale des Organisations de Festivals)
Prof. Armando Moreno, Pres.
4230 Stansbury Ave., Ste. 105
Sherman Oaks, CA 91423
Phone: (818)789-7596
Fax: (818)784-9141
E-mail: morenfidof@aol.com
Home Page: http://www.morenofidof.org

Formerly: (2004) International Federation of Festival Organizations.

• 11593 • **Distant Accords Awards**
For recognition of excellence in festival production. What the Oscar is to the motion picture industry or the Grammy is to the record industry, the Distant Accords Awards are to the festivals and cultural events of the world. Festival organizers, organizations, and artists from around the world who support festivals as a means for a better understanding among nations, people, and generations by the exchange of cultural heritage and cooperation are eligible. A diploma is awarded annually. Established in 1989.

• 11594 • **For Peace and Friendship International Song Contest**
Established in 1996 and proclaimed at the Traditional Annual Assembly in Cannes, France, for excellence in Festival Production, Hospitality, Quality of Artistic Values and promoting FIDOF's Basic aim: "Peace and Friendship through Music and Art."

• 11595 • **Medal for Peace and Friendship through Music and Arts**
To recognize the contribution in supporting the festival movement and promotion of international exchange of cultural activities world-wide. Established 1987.

• 11596 •
International Federation of Leather Guilds
Ernie Wayman, Exec.Dir.
% Ernie Wayman, Exec.Dir.
3117 Babette Dr.
Southport, IN 46227
Phone: (317)787-2586
E-mail: ernie@thewaymans.com
Home Page: http://www.ifolg.org

• 11597 • **Hall of Fame Award**
To recognize outstanding service to the Federation. A plaque is awarded when warranted. Established in 1989.

• 11598 •
International Federation of Operational Research Societies
(Federation International des Societes de Recherche Operationnelle)
Prof. Thomas Magnanti, Pres.
School of Engineering
Massachusetts Inst. of Technology
77 Massachusetts Ave.
Cambridge, MA 02139-4307
Phone: (617)253-6604
Fax: (617)253-8549
E-mail: magnanti@mit.edu
Home Page: http://www.ifors.org

• 11599 • **EURO Golden Medal**
To recognize a prominent person or institution, either for a remarkable role played in the promotion of operational research in Europe, or for an outstanding contribution to the operational research science. A medal is awarded. Established by the Association of European Operational Research Societies within IFORS.

• 11600 • **Operational Research Development Prize**
To recognize the best paper on a developing country problem. The paper must be presented at the triennial world conference.

• 11601 •
International Federation of Ophthalmological Societies
Bruce E. Spivey MD, Sec.Gen.
945 Green St.
San Francisco, CA 94133
Phone: (415)409-8410
Phone: (415)409-8411
Toll-Free: 888-611-1402
Fax: (415)409-8400
E-mail: bruce@spivey.org
Home Page: http://www.icoph.org

• 11602 • Duke-Elder Award
Recognizes special contributions to ophthalmology. A medal is awarded quardrennially.

• 11603 • Jules Francois Award
Award if recognition. A medal is awarded quardennially.

• 11604 • Gonin Award
Recognizes special contributions to ophthalmology. A medal is awarded quadrennially.

• 11605 •
International Federation of Translators
(Federation Internationale des Traducteurs)
Miriam Lee, Sec.Gen.
2021 Ave. Union, Bur. 1108
Montreal, QC, Canada H3A 2S9
Phone: (514)845-0413
Fax: (514)845-9903
E-mail: info@fit-ift.org
Home Page: http://www.fit-ift.org

• 11606 • Pierre Francois Caille Memorial Medal
(Medaille Pierre Francois Caille)
For recognition of outstanding services to the translating profession. Members of the Federation may propose a member for consideration three months before the FIT Congress. A medal and a diploma are awarded every three or four years at the FIT Congress. Established in 1981 in honor of Pierre Francois Caille, founder of FIT in 1953 in France, and a long time president.

• 11607 • FIT - Translation Prize
(Prix FIT - de la Traduction)
For recognition of a literary and a non-literary translation that demonstrates an outstanding contribution to improving the quality of translation. Members of the Federation may propose a member for consideration six months prior to the opening of the FIT Congress. A monetary prize and a diploma are awarded every three years at the FIT Congress. Established in 1970 by Zlatko Gorjan, FIT president. Previously sponsored by Carl-Bertil Nathhorst-Stiftelser, Stockholm. Formerly: FIT C. B. Nathhorst Translation Prize.

• 11608 • FIT Astrid Lindgren Translation Prize
(Prix FIT de la Traduction Astrid Lindgren)
To promote the translation of a work written for children. Members of the Federation may propose a member for consideration six months prior to the opening of a FIT Congress. A monetary prize and a diploma are awarded at the FIT Congress every three or four years. Established in 1981 by Zygm. Stoberski of Poland in honor of Astrid Lindgren, an author of children's books. Sponsored by Astrid Lindgren of Stockholm.

• 11609 •
International Federation of Vexillological Associations
(Federation internationale de associations vexillologiques)
Mr. Charles Spain Jr., Sec.-Gen.
504 Branard St.
Houston, TX 77006-5018
Phone: (713)529-2545
Phone: (713)655-2742
Fax: (713)752-2304
E-mail: sec.gen@fiav.org

• 11610 • Laureate of the Federation
To honor individuals who have made outstanding contributions to vexillology (the study of flag history and symbolism). Selected by vote of the genearl assembly. A plaque is awarded when merited at the Congress of Vexillology. Established in 1969.

• 11611 • Vexillon
To recognize the individual or individuals who, during the preceding two years, have made the most important contribution to vexillology (the study of flags and flag history and symbolism.) Selected by the vote of the FIAV board. A plaque is awarded biennially at the International Congress of Vexillology. Established in 1989.

• 11612 •
International Festival of Films on Art
(Festival International du Film sur l'Art Montreal)
Rene Rozon, Dir.
640 Saint-Paul St. W, Ste. 406
Montreal, QC, Canada H3C 1L9
Phone: (514)874-1637
Fax: (514)874-9929
E-mail: info@artfifa.com
Home Page: http://www.artfifa.com

• 11613 • Montreal International Festival of Films on Art
(Festival International du Film sur l'Art Montreal)
For recognition of outstanding films and videos on art, including painting, sculpture, architecture, design, crafts, fashion, decorative arts, museology, restoration, photography, cinema, literature, dance, music, and theatre. The following prizes may be awarded: (1) Pratt and Whitney Canada Grand Prize; (2) Jury Award; (3) Best Canadian Film Award; (4) National Film Board of Canada Prize for Creativity; (5) Best Profile Award; (6) Best Essay Award. (7) Best Television Film Award; (8) Best Reportage Award; and (9) Best Educational Film Award. Certificates, film, and works of art are awarded annually. Established in 1981 by Rene Rozon.

• 11614 • Pratt & Whitney Canada Grand Prix
To recognize the best film on art. First place winners receive a diploma and a monetary prize of 3,000 francs; gold watches are awarded for second and third place. The festival is held every two years in October. Established in 1992.

• 11615 •
International Fire Buff Associates
Gary M. Heathcote, First VP
955 Regina Dr.
Baltimore, MD 21227
Phone: (410)242-8672
Fax: (410)242-4688
E-mail: gghcote@aol.com
Home Page: http://www.ifba.org

• 11616 • Fireman of the Year
To acknowledge an outstanding fireman serving in the fire department of the city where the group's annual convention is held. The fireman is chosen by the host city Fire Chief. An inscribed plaque and a $100 United States Savings Bond are awarded annually at the convention banquet. Established in 1971.

• 11617 • Henry N. Wilwers Fire Buff of the Year
To recognize an outstanding fire buff within the organization. An inscribed plaque is awarded annually at the convention banquet. Established in 1971.

• 11618 •
International Fire Photographers Association
David Sassaman, Membership Coor.
146 W Caracas Ave.
Hershey, PA 17033-1510
Phone: (717)533-4133
Fax: (610)683-7912
E-mail: membership@ifpaonline.com
Home Page: http://www.ifpaonline.com

• 11619 • Man of the Year
To provide recognition for service of outstanding quality to the Association. Current active members of the Association are eligible. A wall plaque is awarded when merited. Established in 1974 in memory of Ralph E. Fox.

• 11620 • Master Fire Photographer
To provide recognition for excellence in fire photography. Current active members of the Association who have completed various photographic and written requirements, and passed a review by the Admissions Board, are eligible. A certificate and an emblem are awarded annually when merited. Established in 1980.

• 11621 • William G. Nolan Service Award
To recognize an actively involved member for outstanding efforts on behalf of the IFPA. Established in 1983 in honor of Bill Nolan.

• 11622 •
International Fire Service Training Association
Susan F. Walker, Contact
Oklahoma State Univ.
930 N Willis
Stillwater, OK 74078-8045
Phone: (405)744-5723
Toll-Free: 800-654-4055
Fax: (405)744-8204
E-mail: royals@osufpp.org
Home Page: http://www.IFSTA.org

• 11623 • **Everett E. Hudiburg Award**
To honor individuals for significant contributions to the training of firefighters. Anyone who works in the fire service field is eligible to submit an application by March 1. Recipients are selected by secret ballot of the Executive Board. A plaque is awarded annually at the Validation Conference in July. Established in 1972 in memory of Everett E. Hudiburg, a past editor.

• 11624 •
International Flat Earth Research Society
Charles K. Johnson, Pres.
PO Box 2533
Lancaster, CA 93539
Phone: (805)727-1635

Formerly: (1984) International Flat Earth Research Society.

• 11625 • **Honorary Member**
To encourage individuals to know that they do not have to go along with a program and don't have to have "professional" advice in any field. (Self-reliance is a top virtue.) Individuals who have demonstrated common sense and natural logic in doing a good work that benefits others or self and who have gone against the "herd" are eligible. A Certificate of Membership is awarded when the Society is made aware of a deserving individual. Established in 1986 by Charles K. Johnson in honor of Samuel Shenton and Lillian Shenton who headed the Society International from 1943 to 1971 in Dover, England. Formerly: (1986) Seeker of the Truth.

• 11626 •
International Fluid Power Society
Clayton Fryer, Pres.
PO Box 1420
Cherry Hill, NJ 08034-0054
Toll-Free: 800-303-8520
Fax: (856)424-9248
E-mail: info@ifps.org
Home Page: http://www.ifps.org

• 11627 • **Distinguished Achievement Award to Fluid Power Educator**
To recognize an individual with a minimum of ten years experience in teaching fluid power in industry or academia. A plaque is awarded. Established in 1969. Formerly: Outstanding Fluid Power Educator.

• 11628 • **Outstanding Chapter Award**
To recognize outstanding accomplishments during the previous year by active chapters of the Society. A certificate is awarded annually. Established in 1967. Formerly: President's Award.

• 11629 • **Outstanding Industry Leader**
This, the Society's most prestigious award, is given to an individual whose efforts have resulted in a broad based impact on the fluid power industry. Consideration is given to dedication, accomplishment and contributions to the industry; efforts in behalf of one's employer; and support given to industry and professional activities such as FPS, NFPA, and ISO, etc. Plaques are presented. Established in 1976.

• 11630 •
International Foodservice Manufacturer Association
Michael J. Licata, Pres./CEO
2 Prudential Plz., 180 N Stetson, Ste. 4400
180 N Stetson Ave., Ste. 400
Chicago, IL 60601
Phone: (312)540-4400
Fax: (312)540-4401
E-mail: ifma@ifmaworld.com
Home Page: http://www.ifmaworld.com

• 11631 • **Foodservice Operator of the Year**
To recognize lasting and outstanding contributions to the advancement of the food service industry. Awards are given in the following categories: independent restaurant operator, chain full service, chain fast service, health care, elementary and secondary schools, colleges and universities, business and industry/food service management, specialty food services, and hotels and lodging. Any person, worldwide, engaged in the active ownership, management, supervision, or employment of an establishment in one of the nine classes of the food service industry is eligible to receive a Silver Plate Award. The Gold Plate Award, who is designated Food service Operator of the Year, is selected from among the nine Silver Plate winners. The deadline for nominations is in December. Awarded annually in February, with an awards Banquet in May during the National Restaurant Association show in Chicago. Established in 1955.

• 11632 •
International Formalwear Association
Karen A. Hurley, Exec.Dir.
401 N Michigan Ave.
Chicago, IL 60611-4267
Phone: (312)644-6610
Fax: (312)321-4098
E-mail: ifa@sba.com
Home Page: http://www.formalwear.org

• 11633 • **Black Tie Award**
To recognize an individual who has made a significant contribution to the formalwear industry. A plaque is awarded annually at the EXPO Convention & Trade Show.

• 11634 • **Motion Picture Academy Awards/Television Emmy Awards: Black Tie Award**
To recognize actors for innovative use of, and distinguished appearance in, men's formalwear. 323175

• 11635 •
International Franchise Association
Cecilia Bond, Exec.Asst.
1350 New York Ave. NW, Ste. 900
Washington, DC 20005
Phone: (202)628-8000
Phone: (202)662-0780
Fax: (202)628-0812
Fax: (202)628-0812
E-mail: ifa@franchise.org
Home Page: http://www.franchise.org

• 11636 • **Entrepreneur of the Year**
To recognize a prominent and successful franchisor with a track record of innovation and a tenure of achievement in the midst of a growing operation. Nomination deadline varies. The award is given at the discretion of the committee and Board of Directors and is awarded annually. Established in 1982.

• 11637 • **Free Enterprise Award**
To recognize an organization or individual from government, the media, business, or academia that has made significant contributions to the free enterprise system in the United States and elsewhere in the world. The award is given at the discretion of the committee and Board of Directors and is awarded annually. Established in 1982.

• 11638 • **IFA Hall of Fame Award**
To recognize an IFA member who has contributed significantly to the advancement of the art and economic values of franchising, and who has applied his or her expertise for the benefit of the franchising community. The award is given at the discretion of the committee and Board of Directors and is awarded annually. This award is IFA's oldest. Established in 1979.

• 11639 • **IFA Bonny LeVine Award**
To recognize successful women who are franchise entrepreneurs or executives who have best served as mentors and role models for other women. The award is given at the discretion of the committees and Board of Directors and is awarded annually. Established in 1994 to honor of Bonny LeVine, co-founder of PIP Printing.

• 11640 •
International Furnishings and Design Association
Lee K. Coggin FIFDA, Pres.
191 Clarksville Rd.
Princeton Junction, NJ 08550
Phone: (609)799-3423
Fax: (609)799-7032
E-mail: info@ifda.com
Home Page: http://www.ifda.com

Formerly: National Home Fashions League.

• 11641 • **Fellow Recognition**
To recognize extraordinary service to both the Association and the interior furnishings industry. Members of the Association for eight consecutive years are eligible. A certificate and an engraved crystal are awarded annually. Established in 1973.

• 11642 • **Honorary Recognition**
To recognize individuals who have made notable contributions to the interior furnishings field or to socio-environmental improvement. Awarded periodically. Established in 1977.

• 11643 • **Trailblazer Award**
To recognize a person who has been responsible for an innovation that meaningfully alters the way some aspect of the interior furnishings industry functions or is perceived. The awardee need not be a member of the Association. Awarded annually. Established in 1966.

• 11644 •
International Game Fish Association
Rob Kramer, Pres.
IGFA Fishing Hall of Fame & Museum
300 Gulf Stream Way
Dania Beach, FL 33004
Phone: (954)927-2628
Fax: (954)924-4299
E-mail: hq@igfa.org
Home Page: http://www.igfa.org

• 11645 • **International Game Fish Association Awards**
To recognize outstanding achievement in game fishing. The following awards are presented: 1,000 Pound Club - for landing a marlin, shark, or tuna, that weighs 1,000 pounds or more; World Record for Game Fish Award for the heaviest game fish caught on a specific strength line or the heaviest fish caught of a species on any size line that is referred to as an all - tackle world record; 5 to 1 Club - for landing a fish that is five times heavier than the breaking strength of the angler's fishing line; 10 to 1 Club - for landing a fish that is ten times heavier than the breaking strength of the angler's fishing line; 15 to 1 Club - for landing a fish that is 15 times heavier than the breaking strength of the angler's fishing line; 20 to 1 Club - for landing a fish that is 20 times heavier than the breaking strength of the angler's fishing line; and 10 Pound Bass Club - for freshwater bass catches of 10 pounds or more. Largemouth, smallmouth, spotted, and peacock bass are eligible. These awards are open to everyone. A certificate, embroidered patch, and pin are awarded as catches are approved by the association. The World Record for Game Fish Award was established in 1939. Additional awards were established in 1985.

• 11646 •
International Gay and Lesbian Human Rights Commission
Paula Ettelbrick, Exec.Dir.
350 5th Ave., 34th Fl.
New York, NY 10118
Phone: (212)216-1814
Fax: (212)216-1876
E-mail: iglhrc@iglhrc.org
Home Page: http://www.iglhrc.org

• 11647 • **Felipa da Souza Award**
To honor two individuals and one organization that, at great risk or personal cost, have made significant contributions toward securing the human rights and freedoms of sexual minorities.

• 11648 •
International Geographical Union (Union Geographique Internationale)
Prof. Adalberto Vallega, Pres.
% Ronald F. Abler, Sec.-Gen.
National Academy of Sciences
1710 16th St. NW
Washington, DC 20009
Phone: (202)352-6222
Fax: (202)234-2744
E-mail: rabler@aag.org
Home Page: http://www.igu-net.org

• 11649 • **Laureat d'Honneur of the International Geographical Union**
To recognize individuals who have made outstanding contributions to international understanding or cooperation or in the application of geography to worldwide problems. Individuals must be nominated by member countries prior to the International Geographical Congress held every four years. A diploma is awarded every four years at the congress. Established in 1976.

• 11650 •
International Golf Federation
Stephanie Parel, Joint Dep.Sec.
Golf House
PO Box 708
Far Hills, NJ 07931-0708
Phone: (908)234-2300
Fax: (908)234-2178
E-mail: sparel@usga.org
Home Page: http://www.internationalgolffederation.org

Formerly: (2003) World Amateur Golf Council.

• 11651 • **Eisenhower Trophy**
For international men's team competition. A trophy is awarded biennially.

• 11652 • **Espirito Santo Trophy**
For international women's team competition. A trophy is awarded biennially.

• 11653 •
International Good Neighbor Council (Consejo Internacional de Buena Vecindad)
John Chapa, Int'l Pres.
% John Chapa, Int'l Pres.
2828 Beauregard Ave.
San Angelo, TX 76901
Phone: (915)949-7849
E-mail: chapajohn@delinet.com
Home Page: http://www.cibv-ignc.org

• 11654 • **Good Neighbor Award**
To recognize individuals who promote goodwill and understanding among nations of the Western Hemisphere and facilitate communication and cooperation among countries, agencies, and official and private groups with common interests. Nominations are accepted. A medal and plaque are awarded annually. The award commemorates good neighborliness among the nations, through this Organization, founded by Mr. Glenn A. Garrett, former Governor of Texas, and Mr. Jose A. Muguerza, former Governor of Nuevo Leon.

• 11655 •
International Graphoanalysis Society
Greg Greco, Pres.
842 5th Ave.
New Kensington, PA 15068
Phone: (724)472-9701
Fax: (267)501-1931
E-mail: greg@igas.com
Home Page: http://www.igas.com

• 11656 • **International Graphoanalyst of the Year**
For recognition of outstanding performance in furthering the professional prestige and acceptance of the science of graphoanalysis. Society members are eligible. A plaque is presented annually at the IGAS Convention. Established in 1961.

• 11657 •
International Guild of Candle Artisans
Alice Marguardt, Ed.
1640 Garfield
Fremont, NE 68025
E-mail: amgwicks@pionet.net
Home Page: http://www.igca.net

• 11658 • **Candle Artisan of the Year**
To recognize the candle artisan receiving the highest score on total candles entered in competition at the annual IGCA convention. Members are eligible. Award is given only if the minimum number of points in designated classes is met. A plaque is awarded annually in July. Established in 1966.

• 11659 • **Judges Choice Award**
To recognize an outstanding candle artisan, who is considered to be an exemplar of the art, from amongst the blue ribbon winners entered in competition at the annual IGCA convention. Winners are selected by judges of the competition.

• 11660 • **Members Choice Award**
For recognition of an outstanding candle artisan at the annual IGCA convention competition. Winners are selected by IGCA members in good standing at the convention.

• 11661 • **Lois Tollefsen Award**
To recognize new procedures in the art of candle making. New procedures may include molding, formulating, painting, decoration, and new use of wax. Entrants must submit their candles with a card stating "New Technique" and a brief example of the technique thereon. Awarded annually.

• 11662 •
International Guild of Hair Removal Specialists
Vickie L. Mickey, Pres.
1918 Bethel Rd.
Columbus, OH 43220
Phone: (614)457-5614
Toll-Free: 800-830-3247
Fax: (614)457-6884
E-mail: igpc@northstate.net
Home Page: http://www.ighrs.org

• 11663 • **Conference Coordinator Award**
To recognize an individual for organizing the Guild conference. A plaque is awarded biennially at the conference. Established in 1985.

• 11664 • **District Representatives Award**
For recognition of special achievement in serving as District Representatives of the Guild. An award is presented biennially at the conference. Established in 1985.

• 11665 • **Founder and First President Award**
For recognition of achievement. An award is presented biennially at the conference. Established in 1985.

• 11666 • **Dr. Michel Award**
To recognize the individual who did the most to further the cause of electrolysis in the last two years. A plaque is awarded biennially at the conference. Established in 1985.

• 11667 • **Officers Medallion**
For recognition of service on the Board of the Guild. Members serving on the Board of the Guild are eligible. A medallion is awarded biennially at the conference. Established in 1985.

• 11668 • **Outgoing Officer Award**
To recognize an electrologist. A medallion is awarded biennially at the conference. Established in 1985.

• 11669 •
International Handgun Metallic Silhouette Association
Mike Stimson, Pres.
PO Box 901120
Sandy, UT 84070-1120
Phone: (801)733-2423
Fax: (801)733-2424
E-mail: pres@texasairnet.com
Home Page: http://www.ihmsa.org

• 11670 • **Outstanding Service**
Awarded annually for sportsmanship, volunteerism

• 11671 •
International Hearing Society
Cindy J. Helms BC-HIS, Exec.Dir.
16880 Middlebelt Rd., Ste. 4
Livonia, MI 48154-3367
Phone: (734)522-7200
Toll-Free: 800-521-5247
Fax: (734)522-0200
E-mail: chelms@ihsinfo.org
Home Page: http://www.ihsinfo.org

Formerly: (1995) National Hearing Aid Society.

• 11672 • **Leland A. Watson Award**
This, the highest award in the International Hearing Society, is given to recognize individuals who have made outstanding contributions in the hearing aid profession. Recipients are nominated by the Board of Governors. A trophy is awarded when merited. Established in 1960 to honor the achievements made in the hearing health care field by Leland A. Watson.

• 11673 •
International Horn Society
Heidi Vogel, Exec.Sec.
PO Box 630158
Lanai City, HI 96763-0158
Phone: (907)789-5477
Fax: (907)789-5477
E-mail: exec-secretary@hornsociety.org
Home Page: http://www.hornsociety.org

• 11674 • **Performance Scholarships**
To encourage young hornists who have not reached the age of 25 by June 30 of the competition year. Hornists need not be members of IHS. The deadline for applications is March 15. Five winners have the opportunity to perform at an annual IHS Workshop. Each contestant receives free registration and room and board for the week. The first and second place winners receive $300 and $200, respectively. Awarded annually during Workshop Week. Established in 1978 in memory of Max Pottage, Carl Geyer and John Barrows. Additional information is available from Heather Pettit, Newsletter Editor, 839 Coach Rd., Palatine, IL 60074-1831.

• 11675 •
International Hot Rod Association
Aaron Polburn, Pres.
9 1/2 E Main St.
Norwalk, OH 44857
Phone: (419)663-6666
Phone: (419)660-4209
Fax: (419)663-4472
E-mail: comments@ihra.com
Home Page: http://ihra.com

• 11676 • **Bracket World Finals Team Championship**
To recognize the top bracket track team in the nation. The track must be sanctioned by IHRA. Each team member earns points for the team during eliminations at the Bracket World Finals drag race. A plaque is awarded annually at the awards banquet. Established in 1978. Formerly administered by the Professional Drag Racing Association.

• 11677 • **IHRA Pro Alcohol Funny Car World Champion**
To recognize achievement in the Pro Alcohol Funny Car eliminator. The winner must finish first in the final IHRA Pro Alcohol Funny Car points standings, compiled from eleven national events held around the United States. A monetary award, a World Championship Ring, and other gifts are awarded annually at the IHRA World Championship Awards Banquet. Established in 1974.

• 11678 • **IHRA Pro Stock World Championship**
For recognition of competition in the Pro Stock eliminator. The driver must be a member of IHRA to compete. The winner must finish first in the final IHRA Pro Stock points standing, which encompasses eleven national events in the United States. A monetary award, a World Championship Ring, and other gifts are awarded annually at the season's end at the IHRA awards banquet. Established in 1974.

• 11679 • **IHRA Pro Top Fuel Dragster World Champion**
To recognize achievement in the Pro Nitro Dragster eliminator. The winner must finish in first place in the final IHRA Pro Nitro Dragster points standings, which encompasses nine nationals around the United States. A monetary award, a World Championship Ring, and other awards are presented annually at the World Championship awards banquet. Established in 1974. Formerly: IHRA Pro Nitro Dragster World Champion.

• 11680 • **Pro Modified World Champion**
For recognition of competition in the Pro Modified eliminator. Drivers must be members of IHRA. The winner must finish first in the final Pro Modified points standings, which encompass eleven national events in the United States. A monetary prize, a World Championship Ring, and other gifts are awarded annually at the season's end during the IHRA awards banquet. Established in 1990.

• 11681 •
International Hydrofoil Society
John Meyer, Pres.
PO Box 51
Cabin John, MD 20818
Phone: (301)519-9043
Fax: (703)917-0044
E-mail: president@foils.org
Home Page: http://www.foils.org

• 11682 • Mark Thornton Gold Challenge Award
To recognize an individual under 40 years of age who has advanced the science and technology of hydrofoils.

• 11683 •
International Institute of Fisheries Economics and Trade
Ann L. Shriver, Exec.Dir.
Department of Agricultural and Resource Economics
Oregon State University
Corvallis, OR 97331-3601
Phone: (541)737-1439
Phone: (541)737-1416
Fax: (541)737-2563
E-mail: iifet@oregonstate.edu
Home Page: http://oregonstate.edu/Dept/IIFET/

• 11684 • Best Student Paper Award
Recognizes the best paper presented at IIFET conference. Graduate students are eligible. Awarded biennially.

• 11685 • Certified International Financier
Award of recognition. Lenders, brokers, major full-time borrowers are eligible. Awarded annually.

• 11686 • Distinguished Service Award
Recognizes a major contribution in Fisheries Economics. Awarded biennially.

• 11687 •
International Institute of Flint
Pamela Bakken, Exec.Dir.
515 Stevens St.
Flint, MI 48502-1719
Phone: (810)767-0720
Fax: (810)767-0724
E-mail: iif@gfn.org
Home Page: http://www.gfn.org/~iif

• 11688 • Parmalee Scholarship
For undergraduate students majoring in foreign languages, ethnic areas, or international studies. Scholarship awarded annually.

• 11689 •
International Institute of Integral Human Sciences
(Institut International des Sciences Humaines Integrales)
Prof. John Rossner, Pres.
PO Box 1387, Sta. H
Montreal, QC, Canada H3G 2N3
Phone: (514)937-8359
Fax: (514)937-5380
E-mail: info@iiihs.com
Home Page: http://www.iiihs.org

• 11690 • Honorary Fellow of the College of Human Sciences
Award of recognition for distinguished contributions. Awarded periodically.

• 11691 •
International Institute of Wisconsin
Alexander P. Durtka Jr., Pres.
1110 N Old World 3rd St., Ste. 420
Milwaukee, WI 53203
Phone: (414)225-6220
Fax: (414)225-6235
E-mail: iiw@execpc.com
Home Page: http://www.IIWisconsin.org

• 11692 • World Citizen
For those making significant contributions in cultural diversity; one native born citizen, the other a foreign born, naturalized citizen. Recognition award bestowed annually.

• 11693 •
International Isotope Society
Dr. Conrad Raab, Pres.
Merck & Co., Inc.
RY 80R-104
PO Box 2000
Rahway, NJ 07065-0900
Phone: (732)594-6976
Fax: (732)594-6921
E-mail: iis@intl-isotope-soc.org
Home Page: http://www.intl-isotope-soc.org

• 11694 • Melvin Calvin Award
Recognizes scientific achievement. Awarded triennially.

• 11695 • IIS Award
Recognizes distinguished service to the society. Society members are eligible. Awarded triennially.

• 11696 •
International Kart Federation
Jim McMillam, Pres.
1609 S Grove Ave., Ste. 105
Ontario, CA 91761
Phone: (909)923-4999
Fax: (909)923-6940
E-mail: support@ikfkarting.com
Home Page: http://www.ikfkarting.com

Formerly: (1957) Go Kart Club of America.

• 11697 • Duffy Award
This, the highest award of karting, is given for achievement in the Grandnational. Members of IKF who race at the Grandnationals are eligible. The Duffy, a solid bronze statuette on a wooden base, is awarded annually at each of the six Grandnational events. Established in 1979 in honor of Duffy Livingstone, past President of the Board and one of the founders of organized karting. Each year, the Duffy awards are sponsored by advertisers, manufacturers, kart shops, and clubs.

• 11698 •
International Labor Communications Association, AFL-CIO/CLC
Mr. Alec Dubro, Media Coor.
815 16th St. NW
Washington, DC 20006
Phone: (202)974-8039
Phone: (202)974-8036
Fax: (202)974-8038
E-mail: ilca@aflcio.org
Home Page: http://www.ilcaonline.org

Formerly: (1984) International Labor Press Association.

• 11699 • ILCA Film and Broadcast Competition
To recognize achievement by labor organizations in video and audio communications and arts; to increase interest in film, tape, and audio resources now available in the labor movement; and to encourage more use of these communications media. Works shown or broadcast in the previous year are eligible in the following categories: films, television, video, or radio programs produced for informing and/or educating union members and/or the general public; informative television commercials; informative radio commercials to include public service announcements; issue-oriented television commercials on ballot or legislative issues.

• 11700 • ILCA Media Awards Contest
To recognize excellence in the labor press. Member publications may submit entries in the following four categories: (1) General Excellence - for general editorial excellence in international and national union publications with various circulations; state and local AFL-CIO central body publications; local union publications; and regional publications by a branch of a national or international union. A first, second, and third award is presented in each category and, where justified, an Honorable Mention is given. (2) Special Performance - for journalistic efforts in best original cartoon; best original photograph; best graphic; best front page; and various classes of best written articles. Formerly: Labor Press Journalistic Awards Contest.

• 11701 •
International Labor History Association
Ronald C. Kent, Editor
706 Bruce Ct.
Madison, WI 53705
Phone: (608)231-1886

• 11702 • **ILHA Book of the Year**

Recognizes the author of an outstanding labor history. Awarded annually.

• 11703 •

International Labor Rights Fund
Terry Collingsworth, Exec.Dir.
733 15th St. NW, Ste. 920
Washington, DC 20005-2112
Phone: (202)347-4100
Fax: (202)347-4885
E-mail: laborrights@igc.org
Home Page: http://www.laborrights.org

• 11704 • **International Labor Rights Advocate Award**

Recognizes pioneering or outstanding contribution to the extension of labor rights. Awarded periodically.

• 11705 •

International Lacrosse Federation
Peter Hobbs, Pres.
4117 Gilgo E
Gilgo Beach, NY 11702
Phone: (631)630-4433
E-mail: phobbs@shd.com.au
Home Page: http://www.intlaxfed.org/

• 11706 • **Turnbill Trophy**

A trophy is awarded to the world champion quadrennially.

• 11707 •

International Lactation Consultant Association
Jim Smith, Exec.Dir.
1500 Sunday Dr., Ste. 102
Raleigh, NC 27607
Phone: (919)861-5577
Fax: (919)787-4916
E-mail: info@ilca.org
Home Page: http://www.ilca.org

• 11708 • **Manuscript Award**

To recognize the best article printed in the *Journal of Human Lactation.*

• 11709 • **Niles Newton Memorial Award for Outstanding Achievement in Human Lactation**

For recognition of outstanding achievements in the field of human lactation, be that in breastfeeding education, consultation, clinical practice, or research. There are no restrictions on age, sex, nationality, or citizenship. A crystal mounted on a piece of white marble with a nursing mother and baby etched into the front is awarded when merited. Established in 1987.

• 11710 •

International Landslide Research Group
Earl E. Brabb, Pres.
4377 Newland Hights Drive
Rocklin, CA 95765
Phone: (916)315-8811
E-mail: ilrg@mindspring.com
Home Page: http://ilrg.gndci.pg.cnr.it/

• 11711 • **Distinguished Leadership for Landslide Research**

Recognizes leadership in landslide research. Awarded periodically.

• 11712 •

International Laser Display Association
David Lytle, Exec.Dir.
3721 SE Henry St.
Portland, OR 97202
Phone: (502)407-0289
E-mail: david@laserist.org
Home Page: http://www.laserist.org

• 11713 • **ILDA Award**

Recognizes an outstanding laser display. Awarded annually. Inquire for application details.

• 11714 •

International Law Students Association
Michael A. Peil, Exec.Dir.
25 E Jackson Blvd., Ste. 518
Chicago, IL 60604
Phone: (312)362-5025
Fax: (312)362-5073
E-mail: ilsa@ilsa.org
Home Page: http://www.ilsa.org

• 11715 • **Francis Deak Award**

Award of recognition. Inquire for application details.

• 11716 • **Dean Rusk Award**

Recognizes outstanding student writing in student law journals.

• 11717 •

International League of Antiquarian Booksellers
Robert D. Fleck, Pres.
310 Delaware St.
New Castle, DE 19720
Phone: (302)328-7232
Toll-Free: 800-996-2556
Fax: (302)328-7274
E-mail: info@ilab-lila.com
Home Page: http://www.ilab-lila.com

• 11718 • **Quadrennial Prize for Bibliography (Prix quadrennial de Bibliographie)**

To recognize the author of the best work of learned bibliography or of research into the history of books or of typography, and books of general interest on the subject. Authors of any nationality may submit a published or unpublished work in a language which is universally used. A monetary prize of $10,000 US is awarded every four years. Deadline is December 31. Established in 1963.

• 11719 •

International Legal Fraternity Phi Delta Phi
Jeff Wilker, Pres.
1426 21st St. NW
Washington, DC 20036
Phone: (202)223-6801
Toll-Free: 800-368-5606
Fax: (202)223-6808
E-mail: info@phideltaphi.org
Home Page: http://www.phideltaphi.org

• 11720 • **Balfour Scholarship**

For recognition of academic achievement. Any fraternity member who has completed one year of legal study is eligible. Applications must be submitted by November 1. Scholarships of $3,000 each are awarded when merited.

• 11721 • **International Inn of the Year**

To recognize the outstanding student Inn of the Year. Inns are judged on the following criteria: academic excellence, Inn activities, individual member achievement, single project awards, and overall improvement during the academic year. Forms must be submitted by February 13. A key pin is awarded annually.

• 11722 • **J. Will Pless International Graduate of the Year**

To recognize the outstanding law school graduate of the year. Each student Inn selects one candidate by March 15 for the competition. Selection is based on academic achievement, service to the Fraternity, and service to the law school community. An invitation to the biennial convention and a certificate are presented annually to the winner. Each Inn nominee receives a certificate of recognition, and the Inn of the winner receives a plaque.

• 11723 • **A. Frank Vick Outstanding Province President Award**

To recognize a province president for achievement. A plaque and a certificate are awarded biennially at the Fraternity convention.

• 11724 •

International Life Sciences Institute - North America
PhD Robert Fisher PhD, Exec.Dir.
One Thomas Cir., 9th Fl.
Washington, DC 20005
Phone: (202)659-0074
Toll-Free: 800-538-9601
Fax: (202)659-3859
E-mail: rfisher@ilsi.org
Home Page: http://www.ilsina.org

• 11725 • **Future Leader Awards**

To recognize young scientists in the field of nutrition who are in their first academic position and to provide the opportunity for young investigators to conduct exploratory research that might not receive funding from other sources. Recipients are chosen primarily on the basis of their promise as leaders as judged by their senior colleagues. Each award provides a grant of $15,000 annually for a period of two years. Established in 1964.

• 11726 •
International Lightning Class Association
Karen Johnson, Exec.Sec.
PO Box 10747
Murfreesboro, TN 37129
Phone: (615)893-5274
Fax: (615)893-5205
E-mail: office@lightningclass.org
Home Page: http://www.lightningclass.org

• 11727 • Edith Oliver Dusmet World Championship Cup
To recognize the top Skipper in Lightning Class World Championships held biennially and in rotation in North America, Europe, and South America. Members of the association who qualify in district or continent championships are eligible. The Challenge Perpetual Trophy, an antique English cup, is awarded biennially following the championship. Established in 1965 by James Dusmet de Smours of Naples, Italy, in memory of his mother, Edith Oliver Dusmet.

• 11728 • North American Championship Trophy
To recognize the top skipper in the Lightning North American Championships held each year. Members of the association who qualify in district championships are eligible. A trophy, retired by Thomas Allen after winning it three times, was donated and established by Allen as a perpetual trophy. The trophy replaced the original *Internationals Trophy* which was previously retired. Established in 1969.

• 11729 •
International Lilac Society
David P. Gressley, Sec.
3 Paradise Ct.
Cohoes, NY 12047-1422
Phone: (440)946-4400
Phone: (440)602-3855
Fax: (440)602-3857
E-mail: dgressley@holdenarb.org
Home Page: http://lilacs.freeservers.com

• 11730 • Distinguished Recognition Award
To recognize an individual for outstanding service to the Society. Established in 1989.

• 11731 • Honors and Achievement Award
This, the highest award of the Society, is given for recognition of outstanding work, dedication, and service in promoting the lilac or the Society. Individuals may win this award only once. A plaque is awarded as merited. Established in 1972.

• 11732 • Arch McKean Award
To recognize an individual for publicizing the lilac and promoting the Society in the media, television, radio, and newspapers. Established in 1985.

• 11733 • President's Award
To recognize the arboretum, or public or private park or garden for outstanding collections and public display of lilacs, work with promoting the growing and landscape uses of the lilac, outstanding landscaping with lilacs or major research with lilacs. It is an institutional or park-garden award. Its purpose is to encourage the planting of lilacs for public display and education. It is not intended for strictly private gardens no matter how great their excellence. Established in 1972.

• 11734 •
International Linear Algebra Society
Daniel Hershkowitz, Pres.
Department of Mathematics
Pacific Lutheran University
Tacoma, WA 98447
E-mail: jeffrey.stuart@plu.edu
Home Page: http://www.math.technion.ac.il/iic/ILAS.html

• 11735 • Hans Schneider Prize in Linear Algebra
Triennial recognition for research, contribution & achievements.

• 11736 •
International Magnesium Association
Greg Patzer, Exec.VP
1000 N Rand Rd., Ste. 214
Wauconda, IL 60084
Phone: (847)526-2010
Fax: (847)526-3993
E-mail: gpatzer@tso.net
Home Page: http://www.intlmag.org

• 11737 • Application Award
To recognize, on an international level, a magnesium product concept with a wide application potential. Established in 1962. Application recognizes a significant advance resulting in a large volume potential for magnesium. The IMA awards demonstrate a high standard of excellence. The criteria for the selection is creativity, innovation, uniqueness and commercial success. Formerly: (1991) Design and Application Award.

• 11738 • Design Award
To recognize, on an international level, the most creative structural use of the metal magnesium for that year. Cast Products and Wrought Products categories will recognize unique, novel and creative design and development. The design and engineering must demonstrate a significant advance over current practice. Established in 1962. Formerly: (1991) Design and Application Award.

• 11739 • Process Award
To recognize innovation in manufacturing or processing technology. Process recognizes innovation in manufacturing or processing technology of the primary production, conversion in manufacturing, improvements in manufacturing techniques leading to higher quality and reduced costs, innovations in management systems in manufacturing. Awarded as part of the annual Awards of Excellence program. Established in 1962.

• 11740 • Special Award
To recognize, on an international level, a company or individual offering a one-time achievement for the industry. Established in 1962.

• 11741 •
International Masonry Institute
Hazel Bradford, Communications Dir.
The James Brice House
42 East St.
Annapolis, MD 21401
Phone: (410)280-1305
Toll-Free: 800-803-0295
Fax: (301)261-2855
E-mail: hbradford@imiweb.org
Home Page: http://www.imiweb.org

• 11742 • Golden Trowel Award
Award of recognition for union built masonry projects. Awarded periodically.

• 11743 •
International Mathematical Union
(Union Mathematique Internationale)
P. Griffiths, Sec.
Institute for Advanced Study
Einstein Dr.
Princeton, NJ 08540
Phone: (609)734-8259
Fax: (609)683-7605
E-mail: imu@ias.edu
Home Page: http://www.mathunion.org/

• 11744 • Fields Medal
This, the highest honor bestowed on mathematicians, is given for recognition of outstanding achievements in mathematics. Young mathematicians are eligible. A monetary prize and a medal are awarded every four years at the International Congress of Mathematicians. At least two and no more than four medals are awarded. Established by Professor Fields and first awarded in 1936.

• 11745 • Rolf Nevanlinna Prize
For recognition of outstanding achievements in the mathematical aspects of information science. Young mathematicians are eligible. A monetary prize and a medal are awarded every four years at the International Congress of Mathematicians. Established in 1982 with funds provided by the University of Helsinki.

• 11746 •
International Microelectronics and Packaging Society
Michael O˜Donoghue, Exec.Dir.
611 2nd St. NE
Washington, DC 20002
Phone: (202)548-4001
Fax: (202)548-6115
E-mail: imaps@imaps.org
Home Page: http://www.imaps.org

• 11747 • **Corporate Achievement Award**
To recognize a corporation, at whatever division or department level that is appropriate, which has provided significant technical contributions to the hybrid industry while also demonstrating support of ISHM through participation in such activities as corporate membership, symposium exhibition, and individual membership encouragement. Awarded annually. Established in 1970. Formerly: Corporate Recognition Award.

• 11748 • **Fellow of the Society**
To honor and recognize those who have made a significant and continuing contribution to ISHM over the years. Some possible criteria for this award are: (1) membership in ISHM for ten years; (2) service to ISHM as a local or national officer; (3) service to ISHM as a local or national committee member; and (4) presentation of papers at local or national symposia. Awarded annually. Established in 1981.

• 11749 • **Daniel C. Hughes, Jr., Memorial Award**
To recognize an individual for an outstanding technical achievement relating to hybrid microelectronics combined with, as appropriate, outstanding contributions supporting the hybrid microelectronic industry, academic achievement, or support and service to ISHM. Members are eligible to make nominations. Life membership is awarded annually. Established in 1970 to honor Daniel C. Hughes, Jr., who was involved in designing and developing processes and equipment for the electronics industry.

• 11750 • **Technical Achievement Award**
For recognition of outstanding technical achievements and contributions to the microelectronics industry. Members of ISHM in good standing must be nominated by a chapter with solicitations by regional directors. Awarded annually. Established in 1980.

• 11751 •
International Motor Press Association
Slaton White, Pres. Emeritus
4 Park St.
Harrington Park, NJ 07640
Phone: (201)750-3533
Fax: (201)750-2010
E-mail: slaton.white@time4.com
Home Page: http://www.impa.org

• 11752 • **Ken W. Purdy Award**
To recognize an individual for superior automotive writing during the calendar year. Works written and published in English are eligible. A plaque is awarded annually. Established in 1974 in memory of Ken W. Purdy who exemplified what creative automotive journalism should be.

• 11753 •
International Motor Sports Association
H. Doug Robinson, Exec.Dir.
1394 Broadway Ave.
Braselton, GA 30517
Phone: (706)658-2120
Fax: (706)658-2130
E-mail: info@imsaracing.net
Home Page: http://www.imsaracing.net

• 11754 • **Exxon Supreme GT**
To recognize the winners of this production-based series. Awards are given to the winning drivers and manufacturers in two divisions: Grand Touring Supreme 1 (GTS-1) and Grand Touring Supreme 2 (GTS-2). Technician of the Year and Most Improved Driver are also awarded. Established in 1971. Sponsored by Exxon Co.

• 11755 • **Exxon World Sports Car Championship**
To recognize the winning driver and manufacturer champions of this open cockpit sports car racing series. Awards and championships points are given to top finishing drivers and manufacturers in each race. Most Improved Driver and Technician of the Year are also recognized and awarded. Established in 1993, with the first official championship recognized in 1994. Sponsored by Exxon Company, U.S.A.

• 11756 • **Ferrari Challenge**
To recognize the winning drivers of two divisions Ferrari 348s and Ferrari 355s. Jointly organized by Ferrari North America through its authorized dealers and IMSA.

• 11757 • **Slick 50 Pro Series**
To recognize the championship winning drivers in two separate divisions in the series for sports racers: World Sports Racer and International Sports Racer. Established in 1996. Sponsored by Slick 50.

• 11758 • **Street Stock Endurance Championship**
To recognize the winning drivers and manufacturers in this four-class series for high performance, showroom stock-type American, European, and Japanese sports coupes and sedans, with safety and limited performance modifications added. Winning drivers and manufacturers will be awarded championships in Grand Sports, Sports, Touring, and Compact classes. A "Rising Star" award is given in each class to the driver showing the most potential, and "Car of the Year" honors go to the model of car scoring the most points regardless of class. Established in 1985.

• 11759 •
International Motorsports Hall of Fame
PO Box 1018
Talladega, AL 35161
Phone: (256)362-5002
Fax: (256)362-5684
E-mail: cbradford@motorsportshalloffame.com
Home Page: http://www.motorsportshalloffame.com

• 11760 • **International Motorsports Hall of Fame**
To formally and permanently recognize individuals for contributions to the growth of motorsports. Individuals who have been retired from their line of work in motorsports (driver, mechanic, etc.) for at least five years are eligible. Inductees are selected by a group of national and international motorsports media. A large trophy-like award, permanently displayed in the Hall of Fame, and a medallion to the recipient are awarded annually. The Annual Induction Ceremony is held in the spring at the International Motorsports Hall of Fame in Talladega, Alabama. Established in 1983. Since the Hall of Fame opened in 1983, six other Halls of Fame have become part of the display: Alabama Sportswriters Hall of Fame, ARCA Championship Hall of Fame, Western Auto NASCAR Mechanics Hall of Fame, Quarter Midgets of America Hall of Fame, and World Karting Hall of Fame. Sponsored by 76 Corporation.

• 11761 •
International Narcotic Enforcement Officers Association
John J. Bellizzi, Exec.Dir.
112 State St., Ste. 1200
Albany, NY 12207-2079
Phone: (518)463-6232
Fax: (518)432-3378
E-mail: ineoa@iopener.net
Home Page: http://www.ineoa.org

• 11762 • **Anslinger Award**
For recognition of outstanding dedication, achievement, and contribution in combating international drug trafficking and the prevention of drug abuse. Active narcotic officers are eligible. A plaque is awarded when merited at the annual conference. Established in 1978 in honor of Harry J. Anslinger, first U.S. Commissioner of Narcotics.

• 11763 • **Commendation Awards**
To recognize individuals for outstanding contributions in the area of narcotic enforcement.

• 11764 • **INEOA Medal of Valor**
To recognize an individual for having performed his or her duty in the area of narcotic enforcement at a personal risk of self.

• 11765 • **Special Agency Awards**
To recognize individuals nominated by their respective agency, who have distinguished themselves in the performance of their duty in the

area of narcotic enforcement. Individuals active in the following categories are eliglble: Army - U.S.; Border Patrol - U.S.; Coast Guard - U.S.; Customs U.S.; DEA - U.S.; O.S.I. USAF; FBI; I.R.S.; International Law Enforcement; Navy - U.S.; and A.T. & F.

• 11766 • Special Awards of Honor

To recognize individuals who have made outstanding contributions in the area of drug abuse or drug enforcement.

• 11767 • UN/INEOA Law Enforcement Medal

To recognize an individual for an outstanding contribution in the area of international drug control. Open to all. A medal is awarded when merited. Established in 1986.

• 11768 •

International Navigation Association - USA
David C. Scull, Pres.
PO Box 856
Charlotte Hall, MD 20622-0856
Phone: (240)288-5107
Fax: (240)228-5304
E-mail: dscull@erols.com
Home Page: http://www.pianc-aipcn.org/

• 11769 • Jack A. Pierce Award

For outstanding contributions to the navigational community.

• 11770 •

International Newspaper Marketing Association
Eivind Thomsen, Senior VP
10300 N Central Expy., Ste. 467
Dallas, TX 75231-8621
Phone: (214)373-9111
Fax: (214)373-9112
E-mail: inma@inma.org
Home Page: http://www.inma.org

Formerly: (1987) International Newspaper Promotion Association.

• 11771 • Silver Shovel Award

This, INMA's highest honor, recognizes an individual for unselfish devotion to the Association and for significant contributions to the newspaper industry. Members of INMA are eligible. A plaque and a lapel pin are awarded annually at the international conference. Established in 1949.

• 11772 •

International Old Lacers, Inc.
Louise Colgan, Pres.
191 State St.
Framingham, MA 01702-2465
Phone: (510)793-5050
E-mail: ljh@gis.net
Home Page: http://
www.internationaloldlacers.org

• 11773 • International Old Lacers Contest

A contest to create a piece of lace. In 1988, individuals were to make a piece of lace 4 by 5 1/2 inches to use on an all-purpose greeting card. In 1989, a lace doily approximately 8 inches in diameter was made. A monetary award of $50 is presented to the winner. Ribbons are awarded for second and third prize.

• 11774 •

International Order of E.A.R.S.
Lee Pennington, Dir.
651 S 4th St.
Louisville, KY 40202
Phone: (502)245-0643
Fax: (502)254-7542
E-mail: cornislandstorytelling@msn.com
Home Page: http://
www.cornislandstorytellingfestival.org

• 11775 • Director's Award

Recognizes outstanding service to the organization and to storytelling. Awarded annually.

• 11776 • Distinguished Service Citation

Annual award of recognition.

• 11777 • Volunteer of the Year

Recognizes outstanding work by volunteers. Awarded annually.

• 11778 •

International Organization for Chemical Sciences in Development
(Organizacion Internacional de las Ciencias Quimicas para el Desarollo)
P.O. ox 8156
Falls Church, VA 22041
Phone: (703)845-9078
E-mail: iocd@igc.org
Home Page: http://www.iocd.org

• 11779 • International Organization for Chemical Sciences in Development Awards

To recognize chemists and institutions around the world for collaborative programs aimed at strengthening the chemical sciences in developing countries. Fellowships and awards are presented.

• 11780 •

International Organization of Plant Biosystematists
Gonzalo Nieto Feliner, Pres.
Missouri Botanical Garden
PO Box 299
St. Louis, MO 63166-0299
Phone: (314)577-5175
Fax: (314)577-0820
E-mail: nieto@ma-rjb.csic.es
Home Page: http://www.iopb.org

• 11781 • International Organization of Plant Biosystematists Life Membership

To recognize an individual for contributions in promoting the field of biosystematics and developing the International Organization of Plant Biosystematics. A scroll is awarded triennially at the Symposium. Established in 1989. In addition, the triennial IOPB Award is also presented.

• 11782 •

International Ozone Association
Margit Istok, Exec.Dir.
98 Warren Ave.
Quincy, MA 02170-4066
Phone: (203)348-3542
Fax: (203)967-4845
E-mail: mistok@int-ozone-assoc.org
Home Page: http://www.int-ozone-assoc.org

• 11783 • Prix Hallopeau

To recognize further development in the field of ozone and its application. Awarded for original research revealing some unprecedented knowledge of the fundamental aspects of the industrial generation and the uses of ozone. The submitted works should be of a level similar to that of a Doctor's degree thesis. Awarded every two years for a paper presented during the 2 years preceding the Ozone World Congress. Established in honor of Jean Hallopeau, founding member of the IOI and designer-engineer of Compagnie Generale des Eaux.

• 11784 • Honorary President and Honorary Member

Honorary Member and President is awarded to any individual in recognition of his/her outstanding contribution towards furthering the objectives of the Ozone Association.

• 11785 • Morton J. Klein Award

To recognize contributions of the highest order to the International Ozone Association in commemoration of the clear vision, diplomatic proficiency, and leadership which characterized the life of Morton J. Klein. Established in 1995 in honor of Morton J. Klein, who has been associated with the IOA since it was first organized as the International Ozone Institute in 1973.

• 11786 • Harvey M. Rosen Memorial Award

For recognition of the best paper published in *Ozone: Science & Engineering* for the two years of an IOA World Congress. Established in 1989 in honor of Dr. Harvey M. Rosen, who was the prime catalyst behind the establishment of IOA and *Science & Engineering*.

• 11787 •

International Parking Institute
Kim E. Jackson CAPP, Exec.Dir.
PO Box 7167
Fredericksburg, VA 22404
Phone: (540)371-7535
Fax: (540)371-8022
E-mail: jackson@parking.org
Home Page: http://www.parking.org

Formerly: (1996) Institutional and Municipal Parking Congress.

• 11788 • International Parking Awards Competition
To recognize and commend trends toward parking facilities that are aesthetically appealing as well as functional, to encourage excellence in parking design, and to encourage innovation in parking programs and operations. Owners of parking facilities, and owners/operators of parking programs are eligible. Entries may be submitted by the December deadline each year. Awards are made in three categories: best design of a parking facility under 800 spaces, best design of a parking facility with 800 or more spaces, and innovation in a parking operation or program. Plaques and certificates are awarded annually at the IPI convention. A feature article with color photos of winning entries is published in *The Parking Professional* magazine. Established in 1982. Formerly: (1984) IMPC Award for Excellence in Parking Design; (1996) IMPC Award for Excellence in Parking Design and Program Innovation.

• 11789 •
International Partnership for Service-Learning and Leadership
Linda A. Chisholm, Pres.
815 2nd Ave., Ste. 315
New York, NY 10017
Phone: (212)986-0989
Fax: (212)986-5039
E-mail: info@ipsl.org
Home Page: http://www.ipsl.org

• 11790 • Alec and Mora Dickson Scholarship
Awarded for participation in the Master's Degree in International Service program. $2,000-$3,000 is awarded annually.

• 11791 • The Howard A. Berry Scholarship
Two colleges/universities are awarded the honor of selecting a student to receive $1,000 towards and IPS-L semester of the year program. Awarded annually.

• 11792 • The Seymour Eskow Scholarship
Awarded to a community college student for participation in an IPS-L semester or year program. $1,000 is awarded. Awarded annually.

• 11793 • The Sven Groennings Scholarship
Awarded to a Stanford University student or graduate for participation in and IPS-L semester or year program. $1,000 is awarded annually.

• 11794 •
International Peace Academy
Terje Roed-Larsen, Pres.
777 UN Plz., 4th Fl.
New York, NY 10017-3521
Phone: (212)687-4300
Fax: (212)983-8246
E-mail: ipa@ipacademy.org
Home Page: http://www.ipacademy.org

• 11795 • Distinguished Peacekeeper Award
For recognition of outstanding service in the field of peacekeeping. A medal is awarded when merited. Established in 1981. 620661

• 11796 •
International Planned Parenthood Federation, Western Hemisphere Region
Alexander C. Sanger, Chm.
120 Wall St., 9th Fl.
New York, NY 10005
Phone: (212)248-6400
Fax: (212)248-4221
E-mail: info@ippfwhr.org
Home Page: http://www.ippfwhr.org

• 11797 • Rosa Cisneros Award
To acknowledge the contribution that communications professionals and media institutions have made toward increasing public awareness of sexual and reproductive health issues. Nominations of reporters are welcome, for any staff of a communications professional occupation covering North America, Latin America, or the Caribbean. Materials produced or published during the preceding year are considered for the award. Awarded annually. Established in 1989.

• 11798 •
International Platform Association
David Pearl, Dir.Gen.
PO Box 250
Winnetka, IL 60093
Phone: (847)446-4321
Fax: (847)446-7186

• 11799 • Jack Anderson Award
To recognize contributions to investigative reporting. An engraved silver bowl is awarded as merited. Established in 1976. This award honors Jack Anderson, the contemporary investigative journalist. Formerly: Lincoln Steffens Award.

• 11800 • Best Conference Program Award
To honor the top club or association lecture program chairman in the United States. An engraved silver bowl is awarded as merited. Established in 1981. Formerly: (1982) Drew Pearson Award.

• 11801 • Harry Blackstone Award
To recognize the best magic performance of the year. An engraved silver bowl is awarded annually. Established in 1980 in memory of Harry Blackstone, IPA's greatest magician member.

• 11802 • Winston Churchill Award
To recognize an individual whose statements from the platform will most affect the future of the United States. An engraved silver bowl is awarded on special occassions at the Association's convention in July. Established in 1952 in honor of a former IPA member, Winston Churchill, who, through parentage having one foot in Great Britain and the other in the United States, used his great influence to forward mutually advantageous relations between Great Britain and the United States.

• 11803 • George Crile Award
To recognize the individual who has most successfully disseminated new medical discoveries and procedures to the public. A silver bowl is awarded. Established to honor the great father and son combination whose research influenced medical history.

• 11804 • Clarence Darrow Award
For recognition of contributions to the American system of justice. An engraved silver bowl is awarded as merited. Established in 1981. The award commemorates Clarence Darrow, the legal crusader of two centuries ago.

• 11805 • Ralph Waldo Emerson Award
To recognize a person who is a literary immortal and a living legend in his or her time. An engraved silver bowl is awarded as merited. Established in 1981 to honor Ralph Waldo Emerson, the noted philosopher and poet.

• 11806 • International Platform Association Award
To recognize outstanding public service achievements. An engraved silver bowl is awarded annually. Established in 1967.

• 11807 • IPA Top Discovery in the Field of Humor
For recognition of the humorist receiving the best audience vote of five such speakers who have never been presented before to the lecture program chairmen at an IPA convention. One humorist appears each evening for five successive nights at the IPA convention and the winner is decided by audience polls that are taken after each presentation. An engraved silver bowl is awarded as merited. Established in 1982.

• 11808 • Orators Hall of Fame
To recognize "the best orators in history."

• 11809 • Eleanor Roosevelt Award
To recognize outstanding achievement. An engraved silver bowl is awarded annually. Established in 1980 to honor Eleanor Roosevelt, the American humanitarian, writer, and wife of F. D. Roosevelt.

• 11810 • Theodore Roosevelt Award
To recognize excellence in public service. An engraved silver bowl is awarded annually. Established in 1973 in commemoration of former IPA member, President Theodore Roosevelt.

• 11811 • Carl Sandburg Award
To recognize a poet designated "The People's Poet." An engraved silver bowl is awarded annually. Established in 1968 in memory of Carl Sandburg, an American author and long time IPA member.

• 11812 • Glenn Seaborg Award
To recognize an individual who has done the most to increase the public's interest in science. An engraved silver bowl is awarded annually. Established in 1979 to honor Glenn Seaborg, the American chemist.

• 11813 • Lowell Thomas Award
To recognize the outstanding electronic journalist of the year. An engraved silver bowl is awarded annually. Established in 1974.

• 11814 • Mark Twain Award
To recognize that platform performer whose standards of humor most approach those of former IPA member Mark Twain. An engraved silver bowl is awarded annually. Established in 1972 in memory of Samuel Clemens, the American writer.

• 11815 • John Wayne Award
For recognition of a cinema personality who has become a legend in his or her own time. An engraved silver bowl is awarded annually. Established in 1981. The award honors John Wayne, the noted film actor.

• 11816 • Daniel Webster Award
To recognize the most influential words spoken concerning the nation's most important problem. An engraved IPA silver bowl is awarded annually. Established in 1976 in memory of Daniel Webster, the American statesman and author.

• 11817 •
International Polka Association
Kenneth P. Gill, Pres.
4608 S Archer Ave.
Chicago, IL 60632-2932
Toll-Free: 800-TO-POLKA
E-mail: ipa@internationalpolka.com
Home Page: http://www.internationalpolka.com

• 11818 • Joseph Jozwiak Memorial Special Achievement Award
To recognize polka enthusiasts who have graciously extended themselves with specific contributions in benevolence. Awarded annually.

• 11819 • Polka Music Awards
To recognize individuals or groups who excel as artists and performers of polka music. Awards are presented in the following categories: favorite single recording, favorite album, favorite female vocalist, favorite male vocalist, and favorite instrumental group. Selections are based on recordings that are certified by the manufacturer as having been released during the past year, and on evaluation of radio exposure, sales, and public appearances. Individual plaques and medals are awarded annually. Established in 1968.

• 11820 • Polka Music Hall of Fame
To recognize the individual efforts and contributions of personalities involved in the enhancement of polka music. Two living people, one deceased person, and one pioneer are elected every year. Candidates must have been active a minimum of 20 years in various capacities of polka music such as musician, bandleader, radio and TV DJ, vocalist, producer, ballroom operator, recordings, news columnist, or association leadership; must have made outstanding contributions and efforts towards the promotion of polka music; and achieved some degree of national prominence. Monetary prizes, plaques, and a diamond centered lapel pin are awarded annually. Conducted in conjunction with the International Polka Festival. Established in 1968. In 1983, the Pioneer Category was added to honor deserving personalities who have been active in polka music for over 40 years.

• 11821 •
International Precious Metals Institute
Dr. Larry Manziek, Exec.Dir.
4400 Bayou Blvd., Ste. 18
Pensacola, FL 32503-1908
Phone: (850)476-1156
Fax: (850)476-1548
E-mail: mail@ipmi.org
Home Page: http://www.ipmi.org

• 11822 • Henry J. Albert Award
To recognize and encourage outstanding theoretical or experimental contributions to the metallurgy of precious metals. A palladium medal and a certificate are awarded. Established in 1979. Sponsored by Engelhard Corporation.

• 11823 • IPMI Distinguished Achievement Award
To recognize important career contributions to the advancement of precious metals, either technological, economic, or business. A plaque bearing a precious metal medallion is awarded and the recipient is invited to present the award lecture at the IPMI Annual Meeting. Established in 1977.

• 11824 • IPMI Student Award
To recognize and encourage outstanding work by graduate or undergraduate students who have started or plan to do research or development projects in the field of precious metals. Nominations from faculty members must be received by December 6. Three monetary prizes of $3,000 each, in addition, an IPMI Graduate Student Award of $5,000 is presented to the university to support the work of graduate students. The IPMI Graduate Student Award is sponsored by Gemini Industries, Inc. Established in 1980.

• 11825 •
International Psychohistorical Association
Henry Lawton, Sec.
PO Box 314
New York, NY 10024
Phone: (201)891-4980
E-mail: hwlipa@aol.com
Home Page: http://www.geocities.com/athens/acropolis/8623

• 11826 • Evelyn Bauer Prize
To recognize the woman whose work on psychohistory is most outstanding. If the award is given for a book, research paper, or presentation that is delivered elsewhere, the recipient will then give a presentation based upon her work at the annual IPA convention, although the winner need not be a member of the IPA. A monetary award of $100 to $500 is presented annually. Established in 1988 in memory of Evelyn Bauer, a pioneer in the field of psychohistory and a former member of the Executive Committee. Additional information is available from Henry Lawton, M.A., M.L.S., 266 Monroe Avenue, Wyckoff, NJ 07481.

• 11827 • Emilio Bernabei Prize
To recognize an outstanding paper on psychohistory. Preference is given to presentations on dreams. Full-time students who attend the annual IPA convention are eligible. A monetary award of $300 is presented annually. Established in 1988 by Mena and Dominic Potts in memory of Mrs. Potts' father, Emilio Bernabei. Additional information is available from Henry Lawton, M.A., M.L.S., 266 Monroe Avenue, Wyckoff, NJ 07481.

• 11828 • Economic Award
To encourage the psychohistorical study of economics and business. Membership is not required. A monetary award of $500 is presented annually. Established in 1990 by William Joseph.

• 11829 • Rose and Michael David Elovitz Prize
To recognize a full-time graduate student of outstanding promise who presents a paper at the annual IPA convention. A monetary award of $100 is presented annually. Established in 1988 by Paul H. Elovitz in memory of his parents, Rose and Michael David Elovitz. Additional information is available from Henry Lawton, M.A., M.L.S., 266 Monroe Avenue, Wyckoff, NJ 07481.

• 11830 • Azar Kalbache and Zahara Ben Mamou Award
To encourage professional presentations by scholars early in their careers. ABD (all but dissertation) graduate students, recent Ph.D.'s (witin three years), or recent graduates of psychoanalytic institutes (within three years) are eligible. Presentations on family history are welcome. The award is based on a presentation given at the IPA convention. Paper must be submitted by May 1st. Membership is not required. A monetary award of $100 is awarded annually at the convention, or shortly thereafter. Established in 1990 by Adele Aniane Kalbache Brosh in memory of her parents, Azar Kalbach (father) and Azhara Ben Mamou (mother). Additional information is available from Henry Lawton, Secretary, 266 Monroe Avenue, Wyokoff, NY 07481, phone: (201) 891-4980.

• 11831 •
International Public Management Association for Human Resources
Neil Reichenberg, Exec.Dir.
1617 Duke St.
Alexandria, VA 22314
Phone: (703)549-7100
Fax: (703)684-0948
E-mail: membership@ipma-hr.org
Home Page: http://www.ipma-hr.org

• 11832 • **IPMA Award for Excellence**
To recognize the overall quality, accomplishments, and contributions of an agency personnel program that exceeds the normal operation of a "good government personnel program." Any member public agency may be nominated. Established in 1986.

• 11833 • **IPMA Honorary Life Membership**
For recognition of persons who have rendered distinguished service in advancing or upholding the purposes of the International Personnel Management Association. Active members of the Association are eligible. A plaque is awarded annually. Established in 1949.

• 11834 • **Warner W. Stockberger Achievement Award**
To recognize and honor a person in public or private life who has made an outstanding contribution to public personnel management in terms of any of the following: encouraging acceptance of personnel administration principles as an aid to better management; skillful application of personnel administration principles to any group of employees; leadership in favor of sound personnel principles by developing, sponsoring, or promoting progressive legislation strengthening personnel management in the public service; leadership in developing creative responses to new and unusual challenges in personnel management; and distinguished teaching, authorship, or research. A plaque is awarded annually. Established in 1949 to honor Dr. Warner W. Stockberger, a pioneer and leader in federal personnel administration and the first Director of Personnel of the U.S. Department of Agriculture.

• 11835 •
International Publishing Management Association
Carol Kraft, COO
1205 W College St.
Liberty, MO 64068
Phone: (816)781-1111
Fax: (816)781-2790
E-mail: ipmainfo@ipma.org
Home Page: http://www.ipma.org
Formerly: (1986) In-Plant Printing Management Association; In-Plant Management Association.

• 11836 • **James M. Brahney Grant**
To promote education in the field of in-house graphic communications management and to recognize institutions of higher learning that demonstrate excellence in graphic communications educational programs. Nominations are only accepted from IPMA chapters. The nomination deadline is February 1. Five scholarships valued up to $1,000 are presented annually. Established in 1967 and renamed in 1976 to honor James M. Brahney, founder and first president of IPMA. Formerly: (1976) IPMA Educational Award.

• 11837 • **In-House Promotional Excellence Award**
For recognition of creative and superior promotional campaign(s) developed by and used to promote in-house printing and duplicating departments. The deadline for applications is February 1 of each year. Crystal awards are presented for first, second, and third place annually at the Association's educational conference. Established in 1989. Formerly: (1996) Excellence in In-Plant Promotion Award.

• 11838 • **In-Print Award**
To recognize outstanding achievement and craftsmanship in printing by in-house printing and graphic arts departments of government agencies, educational institutions, and private business and industry. Printed materials must have been produced during the previous calendar year to be eligible. Entries must be postmarked by January 31. A plaque and one year membership in IPMA are awarded to first place winners in all categories. Plaques are presented to second place, third place, and Honorable Mention winners. Best of Show winner receives a crystal obelisk. Awarded annually at the Association's educational conference and exhibit. Established in 1962. Co-sponsored by IPMA and *In-Plant Graphics* magazine. Formerly: Fine Printing Awards.

• 11839 • **International Member of the Year Award**
To recognize outstanding contributions to the Association and its members during the preceding year. The IPMA International Member of the Year holds a special place as an industry leader and volunteer leader within the Association. IPMA's 10 members selected as Regional Members of the Year automatically become nominees for International Member of the Year. The deadline for nominations is January 10. Established in 1979.

• 11840 • **International Retired Member of the Year Award**
To honor a retired member for outstanding contributions to the Association and its members during the preceding year. The awardee holds a special place as a retired industry leader and volunteer leader within the Association. IPMA's ten members selected as Regional Retired Member of the Year automatically become nominees for this award. Deadline for nominations is January 10.

• 11841 • **IPMA Fellow Member**
To recognize those individuals who by their actions or achievements have supported the goals of the Association in some extraordinary manner. Members must be nominated by at least 10 other members. The nomination is submitted to IPMA international board of directors, where it must receive unanimous approval to grant Fellow Member status. A plaque is awarded when merited at IPMA's conference. Established in 1981.

• 11842 • **IPMA International Vendor/Associate Member of the Year Award**
To honor a vendor/associate member for outstanding contributions to the Association's goals and activities. The 10 individuals selected as Regional Vendor/Associate Members of the Year automatically become nominees for selection as International Vendor/Associate Member of the Year. The deadline for nominations is January 10. A plaque or special award is presented each year at the annual Association awards banquet. Established in 1988.

• 11843 • **Management Award**
To recognize excellence in the management of in-house printing, graphic arts, and mailing departments that demonstrably produce a significant, favorable impact on the operations and objectives of their parent company or organization. The deadline is February 1 of each year. A plaque is presented annually at the IPMA educational conference. Established in 1985.

• 11844 • **Print on Demand Applications Award**
To honor in-house publishers who have used the innovative printing method of print on demand. Categories are: Primary and Secondary Education, Colleges and Universities, Insurance, Hospitals and Health. Government, and Other. Deadline is February 1. Winners receive a plaque at the annual awards banquet. Established in 1996.

• 11845 • **Print on Demand Award**
To recognize and encourage IPMA members to continue to shift printing processes from conventional to digital methods and to share the benefits that departments have gained through the use of new technology. The award will identify specific applications in industries that lend themselves to On Demand Printing and raise awareness levels on what can be done to implement this technology.

• 11846 •
International Radio and Television Society Foundation
Joyce M. Tudryn, Pres.
420 Lexington Ave., Ste. 1601
New York, NY 10170
Phone: (212)867-6650
Fax: (212)867-6653
Home Page: http://www.irts.org
Formerly: (1995) International Radio and Television Society.

• 11847 • **Foundation Award**
Four awards presented to outstanding individuals for significant achievement in the given year.

Awarded at the IRTS Foundation Newsmaker Luncheon in May. Established in 1994.

• 11848 • **Gold Medal Award**
To recognize distinguished contributions to or achievements in the field of electronic communications. A gold medal is awarded annually. Established in 1960.

• 11849 •
International Reading Association
Alan E. Farstrup, Exec.Dir.
800 Barksdale Rd.
PO Box 8139
Newark, DE 19714-8139
Phone: (302)731-1600
Fax: (302)731-1057
E-mail: pubinfo@reading.org
Home Page: http://www.reading.org

Formed by merger of: International Council for the Improvement of Reading; National Association for Remedial Teaching.

• 11850 • **Advocacy Award**
Recognizes state and provincial councils that demonstrate how they are working to affect educational policy and legislation through effective advocacy at the local, state/provincial and/or nation. Awarded annually.

• 11851 • **Arbuthnot Award**
To honor an outstanding college or university teacher of children's and young adult literature. Nominees must be Association members, affiliated with a college or university, and engaged in teacher and/or librarian preparation at the undergraduate and/or graduate level. The deadline is November 15. Established in 1986, the award offers a $1,000 cash prize. Additional information is available from the Executive Office, International Reading Association.

• 11852 • **Award of Excellence**
For state and provincial associations that have organized and implemented a wide range of programs and activities that serve and support councils and members, contribute to education and support programs and goals of the association. Awarded annually.

• 11853 • **Broadcast Media Awards for Television**
To recognize outstanding reporting and programming on television and cable television that deal with reading and literacy, recognize the value of reading in today's society, and/or promote reading as a lifetime habit. Entries must be oriented toward the general public rather than professionals in reading education, and must be informational, critical, or motivational rather than instructional. Submissions may include, but are not limited to: journalism on reading in the schools, home, and community, including accounts of research and educational practices, daily coverage of reading activities, and appraisal of school reading programs; interview programs on reading in the schools and community, or reading education in general; public service programming that informs about reading, seeks to instill the love of reading, and/or promotes literacy; and entertainment programming that effectively informs about reading, promotes literacy, and/or seeks to instill the love of reading. Entries must have appeared between January 1 and December 31 of the year preceding the award and must reach the selection committee by January 7. Established in 1977. Information on submitting radio entries is available from the Public Information Office, International Reading Association. Formerly: Broadcast Media Awards for Radio and Television.

• 11854 • **Developing Country Grants**
Awarded to members of the association residing in developing countries who seek support for literacy projects in their own countries. Number of grants awarded annually is determined by the amount of donations made each year.

• 11855 • **Dina Feitelson Research Award**
To honor exemplary work published in English in a refereed journal that reports on empirical study investigating aspects of literary acquisition such as phonemic awareness, the alphabetic principle, bilingualism, or cross-cultural studies of beginning reading. A monetary prize of $500 is awarded annually. Deadline is September 15.

• 11856 • **William S. Gray Citation of Merit**
To recognize a nationally or internationally known person for outstanding contributions to the field of reading. The deadline is October 15. Additional information is available from the Executive Office, International Reading Association. Established in 1956. Renamed in 1982 to honor William S. Gray.

• 11857 • **Albert J. Harris Award**
To recognize outstanding published works on the topics of reading disabilities and the prevention, assesment, or instruction of learners experiencing difficulty learning to read. Publications that have appeared in a professional journal or monograph during the year of the award between June 1 and May 31 are eligible. The deadline for submissions is September 15. A monetary award of $500 is presented annually. Established in 1975. Additional information is available from the Research and Policy Division of the International Reading Association.

• 11858 • **Honor Council Program**
For local and special interest councils that organize and conduct well-rounded programs serving the council members, the community, the state/provincial association or affiliate, and the Association. Awarded annually.

• 11859 • **Lee Bennett Hopkins Promising Poet Award**
Given every three years to a promising poet of children's and young adult poetry who has published no more than two books. Entries must be received by December 1. Awarded annually. Established in 1995. The $500 award is supported by a grant from Lee Bennett Hopkins.

• 11860 • **Institute for Reading Research Fellowship**
No additional information available.

• 11861 • **International Citation of Merit**
To recognize an individual clearly visible through international activities in the field of literacy, whose activities are for the benefit of countries other than, as well as, the nominee's country. The deadline is October 15. Awarded biennially in even-numbered years. Established in 1967. Additional information is available from the Executive Office, International Reading Association.

• 11862 • **IRA Children's Book Award**
For recognition of a first or second book, either fiction or nonfiction, by an author who shows unusual promise in the children's book field. Books from any country and in any language copyrighted during the calendar year are considered. Awards are presented in three categories: primary, intermediate, and young adult. Entries in a language other than English must include a one-page abstract in English, and a translation into English of one chapter, or similar selections that in the submitter's estimation is representative of the book. Entries must be received by December 1. A monetary prize of US $500 is awarded annually in each category. The award was first presented in 1975 for a book published in 1974. To submit a book for consideration by the selection committee, send 10 copies to the chair. Additional information is available from the Executive Office, International Reading Association.

• 11863 • **IRA Presidential Award for Reading and Technology**
Honors educators who have made an outstanding contribution to the field of reading education through the use of technology.

• 11864 • **Eleanor M. Johnson Award**
To recognize a current outstanding elementary classroom teacher of reading and language arts. Candidates must be Association members, have a minimum of five years' teaching experience, and be endorsed by four persons. The deadline is November 15. A monetary award of US $1,000 is presented. Established in 1989 to honor Eleanor M. Johnson, founder and editor-in-chief of *Weekly Reader*. Sponsored by *Weekly Reader* Corporation. Additional information is available from the Executive Office, International Reading Association.

• 11865 • **Elva Knight Research Grant**
For research in reading and literacy, that addresses significant questions for the disciplines of literacy research and practice.

• 11866 • Local Council Community Service Award
To recognize a local International Reading Association council for outstanding service to its community and literacy. National affiliates are eligible in countries without local councils. The deadline is November 7. Additional information is available from Council Program Associate, Division of Council and Affiliate Services.

• 11867 • Constance M. McCullough Award
Assists a member of the Association in the investigation of reading-related problems and to encourage international professional development activities that are carried out in countries outside North America. A monetary prize of $5,000 is awarded annually.

• 11868 • Ronald W. Mitchell Convention Travel Grant
Provides funding to allow teachers of children in grades 4 and 5 (ages 10-11) that might not otherwise have the opportunity to attend an IRA annual convention.

• 11869 • Outstanding Dissertation of the Year Award
To recognize the dissertation considered most outstanding in reading or related fields. Studies using any research approach (ethnographic, experimental, historical, survey, etc.) completed between September 1 and August 31 of the award year are eligible. Each study is assessed in the light of this approach, the scholarly qualification of its report, and its significant contributions to knowledge within the reading field. The deadline is October 1. A monetary award of US $1,000 is presented annually and is supported by a grant from Scott Foresman. Established in 1964. Additional information is available from the Research and Policy Division, International Reading Association.

• 11870 • Outstanding Teacher Educator in Reading Award
To recognize an outstanding college or university teacher of reading methods or reading-related courses. Nominees must be International Reading Association members, affiliated with a college or university, and engaged in teacher preparation in reading at the undergraduate and/or graduate levels. Entries must be received by October 15. Additional information is available from the Executive Office, International Reading Association.

• 11871 • Print Media Award
To recognize outstanding reporting in newspapers, magazines, and wire services related to reading. Entries may include in depth studies of reading instruction, discussion of research, or ongoing coverage of reading programs in the community. The contest is limited to professional journalists. The deadline is January 7. Established in 1964. Additional information is available from the Public Information Office, International Reading Association. Formerly: (1970) Annual News Award.

• 11872 • Reading/Literacy Research Fellowship
For researcher residing outside the U.S. or Canada who has experienced exceptional promise in reading research. A monetary prize of $5,000 is awarded.

• 11873 • Helen M. Robinson Grant
To assist doctoral students at the early stages of their dissertation research in the area of reading and literacy. Applicants must be Association members. A monetary prize of $1,500 is awarded annually.

• 11874 • Regie Routman Teacher Recognition Award
To honor an outstanding elementary teacher dedicated to improving teaching and learning through reflective writing about his or her teaching and learning process. All applicants must be association members. Applications must be received by November 1. Awarded annually. Established in 1994. The $1,000 award is supported by a grant from Regie Routman.

• 11875 • Nila Banton Smith Award
To recognize the classroom teacher or reading teacher who has shown leadership in translating theory and current research into practice for developing content and literacy. Applicants be actively teaching students in the 7th through 12th grade range or equivalent. The recipient of this award must have demonstrated excellence at the classroom level, in addition to either the building level or district level. The deadline for nominations is November 15. A monetary award of US $1,000 is awarded annually. Established in 1978. The award honors Nila Banton Smith, the ninth president of the Association. Additional information is available from the Executive Office, International Reading Association.

• 11876 • Special Service Award
To recognize, from time to time, unusual and distinguished service to the International Reading Association. The deadline is October 15. Established in 1966. Additional information is available from the Executive Office, International Reading Association.

• 11877 • Teacher as Researcher Grant
Support teachers in their inquiries about literacy and instruction. Inquire for application details.

• 11878 • Travel Grants for Educators
Provides support to educators from any country for meetings (across continents) sponsored by the association.

• 11879 • Gertrude Whipple Professional Development Grant
Assist a member with the planning and creation of professional development projects, the production of high-quality materials, the marketing and scheduling of meetings and workshops and the logistic support for conducting them.

• 11880 • Paul A. Witty Short Story Award
To recognize the author of an original short story published for the first time during the preceding year in a periodical for children. The short story should serve as a literary standard that encourages young readers to read periodicals. Entries must be submitted by December 1. A stipend of US $1,000 is awarded. Established in 1986. Additional information is available from the Exeuctive Office, International Reading Association.

• 11881 •
International Readings at Harbourfront Centre
235 Queens Quay W
Toronto, ON, Canada M5J 2G8
Phone: (416)973-4760
Fax: (416)954-4323
E-mail: readings@harbourfront.on.ca
Home Page: http://www.readings.org

• 11882 • Harbourfront Festival Prize
To recognize an individual who has made a substantial contribution to the world of books and writing through his or her own writing and/or labours on behalf of other writers. A monetary prize of $10,000 is awarded annually.

• 11883 •
International Recording Media Association
Charles Van Horn, Pres.
182 Nassau St., Ste. 204
Princeton, NJ 08542-7005
Phone: (609)279-1700
Fax: (609)279-1999
E-mail: info@recordingmedia.org
Home Page: http://www.recordingmedia.org

Formerly: (1990) International Tape/Disc Association.

• 11884 • Gold and Platinum Video Awards
To mark the audited sale of videos. For the Gold Award, the sale of a minimum of 125,000 units or a minimum of $9 million at suggested retail price for a theatrical video; and 25,000 units and $1 million at suggested retail price for non-theatrical or music videos is required. For the Platinum award, the sale of a minimum of 250,000 units or a minimum of $18 million at suggested retail price for a theatrical video; and 50,000 units and a minimum of $2 million at suggested retail price for non-theatrical or music video is required. Only U.S. sales are included. Certification is awarded when the requisite sale has been achieved and the company applies for certification. Established in 1980. Formerly: ITA Golden Videocassette Awards.

• 11885 •
International Religious Liberty Association
Dr. John Graz, Sec.Gen.
12501 Old Columbia Pike
Silver Spring, MD 20904-6600
Phone: (301)680-6686
Fax: (301)680-6695
E-mail: rasmussenc@gc.adventist.org
Home Page: http://www.irla.org

• 11886 • **IRLA Award**
Recognizes defense and promotion of religious freedom. Awarded annually.

• 11887 •
International Rescue Committee - USA
George Rupp, Pres./CEO
122 E 42nd St.
New York, NY 10168-1289
Phone: (212)551-3000
Toll-Free: 877-REF-UGEE
Fax: (212)551-3180
E-mail: info@theirc.org
Home Page: http://www.theIRC.org

• 11888 • **Freedom Award**
For recognition of outstanding contributions to human freedom and the cause of refugees. A plaque is awarded as determined by the Board of Directors. Established in 1957.

• 11889 •
International Road Federation
C. Patrick Sankey, CEO
1010 Massachusetts Ave. NW, Ste. 410
Washington, DC 20001
Phone: (202)371-5544
Fax: (202)371-5565
E-mail:
info@internationalroadfederation.org
Home Page: http://www.irfnet.org

• 11890 • **Man of the Year**
For recognition of distinguished contributions to the development of roads and road transport, and in recognition of personal achievements and leadership in the transportation profession. A parchment scroll is awarded annually. Established in 1951.

• 11891 •
International Save the Pun Foundation
Norman Gilbert, Chm.
Box 5040, Sta. A
Toronto, ON, Canada M5W 1N4
Phone: (416)736-7126
Fax: (416)736-7116
E-mail: punpunpun@rogers.com
Home Page: http://www.punpunpun.com

• 11892 • **Punster of the Year**
To recognize a major contribution to the art of word play. Applicants must have contributed materially through any of the arts, including the performing arts, to the use of puns as a form of humor and thus encouraged people to take a greater interest in reading. A framed certificate and international publicity are awarded annually at the foundation's annual dinner. Established in 1988.

• 11893 •
International Sculpture Center
Mary Catherine Johnson, Associate Dir.
14 Fairgrounds Rd., Ste. B
Hamilton, NJ 08619-3447
Phone: (609)689-1051
Fax: (609)689-1061
E-mail: isc@sculpture.org
Home Page: http://www.sculpture.org

• 11894 • **Lifetime Achievement in Contemporary Sculpture**
Annual recognition for achievement in sculpture field.

• 11895 • **Outstanding Sculpture Educator**
For achievement in sculpture field. Recognition is given annually.

• 11896 • **Outstanding Student Achievement in Contemporary Sculpture**
For achievement in sculpture field. Recognition is given annually.

• 11897 • **Patron's Recognition Award**
For achievement in sculpture field. Recognition is given annually.

• 11898 •
International Section of the National Council on Family Relations
Jacki Fitzpatrick CFLE, Chair
3989 Central Ave. NE, Ste. 550
Minneapolis, MN 55421
Phone: (763)781-9331
Toll-Free: 888-781-9331
Fax: (763)781-9348
E-mail: info@ncfr.org
Home Page: http://www.ncfr.org

• 11899 • **Jan Trost Award**
Award of recognition. A plaque is presented annually.

• 11900 •
International Shuffleboard Association
Joe Messier, Pres.
390 Santa Fe Trail
North Fort Myers, FL 33917
Phone: (239)543-1235
Fax: (905)458-7759
E-mail: jhmessier@earthlink.net
Home Page: http://www.trigger.net/~sandy/internat.htm

• 11901 • **Team Awards**
To recognize the winners of men's and women's team events. Individuals of all ages from the United States, Canada, Japan, Australia, and Zimbabwe are eligible. A traveling trophy and an individual plaque are awarded annually at a special inaugural tournament. Established in 1979 by the National Shuffleboard Association.

• 11902 •
International Side-Saddle Organization
Linda Bowlby, Pres.
PO Box 1104
Bucyrus, OH 44820
Phone: (419)284-3176
Phone: (609)476-4598
Fax: (609)476-2977
E-mail: issoaside@aol.com
Home Page: http://www.sidesaddle.com

• 11903 • **National Champion Bronze Statue**
To recognize the U.S. National Champion Side-Saddle Rider each year. A bronze statue is awarded annually. Established in 1974. Formerly: (1995) Empress Elizabeth National Champion.

• 11904 •
International Sign Association
Lauren Dwyer, Membership Mgr.
707 N Saint Asaph St.
Alexandria, VA 22314
Phone: (703)836-4012
Phone: (703)836-4015
Fax: (703)836-8353
E-mail: lauren.dwyer@signs.org
Home Page: http://www.signs.org

Formerly: (1996) National Electric Sign Association.

• 11905 • **Sign Design Competition**
To recognize outstanding sign designs. The Junior Division is open to students enrolled at a vocational, high school, community college, or university; entrants must be sponsored by an ISA member company. The Professional Division is open to all professional sign designers, except for those companies represented by the panel of judges. Specific contest assignments are issued each year. Criteria used in judging include innovation, communication functions, design harmony, and practical completion of assignment. The following prizes are awarded: a monetary award of $2,000 to the winning entry in the Professional Division and $500 in the Junior Division; a second prize of $1,000 in the Professional Division and $300 in the Junior Division; and a third prize of $500 in the Professional Division and $100 in the Junior Division. A plaque depicting the winning design is also presented to the company/school of the first prize winners. In addition to cash awards, non-cash Merit Awards and Honorable Mentions are awarded. Additionally, all winners and their employer companies/schools receive plaques and certificates. Awarded annually at the ISA International Sign Expo. Established in 1946.

• 11906 •
International Silo Association
Joe Shefchik, Pres.
332 Brookview Dr.
PO Box 8264
Luxemburg, WI 54217
Phone: (920)265-6235
E-mail: info@silo.org
Home Page: http://www.silo.org

Absorbed: (1980) National Silo Association.

• 11907 • **Zur Craine Award**
For recognition of an individual who has contributed outstanding service to the silo and silage equipment industry. Nominations are sought from ISA members. A medallion is presented annually. Established in 1959 in memory of Zur Craine who provided 43 years of active participation in the Association and was its first President. Sponsored by the George Whitesides Company of Louisville, Kentucky.

• 11908 • **Honorary Member**
To recognize an individual who has rendered conspicuous and exemplary service to the Association and who deserves recognition and thanks for his voluntary contributions toward its continued success. Nominations by members are accepted. A plaque is presented, usually each year, at the annual convention. Established in 1957.

• 11909 •
International Slurry Surfacing Association
Michael R. Krissoff, Exec.Dir.
3 Church Cir., PMB 250
Annapolis, MD 21401
Phone: (410)267-0023
Fax: (410)267-7546
E-mail: krissoff@slurry.org
Home Page: http://www.slurry.org

• 11910 • **President's Award**
Recognizes innovation and contracting excellence. Awarded annually.

• 11911 •
International Snowmobile Manufacturers Association
Edward Klim, Pres.
1640 Haslett Rd., Ste. 170
Haslett, MI 48840-8607
Phone: (517)339-7788
Fax: (517)339-7798
E-mail: snow@snowmobile.org
Home Page: http://www.snowmobile.org

• 11912 • **International Award of Merit**
Recognizes government officials providing service to the industry. Awarded annually.

• 11913 •
International Soap Box Derby
Jeff Iula, Gen.Mgr.
PO Box 7225
Akron, OH 44306
Phone: (330)733-8723
Fax: (330)733-1370
E-mail: soapbox@aasbd.org
Home Page: http://ndr.org/AASBD1.htm

• 11914 • **All-American Soap Box Derby**
To recognize individuals who have placed in the top nine in each division in the world. The stock division contestants, who are 9 through 16 years old, build cars from kits purchased from All-American headquarters. The Kit Car division gives competitors an opportunity to expand their knowledge and build a more advanced model. The masters division champions, who are 11 through 17 years old, build the more traditional, sleeker, layback cars. Scholarships are given to the top three, and trophies are awarded to the top nine and junior division winners. Presented annually at a ceremony at a local theatre in Akron. Established in 1934.

• 11915 •
International Society for Astrological Research
Raymond A. Merriman, Pres.
PO Box 38613
Los Angeles, CA 90038
Phone: (805)525-0461
Toll-Free: 800-982-1788
Fax: (805)933-0301
E-mail: maitreya@csiway.com
Home Page: http://www.isarastrology.com

• 11916 • **Grants for Astrological Research**
To support astrological research that seeks to validate, test, revise, or improve the current understanding of astrological theory and astrological techniques. The grants are intended to provide funds for items not normally available from the investigator's resources. Allowable items include specialized services, supplies, microfilms or other forms of unique data, payments of informants or subjects, and computer time (only when use of a microcomputer is inadequate or unavailable through ISAR). All persons interested in conducting research on astrology may submit a proposal for evaluation. ISAR membership is considered in the evaluation, but is not a requirement. Grants are awarded for periods of up to 24 months.

• 11917 •
International Society for Augmentative and Alternative Communication
Clare Bonnell, Exec.Dir.
49 The Donway W, Ste. 308
Toronto, ON, Canada M3C 3M9
Phone: (416)385-0351
Fax: (416)385-0352
E-mail: clare.bonnell@isaac-online.org
Home Page: http://www.isaac-online.org

• 11918 • **Bridge School International Award**
To learn and teach augmentative and alternative communication methods in an educational centre of excellence in the United States. Winner will receive exposure to strategies that will ensure that children with severe speech and physical impairments achieve full participation in their communities through the use of augmentative and alternative means of communication. The successful candidate also receives travel and accommodation expenses as well as a salary, and then mentor support after returning home. Awarded annually. Sponsored by Bridge School Foundation.

• 11919 • **Shirley McNaughton Exemplary Communication Award**
To recognize individuals for exemplary communication as instructors. The recipient will be provided a 1-2 week internship opportunity for training in Blissymbolics. A $500 Canadian contribution for travel to the Learning Centre in Bala, Ontario, is also awarded annually.

• 11920 • **WORDS/ISAAC AAC Consumer User Scholarship**
To provide financial assistance to a person who uses Augmentative/Alternative Communication (AAC) to obtain education and/or training at the postsecondary level. Any AAC user using aided and/or unaided AAC systems, or ISAAC member is eligible. Applicants must submit a 300- to 500-word essay addressing what they plan to do with the scholarship and why and where they plan to use the scholarship. Pertinent personal background information, a time schedule for a two-year period educational curriculum, a short curriculum vitae, and two letters of recommendation are also required. A monetary award of $3,000 is awarded at the Biennial ISAAC Conference.

• 11921 • **WORDS/ISAAC Outstanding Consumer User Lecture Award**
To provide recognition to outstanding person who uses Augmentative/Alternative Communication (AAC) and to provide a platform for the users to address consumers and professionals on a subject of their choice. All AAC users using aided and/or unaided AAC systems, and ISAAC members are eligible. Applicants must submit a 500- to 1,000-word essay addressing the chosen topic, an indication of the kind of format they are planning to use, an outline of the content of the lecture, and a statement of intent to attend the biennial conference and to present the lecture if selected. A monetary award of $3,000 is awarded at the biennial conference. Application deadline is February 1.

• 11922 • **Words+ Outstanding Consumer Lecture Award**
To provide a platform for an outstanding person who uses Augmentative and Alternative Communication (AAC) to present a topic using any voice output communication system (speech generating device) in which s/he has special expertise. Lectures highlight an individual's talent (e.g., story telling, humor, creative writing), life

perspective (current events, relationships) or individual scholarly endeavors/expertise. A featured presentation at the ISAAC Biennial Conference and a cash award of $3,000 is awarded annually. Sponsored by Words+ Inc. Formerly: Johnston Distinguished Lecture Award.

• 11923 •
International Society for Burn Injuries
Dr. Ronald Tompkins M.D., Sec.-Treas.
Massachusetts General Hospital
55 Fruit St.
Boston, MA 02114-2696
Phone: (617)726-3447
Fax: (617)367-8936
E-mail: rtompkins@partners.org
Home Page: http://www.worldburn.org

• 11924 • **Tanner-Vandeput Prize for Burn Research**
Recognizes the individual who has made the greatest contribution to burn research. Awarded quadrennially.

• 11925 •
International Society for Developmental Psychobiology
Regina Sullivan, Sec.
McLean Hospital
Department of Psychiatry
115 Mill St.
Belmont, MA 02478
Phone: (540)231-5346
Fax: (540)231-3652
E-mail: rsullivan@ou.edu
Home Page: http://www.isdp.org

• 11926 • **ISDP Dissertation Prize**
To recognize an individual for an outstanding dissertation in developmental psychobiology. Nominees must have successfully completed defense of the doctoral dissertation. Nomination must occur within 12 months of the student's degree date. A plaque is awarded annually at the convention. Established in 1989.

• 11927 • **David Kucharski Young Investigator Award for Research in Developmental Psychobiology**
To recognize individuals for outstanding research in developmental psychobiology. Nominees must be ISDP members who received their Ph.D. or M.D. degree at least four but no more than seven years prior to the nomination. A plaque is awarded annually at the convention. Established in 1989.

• 11928 •
International Society for Education through Art
(Societe Internationale pour l'Education Artistique)
Rachel Mason, Contact
% D. Smith-Shank, Sec.
School of Art
Northern Illinois University
DeKalb, IL 60115
Phone: (815)753-7880
Fax: (815)753-7701
E-mail: u21dls1@wpo.cso.niu.edu
Home Page: http://www.insea.org

• 11929 • **Mahmoud El-Bassioury Award**
To reward long-standing activities in art education. Awarded three times per year.

• 11930 • **International Society for Education through Art Awards**
To promote the exchange of information in the field of art and design education through publications, papers, and conferences.

• 11931 • **Sir Herbert Read Award**
To recognize outstanding service to international art education. Awarded triennially.

• 11932 •
International Society for Heart and Lung Transplantation
Amanda W. Rowe, Exec.Dir.
14673 Midway Rd., Ste. 200
Addison, TX 75001
Phone: (972)490-9495
Fax: (972)490-9499
E-mail: ishlt@ishlt.org
Home Page: http://www.ishlt.org

Formerly: International Society for Heart Transplantation.

• 11933 • **Philip K. Caves Award**
To encourage and reward original work in medical research that offers promise for the future. Applicants must submit an abstract. A monetary award of $1,000 and a certificate are presented annually at the Scientific Sessions. Established in 1982 in honor of Philip K. Caves, who developed and pioneered the technique of transvenous endomyocardial biopsy to be used in the monitoring of cardiac graft tolerance. Limited to individuals who are residents, fellows, or graduate students.

• 11934 •
International Society for Individual Liberty
Vincent H. Miller, Pres./Ed.
836-B Southampton Rd., No. 299
Benicia, CA 94510-1960
Phone: (707)746-8796
Fax: (707)746-8797
E-mail: isil@isil.org
Home Page: http://www.isil.org

Absorbed: (1991) Libertarian International.

• 11935 • **Freedom Torch**
To recognize major contributions to the cause of human liberty around the world. A gold medal is awarded at world conventions. Established in 1986.

• 11936 •
International Society for Iranian Studies
Haideh Sahim MC, Exec.Dir.
109-14 Ascan Ave., Ste. 5J
New York University
50 Washington Square S, Rm. 306
Forest Hills, NY 11375
Phone: (212)995-4689
Fax: (212)955-4144
E-mail: director@iranian-studies.com
Home Page: http://www.iranian-studies.com

• 11937 • **Saidi-Sirjani Memorial Book Prize**
Recognizes an excellent book on topic of Persian studies write secretariat for details. A monetary award is given annually.

• 11938 •
International Society for Performance Improvement
Rick Battaglia, Exec.Dir.
1400 Spring St., Ste. 260
Silver Spring, MD 20910
Phone: (301)587-8570
Fax: (301)587-8573
E-mail: info@ispi.org
Home Page: http://www.ispi.org

Formerly: (1995) National Society for Performance and Instruction.

• 11939 • **Chapter of Excellence Award**
No further information was available for this edition.

• 11940 • **Distinguished Chapter Award**
No further information was available for this edition.

• 11941 • **Outstanding Chapter Communication Products Award**
To recognize an individual chapter's overall performance improvement during the preceding two-year period. Chapters that have excelled in producing programs and publications, have responded to member needs, and have served the profession and the society are eligible. A plaque is awarded annually.

• 11942 • **Outstanding Human Performance Intervention Award**
To recognize outstanding results derived from the application of non-instructional human performance technologies to human performance problems or needs. Research may include, but is not limited to, non-training solutions such as performance appraisal systems, feedback systems, incentive programs, and other performance solutions. Submission deadline is October 15. A plaque is awarded annually.

• 11943 • Outstanding Instructional Communication Award
To recognize an outstanding communication that enables individuals or organizations to achieve excellence in the human performance technologies. The format of the instructional communication is completely open and may include, but is not limited to, book, film, videodisc, videotape, presentations, newsletter, article, or other forms of communication. Submission deadline is October 14. A plaque is awarded annually.

• 11944 • Outstanding Instructional Product or Intervention Award
To recognize outstanding results derived from instructional products and interventions developed through systematic approaches to human performance problems or needs. Submission deadline is October 14. A plaque is awarded annually. Formerly: Outstanding Instructional Product.

• 11945 • Outstanding Performance Aid Award
To recognize outstanding results achieved through the design and implementation of material used on the job to assist the performer in accomplishing a task. Submission deadline is October 14. A plaque is awarded annually.

• 11946 • Outstanding Research Award
To recognize outstanding research in the field of Human Performance Technology or a related field such as adult education, human technology, behavioral psychology, or vocational education. Submission deadline is October 14. A plaque is awarded annually. Formerly: (1996) Outstanding New Systematic Application Award.

• 11947 • Outstanding Student Research Award
To recognize outstanding research conducted by a graduate student in the field of Human Performance Technology or a related field such as adult education, human technology, behavioral psychology, or vocational education. Submission deadline is October 14. A plaque is awarded annually.

• 11948 •
International Society for Pharmaceutical Engineering
Robert Best, CEO
3109 W Dr. Martin Luther King Jr. Blvd., Ste. 250
Tampa, FL 33607
Phone: (813)960-2105
Fax: (813)264-2816
E-mail: customerservice@ispe.org
Home Page: http://www.ispe.org

• 11949 • Affiliate of the Year Award
To recognize outstanding work by one of the affiliates. Criteria include membership growth, number and quality of local activities, participation in international committees, and innovation. Awarded annually.

• 11950 • Chapter Excellence Awards
To recognize outstanding work by one of the North American chapters. Awards are presented in the following categories: Service to the Society/Industry; Membership Services; Chapter Management; Most Improved Chapter; Membership Development, and Student Development. Awarded annually.

• 11951 • Company of the Year Award
To recognize the company who contributed the most to the achievement of ISPE's goals. The company must have members in the Society to be eligible for the award. An engraved plaque is awarded annually at the ISPE annual meeting in November. Established in 1981.

• 11952 • ISPE Distinguished Achievement Award
For untiring guidance, dedication, and loyalty to ISPE. Candidate must be a member of the Society and nominated by a fellow member. A distinctive trophy is awarded annually at the ISPE annual meeting in November. Established in 1990. Formerly: ISPE Engineer of The Year.

• 11953 •
International Society for Philosophical Enquiry
Dr. Robert M. Campbell, Dir. of Admissions
2202 Brampton Rd.
Walnut Creek, CA 94598-2318
Phone: (925)939-2124
Fax: (925)216-7730
E-mail: robcampbell@aya.yale.edu
Home Page: http://www.thethousand.com

• 11954 • Mentor
To recognize an individual for achievements, advancing a field of knowledge, and service to mankind exemplifying the ideals of the Society, which is dedicated to the advancement of human knowledge through personal accomplishment, advanced enquiry, and creative contributions. Non-members are eligible for nomination by a member during January each year. A certificate, honorary membership in the Society, a biography in *TELICOM*, and an invitation to publish papers are awarded when merited.

• 11955 • Whiting Memorial Fund Award
To help advance work relating to the purposes and goals of the Society by recognizing those who have made outstanding contributions to humanity. Recipients are chosen by a vote of the Whiting Memorial Fund Committee. A monetary award and/or a plaque or other commemorative object are awarded annually to one recipient. Established in 1988 to honor the late C. Randolph "Steve" Whiting, first President of the ISPE.

• 11956 •
International Society for the Arts, Sciences and Technology
Roger Malina, Exec.Dir.
211 Sutter St., Ste. 800
San Francisco, CA 94108
Fax: (415)391-2385
E-mail: isast@leonardo.info
Home Page: http://www.leonardo.info

• 11957 • Leonardo Award for Excellence
To recognize excellence in an article published in the society's journal, *Leonardo.* A monetary award of $500 is awarded annually. Established in 1987. Formerly: Coler - Maxwell Medal.

• 11958 • Frank J. Malina - Leonardo Prize for Lifetime Achievement
To recognize an eminent artist who, through a lifetime of work, has achieved a synthesis of contemporary art, science, and technology. Individuals may be nominated by members of the society. A monetary award of $500 is awarded annually. Established in 1985 in honor of Dr. Frank J. Malina, American rocketry pioneer, kinetic artist and, founder of the journal *Leonardo.*

• 11959 • New Horizons Award for Innovation
To recognize new and emerging artists for innovation in new media. A monetary award of $500 and an invitation to publish an article in ISAST's journal, *Leonardo*, are presented annually. Established in 1986.

• 11960 • Makepeace Tsao Leonardo Award
To recognize organizations and artists' groups that increase public awareness of art forms involving science and technology through the sponsoring or curating of exhibitions. Established in 1997.

• 11961 •
International Society for the Study of Human Ideas on Ultimate Reality and Meaning
Institute for URAM
Allen Utke, Pres.
PO Box 38
Pickering, ON, Canada L1V 2R2
Phone: (905)839-3858
Fax: (905)839-3387
E-mail: jperry@chass.utoronto.ca
Home Page: http://matrix.scranton.edu/uram/section2.html

• 11962 • URAM Award for Excellence in Creative Endeavors for Research and Scholarship
To recognize innovative organizations promoting URAM research and scholarship. Candidates must be involved in a creative endeavor for URAM research and scholarship and must be selected by the Governing Council of the Society. A certificate is awarded biennially. Established in 1985.

• 11963 • **URAM Award for Excellence in Creative Scholarly Writing**
To promote creative scholarly writing that deals with the idea of ultimate reality and in-depth meaning of any subject matter. The candidate is selected by the community of the section editors of the URAM journal. A certificate is awarded biennially. Established in 1985.

• 11964 •
International Society for Traumatic Stress Studies
Rick Koepke, Exec.Dir.
60 Revere Dr., Ste. 500
Northbrook, IL 60062
Phone: (847)480-9028
Fax: (847)480-9282
E-mail: istss@istss.org
Home Page: http://www.istss.org

• 11965 • **Chaim Danieli Young Professional Award**
To recognize excellence in service or research in the field of traumatic stress by an individual who has completed training within the last five years. Awarded annually. Established in 1989 by Yael Danieli, Ph.D., in memory of her father.

• 11966 • **Sarah Haley Memorial Award for Clinical Excellence**
To recognize a clinician working in direct service to traumatized individuals whose written and/or verbal communications to the field exemplify the work of Sarah Haley. Awarded annually. Established in 1994.

• 11967 • **Robert S. Laufer PhD Memorial Award for Outstanding Scientific Achievement**
To recognize an individual or group that has made an outstanding contribution to research in the PTSD field. Awarded annually. Established in 1991 by Ellen Frey-Wouters in memory of her husband.

• 11968 • **Lifetime Achievement Award**
The highest honor given by ISTSS, this award recognizes the individual(s) who has made the greatest lifetime contribution(s) to the field of PTSD. Awarded annually. Established in 1985. Formerly: (1994) Pioneer Award.

• 11969 •
International Society for Vehicle Preservation
Walter R. Haessner, Exec.Dir.
PO Box 50046
Tucson, AZ 85703-1046
Phone: (520)622-2201
Fax: (520)792-8501
E-mail: isvp@earthlink.net
Home Page: http://www.aztexcorp.com/root/isvp.html

• 11970 • **IAMA Award**
Recognizes excellence in automotive media. A trophy is awarded annually.

• 11971 •
International Society of Air Safety Investigators
Frank S. Del Gandio, Pres.
107 E Holly Ave., Ste. 11
Sterling, VA 20164
Phone: (703)430-9668
Fax: (703)430-4970
E-mail: isasi@erols.com
Home Page: http://www.isasi.org

• 11972 • **Jerome F. Lederer Award**
To recognize outstanding contributions to technical excellence in accident investigation. Members may submit nominations to the chairman of the awards committee. A plaque is presented annually at the ISASI seminar. Established in 1977 to honor Jerome F. Lederer.

• 11973 •
International Society of Applied Intelligence
Dr. Moonis Ali, Pres.
Texas State University, San Marcos
Department of Computer Science
601 University Dr.
San Marcos, TX 78666-4616
Phone: (512)245-3409
Fax: (512)245-8750
E-mail: cs@txstate.edu
Home Page: http://isai.cs.txstate.edu

• 11974 • **IAE/AIE Best Papers Award**
Recognizes outstanding papers presented at ISAI conference. Awarded annually.

• 11975 •
International Society of Appraisers
Jorge N. Sever, Exec. Dir.
1131 SW 7th St., Ste. 105
Renton, WA 98055
Phone: (206)241-0359
Toll-Free: 888-472-4732
Fax: (206)241-0436
E-mail: isa@isa-appraisers.org
Home Page: http://www.isa-appraisers.org

• 11976 • **Media Award**
Recognizes an article promoting professionals in appraising. Awarded annually.

• 11977 •
International Society of Biometeorology
Dr. Scott Greene, Sec.
Department of Geography
Univ. of Oklahoma
Fuji-Yoshida
Norman, OK 73071
Phone: (405)325-4319
Fax: (405)447-8455
E-mail: jgreene@ou.edu
Home Page: http://www.es.mq.edu.au/ISB

• 11978 • **Biometeorological Research Foundation Award**
To recognize scientists for outstanding research in biometeorology. Awarded triennially. Established in 1971.

• 11979 • **International Society of Biometeorology Honorary Member**
To recognize scientists for outstanding contributions in the field of biometeorology.

• 11980 • **William F. Peterson Foundation Awards**
To recognize outstanding scientists in the fields of animal, human, and plant biometeorology. A gold medal is awarded triennially. Established in 1966. Additional information is available from R.J. Reiter, Dept. of Anatomy, Health Science Center, University of Texas, 7703 Floyd Curve Dr., San Antonio, TX, 78283.

• 11981 •
International Society of Certified Electronics Technicians
Mack Blakely, Exec.Dir.
3608 Pershing Ave.
Fort Worth, TX 76107-4527
Phone: (817)921-9101
Toll-Free: 800-946-0201
Fax: (817)921-3741
E-mail: info@iscet.org
Home Page: http://www.iscet.org

• 11982 • **Chairman's Award**
To recognize an individual or an organization for long and outstanding work promoting ISCET, the CET program, technical training, or technical achievement. Awarded annually when merited. Established in 1985.

• 11983 • **Governor's Award**
To recognize an individual or an organization for exceptional work promoting ISCET, the CET program, technical training, or technical achievement throughout the year. Awarded annually when merited. Established in 1985.

• 11984 • **Technician of the Year Award**
To recognize a technician for outstanding work in the field of electronics. Established in 1976.

• 11985 •
International Society of Chemical Ecology
Dr. Stephen Foster, Sec.
Dept. of Biology
State University of New York ESF
1 Forestry Dr.
Syracuse, NY 13210-2726
E-mail: stephen.foster@ndsu.nodak.edu
Home Page: http://www.chemecol.org

• 11986 • **ISCE Silver Medal**
Award of merit. Awarded annually. Inquire for application details.

Awards are arranged in alphabetical order below their administering organizations

• 11987 • **Silverstein-Simeone Award Lecture**
Award of merit. Awarded annually. Inquire for application details.

• 11988 • **Student Travel Awards**
Awarded annually for merit and need.

• 11989 •
International Society of Dermatology
Torello Lotti MD, Sec.Gen.
138 Palm Coast Pkwy. NE, No. 333
Palm Coast, FL 32137
Phone: (386)437-4405
Fax: (847)429-9545
E-mail: info@intsocdermatol.org
Home Page: http://www.intsocdermatol.org

Formerly: (1984) International Society of Tropical Dermatology.

• 11990 • **Castellani - Reiss Medal and Award**
To recognize the most outstanding work in tropical, geographic ecology of dermatoses, and/or the underlying basic sciences, during the period between World Congresses of the Society. A monetary prize of $1,000, a gold medal, and travel expenses to attend the World Congress are awarded every five years. Established in 1969 in honor of the founders of the Society, Aldo Castellani and Frederick Reiss. Additional information is available from Francisco Kerdel, M.D., Treasurer-General, 1400 NW 12th Ave., 6 South, Dermatology Miami, FL 33136.

• 11991 •
International Society of Explosives Engineers
Jeffrey L. Dean, Exec.Dir. and Gen.Counsel
30325 Bainbridge Rd.
Cleveland, OH 44139-2295
Phone: (440)349-4400
Fax: (440)349-3788
E-mail: isee@isee.org
Home Page: http://www.isee.org

• 11992 • **Blasters Leadership Award**
For distinguished service to the explosives industry. Awarded annually.

• 11993 • **President's Award**
Annual award of recognition.

• 11994 •
International Society of Logistics
8100 Professional Pl., Ste. 111
Hyattsville, MD 20785
Phone: (301)459-8446
Fax: (301)459-1522
E-mail: solehq@sole.org
Home Page: http://www.sole.org

• 11995 • **Chapter Awards**
To recognize chapters that meet the program goals of the Society and standards of excellence through successful and effective activities. Total quality management, rather than peer chapter competition is evaluated. Platinum, Gold, Silver, Bronze, and Copper Awards are presented. In addition, the Society presents a Chapter Newsletter Award to the most outstanding newsletter.

• 11996 • **Distinguished Service Award**
This, the highest honor bestowed on individuals for service to the Society, is given to recognize contributions made over a continuous period of time (at least 10 years). Candidates must have served at least two terms on either the Board of Directors or the Logistics Education Foundation's Board of Governors. Awarded annually at the annual Symposium in August. Established in 1984.

• 11997 • **Eccles Medal**
To recognize outstanding achievements in the development or advancement of logistics education. Members and non-members are eligible. Two awards may be given annually, one to an individual and another to an organization or institution. The award is named for the late Rear Admiral Henry Eccles, famous Navy logistician.

• 11998 • **Fellow**
To recognize a member for professional logistics accomplishments, outstanding contributions to the Society, education, outstanding contributions to the field of logistics, and special honors/recognition in the field. Candidates must have been members for at least five continuous years. An honorary membership is awarded annually.

• 11999 • **Field Awards**
To recognize technical achievement and professional contributions of logisticians. Covering the entire functional spectrum of logistics, the awards focus on specific areas each year. Awarded annually at the annual Symposium in August.

• 12000 • **Founders Medal**
This, the highest honor which the Society can bestow on an individual, is given for recognition of outstanding achievements in logistics engineering, technology, or management that have had a national or international impact. Members and non-members are eligible. Awarded annually in August at the annual Symposium.

• 12001 • **President's Award for Merit**
To recognize individuals who have provided superior service and have contributed significantly to meeting the Society goals during the past year. The President of the Society makes the selection. Awarded annually at the annual Symposium in August.

• 12002 • **Jack L. Williams Space Logistics Medal**
To recognize individuals for outstanding achievements in the field of space logistics through their vision, leadership, and technical excellence. Members and non-members are eligible. Awarded annually. Established in honor of Jack Williams, NASA director, Kennedy Space Center, from 1983 until his death in 1989.

• 12003 • **Young Logistician Award**
To recognize a junior member who exemplifies the continued vitality and growth of the society by his/her own professional development and contributions. Candidates must be 35 years of age or younger who have been members of the Society for less than five years. One winner is selected in each district. Complimentary one-year membership extension is awarded annually. Established in 1991.

• 12004 •
International Society of Meeting Planners
Robert G. Johnson, Exec.Dir.
1224 No. Nokomis NE
Alexandria, MN 56308-5072
Phone: (320)763-4919
Fax: (320)763-9290
E-mail: ismp@iami.org
Home Page: http://www.iami.org/ismp.cfm

• 12005 • **Meeting Facility of the Year**
Recognizes outstanding service to ISMP. Awarded annually.

• 12006 •
International Society of Parametric Analysts
Allison Brown, Service Contractor
PO Box 3185
Town & Country Branch
Chandler, AZ 85244
Phone: (480)917-4747
Phone: (636)262-0269
Fax: (480)792-6930
E-mail: ispaoffice@earthlink.net
Home Page: http://www.ispa-cost.org

• 12007 • **Best Article - *Journal of Parametrics* Award**
To recognize the author(s) of the highest rated article published in the *Journal of Parametrics* during the preceding year. This award is determined by the panel of Journal referees prior to the annual conference in time to invite the winner(s) to attend the conference to receive the award. A monetary prize of $250 and a plaque are presented annually.

• 12008 • **ISPA Keith Bulbridge Award**
To recognize an individual, group, or corporation, whose support has displayed continuing efforts to reflect a dedication to the principles and goals of the Society during prior years. This award is meant to bring activities undertaken as a volunteer effort to the attention of the Society. Nominations are accepted from the general membership only. A plaque is awarded at the annual conference when merited. Established in 1988.

• 12009 • **Conference Speaker Award and Best Workshop Speaker Awards**
To recognize the overall best speaker at the conference and best speaker in each workshop,

respectively. All awards in the category are judged at the annual conference by ballots scored by conference attendees. Tabulation of all ballots and finalization of winners (and overall Conference Speaker Award winner) are performed by the Honors and Awards Committee. Since the highest rated Best Workshop Speaker also wins the Conference Speaker Award, only the Conference Speaker Award plaque is presented to that individual. All awards in this category are presented at the conclusion of all workshops. A plaque is presented to each winner.

• 12010 • Frank Freiman Award

This, the Society's most prestigious medal, is given to recognize outstanding contributions to the theoretical or applied aspects of parametric modeling or cost estimating over a significant amount of time. It is to be awarded in recognition of parametric model building, promotion of parametrics, or application of parametric analysis. Nominations from the membership are accepted. A plaque and citation are presented at the Convention when merited. Established in 1982 in honor of Frank Freiman, a proponent of parametric costing and father of RCA price-leased models. Additional information for this award and others is available from Iva Voldase, Honors and Awards Chair, TRW One Space Park, Bldg. R2, Room 2050, Redondo Beach, CA, 90278. Tel: (310)813-6510.

• 12011 • Parametrician of the Year

To recognize an individual or group who has made outstanding contributions to the profession of parametric cost analysis during prior years. This typifies a leader in the activities of practicing or promoting the use of parametrics. Nominations are accepted from the membership of ISPA members. A plaque is presented at the annual conference when merited. Established in 1981.

• 12012 •
International Society of Phonetic Sciences
Prof. Ruth Huntley Bahr, Pres.
4202 E Fowler Ave., PCD 1017
Dept. of Communication Science and Disorders
University of South Florida
Tampa, FL 33620
Phone: (813)974-3182
Fax: (813)974-0822
E-mail: rbahr@chuma1.cas.usf.edu
Home Page: http://www.isphs.org

• 12013 • Honors of the Association

To recognize outstanding phoneticians who have made material and long-term contributions to the discipline and the Society. A monetary award of $500 and a plaque are awarded every four years. Established in 1979.

• 12014 • Kay Elemetrics Award for Research in Phonetics

For recognition of scientific contributions to the phonetic sciences by leading world phoneticians. Nomination by three or more ISPhS members/officers/fellows is necessary for consideration. A monetary prize of $1000 and a plaque are awarded biennially in even-numbered years. Established in 1983 by the Society and John Crump, President of Kay Elemetrics.

• 12015 • Smith Memorial

To recognize an individual for service or research in applied phonetics. A monetary award of $1,000 DM and a plaque are awarded biennially in odd-numbered years. Established in 1984.

• 12016 •
International Society of Political Psychology
Bruce Dayton, Exec.Dir.
ISPP Central Office
Syracuse Univ.
346 Eggers Hall
Syracuse, NY 13244
Phone: (315)443-4470
Fax: (315)443-9085
E-mail: ispp@maxwell.syr.edu
Home Page: http://ispp.org

• 12017 • Erik H. Erikson Award

Recognizes early career achievements in political psychology. Awarded annually.

• 12018 • Alfred M. Freedman Award

Recognizes the best paper presented at the annual meeting.

• 12019 • Jeanne N. Knutson Award

Recognizes distinguished service to the society.

• 12020 • Harold D. Lasswell Award

Recognizes distinguished scientific contribution to political psychology. Awarded annually.

• 12021 • Nevitt Sanford Award

For distinguished professional contribution to the field. Awarded annually.

• 12022 •
International Society of Psychiatric Mental Health Nurses
Lynette W. Jack, Pres.
7600 Terrance Ave., Ste. 203
1211 Locust St.
Middleton, WI 53562
Phone: (608)836-3363
Toll-Free: 800-826-2950
Fax: (215)545-8107
E-mail: info@ispn-psych.org
Home Page: http://www.ispn-psych.org

• 12023 • Robert O. Gilbert Foundation Research Award

To support the focus of research in mental health or mental illness in children, adolescents and/or their families. Awarded annually with a monetary prize. Established in 1995.

• 12024 •
International Society of Travel and Tourism Educators
Sharon Scott, Pres.
23220 Edgewater
St. Clair Shores, MI 48082-2037
Phone: (586)294-0208
Fax: (586)294-0208
E-mail: joannb@istte.org
Home Page: http://www.istte.org

• 12025 • JTTM Award for Excellence in Travel and Tourism Education

Recognizes the most significant contributions to the field of travel and tourism education during the past year. Individuals and institutions are eligible. Awarded annually.

• 12026 •
International Society of Weekly Newspaper Editors
Dr. Chad Stebbins, Exec.Dir.
Institute of International Studies
Missouri Southern State University
3950 E Newman Rd.
Joplin, MO 64801-1595
Phone: (417)625-9736
Fax: (417)659-4445
E-mail: stebbins-c@mssu.edu
Home Page: http://www.iswne.org

• 12027 • Eugene Cervi Award

To recognize outstanding and aggressive local reporting and/or outstanding reporting of local government. Reporters who work for newspapers published fewer than five days per week are eligible. A bronze statue and expenses paid trip to conference are awarded annually. Established in 1976.

• 12028 • Golden Quill Award

To recognize excellence in editorial writing in weekly newspapers throughout the world. Commercial newspapers published less than five days per week are eligible. The twelve finalists are called the Golden Dozen. The top winner receives a gold plaque and expenses paid trip to annual conference which are awarded annually in July. Established in 1961.

• 12029 •
International Society of Weighing and Measurement
Steve Kendra, Pres.
15245 Shady Grove Rd., Ste. 130
Rockville, MD 20850
Phone: (301)258-1115
Fax: (301)990-9771
E-mail: staff@iswm.org
Home Page: http://www.iswm.org

Formerly: (1985) National Scale Men's Association.

• 12030 • Earl Curl Award

To recognize the Outstanding Local Division of ISWM. A gavel is awarded annually at the Technical Conference. Established in 1961. Sponsored by Nicol Scales, Inc., Dallas, TX.

• 12031 • Miles D. Fishman Memorial Award

To recognize an outstanding young person who has contributed in a significant manner to the promotion of the scale industry, weights and measures, and/or the Society. Members under 40 years of age are eligible. A trophy or plaque is awarded annually at the Technical Conference. Established in 1983 in memory of Miles D. Fishman, an energetic and hard working member of the Society. Sponsored by the Scale Dealers Association.

• 12032 • ISWM Woody Woodland Memorial Award

To honor an individual who has, by his or her own efforts and services, contributed in an outstanding manner to the scale or weighing industry. Selection is be based on any phase of the profession, including weights and measures enforcement, and may be given posthumously. A plaque is awarded annually at the Technical Conference of the Society. Established in 1959 by Mack Rapp in memory of J. E. Woodland, who dedicated his life to the scale industry.

• 12033 • Lady of the Year Award

To encourage active participation in the Society on the part of wives of members and women in the weighing industry, and to recognize the invaluable contributions they have made to the Society and the industry. An honorarium of $100, one dozen roses, and a certificate or plaque are awarded annually at the Technical Conference. Established in 1979.

• 12034 • Mark Pickell Award

To honor an active member of a local division of the Society who has worked to create interest in and strengthen the Society on a local level. A plaque is awarded annually. Established in 1963 to honor Mark W. Pickell, former Secretary-Treasurer of the Society. Sponsored by Spinks Scale Company, Atlanta, Georgia.

• 12035 • Technical Excellence Award

To recognize technical achievement in the weighing industry for discovery or successful application of a principle or concept. The principle must be of a technical nature, must have been introduced within the past 100 years, be unique, represent an improvement to increase efficiency and/or accuracy of weighing equipment, and must have been in use for a reasonable period of time. It must also be of economic significance and foster advancement of the industry. An honorarium of $200, a stylized pyramid shaped ring-handled weight, and a certificate are awarded annually. Established in 1979.

• 12036 •

International Softball Congress
Ken Hackmeister, Exec.Dir.
153 East 200 South, Ste. 10
Farmington, UT 84025
Phone: (801)447-8807
Fax: (801)447-8793
E-mail: iscken@comcast.net
Home Page: http://www.iscfastpitch.com

Formed by merger of: (1958) International Softball League; National Softball Congress.

• 12037 • Bob Welby Memorial Recognition of Service Award

For recognition of special service and/or contributions to the International Softball Congress and fast pitch softball in general. This award is for individuals who do not otherwise qualify for induction into the ISC Hall of Fame. A plaque, placed in the ISC Hall of Fame in Kimberly, Wisconsin, is awarded annually. Established in 1990.

• 12038 • Marvin Casteel Memorial Award

For recognition of the runner-up team in the annual International Softball Congress World Fastpitch Tournament. An elaborate 5-foot trophy is awarded annually. The trophy was renamed in 1989 in memory of long-time ISC administrator Marv Casteel of Ogden, Utah.

• 12039 • Carrol Forbes Memorial Award

For recognition of the best men's fastpitch softball team of the world. The team that wins the International Softball Congress World Fastpitch Tournament is designated the best. An elaborate 6-foot trophy is awarded annually. The ISC World Tournament was established in 1947. The trophy was re-named in 1983 in memory of Carrol Forbes (1909-1982), founder and executor of the ISC. Formerly: (1983) ISC World Championship Trophy.

• 12040 • ISC Hall of Fame

To recognize outstanding softball players, umpires, and administrators. Players must have been out of competition for the past five years or have reached their 40th birthday while still playing. The nominee must have been named to the All-World (American) team at least once during his or her career. A plaque is awarded. At least one individual is inducted each year. Established in 1953.

• 12041 • Rawlings Sporting Goods Company ISC All-World Awards

To recognize the outstanding individuals and teams in softball. Awards are given in the following categories: first team, second team, most valuable player, outstanding pitcher, leading hitters, most runs batted in, team sportsmanship, and best dressed team. Formerly: ISC All-World Awards; (1996) Phillips Petroleum Company ISC All-World Awards.

• 12042 •

International Steel Guitar Convention
Scott (Scotty) DeWitt, Founder
9535 Midland Blvd.
St. Louis, MO 63114-3314
Phone: (314)427-7794
Phone: (314)427-7795
Fax: (314)427-0516
E-mail: scotty@scottysmusic.com
Home Page: http://scottysmusic.com

• 12043 • Steel Guitar Hall of Fame

To recognize players of the steel guitar who have made outstanding musical achievements. Individuals of any age from any country who have devoted their musical life to the steel guitar are eligible. A plaque is awarded annually at the International Steel Guitar Convention. Established in 1978 by DeWitt A. Scott, Sr. to coincide with the International Steel Guitar Convention.

• 12044 •

International Studies Association
Thomas J. Volgy, Exec.Dir.
324 Social Sciences Bldg.
Univ. of Arizona
Tucson, AZ 85721
Phone: (520)621-7715
Phone: (520)621-1208
Fax: (520)621-5780
E-mail: isa@u.arizona.edu
Home Page: http://www.isanet.org

• 12045 • Carl Beck Award

To recognize the best graduate student authored paper in the field of International Studies. The committee looks for original papers that deal with traditional concerns in new and interesting ways or with emergent conditions or problems. A $300 cash prize is awarded annually. The award honors Carl Beck and was established in 1980.

• 12046 • Karl Deutsch Award

To recognize the scholar under the age of forty, or within ten years of the acquisition of a doctoral degree, who is judged to have made, through a body of publications, the most significant contribution to the study of international relations and peace research. A $500 cash prize is awarded annually at the Association's annual convention. Established in 1981 by World Academy of Art and Science and the Peace Science Society (International) to commemorate the life work of Karl W. Deutsch, Stanfield Professor of Peace at Harvard University.

• 12047 • Feminist Theory and Gender Studies Graduate Paper Award

To honor the best feminist theory/gender studies graduate student paper presented at any ISA convention. A monetary prize is awarded annually. Established in 1995.

• 12048 • Harold and Margaret Sprout Award

For recognition of a book or piece of research that the award committee judges to be the best research work published in English in the last two years on international environmental affairs. The responsibility for selection lies with the Environmental Studies Section of the International Studies Association. A $250 cash prize is presented annually. Established in 1972, to honor Harold and Margaret Sprout, two pioneers in the study of international environmental problems.

• 12049 •
International Sunfish Class Association
Terry Beadle, Sec.
PO Box 300128
Waterford, MI 48330-0128
Phone: (248)673-2750
Fax: (248)673-2750
E-mail: sunfishoff@aol.com
Home Page: http://www.sunfishclass.org

• 12050 • **World Champion Award**
Annual awards of recognition. Qualifications are made by country and one week of races.

• 12051 •
International Surfing Association
Fernando Aguerre, Pres.
5580 La Jolla Blvd., Ste. 145
La Jolla, CA 92037
Phone: (858)551-5292
Fax: (858)551-5290
E-mail: surf@isasurf.org
Home Page: http://www.isasurf.org

• 12052 • **Kahuna Award**
Recognizes a supporter of ISA. Awarded annually. Inquire for application details.

• 12053 •
International Swimming Hall of Fame
Bruce Wigo, Pres./CEO
1 Hall of Fame Dr.
Fort Lauderdale, FL 33316
Phone: (954)462-6536
Fax: (954)522-4521
E-mail: bwigo@ishof.org
Home Page: http://www.ishof.org

• 12054 • **International Marathon Swimming Hall of Fame Award**
Recognizes those who have excelled in marathon swimming.

• 12055 • **International Swimming Hall of Fame Gold Medallion Award**
For recognition of a former competitive swimmer for his or her national or international significant achievement in the fields of science, art, business, or government. Selection is made by the Board of Directors of the International Swimming Hall of Fame from a list of distinguished citizens nominated from the world of swimming. There are no restrictions other than that the recipient must be an outstanding adult whose life is an inspiration for swimmers. A gold medallion is awarded annually. Established in 1983 by M. R. "Cy" Young, the Mayor of Fort Lauderdale.

• 12056 • **International Swimming Hall of Fame Honoree**
For recognition of individuals who have distinguished themselves in the sport of swimming, diving, synchronized swimming, water polo, or as a contributor or coach. Competitors who have been out of competition for at least four years and swimming coaches who have given at least 25 years of service are eligible. A laminated plaque and a special International Swimming Hall of Fame blazer crest are awarded annually in May. Established in 1965. Over 400 athletes have been inducted.

• 12057 • **ISHOF Service Award**
Honors the individual who has made many contributions to the International Swimming Hall of Fame. Nominees must have given great service not only to the Hall, but to his or her sport, school, community, and family.

• 12058 • **G. Harold Martin Award**
To honor long and exceptional leadership, insight, dedication, and friendship to theInternational Swimming Hall of Fame. Awarded annually. Established in 1996.

• 12059 • **Presidential Honor Award**
To recognize extraordinary athletic achievement or exceptional endowment of theInternational Swimming Hall of Fame. Awarded annually. Established in 1995.

• 12060 • **Al Schoenfield Media Award**
Recognizes those who have promoted swimming through all forms of the media.

• 12061 • **John K. Williams Jr. International Adaptive Aquatic Award**
To honor an individual who has made significant and substantial contributions to the field of adaptive aquatics (aquatics for persons with disabilities) as a participant, athlete, teacher, instructor, coach, organizer, administrator, or media representative. Awarded annually. Established in 1994.

• 12062 •
International Technology Education Association
Kendall N. Starkweather PhD, Exec.Dir.
1914 Association Dr., Ste. 201
Reston, VA 20191-1539
Phone: (703)860-2100
Fax: (703)860-0353
E-mail: itea@iteaconnect.org
Home Page: http://www.iteaconnect.org

• 12063 • **Academy of Fellows**
This, the highest award the Association bestows, is given to honor an individual who has gained prominence in technology education and who has brought honor to the technology education profession. A citation and membership in the Academy of Fellows are awarded annually.

• 12064 • **Award of Distinction**
To recognize an individual who has distinguished him/herself through accomplishment in the improvement of instruction, research and scholarship, and/or effective teaching. Members of the technology education profession are eligible. A plaque is awarded annually. Established in 1973.

• 12065 • **Distinguished EEA - SHIP Member Award**
To honor an outstanding member of EEA-SHIP who has developed a better and closer working relationship between responsible firms doing business in the education field and educators. Nominations for this award may be made by the Association in cooperation with the Education Exhibitors Association representative. Three names may be submitted to the Special Citation Committee for consideration. Established in 1978.

• 12066 • **Distinguished Technology Educator Award**
To recognize technology educators who have demonstrated a high level of competence and ethical fitness in technology education. Awarded annually.

• 12067 • **Rutherford B. Lockette Humanitarian Award**
To recognize an individual who has put forth outstanding efforts to promote humanistic values while serving as a professional in the technology education field. Established in 1984.

• 12068 • **Meritorious Service Award**
Presented to an individual worthy of commendation for excellence of service to the International Technology Education Association. The recipient must be an ITEA member.

• 12069 • **Prakken Professional Cooperation Award**
To recognize an individual who, through teaching, research, and professional service, has promoted the field of technology education in collaboration with other fields of discipline. To qualify for this award, individuals should be involved with projects that collaborate with other disciplines, such as science, engineering, mathematics, marketing, management, etc. The recipient of the award may be from inside or outside of the field of technology education. Nominees do not need to be members of ITEA. Awarded annually.

• 12070 • **Program Excellence Award**
To recognize technology education classroom teachers at the elementary, middle, or high school levels for their outstanding contributions to the profession and their students through outstanding technology education programs. Awarded annually.

• 12071 • **Special Recognition Citation**
To recognize an individual who has performed outstanding service to or for the Association, or

Awards are arranged in alphabetical order below their administering organizations

to or for technology education. The citation may be made for persons within or outside the technology profession or a commercial and professional organization.

• 12072 • Teacher Recognition Awards

To recognize outstanding technology education teachers in each of the United States and Canadian provinces. Technology education classroom teachers below the college level who are members of the Association are eligible. A certificate and a plaque are presented to each winner. Awarded annually when merited.

• 12073 •

International Tennis Hall of Fame
Mark L. Stenning, CEO
194 Bellevue Ave.
Newport, RI 02840
Phone: (401)849-3990
Toll-Free: 800-457-1144
Fax: (401)849-8780
E-mail: newport@tennisfame.com
Home Page: http://www.tennisfame.com

• 12074 • Samuel Hardy Award

To recognize an individual for long and outstanding service rendered to the sport of tennis. The recipient is selected by the directors of the International Tennis Hall of Fame. The permanent trophy, a large sterling tray, was donated by Samuel Hardy to the USTA. The name of each winner is engraved on the tray. The recipient also receives a suitably inscribed award. Awarded annually at the USTA annual meeting. Established in 1953 in memory of Samuel Hardy, who won numerous events on the French Riviera.

• 12075 • International Tennis Hall of Fame Enshrinement

To recognize achievement in or contribution to the game of tennis. Players who have not been a significant factor in competitive tennis during the previous five years are eligible. Writers, coaches, and administrators are also eligible. A plaque mounted in the Museum's Enshrine Room, an enshrine pin, and a certificate are awarded annually in Newport in July. Established in 1955.

• 12076 • Bill Talbert Junior Sportsmanship Award

To recognize junior tennis players who exemplify the finest qualities of sportsmanship in tournament play. Four players chosen from throughout the United States are selected to receive this award each year.

• 12077 • Tennis Educational Merit Award for Men

To recognize the male teaching professional and/or instructor or administrator who has rendered outstanding service to the tennis educational program through leadership, inspiration, and devotion. The permanent trophy is a large silver bowl, on which the winners name is engraved. A suitably inscribed award is presented annually at the USTA annual meeting. Established in 1967. Formerly: Tennis Educational Merit Award.

• 12078 • Tennis Educational Merit Award for Women

To recognize the female teaching professional and/or instructor or administrator who has rendered outstanding service to the tennis educational program through leadership, inspiration, and devotion. The permanent trophy is a large silver bowl, on which the winner's name is engraved. A suitably inscribed award, is presented each year at the USTA annual meeting. Established in 1972. Formerly: Special Educational Merit Award for Women.

• 12079 •

International THEOS Foundation
Russell McKinnon, Pres.
PO Box 7361
Alexandria, VA 22307
Phone: (703)765-0887
E-mail: md1995@erols.com
Home Page: http://theosfoundation.org

• 12080 • Bea Decker Memorial Outreach Award

For recognition of significant contributions to the field of grief and bereavement, specifically in working with recently widowed people in rebuilding their lives. There are no eligibility requirements. The deadline is one month prior to the annual convention normally held between June and October. A certificate is awarded annually at the convention. Established in 1979 in memory of THEOS founder, Bea Decker.

• 12081 •

International Thermographers Association
100 Daingerfield Rd.
Alexandria, VA 22314-2804
Phone: (703)519-8122
Fax: (703)548-3227
E-mail: ita@printing.org
Home Page: http://www.gain.net/PIA_GATF/ita.html

• 12082 • International Thermographers Association Product Excellence Contest

To recognize outstanding examples of production excellence in the thermography industry. The contest is open to anyone engaged in the production of thermography. Plaques and certificates are awarded annually in 20 entry categories, and presented at the annual International Thermographers Convention. Formerly: International Thermographers Product Excellence Contest.

• 12083 •

International Ticketing Association
Jeffrey Larris, Pres.
330 W 38th St., No. 605
New York, NY 10018
Phone: (212)629-4036
Fax: (212)629-8532
E-mail: info@intix.org
Home Page: http://www.intix.org

Formerly: (1997) Box Office Management International.

• 12084 • Box Office of the Year Award

For recognition of the "team." A plaque is awarded at the annual convention. Established in 1989.

• 12085 • Lifetime Achievement Award

For recognition of outstanding achievement for a career box office manager who has served as a mentor and model for the profession. A crystal trophy is awarded at the discretion of the awards committee. Established in 1987.

• 12086 • Spirit Award

To recognize an active BOMI member who has represented BOMI's spirit of enthusiasm, friendship, participation, and cooperation to colleagues and to the industry. All categories of BOMI members, including systems directors, marketing and group sales directors, box office and business managers, vendors and suppliers, etc., are eligible.

• 12087 • Ticketing Professional of the Year Award

For recognition of contributions to the profession of box office management. Members may be nominated by other members or may nominate themselves. A trophy is awarded annually.

• 12088 •

International Track and Field Coaches Association
George Dales, Pres.
1705 Evanston St.
Kalamazoo, MI 49008
Phone: (269)349-1008
Fax: (269)387-4461
E-mail: cdales@webtv.com

• 12089 • Honorary Member

Inquire for application details.

• 12090 •

International Trade Council
Dr. Peter T. Nelsen, Pres.
3114 Circle Hill Rd.
Alexandria, VA 22305-1606
Phone: (703)548-1234
Fax: (703)548-6216

• 12091 • Exporter of the Year

Recognizes innovations in opening new markets. Awarded annually.

• 12092 •
International Transactional Analysis Association
Ken Foselman PhD, Contact
2186 Rheem Dr., No. B-1
Pleasanton, CA 94588
Phone: (925)600-8110
Phone: (510)625-7724
Fax: (925)600-8112
E-mail: ken@itaa-net.org
Home Page: http://www.itaa-net.org

• 12093 • **Eric Berne Memorial Award**
To give recognition to individuals who have published original and significant contributions to transactional analysis in one of four award categories: (1) theory (2) research (3) practice applications (4) the comparison and or integration of transactional analysis theory or practice with other theories or approaches. For more information contact ITAA. The winner receives an inscribed plaque. This is awarded on an annual basis. Established in 1971.

• 12094 •
International Trumpet Guild
Jeffrey Piper, Pres.-Elect
241 E Main St., No. 247
Westfield, MA 01086-1633
Fax: (413)568-1913
E-mail: info@trumpetguild.org
Home Page: http://www.trumpetguild.org

• 12095 • **Carmine Caruso International Jazz Trumpet Solo Competition**
For recognition of jazz trumpeters under 30 years of age. Monetary prizes of $10,000 and $5,000 are awarded triennially. Sponsored by a grant from the Herb Alpert Foundation.

• 12096 • **Honorary Recognition Awards**
To provide recognition for outstanding trumpeters. Awarded when merited.

• 12097 • **International Trumpet Guild Composition Contest**
To stimulate new compositions for trumpet in different categories each year, such as brass quintet and chamber music. The work must be a new composition written for the contest during the preceding two-year period. It must be unpremiered, although a tape recording of a reading is required with the manuscript and performance time must be 10 to 20 minutes. Monetary prizes of $1,500 and $750 are awarded to the first and second place winners. Awarded annually.

• 12098 • **ITG Student Performance Competitions**
To provide recognition for outstanding student trumpeters in the following categories: ITG Solo Performance Competition, ITG Jazz Improvisation Competition, and ITG Mock Orchestra Audition Competition. Competitions are available to ITG member trumpeters who are under 25 years of age. Monetary awards, certificates, and recognition in the *ITG Journal* are awarded annually to winners of each competition. Established in 1977. In addition, there is an annual ITG Conference Scholarship Competition.

• 12099 • **Ellsworth Smith Solo Performance Competition**
For recognition of trumpeters under 30 years of age. Monetary prizes from $2,000 to $7,000 are awarded biennially. Sponsored by a grant from the Columbus Foundation of Columbus, Ohio.

• 12100 •
International Unicycling Federation
John Foss, Dir.
1560 Baylor Ct.
Eagan, MN 55122-1859
Phone: (425)831-7053
Fax: (425)831-7538
E-mail: jfoss@unicycling.com
Home Page: http://www.unicycling.org/iuf

• 12101 • **World Unicycling Championships**
For recognition of outstanding individual, pairs, or group artistic unicycling performances or fastest speeds for 100m, 400m, and 1,500m races at the Championships. Medals and trophies are awarded biennially. Established in 1984.

• 12102 •
International Union of Pure and Applied Physics - USA
(Union Internationale de Physique Pure et Appliquee)
Judy Frantz, Sec.Gen.
One Physics Ellipse
College Park, MD 20740
Phone: (301)209-3270
Fax: (301)209-0865
E-mail: frantz@aps.org
Home Page: http://www.iupap.org

• 12103 • **Award in Magnetism**
To recognize contributions to magnetism. Awarded every three years. Established in 1991 by the International Commission on Magnetism.

• 12104 • **Boltzmann Medal**
To recognize outstanding achievements in thermodynamics or statistical mechanics. A gold medal is awarded triennially by the International Commission on Statistical Physics.

• 12105 • **ICO Prize**
To recognize outstanding achievements in optics. Awarded annually. Established in 1982. Sponsored by the International Commission for Optics. Additional information is available from Dr. P. Chavel, Institut d'Optique, CNRS, BP 147, F-91403 Orsay Cedex, France. fax:(33-1)69358700. Phone: (33-1)69 35 8741 e-mail:pierre.chavel@iota.u-psud.fr

• 12106 • **ICPE Medal for Physics Teaching**
To improve the teaching of physics at all levels of education and on an international basis, and to recognize an outstanding contribution to physics education. The contribution should be major in scope and impact and should have been extended over a considerable period of time. A medal designed by the Hungarian artist Miklos Borsos is awarded biennially. Established in 1980 by the International Commission on Physics Education. Additional information is available from Prof. P.J. Black, Chairman of IUPAP Com. on Physics Education (C14), School of Education, King's College London, Cornwell House, Waterloo Rd., London SE1 8WA, UK Fax (44-171)872 3182. Phone: (44-171)872 3166. E-mail paul.black@kcl.ac.uk

• 12107 • **London Award**
For recognition of outstanding work in the field of low temperature physics. Awarded by the International Commission on Low Temperature Physics. Established in 1958. Additional information is available from Prof. M. Krusius, Chairman of IUPAP Com. on Low Temperature Physics (C5), Low Temperature Laboratory, Helsinki University of Technology, SF-02150 Espoo, Finland. Fax :(358-9) 451 2969. Phone (358-9) 451 2960. Office phone:(358-9)451 2978 (lab). E-mail:krusius@neuro.hut.fi

• 12108 • **Penning Award Excellence in Low-Temperature Plasma Physics**
To recognize contributions to low-temperature plasma physics. Awarded biennially in odd-numbered years. Established in 1991 by the International Commission on Plasma Physics.

• 12109 • **SunAmco Medal**
To recognize achievements and contributions to metrology, the measurement of atomic masses and fundamental principal constants and the units and nomenclature of physics. A medal is awarded as appropriate. Established in 1990 by IUPAP Commission C2: Sun Amco. Additional information is available from Professor A. H. Wapstra, Secretary, IUPAP Commission C2: SunAmco, National Institute for Nuclear Physics and High Energy Physics, Section K, P.O. Box 41882, NL-1009 DB Amsterdam, Netherlands. Fax: (31-20)592-5155. E-mail: wapstra@nikhefk.nikhef.nl

• 12110 • **Young Author Best Paper Award**
In recognition of the best paper by a young author. Awarded biennially in even-numbered years. Established in 1990 by the International Commission on Semiconductors (C8) and sponsored by the semiconductor industries of USA, Japan, and Europe.

• 12111 •
International Veteran Boxers Association
Scoop Gallello, Pres.
35 Brady Ave.
New Rochelle, NY 10805
Phone: (914)235-6820
Fax: (914)654-9785

• 12112 • Steve Belloise Award
To recognize the boxer who has distinguished himself in and out of the ring as a decent and honest individual and who gave the best at all times.

• 12113 • Boxing Hall of Fame Award
To recognize former boxers who have distinguished themselves in the square circle. Inductees must be retired at least five years. A laminated scroll on a wooden base is awarded annually at the Association's banquet. Established in 1969.

• 12114 • Freddie Fiducia Award
To recognize an individual who has shown leadership and dedication in the field of boxing during the previous year. Members of the Association are eligible. A laminated plaque on a wooden base is awarded each year at the Association's convention. Established in 1969 in memory of Freddie Fiducia, a noted heavyweight boxer from New Jersey who exemplified the true boxer - humane and honest.

• 12115 • Fighter of the Year
To recognize a former boxer who has either distinguished himself in the ring or has surmounted obstacles in life and battled the odds. Former boxers, professional or amateur, are eligible. A laminated scroll on a wooden base is awarded annually. Established in 1970.

• 12116 • Humanitarian Award
To recognize a member of the Association who has shown humane and good treatment to all. A laminated scroll on a wooden base is awarded annually. Established in 1970.

• 12117 • Manager of the Year
To recognize a manager who has shown expertise in handling a boxer. Awarded annually. Established in 1991.

• 12118 • Babe Orlando Award
To recognize an individual who has shown literary interest in boxing. A laminated scroll on a wooden base is presented annually at the Association's convention. Established in 1975 in memory of Babe Orlando of New Jersey, a former boxer and a boxing writer, who was the editor and publisher of the boxing monthly, *The Reporter*.

• 12119 • Joe Poodles, Sr. Award
To honor a former boxer who has devoted his energies to aiding the veteran boxer. Awarded annually. Established in 1982.

• 12120 • Irving Silverman Award
To recognize a former boxer who has shown compassion in aiding the stricken destitute former boxer. Established in 1981 in honor of Irv Silverman, a former boxer and the secretary of IVBA since 1964.

• 12121 • Special Award
To recognize an individual for outstanding dedication to the sport of boxing. Awarded annually. Established in 1983.

• 12122 • Trainer of the Year
To recognize a boxing trainer who has conditioned his boxer to the peak of physical condition to prepare him for defensive as well as offensive ring combat. Awarded annually. Established in 1991.

• 12123 •
International Visitors Council - Columbus
Kevin R. Webb, Exec.Dir.
57 Jefferson Ave.
Columbus, OH 43215
Phone: (614)225-9057
Fax: (614)225-0656
E-mail: info@columbusivc.org
Home Page: http://www.columbusivc.org

• 12124 • Citizen Diplomat Award
For outstanding community volunteerism in international activities. Recognition award bestowed annually.

• 12125 •
International Water Resources Association
Ben Dziegielewski, Exec.Dir.
4535 Faner Hall
Carbondale, IL 62901-4516
Phone: (618)453-6021
Fax: (618)453-6465
E-mail: iwra@siu.edu
Home Page: http://www.iwra.siu.edu

• 12126 • The Best Paper Award
Bestowed to the author of the most outstanding paper published in *Water International* during the year. Awarded annually.

• 12127 • Chow Memorial Endowed Lecturer
Bestowed to an internationally acclaimed expert in a water resources field in recognition of his or her exemplary service to science and humanity.

• 12128 • Crystal Drop Award
Recognition long-term contribution to improving the world's water situation. Bestowed to an individual or an organization. Awarded triennially.

• 12129 • IWRA Distinguished Lecturer
Recognizes ingenuity and resourcefulness in adapting water resources technology in a water management program. Awarded annually.

• 12130 •
International Wheat Gluten Association
G. Peter Bunn III, Gen. Counsel
9300 Metcalf Ave., Ste. 300
Overland Park, KS 66212
Phone: (913)381-8180
Fax: (913)381-8836
E-mail: pbunn@fbolaw.com
Home Page: http://www.fbolaw.com

• 12131 • Best Paper Award
For recognition of the paper having the overall best quality slides, presentation, scientific content, and relevance to wheat gluten uses, or applications and industry products in the promotion and consumption of vital wheat gluten. Any individual presenting a paper pertaining to wheat gluten uses/applications and industry products at the annual meeting of the AACC is eligible. A monetary award of $250 and a plaque are presented annually at the American Association of Cereal Chemists Meeting. Established in 1984 by International Wheat Gluten Association Technical Committee.

• 12132 •
International Wild Waterfowl Association
Ali Lubbock, Sec.
Sylvan Heights Waterfowl
PO Box 36
Scotland Neck, NC 27874
Phone: (252)826-5038
Fax: (252)826-5284
E-mail: wildwaterfowl@hotmail.com
Home Page: http://www.wildwaterfowl.org

• 12133 • Conservation Award
For recognition of conservation efforts.

• 12134 • First Breeding Award
To call attention to and encourage avicultural efforts applied to waterfowl species not bred before in North America. Breeders of waterfowl for young that are progeny of a captive pair and have been reared to fledgling are eligible. A parchment certificate is awarded when merited. Established in 1964.

• 12135 • Lifetime of Service to Aviculture Award
For recognition of service to the field of aviculture throughout a lifetime.

• 12136 • Gerard McQuade Memorial Fund Award
To acknowledge and stimulate the entry of new breeders into aviculture, particularly with waterfowl. Breeders with less than five years experience whose achievements are deemed outstanding are eligible. An inscribed hardwood and bronze plaque are awarded annually if merited. Established in 1975.

• 12137 • Outstanding Achievement Awards
To recognize and encourage unusual avicultural effort by breeders in the categories of : (1) wild duck breeding; (2) wild goose breeding; and (3)

swan breeding. An inscribed hardwood and bronze plaque are awarded annually when merited. Established in 1964.

• 12138 • Justin A. Southwick Memorial Award in Aviculture

To honor illustrious avicultural effort with waterfowl, particularly that directed toward establishing new species in captivity. Members of the Association are eligible. An award, selected for each winner, is presented when merited. Established in 1971.

• 12139 • Waterfowl Breeders Hall of Fame

To recognize individuals who, through extraordinary achievement and dedicated service, have contributed significantly to the preservation and collective knowledge of waterfowl. Members are eligible. A limited edition bronze canvasback statue is presented when merited by vote of the Board of Directors. Established in 1987.

• 12140 •
International Wildlife Film Festival and Media Center
Janet Rose, Exec.Dir.
718 Higgins
Missoula, MT 59801
Phone: (406)728-9380
Fax: (406)728-2881
E-mail: iwff@wildlifefilms.org
Home Page: http://www.wildlifefilms.org

• 12141 • International Wildlife Film Festival

To encourage and recognize excellence in wildlife film making, based on the film's scientific accuracy, artistic vision, and technical merit. Etched glass awards and paper certificates are awarded in the following categories: Television Program; Television Series; Independent Production; Children's Series; Children's Program; News Story; Advertising/Public Service Announcement; Amateur Production; Newcomer Production; Government Agency; Scientific Training; Youth Group; Indigenous People's Program; Conservation and Environmental Program; Point-of-View Program; Human-Wildlife Interactions; Large Format; Presenter/Host Program; and Music Video. The following awards are also given: Best of Festival first, second, and third places; Best of Category (providing there are two or more entries); Merit Award; and Honorable Mention.

• 12142 •
International Wizard of Oz Club
Peter E. Hanff, Pres.
PO Box 26249
San Francisco, CA 94126-6249
E-mail: info@ozclub.org
Home Page: http://www.ozclub.org

• 12143 • L. Frank Baum Memorial Award

To honor an individual who has contributed to furthering the enjoyment of the Oz and Baum books. A wooden plaque is awarded annually. Established in 1961.

• 12144 •
International Women's Media Foundation
Lisa Woll, Exec.Dir.
1625 K St. NW, Ste. 1275
Washington, DC 20006
Phone: (202)496-1992
Fax: (202)496-1977
E-mail: info@iwmf.org
Home Page: http://www.iwmf.org

• 12145 • Courage in Journalism Award

To recognize full or part-time, domestic or foreign writers, editors, photographers, and producers who have demonstrated extraordinary bravery and dedication in pursuing their craft under difficult and dangerous circumstances, official secrecy, oppression, political pressure, or any other professionally intimidating obstacle. A crystal sculpture and a monetary award are presented annually. Established in 1990.

• 12146 • Percy Grainger Medallion

Annual award of recognition for individuals whose achievements in Grainger Scholarship merit the award. Inquire for application details.

• 12147 •
International Wood Products Association
Brent J. McClendon CAE, Exec.VP
4214 King St. W
Alexandria, VA 22302
Phone: (703)820-6696
Fax: (703)820-8550
E-mail: info@iwpawood.org
Home Page: http://www.iwpawood.org

• 12148 • Hall of Fame and Distinguished Service

Recognizes excellence in the imported wood products industry.

• 12149 •
Internet Alliance
Emily T. Hackett, Exec.Dir.
1111 19th St. NW, Ste. 1180
Washington, DC 20035-5782
Phone: (202)861-2476
Phone: (202)329-0017
Fax: (202)955-8081
E-mail: info@internetalliance.org
Home Page: http://www.internetalliance.org

Formerly: Videotex Industry Association.

• 12150 • Design Award

To honor an individual or organization for their commercial work that has made an outstanding contribution to design. Nominations may include all forms of interactive electronic services and are to be judged in the three areas of art direction, copy, and structural design. A plaque is awarded annually. Established in 1984. Formerly: Videotex Design Award.

• 12151 • Distinguished Service Award

To recognize an individual who has made a visible and obvious contribution to the interactive services industry in general and to the ISA in particular. Members must be nominated by another member. A plaque is awarded annually at the ISA Annual Meeting. Established in 1984.

• 12152 • Innovation Award

To recognize an organization or individual who has achieved the greatest innovation in development during the year. The award is open to all, but nominations must be made by a member. A plaque is awarded annually at the ISA Annual Meeting. Established in 1984. Formerly: Videotex Innovation Award.

• 12153 • Outstanding Achievement Award

For recognition of an organization that has established a record of accomplishments for its pioneering efforts, leadership, and measurable successes in the interactive services industry. The award is open to all, but nomination must be made by a member. A plaque is awarded annually at the ISA Annual Meeting. Established in 1984.

• 12154 • Product and Service Awards

The product and service awards are divided into five categories, each offering three awards. In the four following categories, Online and Internet, Interactive Telephone, Interactive Television, and Screen Telephone, awards are given in the areas of: (1) Innovation - based on uniqueness of idea and the extent to which the recipient stands out in the field. Applies to any technology, product or service; (2) Best Application - to consumer acceptance and achievement of the service's business objectives. Applies to any interactive application: information, transaction, communications, or entertainment; and (3) Design - based on the product or service's ease of use, ability to work within the current technology constraints and audio visual appeal. In the fifth category, Interactive Marketing Awards, awards are given in the following areas: (1) Best Online Business-to-Consumer Marketing Application - to any campaign that markets products or services to individual consumers. Award will be based on consumer acceptance and achievement of the campaign's business objectives; (2) Best Interactive Telephone Business-to-Consumer Marketing Application - to any campaign that markets products or services to individual consumers using the telephone. Award will be based on consumer acceptance and achievement of the campaign's business objectives; and (3) Best Business-to-Consumer Multimedia Marketing Application - to any campaign that markets products or services utilizing interactive multimedia (sound, video, photographic images, graphics) methods or tools - offline or in combination with online programs, e.g. public access kiosk programs and compact disc presentations for which advertising and marketing objectives are a primary consideration. Award will be based on consumer acceptance and achievement of the campaign's business objectives.

• 12155 •
Interstate Mining Compact Commission
Gregory E. Conrad, Exec.Dir.
445A Carlisle Dr.
Herndon, VA 20170
Phone: (703)709-8654
Fax: (703)709-8655
E-mail: gconrad@imcc.isa.us
Home Page: http://www.imcc.isa.us

• 12156 • **Kenes C. Bowling National Mine Reclamation Awards**
To recognize outstanding achievements in mined land reclamation and to promote reclamation on a national level. Each year two awards are presented: one for coal and another for non-coal minerals. A third award is also presented (optionally) to a small operator exhibiting outstanding reclamation work. Competition is limited to IMCC member states, with each state authorized to make one nomination in each category. To be eligible, a mining company must have been actively mining/reclaiming the site during the 12-month period prior to the nomination. Criteria considered in judging include: Compliance, Contemporaneous Reclamation, Drainage, Bond Release, and Innovative Practices. Plaques are awarded annually in each category. In addition, honorable mention certificates are presented. Established in 1987 and later named to honor Kenes C. Bowling, Charter Executive Director.

• 12157 • **IMCC National Annual Minerals Education Awards**
To recognize the efforts of those who educate others about the use of minerals and the issues associated with mining, particularly from an environmental perspective, and those who have undertaken special outreach programs to inform the public about mining. Two awards are presented annually: The Mining Awareness Educator Award, which is presented to an individual school or teacher from an IMCC member state, and the Public Outreach Award, which is presented to an industry, environmental, citizen, or other group not associated with schools in an IMCC member state that has achieved excellence in one of several categories of public outreach with mineral education.

• 12158 •
Inventors Clubs of America
Carl Preston, Contact
524 Curtis Rd.
East Lansing, MI 48823
Phone: (517)332-3561
Fax: (404)846-0980

• 12159 • **Creative Arts Award**
For outstanding achievement in the arts, music, sports, technology, movies, computers, or creative endeavors of any type. Individuals or organizations are eligible. The deadline is April 5. A medal or plaque is presented annually in May. Established in 1975 by Alexander T. Marinaccio, founder of the Inventors Clubs of America.

• 12160 • **Honorary Title of Inventor**
To honor outstanding scientists and inventors for their contributions to society and for the betterment of mankind. The deadline is April 5. A medal or plaque is awarded annually in May. Established in 1975 by Alexander T. Marinaccio, founder of the Inventors Clubs of America.

• 12161 • **Humanitarian Award**
To recognize an outstanding humanitarian achievement by any person, group, society, club, or association. The deadline is April 5. A medal or plaque is presented annually in May. Established in 1975 by Alexander T. Marinaccio, founder of the Inventors Clubs of America.

• 12162 • **International Hall of Fame World Award**
To recognize an outstanding contribution to society in the arts or technology for the betterment of mankind. The contribution must be nationally or internationally recognized. Persons from anywhere in the world are eligible. The deadline is April 5. A medal or plaque is presented annually in May. Established in 1975 by Alexander T. Marinaccio, founder of the Inventors Clubs of America.

• 12163 • **New Product Award**
To encourage the development and marketing of new products that help create new jobs and employment. Patented, inventions that have applied for patents, or designs by an inventor anywhere in the world are considered. The deadline is April 5. A medal or a plaque is presented annually in May. Established in 1975 by Alexander T. Marinaccio, founder of the Inventors Clubs of America.

• 12164 • **Special Recognition Award**
To honor the people or organizations who assisted the International Hall of Fame Award winners or do outstanding things, and who, in the opinion of the committee, merit special recognition. The deadline is April 5. A plaque or certificate is presented annually. Established in 1975 by Alexander T. Marinaccio, founder of the Inventors Clubs of America.

• 12165 •
Inventors Workshop International Education Foundation/Entrepreneurs Workshop
Alan A. Tratner, Pres.
1029 Castillo St.
Santa Barbara, CA 93101-3736
Phone: (805)967-5722
Fax: (805)899-4927
E-mail: iwief@inventorsworkshop.org
Home Page: http://inventorsworkshop.org

• 12166 • **Great Idea Contest**
To stimulate inventing, creativity and entrepreneurship, and to reward innovation, uniqueness, cleverness, diligence, and quality in ideas that tend to result in protectable intellectual property. The contest is open to members of IWIEF and the general public, and the contest categories reflect all age groups and educational levels from science to technology to arts. Awards may be given in the following categories: arts, transportation, construction, electrical, energy, agriculture, educational, furniture, food, tools, medical, recreation, chemical, handicapped, ecological, automotive, pollution control, and miscellaneous products. Prizes for first, second, and third place, and honorable mention winners in each category could include: certificates, trophies, preliminary patent/trademark searches, evaluations, books, subscription to *Invent/Lightbulb* Magazine, InvenTech Exhibit Booth, scholarship, donated professional services, and many other possible items. Established in 1989. Co-sponsored by *Invent/Lightbulb* Magazine; Entrepreneurs Workshop International; American Initiative for Creativity, Invention and Entrepreneurship; Foundation for Gifted and Talented Children; and Toy and Game Inventors of America.

• 12167 • **Imagination Fair Great Idea Contest**
Events for youth 6 - 18 years of age.

• 12168 • **Young Eco Inventors Contest With Eco Expo**
Contest is open to children. No further information was available for this edition.

• 12169 •
Investigative Reporters and Editors
Brant Houston, Exec.Dir.
Missouri School of Journalism
138 Neff Annex
Columbia, MO 65211
Phone: (573)882-2042
Fax: (573)882-5431
E-mail: info@ire.org
Home Page: http://www.ire.org

• 12170 • **IRE Awards**
To honor the best examples of investigative reporting in the United States each year and to promote high standards within the profession. Awards are given in the following categories: newspapers over 250,000 newspapers under 200,000 circulation, newspapers between 100,000 - 250,000 circulation, network and syndicated programs, television in the top 20 markets, television below the top 20 markets, radio, books, magazines, and specialty publications. There is also a student category. There are up to three winners in each of the seven categories. The entry deadline is January 15 for the previous year's work. Winners receive certificates, and top winners receive plaques. Winners may also appear as panelists at the national conference. Awarded annually. Established in 1979.

• 12171 • **Thomas Renner Crime Reporting Award**
To recognize the achievement of best investigative reporting in print, broadcast or book form covering organized crime and its impact on society. Eligibility is open to anyone submitting a story. A monetary prize of $1,000 is awarded to the top winner. Certificates and plaques are also awarded annually. Established in 1990 in honor of Tom Renner.

• 12172 •
Investment Dealers Association of Canada (Association Canadienne des Courtiers en Valeurs Mobilieres)
Joseph J. Oliver, CEO & Pres.
121 King St., W, Ste. 1600
121 King St. W, Ste. 1600
Toronto, ON, Canada M5H 3T9
Phone: (416)364-6133
Toll-Free: 877-442-4322
Fax: (416)364-0753
Home Page: http://www.ida.ca

• 12173 • **Award of Distinction**
Recognizes outstanding investment advisors. Awarded annually.

• 12174 •
Investment Education Institute
Richard A. Holthaus, Pres./CEO
PO Box 220
Royal Oak, MI 48068
Phone: (248)583-6242
Toll-Free: 877-275-6242
Fax: (248)583-4880
E-mail: corporate@betterinvesting.org
Home Page: http://www.better-investing.org

• 12175 • **Distinguished Service Award in Investment Education**
To recognize those people who have made an outstanding contribution to investment education. Awards are given in the following categories: Financial Analysts, government, publications, stock market, investor relations, educators/economists, investment clubs, industry, and international. Nominations are made by a committee. Personalized certificates plus wooden shoes, emblematic of the Dutch as our first investors, are presented annually at the National Association of Investors Corporation Congress. Established in 1963 by the National Association of Investors Corporation.

• 12176 •
IODE - Municipal Chapter of Toronto
Charlotte Teeple, Exec.Dir.
40 St. Clair Ave. E, Ste. 205
Toronto, ON, Canada M4T 1M9
Phone: (416)925-5078
Fax: (416)925-5127
Home Page: http://www.bookcentre.ca/awards/award_ind/awards.php?award=iode

• 12177 • **Municipal Chapter of Toronto IODE Children's Book Award**
To encourage the publication of Canadian literature for children. A recently published author and/or illustrator who is a resident of Toronto or the surrounding area is eligible for the award. A monetary award of $1,000 and a certificate are presented annually to the winners. Established in 1974.

• 12178 •
IONS - Institute of Noetic Sciences
James O'Dea, Pres.
101 San Antonio Rd.
Petaluma, CA 94952
Phone: (707)775-3500
Phone: (707)779-8217
Toll-Free: 877-769-4667
Fax: (707)781-7420
E-mail: membership@noetic.org
Home Page: http://www.noetic.org

• 12179 • **Temple Award for Creative Altruism**
To recognize one or more outstanding altruists whose lives and work embody the inspirational light of unselfish service motivated by love. The deadline for nominations is September 15. An award fund of $25,000 is divided among the recipients each year. Established in 1987. For additional information contact Rose Welch at 707779-8238.

• 12180 •
Iowa Bankers Association
John Sorensen, Pres./CEO
8800 NW 62nd Ave.
PO Box 6200
Johnston, IA 50131
Phone: (515)286-4300
Toll-Free: 800-532-1423
Fax: (515)280-4140
E-mail: jsorensen@iowabankers.com
Home Page: http://www.iabankers.com

• 12181 • **John Hughes Scholarship**
For Iowa School of Banking.

• 12182 •
Iowa Horse Industry Council
Peggy Miller, Assoc.Prof.
Iowa State University
119 Kildee Hall
Ames, IA 50011
Phone: (515)294-5260
Fax: (515)294-0018
E-mail: peggy@iastate.edu
Home Page: http://www.iowahorsecouncil.org

• 12183 • **IHIC Scholarship**
For student attending college. Scholarship awarded annually.

• 12184 •
Iowa Hospice Organization
Rebecca Anthony, Exec.Dir.
100 E. Grand Ave., Ste. 120
Des Moines, IA 50309-1800
Phone: (515)288-1955
Fax: (515)283-9366
E-mail: anthonyb@ihaonline.org
Home Page: http://www.iowahospice.org

• 12185 • **Spirit of Hospice Award**
For contribution to hospice care in Iowa; must be nominated by a provider member. Recognition award bestowed annually.

• 12186 •
Iowa League of Cities
Thomas G. Bredeweg, Exec.Dir.
317 6th Ave., Ste. 800
Des Moines, IA 50309-4111
Phone: (515)244-7282
Fax: (515)244-0740
E-mail: mailbox@iowaleague.org
Home Page: http://www.iowaleague.org

• 12187 • **All-Star Community Awards**
For cost savings, community enrichment, intergovernmental cooperation. Recognition award bestowed annually.

• 12188 •
Iowa School of Letters
℅ Iowa Writers' Workshop
Univ. of Iowa
100 Dey House
507 N Clinton St.
Iowa City, IA 52242-1000
Phone: (319)335-0416
Toll-Free: 800-553-IOWA
Fax: (319)335-0420

• 12189 • **Truman Capote Award for Literary Criticism in Memory of Newton Arvin**
For recognition of the best book of general literary criticism written in English in the previous four years. Candidates must be nominated. A $50,000 cash prize is awarded annually. Established in 1994 in memory of Newton Arvin, a critic who taught at Smith College. Sponsored by the Truman Capote Literary Trust.

• 12190 • **Iowa Short Fiction Award**
To encourage writing in the typically American literary genre of the short story by recognizing unpublished authors of book-length short fiction. Manuscripts must be 150 pages or more and the author may not have published a volume of prose fiction previously (but may have published stories in periodicals). Writers who have published a volume of poetry are eligible. Revised manuscripts that have been previously entered may be resubmitted. Manuscripts must be submitted between August 1 and September 30. Award-winning manuscripts will be published by the University of Iowa Press. Established in 1988. Formerly: Iowa School of Letters Award for Short Fiction.

• 12191 • **James A. Michener - Paul Engle Fellowship**
To recognize and provide funding for graduates of the Iowa Writers' Workshop. Applicants must be graduates of the Iowa Writers' Workshop. Grants are awarded to provide time to finish a given work or to prepare it for publication. Awards are presented in two categories: prose - for a novel, or as much as is completed with a

very brief synopsis, or a collection of short stories, or as much as is completed; and poetry candidates are nominated by the poetry faculty members. Entries must be submitted between April 1 and April 15. Monetary awards of $12,000 are presented annually. Established about 1990 by James A. Michener to honor Paul Engle, director of the University of Iowa Writers' Workshop from 1941 to 1966.

• 12192 • John Simmons Short Fiction Award
To encourage writing in the typically American literary genre of the short story by recognizing unpublished authors of book-length short fiction. Manuscripts must be 150 pages or more and the author may not have published a volume of prose fiction previously (but may have published stories in periodicals). Writers who have published a volume of poetry are also eligible. Revised manuscripts that have been previously entered may be resubmitted. Manuscripts must be submitted between August 1 and September 30. Award-winning manuscripts will be published by the University of Iowa Press. Established in 1988 to honor John Simmons, founding director of the University of Iowa Press, as well as an admirer and writer of fine short fiction.

• 12193 •
Irish American Cultural Institute
John P. Walsh, Chm./CEO
1 Lackawanna Pl.
Morristown, NJ 07960
Phone: (973)605-1991
Fax: (973)605-8875
E-mail: info@iaci-usa.org
Home Page: http://www.irishaci.org

• 12194 • Butler Literary Award
To recognize and encourage excellence among writers whose works are in the English and the Irish languages. Fiction, poetry, or drama written in Irish or English is eligible. Monetary prizes totaling $5,000 are awarded annually for writings in English and in Irish in alternate years. Established in 1967.

• 12195 • Four Masters Award
To recognize the outstanding history article in the IACI's journal of Irish Studies, *Eire-Ireland.* A monetary prize of $500 is awarded annually.

• 12196 • Heritage Award
To honor Irish efforts to interpret Irish history and to promote an appreciation of its diversity at the community level in Ireland. A monetary prize of $5,000 is awarded annually.

• 12197 • Irish American Cultural Institute Awards
Recognizes writing in Irish and English and the arts. Writers and Irish artists, painters, musicians, and dramatists are eligible. Awarded annually.

• 12198 • Irish American Cultural Institute Poetry Award
To honor poets whose work has made a signal contribution to Irish letters. A monetary award of $5,000 is presented annually. Established initially 1986 by the O'Shaughnessy family of St. Paul, longtime supporters of the IACI.

• 12199 • Irish Research Funds
To further an appreciation of the Irish-American experience by underwriting primary research and other scholarly efforts. Endowed research funds, one donated by the Irish Institute of New York, another by the Lawrence O'Shaughnessy family of Minnesota, and another by Friendly Sons of St. Patrick of Philadelphia, underwrite scholarly research and other efforts to examine the Irish-American experience. Projects from all disciplines, regardless of historic period or geographic focus, can be considered for these grants. All projects must deal with significant research matters and be directed by competent scholars. Research Fund awards of $1,000 to $5,000 are announced annually in January.

• 12200 • Irish Way Scholarships
Scholarships are awarded annually.

• 12201 • O'Malley Art Award
To recognize and promote Irish achievements in the visual arts, particularly those that have stimulated or guided other Irish artists. A monetary award of $5,000 is awarded annually. Established in 1989 in memory of Ernie O'Malley who, in addition to literary and patriotic activities, was also a notable collector of Irish and world art.

• 12202 • Visiting Fellowship in Irish Studies at University College Galway
A fellowship is awarded annually.

• 12203 •
Irrigation Association
Thomas H. Kimmell, Exec.Dir.
6540 Arlington Blvd.
Falls Church, VA 22042-6638
Phone: (703)536-7080
Fax: (703)536-7019
E-mail: tom@irrigation.org
Home Page: http://www.irrigation.org
Formerly: (1976) Sprinkler Irrigation Association.

• 12204 • Industry Achievement Award
To recognize outstanding contributions to the development of the irrigation industry and products used by it. Individuals from industry firms are eligible. A walnut plaque with anodized brass plate is awarded annually when merited. Established in 1966.

• 12205 • National Water and Energy Conservation Award
To recognize significant achievement in the conservation of water and energy as they relate to irrigation procedures, equipment, methods, and techniques; to bring national recognition to individuals, firms, or agencies working to conserve our natural resources; and to challenge those responsible for irrigation usage in agriculture or in the landscape to reach for and achieve a higher level of excellence. Any individual, firm, government agency (local, state, or federal), civic organization, or university or college division or department that has been active in the promotion of water or energy conservation may qualify for the award. The entry deadline is September 1. A brass bowl on a walnut pedestal is awarded annually in January. Established in 1981.

• 12206 • Partner of the Year
To honor a person or group making exceptional contributions or distinctive accomplishments in areas allied with, related to, or an integral part of the irrigation industry. Awarded annually. Established in 1995.

• 12207 • Person of the Year Award
To recognize individuals who have made outstanding contributions towards the further acceptance of good irrigation practices. Individuals outside the industry are eligible. A walnut plaque is awarded annually. Established in 1952.

• 12208 • Crawford Reid Memorial Award
To recognize individuals who have made significant achievements in the promotion of proper irrigation techniques and procedures, and have brought about major advancement of the industry outside the United States. Any individual active in the irrigation industry outside the United States is eligible. A plaque is awarded from time to time. Established in 1979 in memory of Crawford Reid, the second president of the Association.

• 12209 •
ISA - Instrumentation, Systems, and Automation Society
Dr. James E. Pearson, Exec.Dir.
67 Alexander Dr.
PO Box 12277
Research Triangle Park, NC 27709
Phone: (919)549-8411
Fax: (919)549-8288
E-mail: info@isa.org
Home Page: http://www.isa.org

• 12210 • Douglas H. Annin Award
Recognizes outstanding achievements in design or development of an automatic control system. A monetary award of $1000 is given annually.

• 12211 • E.G. Bailey Award
Recognizes excellence in design, development, or application in instrumentation and control systems in utilities and process control industries. A plaque and monetary award of $1000 are given annually.

• 12212 • **Arnold O. Beckman Founder Award**
Recognizes significant technological contributions to conception and implementation of a new principle of design, development, or application. A plaque and monetary award of $3000 are given annually.

• 12213 • **Distinguished Society Service Award**
Recognizes long standing devoted service and contributions to the ISA. Awarded annually.

• 12214 • **Donald P. Eckman Education Award**
Recognizes contributions to education and training in science, engineering, and technology. A monetary award of $1000 is given annually.

• 12215 • **Excellence in Documentation Award**
Recognizes an outstanding article, paper, or document published by the ISA. A plaque and monetary award of $1000 are given annually.

• 12216 • **Kermit Fischer Environmental Award**
To recognize an individual for outstanding achievement in the conception, design, and/or implementation of an application of instrumentation or control in the field of environmental science. A monetary award of $1,000, a plaque, and a certificate are awarded annually. Established in 1980 in memory of Kermit Fischer.

• 12217 • **Golden Achievement Award**
Recognizes long, dedicated service to the ISA. May be awarded annually.

• 12218 • **Honorary Member**
Recognizes individuals whose support of, and/or contributions to the advancement of the arts and sciences of instrumentation, systems, and automation are deserving of special recognition. May be awarded annually.

• 12219 • **ISA Fellow**
To recognize outstanding achievement in scientific or engineering fields as recognized by ISA peers. Candidate must have five years as ISA senior member and at least 10 years in instrumentation development, application, operation, management, or teaching. Awarded annually. Established in 1959. For more information contact Laura Crumpler at lcrumpler@isa.org.

• 12220 • **Outstanding Division Award**
To recognize a division in the automation and technology or industries and sciences departments for outstanding activities and definitive reporting during the year. The awards were originated to stimulate the improvement of ISA division activities and to encourage documentation of division activities, plans, and achievements.

• 12221 • **Section Performance Award**
Recognizes achievement within the section recognition program or outstanding accomplishment in a particular area of section activity. A plaque and monetary award of $500 are given annually.

• 12222 • **Albert F. Sperry Founder Award**
Recognizes outstanding technical, educational, or philosophical contributions to science and technology. A plaque and monetary award of $3000 are given annually.

• 12223 • **Standards and Practices Award**
Recognizes an ISA Member for outstanding contributions in organizing developing, or administering standards and practices . A plaque and monetary award of $1000 are given annually.

• 12224 • **Student Paper Award for Four and Five Year Students**
To encourage students to study and pursue engineering or scientific careers in instrumentation. Student authors who are enrolled as full-time undergraduates in a four year college or university are eligible. A monetary award of $500, a plaque, and a certificate are awarded annually. Established in 1966.

• 12225 • **Student Paper Award for Two and Three Year Students**
To encourage students to study and pursue engineering or scientific careers in instrumentation. Student authors who are enrolled as full-time undergraduates in a two- to three-year academic program or in a formal instrumentation apprentice or vocational program are eligible. A monetary award of $500, a plaque, and a certificate are awarded annually. Established in 1986.

• 12226 • **UOP Technology Award**
To recognize an outstanding achievement in the conception, design, or implementation of instrumentation and/or process control in an area of activity covered by the scope of the Society;s Automation and Technology Department. A plaque and monetary award of $1000 are given annually.

• 12227 •
Islamic Propagation Centre
Hafiz Mohammed Nafees, Contact
5761 Coopers Ave., Bldg. 6
Mississauga, ON, Canada L4Z 1R9
Phone: (905)874-9179
Fax: (905)874-9179
E-mail: zsyed@ipci-canada.com
Home Page: http://www.ipci-canada.com/aboutus.htm

• 12228 • **Quran Recitation**
Recognizes an individual displaying knowledge of the Quran and Islam. Awarded annually.

• 12229 •
Islamic Research Foundation International
Dr. Ibrahim B. Syed, Pres.
7102 W Shefford Ln.
Louisville, KY 40242-6462
Phone: (502)287-6262
Phone: (502)423-1988
Toll-Free: 800-484-1162
Fax: (502)423-1933
E-mail: irfi@iname.com
Home Page: http://www.irfi.org

• 12230 • **Dr. Tajuddin Ahmed Book Publication Award**
Recognizes an author of a work on the Islamic renaissance, Tafsir of the Qur'an, or understanding of the Qur'an and Hadith in the light of modern knowledge. Awarded annually.

• 12231 • **Essay Competition**
Recognizes the best essays on how the fundamental scientific and medical discoveries and inventions of Muslim scientists laid the foundation for European Renaissance and paved the way for modern scientific discoveries and technical achievements. Awarded annually.

• 12232 • **Travel Grants to Students Coming to USA from Developing Countries**
Annual award of recognition.

• 12233 •
Island Resources Foundation
Bruce Potter, Pres.
1718 P St. NW, Ste. T-4
Washington, DC 20036
Phone: (202)265-9712
Fax: (202)232-0748
E-mail: bpotter@irf.org
Home Page: http://www.irf.org

• 12234 • **Euan P. McFarlane Environmental Award**
To recognize young West Indians who have demonstrated initiative, resourcefulness, and leadership in promoting the conservation of natural and historical resources and the enhancement of the environment in the eastern Caribbean. Any resident of an eastern Caribbean island under the age of 35 who has early in life, often without remuneration or recognition, devoted him or herself to the preservation of the natural and human environment and whose career or avocation demonstrate an appreciation of and adherence to the advancement of environmental stewardship and balanced development in the eastern Caribbean region is eligible. A monetary award of up to $1,000 is presented annually in September. There are no restrictions on the use of the award. Established in 1988 to honor Euan P. McFarlane, who was, until his death in 1983, actively involved in environmental causes in the Caribbean. He was a former treasurer and board member of the Caribbean Conservation Association, a trustee of the Island Resources Foundation, and founding member of the St. Croix Landmarks Society. Funded by Laurance S. Rockefeller.

• 12235 •
Iso and Bizzarrini Owners Club
Jack Freethy, Pres.
2025 Drake Dr.
Oakland, CA 94611
Phone: (510)339-8347
Fax: (510)339-8347

• 12236 • **Annual Meeting Best Of Show Founders Award**
Recognizes service to club. A trophy is awarded annually.

• 12237 •
Israel Humanitarian Foundation
Regina Gottfried, Natl.Exec.Dir.
276 5th Ave., Ste. 404
New York, NY 10001
Phone: (212)683-5676
Toll-Free: 888-434-5IHF
Fax: (212)213-9233
E-mail: regina@ihf.net
Home Page: http://www.ihf.net

• 12238 • **Herbert A. Rothman Award**
Recognizes outstanding service to the foundation. Awarded annually.

• 12239 •
Issue Management Council
Teresa Yancey Crane, Pres.
207 Loudoun St. SE
Leesburg, VA 20175-3115
Phone: (703)777-8450
E-mail: info@issuemanagement.org
Home Page: http://www.issuemanagement.org

Formerly: (1996) The Issue Exchange.

• 12240 • **W. Howard Chase Award for Excellence in Issue Management**
To recognize excellence in applying a process approach to the management of issues. Awarded annually with a Steuban-designed crystal. Established in 1988.

• 12241 •
Italian Charities of America
Rose Sproviero, Pres.
8320 Queens Blvd.
Elmhurst, NY 11373
Phone: (718)478-3100
Fax: (718)478-2665

• 12242 • **Man of the Year**
Annual award of recognition.

• 12243 • **Women of the Year**
Annual award of recognition.

• 12244 •
Italian Cultural Institute of New York
686 Park Ave.
New York, NY 10021-5009
Phone: (212)879-4242
Fax: (212)861-4018
E-mail: direttore@italcultny.org
Home Page: http://www.italcultny.org

• 12245 • **Campana Translation Prize**
To recognize the best translation of contemporary Italian poetry published in the United States. Entries for the prize competition are accepted from American and/or Italian publishers, American universities, American or Italian-American cultural foundations, American scholars of Italian poetry, Italianists, PEN members, and literary agents. Works published during the preceding two years may be submitted by June 30. A monetary prize of $3,000 is awarded biennially. Awarded in collaboration with Columbia University, Department of Italian. Established in memory of the poet, Dino Campana (1885-1932).

• 12246 •
Italian Folk Art Federation of America
Paul Torna, Pres.
PO Box 1192
Rockford, IL 61105
Toll-Free: 800-601-6888
E-mail: paultorna@verizon.net
Home Page: http://www.italian-american.com/ifafa/welcome.htm

• 12247 • **IFAFA Award**
Recognizes services pertaining to Italian involvement in the community. Awarded biennially.

• 12248 •
Italian Historical Society of America
Dr. John J. LaCorte, Pres.
410 Park Ave., Ste. 1530
New York, NY 10022
Phone: (718)852-2929
Fax: (718)855-3925
E-mail: society1@italianhistorical.org
Home Page: http://www.italianhistorical.org

• 12249 • **Meucci Award**
Recognizes exceptional contributions to improve human conditions. Awarded annually.

• 12250 • **Varrazano Award**
Recognizes exceptional contributions to improve human conditions. Awarded annually.

• 12251 •
Italian Sons and Daughters of America
Josephine Donahue, Controller
419 Wood St.
Pittsburgh, PA 15222
Phone: (412)261-3550
Fax: (412)261-9897

• 12252 • **Leonardo da Vinci Award**
Annual award of recognition.

• 12253 • **Man of the Year Award**
Annual award of recognition.

• 12254 • **Michaelangelo Award**
Annual award of recognition.

• 12255 • **Renaissance Award**
Annual award of recognition.

• 12256 •
Italian Wine and Food Institute
Dr. Lucio Caputo, Pres.
PO Box 789
New York, NY 10150-0789
Phone: (212)867-4111
Fax: (212)867-4114
E-mail: iwfi@aol.com
Home Page: http://www.italianwineandfoodinstitute.com

• 12257 • **Special Achievement - Man/Woman of the Year**
Recognizes individuals who have made outstanding contributions to the industry. Awarded annually.

• 12258 •
Italic Institute of America
John Mancini, Chm.
PO Box 818
Floral Park, NY 11001
Phone: (516)488-7400
Phone: (212)268-8085
Fax: (516)488-4889
E-mail: italicone@aol.com
Home Page: http://www.italic.org

Formerly: (2000) Italic Studies Institute.

• 12259 • **ARA Pacis Award (Altar of Peace)**
Recognizes significant contributions by an Italic individual. Awarded annually.

• 12260 •
Italy-America Chamber of Commerce
Franco De Angelis, Sec.Gen.
730 5th Ave., Ste. 600
New York, NY 10019
Phone: (212)459-0044
Fax: (212)459-0090
E-mail: info@italchamber.org
Home Page: http://www.italchambers.net/newyork

• 12261 • **Business and Culture Award**
Recognizes economic achievements in international relations. Awarded annually. Formerly: (2006) Golde Award.

• 12262 •
Izaak Walton League of America
Paul Hansen, Exec.Dir.
707 Conservation Ln.
Gaithersburg, MD 20878
Phone: (301)548-0150
Toll-Free: 800-IKE-LINE
Fax: (301)548-0146
E-mail: general@iwla.org
Home Page: http://www.iwla.org

• 12263 • **"54" Founders Award**
This, the League's highest award, is given to recognize a person, group, or institution for an outstanding contribution to the conservation of America's renewable natural resources. Nominations must be submitted by local chapters or state divisions. Decisions are made by an appointed awards committee made up of members. A bronze plaque and citation are awarded annually as merited. Established in 1949.

• 12264 • **James Lawton Childs Award**
For recognition of the most outstanding conservation program staged by a chapter of the League. Nominations must be submitted by local chapters or state divisions. Decisions are made by an appointed awards committee made up of members. A monetary prize, a trophy, and a citation are awarded annually.

• 12265 • **IWLA Conservation Award**
To recognize a member for outstanding contributions to the conservation work in the League's name. Nominations must be submitted by local chapters or state divisions. Decisions are made by an appointed awards committee made up of members. A framed certificate is awarded annually.

• 12266 • **IWLA Hall of Fame Award**
For recognition of long devotion and service to the League and its objectives resulting in a record of outstanding accomplishment. Nominations must be submitted by local chapters or state divisions. Decisions are made by an appointed awards committee made up of members. Awarded when merited.

• 12267 • **IWLA Honor Roll Award**
To recognize an individual or organization for outstanding contributions to broaden public understanding and appreciation of the natural world. Nominations must be submitted by local chapters or state divisions. Decisions are made by an appointed awards committee made up of members. A citation is awarded annually. Established in 1948.

• 12268 • **Robert C. O'Hair Memorial Award**
For recognition of the chapter having done the most outstanding youth work. Nominations must be submitted by local chapters or state divisions. Decisions are made by an appointed awards committee made up of members. A $100 government bond and a plaque are awarded annually.

• 12269 • **Outdoor Ethics Awards**
To recognize individuals, groups, companies, or institutions that have done outstanding work in outdoor ethics during the past year. Up to five awards are given.

• 12270 • **Save Our Streams Award**
To recognize the SOS program that best demonstrates the principles of environmental education and citizen action in the pursuit of clean water. Nominations must be submitted by local chapters or state divisions. Decisions are made by an appointed awards committee made up of members. A $100 cash award is given.

• 12271 • **Arthur R. Thompson Memorial Award**
For recognition of the most outstanding conservation activity by a division of the League. Nominations must be submitted by local chapters or state divisions. Decisions are made by an appointed awards committee made up of members. A trophy and a citation are awarded annually. Established by the Roanoke, Virginia chapter.

• 12272 •
J-Lab: The Institute for Interactive Journalism
Jan Schaffer, Exec.Dir.
7100 Baltimore Ave., Ste. 101
College Park, MD 20740-3637
Phone: (301)985-4020
Fax: (301)985-4021
E-mail: news@j-lab.org
Home Page: http://www.j-lab.org

• 12273 • **Batten Awards for Innovations in Journalism**
To reward journalism that uses new information ideas and technologies in innovative ways to involve people very actively in critical public issues by showing as well as telling, by providing access to news and information that stirs their imagination and invites participation. Entries from all media are eligible. Encouraged are both top-down and bottom-up innovations, those driven by the news organization, and those that require significant audience participation. The Knight Foundation has funded a $10,000 Grand Prize and up to $5,000 in Special Distinction Awards to be given at the judges' discretion. Awarded annually. Established in honor of James K. Batten, a leader in civic journalism, who died in June 1995. Formerly: (2002) Batten Awards for Excellence in Civic Journalism.

• 12274 •
Jackie Robinson Foundation
Della Britton Baeza, Pres./CEO
3 W 35th St., 11th Fl.
New York, NY 10001-2204
Phone: (212)290-8600
Fax: (212)290-8081
E-mail: general@jackierobinson.org
Home Page: http://www.jackierobinson.org

• 12275 • **Robie Award for Achievement in Industry**
To recognize outstanding corporate leaders who have worked for the advancement of minorities in their company's economic development, and through education initiatives. A medallion is awarded annually at the Awards Dinner. Established in 1980 in memory of Jackie Robinson.

• 12276 • **Robie Humanitarianism Award**
To recognize outstanding individuals who have devoted their lives to the promotion of human dignity and social justice. Individuals who have contributed through their advocacy of human rights and/or social justice to enrich lives and secure a more equitable world are eligible. Awarded annually at the Awards Dinner. Established in 1979 to honor Jackie Robinson.

• 12277 •
Jackson County Literacy Council
Claire Albright, Contact
1713 Kenneth Ave.
Pascagoula, MS 39567
Phone: (228)762-2814
E-mail: cawa41@aol.com

• 12278 • **Tutor Appreciation Awards**
For volunteer hours/100 hours or 500 hours and above. Recognition award bestowed annually.

• 12279 •
Jackson State University
Bureau of Business and Economic Research
P.O. Box 18170
Jackson, MS 39217
Phone: (601)979-2028
Fax: (601)979-2796
E-mail: jsupat@aol.com
Home Page: http://www.jsums.edu

• 12280 • **Research Awards**
Faculty members are eligible. Inquire for application details.

• 12281 •
Jaguar Clubs of North America
Nelson Rath, Admin.Mgr./Treas.
1000 Glenbrook
Anchorage, KY 40223
Toll-Free: 800-258-2524
E-mail: nrath@jcna.com
Home Page: http://www.jcna.com

• 12282 • **Frederic S. Horner Sportsmanship Award**
Award of recognition.

• 12283 • **Andrew Whyte Award**
Recognizes service to the national organization. Awarded annually.

• 12284 •
James Beard Foundation
Dorothy Cann Hamilton, Pres.
167 W 12th St.
New York, NY 10011
Phone: (212)675-4984
Phone: (212)627-2308
Toll-Free: 800-36-BEARD
Fax: (212)645-1438
E-mail: info@jamesbeard.org
Home Page: http://www.jamesbeard.org

• 12285 • **The James Beard Foundation Book Awards**
To recognize outstanding culinary books. Open to all U.S. and Canadian publishers who have released culinary topic books in the previous calendar year. Awards are presented annually for the Best Food Photography, Cookbook of the Year, and the Cookbook Hall of Fame. The original awards program was established in 1966 by R. T. French Company and administered by the International Association of Culinary Professionals. (See separate listing.) The competition split in 1990. Entry deadline is November 19. Additional information is available from M. Young Communications, 80 5th Ave., Ste. 705, New York, NY 10011, telephone: (212) 620-7027; fax: (212) 645-3654. Formerly: R. T. French Tastemaker Awards.

• 12286 • **The James Beard Foundation/ Cervena Council/D'Artagnan Who's Who of Food and Beverage in America**
To recognize significant and lasting achievement in the culinary field. Awarded annually. Established in 1984 by *Cook's* magazine and *Restaurant Business* magazine. Formerly: (1998) James Beard Who's Who of Food and Beverage in America.

• 12287 • **The James Beard Foundation Restaurant Awards**
To recognize chefs, restaurants, and wine professionals for their achievements in the previous year. Awards are presented in the following categories: James Beard Humanitarian Award; Outstanding Chef; Perrier Outstanding Restaurant; Hawaiian Vintage Chocolate Outstanding Pastry Chef; Perrier-Jouet Rising Star Chef of the Year; Hudson Valley Foie Gras Outstanding Wine Service Award; Hudson Valley Foie Gras Outstanding Wine & Spirits Professional; American Express America's Best Chef: Northeast, Mid-Atlantic, Southeast, Midwest, Southwest, California, Northwest, and New York; Outstanding Service Award; and America's Regional Classics Award. Awarded annually. Established in 1990. Formerly: James Beard/Seagram Restaurant Awards; (1998) James Beard/Perrier Jouet Restaurant Awards.

• 12288 • **Journalism Awards**
To recognize journalism and video professionals in the United States and Canada. Awards include separate newspaper and magazine categories for: Restaurant Review/Critique; News Reporting; Feature Reporting; Series Reporting; Diet, Nutrition, and Health; and Wine Writing. Also available is the M. K. Fisher Distinguished Writing Award. Entry deadline is January 15. Awarded annually.

• 12289 • **Restaurant Design and Graphics Awards**
To recognize excellence in restaurant design and graphics for projects executed in the U.S. and Canada. The competition is open to any architect, interior designer or graphic designer who meets the awards criteria. The categories are Best Restaurant Design and Best Restaurant Graphics. Awarded annually.

• 12290 • **Viking Range Awards for Broadcast Media**
To recognize journalism and video professionals in the United States and Canada. Awards include Outstanding TV Food Journalism, Best TV Cooking Show, Best Radio Show on Food, and Best Cooking Video. Entry deadline is January 31. Awarded annually.

• 12291 •
James E. Guinn Former Student Alliance
Ernest Mackey, Chm.
2700 Carnation St.
Fort Worth, TX 76111-2711
Phone: (817)534-5549
Phone: (817)535-2220

• 12292 • **James L. Guinn Awards**
For contribution to community. Recognition award bestowed annually.

• 12293 •
James Joyce Society of Southern Colorado
John Holiday, Founder
PO Box 62482
Colorado Springs, CO 80962
Phone: (719)594-9164

• 12294 • **Freedom of Expression Award**
Recognizes individuals with intellectual courage. Awarded annually.

• 12295 •
Jane Addams Peace Association
Linda B. Belle, Exec.Dir.
777 UN Plz., 6th Fl.
New York, NY 10017
Phone: (212)682-8830
Fax: (212)286-8211
E-mail: japa@igc.org
Home Page: http://www.janeaddamspeace.org

• 12296 • **Jane Addams Children's Book Award**
To promote the cause of peace, social justice, world community, and gender and racial equality to young readers. Children's books that best combine literary merit with themes of world community and social justice and were published in English in the preceding year, are eligible. Winners are announced on April 28 of each year, and an award ceremony with cash gifts is held in New York City the third Friday of October.

• 12297 •
Jane Austen Society of North America
Joan Klingel Ray PhD, Pres.
106 Barlows Run
Williamsburg, VA 23188-9326
Phone: (719)262-4005
Toll-Free: 800-836-3911
Fax: (719)262-4557
E-mail: jray@uccs.edu
Home Page: http://www.jasna.org

• 12298 • **Award for Notable Endeavor ("The Jane")**
Award of recognition. For notably enhancing the knowledge of Jane Austen studies. Awarded periodically.

• 12299 •
Japan America Society
Douglas G. Erber, Exec. Dir.
505 South Flower St., Level C
Los Angeles, CA 90071
Phone: (213)627-6217
Fax: (213)627-1353

• 12300 • **Student Scholarships**
For excellence in US-Japan studies. Monetary award bestowed annually.

• 12301 •
Japan-America Society of Georgia
Mr. Clark T. Wisenbaker, Exec.Dir.
3121 Maple Dr. NE, Ste. 224
Atlanta, GA 30305
Phone: (404)842-1400
Fax: (404)842-1415
E-mail: jasg@mindspring.com
Home Page: http://www.us-japan.org/jasg

• 12302 • **Mike Mansfield Award**
For furthering US-Japan relations. Recognition award bestowed annually.

• 12303 •
Japan Society
Frank L. Ellsworth, Pres.
333 E 47th St.
New York, NY 10017
Phone: (212)832-1155
Fax: (212)755-6752
E-mail: hr@japansociety.org
Home Page: http://www.japansociety.org

• 12304 • **Japan Society Award**
Annual award of recognition.

• 12305 •
Japanese American Citizens League
John Tateishi, Natl.Exec.Dir.
1765 Sutter St.
San Francisco, CA 94115
Phone: (415)921-5225
Fax: (415)931-4671
E-mail: jacl@jacl.org
Home Page: http://www.jacl.org

• 12306 • Ruby Yoshino Schaar Biennium Playwright Award
To encourage talented playwrights to tell the story of the Japanese-American or Japanese-Canadian in North America. Applicants must be playwrights of Japanese descent with American or Canadian citizenship, be sponsored by an active member of JACL or a chapter of the JACL, and have had at least one play presented in a public forum, such as an established theatre, workshop, or formal reading. The deadline for applications is March 15 in even years. Established in 1984 by the New York Chapter of the Japanese American Citizens League.

• 12307 •
Jazz Arts Music Society of Palm Beach
Susan Merritt, Pres.
PO Box 3033
Palm Beach, FL 33480-1233
Phone: (561)835-0382
Fax: (561)835-1363
E-mail: jamspb@aol.com
Home Page: http://www.jamsociety.org

• 12308 • JAMS Scholarship
For a young adult under 25 years of age in school wishing to continue studying jazz. Scholarship awarded annually.

• 12309 •
Jazz World Database
Jan Byrczek, Pres.
341 W 11th St., Ste. 2-G
New York, NY 10014
Phone: (212)581-7188
Fax: (212)253-4160
E-mail: jwd@jazzworlddatabase.com
Home Page: http://
www.jazzworlddatabase.com

Formerly: (1983) International Jazz Federation.

• 12310 • European Young Jazz Artists
To recognize the winning groups in the European Jazz Competitions. Competitions are held each year in Germany, Belgium, Poland, Spain, France and other countries. Monetary prizes and certificates are awarded at each competition. Jazz groups based in Europe whose members are under the age of 30 are eligible. The group must include two to seven musicians and should have been selected by the Jury as the winners of the European Jazz Competition. A monetary award of 5,000 German marks and a trophy plus practical assistance with career development are awarded annually in October. Established in 1982 in association with Leverkusener Jazz Tage, West Germany.

• 12311 •
Jefferson County Historical Commission
Duncan McCollum, Archives and Records Management
100 Jefferson County Pkwy., Ste. 1500
Golden, CO 80419-1500
Phone: (303)271-8446
Fax: (303)271-8452
E-mail: dmccollu@co.jefferson.co.us

• 12312 • Writers' Award Contest
For outstanding local history articles. Monetary award bestowed annually.

• 12313 •
Jellinek Memorial Fund
1091 Westmount Ave.
PO Box 202332
Mississauga, ON, Canada L5E 1X6
Phone: (416)340-3105
Fax: (416)595-9486
E-mail: vcabral@rogers.com

• 12314 • E. M. Jellinek Memorial Award
To recognize scientists who have made outstanding contributions to the advancement of knowledge in the alcohol/alcoholism field. Living scientists, regardless of nationality, may be nominated. A monetary award of $5,000 Canadian and an inscribed bronze bust of E. M. Jellinek are awarded annually and presented at an appropriate international conference selected by the Board of Directors. E.M. Jellinek was one of the founding fathers of the scientific approach to the study of alcohol problems and a prime mover in the development of treatment and rehabilitation programs. The Jellinek Memorial Fund was established and incorporated in 1965. was established in 1955.

• 12315 •
Jesuit Secondary Education Association
Ralph E. Metts SJ, Pres.
1616 P St. NW, Ste. 400
Washington, DC 20036-1418
Phone: (202)667-3888
Fax: (202)387-6305
E-mail: jsea@jsea.org
Home Page: http://www.jsea.org

• 12316 • Ignatian Educator
Recognizes service with Jesuit secondary education. Awarded triennially.

• 12317 •
Jewelers Security Alliance
John J. Kennedy, Pres.
6 E 45th St.
New York, NY 10017
Phone: (212)687-0328
Toll-Free: 800-537-0067
Fax: (212)808-9168
E-mail: jsa2@jewelerssecurity.org
Home Page: http://
www.jewelerssecurity.org

• 12318 • Gold and Silver Shield Awards
Recognizes contribution to crime prevention. Awarded annually.

• 12319 • James B. White JSA Award
Award of recognition. Law enforcement persons are eligible. Awarded annually.

• 12320 •
Jewish Book Council
Miri Pomerantz, Mng.Assoc.
15 E 26th St.
New York, NY 10010
Phone: (212)532-4949
Phone: (212)786-5157
Fax: (212)481-4174
E-mail: jbc@jewishbooks.org
Home Page: http://
www.jewishbookcouncil.org

Formerly: Jewish Book Council/JWB (Jewish Welfare Board).

• 12321 • National Jewish Book Award - Autobiography/Memoir
To recognize the author of an autobiography or a memoir of the life of a Jewish person. A monetary award of $750 to the author and a citation to the publisher and the author are awarded annually. Established in 1989.

• 12322 • National Jewish Book Award - Children's Literature
To honor the most distinguished children's book on a Jewish theme originally written and published in English, or to recognize cumulative contributions to Jewish juvenile literature. Books published in the United States or Canada are eligible. A monetary award of $750 to the author and a citation to the publisher and author are awarded annually. Established in 1952.

• 12323 • National Jewish Book Award - Children's Picture Book
To recognize an author and illustrator of children's books with Jewish themes in which the illustrations are an intrinsic part of the text. Books published in the United States or Canada are eligible. A monetary award of $750 to the author, and a citation to the publisher and the author are presented annually in the spring. Established in 1982.

• 12324 • National Jewish Book Award - Contemporary Jewish Life
To recognize the author of a non-fiction work dealing with the sociology of modern Jewish life. A monetary award of $750 to the author and a citation to the author and the publisher are awarded annually. Established in 1988.

• 12325 • National Jewish Book Award - Fiction
To honor an outstanding work of fiction, either a novel or collection of short stories, that combines high literary merit with an affirmative expression of Jewish values. Books published in the United States or Canada are eligible. A mon-

etary award of $750 to the author and a citation to the publisher and the author are awarded annually. Established in 1948.

• 12326 • National Jewish Book Award - Holocaust

To recognize an outstanding nonfiction book dealing with some aspect of the Nazi holocaust period. Books published in the United States or Canada are eligible. A monetary award of $750 to the author and a citation to the publisher and the author are awarded annually. Established in 1965.

• 12327 • National Jewish Book Award - Israel

To recognize an outstanding nonfiction work concerning the state of Israel. Books published in the United States or Canada are eligible. A monetary award of $750 to the author and a citation to the publisher and the author are awarded annually. Established in 1974.

• 12328 • National Jewish Book Award - Jewish History

To recognize the author of a book on Jewish history, except periods covering the European Holocaust of Judaism and Israel. The award consists of a monetary prize of $750 to the author and a citation to the publisher and the author. Awarded annually. Established in 1973.

• 12329 • National Jewish Book Award - Jewish Thought

To honor a book dealing with some aspect of Jewish thought, past or present, that combines knowledge, clarity of thought, and literary merit, and was originally written in English. Books published in the United States or Canada are eligible. A monetary award of $750 to the author and a citation to the publisher and the author are awarded annually. Established in 1949.

• 12330 • National Jewish Book Award - Scholarship

To recognize an author of a book that makes an original contribution to Jewish learning and enriches the degree of knowledge available. Books published in the United States or Canada are eligible. A monetary award of $750 to the author and a citation to the publisher and the author are presented annually. Established in 1982.

• 12331 • National Jewish Book Award - Sephardic Studies

To recognize the author of a book in Sephardic studies. Books published in the United States or Canada during the preceding year are eligible. A monetary prize of $750 and a citation are awarded annually. Established in 1992. Sponsored by Maurice Amado Foundation.

• 12332 • National Jewish Book Award - Visual Arts

To recognize the author of a book of Jewish art or interest in Jewish art in all forms. Books published in the United States or Canada during the preceding year are eligible. A monetary prize of $750 to the author and a citation to the publisher and the author are awarded annually. Established in 1981.

• 12333 • National Jewish Book Award - Yiddish Literature

To recognize the author of a book of literary merit in the Yiddish language. Works of fiction, poetry, essays, and memoirs are eligible. A monetary prize of $750 to the author and a citation to the publisher and the author are awarded annually. Established in 1980.

• 12334 •
Jewish Community Center Theatre - Eugene S. and Blanche R. Halle Theatre
26001 S Woodland Rd.
Beechwood, OH 44122
Phone: (216)831-0700
Fax: (216)831-7796
E-mail: halletheatre@clevejcc.org
Home Page: http://www.clevejcc.org

• 12335 • American Hero Award

Recognizes heroic acts done for America. Awarded annually.

• 12336 • Dorothy Silver Playwriting Competition Prize

Encourages and produces new plays on the Jewish experience. Applicants may be of any nationality, but must have written an unpublished, unproduced play directly concerned with the Jewish experience and suitable for full-length presentation. Awardee must be in residence during the production of a staged reading of his/her play at the JCC Theatre. One half of the award funds will be paid upon announcement of the prize; the other half will be paid later and may be used to cover travel and residency expenses during the production period. JCC reserves the right to perform the first full-staged production of the winning script following the staged reading, without payment of additional royalties. $1000 is awarded. The manuscript and a self-addressed stamped envelope must be submitted by May 1. Notification is in late summer.

• 12337 •
Jewish Community Centers Association
Miriam Rinn, Comm. Dir.
15 E 26th St.
New York, NY 10010-1579
Phone: (212)532-4949
Fax: (212)481-4174
E-mail: info@jcca.org
Home Page: http://www.jcca.org

Formerly: JWB.

• 12338 • Florence G. Heller Award

To recognize a distinguished career of professional contribution within JWB's fields of work. A monetary award of $500 and a medallion are awarded every two years at the Biennial Convention. Established in 1968 in memory of Florence G. Heller.

• 12339 • JCC Biennial Communications Awards Competition

To recognize outstanding communication materials. Awards for the Jewish Community Centers are based on five levels of the Center's budget. The categories are: multi-media presentations; special events; center brochures; center photos; camp brochures; and camp photos. Military personnel categories are: military/VA chapel bulletins; and military/VA photos. Entries must have been produced within 24 months prior to the entry deadline of September 15. Awarded every two years. Established in 1978.

• 12340 • JCC Program Awards

To recognize Centers which have inaugurated and sustained innovative and original programs. Five Program Awards are presented according to size of the city. Awarded at the Biennial Convention.

• 12341 • Leadership Development Awards

To recognize distinguished leadership potential. Awarded every two years at the JWB Biennial Convention.

• 12342 • Frank L. Weil Awards

To recognize distinguished contributions to three phases of the work embraced by JWB, namely, the Jewish Community Center field, armed services field, and the advancement of North America Jewish culture. Three bronze medallions and scrolls are awarded every two years at the Biennial Convention. Established in 1950 in honor of Frank L. Weil, president of JWB from 1940-1950.

• 12343 •
Jewish Deaf Congress
214-11 85th Ave.
Hollis Hills, NY 11427
Phone: (718)740-0470
Fax: (718)740-4994
E-mail: florsheim@aol.com

• 12344 • Award of Merit

To recognize outstanding involvement within the affiliates for the past two years. The affiliate nominates the year's outstanding worker and he/she is honored at the convention banquet. A certificate is awarded biennially. Established in 1962 by Alexander Fleischman.

• 12345 • Phillip Hanover Memorial Recognition Award

To recognize and honor NCJD presidents upon completion of their term(s) of office. A plaque is awarded biennially. Established in 1988 in memory of Philip hanover, NCJD's first president.

• 12346 • Henry and Anna Papinger Endowment Award

To recognize outstanding leadership and achievement nationwide. The Board selects the honoree from nominations. A monetary award and a plaque are awarded biennially at the

NCJD Convention. Established in 1978 by Anna Plapinger.

• 12347 • Celia Warshawsky Award
To recognize a young person, between 17 and 35 years of age, for services and achievement during the two-year period preceding the biennial Convention. A plaque is awarded biennially at the convention. Established in 1988 by Lenny Warshawsky in memory of Celia Warshawsky.

• 12348 •
Jewish Educators Assembly
Edward Edelstein, Exec.Dir.
300 Forest Dr.
Greenvale, NY 11548
Phone: (516)484-9585
Fax: (516)484-9586
E-mail: jewisheducators@aol.com
Home Page: http://www.jewisheducators.org

• 12349 • JEA Research and Development Fund Award
For recognition of a contribution to the field of Jewish activity. A monetary prize and a plaque are awarded at the convention. Established in 1983.

• 12350 •
Jewish Family and Children's Services of San Francisco, the Peninsula, Marin and Sonoma Counties
Dr. Anita Friedman, Exec.Dir.
Miriam Schultz Grunfeld Professional Bldg.
2150 Post St.
San Francisco, CA 94115
Phone: (415)449-1200
Fax: (415)922-5938
E-mail: chanaa@jfcs.org
Home Page: http://www.jfcs.org

• 12351 • FAMY Awards
For outstanding volunteer service. Recognition award bestowed annually.

• 12352 •
Jewish Federation of Metropolitan Detroit
PO Box 2030
Bloomfield Hills, MI 48303-2030
Phone: (248)642-4260
Fax: (248)642-4985
Home Page: http://www.thisisfederation.org
Formerly: Jewish Welfare Federation of Metropolitan Detroit.

• 12353 • Fred M. Butzel Memorial Award for Distinguished Community Service
To recognize outstanding service to the Jewish community and the Detroit community at large. A plaque is awarded at the Federation's annual meeting in the fall. Established in 1951 in memory of the late Jewish leader, Fred M. Butzel, who devoted his life to serving the underprivileged of Detroit.

• 12354 •
Jewish Foundation for the Righteous
Stanlee Joyce Stahl, Exec.VP
305 7th Ave., 19th Fl.
New York, NY 10001-6008
Phone: (212)727-9955
Fax: (212)727-9956
E-mail: jfr@jfr.org
Home Page: http://www.jfr.org

• 12355 • Recognition of Goodness Award
Recognizes individuals who have demonstrated their commitment to improving the lives of righteous gentiles. Awarded annually.

• 12356 •
Jewish Genealogical Society of Greater Philadelphia
Mark Halpern, Pres.
PO Box 335
Exton, PA 19341-0335
E-mail: jgsgp@comcast.net
Home Page: http://www.jewishgen.org/jgsp

• 12357 • Rabbi Malcolm H. Stern Award
For service and contribution to the field of Jewish genealogy. Recognition award bestowed periodically.

• 12358 •
Jewish Institute for National Security Affairs
Mark Broxmeyer, Chm.
1779 Massachusetts Ave. NW, Ste. 515
Washington, DC 20036
Phone: (202)667-3900
Fax: (202)667-0601
E-mail: info@jinsa.org
Home Page: http://www.jinsa.org

• 12359 • Henry M. Jackson Distinguished Service Award
To honor a public figure for outstanding contributions to the defense of freedom and democracy. The award provides recognition of dedication to a strong U.S. national defense program and recognition of Israel as a strategic ally of the United States. An American Eagle statue is awarded annually in November. Established in 1982 to honor Senator Henry M. Jackson.

• 12360 •
Jewish Labor Committee
Avram Lyon, Exec.Dir.
25 E 21st St.
New York, NY 10010
Phone: (212)477-0707
Fax: (212)477-1918
E-mail: jlcexec@aol.com
Home Page: http://www.jewishlabor.org

• 12361 • Human Rights Award
To advance the struggle for social justice and equal opportunity within the framework of the American labor movement. National trade union leaders, local trade union leaders, and business leaders, who have contributed to the cause of worker right and human rights are eligible. Awarded annually. Established in 1967 by the National Trade Union Council for Human Rights of Jewish Labor Committee.

• 12362 •
The Jewish Museum
Helen Goldsmith Menschel, Dir.
Public Relations
1109 5th Ave.
New York, NY 10128
Phone: (212)423-3200
Fax: (212)423-3232
E-mail: info@thejm.org
Home Page: http://www.jewishmuseum.org

• 12363 • Mayer Sulzberger Award
To recognize people who have made a significant contribution to the perpetuation of art, culture, and education in the context of the Jewish experience. People who have helped to perpetuate a Jewish identity as well as humanist values are considered. A gift of Jewish ceremonial art is awarded at the museum's spring gala as needed. Established in honor of Judge Mayer Sulzberger, whose donation of 26 pieces of Judaica to the Jewish Theological Seminary of America in 1904 laid the groundwork for the Jewish Museum.

• 12364 •
Jewish National Fund
Russell F. Robinson, CEO
42 E 69th St.
New York, NY 10021
Phone: (212)879-9300
Phone: 888-JNF-0099
Toll-Free: 888-JNF-0099
Fax: (212)570-1673
E-mail: communications@jnf.org
Home Page: http://www.jnf.org

• 12365 • Hatikvah Award
To recognize contributions and commitment to a local Jewish community and the state of Israel. A plaque depicting children planting trees is awarded.

• 12366 • Legion of Honor
To recognize individuals of distinction in the Jewish community who have performed significant deeds to benefit the Jewish people and the state of Israel and have demonstrated a commitment to the continuance of good works prior to admission in the Legion of Honor. A medal is awarded.

• 12367 • Shalom Peace Award
To recognize great contributions to the furtherance of the cause of peace in the world. A plaque is presented when merited.

• 12368 • Tree of Life Award
Given in recognition of outstanding community involvement, dedication to the cause of American-Israeli friendship and devotion to peace and the security of human life. This humanitarian

award is the Jewish National Fund's highest honor and is named "Tree of Life" to symbolize the JNF's efforts to reclaim and develop the Land of Israel, to increase the water resources and cover it with green forests.

• 12369 •
Jewish Peace Fellowship
Murray Polner, Chair
Box 271
Nyack, NY 10960-0271
Phone: (845)358-4601
Fax: (845)358-4924
E-mail: jpf@forusa.org
Home Page: http://www.jewishpeacefellowship.org

• 12370 • **Abraham Joshua Heschel Peace Award**
To honor an American Jew for exceptional contributions to peace in the Jewish tradition. Jewish Americans are selected and awarded a plaque biennially. Established in 1984 in memory of Rabbi Abraham Joshua Heschel, Executive Committee member of the Jewish Peace Fellowship and an important spokesperson for peace and justice.

• 12371 •
Jewish Reconstructionist Federation
Daniel G. Cedarbaum, Pres.
7804 Montgomery Ave., Ste. 9
Elkins Park, PA 19027-2649
Phone: (215)782-8500
Fax: (215)782-8805
E-mail: info@jrf.org
Home Page: http://www.jrf.org

Formerly: Jewish Reconstructionist Foundation; Federation of Reconstructionist Congregations and Havurot.

• 12372 • **Kaplan Medal**
For recognition of devotion, hard work, and special accomplishment in furthering the goals of Reconstructionism. A medal is awarded annually. Established before 1966 in honor of Rabbi Mordechai M. Kaplan, founder of Reconstructionism.

• 12373 •
Jewish Theological Seminary
Ismar Schorsch, Pres.
3080 Broadway
New York, NY 10027
Phone: (212)678-8000
Fax: (212)678-8947
Home Page: http://www.jtsa.edu

• 12374 • **Rabbi Max Arzt Distinguished Rabbinic Service Award**
No further information available for this edition.

• 12375 • **Eternal Light Medal**
To recognize leadership and service to Jewish education, religion, and culture. Individuals who demonstrate consecrated efforts to advance and strengthen the community, state, and nation, and the house and the people of Israel are considered. Established in 1967.

• 12376 • **Rabbi Simon Greenberg Rabbinic Achievement Award**
No further information was provided for this edition.

• 12377 • **Herbert H. Lehman Ethics Award**
To recognize a distinguished exemplar of the ancient Jewish quest for ethical and moral truth by which all persons should live. A gold medal is awarded as merited. Established in 1960.

• 12378 • **Louis Marshall Award**
To recognize consecrated service to Judaism, the American Jewish community, and humankind, after the tradition of Louis Marshall, an eminent constitutional lawyer. A gold medal is awarded annually. Established in 1965.

• 12379 • **National Community Service Award**
To recognize Jewish lay leaders for dedication to the principles of Judaism, selfless support of the programs of the Jewish Theological Seminary, and exemplary leadership in endeavors to enrich the spiritual life of the community. Five or six bronze plaques are awarded annually. Established in 1961.

• 12380 • **New Generations Award**
No further information was provided for this edition.

• 12381 • **Rabbinical Service Award of Appreciation**
No further information was provided for this edition.

• 12382 • **Solomon Schechter Medal**
To recognize individuals who have made an extraordinary contribution to Judaism in America. Established in 1959 to honor Solomon Schechter, president of the Seminary from 1902 to 1915.

• 12383 • **Second Century Award**
No further information was provided for this edition.

• 12384 • **Shin Award**
No further information was provided for this edition.

• 12385 •
Jewish War Veterans of the U.S.A.
Herb Rosenbleeth, Exec.Dir.
1811 R St. NW
Washington, DC 20009
Phone: (202)265-6280
Fax: (202)234-5662
E-mail: jwv@jwv.org
Home Page: http://www.jwv.org

• 12386 • **Gold Medal of Merit**
For recognition of contributions by an American to the security and defense of the United States and preservation of its democratic traditions. A gold medal is awarded only when warranted. Established in 1947.

• 12387 • **Commodore Uriah P. Levy Citizen's Award**
For recognition in the field of leadership to the United States. Veterans of good standing who have shown leadership within the community or organization are eligible. A plaque is awarded when warranted. Established in 1983 by the National Memorial Board of Directors in honor of Commodore Uriah P. Levy, the first Jewish Commodore in the United States Navy.

• 12388 • **Colonel Mickey Marcus Award**
For recognition of humanitarian work in a community, state, or country. Veterans, non-veterans, and foreigners are eligible. A plaque is awarded annually in different parts of the country. Established in 1985 in memory of Colonel David "Mickey" Marcus, graduate of West Point, Commissioner of Corrections, New York City, World War II veteran, and first Commander of Israeli forces in 1948.

• 12389 •
Jewish War Veterans of the U.S.A. - National Ladies Auxiliary
Charlene Ehrlich, Pres.
1811 R St. NW
Washington, DC 20009-1603
Phone: (202)667-9061
Fax: (202)667-6689
E-mail: jwv@jwv.org
Home Page: http://www.jwv.org

• 12390 • **Humanity Award**
Award of recognition. For military academies. Awarded annually.

• 12391 •
Jewish Women International
Loribeth Weinstein, Exec.Dir.
2000 M St. NW, Ste. 720
Washington, DC 20036
Phone: (202)857-1300
Toll-Free: 800-343-2823
Fax: (202)857-1380
E-mail: jkarotkin@jwi.org
Home Page: http://www.jewishwomen.org

Formerly: B'nai B'rith Women.

• 12392 • **Perlman Award for Human Advancement**
To recognize an individual or group on an international level for outstanding contributions to human advancement through the furthering of equal justice, human rights, wider opportunity, and a higher quality of life for all. Nominations are accepted. A monetary award of $2,500 and the JWI Perlman Award Sculpture are bestowed biennially at the national convention. Established in 1980 in honor of Anita and Louis Perlman and their efforts in the development of

youth activities, prenatal education, and scientific and medical research.

• 12393 •
Jobs for America's Graduates
Jimmy G. Koeninger PhD, Exec.VP
1729 King St., Ste. 100
Alexandria, VA 22314
Phone: (703)684-9479
Fax: (703)684-9489
E-mail: jimkoeninger@jag.org
Home Page: http://www.jag.org

• 12394 • **National Leadership**
Recognizes significant service to the organization. Awarded annually.

• 12395 •
Jockey Club of Canada
Bridget Brimm, Contact
PO Box 66, Sta. B
Etobicoke, ON, Canada M9W 5K9
Phone: (416)675-7756
Fax: (416)675-6378
E-mail: jockeyclub@bellnet.ca
Home Page: http://www.jockeyclubcanada.com

• 12396 • **Sovereign Award**
To honor champions of the sport of thoroughbred horse racing in Canada. The horse must have made at least three starts during the year in Canada. In addition to Horse of the Year, awards are given in the following categories: (1) E.P. Taylor Award of Merit (not annually); (2) Older Champion Horse or Gelding; (3) Older Champion Filly or Mare; (4) Three Year Old Champion Colt; (5) Three Year Old Champion Filly; (6) Champion Female Turf Horse; (7) Champion Male Turf Horse; (8) Two Year Old Champion Colt; (9) Two Year Old Champion Filly; (10) Outstanding Owner; (11) Outstanding Breeder; (12) Outstanding Trainer; (13) Outstanding Jockey; (14) Outstanding Apprentice Jockey; (15) Outstanding Broodmare of the Year; (16) Outstanding Newspaper Story; (17) Outstanding Photography; (18) Champion Sprinter; (19) Outstanding Feature Story; and (20) Outstanding Film/Video Broadcast. Media submissions must be of Canadian racing content and published/aired during the previous year, November 1 to October 31. Awards of Merit are voted by various organizations in racing. A statue of St. Simon, a famous racehorse, is awarded annually in December to all first time winners. A gold sovereign to attach to the trophy and a plaque are awarded to repeat winners. Established in 1975.

• 12397 •
John F. Kennedy Library Foundation
John Shattuck Jr., CEO
Columbia Point
Boston, MA 02125
Phone: (617)514-1550
Phone: (617)514-1573
Toll-Free: (866)JFK-1960
Fax: (617)436-3395
E-mail: postmaster@jfklfoundation.org
Home Page: http://www.jfklibrary.org

• 12398 • **John F. Kennedy Profile in Courage Award**
To honor President Kennedy by promoting the quality of political courage in public officials. The award is usually given to living Americans who are or were elected officials, although in especially deserving cases, posthumous awards may be considered. A monetary prize of $25,000 and a silver award lantern are presented annually on or around May 29, President Kennedy's birthday. Established in 1989 to commemorate President John F. Kennedy.

• 12399 •
John Pelham Historical Association
Brett Bradshaw, Pres.
PO Box 371
East Berlin, CT 06023-0371
Phone: (860)635-0463
E-mail: info@gallantpelham.org
Home Page: http://www.gallantpelham.org

• 12400 • **Certificate of Appreciation**
To recognize an individual for achievement or support benefiting the Association. A framed certificate is awarded annually at the convention. Established in 1988 to honor Maj. John Pelham, a major in the Confederate army who fought at the battles of Manassas, Antietam, and Fredericksburg.

• 12401 •
John Templeton Foundation
Pamela P. Thompson, VP Communications
300 Conshohocken State Rd., Ste. 500
West Conshohocken, PA 19428
Phone: (610)941-2828
Fax: (610)825-1730
E-mail: info@templeton.org
Home Page: http://www.templeton.org

• 12402 • **The Epiphany Prizes**
To encourage the production of movies that are wholesome, uplifting and inspirational and that result in a greater increase in either man]s understanding or love of God. The top three winners will receive $50,000 in prizes, with the top winner receiving $25,000. The top winner]s script will also be read by top studio executives at Disney, DreamWorks, Fox, and Universal. Formerly: Templeton Prizes for Inspiring Movies and TV.

• 12403 • **Essay Contest in Progress in Religion Through the Sciences**
To stimulate fresh thinking on the interaction between science and religion. An essay contest organized within the nine member schools of The Boston Theological Institute.

• 12404 • **Exemplary Papers in Humility Theology**
To recognize exceptional articles previously published or accepted for publication in a peer reviewed journal recognizing the constructive relationship between theology/religion and the sciences in the following categories: Theology and the natural Sciences, Religion and the Medical Sciences, and Religion and the Human Behavioral Sciences. Monetary prices of $2,000 are awarded.

• 12405 • **Faith & Medicine Competitive Grant Award**
To recognize medical schools offering a model course addressing the long neglected domains of religion and spirituality in medical care. Up to ten awards of $10,000 each are awarded annually. The award is divided equally between the instructor and the school offering the course.

• 12406 • **Honor Roll for Education in a Free Society**
To recognize exemplary enterprise teaching. A prize is offered for Lifetime Teaching and an Outstanding Book of the Year.

• 12407 • **Laws of Life Essay Contest - Christian Education Movement/BT Campus World**
To recognize British secondary students who have written outstanding essays on the laws of life. The on-line essay contest makes use of new technology for both advertising the contest and receipt of submitted essays.

• 12408 • **Laws of Life Essay Contest - Franklin County, Tennessee**
To stimulate thinking about moral and ethical law of life among junior and senior high school students. This biennial contest offers 13 monetary awards for essays. Additionally, a prize is offered for the first place winner's teacher to be used toward book purchases.

• 12409 • **Laws of Life Essay Contest - Nassau, Bahamas**
To stimulate thinking among junior and senior high school students about moral and ethical laws of life. This biennial contest offers 13 monetary awards. Additionally, a prize is offered for the first place winner's teacher to be used toward book purchases.

• 12410 • **Laws of Life Essay Contest - Peale Center for Christian Living**
To encourage young readers to reflect upon the laws of life. Three cash prizes are awarded and wining essays are published in "Plus the Magazine of Positive Living." Hosted twice annually by "Plus the Magazine of Positive Living."

• 12411 • Prize for Outstanding Books in Theology and the Natural Sciences
To recognize outstanding books nominated and selected by an international panel of judges. Winning publications must offer outstanding scholarship in the relationship between theology, and such natural sciences as physics, cosmology, evolutionary biology and genetics. A monetary prize of $10,000 is awarded.

• 12412 • Religion Reporter of the Year Award
To reward excellence in enterprise reporting and versatility in the field of religious writing. A monetary prize of $3,500 is awarded annually.

• 12413 • Science and Religion Course Program
To encourage the development of interdisciplinary courses in science and religion. Up to one hundred awards of $10,000 are offered for instructor and college, university or school of theology hosting the course. Additionally, a complimentary series of workshops are sponsored in science and religion pedagogy.

• 12414 • Templeton Prize for Progress toward Research or Discoveries about Spiritual Realities
To recognize a living person of any religious tradition or movement who has made a unique contribution to progress toward research or discoveries about spiritual realities. The judges consider a nominee's originality in advancing ideas and/or institutions that have deepened the world's understanding of God and of spiritual life and service. The qualities sought in awarding the prize are: freshness, creativity, innovation, and effectiveness. Such contributions may involve new concepts of the spirit, new organizations, new methods of evangelism, new and effective ways of communicating God's wisdom and infinite love, creation of new schools of thought, creation of new structures of understanding the relationship of the Creator to His ongoing creation of the universe, to the physical sciences, the life sciences, and the human sciences, and the releasing of new and vital impulses into old religious structures and forms.

• 12415 • Templeton United Kingdom Project Trust Award
To encourage originality and entrepreneurship in religion. Two awards of 3,000 lire are presented semi-annually throughout Great Britain to both an individual and an organization.

• 12416 •
Johns Hopkins University
William R. Brody, Pres.
Office of the President
242 Garland Hall
3400 N Charles St.
Baltimore, MD 21218
Phone: (410)516-8000
Fax: (410)516-6097
E-mail: wrbrody@jhu.edu
Home Page: http://www.jhu.edu

• 12417 • Albert Schweitzer Prize for Humanitarianism
To advance the cause of humanitarianism in the United States through recognition of exemplary achievement by individuals and organizations in the areas of human service and environment. Nominations of individuals or organizations are solicited by the Board of Trustees and the deadline is July 31. A monetary prize of $15,000 is awarded biannually. Established in 1986 by Dr. Alfred Toepfer, President of the Alexander von Humboldt Foundation to commemorate Dr. Albert Schweitzer. Sponsored by the Alexander von Humboldt Foundation of New York.

• 12418 •
Johnson County Historical Society
Margaret Wieting, Exec.Dir.
PO Box 5081
Coralville, IA 52241
Phone: (319)351-5738
Fax: (319)351-5310
E-mail: johctyhistscty@yahoo.com
Home Page: http://www.jccniowa.org/~jchsweb1

• 12419 • Irving Weber Award
For preservation of local history. Recognition award bestowed annually.

• 12420 •
Lyndon Baines Johnson Library and Museum
Harry Middleton, Dir.
2313 Red River St.
Austin, TX 78705
Phone: (512)721-0200
Fax: (512)721-0170
E-mail: library@johnson.nara.gov
Home Page: http://www.lbjlib.utexas.edu

• 12421 • Grants-in-Aid Program
Defrays living, travel, and related expenses incurred while conducting archival research at the LBJ Library. Applications are reviewed by a special Faculty Committee appointed by the President of the University of Texas at the request of the LBJ Foundation. Prior to submitting a grant-in-aid proposal, applicants must contact the Archives at the above address, to obtain information about materials available in the library on the proposed research topic. Awards are bestowed on a competitive basis. Grant applications for October through March must be received by July 31. Grant applications for April through September must be received by January 31st. For further information, contact Tina Houston by mail at the above address, by telephone at (512) 721-0206, or by e-mail at tina.houston@nara.gov.

• 12422 • D. B. Hardeman Prize
To encourage scholarship on the U.S. Congress and to recognize the best book published on the Congress or one of its members in the preceding year. A monetary award of $1,000 is awarded annually. Established in 1980 by the Lyndon Baines. Johnson Library in memory of D.B. Hardeman, student of the Congress, and aide and associate of House Speaker Sam Rayburn. Additional information is available from Lyndon B. Johnson Library, % Ted Gittinger, 2313 Red River Street, Austin, TX 78705; telephone: (512) 482-5137, ext. 265 or ted.gittinger@nara.gov.

• 12423 •
Join Hands Day
Frederick H. Grubbe, Pres.
1315 W 22nd St., Ste. 400
Oak Brook, IL 60523
Phone: (630)355-6633
Toll-Free: 877-OUR-1DAY
Fax: (630)522-6327
E-mail: actioncenter@joinhandsday.org
Home Page: http://www.joinhandsday.org

• 12424 • Excellence Awards
Recognition is given annually for outstanding projects.

• 12425 •
Joint Baltic American National Committee
Karl Altau, Managing Dir.
400 Hurley Ave.
Rockville, MD 20850-3121
Phone: (301)340-1954
Fax: (301)309-1406
E-mail: jbanc@jbanc.org
Home Page: http://www.jbanc.org

• 12426 • Baltic Freedom Award
To recognize individuals for their commitment to freedom and self-determination for the peoples of Estonia, Latvia, and Lithuania. Individuals who have contributed to the Baltic struggle may be nominated. A framed certificate is awarded annually in June at the Baltic Freedom Day Reception.

• 12427 •
Joint Financial Management Improvement Program
Doris Chew, Actg. Dir.
1990 K St. NW, Ste. 430
Washington, DC 20006
Phone: (202)219-0526
Fax: (202)219-0549
E-mail: doris.chew@gsa.gov
Home Page: http://www.jfmip.gov/jfmip

• 12428 • Donald L. Scantlebury Memorial Award
To recognize senior financial management executives who, through outstanding and continuous leadership in financial management, have been principally responsible for significant economies, efficiencies, and improvements in federal, state, or local government. Federal, state, or local government employees who are senior executives are eligible. Nominations must be submitted by early January. A plaque is awarded annually in March. Established in 1970 and renamed in memory of Donald L. Scantlebury, who was the Chief Accountant of the General Accounting Office and chairman of the JFMIP Steering Committee. Formerly: (1981) Financial Management Improvement Award.

• 12429 •
Joshua Slocum Society International
Ted Jones, Commodore
15 Codfish Hill Rd. Extension
Bethel, CT 06801
Phone: (203)790-6616
Fax: (203)778-9917
E-mail: ted@joshuaslocumsocietyintl.org
Home Page: http://
www.joshuaslocumsocietyintl.org

• 12430 • **J. B. Charcot Award**
For recognition of the most notable use of a working boat or working boat fleet during the previous year. An inscribed plaque is awarded when merited. Established in 1956 in honor of J.B. Charcot, the French explorer, and for the fishing ketch bearing his name.

• 12431 • **Hakluyt Award**
For recognition of the most notable writing dealing with boats. An inscribed plaque is awarded when merited. Established in 1956 in honor of Richard Hakluyt, the compiler of maritime voyages.

• 12432 • **Honorary Member Award**
To recognize individuals who have: (1) circumnavigated in their own vessels under 65 feet; (2) received other Slocum awards; or (3) distinguished themselves in small craft voyaging or seamanship. Honorary Life Memberships are awarded.

• 12433 • **Joshua Trophy**
To recognize the most outstanding voyage in a small boat of one's own design and construction, that not only enhances the lore of bluewater sailing, but also significantly contributes to the technical knowledge of seaworthy small vessels. Established in 1991.

• 12434 • **Northern Light Award**
To recognize the captain and/or crew of a merchant vessels that renders outstanding service to small boats in distress. Awarded when merited. Established in 1987.

• 12435 • **Slocum Award**
For recognition of the most notable single-handed transoceanic passage made during the previous year. An inscribed plaque is awarded when merited. Established in 1956 in honor of the first man to sail around the world alone.

• 12436 • **Spray Trophy**
To recognize the best replica of Slocum's vessel owned or built by a member of the Society.

• 12437 • **Carl H. Vilas Literary Award**
To recognize outstanding articles or photos on cruising by members. Established in 1991 to honor Carl Vilas, a long-time member of the Slocum Society, a member of Cruising Club of America for 50 years, editor of the *Cruising Club of America News* and club historian, and winner of the Nye Trophy.

• 12438 • **Voss Award**
For recognition of the most notable two-man transoceanic passage made during the previous year. An inscribed plaque is awarded when merited. Established in 1956 in honor of the first man to sail around the world with a crew member.

• 12439 •
Joshua's Tract Conservation and Historic Trust
Hugh Hamill, Pres.
PO Box 4
Mansfield Center, CT 06250-0004
Phone: (860)429-9023
Fax: (860)429-9023
E-mail: joshuastrust@snet.net
Home Page: http://
www.joshuaslandtrust.org

• 12440 • **Conservation Award**
For individuals and organizations making substantial contributions to conservation, open space preservation, etc. Recognition award bestowed annually.

• 12441 •
Jostens Inc.
5501 American West Blvd.
Minneapolis, MN 55437
Phone: (952)830-3300
E-mail: janharding@aol.com

• 12442 • **Service and Performance Award**
To recognize outstanding program development and administration carried out in the Baltimore, Maryland, and Delaware areas.

• 12443 •
Journal of Aesthetics and Art Criticism
Department of Philosophy
Susan L. Feagin, Ed.
717 Anderson Hall
Department of Philosophy
Temple University
Philadelphia, PA 19122
Phone: (215)204-2466
Fax: (215)204-2465
E-mail: jaac@temple.edu
Home Page: http://www.temple.edu/jaac

• 12444 • **John Fisher Memorial Prize**
To recognize the development of new voices and talent in the field of aesthetics. Awarded biennially with a monetary prize of $1,00 and publication in the *Journal.* Sponsored by the *Journal* and the American Society for Aesthetics.

• 12445 •
Journal of Consumer Research
University of Wisconsin, Madison
John Deighton, Ed.
School of Business
975 University Ave.
Madison, WI 53706-1323
Phone: (608)265-1146
Fax: (608)265-1147
E-mail: jcr@bus.wisc.edu
Home Page: http://wiscinfo.doit.wisc.edu/jcr

• 12446 • **Robert Ferber Award for Consumer Research**
For recognition of the best article on consumer behavior based on a doctoral dissertation for which a degree was awarded not more than three years prior to the year of the submission. Manuscripts published and eligible for the award in each volume of the journal become candidates for the award. Volumes run from June to March and the judging for the award is completed by June 1. The award consists of a monetary prize of $1,000 for the winner and $500 for honorable mention, an engraved plaque, and presentation of the paper at the Annual Conference of the Association for Consumer Research. Awarded annually. Established in 1978. The award now commemorates Robert Ferber (1922-1981), a marketing research pioneer, founder of the *Journal of Consumer Research* and *Journal of Marketing Research*, author, editor, and Renaissance man. Co-sponsored by the Association for Consumer Research. Formerly: (1982) Consumer Research Award.

• 12447 •
Journalism Education Association
Linda S. Puntney, Exec.Dir.
Kansas State University
103 Kedzie Hall
Manhattan, KS 66506-1505
Phone: (785)532-5532
Phone: (785)532-7822
Toll-Free: (866)532-5532
Fax: (785)532-5563
E-mail: jea@spub.ksu.edu
Home Page: http://www.jea.org
Formerly: (1963) National Association of Journalism Directors.

• 12448 • **Lifetime Achievement Award**
Awarded to retirees for lifetime dedication to journalism education. Established in 1987. Deadline for nomination is July 1.

• 12449 • **Medal of Merit**
To recognize local or national accomplishments in scholastic journalism. Members of JEA who have been active in the association for at least ten years are eligible. Deadline for application is July 1. Pins and certificates are awarded annually at the fall convention. Established in 1967.

• 12450 • **Media Citation**
To honor professional journalists, professional media outlets, or any individual or group making a significant contribution to scholastic journal-

Awards are arranged in alphabetical order below their administering organizations

ism. Nominations are accepted. Up to three wood and metal plaques are awarded annually. Established in 1967. Deadline for application is July 1.

• 12451 • National High School Journalist of the Year

The Sister Rita Jeanne Scholarship, named after JEA's long-time treasurer, recognizes some of the top high school journalists in the country. The contest begins at the state level. Winners from each state Journalists of the Year competition are sent to the national level. Portfolios are judged at the national JEA/NSPA convention each spring, and winners are announced at the awards ceremony which concludes the convention. Scholarship funds are released when a student enrolls in a college journalism program. The top winner receives a $2,000 scholarship and four runners-up receive $1,000 scholarships.

• 12452 • National Yearbook Adviser of the Year

To honor outstanding high school advisers. A nominated adviser (and this nomination can come from any interested persons or groups) must fill out the enclosed application, which must include a copy of the yearbook he or she advised. Student scholarships ($1,000 for the winner, four $500 scholarships for Distinguished Advisers) are awarded to students in the advisers' schools in late May. Established in 1995.

• 12453 • Student Impact Award

For recognition of a secondary school student or team who, through the study and practice of journalism, has made a significant difference in his or her own life, the lives of others, the school attended, or the community in which he or she lives. For further information contact the organization at the above address. Formerly: Special Awards.

• 12454 • Carl Towley Award

This, the association's highest award, is given in recognition of JEA members whose work is unusually beneficial to the field of scholastic journalism and to the organization and who have contributed qualitatively and quantitatively to JEA. The deadline for nominations is July 1. Awarded annually. Established in 1964 in honor of Carl Towley, JEA's first executive secretary.

• 12455 •
Joy in Singing
Paul Sperry, Mus.Dir.
260 W 72nd St., No. 6D
New York, NY 10023
Fax: (212)579-0779
E-mail: info@joyinsinging.org
Home Page: http://www.joyinsinging.org

• 12456 • Joy In Singing Award Recital

To further the careers of young singers and promote the art of the song recital. Individuals who have auditioned in New York City and have an extensive background in the art song literature are eligible. A debut recital in New York City following three preliminary recitals in the suburban areas within a 100 mile radius of New York are awarded annually. Established in 1958 by Winifred Cecil.

• 12457 •
Jozef Pilsudski Institute of America for Research in the Modern History of Poland
Mr. Jacek Galazka, Pres.
180 2nd Ave.
New York, NY 10003-5778
Phone: (212)505-9077
Fax: (212)505-9052
E-mail: info@pilsudski.org
Home Page: http://www.pilsudski.org

• 12458 • Jerzy Lojek Award

To recognize the best book on modern Polish history and the independence movements since 1863 to the present. The recipient is chosen by the jury of the institute. A monetary award is presented annually. Established in 1991 by Danuta and Andrzej Cisek.

• 12459 •
William A. Jump Memorial Foundation
Attn: DAPE-CP-ESO
U.S. Army Incentive Awards Board
300 Army Pentago, Rm. 2C453
Washington, DC 20310
Phone: (703)695-4011
E-mail: marvol.alexander@hqda.army.mil

• 12460 • William A. Jump Award

To recognize outstanding service in administration and notable contributions to the efficiency and quality of the public service. Federal government employees under 37 years of age are eligible. The deadline for nominations is usually the last Friday in February of each year. A golden key and certificate are awarded annually. Established in 1950 in memory of William A. Jump, budget and finance officer of the U.S. Department of Agriculture.

• 12461 •
Junior Achievement
David S. Chernow, Pres./CEO
1 Education Way
Colorado Springs, CO 80906
Phone: (719)540-8000
Fax: (719)540-6299
E-mail: newmedia@ja.org
Home Page: http://www.ja.org

• 12462 • Junior Achievement National Business Hall of Fame

To honor men and women who have made outstanding and enduring contributions to improving the products, processes, efficiences, or the human relations of business. Eligible individuals fall into two categories: the first group is drawn from the long history of United States business (for example, Andrew Carnegie, J. Pierpoint Morgan, Henry Ford, Walt Disney, Eli Whitney); the second group is made up of people who are still living but who no longer occupy the post in which their main contribution was made (for example, Donald T. Regan of Merrill Lynch and fashion designer Liz Claiborne). An etched Tiffany crystal trophy is awarded annually at the National Business Hall of Fame Conference. A biographical plaque is placed in the Hall of Fame, which is housed in a permanent exhibit at the Museum of Science and Industry in Chicago. Established in 1974.

• 12463 •
Junior Achievement of Canada
Simon Romano, Sec.
2275 Lakeshore Blvd. W, Ste. 306
Toronto, ON, Canada M8V 3Y3
Phone: (416)622-4602
Toll-Free: 800-265-0699
Fax: (416)622-6861
E-mail: programs@jacan.org
Home Page: http://www.jacan.org

• 12464 • Canadian Business Hall of Fame

For recognition of outstanding and enduring contributions to improving the products, the processes, the efficiencies, or the human relations of business in Canada. Retired or former business leaders are eligible. Nominations are accepted. Four to six business laureates are honored annually at the Hall of Fame Induction Ceremony and Banquet. Established in 1979.

• 12465 •
Junior Engineering Technical Society
Leann Yoder, Exec.Dir.
1420 King St., Ste. 405
Alexandria, VA 22314-2794
Phone: (703)548-5387
Fax: (703)548-0769
E-mail: info@jets.org
Home Page: http://www.jets.org

• 12466 • JETS National TEAMS Awards

To recognize outstanding student TEAMS determined in a written problem-solving competition related to mathematics and science as applied to real-life engineering situtations. All high schools may compete in the Tests of Engineering Aptitude, Mathematics, and Science Competition. Students form 4-8 member teams and compete at state and national levels. Trophies, plaques, medallions, scientific equipment, and other awards are presented annually. Local awards are presented at the regional and state competition sites. National Awards are announced by The Junior Engineering Technical Society. Established in 1978.

• 12467 •
Junior Golf Association of Mobile
Michael C. Thompson, Chm.
PO Box 70106
Mobile, AL 36670-1106
Phone: (251)473-5550
Fax: (251)473-8026
E-mail: mct@rtbh.com
Home Page: http://jgam.net

• 12468 • The Junior Golf Association of Mobile Scholarship
For academic and civic achievements. Scholarship awarded annually.

• 12469 •
Junior Philatelists of America
Jennifer Arnold, Exec.Sec.
PO Box 2625
Albany, OR 97321-0643
Phone: (541)967-7043
Fax: (541)967-9515
E-mail: exec.sec@jpastamps.org
Formed by merger of: (1976) Junior Philatelic Society of America; American Philatelic Society Writers Unit Junior Division.

• 12470 • JPA H. E. Harris Ribbon
To reward, recognize, and encourage high-quality philatelic exhibits by juniors shown in junior (persons under 21), youth, or general exhibit classes, sections, or divisions. An award ribbon is presented irregularly, but many times (15) per year at large stamp exhibitions whose organizing committees have arranged to present it. Established in 1977 by H.E. Harris & Company, the large Boston philatelic firm, in memory of H.E. Harris, the founder of the firm who provided the initial funding for the award.

• 12471 • JPA Blue Ribbon and Certificate
To recognize and encourage high-quality philatelic exhibits by juniors (persons under 21) shown in junior, youth, and general classes, sections, or divisions of exhibitions. The award is presented at the discretion of judges to the best junior exhibit in the show. A ribbon is given irregularly, but many times per year at smaller stamp exhibitions whose organizing committees have arranged to present it. Established in 1974.

• 12472 •
Juvenile Diabetes Research Foundation International - Central Florida Chapter
279 Douglas Ave., Ste. 1108
Altamonte Springs, FL 32714
Phone: (407)774-2166
Fax: (407)774-2168
E-mail: centralflorida@jdrf.org
Home Page: http://www.jdrf.org/centralflorida

• 12473 • Diabetes Research Grants
For meritorious diabetes research. Grant awarded annually.

• 12474 •
Juvenile Diabetes Research Foundation of Greater Chicago
Amy Franze, Exec.Dir.
500 N. Dearborn, Ste. 305
Chicago, IL 60610
Phone: (312)670-0313
Toll-Free: 800-JDF-CURE
Fax: (312)670-0250
E-mail: afranze@jdrf.org
Home Page: http://www.jdrfillinois.org

• 12475 • Man/Woman of the Year
For significant contributions to the community/diabetes issues. Recognition award bestowed annually.

• 12476 •
Juvenile Welfare Board of Pinellas County
James E. Mills ACSW, Exec.Dir.
6698 68th Ave. N, Ste. A
Pinellas Park, FL 33781-5060
Phone: (727)547-5600
Fax: (727)547-5610
E-mail: jmills@jwbpinellas.org
Home Page: http://www.jwbpinellas.org

• 12477 • Cooperman-Boque Awards
For outstanding human services workers in Pinellas County. Recognition award bestowed annually.

• 12478 •
KA-BAR Knife Collectors Club
Kimberly Johnson, Admin.
200 Homer St.
Olean, NY 14760
Phone: (716)372-5952
Toll-Free: 800-282-0130
Fax: (716)790-7188
E-mail: info@ka-bar.com

• 12479 • Best of Show Award
Award of recognition. For the best collection or best knives at knife shows.

• 12480 •
Kankakee River Valley Chamber of Commerce
Sara Segur, Contact
PO Box 905
PO Box 905
Kankakee, IL 60901
Phone: (815)933-7721
Fax: (815)933-7675
E-mail: sara.segur@krvcc.org
Home Page: http://www.kankakee.org

• 12481 • Athena Award
For outstanding business woman. Recognition award bestowed annually.

• 12482 • Citizen of the Year
For outstanding service to the community. Recognition award bestowed annually.

• 12483 •
Kansas Association of Chiefs of Police
Doyle King, Exec.Dir.
PO Box 780603
Wichita, KS 67278-0603
Phone: (316)733-7300
Fax: (316)733-7301
E-mail: kacp@cox.net
Home Page: http://www.kacp.cc

• 12484 • Awards for Valor
For initiative and bravery. Recognition award bestowed annually.

• 12485 •
Kansas City Artist Association
Janet Simpson, Exec.Dir.
201 Wyandotte
Kansas City, MO 64105
Phone: (816)421-5222
Fax: (816)421-0656
Home Page: http://www.kansascityartistscoalition.org

• 12486 • Dorothy's 60 Award
For K-12 public school art teachers. Monetary award bestowed annually.

• 12487 •
Kansas City Barbeque Society
Carolyn Wells, Exec.Dir.
11514 Hickman Mills Dr.
Kansas City, MO 64134
Phone: (816)765-5891
Toll-Free: 800-963-KCBS
Fax: (816)765-5860
E-mail: kcbs@kcbs.us
Home Page: http://www.kcbs.us

• 12488 • Hall of Flame
To recognize outstanding achievement in the field of barbecue and service to the organization. Awarded annually with a plaque. Established in 1985.

• 12489 • Team of the Year
To recognize the cooking team with highest overall points. Category-specific Teams of the Year are also recognized in Chicken, Ribs, Pork, and Brisket. Awarded annually.

• 12490 •
Kansas Crop Improvement Association
Daryl Strouts, Admin.
2000 Kimball Ave.
Manhattan, KS 66502
Phone: (785)532-6118
Fax: (785)532-6551
E-mail: kscrop@kansas.net
Home Page: http://www.oznet.ksu.edu/kcia

• 12491 • Kansas Premier Seed Grower
Inquire for application details.

• 12492 •
Kansas Dietetic Association
2109 SW Moundview Dr.
Topeka, KS 66614-1235
Phone: (785)357-2803
Fax: (785)357-2801
E-mail: edavis@stormontvail.org

• 12493 • Distinguished Dietitian of the Year
For professional contributions. Recognition award bestowed annually.

Awards are arranged in alphabetical order below their administering organizations

• 12494 • **Young Dietitian of the Year**
For professional contributions. Recognition award bestowed annually.

• 12495 •
Kansas Hearing Aid Association
3200 SW College Ave.
Topeka, KS 66611-2052
Phone: (785)266-4833

• 12496 • **Pioneer Award**
For length of time and type of service to the association. Recognition award bestowed annually.

• 12497 •
Kansas State University
Center for Basic Cancer Research
1 Chalmers Hall
Manhattan, KS 66502
Phone: (785)532-6705
Fax: (785)532-6707
Home Page: http://www.ksu.edu/cancer.center

• 12498 • **Cancer Research Award Program**
Kansas State University undergraduates are eligible. Inquire for application details.

• 12499 •
Kansas Watercolor Society
Carole Ranney, Pres.
PO Box 1796
Hutchinson, KS 67504-1796
Phone: (620)662-1517
E-mail: kws@kansaswatercolor.com
Home Page: http://www.kansaswatercolor.com

• 12500 • **KWS Great 8 Exhibition**
To encourage and recognize excellence in artists for paintings in aqueous media on paper. Artists 18 years and older residing in Colorado, Kansas, Oklahoma, Missouri, Nebraska, Texas and New Mexico are eligible. Only original paintings in primarily aqueous medium on paper are acceptable. Entries may not have been exhibited at the Wichita Art Museum and must be for sale during the exhibit. Monetary and purchase awards totaling $15,000 are presented annually. Established in 1970. A maximum of 3 2" x 2" slides; labeled with the artist's name, title of work, image size, framed size, and number corresponding with entry form must be submitted. Entry fees of $25 for 1 or 2 slides for nonmembers and $20 for members and an additional $5 for a third slide must also be submitted. Deadline April 11. Co-sponsored by the Wichita Art Museum, the Kansas Arts Commission, and the Emprise Bank of Wichita. Formerly: (1996) Five State Exhibition; (2003) Seven State Exhibition.

• 12501 •
Kansas Wildflower Society
Craig C. Freeman, Contact
Univ. of Kansas
2045 Constant Ave.
Lawrence, KS 66047-3729
Phone: (785)864-3453
Fax: (785)864-5093

• 12502 • **Mary Bancroft Memorial Scholarship**
For Kansas college or university student interested in botany. Scholarship awarded annually.

• 12503 •
Kappa Delta Epsilon
Mrs. Barbara M. Jackson, Natl.Pres.
619 34th Ave. E
Tuscaloosa, AL 35404
Toll-Free: 800-779-4106
Fax: (205)822-4106
E-mail: sealark@aol.com
Home Page: http://www.kappadeltaepsilon.org

• 12504 • **Boyd-Orr International Award**
Biennial award of recognition.

• 12505 • **Outstanding Chapter Award**
Biennial award of recognition.

• 12506 • **Scrapbook Award**
Biennial award of recognition.

• 12507 • **Writing Award**
Recognizes writing for KDE's publication *The Current*. Awarded biennially.

• 12508 •
Kappa Delta Pi
Michael P. Wolfe, Exec.Dir.
3707 Woodview Trace
Indianapolis, IN 46268-1158
Phone: (317)871-4900
Toll-Free: 800-284-3167
Fax: (317)704-2323
E-mail: wolfe@kdp.org
Home Page: http://www.kdp.org

• 12509 • **Achieving Chapter Excellence (ACE)**
Annual award of recognition. Awarded to Kappa Delta PI members only.

• 12510 • **Book-of-the-Year Award**
Annual award of recognition to Kappa Delta PI members only.

• 12511 • **Distinguished Dissertation Award**
Annual award of recognition to Kappa Delta PI members only.

• 12512 • **Graduate and Undergraduate Scholarships**
Annual scholarship. For members only.

• 12513 • **National Student Teacher of the Year**
Annual award of recognition to Kappa Delta PI members only.

• 12514 •
Kappa Delta Rho
Joseph Rees II, Exec.Dir.
331 S Main St.
Greensburg, PA 15601
Phone: (724)838-7100
Toll-Free: 800-536-KDR1
Fax: (724)838-7101
E-mail: info@kdr.com
Home Page: http://www.kdr.com

• 12515 • **Ordo Honorium Award**
Recognizes personal accomplishments or exceptional involvement with the fraternity. Awarded annually.

• 12516 •
Kappa Mu Epsilon
Dr. Don Tosh, Pres.
Department of Mathematics & Computer Science
Central Missouri State University
Warrensburg, MO 64093
Phone: (660)543-8929
Phone: (419)372-2636
Fax: (419)372-6092
E-mail: toshd@evangel.edu
Home Page: http://kappamuepsilon.org

• 12517 • **George R. Mach Distinguished Service Award**
Biennial award of recognition.

• 12518 •
Kappa Tau Alpha
Dr. Keith P. Sanders, Exec.Dir.
University of Missouri
School of Journalism
Columbia, MO 65211-1200
Phone: (573)882-7685
Fax: (573)884-1720
E-mail: umcjourkta@missouri.edu
Home Page: http://www.missouri.edu/~ktahq

• 12519 • **Frank Luther Mott - Kappa Tau Alpha Research/Book Award**
For recognition of the best research book in the field of journalism. Books published during the preceding year are eligible for nomination by publishers and authors of the book. Deadline for books bearing a 2005 copyright is December 8. A monetary award of $1,000 and a certificate are awarded annually. Established in 1944.

• 12520 •
Katalysis Partnership
Christina Jennings, Exec.Dir.
1331 N Commerce St.
Stockton, CA 95202
Phone: (209)943-6165
Fax: (209)943-7046
E-mail: jvgontard@katalysis.org
Home Page: http://www.katalysis.org

• 12521 • **Robert E. Graham Development Entrepreneur of the Year Award**
Recognizes the contribution of individuals who have demonstrated significant dedication to the mission of the Partnership. Awarded annually.

• 12522 •
Keats-Shelley Association of America
Dr. Robert A. Hartley, Sec.-Treas.
476 5th Ave.
New York Public Library, Rm. 226
New York, NY 10018
Phone: (212)764-0655
Fax: (813)639-2201
E-mail: rhartley@optonline.net
Home Page: http://www.rc.umd.edu/ksaa/ksaa.html

• 12523 • **Distinguished Scholar Award**
To recognize distinguished books and outstanding careers of publishing on Keats, Shelley, Byron, and members of their circles. Usually awarded to members of the Association, as nominated by a committee of Directors in January. Plaques are presented at the Annual Awards Dinner, held in conjunction with the Modern Language Association convention. Established in 1981.

• 12524 • **Keats - Shelley Association Annual Prize**
To recognize a distinguished article pertaining to the area of the Association's interests, published in the United States or Canada during a single year (June to May). A selection committee of three scholar-critics reviews the nominations. An honorarium of $250 and a plaque are presented annually at the Annual Awards Dinner, held in conjunction with the Modern Language Association convention. Established in 1986.

• 12525 •
Donald Keene Center of Japanese Culture
Greg Pflufelder, Faculty Dir.
507 Kent Hall
MC 3920
Columbia University
New York, NY 10027
Phone: (212)854-5036
Fax: (212)854-4019
E-mail: donald-keene-center@columbia.edu
Home Page: http://www.columbia.edu/cu/ealac/dkc

• 12526 • **Japan-U.S. Friendship Commission Prize for the Translation of Japanese Literature**
To recognize the best translation into English of a Japanese modern work of literature, and the best Japanese classical literary translation. Translators of any nationality are welcome to apply. Translations must be book-length works of Japanese literature such as novels, collections of short stories, literary essays, memoirs, drama, or poetry. Manuscripts, both unpublished and in press, and books published during the preceding 2 years may be submitted. Application deadline is February 1 of each year. Two monetary prizes of $2,500 each are awarded.

• 12527 •
Keene State College
229 Main St.
Keene, NH 03435
Phone: (603)358-2302
Toll-Free: 800-KSC-1909
Fax: (603)358-2257
E-mail: admissions@keene.edu
Home Page: http://www.keene.edu

• 12528 • **Children's Literature Festival Award**
To recognize an author and/or illustrator for continuing distinguished contributions in the field of children's literature. Individuals currently writing and illustrating who have made outstanding contributions over a period of at least ten years are eligible. Nominations are submitted by individuals attending the Children's Literature Festival in October. A monetary award and an engraved pewter Paul Revere bowl are presented. Established in 1985.

• 12529 •
Keep America Beautiful
Becky Lyons, VP
1010 Washington Blvd.
Stamford, CT 06901
Phone: (203)323-8987
Fax: (203)325-9199
E-mail: blyons@kab.org
Home Page: http://www.kab.org

• 12530 • **Iron Eyes Cody Award**
To recognize an outstanding man for a lifetime of achievement who has contributed to the fulfillment of KAB's mission by raising public awareness about litter prevention beautification, solid waste management and public participation to preserve and enhance natural resource and public lands by setting an example for all Americans to follow. The award is named for KAB's internationally famous media spokesman, the "crying Indian" and is given only if judges decide a nominee has contributed substantially in the movement for a cleaner, more beautiful America.

• 12531 • **Mrs. Lyndon B. Johnson Award**
To recognize an outstanding woman for a lifetime of achievement who have contributed to the movement to improve the quality of American life through litter prevention and beautification efforts at the grassroots level. This highly selective award is given only if judges decide a nominee has contributed substantially in the movement for a cleaner, more beautiful America. Established in 1968 to acknowledge the First Lady's many litter prevention and beautification activities.

• 12532 • **Keep America Beautiful National Awards**
To recognize and honor community programs on the local, state and national level that have improved the quality of life. Eligible groups are: non-profit, youth groups and schools, government agencies, business and professional organizations. Category selections includes: Litter Prevention; Beautification; Reduce, Reuse, Recycle; Educational Initiatives; and Take Care of America. The deadline for entries is mid-August each year. First, second, and third place awards are presented each December at the National Awards Dinner in Washington, D.C. Established in 1954. Outstanding participants in other programs are also awarded at the Dinner. First and second prizes are given for the Keep America Beautiful Month Awards, KAB System Awards; National Advisory Council Partnership Award; Federal Highway Administration/Keep America Beautiful, Inc. Awards; Iron Eyes Cody and Mrs. Lyndon B. Johnson Awards; and The Build America Beautiful Award.

• 12533 •
Keep Athens-Clarke County Beautiful
Stacee Farrell, Exec.Dir.
PO Box 1868
Athens, GA 30603-1868
Phone: (706)613-3501
Fax: (706)613-3504
E-mail: sfarrell@co.clarke.ga.us
Home Page: http://keepathensbeautiful.org

• 12534 • **Industry Recycler of the Year Award**
For waste reduction/recycling efforts. Recognition award bestowed annually.

• 12535 •
Kennedy Center Alliance for Arts Education Network
Kathi R. Levin, Dir.
John F. Kennedy Center for the Performing Arts
2700 F St., NW
Washington, DC 20566
Phone: (202)416-8845
Fax: (202)416-8802
E-mail: kcaaen@kennedy-center.org
Home Page: http://www.kennedy-center.org/education/kcaaen

• 12536 • **Creative Ticket National Schools of Distinction Award**
Recognizes individual schools for doing an outstanding job of making the arts an essential part of their students education. Up to 5 awards are given annually.

• 12537 • Kennedy Center Alliance for the Arts Education Network and National School Board Association Award
Recognizes a school board that has demonstrated support for, and commitment to high quality arts education in its school district, community, state, or special jurisdiction. Awarded annually.

• 12538 •
Kennedy Center American College Theater Festival
John F. Kennedy Center for the Performing Arts
2700 F St. NW
Washington, DC 20566
Phone: (202)416-8857
Phone: (202)416-8000
Toll-Free: 800-444-1324
Fax: (202)416-8802
E-mail: skshaffer@kennedy-center.org
Home Page: http://www.kennedy-center.org/education/actf

• 12539 • ACTF Awards for Theatrical Design Excellence
To recognize outstanding student designers by exhibiting their work at the Kennedy Center. Open only to schools, not individual students. Any full-length production entered in the American College Theatre Festival that has one or more of the visual elements designed by a student is eligible. National winners in set design and costume design receive an honorarium of $500 and an all-expenses-paid trip to New York City for seven days to visit the studios of distinguished designers. *Theatre Crafts* magazine and *USITT Journal of Theatre and Technology* publish information on the national set and costume design winners.

• 12540 • ACTF Musical Theatre Award
For recognition of a musical play by college and university students in the Michael Kanin Playwriting Award Program. Open only to schools, not individual students. The musical play must be original and copyrighted. Fifty percent of the creative team must be full-time undergraduate or graduate students of accredited institutions of higher learning. The musical play must be fully produced by a college or university to be considered for the award. Plays are eligible up to one year after the playwright's graduation. Monetary awards of $1,000 each are awarded for music, for the lyrics, for the book, and $1,000 to the college or university producing the musical play. Established in 1980. Formerly: (1989) ASCAP Foundation College Musical Theatre Award.

• 12541 • John Cauble Short Play Award
To encourage young writers to develop the short play form to the full-length play in preparation for the professional world. Open only to schools, not individual students. Two or three outstanding productions of such plays in American colleges will be recognized each year with consideration for presentation at the Kennedy Center. The short play must be original writing, no translations or direct adaptations and approximately 35 minutes in playing time. A monetary award of $1,000, publication and catalog listing by Samuel French, Inc., membership in the Dramatists Guild, and an offer of agency representation by William Morris, Inc. are awarded. Established in 1988. Formerly: (2006) Short Play Awards Program.

• 12542 • Columbia Pictures Television Playwriting Award
To recognize achievements in comedy playwriting by an undergraduate or graduate student. Open only to schools, not individual students. Playwrites who enter the Michael Kanin Playwriting Awards Program are eligible. The winner receives a professional assignment to write a complete teleplay for one of the series produced by Columbia Pictures Television; he/she will be flown to Los Angeles (all expenses paid) to participate in story conferences; and the playwright receives Writers Guild Scale for the completed teleplay, travel expenses, and is installed as a member of the Writers Guild of America. Awarded annually. Established in 1975. Sponsored by Columbia Pictures Television. Formerly: (1986) Columbia/Embassy Television Playwriting Award; Norman Lear Award for Achievement in Comedy Playwriting.

• 12543 • David Library of the American Revolution Award for Playwriting on American Freedom
To recognize an outstanding, original full-length play on the subject of American life and freedom by a student in an undergraduate or graduate program. Open only to schools, not individual students. Plays entered in the Michael Kanin Playwriting Awards Program are eligible. A monetary award of $3,000 is divided among the playwrights winning the Grand Prize and Excellence Awards. Awarded annually. Established in 1974 by a grant from Dr. Sol Feinstone. Supported by the David Library of the American Revolution.

• 12544 • Freedom Forum Playwriting Award
To recognize the best play written on the themes of world peace and international disarmament. First place receives a monetary award of $5,000 a fellowship to the Sundance Theater Lab, and an offer of a contract to publish, license, and market the play. Second place receives $2,500.

• 12545 • Lorraine Hansberry Playwriting Award
To recognize an outstanding, original play on the Black experience in America written by a student in an undergraduate or graduate program. Open only to schools, not individual students. Plays entered in the Michael Kanin Playwriting Awards Program are eligible. The following monetary prizes are awarded: first prize - $2,500 to the playwright and $750 to the drama department presenting the play; and second prize - $1,000 and $500 to the Theater Departments of the college(s) and university(ies) producing the play. Awarded annually. Established in 1977. Funded by Penn State University.

• 12546 • National Student Playwriting Award
To recognize an outstanding, original full-length play or musical written by a student in an undergraduate or graduate program. Production of the winning play is held in Washington, D.C., as part of the ACTF National Festival. (Since 1988, all Festival awards have been part of the Michael Kanin Playwriting Award Program, in honor of the playwright and screenwriter who organized that year's program.) Open only to schools, not individual students. The playwright receives the following: exposure of the play to reviewers, producers, directors, and other professionals, through its presentation in Washington, as well as the attendant national publicity; $2,500 from the William Morris Agency and the offer of an agency management contract; and full membership in the Dramatists Guild and an honorary reception at the Guild offices in New York. In addition, Samuel French, Inc. publishes and distributes the play for stock and amateur production on the basis of its standard professional royalities. Awarded annually. Established in 1974. Sponsored by the William Morris Agency and the Association for Theatre in Higher Education. Formerly: National Award.

• 12547 • Irene Ryan Winners Circle Evening of Scenes
To recognize the best student acting performances during regional and national ACTF competitions. Open only to schools, not individual students. A monetary prize of $500 at the regional level and two $2,500 cash prizes at the national level plus travel expenses are awarded annually. Established in 1972. Sponsored by the Irene Ryan Foundation. Formerly: Irene Ryan Winners Circle Acting Awards.

• 12548 • Jean Kennedy Smith Playwriting Award
Offered for the best student-written script that explores the human experience of living with a disability. The play must comply with the guidelines for scripts entered in the Michael Kanin Playwriting program. The winning playwright will receive a cash award of $2,500, active membership in the Dramatist's Guild, and a fellowship to attend a playwriting program. Awarded annually.

• 12549 •
John F. Kennedy Center for the Performing Arts
Michael M. Kaiser, Pres.
2700 F St. NW
Washington, DC 20566
Phone: (202)467-4600
Phone: (202)416-8000
Toll-Free: 800-444-1324
Home Page: http://www.kennedy-center.org

• 12550 • Fund for New American Plays
To enable nonprofit professional theater organizations across the country to enhance productions of new American plays already scheduled for debut, and to ensure that new works are produced in a manner that reflects the playwright's intentions. Nonprofit professional theater organizations are eligible. Monetary grants

are designed to underwrite special expenses related to collaborative efforts among playwrights, directors and designers; large cast productions; and the participation of guest artists. Established in 1986 by the John F. Kennedy Center for the Performing Arts, the President's Committee on the Arts and the Humanities, and American Express Company. Due to the nature of this award, no submissions from playwrights or theater companies will be solicited or accepted. The Kennedy Center will contact regional theaters directly.

• 12551 • Kennedy Center Friedheim Awards for New Music

To pay tribute to living American composers for meritorious musical compositions in the fields of orchestral and chamber music. The two categories alternate, honoring composers of instrumental orchestral compositions in even-numbered years and composers of instrumental chamber compositions in odd-numbered years. American composers are considered for the awards without restrictions as to age or society membership. To be considered, a work must receive its American premiere between July 1 of the two previous calendar years and June 30 of the award year. Anyone, including the composer, may make a nomination. The deadline is May 15. The following monetary prizes are awarded: first prize - $5,000; second prize - $2,500; third prize - $1,000; fourth prize - $500. Annual presentations are made in October. Established in 1978 in memory of Arthur Friedheim, a distinguished pianist. Funded in part by a grant from the Eric Friedheim Foundation. Additional information is available from Friedheim Awards Coordinator, The Kennedy Center, Washington, DC 20566, (202) 416-8031.

• 12552 • Kennedy Center Honors

To recognize individuals for their distinguished artistic achievements and career contributions to American culture. The primary criterion in the selection of the recipients is artistic achievement as a performer, composer, choreographer, playwright, director or conductor. Honorees are nominated by the Artists Committee in the areas of dance, music, theater, opera, motion pictures and television. Final selection is made by the Kennedy Center Board of Trustees. A unique beribboned medal, created for the Kennedy Center Honors, is awarded each year at an annual celebration consisting of a traditional Board of Trustees dinner and an Honors Gala performance, preceeded by a reception hosted by the President of the United States. Established in 1978. Additional information is available from Laura Langley, phone: (202) 416-8430.

• 12553 •
John F. Kennedy Center for the Performing Arts
Partners in Education Program
Michael M. Kaiser, Pres.
2700 F St. NW
Washington, DC 20566
Phone: (202)416-8806
Fax: (202)416-8860
Home Page: http://www.kennedy-center.org/education/partners

• 12554 • Kennedy Center Alliance for Arts Education Network/National School Boards Association Award

To recognize an outstanding school board in the United States that has demonstrated support for and commitment to high-quality arts education in its school district, community, and state or special jurisdiction. To be nominated, a local school board must demonstrate the following: significant contribution in support of the development of visual arts, dance, music, theater/drama, and creative writing in the district's schools; advocacy for the arts and arts-in-education at the school district, community, and state or special jurisdiction levels; financial support of arts programs in the school district; fulfillment of the responsibilities of effective school board members as prescribed by the NSBA in its Code of Ethics for School Board Members; current membership in its NSBA Federation Member State School Boards Association at the time that the award is made; and willingness to accept the award if it is bestowed and to participate in publicizing it. Nominations may be submitted via their state Alliance for Arts Education by December 1. A plaque/medallion is awarded annually. Established in 1988. Awarded in cooperation with the National School Boards Association. Formerly: (1996) Kennedy Center/National School Boards Association Award.

• 12555 •
Kenosha History Center
Tom Schleif, Exec.Dir.
220 51st Pl.
Kenosha, WI 53140
Phone: (262)654-5770
Fax: (262)654-1730
E-mail: kchs@acronet.net
Home Page: http://www.kenoshahistorycenter.org

• 12556 • Award of Merit

For significant contribution to preserving Kenosha County's history. Recognition award bestowed annually.

• 12557 •
Kent State University
Gerontology Center
College of Continuing Studies
PO Box 5190
Kent, OH 44242-0001
Phone: (330)672-2002
Fax: (330)672-2079
E-mail: david@ccs.kent.edu
Home Page: http://imagine.kent.edu/staff/centers/detail.asp?id=231

• 12558 • Carl I. Brahce Gerontology Award

Annual award of recognition. Kent State University faculty and/or student are eligible.

• 12559 •
Kent State University Alumni Association
Lindsey Hugh Loftus, Exec.Dir.
Williamson Alumni Center
PO Box 5190
Kent, OH 44242-0001
Phone: (330)672-5368
Toll-Free: 888-320-5368
Fax: (330)672-5368
E-mail: alumni@kent.edu
Home Page: http://www.kent.edu/alumni

• 12560 • Distinguished Teaching Awards

Annual award of recognition.

• 12561 •
Kentucky Arts Council
Gerri Combs, Exec.Dir.
Capital Plz. Tower, 21st Fl.
500 Mero St.
Frankfort, KY 40601-1987
Phone: (502)564-3757
Toll-Free: 888-833-2787
Fax: (502)564-2839
E-mail: kyarts@ky.gov
Home Page: http://www.kyarts.org

• 12562 • Kentucky Artists Fellowships

To encourage and support the professional development of Kentucky artists. The award categories alternate annually between writing (poetry, fiction, drama, etc.), choreography, and music composition (even-numbered years) and visual and media arts (odd-numbered years). Individuals who have been residents of Kentucky for at least one year immediately prior to application are eligible. Fellowships of $7,500 each are awarded annually. In addition, Professional Assistance Awards of $1,000 each are presented. Deadline is September 15. Established in 1983. Formerly: (1991) Al Smith Fellowships.

• 12563 •
Kentucky Paralegal Association
Barbie D. Mullins, Pres.
PO Box 2675
Louisville, KY 40201-2675
Fax: (859)281-6480
E-mail: bmullins@mmlk.com
Home Page: http://www.kypa.org

• 12564 • Don Eppler Memorial Scholarship

For student enrolled in paralegal studies. Scholarship awarded annually.

• 12565 •
Kentucky Psychiatric Association
Theresa N. Walton, Exec.Dir.
PO Box 198
Frankfort, KY 40602-0198
Phone: (502)695-4843
Toll-Free: 877-597-7924
Fax: (502)695-4441
E-mail: waltonkpa@aol.com
Home Page: http://www.kypsych.org

• 12566 • **Barry Bingham Media Award**
For outstanding coverage of mental illness issues. Recognition award bestowed annually.

• 12567 •
Kentucky Right to Life Association
Margie Montgomery, Exec.Dir.
134 Breckinridge Ln.
Louisville, KY 40207
Phone: (502)895-5959
Fax: (502)895-7028
E-mail: krla@bellsouth.net
Home Page: http://www.krla.org

• 12568 • **Red Rose-White Rose Award**
For outstanding work in promoting respect for all human life. Recognition award bestowed annually.

• 12569 •
Kentucky Watercolor Society
Carol Wiseman, Exec. Dir.
PO Box 7125
Louisville, KY 40257-0125
Phone: (502)326-9256
Fax: (502)426-4471
E-mail: kwsart@bellsouth.net
Home Page: http://kentuckyartists.com/kws/

• 12570 • **Aqueous USA Exhibition**
To recognize artists with outstanding ability in watercolor painting. Entrants must be over the age of 18. Merit, purchase, and traveling awards are presented annually. For KWS signature membership, eligible artists must have had at least one artistic work accepted for exhibition in at least three Aqueous juried competitions while maintaining continuous membership. Established in 1978. Additional information is available from Aline Barker, 1137 Ash St., Louisville, KY 40217. Formerly: (1998) Aqueous Show.

• 12571 •
Keramos
Dr. Robert W. Schwartz, VP
Dept. of Ceramic Engineering
222 McNutt Hall
University of Missouri-Rolla
Rolla, MO 65409-0330
Phone: (573)341-6025
Fax: (573)341-6934
E-mail: rwschwar@umr.edu
Home Page: http://www.ceramics.org/keramos

• 12572 • **Greaves-Walker Roll of Honor Award**
Recognizes outstanding achievement in field of ceramics. Awarded annually.

• 12573 •
Keren-Or, Inc.
Albert Hornblass MD, Pres.
350 7th Ave., Rm. 200
New York, NY 10001
Phone: (212)279-4070
Fax: (212)279-4043
E-mail: info@keren-or.org
Home Page: http://www.keren-or.org/

• 12574 • **Ray of Light**
Annual award of recognition.

• 12575 •
Kettering - Moraine - Oakwood Chamber of Commerce
Ann-Lisa Rucker, Exec.Dir.
2977 Far Hills Ave.
Kettering, OH 45419
Phone: (937)299-3852
Fax: (937)299-3851
E-mail: info@kmo-coc.org
Home Page: http://www.kmo-coc.org

• 12576 • **Enterprise Spirit Award**
For businesses making contributions to community development. Recognition award bestowed annually. 315536-5231

• 12577 •
Keuka College Alumni Association
Pat Middlebrook, Pres.
Office of Alumni and Family Relations
Keuka Park, NY 14478
Phone: (315)279-5238
Fax: (315)279-5216
E-mail: alumni@mail.keuka.edu
Home Page: http://www.keukaalumni.com/alumni/alumni_association.htm

• 12578 • **Community Service Award**
Annual award of recognition.

• 12579 • **Effective Use of Retirement Award**
Annual award of recognition.

• 12580 • **Professional Achievement**
Annual award of recognition.

• 12581 • **Recent Graduate Award**
Annual award of recognition.

• 12582 • **Service to Keuka**
Annual award of recognition.

• 12583 •
Keweenaw County Historical Society
Peter VanPelt, Pres.
HC-1, Box 265L
Eagle Harbor, MI 49950
Phone: (906)289-4990
Phone: (906)296-2561

• 12584 • **Lauri W. Leskinen Memorial Award**
For historic preservation in Keweenaw County. Recognition award bestowed annually.

• 12585 •
Kilby International Awards Foundation
Victoria Smith Downing, Chm.
PO Box 75-3131
Dallas, TX 75275-3131
Phone: (214)768-3355
Fax: (214)768-1262
E-mail: kilby@kilby.org
Home Page: http://www.kilby.org

• 12586 • **Kilby International Awards**
To celebrate creativity in the human spirit, to acknowledge the power of one creative individual to bring change to the world, and to encourage future gifts for mankind through early recognition of individuals who dare to dream, design, test, and apply ideas in unchartered paths in hope that these efforts will enhance the quality of life for all. Many of the previous winners have gone on to receive other prestigious awards, such as the Nobel Prize, the National Medal of Science, the Bauer Award, and many others. Five to seven winners are announced annually at the Kilby Awards Presentation in November. Additionally, the Jury names a "Kilby Young Innovator" for whom early recognition may become a significant factor in creative freedom. Deadline for nominations is in July. Established in 1989 to honor Jack St. Clair Kilby, inventor of the integrated circuit, commonly called the microchip. Formerly: Jack St. Clair Kilby Awards of Excellence.

• 12587 •
Kindness Incorporated
M. Susan Hess, Pres.
PO Box 7071
Elgin, IL 60121-7071
Phone: (847)888-2750
Phone: (847)697-5543
Fax: (847)742-0461

• 12588 • **No Small Change Award**
For donation canister that gathers the most each year. Recognition award bestowed annually.

• 12589 •
King County Bar Association
Gary A. Maehara, Pres.
1200 5th Ave., Ste. 600
Seattle, WA 98101
Phone: (206)267-7100
Fax: (206)267-7099
E-mail: admin@kcba.org
Home Page: http://www.kcba.org

• 12590 • **Friend of the Legal Profession Award**
For distinguished and meritorious service to the legal profession and justice system. Awarded annually.

• 12591 • Helen M. Geisness Outstanding Lawyer or Non-Lawyer Award
For recognition of exemplary distinguished service on behalf of the Association. Awarded annually.

• 12592 • Outstanding Judge Award
For recognition of distinguished service to the legal profession, the judiciary, and the public in a profession-related activity. Active or retired judges of the Seattle Municipal Court, King County District Court, King County Superior Court, Division I of the Court Appeals, State Supreme Court, U.S. District Court (Western District), Ninth Circuit Court of Appeals, and Bankruptcy Court are eligible. Awarded annually.

• 12593 • Outstanding Lawyer Award
For distinguished and meritorious service to the legal profession and the public in a profession-related activity. Awarded annually.

• 12594 •
Kings County Farm Bureau
Ryan Bertao, Exec.Dir.
870 Greenfield Ave.
Hanford, CA 93230
Phone: (559)584-3557
Fax: (559)584-1614
E-mail: kcfb@kcfb.org
Home Page: http://www.kcfb.org

• 12595 • KCFB Scholarship
For agriculture or home economic major. Scholarship awarded annually.

• 12596 •
Kinsmen and Kinette Clubs of Canada
(Les Clubs Kin du Canada)
Marion E. Price, Exec.Dir.
1920 Hal Rogers Dr.
PO Box KIN
Cambridge, ON, Canada N3H 5C6
Phone: (519)653-1920
Toll-Free: 800-742-5546
Fax: (519)650-1091
E-mail: kinhq@kinclubs.ca
Home Page: http://www.kinclubs.ca

• 12597 • Hal Rogers Endowment Fund
A monetary award is given annually.

• 12598 •
Kitplanes Magazine
Marc Cook, Editor-in-Chief
531 Encinitas Blvd., Ste. 105
Encinitas, CA 92024
Phone: (760)436-4747
Fax: (760)436-4644
E-mail: editorial@kitplanes.com
Home Page: http://www.kitplanes.com

• 12599 • President's Award
To honor the person who manufactures Kit Aircraft and who has brought business integrity, innovation, and high quality to the amateur-built aircraft community. Awarded annually with a trophy and plaque. Sponsored by *Kitplanes Magazines* and Light Aircraft Manufacturers Association. Established in 1991.

• 12600 •
Kiwanis International
Stephen K. Siemens, Pres.
3636 Woodview Trace
Indianapolis, IN 46268-3196
Phone: (317)875-8755
Toll-Free: 800-549-2647
Fax: (317)879-0204
E-mail: kiwanismail@kiwanis.org
Home Page: http://www.kiwanis.org

• 12601 • Robert P. Connelly Heroism Award
To recognize service beyond the call of duty as exemplified by individuals who risked death or physical harm to save the life of another person. The rescuer must have had no official responsibility for the rescue effort, must have performed the act of heroism in a civilian context, and must not be closely related to the person who was rescued. Nominations are accepted only from Kiwanis clubs. A bronze medal on a walnut board is awarded along with a $ 500 U S Savings bond when merited. Established in 1967 as a tribute to Robert P. Connelly, a Kiwanian who lost his life attempting to rescue a crippled woman who had fallen in the path of an onrushing passenger train more than 450 recognized since 1967.

• 12602 •
Klingon Strike Force
Thought Admi Gennie Summers, Contact
104 N Spring St.
Cassville, MO 65625
E-mail: summers@mo-net.com

• 12603 • Commendation and Promotion
Quarterly award of recognition. Selection is based on level of participation.

• 12604 •
John S. Knight Fellowships
James R. Bettinger, Dir.
Bldg. 120, Rm. 424
450 Serra Mall
Stanford University
Stanford, CA 94305-2050
Phone: (650)723-4937
Fax: (650)725-6154
E-mail: knight-info@lists.stanford.edu
Home Page: http://knight.stanford.edu

• 12605 • John S. Knight Fellowships
To promote print and broadcast journalism by enabling top journalists to spend an academic year studying at Stanford University. Individuals with at least seven years experience in print or broadcast journalism are eligible. Twelve United States journalists and six to seven international journalists selected. A stipend is awarded annually. Established in 1966.

• 12606 •
Knowles/Knoles/Noles Family Association
Robert B. Noles, Hist.
133 Acadian Ln.
Mandeville, LA 70471
Phone: (985)845-4688
Fax: (985)845-4698
E-mail: rbnoles@bellsouth.net
Home Page: http://kknfa.org

• 12607 • Knowles Kousin
Recognizes research contributor.

• 12608 •
Korea Veterans Association of Canada
(Association Canadienne des Veterans de la Coree)
Les Peate, Natl.Pres.
8 Moorside
Ottawa, ON, Canada K2C 3P4
Phone: (613)225-0443
Fax: (613)225-9935
E-mail: jlpeate@modenet.com
Home Page: http://www.kvacanada.com

• 12609 • Distinguished Service Star
Annual award of recognition. Only KVA members are eligible.

• 12610 •
Kosciuszko Foundation
Joseph E. Gore, Pres. & Exec.Dir.
15 E 65th St.
New York, NY 10021-6595
Phone: (212)734-2130
Fax: (212)628-4552
E-mail: thekf@aol.com
Home Page: http://www.kosciuszkofoundation.org

• 12611 • Kosciuszko Foundation Doctoral Dissertation Award
To encourage the development of Polish studies in America. An award is given towards publication of a revised doctoral dissertation which has made the most significant contribution to the development of Polish studies in America. Any aspect of literature, linguistics, history, art, or music of Poland, or studies relating to the Polish community in the United States, is included. A monetary prize of up to $2,500 is given when the applicant has found a publisher for his/her work. The award is usually presented annually. Established in 1964.

• 12612 • Kosciuszko Foundation Exchange Program with Poland
To provide opportunities for Polish citizens to study or do research in the United States, and for U.S. citizens to study or do research in Poland. U.S. applicants for studies in Poland must be of Polish origin or Americans of non-Polish descent who are pursuing studies/research relating to Polish subjects. Two exchange programs to Poland are awarded annually.

• 12613 • National Chopin Piano Competition

To encourage highly talented young musicians, of all national backgrounds, to study and perform the works of Polish composers. The Competition is open without restriction to citizens or permanent residents of the United States and to international full-time students with valid student visas. The application deadline is February 20. Applicants must be between the ages of 16 and 22 as of the opening date of the competition. It is expected that applicants will have already demonstrated unusual talent and artistic achievement, and only those ready for a national competition are encouraged to apply. The following monetary prizes in the form of scholarships are awarded annually: first prize - $5,000; second prize $2,500; and third prize - $1,500. The first prize winner is also invited to perform recitals in the U.S. and at the International Chopin Festival in Duszniki-Zdroj, Poland. Established in 1949 on the occasion of the 100th anniversary of the death of Frederic Chopin.

• 12614 • Marcella Sembrich Scholarship in Voice

To encourage highly talented students of voice to study the works of Polish composers. The scholarship is awarded to citizens or legal residents of the United States regardless of ethnic background, who have demonstrated unusual music ability but have not yet made extensive professional appearances. Applicants must be between the ages of 18 and 25. In addition to their applications, a tape of at least twenty minutes in length, including at least one song or aria by a Polish composer, must be submitted. The awards are as follows: First Prize - $1,000, round trip airfare from New York to the International Moniuszko Competition in Warsaw, a recital at the Moniuszko Festival, and an invitation to perform at the Sembrich Memorial Association in Lake George, NY; Second Prize $750; and Third Prize - $500. Application deadline is December 15. Established by Mary F. Koons of Wilkes-Barre, PA, in memory of her sisters, Ann Koons Parrish and Julia Koons Bonin.

• 12615 •
The Koussevitzky Music Foundations
% Brown Raysman Millstein Felder & Steiner LLP
900 3rd Ave.
New York, NY 10022
Phone: (212)895-2367
Fax: (212)895-2900
E-mail: info@koussevitzky.org
Home Page: http://www.koussevitzky.org

• 12616 • Koussevitzky Commissions

To recognize composers. Commissions are awarded annually to composers jointly with the Serge Koussevitzky Music Foundation in the Library of Congress (see separate listing). Applications must be made by performing organizations. Commissions for works for chamber groups range from $12,500 to $17,500.

• 12617 •
Krause Publications
William Bright, Publisher
700 E State St.
Iola, WI 54990-0001
Phone: (715)445-2214
Fax: (715)445-4087
E-mail: brightw@krause.com
Home Page: http://www.krause.com

• 12618 • Coin of the Year Award

An internationally conducted competition to provide recognition of outstanding coin design and marketing efforts worldwide, and to stimulate national governments to greater participation in both areas. Awards are presented in the following categories: Most Historically Significant Coin, Best Silver Coin, Best Crown, Best Trade Coin, Best Gold Coin, Most Artistic Coin, Most Popular Coin, Most Innovative Coinage Concept, Best Contemporary Event Coin, Most Inspirational Coin and Coin of the Year. Plaques are awarded annually. Established in 1984 to recognize 1982 coins. Sponsored by *World Coin News*.

• 12619 • Numismatic Ambassador Award

To recognize enthusiasts whose interests in building the hobby of coin collecting have placed them a cut above their peers. Numismatic Ambassadors have always been more than just collectors. They have gained the respect of all who surround them through unselfish sharing of numismatic knowledge and faithful service to the hobby they so dearly love. Anyone is eligible to be a Numismatic Ambassador. Nominations must be submitted in November to *Numismatic News*. Plaques and medals are awarded annually to not more than twelve individuals. Established in 1974. Sponsored by *Numismatic News*. Additional information is available from Krause Publications.

• 12620 •
KU Queers and Allies (QandA)
Sarah Katheryn, Dir.
Box 13, Kansas Union
Lawrence, KS 66045
Phone: (785)864-3091
E-mail: qanda@ku.edu
Home Page: http://www.ku.edu/~qanda

• 12621 • Gay, Lesbian, Bisexual and Transgender Community Leader Scholarship

For individuals demonstrating strong G.P.A. and community leadership. Scholarship awarded annually.

• 12622 •
La Crosse Area Development Corporation
James P. Hill, Exec.Dir.
712 Main St.
La Crosse, WI 54601
Phone: (608)784-5488
Toll-Free: 888-208-0698
Fax: (608)784-5408
E-mail: ladco@centurytel.net
Home Page: http://www.ladcoweb.org

• 12623 • Coulee Region Entrepreneurial Award

For business plan evaluated on feasibility, potential for growth, job creation, and marketability. Monetary award bestowed annually.

• 12624 • Director's Award

For individual who has performed great service to the organization or who is retiring from the Board of Directors. Recognition award bestowed annually.

• 12625 • Distinguished Service Award

For contributions to the development of the area economy. Recognition award bestowed annually.

• 12626 • President's Award

For a current, major contribution or accomplishment. Recognition award bestowed annually.

• 12627 •
La Leche League International
Marcia Lutostanski, Chair
1400 N Meacham Rd.
Schaumburg, IL 60173-4808
Phone: (847)519-7730
Toll-Free: 800-LA-LECHE
Fax: (847)519-0035
E-mail: llli@llli.org
Home Page: http://www.lalecheleague.org

• 12628 • La Leche League International Award of Achievement

To honor an individual or group for outstanding work or accomplishment in the breastfeeding field. Awarded at LLLI International Conferences, if possible. Established in 1989.

• 12629 • La Leche League International Award of Appreciation

To honor an individual or group whose support of La Leche League has been outstanding. Awarded at LLLI International Conferences, if possible. Established in 1988.

• 12630 • La Leche League International Award of Excellence

To honor an individual or group for outstanding work or accomplishment in the breastfeeding field. Awarded at LLLI International Conferences, if possible. Established in 1988.

• 12631 • La Leche League International Award of Recognition

To honor an individual or group for outstanding work or accomplishment in the breastfeeding field. Awarded at LLLI International Conferences, if possible. Established in 1991.

• 12632 • La Leche League International Founders' Award

To honor individuals or groups for continuous outstanding and exemplary contributions to breastfeeding in the world. Awarded at LLLI International Conferences, if possible. Established in 1988.

• 12633 •
La Salle University
Michael J. McGinniss, Pres.
1900 W Olney Ave.
Philadelphia, PA 19141
Phone: (215)951-1000
Fax: (215)951-1066
Home Page: http://www.lasalle.edu

Formerly: La Salle College.

• 12634 • La Salle Collegian Award

To recognize public service in the field of communications. Awarded periodically by *The Collegian*, the weekly student newspaper of La Salle University. Established in 1949.

• 12635 • Signum Fidei Medal

For recognition of an individual who has made most noteworthy contributions to the advancement of humanitarian principles in keeping with the Christian-Judeo tradition. A plaque with a medal imbedded on top is awarded annually. Established in 1942 by the Alumni Association of La Salle University. The medal derives its name from the motto of the Brothers of the Christian Schools and means "sign of faith."

• 12636 •
La Sertoma International
Pamela E. Martell, Exec.Sec.
21710 S Race
Spring Hill, KS 66083
Phone: (913)686-3000
Fax: (913)686-3000
E-mail: lasertomahq@earthlink.net
Home Page: http://www.lasertoma.org

• 12637 • International Humanitarian Award

To honor an individual for outstanding service to mankind. Non-Sertoman judges select the winner from the 15 winners in each region of Sertoma. A plaque and an expense-paid trip to the Convention are awarded annually. Established in 1954.

• 12638 •
Labor Education and Research Project
7435 Michigan Ave.
Detroit, MI 48210
Phone: (313)842-6262
Fax: (313)842-0227
E-mail: chris@labornotes.org

• 12639 • Troublemaker Awards

Recognizes individual and collective efforts to reform unions and improve working conditions. Awarded biennially.

• 12640 •
Labor Research Association
Jeannine Rudolph, Contact
330 W 42nd St., 13th Fl.
New York, NY 10036
Phone: (212)714-1677
Toll-Free: 800-875-8775
Fax: (212)714-1674
E-mail: jrudolph@lra-ny.com
Home Page: http://www.laborresearch.org

• 12641 • Ernest DeMaio Award for Trade Union Activism

For recognition of rank-and-file trade union members who have made significant contributions to the advancement of working people's struggles. A plaque is awarded annually at a dinner held in the awardee's honor. Established in 1991.

• 12642 • LRA Labor Award

For recognition of those who have made significant contributions to the struggles of labor. Union or political leaders may be selected by the Board of Directors. A plaque is awarded at a dinner held in the awardee's honor. Presented annually. Established in 1976.

• 12643 •
Laboratory of Plasma Studies
369 Upson Hall
Cornell University
Ithaca, NY 14853
Phone: (607)255-0332
Fax: (607)255-3004
E-mail: plasma_studies@cornell.edu
Home Page: http://pc3.lps.cornell.edu

• 12644 • Philip Champney Prize

To recognize exceptional performance of students in Pulsed Power, Intense Particle Beams, or Related Sciences. Awarded annually with a monetary prize of $1,250 and a certificate. Established in 1991.

• 12645 •
Ladies Auxiliary Veterans of Foreign Wars
406 W 34th St.
VFW Bldg.
Kansas City, MO 64111
Phone: (816)561-8655
Fax: (816)931-4753
E-mail: info@ladiesauxvfw.com
Home Page: http://www.ladiesauxvfw.com

• 12646 • Outstanding Young Volunteer of the Year Award

To recognize and encourage volunteerism at a young age. Students between age 12 and 15 are eligible if they are U.S. citizens and attend school in the same state as the sponsoring Auxiliary. A $5,000 U.S. savings bond and travel expenses are awarded annually. Established in 1991.

• 12647 • Voice of Democracy Scholarship Program

To give high school students the opportunity to voice their opinions about their responsibility to the United States, to convey them via the broadcast media to all of America, and to recognize outstanding broadcast scripts. Students in grades 10-12 in public, parochial, and private schools in the United States and overseas are eligible to compete. Former national and/or first place state winners are not eligible to compete again. Participants are judged on their interpretation of the announced theme. The script must not be less than three minutes nor longer than five minutes. The national first place winner receives a $25,000 scholarship. Awarded annually in Washington, D.C. in March. Established in 1946.

• 12648 • Young American Creative Patriotic Art Competition

To encourage young Americans to develop patriotic art and contribute to the culture and history of the United States. Students in grades 9-12 may submit artwork on paper or canvas in watercolor, pencil, pastel, charcoal, tempera, crayon, acrylic, pen-ink, or oil. Art is judged on local, state, and national levels. Only state winners may enter the national competition. Prior first and second place national winners may not compete again. The following national awards are presented: first prize - $10,000, second prize - $5,000, third prize - $2,500. First prize includes a plaque and an all-expense paid trip to the Ladies Auxiliary National Convention. Second and third place winning entries will be featured in the Magazine and on the web site.

• 12649 •
Ladies Professional Golf Association
Rae F. Evans, Chair
100 International Golf Dr.
Daytona Beach, FL 32124-1092
Phone: (386)274-6200
Fax: (386)274-1099
E-mail: feedback@fanslpga.com
Home Page: http://www.lpga.com

• 12650 • Patty Berg Award

To recognize outstanding contributions to women's golf. Any person, a member or non-member, may be nominated. The selection committee is composed of, by appointment from the Commissioner's office, a Hall of Fame member, past President, member of a sponsor association, Board of Directors member, and media representative. The Berg Trophy is a spiral structure of clear crystal mounted on a black leather base. The crystal is a Steuben called "Tetrahedra." Awarded when merited. Established in

1979 to honor Patty Berg and recognize her diplomacy, sportsmanship, goodwill, and contributions to the game.

• 12651 • **Budget Service Award**
To honor a LPGA player for contributions and services to junior golf. Awarded annually. Established in 1991 by Budget Rent a Car, which donates $5,000 to the LPGA Junior Golf Program in conjunction with this award.

• 12652 • **Coach of the Year**
To honor a woman golf professional who is actively engaged in the teaching and coaching of golf at the college or high school level. Members in good standing of the LPGA Teaching and Club Professional Division, presently serving in the position of head coach at an accredited educational institution, who have demonstrated responsibility in the areas of coaching, recruiting, program development, instruction, tournament organization, and professional involvement in associations governing athletics are eligible. Awarded annually. Established in 1981. Sponsored by Steuben.

• 12653 • **Commissioner's Award**
To honor an individual or organization who has contributed uniquely to the LPGA and its members, who has furthered the cause of women's golf, and whose character and standards are of the highest order. Established in 1991.

• 12654 • ***Golf Digest* - LPGA Founders Cup**
To recognize altruistic contributions to the betterment of society by a LPGA member. Nomination balloting is open to all members of the LPGA and determines the finalists. Established in 1981 to commemorate the 30th anniversaries of *Golf Digest* and the LPGA.

• 12655 • **Ellen Griffin Rolex Award**
To recognize an individual, male or female, who has made a major contribution to the teaching of golf and who has demonstrated in teaching the spirit, love, and dedication to the golf student, teaching skills, and the game of golf. Awarded annually. Established in 1989 by the LPGA Teaching and Club Professional Division in honor of Ellen Griffin, a dedicated golf teacher.

• 12656 • **LPGA Hall of Fame**
To honor the best professional women golfers. Association members in good standing for 10 consecutive years who have won 30 official Tour events including two major championships, or 35 official Tour events with one major championship, or 40 official Tour events are eligible. Established in 1951 after being a part of the Women's Golf Hall of Fame since 1950.

• 12657 • **William and Mousie Powell Award**
To recognize an LPGA member who, in the opinion of her playing peers by her behavior and deeds, best exemplifies the spirit, ideals, and values of the LPGA. The Powell Award trophy is permanently displaiyed at the LPGA headquarters. A bracelet designed by Tiffany's is awarded to each winner. Established in 1986.

• 12658 • **Professional of the Year**
To recognize a woman professional who manages a total golf program. An individual must manage a shop, have shown exceptional leadership and dedication to the game, and have been active in LPGA Teaching and Club Professional Division sectional and national events, tournament supervision, and promotion of junior and women's golf to be eligible. Awarded annually. Established in 1980. Sponsored by Steuben.

• 12659 • **Rolex Player of the Year**
To recognize the player who, during the current Tour year, has had the most consistent and outstanding record. Members of LPGA are eligible. Points are awarded to the top five finishers in each official LPGA tournament. The honoree's name is inscribed on a permanent trophy - an Irish silver cup made in the 1900s in Dublin. Awarded annually. Established in 1966. Sponsored by Rolex Watch U.S.A., Inc.

• 12660 • **Rolex Rookie of the Year**
To recognize a player who, in her first season, accumulates the most points, awarded in each domestic event, by the end of the last domestic event of the season. Points are doubled for the four major championships. A Georgian silver cup is awarded annually. Established in 1962. Sponsored by Rolex Watch U.S.A. Inc. Formerly: (1995) Gatorade Rookie of the Year.

• 12661 • **Samaritan Award**
To honor the touring member of the LPGA who, during her last four years, has most clearly demonstrated the selfless qualities of a "good samaritan" by humanitarian, charitable efforts to improve human health and alleviate physical suffering. Established in 1984.

• 12662 • **Teacher of the Year**
To recognize the woman teaching professional who has best exemplified her profession during the year. Nominations are made by the LPGA Teaching and Club Professional Division members and then screened before being submitted for final vote. Awarded annually. Established in 1958.

• 12663 • **Vare Trophy**
To recognize the player with the lowest scoring average at the end of each year. Vare Trophy scoring averages are computed on the basis of a player's total yearly score in official LPGA tournaments divided by the number of offical rounds she played during the year. A player must compete in 70 official rounds of tournament competition during the LPGA tour year. The trophy is awarded annually. The Vare Trophy was presented to the Ladies Professional Golf Association by Betty Jameson in 1952 in honor of the great American player, Glenna Collett Vare.

• 12664 •
Lake City Area Chamber of Commerce
Catherine Ditmar, Exec.Dir.
212 S Washington St.
PO Box 150
Lake City, MN 55041
Phone: (651)345-4123
Fax: (651)345-4195
E-mail: lcchamber@earthlink.net
Home Page: http://www.lakecity.org

• 12665 • **Water Ski Days Queen**
For person skiing as Lake City Youth Ambassador. Scholarship awarded annually.

• 12666 •
Lakeshore Humane Society
Linda Willman, Dir.
1551 N 8th St.
Manitowoc, WI 54220
Phone: (920)684-5401
Fax: (920)684-5885
E-mail: lakeshorehumane@sbcglobal.net
Home Page: http://lhs.petfinder.com

• 12667 • **Certificate of Appreciation**
For volunteers or promoters of the humane treatment of animals. Recognition award bestowed annually.

• 12668 •
Lamaze International
Linda L. Harmon, Exec.Dir.
2025 M St., NW, Ste. 800
Washington, DC 20036-3309
Phone: (202)367-1128
Toll-Free: 800-368-4404
Fax: (202)367-2128
E-mail: info@lamaze.org
Home Page: http://www.lamaze.org

• 12669 • **Elisabeth Bing Award**
To honor members who have made outstanding contributions in the field of childbirth education, either within ASPO/Lamaze's programs or apart from them. The recipient must be a professional childbirth educator member and must be recognized nationally for his or her efforts. Criteria considered include length of and variety of service, leadership positions held, and innovative initiatives. A plaque is awarded annually. Established in 1975. Renamed in 1983 to honor Elisabeth Bing, a founding member of ASPO/Lamaze in 1960. Formerly: (1983) Distinguished Service Award.

• 12670 • **Irwin Chabon Award**
For recognition of an individual's dedication to the principles of ASPO/Lamaze and for efforts on behalf of childbirth education, especially at the national level. The recipient must be a Provider member. Criteria considered include length and variety of service, leadership positions held, and innovative initiatives. A plaque is awarded annually. Established in 1977 to honor Irwin Chabon, an early ASPO/Lamaze Board member and, in the 1960s, the first physician to write a book on psychoprophylaxis.

• 12671 • **Chapter of the Year**
To recognize an outstanding ASPO/Lamaze chapter. Evaluation takes into account the chapter's management of its finances, organization, public information, programs, and membership. A plaque is awarded annually. Established in 1981.

• 12672 • **Chapter Program of the Year**
For recognition of an outstanding ongoing program in a chapter for qualities such as purpose, finances, impact, and novelty. Possible nominations include: postpartum or exercise groups, continuing education requirements program, teacher proficiency evaluation, and an attempt to change a hospital policy. A plaque is awarded annually. Established in 1980.

• 12673 • **Chapter Volunteer of the Year**
To recognize an outstanding volunteer for length of service, variety of service, leadership positions held, and innovative initiatives. A plaque is awarded annually. Established in 1981.

• 12674 • **Marjorie Karmel Award**
For recognition of an individual's dedication to the principles of ASPO/Lamaze and efforts on behalf of the organization, especially at the national level. The recipient should be a Parent member. Criteria considered are: length and variety of service, leadership positions held, and innovative initiatives. A plaque is awarded annually. Established in 1977 to honor Marjorie Karmel, who wrote *Thank You, Dr. Lamaze*, thus symbolizing the love and dedication toward the promotion of psychoprophylaxis, family-centered maternity care, and parenting concerns.

• 12675 • **Lamaze Childbirth Educator Program Scholarship**
For members enrolled in Lamaze Childbirth Educator Program who demonstrate financial need. Awarded annually.

• 12676 • **President's Award**
Annual award of recognition.

• 12677 • **Research Award**
To honor the person or organization that has contributed significantly through research in the field of childbirth education and related subjects. Criteria considered are length and variety of service, leadership positions held, and innovation. Any individual or organization is eligible. The nature of this award will be determined by the Board of Directors. Established in 1978.

• 12678 • **Special Recognition Award**
For recognition of a deserving individual or program that does not fit into any of the other award categories, such as creating a chapter exhibit, or developing a special event or a program for a one-time presentation at a hospital, school, or a special chapter meeting. Criteria considered include leadership, design, novelty, and impact. A plaque is awarded annually. Established in 1981.

• 12679 •
Lambda Kappa Sigma
Joan E. Rogala CAE, Exec.Dir.
20110 Glenoaks Dr.
Brookfield, WI 53045
Phone: (262)784-8405
Toll-Free: 800-557-1913
Fax: (414)784-8406
E-mail: lks@lks.org
Home Page: http://www.lks.org

• 12680 • **Award of Merit**
To recognize alumni members who have distinguished themselves by reason of academic achievement, professional advancement, community service, organizational work or commercial endeavor. Nominations may be submitted by April 30. The Grand Council selects the recipient. A certificate is awarded biennially at the Convention. Established in 1960.

• 12681 • **Distinguished Service Citation**
To recognize outstanding service to the fraternity by an alumni member. Nominations may be submitted by April 30. The Grand Council selects the recipient. An engraved plaque or trophy is awarded biennially at the Convention. Established in 1974.

• 12682 •
Lambda Literary Foundation
Charles Flowers, Exec.Dir.
392 Central Park W
Suite 11M
New York, NY 10025
E-mail: asklambda@earthlink.net
Home Page: http://www.lambdaliterary.org

• 12683 • **Lambda Literary Awards**
To promote and to recognize excellence in the area of gay and lesbian writing and publishing. Only gay and lesbian books published (copyrighted) in the previous calendar year in the United States are eligible. Nominations are accepted and solicited nationally. The nomination deadline is February 21. A transparent engraved plaque in the shape of a book is awarded annually at the American Booksellers Convention to each winner. Established in 1989.

• 12684 •
Lamoille County Planning Commission
Michele Boomhower, Ed.
PO Box 1009
Morrisville, VT 05661
Phone: (802)888-4548
Fax: (802)888-6938
E-mail: lcpc@lcpcvt.org
Home Page: http://www.lcpcvt.org

• 12685 • **Jim Marvin Award**
For community service/project design. Recognition award bestowed annually.

• 12686 •
Lancaster Historical Society
Theresa L. Wolfe, Pres.
40 Clark St.
Lancaster, NY 14086
Phone: (716)681-7719
Phone: (716)683-4679

• 12687 • **Louise Keysa Scholarship**
For excellence in social studies. A monetary prize of $250 is awarded annually.

• 12688 •
Land Improvement Contractors of America
Eileen Levy, Publisher
3080 Ogden Ave., Ste. 300
Lisle, IL 60532
Phone: (630)548-1984
Fax: (630)548-9189
E-mail: nlica@aol.com
Home Page: http://www.licanational.com

• 12689 • **Contractor of the Year**
To recognize achievement in the field of land improvement contracting nationwide. Members are eligible. A plaque is awarded annually at the LICA National Convention. Established in 1964.

• 12690 •
Lannan Foundation
Jaune Evans, Exec.Dir.
313 Read St.
Santa Fe, NM 87501-2628
Phone: (505)986-8160
Fax: (505)986-8195
E-mail: info@lannan.org
Home Page: http://www.lannan.org

• 12691 • **Lannan Literary Awards**
To recognize work of the highest literary merit in fiction, poetry, and nonfiction, and to increase the level of critical acclaim paid to English-language writers whose work represents exceptional literary achievement. The Foundation is particularly interested in work that calls attention to essential humanistic values in creative, skillful, and provocative ways, recognizing young, emerging, and venerated writers alike. Candidates are first recommended by a select group of writers, literary scholars, and editors. Nominators are geographically dispersed and serve anonymously. Applications from any other source are not accepted. The final determination of prize winners is left to the Foundation's Literary Arts Committee. Established in 1989.

• 12692 •
Laser Institute of America
Peter M. Baker, Exec.Dir.
13501 Ingenuity Dr., Ste. 128
Orlando, FL 32826
Phone: (407)380-1553
Toll-Free: 800-345-2737
Fax: (407)380-5588
E-mail: lia@laserinstitute.org
Home Page: http://www.laserinstitute.org

• 12693 • **Arthur L. Schawlow Award**

To recognize individuals who have made distinguished contributions in application of lasers for science, industry, or education. Nominations are accepted. A $1,000 honorarium, a three inch silver medal, and a citation are awarded annually at the conference. Established in 1975, and renamed in 1982 in honor of the late Arthur L. Schawlow, Nobel Laureate in physics. Formerly: (1982) Laser Institute of America Honored Speaker Award.

• 12694 •

Albert and Mary Lasker Foundation
Neen Hunt, Pres.
Albert Lasker Medical Research Awards Program
110 E 42nd St., Ste. 1300
New York, NY 10017
Phone: (212)286-0222
Fax: (212)286-0924
E-mail: info@laskerfoundation.org
Home Page: http://www.laskerfoundation.org

• 12695 • **Mary Woodard Lasker Award for Public Service in Behalf of Medical Research**

To recognize outstanding research by an individual or a group that contributes clinically to the alleviation or elimination of one of the major medical causes of disability or death, and which also may result in prolongation of the prime of life. A monetary award of $25,000, a statuette of the Winged Victory of Samothrace, and a citation are awarded annually. Established in 1963; renamed in 1996. Formerly: (1996) Albert Lasker Public Service Award.

• 12696 • **Albert Lasker Award for Special Achievement in Medical Research**

To recognize extraordinary achievement in medical research, which has unprecedented impact on the progress of medical science. Established in 1997.

• 12697 • **Albert Lasker Basic Medical Research Award**

For recognition of an investigator or investigating group that has made fundamental biological and medical investigations which provide techniques, information, or concepts that are prerequisite to the elimination of the major causes of disability and death, and may also prolong the prime of life. A monetary award of $50,000, a statuette of the Winged Victory of Samothrace, and a citation are awarded annually. Established in 1962.

• 12698 •

Latin American Studies Association
Sonia E. Alvarez, Pres.
946 William Pitt Union
University of Pittsburgh
Pittsburgh, PA 15260
Phone: (412)648-7929
Fax: (412)624-7145
E-mail: lasa@pitt.edu
Home Page: http://lasa.international.pitt.edu

• 12699 • **Media Medal**

Recognizes outstanding media coverage of Latin America. Given every eighteen months to recognize journalistic contributions to the analysis and public debate about Latin America in the United States and in Latin America, as well as breakthrough journalism. Both print and electronic medias are eligible.

• 12700 • **Premio Iberoamericano Book Award**

For an outstanding book on Latin America in the social sciences and humanities, published in Spanish or Portuguese in any country. No book may compete more than once. Books are judged on the quality of research, analysis, and writing, and the significance of their contribution to Latin American Studies. Awarded annually.

• 12701 • **Kalman Silvert Award**

Recognizes lifetime contribution to the study of Latin America. Awarded periodically.

• 12702 • **Bryce Wood Book Award**

To recognize the outstanding book on Latin America in the social sciences and humanities published in English. Books will be judged on the quality of the research, analysis, and writing, and the significance of their contribution to Latin American studies. The selection will be made one month before the association's international congress. Awarded periodically.

• 12703 •

Latin Liturgy Association
Mr. James F. Pauer, Pres.
PO Box 16517
Rocky River, OH 44116
Phone: (718)979-6685
Fax: (718)667-7128
E-mail: jfpauer@juno.com
Home Page: http://www.latinliturgy.com

• 12704 • **Domus Dei**

Recognizes service to the Latin Liturgy. Awarded biennially.

• 12705 •

Latino American Management Association
Stephen Denlinger, CEO
419 New Jersey Ave. SE
Washington, DC 20003
Phone: (202)546-3803
Fax: (202)546-3807
E-mail: lamausa@bellatlantic.net
Home Page: http://www.lamausa.com

• 12706 • **Businessperson of the Year**

Recognizes outstanding contributions to the Hispanic community. Business executives are eligible. Awarded annually.

• 12707 • **Corporate Advocate Leadership Award**

Recognizes a corporation that has shown exemplary leadership in its commitment to the Hispanic business community. Awarded annually.

• 12708 • **Entrepreneur of the Year**

Recognizes superior entrepreneurial skills. Business owners are eligible. Awarded annually.

• 12709 • **Government Advocate Leadership Award**

Recognizes an increase in the Government's use of Hispanic business products and services. Outstanding public sector individuals are eligible. One award is given annually.

• 12710 • **Hispanic Leadership Award**

Recognizes a dramatic impact on the Hispanic business community. Individuals are eligible. Awarded annually.

• 12711 • **Rising Star Leadership Award**

Recognizes skills that signal great potential for future distinction. Business owners and corporate mangers are eligible. Awarded annually.

• 12712 •

Latino Gerontological Center
(Centro Gerontologico Latino)
Mario E. Tapia, Pres. & CEO
75 Maiden Ln., Ste. 208
New York, NY 10038
Phone: (212)402-5474
Fax: (212)480-9734
E-mail: info@gerolatino.org
Home Page: http://www.gerolatino.org

• 12713 • **Golden Age Award**

Recognizes an individual who has made significant contributions to Latino-Hispanic communities throughout the world. Awarded annually.

• 12714 •
Latrobe Area Chamber of Commerce
Andrew M. Stofan, Pres.
326 McKinley Av. Ste. 102
PO Box 143
Latrobe, PA 15650
Phone: (724)537-2671
Fax: (724)537-2690
E-mail: info@latrobearea.com
Home Page: http://www.latrobearea.com

• 12715 • **Community Service Award**
For unselfish service to the community. Recognition award bestowed annually.

• 12716 •
Laubach Literacy of Canada
Lilla Sinanan, Dir. of Mktg.
70 Crown St., Ste. 225
St. John, NB, Canada E2L 2X6
Phone: (506)634-1980
Toll-Free: 877-634-1980
Fax: (506)634-0944
E-mail: newreadersbookstore@nb.aibn.com
Home Page: http://www.laubach.ca

• 12717 • **Laubach Literacy of Canada Award**
Recognizes volunteer contributors. Awarded periodically.

• 12718 •
Law and Society Association
Ronald M. Pipkin, Exec. Officer
205 Hampshire House
131 County Cir.
Univ. of Massachusetts
Amherst, MA 01003-9257
Phone: (413)545-4617
Fax: (413)577-3194
E-mail: exec_office@lawandsociety.org
Home Page: http://www.lawandsociety.org

• 12719 • **Article Prize**
To recognize an article published in the previous two years in a major journal of sociolegal scholarship that is an outstanding contribution to sociolegal scholarship. Awarded annually. Established in 1998.

• 12720 • **Hurst Prize**
For recognition of an outstanding contribution to American legal history. Nominations are accepted. A monetary award of $500 is awarded biennially as merited. Established in 1980 in honor of J. Willard Hurst, and first awarded in 1982.

• 12721 • **Herbert Jacob Book Prize**
To recognize the author(s) of a book published in the last two years that is a major contribution to sociolegal scholarship. Awarded annually. Established in 1996. Formerly: (1997) Book Prize.

• 12722 • **Kalven Prize**
For recognition of a scholarly contribution to the field of law and society. Nominations are accepted. A monetary award of $500 is presented biennially. Established in 1981 in honor of Harry J. Kalven Jr., and first awarded in 1983.

• 12723 •
Law Enforcement Memorial Association
Sgt. Ronald C. Van Raalte, Pres.
PO Box 72835
Roselle, IL 60172-0835
Phone: (847)409-8961
Fax: (847)524-1369
E-mail: forgottenheroes@aol.com
Home Page: http://www.forgottenheroes-lema.org

• 12724 • **Alan J. Vargo Memorial**
To recognize individuals who make extraordinary contributions to the mission of the association. A plaque is awarded as merited. Established in 1992.

• 12725 •
Law of Polk County
Erin Rice, Pres.
PO Box 65502
West Des Moines, IA 50265-0502
E-mail: wdmbrennans@aol.com

• 12726 • **Cristine Swanson Wilson Memorial Scholarship**
For law students. Scholarship awarded annually.

• 12727 •
Lawyers Alliance for World Security
Jack Mendelsohn, VP/Exec.Dir.
1901 Pennsylvania Ave. NW, Ste. 201
Washington, DC 20006
Phone: (202)745-2450
Fax: (202)667-0444
E-mail: info@lawscns.org
Home Page: http://www.cdi.org/LAWS/

• 12728 • **W. Averell Harriman Award**
Recognizes significant contribution to the cause of peace. Awarded annually.

• 12729 •
Lay Carmelite Order of the Blessed Virgin Mary of Mount Carmel
Rev. John Benedict Weber, Dir.
8501 Bailey Rd.
Darien, IL 60561-8417
Phone: (630)969-5050
Home Page: http://carmelnet.org/toc/toc.htm

• 12730 • **Certificate of Appreciation Award**
Recognizes those who have given outstanding service to the organization. Awarded biennially.

• 12731 •
LDA Publishers
Elaine M. Sprance, Ed.
29-33 200th St., Ste. B-11
Bayside, NY 11361
Phone: (718)224-9484
Toll-Free: 888-388-9887
Fax: (718)224-9487
E-mail: elaine@ldadirect.com
Home Page: http://www.ldapublishers.com

Formerly: Library Directory Associates Publishers.

• 12732 • **LDA Award for Excellence in Library Achievement**
To call attention to the importance of Long Island (NY) libraries, librarians, and their work. The following criteria are considered: outstanding achievement in developing and publishing library materials; long and distinguished service in the advancement of librarianship; an original contribution for promoting the library; progressive legislative activity; promoting of intellectual freedom; and creative, innovative utilization of technologies. Librarians, trustees, support staff, friends of the library, vendors, and publishers may be nominated by April 15. A plaque is awarded annually at the Long Island Libraries Conference. Established in 1978.

• 12733 •
Le Mars Community School District Alumni Association
Carolyn Vance, Contact
Plymouth County Historical Museum
335 1st Ave. SW
Le Mars, IA 51031-2261
Phone: (712)546-7650
E-mail: lcsdalumni@multivance.com

• 12734 • **Decades of Excellence Crystal Bell Teacher Award**
For teachers in LCSD school system. Monetary award.

• 12735 •
Leaders' Forum
Karen Nelson, Exec.Dir.
759 N. Milwaukee, Ste. 301
Milwaukee, WI 53202
Phone: (414)224-0554
Fax: (414)224-0812

• 12736 • **Impact Award**
For corporate progress toward recruitment and retention of AA professionals; citizenship and support of same. Recognition award bestowed annually.

• 12737 •
Leadership Conference on Civil Rights
Wade Henderson, Exec.Dir.
1629 K St. NW, 10th Fl.
Washington, DC 20006
Phone: (202)466-3311
Fax: (202)466-3435
E-mail: webmaster@civilrights.org
Home Page: http://www.civilrights.org

• 12738 • **Hubert H. Humphrey Civil Rights Award**
For recognition of selfless devotion to the cause of equality. Recipients of the award are selected by officers of the organization with suggestions made by the Executive Committee. A medallion, encased in lucite, is presented at the Annual Meeting. Established in 1978 in memory of Hubert H. Humphrey, a former Minnesota Senator and Vice President of the United States.

• 12739 •
Leadership Fort Wayne
Jane Wilks, Exec.Dir.
2101 Coliseum Blvd. E
Fort Wayne, IN 46805-1445
Phone: (260)481-6112
Fax: (260)481-4116
E-mail: wilks@ipfw.edu
Home Page: http://www.leadershipfortwayne.org

• 12740 • **Youth as Resources**
For community service projects by youth. Grant awarded semiannually.

• 12741 •
League of American Theatres and Producers
Alan Cohen, Contact
226 W 47th St.
New York, NY 10036
Phone: (212)764-1122
Phone: (212)703-0200
Fax: (212)719-4389
E-mail: fanclub@broadway.org
Home Page: http://www.livebroadway.com

Formerly: (1985) League of New York Theatres and Producers, Inc..

• 12742 • **Antoinette Perry Awards (Tony Awards)**
To recognize outstanding theatrical achievement in the Broadway theatre. Legitimate theatrical productions opening in an eligible Broadway house with 499 or more seats during the Tony season (May to May) are eligible for nomination. Awards are presented in the following creative categories: Best Play - awards to the author and producer; Best Musical - award to the producer; Best Book of a Musical; Best Original Score of a Musical written for the theater; Best Revival of a Play or a Musical - award to the producer; Best Actor in a Play; Best Actress in a Play; Best Featured Actor in a Play; Best Featured Actress in a Play; Best Actor in a Musical; Best Actress in a Musical; Best Featured Actor in a Musical; Best Featured Actress in a Musical; Best Direction of a Play; Best Direction of a Musical; Best Scenic Design; Best Costume Design; Best Lighting Design; and Best Choreography. Tony Awards - a silver medallion embossed with masks of comedy and tragedy mounted on black lucite-base, are awarded annually in each category. Established in 1947 in honor of Antoinette Perry of the American Theatre Wing.

• 12743 •
League of Canadian Poets
Joanna Poblocka, Exec.Dir.
920 Yonge St., Ste. 608
Toronto, ON, Canada M4W 3C7
Phone: (416)504-1657
Fax: (416)504-0096
E-mail: info@poets.ca
Home Page: http://www.poets.ca

• 12744 • **Gerald Lampert Memorial Award**
To recognize the best first book of poetry published during the preceding year. Canadian citizens or landed immigrants who have been published by a professional publisher (not self-published) during the preceding year are eligible. A monetary prize of $1,000 Canadian is awarded each year at the League's annual general meeting. Established in 1979 in memory of Gerald Lampert, an arts administrator who organized writers' tours and took a particular interest in the work of new writers.

• 12745 • **Pat Lowther Memorial Award**
For recognition of the best book of poetry written by a woman and published during the preceding year. Canadian citizens or landed immigrants whose books have been published by a professional publisher (not self-published) are eligible. A monetary prize of $1,000 Canadian is awarded annually at the League's annual general meeting. Established in 1976 in memory of Pat Lowther, former president of the League whose life ended tragically.

• 12746 •
League of Composers - International Society of Contemporary Music
Sebastian Zubieta, Exec.Co-Dir.
% Farrin & Zubieta
875 W 181st St., Ste. 4D
New York, NY 10033
Phone: (718)442-5225
E-mail: info@league-iscm.org
Home Page: http://www.league-iscm.org

• 12747 • **National Composers' Competition**
To provide recognition for outstanding American compositions. U.S. citizens may submit compositions. The winner is awarded a performance of the composition in New York, and an official submission to the ISCM World Music Days. Awarded annually. Established in 1976. Deadline for application is mid-March and carries an entry fee of $20.

• 12748 •
League of Minnesota Cities
Jim Miller, Exec.Dir.
145 Univ. Ave. W
St. Paul, MN 55103
Phone: (651)281-1200
Phone: (651)281-1290
Toll-Free: 800-925-1122
Fax: (651)281-1299
Home Page: http://www.lmnc.org

• 12749 • **C.C. Ludwig Award**
For outstanding service of elected/appointed city officials. Recognition award.

• 12750 • **City Achievement Award**
For annual adjudicated projects. Recognition award.

• 12751 •
League of Women Voters of Arkansas
Stephanie Johnson, Pres.
The Executive Bldg.
2020 W Third, No. 504
Little Rock, AR 72205-0000
Phone: (501)376-7760
Fax: (501)975-4670
E-mail: msstephjohnson@aol.com
Home Page: http://www.lwv-arkansas.org

• 12752 • **Horizon Award**
For individuals and organizations enhancing the quality of life in Arkansas and strengthening the democratic process. Recognition award bestowed biennially.

• 12753 •
League of Women Voters of Oklahoma
500 N Broadway, Ste. 125
Oklahoma City, OK 73102
Phone: (405)232-8683
Fax: (405)236-8683
E-mail: lwvokla@aol.com
Home Page: http://www.lwvok.org

• 12754 • **Making Democracy Work Award**
For someone who has furthered citizen involvement in government. Recognition award bestowed annually.

• 12755 •
The Leakey Foundation
Roccie Hill, Exec.Dir.
1002A O'Reilly Ave.
PO Box 29346
San Francisco, CA 94129-0346
Phone: (415)561-4646
Fax: (415)561-4647
E-mail: info@leakeyfoundation.org
Home Page: http://www.leakeyfoundation.org

• 12756 • L. S. B. Leakey Foundation Prize for Multidisciplinary Research on Ape and Human Evolution

To reward intellectual achievement and express appreciation for multidisciplinary research performed with courage and perseverance in the fields of ape and human evolution. The award honors a scientist (scientists) for achievement transcending the boundaries of his or her discipline and linking widely differing branches of science. Nominations may be submitted by January 1. A monetary award of $25,000 and a medal are presented every two or three years. Established in 1990 to honor Louis Leakey for his extraordinary contribution to science by creating a web of inquiries into the relationships between the study of great apes and hunter-gatherers as they relate to the study of human origins. Please contact the Foundation for further information.

• 12757 •
Learning Disabilities Association of Arkansas
Stacy Mahurin, Co-Pres.
7509 Cantrell Rd., Ste. 103C
Little Rock, AR 72207
Phone: (501)666-8777
Phone: (501)666-4070
Fax: (501)666-4070
E-mail: info@ldaarkansas.org

• 12758 • Norman Scholarship

To assist young adults with learning disabilities with independent living skills. Recognition award bestowed annually.

• 12759 •
Learning Disabilities Association of California
Georgia Abi-Nader, Pres.
PO Box 601067
Sacramento, CA 95860
Phone: (916)725-7881
Toll-Free: (866)532-6322
Fax: (916)725-8786
Home Page: http://www.ldaca.org

• 12760 • John Arena Memorial Scholarship

For post-secondary student with learning disabilities. Scholarship awarded annually.

• 12761 •
Leavenworth Area Development
Lynn McClure, Exec.Dir.
1298 Eisenhower Rd.
Leavenworth, KS 66048
Phone: (913)727-6111
Phone: (913)727-2706
Fax: (913)727-5515
E-mail: lynnm@lvarea.com
Home Page: http://www.lvarea.com

• 12762 • Economic Development Volunteer

For work in economic development. Recognition award bestowed annually.

• 12763 •
Lefthanders International
Dean R. Campbell, Publisher & Pres.
PO Box 723
Manhattan, KS 66505-0723
Fax: (913)232-3999

• 12764 • Lefthanders of the Year Awards

To recognize outstanding lefthanded individuals in the following categories: public personality, entertainment, music, sports, and past favorites. To be considered, an individual must be left handed and have made a significant achievement during the previous year. The readers of *Lefthander Magazine* make the selection. An overall winner is chosen from the winners in each of the categories. Trophies and a feature of the winners in *Lefthander Magazine* are awarded annually each January. Established in 1976.

• 12765 •
Legal Aid Society of the Orange County Bar Association
Mary Anne DePetrillo, Exec.Dir.
100 E Robinson St.
Orlando, FL 32801
Phone: (407)841-8310
Fax: (407)648-9240
E-mail: mdepetrillo@legalaidocba.org
Home Page: http://legalaidocba.org/

• 12766 • Pro Bono Service Awards

For service to clients. Recognition award bestowed annually.

• 12767 •
Legal Momentum: Advancing Women's Rights
Kathy J. Rodgers, Pres.
395 Hudson St.
New York, NY 10014
Phone: (212)925-6635
Fax: (212)226-1066
E-mail: peo@legalmomentum.org
Home Page: http://www.legalmomentum.org

• 12768 • BUDDY Award (Bringing Up Daughters Differently)

The BUDDY Awards (Bringing Up Daughters Differently) honor families who bring up daughters to achieve their full potential. The event demonstrates a powerful combination of individual courage and success, a commitment to diversity, and the ideals of women's equality. Each recipient (there are four annually, chosen from the African-American, Hispanic-Latina, Asian-American, and white communities of Los Angeles) receives a plaque with a framed graphic describing the event and the BUDDY principles.

• 12769 • Equal Opportunity Award

To recognize leaders in business and fashion who advance women's equality in the corporate community. A crystal sculpture of a primitive folk art doll with symbolic meaning is awarded annually to numerous recipients at an honoree dinner in New York City. Established in 1979.

• 12770 • Muriel Fox Communications Award

To recognize an especially noted leader in business or fashion who advances women's equality in the corporate community. A crystal sculpture of a primitive folk art doll with symbolic meaning is given at the Equal Opportunity Awards (see separate entry) honoree dinner held in New York City. The award is also known as The Foxy. Awarded annually. Established in 1991.

• 12771 •
Legion of Valor of the United States of America
Philip J. Conran, Adj.
4706 Calle Reina
Santa Barbara, CA 93110-2018
Phone: (805)692-2244
E-mail: pconran@cox.net
Home Page: http://www.legionofvalor.com

• 12772 • Legion of Valor Bronze Cross for Achievement

To encourage ROTC cadets at all levels (college, military school, and high school) to achieve scholastic excellence in both military and academic subjects, and to stimulate development of leadership. Cadets of the Army, Navy, Air Force, and Marine Corps ROTC who stand at least in the upper fourth of their class and are recommended by the senior military officer of the ROTC unit are eligible. Recommendations are endorsed by civilian officials of the educational institution concerned, endorsed at senior military levels and approved at Legion of Valor headquarters. About 40 bronze crosses bearing the emblem of the Legion of Valor are presented annually. Established in 1958.

• 12773 • Legion of Valor Silver Cross for Valor

To recognize individuals for civilian acts of gallantry which, under conditions of extreme hazard, result in the preservation of life. A certificate and silver cross are awarded as merited. Established in 1957.

• 12774 •
Lemelson-MIT Program
Massachusetts Institute of Technology
Michael McNally, Lemelson-MIT Program Officer
School of Engineering
77 Massacheusetts Ave. Bldg. E 60-215
Cambridge, MA 02139
Phone: (617)253-3352
Fax: (617)258-8276
E-mail: invent@mit.edu
Home Page: http://web.mit.edu/invent/

• 12775 • $30,000 Lemelson-MIT Student Prize

An annual $30,000 cash prize presented to an MIT senior or graduate student who has created or improved a product or process, applied a technology in a new way, redesigned a system or in other ways demonstrated remarkable inventiveness.

• 12776 • $100,000 Lemelson-MIT Lifetime Achievement Award
Annual award which honors a remarkable individual for his or her life-long commitment to improving society through invention in the fields of medicine and healthcare, computing and telecommunications, energy and environment, consumer products or industrial products.

• 12777 • $500,000 Lemelson-MIT Prize
An annual prize that recognizes an individual who has a rich history of inventiveness and creativity and a proven commitment to inspiring others in the fields of medicine and health care, computing and telecommunications, energy and environment, consumer products or industrial products.

• 12778 •
Lentz Peace Research Association
Ms. Miranda Duncan, Contact
One University Blvd.
8001 Natural Bridge Rd.
Rm. 362, Social Science and Business Bldg.
St. Louis, MO 63121-4400
Phone: (314)516-6040
Phone: (314)516-5753
Fax: (314)516-5268
E-mail: duncanm@missouri.edu
Home Page: http://www.umsl.edu/services/cis/research/theodore_lentz.html

Formerly: Peace Research Laboratory.

• 12779 • Lentz International Peace Research Award
To honor outstanding contributions to the field of peace research, to encourage others to engage in peace research, and to popularize the field of peace research. A panel of international judges selects the awardee. A monetary award of $1,000, a replica of a prismatic sculpture created by Fred Dreher, and travel expenses are awarded biennially. The recipient participates in a seminar previous to the reception where the presentation is made, and speaks at the reception. Established in 1972 in the name of Dr. Theodore F. Lentz to recognize and honor his unselfish and untiring zeal in the promotion of peace research.

• 12780 •
Leominster Historical Society
Thomas Tucker, Pres.
17 School St.
Leominster, MA 01453-3124
Phone: (978)537-5424

• 12781 • History Prize
For highest grade in U.S. history in high school. Monetary award bestowed annually.

• 12782 •
Les Amis d'Escoffier Society
% Castle Restaurant
1230 Main St.
Leicester, MA 01524
Phone: (508)892-9090
E-mail: info@castlerestaurant.com
Home Page: http://www.castlerestaurant.com/les_amis_descoffier_society.htm

• 12783 • Amis d'Escoffier Society Awards
To recognize achievement and contributions in upgrading the image of the professional culinarian, restaurateur, hotelier, and club manager. Any individual who appreciates fine dining, the best foods and wines, and believes in live and let live is eligible. A medal is awarded annually to each Chapter. Established in 1936 by Joseph Donon to honor August Escoffier.

• 12784 •
Leukemia and Lymphoma Society
Dwayne Howell PhD, Pres./CEO
1311 Mamaroneck Ave.
White Plains, NY 10605
Phone: (914)949-5213
Toll-Free: 800-955-4572
Fax: (914)949-6691
E-mail: infocenter@leukemia-lymphoma.org
Home Page: http://www.lls.org

Formerly: (1954) DeVilliers Foundation.

• 12785 • Chairman's Citation
To recognize outstanding accomplishments within the chapter in the areas of fund raising, program efforts or volunteer leadership. It is usually presented by the President of the local Board on behalf of the Chairman of the National Board of Trustees, and is accompanied by a letter signed by the Chairman of the Board. Recipients are usually those persons and/or organizations that have already received the highest award a chapter can bestow locally and who deserve national recognition for their efforts. Established in 1990.

• 12786 • William Dameshek Award
To recognize an individual or organization who has aided the society in an outstanding way by helping focus national attention on leukemia and related diseases. Established in 1969 in honor of Dr. Dameshek, president for medical and scientific affairs for several years.

• 12787 • DeVilliers Award
To honor scientific achievements in the advancement of research into leukemia, lymphoma and myeloma. Award winners receive a grant of $100,000 over a two-year period to support a research fellow in the laboratory of the honoree. Established in 1953 in memory of Robert de Villiers who died from leukemia in 1949, and whose family established the de Villiers Foundation, the forerunner of the Leukemia Society.

• 12788 • Journalism Awards
To recognize the efforts of outstanding American journalists who have helped educate the public about the advancements that have been made in cancer treatment through leukemia research. Awards are presented in four categories: newspapers, magazines, radio, and TV. Entries must be original works calling attention to the advancements in leukemia research either through stories or programs about research programs, specific or groups of patients, cancer clinics or hospitals, or related stories. A certificate is presented to winners. Entries may be submitted by June 1. Awarded annually during the Society's national annual meeting in October. Established in 1986.

• 12789 • Dr. John J. Kenny Award
To honor medical persons who have contributed significantly to the Society's research, professional education or patient aid program. The award is named for Dr. John J. Kenny, a former Vice Chairman of Medical and Scientific Affairs. Established in 1980.

• 12790 • Kenneth B. McCredie
To recognize the long-term commitment of individuals, groups, organizations or companies who have significantly supported the Leukemia Society of America for at least five years and raised more than $1 million. Established in 1991 in memory of Dr. Kenneth B. McCredie, who served as chief of developmental therapeutics at M.D. Anderson Hospital and provided vital leadership for the Leukemia Society's medical and other major programs for over ten years.

• 12791 • Media Awards
To honor outstanding efforts in educating the public about leukemia and its related cancers, specific or groups of patients, cancer clinics or hospitals, Society activities and events or related stories. A certificate is presented to winners in print, television, radio, and new media categories. Established in 1986. Formerly: Leukemia Society of America Journalism Awards.

• 12792 • National Leadership Award
To honor past or present members of the Society's national board of trustees who have significantly served as national leaders of the Society, and, by their leadership, advanced the overall stature and programs of the Society and helped position it as one of America's top volunteer health agencies. Established in 1985.

• 12793 • Return of the Child Award
To recognize an individual, organization or institution which has made a major and lasting scientific or humanitarian contribution to better understanding the management and/or treatment of leukemia and related cancers. The award portrays the Biblical story of Abraham and Isaac and Abraham's joy when his son is returned to him. The award is a reproduction of a sculpture by Leukemia Society Trustee Emeritus William T. Kieffer, Jr.

• 12794 • Michael Schoenbrun Award
To honor an individual or organization that has significantly increased the public's knowledge about the Society's mission and programs, or leukemia and its related cancers, through the television and/or motion picture media, whose contributions to the Society are both prodigious and practical. Originally presented as a tribute to the late Michael Schoenbrun, a Society trustee from 1980 until 1990. Established in 1993.

• 12795 • Special Recognition Award
To honor individuals and organizations who have significantly supported the national programs of the Society in a variety of ways. Established in 1983.

• 12796 • Spiral of Life Award
To honor lay persons (other than recognizable public figures) who have contributed personal and special talents that have made an outstanding national contribution to the Society's programs. Established in 1979.

• 12797 •
Leukemia and Lymphoma Society of America, Northern Florida Chapter
Eden Carr, Exec.Dir.
9143 Phillips Hwy., Ste. 130
Jacksonville, FL 32256
Phone: (904)538-0721
Toll-Free: 800-868-0072
Fax: (904)538-9245
Home Page: http://www.leukemia.org

• 12798 • Patient Aid
For diagnosis of leukemia, lymphoma, hodgkins disease, or myeloma. Monetary award bestowed monthly.

• 12799 •
Lewis and Clark Trail Heritage Foundation
Carol A. Bronson, Exec.Dir.
600 Central Ave., Ste. 327
Great Falls, MT 59403
Phone: (406)454-1234
Toll-Free: 888-701-3434
Fax: (406)771-9237
E-mail: membership@lewisandclark.org
Home Page: http://www.lewisandclark.org

• 12800 • Appreciation Award
For recognition of the gracious support in the form of deeds, words, or funds given to the Foundation in its endeavors to preserve and perpetuate the lasting historical worth of the 1803-1806 Lewis and Clark Expedition. This award may be presented to any individual or entity. A framed parchment certificate is presented at the annual meeting in August. Established in 1981.

• 12801 • Award of Meritorious Achievement
For outstanding contributions in bringing to this nation a greater awareness and appreciation of the Lewis and Clark Expedition. The award may be presented to any individual or entity. A walnut plaque with an etched metal citation is presented at the annual meeting in August. Established in 1972.

• 12802 • Distinguished Service Award
For outstanding contributions toward furthering the purpose and objectives of the Foundation. This award may be presented only to a member of the Foundation. A walnut based plaque with an etched metal citation is presented at the annual meeting in August. Established in 1978.

• 12803 • Youth Achievement Award
For recognition of a person or group of persons under the age of 21 who has increased knowledge of the Lewis and Clark Expedition through outstanding composition, art, drama, photography, site preservation and enhancement, or other significant contribution. A parchment certificate is presented at the annual meeting in August. Established in 1983.

• 12804 •
Libertarian Futurist Society
Victoria L. Varga, Dir.
650 Castro St., Ste. 120-433
Mountain View, CA 94041
Phone: (585)582-1068
E-mail: vvarga1@rochester.rr.com
Home Page: http://www.lfs.org

• 12805 • Hall of Fame
To recognize novels that demonstrate the value of human freedom. Novel-length fiction published at least five years previously is considered. A one-tenth ounce gold coin with the image of economist F.A. Hayak on its face is awarded annually. Established in 1982.

• 12806 • Prometheus Award
To recognize novels that demonstrate the value of human freedom. Novel-length fiction published in the previous year is considered. A one-half ounce gold coin with the image of economist F.A. Hayak on its face is awarded annually. Established in 1982.

• 12807 •
Libertarian Party of California
Aaron Starr, Chm.
14547 Titus St., Ste, 214
Panorama City, CA 91402-4935
Phone: (818)782-8400
Toll-Free: 877-884-1776
Fax: (818)782-8488
E-mail: office@ca.lp.org
Home Page: http://www.ca.lp.org/

• 12808 • Karl Brey Award
For behind-the-scenes activism. Monetary award bestowed annually.

• 12809 •
Liberty Bell Wanderers
Mr. Ronald A. Nelson, Pres.
2 Alexis Dr.
Ambler, PA 19002
Phone: (215)699-9246
E-mail: lbwanderers@aol.com
Home Page: http://hometown.aol.com/lbwvolks1/LBW.html

• 12810 • Achievement Award
For completion of required number of walking events. Recognition award.

• 12811 •
Liberty Seated Collectors Club
John W. McCloskey, Pres.
5718 King Arthur Dr.
Kettering, OH 45429
Phone: (937)434-4035

• 12812 • Kamal M. Ahwash Literary Award
To recognize an outstanding article in *Gobrecht Journal*, a journal that publishes original research articles on nineteenth century silver coinage of the United States. Members who contributed articles to the journal during the past year are eligible. A plaque is presented annually. Established in 1982 in honor of Kamal M. Ahwash, the first president of LSCC.

• 12813 •
Library Administration and Management Association
Lorraine Olley, Exec.Dir.
50 E Huron St.
Chicago, IL 60611-2795
Phone: (312)280-5036
Toll-Free: 800-545-2433
Fax: (312)280-5033
E-mail: lama@ala.org
Home Page: http://www.ala.org/lama

• 12814 • Best of Show Awards
Recognizes public relations materials produced by libraries during the previous year. Materials in the following categories are accepted: Annual Reports; Bibliographies/Booklists; Calendars of Events; Newsletters, and materials promoting programs on diversity, fund-raising, programs and special events, original children's young adult, or adult summer reading clubs, services available, print materials about the internet or the organizations web site are also eligible. Materials will be accepted between March 9 and April 6. All materials should be sent to Sherril Smit, Assistant to the Director, Public Libraries of Saginaw, 505 Jones St., Saginaw, MI 48067.

• 12815 • Certificate of Achievement
Recognizes contribution to the goals of LAMA. Nominees must be individual members of the association. Nomination deadline is December 1. Completed nomination form should be sent to Karen Muller, Exec. Dir., at the above address.

• 12816 • John Cotton Dana Library Public Relations Awards

To recognize libraries or library organizations of all types for outstanding public relations programs. All libraries, agencies, and associations promoting library service are eligible. Institutions represented by John Cotton Award judges and organizational unites of the American Library Association and H. W. Wilson Co. are not eligible. Two copies of the official application form, with the original signed by the Library Director; a concise summary of the project; and a concise description of the project, including needs assessment, planning, implementation and evaluation phases must be submitted in a binder or presentation book. Formerly: John Cotton Dana Publicity Award.

• 12817 • LAMA Cultural Diversity Grant

Recognizes cultural diversity programs. Applicants must be LAMA unit or individual members. Four copies of a description of the proposed project, including outcomes and target audience; explanation of how this project meets the LAMA cultural diversity goals; description of the need for the project; evidence of support and commitment to complete the project; a description of the target audience; a description of how the project will be evaluated; and a proposed budget must be submitted. A statement of endorsement from the Committee Chair and Section Chair may also be submitted. Application deadline is December 1.

• 12818 • LAMA President's Award

Recognizes contributions to the goals of LAMA. Nominees must be individuals who are not members of LAMA. Nomination deadline is December 1. Completed forms must be sent to Karen Muller, Exec. Dir., at the above address.

• 12819 • Library Buildings Award Program

To encourage excellence in the architectural design and planning of libraries. Awards for distinguished accomplishments in library architecture by an American architect are made to all types of libraries in the United States and abroad. Awards are given in the following categories: new buildings, additions, renovations/restorations, conversions to library use, and interior redesign and refurnishing. Submission are made in the following two part method: An entry slip and fee $200 for each building entered must be submitted to the American Institute of Architects at the address below. Upon receipt of the slip and fee, a receipt and submission package will be forwarded to the applicants. All materials must be enclosed in a uniform 8 x 11 binder with transparent window sleeves for displaying 24 inserts, back to back. This binder will be included in the packet sent by the AIA. Entry slip submission deadline is November 17. Project submission deadline is December 15. Certificates are presented to the architects and the directors of all winning libraries during the ALA Annual Conference. Administered jointly by the American Institute of Architects, Library Buildings Awards Program, 1735 New York Ave., NW, Washington, DC 20006-5292. and the Library Administration and Management Association Division of the American Library Association.

• 12820 • Recognition of Group Achievement Award

Recognizes committee or task force teamwork supporting the goals of the association. Application deadline is December 1. Completed material should be sent to Karen Muller, Exec. Dir. at the above address.

• 12821 • Student Writing and Development Award

Recognizes an article on a topic relating to library administration and management and enhances the professional development os students of library and information studies. Applicants must be students enrolled in a library and information studies graduate program at an ALA accredited school; be a current student member of ALA and LAMA or join prior to acceptance of the award. Selection is based on the quality and appropriateness of the manuscripts based on relevance to the announced theme, applicability to more than one library setting, originality, persuasiveness of arguments, quality of writing, clarity of presentation, and contribution to the continuing education of the LAMA membership. An original manuscript of 4000 to 6000 words, a completed application form signed by the Dean or Director of the ALA accredited program of library and information studies in which the applicant is enrolled must be submitted in print form and on diskette. Application deadline is March 31. All material should be sent to Shonda Russell at the above address.

• 12822 •
Library and Information Technology Association
Mary C. Taylor, Exec.Dir.
50 E Huron St.
Chicago, IL 60611-2795
Phone: (312)280-4268
Phone: (312)280-4267
Toll-Free: 800-545-2433
Fax: (312)280-3257
E-mail: lita@ala.org
Home Page: http://www.lita.org

• 12823 • LITA/Gaylord Award for Achievement in Library and Information Technology

To recognize distinguished leadership and achievement in library and information technology, notable development or application of technology, superior accomplishments in research or education, or original contributions to the literature of the field. A monetary award of $1,000 and a certificate are awarded annually. Established in 1979. Sponsored by Gaylord Brothers, Inc. Formerly: LITA Award for Achievement in Library and Information Technology.

• 12824 • Frederick G. Kilgour Award for Research in Library and Information Technology

Recognizes research into the development of information technologies. The focus is on works showing promise of a positive and substantive impact on any aspect of the publication, storage, retrieval and dissemination of information, or the processes by which information and data is manipulated and managed. Preference is given to completed research over works in progress. Applicants must be ALA members. $2000 and expenses to the ALA conference are awarded. Sponsored by OCLC Online Computer Center, Inc. Established in 1998.

• 12825 • LITA/Christian Larew Memorial Scholarship in Library and Information Technology

Encourages people to entry the library science field. Applicants must show academic excellence, leadership, and a vision in pursuit of library and information technology. $3000 is awarded annually. Established in 1999.

• 12826 • LITA/Endeavor Student Writing Award

Recognizes student writing in the field of libraries and information technology. Works must be unpublished and written by a student enrolled in an ALA-accredited library and information studies graduate program. $1000 and a certificate are awarded. Application deadline is March 31. Established in 2000.

• 12827 • LITA/GEAC Scholarship in Library and Information Technology

To encourage the entry of qualified persons into the library automation field who plan to follow a career in the field and who evidence leadership in, and a strong commitment to, the use of automated systems in libraries. A monetary award of $2,500 is made to a student at the master's degree level in an ALA-accredited program in library and information science, with emphasis on library automation.

• 12828 • LITA/Library Hi Tech Award

To recognize an individual or institution for a single seminal work or a body of work that demonstrates outstanding communication for continuing education of practitioners in library of information technology. Print and non-print publications, including articles, books, course plans or actual courses, visual media, hypermedia, and others must have been completed or ongoing during the five-year period preceding the presentation of the award. The deadline for nominations is December 15. A $1,000 stipend and a plaque are awarded each year at the LITA President's Program during the annual conference of the American Library Association. Established in 1993.

• 12829 • LITA-LSSI Minority Scholarship in Library and Information Technology

To encourage a member of principal minority groups with a strong commitment to library automation to choose library automation as a career. U.S. or Canadian citizens who are enrolled at or accepted in an ALA-accredited master's degree program and who are members of a principal minority may apply by April 1. A scholarship of $2,500 is awarded annually, usually midsummer. Established in 1994.

• 12830 • LITA/OCLC Minority Scholarship in Library and Information Technology

To encourage a member of principal minority groups with a strong commitment to library automation to choose library automation as a career. U.S. or Canadian citizens who are enrolled at or accepted in an ALA-accredited master's degree program and who are members of a principal minority may apply by April 1. A scholarship of $3,000 is awarded annually, usually midsummer. Established in 1990.

• 12831 •
Library of Congress
101 Independence Ave. SE
Washington, DC 20540-1610
Phone: (202)707-5000
Fax: (202)707-9199
E-mail: pao@loc.gov
Home Page: http://www.loc.gov

• 12832 • Rebekah Johnson Bobbitt National Prize for Poetry

To recognize an American poet for the best book of poetry published during the preceding two years. With this award, the United States joins Great Britain, France, and other countries in honoring poetry by presenting a prize on behalf of the nation. Submissions are only accepted from publishers. Authors must be living U.S. citizens. Authors' first poetry books or books composed of new work qualify; collected and selected works qualify only if they include at least 30 new poems previously unpublished in book form. To be considered for this Prize, a "book" is defined as a collection of printed leaves that have been folded, secured by adhesive along the binding edge (perfect binding; no saddle-stitched or stapled binding), and bound. It must be published in a standard edition of not less than 1,000 copies. A monetary award of $10,000 is presented at an invitational reception, followed by a public reading by the author from the winning book. Awarded biennially in even-numbered years. Established in 1990 by the family of the late Rebekah Johnson Bobbitt of Austin, Texas. Additional information is available from Jennifer Rutland, Poetry Office, phone: (202) 707-5394.

• 12833 • J. Franklin Jameson Fellowship in American History

To recognize an outstanding American historian and to support significant scholarly research by young students of American history and culture in the collection at the Library of Congress. Established in 1978 to honor J. Franklin Jameson, a founder of the American Historical Association, Chief of the Library's Manuscript Division (1928-37), and first incumbent in the Library's Chair of American History. Supported jointly by the Library of Congress and the American Historical Association.

• 12834 • Poet Laureate, Consultant in Poetry

To recognize an outstanding American poet. The Poet Laureate seeks to raise national consciousness to a greater appreciation of the reading and writing of poetry. The Laureate receives a $35,000 annual stipend funded by a gift from Archer M. Huntington.

• 12835 •
Library Public Relations Council
Kay Cassell, Membership Chm.
2565 Broadway, No. 532
New York, NY 10025
E-mail: info@libraryprcouncil.org

• 12836 • "L. PeRCy" Awards

For recognition of outstanding publicity materials produced by libraries. The awards are given in two divisions, libraries serving areas of 65,000 population and up, and libraries serving populations of less than 65,000. Awards are presented in categories determined each year. Awards are presented annually at the American Library Association Convention. Formerly: Library Public Relations Council Award.

• 12837 • Share the Wealth Packets

To recognize innovative and effective public relations work by libraries. Certificates of Merit are awarded, and packets of selected items are sent to all members and are on view at the ALA annual meeting.

• 12838 •
Liederkranz Foundation
Dr. Hans G. Hachmann, Pres.
6 E 87th St.
New York, NY 10128
Phone: (212)534-0880
Fax: (212)828-5372
E-mail: info@liederkranznycity.org
Home Page: http://www.liederkranznycity.org

• 12839 • Liederkranz Scholarship Awards Competitions

To encourage the career development of singers. Age requirements are: general voice ages 20-35; Wagnerian voice ages 25-45. Entries must be post marked by November 15th. Between 1000 and 6000 are awarded annually. Applications must be requested by October. A self-addressed envelope must be included with application requests.

• 12840 •
Life Coalition International
(Te Roopu Whaka Waihanga Iwi O Aotearoa)
Keith Tucci, Contact
PO Box 360221
Dept. of Geography
University of Waikato
Private Bag 3105
Melbourne, FL 32936-0221
Phone: (321)726-0444
E-mail: patatlci@yahoo.com
Home Page: http://www.lifecoalition.com

• 12841 • Statistics New Zealand/Jacoby Prize

Recognizes the best essay written during a course of university study on a population topic. Awarded annually. The cash prize is $250 with a copy of the latest New Zealand official yearbook and demographic trends, plus a year's membership of Panz and publication of the winning essay in the New Zealand population review. Formerly: (2004) Jacoby Prize.

• 12842 •
Life Office Management Association
Thomas P. Donaldson, Pres.
2300 Windy Ridge Pky., Ste. 600
Atlanta, GA 30339-8443
Phone: (770)951-1770
Toll-Free: 800-275-5662
Fax: (770)984-0441
E-mail: marketing@loma.org
Home Page: http://www.loma.org

• 12843 • Excellence in Education Award

For recognition of outstanding achievement in developing human resources through the Fellow, Life Management Institute (FLMI) Insurance Program. Participating LOMA member companies and their educational representatives responsible for on-site administration of the FLMI Program are nominated. Awards are presented to both the participating company and the company educational representative at the annual conference held in September. Established in 1991.

• 12844 • FLMI Insurance Education Award

For recognition of a significant national contribution to insurance education. Distinguished insurance educators or administrators connected with insurance education programs are nominated for lifelong and enduring contributions to the enhancement of insurance education. A plaque and transportation to LOMA's annual conference are awarded at the annual conference. Awarded annually when merited. Established in 1980.

• 12845 • Outstanding Society Awards

For recognition of fellow societies that demonstrate outstanding performance in the areas of society management, society membership, communication, educational support of students, continuing education, and community service. Individual societies petition LOMA for the awards based upon society activity for the year. Awards for the previous calendar year are presented each spring. Established in 1987.

Awards are arranged in alphabetical order below their administering organizations

• 12846 •
Lifespan/Tufts/Brown Center for AIDS Research
The Miriam Hospital
Brown University
CFAR Immunology Center, RISE Bldg.
164 Summit Ave.
Providence, RI 02906
Phone: (401)793-4068
Fax: (401)793-4704
E-mail: vgodleski@lifespan.org
Home Page: http://www.ltbcfar.org

• 12847 • **Developmental Awards**
Faculty at Brown or Tufts are eligible. Inquire for application details.

• 12848 •
Lighter-Than-Air Society
Joseph C. Huber Jr., Chm.
526 S Main St., Ste. 232
Akron, OH 44311
Phone: (330)535-5827
Phone: (330)535-0100
Fax: (330)668-1105
E-mail: suggest@blimpinfo.com
Home Page: http://www.blimpinfo.com

Formerly: Wingfoot Lighter than Air Society.

• 12849 • **Achievement Award**
To recognize an individual or team who has succeeded in some outstanding lighter than air endeavor during the previous year. A plaque is awarded annually. Established in 1954. Other awards presented by the Society are the Van Orman Trophy, the Lambacher Trophy, the Montgolfier Trophy and Honorary Life Member.

• 12850 •
James F. Lincoln Arc Welding Foundation
Carl Peters, Exec.Dir.
PO Box 17188
Cleveland, OH 44117-1199
Phone: (216)481-4300
Fax: (216)486-1751
Home Page: http://www.jflf.org

• 12851 • **Awards for Achievement in Arc Welded Design, and Engineering and Fabrication**
For recognition of innovative ideas in welded design, engineering, fabrication, or welding procedures and processes that reduce costs or achieve other noteworthy design objectives. Criteria considered for the award are: ingenuity and innovation, practicality, results achieved, and the contribution of arc welding. Individuals or groups of no more than three persons working as a design, engineering, research, fabricating, production, or maintenance group must submit an entry by May 1. Government officials are ineligible. Monetary awards ranging from $500 to $10,000 are presented, including Best of Program Award - $10,000; Gold Award - $5,000; two Silver Awards - $2,500 each; three Bronze Awards - $1,500 each; and 15 Merit Awards - $500 each. Awarded annually. Established in 1934. Formerly: James F. Lincoln Arc Welding Design and Engineering Awards Program.

• 12852 •
Lincoln Center for the Performing Arts
Reynold Levy, Pres.
140 W 65th St.
New York, NY 10023
Phone: (212)875-5000
Fax: (212)875-5185
E-mail: webmaster@lincolncenter.org
Home Page: http://www.lincolncenter.org

• 12853 • **Directors Emeriti Award**
To recognize one or more staff members and a volunteer for outstanding and dedicated service to Lincoln Center for the Performing Arts. Two monetary prizes of $5,000 each are awarded annually. Established in 1987 by Lawrence Wien, past Chairman of the Directors Emeriti Council.

• 12854 • **Avery Fisher Career Grants**
To give professional assistance and recognition to talented instrumentalists who have potential for solo careers. A monetary award of $10,000 is made available to each recipient to be used for specific needs in the furtherance of their careers. Applicants must be U.S. citizens. Up to five Grants may be given each year.

• 12855 • **Avery Fisher Prize**
To recognize artists for outstanding achievement and excellence in music. A monetary award of $25,000 is given to solo instrumentalists who are U.S. citizens. There is no specific age limit. A marble plaque in Avery Fisher Hall bears the names of all Prize recipients.

• 12856 • **Martin E. Segal Award**
To help inspire Lincoln Center's deep commitment to developing new works, to support today's creative young performers and further their studies, and to build the audiences of tomorrow. Consideration is given to artists within the Lincoln Center family or a program generated by a Lincoln Center constituent. Two monetary prizes of $5,000 each are awarded annually in May. Established in 1986 in honor of Martin E. Segal, Lincoln Center Chairman Emeritus.

• 12857 •
Lincoln Forum
Annette Westerby, Admin.
14 Blue Heron Dr. W
Greenwood Village, CO 80121
Phone: (401)364-3642
Phone: (303)721-6681
Fax: (401)222-1351
E-mail: anetwest@earthlink.net
Home Page: http://www.thelincolnforum.org

• 12858 • **Chuck and Linda Pratt Essay Award of the Lincoln Forum**
Based on essay competition. Monetary award bestowed annually.

• 12859 •
Lincoln Group of New York
Joseph Edward Garrera, Pres.
PO Box 220
Newton, NJ 07860
Phone: (973)383-9304
Phone: (973)383-7178
Fax: (973)383-7178
Home Page: http://www.lincolngroupny.org

• 12860 • **National Award of Achievement**
For best Lincoln accomplishment in the country each year. Recognition award bestowed annually.

• 12861 •
Lincoln Lancaster Women's Commission
Bonnie Coffey, Dir.
440 S 8th St., Ste. 100
Lincoln, NE 68508-2294
Phone: (402)441-7716
Fax: (402)441-6824
E-mail: bcoffey@ci.lincoln.ne.us

• 12862 • **Erasmus Correll Award**
For outstanding feminist activities by a male. Recognition award bestowed annually.

• 12863 • **Alice Paul Award**
For outstanding feminist activists. Recognition award bestowed annually.

• 12864 • **Women's Artist Award**
For outstanding female artists. Recognition award bestowed annually.

• 12865 •
Lincoln University of Missouri
Department of Communications
Don Govang, Awards Chair
820 Chestnut St.
Jefferson City, MO 65101
Phone: (573)681-5196
Toll-Free: 800-521-5052
Fax: (573)681-5040
E-mail: govangd@lincolnu.edu

• 12866 • **Unity Awards in Media**
To recognize the media for excellence in reporting on issues affecting the rights and well-being of the handicapped and/or minorities. Entries may be submitted from print and broadcast media in the United States in the following categories: reporting of economics, editorial writing, education, investigative reporting, and politics and public affairs/social issues reporting. The contest is open to any print or broadcast person working for a recognized daily, weekly, monthly or quarterly publication including newspapers and magazines as well as radio and television stations. Submissions are evaluated in both regional and national categories. A trophy is presented annually. Established in 1949 by Armistead S. Pride, Professor Emeritus of Journalism and former Head of the Department. Formerly: (1974) Headliner Awards.

• 12867 •
Linguistic Association of Canada and the United States
Lilly Lee Chen, Sec.-Treas.
Center for the Study of Languages, MS 36
Rice University
Houston, TX 77251-1892
Phone: (713)348-2820
Fax: (713)348-5846
E-mail: lchen@ruf.rice.edu
Home Page: http://www.lacus.org

• 12868 • **Presidents' Prize**
To recognize the paper presented at the Association's Annual Forum meeting that makes the greatest contribution to knowledge by a single author who has not yet achieved tenure. An author must be a member of the Association and must submit a paper abstract in the normal manner. If the paper is selected to be presented at the annual meeting, and the author has not yet achieved tenure at that time, his paper will automatically be considered for the prize. A monetary prize of $500 and a certificate are awarded annually when merited at the Forum meeting in August. A certificate is also awarded for the President's Commendation. Established in 1986.

• 12869 •
Link Foundation
Dr. Cheryl Dimick, Contact
PO Box 6005
Dartmouth College
Binghamton, NY 13902-6005
Phone: (603)646-2674
Phone: (607)777-6757
Fax: (407)658-5059
E-mail: thompson@ist.ucf.edu
Home Page: http://www.binghamton.edu/home/link/link.html

• 12870 • **Link Foundation Energy Fellowship Program**
To foster energy research; to enhance both the theoretical and practical knowledge and application of energy research; and to disseminate the results of that research through lectures, seminars, and publications. Preference is shown to proposals dealing directly with energy and exploring ideas not yet fully tested rather than to developed programs already in progress. However, in keeping with the founders' philosophy, ideas that can be implemented in the relatively near term are given first priority. Doctoral students may apply. The deadline for application is December 1. A grant of $25,000 is awarded towrads a 2-year fellowship for students working towards a Ph.D.

• 12871 •
Lipizzan Association of North America
Mrs. Sandy Heaberlin, Dir.
PO Box 1133
Anderson, IN 46015-1133
Phone: (765)644-3904
Fax: (765)641-1205
E-mail: lipizzan@lipizzan.org
Home Page: http://www.lipizzan.org

• 12872 • **United States Dressage Federation All Breed Award**
Annual award of recognition.

• 12873 •
Literary Translators Association of Canada (Association des Traducteurs et Traductrices Litteraires du Canada)
Kathleen Merken, Membership Sec.
Concordia University-SB 335
1455 de Maisonneuve Blvd. W
Montreal, QC, Canada H3G 1M8
Phone: (514)848-8702
E-mail: info@attlc-ltac.org
Home Page: http://www.attlc-ltac.org

• 12874 • **John Glassco Translation Prize**
Recognizes a translator of a full-length novel into English or French. Awarded annually.

• 12875 •
Lithuanian American Roman Catholic Women's Alliance
Dale Murray, Pres.
3005 N 124th St.
Brookfield, WI 53005
Phone: (262)786-7359
Phone: (630)573-0066
Fax: (262)786-7359

• 12876 • **Outstanding Lithuanian Woman Award**
For national recognition of contributions to Lithuanian causes and the community. Activities considered include religion, human rights, cultural and community contributions, and professional development. Non-members may be recommended. A plaque is awarded biennially. Established in 1977. Formerly: (1992) Lithuanian Catholic Women.

• 12877 •
Little Big Horn Associates
Joan Croy, Sec.-Treas.
6200 Blanchett Rd.
Newport, MI 48166
Phone: (304)744-4263
Phone: (304)345-1400
Fax: (304)343-1826
E-mail: lbha@cox.net
Home Page: http://www.lbha.org

• 12878 • **John M. Carroll Literary Award**
To recognize the author of a book on "Custeriana," the life and times of Gen. George A. Custer. The author must have done original research which provides new evidence, new concepts, and historical accuracy as primary factors in the book. Books copyrighted or made generally available during the award year are eligible. A plaque is awarded annually at the convention. Established in 1983.

• 12879 • **Dr. Lawrence A. Frost Award**
To recognize the author of an outstanding article appearing in Little Big Horn Associates' publications, *Research Review* or *Newsletter*. Articles must relate to Gen. George A. Custer, his life or his times, and contain evidence of original historical research or new concepts and must have appeared in the above publications during the year of the award. A plaque is awarded annually at the convention. Established in 1983.

• 12880 •
Little Mouse Club
Wanda Wilson, Founder & Facilitator
603 Brandt Ave.
New Cumberland, PA 17070
Phone: (717)774-1778
Fax: (717)712-0811
E-mail: littlemouseclub@yahoo.com
Home Page: http://www.geocities.com/Heartland/Ranch/3220/main.html

• 12881 • **Best American Mouse Award**
Semiannual award of recognition. A trophy and rosette ribbon are presented.

• 12882 • **Best English Mouse Award**
Semiannual award trophy and Rossette Ribbon are awarded.

• 12883 • **Best In Show Award**
Semiannual award rosette ribbon and trophy are awarded.

• 12884 • **Best Pet Mouse Award**
Semiannual award of recognition. A trophy and rosette ribbon are presented.

• 12885 •
Little People of America
Tricia Mason, Pres.
5289 NE Elam Young Pkwy., Ste. F-100
Hillsboro, OR 97124
Phone: (503)846-1562
Toll-Free: 888-LPA-2001
Fax: (503)846-1590
E-mail: info@lpaonline.org
Home Page: http://www.lpaonline.org

• 12886 • **Distinguished Service Award**
Recognizes service and outstanding contributions to LPA. Awarded annually.

• 12887 •
Little Theatre of Alexandria
Russell Wyland, Pres.
600 Wolfe St.
Alexandria, VA 22314
Phone: (703)683-5778
Fax: (703)683-1378
E-mail: asklta@thelittletheatre.com
Home Page: http://www.thelittletheatre.com

• 12888 • **Little Theatre of Alexandria National One-Act Playwriting Competition**
For recognition of excellence in writing one-act plays. Original, unpublished, unproduced one-act play scripts are eligible. All scripts must be postmarked by May 31st and include a $20 registration fee. Only stage plays are eligible.

Scripts are evaluated on concept, structure, character development and dialogue. Preference is given to scripts that have a running time of 20 to 60 minutes, those with few scenes and only one set, and when a precis of the play precedes abstract works. The following monetary awards are presented: first prize - $350; second prize - $250; and third prize - $150. Established in 1978 by A. Weisbrod, founder. Formerly: (1985) Weisbrod One-Act Competition.

• 12889 •
Live Free Inc.
6672 Baltimore Pike
Littlestown, PA 17340
Toll-Free: 800-707-0302
Fax: (717)359-0220
E-mail: livefree@livefreeonline.com
Home Page: http://www.livefreeonline.com

• 12890 • **Life and Freedom Award**
To recognize an individual who has made an outstanding contribution to the preservation of human life and individual freedom through survival/self-sufficiency research and education. Normally only members of Live Free are eligible, but in special cases, non-members are eligible. A certificate is awarded annually when merited. Established in 1978.

• 12891 •
Live Theatre League of Tarrant County
Linda M. Lee, Treas.
3505 W Lancaster Ave.
Fort Worth, TX 76107
Phone: (817)731-2238
Fax: (817)731-2239
E-mail: livetheatreleague@yahoo.com
Home Page: http://www.livetheatreleague.org

• 12892 • **Elston Brook Lifetime Achievement Award**
For service to theater. Recognition award bestowed annually.

• 12893 • **Corporate Award**
For service to theater. Recognition award bestowed annually.

• 12894 • **Patron of the Year Award**
For service to theater. Recognition award bestowed annually.

• 12895 •
Livestock Publications Council
Diane E. Johnson, Exec.Dir.
910 Currie St.
Fort Worth, TX 76107
Phone: (817)336-1130
Fax: (817)232-4820
E-mail: dianej@flash.net
Home Page: http://www.livestockpublications.com

• 12896 • **Forrest Bassford Student Award**
To recognize achievements of sophomore and junior college students majoring in agricultural journalism. A $1,500 CME scholarship, a plaque, travel expenses to attend and participate in the Council's annual meeting, workshop, and Publications Contest Illustrated Critique are awarded annually. Up to three other students each receive $500 travel scholarship to attend the Ag Publications Summit. Established in 1985.

• 12897 • **Hall of Fame Award**
To honor distinguished livestock publishing leaders with induction into a Hall of Fame. This honor is reserved for those who have adhered to high standards of professionalism in all aspects of their endeavors. Length of service, while important, is not the dominant criterion for this honor. More important are such factors as industry and professional leadership, quality and importance of editorial content, quality of writing and graphics, efficiency of distribution, reputation for integrity, and personnel development. Established in 1990.

• 12898 • **Headliner Award**
To recognize an individual from outside the livestock publishing field for actions that have produced positive changes in livestock production and marketing, or in product marketing (i.e. meat, milk, wool, etc.) within the last five years. Awarded annually. Established in 1980.

• 12899 •
Livingston County Council on Alcohol and Substance Abuse
Rodney V. Evans MPS, Exec.Dir.
Holcomb Bldg. Ste. 2
30 Commercial St.
Geneseo, NY 14454
Phone: (585)243-9210
Phone: (585)243-9236
Fax: (585)243-9235
E-mail: edlccasa@frontiernet.net
Home Page: http://www.casa-livingston.org

• 12900 • **Community Service Award**
For individual who demonstrates commitment to support mission of agency. Recognition award bestowed annually.

• 12901 •
Locus Publications
Mark R. Kelly, Ed.
PO Box 13305
Oakland, CA 94661
Phone: (510)339-9196
Phone: (510)339-9198
Fax: (510)339-8144
E-mail: locus@locusmag.com
Home Page: http://www.locusmag.com

• 12902 • **Locus Awards**
To recognize outstanding science fiction. The readers of *Locus* vote for the winners. Awards are presented in the following categories: Anthology, Art Book, Artist, Collection, Fantasy Novel, First Novel, Magazine, Nonfiction, Novelette, Novella, Publisher, Science Fiction Novel, Short Story, Horror Novel/Dark Fantasy, and Editor. A trophy and a subscription to *Locus* are awarded annually at a banquet July 4th weekend. Established in 1971.

• 12903 •
The Loft Literary Center
Linda Myers, Exec.Dir.
1011 Washington Ave. S, Ste. 200
Minneapolis, MN 55415
Phone: (612)215-2575
Fax: (612)215-2576
E-mail: loft@loft.org
Home Page: http://www.loft.org
Formerly: (2003) The Loft, A Place for Writing and Literature.

• 12904 • **Loft Creative Nonfiction Award**
To provide six area writers with the opportunity to work with a nationally-known creative prose writer. During the four week program, the resident writer works with the area writers in an intensive seminar and participates in panels and readings in the Twin Cities and elsewhere in the state. Midwest writers who live close enough to the Twin Cities to participate fully in the four-week program are eligible. Six monetary stipends of $250 each are awarded annually. Established in 1985.

• 12905 • **Loft Mentor Series Award**
To provide twelve area writers of poetry and fiction with advanced criticism and professional development opportunities by bringing four nationally-known writers to the Twin Cities for three-day residencies, and having a local mentor work with the program group for the year. The mentors give public readings (with the mentor series winners) and workshops, and work extensively with the contest winners. Minnesota writers are eligible. Twelve monetary stipends of $500 each are awarded annually to the winners. Established in 1979.

• 12906 • **McKnight Artist Fellowships for Writers**
To recognize Minnesota writers and to give Minnesota writers of demonstrated ability an opportunity to work for a concentrated period of time on their writing. Writers who are residents of Minnesota (as determined by income tax return or driver's license) may apply. Five "Loft Awards" of $25,000 each are awarded annually, in prose and poetry. Established in 1981. Formerly: (1997) Loft-McKnight Award.

• 12907 •
Log Cabin Society of Michigan
Ms. Virginia M. Handy, Contact
3503 Rock Edwards Rd.
Sodus, MI 49126-8700
Phone: (269)925-3836
Fax: (269)925-3836
E-mail: logcabincrafts@qtm.net
Home Page: http://www.qtm.net/logcabincrafts

• 12908 • Lenehan Log Cabin Photography Competition

For high quality photos of log cabins suitable for publication in state and national periodicals and books, and for calendars. Monetary award bestowed annually.

• 12909 •
London Club
Dennis A. Baranski, Chm.
214 North 2100
Lecompton, KS 66050

• 12910 • London Club Award

To recognize research by a member in the field of unsolved crime. A plaque is awarded irregularly. Established in 1975.

• 12911 •
Long Branch Historical Association
JoAnn Levin, Corresponding Sec.
475 Bath Ave.
Long Branch, NJ 07740-6034
Phone: (732)229-9258
Fax: (732)229-2003

• 12912 • Black History Month Contest

For school children in Long Branch who write the best essay on African American contributions and their effects on his/her life. Monetary award bestowed annually.

• 12913 •
Long Island University, Brooklyn Campus
Gale Stevens Haynes, Provost
1 University Plz.
Brooklyn, NY 11201-8423
Phone: (718)488-1011
Fax: (718)780-4065
Home Page: http://www.brooklyn.liu.edu

• 12914 • Martin Luther King Award

No further information was provided for this edition.

• 12915 • George Polk Awards

To recognize journalistic achievement in print and broadcast journalism. In print journalism, awards are given in the following categories: (1) foreign reporting; (2) national reporting; (3) local reporting; (4) regional reporting; (5) metropolitan reporting; (6) business or economic reporting; (7) environmental reporting; (8) special publications; (9) photojournalism; (10) medical reporting; and (11) political reporting. In broadcast journalism, awards are given in the following categories: (1) network television reporting; (2) local television reporting; and (3) documentaruy reporting. In addition, the Career Award is presented. Plaques are awarded annually. Established in 1948 by Long Island University to honor George Polk, a CBS correspondent who was slain in 1948 during the Greek Civil War while trying to reach insurgent leaders for an interview. Formerly: George Polk Memorial Awards.

• 12916 •
LoonWatch
Sigurd Olson Environmental Institute
Northland College
1411 Ellis Ave.
Ashland, WI 54806-3999
Phone: (715)682-1699
Fax: (715)682-1218
E-mail: loonwatch@northland.edu
Home Page: http://www.northland.edu/soei/loonwatch.asp

• 12917 • Sigurd T. Olson Common Loon Research Award

To provide funds for research on Common Loons in the Lake Superior-Lake Michigan region of the United States and Canada. The award is granted on the basis of the project's potential to better understand and manage Upper Great Lakes populations of Common Loons. Proposals must be submitted by January 10. A monetary award of up to $1,000 is presented annually. Established in 1986.

• 12918 •
Lucille Lortel Theatre
George Forbes, Exec.Dir.
322 8th Ave., 21st. Fl.
New York, NY 10001
Phone: (212)924-2817
Fax: (212)989-0036
E-mail: nbeer@lortel.org
Home Page: http://www.lortel.org

• 12919 • Lucille Lortel Award

To recognize outstanding achievement Off-Broadway. Members of the New York Off-Broadway theatre community are eligible. An etched trophy is awarded annually. Established in 1986 to honor Lucille Lortel. Sponsored by the League of Off-Broadway Theatres and Producers.

• 12920 •
Los Alamos National Laboratory
Manuel Lujan, Jr. Neutron Scattering Center
Mail Stop H805
PO Box 1663
Los Alamos, NM 87545
Phone: (505)665-0630
Fax: (505)665-2676
E-mail: lansce-users@lanl.gov
Home Page: http://lansce.lanl.gov/lujan/index_lujan.htm

• 12921 • Rosen Prize

Awarded for outstanding thesis.

• 12922 •
Los Angeles Advertising Agencies Association
Susan Franceschini, Exec.Dir.
4223 Glencoe Ave., Ste. C-100
Marina del Rey, CA 90292
Phone: (310)823-7320
Fax: (310)823-7325
E-mail: submissions@laaaa.com
Home Page: http://www.laaaa.com

Formerly: (2002) Western States Advertising Agencies Association.

• 12923 • Advertising Leader of the Year Award

For outstanding contributions to the advertising industry in the Los Angeles community. A plaque, silver bowl, or other appropriate piece is awarded annually. Established in 1957.

• 12924 •
Los Angeles Athletic Club
Steve Hathaway, Gen.Mgr.
431 W 7th St.
Los Angeles, CA 90014
Phone: (213)625-2211
Toll-Free: 800-421-8777
Fax: (213)892-0646
E-mail: laac@laac.net
Home Page: http://www.laac.com

• 12925 • John R. Wooden Award

To recognize the nation's most outstanding collegiate male basketball player, the Collegiate All-American Team, and the Southern California area High School Most Valuable Players. Recipients are selected by a panel of 1,000 sportscasters and sportswriters from 50 states. The top fifteen candidates on the ballot are selected by the National Advisory Board according to the criteria. Emphasis is placed on scholastic merits and being the complete player. The following awards are presented: All American Trophy and All American jackets are presented to ten top members of the All American Team and a monetary prize of $2,000 to the school of the top four players who attend the event for the general scholarship fund; the John R. Wooden Trophy to the Outstanding Collegiate Basketball Player - a five figured bronze trophy, a monetary prize of $4,000 to the school's general scholarship fund, and a duplicate trophy to the school are awarded to the male Player of the Year; and the John R. Wooden Most Valuable High School Player Award - plaques and monetary prizes of $500 to each recipient's school for their athletic fund are awarded to outstanding players in five California Southern Section Divisions and two Los Angeles City Divisions. Awarded annually. Established in 1976 to honor UCLA Coach John R. Wooden, a two time inductee of the Basketball Hall of Fame.

• 12926 •
Los Angeles Conservancy
523 W 6th St., Ste. 826
Los Angeles, CA 90014-1218
Phone: (213)623-2489
Phone: (213)430-4219
Fax: (213)623-3909
E-mail: info@laconservancy.org
Home Page: http://www.laconservancy.org

• 12927 • **Preservation Award**
For noteworthy restoration of an historical building. Recognition award bestowed annually.

• 12928 •
Los Angeles Public Library
Evelyn Hoffman, Exec.Dir/
630 W 5th St.
Los Angeles, CA 90071
Phone: (213)228-7000
Fax: (213)228-7069
E-mail: children@lapl.org
Home Page: http://www.lapl.org

• 12929 • **FOCAL Award**
To recognize an author or illustrator for excellence in a creative work which enriches a child's appreciation for and knowledge of California. The FOCAL Award is a hand-crafted puppet representing one of the characters in the honoree's work. A duplicate puppet is presented to the Children's Literature Department of the Los Angeles Public Library. Presented annually. Established in 1980.

• 12930 •
***Los Angeles Times* Book Prizes**
Tom Crouch, Administrator
202 W 1st St.
Los Angeles, CA 90012
Phone: (213)237-5775
Toll-Free: 800-LA-TIMES
E-mail: tom.crouch@latimes.com
Home Page: http://www.latimes.com/bookprizes

• 12931 • ***Los Angeles Times* Book Prizes**
To honor achievement in literature by recognizing writers who have demonstrated outstanding craftsmanship and vision. The best book and four finalists are selected in each of nine categories: biography; current interest; fiction; first fiction (the Art Seidenbaum Award, named for the late founder of the book prize program); history; mystery/thriller; poetry; science and technology; and young adult fiction. In addition, the Robert Kirsch Award, named for the late Times book critic, recognizes an outstanding body of work by an author living in and/or writing about the American West. Hardcover or soft-cover books having their first U.S. publication between January 1 and December 31 each year are eligible. This U.S. publication must be in English, but English does not have to be the original language of the work. Writers, who may be of any nationality, should be alive at the time of their book's qualifying American publication, although eligibility is also extended to significant new translations of the work of deceased writers. Nominations and selections are made by independent, appointed panels of judges; submissions are not accepted. A citation and $1000 are awarded annually in April of the following year to each category winner and to the Kirsch Award recipient. Established in 1980.

• 12932 •
Louisiana Grain and Feed Association
Brent Bordelon, Pres.
PO Box 12360
Alexandria, LA 71315-2360
Phone: (318)442-0971
Fax: (318)443-2802

• 12933 • **LGFF Scholarship Award**
For graduating H.S. senior with parent working for member companies in state of LA. Scholarship awarded annually.

• 12934 •
Louisiana Library Association
Beverly E. Laughlin, Exec.Dir.
421 S 4th St.
Eunice, LA 70535
Phone: (337)550-7890
Toll-Free: 877-550-7890
Fax: (337)550-7846
E-mail: office@llaonline.org
Home Page: http://www.llaonline.org

• 12935 • **Alex P. Alain Intellectual Freedom Award**
To recognize the contribution of an individual or group in actively promoting intellectual freedom in Louisiana. An engraved plaque; cash awards provided by Social Issues Resources Series, Inc. in the amount of $500 to the award recipient and $500 for materials to the library of the recipient's choice; and expenses to attend the conference are awarded annually. Established in 1991. Sponsored by Social Issues Resources Series. Formerly: Intellectual Freedom Award.

• 12936 • **Anthony H. Benoit Mid-Career Award**
To recognize a Louisiana librarian with ten to twenty years of professional experience who has made outstanding contributions to the field of librarianship. An engraved plaque is awarded annually. Established in 1979. Sponsored by the New Members Round Table. Renamed in 1992 to honor the memory of Anthony H. Benoit, 1984-85 LLA President. Formerly: NMRT Mid-Career Award.

• 12937 • **Essae M. Culver Distinguished Service Award**
To recognize a professional member of the Louisiana Library Association whose service and achievements have been of particular value to Louisiana librarianship. An engraved medallion is awarded when merited. Established in 1964 in honor of Essae M. Culver, the first Louisiana state librarian.

• 12938 • **Lucy B. Foote Award**
To honor an LLA member who has made a substantial contribution to the library profession through the field of special librarianship. An engraved plaque is awarded annually. Established in 1981 in honor of Lucy B. Foote (1893-1973), a pioneering bibliographer of Louisiana state documents. Sponsored by the Subject Specialists Section.

• 12939 • **Sue Hefley Educator of the Year Award**
To recognize an educator other than a school librarian (i.e., school superintendent, principal, building supervisor, administrator, etc.) who is directly responsible for a school or group of schools at the elementary or secondary level who shows outstanding support of the school library. Individuals may be nominated by LASL/LLA members by February 1. A plaque is awarded annually when merited. Established in 1972. Renamed in 1982 for Sue Hefly, former State Supervisor of School Libraries. Sponsored by the Louisiana Association of School Librarians. Formerly: (1982) LASL Educator's Award.

• 12940 • **Margaret T. Lane Award**
To recognize an individual or organization that has made a significant contribution in advancing access to, or use of, government information in Louisiana. Nominees must be characterized by the following: Actively participates in organizations devoted to the promotion and enhancement of access to government information; fosters the use of government information; has impacted the use through research and publication, the implementing of new programs and services, or other means; and serves as a model for other librarians. An engraved plaque is awarded annually when merited.

• 12941 • **Louisiana Literary Award**
To encourage more and better literature about the state of Louisiana by recognizing the author of an outstanding book published during the preceding year that deals with a Louisiana subject. A monetary award of $250 and a bronze medal are awarded each year at the annual conference. Established in 1948.

• 12942 • **Modisette Award**
To encourage improvement of conditions in the public and school library and trustee fields by encouraging high standards in each field. The award is given in five categories: (1) public library, (2) library trustees, (3) elementary school library, (4) middle school library (5) junior-senior high library. A certificate is awarded annually if merited. Established in 1944 (school and public); and 1953 (trustee) in honor of James Oliver Modisette, educator, lawyer, and President of the Association.

• 12943 • **Outstanding Academic Librarian Award**
To recognize an individual who has made an especially significant contribution to further the development of academic libraries, librarians, or librarianships within Louisiana. Candidate must be a currently active academic librarian (on rare

occasions non-librarians have been honored); contributions must be of value to libraries or librarians as a whole; and nominations must be made by a current member of LLA. Nominees should be characterized by the following: actively participates in activities that enhances the ability of academic librarians to improve library usage; Conducts research which enriches the ability of library users to more fully utilize current information; and serves as a model for the potential to further the impact academic libraries have on the education and or livelihood of Louisiana's students and residents. An engraved plaque and certificate are awarded.

• 12944 • **School Library Media Specialist Award**
To give recognition to a school library media specialist who has demonstrated through action and philosophy a dedication to the mission and goals of the media specialist profession. Candidates must be building level media specialists for at least two years, employed by the state of Louisiana, and be members in good standing of the Louisiana Association of School Librarians. A plaque is awarded annually.

• 12945 •
Louisiana Preservation Alliance
Sandra Byrd, Office Mgr.
263 3rd St., Ste. 302
PO Box 1587
Baton Rouge, LA 70821
Phone: (225)344-6001
Fax: (225)344-7176
E-mail:
lapreservationalliance@inetmail.att.net
Home Page: http://
www.lapreservationalliance.org

• 12946 • **LPA Honor Awards**
For significant work in historic preservation. Recognition award bestowed annually.

• 12947 •
Louisiana Psychiatric Medical Association
PO Box 15765
New Orleans, LA 70175
Phone: (504)891-1030
Toll-Free: 800-438-6471
Fax: (504)891-1077
E-mail: lpma@lpma.net
Home Page: http://www.lpma.net

• 12948 • **Bick Award**
For medical school graduate who demonstrates outstanding promise in psychiatry in three medical schools: Tulane, LSU in New Orleans, and LSU in Shreveport. Monetary award bestowed annually.

• 12949 •
Louisiana State Paralegal Association
Gail P. Seale, Pres.
PO Box 2055
Monroe, LA 71207
Phone: (318)387-8000
Fax: (318)387-8200
E-mail: gseale@la-paralegals.org
Home Page: http://www.la-paralegals.org

• 12950 • **Rochelle Scholarship**
For paralegal student at accredited university in Louisiana. Scholarship awarded annually.

• 12951 •
Louisiana State University
Herbarium
Department of Biological Sciences
202 Life Sciences Bldg.
Baton Rouge, LA 70803-1715
Phone: (225)578-2601
Fax: (225)578-2597
E-mail: leu@isu.edu

• 12952 • **Bernard Lowy Fund**
For the study of Latin American Tropical Botany. Inquire for application details.

• 12953 •
Louisiana State University
Kresge Hearing Research Laboratory of the South
533 Bolivar St., 5th Fl.
Dept. of Otorhinolaryngology
New Orleans, LA 70112
Phone: (504)568-4785
Fax: (504)568-4460
E-mail: rbobbin@lsuhsc.edu
Home Page: http://www.kresgelab.org

• 12954 • **Annual Prize for Hearing Research**
$5000 is awarded annually. Inquire for application details.

• 12955 • **Special Ad Hoc Awards**
Annual award of recognition. Inquire for application details.

• 12956 •
Louisiana State University
U.S. Civil War Center
Raphael Semmes Dr.
Baton Rouge, LA 70803
Phone: (225)578-3151
Fax: (225)578-4876
E-mail: lwood@lsu.edu
Home Page: http://www.cwc.lsu.edu

• 12957 • **Michael Shaara Award**
For civil war fiction. Inquire for application details.

• 12958 •
Louisiana Turfgrass Association
Dr. Tom Koske, Recording Sec.
PO Box 25100
Baton Rouge, LA 70894-5100
Phone: (225)578-2222
Fax: (225)578-0773
E-mail: tkoske@agctr.lsu.edu

• 12959 • **Turf Research**
For committee evaluation. Grant awarded annually.

• 12960 • **Turf Scholarship**
For committee evaluation. Scholarship awarded annually.

• 12961 •
Love Creek Productions
162 Nesbit St.
Weehawken, NJ 07087-6817
E-mail: creekread@aol.com

• 12962 • **Love Creek Mini Festival**
To encourage the development of and to recognize the excellence of emerging playwrights by providing the opportunity for scripts to be judged on their merits in performance. Scripts must concern a theme that is announced each year; be written in English, unpublished, and unproduced in New York City in the past year; contain at least two characters and run less than 40 minutes; and be accompanied by a letter giving permission for production, and stating whether Equity showcase is acceptable, if selected as a finalist; produced as part of short play festival. A monetary prize is awarded at the conclusion of the season to the best script in overall festival. Produced as part of Short Play Festival depending on number of entries. Established in 1988.

• 12963 • **Love Creek Short Play Festival**
To encourage the development of and to recognize the excellence of emerging playwrights by providing the opportunity for scripts to be judged on their merits in performance. Scripts must be in English, unpublished, and unproduced in New York City in the past year; must contain at least two characters and run less than 40 minutes; and must be accompanied by a letter giving permission for production and stating whether an Equity showcase is acceptable, if selected as a finalist. Include SASE for return/response if script not chosen. A monetary award is presented to the overall festival winner at the conclusion of the season. Finalists receive a mini-showcase production. Submissions accepted throughout the year. Established in 1985.

• 12964 •
Loveland Beagle Club
Frank G. Stowell, Corresponding Sec.
2285 Jonathan Ct.
Cincinnati, OH 45255
Phone: (513)688-7887
E-mail: fgstow1@aol.com

• 12965 • **Dog of the Year**
For best trained dog. Recognition award bestowed annually.

• 12966 •
Loyola University Chicago
Michael J. Garanzini, Pres.
Dept. of P.R.
6525 Sheridan Rd.
Chicago, IL 60626
Phone: (773)274-3000
E-mail: loyolanow@luc.edu
Home Page: http://www.luc.edu

• 12967 • **Civic Award Citation**
For dedicated service in the Chicago community and outstanding examples of responsible citizenship to present and future generations. Awarded annually. Established in 1956.

• 12968 • **Damen Award**
To honor an individual who has distinguished himself through his dedication to God, society, and the nation. Awarded annually. Established in 1957 in honor of Fr. Damen, first president of Loyola.

• 12969 • **Founder's Day Alumni/Alumnae Citations**
For distinguished service to Loyola University, Church, community or profession and for exemplifying the ideals of Jesuit education. Awarded annually. Established in 1956.

• 12970 • **Loyola Camellia**
To recognize distinguished women for dedicated and responsible participation in the community's social, cultural or educational programs. Awarded annually. Established in 1965.

• 12971 • **President's Medallion**
To recognize outstanding service to Loyola University.

• 12972 • **Siedenburg Award**
For recognition of extraordinary voluntary contributions of time and talents to the well-being of Loyola University and its graduates. Members of the Chicago community who have generously served Loyola are eligible. A plaque is awarded annually. Established in 1973.

• 12973 • **Stritch Medal**
To recognize a physician or medical researcher who exhibits to a high degree professional competence, resourcefulness, loyalty, benevolence, and dedication. Awarded annually. Established in 1960.

• 12974 • **Sword of Loyola**
To honor local, national or international individuals exemplifying the ideals of Saint Ignatius of Loyola - courage, dedication and service. Awarded annually. Established in 1964.

• 12975 •
Lumbermen's Association of Texas
816 Cong. Ave., Ste. 1250
Austin, TX 78701
Phone: (512)472-1194
Fax: (512)472-7378
E-mail: latadmin@lat.org
Home Page: http://www.lat.org

• 12976 • **Associate of the Year**
For service to industry, community, customers. Recognition award bestowed annually.

• 12977 • **Lumberman of the Year**
For service to industry, community, customers. Recognition award bestowed annually.

• 12978 •
Lupus Foundation of America
Sandra Reymond, Pres./CEO
2000 L St. NW, Ste. 710
Washington, DC 20036
Phone: (202)349-1155
Toll-Free: 800-558-0121
Fax: (202)349-1156
E-mail: info@lupus.org
Home Page: http://www.lupus.org

• 12979 • **Five Year Research Support Program**
Available to junior investigators, defined as assistant professor and below if in academic medicine. The research must be conducted in the United States, and the research must consist of clinical, basic or psychological research related to the causes, treatments, prevention, or care for lupus. The award is $25,000 for up to two years. The deadline is April 1 each year, and the award is issued on October 1. Formerly: (2006) Research Grant of the Lupus Foundation of America.

• 12980 • **Fleur-de-Lis Awards**
For recognition of doctors and hospitals for major contributions to Lupus research, public awareness, and patient support; directors who have contributed much in the way of time, energy, and their own money on behalf of Lupus work; outgoing presidents who have served for more than a year to build a successful Chapter; officers who have served for two years or more; businesses that have provided help in reaching the goals of the Society; other organizations for promoting Lupus education, research, and awareness; and individuals who have made an outstanding contribution on behalf of the Society's objectives. A plaque is awarded. First awarded in 1977.

• 12981 • **National Lupus Hall of Fame**
To honor those who have distinguished themselves with continuous service and dedication in the fight against Lupus on behalf of Lupus patients and their families. Nominations must be submitted by May 1. Established in 1984. Formerly: Recognition Award.

• 12982 •
Lupus Foundation of America, Arizona Area Coordinator
12630 N. 21st Ave.
Phoenix, AZ 85029
Phone: (602)870-7622
E-mail: lupusaz@aol.com

• 12983 • **Lifetime Achievement Award**
For fifteen years service on local and national levels. Recognition award bestowed annually.

• 12984 •
Lupus Foundation of America, Arkansas Chapter
Jamesetta Smith, Pres.
220 Mockingbird
Hot Springs, AR 71913
Phone: (501)525-9380
Toll-Free: 800-294-8878
Fax: (501)525-9380
E-mail: lupusarkhs@cs.com
Home Page: http://www.cmcnetwork.org/lupus/

• 12985 • **Volunteer of the Year**
For volunteers and special services. Recognition award bestowed annually.

• 12986 •
Lupus Foundation of Minnesota
Bill Jenison, Pres.
The Atrium Ste. 135
2626 E 82nd St.
Bloomington, MN 55425
Phone: (952)746-5151
Toll-Free: 800-645-1131
Fax: (612)375-0102
E-mail: info@lupusmn.org
Home Page: http://www.lupusmn.org

• 12987 • **Research Award**
For research in lupus. Monetary award bestowed annually.

• 12988 •
Lutheran Education Association
Jonathan C. Laabs Ed.D, Exec.Dir.
7400 Augusta St.
River Forest, IL 60305
Phone: (708)209-3343
Fax: (708)209-3458
E-mail: lea@lea.org
Home Page: http://www.lea.org

• 12989 • **Christus Magister Award**
To honor the Lutheran Educator of the Year. Educators, pastors, laymen and laywomen of the Lutheran Church-Missouri Synod, who need not be members of the Association, are eligible. Lutheran educators are considered for outstanding contributions to Lutheran education at any level - early childhood, elementary, secondary, higher education - or in any educational agency, in one or more of these appropriate areas: classroom teaching, administration, supervision, parish education, research, publication, or educa-

tional leadership. Such service or contribution should be recognized as having current significance at the parish, area, district or synodical level. The deadline for nominations is November 1. The awardee receives an inscribed bronze medallion mounted on a wood plaque. Awarded annually at the Convention. Established in 1965.

• 12990 • Ellen Waldschmidt Award
For recognition of outstanding service or contribution to the Association. An art piece is awarded annually. Established in 1985 in honor of Ellen Waldschmidt, office manager of the Association for 20 years.

• 12991 •
Lutheran Historical Conference
Marvin A. Huggins, VP
Concordia Historical Institute
801 DeMun Ave.
St. Louis, MO 63105
Phone: (314)505-7921
Phone: (314)505-7901
Fax: (314)505-7901
E-mail: luthhist@luthhist.org
Home Page: http://www.luthhist.org

• 12992 • Distinguished Service Award
To recognize outstanding contributions in the writing of church history, archival work, and library work. Nominations are made by the Awards Committee. An inscribed certificate is awarded biennially when merited during the convention. Established in 1974.

• 12993 •
Lutherans Concerned/Great Lakes
801 S Forest Ave.
Ann Arbor, MI 48104
Phone: (734)996-2439
E-mail: lgreatlakes@lcna.org
Home Page: http://www.lcna.org

• 12994 • Angel Award
For efforts on behalf of lesbian and gay Lutherans. Recognition award bestowed biennially.

• 12995 •
Lutherans Concerned/North America
Emily Eastwood, Exec.Dir.
PO Box 4707
St. Paul, MN 55104-0707
Phone: (651)665-0861
Fax: (651)665-0863
E-mail: membership@lcna.org
Home Page: http://www.lcna.org

• 12996 • Jim Siefkes Justice Maker Award
To recognize superior, tireless efforts of an individual on behalf of gay and lesbian people in Lutheran church bodies in North America. The impact of these efforts must be national or international in scope and carried out over a period of years. A plaque is awarded every two years at the biennial assembly. Members of Lutherans Concerned may nominate candidates; recipient is chosen by the board of directors. Deadline is April 1 of even years. Award is giving in honor of the Rev. Jim Siefkes, who organized the original conference which created Lutherans Concerned.

• 12997 •
LV of Harrison County
Amy Quinn, Contact
104 E Main St., Ste. 3A
153 W. Main St., Ste. 214
Clarksburg, WV 26301
Phone: (304)624-0533
E-mail: literacyvol@ntelos.net

• 12998 • Ethel Minter Award
For student making most progress. Recognition award bestowed annually.

• 12999 •
Lynchburg Historical Foundation
Sally A. Schneider, Exec.Dir.
PO Box 248
Lynchburg, VA 24505-0248
Phone: (434)528-5353
Fax: (434)528-9413
E-mail: lhfi@centralva.net

• 13000 • Merit Award
For restoration projects. Recognition award bestowed annually.

• 13001 • Preservationist of the Year
For individual who has worked diligently for preservation. Recognition award bestowed annually.

• 13002 •
The Lyric Theatre
Susan Mattingly, Exec.Dir.
135 College Ave.
PO Box 665
Blacksburg, VA 24063
Phone: (540)951-4771
E-mail: thelyric@centerbind.com
Home Page: http://www.thelyric.com

• 13003 • *The Lyric* Annual Awards
To recognize achievement in writing poetry. The poet's work must have appeared in issues of the current year's *The Lyric* magazine. The following prizes are awarded annually: Fluvanna Prize - $50; *The Lyric* Memorial Prize - $100; New England Prize - $50; Margaret Haley Carpenter Prize - $50; Roberts Memorial Prize $100; Virginia Prize - $50; Louise Hajek Prize - $50. Also gives annual honorable mention prizes, consisting of one-year subscriptions to *The Lyric*.

• 13004 • Quarterly Awards
To recognize achievement in poetry writing. Poets whose work appeared in *The Lyric* magazine are eligible. A monetary prize of $50 is awarded quarterly.

• 13005 •
John D. and Catherine T. MacArthur Foundation
Jonathan F. Fanton, Pres.
140 South Dearborn St.
Chicago, IL 60603
Phone: (312)726-8000
Fax: (312)920-6259
E-mail: 4answers@macfound.org
Home Page: http://www.macfound.org

• 13006 • MacArthur Fellows
The MacArthur Fellows program is a talent search designed to encourage discoveries or other significant contributions to society by American citizens or residents. By supporting these Fellows, highly talented individuals working in a wide range of fields, the Foundation means to honor creative persons everywhere. Individuals cannot apply for a MacArthur Fellowship. Instead, names are proposed to the Foundation by a group of more than 100 designated nominators in a variety of professions and areas of the country. They serve anonymously for one year. Their nominations are reviewed by a 12-member selection committee, which meets eight or nine times a year. Final approval for MacArthur Fellowships comes from the Foundation's Board of Directors. There is no annual quota of Fellows and no predetermined time for naming them. MacArthur Fellowships have no strings attached. Recipients are free to use the awards as they wish. The MacArthur Foundation imposes no reporting requirements or restrictions on MacArthur Fellows. Grants ranging from $150,000 to $375,000 over five years, depending on the age of the recipient (the older winners receiving larger grants) are awarded. About 25 Fellows are selected each year. The Fellows also receive comprehensive health insurance. The Foundation began operations after the death of John D. MacArthur in 1978, and the Fellows Program was instituted in 1981. Formerly: (1986) MacArthur Prize Fellows.

• 13007 •
The MacDowell Colony
Cheryl Young, Exec.Dir.
163 E 81st St.
New York, NY 10028
Phone: (212)535-9690
Fax: (212)737-3803
E-mail: info@macdowellcolony.org
Home Page: http://www.macdowellcolony.org

• 13008 • Edward MacDowell Medal
To recognize an outstanding contribution to the arts. American artists are eligible by nomination. Applications not accepted. The award is rotated among visual artists, architects, writers, composers, filmmakers, and interdisciplinary artists who are selected by independent committees of peers including, where possible, previous winners. A bronze medal is awarded annually at the Colony in August. Established in 1960 to commemorate the 100th birthday of the noted composer, Edward MacDowell. 297742 SME UR

• 13009 •
Machine Vision Association of the Society of Manufacturing Engineers
Nancy S. Berg, Exec.Dir./Gen.Mgr.
One SME Dr.
PO Box 930
Dearborn, MI 48121-0930
Phone: (313)271-1500
Toll-Free: 800-733-4763
Fax: (313)425-2861
E-mail: service@sme.org
Home Page: http://www.sme.org/mva

• 13010 • **Chairman's Award**
To recognize outstanding contributions to the Association and/or the field of machine vision through significant achievements and/or leadership. The achievements may consist of a single outstanding accomplishment or several significant accomplishments in one or several areas of activity. Recipients must be MVA/SME members or members of affiliate member companies. A plaque is awarded biennially at the MVA/SME Machine Vision Conference. Established in 1986. Formerly: (1990) President's Award.

• 13011 •
Madison County Tourism
Jim Walter, Exec.Dir.
PO Box 1029
Brooks Hall, Rte. 20
Morrisville, NY 13408
Phone: (315)684-7320
Toll-Free: 800-684-7320
Fax: (315)684-7348
E-mail: info@madisontourism.com
Home Page: http://www.madisontourism.com

• 13012 • **Student Intern Scholarship Award**
For student of travel/tourism/hospitality, who interns in tourism office. Scholarship awarded annually.

• 13013 •
Magazine Publishers of America
Nina Link, Pres.
810 7th Ave., 24th Fl.
New York, NY 10019
Phone: (212)872-3700
Fax: (212)888-4217
E-mail: mpa@magazine.org
Home Page: http://www.magazine.org

Formerly: (1987) Magazine Publishers Association.

• 13014 • **Henry Johnson Fisher Award**
To recognize a magazine leader who has gained distinction through significant and long-standing contributions to the magazine industry. An honorarium of $10,000 which is presented to the recipient(s) or to a designated project or charity by *Times Mirror* Magazines, Inc., which acquired *Popular Science* in 1967. A representation of the actual award, a clear crystal Steuben urn, "The Arts" is also awarded annually. Established in 1964 by Popular Science Publishing Company in memory of Henry Johnson Fisher, for 65 years of service to the magazine profession.

• 13015 • **MPA Kelly Awards**
To recognize and encourage excellence in magazine advertising creativity. Any advertising campaign is eligible if it appears during the current year in consumer magazines published in the United States, regardless of product or service advertised, size or coloration. A monetary prize of $100,000 is awarded annually. The winning campaign is announced at an award dinner during which the campaigns of all 25 finalists are presented. In addition to the cash prize, which is to be allocated to members of the winning agency's creative department by its director, a trophy is awarded. The remaining Kelly Award finalists also receive trophies. Established in 1981 in memory of Stephen E. Kelly, a former MPA president. Formerly: (1987) Stephen E. Kelly Award.

• 13016 •
Judah L. Magnes Museum
Terry Pink Alexander, Exec.Dir.
2911 Russell St.
Berkeley, CA 94705
Phone: (510)549-6950
Fax: (510)849-3673
E-mail: info@magnes.org
Home Page: http://www.judahmagnesmuseum.org

• 13017 • **Anna Davidson Rosenberg Award for Poems on the Jewish Experience**
To recognize and encourage poetry in English on the Jewish experience. Original, unpublished poems must be submitted with an entry form from April 15 to August 31 each year. Poems may not be sent by fax nor by email. Send self-addressed, stamped envelope by July 30 for required entry form. Monetary awards, certificates, and a reading at the museum are awarded annually. Honorable mention awards, senior awards, youth awards, emerging poet awards.

• 13018 •
The Magnolia Society
Roberta Davids Hagen, Sec.
6616 81st St.
Cabin John, MD 20818
Phone: (301)320-4296
Fax: (301)320-4296
E-mail: rhagen6902@aol.com
Home Page: http://www.magnoliasociety.org

• 13019 • **D. Todd Gresham Award**
To recognize accomplishments in the fields of botany and horticulture relative to Magnolias and other plants of the family Magnoliaceae. A plaque is awarded at the annual meeting. Established in 1981 to commemorate D. Todd Gresham.

• 13020 •
Mahomet Chamber of Commerce
Chuck Thompson, Pres.
202 NE St.
PO Box 1031
Mahomet, IL 61853-1031
Phone: (217)586-3165
Fax: (217)586-1816
E-mail: mahchbrcomm@netscape.net
Home Page: http://www.mahometchamberofcommerce.com

• 13021 • **Mahomet Chamber of Commerce Scholarship**
For graduate of Mahomet/Seymour high school. Scholarship awarded annually.

• 13022 •
Mail Systems Management Association
Chuck Zeikle, Pres.
JAF Bldg.
PO Box 2155
New York, NY 10116-2155
Toll-Free: 800-955-6762
E-mail: fahyb@aol.com
Home Page: http://www.msmanational.org

• 13023 • **Chapter of the Year Award**
To recognize the chapter that best upholds the standards and mission statement of MSMA. Qualifications for consideration include educational programs, network relations, participation in industry activities, timely communication to members, and maintaining and sustaining membership and development. Awarded annually.

• 13024 • **Manager of the Year Award**
To recognize any member's outstanding contribution(s) to the profitability of their company and profession over the past year. Nominations can be made by any member. All nominations must be submitted by December 31. Awarded annually.

• 13025 • **MSMA Distinguished Service Award**
To recognize an individual's extraordinary efforts throughout the previous year. Presented to a member who has made significant contributions towards the advancement and benefit of either their local chapter or the national association. A committee appointed by the National Board of Directors selects the member to be honored by January of each year. A plaque and life membership are presented at the Annual Conference MailCom. The deadline for applications is December 31. Established in 1982. Formerly: Mail System Management Hall of Fame.

• 13026 •
Mailing and Fulfillment Service Association
David A. Weaver, Pres. and CEO
1421 Prince St., Ste. 410
Alexandria, VA 22314-2814
Phone: (703)836-9200
Toll-Free: 800-333-6272
Fax: (703)548-8204
E-mail: mfsa-mail@mfsanet.org
Home Page: http://www.masa.org

• 13027 • **Leo G. Bill Bernheimer, Jr. Award**
For recognition of exceptional dedication and service to the Association. Members are eligible. A plaque is awarded annually at the convention. Established in 1963 in honor of Jeanette Robinson Hinderstein, full-time executive secretary of the Association for 25 years and re-named in memory of Bill Bernheimer, former president of the Association. Formerly: (1976) Jeanette Robinson Hinderstein Award.

• 13028 • **Henry Hoke, Sr. Award**
For recognition of the best single promotion for a client or one's company. Members are eligible. A plaque is awarded annually at the convention. Established in honor of Henry Hoke, Sr., a pioneer and innovator in direct mail advertising.

• 13029 • **L. U. "Luke" Kaiser Educational Award**
For recognition of the best contribution to education in the mailing industry. Members are eligible. A bowl is awarded annually at the conference. Established in 1978 in honor of Luke Kaiser, mailing industry pioneer.

• 13030 • **Miles Kimball Medallion**
For recognition of the most outstanding contribution to advancement of the direct mail industry. Non-members are eligible. A plaque is awarded annually at the convention. Established in 1952 in honor of Miles Kimball, a leading exponent of direct mail advertising as a profession.

• 13031 • **Mailing Industry Ingenuity Award**
For recognition of excellence in problem solving in any area of direct mail design or production. Members are eligible. A plaque is awarded annually at the convention.

• 13032 • **MASA President's Plaque**
For recognition of the best mail campaign for a client. Members are eligible. A plaque is awarded annually at the convention. Established in memory of Gorden E. Small, first elected MASA president.

• 13033 • **John Howie Wright Cup**
For recognition of the best self-promotion mailing campaign. Members are eligible. A plaque is awarded annually at the convention. Established in honor of John Howie Wright, an original member of MASA.

• 13034 •
Maine Hospice Council
693 Western Ave., Ste. 3
PO Box 2239
Manchester, ME 04351
Phone: (207)626-0651
Toll-Free: 800-438-5963
Fax: (207)622-1274
E-mail: info@mainehospicecouncil.org
Home Page: http://www.mainehospicecouncil.org

• 13035 • **Friend of the Maine Hospice Council**
For volunteer who has given time, energy and effort toward the mission of the Maine Hospice Council. Recognition award bestowed annually.

• 13036 •
Maine Journeymen
Richard McCrory, Treas.
533 Post Rd.
Bowdoinham, ME 04008-4448
Phone: (207)666-5672
E-mail: snackman@gwi.net

• 13037 • **Joe Asali Scholarship Award**
For high school graduate entering mechanical engineering field. Scholarship awarded annually.

• 13038 •
Maine Oil Dealers Association
Jamie Py, Pres.
25 Greenwood Rd.
PO Box 249
Brunswick, ME 04011-0249
Phone: (207)729-5298
Fax: (207)721-9227
E-mail: oilman@meoil.com
Home Page: http://www.meoil.com

• 13039 • **Sanford-Springvale Rotary Club Scholarship Fund**
For students with financial need, good academic record-going to college or vocational school. Scholarship awarded annually.

• 13040 •
Maine Space Grant Consortium
Dr. Terry Shehata, Exec.Dir.
87 Winthrop St., Ste. 200
Augusta, ME 04330
Phone: (207)397-7223
Toll-Free: 877-397-7223
Fax: (207)622-4548
E-mail: shehata@msgc.org
Home Page: http://www.msgc.org

• 13041 • **Maine Space Grant Consortium Internships**
For undergraduate students in research, business, government, and industry. Awarded annually. Inquire for application details.

• 13042 •
Malahat Review
John Barton, Ed.
University of Victoria
PO Box 1700
Stn. CSC
Victoria, BC, Canada V8W 2Y2
Phone: (250)721-8524
Fax: (250)721-8524
E-mail: malahat@uvic.ca
Home Page: http://web.uvic.ca/malahat

• 13043 • **Long Poem Prize**
To recognize a poet for a long poem or a cycle of poems. Unpublished works of a maximum of 20 pages must be submitted by March 1. Two monetary awards of $400 each, plus payment for publication are awarded alternately with the Novella Prize. Established in 1987.

• 13044 • **Novella Prize**
To recognize an author of a novella. Unpublished works up to 30,000 words must be submitted by March 1. A monetary award of $500, plus payment for publishing, are awarded in even-numbered years (alternates with the Long Poem Prize).

• 13045 •
Malice Domestic
Louise Leftwich, Awards Chair
PO Box 31137
Bethesda, MD 20824-1137
Phone: (703)613-6625
Fax: (703)613-6003
E-mail: agathas@malicedomestic.org
Home Page: http://www.malicedomestic.org

• 13046 • **Agatha Awards**
Awarded for the best novel, first mystery novel, nonfiction, short story, and children's/young adult published in the previous year. To be eligible, a book must have been published in the U.S. between January 1 and December 31 of the previous year, and must be a Malice Domestic book. The award is a teapot with Malice's skull and crossbones on the side. All nominees receive a certificate. Awarded annually.

• 13047 •
Maltese-American Benevolent Society
Carmen Nino, Pres.
1832 Michigan Ave.
Detroit, MI 48216
Phone: (313)961-8393
Fax: (313)961-2050

• 13048 • **Member of the Year Award**
For recognition of outstanding and dedicated service to the society. A plaque is awarded annually. Established in 1977.

• 13049 • **George Zammit Award**
To reward voluntary services to the club's bingo program. Awarded as merited.

• 13050 •
Manhattan College
Thomas Scanlan, Pres.
Corporate & Foundation Relations
Sears Hall
Manhattan College Pky.
Riverdale, NY 10471
Phone: (718)862-7200
Toll-Free: 800-MC2-XCEL
Fax: (718)862-8019
E-mail: chrisstogel@manhattan.edu
Home Page: http://www.manhattan.edu

• 13051 • **Manhattan College De La Salle Medal**
To recognize an individual for significant contributions to the moral, cultural or educational life of the nation. A gold-plated medal mounted in sculpted, burnished silver-toned metal is awarded annually. Established in 1951 in memory of John Baptist De La Salle, founder of the Institute of the Brothers of the Christian Schools. Formerly: Saint La Salle Medal.

• 13052 • **Manhattan College Pacem in Terris Medal**
To recognize those individuals and organizations who best represent the vision and program for peace as stated in Pope John XXIII's encyclical letter, Pacem in Terris, (Peace on Earth) emphasizing the need for universal human rights, disarmament, and responsible world governance. Individuals and organizations are selected by Manhattan College. A bronze medal is awarded when merited. Established in 1988 by the Peace Studies Program of Manhattan College to commemorate the 25th anniversary of Pope John XXIII's encyclical "Pacem in Terris" and the 40th anniversary of the Universal Declaration of Human Rights. Additional information is available from the Peace Studies Program, Manhattan College.

• 13053 •
Manitoba Psychological Society
Dr. Jennifer Frain, Pres.
PO Box 151 RPO Corydon
Winnipeg, MB, Canada R3M 3S7
Phone: (204)488-7398
Fax: (204)487-0784
E-mail: jfrain@newdirections.mb.ca
Home Page: http://www.mps.mb.ca

• 13054 • **Clifford J. Robson Award**
To recognize distinguished service to psychology in Manitoba. Members of the Psychological Association of Manitoba and members of the Manitoba Psychological Society are eligible. A plaque is awarded at the annual general meeting.

• 13055 •
Mankato Area Environmentalists
Katy Wortel, Contact
1411 Pohl Rd.
Mankato, MN 56001-5751
Phone: (507)345-4494
Fax: (507)345-6679
E-mail: enviros@hickorytech.net
Home Page: http://www.hickorytech.net/~enviros

• 13056 • **Earth Keeper of the Year**
For service above and beyond the call of duty for the good of the environment. Recognition award bestowed periodically.

• 13057 •
Manning, Selvage and Lee
Mark Hass, CEO
1675 Broadway
New York, NY 10019
Phone: (212)468-4200
Fax: (212)468-4007
E-mail: mark.hass@mslpr.com
Home Page: http://www.mslpr.com

• 13058 • **Friskies Canine Frisbee Disc World Championships**
To recognize dog/owner teams for their Frisbee sport ability. Judging is based on showmanship, leaping ability, degree of difficulty, and execution. The "top dog" and runner-up teams from the seven Regional Finals will receive an expense-paid trip to Washington, D.C., to compete in the Friskies Canine Frisbee disc World Finals. In addition, the canine champion will receive a year's supply of Friskies dog foods and treats.

• 13059 •
Manomet Center for Conservation Sciences
PO Box 1770
Manomet, MA 02345
Phone: (508)224-6521
Fax: (508)224-9220
E-mail: info@manomet.org
Home Page: http://www.manomet.org
Formerly: (1995) Manomet Bird Observatory.

• 13060 • **Kathleen S. Anderson Research Grant**
To encourage significant avian research in areas of interest to Kathleen Anderson and Manomet Center for Conservation Sciences, and to support promising biologists in their work. Projects are considered in one or more of the following areas: migration, feeding ecology, habitat fragmentation, populations, competition, shorebirds, and endangered species. All proposed projects must take place in the Americas, and work based at Manomet is encouraged. Any person, of any age, beginning a career in biology is eligible. Enrollment in an academic program is desirable, but not required. Proposals are due December 1. Monetary awards are presented annually in March. Established in 1985 to honor Kathleen S. Anderson, Director Emeritus of MO.

• 13061 •
March of Dimes Birth Defects Foundation, Central Texas Area Chapter
Judy A. Schaffer, Contact
Central Division
6 W French Ave., Ste. 202
Temple, TX 76501-3207
Phone: (254)774-7277

• 13062 • **Community Service Grant**
For issues relating to maternal and child health, specifically prevention of birth defects. Grant awarded annually.

• 13063 •
Guglielmo Marconi International Fellowship Foundation
Darcy Gerbarg, Exec.Dir.
Fu Foundation School of Engineering and Applied Science
Columbia University
500 Mudd Bldg.
500 W 120th St.
New York, NY 10027
Phone: (212)854-7676
Fax: (212)854-9191
E-mail: info@marconifoundation.org
Home Page: http://www.marconifoundation.org

• 13064 • **The Marconi Prize**
To recognize individuals who have made a significant contribution to the advancement of the technology of communications through scientific or engineering discoveries, inventions, or innovations. The Fellowship invites nominations of individuals whose work in the fields of communication science and technology exemplifies the technical creativity and concern for human welfare of Guglielmo Marconi. The annual nomination deadline is July 31. A monetary grant of $100,000 and a trophy, created by Otello Guarducci, are awarded annually. Established in 1974 by Gioia Marconi Braga, daughter of Guglielmo Marconi. The award commemorates Marconi's contributions to scientific invention, engineering and technology, and his commitment to their use for the betterment of the human condition. Sponsored by numerous corporations and organizations concerned with furthering advances in communications. Formerly: (2004) Marconi International Fellowship.

• 13065 •
Marijuana Anonymous World Services
Catherine Baker, Contact
PO Box 2912
Van Nuys, CA 91404
Toll-Free: 800-766-6779
E-mail: office@marijuana-anonymous.org
Home Page: http://www.marijuana-anonymous.org/

• 13066 • **National Golden Target Award**
For excellence in public relations at the national level. Awarded annually.

• 13067 • State Award for Excellence
For excellence in public relations at the state level. Awarded annually.

• 13068 •
Marine Corps Aviation Association
Lt.Col. R. Art Sifuentes USMC, Exec.Dir.
715 Broadway St.
PO Box 296
Quantico, VA 22134
Phone: (703)630-1903
Toll-Free: 800-280-3001
Fax: (703)630-2713
E-mail: mcaa@flymcaa.org
Home Page: http://www.flymcaa.org

Absorbed: (1972) First Marine Aviation Force Veterans' Association.

• 13069 • Commandant's Aviation Trophy
To recognize the most outstanding accomplishment of all assigned tasks by a squadron. All Marine fixed-wing, helicopter, transport, and training squadrons, regular or reserve, are eligible. The permanent trophy is a plaque mounted on a pedestal bearing the Marine Corps emblem. An MCAA Fighting Hawk trophy is presented for permanent retention at the annual reunion of the MCAA. Established in 1969.

• 13070 • Alfred A. Cunningham Award (Marine Aviator of the Year)
To recognize the most outstanding contribution to Marine aviation in combat, R&D, weapons employment, or to overall Marine aviation. All Marine aviators, regular or reserve, are eligible. The permanent trophy is a gold replica of the Earth set on a pedestal and mounted with a biplane. An MCAA Fighting Hawk trophy is presented for permanent retention at the annual reunion of the MCAA. Established in 1962 in memory of Alfred A. Cunningham, aviator.

• 13071 • Donald E. Davis Award
To recognize the Marine Aviation Logistics Squadron of the Year, which demonstrates the highest degree of leadership, logistical expertise, innovation, and superior accomplishment in support of Marine aviation. All Marine Aviation Logistics squadrons, regular or reserve, are eligible. Awarded annually. Sponsored by Reflectone, Inc.

• 13072 • Jack W. Demmond Award
To honor and recognize the Aviation Ground Marine of the Year. All enlisted Marines serving in Marine Aviation, regular or reserve, are eligible. Awarded annually. Established in 1995. Sponsored by OC Incorporated.

• 13073 • Edward C. Dyer Award
To recognize the Marine Medium Helicopter Squadron of the Year. All CH-46E and CH/RH-53D squadrons are eligible. Awarded annually. Sponsored by Boeing Defense & Space Group.

• 13074 • Edward S. Fris Award (Command and Control Unit of the Year)
To recognize the most outstanding contribution to Marine aviation by a unit of the MACCS to include MACG Dets. The permanent trophy is an onyx and chrome trophy depicting the various units of the Marine Air Control Group. An MCAA Fighting Hawk trophy is presented for permanent retention at the annual reunion of the MCAA. Established in 1985. Sponsored by Raytheon Electronic Systems Company.

• 13075 • Robert F. Gibson Award (Marine Air Command and Control Officer of the Year)
To recognize the most outstanding contribution to Marine aviation by an officer serving in a MACCS unit. All officers from any unit in the MACCS, regular or reserve, are eligible. The permanent trophy is a large cut glass trophy on a walnut base with the unit emblem of an MACG fixed to each corner. An MCAA Fighting Hawk trophy is presented for permanent retention at the annual reunion of the MCAA. Established in 1972. Sponsored by Litton Data Systems.

• 13076 • John P. Giguere Award
To recognize the Marine Light/Attack Helicopter Squadron of the Year. All HML/A squadrons, regular or reserve, are eligible. Awarded annually. Established in 1995. Sponsored by Bell Helicopter Textron.

• 13077 • Gaines G. Gilbert Award
To recognize the Aviation Ordnance Marine of the Year. Awarded annually.

• 13078 • Robert M. Hanson Award (Fighter/Attack Squadron of the Year)
To recognize the most outstanding fighter/attack squadron. All Marine F/A-18A C/D squadrons, regular or reserve, are eligible. The permanent trophy is a winged man on a pedestal bearing the Marine Corps emblem. An MCAA Fighting Hawk trophy is presented for permanent retention at the annual reunion of the MCAA. Established in 1988 in memory of Capt. Robert M. Hanson, USMC fighter ace and Medal of Honor winner, killed in WWII after shooting down 25 enemy aircraft. Sponsored by McDonnell Douglas Aerospace.

• 13079 • James E. Hatch Award
To recognize the Marine Wing Support Squadron of the Year. Awarded annually. Established to recognize the MWSS which demonstrates the highest degree of support to an Aviation Combat Element (ACE) by furnishing essential aviation ground support and service.

• 13080 • Earle Hattaway Award (Marine Aviation Ground Officer of the Year)
To recognize the most outstanding contribution to Marine aviation in combat, R&D, or overall Marine aviation. All Marine aviation ground officers, regular or reserve, are eligible. The permanent trophy is a silver cup with a winged man mounted on a pedestal. An MCAA Fighting Hawk trophy is presented for permanent retention at the annual reunion of the MCAA. Established in 1972. Sponsored by Rolls Royce, Inc.

• 13081 • The Kenneth A. Innis Award (Aviation Command and Control Marine of the Year)
To recognize the most outstanding contribution to Marine aviation by an enlisted Marine serving in a MACCS unit. All enlisted personnel from any unit in the MACCS, regular or reserve, are eligible. A trophy is presented at the annual reunion of the MCAA. Established in 1988. Sponsored by Lockheed Martin Tactical Defense Systems.

• 13082 • James MaGuire Award (Exceptional Achievement)
To recognize the most significant contribution in a professional manner to enhance Marine aviation not otherwise recognized by a Marine aviation award. All Marine aviation personnel/units, regular or reserve, are eligible. The permanent trophy is a large silver cup surmounted by an eagle. An MCAA Fighting Hawk trophy is presented for permanent retention at the annual reunion of the MCAA. Established in 1974. Sponsored by Lockheed Martin Fairchild Systems.

• 13083 • Keith B. McCutcheon Award (Marine Heavy Helicopter Squadron of the Year)
To recognize the most outstanding Marine heavy helicopter squadron. All Marine CH-53E squadrons, regular or reserve, are eligible. The permanent trophy is a silver cup mounted on a pedestal surrounded by four columns topped with an eagle. An MCAA Fighting Hawk trophy is presented for permanent retention at the annual reunion of the MCAA. Established in 1972 in memory of Gen. Keith B. McCutcheon, the pioneer Marine Corps helicopter pilot. Sponsored by Sikorsky Aircraft.

• 13084 • Royal N. Moore Award
To recognize the Electronic Warfare Squadron of the Year. All EA-6B squadrons, regular or reserve, are eligible. Awarded annually. Sponsored by Northrop Grumman Electronic Systems and Integration Division.

• 13085 • James E. Nicholson Award (Marine Non-Commissioned Officer Leadership Award)
To recognize the most significant example of leadership demonstrated by an enlisted Marine over an extended period, such as a deployment. All enlisted Marines serving within Marine aviation, regular or reserve, are eligible. The permanent trophy is a silver bowl engraved with the likeness of James E. Nicholson. An MCAA Fighting Hawk trophy is presented for permanent retention at the annual reunion of the MCAA. Established in 1977 to honor James E. Nicholson. Sponsored by Hughes Aircraft Company.

• 13086 • Danny Radish Award (Marine Enlisted Aircrew of the Year)
To recognize the most outstanding contribution to Marine aviation by an enlisted aircrew mem-

ber. Any unlisted aircrew member, fixed wing or rotary-wing, regular or reserve, is eligible. The permanent trophy is a silver cup with four eagles and a figure. An MCAA Fighting Hawk trophy is presented for permanent retention at the annual reunion of the MCAA. Established in 1972. Sponsored by GEC Marconi Avionics.

• 13087 • Robert Guy Robinson Award (Marine Naval Flight Officer of the Year)
To recognize the most outstanding contribution to Marine aviation in combat, R&D, weapons employment, or to overall Marine aviation. All Marine Naval Flight Officers, regular or reserve, are eligible. The permanent trophy is a silver cup set on a pedestal and surmounted with a sphere. An MCAA Fighting Hawk trophy is presented for permanent retention at the annual reunion of the MCAA. Established in 1971 to honor 1st Lt. Robert Guy Robinson, WWII Medal of Honor winner, and pioneer in the Naval Flight Officer field. Sponsored by Northrop Grumman Corporation.

• 13088 • Pete Ross Safety Award
To recognize the reserve fighter or attack squadron with the best aviation safety record over the past year. The permanent trophy is a silver cup mounted on wood base, surmounted by a silver F9F Panther. An MCAA Fighting Hawk trophy is presented for permanent retention at the annual reunion of the MCAA. Established in 1980 in memory of 1st Lt. Joseph "Pete" Ross, killed while on active duty for training with the Marine Corps Reserve. Sponsored by the Ross Family.

• 13089 • Lawson H. M. Sanderson Award (Attack Squadron of the Year)
To recognize the most outstanding Marine attack squadron. All Marine AV-8B squadrons, regular or reserve, are eligible. The permanent trophy is silver with a biplane and winged figure. An MCAA Fighting Hawk trophy is awarded for permanent retention at the annual reunion of the MCAA. Established in 1979 to honor Lawson H. M. Sanderson, the father of Marine close air support. Sponsored by British Aerospace.

• 13090 • Silver Hawk Award
To recognize the senior Marine Naval aviator on active duty whose date of designation precedes that of any other Marine Naval aviator. The permanent trophy is a granite block surmounted with silver hawk with the MCAA logo and a set of Naval Aviator's Wings are attached. An MCAA Fighting Hawk trophy is presented for permanent retention at the annual reunion of the MCAA. Established in 1972. Sponsored by Boeing Co.

• 13091 • Kenneth W. Southcomb Award
To honor and recognize the Aviation Supply Marine of the Year. Any enlisted Marine in aviation supply billets is eligible. Awarded annually. Established in 1995. Sponsored by AAR Cadillac Manufacturing, Inc.

• 13092 • Willie D. Sproule Award (Aviation Maintenance Marine of the Year)
To recognize the most outstanding contribution to Marine aviation by an enlisted Marine serving in a maintenance billet. All Marine maintenance billets, regular or reserve, are eligible. The permanent trophy is a pair of crossed silver wrenches mounted on a pedestal bearing the emblem of the MCAA. An MCAA Fighting Hawk trophy is presented for permanent retention at the annual reunion of the MCAA. Established in 1972. Sponsored by Lockheed Martin Aeronautics.

• 13093 • Paul G. Vess Award (Avionics Marine of the Year)
To recognize the most outstanding contribution to Marine aviation as an electronic technician. All Marine aviation electronic technicians, regular or reserve, are eligible. The permanent trophy is a silver cup mounted on a wooden base with a winged figure adorning the cup. An MCAA Fighting Hawk trophy is awarded for permanent retention at the annual reunion of the MCAA. Established in 1977. Sponsored by Sander's, a Lockheed Martin Company.

• 13094 • Henry Wildfang Award
To recognize the Marine Aerial Refueler Squadron of the Year. Awarded annually.

• 13095 •
Marine Corps Heritage Foundation
Ret. BGen Ron Christmas USMC, Pres.
307 5th Ave.
Quantico, VA 22134
Phone: (703)640-7965
Toll-Free: 800-397-7585
Fax: (703)640-9546
E-mail: info@marineheritage.org
Home Page: http://www.marineheritage.org

• 13096 • Sgt. Maj. Dan Daly Award
For recognition of writing pertinent to Marine Corps history for a Marine Corps post or station periodical during the preceding year by an enlisted author. A monetary prize of $1,000 and a plaque are awarded annually. Sponsored by the Marine Corps Association's *Leatherneck Magazine.*

• 13097 • Geiger Award
For recognition of the best Marine Corps aviation-related article published in the *Marine Corps Gazette*. A monetary award of $1,000 and a bronzed plaque are awarded annually. Established in 1983 in memory of Marine Corps General Roy S. Geiger through a donation by Col. G.F. Robert Hanke in memory of his father, Ralph Hanke, Wing Commander, Royal Air Force.

• 13098 • General Wallace M. Greene, Jr., Award
For recognition of the best nonfiction book pertinent to Marine Corps history written in the preceding three calendar years. A monetary prize of $1,000 and a plaque are awarded annually in the fall. Established in 1987 in honor of General Wallace M. Greene, USMC, 23d Commandant of the Marine Corps.

• 13099 • Colonel Robert D. Heinl, Jr., Memorial Award in Marine Corps History
For recognition of the best article pertinent to Marine Corps history published in a given year. A monetary award of $1,000 and a bronzed plaque are presented annually. Honorable mention winners receive a plaque. Established in 1980 in memory of Colonel Robert D. Heinl, Jr., USMC (Ret), a founder of the Marine Corps Historical Foundation.

• 13100 • Magruder Award for Museology (Museum Displays)
To recognize an individual, group, or exhibit for an outstanding display on a Marine Corps related topic. Established in 1988 and named for Colonel John Magruder III, the first director of the Marine Corps Museum.

• 13101 • Colonel John W. Thomason, Jr. Award
For recognition of excellence in the fine or applied arts, including photography, in depicting the historical or contemporary Marine Corps. The award may be given for a single work, a series or group of works, or for life-long accomplishments. A plaque is awarded annually. Established in 1987 in memory of Col. John W. Thomason, Jr., USMC.

• 13102 •
Marine Corps Mustang Association
David P. Brunstad, Business Mgr.
6020 Stage Rd., Ste. No. 42-242
101 Rte. 130 S
Memphis, TN 38134-8377
Phone: (866)937-6262
Toll-Free: (866)937-6262
Fax: (866)939-6262
E-mail: mustangbusmgr@aol.com
Home Page: http://www.marinecorpsmustang.org

• 13103 • Mustang Spirit Award
To recognize a Warrant Officer from each basic class who displays qualities of a Marine "Mustang" as exhibited by attitude, leadership and spirit. A plaque and $300 uniform allowance are awarded to one or more recipients annually. Established in 1990.

• 13104 •
Marine Corps Reserve Association
Richard H. Esau Jr., Exec.Dir.
337 Potomac Ave.
Quantico, VA 22134
Phone: (703)630-3772
Toll-Free: 800-927-6270
Fax: (703)630-1904
E-mail: mcra@mcrassn.org
Home Page: http://www.mcrassn.org

• 13105 • Awards of Recognition
One recognizes outstanding units of the Selected Marine Corps Reserve. Another recog-

nizes an outstanding individual who best supports the objectives of the association.

• 13106 • MCJROTC Awards
Award of recognition. MCJROTC units nationally are eligible. Awarded annually.

• 13107 •
Marine Technology Society
Dr. Jerry Streeter, Pres.
5565 Sterrett Pl., Ste. 108
Columbia, MD 21044
Phone: (410)884-5330
Fax: (410)884-9060
E-mail: mtsmbrship@erols.com
Home Page: http://www.mtsociety.org

• 13108 • Compass Distinguished Achievement Award
To stimulate the conception, design, development, and application of new equipment and techniques in oceanographic exploration, research and survey, undersea defense, ocean transportation, fisheries, marine mining and minerals recovery, pollution control, desalination, and education leading to greater utilization of the knowledge and resources of the world's oceans; and to acknowledge and honor those individuals making significant and outstanding contributions in these areas of oceanography and marine technology. Selection is based on outstanding individual accomplishments. Although the field is exceedingly complex in terms of science, technology, economics, research, engineering, law, manufacturing, etc., and candidates may be best known for their work in one of the many areas involved, the criteria for selection are recognizable achievements and definable contributions to as much of the total field as possible. A silver scroll plaque engraved with the replica of a compass with an inscription, a Rolex watch, and a certificate are awarded annually. Established in 1966 by Compass Publications Inc.

• 13109 • Compass Industrial Award
To honor those industrial firms making significant and outstanding contributions in the areas of oceanography and marine technology. Selection is based on the total contribution of a company to the field of oceanography, marine technology, and undersea defense. Activities considered for this award include development of a specific hardware package or system for use in the field of oceanography, operation of a specific survey or ocean research project at sea or onshore, administration of a government research project, manufacturing and marketing of specific equipment, introduction of new concepts and techniques, and demonstration of outstanding leadership in the field. A certificate and silver scroll plaque engraved with the replica of a compass and with an inscription are awarded annually. Established in 1966 by Compass Publications Inc.

• 13110 • Compass International Award
To honor those individuals, companies, or organizations throughout the world who have made significant and outstanding contributions in oceanography and marine technology. An individual, company, or organization from any country or territory outside the United States of America may be considered. A certificate and silver scroll plaque engraved with the replica of a compass and with an inscription are awarded annually. Established in 1980 by Compass Publications, Inc.

• 13111 • Lockheed/Martin Ocean Engineering Award
To recognize individual achievement in marine science, engineering, and technology. A monetary award of $2,500, a plaque from Lockheed Missile and Space System Corporation, and a certificate are awarded annually. Established in 1969. Sponsored by the Lockheed Corporation. Formerly: (1990) Lockheed Award for Ocean Science and Engineering.

• 13112 • MTS Special Commendation
For recognition of an outstanding accomplishment through individual or team management leading to significant advances in marine affairs. Open to anyone in management, public service, or the social science fields. Awarded annually. Established in 1966.

• 13113 •
Mariological Society of America
Rev. Thomas A. Thompson SM, Exec.Sec.
Marian Library
Univ. of Dayton
Dayton, OH 45469-1390
Phone: (937)229-4294
Fax: (937)229-4258
E-mail: cecilia.mushenheim@notes.udayton.edu
Home Page: http://www.mariologicalsocietyofamerica.us

• 13114 • Cardinal John J. Wright Mariological Award
For recognition of a valuable contribution to the field of Marian studies. A monetary gift and a citation are awarded by a standing committee. Established in 1950 as the Marian Award for Priests, the award changed its name to the Mariological Award in 1952 and was renamed the Cardinal John J. Wright Mariological Award in 1969 in honor of this early member of the society who served as its Episcopal Chairman from 1951 until his death in 1979. Formerly: (1952) Mariological Award; (1950) Marian Award for Priests.

• 13115 •
Marion County Bar Association
Nathaniel Lee, Chm.
617 Indiana Ave., 2nd Fl.
Indianapolis, IN 46202
Phone: (317)634-3950
Phone: (317)631-5151
Fax: (317)636-0600

• 13116 • Rufus C. Kuykendall
For members of the bar association. Recognition award bestowed annually.

• 13117 •
Marketing and Advertising Global Network
Albert W. Dudreck, Exec.Dir./Controller
PO Box 38653
Pittsburgh, PA 15238
Phone: (412)968-5755
Fax: (412)968-5763
E-mail: mxdirector@verizon.net
Home Page: http://www.magnetglobal.org

• 13118 • Indie Awards Competition
Recognizes a body of work for each agency's previous year. Awarded annually.

• 13119 •
Marketing Science Institute
Marni Zea Clippinger, COO
1000 Massachusetts Ave.
Cambridge, MA 02138-5396
Phone: (617)491-2060
Fax: (617)491-2065
E-mail: msi@msi.org
Home Page: http://www.msi.org

• 13120 • Alden G. Clayton Doctoral Dissertation Proposal Award
To stimulate and support research by doctoral students on subjects of importance and relevance to marketing practitioners. Doctoral students in marketing or related fields may submit proposals dealing with specified topics. The deadline for submitting proposals usually falls in the middle to the end of July. A monetary award of $5,000 is awarded annually to up to five winners. Established in 1984 to honor Alden G. Clayton, former MSI president who retired in 1986 after more than a decade of leadership at the Institute. For complete guidelines visit: http/www.msi.org/research_competitions.cfm and then click on the AGC Competition. Formerly: (1987) MSI Annual Doctoral Dissertation Proposal Award.

• 13121 •
Marlowe Society of America
Prof. Bruce E. Brandt, Pres.
Dept. of English, Box 504
South Dakota State Univ.
Brookings, SD 57007-1397
Phone: (605)688-4058
Fax: (605)688-5192
E-mail: bruce.brandt@sdstate.edu
Home Page: http://web.ics.purdue.edu/~pwhite/marlowe

• 13122 • Roma Gill Prize
To recognize the best work of scholarship on Chrisopher Marlowe published within the Award period. A monetary prize is awarded every two years. There is also a possible honorable mention award. Established in 1985 to honor Roma Gill, a distinguished Marlowe Scholar.

• 13123 •
Marquette University
Department of Journalism
John Smith, Dean
1131 W Wisconsin Ave.
PO Box 1881
Milwaukee, WI 53201-1881
Phone: (414)288-1705
Fax: (414)288-3099
E-mail: 6974thornw@mu.edu
Home Page: http://www.marquette.edu/comm/departments/journalism.html

• 13124 • **By-Line Award**
For recognition of the performance of competent journalism through the years and the acceptance and fulfillment of professional responsibility. Alumni of the journalism program of Marquette University are eligible. The award is not presented for a specific book, movie, news report, or magazine article; it is given for performance through the years. Among newspaper men and women, the by-line signifies technical excellence and personal responsibility, two qualities that determine good and faithful practice in all fields of journalism: broadcasting, film, advertising, public relations, and management. An engraved copper printing plate is awarded annually. Established in 1946.

• 13125 • **Professional Excellence in Religious Communication Award**
To recognize alumni who have been outstanding professionals in the field of religious communication. Alumni of the College of Communication, with a distinguished career in some phase of religious communication are considered. A plaque is awarded periodically. Established in 1986 on the occasion of the 75th anniversary of the College of Journalism.

• 13126 •
Maryknoll Fathers and Brothers
John Sivalon, Superior Gen.
PO Box 304
Maryknoll, NY 10545-0307
Phone: (914)941-7590
Toll-Free: 888-627-9566
Fax: (914)923-0733
E-mail: mkweb@maryknoll.org
Home Page: http://www.maryknoll.org

• 13127 • **Maryknoll Mission Award**
Recognizes those who exemplify Maryknoll values and global vision. A monetary award is given annually.

• 13128 •
Maryknoll Lay Missioners
Howard Schwartz, Media Relations Dir.
PO Box 307
Maryknoll, NY 10545-0307
Phone: (914)762-6364
Toll-Free: 800-818-5276
Fax: (914)762-7031
E-mail: info@mklm.org
Home Page: http://laymissioners.maryknoll.org

• 13129 • **Maryknoll Student Essay Contest**
Essay contest organized by Maryknoll magazine for 500-750 word essays based on a Christian theme that changes each year. Judging is divided into two divisions of grades 6-8 and 9-12. First prize is $1,000, second prize is $300, and third prize is $150. The dead line for submissions is early December. Contact Maryknoll for an application and for the current theme.

• 13130 •
Maryland Association of Private Career Schools
Ron Beall, Contact
Lincoln Tech. Institute
9325 Snowden River Pkwy.
Columbia, MD 21045
Phone: (410)290-7100
Fax: (410)309-6076

• 13131 • **MAPCS Scholarship Program**
For graduating high school seniors. Scholarship awarded annually.

• 13132 •
Maryland Jockey Club
% Pimlico Race Course
5201 Park Heights Ave.
Baltimore, MD 21215
Phone: (410)542-9400
Fax: (410)466-5622
E-mail: jgagliano@marylandracing.com
Home Page: http://www.marylandracing.com

• 13133 • **Eugene (Butch) Eseman Award**
To recognize the apprentice jockey at Pimlico Race Course who wins the most races during the racing season. A horse and jockey statuette and nameplate on a perpetual plaque are awarded annually. Established in 1978.

• 13134 • **National Jockeys Hall of Fame**
For recognition of outstanding jockeys. Portraits of the members painted by Baltimore artist Henry Cooper are displayed in the Hall of Fame dining room at Pimlico. Established in 1955.

• 13135 • **Old Hilltop Award**
To honor members of the sports media who have covered the sport of Thoroughbred racing with excellence and distinction. A Pimlico pewter plate and nameplate on a perpetual plaque are awarded annually. Old Hilltop is the nickname that historic Pimlico has been called since the turn of the century. Established in 1976.

• 13136 • **Preakness Stakes**
For recognition of the winner of the race of 3-year-old horses at Pimlico. This race, the second event in the Triple Crown which includes the Kentucky Derby and the Belmont Stakes, is held annually on the third Saturday in May. The Preakness Purse is one million dollars. Established in 1873.

• 13137 • **David F. Woods Memorial Award**
For recognition of the media person writing the best Preakness story of the year. All members of the media are eligible. A pewter bowl, which is a copy of the Annapolis Racing Trophy of 1743, is awarded at Alibi Breakfast at Pimlico. Established in 1982 in memory of David F. Woods, the former public relations director of Pimlico Race Course.

• 13138 •
Mason Contractors Association of America
Michael Adelizzi, Exec.Dir.
33 S Rosell Rd.
Schaumburg, IL 60193
Phone: (847)301-0001
Toll-Free: 800-536-2225
Fax: (847)301-1110
E-mail: madelizzi@masoncontractors.org
Home Page: http://www.masoncontractors.org

• 13139 • **International Excellence in Masonry Award**
Award of recognition. Contractors and architects are eligible. Awarded annually.

• 13140 •
Masonic Lodge No. 246
Raymond Atwood, Contact
8120 Main St.
Garrettsville, OH 44231
Phone: (330)527-2675
E-mail: gareettsville-246@masonic-lodges.org
Home Page: http://www.masonic-lodges.org/garrettsville-246

• 13141 • **President Garfield Humanitarian Award**
Based on grades, leadership, and need. Scholarship awarded annually.

• 13142 •
The Masquers
Bob Goshay, Pres.
105 Park Pl.
Point Richmond, CA 94801-3922
Phone: (510)232-3888
E-mail: info@masquers.org
Home Page: http://www.masquers.org

• 13143 • **George Spelvin Award**
To recognize someone in the theatre industry for outstanding achievement. A statue is awarded biannually. Established in 1949.

• 13144 •
Massachusetts Association for Children With Learning Disabilities
Teresa Allisa Citro, Exec.Dir.
PO Box 142
PO Box 142
Weston, MA 02493
Phone: (781)890-5399
Fax: (781)890-0555
E-mail: info@worldwide.org
Home Page: http://www.ldam.org

• 13145 • **Samuel Kirk Award**
For an outstanding educator. Recognition award bestowed annually.

• 13146 •
Massachusetts Association of School Business Officials
John A. Crafton, Exec.Dir.
84 Brick Kiln Rd.
Chelmsford, MA 01824
Phone: (978)452-7044
Fax: (978)452-7114
E-mail: masbo@mec.edu
Home Page: http://www.masbo.org

• 13147 • **President's Award**
For recognition of individual for outstanding contribution to their district, community, profession and/or to MASBO. Monetary award bestowed annually.

• 13148 •
Massachusetts Audubon Society
Taber D. Allison, VP
208 S Great Rd.
Lincoln, MA 01773
Phone: (781)259-9500
Toll-Free: 800-AUD-UBON
Fax: (781)259-8899
E-mail: webmaster@massaudubon.org
Home Page: http://www.massaudubon.org

• 13149 • **Audubon A Award**
For Massachusetts citizens, media, government officials, or group for exemplary citizen action work. Recognition award bestowed annually.

• 13150 • **Conservation Teacher of the Year**
For Massachusetts elementary, middle, and secondary school teachers. Recognition award bestowed annually.

• 13151 •
Massachusetts Conveyancers Association
Daniel J. Ossoff, Pres.
50 Cong. St., Ste. 600
Boston, MA 02109-4075
Phone: (617)854-7555
Toll-Free: 800-496-6799
Fax: (617)854-7570
E-mail: graham@massrelaw.org
Home Page: http://www.massrelaw.org/

• 13152 • **Richard B. Johnson Memorial Award**
For lifelong contributions to the conveyancing bar. Recognition award bestowed periodically.

• 13153 •
Massachusetts Council for the Social Studies
George G. Watson Jr., Exec.Sec.
7 Ambrosia Ln.
Pocasset, MA 02559-1921
Phone: (781)933-8868
Home Page: http://www.masscouncil.org

• 13154 • **Elementary Teachers of Excellence in Social Studies**
For exemplary teacher (K-6) of social studies. Recognition award bestowed annually.

• 13155 • **High School Teachers of Excellence in Social Studies**
For exemplary teacher (9-12) of social studies. Recognition award bestowed annually.

• 13156 • **Middle School Teachers of Excellence in Social Studies**
For exemplary teacher (7-9) of social studies. Recognition award bestowed annually.

• 13157 • **Supervisor of Excellence in Social Studies**
For exemplary supervision of social studies. Recognition award bestowed annually.

• 13158 •
Massachusetts Forestry Association
PO Box 1096
Belchertown, MA 01007-1096
Phone: (413)323-7326
Fax: (413)323-9594

• 13159 • **John Lambert, Jr. Forest Stewardship Award**
For individual demonstrating most concern for the Massachusetts woodlands. Recognition award bestowed annually.

• 13160 • **Massachusetts Tree Farmer of the Year**
For tree farmer promoting good forest management. Recognition award bestowed annually.

• 13161 •
Massachusetts Lodging Association
Mr. Arthur Canter, Pres. and CEO
7 Liberty Sq., Ste. 200
Boston, MA 02109-4821
Phone: (617)720-1776
Toll-Free: 800-662-0272
Fax: (617)720-1305
E-mail: info@masslodging.com
Home Page: http://www.masslodging.com

• 13162 • **Francois L. Nivaud Award**
For high school student in the hospitality program in the state of Massachusetts. Scholarship awarded annually.

• 13163 •
Massachusetts Paralegal Association
Cindy Quinn, Pres.
PO Box 1381
Marblehead, MA 01945
E-mail: massachusetts@paralegals.org
Home Page: http://www.massparalegal.org

• 13164 • **Outstanding Paralegal Award**
For MPA members, 5 years experience as paralegal, nomination. Recognition award bestowed annually.

• 13165 • **Pro Bono Award**
For dedication to helping those less fortunate. Recognition award bestowed annually.

• 13166 •
Massachusetts Science Educators Hall of Fame
Thomas L. Maccarone, Pres.
Web Services
Boyden Hall
Bridgewater State Coll.
Bridgewater, MA 02325
E-mail: webteam@bridgew.edu
Home Page: http://www.bridgew.edu/MHFSE/

• 13167 • **Science Educator's Hall of Fame**
For teacher for distinguished service. Recognition award bestowed annually.

• 13168 •
Massachusetts Society of Professional Engineers
Susan D'Olimpio, Administrator
Engineering Center
One Walnut St.
Boston, MA 02108-3616
Phone: (617)227-5551
Fax: (617)227-6783
E-mail: mspe@engineers.org
Home Page: http://www.mspe.com

• 13169 • **Young Engineers of the Year**
For engineers age 35 or under. Recognition award bestowed annually.

• 13170 •
Massachusetts Sports Commission
Jonathan Paris, Dir. of Events and Marketing
1 FleetCenter Pl., Ste. 200
Boston, MA 02114
Phone: (617)624-1237
Fax: (617)624-1237
E-mail: info@masports.org
Home Page: http://www.masports.org

• 13171 • Grants for Girls
For grassroots girls' sports programs in MA for girls aged 9 to 18. Grant awarded annually.

• 13172 •
Master of Professional Writing Program
Dr. James Ragan, Program Dir.
University of Southern California
WPH 404
Los Angeles, CA 90089-4034
Phone: (213)740-3252
Fax: (213)740-5775
E-mail: mpw@usc.edu
Home Page: http://www.usc.edu/dept/LAS/mpw

• 13173 • Ann Stanford Poetry Prize
For recognition of an outstanding poem or group of poems. Up to five poems may be submitted by April 15. A monetary award of $1,000 for first prize, $200 second prize, and $100 third prize and publication of winning entries in the *The Southern CA Anthology* are awarded annually. Established in 1988 by *The Southern CA Anthology* to honor Ann Stanford. There is a $10 entry fee. All entrants receive a free copy of the SCA.

• 13174 •
Master Printers of America
100 Daingerfield Rd.
Alexandria, VA 22314
Phone: (703)519-8000
Fax: (703)548-4165
E-mail: erp@printing.org
Home Page: http://www.gain.org

• 13175 • Certificate of Craftsmanship
For recognition of printing trade skills in a particular craft. Employees of a non-union member of Master Printers of America, a department of Printing Industries of America, are eligible. A certificate, laminated miniature, and lifetime magazine subscription are awarded. Established in 1950. Administrative Achievement Awards and Production Services Awards are also presented. Over 60,000 individuals have been certified.

• 13176 •
Master's Men Ministry
National Associaton of Free Will Baptists
PO Box 5002
Antioch, TN 37011-5002
Phone: (615)760-6141
Toll-Free: 877-767-8039
Fax: (615)731-0771
E-mail: masters@nafwb.org
Home Page: http://nafwb.org/mm

• 13177 • Layman of the Year
To recognize an outstanding Free Will Baptist layman for his accomplishment in a given year. Nominations are accepted from pastors of each local church. A plaque is awarded annually. Established in 1957.

• 13178 •
Mastiff Club of America
Jodi LaBombard, Membership Sec.
30 Blue Heron Dr.
Rochester, NY 14624
Phone: (585)594-5354
Fax: (352)787-3293
E-mail: merbership-secretary@mastiff.org
Home Page: http://mastiff.org

• 13179 • John Brill Trophy
To recognize a member who has contributed the most to the Club. A trophy is presented annually. Established in 1978 by Mrs. Patty Brill.

• 13180 •
Materials Research Society
John B. Ballance, Exec.Dir.
506 Keystone Dr.
Warrendale, PA 15086-7573
Phone: (724)779-3003
Fax: (724)779-8313
E-mail: info@mrs.org
Home Page: http://www.mrs.org

• 13181 • Graduate Student Award
To recognize a graduate student for a major potential contribution to materials science, based on current research on a project related to symposia presented at the fall or spring meetings of the society. Completed applications must be received at least 90 days prior to first day of MRS meeting. Full-time graduate students (not post-doctoral) must be endorsed by their faculty advisors. A monetary award of $400, a plaque, and waived registration fees are awarded annually to approximately 10 students at the spring meeting and 15 students at the fall meeting. Established in 1980.

• 13182 • MRS Medalist Program
To recognize outstanding recent achievements in materials research. A specific discovery or advancement expected to have a major impact on the progress of any materials-related field is considered. Open to scientists and engineers who have, in recent years, been responsible for major advances in any materials-related field of research. A nominee need not be a member of the Materials Research Society, and nominees of any national origin or citizenship are eligible. The deadline is June 1. A monetary award of $5,000, a medal, and travel expenses are awarded. Each medalist is invited to present a general-interest talk describing his or her work featured within the structure of the society's fall meeting. Established in 1990.

• 13183 • Outstanding Young Investigator Award
To recognize outstanding, interdisciplinary scientific work in materials research by a young scientist or engineer. The awardee must also show exceptional promise as a developing leader in the materials area. A nominee must be a young scientist or engineer who has contributed in an outstanding and innovative way to the progress of materials research; the work should have a significant interdisciplinary aspect. The nominee must be under 36 years of age and need not be a member of the society. Individuals of any national origin or citizenship are eligible. The deadline is October 3. A monetary award of $5,000, a presentation trophy, and a certificate are presented. The awardee is invited to present a general-interest talk to be featured within the structure of the society's spring meeting, reasonable travel expenses to attend the meeting will be reimbursed. Established in 1990.

• 13184 • The David Turnbull Lectureship
To recognize the career of a scientist who has made outstanding contributions to understanding materials phenomena and properties through their research, writing, and lecturing, as exemplified by the life of David Turnbull. A $5,000 honorarium and a citation plaque are awarded annually. In addition, the recipient will give a technical lecture at a designated session of the MRS Fall Meeting, and will provide a manuscript of the lecture suitable for publication in the *Journal of Materials Research.* The registration fee and reasonable travel expenses to the MRS fall meeting will be reimbursed. Additional funds will be provided for travel expenses to enable the recipient to address MRS Sections and University Chapters, and/or participate in production of a video version of the lecture. Nominations must be submitted by June 1.

• 13185 • Von Hippel Award
To recognize outstanding contributions to materials science, particularly in an interdisciplinary manner. Individuals who have demonstrated particularly significant contributions in materials research of a fundamental nature are eligible. Nominations must be submitted by June 1. A monetary award of $10,000, travel expenses to the fall meeting of the society, and an engraved ruby laser crystal are awarded annually. The recipient delivers the von Hippel lecture. Established in 1974 to honor Arthur R. von Hippel, Professor Emeritus, Massachusetts Institute of Technology.

• 13186 •
Mathematical Association of America
Tina H. Straley, Exec.Dir.
1529 18th St. NW
Washington, DC 20036-1358
Phone: (202)387-5200
Toll-Free: 800-741-9415
Fax: (202)265-2384
E-mail: maahq@maa.org
Home Page: http://www.maa.org

• 13187 • Carl B. Allendoerfer Awards
To recognize outstanding expository writing on mathematics. Articles published in *Mathematics Magazine* are eligible. Two monetary prizes of $500 are awarded annually. Established in 1976 in honor of Carl B. Allendoerfer, the twenty-sixth president of the MAA.

• 13188 • Beckenback Book Prize
To recognize the author of a distinguished book published by the Association. A monetary prize of $1,000 is awarded when merited. Established

in 1986, the award succeeds the former MAA Book Prize established in 1982.

• 13189 • **Certificate of Merit**
To recognize an individual for some special work or service associated with mathematics or the wider mathematical community. Awarded at irregular intervals.

• 13190 • **Chauvenet Prize**
To recognize the author of a noteworthy paper published in English, which is in the range of profitable reading for members of the Association. A monetary award of $1,000 and a certificate are awarded annually at the January meeting. Established in 1925 and named for William Chauvenet, a mathematics professor at the U.S. Naval Academy and made available through a gift in the same year from J.L. Coolidge, then MAA President.

• 13191 • **Lester R. Ford Awards**
To recognize outstanding expository writing. Authors of articles published in *The American Mathematical Monthly* are eligible. A maximum of five monetary prizes of $500 are awarded annually at the summer meeting. Established in 1964 to honor Lester R. Ford Sr., the twenty-first president of the MAA.

• 13192 • **Yueh-Gin Gung and Dr. Charles Y. Hu Award for Distinguished Service to Mathematics**
To recognize distinguished service to mathematics other than the creation of new mathematics. A monetary prize of $4,000, a certificate, and a silver cup are awarded annually at the January meeting. Established in 1960, and revised in 1988 and made possible by the late Dr. Hu and his wife, Yueh-Gin Gung. Formerly: (1987) Award for Distinguished Service.

• 13193 • **Deborah and Franklin Tepper Haimo Award for Distinguished College or University Teaching of Mathematics**
To recognize college or university teachers of mathematics who have been widely recognized as extraordinarily successful. A monetary prize of $1,000 and a certificate are awarded to as many as three recipients at the Annual Meeting of the Association.

• 13194 • **Merten Hasse Prize**
To recognize a mathematician younger than 40 years of age at the time of publication for expository writing appearing in an Association publication. A monetary prize of $1,000 and a certificate is awarded biennially in odd-numbered years at the Summer Meetings of the Association. Established in 1987 and named after Merten M. Hasse, who was a former teacher of the anonymous donor.

• 13195 • **Hedrick Lectureship**
To recognize an individual for a significant contribution to the field of mathematics. A certificate and appropriate publicity are awarded annually in August. The recipient presents a lecture at the annual Board of Governors' meeting the following August. The award is anmed after the first president of the MAA.

• 13196 • **George Polya Award**
To recognize outstanding expository writing on mathematics. Articles published in *The College Mathematics Journal* are eligible. Two monetary prizes of $500 are awarded annually. The George Polya Lectureship is also awarded. Established in 1978 to honor George Polya, distinguished teacher and writer.

• 13197 • **Edyth May Sliffe Awards for Distinguished Junior High and High School Mathematics Teaching**
To recognize junior high and high school mathematics teachers whose teams achieved the top scores on standardized mathematics examinations. Monetary prizes ranging from $200 to $750 are awarded annually. The award is named after a high school mathematics teacher in Emeryville, California. Awarded annually to numerous recipients. Established first as an award for high school teachers only; in 1994 the award was extended to junior high school teachers.

• 13198 •
Mathematical Programming Society
Rolf H. Mohring, Chm.
3600 University City Science Ctr.
Philadelphia, PA 19104-2688
Phone: (215)382-9800
Fax: (215)386-7999
E-mail: service@mathprog.org
Home Page: http://www.mathprog.org

• 13199 • **Dantzig Prize**
For recognition of original work in mathematical programming. Prizes are awarded triennially. Established in 1981 by the MPS and the Society of Industrial and Applied Mathematics (SIAM) in honor of George B. Dantzig.

• 13200 • **Fulkerson Prize**
For recognition of outstanding papers in the field of discrete mathematics. Up to three monetary awards of $1500 each are presented triennially at the International Symposium of the MPS. Established in 1981 by MPS and the American Mathematical Society in honor of Ray Fulkerson.

• 13201 • **Orchard-Hays Prize**
For recognition of achievement in the field of computational mathematical programming. An award of $1500 will be made triennially at the International Symposium of the MPS.

• 13202 •
Mathematics Research Center
(Centre de recherches mathematiques, Universite de Montreal)
McGill University
845 Sherbrooke St., W., Rm. 504
Montreal, QC, Canada H3A 2T5
Phone: (514)398-4456
Fax: (514)398-4768
E-mail: vinet@vpa.mcgill.ca
Home Page: http://www.crm.umontreal.ca

• 13203 • **ACP-CRM/CAP-CRM Prize in Theoretical and Mathematical Physics**
To recognize exceptional achievements in theoretical and mathematical physics. The main selection criterion is research excellence. A commemorative medal and a monetary prize of $2,000 are awarded annually. Established in 1995. Formerly: .

• 13204 • **Andre Aisenstadt Prize**
To recognize young Canadian researchers in the mathematical sciences. Awarded annually with a monetary prize of $3,000 and a medal. Established in 1991.

• 13205 • **CRM-Fields-PIMS Prize**
To honor a candidate on the basis of outstanding contributions to the advancement of research in the mathematical sciences. Awarded annually with a monetary prize of $5,000. Established in 1994.

• 13206 •
Mature Market Resource Center
Pat Ford, Associate Dir.
1850 W Winchester Rd., Ste. 213
Libertyville, IL 60048
Phone: (847)816-8660
Toll-Free: 800-828-8225
Fax: (847)816-8662
E-mail: seniorprograms@aol.com
Home Page: http://www.seniorprograms.com

• 13207 • **National Mature Media Awards Program**
To recognize advertising, marketing, and educational materials produced by hospitals, financial institutions, housing communities, community organizations, and other groups that produce information resources for adults 50 years and older. Materials must have been developed or produced during the year preceding the award. Deadline for application is spring. Gold, silver, bronze, and merit awards are bestowed annually in more than 30 categories. Winning entries are displayed at a national aging conference. Established in 1991.

• 13208 •
MC Sailing Association
Herman Van Beek, Exec.Sec.
2816 Biscayne Dr.
Plano, TX 75075
Phone: (972)596-9524
Fax: (509)692-3503
E-mail: secretary@mcscow.org
Home Page: http://www.mcscow.org

• 13209 • **MC National Championship Regatta**
For recognition of winning regatta sailors in one design class scow. The following trophies are awarded: (1) MC Nationals Perpetual Trophy - to the overall winner of the fleet; (2) Women's Perpetual Trophy - to the top woman winner, regular fleet; and (3) Masters - to individuals over 50 years of age by January 1 of the race year and Grand Masters (over 60). Awarded annually in July. Established in 1970.

• 13210 •
McClelland & Stewart, Ltd.
75 Sherbourne St., 5 Fl.
Toronto, ON, Canada M5A 2P9
Phone: (416)598-1114
Toll-Free: 800-788-1074
Fax: (416)598-7764
E-mail: mail@mcclelland.com
Home Page: http://www.mcclelland.com

• 13211 • **Journey Prize**
To recognize and support new and emerging Canadian writers of short fiction. Short stories and excerpts from a novel in progress that have been selected for inclusion in the annual *Journey Prize Stories*, published by McClelland & Stewart, during the previous year are considered. Nominations must be submitted by editors of Canadian literary journals. A monetary prize of $10,000 is awarded annually to one writer included in the Anthology. In addition, the journal that first published and submitted the winning story receives $2,000 from McClellard and Stewart. Established in 1989 with funds provided by James A. Michener's donation of all Canadian royalty earnings from his 1988 best selling novel, Journey.

• 13212 •
McCord Museum of Canadian History
Dr. Victoria Dickenson, Exec.Dir.
690 Sherbrooke St. W
Montreal, QC, Canada H3A 1E9
Phone: (514)398-7100
Fax: (514)398-5045
E-mail: info@mccord.mcgill.ca
Home Page: http://www.mccord-museum.qc.ca

• 13213 • **Marie-Paule Nolin Award**
Funding for internship in McCord Museum Costume and Textile collection.

• 13214 •
McDowell Sonoran Land Trust
PO Box 14365
Scottsdale, AZ 85267-4365
Phone: (480)998-7971
Fax: (480)994-3321
E-mail: preserve@mslt.org
Home Page: http://www.mslt.org

• 13215 • **Arizona Heritage Grant**
For environmental education programs. Monetary award bestowed triennially.

• 13216 •
Donald McGannon Communication Research Center
Faculty Memorial Hall, 4th Fl.
Fordham University
Bronx, NY 10458
Phone: (718)817-4195
Fax: (718)817-5043
E-mail: mcgctr@fordham.edu
Home Page: http://www.fordham.edu

• 13217 • **Communication Policy Research Award**
To recognize published research with social and ethical relevance for communication policy. The methodology of the research can be philosophical, historical, statistical, or scientific. Original research published in the prior or present year, or accepted for future publication in any book must be submitted by January 15. A monetary award of $2,000 is presented annually for the best authored book. Established in 1987.

• 13218 •
McGill University
Gault Nature Reserve
Martin Lechowicz, Dir.
Gault House
422 Chemin des Moulins
Mont-Saint-Hilaire, QC, Canada J3G 4S6
Phone: (450)467-1755
Fax: (450)467-8015
E-mail: info.gault@mcgill.ca
Home Page: http://www.mcgill.ca/gault

• 13219 • **Summer Stipends**
Awarded to undergraduate research assistants. Inquire for application details.

• 13220 •
The McGraw-Hill Companies, Inc.
Harold McGraw III, Chmn, Pres. and CEO
1221 Avenue of the Americas
New York, NY 10020
Phone: (212)512-2000
Toll-Free: (866)436-8502
Fax: (212)512-3840
E-mail: webmaster@mcgraw-hill.com
Home Page: http://www.mcgraw-hill.com

• 13221 • **Harold W. McGraw, Jr. Prize in Education**
To recognize individuals who have made significant contributions to the advancement of knowledge through education. The prize honors individuals whose accomplishments are making a difference today, and whose programs and ideas can serve as effective models for the education of future generations of Americans. Only individuals who are presently committed to the cause of education are eligible. Institutions, boards, organizations and other groups are not. Nominees need not be professional educators, nor is eligibility limited to traditional educational achievement. Individuals may be nominated in the areas of teaching, administration, policy planning, business, government, publishing and adult education. Each year, a Nominating Committee, consisting of leaders in the educational community across the country, submit nominations to the Board of Judges. In addition, the Board of Judges considers nominations received directly, if they meet eligibility requirements, and include references from the educational community. The following criteria are used for consideration: (1) Prize winners must have made a significant impact in their fields relating to the advancement of knowledge through education; (2) Prize winners must have displayed a sense of innovation in attempting to creatively change, improve, enhance or further a specific area of education; (3) Individuals may be nominated for lifetime achievement; (4) Winners from teaching, administration or policy planning must have instituted or enhanced curriculums, developed exceptional programs, changed or improved policy; and (5) Winners from the business sector must display a sense of commitment beyond financial contributions, and must have taken a significant leadership role in furthering a specific aspect of education. Up to three monetary prizes of $25,000 each are awarded annually. Established in 1988 in honor of the Centennial celebration of McGraw-Hill and Harold W. McGraw, Jr., chairman emeritus, McGraw Hill, Inc. Hill, Inc.

• 13222 •
McHenry County Historical Society
Nancy J. Fike, Admin.
6422 Main St.
Union, IL 60180
Phone: (815)923-2267
Fax: (815)923-2271
E-mail: info@mchsonline.org
Home Page: http://www.mchsonline.org

• 13223 • **Leta Clark Elementary Teacher Scholarship**
For McHenry County high school senior planning to become elementary teacher. Monetary award bestowed annually.

• 13224 •
McNeill Street Pumping Station Preservation Society
Bob Hopkins, Sec.-Treas.
PO Box 957
Shreveport, LA 71163-0957
Phone: (318)221-3388
Phone: (318)221-8312
Fax: (318)424-6508
Home Page: http://www.mcneillstreet.org

• 13225 • **Honorary Society Membership**
For service to the society and its mission. Recognition award bestowed periodically.

• 13226 •
Meadville Area Family YMCA
Mary Lee McQuiston, Dir.
356 Chestnut St.
Meadville, PA 16335
Phone: (814)336-2196
Fax: (814)336-6012

• 13227 • **George Barco Volunteer of the Year**
For volunteer service to the YMCA. Recognition award bestowed annually.

• 13228 •
Mechanical Contractors Association of the Capital District
Ralph R. Zeto, Exec.Dir.
6 Airline Dr.
Albany, NY 12205
Phone: (518)869-0582
Fax: (518)869-0583
E-mail: ralphzeto@msn.com

• 13229 • **Richard P. Walsh Scholarship**
For scholastic ability. Scholarship awarded annually.

• 13230 •
Media Alliance
Jeff Pearlstein, Exec.Dir.
942 Market St., Ste. 503
San Francisco, CA 94102
Phone: (415)546-6334
Fax: (415)546-6218
E-mail: info@media-alliance.org
Home Page: http://www.media-alliance.org

• 13231 • **Mitford Memorial Scholarship**
For outstanding youth journalist. Scholarship awarded annually.

• 13232 •
***Media and Methods* Magazine**
Michele Sokoloff, Publisher
1429 Walnut St.
Philadelphia, PA 19102
Phone: (215)563-6005
Toll-Free: 800-555-5657
Fax: (215)587-9706
E-mail: michelesok@media-methods.com
Home Page: http://www.media-methods.com

• 13233 • ***Media and Methods* Magazine Awards Portfolio Competition**
Recognizes and features outstanding instructional technologies for K-12 classrooms and library use. Honors the commitment and creativity of the producers, manufacturers, and distributors who are making a significant contribution to excellence in education. Entries should serve the instructional presentation equipment needs of teachers, administrators, and students in public and private schools. A special award seal for one year's use, a framed certificate, and a published recognition in the May/June issue are awarded to the winning companies. Formerly: *Media and Methods* Maxi Awards.

• 13234 •
Media Human Resources Association
Johnny C. Taylor Jr., Senior VP
1800 Duke St.
Alexandria, VA 22314-1943
Phone: (703)548-3440
Phone: (703)548-6999
Toll-Free: 800-283-SHRM
Fax: (703)535-6490
E-mail: shrm@shrm.org
Home Page: http://www.shrm.org

• 13235 • **John D. Blodger Diversity Award**
Recognizes advances in the concept of diversity within the media industry. Awarded annually.

• 13236 • **Catalyst Award**
To recognize outstanding human resource management in the media industry. Nominations may be submitted by MHRA members and by publisher presidents who have MHRA members on staff. The deadline for nominations is April 1. A glass sculpture from Frable Gallery, Atlanta, is awarded annually when merited at the annual conference. Established in 1990.

• 13237 •
The Media Project
Melissa Havard, Contact
269 S Beverly Dr., Ste. 721
Beverly Hills, CA 90212
Phone: (310)234-0454
Fax: (310)441-6553
E-mail: healthytv@themediaproject.com
Home Page: http://www.themediaproject.com

Formerly: (1995) Center for Population Options (California).

• 13238 • **SHINE (Sexual Health in Entertainment) Awards**
To recognize outstanding portrayals of sexuality, reproductive health, and family planning issues in entertainment and public affairs programming. Work must be aired nationally. Eligible topics include, but are not limited to pregnancy, HIV and AIDS, contraception, sexual education, and healthy relationships. Awards are presented in the following 12 categories: comedy, daytime drama, drama, entertainment special, informational/documentary, scene stealer, series storyline, youth episodic, youth informational/documentary, Latino broadcast novela, Latino broadcast series, Latino broadcast talk/variety. Two additional awards are presented: Special Corporate Achievement Award and Special Latino Award for Excellence. Awards are presented annually at a gala awards ceremony in October in Los Angeles. Formerly: Nancy Susan Reynolds Media Awards.

• 13239 •
Median Iris Society
Perry Dyer, Pres.
6401 Cedar Rd.
Iuka, IL 62849
Phone: (618)822-6584
E-mail: erni@midwest.net
Home Page: http://www.medianiris.com

• 13240 • **Median Iris Awards**
For recognition of superiority in a specific category of median irises. The iris must previously have won an Award of Merit from the American Iris Society, and must meet the criteria for the category. Medals are presented in the following categories: Standard Dwarf Bearded - Cook - Douglas Medal, named for the two originators of the type, Paul H. Cook and Geddes Douglas; Intermediate Bearded - the Hans and Jacob Sass Medal, named for the famed brothers whose imagination carried them far with this class when it was of little repute in contrast to the expanding size and color variety of the tall beardeds; the Border Bearded - the Knowlton Medal, named for Harold Knowlton, former president of the American Iris Society; and the Williamson-White Medal for the Miniature Tall Bearded class named for two early workers in this field, Mary Williamson and Alice White. Winners of these medals qualify to compete for the Dykes Medal, the most coveted honor in irisdom. The Dykes Medal is presented by the British Iris Society. Awarded annually when merited at the American Iris Society Convention. The awards were established earlier but given medal status in 1966, and 1993 in the case of the Miniature Tall Bearded class. Additional information is available from the American Iris Society, 3110 Kirkham Drive., Glendale, CA 91206-1128.

• 13241 •
Medical Dental Hospital Business Associates
Jennifer English Lynch, Exec.Dir.
8201 Greensboro Dr., 3rd Fl.
McLean, VA 22102
Phone: (703)610-9016
Toll-Free: 888-751-0481
Fax: (847)227-4771
E-mail: jlynch@mdhba.org
Home Page: http://www.mdhba.org

• 13242 • **Elmer Award**
To recognize MDHBA members selected by the past Presidents Council as having made the most significant contribution to organizational activities. Established in 1981 in honor of member, Elmer Uffman, in recognition of his contributions to the medical economics profession and MDHBA.

• 13243 • **Robert T. Hellrung Award**
To recognize an individual for major contributions to the Association during his or her term in office. Awarded annually. Established in 1977 in honor of Robert T. Hellrung for his contributions to the medical economics profession and to MDHBA.

• 13244 • Lifetime Achievement Award
Award of recognition.

• 13245 • Pinnacle Award
Recognizes member agencies who have received recognition from clients. Awarded annually.

• 13246 •
Medical Education for South African Blacks
Saul Levin, Pres./CEO
2370 Champlain St. NW, Ste. 12
Washington, DC 20009-2633
Phone: (202)222-0050
Toll-Free: (866)MESABO06
Fax: (202)222-0202
E-mail: mesab@mesab.org
Home Page: http://www.mesab.org

• 13247 • Award for Service
Recognizes persons who have an outstanding record of service to the community, especially disadvantaged elements of the community, with emphasis on work in the U.S. and South Africa. Awarded annually.

• 13248 •
Medical Fitness Association
Cary Wing EdD, Exec.Dir.
PO Box 73103
Richmond, VA 23235-8026
Phone: (804)327-0330
Fax: (804)327-1630
E-mail: info@medicalfitness.org
Home Page: http://medicalfitness.org

• 13249 • Distinguished Service
To recognize those who have displayed significant leadership in the profession. Recipients of these awards reflect outstanding accomplishments in their professional and personal lives. Two awards are offered, one for Management Excellence in Hospital Health and Fitness Center Leadership (CEO/Administrator), and one for Management Excellence in Hospital Health and Fitness Center Operations (non-CEO). Both awards are presented annually at the MFA annual conference. Any member of MFA may nominate himself/herself or another individual for this award. The nominee must be currently employed in a full-time capacity as the chief executive officer (president/administrator) of a hospital or health system, or as the manager of the hospital's fitness center; must be in the position for at least one year prior to nomination, and a member of MFA for at least two years. Established in 1995.

• 13250 •
Medical Library Association
Carla J. Funk, Exec.Dir.
65 E Wacker Pl., Ste. 1900
Chicago, IL 60601-7298
Phone: (312)419-9094
Fax: (312)419-8950
E-mail: info@mlahq.org
Home Page: http://www.mlanet.org

• 13251 • Estelle Brodman Award for the Academic Medical Librarian of the Year
To recognize both significant achievement and potential for leadership and continuing excellence at mid-career in the area of academic health sciences librarianship. Awarded annually. Established in 1986 by Irwin H. Pizer to recognize Dr. Brodman's exemplary career as an educator, seminal thinker, able administrator, technological innovator, and skillful practitioner.

• 13252 • Lois Ann Colaianni Award for Excellence and Achievement in Hospital Librarianship
This award is given to a member of the association who has made significant contributions to the profession through overall distinction or leadership in hospital library administration or service; production of a definitive publication related to hospital librarianship, teaching, research, advocacy, or the development or application of innovative technology to hospital librarianship. Awarded annually. Established in 1991.

• 13253 • Cunningham Memorial International Fellowship
To provide for observation and supervised work in one or more medical libraries in the United States or Canada. Medical librarians from outside the United States and Canada are eligible to apply by December 1. A monetary award of $6,000 and an additional $2,000 for travel within the United States or Canada are awarded annually. Established in 1967 to honor Eileen Roach Cunningham, librarian at Vanderbilt University and forerunner of the International Cooperation Committee.

• 13254 • Louise Darling Medal for Distinguished Achievement in Collection Development in the Health Sciences
To recognize individuals, institutions, or groups of individuals who have made significant contributions to health sciences librarianship through overall distinction or leadership in collection development, distinctive publishing, teaching in collection development, development of outstanding national resources, or other collection development related activities. Awarded annually. Established in 1987 by Ballen Booksellers International, Inc., to recognize Louise Darling's significant accomplishment in collection development in the health sciences, in particular the development of the collection at the University of California, Los Angeles, and the exemplary collection development policy, "An Outline of Suggested Acquisitions for the Biomedical Library." It continues to be supported by Blackwell North America, Inc. Deadline for nominations is November 1.

• 13255 • Janet Doe Lectureship
To select an individual to present a lecture on either the history or philosophy of medical librarianship. This lecture honors Janet Doe, Librarian Emerita of the New York Academy of Medicine, past president of MLA, and editor of the first two editions of the *Handbook of Medical Library Practice*. Membership contributions insure the continuance of the lectureship as a highlight of the association's annual meeting. The lectureship offers an honorarium and travel expenses to the individual selected to present the lecture. The lecture is subsequently published in the *Bulletin of the Medical Library Association*. Established in 1966 by an anonymous donor. Deadline for nominations is November 1.

• 13256 • Fellows and Honorary Members
Fellowship is conferred on regular MLA members in recognition of outstanding and sustained contributions to the advancement of the purposes of MLA. Honorary membership is conferred on individuals, not formerly MLA members, who have made outstanding contributions to the advancement of the purposes of the association. Awarded annually.

• 13257 • Murray Gottlieb Prize
For recognition of an outstanding unpublished essay on the history of American medicine and allied sciences by a health sciences librarian. A monetary prize of $100 is awarded annually. Established in 1956 by Robert and Jo Grimes of the Old Hickory Bookshop, Brinklow, Maryland. Given in memory of Murray Gottlieb, a New York antiquarian book dealer. Deadline to submit papers is November 1.

• 13258 • ISI Frank Bradway Rogers Information Advancement Award
To recognize an MLA member or small group of members for an outstanding contribution to the application of technology to the delivery of health sciences information. Awarded annually. Established in 1973. Sponsored by the Thomson Scientific. Deadline for nominations is November 1. Formerly: Frank Bradways Rogers Information Advancement Award.

• 13259 • Joseph Leiter Lectureship
To recognize lecturers chosen for their ability to discuss subjects related to biomedical communications. The lecture is presented biennially at the association's annual meeting and in alternate years at NLM. Established in 1983 to stimulate intellectual liaison between the Medical Library Association and the National Library of Medicine.

• 13260 • Majors/MLA Chapter Project of the Year Award
This is a general award for excellence, innovation, and contribution to the profession of health sciences librarianship, demonstrated through special projects beyond the normal operational programming of an MLA chapter. Awarded annually. Sponsored by Majors Scientific Books Inc. Established in 1995.

• 13261 • John P. McGovern Award Lectureship
To select an individual of significant national or international stature to present a lecture on a topic of importance to health sciences librarianship at the annual meetings of the association. Established in 1983 in honor of John P. McGov-

ern, M.D., noted physician, educator, author, and medical historian.

• 13262 • MLA Award for Distinguished Public Service

To recognize individuals whose exemplary actions have served to advance the health, welfare, and intellectual freedom of the public. Nominees are not limited to members of the library and information science profession, nor to the membership of the association. Awarded annually. Established in 1988.

• 13263 • MLA Research, Development and Demonstration Projects Awards

To support research, development, and demonstration projects that will help to promote excellence in the field of health science librarianship and information science. (Grants will not be given to support activities that are operational in nature or have only local usefulness.) Candidates must be individual members of the MLA, be practicing medical librarians, hold graduate degrees in library science, have at least two years experience at the professional level, and be citizens or permanent residents of the United States. Monetary awards are presented annually when merited. Established in 1985. Deadline to submit applications is December 1. Awards range from $100 to $1000.

• 13264 • MLA Scholarships and Fellowships

To assist qualified students in graduate library science programs and to enable practicing health sciences librarians to take advantage of opportunities for continuing professional development. The following programs are offered: Continuing Education Grant; MLA Scholarship for Minority Students - African-American, Hispanic, Asian, Native American, or Pacific Island American individuals who wish to study medical librarianship are eligible for a $2,000 scholarship; ISI, MLA Scholarship; and MLA Doctoral Fellowship. The awards are presented each year at the annual meeting. Deadline to submit applications is Decemeber 1.

• 13265 • Marcia C. Noyes Award

This, the association's highest professional distinction, is given for recognition of lasting outstanding contributions to medical librarianship. Nominations are accepted. Awarded annually when merited. Established in 1947 in memory of Marcia C. Noyes (1869-1946), one of MLA's charter members. Deadline to submit nominations is November 1.

• 13266 • President's Award

To recognize a notable or important contribution made during the past association year by an MLA member. The contribution must have enhanced the profession of medical librarianship and furthered the objectives of the MLA. Selection is made by the officers and Board of Directors of the association. Established in 1982.

• 13267 • Rittenhouse Award

To recognize the distinguished work of library students and library interns who are interested in medical librarianship. Unpublished manuscripts applicable to medical librarianship written by a student in an MLA-approved medical library course, or a trainee in an MLA-approved internship program are eligible. A monetary prize of $500 is awarded annually. Established in 1967. Sponsored by Rittenhouse Book Distrbutors, Inc., Philadelphia, PA. Deadline to submit papers is November 1.

• 13268 •
Medical Mycological Society of the Americas
Ms. Annette Fothergill, Sec.-Treas.
2501 Timberline Dr.
Austin, TX 78746
Phone: (512)458-7566
Fax: (512)458-7697
E-mail: jim.harris@tdh.state.tx.us

• 13269 • Rhoda Benham Award

To recognize meritorious contributions to the field of medical mycology. Members may submit nominations. A medal is awarded annually at the annual meeting. Established in 1967 in memory of Dr. Rhoda Benham. For further information, contact William G. Merz, Secretary-Treasurer.

• 13270 • Billy H. Cooper Memorial Meridian Award

To recognize distinguished contributions to the area of clinical mycology. Members under 50 years of age are eligible. A monetary award of $500 and a plaque are presented annually at the annual meeting. Established in 1982 in memory of Dr. Billy H. Cooper.

• 13271 •
Medical Society of the State of New York
PO Box 5404
Lake Success, NY 11042-5404
Phone: (516)488-6100
Fax: (516)488-1267
E-mail: mssny@mssny.org
Home Page: http://www.mssny.org

• 13272 • Albion O. Bernstein, M.D. Award

To recognize a physician or scientist for outstanding achievement in medicine. Physicians or scientists in the United States or Canada under the age of 50 are eligible. A $2,000 stipend and a scroll are awarded annually at the House of Delegates Meeting. Established in 1962 by the late Morris T. Bernstein to perpetuate the memory of his son, a physician who tragically lost his life while responding to a medical call.

• 13273 •
Medieval Academy of America
Richard K. Emmerson, Exec.Dir./Ed.
104 Mt. Auburn St., 5th Fl.
Cambridge, MA 02138
Phone: (617)491-1622
Fax: (617)492-3303
E-mail: speculum@medievalacademy.org
Home Page: http://
www.medievalacademy.org

• 13274 • John Nicholas Brown Prize

For recognition of a first book or monograph on a medieval subject, judged to be of outstanding quality, by an author resident in North America. The selection of the winner is made by a committee appointed by the President of the Academy. Works on any aspect of medieval studies published in the fourth year prior to the competition are considered. A monetary prize of $1,000 is presented each year at the annual meeting. Established in 1978 and named after John Nicholas Brown, one of the founders of the Medieval Academy.

• 13275 • Van Courtlandt Elliott Prize

To recognize a young scholar publishing his or her first article (not less than five pages in length) in the field of medieval studies. Articles appearing in any journal (American, European, or other) published two years prior to the competition are considered, provided the authors are residents of North America. The committee awards a single prize of $500. Established in 1971 in memory of Dr. Van Courtlandt Elliott.

• 13276 • Haskins Medal

To recognize a distinguished publication of outstanding importance in the field of medieval studies. Books by scholars having professional residence in North America that have been published within the six years prior to the award are considered. A medal is presented annually. Established in 1940 in memory of Charles Homer Haskins, one of the founders of the Academy and its second President.

• 13277 •
Meeting Professionals International
Colin Rorrie PhD, Pres./CEO
3030 LBJ Freeway, Ste. 1700
Dallas, TX 75234-2759
Phone: (972)702-3000
Fax: (972)702-3070
E-mail: feedback@mpiweb.org
Home Page: http://www.mpiweb.org

• 13278 • Chapters of the Year

For recognition of the chapters that reflects progress and professionalism in the meeting industry. The following criteria are considered: Educational Programs; Membership Growth and Retention; Administrative Capabilities, Communications including Public Relations/Marketing; Special Activities; and Community Service. Two plaques are awarded annually; one for chapters with up to 250 members and the other for chapters with over 250 members. Established in 1981.

• 13279 • **Global Paragon Awards**
To recognize exceptional and distinctive global meetings. The entire meeting industry, both corporate and association sectors, is eligible to compete for this premier award which recognizes excellence in the planning and delivery of meetings throughout the world. A total of two awards are presented; one for meetings which cost up to $1000 per attendee and another for those costing over $1000 per attendee. Both exclude transportation costs. The two categories are divided into budgetary levels based on the total cost per attendee to produce the meeting in question. Winners receive a Galway Crystal Trophy. Established in 1994.

• 13280 • **Industry Award**
To recognize contributions resulting in the continued elevation of professionalism, standards, and recognition of the meeting industry. Established 1984.

• 13281 • **Marion Kershner Memorial Chapter Leader Award**
Presented annually to a member who motivates others, stimulates volunteer functions and acts as a catalyst to cause exceptional results that influence the life of that individual's respective MPI chapter. Winner receives a crystal gavel. Awarded annually. Established in 1990. Formerly: (1997) Chapter Leader of the Year.

• 13282 • **MPI Planner of the Year**
Presented annually to a member of MPI in recognition of outstanding association/industry contributions, leadership and professionalism. The award is based on MPI service at the International and chapter levels, presentations relating to the industry, articles written for the hospitality industry press and industry recognition received. A Waterford bowl is awarded. Established in 1974. Formerly: (1976) Buzz Bartow Memorial Award.

• 13283 • **MPI Supplier of the Year**
Presented annually to a member of MPI in recognition of outstanding association/industry contributions, leadership and professionalism. The award is based on MPI service at the International and chapter levels, presentations relating to the industry, articles written for the hospitality industry press and industry recognition received. A Waterford bowl is awarded. Established in 1974. Formerly: (1976) Buzz Bartow Memorial Award.

• 13284 • **President's Award**
For contributions beyond the call of duty to MPI by substantially increasing the association's progression and recognition within the meeting industry. A plaque is awarded annually. Established in 1984.

• 13285 • **Tomorrow's Leaders of MPI Award**
Presented annually to MPI members who have made contributions to the association at the international and/or chapter level(s). MPI's newest award category, recipients also reflect the key goal of professionalism as stated in the association's strategic plan. Recipients must be members for less than four years. A Tiffany crystal disc is awarded annually. Established in 1995.

• 13286 •
Meetings and Conventions
Loren G. Edelstein, Exec.Dir.
% Northstar Travel Media LLC
500 Plaza Dr.
Secaucus, NJ 07094-3626
Phone: (201)902-2000
Fax: (201)319-1716
E-mail: ledelstein@ntmllc.com
Home Page: http://www.meetings-conventions.com

• 13287 • **Gold Awards**
To honor hotels internationally for exemplary service and facilities. Winners are elected by readers of *Meetings and Conventions* magazine. Plaques are awarded annually. Established in 1978. Gold Platter, Gold Service, and Gold Key Awards are presented.

• 13288 •
Melpomene Institute
Rachel Seidman, Dir.
1010 University Ave. W, Ste. 205
St. Paul, MN 55104
Phone: (651)642-1951
Fax: (651)642-1871
E-mail: info@melpomene.org
Home Page: http://www.melpomene.org

Formerly: (2002) Melpomene Institute for Women's Health Research.

• 13289 • **Melpomene Outstanding Achievement Award**
To recognize a woman who, by example, outreach, and continuing endeavors serves as a role model for girls and women of all ages who seek to make physical activity a part of their life. Awarded biennially. Established in 1986.

• 13290 •
Memorial Foundation for Jewish Culture
Dr. Jerry Hochbaum, Exec.VP
50 Broadway, 34th Fl.
New York, NY 10004-1690
Phone: (212)425-6606
Fax: (212)425-6602
E-mail: office@mfjc.org
Home Page: http://www.mfjc.org

• 13291 • **International Doctoral Scholarship for Studies Specializing in Jewish Fields**
To help train qualified individuals for careers in Jewish scholarship and research and to help Jewish educational, religious, and communal workers obtain advanced training for leadership positions. Any graduate student specializing in a Jewish field who is officially enrolled or registered in a doctoral program at a recognized university is eligible to apply. Priority is given to applicants who are at the dissertation level. Applications must be requested in writing and completed forms submitted by October 31. Grants range from $2,000 to $5,000 a year.

• 13292 • **International Fellowships in Jewish Studies**
To assist well-qualified individuals in carrying out an independent scholarly, literary, or art project, in a field of Jewish specialization that makes a significant contribution to the understanding, preservation, enhancement, or transmission of Jewish culture. Any qualified scholar, researcher, or artist who possesses the knowledge and experience to formulate and implement a project in a field of Jewish specialization may apply for support. Applications must be requested in writing and completed forms submitted by October 31. Fellowships range from $1000 to $5000 a year.

• 13293 •
Menlo Park Chamber of Commerce
Fran Dehn, Pres./CEO
1100 Merrill St.
Menlo Park, CA 94025-4386
Phone: (650)325-2818
Fax: (650)325-0920
E-mail: info@menloparkchamber.com
Home Page: http://www.menloparkchamber.com

• 13294 • **Golden Acorn Award**
For volunteerism. Recognition award bestowed annually.

• 13295 • **Jerry Jacob Scholarship**
For business excellence. Scholarship awarded annually.

• 13296 •
Mental Health Association of the Piedmont
Sharon Fields McCormick, Exec.Dir.
153 N. Spring St.
Spartanburg, SC 29306
Phone: (864)582-3104
Fax: (864)582-3322

• 13297 • **Davenport Distinguished Service Award**
For service/advocacy/education in field of mental health. Recognition award bestowed annually.

• 13298 •
Merchandise Mart Properties, Inc.
200 World Trade Ctr., Ste. 470
Chicago, IL 60654
Phone: (312)527-7613
Toll-Free: 800-677-MART
Fax: (312)527-7782
Home Page: http://www.merchandisemart.com

• 13299 • **Merchandise Mart Hall of Fame**
To recognize outstanding American merchants whose contributions to merchandising have had continuing and far-reaching impact on the nation's economy. Individuals who have contrib-

uted most significantly to the American system of distribution through merchandising innovations, civic or community leadership, enlightened human relations and financial success are eligible. A bronze bust of each man elected is installed on The Merchandise Mart Plaza. Awarded when merited. Established in 1953 by the late Joseph P. Kennedy, former Ambassador to Great Britain and owner of The Merchandise Mart.

• 13300 •
Mercy Corps
Neal Keny-Guyer, CEO
Dept. W
PO Box 2669
Portland, OR 97208-2669
Phone: (503)796-6800
Toll-Free: 800-292-3355
Fax: (503)796-6844
E-mail: info@mercycorps.org
Home Page: http://www.mercycorps.org

• 13301 • **Humanitarian of the Year**
Recognizes an individual who has made significant contributions to the poor. Awarded annually.

• 13302 •
Merrimack Valley Chamber of Commerce
Joseph J. Bevilacqua, Pres.
264 Essex St.
Lawrence, MA 01840-1496
Phone: (978)686-0900
Fax: (978)794-9953
E-mail:
thechamber@merrimackvalleychamber.com
Home Page: http://
www.merrimackvalleychamber.com

• 13303 • **Wilkinson Award**
For citizenship and community service. Recognition award bestowed annually.

• 13304 •
Mesa Arts Center
Gerry Fathauer, Exec.Dir.
1 E Main St.
PO Box 1466
Mesa, AZ 85211-1466
Phone: (480)644-6501
Fax: (480)644-2901
E-mail:
artscenterinfo@mesaartscenter.com
Home Page: http://
www.mesaartscenter.com

• 13305 • **Mesa Contemporary Arts**
Presents national juried contemporary art exhibitions throughout the year. Monetary and purchase awards totaling up to $2,000 per exhibit are presented. The gallery was established in 1981, and is sponsored by the City of Mesa.

• 13306 •
Metal Construction Association
Pam Oddi, Administrator
4700 W Lake Ave.
Glenview, IL 60025-1485
Phone: (847)375-4718
Fax: 877-665-2234
E-mail: mca@metalconstruction.org
Home Page: http://
www.metalconstruction.org

• 13307 • **MCA Annual Merit Awards Program**
To recognize and celebrate the most successful buildings, products, and systems turned out each year by the metal construction industry. The awards are given for advancement of the objectives of the industry and to expand the role of metal in construction. Projects completed during the previous two-year period may be submitted in four categories: commercial, industrial, institutional and residential. The deadline is October 19. Three types of awards are presented: Award of Merit, Honor Award, and Scholarship Award, $1,000 scholarships to outstanding honorees from the Honor Award category. The scholarships are given to accredited architectural, engineering, or trade schools or students of the honorees' choice. Awarded annually.

• 13308 •
Metal Powder Industries Federation
C. James Trombino, Exec.Dir./CEO
105 College Rd. E
Princeton, NJ 08540-6692
Phone: (609)452-7700
Fax: (609)987-8523
E-mail: info@mpif.org
Home Page: http://www.mpif.org

• 13309 • **Automotive Achievement Award**
To recognize individuals contributing to the expansion of automotive powder metal applications. Candidates must be active employees of automotive OEM manufacturers and/or first tier suppliers. The deadline for submissions is September 30. A certificate and citation are awarded when merited during the Society of Automotive Engineers' Annual Conference and Exposition.

• 13310 • **Automotive Innovation Award**
To recognize innovative powder/metal designs, processes and materials used in automobile applications. Awarded annually by the President of the Metal Powder Industries Federation at the Society of Automotive Engineers' Annual Conference and Exposition.

• 13311 • **Distinguished Service to Powder Metallurgy Award**
To recognize individuals who devote the major part of their working careers to one or more segments of the field of powder metallurgy and whose long-term contributions and achievements are such that, in the minds of their peers, they deserve special recognition for outstanding and distinguished service. Individuals who are U.S. or Canadian residents for 15 years prior to the award and with 25 years of service to the industry are eligible. Ten to twelve plaques are awarded biennially, in odd-numbered years. Established in 1967.

• 13312 • **Outstanding Technical Paper Award**
To recognize authors for excellence in scientific and technical written communications from those papers presented and submitted for publication from the annual technical conference organized by the Metal Powder Industries Federation and APMI International; to enhance the quality of technology transfer in the P/M literature by increasing the professional level of papers submitted for the conference; and to enhance and promote the science and technology of powder metallurgy products, processes, and materials. Papers must be scientifically or technically new, innovative, or a constructive review; have long-term reference value; have professional integrity; and have clear organization in writing, graphics, and logic. Awarded annually. Established in 1993.

• 13313 • **Powder Metallurgy Design Competition**
To recognize outstanding applications of powder metallurgy such as cost saving, reliability, strength, and ability to perform in demanding applications. Member companies of the Federation are eligible for consideration in the categories of ferrous, non-ferrous, injection molded, stainless steel, advanced particulate materials, and overseas. The following prizes are awarded: Grand Prizes, and Awards of Distinction. Plaques are awarded annually. Established in 1964.

• 13314 • **Powder Metallurgy Pioneer Award**
To recognize outstanding individuals in all aspects of the broad fields of powder metallurgy who have been constructive in the pioneering development and advancement of the industry. Members are eligible. Awarded every four years. Established in 1961.

• 13315 •
Metropolitan Area Planning Council
David C. Soule, Exec. Dir.
60 Temple Pl.
Boston, MA 02111
Phone: (617)451-2770
Fax: (617)482-7185
Home Page: http://www.mapc.org

• 13316 • **Charles Eliot II Award**
For excellence in regional planning. Recognition award bestowed annually.

Awards are arranged in alphabetical order below their administering organizations

• 13317 •
Metropolitan Opera
Ann Coughlin, Company Admin.
Lincoln Center
New York, NY 10023
Phone: (212)799-3100
Fax: (212)870-7606
E-mail: ncouncil@mail.metopera.org
Home Page: http://www.metopera.org

• 13318 • **Metropolitan Opera National Council Auditions**
To discover new talent for the Metropolitan Opera and to find, assist, and encourage young singers in preparation for their careers. Women and men between 20 and 30 years of age are eligible. District auditions take place from September through February and regional auditions usually take place by the end of February. The following awards are granted in each Region: first place - $800, Mrs. Edgar Tobin Award; second place - $600, Metropolitan Opera National Council Award; and third place - $400, Metropolitan Opera National Council Award. Regional winners go on to New York to compete in the Semi Finals and Grand Finals Concert. Each semi-finalist not selected to advance to the Grand Finals Concert receives $1,500; National Finalists receive $5,000 and National Winners receive $15,000.

• 13319 • **Verdi Medal of Achievement**
For recognition of achievement in opera. A medal is presented annually. Established in 1976 by Betti Richard, a sculptor. In addition, an auditions program is held.

• 13320 •
Metropolitan Opera Guild
Rudolph S. Rauch, Managing Dir.
70 Lincoln Center Plz., 6th Fl.
New York, NY 10023
Phone: (212)769-7000
Fax: (212)769-7007
E-mail: info@metguild.org
Home Page: http://www.metopera.org

• 13321 • **Belmont Medal**
To recognize an individual for very distinguished service to the Metropolitan Opera Guild. A medal is awarded from time to time and is normally presented at a meeting of the Guild Board. Established in 1980 in memory of Eleanor Robson Belmont, who founded the Metropolitan Opera Guild in 1935.

• 13322 •
MG Drivers Club of North America
Richard F. Miller, Club Dir.
18 George's Pl.
Clinton, NJ 08809-1334
Phone: (908)713-6251
Fax: (908)713-6251
E-mail: mgdriversclub@hotmail.com
Home Page: http://www.mgdriversclub.com

• 13323 • **Cecil Kimber Enthusiasts Award**
For significant contribution to the MG Marque. A trophy awarded annually.

• 13324 •
Miami Beach Film Society
Dana Keith, Founder/Dir.
512 Espanola Way
Miami Beach, FL 33139
Phone: (305)673-4567
Fax: (305)534-5196
E-mail: info@mbcinema.com
Home Page: http://www.mbcinema.com

• 13325 • **MBFS**
For excellent contribution to film industry. Recognition award bestowed annually.

• 13326 •
Michael E. DeBakey International Surgical Society
Kenneth L. Mattox MD, Sec.-Treas.
1 Baylor Plz.
Department of Surgery
Houston, TX 77030
Phone: (713)798-4557
Fax: (713)796-9605
E-mail: mediss04@aol.com
Home Page: http://www.mediss.org

• 13327 • **Michael E. DeBakey Award**
To recognize outstanding achievement in the field of cardiovascular surgery. A monetary award of $25,000 and a miniature bronze statue of Dr. DeBakey are awarded biennially. Established in 1978.

• 13328 •
Michener Awards Foundation
(Fondation des Prix Michener)
David Humphreys, Pres.
130 Albert St., Ste. 1620
Ottawa, ON, Canada K1P 5G4
Phone: (613)230-3155
Fax: (613)236-2556
E-mail: info@michenerawards.ca
Home Page: http://www.michenerawards.ca

• 13329 • **Michener-Deacon Fellowship (Prix Michener de Journalism)**
To recognize the print or broadcasting medium judged to have performed the outstanding example of objective, hard-hitting, and meritorious public service journalism in Canada in the preceding year. Eligible for the award are: newspapers - daily, weekly, or with other publication intervals; periodicals; radio and television stations; news agencies; and radio and television networks. Entries may be submitted by the end of January. A metal sculpture on a marble base is awarded annually. Established in 1970 by the Federation of Press Clubs of Canada to honor the Rt. Hon. Roland C. Michener, P.C., C.C. Formerly: (2006) Michener Award.

• 13330 • **Michener Four-Month Fellowships (Bourses de quatre mois)**
To encourage advancement in the field of Canadian journalism by rewarding career journalists who are interested in studies or projects that benefit the Canadian community. Canadian citizens or residents of Canada are eligible for the $25,000 award for a study leave of four months. Entries must be submitted in February. Established in 1987 to honor the Rt. Hon. Roland C. Michener, P.C., C.C. and the benefactor Paul S. Deacon.

• 13331 •
Michigan Association for Infant Mental Health
Deborah Weatherston PhD, Exec.Dir.
The Guidance Center
Insititute for Children, Youth, and Families
13101 Allen Rd.
Southgate, MI 48195
Phone: (734)785-7700
Fax: (734)287-1680
E-mail: dkahraman@guidance-center.org
Home Page: http://www.mi-aimh.msu.edu

• 13332 • **Selma Fraiberg Award**
For service to infants and families. Recognition award bestowed annually.

• 13333 • **Betty Tableman Award**
For service to infants and families. Recognition award bestowed annually.

• 13334 •
Michigan Association for the Education of Young Children
Keith Myers, Exec.Dir.
4572 S Hagadorn Rd., Ste. 1-D
East Lansing, MI 48823-5385
Phone: (517)336-9700
Toll-Free: 800-336-6424
Fax: (517)336-9790
E-mail: miaeyc@miaeyc.org
Home Page: http://www.miaeyc.org

• 13335 • **Betty Garlick Lifetime Achievement Award**
For lifelong commitment to Michigan's children. Recognition award bestowed annually.

• 13336 •
Michigan Association of Metal Finishers
2565 Industrial Row Dr.
Troy, MI 48084
Phone: (248)435-3428
Fax: (248)288-5400

• 13337 • **Award of Merit**
For outstanding service of a local or national nature. Recognition award bestowed annually.

• 13338 •
Michigan Competing Band Association
Mack W. Pittard, Exec.Dir.
10237 N Seymour Rd.
Montrose, MI 48457-9014
Phone: (810)639-2442
Fax: (810)639-3786
E-mail: greenb@huronvalley.k12.mi.us
Home Page: http://www.michcompband.org

• 13339 • **MCBA Scholarship**
For Michigan high-school senior majoring in music at college or university in the next year; honors, awards, proficiency scores on state exams, and recommendation. Scholarship awarded annually.

• 13340 •
Michigan Concrete Paving Association
Robert J. Risser Jr., Exec.Dir.
2111 Univ. Park Dr. Ste. 550
Okemos, MI 48864
Phone: (517)347-7720
Toll-Free: 877-517-6272
Fax: (517)347-7740
E-mail: mcpa@miconcpave.com
Home Page: http://www.durableroads.com

• 13341 • **Concrete Paving Awards**
For job done in previous construction season. Recognition award bestowed annually.

• 13342 •
Michigan Department of State Police
714 S Harrison Rd.
East Lansing, MI 48823
Phone: (517)332-2521
E-mail: msp_webmaster@michigan.gov
Home Page: http://www.michigan.gov/msp

• 13343 • **Civilian of the Year Award**
To recognize accomplishments on and off the job and for efforts to continue the department's tradition of service through excellence, integrity, and courtesy. Awarded annually.

• 13344 • **Carl A. Gerstacker Trooper of the Year Award**
To honor troopers who perform above and beyond the call of duty. Awarded annually. Established in 1961.

• 13345 • **Donald S. Leonard Award**
Given annually to an enlisted member of the Michigan State Police for excellence in academics. Awarded annually.

• 13346 • **Motor Carrier Officer of the Year**
To honor the motor carrier officer who typifies outstanding service, accomplishment, and achievement and who best upholds the department's tradition of service through excellence, integrity, and courtesy. Awarded annually.

• 13347 •
Michigan Hackney and Shetland Club
Lambert Schut Jr., Contact
6108 64th Ave.
Hudsonville, MI 49426
Phone: (616)669-5080
Phone: (616)875-7151
Fax: (616)875-7127

• 13348 • **Michigan Hall of Fame**
For years spent promoting the breeds. Recognition award bestowed annually.

• 13349 • **Eugene Palmer Memorial Trophy**
For class champion at show. Trophy awarded annually.

• 13350 •
Michigan Humane Society
Cal Morgan, Exec.Dir.
7401 Chrysler Dr.
Detroit, MI 48211
Phone: (313)872-3400
Fax: (313)872-6698
Home Page: http://www.michiganhumane.org

• 13351 • **Show a Little Heart**
For outstanding service to animals. Recognition award bestowed annually.

• 13352 •
Michigan Mosquito Control Association
Thomas Putt, Pres.
PO Box 366
Bay City, MI 48707
Phone: (989)687-5044
Fax: (989)687-7914
E-mail: info@mimosq.org
Home Page: http://www.mimosq.org/

• 13353 • **MMCA Annual Scholarship**
For science major, undergrad. Scholarship awarded annually.

• 13354 •
Michigan Outdoor Writers Association
Nancy Mathews, Contact
E 4624 M35
Escanaba, MI 49829
Phone: (906)789-0546
E-mail: info@mioutdoorwriters.org

• 13355 • **U.S. Outdoor Travel Film Festival**
For recognition of excellence in outdoor-travel films. Awards are given in the following categories: fishing; hunting; boating and water sports; outdoor-travel adventure, travel, recreation; best outdoor documentary (birds, trees, bees, water, life of species, threat to it, etc.); how-to-do-it; most unusual treatment of an outdoor subject; best ecology documentary; junior sportsman; most unusual travel film; and best air travel film. State and federal government agencies, trade and manufacturing associations, business firms, film production companies, ad agencies, outdoor and travel promotion groups, and individuals are eligible. Film must be received by judges by the first Friday in December. First-prize awards and certificates of excellence for films of merit are awarded. Public designation and advertisement of winning films as "Teddys" by winners is encouraged and assisted by MOWA. MOWA itself publicizes the results. The name "Teddy" instead of "Oscar" was chosen to honor the late, great conservation-minded President Theodore Roosevelt. Winners receive shadow box trophies with a miniature of the bust of Roosevelt in his Washington memorial by Gutzon Borglum.

• 13356 •
Michigan Sea Grant
Don Scavia, Dir.
401 E Liberty St., Ste. 330
University of Michigan
Ann Arbor, MI 48104-2298
Phone: (734)763-1437
Fax: (734)647-0768
E-mail: msgweb@umich.edu
Home Page: http://www.miseagrant.umich.edu

• 13357 • **Great Lakes Commission - Sea Grant Fellowship**
Advances the environment quality and sustainable economic development goals of the Great Lakes states. Fellowship is good for one year. Inquire for application details.

• 13358 • **Knauss Marine Policy Fellowship**
Matches graduate students with hosts in the legislative branch, or other institutions in Washington, D.C. Sponsored by the National Sea Grant College Program and NOAA. Each fellowship lasts one year.

• 13359 •
Michigan Space Grant Consortium
Prof. Alec D. Gallimore, Dir.
2106 Space Research Bldg.
University of Michigan
2455 Hayward St.
Ann Arbor, MI 48109-2143
Phone: (734)764-9508
Fax: (734)763-0437
E-mail: blbryant@umich.edu
Home Page: http://www.umich.edu/~msgc

• 13360 • **Research Seed Grant Program**
For junior faculty or research scientists at affiliate institutions.

• 13361 •
Michigan Towing Association
David E. Jerome, Exec.Sec.
PO Box 220
436 N. Center St.
Northville, MI 48167-0220
Phone: (248)348-4433
Fax: (248)348-7364
E-mail: jasoffice@jeromeaustin.com
Home Page: http://www.michtow.org

• 13362 • **William Dendinger Driver of the Year**
For driving competition. Recognition award bestowed annually.

• 13363 •
Michigan United Conservation Clubs
Amanda Hathaway, Public Relations Mgr.
PO Box 30235
2101 Wood St.
Lansing, MI 48912-3785
Phone: (517)371-1041
Toll-Free: 800-777-6720
Fax: (517)371-1505
E-mail: mucc@mucc.org
Home Page: http://www.mucc.org

• 13364 • **Ben East Prize**
To recognize writers and reporters for excellence in reporting on conservation, environmental affairs, and outdoor recreation in Michigan. Writers and reporters in all media - daily or weekly newspapers, magazines, books, radio, and television - may be nominated by individual reporters, publishers, broadcasters, or by any other person. The deadline for submitting nominations is March 15. A monetary award of $1,000 and a plaque are awarded annually in two categories: print and broadcasting. Established in 1977 to honor Ben East, dean of Michigan outdoor reporters.

• 13365 •
Micronet R & D
C.A.T. Salama, Prog.Ldr.
10 King's College Rd.
University of Toronto
Toronto, ON, Canada M5S 3G4
Phone: (416)978-8658
Fax: (416)978-4516
E-mail: micronet@vrg.utoronto.ca
Home Page: http://www.micronetrd.ca

Formerly: (2004) Microelectronic Devices, Circuits, and Systems.

• 13366 • **Best Student Paper Award**
Recognizes the best student paper presented at the Annual Workshop.

• 13367 •
Mid-America Publishers Association
Jan Nathan, Exec.Dir.
% PMA, the Independent Book Publishers Association
627 Aviation Way
Manhattan Beach, CA 90266
Phone: (310)372-2732
Fax: (310)374-3342
E-mail: info@pma-online.org
Home Page: http://www.pma-online.org

• 13368 • **Mid-America Publishers Association (MAPA) Awards Program**
To recognize outstanding published titles. Award categories include: artistic, literary, marketing, and other. Applications due by June 1.

• 13369 •
Mid-America Regional Council
David A. Warm, Exec.Dir.
600 Broadway, Ste. 300
Kansas City, MO 64105
Phone: (816)474-4240
Fax: (816)421-7758
E-mail: dwarm@marc.org
Home Page: http://www.marc.org

• 13370 • **Regional Leadership Award**
For outstanding contributions toward achieving regional excellence. Recognition award bestowed annually.

• 13371 •
Mid-Atlantic States Association of Avian Veterinarians
Keath L. Marx DVM, Exec.Dir.
Memorial Bldg., Ste. 291
610 N. Main St.
Blacksburg, VA 24060-3311
Phone: (540)951-2559
Fax: (540)953-0230
E-mail: office@masaav.org
Home Page: http://www.masaav.org

• 13372 • **Pamela Slack Award for Excellence**
For veterinary college junior. Scholarship awarded annually.

• 13373 • **E. L. Stubbs Research Grant**
For researchers in avian medicine and surgery. Grant awarded periodically.

• 13374 •
Mid-West Truckers Association
Donald Schaefer, Exec.VP
2727 N Dirksen Pky.
Springfield, IL 62702
Phone: (217)525-0310
Fax: (217)525-0342
E-mail: info@mid-westtruckers.com
Home Page: http://www.mid-westtruckers.com

• 13375 • **Outstanding Associate Business Member of the Year**
To recognize an associate business member's support of, and involvement with, the Association. Candidates are nominated by the executive board, and the Executive Vice President selects the winner. A plaque and a truck clock are awarded each year during the annual convention. Established in 1983.

• 13376 • **Outstanding Member of the Year**
To recognize members for outstanding contributions to the activities of the Association. Candidates are nominated by the representative and executive board, and winners are selected by the Executive Vice President. A plaque and a truck clock are awarded each year during the annual convention to a member in the northern, central, and southern regions. Established in 1977.

• 13377 • **Safe and Courteous Driver of the Year**
To recognize drivers for their safe driving over the years. Truck drivers with few traffic violations and/or accidents over a period of years are considered. First and second place prizes are awarded each year at the annual convention, including monetary prizes, plaques, watches, and various other gifts. Established in 1990. Sponsored by Mid-West Truckers Association, Northland Insurance Company, and Clemens & Associates Insurance Agency.

• 13378 •
Middle East Report
Middle East Research and Information Project
Chris Toensing, Exec.Dir.
1500 Massachusetts Ave. NW, Ste. 119
Washington, DC 20005
Phone: (202)223-3677
Fax: (202)223-3604
E-mail: ctoensing@merip.org
Home Page: http://www.merip.org

• 13379 • **Philip Shehadi New Writers Award**
To recognize new thinking on the Middle East and to provide a forum for the growing numbers of writers and students specializing in the Middle East. Winners receive $500 and publication in Middle East Report.

• 13380 •
Middle East Studies Association of North America
Mark J. Lowder, Asst.Dir.
1219 N Santa Rita Ave.
University of Arizona
Tucson, AZ 85721
Phone: (520)621-5850
Fax: (520)626-9095
E-mail: mesana@U.arizona.edu
Home Page: http://fp.arizona.edu/mesassoc/

• 13381 • **Albert Hourani Book Award Competition**
For a published book in Middle East studies. Awarded annually.

• 13382 • **Malcolm H. Kerr Dissertation Award competition**
Recognizes outstanding work in the humanities and social sciences. Awarded annually.

• 13383 • **Mentoring Award**
Annual award of recognition.

• 13384 • **Service Award**
Annual award of recognition.

• 13385 •
Middle Georgia Historical Society
Lucia C. Carr, Exec.Dir.
Sidney Lanier Cottage
PO Box 13358
Macon, GA 31208-3358
Phone: (478)743-3851
Fax: (478)745-3132

• 13386 • **History of Macon Award**
For student project at Winship History, Geography Magnet School. Trophy awarded annually.

• 13387 •
Middletown Pee Wee Football League
Dan H. Bremer, Treas.
PO Box 921
Middletown, OH 45042
Phone: (513)422-3973
E-mail: jettieb1@hotmail.com
Home Page: http://infosports.net/mpwfc/

• 13388 • **Middletown Pee Wee Football Scholarship Award**
For active participation in football or cheerleading as high school senior and carrying good GPA. Scholarship awarded annually.

• 13389 •
Midland-Odessa Symphony & Chorale, Inc.
M. Wade Kelley, CEO
3100 LaForce Blvd.
PO Box 60658
Midland, TX 79711
Phone: (432)563-0921
Fax: (432)617-0087
E-mail: symphony@mosc.org
Home Page: http://www.mosc.org

• 13390 • **National Young Artist Competition**
To encourage performing careers in music. Individuals under the age of 29 are eligible. The competition will be held among three categories - Piano, Strings, and Winds and Percussion. A monetary award of $3,500, the Lara Hoggard Performance Medallion and a solo appearance with the Midland-Odessa Symphony will be given to the overall winner of the competition. Two other finalists will receive $2,000, and $2,500 and will be awarded at the discretion of the jurors. Established in 1963.

• 13391 •
Midwest Archives Conference
Menzi Behrnd-Klodt, Sec.
7422 Longmeadow Rd.
Madison, WI 53717
Phone: (608)827-5727
Fax: (608)827-5727
E-mail: menzi.behrnd-klodt@americangirl.com
Home Page: http://www.midwestarchives.org

• 13392 • **Emeritus Membership**
To recognize distinguished members of the archival profession upon their retirement, particularly those who have made a significant and substantial contribution to the Midwest Archives Conference during his or her archival career. Individuals who have retired from full-time professional responsibilities are considered. Entries must be submitted by January 31. Complimentary membership benefits are awarded annually. Established in 1975.

• 13393 • **Margaret Cross Norton Award**
To recognize excellence in professional literature on the subject of archives; specifically, to recognize the best article appearing in the previous two years of the journal *Archival Issues*. A monetary award of $250 and a certificate are presented biennially at the annual business meeting in odd-numbered years. Established in 1985 in memory of Margaret Cross Norton, a pioneer in the American archival profession and the first state archivist of Illinois (1922-1957).

• 13394 • **President's Award**
To recognize significant contributions to the archival profession by individuals or institutions not directly involved in archival work, but knowledgeable about its purposes and value. The candidate - an individual, institution, or organization - must not be directly involved in archival work, but must have contributed to the profession through such areas as legislation, publicity, advocacy, or long-term fiscal support. Up to three certificates are awarded annually at the organization's business meeting. Established in 1986.

• 13395 •
Midwest Center for Nonprofit Leadership
University of Missouri—Kansas City L.P. Cookingham Institute of Public Affairs
Bloch School Rm. 310
5100 Rockhill Rd.
Kansas City, MO 64110-2499
Phone: (816)235-2305
Toll-Free: 800-474-1170
Fax: (816)235-1169
E-mail: mcnl@umkc.edu
Home Page: http://www.mcnl.org

• 13396 • **Edward A. Smith Awards**
For excellence in nonprofit leadership.

• 13397 •
Midwest Roofing Contractors Association
Tom Knight, Exec.Dir.
4840 Bob Billings Pkwy., Ste. 1000
Ste. 1000
Lawrence, KS 66049-3862
Phone: (785)843-4888
Toll-Free: 800-497-6722
Fax: (785)843-7555
E-mail: mrca@mrca.org
Home Page: http://www.mrca.org

• 13398 • **MRCA Foundation Scholarship Grants**
For students entering construction field. Scholarship awarded annually.

• 13399 •
Military Audiology Association
CDR Kelly Paul, Pres.
5137 Clavel Terr.
Rockville, MD 20853
E-mail: kspaul@mar.med.navy.mil
Home Page: http://www.militaryaudiology.org

• 13400 • **Elizabeth Guild Award**
Recognition is given annually.to an outstanding audiologist.

• 13401 • **Founder's Award**
Annual recognition of a member for overall excellence to advancing profession.

• 13402 •
Military Chaplains Association of the U.S.A.
David E. White, Exec.Dir.
PO Box 7056
Arlington, VA 22207-7056
Phone: (703)276-2189
Fax: (703)276-2189
E-mail: chaplains@mca-usa.org
Home Page: http://www.mca-usa.org

• 13403 • **Distinguished Service Award**
To recognize outstanding service in the practice of chaplaincy. Awarded annually to those who are recognized leaders in chaplaincy and help set the standard of excellence in the practice of chaplaincy. Winners are selected by the Chief of Chaplains of each service: the Air Force, Army, Civil Air Patrol, Coast Guard, Marine Corps, Navy, and Veteran's Administration. Established in 1991.

• 13404 • **National Citizen of the Year**
To recognize, honor, and cite a citizen of achievement who is also faithful in religious duties. Selection is made by the sponsoring convention chapter, with final approval made by the National Executive Committee. A framed citation in a manuscript is awarded annually. Not always given at convention. Established in 1948.

Awards are arranged in alphabetical order below their administering organizations

• 13405 •
Military Operations Research Society
Brian D. Engler, Exec.VP
1703 N Beauregard St., No. 450
Alexandria, VA 22311-1717
Phone: (703)933-9070
Fax: (703)933-9066
E-mail: morsoffice@mors.org
Home Page: http://www.mors.org

• 13406 • **Richard H. Barchi Prize**
For recognition of the best paper presented at the annual symposium. The paper must exhibit professional quality and be a contribution to military operations research. A monetary prize of $1000 and a certificate are awarded annually. Established in 1983 in honor of Richard H. Barchi, a former board member.

• 13407 • **David Rist Prize**
For recognition of the best implemented study in the field of military operations research. To be considered, an entry must: be an original and self-contained contribution to the systems analysis or operations research of an implementation; demonstrate an application of analysis or methodology, either actual or prospective; prove recognizable new insight into the problem or its solution; have impact on major decisions; and be used by a client organization. Two cash prizes are awarded: $3,000 for the winner and $1,000 for honorable mention. Established in 1965 in honor of David Rist, a former board member. Formerly: MORS Prize.

• 13408 • **Clayton J. Thomas Award**
Recognizes members of the profession who have excelled in individual achievement and have expanded the application of military operations research techniques and improved its set of analytical tools. Selection is based on service over time to the profession; enhancement of the image and substance of military operations research as a unique scientific discipline and a means for providing technically sound alternatives to defense decision makers; and sustained, outstanding performance as a practitioner in military operations research, resulting in important improvements to tools and application of analytical capabilities; extension of individual knowledge and talents to others in the profession leading to improvement of analytic capabilities. Established in 1999 as a tribute to Clayton J. Thomas, a respected colleague who has give and continues to give so much of enduring value to the military operations research community.

• 13409 • **John K. Walker, Jr. Award**
Recognizes the authors of the best technical article published in *PHALANX* during the previous calendar year. Articles should expand the application of military operations research techniques, improve the set of analytical tools, and communicate the results of the work to the broader analytic community. Awarded annually. Established in honor of John K. Walker, Jr., a respected colleague, *PHALANX* editor for twelve years, and *PHALANX* editor emeritus for seven years, who by his long-term involvement with the Military Operations Research Society gave so much of enduring value to the military operation research community.

• 13410 • **Vance R. Wanner Award**
Exists to enhance the profession of military operations research. Awarded annually to recognize consistent, sustained contributions and dedication to the military operations research profession. Established in 1978 in honor of the first executive secretary of the society.

• 13411 •
Military Order of Foreign Wars of the United States
Col. Duane H. Bartrem, Commander Gen.
5985 Austin Way
Grand Ledge, MI 48837
Phone: (517)627-9072
Phone: (610)622-2041
E-mail: dhbartrem@aol.com
Home Page: http://www.foxfall.com/mofw.htm

• 13412 • **U.S. Air Force Academy Physics Award**
To recognize the most proficient cadet in the field of physics. A Bronze Eagle is awarded.

• 13413 • **U.S. Coast Guard Academy Most Proficient Cadet in Handling a Sailing Vessel**
A pair of binoculars is awarded.

• 13414 • **U.S. Military Academy General Management Award**
To recognize general management. A wristwatch and a crossed saber plaque are awarded.

• 13415 • **U.S. Naval Academy Mathematics Award**
To recognize excellence in mathematics. A wristwatch and plaque is awarded.

• 13416 • **US Merchant Marine Academy Award**
A pair of binoculars is awarded.

• 13417 •
Military Order of the World Wars
Col. Jack B. Jones, Commander-in-Chief
435 N Lee St.
Alexandria, VA 22314
Phone: (703)683-4911
Toll-Free: 877-320-3774
Fax: (703)683-4501
E-mail: moww@comcast.net
Home Page: http://www.militaryorder.net

• 13418 • **Award of Merit**
To recognize outstanding ROTC Cadets at both the college and high school levels. A medal is presented for three grades: gold medal for college junior; silver medal for college sophomore; and bronze medal for college freshman and all high school junior ROTC. Awarded annually. Established in 1939.

• 13419 • **Distinguished Service Award**
To recognize an American citizen who has made a notable contribution to national defense or the preservation of U.S. Constitutional liberties. Awarded annually since its inception in 1963.

• 13420 •
Milkweed Editions
Daniel Slager, Editor-in-Chief
Open Book Bldg., Ste. 300
1011 Washington Ave. S
Minneapolis, MN 55415-1246
Phone: (612)332-3192
Toll-Free: 800-520-6455
Fax: (612)215-2550
E-mail: webmaster@milkweed.org
Home Page: http://www.milkweed.org
Formerly: (1985) Milkweed Chronicle.

• 13421 • **Milkweed National Fiction Prize**
To promote to a national audience the best new manuscripts of fiction (novel, short story collection, novella, or combination of short stories and one or more novella). The award will go to the manuscript of high literary quality that best embodies human values and contributes to cultural understanding. The winner will receive a $5,000 cash advance on any royalties agreed upon in the contractual arrangement negotiated at the time of acceptance. All manuscripts received for publication by Milkweed Editions are automatically entered into the competition. Works previously published as a book are not eligible, but individual stories or novellas previously published in magazines or anthologies are eligible. Established in 1986.

• 13422 • **Milkweed Prize for Children's Literature**
To promote manuscripts of juvenile fiction of high literary quality that embody human values and contribute to cultural understanding. The award will go to the best novel for children 8-13 years old that Milkweed Editions accepts for publication by a writer not previously published by Milkweed. The winner will receive a $5,000 cash advance on any royalties agreed upon in the contractual arrangement negotiated at the time of acceptance. All children's manuscripts received are automatically entered into the competition. Previously published work, picture books, collections of stories, and retellings of legends or folktales are not eligible. Established in 1993.

• 13423 •
Millbrook Society
Capt. David T. Shannon Jr., Exec.Dir.
PO Box 506
Hatboro, PA 19040
Phone: (215)957-1877
E-mail: milbrook@voicenet.com
Home Page: http://www.millbrooksociety.org

• 13424 • Millbrook-Proctor and Gamble Student Service

For student volunteer with a minimum of 500 hrs. service at graduation. Scholarship awarded annually.

• 13425 •
John William Miller Fellowship Fund
The Library, Williams College
Williamstown, MA 01267
Phone: (413)597-2504
Fax: (413)597-4106
E-mail: jwmillerfund@hotmail.com
Home Page: http://www.williams.edu/resources/miller/contents.html

• 13426 • John William Miller Essay Prizes and Research Fellowships

Established, in conjunction with Williams College, to advance study of the philosophy of John William Miller. A monetary prize of $1,000 is awarded annually for the best essay published in a recognized journal on some aspect of Miller's work. Established in 1985. In addition, fellowships of up to $20,000 are awarded to support research on Miller's philosophy leading to book-length publication.

• 13427 •
Mills County Historical Society
Carrie Merritt, Exec. Officer
Box 255
Glenwood, IA 51534
Phone: (712)527-5038
Phone: (712)527-9221
E-mail: carriemerritt@hotmail.com

• 13428 • Chamber of Commerce

For community service. Recognition award bestowed annually.

• 13429 •
Mind Science Foundation
Joseph Dial, Exec.Dir.
117 W El Prado Dr.
San Antonio, TX 78212
Phone: (210)821-6094
Fax: (210)821-6199
E-mail: info@mindscience.org
Home Page: http://www.mindscience.org

• 13430 • Imagineer Awards

To reward 3-7 previously unrecognized visionaries who have come up with a new idea (or a new form for an existing one) that has potential for benefiting the community and society in general. Bexar County residents are eligible. Nominations are submitted annually in the spring. Winners receive a research stipend of $2,000 and are honored at a dinner in the fall. For deadline and award dates contact MSF.

• 13431 •
Mineralogical Society of America
Dr. J. Alexander Speer, Exec.Dir.
3635 Concord Pkwy., Ste. 500
Chantilly, VA 20151-1125
Phone: (703)652-9950
Fax: (703)652-9951
E-mail: ejohnson@minsocam.org
Home Page: http://www.minsocam.org

• 13432 • *American Mineralogist* Undergraduate Award

To recoignize outstanding students who have shown an interest and ability in their discipline of mineralogy. The AMU awards allow MSA to join with the individual faculty to formally recognize outstanding students. A certificate is presented at an awards ceremony at his or her university or college. In addition, each recipient receives a complimentary student membership, including the *American Mineralogist*. Awarded twice each year to several recipients.

• 13433 • Crystallographic Research Grant

For research in crystallography, mineral physics or chemistry, and mineralogy. Winning criteria include the qualifications of the applicant; the quality, innovativeness, and scientific significance of the research; and the likelihood of success of the project. Students, both graduate and undergraduate, are eligible, provided that they are at least 25 years of age but younger than 36 years of age on the date of the award. The deadline for applications is June 1. A monetary prize of $5,000 is awarded annually and announced at the annual fall meeting. Established in 1974, and funded by the Edward H. Kraus Crystallographic Research Fund with contributions from members of the Mineralogical Society of America.

• 13434 • Distinguished Public Service Medal

To recognize important contributions to furthering the vitality of the geological sciences, especially but not necessarily in the fields of mineralogy, geochemistry, petrology, and crystallography. Candidates should not be involved in original scientific research, but rather provide public service through such activities as public awareness, testimony to state and federal government, and education. The award is open to citizens of the U.S. or abroad. A silver medal is awarded annually when merited. Established in 1990.

• 13435 • Grant for Student Research in Mineralogy and Petrology

For research in the fields of either mineralogy or petrology. Winning criteria include the qualifications of the applicant; the quality, innovativeness, and scientific significance of the research; and the likelihood of success of the project. Students, both graduate and undergraduate, are eligible. The deadline for applications is June 1. Two monetary prizes of up to $5,000 are awarded annually. Established in 1981.

• 13436 • Mineralogical Society of America Award

For recognition of outstanding published contributions to the science of mineralogy. Work must be published prior to the candidate's 35th birthday or within seven years of the awarding of a PhD. A certificate and life membership are awarded annually. Established in 1951.

• 13437 • Roebling Medal

For recognition of scientific eminence as represented by scientific publication of outstanding original research in mineralogy, petrology, and crystallography. The award is open to researchers in the U.S. or abroad. A gold medal and life membership are awarded annually. Established in 1937 in honor of Col. Washington A. Roebling (1837-1926), an engineer and friend of the society.

• 13438 • Undergraduate Award for Outstanding Students in Mineralogy

To recognize outstanding students who have shown an interest and ability in the discipline of mineralogy. The AMU Awards allow MSA to join with the individual faculty to formally recognize outstanding students. A certificate is presented at an awards ceremony at his or her university or college. In addition, each recipient receives a complimentary student membership.

• 13439 •
Minerals, Metals, and Materials Society
Alexander R. Scott, Exec.Dir.
184 Thorn Hill Rd.
Warrendale, PA 15086-7514
Phone: (724)776-9000
Toll-Free: 800-759-4867
Fax: (724)776-3770
E-mail: tmsgeneral@tms.org
Home Page: http://www.tms.org

Formerly: (1988) Metallurgical Society.

• 13440 • Application to Practice Award

To recognize an individual who has demonstrated outstanding achievement in transferring research results or findings in some aspect of the fields of metallurgy and materials into commercial production and practical use as a representative of an industrial, academic, governmental, or technical organization. Nominations must be submitted by October 31. A black marble pillar is awarded annually. Established in 1985.

• 13441 • John Bardeen Award

To recognize an individual who has made outstanding contributions and is a leader in the field of electronic materials. Criteria for award is an established record of research and publications in the field of electronic materials and recognition of the quality and relevance of work that has had or is likely to have a significant and lasting impact in the field of electronic materials. A medal and a plaque in a walnut book are awarded annually.

• 13442 • Distinguished Service Award
To recognize a member's outstanding contributions to TMS. Must be a member of TMS, and exhibit exceptional devotion of time, effort, thought and action toward furthering the Society's mission through administrative/functional activities. Presented for ten or more years of service at the Society level in membership development, local sections, student chapters, education and professional affairs, or other Society-level activities. A medal and engraved plaque are awarded annually. Nominations must be submitted by October 31.

• 13443 • Educator Award
To recognize an individual who has made outstanding contributions to education in metallurgical engineering and/or materials science and engineering. The award is not limited to classroom teachers, but also recognizes contributions through writing of textbooks, building of strong academic programs, outreach to high school students, or innovative ways of educating the general populace. Nominations must be submitted by October 31. A black marble pillar is awarded annually.

• 13444 • Extraction and Processing Distinguished Lecture Award
To recognize an eminent individual in the field of non-ferrous extraction and processing metallurgy. The recipient will be invited to present a comprehensive lecture at the Society's annual meeting. Awarded when merited with the presentation of a black marble pillar with glass insert. Nominations must be submitted by March 31 each year. Established in 1955.

• 13445 • Extraction and Processing Science Award
To recognize a paper, or series of closely related papers with at least one common author, that represents a notable contribution to the scientific understanding of extraction and processing metallurgy, with an emphasis on nonferrous metals. The paper(s) must have been published in *JOM, Metallurgical Transactions A* or *B,* or any other appropriate AIME publication within the previous two-year period. A black marble pillar with glass insert is awarded annually. Nominations must be submitted by March 31 each year. Established in 1955. Formerly: (1970) Extractive Metallurgy Division Best Paper Award.

• 13446 • Extraction and Processing Technology Award
To recognize a paper, or series of closely related papers with at least one common author, that represents a notable contribution to the advancement of the technology of extraction and processing metallurgy, with an emphasis on nonferrous metals. The paper(s) must have been published in *Metallurgical Transactions A* or *B,* or any other appropriate AIME publication within the previous two-year period. A black marble pillar with glass insert is awarded annually. Nominations must be submitted by March 31 each year. Established in 1955. Formerly: (1970) Extractive Metallurgy Division Best Paper Award.

• 13447 • Fellow Award
To recognize outstanding contributions by a member to metallurgical science and technology with strong consideration of outstanding service to the Society. Candidates must be a full member of the Society for at least five continuous years, and must have a good personal reputation and distinction as an eminent authority in some aspect of the practice of metallurgy. The maximum number of living fellows cannot exceed one hundred. A certificate and a specially-designed membership pin are awarded when merited. Established in 1963. Nominations must be submitted by October 31 each year. Formerly: Fellows of the Metallurgical Society of AIME; Fellow of the Metallurgical Society.

• 13448 • Robert Lansing Hardy Medal Award
To recognize a young person in the broad fields of metallurgy or materials science for exceptional promise of a successful career. Candidates must be members of the Society under 35 years of age by December 31 of the year in which the original nomination is made are eligible. Nominations must be submitted by October 31. A medal and a plaque in a walnut book are awarded annually. Nominations must be submitted by October 31 each year. Established in 1955 by Arthur C. Hardy in memory of his son, Robert, a young man of great promise in the field of physical metallurgy who died at the age of 25.

• 13449 • William Hume-Rothery Award
To recognize an outstanding scientific leader for scholarly contributions to the science of alloys. The recipient will participate with the Alloy Phase Committee in organizing the symposium held in conjunction with the Society's annual meeting. Nominations must be submitted by October 31. An engraved plaque in a walnut book is awarded annually. Established in 1972 by the Institute of Metals Division of The Metallurgical Society of AIME.

• 13450 • Institute of Metals Lecturer and Robert Franklin Mehl Award
To recognize an outstanding scientific leader. The recipient will be invited to present a lecture at the materials science and application of metals program at the Society's annual meeting. A medal and a plaque in walnut book are awarded annually. Established in 1921. The Robert Franklin Mehl Award was added in 1972.

• 13451 • Leadership Award
To recognize an individual who has demonstrated outstanding leadership in the national and international materials community as a representative of an industrial, academic, governmental, or technical organization. Nominations must be submitted by October 31. A black marble pillar is awarded annually. Established in 1985.

• 13452 • Light Metals Award
To recognize a paper published in the preceding year's volume of *Light Metals.* The paper must also be presented during the annual meeting in the same year that it appears in *Light Metals.* Papers that exemplify the application of science to the solution of a practical problem, are technological in nature, and present new and significant information are considered. Nominations must be submitted by March 31. A black marble award is presented during the annual meeting of the Society.

• 13453 • Light Metals Distinguished Service Award
To recognize an individual whose continuous service to TMS Light Metals Division activities has clearly facilitated TMS's capability to serve its aluminum-oriented members and their supporting organizations. Must be a full member of TMS for a minimum of ten years, active in the aluminum industry or related entities for a minimum of twenty years, must have a record of consistently and proactively advancing the service capability of the Light Metals Division and to be of the highest personal integrity and competence level. An engraved aluminum/sandstone piece is awarded annually.

• 13454 • Light Metals Division *JOM* Best Paper Award
To recognize the most notable paper published in the preceding year's *JOM.* The paper should be of direct interest to the Light Metals Division and related industries, readable by the non-specialist, usable by the practitioners, informative and contemporary, well-referenced, and not focusing on a particular technology. An engraved plaque is awarded annually.

• 13455 • Light Metals Technology Award
To recognize an individual who has demonstrated outstanding long term service to the world's light metals industry by consistently providing technical/operating knowledge or information to the industry and by doing so has enhanced the competitiveness of the industry. The knowledge/information provided must be readily available to the industry and advance the competitiveness of the industry against other materials. An engraved plaque is awarded annually by the Light Metals Division.

• 13456 • Champion H. Mathewson Award
To recognize a paper, or series of closely related papers with at least one common author, that represents a notable contribution to metallurgical science. The paper(s) must have been published in *Metallurgical Transactions A* or *B,* or any other appropriate AIME publication within the previous two-year period. A medal and plaque in walnut book are awarded annually. Nominations must be submitted by October 31 each year. Established in 1950 to honor Champion H. Mathewson, noted scientist and teacher, and president of AIME in 1943. Formerly: Institute of Metals Division Award.

• 13457 • Structural Materials Distinguished Materials Scientist/Engineer Award
To recognize an individual who has made a long lasting contribution to the fundamental under-

standing of microstructure, properties and performance of structural materials for industrial applications. Must be a member of TMS for at least five years, have made prolonged contributions to the science of structural materials with research, demonstrate direct input on commercial processes and products and have superior standing among peers. A mahogany book with medal is awarded annually by the Structural Materials Division.

• 13458 • Structural Materials Distinguished Service Award

To recognize an individual whose dedication and commitment to the Structural Materials Division has made a demonstrable difference to the objectives and capabilities of the division and society. Must be a member of TMS for a minimum of ten years, active in the field of structural materials and a recognized leader through contributions to industry, academia and/or government through technical presentation, publication, etc. An engraved plaque and a citation are awarded annually by the Structural Materials Division.

• 13459 • TMS/ASM Joint Distinguished Lectureship in Materials and Society Award

To recognize an individual experienced in a policy-making role in the field of materials engineering for the U.S. and its industries; an eminent individual with an overview of technology and society affected by development in materials engineering; a person associated with government, industry, research, or education. The recipient will be invited to present a lecture that will clarify the role for materials engineering in technology and in society in its broadest sense, to present an evaluation of progress made in developing new technology for the ever changing needs of technology and society, and to define new frontiers for materials engineering. Nominations must be submitted by April 1 each year. A certificate with citation is awarded at the joint fall meeting of the societies. Established in 1970 by the Minerals, Metals & Materials Society (formerly The Metallurgical Society) and ASM International. Formerly: The Metallurgical Society.

• 13460 •
Miniature Piano Enthusiast Club
Janice E. Kelsh, Exec.Dir.
633 Pennsylvania Ave.
Hagerstown, MD 21740
Phone: (301)797-7675
Fax: (301)827-7029
E-mail: mpec2000@hotmail.com
Home Page: http://www.angelfire.com/music2/miniaturepianoclub

• 13461 • MPEC Award

To recognize individuals who submit, via photo, the most unique and original miniature piano collection. Awarded every two years. Established in 1991.

• 13462 •
Mining and Metallurgical Society of America
Robert W. Schafer, Pres.
476 Wilson Ave.
Novato, CA 94947-4236
Phone: (415)897-1380
Phone: (415)897-1380
Fax: (415)897-1380
E-mail: info@mmsa.net
Home Page: http://www.mmsa.net

• 13463 • Gold Medal Award

For recognition of conspicuous professional or public service in the advancement of the science of mining and metallurgy or of economic geology, for the betterment of the conditions under which these industries are carried on, and for the protection of the health and safety of workmen in the mines and in metallurgical establishments. The recipient need not necessarily be a member of the society. Awarded when merited. Established in 1914.

• 13464 •
Minnesota Advocates for Human Rights
Robin Phillips, Exec.Dir.
650 3rd Ave. S, No. 550
Minneapolis, MN 55402-1940
Phone: (612)341-3302
Phone: (612)341-9845
Fax: (612)341-2971
E-mail: hrights@mnadvocates.org
Home Page: http://www.mnadvocates.org

• 13465 • Minnesota Awards for Human Rights

To recognize outstanding contributions to the area of international human rights. Any individual or group concerned with promoting international human rights is eligible. A plaque and travel expenses are awarded annually. Established in 1985. Formerly: (1997) Minnesota International Human Rights Award.

• 13466 •
Minnesota Association of Townships
David A. Fricke, Exec.Dir.
Edgewood Professional Bldg.
PO Box 267
PO Box 267
St. Michael, MN 55376
Phone: (763)497-2330
Toll-Free: 800-228-0296
Fax: (763)497-3361
E-mail: info@mntownships.org
Home Page: http://www.mntownships.org

• 13467 • Township Leader of the Year

For Minnesota township officer. Recognition award bestowed annually.

• 13468 •
Minnesota Concrete Masonry Association
Mike Johnsrud, Exec.Dir.
12300 Dupont Ave. S
Burnsville, MN 55337
Phone: (952)707-1976
Fax: (952)707-1251
E-mail: mjohnsrud@mcma.net
Home Page: http://www.mcma.net

• 13469 • Minnesota Masonry Project Awards

For outstanding concrete masonry projects. Recognition award bestowed annually.

• 13470 •
Minnesota Conservation Federation
Ken Hiemenz, Pres.
551 Snelling Ave. S, Ste. B
St. Paul, MN 55116-1525
Phone: (651)690-3077
Toll-Free: 800-531-3077
Fax: (651)690-2208
E-mail: mncf@mtn.org
Home Page: http://www.mncf.org

• 13471 • Conservationist of the Year

For accomplishments and efforts. Recognition award bestowed annually.

• 13472 •
Minnesota Funeral Directors Association
Mr. Kelly F. Guncheon CAE, Exec.Dir.
10800 County Rd. 15
Plymouth, MN 55441
Phone: (763)398-0115
Fax: (763)398-0118
E-mail: info@mnfuneral.org
Home Page: http://www.mnfuneral.org

• 13473 • Robert C. Slater

For residents enrolled in mortuary science. Scholarship.

• 13474 •
Minnesota Historical Society
Nina Archabal, Dir.
Publications & Research Dept.
345 W Kellogg Blvd.
St. Paul, MN 55102-1906
Phone: (651)296-6126
Fax: (651)297-1345
Home Page: http://www.mnhs.org

• 13475 • Theodore C. Blegen Award

To honor the best article written by a staff member appearing in *Minnesota History,* the society's quarterly magazine. A monetary award of $600 and a certificate are awarded at the annual meeting of the society. Established in 1970 in honor of Theodore C. Blegen, historian and former superintendent of the society, editor of the journal, and dean of the graduate school, University of Minnesota.

• 13476 • Solon J. Buck Award
To honor the author of the best article appearing in *Minnesota History,* the society's quarterly magazine, during the calendar year preceding the award. A monetary award of $600 and a certificate are awarded annually at the annual meeting of the society. Established in 1954 in honor of Solon J. Buck, former director of the society and later Archivist of the United States.

• 13477 •
Minnesota Holstein Association
Chad Popp, Exec.Sec.
411 28th Ave. S
Waite Park, MN 56387-1088
Phone: (320)259-0637
Fax: (320)259-0009
E-mail: mnholstein@cloudnet.com
Home Page: http://www.cloudnet.com/~mnholstein

• 13478 • Distinguished Young Couple
For members of MHA who have made a significant contribution to the industry. Recognition award bestowed annually.

• 13479 • Longtime Meritorious Service
For member of MHA who has made a significant contribution to the industry. Recognition award bestowed annually.

• 13480 • Person of the Year
For member of MHA who has made a significant contribution to the industry. Recognition award bestowed annually.

• 13481 •
Minnesota Psychological Association
Rebecca Buller, Exec.Dir.
1711 W County Rd., B No. 310N
Roseville, MN 55113-4036
Phone: (651)697-0440
Toll-Free: 800-417-3660
Fax: (651)697-0439
E-mail: psychexec@aol.com
Home Page: http://mnpsych.org

• 13482 • Walter D. Mink Award
For outstanding undergraduate teacher. Recognition award bestowed annually.

• 13483 • Donald G. Paterson Award
For outstanding undergraduate senior in psychology. Monetary award bestowed annually.

• 13484 •
Minnesota Stroke Association, NSA Chapters
Kathleen Miller, Exec.Dir.
13705 26th Ave. N, Ste. 106
Minneapolis, MN 55441
Phone: (763)553-0088
Toll-Free: 800-647-4123
Fax: (952)475-9325
E-mail: mnstroke@covad.net
Home Page: http://www.strokemn.org

• 13485 • Sister Kenny Institute International Art Show for Artists with Disabilities
For artwork by Minnesota stroke survivor. Monetary award bestowed annually.

• 13486 •
Minnewaukan Community Club
Richard Peterson, Sec.-Treas.
PO Box 98
Minnewaukan, ND 58351-0098

• 13487 • Citizen of the Year
For community leadership and accomplishments. Recognition award bestowed annually.

• 13488 • Hall of Fame
For community leadership and accomplishments. Recognition award bestowed annually.

• 13489 •
Minot State University
Northwest Art Center
David Fuller, Pres.
Gallery Dir.
500 University Ave. W
Minot, ND 58707
Phone: (701)858-3264
Toll-Free: 800-777-0750
Fax: (701)858-3894
E-mail: nac@mindotstateu.edu
Home Page: http://www.misu.nodak.edu/nac

• 13490 • Americas 2000: All Media Competition
To recognize works in a traditional or experimental medium. All works must be original and not measure over 60 inches in any direction. Work must be ready to exhibit, completed within the last two years, and not previously exhibited in an Americas 2000 exhibition. Five entries are allowed per artist. The Best of Show Award includes a Solo Exhibition and an invitation to the Best of the Best exhibition. Cash and Purchase Awards are also awarded. Held annually.

• 13491 • Americas 2000 Paper Works Competition
To recognize artists and to encourage professional development. Works in any medium, traditional or experimental, on or of paper, including photographs, are eligible. All works must be original and not measure over 60 inches in any direction. Work must be ready to exhibit, completed within the last two years, and not previously exhibited in an Americas 2000 exhibition. The Best of Show Award includes a solo exhibition and invitation to the Best of the Best exhibit. Cash and Purchase Awards are also awarded. Five entries are allowed per artist. Deadline for entry is November 1st of each year. Established in 1969. Formerly: National Print and Drawing Exhibition; National Works on Paper Exhibition.

• 13492 •
Miracle Flights for Kids
Ann McGee, Natl.Pres.
2756 N Green Valley Pkwy., No. 115
Green Valley, NV 89014-2120
Phone: (702)261-0494
Toll-Free: 800-FLY-1711
Fax: (702)261-0497
E-mail: info@miracleflights.org
Home Page: http://www.miracleflights.org

• 13493 • Award of Gratitude
Recognizes outstanding community service. Awarded periodically.

• 13494 •
Miss America Organization
Art McMaster, Acting Pres./CEO
Two Miss America Way, Ste. 1000
Atlantic City, NJ 08401
Phone: (609)345-7571
Fax: (609)345-6079
E-mail: info@missamerica.org
Home Page: http://www.missamerica.org
Formerly: (1989) Miss America Pageant.

• 13495 • Miss America
To provide educational and career opportunities for young, talented, attractive American women. To qualify, a participant must be between the ages of 17 and 24, be a citizen of the United States, meet character criteria as set forth by the Organization, and have the time and good health to meet the job requirements. Additionally, contestants must first win a local competition and then compete to represent her state. Preliminary competition categories are Artistic Expression (talent), Presentation and Community Achievement (interview), Presence and Poise (evening wear), and Lifestyle and Fitness (swimsuit). The final night of competition includes the Lifestyle and Fitness, Presence and Poise, Peer Respect and Leadership, Artistic Expression, and Top Five Knowledge and Understanding competitions. The winner embarks on a year-long national speaking tour, addressing diverse audiences, increasing awareness, and promoting her chosen platform. More than $40,000,000 in educational scholarship funds is available annually at the local, state, and national pageants. Each year's Miss America receives a $50,000 scholarship, with additional scholarships awarded to the runners-up and to the winners of specific competitions. The National Pageant is held each year in Atlantic City, New Jersey, during September. It was first conducted in 1921.

• 13496 • Miss America Women's Achievement Award
To recognize American women who demonstrate exemplary commitment to a cause or issue of benefit to American society and who serve as role models for others. A $25,000 grant and a commemorative crystal sculpture, created by Waterford, are awarded annually. Established in 1989. Sponsored by the Miss America Foundation.

• 13497 •
Miss Universe
Paula M. Shugart, Pres.
1370 Avenue of the Americas, 16th Fl.
New York, NY 10019
Phone: (212)373-4999
Fax: (212)315-5378
E-mail: missupr@missuniverse.com
Home Page: http://www.missuniverse.com

Formerly: (1991) Madison Square Garden Television Productions.

• 13498 • **Miss Teen USA**
The Miss Teen USA Pageant is an annual competition for female teenagers from the 50 states and the District of Columbia. United States citizens between the ages of 15 and 19 who have been residents of the state they represent for at least six months prior to the state pageant are eligible. Contestants must be in good health, have good moral character, and have never been married or given birth. MISS TEEN USA receives a prize package of approximately $150,000. Nine other semi-finalists are recognized, including Miss Photogenic and Miss Congeniality. Established in 1983. Sponsors change annually.

• 13499 • **Miss Universe**
The Miss Universe Pageant is an annual competition for women from around the world. Women between the ages of 18 and 26 who are citizens of the country they represent are eligible. Contestants must be in good health, have good moral character, and have never been married or given birth. Miss Universe receives approximately $250,000 in cash and prizes and an exciting and glamorous year of international travel. Nine other semi-finalists are recognized. Established in 1952. Sponsors change annually.

• 13500 • **Miss USA**
The Miss USA Pageant is an annual competition for women, with delegates from the 50 states and the District of Columbia competing for the crown and the honor of representing the United States in the Miss Universe Pageant. United States women between the ages of 18 and 26 who have been residents of the state they represent for at least six months prior to the state pageant are eligible. Contestants must be in good health, have good moral character, and have never been married or given birth. Miss USA receives approximately $200,000 in cash and prizes. Nine other semi-finalists are recognized, including Miss Congeniality and Miss Photogenic. Established in 1952. Sponsors change annually.

• 13501 •
Mississippi-Alabama Sea Grant Consortium
Dr. LaDon Swann, Dir.
Caylor Bldg., Ste. 200
703 E Beach Dr.
PO Box 7000
Ocean Springs, MS 39566-7000
Phone: (228)818-8836
Fax: (228)818-8841
E-mail: swanndl@auburn.edu
Home Page: http://www.masgc.org

• 13502 • **Mississippi-Alabama Sea Gran Consortium Grants**
Approximately fifteen awarded each year. Inquire for application details.

• 13503 •
Mississippi Association of Public Accountants
Jo M. Allen, Exec.Sec.-Treas.
PO Box 907
PO Box 907
Carthage, MS 39051
Phone: (601)267-6990
Toll-Free: 800-321-1276
Fax: (601)267-4887
E-mail: jomallen@netdoor.com
Home Page: http://www.msapa.org

• 13504 • **Neil Magruder Scholarship**
For college junior or senior accounting major; good grades. Scholarship awarded annually.

• 13505 •
Mississippi Historical Society
PO Box 571
Jackson, MS 39205-0571
Phone: (601)359-6850
Fax: (601)359-6975
E-mail: mhs@mdah.state.ms.us
Home Page: http://www.mdah.state.ms.us/admin/mhistsoc.html

• 13506 • **Willie D. Halsell Prize**
To recognize the author of the best article published in *The Journal of Mississippi History* during the previous calendar year. A monetary award of $200 is presented annually at the annual meeting of the society in March. Established in 1976 to honor Willie D. Halsell, Special Collections Librarian at Mississippi State University and Bibliographical Editor of *The Journal of Mississippi History* (1957-1974).

• 13507 • **McLemore Prize**
To recognize distinguished scholarly books on a topic in Mississippi history or biography. Published works of original scholarship are given preference over edited works. Entries must be submitted by January 1. A monetary award of $700 is presented annually, if merited, at the annual meeting of the society in March. Established in 1980 to honor Richard A. McLemore, former president of the Mississippi Historical Society and former director of the Mississippi Department of Archives and History and his wife, Nannie Pitts McLemore, also a former president of the Mississippi Historical Society.

• 13508 • **Glover Moore Prize**
To recognize the best master's thesis on a topic in Mississippi history or biography. A monetary award of $300 is awarded when merited. Deadline for entries is January 1. Established in 1989.

• 13509 • **Franklin L. Riley Prize**
To recognize the best doctoral dissertation on a topic in Mississippi history or biography. Entries must be submitted by December 1. A monetary award of $500 is presented biennially, if merited, at the annual meeting of the society in March. Established in 1980 to honor Franklin L. Riley, whose work led to the creation of the Mississippi Department of Archives and History.

• 13510 • **Dunbar Rowland Award**
To honor individuals who have made a major contribution to the preservation and interpretation of Mississippi history. Nominations must be submitted by January 1. A framed certificate plus travel expenses are awarded periodically, when merited, at the annual meeting of the society in March. Established in 1989 to honor Dunbar Rowland, first director of the Mississippi Department of Archives and History, 1902-1937.

• 13511 • **B. L. C. Wailes Award**
To honor a distinguished historian of national reputation who is a native Mississippian or who has spent a portion of his or her professional career in Mississippi. Nominations must be submitted by January 1. A framed certificate plus travel expenses are awarded periodically, when merited, at the annual meeting of the society in March. Established in 1989 to honor B.L.C. Wailes, scholar, naturalist, state geologist, and founder of the Mississippi Historical Society in 1858.

• 13512 •
Mississippi State Medical Association
William F. Roberts, Exec.Dir.
408 W. Parkway Pl.
PO Box 2548
Ridgeland, MS 39157-6010
Phone: (601)853-6733
Fax: (601)853-6746

• 13513 • **MSMA Community Service Award**
For outstanding civic and community service. Monetary award bestowed annually.

• 13514 •
Mississippi State University
Cobb Institute of Archaeology
PO Drawer AR
College of Arts & Sciences
MSU Mail Stop 9541
Mississippi State, MS 39762
Phone: (662)325-3826
Fax: (662)325-8690
E-mail: jds1@msstate.edu
Home Page: http://www.cobb.msstate.edu

• 13515 • **Undergraduate Research Assistantships**
For archeology students. Awarded annually. Inquire for application details.

• 13516 •
The University of Southern Mississippi School of Library and Information Science
M.J. Horton, Dir.
118 College Dr., No. 5146
Hattiesburg, MS 39406-0001
Phone: (601)266-4228
Fax: (601)266-5774
E-mail: slis@usm.edu
Home Page: http://www-dept.usm.edu/~slis

• 13517 • **University of Southern Mississippi Medallion**
For recognition of distinguished service to children's literature by an author or illustrator. Selection is based on a sustained quality of work over a period of time. Nominations may be made by publishers, authors, illustrators, professors or others. A committee composed of authors, librarians, and children's literature experts makes the final selection. Sterling silver medallions are struck each year bearing a profile of the recipient on one side and a representative book character on the other. These are presented to the winner, and retained in the permanent collection of the Grummond Collection at USM. Awarded annually at the Annual Fay B. Kaigler Children's Book Festival held each Spring. Established in 1969.

• 13518 •
Mississippi Urban Forest Council
Donna Yowell, Exec.Dir.
164 Trace Cove Dr.
Madison, MS 39110
Phone: (601)856-1660
Fax: (601)359-1349
E-mail: dyowell@aol.com

• 13519 • **Urban and Community Forestry Award**
For outstanding efforts to enhance the livability of MS cities and towns with tree programs or projects. Recognition award bestowed annually.

• 13520 •
Missouri Archaeological Society
Bob Grant Jr., Pres.
Museum Support Ctr.
101A Rock Quarry Rd.
Columbia, MO 65211-3170
Phone: (573)882-3544
Toll-Free: 800-472-3223
Fax: (573)882-9410
E-mail: galenm@missouri.edu
Home Page: http://coas.missouri.edu/mas

• 13521 • **Honorary Member**
To recognize distinguished members who have made selfless contributions to the Society's programs or objectives. Selection is made by the Board of Directors. For honorary life members, the award consists of free membership and publications for life. For specific year honorary members, the award consists of free memberships and publications for a year and a letter of award. Presented at the annual meeting. Established in 1983.

• 13522 • **Erwin T. Koch Award**
To honor the individual selected to be the speaker at the annual meeting banquet of the Society. A monetary award is provided by the Erwin T. Koch Trust Fund. Established by Erwin Koch of St. Louis, Missouri, philanthropist, life member of the Society, and former trustee.

• 13523 • **Jesse Wrench Scholarship**
To recognize an archaeology student at the University of Missouri-Columbia. The recipient of the annual $600-$1,000 award will participate in a research mentorship with a professor in the Anthropology department. Named in honor of Jesse Wrench, the first president of the Society.

• 13524 •
Missouri Association of Meat Processors
Ronnie Alewel, Exec.Sec.
1770 Cedar Ln.
Sedalia, MO 65301
Phone: (660)827-0005
Fax: (660)827-0005
E-mail: info@missourimeatprocessors.com
Home Page: http://missourimeatprocessors.com

• 13525 • **Hall of Fame Outstanding Service**
For individual attending Missouri University School of Agriculture. Scholarship awarded annually.

• 13526 •
Missouri Association of School Librarians
Susan Rundel, Pres.
925 Madison
Jefferson City, MO 65101
Phone: (573)893-4155
Fax: (573)632-6678
E-mail: masl_org@earthlink.net
Home Page: http://www.maslonline.org

• 13527 • **Show Me Award**
For recognition of an outstanding book written by a living author in the United States for children in grades one through three and published during the two previous years. The winning title is chosen by a vote of the children of Missouri in grades one through three in the spring. Awarded annually.

• 13528 • **Mark Twain Award**
For recognition of an outstanding book written by an author living in the United States for children in grades four through eight and published during the two previous years, and to provide fresh reading motivation to the children of Missouri. The winning title is chosen by a vote of the children of Missouri in grades four through eight in the spring. An antique bust of Mark Twain, designed by Missouri artist Barbara Shanklin and mounted on Missouri walnut, is awarded annually at the Spring Conference. Established in 1971 by MASL and the Missouri Library Association.

• 13529 •
Missouri Bass Federation
George Thomlinson, Pres.
28 Mill Race Dr.
St. Peters, MO 63376
Phone: (314)922-0755

• 13530 • **Bradley Brooks Moore Scholarship**
For member or relative seeking a science related major. Scholarship awarded annually.

• 13531 •
Missouri Dental Association
Jacob J. Lippert, Exec.Dir.
3340 Amer. Ave.
Jefferson City, MO 65109
Phone: (573)634-3436
Fax: (573)635-0764
E-mail: jake@modental.org
Home Page: http://www.modental.org

• 13532 • **Dentist of the Year**
For service to profession. Recognition award bestowed annually.

• 13533 • **Distinguished Service**
For service to profession. Recognition award bestowed annually.

• 13534 •
Missouri Department of Elementary and Secondary Education
PO Box 480
Jefferson City, MO 65102
Phone: (573)751-4212
Fax: (573)751-8613
E-mail: pubinfo@dese.mo.gov
Home Page: http://dese.mo.gov

• 13535 • **Missouri Teacher of the Year Program**
To honor a teacher (pre-kindergarten through 12th grade) for excellence in the teaching of elementary and secondary education in public schools. Awarded annually.

• 13536 •
Missouri Hotel and Lodging Association
129 E High St., Ste. A
Jefferson City, MO 65101-5401
Phone: (573)636-2107
Toll-Free: 800-462-4756
Fax: (573)635-4890
E-mail: info@lodgingmissouri.com
Home Page: http://www.lodgingmissouri.com

• 13537 • **John K. Bryan Scholarship**
For students in the hotel/restaurant program at University of Missouri. Scholarship awarded annually.

• 13538 •
Missouri Rural Foundation
Charlene Odle-Winsor, Pres.
301 W. High St., Rm. 770
PO Box 118
Jefferson City, MO 65102-0118
Phone: (573)751-1238
Phone: (660)747-2707
Toll-Free: 800-474-1170
Fax: (573)526-5550

• 13539 • **Missouri Rural Foundation Awards**
For education, telecommunications, and housing; based upon need. Grant awarded annually.

• 13540 •
Missouri Sheriffs Association
229 Madison St.
Jefferson City, MO 65101-3278
Phone: (573)635-5925
Fax: (573)635-2128
E-mail: jvermeersch@earthlink.net

• 13541 • **John Dennis Scholarship**
For Missouri senior attending Missouri college or university needing financial assistance; upper 50% of graduating class; someone active in extra-curricular activities. Scholarship awarded annually.

• 13542 •
Missouri Southern International Piano Competition
Vivian Leon, Dir.
3950 E Newman Rd.
Missouri Southern State University
Joplin, MO 64801-1595
Phone: (417)625-9755
Fax: (417)625-9798
E-mail: msipc@mssu.edu
Home Page: http://www.mssu.edu/msipc

• 13543 • **Missouri Southern International Piano Competition**
To recognize outstanding international pianists and to bring outstanding talent to perform for the community. Individuals 18 to 30 years of age may apply to the Senior Division; individuals 17 and under may apply to the Junior Division. The following monetary awards are presented: Senior Division, first place - $10,000 plus Carnegie Recital Hall Debut; second place - $5,000; third place - $3,000; and other finalists - $2,000; Junior Division, first place - $3,000; second place - $2,000; third place $1,500; and other finalists - $1,000. This event is held biennially.

• 13544 •
Mixed Blood Theatre Company
Jack Reuler, Artistic Dir.
1501 S 4th St.
Minneapolis, MN 55454
Phone: (612)338-0937
Fax: (612)338-1851
E-mail: robin@mixedblood.com
Home Page: http://www.mixedblood.com

• 13545 • **Mixed Blood versus America**
For recognition of the best original unproduced script of a play submitted to the contest entitled "Mixed Blood versus America." The playwright must have had one previous production. (Send for guidelines.) The deadline for submissions is March 15. A monetary prize of $2,000 plus production of the script are awarded annually. Established in 1984.

• 13546 •
Mobile Opera Guild
Jerome Shannon, Artistic Dir.
257 Dauphin St.
Mobile, AL 36660-1633
Phone: (251)432-6772
Phone: (251)476-7377
Fax: (334)476-7377
E-mail: info@mobileopera.org
Home Page: http://www.mobileopera.org/guild.php

• 13547 • **Rose Palmai-Tenser Scholarship**
To encourage further study in the field of opera. Legal residents of the U.S. who are between 21 and 35 years of age may apply no later than mid-March. A first prize of $3,500, second prize of $2,000, and third prize of $1,000 are awarded annually. Established in 1966 by Mobile Opera Guild in honor of Madama Rose Palmai-Tenser, founder and artistic director of the Mobile Opera. Additional information is available from Mrs. Sylvia Posey or Mrs. Deena Hill, Scholarship Chairpersons.

• 13548 •
Mobile Post Office Society
Douglas N. Clark, Sec.
PO Box 427
Marstons Mills, MA 02648-0427
Phone: (508)428-9132
Phone: (508)548-2466
E-mail: dnc@math.uga.edu
Home Page: http://www.eskimo.com/~rkunz/mposhome.html

• 13549 • **Charles L. Towle Award**
Recognizes the best exhibit at the society's annual convention. A medal is awarded annually.

• 13550 •
The Mobius Awards
Kristen Gluckman, Exec.Dir.
713 S Pacific Coast Hwy., Ste. A
Redondo Beach, CA 90277-4233
Phone: (310)540-0959
Fax: (310)316-8905
E-mail: mobiusinfo@mobiusawards.com
Home Page: http://www.mobiusawards.com

• 13551 • **Mobius Advertising Awards**
To recognize outstanding television and radio commercials as well as print advertising and package designs. Invited for entry are television, cinema, in-flight, cable, and radio commercials produced, screened, or aired in the past 12 months. Consumer and trade print advertising, including newspapers, magazines, brochures, books, outdoor, and direct mail is also invited along with packaging for all types of products including carry-out and promotional packaging. Deadline is October 1 of each year. Awarded annually.

• 13552 •
Model A Restorers Club
Mick Isbell, Pres.
6721 Merriman Rd.
Garden City, MI 48135
Phone: (734)427-9050
Fax: (734)427-9054
E-mail: talk@modelaford.org
Home Page: http://www.modelaford.org

• 13553 • **Ken Brady Award**
To recognize an individual who gave unsparingly of his time and energy to the club. Members are eligible. A trophy and name engraved on a permanent plaque in the national office are awarded annually at the national convention. Established in 1978 in honor of Ken Brady, a former president of the organization.

• 13554 • **George De Angelis Award**
To recognize an outstanding individual who has prepared and written a technical article on the Model A Ford for the Model A Restorers Club. A trophy and name engraved on a permanent plaque in the national office are awarded annually. Established in 1984 to honor George De Angelis, former editor of the *Model A News*.

• 13555 • **Winner's Circle National Winners**
To recognize members for outstanding Model A restoration. The following awards are presented: Henry Ford Award of Excellence, Master Restoration Award, MARC of Excellence, First Place, Second Place, Third Place, and MARC of Recognition.

• 13556 •
Model "T" Ford Club of America
Jay G. Klehfoth, Exec.Dir.
PO Box 126
Centerville, IN 47330-0126
Phone: (765)855-5248
Fax: (765)855-3428
E-mail: admin@mtfca.com
Home Page: http://www.mtfca.com

• 13557 • **Walter Rosenthal Award**
For recognition of outstanding efforts to promote the hobby of restoring Model T Fords. Members of the Club are eligible. A large perpetual trophy is passed on from year to year, and a plaque is given to the year's honoree at the end of the year. Awarded annually in January. Established in 1969.

• 13558 •
Modern Language Association of America
Rosemary G. Feal, Exec.Dir.
26 Broadway, 3rd Fl.
New York, NY 10004-1789
Phone: (646)576-5000
Fax: (646)458-0300
E-mail: execdirector@mla.org
Home Page: http://www.mla.org

• 13559 • **Morton N. Cohen Award for a Distinguished Edition of Letters**
To recognize a distinguished edition of letters. Authors and editors can apply regardless of the fields they represent, and membership in the MLA is not required. At least one volume of the edition must have been published during the preceding two-year period. The deadline is May 1. Submit four copies of each eligible volume. A monetary award of $1,000 and a certificate are presented biennially in odd-numbered years at the convention. Established in 1989 by a gift from Morton N. Cohen, professor emeritus of English of the City University of New York.

• 13560 • **Katherine Singer Kovacs Prize**
To recognize an outstanding book published in English in the field of Latin American and Spanish literatures and cultures. Original, broadly interpretive books that enhance understanding of the interrelations among literature, the arts, and society, and that offer fresh perspectives on the field are considered. Six copies of each competing book must be submitted by May 1. A monetary award of $1,000 and a certificate are presented annually at the convention. Established in 1990 to honor Katherine Singer Kovacs, a specialist in Spanish and Latin American literature and film.

• 13561 • **James Russell Lowell Prize**
To recognize a member for an outstanding scholarly book, specifically a literary or linguistic study, a critical edition of an important work, or a critical biography. Books published during the preceding year must be submitted by March 1. A monetary award of $1,000 and a certificate are awarded annually at the convention. Established in 1969 in honor of James Russell Lowell.

• 13562 • **Howard R. Marraro Prize**
To recognize members for distinguished scholarly book or essay on any phase of Italian literature or comparative literature. Works published during the preceding year must be submitted by May 1 of even-numbered years. Monetary award of $1,000 and certificate are presented biennially at the annual convention in December. Established in 1973 in honor of Howard R. Marraro. From 1996 to 2000, it was awarded jointly with the Aldo and Jeanne Scaglione Prize for Italian Literary Studies, which is now awarded separately in odd-numbered years.

• 13563 • **Kenneth W. Mildenberger Prize**
To recognize an outstanding scholarly book in the fields of language, culture, literacy, or literature with strong application to the teaching of languages other than English. Open to members and non-members. Seven copies of book must be submitted by May 1. A monetary prize of $1,000, a certificate, and one year's membership in the Association are awarded at the convention. Established in 1980 in honor of Kenneth W. Mildenberger.

• 13564 • **Prize for a Distinguished Bibliography**
To recognize an outstanding enumerative or descriptive bibliography published in serial, monographic, book, or electronic format. The prize will be given without regard to the language of the compiler or of the text presented in the bibliography, as long as it falls within the subject scope of the MLA. A multivolume bibliography is eligible if at least one volume was published during the preceding two-year period. A monetary award of $1000 and a certificate are presented biennially in even-numbered years at the convention.

• 13565 • **Prize for a Distinguished Scholarly Edition**
To recognize an outstanding scholarly edition. A multivolume edition is eligible if at least one volume was published during that period. The prize will be given without regard to the field or language either of the editor or of the text presented in the edition. Four copies must be received by May 1. A monetary award of $1000 and a certificate are presented biennially in odd-numbered years at the convention.

• 13566 • **Prize for a First Book**
To honor an outstanding scholarly work published in the year prior to the award year as the first book-length publication by a current member of the association. To qualify, a book must be a literary or linguistic study, a critical edition of an important work, or a critical biography. Studies dealing with literary theory, media, cultural history, and interdisciplinary topics are eligible; books that are primarily translations are not. The award, which consists of $1000 and a certificate, is presented at the association's annual convention. Established in 1993.

• 13567 • **Prize for Independent Scholars**
To recognize and encourage the achievements and contributions of independent scholars. Open to members and non-members, this prize is awarded for a distinguished scholarly book in the field of English or another modern language or literature. Authors must not be enrolled in a program leading to an academic degree and can not hold a tenured, tenure-accruing, or "tenure-track" position in a postsecondary educational institution. Six copies of each competing book published during the preceding year must be submitted by May 1. A monetary award of $1,000, a certificate, and one year's membership in the Association are awarded annually at the convention. Established in 1983.

• 13568 • **Lois Roth Award for a Translation of a Literary Work**
To recognize an outstanding translation into English of a book-length literary work. Five copies must be received by April 1. A monetary award of $1000 and a certificate are presented biennially in odd-numbered years at the convention.

• 13569 • **Aldo and Jeanne Scaglione Prize for a Translation of a Literary Work**
To recognize an outstanding translation into English of a book-length literary work. Submit five copies of each competing book. The deadline is May 1. A monetary award of $1,000 and a certificate are presented biennially in even-numbered years at the convention.

• 13570 • **Aldo and Jeanne Scaglione Prize for a Translation of a Scholarly Study of Literature**
To recognize an outstanding translation into English of a book-length work of literary history, literary criticism, philology, and literary theory. Submit four copies of each competing book. The deadline is May 1. A monetary award of $1,000 and a certificate are presented biennially in odd-numbered years at the convention.

• 13571 • **Aldo and Jeanne Scaglione Prize for Comparative Literary Studies**
To recognize outstanding scholarly work in the field of comparative literary studies, involving at least two literatures. The committee solicits entries of books published by current members in the previous calendar year. Works of literary history, literary criticism, philology, and literary theory are eligible, as are works dealing with literature and other arts and disciplines, including cinema; books that are primarily translations are not. An award of $1,000 and a certificate are presented at the association's annual convention. Established in 1992.

• 13572 • **Aldo and Jeanne Scaglione Prize for French and Francophone Studies**
To recognize outstanding scholarly works in the field of French or francophone linguistic or literary studies. The committee solicits entries of books published by current members of the association in the previous calendar year. Works of literary history, literary criticism, philology, and literary theory are eligible; books that are primarily translations are not. An award of $1,000 and a certificate are presented at the association's annual convention. Established in 1992.

• 13573 • **Aldo and Jeanne Scaglione Prize for Italian Literary Studies**
From 1996 to 2000, this award was presented jointly with the Howard R. Marraro Prize. Now awarded separately in odd-numbered years.

• 13574 • **Aldo and Jeanne Scaglione Prize for Studies in Germanic Languages and Literatures**
To recognize outstanding scholarly work on the linguistics or literatures of the Germanic languages, including Danish, Dutch, German, Icelandic, Norwegian, Swedish, and Yiddish. Works of literary history, literary criticism, philology, and literary theory published in the previous two years are eligible; books that are primarily translations are not. Open only to members of the MLA. An award of $1,000 and a certificate

are presented biennially in odd-numbered years at the association's annual convention. Established in 1992.

• 13575 • Aldo and Jeanne Scaglione Prize for Studies in Slavic Languages and Literatures

To recognize an outstanding scholarly work on the linguistics or literatures of the Slavic languages. Works of literary history, literary criticism, philology, and literary theory are eligible; books that are primarily translations are not. Books published in the previous two years are eligible. A monetary prize of $1000 and a certificate are presented in even-numbered years at the association's annual convention. Established in 1993.

• 13576 • Mina P. Shaughnessy Prize

To recognize an outstanding scholarly book in the fields of language, culture, literacy, or literature with a strong application to the teaching of English. Books published by members or nonmembers in the previous calendar year must be nominated by May 1. A monetary award of $1,000, a certificate, and one year's membership in the Association are awarded annually at the convention. Established in 1980 in honor of Mina P. Shaughnessy.

• 13577 •

Modern Plastics

Kevin O]Grady, Group Publisher
Canon Communications LLC
11444 W Olympic Blvd., Ste. 900
Los Angeles, CA 90064
Phone: (310)445-4200
E-mail: jsloan@modplas.com
Home Page: http://www.modplas.com

• 13578 • Best of Conference Paper Award

To recognize and encourage outstanding contributions to the literature of reinforced plastics/composites by rewarding the authors of the best paper presented at the Society of the Plastic Industry's Composites Institute Conference. A monetary award and an engraved walnut plaque are awarded annually. Established in 1968 in conjunction with the Society of the Plastics Industry, Inc.

• 13579 •

Monett Chamber of Commerce
Suzy McElmurry, Exec.Dir.
PO Box 47
PO Box 47
Monett, MO 65708-0047
Phone: (417)235-7919
Fax: (417)235-4076
E-mail: chamber@monett-mo.com
Home Page: http://www.monett-mo.com

• 13580 • Pride and Progress

For service to the community. Recognition award bestowed annually.

• 13581 •

Money for Women/Barbara Deming Memorial Fund
PO Box 630125
Bronx, NY 10463

• 13582 • Money for Women/Barbara Deming Memorial Fund Grants

To provide grants to individual feminists in the arts (artists, writers of fiction, nonfiction, and poetry). The Fund does not give educational assistance, monies for personal study or loans, monies for dissertation or research projects, grants for group projects, business ventures or self publication. Citizens of the United States or Canada should send SASE for application. The deadlines for application are June 30 and December 31. Grants up to $1,500 are awarded biannually.

• 13583 •

Thelonious Monk Institute of Jazz
Thomas R. Carter, Pres.
5225 Wisconsin Ave. NW, Ste. 605
Washington, DC 20015
Phone: (202)364-7272
Fax: (202)364-0176
E-mail: info@monkinstitute.com
Home Page: http://www.monkinstitute.com

• 13584 • Thelonious Monk International Jazz Competition

To recognize the outstanding jazz musicians from around the world. The competition features a different instrument each year; there are no age limits but contestants may not have recorded as a leader for a major record label. Applications must be submitted by September 1. The following monetary awards are presented: first place - $20,000; second place $10,000; and third place - $5,000. Fifty percent of prize monies is paid directly toward winners' musical studies; remaining monies must be applied toward music study expenses or directly toward promotion of winner's careers. The competition is held annually. Established in 1987 as a jazz piano competition. Formerly: (1990) Thelonious Monk International Jazz Piano Competition; Thelonious Monk International Jazz Instrumental Competition.

• 13585 •

Montana Arts Council
Arlynn Fishbaugh, Exec.Dir.
316 N Park Ave., Ste. 252
PO Box 202201
Helena, MT 59620-2201
Phone: (406)444-6430
Fax: (406)444-6548
E-mail: mac@mt.gov
Home Page: http://www.art.state.mt.us

• 13586 • Individual Artist Fellowship

To recognize, reward, and encourage professional Montana artists who demonstrate creativity, skill, and excellence. Awards are presented in literature, music, theatre, dance, visual arts, crafts, photography, opera/music theater, and media arts. Non-students over 18 years old who reside in Montana are eligible. Please see web site for deadlines. Fellowships of $5000 are awarded for each category in alternate fiscal years. Established in 1984.

• 13587 •

Montana Mental Health Association
Charles McCarthy, Exec.Dir.
25 S Ewing St., Ste. 206
Helena, MT 59601
Phone: (406)442-4276
Toll-Free: 800-823-6426
Fax: (406)442-4986
E-mail: mmha@qwest.net
Home Page: http://www.mhamontana.org

• 13588 • Minneapolis Foundation

For educational pursuits. Grant awarded annually.

• 13589 •

Montana Society of Certified Public Accountants
33 S Last Chance Gulch, Ste. 2B
PO Box 138
Helena, MT 59601
Phone: (406)442-7301
Toll-Free: 800-272-0307
Fax: (406)443-7278
Home Page: http://www.mscpa.org

• 13590 • Junior Scholarship

For outstanding junior accounting student. Scholarship awarded annually.

• 13591 •

Montana Wholesale Distributors Association
Mark Staples, Exec.Dir.
PO Box 1018
Helena, MT 59624
Phone: (406)443-4345
E-mail: atedesco@initco.net

• 13592 • Candy Salesman of the Year

For sales efforts/results. Recognition award bestowed annually.

• 13593 • Lou Gordon Humanitarian Award

For community service. Recognition award bestowed annually.

• 13594 •

Monticello
PO Box 316
Charlottesville, VA 22902
Phone: (434)984-9822
Fax: (434)977-7757
E-mail: publicaffairs@monticello.org
Home Page: http://www.monticello.org

• 13595 • Thomas Jefferson Memorial Foundation Award in Law

To recognize an outstanding member of the legal profession. An honorarium of $3,000 a medal, and travel expenses are awarded annually at the University of Virginia Founder's Day Ceremony. The recipient delivers a lecture at the School of Law. Established in 1977. Cosponsored with the University of Vargini**a.

• 13596 • Thomas Jefferson Memorial Foundation Medal in Architecture

To recognize excellence in architecture in the world. An honorarium of $5,000, a medal, and travel expenses to attend the awards ceremony and present a lecture are awarded annually at the University of Virginia. The award is presented on April 13 at an official University ceremony celebrating Thomas Jefferson's birthday. Established in 1966 through the School of Architecture of the University of Virginia.

• 13597 •
Montreal International Festival of New Cinema
(Festival International du Nouveau Cinema et de la Video Montreal)
3530 Saint-Laurent Blvd., Ste. 304
Montreal, QC, Canada H2X 2V1
Phone: (514)847-9272
Fax: (514)843-4631
E-mail: info@nouveaucinema.ca

• 13598 • Montreal International Festival of New Cinema and Video
(Festival du Nouveau Cinema de Montreal)

To discover and promote outstanding films and videos produced each year in every part of the world. The festival is held over 10 days each summer. Films and videos are selected on the basis of their originality and for the significant contribution they make to develop a new language in the field of creative audiovisual expression. Selection criteria include the innovative qualities of a work's content, structure and form, advancing as they do communication and cultural exchange through these media. Films and videos must not have been shown in Quebec. Film or video in its original version and subtitled in French (preferably) or in English may be submitted by March 14. The Montreal International Festival of New Cinema and Video is non-competitive. However, awards and prizes for the best film (feature and short subject categories), best documentary, people's choice, and innovation are offered independently by the Quebec Film Critics Association and an international jury of video specialists. These awards are supplemented by monetary prizes provided by Canadian corporations.

• 13599 •
Montreal International Fireworks Competition
Parc Jean-Drapeau
Pavillon du Canada
1, Circuit Gilles-Villeneuve
Montreal, QC, Canada H3C 1A9
Phone: (514)872-6120
Fax: (514)872-5691
E-mail: clientele@parcjeandrapeau.com
Home Page: http://www.parcjeandrapeau.com

• 13600 • Montreal International Fireworks Competition

For recognition of the best fireworks display presented during the yearly competition in Montreal. Recipients are determined by a People's Jury. A Jupiter Award trophy is awarded annually. Established in 1985. Produced by le parc jean-Drapeau.

• 13601 •
Montreal Neurological Institute and Hospital
(Institut et Hospital Neurologiques de Montreal)
David R. Colman, Dir.
3801 University St.
Montreal, QC, Canada H3A 2B4
Phone: (514)398-6644
Fax: (514)398-8248
E-mail: info.mni@mcgill.ca
Home Page: http://www.mni.mcgill.ca

• 13602 • Jeanne Timmins Costello Fellowships

For recognition of research and study in clinical and basic neuroscience. Candidates must have M.D. or Ph.D. degrees, and apply within four years of receipt of degree. Those with M.D. degrees will ordinarily have completed clinical studies in neurology or neurosurgery. Individuals may apply by October 31 each year. Four fellowships of C$25,000 are awarded annually.

• 13603 • Preston Robb Fellowship

To support the training of a clinical fellow to work jointly with a basic and a clinician scientist from the Institute. Candidates must have an M.D. degree with clinical studies in neurology or neurosurgery. One year stipend of $25,000 Canadian is awarded annually.

• 13604 •
Montreal Symphony Orchestra
(Orchestre Symphonique de Montreal)
Madeleine Careau, Gen.Mgr.
260 de Maisonnevue Blvd. W, 2nd Fl.
Montreal, QC, Canada H2X 1Y9
Phone: (514)842-9951
Fax: (514)847-0728
Home Page: http://www.osm.ca

• 13605 • Concours OSM

To encourage the development of young Canadian musicians. Canadian citizens or landed immigrants are eligible for the awards in the following music and age categories: Winds, 16-25 years of age; Voice, 18-30 years of age; Piano Class A, 18-25 years of age; Piano Class B, age 17 and under; Strings Class A, 18-25 years of age, except for double-bass; and Strings Class B, age 17 and under. The deadline is November 1. The award consists of a scholarship and concert with the orchestra for first prize, and scholarships for second and third prizes. Monetary awards totaling C$15,500 are presented. Awarded annually in alternate years for piano/voice and strings/winds. Established in 1935 by Mrs. Athanase David.

• 13606 •
Montreal World Film Festival
(Festival des Films du Monde - Montreal)
1432 rue de Bleury
Montreal, QC, Canada H3A 2J1
Phone: (514)848-3883
Fax: (514)848-3886
E-mail: info@ffm-montreal.org
Home Page: http://www.ffm-montreal.org

• 13607 • Montreal World Film Festival

To encourage cultural diversity and understanding between nations, to foster the cinema of all continents by stimulating the development of quality cinema, to promote filmmakers and innovative works, to discover and encourage new talents, and to promote meetings between cinema professionals from around the world. The following awards are presented in the World Competition: Grand Prix of the Americas for the best film, Special Grand Prix of the Jury, Best Director, Best Screenplay, Best Artistic Contribution (awarded to a technician), Best Actress, Best Actor, and Innovation Award. Other competitions include the First Films World Competition, Hors Concours, Focus on World Cinema, Documentaries of the World, Cinema Under the Stars, and Canadian Student Film Festival. Trophies are awarded annually. Deadline is June of each year. Established in 1977 by Serge Losique.

• 13608 • Prix des Montreal

To recognize a director of a first fiction feature film. Established in 1990 by the Fondation du Festival des Films du Monde.

• 13609 •
Jenny McKean Moore Fund for Writers
Dept. of English
Rome Hall, Ste. 760
801 22nd St. NW
George Washington University
Washington, DC 20052
Phone: (202)994-6180
Fax: (202)363-8628
Home Page: http://www2.gwu.edu/~english/cw.htm

• 13610 • Jenny McKean Moore Writer-in-Washington

To encourage development in creative writing. Individuals with strong published writing and teaching experience are eligible. Genre is specified each year. The deadline is November 15. A teaching position for one academic year is awarded annually. Established in 1973 in honor of Jenny McKean Moore.

• 13611 •
Mortar Board
Diane M. Selby, Exec.Dir.
1200 Chambers Rd., Ste. 201
Columbus, OH 43212
Phone: (614)488-4094
Toll-Free: 800-989-6266
Fax: (614)488-4095
E-mail: mortar-board@osu.edu
Home Page: http://www.mortarboard.org

• 13612 • Mortar Board Chapter Citation Award
To recognize an important contribution of an individual to a Mortar Board chapter or the community where it is located. A chapter citation certificate is awarded by individual chapters annually, if desired.

• 13613 • Mortar Board Honorary Member
To recognize a distinguished contribution toward the advancement of the goals and purpose of Mortar Board within the college or university and community or region. A Mortar Board membership certificate is awarded when merited.

• 13614 • National Citation
To recognize distinguished contributions to the nation within the ideals of scholarship, service, and leadership and to promote equal opportunities among all peoples while emphasizing the advancement of the status of women. Presented to no more than two persons at one time at the annual national conference. Established in 1973.

• 13615 •
Moss-Thorns Gallery of Art
Dept. of Art
Fort Hays State University
600 Park St.
Hays, KS 67601-4000
Phone: (785)628-3478
Fax: (785)628-4087
Home Page: http://www.fhsu.edu/admissions/vr/museum_1.shtml

• 13616 • Great Plains National Exhibition
For recognition of outstanding two-dimensional work in the field of art. Open to all artists, 18 years or older, who live in the United States. Submitted works are selected by a jury for national exhibition. A Juror's Award and Purchase Awards totaling $2,000 are presented annually. Established in 1975; renamed in 1995. Formerly: Kansas National Small Painting, Drawing, and Print Exhibition; (1998) Great Plains National Exhibition of Small, Two-Dimensional Works.

• 13617 •
Mothers Against Munchausen Syndrome by Proxy Allegations
Lisa Dower, Admin.Mgr.
1407 Ranch Dr.
Senatobia, MS 38668
Fax: (662)562-6669
E-mail: renitaabrown@hotmail.com
Home Page: http://www.msbp.com/

• 13618 • John Guice Award
Recognizes significant impact on both the advancement of the association and the industry at large in Australia. Participants are nominated by the branches . Awarded biennially. Established in recognition of the contribution and efforts of the late John Guice.

• 13619 • Lifetime Membership Award
No additional information available at this time.

• 13620 • Student Prize Essay/Project
Final year students currently enrolled in a tertiary institution are eligible. Essay topic is waste management. The essay/project must be a minimum of 2,500 words. It may be in the format of a case study, research project, outline of a model, or essay/project. It must be fully referenced. The interpretation of the topic is up to individual students. The essay/project may be of a technical nature or address other issues such as policy or social issues in relation to the topic.

• 13621 •
Motion Picture Theatre Associations of Canada
(Associations des proprietaires de cinemas du Canada)
Adina Lebo, Exec.Dir.
146 Bloor St. W
Toronto, ON, Canada M5S 1P3
Phone: (416)969-7057
Fax: (416)964-6007
E-mail: mptac.ca@ca.inter.net
Home Page: http://www.mptac.ca

• 13622 • Show Canada Showmanship Awards
Awarded periodically for outstanding film promotions. Inquire for application details.

• 13623 •
Motor and Equipment Manufacturer Association
Christopher M. Bates, Pres./CEO
10 Laboratory Dr.
PO Box 13966
Research Triangle Park, NC 27709-3966
Phone: (919)549-4800
Fax: (919)549-4824
E-mail: info@mema.org
Home Page: http://www.mema.org

• 13624 • Triangle Award
Award of recognition for industry service. Awarded periodically.

• 13625 •
Motor Trend
Petersen Publishing Company
8490 Sunset Blvd.
Los Angeles, CA 90069
Phone: (213)782-2220
Fax: (213)782-2355
Home Page: http://www.motortrend.com

• 13626 • *Motor Trend* Car of the Year
To recognize the domestic car that represents the year's biggest leap forward. Cars are tested for new approaches, innovation, and stylistic daring - aspects that describe the most significant ideal car of the year. Cars and minivans that are projected to sell at least 5,000 units during the model year are eligible; customs and exotic specialty vehicles are not eligible. Nominees are tested for acceleration, braking, lateral acceleration, slalom, interior noise levels, on-the-road driving performance, quality of assembly, overall design, and value. Fuel economy numbers from the Environmental Protection Agency are evaluated. Awarded annually. Established in 1949 to demonstrate that America can build cars that rank in the world's highest echelons.

• 13627 • *Motor Trend* Import Car of the Year
To recognize the most significant imported vehicle of the year. Nominees are examined in: (1) instrumented runs to establish acceleration and braking results; (2) slalom times; (3) skidpad circuits for lateral acceleration; (4) real-world driving experience encompassing highway, city streets, mountainous conditions and stop-and-go events; (5) interior noise levels, and other evaluations. Cars and minivans are evaluated for styling and design, quality control, comfort and convenience, chassis dynamics, dollar value, acceleration, handling, ride and drive, and fuel economy. Awarded annually. Established in 1976.

• 13628 • *Motor Trend* Truck of the Year
For recognition of the most outstanding personal-use street pickup truck or sport/utility vehicle in the American market. To be eligible for consideration, the vehicle must be on sale to the public by January 1 of the year's award. Each eligible truck must be expected to sell 2,000 or more units in the North American market. Nominees may be domestically built or imported. The tests are divided into two phases - objective and subjective with instrumented testing of performance, braking, handling, and interior noise levels. Quality of assembly, overall design, and driving comfort are among the myriad categories scored. The winner is announced in the January issue of *Motor Trend* magazine. Awarded annually. Established in 1989.

• 13629 •
Motorcycle Safety Foundation
Tim Buche, Pres.
2 Jenner St., Ste. 150
Irvine, CA 92618-3806
Phone: (949)727-3227
Toll-Free: 800-446-9227
Fax: (949)727-4217
E-mail: msf@msf-usa.org
Home Page: http://www.msf-usa.org

• 13630 • Motorcycle Safety Foundation Awards Program
To recognize significant contributions by individuals and organizations in the field of motorcycle safety. The following awards are presented: Award of Excellence, Outstanding State Program, Outstanding RiderCoach Trainer, Outstanding RiderCoach, Outstanding Community Training Sponsor, Outstanding Dealer/Retailer, Outstanding Military Base, Outstanding Motorcycle Club or Event, Outstanding Motorcycle

Safety Support, Outstanding Media or Entertainment Award, and the Public Awareness Award. Established in 1979.

• 13631 •
Mounds View High School Alumni Association
% Mounds View High School
1900 Lake Valentine Rd.
Arden Hills, MN 55112
Phone: (651)639-6133
Home Page: http://www.moundsviewschools.org/moundsview/alumni

• 13632 • Distinguished Alumni Award
To honor the outstanding contributions graduates make in their communities, society, professions, or vocations. Nominees must have graduated at least 10 years ago. Awarded annually. Established in 1995.

• 13633 •
Mount Desert Island Biological Laboratory
John N. Forrest Jr., Dir.
Old Bar Harbor Rd.
PO Box 35
Salisbury Cove, ME 04672
Phone: (207)288-3605
Fax: (207)288-2130
E-mail: mdibl_info@mdibl.org
Home Page: http://www.mdibl.org

• 13634 • NSF-REV
New Investigator Awards Inquire for application details.

• 13635 •
Mount Rogers Planning District Commission
Thomas Taylor, Exec. Dir.
1021 Terrace Dr.
Marion, VA 24354
Phone: (276)783-5103
Toll-Free: 800-628-4583
Fax: (276)783-6949
E-mail: staff@mrpdc.org
Home Page: http://www.mrpdc.org

• 13636 • Regional Service Award
For service provider in the region. Recognition award bestowed biennially.

• 13637 • Regional Service Award for the Disabled
For service provider in the region. Recognition award bestowed biennially.

• 13638 •
Mount Vernon Genealogical Society
Ed Schott, Pres.
1500 Shenandoah Rd.
Alexandria, VA 22308
Phone: (703)780-9284
Phone: (703)765-4645
E-mail: mvgs@mindspring.com
Home Page: http://www.mindspring.com/~mvgs/

• 13639 • Certificate of Merit
For outstanding contributions. Recognition award bestowed annually.

• 13640 •
Mountain West Center for Regional Studies
Elaine Thatcher, Prog. Dir.
0735 Old Main Hill
Utah State University
Logan, UT 84322-0735
Phone: (435)797-3630
Fax: (435)797-3899
E-mail: mwc@cc.usu.edu
Home Page: http://www.usu.edu/mountainwest

• 13641 • Evans Biography Award
To encourage fine writing about the people who helped shape the growth and character of the American West, Utah, and "Mormon Country" (Intermountain West, Southern Canada, and Northern Mexico). Author and subject need not be affiliated with the Church of Jesus Christ of Latter-day Saints. Submissions may be of four topics: (1) Biography, autobiography, or edited memoir of someone who lived a significant portion of his or her life in this geographic region; (2) Historical text in which the biographical material concerning the principals is extensive and significant; (3) Collection of biographical portraits in which the individuals fit a unifying theme and understanding; (4) Biography or history with significant biographical content dealing with nineteenth-century Mormon history, including the Palmyra, Kirtland, Nauvoo, and exodus periods. Submissions must be received by December 1st, and must have been published in the preceding twelve months. A monetary prize of $10,000 is awarded annually and announced in August. Established in 1983 by the Evans Family in honor of David Woolley and Beatrice Cannon Evans.

• 13642 • Evans Handcart Award
For distinguished biographies on persons who lived a significant portion of their lives in what might be termed "Mormon Country". All book-length biographies must be published at the time of submission. Submission deadline is December1. $1,000 is awarded annually. Established in 1986.

• 13643 • Thomas J. Lyon Book Award
To honor outstanding single-author scholarly books on the literature and culture of the American West. Awarded annually.

• 13644 •
Mountaineers Books
Hally Swift, Dir. of Finance
1001 SW Klickitat Way, Ste. 201
Seattle, WA 98134
Phone: (206)223-6303
Fax: (206)223-6306
E-mail: mbooks@mountaineersbooks.org
Home Page: http://www.mountaineersbooks.org

• 13645 • Barbara Savage "Miles From Nowhere" Memorial Award
To honor the memory of Barbara Savage, author of "Miles From Nowhere" and to encourage non-fiction adventure writing in the genre of her book. Manuscripts must be a compelling non-fiction account of a personal outdoor Adventure. Only book-length (45,000 - 70,000 words) original works, previously unpublished in the English language will be considered. The author must hold all right to the work. A cover letter, including author's full legal name, brief biography and a statement of previous credits must also be submitted. Entries must be received by March 1. A monetary award of $3,000, a $12,000 guaranteed advance against royalties, and publication of the book by the Mountaineers are awarded. Established in 1990 in memory of Barbara Savage. This is biennial award-entries are considered in even-numbered years.

• 13646 •
Mountainfilm
Jamie Morrison, Gen.Mgr.
109 E Colorado Ave., Ste. 1
PO Box 1088
Telluride, CO 81435
Phone: (970)728-4123
Fax: (970)728-6458
E-mail: contact@mountainfilm.org
Home Page: http://www.mountainfilm.org

• 13647 • Mountainfilm in Telluride
To recognize outstanding mountain-inspired film art. Awards are presented in the following categories: Best of Festival, Best Mountain Climbing Film, Best Environmental Film, Best Global Consciousness Film, Best Humanitarian Film, Best Sports Documentary, Best Feature Documentary, Best Adventure Film, and Best Narrative Film. Also presented are Special Jury Awards, Aspiring Filmmaker Award, Citizen Activism Award, and Kid's Film Awards. Awarded annually. Established in 1979.

• 13648 •
Mountainview Women's Nine Hole Golf Association
Marilyn Bertke, Pres.
38691 S. Mountain View Blvd.
Tucson, AZ 85739-1052
Phone: (520)818-1592
E-mail: mnhoward1@msn.com
Home Page: http://mountainviewniners.com

• 13649 • **Club Championship President's Cup**
For golf scores. Recognition award bestowed annually.

• 13650 • **Low Gross**
For golf scores. Recognition award bestowed annually.

• 13651 • **Low Net**
For golf scores. Recognition award bestowed annually.

• 13652 • **Rookie of the Year**
For golf scores. Recognition award bestowed annually.

• 13653 •
Mr. Blackwell
531 S Windsor Blvd.
Los Angeles, CA 90005
Phone: (213)933-8136
Fax: (213)933-8137

• 13654 • **Fabulous Fashion Independents**
To recognize women whose clothes Mr. Blackwell admires. Announced annually at a news conference by Mr. Blackwell. Established in 1960. Formerly: Best-Dressed Women.

• 13655 • **Worst-Dressed Women**
To recognize the women who have violated fashion's prime purpose, that of glorifying womenhood. Mr. Blackwell's list of the Ten Worst-Dressed Women is announced annually at a news conference held in the drawing room of his Windsor-Square town house. Established in 1960. In 1987 Mr. Blackwell's Hall of Fame was established. In 1989 the Fashion Fiasco of the Year was established.

• 13656 •
MTM Association for Standards and Research
Dirk J. Rauglas, Exec.Dir.
1111 E Touhy Ave.
Des Plaines, IL 60018
Phone: (847)299-1111
Fax: (847)299-3509
E-mail: webmaster@mtm.org
Home Page: http://www.mtm.org

• 13657 • **Fellow Award**
For recognition of noteworthy dedication and sustained service on behalf of the MTM Association for Standards and Research. Candidate must have a minimum of six years of active committee and/or board membership to be considered. A plaque is presented annually. Established in 1978.

• 13658 • **President's Award**
To recognize an individual for outstanding accomplishments and contributions in furthering the objectives of the MTM Association for Standards and Research and in support of the MTM System. A plaque is presented annually. Established in 1971.

• 13659 •
Mu Phi Epsilon Foundation
Gerri Flynn, Exec.Sec-Treas.
4202 Atlantic Ave., Ste 202
Long Beach, CA 90807-2826
Phone: (562)424-9799
Toll-Free: 888-259-1471
Fax: (562)424-9778
E-mail: mpeieo@aol.com
Home Page: http://home.muphiepsilon.org/

• 13660 • **Mu Phi Epsilon International Competition**
To offer opportunities for recital and concert experience to outstanding young artist-members of Mu Phi Epsilon ready to pursue performing careers, as a way of bridging the gap between advanced studies and professional concertizing; and to enable chapters of the Fraternity throughout the United States and Canada to present these young artists in professional concerts or recitals. Instrumentalists must be 18-35 years of age; vocal applicants must be 18-40 years of age. Applicants must have appeared in solo recitals and/or with orchestra. Winner(s) are awarded a two-year contract for expense-paid concert/recital appearances sponsored by the Mu Phi Epsilon Foundation and chapters of Mu Phi Epsilon. In addition, local and national publicity, an honorarium for each concert performed and an appearance at the International Convention of Mu Phi Epsilon are awarded. All finalists receive Claudette Sorel cash awards. Awarded triennially in the convention year. Established in 1964. Additional information is available from Dr. Jeanine Wagner, Chairman, 2706 Sunset Dr., Carbondale, IL 62901. Formerly: Sterling Staff Competition.

• 13661 •
Mu Phi Epsilon International
Gloria Debatin, Exec.Sec-Treas.
4705 N Sonora Ave., Ste. 114
Fresno, CA 93722-3947
Phone: (559)277-1898
Toll-Free: 888-259-1471
Fax: (559)277-2825
E-mail: mpeieo@aol.com
Home Page: http://home.muphiepsilon.org

• 13662 • **Mu Phi Epsilon Annual Grants and Scholarships**
For recognition of achievement in music and contributions to Mu Phi Epsilon, an international professional music fraternity. The following grants are awarded: Grant-in-Aid, Merle Montgomery Doctoral Grant, Mabel Henderson Memorial Grant for Foreign Experience, Helen Haupt Alumni Chapter Project Grants, Lillian Harlan Ramage Grant for Graduate Study in Composition, Ellen Jane Lorenz Porter Grant for Graduate Work in Composition, and Ruth Dean Morris Scholarship. The following scholarships are awarded: Gerke Collegiate Artist Scholarships, Jazz Scholarship, Edythe G. Burdin Scholarship, Madge Cathcart Gerke Scholarship, Hazel B. Morgan Scholarship, Nadine Williams Scholarship, La Verne Jackson Memorial Music Therapy Scholarship, Bernstein-Crosman Scholarship, Eleanor B. Weiler and Mildred B. Frame Piano Scholarship Fund, Helen Haupt Piano Scholarship, Alberta Denk Scholarship for Violin, Viola, Cello, Elizabeth Boldenweck Voice Scholarship, Mikanna Clark Taurman Voice Scholarship, Sara Eikenberry Voice Scholarships, Ines Pratt Jamison Scholarship, and Brena Hazzard Voice Scholarship.

• 13663 •
Multi-Level Marketing International Association
Doris Wood, Pres. Emeritus/CEO
119 Stanford Ct.
Irvine, CA 92612
Phone: (949)854-0484
Fax: (949)854-7687
E-mail: info@mlmia.com
Home Page: http://www.mlmia.com

• 13664 • **Distributor of the Year Award**
Annual award of recognition.

• 13665 • **Hall of Fame**
Periodic award of recognition.

• 13666 • **International Company Award**
Periodic award of recognition.

• 13667 • **MLM Company of the Year**
Annual award if recognition.

• 13668 • **Supplier of the Year**
Annual award of recognition.

• 13669 • **Support Company of the Year**
Annual award of recognition.

• 13670 •
Multiple Sclerosis Society of Canada (Societe Canadienne de la Sclerose en Plaques)
North Tower
175 Bloor St. E, Ste. 700
Toronto, ON, Canada M4W 3R8
Phone: (416)922-6065
Toll-Free: 800-268-7582
Fax: (416)922-7538
E-mail: info@mssociety.ca
Home Page: http://www.mssociety.ca

• 13671 • **John Alexander Media Award**
Annual monetary award.

• 13672 •
Muncie Obedience Training Club
Susan Armstrong, Sec.
8201 W Adaline St.
Yorktown, IN 47396-1405
Phone: (765)759-7745
Phone: (765)288-4863
E-mail: muncieobed@hotmail.com
Home Page: http://groups.msn.com/ MuncieObedienceTrainingClub/

• 13673 • **May McCommon Memorial Trophy**
For top score at obedience trial. Recognition award bestowed annually.

• 13674 •
Municipal Art Society of New York
457 Madison Ave.
New York, NY 10022
Phone: (212)935-3960
Home Page: http://www.mas.org

• 13675 • **Certificates of Merit**
To acknowledge contributions by organizations and individuals to the quality of life in New York City. Members nominate candidates. Certificates are awarded annually, usually in the spring.

• 13676 • **W. Allison and Elizabeth Stubbs Davis Award**
To recognize an employee of the New York City Department of Parks and Recreation for exceptional dedication in the service of the city's parks. The recipient is honored with a Certificate of Merit and $500. Established to honor the parents of former Parks Commissioner Gordon J. Davis.

• 13677 • **Brendan Gill Prize**
To recognize the creator of a specific work—such as a book, essay, musical composition, play, painting, sculpture, architectural design, film, or choreographic work—completed in the previous year that best captures the spirit and energy of New York City. Anonymous nominations or suggestions are welcome by December 15. A monetary prize of $5,000 and a Steuben glass trophy are awarded annually. Established in 1987 in honor of Brenda Gill - author, journalist, and civic leader.

• 13678 • **Ralph C. Menapace Fellowship in Urban Land Use Law**
To provide an opportunity for a recent law graduate to spend two years acquiring first-hand experience in preservation, zoning legislation, litigation, and practice before New York's regulatory bodies. Named in honor of Ralph C. Menapace, Jr., a distinguished member of the Bar, active civic leader, and past president of the Society who died in 1984.

• 13679 • **New York Preservation Awards**
To recognize outstanding examples of historic preservation and to encourage others in this pursuit. Winners are selected in three categories: commercial structure, residential structure, and nonprofit institutional structure. Property owners who have completed restoration of building exterior or interior spaces open to the public during the preceding year are eligible to enter. A monetary prize of $1,000 and a plaque are awarded to the institutional nonprofit recipient, and plaques are awarded in the other two categories. Awarded annually. Established in 1988 by The Municipal Art Society and the Williams Real Estate Company.

• 13680 • **Jacqueline Kennedy Onassis Medal**
To recognize an individual for exemplary contribution to the cultural life of New York City. A medal, designed in 1892 by Daniel Chester French, is awarded each year. Formerly: (1996) President's Medal.

• 13681 • **Elliot Willensky Fund**
To support projects in sympathy with Mr. Willensky's vision of an ever-changing, delightful, and surprising New York City. A monetary prize of $1,000 is awarded annually. Established in memory of the late architect, author, and vice-chairman of the New York City Landmarks Preservation Commission. The fund is governed by an independent committee under the auspices of the Municipal Art Society. Awarded annually. Established in 1990.

• 13682 •
Muscular Dystrophy Association
Bob Mackle, Dir. Public Information
3300 E Sunrise Dr.
Tucson, AZ 85718
Phone: (520)529-2000
Toll-Free: 800-344-4863
Fax: (520)529-5300
E-mail: mda@mdausa.org
Home Page: http://www.mdausa.org

• 13683 • **MDA Broadcast Journalism Awards**
To encourage and recognize original television programming that increases public understanding of neuromuscular disease and stimulates public support of MDA's efforts to conquer these disorders and help people affected by them. Awards are presented in ten categories: news, public affairs, special event promo, Telethon profile feature, Telethon news feature, Telethon special event feature, Telethon memorial feature, Telethon music video, Telethon promo, and Telethon local segment intro. Established in 1979.

• 13684 •
Muscular Dystrophy Association, Lafayette
Kelly Allgood, District Dir.
1819 W Pinhook Rd., No. 111
Lafayette, LA 70508
Phone: (337)234-0088
Phone: (337)433-1890
Fax: (337)269-0103
E-mail: lafayetteladistrict@mdausa.org

• 13685 • **Personal Achievement Award**
For outstanding achievement by an individual with a neuromuscular disease. Recognition award bestowed annually.

• 13686 •
Museum of Comparative Zoology
Harvard University
26 Oxford St.
Cambridge, MA 02138
Phone: (617)495-3045
Fax: (617)496-5667
E-mail: jmccarthy@mcz.harvard.edu
Home Page: http://www.mcz.harvard.edu

• 13687 • **Ernst Mayr Grants**
Recognizes outstanding work in animal systematics.

• 13688 •
Museum of New Mexico
Shay Cannedy, Pub. Relations
107 W Palace Ave.
PO Box 2087
Santa Fe, NM 87504-2087
Phone: (505)476-1250
Fax: (505)476-5076
E-mail: emartinez@mnm.state.nm.us
Home Page: http:// www.museumofnewmexico.org

• 13689 • **New Mexico Juried Exhibition**
To recognize outstanding fine art and fine craft in all media, including paintings, prints, drawings, photography, sculpture, video, and multimedia. Purchase awards are made for the Museum of New Mexico's permanent collection. Awarded in alternate years with the Southwest juried exhibition. Formerly: Biennial Exhibition Awards; (1998) New Mexico Fine Arts Competition.

• 13690 • **Southwest Juried Exhibition**
To recognize outstanding fine art and craft in all media, including paintings, prints, drawings, photography, sculpture, video and multi-media. Residents of New Mexico, Arizona, Utah, Southern California, Colorado, Texas, Nevada, and Oklahoma are eligible. Purchase awards are made for the Museum of New Mexico's permanent collections. Established by the Museum of Fine Arts, which is a unit of the Museum of New Mexico system. Awarded in alternate years with the New Mexico juried exhibition. Formerly: Biennial Exhibition Awards; (1998) Southwest Fine Arts Competition.

• 13691 •
Museum of Science, Boston
Carole McFall, Press. Off.
Community Relations
Science Park
Boston, MA 02114
Phone: (617)723-2500
Fax: (617)589-0454
E-mail: information @mos.org
Home Page: http://www.mos.org

• 13692 • **Walker Prize**
To recognize a scientist or researcher who has meritoriously published scientific investigation and discovery in any scientific field. Individuals anywhere in the world are eligible. A $7,500 honorarium is awarded annually. Established in 1864 by Dr. William J. Walker, a prominent Boston physician and businessman.

• 13693 • **Bradford Washburn Award**
To recognize an outstanding contribution toward public understanding of science, appreciation of its fascination, and of the vital role it plays in all our lives. Individuals anywhere in the world are eligible. An honorarium of $10,000 and a golden medal are awarded annually. Established in 1964 in honor of former Museum Director, Bradford Washburn.

• 13694 •
Museum of the City of New York
Susan Henshaw Jones, Pres.
1220 5th Ave.
New York, NY 10029
Phone: (212)534-1672
Fax: (212)423-0758
E-mail: mcny@interport.net
Home Page: http://www.mcny.org

• 13695 • **Historic New York City Business Award**
To recognize a corporation, business, firm, or industry that has made significant contributions to the betterment of New York City and its people for at least fifty years. A plaque is awarded annually at a gala benefit dinner.

• 13696 • **Twenty-Four Dollar Award**
To honor a citizen of New York who has made an outstanding contribution to the City. Individuals who are not political officeholders, but helped the City by gifts or service, and leadership are eligible. A plaque with 24 silver dollars is awarded annually at a cocktail reception. Established in 1971. The award is named for the nineteenth century equivalent of the Dutch purchase price of Manhattan Island, which was sixty guilders worth of trading goods. Formerly: $24 Citizenship Award.

• 13697 •
Music Center of Los Angeles County
Catherine Babcock, Media Relations
135 N Grand Ave.
Los Angeles, CA 90012
Phone: (213)972-7211
Fax: (213)975-9785
E-mail: general@musiccenter.org
Home Page: http://www.musiccenter.org

• 13698 • **Music Center Spotlight Awards**
To recognize and reward outstanding young talent. Southern California High school age students in the performing arts fields of dance, vocal, and instrumental music may apply. A monetary award of $5,000 to the first place winner, $2,500 to runners-up, a trophy, and a chance to perform on the stage of the Dorothy Chandler Pavilion are awarded annually. Established in 1988 by Walter Grauman, Executive Producer. Sponsored by Pacific Bell Foundation. Formerly: (1990) WinterFest Spotlight Award.

• 13699 •
Music Distributors Association
13610 92nd St.
Alto, MI 49302
Phone: (616)765-9912
Fax: (616)765-3479
E-mail: gplummer@iserv.net
Home Page: http://
www.musicdistributors.org

Formerly: (1977) National Association of Musical Merchandise Wholesalers.

• 13700 • **Industry Leadership Award**
To recognize extraordinary support and encouragement of music wholesalers and the Association. Any active member of the musical instrument industry may be nominated by Association members. The Executive Committee and Officers select the winner. A plaque is awarded annually or biennially at the convention. Established in 1977.

• 13701 •
Music Teachers National Association
Dr. Gary L. Ingle, Exec.Dir.
441 Vine St., Ste. 505
Cincinnati, OH 45202-2811
Phone: (513)421-1420
Toll-Free: 888-512-5278
Fax: (513)421-2503
E-mail: mtnanet@mtna.org
Home Page: http://www.mtna.org

• 13702 • **Chamber Music Competition**
To provide a forum for outstanding chamber music performers. Contestants must be between the ages of 18 and 26. Ensembles can range between 3 and 6 players among any combination (excluding piano only) of brass, piano, string, and wind instruments. Held annually.

• 13703 • **MTNA Collegiate Artist Competition**
To recognize outstanding musical accomplishment on the collegiate level. A monetary prize is awarded to each national winner in piano, voice, organ, strings, woodwinds, brass, percussion, and classic guitar. In addition, a merit award and a certificate are presented to each student participating in the national competitions, and a winner's certificate to each national winner and his teacher. Awarded annually. Sponsored in part by Sternway & Sons, Slingofand Drum Co., and Gibson Musical Rasturants.

• 13704 • **MTNA Junior High School Piano Competition**
To recognize outstanding piano performance at the junior high school level. Full-time students in grade 7, 8, or 9 who are studying with a current member of MTNA for six of the nine months preceding the state auditions are eligible. The national winner receives a monetary award, a certificate, and a plaque. The winner's teacher receives a certificate. Division winners receive a certificate, and a plaque. Awarded annually. Sponsored in part by Baldwin Piano and Organ Company, Cincinnati, OH.

• 13705 • **MTNA Junior Performance Competitions**
To recognize outstanding musical accomplishment on the junior high school level. Categories include piano, string, woodwind, and brass. National winners receive a monetary award, a plaque, and a certificate. Winners' teachers receive a monetary award and a plaque. All students participating in the national auditions receive a merit award.

• 13706 • **MTNA Senior Performance Competition**
To recognize outstanding musical accomplishment on the high school level. Categories include brass, piano, string, voice, and woodwinds. A monetary award and a certificate are presented to each national winner; and a monetary prize and a certificate are presented to the winners' teachers. In addition, a merit award and a certificate are presented to each student participating in the national auditions. Awarded annually. Sponsored in part by Yamaha Music Corporation of America.

• 13707 • **MTNA-Shepherd Distinguished Composer of the Year Award**
For recognition of achievement in the field of musical composition. The composition must have been commissioned by an MTNA state affiliate. A tape and score should be submitted to the MTNA national office by December 1 of the year commissioned. A performance of the winning composition, a monetary award, and a plaque are presented annually at the MTNA national convention. Established in 1976.

• 13708 • **MTNA Student Composition Competition**
To recognize outstanding achievement in musical composition on the elementary, junior, high school, and collegiate levels. Composers studying with an active MTNA member may enter the state competitions. The winners of the state go to the regional contests, and the regional winner proceeds to the national level. Additionally, each winner and his teacher receive a certificate, and the winning composition is performed at the national convention. Awarded annually. Formerly: MTNA National Student Composition Contest.

• 13709 •
Musica Sacra
PO Box 38-1336
Cambridge, MA 02238-1336
Phone: (617)349-3400
Fax: (212)529-2861
E-mail: info@musicasacra.org
Home Page: http://www.musicasacra.org

• 13710 • **MUSICA SACRA Bach Vocal Competition**
To recognize outstanding vocalists. There are no age restrictions. Tapes of late Baroque arias, including at least one by J.S. Bach, must be submitted in January. Selected finalists must be prepared to sing three Late Baroque arias that also include at least one by J.S Bach. Related recitatives are optional. An appearance in MUSICA SACRA'S season with a paid entry fee of $600 is awarded for first prize. A monetary award of $200 is presented for second prize. Established in 1986.

• 13711 •
Musical Arts Society of New Orleans
Shearon Horton, Dir.
PO Box 19599
New Orleans, LA 70179-0599
Phone: (504)525-0717
Fax: (504)525-0717
E-mail: director@masno.org
Home Page: http://www.masno.org

• 13712 • **New Orleans International Piano Competition**
To provide an opportunity for the most gifted and communicative musicians to further their careers, and to provide an opportunity to discover great music through some of the finest pianistic talents. Open to all pianists of any age and nationality. The deadline for entry is March 1. The following awards are presented: First Prize - $16,000 including paid performances as soloists and with renowned symphonies and orchestras; Second Prize - $6,000 including two paid performances; Third Prize - $3,000 and a paid performance. Semifinalists receive a $600 monetary prize. Awarded annually. Established in 1989.

• 13713 •
Musical Club of Hartford
E.B. Storrs Scholarship Committee
38 Nott St.
Wethersfield, CT 06109-1828
Phone: (860)667-9151
E-mail: amayo@prodigy.net
Home Page: http://www.musical-club-of-hartford.org

• 13714 • **Evelyn Bonar Storrs Memorial Piano Scholarships**
To provide scholarships for talented and advanced students of piano. To qualify, high school students must be living or studying music in Connecticut. Recipients are selected annually through recommendations of the Piano Faculty, including the Chairman of several Connecticut schools including: Hartt School of Music, (Univ. of Hartford), University of Connecticut, and Hartford Conservatory. First prize is a $500 scholarship; second prize is a $300 scholarship; third prize is a $200 scholarship. Application deadline is April 15. Established in the will of Evelyn Bonar Storrs, a 70-year member of Musical Club of Hartford.

• 13715 •
Musicians AFM Local 7
Frank Amoss, Pres.
2050 S Main St.
Santa Ana, CA 92707
Phone: (714)546-8166
Fax: (714)662-0279
E-mail: info@ocmusicians.org
Home Page: http://www.ocmusicians.org

• 13716 • **B. Douglas Sawtelle Scholarship**
For musical excellence. Monetary award bestowed annually.

• 13717 •
Muttart Diabetes Research & Training Centre
Brenda Bohne, Admin. Asst.
458 Heritage Medical Research Centre
University of Alberta
Edmonton, AB, Canada T6G 2S2
Phone: (780)492-6855
Fax: (780)492-4666
E-mail: bbohne@ualberta.ca

• 13718 • **Dr. Gordon D. Brown Memorial Training Award in Diabetes**
To honor a phase I or phase II medical student to gain experience in clinical diabetes and diabetes-related research. A 12-week summer studentship is awarded annually with a stipend support. Established in 1984.

• 13719 • **J.B. Collip Diabetes Studentship**
To recognize academic standing, research potential, and career goals. Awarded every two or three years with stipend support to a graduate Student in a Ph.D. or Masters' program. Established in 1983.

• 13720 •
Mycological Society of America
Kay Rose, Contact
Allen Marketing & Management
810 E 10th St.
Lawrence, KS 66044
Phone: (785)843-1235
Toll-Free: 800-627-0629
Fax: (785)843-1274
E-mail: krose@allenpress.com
Home Page: http://www.msafungi.org

• 13721 • **C.J. Alexopoulos Prize**
To recognize outstanding contributions to mycology by younger researchers, based on quality, originality, and quantity of their published work. Individuals who are current members of MSA and who have completed their last degree within the past ten years are eligible. A monetary prize equal to the annual interest on the Alexopoulos Fund and an engraved plaque are awarded annually. Established in 1978.

• 13722 • **Annual Lecturer Award**
To recognize an eminent mycologist. The awardee has the responsibility of presenting a lecture at the Society's annual meeting. An honorarium of $1,000 is awarded annually. Established in 1950.

• 13723 • **Distinguished Mycologist Award**
To recognize outstanding contributions in the field of mycology. Members of the Society whose degrees were awarded at least 20 years prior to the award year are eligible. Nominees are evaluated on the basis of quality, originality, and quantity of their published research, and on the basis of service to the MSA or to the field of mycology in general. An engraved plaque is awarded annually. Established in 1981.

• 13724 • **Graduate Fellowships in Mycology**
To recognize and support outstanding student research in mycology. Applicants must be student members of the MSA and be candidates for the Ph.D. degree in residence at an American or Canadian university. Awarded annually are two graduate fellowships of $2,000, one Memorial NAMA Fellowship of $2,000, and one Backus Award of $1,000. Established in 1967.

• 13725 • **Graduate Research Prizes**
To recognize outstanding student research contributions. Awards are presented in two categories: oral presentation and poster presentation. Graduate students whose works are judged best at the annual meeting of the Society are eligible. A maximum of two monetary prizes of $100 are awarded annually in each category. Established in 1971.

• 13726 • **William H. Weston Award for Teaching Excellence**
To recognize an individual who has demonstrated teaching excellence in mycology at the undergraduate and/or graduate level. Nominees must be current members of the MSA. An inscribed plaque is awarded annually when warranted. Established in 1980.

• 13727 •
Mystery Readers International
Janet A. Rudolph, Dir./Ed.
PO Box 8116
Berkeley, CA 94707-8116
Phone: (510)845-3600
Fax: (510)845-1975
E-mail: janet@mysteryreaders.org
Home Page: http://www.mysteryreaders.org

• 13728 • **Macavity Awards**
To recognize excellence in the mystery writing field. A certificate is awarded annually to the recipient in each of four categories. Established in 1986.

• 13729 •
Mystery Writers of America
Margery Flax, Office Mgr.
17 E 47th St., 6th Fl.
New York, NY 10017
Phone: (212)888-8171
Fax: (212)888-8107
E-mail: mwa@mysterywriters.org
Home Page: http://www.mysterywriters.org

• 13730 • **Robert L. Fish Memorial Award**
For recognition of the best first mystery or suspense short story by an American author whose fiction has not been previously published. The deadline for submissions is November 30 of each year. A monetary prize of $500 and a plaque are presented in New York at the Edgar Awards Banquet. Established in 1984 in memory of Robert L. Fish, novelist and short story writer.

• 13731 • **Grandmaster Award**
To recognize important contributions to the mystery field over time, as well as a significant output of consistently high quality. Awarded annually at the discretion of the Board of Directors. Applications not accepted. Established in 1954.

• 13732 • **Edgar Allan Poe Awards (Edgars)**
To recognize an author for outstanding contributions in mystery, crime, and suspense writing. Awards are given in the following 13 categories: best novel, best first novel by an American author, best paperback original, best critical/biographical study, best fact crime, best short story, best children's mystery, best young adult mystery, best motion picture screenplay, best television feature or miniseries teleplay, best television series episode teleplay, best play, and the Mary Higgins Clark Award. All books, short stories, television shows, and films in the mystery, crime, suspense, and intrigue fields are eligible in their respective category if they were copyrighted and published or shown for the first time in the United States during the previous year. Nominees for best short story are eligible if the story first appeared in a book published in the United States during the calendar year, or a magazine published in the United States bearing a cover date of this calendar year. In all book categories, date of publication takes precedence over copyright date. The deadline for submissions is December 1 of each year. All nominees receive a scroll, and the winner in each category is awarded a ceramic bust of Edgar Allan Poe. In addition, the following awards are presented on occasion: Raven Award, for nonwriting achievements in the mystery field; and Ellery Queen Award, awarded to an outstanding mystery editor or writing team. Established in 1946.

• 13733 •
Mystic Seaport
Douglas H. Teeson, Pres.
PO Box 6000
75 Greenmanville Ave.
Mystic, CT 06355-0990
Phone: (860)572-0711
Phone: (860)572-5315
Toll-Free: 888-973-2767
Fax: (860)572-5326
E-mail: info@mysticseaport.org
Home Page: http://www.visitmysticseaport.com

• 13734 • **Gerald E. Morris Prize Article Contest**
To encourage research and publication in the field of American maritime history. Accurate scholarship demonstrating original research and, when appropriate, the use of primary source material is considered. Articles may take the form of biographical, literary, musical, or scientific discussions that relate to America's waterborne history; explications of economic or social history; studies of trades, maritime communities, or racial or ethnic group participation; or explanations of forms of maritime technology. However, works of fiction and studies of naval operations are excluded. The deadline for application is December 1. A monetary prize of $500 and publication in the *Log of Mystic Seaport* are awarded annually. Established in 1980 by Gerald E. Morris, former librarian of the G. W. Blunt White Library at Mystic Seaport. Sponsored by the Fellows of the G. W. Blunt White Library. Formerly: *Log of Mystic Seaport* Prize Article Contest.

• 13735 • **A.G Vietor Maritime Research Award**
To recognize a person who has made a significant contribution in the maritime research field. The award will be made for maritime research or publication. Forms of this research might include biography, literary, musical or scientific discussions, studies of trades or communities, fiction, or explanations of forms of maritime technology. The recipient of the award will be announced at the annual spring meeting of the Fellows and will receive a cash award of $1,000 from the Acorn Foundation. The winner will also be named an honorary Fellow for the year and have their name added to a plaque in the Library. Awarded annually.

• 13736 •
Mystic Valley Railway Society
W. Russell Rylko, Pres.
PO Box 365486
Hyde Park, MA 02136-0009
Phone: (617)361-4445
Fax: (617)361-4451
E-mail: info@mysticvalleyrs.org
Home Page: http://www.mysticvalleyrs.org

• 13737 • **Railroad Calendar Color Slide Contest**
To encourage members to share and preserve the New England Railroad heritage in color photography. Applicants must be members, and images must be taken within the six New England states. Deadline is December 31st of each year. Monetary awards are $125 for images that will appear on the calendar's front or back cover, and $75 for those that will appear on the monthly pages. Established in 1980.

• 13738 •
Mythopoeic Society
Edith Crowe, Corresponding Sec.
PO Box 320486
San Francisco, CA 94132-0486
E-mail: edith.crowe@sjsu.edu
Home Page: http://www.mythsoc.org

Absorbed: (1972) Tolkien Society of America.

• 13739 • **Mythopoeic Fantasy Awards**
For recognition of an outstanding work of fantasy "in the spirit of the Inklings" published during the previous year. Awards are given in two categories: adult literature and children's literature. Trophies are awarded annually at the Society conference. Established in 1971.

• 13740 • **Mythopoeic Scholarship Awards**
Awards given in Inklings Studies for recognition of an outstanding scholarly work on J.R.R. Tolkien, C.S. Lewis, Charles Williams, or their impact on literature, society, etc., published during the previous three years. Awards are also given in Myth and Fantasy Studies for recognition of an outstanding scholarly work on other mythopoeic authors or on the general fields of myth and fantasy criticism. Trophies are awarded annually at the Society conference. Established in 1971.

• 13741 •
NACE International: The Corrosion Society
Tony Keene, Exec.Dir.
1440 S Creek Dr.
PO Box 201009
Houston, TX 77084-4906
Phone: (281)228-6200
Toll-Free: 800-797-6223
Fax: (281)228-6300
E-mail: firstservice@nace.org
Home Page: http://www.nace.org

Formerly: (1995) National Association of Corrosion Engineers.

• 13742 • **R. A. Brannon Award**
To recognize outstanding work by a current member of NACE in any area of activity at the national level of the organization. The work should clearly show some degree of excellence beyond the normal performance expected of an individual in the execution of the duties of an office or an assignment, whether it be an elected or appointed position. A past president is not eligible until five years have passed following his or her term of office. Nomination deadline is June 30. Walnut book plaques are awarded annually when merited. Established in 1973 in honor of R. A. Brannon, the first president of NACE.

• 13743 • A. B. Campbell Award
To recognize the most outstanding manuscript published in *Materials Performance* or *Corrosion* (NACE journals) during the previous year by an author under 35 years of age. Selection criteria includes author contribution, as well as technical excellence and significance of the paper. Nomination deadline is June 30. A monetary award of $1,000 is presented annually. Established in 1953.

• 13744 • Distinguished Service Award
To recognize distinguished service to NACE by an elected or appointed member for duties, responsibilities, or assignments performed at the section, region, or national level. A past president is not eligible for the award. A maximum of 10 awards are given in any year. Awarded annually. Nomination deadline is June 30. Established in 1969.

• 13745 • T. J. Hull Award
To recognize an individual for an outstanding contribution to NACE in the field of publications. Nomination deadline is June 30. Established in 1987 and named for T. J. Hull, retired executive director of the Association.

• 13746 • Frank Newman Speller Award
To recognize a contribution to corrosion engineering, such as the development or improvement of a method, process, apparatus or equipment, or material that facilitates the control of corrosion or makes it less costly. An individual who has made a recognized national or international contribution to corrosion engineering through some form of education or works may qualify. The nominee must be living, but need not be a member of NACE. Nomination deadline is June 30. A walnut book plaque is awarded annually when merited. Established in 1946 in honor of Frank Newman Speller.

• 13747 • Technical Achievement Award
For recognition of distinguished technical achievement in corrosion engineering. The achievement must have had significant impact on the practice of corrosion engineering or the enhancement of the profession. Recognized achievements may be in the areas of research, engineering, or education. Talks given, papers published, awards received, books written, patents, educational activities, and technical committee activities are considered in evaluating the technical achievements of the nominee. A maximum of five awards may be given by the Association in any year. Nomination deadline is June 30. Established in 1986.

• 13748 • Willis Rodney Whitney Award
To recognize a significant contribution to corrosion science, such as the development or improvement of a theory that provides a more fundamental understanding of corrosion phenomena and/or the prevention of corrosion. An individual who has made a recognized national or international contribution to corrosion science through some form of education or work that leads to a better understanding of the science of corrosion may qualify. The nominee must be living, but need not be a member of NACE. Nomination deadline is June 30. Walnut book plaques are awarded each year when merited at the annual conference banquet. Established in 1946 in honor of Willis Rodney Whitney.

• 13749 •
Naismith Memorial Basketball Hall of Fame
John L. Doleva, Pres. & CEO
1000 W Columbus Ave.
Springfield, MA 01105
Phone: (413)781-6500
Toll-Free: 877-4HO-OPLA
Fax: (413)781-1939
E-mail: info@hoophall.com
Home Page: http://www.hoophall.com

• 13750 • John W. Bunn Award
To honor an international or national figure for lifetime contributions to the game of basketball. Awarded annually. A trophy is permanently displayed in the Basketball Hall of Fame. Established in 1973 in honor of John W. Bunn, the first chairman of the Basketball Hall of Fame Committee (1949-1969).

• 13751 • Curt Gowdy Media Award
Established by Basketball Hall of Fame trustees to single out a member of the electronic and print media for outstanding contributions to basketball. The awards are presented each fall at a dinner during the Basketball Hall of Fame's Enshrinement Weekend. Established in 1990 to honor Curt Gowdy, who served as president of the Basketball Hall of Fame for seven consecutive one-year terms (1978-85).

• 13752 • Frances Pomeroy Naismith Award
To honor an outstanding senior male college Division I senior who is six feet tall or under, as well as a female senior five-foot-eight or under, who have exhibited outstanding skill, character, leadership, and loyalty. The men's award winner is selected by a panel from the National Association of Basketball Coaches, and the women's award winner is selected by the Women's Basketball Coaches Association. Wood plaques are awarded annually. Established for men in 1969 and for women in 1984 by James S. Naismith, son of the founder of basketball, in memory of his daughter-in-law, Frances Pomeroy Naismith.

• 13753 •
NAMI Kansas-The Alliance on Mental Illness
Karen Manza, Exec.Dir.
112 SW 6th, Ste. 505
PO Box 675
Topeka, KS 66601-0675
Phone: (785)233-0755
Toll-Free: 800-539-2660
Fax: (785)233-4804
E-mail: namikansas@nami.org
Home Page: http://www.namikansas.org

• 13754 • NAMI Kansas Award of Appreciation
For active supporter/advocate/activist promoting organization's mission, goals and objectives Scholarship awarded annually.

• 13755 •
Nash Car Club of America
Jim Bracewell, Membership Chm.
1 N 274 Prarie
Glen Ellyn, IL 60137
Phone: (630)469-5848
Fax: (608)647-6430
E-mail: bracewell@nashcarclub.org
Home Page: http://www.nashcarclub.org

• 13756 • Thomas B. Jeffery Award
To recognize a member for an outstanding contribution to the club on a national level. A plaque is awarded annually at the Grand NASHional Meet. Established in 1972 by Charles Rizzo, Kenosha, WI, in honor of Thomas B. Jeffery.

• 13757 •
Nashville Film Festival
Sallie Mayne, Mng.Dir.
161 Rains Ave.
PO Box 24330
Nashville, TN 37202-4330
Phone: (615)742-2500
Fax: (615)742-1004
E-mail: info@nashvillefilmfestival.org
Home Page: http://www.nashvillefilmfestival.org

• 13758 • Nashville Film Festival
To showcase the nation's best independent films and videos, and to encourage and promote their wider appreciation. Citizens of any country are eligible to submit 35mm and 16mm film and 3/4-inch video entries of any length by November 4. Films in the following genres are considered: feature narrative, documentary feature, documentary short, short narrative, college student short narrative, animation, college student animation, experimental, music video, and young filmmaker. Monetary prizes are presented to the winner in each category. Awarded annually at the festival held in Nashville, TN. Established in 1969. Formerly: Sinking Creek Film Celebration.

• 13759 •
Nashville Songwriters Association International
Barton Herbison, Exec.Dir.
1701 W End Ave., 3rd Fl.
Nashville, TN 37203-2601
Phone: (615)256-3354
Toll-Free: 800-321-6008
Fax: (615)256-0034
E-mail: nsai@nashvillesongwriters.com
Home Page: http://www.nashvillesongwriters.com

• 13760 • Nashville Songwriters Association International Awards

To recognize songwriters and their songs. The following awards are presented annually: (1) Song of the Year; (2) Songwriter of the Year; (3) Songwriter/Artist of the Year; (4) Songwriter Achievement Award; and (5) The Maggie Cavender Award of Service. Certificates, trophies and plaques are awarded annually. Established in 1970.

• 13761 •
NASSTRAC
Brian Everett, Exec.Dir.
380 Industrial Blvd.
Waconia, MN 55387
Phone: (952)442-8850
Fax: (952)442-3941
E-mail: brian@nasstrac.org
Home Page: http://www.nasstrac.org

Formerly: (1985) National Small Shipments Traffic Conference.

• 13762 • NASSTRAC Awards Program

To recognize members and member companies for outstanding distribution programs and service. The following awards are presented annually: Member of the Year, sponsored by NASSTRAC; Carrier of the Year (with National, Multi-Regional, and Regional categories), sponsored by Logistics Management Magazine; and LTL Program of the Year, sponsored by Distribution Magazine.

• 13763 •
George Jean Nathan Trust
English Dept.
Goldwin Smith Hall
Cornell University
Ithaca, NY 14853
Phone: (607)255-6801
Fax: (607)255-6661
E-mail: english_chair@cornell.edu
Home Page: http://www.arts.cornell.edu/english/nathan/index.html

• 13764 • George Jean Nathan Award for Dramatic Criticism

To recognize outstanding drama criticism or reviews by U.S. citizens published in books, newspapers, magazines, and other periodicals, or in electronic form, or broadcast on television or radio originating in the United States. The award is one of the most distinguished in the American theatre. The award selection is made jointly by the chairs of the English departments of Cornell, Princeton, and Yale universities. The entry deadline is September 30. A monetary award of $10,000 and a trophy are awarded annually. Established in 1958 in memory of George Jean Nathan, whose objective it was to encourage and assist in developing the art of drama criticism and the stimulation of intelligent playgoing.

• 13765 •
Nation Institute
Hamilton Fish, Pres.
33 Irving Pl., 8th Fl.
New York, NY 10003
Phone: (212)209-5400
Fax: (212)982-4022
E-mail: instinfo@nationinstitute.org
Home Page: http://www.nationinstitute.org

• 13766 • I. F. Stone Award

For recognition of the article that represents the most outstanding example of journalism in the unique intellectual and investigative tradition of the late I. F. Stone. Open to all undergraduate students enrolled in a United States college. Articles may be submitted by the writers themselves or nominated by editors of student publications or faculty members. While entries originally published in student publications are preferred, unpublished articles also are considered, provided they were not written as part of a student's regular course work. All entries must have been written or published during the previous school year. Each writer, editor of a student publication, or faculty member may submit up to three separate entries. Investigative articles are particularly encouraged. The deadline for submissions is June 30. The winning article may be published in *the Nation* at the discretion of the editor. The award comes with a cash prize. Established in 1990 in memory of I. F. Stone (1907-1989), former Washington editor of *The Nation*, and perhaps best known as the editor, publisher, and writer of the muckraking *I. F. Stone's Weekly*, which was published from 1953 to 1971.

• 13767 •
National Academic Advising Association
Roberta Flaherty, Exec.Dir.
Kansas State Univ.
2323 Anderson Ave., Ste. 225
Manhattan, KS 66502-2912
Phone: (785)532-5717
Fax: (785)532-7732
E-mail: nacada@ksu.edu
Home Page: http://www.nacada.ksu.edu

• 13768 • NACADA Student Research Award

To recognize student research that significantly adds to the body of knowledge on academic advising. Any current NACADA member who is completing or has recently (within one year) completed research at the M.S., Ed.D., or Ph.D. level is eligible. A monetary award of $500 and a plaque are awarded annually at the National Conference in October. Established in 1983. Visit www.nacada.ksu.edu/Awards/index.htm for more information.

• 13769 • Outstanding Advising Awards

To recognize individual advisors, faculty advisors, and advising administrators who have demonstrated the qualities associated with outstanding academic advising and/or advising administration. Awards are presented at the NACADA Annual Conference in October.

• 13770 • Outstanding Advising Program Awards

To recognize programs that can document innovative and/or exemplary practices that have resulted in the improvement of their academic advising services. A plaque is awarded to one or more recipients at the NACADA Annual Conference in October.

• 13771 • Pacesetter Award

To recognize chief executive officers, provosts, and chief academic or student affairs officers who exemplify a commitment to advising and are true advocates for students and advisors. Nominees must not have direct involvement with or responsibility for the administration of advisors or advising. A plaque is presented at the National Conference in October of each year.

• 13772 • Service to NACADA Award

To recognize a current member of NACADA for outstanding service to the organization. Nominees must have a history of involvement and membership in the organization. Previous winners are not eligible. A plaque is awarded annually at the National Conference in October. Established in 1984. Formerly: (1986) Special Award for Dedicated Service.

• 13773 •
National Academy
Annette Blaugrund PhD, Dir.
1083 5th Ave.
New York, NY 10128
Phone: (212)369-4880
Fax: (212)360-6795
E-mail: ppineda@nationalacademy.org
Home Page: http://www.nationalacademy.org

Formerly: (1997) The National Academy of Design; The National Academy.

• 13774 • Agop Agopoff Award

For recognition of a classical work of art in sculpture. A monetary award of $100 is awarded annually at the Academy's Exhibition. Established in 1986.

• 13775 • Benjamin Altman (Figure) Prize

For recognition of achievement in figure paintings in oil by native born Americans. Monetary prizes of $3,000 and $1,500 are awarded annually at the Academy's Exhibition. Established in 1915.

• 13776 • Benjamin Altman (Landscape) Prize

For recognition of achievement in landscape paintings in oil by American born citizens. Monetary prizes of $3,000 and $1,500 are awarded annually at the Academy's Exhibition. Established in 1916.

• 13777 • Anonymous Prize

To recognize an outstanding print at the Academy's Exhibition. A monetary award of $250 is presented. Established in 1950.

• 13778 • Helen Foster Barnett Prize
For recognition of an outstanding work of sculpture by an artist under 35 years of age who has not previously received the award. A monetary prize of $500 is presented annually when merited at the Academy's Exhibition. Established in 1908.

• 13779 • Paul and Margaret Bertelsen Prize
For recognition of a portrait in any medium. A monetary prize of $400 is awarded at the Academy's Exhibition. Established in 1987.

• 13780 • Cannon Prize
For recognition of outstanding painting in watercolor by an American artist. A monetary prize of $400 is awarded annually at the Academy's Exhibition. Established in 1951.

• 13781 • Emil and Dines Carlsen Award
For recognition of the best still life exhibited at the Annual Exhibition of the Academy. A monetary prize of $1,000 is awarded annually. Established in 1977.

• 13782 • Andrew Carnegie Prize
For recognition of notable achievement in oil, other than a portrait, by an American artist. A monetary prize of $1,000 is presented annually at the Academy's Exhibition. Established in 1901.

• 13783 • Certificates of Merit
For recognition of outstanding achievement in painting, sculpture, graphic arts, and watercolor. Awarded when merited. Established in 1974.

• 13784 • Thomas B. Clarke Prize
For recognition of the most outstanding figure composition painted in the United States by an American citizen without limitation of age. Members of the National Academy of Design are not eligible. A monetary prize of $300 is awarded annually. Established in 1884.

• 13785 • Gladys Emerson Cook Prize
For recognition of the best animal sketch or painting. A monetary prize of $200 is awarded annually. Established in 1980.

• 13786 • Ralph Fabri Prize
For recognition of outstanding work in graphic arts. A monetary prize of $200 is awarded annually at the Academy's Exhibition. Established in 1976.

• 13787 • George Hitchcock Landscape in Sunlight Prize
To recognize a painting of a landscape in sunlight by an artist under 40 years of age. A monetary prize of $750 awarded triennially. Established in 1990.

• 13788 • Artists Fund Malvina Hoffman Prize
For recognition of the finest sculpture in the Exhibition. A monetary prize of $400 is awarded annually at the Academy's Exhibition. Established in 1969.

• 13789 • Joseph S. Isidor Memorial Medal
For recognition of an outstanding figure composition painted in oil. American artists are eligible. A gold medal is awarded annually when merited at the Academy's Exhibition. Established in 1907.

• 13790 • Isaac N. Maynard Prize
For recognition of an outstanding achievement in oil portrait painting. A monetary prize of $100 is presented each year at the Academy's Exhibition. Established in 1913.

• 13791 • Leo Meissner Prize
For recognition of an outstanding achievement in a print. A monetary prize of $200 is awarded annually. Established in 1979.

• 13792 • Adolph and Clara Obrig Prize
For recognition of two outstanding paintings in watercolor by American artists. Monetary prizes of $450 and $300 are awarded annually at the Academy's Exhibition. Established in 1951.

• 13793 • Adolph and Clara Obrig Prize for Painting in Oil
For recognition of an outstanding painting in oil by an American artist. A monetary prize of $600 is presented annually at the Academy's Exhibition. Established in 1933.

• 13794 • Edwin Palmer Memorial Prize
For recognition of the most outstanding marine painting. A monetary prize of $2,000 is awarded annually. Established in 1929.

• 13795 • William A. Paton Prize
For recognition of an outstanding painting in watercolor by an American born citizen who was a resident of the United States for three years prior to the award. A monetary prize of $1,000 is awarded annually at the Academy's Exhibition. Established in 1967.

• 13796 • Thomas R. Proctor Prize
For recognition of an outstanding portrait in oil or sculpture. A monetary prize of $500 is awarded annually at the Academy's Exhibition. Established in 1904.

• 13797 • William P. and Gertrude Schweitzer Prizes
For recognition of the best watercolor in the exhibition. A monetary award of $2,000 is given. For recognition of excellence in watercolor. A monetary award of $1,500 is given. Established in 1987.

• 13798 • Mikhail and Ekateryna Shatalov Award
To recognize an artist who has painted a romantic realist landscape executed in a free manner. A monetary prize of $350 is awarded. Established in 1983.

• 13799 • Ellin P. Speyer Memorial Prize
For recognition of an outstanding painting or piece of sculpture portraying an act of humaneness towards animals, or a painting or piece of sculpture of animals. A monetary prize of $400 is presented annually at the Academy's Exhibition. Established in 1922.

• 13800 • S. J. Wallace Truman Prize
For recognition of an outstanding landscape painting in oil by an artist under 35 years of age. A monetary prize of $850 is presented annually at the Academy's Exhibition. Established in 1941.

• 13801 • Harry Watrous Award
For recognition of outstanding work in sculpture. A monetary prize of $500 is awarded annually at the Academy's Exhibition. Established in 1916. Formerly: (1997) Elizabeth N. Watrous Gold Medal.

• 13802 •
National Academy of Education
Amy Swauger, Exec.Dir.
New York University
School of Education
726 Broadway, 5th Fl.
New York, NY 10003-9580
Phone: (212)998-9035
Fax: (212)995-4435
E-mail: nae.info@nyu.edu
Home Page: http://www.nae.nyu.edu

• 13803 • NAE/Spencer Postdoctoral Fellowship Program
To promote scholarship in the United States and abroad on matters relevant to the improvement of education in all of its forms, and to encourage professional development among scholars in the early stages of their academic careers. Applicants must have received their Ph.D., Ed.D., or equivalent research degree within the last six years. Applications from persons in all disciplines are accepted until the deadline of November 10. Up to 20 fellowships of $55,000 for one academic year of research or $27,500 for each of two contiguous years at half-time are announced in May. Established in 1985 by the Spencer Foundation and National Academy of Education.

• 13804 •
National Academy of Engineering
William A. Wulf, Pres.
500 Fifth St. NW
NAS 309
Washington, DC 20001
Phone: (202)334-3200
Fax: (202)334-2290
E-mail: wwulf@nae.edu
Home Page: http://www.nae.edu

• 13805 • **Arthur M. Bueche Award**
The Arthur M. Bueche (Bee'-kuh) Award honors an engineer who has shown dedication in science and technology, as well as active involvement in determining U.S. science and technology policy, promoting technological development, and contributing to the enhancement of the relationship between industries, government, and universities. Recipient receives a $2,500 cash award during NAE's annual meeting in October. NAE members and non-members are eligible. Established in 1982.

• 13806 • **Charles Stark Draper Prize**
Honors an engineer whose accomplishment has significantly impacted society by improving the quality of life, providing the ability to live freely and comfortably, and/or permitting the access to information. Awarded annually to recognize achievements in all engineering disciplines. Recipient receives a $500,000 cash award. NAE members and non-members worldwide are eligible.

• 13807 • **Founders Award**
To honor an outstanding NAE member or foreign associate who has upheld the ideals and principles of the NAE through professional, educational, and personal achievement and accomplishment. Founding members of the NAE are not eligible. Recipient receives a cash award of $2,500 and a gold medal imprinted with a replica of the NAE seal during the annual meeting in October. Established in 1965. Formerly: Founders Medal.

• 13808 •
National Academy of Neuropsychology
Robert W. Elliott PhD, Pres.
2121 S Oneida St., Ste. 550
Denver, CO 80224-2594
Phone: (303)691-3694
Fax: (303)691-5983
E-mail: office@nanonline.org
Home Page: http://www.NANonline.org

• 13809 • **Distinguished Neuropsychologist Award**
To recognize outstanding contributions to the field of neuropsychology. Recipients are nominated by the Academy. A plaque and travel opportunities are awarded each year at the annual conference. Established in 1989.

• 13810 •
National Academy of Opticianry
Jim Iciek Jr., Exec.Dir.
8401 Corporate Dr., Ste. 605
Landover, MD 20785
Phone: (301)577-4828
Toll-Free: 800-229-4828
Fax: (301)577-3880
E-mail: info@nao.org
Home Page: http://www.nao.org

• 13811 • **Education Achievement Award**
To recognize educators whose contributions to opticianry education can be described as major and noteworthy and or who have made, or are making, significant contributions to the education of opticians. Nominations are accepted from the industry.

• 13812 • **Beverly Myers Nelson Achievement Awards**
To recognize individuals who have made meritorious contributions or who have rendered outstanding services to the field of ophthalmic optics, particularly prescription opticianry, or to undertakings and interests germane thereto. Nominations are accepted from the industry. A certificate is awarded annually at the annual business meeting. Established in 1951 by Leslie W. Myers in memory of his daughter, Beverly Myers Nelson.

• 13813 • **Beverly Myers Nelson Student Awards**
To recognize outstanding second-year students enrolled in opticianry programs accredited by the Commission on Opticianry Accreditation. Submitted students papers are rated for first, second and third place awards. Established in 1975 by Leslie W. Myers in memory of his daughter, Beverly Myers Nelson.

• 13814 • **The National Academy Hall of Fame Award Program**
To recognize individuals whose contributions to the vision care of the public can be described as "major" and "noteworthy" and/or who have made or are making significant contributions to ophthalmic dispensing. Nominations are accepted form the industry.

• 13815 •
National Academy of Popular Music
Bob Leone, Project Dir.
330 W 58th St., Ste. 411
New York, NY 10019-1827
Phone: (212)957-9230
Phone: (212)957-9229
Fax: (212)957-9227
E-mail: info@songwritershalloffame.org
Home Page: http://www.songwritershalloffame.org

• 13816 • **Songwriters Hall of Fame**
To honor and highlight the accomplishments of songwriters in all music genres. Individuals with 20 years of successful songwriting are eligible. A lucite square with an embedded gold medallion is awarded to the individuals inducted into the Hall of Fame. The Hall of Fame also presents the following three awards annually when merited: Johnny Mercer Award; Patron of the Arts Award; The Sammy Cahn Lifetime Achievement Award; and Abe Olman Publishers Award. On occasion, a Hitmaker Award, a Board of Directors Award, and Special Song Citations may also be presented. Established in 1969.

• 13817 •
National Academy of Public Administration
William Shields, VP, Administration
1100 New York Ave. NW, Ste. 1090E
Washington, DC 20005-3934
Phone: (202)347-3190
Fax: (202)393-0993
E-mail: academy@napawash.org
Home Page: http://www.napawash.org

• 13818 • **Louis Brownlow Book Award**
To recognize the author of an outstanding book on a topic of wide contemporary interest to both practitioners and scholars in the field of public administration. Books published within the last two years are eligible. Nominations may be submitted by publishers, individuals, or professional associations with an interest in the subject matter by May 31. A plaque is awarded annually in November. Established in 1968.

• 13819 • **National Public Service Awards**
To honor public service practitioners whose careers exhibit the highest standard of excellence, dedication, and accomplishment; to provide recognition for outstanding individuals; and to underscore the need to have creative and highly skilled individuals as managers of complex and demanding government functions. Public service practitioners who currently work or have spent the primary part of their careers working in public service, have made outstanding contributions on a sustained basis rather than having performed a single exceptional deed, and have accomplished or caused to be accomplished significant programs or projects within their areas of responsibility to the ultimate benefit of the general public. Award winners are selected from all levels of public service - local, state, and federal governments, and international and nonprofit organizations. Individuals who have retired from a public service career are not eligible. Nominations are solicited from the entire public service community and are accepted from individuals, government units, professional groups, the business community, nonprofit organizations, and educational groups. The deadline is October 15. Up to five trophies are presented annually at an awards ceremony in April. Established in 1983. Administered jointly with the American Society for Public Administration (ASPA).

• 13820 • **Herbert Roback Scholarship**
To encourage college students to pursue careers in public service. Two scholarships of $7,500 each are awarded annually in November for graduate study in public administration, public and international affairs, and/or political science at Maxwell School at Syracuse University,

Brandeis University, Woodrow Wilson School at Princeton, John Jay College at CUNY, Albany/SUNY, New York University, or any metropolitan Washington DC area college. Nomination deadline is May 31. Established in 1979 to honor Herbert Roback.

• 13821 •
National Academy of Recording Arts and Sciences
Neil Portnow, Pres.
3402 Pico Blvd.
Santa Monica, CA 90405
Phone: (310)392-3777
Fax: (310)399-3090
E-mail: memservices@grammy.com
Home Page: http://www.grammy.com

• 13822 • **Grammy Awards**
To recognize and honor the best in the recording arts and sciences based on artistic or technical achievement, not sales or chart positions. Winners are determined through nomination and final voting stages by voting members. Awards are given for performances in 31 fields (pop, gospel, classical, etc.) and 108 categories within those fields. Additional awards include Record of the Year, Song of the Year, and Best New Artist. Nominees need not be members. A Grammy - a golden statuette that is a composite design of early gramophones - is awarded annually at the Grammy Awards Show on prime-time TV. Established in 1958.

• 13823 • **Hall of Fame Awards**
To honor early recordings of lasting, qualitative or historical significance which were released more than 25 years ago. Winners are selected annually. Established in 1973.

• 13824 •
National Academy of Sciences
Bruce M. Alberts, Pres.
505 Fifth St. NW
Washington, DC 20001
Phone: (202)334-2000
Fax: (202)334-2158
E-mail: webmailbox@nas.edu
Home Page: http://www.nasonline.org

• 13825 • **Alexander Agassiz Medal**
To recognize an outstanding original contribution in the science of oceanography. A monetary prize and a medal are presented approximately every three years. Established in 1913 by Sir John Murray in honor of his friend, Alexander Agissiz.

• 13826 • **Arctowski Medal**
To recognize studies in solar physics and solar-terrestrial relationships. A monetary prize, plus an additional amount to an institution of the recipient's choice, and a medal are presented every three years. Established in 1969 through the Henryk Arctowski Fund by the bequest of Mrs. Jane Arctowska.

• 13827 • **Award for Behavioral Research Relevant to the Prevention of Nuclear War**
To recognize basic research in any field of cognitive or behavioral science that has employed rigorous formal or empirical methods, optimally a combination of these, to advance our understanding of problems or issues relating to the risk of nuclear war. Prize awarded approximately every three years. Established by gift of William K. and Katherine W. Estes.

• 13828 • **John J. Carty Award for the Advancement of Science**
To recognize noteworthy and distinguished accomplishments in any field of science within the scope of the charter of the Academy. A monetary prize and a medal are awarded every one to three years. Specific fields are designated by the Council of the NAS for each presentation. Established in 1930 by the American Telephone and Telegraph Company.

• 13829 • **Comstock Prize in Physics**
To recognize a recent innovative discovery or investigation in electricity, magnetism, or radiant energy. Bona fide residents of North America are eligible. A monetary prize is presented every five years. Established in 1913 through the Cyrus B. Comstock Fund.

• 13830 • **Arthur L. Day Prize and Lectureship**
To recognize a scientist making new contributions to the physics of the Earth whose four to six lectures would prove a solid, timely, and useful addition to the knowledge and literature in the field. The award consists of a monetary prize plus costs of the lecture program and publication of the resulting manuscript. Awarded approximately every three years. Established in 1972.

• 13831 • **Henry Draper Medal**
To recognize outstanding investigations in astronomical physics. A monetary prize and a medal are presented every four years. Established in 1833 by Mrs. Henry Draper.

• 13832 • **Daniel Giraud Elliot Medal**
To recognize meritorious work in zoology or paleontology published in a three- to five-year period. A monetary prize and a medal are awarded approximately every four years. Established in 1917 by a gift from Margaret Henderson Elliot.

• 13833 • **Gibbs Brothers Medal**
To recognize outstanding contributions in the field of naval architecture and marine engineering. A monetary prize and a medal are presented biennially. Established in 1965 by a gift from William Francis and Frederick H. Gibbs.

• 13834 • **Jessie Stevenson Kovalenko Medal**
To recognize important contributions to medical science. A monetary prize and a medal are presented approximately every three years. Established in 1949 by a gift from Michael S. Kovalenko.

• 13835 • **Richard Lounsbery Award**
To recognize extraordinary scientific achievement by French and American scientists in biology and medicine. This award is intended to stimulate research and to encourage reciprocal scientific exchanges between the United States and France. A monetary prize, an additional stipend for travel and related expenses of research in the opposite country, and a medal are awarded annually, in alternate years to a French and an American scientist. Established in 1978 by Vera Lounsbery in honor of her husband.

• 13836 • **NAS Award for Chemistry in Service to Society**
To recognize contributions to chemistry, either in fundamental science or its application, that clearly satisfy a societal need. Awarded approximately every two years. Established in 1981 by E. I. du Pont de Nemours and Company.

• 13837 • **NAS Award for Initiatives in Research**
To recognize innovative young scientists and to encourage research likely to lead toward new capabilities for human benefit. Promising young scientists, preferably under 35 years of age, who are citizens of the United States are eligible. A monetary prize is awarded annually. The field of presentation rotates among the physical sciences, engineering, and mathematics. Established in 1980 by AT & T Bell Telephone Laboratories in honor of William O. Baker.

• 13838 • **NAS Award for Scientific Reviewing**
To recognize authors whose reviews have synthesized extensive and difficult material, rendering a significant service to science and influencing the course of scientific thought. Cumulative efforts in writing reviews, usually over a period of years rather than for a specific article, are considered. The field of award rotates among the biological, physical, and social sciences. A monetary prize is awarded annually. Established in 1977 in honor of J. Murray Luck. Sponsored by Annual Reviews Inc. and the Institute for Scientific Information. Formerly: James Murray Luck Award.

• 13839 • **NAS Award for the Industrial Application of Science**
To recognize original scientific work of intrinsic scientific importance and with significant, beneficial applications in industry. A monetary award is presented triennially. Established in 1990 by the International Business Machines Corporation in honor of Ralph E. Gomory.

• 13840 • **NAS Award in Aeronautical Engineering**
To recognize outstanding contributions to aeronautical engineering. A monetary prize is awarded every five years. Established in 1948 by Professor and Mrs. Jerome C. Hunsaker.

• 13841 • NAS Award in Chemical Sciences
To recognize innovative research in the chemical sciences that contributes, in the broadest sense, to the better understanding of the natural sciences and to the benefit of humanity. Researchers with broad fundamental impact are eligible. A monetary prize and a medal are awarded annually. Established in 1978. Supported by the Merck Company Foundation.

• 13842 • NAS Award in Mathematics
To recognize an individual for excellence of research in the mathematical sciences published within the preceding ten years. A monetary award is presented every four years. Established in 1988 by the American Mathematical Society in commemoration of its centennial.

• 13843 • NAS Award in Molecular Biology
To recognize a recent notable discovery in the field of molecular biology by a young scientist who is a citizen of the United States. A monetary prize of is awarded annually. Supported by Prizer Inc. Formerly: (1988) USX Foundation Award in Molecular Biology; (1987) United States Steel Foundation Award in Molecular Biology.

• 13844 • NAS Award in the Neurosciences
To recognize extraordinary contributions to progress in the fields of neuroscience, including neurochemistry, neurophysiology, neuropharmacology, developmental neuroscience, neuroanatomy, and behavioral and clinical neuroscience. A monetary prize and a medal are awarded approximately every three years. Established in 1987 by the FIDIA Research Foundation.

• 13845 • Public Welfare Medal
To recognize distinguished contributions in the application of science to the public welfare. The medal is presented annually. Established in 1913 at the suggestion of George F. Becker and initially supported by the Marcellus Hartley Fund.

• 13846 • Robertson Memorial Lecture
To publicize the work of a distinguished scientist from anywhere in the world. Every three years, a recipient is awarded a monetary prize as well as an invitation to lecture on his or her work and its international aspects. The field of presentation rotates among the biological, physical, and social sciences. Established in 1962 in memory of Howard P. Robertson.

• 13847 • Gilbert Morgan Smith Medal
To recognize excellence in published research on marine or freshwater algae. A monetary prize and a medal are awarded triennially. Established in 1975. Established through the Helen P. Smith Fund in honor of her husband.

• 13848 • J. Lawrence Smith Medal
To recognize outstanding investigations of meteoric bodies. A monetary prize and a medal are presented every three years. Established in 1884 by a gift from Sarah Julia Smith.

• 13849 • Mary Clark Thompson Medal
To recognize outstanding services to geology and paleontology. Preference is given to American scholars. A monetary prize and a medal are presented every three to five years. Established in 1919.

• 13850 • Troland Research Awards
To recognize unusual achievement and to further empirical research in psychology regarding the relationships of consciousness and the physical world. Two monetary prizes are awarded annually to young investigators (age 40 or younger). Funds are to be used by the awardee to support his or her research within the broad spectrum of experimental psychology, including, for example, the topics of sensation, perception, motivation, emotion, learning, memory, cognition, language, and action. For both awards, preference will be given to experimental work taking a quantitative or other formal approach, and/or to experimental research seeking physiological explanations. Established in 1983 at the bequest of Leonard T. Troland.

• 13851 • Selman A. Waksman Award in Microbiology
To recognize outstanding achievement in microbiology. A monetary prize is presented biennially. Established in 1968 by the Foundation for Microbiology. Formerly: National Academy of Sciences Award in Microbiology.

• 13852 • Charles Doolittle Walcott Medal
To stimulate research in pre-Cambrian or Cambrian life and history. A monetary prize and a medal are presented once every five years. Established in 1928 by Mary Vaux Walcott.

• 13853 • G. K. Warren Prize
To recognize noteworthy and distinguished accomplishment in fluviatile geology and closely related aspects of the geological sciences. A monetary prize is awarded approximately every four years. Established in 1961 by Emily B. Warren in memory of her father.

• 13854 • James Craig Watson Medal
To recognize contributions to the science of astronomy. A monetary prize and a medal are presented approximately every three years. Established in 1887.

• 13855 •
National Academy of Sciences
Institute of Medicine
2101 Constitution Ave. NW
Washington, DC 20418
Phone: (202)334-2383
Fax: (202)334-3862
E-mail: hppf@nas.edu

• 13856 • Robert Wood Johnson Health Policy Fellowships
To develop the capacity of outstanding mid-career health professionals in academic and community-based settings to assume leadership roles in health policy and management. The fellowships are intended to provide opportunities for mid-career professional people to gain an understanding of the health policy process and to contribute to the formulation of new policies and programs. Six Fellows participate each year in a one-year program of orientation and full-time working experience in the nation's capital. Fellows have been selected from faculty in medicine, dentistry, the biomedical sciences, nursing, public health, health services administration, the allied health professions, economics and other social sciences; and organized delivery systems such as HMOs and other community-based providers and institutions. Nominations must be submitted by November 18. Established in 1973. Sponsored by The Robert Wood Johnson Foundation.

• 13857 • Gustav O. Lienhard Award
To recognize individuals for outstanding achievement in improving health care services in the United States. There are no eligibility limits with respect to the education and profession of individuals who may be nominated. Selection criteria include: achievement in the area of personal health services; achievement of national scope; innovative, creative, and pioneering achievement; unique contributions to that achievement; positive change over a sustained period; a qualitative and quantitative impact; and success in overcoming barriers, based on resources available. Individuals or groups may submit nominations by April 30. A monetary award of $25,000 and a medal are presented annually by the Institute of Medicine at its October annual meeting in Washington, D.C. Established in 1986 to honor Gustav Lienhard, chairman of the Robert Wood Johnson Foundation's board of trustees from 1971 to 1986.

• 13858 •
National Academy of Sports
Howard Hillman, Pres.
220 E. 63rd St.
New York, NY 10021
Phone: (212)838-2980
Fax: (212)838-3980

• 13859 • Academy Award of Sports
To honor the nation's top athletes and teams. A gold star on a walnut base is awarded annually. Established in 1963.

• 13860 •
National Academy of Television Arts and Sciences
Todd Leavitt, Pres.
5220 Lankershim Blvd.
North Hollywood, CA 91601-3109
Phone: (818)754-2810
Phone: (818)754-2800
Fax: (818)761-2827
E-mail: todd@emmys.org
Home Page: http://www.emmyonline.org

• 13861 • **Daytime Emmy Awards**
For recognition of outstanding daytime program and individual achievements that advance the arts and sciences of television. Gold Emmy statuettes are awarded annually in each of 58 categories, including acknowledgements for series, performers, and all other technical and creative areas of production. Established in 1974. The awards ceremony is broadcast on national television each April.

• 13862 • **Emmy Awards**
For recognition of outstanding achievements that advance the arts and sciences of primetime television. Gold Emmy statuettes are awarded annually in 94 categories, as well as in the Creative Arts Emmy Awards and the Los Angeles Area Emmy Awards. The awards are administered by three sister organizations: the National Academy of Television Arts and Sciences, the Academy of Television Arts and Sciences, and the International Academy of Television Arts and Sciences. Established in 1949.

• 13863 • **News and Documentary Emmy Awards**
To recognize news and documentary programs, program segments, news and documentary writers, directors, and technical and design craftspersons. To be eligible, a program or report must have aired nationally, in the proper eligibility year, and fit in one of 36 categories. A gold Emmy statuette is awarded annually.

• 13864 • **Public and Community Service Emmy Awards**
To recognize a local television station or a cable company in the United States for a programming campaign that provides an example of outstanding service to its community. In addition, two awards for Outstanding Public Service Announcement are also presented each year, as well as an award for public service announcements in a sponsored commercial. Winners for the gold Emmy statuettes are selected by a panel of judges composed of community leaders, clergy, educators, businesspeople, and artists. Established in 1962.

• 13865 • **Sports Emmy Awards**
To recognize producers and individuals in national network and syndicated sports programming for outstanding achievements in sports television coverage. Gold Emmy awards are presented in 27 categories each year. In addition, the Sports Lifetime Achievement Award is presented. Established in 1950.

• 13866 • **Technical Engineering Achievement Awards**
To recognize developments and/or standardization in engineering technologies that are either so extensive an improvement on existing methods or so innovative in nature that they materially affect the transmission, recording, or reception of television. The award may be given to an individual, a company, or a scientific or technical organization responsible for the development. The awards are given in two categories: the area focusing on the historical definition of television, linearly produced and delivered in a real-time broadcast manner; and the other encompassing on such advanced media as non-linear creation and distribution, point-to-point delivery, one- and two-screen television technologies, and gaming for television delivery. A gold Emmy statuette is awarded annually when merited. Established in 1948.

• 13867 •
National Accreditation Council for Agencies Serving the Blind and Visually Impaired
Steven K. Hegedeos, Exec.Dir.
21475 Lorain Rd.
Cleveland, OH 44126
Phone: (440)409-0340
Fax: (440)409-0173
E-mail: shegedeos@nacasb.org
Home Page: http://www.nacasb.org

• 13868 • **Distinguished Service Award**
To recognize individuals who have demonstrated a sustained commitment to standards and accreditation, outstanding leadership in the field of work with the blind, and devoted service to blind and visually handicapped Americans. A certificate was awarded when merited. Established in 1982.

• 13869 • **NAC Award**
To encourage professional and citizen leadership toward higher standards in the field of work with the blind and visually handicapped, and to make the public more aware of the importance of high standards of service. Leadership by a professional or volunteer above and beyond the call of duty was the basis for selection. An engraved design of Steuben glass was awarded from time to time. Established in 1969.

• 13870 • **Service Award**
To recognize individuals who have rendered outstanding service to blind and visually handicapped Americans by advancing the application of standards in the accreditation process. A certificate was awarded when merited. Established in 1971.

• 13871 •
National Action Committee on the Status of Women
(Comite Canadien d'Action sur le Statut de la Femme)
Denise Campbell, Pres.
234 Eglinton Ave. E., Ste. 203
Toronto, ON, Canada M4P 1K5
Phone: (416)932-1718
Fax: (416)932-0646
E-mail: nac@web.net
Home Page: http://www.nac-cca.ca

• 13872 • **Woman of Courage**
Annual award of recognition.

• 13873 •
National Action Council for Minorities in Engineering
Nadine Dennis, Dir. Development
Reginald H. Jones Award
440 Hamilton Ave., Ste. 302
White Plains, NY 10601-1813
Phone: (914)539-4010
Fax: (914)539-4032
E-mail: webmaster@namce.org
Home Page: http://www.nacme.org

• 13874 • **Reginald H. Jones Distinguished Service Award**
To recognize individuals whose efforts have resulted in increased minority participation in the nation's engineering workforce. A plaque and a $10,000 honorarium donated in the name of the recipient to a tax-exempt organization working in the minority engineering effort are awarded annually at the NACME Forum. Established in 1983 to honor Reginald H. Jones, former chairman and CEO of the General Electric Company, whose pioneering leadership helped initiate the minority engineering effort.

• 13875 •
National Aeronautic Association
David L. Ivey, Pres.
1737 King St., Ste. 220
Alexandria, VA 22314
Phone: (703)527-0226
Toll-Free: 800-644-9777
Fax: (703)527-0229
E-mail: naa@naa.aero
Home Page: http://www.naa-usa.org

Formerly: (1922) Aero Club of America.

• 13876 • **Frank G. Brewer Trophy**
For recognition of outstanding contributions of enduring value to aerospace education and training of youth in the United States. Individuals, groups, and organizations may be nominated. The nomination period is December 1 through February 28. A trophy is awarded annually. Established in 1943 by Frank G. Brewer, in honor of his two sons and the half million other youths put into the air by World War II.

• 13877 • **Robert J. Collier Trophy**
For recognition of "the greatest achievement in aeronautics or astronautics in America, with respect to improving the performance, efficiency, and safety of air or space vehicles, the value of which has been thoroughly demonstrated by actual use during the preceding year." Individuals, groups, and organizations are eligible. The nomination period is November 1 through January 31. A trophy is awarded annually. Established in 1910 by Robert J. Collier. Formerly: (1944) Aero Club of America Trophy.

• 13878 • **Elder Statesman of Aviation Award**
To honor outstanding Americans over the age of 60 who have made contributions of significant value to aviation. Applicants must be citizens of the United States; have been actively identified with aeronautics for at least 15 years; made

contributions of significant value to aeronautics; and exhibit qualities of patriotism, integrity, and a moral courage. Nomination period is April 1 through June 30. A certificate is presented annually. Established in 1954.

• 13879 • Mackay Trophy

For recognition of the "most meritorious flight of the year" by an Air Force person, persons, or organizations. The Chief of Staff of the U.S. Air Force selects the winner from nominees submitted. The Mackay Trophy, awarded annually, is the oldest award intended exclusively for members of the United States Air Force. It is on permanent display at the National Air and Space Museum in Washington, D.C. Deadline for nominations is January 31 of the year following the flight. Established in 1912 by Clarence H. Mackay, a wealthy industrialist, communications pioneer, and aviation enthusiast.

• 13880 • Wright Brothers Memorial Trophy

For recognition of "significant public service of enduring value to aviation in the United States." Living American citizens who, as civilians, have rendered some personal and direct service as an officer or employee of the federal, state, or local government, with or without compensation, are eligible. The nomination period is June 1 through August 31. A trophy is awarded annually on the anniversary of the historic first flight. Established in 1948 in memory of Orville and Wilbur Wright.

• 13881 • Katharine Wright Memorial Award

To honor a "woman who has provided encouragement, support, and inspiration to her husband and was thus instrumental in his success, or who made a personal contribution to the advancement of the art, sport, and science of aviation and space flight over an extended period of time." Nominations are accepted from aviation organizations and interested individuals throughout the United States between January 1 through March 31. A certificate is awarded each year at the annual meeting of The Ninety-Nines, Inc. in July. Established in 1981 by Gates Learjet Corporation in memory of Katharine Wright, sister of Orville and Wilbur Wright. Administration of this award was transferred to NAA in 1990. The trophy is on display at the offices of The Ninety-Nines, Inc. in Oklahoma City, OK.

• 13882 •
National Aeronautics and Space Administration
Cathie Lane, Contact
Incentive Awards Board
NASA Headquarters, Code FPP
300 E St. SW
Washington, DC 20546
Phone: (202)358-1213
Fax: (202)358-3039
E-mail: cathie.lane-1@nasa.gov
Home Page: http://nasapeople.nasa.gov

• 13883 • Certificate of Appreciation

To recognize an employee for an outstanding accomplishment that has contributed substantially to the mission of NASA. A framed certificate bearing the official seal of NASA and signed by the Administrator is awarded when merited.

• 13884 • Congressional Space Medal of Honor

This, the highest honor that NASA confers, is given to recognize a distinguished astronaut who, in the performance of duties, displayed exceptionally meritorious efforts and contributed to the welfare of the nation and mankind. The United States Executive Office of the President may award in the name of Congress a medal of appropriate design. Established in 1969.

• 13885 • Distinguished Public Service Medal

This, the highest honor that NASA confers to a non-government individual, recognizes individuals whose distinguished accomplishments contributed substantially to the NASA mission. The contribution must be so extraordinary that other forms of recognition by NASA would be inadequate. Individuals who are neither employees of the federal government nor employees during the period that the service was performed are eligible. A medal and a framed certificate bearing the official seal of NASA and signed by the administrator are awarded annually when merited.

• 13886 • Distinguished Service Medal (NASA Medal)

To recognize an individual in the federal service who, by distinguished service, ability, or courage, has personally made a contribution representing substantial progress to the NASA mission in the interests of the United States. The contribution must be so extraordinary that the other forms of recognition by NASA would be inadequate. A medal and a framed certificate bearing the official seal of NASA and signed by the administrator are awarded annually when merited.

• 13887 • Equal Employment Opportunity Medal

To recognize an individual, either government employee or civilian, for outstanding achievement and material contribution to the goals of the Equal Employment Opportunity programs either within government or within community organizations or groups. A medal and a framed certificate bearing the official seal of NASA and signed by the administrator are awarded annually when merited.

• 13888 • Exceptional Achievement Medal

For recognition of a significant, specific accomplishment or substantial improvement in operations, efficiency, service, financial savings, science, or technology that contribute to the mission of NASA. NASA employees and employees of other federal agencies may be nominated. A gold medal and a framed certificate bearing the official seal of NASA, and signed by the administrator are awarded annually when merited. Established in 1991.

• 13889 • Exceptional Administrative Achievement Medal (EAAM)

Awarded to an individual in the Feder service (NASA Classification 500 Group clerical/assistant and related support positions only) for a Significant, specific accomplishment or contribution characterized by Unusual initiative or creativity that demonstrates a substantial Improvement in administrative support contributing to the mission of NASA. A medal is awarded.

• 13890 • Exceptional Bravery Medal

To recognize an individual, either government employee or civilian, for exemplary and courageous handling of an emergency in NASA program activities by an individual who, independent of personal danger, acted to prevent the loss of human life or government property. A medal and a framed certificate bearing the official seal of NASA and signed by the administrator are awarded annually when merited.

• 13891 • Exceptional Engineering Achievement Medal

To recognize an individual, either government employee or civilian, for exceptional engineering contributions toward achievement of the NASA mission. This award may be given for individual efforts that have resulted in a contribution of fundamental importance in the field or have significantly enhanced understanding of the field. A medal and framed certificate bearing the official seal of NASA and signed by the administrator are awarded annually when merited.

• 13892 • Exceptional Scientific Achievement Medal

To recognize an individual, either government employee or civilian, for an unusually significant scientific contribution toward achievement of the NASA mission. This award may be given for individual efforts that have resulted in a contribution of fundamental importance in the field or have significantly enhanced understanding of the field. A medal and a framed certificate bearing the official seal of NASA and signed by the administrator are awarded annually when merited.

• 13893 • Exceptional Service Medal

To recognize a government employee for significant sustained performance characterized by unusual initiative or creative ability that clearly demonstrates substantial improvement in engineering, aeronautics, space flight, administration, support, or space-related endeavors that contribute to the mission of NASA. A medal and a framed certificate bearing the official seal of NASA and signed by the Administrator are awarded annually when merited.

• 13894 • Exceptional Technology Achievement Medal (ETAM)

Awarded to government and non-government individuals for technology contributions achieved in one of the following: Early Technology development significantly contributing to the NASA mission, Exemplary collaborative effort in achieving significant technology transfer, or Exceptional utilization of a NASA-developed technology resulting in a Significant commercial application

• 13895 • Group Achievement Award
To recognize a group of government employees or a group comprised of both government and non-government personnel for outstanding accomplishment through the coordination of many individual efforts and has contributed substantially to the accomplishment of the mission of NASA. A framed certificate bearing the official seal of NASA and signed by the administrator is awarded annually when merited.

• 13896 • George M. Low Award
To recognize current NASA prime contractors and subcontractors in the aerospace industry who have demonstrated sustained excellence and outstanding technical and managerial achievements in quality and performance on NASA-related contracts or subcontracts in four categories: large business product, large business service, small business product, and small business service. The objectives of this award are to increase public awareness of the importance of quality and productivity to the nation's aerospace program and industry in general to encourage domestic business to continue efforts to enhance quality, increase productivity, and thereby strengthen competitiveness; and to provide the means for sharing the successful methods and techniques used by the applicants with other American enterprises. Winning organizations will receive the George M. Low Trophy; finalists will receive a George M. Low Plaque. Established in 1985 and renamed in 1990 in memory of George M. Low, who greatly contributed to the early development of NASA Space Programs during his 27 years of Government service.

• 13897 • Outstanding Leadership Medal
To recognize a government employee for notably outstanding leadership that has had a pronounced effect upon the technical or administrative programs of NASA. The leadership award may be given for an act of leadership, for sustained contributions based on an individual's effectiveness, for the productivity of the individual's program, or demonstrated ability to develop the administrative or technical talents of other employees. A medal and a framed certificate bearing the official seal of NASA and signed by the administrator are awarded annually when merited.

• 13898 • Public Service Group Achievement Award
To recognize a group of non-government employees for outstanding accomplishment that has contributed substantially to the mission of NASA. A framed certificate bearing the official seal of NASA and signed by the administrator is awarded annually when merited.

• 13899 • Public Service Medal
To recognize an individual for exceptional contributions to the mission of NASA. Individuals who were neither employees of the federal government nor employees during the period that the service was performed are eligible. A medal and a framed certificate bearing the official seal of NASA and signed by the administrator are awarded annually when merited.

• 13900 • Space Flight Medal
To recognize significant achievement or service during individual participation in a Space Transportation System flight mission as a flight crew member (civilian and military astronaut, pilot, mission specialist, payload specialist, or other space flight participant). The NASA Space Flight Cluster is awarded for subsequent flights.

• 13901 •
National Agricultural Aviation Association
Andrew Moore, Exec.Dir.
1005 E St. SE
Washington, DC 20003-2847
Phone: (202)546-5722
Fax: (202)546-5726
E-mail: information@agaviation.org
Home Page: http://www.agaviation.org

• 13902 • Agrinaut Award
To recognize the agricultural aircraft operator or operating organization that has made an outstanding contribution in the field of agricultural aircraft operations. The recipient of the award must have been actively engaged in commercial agricultural application with an agricultural aircraft and the achievement cited must have contributed to the "state-of-the-art" for the benefit of the agricultural aircraft industry as a whole. A freestanding cup inscribed with the award winner's achievements is awarded annually. Established in 1967 by Agrinautics of Las Vegas, Nevada, and by the NAAA under procedures established for noting new operating techniques, new and novel equipment, new successful crop applications, or other contributions.

• 13903 • Allied Industry Individual Award
To recognize NAAA members or staff and/or an allied industry individual who has significantly contributed their efforts for the benefit of the allied industry and its exhibit efforts. Nominations are made by allied industry members only, and award recipients are selected by the allied industry directors on the NAAA Board. Awarded annually. Established in 1978.

• 13904 • Delta Air Lines Puffer Award
To recognize an individual who has made an outstanding contribution to the design of agricultural aircraft and/or related equipment. An engraved three-color plaque emblazoned with the Delta Air Lines emblem, which was first used as the trademark of Delta Air Corporation at Monroe, Louisiana, is awarded annually. Established in 1972. Sponsored by Delta Air Lines.

• 13905 • John Robert Horne Memorial Award
To recognize a pilot with five years or less experience in the agricultural aviation industry who has an exemplary safety record and/or has contributed to safety in agricultural aviation. A wall plaque inscribed with the recipient's name and year is awarded annually. Established in 1980 by John and Jewell Horne in memory of their son, John Robert Horne.

• 13906 • Larsen-Miller Community Service Award
For recognition of outstanding contributions by a member to his community. An engraved plaque commemorating the achievement is awarded when merited. Established in 1974 by the Arizona Agricultural Aviation Association in honor of Randy Larsen and Paul Miller, an operator and flagman, who lost their lives trying to rescue three victims of an automobile accident.

• 13907 • William O. Marsh Safety Award
For recognition of significant achievements in safety, safety education, or an outstanding operational safety program. A bronze wood-mounted wall plaque inscribed with the year and achievement of the recipient is awarded annually. Established in 1972 by Fairfax Underwriters Services, Inc. in memory of William O. "Bill" Marsh.

• 13908 • Most Active Woman Award
To recognize an outstanding contribution of a woman who is active in the affairs of the industry or the Association. Presented annually. Established in 1971 by Mrs. Shirley Carroll in memory of her son, William Carroll.

• 13909 • NAAA Falcon Club
To recognize individuals who, through personal effort and dedication, have made substantial contributions to the agricultural aviation industry and its national association. A club pin is presented at the discretion of the current NAAA president. Established in 1982 by NAAA president, Roy Wood.

• 13910 • Outstanding Service Awards
For recognition of service to the commercial agricultural aviation industry or to the Association. A bronze wood-mounted wall plaque inscribed with the recipient's name and the year is awarded annually to one or more recipients. Established in 1967.

• 13911 • Related Industry Award
For recognition of outstanding contributions by an allied industry member and his company. An engraved plaque commemorating the achievement is awarded annually. Established in 1969.

• 13912 •
National Agricultural Center and Hall of Fame
630 Hall of Fame Dr.
Bonner Springs, KS 66012
Phone: (913)721-1075
Fax: (913)721-1202
E-mail: info@aghalloffame.com
Home Page: http://aghalloffame.com

• 13913 • **Agricultural Hall of Fame**
To honor individuals who have helped make this nation great by their outstanding contributions to the establishment, development, advancement, or improvement of agriculture in the United States. Farmers, farm women, farm leaders, teachers, scientists, inventors, governmental leaders, and other individuals are eligible. Usually, candidates must have been deceased at least ten years. A unanimous vote by the board of governors may declare a living person (or person deceased less than 10 years) as an eligible candidate. Portraits of recipients are hung in the Hall of Honorees. Awarded only when merited. Established in 1960.

• 13914 • **Special Recognition Awards**
No further information was available for this edition.

• 13915 • **Volunteer of the Year Award**
No further information was available for this edition.

• 13916 •
National Air Transportation Association
James K. Coyne, Pres.
4226 King St.
Alexandria, VA 22302
Phone: (703)845-9000
Toll-Free: 800-808-6282
Fax: (703)845-8176
E-mail: info@nata-online.org
Home Page: http://www.nata.aero

• 13917 • **Aviation Journalism Award**
To recognize an author or publication that excels in consumer education or editorial support that is beneficial to the FBO/Air Charter industry at the regional or national level. Nominations should include a copy of the article, periodical, book, or presentation. The recipient need not be a member of NATA. Deadline is March 1. One monetary award of $500 is presented annually.

• 13918 • **Distinguished Service Award**
To recognize an individual, group of individuals, or organization for outstanding service or contribution to General Aviation. Recognizes recent accomplishments of those still active in the day-to-day business of general aviation. Recipient need not be a member of NATA. Deadline is March 1. One monetary award of $1,000 is presented annually.

• 13919 • **Excellence in Pilot Training Award**
To recognize an individual, a group of individuals, or an organization for outstanding contributions in safety, professionalism, leadership, and excellence in the field of pilot training. The recipient must be a certified flight instructor (CFIAI, ASMEL minimum); be an employee of or conduct a full-time flight training business in accordance with FAR Part 61 or Part 141; and be directly connected to the field of pilot training for a period of not less than 10 years. Deadline is March 1. A monetary prize of $1,000 is awarded annually. Sponsored by Jeppesen Sanderson, Inc., an NATA Associate Member Company.

• 13920 • **General Aviation Service Technician Award**
To recognize an employee of an NATA Regular Member company who is judged to be the best in elevating the professional status of general aviation service companies with regard to promotion of safety, customer service, productivity, and innovative ideas. Eligible nominees must be a licensed Airframe and Powerplant Mechanic or a Radio Repairman for a period of not less than 20 years. Deadline is March 1. A certificate and monetary award of $1,000 are presented annually. Sponsored by the Aircraft Technical Publishers, an NATA Associate Member company.

• 13921 • **William A. "Bill" Ong Memorial Award**
For recognition of extraordinary achievement and extended meritorious service to the General Aviation industry, which includes corporate jets, air charter planes, helicopters, and other smaller aircraft. Nominees should have devoted a lifetime of service to the General Aviation industry and no longer be actively involved in the day-to-day business activities. Recipient need not be a member of NATA. One monetary award of $1000 is presented annually. Deadline is March 1. Established in memory of William A. Ong, the Association's first voluntary president from 1940 through 1942.

• 13922 •
National Alliance for Research on Schizophrenia and Depression
Constance E. Lieber, Pres./CEO
60 Cutter Mill Rd., Ste. 404
Great Neck, NY 11021
Phone: (516)829-0091
Phone: (516)829-5576
Toll-Free: 800-829-8289
Fax: (516)487-6930
E-mail: info@narsad.org
Home Page: http://www.narsad.org

• 13923 • **Distinguished Investigator Award**
Recognizes research relevant to schizophrenia, major affective disorders, or other serious mental illnesses. Applicants must be full professors or equivalent. Up to $100,000 for one year is awarded. Application deadline is May 15. Formerly: (1997) Established Investigator Award.

• 13924 • **Independent Investigator Award**
Recognizes research relevant to schizophrenia, major affective disorders, or other serious mental illnesses. Applicants must be associate professors or the equivalent. $50,000 per year for two years is awarded (maximum award is $100,000). Awarded annually.

• 13925 • **Young Investigator Award**
Recognizes research relevant to schizophrenia, major affective disorders, or other serious mental illnesses. Applicants must have a doctoral level degree and be employed in research training or be in a faculty or independent research position. Up to $30,000 per year for up to 2 years is awarded. Application deadline is July 25.

• 13926 •
National American Legion Press Association
George W. Hooten, Exec.Dir.
PO Box 1055
Indianapolis, IN 46206
Phone: (404)377-5602
E-mail: geonalpa@mindspring.com
Home Page: http://www.nalpa.legion.org

• 13927 • **Best Publication Awards**
To recognize publications that best exemplify excellence in journalism. Categories include Mary B. Howard Plaque, Emerson O. Mann Plaque, Al Weinberg Plaque, R. C. Mann Plaque, George W. Hooten Plaque, and William E. Rominger Plaque. Awarded annually.

• 13928 • **R. C. Cann Plaque**
To recognize outstanding publications produced at small posts (up to 250 members) and all other unit/squadrons (SAL, Auxiliary, etc.) Awarded annually. Established in 1957.

• 13929 • **NALPA Past President Award**
To recognize an individual for outstanding service to his community or the nation in any field of endeavor. Awarded annually.

• 13930 •
National Amputee Golf Association
Bob Wilson, Exec.Dir.
11 Walnut Hill Rd.
Amherst, NH 03031-1713
Phone: (603)672-6444
Toll-Free: 800-633-6242
Fax: (603)672-2987
E-mail: info@nagagolf.org
Home Page: http://www.nagagolf.org

• 13931 • **Certificate of Appreciation**
For recognition of outstanding contributions to NAGA and the encouragement of amputee rehabilitation, both mental and physical through the medium of golf. A framed certificate (plaque) is awarded annually. Established in 1981.

• 13932 • Most Improved Golfer
For recognition of individuals who have improved their playing ability in a specified event over the previous year. An engraved plate is awarded at regional and local tournaments by NAGA annually. Established in 1988.

• 13933 • National Amputee Golf Champion (Men and Women)
To recognize excellence in the golf competition. Amputees who have lost a hand or foot or combination thereof at a major joint are eligible. An engraved Armetel plate is awarded annually. Established in 1948.

• 13934 • Perseverance Award
For recognition at the National and National Senior Amputee championships to a man or woman who exemplifies the meaning of the word. To keep at something in spite of difficulties. Awarded as needed annually. A marble and glass trophy is awarded. Established in 2000.

• 13935 •
National Animal Control Association
John Mays, Exec.Dir.
PO Box 480851
Kansas City, MO 64148-0851
Phone: (913)768-1319
Fax: (913)768-1378
E-mail: naca@interserv.com
Home Page: http://www.nacanet.org

• 13936 • Animal Control Employee of the Year
To recognize individuals within the field of animal control management who have went above and beyond the call of duty within the profession of animal control.

• 13937 • Diane Lane Memorial Award
Given to individuals in the field of animal control who have went above and beyond the call of duty within the profession.

• 13938 • Bill Lehman Memorial Award
Given to individuals within the field of animal control who have went above and beyond the call of duty in the profession of animal control.

• 13939 • Outstanding Animal Control Agency of the Year
To recognize individuals within the field of animal control who have given above and beyond the call of duty to the professionalization of animal control.

• 13940 • Outstanding Sate Association Award
Presented to individuals who have went above and beyond the call of duty in the profession of animal control.

• 13941 • R.D. 'Bob' Ward Memorial Posthumous Award
Given to individuals who have went above and beyond the call of duty within the field of animal control.

• 13942 •
National Apostolate for Inclusion Ministry
Rev. Ray Daull, Pres.
PO Box 218
Riverdale, MD 20738-0218
Phone: (301)699-9500
Toll-Free: 800-736-1280
E-mail: qnafim@aol.com
Home Page: http://www.nafim.org

• 13943 • Early Career Award
To recognize individuals early in their career who have contributed significantly to the field of psychosomatic medicine. Awarded annually with a cash award of $1,000 and a plaque.

• 13944 • Leadership Award
To recognize an outstanding leader in the field of mental retardation. Awarded annually with a plaque. Established in 1974.

• 13945 • Program Award
To recognize significant achievements of a program serving people with mental retardation. Awarded annually with a plaque. Established in 1974.

• 13946 • Service Award
To recognize outstanding contribution to field of mental retardation made by an individual over a long period of time. Awarded annually with a plaque. Established in 1974.

• 13947 • Youth Award
To recognize significant contributions to the field of mental retardation by a person younger than 22 years. Awarded annually with a plaque. Established in 1974.

• 13948 •
National Arbor Day Foundation
John Rosenow, Pres.
100 Arbor Ave.
Nebraska City, NE 68410
Phone: (402)474-5555
Toll-Free: 888-448-7337
Fax: (402)474-0820
E-mail: member.service@ardorday.org
Home Page: http://www.arborday.org

• 13949 • Arbor Day Awards
To recognize the outstanding accomplishments of individuals, organizations, corporations, and institutions whose work has furthered the Arbor Day ideal. The following awards are presented: J. Sterling Morton Award - the highest honor of the foundation, to an individual who pursues the Arbor Day ideal on the national or international level; Frederick Law Olmsted Award - to individuals who work as tree planters on the state or regional level; Lawrence Enersen Award - to individuals whose life's work exemplifies commitment to tree planting and conservation in community improvement; Lady Bird Johnson Award - to an individual, group, organization, or governmental body for roadside beautification; Good Steward Award - to individuals who have best cared for and used land wisely; Project Awards; Education Awards; Media Awards; Celebration Awards; and Promise to the Earth Award. Honorees are presented an Arbor Day Award plaque and may use the Arbor Day recognition trademark until the following year's winners are announced. Awarded annually at a banquet. Established in 1972. Formerly: .

• 13950 • Building with Trees Awards of Excellence
Recognizes the efforts exemplifying the Building With Trees concepts. Residential, commercial, retail, industrial, public, and mixed-use projects of all sizes are eligible. In addition to awards for overall projects, special awards may be given for areas of particular merit. Awarded annually.

• 13951 •
National Archery Association of the United States
Bradley R. Camp, Exec.Dir.
1 Olympic Plz.
Colorado Springs, CO 80909-5778
Phone: (719)866-4576
Fax: (719)632-4733
E-mail: info@usarchery.org
Home Page: http://www.usarchery.org

• 13952 • National Target Championships
For recognition of men and women champion amateur archers. The men's champion is determined by the highest aggregate score in two international rounds (competitions) at the annual NAA Championship Tournament which requires the shooting of 72 arrows at a 122 cm. target face at 90 and 70 meters and 72 arrows at an 80 cm. face at 50 and 30 meters. The women's champion is determined by the highest aggregate score in two international rounds (competitions) at the annual NAA Championship Tournament which requires the shooting of 72 arrows at a 122 cm. target face at 70 and 60 meters and 72 arrows at an 80 cm. face at 50 and 30 meters. Established in 1946. Note: The above is a basic format which may change from time to time.

• 13953 • Shenk Award
To recognize male and female amateur archers in the Olympic Bow Division with the highest cumulative scores in the U.S. Indoor, Field, and Target Championships. A trophy is awarded annually at the awards banquet. Established in 1980 to honor former NAA president Clayton Shenk.

• 13954 • Thompson Award
To recognize an individual for outstanding and meritorious service to the sport of archery without expectation of reward. A medal is awarded as merited. Established in 1939 in honor of NAA's first president, J. Maurice Thompson.

• 13955 •
National Art Education Association
Dr. Thomas A. Hatfield, Exec.Dir.
1916 Association Dr.
Reston, VA 20191-1590
Phone: (703)860-8000
Fax: (703)860-2960
E-mail: thatfield@naea-reston.org
Home Page: http://www.naea-reston.org

• 13956 • **Manuel Barkan Memorial Award**
For recognition of a contribution of scholarly merit to the field of art education. Contributors of articles to *Art Education* or *Studies in Art Education* are considered for articles published within the calendar year preceding the conference year. Awarded annually. Nomination deadline is October 1. Established in honor of Dr. Manuel Barkan.

• 13957 • **Committee on Multiethnic Concerns J. Eugene Grisby, Jr. Award**
To honor individuals who have made distinguished contributions to the profession of art education in scholarly writing, research, professional leadership, teaching, and/or community service. Active NAEA members and non-members may be nominated. Deadline for nominations to COMC Award chair is October 1. Awarded annually.

• 13958 • **Design Standards Award**
To recognize exemplary school art facilities which meet or exceed the standards of the NAEA. Award is offered for the school year. Elementary, middle/junior, and senior high schools are eligible. Awarded annually.

• 13959 • **Distinguished Service Award (Outside the Profession)**
For recognition of individuals or groups for outstanding achievements and contributions to art education by persons outside the profession. Administrators, politicians, teachers of other disciplines, and school board members are eligible for nomination to awards coordinators before October 1.

• 13960 • **Distinguished Service Award (Within the Profession)**
For recognition of outstanding achievement, contribution, and service to the field of art education and to national and state/province art education associations. Active NAEA members are eligible for nomination by October 1.

• 13961 • **Marion Quin Dix Leadership Award**
For recognition of outstanding contributions and service to the profession by a state/province association officer in the performance and/or development of specific programs, goals, or activities at the state/province association level. Officers must be nominated to the President-Elect by October 1. Established in honor of NAEA's third president, Marion Quin Dix.

• 13962 • **Higher Education Student Achievement Award**
To recognize excellence in student artistic involvement at the college/university level. Active student members of a college/university chapter may be nominated. Deadline for nominations is October 1. Awarded annually.

• 13963 • **Lowenfeld Award**
To recognize an individual who has made significant contributions to art education over the years. The recipient presents the "Lowenfeld Lecture" at the national convention. Deadline for nominations is October 1. Established in 1960 by friends and former students of Viktor Lowenfeld.

• 13964 • **National Art Educator Award**
To recognize an NAEA member for outstanding achievements and service of national significance during previous years. Deadline for nominations is October 1. Formerly: (1997) NAEA Art Educator of the Year.

• 13965 • **National Art Honor Society Sponsor Award**
To recognize the dedication of an NAEA member who sponsors an outstanding National Art Honor Society chapter. Deadline for nominations is October 1.

• 13966 • **National Division Art Educator Award**
To recognize one outstanding NAEA member from each of the six divisions for outstanding service and achievement of national significance during previous years. The divisions are elementary, secondary, middle level, higher education, supervision/administration, and museum education. Nominees must spend at least 51 percent of their working day in the job division for which they have been nominated. Division award nominees are generally, but not exclusively, taken from the present and previous years' regional division award recipients. Division members at-large may be nominated as well. Formerly: (1997) National Division Art Educator of the Year.

• 13967 • **National Junior Art Honor Society Sponsor Award**
To recognize the dedication of an NAEA member who sponsors an outstanding National Junior Art Honor Society chapter. Nominations must be made to the National Secretary Division Director-elect by October 1. Awarded annually.

• 13968 • **Presidential Citation Award**
To recognize a state/province association that has demonstrated superior achievements of a specific goal that contributes to the improvement of art education as a profession. State/province art education associations are eligible for nomination by October 1.

• 13969 • **Program Standards Award**
To recognize outstanding achievements of elementary and secondary school art programs that meet or exceed program standards in the NAEA *Purposes, Principles and Standards for School Art Programs* booklet. Public or private elementary, middle/junior, and senior high schools are eligible to apply throughout the school year.

• 13970 • **Regional Division Art Educator Award**
To honor one outstanding NAEA member from each of the six divisions within each of the four geographic regions. This award recognizes exemplary contributions, achievements, and service at a regional level. The regions are Eastern, Western, Southeastern, and Pacific, and the divisions are elementary, secondary, middle level, higher education, supervision/administration, and museum education. Nominees must spend at least 51 percent of their working day in the job division for which they have been nominated. Deadline for nominations is October 1. Formerly: (1997) Regional Division Art Educator of the Year.

• 13971 • **Retired Art Educator Award**
To recognize continuous outstanding service to art education by an individual after retirement through teaching, professional leadership, and/or community service.

• 13972 • **Secondary Art Achievement Award**
For recognition of originality and quality of art work by members of high school NAHS chapters. Teachers may send nominations to the National Secondary Division Director-elect. A certificate is presented at the national conventions. Formerly: .

• 13973 • **State/Province Art Educator Award**
To honor the outstanding NAEA member in each state/province whose service and contribution to art education merit state/province-wide recognition and acclaim. Nominees must be active NAEA members in the state/province in which they are nominated. Individual members must submit nominations to their state/province association presidents or awards chair. Awarded annually. Formerly: (1997) State/Province Art Educator of the Year.

• 13974 • **State/Province Association Newsletter Award**
For recognition of excellence in the development and publication of a state/province art education association or special interest groups newsletter. Three copies of newsletter issues published in the previous calendar year must be submitted by February 1. Awards are presented at the annual convention. Formerly: NAEA State/Province Newsletter Editor Award.

• 13975 • **Student Chapter Sponsor Award of Excellence**
To recognize dedication to the development of future professional members of the NAEA through sponsorship of an outstanding student chapter group at the college/university level.

Nominations must be made by October 1. Formerly: .

• 13976 • **Youth Art Month Award**
To recognize outstanding achievements in the promotion of art education. State/province associations and Youth Art Month chairs are eligible. Awarded annually. Administered by the Council for Art Education, Inc.

• 13977 •
National Art Materials Trade Association
Katharine Coffey, Exec.Dir.
15806 Brookway Dr., Ste. 300
Huntersville, NC 28078
Phone: (704)892-6244
Toll-Free: 800-746-2682
Fax: (704)892-6247
E-mail: info@namta.org
Home Page: http://www.namta.org

• 13978 • **Excellence in Communication Award**
To encourage professional development in visual communications in art materials, newsletters, catalogs, print ads, and point-of-purchase promotions. Winning pieces are held up as industry standards. Members are eligible. A plaque and publicity are awarded annually. Established in 1985 by NAMTA's Business Management Committee.

• 13979 • **NAMTA Hall of Fame Award**
To recognize business and industry achievements and contributions to the art materials industry. Members are eligible. A plaque is awarded at the annual convention. Established in 1959.

• 13980 • **Outstanding Booth Awards**
To encourage professional development of art materials marketing, presentation, and promotion for trade shows. Members who exhibit at NAMTA's annual convention and trade show are eligible. A plaque and publicity are awarded at the annual convention. Established in 1984.

• 13981 •
National Arts Centre Orchestra
Peter Herrndorf, Pres. and CEO
Sta. "B"
PO Box 1534
Ottawa, ON, Canada K1P 5W1
Phone: (613)947-7000
Fax: (613)943-1400
E-mail: cdeacon@nac-cna.ca
Home Page: http://www.nac-cna.ca/en/naco

• 13982 • **Bursary Competition**
To provide recognition and financial support to a young Canadian musician who is following a program of study designed to further a career as a professional orchestral musician. Music students aged 16 to 24 whose family residence is in the National Capital Region (NCR), or who have been following a recognized course of music study in the NCR in preparation for careers as professional orchestral musicians, are eligible. The grand prize winner receives an award of $6,000. Other awards include the Harold Crabtree Foundation Award ($5,000); the NAC Orchestra Association Award ($3,000); the Vic Pomer Award ($1,500); and the Piccolo Prix ($500). Established in 1981.

• 13983 •
National Arts Club
15 Gramercy Park S
New York, NY 10003
Phone: (212)475-3424
Fax: (212)475-3692
E-mail: nacnewyork@aol.com
Home Page: http://www.nationalartsclub.org

• 13984 • **Citations of Merit**
For recognition of outstanding contributions to the arts. Awarded when merited.

• 13985 • **Gold Medal of Excellence for Photography**
For recognition of outstanding contributions to photography. A medal is awarded annually. Established in 1993.

• 13986 • **Gold Medal of Honor for Dance**
To honor exceptional contributions to dance. A medal is awarded annually. Established in 1993.

• 13987 • **Gold Medal of Honor for Design**
To recognize outstanding contributions to design. Established in 1991.

• 13988 • **Gold Medal of Honor for Education**
For recognition of exceptional contributions to arts education. A medal is awarded annually. Established in 1994.

• 13989 • **Gold Medal of Honor for Film/Video**
To recognize outstanding contributions to film and video. A medal is awarded every one to three years. Established in 1988.

• 13990 • **Gold Medal of Honor for Theater/Drama**
To recognize outstanding contributions to theater/drama. A medal is awarded annually. Established in 1973.

• 13991 • **Gold Medal of Honor for Visual Arts**
To recognize outstanding contributions to art. A medal is awarded annually at an awards dinner. Established in 1958.

• 13992 • **Kesselring Prize**
To provide financial aid to promising playwrights. Nominees may be submitted and sponsored by invited repertory theaters and/or other qualified institutions. A monetary prize of $10,000 to the winner and honorable mention awards of $5,000 each are awarded annually. A supplementary award may be declared consisting of a professional staged reading of a winning work. Established in 1980 to honor Joseph Otto Kesselring, actor, author and producer of vaudeville sketches. Formerly: Joseph Kesselring Fund Award.

• 13993 • **Medal of Honor for Literature**
To recognize outstanding contributions to literature, including novels, poetry, plays, memoirs, and biographies. A medal is awarded annually at an awards dinner. Established in 1968.

• 13994 • **Medal of Honor for Music**
To recognize accomplishment in any field of music and any form of artistry, as well as occasional recognition of philanthropy and support. A medal is awarded annually at an awards dinner. Established in 1957.

• 13995 • **Richard Seyffert Memorial Award**
For recognition of outstanding artistic achievement. A monetary award and a plaque are awarded annually. Established in 1989.

• 13996 •
National Asphalt Pavement Association
Mike Acott, Pres.
NAPA Bldg.
5100 Forbes Blvd.
Lanham, MD 20706
Phone: (301)731-4748
Toll-Free: 888-468-6499
Fax: (301)731-4621
E-mail: webmaster@hotmix.org
Home Page: http://www.hotmix.org

• 13997 • **Brochure Award**
To encourage more hot mix asphalt producing firms to publish brochures describing their firm and their products, to recognize those firms already having produced a company brochure, and to select the best brochure(s) published during a calendar year. Any hot mix asphalt producing firm providing both manufacturing and laydown services, manufacturing only, or laydown only service may enter by October 10. The competition is not open to firms producing equipment, materials, or services used in the production or placement of hot mix asphalt. Brochures are judged on overall appearance, attractiveness, and purpose. Brochures selected as the most outstanding for the year are displayed at the NAPA Annual Convention and recognition plaques are presented during the convention. Established in 1984.

• 13998 • **Ecological Award**
To publicly recognize those hot mix asphalt firms displaying a strong sense of public responsibility through awareness of environmental control and facility appearance, resulting in their becoming a better industrial community member and projecting a more positive image of their operation and their industry. Awards are given in two categories: HMA facilities less than five years old and HMA facilities operating at one location for

more than five years. Entries must be submitted by October 10. Established in 1971. Sponsored by *Roads & Bridges* magazine.

• 13999 • Hot Mix Asphalt Hall of Fame

To recognize and honor those individuals who have made significant and lasting national contributions to the hot mix asphalt industry leading to innovations in the production and placement of hot mix asphalt, in the usage of hot mix asphalt as a paving material, and in the general advancement and recognition of the industry. Individuals who have been active in the hot mix industry affiliated with hot mix asphalt producing and placement firms, with manufacturers and suppliers of equipment and services to the industry, public works agencies, educational/trade institutions, consultants, and governmental agencies are considered. To be eligible, however, an individual must no longer be active in one of the above capacities. Nominations may be made at any time by any individual. Individuals inducted into the Hall of Fame receive an inscribed medallion, displayed in a special Hot Mix Hall of Fame display area in the headquarters office of the National Asphalt Pavement Association.

• 14000 • Quality in Construction Award

To recognize outstanding quality in hot mix asphalt paving throughout the United States. Recipients are owners or contractors of all projects that exhibit exemplary quality. All types of pavement are eligible, including roads, highways, airports, and commercial. Highway pavements above 50,000 tons that win the Quality in Construction Award in the current year may be eligible for the Sheldon G. Hayes Award in the following year. The nomination should be submitted by the company that built the pavement by October 14. Formerly: Pavement Awards.

• 14001 •
National Association for Cave Diving
Debra A. Green, Oper.Mgr.
PO Box 14492
Gainesville, FL 32604
Phone: (352)331-7666
Toll-Free: 888-565-6223
E-mail: manager@safecaving.org
Home Page: http://www.safecavediving.com

• 14002 • Steve Gerrad Outstanding Service Award

To recognize levels of cave diving executed safely. Awarded upon approval. Established in 1990.

• 14003 • Bill McFaden Cartography Award

To recognize expertise in underwater cave cartography. Awarded annually with a plaque. Established in 1990.

• 14004 •
National Association for Equal Opportunity in Higher Education
Lezli Baskerville, Pres.
8701 Georgia Ave., Ste. 200
Silver Spring, MD 20910
Phone: (301)650-2440
Fax: (301)495-3306
Home Page: http://www.nafeo.org

• 14005 • Distinguished Alumni Citation of the Year

To recognize distinguished alumni. Three hundred certificates are awarded annually at the National Conference on Blacks in Higher Education. Eligible candidates must be alumni of member institutions.

• 14006 • Leadership Award

To recognize outstanding leadership. One to three designer awards are presented annually at the National Conference on Blacks in Higher Education. Eligible candidates must be nominated by members and will be selected by Conference Committee.

• 14007 • Research Achievement Award

To recognize outstanding achievement in research. One plaque is awarded annually at the National Conference on Blacks in Higher Education. Eligible candidates must be nominated by the president of member institutions.

• 14008 •
National Association for Ethnic Studies
Larry Estrada, Pres.
Western Washington University
516 High St., MS 9113
4701 W Thunderbird Rd., MC3051
Bellingham, WA 98225
Phone: (360)650-2349
Fax: (360)650-2690
E-mail: naes@wwu.edu
Home Page: http://www.ethnicstudies.org

• 14009 • Charles C. Irby Distinguished Service Award

To recognize members who have distinguished themselves in the field of ethnic studies and has contributed to the goals of the organization. These individuals should have shown exemplary leadership skills in NAES and be committed to organizational goals. Awarded annually. Established in 1988 to commemorate the work of Charles C. Irby, one of the founding members of the NAES, president, and editor of all publications.

• 14010 • Ernest M. Pon Memorial Award

To recognize Asian/Asian American leaders and community organizations for outstanding service. Non-profit Asian/Asian American community/national organizations and outstanding Asian/Asian American community leaders are eligible. A plaque and a small stipend are awarded annually. Established in 1986 by Barbara L. Hiura to honor the work of Ernest M. Pon.

• 14011 •
National Association for Gifted Children
Peter D. Rosenstein, Exec.Dir.
1707 L St. NW, No.550
Washington, DC 20036
Phone: (202)785-4268
Fax: (202)785-4248
E-mail: nagc@nagc.org
Home Page: http://www.nagc.org

Formerly: (1976) Association of Professors of Higher Education.

• 14012 • Dissertation of the Year Award

To recognize the most significant doctoral dissertation completed within the last 12 months ending May 31, prepared in any discipline that is concerned with the study of higher education. Dissertations may focus on the social context, administration, teaching and learning, instructional studies, or planning of higher education. Nominations are accepted from faculty members. A certificate, travel expenses to attend the Annual Conference, and approximately $500 worth of books donated by Jossey-Bass Publishers are awarded annually. Established in 1976. Formerly: (1984) Distinguished Dissertation Award in Higher Education.

• 14013 •
National Association for Girls and Women in Sport
Athena Yiamouyiannis, Exec.Dir.
1900 Association Dr.
Reston, VA 20191-1598
Phone: (703)476-3400
Toll-Free: 800-213-7193
Fax: (703)476-9527
E-mail: nagws@aahperd.org

• 14014 • Wade Trophy

To recognize the top player in women's collegiate basketball. Candidates must be members of the NCAA Division I Kodak/WBCA All-America Team, have proven skill in basketball as evidenced by game and season statistics, demonstrate leadership and character, and be a positive role models for women in sport. The trophy is permanently displayed in the Basketball Hall of Fame in Springfield, MA. Established in 1978 to honor Lily Margaret Wade, a member of the National Basketball Hall of Fame who dedicated her life to women's athletics, education, and basketball. Presented annually. Cosponsored by the Women's Basketball Coaches Association.

• 14015 •
National Association for Humane and Environmental Education
Bill DeRosa, Exec.Dir.
67 Norwich Essex Tpke.
PO Box 362
East Haddam, CT 06423-1736
Phone: (860)434-8666
Fax: (860)434-9579
E-mail: nahee@nahee.org
Home Page: http://www.nahee.org

Formerly: (1989) National Association for the Advancement of Humane Education.

• 14016 • National Kind Teacher Award

Recognizes a K-6 classroom teacher who effectively and innovatively incorporates lessons about kindness to people, animals, and the environment into his/her curriculum. Prize includes an award plaque, a feature story in *KIND Teacher,* and a package of humane education resources. Established in 1981 in honor of Jacques Sichel, former board member of The Humane Society of the United States, who was an active proponent of humane education.

• 14017 •

National Association for Industry-Education Cooperation
Dr. Donald M. Clark, Pres./CEO
235 Hendricks Blvd.
Buffalo, NY 14226-3304
Phone: (716)834-7047
Fax: (716)834-7047
E-mail: naiec@pcom.net
Home Page: http://www2.pcom.net/naiec

Formerly:.

• 14018 • Educational Sponsorship Award

To recognize an industrial firm, trade, or professional association for creative and effective cooperation with public/postsecondary schools in improving any subject area in academic and vocational education. Projects may include sponsored materials, training programs, work/education and economic development, or other exemplary industry-education collaborative efforts directed at school improvement. The entry deadline is December 31. A plaque and a citation are awarded each year at the Annual NAIEC Showcase Conference. Established in 1964.

• 14019 • Utilization Award

To recognize an educator for his/her skill and success in using industry-sponsored resources for education. Criteria include ingenuity, selectivity, appropriateness, and effectiveness in furthering school improvement through industry-education joint efforts. The entry deadline is December 31. A plaque and a citation are awarded yearly at the Annual NAIEC Showcase Conference. Established in 1964.

• 14020 •

National Association for Interpretation
Tim Merriman, Exec.Dir.
PO Box 2246
Fort Collins, CO 80522
Phone: (970)484-8283
Toll-Free: 888-900-8283
Fax: (970)484-8179
E-mail: naiexec@aol.com
Home Page: http://www.interpnet.com

Formed by merger of: Association of Interpretive Naturalists; Western Interpretation Association.

• 14021 • Fellow Award

To recognize a member who has exhibited excellence in the field in any of a number of categories. A plaque is awarded to one member annually. Established in 1988.

• 14022 • Honorary Member

To recognize non-members who have rendered nationally-recognized service or given prestige to the profession. A plaque is awarded when merited. Established in 1988.

• 14023 • Meritorious Service Award

To recognize members who have performed exceptional services for the Association. A plaque is awarded. Established in 1988.

• 14024 • Special Award

To recognize exceptional work in the field of interpretation or service to the profession that may not fit in one of the standard award categories. Members or non-members are eligible. A plaque is awarded. Established in 1988.

• 14025 •

National Association for Pupil Transportation
Michael Martin, Exec.Dir.
1840 Western Ave.
Albany, NY 12203-0647
Phone: (518)452-3611
Phone: (518)452-3611
Toll-Free: 800-989-NAPT
Fax: (518)218-0867
E-mail: info@napt.org
Home Page: http://www.napt.org

• 14026 • NAPT Distinguished Service Award

To recognize individuals who have achieved national recognition for their dedication to pupil transportation. Candidates must have a minimum of five years experience in pupil transportation, must be in an administrative, managerial, or supervisory capacity, and be actively engaged in the daily operation of pupil transportation. A plaque is awarded annually at the annual conference. Established in 1981. Formerly: (1985) Transportation Administrator of the Year.

• 14027 •

National Association for Recreational Equality
Dr. Reeve Brenner, Founder/Pres.
785 E Rockville Pike, PMB 504
Rockville, MD 20852
Phone: (301)309-0260
Toll-Free: 800-933-0140
Fax: (301)309-0263
E-mail: info@bankshot.com
Home Page: http://www.bankshot.com

• 14028 • Arial Anaker Award

Recognition is given annually for good sportsmanship.

• 14029 •

National Association for Research in Science Teaching
Marilyn Estes, Admin.Asst.
University of Missouri-Columbia
303 Townsend Hall
Columbia, MO 65211-2400
Phone: (573)884-1401
Fax: (573)884-2917
E-mail: narst@missouri.edu
Home Page: http://www2.educ.sfu.ca/narstsite

• 14030 • Distinguished Contributions to Science Education Through Research Award

To recognize and reward individuals who have made significant contributions to science education through research. Contributions may be of several types including, but not limited to: empirical, philosophical or historical research, evaluative studies, policy-related research, and studies reflecting new techniques to be applied in research. The recipient should have contributed over a period of at least 20 years since receiving his/her doctorate and should be at the pinnacle of his/her career. A plaque is awarded when a deserving person is nominated.

• 14031 • Early Career Research Award

To recognize superior contributions of research and scholarship in science education during the initial five years of a career. A plaque is awarded at the Annual Meeting.

• 14032 • Journal of Research in Science Teaching Award JRST Award

To recognize the best research article published in *The Journal of Research in Science Teaching (JRST)* in the previous year and to honor the author of the article. Every article published in *JRST* is automatically considered for the award. An engraved wall plaque and certificate are awarded each year at the Association's annual meeting.

• 14033 • Outstanding Dissertation Award

To recognize superior research in a doctoral dissertation in science education. A plaque is awarded at the Annual Meeting.

• 14034 • Outstanding Masters Thesis Award

To recognize superior research in a Master's Thesis judged to have the greatest significance in the field of science education.

• 14035 • Outstanding Paper Award

To recognize that paper or research report presented at the annual meeting judged to have the greatest significance and potential in the field of science education. Criteria include conceptual/theoretical aspects, research approach, presentation and interpretation of research, conclusions, craftsmanship/communication, significance of the study, and creativity. An engraved wall plaque and certificate are awarded each year at the Association's annual meeting.

• 14036 •
National Association for Search and Rescue
Randy Servis, Pres./Chm.
PO Box 232020
Centreville, VA 20120-2020
Phone: (703)222-6277
Toll-Free: 877-893-0702
Fax: (703)222-6277
E-mail: info@nasar.org
Home Page: http://www.nasar.org

• 14037 • **Lois Clark McCoy Service Award**
To recognize the individual or unit who made the most significant contribution to the Association. A pewter bowl and a plaque are awarded when merited. Established in 1985. Formerly: (2002) NASAR Service Award.

• 14038 • **Hal Foss Award**
To recognize the individual or organization that has made the most significant contribution to search and rescue on a national basis. Consideration is given, but not limited, to the following factors: exceptional performance in the organization; establishment and maintenance of professional standards of SAR performance; individual daring, skill, and perseverance while performing an especially outstanding SAR task; continuing SAR training programs and mission preparedness; and length of service to and relation with the local community. A plaque is presented annually at the National Conference. Established in 1974 in honor of Hal Foss, Washington State SAR coordinator and principal founder of NASAR.

• 14039 • **State/Canadian Province SAR Award**
To recognize the individual or organization that has made the most significant contribution to search and rescue within a NASAR member state or province. Consideration is given, but not limited, to the following factors: exceptional performance in the organization; establishment and maintenance of professional standards of SAR performance; individual daring, skill, and perseverance while performing an especially outstanding SAR task; continuing SAR training programs and mission preparedness; and length of service to and relations with the local community. A plaque is presented when merited at the National Conference. Established in 1974.

• 14040 • **Valor Award**
To recognize a person who, by being involved in a life-saving SAR effort, exemplifies the selfless, perhaps risky, commitment embodied in the motto of NASAR: "That Others May Live". It is not presented posthumously. Three criteria are considered: 1. The nominee's actions were beyond reasonably expected search and rescue (SAR) behavior; 2. the nominee alleviated a situation in which a "victim" was in substantial peril, with the high potential for life-threatening injury or death; and 3. the nominee placed himself or herself in a situation potentially resulting in serious injury or death, though not exceeding the bounds of good judgment. A plaque is presented periodically at the Annual Conference. Established in 1977 by the San Diego Mountain Rescue Team in memory of two members killed in unrelated accidents. Formerly: (1990) Zimmerman-Rand Valor Award.

• 14041 • **Bob Wright Award**
To recognize significant contributions by a national leader of young people to the field of search and rescue education. The award includes an educational stipend or scholarship for the recipient of his/her choice. Awarded annually when merited. Established in 1993 in memory of Bob Wright, a NASAR life member and volunteer youth leader.

• 14042 •
National Association for Sport and Physical Education
Charlene Burgeson, Exec.Dir.
1900 Association Dr.
Reston, VA 20191-1598
Phone: (703)476-3400
Toll-Free: 800-213-7193
Fax: (703)476-8316
E-mail: naspe@aahperd.org
Home Page: http://www.naspeinfo.org

• 14043 • **Teacher of the Year Awards**
To recognize outstanding teaching performance and the ability to motivate youth to participate in a lifetime of physical activity at the elementary, middle, and high school levels. To be eligible, the candidate must be a current member of NASPE, have a degree in and certification as a full-time physical education teacher, have a minimum of five years teaching experience, and devote at least 60 percent of total teaching responsibility to physical education classes. Winners conduct a quality physical education program as reflected in NASPE standards; utilize various innovative teaching methodologies; serve as positive role models; participate in professional development opportunities; and serve the profession through leadership, presentations, and/or writing. Self application and nomination by colleagues begins at the State AHPERD level. State winners at each grade level move on to District competition. District winners compete for national recognition at the AAHPERD National Convention each spring. Formerly: (2004) Elementary, Middle, and Secondary School Physical Education Teacher of the Year.

• 14044 •
National Association for Stock Car Auto Racing
Mike Helton, Pres.
1801 W Intl. Speedway Blvd.
PO Box 2875
Daytona Beach, FL 32120
Phone: (386)253-0611
Fax: (386)258-7646
E-mail: nascar@turner.com
Home Page: http://www.nascar.com

• 14045 • **NASCAR Championships**
For recognition of stock car race drivers based on points earned in various categories and races. Cars are not to be specially-made but are stock production models. Three categories of races are held: Nextel Cup, Busch Series, and Craftsman Truck Series. Prizes total more than $30 million annually. The first recognized stock car race in the United States is considered to have been the match contest between automobile manufacturers Henry Ford and Alexander Winston in Detroit, held in either 1899 or 1900, which Henry Ford won.

• 14046 •
National Association for the Advancement of Colored People
Dennis C. Hayes, Pres./CEO
4805 Mt. Hope Dr.
Baltimore, MD 21215
Phone: (410)521-4939
Toll-Free: 877-NAA-CP98
Fax: (410)358-3818
Home Page: http://www.naacp.org

• 14047 • **Kelly M. Alexander, Sr., NAACP State Conference President's Award**
To recognize a State Conference president for outstanding achievement in the following areas: (1) programs; (2) membership; (3) fund raising; (4) growth of branches; (5) leadership; and (6) youth and college leadership development. Nominations may be submitted by December 31. A monetary award of $1,000 and a gold medal are awarded annually. Established in 1987 to honor Kelly M. Alexander, Sr., who served as a State Conference President for 27 years and chairman of the NAACP Board of Directors.

• 14048 • **William Edward Burghardt Du Bois Medal**
To recognize individuals who are not citizens of the United States for exceptional contributions to the protection of human rights and furtherance of international understanding, fraternity and fundamental freedoms. Men or women whose lives exemplify the tradition of service to mankind; who perform extraordinary acts of moral courage; and whose work promotes civil rights and democratic principles are eligible. Nominations may be submitted by May 15. A medal is awarded annually. Established in 1985.

• 14049 • **Image Awards**
To recognize outstanding achievements and performances of people of color in the arts as well as those individual or groups who promote social justice. Awards are presented in 36 categories in movies, television, music, and literature. Additionally, honorary awards include the Chairman's Award, President's Award, and the Image Awards Hall of Fame. The annual award show is broadcast nationally each February by the NAACP Hollywood Bureau. Established in 1979.

• 14050 • **Spingarn Medal**
To recognize the highest achievement of an American Negro. The purpose of the medal is twofold: to call the attention of the American people to the existence of distinguished merit and achievement among American Negroes;

Awards are arranged in alphabetical order below their administering organizations

and to serve as a reward for such achievement, and as a stimulus to the ambition of colored youth. Men and women of African descent and American citizenship who shall have made the highest achievement during the preceding year or years in any honorable field of human endeavor are eligible. Nominations may be submitted by January 1. A gold medal is presented at the annual convention of the National Association for the Advancement of Colored People, and the presentation speech is delivered by a distinguished citizen. Established in 1914 by the late J.E. Spingarn, then Chairman of the Board of Directors of the National Association for the Advancement of Colored People. The award honors Joel E. Spingarn, President of the NAACP, 1930-1939.

• 14051 •
National Association for the Advancement of Psychoanalysis
Margery Quackenbush, Exec.Dir.
80 8th Ave., Ste. 1501
New York, NY 10011-1501
Phone: (212)741-0515
Phone: (212)741-0516
Fax: (212)366-4347
E-mail: info@naap.org
Home Page: http://www.naap.org

• 14052 • **Gradiva Awards**
To recognize the best published, produced, or publicly exhibited works that advance psychoanalysis. Awards are presented in the following categories: Article, Book, Motion Picture, Television Program, Stage Production (including revival), Poem, Art work (any media), Children's Literature, New Media, Song or Musical Composition, and Student Article. Each winner receives a brass plaque etched with the image of Gradiva that is based on a Pompeiian relief similar to one that hung in Sigmund Freud's office. Awarded annually. Established in 1994.

• 14053 •
National Association for the Specialty Food Trade
John Roberts, Pres.
120 Wall St., 27th Fl.
New York, NY 10005
Phone: (212)482-6440
Fax: (212)482-6459
E-mail: custserv@fancyfoodshows.com
Home Page: http://www.specialtyfood.com

• 14054 • **Edward T. Sajous Achievement Award**
To honor a member, past or present, for outstanding service. A silver bowl or plaque is awarded annually. Established in 1974.

• 14055 • **Ronald C. Schmitz Silver Spoon Award**
To honor an individual or corporation that has promoted the interest of fine foods. A silver spoon in lucite is awarded annually. Established in 1962.

• 14056 •
National Association for Vocational Education Special Needs Personnel
% Teresa Bohannon
Tulsa Technology Ctr.
3420 S Memorial Dr.
Tulsa, OK 74147-7200
E-mail: tbohanno@tulsatech.org

• 14057 • **Direct Vocational Special Needs Support Person of the Year**
To recognize administrative or non-classroom persons who have made a major contribution to the development and/or growth of vocational/technical special needs education. Nominees could include: local/area administrators of vocational/technical education special needs programs; state administrators of vocational education special needs programs; vocational/technical education special needs teacher educators. A plaque is awarded annually.

• 14058 • **Indirect Provider of Major Support Services and Contributions to the Field of Vocational Special Needs Education Award**
To recognize friends of vocational/technical special needs education who have made a major contribution to the development and/or growth of vocational/technical special needs education. Nominees might include private employers, advisory committee members, state or national legislators, individuals who has been usually supportive of vocational/technical special needs education, or local school district administrators. A plaque is awarded annually.

• 14059 • **Outstanding Vocational Special Needs Teacher of the Year**
To recognize an outstanding classroom teacher or job placement coordinator working with identified special needs students in vocational/technical education programming. University professors and administrative/guidance personnel are not eligible. A plaque and $500 gift certificate is awarded annually.

• 14060 •
National Association of Academic Advisors for Athletics
Sandy Meyer, Pres.
PO Box A-7
College Station, TX 77844-9007
Phone: (979)862-4310
Fax: (979)862-2461
E-mail: n4a@athletics.tamu.edu
Home Page: http://www.nfoura.org

• 14061 • **Award for Distinguished Service to N4A**
Recognizes an individual who has maintained continuous membership for five years.

• 14062 • **N4A National Academic Achievement Award**
To recognize student-athletes who have overcome physical, intellectual, and/or emotional deficiencies and gone on to noteworthy academic and athletic achievements. Individuals must have completed 36 semesters of 48 quarter hours, have a 2.00 GPA and be a letter winner in their sport. Plaques are awarded annually to the top ten student-athletes nationally and certificates of recognition are awarded to national and regional honorees at the national convention. Established in 1989.

• 14063 •
National Association of Academies of Science
Dr. Kathleen Donovan, Pres.
Department of Psychology
University of Central Oklahoma
100 N University Dr.
Edmond, OK 73034
Phone: (405)974-5422
Fax: (405)755-8799
E-mail: kdonovan@ucok.edu
Home Page: http://astro.physics.sc.edu/NAAS

• 14064 • **Distinguished Service Award**
To honor individuals for faithful service to the Association, the American Association for the Advancement of Science, and to their state Academies of Science. One to three certificates are awarded annually. Established in 1962.

• 14065 •
National Association of African-American Sportswriters and Broadcasters
Clyde Davis, Pres.
308 Deer Park Ave.
Dix Hills, NY 11746
Phone: (631)462-3933
E-mail: clydesports@aol.com

• 14066 • **Niles Davis Award**
To support African-American graduates who attend college majoring in either sports medicine, law, journalism, or management. Student must maintain a B-plus average. Awarded annually with a four-year scholarship. Established in 1995.

• 14067 •
National Association of Animal Breeders
Dr. Gordon A. Doak, Pres.
PO Box 1033
Columbia, MO 65205
Phone: (573)445-4406
Fax: (573)446-2279
E-mail: naab-css@naab-css.org
Home Page: http://www.naab-css.org

• 14068 • **Distinguished Service Award**
To recognize individuals who have made significant long-term contributions to the furtherance of the artificial insemination industry. Nominees must be living and currently active in their field of work at the time of nomination. A plaque is presented at the annual convention. Established in 1979.

• 14069 • Member Director Award
To recognize an individual who has made significant long-term contributions to the artificial insemination industry. The award is based on the influence the individual has had on the artificial insemination industry, not necessarily just service to the Association. Nominees must have been active members within the past two years of a Board of Directors (cooperative or private) of an NAAB regular member. A plaque is presented at the annual convention. Established in 1985.

• 14070 • NAAB Research Award
To recognize individuals who have made valuable long-term contributions to the science of artificial insemination, physiology, or animal breeding in the United States. The award is based on, but not limited to, original published research and teaching. The cumulative contribution of the nominee's research to the industry is a primary consideration. Nominees must be living and currently active in their field of work at the time of nomination. A monetary prize of $1,000 and a plaque are awarded annually. Established in 1970.

• 14071 •
National Association of Anorexia Nervosa and Associated Disorders
Vivian Hanson Meehan RN, Pres./Founder
Box 7
Highland Park, IL 60035
Phone: (847)831-3438
Fax: (847)433-4632
E-mail: anad20@aol.com
Home Page: http://www.anad.org

• 14072 • ANAD Award
For recognition of exceptional achievement in and contributions to the field of eating disorders, especially anorexia nervosa and bulimia. Contributions may be for research, leadership, and humanitarian considerations. A plaque is presented when merited. Established in 1976.

• 14073 • ANAD Service Awards
To recognize outstanding volunteer contributions to the Association.

• 14074 • Women Helping Women Awards
To recognize contributions in the eating disorders field that especially benefit women. Established in 1993.

• 14075 •
National Association of Attorneys General
Lynne Ross, Exec.Dir.
750 First St. NE, Ste. 1100
Washington, DC 20002
Phone: (202)326-6000
Fax: (202)408-7014
E-mail: support@naag.org
Home Page: http://www.naag.org

• 14076 • Kelley - Wyman Award
To annually recognize the Attorney General who has done the most to advance the objectives of the Association to help make the United States of America a better place to live for all. Established in 1956 by the Honorable Louis C. Wyman, former Attorney General of New Hampshire, in memory of his father, Louis E. Wyman; the award was renamed in recognition of Frank J. Kelley, former Attorney General of Michigan who served for 37 years. Formerly: (2000) Wyman Memorial Award.

• 14077 • C. Raymond Marvin Award
To recognize those individuals within the offices of the attorneys general who have demonstrated outstanding leadership, expertise, and achievement in advancing the objectives of the association. Selection is by nomination. A plaque is awarded annually at the summer meeting. Established in 1987 by C. Raymond Marvin, former Executive Director of the Association.

• 14078 •
National Association of Bar Executives
Jill Werner, Staff Dir.
ABA Div. for Bar Services
321 N Clark, Ste. 2000
Chicago, IL 60610
Phone: (312)988-5360
Fax: (312)988-5492
E-mail: nabc@abanet.org
Home Page: http://www.nabenet.org

• 14079 • Bolton Award for Professional Excellence
To recognize a NABE member who upholds the highest standards of professionalism and character. Recipient must also have demonstrated service to NABE and the profession. A plaque is awarded at the Annual Meeting. Established in 1978 in honor of Frederick Hershey Bolton.

• 14080 •
National Association of Basketball Coaches
James A. Haney, Exec.Dir.
1111 Main St., Ste. 1000
Kansas City, MO 64105-2136
Phone: (816)878-6222
Fax: (816)878-6223
E-mail: jim@nabc.com
Home Page: http://nabc.collegesports.com

• 14081 • Coach of the Year
To recognize the outstanding coaches in Divisions I, II, and III, NAIA and Junior College. Awarded annually at the NABC banquet in March. Formerly: Kodak Coach of the Year.

• 14082 • Defensive Player of the Year
To recognize the defensive player of the year. Awarded annually at the NABC banquet in March. Established in 1987. Formerly: (1996) Hank IBA Defensive Player of the Year.

• 14083 • Division I Player of the Year
To honor the nation's outstanding collegiate basketball player in Division I. A trophy is presented annually at the convention. Established in 1975. Formerly: (1996) Eastman Award.

• 14084 • Division II Player of the Year
To honor the nation's outstanding collegiate basketball player in Division II. Awarded annually in March at the NCAA Division II Championship. Established in 1983. Formerly: (1991) Spalding Player of the Year.

• 14085 • Division III Player of the Year
To honor the nation's outstanding collegiate basketball player in Division III. Awarded annually in March at the Division III Championship. Established in 1983.

• 14086 • Golden Anniversary Award
To honor basketball coaches. Awarded annually at the NABC banquet in March. Formerly: (1996) Balfour Silver and Golden Anniversary Award.

• 14087 • Metropolitan Award
Awarded annually at the NABC banquet in March. Established in 1941.

• 14088 • Cliff Wells Appreciation Award
To honor an individual who has had great impact on and assisted the NABC to move forward with its objectives and goals. Established in 1974.

• 14089 •
National Association of Biology Teachers
Wayne Carley, Exec.Dir.
12030 Sunrise Valley Dr., Ste. 110
Reston, VA 20191
Phone: (703)264-9696
Toll-Free: 800-406-0775
Fax: (703)264-7778
E-mail: office@nabt.org
Home Page: http://www.nabt.org

• 14090 • Award for Excellence in Encouraging Equity
In recognition of efforts to encourage, promote, and strive for equity in the educational community. All NABT members are eligible for the award and may nominate themselves or others. Nominations must be submitted by March 15, and completed application packets must be submitted by May 1. A plaque and an honorarium will be presented at the Section Breakfast Meeting at the NABT National Convention. Awarded annually.

• 14091 • Biotechnology Teaching Award
To recognize a secondary school teacher or undergraduate college biology instructor who has successfully demonstrated outstanding and creative teaching of biotechnology in the classroom. The award may be given for either a short-term series of activities or a long integration of biotechnology into the curriculum. The lessons must include active laboratory work and encompass major principles as well as processes of

biotechnology. Topics may include any aspect of basic DNA, protein biotechnology or immunology, or applied biotechnology in areas such as medical, forensic, plant, and environmental biotechnology. Criteria for selection include creativity, scientific accuracy and currency, quality of laboratory practice and safety, ease of replication, benefit to students, and potential significance beyond the classroom. A monetary award of $500, a plaque, and a complimentary one-year membership in NABT are awarded at the national convention. Established in 1991.

• 14092 • Distinguished Service Award

To honor a nationally recognized scientist who has made significant contributions to biology education through research, writing, and teaching. Nominations must be submitted by May 1. A framed certificate and specially prepared citation are awarded at the annual banquet. Established in 1988.

• 14093 • Four-Year College Biology Teaching Award

To recognize creativity and innovation in undergraduate college biology teaching. These innovations may include, but are not limited to, curriculum design, teaching strategies, and laboratory utilization, and must have been implemented in the classroom and demonstrated to be effective. Entrants must be members of NABT. Nomination deadline is March 15. A monetary award of $1,000, a plaque, and a complimentary one-year membership in NABT are awarded at the national convention. Established in 1991. Sponsored by Benjamin/Cummings Publishing Company.

• 14094 • Melody Hall Memorial Award

To recognize an outstanding elementary/middle school life science or biology educator (grades 5-8) from the metropolitan area surrounding the site of that year's NABT Annual Convention. A certificate, a one-year complimentary NABT membership, and complimentary registration at the NABT Convention is awarded annually. NABT members may nominate themselves or others, and nominations must be submitted by May 1. Established in memory of Melody Hall, who served NABT for many years as OBTA Director of Georgia and Chair of the Elementary/Middle School Section. Sponsored by the Melody Hall Memorial Fund.

• 14095 • Honorary Membership

To recognize individuals who have achieved distinction in teaching, research, or service in the biological sciences. Nominations are based on the following criteria: the candidate should be nationally or regionally known in the field of biology education; ongoing contributions for ten years or more; contributions that have had an impact for the last ten years; contributions that have had an impact on young people, either directly or indirectly; and the candidate should be a model for others in biology education. Winners receive lifetime membership in the association, awarded at the annual banquet when merited. Nominations must be submitted by May 1. Established in 1964.

• 14096 • Middle School Teaching Award

To recognize a middle school/junior high teacher who incorporates an innovative life science activity or life science unit in his/her science teaching. All middle school/junior high (grades 5-8) science teachers who include life science lessons/units in their current classroom teaching are eligible to receive this award. Teachers are judged on the following criteria: teaching ability, level of participation in school and community affairs, inventiveness, initiative, and student-teacher relationships. Teachers must be nominated by a supervisor or colleague by March 15, and nominees must submit a completed application package by May 1. A Power Macintosh computer, a plaque, and a complimentary one-year NABT membership are awarded annually at the NABT National Convention. Sponsored by Apple Computer, Inc.

• 14097 • Outstanding Biology Teacher Award

To recognize outstanding performance in the classroom and to bring this type of performance to the attention of the general public. Teachers of biology/life science for grades seven through 12 in each state of the United States, Washington DC, Canada, Puerto Rico, and overseas territories are eligible to be nominated by February 1. Membership in NABT is not required, but nominees must have at least three years of public, private, or parochial school teaching experience. Certificates and a pair of binoculars are awarded annually at a special event during the national convention. Established in 1960.

• 14098 • Outstanding New Biology Teacher Achievement Award

To recognize outstanding teaching by a biology teacher (grades 7-12) within the first three years of his or her career to encourage beginning teachers to develop original and outstanding programs and techniques and to make a contribution to the profession. A monetary award of $500 to attend the NABT convention and for purchase of biological supplies and equipment are awarded annually.

• 14099 • Two-Year College Biology Teaching Award

To recognize excellence in two-year college biology teaching. The primary criterion for the award is skill in teaching, although serious consideration is given to scholarship, usually demonstrated through publications or innovative techniques relating to teaching strategies, curriculum design, or laboratory utilization. Nominees must be current members of NABT. Nomination deadline is March 15. A monetary award of $1,000, a plaque, and a complimentary one-year membership in NABT are awarded at the national convention. Established in 1990. Sponsored by McGraw-Hill Companies Inc.

• 14100 •
National Association of Black Journalists
Tangie Newborn, Exec.Dir.
8701A Adelphi Rd.
Adelphi, MD 20783-1716
Phone: (301)445-7100
Fax: (301)445-7101
E-mail: nabj@nabj.org
Home Page: http://www.nabj.org

• 14101 • Salute to Excellence Awards

To recognize outstanding news stories and photographs that highlight African American people or programs and issues of special concern to the Black community. Entries are judged for impact, sensitivity, quality, and significance. An entry can be a single news story, photo, or TV or radio program, or a series of stories, photos, or TV or radio programs on a related subject. Newspaper entries for each category are grouped and judged according to circulation; television entries for each category are judged based on market ranking. The following special awards are also presented: Journalist of the Year Award, Lifetime Achievement Award, Emerging Journalist of the Year Award, Ida B. Wells Award, and the Community Service Award Established in 1975.

• 14102 • Ida B. Wells Award

For recognition of exemplary leadership in providing minorities with employment opportunities in journalism. Applications or nominations showing the leadership and achievements reflected in the purpose of the award are accepted from anyone. An original bust of Ida B. Wells with inscription of the winner's exemplary achievements is awarded, as well as up to $10,000 in journalism scholarships for minorities. Deadline is May 1. Awarded annually at the convention of one of the sponsoring organizations: National Association of Black Journalists, National Conference of Editorial Writers, and National Broadcast Editorial Association. Established in 1983 by Michael Richardson and Samuel Adams. The award honors Ida B. Wells (1866-1932), pioneer black editor and anti-lynching leader. She was co-owner of a newspaper, a candidate for Congress, and a founding member of the NAACP.

• 14103 •
National Association of Boards of Pharmacy
Carmen A. Catizone MS, Exec.Dir./Sec.
1600 Feehanville Dr.
Mount Prospect, IL 60056
Phone: (847)391-4406
Fax: (847)391-4502
E-mail: custserv@nabp.net
Home Page: http://www.nabp.net

• 14104 • Lester E. Hosto Distinguished Service Award

To recognize individuals for outstanding contributions to the protection of the public health that have greatly furthered the goals and objectives of the Association. A mounted plaque is presented annually. Established in 1976.

• 14105 •
National Association of Broadcasters
Edward O. Fritts, CEO/Pres.
1771 N St. NW
Washington, DC 20036
Phone: (202)429-5300
Fax: (202)429-4199
E-mail: nab@nab.org
Home Page: http://www.nab.org

• 14106 • **Hugh Malcolm Beville, Jr. Award**
To honor the most significant contribution of an individual to the advancement of U.S. broadcast audience research. Contributions to all phases of the research process are considered, including design, execution, analysis, and reporting, as well as advancing knowledge and understanding of the broadcast audience research process as a whole. A plaque is awarded at the annual convention. Established in 1989 in memory of "Mal" Beville, often termed "the dean of broadcast research." Co-sponsored by the Broadcast Education Association.

• 14107 • **Belva B. Brissett Award**
To recognize a broadcaster who has made a significant contribution to the advocacy and advancement of over-the-air broadcasting through the federal regulatory process. A plaque is awarded when appropriate at the Broadcasters' Law and Regulation Conference held in conjunction with the association's spring convention. Established in 1992 in memory of Belva B. Brissett, NAB senior vice president, regulatory affairs.

• 14108 • **Broadcasting Hall of Fame**
To recognize and honor those personalities or programs that have made a significant and lasting contribution to the broadcasting industry, with separate categories for radio and television. Plaques, which are displayed at NAB headquarters, are awarded annually at the NAB spring convention. Established in 1976. Formerly: (1988) Radio Broadcasting Hall of Fame.

• 14109 • **Grover C. Cobb Memorial Award**
To recognize a broadcaster or public servant who demonstrates unusual dedication to improving broadcasting's relationship with the federal government. A plaque and a grant are awarded when appropriate at the Association's spring convention. Established in 1976 in memory of Grover C. Cobb, NAB senior vice president, government relations.

• 14110 • **Crystal Radio Awards**
To recognize 10 radio stations for year-round commitment to excellence in local community service. Trophies are awarded annually at the Association's spring convention. Established in 1987.

• 14111 • **Distinguished Service Award**
To recognize a broadcaster who has made a contribution to the American system of broadcasting, by virtue of individual achievement or continuing service. A crystal sculpture is awarded annually at the Association's spring convention. Established in 1953.

• 14112 • **Engineering Achievement Awards**
To recognize individuals who have made a single contribution or multiple contributions that have significantly advanced the state of broadcast engineering. These contributions may include inventions, the development of new techniques, the dissemination of technical knowledge and literature, or leadership in broadcast engineering affairs. Candidates must be or have been an owner, officer, or employee of any company, subsidiary, or division whose primary business is broadcasting, or is directly in support of broadcasting, including employees of the federal government directly engaged in broadcast engineering work. Established in 1959. Beginning in 1991, separate awards are made for Engineering Achievement in Radio and Engineering Achievement in Television. Formerly: (1991) Engineering Award.

• 14113 • **International Broadcasting Excellence Award**
To recognize broadcasters outside the United States who have demonstrated exceptional leadership in advancing the broadcast industry and the services they provide to their community and audiences. A crystal trophy is presented at the invitation only International Leadership Dinner held at NAB's annual spring industry convention. Two awards are presented annually. Established in 1995.

• 14114 • **Wally Jorgenson Award**
To recognize outstanding leadership within TARPAC (Television and Radio Political Action Committee). Presented by the trustee or congressional Club member who has made the most significant contribution to the success of NAB's political action committee. A marble trophy is awarded during NAB conventions in Las Vegas. Established in 1997.

• 14115 • **Marconi Radio Awards**
To honor radio stations and air personalities for their overall excellence in radio broadcasting. Awards are presented in 22 categories based on size and format, as well as for Legendary Station of the Year and Network/Syndicated Personality of the Year. All NAB member radio stations are eligible. Trophies are awarded annually at the fall Radio Convention. Established in 1989 and named for Guglielmo Marconi, inventor of the wireless.

• 14116 • **National Radio Award**
To recognize an individual who has made a significant or ongoing contribution to the radio industry either as a performer or in any leadership capacity. A trophy is awarded annually at the fall Radio Convention. Established in 1984.

• 14117 • **Service to Children Television Awards**
To recognize outstanding achievement in locally-produced children's television programming and outreach activities. Separate awards are presented in the Small Market and Medium/Large Market categories. Awarded annually in Washington DC. Established in 1985.

• 14118 • **Spirit of Broadcasting Award**
To recognize an individual or organization for outstanding contributions to the professional standards and vitality of the broadcasting industry. A trophy is awarded when merited at the Association's spring convention. Established in 1984.

• 14119 •
National Association of Catholic Chaplains
Kathy Eldridge, Dir. of Operations
PO Box 070473
Milwaukee, WI 53207-0473
Phone: (414)483-4898
Fax: (414)483-6712
E-mail: info@nacc.org
Home Page: http://www.nacc.org

• 14120 • **Distinguished Service Award**
To recognize individuals who have made outstanding contributions to the Association. The recipient must be an NACC member to be eligible, and must be present to receive the award. A plaque is awarded when merited at the Convention. Established in 1974. Formerly: (1985) Diplomate Award.

• 14121 • **Outstanding Colleague Award**
To recognize individuals who have made continuing contributions to the NACC nationally or to the field of pastoral care for at least five years. The recipient must be a member of the NACC or of a participating organization in the Network on Ministry in Specialized Settings. Up to three awards may be bestowed each year at the National Convention. Established in 1993.

• 14122 • **Prestigious Award**
To recognize individuals who have made an outstanding and long lasting contribution to the field of pastoral care or to the NACC. The recipient need not be a member of the NACC or the Network (though may be) and shall be able to be present to receive the award personally.

• 14123 •
National Association of College and University Business Officers
James E. Morley Jr., Pres./CEO
2501 M St. NW, Ste. 400
Washington, DC 20037-1308
Phone: (202)861-2500
Toll-Free: 800-462-4916
Fax: (202)861-2583
E-mail: james.morley@nacubo.org
Home Page: http://www.nacubo.org

Awards are arranged in alphabetical order below their administering organizations

• 14124 • Management Achievement Award

To recognize the achievements of colleges and universities in improving the quality of higher education programs and services. Judging is based on the following criteria: leadership, information and analysis, strategic and operational planning, human resource development and management, educational and business-process management, institutional performance results, and satisfaction of those receiving services. Monetary prizes from $1,000 to $10,000 are awarded. Sponsored by Barnes and Noble Bookstores, Inc.

• 14125 • Process Improvement Award

To recognize college and university process improvement through re-engineering, redesign, or restructuring. Initiatives submitted in this award category can be specific programs, projects, or activities. The award recognizes such factors as reduction of cycle time, process simplification, improvements in productivity, and enhanced customer service and satisfaction. Applications must reflect programs that have been in place for at least 12 months. Four scoring categories are involved totaling 1,000 points: management commitment and employee involvement, process documentation and benchmarking, process simplification and cycle-time reduction, and customer input and feedback.

• 14126 • Resource Enhancement Award

To recognize initiatives taken by colleges and universities that reduce costs, increase revenues, or improve productivity. Judging is based on the following criteria: originality, portability, process documentation of resource enhancements, results, and quality of application. Monetary prizes from $1,000 to $10,000 are awarded. Sponsored by Barnes and Noble Bookstores, Inc.

• 14127 •

National Association of College and University Food Services
Joseph Spina PhD, Exec.Dir.
Manly Miles Bldg.
Michigan State Univ.
1405 S Harrison Rd., Ste. 305
East Lansing, MI 48824-5242
Phone: (517)332-2494
Fax: (517)332-8144
E-mail: webmaster@nacufs.org
Home Page: http://www.nacufs.org

• 14128 • Daryl Van Hook Industry Award

To recognize an industry member for outstanding contributions to NACUFS. Awarded annually. Established in 1992. Formerly: Industry Appreciation Award.

• 14129 • Loyal E. Horton Dining Awards

To encourage colleges and universities to employ innovations in menu, presentation, special event planning, and new concepts for student dining. The award provides an avenue for sharing dining ideas and creative presentations among dining services. Gold, silver, and bronze medals are given in each of six categories: Residence Hall Dining - Theme Dinner; Residence Hall Dining - Single Stand-Alone Concept/Outlet; Residence Hall Dining - Multiple Concepts/Outlets; Catering - Standard Menu; Catering - Special Event; Retail Sales - Single Stand-Alone Concept/Outlet; Retail Sales - Multiple Concepts/Outlets. Awarded annually. Established in 1973. Formerly: (1995) Dining Idea Exchange Contest.

• 14130 • Richard Lichtenfelt Award

For recognition of outstanding volunteer service to NACUFS on the national level. The recipient of the award is selected by the National President. Awarded annually at the National Conference. Named in honor of Richard Lichtenfelt, NACUFS's first president.

• 14131 • Theodore W. Minah Distinguished Service Award

For recognition of outstanding and enduring contributions to the institutional food service industry and to the Association. The contribution may take the following forms: Association offices held and committees served; articles and manuscripts written, published or unpublished; length of service in college/university foodservice; contributions to formal educational programs; inventions and innovations to the foodservice industry; and contributions to allied food industries, such as school lunch programs, dietetics in hospitals, or mental health institutions; or outstanding ability in college food service operation. A silver bowl, platter, and ladle are awarded annually. Established in 1967.

• 14132 • Regional Presidents Award

To recognize members at the National Conference for outstanding service to NACUFS on the regional and/or national level. The names of the recipients of these awards are submitted by the Regional Presidents to the Executive Board for approval.

• 14133 •

National Association of College Auxiliary Services
Dr. Bob Hassmiller CAE, Exec.Dir.
7 Boar's Head Ln.
Charlottesville, VA 22903-4610
Phone: (434)245-8425
Fax: (434)245-8453
E-mail: info@nacas.org
Home Page: http://www.nacas.org

• 14134 • Golden Award

To recognize outstanding campus leadership, activities, and/or programs promoting cultural awareness and inclusion. Any current individual member, institution, or business partner in good standing is eligible. This award recognizes exemplary and outstanding service to cultural awareness in the profession of college auxiliary management and the promotion of inclusion in an on-going fashion, through leadership in the areas of cultural diversity and equality. Awarded annually. Established in 1992 in honor of Edwin R. "Bob" Golden for his foresight in acknowledging the need for attention to issues of cultural diversity in the Association.

• 14135 • Outstanding Service Award

To recognize outstanding service to the association, its members, and the profession of college auxiliary services. A certificate is awarded annually. Established in 1969.

• 14136 • Silver Torch Award

To recognize and honor retired or retiring members who have had a continuing positive influence on the Association and on the profession. Awarded when merited.

• 14137 •

National Association of Community Health Centers
Tom Van Coverden, Pres./CEO
7200 Wisconsin Ave., Ste. 210
Bethesda, MD 20814
Phone: (301)347-0400
Fax: (301)347-0459
E-mail: contact@nachc.com
Home Page: http://www.nachc.com

• 14138 • National Association of Community Health Centers Awards

To recognize individuals who, through consistent support, dedication, and a high level of involvement, have made significant contributions to the community health center movement. The following awards are presented: John Gilbert Award, Aaron L. Brown Memorial Public Service Award, Samuel U. Rodgers Achievement Award, Ethel Bond Memorial Consumer Award, Louis S. Garcia Community/Migrant Health Service Award; plus two Clinical Awards: Education & Training, and Innovative Research Award. Awarded annually.

• 14139 •

National Association of Competitive Mounted Orienteering
Mr. Walter H. Olsen, Exec.Dir.
503 171st Ave. SE
Tenino, WA 98589-9711
Phone: (360)264-2727
Phone: (360)264-5192
Toll-Free: 800-354-7264
Fax: (360)264-4890
E-mail: arabnacmo@thurston.com
Home Page: http://www.nacmo.org

• 14140 • Horse Awards

Applicants must be active members of the association. Awards are given in the following areas: 200 and 400 points certificates are given; 600 points an embroidered halter is given; 800 points an embroidered stable sheet is given; 1000 points a blothauc halter-bridge in NACMO colors is given.

• 14141 • National High Point Awards

To recognize high points gathered in the sport of mounted orienteering. Categories include team, National High Point Male Rider, and National High Point Female Rider. In addition, state youth division awards and a National Sportsmanship award are given yearly. In each state, plaques are awarded at the association's annual meeting. Established in 1981.

• 14142 • **Ride Managers**
Applicants must be active members of the association. Awards are given in the following areas: 5 rides a patch is given; 10 rides a chevron and eligibility to purchase an NACMO jacket is given; 20 rides lifetime membership and a patch are given.

• 14143 • **Rider Awards**
Applicants must be active members of the association. Awards are given in the following areas: for 50, 150, and 300 points a certificate is given; for 500 points a patch and eligibility to purchase NACMO jackets is given; for 750 points a chevron is given; for 1000 points a chevron and a wooden directors chair with logo are given.

• 14144 • **State Awards and National Awards**
Applicants must be active members of the association; have resided in the state for more than half of the NACMO year; and may compete at any NACMO sanctioned ride anywhere; must compete as an individual (lone rider) or team on all rides; must compete as an individual (lone rider) or team against all others throughout the sport on five highest rides. There must be more than one state, territory, province or country included.

• 14145 •
National Association of Composers, U.S.A.
Dr. Deon Nielsen Price, Pres.
PO Box 49256, Barrington Sta.
Los Angeles, CA 90049
Phone: (310)838-4465
Fax: (310)838-4465
E-mail: nacusa@music-usa.org
Home Page: http://www.music-usa.org/nacusa

Formerly: (1975) National Association of American Composers and Conductors.

• 14146 • **Citations**
To recognize distinguished service to American music. Awarded periodically. Established in 1938.

• 14147 • **Young Composers' Competition**
To recognize outstanding compositions by NACUSA members who are American citizens between the ages of 18 and 30. Compositions not exceeding 15 minutes in length and not requiring more than five players must be submitted by November 30. Compositions submitted must not have been previously published nor have won any other musical competition. First prize is a monetary award of $400 and a possible performance at a NACUSA concert; second prize is $200 and a possible performance at a NACUSA concert. Awarded annually. Established in 1979.

• 14148 •
National Association of Conservation Districts
Krysta Harden, CEO
509 Capitol Ct. NE
Washington, DC 20002-4937
Phone: (202)547-6223
Fax: (202)547-6450
E-mail: krysta-harden@nacdnet.org
Home Page: http://www.nacdnet.org

• 14149 • **Business Conservation Leadership Award**
To recognize a local business, a business corporation, or a unit of such a corporation that has planned and carried out impressive land, water, and related resource management practices on its property in cooperation with a local conservation district, or provided financial, personal, or other assistance to a district, state, or national conservation program. A plaque is awarded annually at the annual meeting. Established in 1975.

• 14150 • **Conservation Tillage Awards**
To recognize outstanding contributions to conservation tillage. Nominations are accepted. Two monetary prizes of $500 each are presented to the Conservation Tillage Information Center for work in promoting the use of conservation tillage. The Information Center, (202)347-4735, is a special project of the National Association of Conservation Districts. A plaque is awarded each year at the CTIC annual meeting. Established in 1984 by Chevron Chemical Company and *Agrichemical Age*.

• 14151 • **Distinguished Service Award**
To recognize a member for significant contributions to the conservation and proper management of our nation's natural resources. Nominations are accepted by November 18. A plaque is awarded annually. Established in 1962.

• 14152 • **District Newsletter Contest**
To encourage conservation districts to further their educational and information efforts through regularly published newsletters. Selection is based on readability, regularity, timely and varied coverage of conservation activities, and broad circulation of the newsletter. The following prizes are awarded: first place national winner - $500; second place national winner - $300; and third place national winner - $200; first place regional winners - $150 each; and runner-up regional winners - $50 each. Established in 1957. Co-sponsored by the Farm and Industrial Equipment Institute.

• 14153 • **Excellence in Communications Awards**
To recognize two conservation districts for their outstanding overall communications efforts. Districts are judged on their effective and successful use of one or more media types to achieve a desired outcome. Media types can include any combination of newsletters, special publications, broadcast media, print media, websites, and public information campaigns. Judging criteria include subject matter, creativity, clarity and simplicity, overall quality and attractiveness, call to action, and effective use of media. Nomination deadline is November 18. Each year, the winner receives a monetary award of $1,000 and the runner-up receives $500. Established in 1968. Co-sponsored by the Association of Equipment Manufacturers.

• 14154 • **Farm Management Conservation Award**
To recognize accomplishments that farm management companies have made in the area of soil and water conservation; to facilitate closer working relationships between conservation districts and farm management companies; and to heighten their understanding and overall awareness of the need to conserve and protect this nation's soil, water, and related natural resources. Any farm management company with a majority of their farm managers belonging to the American Society of Farm Managers and Rural Appraisers is eligible to compete in the award program. Nominations must be endorsed by at least one of the conservation districts where the company currently manages land. Award winners receive a plaque and an expense-paid trip to the NACD national convention where they are recognized. Awarded annually. Established in 1988. Sponsored by The American Society of Farm Managers and Rural Appraisers, Pioneer Hi-Bred International, Inc., and National Association of Conservation Districts. Additional information is available from Pioneer Hi-Bred International, Inc., Farm Manager Coordinator, 4401 Westown Pkwy., West Des Moines, IA 50265, or American Society of Farm Managers and Rural Appraisers, 950 S. Cherry St., Ste. 106, Denver, CO 80222.

• 14155 • **Goodyear Conservation Awards**
To recognize conservation districts judged to have the most outstanding resource management programs in their respective states. Selection is based on a comparison of the actual achievements of a conservation district, as compared to a work plan filed earlier in the year. Representatives of the Grand Awards winners and the outstanding cooperator from each award-winning district receive an expense-paid, vacation-study trip to the 12,000-acre Goodyear Farms for their conservation efforts. Established in 1947 by Goodyear Tire and Rubber Company and NACD.

• 14156 • **NACD - ICI Americas Conservation District Awards**
To offer national recognition to conservation districts for outstanding programs in conservation education. Educational programs carried out by conservation districts in each state, including Puerto Rico and the Virgin Islands, are eligible. From state winners, regional district winners are judged and recognized. The top two national winning districts are recognized with a prestigious plaque that is presented at the opening general session of the NACD annual convention. The national first place district receives $500 for travel expenses to the convention. The

national first place district has the opportunity to present its program before the Education and Youth discussion forum at the NACD convention. The winners in each of the seven NACD Regions receive monetary awards of $200. A certificate and plaque are presented to each state level winner. Awarded annually. Established in 1972. Co-sponsored by the Allis Chalmers Corporation. Formerly: NACD Deutz/Allis Chalmers Conservation District Awards.

• 14157 • NACD - ICI Americas Conservation Teacher Awards
To offer national recognition of teachers for outstanding programs in conservation education. The program is open to all full-time classroom teachers in Grades K-12. The nomination deadline is March 31. The following awards are presented annually: the national first place teacher receives a monetary prize of $1,000 and an expense paid trip to the NACD national convention where the award is made; and the national second place teacher receives a monetary award of $500. Plaques are also awarded annually. Established in 1972. Co-sponsored by the Allis Chalmers Corporation. Formerly: NACD - Allis Chalmers Conservation Teacher Awards.

• 14158 • Professional Service Award
To recognize employees of conservation districts, state associations, or state or federal agencies for exceptional service in furthering the cause of conservation districts and assisting the programs of NACD. Awarded each year at the annual meeting. Established in 1981.

• 14159 • Special Recognition Award
To recognize outstanding contributions, dedicated service, or exceptional achievement by an individual, organization, or corporation chosen by the Board. An award in this category is not necessarily made each year, and nominations are not sought from state associations in the regular awards program. A plaque is awarded when merited. Established in 1980.

• 14160 • Special Service Award
To recognize a soil and water conservation district leader or an American closely allied with the organized district movement for outstanding contributions to the NACD and its objectives. A plaque is awarded each year at the annual meeting. Established in 1963.

• 14161 •
National Association of Consumer Agency Administrators
Elizabeth Owen, Exec.Dir.
2 Brentwood Commons, Ste. 150
750 Old Hickory Blvd.
Brentwood, TN 37027
Phone: (615)371-6125
Toll-Free: (866)SAY-NACAA
Fax: (202)347-2563
E-mail: eowen@nacaa.net
Home Page: http://www.nacaa.net

• 14162 • Achievement in Consumer Education Awards
To recognize outstanding consumer education efforts by government, industry, and the media. At an annual conference in May or June, plaques are awarded in the areas of television, radio, print, and innovative programs.

• 14163 • Agency of the Year Award
To recognize outstanding performance of a NACCA member agency, either through long-term efforts or by virtue of a significant program or other success. Other criteria include a successful and beneficial enforcement action or an outstanding education or outreach program. Awarded annually.

• 14164 •
National Association of Counties
Larry E. Naake, Exec.Dir.
440 1st St. NW, Ste. 800
Washington, DC 20001
Phone: (202)393-6226
Phone: (202)942-4287
Fax: (202)393-2630
E-mail: tgoodman@naco.org
Home Page: http://www.naco.org

• 14165 • Achievement Awards
To recognize innovative county government programs called County Model Programs. Members of NACo must submit entries in one of the following 21 categories: arts and historic preservation; children and youth; citizen education and public information; community/economic development; county administration and management; court administration and management; criminal justice and public safety; emergency management and response; employment and training; environmental protection and energy; financial management; health; human services; information technology; libraries; parks and recreation; personnel management, employee training, and employee benefits; planning; risk management; transportation; and volunteers. Application deadline is February 11. A certificate is awarded to each recipient at the annual conference, usually in July. Established in 1970.

• 14166 • Joe Cooney Award
To recognize an individual who has made a substantial contribution to innovative excellence in employment and training. Individuals working below the level of top agency management are eligible.

• 14167 • Distinguished Service Award for Elected County Official
To recognize the role county local officials play in the effectiveness of public/private partnership's ability to work together for a common goal. Awarded annually at the Association's conference. Deadline is August 15.

• 14168 • JTPA Awards for Excellence
To recognize the many successes of the Job Training Partnership Act. Private industry councils, service providers, grant recipients, or state agencies may submit entries. Programs will be judged on the following criteria: Innovation, Ongoing Activities, Transferability, Tangible Results, and Cost Effectiveness. A plaque is awarded at the annual Employment Policy and Human Resources Conference.

• 14169 •
National Association of County Agricultural Agents
Glen Rogers, Pres.
252 N Park St.
Decatur, IL 62523
Phone: (217)876-1220
Fax: (217)877-5382
E-mail: nacaaemail@aol.com
Home Page: http://www.nacaa.com

• 14170 • Achievement Award
To recognize outstanding service in cooperative extension. Members of the association with less than ten years of service in the area are eligible. A certificate is awarded annually in each state of the United States. Established in 1972.

• 14171 • Distinguished Service Award
To recognize distinguished contributions to cooperative extension programs in local areas. Members of the association who have had ten years or more of experience with cooperative extension service are eligible. The number of members per state determines the number of awards presented. A certificate is awarded annually.

• 14172 •
National Association of County and City Health Officials
John M. Auerbach MBA, Exec.Dir.
1100 17th St. NW, 2nd Fl.
Washington, DC 20036
Phone: (202)783-5550
Fax: (202)783-1583
E-mail: john_auerbach@bphc.org
Home Page: http://www.naccho.org

• 14173 • Award for Excellence in Environmental Health
For national recognition of outstanding, significant, and innovative activities and programs of local health departments in the area of environmental health. A plaque and travel expenses to attend the awards lunch are awarded annually. Two runners-up also receive certificates. Established in 1990.

• 14174 • Award for Excellence in Multicultural Health
For national recognition of outstanding, significant, and innovative approaches by local health departments in assuring access to culturally competent health care services for racial and/or cultural and linguistic minorities. A plaque and travel expenses to attend the awards lunch are bestowed annually. Two runners-up also receive certificates. Established in 1994.

• 14175 • J. Howard Beard Award
For recognition of achievement in implementing innovative programs to address public health problems or issues. Association membership is required. A plaque is awarded annually. Established in 1986. Renamed in 1989 to honor J. Howard Beard. Formerly: (1989) NACHO Achievement Award.

• 14176 • Jim Parker Memorial Award
To recognize and encourage innovations to established and/or improved collaborations between state and local health departments. A plaque and travel expenses to attend the awards lunch are bestowed annually. Two runners-up receive certificates. Established in 1983. Cosponsored by the Association of State Territorial and Health Officials, the Centers for Disease Control and Prevention, and the Association of State and Territorial Local Liaison Officials.

• 14177 • Primary Care Award
For national recognition of outstanding, significant, and innovative approaches by local health departments in assuring access to primary care services for medically underserved populations. Local health department officials who are members of the Association are eligible. A plaque and travel expenses to attend the awards lunch are awarded annually. Two runners-up are also presented with certificates. Established in 1990.

• 14178 •
National Association of County Engineers
A.R. Giancola, Exec.Dir.
440 1st St. NW
Washington, DC 20001
Phone: (202)393-5041
Fax: (202)393-2630
E-mail: nace@naco.org
Home Page: http://www.countyengineers.org

• 14179 • County Engineer of the Year Awards
To recognize county engineers for application of efficient engineering management principles and standards for the economic design, construction, maintenance, and operation of public works facilities. The Rural County Engineer of the Year Award is presented to the engineer representing a county with a population of 100,000 or less, and the Urban County Engineer of the Year Award is for populations greater than 100,000. Members of the Association are eligible. Engraved plaques are awarded annually at the NACE Annual Management and Technical Conference. Established in 1965.

• 14180 •
National Association of County Information Officers
Roger W. Kortekaas, Contact
600 E 4th St.
Charlotte, NC 28202
Phone: (704)336-2597
Fax: (704)336-6600
E-mail: korterw@co.mecklenburg.nc.us
Home Page: http://www.nacio.org
Formerly: National Association of Counties.

• 14181 • Awards of Excellence
To recognize the work of county public information officers and their staffs. Individuals working in county public information offices or performing public information duties for county governments are eligible. Awards are presented in a variety of categories among: annual reports, brochures, internal and external publications, writing, graphic design, photography, audio visual productions, special projects, computer media. A Best of Show winner is also selected. Plaques and certificates naming the winner and the employing county are awarded annually. Established in 1971.

• 14182 •
National Association of Credit Management
Robin Schauseil CAE, Pres./COO
8840 Columbia 100 Pkwy.
100 Parkway
Columbia, MD 21045
Phone: (410)740-5560
Toll-Free: 800-955-8815
Fax: (410)740-5574
E-mail: nacm_info@nacm.org
Home Page: http://www.nacm.org

• 14183 • National Credit Executive of the Year
For recognition in the business credit community. Active Certified Credit Executives (CCEs) Members of the association are eligible and are judged by the Honors and Awards Committee. Established in 1985.

• 14184 •
National Association of Criminal Defense Lawyers
Ralph Grunewald, Exec.Dir.
1150 18th St. NW, Ste. 950
Washington, DC 20036
Phone: (202)872-8600
Fax: (202)872-8690
E-mail: assist@nacdl.org
Home Page: http://www.criminaljustice.org

• 14185 • Robert C. Heeney Memorial Award
To recognize the member who best exemplifies the goals and values of the Association and the legal profession in general. A plaque and a certificate are awarded annually. Established in 1981 in memory of Robert C. Heeney, the 18th president of the Association.

• 14186 • Presidential Commendation
To recognize and reward contributions to the improvement of the criminal justice system and the defense of individual liberties. A parchment is awarded at the discretion of the President.

• 14187 •
National Association of Diaconate Directors
Deacon Daniel Peterson, Pres.
2136 12th St., Ste. 105
Rockford, IL 61104
Phone: (815)965-2100
Fax: (815)965-1569
E-mail: info@nadd.cc
Home Page: http://www.nadd.cc

• 14188 • NADD Award
To recognize an individual, organization, or group which has made a significant contribution to the Diaconate movement in the United States. A plaque is awarded each year at the annual convention. Nominations are made by members of the Executive Board. Established in 1978.

• 14189 • Bart O'Leary Award
To recognize outstanding service to the NADD. A plaque is usually awarded at the annual convention. Nominations are made by members of the Executive Board. Established in 1990.

• 14190 • Philbin Award
To recognize the contribution of a Director of a Permanent Diaconate Program to the Permanent Diaconate on a national and/or local level. A plaque is usually awarded at the annual convention. Nominations are made by members of the Executive Board. Established in 1978 for Father William Philbin.

• 14191 • Recognition Award
To recognize the contributions of individuals serving the association in leadership roles. Nominations are made by members of the Executive Board. A plaque is usually awarded at the annual convention. Established in 1992.

• 14192 • Special Award
To recognize the contributions made to Diaconate by an individual. A plaque is usually awarded at the annual convention. Nominations are made by members of the Executive Board. Established in 1978.

• 14193 •
National Association of Diocesan Ecumenical Officers
Rev. Robert B. Flannery, Pres.
St. Francis Xavier Church
303 S Poplar St.
Carbondale, IL 62901
Phone: (618)457-4556
Fax: (618)457-7368
E-mail: rbflan@globaleyes.net
Home Page: http://www.nadeo.org

Awards are arranged in alphabetical order below their administering organizations

• 14194 • James Fitzgerald Award
To recognize a person or organization whose contribution to the work of Christian unity and Interfaith relations has made an impact on the ecumenical endeavor on the national, regional, or local scene. A committee makes a recommendation from the list of nominees to the NADEO Board. A plaque is awarded annually at the NADEO luncheon, held during the National Workshop on Christian Unity. Established in 1979 in honor of James Fitzgerald, an original founding member of NADEO. Formerly: (1987) NADEO Annual Award for Ecumenism; (1983) James Fitzgerald Award for Ecumenism.

• 14195 •
National Association of Display Industries
Klein Merriman, Sec.
3595 Sheridan St., Ste. 200
Hollywood, FL 33021
Phone: (954)893-7225
Fax: (954)893-8375
E-mail: nadi@nadi-global.com
Home Page: http://www.nadi-global.com

• 14196 • Annual Display Award
To recognize an outstanding individual in the field of visual merchandising. Applicants must be active members of the community and well-respected in the industry for talent and professionalism. Awards are given in the following categories: (1) Visual Merchandiser (Mass Merchandiser); (2) Visual Merchandiser (Full Line Department Store or Chain); (3) Visual Merchandiser (Department Store or Chain); (5) Retail Management (Industry or Fine Arts); (4) Visual Merchandiser (Specialty Store or Specialty Store Chain); and (6) Store Planning (In-Store or Consultant). An engraved crystal disc, set in a silver-trimmed leather presentation case designed by Tiffany's, is awarded annually in conjunction with the December Trade Show. Established in the early 1960s.

• 14197 • Founders Award
To recognize upper management retail executives whose support and leadership in the field of visual merchandising is especially outstanding. A crystal globe, set on an engraved sterling silver stand, designed by Tiffany, is awarded when deemed appropriate. Established in the early 1980s. The award commemorates the founding fathers of NADI.

• 14198 • Hall of Fame
To induct the most recognized visual merchandising talents into the NADI Hall of Fame. Applicants who show continued achievement in the visual merchandising field are eligible. A crystal globe, set on an engraved sterling silver stand, designed by Tiffany, is awarded annually at the spring trade show. Established in the early 1960s.

• 14199 •
National Association of Dramatic and Speech Arts
Jacqueline K. Davis, Pres.
PO Box 561
Grambling, LA 71245
Phone: (281)618-5548
Fax: (281)618-5455
E-mail: info@nadsa.com
Home Page: http://www.nadsa.com

• 14200 • S. Randolph Edmonds Playwriting Award
To honor the best play written on the black experience. Established in 1975 by S. Randolph Edmonds, founder of NADSA.

• 14201 • Lifetime Achievement Award
To recognize an individual for contributions in the area of dramatic and speech arts on the national level. Members or special people may be nominated by February 15 of the year prior to the award. A plaque is awarded annually at the conference. Established in 1984 by Dr. H.D. Flowers, II. Formerly: NADSA Special Recognition.

• 14202 • NADSA Outstanding Service Award
To recognize an individual for outstanding service to the Association. Members may be nominated by February 15 of the year prior to the award. A plaque is awarded annually at the conference. Established in 1984 by Dr. H.D. Flowers, II.

• 14203 • NADSA Research Award
To recognize an individual for research in the area of dramatic and speech arts. Members may be nominated by February 15 of the year prior to the award. A plaque is awarded annually at the conference. Established in 1984 by Dr. H.D. Flowers, II.

• 14204 • NADSA Scholar Award
To recognize an individual for scholarly achievement in the area of dramatic and speech arts. Members may be nominated by February 15 of the year prior to the award. A plaque is awarded annually at the conference. Established in 1984 by Dr. H.D. Flowers, II.

• 14205 •
National Association of Elementary School Principals
Dr. Vincent L. Ferrandino, Exec.Dir.
1615 Duke St.
Alexandria, VA 22314
Phone: (703)684-3345
Toll-Free: 800-386-2377
Fax: (703)396-2377
E-mail: naesp@naesp.org
Home Page: http://www.naesp.org

• 14206 • Distinguished Service Awards
To honor an individual who has made a vital and enduring contribution to the well-being and progress of education or children. Two separate awards are presented: Distinguished Service to Children Award for dedicated advocacy on behalf of improving the lives of children and youth nationally and/or globally; and the Distinguished Service to Education Award for contributions that have resulted in improvements in the education of children and youth nationally and/or globally. A plaque is awarded annually at the convention. Established in 1982. Formerly: Award for Distinguished Service to Children.

• 14207 • National Distinguished Principal Award
To honor exemplary elementary and middle school principals who set the pace, character, and quality of the education children receive during their early school years. One principal is chosen annually from each of the 50 states and the District of Columbia, with additional awards for private K-8 schools, Department of Defense Dependents' Schools, and Department of State Overseas Schools. The two-day awards ceremony takes place in Washington DC each fall. Established in 1984. Co-sponsored by the U.S. Department of Education.

• 14208 •
National Association of Emergency Medical Technicians
Ken Bouvierre, Pres.
PO Box 1400
Clinton, MS 39060-1400
Phone: (601)924-7744
Toll-Free: 800-34N-AEMT
Fax: (601)924-7325
E-mail: info@naemt.org
Home Page: http://www.naemt.org

• 14209 • EMT-Paramedic Emergency Medical Service of the Year Award (ALS Service of the Year Award)
To recognize an EMS system that exemplifies outstanding professionalism and service to the community it serves. Any EMS system at the paramedic level, except those in which NAEMT leadership personnel participate, may be nominated. A plaque and a $1,000 stipend are awarded at the annual awards banquet. Established in 1985. Co-sponsored by Zoll Medical Corp.

• 14210 • J. D. Farrington Award of Excellence
To recognize an individual for significant contributions to emergency medical service development. Nominations are made by the NAEMT Board of Directors. A plaque is awarded when merited. Established in 1977.

• 14211 • A. Roger Fox Founder's Award
To recognize an NAEMT member for significant contributions to the Association. Nominations are made by the NAEMT Board of Directors. A plaque is awarded when merited. Established in 1978.

• 14212 • Governor's National Leadership Award
To recognize a member who has helped the Association grow. Nominations are made by the NAEMT Board of Governors. A plaque is awarded when merited. Established in 1981. Formerly: Stephen A. Frew National Leadership Award.

• 14213 • Jeffrey S. Harris State Leadership Award
To recognize a member of an NAEMT state affiliate organization that most helps the state grow and progress. Members of the NAEMT state affiliated organizations are eligible. Nominations may be made by the NAEMT Board of Governors. A plaque is awarded when merited. Established in 1981.

• 14214 • William Klingensmith EMS Administrator of the Year Award
To recognize an administrator who has made a significant contribution to the EMS administration on the local, state, or national level. Any EMS administrator whose primary responsibility is the direction of individuals involved in the delivery of prehospital care may be nominated. A plaque and a $1,000 stipend are awarded annually. Established in 1988 in honor of William Klingensmith, former NAEMT secretary and governor. Co-sponsored by Merginet.com, a division of Moore Medical Corp.

• 14215 • Asmund S. Laerdal Award for Excellence (EMT-Paramedic of the Year Award)
To recognize an EMT-Paramedic who has contributed significantly to EMS at the community, state, or national level. Any paramedic whose primary responsibility is providing direct patient care is eligible. A stipend of $1,000 and a carved Norwegian crystal are awarded annually. Established in 1984. Named in honor of Asmund S. Laerdal, founder of the Laerdal Co. Co-sponsored by the Laerdal Medical Corp.

• 14216 • Rocco V. Morando Lifetime Achievement Award
To recognize an individual whose contribution to prehospital care has been consistent and long-lasting, representing in effect a lifetime of outstanding service to the profession and the public. Nominations are made by the NAEMT Board of Directors. A plaque is awarded when merited. Established in 1984.

• 14217 • Robert E. Motley EMT of the Year Award
To recognize an EMT who has significantly contributed to EMS at the community, state, or national level. Any basic or intermediate EMT whose primary responsibility is providing direct patient care is eligible. A stipend of $1,000 and a plaque are presented annually at the awards banquet. Established in 1978. Co-sponsored by JEMS Communications.

• 14218 • Presidential Leadership Award
To recognize individuals who have demonstrated outstanding support for the NAEMT and/or EMS. Nominations are accepted and the winner is selected by the President of NAEMT. A plaque is presented when merited. Established in 1977.

• 14219 • Leo R. Schwartz Emergency Medical Service of the Year Award (BLS Service of the Year Award)
To recognize an EMS system that exemplifies outstanding professionalism and service to the community it serves. Any EMS system at the basic or intermediate level except those in which NAEMT leadership personnel participate may be considered. A stipend of $1,000 and a plaque are awarded annually at the awards banquet. Established in 1979 in honor of Leo R. Schwartz, former chief of the National Highway Traffic Safety Administration who designed the EMS Star of Life. Co-sponsored by *EMS Magazine.*

• 14220 • Mary Ann Talley EMS Instructor/Coordinator of the Year Award
To recognize an outstanding instructor of an ongoing training program for basic/intermediate EMTs or paramedics who is approved by the state EMS lead agency. Any state approved instructor/coordinator who is a member of NAEMT is eligible. A plaque and a $1,000 stipend are awarded annually. Established in 1983 in honor of Mary Ann Talley, program director of the EMS Training Department at the University of South Alabama in Mobile. Co-sponsored by Mosby.

• 14221 •
National Association of Federal Credit Unions
Fred R. Becker Jr., Pres./CEO
3138 10th St. N
Arlington, VA 22201-2149
Phone: (703)522-4770
Toll-Free: 800-336-4644
Fax: (703)524-1082
E-mail: fbecker@nafcu.org
Home Page: http://www.nafcu.org

• 14222 • Innovation Showcase Award
To recognize innovative, transferable ideas that have been implemented by NAFCU member credit unions to improve member service, credit union health, or operations. The winners' innovations are showcased at NAFCU's Credit Union Technology Forum and Trade Show and a plaque is presented to credit unions during the opening session of the program. Winning innovations are also featured in NAFCU's bi-monthly magazine, The Federal Credit Union. Deadline for entry is December 31. Established in 1995.

• 14223 • NAFCU Awards Program
To recognize outstanding Federal credit unions, volunteers, and professionals. Dedicated volunteers, experienced professionals, and innovative federal credit unions that have made contributions to the industry and have upheld the spirit of cooperativeness are eligible. Credit unions must be members of NAFCU. The deadline for nominations is March 5. Each award is divided into two asset categories: below $75 million and $75 million and above. A plaque is presented to the credit unions submitting winning entries for Volunteer of the Year, Professional of the Year, and Federal Credit Union of the Year at a special awards luncheon at the annual conference. Winners are also featured in NAFCU's bi-monthly magazine, "The Federal Credit Union", and the weekly newsletter, "Update". Established in 1975.

• 14224 • Quarter-Century Honor Roll
To recognize individuals, both paid and volunteer, who have dedicated 25 years of service or more to the credit union community. Individuals who have unselfishly contributed much effort to ensure the success of the credit union movement are eligible. Credit Unions can also submit honorees posthumously. A Quarter-Century Honor Roll certificate signed by the president of NAFCU is forwarded to the Board of Directors at the individual's credit union for appropriate presentation. Those accepted into the Quarter-Century Honor Roll are also acknowledged by NAFCU's bi-monthly magazine, *The Federal Credit Union,* which periodically publishes an Honor Roll list. Established in 1986.

• 14225 •
National Association of Federal Veterinarians
Dr. Joe Yearous, Pres.
1101 Vermont Ave. NW, Ste. 710
Washington, DC 20005
Phone: (202)289-6334
Fax: (202)842-4360
E-mail: dboyle@nafv.org
Home Page: http://users.erols.com/nafv
Formerly: (1943) National Association of the Bureau of Animal Industry Veterinarians.

• 14226 • Dr. Daniel E. Salmon Award
To recognize outstanding contributions and notable service in the public's interest by a federally employed veterinarian, and to encourage junior veterinarians to continue excellence in their performance and to aspire for public service as a lifelong career. A veterinarian who is a career employee of the federal government, GS13 or below (or military rank of 0-4 or below), or who has no more than 10 years of service, and who has demonstrated sustained significant contributions over a period of five years or more in federal programs involving public health, consumer protection, or animal health and welfare is eligible. A monetary prize of $500 and a plaque are awarded annually at the USDA honor awards ceremony. Established in 1984 in honor of Dr. Daniel E. Salmon, a world renowned veterinary scientist and the first director of the USDA Bureau of Animal Industry, which celebrated its centennial in 1984.

• 14227 •
National Association of Federally Licensed Firearms Dealers
Andrew Molchan, Pres.
2400 E Las Olas Blvd., No. 397
Fort Lauderdale, FL 33301
Phone: (954)467-9994
Fax: (954)463-2501
E-mail: info@amfire.com
Home Page: http://www.amfire.com

• 14228 • **Award of Merit**
For recognition of product innovation for outdoor products (knives, guns, archery, etc.). Products that have been produced and marketed during the preceding year are considered. A plaque is awarded annually at the Firearms Trade Expo. Established in 1974.

• 14229 •
National Association of Fire Investigators
Heather Kennedy, Dir. of Membership Svcs.
857 Tallevast Rd.
Sarasota, FL 34243
Phone: (941)359-2800
Toll-Free: 877-506-NAFI
Fax: (941)351-5849
E-mail: info@nafi.org
Home Page: http://www.nafi.org

• 14230 • **Man of the Year**
To recognize significant contributions to the fire investigation profession and NAFI. Firefighters, police officers, attorneys, insurance adjusters, claimspeople, fire experts, fire marshals in the military, or full-time fire investigators may be nominated. An engraved plaque is awarded annually when merited. Established in 1969. Formerly: Fire Investigator of the Year.

• 14231 •
National Association of First Responders
Henry Weir Jr., Pres.
5334 Armadillo Ave.
Orange Beach, AL 36561-4211
Phone: (251)981-3383
Phone: (251)979-6592

• 14232 • **National Association of First Responders Awards**
To recognize members of the association or other citizens for outstanding contributions, dedication, and support to the association or for deeds of high character, such as lifesaving. Individuals may be nominated by members or the general public for any deed during the year. The following awards are presented: President's Award, Lifesaving or Merit Award, EMT - Paramedic of the Year, First Responder Award, and Leadership Award. A medal, trophy or plaque is awarded when merited and at conventions. Established in 1984. Contact Henry Weir Jr. at the above address.

• 14233 •
National Association of Fleet Administrators
Phillip E. Russo CAE, Exec.Dir.
100 Wood Ave. S, Ste. 310
Iselin, NJ 08830
Phone: (732)494-8100
Fax: (732)494-6789
E-mail: info@nafa.org
Home Page: http://www.nafa.org

• 14234 • **Distinguished Service Award**
To recognize a member's distinguished service to and support of NAFA, to the profession, to an outside organization in the field of education or government that benefited the profession, and for special recognition of a person outside NAFA's membership who has made a significant contribution to the profession of fleet management. Nominations may be made by members. Plaques are awarded at the annual conference. Established in 1970.

• 14235 •
National Association of Foreign-Trade Zones
Dr. Willard M. Berry, Exec.Dir.
1000 Connecticut Ave. NW, Ste. 1001
Washington, DC 20036
Phone: (202)331-1950
Fax: (202)331-1994
E-mail: info@naftz.org
Home Page: http://www.naftz.org

• 14236 • **Person of the Year**
For recognition of a contribution to U.S. international trade development. A globe is awarded annually. Established in 1985.

• 14237 •
National Association of Geoscience Teachers
Dr. Ian MacGregor, Exec.Dir.
31 Crestview Dr.
Western Washington University
PO Box 5443
Napa, CA 94558
Phone: (707)427-8864
Fax: (707)427-8864
E-mail: nagt@gordonvalley.com
Home Page: http://www.nagt.org

• 14238 • **Neil A. Miner Award**
To recognize an individual for exceptional contributions to the stimulation of interest in the earth sciences. The deadline for nominations is April 1. A plaque is presented annually at the Association's annual meeting. Established in 1952 in memory of Neil A. Miner, for his unselfish outlook on life, and for his personal philosophy, which inspired fellow teachers as well as students.

• 14239 • **Outstanding Earth Science Teacher Award**
To recognize exceptional contributions to the stimulation of interest in the earth sciences at the secondary level. Middle school and high school teachers are eligible. Eleven national finalists are selected, one from each NAGT regional section. Nomination deadline is June 1. Each winner is awarded a walnut plaque, $500 in travel funds, $500 in classroom improvement funds, as well as other prizes. Established in 1971.

• 14240 • **James H. Shea Award**
For recognition of exceptional contributions in writing and/or editing earth science materials that are of interest to the general public and/or teachers of earth science. The submission deadline is May 1. A plaque is presented at the Association's annual meeting. Established in 1991 in honor of the current and long-time editor of the *Journal of Geoscience Education.*

• 14241 •
National Association of Government Communicators
David Matusik APR, Pres.
10366 Democracy Ln., Ste. B
Fairfax, VA 22030
Phone: (703)691-0037
Fax: (703)706-0866
E-mail: info@nagc.com
Home Page: http://www.nagc.com

• 14242 • **Blue Pencil Awards**
To recognize the best in writing, publications, print-related projects and programs, and campaigns produced by government communicators by or for government agencies. Awards are given in 40 categories among publications, media relations, photography, visual communications, shoestring budget media, and special communications. Application deadline is mid-December. Awards are presented at a special banquet held each spring during NAGC's annual conference. Established in 1976.

• 14243 • **Gold Screen Awards**
To recognize outstanding audio-visual, broadcast, or electronic-related components and programs produced by government communicators by or for government agencies. Awards are given in 16 categories among audio, video, DVDs, CDs, web pages, e-newsletters, multimedia, and other broadcast or electronic-related components and programs. Application deadline is mid-December. Awards are presented at a special banquet held each spring during NAGC's annual conference. Established in 1976.

• 14244 • **Government Communicator of the Year**
To recognize an individual for outstanding work in the field of communications. Open to anyone in government communications. Recipients are chosen by an association committee. A plaque is awarded annually. Established about 1980.

• 14245 •
National Association of Health Underwriters
Janet Trautwein CAE, Exec.VP/CEO
2000 N 14th St., Ste. 450
Arlington, VA 22201
Phone: (703)276-0220
Fax: (703)841-7797
E-mail: info@nahu.org
Home Page: http://www.nahu.org

• 14246 • **Harold R. Gordon Memorial Award**
To recognize an individual for significant contributions to the development and progress of the health insurance business either during the year or over a sustained period of time. Application deadline is April 5. A plaque and certificate are awarded annually. Established in 1948 in memory of Harold R. Gordon, the first director of the Health Insurance Association of America.

• 14247 • **Leading Producer Round Table Awards**
To honor members for health and disability insurance sales achievement. Applications must be submitted by March 31. Certificates are awarded annually. Established in 1942.

• 14248 •
National Association of Hispanic Journalists
Ivan Roman, Exec.Dir.
1000 National Press Bldg.
529 14th St. NW
Washington, DC 20045-2001
Phone: (202)662-7145
Toll-Free: 888-346-NAHJ
Fax: (202)662-7144
E-mail: nahj@nahj.org
Home Page: http://www.nahj.org

• 14249 • **Guillermo Martinez-Marquez Journalism Award**
To promote and recognize the professional successes of NAHJ members/Hispanic journalists in the United States, Puerto Rico and other U.S. territories. Any Hispanic journalist in either English-language or Spanish-language media (print, television, radio) is eligible. Work produced during the previous calendar year may be submitted by February 28. Awards are presented in three categories: (1) Print media; (2) Television news; and (3) Radio news. Prizes for winners in each category and one monetary prize of $1,000 are awarded annually at the national convention. Established in 1986 to honor Guillermo Martinez-Marquez.

• 14250 • **Photojournalism Award**
To recognize excellence in photography by NAHJ members/Hispanic photojournalists throughout the United States, Puerto Rico, and other territories. Hispanic photojournalists in either English- or Spanish-language media are eligible. Published and non-published photos taken during the previous calendar year may be submitted by February 28. Awards are presented in the following categories: (1) News; (2) Feature; (3) Sports; (4) Portrait/Personality; (5) Illustration; and (6) Picture Story. $500 and a prize are awarded annually at the national conference. Established in 1989.

• 14251 •
National Association of Hispanic Nurses
Rudy Valenzuela RN, Pres.
1501 Sixteenth St. NW
Washington, DC 20036
Phone: (202)387-2477
Fax: (202)483-7183
E-mail: info@thehispanicnurses.org
Home Page: http://www.thehispanicnurses.org

• 14252 • **Henrietta Villaescusa Community Service Award**
To honor Hispanic nurses who have contributed to the improvement of health in the Hispanic community. Awarded annually.

• 14253 • **Janie Menchaca Wilson Leadership Award**
To honor Hispanic nurses who have distinguished themselves as nursing leaders.

• 14254 •
National Association of Home and Workshop Writers
Dan Ramsey, Pres.
3201 Primrose Dr.
Willits, CA 95490
Phone: (707)459-6722
Fax: (775)234-7361
E-mail: writer@danramsey.com
Home Page: http://www.nahww.org

• 14255 • **Vaughan and Bushnell Awards (Golden Hammer Awards)**
To recognize excellence in how-to writing by home and workshop writers. The contest includes books, magazines, short subjects, electronic media, and video scripts. Prizes of cash and tools are awarded annually. Established in 1991. Sponsored by Vaughan & Bushnell Manufacturing Co. Formerly: NAHWW/Stanley Awards (Stanleys). 89-2600

• 14256 •
National Association of Home Builders
Jerry Howard, Exec.VP/CEO
1201 15th St. NW
Washington, DC 20005
Phone: (202)266-8200
Toll-Free: 800-368-5242
Fax: (202)266-8400
E-mail: info@nahb.com
Home Page: http://www.nahb.org

• 14257 • **Associate Remodeler of the Year Award**
To recognize suppliers, manufacturers, and other outside industry traders in the Association for state and local Remodelers Council activity, business longevity, honors and awards, and community service. A certificate and publicity are awarded.

• 14258 • **Best in American Living Awards**
To recognize individuals across the United States who produce homes which illustrate design quality, success in the marketplace, and exemplify the "Best in American Living." Open to builders, architects, designers, developers, land planners, and interior designers nationwide. Homes completed or for which the first model opened during the preceding year are eligible. The deadline is July 15. Entries can win nationally, in the category entered, or on a regional/local level. Judges select finalists in each category, from which Grand, Merit, and Honorable Mention Awards may be chosen. Best in Region Awards and House of the Year are also presented. Awarded annually. Established in 1983.

• 14259 • **National Housing Hall of Fame**
To honor individuals who have made a significant, lasting, and national contribution to the housing industry. Both applications and nominations are accepted. Members are selected from the categories of builder/developer, government, and housing related (all other sectors of the building industry). A plaque is installed in the National Housing Hall of Fame, and a personal memento is presented to the awardee at the NAHB Spring Board of Directors Meeting in Washington, D.C. Awarded annually. Established in 1976.

• 14260 • **Remodeler of the Month/Year Awards**
To recognize exemplary NAHB involvement at any level, superior business management, and an outstanding contribution to the remodeling industry. Nominees must be members of the NAHB Remodelers Council. The 12 winners of the "Remodeler of the Month Award" compete for the "Remodeler of the Year Award". A certificate is awarded. Established in 1983. Sponsored by *Qualified Remodeler* magazine.

• 14261 • **Renaissance Awards**
For recognition of excellence in design and construction of residential and nonresidential remodeling and renovation projects. Remodeling and renovation projects must be completed after January 1 of the year preceding the year of the competition. Awards are given in three categories: Grand, Merit, and Honorable Mention. A plaque or framed photo and silk screened award are awarded annually at the convention or educational conference. Established in 1983. Sponsored by *Remodeling* magazine. Additional information is available from the NAHB's Remodelors Council, (202) 822-0216.

• 14262 •
National Association of Housing and Redevelopment Officials
Saul N. Ramirez Jr., Exec.Dir.
630 Eye St. NW
Washington, DC 20001
Phone: (202)289-3500
Toll-Free: 877-866-2476
Fax: (202)289-8181
E-mail: nahro@nahro.org
Home Page: http://www.nahro.org

• 14263 • **M. Justin Herman Memorial Award**
To recognize an individual for an outstanding contribution to the quality of life through service in the fields of housing or community development. Awards are made on the basis of either national contributions or for specific local achievements. The nominee need not be a member of NAHRO. Each nominee must have demonstrated an outstanding contribution to the nation's effort to achieve the goal of "a decent home and a suitable living environment for every American family." Nominations must be submitted by July 1. Established in 1975 to honor M. Justin Herman and provide a living acknowledgment for the standard of excellence he established in the field of housing and community development and the contributions he made to the beauty and vigor of San Francisco.

• 14264 • **John D. Lange International Award**
To recognize an individual in the housing and community development field who has made an outstanding contribution toward international understanding and exchange of international experience. Nominations must be submitted by July 1. Established in 1983 to honor John D. Lange, Executive Director of NAHRO from 1951 to 1970, who participated actively throughout his professional career in international exchange and, in his retirement, carried out executive service assignments in Argentina, Indonesia, and the Philippines. Sponsored by the NAHRO International Committee.

• 14265 • **C. F. "Buzz" Meadows Memorial Award**
To recognize an individual for an outstanding contribution in the field of public procurement and/or contract administration. Individuals who work for a local public agency or a state or federal agency must be nominated by July 1. Established in 1987 to honor C.F. "Buzz" Meadows, a former HUD official who was responsible for the Consolidated Supply Program. Sponsored by the NAHRO Manufacturers and Suppliers Council.

• 14266 • **NAHRO Agency Awards of Excellence in Housing and Community Development**
To recognize outstanding achievement in housing and community development programs throughout the country. Entrants are submitted by the NAHRO regional juries from among the National Award of Merit categories (see separate entry). The Awards of Excellence recognize outstanding achievement in project design and program or administration innovation that provides a model for other agencies. It is expected that, in most cases, the agency will have expanded its role and effectiveness beyond what is being accomplished by a well-operated agency.

• 14267 • **NAHRO Agency Awards of Merit in Housing and Community Development**
To give national recognition to meritorious housing and community development projects, programs, and services provided by NAHRO agency members throughout the country; to provide additional opportunities to inform the public of the best in housing and community development; and to create a resource bank of information on significant, innovative activities performed by housing and redevelopment agencies and community development departments. Awards are presented in Project Design, Program Innovation, and Administrative Innovation. Entries must be submitted by February 15. Awarded at the summer conference.

• 14268 • **Frederic M. Vogelsang Memorial Manuscript Award**
To recognize informed, timely analysis and innovative thinking on the major issues facing low-income housing and community revitalization policies and programs. Manuscripts not exceeding 20 pages must be submitted by July 1. A monetary award of $500 and publication of the manuscript in *Journal of Housing* are awarded. Established in 1983 to honor Frederic Vogelsang, a 20-year NAHRO staff member and former *Journal of Housing* editor.

• 14269 • **Elizabeth Wells Memorial Award**
To recognize a currently serving commissioner, or one who has served within the past 12 months, for excellence as an advocate in developing the financial, political, and community support necessary to ensure the continuation and expansion of housing or community development programs. Individual members of the association must be nominated by July 1. Established in 1987 to honor Elizabeth Wells and provide living acknowledgment of the outstanding contributions she made to the housing field as a member of the Board of Commissioners of the King County Housing Authority and as a member and the first vice president of NAHRO's National Commissioners' Committee.

• 14270 •
National Association of Independent Fee Appraisers
Laura Rudzinski IFA, Exec.VP
401 N Michigan Ave., Ste. 2200
Chicago, IL 60611
Phone: (312)321-6830
Fax: (312)673-6652
E-mail: info@naifa.com
Home Page: http://www.naifa.com

• 14271 • **Appraiser of the Year Award**
To recognize the member who has contributed the most to the local and national Association in the year of the current convention session. A wooden plaque is awarded annually in September at the national convention. Established in 1964 by V. G. Bob Warner of the New Orleans, Louisiana, chapter of the Association.

• 14272 • **Public Relations Award**
No further information was available for this edition.

• 14273 •
National Association of Independent Resurfacers
Nancy Surprenant, Exec.Sec.
5806 W 127th St.
Alsip, IL 60803
Phone: (708)371-8237
Fax: (708)371-8283
E-mail: nairbowlanecare@msn.com
Home Page: http://www.nairbowl.org

• 14274 • **Tom Nonnenmacher Industry Service Award**
This, NAIR's most prestigious honor, recognizes an individual for his or her outstanding service and dedication to the Association and to the bowling industry. A plaque is awarded annually at the Convention. Established in 1976 and renamed in 1985 to honor Tom Nonnenmacher, NAIR's first president.

• 14275 •
National Association of Industrial and Office Properties
Thomas J. Bisacquino, Pres.
2201 Cooperative Way, 3rd Fl.
Herndon, VA 20171
Phone: (703)904-7100
Toll-Free: 800-666-6780
Fax: (703)904-7942
E-mail: bisacquino@naiop.org
Home Page: http://www.naiop.org

• 14276 • **Developer of the Year**
To recognize a commercial real estate development firm for leadership in the industry, active support of the industry, and active support of the local community. Criteria include: outstanding quality of products and services; demonstrated support of local community; active support of the industry through NAIOP; leadership in the real estate and general business communities; financial consistency and stability; and demonstrated ability to adapt to market conditions. A trophy is presented annually. Established in 1979. Formerly: NAIOP Man of the Year Award.

• 14277 • **Literature and Video Awards**
For recognition of the most outstanding promotional literature and videos in the industry. Awards are given in the following categories: (1) Industrial Park Brochure; (2) Industrial Building Brochure; (3) Office Park Brochure; (4) Office Building Brochure; (5) General Information Brochure; (6) Video Cassettes; (7) Mixed-Use Park Brochure; (8) Newsletters; and (9) Electronic Marketing. A certificate and ribbon are presented annually in October. Established in 1978. Formerly: Literature of the Year Awards.

• 14278 •
National Association of Intercollegiate Athletics
Steve Baker, Pres./CEO
PO Box 1325
Olathe, KS 66051
Phone: (913)791-0044
Fax: (913)791-9555
E-mail: kdee@naia.org
Home Page: http://www.naia.org

• 14279 • **Administrator of the Year**
To recognize the outstanding accomplishments of an athletics administrator. Each conference/section of the NAIA may nominate one male and one female administrator for achievements during the immediate previous year. A laminated plaque is presented to the awardee and hand-lettered certificates are presented to the other nominees.

• 14280 • **All-America Awards**
To recognize outstanding athletes in the various sports in which the program is active. The All-America Selection Committee of each Coaches Association/Sports Section recommends procedures for selection and the implementation of the All-America program in their sport to the NAIA. A printed certificate is presented to the athlete and institution. Awarded annually.

• 14281 • **All-America Scholar-Athlete Awards**
To recognize the most outstanding scholar-athletes in the various sports in which the program is active. Individuals must have a 3.5 (4.0 scale) minimum grade point average, be juniors or seniors and have been in attendance at least one term at the school making the nomination, and be varsity participants. Printed certificates are presented to the athlete and institution. Awarded annually. Formerly: NAIA Academic All-America Awards.

• 14282 • **All-Tournament Teams/ Outstanding Athlete Award**
All Tournament Teams are selected at most of the NAIA national events (where appropriate). In addition, an outstanding athlete may be selected. The selection is based primarily upon athletic skill and is usually by vote of the media and/or tournament committee members present at the event. Plaques are presented.

• 14283 • **Awards of Merit**
To recognize those persons who have served the NAIA and/or intercollegiate athletics in exemplary fashion and who do not fall under the classification of the Hall of Fame. Members of advisory committees who render outstanding service, Regional Chairs, Regional Eligibility Chairs, Regional Information Directors, NAIA Coaches Association/Sports Section Presidents/Chairs who perform their duties with distinction and skill, and others whose service to the NAIA is exceptional are eligible. A laminated plaque is presented.

• 14284 • **Coach of the Year Award**
All sports that conduct a National Championship have the opportunity to elect a Coach of the Year. Selection is based on outstanding coaching records, including proven high principles and ethics in the performance of the coaching profession, a high degree of respect and good will achieved among fellow coaches, and a demonstrated devotion to the principles and philosophy of the NAIA. A walnut plaque is usually awarded.

• 14285 • **Distinguished Alumnus Award**
To recognize former students who have been involved in intercollegiate athletics at NAIA member institutions and who have achieved national or international distinction characterized by universal humanitarian endeavors and civic concern. Nominees must have attained outstanding achievement in their chosen fields, but not necessarily athletics. A bronze plaque is awarded periodically. Established in 1963.

• 14286 • **A. O. Duer Scholarship Award**
To recognize a junior student athlete in any sport who has excelled in scholarship, character, and citizenship. Students must be juniors attending an undergraduate institution and have an overall grade point average of at least 3.75 on a 4.0 scale. A monetary award of $1,000 is presented annually to the student's institution and a plaque to the honoree. Established in 1967 in honor of A. O. Duer, former NAIA Executive Secretary who served the association for 26 years.

• 14287 • **Hall of Fame Program**
To honor men and women for outstanding service to intercollegiate athletics in a variety of sports and the NAIA over a period of years. The program honors men and women who have met the criteria in three categories: meritorious service, coaches, and athletes. Nominations are accepted. A laminated plaque for the recipient and a Hall of Fame Certificate to the member school are presented annually. Established in 1952.

• 14288 • **Frank Hesselroth Leadership Award**
To honor an outstanding junior men's or women's basketball player who exhibits outstanding qualities in academics, playing ability, and campus and community leadership. Students must be juniors at the undergraduate level and have an overall grade point average of at least 3.0 on a 4.0 scale. A monetary award of $1,000 is presented to the student's institution and a revere bowl is presented to the award winner during the men's or women's basketball championship banquet. Established in 1983 to recognize Frank Hesselroth, founder of the honorary coach program for the NAIA basketball championship.

• 14289 • **Emil S. Liston Award**
To recognize a junior men's or women's basketball player who has shown high athletic and scholastic achievement. Students must be juniors at an undergraduate institution and have an overall grade point average of at least 3.5 on a 4.0 scale. A monetary award of $1,000 is presented annually to the student's institution and a plaque to the honoree. Established in 1950 in honor of Emil S. Liston, the first Executive Secretary of NAIA.

• 14290 • **NAIA - SIDA All-Sports Championship Awards**
To recognize the top four All-Sports Champions in the NAIA in both the men's and women's divisions. Points are awarded based upon the order of team position in all NAIA National Championships. (An exception is football, where the top 20 teams in each division, as determined by the final NAIA rating, are awarded points). Trophies are presented. Awarded annually.

• 14291 • **NAIA-SIDA Top Web Sites of the Year**
To recognize the most impressive web sites of NAIA schools.

• 14292 • **Ike Pearson Award**
To recognize a sports information director who has contributed outstanding service to his or her institution and to the NAIA at both the conference and national level. A plaque is presented annually. Nomination deadline is March 1. Established in memory of Clarence "Ike" Pearson, who served as the chief of statistical services for the NAIA National Basketball Championship for 29 consecutive years prior to his death in November 1976. Co-sponsored by the Sports Information Directors Association.

• 14293 • **Gary Spitler Memorial Award**
Established in memory of Gary Spitler for overall excellence in publications. Awarded annually.

• 14294 •
National Association of Jewelry Appraisers
Ms. Gail Brett Levine GG, Exec.Dir.
PO Box 18
Rego Park, NY 11374-0018
Phone: (718)896-1536
Fax: (718)997-9057
E-mail: naja.appraisers@netzero.net
Home Page: http://www.najaappraisers.com

• 14295 • **Outstanding Contribution Award**
For recognition of contributions to NAJA. Members may be nominated. A plaque is presented when appropriate. Established in 1983.

• 14296 • **Person of the Year Award**
For recognition of contributions and dedication by members to the NAJA. A plaque is presented when appropriate. Established in 1983. Formerly: (1995) Man of the Year.

Awards are arranged in alphabetical order below their administering organizations

• 14297 •
National Association of Left-Handed Golfers
Wallace Jones, Sec.-Treas.
3249 Hazelwood Dr. SW
Atlanta, GA 30311
Phone: (404)696-1763
Toll-Free: 800-844-6254
Fax: (404)691-5549
E-mail: nalg@mindspring.com
Home Page: http://www.nalg.org

• 14298 • **Board of Governors Trophy**
For recognition of distinguished or outstanding service to the association in the past years. A trophy is awarded. Established in 1964.

• 14299 • **Hall of Fame**
To recognize distinguished members of NALG who have a fine playing record, good character and reputation, and have made substantial contributions to state, regional, and national activities of the association. A distinctive crest is awarded as merited. Established in 1961.

• 14300 • **Waltke Trophy**
To recognize the amateur champion who has the low gross score - 72 holes during four days. Lefty golfers over the age of 18 are eligible. A trophy is awarded annually. Established in 1936 in honor of lefty Richard H. Waltke of St. Louis, who was responsible for the purchase of the first trophy.

• 14301 •
National Association of Legal Investigators
Robert Townsend, Natl.Dir.
PO Box 3330
PO Box 905
Dana Point, CA 92629
Phone: (949)495-0089
Toll-Free: 800-266-6254
Fax: (949)495-0580
E-mail: info@nalionline.org
Home Page: http://www.nalionline.org

• 14302 • **Editor-Publisher Award**
For recognition of work published in the official journal of NALI quarterly, *The Legal Investigator.* The author of each article submitted must be an active or retired member of NALI in good standing. Three plaques are awarded at the annual convention. Established in 1983.

• 14303 •
National Association of Metal Finishers
David Barrack CAE, Interim Exec.Dir.
3660 Maguire Blvd., Ste. 250
Orlando, FL 32803
Phone: (407)281-6445
Fax: (407)281-7345
E-mail: info@namf.org
Home Page: http://www.namf.org

• 14304 • **Award of Merit**
To recognize individuals from member companies for outstanding service of a local and/or national nature. Up to eight awards may be presented each year. Nomination deadline is October 26.

• 14305 • **Award of Special Recognition**
To recognize individuals or organizations, not from member companies, for their invaluable assistance to and support of the job metal finishing industry. Over the years, these awards have gone to government officials, an industry supplier, and a trade association. Nomination deadline is October 26. Awarded at the annual convention when merited.

• 14306 • **Honorary Member**
For recognition of an individual who is a nonmember of the association and who has contributed substantially to NAMF over an extended period of time. This is an honorary award and carries with it no rights (such as voting), nor any obligations (such as dues). Nominations for honorary members must come from a NAMF member, and are due by October 26. Awarded at the annual convention when merited.

• 14307 • **Life Member**
To recognize an individual who has been a member of the Association for at least ten years and who has contributed to the metal finished industry through significant national involvement. Nominee must be in good membership standing in any related predecessor organization(s) and be retired from the metal finishing field. Candidates are selected by unanimous vote of the Board of Directors of this Association. Awarded at the annual convention when merited.

• 14308 • **Outstanding Achievement Award**
To recognize an active board member, a past member, or a non-board member who has made outstanding contributions to NAMF. The award acknowledges a single individual whose efforts to improve and strengthen NAMF is considered by the Board of Directors as being representative of distinguished and notable contributions. Award can be given for a single contribution, or for long term service.

• 14309 • **Silvio C. Taormina Memorial Award**
This, NAMF's top award, is given to recognize a management individual who has performed the most outstanding service to the finishing industry, nationally and/or internationally. Nomination deadline is October 26. Awarded at the annual convention when merited.

• 14310 •
National Association of Negro Business and Professional Women's Clubs
Peola Smith-Smith, Pres.
1806 New Hampshire Ave. NW
Washington, DC 20009
Phone: (202)483-4206
Fax: (202)462-7253
E-mail: nanbpwc@aol.com
Home Page: http://www.nanbpwc.org

• 14311 • **Crystal Award**
To recognize a woman who has demonstrated outstanding accomplishment as a producer of goods or services business. The woman must be a business owner.

• 14312 • **National Achievement Award**
For recognition of achievement by a woman. The nominee shall have effectuated the lives of an astounding number of individuals or a group during this time element. Up-to-date date should be documented by recent clippings recognized by individuals and/or groups fully aware of, and/or benefiting from, said accomplishment, individuals should be engaged in same or related endeavor at time of consideration. Material submitted must be typed.

• 14313 • **National Appreciation Award**
For recognition for service to the Association. Members are eligible. Awarded annually at the Convention. Shall be presented to a women who has performed outstanding deeds or services, valuable and/or unselfish deed(s) or act(s) of heroism to The National Association of Negro Business and Professional Women's Clubs, Inc. The nominee whall be achieved for the organization improved conditions which may or may not not be related to the nominee's vocational or professional endeavors. The services and deeds contributed by the nominee shall have an observable impact upon the organization within the recent two years of nomination. All material must be typed and supporting data fully documented.

• 14314 • **National Community Service Award**
To recognize an oustanding woman, non-member, who resides in the city where the convention is held for a contribution to the community. Shall be presented to a women who has performed outstanding deeds or services, valuable and/or unselfish deed(s) or act(s) of heroism. A plaque is awarded annually at the convention. The nominee's deeds, service or heroism shall have affected the lives of a significant number of individuals or groups with these stated causes well known to the community within a recent two year period. The awardee is selected by the hostess club(s): other clubs do not submit nominations. Material must be typed and fully documented.

• 14315 • **National Youth Award**
For recognition of achievement. Outstanding young women under 30 years of who has contributed outstanding community service and/or been actively participating in varied affairs which benefit the needs of other individuals and/or that state. The nominee shall have demonstrated these contributions within the recent two years. Material must be typed.

• 14316 •
National Association of Neonatal Nurses
Brandon Dybala, Admin.
4700 W Lake Ave.
Glenview, IL 60025-1485
Phone: (847)375-3660
Toll-Free: 800-451-3795
Fax: 888-477-6266
E-mail: info@nann.org
Home Page: http://www.nann.org

• 14317 • **Robyn Main Excellence in Clinical Practice Award**
To recognize and encourage excellence in the provision of direct patient care by neonatal nurses. Nominees must be NANN members who provide direct patient care as staff nurses. Selection will be based on the nominee's ability to maintain currency in clinical knowledge; demonstration of expert communication skills; practice models of family-centered care; meticulous attention to details in daily practice; facilitate an interdisciplinary plan of care for patients; act as an excellent role model. A $500 educational stipend, an award, and the Robyn Main sculpture are awarded.

• 14318 • **SIG Leadership Award**
To recognize excellence in leadership, mentorship, and clinical practice of neonatal nurses in advanced practice roles (CNS, NNP, or Manager). Membership in the National Association of Neonatal Nurses and a Specialty Interest Group (SIG) are required. A plaque, $500 cash reward, travel expenses, conference registration, and hotel accommodations at the Association meeting are awarded annually. Established in 1991 by Lynn E. Lynam. Formerly: SIG Excellence in Advanced Practice Award.

• 14319 •
National Association of Pastoral Musicians
Dr. J. Michael McMahon, Pres.
962 Wayne Ave., Ste. 210
Silver Spring, MD 20910-4461
Phone: (240)247-3000
Fax: (240)247-3001
E-mail: npmpres@npm.org
Home Page: http://www.npm.org

• 14320 • **NPM Scholarships**
To assist with the cost of educational formation for pastoral musicians. Members who are enrolled in some form of educational program (degree or continuing education, full- or part-time studies) related to the field of pastoral music are eligible. Recipients should intend to work for at least two years in the field of pastoral music following graduation or program completion. Approximately $30,000 in scholarships is available each year, with individual scholarships ranging from $500 to $4,500. Application deadline is March 3. Established in 1985.

• 14321 •
National Association of Pediatric Nurse Practitioners
Karen Kelly Thomas, Exec.Dir.
20 Brace Rd., Ste. 200
Cherry Hill, NJ 08034-2634
Phone: (856)857-9700
Fax: (856)857-1600
E-mail: info@napnap.org
Home Page: http://www.napnap.org

• 14322 • **Loretta C. Ford Distinguished Fellow Award**
To honor an active member who best exemplifies contributions to the expansion or improvement of pediatric health care and the advancement of the profession of Pediatric Nurse Practitioner at the local community, state, and/or regional level. Nomination deadline is December 30. A plaque and travel expenses to attend the annual conference are awarded annually. Established in 1980.

• 14323 • **Henry K. Silver Memorial Award**
To honor an active member who best exemplifies contributions to the expansion or improvement of pediatric health care and the advancement of the profession of Pediatric Nurse Practitioner at the national and/or international level. Nomination deadline is December 30. Established in 1979 to honor Dr. Henry K. Silver, who was instrumental in establishing the first PNP program.

• 14324 •
National Association of Personal Financial Advisors
Jamie Milne, Chair
3250 N Arlington Heights Rd., Ste. 109
Arlington Heights, IL 60004
Phone: (847)483-5400
Phone: 888-333-6659
Toll-Free: 800-366-2732
Fax: (847)483-5415
E-mail: info@napfa.org
Home Page: http://www.napfa.org

• 14325 • **Distinguished Service Award**
To recognize significant contributions to the advancement of the practice of fee-only financial planning and advising. Awarded annually at the convention. Established in 1989. Formerly: (1989) Financial Planner of the Year.

• 14326 • **Doctoral Awards Program**
To identify and encourage the research of younger scholars in the field of higher education administration. Theses completed and accepted during the year ending June 30 must be submitted by March 31. Two awards are presented: Dr. Leo and Margaret Goodman-Malamuth AAUA Foundation Award and Dr. Donald A. Gatzke AAUA Foundation Award. Awarded annually. The first research awards were presented in 1983.

• 14327 •
National Association of Photo Equipment Technicians
Renee Miastkowski, Pres.
1062 Tower Ln.
Tower Ln. Business Park
Bensenville, IL 60106-1027
Phone: (630)595-2525
Fax: (630)595-2526
Home Page: http://www.pmai.org/sections/napet.htm

• 14328 • **La Croix Award**
For recognition of achievement or contribution to the photo equipment repair industry. Officers of the Association make nominations and the members vote. A trophy is awarded biennially. Established in 1976 in honor of George La Croix.

• 14329 •
National Association of Pipe Coating Applicators
Merritt B. Chastain Jr., Mng.Dir.
AmSouth Bank Bldg.
333 Texas St., Ste. 717
Shreveport, LA 71101-3673
Phone: (318)227-2769
Fax: (318)222-0482
Home Page: http://www.napca.com

• 14330 • **Hall of Fame Award**
For recognition of individuals who have contributed greatly to the advancement of the association and the pipe coating industry. The individual does not have to be a member of the association and may be living or deceased. Awarded annually when merited at the convention upon vote of a special committee. Established in 1972.

• 14331 •
National Association of Printing Ink Manufacturer
James E. Coleman, Exec.Dir.
581 Main St.
Woodbridge, NJ 07095-1104
Phone: (732)855-1525
Fax: (732)855-1838
E-mail: napim@napim.org
Home Page: http://www.napim.org

• 14332 • **Ault Award**
This, the highest award the industry bestows on its peers, is given to recognize outstanding contributions to the progress of the printing ink industry through science and technology. Nominations must be made by ink manufacturers of the United States or Canada. A bronze medallion and an engraved plaque are awarded annually. Established in 1954 in memory of L.A. Ault, an early leader in the industry and a founder of the Ault and Wiborg Company.

• 14333 • **Printing Ink Pioneer Award**
To recognize long-term members of the industry who have faithfully served their companies and the association for many years. NAPIM members are eligible. An engraved plaque is awarded. Established in 1956.

• 14334 • Technical Achievement Award
To recognize and honor an ink maker who has made an outstanding technical contribution to the printing ink industry. Technical achievement in the form of research, development, or other technology in any segment of the ink industry is the predominant characteristic sought in determining eligibility. Individuals who have served in the industry for a minimum of 15 years may be nominated. An engraved plaque and an engraved medallion are awarded annually. Established in 1982.

• 14335 • Technical Associate Member Service Award
To recognize and honor an outstanding individual who, as a supplier to the printing ink industry, has played a major role in the progress of printing ink technology. Established in 1995.

• 14336 •
National Association of Produce Market Managers
James Farr, Sec.
PO Box 291284
Columbia, SC 29229
Phone: (404)675-1782
Fax: (404)362-4564
E-mail: sbrannon@mfcq.state.md.us
Home Page: http://www.napmm.com

• 14337 • Market Manager of the Year
To recognize a market manager for outstanding performance in his job and for substantial contributions to the growth of the fresh fruit and vegetable movement throughout the market. A plaque is awarded annually. Established in 1954.

• 14338 •
National Association of Professional Baseball Leagues
Mike Moore, Pres./CEO
PO Box A
St. Petersburg, FL 33731
Phone: (727)822-6937
Fax: (727)821-5819
E-mail: admin@minorleaguebaseball.com
Home Page: http://www.minorleaguebaseball.com

• 14339 • John H. Johnson President's Trophy
To honor the pro baseball team that is run as a top notch business operation. Any club that is a member of NAPBL is eligible. A trophy is awarded annually. Established in 1974.

• 14340 • League Executive of the Year Awards
To recognize the most outstanding overall job of minor league club operation. Club operators in each minor league are eligible. A trophy is awarded annually. Established in 1964.

• 14341 • Larry MacPhail Trophy
To recognize outstanding achievements in the promotion of a minor league baseball team. Clubs in all of the minor leagues are eligible. A trophy is awarded annually. Established in 1959.

• 14342 •
National Association of Professional Insurance Agents
400 N Washington St.
Alexandria, VA 22314
Phone: (703)836-9340
Fax: (703)836-1279
E-mail: piaweb@pianet.org
Home Page: http://www.pianet.com

• 14343 • Company Award of Excellence
To honor companies for their commitment to the Association, to the American Agency System, and to furthering the interests of and creating a better business environment for professional independent insurance agents. Nominations are accepted from companies and PIA member-agents. Award is presented annually at a special presentation held in conjunction with the annual convention.

• 14344 • Company Representative of the Year
To honor an insurance company representative for outstanding contributions to the progress of his or her company, community, and the insurance industry. Awarded annually at a special awards presentation. Established in 1957.

• 14345 • Professional Agent of the Year
To honor an outstanding PIA agent who has contributed greatly toward the progress of his or her association, community, and the insurance industry in general. Insurance agents who are also members of the association are eligible. The title "Agent of the Year" is bestowed upon the honorees by the respective state or regional Association. A trophy is awarded to the national winner and certificates to state/regional winners during a special awards ceremony at the annual convention. Established in 1957.

• 14346 •
National Association of Professional Organizers
Louise S. Miller, Exec.Dir.
4700 W Lake Ave.
Glenview, IL 60025
Phone: (847)375-4746
Fax: (770)263-8825
E-mail: hq@napo.net
Home Page: http://www.napo.net

• 14347 • Organizing Excellence Award
For recognition of achievement and contribution to the field of professional organizing, and for contributions to NAPO. Awards are presented in four categories: (1) Business; (2) Education; (3) Home and Family; and (4) Profession. A trophy or plaque is awarded at the annual convention. Established in 1987.

• 14348 •
National Association of Railroad Passengers
Ross B. Capon, Exec.Dir.
900-2nd St. NE, Ste. 308
Washington, DC 20002
Phone: (202)408-8362
Fax: (202)408-8287
E-mail: narp@narprail.org
Home Page: http://www.narprail.org

• 14349 • Dr. Gary Burch Memorial Safety Award
To recognize the railroad employee who has done the most to improve the overall safety of railroad passengers. Any railroad employee nominated by his/her employer is eligible. A monetary award of $1,000 plus a plaque is presented annually. Established in 1994 in memory of Dr. Gary Burch.

• 14350 • George Falcon Golden Spike Award
To recognize celebrities, elected officials and other individuals who have made important contributions to the rail passenger cause. A golden spike mounted on a wooden plaque with a brass inscription plate is awarded annually. Established in 1965 by George Falcon, publisher of *Key* magazine, and an active early member of the Association.

• 14351 •
National Association of Real Estate Editors
Mary Doyle-Kimball, Exec.Dir.
1003 NW, 6th Terr.
Boca Raton, FL 33486
Phone: (561)391-3599
Fax: (561)391-0099
E-mail: madkimba@aol.com
Home Page: http://www.naree.org

• 14352 • Real Estate Journalism Competition
To recognize individuals for excellence in reporting on housing and real estate. All full-time print and broadcast journalists are eligible. Awards are presented in 11 individual entry categories and 9 team/group entry categories. Entries are judged on clarity of writing, objectivity, originality, depth of reporting, and design, if applicable. First place category winners each receive a monetary award of $250. Additionally, the Best Overall Entry by an Individual receives a cash award of $1,250, and the recipient of the James D. Carper Award for Best Entry by a Young Journalist receives a cash award of $250. Awarded annually at the November business meeting. Nomination deadline is February 5. Established in 1949.

• 14353 •
National Association of Realtors
Terrence M. McDermott, Exec.VP
430 N Michigan Ave.
Chicago, IL 60611
Toll-Free: 800-874-6500
Fax: (312)329-5960
E-mail: infocentral@realtors.org
Home Page: http://www.realtor.org

• 14354 • **Distinguished Service Award**
To honor Realtors who have been recognized as local leaders and whose involvement in political and community activities have been extraordinary for at least 25 years. The person may not have served as president of the Association. An engraved statuette, plaque, and jeweled lapel pin are awarded annually. Nomination deadline is February 16. Established in 1979.

• 14355 • **Realtor of the Year**
For recognition of the most successful Realtor in each of the 50 United States, the District of Columbia, Puerto Rico, the Virgin Islands, and Guam. Awarded annually and honored at the national convention of the Association.

• 14356 •
National Association of Recording Merchandisers
Jim Donio, Pres.
9 Eves Dr., Ste. 120
Marlton, NJ 08053
Phone: (856)596-2221
Fax: (856)596-3268
E-mail: donio@narm.com
Home Page: http://www.narm.com

• 14357 • **Advertising and Marketing Awards**
To recognize excellence in all forms of industry advertising and marketing. NARM member retailers, wholesalers, and entertainment software suppliers are eligible for outstanding achievements in newspaper, magazine, radio, and television advertising; website and e-mail promotions; direct mail pieces; point-of-purchase materials; special media; and overall advertising and marketing campaigns. Plaques are awarded annually at the convention. Established in 1980.

• 14358 • **Best Seller Awards**
For recognition by the industry of actual over-the-counter sales to the consumer of records and pre-recorded tapes. Nominations may be made by NARM regular members for the best selling product in the calendar year beginning January 1 and ending December 31. The deadline for ballots is February 1. Awards are given in the following categories: (1) Best Selling Single (45 RPM); (2) Best Selling Single (12 inch); (3) Best Selling Movie or TV Soundtrack; (4) Best Selling Original Cast Album; (5) Best Selling Country Album by a Male Artist; (6) Best Selling Country Album by a Female Artist; (7) Best Selling Country Album by a Group; (8) Best Selling Black Music Album by a Male Artist; (9) Best Selling Black Music Album by a Female Artist; (10) Best Selling Black Music Album by a Group; (11) Best Selling Jazz Album; (12) Best Selling Gospel/Spiritual Album; (13) Best Selling Classical Album; (14) Best Selling Children's Product; (15) Best Selling Album by a Female Artist; (16) Best Selling Album by a Male Artist; (17) Best Selling Album by a Group; (18) Best Selling Album; (19) Best Selling Album by a New Artist; (20) Best Selling Foreign Language Album; (21) Best Selling Videocassette merchandised as Music Video; (22) Best Selling Comedy Album; and (23) Best Selling Rap Album. Plaques are awarded annually at the convention. Formerly: Gift of Music Best Seller Awards.

• 14359 • **Harry Chapin Memorial Humanitarian Award**
To recognize efforts by the music industry and its members to enrich and improve the quality of life around the world. An individual(s) whose primary field of endeavor is within the music industry and whose efforts are deemed to have met the awards purpose is eligible for consideration. A plaque is awarded when merited. Established in 1983 in memory of Harry Chapin. Formerly: (1983) Humanitarian Award.

• 14360 • **Display Contest**
To recognize individuals from retail record stores for photos of windows or in-store displays using NARM merchandising materials. The following contests are held: (1) Grammy Awards Show Display Contest; (2) Country Music Association Awards Show Display Contest; and (3) American Music Awards Display Contest. Monetary awards are presented.

• 14361 • **Mickey Granberg Award**
To recognize individuals for outstanding contributions to the independent distribution network. Awarded when merited. Established in 1987 and named for Mickey Granberg, NARM Executive Vice President.

• 14362 • **Independent Distributors Best Seller Awards - Indie Best Sellers**
For recognition by the industry of best sellers through independent distributors. Nominees are based o the ballot of the NARM Independent Distributors Advisory Committee; and winners are selected from the votes of the NARM Regular Members, based on their sales between July 1 and June 30. Awards are presented in the following categories: (1) Best Selling Single - (7 inch); (2) Best Selling Single - (12 inch); (3) Best Selling Catalog; (4) Best Selling New Artist; and (5) Best Selling Album. Established in 1986.

• 14363 • **Music Educator of the Year Award**
No further information was available for this edition.

• 14364 • **Presidential Award**
For recognition of sustained creative achievement in and contribution to the field of music. The President of the Association sets the criteria for the award. A plaque is awarded when merited at the annual convention. Established in 1964.

• 14365 • **Retailer of the Year Award**
For recognition of retailing excellence. Retailers who are members of NARM are eligible. The following criteria are considered: (1) artist development; awareness of new product; (2) cooperation with manufacturers/distributors regarding merchandising programs; (3) communication with all levels of manufacturer/distributor; (4) fiscal responsibility; (5) merchandising tie-ins with national TV shows; (6) overall creative merchandising; (7) proper training and quality of personnel; (8) retail advertising and in-store tie-ins; and (9) tour awareness and support. Members of the Manufacturing Advisory Council make the selection. Awards are given in two categories: (1) small retailer - 1 to 15 stores; and (2) large retailer - 16 or more stores. A gold punch bowl is awarded annually at the convention. Established in 1973. Formerly: (1988) Merchandiser of the Year Award.

• 14366 • **Wholesaler of the Year Award**
To recognize a wholesaler for: (1) communication with all levels of manufacturers/distributors; (2) cooperation with all manufacturers/distributors re merchandising programs and contests; (3) fiscal responsibility; (4) maximization of advertising and tie-in with in-store display; (5) maximization of best sellers and key catalogue; (6) merchandising tie-in with national TV shows, major motion pictures and/or special events; (7) overall creative merchandising and marketing; (8) proper training and quality of personnel; (9) tour awareness and support; and (10) willingness to stock, promote, advertise and merchandise not only the hits, but to act early on product that makes sense for a particular market, e.g., Country, Black. Established in 1985.

• 14367 •
National Association of Rocketry
Mark Bundick, Pres.
PO Box 177
Altoona, WI 54720
Phone: (715)832-1946
Toll-Free: 800-262-4872
Fax: (715)832-6432
E-mail: nar-hq@nar.org
Home Page: http://www.nar.org

Formerly: (1958) Model Missiles Association.

• 14368 • **H. Galloway Spacemodeling Service Award**
To recognize an individual(s) who has made a significant contribution to the hobby of spacemodeling (model rocketry). Nominations must be made in writing by an adult member of the National Association of Rocketry by July 15. A framed aerospace photograph (e.g., Space Shuttle) with an engraved gold card is presented annually during the U.S. Spacemodeling Championships. Established in 1978 in honor of Howard Galloway, a longtime beloved member of the Association. Co-sponsored by Rockwell International, Downey, CA.

• 14369 •
National Association of Scholars
Stephen H. Balch, Pres.
221 Witherspoon St., 2nd Fl.
Princeton, NJ 08542-3215
Phone: (609)683-7878
Fax: (609)683-0316
E-mail: nasonweb@nas.org
Home Page: http://www.nas.org

• 14370 • **Barry R. Gross Memorial Award**
To recognize an NAS member for outstanding service to the cause of academic reform. A monetary award of $1,000, a plaque and travel expenses to attend the national conference and present a speech are awarded. Established in 1996 to honor the memory of Barry R. Gross, who was NAS National Program Officer and Treasurer.

• 14371 • **Sidney Hook Memorial Award**
The Sidney Hook Memorial Award is granted to an individual for distinguished contributions to the defense of academic freedom and the integrity of academic life. A monetary award of $2,500, a plaque, and travel expenses to attend the national conference and present a speech are awarded. Established in 1989 to honor the memory of Dr. Sidney Hook.

• 14372 • **Peter Shaw Memorial Award**
To recognize exemplary writing on issues pertaining to higher education and American intellectual culture. A monetary award of $1,000, a plaque and travel expenses to attend the national conference and present a speech are awarded. Established to honor the memory of Peter Shaw who was editor of *Academic Questions* and National Chairman of the NAS.

• 14373 •
National Association of Schools of Public Affairs and Administration
Laurel McFarland, Exec.Dir.
1120 G St. NW, Ste. 730
Washington, DC 20005
Phone: (202)628-8965
Fax: (202)626-4978
E-mail: naspaa@naspaa.org
Home Page: http://www.naspaa.org

• 14374 • **ASPA/NASPAA Distinguished Research Award**
To recognize the research of an individual whose published work has had a substantial impact on the thought and understanding of public administration. (It is not intended to honor lifetime contributions to the field or a recent book.) The nominee must be living, but need not be an ASPA member. Nominations must be submitted by June 30th. A monetary award of $500 and a plaque are presented at the annual conference in October. Awarded jointly with the American Society for Public Administration.

• 14375 • **NASPAA Annual Dissertation Award**
To recognize significant research in the field of public administration and public affairs. Dissertations written during the previous year by students at NASPAA member institutions must be submitted by June 30. A monetary award of $500, plus $250 travel allowance, and a plaque are awarded at the annual conference in October. Established in 1981.

• 14376 • **Elmer B. Staats Public Service Career Awards**
To recognize faculty who inspire students to pursue a public service career, and to publicize public service careers and methods of encouraging student interest and participation. Any faculty member in a NASPAA member program with at least one year of teaching experience is eligible. Candidates may be nominated by any individual who is a student, graduate, faculty, colleague, or employer of program graduates. The deadline is June 30. A monetary award of $1,000 and a plaque are presented at the annual conference in October of odd years.

• 14377 • **Leslie A. Whittington Excellence in Teaching Award**
To recognize faculty at NASPAA's institutions who make outstanding contributions to education for public service over a sustained period of time. Nominees must have demonstrated excellence in teaching and sustained contributions to education for public service, such as content and presentation of courses and quality of advising impact of faculty on students and their public service careers. The deadline for entry is June 30. A monetary award of $500 and a plaque are presented at the annual NASPAA conference in October.

• 14378 • **Alfred M. Zuck Public Courage Award**
To affirm NASPAA's commitment to and respect for bold and unselfish acts to advance the public interest. The NASPAA public courage award will be presented to a graduate of a NASPAA program who has made important contributions in public service to advance the public enterprise at the cost of significant risk to personal advancement. Recipients should be practitioners who have shown courage whether or not they have achieved notable success in customary career recognition terms. The award of $500 and a plaque will be presented at the October NASPAA Annual Conference in even-numbered years. Formerly: NASPAA Public Courage Award.

• 14379 •
National Association of Science Writers
Diane McGurgan, Exec.Dir.
PO Box 890
Hedgesville, WV 25427
Phone: (304)754-5077
Fax: (304)754-5076
E-mail: diane@nasw.org
Home Page: http://www.nasw.org

• 14380 • **Science-in-Society Journalism Awards**
To honor and encourage outstanding investigative and interpretive reporting about the sciences and their impact on the quality of life, both good and bad. Emphasis is placed on the kind of critical, probing article that would otherwise not receive an award from an interest group. Awards are given in five categories: newspapers, magazines, broadcasting, books, and websites. Material must be presented in English, intended for the lay person, and first broadcast or published in North America. Entries must be postmarked by February 1. Monetary prizes of $1,000 and certificates of recognition are awarded annually in each category. Publishers/broadcasters of winning entries also receive certificates of recognition. Established in 1972.

• 14381 •
National Association of Scientific Materials Managers
Joanne Brown CSMM, Pres.
Wabash College
Chemistry Department
301 W Wabash Ave.
Crawfordsville, IN 47933
E-mail: barkerp@wabash.edu
Home Page: http://www.naosmm.org

• 14382 • **Outstanding Scientific Materials Managers Award**
To recognize achievement in the advancement of the profession through distinguished operational, educational, or administrative activity, and participation in NAOSMM meeting programs or service on NAOSMM's board or committees. Members of the Association are eligible and may be nominated by a committee, an immediate supervisor, administrator, or other members. A monetary award of $50 and a plaque are awarded annually at the National Conference and Trade Show. Established in 1983. Additional information is available from Kevin Mautte, President.

• 14383 •
National Association of Secondary School Principals
Dr. Gerald N. Tirozzi, Exec.Dir.
1904 Association Dr.
Reston, VA 20191-1537
Phone: (703)860-0200
Toll-Free: 800-253-7746
Fax: (703)476-5432
Home Page: http://www.principals.org

• 14384 • **Benjamin Fine Awards**
For recognition of balanced professional reporting that: (1) explains complex educational issues leading to a better public understanding of education; (2) describes ways in which individuals and community organizations can effectively work with schools to increase educational opportunities for students; (3) examines effective educational offerings in schools and school districts; and (4) discusses significant trends in school and community relationships. Awards are presented in the four areas of: single article, editorial column, series, and supplement in each

of the following five categories: (1) magazines; (2) non-daily newspapers of any circulation; (3) daily newspapers with a circulation of 100,000 or fewer; (4) daily newspapers with a circulation of 100,001 or above (and articles by wire service reporters); and (5) education trade publications. Professional newspaper and magazine reporters and editors are eligible. Nominations may be made by NASSP members, the news media, the general public, or oneself. Only professionally-produced publications are eligible to be nominated. A monetary award of $1,500 and a plaque are presented to the Grand Prize winner. Plaques for winners and certificates for honorable mention are also awarded annually at the convention. Established in 1981 to honor Benjamin Fine, former education editor, *The New York Times.*

• 14385 • National Honor Society Scholarship Program
To provide recognition for 200 high school seniors who are members of National Honor Societies. The award is based on scholarship, leadership, service, and character. Scholarships of $1,000 s presented annually to each winning student. Nomination deadline is January 21. Established in 1946.

• 14386 • Principal's Leadership Award
To recognize student leaders from the senior class. Nominees are selected on the basis of their leadership skills, participation in service organizations and clubs, achievements in the arts and sciences, employment experience, and academic record. Scholarships of $1,000 are awarded to 100 outstanding seniors from all 50 states, the District of Columbia, and Puerto Rico. Nomination forms are mailed to all high school principals; nomination deadline is December 2. Established in 1987. Sponsored by Herff Jones, Inc., and administered by the NASSP Division of Student Activities.

• 14387 •
National Association of Social Workers
Elvira Craig de Silva ACSW, Pres.
750 First St. NE, Ste. 700
Washington, DC 20002-4241
Phone: (202)408-8600
Toll-Free: 800-638-8799
Fax: (202)336-8313
E-mail: info@naswdc.org
Home Page: http://www.naswdc.org

• 14388 • Knee/Whitman Lifetime Achievement Award
To recognize a member who has contributed to the profession of social work. This person will be a role model of leadership and dedication to social work, having a history of significant contribution to the profession through direct service, social work administration, or through teaching, writing, lecturing, etc. A plaque and an expense-paid trip to receive the award at the conference are presented annually. Established in 1988.

• 14389 • National Public Citizen of the Year
To honor an outstanding member of the community - who is not a social worker - whose accomplishments exemplify the values and mission of professional social work. The recipient must make a significant contribution to an area of concern to the social work profession, act with courage, demonstrate outstanding leadership, and exemplify social work values and ethics. A plaque is awarded annually. Established in 1973.

• 14390 • National Social Worker of the Year
To honor a member who exemplifies the best of the profession's values and achievements through specific accomplishments. The recipient must be a member of the Association, make a demonstrable difference to an area of concern to the social work profession, demonstrate outstanding leadership, contribute to a positive image for the profession, and act with courage. A plaque is awarded annually. Established in 1968 in memory of Howard F. Gustafson, former President of the Association.

• 14391 • President's Award
To recognize individuals, groups, or organizations whose contributions to society or the social work profession are deemed outstanding and are in consonance with the priorities of the Association. The NASW President makes a single selection during any calendar year subject to approval by the Board of Directors. The award need not be made annually. Established in 1988.

• 14392 •
National Association of Social Workers, Kansas Chapter
Jayhawk Towers
700 SW Jackson St., Ste. 801
Topeka, KS 66603-3740
Phone: (785)354-4804
Toll-Free: 800-776-4806
Fax: (785)354-1456
E-mail: knasw@birch.net
Home Page: http://www.knasw.com

• 14393 • Social Worker of the Year; Public Citizen of the Year
For exemplary work toward improving people's well-being. Recognition award bestowed annually.

• 14394 •
National Association of State Chief Information Officers
Mr. Doug Robinson, Exec.Dir.
201 E Main St., Ste. 1405
Lexington, KY 40507
Phone: (859)514-9153
Fax: (859)514-9166
E-mail: nascio@amrms.com
Home Page: http://www.nascio.org

Formerly: (2002) National Association of State Information Resource Executives.

• 14395 • NASIRE Recognition Awards for Outstanding Achievement in the Field of Information Technology
To recognize systems, programs, services, or procedures that have made an important contribution to the operation of state government. Members are eligible. Plaques are awarded at the annual meeting. Formerly known as State Achievement Awards.

• 14396 •
National Association of State Procurement Officials
Matthew Trail, Associate Dir.
201 E Main St., Ste. 1405
Lexington, KY 40507
Phone: (859)514-9159
Phone: (606)231-1963
Fax: (859)514-9188
E-mail: lpope@amrinc.net
Home Page: http://www.naspo.org

Formerly: (1998) National Association of State Purchasing Officials.

• 14397 • Cronin Club Award
For recognition of outstanding cost cutting initiatives in state purchasing. Any of the 50 states' purchasing agencies is eligible. A plaque is awarded annually to the first-, second-, and third-place winners. Established in 1985 and named for by George Cronin, the first NASPO president.

• 14398 •
National Association of State Units on Aging
Daniel A. Quirk PhD, Exec.Dir.
1201 15th St. NW, Ste. 350
Washington, DC 20005
Phone: (202)898-2578
Toll-Free: 800-677-1116
Fax: (202)898-2583
E-mail: dquirk@nasua.org
Home Page: http://www.nasua.org

• 14399 • Louise B. Gerrard Award
To recognize the meritorious contributions of individuals committed to enhancing the quality of life of rural older Americans through improvements in policy, planning, advocacy, or services. Practitioners, researchers, educators, service providers, administrators, or public officials at the Federal, state, or local levels whose exemplary efforts reflect improvement in the lives of the rural elderly are eligible. Established in 1980 in honor of Louise B. Gerrard, former Executive Director for the West Virginia Commission on Aging, whose pioneering efforts in the development of the Aging Network have impacted the lives of millions of older Americans, especially rural older persons.

• 14400 •
National Association of Store Fixture Manufacturer
Klein Merriman, Exec.Dir.
3595 Sheridan St., Ste. 200
Hollywood, FL 33021
Phone: (954)893-7300
Fax: (954)893-7500
E-mail: nasfm@nasfm.org
Home Page: http://www.nasfm.org

Formerly: SID Award (Store Interior Design Award).

• 14401 • Retail Design Awards
To encourage interest in and understanding of the profession of store design, individual, and store fixture design, and to give proper recognition to individuals and organizations for making outstanding contributions to the profession. Designers, retailers, and store fixture manufacturers are eligible. Crystal awards are presented during NASFM's Awards Reception held in conjunction with GlobalShop. Formerly: SID Award (Store Interior Design Award).

• 14402 •
National Association of Student Personnel Administrators
Gwendolyn Jordan Dungy, Exec.Dir.
1875 Connecticut Ave. NW, Ste. 418
Washington, DC 20009
Phone: (202)265-7500
Fax: (202)797-1157
E-mail: office@naspa.org
Home Page: http://www.naspa.org

• 14403 • Scott Goodnight Award for Outstanding Performance as a Dean
To recognize deans who have demonstrated the following: sustained professional service in student affairs work; high-level competency in administrative skills; merited stature among and support of students, faculty, and fellow administrators on their campuses; innovative response in meeting varied and emerging needs of students; effectiveness in the development of junior staff members; and significant contributions to the field through publications of professional involvement and leadership in community and university affairs. Nominations may be made by individual NASPA members. In addition, each region may make a recommendation to the Awards Committee through the regional vice president. Application deadline is November 1. Established in 1965.

• 14404 • Melvene D. Hardee Dissertation of the Year Award
To encourage high-quality research relevant to the field of college student affairs administration. It is awarded to an outstanding doctoral student in, or intending to enter, student affairs work. Nominees must have completed their dissertations and had their degrees conferred no more than 12 months prior. Nominees must submit a completed application form, a release form signed by a professor, and an abstract of the dissertation by September 16. Established in 1977 and renamed in 1986 in honor of Melvene D. Hardee, professor emerita at Florida State University.

• 14405 • Outstanding Contribution to Higher Education Award
For recognition of individuals who have rendered service with national impact in programs, policies, or research, and who have made a contribution to the broad reach of higher education. Current board members of NASPA are not eligible. Nomination deadline is November 1. Established in 1969.

• 14406 • Outstanding Contribution to Literature or Research Award
To recognize individuals who have demonstrated professional commitment to student affairs administration. Their publication, research, and/or literature are judged by how well it is utilized by practicing student affairs administrators. The materials should be applicable to national use and not restricted to local or regional application. The deadline for nominations is November 1. Established in 1968.

• 14407 • Regional Awards
Each of the seven regions of the national Association has its own procedures for nominating and selecting its award recipients. Regional award recipients are recognized at such regional events as the regional conference or regional business meetings.

• 14408 • Robert H. Shaffer Award for Academic Excellence as a Graduate Faculty Member
To recognize tenured faculty members who are teaching full-time in a graduate preparation programs in student affairs. Nominees must be a personal inspiration to graduate students, have served on doctoral committees, have made significant contributions to professional associations, and have distinguished records of scholarly achievement, including publication in relevant literature. Nomination deadline is November 1. Established in 1986 to honor the contributions of Robert H. Shaffer, dean and professor emeritus at Indiana University.

• 14409 • Fred Turner Award for Outstanding Service to NASPA
To recognize members who have demonstrated continuous NASPA membership for 10 years or more and who have served in a leadership role at the state, regional, or national levels of NASPA. Nomination deadline is November 1. Established in 1972 in honor of Fred Turner, one of NASPA's most distinguished past presidents.

• 14410 •
National Association of Teachers of Singing
Dr. William A. Vessels, Exec.Dir.
4745 Sutton Park Ct., Ste. 201
Jacksonville, FL 32224
Phone: (904)992-9101
Fax: (904)992-9326
E-mail: info@nats.org
Home Page: http://www.nats.org

• 14411 • Artist Awards
To select young singers whose artistry fits them to embark on professional careers, and to encourage these young artists to carry on the tradition of fine singing as professional artists. Recipients must be between the ages of 21 to 35 and must have studied for at least one year with a teacher who is a member of the Association. The following monetary prizes are awarded: (1) First place awards totaling $10,000; (2) Second place $4,000; (3) $17,500 in other foundation awards. Awarded at the national convention held every 2 years. Established in 1955. Inquire for application details.

• 14412 •
National Association of Television Program Executives
Rick Feldman, Pres./CEO
5757 Wilshire Blvd., Penthouse 10
Los Angeles, CA 90036-3681
Phone: (310)453-4440
Fax: (310)453-5258
E-mail: info@natpe.org
Home Page: http://www.natpe.org

• 14413 • Creative Achievement Award
To honor an individual who has exhibited a lifetime of distinguished achievement in television. Presented when merited. Established in 1965. Formerly: (1999) Lifetime Achievement Award.

• 14414 •
National Association of the Holy Name Society
Richard Wieand, Pres.
PO Box 12012
Baltimore, MD 21281-2012
Phone: (410)325-1524
Toll-Free: (866)624-6711
Fax: (410)325-1524
E-mail: nahns@juno.com
Home Page: http://www.holynamesociety.info

• 14415 • Distinguished Service Award
To recognize distinguished service by a lay person or clerical member. Established in 1977.

• 14416 • Louis C. Fink Literary Award
To recognize outstanding newsletter publication expressing/advertising the ideals of the Holy Name Society. Established in 1988.

• 14417 • Humanitarian Award
To recognize distinguished service by a lay person or clerical member. Established in 1985

• 14418 • Keystone Award
To recognize a parish unit being a keystone of the holy name movement. Established in 1999.

• 14419 • Father McKenna Award
To recognize a member of the clergy for distinguished service to Holy Name. An inscribed plaque is awarded biennially. Established in 1950 to honor Father McKenna, an early suc-

cessful Dominican preacher for Holy Name in the United States.

• 14420 • Medallion Circle Award
To honor ecclesiastics and lay members who have singularly contributed to the enrichment of the Holy Name Society. Established in 1963.

• 14421 • Presidential Award
To recognize an individual for efforts to promote reverence for the Name of God. Selected by the President of the Society. A citation is awarded biennially. Established in 1986.

• 14422 • Shield of Blessed Gregory X Crusader
To recognize a member of the hierarchy for efforts to promote reverence for the Name of God. An inscribed plaque is awarded biennially. Established in 1930.

• 14423 • Vercelli Medal
To recognize a lay member, active on the national diocesan, for outstanding service. A gold medal is awarded biennially. Established in 1947 in memory of the founder of the Holy Name Society (in 1274) as a confraternity of the Roman Catholic Church.

• 14424 •
National Association of the Physically Handicapped
Bernadette Travis, Pres.
1375 Dewitt Dr.
Akron, OH 44313
Phone: (330)724-1994
Phone: (330)724-1994
Toll-Free: 800-743-5008
E-mail: trumanjm@aol.com
Home Page: http://www.naph.net

• 14425 • Certificate of Merit
To recognize outstanding service to the physically handicapped through efforts to advance the social, economic, and physical welfare of handicapped persons. Employers and other groups showing an interest in members of the Association are eligible. Engraved certificates are awarded during National Employ the Physically Handicapped Week each year. Established in 1961.

• 14426 • NAPH Medallion
To recognize outstanding service to the physically handicapped. Members of the Association are eligible. An engraved gold medal is awarded annually at the National Convention. Established in 1961.

• 14427 •
National Association of the Remodeling Industry
Gwen Biasi, Dir. of Marketing
780 Lee St., Ste. 200
Des Plaines, IL 60016
Phone: (847)298-9200
Toll-Free: 800-611-NARI
Fax: (847)298-9225
E-mail: info@nari.org
Home Page: http://www.nari.org

Formed by merger of: National Home Improvement Council; National Remodeling Association.

• 14428 • Certified Remodeler (CR) "Superstar" Award
To recognize those who have demonstrated outstanding use of, promotion, and/or support for the NARI Certification Program. Up to three awards are presented. No entry fee required. Entry deadline is December 1.

• 14429 • Contractor of the Year Awards (CotY Awards)
In recognition of excellent workmanship and professional achievements. CotY Awards are given in 26 categories based on project size and function. Only NARI contractor members are eligible. All entries are judged on problem solving, functionality, aesthetics, craftsmanship, innovation, degree of difficulty, and entry presentation. A project may be entered in one category only. Winners are announced at the Evening of Excellence awards event each year. Entry deadline is December 2. Established in 1942.

• 14430 • Distributor of the Year Award
To recognize distributors who have demonstrated a strong commitment to NARI, the professional remodeling industry, and the community or communities in which they do business. Entry deadline is December 1. Awarded annually.

• 14431 • Excellence in Advertising Awards
To recognize the best print and broadcast advertisements. A total of four awards are given: Advertising/Print (gross sales volume under $1 million), Advertising/Print (gross sales volume $1 million or over), Advertising/Broadcast (gross sales volume under $1 million), and Advertising/Broadcast (gross sales volume $1 million and over). No entry fee required. Entry deadline is December 1.

• 14432 • Henry Fenderbosch Leadership Award
To recognize past and present NARI members for meritorious service to NARI and the remodeling industry. Individuals who have shown exceptional leadership, devotion, dedication, and accomplishment on behalf of NARI on the national level may be nominated by December 2. Established in 1986 in honor of the late Henry Fenderbosch, NARI president and chairman of the board.

• 14433 • Government Affairs Award
To recognize members who have demonstrated active involvement in either promoting NARI-sponsored and/or have supported legislation or defeating legislation detrimental to the professional remodeling industry. Entrants may be active on any or all levels of government affairs including federal, state, county, and city. Entry deadline is December 1. Awarded annually.

• 14434 • Harold Hammerman Spirit of Education Award
To recognize excellence in training and education in the construction industry. Any individual whose work is related to the remodeling and building industries and who can demonstrate that he or she has training and educated others, whether it be for a profit business or a nonprofit program in the industry, is eligible. Individuals are judged based on their excellence in the training and educating of others in the following categories: advertising, design, specification and contract writing, building codes, sales training, estimating, production methods, management, public relations, legislation, and financing. Entry deadline is December 2. Established in 1978 by Harold Hammerman.

• 14435 • Peter H. Johnson Image Award
To recognize a member company that has promoted the image of the professional remodeling industry through civic or charitable projects, public relations efforts, legislative activities, etc. Entry deadline is December 1. Awarded annually.

• 14436 • Local Chapter Community Project Award
To recognize a chapter for work done as a community project to enhance the community and increase awareness of NARI, both locally and nationally. Entry deadline is December 1. Awarded annually.

• 14437 • Local Chapter Excellence Award
To recognize a chapter for work done, other than a specific community project, that impacted the community in a positive manner and enhanced the consumer awareness of NARI, both in the local community and nationally. Entry deadline is December 1. Awarded annually.

• 14438 • Local Chapter President Award
To recognize a local chapter president who has demonstrated outstanding leadership in the broad range of service to his or her chapter. Entry deadline is December 1. Awarded annually.

• 14439 • Professionalism Award
To recognize nonpaid NARI members who have shown exceptional leadership, devotion, dedication, and accomplishment through their efforts to promote NARI as a professional organization at the local level. Entry deadline is December 1. Awarded annually.

• 14440 •
National Association of Theatre Owners
MaryAnn Anderson, VP/Exec.Dir.
750 First St. NE, Ste. 1130
Washington, DC 20002
Phone: (202)962-0054
Fax: (202)962-0370
E-mail: nato@natodc.com
Home Page: http://www.natoonline.org

• 14441 • **NATO Awards**
To recognize outstanding stars, producers, directors, screen writers and other individuals connected with the film industry. Awards are presented annually in the following categories: Stars of the Year (male/female), Screen Writer of the year; Male/Female Stars of Tomorrow; Director of the Year; and Producer of the Year. Trophies are awarded annually at the Convention. In addition, other awards for special merit or longstanding achievement are awarded when merited. Established in 1954.

• 14442 •
National Association of Towns and Townships
Allen R. Frischkorn Jr., Exec.Dir.
444 N Capitol St. NW, Ste. 397
Washington, DC 20001-1202
Phone: (202)624-3550
Phone: (202)624-3553
Fax: (202)624-3554
E-mail: natat@sso.org
Home Page: http://www.natat.org/natat

• 14443 • **American Community Leadership Award**
To recognize town, township, or small community officials whose community service exhibits the highest standards of dedication, ability, creativity and leadership. Local officials currently in office may be nominated by June 15. A $10,000 grand prize; 100-$5,000 prizes and/up to 350-$1,000 prizes. Formerly: (1990) Dave Durenberger Grassroots Government Leadership Award; Grassroots Government Leadership Award.

• 14444 •
National Association of Towns and Townships
National Center for Small Communities
Allen R. Frischkorn Jr., Exec.Dir.
444 N Capitol St. NW, Ste. 397
Washington, DC 20001-1202
Phone: (202)624-3550
Phone: (202)624-3553
Fax: (202)624-3554
E-mail: natat@sso.org
Home Page: http://www.natat.org/natat

• 14445 • **Small Town America Hall of Fame**
To recognize and honor individuals, corporations, and foundations who have achieved special prominence or who have distinguished themselves in the small town America arena. A plaque is awarded periodically. Established in 1987.

• 14446 •
National Association of Traveling Nurses
L. David Stoller, Chm.
PO Box 35215
Chicago, IL 60707-0215
Phone: (708)453-0080
Fax: (708)453-0083
E-mail: natn@rentamark.com
Home Page: http://www.travelingnurse.org

• 14447 • **Nurse of the Year**
To recognize the traveling nurse. Awarded annually with a plaque. Established in 1970.

• 14448 •
National Association of Underwater Instructors
Jim Bram, Pres.
1232 Tech Blvd.
PO Box 89789
Tampa, FL 33619-7832
Phone: (813)628-6284
Toll-Free: 800-553-6284
Fax: (813)628-8253
E-mail: nauihq@nauiww.org
Home Page: http://www.naui.org

• 14449 • **Dr. Charlie Brown Memorial Award**
To recognize individuals for voluntary contributions or service toward sport diving or sport diving safety. Nominees are usually not employed in the diving field, and need not be a member of NAUI. A trophy, plaque, and blazer crest are awarded annually at the NAUI awards ceremony. Nomination deadline is December 31. Established in 1986 by Robert Widmann and Mike Williams, NAUI instructors, in honor of Dr. Charles V. Brown, M.D., for his voluntary work in sport diving.

• 14450 • **Leonard Greenstone Diving Safety Award**
For significant contributions to safety in all aspects of diving. The award is intended to encourage development of all forms of safety programs, equipment, and devices which would eliminate injuries or loss of life relating to underwater activities. Membership is not required. Nominations are accepted. An honorarium of $1,000 and the Poseidon Trophy, which is to be retained by the recipient during the year of his or her award, are presented when merited. Awarded annually. Established in 1974 by Leonard Greenstone, a diver for more than three decades. Additional information is available from Leonard Greenstone, 6029 Venice Blvd., Los Angeles, CA 90034.

• 14451 • **Service Awards**
To recognize members for outstanding performance and service to NAUI and sport diving. Outstanding Service Award and Continuing Service Awards are presented annually. Nomination deadline is December 31. Established in 1975.

• 14452 •
National Association of University Women
Ezora J. Proctor, Pres.
1001 E St. SE
Washington, DC 20003-2847
Phone: (202)547-3967
E-mail: Information@NAUW.org

• 14453 • **National Association of University Women National Fellowship**
To provide a fellowship for study for a doctoral degree. Applications are accepted. A fellowship of $2,500 is awarded annually. Additional information is available from the Fellowship Chairperson, 1501 11th Street, N.W., Washington, DC, 20009.

• 14454 •
National Association of Women and the Law
(Association Nationale de la Femme et du Droit)
Bonnie Diamond, Exec.Dir.
1066 Somerset St. W, Ste. 303
Ottawa, ON, Canada K1Y 4T3
Phone: (613)241-7570
Fax: (613)241-4657
E-mail: info@nawl.ca
Home Page: http://www.nawl.ca

• 14455 • **NAWL Trust for Research & Education - Essay Competition**
Open to students in post-secondary schools. Monetary awards are given annually.

• 14456 •
National Association of Women Artists
Ann Chennault, Office Mgr.
80 5th Ave., Ste. 1405
New York, NY 10011
Phone: (212)675-1616
Phone: (212)675-8257
Fax: (212)675-1616
E-mail: nawomena@msn.com
Home Page: http://www.nawanet.org

• 14457 • **Annual Exhibition Awards**
To encourage women in the arts and to provide a means of showing their works. Only members of the Association may submit works of art in the categories of Works on Canvas, Works on Paper, Sculpture, Printmaking, Photography, and Computer Graphics. An invited Jury of Awards makes the final selections. Medals of Honor and monetary prizes totaling $10,000 are awarded annually in the spring.

• 14458 •
National Association of Women Judges
Drucilla Stender Ramey Esq., Acting Exec.Dir.
1112 16 St. NW, Ste. 520
Washington, DC 20036-4807
Phone: (202)393-0222
Fax: (202)393-0125
E-mail: nawj@nawj.org
Home Page: http://www.nawj.org

• 14459 • Honoree of the Year Award
To recognize individuals who have assisted women judges to become more proficient in their professions to solve the legal, social and ethical problems associated with the profession; assisted in increasing the number of women judges; and addressed important issues affecting women judges. Individuals, male or female, judges or non-judges, may be nominated. A plaque and other appropriate gifts are awarded at the annual conference in the fall. Established in 1982. Formerly: Judge of the Year Award.

• 14460 •
National Athletic Trainers' Association
Eve Becker-Doyle CAE, Exec.Dir.
2952 Stemmons Fwy.
Dallas, TX 75247-6196
Phone: (214)637-6282
Toll-Free: 800-879-6282
Fax: (214)637-2206
E-mail: ebd@nata.org
Home Page: http://www.nata.org

• 14461 • Honorary Membership Award
To recognize continued assistance in the field of sports medicine and progress of the athletic trainer. Individuals who are not trainers are eligible. A plaque is awarded annually. Established in 1965.

• 14462 • Twenty-Five Year Award
To recognize individuals who have completed 25 years as athletic trainers. A certificate is awarded annually at the association's National Convention. Established in 1960.

• 14463 •
National Auctioneers Association
Robert A. Shively CAE, Exec.Dir.
8880 Ballentine
Overland Park, KS 66214-1985
Phone: (913)541-8084
Fax: (913)894-5281
E-mail: bob@auctioneers.org
Home Page: http://www.auctioneers.org

• 14464 • Advertising Awards
For recognition of achievement by members in various categories of auction advertisement. A plaque is awarded annually at the convention. Established in 1976.

• 14465 • Hall of Fame Award
To recognize longstanding members who have made contributions to auctioneering. Criteria include contributions made to the auction profession, involvement with the Association, involvement in state auctioneers associations, and community involvement and activities. Selection of members is made by former recipients of the Hall of Fame Award. A plaque with an engraved reproduction of the winner and an inscription is awarded. A maximum of three awards are presented annually. Established in 1961.

• 14466 • International Auctioneers Championship
To promote the auction method of marketing and emphasize the importance of the auctioneer as an effective marketing specialist. Members of the association who are at least 18 years of age are eligible. Entrants in the men's and women's divisions are judged on style, chant, presence, and persuasive sales ability by a panel of auctioneer judges. Contestants showcase their vocal skills by auctioning off three items each, and then demonstrate general communication skills during an interview. Each winner receives a trophy, a ring, and $10,000 in prize money. Awarded annually at the convention. Established in 1988.

• 14467 •
National Audubon Society
John Flicker, Pres./CEO
700 Broadway
New York, NY 10003
Phone: (212)979-3000
Fax: (212)979-3188
E-mail: audubonathome@audubon.org
Home Page: http://www.audubon.org

• 14468 • Audubon Medal
To honor individual achievement in the field of conservation and environmental protection. Achievements of national or international significance are considered. Audubon directors and staff are not eligible. A bronze medal is awarded annually during the Centennial Audubon Medal Dinner. Established in 1947.

• 14469 • Charles H. Callison Award
To recognize chapters, individual volunteers, staff, and board directors who have made an outstanding contribution to conservation advocacy. A plaque is awarded to one professional and one volunteer annually. Established in 1994.

• 14470 •
National Auto Auction Association
Jim DesRochers, Pres.
5320-D Spectrum Dr.
Frederick, MD 21703-7337
Phone: (301)696-0400
Phone: (510)760-6412
Fax: (301)631-1359
E-mail: naaa@naaa.com
Home Page: http://www.NAAA.COM

• 14471 • Hall of Fame
For recognition of contributions above and beyond what is ordinarily expected with regard to the auto auction industry and the association. One nominee is from the owners and managers of member auctions, and one is from a related industry, such as manufacturers representatives, guidebook publishers, or fleet and leasing entities. Wall plaques are awarded annually at the national convention. Established in 1968.

• 14472 •
National Aviation Hall of Fame
Ron Kaplan, Exec.Dir.
1100 Spaatz St.
PO Box 31096
Dayton, OH 45437
Phone: (937)256-0944
Fax: (937)256-8536
E-mail: rkaplan@nationalaviation.org
Home Page: http://www.nationalaviation.org
Formerly: Aviation Hall of Fame.

• 14473 • Milton Caniff Spirit of Flight Award
To recognize a group or organization for outstanding contributions or service to America's aviation heritage. Awarded annually. Established in 1981. Formerly: Spirit of Flight Award.

• 14474 • Gold Medal of Honor and Achievement
For recognition of outstanding contributions to aviation and space by enshrinement in the National Aviation Hall of Fame. A gold medal is awarded annually. Established in 1962. Formerly: Aviation Hall of Fame Gold Medal of Honor and Achievement.

• 14475 • Hall of Fame Award
To honor and recognize United States citizens and residents who have significantly contributed to advancements in air and space flights. Nominees may include aviation leaders, pilots, teachers, scientists, engineers, inventors, and governmental leaders, among others. Nominees must be United States citizens or residents. No person shall be honored for achievement attained less than five years prior to nomination date. A plaque with a statement of the recipient's accomplishments is hung in the National Aviation Hall of Fame. Four to eight individuals are inducted annually. Nomination deadline is August 1. Established in 1962. Formerly: Aviation Hall of Fame Award.

• 14476 • Silver Medal of Outstanding Service
To honor members of the National Aviation Hall of Fame and others who have rendered outstanding service to the organization. A silver medal is awarded annually. Established in 1962. Formerly: Aviation Hall of Fame Silver Medal of Outstanding Service.

• 14477 •
National Ballet of Canada
Kevin Garland, Exec.Dir.
470 Queens Quay W
Toronto, ON, Canada M5V 3K4
Phone: (416)345-9686
Fax: (416)345-8323
E-mail: info@national.ballet.ca
Home Page: http://www.national.ballet.ca

• 14478 • Erik Bruhn Prize
To recognize and encourage outstanding talent in young dancers. Dancers must be members of

qualifying companies and between the ages of 18 and 23 on the date of the competition. Companies designated by the prize's founder and administrators as qualifying include the National Ballet of Canada, the Royal Ballet, the Royal Danish Ballet, and American Ballet Theatre. Each company selects one male and one female participant. A monetary award of $15,000 is divided equally between the winning male and female dancers, and each receives a commemorative sculpture. Medals are awarded to all other dancers. Awarded annually in May in 1988 and 1989, and biennially thereafter. Established in 1986 by the late Erik Bruhn, then Artistic Director of the National Ballet of Canada. The award honors the illustrious and exemplary career of Erik Bruhn, that it might be an inspiration for all future dancers.

• 14479 •
National Band Association
Linda Moorhouse, Pres.
118 College Dr., No. 5032
Hattiesburg, MS 39406-0001
Phone: (601)297-8168
Fax: (601)266-6185
E-mail: info@nationalbandassociation.org
Home Page: http://
www.nationalbandassociation.org

• 14480 • AWAPA (Academy of Wind and Percussion Arts) Award
This, the highest honor bestowed by American band conductors upon an individual, is given to recognize significant and outstanding contributions in furthering the excellence of bands and band music. An engraved scroll, a medallion, and a nine-inch silver statuette are awarded annually. Established in 1960.

• 14481 • Band Booster Award
To honor outstanding service by members to band booster organizations. A certificate is awarded annually.

• 14482 • Certificate of Merit for Marching Excellence
To recognize outstanding marching band directors. A certificate is awarded annually. Established in 1983.

• 14483 • Citation of Excellence
To recognize outstanding contributions by concert band directors. Approximately 40 engraved scrolls are awarded annually. Established in 1968.

• 14484 • Hall of Fame of Distinguished Band Conductors
To honor individuals, living and deceased, for outstanding service to the field of wind band music as conductors. Individuals at least 65 years of age, or people who are deceased are eligible. The award consists of enshrinement in the NBA Hall of Fame of Distinguished Band Conductors at Troy State University, a portrait, and memorabilia. Awarded annually. Established in 1980.

• 14485 • High School Jazz Student Award
To recognize outstanding young jazz musicians. Seniors, juniors, and sophomores are eligible. A certificate is awarded annually.

• 14486 • Music Campers Citation
To recognize the achievements of top summer music campers. A certificate is awarded annually in the summer.

• 14487 • Outstanding Band Musician Award
To recognize band members who display outstanding musicianship, citizenship, and leadership. A certificate is awarded annually.

• 14488 • Outstanding Jazz Educator Award
To recognize outstanding jazz educators. A certificate is awarded annually.

• 14489 •
National Bar Association
Kim M. Keenan, Pres.
1225 11th St. NW
Washington, DC 20001
Phone: (202)842-3900
Fax: (202)289-6170
E-mail: headquarters@nationalbar.org
Home Page: http://www.nationalbar.org

• 14490 • Equal Justice Award
To recognize an individual for contributions and quest for equal justice that have added substance to the guarantees of the U.S. Constitution. Awarded annually. Established in 1977.

• 14491 • Gertrude E. Rush Award
To recognize individuals who have demonstrated leadership ability in the community within their profession; a pioneer spirit in the pursuit of civil and human rights; and excellence in legal education and perseverance in the law, public policy, or social activism. Nominations are accepted. A trophy is awarded annually during the NBA Mid-Year Conference. Established in 1982 in honor of Gertrude Rush, NBA's only female co-founder.

• 14492 • C. Francis Stradford Award
To recognize a person who has performed outstanding service in the furtherance of the association's objectives. Nominations are accepted by June 1. A plaque is presented at the NBA Annual Convention each summer. Awarded in honor of C. Francis Stradford, NBA co-founder.

• 14493 •
National Baseball Hall of Fame and Museum
Dale Petroskey, Pres.
PO Box 590
Cooperstown, NY 13326
Phone: (607)547-7200
Phone: (607)547-7200
Toll-Free: 888-425-5633
Fax: (607)547-2044
Home Page: http://
www.baseballhalloffame.org

• 14494 • Ford C. Frick Award
To honor a broadcaster for major contributions to the game of baseball. A scroll is awarded annually. Established in 1978 to honor Ford C. Frick, veteran broadcaster, baseball commissioner, and National League president.

• 14495 • Hall of Fame
To honor baseball's great players, executives, managers, and umpires whose careers combine outstanding playing ability, integrity, sportsmanship, character, and distinguished contribution to the teams or leagues for which they played or managed as well as to the sport itself. Annual elections are made by the Baseball Writers Association of America. Eligible candidates must have been active in the Major Leagues during a period beginning 20 years before and ending five years prior to election; have played in each of 10 Major League championship seasons; and must not appear on Baseball's ineligible list. Recipients receive a ring, and a bronze plaque is displayed in the Hall of Fame. Established in 1936.

• 14496 • J. G. Taylor Spink Award
To honor a sportswriter for meritorious contributions to baseball writing. A scroll is presented annually. Established in 1962 to honor J. G. Taylor Spink, founder of *The Sporting News*. Administered by the Baseball Writers Association of America.

• 14497 •
National Basketball Association
David J. Stern, Commissioner
645 5th Ave., 10th Fl.
New York, NY 10022
Phone: (212)826-7000
Toll-Free: 800-NBA-0548
Fax: (212)826-0579
E-mail: fanrelations@nba.com
Home Page: http://www.nba.com

Absorbed: (1976) American Basketball Association.

• 14498 • All-Defensive Team
To select an all-defensive team. Selection is made by the league's 30 head coaches. Each head coach is asked, at the conclusion of the regular season, to select first and second All-Defensive teams by position, with the provision that a coach could not vote for one of his own players. Awarded annually. Established in 1968.

• 14499 • All-NBA Team
To select an All-NBA team. Selection is made of outstanding professional basketball players by a nationwide panel of 122 sports writers and broadcasters. Three teams are selected: 1st, 2nd, and 3rd All-NBA teams. Awarded annually. Established in 1946.

• 14500 • Coach of the Year - Red Auerbach Trophy
To recognize the NBA Coach of the Year. Voting is conducted by a nationwide panel of sports writers and broadcasters. Awarded annually. Established in 1962. Formerly: .

• 14501 • Defensive Player of the Year
To recognize the most outstanding defensive basketball player of the year. Players are voted upon by a nationwide panel of 125 sportswriters and broadcasters throughout the United States and Canada. Awarded annually. Established in 1982.

• 14502 • Executive of the Year
To recognize the NBA Executive of the Year. Selection is made by *The Sporting News*. Awarded annually. Established in 1972.

• 14503 • got milk? All-Rookie Team
To select an All-Rookie team. The individuals selected are voted upon without regard to position. Selection is made by the league's 30 head coaches. Each head coach is asked, at the conclusion of the regular season, to select first and second All-Rookie teams by position, with the provision that a coach could not vote for one of his own players. Awarded annually. Established in 1962. Formerly: NBA All-Rookie Team.

• 14504 • got milk? Rookie of the Year - Eddie Gottlieb Trophy
To recognize the most outstanding first-year player in the NBA. Selection is made by a vote of sportswriters and broadcasters throughout the United States and Canada. Awarded annually. Established in 1952. Formerly: .

• 14505 • J. Walter Kennedy Citizenship Award
To recognize a player or coach for outstanding service and dedication to the community. Selection is made by the Professional Basketball Writers Association. Awarded annually. Established in 1974 in honor of J. Walter Kennedy, the second commissioner of the NBA.

• 14506 • Most Improved Player
To recognize an up-and-coming player who has made a dramatic improvement in his game from the previous season(s). Players are voted upon by a nationwide panel of 123 sportswriters and broadcasters throughout the United States and Canada. Awarded annually. Established in 1986.

• 14507 • Most Valuable Player Award - Maurice Podoloff Trophy
To recognize the Most Valuable Player in the NBA each year for his regular season accomplishment. Players are voted upon by a nationwide panel of 127 sportswriters and broadcasters throughout the United States and Canada. Awarded annually. Established in 1956 in honor of the former league commissioner, Maurice Podoloff.

• 14508 • Sixth Man Award
To recognize top basketball players who are non-starters. Players are voted upon by a nationwide panel of 125 sportswriters and broadcasters throughout the United States and Canada. Awarded annually. Established in 1983.

• 14509 • World Championship - Larry O'Brien Trophy
The final basketball series of the season for NBA teams determines the winning team. Participating teams are determined by playoff competition. The top 16 teams (8 from both the Eastern and Western Conferences compete) plays. Awarded annually to the winning team. Established in 1978 and renamed in 1984 in honor of the late former NBA commissioner Larry O'Brien.

• 14510 •
National Beep Baseball Association
Jeana Weigand, Sec.
5568 Boulder-Crest St.
Columbus, OH 43235
Phone: (614)442-1444
E-mail: secretary@nbba.org
Home Page: http://www.nbba.org

• 14511 • Jim Quinn Award
To recognize an individual's outstanding contribution to and promotion of sport of beep baseball. Awarded annually with a plaque. Established in 1981.

• 14512 •
National Biplane Association
Charles W. Harris, Expo Chm.
PO Box 470350
Tulsa, OK 74147-0350
Phone: (918)665-0755
Fax: (918)665-0039
Home Page: http://www.nationalbiplaneassn.org

• 14513 • Chairman's Award
Recognition is given annually biplanes.

• 14514 • Grand Champion
Annual recognition of Biplanes.

• 14515 • Robert P. Moore Memorial Award
For biplanes. Recognition is given annually.

• 14516 • Reserve Grand Champion
For biplanes. Recognition is given annually.

• 14517 •
National Bison Association
Dave Carter, Exec.Dir.
1400 W 122nd Ave., Ste. 106
Westminster, CO 80234
Phone: (303)292-2833
Fax: (303)292-2564
E-mail: info@bisoncentral.com
Home Page: http://www.bisoncentral.com
Formerly: (1997) National Buffalo Association.

• 14518 • Buffalo Hall of Fame
To recognize those persons who have been instrumental in the comeback of the American buffalo in the historic category (at the turn of the century) and in the current category ("here and now"). Nominations may be made for both categories by August 5. A plaque is presented to the winner in each category at an annual award ceremony in September. Established in 1980.

• 14519 • Restaurant Award of Excellence
To recognize restaurants that do an outstanding job of introducing the general public to the savory delights of buffalo meat. The restaurant must prepare and serve buffalo in such a way that people are so impressed they want to eat it again. A plaque is awarded annually, generally in the summer. Established in 1982.

• 14520 •
National Black Police Association
Marcus G. Jones, Natl.Chm.
3251 Mt. Pleasant St. NW
Washington, DC 20010-2103
Phone: (202)986-2070
Fax: (202)986-0410
E-mail: nbpanatofc@worldnet.att.net
Home Page: http://www.blackpolice.org

• 14521 • Achievement Award
To recognize outstanding achievement by a citizen of national status (Congressman, lawyer, judge, mayor, medical researcher, educator, etc.), or a former police officer or NBPA member who enters another field and achieves recognition in his or her new field of endeavor. A plaque is awarded annually.

• 14522 • Law Enforcement Award
To recognize a professional law enforcement person, or one associated with the field of law enforcement in related capacity of national status. Individuals who have contributed greatly to improving the profession itself, instituted successful crime prevention programs, provided leadership in closing difficult criminal cases of national concern, and provided leadership in striking down the historical vestiges of discrimination within law enforcement are eligible. A plaque is awarded annually.

• 14523 • Renault Robinson Award
To recognize a member who has served the black community during the year. A plaque is awarded annually. Established to honor Renault Robinson, for his courageous efforts to provide equal rights and justice to all citizens and for being outspoken on equal employment opportunities for black police officers nationwide.

• 14524 • Willie Smoot Organizational Meritorious Award
To recognize a chapter member organization for developing an Outreach Program that resulted in a positive impact upon the community served and demonstrated dedication to the principles for which the NBPA was founded. A plaque is awarded annually.

• 14525 •
National Black Programming Consortium
Mable Haddock, Pres./CEO
68 E 131st St., 7th Fl.
New York, NY 10037
Phone: (212)234-8200
Fax: (212)234-7032
E-mail: info@nbpc.tv
Home Page: http://www.nbpc.tv

• 14526 • "Prized Pieces" International Film and Video Festival
To recognize issue-based, socially conscious films that address global human rights from a uniquely black perspective. Filmmakers and screenwriters receive monetary prizes of up to $2,500. Application deadline is July 30. Established in 1981.

• 14527 •
National Board for Certification in Hearing Instrument Sciences
16880 Middlebelt Rd., Ste. 3
Livonia, MI 48154
Phone: (734)522-2900
Fax: (734)522-0900
E-mail: info@hearingnbc.org
Home Page: http://www.hearingnbc.org

• 14528 • Marylene Freshley Award
To recognize outstanding services for education, recruitment, and growth of Board Certification in hearing instrument sciences. Candidates must be Board Certified in hearing instrument sciences. A plaque is awarded. Established in 1988 by the NBC-HIS Board of Directors to honor the courage and tireless efforts displayed by Marylene Freshley in establishing the Board Certification program.

• 14529 •
National Book Critics Circle
Rebecca Miller, Pres.
360 Park Ave. S
New York, NY 10010
Phone: (973)744-9045
E-mail: miller@reedbusiness.com
Home Page: http://www.bookcritics.org

• 14530 • National Book Critics Circle Awards
To recognize books in five categories: fiction, general nonfiction, biography/autobiography, poetry, and criticism. Nominations must be made by members of the NBCC and by the group's board of directors. Eligible titles are books written in the English language by American authors and published for the first time in the United States during the previous calendar year. Collected works must contain substantial material not previously published in book form. No book written or edited by a current NBCC director is eligible. Scrolls are awarded annually. Additionally, the Ivan Sandrof Lifetime Achievement Award is presented at their discretion and an annual Nona Balakian Citation for Excellence in Reviewing Award is presented to a member of the organization. Established in 1974.

• 14531 •
National Book Foundation
Harold Augenbraum, Exec.Dir.
95 Madison Ave., Ste. 709
New York, NY 10016
Phone: (212)685-0261
Fax: (212)213-6570
E-mail: nationalbook@nationalbook.org
Home Page: http://www.nationalbook.org

• 14532 • National Book Awards
To honor American books of the highest literary merit. For decades these award-winning books have earned a permanent place in world literature, a distinction made possible by the participation of discerning and dedicated judges and the faithful support of the American publishing industry. Awards are given in four categories: fiction, nonfiction, poetry, and young people's literature. Full-length books, collections of short stories and essays by one author, and collected and selected poems written by one author are eligible, provided they were scheduled for publication in the United States between December 1 and November 30. In each category, a cash prize of $10,000 is awarded to the winner and $1,000 to each finalist. Awarded annually. Established in 1950.

• 14533 •
National Broadcasting Society - Alpha Epsilon Rho
Jim Wilson, Exec.Dir.
PO Box 4206
Chesterfield, MO 63006
Phone: (314)469-1943
Toll-Free: (866)272-3746
Fax: (314)469-1948
E-mail: nbsaerho@swbell.net
Home Page: http://www.nbs-aerho.org

• 14534 • Advisor of the Year
To recognize a chapter advisor who has provided the strongest and most meaningful leadership to his or her chapter. Selection is made by the Executive Council. Awarded annually at the National Convention.

• 14535 • Advisory Board Member of the Year
To recognize a member of the National Advisory Board who has made the most significant contribution to the betterment of the Society. Awarded when merited.

• 14536 • Chapter of the Year
This, the Society's highest award, is given to recognize the non-rookie chapter that has made the most significant contribution to the Society on a local, regional, or national basis. Selection is made by the Executive Council. Awarded annually at the National Convention.

• 14537 • Member of the Year
To recognize a non-rookie member who has, by his or her own individual efforts, made significant contributions to the betterment of the Society. Selection is made by the Executive Council. Awarded annually at the National Convention.

• 14538 • Most Improved Chapter of the Year
To recognize the chapter that has made the most significant improvement in Society activities during the past year. Awarded annually.

• 14539 • National Student Production Awards Competition
To encourage and reward students for their audio, video, and film production accomplishments. Students enrolled in any college, university, junior college, or trade school offering courses in broadcasting or film may enter. There are four general categories for the competition: video information, video entertainment, audio information, and audio entertainment. These four categories have several subcategories. The entry deadline is January 4. Certificates are awarded each year at the National Convention of AERho. Established in 1963.

• 14540 • Professional Development Coordinator of the Year
To recognize the student or professional member of a chapter for the most significant job in acquiring professional membership and maintaining strong liaison with the professional and alumni members of his or her chapter. Selection is made by the Executive Council. Awarded annually at the National Convention.

• 14541 • Professional Member of the Year
To recognize a professional member who has advanced the art and science of broadcasting and has made significant contributions to the academic and professional aspects of the Society. Formerly: Concerned Broadcaster of the Year.

• 14542 • Public Relations Coordinator of the Year
To recognize the Chapter Public Relations Coordinator who has conducted the most significant and successful promotional campaigns and

activities for their local chapter in the year of the award.

• 14543 • Region of the Year

To recognize an individual region that has, as a total entity, made the most significant contributions to the betterment of the goals of the Society. Selection is made by the Executive Council. Awarded annually at the National Convention.

• 14544 • Regional Representative of the Year

To recognize the regional representative who has made the most significant contribution and provided the greatest assistance to his or her region. Selection is made by the Executive Council. Awarded annually at the National Convention.

• 14545 • Rookie Chapter of the Year

To recognize the rookie chapter that has made the most significant growth and overall development during its first year of existence. Selection is made by the Executive Council. Awarded annually at the National Convention.

• 14546 • Rookie Member of the Year

To recognize a member of a rookie chapter who has made the most significant contribution during the first year of participation in the activities of the Society. Selection is made by the Executive Council. Awarded annually at the National Convention.

• 14547 • State Coordinator

To recognize the state coordinator who has made the most significant contribution to the chapters within his/her own state. Selection is made by the Executive Council. Awarded annually at the National Convention.

• 14548 •
National Building Museum
Chase Rynd, Exec.Dir.
401 F St. NW
Washington, DC 20001
Phone: (202)272-2448
Fax: (202)272-2564
E-mail: crynd@nbm.org
Home Page: http://www.nbm.org

• 14549 • Honor Award

To recognize individuals or organizations that have significantly and positively influenced the formation of the built environment. The award honors contributions to the world of design, construction, preservation, land use, as well as civic leaders. Awarded annually. Established in 1985.

• 14550 •
National Burglar and Fire Alarm Association
Merlin Guilbeau, Exec.Dir.
2300 Valley View Ln., Ste. 230
Irving, TX 75062
Phone: (214)260-5970
Toll-Free: 888-447-1689
Fax: (214)260-5979
E-mail: webmaster@alarm.org
Home Page: http://www.alarm.org

• 14551 • Chartered State Association Executive Director of the Year

To recognize the CSA executive director who best exemplifies the practice of association management principles in relation to the alarm industry. Awarded annually.

• 14552 • Chartered State Association of the Year

To recognize outstanding achievements in the advancement of the goals of the burglar and fire alarm industry. One of NBFAA's autonomous Chartered State Associations is chosen each year to receive the award.

• 14553 • Chartered State Association President of the Year

To recognize a Chartered State Association president for outstanding contribution to the growth of his/her own association and for significant contributions to the advancement of the national association. Awarded annually.

• 14554 • Fire Fighter of the Year

No further information was available for this edition.

• 14555 • Sara E. Jackson Memorial Award

To honor a committee chair in the NBFAA for outstanding leadership and dedicated service to the alarm industry. A plaque is awarded annually at the convention. Established in 1984 by the family of Sara E. Jackson, a past president of NBFAA.

• 14556 • Police Officer of the Year

No further information was available for this edition.

• 14557 • Morris F. Weinstock Award

To honor a member of the Association for an outstanding achievement and for involvement in the continued efforts towards the advancement of the burglar and fire alarm industry and to the benefit of the entire Association and its membership. An engraved wood and brass wall plaque in the shape of the United States is awarded annually at the Association's convention. Established in 1970 in memory of Morris F. Weinstock, a founding father of the Association, by his family.

• 14558 •
National Burglar and Fire Alarm Association
National Training School (NTS)
Merlin Guilbeau, Exec.Dir
8300 Colesville Rd., Ste. 750
Silver Spring, MD 20910
Phone: (301)585-1855
Fax: (301)585-1866
E-mail: webmaster@alarm.org
Home Page: http://www.alarm.org

• 14559 • Instructor of the Year

To honor the NTS instructor judged to be superior in breadth of knowledge and skills of presentation. Awarded annually.

• 14560 • Professional Alarm Technician of the Year

To recognize the alarm installer who best exemplifies the combination of technical expertise and professionalism supported by NTS.

• 14561 •
National Business Aviation Association
John W. Olcott, Pres.
1200 18th St. NW, Ste. 400
Washington, DC 20036-2506
Phone: (202)783-9000
Fax: (202)331-8364
E-mail: info@nbaa.org
Home Page: http://www.nbaa.org

Formerly: (1998) National Business Aircraft Association.

• 14562 • Aviation Maintenance Department Safety Award

To honor the personnel who maintain NBAA-member company airplanes. The company of the winning department must also qualify for the Corporate/Commercial Business Flying Safety Award. A certificate is awarded annually. Established in 1974.

• 14563 • Aviation Support Services Safety Award

To recognize aviation support services personnel, such as flight attendants, dispatchers, schedulers, clerical assistants, aircraft refuelers/cleaners, and repairmen. Individuals employed by NBAA member companies primarily for support of corporate/business flight operations are eligible for individual awards. Only accident-free years of employment primarily in support of corporate/business flight operations are counted. Employment by the military, air carriers, commuters, personal employment, and flight schools not specifically dealing with corporate/business flight operations are not considered. A certificate of recognition is presented annually.

• 14564 • Corporate/Commercial Business Flying Safety Awards

To honor NBAA-member companies whose aircraft have flown in excess of three or more consecutive accident-free years. A certificate is awarded annually. Established in 1953.

• 14565 • John P. "Jack" Doswell Award
To recognize those who have made a definite contribution to the aims, goals and objectives of business aviation. Awarded annually. Established in 1987 by NBAA. It is named for John P. "Jack" Doswell who, despite the personal challenges of a debilitating illness, made a lasting contribution to the improvement of business aviation and its users.

• 14566 • Gold Wing Award for Excellence In Journalism
To honor excellent, accurate and insightful reporting on business aviation issues. Presented each year in both trade and non-trade categories and will include both broadcast and print coverage. The Association also selects annually a member of the press to receive its Platinum Wing Award in recognition of lifetime achievement in business aviation reporting.

• 14567 • Maintenance/Avionics Technician Safety Award
For recognition of member companies' technicians who have been employed three or more years in support of corporate/business flight operations. A certificate is awarded annually. Established in 1984.

• 14568 • Meritorious Service to Aviation Award
This award, one of the most prestigious in aviation, is given to those individuals who, by virtue of a lifetime of personal dedication, have made significant identifiable contributions that have materially advanced aviation interests (not necessarily confined to business aviation). A citation is awarded annually. Nomination deadline is February 25. Established in 1950.

• 14569 • Pilot Safety Award
To honor pilots employed by NBAA-member companies who have flown corporate aircraft in excess of 1,500 accident-free hours. A certificate is awarded annually. Established in 1953.

• 14570 •
National Business Education Association
Dr. Janet M. Treichel, Exec.Dir.
1914 Association Dr.
Reston, VA 20191-1596
Phone: (703)860-8300
Fax: (703)620-4483
E-mail: nbea@nbea.org
Home Page: http://www.nbea.org

• 14571 • Collegiate or University Teacher of the Year
To recognize outstanding contributions to business education by a senior college or university business teacher. Nominations of members are due by December 1. A one-year professional membership in NBEA; a one year subscription to *Business Education Forum, Keying In,* and *NBEA Yearbook;* and a plaque are presented annually at the NBEA Convention. Established in 1978.

• 14572 • Distinguished Service Award
To recognize outstanding contributions to business education by an institution, organization, business firm, government agency, or an individual associated with any of these groups. Nominations are due December 1. A one-year professional membership in NBEA; a one year subscription to *Business Education Forum, Keying In,* and *NBEA Yearbook;* and a plaque are presented annually at the NBEA Convention. Established in 1979.

• 14573 • Distinguished Service Award for an Administrator or Supervisor
To recognize outstanding contributions to business education by an administrator or supervisor. The nominee must be an NBEA member, and an administrator or supervisor of business education. Nominations are due by December 1. A one-year professional membership in NBEA; a one year subscription to *Business Education Forum, Keying In,* and *NBEA Yearbook;* and a plaque are presented annually at the NBEA Convention. Established in 1978.

• 14574 • Postsecondary Teacher of the Year
To recognize outstanding contributions to business education by a postsecondary business teacher who does not teach at a senior college. The nominee must be an NBEA member, and nominations are due by December 1. A one-year professional membership in NBEA; a one year subscription to *Business Education Forum, Keying In,* and *NBEA Yearbook;* and a plaque are presented annually at the NBEA Convention. Established in 1978.

• 14575 • Secondary Teacher of the Year
To recognize outstanding contributions to business education by a secondary business teacher. Nominations of members are due by December 1. A one-year professional membership in NBEA; a one year subscription to *Business Education Forum, Keying In,* and *NBEA Yearbook;* and a plaque are presented annually at the NBEA Convention. Established in 1978.

• 14576 •
National Cable and Telecommunications Association
Brian Dietz, Sr.Dir., Commun.
1724 Massachusetts Ave. NW
Washington, DC 20036
Phone: (202)775-3550
Fax: (202)775-3675
E-mail: webmaster@ncta.com
Home Page: http://www.ncta.com

• 14577 • Distinguished Vanguard Awards for Leadership
These, the most prestigious of NCTA's National Awards, are given to recognize the best and the brightest individuals in the cable television industry. Each year two awards are presented: The Larry Boggs Award, established in 1965 to honor a man; and The Idell Kaitz Award, established in 1973 to honor a woman. Nominees should meet the following criteria: exhibit outstanding leadership qualities, make significant contributions to the growth and development of cable television on the national level, and be NCTA members. The deadline for nominations is March 21. The awards honor Larry Boggs, who pioneered the development of the cable industry, and Idell Kaitz, whose representation of the industry made a significant impact on policy makers.

• 14578 • Vanguard Award for Associates and Affiliates
For recognition of indispensable contributions of the cable industry's equipment manufacturers and service suppliers. Nominees should meet the following criteria: exhibit outstanding leadership qualities, make significant contributions to the growth and development of cable TV on the national level, and be a NCTA Associate member. Nomination deadline is March 21. A plaque is awarded annually in memory of Robert H. Beisswenger, who was president of Jerrold Electronics. Established in 1975 as the Robert H. Beisswenger Memorial Award. Formerly: (1986) Associates Award; Robert H. Beisswenger Memorial Award.

• 14579 • Vanguard Award for Marketing
To honor an individual who has been instrumental in the development of a unique marketing approach that significantly enhances cable's public image and increases subscriber penetration. Nominees should meet the following criteria: provide leadership in the development of marketing concepts that lead to significant advancement in consumer awareness of cable television and increased subscribership; contribute through industry sponsored events and/or promote by other means marketing concepts that benefit the industry; and be NCTA Members. Nomination deadline is March 21. Awarded annually. Established in 1984. Formerly: (1986) Marketing Award.

• 14580 • Vanguard Award for Programmers
To recognize the innovation, leadership, and individual achievement of NCTA's programmer members. Nominees should meet the following criteria: exhibit outstanding leadership qualities; make significant contributions to the continuing growth and development of cable television programming on the national level; and be an NCTA Programmer member. Nomination deadline is March 21. Awarded annually. Established in 1988.

• 14581 • Vanguard Award for Public Relations
To recognize an individual who has significantly enhanced the status of the cable industry as a community leader, a state advocate, or a national contributor. Nominees should meet the following criteria: significantly contribute to the cable industry's national agenda through effectiveness in community and/or government relations at the national, state, or local level; provide leadership in the development of concepts that lead to significant advancement in positive public awareness of cable television; and be an

NCTA member. Awarded annually. Established in 1994. Formerly: (1999) Vanguard Award for Public Relations/Vanguard Award for State/Regional Association Leadership.

• 14582 • Vanguard Award for Science and Technology

To honor engineers who have been active and imaginative forces in product improvement, design, and development of engineering techniques that benefit the cable television industry. Nominees should meet the following criteria: be involved in technical development and/or system operations; make significant contributions to the continuing technical advancement of the industry through manufacturing, design, application, and implementation; and be NCTA members. Nomination deadline is March 21. Awarded annually. Established in 1973. In 1984 the Engineering Awards for Outstanding Achievement in Operations and Development were combined in the Science and Technology Award.

• 14583 • Vanguard Award for Young Leadership

To recognize those individuals who are challenged by the tremendous potential of cable television and take the risks to make their dreams a reality. Nominees should meet the following criteria: be 40 years of age or under; exhibit outstanding leadership qualities; make significant contributions to the growth and development of cable television on the national level; and be NCTA members. Awarded in the memory of Jerry Greene, who was the founder of Harriscope Cable Corporation and chief financial officer of its successor companies, Warner Cable and Cyprus Communications. Nomination deadline is March 21. Awarded annually. Established in 1978 as the Jerry Greene Memorial Award. Formerly: (1986) Challenger Award; Jerry Greene Memorial Award.

• 14584 •
National Cancer Institute of Canada
(Institut National du Cancer du Canada)
Michael Wosnick, Executive Director
10 Alcorn Ave., Ste. 200
Toronto, ON, Canada M4V 3B1
Phone: (416)961-7223
Fax: (416)961-4189
E-mail: ncic@cancer.ca
Home Page: http://www.ncic.cancer.ca

• 14585 • NCIC Awards for Excellence in Cancer Research

Four independent awards recognizing outstanding achievements in cancer research and control: Robert L. Noble Prize, O. Harold Warwick Prize, William E. Rawls Prize and Terry Fox Young Investigator Award. All four are awarded annually.

• 14586 •
National Carousel Association
Terry I. Blake, Exec.Sec.
PO Box 4333
Evansville, IN 47724-0333
Phone: (812)428-3675
E-mail: terrybnca@juno.com
Home Page: http://www.nca-usa.org

• 14587 • Certificate of Appreciation

To recognize the preservation of a carousel, or work that advances the knowledge and appreciation of the hand-carved wooden carousel. Nominations of individuals, cities, parks, or organizations are accepted. There is no deadline. Four to six plaques may be awarded annually. Established in 1980 by Frederick Fried, the cofounder of NCA.

• 14588 •
National Cartoonists Society
Steve McGarry, Pres.
1133 W Morse Blvd., Ste. 201
PO Box 713
Winter Park, FL 32789
Phone: (407)647-8839
Fax: (407)629-2502
E-mail: becca@crowsegal.com
Home Page: http://www.reuben.org

• 14589 • ACE Award

The "Amateur Cartoonist Extraordinaire" Award is presented to an individual who could have become a cartoonist, but choose to take another career path (such as a famous actor/actress, public official, etc.). An honorary plaque is presented when merited. Established in 1961.

• 14590 • Category Awards

For recognition of distinguished attainment by professional cartoonists for published works in the following categories: advertising illustration, animation, comic books, editorial cartoons, magazine feature/magazine illustration, animation feature, newspaper illustration, animation television, gag cartoons, newspaper panels, book illustration, greeting cards, and newspaper strips. Submissions are not accepted. The best in each category is awarded a silver plaque. Awarded annually. Established in 1956.

• 14591 • Reuben Award

To honor the outstanding cartoonist of the year. Professional cartoonists are eligible. Submissions are not accepted. The Reuben, a bronze statuette designed by the late Rube Goldberg, is awarded annually in April. Established in 1946 in memory of Rube Goldberg, the first NCS President. Formerly: Rube Goldberg Award.

• 14592 • Silver T-Square

In recognition of outstanding service to the profession or the Society. A silver T-square is awarded as merited. Submissions are not accepted. Established in 1948.

• 14593 •
National Catalog Managers Association
Mark Seng, Pres.
7101 Wisconsin Ave., Ste. 1300
Bethesda, MD 20814-3415
Phone: (301)654-6664
Fax: (301)654-3299
E-mail: ncma@aftermarket.org
Home Page: http://www.ncmacat.org

• 14594 • Catalog of the Year Awards

For recognition of an automotive aftermarket catalog conforming to the high standards set forth by the association. The criteria considered include layout, typography, paper, ease of use, and many other catalog specifications. Five plaques are awarded annually at the association conference. Established in 1977.

• 14595 •
National Catholic Band Association
John Badsing, Sec.-Treas.
3334 N Normandy
Chicago, IL 60634-3716
Phone: (773)282-9153
E-mail: info@catholicbands.org
Home Page: http://www.catholicbands.org

Formerly: National Catholic Bandmasters' Association.

• 14596 • Adam P. Lesinsky Award

To recognize significant contributions to music in the Catholic schools on a national level. An inscribed plaque is awarded annually when merited at the Association's national conference. Established in 1975.

• 14597 • NCBA Service Award

To recognize a member for notable achievement in leadership involving service to other members. A certificate is presented. Established in 1985.

• 14598 • Robert F. O'Brien Award

To recognize a graduating senior who has demonstrated unusual leadership, dedication, and loyalty to his or her band as well as continual development as a musician. Awarded annually. Established in 1991 in honor of Robert F. O'Brien, founder of the Association.

• 14599 • President's Award

For recognition of outstanding contributions to the work of the NCBA in a single event. A plaque is awarded when merited at the national conference. Established in 1985.

• 14600 • Charles R. Winking Award

For recognition of outstanding contributions to the field of wind band conducting. A plaque is awarded annually when merited at the national conference. Established in 1985 in memory of the work of Charles R. Winking.

• 14601 • **Reverend George C. Wiskirchen Jazz Award**

To honor the outstanding jazz musician in a band program. Awarded annually. Established in 1993.

• 14602 •

National Catholic Development Conference
Sister Georgette Lehmuth OSF, Pres./CEO
86 Front St.
Hempstead, NY 11550-3667
Phone: (516)481-6000
Toll-Free: 888-879-6232
Fax: (516)489-9287
E-mail: glehmuth@ncdusa.org
Home Page: http://www.ncdcusa.org

• 14603 • **Good Samaritan Award**

To recognize an individual whose accomplishments exemplify the concern for humankind as manifested by the Good Samaritan parable. Any person, lay or religious, member or nonmember, who is active in service having impact on the needy is eligible. A monetary prize and a bronze statue depicting the parable of the good Samaritan are awarded annually. Established in 1968.

• 14604 • **Robert F. Morneau Distinguished Service Award**

To recognize an individual who has made an unusually significant contribution to the cause of religious and charitable fundraising in the nonprofit sector. To be eligible, an individual must have been a member of the NCDC for at least seven years, and have provided service to Catholic fundraising profession for a minimum 10 years. A plaque with a bronze sculpture depicting Jesus washing the feet of the disciples is awarded annually. Established in 1975. The George T. Holloway Distinguished Service Award is a similar award presented to individuals providing religious fundraising services in the corporate sector.

• 14605 •

National Catholic Educational Association
Dr. Claire Helm, VP Operations
1077 30th St. NW, Ste. 100
Washington, DC 20007
Phone: (202)337-6232
Fax: (202)333-6706
E-mail: nceaadmin@ncea.org
Home Page: http://www.ncea.org

• 14606 • **Board of Directors Awards**

To recognize individuals or organizations that support Catholic education. Four awards are presented annually: C. Albert Koob Merit Award, John F. Meyers Award, Catherine T. McNamee CSJ Award, and Leonard F. DiFiore Parental Choice Advocate Award.

• 14607 • **Catholic Secondary Education Award**

To recognize secondary educators for their significant contributions to Catholic secondary education in the United States. Outstanding school personnel associated with Catholic secondary education with demonstrable achievements in Catholic secondary education at the local, diocesan, state, or national level may be nominated by NCEA members. Plaques are presented annually at the convention. Established in 1983.

• 14608 • **O'Neil D'Amour Award**

To recognize an individual for outstanding contribution of statewide, regional, national, or international significance to boards of Catholic education. Individuals, lay or religious, Catholic or non-Catholic, professional or nonprofessional educators, are eligible. Awarded annually. Established in 1977.

• 14609 • **Distinguished Principal Awards**

No further information was provided for this edition.

• 14610 • **Elementary Departmental Award in Recognition of Commitment to Catholic Elementary Education**

To recognize outstanding commitment to Catholic elementary education. Selection is based on the following criteria: the nominee must have made a major contribution to Catholic education; the contribution(s) must relate to at least one of the objectives of the Department of Elementary Schools; the nominee shall not be a member of DESEC or of the NCEA staff but may be a former member; and the nominee should have had experience in elementary education. A plaque and a citation are awarded annually during the convention. Established in 1979.

• 14611 • **Exhibitor Awards**

No further information was provided for this edition.

• 14612 • **Miriam Joseph Farrell Distinguished Teacher Award**

To give public recognition to the excellence of Catholic elementary school teachers. The nominee must be a teacher: in a Catholic elementary school(s) for at least ten years; with a clear, integrated philosophy of Catholic education; held in high regard by peers, students, and parents; and be an individual or institutional member of the NCEA Department of Elementary Schools. Entry deadline is November 1. Awarded annually during the national convention to twelve individuals, one from each region. Established in 1982 in memory of the Catholic elementary educator, Sister Miriam Joseph Farrell, P.B.V.M. Sponsored by Mutual of America.

• 14613 • **C. Albert Koob Award**

To recognize an outstanding contribution to Catholic education in America. Individuals, lay or religious, Catholic or non-Catholic, professional or non-professional, are eligible. The awardee is selected by the NCEA Board of Directors. An engraved plaque is awarded annually. Nomination deadline is November 11. Established in 1968 and renamed to honor Reverend C. Albert Koob, O. Pream, a former NCEA President (1966-1974). Formerly: (1975) NCEA Merit Award.

• 14614 • **Bishop Loris Lane Award**

To honor a person for an outstanding contribution to the work of priestly formation in the Roman Catholic community of the United States. Nomination is by members of the Executive Committee of the NCEA Seminary Department and general election is by the Committee. A plaque is awarded annually. Established in 1984 in honor of Bishop Loris Lane, former leader in the Program for Priestly Formation.

• 14615 • **John F. Meyers Award**

To recognize outstanding support of Catholic education. Institutions or individuals, lay or religious, professional or non-professional, are eligible. The awardee is selected by the NCEA Board of Directors. An engraved plaque is awarded when merited. Nomination deadline is November 11. Established in 1986 in honor of Msgr. John Francis Meyers, former NCEA President (1976-86).

• 14616 • **Mustard Seed Awards**

To recognize parishes that excel in parental involvement in their faith formation programs. This award is given to the parish, represented by the pastor, and to the parish religious education director, whose responsibility is for leading, implementing and facilitating parental participation and leadership. Criteria include: level/proportion of parental participation; ways parents offer significant input, leadership or direction setting; ways parish supports, facilitates and empowers family catechesis; and ways parish provides education/information opportunities for parents. Awarded to several recipients each year.

• 14617 • **NABE Board Member of the Year**

To recognize an active board member who has made an outstanding contribution to the local Catholic board movement. Both professional educators and non-professional board members are eligible. Nominations from NABE members are accepted. A plaque with citation and gavel are awarded annually at the Convention of the National Catholic Educational Association, NABE Awards session. Established in 1975. Sponsored by the National Association of Boards of Education/NCEA.

• 14618 • **NABE Executive Officer of the Year**

To honor a currently serving executive officer, pastor or vicar to a Catholic board who demonstrates a high level of skill in and dedication to nurturing the policy process, especially by helping board members to develop the skills for making decisions in the context of a Christian community. Nominations may be made by a nonprofessional educator who is a member of the nominee's board. An engraved bowl is awarded at the NCEA/NABE Convention when merited. Established in 1984.

• 14619 • **NABE Honor Roll of Outstanding Members**

To recognize active board members who have made outstanding contributions to the local Catholic board movement. Both professional educators and non-professional board members are eligible. Nominations are accepted from NABE members. A certificate is awarded annually if merited at the NABE Awards Reception at the national Convention. Established in 1975. Sponsored by the National Association of Boards of Education/NCEA.

• 14620 • NCEA Presidential Award
To honor individuals who have contributed in an outstanding way to Catholic education at the diocesan level. Any person who, through service or achievement, has made an outstanding contribution to Catholic education at the diocesan level is eligible. Nominations from diocesan offices of education may be submitted at any time. A printed scroll is awarded. Established in 1973.

• 14621 • Parent Organization Recognition Awards
To recognize outstanding achievement in the parent-school partnership in the cause of Catholic education. Awards are given in the following categories: most original fund-raising event; most creative program; most effective community-building sessions or series; and successful creation of a federation of local parent organizations. Members of NCEA's Parents Office are eligible. A certificate is awarded annually at the awards program at the NCEA convention. Established in 1978. Sponsored by the NCEA Parents Office.

• 14622 • Parent Partnership Awards
No further information was provided for this edition.

• 14623 • Religious Education Excellence Awards
To recognize parish catechetical directors whose programs exemplify outstanding qualities in serving children, parents, and adults. Awarded annually.

• 14624 • Elizabeth Ann Seton Award
To recognize the accomplishments of leaders who have made a significant difference in American education and/or Catholic education. A scholarship of $1,000 is made in the recipient's name to an outstanding Catholic student. A medallion is presented to four or five individuals each year at the Seton Awards Gala in September. Established in 1990.

• 14625 • Saint Elizabeth Ann Seton Award
To recognize an individual whose personal or professional philanthropy or volunteer service has impacted Catholic education in particular or U.S. education and our country's youth in general. Individuals of any creed or religion are eligible. Each year, a recipient is awarded a certificate and a $1,000 scholarship presented in his/her honor to a deserving Catholic school student from the local community. Established in 1981 in honor of St. Elizabeth Ann Seton's lifelong dedication to teaching.

• 14626 •
National Catholic Pharmacists Guild of the United States
John Paul Winkelmann, Exec.Dir./Co-Pres.
1012 Surrey Hills Dr.
St. Louis, MO 63117-1438
Phone: (314)645-0085

• 14627 • Award of Merit Certificate
For recognition of support and assistance to the guild by fellows or life members of the guild and/or others. Several certificates are awarded annually. Established in 1969.

• 14628 • Catholic Pharmacist of the Year
This, the highest award of the guild, is given to honor a guild member who has rendered exceptionally outstanding services to the guild, the Catholic Church, and the pharmacy profession. An engraved brass plaque mounted on a walnut board is usually awarded. Established in 1968.

• 14629 • For Church and Profession (of Pharmacy) Award
(Pro Ecclesia et Professione (Pharmaciae))
To honor guild members and others who have rendered outstanding services to the guild, the Catholic Church, and the pharmacy profession. A plaque is usually awarded. Established in 1966.

• 14630 • Honorary Founder of the Guild
An extraordinary award that was presented twice during 1987, the twenty-fifth anniversary of the NCPG.

• 14631 • Honorary President of the Guild
To give special recognition to a guild member for outstanding service to the guild. An Award of Merit certificate is awarded. Established in 1973.

• 14632 •
National Caucus and Center on Black Aged
Karyne Jones, Pres./CEO
1220 L St. NW, Ste. 800
Washington, DC 20005
Phone: (202)637-8400
Fax: (202)347-0895
E-mail: info@ncba-aged.org
Home Page: http://www.ncba-aged.org

• 14633 • Jean Camper Cahn Award
To recognize increasing minority participation in programs and services for the aging.

• 14634 •
National Center for Public Policy Research
Amy Moritz Ridenour, Pres.
501 Capitol Ct. NE
Washington, DC 20002
Phone: (202)543-4110
Fax: (202)543-5975
E-mail: info@nationalcenter.org
Home Page: http://www.nationalcenter.org

• 14635 • Winston Churchill Memorial Award
To recognize the person who has made the greatest and most selfless contribution to the formation of a public policy that protects and promotes freedom and human rights. A plaque is awarded at a presentation with guests and the press. Established in 1982 in memory of the former British Prime Minister, Winston Churchill.

• 14636 •
National Center for Public Productivity
Rutgers, The State University of New Jersey
Graduate Department of Public Administration
360 King Blvd., Hill Hall 701
Newark, NJ 07102
Phone: (973)353-5093
Fax: (973)353-5907
E-mail: ncpp@andromeda.rutgers.edu
Home Page: http://www.andromeda.rutgers.edu/~ncpp/

• 14637 • Exemplary State and Local Awards Program
To recognize public initiatives that improve the quality of government services and operations. Awarded annually with a plaque. Established in 1989.

• 14638 • New Jersey Exemplary State and Local Awards
To recognize public initiatives within the State of New Jersey that improve the quality of government services and operations. Awarded annually with a plaque. Established in 1993.

• 14639 •
National Center for State Courts
Chuck Ericksen, Exec.Dir.
300 Newport Ave.
Williamsburg, VA 23187
Phone: (757)259-1528
Toll-Free: 800-616-6160
Fax: (757)564-2108
E-mail: icm@ncsc.dni.us
Home Page: http://www.ncsconline.org/

• 14640 • Warren E. Burger Award
To honor individuals for outstanding accomplishments in the field of court management. The call for nominations is usually issued in February. A plaque is awarded annually. Established in 1974 to honor Chief Justice (Retired) of the United States, Warren E. Burger. Additional information is available from Charles A. Ericksen, Institute for Court Management.

• 14641 • Distinguished Service Awards
To recognize individuals who have made significant, long-standing contributions to the improvement of the justice system and who have supported the mission of the National Center. Awards are presented in four categories: present/former state court judge; present/former non-judge court employee; lawyer or lay person; and Special Award. An engraved pewter plate

and a bound resolution are awarded annually. Established in 1984.

• 14642 • Paul C. Reardon Award
To recognize an individual who has dedicated himself or herself to the goals and mission of the National Center for State Courts. Awarded annually. Established in 1989 in memory of Paul C. Reardon, first president of the National Center.

• 14643 • William H. Rehnquist Award for Judicial Excellence
To recognize a state court judge for outstanding achievements in judicial excellence in accordance with criteria. Awarded annually. Established in 1996.

• 14644 •
National Centre for Audiology
Prudence Allen, Dir.
Elborn College, Rm. 2262
1201 Western Rd.
University of Western Ontario
London, ON, Canada N6G 1H1
Phone: (519)661-3901
Fax: (519)661-3805
E-mail: jamieson@nca.uwo.ca
Home Page: http://www.uwo.ca/nca

Formerly: UWO - Faculty of Applied Health Science.

• 14645 • Alexander Graham Bell Student Prize in Speech Communication and Behavioral Acoustics
To recognize a graduate student at a Canadian academic institution for outstanding research in the field of speech communication or behavioral acoustics. A monetary prize of $800 is awarded annually. Established in recognition of Bell's lifelong interest in hearing and hearing loss and his strong ties to Canada, both in Ontario during his early career, and in Nova Scotia, later in life.

• 14646 •
National Cervical Cancer Coalition
Hollis Forster, Exec.Dir.
2625 Alcatraz Ave., Ste. 282
Berkeley, CA 94705
Phone: (818)909-3849
Toll-Free: 800-685-5531
Fax: (818)780-8199
E-mail: info@nccc-online.org
Home Page: http://www.nccc-online.org

• 14647 • NCCC Focus Award
Recognizes outstanding websites.

• 14648 •
National Chamber of Commerce for Women
R. Wright, Exec.Dir.
10 Waterside Plz., Ste. 6H
New York, NY 10010
Phone: (212)685-3454
Phone: (212)685-4581
Fax: (212)685-4547
E-mail: nccw@aol.com

• 14649 • Elizabeth Lewin Award
To recognize women entrepreneurs whose business success is due to management and marketing skill, not to money infusions. Active members of the Chamber who use the NCCW Infobank are eligible. Free advertising in the bimonthly publication *ENRICH* is awarded annually. Established in 1977 in memory of Elizabeth Lewin, a woman entrepreneur who succeeded in a man's world.

• 14650 • Scholarships and Research Grants, Behavioral Studies
For recognition and encouragement of research that examines organizational behavior or business ethics. Established in 1981. Formerly: Woman of the Year.

• 14651 •
National Child Labor Committee
Jeffrey Newman, Exec.Dir.
1501 Broadway, Ste. 403
New York, NY 10036
Phone: (212)840-1801
Fax: (212)768-0963
E-mail: nclckapow@aol.com
Home Page: http://www.kapow.org/nclc.htm

• 14652 • Lewis Hine Awards
For recognition of unique, dedicated, and largely unheralded volunteer service or professional work on behalf of America's children and youth. Ten winners are selected annually, five professionals and five volunteers, from local communities nationwide. Individuals may be nominated by corporate, governmental or non-profit executives. Winners receive a monetary prize of $1,000 each. Recipients are brought to New York for the Awards ceremony. Established in 1985 in honor of Lewis Hine, an early twentieth century photographer of children and child labor, whose now-famous body of work raised a nation's conscience and improved the lives of millions of young people.

• 14653 •
National Christian College Athletic Association
Dan Wood, Exec.Dir.
302 W Washington St.
Greenville, SC 29601-1919
Phone: (864)250-1199
Fax: (864)250-1141
E-mail: info@thenccaa.org
Home Page: http://www.thenccaa.org

• 14654 • All-Tournament Team
To recognize outstanding student athletes. Selection is based on criteria set forth by each sport.

• 14655 • Championship Banners
To recognize the winning school of the national championships. Plaques are presented for second through fourth places.

• 14656 • Coach of the Year
To recognize outstanding coaches at both the district and national levels. All sports that conduct a National Championship have the opportunity of selecting a National Coach of the Year. Criteria and method of selection shall be recommended by the coaches within each sport. Awarded annually.

• 14657 • Hall of Fame
To recognize individuals who have given outstanding leadership and/or service to the NCCAA. Awarded to one or more recipients annually. Established in 1991.

• 14658 • Susan R. Hellings Award
To honor the outstanding female volleyball player (Division I) selected from the NCCAA member colleges. Athletes in their junior or senior year who excel on an outstanding team, are excellent students, demonstrate leadership ability, and have a clear Christian testimony both on and off the court are eligible. An award to commemorate the occasion is presented annually to the recipient and to the institution she represents. Established in 1986. The award honors Susan R. Hellings who played volleyball in the mid 1970's at Houghton College.

• 14659 • Louisville Slugger
To recognize the eight baseball coaches who participated in the NCCAA National Baseball Tournament. Awarded annually at the American Baseball Coaches Association national meeting.

• 14660 • Pete Maravich Memorial Award
To recognize the outstanding Christian male basketball player from the NCCAA for Division I (Christian Liberal Arts Colleges) and Division II (Bible Colleges). Nominees must possess a vital Christian testimony and exhibit outstanding leadership qualities. A plaque is awarded. Established in 1989 to honor Pete Maravich, a former NCAA Basketball All-American and NBA player.

• 14661 • Meritorious Service Award
To recognize individuals who, over a period of years, exhibit a dedication and special service to the NCCAA. Their effort must have made a significant contribution to the welfare of the association and be so recognized by the participating colleges as a whole. Examples of persons qualifying for the Meritorious Service Award are: members of the Advisory Committee who render service beyond the call of duty; national officers, district officers, Christian lay-leaders who have given sacrificially to the association; and others whose service to the NCCAA is exceptional. The award is presented at the annual meeting luncheon.

• 14662 • Outstanding Player
To recognize an outstanding student athlete at the National Championship.

• 14663 • Ben Peterson Christian Sportsmanship Award
To recognize an NCCAA wrestler who is a junior or senior attending the NCCAA National Championships. The following criteria are taken into consideration: academics, christian service, college activities/awards (in addition to wrestling), team influence/leadership, wrestling record (career and present year), and personal discipline/lifestyle. The wrestling coaches present at the National Championship make the selection for this award. Coaches may not vote for their own nominee.

• 14664 • Scholar-Athlete
To recognize a student athlete for outstanding academic performance.

• 14665 • Sports Ministries Award
To recognize member institutions having significant spiritual outreach through the utilization of athletic ministries. All institutions wishing to be considered for this award should send a detailed summary of their outreach ministries program to the NCCAA Executive Director by November 1 of each year. The award is given to the representative of the institution at the annual meeting luncheon.

• 14666 • Student-Athlete of the Week
To recognize one player in each sport, both Divisions I and II, chosen from the list of nominees submitted by all sanctioned sports each week.The student-athlete should exemplify the Christian ideals held by the NCCAA.The sanctioned national tournament sports are: baseball, men's and women's basketball, men's and women's cross-country, men's golf, men's and women's indoor track and field, men's and women's soccer, softball, men's tennis, men's and women's track and field and women's volleyball. Awarded every week in each sport.

• 14667 • Wheeler Cross Country Award
To recognize the outstanding Christian male and female cross country participants of the nation. Nominees must be team members of a Christian college recognized by the NCCAA and possess a vital Christian testimony. Junior and senior students in good academic standing who participate in the national meet the year of the award may be nominated by their coach. A plaque is awarded to each recipient and a trophy is awarded to each recipient's institution. Established in 1987. Sponsored by John and Joanne Wheeler.

• 14668 • Wheeler Track and Field Awards
To recognize the outstanding Christian male and female track and field participants of the nation. Nominees must be team members of a Christian college recognized by the NCCAA and possess a vital Christian testimony on and off the track. Junior and senior students in good academic standing who participate in the national meet the year of the award may be nominated by their coach. A plaque is awarded to each recipient and a trophy is awarded to each recipient's institution. Established in 1984. Sponsored by John and Joanne Wheeler.

• 14669 • Wilhelmi-Haskell Stewardship Award
To recognize individuals who, over a period of years, have exhibited dedicated work and loyal support of the NCCAA program and ministry. The recipient is recommended by the Executive Director or the Director of Advancement. This award is presented at the annual meeting luncheon.

• 14670 • Wittnauer NCCAA Player of the Year
To recognize the outstanding Christian soccer player of the nation. Junior or senior students in good academic standing who are team members of a Christian College recognized by the NCCAA and who exhibit outstanding leadership qualities including Christian service activities are eligible. Athletes may be nominated by their soccer coach by November 1. Established in 1987. Sponsored by Kay Jewelers. Formerly: (1997) Kay Jeweler's/J.B. Robinson Award.

• 14671 •
National Citizens' Coalition
Miriam Alford, Dir.
27 Queen St. E, Ste. 501
Toronto, ON, Canada M5C 2M6
Phone: (416)869-3838
Fax: (416)869-1891
E-mail: ncc@morefreedom.org
Home Page: http://www.morefreedom.org

• 14672 • Colin M. Brown Freedom Medal
To recognize an individual for an outstanding contribution to the advancement and defense of basic political and economic freedoms. The deadline for nominations is June 30. A framed silver medal is awarded at an annual dinner held in November. Established in 1987 by Colin M. Brown, founder of the organization.

• 14673 •
National Civic League
Christopher T. Gates, Pres.
1445 Market St., Ste. 300
1445 Market, Ste. 300
Denver, CO 80202
Phone: (303)571-4343
Toll-Free: 800-864-8622
Fax: (303)571-4404
E-mail: ncl@ncl.org
Home Page: http://www.ncl.org

Formerly: (1981) National Municipal League.

• 14674 • All-America City Awards
To encourage and recognize civic excellence in all major areas of community improvement. Cities, towns, counties, neighborhoods, and regions where citizens, government, business, and voluntary organizations pull together to address local critical issues are eligible. Selection criteria include: participation of the public, private, and nonprofit sectors and key constituencies to the maximum extent possible; recognition and involvement of diverse segments and perspectives (ethnic, racial, socio-economic, age, etc.) in community decision-making; creative use and leveraging of community resources; significant and specific community achievements; projects that address the community's most important needs; cooperation across jurisdictional boundaries; clear demonstration of project results and impacts (i.e., dollars raised or number of people affected); projects that have significantly improved the community within the last three years and have the potential to continue improving the quality of life; and documentation of the ways in which the lives of children and youth have been tangibly improved. A plaque is awarded annually in the spring to ten U.S. communities. Established in 1949. Formerly: .

• 14675 •
National Classification Management Society
Sharon K. Tannahill, Exec.Dir.
994 Old Eagle School Rd., Ste. 1019
Wayne, PA 19087-1866
Phone: (610)971-4856
Fax: (610)971-4859
E-mail: info@classmgmt.com
Home Page: http://www.classmgmt.com

• 14676 • Donald B. Woodbridge Award
For recognition of excellence in the general field of classification management. Nominations must be submitted by November 1 by an individual, chapter, or area. A mounted plaque is presented when merited at the annual National Seminar. Established in 1980 in honor of Donald B. Woodbridge, a past president and founder of NCMS.

• 14677 •
National Coalition of 100 Black Women
Leslie A. Mays, Pres.
38 W 32nd St., Ste. 1610
New York, NY 10001-3816
Phone: (212)947-2196
Fax: (212)947-2477
E-mail: nc100bw@aol.com
Home Page: http://www.ncbw.org

• 14678 • Candace Award
To recognize leadership and achievements of black women in various fields of endeavor. Named after the ancient Ethiopian word for queen.

• 14679 •
National Coffee Association of U.S.A.
Robert F. Nelson, Pres./CEO
15 Maiden Ln., Ste. 1405
New York, NY 10038-4003
Phone: (212)766-4007
Fax: (212)766-5815
E-mail: djpecheco@ncausa.org
Home Page: http://www.ncausa.org

• 14680 • Silver Service/Silver Cup Awards

To recognize an operator member of the Association who makes extraordinary professional strides which reflect positively upon himself and the industry. Candidates may be nominated by their peers and competitors who acknowledge them as leaders in a progressive industry. Candidates must be: an NCSA member in good standing; either an owner or branch manager of a coffee service company; a coffee service operator for a minimum of four years; active in efforts to improve the industry; and able to submit recommendations from one competitor and two suppliers. Engraved plaques and a silver coffee service are awarded annually. Established in 1975.

• 14681 •
National College of District Attorneys
Robert S. Fertitta, Dean
University of South Carolina Law School
1600 Hampton St., Ste. 414
937 Assembly St.
Columbia, SC 29208
Phone: (803)544-5005
Fax: (803)544-5301
E-mail: kuhn@law.law.sc.edu
Home Page: http://www.law.sc.edu/ncda

• 14682 • Distinguished Faculty Award

To recognize outstanding contributions to the continuing education of prosecuting attorneys. Candidate must have lectured for the college at Houston for at least three years to be considered for the award. A plaque is presented annually. Established in 1976.

• 14683 • Lecturer of Merit

To recognize members who have lectured at numerous courses, contributed written course materials, and have demonstrated a particular interest and ability in continuing legal education. Established in 1979.

• 14684 •
National Collegiate Athletic Association
Myles Brand, Pres.
PO Box 6222
700 W Washington St.
Indianapolis, IN 46206-6222
Phone: (317)917-6222
Fax: (317)917-6888
Home Page: http://www2.ncaa.org

• 14685 • Award of Valor

To recognize a coach or administrator currently associated with intercollegiate athletics or a current or former varsity letter-winner at an NCAA institution who, when confronted with a situation involving personal danger, averted or minimized potential disaster by courageous action or noteworthy bravery. Nomination deadline is August 1. Awarded when merited. Established in 1974.

• 14686 • National College Football Champions

Through an NCAA conducted national championship competition for Divisions I-AA, II, and III, an official national champion team is selected each year. An unofficial national champion in I-A is selected by the Associated Press (AP) poll of sportswriters and the United Press International (UPI) poll of football coaches. The AP poll originated in 1936; the UPI poll in 1950.

• 14687 • NCAA National Championships

The NCAA sponsors 80 national championships annually in 37 sports for its member institutions. It oversees tournaments to determine team and individual National Collegiate Champions in the following men's and women's sports: baseball, basketball, bowling, cross country, fencing, field hockey, football, golf, gymnastics, ice hockey, lacrosse, rifle, rowing, skiing, soccer, softball, swimming and diving, tennis, track and field, volleyball, water polo, and wrestling. To be eligible to enter a team or individual in NCAA championship competition, an institution must be an active member in good standing in the appropriate division or have its sport so classified and be eligible under the rules of the intercollegiate athletics conference of which it is a member.

• 14688 • Theodore Roosevelt Award

This, the Teddy Award, the highest individual honor the Association can bestow, is given to an individual for whom competitive athletics in college and attention to physical well-being thereafter have been important factors in a distinguished career of national significance and achievement. More specifically, the Teddy Award is presented annually to a distinguished citizen of national reputation and outstanding accomplishment who, having earned a varsity athletics award in college, has by a continuing interest and concern for physical fitness and competitive sport and by personal example exemplified most clearly and forcefully the ideals and purposes to which collegiate athletics programs and amateur sports competitions are dedicated. Nomination deadline is August 1. Established in 1967.

• 14689 • Silver Anniversary Award

To recognize six distinguished former student athletes on their silver (25th) anniversary as colleges graduates. The recipient must have been a varsity letter-winner at an NCAA member institution. Eligibility must have been completed 25 years before the Convention date, and the recipient must be able to attend the honors program. Selection criteria consist of athletic achievement, campus activities, professional accomplishment, and contributions to professional organizations and to charitable and civic activities. Nomination deadline is August 1. Established in 1973. Formerly: College Athletics Top Ten.

• 14690 •
National Collegiate Athletic Association Division 1 Track Coaches Association
Myles Brand, Contact
PO Box 6222
700 W. Washington St.
Indianapolis, IN 46206-6222
Phone: (317)917-6222
Fax: (317)917-6888
Home Page: http://www.ncaa.org/wps/portal

• 14691 • Academic Athletes of the Year (All Academic Team)

To recognize outstanding athletes. Plaques and certificates are presented biannually at the site of the NCAA Championships. Established in 1964.

• 14692 • All American Awards

To recognize the top 8 place winners in indoor and outdoor track. Plaques and certificates are presented biannually at the site of the NCAA Championships. Established 1964.

• 14693 • District Coach of the Year

To recognize an outstanding NCAA Division 1 indoor and outdoor track coach of the year. Plaques and certificates are awarded biannually at the site of the NCAA Championships. Established in 1964.

• 14694 • Honorary Membership (Outstanding Contributors)

To recognize exceptional contributions to the Association. Plaques and certificates are presented biannually at the site of the NCAA Championships. Established in 1964.

• 14695 • National Coach of the Year

To recognize an outstanding NCAA Division 1 indoor and outdoor track coach. Plaques and certificates are presented biannually at the site of the NCAA Championships. Established in 1964.

• 14696 • Outstanding Male and Female Athlete of the Year

To recognize outstanding athletic achievements by men and women. Plaques and awards are presented biannually at the site of the NCAA Championships. Established 1964.

• 14697 •
National Commission on Correctional Health Care
Edward A. Harrison, Pres.
1145 W Diversey Pkwy.
Chicago, IL 60614
Phone: (773)880-1460
Fax: (773)880-2424
E-mail: info@ncchc.org
Home Page: http://www.ncchc.org

• 14698 • Bernard P. Harrison Award of Merit
To honor an individual for a significant contribution to correctional health care. Individuals may be nominated for a single event or a series of accomplishments. A plaque is awarded annually at the national conference in the fall. Established in 1986 and named in 1990 in honor of Bernard P. Harrison, J. D., who founded the commission and served as its first president. Formerly: (1991) Award of Merit.

• 14699 • Poetry and Poster Contest
Recognizes talent in art and poetry for incarcerated youth. Selection is based on exceptional skills in either their artistic or poetic abilities. Judging is done by a panel with backgrounds in psychiatry, journalism, art therapy, poetry, English literature, and HIV programming. Winners are selected in the following categories: ages 14 and under (first, second, and third place); ages 15-17 (first, second, and third place); and ages 18-21 (first, second and third place). Established in 2001.

• 14700 •
National Committee on American Foreign Policy
Monica Scott, Program Dir.
320 Park Ave., 8th Fl.
New York, NY 10022-6839
Phone: (212)224-1120
Fax: (212)224-2524
E-mail: contact@ncafp.org
Home Page: http://www.ncafp.org

• 14701 • William J. Flynn Initiative for Peace Award
To recognize an individual who worked tirelessly to resolve a conflict that has affected the national interests of the United States. Established in 1987. Formerly: (2001) Initiative for Peace Award.

• 14702 • Human Rights Award
Special human rights award. Established in 1987, it was first presented to Elie Wiesel.

• 14703 • George F. Kennan Award for Distinguished Public Service
To recognize an American who has served the United States in an exemplary way and has made a seminal contribution to defining and illuminating the national interest of the United States. A crystal dome is awarded. Established in 1994 in honor of George F. Kennan, a scholar, diplomat, and statesman.

• 14704 • Hans J. Morgenthau Award
To recognize an individual whose efforts have contributed to the advancement of the national interests of the United States and to the achievement of U.S. foreign policy objectives within the framework of political realism. United States and foreign citizens are eligible. Established in 1981 in honor of Hans J. Morgenthau, a scholar and founder of the organization. Formerly: Hans J. Morgenthau Memorial Award.

• 14705 •
National Communication Association
Roger Smitter, Dir.
1765 N St. NW
Washington, DC 20036
Phone: (202)464-4622
Fax: (202)464-4600
E-mail: smorreale@natcom.org
Home Page: http://www.natcom.org

Formerly: (1970) Speech Association of America; Speech Communication Association.

• 14706 • Samuel L. Becker Distinguished Service Award
To recognize an individual who has made outstanding contributions to both SCA and the profession. The deadline for nominations is April 15. An engraved plaque is awarded annually. Established in 1971. Formerly: (1998) SCA Distinguished Service Award.

• 14707 • Donald H. Ecroyd Award for Outstanding Teaching in Higher Education
To honor a member who exemplifies superlative teaching in higher education. Individuals with Master's degrees or higher in the speech communication discipline who hold full-time teaching assignments are eligible. A plaque and a monetary prize of $500 is awarded annually. Established in 1988.

• 14708 • Douglas W. Ehninger Distinguished Rhetorical Scholar Award
To honor scholars who have executed research programs in rhetorical theory, rhetorical criticism, and/or public address studies. The award is given to a person, who, through multiple publications and presentations around a rhetorical topic or theme, demonstrates intellectual creativity, perseverance, and impact on academic communities. Members of the Association must be nominated by April 15. A plaque and a monetary award of $500 is presented annually. Established in 1986.

• 14709 • Golden Anniversary Monograph Awards
To recognize the authors of outstanding monographs or articles in the speech communication arts and sciences. Members of the Association are eligible. The deadline for nominations is April 15. Up to three monetary awards of $200 are awarded annually. The Diamond Anniversary Book Award is also presented annually. Established in 1964. Formerly: (1987) SCA Golden Anniversary Fund Awards.

• 14710 • Franklyn S. Haiman Award for Distinguished Scholarship in Freedom of Expression
To recognize members for outstanding published research on freedom of expression. The body of scholarship that has appeared in the *Free Speech Yearbook* or other journals, books, or monographs within the past three years is eligible. Awarded annually. Established in 1976. Formerly: (1988) Herbert A. Wichelns Freedom of Speech Award; (1990) Haiman Award.

• 14711 • Lilla A. Heston Award for Outstanding Scholarship in Interpretation and Performance Studies
To recognize an author of published research and creative scholarship in interpretation and performance studies. The scholarship recognized by the award is to be broadly defined to include the spectrum of scholarship expressed by *Text and Performance Quarterly*. While *TPQ* is to serve as a model for defining the scope of the award, the scholarship recognized by the award may be published in any SCA journal; in a major research or literary journal of another association or organization; in book or monograph form; or published in other than a print media, such as but not limited to live performance, film, video tape, photography, audio tape, and radio. Scholarship published during the previous three-year period is eligible. A monetary award of $1,000 and a plaque are presented annually. Established in 1990 to honor Lilla A. Heston, teacher, scholar, performer, director, editor, and administrator whose work brought credit to the entire field of speech communication.

• 14712 • Robert J. Kibler Memorial Award
To recognize an individual for the qualities epitomized by the personal and professional life of Robert J. Kibler, the late Professor of Communications at Florida State University. These included dedication to excellence, commitment to the profession, concern for others, vision of what could be, acceptance of diversity, and forthrightness. The deadline for nominations is April 15. A plaque is awarded annually. Established in 1979 to honor Dr. Robert J. Kibler, Professor of Communication at Florida State University.

• 14713 • Gerald R. Miller Outstanding Doctoral Dissertation Award
To recognize outstanding doctoral dissertations in any of the communication arts and sciences. The deadline for nominations is April 15. Up to three awards of $200 each are awarded annually. Established in 1971.

• 14714 • Marcella E. Oberle Award for Outstanding Teaching in Grades K-12
To recognize teachers in kindergarten through senior high school level who have exhibited both outstanding teaching and a commitment to teaching and the speech communication profession. The nominee must be considered an outstanding teacher by supervisors, colleagues, and students, and must be committed to high standards and quality education, and utilize innovative and/or exemplary teaching practices. The nominee also is expected to perform community service activities and to contribute favorably to the speech communication profession and to have helped make speech communication an integral part of his or her school district. A monetary award of $250 is presented annually. Established in 1989 to honor Marcella Oberle.

• 14715 • Karl R. Wallace Memorial Award
To foster and promote philosophical, historical, or critical scholarship in rhetoric and public dis-

course. Individuals who have recently received a PhD degree or who will receive the degree soon after the award are eligible. The deadline for nominations is April 15. A plaque and a monetary prize of $1,200 are awarded annually. Established in 1976 in memory of Karl Wallace, the distinguished rhetorical scholar.

• 14716 • James A. Winans/Herbert A. Wichelns Memorial Award for Distinguished Scholarship in Rhetoric and Public Address

To recognize members who authored an outstanding scholarly book on rhetoric and/or public address. The deadline for nominations is April 15. A plaque and a monetary prize of $1,000 are awarded annually. Established in 1966 by students, colleagues, and admirers of James Winans and Herbert Wichelns, two distinguished Cornell University professors.

• 14717 • Charles H. Woolbert Research Award

To recognize a member whose research has proven to be particularly seminal. Individuals who have published journal articles or book chapters that have stood the test of time and that have become the stimulus for new conceptualizations of speech communication phenomena are eligible. When first published, the article or chapter to be honored may well not have been seen to be as heuristic as it later became. Thus, the Woolbert Award is reserved for articles that at the time of the award are in their tenth through fifteenth years in print and have not previously received an SCA sponsored award. The nominations deadline is April 15. An engraved plaque is awarded annually. Established in 1980 in honor of Charles Woolbert, one of the field's earliest and most distinguished social scientists.

• 14718 •
National Confectionery Sales Association
Teresa M. Tarantino, Exec.Dir.
10225 Berea Rd., Ste. B
Cleveland, OH 44102
Phone: (216)631-8200
Fax: (216)631-8210
E-mail: ttarantino@mail.propressinc.com
Home Page: http://www.candyhalloffame.com

• 14719 • Candy Hall of Fame

To recognize outstanding individuals who have distinguished themselves by their dedication and loyalty to the furtherance of the image of the candy industry. Sales representatives, candy manufacturers, national candy sales managers, and candy merchandisers are eligible for nomination. They must be 45 years of age or older, and have at least 20 years of service in the industry. A plaque is awarded annually and the inductee's name is listed on a Candy Hall of Fame Plaque on permanent display at Chocolate World, Hershey, Pennsylvania. Established in 1971 by Arthur Sarnow and Robert J. Pearsall, co-founders.

• 14720 •
National Conference of Puerto Rican Women
Lydia M. Sosa, Nat.Pres.
5 Thomas Cir. NW
Washington, DC 20005
Phone: (202)387-4716
E-mail: webmaster@wannagetaway.com

• 14721 • National Conference of Puerto Rican Women Award

For recognition of outstanding service to the advancement of Puerto Rican and Hispanic women. Awards are presented at the annual conference. Established in 1972.

• 14722 •
National Conference of Women's Bar Associations
Pamela L. Nicholson, Exec.Dir.
PO Box 82366
Portland, OR 97282-0366
Phone: (503)657-3813
Fax: (503)657-3932
E-mail: info@ncwba.org
Home Page: http://www.ncwba.org

• 14723 • Public Service Award

To recognize solutions offered by Women's Bar Associations to problems facing the less fortunate. Women's bar associations are eligible. A plaque is awarded annually at the annual meeting. Established in 1985.

• 14724 •
National Conference on Peacemaking and Conflict Resolution
Ann Yellott, Admin./Network Coor.
3070 Bristol Pike, Ste. 116
Bensalem, PA 19020
Phone: (520)670-1541
Toll-Free: 877-397-3223
Fax: (215)245-6994
E-mail: peaceweb@apeacemaker.net
Home Page: http://www.apeacemaker.net

• 14725 • Margaret S. Herrman Founder's Award

To recognize significant contributions to the PeaceWeb and the field of peacemaking and conflict resolution. A plaque is awarded at the PeaceWeb biennial conference. Established in 1991.

• 14726 •
National Constables Association
Bruce Speight, Natl.Dir. of Communications
16 Stonybrook Dr.
Levittown, PA 19055-2217
Phone: (215)547-6400
Phone: (318)256-0195
Toll-Free: 800-272-1775
Fax: (215)943-0979
E-mail: ntlconstable@lycos.com
Home Page: http://www.angelfire.com/la/nationalconstable

• 14727 • Community-Constable Partnership Award

To recognize the community, city, or local municipality which has given positive recognition to the position of the Constable. Awarded annually.

• 14728 • Constable of the Year

To recognize the activities and accomplishments that have brought recognition, dignity, and status to the position of a selected Constable. Awarded annually.

• 14729 • Extraordinary Service/Hero Award

To honor the service beyond the call of duty, such as an act or heroism or total devotion to a specific achievement. Awarded annually.

• 14730 • Fighter Against Drug Abuse

To recognize the Constable whose personal efforts have had a substantive input against the abuse of drugs. Awarded annually.

• 14731 • Outstanding Service to the Constable System by a Non-Constable Award

To recognize the non-constable person whose activities have brought positive recognition to the position of Constable. Awarded annually.

• 14732 •
National Consumers League
Linda Golodner, Pres./CEO
1701 K St. NW, Ste. 1200
Washington, DC 20006
Phone: (202)835-3323
Fax: (202)835-0747
E-mail: info@nclnet.org
Home Page: http://www.nclnet.org

• 14733 • Florence Kelley Consumer Leadership Award

For recognition of individuals who have emulated Kelley's approach to improving the welfare of all consumers. A framed certificate featuring Kelley's portrait is presented annually. Established in 1995.

• 14734 • Trumpeter Award

For recognition of contributions by consumer advocates. Awardee is determined by the Board of Directors. A framed certificate featuring a trumpet is presented annually. Established in 1973. Formerly: (1976) Distinguished Citizen Award.

• 14735 •
National Corn Growers Association
Rick Tolman, CEO
632 Cepi Dr.
Chesterfield, MO 63005
Phone: (636)733-9004
Fax: (636)733-9005
E-mail: corninfo@ncga.com
Home Page: http://www.ncga.com

• 14736 • **National Corn Yield Contest**
To encourage the development of new and innovative management practices and to show the importance of using sound cultural practices in U.S. corn production. Entrants must hold a membership in the National Corn Growers Association. The contest entry must be at least 10 acres of one corn hybrid in one continuous plot. Trophies are awarded to the first, second, and third place National and State winners in each of the nine contest classes. Awarded annually. Application deadline is August 1.

• 14737 •
National Corvette Restorers Society
Gilbert Scrivner, Pres.
6291 Day Rd.
Cincinnati, OH 45252-1334
Phone: (513)385-8526
Phone: (513)385-6367
Fax: (513)385-8554
E-mail: ncrscincy@aol.com
Home Page: http://www.ncrs.org

• 14738 • **Duntov Mark of Excellence Award**
To recognize individuals for the preservation and restoration of corvettes dating from 1953 to 1982. Society members are eligible. Corvette owners must restore the vehicle to NCRS judging specifications and attain at least 97 out of 100 points (at two national or regional NCRS events) and present the car for a performance test, which must be passed. A plaque and a certificate are awarded annually at the national convention. Established in 1985 in honor of Zora Arkus-Duntov, chief engineer for the Chevrolet Corvette for many years.

• 14739 • **Folz Memorial Award**
To recognize the farthest driven 1953-1982 Corvette of the national convention that achieves a minimum judging score of 94 points out of 100, including mileage points. Members are eligible. A plaque is awarded annually at the national convention. Established in 1988 in memory of the late Sam Folz of Kalamazoo, Michigan, a founder of NCRS.

• 14740 •
National Cosmetology Association
Josephine Zeppieri, Pres.
401 N Michigan Ave., 22 Fl.
Chicago, IL 60611
Phone: (312)527-6765
Fax: (312)464-6118
E-mail: nca1@ncacares.org
Home Page: http://www.salonprofessionals.org

Formerly: (1986) National Hairdressers and Cosmetologists Association.

• 14741 • **American Image Enhancement Award**
To recognize a person or an entity who has contributed to the enhancement of the image of a particular segment of the population, such as the young, elderly, etc. A Lenox crystal obelisk is awarded to the celebrity and to that winner's NCA member cosmetologist. Established in 1987.

• 14742 • **Female Style Maker of the Year**
To recognize a nationally known female figure for her lifestyle, fashion sense, and degree of public influence. Criteria for consideration are public visibility within the arts, politics, or any other social area. The winner is selected from a field of ten nominees through a membership balloting procedure. She also becomes national spokesperson for Look Good...Feel Better, a program that helps female cancer patients overcome the appearance-related effects of treatment. The award is presented annually in July at the NCA National Convention. Established in 1974. Formerly: (1987) Top Ten Female Style Makers of the Year.

• 14743 • **Male Style Maker of the Year**
To recognize a nationally known male figure for his lifestyle, fashion sense, and degree of public influence. Criteria for consideration are public visibility in the arts, politics, or any other social area. The winner is selected from a field of ten noninees through a membership balloting procedure. The award is presented annually in July at the NCA National Convention. Established in 1984.

• 14744 •
National Costumers Association
Jennifer Skarstedt, Sec.-Treas.
121 N Bosart Ave.
Indianapolis, IN 46201
Phone: (317)351-1940
Toll-Free: 800-NCA-1321
Fax: (317)351-1941
E-mail: office@costumers.org
Home Page: http://www.costumers.org

• 14745 • **Grand International Trophy for Excellence of Design and Fabric**
To recognize excellence of design and fabrics. A trophy is awarded annually at the national convention.

• 14746 • **Major Harrelson Service Award**
To recognize members for distinguished dedication and service to the association. A walnut plaque with an engraved gold plate is awarded when merited at the national convention. Established in 1956.

• 14747 •
National Council for Adoption
Thomas Atwood, Pres.
225 N Washington St.
Alexandria, VA 22314-2561
Phone: (703)299-6633
Fax: (703)299-6004
E-mail: ncfa@ncfa-usa.org
Home Page: http://www.adoptioncouncil.org

Formerly: National Committee for Adoption.

• 14748 • **Adoption Hall of Fame Award**
To recognize outstanding contributions. A Tiffany crystal is awarded annually. Established in 1983.

• 14749 • **Friend of Adoption**
To recognize individuals for a significant impact upon and contribution to the field of adoption. A plaque is awarded annually at the annual meeting. Established in 1980.

• 14750 •
National Council for Community Behavioral Healthcare
Linda Rosenberg, Pres./CEO
12300 Twinbrook Pkwy., Ste. 320
Rockville, MD 20852
Phone: (301)984-6200
Fax: (301)881-7159
E-mail: lindar@nccbh.org
Home Page: http://www.nccbh.org

• 14751 • **Awards of Excellence**
To recognize innovation and achievement in fundraising and business development; special programming for children with a serious emotional disturbance or chemical addiction problem and adults and seniors with a serious mental illness or chemical addiction; public policy achievements; and community behavioral health provider organizational achievement in meeting the demands of the health care environment. Recipients must be NCCBH member organizations. Plaques are awarded each year at the NCCBH Annual Training Conference. Established in 1975.

• 14752 •
National Council for Continuing Education and Training
Wayne Williams, Pres.
PO Box 130623
Carlsbad, CA 92013-0623
Phone: (760)753-8375
Fax: (760)942-7296
E-mail: wwilliam@tcc.ctc.edu
Home Page: http://www.nccet.org

Formerly: National Council on Community Services for Community and Junior Colleges; National Council on Community Services and Continuing Education.

• 14753 • **National Leadership Award**
To recognize an individual for achievement in the continuing education and workforce training field. Awards are given in the following categories: Inside the Field: to recognize a community college administrator, American Association of Community Colleges staff or board member, NCCET member, or leader whose work in community services, continuing education, and/or learning technologies has been national in impact and significance; Outside the Field: to recognize an individual who has contributed to the field of community services, continuing education, workforce development, and/or learning technologies who is affiliated with another higher education segment, government, other educational organization, business and indus-

Awards are arranged in alphabetical order below their administering organizations

try, mass media, or public organizations; and Exemplary Service: to recognize outstanding service to the NCCET by board members, chairpersons, and regional and functional directors (exclusive of the president). Nominations may be made by the Board of Directors, and must be submitted by December 10. Plaques are awarded to the National and Regional winners annually at the American Association of Community and Colleges convention in April. Established in 1970. Formerly: National Person of the Year Award.

• 14754 • President's Leadership Award
To recognize an individual for achievement and/or contribution to the continuing education and workforce training field. A plaque is awarded annually at the American Association of Community Colleges convention. Established in 1985.

• 14755 • Regional Leadership Award
To recognize an individual's contribution to continuing education and workforce training known to a significant number of people and/or institutions in the area. The influence must have extended over a significant time period, i.e., two to five years. Regional representatives from the ten areas are responsible for the nomination process and selection. Plaques are awarded annually at the American Association of Community Colleges convention in April. Established in 1970. Formerly: Regional Person of the Year Award.

• 14756 •
National Council for Eurasian and East European Research
910 17th St. NW, Ste. 300
Washington, DC 20006
Phone: (202)822-6950
Fax: (202)822-6955
E-mail: dc@nceeer.org
Home Page: http://www.nceeer.org

• 14757 • Research Contracts
Selection is based on the results of a national competition. Inquire for competition details.

• 14758 •
National Council for GeoCosmic Research
Liane Thomas Wade, Exec.Sec.
8810C Jamacha Blvd., No. 183
Spring Valley, CA 91977
Phone: (619)303-9236
E-mail: execdir@geocosmic.org
Home Page: http://www.geocosmic.org

• 14759 • Sisyphus Award
To recognize members for service to the Council and its goals furthering the study of the interaction of man and the Universe. A trophy is awarded triennially at the convention. Established in 1989.

• 14760 •
National Council for Geographic Education
Dr. Michal L. LeVasseur, Exec.Dir.
206A Martin Hall
Jacksonville State Univ.
Jacksonville, AL 36265-1602
Phone: (256)782-5293
Fax: (256)782-5336
E-mail: ncge@ncge.org
Home Page: http://www.ncge.org

• 14761 • College/University Excellence of Scholarship Award
To honor the outstanding graduating senior geography major from each college and university in North America making a nomination. A certificate is awarded annually. Co-sponsored by the Association of American Geographers.

• 14762 • Cram Scholarships
Awarded by the NCGE and the George F. Cram Co. for K-12 teachers for exemplary materials presentations at the annual meeting. A monetary prize of $750 is awarded annually.

• 14763 • Distinguished Mentor Award
To recognize up to three professors who are associated with a Ph.D. granting institution and who have aided geographers who are presently active in geographic education. Plaques are awarded at the NCGE annual meeting.

• 14764 • Distinguished Teaching Achievement Awards
For recognition of outstanding teaching of geography. Two separate awards are given: the College/University Distinguished Teaching Achievement Award and the K-12 Distinguished Teaching Achievement Award. Plaques and a one-year membership in the Association are awarded annually at the council's convention banquet.

• 14765 • Geographic Education Dissertation Award
To recognize outstanding doctoral research. First prize of $300 and second prize of $100 is awarded annually.

• 14766 • *Journal of Geography* Awards
To encourage and reward good writing and good ideas in the teaching of geography by recognizing the authors of the following: best article related to elementary teaching in the *Journal,* best article related to secondary teaching published in the *Journal,* and best content article published in the *Journal.* A plaque is awarded every two years, alternating between the three education levels: elementary, secondary, and college/university. The award for the best content article is presented annually. Nomination deadline is June 15.

• 14767 • George J. Miller Distinguished Service Award
This, the highest award given by the NCGE, honors an individual for the quality and character of contributions to geographic education. Service to the NCGE is not the sole criteria for this award. Instead, service to geographic education is primary, and may include research, papers and publications, teaching, grants, service as a role model, lobbying on behalf of geographic education, training of teachers, development of curriculum materials, and administrative activities. Nomination deadline is March 1. A plaque is awarded annually at the council's convention banquet.

• 14768 • Publication Award
To recognize and encourage interest in geographic education among non-geographers by recognizing the best article on geographic education in a non-geographic magazine. A plaque is awarded annually at the council's convention banquet.

• 14769 • Women in Geography Education Scholarship
To recognize an outstanding female student with a major in geographic education. A scholarship of $300 and travel expenses of $300 are awarded annually.

• 14770 •
National Council for Interior Design Qualification
Jeffrey F. Kenney, Exec.Dir.
1200 18th St. NW, No. 1001
Washington, DC 20036-2506
Phone: (202)721-0220
Fax: (202)721-0221
E-mail: info@ncidq.org
Home Page: http://www.ncidq.org

• 14771 • Louis S. Tregre Award
To recognize diligent and consistent volunteer work to further the goals of NCIDQ. A crystal trophy is awarded at the Annual Meeting. Established in 1991, in honor of Louis S. Tregre, founding director and chairman emeritus.

• 14772 •
National Council for Marketing and Public Relations
Becky Olson, Exec.Dir.
PO Box 336039
Greeley, CO 80633
Phone: (970)330-0771
Fax: (970)330-0769
E-mail: bolson@ncmpr.org
Home Page: http://www.ncmpr.org

Formerly: National Council for Community Relations.

• 14773 • Communicator of the Year Award
For recognition of outstanding public relations leadership and management at two-year colleges. Nominations must be made by a public information officer or president and endorsed by the nominee's chief executive officer. The nominee must be a member of NCMPR. Areas to be considered for nominations include, but are not limited to, the following: (1) Effective management/development of a project that has local,

regional or national impact; (2) Examples of technical skills in publications, advertising, media as evidenced in a campaign or cited by awards; (3) Improvement of communications within the institution; and (4) Professional development activities, including academic studies, workshops, publications, consultations. Special emphasis is placed on contributions to NCMPR. It is awarded annually in each of NCMPR's seven districts, and district recipients automatically become a nominee for the national award, which is presented at the national conference. Established in 1980. Formerly: (1985) Practitioner of the Year.

• 14774 • Pacesetter of the Year Award

To recognize a community college president or CEO who has demonstrated special leadership and support in marketing and public relations. Nominations must be made by an NCMPR member. Areas to be considered for nominations include, but are not limited to, the following: (1) Programs, plans, and activities related to community college advancement at the local, regional, or national level; (2) Participation in civic and service groups at executive level; (3) Contributions to, and support of, the public relations office; and (4) Development/administering of educational programs that demonstrate vision, planning, and executive leadership. It is awarded annually in each of NCMPR's seven districts, and district recipients automatically become a nominee for the national award, which is presented at the national conference. Established in 1980.

• 14775 • Paragon Awards

To recognize outstanding achievement in communications at community, junior, and technical colleges. The entry/entries must have been published, broadcast, displayed, and used for the first time between December 1 and November 30 of the year preceding the award. Entries must be essentially new designs and publications. Awards are presented in various subcategories among the larger categories of printed publications, advertising, video entries, writing, visual arts, electronic media, and promotional campaigns. A first, second, and third place may be awarded in each category. Established in 1985.

• 14776 • D. Richard Petrizzo Award for Career Achievement

To recognize an NCMPR professional for career accomplishments in college marketing and public relations. Criteria include: (1) Career accomplishments in the two-year college marketing and public relations field, including quality, creativity and impact of the professional work on the institution and community; (2) Exhibited knowledge and skills as a top practitioner, demonstrated in exemplary public relations and marketing programs under their leadership; and (3) Service contributions to the profession, including service to professional organizations (NCMPR and others), impact on developing the professionalism and recognition of the two-year marketing/public relations field, contributions to expanding understanding of the two-year college mission and accomplishments, and contributions to working with newcomers and others in the field. Nominees must have served at least ten years in a marketing/public relations capacity at one or more junior, community, technical, and related institutions. A trophy is awarded annually. Established in 1990 to honor D. Richard Petrizzo, a former NCMPR president who helped shape the organization in its early years.

• 14777 •
National Council for the Social Studies
Susan Griffin, Exec.Dir.
8555 16th St., Ste. 500
Silver Spring, MD 20910
Phone: (301)588-1800
Toll-Free: 800-683-0812
Fax: (301)588-2049
E-mail: ncss@ncss.org
Home Page: http://www.ncss.org

• 14778 • Defense of Academic Freedom Award

To recognize an individual who has distinguished himself/herself in defending the principles of academic freedom in specific controversies, in fostering academic freedom through advocacy, and in defending or advocating the freedom to teach and learn. This defense or advocacy of academic freedom must be related to the teaching of social studies. Persons eligible include classroom teachers, professionals in other areas of education, students, parents, community groups, and members of other organizations. NCSS membership is not required. The deadline for nomination is March 21. A monetary award of $1,500, a commemorative gift, and presentation at the Annual Conference are awarded annually.

• 14779 • Exemplary Research in Social Studies Award

To recognize and encourage scholarly inquiries into significant issues and possibilities for social studies education. The award is given for published research of an empirical, theoretical, or philosophical nature. The research must have social education as its central focus, employ rigorous research standards, advance conception of social education and knowledge of teaching and learning in social education, and attend to social, political, and ethical concerns. Deadline is May 1. Awarded annually.

• 14780 • Fund for the Advancement of Social Studies Education (FASSE) Grant

To encourage diverse and innovative projects in social studies education related to a theme determined by the FASSE Board. The FASSE Board offers two grants up to $1,000 each from among the following categories: K-5, 6-9, 10-12, and college/university (teacher education). NCSS membership is required. The proposal deadline is postmarked March 21. Formerly: (1995) Achievement of Social Studies Education General Grant.

• 14781 • Jean Dresden Grambs Distinguished Career Research in Social Studies Award

To recognize a social studies professional who has made extensive contributions to knowledge concerning significant areas of social studies education through meritorious research. The candidate's research must span ten or more years, focus on social studies education, employ rigorous standards, advance knowledge of teaching and learning in social education, and attend to social, political, and ethical concerns. Submission deadline is May 1. A commemorative gift, presentation at the Annual Conference, and a one-year comprehensive membership in NCSS are presented biennially in odd-numbered years.

• 14782 • Grant for Geographic Literacy

To encourage unique and innovative social studies education projects by teachers and researchers. This grant strives to promote geography education in the schools; to enhance the geographic literacy of students at the classroom, district, or statewide level; and to encourage the integration of geography into the social studies curriculum/classroom. Selection is based on the strength of the program's rationale, the feasibility of its implementation, the number of teachers and students served, and its potential for continuation after initial implementation. The deadline for applications is March 21. A grant of $2,500, a commemorative gift, and presentation at the Annual Conference is awarded annually. Co-sponsored by the George F. Cram Co.

• 14783 • Christa McAuliffe Reach for the Stars Award

To recognize a social studies teacher or teacher-educator who best exemplifies a unique ambition or dream that under ordinary circumstances may not be fulfilled. Applications may be submitted by social studies teachers or social studies teacher-educators currently engaged in full-time work with students and are current members of the Council. Applicants must provide a description of the project, list of instructional responsibilities, and a plan for reporting to the membership of NCSS the realization of the applicant's dream. NCSS membership is required. The deadline for submissions is postmarked May 1. A monetary award of $1,500, a commemorative gift, and presentation at the Annual Conference are awarded annually. Established in 1986 in memory of Christa McAuliffe, an innovative social studies teacher who was the first classroom teacher to participate in space flight.

• 14784 • Larry Metcalf Exemplary Dissertation Award

For recognition of doctoral research that focuses on social education, employs rigorous research standards, advances conception of social education and knowledge of teaching and learning in social education, and attends to social, political, and ethical concerns. A monetary prize of $250 is awarded biennially in odd-numbered years.

• 14785 • James Michener Prize in Writing Award

To recognize and honor persons who through their writing have enhanced the social studies profession through: (1) a career devoted to writing of and about social studies; (2) a body of work that has made the social studies come alive through fiction, non-fiction, children's literature, young adult literature, poetry, or other works; (3) works in history or the social sciences which have contributed to the evolution of the social studies profession; or (4) works that affect the understanding, growth, and future of the society. A monetary award of $5,000, a commemorative gift, Annual Conference recognition and one-hour session presentation are awarded every five years. Deadline is June 1.

• 14786 • Outstanding Elementary Social Studies Teacher of the Year Award
To recognize exceptional classroom social studies teachers for grades K-6 who teach social studies regularly and systematically. Nominee must be a member of NCSS and must have demonstrated an exceptional abilities in at least six of the following seven categories: develop and/or use instructional materials creatively and effectively; incorporate innovative and verified effective instructional strategies and techniques; utilize new scholarship from history, the social sciences, or other appropriate fields; utilize the ten interrelated themes identified in NCSS curriculum standards; foster a spirit of inquiry and the development of skills related to acquiring, organizing, processing, and using information and making decisions related to both domestic and international matters; foster the development of democratic beliefs and values, and the skills needed for citizen participation appropriate to elementary age classroom, school, and community settings; and show evidence of professional involvement in such activities as workshops, curriculum development, and committees. The deadline for nomination is April 1. A monetary award of $2,500, a commemorative gift, presentation at the Annual Conference, and a one-year comprehensive membership in NCSS are awarded annually.

• 14787 • Outstanding Middle Level Social Studies Teacher of the Year
To recognize a middle level (grades 5-8) classroom social studies teacher who has demonstrated an exceptional ability to develop and/or use instructional materials creatively and effectively; incorporate innovative and/or verified effective instructional strategies and techniques; utilize new scholarship from history, the social sciences, or other appropriate fields; utilize the ten interrelated themes identified in NCSS Curriculum Standards; foster a spirit of inquiry and the development of skills related to acquiring, organizing, processing, and using information and making decisions related to both domestic and international matters; foster development of democratic beliefs and values, and the skills needed for citizen participation appropriate to middle school age youth in classroom, school, and community settings; and show evidence of professional involvement through activities such as workshops, curriculum development, committees, and other association activities. Nominees must have maintained current NCSS membership status for at least two consecutive years prior to the nomination date. Self nominations are not accepted. The deadline for nomination is postmarked April 1. A monetary award of $2,500 is bestowed annually. Co-sponsored by *Scholastic, Inc.*

• 14788 • Outstanding Secondary Social Studies Teacher of the Year
To recognize two exceptional classroom social studies teachers for grades 7-12 who teach social studies regularly and systematically. Nominee must be a member of NCSS and must have demonstrated an exceptional abilities in at least six of the following seven categories: develop and/or use instructional materials creatively and effectively; incorporate innovative and verified effective instructional strategies and techniques; utilize new scholarship from history, the social sciences, or other appropriate fields; utilize the ten interrelated themes identified in NCSS curriculum standards; foster a spirit of inquiry and the development of skills related to acquiring, organizing, processing, and using information and making decisions related to both domestic and international matters; foster the development of democratic beliefs and values, and the skills needed for citizen participation appropriate to secondary age classroom, school, and community settings; and show evidence of professional involvement in such activities as workshops, curriculum development, and committees. The deadline for nomination is April 1. A monetary award of $2,500, a commemorative gift, presentation at the Annual Conference, and a one-year comprehensive membership in NCSS are awarded annually.

• 14789 • Social Studies Programs of Excellence
For recognition of two outstanding social studies programs at the district, elementary, middle/junior high, senior high, or teacher education (pre- and in-service) levels. Eligible programs must be currently implemented and complete social studies programs, not single courses or parts of a program, and be consistent with NCSS Standards for the Preparation of Social Studies Teachers or the themes identified in NCSS Curriculum Standards. Up to five state winners, one in each category, may be selected; states may then nominate up to two programs for national consideration. To be considered for the national award, materials must be received from state coordinators. State deadlines vary; national deadline is June 30. Awarded annually. Co-sponsored by MetLife Resources.

• 14790 • Spirit of America Award
To recognize an individual in or outside of the social studies profession who has made a significant or special contribution that exemplifies the American Democratic Spirit that would not be recognized by any other NCSS award. Nominations may be made by anyone in the social studies profession and postmarked by March 21. A commemorative plaque is awarded annually. Co-sponsored by the Social Studies School Service.

• 14791 • Carter G. Woodson Book Award
To recognize the most distinguished social science books appropriate for young readers that depict ethnicity in the United States. The award is intended to encourage the writing, publishing, and dissemination of outstanding social science books for young readers that treat topics related to ethnic minorities and race relations sensitively and accurately. The deadline for nominations is February 1. A plaque and medallion is awarded annually for an elementary (K-6) book and a middle (5-8) or secondary (7-12) book. Established in 1974 in honor of Carter G. Woodson, the black historian and educator who founded and edited the *Journal of Negro History.*

• 14792 •
National Council of Commercial Plant Breeders
Roger McBroom, Pres.
225 Reinekers Ln., Ste. 650
Alexandria, VA 22314
Phone: (703)837-8140
Fax: (703)837-9365
Home Page: http://www.nccpb.org

• 14793 • Graduate Student Plant Breeding Award
To support a graduate student currently pursuing an advanced degree in Plant Breeding at a U.S. university. The award will be made based on (1) significance and originality of basic or applied plant breeding thesis research; (2) strong scholastic achievement in graduate level plant breeding and related coursework; (3) evidence of integrity, professionalism, and effective leadership skills as determined by peer, Graduate Advisor, and Graduate Faculty evaluations. A monetary prize of $2,500 is awarded annually.

• 14794 • Private Plant Breeding Award
For recognition of significant contributions to plant science through basic, applied, or developmental research in plant breeding and genetics during their careers in the private sector. A monetary award of $1,500, a plaque, and a certificate are awarded annually. Established in 1985.

• 14795 • Public Plant Breeding Award
For recognition of outstanding contributions to the advancement of plant breeding and genetics in the public sector. Nomination deadline is May 20. A monetary award of $1,500 and an engraved plaque are awarded annually. Established in 1962.

• 14796 •
National Council of Examiners for Engineering and Surveying
Betsy Brown, Exec.Dir.
280 Seneca Creek Rd.
PO Box 1686
Clemson, SC 29633-1686
Phone: (864)654-6824
Toll-Free: 800-250-3196
Fax: (864)654-6033
E-mail: pfenno@ncees.org
Home Page: http://www.ncees.org

Formerly: (1989) National Council of Engineering Examiners.

• 14797 • Distinguished Service Award
To recognize service by members to State Regulatory Boards, and NCEES through performance on committees and/or as officers. Five awards per year are usually presented. A certificate and a medallion are awarded. In addition, one Distinguished Service Award with Special Commendation is awarded annually. Established in 1938. Formerly: (1980) Distinguished Service Certificate.

• 14798 • Meritorious Service Award
To recognize Member Board and NCEES employees for outstanding service of a nature furthering the effectiveness of the Council in carrying out its objectives. Established in 1992.

• 14799 •
National Council of Farmer Cooperatives
Jean-Mari Peltier, Pres.
50 F St. NW, Ste. 900
Washington, DC 20001
Phone: (202)626-8700
Fax: (202)626-8722
E-mail: jmpeltier@ncfc.org
Home Page: http://www.ncfc.org
Formerly: American Institute of Cooperation.

• 14800 • Cooperative Month Awards
To recognize individuals demonstrating support for the ideals of cooperation. Awards are given in seven categories: cooperative statesmanship, communications, education, public service, international, career, and cooperative month theme. Awarded annually in October by the National Coordinating Committee for October Cooperative Month.

• 14801 • Graduate Awards
For recognition of outstanding graduate theses and dissertations written on topics concerned with aspects of economics, finance, operation, law, or structure of American agricultural cooperatives. Any graduate student in economics, business, communications, sociology, or another relevant field who has an agricultural vocational objective is eligible to submit applications by April 15. The following awards are presented: Edwin G. Nourse Award - $1,500 for the best doctoral dissertation; Kenneth D. Naden Award - $1,000 for the best master's thesis; and E. A. Stokdyk Award - $600 for a runner-up master's thesis. Awarded annually.

• 14802 • Undergraduate Awards
To recognize undergraduates who write outstanding term papers on topics concerned with agricultural cooperatives. Papers submitted must deal with issues affecting the operations of American agricultural cooperatives. Undergraduate students in their junior or senior year at a college or university, or second-year students at a junior or community college may submit papers by June 1. Five monetary awards of $200 each are presented annually.

• 14803 •
National Council of La Raza
Janet Murguia, Pres.
Raul Yzaguirre Bldg.
1126 16th St., NW
Washington, DC 20036
Phone: (202)785-1670
Fax: (202)289-8173
Home Page: http://www.nclr.org

• 14804 • Affiliate of the Year Award
For recognition of an NCLR affiliate for its exemplary work in serving its local community and for supporting NCLR's policy and programmatic initiatives. Selection criteria include the programmatic and advocacy capability of the organization; the initial impact of its work; and the long-range potential impact. A monetary award of $25,000 is presented annually at the annual conference. In addition, three regional honorees, representing the Western, Central, and Eastern regions, each receive a cash award of $5,000. Established in 1980. Sponsored by the Ford Motor Co.

• 14805 • Maclovio Barraza Leadership Award
To recognize individuals who have made specific and identifiable contributions of major significance in promoting the interests of Hispanics in the United States on a local or regional level. Excluded from consideration are those who, at the time of the nomination or receipt of the Award, are members of the NCLR Board of Directors, or are employees of NCLR. Nominees need not be Hispanic. The contribution cited in a nomination should either be recent or have important contemporary relevance to Hispanic Americans. Nomination deadline is September 30. Awarded at the annual Conference. Established in 1981.

• 14806 • Graciela Olivarez La Raza Award
To recognize individuals or groups/organizations that have demonstrated a superior commitment to, and made a significant contribution towards, promoting the interests of Hispanic Americans in the United States on a national level. Excluded from consideration are those who, at the time of the nomination or receipt of the award, are members of the NCLR Board of Directors, or employees of the National Council of La Raza. Nominees need not be Hispanic. The contribution cited in a nomination should either be recent or have important contemporary relevance to Hispanic Americans. Nomination deadline is September 30. Awarded at the annual Conference. Established in 1978.

• 14807 • President's Award
To recognize an individual for outstanding contributions in furthering the goals, philosophy, and mission of the National Council of La Raza and dedication to Hispanic issues and concerns.

• 14808 • Ruben Salazar Award for Communications
To recognize persons, groups, or organizations that have made significant contributions towards promoting a positive, accurate portrayal of Hispanic culture, aspirations, and concerns. Contributions may be in any one of, or a combination of, the following: (1) Print media; (2) Electronics Media (Television, Radio); (3) Films; and (4) Theatre. Excluded from consideration are those who, at the time of the nomination of receipt of the award, are members of the Council of La Raza Board of Directors, or employees of the National Council of La Raza. Nominees need not be Hispanic; however, the contributions cited in a nomination should be either recent or have important contemporary relevance to Hispanic Americans. Nomination deadline is September 30. Awarded at the annual conference. Established in 1979.

• 14809 •
National Council of Less Commonly Taught Languages
Antonia Folarin Schleicher PhD, Exec.Dir.
National African Language Resource Ctr.
4231 Humanities Bldg.
455 N Park St.
Madison, WI 53706
Phone: (608)265-7905
Fax: (608)265-7904
E-mail: ncolctl@mailplus.wisc.edu
Home Page: http://www.councilnet.org

• 14810 • A. Ronald Walton Award
Recognizes a career of distinguished service to the LCTLs. Awarded annually.

• 14811 •
National Council of Secondary School Athletic Directors
Dr. Dave Lutes, Chm.
1900 Association Dr.
Reston, VA 20191-1598
Phone: (703)476-3400
Toll-Free: 800-213-7193
Fax: (703)476-8316
E-mail: naspe@aahperd.org
Home Page: http://www.aahperd.org/naspe

• 14812 • Athletic Director of the Year Award
To recognize secondary school athletic directors who exemplify the highest standards of their profession and have made significant contributions to their schools and communities. Selection is based on the candidate's impact on the lives of students and their use of athletics as a catalyst to achieve some demonstrable progress in the social and cultural environment of the school and community. Both applications and nominations are accepted. The following prizes are awarded: 50 state awards - recipients are selected on the basis of their contributions to schools and communities; five regional awards - winners are selected from among the state recipients; and a National Athletic Director of the Year, who is selected from the recipients of the regional awards by a panel of nationally known individuals interested in sports and education.

Nomination deadline is November 15. A plaque is awarded annually. Established in 1971. Cosponsored by Educational Communications Inc.

• 14813 •
National Council of Senior Citizens
8403 Colesville Rd., Ste. 1200
Silver Spring, MD 20910-3314
Phone: (301)578-8837
Fax: (301)578-8999

• 14814 • Award of Merit/Distinguished Service Award
To recognize lawmakers (usually one U.S. Representative and one U.S. Senator) who have consistently demonstrated dedication and commitment to America's elderly by outstanding work on their behalf in the U.S. Congress or State Legislatures. Also, used on occasion to honor NCSC members, club leaders and other supporters for outstanding work to achieve NCSC's goal of "a better life for older people. . .and for people of all ages." A certificate and framed citation are awarded when merited. Established in 1963.

• 14815 • Jacob Clayman Award
To honor outstanding advocacy on behalf of the nation's elderly. Established in 1992 to honor NCSC's longtime president Jacob Clayman, a champion of seniors, working men and women, consumers, and minorities, and a pioneer in civil rights.

• 14816 • Community Service Award/ Certificate of Merit
To recognize individuals for community service. A certificate and a framed citation are awarded in recognition of dedication and commitment to improving the quality of life for Americans of all ages, and are usually given to activists at the grassroots level. Established in 1968.

• 14817 • Nelson Cruikshank Award
To honor outstanding service on behalf of older people. A designed glass obelisk with the NCSC logo etched on it and a certificate are awarded. Established in 1990 in memory of Nelson Cruikshank, NCSC's third president, who was a champion of Social Security and a pioneer in the battle to win Medicare. Cruikshank was also instrumental in founding the National Council of Senior Citizens.

• 14818 • Claude Pepper Award
To honor outstanding service on behalf of America's older people. A designed glass plate with Claude Pepper's portrait etched on it and a certificate are awarded. Established in 1989 in memory of the late Claude Pepper, Democratic Representative from Florida, who served for many years as Chairman of the House Aging Committee and was a well-known champion of the elderly, fighting for Social Security, Medicare/Medicaid, and the Older Americans Act.

• 14819 •
National Council of Social Security Management Associations
Ron Buffaloe, Pres.
1816 E Innes St.
Salisbury, NC 28146
Phone: (704)633-9523
Fax: (704)633-6797
E-mail: president@ncssma.org
Home Page: http://www.ncssma.org

• 14820 • Joseph P. Collins Award
This, the highest award presented by the National Council, is given to recognize the member who, during the preceding year, has done the most to further the objectives of the National Council. To be eligible, an individual must be a member in good standing of a Regional Association that in turn is a member of the National Council. The award is made for a single act during the preceding year or for sustained performance over a period of time extending into the year preceding the award. The act or performance must have had a substantial effect in furthering one or more of the objectives of the National Council. Nominations can be accepted from: any regional association that is a member of the Council; the National Council Executive Committee, acting as a body; or any group of ten members involving at least three Regional Associations, acting as a body. An inscribed silver Revere bowl and expenses are presented annually at the annual banquet. Established in 1978 in memory of the first President of the Council, Joseph P. Collins.

• 14821 • Community Service Award
To recognize management association members for their involvement in community affairs, volunteer services, civic clubs, and humanitarian deeds. Each regional association may nominate one member annually. A plaque is awarded annually in October. Established in 1986.

• 14822 • Special Achievement Award
To recognize individuals who have made significant contributions to the objectives and achievements of the National Council. These may be for service over a long period of time or for a significant single contribution. Members in good standing of a regional association, non-member employees of the Social Security Administration, or individuals outside the Social Security Administration are eligible. Nominations may be made at any time by a Regional Association or by the National Council Executive Committee. Framed certificates, resolutions of appreciation, or plaques are awarded when merited.

• 14823 •
National Council of Supervisors of Mathematics
Linda Gojak, Pres.
PO Box 150368
Lakewood, CO 80215-0368
Phone: (303)274-5932
Fax: (303)274-5932
E-mail: ncsm@mathforum.org
Home Page: http://www.ncsmonline.org

• 14824 • Glenn Gilbert National Leadership Award
To recognize an individual for a unique and dedicated contribution to mathematics education. Individuals who have demonstrated leadership and made significant contributions to mathematics education are eligible. The deadline is February 1. A plaque and life membership in the council are awarded annually. Established in 1982 in memory of Glenn Gilbert.

• 14825 •
National Council of Teachers of English
Kent Williamson, Exec.Dir.
1111 Kenyon Rd.
Urbana, IL 61801-1096
Phone: (217)328-3870
Toll-Free: 800-369-6283
Fax: (217)328-0977
E-mail: public_info@ncte.org
Home Page: http://www.ncte.org

• 14826 • Achievement Awards in Writing
To encourage high school juniors in their writing and to recognize publicly some of the best student writers in the nation. A maximum of 876 awards is possible. Certificates are awarded annually. Established in 1957.

• 14827 • Award for Excellence in Poetry for Children
To recognize and foster excellence in children's poetry by encouraging its publication and by exploring ways to acquaint teachers and children with poetry through such means as publications, programs, and displays. Criteria include literary merit, poet's contributions, evolution of the poet's work, and its appeal to children. Living American poets are eligible. A plaque is awarded every three years. Established in 1977.

• 14828 • CCCC Richard Braddock Award
To recognize the best article on writing or the teaching of writing in *College Composition and Communication,* the official journal of the Conference on College Composition and Communication, a constituent organization of NCTE. A certificate is awarded annually. Established in 1975 in honor of the late Richard Braddock, chair of CCCC in 1967.

• 14829 • CEE James N. Britton Award for Inquiry within the English Language Arts
To encourage English language teacher development by promoting reflective inquiry in which teachers raise questions about teaching and learning in their own teaching/learning settings. Entries must have been published by an English language arts teacher at any level, preschool through university; published in any format during the two-year time period under consideration; and focused on a systematic study of any aspect of the inquirer's own teaching, including collaborative research with other practitioners. Nomination deadline is May 1. Certificates are awarded annually by the Conference on English Education, a constituent group of NCTE. Estab-

lished in 1989 in honor of James N. Britton, a leading researcher in English language arts.

• 14830 • CEE Richard A. Meade Award

To recognize published research that investigates English/language arts teacher development at any educational level, of any scope, and in any setting. Nomination deadline is May 1. Certificates are awarded annually by the Conference on English Education, a constituent organization of NCTE. Established in 1988 in honor of Richard Meade, a founder of CEE known for his research in the teaching of composition and in teacher preparation.

• 14831 • Distinguished Service Award

To recognize persons who have exhibited valuable professional service to the profession, scholarly or academic distinction, distinctive use of the language, and excellence in teaching. Members of the Council are eligible. A silver platter, a plaque, and a complimentary lifetime in NCTE are awarded when merited. Established in 1950. Formerly: (1969) W. Wilbur Hatfield Award.

• 14832 • Doublespeak Award

An ironic tribute to public speakers who have perpetuated language that is grossly deceptive, evasive, euphemistic, confusing, or self-centered. The words must originate from an American. Nomination deadline is September 15. Past recipients include the tobacco industry, the U.S. Department of Defense, and Justice Clarence Thomas. Awarded annually. The award is named after the Big Brother governmental language described in George Orwell's "1984." Established in 1974.

• 14833 • Paul and Kate Farmer Award

For recognition of outstanding articles written by classroom teachers and appearing in the *English Journal*. Senior high school teachers (grades 9-12) and junior high school teachers (grades 6-9) who publish articles in the *English Journal* between September and July of any given school year are eligible. A monetary award, a plaque, and a certificate are awarded to two recipients annually. Established in 1980 in honor of Paul and Kate Farmer, founders and donors.

• 14834 • Rewey Belle Inglis Award

To honor an outstanding woman for achievement in English and/or English education. Awarded annually by Women in Literacy and Life Assembly, a constituent group of NCTE. Established in 1989 in honor of the first woman president of the National Council of Teachers of English.

• 14835 • Orbis Pictus Nonfiction Award

To promote and recognize excellence in the writing of nonfiction for children. Criteria include accuracy, organization, design, and style. Nomination deadline is November 30. Awarded annually. Established in 1989 to commemorate the work of John Comenius, *Orbis Pictus: The World in Pictures*, published in 1657 and considered to be the first book actually planned for children.

• 14836 • George Orwell Award for Distinguished Contribution to Honesty and Clarity in Public Language

To recognize writers who have made outstanding contributions to the critical analysis of public discourse. Nominees must be American authors, editors, or producers of print or non-print work that contributes to honesty and clarity in public language. Nomination deadline is September 15. A certificate is awarded annually. Established in 1975.

• 14837 • Program to Recognize Excellence in Student Literary Magazines

To recognize students, teachers, and schools producing excellent literary magazines; to improve the quality of such magazines; and to encourage all schools to develop literary magazines, seeking excellence in writing and schoolwide participation in production. All senior high, junior high, and middle schools throughout the United States, Canada, Virgin Islands, and American schools abroad are eligible. Entries must be submitted by June 30. Entries are judged on literary content/quality, content variety, editing and proofreading, artistic quality, and front matter and pagination. Awarded annually. Established in 1984.

• 14838 • Promising Researcher Award

To recognize individuals who have completed dissertations, theses, or initial, independent studies up to three years after the dissertation. Entries should be related to the teaching of English or the language arts and should have employed a recognized research approach. Application deadline is March 1. Awarded annually. Established in 1970 in memory of Bernard O'Donnell.

• 14839 • Promising Young Writers Program

To recognize outstanding eighth-grade writers in the U.S., Canada, and the Virgin Islands. Students must be nominated by their schools; schools may nominate more than one student if their enrollment meets certain criteria. The number of winners per state may not exceed the number of Congressional Representatives of that state. Certificates of Recognition are awarded to winners; Certificates of Participation are awarded to all participants. Awarded annually. Established in 1986.

• 14840 • David H. Russell Award for Distinguished Research in the Teaching of English

For recognition of outstanding published research in English that has had or should have an important impact on the teaching of English with valid implications for classroom teachers. Authors of works of scholarship or research in language, literature, rhetoric, pedagogy, or learning that is published during the previous five years are eligible. Nomination deadline is March 1. A monetary award and a plaque are awarded annually. Established in 1963 in honor of David H. Russell, president of NCTE in 1963. Formerly: (1966) Distinguished Research Award.

• 14841 • James R. Squire Award

To recognize outstanding service, not only to the stature and development of NCTE and the discipline that it represents, but also to the profession of education as a whole, internationally as well as nationally. A plaque, platter/sculpture, and a complimentary lifetime membership in NCTE are awarded when merited. Established in 1967. Formerly: (1999) Executive Committee Award.

• 14842 • Teacher-Researcher Grants

To financially assist teachers in research on student learning in their classrooms. Awarded annually by the NCTE Research Foundation. Established in 1984.

• 14843 • Technical and Scientific Communication Award

To recognize publications in the field of technical and scientific communications. The six award categories are: best article on philosophy or theory of technical or scientific communication; best article reporting historical research or textual studies in technical or scientific communication; best article on methods of teaching technical and scientific communication; best article reporting qualitative or quantitative research in technical or scientific communication; best collection of essays; and best book. Submission deadline is June 15. Certificates are awarded annually. Established in 1981.

• 14844 • TETYC Best Article of the Year Award

To recognize the best article, from the previous publication year, in *Teaching English in the Two-Year College*, an NCTE quarterly publication. A certificate is awarded annually. Established in 1982.

• 14845 •
National Council of Teachers of English Assembly on Literature for Adolescents
Kent Williamson, Exec.Dir.
1111 Kenyon Rd.
Urbana, IL 61801-1096
Phone: (217)328-3870
Toll-Free: 800-369-6283
Fax: (217)328-0977
E-mail: public_info@ncte.org
Home Page: http://www.ncte.org

• 14846 • ALAN Award

For recognition of significant contributions to the field of adolescent literature. Publishers, authors, librarians, scholars, and editors are eligible. A plaque is awarded annually. Established in 1974.

• 14847 •
National Council on Alcoholism and Drug Dependence
Stacia Murphy, Pres.
20 Exchange Pl., Ste. 2902
New York, NY 10005-3201
Phone: (212)269-7797
Toll-Free: 800-622-2255
Fax: (212)269-7510
E-mail: national@ncadd.org
Home Page: http://www.ncadd.org

Formerly: (1991) National Council on Alcoholism.

• 14848 • **Bronze Key Award**
To recognize an individual who has made an outstanding contribution in the field of alcoholism or to NCADD at a regional, state, or local level. The recipient is determined by the NCADD affiliate as appropriate.

• 14849 • **Gold Key Award**
To recognize an individual who has made an outstanding contribution in the field of alcoholism on a national level. Although such contribution may have been of a brief duration, it will have been highly visible and improved national recognition of alcholism and other drugs problems and further general understanding that these are treatable and preventable conditions. The recipient is determined by the National Board of NCADD. The award ordinarily is given to only one person each year and is presented at the NCADD Annual Meeting. Established in 1959.

• 14850 • **Humanitarian Award**
To recognize an major national figures who have made a brief or one-time contribution to the continuning work of NCADD or the field of alcoholism and other drugs or private citizens who have furhtered the cause and mission of NCADD through a major contribution of national magnitude. Awarded when merited. Established in 1978.

• 14851 • **Marty Mann Founder's Award**
To recognize an individual of national prominence in the field of alcoholism and other drug problems whose life work strongly reflects energy, dedication, and focus exemplified by NCADD's founder Mrs. Marty Mann. The award recognizes at least ten years of exceptional contributions to public and professional education on alcoholism and other drug problems as treatable and preventable conditions and as major public health concerns. A desk-top object bearing the likeness of Marty Mann, the NCADD logo, and an engraved metal plate are awarded at the NCADD Annual meeting. Established in 1987 to honor Marty Mann, the founder of National Council on Alcoholism and Drug Dependence.

• 14852 • **Silver Key Award**
To recognize an individual who has made an outstanding contribution to the work of the NCADD or in support of the mission and programs at a national level. The recipient is determined by the National Board of NCADD. The award ordinarily is given to only one person each year and is presented at the NCADD Annual Meeting. Established in 1971.

• 14853 • **R. Brinkley Smithers Award**
To honor an individual for voluntary service in the cause of controlling, reducing, and preventing alcoholism and other drug problems and in promoting public and professional understanding of alcoholism and other drug problems as treatable and preventable conditions. A desktop object bearing a likeness of R. Brinkley Smithers, the NCADD logo, and an engraved metal plate are presented at the NCADD Annual Meeting. Established in 1986 to honor R. Brinkley Smithers for his pioneering contributions to the alcoholism movement in the United States.

• 14854 •
National Council on Alcoholism and Drug Dependence Greater Detroit Area
4777 Outer Dr., 4th Fl.
Detroit, MI 48234
Phone: (313)369-5400
Fax: (313)369-5415
E-mail: detroit.mi@ncadd.org

• 14855 • **Lamplighter of the Year**
For outstanding accomplishments in combating substance abuse. Recognition award bestowed annually.

• 14856 •
National Council on Economic Education
Robert F. Duvall PhD, Pres. & CEO
1140 Avenue of the Americas, 2nd Fl.
New York, NY 10036
Phone: (212)730-7007
Toll-Free: 800-338-1192
Fax: (212)730-1793
E-mail: rduvall@ncee.net
Home Page: http://www.ncee.net

• 14857 • **NCEE/Nasdaq National Teaching Awards**
For recognition of outstanding economic education teaching practices in the current year and to stimulate improvements in economic education teaching practices. Educators in public, private, and parochial schools teaching in the following categories are eligible: primary level - grades K-3; intermediate level - grades 4-6; junior high school level - grades 7-9; high school level - grades 10-12. Five regional winners receive $10,000 each. Grand Prize Winner receives a total of $25,000. Applications available online. The deadline is July 31. Co-sponsored by the Nasdaq Educational Foundation Formerly: (2004) National Awards for Teaching Economics.

• 14858 •
National Council on Family Relations
Michael L. Benjamin, Exec.Dir.
3989 Central Ave. NE, No. 550
Minneapolis, MN 55421
Phone: (763)781-9331
Toll-Free: 888-781-9331
Fax: (763)781-9348
E-mail: info@ncfr.org
Home Page: http://www.ncfr.org

• 14859 • **Ernest W. Burgess Award**
For recognition of outstanding scholarly achievement during the course of a career in the study of families. Nominees must be current members of NCFR. A plaque and monetary prize of $1,000 are awarded biennially in even-number years. Established in 1962 in honor of Burgess, co-founder of NCFR.

• 14860 • **Distinguished Service to Families Award**
For recognition of exceptional leadership and/or service to improve family living. National leaders in the family field, political figures, entertainers, and volunteers are eligible. If the award winner is in the policy field, the award is dubbed the Dr. Harold Feldman Award; if the recipient is in a health field, it is dubbed the Dr. Fred Bozett Award. A monetary prize of $1,000 and a plaque are awarded biennially in odd-numbered years. Established in 1974.

• 14861 • **Reuben Hill Award**
To recognize the author(s) of the best research article published during the year. Nominees must be current members of NCFR. A plaque is given to the author of the award-winning article, and a monetary prize of $1,000 is divided among all the authors. Awarded annually. Sponsored by the Research and Theory Section of NCFR. Established in 1980.

• 14862 • **Media Awards Competition**
To promote excellence in videos concerned with family-related subjects and to promote the production of well done family related films by recognizing an outstanding film, filmstrip, or videocassette in this area. The deadline is April. Awards are presented in the following categories: (1) Addiction/Substance Abuse; (2) Aging; (3) Contemporary Social Issues; (4) Families with Special Needs; (5) Family Violence/Abuse; (6) Human Development Across the Life Span; (7) Marital and Family Issues and Communications; (8) Mental Health, Stress, Transition, and Crisis Management; (9) Diverse Family Systems; (10) Parenting Issues; (11) Sexuality and Sex Role Development; (12) Teenage Pregnancy and Sexuality; (13) STD/AIDS; (14) Other PSAs. A certificate is awarded annually. Established in 1969.

• 14863 • **Ernest Osborne Award**
For recognition of excellence in the teaching of family studies. Nominees must be current members of NCFR. A plaque and a monetary prize of $1,000 are awarded biennially during odd-num-

bered years. Established in 1966 in honor of Osborne, a three-time president of NCFR.

• 14864 • Student Award
To foster excellence in family related studies, and to encourage the potential of future contributions to this field. Graduate student members of the NCFR are eligible. A plaque and a monetary prize of $1,000 are awarded annually. Established in 1970.

• 14865 •
National Council on Public History
David G. Vanderstel, Exec.Dir.
327 Cavanaugh Hall - IUPUI
425 University Blvd.
425 University Blvd.
Indianapolis, IN 46202
Phone: (317)274-2716
Fax: (317)278-5230
E-mail: ncph@iupui.edu
Home Page: http://www.ncph.org

• 14866 • G. Wesley Johnson Award
For recognition of the best article published during the preceding year in *The Public Historian.* All articles published in a single volume (four issues) are eligible and are automatically considered. A monetary prize of $250 and a certificate are awarded annually in April. Established in 1986 by History Associates, Inc. The award was renamed in 1987 to honor G. Wesley Johnson, former editor of *The Public Historian.* For more information, contact: Lindsey Reed, Managing Editor, Department of History, University of California, Santa Barbara, CA 93106. Formerly: (1987) Journal Award.

• 14867 • Robert Kelly Memorial Award
Established to perpetuate the legacy and memory of Dr. Robert Kelly, a founder of the public history movement. Honors distinguished and outstanding achievements by individuals, institutions, non-profit or corporate entities for having made significant inroads in making history relevant to the lives of people outside of academia. A cash prize of $500 and framed certificate are awarded biennially in even-numbered years.

• 14868 •
National Council on the Aging
Dr. James Firman, Pres./CEO
300 D St. SW, Ste. 801
Washington, DC 20024
Phone: (202)479-1200
Toll-Free: 800-373-4906
Fax: (202)479-0735
E-mail: info@ncoa.org
Home Page: http://www.ncoa.org

• 14869 • Geneva Mathiasen Award
To recognize an individual for major contributions to NCOA and its programs. Awarded annually. Established to honor Geneva Mathiasen, an NCOA founder and Executive Director (1950-1969).

• 14870 • Ollie A. Randall Award
To recognize an individual who has made singular and outstanding contributions toward advancing the cause of the aging in accordance with the Council's philosophy of enabling the older person to live a dignified, healthy, and productive life. A Steuben glass trophy is awarded annually. Established in 1964 to honor Ollie A. Randall, an NCOA founder.

• 14871 •
National Council on U.S.-Arab Relations
Dr. John Duke Anthony, Pres./CEO/ Founder
1730 M St. NW, Ste. 503
Washington, DC 20036
Phone: (202)293-6466
Fax: (202)293-7770
E-mail: info@ncusar.org
Home Page: http://www.ncusar.org

• 14872 • Joseph J. Malone Fellowship in Arab and Islamic Studies
To provide educators with the opportunity to gain and expand their knowledge about the Arab world through travel - study visits of two weeks - that they may apply this to their teaching and outreach. The program is limited to outstanding educators, administrators, and community leaders. Established in 1984 in memory of Joseph J. Malone, an educator, historian, and author. Formerly: Joseph J. Malone Post-Doctoral Fellows Program.

• 14873 •
National Court Appointed Special Advocate Association
Michael S. Piraino, CEO
100 W Harrison St., Ste. 500
North Tower
Seattle, WA 98119
Phone: (206)270-0072
Phone: 800-414-CASA
Toll-Free: 800-628-3233
Fax: (206)270-0078
E-mail: inquiry@nationalcasa.org
Home Page: http://www.nationalcasa.org

• 14874 • G. F. Bettineski Child Advocate of the Year Award
To recognize a child advocate who is representative of inspirational volunteer service on behalf of abused and neglected children. An individual associated with the National CASA Association who has made a significant voluntary contribution toward advocacy for abused and neglected children is eligible. A plaque, or other recognition piece, conference registration, and travel to the annual conference are awarded annually. Active CASA/GAL volunteers may be nominated by December 15. Established in 1986 in memory of George F. Bettineski, a child advocate who served as a guardian ad litem in the King County Juvenile court in Seattle, Washington.

• 14875 • Judge of the Year Award
To recognize a juvenile court judge who has demonstrated exceptional leadership, made significant contributions on behalf of children's issues, and supported and promoted CASA programs and volunteers. Judges are nominated for the award by CASA volunteers and staff. Sitting judges may be nominated by December 15. A plaque or other recognition piece and expenses to attend the National Conference are awarded annually in the spring. Established in 1989.

• 14876 • Kappa Alpha Theta Program Director of the Year Award
To recognize the CASA/GAL Program Director who has: taken significant action to establish a new CASA program or enhance an existing program, played an active role in heightening community awareness of problems of abused and neglected children and how CASA helps, and demonstrated outstanding leadership qualities. Current directors of state or local CASA/GAL offices holding program membership in National CASA may be nominated by December 15. A monetary award of $4,000 is presented annually in the spring. Established and sponsored by the Kappa Alpha Theta Foundation.

• 14877 •
National Court Reporters Association
Mark J. Golden CAE, Exec.Dir./CEO
8224 Old Courthouse Rd.
Vienna, VA 22182-3808
Phone: (703)556-6272
Toll-Free: 800-272-6272
Fax: (703)556-6291
E-mail: msic@ncrahq.org
Home Page: http://www.ncraonline.org

Formerly: National Shorthand Reporters Association.

• 14878 • CASE Award of Excellence
To recognize outstanding educators in the field of court reporting. Awarded annually. Established in 1987. Sponsored by Council on Approved Student Education. Formerly: Award of Excellence for Distinguished Educators.

• 14879 • Distinguished Service Award
To recognize outstanding service to the profession. Members of the Association are eligible. A bronze scroll/plaque is awarded annually and the recipient's name is added to a silver bowl on display at NCRA headquarters. Established in 1960.

• 14880 • Fellow of the Academy of Professional Reporters
To recognize outstanding and extraordinary qualifications and experience in the field of shorthand reporting. Professional members who have been in the active practice of court reporting for ten years and who have attained distinction as measured by performance are eligible. A certificate and pin are awarded to one or more recipients annually. Established in 1975.

• 14881 •
National Court Reporters Foundation
B.J. Shorak, Deputy Exec.Dir.
8224 Old Courthouse Road
Vienna, VA 22182-3808
E-mail: msic@ncrahq.org
Home Page: http://www.ncraonlone.org/foundation/index.shtml

• 14882 • **Santo J. Aurelio Award for Altruism**
Given to a NCRA member who have demonstrated altruistic behavior and unselfish regard to others. Established in 1996 by Mrs. Josephine C. Aurelio in honor of her husband, Santo J. Aurelio. Sponsored by the NCRF.

• 14883 • **National Court Reporters Foundation Scholarships**
To recognize outstanding court reporting by students attending NCRA-approved court reporter education programs. Students entering the second year of a program who have attained exemplary academic records are eligible to submit essays on a predetermined subject. Awards include: Student with a Disability Scholarship, First-Year Student Scholarship, Frank Sarli Memorial Scholarship, and the William E. Weber Scholarship. Awarded annually. Established in 1982. Formerly: NSRA Heritage Foundation Scholarships Fund.

• 14884 • **New Professional Reporter Grant**
$2,000 grant presented to a current NCRA member who is a new employee, working in his or her first year out of school. Sponsored by the NCRF.

• 14885 •
National Cowboy and Western Heritage Museum
Charles P. Schroeder, Exec.Dir.
1700 NE 63rd St.
Oklahoma City, OK 73111
Phone: (405)478-2250
Fax: (405)478-4714
E-mail: info@nationalcowboymuseum.org
Home Page: http://www.nationalcowboymuseum.org

Formerly: (2000) National Cowboy Hall of Fame and Western Heritage Center.

• 14886 • **Prix de West Invitational Exhibition**
To recognize outstanding quality in Western Art in oil, watercolor, pastel, drawing, or sculpture. Academy members and invited guest artists may enter. A number of awards are presented annually, including the Prix de West Purchase Award ($5,000); Frederic Remington Painting Award ($3,000); James Earle Fraser Sculpture Award ($3,000); Express Ranches the Great American Cowboy Award ($3,000); Robert Lougheed Memorial Award ($3,000); Major General and Mrs. Don D. Pittman Wildlife Art Award ($3,000); and Nona Jean Hulsey Rumsey Buyers' Choice Award ($3,000). Established in 1973. Formerly: (1995) National Academy of Western Art Exhibition.

• 14887 • **Western Heritage Awards (Wrangler Award)**
To recognize outstanding quality in portraying the Old West in Western films, television, literature, and music. Awards are given in 15 categories. Individuals, organizations, and companies are eligible. Nominations must be submitted by November 30. The Wrangler, an original bronze sculptures, is awarded in each category annually. Established in 1960.

• 14888 •
National Cutting Horse Association
Bill Riddle, Pres.
260 Bailey Ave.
Fort Worth, TX 76107-1862
Phone: (817)244-6188
Fax: (817)244-2015
E-mail: bri6622180@aol.com
Home Page: http://www.nchacutting.com

• 14889 • **Horse Hall of Fame**
To recognize outstanding cutting horses. To be inducted, a horse must first win $150,000 in NCHA Open Championship contests. Upon induction, a gold certificate is issued to the owner of the horse and a plaque is hung on the walls of the Association office. Established in 1962.

• 14890 •
National Dairy Shrine
Maurice E. Core, Exec.Dir.
1224 Alton Darby Creek Rd.
Columbus, OH 43228-9792
Phone: (614)878-5333
Fax: (614)870-2622
E-mail: shrine@cobaselect.com
Home Page: http://www.dairyshrine.org

Formerly: Dairy Shrine.

• 14891 • **Distinguished Dairy Cattle Breeder Award**
To recognize an active, outstanding dairy cattle breeder excelling in the management of a dairy breeding herd. Awarded annually. Established in 1973.

• 14892 • **Guest of Honor Award**
To recognize contemporary dairy leaders for outstanding accomplishments and contributions to the dairy industry. One individual is selected annually. Established in 1949.

• 14893 • **Pioneer Award**
To recognize pioneers of the dairy industry who gave greatly to the industry. Pictures and biographies of those selected are preserved by Dairy Shrine. Three or four (living or deceased) are honored annually.

• 14894 •
National Dance Association
Ms. Colleen Dean, Program Administrator
1900 Association Dr.
Reston, VA 20191-1599
Phone: (703)476-3464
Phone: (703)476-3436
Toll-Free: 800-213-7193
Fax: (703)476-9527
E-mail: nda@aahperd.org
Home Page: http://www.aahperd.org/nda

Formerly: (1979) Dance Division.

• 14895 • **Heritage Award**
To honor an individual for contributions of national or international significance, over a long period of years, to dance in one or more of the following categories: teaching excellence; establishment or administration of a functioning dance department, center, or program; research or publication; consulting; choreography; performance; notation; or related arts. Nominations are accepted at any time. A plaque is awarded annually when merited at the Dance Heritage Luncheon. Established in 1963.

• 14896 • **K-12 Dance Educator of the Year**
To recognize exemplary dance educators in grades K-12. Candidates must be dance teachers with a minimum of three years' teaching experience, and must show evidence of effective teaching in regards to creativity, balanced and sequential curriculum, cultural impact, and professional commitment. District educators and state educators are recognized. These finalists are interviewed and a national honoree is selected at the national convention. A plaque is awarded. Established in 1988.

• 14897 • **Outstanding Student Recognition Awards**
To recognize outstanding dance students who have made an impact to their faculties and departments. At least one recipient can be honored in each of the following categories: graduate students, dance major, dance minor, and dance emphasis. Certificates are awarded annually at the national convention. Established in 1989.

• 14898 • **Scholar/Artist Award**
To recognize individuals for contributions to dance through scholarly writing, research, and/or creative work, including choreography. The honoree delivers a presentation and receives a plaque at the national convention. Established in 1977.

• 14899 • **Student Literary Award**
To recognize outstanding student writing on dance and dance education by collegiate students of dance. One undergraduate and one graduate student are honored each year. Candidates must be enrolled in a dance course at the time of entrance and be sponsored by a member of the dance faculty. The selected manuscripts are published in the Association's newsletter, and honorees receive a certificate and one-year

complimentary student membership in the Association. Established in 1990.

• 14900 •
National Defense Industrial Association
Lt. Gen Lawrence P. Farrell Jr., Pres.
2111 Wilson Blvd., No. 400
Arlington, VA 22201-3061
Phone: (703)522-1820
Phone: (703)247-2550
Fax: (703)522-1825
E-mail: info@ndia.org
Home Page: http://www.adpa.org

Formerly: (1997) National Security Industrial Association.

• 14901 • **Defense Industry Award**
Award of recognition. Awarded biennially.

• 14902 • **ROTC Award**
Award of recognition for an ROTC member. Inquire for additional information.

• 14903 •
National Defense Transportation Association
LTG Kenneth R. Wykle, Pres.
50 S Pickett St., Ste. 220
Alexandria, VA 22304-7296
Phone: (703)751-5011
Fax: (703)823-8761
E-mail: info@ndtahq.com
Home Page: http://www.ndtahq.com

• 14904 • **Department of Defense Distinguished Service Award**
To recognize a Senior Executive of the Department of Defense who has made outstanding contributions to NDTA programs and national security. Awarded annually.

• 14905 • **Department of Defense Distinguished Service Award**
For recognition of a Senior Executive of the Department of Defense for outstanding contribution to NDTA programs and national security. The nominee's achievements must have been executed beyond normal duty requirements and should demonstrate unusual dedication to the aims and objectives of NDTA. Established in 1966.

• 14906 • **National Transportation Award**
For recognition of significant accomplishments in the field of defense transportation and to emphasize the importance of transportation as an instrument of national defense. Members of the transportation industry within the United States, other than employees, representatives, or organizations of the United States government, are eligible. The name of the awardee is engraved on the Grand Trophy which is permanently based at NDTA headquarters. A sterling silver Paul Revere bowl and replica of the Grand Trophy are presented to the winning candidate. Awarded annually at the annual forum. Established in 1949.

• 14907 • **NDTA Distinguished Service Award**
To recognize government, military, and civilian personnel for their actions, dedication, and assistance in furthering the aims and objectives of the association. National achievements are emphasized over those of a regional or local scope. Any active member of NDTA is eligible. The deadline for nominations is May 15. Presented annually at the NDTA forum.

• 14908 • **President's Award**
For recognition of an organization, government agency, or individual who has responded in a constructive manner to a major critical current issue confronting the transportation industry. The issue may be local in nature if it has national implications. Nomination deadline is May 15. A trophy is awarded when merited. Established in 1974.

• 14909 •
National Democratic Institute for International Affairs
Kenneth D. Wollack, Pres.
2030 M St. NW, 5th Fl.
Washington, DC 20036-3306
Phone: (202)728-5500
Fax: (202)728-5520
E-mail: contact@ndi.org
Home Page: http://www.ndi.org

• 14910 • **W. Averell Harriman Democracy Award**
To recognize an individual or organization from the United States or abroad that has demonstrated a commitment to democracy and human rights. Criteria include: sustained commitment, moral integrity, involvement in the political process, representative of a larger political movement, and affiliation to NDI's work. A crystal globe is awarded annually. Established in 1985 to pay tribute to Governor W. Averell Harriman's legacy to the Democratic Party and his dedication to democracy and internationalism.

• 14911 •
National Derby Rallies
Terry Henry, Membership Coor.
6644 Switzer Ln.
Shawnee, KS 66203
Phone: (913)962-0706
E-mail: info@ndr.org
Home Page: http://www.ndr.org

• 14912 • **Championship Awards**
For recognition of achievement in construction and design of gravity race cars. Five divisions make up NDR's racing program. Criteria for participating in each division remain based primarily upon the type of race car being used. Awards are given in the following divisions: Stock, Super Stock, AA Scottie, Scottie Pro, and the exhibition Senior division. In addition, various awards are given for non-race participation, such as the Outstanding NDR Family, Mark Cole Sportsmanship Award, Bob Turner Award, Cox Family Rookie of the Year Award, Gary Burdgick Award, and Best Decorated Stock and Super Stocks. Presented annually each summer. Established in 1978 in memory of Gary Bardgick.

• 14913 •
National DeSoto Club
Jim Reese, Membership Sec.
PO Box 1204
Tallevast, FL 34270
E-mail: firedome@shelteringoaks.com
Home Page: http://www.desoto.org

• 14914 • **Hernando DeSoto Award**
To honor the member who excelled in promoting the National DeSoto Club or the DeSoto Marque during the previous calendar year. The winner's name is engraved on a plaque. Awarded annually at the national convention. Established in 1986 to honor Hernando DeSoto.

• 14915 •
National District Attorneys Association
Velva Walter, Dir., Media Relations
99 Canal CN Plz., Ste. 510
Alexandria, VA 22314
Phone: (703)549-9222
Fax: (703)836-3195
E-mail: jean.holt@ndaa-apri.org
Home Page: http://www.ndaa.org

Formerly: (1959) National Association of County and Prosecuting Attorneys.

• 14916 • **President's Award**
For recognition of service and dedication to the public as prosecutor, to the Association and/or as a member of the Board. A plaque is awarded when merited at the convention. Established in 1956.

• 14917 •
National Duckpin Bowling Congress
Sue Burucker, Exec.Dir./Sec.
4991 Fairview Ave.
Linthicum, MD 21090
Phone: (410)636-2695
Phone: (410)444-4058
Fax: (410)636-3256
E-mail: nationalduckpin@aol.com
Home Page: http://ndbc.org

• 14918 • **National Trophy**
To recognize the top ranked male and top ranked female in duckpin bowling. Given to sanctioned members of the National Duckpin Bowling Congress who have the highest total average score for the previous year. A crystal and bronze original artwork trophy in a lucite case is awarded annually. The award is announced in November and awarded in April at the annual meeting. Formerly: (1984) National Ranking Award.

• 14919 •
National Economic Association
Dr. Philip N. Jefferson, Pres.
Swarthmore Coll.
Dept. of Economics
500 College Ave.
Swarthmore, PA 19081
Phone: (610)690-6856
Fax: (610)328-7352
E-mail: pjeffer1@swarthmore.edu
Home Page: http://www.ncat.edu/~neconasc

• 14920 • Samuel Z. Westerfield Award
To recognize and encourage scholarly work by African American economists. Selection is based on outstanding contributions as both a scholar and an economist. A plaque is awarded periodically, usually biennially. Established in 1973 in honor of Samuel Z. Westerfield, a distinguished economist and former Ambassador to Liberia.

• 14921 •
National Electrical Manufacturer Association
Evan Gaddis, Pres.
1300 N 17th St., Ste. 1847
Rosslyn, VA 22209
Phone: (703)841-3200
Fax: (703)841-5900
E-mail: webmaster@nema.org
Home Page: http://www.nema.org

Formerly: National Lighting Bureau.

• 14922 • National Lighting Awards Program
To recognize projects in which lighting has been used to enhance human productivity, improve security, stimulate retail sales, or to otherwise achieve the "bottom line" benefits of effective electric illumination. Anyone associated with a successful lighting project may enter. Deadlines for submission are subject to change each year, usually by mid-October. Those submitting the most effective submissions are selected to be authors of articles which appear in national trade magazines. Awarded annually. Established in 1978.

• 14923 •
National Electrical Manufacturer Representatives Association
Henry P. Bergson, Pres.
660 White Plains Rd., Ste. 600
Tarrytown, NY 10591-1504
Phone: (914)524-8650
Fax: (914)524-8655
E-mail: nemra@nemra.org
Home Page: http://www.nemra.org

• 14924 • Thomas F. Preston Manufacturer of the Year Award
Bestowed annually upon an individual from an electrical manufacturing company who has demonstrated commitment and support to the independent manufacturers' representatives that market the products produced by his or her organization. Recipients are members of the NEMRA Manufacturers Group (NMG) and must be nominated by a NEMRA representative member. An engraved clock is awarded at the annual NEMRA Conference. Established in 1979. Formerly: (1987) NEMRA Manufacturer of the Year.

• 14925 •
National Electronics Service Dealers Association
Mack Blakely, Exec.Dir.
3608 Pershing Ave.
Fort Worth, TX 76107-4527
Phone: (817)921-9061
Fax: (817)921-3741
E-mail: info@nesda.com
Home Page: http://www.nesda.com

Formerly: National Electronics Sales and Service Dealers Association.

• 14926 • NESDA Awards
To recognize individuals for significant contributions to the industry or the association. The following awards are presented: Person of the Year, M. L. Finneburgh Sr. Award of Excellence, Leo Shumavon Award, Richard Mildenberger Outstanding NESDA Officer Award, Outstanding Committee Chairperson, Outstanding Associate President, National Friend of Service Award, State or Regional Friend of Service Award, Everett Pershing Memorial Membership Award, and Associate Leadership Excellence Award. Members must submit nominations by June 1. Awarded annually at the convention during the first week in August.

• 14927 •
National Endowment for Democracy
Carl Gershman, Pres.
1101 15th St. NW, Ste. 700
Washington, DC 20005
Phone: (202)293-9072
Fax: (202)223-6042
E-mail: info@ned.org
Home Page: http://www.ned.org

• 14928 • NED Democracy Award
Presented to an outspoken advocate of human rights who exhibits leadership and courage.

• 14929 •
National Endowment for the Arts
Eileen B. Mason, Senior Deputy Chm.
1100 Pennsylvania Ave. NW
Washington, DC 20506-0001
Phone: (202)682-5400
E-mail: masone@arts.endow.gov
Home Page: http://www.arts.gov

• 14930 • Grants for Arts Projects
To support excellence in the arts, both new and established, bringing the arts to all Americans and providing leadership in arts education. In most cases, funding is limited to organizations, not individuals. Grants are offered in a variety of disciplines, including: arts education, dance, design, folk and traditional arts, literature, local arts agencies, media arts, multidisciplinary arts, museums, music, musical theater, opera, presenting, state and regional, theater, and visual arts. Awarded annually. Formerly: (2004) National Endowment for the Arts Programs.

• 14931 • Jazz Masters Fellowships
The highest honor that the United States bestows upon jazz musicians. Awards are categorical; e.g., a rhythm instrumentalist, pianist, solo instrumentalist, vocalist, and an arranger or composer will be honored each year. In addition, the A. B. Spellman Jazz Masters Award is given to a jazz advocate; that is, an individual who has made major contributions to the appreciation, knowledge, and advancement of the American jazz art form. Recipients of these one-time awards are nominated by the jazz community and the general public. Recipients must be citizens or permanent residents of the United States; posthumous fellowships will not be awarded. Up to five monetary awards of $25,000 are given annually. Established in 1970, and expanded to become part of the Jazz Masters Initiative in 2005. Formerly: (2004) American Jazz Masters Fellowship Awards.

• 14932 • National Heritage Fellowships
To recognize lifetime achievement, artistic excellence, and contributions to our nation's folk and traditional arts heritage. Individuals nominated should be worthy of national recognition, have a record of ongoing artistic accomplishment, and be actively participating in their art form either as a practitioner or teacher. A number of fellowships are awarded, including the Bess Lomax Hawes NEA National Heritage Award. Fellowships are not open to application, but are awarded on the basis of nomination from the public. Nomination deadline is October 1. Each award is $20,000.

• 14933 • National Medal of Arts
To individuals or groups who, in the President's judgment, are deserving of special recognition by reason of their outstanding contributions to the excellence, growth, support, and availability of the arts in the United States. Up to 12 recipients each year are awarded a medal designed by sculptor Robert Graham. Established by the U.S. Congress in 1984.

• 14934 •
National Endowment for the Humanities
Bruce Cole, Chm.
1100 Pennsylvania Ave. NW
Washington, DC 20506
Phone: (202)606-8400
Toll-Free: 800-NEH-1121
Fax: (202)606-8282
E-mail: info@neh.gov
Home Page: http://www.neh.fed.us

• 14935 • Charles Frankel Prize
Recognize persons for outstanding contributions to the public's understanding of humanities.

• 14936 • The Jefferson Lecture Award
For individual who has made significant scholarly contributions to the humanities. Recognition is given.

• 14937 • Jefferson Lecture in the Humanities
This award is the highest official honor that the federal government bestows for distinguished intellectual achievement in the humanities. It recognizes an individual who has made significant scholarly contributions to the humanities and who has the ability to communicate the knowledge and wisdom of the humanities in a broadly appealing manner. Traditionally delivered each spring, the lecture is attended by scholars, professionals in the humanities, and interested members of the public. A monetary prize of $10,000 is awarded annually. Established in 1972.

• 14938 • National Endowment for the Humanities Grant Programs
The National Endowment for the Humanities is an independent federal government grant-making agency to support research, education, and public programs in the humanities. The term *humanities* includes, but is not limited to, the study of the following disciplines: history; philosophy; languages; linguistics; literature; archaeology; jurisprudence; the history, theory, and criticism of the arts; ethics; comparative religion; and those aspects of the social sciences that employ historical or philosophical approaches. Grants are made through seven divisions: Challenge Grants, Education Programs, Preservation and Access, Public Programs, Research Programs, Federal/State Partnerships, and *We the People.* Established in 1965.

• 14939 • National Humanities Medal
Recognition is given to individuals or groups whose work has deepened the nation's understanding of the humanities.

• 14940 •
National Environmental Health Association
Nelson E. Fabian, Exec.Dir.
720 S Colorado Blvd., Ste. 970, S Tower
Denver, CO 80246-1925
Phone: (303)756-9090
Fax: (303)691-9490
E-mail: staff@neha.org
Home Page: http://www.neha.org

Formerly: (1970) National Association of Sanitarians.

• 14941 • A. Harry Bliss Editors' Award
To recognize exemplary contributions to the editorial content - writers, peer reviewers, and other assistance - of the *Journal of Environmental Health.* A plaque is awarded annually when merited. Established in 1969. Formerly: .

• 14942 • Certificate of Merit
To recognize accomplishments of one outstanding professional member from each affiliate of the Association. A certificate is awarded annually. Established in 1965.

• 14943 • Food Industry Award
To recognize an outstanding professional whose work in food science is exemplary. Anyone is eligible. A plaque is presented at the annual conference. Established in 1974.

• 14944 • Honorary Member
To recognize individuals who have attained high standing in employment and organization activities. Established in 1937.

• 14945 • Walter S. Mangold Award
This, the highest honor bestowed by NEHA, is presented for outstanding contributions to the preservation of the environment by an environmental health professional. Nominees must be members of NEHA and be actively engaged in the field of environmental health. Nominations may be submitted by March 15. A cash honorarium and a crystal and marble statue are awarded annually. Established in 1955 to honor the work of Walter S. Mangold in developing the education and professionalism of environmental health specialists.

• 14946 • Past Presidents' Award
To recognize an individual for longstanding service and contributions to NEHA and to the environmental health profession. A plaque is awarded annually.

• 14947 • Presidential Citation
To recognize distinguished service in the field of environmental health and service to NEHA. A certificate is awarded as merited. Established in 1957.

• 14948 • Sabbatical Exchange Program
To provide an opportunity for two members to spend two-to-four-week sabbaticals in either England or Canada observing, questioning, and sharing environmental health practices and information. Applicant must be a NEHA member at the time of application and while on the sabbatical. Two awards are given annually, one each to England and Canada. For a four-week sabbatical, the stipend is $4,000, plus round trip airfare up to $1,000. Stipends are adjusted accordingly for a two-week sabbatical, which is the minimum to be taken. A commemorative plaque is also awarded. Co-sponsored by Chartered Institute of Environmental Health and Canadian Institute of Public Health Inspectors.

• 14949 •
National Environmental, Safety and Health Training Association
Charles L. Richardson, Exec.Dir.
5320 N 16th St., Ste. 114
Phoenix, AZ 85016-3241
Phone: (602)956-6099
Phone: (602)956-6998
Fax: (602)956-6399
E-mail: info@neshta.org
Home Page: http://www.neshta.org

• 14950 • Environmental Education Award
To recognize an individual for contributions to environmental training that are of regional, national, or international scope or significance. Active NESHTA members are eligible. A plaque is presented annually at the National Conference in August. Established in 1979.

• 14951 • George A. Kinias Service Award
For recognition of special service to the industry of environmental training or to the Association. A plaque and recognition at the annual conference are awarded annually when merited. Established in 1987 in honor of George A. Kinias, first President, founding member, and Executive Director of the Association. Formerly: (1989) NETA Special Service Award.

• 14952 • President's Award for the Outstanding Conference Paper
To encourage and recognize the use of written papers in conjunction with presentations made at the NESHTA annual conference. Authors need not be members of NESHTA to be eligible. A certificate is awarded annually. Established in 1990.

• 14953 • Trainer of the Year Award
To recognize the efforts of the "grassroots" environmental trainer actively involved in training delivery and making an impact at the local level. Active NESHTA members are eligible. A plaque is presented annually at the National Conference in August. Established in 1983.

• 14954 •
National Ethnic Coalition of Organizations
Rosemarie Taglione, Exec.Dir.
232 Madison Ave., Ste. 900
New York, NY 10016-2901
Phone: (212)755-1492
Fax: (212)755-3762
E-mail: neco1492@aol.com
Home Page: http://www.neco.org/awards/index.html

• 14955 • Ellis Island Medals of Honor
To recognize outstanding professional and patriotic contributions of ethnic American citizens from all backgrounds. Between 80 and 100 medalists are selected from more than 15,000 nominations received. The medals were conceived to pay tribute to the immigrant experience, remarkable individual achievement, and, above all, the spirit that makes America unique among nations. Awarded annually. Established in 1986.

Awards are arranged in alphabetical order below their administering organizations

• 14956 •
National Eye Research Foundation
Andrew K. Kin, Exec.Dir.
910 Skokie Blvd., No. 207A
Northbrook, IL 60062
Phone: (847)564-4652
Toll-Free: 800-621-2258
Fax: (847)564-0807
E-mail: info@nerf.org
Home Page: http://www.nerf.org

• 14957 • Leo Award
To recognize outstanding contributions to the eye care field. A trophy is awarded in August at the Annual Post-Graduate Congress. Established in honor of Leo, the rabbit who was the subject used in the original contact lens research. Established in 1993.

• 14958 •
National Family Partnership
Ileana Reyes, Contact
2490 Coral Way, Ste. 501
Miami, FL 33145
Phone: (305)856-4886
Toll-Free: 800-705-8997
Fax: (305)856-4815
E-mail: ireyes@informedfamilies.org
Home Page: http://www.nfp.org

Formerly: (1995) National Federation of Parents for Drug-Free Youth.

• 14959 • National Recognition Award
For recognition of outstanding service and selfless contribution to the support, development, and growth of the National Parent Movement. Selection is by nomination. A plaque is awarded annually. Established in 1981.

• 14960 •
National Farm-City Council
Marsha Purcell, Sec.-Treas.
1501 E Woodfield Rd., Ste. 300W
Schaumburg, IL 60173-5422
Phone: (847)969-2974
Fax: (847)969-2752
E-mail: marshap@fb.org
Home Page: http://www.farmcity.org

• 14961 • Farm-City Award
To recognize individuals or corporations for efforts to bring about better understanding between the rural and urban segments of American society. Certificates are awarded annually after the observance of National Farm-City Week, the week ending Thanksgiving Day.

• 14962 •
National Federation of Abstracting and Information Services
Bonnie Lawlor, Exec.Dir.
1518 Walnut St., Ste. 1004
Philadelphia, PA 19102-3403
Phone: (215)893-1561
Fax: (215)893-1564
E-mail: nfais@nfais.org
Home Page: http://www.nfais.org

• 14963 • Miles Conrad Award/Lecturer
To recognize outstanding contributions in the field of abstracting and indexing. The awardee presents a lecture at the Federation's convention on a suitable topic with emphasis on abstracting and indexing activities above the level of any individual organization. Awarded annually. Established in 1965 in memory of G. Miles Conrad, first President of the Federation.

• 14964 • Ann Marie Cunningham Memorial Award
Recognizes volunteer efforts on behalf of NFAIS. Awarded annually.

• 14965 •
National Federation of Democratic Women
Dr. Barbara Mansfield, Pres.
PO Box 72
Bastrop, LA 71221
Phone: (318)281-2356
Fax: (318)281-2736
E-mail: blmansfield@cox.net
Home Page: http://nfdw.com

• 14966 • Humanitarian Award
To honor those who have made significant contributions to the cause of human and/or civil rights. Nominees must have demonstrated support of NFDW, possess leadership qualities, and have proven success in achieving human and/or civil rights. The nominee can be either male or female.

• 14967 • Outstanding Elected Democratic Woman Holding Public Office
To recognize a current statewide, regional, or national woman office holder who has demonstrated support of the Federation, the Democratic Party, and its principles and commitment to the success of other Democratic women. Established in 1987. In addition, special awards are presented at the Convention.

• 14968 • Outstanding NFDW Member of the Year
For recognition of an active member who has made a significant contribution to the growth, development, and promotion of the Federation. Members of national scope and stature are eligible. A certificate is awarded annually at the Convention. Established in 1985.

• 14969 •
National Federation of Music Clubs
Jennifer Keller, Exec.Dir.
1336 N Delaware St.
Indianapolis, IN 46202-2481
Phone: (317)638-4003
Fax: (317)638-0503
E-mail: info@nfmc-music.org
Home Page: http://www.nfmc-music.org

• 14970 • Competitive Awards
For recognition of outstanding music performances. More than $750,000 in competition and award prizes are offered on the local, state, and national level. Awards are given in several age and artistic categories, such as Young Artist, Duo-Piano, Student Auditions and Awards, Junior Composers, Senior Division, and Summer Music Centers Awards. Frequency varies by award. Formerly: (1997) National Federation of Music Clubs Awards and Scholarships.

• 14971 •
National Federation of Press Women
Tonda Rush, Pres.
PO Box 5556
Arlington, VA 22205
Phone: (703)534-2500
Toll-Free: 800-780-2715
Fax: (703)534-5751
E-mail: presswomen@aol.com
Home Page: http://www.nfpw.org

• 14972 • Communicator of Achievement Award
To recognize a member for exceptional achievement in the communications field and for services to NFPW and the community. Nomination deadline is May 1. First- and second-place awards are presented annually. Formerly known as Woman of Achievement Award. Established in 1957.

• 14973 • Honorary Member
To recognize a woman for an outstanding contribution in the field of communications. Awarded occasionally when merited. Established in 1971.

• 14974 • President's Award
For recognition of individuals who have wielded a powerful nationwide influence through their communications skills. Awarded when merited. Established in 1982.

• 14975 • Sweepstakes Winner
To improve professional skills by recognizing excellence in communicating. Entrants must be professional, student, or retired members of NFPW. Awarded annually to the top winner in the NFPW Communications Contest, in which 76 subcategories exist within the larger categories of print media; photography; radio/television; World Wide Web; advertising; public relations, promotion, publicity; speeches; collegiate communications; achievement and research; and books, fiction, and verse. Established in 1969.

• 14976 •
National Federation of State High School Associations
Robert F. Kanaby, Exec.Dir.
NFHS Distribution Ctr.
1802 Alonzo Watford Sr. Dr.
Indianapolis, IN 46202
Phone: (317)972-6900
Fax: (317)822-5700
E-mail: sloomis@nfhs.org
Home Page: http://www.nfhs.org

Formerly: (1970) National Federation of State High School Athletic Associations.

Awards are arranged in alphabetical order below their administering organizations

• 14977 • Distinguished Service Awards
To recognize an individual for a record of long-standing service and dedication to the National Federation within a specific sport, or for a significant contribution to high school activity programs. Established in 1950.

• 14978 • National Federation Citations
To recognize individuals whose contributions have impacted high school activity programs through their association with one of the following groups of professionals: athletic directors; coaches; officials; music adjudicators and directors; and speech, drama, and debate directors. A long-standing and distinguished record of involvement with high school activity programs at the local and state levels, and the admiration and respect of their colleagues are also factors in determining recipients.

• 14979 • National High School Sports Hall of Fame Awards
To recognize individuals who have had distinguished careers as high school athletes, coaches, officials, administrators, or sports media or medicine contributors. Although the committees cannot ignore what a person accomplishes later in life, the most important criterion is high school experience. Inductees are presented awards and medallions at the annual Hall of Fame Induction Ceremony, held each summer in conjunction with the annual meeting. Established in 1982.

• 14980 •
National Federation of State High School Associations
National Federation Interscholastic Coaches Association
Robert F. Kanaby, Exec.Dir.
PO Box 690
PO Box 20626
Indianapolis, IN 46206
Phone: (317)972-6900
Fax: (317)822-5700
Home Page: http://www.nfhs.org

Formerly: National Federation Interscholastic Officials Association.

• 14981 • Award of Merit
This, the Association's highest award, is given for outstanding contributions to the organization. Nominations may be submitted by May 1. Awarded when merited. Established in 1979.

• 14982 • Distinguished Service Award (Coaching)
For recognition of achievement in coaching or a contribution to coaching. Individuals who have given long and distinguished service are eligible. A plaque is awarded annually in the fall. Established in 1982 by the NFICA Board of Directors. Formerly: Distinguished Service Award (Officiating).

• 14983 • Distinguished Service Awards
To recognize individuals for special contributions to the Association. Awards are given in the following categories: (1) Interscholastic administrators - for contributions at the state and national level. Members are eligible, and judged by length of service in athletic administration; and (2) Individuals outside the field of interscholastic athletic administration - for contributions to interscholastic athletics meriting national recognition, extending beyond the local community level. Presence at the award ceremony is requested. Awarded annually at the National Conference in December. Established in 1979.

• 14984 • National Federation Interscholastic Coaches Association Annual Awards
For recognition of outstanding high school coaches. At the state level, NFICA certificates are awarded to active high school coaches for recent, significant achievement in their sport. At the sectional level, walnut Distinguished Service Award plaques are awarded to one active coach in each of the eight NFICA sections. This award is given in recognition of the coach's contribution to high school sports over a long and distinguished career. All states in each NFICA Section may nominate one active coach per year for this prestigious honor. At the sectional level, a similar Distinguished Service Award plaque is given to one contributor in each of the eight NFICA sections. This award signifies a great contribution to high school sports over a long and distinguished career in a field outside actual coaching. Again, all states in each NFICA section may nominate one person per year for this honor. In addition, the National High School Hall of Fame annually considers nominees for induction. Formerly: National Federation Interscholastic Officials Association.

• 14985 • NFICA Certificates for Each State
To recognize outstanding high school coaches and officials for recent, significant achievement. The following certificates are awarded: NFICA Outstanding Coach; and NFIOA Outstanding Official. In addition, NFIOA and NFICA Contributor Awards are given to individuals not actively coaching or officiating.

• 14986 •
National Federation of State Poetry Societies
Budd Powell Mahan, Pres.
7059 Spring Valley Rd.
Dallas, TX 75254
Phone: (352)746-2919
Fax: (352)746-7817
E-mail: bmahan@airmail.net
Home Page: http://nfsps.com

• 14987 • Alabama State Poetry Society Award
To recognize the subject of death in poetry. Any form is acceptable, with a 50 line limit. First prize is $75, second prize is $50, and third prize is $25. Awarded annually. Sponsored by the Alabama State Poetry Society.

• 14988 • All Poets Award
To recognize poems of any subject and any form with a 75-line limit. First prize is $50, 2nd prize is $25, and 3rd prize is $15, with two honorable mentions of $5. Awarded annually. Sponsored by Lakeshore Publishing.

• 14989 • Annual Contests
To recognize the importance of poetry to the national cultural heritage. Fifty poetry contests with cash prizes totaling $6,000 are held annually. Some contests are open only to members of NFSPS. The entry deadline is March 15. A list of winners appears in the NFSPS *Strophes* in August. Among the awards presented are the Winners' Circle Award, Poetry Society of Texas Award, Futuristic Award, Power of Women Award, Amelia Reynolds Long Memorial Award, and Our American Indian Heritage Award. Established in 1959.

• 14990 • Arizona State Poetry Society Award
To honor the memory of Dorothy Greenlee. Awards are given for any subject, any form, with a line limit of 32. First prize is $35, second prize is $25 and third prize is $15. Entries must be postmarked by March 15. Sponsored by the Arizona State Poetry Society.

• 14991 • Columbine Poets of Colorado Award
Awards are given for poetry on any subject, in any form, with a limit of 30 lines. First prize is $50, second prize is $30, and third prize is $20. Awarded annually. Sponsored by Columbine Poets of Colorado.

• 14992 • Connecticut Poetry Society Award
Awards are given for poetry on the subject of lunch, in any form, with a line limit of 40. First prize is $25, second prize is $20, and third prize is $15. Awarded annually. Sponsored by the Connecticut Poetry Society.

• 14993 • Florida State Poets Association, Inc. Award
To recognize the narrative subject of poetry in any form. There is a limit of 40 lines. First prize is $100, second prize is $50, and third prize is $25. Awarded annually. Sponsored by the Florida State Poets Association.

• 14994 • Founders Award
To honor poetry in memory of Mary B. Wall. Poetry may be of any subject and any form, with a limit of four poems per contestant. First prize is $1,500, 2nd prize is $500, and 3rd prize is $250. Awarded annually.

• 14995 • Futuristic Award
Awards are given for optimistic, sensitive, and persuasive poems concerning the year 2056 A.D. Traditional meter and rhyme required; poems must be limited to 32 lines. First prize is $100, second prize is $60, and third prize is $40. Awarded annually. Sponsored by Walt Morgan.

• 14996 • **Georgia Poetry Society Award**
To recognize poems of any serious or dramatic subject. The form must be Keatsian Ode, making judicious use of slant rhyme (without overusing exact rhyme). There is a line limit of 30. Open to members only. First prize is $50, second prize is $35, and third prize if $15. Awarded annually.

• 14997 • **Dorman John Grace Memorial Award**
Awards are given for poetry on any subject in the form of traditional Sonnet. Open to members only. First prize is $25, second prize is $20, and third prize is $15. Awarded annually. Sponsored by the Pennsylvania Poetry Society.

• 14998 • **Joseph V. Hickey Memorial Award**
Awards are given for narrative poems on the subject of inanimate objects with a limit of 40 lines. First prize is $90, second prize is $65, and third prize is $45. Awarded annually. Sponsored by Joseph V. Hickey's wife, Madelyn Eastlund.

• 14999 • **Humorous Poetry Award**
Awards are given for rhymed poetry on any subject, with a 16-line limit. First prize is $35, second prize is $25, and third prize is $15. Awarded annually. Sponsored by Colleen Stanley Bare.

• 15000 • **Indiana State Federation of Poetry Clubs Award**
Awards are given for poetry in any form and any subject. Poems must be limited to 42 lines. First prize is $50, second prize is $35, and third prize is $25. Awarded annually. Sponsored by Indiana State Federation of Poetry Clubs, Poets' Study Club of Terre Haute, and the Anderson Poetry Club.

• 15001 • **Iowa Poetry Association Award**
Awards are given for poems for children. Poems may be of any form, with a 32-line limit. First prize is $25, second prize is $20, and third prize is $15. Awarded annually. Sponsored by the Iowa Poetry Association.

• 15002 • **Kentucky State Poetry Society Award**
Awards are given for poetry in any form, any subject. Poems must have a 28 line limit. First prize is $25, second prize is $20, and third prize is $15. Awarded annually.

• 15003 • **League of Minnesota Poets Award**
Awards are given for free verse poems on any subject with a 45-line limit. First prize is $50, second prize is $30, and third prize is $20. Awarded annually. Sponsored by the League of Minnesota Poets.

• 15004 • **Lighten Your Life Award**
Awards are given on any humorous subject, in any rhyming form, within 12 lines. First prize is $25, second prize is $20, and third prize is $15. Awarded annually. Sponsored by Wanda Blaisdell.

• 15005 • **Ben Lomond Poets Award**
Awards are given for poems on the subject of mountains, in any form, with a line limit of 40. First prize is $25, second prize is $20, and third prize is $15. Awarded annually. Sponsored by Ben Lomond Poets.

• 15006 • **Amelia Reynolds Long Memorial Award**
To recognize the subject of "On the Light Side" in poetry in any form. There is a limit of 32 lines. First prize is $50, second prize is $30, and third prize is $20. Awarded annually. Sponsored by the Amelia Reynolds Long Memorial Fund.

• 15007 • **Louisiana State Poetry Society Award**
Awards are given for traditional or modern Haiku. Poems can be of any subject with a 3-line limit. First prize is $25, second prize is $20, and third prize is $15. Awarded annually. Sponsored by the Louisiana State Poetry Society.

• 15008 • **Massachusetts State Poetry Society Award**
Awards are given for poems on any subject, and of any form. Poems must have a line limit of 40. First prize is $25, second prize is $20, and third prize is $15. Awarded annually. Sponsored by the Massachusetts State Poetry Society.

• 15009 • **Minute Award**
Awards are given for poems written using the "Minute" method. A Minute is a 60-syllable, 12-line poem written in strict iambic meter, with a syllable count of 8, 4, 4, 4, 8, 4, 4, 4, 8, 4, 4, 4, and rhymed a, a, b, b, c, c, d, d, e, e, f, f, capitalized and punctuated like prose and capturing a minute in time. First prize is $25, second prize is $20, and third prize is $15. Awarded annually. Sponsored by Verna Lee Hinegardner.

• 15010 • **Mississippi Poetry Society Award**
Awards are given for poetry on any subject in the form of gloss (iambic tetrameter or iambic pentameter). There is a line limit of 24. First prize is $25, second prize is $20, and third prize is $15. Awarded annually. Sponsored by the Mississippi Poetry Society.

• 15011 • **Missouri State Poetry Society Award**
Awards are given for poetry on the subject of food in any form, with a limit of 40 lines. First prize is $35, second prize is $25, and third prize is $15. Awarded annually.

• 15012 • **Jack Murphy Memorial Award**
To honor the memory of Jack Murphy, who served as president of NFSPS and the Poetry Society of Texas. Applicants must be members of NFSPS. Awards are given for any subject and any form. Poems must be limited to 40 lines. First prize is $100, second prize is $60, and third prize is $40. Entries must be postmarked by March 15. Sponsored by Pat and Don Stodghill.

• 15013 • **Music Award**
Awards are given for sonnets expressing the spiritual impact of great music. First prize is $75, second prize is $30, and third prize is $20. Awarded annually. Sponsored by Pearl Hand Cockrell.

• 15014 • **Nebraska State Poetry Society Award**
Awards are given for poetry on the subject of storms, in any form, with a line limit of 30. Open to members only. First prize is $25, second prize is $20, and third prize is $15. Awarded annually. Sponsored by the Nebraska State Poetry Society.

• 15015 • **Nevada Poetry Society Award**
Any form of humorous or satirical poetry with a line limit of 40. First prize is $100, second prize is $60 and third prize is $40. Awarded annually.

• 15016 • **New Jersey Poetry Society Award**
Awards are given for poetry on any subject, in any form, with a line limit of 40. First prize is $25, second prize is $20, and third prize is $15. Awarded annually. Sponsored by the New Jersey Poetry Society.

• 15017 • **New York Poetry Forum Award**
Awards are given on the subject of The Art of Poetry. Poems may be of any form, with a 40 line limit. First prize is $50, second prize is $30, and third prize is $20. Awarded annually.

• 15018 • **Ohio Award**
Awards are given for poetry on any subject, in any form, with a limit of 40 lines. First prize is $50, second prize is $25, and third prize is $15. Awarded annually.

• 15019 • **Our American Indian Heritage Award**
Awards are given on any subject of poetry about American Indians, past or present. Poems may be of any form, with a line limit of 40. First prize is $35, second prize is $25, and third prize is $15. Awarded annually. Sponsored by the New Mexico State Poetry Society. Formerly: Our Native American Heritage Award.

• 15020 • **Plains Poets Award**
Awards are given on the subject of rain. Poems may be of any form, with a 30-line limit. First prize is $50, second prize is $35, and third prize is $15. Awarded annually. Sponsored by Sy and Carlee Swann.

• 15021 • **Poetry Society of Michigan Award**
Awards are given for poetry on any subject in Villanelle form. First prize is $25, second prize is

$20, and third prize is $15. Awarded annually. Sponsored by the Poetry Society of Michigan.

• 15022 • Poetry Society of Oklahoma Award
Awards are given for poetry on a humorous subject in good taste. Poems may be any form, with a line limit of 20. First prize is $25, second prize is $20, and third prize is $15. Awarded annually. Sponsored by the Poetry Society of Oklahoma.

• 15023 • Poetry Society of Tennessee Pirouette Award
Awards are given for poetry on any subject in the Pirouette form (created by Chuck Belcher), consisting of a 10-line free verse with a turnaround, a sharp reversal of thought in the middle. Each line contains six syllables. First prize is $25, second prize is $20, and third prize is $15. Awarded annually. Sponsored by the Poetry Society of Tennessee.

• 15024 • Poetry Society of Texas Award
Awards given for any subject and form of poetry, with a 40-line limit. First prize is $125, 2nd prize is $50, and 3rd prize is $25. Awarded annually. Sponsored by the Poetry Society of Texas.

• 15025 • Poets' Roundtable of Arkansas Award
Awards are given for poetry on any subject, and any form, with a line limit of 40. Open to members only. First prize is $25, second prize is $20, and third prize is $15. Awarded annually. Sponsored by the Poets' Roundtable of Arkansas.

• 15026 • Power of Woman Award
To honor the memory of Barbara Stevens, who served as president of NFSPS. Any form of poetry with a limit of 50 lines may be entered. First prize is $100, second prize is $75, and third prize is $25. Awarded annually. Sponsored by Susan and Christina Chambers.

• 15027 • Morton D. Prouty and Elsie S. Prouty Memorial Award
To honor the memory of Elsie S. Prouty and Morton D. Prouty, Jr., who served as NFSPS treasurer and Poet Laureate of Alabama. Awards are given for poems on nature, any form, with a 40-line limit. First prize is $50, second prize is $25, and third prize is $15. Awarded annually.

• 15028 • Save Our Earth Award
To honor the memory of David F. Balph. Awards are given on poetry with the subject of environmental issues. Poems may be any form, with a line limit of 40. First prize is $25, second prize is $20, and third prize is $15. Awarded annually. Sponsored by Martha H. Balph.

• 15029 • William Stafford Memorial Award
To honor the memory of William Stafford, Oregon's late poet laureate and twice honorary chancellor of NFSPS. Awards are given for any subject or form, with a limit of 40 lines. First prize is $50, second prize is $30, and third prize is $20. Awarded annually. Sponsored by the Oregon State Poetry Association.

• 15030 • Barbara Stevens Memorial Award
Awards are given on any serious theme, any from, with a line limit of 12. First prize is $25, second prize is $20, and third prize is $15. Awarded annually. Sponsored by the South Dakota Poetry Society.

• 15031 • Don R. Stodghill Award
Awards are given for poetry on any subject, in any form, with a limit of 16 lines. First prize is $50, second prize is $30, and third prize is $20. Awarded annually to honor the service of Don R. Stodghill to NFSPS and the Poetry Society of Texas. Sponsored by Budd Powell Mahan.

• 15032 • Student Award
Awards are given for any form of poetry, any subject. There is a 32-line limit. Students in grades 9 through 12 are eligible. First prize is $50, second prize is $30, and third prize is $20. There are also seven honorable mentions of $5 each. Awarded annually. Sponsored by Kay Kinnaman Sims and Ralph Hammond.

• 15033 • Two Ladies from Texas Award
Awards are given for poems on the subject of cats—their endearing habits, intelligence, loyalty, beauty, etc. Any form is permitted with a limit of 40 lines. Open to members only. First prize is $50, second prize is $30, and third prize is $20. Awarded annually. Sponsored by Nancy Baass and Mildred Vorpahl Baass.

• 15034 • Utah State Poetry Society Award
To recognize the subject of heritage in poetry. Poems must fall within a 50 line limit. First prize is $100, second prize is $60, and third prize is $40. Awarded annually.

• 15035 • West Virginia Poetry Society Award
Awards are given on poetry for the subject of Appalachia - the history, heritage, home life, or gifts of nature. Any form is allowed, with a line limit of 40. First prize is $50, second prize is $30, and third prize is $20. Awarded annually. Sponsored by West Virginia Poetry Society.

• 15036 • Winners' Circle Award
To recognize poems of any subject and any form with an 80 line limit. First prize is $400, 2nd prize is $300, and 3rd prize is $245. Awarded annually.

• 15037 • WYOpoets Award
Awards are given for poetry on the subject of wildlife, in any form, with a line limit of 50. Open to members only. First prize is $25, second prize is $20, and third prize is $15. Awarded annually. Sponsored by WYOpoets of Wyoming.

• 15038 •
National Federation of the Blind
Marc Maurer, Pres.
1800 Johnson St.
Baltimore, MD 21230
Phone: (410)659-9314
Fax: (410)685-5653
E-mail: nfb@nfb.org
Home Page: http://www.nfb.org

• 15039 • National Federation of the Blind Scholarship Program
To recognize outstanding achievement by blind scholars. Applicants must be legally blind and be pursuing or planning to pursue a full-time post secondary course of study. Awarded on the basis of academic achievement, service to the community, and financial need. The deadline for applications is March 31. Thirty scholarships ranging in value from $3,000 to $12,000 are presented annually, including: Kenneth Jernigan Scholarship - $12,000 given by the American Action Fund for Blind Children and Adults; National Federation of the Blind Scholarships - two for $4,000, five for $2,500, and nine for $2,000; Anne Pekar Memorial Scholarship - $4,000 awarded in memory of Anne Parker by her parents; Charles and Melva T. Owen Memorial Scholarship - $3,000; Howard Brown Rickard Scholarship - $2,500 awarded to a student of law, medicine, engineering, architecture, or the natural sciences; Frank Walton Horn Memorial Scholarship - $2,500 awarded by Mr. and Mrs. Charles E. Baranum, the mother and stepfather of Catherine Horn Randall. Preference is given to those studying architecture or engineering; National Federation of the Blind Humanities Scholarship - $2,500 awarded to a student of traditional humanities, such as art, English, foreign languages, history, philosophy, or religion; National Federation of the Blind Educator of Tomorrow Award - $2,500 awarded to an individual planning to pursue a career in elementary, secondary, or post secondary teaching; Hermoine Grant Calhoun Scholarship - $2,000 awarded to a woman and established by Dr. Isabelle Grant in memory of her daughter; Kuchler-Killian Memorial Scholarship - awarded in memory of Charles Albert and Alice Helen Kuchler by their daughter, Junerose Killian, a dedicated member of the National Federation of the Blind of Connecticut; and Ellen Setterfield Memorial Scholarship - $2,000, established by Roy Landstrom. Expenses to attend the national convention in July where the awards are presented are also provided. Awarded annually.

• 15040 • Newel Perry Award
To honor an individual who has made an outstanding contribution to the welfare of the blind. Members of the Federation are not eligible. A brass plate mounted on a walnut plaque is awarded as merited. Established in 1973.

• 15041 • Jacobus TenBroek Award
To honor the member who has made an outstanding contribution to the NFB and to the welfare of the blind. A brass plate mounted on a walnut plaque is awarded as merited. Established in 1955.

• 15042 •
National Federation of the Blind of South Dakota
Karen S. Mayry, Pres.
919 Main, Ste. 15
Rapid City, SD 57701
Phone: (605)348-8418
Toll-Free: 800-558-1843

• 15043 • **Anna Marklund Scholarship**
For an individual who is legally blind. Scholarship awarded annually.

• 15044 •
National Field Archery Association
Marihelen Rogers, Exec.Sec.
31407 Outer I-10
Redlands, CA 92373
Phone: (909)794-2133
Toll-Free: 800-811-2331
Fax: (909)794-8512
E-mail: nfaarchery@aol.com
Home Page: http://www.NFAAarchery.com

• 15045 • **National Field Archery Championship**
To recognize the champion in field archery competition. The competition is held in three main tournament rounds: the Field Round, the Hunter's Round, and the Animal Round. In the Field Round, the target distances vary from 15 to 80 yards; in the Hunter's Round, the distances average one-third less; and in the Animal Round, the distances are even shorter and the target faces are drawings or cutouts of animals. Amateur and professional men and women are eligible to participate. The championship is held annually. Established in 1946.

• 15046 •
National Fishing Lure Collectors Club
Colby Sorrells, Sec.-Treas.
PO Box 509
Mansfield, TX 76063
Phone: (817)473-6748
Fax: (417)338-4427
E-mail: texasbassbugger@yahoo.com
Home Page: http://www.nflcc.com

• 15047 • **Honorary Membership Award**
To honor and give recognition to individuals who were part of the pre-1960 fishing tackle era and who made significant contributions to the history and development of fishing tackle. Individuals must still be living and be at least 65 years old. Nominations may be submitted to the selection committee chairman by June 1 of each year. An Honorary Member Certificate is awarded annually at the July National Meeting. Recipients are designated Old Tackle Makers and receive life membership and a certificate. Established in 1984.

• 15048 •
National Flag Foundation
Joyce J. Doody, Exec.Dir.
Flag Plz.
1275 Bedford Ave.
Pittsburgh, PA 15219
Phone: (412)261-1776
Toll-Free: 800-615-1776
Fax: (412)261-9132
E-mail: flag@americanflags.org
Home Page: http://www.americanflags.org
Formerly: (1972) Flag Plaza Foundation.

• 15049 • **Captain William Driver Award**
For recognition of the finest presentation at the annual meeting of the North American Vexillological Association. A Certificate of Commendation and small honorarium are presented annually in October at the NAVA Meeting. Established in 1969 by National Flag Foundation in honor of Captain Driver, the man who nicknamed the U.S. Flag "Old Glory", the best turned public relations phrase in history.

• 15050 • **Flags of America Award**
To recognize scouts who participate in and conduct the "Historic Flag Ceremony" at Flag Plaza, and to recognize distinguished American patriots. Scouts or youth participants in the historic flag ceremony, or individuals selected for special recognition by the NFF Board of Directors, are eligible. A multi-colored gold framed flag chart depicting 36 historic flag scenes, the most complete and colorful depiction of the history of the American Flag on one piece of paper in print in the world today, is awarded. Established in 1968 by the Greater Pittsburgh Council, Boy Scouts of America, and National Flag Foundation.

• 15051 • **Great American Artificer Award**
To recognize distinguished American patriots. Nominations may be made by members of the Board of Directors of the Foundation with unanimous approval of the entire Board. A plaque/certificate and a hand-drawn nail tie-clasp are awarded periodically. Established in 1968 in honor of the early American Artificer, the citizen-soldier who hewed and built the colonies into a nation.

• 15052 • **New Constellation Award**
The award is a reminder of the heroic achievements of the forefathers of America in uniting the colonies, winning the War for Independence, and forging a fledgling nation dedicated to the ideals of equality, liberty, and justice.

• 15053 •
National Fluid Power Association
Linda Western, Exec.Dir.
3333 N Mayfair Rd., Ste. 211
Milwaukee, WI 53222-3219
Phone: (414)778-3344
Fax: (414)778-3361
E-mail: nfpa@nfpa.com
Home Page: http://www.nfpa.com

• 15054 • **Fluid Power Achievement Award**
To honor an individual for an outstanding contribution to fluid power through exceptional efforts, commitment and dedication, or through a more specific achievement in the areas of research, design, systems application, and/or education. The achievement can include an invention, a breakthrough in fluid power technology, a novel application that opens new markets, or an ongoing effort to teach future generations about fluid power. Contributions will also have had a broad-based, positive impact on the industry. Residents of the United States, its territories or possessions, who have been or are currently active in the industry may be nominated. Established in 1961.

• 15055 • **Standards Development Awards**
To recognize an individual for leadership in the fluid power industry, as exhibited through the individual's efforts as chairperson of a group responsible for development of an industry standard. A plaque with an inscribed plate is awarded when merited. Established in 1970.

• 15056 •
National Flute Association
Phyllis Pemberton, Exec.Dir.
26951 Ruether Ave., Ste. H
Santa Clarita, CA 91351
Phone: (661)250-8920
Fax: (661)299-6681
E-mail: nationalflute@aol.com
Home Page: http://www.nfaonline.org

• 15057 • **Convention Performers Competition**
Competition is open to all professional flutists and flute teachers. Winners are limited to two consecutive convention performances on the Newly Published Music concert. Held biennially in odd-numbered years.

• 15058 • **High School Flute Choir Competition**
To provide outstanding high school students the opportunity to perform at NFA conventions. Held annually.

• 15059 • **High School Soloist Competition**
To recognize outstanding flutists. Contestants must be in grades nine through 12 or the equivalent, and between the ages of 14 and 19. Monetary awards of $400, $250, and $150 are presented. In addition, the Geoffery Gilbert Prize of $400 is presented to the first place winner to be used for flute study with a teacher who is a member of the Association. Awarded annually at the national convention. Established in 1987.

• 15060 • **Jazz Flute Masterclass**
Masterclass is open to any flutist who is an undergraduate or graduate student. Three entrants will be selected to perform in a Masterclass taught by a prominent jazz performer/

Awards are arranged in alphabetical order below their administering organizations

teacher. Competition is held biennially in odd-numbered years.

• 15061 • Masterclass Performers Competition

The competition is open to any flutist who is an undergraduate or graduate student at a college, university, or conservatory. All candidates must be current members of the NFA and currently studying with a flute teacher who is also an NFA member. Held annually.

• 15062 • Orchestral Audition and Masterclass Competition

Competition is open to flutists under the age of 27 who are capable of demonstrating a high level of playing ability. Competition has two sections: a mock audition, followed by a masterclass. Three applicants will be chosen to perform a mock audition at the convention where prizes of $1,000, $500, and $400 will be awarded. Held annually.

• 15063 • Professional Flute Choir Competition

Competition is open to all professional flutist and flute teachers. A Flute Choir consisting of a minimum of fourteen players will be selected to perform at the annual convention. Held annually.

• 15064 • Young Artist Competition

To recognize outstanding member flutists under the age of 30. Six semi-finalists are selected on the basis of their taped preliminary auditions to compete at the NFA Convention. Three finalists are chosen and presented in a convention recital. Previous first prize winners in this competition are ineligible to compete again. The applications deadline is April 1. Monetary prizes of $2,000, $1,000, and $500 are awarded annually. In addition, a monetary award of $100 is presented to each semifinalist who is not chosen as a finalist. Established in 1974.

• 15065 •
National Football Foundation and College Hall of Fame
Michael Russo, Contact
22 Maple Ave.
Morristown, NJ 07960-5215
Phone: (973)829-1933
Toll-Free: 800-486-1865
Fax: (973)829-1737
E-mail: membership@footballfoundation.com
Home Page: http://www.footballfoundation.com

Formerly: (1995) National Football Foundation and Hall of Fame.

• 15066 • Asa S. Bushnell Trophy

To recognize the college division championship football team of the National Collegiate Athletic Association Division II. Established in 1975.

• 15067 • College Football Hall of Fame

To recognize those college players and coaches whose deeds and lives during and after their playing and coaching days have been exemplary and inspiring. Inductions are made yearly. Established in 1958.

• 15068 • Distinguished American Award

To recognize an outstanding person who has maintained a lifetime of interest in the game and who, over a long period of time, has exhibited enviable leadership qualities and made a significant contribution to the betterment of amateur football in the United States. Recipients need not be former coaches or players. Awarded when merited. Established in 1966.

• 15069 • Dwight D. Eisenhower Trophy

To recognize the champion football team of the National Association of Intercollegiate Athletics Division I. A silver bowl is awarded annually. Established in 1972.

• 15070 • Gold Medal

This, the highest individual honor that the Foundation bestows, is given to recognize a person who has significantly contributed to college football and has achieved success in an industrial, business, financial, educational, professional, or related career. American citizens who have contributed notably in public service to the welfare of their country and fellow citizens are eligible. Awarded annually. Established in 1958.

• 15071 • John F. Kennedy Trophy

To recognize the college division championship football team of the National Collegiate Athletic Association Division I-AA. A silver bowl is awarded annually at the Foundation's Hall of Fame/NCAA Luncheon. Established in 1972.

• 15072 • MacArthur Trophy

To recognize the outstanding college football team of the season, which is the BCS National Champion. A silver bowl, designed by Tiffany and Company, that represents a stadium with rows of seats carved in relief, is awarded annually. Established in 1959 by an anonymous donor in memory of the former General of the Army, Douglas MacArthur.

• 15073 • National Scholar-Athlete Awards

To recognize a select group of college seniors who have demonstrated outstanding academic success, exemplary community leadership, and superior football performance. The National Football Foundation selects fifteen scholar-athletes who will each be awarded graduate fellowships of $18,000. One outstanding candidate - the Scholar-Athlete of the Year - will be awarded the Draddy Trophy, a grant of an additional $7,000. Ten additional scholarship awards are available: Harold Alfond Scholar-Athlete Award, E. Douglas Kenna Scholar-Athlete Award, Jefferson Walker Kirby Scholar-Athlete Award, William Pearce/Joseph V. Paterno Scholar-Athlete Award, Robert A. Simms Scholar-Athlete Award, Coach Eddie Robinson Scholar-Athlete Award, Coach Lou Saban Scholar-Athlete Award, National Football League Scholar-Athlete Award, John M. MCConnell Scholar-Athlete Award, and the Florida Citrus Sports Scholar-Athlete Award. Established in 1959.

• 15074 • Outstanding Contribution to Amateur Football Award

To provide national recognition to an individual whose efforts and activities in support of the Foundation and its goals have been of national significance. Individuals motivated out of a pure love for the game and a desire to help young people to play well are considered. Awarded annually. Established in 1974.

• 15075 • Outstanding Football Official Award

To honor an outstanding amateur official for officiating abilities demonstrated in intercollegiate competition, sportsmanship, integrity, character, and contribution to the sport of football. Awarded annually. Established in 1984.

• 15076 • Theodore Roosevelt Trophy

To recognize the college division championship football team of the National Association of Intercollegiate Athletics Division II. Established in 1979.

• 15077 • Amos Alonzo Stagg Trophy

To recognize the college division championship football team of the National Collegiate Athletic Association Division III. Established in 1978.

• 15078 •
National Football Foundation and College Hall of Fame, Valley of the Sun Chapter
Lew Shaw, Exec.Dir.
14211 N 57th Way
Scottsdale, AZ 85254-3020
Phone: (602)996-7678
Fax: (602)494-9636
E-mail: footballhoff@cox.net
Home Page: http://www.azfootballhoff.org

• 15079 • Distinguished Arizonan Award

Former player or individual who has made significant contributions to the game in Arizona. Recognition award bestowed annually.

• 15080 • Outstanding Coach's Award

For amateur coach. Recognition award.

• 15081 • Scholar-Athlete Awards

For two college and 11 high school football players. Scholarship awarded annually.

• 15082 • Jack Stewart Award

For contribution to amateur football in Arizona: football official. Recognition award bestowed annually.

• 15083 •
National Football League
Paul Tagliabue, Commissioner
280 Park Ave.
New York, NY 10017
Phone: (202)450-2000
Toll-Free: 877-635-7467
Fax: (202)681-7575
E-mail: customer_service@nflshop.com
Home Page: http://www.nfl.com

• 15084 • **George S. Halas Trophy**
To recognize the winner of the National Football Conference Championship. Established in 1984. First awarded January 6, 1985.

• 15085 • **Lamar Hunt Trophy**
To recognize the winner of the American Football Conference Championship. Established in 1984. First awarded January 6, 1985.

• 15086 • **Offensive and Defensive Linemen of the Year**
To recognize the year's outstanding linemen. Awarded annually. Established in 1986. Sponsored by Miller Lite.

• 15087 • **Pete Rozelle Trophy**
Since Super Bowl I in 1967 A select group of sportswriters at the game select the most valuable player in the Super Bowl. The Pete Rozelle Trophy was first awarded in 1990 following Super Bowl XXIV in honor of Pete Rozelle. Formerly: (1989) Super Bowl Most Valuable Player.

• 15088 • **Super Bowl**
The Super Bowl is the world championship football game played each year between the champions of the two Conferences - the American Football Conference and the National Football Conference. Beginning with Super Bowl V, the trophy presented for permanent possession of the winning team was known as the Vince Lombardi Trophy. Individual players also receive monetary bonuses: $48,000 each to those on the winning team; and $29,000 each to those on the losing team. The first Super Bowl was played on January 15, 1967.

• 15089 • **True Value Man of the Year**
To recognize an NFL Player for his charitable work in the community. A plaque is awarded annually. Established in 1970. Sponsored by True Value.

• 15090 •
National Football League Players Association
Eugene Upshaw Jr., Exec.Dir.
2021 L St. NW, Ste. 600
Washington, DC 20036
Phone: (202)463-2200
Toll-Free: 800-372-2000
Fax: (202)857-0380
E-mail: webmaster@nflplayers.com
Home Page: http://www.nflpa.org

• 15091 • **JB Awards**
To recognize outstanding active players in the American Football Conference and the National Football Conference of the National Football League. Recipients are determined by a vote of the players - offensive players vote for defensive players and defensive players vote for offensive players. Nine awards are presented to one NFC and one AFC player annually, including Special Teams Player of the Year; Offensive Rookie of the Year; Most Valuable Player; and Linebacker of the Year. Established in 1973. Co-sponsored by Players Inc. and James Brown of the Fox Network's "NFL Sunday."

• 15092 • **Outstanding Offensive and Defensive Linemen of the Year Awards**
To honor the outstanding offensive and defensive linemen of the year in the NFL. Active NFL players are eligible and are selected by a vote of the players who played against them during the season. Three-foot trophies are awarded annually. Established in 1974.

• 15093 • **Byron "Whizzer" White Humanitarian Award**
To honor the NFL player who is outstanding in service to his community and fellow man. Active NFL players are eligible and are nominated by a vote of their teammates. A statue of Bryon White, in football uniform with nameplate, is awarded annually. Established in 1967 to honor Byron White, former NFL player and a Supreme Court Justice.

• 15094 •
National Forensic Association
Prof. Larry Schnoor, Pres.
107 Agency Rd.
Mankato, MN 56001-5053
Phone: (507)387-3010
Fax: (507)387-3068
E-mail: lgene9535@aol.com
Home Page: http://cas.bethel.edu/dept/comm/nfa

• 15095 • **National Forensic Association Awards**
To recognize colleges and college students competing in a variety of speaking events. The following five awards are presented: (1) National Championships in Individual Events, where first-place winners are recognized in the categories of: extemporaneous speaking, prose interpretation, after dinner speaking, rhetorical criticism, informative speaking, poetry interpretation, impromptu speaking, persuasive speaking, and duo interpretation; (2) Top Ten Schools, where the Top Ten Schools are recognized and the Top School is considered to be the National Champion; (3) Top 15 Speakers, which recognizes the best overall speakers; (4) Founder's Trophy, which recognizes a school for success over the years; and (5) Sweepstakes Awards, which recognize schools in four categories based on size of entry in the following Divisions: Open; Presidents I; Presidents II; and Presidents III. Trophies and plaques are presented annually. Established in 1973 by Dr. Seth C. Hawkins.

• 15096 •
National Forensic League
J. Scott Wunn, Exec.Sec.
125 Watson St.
PO Box 38
Ripon, WI 54971
Phone: (920)748-6206
Phone: (920)748-6896
Fax: (920)748-9478
E-mail: nfl@centurytel.net
Home Page: http://nflonline.org

• 15097 • **Phyllis Flory Barton Top Debate Speaker Award**
For recognition of the high point debater in the National Tournament Preliminary Rounds. A trophy and $250 scholarship are presented annually. Established in 1986 in memory of Phyllis Barton.

• 15098 • **Ralph E. Carey Distinguished District Chair Awards**
To recognize outstanding service by NFL district directors. NFL members who are chairpersons of NFL districts are eligible. A trophy and other awards are awarded annually. Established in 1991 in memory of Ralph E. Carey.

• 15099 • **Diamond Key Award**
To recognize a speech and debate coach who has coached students to excellence. Members of the National Forensic League who have five years coaching experience are eligible for the following awards: First Diamond Coach - 1,500 coaching points; Second Diamond Coach - 3,000 coaching points; Third Diamond Coach - 6,000 coaching points; Fourth Diamond Coach - 10,000 coaching points; Fifth Diamond Coach - 13,000 coaching points; Sixth Diamond Coach - 16,000 coaching points; Seventh Diamond - 19,000 coaching points; Eighth Diamond Coach - 22,000 coaching points; and Ninth Diamond Coach - 25,000 coaching points. A pin or key inserted with diamonds is awarded. Established in 1933.

• 15100 • **Distinguished Service Key**
To honor coaches for outstanding service to the league. NFL member coaches who accumulate 20 citations are eligible. A key is awarded when earned. In addition, coaches who accumulate 50 citations are awarded a Distinguished Service Plaque. Additional plaques are awarded for each of the 50 citations.

• 15101 • **Hall of Fame**
For recognition of an outstanding career in speech communication education. Members of the league with 25 years of service are eligible. Plaques are awarded annually. Established in 1978.

• 15102 • **Pi Kappa Delta/Bruno E. Jacob Trophy**
To recognize the school that has accumulated the largest number of cumulative rounds earned at the national tournament. Any full charter or affiliated chapter with the National Forensic League is eligible. A trophy is awarded annually

at the national tournament. Established in 1936. Formerly: (1978) Delta Sigma Rho - Tau Kappa Alpha Trophy; (1997) Bruno E. Jacob Trophy.

• 15103 • Leading Chapter Award
To honor the chapter in each district that accumulates the largest number of new degrees on a cumulative basis. A plaque is awarded annually. Established in 1931.

• 15104 • Lincoln Financial Group Awards of Excellence
To recognize the schools who meet a standard of excellence at the National Speech Tournament. Formerly: (1998) Phillips Petroleum Performance Award; Sweepstakes Trophy; .

• 15105 • Harland B. Mitchell National Debate Trophy
To recognize the team winning the final round of cross-examination debate at the national tournament. Members at an NFL chapter school or affiliated school who qualified for the nationals by winning the district debate tournament are eligible. A trophy is awarded annually. Established in 1979 to honor Harland B. Mitchell, by his former debate students at Seminole High School, Seminole, OK.

• 15106 • Senator Karl E. Mundt Trophy
To recognize a school for outstanding achievement over several years at the National Student Congress. Membership in an NFL chapter or an affiliated school is required. A trophy is awarded annually. Established in 1955.

• 15107 • National Awards
To recognize individuals for outstanding performance at the National Speech Tournament. Awards are presented in the following categories: Henry J. Kaiser Policy Debate; Barbara Jordan Youth Debates on Health; Lincoln Financial Group Lincoln Douglas Debates; Patrick Henry Memorial Oratorical Contest; Lanny D. Naegelin Dramatic Interpretation Contest; Public Employees Roundtable Contest in U.S. Extempore Speaking; and the Dacor/ASPA Contest in Foreign Extempore Speaking. Members of an NFL chapter school or affiliated school who qualify for the nationals by placing at the district tournament are eligible. Trophies are awarded annually to the top 60 contestants in each category. In addition, students who were eliminated in the early rounds may be awarded national honors in the following consolation events: Impromptu Speaking, Prose Reading, Poetry Reading, Commentary, Expository Speaking, and Storytelling. The nationals were established in 1931; no tournaments were held from 1942 to 1946.

• 15108 • John C. Stennis Student Congress Awards
To recognize a Senator and a Representative for outstanding contribution to Student Congress debate. Members of an NFL chapter school who are elected from district congresses are eligible. Trophies and scholarships are awarded annually. Established in 1938.

• 15109 •
National Forum for Black Public Administrators
John E. Saunders III, Exec.Dir.
777 N Capitol St. NE, Ste. 807
Washington, DC 20002
Phone: (202)408-9300
Toll-Free: 888-766-9951
Fax: (202)408-8558
E-mail: jsaunders@nfbpa.org
Home Page: http://www.nfbpa.org

• 15110 • Hall of Fame Award
To recognize and honor African Americans in public service whose accomplishments are noteworthy of emulation and who serve as a source of inspiration and encouragement to others in public management. Applicants are selected by nomination. A bronze medal is awarded at the annual conference. Established in 1991.

• 15111 • Marks of Excellence Award
To recognize African American public administrators with outstanding cumulative years of public service and who have demonstrated superior management ability, outstanding dedication to public service leadership, and a laudable commitment to the community. Applicants are selected by nomination. A bronze statue is awarded annually at the convention. Established in 1984.

• 15112 •
National Forum of Greek Orthodox Church Musicians
Dr. Vicki Pappas PhD, Natl. Chair
1700 N Walnut St., No. 302
Bloomington, IN 47404
Phone: (812)855-8248
Fax: (812)855-9630
E-mail: pappas@indiana.edu
Home Page: http://www.goarch.org/en/archdiocese/affiliates/nfcm.asp

• 15113 • Archbishop Iakovos' Years of Service Award
To honor those persons who have served as choir directors in Greek Orthodox churches for 25 or more years. A specially designed 25-year pin depicting St. Romanos the Methodist, the patron saint of church musicians, and a certificate of recognition are awarded annually in October, on National Church Music Sunday. Established in 1988.

• 15114 • Patriach Athenagoras Diocesan Service Award
To recognize those church musicians who have made distinguished contributions in their respective dioceses, choir federations, and parish choirs. Each diocese's Choir Federation may nominate up to three individuals per year. The medals are awarded at appropriate diocesan functions. Established in 1996.

• 15115 • St. Romanos the Melodist Medallion
To recognize church musicians of the Greek Orthodox Church who have made exemplary national contributions to the development and perpetuation of Greek Orthodox liturgical music. Individuals are nominated by the regional choir federation and/or the National Forum Coordinating Committee. The Medallion of St. Romanos the Melodist, the patron saint of church musicians, is awarded biennially in conjunction with the Clergy-Laity Congress of the Greek Orthodox Archdiocese of North and South America. Established in 1980.

• 15116 •
National Foundation for Advancement in the Arts
Ms. Vivian Orndorff, Dir. of Programs
444 Brickell Ave., P-14
Miami, FL 33131
Phone: (305)377-1140
Toll-Free: 800-970-ARTS
Fax: (305)377-1149
E-mail: info@nfaa.org
Home Page: http://nfaa.artsawards.org

• 15117 • Arts Recognition and Talent Search (ARTS)
For recognition of talented young American artists in every art form, including dance, music, jazz, photography, theater, visual arts, voice, film and video, and writing. Students must be 17 or 18 years of age or a graduating high school senior, and be U.S. citizens or residents (jazz is open to musicians from around the world). Approximately $3 million in college scholarship awards is available. Finalists receive awards ranging from $250 to $10,000; honorable mention awards receive $100 each; Merit Awards receive a certificate. Awarded annually. In addition, NFAA nominates up to 50 ARTS finalists to be named one of the 20 Presidential Scholars in the Arts, sponsored by the White House. Established in 1981.

• 15118 • Career Advancement of Visual Artists (CAVA)
To provide emerging, professional visual artists with unencumbered time and space to develop their art in a supportive environment, and to provide opportunities to interact with professionals in their field. Open to all visual artists who have not worked professionally for more than five years, who are U.S. citizens or permanent residents of the United States, and have completed their schooling and have not been enrolled in a formal course of study for at least one year. The award includes a four month residency, renewable for three years, with housing and studio space; $1,000 per month stipend; funds for art supplies; and an exhibition with catalogue for national distribution. Awarded annually. Established in 1988.

• 15119 •
National Foundation for Infectious Diseases
Carol J. Baker MD, Pres.-Elect
4733 Bethesda Ave., Ste. 750
Bethesda, MD 20814
Phone: (301)656-0003
Fax: (301)907-0878
E-mail: info@nfid.org
Home Page: http://www.nfid.org

• 15120 • **Hoechst Marion Roussel Postdoctoral Fellowship in Nosocomial Infection Research and Training**
To encourage and assist a qualified physician trainee researcher to become a specialist and investigator in the field of nosocomial infections. Priority is given to the study of gram positive nosocomial infectious diseases and to applicants with no outside grant support. The fellowship is awarded to an individual meeting the eligibility requirements for one year. The applicant must be a physician and a citizen of the United States. He or she must demonstrate aptitude and accomplishment in research and must confirm arrangements for conduct of the proposed research in a recognized host laboratory. The applicant must be sponsored by a university-affiliated medical center. The fellowship may not be awarded if the applicant has received or will receive a major fellowship, research grant, or traineeship from the federal government or another foundation in excess of the amount of this award. Applications must be postmarked no later than January 13. Selection criteria include, but are not limited to, applicant's record of scholarship performance and professional qualifications; scientific merit of the research project proposed; validity of clinical research rationale; and adequacy of facilities available to the applicant, host department, and host institution. A stipend of $21,000 for the year with an additional $1,000 for travel and supplies is awarded annually. Sponsored by Hoechst Marion Roussel. Formerly: NFID - Marion Murrell Dow, Inc. Postdoctoral Fellowship in Nosocomial/Gram Positive Infection Research and Training.

• 15121 • **Pfizer Mycology Postdoctoral Fellowship/John P. Utz Award**
To encourage outstanding physicians to select careers in medical mycology and opportunistic pathogens. Priority will be given to fellows in or entering infectious diseases training. Each applicant must demonstrate aptitude and training in research and must confirm arrangements for the proposed research in a recognized host laboratory. The applicant must be sponsored by a university-affiliated medical center. The award amount is $55,000 for one year. Application deadline is February 15. Awarded annually.

• 15122 • **Postdoctoral Fellowship in Emerging Infectious Diseases**
To encourage and assist a qualified physician to become a recognized authority on emerging infectious diseases and epidemiology. The fellowship is awarded for one year to individuals who are physicians and citizens of the United States, and who have completed an infectious diseases fellowship. The fellowship includes a $50,000 stipend. Sponsored by NFID, CDC, and Merck & Co., Inc.

• 15123 • **Postdoctoral Fellowship in Infectious Disease Training and Herpes Virus Research**
To encourage and assist a qualified physician researcher to become a specialist and investigator in the field of viral infections, notably those due to Herpes viruses (CMV, EB, H. simplex, and V. zoster). Priority is given to the study of Herpes viruses, especially as they might pertain to AIDS and HIV infections, and to those applicants with no outside grant support. The fellowship is awarded to an individual meeting the eligibility requirements for a period of one year. The applicant must be a physician and a citizen of the United States. He or she must demonstrate aptitude and accomplishment in research and must confirm arrangements for conduct of the proposed research in a recognized host laboratory. The applicant must be sponsored by a university-affiliated medical center. Applicants receiving or to be awarded grants in the same academic year in excess of the amount of this award are not eligible. Applications must be postmarked no later than January 13. Selection criteria include, but are not limited to, applicant's record of scholarship performance and professional qualifications; scientific merit of the research project proposed; validity of clinical research rationale; and adequacy of facilities available to the applicant, host department, and host institution. A stipend of $23,000 for the year with an additional $1,000 for travel and supplies is awarded annually. Formerly: NFID - Actra USA, Inc. Postdoctoral Fellowship in Infectious Disease Training and Herpes Virus Research.

• 15124 • **Postdoctoral Fellowships in Infectious Diseases**
To encourage and assist young qualified physicians to become specialists and investigators in the field of infectious diseases. Fellowships are open to individuals who are enrolled in accredited graduate training programs in infectious diseases. Selection criteria will include but not be limited to the applicant/s scholarship performance and professional qualifications, scientific merit of the proposed project, validity of the research rationale, and adequacy of the facilities available to the applicant. Postdoctoral fellows who hold another comparable fellowship are not eligible. Application deadline is February 15. Specific fellowships are the Colin L. Powell Minority Postdoctoral Fellowship in Tropical Disease Research ($30,000 for one year); Pfizer Mycology Postdoctoral Fellowship/John P. Utz Award ($55,000 for one year); and Ellison Postdoctoral Fellowship in International Infectious Diseases ($40,000). Awarded annually. Formerly: Eli Lilly Fellowship in Infectious Diseases.

• 15125 • **Young Investigator Awards**
To assist young investigators who are beginning their research. Candidates must have a medical or equivalent doctoral level degree; be young, unestablished investigators; and should not be more than three years out of a training program. The candidates also must be assured of a faculty position at a U.S. institution. Selection of awardees includes consideration of each applicant/s commitment to clinical and laboratory investigation, the research program envisioned by the applicant, and creativity, originality, and excellence in prior performance. Application deadline is February 15. The recipient of the Association of Subspecialty Professors Young Investigator Award in Geriatrics receives a grant of $100,000 over two years, and the recipient of the Wyeth Young Investigator Award in Vaccine Development receives $60,000 over two years. Awarded annually. Formerly: NFID - Burroughs Welcome Fund Young Investigator Awards.

• 15126 •
National Friends of Public Broadcasting
% WETA Friends of 13
University of Maryland
College Park, MD 20742
Phone: (301)405-1000
E-mail: webmaster@itd.umd.edu
Home Page: http://www.umd.edu

• 15127 • **Elizabeth Campbell Outstanding Public Broadcasting Award**
To recognize outstanding volunteers in public broadcasting who demonstrate leadership, effectiveness, and unselfish devotion to the cause of public broadcasting. Nominations are accepted. Awarded annually. Named in honor of Elizabeth Campbell, a founding member of the National Friends and an outstanding volunteer at WETA in Washington, D.C.

• 15128 • **Charlotte Hill Volunteers in Fund-Raising Award**
For recognition of the station or stations that demonstrate creativity and effectiveness in the use of volunteers in fund raising. Nominations are accepted. Awarded annually. Established to honor Charlotte Hill, past chairperson of NFPB and a dedicated volunteer at WTTW in Chicago. Formerly: (1989) Volunteers in Fund Raising Awards.

• 15129 • **Jan Mitchell Community Development Award**
To recognize the station or Friends groups with the most outstanding projects or campaign to raise community awareness and appreciation. Nominations are accepted. Awarded annually. Named in honor of Charlotte Hill, past chairperson of the National Friends, and a dedicated volunteer at KLVX in Las Vegas. Formerly: (1989) Charlotte Hill Community Development Awards.

• 15130 • **Elaine Peterson Distinguished Service Award**
To recognize volunteers for significant contributions to their communities through exceptional service to their stations. Awarded from time to time. Established in honor of Elaine Peterson, past chairperson and senior trustee of NFPB, and a dedicated volunteer at WMVS in Milwaukee.

• 15131 •
National Frozen and Refrigerated Foods Association
Nevin B. Montgomery, Pres./CEO
PO Box 6069
PO Box 6069
Harrisburg, PA 17112
Phone: (717)657-8601
Fax: (717)657-9862
E-mail: info@nfraweb.org
Home Page: http://www.nfraweb.org

Formerly: (2002) National Frozen Food Association.

• 15132 • Golden Penguin Awards
To recognize outstanding promotion and merchandising of frozen foods during March National Frozen Food Month. Any NFFA-member company or individual actively involved in the frozen food industry is eligible. Membership in the association is not required for certain categories, call NFFA for details. Golden Penguin Awards are presented in the following categories: Allied Services, Foodservice Operation, Corporate Foodservice Distributor, Foodservice Brokerage/ Direct Sales, Foodservice Distributor, Foodservice Frozen Food Organization, Foodservice Manufacturer, Non-Commerical Foodservice Operation, School Foodservice Operation, Trade Media, Retail Manufacturer, Retail Brokerage/Direct Sales, Retail Distributor, Retail Corporate Wholesaler, Retail Wholesaler Division, Retail Cooperative, Retail Buying Group, Retail Chain, Overall Store Effort, Retail Display, Convenience Store, Military Broker, Military commissary, Military Commissary Display, Allied Services, Trade Media, Consumer Media, Retail Frozen Food Organization. Golden Penguin Awards are presented to winners. Runner-up Silver Penguin trophies are also awarded. Golden penguins are awarded annually at the National Frozen Food Convention.

• 15133 •
National Funeral Directors Association
Fay Spano, Public Relations Dir.
13625 Bishops Dr.
Brookfield, WI 53005-6607
Phone: (262)789-1880
Phone: (262)814-1549
Toll-Free: 800-228-6332
Fax: (262)789-6977
E-mail: nfda@nfda.org
Home Page: http://www.nfda.org

• 15134 • Pursuit of Excellence Award
To recognize outstanding member funeral homes in the United States. Applicant must qualify in each of the following categories: Educational programs; Compassionate service programs; Community and professional service activities; Library or media resource activities; Attendance at professional conferences, seminars, and meetings; Special in-house programs formulated by the funeral home; Technical skills activities; and Individual funeral home service and public relations programs. Plaques are awarded annually at the Convention. Established in 1981 for the Association's centennial celebration.

• 15135 •
National Garden Clubs
Mrs. Kitty Larkin, Pres.
4401 Magnolia Ave.
St. Louis, MO 63110-3492
Phone: (314)776-7574
Fax: (314)776-5108
E-mail: headquarters@gardenclub.org
Home Page: http://www.gardenclub.org

• 15136 • Exemplary Journalism Award
For recognition of outstanding journalism in the field of horticulture on an announced theme. Any journalist may enter published or broadcast material by June 1. A plaque is awarded annually. Established in 1980.

• 15137 •
National Genealogical Society
Diane O'Connor, Exec.Dir.
3108 Columbia Pke., Ste. 300
Arlington, VA 22204-4304
Phone: (703)525-0050
Toll-Free: 800-473-0060
Fax: (703)525-0052
E-mail: ngs@ngsgenealogy.org
Home Page: http://www.ngsgenealogy.org

• 15138 • Award for Achievement: Individual
To recognize an individual for exceptional contributions to the field of genealogy over a period of five or more years that have resulted in significantly aiding research or furthering interest in genealogy. A certificate is presented at the NGS Conference. Established in 1991.

• 15139 • Award for Achievement: Organization
To recognize a nonprofit genealogical or historical organization for exceptional contributions to the field of genealogy over a period of five or more years that have resulted in significantly aiding research or furthering interest in genealogy. A certificate is presented at the NGS Conference. Established in 1991.

• 15140 • Award for Excellence: Genealogical Methods and Sources
To recognize a specific, significant single contribution in the form of a book, an article, or a series of articles published during the past five years that discusses genealogical methods and sources and serves to foster scholarship and/or advance or promote excellence in genealogy. A certificate is presented at the NGS Conference. Established in 1991.

• 15141 • Award for Excellence: Genealogy and Family History
To recognize a specific, significant single contribution in the form of a family genealogy or family history book published during the past five years that serves to foster scholarship and/or otherwise advances or promotes excellence in genealogy. A certificate is presented at the NGS Conference. Established in 1991.

• 15142 • Award for Excellence: *National Genealogical Society Quarterly*
To recognize a specific, significant single contribution in the form of an article or a series of articles that serves to foster scholarship and/or advance or promote excellence in genealogy. Articles accepted by the *National Genealogical Society Quarterly* editors and published during the past year are eligible. A certificate is presented at the NGS Conference. Established in 1991.

• 15143 • Award of Merit
To recognize distinguished work in American genealogy by individuals and organizations. A nominee need not be a member of NGS. This award may be presented to an individual more than once. Established in 1956.

• 15144 • Certificate of Appreciation
To recognize an individual or organization that has made a large financial gift (benefactor) to the Society for the support of its programs, or to recognize exceptional or long-term volunteer service in support of the Society's programs. A nominee need not be a member of NGS. May be presented to an individual or an institution more than once. The nominee receives a certificate. Awards are presented at the NGS Conference and also at the Volunteer Appreciation Day held at the Society's headquarters.

• 15145 • Distinguished Service Award
To recognize dedication of the work of the Society. A nominee must have been a member of NGS for at least three years. May be presented to an individual more than once.

• 15146 • Family History Writing Contest Award of Excellence
To recognize members who have put together an outstanding three-generation family history beginning with a progenitor who lived in an American colony or state. The genealogy should place ancestors in historical context in addition to presenting genealogical data that is well-documented. Manuscripts are placed in the NGS library for public reading and access. An expense-paid trip to the NGS Conference and publication in the "NGS Quarterly" are awarded.

• 15147 • Fellow of the National Genealogical Society
This, NGS's most prestigious award, is given to recognize outstanding work in the field of genealogy or the related fields of history, biography, or heraldry, in addition to outstanding service to the Society. A nominee must have been a member of the NGS for at least 5 years. A certificate and a gold pin are awarded. Established in 1955.

• 15148 • Honorary Member (Individual)
To recognize outstanding contributions to the field of genealogy or to NGS. A nominee need

Awards are arranged in alphabetical order below their administering organizations

not be a member of NGS. An Honorary Member receives a certificate and the privileges of life membership.

• 15149 • Honorary Member (Institutional)
To recognize an organization which has served as a sponsoring organization for an NGS Conference in the States. The Institution receives a certificate, presented at the NGS Conference, and the privileges of life membership.

• 15150 • National Genealogy Hall of Fame
To honor deceased American men and women who made significant contributions to the field of genealogy in the United States. NGS affiliation is not required to nominees, nominating societies, or electors. One nominee is elected annually and announced at the NGS Conference. Portraits of elected individuals are displayed in the Octagon Room at the Glebe House, the Society's headquarters.

• 15151 • Newsletter Competition
To recognize interest, variety, and originality; quality of writing and editing; attractiveness and readability of pages; and overall makeup of an outstanding genealogical newsletter. Awarded to two classes: Class I - genealogical societies; and Class II - family associations. Open only to genealogical societies and family associations which publish newsletters. A certificate, one-year membership in the Society, and a feature in the NGS Newsletter are awarded.

• 15152 • Rubincam Youth Award
To recognize the best three-generation, single-line genealogy submitted by those 18 years of age or younger. The work must be original and unpublished and may be of the applicant's family or any other family with at least three generations of descendants. Selection is based on content and depth of research, documentation, writing, punctuation, and spelling. Proper footnote citations are also considered. The deadline for entries is March 1. A certificate, one-year membership, and $500 monetary prize are awarded annually. Established to honor Milton Rubincam for his many years of service to the Society.

• 15153 •
National Geographic Society
John Fahey, Pres.
1145 17th St. NW
Washington, DC 20036
Phone: (202)857-7000
Toll-Free: 800-647-5463
Fax: (202)775-6141
E-mail: askngs@nationalgeographic.com
Home Page: http://www.nationalgeographic.com

• 15154 • Alexander Graham Bell Medal
To recognize extraordinary achievement in geographic research, broadly construed. A gold medal is awarded irregularly. Established in 1980 in honor of Alexander Graham Bell, the noted inventor, and second president of the Society.

• 15155 • Franklin L. Burr Award
To recognize especially meritorious work in the field of geographic science. Leaders of Society's expeditions and researches are eligible. A monetary award and a certificate are awarded irregularly. Established in 1933 by Mary C. Burr in memory of her father.

• 15156 • Grosvenor Medal
To recognize exceptional service to geography by a Society officer or employee. A gold medal is awarded irregularly. Established in 1949 in honor of Gilbert Hovey Grosvenor, the 55-year Society President and Editor.

• 15157 • Arnold Guyot Memorial Award
To recognize outstanding scientific investigations in geology or paleontology. Awarded irregularly. Established in 1968.

• 15158 • Hubbard Medal
To recognize distinction in exploration, discovery and research. A gold medal is awarded irregularly. Established in 1906 in memory of Gardiner Greene Hubbard, the first President of the Society.

• 15159 • John Oliver La Gorce Medal
To recognize accomplishment in geographic exploration or in the sciences, or for public service to advance international understanding. A gold medal is awarded irregularly. Established in 1967 in honor of John Oliver La Gorce, a former Society President and Editor. Formerly: Special Gold Medal.

• 15160 • National Geographic Society Centennial Award
Fifteen "Pioneers of Discovery" were honored at the centennial celebration of the National Geographic Society in November, 1988. The honorees are scientists, adventurers and explorers, and have all had long associations with the National Geographic Society.

• 15161 • Special National Geographic Society Award
To recognize notable contributions to science. Awarded as merited. Established in 1968.

• 15162 • White Space Trophy
To recognize a member of the U.S. Air Force, military or civilian, who has made the year's most significant contribution to progress in aerospace. A trophy is awarded annually at a luncheon. Established in 1961 by Dr. Thomas W. McKnew, chairman emeritus of the NGS Board of Trustees. The award honors Gen. Thomas D. White, Champion of the role of the U.S. Air Force in space. Additional information is available from Susan Norton, NGS.

• 15163 •
National Glass Association
Philip J. James CAE, Pres./CEO
8200 Greensboro Dr., Ste. 302
McLean, VA 22102-3881
Phone: (703)442-4890
Toll-Free: (866)DIAL-NGA
Fax: (703)442-0630
E-mail: administration@glass.org
Home Page: http://www.glass.org

• 15164 • Award for Community Service
To recognize an individual NGA member who has contributed substantially to his or her community and to the public good. Members of the Association may be nominated by an industry member. Established in 1980. Formerly: E. Hank Siesel Award for Community Service.

• 15165 • Glass Professional of the Year
To honor the glass professional who has been a principal force in consistently promoting the highest standard of professional involvement in the glass industry. Members of the Association may be nominated by December 31st. Formerly: Glass Dealer of the Year.

• 15166 •
National Golf Foundation
Dr. Joseph F. Beditz, CEO & Pres.
1150 S U.S. Hwy. 1, Ste. 401
Jupiter, FL 33477
Phone: (561)744-6006
Toll-Free: 800-733-6006
Fax: (561)744-6107
E-mail: info@ngf.org
Home Page: http://www.ngf.org

• 15167 • The Graffis Award
For recognition of outstanding contributions to the game and business of golf in the tradition of Herb and Joe Graffis, who co-founded the NGF in 1936. A plaque is awarded annually. Established in 1977 as the Herb Graffis and Joe Graffis Awards, which were combined in 1992. Formerly: (1992) Herb Graffis Award; (1992) Joe Graffis Award.

• 15168 • Jack Nicklaus Golf Family of the Year Award
To recognize families who have made substantial contributions to the game and exemplify the ideals of golf and family. A plaque is awarded annually. Established in 1986. Formerly: (1992) Jack Nicklaus Family Award.

• 15169 •
National Governors Association
Raymond C. Scheppach, Exec.Dir.
Hall of States
444 N Capitol St. NW, Ste. 267
Washington, DC 20001-1512
Phone: (202)624-5300
Fax: (202)624-5313
E-mail: webmaster@nga.org
Home Page: http://www.nga.org

Awards are arranged in alphabetical order below their administering organizations

• 15170 • Distinguished Service Awards
To recognize distinguished service to state government by key state officials and private citizens. Each candidate is nominated by their governor. Three awards are given for state officials, three for private citizens, and two for distinguished service to the arts. Awards are presented at the NGA annual meeting. Established in 1976. In 1980, the arts category was added.

• 15171 •
National Grange
William Steel, Pres./Master
1616 H St. NW
Washington, DC 20006
Phone: (202)628-3507
Toll-Free: 888-4GR-ANGE
Fax: (202)347-1091
E-mail: info@nationalgrange.org
Home Page: http://www.nationalgrange.org

• 15172 • Community Service Award
To encourage every Subordinate Grange to assume a productive leadership role in community improvement, community service, and community development by recognizing outstanding community service projects. Any project carried out or started between September 1 of the previous year and August 31 of the award year that benefits the community is eligible. The deadline is March 31. Monetary awards and certificates are presented to state and national winners annually. Established in 1960.

• 15173 •
National Grocers Association
Thomas K. Zaucha, Pres./CEO
1005 N Glebe Rd., Ste. 250
Arlington, VA 22201-5758
Phone: (703)516-0700
Fax: (703)516-0115
E-mail: info@nationalgrocers.org
Home Page: http://www.nationalgrocers.org

• 15174 • Grocers Care Awards
To recognize independent grocers and their wholesalers for commitment to the community and support of National Grocers Week. Flags and certificates are awarded annually. Established in 1988.

• 15175 •
National Guard Association of the United States
Ret.Brig.Gen Stephen M. Koper, Pres.
1 Massachusetts Ave. NW
Washington, DC 20001
Phone: (202)789-0031
Fax: (202)682-9358
E-mail: ngaus@ngaus.org
Home Page: http://www.ngaus.org

• 15176 • National Guard Association of the United States Awards Program
To recognize individuals and organizations who by superior performance, acts of heroism, or service of a meritorious nature make a contribution to the goals of the association, to the purpose and effectiveness of the National Guard, or to the stability and security of the United States. The following awards are presented: (1) Army National Guard Unit Awards - Major Gen. Milton A. Reckord Trophy, Pershing Plaque, and Certificate of Victory; (2) Air National Guard Unit Awards - Spaatz Trophy, Distinguished Flying Unit Plaques, Mission Support Trophy, Distinguished Mission Support Plaques, William W. Spruance Safety Award; and (3) NGAUS Individual Awards - Harry S. Truman Award, Montgomery Medal, Meritorious Service Award and Certificate, Distinguished Service Medal, Valley Forge Cross for Heroism, Valley Forge Certificate, Charles Dick Medal of Merit, Patrick Henry Award, and Garde Nationale Trophy. Awards are presented during the association's annual general conference. The Awards Program was established in 1936.

• 15177 • Harry S. Truman Award
This, the highest award conferred upon an individual by the association, is given for recognition of sustained contributions of exceptional and far-reaching magnitude to the defense and security of the United States. A trophy comprised of 13 pewter sculpted minutemen, representing the 13 original colonies, is awarded when merited. Established in 1968 in memory of the former President of the United States, Harry S. Truman.

• 15178 •
National Guild of Community Schools of the Arts
Jonathan Herman, Exec.Dir.
520 Eighth Ave., Ste. 302
New York, NY 10018
Phone: (212)268-3337
Fax: (212)268-3995
E-mail: info@nationalguild.org
Home Page: http://www.nationalguild.org

• 15179 • President's Award
To recognize outstanding achievement by a person who has given exceptional service to the National Guild and to the community school movement. Nominations should be received before July 31. Awarded annually. Established in 1989.

• 15180 • Colonel Samuel Rosenbaum Memorial Award
To recognize an individual whose work exemplifies and promotes the ideals of the National Guild and its membership. The award is not usually given to a professional musician or artist. The deadline for nominations is July 31. A sculptured stone with an engraved plaque is awarded annually at the national conference of the Guild. Established in the early 1970s in memory of Colonel Samuel Rosenbaum, a former Trustee of the Music Performance Trust Funds and a lifelong supporter of the National Guild.

• 15181 •
National Gymnastics Judges Association
Butch Zunich, Pres.
2302 Sand Point
Univ. of Nebraska
Champaign, IL 61822
Phone: (217)359-4866
Phone: (217)384-8517
Fax: (217)384-8550
E-mail: zunich@ngja.org
Home Page: http://www.ngja.org

• 15182 • Frank J. Cumiskey Hall of Fame
To honor those who have made an outstanding contribution to officiating and as leaders in the Association. Nominees must be over the age of 40 and have made significant contributions to the sport, including election to national office as well as judging an Olympic or World Championship event. Elections are held every other year. A plaque is awarded to those elected at the annual USA Gymnastics Congress. Established in 1970.

• 15183 • Regional Judge of the Year Award
To honor an outstanding candidate from each of the four regions, usually a developing judge. Awarded annually.

• 15184 • Service Award
To honor outstanding service to the association. Award is presented by the President. Award is not necessarily given annually.

• 15185 •
National Hardwood Lumber Association
Paul Houghland Jr., Exec.Mgr.
PO Box 34518
6830 Raleigh-LaGrange Rd.
Memphis, TN 38184-0518
Phone: (901)377-1818
Fax: (901)382-6419
E-mail: info@nhla.org
Home Page: http://www.natlhardwood.org
Formerly: (1995) Hardwood Research Council.

• 15186 • Outstanding Research Award
To recognize achievement, promote awareness of hardwood research and encourage professional development in the broad field of hardwood forestry, utilization, and product manufacturing. A monetary award of $2,000, a plaque, and travel expenses are awarded annually at the Hardwood Symposium. Established in 1985.

• 15187 •
National Headache Foundation
Seymore Diamond MD, Exec.Chm.
820 N Orleans, Ste. 217
Chicago, IL 60610
Toll-Free: 888-NHF-5552
Fax: (773)525-7357
E-mail: info@headaches.org
Home Page: http://www.headaches.org

Formerly: (1986) National Migraine Foundation.

• 15188 • **Seymour Diamond Clinical Fellowship in Headache Education**
To encourage, provide for, and engage physicians toward the clinical management of headache patients. This is an individualized hands-on approach at a headache clinic mutually selected between the committee and the applicant. The objectives are to develop competence in the management of common and complex headache problems, to publish a research paper keyed to the treatment of headache, and to prepare applicant for a career in treating headache patients. A certificate will be awarded upon successful completion of one-year fellowship. The stipend for one year will be $40,000. Applicant will be a graduate of an approved medical school in the United States and be at least post graduate year four. A personal interview may be requested.

• 15189 • **Layman Support Award**
To recognize the layperson who has given unselfishly of his or her time, offered guidance, and provided support to further the goals of the National Headache Foundation. Established in 1989.

• 15190 • **Media Support Award**
To recognize a member of the media who has given unselfishly of his or her time, offered guidance, and provided support to further the goals of the National Headache Foundation. Candidates are selected by committee. Established in 1989.

• 15191 • **National Headache Foundation Lectureship Award**
To recognize an individual for a professional contribution to the field of headache study. A plaque is presented. Established in 1979.

• 15192 • **Professional Support Award**
To recognize an industry professional who has given unselfishly of his or her time, offered guidance, and provided support to further the goals of the National Headache Foundation. Candidates are selected by committee. A plaque is awarded. Established in 1989.

• 15193 •
National Headliner Awards
Michael R. Schurman, Exec.Dir.
226 Mt. Vernon Ave.
PO Box 239
Northfield, NJ 08225
Phone: (609)646-8896
Fax: (609)646-8826
E-mail: infoheadliners@aol.com
Home Page: http://www.nationalheadlinerawards.com

Formerly: (1998) National Headliner Club.

• 15194 • **National Headliner Awards**
To recognize outstanding achievement in journalism in the areas of reporting, writing, photography, graphics, and TV and radio broadcasting. Awards are presented in two main categories, print and broadcast. In each category, first-, second- and third-place awards are presented in various subcategories among newspapers, magazines, photography, radio, and television. Medallions are presented during the awards weekend in Atlantic City. Established in 1934.

• 15195 •
National Hearing Conservation Association
Karen Wojdyla, Exec.Dir.
7995 E Prentice Ave., Ste. 100
Greenwood Village, CO 80111
Phone: (303)224-9022
Fax: (303)770-1614
E-mail: nhca@gwami.com
Home Page: http://www.hearingconservation.org

• 15196 • **Media Award**
To recognize efforts to inform the public about noise, hearing conservation, and hearing health. A plaque is presented when merited at the NHCA Annual Conference. Established in 1991.

• 15197 • **Outstanding Hearing Conservationist Award**
To recognize outstanding contributions to, or achievement within, the field of hearing conservation. A plaque is awarded at the NHCA Annual Conference. Established in 1990.

• 15198 • **Outstanding Lecture Award**
To provide incentive to speakers to deliver high-quality, informative, and polished lectures. A monetary award and certificate are presented at the NHCA Annual Conference. Established in 1990.

• 15199 • **Michael Beall Threadgill Award**
To honor those who have significantly contributed to the growth and excellence of the Association. A plaque is awarded at the NHCA Annual Conference. Established in 1985 in memory of Michael Beall Threadgill. Formerly: Award for Outstanding Leadership and Service to NHCA.

• 15200 •
National Hemophilia Foundation
Alan Kinniburgh PhD, CEO
116 W 32nd St., 11th Fl.
New York, NY 10001
Phone: (212)328-3700
Toll-Free: 800-42-HANDI
Fax: (212)328-3777
E-mail: info@hemophilia.org
Home Page: http://www.hemophilia.org

• 15201 • **Awards of Distinction in Programs**
To recognize outstanding programs in health education, outreach, and communications initiatives within the bleeding disorders community. Each chapter or association receiving an award will be given a $1,000 incentive award to enhance, continue, or make available to other chapters or associations the program for which the award is granted. Application deadline is August 19. Awarded annually at the National Meeting.

• 15202 • **Dr. Kenneth Brinkhous Physician of the Year Award**
To honor distinguished clinical investigators who have made major contributions to the advancement of the care of patients with hemophilia and related bleeding disorders. The recipient should be an individual with a strong public record of accomplishment in patient care and at least one of the following: (1) development and/or application of innovative therapy for patients with bleeding disorders; or (2) important clinical observations in patients with bleeding disorders. Established in 1991.

• 15203 • **Corporate Leadership Award**
To honor outstanding corporate leadership which fosters commitment to the spirit of volunteerism on a national level. Established in 1984.

• 15204 • **Joseph D. Early Advocate of the Year Award**
To recognize health professionals for outstanding work related to advocacy and the bleeding disorders community. Individuals and teams at hemophilia treatment centers, chapters, or elsewhere who work with patients, sexual partners and families affected by HIV and hemophilia are eligible. Consideration will be given for achievements in one or more of the following areas: (1) development and coordination of innovative and creative approaches to prevention of HIV transmission and health promotion; (2) programs such as educational programs, counseling, outreach programs; or (3) documentation of program effectiveness. Established in 1991.

• 15205 • **Mary M. Gooley Humanitarian of the Year Award**
To recognize an individual who has made an outstanding, long-term national contribution in multiple areas on behalf of individuals affected by bleeding disorders. A plaque is awarded annually when merited. Established in 1969.

Awards are arranged in alphabetical order below their administering organizations

• 15206 • Government Achievement Award
For recognition of governmental action which has contributed significantly to the development of, or advocacy for, regional or statewide development or administration of hemophilia-related legislation. Established in 1988.

• 15207 • Robert Lee Henry Volunteer of the Year Award
To recognize an individual whose volunteer work for NHF has contributed significantly to its mission and goals. Established in 1972 in recognition of the founder of NHF. Formerly: Volunteer of the Year Award.

• 15208 • Dr. L. Michael Kuhn Advocate of the Year Award
To recognize individuals for governmental action which has contributed significantly to the development of, or advocacy for regional or statewide development of hemophilia-related legislation which has a national impact. A certificate is awarded when merited. Established in 1974.

• 15209 • Nurse of the Year Award
To recognize an individual who has demonstrated outstanding service to the bleeding disorders community over and above the responsibilities as a treatment center nurse. This person must have worked with patients with bleeding disorders and their families for at least two years, and be a member of the National Hemophilia Foundation's Nursing Network. Nominations are evaluated by a subcommittee of the Nursing Executive Committee and recommendations forwarded to the NHF Awards Committee for final approval. Up to three selections are made. Nurses may only receive this award once during their career. Established in 1991.

• 15210 • Outstanding Chapter Leadership Award
To honor individuals and organizations who have made outstanding contributions toward attaining chapter goals. Nominees are chosen locally by NHF chapters and are considered for additional recognition at the NHF Annual Meeting. Eligibility is limited to participating chapters, and each chapter is limited to one recommendation except under exceptional circumstances. Established in 1975.

• 15211 • Outstanding Chapter Newsletter Award
To honor the Chapter of the Foundation which has produced the most outstanding newsletter, based on graphics, content, and design. Two awards may be given: one award for a chapter newsletter produced by volunteers only; and another produced by paid staff. Established in 1989.

• 15212 • Judith Graham Pool Postgraduate Research Fellowships in Hemophilia
To provide funds for clinical or basic research on the biochemical, genetic, hematologic, orthopedic, psychiatric, or dental aspects of the hemophilias or von Willebrand's Disease. Other permissible areas include research into rehabilitation, therapeutic modalities, AIDS research with respect to the hemophilias, or social features of these disorders. United States citizens are eligible. Doctoral degree holders (M.D., Ph.D., D.V.M.) in post graduate training programs may submit applications by December 15. Fellowships of up to $35,000 are awarded through medical and graduate schools. Established in 1971 in honor of Dr. Judith Graham Pool who discovered cryoprecipitate. Additional information is available from Charla Andrews, Director of Research.

• 15213 • Dr. Murray Thelin Researcher of the Year Award
To recognize scientists for major contributions to research on bleeding disorders. A plaque is awarded annually when merited. Established in 1966.

• 15214 • Ryan White and Loras Goedken Meritorious Service Awards
To recognize an individual or group of individuals whose outreach efforts have made an outstanding contribution toward improved understanding of hemophilia and HIV/AIDS. These awards, one given to an adult and the other to a young adult under 25 years of age, recognize efforts resulting in positive dialog and action both within the hemophilia community and among other groups, such as school children and parents, especially those efforts which have improved relations among these groups or have offered unique insight into the future of hemophilia and AIDS. Established in 1991.

• 15215 •
National Hereford Hog Record Association
Ruby Schrecengost, Sec.-Treas.
22405 480th Ave.
Flandreau, SD 57028
Phone: (605)997-2116
Fax: (605)997-2116

• 15216 • Grand Champion and Reserve Grand Champion Boar and Gilt
To encourage more breeders to compete in the National Show and Sale. Four trophies, gifts, and ribbons are awarded annually. Established in 1934.

• 15217 • Hog Promoter of the Year
To recognize the member earning the most points for promoting the Hereford Hog during the year. A trophy is awarded. Established in 1985.

• 15218 • Junior Showmanship
To encourage boys and girls to develop an interest in raising purebred stock. Individuals under 18 years old who are junior members of the National Association at the time of the show are eligible. The hog must be registered in their name. A trophy is awarded to a boy or a girl annually in both the junior division. Established in 1950.

• 15219 • King Contest
To honor a young man and help promote pork. Awardee must be single, between the ages of 14 and 21, and a junior member or the son of a life member. A trophy is awarded annually. Established in 1983.

• 15220 • Most Registrations
To encourage more breeders to register more hogs. A trophy is awarded annually. Established in 1960.

• 15221 • Queen Contest
To honor a young lady and help promote pork. Awardee must be single, between the ages of 14 and 21, and a junior member or the daughter of a life member. A sash, tiara, and a trophy are presented each year at the annual banquet. Established in 1966.

• 15222 •
National High School Athletic Coaches Association
Dick Galiette, Exec.Dir.
PO Box 4342
Hamden, CT 06514-2262
Phone: (203)288-7473
Fax: (203)288-8224
E-mail: office@hscoaches.org
Home Page: http://www.hscoaches.org

• 15223 • Coaches of the Year
To recognize coaches for outstanding contributions to the high school coaching profession, dedication to the highest and best in amateur athletics, and an outstanding overall coaching record. Recognition is given in the following areas: baseball, boys' basketball, girls' basketball, boys' cross country, girls' cross country, football, golf, boys' soccer, girls' soccer, softball, swimming, boys' track, girls' track, volleyball, wrestling, and special sports (category varies each year). The Athletic Director of the Year award is also presented. A mounted certificate and a ring are awarded annually. Established in 1968. Formerly: Wilson National High School Coaches - AD of the Year.

• 15224 •
National High School Band Directors Hall of Fame
Dr. Oliver C. Boone PhD, Exec.Dir.
Crawford County High School
PO Box 98
Roberta, GA 31078
Phone: (386)252-0381
Fax: (386)252-0381
E-mail: oboone9007@mchsi.com
Home Page: http://www.mwcleveland.com/hsbanddirectorshalloffame

Formerly: National High School Band and Choral Directors Hall of Fame.

• 15225 • Hall of Fame and Band of the Year Award
To recognize and honor outstanding high school bands in the United States. Individuals with acceptable educational and professional creden-

tials are requested to direct a performance of an assigned musical composition. Bands that receive exposure on national television performing in a major event and are judged by the National High School Band Institute's scout are eligible to participate in the contests. A plaque/trophy is awarded annually. Established in 1985.

• 15226 • National High School Band Director of the Year

To recognize and honor outstanding high school band directors. Candidates receive invitations from the National High School Band Hall of Fame nominating committee. A trophy/plaque and membership in the National High School Band Directors Hall of Fame are awarded annually. Established in 1985. In addition, a Jazz Band Director of the Year is selected.

• 15227 •
National High School Band Directors Hall of Fame
College Division
Dr. Oliver C. Boone, Dir.
℅ Crawford County High School
400 E Agency St.
PO Box 98
Roberta, GA 31078
E-mail: oboone@crawford.k12.ga.us
Home Page: http://www.banddirectorshalloffame.homestead.com

Formerly: National Band and Choral Directors Hall of Fame.

• 15228 • National College Band and Choral Directors Hall of Fame Band of the Year

To recognize and honor outstanding college bands in the United States. Bands that receive exposure on national television performing in a major event and are judged by the National College Band and Choral Directors Hall of Fame Scouts are eligible by invitation to participate in band competitions. A plaque/trophy is awarded annually. Established in 1985.

• 15229 • National College Band Director of the Year

To recognize and honor outstanding college band directors. A plaque/trophy and membership in the National College Band and Choral Directors Hall of Fame are awarded annually.

• 15230 • National College Choral Director of the Year

To recognize and honor outstanding college choral directors. A plaque/trophy and membership in the National College Band and Choral Directors Hall of Fame are awarded annually. Established in 1985.

• 15231 • National College Choral Directors Hall of Fame Choir of the Year

To recognize and honor outstanding college choral groups. By invitation, candidates perform special choral assignments. A plaque/trophy is awarded annually. Established in 1985.

• 15232 •
National High School Rodeo Association
Kent Sturman, Exec.Dir.
12001 Tejon St., Ste. 128
Denver, CO 80234
Phone: (303)452-0820
Toll-Free: 800-46-NHSRA
Fax: (303)452-0912
E-mail: info@nhsra.org
Home Page: http://www.nhsra.org

• 15233 • National High School Finals Rodeo

For recognition of the finalists in twelve different rodeo events. High school students who are members of the association are eligible. National World's Champions are named in the following events: Saddle Bronc Riding, Bareback Riding, Bull Riding, Team Roping, Calf Roping, Steer Wrestling, Boys' Cattle Cutting, Girls' Cattle Cutting, Goat Tying, Pole Bending, Barrel Racing, and Breakaway Roping. The team accumulating the most points overall claims the Carhartt National Team Award. An All-Around Cowboy and Cowgirl, and All-Around Rookie Cowboy and Cowgirl are recognized for accumulating the most points in the finals. A Rodeo Queen Contest is also held.

• 15234 •
National Hockey League Players' Association
Robert W. Goodenow, Exec.Dir.
777 Bay St., Ste. 2400
Toronto, ON, Canada M5G 2C8
Phone: (416)313-2300
Fax: (416)313-2301
Home Page: http://www.nhlpa.com

• 15235 • Lester B. Pearson Award

Bestowed to the outstanding NHL player of the season. Awarded annually.

• 15236 •
National Home Furnishings Association
Steve DeHaan, Exec.VP
3910 Tinsley Dr., Ste. 101
PO Box 2396
High Point, NC 27265-3610
Phone: (336)886-6100
Toll-Free: 800-888-9590
Fax: (336)801-6102
E-mail: info@nhfa.org
Home Page: http://www.nhfa.org

• 15237 • Willis Award of Merit

To encourage and promote cooperation, understanding, the exchange of ideas, and to lend dignity and purpose to the Association. Awarded annually. Established in 1954 by the Willis Family of Virginia Beach, Virginia, as a memorial to John Willis, Jr., and his son, Benjamin J. Willis, Sr.

• 15238 •
National Horseshoe Pitchers Association of America
Dick Hansen, Contact
3058 S. 76th St.
Franksville, WI 53126
Phone: (262)835-9108
Fax: (707)538-3128
E-mail: nhpa.sec.trea@worldnet.att.net
Home Page: http://www.horseshoepitching.com

• 15239 • Achievement Awards

For recognition of outstanding local or statewide contributions to the sport of horseshoe pitching during the preceding year. Awarded annually during the World Tournament. Multiple recipients may be honored each year. Established in 1957.

• 15240 • Horseshoe Hall of Fame

To honor outstanding individuals in the game of horseshoe pitching, dating back to 1909. Selections are made in three categories: (1) Players - those who, with distinguished outstanding performance in World Tournament Championship play, have brought prestige to the art of horseshoe pitching; (2) Promoters/Organizers - those who have made significant and beneficial contributions to the Association in an administrative capacity; and (3) Players/Organizers - a combination of a good player and a worthy conscientious administrator, organizer, or officer in the NHPA. Ten years minimum service as an NHPA member is required. One to three individuals may be elected annually. Established in 1965.

• 15241 • Regional Director of the Year

To honor regional directors who display the attitude and initiative of fulfilling their duties of upholding the image and extending the recognition of the NHPA. Winners receive the Gene and Mary Van Sant Memorial Award. Awarded annually. Established in 1990.

• 15242 • Special Recognition and Presidential Awards

To recognize contributions to the game and NHPA for a specific activity or extraordinary longevity. Awarded when merited. Established in 1974.

• 15243 • Stokes Memorial Award

This, the second most valuable award the game offers outside the World Title, is given to recognize individuals who have done the most during the preceding three to five years to promote, foster, and build the sport of horseshoe pitching. A plaque is awarded annually. Established in 1958 in memory of Arch Stokes, a beloved and important figure in the history of horseshoe pitching.

• 15244 • World Horseshoe Tournament

For recognition of outstanding performances in horseshoe pitching tournaments in the following categories: men, women, elders (over 70 years of age), senior men (over 60 years of age), senior women (over 60 years of age), junior boys (under 17), and junior girls (under 17). Held annually.

• 15245 •
National Housing Conference
Conrad Egan, Pres./CEO
1801 K St. NW, Ste. M-100
Washington, DC 20006-1301
Phone: (202)466-2121
Fax: (202)466-2122
E-mail: nhc@nhc.org
Home Page: http://www.nhc.org

• 15246 • **Carl A.S. Coan, Sr. Award**
For recognition of outstanding commitment and leadership in the effort to provide decent, safe, and affordable housing throughout the nation. Awarded annually. Established in 1984 in memory of Carl A.S. Coan, Sr. who played a major role in the development of housing and community development legislation, especially as staff director of the Senate Subcommittee on Housing and Urban Affairs.

• 15247 • **Housing Person of the Year Award**
To recognize individuals or organizations that have made significant contributions to the goal of increased affordable housing and strong, healthy communities throughout the nation. Established in 1973 and awarded annually. Formerly: (1995) Honor Roll of Housing.

• 15248 • **Nathaniel S. Keith Award**
For recognition of outstanding service on behalf of housing and community development. Established in 1975 in memory of Nathaniel S. Keith, who was involved in housing and urban renewal during his years of service in senior positions in the federal government and private industry.

• 15249 •
National Humanities Center
Geoffrey Harpham, Pres./Dir.
PO Box 12256
PO Box 12256
Research Triangle Park, NC 27709-2256
Phone: (919)549-0661
Fax: (919)990-8535
E-mail: lmorgan@ga.unc.edu
Home Page: http://www.nhc.rtp.nc.us

• 15250 • **Fellowship**
To support advanced post-doctoral study in the humanities. By encouraging excellence in scholarship, the Center seeks to insure the continuing strength of the liberal arts in higher education and to affirm the importance of the humanities in American life. Open to humanistic scholars of all nations who hold doctoral degrees or have equivalent professional accomplishments. Applications must be submitted by October 15. A stipend and travel expenses are awarded annually. Established in 1978.

• 15251 •
National Hypertension Association
William M. Manger MD, Chm.
324 E 30th St.
New York, NY 10016
Phone: (212)889-3557
Phone: (212)889-3558
Fax: (212)447-7032
E-mail: nathypertension@aol.com
Home Page: http://
www.nathypertension.org

• 15252 • **National Hypertension Association Recognition Award**
To recognize individuals who have made an outstanding contribution to the field of hypertension by scientific investigation, public service, prevention, or support of the endeavors of the National Hypertension Association. A crystal Octron (an eight-sided crystal suggesting the Octagonal Page Mosaic Theory of hypertension), designed by Lloyd Atkins for Steuben, is awarded periodically. Established in 1985 to honor Irvine H. Page, M.D., the most distinguished scientist in hypertensive research.

• 15253 •
National Independent Automobile Dealers Association
Michael R. Linn, Exec.VP/CEO
2521 Brown Blvd.
Arlington, TX 76006
Phone: (817)640-3838
Toll-Free: 800-682-3837
Fax: (817)649-5866
E-mail: mike@niada.com
Home Page: http://www.niada.com

• 15254 • **National Quality Dealer Award**
This, the most prestigious award of the Association, is given to recognize members who have distinguished themselves not only in their dealership, but also in community affairs with an emphasis on contributions made to the social, economic, religious, and civic lives of their community, state, and nation. Members must be nominated by an affiliated state organization. A plaque and an appropriate medallion are awarded annually at the convention. Established in 1976.

• 15255 •
National Indian Health Board
J.T. Petherick, Exec.Dir.
101 Constitution Ave. NW, Ste. 8-B02
Washington, DC 20001
Phone: (202)742-4262
Fax: (202)742-4285
E-mail: jpetherick@nihb.org
Home Page: http://www.nihb.org

• 15256 • **Consumer Conference Awards**
To recognize achievements in helping improve the health status of American Indian/Alaskan Native people. Awards include the Jake White Crow Award, National Impact Award, Area/Regional Impact Award, and the Local Impact Award. Presented annually. Established in 1972.

• 15257 •
National Industries for the Blind
Jim Gibbons, Pres./CEO
1310 Braddock Pl.
Alexandria, VA 22314-1691
Phone: (703)310-0500
Fax: (703)998-8268
E-mail: info@nib.org
Home Page: http://www.nib.org

• 15258 • **Robert B. Irwin Award**
To recognize an individual for significant contributions to an area related to sheltered workshop employment for blind persons. A plaque is awarded annually at the National Sales Meeting of The General Council of Workshops for the Blind. Established in 1953 in memory of Dr. Robert B. Irwin, who pioneered and led the way for creating employment opportunities for the blind.

• 15259 • **Peter J. Salmon Award - Blind Worker of the Year**
To recognize an outstanding blind worker employed in an NIB Workshop below the administrative level. Each local Workshop selects a Blind Worker of the Year and the NIB selects the national winner for the Peter J. Salmon Award. A plaque is awarded at the Annual Meeting of the General Council of Workshops for the Blind. Established in 1968 in memory of Dr. Peter J. Salmon, who was instrumental in the establishment of NIB.

• 15260 •
National Institute of American Doll Artists
Kathryn Walmsley, Pres.
8320 Maplewood St.
Lenexa, KS 66215
Phone: (913)894-2382
Fax: (913)888-5167
E-mail: rewbird@aol.com
Home Page: http://www.niada.org

• 15261 • **Helen Bullard Scholarship**
Awarded to outstanding doll artists. Helps defray costs of attending the annual conference. Established in 1998.

• 15262 • **Patron Honor Award**
To recognize unusual services by a patron of the organization. An inscribed scroll is awarded annually. Established in 1963.

• 15263 • **Pat Stall Memorial Award**
To recognize unusual services by an Honor Patron. First awarded in 1993. Established in 1989.

• 15264 •
National Institute of Governmental Purchasing
Belinda Reutter, Dir. Member Services
151 Spring St.
Herndon, VA 20170-6214
Phone: (703)736-8900
Toll-Free: 800-FOR-NIGP
Fax: (703)736-9644
E-mail: membership@nigp.org
Home Page: http://www.nigp.org

• 15265 • **Buyer of the Year Award**
To recognize outstanding public purchasers for contributions to the public procurement profession, professional development and certification, the entity he/she serves, the NIGP chapter, and NIGP as a whole. The individuals considered for this award are limited to the rank and file buyers, and does not include supervisory and management professionals in the organization. Awarded annually. Formerly: .

• 15266 • **Chapter of the Year Award**
To recognize outstanding chapters based on service to the profession, service to NIGP, membership recruitment, member services, and overall operations. Awards are presented in three categories: Large Chapters (151 or more members), Mid-sized Chapters (61-160 members), and Small Chapters (less than 60 members). Awarded annually. Established in 1983.

• 15267 • **Distinguished Service Awards**
To recognize public purchasing executives and other individuals who have provided extraordinary service to their government entity, the community, NIGP, or the purchasing profession. The awards, in the form of framed certificates, are presented annually at the NIGP Forum and Products Exposition. Established in 1950.

• 15268 • **Albert H. Hall Memorial Award**
This, the highest form of recognition offered by NIGP, is given to recognize a former or present member who has made outstanding contributions to NIGP over an extended period of time. Candidates should be involved in promoting professional purchasing, be active participants and promoters in education and professional development programs, and be active leaders in public purchasing organizations. An engraved crystal urn on a lighted base is presented annually at the NIGP Forum and Products Exposition. Established in 1977 in memory of Albert H. Hall, the founder and Executive Vice President of NIGP from 1944 to 1975. Formerly: (1977) NIGP Fellow Award.

• 15269 • **Manager of the Year Award**
To recognize an outstanding purchasing manager for contributions to the public procurement profession, professional development and certification, the entity he/she serves, the NIGP chapter, and NIGP as a whole. The individuals considered for this award are limited to the supervisory and management professionals in the organization. Awarded annually. Formerly: (1997) Purchasing Manager of the Year Award.

• 15270 •
National Institute of Nursing Research
NIH Bldg. 31, Rm. 5B-10
31 Center Dr.
Bethesda, MD 20892-2178
Phone: (301)496-0207
Fax: (301)480-8845
E-mail: info@ninr.nih.gov
Home Page: http://www.nih.gov/ninr

• 15271 • **Career Development Awards**
Provides support for doctorally prepared nurses, including targeted awards for minority nurses.

• 15272 • **National Research Service Awards**
Provides predoctoral and postdoctoral research training support for nurses.

• 15273 • **Research Awards**
Provides support for the conducting of Research in areas compatible with the NINR mission.

• 15274 •
National Intercollegiate Soccer Officials Association
Dr. Raymond Bernabei, Exec.Dir.
541 Woodview Dr.
Longwood, FL 32779-2614
Phone: (407)862-3305
Fax: (407)862-8545
E-mail: information@nisoa.com
Home Page: http://www.nisoa.com

• 15275 • **Dr. Raymond Bernabei Honor Award**
To recognize outstanding achievement in college soccer officiating and contributions made to the association and its members. Eligible candidates must have 10 years of meritorious service to soccer, be known by their products and writings, and have assisted the NISOA. One trophy is awarded at the Annual Convention in July. Established in 1966.

• 15276 • **Hall of Fame Award**
To recognize an individual that has dedicated himself/herself to the development of the game by personal action and words. A nominee must be of unquestionable moral character, able to demonstrate outstanding leadership ability and be an outstanding citizen. Nominee should be a member of NISOA for at least ten years; be a member of good standing for five or more consecutive years; serve NISOA in some official capacity for at least five years. Nominees should have officiated for at least ten years with a high rating on a college level and/or officiated several regional or national play-off games. No more than two individuals will be inducted annually. Established in 1973.

• 15277 • **Interscholastic Member Recognition Award**
To recognize one interscholastic soccer referee who is a member of NISOA. Established in 1992.

• 15278 • **National Merit Award**
Given to an individual currently active in college coaching and an individual currently active in high school coaching, whose reputations are recognized by officials as praiseworthy and reflective of the highest standards of professional and ethical behavior. Candidates should be currently active at any level of the game; a member of the NSCAA for a minimum of five years; have a minimum of five years coaching experience; and have earned a reputation for fairness, honesty and integrity in his/her relationship with athletes, fellow coaches and soccer officials. Award is presented annually at the NSCAA Awards Banquet. Established in 1986. in 1986.

• 15279 • **Recognition Award**
To recognize an individual who has contributed to the welfare of soccer and who would not be considered likely to receive the Annual NISOA Honor Award. No more than three awards are given annually. Submit nominee to Awards Chairman by September 30. Established in 1965.

• 15280 • **Robert Sumpter Excellence in Teaching Award**
Candidates should be a member of NISOA for ten years or more; have served as NISOA Clinician for eight years or more; and demonstrate the traits personifying Robert Sumpter of honesty, integrity, scholastic, trustworthiness, and promotes service first. Awardee is provided with two nights lodging at the Annual NISOA Convention where the award will be presented. Awarded annually. Established in 1995.

• 15281 •
National Interscholastic Swimming Coaches Association of America
Arvel McElroy, Contact
Loathe South High School
Olathe, KS 60602
Phone: (913)780-7160
Phone: (785)841-6624
Fax: (913)780-7170
E-mail: president@nisca.net
Home Page: http://www.nisca.net

• 15282 • **Hall of Fame Award**
This, the highest award of NISCA, is given for leadership in interscholastic aquatics. To be considered for this award, a NISCA member must have: served aquatics in swimming, diving, and/or water polo for at least 20 years; been a NISCA member in good standing for at least 10 years; had above average success as a competitive aquatic coach; and shown leadership at the local or national level in interscholastic aquatics. Awarded annually. The recipient's name is engraved on the permanent NISCA trophy displayed at the International Swimming Hall of Fame in Fort Lauderdale, Florida, and an individual award is presented. Established in 1972.

• 15283 • **National Collegiate and Scholastic Swimming Trophy**
To recognize coaches who have made significant contributions to swimming as a competitive

sport, including protecting oneself and other in emergencies and as a healthful recreational activity in the province of undergraduate and scholastic education in the United States. A trophy is awarded annually. Established in 1969. Cosponsored by the College Swimming Coaches Association.

• 15284 • Outstanding Service Awards
To recognize members of NISCA who have achieved greatness through outstanding efforts and contributions to aquatic sport in the United States. To be considered for this award, a NISCA member must have: served aquatics in swimming, diving, and/or water polo for at least 15 years; been a NISCA member in good standing for at least 10 years; had above average success as a competitive aquatic coach; and shown leadership at the local or national level in interscholastic aquatics. Awarded annually. Established in 1971.

• 15285 •
National Intramural-Recreational Sports Association
Dr. Kent J. Blumenthal CRSS, Exec.Dir.
4185 SW Research Way
Corvallis, OR 97333-1067
Phone: (541)766-8211
Fax: (541)766-8284
E-mail: nirsa@nirsa.org
Home Page: http://www.nirsa.org

• 15286 • 25 Year Award
To recognize any association member of 15 years who has coached for 25 years. Members must apply to the association professional Awards Chairman.

• 15287 • Appreciation Award
To recognize an individual, corporation, or company that donates time and money to sponsor an association program such as the national convention, national meeting, and awards program.

• 15288 • Completion of Service Award
To recognize a member who has retired from both teaching and coaching. Members must apply to the association professional Awards Chairman.

• 15289 • Honorary Membership Award
For outstanding and/or long term contribution in support of the association. It is the highest award available to a non-association member.

• 15290 • Life Membership Award
To honor regular members for signal and distinguished service to the association and aquatic sports over an extensive period of time. It is the highest award available to an association member.

• 15291 • Power Point Rankings Award
Consists of a special plaque awarded to the winner of each class at the association's national convention.

• 15292 • Special Service Award
To honor a regular member for service of a special nature rendered to the association for a period of at least four years.

• 15293 •
National Italian American Bar Association
Cirino M. Bruno, Pres.
PMB 932
2020 Pennsylvania Ave. NW
Washington, DC 20006-1846
Phone: (212)269-1400
Fax: (212)809-5449
E-mail: niaba@niaba.org
Home Page: http://www.niaba.org

• 15294 • Distinguished Public Service
Recognition is given.

• 15295 • Pro Bono Award
Recognition is given.

• 15296 •
National Jewish Committee on Scouting
Rabbi Peter Hyman, Chm.
PO Box 152079
Irving, TX 75015-2079
Phone: (610)356-5165
Fax: (610)356-6713
E-mail: peh51@aol.com
Home Page: http://www.jewishscouting.org

• 15297 • Aleph Award
To recognize Jewish study on the part of Cub Scouts of the Jewish faith. An open Torah scroll with an eternal light superimposed is awarded. Established in 1971.

• 15298 • Etz Chaim (Tree of Life) Award
To recognize older Scouts in high school (age 14-17) and registered Explorers (age 14-20) and to encourage the young adult to discover possible adult Jewish roles in the context of family, community, and Jewish people.

• 15299 • Maccabee Award
To recognize Jewish study on the part of Tiger Cubs of the Jewish Faith. The requirements are subdivided into six categories: Jewish names, Jewish holidays, Jewish terms, Jewish symbols and objects, Jewish community helpers, and Jewish heroes.

• 15300 • Shofar Award (Ram's Horn)
To recognize outstanding service by adults in the promotion of scouting among Jewish youth.

• 15301 • Ner Tamid Award
To recognize Jewish study on the part of Boy Scouts and Explorers of the Jewish faith. The Ner Tamid emblem is awarded.

• 15302 •
National Jewish Girl Scout Committee
Adele Wasko, Field Chm.
33 Central Dr.
Bronxville, NY 10708-4603
Phone: (914)738-3986
Phone: (718)252-6072
Fax: (914)738-6752
E-mail: njgsc@aol.com
Home Page: http://www.njgsc.org

• 15303 • Ora Award
To recognize outstanding efforts by adults in extending Girl Scouting in the Jewish community, as well as contributions toward encouraging international relationships with the Israel Boy and Girl Scouts Federation. The award is given nationally and internationally to any adult who fulfills the purpose of the award. Nominations may be submitted to the Committee. A silver pin on a blue drape and a certificate are awarded. Established in 1977.

• 15304 •
National Junior College Athletic Association
Wayne Baker, Exec.Dir.
1755 Telstar Dr., Ste. 103
Colorado Springs, CO 80920
Phone: (719)590-9788
Fax: (719)590-7324
E-mail: wbaker@njcaa.org
Home Page: http://www.njcaa.org

• 15305 • Academic Team-of-the-Year
Honors an athletic team for each sport based on grade point averages. Deadline for football, soccer, cross country, and volleyball is February 15; June 15 for all others. Must have minimum 3.0 GPA to be nominated. Awarded annually.

• 15306 • Achievement Award
To recognize individuals who have displayed outstanding athletic ability in national, Olympic, or international competition, and who possess excellent ethical character. The nominees must be out of junior college for at least five years. Nominations must be made by January 15. Three awards may be presented annually.

• 15307 • All-American Awards
To recognize the most outstanding junior college athletes in their sport regardless of geographic location. All-American teams include: baseball (men); basketball (men); basketball (women); bowling (women); bowling (men); cross country (women); cross country (men); field hockey (women); football (men); golf (men); ice hockey (men); lacrosse (men); marathon (women); marathon (men); soccer (women); soccer (men); softball fast pitch (women); softball slow pitch (women); swimming and diving (women); swimming and diving (men); tennis

(women); tennis (men); indoor track and field (men); indoor track and field (women); outdoor track and field (women); outdoor track and field (men); volleyball (women); and wrestling (men). Nominees for the Distinguished Academic All-American Award must have an accumulative grade point average of 3.8 and nominees for the Academic All-American By Sport Award must have an accumulative grade point average of 3.6 or better on a 4.0 scale for 60 quarter hours or 45 semester hours. Awarded annually. Nomination deadline is June 15.

• 15308 • Appreciation Award
Given to individuals and institutions at the discretion of the Executive Director of the NJCAA.

• 15309 • Coaches Association Awards
Bestows awards in baseball, women's and men's basketball, bowling, cross country, lacrosse, golf, soccer, swimming, men's tennis, indoor and outdoor track and field, volleyball, and wrestling.

• 15310 • Betty Jo Graber Female Student-Athlete-of-the-Year
To honor a female student-athlete-of-the-year. The student is nominated by her athletic director, with approval from the college president. Selection is based on athletic ability and achievement. The student-athlete must have a minimum 2.0 GPA, have completed her second year of NJCAA competition, and have achieved NJCAA All-American status at least one year in her sport. Nominations are due June 30. The award winner will be honored in the September issue of the *JUCO Review.*

• 15311 • Loyalty Award
To recognize an active athletic director at a member college who has worked to uphold the ideals of the NJCAA and demonstrate leadership in an athletic program exemplifying excellence both on the field and in the classroom. Nomination deadline is January 15. Awarded annually.

• 15312 • Merit Award
To recognize former junior college athletes who have distinguished themselves and are recognized nationally for their achievements in a variety of appropriate fields. Nominations must be made by January 15. Three awards may be presented annually.

• 15313 • Lea Plarski Award
To recognize a male and female student-athlete. The student-athlete will be nominated for this award by his/her athletic director, with approval from the college president. The criteria for selection are based on sportsmanship, leadership, community service, academic excellence, athletic ability and achievement, and other activities within the college. Nomination deadline is April 15. The two award winners will be honored in the September issue of the *JUCO Review.*

• 15314 • David Rowlands Male Student-Athlete-Of-The-Year
To honor a male student-athlete-of-the-year. The student is nominated by his athletic director, with approval from the college president. Selection is based on athletic ability and achievement. The student-athlete must have a minimum 2.0 GPA, have completed his second year of NJCAA competition, and have achieved NJCAA All-American status at least one year in his sport. Nominations are due June 30.

• 15315 • Service Award
For recognition of individuals (most often not athletes, but instead, Deans, Presidents, etc.) who have made significant contributions to junior college athletics on a national level for an extended period of time. Nominations must be made by January 15. Each year, one of these awards is reserved for a member of the news media; if there is not a qualified candidate from the media, another qualified candidate may be considered. A total of four may be awarded annually.

• 15316 • Special NJCAA Awards
Special awards are presented in many sport categories. In baseball, each member of the NJCAA All-American Baseball Team receives a Hillerich and Bradsby Company Trophy Bat. This award is also presented to the 10 coaches of the district championship teams. Other baseball awards include the Rawlings Big Stick Award, which is given for times at bat, the Homa S. Thomas Sportsmanship Award, the Robert Purkey, Jr. Memorial Outstanding Pitcher Award, the Best Defensive Player Award, and the Preston Walker Most Valuable Player Award. Women's basketball awards include the Kodak All-American Team, Champion Outstanding Player of the Year, and Converse Coach of the Year Awards. Awards for men's basketball are the Charles Sesher Sportsmanship Award, the V. C. "Bub" Obee Small Player Award, the William French Most Valuable Player Award, and the Coach of the Tournament Award. For cross country, the Cross Country Journal Award is awarded to the college with the best combined team placing of men's and women's teams in National Championships. In swimming, the National Aquatic Service, Inc. - Annual Service Recognition Award and NJCAA Swimming and Diving Coaches Association awards for a variety of achievements are given.

• 15317 • Reed K. Swenson Leadership Award
To recognize outstanding Americans who have contributed, in general, to the intercollegiate athletic scene. Nominations must be made by January 15 to the Chairman of the Committee on Service and Recognition. Awarded annually. Formerly: Moral Leadership Award.

• 15318 •
National Kidney Foundation
John Davis, Chief Exec. Officer
30 E 33rd St.
New York, NY 10016
Phone: (212)889-2210
Toll-Free: 800-622-9010
Fax: (212)689-9261
E-mail: info@kidney.org
Home Page: http://www.kidney.org

• 15319 • Chairman's Award
For recognition of a person or group that has demonstrated outstanding concern and dedication to the National Kidney Foundation. The chairman selects recipients of this award. Presented annually at the Foundation's Annual Meeting. Established in 1973.

• 15320 • Distinguished Service Award
For recognition of an individual who has rendered a noteworthy contribution on behalf of the programs of the Kidney Foundation. The deadline is August 29. Presented annually at the Foundation's Annual Meeting. Established in 1970.

• 15321 • Health Advancement Award
For recognition of an individual or organization that has significantly aided the National Kidney Foundation in promoting its programs of public and professional education. The deadline for nominations is August 29. Presented annually at the Foundation's Annual Meeting. Established in 1971.

• 15322 • David M. Hume Memorial Award
For recognition of an individual who has significantly contributed to furthering the understanding of kidney diseases, kidney transplants, or the physiology of the kidney. This award is the highest honor the Foundation bestows on a medical professional. The deadline for nominations is August 29. Presented annually at the Foundation's Annual Meeting. Established in 1974 in memory of Dr. David M. Hume, a member of the team that performed the first successful kidney transplant with twins.

• 15323 • President's Award
For recognition of an individual or group that has demonstrated outstanding concern for and dedication to the National Kidney Foundation. The President selects the recipient of this award. Presented annually at the Foundation's Annual Meeting. Established in 1969.

• 15324 • Public Service Award
For recognition of an individual, an individual program, a series of programs, or an article or series of articles that has successfully heightened the public awareness of kidney disease, its related problems, or any programs in which the Kidney Foundation is actively involved. This award may be presented to both broadcast and print media. The deadline for nominations is August 29. Presented annually at the Foundation's Annual Meeting. Established in 1969.

• 15325 • Donald W. Seldin Award
To recognize excellence in clinical research in nephrology. Presented at the Annual Spring Clinical Meeting in April. Awarded annually.

• 15326 • Trustees' Award
For recognition of an individual or group that has performed an important service to the Kidney Foundation. This award is conferred at the recommendation of the Trustees. Presented annually at the Foundation's Annual Meeting. Established in 1969.

• 15327 • Volunteer Service Award
For recognition of an individual who has continually promoted the programs of the Kidney Foundation by involving outside organizations in service projects. The deadline for nominations is August 29. Presented annually at the Foundation's Annual Meeting. Established in 1969.

• 15328 • Martin Wagner Memorial Award
For recognition of an individual who has, over several years, rendered distinguished service to the National Kidney Foundation. This award is the highest honor that can be given to a volunteer. The deadline for nominations is August 29. Presented annually at the Foundation's Annual Meeting. Established in 1974 in memory of Martin Wagner, a dedicated volunteer, who was one of the Founders of the National Kidney Foundation.

• 15329 •
National Kidney Foundation of Arkansas
Holly Whitcombe, Exec.Dir.
PO Box 453
Little Rock, AR 72203-0453
Phone: (501)664-4343
Phone: (501)664-8765
Toll-Free: 877-254-3639
Fax: (501)664-7145
E-mail: nkf@aristotle.net
Home Page: http://kidneyar.org

• 15330 • J.D. Chastain Renal Research Award
For kidney disease research in Arkansas. Grant awarded annually.

• 15331 •
National Kidney Foundation of Ohio
Orelle Jackson, Exec.Dir.
1373 Grandview Ave., Ste. 200
Columbus, OH 43212-2804
Phone: (614)481-4030
Phone: (614)481-4080
Toll-Free: 800-242-2133
Fax: (614)481-4038
E-mail: info@nkfofohio.org
Home Page: http://www.nkfofohio.org

• 15332 • Mary Jo Cosio, RN Award
For renal disease research. Grant awarded annually.

• 15333 •
National League of American Pen Women
Anna Di Bella, Contact
1300 17th St. NW
Washington, DC 20036-1973
Phone: (202)785-1997
Fax: (202)452-6868
E-mail: info@americanpenwomen.org
Home Page: http://www.americanpenwomen.org

• 15334 • Mature Women Scholarship Grant
To encourage the development of women in the fields of art, letters, and music. Women over the age of 35 who are United States citizens, neither members nor past members of the league nor the immediate family of members are eligible. Three monetary awards of $1,000 each are presented biennially in even-numbered years in art, letters, and music to further their creative purposes. Send a SASE for requirements. Deadline for entries is October 1 of odd numbered years. Awarded in April of even-numbered years. Established in 1974.

• 15335 •
National Legal Aid and Defender Association
Clinton Lyons, Exec.Dir.
1140 Connecticut Ave. NW, Ste. 900
Washington, DC 20036
Phone: (202)452-0620
Fax: (202)872-1031
E-mail: info@nlada.org
Home Page: http://www.nlada.org

• 15336 • Emery A. Brownell Media Award
To give national recognition to newspapers, films, and radio and television stations that have informed the public of the crucial role played by civil or defender organizations in ensuring equal justice under law. Legal publications are not eligible. The deadline for nominations is August 1. A plaque is awarded biennially in even-numbered years. Established in 1963 in memory of Emery Brownell, Executive Director of the association from 1940-1961. Formerly: Emery A. Brownell Press Award.

• 15337 • Clara Shortridge Foltz Award
To recognize a public defender program or defense delivery system for outstanding achievements in the provision of indigent defense services. The deadline for nominations is August 1. A plaque is awarded biennially in odd-numbered years. Established in 1985 to honor Clara Shortridge Foltz, the founder of the nation's public defender system. Co-sponsored by the American Bar Association's Standing Committee on Legal Aid and Indigent Defendants.

• 15338 • Mary Ellen Hamilton Award
To commend a non-attorney who, on a compensated or volunteer basis, has provided extraordinary service or support to the provision of legal services to the poor. The deadline for nominations is August 1. A plaque is awarded biennially in odd-numbered years. Established in 1981. In 1985, the award was named in honor of one of the founders of the National Clients Council and the Alliance for Legal Rights. Formerly: (1984) Special Award.

• 15339 • Reginald Heber Smith Award
To recognize the dedicated services and outstanding achievements of civil or indigent defense attorneys while employed by the organization supporting such services. The award may be given up to two years following the attorney's termination of employment with the organization. The deadline for nominations is August 1. A plaque is awarded annually. Established in 1957 in honor of Reginald Heber Smith, a former counsel for the Boston Legal Aid Society and the author of *Justice and the Poor*, published by the Carnegie Foundation in 1919.

• 15340 • Arthur von Briesen Award
To honor an attorney not employed by a legal services or defender program who has made substantial volunteer contributions to the delivery of legal services and/or indigent defense representation. The deadline for nominations is August 1. A plaque is awarded biennially in even-numbered years. Established in 1961 in honor of the first president of NLADA.

• 15341 •
National Legislative Council for the Handicapped
PO Box 262
Taylor, MI 48180

• 15342 • Public Service Award
For recognition of public service to the handicapped or senior citizens in a field of activity such as life saving, health, living conditions, barrier free society, and rehabilitation programs. An individual may be recognized for his or her activities in volunteer work for the handicapped or senior citizens, or a firm or company may be nominated for consideration by the awards committee. Plaques and certificates are awarded annually. Established in 1977 by Gerald T Harris, National Chairperson.

• 15343 •
National Lesbian and Gay Journalists Association
Pamela Strother, Exec.Dir.
1420 K St. NW, Ste. 910
Washington, DC 20005
Phone: (202)588-9888
Fax: (202)588-1818
E-mail: info@nlgja.org
Home Page: http://www.nlgja.org

• 15344 • Crossroads Market/NLGJA Print Awards
For recognition of excellence in print journalism on issues concerning the gay and lesbian community. Eligible work must have appeared during the year prior to presentation of the award in newspapers or magazines published in the United States. An award of $2,500 is given an-

Awards are arranged in alphabetical order below their administering organizations

nually at the NLGJA conference held in September. The award was established in 1994.

• 15345 •
National Lubricating Grease Institute
Chuck Hitchcock, Gen.Mgr.
4635 Wyandotte St.
Kansas City, MO 64112
Phone: (816)931-9480
Fax: (816)753-5026
E-mail: nlgi@nlgi.org
Home Page: http://www.nlgi.com

• 15346 • **Authors' Award**
To recognize the author(s) of a paper of special significance to any aspect of the grease industry that is presented at the annual meeting of the Institute. An engraved silver bowl is awarded annually. Established in 1963.

• 15347 • **Award for Achievement**
This, the institute's highest award, recognizes outstanding contributions to the growth and development of the Institute. An engraved clock is awarded during the annual meeting. Established in 1952.

• 15348 • **Chevron U.S.A. Marketing Award**
To recognize the author of the best marketing paper presented at the annual meeting that can serve as a reference for the proper selection and application of greases. A monetary award of $100 and a plaque are awarded annually. Established in 1980.

• 15349 • **Clarence E. Earle Memorial Award**
To recognize the author(s) of an outstanding paper on any phase of the manufacturing of grease presented at the annual meeting of the Institute. A monetary award of $200 and a plaque are awarded annually when merited. Established in 1965 by the Cyprus Foote Mineral Company and the Institute.

• 15350 • **Fellows Award**
For recognition of outstanding work in the technical development of greases, grease tests, grease usage, and/or promotion of grease sales within the auspices of the Institute. A plaque is awarded at the annual meeting of the Institute. Established in 1975.

• 15351 • **Honorary Membership**
To recognize an individual who has served the Institute in some outstanding capacity over a period of years and is not a representative of a member company. A silver tray is presented at the annual meeting of the Institute. Established in 1955.

• 15352 • **Meritorious Service Trophy**
For recognition of three or more years of service on the Board of Directors, outstanding participation on Technical Committee projects, or contributions to the welfare of the Industry or the Institute. Active members and individuals not actively involved in the Institute are eligible. A plaque is awarded at the annual meeting of the Institute. Established in 1980.

• 15353 • **Pioneer Trophy**
Recognizes those who, through their farsightedness, enterprise, and innovation, pioneered significant and lasting improvements in the Institute. Awarded only on singular occasions; bronze eagle on marble given at annual meeting. Established in 1991.

• 15354 •
National Magazine Awards Foundation
425 Adelaide St. W, Ste. 700
Toronto, ON, Canada M5V 3C1
Phone: (416)828-9011
Fax: (416)504-0437
E-mail: info@nmaf.net
Home Page: http://www.nmaf.net

• 15355 • **National Magazine Awards**
For recognition of outstanding contributions to magazines. Awards are presented annually in 33 subcategories among written, integrated, and visual categories. Additionally, the Foundation Award for Outstanding Achievement, the Alexander Ross Award for Best New Magazine Writer, Best Student Writer Award, and the President's Medal are presented. Open to Canadian magazines published at least twice a year in English, French, or a combination of both. The annual competition closes in early January, and a magazine awards presentation dinner is held in April or May. Awards are gold or silver scrolls with $1,500 and $500 cash prizes respectively. Established in 1978.

• 15356 •
National Marine Educators Association
Sarah Schoedinger, Pres.
PO Box 1470
Ocean Springs, MS 39566-1470
Phone: (228)818-8810
Fax: (228)818-8894
E-mail: johnette.bosarge@usm.edu
Home Page: http://www.marine-ed.org

• 15357 • **James Centorino Award**
For recognition of distinguished performance in marine education by professionals who are not classroom teachers. Only NMEA members are eligible. Nomination deadline is May 1. A plaque and a complimentary one-year membership in NMEA are awarded annually.

• 15358 • **Honorary Member**
This, the highest recognition bestowed by NMEA, is given to individuals in recognition of a distinguished career in teaching, research, or service in marine education. Individuals must be model professionals who are nationally known in the field. Nomination deadline is May 1. Awarded when merited.

• 15359 • **Marine Education Award**
For recognition of work in any aspect of marine education at the local or national level. Members or non-members of NMEA are eligible. Nomination deadline is May 1. A complimentary one-year membership in NMEA is awarded annually.

• 15360 • **Outstanding Teacher Award**
For recognition of effective and innovative classroom teaching at any level. Only NMEA members are eligible. The candidate's classroom environment, innovative materials and activities used and/or developed, integration of marine topics into various subject areas, evidence of superior performance by candidate's students, and participation in NMEA are considered. Nomination deadline is May 1. A plaque and a complimentary one-year membership in NMEA are awarded annually.

• 15361 • **President's Award**
To recognize a member for outstanding contributions to NMEA and/or to marine education. The President of NMEA makes the selection; however, recommendations from members are welcome. A plaque and a complimentary one-year membership in NMEA are awarded annually.

• 15362 •
National Marine Manufacturers Association
Thomas J. Dammrich, Pres.
200 E Randolph Dr., Ste. 5100
Chicago, IL 60601
Phone: (312)946-6200
Fax: (312)946-0388
E-mail: webmaster@nmma.org
Home Page: http://www.nmma.org

• 15363 • **Charles F. Chapman Memorial Award**
For recognition of individuals or groups within the marine industry who have made outstanding contributions to the sport of boating for the benefit of the recreational boating industry and boating public. Consideration is given to time and effort given to establishing or promoting a boating program or activity; ability to organize and effectively bring about changes in community groups; originality in setting new directions which help solve problems or otherwise facilitate enjoyment of boating; and accomplished knowledge and skills. The award, consisting of a medallion and $1,000 to be donated to a worthy marine-oriented organization of the recipient's choice, is presented each year at the Miami International Boat Show. Established in 1977 in honor of Charles Chapman, former editor and publisher of *MotorBoating & Sailing* magazine.

• 15364 • **Director's Award**
To recognize an individual who best communicates the pleasures of recreational boating to non-traditional boating audiences through newspaper or magazine articles, radio or television broadcasting, films, books, or widespread electronic methods. A monetary award of $2,500 and a certificate are awarded annually at the International Boat Show in Miami in February.

• 15365 •
National Marine Representatives Association
Jim Hannan, Pres.
PO Box 360
Gurnee, IL 60031
Phone: (847)662-3167
Fax: (847)336-7126
E-mail: info@nmraonline.org
Home Page: http://www.nmraonline.org

• 15366 • **Mel Barr Award**
For recognition of outstanding service to the marine industry. Candidates are selected by a panel of the past presidents of the Association. A trophy is presented annually at the NMRA Annual Meeting in September. Established in 1967 in memory of Mel Barr, the first president and founder of NMRA, by his family. Co-sponsored by *Boating Industry* magazine.

• 15367 •
National Medical Fellowships
Vivian Fox, Pres./CEO
5 Hanover Sq., 15th Fl.
New York, NY 10004
Phone: (212)483-8880
Fax: (212)483-8897
E-mail: info@nmfonline.org
Home Page: http://www.nmfonline.org

• 15368 • **C. R. Bard Foundation Prize**
Awarded to a senior medical student who will practice in the field of cardiology or urology.

• 15369 • **Ralph W. Ellison Memorial Prize**
Presented to a graduating medical student for outstanding academic achievement, leadership, and potential for distinguished contributions to medicine. A certificate and $500 stipend are awarded annually. Established in 1994.

• 15370 • **JNMA Awards for Medical Journalism**
To recognize demonstrated skill in journalism and academic achievement by medical students of African-American descent. Students must be United States citizens attending an accredited M.D. or D.O. degree granting schools in the United States and be nominated by their medical school deans. Candidates must also submit copies of work that demonstrate their skill in journalism. Three monetary awards of $2,500 are presented annually.

• 15371 •
National Mental Health Association
Michael Faenza, CEO/Pres.
2001 N Beauregard St., 12th Fl.
Alexandria, VA 22311
Phone: (703)684-7722
Toll-Free: 800-969-NMHA
Fax: (703)684-5968
E-mail: infoctr@nmha.org
Home Page: http://www.nmha.org

• 15372 • **Clifford W. Beers Award**
To recognize a consumer of mental health services in either an inpatient or outpatient setting who best fits the image of Clifford W. Beers in efforts to improve conditions for and attitudes towards individuals with mental illness. Awarded annually. Established in 1976 in honor of Clifford W. Beers, founder of the mental health citizens' advocacy movement in the United States.

• 15373 • **Sandy Brandt Volunteer Service Award**
To recognize the unlimited hours of service and continuing commitment to the mission of the Mental Health Association contributed by volunteers. The nominee must be a member of an NMHA affiliate, have a history of service as a mental health volunteer, have performed in a volunteer capacity to implement the mission/programs of the Association. A plaque, and expenses paid in full to attend the annual meeting are awarded at the Association's Annual Meeting. Named in honor of Sandy Brandt, long-time volunteer for the Mental Health Association for over three decades.

• 15374 • **Ruth P. Brudney Award**
To recognize significant contributions made to the care and treatment of people with mental illnesses by practicing professionals in the field of social work. The nominee must hold a master's level (or higher) degree in social work, hold a professional position in an organization that provides/manages social work services to people with mental illnesses. A plaque and all expenses paid to attend the annual meeting are awarded at the Association's Annual Meeting. Established in 1986 through a gift of George Brudney in memory of his wife, Ruth, a psychiatric social worker.

• 15375 • **Tipper Gore "Remember the Children" Award**
To recognize an individual who has dedicated their career to improving the lives of children and their families. Awarded annually.

• 15376 • **Katherine Hamilton Volunteer of the Year Award**
To recognize outstanding personal volunteer service to people with serious mental illnesses. The nominee must be an immediate relative of a person with a mental illness who is not an NMHA staff person or relative or member of the Board of Indiana Mental Health Memorial Foundation or close relative. A grant of $2,000 for a mental health project, a plaque, and expenses paid to the annual meeting are awarded annually at the Association. Established in 1987 by the Indiana Mental Health Foundation in memory of Katherine Hamilton who left the bulk of her estate to MHA in Indiana. Sponsored by the Indiana Mental Health Memorial Foundation.

• 15377 • **William R. McAlpin, Jr. Mental Health Research Achievement Award**
To recognize a researcher in the field of mental illness research whose work is considered by a panel of judges to: (1) offer significant promise in increasing scientific knowledge in the understanding of one or more of the mental illnesses; (2) expand opportunities for continued avenues of research activities in related scientific fields or areas; and (3) meet the highest standards for scientific research. A monetary prize of $5,000 and a gold medallion on a walnut plaque are awarded annually. Established in 1972 in memory of William R. McAlpin, Jr. who was devoted to the cause of mental health and the advancement of mental illness research.

• 15378 • **Mental Health Media Awards**
To honor representatives of the media for outstanding contributions in the coverage of mental health issues. These contributions may be in the form of continuous mental health coverage during the year, a series of mental health articles or programs, or the production of a public service announcement. Awards are given in the following categories: daily newspapers with circulation over 500,000; daily newspapers with circulation between 250,000 and 500,000; daily newspapers with circulation between 100,000 and 250,000; daily newspapers with circulation under 100,000; other publications, including non-daily newspapers and magazines; local radio or television stations for news and entertainment programs; national radio or television networks and cable systems for news or entertainment programs; and radio or television public service announcements. The Helen Carringer Mental Health Journalism Award is presented to the best in show in the print categories. The Mental Health Broadcast Media Award is presented to the best in show in the electronic categories. Awarded annually.

• 15379 • **Lela Rowland Prevention Award**
To increase the understanding of primary prevention in the mental health field, to arouse interest in prevention possibilities, to demonstrate the existence of credible programs, and to recognize and reward those who develop effective programs in this area of concern. A monetary award of $2,000 and a plaque are awarded. Established in 1976 in honor of Lela Rowland, who worked closely with her husband over a long career in mental health and the Association.

• 15380 •
National Military Fish and Wildlife Association
Jim Bailey, Pres.
93 Windmill Rd.
Conowingo, MD 21918
Phone: (443)655-0917
E-mail: jim.bailey@nmfwa.org
Home Page: http://www.nmfwa.org

• 15381 • **Special Act Award**
To recognize an individual for achievement and outstanding contribution to the Department of Defense's wildlife law enforcement program. Individuals may be nominated for contributions to the Department of Defense Natural Resources program. A plaque and a certificate are awarded annually at the awards banquet. Established in 1988.

• 15382 •
National Military Intelligence Association
Debra Davis, Contact
PO Box 479
Hamilton, VA 20159
Phone: (540)338-1143
Fax: (703)738-7487
E-mail: nmia@adelphia.net
Home Page: http://www.nmia.org

• 15383 • **Academic Excellence Awards - Joint Military Intelligence College**
To recognize scholarship in the field of military intelligence. Two awards are presented annually: (1) Postgraduate Intelligence Program; and (2) Senior Enlisted Intelligence Program - DIC/Defense Intelligence Agency. Selection is made by the faculty/administration of DIC/DIA. Certificates and plaques are awarded annually at DIC graduations. In addition, awardees receive a one-year free membership in the Association and a subscription to newsletters and the *American Intelligence Journal.* Established in 1983. Formerly: (1985) Excellence in Military Scholarship.

• 15384 • **National Military Intelligence Association Annual Awards**
To recognize outstanding accomplishments in the field of military intelligence. The following awards are presented: (1) U.S. Army: Lt. Col. Arthur D. Nicholson Award; (2) U.S. Army Reserve: Col. Carl Eifler Award; (3) U.S. Navy: Vice Admiral Rufus L. Taylor Award; (4) U.S. Navy Reserve: Naval Reserve Award; (5) Air Force: Major General Jack E. Thomas Award; (6) Marine Corps: Col. Donald G. Cook Award; (7) Marine Corps Reserve: Col. James L. Jones Award; (8) Coast Guard: Admiral Frederick C. Billard Award and the Lt. Charles S. Root Award; (9) Defense Intelligence Agency: John T. Hughes Award; (10) National Security Agency: Major Gen. John E. Morrison Jr. Award; (11) Central Intelligence Agency: Lt. General Vernon A. Walters Award; (12) National Imagery and Mapping Agency: William F. Lackman Jr. Award; and (13) National Reconnaissance Office: Jimmie D. Hill Award. Selections are made by the Intelligence Service Chiefs/DIA Director. A certificate and a plaque are annually at the annual NMIA banquet. In addition, awardees are given one-year free membership in NMIA and a subscription to newsletters and the *American Intelligence Journal.* Established in 1985.

• 15385 •
National Mining Association
Jack N. Gerard, Pres./CEO
101 Constitution Ave. NW, Ste. 500 E
Washington, DC 20001-2133
Phone: (202)463-2600
Fax: (202)463-2666
E-mail: craulston@nma.org
Home Page: http://www.nma.org

Formerly: (1995) American Mining Congress.

• 15386 • **Distinguished Service Award**
To recognize an individual for distinguished service to the mining, metallurgical, and/or mineral processing industries. Nominations must be submitted by October 15. A bronze sculpture is awarded. Established in 1986.

• 15387 • **Sentinels of Safety**
This, the most prestigious award in the mining industry, is given to recognize superior occupational injury prevention programs by maintaining no work-related disabling injuries. Mines must have sustained a disability/injury-free year with highest number of hours worked in eight categories of mining methods: underground coal mines, underground metal mines, underground nonmetal mines, surface coal mines, open pit metal/nonmetal mines, quarry, bank or pit, and dredge. A trophy is awarded annually. Established in 1923 by the U.S. Bureau of Mines and Explosives Engineers. Awarded jointly with the Mine Safety and Health Administration.

• 15388 •
National Minority Supplier Development Council
Harriet R. Michel, Pres.
1040 Ave. of the Americas, 2nd Fl.
New York, NY 10018
Phone: (212)944-2430
Fax: (212)719-9611
E-mail: nmsdc1@aol.com
Home Page: http://www.nmsdcus.org

• 15389 • **Minority Business Leadership Awards**
For recognition of long-term achievement in minority business development. Two awards are presented to minority business owners for exemplary business accomplishments and community service; one award is presented to the CEO of a corporation in recognition of more than two decades' work of meaningfully increasing corporate purchasing from minority-owned businesses. Recipients are approved by the Executive Committee. Tiffany crystal is presented annually to the recipients at the annual recognition Dinner-Dance held in May. Established in 1989.

• 15390 • **National Minority Supplier Development Council Awards**
To recognize individuals and organizations that have made exceptional contributions to minority business development through outstanding leadership and achievements. The following awards are presented: Corporation of the Year, Supplier of the Year Award, MBE Coordinator of the Year, and Council of the Year. Tiffany crystal is presented annually to the recipients at the annual recognition banquet held in October. Established in 1972. Formerly: (2004) National Minority Supplier Development Council Conference.

• 15391 •
National Mother's Day Committee
Karen Murray, Chair
47 W 34th St., Ste. 534
New York, NY 10001
Phone: (212)594-6421
Fax: (212)594-9349
E-mail: fdcmdc@att.net
Home Page: http://www.momanddadday.com

Formerly: National Committee for the Observance of Mother's Day.

• 15392 • **Outstanding Mother Award**
To recognize a mother who serves as a role model to influence the American public with a perception of contemporary motherhood as a vital and growing factor in our social fabric. Candidates must be biological, adoptive, or foster mothers with a good record of interest in children's related activities, not just in the family, but in the community; be involved in some aspect of public service; and have a tradition of solid family ties. A sculpture, designed by Henry Dunay, is presented annually in April. Established in 1979.

• 15393 •
National Multiple Sclerosis Society
Joyce M. Nelson, Pres./CEO
733 3rd Ave.
New York, NY 10017
Phone: (212)986-3240
Toll-Free: 800-FIG-HTMS
Fax: (212)986-7981
E-mail: info@nmss.org
Home Page: http://www.nmss.org

• 15394 • **The Norman Cohn Hope Award**
This, the Society's highest honor, is awarded by the National Board of Directors to the Chapters' volunteer of the year. A Tiffany crystal paperweight engraved with the Society logo and Norman Cohn's name is awarded annually. Formerly: Chapter Hope Chest Award.

• 15395 • **Congressman of the Year**
To recognize members of Congress with distinguished records of support for medical research, rehabilitation services, and legislation affecting people with multiple sclerosis. Incumbent U.S. Representatives and U.S. Senators are nominated by March 1 by any chapter of the Society or other source. The awardees are a Representative and Senator chosen by the Society's Government Relations Committee and the Board of Directors. A Society grant for current research investigation is often named for the recipient. Awarded annually. Established in 1984.

• 15396 • **John Dystel Prize**
To recognize a researcher's outstanding contributions to furthering the understanding, treatment, and prevention of multiple sclerosis. All investigators who are actively engaged in fundamental or clinical research related to multiple sclerosis are eligible. A monetary prize of $15,000 is awarded at the annual meeting. Co-

sponsored by the American Academy of Neurology. Established in 1994.

• 15397 • Governor of the Year

To recognize Governors with distinguished records of leadership in support of medical research, rehabilitation services, and legislation affecting people with multiple sclerosis. Incumbent Governors must be nominated by September 1. A Society grant for current research investigation is frequently named for the recipient. Awarded annually. Established in 1985.

• 15398 • Mother/Father of the Year Award

To honor parents who have multiple sclerosis and who courageously make the most of life despite the obstacles imposed by the disease. The candidate, a parent with MS who has outstanding parenting skills, must be nominated by a local chapter and selected by a national committee. Plaques are presented annually. Established in 1954.

• 15399 • MS Achievement Award

To recognize and honor a person with multiple sclerosis who has demonstrated outstanding personal and/or professional achievement in his/her life despite the obstacles imposed by the disease. Nominee must have received this award at the chapter and area level to be considered at the national level. A plaque is presented annually. Established in 1979. Formerly: (1983) MS Patient Achievement Award.

• 15400 • MS Public Education Awards

To recognize editors, writers, and program directors who have enhanced public understanding about MS and the ways in which people with MS and their families cope with the disease. Monetary prizes are awarded for the best print and broadcast entries annually. Established in 1974.

• 15401 • Outstanding Volunteer Service Award

This, the highest and most prestigious volunteer award, is given for recognition at the national level of volunteer and philanthropic contributions to the Society. Awards are given in three categories: Outstanding Individual Volunteer Award, Outstanding Corporate Volunteer Award. Outstanding Club/Organization Volunteer Award. A plaque is awarded in each category. Established in 1961. Formerly: Volunteer of the Year Award.

• 15402 • Ralph I. Straus Award

For recognition of the scientist(s) of any nationality whose published research shall have resulted in the development of an effective and specific method of preventing or arresting multiple sclerosis in humans. Nominations must have the approval of the Medical Advisory Board of NMSS and of a special award committee. A monetary award of an amount not less than the most recently awarded Nobel Prize in Physiology or Medicine is presented. Established in 1973 in honor of Ralph I. Straus, philanthropist and former president of the Society whose mother had MS.

• 15403 •

National Museum of Racing and Hall of Fame
Peter H. Hammell, Dir.
191 Union Ave.
Saratoga Springs, NY 12866-3566
Phone: (518)584-0400
Toll-Free: 800-562-5394
Fax: (518)584-4574
E-mail: nmrinfo@racingmuseum.net
Home Page: http://www.racingmuseum.org

• 15404 • Hall of Fame

To recognize achievement in thoroughbred racing. Awards are given to trainers, jockeys, and horses. Candidates are selected from: horses that have been retired from racing 5 years, trainers who have practiced their profession in thoroughbred racing for 25 years, and jockeys who have ridden at least 20 years. Selections are made by a committee made up of approximately 130 sports writers and radio and television racing announcers. A walnut plaque is awarded annually during the summer race meet in Saratoga. Established in 1955.

• 15405 •

National Music Council
Dr. David Sanders, Dir.
425 Park St.
Upper Montclair, NJ 07043
Phone: (973)655-7974
Phone: (973)655-7974
Fax: (973)655-5432
E-mail: sandersd@mail.montclair.edu
Home Page: http://www.musiccouncil.org

• 15406 • American Eagle Award

For recognition of distinguished service and achievement in American music. Trophies are awarded annually at an awards luncheon following the general membership meeting for classical and poplar music. Established in 1982.

• 15407 •

The National Music Festival
3954 Parkdale Rd.
Saskatoon, SK, Canada S7H 5A7
Phone: (306)343-1835
Fax: (306)373-1390
E-mail: national.festival@sasktel.net
Home Page: http://www.fcmf.org/National%20Music%20Festival.htm

Formerly: Federation of Canadian Music Festivals.

• 15408 • The National Music Festival

To provide a showcase for Canada's finest young classical musicians. First prize in each category - $1,500; second prize - $1,000; third prize - $500; Grand Award $5,000. Formerly: CIBC National Music Festival.

• 15409 •

National Newspaper Association
Brian Steffens, Exec.Dir.
PO Box 7540
Columbia, MO 65205-7540
Phone: (573)882-5800
Toll-Free: 800-829-4662
Fax: (573)884-5490
E-mail: briansteffens@nna.org
Home Page: http://www.nna.org

• 15410 • Amos Award

To recognize a working newspaperman who has provided distinguished service and leadership to the community press and his community. Active, working men associated with a non-metropolitan newspaper, a past officer, former board member, or state association manager may be nominated by June 1 of the awarding year. A plaque is awarded annually at the Convention. Established in 1938 in memory of General James O. Amos of Ohio, a pioneering newsman.

• 15411 • Better Newspaper Contest

To promote excellence among the newspaper members of the Association. Entries are judged within 37 categories. The deadline for receipt of entries is March 31. Plaques for first, second, and third place, as well as honorable mention certificates, are awarded annually at the Convention. Established before 1929. A separate event, the Better Newspaper Advertising Contest, is held concurrently.

• 15412 • McKinney Award

To recognize a working newspaperwoman who has provided distinguished service and leadership to the community press and her community. Active, working women associated with a non-metropolitan newspaper, a past officer, former board member, or state association manager may be nominated by June 1 of the awarding year. A plaque is awarded annually at the Convention. Established in 1966 in memory of Emma McKinney, an Oregon pioneering newswoman.

• 15413 •

National Newspaper Publishers Association
Darryl Gale, Office Mgr.
3200 13th St. NW
Washington, DC 20010
Phone: (202)588-8764
Fax: (202)588-5029
E-mail: membership@nnpa.org
Home Page: http://www.nnpa.org

• 15414 • Distinguished Service Award

Recognizes significant contribution to black advancement. Black leaders are eligible. Contributions must have been made during the previous year. Awarded annually.

• 15415 •
National Notary Association
Milton G. Valera, Pres.
9350 DeSoto Ave.
PO Box 2402
Chatsworth, CA 91313-2402
Phone: (818)739-4000
Toll-Free: 800-876-6827
Fax: (818)700-1830
E-mail: info@nationalnotary.org
Home Page: http://www.nationalnotary.org

Formerly: (1965) California Notary Association.

• 15416 • **March Fong Eu Achievement Award**
To recognize the person who has done the most to improve the standards, image, and quality of the office of Notary Public. A trophy, travel expenses to attend the conference, and national publicity are awarded annually. Established in 1979 and named for its first recipient.

• 15417 • **Notary of the Year Award**
To honor a notary public who has demonstrated exemplary service to the public in any or all of the following areas: overall performance as a Notary Public, initiative and public-spiritedness, service to the disadvantaged, high ethical standards, introduction of highly effective procedures, and accomplishments that set an example for Notaries and other public officials. A trophy, travel expenses to attend the annual conference, and a profile in *The National Notary* magazine are awarded annually at the national conference. Established in 1989.

• 15418 •
National Ocean Industries Association
Tom Fry, Pres.
1120 G St. NW, Ste. 900
Washington, DC 20005
Phone: (202)347-6900
Fax: (202)347-8650
E-mail: tom@noia.org
Home Page: http://www.noia.org

• 15419 • **Award for Excellence in Environmental Conservation**
To recognize those projects and actions the ocean industries undertake to ensure that offshore oil and gas operations are compatible with the coastal and marine environments. Any project or activity that was conducted between January 1 and December 31 of the preceding year may be nominated. Nominations are judged by a selection committee of representatives from the federal government and national environmental conservation organizations. Nominations must meet the following selection criteria: the program of the nominated company must meet all requirements of laws and regulations; nominee's achievements must serve to protect and enhance the nation's marine and coastal environments, including wetlands; documentation and endorsements must accompany the nominations from outside organizations such as state and local government entities and environmental conservation organizations; a strong commitment to protecting and enhancing the environment must be exhibited by the nominee's contribution of time, effort, and resources; and the program must serve as a model for others to follow and as an educational tool to inspire and inform other companies and individuals as well as the public at large. The deadline for entries is January 31. A plaque is awarded annually. Established in 1991.

• 15420 • **Safety in Seas Award**
To recognize excellence among those individuals or organizations that, by their actions, design, or influence, have contributed to improving the safety of life offshore. Membership in the association is necessary. The following criteria are considered: the nominated product, program, or organization should be creative and innovative; the nomination should be for a significant safety achievement, not simple recognition of a company "doing its job"; tangible results should be demonstrated or be reasonably anticipated; and the nominated product, program, or organization should be an inspiration or example to other industry members. It should be translatable to other companies or, in the case of a product, be useful to a wide segment of the industry. Nomination deadline is February 10. A medallion, created by sculptor J. Seward Johnson, Jr., is awarded each year at the annual meeting in April. Established in 1978. Co-sponsored by Compass Publications Inc. and *Sea Technology Magazine.*

• 15421 •
National Office Paper Recycling Project
David Gatton, Contact
1620 Eye St. NW
Washington, DC 20006
Phone: (202)293-7330
Toll-Free: 800-USM-AYOR
Fax: (202)293-2352
E-mail: jwelfley@usmayors.org
Home Page: http://www.usmayors.org/uscm/uscm_projects_services/environment/national_paper_rec ycling_project.html

• 15422 • **Grand Challenge Award**
To recognize the achievements of member organizations, businesses, or government agencies who best exemplify office recycling efforts beyond that which is required by job or law stipulations. Awarded annually with trophies and certificates. Established in 1995.

• 15423 • **National Leadership Awards**
To recognize the achievements of member organizations, businesses, or government agencies who best exemplify office recycling efforts beyond that which is required by job or law stipulations. Awarded annually with trophies and certificates. Established in 1995.

• 15424 • **Recycler of the Year Award**
To recognize the achievements of member organizations, businesses, or government agencies who best exemplify office recycling efforts beyond that which is required by job or law stipulations. Awarded annually with trophies and certificates. Established in 1995.

• 15425 •
National Opera Association
Robert Hansen, Exec.Sec.
PO Box 60869
Canyon, TX 79016-0869
Phone: (806)651-2857
Fax: (806)651-2958
E-mail: rhansen@mail.wtamu.edu
Home Page: http://www.noa.org

• 15426 • **Chamber Opera Competition**
To encourage composers to write chamber operas suitable for use by universities and colleges. A full production of the winner's opera with orchestra, sets, costumes, etc. is given at the NOA convention. Submission deadline is June 30 of even-numbered years. Awarded biennially at the convention. Established in 1984.

• 15427 • **Dissertation Competition**
To recognize outstanding dissertations on operatic subjects. Degree granting institutions are invited to submit one nomination for the competition. Nomination deadline is June 1. Winners receive a certificate, an invitation to read a paper derived from the dissertation at the National Convention, and publication in the *Opera Journal.* Awarded biennially.

• 15428 • **Opera Production Competition**
To encourage and reward creative, high quality opera productions in small professional opera companies and such opera training programs as academic institutions, music conservatories, summer opera training programs, and opera outreach programs. Each year winners will show an excerpt of their production at the annual NOA convention. Application deadline is September 15. Established in 1984.

• 15429 • **Scholarly Paper Competition**
To recognize outstanding achievement in scholarly writing and research related to opera history, performance, or production. A $500 cash prize, invitation to read the paper at the Annual Convention, and publication in the *Opera Journal* are awarded annually.

• 15430 • **Vocal Competition**
To encourage young singers to continue their studies toward an operatic career. The competition consists of two categories: Artist and Scholarship. The Artist Division is open to singers aged 25 to 40. Among other cash prizes ranging from $500 to $2,000, the Artist Division awards three main prizes: Todd Duncan Legacy Award, Clifford E. Bair Endowment Award, and Marjorie Gordon Award, along with a grant scholarship by the American Institute of Musical Studies for summer study in Austria for the first place winner. The Scholarship Division is open to singers aged 18 to 24 who are enrolled in undergraduate or graduate programs, and whose teacher, opera director, or institution is a member of NOA. In addition to various cash prizes ranging from

$500 to $2,000, the Scholarship Division awards the Nick Vrenios Memorial Award and the Constance Eberhardt Memorial Awards, as well as a grant scholarship by the American Institute of Musical Studies for summer study in Austria for the first place winner. Presented annually at the Fall Convention. Established in 1979.

• 15431 •
National Organization for Human Service Education
Georgiana Glose, Pres.
5601 Brodie Ln., Ste. 620-215
Austin, TX 78745
Phone: (512)692-9361
Fax: (512)692-9445
E-mail: ftg_snap@hotmail.com
Home Page: http://www.nohse.org

Formerly: National Organization of Human Service Educators.

• 15432 • **Miriam Clubok Award**
To recognize a member of NOHS who has provided outstanding leadership in support of the organization's mission, goals, and objectives. Nomination deadline is May 15. Awarded annually. Established in 1986.

• 15433 • **Lenore McNeer Award**
For recognition of demonstrated leadership and advocacy in the field of human services. Candidate may or may not be a member of NOHS. Nomination deadline is May 15. A plaque is presented at the Annual Convention. Established in 1981 in memory of Lenore McNeer.

• 15434 • **Outstanding Contribution by an Organization**
To recognize an organization, agency, or company for support of NOHS and its missions, goals, activities, and objectives; as well as demonstrated commitment to human service education. Nomination deadline is May 15. Awarded annually. Established in 1986.

• 15435 • **Outstanding Human Service Student**
To recognize a student member of NOHS for outstanding scholarship, leadership, and commitment to NOHS's goals and to the profession. Nomination deadline is May 15. Awarded annually. Established in 1987.

• 15436 • **President's Award**
To recognize a special contribution or effort to assist NOHS in achieving its missions. Awarded annually when merited. Established in 1986.

• 15437 •
National Organization for Men
Dr. Warren Farrell, Co-Pres.
30 Besey St.
New York, NY 10007
Phone: (760)753-5000
Phone: (510)655-2777
Fax: (212)791-3056
E-mail: warren@warrenfarrell.com
Home Page: http://www.orgformen.org

• 15438 • **Wimps, Grumblers, and Grousers Award**
To recognize those individuals who have most adversely affected men and family issues during the past year. A lithograph is awarded annually by the end of December. Established in 1983 by Sidney Siller, founder of the Organization.

• 15439 •
National Organization for Rare Disorders
Susan Olivo, Development Associate
55 Kenosia Ave.
PO Box 1968
Danbury, CT 06813-1968
Phone: (203)744-0100
Toll-Free: 800-999-6673
Fax: (203)798-2291
E-mail: orphan@rarediseases.org
Home Page: http://www.rarediseases.org

• 15440 • **National Organization for Rare Disorders Awards**
To recognize individuals and corporations for outstanding contributions on behalf of individuals with rare diseases - any disorder affecting less than 200,000 Americans. Recipients are nominated and chosen by the Board of Directors. Three awards are presented annually: Humanitarian Award, Outstanding Service to the Public Health Award, and Corporate Awards for orphan drug development. Plaques are awarded annually at the NORD's Tribute Banquet. Established in 1986.

• 15441 •
National Organization for Victim Assistance
Jeannette M. Adkins Ph.D., Exec.Dir.
510 King St., Ste. 424
Alexandria, VA 22314
Phone: (703)535-NOVA
Toll-Free: 800-TRY-NOVA
Fax: (703)535-5500
E-mail: jeannette@trynova.org
Home Page: http://www.trynova.org

• 15442 • **Tadini Bacigalupi Program of Distinction Awards**
To honor three prominent victim services programs. Awarded annually. Established in 1981 in honor of Tadini Bacigalupi, Jr., one of NOVA's founders and to recognize his commitment to local grassroots and service programs. Formerly: (1982) NOVA Program of Distinction Awards.

• 15443 • **Morton Bard Allied Professional Award**
To recognize outstanding contributions to the support of victim rights and services by a professional who is not involved in direct victim assistance work. Awarded annually. Established in 1989.

• 15444 • **John J. P. Dussich Founder's Award**
For recognition of outstanding contributions to the organization. Awarded annually, if merited. Established in 1980 in honor of John P. Dussich, a founder and the first executive director of NOVA, 1975-1979.

• 15445 • **Margery Fry Award**
To recognize an individual who has given outstanding service as a victim assistance practitioner. Awarded annually. Established in 1978 in honor of Margery Fry, an English social worker instrumental in the victim compensation and battered women movement.

• 15446 • **H. John Heinz Award**
To recognize public officials or employees in federal government for leadership in establishing victim services and rights. Awarded by decision of the Board to no more than one person each year when merited. Named in honor and memory of Senator H. John Heinz III.

• 15447 • **Donald E. Santarelli Award for Public Policy**
For recognition of outstanding service to the victims' movement in the public policy arena. Awarded annually. Established in 1977 in honor of Donald E. Santarelli, former administrator of the Law Enforcement Assistance Administration.

• 15448 • **Stephen Shafer Award**
For recognition of outstanding research contributions to the victims' movement. Awarded annually. Established in 1979 in honor of Stephen Shafer, researcher and academic.

• 15449 • **Edith Surgan Award**
To recognize an outstanding leader of the self-help or activist groups in the victims' movement. Awarded annually. Established in 1984 in honor of Edith Surgan, the founder of Crime Victims Assistance Organization and the chair of NM Crime Victims Reparation Commission.

• 15450 • **Volunteer of the Year Award**
To recognize those volunteering for the NOVA organization. Awarded annually. Established in 1983.

• 15451 •
National Organization for Women, East End Chapter
Marilyn Fitterman, Pres.
PO Box 562
Wainscott, NY 11975
Phone: (631)329-0123
E-mail: eastendnow@aol.com
Home Page: http://www.now.org

• 15452 • **Essay Contest**
For best essay submitted by student of a local high school. Monetary award bestowed annually.

• 15453 •
National Organization of Black Law Enforcement Executives, Central Virginia Chapter
Morris Roberson, Pres.
PO Box 26851
Richmond, VA 23261-6851
Phone: (804)598-1537
Fax: (804)598-1569
E-mail: morris.roberson@worldnet.att.net
Home Page: http://noblecvc.org

• 15454 • **NOBLE Central Virginia Chapter**
For graduating high school student pursuing studies in criminal justice. Scholarship awarded annually.

• 15455 •
National Organization of Single Mothers
Andrea Engber, Dir./Founder
11111 Jim Sossomer Rd.
Midland, NC 28107
Phone: (704)888-6667
Home Page: http://www.singlemothers.org

• 15456 • **Complete Single Mother Award**
Recognition is given annually to a single mom.

• 15457 •
National Organization on Disability
Michael R. Deland, Pres. & Chm.
910 16th St. NW, Ste. 600
Washington, DC 20006
Phone: (202)293-5960
Fax: (202)293-7999
E-mail: ability@nod.org
Home Page: http://www.nod.org
Formerly: (1981) United States Council for IYDP.

• 15458 • **Community Partnership Program Accessible America Award**
To recognize towns, cities, and counties whose disability programs have demonstrated, through creative, in-depth activities, the most significant progress in increasing the participation of persons with disabilities in their communities in the previous year. Cities, towns, townships, and counties, military installations, and Native American Tribes located anywhere in the United States and its territories are eligible to enter. Award prizes total $55,000, with $25,000 awarded to the Grand Prize winner. Nomination deadline is October 31. Sponsored by United Parcel Service (UPS).

• 15459 •
National Organization Taunting Safety and Fairness Everywhere
Dale Lowdermilk, Exec.Dir./Founder
PO Box 5743WS
Montecito
Santa Barbara, CA 93150
Phone: (805)969-6217
Phone: (805)966-0611
E-mail: dale93150@aol.com
Home Page: http://www.notsafe.org

• 15460 • **Stir-the-Pot Award**
To recognize individuals who face bureaucratic overregulation without backing down or being intimidated with red tape. Nominations of newsworthy or noteworthy performances that expose regulatory excess at the state, local, or national level are considered. A certificate of recognition and national press release are awarded annually. Established in 1987.

• 15461 •
National Orientation Directors Association
LeeAnn Melin, Exec.Sec.-Treas.
University of Michigan - Flint
375 University Center
Flint, MI 48502-1950
Phone: (810)424-5513
Fax: (810)762-3023
E-mail: nodahomeoffice@umflint.edu
Home Page: http://www.nodaweb.org

• 15462 • **Outstanding Contributions to the Orientation Profession Award**
Recognizes contributions and/or publications in the field of orientation, retention, and transitions. Selection is based on the significance of the research and/or publication; outstanding leadership; merited stature; and how innovative and effective the contribution is to fostering the advancement of the profession. A completed nomination form (available online) and a nomination statement must be submitted..

• 15463 • **Norman K. Russell Scholarship**
To recognize and assist graduate students who have demonstrated a strong commitment to orientation, retention, and transition; who will contribute to the enhancement of the orientation field; and who are currently enrolled as a graduate student in orientation-related fields. Three $1,000 scholarships are awarded annually at the national conference. Formerly: (1981) NODA Scholarship.

• 15464 •
National Outdoor Book Awards
Ron Watters, Chm.
Box 8128
Idaho State University
Pocatello, ID 83209
Phone: (208)282-3912
Fax: (208)282-4600
E-mail: wattron@isu.edu
Home Page: http://www.isu.edu/outdoor/books

• 15465 • **National Outdoor Book Awards**
To recognize the work of outstanding writers and publishers of outdoor books. Books may be nominated in one of nine categories including: History/Biography, Outdoor Literature, Children's Books, Nature, Instructional Texts, Adventure Guidebook, Nature Guidebook, and Design/Artistic Merit. In addition, the Outdoor Classic Award is given annually to books which over a period of time have proved to be exceptionally valuable works in the outdoor field. To be nominated, books must have been released in the previous or current year.

• 15466 •
National Paint and Coatings Association
J. Andrew Doyle, Pres.
1500 Rhode Island Ave. NW
Washington, DC 20005-5597
Phone: (202)462-6272
Fax: (202)462-8549
E-mail: npca@paint.org
Home Page: http://www.paint.org

• 15467 • **Allen W. Clark Award**
To recognize outstanding community service work by a local paint and coating association through the NPCA's "Picture It Painted" campaign. The project considered must be of benefit to the community, showcase an industry product, and be organized and managed by the local association. An engraved plaque and cash award are presented during the NPCA Annual Meeting in the fall. Established in 1982 in honor of Allen W. Clark, creator of the Clean Up - Paint Up - Fix Up Campaign and founder of the *American Paint and Coatings Journal.*

• 15468 • **Gold Star Award**
To recognize and award a local association's efforts to provide exemplary service to its own membership and to further the goals of NPCA and the industry in the region. Awards are made to three locals based on their size: small, medium, or large.

• 15469 • **George Baugh Heckel Award**
This, the Association highest honor, is given in recognition of an individual who has contributed significant time and energy over the past year to the advancement of NPCA goals. The award is bestowed at the Association's Annual Meeting. Deadline for nominations is June 1.

• 15470 • Industry Achievement Award
To recognize specific contributions to the paint and coatings industry. A certificate is presented at the NPCA Annual Meeting. Established in 1983.

• 15471 • Industry Statesman Awards
To recognize those who have contributed lifelong, dedicated service to the paint industry and NPCA. Awards are given at the Association's Annual Meeting to one or more recipients. Deadline for nominations is June 1.

• 15472 • Pollution Prevention Award
To recognize outstanding achievement by NPCA members in protecting the environment through waste minimization and/or toxic reduction technologies or practices employed in their manufacturing processes. Awards are presented at the Association's Annual Meeting. Developed by NPCA's Water Quality/Waste Management Committee and endorsed by the Association's Executive Committee and Board of Directors in 1990.

• 15473 • Safety Awards
To recognize NPCA member company plants for outstanding employee safety records. The awards recognize superior safety performance by members of the paint industry, and allow NPCA to compile overall industry safety statistics. The following awards are presented to one or more recipients: Safety Awards of Excellence, Safety Awards of Honor, Safety Awards of Commendation, and Safety Awards of Merit. Awarded annually.

• 15474 •
National Paperbox Association
Scott Miller, Exec.VP
113 S West St., 3rd Fl.
Alexandria, VA 22314-2858
Phone: (703)684-2212
Fax: (703)683-6920
E-mail: npahq@paperbox.org
Home Page: http://www.paperbox.org

Formerly: National Paperbox and Packaging Association.

• 15475 • Packaging Competition Awards
To recognize significant achievement in the development and manufacturing of rigid boxes and folding cartons. Only members are eligible. A Best of Show Award is presented to the most outstanding rigid box and folding carton. Awarded annually. Established in 1950.

• 15476 •
National Park Academy of the Arts
Abi Garaman, Chm.
PO Box 608
Jackson Hole, WY 83001
Toll-Free: 800-553-2787
Fax: (307)739-1199
E-mail: info@artsfortheparks.com
Home Page: http://www.artsfortheparks.com

• 15477 • Arts for the Parks Competition
To recognize artists whose paintings best capture the "essence" and diversity of the landscape, wildlife, and history of our National Park system. Each year a monetary award of $25,000 is presented to the winner, with other cash prizes awarded to regional and category winners. Established in 1986.

• 15478 • Awards of Merit
Recognizes historical, marine, and landscape art. Three monetary awards are given.

• 15479 • Founder's Favorite Winner Award
Recognizes paintings that capture the essence and diversity of the landscape, wildlife, and history of our National Park system. All artists are eligible. A monetary award is given annually.

• 15480 • Grand Prize Winner Award
Recognizes artists whose paintings best capture the essence and diversity of the landscape, wildlife, and history of our National Park system A monetary prize is given annually.

• 15481 • Judges Award of Merit
Recognizes artists whose painting best capture the essence and diversity of the landscape, wildlife, and history of our National Park system. A monetary prize is given annually.

• 15482 • Regional Awards
Recognizes paintings that best capture the essence and diversity of the landscape, wildlife, and history of our National Park system. All artists are eligible. A monetary prize is given annually.

• 15483 • U.S. Art Magazine Award of Merit
Recognizes paintings that best capture the essence and diversity of the landscape, wildlife, and history of our National Park system. All artists are eligible. A monetary prize is given annually.

• 15484 • Wildlife Category Award of Merit
Recognizes paintings that capture the essence and diversity of the landscape, wildlife, and history of our National Park system. All artists are eligible. A monetary award is given annually. Established in 1986.

• 15485 •
National Parkinson Foundation
Daniel Arty, Pres.
1501 NW 9th Ave.
Bob Hope Parkinson's Research Center
Bob Hope Rd.
Miami, FL 33136-1494
Phone: (305)243-6666
Toll-Free: 800-327-4545
Fax: (305)243-5595
E-mail: contact@parkinson.org
Home Page: http://www.parkinson.org

• 15486 • Distinguished Service Award
To recognize individuals who go above and beyond the call of duty to assist the foundation with their important efforts. Nominations may be submitted by December. A plaque is awarded annually at the Gala for Hope in February. Established in 1984.

• 15487 • Humanitarian Award
To recognize an individual who has provided outstanding leadership and support to philanthropic, social, and community organizations. Nominations may be submitted by October. A plaque and gift are awarded annually at the Gala for Hope in February. Established in 1983.

• 15488 •
National Parks Conservation Association
Thomas Kiernan, Pres.
1300 19th St. NW, Ste. 300
Washington, DC 20036
Phone: (202)223-6722
Toll-Free: 800-NAT-PARKS
Fax: (202)659-0650
E-mail: npca@npca.org
Home Page: http://www.eparks.org

Formerly: (1970) National Parks Association.

• 15489 • Marjory Stoneman Douglas Award
To recognize an individual for an outstanding effort that results in the protection of a unit or a proposed unit of the National Park System. A monetary award of $5,000 and an engraved pewter bowl are presented annually at an NPCA event. The award is named in honor of Marjory Stoneman Douglas for her many years of dedication to preserving the fragile ecosystem of the Florida Everglades. Established in 1986.

• 15490 • Stephen Tyng Mather Award
To recognize individuals who put principle before personal gain in the preservation of natural and/or archaeological resources. Any federal employee who has been employed for two years or more in the preservation or management of natural and archaeological resources may be nominated. A monetary award of $2,500 a certificate, and travel allowance to the ceremony are presented annually at the March Board Meeting. Established in 1983 in honor of Stephen T. Mather, the first director of the National Park Service and co-founder of NPCA.

• 15491 • William Penn Mott Jr. Park Leadership Award
For recognition of outstanding contribution by a member of Congress or other public official to the preservation and/or protection of the National Parks who stands as a strong advocate of the National Park System. Nominations are accepted. A certificate and framed print is presented annually. Established in 1980. In 1992, the award was renamed for William Penn Mott, former director of the National Park Service.

• 15492 • **Freeman Tilden Award**
To recognize the best National Park Service interpreter, to encourage greater efforts by other interpreters in the Park Service, and to reward the quality of the interpretive efforts of an individual. Seasonal or full-time National Park Service employees working in the field of interpretation are eligible. National winners are selected from ten regional winners who are awarded a commemorative plaque and lithograph of Freeman Tilden at appropriate ceremonies in their region. The overall winner is awarded a monetary prize of $2,500, a replica of a bust of Freeman Tilden, and a travel allowance for the winner and spouse to the award ceremony. Presented annually in the fall. Established in 1982 by KC Publications, the National Park Service, and NPCA. The award honors Freeman Tilden, the father of interpretation.

• 15493 •
National Peach Council
Charles Walker, Managing Dir.
12 Nicklaus Ln., Ste. 101
Columbia, SC 29229
Phone: (803)788-7101
Fax: (803)865-8090
E-mail: peachcouncil@att.net
Home Page: http://www.nationalpeach.org

• 15494 • **Achievement Award**
For recognition of outstanding contributions to the peach industry or the National Peach Council. A sculptured glass peach on a wooden base with a plaque is awarded when merited at the Annual Convention. Established in 1968.

• 15495 • **Carroll R. Miller Award**
To encourage and recognize noteworthy research relating to improved marketing and utilization of peaches and/or peach products. Awarded annually. Established in 1972 in memory of Carroll Miller, a founding member and first president of NPC.

• 15496 •
National Pest Control Association
8100 Oak St.
Dunn Loring, VA 22027
Phone: (703)573-8330
Toll-Free: 800-678-6722
Fax: (703)573-4116
Home Page: http://www.urbanwildlifesociety.org/UWS/BrdCtrl/NatlPestAssnHabtatMod.html

• 15497 • **Committee of the Year Award**
To recognize and reward committee members who have made outstanding contributions to a productive committee of the Association. A walnut engraved plaque is awarded annually at the national convention. Established in 1973.

• 15498 • **Committee Person of the Year Award**
To recognize and reward an outstanding committee person for contributions to the Association. A walnut engraved plaque is awarded annually. Established in 1979.

• 15499 •
National Pig Carvers Association
Ron Harper, Dean
2035 Willow Glen Rd.
Fallbrook, CA 92028
Phone: (760)723-5122
E-mail: rharper@tfb.com

• 15500 • **Member of the Year Award**
To recognize members who best demonstrate commitment to the goals and aims of the organization. Presented annually with a trophy. Established in 1992.

• 15501 •
National Pigeon Association
Pat Avery, Co-Sec.-Treas.
PO Box 439
Newalla, OK 74857-0499
Phone: (405)386-6884
Fax: (405)386-5541
E-mail: james4bird@aol.com
Home Page: http://www.npausa.com

• 15502 • **Hall of Fame**
To recognize efforts on behalf of the Association and outstanding work in the breeding and exhibiting of pigeons. Applicants must have bred and exhibited pigeons for at least ten years and have been an association member for at least ten years. A plaque is awarded annually. Established in 1957.

• 15503 • **Master Breeder Award**
To recognize work in the breeding of pigeons and efforts to improve the breed. Individuals capable of breeding pigeons to a particular standard for at least ten years are eligible for the award. A certificate is awarded annually. Established in 1930.

• 15504 • **Master Judge Award**
Recognizes the importance of qualified judges. Awards are given for All Breed Master Judge and Special Breed Master Judge annually. Established in 1990.

• 15505 • **Outstanding Service Award**
To recognize an outstanding member for service rendered during the past year. A plaque is awarded annually. Established in 1978.

• 15506 •
National Playwrights Conference
Eugene O'Neill Memorial Theatre Center
234 W 44th St., Ste. 901
New York, NY 10036
Phone: (212)382-2790
Fax: (212)921-5538

• 15507 • **Eric Kocher Playwrights Award**
Awarded to a playwright for an internationally focused work that shows depth and originality.

• 15508 • **National Playwrights Conference and New Drama for Media Project**
To develop talented writers by offering them the opportunity to work on their plays together with other talented professional theater and media artists. Adaptations are not eligible. Playwrights must be United States citizens or permanent residents. Collaborations and one-act plays are eligible. All submissions must be previously unproduced and not currently under option. Playwrights are limited to one submission of an original play for the theater and/or one submission of an original script work for media. The period for submissions is September 15 to November 15. Up to twelve plays are selected annually for staging. The Charles MacArthur Fellowship, established by Helen Hayes in memory of her husband, is also awarded. Playwrights are required to remain in residence for the duration of the conference. Send an SASE in August to receive the submission guidelines. The New Drama for Media Project was established in 1977. Formerly: National Playwrights Conference and New Drama for Television Project.

• 15509 • **O'Neill Awards**
To enable American playwrights to work on their plays together with other theater or media artists. Applicants must be U.S. citizens or permanent residents who have written an original script for theater, television, or screen. Submissions must not have been previously produced. Awards are tenable at the National Playwrights Conference during the summer. Award recipients work on the development of their scripts with theatre professionals, and participate in the production of their plays. The award is $1,000 plus transportation and room and board for four weeks.

• 15510 • **Harold and Mimi Steinberg Prize**
Awarded as the last money investment in a play developed at the conference and deemed to have excellent commercial potential. The award consists of $100,000.

• 15511 •
National Poetry Association
934 Brannan St. 2nd Fl
San Francisco, CA 94103
Phone: (415)552-9261
Fax: (415)552-9271
E-mail: info@internationalpoetrymuseum.org
Home Page: http://www.nationalpoetry.org

• 15512 • **Cin(E)-Poetry Festival**
To recognize the effective use of film and videography as a vehicle for poetry - the dynamic use of word and image to achieve a unity of mood. Poetry films and video poems that incorporate a verbal poetic statement in narrated or captioned form are eligible. Entries must be submitted by November 1. Monetary awards vary; certificates and a college exhibition tour are presented. Established in 1975 by Herman Berland. Sponsored by the Literary Television. Formerly: Poetry Film Festival.

• 15513 •
National Press Club
Richard Dunham, Pres.
National Press Bldg.
529 14th St. NW
Washington, DC 20045
Phone: (202)662-7500
Phone: (202)662-7511
Fax: (202)662-7512
E-mail: info@press.org
Home Page: http://www.press.org

• 15514 • **John Aubuchon Freedom of the Press Award**
To recognize members of the print and broadcast media and those who have promoted and/or protected freedom of the press. Awards are presented in two categories: national and international. Entries are limited to work that was published and/or broadcast for dissemination during the preceding year or for activities during the same period that promoted and/or protected freedom of the press. Application deadline is April 1. A monetary prize of $1,000 is awarded annually in each category. Established in 1989.

• 15515 • **Consumer Journalism Award**
To recognize excellence in reporting on consumer subjects. Professional journalists are eligible for material in four categories: newspapers, periodicals (including online reporting), television, and radio. Judges look favorably on solution-oriented or strategic-oriented pieces that prompt action by consumers, the community, the government, or an individual. Application deadline is April 1. A monetary award of $500 is presented for each category. Awarded annually. Established in 1973.

• 15516 • **Robin Goldstein Award for Washington Regional Reporting**
To recognize reporters who demonstrate excellence and versatility in covering Washington from a local angle for hometown newspapers. Entrants must be full-time professional reporters. Entries may include up to six articles or columns. Special attention will be paid to diversity of subject and style. Application deadline is April 1. A monetary prize of $1,000 is awarded annually. Administered by the National Press Foundation.

• 15517 • **Edwin M. Hood Award for Diplomatic Correspondence**
To recognize excellence in reporting on United States diplomatic and foreign policy issues in two categories: print/online and broadcast. Professional journalists who report on American diplomatic affairs are eligible. Application deadline is April 1. A monetary award of $500 is presented for each category. Awarded annually. Established in 1981.

• 15518 • **Annual National Press Club Sandy Hume Memorial Award for Excellence in Political Journalism**
Annual award of recognition. Inquire for more information on this award. Formerly: (2006) Political Journalism Award.

• 15519 • **Robert L. Kozik Award for Environmental Reporting**
To recognize excellence in environmental reporting on a local, national, or international level in two categories: print/online and broadcast. Open to professional journalists. Application deadline is April 1. The Kozik Medal and a monetary prize of $500 are awarded annually in each category. Established in 1991 by the late Franklin E. Kozik to recognize journalists' accomplishments in the field, call attention to the environment, and memorialize his son Robert, who died of cancer in 1989 at age 35.

• 15520 • **Newsletter Journalism Award**
To recognize excellence in newsletter journalism. Two awards are presented annually in two categories: Analytical/interpretive reporting piece and Exclusive story. Entries must be published by an independent newsletter and serve the audience and mission of the newspaper. The competition is open to professional journalists who receive at least 50 percent of their wages from journalistic activities, either independently or as employees of independent, for-profit newsletters. Application deadline is April 1. A monetary award of $2,000 is presented in each category. Established in 1987.

• 15521 • **Online Journalism Award**
Annual award of recognition. Inquire for more information on this award.

• 15522 • **Annual Arthur Rose Award for Press Criticism**
Annual award of recognition. Inquire for more information on this award.

• 15523 • **Annual National Press Club Joseph D. Ryle Award for Excellence in Writing on the Problems of Geriatrics**
Annual award of recognition. Inquire for more information on this award.

• 15524 • **Washington Correspondence Award**
To honor the work of reporters who cover Washington for the benefit of hometown audiences. The contest focuses on Washington reporting of events, issues, and politics of importance to a city, state, or region. Professional journalists accredited in Washington are eligible. Entries must consist of a single report or series on one topic that is neither for national reporting nor for a body of work. Application deadline is April 1. A monetary award of $1,000 is presented annually. Established in 1978.

• 15525 •
National Press Foundation
Donna Washington, Dir. of Operations
1211 Connecticut Ave. NW, Ste. 310
Washington, DC 20036
Phone: (202)663-7280
Fax: (202)530-2855
E-mail: donna@nationalpress.org
Home Page: http://www.nationalpress.org

• 15526 • **Clifford K. and James T. Berryman Award for Editorial Cartoons**
To recognize editorial cartoonists of newspapers and magazines for work that exhibits power to influence public opinion, as well as be of good quality and have a striking effect. Application deadline is October 3. A monetary award of $2,500 and an etched crystal vase are presented annually at the awards dinner. Established in 1991 by Florence Berryman in memory of her father and brother, both Pulitzer Prize winning cartoonists.

• 15527 • **Editor of the Year Award**
To recognize an editor who has realized significant journalistic achievements that enhance the quality of journalism in the United States. Newspaper, periodical, and newsletter editors at any level are eligible for nomination by their superiors or other representatives. Applications are not accepted; recipient is selected by the NPF Board. A monetary award and an etched crystal vase are awarded annually at the awards dinner. Established in 1984.

• 15528 • **Kiplinger Distinguished Contributions to Journalism Award**
To honor persons who have, through their vision and leadership, strengthened American journalism and furthered the efforts to establish quality in American journalism. Applications are not accepted; recipient is selected by the NPF Board. An etched crystal vase is awarded annually at the awards dinner. Established in 1984 to honor Willard Kiplinger.

• 15529 • **Sol Taishoff Award for Excellence in Broadcast Journalism**
To recognize an active broadcaster for accomplishment in field reporting, producing, writing, or work at the anchor desk. Applications are not accepted; recipient is selected by the NPF Board. A monetary award and an etched crystal vase are awarded annually at the awards dinner. Established in 1984 in memory of Sol Taishoff, editor and publisher of *Broadcasting Magazine.*

• 15530 •
National Press Photographers Association
Greg Garneau, Exec.Dir.
3200 Croasdaile Dr., Ste. 306
Durham, NC 27705
Phone: (919)383-7246
Fax: (919)383-7261
E-mail: info@nppa.org
Home Page: http://www.nppa.org

• 15531 • **Association Fellowship Award**
To recognize an individual for continuous outstanding service in the interests of press photography and for outstanding technical achievement in photography. Awarded annually. Established in 1948.

• 15532 • **Joseph Costa Award**
To recognize an individual for outstanding initiative, leadership, and service in advancing the goals of NPPA. Awarded annually. Established in 1954 in honor of Joseph Costa, a founder of

NPPA and the first President and Chairman of the Board.

• 15533 • Ernie Crisp Television News Photographer of the Year
This award is the highest honor in television news photography. Presented annually. Established in 1954. Formerly: Newsfilm Cameramen of the Year.

• 15534 • Robin F. Garland Educator Award
For recognition of outstanding service as a photojournalism educator. Awarded annually. Established in 1974 in memory of Robin F. Garland, a picture editor and war correspondent for the *Saturday Evening Post*.

• 15535 • Jim Gordon Editor of the Year Award
To recognize an editor of an outstanding newspaper, magazine, video, movie, Web site, book, or other publication or broadcast that supports and promotes strong photojournalism, and best use of photography, and whose individual dedication and efforts have moved photojournalism's standards forward while also advancing the best interests of all photographers. A citation is awarded annually. Established in 1958.

• 15536 • Humanitarian Award
To recognize an individual for playing a key role in saving lives or in rescue situations. Established in 1985.

• 15537 • J. Winton Lemen Award
To recognize continuing outstanding service in the interests of press photography and for outstanding technical achievement in photography. Awarded annually. Established in 1948 to honor J. Winton Lemen, a charter member of the NPPA.

• 15538 • Kenneth P. McLaughlin Award of Merit
For recognition of individuals rendering continuing outstanding service in the interests of news photography, whether or not they are members of the profession. Awarded annually. Established in 1950 in memory of Kenneth P. McLaughlin, a photographer for the *San Francisco Chronicle* and third President of the NPPA.

• 15539 • Sam Mellor Award
To recognize the regional associate director judged to be the most outstanding in the performance of duties. A citation was awarded annually from 1958-1975 and resumed in 1983. Established in memory of Samuel Mellor, a photographer for the *New York Post* until his death in 1954.

• 15540 • Military Photographer of the Year
For recognition of the outstanding military photographer of the year. Awarded annually. Established in 1961.

• 15541 • NPPA Citations
For recognition of special contributions advancing photojournalism. Awarded annually. Established in 1948.

• 15542 • Outstanding Publication Award
To recognize the production of the most outstanding regional or chapter publication, either in print or online. Awarded annually. Established in 1969. Formerly: Outstanding Newsletter Award.

• 15543 • Picture Editor of the Year
To recognize a picture editor for outstanding accomplishments. Established in 1985.

• 15544 • Pictures of the Year Competition
To recognize photojournalists for their skills and creativity in visual communication. The contest divisions include newspaper, magazine, and editing. The highest honors go to the Newspaper Photographer of the Year, the Magazine Photographer of the Year, and the winner of the Canon Photo Essay Award. Individual category awards of $100 and a plaque for first place, plaques for second and third place, and a parchment certificate for Awards of Excellence are given in the following categories: (1) Newspaper Division: spot news; general news; feature picture; sports action; sports feature; portrait/personality; pictorial; editorial illustration; fashion illustration; food illustration; news picture story; feature picture story; sports portfolio-one week's work; (2) Magazine Division: news or documentary picture; feature picture; sports picture; portrait/personality; pictorial; science/natural history; illustration; picture story; sports portfolio; science/natural history; illustration; picture story; sports portfolio; (3) Newspaper Editing Awards: (a) Newspapers: Newspaper Picture Editing Award-team; Newspaper Picture Editing Award-individual; Best Use of Photography by a Newspaper with a circulation: under 25,000; 25,000 to 150,000; over 150,000; and zoned editions; (b) Individual categories: news page; feature page; sports page; series or special section; newspaper-produced Magazine Picture Editing Award; and (c) Magazines: Best Use of Photography by a Magazine. Established in 1943.

• 15545 • President's Award
For recognition of special services to the NPPA. Selection is made at the discretion of the Association's president. Awarded annually to one or more recipients, when merited. Established in 1957.

• 15546 • Regional Television Photographer of the Year
To recognize television photographers and to promote, encourage, and teach the highest levels of photojournalism and ethics. The award is given to the annual winner of the Television Quarterly Clip Contest, a competition held every three months for NPPA members. The contest has four categories: spot news, general news, 48-hour feature, and in-depth reporting. Judges choose a first, second, and/or third place winner, and the Regional Television Photographer of the Year will be awarded to the entrant in each of the 11 regions who accumulates the most points during the year. Awarded annually. Established in 1980.

• 15547 • Special Citations
To recognize an individual or organization for significant contributions that advance the interests of photojournalism. Awarded annually to one or more recipients. Established in 1961.

• 15548 • Joseph A. Sprague Memorial Award
This is the highest honor in the field of photojournalism. Two awards are given each year: to a working photojournalist who advances, elevates, or attains unusual recognition for the profession of photojournalism by conduct, initiative leadership, skill, and devotion to duty; and to an individual, not a working photojournalist, for unusual service or achievement beneficial to photojournalism or for an outstanding technology advance in equipment or processes of photojournalism. Plaques, rings, and citations are awarded annually in both categories. Established in 1949 in memory of Joseph A. Sprague, who designed several cameras.

• 15549 • Television Newsfilm Awards
For recognition of excellence in news coverage by cameramen. Photographers who produce films in the following classes are eligible: spot news, general news, feature, news special, news documentary, and team filming. A plaque is awarded annually. Established in 1942.

• 15550 • Burt Williams Award
To recognize a news photographer for completion of forty years of service in press photography. Individuals, whether or not they are members of the association, are eligible. Established in 1955 in memory of Burt Williams, a founder and first national secretary of the NPPA.

• 15551 •
National Propane Gas Association
Richard R. Roldan, Pres./CEO
1150 17th St. NW, Ste. 310
Washington, DC 20036-4623
Phone: (202)466-7200
Fax: (202)466-7205
E-mail: info@npga.org
Home Page: http://www.npga.org
Formerly: National LP-Gas Association.

• 15552 • Distinguished Service Award
For recognition of outstanding contributions to the propane gas industry. Nominations are accepted. A scroll and medal are awarded at the Annual Meeting when merited. Established in 1950.

• 15553 • Bill Hill Memorial Award
For recognition of significant contributions in the area of public affairs that have real benefit for the propane gas industry. Members are eligible. The deadline for nominations is December 31. A plaque and a monetary contribution in the recipient's name to an educational or scientific institute are awarded annually when merited. Established in 1981 in memory of William C. Hill.

• 15554 • Marketing Achievement Awards
To recognize NPGA's affiliated state associations, marketer, and supplier members who have made outstanding contributions to the propane gas industry, their community, and company through print, radio, and television advertising, public relations and media materials, community events and trade shows, and other marketing materials. The deadline for entry is March 14. Awards are presented each year at the Annual Meeting. Established in 1984. In 1995, the Grand Marketing Achievement Award was established to recognize entrants who have successfully tracked the results of their programs.

• 15555 • Safety Award
To recognize an individual, a small company, or a branch establishment for distinguished service to the cause of safety in the propane-gas industry. Both members and public service individuals are eligible. The deadline for nominations is December 31. A plaque is awarded when merited at the Annual Meeting. Established in 1959.

• 15556 • State Director of the Year Award
To recognize a State Director who has been most effective in carrying out his responsibilities during the course of the previous year. Nominations by members are accepted. A plaque is presented at the Annual Meeting. Awarded annually when merited. Established in 1983.

• 15557 •
National Property Management Association
Bonnie Schlag, Exec.Dir.
1102 Pinehurst Rd.
Dunedin, FL 34698
Phone: (727)736-3788
Fax: (727)736-6707
E-mail: hq@npma.org
Home Page: http://www.npma.org

• 15558 • Chapter of the Year
To recognize the chapters that have provided the most effort in assisting the NPMA to achieve its overall objectives. Award designations are divided into categories based on the size of the chapter. A plaque and monetary award of $1,000 are awarded annually to each winner. Established in 1991.

• 15559 • Federal Property Person of the Year
To recognize individual achievements and accomplishments in the field of property management by an employee of the federal government. Members and nonmembers are eligible. A plaque is awarded annually. Established in 1989.

• 15560 • Jack Griffiths Property Person of the Year
To recognize individual achievements and accomplishments in the field of property management. Only NPMA members are eligible. A large plaque is awarded annually. Established in 1976.

• 15561 •
National PTA - National Congress of Parents and Teachers
Warlene Gary, CEO
541 N Fairbanks Ct.
Chicago, IL 60611-3396
Phone: (312)670-6782
Toll-Free: 800-307-4PTA
Fax: (312)670-6783
E-mail: info@pta.org
Home Page: http://www.pta.org

• 15562 • Advocates for Children Award
To recognize local units that demonstrate a commitment to the objectives of the PTA by encouraging and strengthening parent involvement and advocacy for all children. Eight local unit presidents - one from each of the eight PTA regions - and the schools' principals are awarded expense-paid trips to the National PTA convention and plaques. Sponsored by World Book, Inc.

• 15563 • Phoebe Aperson Hearst/ National PTA Excellence in Education Partnership Award
To recognize a local PTA whose collaborative efforts with parents, families, educators, and community members promote parent/family involvement in ongoing programs that encourage student success. Local PTAs in good standing may submit applications to their state PTA, which may submit one application for national consideration. The national winner receives a monetary award of $2,000 and two expense-paid trips to the National PTA convention. Four honorable mentions receive a plaque and $500 each. Awarded annually. Sponsored by the William Randolph Hearst Foundation.

• 15564 • Membership Awards
To recognize local units, councils, districts and/ or regions, and state PTAs reporting a membership increase.

• 15565 • Reading/Literacy Award
To recognize a local unit that has conducted an outstanding reading program during the year. Projects that have a strong element of parent involvement are considered. Applications may be submitted by April 1. A monetary award of $500, an expense-paid trip for the local unit president to the National PTA convention, and 200 books for the school library are awarded annually. Sponsored by Scholastic and American Greetings.

• 15566 • Student Involvement Award
To recognize local units with student involvement, to inspire units that have student involvement to improve and enhance their programs, and to further the National PTA's goal of increasing effective student involvement. Applications may be submitted by April 1. A monetary award of $500, an expense-paid trip to the National PTA Convention for one adult and one PTA/ PTSA student representative, and two commemorative gifts are awarded.

• 15567 •
National Quality Institute
(Institut national de la qualite)
Allan Ebedes, Pres. and CEO
2275 Lake Shore Blvd. W, Ste. 307
Toronto, ON, Canada M8V 3Y3
Phone: (416)251-7600
Toll-Free: 800-263-9648
Fax: (416)251-9131
E-mail: awards@nqi.ca
Home Page: http://www.nqi.ca

• 15568 • Canada Awards for Excellence (Prix Canada pour l'excellence)
Recognizes the outstanding achievement of excellence through quality and workplace wellness. Open to organizations from all sectors. CAE recognition is achieved by those organizations that have met the NQI Criteria. NQI's Progressive Excellence Program (PEP) rewards excellence at four different stages, the Last stage at the level of the CAE. Submissions may be made by applicants whose primary activities are conducted wholly or principally in Canada or from a Canadian base of operations. Trophies and certificates, as well as export assistance and media attention, are awarded annually in the fall. Established in 1984. Formerly sponsored by Industry Canada. Formerly: (1995) Canada Awards for Business Excellence.

• 15569 •
National Railroad Construction and Maintenance Association
Chuck Baker, Exec.Dir./VP
122 C St. NW, Ste. 850
Washington, DC 20001
Phone: (202)715-2920
Toll-Free: 800-883-1557
Fax: (202)318-0867
E-mail: info@nrcma.org
Home Page: http://www.nrcma.org

• 15570 • Member of the Year
No further information was provided for this edition.

• 15571 • Safe Contractor of the Year Awards
Recognizes an outstanding active safety program. Applicants must be member contractors. Awarded annually.

• 15572 •
National Ramah Commission
Rabbi Sheldon Dorph, Dir.
3080 Broadway
New York, NY 10027
Phone: (212)678-8881
Fax: (212)749-8251
E-mail: ramah@jtsa.edu
Home Page: http://www.campramah.org

• 15573 • **Ramah Leadership Award**
Awarded annually to entering college freshmen for service to Ramah camps.

• 15574 •
National Recreation and Park Association
John A. Thorner, Exec.Dir.
22377 Belmont Ridge Rd.
Ashburn, VA 20148-4501
Phone: (703)858-0784
Fax: (703)858-0794
E-mail: info@nrpa.org
Home Page: http://www.nrpa.org

• 15575 • **Robert W. Crawford Young Professional Award**
To recognize young park and recreation professionals who exemplify innovative and pioneering leadership in the planning, development, and programming of a wide variety of creative community leisure opportunities. To be eligible, an individual must be an active member of NRPA and the state recreation association, be under 35 years of age, and have national and/or state certification. A plaque is awarded annually. Established in 1991 in memory of Robert W. Crawford.

• 15576 • **Dorothy Mullen National Arts and Humanities Award**
To honor the most innovative and effective arts and humanities programs across the nation. Entries are judged on the basis of content, innovation, contribution to community, and expansion of interest in the arts and humanities, among other criteria. Open to all NRPA agencies and members. Awards are presented in the following categories: Class I - populations of 500,000 or more; Class II - 200,000 to 499,999; Class III - 75,000 to 199,999; Class IV - 25,000 to 74,999; and Class V - 24,999 and under. Awarded annually.

• 15577 • **National Award for Media Excellence**
To recognize a writer, artist, reporter, publisher, or media corporation/owner who has significantly contributed to the public's understanding and awareness of public parks, recreation, and conservation programs. This could be achieved through such media as general circulation books, magazines, newspapers, news collection organizations, broadcast stations, anthologies of photographs or art works, mass circulation films, or other outlets. Awarded annually. Established in 1984.

• 15578 • **National Congressional Award**
To recognize a member of the U.S. Senate or House of Representatives who has demonstrated continuing national leadership in efforts to improve and/or protect the quality and quantity of leisure opportunities through park, recreation, and conservation programs and projects. One or more awards are presented annually.

• 15579 • **National Corporate Humanitarian Award**
To recognize a corporation or foundation that has made significant and consistent contributions to the recreation, parks, and conservation field by the sponsorship, creation, or implementation of a program or project. The scope of the program or project must have been consistently displayed over a minimum of five years on the local, state, or national level. Awarded annually. Established in 1983.

• 15580 • **National Distinguished Professional Award**
To recognize a professional in the field who, through inspiration, incentive, and leadership, has made noteworthy contributions over a period of time to the park, recreation, and conservation movement. Individuals who have been active at the professional level for at least 15 years and have been members of NRPA for at least ten years are eligible. Up to two awards may be presented annually.

• 15581 • **National Humanitarian Award**
To recognize an individual or organization whose concern for and dedication to humanity has been expressed through park, recreation, and conservation efforts that have enriched the lives of people in neighborhoods, communities, states, or the nation. One award is presented annually.

• 15582 • **National Literary Award**
To recognize a writer or publisher who has made the most significant contribution to the understanding of new innovations or refined philosophic thoughts and tenets, trends, or research in parks, recreation, and conservation. The literature must be of national significance and should have a major impact, such as stirring professional awareness and opinion or creating new concepts in parks, recreation, and conservation. Awarded annually when merited.

• 15583 • **National Voluntary Service Award**
To recognize a citizen or organization whose voluntary contributions of time and effort over a period of years have improved the quality and quantity of leisure opportunities through park, recreation, and conservation programs and projects in neighborhoods, communities, states, or the nation. No more than three awards are given annually.

• 15584 • **Theodore and Franklin Roosevelt Award for Excellence in Recreation and Park Research**
To recognize an individual whose contributions to recreation and basic or applied research have significantly advanced the cause of the recreation movement, and whose dedication to the field parallels the same dedication and zeal toward parks, recreation, and conservation that was exhibited by the two former presidents after whom the award is named. A monetary award of $1,500 and a plaque are awarded annually. Established in 1981.

• 15585 • **Ralph C. Wilson Award**
To recognize an individual whose long-term service and dedication to the NRPA's boards, committees, regional councils, and volunteer initiatives have been exemplary and have advanced the cause of parks, recreation, and conservation. Open to members of NRPA. Awarded annually. Established in 1989 to honor Ralph C. Wilson, one of the association's most distinguished leaders, for his devotion to NRPA and his significant influence in shaping a strong citizen and professional national advocate organization.

• 15586 •
National Recreational Vehicle Owners Club
K.W. Stephens, Natl.Dir.
Jack's Branch Rd.
PO Box 520
Gonzalez, FL 32560-0520
Phone: (850)937-8354
Toll-Free: 800-281-9186
Fax: (850)937-8356
E-mail: nrvockws@spydee.net
Home Page: http://www.nrvoc.com

Formerly: (2003) National RV Owners Club.

• 15587 • **Member of the Year Award**
To recognize contribution of time and talent to the field of "RVing" or RV camping and travel. Nomination of members is made by the membership. A plaque and travel are awarded annually at the convention. Established in 1987.

• 15588 •
National Recycling Coalition
Kate Krebs, Exec.Dir.
1325 G St. NW, Ste. 1025
Washington, DC 20005
Phone: (202)347-0450
Fax: (202)347-0449
E-mail: info@nrc-recycle.org
Home Page: http://www.nrc-recycle.org

• 15589 • **National Recycling Coalition Annual Awards**
To recognize outstanding recycling achievements, publicize success stories, and help raise the caliber of recycling across the country. Candidates must by nominated by NRC members. The following awards are presented to public, private, and joint efforts: Best Rural Program, Best Regional Program, Best Urban Program, Best Recycling Innovation, Procurement Award, Public Education Award, and Most Innovative

Local Market Development Award. The Fred Schmitt Award for Outstanding Corporate Leadership is presented to a company. The Tim McClure Award for Outstanding Environmental and Community Leadership is presented to an organization. The Beth Brown Boettner Award for Outstanding Public Education is given to a governmental body. Recycler of the Year is awarded to an individual. Selection criteria for the awards include the following: significant recycling, waste reduction, or diversion from disposal; participation rates and recovery of recyclable materials from residential or commercial sources; number/type of materials collected; length of time the program has been in operation; public outreach efforts; applicability to other communities and/or business; and efforts that strengthen local market conditions. Awarded annually.

• 15590 •
National Rehabilitation Association
633 S Washington St.
Alexandria, VA 22314
Phone: (703)836-0850
Fax: (703)836-0848
E-mail: info@nationalrehab.org
Home Page: http://www.nationalrehab.org/website/index.html

• 15591 • **W. F. Faulkes Award**
To recognize technical and/or professional achievement in the field of rehabilitation. Individuals or organizations that have in the preceding years made major contributions of national importance to the increase of knowledge in the field of rehabilitation or to the development of techniques or methods in the application of such knowledge or to the prevention of disability are eligible. Eligibility for this award would be: (1) the author of a notable technical treatise on rehabilitation; (2) a physician or medical school that has discovered a new technique useful in rehabilitating certain groups of persons with disabilities; (3) a research scientist or laboratory whose work has led to the discovery of a preventive or cure for a handicapping condition; and (4) a rehabilitation worker who has put into practice a new rehabilitation technique or method which has had, nationally, an important effect on rehabilitation practice. The deadline for nominations is August 1. Established in 1954 to honor W.F. Faulkes, the Association's founder and first president.

• 15592 • **Belle Greve Memorial Award**
To recognize an individual who has shown unusual initiative or creativity in the development and/or administration of a service program of demonstrated value for persons with disabilities. The program concerned must have contributed to an increased public awareness of the problems of persons with disabilities. Eligibility for this award would be the administrator of a rehabilitation or closely allied program, the director of a workshop or other rehabilitation facility, a research worker, caseworker or supervisor whose efforts have largely been responsible for the development of a new or original program of services, or any person in a program or facility that has significantly participated in its development in untried areas, although not personally involved in direct services to individuals. The deadline for nominations is August 1. Awarded annually. Established by the Ohio Chapter to honor Belle Greve, founder of the Cleveland Rehabilitation Center.

• 15593 • **Organizational Award**
To recognize a national organization with an outstanding record of service to persons with disabilities. The organization may be one whose principle objectives are in the rehabilitation field or one which, regardless of its major objectives, has demonstrated effective concern for the care, treatment, education or rehabilitation of persons with disabilities. Eligible for this award are organizations that have made a contribution to the well-being or rehabilitation of persons with disabilities in activities over and beyond the purpose for which the organization was established. Nominees eligible for the award are an organization that has established a unique service program to better serve persons with disabilities, an organization that has, through its initiative and creativity, developed programs which have contributed significantly to the rehabilitation movement on a national basis, and organizations that have acted as a catalyst in the community to better integrate, coordinate and develop services to persons with disabilities. The award recipient may be nominated for its past or present program of activities and for its contribution during the preceding year or for a major contribution in preceding years. The deadline for nominations is August 1. Awarded annually.

• 15594 • **President's Award**
To recognize outstanding achievement in behalf of persons with disabilities. Individuals or organizations whose activities in the preceding years have made a major contribution to the rehabilitation of persons with disabilities on a nationwide basis, in an area not generally considered technical, are eligible. Eligible for this award are members of Congress who have demonstrated a leadership role in the development and/or passage of legislation which increases rehabilitation opportunities for persons with disabilities, employers who have made intelligent and persistent efforts to provide employment opportunities for persons with disabilities and have inspired others to do likewise, members of a profession or other group whose zeal for rehabilitation have heightened the interest and enlarged the contribution of that profession or group, or people with disabilities whose examples or whose concern for persons with disabilities has so inspired others as to effect a nationwide impact upon rehabilitation. The deadline for nominations is August 1.

• 15595 • **Max T. Prince Meritorious Service Award**
To recognize an individual who has demonstrated years of faithful service and leadership to NRA through any segment or combination of segments of association activities or life. Emphasis is placed on both the length of service and levels of service, and is given to persons showing outstanding service or leadership, both qualitatively and quantitatively. Sustained membership in the Association is required. Members who have demonstrated a lifetime or near lifetime of service to persons with disabilities are eligible. Such services, however, while affecting large numbers of persons with disabilities, need not necessarily be national in geographical scope but must be very substantial in number. The services may be of a direct or indirect nature. Outstanding clinicians and administrators and other persons within the rehabilitation movement, broadly defined, are eligible for this award. The deadline for nominations is August 1. Awarded annually.

• 15596 • **Public Service Award**
To recognize an individual or organization that has demonstrated leadership in improving rehabilitation services at the federal, state, or local levels. Those eligible include individuals or organizations who have exercised creative and effective political leadership over a period of years on behalf of rehabilitation programs and individuals with disabilities at the federal, state, or local levels. The deadline for nominations is August 1. Awarded when merited. Established in 1981. Formerly: Legislative Service Award.

• 15597 • **E. B. Whitten Silver Medallion Award**
To recognize individuals who have exercised notable leadership in removing environmental and legal barriers and in helping to overcome discrimination of persons with disabilities. The contribution of the individual may have been made nationally or locally, and must have been of such stature as to influence action on a regional or national basis. The deadline for nominations is August 1. Awarded annually. Established in 1974 to honor E.B. Whitten, the NRA's first executive director, who served for over 25 years.

• 15598 •
National Rehabilitation Association Vocational Evaluation and Work Adjustment Association
9612 Mennonite Rd.
Wadsworth, OH 44281
Phone: (216)336-8090

• 15599 • **Paul R. Hoffman Award**
For recognition of innovation and creativity in service to persons with disabilities through professional or technical achievements in vocational evaluation and/or work adjustment. Members and nonmembers are eligible for nomination. A plaque is awarded annually at the convention. Established in 1974 in honor of Paul R. Hoffman.

• 15600 • **Past President's Best Practices Award**
To recognize an agency or program that serves as a model for service to individuals with disabilities. A plaque is presented at the National Rehabilitation Association Conference. Established in 1992.

• 15601 • **VEWAA Service Award**
To recognize a member who has made a significant contribution to the Association. A plaque is awarded annually to one or more recipients at the convention. Established in 1979.

• 15602 •
National Rehabilitation Counseling Association
Dr. Betty Hedgeman, Admin.
PO Box 4480
Manassas, VA 20108
Phone: (703)361-2077
Fax: (703)361-2489
E-mail: nrcaoffice@aol.com
Home Page: http://nrca-net.org

• 15603 • **Counselor of the Year Award**
To recognize a rehabilitation counselor who has made an outstanding contribution to improve services or more effective use of existing resources and approaches for people with disabilities. Awards are presented at the state and regional levels. Eligible nominees must be members of NRCA, employed as a full-time counselor working with a caseload of persons with disabilities, and a Certified Rehabilitation Counselor. The national winner is selected from the pool of regional winners. A plaque is awarded annually. Established in 1965.

• 15604 • **National Citation Awards**
To recognize meritorious service or significant achievements in the field of rehabilitation counseling services of the disabled on a local, state, regional, or national level. Nomination deadline is May 15. Awarded annually. Established in 1960.

• 15605 • **National Distinguished Service Award**
To recognize unusual or significant professional or technical achievement in the rehabilitation counseling field or in providing services to the disabled on a national basis. Nomination deadline is May 15. Awarded annually. Established in 1960.

• 15606 • **NRCA Fellow**
To recognize NRCA members who have shown exceptional dedication, performance, and expertise as rehabilitation counselor practitioners. Members meeting the above criteria who have been members of NRCA for ten of the past fifteen years, and are presently a Certified Rehabilitation Counselor are eligible to apply or have nominations made by others by November 1. Awarded annually.

• 15607 • **Harley B. Reger Memorial Award**
To recognize the state NRCA branch with the greatest achievement. Nominations must be submitted to the regional branch by May 15, and national nominations from regional branches must be received by June 15. Awarded annually. Established in memory of Harley B. Reger, a former NRCA President and leader during the formative years of the Association.

• 15608 •
National Rehabilitation Hospital
Edward B. Healton, Med.Dir.
Communications & Development
102 Irving St. NW
Washington, DC 20010-2949
Phone: (202)877-1000
Fax: (202)829-5161
E-mail: info@hrhrehab.org
Home Page: http://www.nrhrehab.org
Awards discontinued.

• 15609 • **Victory Awards**
Celebrates the victory of the human spirit and honors individuals who best exemplify exceptional strength and courage in the face of adversity. Fields honored include arts and entertainment, sports, politics, community leaders, advocates for disability rights, champion athletes, teachers, parents, and students. Established in 1986.

• 15610 •
National Religious Broadcasters
Dr. Frank Wright, Pres./CEO
9510 Technology Dr.
Manassas, VA 20110
Phone: (703)330-7000
Fax: (703)330-7100
E-mail: adunlap@nrb.org
Home Page: http://www.nrb.org

• 15611 • **Board of Directors' Award**
To recognize a distinguished individual who, while an avowed Christian, may not necessarily be in the field of electronic communications. The deadline for nomination is September 30. A plaque is awarded annually at the national convention. Established in 1988.

• 15612 • **Chairman's Award**
To recognize an individual, organization, agency, music or publishing company, etc., that has made a deserving contribution to religious broadcasting. The deadline for nomination is September 30. A plaque is awarded annually at the national convention. Established in 1988.

• 15613 • **Distinguished Service Award**
To recognize an individual or organization for outstanding contributions to the field of broadcasting. The deadline for nomination is September 30. A plaque is awarded annually at the national convention. Established in 1972 in memory of William Ward Ayer, NRB's founding President.

• 15614 • **Milestone Award**
To recognize an individual or organization for 50 years of continuous service in religious broadcasting. The deadline for nominations is September 30. A plaque is awarded annually at the national convention. Established in 1976.

• 15615 • **Radio Program Producer of the Year**
To recognize the most deserving U.S. religious radio program producer. The deadline for nominations is September 30. A plaque is awarded annually at the national convention. Established in 1988. Formerly: (1988) Award of Merit.

• 15616 • **Radio Station of the Year**
To recognize the most deserving religious radio station in the United States. The deadline for nomination is September 30. A plaque is awarded annually at the national convention. Established in 1988. Formerly: (1988) Award of Merit.

• 15617 • **Religious Broadcasting Hall of Fame Award**
To recognize a Christian broadcaster who has achieved wide recognition in the field of religious electronic media with the highest standards. The deadline for nomination is September 30. A plaque is awarded annually at the national convention. Established in 1975.

• 15618 • **Television Program Producer of the Year**
To recognize the most deserving U.S. religious TV program producer. The deadline for nomination is September 30. A plaque is awarded annually at the national convention. Established in 1988.

• 15619 •
National Religious Vocation Conference
Bro. Paul Bednarczyk CSC, Exec.Dir.
5420 S Cornell Ave., No. 105
Chicago, IL 60615-5604
Phone: (773)363-5454
Fax: (773)363-5530
E-mail: nrvc@aol.com
Home Page: http://nrvc.net

• 15620 • **Harvest Award**
For recognition of a significant contribution to vocation ministry in the Catholic Church in the U.S. Persons or groups who are not members of the Conference are eligible. A plaque is awarded biennially at the national convention. Established in 1981 by the National Conference of Religious Vocation Directors. Formerly: John Paul II Award.

• 15621 •
National Research Council
Ralph J. Cicerone, Chm.
500 Fifth St. NW
Washington, DC 20001
Phone: (202)334-2000
Home Page: http://www.nationalacademies.org

• 15622 • **Ford Foundation Postdoctoral Diversity Fellowships**
To provide for one-year postdoctoral fellowships to teacher-scholars preparing for or already engaged in college or university teaching and research. Awards are made in the behavioral and

social sciences, humanities, engineering, mathematics, physical sciences, and biological sciences, or for interdisciplinary programs comprised of two or more eligible disciplines. Applicants must be U.S. citizens or nationals who are members of the following minority groups: Native American Indian or Alaskan Native (Eskimo or Aleut), Black/African American, Mexican American/Chicano/Chicanas, Native Pacific Islander (Micronesian or Polynesian), and Puerto Rican; must have received a Ph.D. or an Sc.D. degree by the application deadline; and must not have held the degree for longer than seven years by the application deadline. Application deadline is November 15. A stipend of $40,000 is awarded to approximately 24 postdoctoral fellows each year. The National Research Council also offers the Ford Foundation Predoctoral and Dissertation Minority Fellowships.

• 15623 • **Research Associateship Programs**
To provide postdoctoral scientists and engineers of unusual promise and ability opportunities for research on problems, largely of their own choice, that are compatible with the research interests of the sponsoring laboratories; and to contribute thereby to the overall research effort of these laboratories and to the national scientific and technological welfare. Research opportunities are available in the following major disciplines: Chemistry; Earth and Atmospheric Sciences; Engineering, Applied Sciences, and Computer Science; Life, Medical, and Behavioral Sciences; Mathematics; Physics; and Space and Planetary Sciences. The National Research Council in cooperation with participating federal laboratories offers approximately 450 awards for independent scientific research. Recipients are free to work on problems of their own choice as guest investigators at the federal laboratories. Many of the programs are open to experienced senior scientists as well as to recent PhDs. Stipends begin at $27,150 for Regular Research Associateships and at $35,000 for Senior Research Associateships. Deadline for application is February 1. Awarded annually.

• 15624 •
National Restaurant Association
Steven C. Anderson, Pres./CEO
1200 17th St., NW
Washington, DC 20036
Phone: (202)331-5900
Toll-Free: 800-424-5156
Fax: (202)331-2429
E-mail: info@dineout.org
Home Page: http://www.restaurant.org

• 15625 • **American Culinary Classic**
One of the largest culinary competitions of its kind in America, it recognizes chefs, apprentices, students, and culinarians for outstanding food preparation. The event is held at the annual NRA Show. Awards are given in Professional and Student categories. Gold, silver, and bronze medals are awarded. Other awards presented are: Best of Show, Best Entry for Junior Culinarian, Most Original Piece of Show, and Grand Prize for Pastry. Established in 1971. Winners often participate in the Culinary Olympics in Frankfort, Germany, with the winners of the other regional competitions: Culinary World Cup (Luxembourg); Salon Culinaire Mondial (Basel, Switzerland); Food & Hotel Asia Competition (Singapore); Hotelympia (London); Culinary Masters (Canada); and Chef Ireland (Ireland). Formerly: Culinary Arts Salon.

• 15626 • **Great Menu Contest**
To recognize an owner or manager of a foodservice operation for outstanding restaurant menus based on imagination, design, and merchandising power. Awards are given in the following categories: restaurant average per person check less than $8; between $8 and $15; over $15; specialty; banquet/catering; institutional foodservice; most imaginative; best design; and greatest merchandising power. The menus are judged by a panel of designers, food writers, and editors. The judges select first, second, and third place winners who receive plaques and menu stickers. Awarded annually. Established in 1963. Formerly: Menu Idea Exchange Award.

• 15627 • **Hennessy Awards**
To recognize and commend those special United States Air Force bases that excel in the management, preparation, and service of food to their personnel. Awards are given in each of the following categories: single-unit base, multiple-unit base, Air Force Reserve Unit, Air National Guard, Missile Feeding Operation, and Foodservice Small Site. In addition, the Hennessy Travelers Association Award of Excellence is presented. The John L. Hennessy Trophy, consisting of a silver bowl mounted on a pedestal encircled by three silver standing eagles with outstretched wings, is presented in each category. Awarded annually. Established in 1956 in conjunction with the U.S. Air Force. The award honors John Lawrence Hennessy for his contribution to the advancement of military foodservice.

• 15628 • **Ice Carving Classic**
To recognize three-person teams for transforming huge blocks of ice into magnificent works of art. The event is held at the annual NRA Show. The competition pits master ice carvers from around the world against one another in three events: compulsory figures, to be completed in one hour; free-style individual blocks, two hours; and team multiple blocks, three hours. Established in 1988 in cooperation with the National Ice Carving Association.

• 15629 •
National Restaurant Association Educational Foundation
Mary M. Adolf, Pres./COO
175 W Jackson Blvd., Ste. 1500
Chicago, IL 60604-2814
Phone: (312)715-1010
Toll-Free: 800-765-2122
E-mail: info@nraef.org
Home Page: http://www.nraef.org

Formerly: (1998) National Restaurant Association Foundation.

• 15630 • **Ambassador of Hospitality Award**
To honor industry representatives for extraordinary support in the advancement of professionalism through education. Members of the College of Diplomats are eligible. Awards are presented at the annual National Restaurant Association Show. Established in 1987. Formerly: (1998) Ambassador Award of Hospitality.

• 15631 • **College of Diplomats Award**
To recognize the contributions of restaurant/hospitality industry leaders and to pay tribute to the professionalism of operators, manufacturers, employees, students, educators, and publishers. Three awarded annually. Established in 1974. Formerly: (1991) Salute to Excellence Awards.

• 15632 •
National Retail Federation
Tracy Mullin, Pres./CEO
325 7th St. NW, Ste. 1100
Washington, DC 20004
Phone: (202)783-7971
Toll-Free: 800-NRF-HOW2
Fax: (202)737-2849
E-mail: mullint@nrf.com
Home Page: http://www.nrf.com

Formerly: (1995) National Retail Merchants Association.

• 15633 • **American Spirit Award**
To recognize a retailer or retail firm for a tradition of humanitarianism or long term commitment to charitable causes. Awarded annually.

• 15634 • **Distinguished Service Award**
To recognize an outstanding retailer for his or her distinguished service in promoting and increasing the stature of the industry, for support of and participation in state retail associations, for inspirational leadership, and for significant contributions to retailing and to NRF. Five awards are presented annually.

• 15635 • **Gold Medal Award**
This, the NRF's highest honor, is given in recognition of an outstanding industry leader whose career contributions have made a distinct impression in the field of retailing. An engraved gold medal is awarded annually. Established in 1929.

• 15636 • **International Retailer of the Year**
To recognize distinguished service to retailing by an individual retailer outside the United States for excellence both in his/her native country and internationally. A mounted plaque is awarded annually. Established in 1968.

• 15637 • **Leadership in Public Service Award**
To recognize a key public figure whose actions or efforts have contributed in a major way to the

public good and to the economic health of the retail industry. Awarded annually.

• 15638 • **Silver Plaque Award**
To recognize a prominent industry executive who is well established in his or her field and who has made a major contribution to the industry or to NRF. Mounted plaques are awarded annually. Established in 1929.

• 15639 • **Small Retailer of the Year Award**
To recognize a small store retailer who has carved out a unique position in his or her market. A mounted plaque is awarded annually. Established in 1971.

• 15640 • **J. Thomas Weyent Lifetime Achievement Award**
To recognize state retail association executives who have given more than 25 years of service to retailing as the head of one of NFR's member state retail associations.

• 15641 •
National Reye's Syndrome Foundation
Ms. Kathleen Rohrbaugh, Office Mgr.
426 N Lewis
PO Box 829
Bryan, OH 43506
Phone: (419)636-2679
Toll-Free: 800-233-7393
Fax: (419)636-9897
E-mail: nrsf@reyessyndrome.org
Home Page: http://www.reyessyndrome.org

• 15642 • **The John Dieckman Distinguished Educational Award of Honor**
To recognize continued support, dedication, and enthusiasm toward increasing awareness of Reye's Syndrome. Each June, a plaque is awarded to a volunteer helping the Reye's Syndrome Foundation. Established in 1985.

• 15643 • **Elaine J. Lasky Humanitarian Service Award**
To recognize outstanding personal effort, dedication, and commitment toward the eventual elimination of Reye's Syndrome. A plaque and pendant are awarded each June at the Foundation's Annual Meeting. Established in 1985.

• 15644 •
National Rifle Association of America
Wayne LaPierre, Exec.VP
11250 Waples Mill Rd.
Fairfax, VA 22030
Phone: (703)267-1600
Toll-Free: 877-NRA-2000
E-mail: membership@nrahq.org
Home Page: http://www.mynra.com

• 15645 • **Intercollegiate Pistol Championships**
To determine the individual and team champions in Intercollegiate Free Pistol, Standard Pistol, Open Air Pistol, Women's Air Pistol, and Women's Sport Pistol categories. To qualify for invitation, teams and individuals must have scored adequately in the annual NRA Intercollegiate Pistol Sectionals held throughout the U.S. Held annually.

• 15646 • **National Championships**
To recognize the winners of national championship events (indoor and outdoor over U.S. courses of fire) in the following categories: action pistol, black powder rifle, collegiate, high power rifle, high power rifle long range, indoor pistol, outdoor pistol, indoor smallbore rifle, outdoor smallbore rifle, police pistol, and silhouette. Dozens of trophies are awarded each year, including the Bianchi Cup, Castle Trophy, Art Sievers Trophy, and Lee O. Wright Memorial Trophy.

• 15647 • **National Police Shooting Championships**
To recognize the winners of police shooting events. Law enforcement and security officers from around the world can participate. More than $250,000 in prizes is awarded for various categories of competition. The following trophies are awarded: Anheuser Busch Trophy, Harry Reeves Trophy, National Border Patrol Trophy, 3 Police Revolver Distinguished, two Police Semi-Auto Distinguished, Mary C. Camp Memorial Trophy, Francis J. McGee Trophy, National Police Pistol Team Trophy, Revolver Team Trophy, National Sheriff's Association Trophy, John M. Schooley World Team Trophy, William B. Ruger World Team Trophy, Sobel Trophy, and Washington State Reserve Police Association Trophy. Held annually.

• 15648 •
National Rural Health Association
Alan Morgan, Interim CEO
1 W Armour Blvd., Ste. 203
Kansas City, MO 64111-2087
Phone: (816)756-3140
Fax: (816)756-3144
E-mail: mail@nrharural.org
Home Page: http://www.nrharural.org

Formed by merger of: (1986) National Rural Health Care Association; American Rural Health Association.

• 15649 • **Distinguished Educator Award**
To recognize education and curriculum development dedicated to the needs of rural practioners with the potential to encourage, assist, enhance, expand and improve rural health careers. Nominees are reviewed by the scope of their accomplishments, the significance of their work to rural health, the sophistication of the scholarly effort, and evidence of the outcome of their work in rural health. Formerly: (1996) Education Excellence Award.

• 15650 • **Distinguished Researcher Award**
To recognize health services research and basic scientific inquiry specific to rural health needs with the potential to make long-lasting contributions by guiding public policy and health care planning toward a rural focus. Criteria considered in giving the award include the scope of accomplishments, significance of the work to rural health, sophistication of scholarly effort, and evidence of outcome of the work. Formerly: (1996) Research Excellence Award.

• 15651 • **Louis Gorin Award for Outstanding Achievement in Rural Health Care**
To recognize individuals for creativity, unselfishness, compassion, and cooperative attitude in seeking ways to provide lasting contributions to rural health care. A plaque is awarded annually at the annual conference. Established to honor Louis Gorin, a federal employee for over 25 years who served as Deputy Associate Bureau Director for Rural Health.

• 15652 • **Outstanding Rural Health Practice**
To recognize a community oriented rural health care delivery practice which has improved access to rural people through innovative, comprehensive approaches. Factors taken into consideration include: outreach efforts; preventive health and educational programs; quality and efficiency of care; and strong community support and involvement. A plaque is awarded annually at the annual conference.

• 15653 • **Outstanding Rural Health Program**
To recognize a statewide or regional program which promotes or facilitates the development of rural health care delivery systems. Factors taken into consideration include: coordination; networking; innovation; and lasting impact. A plaque is awarded annually at the annual conference.

• 15654 • **Rural Health Practitioner of the Year**
To recognize a direct service provider for leadership in bringing health services to rural populations. Factors taken into consideration include providing outstanding care; involvement in the community; and lasting contribution to the rural health care system. A plaque is awarded annually at the annual conference.

• 15655 •
National Safety Council
Alan McMillan, Pres.
1121 Spring Lake Dr.
Itasca, IL 60143-3201
Phone: (630)285-1121
Toll-Free: 800-621-7619
Fax: (630)285-1315
E-mail: info@nsc.org
Home Page: http://www.nsc.org

Formerly: (1945) Film Safety Awards Committee.

• 15656 • **Million Mile Club Award**
To provide recognition for extraordinary achievement in professional driving. Eligibility for the Million Mile Club Award is exclusive -

enrollment is open only to professional drivers who have achieved at least 1,000,000 miles or 30 years of accident-free driving. Organizations that are members of the National Safety Council and various co-sponsoring organizations are welcome to sponsor their qualified drivers for enrollment. A plaque and lapel pin are awarded when merited.

• 15657 • National Fleet Safety Contests
These competitive contests are designed to promote safe driving and also serve as a means of collecting motor vehicle fleet accident statistics. The programs are open to all Council members and co- sponsor members with fleets operating in the United States or Canada. The contests operate from January 1 - December 31 of each year. Data is submitted on a monthly basis and awards are given on an annual basis. There are five different awards: (1) First Place - a mounted plaque to the fleet having the lowest number of accidents per 1,000,000 vehicle-miles in each group; (2) Second Place - an unmounted engraved plate to the fleet having the second lowest number of accidents per 1,000,000 vehicle-miles in each group; (3) Third Place - an unmounted engraved plate for third place which is determined in the same manner as the first and second place winners. But, there must be at least thirty fleets participating in a group in order to issue a third place award; (4) Perfect Record - to every fleet that completes the year without an accident; and (5) Certificate of Achievement - to each fleet that meets the criteria for reduction of their accident rate. Additional information is available from Rachael Corp.

• 15658 • Occupational Safety/Health Award Program
A non-competitive safety incentive and recognition award program designed to promote the reduction and elimination of occupational injuries and illnesses. The program is available to all employer members of the National Safety Council. Records submitted for evaluation are required to be kept according to the Recordkeeping Requirements under the Occupational Safety and Health Act of 1970 (Revised 1978) by the U.S. Department of Labor. The program recognizes every organization that completes a calendar year with a perfect record (without a case involving days away from work or death). Organizations with non-perfect records may also earn recognition if they meet certain criteria. There are five levels of recognition under this program: (1) Distinguished Achievement in Occupational Safety and Health Award - three are given out each year. They are presented to the small, medium, and large company that has attained the best occupational safety performance. This is the highest honor presented to an industrial organization by the National Safety Council; (2) Award of Honor - earned by (a) accumulating 3,000,000 or more perfect employee-hours; (b) establishing the Best Record in a specific Standard Industrial Classification; or (c) reducing the incidence rates as required; (3) Award of Merit - earned by accumulating between 1,000,000 and 2,999,999 perfect employee-hours or by reducing the incidence rates as required; (4) Award of Commendation - to an organization that accumulates between 200,000 and 999,999 perfect employee-hours; and (5) President's Citation Award - to an organization that has attained a perfect record of less than 200,000 employee-hours. Interim awards are given for safety achievements that are attained within a given year. An organization must have a minimum of 1,000,000 perfect employee-hours and meet other specific requirements. Awarded annually.

• 15659 • Occupational Safety/Health Contests
A competitive award program designed to promote accident prevention by providing award recognition for a good safety performance. The program is a service available to all employer members of the Council and any co-sponsor organizations. The contest operates from January 1 - December 31 of each year. Data is submitted on a monthly basis and awards are given on an annual basis. For purposes of comparability, each industry contest is subdivided into divisions according to the specific product being produced. These divisions correspond with the Standard Industrial Classification Manual (SIC). Contestants are further separated within division by size group. Awards are given based upon rank within each size group. The unit having the lowest incidence rate per 100 full time employees is ranked first. The following awards are given in each size group: (1) First Place - a mounted plaque; (2) Second Place - an unmounted engraved plate; and (3) Third Place - an unmounted engraved plate.

• 15660 • Safe Driver Award Program
This, the recognized trademark of the professional driving industry, is given to those who have proven their skills as accident-free drivers. Member organizations of the Council enrolled in the Motor Fleet Safety Service are eligible. Participating organizations certify drivers to receive wallet certificates designating the number of years of safe driving service. Awarded when merited.

• 15661 •
National Safety Council, Northern Ohio Chapter
Larry Kingston, Exec.Dir.
25 E Boardman St., Ste. 338
Youngstown, OH 44503
Phone: (330)747-8657
Toll-Free: 800-715-0358
Fax: (330)747-6141
E-mail: info@nscnohio.org
Home Page: http://www.nscnohio.org

• 15662 • Medallion Award
For person working for safer environments. Recognition award bestowed annually.

• 15663 •
National Scholastic Press Association
Tom E. Rolnicki, Exec.Dir.
2221 University Ave. SE, Ste. 121
Univ. of Minnesota
Minneapolis, MN 55414
Phone: (612)625-8335
Fax: (612)626-0720
Home Page: http://www.studentpress.org

• 15664 • All American Hall of Fame
Recognizes outstanding school newspapers, yearbooks, and magazines. Awarded when merited. Recipients receive a plaque and have their name added to the national Hall of Fame plaques. Established in 1987.

• 15665 • Pacemaker Award
Recognizes general excellence of newspapers, yearbooks, newsmagazines, and literary magazines. Awarded annually.

• 15666 •
National School Public Relations Association
Richard D. Bagin APR, Exec.Dir.
15948 Derwood Rd.
Rockville, MD 20855-2123
Phone: (301)519-0496
Fax: (301)519-0494
E-mail: nspra@nspra.org
Home Page: http://www.nspra.org

• 15667 • Gold Medallion Award
To recognize excellence in educational public relations programs. Entries may come from public and private schools; vocational-technical schools beyond 12th grade; two-year community colleges; state/national education groups; and public relations agencies, consultants, or private businesses serving such schools and colleges. Application deadline is April 14. Winners receive gold medallions at the NSPRA Annual Seminar. Awarded annually. Established in 1982.

• 15668 • Golden Achievement Award
To recognize exemplary public relations activities, programs, and projects. All public and private schools and institutions are eligible. Programs must demonstrate analysis, planning, execution, and communication, and evaluation. Entries must have been underway or completed during the 12 months preceding the program. Application deadline is March 17. Winners receive certificates, letters of commendation sent to their district or agency, and their names listed in an NSPRA publication. Awarded annually.

• 15669 • Publications and Electronic Media Awards
To recognize outstanding education publications and electronic media programs - radio/TV/cable, Internet web sites, slide productions, and videotape. The contest is open to all public or private schools or districts, including special schools such as vocational-technical institutes; regional or county education service agencies;

education agencies; and private businesses serving as partners with those organizations. Prizes are awarded according to type of publication, type, and size of institution. Application deadline is March 17. Award of Excellence winners receive a plaque, and winners of Merit and Honorable Mention awards receive certificates. Awarded annually. Established in 1972. Formerly: Annual School and College Publications Contest.

• 15670 •
National School Transportation Association
John Corr, Pres.
113 S West St., 4th Fl.
Alexandria, VA 22314
Phone: (703)684-3200
Toll-Free: 800-222-NSTA
Fax: (703)684-3212
E-mail: info@yellowbuses.com
Home Page: http://www.yellowbuses.org

• 15671 • **Distinguished Service Award**
Recognizes contractors who offer excellence of service. Either a state contractors association or an individual NSTA member may nominate a candidate. Nominations must be received by March 1. One award is presented at the annual convention. Established in 1992.

• 15672 • **Golden Merit Award**
To honor excellence of service, safety, and outstanding demonstration of community responsibility by NSTA-member private school bus contractors throughout the United States. Individuals and companies are eligible. Nominees must be both members in good standing of the Association and a school bus contractor for at least five consecutive years. Awards are based on recommendations from the superintendents of schools, insurance carriers, and state Directors of Pupil Transportation. Nominations must be received by April 15. A commendation on parchment is awarded annually at the Association's National Convention. No more than 10 awards are presented in any given year. Established in 1969.

• 15673 • **Hall of Fame Award**
To recognize excellence in long-term efforts on behalf of pupil transportation. Nominees must be both members in good standing of the Association and school bus contractors for at least 10 consecutive years and be members of the state contractors association or have met these requirements at the time of leaving the pupil transportation industry. Either a state contractors association or an individual NSTA contractor member may nominate candidates. Awarded annually at the Association's National Convention. No more than three awards are presented in any given year. Established in 1992.

• 15674 •
National Schools Committee for Economic Education
John E. Donnelly Ph.D., Exec.Dir.
330 E 70th St., Ste. 5J
New York, NY 10021-8641
Phone: (212)535-9534
Fax: (212)535-4167
E-mail: info@nscee.org
Home Page: http://www.nscee.org

• 15675 • **Certificate for Outstanding Service**
Award of recognition. Educators are eligible.

• 15676 •
National Science Foundation
Dr. Arden L. Bement Jr., Dir.
4201 Wilson Blvd.
Arlington, VA 22230
Phone: (703)292-5111
Toll-Free: 800-877-8339
Fax: (703)292-9089
E-mail: info@nsf.gov
Home Page: http://www.nsf.gov

• 15677 • **Vannevar Bush Award**
Recognizes outstanding contribution toward the welfare of mankind and the nation. Applicants must be senior statesperson and a U.S. citizen. Applicants must also meet two of the following criteria: have made distinguished public service activity through science and technology; pioneered the exploration, charting and settlement of new frontiers in science, technology, education, and public service; shown leadership and creativity that inspired careers in science and technology; contributed to the welfare of the Nation and mankind through activities in science and technology; or shown leadership and creativity that has assisted in history making advances in the Nation's science, technology, and education. A bronze medal is awarded annually. A letter of nomination, curriculum vitae, and brief citation summarizing the nominee's contributions must be submitted. Nominations remain active for three years, including the year of nomination. Established in 1980 to honor Dr. Vannevar Bush, a scientist, adviser to presidents and a force behind the establishment of the Foundation. Contact Susan E. Fannoney at the above address for additional details.

• 15678 • **National Medal of Technology**
The highest honor bestowed by the President of the United States to America's leading innovators. First awarded in 1985, the medal is given annually to individuals, teams, or companies for accomplishments in the innovation, development, commercialization, and management of technology, as evidenced by the establishment of new or significantly improved products, processes, or services. In the case of individual winners, U.S. Citizenship is a requirement, companies must be more than fifty percent owned by American Citizens and Members of the National Medal of Technology Steering and Evaluation committees cannot receive the award until at least three years after their service has ended. All finalists will be subject to a full FBI security check, and all discoveries may be used in making the final consideration for the award. The original and 14 copies of the entire nomination package must be submitted. Each nomination package must be contained in no larger than one and a half-inch, three-ring binder. The cover of the binder will be a page one of the nomination form, and the name of the nominee must be printed across the binder spine. Nomination packages not meeting these specifications will not be considered. At least six letters of recommendation or support must accompany the submission. Letters should be from individuals who have first-hand knowledge of the cited achievements. These letters should be addressed to the nominator or the director of the National Medal of Technology. The letters must be copied on blue paper and included in each of the 14 copies of the nomination package. The original letters should be included with the original nomination package. Original letters are not required with resubmission. All information considered proprietary should be marked, and they will be provided confidentially to the extent allowed by the Freedom of Information Act. The nominations are accepted in the categories of Product and Process Innovation, Technology Transfer, Advanced Manufacturing Technology, Technology Management, Human Resources Development, and Environmental Technology, and all nominations should be sent by express or registered mail to: Director, National Medal and Technology, Technology Administration, Room 4226, U.S. Department of Commerce, 1401 Constitution Ave. NW, Washington D.C. 20230.

• 15679 • **President's National Medal of Science**
To honor individuals deserving of special recognition by reason of their outstanding contributions to knowledge in the physical, biological, mathematical, engineering, social, or behavioral sciences. A 12-member committee of scientists and engineers are selected by the President of the U.S. to administer the award. Selection is based on the impact of the work; effect of achievement on future scientific thought; service and contribution to science; peer recognition; contribution to industry and innovation; influence on education. Applicants must be U.S. citizen or permanent residents who have applied for citizenship. Nomination deadline is November 30. Established in 1959.

• 15680 • **Public Service Award**
Recognizes increased public understanding of science or engineering. People or organizations, including companies, organizations, or corporations are eligible. U.S. Government members are not eligible. Selection is based on increased public understanding of the processes of science and engineering through scientific discovery, innovation, and communication to the public; encouragement of others to help raise the public understanding of science and technology; promotion of engagement of scientists and engineers in public outreach and scientific literacy; contributions to the development of broad science and engineering policy and it support; influence and encouragement in the next generation of scientists, and engineers; achievement of recognition outside of the nominee's area of spe-

cialization; and the fostering of awareness of science and technology among broad segments of the population. A summary of the nominees activities must be submitted by fax or mail. Email nominations can not be accepted. Nomination deadline is September 30. Established in 1996. Contact Susan E. Fannoney at the above address for additional details.

• 15681 • **Alan T. Waterman Award**
Recognizes an outstanding research in the fields of science or engineering. Applicants must be young researchers 35 years old or younger; U.S. citizens or permanent residents; and not more than 7 years beyond receipt of the Ph.D. degree by December 31 of the year in which they are nominated. Selection is based on originality, innovation, and impact on the field. A medal and a grant of $500,000 over a three year period are awarded annually. Grant must be used for advanced study in the mathematical, physical, medical, biological, engineering, social or other sciences at the institution of the recipient's choice. Established in 1975. Contact Susan E. Fannoney at the above address for additional details.

• 15682 •
National Science Teachers Association
Michelle Butler, Mgr.
1840 Wilson Blvd.
Arlington, VA 22201-3000
Phone: (703)243-7100
Toll-Free: 800-722-6782
Fax: (703)243-3924
E-mail: mbutler@nsta.org
Home Page: http://www.nsta.org

• 15683 • **Robert H. Carleton Award**
Recognizes outstanding contributions to science education. K-college-level science educations who are NSTA members are eligible. Contribution must be on a national level. $5000, a medallion, a formal citation, and expenses to attend the NSTA's National Convention are awarded annually. Funding provided by Dow Chemical Co.. Application deadline is November 15. Guidelines and nomination form are available at http://www.nsta.org/programs/carleton.shtml.

• 15684 • **CIBA Specialty Chemicals Exemplary Middle Level and High School Principal Awards**
Recognizes leadership in the development, implementation, and maintenance of outstanding science program. Full-time middle level and high school principals are eligible. Selection is based on staff development support; promotion of a positive relationship between the program and the community; and the advocacy of the development of skills and attitudes toward science among children and teachers. Application deadline is October 15th. A monetary prize of $2,000, up to $500 for travel expenses to attend the National Convention, and a one-year NSTA membership are awarded annually. Established in 1979. Sponsored by the CIBA Specialty Chemicals Education Foundation. Formerly: (1997) CIBA-GEIGY Exemplary Middle Level and High School Science Teaching Award.

• 15685 • **CIBA Specialty Chemicals Exemplary Middle Level and High School Science Teaching Awards**
To recognize exemplary science teaching performance. Full-time middle level and high school science teachers are eligible. Selection is based on creative use of teaching materials; design and use of innovative teaching plans; and development and implementation of department, school, or school-community programs. Application deadline is October 15. A monetary prize of $2,000, up to $500 for travel expenses to attend the National Convention, and a one-year NSTA membership are awarded annually to one middle school and one high school teacher. Established in 1975. Sponsored by the CIBA Specialty Chemicals Education Foundation.

• 15686 • **Craftsman/NSTA Young Inventors Awards**
Encourages the combination of creativity and imagination with science, technology, and mechanical ability to invent or modify an existing tool. 2-8 grade students attending school in the United States or one of its Territories are eligible. Students must work independently in conceiving and designing the award. Guidance from a teacher-advisor, parent or significant adult in the actual development of the tool is allowed. A completed form, signed by the student parent, and teacher-advisor, inventor's log, 3-7 pages, a diagram of the tool, and a photograph of the student demonstrating the tool must be submitted. Two national awards consisting of a $10,000 United States Series EE Savings Bond are awarded. 10 national finalists awards of $5000 United States Series EE Savings Bonds are also awarded. In addition the winning teachers and schools receive prizes. Regional Savings Bonds prizes are also given. Every student entering will receive a certificate and a small gift. Application deadline is March 14. Late or faxed entries will not be accepted. Additional information is available at http://www.nsta.org/programs/craftsman.

• 15687 • **Distinguished Informal Science Education Award**
Recognizes contribution to the advancement of science education in an informal or nontraditional setting, such as a science-technology center, museum, or community science center. NSTA members who are not classroom teachers are eligible. A formal citation, three nights' hotel accommodation, and $200 toward expenses to attend the NSTA National Convention are awarded annually. Application deadline is October 15.

• 15688 • **Distinguished Service to Science Education Award**
Recognizes the advancement of science education and teaching. NSTA members showing long-term dedication to science, including leadership and scholarly endeavor, are eligible. The number of awards given each year varies per judge. Formal citation, three nights' hotel accommodation, and $500 toward travel expenses to attend the National Convention are awarded annually. Application deadline is October 15th. Established in 1967.

• 15689 • **Distinguished Teaching Award**
Recognizes contributions to the field of science teaching. NSTA members who teach at any level between kindergarten and college are eligible. The number of awards given each year varies per judge. A formal citation, three nights' hotel accommodation, and $500 for travel are awarded annually. Application deadline is October 15th. Established in 1987.

• 15690 • **Gustav Ohaus Award for Innovations in Science Teaching**
To encourage and honor science teachers who have demonstrated continual innovation in one of the following areas: new curriculum design, instructional methods or techniques, unique organization, administrative patterns, new approach to laboratory activities, or other enhanced learning activity for students. Science teachers in elementary, middle school, and high school levels are eligible. Application deadline is October 15. A monetary prize of $1,500 and travel expenses of $1,500 are awarded annually. Sponsored by the Ohaus Corp.

• 15691 • ***Science Screen Report* Award**
To recognize a teacher who has creatively used commercially available films or videotapes in the development of a unit or theme in science. K-12 science teachers are eligible. A monetary prize of $1,000 and up to $500 for travel expenses to attend the NSTA National Convention are awarded annually. Established in 1986. Sponsored by *Science Screen Report*, Inc.

• 15692 • **Science Teaching Award**
Recognizes positive impact on students, schools, and/or community. K-12 classroom science teachers are eligible. $10,000 and expenses to attend the NSTA's National Convention are awarded annually. Two finalists also receive expenses to attend the convention. Sponsored by the Shell Oil Co. Application deadline is November 15. Nomination form and requirements are available at http://www.nsta.org/programs/shelloil.shtml.

• 15693 • **Toshiba/NSTA ExploraVision Awards**
Encourages students to work as teams using imagination along with tools of science to create new technology. Full-time K-12 grade students who are United States or Canadian citizens living in the United States, U.S. Territories, or Canada are eligible. Entries can be made in the categories of Primary Level (Grades K-3); Upper Elementary Level (Grades 4-6); Middle Level (Grades 7-9); and High School Level (Grades 10 -12). Projects submitted must simulate a research and development team of two to four members identifying a current technology and making possible enhancements to it. Each team must submit a project description, including an overview of the present technology selected, the history of the technology, the team's vision for

the technology's future, breakthrough needed to make the vision come true, and consequences of the new technology on society. The following awards are given in each grade level category: Four student-member first-place teams receive a U.S. EE Savings Bonds worth $10,000 on maturity; four second-place teams receive U.S. EE Savings Bonds worth $5,000 at maturity; (Canadian winners receive Canadian Bond worth the equivalent of the above U.S. Bonds); and 24 regional winning teams receive a Toshiba laptop computer. All national finalist team members and a parent or guardian also receives travel to the Awards ceremony. Coaches and mentors receive travel expenses to the Awards Ceremony. Awarded annually.

• 15694 • **Toyota Tapestry Grant**
Encourages the development of science projects that can be implemented in a school district over a one-year period. K-12 level science teachers are eligible. Selection criteria is based on creativity, level of risk-taking, visionary quality, and novelty of presentation of the subject of science. 50 grants of up to $10,000 each and at least 20 mini-grants of $2500 are awarded.

• 15695 •
National Scrabble Association
John D. Williams Jr., Exec.Dir.
PO Box 700
403 Front St.
Greenport, NY 11944
Phone: (631)477-0033
Fax: (631)477-0294
E-mail: info@scrabble-assoc.com
Home Page: http://www.scrabble-assoc.com

Formerly: Scrabble Players.

• 15696 • **National Scrabble Championship**
To recognize the best Scrabble game players in North America. Members who have played in at least one rated tournament are eligible to compete. Numerous awards are presented, including: $25,000 to the grand prize winner, monetary prizes for the first- through sixth-place winners in each of six divisions; additional prizes for the seventh- through tenth-place winners in certain divisions; awards for the highest rounds and highest games; highest placing senior; highest play by someone 18 years or under; and others. Held annually. Co-sponsored by Milton Bradley Co.

• 15697 •
National Sculpture Society
Gwen Pier, Exec.Dir.
237 Park Ave.
New York, NY 10017
Phone: (212)764-5645
Fax: (212)764-5651
E-mail: nss1893@aol.com
Home Page: http://www.nationalsculpture.org

• 15698 • **Annual Exhibition Awards**
To recognize works at the annual exhibition. Open to all sculptors who are U.S. citizens or are working in the United States. Dozens of awards are presented, including the Gold, Silver, and Bronze medals for sculpture; Maurice B. Hexter Prize; Joyce and Elliot Liskin Foundation Award; John Cavanaugh Memorial Prize; Agop Agopoff Memorial Prize; Margaret Hexter Prize; Edith H. and Richmond Proskauer Prize; Bedi-Makky Foundry Prize; Barrett-Colea Foundry Prize; Joel Meisner Foundry Award; Leonard J. Meiselman Prize; Therese and Edwin H. Richard Memorial Prize; Tallix Foundry Prize; Pietro and Alfrieda Montana Memorial Prize; C. Percival Dietsch Sculpture Prize; Mildred Victor Memorial Prize; John Spring Art Founder Award; Lindsay Morris Memorial Prize; and Mrs. Louis Bennett Prize. Awarded annually.

• 15699 • **Alex J. Ettl Grant**
To recognize a figurative or realist sculptor who has demonstrated a commitment to sculpting and outstanding ability in his or her life's work. Professional members of the National Sculpture Society are not eligible. An unrestricted monetary grant of $4,000 is awarded annually. Application deadline is January 10. Established in 1988.

• 15700 • **Henry Hering Medal**
For recognition of outstanding collaboration between architect, owner, and sculptor in the distinguished use of sculpture in an architectural project. For the medal, not only are fine architectural projects sought, but the sculpture must be figurative, representational, or any style in which the object is recognizable. Nominations for the award must be in the form of portfolios describing the nature of the project and must include photographs clearly showing the building or buildings, the site of sculpture, and close-up photos of the sculpture itself. The deadline for submissions is January 10. Presented annually. The winning entry receives three medals - one each for architect, owner, and sculptor - and a hand-lettered citation.

• 15701 • **Young Sculptor Awards**
To recognize young and emerging sculptors who demonstrate excellence in creating figurative or realist work. Any young or emerging sculptor currently residing in the United States is eligible. The Young Sculptor Awards are presented on the first day of the National Sculpture Competition. They include: Dexter Jones Award ($1,000) for sculpture in bas-relief; Roger T. Williams Prize ($750) for an expressive figurative work outside the classical tradition; Edward Fenno Hoffman Prize ($350) for uplifting work; and the Gloria Medal, a medal designed by C. Paul Jennewein for a meritorious body of work. Held annually. Established in 1978. Co-sponsored by the Lyme Academy College of Fine Arts and the Pennsylvania Academy of Fine Arts. Formerly: ; .

• 15702 •
National Security Council
Stephen Hadley, Advisor
The White House
1600 Pennsylvania Ave. NW
Washington, DC 20500
Phone: (202)456-1414
Fax: (202)456-2461
E-mail: president@whitehouse.gov
Home Page: http://www.whitehouse.gov/nsc

• 15703 • **National Security Medal**
To recognize individuals without regard to nationality, including members of the armed forces of the United States, for distinguished achievement or outstanding contribution on or after July 26, 1947, in the field of intelligence relating to the national security. This contribution may consist of either exceptionally meritorious service performed in a position of high responsibility or of an act of valor requiring personal courage of a high degree and complete disregard of personal safety. Recommendations may be submitted to the Executive Secretary of the National Security Council by any individual having personal knowledge of the facts of the exceptionally meritorious conduct or act of valor. A medal is awarded by the President of the United States, or, under regulations approved by him, by such person or persons as he may designate. A medal and a monetary award of $3,000 are awarded when merited. Established in 1953.

• 15704 •
National Shellfisheries Association
David Bushek, Treas.
PO Box 302
VIMS Eastern Shore Lab.
Accomac, VA 23301
Phone: (757)787-2198
Fax: (757)787-5831
E-mail: nlewis@dmv.com
Home Page: http://www.shellfish.org

• 15705 • **David Wallace Award**
To recognize an individual whose actions most demonstrate the principles and actions concerned with programs in shellfisheries, aquaculture, and conservation. Members are eligible. A plaque is awarded when merited. Established in 1982.

• 15706 •
National Soccer Coaches Association of America
James Sheldon, Exec.Dir.
6700 Squibb Rd., Ste. 215
Mission, KS 66202-3252
Phone: (913)362-1747
Toll-Free: 800-458-0678
Fax: (913)362-3439
E-mail: info@nscaa.com

• 15707 • **All-America Awards**
To recognize outstanding male and female scholar-athletes. The High School Scholar All-America Award is given to a high school senior with a 3.75 grade point average who has

excelled in soccer. The College Scholar All-America Award is awarded to a college junior or senior with a 3.3 grade point average who is not only an excellent soccer player, but is also a starter at least 50 percent of the time. Nominations by soccer coaches who are members of the NSCAA are accepted until October 28. Awarded annually. Established in 1946.

• 15708 • Coach of the Year Award
To recognize the outstanding coach of the year, both men and women. Seven awards are presented on a national level for college, junior college, high school and youth. National winners receive round trip airfare to the Awards Banquet, and a plaque. Regional awards are presented as follows: college, high school, and youth awards, and each receives a plaque. Awarded annually. Established in 1973. Sponsored by Adidas.

• 15709 • Honor Award
To recognize long and devoted service to the game of soccer. Coaches, administrators, officials, or other individuals, excluding active players, are eligible. An engraved trophy is awarded annually. Established in 1942.

• 15710 • Letter of Commendation
To recognize persons, other than players, who have demonstrated exemplary service or contribution to the NSCAA or to the game of soccer in general. Awarded annually. Established in 1956.

• 15711 •
National Society, Daughters of the American Revolution
Linda Tinker Watkins, Pres.Gen.
1776 D St. NW
Washington, DC 20006-5303
Phone: (202)628-1776
Phone: (202)628-4780
Fax: (202)879-3252
E-mail: feedback@dar.org
Home Page: http://www.dar.org

• 15712 • Outstanding Junior Member Contest
To recognize DAR Junior Members between the ages of 18 and 35 who have contributed to DAR work, and promoted historic, educational, and patriotic ideals through community service. The national winner is presented at the Continental Congress of the National Society each April. Established in 1963.

• 15713 • Outstanding Teacher of American History
To recognize an outstanding teacher in the field of American history (and related fields, such as social studies, government, and citizenship) in public, private, and parochial schools, grades 6-12. Teachers providing outstanding service in stimulating understanding of American History, thereby encouraging a spirit of patriotism and loyal support of the United States and its constitutional government, are eligible. Nominations may be submitted by January 15. A monetary award of $3,000 is presented to the national winner at the Continental Congress of the National Society each April. Established in 1983.

• 15714 •
National Society for Histotechnology
Vincent Della Speranza, Pres.
4201 Northview Dr., Ste. 502
Bowie, MD 20716-2604
Phone: (301)262-6221
Fax: (301)262-9188
E-mail: histo@nsh.org
Home Page: http://www.nsh.org

• 15715 • Educational Scholarships
To assist students who are pursuing advanced education and knowledge within the profession of histotechnology and/or actively working toward academic status that may provide eligibility to take the Histotechnologist (HTL) Certification Examination. The awards committee chooses the recipient of each scholarship based on the sincere effort of the applicant and not necessarily upon academic merit. Five $1,000 educational scholarships are awarded each year: Dezna C. Sheehan Memorial Educational Scholarship, Robert A. Clark Memorial Educational Scholarship (sponsored by Sakura Finetek, USA, Inc.), Leonard Noble Educational Scholarship (sponsored by Cardinal Health), Richard-Allan Educational Scholarship (sponsored by Richard-Allan Scientific), and Fisher Diagnostics/Fisher Healthcare Educational Scholarship. Awarded annually.

• 15716 • William J. Hacker Memorial Award
For recognition of the best scientific paper or presentation of a scientific paper relating to microwave technology. A monetary award of $500 and a plaque are awarded annually. Established in 1984. Sponsored by Hacker Instruments, Inc., Fairfield, NJ.

• 15717 • Histotechnologist of the Year Award
To recognize the histologic technician/histotechnologist who best exemplifies the qualities of dedication and service to the profession of histotechnology. Such a person is not confined to any age group. Their dedication may be reflected in a variety of ways, but they are generally recognized as having provided an example to members of NSH. Nominations (normally by regions) for this award should be sent to the chairperson of the awards committee. Nominees must be current members of NSH, with a membership in excess of one calendar year. A grant of $1,000 is awarded annually. Sponsored by Thermo Electron Corp.

• 15718 • Lee G. Luna Foreign Travel Scholarship
To provide for a scholarship to support costs to travel, attend, or study abroad (outside the USA). The applicant/nominee must be an NSH member who has been active for at least two consecutive years immediately prior to application/nomination and whose primary job description is the performance of histopathologic techniques. A scholarship of $3,000 and an inscribed copy of Mr. Luna's book entitled *Histopathologic Methods and Color Atlas of Special Stains and Tissue Artifacts* are awarded annually. Sponsored by Surgipath Medical Industries Inc.

• 15719 • J. B. McCormick, M.D. Award
For recognition of outstanding and exceptional service to the Society. Selection of the recipient for this award is made by the awards committee in consultation with Dr. J. B. McCormick, the award's sponsor. The award, presented when merited, consists of a functioning replica of an 1800 Liberkuhn Compass Microscope and an eight-book boxed set of *The Science Heritage Library*.

• 15720 • Newsletter of the Year Award
For recognition of the state newsletter that best satisfies the following criteria: reflects state, regional, and national news; benefits the histology laboratory and is fully referenced (some articles should originate from the state); has an attractive format; and edited so that all entries are clear and to the point. A monetary award of $500 is awarded annually. Sponsored by Hacker Instruments.

• 15721 • Rosemary and Donald Ostermeier Memorial Award
To recognize an individual who best embodies the qualities of dedication and devotion to their patients, profession, co-workers, staff, and place of employment. Nominees must be certified in histology and be current members of NSH, with membership of at least five years prior to nomination. A monetary prize of $500 and a plaque are awarded annually.

• 15722 • Student Scholarships
To recognize deserving students in approved schools of histotechnology. Academic ability and financial need are the main criteria for selecting each recipient. Three $500 student scholarships are awarded each year: Irwin S. Lerner Student Scholarship (sponsored by Thermo Electron Corp.), Sigma Diagnostics Student Scholarship (sponsored by Sigma Diagnostics Inc.), and Sakura Finetek Student Scholarship (sponsored by Sakura Finetek U.S.A. Inc.). Awarded annually.

• 15723 •
National Society for Park Resources
Steven R. Neu, Pres.
% National Recreation and Park Association
22377 Belmont Ridge Rd.
Ashburn, VA 20148
Phone: (703)858-0784
Fax: (703)858-0794
E-mail: info@npra.org
Home Page: http://www.nrpa.org/content/default.aspx?documentId=529

• 15724 • Best of *Grist* Awards
For recognition of the best contributions to Park Practice Program's *Grist* publication. Three monetary prizes and certificates are conferred annually at the NSPR Banquet held at the time

of the National Recreation and Park Association Congress. Established in 1952.

• 15725 • William Penn Mott, Jr. Awards Program

For recognition of outstanding accomplishments in the field of parks and recreation, and for service to the society. The two award categories are: Award for Excellence and Award for Meritorious Service. Nominations must be made by active members of NSPR by July 1. A laminated certificate on a plaque is awarded annually. Established in 1971 in honor of the Golden Anniversary Year of the National Conference on State Parks. Formerly: Founders Award Program.

• 15726 • National Student Award for Excellence

For recognition of scholastic excellence among undergraduate students pursuing study related to park and outdoor recreation resource management. Certificates are awarded annually at the NSPR. Banquet held at the time of the National Recreation and Park Association Congress.

• 15727 •
National Society of Artists
Adelyn Cooper, Pres.
PO Box 1885
Dickinson, TX 77539-1885
Phone: (281)334-0645
E-mail: thecoopers@whiteserv.com
Home Page: http://www.nsartists.org

• 15728 • National Society of Artists Awards

To recognize excellence in the field of fine arts, including painting, drawing, sculpture, and photography. Recipients must be at least 18 years of age and residents of the continental U.S. or Canada. Each year, two shows are held: the Open Juried Show and the Membership Show. Numerous awards are presented in a variety of categories at each show. Established in 1985 by Gay Paratore-Zarzana.

• 15729 •
National Society of Arts and Letters
Barbara H. Branscum, Pres.
4227 46th St., NW
Washington, DC 20016
Phone: (202)363-5443
Fax: (202)686-8287
E-mail: summs@ix.netcom.com
Home Page: http://www.arts-nsal.org

• 15730 • Estelle Campbell Award

Established to recognize Estelle Campbell, a long time member and generous benefactor. Awarded to the second place winner.

• 15731 • Catherine A. M. Cavanaugh Award

Designed to be given in the literature category. Established in the name of the writer who is a loyal, long time member of NSAL.

• 15732 • Mary Perry Fife Memorial Award

A memorial award given in the category of dance.

• 15733 • National Society of Arts and Letters First Place Award

Established in memory of Mollie Davis Nicholson and Francesca Falk Miller Nielson, founders of the Society who established its perpetual financial support for the recognition of gifted young American artists. An award of $10,000 is given annually.

• 15734 • Mollie Davis Nicholson Award

Contributed by Dorothy Nicholson Stabell in memory of her mother.

• 15735 • Dorothy and Bruce Strong Award

Contributed by Dorothy and Bruce Strong.

• 15736 •
National Society of Biomedical Equipment Technicians
% Association for the Advancement of Medical Instrumentation
1110 Glebe Rd. Ste. 220
Arlington, VA 22201-4795
Phone: (703)525-4890
Toll-Free: 800-332-2264
Fax: (703)276-0793
Home Page: http://www.aami.org

• 15737 • SBET/Renshaw-Heilman BMET of the Year Award

To recognize a biomedical equipment technician who exhibits individual dedication, achievement, and excellence in the field of biomedical equipment technology. Individuals employed in the biomedical field and involved in local, state, or national organizations relating to biomedical technology are eligible. Nominations must be received by March 1. A monetary award of $1,000 and an engraved plaque are awarded annually at the AAMI Annual Meeting & Exposition. Established in 1990 with the support of Renshaw-Heilman and Associates. Sponsored by the Replacement Parts Industries, Inc.

• 15738 •
National Society of Insurance Premium Auditors
Brad L. Feldman MPA, Exec.Dir.
PO Box 1896
Columbus, OH 43216-1896
Phone: (614)221-9266
Toll-Free: 888-846-7472
Fax: (614)221-2335
E-mail: nsipa@nsipa.org
Home Page: http://www.nsipa.org

• 15739 • Distinguished Graduate Award in Premium Auditing

For recognition of achievement of the highest grade average in the national examinations leading to the Associate in Premium Auditing Program of the Insurance Institute of America. A monetary award of $500 and a plaque are presented annually. Established in 1982 by the Insurance Institute of America.

• 15740 • Betty Gerdes Distinguished Service Award

To recognize a member for special efforts in furthering the goals of the Society and increasing the professionalism of insurance premium auditing. Nomination deadline is March 15. A plaque is awarded annually. Established in 1979.

• 15741 •
National Society of Newspaper Columnists
Luenna H. Kim, Exec.Dir.
1345 Fillmore St., Ste. 507
San Francisco, CA 94115
Phone: (415)563-5636
Fax: (415)563-5403
E-mail: director@columnists.com
Home Page: http://www.columnists.com

• 15742 • Column Writing Contest

For recognition of outstanding daily or weekly newspaper columnists in the fields of general interest, humor, notes/items, and online columns. Individuals must write a weekly or daily column for a newspaper, and may be staff, syndicated, self-syndicated, or contributing. Members and nonmembers may submit entries by March 3. Cash prizes are awarded to first, second, and third place winners each year. Established in 1974 by Richard Des Ruisseaux.

• 15743 •
National Society of Painters in Casein and Acrylic
Douglas Wiltraut, Pres.
969 Catasauqua Rd.
Whitehall, PA 18052
Phone: (610)264-7472
E-mail: psychoanalyze@softhome.net
Home Page: http://www.bright.net/~paddy-o/art/nspca.htm

• 15744 • NSPCA Annual Exhibition

To recognize outstanding works of art at the Society's annual exhibition. Approximately 20 monetary awards and medals are awarded annually. Established in 1954.

• 15745 •
National Society of Professional Engineers
Kathryn A. Gray Jr., Pres.
1420 King St.
Alexandria, VA 22314
Phone: (703)684-2800
Toll-Free: 888-285-6773
Fax: (703)836-4875
E-mail: memserv@nspe.org
Home Page: http://www.nspe.org

• 15746 • Distinguished Service Award

To recognize members for exceptional technical contributions to the engineering profession, and for their contributions to their communities and to NSPE. The nomination deadline is January

31. The NSPE Honor Awards Committee selects the recipient. A plaque is awarded at the annual meeting. Established in 1972.

• 15747 • Federal Engineer of the Year Award

To provide recognition for the accomplishments of engineers who serve the federal government. Any federal agency is eligible to participate if it employs at least 50 engineers worldwide. Any individual presently engaged in the practice of engineering either as a manager or technical employee and who is an engineer by education (accredited engineering degree or state engineering license - P.E.) may be nominated. The award is judged primarily on engineering achievements, as well as on educational and collegiate accomplishments, professional and technical society participation, civic and humanitarian activities, awards or honors received, and registration and continuing competence during the last three years. Judging is performed by a select panel appointed by NSPE. The deadline for nominations is February 1. Plaques are awarded annually. Established in 1980. Co-sponsored by Professional Engineers in Government, a division of NSPE.

• 15748 • New Product Award

To stimulate and recognize the full spectrum of benefits that come from the research and engineering of new products. Nominations are grouped according to size of manufacturing company, with selected winners in four employment categories: small, medium, large, and mega-sized. Judging is based on the following criteria: economic contribution, including sales and number of jobs created; ingenuity in use of engineering principles and materials; and improved function in savings, productivity, energy, and safety. The entry deadline is February 15. An engraved plaque is presented during the annual meeting. Established in 1983. Co-sponsored by Professional Engineers in Industry, a division of NSFE.

• 15749 • NSPE Award

This, the highest award of NSPE, is given to an engineer who has made outstanding contributions to the engineering profession, public welfare, and/or humankind. Any engineer of recognized standing who is a citizen of the United States, preferably licensed, is eligible for nomination. Nominations may be made by any member in good standing but must be approved by the candidate's state society. Preference is given to candidates who have consistently promoted the social and professional interests of the engineer. The nomination deadline is January 31. The NSPE Honor Awards Committee selects the recipient. An engraved bronze plaque mounted on a walnut base is awarded at the annual meeting. Established in 1949.

• 15750 • PEI Distinguished Service Award

To recognize an individual who has made an outstanding contribution of national scope to advance the causes of the individual engineer in industry or Professional Engineers in Industry (NSPE-PEI) Practice Division. Major consideration is given to the manner and extent to which engineers in industry have been enriched as a result of the nominee's influence and contributions. The recipient need not be an NSPE member, an engineer, nor be in the engineering profession. The nomination deadline is January 1. An engraved plaque is presented at the NSPE annual meeting. Established in 1972.

• 15751 • PEPP Chairman's Award

To recognize a person or organization that has contributed to the engineering profession, the practice of consulting professional engineers, and the public understanding of the role that the professional engineer in private practice plays in advancing the quality of life. Selection is by the PEPP chairman. Individuals or organizations recognized for efforts, commitment, and dedication that impact the consulting engineering profession are eligible. The award is presented at the NSPE winter meeting.

• 15752 • PEPP Merit Award

To recognize PEPP members who have made outstanding contributions to the practice division. All PEPP members, except current officers of NSPE/PEPP or members of the awards committee, are eligible. Nominations may be made by a PEPP division, PEPP officers, committee chairmen, or an individual member of PEPP. Nominations must be received by February 1. A plaque is presented at the annual meeting of the PEPP Board of Governors.

• 15753 • Private Practice Professional Development Award

To recognize engineering firms for outstanding contributions to the advancement and improvement of the engineering profession through its employment policies and practices. A private practice employer is considered to be a for-profit firm or branch office of a firm whose primary function is to provide engineering design or consulting services for infrastructure, facilities, or processes to clients. Excluded are firms that provide both design and construction services, wholly owned firms supplying design services to a single parent organization, and research and development firms. Criteria include engineering personnel/licensure, recruitment, employment, professional development, and special employment practices. The nomination deadline is April 30. A silver revere bowl is awarded at the annual meeting. Established in 1968.

• 15754 • Professional Development Awards

To recognize employers in industry, private practice, and construction. Recipients in each category are those judged to have the most outstanding record of advancement and improvement of the engineering profession by the development and use of forward-looking engineering employment practices in accordance with highest professional standards. Nominations may be originated by local chapters of practice divisions but must be submitted by state societies. Each state society may submit only one nomination per year in each employment category. The NSPE Professional Development Awards Committee selects the award recipients. The nomination deadline is December 1. The award is a bronze plaque mounted on wooden shields, engraved with the type/category of the award, the name of the winning company/institution/agency and the reasons for its selection. Presented each year at the annual meeting. Established in 1960.

• 15755 • QBS Award

To recognize the public agencies that make exemplary use of the QBS (Qualifications-Based Selection) methods to procure the professional services of consulting engineering firms at the state and local levels. An award is presented in each of two categories: government sector and non-government sector. Nominations are due by November 17. A mounted eagle with brass plate is awarded annually.

• 15756 • Young Engineer of the Year Award

To honor an outstanding young engineer who has made outstanding contributions to the engineering profession and their communities during the early years of their careers. Selection is based on educational and collegiate achievements, professional and technical society activities, civic and humanitarian activities, continuing competence, and engineering achievements. Any licensed (P.E. or E.I.) NSPE member in good standing who is age 35 or under is eligible for nomination. The nomination deadline is January 31. The NSPE Honor Awards Committee selects the recipient. An engraved bronze plaque is presented at the annual meeting. Established in 1970.

• 15757 •

National Society of Professional Surveyors
Patricia A. Canfield, Exec. Administrator
6 Montgomery Village Ave., Ste. 403
Gaithersburg, MD 20879-3546
Phone: (240)632-9716
Fax: (240)632-1321
E-mail: pat.canfield@acsm.net
Home Page: http://www.acsm.net/nsps/index.html

• 15758 • Excellence in Professional Journalism

To encourage and recognize excellence in professional journalism by American Congress on Surveying and Mapping affiliate societies. A plaque is awarded annually in each category. Established in 1982.

• 15759 • Most Interesting Surveying Project of the Year Award

To recognize individuals, companies, governmental units, or state associations having knowledge of interesting projects and the ability to provide documentation of the project, including technical information, releases, photographs, and a record of the personnel and equipment involved. Members of NSPS or affiliates are eligible. The project need not have occurred within the last year. Projects must be submitted by December 31. A Pentax camera, plaque, and 1,000 reprints of the resulting published article are awarded. Sponsored by Pentax Corp.

• 15760 • NSPS Scholarship
To recognize outstanding surveying students and to encourage qualified candidates to pursue an undergraduate degree in surveying. Qualified applicants must be enrolled full-time at an institution with a degree program in surveying. The application deadline is January 1. A monetary award of $1,000 and a certificate are presented to each of two recipients at the ACSM Annual Meeting.

• 15761 • Student Project of the Year Award
To encourage and recognize students who participate, research, and write about surveying projects. Any undergraduate student enrolled in a surveying or surveying related program is eligible for this award. Papers may be submitted by December 31. A plaque, $500 honorarium, and travel and lodging expenses to attend the Spring Convention are awarded annually. Sponsored by C&G Software Systems, Inc.

• 15762 • Surveying Excellence Award
To recognize and honor a person who has performed outstanding service to the development and advancement of the surveying profession. Candidates, who don't necessarily have to be surveyors or members of NSPS or American Congress on Surveying and Mapping (ACSM), must be nominated by an ACSM affiliate section or two NSPS members by December 31. A plaque and $500 honorarium are awarded annually. Sponsored by P.O.B. Publishing Co.

• 15763 •
National Society, Sons of the American Revolution
Roland G. Downing, Pres.Gen.
1000 S 4th St.
Louisville, KY 40203
Phone: (502)589-1776
Fax: (502)589-1671
E-mail: rdowning@udel.edu
Home Page: http://www.sar.org

• 15764 • Bronze Good Citizenship Medal
To recognize minors and adults for noteworthy achievements in their school, community, or state. A bronze medal and certificate are awarded when merited. Established in 1950.

• 15765 • Certificate of Appreciation
To recognize an individual who has rendered notable service to the society. Awarded irregularly. Established in 1984.

• 15766 • Certificate of Distinguished Service
To recognize an individual for outstanding personal service exemplifying the finest American ideals. Awarded irregularly. Established in 1984.

• 15767 • Daughters of Liberty Medal
To recognize women who have rendered outstanding service to the SAR. A bronze medal is awarded irregularly. Established in 1989.

• 15768 • Distinguished Patriot Award
To recognize a United States citizen for outstanding patriotism. Awarded annually. Established in 1987.

• 15769 • Flag Certificate
To recognize and individual or business for display of the United States flag. Awarded irregularly. Established in 1984.

• 15770 • Gold Good Citizenship Medal
To recognize an individual of national prominence for outstanding loyalty to the principles and ideals of the Constitution and Bill of Rights of the United States. A ten-carat gold medal is awarded when merited. Established in 1950.

• 15771 • Heroism Medal
To recognize individuals outside of law enforcement and fire fighting fields who face imminent danger to save another individual. A bronze medal is awarded irregularly. Established in 1988.

• 15772 • International Medal
To recognize foreign dignitaries or a non-citizen of the United States for outstanding service to the world community. A gold medal is presented irregularly. Established in 1992.

• 15773 • Law Enforcement and Fire Safety Commendation Medal
To recognize individuals involved in the fire prevention and fire fighting fields. Given for outstanding service in the line of duty. A bronze medal is awarded irregularly. Established in 1993.

• 15774 • Law Enforcement Commendation Medal
For recognition of exceptional service by police, state troopers, and officers of the court. A gold-filled enamel medal is awarded when merited. Established in 1968.

• 15775 • Liberty Medal
To recognize a member for sponsoring ten new members into the society. A bronze medal is awarded annually to all members who attain this goal. Established in 1987.

• 15776 • Medal of Appreciation
To recognize members of the Daughters of the American Revolution who have rendered outstanding service to the SAR. A gold-filled medal is awarded when merited. Established in 1955.

• 15777 • Meritorious Service Medal
For recognition of outstanding service to the SAR at national, state, or chapter levels. Only members are eligible. Established in 1952.

• 15778 • Minuteman Medal
This, the society's highest award, is given to recognize outstanding service by members to the SAR. As many as six sterling silver medals are awarded annually. Established in 1950.

• 15779 • Outstanding Citizenship Award
To recognize individuals for the highest ideals of character and citizenship. A lapel pin and certificate are awarded irregularly. Established in 1990.

• 15780 • Patriot Medal
For recognition of outstanding service to the SAR at state and local levels. Only members are eligible. Each state is limited to two awards annually. A sterling silver medal is awarded. Established in 1960.

• 15781 • ROTC Medals
To recognize an outstanding cadet at the high school level and college level. The bronze medal is awarded to high school cadets irregularly. The silver medal is awarded to college cadets irregularly. Established in 1954.

• 15782 • Scholarship Contests
To recognize outstanding young people. Three scholarship contests are held: Joseph S. Rumbaugh Historical Oration Contest - open to all sophomore, junior, and senior high school students; Arthur M. and Berdena King Eagle Scout Scholarship - open to Eagle Scouts; and George S. and Stella M. Knight Essay Contest - open to college freshmen and sophomores. The national winners of these programs are announced at the SAR Annual Congress.

• 15783 • Silver Good Citizenship Medal
To recognize outstanding service by an adult to his state or community over a long period of time in several organizations. A sterling silver medal is awarded when merited. Established in 1950.

• 15784 • War Service Medal
To recognize SAR members for service in the United States Armed Forces during war or an emergency recognized by Congress. A certificate and medal are awarded when merited.

• 15785 • Martha Washington Medal
To recognize women who have rendered outstanding service to the society. A gold-filled medal is awarded when merited. Established in 1971.

• 15786 •
National Sojourners
Nelson O. Newcombe, Sec.-Treas.
8301 E Boulevard Dr.
Alexandria, VA 22308-1399
Phone: (703)765-5000
Fax: (703)765-8390
E-mail: nationalsoj@juno.com
Home Page: http://www.nationalsojourners.org

Awards are arranged in alphabetical order below their administering organizations

• 15787 • Sojourners ROTC Awards
To recognize individuals who have most encouraged and demonstrated the ideals of Americanism by deed and/or conduct, and who has demonstrated potential for outstanding leadership. One member of each unit of the Reserve Officer Training Corps (ROTC) or Junior ROTC is awarded with a medal and certificate annually. Established in 1970.

• 15788 •
National Space Club
Rory M. Heydon, Exec.Dir.
2025 M St. NW, Ste. 800
Washington, DC 20036
Phone: (202)973-8661
E-mail: info@spaceclub.org
Home Page: http://www.spaceclub.org

• 15789 • Dr. Robert H. Goddard Scholarship
To stimulate the interest of talented students in the opportunity to advance scientific knowledge through space research and exploration. Applicants must be U.S. citizens, be at least juniors of accredited universities, and have the intention of pursuing undergraduate or graduate studies in science or engineering during the interval of the scholarship. Application deadline is January 6. Each year, a scholarship of $10,000 and travel and lodging expenses to the Goddard Memorial Dinner is awarded. Established in honor of Dr. Robert Goddard, America's rocket pioneer.

• 15790 •
National Speakers Association
Rick Jakle CSP, Pres.
1500 S Priest Dr.
Tempe, AZ 85281
Phone: (480)968-2552
Fax: (480)968-0911
E-mail: info@nsaspeaker.org
Home Page: http://www.nsaspeaker.org

• 15791 • Cavett Award
This, the highest award given by the NSA, is presented to the member whose accomplishments over the years have reflected outstanding credit, respect, honor, and admiration in the NSA and in the speaking profession. Awarded annually. Established in 1973.

• 15792 • Council of Peers Award for Excellence/Speaker Hall of Fame
For recognition of a lifetime of speaking excellence and professionalism. Candidates are judged in seven categories: material, style, experience, delivery, image, professionalism, and communication. The number of new awards each year is limited to five. A statue is awarded annually at the Convention. Established in 1977. Formerly: Continuare Protessus Articulatus Excellare.

• 15793 •
National Speleological Society
B. Scott Fee, Pres.
2813 Cave Ave.
Huntsville, AL 35810-4431
Phone: (256)852-1300
Fax: (256)851-9241
E-mail: nss@caves.org
Home Page: http://www.caves.org

• 15794 • Lew Bicking Award
To recognize an individual member who, through specific actions, has demonstrated a dedication to the thorough exploration and mapping of a cave or group of caves. A monetary award and a certificate are presented annually.

• 15795 • Certificate of Merit
To recognize individuals or organizations for specific accomplishments in cave exploration, study, or conservation. Emphasis is on recent accomplishments. Up to three certificates are awarded annually.

• 15796 • Fellow of the Society
To recognize an individual for service in the field of speleology, whether in research, exploration, conservation, or administration. Emphasis is usually on continued service over a period of time. The total number of fellows is limited to 10 percent of the society membership. Established in 1967.

• 15797 • Group and Grotto Conservation Award
To recognize an individual who has demonstrated an outstanding dedication to the cause of cave conservation and management. A certificate and a monetary award of $100 are presented annually. Established in 1973 to award international organizations; beginning in 1994, the award was presented to individuals.

• 15798 • Peter M. Hauer Spelean History Award
To recognize a member who, over time, has demonstrated outstanding dedication to the conservation of caves. A monetary award and certificate are presented annually. Established in 1979 by friends of Peter M. Hauer and The American Spelean Historical Association.

• 15799 • Honorary Member
To recognize individual contributions to the field of speleology. One life membership in the society is awarded annually.

• 15800 • James G. Mitchell Award
To recognize the best scientific paper presented at any of the sessions of the annual convention by a member (or members) of the Society aged 25 years or younger. A monetary award and a certificate are presented annually. Established in 1969.

• 15801 • Research Grant
A grant is awarded. Inquire for additional information.

• 15802 • William J. Stephenson Award for Outstanding Service
To recognize an individual for outstanding service to speleology and the society. One life membership in the Society is awarded annually.

• 15803 • Ralph W. Stone Graduate Fellowship
To recognize a graduate student on cave-related thesis research. NSS members currently pursing graduate studies anywhere in the world are eligible. A monetary award of $1,700 from the Ralph W. Stone Research Fund is awarded annually at the convention. Established in 1989.

• 15804 •
National Spinal Cord Injury Association
Marcie Roth, Exec.Dir.
6701 Democracy Blvd., Ste. 300-9
Bethesda, MD 20817
Phone: (301)214-4006
Toll-Free: 800-962-9629
Fax: (301)881-9817
E-mail: info@spinalcord.org
Home Page: http://www.spinalcord.org

• 15805 • Elmer C. Bartels Leadership Recognition Award
To recognize individuals who exemplify Bartel's personal philosophy, leadership style, and commitment to the field of improving the lives of individuals with disabilities. To be eligible, an individual must be a person with a disability who meets the following criteria: has been involved in the disability community for a minimum of fifteen years; has made a significant and identifiable contribution on behalf of the disability community in the vocational rehabilitation field and the independent living or disability rights movements; has been recognized in the community as a positive role model; and fosters, nurtures, and encourages potential leaders from the disability community to take on leadership roles in the future. A monetary prize and trophy are awarded annually at a leadership dinner. Established in 1990 in honor of Elmer C. Bartels, Commissioner, Massachusetts Rehabilitation Commission.

• 15806 •
National Sporting Clays Association
Don Snyder, Exec.Dir.
5931 Roft Rd.
San Antonio, TX 78253
Phone: (210)688-3371
Toll-Free: 800-877-5338
Fax: (210)688-3014
E-mail: nssa@nssa-nsca.com
Home Page: http://www.mynsca.com
Formerly: (1995) National Skeet Shooting Association.

• 15807 • World Skeet Shooting Championships
To recognize winners of skeet shooting tournaments in the following categories: (1) 550 high overall; (2) 12 gauge shotshells with 250 clay targets; (3) 20 gauge shotshells with 100 clay targets; (4) 28 gauge shotshells with 100 clay targets; and (5) .410 gauge shotshells with 100 clay targets. In all events, awards for listed winners are of the following description: (1) Champion - Gold medal enhanced with gauge color; (2) Runner-up - Silver medal enhanced with gauge color; (3) Third - Bronze medal enhanced with gauge color; (4) Class First - Gold medal; (5) Class Second - Silver medal; (6) Third, fourth and fifth in class - Bronze medal. Individual Competitions feature the following categories: (1) Industry; (2) Wheelchair; (3) Novice; (4) IMSA; (5) Military; (6) Retired Military; (7) Veteran; (8) Hunter; (9) Lady; (10) Senior; (11) Ducks Unlimited; (12) Sub-Senior; (13) NRA; and (14) Sub-Sub-Senior. Team Competition features the following teams: (1) Family; (2) Military-Civilian Team; (3) Sub-Sub-Senior; (4) Sub-Senior; (5) Senior; (6) Veteran; (7) Military Two-Man Teams; (8) Husband and Wife Team; (9) Two-Man Teams; (10) World Military Five-Man Team; (11) Zone Five-Man Team-12 Ga Only; (12) Five-Man Team; (13) Five-Lady Team; and (14) Five-Man Club - 12 Ga Only. The Championships are held annually.

• 15808 •
National Sports Law Institute
Joseph D. Kearney, Dean
Sensenbrenner Hall
11003 W Wisconsin Ave.
Marquette University Law School
PO Box 1881
Milwaukee, WI 53201-1881
Phone: (414)288-7090
Fax: (414)288-6403
E-mail: matt.mitten@mu.edu
Home Page: http://law.marquette.edu

• 15809 • Master of the Game Award
Honors an individual who has made substantial contributions to the sports industry at the national level and who exemplifies the highest level of professionalism in his or her field. Awarded annually if merited. Established in 1992.

• 15810 • Joseph E. O'Neill Award
Given to an individual in the sports industry who has made a significant contribution to the field and done so while exemplifying the highest ethical standards. Awarded annually when merited. Established in 1992.

• 15811 •
National Sportscasters and Sportswriters Association
Barbara C. Lockert, Program Coor.
322 E Innes St.
Salisbury, NC 28144
Phone: (704)633-4275
Fax: (704)633-2027
Home Page: http://www.nssahalloffame.com

• 15812 • Hall of Fame
To recognize top sports reporters. The award consists of a granite plaque with picture and engraved signature.

• 15813 • National Sportscaster and Sportswriter of Year
To honor the top national sportswriter and sportscaster. The award consists of a shield board of walnut with the NSSA medallion. Awarded annually. Established in 1959.

• 15814 •
National Spotted Saddle Horse Association
Donna West Fletcher, Mgr.
PO Box 898
108 N Spring St.
Murfreesboro, TN 37133-0898
Phone: (615)890-2864
Fax: (615)890-2864
E-mail: nssha898@aol.com
Home Page: http://www.nssha.com

• 15815 • Horse of the Year Awards
For recognition of the outstanding horse of the year in different categories. Standings are calculated from points earned at all NSSHA shows during the year. Dozens of awards are given, including the Juvenile Horse of the Year, Weanling of the Year, Yearling of the Year, Amateur Horse of the Year, and Trainer of the Year. Awarded annually at the Awards Banquet. In addition, the following awards are presented at the World Championship Show: Title Winners in 90 categories, NSSHA World Grand Champion, J. W. Fann Memorial Challenge Trophy, Charles Lamb Memorial Trophy, Ricky's Red Rose Challenge Trophy, Lynn Jordan Memorial Challenge Trophy, Juvenile Stake Challenge Trophy, Lady Riders Challenge Trophy, Penny West Lee Memorial Trophy for the lead line.

• 15816 • Outstanding Promoter Award
To recognize individuals who are outstanding in the promotion of spotted saddle horses. Anyone over 18 years of age is eligible. A silver engraved piece is awarded annually at the awards banquet. Established in 1980.

• 15817 •
National Steeplechase Association
William Gallo Jr., Dir.
400 Fair Hill Dr.
Elkton, MD 21921
Phone: (410)392-0700
Fax: (410)392-0706
E-mail: info@nationalsteeplechase.com
Home Page: http://www.nationalsteeplechase.com

• 15818 • F. Ambrose Clark Memorial Award
To recognize a person who has encouraged and promoted steeplechase racing over a period of time. A bronze medallion is awarded periodically. Established in 1964.

• 15819 •
National Stereoscopic Association
Mr. Lawrence Kaufman, Pres.
PO Box 86708
Portland, OR 97286
Phone: (951)736-8918
E-mail: kaufman3d@earthlink.net
Home Page: http://www.stereoview.org

• 15820 • Edward B. Berkowitz Memorial Award
For recognition of the best article published in *Stereo World* magazine during the previous publication year. A select awards committee recommends and chooses the best article every year. A plaque is awarded annually. Established in 1983 in honor of Edward B. Berkowitz, stereoscopic photographer and collector who had several articles published in *Stereo World.*

• 15821 •
National Stroke Association
Sharon Geris, Communications Dir.
9707 E Easter Ln.
Englewood, CO 80112
Phone: (303)649-9299
Toll-Free: 800-STR-OKES
Fax: (303)649-1328
E-mail: info@stroke.org
Home Page: http://www.stroke.org

• 15822 • Award of Hope and Courage
To recognize stroke survivors and other individuals who by example or service have been a source of hope and courage for those with disabling after-effects from a stroke. A plaque is presented with award. Established in 1985.

• 15823 • Community Education Award
For medical facilities and community organizations. A grant is awarded annually.

• 15824 • Research Fellowship Award in Cerebrovascular Disease
Recognizes doctors dedicated to the field of stroke as a career. A fellowship is awarded annually.

• 15825 •
National Student Campaign Against Hunger and Homelessness
Jennifer Hecker, Dir.
233 N Pleasant St., Ste. 32
Amherst, MA 01002
Phone: (413)253-6417
Toll-Free: 800-NO-HUNGR
Fax: (413)256-6435
E-mail: info@studentsagainsthunger.org
Home Page: http://www.nscahh.org

• 15826 • Bronze Medal Award
To recognize the school that has the best overall performance in the annual work-a-thon, the Hunger Cleanup. Awarded annually with a plaque. Formerly: The Marquette Excellence Award.

• 15827 • Gold Medal Award
To recognize the school that has the best overall performance in the annual work-a-thon, the Hunger Cleanup Awarded annually with a plaque. Formerly: Director's Choice Award.

• 15828 • Rookie of the Year
To recognize the school that has the best overall performance in the annual work-a-thon, the Hunger Cleanup. Awarded annually with a plaque. Formerly: Most Participants Award.

• 15829 • Silver Medal Award
To recognize the school that has the best overall performance in the annual work-a-thon, the Hunger Cleanup. Awarded annually with a plaque. Formerly: Hunger Cleanup Rookie of the Year.

• 15830 •
National Swine Improvement Federation
Kenneth J. Stalder PhD, Sec.-Treas.
Department of Animal Science
Iowa State University
109 Kildee Hall
Ames, IA 50011-3150
Phone: (515)294-4683
Fax: (515)294-5698
E-mail: stalder@iastate.edu
Home Page: http://www.nsif.com

Formerly: (1975) National Association of Swine Test Stations.

• 15831 • Distinguished Service Award
To recognize individuals who have excelled and given leadership to the field of swine performance testing. Individuals must be nominated by member organizations. A plaque is awarded annually. Established in 1993.

• 15832 • Graduate Student
Recognizes outstanding research in swine genetics. Individuals must be nominated by member organizations. A plaque is awarded annually. Established in 1993.

• 15833 •
National Symphony Orchestra Association
Rita Shapiro, Exec.Dir.
JFK Center for the Performing Arts
2700 F St. NW
Washington, DC 20566
Phone: (202)416-8000
Phone: (202)467-4600
Toll-Free: 800-444-1324
Fax: (202)416-8105
Home Page: http://www.kennedy-center.org/nso

• 15834 • Young Soloists' Competition
To encourage and foster the development of young performing artists in the Washington metropolitan area. The competition is held in two divisions: High School Division - a piano and instrumental competition for students in grades 10-12 who are residents of, or studying with an instrumental teacher; and College Division - a piano, instrumental, and vocal competition open to high school graduates currently studying music. Pianists and instrumentalists through age 23, and singers through age 26, are eligible to apply. Competitors in both Divisions must be studying within the metropolitan Washington Council of Governments (District of Columbia, Arlington, Charles, Fairfax, Frederick, London, Montgomery, Prince George's and Prince William Counties), or Washington residents studying music in the COG area or (2) Washington area residents studying elsewhere. All finalists are awarded the Milton W. King Memorial Certificate. Winners perform with the National Symphony Orchestra in a non-subscription concert, and awarded a cash prize of $1,000 and a complimentary one-year membership in the Association. Established in 1973 by Murray Sidlin, then Exxon/Arts Endowment Conductor.

• 15835 •
National Tattoo Association
Florence Makofske, Sec.-Treas.
485 Business Park Ln.
Allentown, PA 18109-9120
Phone: (610)433-7261
Phone: (610)433-9063
Fax: (610)433-7294
E-mail: curt@nationaltattoo.com
Home Page: http://www.nationaltattooassociation.com

Formerly: (1983) National Tattoo Club of the World.

• 15836 • Best Black/Gray Back Piece
To provide recognition at the association's annual convention. Plaques and trophies are presented annually. Established in 1979.

• 15837 • Best Black/Gray Tattoo
To provide recognition at the association's annual convention. Plaques and trophies are presented annually. Established in 1979.

• 15838 • Best Black/White Design Sheet
To provide recognition at the association's annual convention. Plaques and trophies are presented annually. Established in 1979.

• 15839 • Best Colored Back Piece
To provide recognition at the association's annual convention. Plaques and trophies are presented annually. Established in 1979.

• 15840 • Best Colored Design Sheet
To provide recognition at the association's annual convention. Plaques and trophies are awarded annually. Established in 1979.

• 15841 • Best Cover-Up Tattoo
To provide recognition at the association's annual convention. Plaques and trophies are awarded annually. Established in 1979.

• 15842 • Best Large Tatoo/Female
To provide recognition at the association's annual convention. Plaques and trophies are awarded annually. Established in 1979.

• 15843 • Best Large Tattoo/Male
To provide recognition at the association's annual convention. Plaques and trophies are awarded annually. Established in 1979.

• 15844 • Best Portrait Tattoo
To provide recognition at the association's annual convention. Plaques and trophies are awarded annually. Established in 1979.

• 15845 • Best Sleeve
To provide recognition at the association's annual convention. Plaques and trophies are awarded annually. Established in 1979.

• 15846 • Best Tattooed Female
Provides recognition at the association's annual convention. Plaques and trophies are awarded annually. Established in 1979.

• 15847 • Best Tattooed Male
Provides recognition at the association's annual convention. Plaques and trophies are awarded annually. Established in 1979.

• 15848 • Best Tattooist
Provides recognition at the association's annual convention. Plaques and trophies are awarded annually. Established in 1979.

• 15849 • Best Traditional Tattoo
Provides recognition at the association's annual convention. Plaques and trophies are awarded annually. Established in 1979.

• 15850 • Best Unique Tattoo
Provides recognition at the association's annual convention. Plaques and trophies are awarded annually. Established in 1979.

• 15851 • Bob Show Golden Age Award
Provides recognition at the association's annual convention. Applicants must have been in the profession for at least 40 years. Plaques and trophies are awarded annually. Established in 1979.

• 15852 • Fine Art Award
Provides recognition at the association's annual convention. Plaques and trophies are awarded annually. Established in 1979.

• 15853 • Most Realistic Tattoo
Provides recognition at the association's annual convention. Plaques and trophies are awarded annually. Established in 1979.

Awards are arranged in alphabetical order below their administering organizations

• 15854 • **Nicest Studio Award**

Provides recognition at the association's annual convention. Plaques and trophies are awarded annually. Established in 1979.

• 15855 • **Elizabeth Weinzirl Award**

Recognizes enthusiasm in the field. Plaques and trophies are awarded at the association's annual convention. Established in 1979.

• 15856 •

National Taxpayers Union
John Berthoud, Pres.
108 N Alfred St.
Alexandria, VA 22314
Phone: (703)683-5700
Toll-Free: 800-829-4258
Fax: (703)683-5722
E-mail: ntu@ntu.org
Home Page: http://www.ntu.org

• 15857 • **Taxpayer's Friend Award**

To educate the public about the spending attitudes of members of the United States Congress, and to recognize those in Congress who are working to limit federal spending and restore control over the budget, as well as those who are failing to do so. Every year, NTU rates congresspersons on each vote that affects taxes, spending, and debt, then assigns weights to these votes, reflecting the importance of each vote's effect on federal spending. Awarded annually to one or more recipients from the Senate and the House of Representatives. Established in 1979.

• 15858 •

National Telecommunications Cooperative Association
Michael E. Brunner, CEO
4121 Wilson Blvd., Ste. 1000
Arlington, VA 22203
Phone: (703)351-2000
Fax: (703)351-2001
E-mail: publications@ntca.org
Home Page: http://www.ntca.org

Formerly: (2003) National Telephone Cooperative Association.

• 15859 • **Best Subscriber Communication Program**

To recognize outstanding achievement in subscriber relations through the development of a well-rounded subscriber information program. The program should include components such as newsletters and other publications, community meetings, media relations, and employee-customer relations training. The company must be a member telco of NTCA to be eligible. A plaque is presented at the annual meeting in January or February. Established in 1982.

• 15860 • **Heroism Award**

This award honors examples of true humanitarianism in which an individual acts without self-regard to come to the aid of others in a life-threatening situation. The candidate's company must be a member telco of NTCA. Established in 1986.

• 15861 • **Key Employee Award**

To recognize an individual for outstanding achievement in developing and carrying out creative marketing strategies and techniques. Employees are considered for such projects as the formation of telco subsidiaries and the marketing of news services. The candidate's company must be a member telco of NTCA. Established in 1986.

• 15862 • **Lifetime Achievement Award**

To recognize the contributions of federal legislators that have advocated the cause of rural telephony throughout their tenure. A plaque is presented at the annual meeting. Established in 1982.

• 15863 • **Management Achievement Award**

For recognition of outstanding and innovative management achievement on the national, state, and local levels. This category includes excellence in all-around telephone system administrative management and ground-breaking efforts in specific areas. The candidate's company must be a member telco of NTCA and the candidate must hold the position of manager. A plaque is presented at the annual meeting in January or February. Established in 1982.

• 15864 • **Marketing Achievement**

To recognize outstanding achievement in developing and implementing marketing strategies and techniques. The focus is on projects such as the use of modular construction, the phone store concept, or the marketing of vertical services. The candidate's company must be a member telco of NTCA. A plaque is presented when merited at the annual meeting in January or February. Established in 1982.

• 15865 • **Public Relations Achievement**

For recognition of outstanding public relations achievement which has had a significant impact on a national, regional, or local level. Projects gaining national media attention for extension of service to remote areas and for the development of subscriber information are eligible. The candidate's company must be a member telco of NTCA. A plaque is presented when merited at the annual meeting in January or February. Established in 1982.

• 15866 • **Special Achievement Award**

For recognition of achievement in areas such as public service, statesmanship, or education. The candidate's company must be a member telco of NTCA. A plaque is presented at the annual meeting in January or February. Established in 1982.

• 15867 •

National Telemedia Council
Marieli Rowe, Contact
120 E Wilson St.
Madison, WI 53703
Phone: (608)257-7712
Fax: (608)257-7714
E-mail: ntc@danenet.wicip.org
Home Page: http://danenet.wicip.org/ntc

Formerly: (1983) American Council for Better Broadcasts.

• 15868 • **Jessie McCanse Award**

To recognize individual contribution to the field of media literacy, over a sustained period of at least 10 years. Awarded annually. Established on December 13, 1987, on the occasion of the 90th birthday of Jessie McCanse, co-founder of the National Telemedia Council.

• 15869 •

National Theatre Conference
Dr. Carole Brandt, Pres.
Southern Methodist University
Meadows School of the Arts
6101 Bishop Blvd.
Dallas, TX 75205
Phone: (214)768-2880
Fax: (214)768-2228
E-mail: cbrandt@smu.edu

• 15870 • **NTC Citation**

For recognition of distinguished service to the non-professional theater. An inscribed walnut plaque is awarded annually. Established in 1968.

• 15871 •

National Therapeutic Recreation Society
Jeff Witman MS, Pres.
22377 Belmont Ridge Rd.
Ashburn, VA 20148-4501
Phone: (703)858-0784
Toll-Free: 800-626-6772
Fax: (703)858-0794
E-mail: ntrsnrpa@nrpa.org
Home Page: http://www.nrpa.org/content/default.aspx?documentId=530

• 15872 • **Distinguished Service Award**

To recognize a member for outstanding service to the Society and for contributions and leadership in the field of therapeutic recreation. Nominees must be current members with at least a ten-year membership history. A plaque is awarded annually when merited at the Congress for Recreation and Parks. Established in 1969.

• 15873 • **Individual Citation**

To recognize an individual who is not a member of the Society for an outstanding contribution to therapeutic recreation and/or service to persons with disabilities. A plaque is awarded annually at the Congress for Recreation and Parks. Established in 1969.

• 15874 • Member of the Year
To recognize a member for a significant contribution in the field of therapeutic recreation during the preceding year. Nominees must be current members with at least a five-year membership history. A plaque is awarded annually at the Congress for Recreation and Parks. Established in 1980.

• 15875 • Meritorious Service Award
To recognize a member for exemplary behavior displayed through creativity and originality in programs, leadership, and contributions. Awarded to up to three members annually.

• 15876 • Organization and Institution Citations
To recognize organizations and institutions for contributions to the field of therapeutic recreation. Organizations whose major purpose is to advocate, promote, and/or support the delivery of services to persons with disabilities, including any public, private, or voluntary agency or group organized under a local or state charter, permit, certificate of incorporation, etc., such as scouting or other youth groups; Y's or other community-based recreation agencies, senior citizen clubs, women's and men's service clubs and organizations are eligible. Institutions which are primarily residential in nature but which also provide day care or outreach services and whose purpose is to provide health, treatment, rehabilitation, or other human services, including recreation/therapeutic recreation to persons with disabilities are also eligible. A plaque is awarded annually to one organization and one institution at the Congress for Recreation and Parks. Established in 1971.

• 15877 • Presidential Citations and Awards
To recognize outstanding contributions to individuals with disabilities. Awarded annually to one or more recipient when merited. The first awards were presented in 1989.

• 15878 • Research Awards
To recognize one professional NTRS member and one graduate or undergraduate student whose research efforts have enhanced the body of knowledge and/or practice of therapeutic recreation. To be eligible for the Professional Research Award, the candidate must be a member with a minimum of a bachelor's degree in therapeutic recreation or recreation with an option in therapeutic recreation by at least one person conducting the research. The Doris L. Berryman Student Research Award is open to students who are sponsored by a current NTRS member. Awarded annually.

• 15879 •
National Threshers Association
David Schramm, Pres.
22343 Lemoyne Rd.
Luckey, OH 43443
Phone: (419)833-6371
Fax: (734)888-2135
E-mail: daveschramm@earthlink.net
Home Page: http://nationalthreshers.com

• 15880 • John F. Limmer Award for Best Restored Steam Engine
To recognize the best restored steam traction engine. Engines exhibited at the annual National Threshers Reunion are eligible. A trophy is awarded annually in June. Established in 1968. Formerly: (1976) Glenn Shepard Award.

• 15881 •
National Tractor Pullers Association
Loy Thomas, Pres.
6155-B Huntley Rd.
Columbus, OH 43229
Phone: (614)436-1761
Fax: (614)436-0964
E-mail: gregg@ntpapull.com
Home Page: http://www.ntpapull.com

• 15882 • Four Wheel Drive Truck Puller of the Year
To recognize the puller best representing overall skill, sportsmanship, and support of pulling as demonstrated to pullers and fans alike, on and off the track. Nominations are accepted and voted upon by the membership. A monetary award and plaque are presented annually. Established in 1978. Formerly: Truck Puller of the Year.

• 15883 • Grand National Pulling Circuit Rookie of the Year
To recognize a new puller for his achievements. Nominations are accepted and voted upon by the membership. A plaque is presented annually. Established in 1980.

• 15884 • Hooker of the Year
To recognize the puller who has hooked the most times with a single vehicle. The trophy rotates from year to year and is presented by the Pickle Road Gang, Akron, Ohio. Established in 1977.

• 15885 • Mini Rod Puller of the Year
To recognize a puller who best represents overall skill, sportsmanship, and support of pulling as demonstrated to pullers and fans alike, on and off the track. Nominations are accepted and voted upon by the membership. A plaque is presented annually. Established in 1977.

• 15886 • Mini Sled of the Year
To recognize the NIPA licensed mini sled each year that the competing membership feel has done an outstanding job of performance. A plaque is presented annually. Established in 1985.

• 15887 • Pro Stock Puller of the Year
To recognize the puller best representing overall skill, sportsmanship, and support of pulling as demonstrated to pullers and fans alike, on and off the track. Nominations are accepted and voted upon by the membership. A plaque is presented. Established in 1982.

• 15888 • Pull of the Year
To recognize the top pull of the year selected by NTPA competing members. A plaque is presented annually. Established in 1980.

• 15889 • Pulling Family of the Year
To recognize a family who is involved in pulling as a family, whether it be support from home or support of the entire family at the event. Established in 1985.

• 15890 • Pulling Hall of Fame
To honor the innovators of truck and tractor pulling. Current members of the Hall of Fame are responsible for electing new members. Established in 1980.

• 15891 • Super Stock Puller of the Year
To recognize the puller best representing overall skill, sportsmanship, and support of pulling as demonstrated to pullers and fans alike, on and off the track. Nominations are accepted and voted upon by the membership. A plaque is presented annually. Established in 1973.

• 15892 • Two Wheel Drive Puller of the Year
To recognize the truck puller presenting the best overall example of skill, sportsmanship, and support of truck pulling demonstrated to pullers and fans alike, on and off the track. A plaque is presented annually. Established in 1985.

• 15893 • Unlimited Modified Puller of the Year
To recognize the puller best representing overall skill, sportsmanship, and support of pulling as demonstrated to pullers and fans alike, on and off the track. Nominations are accepted and voted upon by the membership. A monetary award and plaque are presented annually. Established in 1972. Formerly: (1977) Puller of the Year.

• 15894 •
National Traditional Country Music Association
Bob Everhart, Pres.
PO Box 492
Anita, IA 50020
Phone: (712)762-4363
E-mail: bobeverhart@yahoo.com
Home Page: http://www.oldtimemusic.bigstep.com

• 15895 • American Heritage Award
For recognition of performers, entertainers, and other individuals who have promoted, perpetuated, and/or performed American traditional

acoustic country music. The selection process is arranged by the President of the Association. A plaque may be awarded each year over Labor Day weekend at the annual Old-Time Country Music Festival. Established in 1976 by Robert Everhart.

• 15896 • America's Old-Time Country Music Hall of Fame
To honor individuals who have actively participated in the promotion, preservation, and performance of traditional country music. Performers or promoters of country music throughout the world. A plaque and a permanent honor in the Pioneer Music Museum in Anita, Iowa, are awarded annually. Established in 1976. Formerly: Iowa Country Music Hall of Fame.

• 15897 • America's Old-Time Fiddler's Hall of Fame
To honor those individuals most closely associated with the art of old-time fiddling - the presentation, the promotion, and the playing of old-time fiddle music. A plaque and permanent honor Hall of Fame, located in the Pioneer Music Museum in Anita, Iowa, are awarded annually. Established in 1987.

• 15898 • National Traditional Music Performer Award
This, a "people's choice" award, honors those who are active in the performance and promotion of traditional acoustic music in all its many forms. A nomination and voting process is conducted entirely with public input on a national scale. Awards are given in the following categories: accordion, autoharp, band, banjo, bass, clogdance, dobro, entertainer of the year, fiddle, gospel, guitar, hammer dulcimer, harmonica, lap dulcimer, mandolin, piano, songwriter, spoons & bones, storyteller, vocalist, and yodeler. Plaques are awarded annually. Established in 1991.

• 15899 •
National Traditionalist Caucus
Donald P. Rosenberg, Chm./Founder
PO Box 971, GPO
New York, NY 10116-0971
Phone: (212)685-4689
Fax: (212)481-6780
E-mail: info@ntcamerica.org
Home Page: http://www.ntcamerica.org

• 15900 • Advancement and Preservation of Civilization Award
To recognize and salute individuals who have contributed significantly to the pro-family cause and/or to our national strength and independence. Contributions of a political, ideological, moral, cultural, social, and educational nature are considered. A framed certificate is awarded twice a year. Established in 1974.

• 15901 • Reach for the Stars Award
Recognizes positive role models for children. Nominees must be young Hollywood entertainers. Awarded annually.

• 15902 •
National Transportation Week
Rosemary Cross, Exec.Dir.
Crowchild Sq.
5403 Crowchild Trl. NW, Ste. 201
Calgary, AB, Canada T3B 4Z1
Phone: (403)247-4115
Fax: (403)541-0915
E-mail: ntwsnt@igs.net
Home Page: http://www.ntweek.org

• 15903 • Award of Achievement
To recognize an individual for innovative achievement that has brought about positive and measurable developments of significant and lasting benefit to transportation in Canada. Nominations must be submitted by March 1. Plaques are awarded annually and are presented at a special ceremony on National Transportation Day, which is the inaugural event of NTW celebrations across Canada. Established in 1987.

• 15904 • Award of Excellence
To recognize an individual who has made within recent years an outstanding contribution to the transportation industry within such varied areas as policy, safety, education, or corporate function. Nominations must be submitted by March 1. Plaques are awarded annually and are presented at a special ceremony on National Transportation Day, which is the inaugural event of NTW celebrations across Canada. Established in 1976. Formerly: (1985) Award of Merit.

• 15905 • Award of Valor
To recognize an individual for an exemplary act of bravery in perilous circumstances either in the defense of life or protection of property during the preceding year. Nominations must be submitted by March 1. Awarded annually at a special ceremony on National Transportation Day, which is the inaugural event of NTW celebrations across Canada. Established in 1979.

• 15906 • Transportation Person of the Year
This, the highest award presented by NTW, recognizes an individual who has assumed a leadership role that has improved and advanced the transportation industry or any one of its many modes. Nominations must be submitted by March 1. Plaques are awarded annually at a special ceremony on National Transportation Day, which is the inaugural event of NTW celebrations across Canada. Established in 1970.

• 15907 •
National Trappers Association
Steve Fitzwater, Pres.
524 5th St.
PO Box 632018
Bedford, IN 47421-2247
Phone: (812)277-9670
Fax: (812)277-9672
E-mail: ntaheadquarters@nationaltrappers.com
Home Page: http://www.nationaltrappers.com

• 15908 • Benefactor Award
To recognize an outstanding benefactor of the NTA. Nominations are accepted a year in advance. Established in 1981.

• 15909 • Certificate of Appreciation
For recognition of those whose contributions to the betterment of the image of the trapper have been outstanding.

• 15910 • Director of the Year
To recognize a director for an outstanding contribution to the trappers' cause. Awarded annually. Established in 1980.

• 15911 • Leadership Award
To recognize a person who has done an outstanding job in a position of leadership. Established in 1978.

• 15912 • President's Award
This special award by the President of the association is presented to an individual who has done an outstanding job in promoting the trappers' cause. A trophy is awarded. Established in 1976.

• 15913 • Dave Reed Memorial Award
For recognition of the state trappers association judged to have the best display at the NTA Convention. Established in 1979 in memory of Dave Reed, a former NTA treasurer, who played an important role during the early years of NTA's existence.

• 15914 • Trapper/Conservationist Award
For recognition of very unusual and outstanding contributions to the trappers' cause. This award is usually presented to a public figure. Nominations are accepted a year in advance. A trophy is awarded. Established in 1971.

• 15915 • Trapper of the Year
For outstanding efforts in the preservation of the art of trapping and of the fur industry through education of others, teaching of conservation, and putting into practice that which one teaches. The following awards are given: Trapper of the Year (East) and Trapper of the Year (West). Trophies are awarded. Established in 1971.

• 15916 •
National Trust for Historic Preservation
Richard Moe, Pres.
1785 Massachusetts Ave. NW
Washington, DC 20036-2117
Phone: (202)588-6000
Toll-Free: 800-944-6847
Fax: (202)588-6059
E-mail: feedback@nthp.org
Home Page: http://www.nationaltrust.org

• 15917 • Louise du Pont Crowninshield Award
This, the oldest and highest award given by the National Trust, is presented to an individual or

organization when there is indisputable evidence of superlative leadership achievement in the preservation and interpretation of our national heritage of buildings, structures, districts, sites, cultural landscapes and objects of historical and cultural significance. Nominations must be made by someone other than the nominee and should be directed to the Vice President for Programs, Services and Information. Winners are selected by a special committee of the Board of Trustees. A monetary prize and a citation are awarded annually during National Historic Preservation Week in May. Established in 1959 as a memorial to Louise Evelina du Pont Crowinshield.

• 15918 • **Great American Main Street Award**
To recognize exceptional accomplishments in revitalizing America's historic and traditional downtowns and neighborhood commercial districts. Any individual, organization, or agency may submit an entry by October 31. Five monetary prizes of $2,500 are awarded to communities to be used in the furtherance of revitalization processes. Awarded annually. Established in 1995.

• 15919 • **National Preservation Honor Awards**
To recognize projects demonstrating outstanding commitment to excellence in historic preservation. Any aspect of preservation, restoration, rehabilitation, or redevelopment of our architectural and maritime heritage that is exemplary is eligible. Candidates and their projects must be in the United States or its territories. Projects must have been completed within the last three years. The nominations deadline is May 1. A plaque is presented to one or more recipients each year. Awarded at the National Trust's annual conference each October.

• 15920 •
National Turf Writers Association
Dan Liebman, Sec.-Treas.
1244 Meadow Lane
Frankfort, KY 40601
Phone: (502)875-4864
Fax: (606)276-4450
E-mail: dliebman@bloodhorse.com

• 15921 • **Mr. Fitz Award**
Recognizes meritorious service to the racing industry. Awarded annually. Established in 1981 to honor James E. "Sunny Jim" Fitzsimmons, noted trainer who won purses in excess of $13,000,000.

• 15922 • **Walter Haight Award**
For recognition of lifetime achievement in the field of turf writing. Members of the Association nominate and elect individuals for the award. A plaque is awarded annually. Established in 1972 to honor Walter Haight, racing columnist for the *Washington Post*.

• 15923 • **Joe Palmer Award**
To recognize outstanding contributions that typify the spirit of racing. Individuals are nominated and elected by the membership. A plaque is awarded annually. Established in 1964 to honor Joe Palmer, racing editor for the *New York Herald*.

• 15924 •
National Urban League
Marc H. Morial, Pres./CEO
120 Wall St., 8th Fl.
New York, NY 10005
Phone: (212)558-5300
Fax: (212)344-5332
E-mail: info@nul.org
Home Page: http://www.nul.org

• 15925 • **Equal Opportunity Day Award**
To recognize individuals and corporations that perpetuate the principle of equal opportunity and exhibit leadership qualities that result in notable contributions to the cause of equal rights. A plaque is awarded annually. Established in 1957.

• 15926 • **Labor Affairs Award**
To recognize organized labor's commitment to forging links and strengthening bonds between the trade union movement and the black community. Two plaques are awarded annually. Established in 1986.

• 15927 • **Living Legends Award**
To recognize Black Americans who have made a significant contribution in their particular field of endeavor. Ten trophies are awarded annually. In addition, Special Legend Awards are presented posthumously. Established in 1987.

• 15928 • **Ann Tanneyhill Award**
To recognize an employee of the National Urban League with ten years or more of service for excellence and extraordinary commitment to the Urban League Movement. A monetary award of $1,000 and a plaque are presented annually. Established in 1970.

• 15929 •
National Vocational Technical Education Foundation
Kimberly A. Green, Exec.Dir.
444 N Capitol St. NW, No. 830
Washington, DC 20001
Phone: (202)737-0303
Fax: (202)737-1106

• 15930 • **Outstanding Business, Industry, Organization, or Individual Contribution Award**
To recognize a business, industry, organization, or individual who has demonstrated exceptional commitment, dedication, and involvement with vocational-technical education through public and private sector partnerships. Five plaques are awarded annually in December. Eligible candidates must have a history of and be an active participant in a partnership program that promotes, expands, or improves vocational-technical education and its link with workforce preparation. Established in 1991 by the National Association of State Directors of Vocational Technical Education (NASDVTE).

• 15931 •
National Water Resources Association
Norm M. Semanko, Pres.
3800 N Fairfax Dr., Ste. 4
Arlington, VA 22203
Phone: (703)524-1544
Fax: (703)524-1548
E-mail: nwra@nwra.org
Home Page: http://www.nwra.org

• 15932 • **Distinguished Service Award**
To recognize individuals in federal and state government for significant contributions to the development and conservation of our nation's water resources. A plaque is awarded annually when merited. Established in 1987.

• 15933 • **Water Statesman of the Year**
For recognition of contributions to the development of water and water resources. A silver ice bucket is awarded annually when merited. Established in 1969.

• 15934 •
National Water Safety Congress
Cecilia Duer, Exec.Dir.
PO Box 1632
Mentor, OH 44061
Phone: (440)209-9805
E-mail: nationalwatersafetycongress@yahoo.com
Home Page: http://www.watersafetycongress.org

• 15935 • **Award of Merit**
To recognize individuals, organizations, firms, or agencies that have made a significant contribution or an outstanding effort to enhance or promote water safety at the local or state level. An engraved lucite plaque is awarded to each of 30 recipients annually. Established in 1952.

• 15936 • **National Award**
For recognition of an individual, organization, firm, or agency that has contributed the most to water safety programs on a national scale for an extended period of time, usually several years. An engraved metal or metal and wood combination plaque is awarded annually. Established in 1954.

• 15937 • **President's Award**
To recognize a board member who has contributed the most to the organization's program during the past year. An engraved metal plaque is awarded annually. Established in 1974.

• 15938 • **Regional Awards**
To recognize individuals, organizations, firms, or agencies that have contributed the most to water safety issues or program within each of the six

Awards are arranged in alphabetical order below their administering organizations

regions. An engraved lucite plaque is awarded to each region annually. Established in 1960.

• 15939 •
National Watercolor Society
Loa Sprung, Third VP
915 S Pacific Ave.
San Pedro, CA 90731
Phone: (310)831-1099
Phone: (310)831-1099
Toll-Free: 800-486-8670
E-mail: nws-website@cox.net
Home Page: http://www.nws-online.org

Formerly: (1975) California National Watercolor Society.

• 15940 • **Annual Exhibition**
To recognize excellence and encourage further development in water media. Artists may submit a slide of a painting for the Annual Exhibit; if accepted, the artist is then asked to submit three paintings (in watermedia) to be eligible for membership. Monetary awards, plaques and certificates are awarded annually at the Annual Exhibition and the Signature Exhibit. Established in 1920. Additional information is available from Joan Folger Fey, historian for the National Watercolor Society, 3511 Manhatten Ave., Manhatten Beach, CA 90266.

• 15941 • **National Watercolor Society Arts and Humanities Award**
To recognize individuals for outstanding contributions to water media. Awarded annually. Established in 1920.

• 15942 •
National Wheelchair Basketball Association
Todd Hatfield, Prog.Mgr.
6165 Lehman Dr., Ste. 101
Colorado Springs, CO 80918
Phone: (719)266-4082
Fax: (719)266-4082
E-mail: toddhatfield@nwba.org
Home Page: http://www.nwba.org

• 15943 • **Hall of Fame**
To honor individuals who have contributed significantly to the sport and the Association either as players, supportive personnel (administrator, coach, etc.), or both. Established in 1973.

• 15944 • **Most Valuable Player**
For recognition of the player judged most valuable to his team during the annual NWBA national tournament. Players on a competing team at the annual national wheelchair basketball tournament are eligible for the award. A plaque or trophy is presented annually. Established in 1970.

• 15945 • **Captain James S. Ure Award for Sportsmanship**
For recognition of a player judged by team representatives and officials as displaying outstanding team spirit and sportsmanship during the annual National Wheelchair Basketball Tournament. Players on a team competing in the annual NWBT may be nominated. A plaque or trophy is presented annually. Established in 1961 in honor of Captain James S. Ure, a highly decorated fighter pilot who was shot down during the Korean conflict.

• 15946 •
National Whistleblower Center
Kris Kolesnik, Exec.Dir.
PO Box 3768
Washington, DC 20027
Phone: (202)342-1902
Fax: (202)342-1904
E-mail: whistle@whistleblowers.org
Home Page: http://www.whistleblowers.org

Formerly: (1995) Northwest Environmental Advocates.

• 15947 • **Awards for Courage**
To recognize whistleblowers who risk their job, career, and livelihood to protect the public health and safety. A plaque is awarded biennially to workers in both private industry and government. Established in 1990.

• 15948 •
National Wild Turkey Federation
Rob Keck, CEO
PO Box 530
770 Augusta Rd.
Wild Turkey Ctr.
Edgefield, SC 29824-0530
Phone: (803)637-3106
Toll-Free: 800-THE-NWTF
Fax: (803)637-0034
E-mail: jfelkins@nwtf.net
Home Page: http://www.nwtf.org

• 15949 • **Roger M. Latham Sportsman Service Award**
To recognize a non-professional for outstanding contributions to the wild turkey resource in the United States. State chapters of the NWTF may make nominations. A plaque is awarded annually at the convention to up to five recipients. Established in 1983 in memory of Roger M. Latham, a wild turkey author and conservationist.

• 15950 • **Henry S. Mosby Award**
To recognize outstanding professional wildlife biologists for significant contributions to the research and management of the wild turkey. Professional wild turkey biologists who have made long term sustained contributions to wild turkey research and management or singular actions resulting in significant contributions to wild turkey management are eligible. A plaque is awarded at the annual convention banquet. Established in 1987 by NWTF Board of Directors in memory of Dr. Henry S. Mosby who devoted 40 years to the wildlife profession as a wildlife biologist, researcher, educator, and administrator.

• 15951 •
National Wildlife Federation
Larry Schweiger, Pres./CEO
11100 Wildlife Center Dr.
Reston, VA 20190-5362
Phone: (703)438-6000
Toll-Free: 800-822-9919
E-mail: info@nwf.org
Home Page: http://www.nwf.org

• 15952 • ***National Wildlife* Photo Contest**
To recognize amateur and aspiring photographers. Photographers aged 18 and older may submit up to five entries that show animal behavior, portraits of wildlife in natural habitat, plant life, natural landscapes, or people interacting with nature. The deadline for entry is July 15. Winning photos earn a monetary prize and will appear in the December-January issue of *National Wildlife;* finalists receive a certificate of merit and a NWF calendar.

• 15953 •
National Wildlife Rehabilitators Association
Lisa Borgia, Exec.Dir.
14 N 7th Ave.
St. Cloud, MN 56303-4766
Phone: (320)259-4086
E-mail: nwra@nwrawildlife.org
Home Page: http://www.nwrawildlife.org

• 15954 • **Lifetime Achievement Award**
To recognize an individual who has contributed to the field of rehabilitation of wildlife in a major way for many years. Nominations must be submitted by October 1. A monetary award of $100, a plaque, and free registration at the NWRA conference are awarded annually. Established in 1984.

• 15955 • **NWRA Grants**
To support research projects in the field of wildlife rehabilitation. Grants of up to $5,000 are awarded annually. Grant proposals must be submitted by October 1 each year. Established in 1984.

• 15956 • **Significant Achievement Award**
To recognize an individual for a significant contribution to the field of rehabilitation of wildlife in the past two years. Nominations must be submitted by October 1 each year. A monetary award of $100, a plaque, and free registration at the NWRA conference are awarded annually. Established in 1984.

• 15957 •
National Woman's Party
Amy Conroy, Exec.Dir.
Sewall-Belmont House & Museum
144 Constitution Ave. NE
Washington, DC 20002-5608
Phone: (202)546-1210
Fax: (202)546-3997
E-mail: info@sewallbelmont.org
Home Page: http://www.sewallbelmont.org

• 15958 • Alice Award
To honor a distinguished woman who has made an outstanding contribution in breaking barriers and setting new precedents for women. A plaque is awarded when merited. Established in 1985 in honor of Alice Paul, a suffragist, human rights activist, and founder of the Party. Formerly: (2003) Alice Paul Award.

• 15959 •
National Women's Hall of Fame
Billie Luisi-Potts, Exec.Dir.
76 Fall St.
Seneca Falls, NY 13148
Phone: (315)568-8060
Fax: (315)568-2976
E-mail: greatwomen@greatwomen.org
Home Page: http://www.greatwomen.org

• 15960 • National Women's Hall of Fame
To honor American women of achievement and struggles in the fields of arts, athletics, business, education, government, the humanities, philanthropy, and science that have been of great value to the development of their country. Nominations of women whose achievements are of national significance and enduring value and whose efforts promote the progress and freedom of women are accepted. Living honorees receive a Steuben Star Crystal. Presented annually at a mid-July ceremony. Established in 1973.

• 15961 •
National Women's Political Caucus
Llenda Jackson-Leslie, Pres.
1634 Eye St. NW, Ste. 310
Washington, DC 20006
Phone: (202)785-1100
Fax: (202)785-3605
E-mail: info@nwpc.org
Home Page: http://www.nwpc.org

• 15962 • Martin Abzug Memorial Award
To recognize the spouse of a feminist leader whose constant support reflects his personal commitment to the goals and ideals of the Caucus. Awarded when merited. Established to honor Martin Abzug, husband and friend whose advice, aid, and staunch support helped the Honorable Bella Abzug through many political struggles and triumphs.

• 15963 • Exceptional Media Merit Award
To recognize journalists for outstanding coverage of issues of particular importance to women. EMMA awards are presented in several categories, encompassing print and electronic media. Established in 1987.

• 15964 •
National Women's Studies Association
Loretta Younger, Natl.Exec.Admin.
7100 Baltimore Ave., Ste. 502
College Park, MD 20740
Phone: (301)403-0525
Phone: (301)403-0524
Fax: (301)403-4137
E-mail: nwsaoffice@nswa.org
Home Page: http://www.nwsa.org

• 15965 • The Abafazi-Africana Women's Studies Essay Award
To discover, encourage, and promote the intellectual development of emerging black women scholars who engage in critical theoretical discussions and/or analyses about feminist/womanist issues among women of color. Two $ 400 awards will be given to an undergraduate and graduate student respectively. Scholarly essays may be on any subject relevant to black girl children, women's issues and/or experiences in the U.S. or throughout the diaspora.

• 15966 • Illinois - NWSA Graduate Scholarship Award
$1, 000 is awarded to a student who will be engaged in the research or writing stages of a Master's Thesis or Ph.D. Dissertation in the interdisciplinary field of Women's Studies. The Research project must be on women and must enhance the NWSA mission. Applicants must be members of NWSA at the time of application.

• 15967 • Jewish Prize
For graduate student who is enrolled for the fall semester and whose area research is Jewish Women's Studies. $ 1,000 is awarded.

• 15968 • Lesbian Caucus Prize
Awarded to graduate student who has a special interest in the lives, work, and culture of Lesbian women. A prize of $500 is awarded annually.

• 15969 •
National Wood Flooring Association
Edward S. Korczak CAE, Exec.Dir.
111 Chesterfield Industrial Blvd.
Chesterfield, MO 63005
Phone: (636)519-9663
Toll-Free: 800-422-4556
Fax: (636)519-9664
E-mail: info@nwfa.org
Home Page: http://www.woodfloors.org

• 15970 • Craftsman Degree
Recognizes individuals who have achieved 25 credits for education, achievement and service, or which 15 must be in education. Awarded to numerous recipients annually.

• 15971 • Floor of the Year Contest
To recognize quality work in the wood flooring industry as well as professional pride and craftsmanship. Applicant must be a NWFA member. Awards are presented in residential and commercial categories. First place trophies made of walnut and second and third place trophies made of cherry are awarded annually at the convention. Established in 1990. Additional information is available from *Hardwood Floors* magazine, 1842 Hoffman St., Ste. 201, Madison, WI 53791.

• 15972 • Honorary Vanguard Degree
Recognizes individuals who have been nominated by an NWFA member, and who are approved by a two-thirds vote of the NWFA Board of Directors. Awarded to numerous recipients annually.

• 15973 • Master Craftsman Degree
Recognizes individuals who have received the Craftsman Degree, who have attended or served as an instructor at an NWFA Advance School, and/or have received an NWFA Floor of the Year Award, and who have earned 25 credits, of which 15 are for achievement. Awarded to numerous recipients annually.

• 15974 • Vanguard Degree
Recognizes individuals who have earned 25 credits, of which 15 are for service and/or achievement to the industry. Awarded to numerous recipients annually.

• 15975 •
National Woodland Owners Association
Dr. Keith A. Argow, Pres.
374 Maple Ave. E, Ste. 310
Vienna, VA 22180
Phone: (703)255-2700
Toll-Free: 800-476-8733
Fax: (703)281-9200
Home Page: http://www.nationalwoodlands.org/

• 15976 • Award for Outstanding Forestry Legislation
To recognize innovative, effective state legislation with an unusually positive impact on private woodland owners and on forest practice. Awarded annually. Established in 1985.

• 15977 • Award for Outstanding Forestry Magazine of an Affiliated State Woodland Owner Association
To recognize practical information to woodland owners, based on format, layout, quality of production, and timeliness of information. Awarded annually. Established in 1991.

• 15978 • Forest Stewardship State of the Year
To recognize the innovation of a program, partnerships involved, and the number of landowners served based on data from the U.S. Forest Service annual review. Awarded annually. Established in 1992.

• 15979 • National Woodland Owners Award of Merit
To recognize outstanding service or contributions to non-industrial private forestry. Awarded when merited. Established in 1991.

Awards are arranged in alphabetical order below their administering organizations

• 15980 • Outstanding Forestry Extension Publication Award

To recognize the writing, layout, timeliness, and practicality of a publication dealing with innovative technology transfers to landowners. Awarded annually. Established in 1991.

• 15981 • Outstanding Forestry Extension Video Award

To recognize the writing, layout, timeliness, and practicality of a video dealing with innovative technology transfers to landowners. Awarded annually. Established in 1992.

• 15982 •

National Wrestling Coaches Association
Mike Moyer, Exec.Dir.
PO Box 254
Manheim, PA 17545-0254
Phone: (717)653-8009
Fax: (717)653-8270
E-mail: mmoyer@nwca.cc
Home Page: http://www.nwcaonline.com

• 15983 • Coach of the Year Awards

To honor the outstanding coaching performance by a coach each year. Awarded annually. Established in 1958. Starting in 1974, a Coach of the Year was recognized in each division: Division I, Division II, and Division III. Additional Coach of the Year awards are given to assistant college coaches, California community college coaches and assistant coaches, junior college coaches, college division coaches, distinguished prep coaches, and high school coaches.

• 15984 • Most Outstanding Wrestler

To honor the top collegiate wrestler at the NCAA National Tournament. Awarded annually. Established in 1958.

• 15985 •

National Wrestling Hall of Fame & Museum
Lee Roy Smith, Exec.Dir.
405 W Hall of Fame Ave.
Stillwater, OK 74075
Phone: (405)377-5243
Fax: (405)377-5244
E-mail: info@wrestlinghalloffame.org
Home Page: http://www.wrestlinghalloffame.org

• 15986 • Hall of Outstanding Americans

To recognize a former wrestler who has earned national or international stature or acclaim in a profession or field of endeavor not related to wrestling, including politics, government, and the military; arts and humanities - music, theater, and literature; science, technology, and medicine; business and industry; philanthropy; and other sports at the Olympic or professional level. Nominations are accepted from the general public. Awarded during Honors Weekend. Established in 1991. Formerly: Hall of Distinguished Americans.

• 15987 • Medal of Courage

To recognize a wrestler or former wrestler who has overcome insurmountable challenges. This award is presented annually during the Honors Weekend. Established in 1996.

• 15988 • National Wrestling Hall of Fame Distinguished Member

To recognize an individual who has made a significant impact on the history of wrestling as an athlete, coach, and/or contributor to the sport. Each Distinguished Member is recognized in the national museum by a granite plaque, and the "take home" award, a smaller plaque, also in granite. Awarded annually. Established in 1976.

• 15989 • Order of Merit

To recognize individuals for extraordinary national and/or international contributions and service to the sport of wrestling above and beyond athletic achievement or coaching success. The recipient is selected annually by the Distinguished Members of the National Wrestling Hall of Fame and the award is presented during the Honors Weekend. Established in 1991.

• 15990 • Dave Schultz High School Excellence Award

To recognize a high school senior with selection based equally on outstanding wrestling achievement, scholastic achievement and citizenship. This award is presented on the state level, with five regional winners chosen from the state winners, and a national winner chosen from the regional winners. The Regional and National awards annually are presented during the Honors Weekend. Established in 1996.

• 15991 •

National Writers Association
Sandy Whelchel, Exec.Dir.
10940 S Parker Rd., No. 508
Parker, CO 80134
Phone: (303)841-0246
Fax: (303)841-2607
E-mail: execdirsandywhelchel@nationalwriters.com
Home Page: http://www.nationalwriters.com

• 15992 • Nonfiction Contest

To encourage the creative form of nonfiction writing and to recognize those who excel in this field. Unpublished nonfiction or book proposals including two chapters not to exceed 5,000 words in the English language may be submitted between October 1 and December 31. Monetary prizes and certificates are awarded in June. Established in 1991. Formerly: (1996) NWC Nonfiction Contest.

• 15993 • Novel Manuscript Award

To develop creative skills, to recognize and reward outstanding ability, and to increase the opportunity for publication. Unpublished book-length manuscripts written in English may be submitted between December and April each year. A monetary prize and a certificate are awarded annually, in June. Established in 1974. Formerly: (1998) NWC Novel Manuscript Award.

• 15994 • Poetry Award

To encourage the writing of poetry and to recognize outstanding poets. Poems written in English that do not exceed 40 lines may be submitted between July 1 and September 30. A monetary prize and certificate are awarded annually in June. Established in 1942. Formerly: (1998) NWC Poetry Award.

• 15995 • Screenplay Contest

To encourage writers of screenplays and recognize outstanding screenwriters. Only unpublished, unproduced scripts are eligible. Submissions are accepted October 1 through January 1. Monetary prizes and certificates are awarded annually in June. Established in 1998.

• 15996 • Short Story Award

To encourage writers of short stories, and to recognize outstanding creative fiction writing. Unpublished fiction written in English that does not exceed 5,000 words may be submitted between April 1 and June 30. Monetary prizes and certificates are awarded annually in June. Established in 1942. Formerly: (1998) NWC Short Story Award.

• 15997 •

National Writers Union
Chris Zic, Exec.Dir.
113 Univ. Pl. 6th Fl.
New York, NY 10003
Phone: (212)254-0279
Fax: (212)254-0673
E-mail: nwu@nwu.org
Home Page: http://www.nwu.org

• 15998 • Bellwether Prize for Social Justice Fiction

To recognize a literary novel whose content addresses issues of social justice. In addition to the cash award of $25,000, the book will be published by a major publisher. Writers who have not published a novel that has sold more than 10,000 copies can submit for the prize. The award, which is awarded in even-numbered years, is administered by the National Writers United Service Organization.

• 15999 •

National Writers Workshop
Linda Jensen, Contact
℅ The Oregonian
801 3rd St.
St. Petersburg, FL 33701
Phone: (727)827-9494
Fax: (727)821-0583
E-mail: info@poynter.org
Home Page: http://www.oregonian.com/nww

Formerly: (1992) American Film Institute Alumni Association Writers Workshop; Writers Workshop.

• 16000 • Ethnic Minorities Screenwriting Competition
To discover and promote talented new ethnic minority screenwriters. Television pilots and on-going television series are not acceptable. Five exceptional writers are chosen. Submissions are accepted from September 1 to January 31. A monetary prize of $500 is awarded annually. Established in 1990. Sponsored by Quincy Jones/ David Salzman Productions, Norman Jewison, Robin and Marsha Williams, Universal, Dan Petrie, Jr., Oliver Stone, and Lawrence Kasdan.

• 16001 • Screenwriter's Contest Award and Promotion
To recognize outstanding writers and to bring them to the attention of the Hollywood film-making community. Scripts for television pilots and on-going television series are not eligible. Each year five to six writers will receive a cash award of $500, and development, presentation, and promotion of their screenplay (total cost of $3,500) will be provided by the Workshop's sponsors. Following presentation/critical discussion, writers will do a rewrite incorporating valid suggestions from moderators and the audience. All screenplays presented will be made available to motion picture industry members and industry feedback will be communicated to the writer. Established by Willard Rodgers, founder/ director.

• 16002 •
National Young Farmer Educational Association
Gordon Stone, EVP
PO Box 20326
Montgomery, AL 36120
Phone: (334)213-3276
Fax: (334)213-3276
E-mail: natloffice@nyfea.org
Home Page: http://www.nyfea.org

Formerly: (1994) National Young Farmer Educational Association.

• 16003 • Farm and Ranch Management Award
To stimulate members to learn and improve their business management skills. The contest tests competitors' skills through one or more management exercises comprising the following areas: decision making; resource acquisition and transfer; farm management tools for planning and analysis; taxes and management; risk and uncertainty; and management in today's environment. Awarded annually.

• 16004 • Outstanding Young Farmer Advisor
To recognize an advisor for dedication, service, and achievements in adult agricultural education. Each applicant must be a current active member of the National Vocational Agricultural Teachers' Association. A monetary award, life membership in the National Young Farmer Educational Association, and a plaque are awarded annually at the National Institute. Established in 1990.

• 16005 • Spokesperson for Agriculture
This award has four objectives: to provide an educational program that inspires participation from a majority of NYFEA chapters; to enhance public speaking skills of young men and women; to further educate the public about agricultural issues at a national and global level; and to provide a rewarding and fun-filled experience for contestants, advisors, and sponsors. NYFEA members who will be over the age of 18 on the day of the national contest, and who have not previously won the contest, are eligible to participate. Competitors must present a prepared five-minute statement on a current agricultural or environmental topic that will provide a positive perspective of agriculture/renewable resources to an audience of consumers and producers. Winners will be part of a media tour and national media campaign to communicate the message of agriculture to the public. Awarded annually.

• 16006 •
The Nationalist Movement
Richard Barrett, First Officer
PO Box 2000
Learned, MS 39154
Phone: (601)885-2288
Phone: (601)373-3847
E-mail: crosstar@nationalist.org
Home Page: http://www.nationalist.org

Formed by merger of: (1989) Forsyth County Defense League.

• 16007 • Patriot of the Nation
To recognize outstanding contributions to the unity, liberty, democracy, and victory of the American people, the American nation, and the American way of life. A pro-majority individual with distinguished service to the country, people, and way of life is eligible. A certificate is awarded periodically. Established in 1987 by the Forsyth County Defense League in honor of the uprising against the pro-minority "January Invasion" of Forsyth County, GA in January, 1987.

• 16008 •
Nation's Restaurant News
Lebhar-Friedman Inc.
425 Park Ave.
New York, NY 10022
Phone: (212)756-5000
Toll-Free: 800-216-7117
Fax: (212)756-5125
E-mail: info@lf.com
Home Page: http://www.nrn.com

• 16009 • Fine Dining Hall of Fame
To recognize top U. S. restaurants judged according to their food, service, and decor. Approximately ten restaurants are inducted each year at a special awards luncheon during the National Restaurant Show in Chicago.

• 16010 • Golden Chain Award
To recognize outstanding leadership and achievement of foodservice operators. Six awards are presented annually at the Multi-Unit Foodservice Operators (MUFSO) conference.

• 16011 • Hot Concepts! Awards
To recognize those restaurateurs who implement fresh restaurant concepts with broad consumer appeal. Criteria for selection include being a forward-thinking company with emerging growth potential; developing a new, clearly-defined concept that appeals to consumers and positions the company at the leading edge of the foodservice industry; and operating at least 5 stores or having a presence in at least 3 markets. Awards are presented in various categories annually.

• 16012 • MUFSO Innovator Award
To recognize creative leadership and innovation that impacts on the foodscience industry. Awarded annually at the Multi-Unit Foodservice Operator's (MUFSO) Conference.

• 16013 • Operator of the Year
To recognize an innovative service chain executive for contributions to his or her service chain and to the foodservice industry. The recipient is selected from the pool of Golden Chain Award winners. A trophy is awarded annually in the fall at *Nation's Restaurant News'* annual Multi-Unit Foodservice Operators (MUFSO) conference. Established in 1971.

• 16014 • Pioneer of the Year
To recognize the lifetime achievement of an innovative foodservice pioneer. Awarded annually at the Multi-Unit Foodservice Operators (MUFSO) conference.

• 16015 •
Native Prairies Association of Texas
John H. Pickett, Pres.
PO Box 210
Georgetown, TX 78627-0210
Phone: (254)897-3646
E-mail: jdpick@charter.net
Home Page: http://www.texasprairie.org

• 16016 • Arnold Davis Prairie Restoration Award
For outstanding efforts in reconstruction of TX prairies. Recognition award bestowed periodically.

• 16017 • E.J. Dyksterhuis Memorial Award
For outstanding scientific contributions. Recognition award bestowed periodically.

• 16018 • R.C. Mauldin Award
For outstanding education contributions. Recognition award bestowed periodically.

• 16019 •
Natural Resources Defense Council
40 W 20th St.
New York, NY 10011
Phone: (212)727-2700
Fax: (212)727-1773
E-mail: nrdcinfo@nrdc.org
Home Page: http://www.nrdc.org

Awards are arranged in alphabetical order below their administering organizations

• 16020 • Environmental Award

To recognize distinguished individuals for their service to the environment. An antique print is awarded annually. Established in 1972.

• 16021 •
Natural Sciences and Engineering Research Council of Canada
(Conseil de recherches en sciences naturelles et en genie du Canada)
350 Albert St.
Ottawa, ON, Canada K1A 1H5
Phone: (613)995-6295
Fax: (613)992-5337
Home Page: http://www.nserc-crsng.gc.ca/

Formerly: (1978) National Research Council of Canada.

• 16022 • Doctoral Prizes

In recognition of high quality research conducted by up to four students completing their doctoral degrees in science and engineering at Canadian universities. Each year, the Deans of Graduate Studies are invited to nominate eligible candidates from their own university. Each university may nominate one candidate for each of the two categories: natural science and engineering. In addition to the quality of their research, students are judged on their academic record, potential for a research career, and overall contributions as a student. The selection committee evaluates the significance of the student's contribution to knowledge, as well as the manner in which the results have been communicated. For engineering nominees, consideration is also given to the potential for practical application of the research.

• 16023 • Gerhard Herzberg Canada Gold Medal for Science and Engineering

To recognize Canada's most outstanding scientists and engineers and to raise public awareness about the major contributions that Canada's top researchers make to international science and technology, and to bettering people's lives. It is awarded annually to an individual who has demonstrated sustained excellence and influence in research for a body of work conducted in Canada that has substantially advanced the natural sciences or engineering fields. The recipient is awarded a medal and a monetary prize $1 million to use for his/her own university-based research or to establish research scholarships, fellowships, or chairs. Established in 1991 in honor of Dr. Gerhard Herzberg, Canada's 1971 Nobel Prize winner in chemistry.

• 16024 • Michael Smith Awards for Science Promotion

To honor individuals and organizations that make an outstanding contribution to the promotion of science in Canada, through activities encouraging popular interest or developing science abilities. Up to five recipients may be selected each year. A medal, framed citation, and monetary prize ($5,000 for individuals; $10,000 for organizations) are awarded annually.

• 16025 • Steacie Memorial Fellowships (Bourses Commemoratives E. W. R. Steacie)

To enhance the career development of outstanding and highly promising scientists and engineers who are staff members of Canadian universities. Candidates must be nominated by senior members of the Canadian science and engineering community. Candidates should have obtained their doctorate within the last twelve years and be principal investigators on any research grant from NSERC. The fellowships permit young researchers to devote all their time to research, by freeing them of teaching and administrative duties for a period of up to two years. Recipients receive their normal university salary and are invited to submit a request for a supplement to their NSERC Research Grant. Up to six fellowships are awarded annually for a two-year period. Includes a contribution to the university of $90,000 per year toward the Fellow's salary. Nomination deadline is July 1. Established in memory of Dr. Edgar W.R. Steacie, a physical chemist and former President of the National Research Council of Canada, who did much to encourage young researchers.

• 16026 •
Nature Canada
(Federation Canadienne de la Nature)
Mark Dorfman, Chair
28 Alberta St., Ste. 900
Ottawa, ON, Canada K1P 6A4
Phone: (613)562-3447
Toll-Free: 800-267-4088
Fax: (613)562-3371
E-mail: info@naturecanada.ca
Home Page: http://www.cnf.ca

• 16027 • Affiliate Award

To honor a CNF affiliate organization that has contributed significantly in the areas of public awareness of conservation issues, protection and/or management of natural areas, or environmental action. Work on either a CNF program or a program that supports CNF objectives is considered. Established in 1988.

• 16028 • Douglas H. Pimlott Conservation Award

This, the most prestigious award of the Federation, is given to recognize an individual for an outstanding contribution to Canadian conservation, either by completing conservation projects of national significance, or by advancing conservation goals through exceptional long-term efforts. Members may submit nominations. Established in 1979 to honor Douglas H. Pimlott, a founding director of CNF and president in 1972 and 1973.

• 16029 • Volunteer Award

To recognize individuals for outstanding voluntary contributions to a project of the Canadian Nature Federation. Up to five awards are presented annually.

• 16030 •
Nature Conservancy
Steve J. McCormick, Pres.
4245 Fairfax Dr., Ste. 100
Arlington, VA 22203-1606
Phone: (703)841-5300
Toll-Free: 800-628-6860
Fax: (703)841-1283
E-mail: comment@tnc.org
Home Page: http://www.nature.org

• 16031 • John and Harriet Dunning Award

To recognize contributions to the protection of South American forest systems.

• 16032 • Oak Leaf Award

This, the highest honor from the Conservancy, is given in recognition of dedicated service by a volunteer or group of volunteers whose service has significantly benefited the Conservancy's local, divisional, or global programs. An oak leaf pin and a plaque are awarded to one or more recipients annually. Established in 1963.

• 16033 • President's Conservation Achievement Award

To recognize exceptional support by individuals, governmental or non-governmental entities, corporations, foundations, or other nonprofit organizations that have worked in partnership with the Conservancy to advance biodiversity protection. An inscribed framed photograph is awarded annually. Established in 1984. Formerly: President's Public Service Award.

• 16034 • President's Stewardship Award

To recognize progress in protecting the ecological integrity of natural areas and the vital elements they harbor. Two awards are presented: Individual award - to an individual volunteer for outstanding stewardship practices that support the objectives of the Conservancy's national stewardship programs; and the Group award - to a local volunteer management group (e.g., preserve committee, scientific advisory group). An inscribed framed photograph representative of an area or element that benefited from the recipient's contributions and activities is awarded at the December national Board of Governors' meeting.

• 16035 •
Nature Conservancy of Minnesota
Rob McKim, Divisional & State Dir.
1101 W River Pkwy., Ste. 200
Minneapolis, MN 55415-1291
Phone: (612)331-0750
Phone: (612)331-0700
Fax: (612)331-0770
E-mail: minnesota@tnc.org
Home Page: http://www.tnc.org

• 16036 • Katherine Ordway Stewardship Award

For research and stewardship of biological diversity. Grant awarded semiannually.

• 16037 •
Nature Saskatchewan
Attila Chanady, Pres.
1860 Lorne St., Rm. 206
Regina, SK, Canada S4P 2L7
Phone: (306)780-9273
Toll-Free: 800-667-4668
Fax: (306)780-9263
E-mail: info@naturesask.ca
Home Page: http://www.naturesask.com

Formerly: (1995) Saskatchewan Natural History Society.

• 16038 • **Conservation Award**
To recognize an individual for outstanding contribution to conservation, either for a specific project or work conducted over a period of years. Nominations may be submitted by July 31. An inscribed certificate is awarded at the organization's annual meeting. Established in 1988.

• 16039 • **Fellows Award**
This class of membership is recognized as an honor to the recipient, recognizing extensive and continuing contribution of time over many years to the Society and its objectives. Awarded annually. Established in 1987.

• 16040 • **Larry Morgotch Memorial Award**
To recognize a member for an outstanding slide presentation on natural history. Awarded annually.

• 16041 • **Cliff Shaw Award**
To recognize an outstanding article or series of articles published in the *Blue Jay.* Awarded annually.

• 16042 • **Volunteer of the Year Award**
To honor a member who, over the course of the previous 12 months, has volunteered significant time and energy to promote the objectives and aims of the Society. Awarded annually.

• 16043 •
Walter W. Naumburg Foundation
Lucy Rowan Mann, Exec. Dir.
60 Lincoln Center Plz.
New York, NY 10023-6588
Phone: (212)874-1150
Fax: (212)724-0263
Home Page: http://www.naumburg.org

• 16044 • **Naumburg Chamber Music Award**
To encourage and assist young, less-established, and serious ensembles toward functioning careers. A maximum of two groups are chosen each year and the winners are awarded a fully-funded New York appearance at Alice Tully Hall. Established in 1965 and usually awarded annually since 1971.

• 16045 • **Naumburg International Competition**
To select a young performer at the beginning of his or her career whose talent is so outstanding that a Naumburg prize might launch an important career. Musicians of every nationality between 17 and 33 years of age are eligible. The competition rotates each year between the disciplines of piano, voice, and violin. Prizes are given for first, second, and third place, and an honorable mention is recognized. Held annually. Established in 1926.

• 16046 •
Nautical Research Guild
31 Water St., Ste. 7
Cuba, NY 14727
Phone: (585)968-8111
E-mail: nrg@a-znet.com
Home Page: http://www.naut-res-guild.org

• 16047 • **Howard I. Chapelle Award for Nautical Research**
Recognizes outstanding nautical research. Hel in conjunction with major ship model events. Awarded periodically.

• 16048 • **Editor's Choice Award**
Awarded annuall. Inquire for application details.

• 16049 •
Naval Enlisted Reserve Association
Capt. Dave Davidson, Exec.Dir.
6703 Farragut Ave.
Falls Church, VA 22042-2189
Phone: (703)534-1329
Toll-Free: 800-776-9020
Fax: (703)534-3617
E-mail: members@nera.org
Home Page: http://www.nera.org

• 16050 • **Seventeen Seventy-Six Award ("1776 Award")**
For recognition of service to the nation, the navy, the community, and the association. All members of the association are eligible. An individual plaque is awarded annually at the national conference. The selectee's name is inscribed on a perpetual plaque at headquarters. Established in 1972 by Maj. Gen. John Patton, USAFR (Ret.)

• 16051 •
Naval Submarine League
Capt. C. Michael Garverick, Exec.Dir.
PO Box 1146
Annandale, VA 22003
Phone: (703)256-0891
Toll-Free: 877-280-7827
Fax: (703)642-5815
E-mail: nslops@cavtel.net
Home Page: http://www.navalsubleague.com

• 16052 • **Active Duty Literary Prize**
To stimulate U.S. Naval Personnel to express their ideas, professional knowledge, and perspectives in writing. Active duty personnel in the U.S. Naval Service are eligible. A monetary prize is awarded annually in the spring. Established in 1990.

• 16053 • **Jack N. Darby Award for Inspirational Leadership and Excellence of Command**
To recognize a submarine officer who has displayed exceptional leadership in command. Members of the U.S. Navy Submarine Service are eligible. A monetary award, a plaque, and a citation are awarded annually at the Symposium. Established in 1987 in honor of Rear Admiral Jack N. Darby, who died while serving as Commander Submarine Force, U.S. Pacific Fleet.

• 16054 • **Literary Honorarium Award**
To acknowledge outstanding articles published in the *Submarine Review.* A monetary prize is awarded annually in June. Established in 1984.

• 16055 • **NROTC Essay Contest**
To stimulate future U.S. Naval Officers to develop writing skills and to express their ideas, professional knowledge, and perspectives. Midshipmen enrolled in the Naval Reserve Officers Training Corps at colleges and universities throughout the United States are eligible. A monetary award, a certificate, and a one-year complimentary membership in the Naval Submarine League are awarded annually in the spring. Established in 1990. Co-sponsored by the U.S. Navy Chief of Education and Training.

• 16056 • **Levering Smith Award for Submarine Support Achievement**
To recognize specific or continuing submarine support actions that have most contributed to the furtherance of the spirit or fighting mettle of the submarine force. Navy service members (officer or enlisted) lieutenant commander or junior are eligible. A monetary award, a plaque, and a citation are awarded annually at the Symposium. Established in 1986 in honor of Vice Admiral Levering Smith, who developed missiles for the U.S. Fleet Ballistic Missile Submarines.

• 16057 • **Submarine/ASW Writing Award**
To advance knowledge in the Naval and Maritime Services. Authors of articles which have been published during the preceding fiscal year, April 1 through March 30, are eligible. A monetary prize is awarded annually at the NSL business meeting in June. Established in 1991. Co-sponsored by the United States Naval Institute.

• 16058 • **Frederick B. Warder Award for Outstanding Achievement**
To recognize a specific action, contribution, or continuing performance that most positively influences the reputation, readiness, or future well-being of the submarine force. Government employees, civilian or military, are eligible. A monetary award, a plaque, and a citation are awarded annually at the Symposium. Established in 1986 in honor of Rear Admiral Frederick B. Warder, a submarine hero of World War II.

• 16059 •
NCSJ: Advocates on Behalf of Jews in Russia, Ukraine, the Baltic
Mark Levin, Exec.Dir.
2020 K St. NW, Ste. 7800
Washington, DC 20006
Phone: (202)898-2500
Fax: (202)898-0822
E-mail: ncsj@ncsj.org
Home Page: http://www.ncsj.org

• 16060 • **Soviet Jewry Freedom Awards**
To recognize individuals or groups for outstanding activity and commitment on behalf of the struggle of Soviet Jews to attain their basic human rights. A bronze plaque on an inscribed wood base is awarded periodically at the National Policy Conference of the National Conference on Soviet Jewry. Established in 1973.

• 16061 •
Nebraska Dressage Association
Cynthia Johnson, Pres.
PO Box 22036
Lincoln, NE 68542
Phone: (402)435-7561
Phone: (402)440-7127
Fax: (402)733-4470
E-mail: cindyj@nebraska.com
Home Page: http://members.cox.net/nda/NDA_Home.html

• 16062 • **Horse and Rider Awards**
For performance in sanctioned dressage shows. Trophy awarded annually.

• 16063 •
Nebraska Hospice and Palliative Care Association
Jonathan Krutz, Exec.Dir.
21203 A St.
Eagle, NE 68347
Phone: (402)540-3128
Phone: (308)389-5376
E-mail: nebraskahospice@aol.com

• 16064 • **Nebraska Hospice Volunteer of the Year**
For nominated by local Hospice member. Scholarship awarded annually.

• 16065 •
Nebraska Humanities Council
Jane Renner Hood, Exec.Dir.
215 Centennial Mall S, Ste. 500
Lincoln, NE 68508
Phone: (402)474-2131
Fax: (402)474-4852
E-mail: nhc@nebraskahumanities.org
Home Page: http://www.nebraskahumanities.org

• 16066 • **Sower Award**
For an individual, community, and organization that have made outstanding contributions to humanities. Recognition award bestowed annually.

• 16067 •
Nebraska Library Association
Maggie Harding, Exec.Dir.
PO Box 98
Crete, NE 68333-0098
Phone: (402)826-2636
Fax: (402)826-2636
E-mail: gh12521@alltel.net
Home Page: http://www.nebraskalibraries.org

• 16068 • **Golden Sower Awards**
To encourage the development of an appreciation among Nebraska's children for excellence in writing and beauty in illustrations. Authors and illustrators of fiction living in the United States must be nominated by teachers, students, and library/media specialists by August 15. Titles published during the preceding five-year period are considered. Awards are presented in three categories: Primary - picture book for grades K-3; Intermediate - novel for grades 4-6; and Young Adult - novel for grades 6-9. A walnut plaque is awarded to one recipient in each category each year. The award replicates the statue of the "Sower" on top of the State Capitol building in Lincoln, Nebraska. Established in 1980 by Dr. Denise C. Storey and Dr. Karla Hawkins Wendelin at the University of Nebraska-Lincoln.

• 16069 • **Meritorious Service Award**
For recognition of contributions toward the improvement of library services on a local, regional, or a statewide basis. The nominee may be an individual, a corporation, or a civic organization. A plaque is awarded annually. Established in 1961.

• 16070 • **Mari Sandoz Award**
To recognize an individual who has made a significant contribution to the Nebraska book world through writing, film production, or related activity. Authors, illustrators, reviewers for television, movies or children's books, and librarians with ties to Nebraska, now or in the past, are eligible. A plaque with a bronze medal in the shape of the state of Nebraska is awarded annually when merited. Established in 1969.

• 16071 • **Trustee Citation Award**
For recognition of a contribution toward the implementation of sound, efficient library policies resulting in the advancement of library service within the community; contribution toward the strengthening of library services outside the area of the local community; and effectiveness in serving jointly as the library's spokesman to the community, and the community's spokesman to the library. A plaque is awarded annually. Established in 1970.

• 16072 •
Nebraska Poultry Industries
Susan S. Joy, Gen.Mgr.
University of Nebraska
A103 Animal Sciences
PO Box 830908
Lincoln, NE 68583-0908
Phone: (402)472-2051
Fax: (402)472-4607
E-mail: egg-turkey@unl.edu
Home Page: http://nepoultry.org

• 16073 • **Sarah Louise Gruver Memorial Scholarship**
For any student whose parent/guardians are involved in some aspect of the commercial poultry production industry in Nebraska. Scholarship awarded annually.

• 16074 •
The Nebraska Review
Neil Azevedo, Ed.
WFAB 212
University of Nebraska
Omaha, NE 68182-0324
Phone: (402)554-3159
Fax: (402)614-2026
E-mail: tnr@zoopress.org
Home Page: http://www.zoopress.org/nebraskareview

• 16075 • **TNR Awards in Fiction and Poetry**
To recognize superior writing in fiction and poetry. Applicants for the fiction award should submit a manuscript of 5,000 words or less, and applicants for the poetry award must not submit more than five poems or six pages. The deadline is September 1 to November 30 with an entry fee of 10.00 per story or packet of poems. All entrants receive a one-year subscription to the magazine. Open submission is January 1 - April 15. Monetary awards of $500 for fiction and $500 for poetry and publication in the *The Nebraska Review* are awarded annually. Established in 1987.

• 16076 •
Nebraska State Genealogical Society
PO Box 5608
Lincoln, NE 68505

• 16077 • **Outstanding Genealogists**
For outstanding work in genealogy or history preservation. Recognition award bestowed annually.

• 16078 •
Nebraska Sustainable Agriculture Society
Paul Rohrbaugh, Exec.Dir.
PO Box 736
Hartington, NE 68739
Phone: (402)254-2289
Phone: (402)869-2396
Fax: (402)869-2288
E-mail: jillw@hartel.net
Home Page: http://www.nebsusag.org

• 16079 • Research and Education Award
For significant contributions to sustainable agriculture in Nebraska. Recognition award bestowed annually.

• 16080 • Stewardship Award
For significant contributions to sustainable agriculture in Nebraska. Recognition award bestowed annually.

• 16081 •
Neighborhood Watch
Mary McIlvaine, Prog.Dir.
800 Center St., Ste. 316
Racine, WI 53403
Phone: (262)637-5711
Fax: (262)636-9575
E-mail: rnw@rootcom.net

• 16082 • Shared Vision Award
For individual and/or group showing leadership and activism in neighborhoods. Recognition award bestowed annually.

• 16083 •
Nevada Association of School Boards
201 S. Roop St., Ste. 102
Carson City, NV 89701-4779
Phone: (775)885-7466
Toll-Free: 877-987-6382
Fax: (775)883-7398
E-mail: nvasb@nsn.k12.nv.us

• 16084 • Distinguished Service Award
For school board, school board member, and administrator. Recognition award bestowed annually.

• 16085 •
New Baltimore Historical Society
Richard Gonyeau, Pres.
51065 Washington
New Baltimore, MI 48047
Phone: (586)725-4755
E-mail: ejllanne@cs.com
Home Page: http://www.newbaltimorehistoricalsociety.org

• 16086 • Award of Appreciation
For a member who exemplifies outstanding service to the society. Recognition award bestowed annually.

• 16087 • Award of Merit
To a member, organization, or business that promotes/supports local history. Recognition award bestowed annually.

• 16088 •
New Brunswick Institute of Agrologists
Charles Briggs, Pres.
PO Box 3479, Sta. B
Fredericton, NB, Canada E3H 5H2
Phone: (506)459-5536
Fax: (506)454-7837
E-mail: duncan.fraser@gnb.ca
Home Page: http://www.nbagrologists.nb.ca

• 16089 • Agricultural Initiative Award
To recognize significant contributions in any agrology field, private or public, by an individual working in New Brunswick agriculture. Members of the Institute who are under 40 years of age and have not received an AIC National Award are eligible. A plaque is awarded annually. Established in 1979.

• 16090 • Agricultural Leadership Award
To recognize outstanding achievement by a New Brunswick farmer as a leader in the industry. Agricultural producers operating a farm in New Brunswick are eligible; this includes owner-operators of farm units, managers of cooperative partnerships or institutional/corporate farms, and part- or full-time farmers in any field of agricultural production. A trophy is awarded annually. Established in 1979 in honor of Louis Hebert, first farmer in Canadian recorded history (1604).

• 16091 • Agricultural Organization of the Year Public Sector
For recognition of outstanding performance by an agricultural organization in the public sector. Departments, branches, sections, units, and services are eligible for the public sector award. Awarded annually. Established in 1989.

• 16092 •
New Canaan Historical Society
Janet Lindstrom, Exec.Dir.
13 Oenoke Ridge
New Canaan, CT 06840
Phone: (203)966-1776
Fax: (203)972-5917
E-mail: newcanaan.historical@snet.net
Home Page: http://www.nchistory.org

• 16093 • Bayles Award
For high school junior excelling in history scholarship. Recognition award bestowed annually.

• 16094 •
New Delta Review
Craig Brandhorst, Editor-in-Chief
English Dept.
214 Allen Hall
Louisiana State University
Baton Rouge, LA 70803
Phone: (225)578-4079
Fax: (504)388-4129
E-mail: new-delta@lsu.edu
Home Page: http://www.english.lsu.edu/journals/ndr

• 16095 • Matt Clark Prize
To recognize achievement in both fiction and poetry. The competition is open to all previously unpublished works. The first place winner in each category receives a monetary award of $100 and publication in the *New Delta Review*. Second- and third-place winners are recognized in the Summer edition of the magazine. Entry deadline is February 28. Awarded annually.

• 16096 •
New Dramatists
Joel K. Ruark, Exec.Dir.
424 W 44th St.
New York, NY 10036
Phone: (212)757-6960
Fax: (212)265-4738
E-mail: newdramatists@newdramatists.org
Home Page: http://newdramatists.org

• 16097 • L. Arnold Weissberger Playwriting Award
To recognize outstanding achievement in playwriting. Plays must be nominated by a theater professional. A monetary award of $5,000 is presented annually. Established in 1987 by the Weissberger estate in memory of L. Arnold Weissberger, a lawyer and long-time New Dramatists Board Chairman.

• 16098 •
New England Council
98 N. Washington St., Ste. 201
Boston, MA 02114
Phone: (617)723-4009
Fax: (617)723-3943
E-mail: newenglandcouncil@msn.com
Home Page: http://www.newenglandcouncil.com

• 16099 • New Englander of the Year Awards
To recognize New Englanders who have demonstrated commitment and contributions in their fields of work as well as leadership and impact on the New England region's quality of life and economy. One award is given to a leader in the private sector, one in the public sector, and one to an institution or public organization. Awarded annually. Established in 1964.

• 16100 •
New England Historic Genealogical Society
Ralph J. Crandall, Exec.Dir.
One Watson Pl., Bldg. 4
PO Box 5089
Framingham, MA 01701
Phone: (617)536-5740
Phone: (508)877-5750
Toll-Free: 888-296-3447
Fax: (617)536-7307
E-mail: membership@nehgs.org
Home Page: http://www.newenglandancestors.org

• 16101 • Coddington Award of Merit
For genealogical excellence. Recognition award bestowed periodically.

Awards are arranged in alphabetical order below their administering organizations

• 16102 •
New England Mountain Bike Association
Philip Keyes, Exec.Dir.
PO Box 2221
Acton, MA 01720-6221
Toll-Free: 800-576-3622
Fax: (717)326-8243
E-mail: pk@nemba.org
Home Page: http://www.nemba.org

• 16103 • **NEMBA Trail Grant**
For benefit to New England trails. Grant awarded biennially.

• 16104 •
New England Pest Management Association
Walter Perry, Exec.Dir.
76 S State St.
Concord, NH 03301-3520
Phone: (603)228-2118
Toll-Free: (866)386-3762
Fax: (603)228-1231
E-mail: clough@choiceonemail.com
Home Page: http://www.nepma.org

• 16105 • **Bart Eldredge Award**
For performance plus longevity. Recognition award bestowed annually.

• 16106 • **Mark Weintraub Scholarship**
For academic and civic performance relative to NEPCA. Monetary award bestowed annually.

• 16107 •
New England Poetry Club
137 W Newton St.
Boston, MA 02118
Phone: (617)423-9585
E-mail: info@nepoetryclub.org
Home Page: http://www.nepoetryclub.org

• 16108 • **Rosalie Boyle/Norma Farber Award**
To recognize a poem in traditional form, including sonnet, villanelle, and sestina. Original, unpublished poems written in English by a member are eligible. Entry deadline is June 30. A monetary prize of $100 is awarded each year. Established in memory of two former club members.

• 16109 • **Barbara Bradley Award**
To recognize a lyric poem under 21 lines written by a woman. Original, unpublished poems written in English by a member or nonmember are eligible. Entry deadline is June 30. A monetary award of $200 is presented annually.

• 16110 • **Ruth Berrien Fox Award**
To encourage the writing of poetry by Massachusetts high school students. Original, unpublished poems written in English by a member or nonmember are eligible. Entry deadline is June 30. A monetary prize of $100 is awarded annually. Established in 1970 by Dr. Henry Fox in memory of his wife.

• 16111 • **Golden Rose Award**
This, the most significant award of the Poetry Club, is given to honor a poet who has done the most for the art in the past year or in his/her lifetime. Poets with New England ties, whether member or nonmember, are eligible. A handmade gold rose is awarded annually. Established in 1920 by the Reverend Eugene Shippen of the Second Unitarian Church of Boston.

• 16112 • **John Holmes Award**
For recognition of outstanding poetry efforts on the part of New England college students. Original, unpublished poems written in English by a member or nonmember are eligible. Entry deadline is June 30. A monetary prize of $100 is awarded each year.

• 16113 • **Firman Houghton Award**
To recognize a lyric poem. Original, unpublished poems written in English by a member or nonmember are eligible. Entry deadline is June 30. A monetary prize of $250 is awarded. Established in memory of Firman Houghton, a former President of the Club.

• 16114 • **Erika Mumford Prize**
To recognize a poem in any form about travel, other lands or cultures, or inspired by the foreign influence. Original, unpublished poems written in English by a member or nonmember are eligible. Entry deadline is June 30. A monetary award of $250 is presented.

• 16115 • **May Sarton Award**
To recognize a poet whose work is an inspiration to other poets. Recipients are selected by the board. Awarded when merited. Established in 1987.

• 16116 • **Daniel Varoujan Award**
To recognize an unpublished poem (not a translation) worthy of the art of Daniel Varoujan, an Armenian poet killed by the Turks in 1915. A monetary prize of $1,000 is awarded annually. Established in 1980 by Diana Der-Hovanessian.

• 16117 • **Gretchen Warren Award**
For recognition of the best published poem by a member of the Club. Entry deadline is June 30. Awarded annually.

• 16118 •
New England Press Association
Brenda Reed, Exec.Dir.
360 Huntington Ave., 428CP
Boston, MA 02115
Phone: (617)373-5610
Fax: (617)373-5615
E-mail: info@nepa.org
Home Page: http://www.nepa.org

• 16119 • **Horace Greeley Award**
To recognize a newspaper or an individual performing outstanding service to the general public. Service above and beyond the normal function of writing, publishing, or editing a newspaper is considered. Excellence, dedication, courage, and effectiveness in serving the public interest are the major determining factors in the selection of candidates to receive this award. Nominees need not be employed by a NEPA member newspaper, but must be employed, or have been employed, by a New England newspaper of general circulation. A suitable plaque, scroll, or certificate is awarded annually when merited. Established in 1966 to honor Horace Greeley, one of the greatest and most dedicated journalists in the history of American journalism.

• 16120 •
New England Regional Genetics Group
Mary-Frances Garber CGC, Exec.Asst.
PO Box 920288
Needham, MA 02492
Phone: (781)444-0126
Fax: (781)444-0127
E-mail: mfgnergg@verizon.net
Home Page: http://www.nergg.org

• 16121 • **Allen Crocker Award**
For public health genetics involvement. Recognition award bestowed annually.

• 16122 •
New England Theatre Conference
Tom Mikotowicz, Pres.
215 Knob Hill Dr.
198 Tremont St.
Hamden, CT 06518
Phone: (617)851-8535
Fax: (203)288-5938
E-mail: mail@netconline.org
Home Page: http://netconline.org

• 16123 • **Award for Outstanding Creative Achievement in the American Theatre**
To honor a theatre personality who has made outstanding creative achievement in the American Theatre. Actors, designers, playwrights, directors, producers, and drama critics are eligible. Nominations accepted by letter. An engraved Paul Revere Bowl is awarded annually at the Fall Convention. Established in 1957.

• 16124 • **John Gassner Memorial Playwriting Award**
To recognize and encourage new playwrights. Original, unproduced and unpublished full-length plays are eligible. The contest is open to all New England residents and all members of the Theatre Conference. Send a stamped, self-addressed envelope for guidelines. A monetary award, staged reading of portions of the winning plays, and the referral of the winning plays to play publishing companies are awarded annually at the Fall Convention. A cash prize of $1,000 for first place and $500 for second place are presented. Established in 1967 in memory of John Gassner (1903-1967), educator and author, in appreciation of his lifelong dedication to all aspects of the profession and academic theatre.

• 16125 • Moss Hart Memorial Award
To encourage production of plays that stress the virtues of freedom and human dignity, and accent the positive virtues of courage, faith, and hope. Any children's, secondary school, college, community, or professional theatre in New England is eligible. An engraved trophy that is retained for one year, and a permanent plaque are awarded annually at the Fall Convention. Up to five divisional awards may also be presented in the Children and Youth, Secondary School, College/University, Community, and Professional Theatre divisions. Established in memory of Moss Hart, dramatist and director, for his wit and sensitivity, his unconquerable enthusiasm for life, and his work in the theatre.

• 16126 • Host Awards
To recognize time and efforts by theatres and institutions that host various New England state and regional drama festivals (high school, college and community theatre festivals). Any theatre group, educational institution, or other organization/facility that hosts an annual drama festival in New England is eligible. Engraved plaques are awarded annually at the various festivals. Established in 1985.

• 16127 • Regional Awards
To honor personalities or organizations in New England for a specific contribution in a particular theatre area and to focus public attention and offer needed recognition to creative theatre achievement. Engraved plaques are awarded to one or more recipients each year at the fall convention. Established in 1957.

• 16128 • Special Awards
To recognize and reward innovations or advancements in the interests of theatre on a national level. Both individuals and organizations are eligible. Engraved plaques are awarded to one or more recipients each year at the fall convention. Established in 1957.

• 16129 • Jack Stein Make-up Award
To encourage and reward excellence in theatrical make-up in a theatre production. Awards are given to a college theatre group in New England presenting work at the regional festivals. An engraved plaque is awarded. Established in 1976 in honor of Jack Stein, a nationally known make-up artist.

• 16130 •
New England Water Works Association
Mr. Raymond J. Raposa, Exec.Dir.
125 Hopping Brook Rd.
Holliston, MA 01746
Phone: (508)893-7979
Fax: (508)893-9898
E-mail: rraposa@newwa.org
Home Page: http://www.newwa.org

• 16131 • Award of Merit
To recognize a member for outstanding service to the Association, outstanding service to a water utility, or outstanding contribution to water works practice. Awarded annually. Established in 1967.

• 16132 • Dexter Brackett Memorial Award
To recognize the most meritorious paper published in the *Journal of the New England Water Works Association* during the previous year. Authors must be members of the Association and papers must be presented at a meeting of the Association. A medal is awarded annually. Established in 1916 in memory of Dexter Brackett, an eminent water works engineer.

• 16133 • Francis X. Crowley Scholarship
To recognize a student majoring in civil or environmental engineering or business administration at a four-year college or university. The award may be given to a student with another major at the discretion of the committee if the alternate course of study is beneficial to the water works industry. A scholarship of $3,000 is awarded annually. Established in 1990.

• 16134 • Distinguished Drinking Water Public Involvement Award
To recognize individuals or organizations who have significantly contributed in one of the following areas: created or expanded a public education or information program about drinking water that impacts New England or serves as a model for other similar organizations or individuals in the protection, promotion, and/or nurturing of public water supply; have a key involvement in the development of public policy that will conserve, nurture, protect, or improve public drinking water supplies; or has made a significant effort to share programs as described. Awarded annually. Established in 1993.

• 16135 • Drinking Water Protection Business Awards Program
To recognize any size business for their outstanding contributions to drinking water source protection. Established in 1996.

• 16136 • Kenneth O. Hodgson Distinguished Service Award
To provide recognition for outstanding service to the Association and the waterworks industry by a member from the supplier service, manufacturing, or contracting area and also to recognize members from the service community who have provided exemplary service and dedication to furthering the ideals of the Association. Awarded annually. Established in 1990 in honor of Kenneth O. Hodgson, who demonstrated dedication, service, and commitment through his years with the Association.

• 16137 • Honorary Member
To recognize a person of eminence in some branch of water works practice or water works engineering or a member who has been outstanding in the promotion of the welfare of the Association or of the profession of water supply. No more than 25 honorary members are recognized at any one time. Awarded when merited. Established in 1886.

• 16138 • Elson T. Killam Memorial Scholarship
To provide a scholarship to a qualified candidate on the basis of merit, character, and need. Full-time civil or environmental engineering students at four-year colleges or universities are eligible. A scholarship in the amount of $1,500 is awarded annually. Established in 1989.

• 16139 • NEWWA Scholarships
To provide scholarships to qualifying candidates on the basis of merit, character, and need. These scholarships are awarded to members and student members of the NEWWA, with preference given to applicants whose programs are considered by the scholarship committee as beneficial to water works practices in New England. Each year, the following scholarships are awarded: George E. Watters Memorial Scholarship ($5,000), Francis X. Crowley Scholarship ($3,000), Elson T. Killam Memorial Scholarship ($1,500), and the Joseph Murphy Scholarship ($1,500). Additional scholarships may be awarded periodically. Established in 1956.

• 16140 • Past Presidents' Award
To recognize a meritorious paper published in the Association's journal during the previous year. Papers must meet one of the following conditions: meet the requirements of the Dexter Brackett Award (see separate entry); be prepared by individual members of the Association, submitted as a contribution to the Journal, but not presented at a meeting of the Association; or papers prepared by a group of authors, all of whom are members of the Association, and presented at a meeting of the Association. A plaque is awarded annually in honor of all past presidents of NEWWA. Established in 1949. Formerly: Commemorative Award.

• 16141 • Trans Atlantic Reciprocal Award
The reciprocal award of diplomas by the Institution of Water Environmental Management (British) and the New England Water Works Association is intended to foster cordial relations between the two organizations and to stimulate the exchange of knowledge and experience relating to the practice of water works. Awarded every four years. Established in 1948. Formerly: (1988) IWES Award; IWEM Award.

• 16142 • Water Works State Leadership Award
Presented to a State Association member by the President of NEWWA to re cognize the contributions of the recipient to his or her State Association and to the water works profession, in general. Established in 1996.

• 16143 •
New England Wild Flower Society
Ms. Gwen Stauffer, Exec.Dir.
180 Hemenway Rd.
Framingham, MA 01701-2699
Phone: (508)877-7630
Fax: (508)877-3658
E-mail: newfs@newfs.org
Home Page: http://www.newfs.org

Formerly: (1969) New England Wildflower Preservation Society.

• 16144 • Award for Outstanding Service to the Society
To recognize an individual, corporation, or group that is a member of the Society for exceptional and longstanding contribution to the welfare of the Society. Preference is given to personal service beyond financial donation. Nominations may be submitted by members of the Society. Previous winners of the award are not eligible. Awarded annually.

• 16145 • Conservation Award
To recognize an individual or a group for outstanding achievement in furthering the conservation of temperate North American plants and their habitats throughout the New England region and beyond. Nomination deadline is April 30. A gift is presented at each Annual Meeting. Established in 1964. Formerly: (1983) Conservation Medal.

• 16146 • Education Award
To recognize an individual or a group for original and significant work that promotes public understanding and appreciation of temperate North American plants. Eligible works include publications, course development, and works of art on public display. Nomination deadline is April 30. A framed certificate is awarded annually.

• 16147 • Homer Lucas Landscape Award
To recognize an individual, organization, or agency responsible for designing and/or maintaining a landscape for public enjoyment (such as parks, public gardens, roadside areas, or nature centers) that displays wildflowers or other temperate North American native plants for aesthetic and educational benefit. The area must be at least three years old prior to evaluation and exhibit excellence of design and maintenance in all seasons. Nomination deadline is April 30. Awarded annually.

• 16148 • State Awards
To recognize an individual, group, or organization within the six New England states for significant contribution to the preservation of native plants and/or their habitat within that state. Preference is given to work that has impact throughout a state. One award may be presented for each of the six New England states each year. Nomination deadline is April 30.

• 16149 • Kathryn S. Taylor Award for Private Gardens
For recognition of a privately-owned garden of any size displaying significant use of wildflowers and other temperate North American native plants. The garden must be at least three years old and exhibit excellence of design and maintenance in all seasons. Finalist gardens, selected from descriptive materials and photographs, are visited by a panel of judges during the twelve-month period preceding presentation of the award. Nomination deadline is April 30. Awarded annually.

• 16150 •
New Hampshire Association of Broadcasters
B. Allan Sprague, Pres.
707 Chestnut St.
Manchester, NH 03104
Phone: (603)627-9600
Fax: (603)627-9603
E-mail: als@nhab.org
Home Page: http://www.nhab.org

• 16151 • Golden Mike Awards
For excellence in broadcasting. Recognition award bestowed annually.

• 16152 •
New Hampshire Golf Association
Gary Philippy, Exec.Dir.
15 W Rd.
Canterbury, NH 03224
Phone: (603)783-4554
Fax: (603)629-9797
E-mail: info@nhgolfhouse.org
Home Page: http://www.nhgolf.com

• 16153 • Player of Year
For most tournament points. Recognition award bestowed annually.

• 16154 •
New Hampshire Nurse Practitioner Association
Sally Becker, Admin.Dir.
PO Box 833
Concord, NH 03302
Phone: (603)648-2233
Toll-Free: 800-796-6717
Fax: (603)648-2466
E-mail: nhnpa@tds.net
Home Page: http://www.npweb.org

• 16155 • Nurse Practitioner of the Year
For service and professionalism. Recognition award bestowed annually.

• 16156 •
New Hampshire Pharmacists Association
2 Eagle Square, Ste. 400
Concord, NH 03301-4956
Phone: (603)229-0292
Fax: (603)224-7769

• 16157 • NHPA Scholarship Trust Fund
For third year NH resident studying pharmacy. Scholarship awarded annually.

• 16158 •
New Hampshire School Transportation Association
Richard H. Clough CAE, Exec.Dir.
76 S State St.
Concord, NH 03301-3520
Phone: (603)228-1231
Fax: (603)228-2118
E-mail: clough@choiceonemail.com
Home Page: http://www.nhsta.org

• 16159 • Driver of the Year
For outstanding performance as a school bus driver. Recognition award bestowed annually.

• 16160 •
New Hanover - Pender County Medical Society
Bonnie Jeffreys Brown, Exec.Dir.
5300 Greenleaf Dr.
Wilmington, NC 28403
Phone: (910)790-5800
Fax: (910)790-5600
E-mail: nhpcmeds@earthlink.net

• 16161 • New Hanover-Pender Co. Medical Society Premedical Scholarship
For senior student at U of NC at Wilmington with outstanding credentials who plans to go into medicine. Scholarship awarded annually.

• 16162 •
New Jersey Center for Visual Arts
68 Elm St.
Summit, NJ 07901
Phone: (908)273-9121
Fax: (908)273-1457
Home Page: http://njmuseums.com/njcva

Formerly: Summit Art Center.

• 16163 • Annual Art Show
To recognize individual art work in crafts, photography, painting, and sculpture. There are approximately five cash awards and one Best In Show award.

• 16164 • International Juried Show
To encourage excellence in all branches of fine arts and crafts. Monetary prizes are awarded annually. Established in 1964.

• 16165 • Ann G. Stein Memorial Arts Person of the Year Award
To recognize the person who in the previous year or series of years, has done the most to further the role of the arts locally, regionally, and in New Jersey by exemplary fulfillment of any of the following criteria: creating significant works of art; innovatively and inspirationally teaching the arts; encouraging, in a leadership role, the support that corporations, foundations, government, other public interest organizations and

private citizens provide for arts activities; participating as an outstanding volunteer in organizations whose mission is to enrich our knowledge, understanding, and appreciation of the arts; promoting the development of educational programs that integrate the arts into the curriculum; and effectively managing and leading an arts organization, community project, private business sector project or a government program that increases the ability of our community to benefit from the arts. Recipients receive an original work of art, created by Dorothy Gillespie of Gillespie Gallery, NYC, suitable for display, their name added to a prominent, permanent plaque installed in the Art Center, an appropriate public award ceremony, and publicity generated in the press featuring pictures of the recipient along with articles about their history of impact on the arts. Awarded annually.

• 16166 •
New Jersey Forest Stewardship Committee
David Edelman, Supv. Forester, Forest Steward.Coor.
New Jersey Forest Service
PO Box 402
Trenton, NJ 08625
Phone: (609)984-3860
Fax: (609)984-0378
Home Page: http://www.state.nj.us/dep/forestry/service/

• 16167 • **Outstanding Forest Steward of the Year**
For quantity and quality of stewardship practices implemented on the land owner's property. Recognition award bestowed annually.

• 16168 •
New Jersey Historical Commission
Dr. Marc Mappen, Exec.Dir.
225 W State St., 4th Fl.
PO Box 305
Trenton, NJ 08625-0305
Phone: (609)292-6062
Fax: (609)633-8168
E-mail: njhc@sos.state.nj.us
Home Page: http://www.newjerseyhistory.org

• 16169 • **Alfred E. Driscoll Prize**
To recognize the author of an outstanding doctoral dissertation on any topic in New Jersey history. A monetary prize of $1,000 is awarded biennially in even-numbered years. Established in 1975 as a fellowship; re-established in 1981. The award honors Alfred E. Driscoll, governor of New Jersey, 1947-54. Formerly: (1981) Governor Alfred E. Driscoll Fellowship.

• 16170 • **Richard P. McCormick Prize**
To recognize the author of an outstanding scholarly work on New Jersey history. Work published within the preceding two years may be nominated or submitted by the author by January 2. A monetary prize of $1,000 is awarded biennially in odd-numbered years. Established in 1983 to honor Richard P. McCormick, professor emeritus, Rutgers University.

• 16171 •
New Jersey Hospice and Palliative Care Organization
Don Pendley, Pres.
175 Glenside Ave.
Scotch Plains, NJ 07076
Phone: (908)233-0060
Fax: (908)233-1630
E-mail: info@njhospice.org
Home Page: http://www.njhospice.org

• 16172 • **Hospice Team Awards**
For excellence of service. Trophy awarded annually.

• 16173 • **Spirit of Hospice Awards**
For excellence of service. Trophy awarded annually.

• 16174 •
New Jersey Humanist Network
Lisa Ridge, Pres.
PO Box 8212
Somerville, NJ 08876
Phone: (732)658-6440
Home Page: http://www.njhn.org/

• 16175 • **Humanist Music Award**
For original composition about humanist issues. Monetary award bestowed annually.

• 16176 •
New Jersey Intellectual Property Law Association
Thomas D. Hoffman, Pres.
269 29th St.
St. Avalon, NJ 08202
Phone: (609)368-4571
Fax: (609)368-4571
E-mail: wendywords@comcast.net
Home Page: http://www.njipla.com

Formerly: New Jersey Patent Law Association; Intellectual Property Law Association.

• 16177 • **Jefferson Medal**
To honor an individual for an exceptional contribution in either the patent, trademark, or copyright field. A gold medal and plaque are awarded annually at the Jefferson Medal Dinner. Established in 1951 in cooperation with the New Jersey State Bar Association.

• 16178 •
New Jersey Library Association
Cathy Delneo, Pres.
PO Box 1534
Trenton, NJ 08607
Phone: (609)394-8032
Fax: (609)394-8164
E-mail: cdelneo@hublib.lib.nj.us
Home Page: http://www.njla.org

• 16179 • **Garden State Children's Book Awards**
To recognize outstanding books for the early and middle grades. The winners are chosen by a committee of the Children's Services Section of the Association on the basis of literary merit and popularity with readers. A three-year lapse is allowed in order to determine this popularity. The awards are given in four categories: (1) Easy-to-Read books; (2) Easy-to-Read series books; (3) Children's Fiction - for grades 2-5; and (4) Children's Nonfiction - for grades 2-5. Each year, awards are given to both authors and illustrators. Established in 1977.

• 16180 • **Garden State Teen Book Awards**
To give recognition to books published for teens. The nominees are selected by a committee from the New Jersey Library Association on the basis of literary merit. New Jersey teens select the winners. A three-year lapse since publication is allowed in order to determine popularity. The awards are given in three categories: Fiction, Grades 6-8; Fiction, Grades 9-12; and Non-Fiction. Awarded annually. Established in 1977.

• 16181 • **Library Service Awards**
To recognize contributions to library and community in the state of New Jersey. Two awards are given: one to an individual and one to a friends/volunteer/community group. Nominees may be any person or group associated with library services including but not limited to library staff members. An engraved momento is awarded annually. Established in 1976 to honor an individual; in 1986, the group award was added.

• 16182 • **Trustee Recognition Award**
To honor an individual in the state of New Jersey for promoting the use of the library and developing recognition of its place in the community, the county, the state or the nation. Equal consideration is given to trustees of small, medium or large libraries, to entire Boards, and to individuals. Awarded annually. Established in 1957.

• 16183 •
New Jersey Literary Hall of Fame
% Alumni Office
NJ Institute of Technology
323 Martin Luther King Jr. Blvd.
Newark, NJ 07102-1982
Phone: (201)596-3441
Home Page: http://www.library.njit.edu/archives/lit-hall

• 16184 • **The Michael**
To honor outstanding authors from New Jersey. Authors who sell 1,000,000 copies of their books, who are awarded national/international awards, or who were on the *New York Times* best-seller list for ten weeks are eligible. The Michael, designed by Michael Graves, is awarded biennially. Established in 1976 by Dr. Herman A. Estrin.

• 16185 •
New Jersey Symphony Orchestra
Stephen Sichak Jr., Interim Pres. and CEO
Education Dept.
2 Central Ave., 3rd Floor
Newark, NJ 07102
Phone: (973)624-3713
Toll-Free: 800-255-3476
Fax: (973)624-2115
E-mail: maraujo@njsymphony.org
Home Page: http://www.njsymphony.org

• 16186 • **Young Artists Auditions Competition**
To identify and encourage gifted young musicians. Applicants may audition on piano, strings, woodwinds, brass, or other orchestral instruments. Applicants must be 19 years old or younger, and must be either legal residents of New Jersey (although they may be attending schools elsewhere) or full-time residential students at a college or university in New Jersey. Applications must be postmarked no later than December 1. Four monetary awards are presented: Henry Lewis Award ($10,000), Judith Nachison Award ($5,000), NJSO League Volunteer Award ($3,000), and Conductor's Award ($2,000). Awarded annually. Established in 1975.

• 16187 •
New Jersey Tenants Organization
Bonnie Shapiro, Admin.Dir.
389 Main St.
Hackensack, NJ 07601
Phone: (201)342-3775
Fax: (201)342-3776
E-mail: info@njto.org
Home Page: http://www.njto.org/

• 16188 • **Ronald B. Atlas Award**
For outstanding tenant activist. Recognition award bestowed annually.

• 16189 •
New Letters
Robert Stewart, Editor-in-Chief
University House
5101 Rockhill Rd.
University of Missouri-Kansas City
Kansas City, MO 64110-2499
Phone: (816)235-1168
Fax: (816)235-2611
E-mail: newletters@umkc.edu
Home Page: http://www.newletters.org

• 16190 • ***New Letters* Writing Awards**
To discover and encourage new writers and to recognize and reward good writing. All entries must be previously unpublished. The following awards are presented annually: Alexander Patterson Cappon Prize for Fiction - a monetary award of $1,000 and publication for the best short story; *New Letters* Prize for Poetry - $1,000 and publication for the best group of three to six poems; and Dorothy Churchill Cappon Prize for Essay - $1,000 for the best essay. Established in 1986.

• 16191 •
New Mexico Art League
3407 Juan Tabo NE
Albuquerque, NM 87111
Phone: (505)293-5034
E-mail: sunspinner1@aol.com

• 16192 • **National Small Painting Exhibition**
To recognize visual artists and to cultivate and promote the arts nationally. Open to all artists over 18 years of age who reside in the United States and its territories. Original works produced in the preceding three year period in oil (including acrylic in oil technique), watercolor, pastel, graphics, or mixed media and have not been previously submitted in the exhibition are eligible. Image size is limited to a maximum of 16 x 20 inches excluding frame and a minimum is 8 x 10 inches. The deadline for receipt of entries is November 27. The following monetary prizes are awarded: Best of Show - $500; first prize - $200; second prize - $100; third prize - $75; and purchase awards in each medium. Ribbons are awarded for honorable mention. Established in 1966.

• 16193 •
New Mexico Library Association
Linda O'Connell, Admin.Asst.
Box 26074
Albuquerque, NM 87125
Phone: (505)400-7309
Fax: (505)899-7600
E-mail: nmla@worldnet.att.net
Home Page: http://www.nmla.org

• 16194 • **Land of Enchantment Book Awards**
To encourage the children of New Mexico to read more and better books. This award is presented in odd years by the New Mexico Reading Association conference and in even years by the New Mexico Library Association conference. The winner is chosen by New Mexico children in grades four through eight, from a master list chosen by a selection committee. Awards are given for children's list and young adults list. Established In 1981.

• 16195 •
New Mexico Museum of Space History
Mark Santiago, Exec.Dir.
PO Box 5430
Alamogordo, NM 88311-5430
Phone: (505)437-2840
Toll-Free: 877-333-6589
Fax: (505)434-2245
E-mail: msantiago@dca.state.nm.us
Home Page: http://www.spacefame.org

• 16196 • **International Space Hall of Fame**
For recognition of space pioneers. The following criteria are considered: outstanding achievement that clearly and obviously advanced either rocketry, space flight, space science, or space engineering; or a lifelong career with a pattern of achievement that significantly and obviously advanced either rocketry, space flight, space science, or space engineering. Contributions do not necessarily have to be international in scope. The inductee may be living or deceased. Selection is made without regard for political ideology or nationality. Group awards are permissible. Scientists, astronauts, engineers, administrators, or even visionaries are eligible. A plaque and permanent placement in the International Space Hall of Fame are awarded annually at the induction ceremony on or about the first Saturday in October. Established in 1976 by the state of New Mexico to honor space pioneers.

• 16197 •
New Rivers Press
Minnesota State University, Moorhead
Wayne Gudmundson, Dir.
1104 7th Ave. S
Moorhead, MN 56563
Phone: (218)299-5870
E-mail: nrp@mnstate.edu
Home Page: http://appserv.mnstate.edu/newriverspress/nrp-2

• 16198 • **Minnesota Voices Project**
To publish and encourage new and emerging authors of poetry, short fiction, novellas, personal essays, and memoirs. Three prizes of $1,000 each and a standard royalty contract are awarded annually. Established in 1981 by C.W. Truesdale.

• 16199 •
New School University
Bob Kerrey, Pres.
66 W 12th St.
New York, NY 10011
Phone: (212)229-5600
Fax: (212)229-8935
E-mail: webmaster@newschool.edu
Home Page: http://www.newschool.edu

• 16200 • **Fiorello H. La Guardia Award**
To honor those people or organizations that have made major contributions to the growth and well-being of New York City. A plaque is generally presented annually at a dinner in the spring. Established in 1973 in memory of Fiorello H. LaGuardia, a former mayor of New York City.

• 16201 •
New West Symphony
Kenneth Hopper, Exec.Dir.
Thousand Oaks Civic Arts Plz., Ste. D
2100 E Thousand Oaks Blvd.
Thousand Oaks, CA 91362-7610
Phone: (805)497-5800
Fax: (805)497-5839
E-mail: bchess@symphony.org
Home Page: http://www.newwestsymphony.org

Formerly: (1995) Ventura County Symphony Association.

• 16202 • Discovery Artist Award
To recognize exceptional musical talent. Preprofessional musicians under the age of 21 (voice to age 25) who are residents of Ventura County, California are eligible. An opportunity to perform with the New West Symphony and solo recital engagements are presented annually. Established in 1967. Formerly: Young Artist Award.

• 16203 •
New York Academy of Sciences
Ellis Rubenstein, Pres./CEO
2 E 63rd St.
New York, NY 10021
Phone: (212)838-0230
Toll-Free: 800-843-6927
Fax: (212)888-2894
E-mail: erubinstein@nyas.org
Home Page: http://www.nyas.org

• 16204 • Heinz R. Pagels Human Rights of Scientists Award
To recognize scientists for contributions to safeguard or advance the human rights of scientists throughout the world. A certificate of citation is awarded annually to one or more recipients. Established in 1979.

• 16205 •
New York American Marketing Association
Erica Stoppenbach, Dir.
116 E. 27th St., 6th Fl.
New York, NY 10016
Phone: (212)687-3280
Toll-Free: 888-467-7249
Fax: (212)557-9242
E-mail: sdemnisky@nyama.org
Home Page: http://www.effie.org

• 16206 • Effie Awards
For recognition of effective advertising campaigns. The Effie is a unique award because it recognizes the team effort of client and agency. Campaigns must currently be running to be considered. Awards are given in more than 40 categories. Gold, silver and bronze E statuettes are awarded annually. The Grand Effie is given for the most effective campaign in all categories. Established in 1969.

• 16207 •
New York Biology Teachers Association
John Cunningham, Editor
PO Box 360192
Brooklyn, NY 11236-0192
Phone: (718)965-0471
E-mail: cleverpig@msn.com
Home Page: http://www.nybta.org

• 16208 • Burgdorf Award
For students who win a research science competition. Recognition award bestowed annually.

• 16209 •
New York Board of Trade
Charles H. Falk, Pres./CEO
World Financial Ctr.
1 N End Ave., 13th Fl.
New York, NY 10282
Phone: (212)748-4000
Phone: (212)748-4094
Toll-Free: 877-877-8890
E-mail: webmaster@nybot.com
Home Page: http://www.nybot.com

• 16210 • Business Speaks Award
For recognition of leadership, dedication, and service to the New York business community and to the nation. A trophy is awarded annually at the November Business Speaks Dinner. Established in 1945.

• 16211 • Textile Section Award
To recognize an outstanding leader in the textile industry. A sterling silver tray is awarded annually in November. Established in 1950 by the Textile Section of the New York Board of Trade.

• 16212 •
New York Botanical Garden
Institute of Systematic Botany
Gregory Long, Pres. and CEO
Bronx River Pky. at Fordham Rd.
Bronx, NY 10458-5126
Phone: (718)817-8700
Fax: (718)562-6780
E-mail: dws@nybg.org
Home Page: http://www.nybg.org

• 16213 • Rupert Barneby Award
Recognizes outstanding research on legumes.

• 16214 • Henry Gleason Award
Inquire for application details.:

• 16215 •
New York Civil Liberties Union
Dhevi Kumar, Contact
125 Broad St.
New York, NY 10004
Phone: (212)344-3005
Fax: (212)344-3318
Home Page: http://www.nyclu.org

• 16216 • Joe Callaway Prize for the Defense of the Right to Privacy
To recognize, encourage, and reward an individual or group that has "contributed significantly during the preceding year to the defense or advancement of personal privacy rights against intrusion by government or others." A monetary prize of $5,000 is awarded annually. Established in 1992 by Joe Callaway.

• 16217 • Florina Lasker Civil Liberties Award
To recognize an individual, organization, or group that has, by word or action, displayed consistent and outstanding courage and integrity in the defense of civil liberties, whether in the performance of duty, or above and beyond the requirements of duty, and by so doing has made a significant and constructive contribution to civil liberties. A monetary award of $1,000 and a plaque are awarded annually. Established in 1957.

• 16218 •
New York Community Trust
Lorie A. Slutsky, Pres.
Oscar Williams & Gene Derwood Fund
909 3rd Ave., 22nd Fl.
New York, NY 10022
Phone: (212)686-0010
Fax: (212)532-8528
E-mail: info@nycommunitytrust.org
Home Page: http://www.nycommunitytrust.org

• 16219 • Oscar Williams and Gene Derwood Award
To recognize a needy or worthy artist or poet. This award is not open to individual nominations or applications. Monetary prizes, which vary, are awarded annually if merited. First presented in 1975. Supported by the estate of Oscar Williams, a noted poet-anthologist who died in 1964. He and his wife, poet-artist Gene Derwood, spent most of their lives encouraging artists.

• 16220 •
New York Festivals
Tara Dawn, Exec.Dir.
7 W 36th St., 14th Fl.
New York, NY 10018
Phone: (212)643-4800
Fax: (212)643-0170
E-mail: infonewsletteryorkfestivals.com
Home Page: http://www.newyorkfestivals.com

• 16221 • International Design, Print and Outdoor Advertising Awards
For recognition of creative excellence in package design and collateral, and in magazine, newspaper, poster, billboard, and transit advertising. All ads run or released during the year preceding the entry deadline, which is March 15. Awards are presented in dozens of categories each year. A Grand Award trophy is awarded for the most outstanding Gold Medal winner in each main category group. Gold medals are awarded in each category within those groups and certificates are presented to finalists. Awarded annually in June. Established in 1984. Formerly: International Advertising Festival of New York.

• 16222 • International Radio Programming and Promotion Awards
Recognizes work in news, information, entertainment, and on-air talent programming and promotion. All professional spots, programs, and features are eligible to compete, provided that they were produced or first aired within 12 months of the competition. Entries are judged on production value, organization, presentation, creativity, and use of the medium. Awards are given in dozens of categories each year. Entry

deadline is March 15. Established in 1982. Formerly: International Radio Festival of New York.

• 16223 • International Television Programming and Promotions Awards
Recognizes the best in news, documentaries, information, and entertainment programming, as well as in music videos, infomercials, promotion spots, openings, and IDs. Awards are given in dozens of categories each year. Entry deadline is September 23. Formerly: International Film and Television Festival of New York.

• 16224 •
New York Financial Writers' Association
Jane Reilly, Exec.Mgr.
PO Box 338
Ridgewood, NJ 07451-0338
Phone: (201)612-0100
Fax: (201)612-9915
E-mail: nyfwa@aol.com
Home Page: http://www.nyfwa.org

• 16225 • Elliott V. Bell Award
To recognize significant long-term contributions to the profession of financial journalism. The awardee is selected by the association's award committee. A plaque is presented annually at the association's annual Awards Dinner. Established in 1976 in honor of Elliot V. Bell, the first president of the association.

• 16226 •
New York Flute Club
David Wechsler, Pres.
Park West Finance Section
PO Box 20613
New York, NY 10025-1515
E-mail: info@nyfluteclub.org
Home Page: http://www.nyfluteclub.org

• 16227 • Young Artist Competition
To encourage professional development and provide an opportunity for young flutists to perform. Flute Club members between 18 and 27 years of age are eligible. First-, second-, and third-place winners receive a certificate, a cash honorarium, and a performance opportunity. Awarded annually. Established in the 1960s.

• 16228 •
New York Foundation for the Arts
Theodore S. Berger, Exec.Dir.
155 Avenue of the Americas, 14th Fl.
New York, NY 10013-1507
Phone: (212)366-6900
Fax: (212)366-1778
E-mail: nyfainfo@nyfa.org
Home Page: http://www.nyfa.org

• 16229 • Artists' Fellowships
To encourage professional development and to provide fellowships to creative artists living or working in New York state. Grants are awarded in 16 artistic disciplines, with applications accepted in eight categories that change on a yearly basis. All applicants must be at least 18 years of age, and must have resided in New York State for the two years immediately prior to application. Graduate or undergraduate matriculated students enrolled in a degree program at the time of application may not apply. Fellowships of $7,000 are awarded annually. Established in 1985.

• 16230 •
New York Genealogical and Biographical Society
Harry Macy, Dir. of Publications
122 E 58th St.
New York, NY 10022-1939
Phone: (212)755-8532
Fax: (212)754-4218
E-mail: publications@nygbs.org
Home Page: http://www.newyorkfamilyhistory.org

• 16231 • Book Award
For the best compiled N.Y. genealogy. Recognition award bestowed annually.

• 16232 •
New-York Historical Society
Louise Mirrer PhD, Pres./CEO
170 Central Park W
New York, NY 10024
Phone: (212)873-3400
Fax: (212)874-8706
E-mail: mkettl@nyhistory.org
Home Page: http://www.nyhistory.org

• 16233 • Historymaker Award
For distinguished New Yorker. Medal awarded annually.

• 16234 •
New York International Ballet Competition
Ilona Copen, Exec.Dir.
250 W 57th St.. Ste. 1023
New York, NY 10107
Phone: (212)956-1520
Fax: (212)586-8406
E-mail: nyibc@nyibc.org
Home Page: http://www.nyibc.org

• 16235 • New York International Ballet Competition
For recognition of the best ballet dancers chosen to participate in NYIBC. The biennial competition held on odd years is open to female ballet dancers 17 to 23 years of age and male ballet dancers 18 to 24 years of age from all countries. During the first two weeks, three pas de deux and classes are taught by world renowned teachers and coaches. During the third week, three competition rounds (four performances), an Awards Ceremony and Gala Performance are held at Lincoln Center for the Performing Arts. All performances are open to the public. Gussie and Samuel Arbuse Gold Medals, Silver Medals, and Bronze Medals are awarded to the best dancers. Also awarded are the Lefkowitz Award for excellence in partnering, the Igor Youskevitch Award of a one-year contract with the American Ballet Theatre, and the Arpino Award of a one-year contract with the Joffrey Ballet.

• 16236 •
New York Library Association
Michael J. Borges, Exec.Dir.
252 Hudson Ave.
Albany, NY 12210-1802
Phone: (518)432-6952
Phone: 800-852-6952
Toll-Free: 800-252-6952
Fax: (518)427-1697
E-mail: info@nyla.org
Home Page: http://www.nyla.org

• 16237 • Lake Placid Education Foundation / NYLA Scholarship
For masters of library science student. Scholarship awarded annually.

• 16238 •
New York Oil Heating Association
John D. Maniscalco, Exec.VP
14 Penn Plaza, Ste. 1102
New York, NY 10122
Phone: (212)695-1380
Fax: (212)594-6583
E-mail: info@nyoha.org
Home Page: http://www.nyoha.org

• 16239 • Peter F. Heaney Memorial Scholarship
For college education advancement. Monetary award bestowed annually.

• 16240 •
New York Press Club
Rich Lamb, Pres.
330 W 42nd St., 9th Fl.
New York, NY 10036-6902
Phone: (212)563-2130
Fax: (212)563-2487
E-mail: mailbox@newyorkpressclub.org
Home Page: http://www.newyorkpressclub.org

• 16241 • Art Award
To recognize the best journalistic effort in the visual arts - print or television. Such excellence may be depicted by a published illustration with a news story or magazine article, an independent illustration, or art as part of a television news program. A plaque is awarded annually at the Awards and Installation Dinner in June. Established in 1981.

• 16242 • Nellie Bly Cub Reporter Award
For recognition of the best journalistic effort, electronic or print, by an individual with three years' experience or less. A letter from the editor attesting to the reporter's tenure must accompany the story. The deadline for nominations is April. A plaque is awarded annually at the Awards and Installation Dinner in June. Established in 1974 and renamed in Nellie Bly's honor in 1979. Formerly: .

• 16243 • Business Award
To recognize excellence in a story or series representing business, finance, trends, or management. Held as part of the annual Journalism Awards program, it is open to individuals and/or legitimate news organizations located within the tri-state area. A mahogany, shield-shaped plaque is awarded to one recipient in each category of print, radio, television, and web journalism. Established in 1996. Formerly: (1998) New York Press Club/AT&T Award.

• 16244 • Byline Awards
For recognition of best deadline reporting of a news story breaking in the New York metropolitan area. The item must have been a spot news report, written or broadcast against a deadline and must have been an event that received major play in the metropolitan media. Awards are presented in three categories: radio; television; and print. A mahogany, shield-shaped plaque with appropriate, factual plate is awarded annually. Established in the mid 1950s.

• 16245 • Feature Photo Award
To recognize the photo that represents excellent feature treatment of a human interest item, background or series. The deadline for nominations is April. A mahogany, shield-shaped plaque is awarded annually at the Awards and Installation Dinner in June. Established in 1984.

• 16246 • Feature Stories Awards
To recognize an outstanding story or series of articles representing excellent feature treatment of a human interest item or a background article or series. Awards are presented in five categories: news organization, television, radio, magazine, and online. A mahogany, shield-shaped plaque is awarded annually at the Awards and Installation Dinner in June. Established in the mid-1950s.

• 16247 • Feature Video Photo Award
For recognition of the best electronic news photography that represents excellent feature treatment of a human interest item, a background article, or series by an individual or TV crew. The deadline for entry is April. A mahogany, shield-shaped plaque is awarded annually. Established in 1992.

• 16248 • Gold Typewriter Award
This, the highest journalism award given by the New York Press Club, is awarded for recognition of a story or series constituting outstanding public service, enterprise, or investigative reporting. Eligible journalists include reporters, rewritemen, editors, columnists, feature department writers, and full-time special writers. A large shield-shaped mahogany plaque is awarded annually at the Awards and Installation Dinner in June. Established in the 1950s.

• 16249 • Rev. Mychal Judge Heart of New York Awards
For recognition of the best story, series, or presentation most complimentary to and about New York. Awards are presented in three categories: radio, television, and print. A mahogany plaque shaped like an apple, for the Big Apple, is awarded annually at the Awards and Installation Dinner in June. Established in 1975.

• 16250 • Spot News Photo Award
For recognition of a photographer of a news story or event breaking in the metropolitan area. The deadline for nominations is April. A mahogany, shield-shaped plaque is awarded annually at the Awards and Installation Dinner in June. Established in 1984.

• 16251 • Spot News Video Award
For recognition of a breaking story in the metropolitan area by an individual or TV crew. The deadline for entry is April. A mahogany, shield-shaped plaque is awarded annually. Established in 1992.

• 16252 •
New York Public Library
5th Ave. & 42nd St.
New York, NY 10018
Phone: (212)930-0800
E-mail: aabbott@nypl.org
Home Page: http://www.nypl.org

• 16253 • Brooke Russell Astor Award
To honor an unsung hero or heroine whose unrelenting efforts and tireless dedication to the city of New York have contributed substantially to its betterment, particularly in the areas of literature, culture, education, or civic/community service. The winner receives a monetary prize of $10,000; Special Mentions each receive $2,500. Awarded annually. Established in 1987 as tribute to Mrs. Astor, noted philanthropist, president of the Vincent Astor Foundation, and Honorary Chairman of the Library's Board of Trustees.

• 16254 • Helen B. Bernstein Book Award for Excellence in Journalism
To honor journalists and their unique role in drawing the attention of the public to important current issues. To be eligible, a book must be an outgrowth of the author's work as a journalist. The winner receives a monetary prize of $15,000; the other finalists each receive $1,000. Awarded annually. Established in 1987 to honor Helen B. Bernstein, contributing writer to several publications, by Joseph Frank Bernstein on their 40th anniversary.

• 16255 • Minerva Awards
To honor valedictorians from all New York City high schools. Valedictorians receive a set of reference books donated by publishers at an event at the library. Awarded annually. Established in 1982.

• 16256 •
New York Racing Association
PO Box 90
Jamaica, NY 11417
Phone: (718)641-4700
Fax: (516)354-8560
E-mail: nyra@nyrainc.com
Home Page: http://www.nyra.com

• 16257 • Belmont Stakes
A one-mile-and-a-half thoroughbred horse race for three-year-olds held annually at Belmont Park in June. The Belmont field is limited to sixteen starters. The winning owner is presented with the August Belmont Memorial Cup, to be retained for one year, as well as a trophy for permanent possession. The winning trainer and jockey receive trophies. The winner receives 60 percent of the purse, 20 percent to second place, 11 per cent to third, 6 percent to fourth, and 3 percent to fifth. This race is the third leg of the Triple Crown. Any horse that sweeps the Kentucky Derby, Preakness Stakes, and Belmont Stakes becomes a Triple Crown Champion. Established in 1867.

• 16258 •
New York Road Runners
9 E. 89th St.
New York, NY 10128
Phone: (212)860-4455
E-mail: membership@nyrr.org
Home Page: http://www.nyrr.org

• 16259 • Abebe Bikila Award
For recognition of outstanding contribution to long distance running, particularly through a spirit of deep commitment to the sport. Awarded annually at the UN Plaza in New York on the day preceding the New York City Marathon. Established in 1978 in memory of Abebe Bikila of Ethiopia, twice winner of the Olympic Marathon.

• 16260 • ING New York City Marathon
An annual marathon held the last Sunday in October or the first Sunday in November in New York City. The 26.2 mile course begins on the Staten Island side of the Verrazano Bridge and ends at the Tavern on the Green in Central Park. More than 36,000 participants cross five bridges and run in all five boroughs of New York City. The race is open to runners of all abilities who are at least 18 years of age on the day of the race. The men's and women's winners receive luxury cars. Awards are presented to top finishers in all age groups and top teams. Medals are awarded to all finishers. In addition, women finishers receive roses. Established in 1969 as the Cherry Tree Marathon held in the Bronx; reorganized in 1970 as the New York City Marathon. Formerly: Cherry Tree Marathon.

• 16261 •
New York Shipping Association
Frank M. McDonough, Pres.
100 Wood Ave. S. Ste. 304
Iselin, NJ 08830-2716
Phone: (732)452-7800
Fax: (732)452-6315
E-mail: bfedorko@nysanet.org
Home Page: http://www.nysanet.org

• 16262 • **Safety Awards**
To recognize terminal operators and longshoremen for safety achievements. Awarded annually to one or more recipients.

• 16263 •
New York Society for Ethical Culture
Robert Liebeskind, Exec.Dir.
2 W 64th St.
New York, NY 10023
Phone: (212)874-5210
Fax: (212)595-7258
E-mail: info@nysec.org
Home Page: http://www.nysec.org

• 16264 • **Ethical Humanist Award**
This, the Society's highest honor, is given to individuals who have acted with extraordinary moral courage, fully aware of the potential cost to their own life, career, or reputation, without regard for the sanction or acclaim of his/her peers or of society, and whose actions have had broad humanizing implications are eligible. Nominations may be made by the Society only. A plaque is awarded when merited. Established in 1970.

• 16265 •
New York Society of Architects
Harold Kahn, Pres.
299 Broadway, Ste. 206
New York, NY 10007
Phone: (212)385-8950
Fax: (212)385-8961
E-mail: nysarch@aol.com
Home Page: http://www.nysarch.com

• 16266 • **Fred L. Liebmann Book Award**
To encourage professional development of architectural students. Students who are in the second year of architectural studies at the following New York City Schools of Architecture are eligible: The Cooper Union, Pratt Institute, New York Institute of Technology, Columbia University, and City College of CUNY. Scholarly or historical architectural books are awarded annually. Established in 1986 by Fred L. Liebmann, R.A., President of NYSA in 1966 and 1967 and winner of the Sidney L. Strauss Award in 1973.

• 16267 • **Lifetime Achievement Award**
In recognition of architects who have made significant achievements in design, architecture, and professionalism. Awarded when merited.

• 16268 • **Sidney L. Strauss Award**
For recognition of outstanding achievement by an architect or others for the benefit of the architectural profession during the previous five years. Nominations may be made by the affiliates of NYSA. A certificate is awarded annually. Established in 1949 in memory of Sidney L. Strauss, former president of NYSA, 1944-45.

• 16269 •
New York State Association for Solid Waste Management
Jeffrey Bouchard, Pres.
PO Box 13461
Albany, NY 12212-3461
Phone: (315)736-5501
Phone: (516)677-5790
E-mail: nywaste@erols.com
Home Page: http://www.newyorkwaste.org

• 16270 • **Solid Waste Manager of the Year**
For significant contribution to integrated solid waste management. Recognition award bestowed annually.

• 16271 •
New York State Association of Criminal Defense Lawyers
Patricia Marcus, Exec.Dir.
245 5th Ave., 19th Fl.
New York, NY 10016
Phone: (212)532-4434
Fax: (212)532-4668
E-mail: info@nysacdl.org
Home Page: http://www.nysacdl.org

• 16272 • **Hon. William J. Brennan Award for Outstanding Jurist**
To recognize an individual for an unwavering commitment to civil rights and individual liberties. A crystal block is awarded annually. Established in 1990.

• 16273 •
New York State Association of Library Boards
Dr. Norman J. Jacknis, Pres.
388 Broadway, 4th Fl.
PO Box 11048
Albany, NY 12211
Phone: (518)445-9505
Fax: (518)426-8240
E-mail: nysalb@nycap.rr.com
Home Page: http://www.nysalb.org

• 16274 • **Velma Moore Award**
To recognize an individual who has made exemplary contributions to the development of library service in New York State. Criteria for the award are: service to state and national library organizations, service in the legislative area, service on state study committees, promotional services at the state level, and service to local and county libraries and to library systems. Nomination deadline is August 15. A $750 honorarium is awarded annually to the library of the winner's choice. Established in 1962 by the Liberty Trustees Foundation of New York State in memory of Velma K. Moore, one of the charter members of the foundation who worked actively for the improvement of library services in New York State from 1947 until her death in 1961.

• 16275 •
New York State Council on the Arts
Richard J. Schwartz, Chm.
175 Varick St.
New York, NY 10014-4604
Phone: (212)627-4455
E-mail: helpdesk@nysca.org
Home Page: http://www.nysca.org

• 16276 • **Governor's Arts Awards**
To recognize and honor artists, actors, patrons, arts organizations, small businesses, local government entities, and arts in education activities for their achievements in the arts in the state of New York. Nominations are made by the public, selected by the Council, and then confirmed by the Governor. Established in 1966 by Governor Nelson A. Rockefeller.

• 16277 •
New York State Court Reporters Association
Larry Donnelly, Exec.Dir.
734 Franklin Ave., No. 319
Garden City, NY 11530
E-mail: nyscra@nyscra.org
Home Page: http://www.nyscra.org

• 16278 • **Horizon Award**
Based on need and merit for students of court reporting. Scholarship awarded annually.

• 16279 •
New York State Department of Health Wadsworth Center
PO Box 509
Empire State Plz.
Albany, NY 12201-0509
Phone: (518)474-7592
Fax: (518)474-3439
E-mail: lawrence.sturman@wadsworth.org
Home Page: http://www.wadsworth.org

• 16280 • **Brown-Hazen Lectureship for Research Excellence in Life Sciences**
For creative contribution to basic research by a young scientist.

• 16281 • **Herbert W. Dickerman Lectureship**
For creative contribution to basic research.

• 16282 •
New York State Fair Old Timers Club
Elizabeth Dishaw, Sec.
294 Kenyon Rd.
Mexico, NY 13114
Phone: (315)699-2297

• 16283 • Old Timers
For exhibiting, working, judging or officer of club. Recognition award bestowed annually.

• 16284 •
New York State Health Facilities Association
Richard J. Herrick, Pres./CEO
33 Elk St., Ste. 300
Albany, NY 12207-1010
Phone: (518)462-4800
Fax: (518)426-4051
E-mail: info@nyshfa.org
Home Page: http://www.nyshfa.org

• 16285 • Nurse of the Year
For nomination by member facilities. Recognition award bestowed annually.

• 16286 • Volunteers of the Year
For nomination by member facilities. Recognition award.

• 16287 •
New York State Historical Association
Dr. Thomas Costello, VP
PO Box 800
Cooperstown, NY 13326
Phone: (607)547-1450
Phone: (607)547-1400
Toll-Free: 888-547-1450
Fax: (607)547-1404
E-mail: costello@nysha.org
Home Page: http://www.nysha.org

• 16288 • Dixon Ryan Fox Manuscript Prize
To recognize the best unpublished, book-length monograph dealing with some aspect of the history of New York State. Manuscripts may deal with any aspect of New York Sate history. Biographies of individuals whose careers illuminate aspects of the history of the state are eligible, as are manuscripts dealing with such cultural matters as literature and the arts, provided that in such cases the methodology is historical. Works of fiction and works of article length are not eligible. A monetary prize of $3,000 is awarded annually. Established in 1973.

• 16289 • Kerr History Prize
To honor the two articles appearing in *New York History*, the quarterly journal of the New York State Historical Association. A monetary award of $1,000 for first prize is given annually. Established in 1969 by Paul S. Kerr, Treasurer of NYSHA.

• 16290 • Henry Allen Moe Prize for Catalogs of Distinction in the Arts
To foster and recognize scholarship in art history and decorative arts studies in the form of published catalogues of exhibitions or collections. Catalogs treating collections located or exhibited in New York State are eligible. Monetary prizes are awarded each year in New York City. Established in 1983 by Mrs. Henry Allen Moe in memory of Henry Allen Moe, scholar and humanist, who was president of the New York State Historical Association for many years.

• 16291 •
New York State Society of CPAs
Louis Grumet, Exec.Dir.
3 Park Ave., 18th Fl.
New York, NY 10016
Phone: (212)719-8300
Toll-Free: 800-633-6320
Fax: (212)719-3364
E-mail: ckaravites@nysscpa.org
Home Page: http://www.nysscpa.org

• 16292 • Excellence in Financial Journalism
To recognize financial journalists who contribute to a better understanding of business topics in print, television, radio and wire services/syndicates. Entries are judged by a panel of certified public accountants on: accuracy and thorough research, the ability to communicate an understanding of the topic, and the fair and balanced representation of the issue(s). Articles must be printed or items broadcasted, between January 1 and December 31. The deadline is February 1. Awards are presented at the annual dinner in May. Established in 1982.

• 16293 •
New York State Writers Institute
William Kennedy, Exec.Dir.
New Library, LE 320
State University of New York, Albany
Albany, NY 12222
Phone: (518)442-5620
Fax: (518)442-5621
E-mail: writers@uamail.albany.edu
Home Page: http://www.albany.edu/writers-inst

• 16294 • Edith Wharton Citation of Merit for State Author
To recognize a New York State fiction writer for a lifetime of works of distinction. Fiction writers living in New York State are nominated by an advisory panel of distinguished authors. An honorarium of $10,000 is awarded biennially in even-number years. The recipient must give two public readings a year, for two years. Established in 1986 in memory of Edith Wharton, acknowledged as one of the great novelists in the history of American literature.

• 16295 • Walt Whitman Citation of Merit Award for State Poet
To recognize a New York State poet for a lifetime of works of distinction. Poets residing in New York State are nominated by an advisory panel of distinguished authors. The recipient must give two public readings a year, for two years. An honorarium of $10,000 is awarded biennially in even-number years. Established in 1981 in memory of the renowned American poet.

• 16296 •
The New York Times
Scott H. Heekin-Canedy, Pres. and Gen. Mgr.
229 W 43rd St.
New York, NY 10036
Phone: (212)556-1234
Fax: (212)556-7389
E-mail: public@nytimes.com
Home Page: http://www.nytimes.com

• 16297 • Best Illustrated Children's Books of the Year
To encourage quality art expression for young people. Books must have been published in the year of the judging. An honorary award is presented annually, and the names of the 10 winners and samples of the work appear in the November *Children's Books Supplement* of *The New York Times.* Established in 1952.

• 16298 •
New York University
Office for University Development and Alumni Relations
25 W 4th St.
New York, NY 10012
Phone: (212)998-6900
Fax: (212)995-4020
E-mail: alumni.info@nyu.edu
Home Page: http://www.nyu.edu/alumni

• 16299 • Albert Gallatin Medal
To recognize an individual for outstanding contributions to society. Graduates, honorary alumni, or members of the New York University family are eligible. A bronze medallion is awarded annually. Established in 1957.

• 16300 •
New York University
Office of Publications
Dr. John Sexton, Pres.
25 W 4th St., 5th Fl.
New York, NY 10012
Phone: (212)998-6840
Fax: (212)995-4021
Home Page: http://www.nyu.edu

• 16301 • Elmer Holmes Bobst Literary Awards
To recognize significant literary accomplishments in fiction and poetry. The Awards recognize vital and enduring contributions to literature, as well as promising new work by emerging writers. No applications are accepted. Monetary prizes of $1,000 each are presented annually. These annual awards were established to mark the 10th anniversary of New York University's Elmer Holmes Bobst Library. Established in 1983 by Mrs. Bobst in memory of her husband, a former chairman of Warner-Lambert.

• 16302 • Ralph J. Gleason Music Book Awards
To recognize outstanding music books. Awarded annually.

• 16303 • Delmore Schwartz Memorial Poetry Award

To recognize the special distinction or promise of a young or unrecognized poet who has published no more than one book of poetry, or of a mature but insufficiently recognized poet. No applications are accepted. A monetary prize of $1,000 is awarded at irregular intervals by a committee of poets: Mona Van Duyn; Theodore Weiss; and M.L. Rosenthal. Applications and inquiries are not invited. Established in 1968 by the J.M. Kaplan Foundation and various individual donors.

• 16304 • University Medal

To recognize distinguished visitors to the University who have made significant contributions in the arts, literature, science, government and diplomacy. No applications are accepted. An engraved gold medal is awarded as merited. Established in 1956.

• 16305 •
New York University Alumni Association
Adrienne A. Rudnick, Exec.Dir.
25 W 4th St., 5th Fl.
New York, NY 10012
Phone: (212)998-6912
Fax: (212)995-4779
E-mail: alumni.info@nyu.edu
Home Page: http://www.nyu.edu/alumni

Formerly: (1997) Alumni Federation of New York University.

• 16306 • Great Teachers Award

For recognition of a singular accomplishment in leading students to knowledge and understanding, and of dedication and intellectual integrity representative of the highest ideals of the teaching profession. Individuals who have taught at least one course at New York University during the academic year are eligible. Three awards are given annually, each consisting of an honorarium of $2,500 and a framed citation. Established in 1959.

• 16307 • Eugene J. Keogh Award for Distinguished Public Service

To recognize individuals for outstanding public service. A gilded medallion is awarded annually. Established in 1987 to honor Eugene J. Keogh, the former U.S. Congressman.

• 16308 •
New York Urban League
Darwin M. Davis, Pres. and CEO
204 W 136th St.
New York, NY 10030
Phone: (212)926-8000
Fax: (212)283-4948
Home Page: http://www.nyul.org

• 16309 • Frederick Douglass Award

To recognize New Yorkers for distinguished leadership in the fight for equal opportunity. Engraved medallions are awarded to one or more recipients annually. Established in 1966 to honor Frederick Douglass, father of the Protest Movement.

• 16310 • Whitney M. Young, Jr. Memorial Scholarship

To provide scholarship assistance for disadvantaged New York City students. Recipients are selected on the basis of academic promise and admission to college. Scholarships in the amount of up to $2,500 are awarded to 10 students each year. Established in 1973. Funded by revenue from the annual Whitney M. Young, Jr. Memorial Football Classic.

• 16311 •
New York Women in Communications, Inc.
Maria Ungaro, Exec.Dir.
355 Lexington Ave., 17th Fl.
New York, NY 10017-6003
Phone: (212)297-2133
Fax: (212)370-9047
E-mail: nywicpr@nywic.org
Home Page: http://www.nywici.org

• 16312 • Matrix Award

This, one of the industry's most prestigious awards, is given to honor the outstanding achievements of women who work in the New York area in the field of communications based on a high degree of professional competence in the fields of books, advertising, newspapers, magazines, broadcasting, public relations, and arts and entertainment. Nominations are accepted. The deadline is usually the end of October to early November. A symbolic matrix (a metal mold used to cast type for printed material which represents the beginning of mass communication) in a shadow box is awarded yearly at the New York Women in Communications' annual matrix awards luncheon. Established in 1970.

• 16313 •
Newark Black Film Festival
The Newark Museum
49 Washington St.
Newark, NJ 07102
Phone: (973)596-6550
Toll-Free: 800-768-7386
Fax: (973)642-0459
Home Page: http://www.newarkmuseum.org/nbff

• 16314 • Paul Robeson Awards

For recognition of excellence in independent filmmaking. The Newark Black Film Festival screens films by black filmmakers and films featuring the history and culture of black people in America and elsewhere. Films completed in the two-year period between awards may be entered in the following categories: documentary, long narrative, short narrative, and experimental. A monetary prize is awarded biennially in even-numbered years. Established in 1985 in honor of Paul Robeson, activist, scholar, performer, and athlete.

• 16315 •
Newberry Library
David Spadafora, Pres.
Committee on Awards
60 W Walton St.
Chicago, IL 60610
Phone: (312)943-9090
Fax: (312)255-3680
E-mail: research@newberry.org
Home Page: http://www.newberry.org

• 16316 • Weiss/Brown Publication Subvention Award

To recognize authors of scholarly books already accepted for publication. Subject matter must cover European civilization before 1700 in the areas of music, theater, French or Italian literature or cultural studies. A monetary award of up to $15,000 will be awarded to subsidize publication costs. Supported by the Roger W. Weiss and Howard Mayer Brown Fund.

• 16317 •
Newcomen Society of the United States
Leighton A. Wildrick, Pres./CEO
211 Welsh Pool Rd., Ste. 240
Exton, PA 19341-1321
Phone: (610)363-6600
Toll-Free: 800-466-7604
Fax: (610)363-0612
E-mail: info@newcomen.org
Home Page: http://www.newcomen.org

Awards discontinued. Formerly: (1983) Newcomen Society in North America.

• 16318 • Harvard-Newcomen Postdoctoral Fellowship

To recognize graduate students in the field of business history. A fellowship valued at approximately $60,000 is awarded to one recipient each year to provide the opportunity to spend a year in residence at the Harvard Business School working with business historians and conducting research. During the appointment, fellows generally complete a book on business history. Administered by Harvard Business School. Established in 1949.

• 16319 •
Newfoundland Club of America
PO Box 2614
Cheyenne, WY 82003
E-mail: newftide@usa.net
Home Page: http://www.newfdogclub.org

• 16320 • Gaines Medal for Good Sportsmanship

To recognize and honor a Club member for good sportsmanship. The medal honors the person who competes fairly and works for the advancement of the sport without regard to personal honors. Members of the Club may be nominated. Currently seated Board Members are ineligible. A bronze medal is awarded annually. Established in 1979. Sponsored by the Gaines Dog Research Center.

• 16321 •
Newsday
Timothy P. Knight, Publisher, Pres. and CEO
235 Pinelawn Rd.
Melville, NY 11747-4250
Phone: (631)843-4000
E-mail: delivery@newsday.com
Home Page: http://www.newsday.com

• 16322 • **George Oppenheimer/*Newsday* Playwriting Award**
To recognize outstanding achievement in playwriting. American playwrights whose works are produced in New York City or Long Island are eligible. Play must be a first-production. Applications are not accepted for this award. A monetary prize of $5,000 and an Oppy Award trophy are presented annually in November. Established in 1979 in memory of George Oppenheimer, drama critic for *Newsday* from 1963 until his death in 1977.

• 16323 •
Newsletter and Electronic Publishers Association
Patricia M. Wysocki, Exec.Dir.
1501 Wilson Blvd., Ste. 509
Arlington, VA 22209-2403
Phone: (703)527-2333
Toll-Free: 800-356-9302
Fax: (703)841-0629
E-mail: nepa@newsletters.org
Home Page: http://www.newsletters.org

• 16324 • **Newsletter Journalism Awards**
Recognizes editorial excellence in newsletter journalism. Awarded annually.

• 16325 •
Newsletter and Electronic Publishers Foundation
Patti Wysocki, Exec.Dir.
1501 Wilson Blvd., Ste. 509
Arlington, VA 22209
Phone: (703)527-2333
Toll-Free: 800-356-9302
Fax: (703)841-0629
E-mail: nepa@newsletters.org
Home Page: http://www.newsletters.org

Formerly: Newsletter Association.

• 16326 • **Journalism Awards**
To recognize editorial excellence in subscription newsletter journalism. Awards are given in the following categories: Best Spot News or Exclusive Single-News Story; Best Single-Topic Newsletter; Best Instructional Reporting; Best Looseleaf Publication; Best Interpretive or Analytical Reporting; Best Financial Advisory Newsletter; and Investigative Reporting. Entrants do not have to be members of the NPA. To be eligible, stories submitted must have been published during the previous year. Multiple entries within individual categories and in several separate categories are permitted. Certificates are awarded annually to first-, second-, and third-place winners, as well as honorable mentions. Established in 1975. Formerly: Newsletter Association Journalism Awards.

• 16327 •
Newspaper Association of America
Jay R. Smith, Chm.
1921 Gallows Rd., Ste. 600
Vienna, VA 22182-3900
Phone: (703)902-1600
Phone: (703)902-1868
Toll-Free: 800-656-4622
Fax: (703)917-0636
E-mail: schij@naa.org
Home Page: http://www.naa.org

• 16328 • **Circulation Federation Awards**
To recognize the winner of the Circulation Promotion Competition. Awards include the Lifetime Achievement Award, Merchandiser of the Year Award, Newspaper Carrier of the Year Award, and Sales Executive of the Year Award. Awarded annually. Formerly: Circulation Council Awards.

• 16329 • **Classified Federation Awards**
To recognize outstanding classified managers. The following awards are presented: Advertiser of the Year Award, Eric Anderson Lifetime Achievement Award, James M. McGovern Award, and the CAMEO Award (Classified Advertising Managers Executive Order Award). Winners are featured in the *Best of the Best* book. Awarded annually. Formerly: Classified Council Awards.

• 16330 • **Cooperative Marketing and Sales Council Awards**
To recognize the winners of the Co-op Tearsheet Competition and the Share-an-Idea Competition. Award winners will be featured in the *Cooperative Marketing and Sales Ideas Book.*

• 16331 • **DANDY Awards**
To encourage and recognize excellence in automotive newspaper advertising, especially by dealers. Awards are presented in several categories; the Best of Show award carries a monetary prize of $25,000. Established in 1972. Beginning in 2003, the DANDY Awards became a division of NAA's ATHENA Award (Award to Honor Excellence in Newspaper Advertising) program.

• 16332 • **Market Development and Promotion Federation Awards**
To recognize the winners of the Promotion and Market Development Competition. Awards include the Lifetime Achievement Award and the Marketing Master Award. Winners are featured in the *Promotion and Market Development Successes* book. Awarded annually. Formerly: Market Development and Promotion Council Awards.

• 16333 • **McGovern Award**
To recognize the publisher of a newspaper that has shown the most interest, dedication and support to newspaper classified advertising. Publishers or presidents of daily newspapers are eligible. A plaque is awarded annually when merited. Established in 1947.

• 16334 • **National Council Awards**
To recognize the winners of the NAA Tearsheet Competition. Award winners will be featured in the *Sales and Ideas Book.* Co-sponsored by the Retail Council.

• 16335 • **Research Council Awards**
To recognize excellence and professionalism in newspaper research. Members are eligible for the Research Award of Merit and the Gerald Zarwell Award. Any single example of research, sampling or special contribution to newspaper research or technology completed within the previous three years may be submitted by July 15. A plaque is awarded annually when merited at the fall conference. Established in 1984 by the Newspaper Research Council and the *San Jose Mercury News.*

• 16336 •
Newspaper Association of America Foundation
Margaret G. Vassilikos, SVP
1921 Gallows Rd., Ste. 600
Vienna, VA 22182
Phone: (703)902-1600
Fax: (703)902-1751
E-mail: margaret.vassilikos@naa.org
Home Page: http://www.naafoundation.org

Formerly: American Newspaper Publishers Association Foundation.

• 16337 • **NAA Foundation - Associated Collegiate Press Pacemakers Awards**
To honor excellence in collegiate journalism. Six student newspapers are selected for overall content and appearance with an emphasis on quality of writing, design, and coverage. Plaques are awarded annually. Supervised by Associated College Press, 620 Rarig Center, 330 South 21st Avenue, Minneapolis, MN 55455-0478. Formerly: ANPA Foundation - Associated Collegiate Press Pacemakers Awards.

• 16338 • **NAA Foundation - International Circulation Managers Association C. K. Jefferson Award**
To recognize an instructor of a Newspaper in Education credit-granting course sponsored by a newspaper and a college, university, or regional or state teacher education center. The scholarship was established in 1989 to honor C. K. "Ken" Jefferson, a former circulation director at the Des Moines Register and a founder of the NIE program. Sponsored by International Circulation Managers Association. Formerly: ANPA Foundation - International Circulation Managers Association C. K. Jefferson Award.

• 16339 • NAA Foundation - National Scholastic Press Association Pacemaker Awards
To encourage vital high school journalism by honoring outstanding high school newspapers. Plaques are awarded annually to six high school newspapers. Administered by the National Scholastic Press Association, 620 Rarig Center, 330 South 21st Avenue, Minneapolis, MN 55455-0478. Formerly: ABOA Foundation - National Scholastic Press Association Pacemaker Awards.

• 16340 • NAA Foundation - Newspaper in Education Program Excellence Award
To honor overall excellence in Newspaper in Education programs at newspapers in North America. Winners are selected in categories related to newspapers' circulation size. Awards are presented at the annual Newspaper in Education Conference, held in the spring. Formerly: ANPA Foundation - Newspaper in Education Program Excellence Award.

• 16341 • National Newspaper Association - Quill and Scroll Award
To recognize excellence in high school journalism in the following divisions: editorial, editorial cartoon, news story, photography/news feature, photography/sports, feature story, in-depth reporting/individual, in-depth reporting/team, advertisement, and sports story. Members of the Quill and Scroll Society are eligible. A plaque is awarded by local daily newspaper executives in ceremonies in their own communities annually. Established by Quill and Scroll Society, School of Journalism, University of Iowa, Iowa City, IA 52242.

• 16342 •
The Newspaper Guild-CWA
Andrew Zipser, Contest Admin.
501 3rd St. NW, Ste. 250
Washington, DC 20001-2760
Phone: (202)434-7177
Fax: (202)434-1472
E-mail: guild@cwa-union.org
Home Page: http://www.newsguild.org

• 16343 • Heywood Broun Award
To encourage and recognize individual journalistic achievement by members of the working media, particularly if it helps to right a wrong or correct an injustice. Journalists working on behalf of newspapers, news services, websites, magazines, and radio and television stations in the United States, Canada, and Puerto Rico are eligible, whether Guild members or not. Entries must be postmarked by the last Friday in January. A monetary award of $5,000 to the winner and two runner-up awards of $1,000 are presented annually. Established in 1941 in honor of Heywood Broun, the Guild's founding president and a newspaper columnist who championed the poor, weak, and oppressed.

• 16344 •
Newton Lions Club
John Neil Fraser, Esquire
16 Gay St.
Newtonville, MA 02460-0000
Phone: (617)332-4487
E-mail: dinglepaws@aol.com

• 16345 • Larry Kadis Memorial Scholarship
For local high school seniors. Scholarship awarded annually.

• 16346 •
NGO Committee on Disarmament, Peace and Security
Vernon C. Nichols, Pres.
777 United Nations Plz., Rm. 3-B
New York, NY 10017
Phone: (212)687-5340
Fax: (212)687-1643
E-mail: disarmtimes@igc.pc.org
Home Page: http://disarm.igc.org/

• 16347 • Pomerance Award
Recognizes service in the field of disarmament in the UN context. Individuals and groups are eligible.

• 16348 •
Niagara University
Joseph L. Levesque, Pres.
Niagara University, NY 14109
Phone: (716)285-1212
Toll-Free: 800-778-3450
Home Page: http://www.niagara.edu

• 16349 • Caritas Medal
To honor contemporary leaders who exemplify the charity of St. Vincent de Paul in an extraordinary way. A bronze medal is awarded annually. Established in 1965 in honor of St. Vincent de Paul, founder of the Vincentian Community of Priests and Brothers.

• 16350 • Dunleavy Award
To honor an individual who has succeeded eminently in his/her field or profession, performed outstanding charitable service, and demonstrated consistent loyalty to Niagara University. A sculpture is awarded annually. Established in 1982 in honor of Francis J. and Albina Dunleavy. Mr. Dunleavy is an alumnus and former Trustee of Niagara University and the retired president of ITT.

• 16351 • Founders Award
To recognize friends of Niagara University with affection, respect, and admiration for their service to the university and the community. Awarded annually when merited.

• 16352 • Medal of Honor
To honor members of the University community who manifest exceptional service over an extended period of time. Established in 1986 by the Board of Trustees.

• 16353 • President's Medal
This, the University's highest honor, is presented to recognize an individual who has given extraordinary service to the University. Nominations must be made by the Trustees of Niagara University. A medal is awarded on an ad hoc basis with no scheduled time or occasion for the presentation. Established in 1970.

• 16354 •
Nieman Foundation
Bob Giles, Curator
Harvard University
1 Francis Ave.
Lippmann House
Cambridge, MA 02138
Phone: (617)495-2237
Fax: (617)495-8976
E-mail: giles@fas.harvard.edu
Home Page: http://www.nieman.harvard.edu

• 16355 • Christopher J. Georges Fellowship
Awarded to a young journalist for an independent reporting project on an issue of enduring social value that documents the human impact of public policy. 10,000 is awarded annually. Contact Melinda Grenier, melinda_grenier@harvard.edu for more information.

• 16356 •
Nieman Foundation for Journalism at Harvard University
Ellie Lottero, Admin.Dir.
Walter Lippmann House
1 Francis Ave.
Cambridge, MA 02138
Phone: (617)495-2237
Fax: (617)495-8976
E-mail: christina_andujar@harvard.edu
Home Page: http://www.nieman.harvard.edu

• 16357 • Louis M. Lyons Award
For recognition of conscience and integrity in journalism. Full-time print or broadcast journalists, domestic or foreign, are eligible for work done in the preceding year. Winners are selected by the current class of Niemen Fellows. An honorarium of $1,000 is awarded annually. Established in 1964 by the Nieman Fellows Class of 1964 in honor of the late Louis M. Lyons, curator of the Nieman Foundation for 25 years.

• 16358 • Nieman Fellowships for Journalists
To provide a mid-career sabbatical for working newspeople to study in the fields of their choice for an academic year at Harvard University. No course credits are given or degree granted for work done during the year. Applicants must meet the following criteria: be full-time staff or free-lance jounalists with the general-interest media; have at least five years of experience; and obtain employer's consent for a leave of absence for the term of Fellowship. Approximately 12 Fellowships are awarded annually to

U.S. journalists (deadline is January 31); from 10 to 12 are awarded to foreign journalists (deadline is March 1). Established in 1938 to honor Lucius Nieman, founder of *The Milwaukee Journal*.

• 16359 •
Nimrod: International Journal of Prose and Poetry
Francine Ringold, Editor-in-Chief
600 S College Ave.
University of Tulsa
Tulsa, OK 74104-3189
Phone: (918)631-3080
Fax: (918)631-3033
E-mail: nimrod@utulsa.edu
Home Page: http://www.utulsa.edu/nimrod

• 16360 • **Pablo Neruda Prize for Poetry**
To recognize outstanding achievement in poetry. No previously published works, works accepted for publication, or dual submissions are eligible. Entries must be submitted by April 30. A monetary prize of $2,000 for first prize and $1,000 for second prize are awarded annually; honorable mentions are also recognized. Established in 1978 in honor of Pablo Neruda.

• 16361 • **Katherine Anne Porter Prize for Fiction**
For recognition of outstanding achievement in short fiction. No previously published works, works accepted for publication, or dual submissions are eligible. Manuscripts must be submitted by April 30. A monetary prize of $2,000 for first prize and $1,000 for second prize are awarded annually; honorable mentions are also recognized. Established in 1978 in honor of Katherine Anne Porter.

• 16362 •
Nine Lives Associates
Dr. Richard W. Kobetz, Dir.
Executive Protection Institute
PO Box 802
Berryville, VA 22611-0802
Phone: (540)554-2540
Phone: (540)554-2547
Fax: (540)554-2558
E-mail: info@personalprotection.com
Home Page: http://www.personalprotection.com

• 16363 • **Award for Outstanding Achievement**
For recognition of professional achievement in the field of professional personal protection and personal goals. Members of Nine Lives Associates with recognized achievements may be nominated by the committee by November 1 each year. An engraved plaque is awarded at the annual conference banquet. Established in 1986 in memory of John M. Beach, member of the association.

• 16364 •
Ninety-Nines, International Organization of Women Pilots
Jody McCarrell, Pres.
4300 Amelia Earhart Rd.
Oklahoma City, OK 73159
Phone: (405)685-7969
Toll-Free: 800-994-1929
Fax: (405)685-7985
E-mail: 1hq99s@cs.com
Home Page: http://www.ninety-nines.org

• 16365 • **Ninety-Nines NIFA Awards**
To encourage active participation by women in aviation. Female university students in good standing who have Private Pilot Certificates are eligible. The following prizes are awarded: first place - a monetary prize of $200 and the Gold Amelia Earhart Medal; second place - $150 and the Silver Amelia Earhart Medal; and third place - $100 and the Bronze Amelia Earhart Medal. In addition, the Top Female Pilot award is presented. Awarded annually. Established in the late 1940s.

• 16366 •
North Alabama Tourist Association
E. Cameron Reeder, Exec.Dir.
25062 North St.
PO Box 1075
Mooresville, AL 35649-1075
Phone: (256)350-3500
Toll-Free: 800-648-5381
Fax: (256)350-3519
E-mail: info@northalabama.org
Home Page: http://www.northalabama.org

• 16367 • **Peak Award**
For tourism achievers in north Alabama. Recognition award bestowed annually.

• 16368 •
North American Academy of Liturgy
% Rev. Richard Rutherford, CSC
University of Portland
500 N Willamette Blvd.
Portland, OR 97203-5798
E-mail: ruther@up.edu

• 16369 • **Berakah Award**
To recognize distinguished contributions by members to the study and the renewal of the liturgy. Nominations from the membership are accepted. A framed parchment with a text indicating the awardee's contribution to the liturgy is presented annually. Established in 1976. The name of the award, "Berakah," is the Hebrew word for blessing, or a prayer of blessing.

• 16370 •
North American Association for Environmental Education
William H. Dent Jr., Exec.Dir.
2000 P St. NW, Ste. 540
Washington, DC 20036
Phone: (202)419-0412
Fax: (202)419-0415
E-mail: email@naaee.org
Home Page: http://www.naaee.org
Formerly: National Association for Environmental Education.

• 16371 • **Jeske Award**
Annual award of recognition. Given through peer review.

• 16372 • **Outstanding Affiliate Award**
Annual award of recognition. Given through peer review.

• 16373 • **Outstanding Individual at the Local Level**
Annual award of recognition. Selection is made by peer review.

• 16374 • **Outstanding Individual at the National/International Level**
Annual award of recognition. Selection is made through peer review.

• 16375 • **Outstanding Organization at the Local Level**
Annaul award of recognition. Selection is made through peer review.

• 16376 • **Outstanding Organization at the National/International Level**
Award of recognition.

• 16377 • **Outstanding Service to Environmental Education Award**
To recognize both individuals and organizations for efforts in promoting and providing environmental education leadership and the local, regional, and global levels. Plaques are presented annually.

• 16378 • **President's Award**
Recognizes outstanding environmental educators and organizations. Awarded annually.

• 16379 •
North American Association for the Diaconate
Susanne Watson Epting, Exec.Dir.
Executive Office
815 2nd Ave.
New York, NY 10017
Phone: (646)486-7672
Phone: (401)737-6681
Fax: (253)648-6298
E-mail: director@diakonoi.org
Home Page: http://www.diakonoi.org

• 16380 • St. Stephen Recognition of Diaconal Ministry
Award of recognition. Given biennially on the recommendation of the diocese. Established in 1995.

• 16381 •
North American Association of Christians in Social Work
Rick Chamiec-Case, Exec.Dir.
PO Box 121
Botsford, CT 06404-0121
Phone: (203)270-8780
Toll-Free: 888-426-4712
Fax: (203)270-8780
E-mail: info@nacsw.org
Home Page: http://www.nacsw.org

• 16382 • Distinguish Service to Social Work
Annual award of recognition.

• 16383 • Distinguished Service to Social Welfare
Recognizes distinguished service to the association. Awarded annually.

• 16384 •
North American Association of Food Equipment Manufacturers
Deirdre T. Flynn, Exec.VP
161 N Clark St., Ste. 2020
Chicago, IL 60601
Phone: (312)821-0201
Toll-Free: 800-336-0019
Fax: (312)821-0202
E-mail: info@nafem.org
Home Page: http://www.nafem.org

• 16385 • William W. Carpenter Award
To recognize an individual's commitment to excellence, leadership, and integrity in the food service industry. The recipient of the award should have been active in the commercial foodservice industry for a minimum of 20 years; have been active in, and made continuous and outstanding contributions to, NAFEM; have held at least one elective office in NAFEM; be a successful business leader; have achieved personal recognition from his/her peers; no longer be a director or officer of NAFEM at the time the award is voted on for presentation. Awarded when merited.

• 16386 • Doctorate of Food Service Award
Recognizes individuals who have contributed to the industry. A medallion is presented during the NAFEM trade show, and the recipients are recognized at the All Industry Awards Banquet.

• 16387 • President's Award
To recognize NAFEM members who have worked for NAFEM and are neither Board members nor Officers. The President recommends the recipient or candidates; the Board determines the winner. Awarded when merited. Formerly: (1987) Award of Merit.

• 16388 •
North American Association of State and Provincial Lotteries
Thomas Shaheen, Pres.
2775 Bishop Rd., Ste. B
Willoughby Hills, OH 44092
Phone: (216)241-2310
Fax: (216)241-4350
E-mail: nasplhq1@aol.com
Home Page: http://www.naspl.org

• 16389 • Batchy, Hickey, and Powers Award
Recognizes the best TV, radio and print lottery ads. Awarded annually.

• 16390 •
North American Association of Summer Sessions
Michael U. Nelson, Exec.Sec.
43 Belanger Dr.
Dover, NH 03820-4602
Phone: (603)740-9880
Fax: (603)742-7085
E-mail: naass@aol.com
Home Page: http://www.naass.org

Formerly: (1975) National Association of Summer Sessions.

• 16391 • Creative and Innovative Awards
To recognize innovative and creative summer programs offered by member institutions. Awards are presented for three programs: credit, non-credit, and administrative programs. Entries are judged on creativity, uniqueness, and benefit to students, the institution, and/or the community. Nomination deadline is September 23. Plaques are awarded annually at the national conference. Established in 1978.

• 16392 •
North American Association of Wardens and Superintendents
Arthur Leonardo, Exec.Dir.
PO Box 11037
Albany, NY 12211-0037
Phone: (518)786-6801
E-mail: elart26@aol.com
Home Page: http://corrections.com/naaws

Formerly: (1976) American Association of Wardens and Superintendents.

• 16393 • Warden of the Year
To recognize an individual for outstanding administration of a correctional institution, and/or the field of corrections. Wardens, superintendents, or chief administrative officers of a prison or jail who are members of the American Correctional Association and NAAWS are eligible. A plaque is awarded annually at the conference. Established in 1980.

• 16394 •
North American Bluebird Society
Lisa Bulick, Exec.Dir.
PO Box 244
Wilmot, OH 44689
Phone: (330)359-5511
Toll-Free: 888-235-1331
Fax: (330)359-5455
E-mail: info@nabluebirdsociety.org
Home Page: http://www.nabluebirdsociety.org

• 16395 • NABS Research Grants
Recognizes outstanding contribution to the field of bluebird conservation. The following awards are presented: Bluebird Research Grants, General Research Grants; and Student Research Grants. Available to student, professional, or individual researchers for a suitable research project. Monetary awards are awarded annually. Established in 1984.

• 16396 •
North American Catalysis Society
John N. Armor, Pres.
7201 Hamilton Blvd.
Allentown, PA 18195-1501
Phone: (610)481-5792
E-mail: armorjn@apci.com
Home Page: http://www.nacatsoc.org

• 16397 • Robert Burwell Lectureship in Catalysis
For recognition of substantial contributions to one or more areas in the field of catalysis with emphasis on discovery and understanding of catalytic phenomena, catalytic reaction mechanisms, and identification and description of catalytic sites and species. Selection is based on contributions to the catalytic literature and the current timeliness of these research contributions. The recipient will be requested to visit and lecture to each of the individual affiliated clubs/societies with which mutually satisfactory arrangements can be made, and prepare a review paper(s) for publication covering these lectures. A prize of $5,000 and a plaque are awarded. An additional $4,500 is available to cover travel expenses.

• 16398 • F. G. Ciapetta Lectureship in Catalysis
To recognize an individual for substantial contributions to one or more areas in the field of catalysis with emphasis on industrially significant catalysts, catalytic processes, and the discovery of new catalytic reactions and systems of potential industrial importance. Selection is based on contributions to the catalytic literature and the current timeliness of these research contributions. Individuals without regard to age, sex, nationality, or affiliation are eligible. An honorarium of $5,000 and a plaque are awarded biennially in even-numbered years. An additional $4,500 is available to cover traveling expenses to visit and lecture to each of the affiliated clubs/societies. The recipient may be invited to prepare a review paper for publication. Established about 1987. Co-sponsored by the Davison Chemical Division of W. R. Grace and Company.

• 16399 • Paul H. Emmett Award in Fundamental Catalysis

To recognize and encourage individual contributions in the field of catalysis, with emphasis on discovery and understanding of catalytic phenomena, proposal of catalytic reaction mechanisms, and identification of and description of catalytic sites and species. Individuals 45 years of age and younger must be nominated by September in even-numbered years. A monetary award of $3,000 and a plaque are awarded. An additional $500 is available for otherwise unreimbursed travel expenses. Sponsored by the Davison Chemical Division of W. R. Grace and Company.

• 16400 • Eugene J. Houdry Award in Applied Catalysis

To recognize and encourage individual contributions in the field of catalysis with emphasis on the development of new and improved catalysts and processes representing outstanding advances in their useful application. Nominations must be submitted by September 1 in even-numbered years. A monetary award of $3,000 and a plaque are awarded. An additional $500 is available for otherwise unreimbursed travel expenses. Sponsored by Sud-chemie, Inc.

• 16401 •

North American Colleges and Teachers of Agriculture

Marilyn B. Parker, Sec.-Treas.
151 W 100 S
Rupert, ID 83350
Phone: (208)436-0692
Fax: (208)436-1384
E-mail: nactasec@pmt.org
Home Page: http://www.nactateachers.org

Formerly: (2003) National Association of Colleges and Teachers of Agriculture.

• 16402 • Distinguished Educator Award

To recognize outstanding educators in post-secondary level agriculture who do not qualify currently as teachers because of their role in higher education. Members of the Association who have ten years or more of service to post-secondary education in agriculture are eligible. Established in 1976.

• 16403 • Distinguished Teacher Award

To recognize an outstanding teacher. Selection is made from nominees who have been NACTA members for five years and annually submit to student evaluation. A monetary prize of $1,000 and a plaque are awarded annually. Established in 1969 and sponsored by Mr. and Mrs. M.E. Ensminger of the Agriservices Foundation, and the Interstate Printers and Publishers, Inc.

• 16404 • Graduate Student Teaching Award

Recognizes and rewards graduate students who excel as teachers in the agricultural disciplines. Applicants must be graduate student members of NACTA or a graduate student covered by an institutional membership; have been involved in classroom instruction, including laboratory and discussion sections, for a minimum of one year or the equivalent; and must be a graduate student in good academic standing. An essay by the nominee on his or her teaching philosophy (limited to five typewritten double-spaced pages); statements of support from three to eight current or former students and from a faculty director; a complete description of his or her teaching involvement; statements of support from administrators directly involved in the teaching activities; statement of support from peers having knowledge about nominee's teaching activities; and statement about nominee's involvement in the activities related to teaching but taking place outside of the classroom must be submitted.

• 16405 • E. B. Knight *NACTA Journal* Award

To recognize an outstanding article published in the *NACTA Journal* during the previous year. A monetary award of $100 and a plaque are awarded annually. Established in 1968.

• 16406 • NACTA John Deere Awards

To recognize outstanding teachers and programs of agricultural business, technology, and/or management in post-secondary schools and colleges. Special emphasis is placed on preparation of students for employment in the areas of management, sales, service, processing, and production but not exclusive of total program thrust. Criteria evaluated include: instructor's teaching philosophy; administrative officer evaluation; three-year placement record; evaluations by current students and alumni; and continued professional development of the faculty member.A $500 stipend and plaque for the instructor and a $500 stipend for the instructor's institution are presented annually at the NACTA Conference.

• 16407 • Outstanding Teacher Award

Applicants must have a minimum of four years and a maximum of eight years of having at least a 50% teaching assignment and must be a member of or in an institution member of the AASCARR. A plaque and $500 cash are awarded annually.

• 16408 • Teacher Fellow Award

To recognize outstanding achievement by a teacher of post-secondary level agriculture for the past five years. To qualify, a NACTA member must have been on a full-time appointment involving at least 25 percent teaching for a minimum of 5 of the past 7 years. Criteria included in the evaluation are the instructor's teaching philosophy; evaluations submitted by current students, alumni, administrative officers, and peers; a self-evaluation; and such factors such as availability to students, teaching innovations, and departmental/institutional activity.A plaque is awarded annually.

• 16409 • Tressler - VNR/AVI Teacher Award

To recognize outstanding achievement in teacher-research by a teacher who need not be primarily engaged in the teaching of agricultural science. A plate or plaque and a stipend are awarded. Established in 1982 in memory of Dr. Donald K. Tressler who was chairman of the AVI Publishing Company. Sponsored by the AVI Publishing Company.

• 16410 •

North American Conference on British Studies

Philip Harling, Contact
University of Kentucky
231 Patterson Office Tower
Lexington, KY 40506
Phone: (859)257-1246
Fax: (859)323-3885
E-mail: harling@uky.edu
Home Page: http://www.nacbs.org

Formerly: (1981) Conference on British Studies.

• 16411 • Albion Book Prize/NACBS Book Prize

For recognition of the best book published anywhere by a North American scholar on any aspect of British Studies from 1800 to the present. The author must be an American or Canadian citizen. Nominations from authors or publishers may be submitted by April 1. A monetary prize of $500 is awarded annually. Established in 1980. Formerly: British Council Book Prize.

• 16412 • Dissertation Year Fellowship

To support dissertation research in the British Isles on any topic of British (including Irish, Scottish, and Imperial) history. Each department may nominate one candidate, who must be a U.S. or Canadian citizen or permanent resident; enrolled in a PhD program in a U.S. or Canadian institution; and completed all degree requirements except the dissertation. The Fellowship consists of a $6,000 stipend; the runner-up receives a $2,000 travel grant. Awarded annually. Established in 1988.

• 16413 • Walter D. Love Prize in History

To recognize the author of the best journal article or published paper of similar length and scope in any field of British history from the Anglo-Saxon conquest to the present, including the history of the Empire and the Commonwealth. The author must be a North American scholar who is a citizen or permanent resident of the United States or Canada. Nominations from authors or publishers must be submitted by April 1. A monetary prize of $150 is awarded at annually. Established in 1981 to perpetuate the memory of Walter D. Love.

• 16414 • NACBS-Huntington Library Fellowship

To aid in dissertation research in British Studies using the collections of the Huntington Library. Applicants must be U.S. or Canadian citizens or permanent residents thereof, and must be enrolled in a PhD program in a U.S. or Canadian institution. Nominations and applications are accepted until November 15. The amount of the fellowship is $2,000. A requirement for holding the fellowship is that the time of tenure be spent in residence at the library. The time of residence varies, but may be as brief as one month. Awarded annually. Established in 1989.

• 16415 • John Ben Snow Foundation Prize
To recognize a North American author for the best book in any field of British Studies dealing with the period from the Middle Ages through the Eighteenth century. The author must be a North American scholar who is a citizen or permanent resident of the United States or Canada. Books may be published anywhere in the world. Nominations from authors or publishers must be submitted by April 1. A monetary prize of $500 is awarded annually. Established in 1983.

• 16416 •
North American Council on Adoptable Children
Joe Kroll, Exec.Dir.
970 Raymond Ave., Ste. 106
St. Paul, MN 55114
Phone: (651)644-3036
Fax: (651)644-9848
E-mail: info@nacac.org
Home Page: http://www.nacac.org

• 16417 • Adoption Activist Awards
For recognition of outstanding contributions toward achieving the goal of providing permanent, loving homes for waiting children, either by personal example or by working for institutional change on a local, state, or regional level. Individuals must be nominated by November 1. Awarded annually. Established in 1985. Formerly: Adopt-Action Service Award.

• 16418 • Child Advocate of the Year
For recognition of service and achievement on the behalf of the children of North America who need permanent adoptive families; and to serve as an inspiration to others to do more and work harder for children. Individuals of national or international distinction in the areas of legislative, philanthropic, judicial, media, professional, or volunteers who have demonstrated great effort in the cause and benefits of children must be nominated by November 1. A plaque is awarded annually. Established in 1978.

• 16419 • Friend of Children Award
To recognize an individual of national distinction who is involved in the field of intercountry adoption. Individuals who have demonstrated effort at the international level to the cause and benefits of children must be nominated by November 1. A plaque is awarded annually. Established in 1982.

• 16420 •
North American Die Casting Association
Daniel Twarog CAE, Pres.
9701 W. Higgins Rd., Ste. 880
Rosemont, IL 60018
Phone: (847)292-3600
Fax: (847)292-3620
E-mail: nadca@diecasting.org
Home Page: http://www.diecasting.org

Formed by merger of: (1989) American Die Casting Institute; Society of Die Casting Engineers.

• 16421 • Company Safety Awards
To recognize outstanding safety programs in the die casting industry. Awarded at the annual meeting.

• 16422 • Distinguished Life Member
To recognize active members of NADCA for many years of service to the industry. Established in 1964.

• 16423 • Doehler Award
To recognize contributions to the advancement of the die casting industry or to the art of die casting as represented by technical achievement, advancements in plant operations, or other activities, not primarily of a scientific or operational nature, which result in the enhancement of the reputation and acceptability of die casting. Individuals, groups, educational institutions, or technical and scientific societies or committees thereof, are eligible. Nominees are eligible for the award whether or not engaged in the die casting business and whether or not in the employ of a member of the North American Die Casting Association. A cash honorarium of $3,000 and a plaque are awarded annually. Established in 1949 through a grant of the Doehler-Jarvis Corporation.

• 16424 • Gullo and Treiber Award
To recognize marketing or sales activity advancing the expansion of knowledge of die casting. Established in 1969 by Chicago White Metal Casting, Inc.

• 16425 • International Award
To recognize an individual(s) responsible for a significant contribution to the die casting industry. This may be in the form of a process, technique, equipment or machinery design, alloys or any related area that enhances die casting internationally. Established in 1981.

• 16426 • Edward A. Kruszynski Achievement Award
To recognize an individual for achieving prominence through stimulation of broad usage of die castings, creative application of scientific principles to the die casting process, development of new process techniques, accomplishment in product design and encouragement of education programs. Established in 1960 and renamed in 1987.

• 16427 • David Laine Memorial Scholarship Program
To provide scholarships on the basis of academic excellence to university students, registered with the Foundry Educational Foundation, who are pursuing a career in the die casting industry. Awarded at the annual meeting in conjunction with FEF. Established in 1975.

• 16428 • Austin T. Lillegren Award
To recognize members for loyal and extraordinary service. Awarded annually. Established in 1960 in memory of Austin T. Lillegren, whose devotion and leadership exemplified unselfish service.

• 16429 • Membership Enrichment Award
To recognize active members who have demonstrated expertise at recruiting new Society members and advancing NADCA's position in the industry. Established in 1983.

• 16430 • Merit Award
To recognize active members who have demonstrated outstanding, ongoing contributions to NADCA. Established in 1981.

• 16431 • Nyselius Award
To recognize a contribution to the industry of a significant technical accomplishment or device. Established in 1965 by the Nyselius Foundation.

• 16432 • Special Service Award
To recognize members who have provided "above and beyond" service to NADCA and its membership. Established in 1983.

• 16433 •
North American Fruit Explorers
Jill Vorbeck, Contact
1716 Apples Rd.
Chapin, IL 62628-4048
Phone: (217)245-7589
Home Page: http://www.nafex.org

• 16434 • Milo Gibson Award
To recognize outstanding achievements or contributions in the field of pomology. Members and non-members from any country may be nominated. A hand-turned fruitwood bowl crafted by John English of Bloomington is presented annually at the convention. In addition, a Service Award is presented when merited to members for outstanding contributions to NAFEX. Established in 1977 by Dr. George Darrow in honor of Milo D. Gibson, founder and editor of *NAFEX*.

• 16435 •
North American Gladiolus Council
Cliff Hartline, Pres.
8401 SE Strawberry Ln.
Milwaukie, OR 97267-5412
Phone: (503)656-9270
Fax: (419)435-5061
E-mail: rgmglads@gwi.net
Home Page: http://www.gladworld.org

• 16436 • Ray Dittus Award
To recognize the hybridizer of the selected cultivar at the upcoming convention. Awarded to cultivars introduced in the previous five years. Entries are judged by at least two NACG judges. The cultivar receiving the most points wins.

• 16437 • Gold Medal Awards
For recognition of outstanding work with gladiolus. Nominations must be submitted by July 1. Officers of the council, hybridizers, and promoters of gladiolus are eligible. A gold medal is awarded at the convention in January. Established in 1945.

• 16438 •
North-American Interfraternity Conference
Jon Williamson, Exec.VP
3901 W 86th St., Ste. 390
Indianapolis, IN 46268-1791
Phone: (317)872-1112
Fax: (317)872-1134
E-mail: nic@nicindy.org
Home Page: http://www.nicindy.org

• 16439 • Gold and Silver Medals
For recognition of outstanding fraternity men. The following criteria are considered: distinguished service to fraternity youth; a life devoted to service to the fraternity movement; personification of the goal and ideal of service to youth; champion of efforts to raise fraternity standards; freely given time, effort, and energy; and promotion of sound educational attainment of positive advantages of youth; and represents the composite aim of all fraternity leaders and workers to improve the service of the fraternity and educational systems. No director of the conference or fraternity staff member is eligible for either of the awards for a period of three years after having completed his term of service. A gold and silver medal are awarded annually in April. The gold medal was established in 1940 and the silver medal in 1980.

• 16440 •
North American Lily Society
Linda Smith, U.S. VP
1419 Anglers Rd.
Beaufort, MO 63013-1712
Phone: (573)484-3157
Fax: (573)484-4481
E-mail: lkscrosk@yhti.com
Home Page: http://www.lilies.org

• 16441 • Slate - MacDaniels Award
To recognize a member or non-member for outstanding contribution to the society. A silver medal is awarded annually. Established in 1983.

• 16442 • E. H. Wilson Award
To recognize a member or non-member for outstanding contribution to the NALS and the genus Lilium. A silver medal is awarded annually. Established in 1959.

• 16443 •
North American Manx Association
Bradley Predergast, Pres.
4960 Cherry Ave.
Santa Maria, CA 93455
Phone: (650)961-6117
E-mail: jarmode@yahoo.com
Home Page: http://www.isle-of-man.com/interests/genealogy/nama

• 16444 • Heritage Award
Recognizes outstanding achievement in Manx language, music, arts and crafts by Manx youth. Awarded annually.

• 16445 •
North American Model Boat Association
Alan Hobbs, Pres.
1815 Halley St.
San Diego, CA 92154
Phone: (619)424-6380
Phone: (406)468-2706
Fax: (619)424-8845
E-mail: cathieg@ix.netcom.com
Home Page: http://www.namba.com

• 16446 • NAMBA Hall of Fame
For recognition of outstanding service to and promotion of model boating and to the Association. Deadline for nominees is May 1st of each year. Established in 1981.

• 16447 •
North American Mustang Association and Registry
Ellen Nelson, Pres.
PO Box 850906
Mesquite, TX 75185-0906
Phone: (972)289-9344

• 16448 • All Around NAMAR Mustang
To recognize the NAMAR mustang that has earned the most points in Halter, Western Pleasure, English Pleasure, and Trail. Mustangs must be registered with NAMAR. Recognition in the NAMAR newsletter and various prizes donated by sponsors are awarded annually at the End of Year Show. Awards are given to the Mustang with the most points in total and in each category. Established in 1986.

• 16449 •
North American Mycological Association
Judy Roger, Exec.Sec.
6615 Tudor Ct.
Gladstone, OR 97027-1032
Phone: (503)657-7358
E-mail: execsec@namyco.org
Home Page: http://www.namyco.org

• 16450 • Award for Contributions to Amateur Mycology
To recognize an outstanding amateur mycologist for work in the areas of local club leadership, workshops, lectures, leading forays, and contributions to taxonomy or toxicology of fungi. Amateur mycologists who are members may be nominated no later than April 1. A plaque and lifetime membership in the association is awarded annually. Established in 1961.

• 16451 •
North American Patristics Society
Clayton N. Jefford, Sec.-Treas.
St. Meinrad School of Theology
200 Hill Dr.
St. Meinrad, IN 47577
Phone: (812)357-6631
Fax: (812)357-6964
E-mail: cjefford@saintmeinrad.edu
Home Page: http://www.patristics.org

• 16452 • Best First Article Award
To recognize the author of an outstanding scholarly article in the area of the study of early Christianity published prior to or in the year for which the award is made. Entries must be the first scholarly piece published by members. A monetary prize of $250 is awarded annually. Established in 1975.

• 16453 •
North American Peruvian Horse Association
Arlynda Castro, Contact
3077 Wiljan Ct., Ste. A
Santa Rosa, CA 95407
Phone: (707)579-4394
Fax: (707)579-1038
E-mail: info@napha.net
Home Page: http://www.pphrna.org

• 16454 • Annual High Point Awards
For recognition of outstanding horses. The following awards are given: (1) High Point Trail Horse - for recognition of the horse which has garnered the most points in organized, competitive or endurance trail rides. Established in 1987; (2) High Point Parade Horse or Group - for recognition of the horse or group which has garnered the most points in judged parades. Established in 1987; and (3) High Point Open Show Horse for recognition of the horse which has garnered the most points in Open Horse Shows or Classes. Awarded annually. The award presented varies. Established in 1991.

• 16455 • High Point Performance Horse Awards
For recognition of show horses that have achieved the most points in the Performance Divisions of Association-approved shows. Given to the High Point Horse (mare, stallion, or gelding) as well as the High Point Gelding. Awarded annually. Established in 1977.

• 16456 • Medallion de Bronce
For recognition of show horses that have achieved 3,000 points in the Performance Divisions of Association-approved shows or that have been three-times High Point Performance Horse of the National Show. A traditional Peruvian stirrup with a bronze medal is presented as merited. Established in 1977.

• 16457 • Medallion de Oro
For recognition of show horses that have achieved 3,000 points in approved shows or that have been "Laureado" at the National Show (i.e., three times Champion of Champions). This is a lifetime award. Registration with the Association is required. A traditional Peruvian stirrup and a Gold Medal are presented as merited.

• 16458 • Medallion de Plata
For recognition of the annual high point winners in Association-approved shows. Categories include stallion, mare, gelding, colt, and filly. A traditional Peruvian stirrup and Silver Medallion are presented annually to five winners. Established in 1977.

• 16459 • Regional Medallions
For recognition of show horses who have garnered the most points in Association-approved shows in each of four zones. A plaque with a silver medal is presented annually. Established in 1990.

• 16460 •
North American Snowsports Journalists Association
Steven Threndyle, Exec.Sec.
460 Sarsons Rd.
Kelowna, BC, Canada V1W 1C2
Phone: (250)764-2143
Fax: (250)764-2145
E-mail: nasja@shaw.ca
Home Page: http://www.nasja.org

Formerly: (1990) United States Ski Writers Association.

• 16461 • Harold S. Hirsch Award for Excellence in Broadcasting
For recognition of outstanding ski broadcasting. Members are eligible to enter work by April 15. A plaque or trophy is awarded annually. Established in 1984.

• 16462 • Harold S. Hirsch Award for Excellence in Ski Photography
For recognition of outstanding ski photography. Members are eligible to enter work by April 15. A silverplated plaque or trophy is awarded annually. Established in 1984.

• 16463 • Harold S. Hirsch Award
To recognize excellence in media coverage of winter snow sports. Articles written during the previous ski season by members of USSWA are eligible. A plaque or trophy is awarded annually. Established in 1963 by Harold S. Hirsch, one of the early manufacturers of ski clothing and accessories.

• 16464 • Lifetime Achievement Award
To honor an individual for a lifetime in ski competition, skiing innovation, equipment design, or any other skiing accomplishment or endeavor deemed noteworthy. A plaque is awarded annually.

• 16465 • Member Awards
To recognize outstanding productivity by members. Awarded as merited.

• 16466 • Outstanding Competitor Award
To recognize the competitor, amateur or professional, who has contributed the most to American skiing during the past year. A trophy or plaque is presented annually. Established in 1967.

• 16467 • The Carson White Golden Quill Award
To recognize an individual who has made great contributions to snow sports. A plaque or trophy is awarded annually if merited. Established in 1965. Formerly known as the Golden Quill Award. Renamed in 1995 to honor Carson White.

• 16468 •
North American Society for Oceanic History
Dr. John B. Hattendorf, Pres.
PO Box 18108
Washington, DC 20374-0571
Phone: (202)707-1409
Home Page: http://www.ecu.edu/nasoh/

• 16469 • John Lyman Book Awards
To recognize the authors of books published during the past year that have made the most significant contributions to naval and maritime literature. Awards are presented in the following six categories: Canadian naval and maritime history, U.S. naval history, U.S. maritime history, science and technology, reference works and published primary sources, and biography and autobiography. A commemorative plaque, a citation, and notice in the Society's newsletter are awarded annually at the awards dinner of the national convention. Established in 1978 in honor of Dr. John Lyman (1915-1977), a founder of NASOH.

• 16470 •
North American Society for Sport History
Ronald A. Smith, Sec.-Treas.
PO Box 1026
121 Dale St.
Lemont, PA 16851-1026
Phone: (814)238-1288
Fax: (814)238-1288
E-mail: secretary-treasurer@nassh.org
Home Page: http://nassh.org

• 16471 • NASSH Book Award
To recognize the best book on sport history. Any book on sport history in the English language is eligible. A monetary award of $500 and a certificate are awarded annually. Established in 1988.

• 16472 •
North American Society for Sport Management
Robin Ammon, Contact
W Gym 014
Slippery Rock University
Slippery Rock, PA 16057
Phone: (724)738-4812
Fax: (724)738-4858
E-mail: nassm@sru.edu
Home Page: http://www.nassm.org

• 16473 • Earle F. Zeigler Lecture Award
This, the Society's most prestigious award, is given to recognize individuals who have made a scholarly contribution to the development of the field. Eligible nominees must be members and outstanding supporters of NASSM, and have a minimum of 10 years of service as a teacher, supervisor, and/or administrator. Nomination deadline is October 1. A plaque and the opportunity to present a scholarly address at the annual meeting are awarded each year. Established in 1988 to honor Dr. Earle F. Zeigler.

• 16474 •
North American Society for the Psychology of Sport and Physical Activity
Alan L. Smith PhD, Sec.-Treas.
Purdue Univ.
Lambert Fieldhouse
800 W Stadium Ave.
West Lafayette, IN 47907-2046
Phone: (765)496-6002
Fax: (765)496-1239
E-mail: alsmith@cla.purdue.edu
Home Page: http://www.naspspa.org

• 16475 • Distinguished Scholar Award
To recognize outstanding long-term contributions in the research areas of motor learning/control, motor development, or sport psychology. Each year, a plaque and $500 is awarded when merited at the Society's annual conference. Established in 1982.

• 16476 • Early Career Distinguished Scholar Award
To recognize outstanding achievements of scholars who are still in the early stage of their scientific careers. Each year $200, a plaque, and conference registration are awarded when merited at the Society's annual conference. Established in 1982.

• 16477 • President's Award
To recognize those who have made significant contributions to the development and growth of the North American Society for the Psychology of Sport and Physical Activity. Candidates must be current or previous members of NASPSPA. A plaque is awarded when merited at the Society's annual conference. Established in 1990.

• 16478 •
North American Trail Ride Conference
Lourie Dinatale, Exec. Administrator
PO Box 224
Sedalia, CO 80135
Phone: (303)688-1677
Fax: (303)688-3022
E-mail: natrc@natrc.org
Home Page: http://www.natrc.org

• 16479 • **Appreciation Certificates for Service to NATRC**
To recognize outstanding service to NATRC. Awards are given in the following categories: National, Region I, Region II, Region III, Region IV, Region V, and Region VI. A certificate is awarded.

• 16480 • **Breed Awards**
To recognize outstanding achievement. Awards are given in the following categories and are listed with their sponsors: High Point Arabian International Arabian Horse Association; High Point 1/2 Arabian International Arabian Horse Association; High Point Appaloosa - Appaloosa Horse Club; High Point American Quarter Horse - American Quarter Horse Association; High Point Fino - Paso Fino Owners and Breeders Association; High Point American Indian Horse - American Indian Horse Registry; High Point Pony of America - Pony of America Association; and High Point American Saddlebreed - American Saddlebred Horse Association. Awarded when applicable and sponsored.

• 16481 • **Polly Bridges Memorial Award**
To recognize the rider who has the highest average horsemanship score rather than the highest number of points. A perpetual sculpture is awarded annually. Established in 1986.

• 16482 • **Cumulative Mileage Awards**
To recognize horses and riders for cumulative mileage completed. The following awards are presented: 1,000 Mile Horse - awarded to horses completing 1,000 miles; mileage chevrons in increments of 250 miles are awarded to riders; and mileage medallions will be awarded to horses and riders achieving the following levels of mileage: 4,000 miles - bronze; 7,000 miles - silver; 10,000 miles - gold; and 15,000 miles - diamond.

• 16483 • **High Point Horsemenship Award**
To recognize riders with the high scores in each Open Class (i.e., heavyweight, lightweight, and junior). A silver bowl is awarded for first place and ribbons are awarded for first through sixth place annually.

• 16484 • **Junior Grand Champion**
To recognize the horse ridden by a junior that has the highest average score, rather than the highest number of points. An embroidered satin jacket is awarded annually.

• 16485 • **Junior High Average Horsemanship**
To recognize the Junior rider who has the highest average horsemanship score, rather than the highest number of points. An embroidered satin jacket is awarded annually.

• 16486 • **Junior National Championship**
To recognize junior national champions in each of the six regions. A sterling silver buckle or horse blanket is awarded annually.

• 16487 • **Jim Menefee Memorial Award**
To recognize the horse and rider combination that has the highest number of total points for horse and horsemanship. A perpetual sculpture is awarded annually. Established in 1979.

• 16488 • **NATRC Honorary Lifetime Membership**
To recognize a member with honorary lifetime membership. A trophy and a certificate are awarded.

• 16489 • **NATRC National Champions**
To recognize national champions in each of the six regions. A sterling silver buckle or horse blanket is awarded annually. Each award has a variety of sponsors.

• 16490 • **NATRC Ride Awards**
To recognize outstanding accomplishments in the following categories: Heavyweight Horse, Lightweight Horse, and Junior Horse. A silver bowl is awarded for both horse and horsemanship first place; horse blankets for first and second place horse; and ribbons for first through sixth places.

• 16491 • **Presidents Cup**
To recognize the overall high point horse in the Open Division. A silver bowl, silver buckle, horse blanket, and ribbon are awarded annually. Established in 1961. Formerly: (1998) National Sweepstakes Champion.

• 16492 • **Regional Horse Awards**
To recognize horses in each Open Division (i.e., heavyweight, lightweight, and junior) for points accumulated within the region of the horse and rider's residence. A silver bowl for first place and ribbons for first through sixth place are awarded annually.

• 16493 • **Bev Tibbitts Grand Champion Horse Award**
To recognize the horse that has the highest average score, rather than the highest number of points. A perpetual sculpture is awarded annually. Established in 1975.

• 16494 •
North American Travel Journalist Association
Elizabeth Beshear, Exec.Dir.
531 Main St., No. 902
El Segundo, CA 90245
Phone: (310)836-8712
Fax: (310)836-8769
E-mail: info@natja.org
Home Page: http://www.natja.org

Formerly: (2004) East-West News Bureau.

• 16495 • **NATJA Awards Competition**
Recognizes service to the public relating to the hospitality industries. Companies and organizations are eligible. Awarded annually. Formerly: (2004) Magic Lantern.

• 16496 •
North American Vexillological Association
Peter Ansoff, Pres.
1977 N Olden Ave. Ext.
PMB 225
Trenton, NJ 08618-2193
E-mail: pres@nava.org
Home Page: http://www.nava.org

• 16497 • **Whitney Award**
To honor outstanding contributions to the field of vexillology (the study of flags) and/or to the Association by a member. A trophy is awarded by the executive board when merited. Established in 1992 in honor of Dr. Whitney Smith, father of vexillology.

• 16498 •
North American Warmblood Association
2400 Faussett Rd.
Howell, MI 48843
Phone: (517)546-5280

• 16499 • **North American Warmblood Association Awards**
To recognize achievement in dressage. Awards are presented in the following categories: Training Level Champion; Second Level Champion; Fourth Level Champion; Prix St. George Champion; AHSA International 2 Champion; and Grand Prix Champion. A medal and certificate are awarded annually. Established in 1986.

• 16500 •
North Carolina Agribusiness Council
Megan E. Henderson, Mgr. of Member Services
3701 National Dr., Ste. 211
Raleigh, NC 27612-4864
Phone: (919)782-4063
Fax: (919)782-4064
Home Page: http://www.ncagribusiness.com/

• 16501 • **Governors Award**
For distinguished service to the agribusiness industry. Recognition award bestowed annually.

• 16502 •
North Carolina Arts Council
Department of Cultural Resources
Raleigh, NC 27699-4632
Phone: (919)733-2111
Fax: (919)733-7897
E-mail: ncarts@ncacmail.net
Home Page: http://www.ncarts.org

• 16503 • **Folk Heritage Award**
To honor traditional folk artists who have made significant lifetime contributions to North Carolina's cultural heritage. Nominations are due by April 1. A monetary award of up to $5,000 is presented annually. Established in 1989.

• 16504 •
North Carolina Association of County Commissioners
C. Ronald Aycock, Exec.Dir.
215 N. Dawson St.
PO Box 1488
Raleigh, NC 27603
Phone: (919)715-2893
Fax: (919)733-1065
E-mail: ncacc@ncacc.org
Home Page: http://www.ncacc.org

• 16505 • **Ketner Productivity Awards**
For cost savings innovation by counties. Monetary award bestowed annually.

• 16506 • **Outstanding County Program Awards**
For innovative programs in four categories. Recognition award bestowed annually.

• 16507 •
North Carolina Dept. of Agriculture & Consumer Services
Steve Troxler, Commissioner
1001 Mail Service Center
Raleigh, NC 27699-1001
Phone: (919)733-7125
Fax: (919)733-0999
Home Page: http://www.agr.state.nc.us

• 16508 • **NAMO Marketing Award**
To recognize an individual or a firm that has developed and carried out some outstanding innovation in marketing on a national basis. A plaque is awarded annually when merited. Established in 1974. For further information, contact M. Wayne Miller.

• 16509 •
North Carolina Herpetological Society
Jeff Beane, Newsletter Ed.
North Carolina State Museum of Natural Sciences
11 W. Jones St.
Raleigh, NC 27601
Phone: (919)733-7450
Phone: (919)779-0996
Fax: (919)733-1573
E-mail: ncherps@juno.com
Home Page: http://www.ncherps.org

• 16510 • **NCHS Grants in Herpetology**
For conservation, education, or research projects; membership required. Grant awarded annually.

• 16511 •
North Carolina Library Association
1811 Capital Blvd.
Raleigh, NC 27604
Phone: (919)839-6252
Fax: (919)839-6253
E-mail: nclaonline@ibiblio.org
Home Page: http://www.nclaonline.org

• 16512 • **NCLA Distinguished Library Service Award**
For distinguished professional library service in NC, significant service or other professional contributions provided during either a short or long term, and service resulting in regional or national impact. Recognition award bestowed biennially.

• 16513 • **NCLA/SIRS Intellectual Freedom Award**
For active promotion of intellectual freedom. Monetary award bestowed biennially.

• 16514 • **Ray Moore Award**
For author of best article in North Carolina libraries. Recognition award bestowed biennially.

• 16515 •
North Carolina Literary and Historical Association
Jeffrey J. Crow PhD, Deputy Sec.
4610 Mail Service Ctr.
Raleigh, NC 27699-4610
Phone: (919)807-7280
Fax: (919)733-8807
E-mail: ahweb@ncmail.net
Home Page: http://www.ah.dcr.state.nc.us

• 16516 • **American Association of University Women Award in Juvenile Literature**
For recognition of the creative activity in writing juvenile literature and to stimulate interest in worthwhile literature written on the juvenile level. Eligible recipients must have been residents of North Carolina for the preceding three years. Application deadline is July 15. A silver cup is awarded annually. Established in 1953 by the North Carolina Chapter of the American Association of University Women.

• 16517 • **Robert D. W. Connor Award**
To stimulate interest in the publication of articles of high quality in the field of North Carolina history. Authors of articles published in the *North Carolina Historical Review* during the previous year are eligible, provided they were residents of North Carolina for the preceding three years. Application deadline is July 15. A monetary prize of $250 and a certificate are awarded annually. Established in 1953 by the Historical Society of North Carolina.

• 16518 • **Christopher Crittenden Memorial Award**
For outstanding contributions to the advancement of North Carolina history. Individuals, organizations, institutions, corporate bodies, or other groups engaged in the study, writing, teaching, preservation, restoration, or dissemination of knowledge pertaining to North Carolina history are eligible, provided they were residents of North Carolina for the preceding three years. Application deadline is July 15. A silver goblet is awarded annually. Established in 1970 in memory of Dr. Christopher Crittenden.

• 16519 • **R. Hunt Parker Memorial Award**
To recognize an individual for a significant lifetime contribution to North Carolina literature. Eligible recipients must have been residents of North Carolina for the preceding three years. Application deadline is July 15. Awarded annually. Established in 1987.

• 16520 • **Sir Walter Raleigh Award for Fiction**
For recognition of outstanding works of fiction, including the novel, drama, and short story. Residents of North Carolina are eligible. Application deadline is July 15. A statuette and cup are awarded annually. Established in 1952 by the Historical Book Club of North Carolina.

• 16521 • **Roanoke-Chowan Award for Poetry**
For recognition of distinguished works of poetry and to stimulate an interest in the literature of North Carolina. Residents of North Carolina are eligible. Application deadline is July 15. A silver cup is awarded annually. Established in 1953 by the Roanoke-Chowan Group of Writers and Allied Artists.

• 16522 •
North Carolina Utility Contractors Association
Jim Lowry, Exec.Dir.
130 Mine Lake Ct., Ste. 100
Raleigh, NC 27615-6417
Phone: (919)845-7733
Fax: (919)882-9629
E-mail: info@ncuca.org
Home Page: http://www.ncuca.org

• 16523 • **Safety Award**
For safety records. Recognition award bestowed annually.

• 16524 •
North Dakota Long Term Care Association
1900 N. 11th St.
Bismarck, ND 58501
Phone: (701)222-0660
Fax: (701)223-0977

• 16525 • **Allen Ergen Scholarship**
For nursing students. Scholarship awarded annually.

• 16526 •
North Dakota Lutherans for Life
Kristin Erickson, Pres.
PO Box 428
102 11th St. SE
Cooperstown, ND 58425
Phone: (701)797-3122
Toll-Free: 888-364-LIFE
E-mail: mjerickson@mlgc.com
Home Page: http://www.lutheransforlife.org

• 16527 • **Jean Garton Award**
For individual who is active in educating others about the sanctity of human life, as well as assisting those involved in sanctity of life issues and crises. Recognition award bestowed annually.

• 16528 •
North Dakota Tourism Department
Sara Otte Coleman, Dir.
PO Box 2057
PO Box 2057
Bismarck, ND 58503-2057
Phone: (701)328-2525
Phone: (701)328-2526
Toll-Free: 800-435-5663
Fax: (701)328-4878
E-mail: tourism@state.nd.us
Home Page: http://www.ndtourism.com

• 16529 • **Tourism Award**
For person or company nominated by peers who excels in tourism industry. Recognition award bestowed annually.

• 16530 •
North Penn Beagle Club
Ronald W. Reichardt, Sec.
365 Rich Hill Rd.
Sellersville, PA 18960-3203
Phone: (215)538-1178
E-mail: snap8333@msn.com

• 16531 • **AKC Licensed Field Trail for Championship Points**
For performance. Recognition award bestowed annually.

• 16532 •
North San Antonio Chamber of Commerce
Mr. E. Duane Wilson, Pres. and CEO
12930 Country Pkwy.
San Antonio, TX 78216-2004
Phone: (210)344-4848
Fax: (210)525-8207
E-mail: deb@northsachamber.com
Home Page: http://www.northsachamber.com

• 16533 • **Athena Award**
For women in business. Recognition award bestowed annually.

• 16534 •
Northcoast Environmental Center
Tim McKay, Exec.Dir.
575 H St.
Arcata, CA 95521
Phone: (707)822-6918
Fax: (707)822-0827
E-mail: nec@yournec.org
Home Page: http://www.necandeconews.to

• 16535 • **Bouquet of the Month**
For contributions to the environment. Recognition award bestowed monthly.

• 16536 •
Northcote Parkinson Fund
John Train, Chm.
67A E 77th St.
New York, NY 10021
Phone: (212)737-1011
Fax: (212)737-6459
E-mail: abslone@compuserve.com
Home Page: http://www.biblia.org/northcote.html

• 16537 • **Civil Courage Prize**
Awarded to individuals exhibiting civil courage. It may be awarded posthumously, and should not ordinarily reflect current political concerns. The award can be $50,000 for a living recipient, or, for a posthumous award, a brief biography will be commissioned, if appropriate.

• 16538 •
Northeast Catholic Alumni Association
Leonard F. Knobbs, Exec.Sec./Treas.
1840 Torresdale Ave.
Philadelphia, PA 19124
Phone: (215)289-4994
Phone: (215)289-4995
Fax: (215)289-9336
E-mail: necathalum@aol.com

• 16539 • **Outstanding Achievement Award**
For a non-alumnus individual or organization that has distinguished themselves in a particular field of endeavor. Recognition award bestowed annually.

• 16540 • **Outstanding Alumnus Award**
To an alumnus individual or organization that has distinguished themselves in a particular field of endeavor. Recognition award bestowed annually.

• 16541 •
Northeast Louisiana Arts Council
Thomas F. Usrey, Exec.Dir.
2305 N 7th St.
West Monroe, LA 71291
Phone: (318)396-9520
Fax: (318)396-6837
E-mail: artsmanne@aol.com
Home Page: http://www.ulm.edu/~nlac/

• 16542 • **NLAG Regrant Program**
For artistic excellence. Grant awarded annually.

• 16543 •
Northeast Modern Language Association
Prof. Josephone McQuail, Exec. Dir.
Dept. of English
Tennessee Technological University
Cookeville, TN 38505
Phone: (931)372-6207
Fax: (931)372-3484
E-mail: jmcquail@tntech.edu
Home Page: http://www.nemla.org

• 16544 • **NEMLA Book Prize**
For recognition of the best unpublished manuscript written by a member. Two awards are given: one for the best book-length manuscript in American or British literature and/or cultural studies; and one for the best book-length manuscript on any subject in foreign language, literature, and/or culture. Each winner will receive a cash prize of $100 and publication by the Ohio University Press and the Fairleigh Dickinson University Press. Application deadline is October 31. Awarded annually. Established in 1986.

• 16545 •
Northeast Nebraska Economic Development District
Renay Robison-Scheer, Exec.Dir.
111 S. 1st St.
Norfolk, NE 68701
Phone: (402)379-1150
Fax: (402)379-9207
E-mail: renay@nenedd.org
Home Page: http://www.nenedd.org

• 16546 • **Collaborative Community Award**
For initiated regional or multi community program or project. Recognition award bestowed annually.

• 16547 •
Northeastern Loggers Association
Joseph E. Phaneuf, Exec.Dir.
PO Box 69
Old Forge, NY 13420
Phone: (315)369-3078
Toll-Free: 800-318-7561
Fax: (315)369-3736
E-mail: jphaneuf@nothernlogger.com
Home Page: http://www.northernlogger.com

• 16548 • **Northeastern Loggers' Association Awards Program**
To recognize significant achievement of individuals and companies in forestry and wood utilization. Nine awards are given: Outstanding Logging Operator, Outstanding Sawmill Operator, Outstanding Service to the Forest Industry, Outstanding Management of Resources, Outstanding Leadership in the Industry, Outstanding Contribution to Forest Industry Education, Outstanding Use of Wood, Outstanding Contribution to Safety, and Outstanding Industry Activist.

Nominees need not be members of NLA, but must reside in or conduct business in the Northeastern or Lake States Region of the United States as delineated by the USFS. The deadline for nominations is January 31. Presented at the annual Northeastern Loggers Congress. Established in 1955.

• 16549 •
Northeastern Lumber Manufacturer Association
Jeff Easterling, Pres.
PO Box 87A
272 Tuttle Rd.
Cumberland, ME 04021
Phone: (207)829-6901
Fax: (207)829-4293
E-mail: info@nelma.com
Home Page: http://www.nelma.org

• 16550 • **Honorary Life Member**
To recognize individuals for outstanding contributions to the northeastern lumber producing industry. A hand-carved plaque is awarded. Established around 1940.

• 16551 •
Northern Arizona Celtic Heritage Society
Martha Shidgler, PR Officer
116 W. Cottage Ave.
Flagstaff, AZ 86001-5564
Phone: (928)779-3817
Phone: (928)556-3161
Fax: (928)779-3812
E-mail: piobair@infomagic.net

• 16552 • **William C. Dunlop Piping Scholarship**
For interest in and devotion to Celtic culture and heritage. Scholarship awarded annually.

• 16553 •
Northern Kentucky University
Department of Theatre and Dance
Fine Arts, Ste. 206
Nunn Dr.
Highland Heights, KY 41099
Phone: (606)572-6362
Toll-Free: 800-637-9948
Fax: (606)572-6057
E-mail: conger@nku.edu
Home Page: http://www.nku.edu/~theatre

• 16554 • **Year End Series Festival of New Plays**
To recognize outstanding playwrights. Full-length plays, adaptations, and musicals that have not had previous professional or university productions may be submitted. One-acts, children's theatre, or reader's theatre pieces are not considered. Four selected playwrights each receive a monetary prize of $500 and an expense paid visit to Northern Kentucky University to see its plays in production. Awarded biennially in odd-numbered years; entries accepted between August and October in even-numbered years. Established in 1983.

• 16555 •
Northern Plains Botanic Garden Society
Larry Fischer, Pres.
PO Box 3031
Fargo, ND 58108-3031
Phone: (701)239-4444

• 16556 • **FM Foundation Downtown Beautification Grant**
For project merit. Monetary award bestowed annually.

• 16557 •
Northwest Business for Culture and the Arts
Virginia Willard, Exec.Dir.
224 NW 13th Ave., Ste. 303
Portland, OR 97209
Phone: (503)228-2977
Fax: (503)248-1808
E-mail: info@nwbca.org
Home Page: http://www.nwbca.org

• 16558 • **Breakfast of Champions**
For giving personally and corporately to arts and culture. Recognition award bestowed three times per year.

• 16559 •
Northwest Film Center
Portland Art Museum
1219 SW Park Ave.
Portland, OR 97205
Phone: (503)221-1156
Fax: (503)294-0874
E-mail: info@nwfilm.org
Home Page: http://www.nwfilm.org
Formerly: Northwest Film Study Center.

• 16560 • **Northwest Film and Video Festival**
To recognize outstanding independent film makers who are permanent residents of Alaska, British Columbia, Idaho, Montana, Oregon, or Washington. Entries may be short films, features, or documentaries. The deadline is August 1. Monetary awards, lab service awards, and public screenings are presented annually. Additionally, the festival tours nationally and the winners receive rental fees. Established in 1972.

• 16561 • **Portland International Film Festival**
To recognize excellence in international films as well as American features, documentaries, and short films. The deadline for entries is October 31. Held annually. Established in 1977.

• 16562 • **Young People's Film and Video Festival**
To identify and celebrate artistic excellence, technical achievement, and originality in work created by young artists. Applicants must be in grades K-12 and must reside in Oregon, Washington, Idaho, Montana, Utah, or Alaska. A public screening of works is held and the winning programs are aired over public television. Certificates are awarded to the winners. Presented annually. Established in 1977. Formerly: (1978) Young Filmmakers Festival.

• 16563 •
Northwest Regional Spinners Association
Ann Klinect, Pres.
21 Nash Rd.
White Salmon, WA 98672
Phone: (509)493-4241
E-mail: dizzysheep@mac.com
Home Page: http://www.nwrsa.org

• 16564 • **Lee Kirschner-Lewis Study Grant**
For members and associates to expand the knowledge of the craft of hand spinning through research and study. Grant awarded annually.

• 16565 •
Northwestern University
Center for International and Comparative Studies
618 Garrett Pl.
Evanston, IL 60208-4135
Phone: (847)467-2770
Fax: (847)467-1996
E-mail: jgibson@northwestern.edu
Home Page: http://www.cas.northwestern.edu/cics/

• 16566 • **CICS Graduate Research Awards**
Inquire for application details.

• 16567 • **Harold Guetzkow Prize**
Recognizes outstanding undergraduate research. Northwestern University students are eligible.

• 16568 •
Northwestern University
Office of the Provost
Lawrence B. Dumas, Provost
% Office of the Provost
633 Clark St.
Evanston, IL 60208
Phone: (847)467-6443
Fax: (847)491-4434
E-mail: nemmers@northwestern.edu
Home Page: http://www.northwestern.edu/provost

• 16569 • **Erwin Plein Nemmers Prize in Economics**
To recognize persons with careers of outstanding achievement in the discipline, as demonstrated by major contributions to new knowledge or the development of significant new modes of analysis. Awarded in even numbered years with a monetary prize of $150,000. Nominations must be received by December 1 of odd-numbered years. Established in 1994.

• 16570 • Frederic Esser Nemmers Prize in Mathematics
To recognize persons with careers of outstanding achievement in the discipline, as demonstrated by major contributions to new knowledge or the development of significant new modes of analysis. Awarded in even numbered years with a monetary prize of $150,000. Nominations must be received by December 1 of odd-numbered years. Established in 1994.

• 16571 •
Northwood University
2600 Military Trail
West Palm Beach, FL 33409-2911
Phone: (561)478-5500
Fax: (561)697-9495
E-mail: fladmit@northwood.edu
Home Page: http://www.northwood.edu

• 16572 • Distinguished Women's Awards
To honor women for outstanding achievement and high ideals in the fields of business, that arts, public service, education, the media, entrepreneurship, volunteerism, and philanthropy. Nominations are accepted by anyone familiar with the nominee's qualifications. One or more women are selected to receive a medal designed by sculptor Giulio Tamassy and a book entitled *Distinguished Women* at the annual recognition luncheon. Established in 1970 by the co-founder of Northwood University, Dr. Arthur E. Turner, and the College Board of Trustees.

• 16573 • Outstanding Business Leader Awards
To recognize leaders in the American entrepreneurial system. Nominations are accepted by anyone familiar with the nominee's qualifications. Criteria used in the selection of awardees include contribution to the philosophy of private enterprise, support of the integration of business and the arts, contribution to education, economic innovation, creative marketing ideas, community involvement, religious leadership, philanthropic contributions, as well as business success. Selection is made by the Board of Trustees. A trophy is presented annually to one or more recipients in January. Established in 1981.

• 16574 •
Northwood University, Michigan Campus
4000 Whiting Dr.
Midland, MI 48640-2398
Phone: (989)837-4200
Fax: (989)837-4111
E-mail: mibusoff@northwood.edu
Home Page: http://www.northwood.edu

• 16575 • Achievement in the Arts Award
To honor men and women of outstanding talent and achievement in the performing, visual, and musical arts fields. Individuals who have reached artistic pinnacles and who have inspired and encouraged young artists and performers by their performances or activities on behalf of talented youth are eligible. A framed citation is awarded annually at a ceremony traditionally held at the Players Club in New York City. Works related to the awardee's own field are performed as part of the program of events. Established in 1977.

• 16576 • Automotive Aftermarket Education Award
To recognize noteworthy efforts to improve education, communication, and progress in the automotive aftermarket field. Nominees who are affiliated with the automotive replacement industry and have shown substantial dedication over a number of years to the education process and the field of automotive replacement marketing are considered. A certificate is presented annually to one or more recipients at the convention. Established in 1975. Formerly: Automotive Replacement Management Award.

• 16577 • Dealer Education Award
To recognize individuals in the automotive marketing field who have made noteworthy contributions to public or private education on any level, inside or outside of the industry. Nominees who are affiliated with the automotive marketing industry and have shown substantial dedication over a number of years to the educational process are considered. Awarded annually to one or more recipients at the convention. Established in 1972. Formerly: Automotive Dealer Education Award.

• 16578 • Alden B. Dow Creativity Center Summer Residency Fellowships
To encourage individual creativity. Applications are accepted from individuals in all disciplines with various areas of interest, including the arts, humanities, and sciences. Project ideas must be new and innovative and have the potential for impact in their fields. A stipend, travel expenses, and room and board are awarded annually. Application deadline is December 31. Established in 1979 by Alden B. Dow, architect laureate of Michigan.

• 16579 • Outstanding Alumni Achievement Award
To honor Northwood University graduates who have excelled in their chosen field and/or have given special service in support of their University. Presented annually in a fall (usually October) ceremony held near the Michigan campus. Graduates from all branches and levels of University are eligible.

• 16580 • Arthur E. Turner Entrepreneur Award
Entrepreneurs who have succeeded at an early age (generally under 40) are honored for the role model they set to the economic and student communities. The originating award was held fall 1996 in Palm Beach, Florida. Future awards will be held annually throughout the nation.

• 16581 •
Norwalk Grassroots Tennis
Arthur J. Goldblatt, Contact
15 Eastwood Rd.
Norwalk, CT 06851-1111
Phone: (203)229-0200
Phone: (203)846-0591
Fax: (203)229-0200
E-mail: goldblatts@worldnet.att.net

• 16582 • Arthur Ashe Award
For most improved player. Recognition award bestowed annually.

• 16583 •
NSF International
789 N Dixboro Rd.
PO BOX 130140
Ann Arbor, MI 48113-0140
Phone: (734)769-8010
Toll-Free: 800-NSF-MARK
Fax: (734)769-0109
E-mail: info@nsf.org
Home Page: http://www.nsf.org

• 16584 • Walter F. Snyder Award
To recognize an individual for achievements in attaining environmental quality, based on peer recognition, for contributions to public health and for leadership in securing actions on behalf of environmental goals. A plaque and a certificate are awarded annually. Established in 1971 and co-sponsored by the National Environmental Health Association.

• 16585 • Spes Hominum Award
For recognition of support to the corporation, its objectives and programs based upon long standing service to the corporation, devotion to environmental quality objectives, and support of NSF philosophy and methodology in solving environmental problems. A person not currently serving on the staff or as an officer is eligible. A medallion embedded in lucite and a framed certificate are awarded annually. Established in 1969.

• 16586 •
NSU Club of America
Terry Stuchlik, Contact
2909 Utah Pl.
Alton, IL 62002
Phone: (618)462-9195
E-mail: stuchlik@ewgateway.org
Home Page: http://members.aol.com/trochoids/14.htm

• 16587 • The Order of NSU
To honor for action above and beyond the call of duty in keeping the NSU Marque alive. Awarded annually with one year membership recognition and club patch. Established in 1976.

• 16588 •
Nuclear Age Peace Foundation
David Krieger, Pres.
PMB 121
1187 Coast Village Rd., Ste. 1
Santa Barbara, CA 93108-2794
Phone: (805)965-3443
Fax: (805)568-0466
E-mail: dkrieger@napf.org
Home Page: http://www.wagingpeace.org

• 16589 • **Distinguished Peace Leadership Award**
To recognize individuals who demonstrate dedicated and courageous leadership in the cause of peace. An award is presented annually. Established in 1984.

• 16590 • **Barbara Mandigo Kelly Peace Poetry Awards**
To encourage poets to explore and illuminate some aspect of peace and the human spirit. Contest is open to people worldwide. All poems must be the original work of the poet, unpublished and in English. Up to three poems may be submitted with a maximum of forty (40) lines per poem. A monetary prize of $1000 is awarded to adult contestants. Two monetary prizes of $200 are awarded in the youth category, one between the ages of 13 to 18 and one to 12 years old and younger. Submissions must be postmarked before July 1. Awarded annually. Established in 1996.

• 16591 • **Swackhamer Peace Essay Contest**
To encourage young people to consider the problems of war and peace, and make suggestions for constructive solutions. Outstanding essays by high school students on an annual theme related to peace in the nuclear age are eligible. A monetary award is presented annually. Submissions must be postmarked by June 1. Established in 1985 in honor of Austin H. and Florence Anderson Swackhamer.

• 16592 • **World Citizenship Award**
Presented to individuals of high distinction who have acted for the benefit of all humanity. An award is presented annually. Established in 1998.

• 16593 •
Nuclear Energy Institute
Joe Colvin, CEO & Pres.
1776 I St. NW, Ste. 400
Washington, DC 20006-3708
Phone: (202)739-8000
Fax: (202)785-4019
E-mail: webmaster@nei.org
Home Page: http://www.nei.org

Formerly: (1987) Atomic Industrial Forum.

• 16594 • **Henry DeWolf Smyth Statesman Award**
To recognize outstanding service in developing and guiding the uses of atomic energy in constructive channels. The recipient must be the joint selection of the two sponsoring organizations. A gold-plated bronze medal is awarded when merited. Established in 1972 and named in honor of Henry DeWolf Smyth of Princeton University, the first recipient of the award. Co-sponsored by the American Nuclear Society.

• 16595 •
Oak Lawn Soccer Club
Bryan Chambless, Pres.
PO Box 190433
Dallas, TX 75219-0995
Phone: (214)366-2565
E-mail: info@oaklawnsoccerclub.org
Home Page: http://
www.oaklawnsoccerclub.org

• 16596 • **OLSC Youth Grant**
For those with financial need and community service experience. Grant awarded annually.

• 16597 •
Oak Ridge Associated Universities
Dr. Ronald D. Townsend, Pres.
OAB-44
PO Box 117
Oak Ridge, TN 37831-0117
Phone: (865)576-3146
Fax: (865)241-2923
E-mail: phillipc@orau.gov
Home Page: http://www.orau.org

Awards discontinued.

• 16598 • **Office of Civilian Radioactive Waste Management Graduate Fellowship Program**
Award includes payment of tuition and fees not to exceed $8,000 per year; monthly stipend of $1,200 throughout the academic year; 1 required summer parcticum at a U.S. Department of Energy National Laboratory. Fellowships is renewable for eligible participants. Applicants must be U.S Citizens or P.R.A.s; students with undergraduate degrees in the physical and life sciences, mathematics, or engineering including graduate students who have not progressed to the point of having an approved theses or dissertation topic; attend a participating University. Application deadline is January 29. Contact Colleen Babcock, (865)576-9272 or e-mail babcocke@orau.gov for applications. Applications are also available at http://www.orau.gov/orise/edu/uggrad/civfel1.htm.

• 16599 • **Office of Civilian Radioactive Waste Management Historically Black Colleges and Universities Undergraduate Scholarship Program**
Promotes education in science, math, engineering, engineering technology, or social science. Award includes payment of tuition and fees not to exceed $8000 per year; monthly stipend of $600 throughout the academic year; required summer internship at U.S. Department of Energy sites. Renewable for eligible participants. Applicants must be U.S. Citizens; Junior or Senior in college at the time pf protram participation; attend an Historically Black College or University; be enrolled full-time in one of the eligible academic areas. Deadline for entry is January 29. Contact Rose Etta Cox (865)576-9279 or e-mail cosre@orau.gov for applications. Applications also available at http://www.orau.gov/orise/edu/uggrad/ocrapp.htm.

• 16600 •
Oak Ridge National Laboratory
P.O. Box 2008
Oak Ridge, TN 37831
Phone: (865)574-4160
Home Page: http://www.ornl.gov

• 16601 • **Frank H. Spedding Award**
To recognize excellence an achievement in research centered on the science and technology of rare earth materials. A plaque and travel expenses to the conference are awarded biennially in even-numbered years. Established in 1979.

• 16602 •
Oboe International
PO Box 1335, Ansonia Sta.
New York, NY 10023-1335

• 16603 • **New York International Competition for Solo Oboists**
To foster the growth, re-establishment of, and public interest in the oboe as a solo musical instrument. Oboists between 18 and 30 years of age are eligible. The following awards are presented: (1) First Prize - $1,500, a New York solo recital in Weill Recital Hall at Carnegie Hall, recital and orchestral appearances throughout the United States, and an oboe; (2) Second Prize - $1,000 and an oboe; (3) Third Prize - $500 and an oboe; and (4) each semifinalist receives a gift certificate donated by a sponsoring oboe accessory dealer. Established in 1986. Formerly: (1991) Lucarelli International Competition for Solo Oboe Players.

• 16604 •
Occupational and Environmental Medical Association of Canada
(Association canadianne de la mecence du travail et de l'environnement)
Lise Jamieson CAE, Exec.Sec.
1147 Lawson Rd.
London, ON, Canada W6G 5K1
Phone: (519)439-7970
Fax: (519)439-8840
E-mail: oemac@oemac.org
Home Page: http://www.oemac.org

• 16605 • **Meritorious Service Award**
For outstanding service in the field of occupational and environmental medicine. Awarded annually.

• 16606 •
Ocean Conservancy
Roger T. Rufe Jr., Pres./CEO
2029 K St.
Washington, DC 20006
Phone: (202)429-5609
Toll-Free: 800-519-1541
Fax: (202)872-0619
E-mail: info@oceanconservancy.org
Home Page: http://www.oceanconservancy.org

• 16607 • **Paid Internships**
Graduate students are eligible. Inquire for application details.

• 16608 •
Ochsner Clinic Foundation
Patrick J. Quinlan, CEO
1514 Jefferson Hwy.
New Orleans, LA 70121
Phone: (504)842-3000
Toll-Free: 800-874-8984
Fax: (504)842-3258
E-mail: efrohlich@ochsner.org
Home Page: http://www.ochsner.org

• 16609 • **Alton Ochsner Award Relating Smoking and Health**
To recognize an individual for outstanding and exemplary original scientific investigations that relate tobacco consumption and health. Clinical investigators or scientists in the basic sciences areas without regard to age, race, sex, or nationality are eligible. The work may be clinical, fundamental, epidemiological, or preventive in nature. The prime criterion for selection is the scientific impact of the work on this major health problem. A monetary award of $15,000, a medal, and a scroll are awarded annually. Established in 1986 for Alton Ochsner, M.D., the first physician to relate cigarette smoking to lung cancer and one of the founders of the Ochsner Medical Institutions.

• 16610 •
Offender Aid and Restoration/USA
Cristina Biebescheimer, Chm.
1400 N Uhle St., Ste. 704
Arlington, VA 22201
Phone: (703)228-7030
Fax: (703)228-3981
E-mail: info@oaronline.org
Home Page: http://www.oaronline.org

• 16611 • **L. Harold DeWolf Award**
For recognition of distinguished contributions to community corrections in America. A nationally renowned person who has contributed to making the criminal justice system more equitable and just must be nominated by an ad hoc committee of the Board of Directors of OAR/USA. Established in 1977 in memory of Dr. L. Harold DeWolf, theologian and author.

• 16612 • **Jay Worrall Public Official Award**
To recognize outstanding contributions in community services in community criminal justice. Local figures are eligible. Established to honor Jay Worrall, the founder of OAR.

• 16613 •
Office of Strategic Services Society
6723 Whittier Ave., Ste. 303A
McLean, VA 22101
Phone: (703)356-6667
E-mail: oss@osssociety.org
Home Page: http://www.osssociety.org

Formerly: (2003) Veterans of the Office of Strategic Services in World War II.

• 16614 • **William J. Donovan Award**
To recognize an individual for distinguished service in the interest of the democratic process and the cause of freedom. A medal carrying the likeness of General Donovan is awarded. Established by the Veterans of OSS in memory of William J. Donovan, the major general who founded the Office of Strategic Services in World War II. Sponsored by the William J. Donovan Memorial Foundation.

• 16615 •
Office of the Americas
Theresa Bonpane, Exec.Dir.
8124 W 3rd St., Ste. 202
Los Angeles, CA 90048-4309
Phone: (323)852-9808
Fax: (323)852-0655
E-mail: ooa@igc.org
Home Page: http://www.officeoftheamericas.org

• 16616 • **Office of the Americas Peace & Justice Award**
Recognizes dedication to peace and justice in the Americas. Awarded annually.

• 16617 •
Official Gilligan's Island Fan Club
Louie Knaiger, Pres.
12429 Dormouse Rd.
San Diego, CA 92129
E-mail: thurshowell@aol.com
Home Page: http://www.gilligansisle.com/main.html

• 16618 • **Globe International Gold Award**
Recognizes website graphics, artwork and information. Awarded biennially.

• 16619 •
Oglebay Institute
Mark R. Williams, Pres.
1330 National Rd.
Wheeling, WV 26003
Phone: (304)242-4200
Fax: (304)242-7747
E-mail: inspire@oionline.com
Home Page: http://www.oionline.com

• 16620 • **Towngate Theatre National Playwriting Contest**
To provide an opportunity to produce a good play that some producers may reject on the basis of subject matter. Contestants are not limited to "crowd pleaser" plays and are welcome to submit scripts of a more serious and thoughtful nature. All full-length, non-musical plays that have never been professionally produced or published are eligible. The deadline for entry is Dec. 31. Contestants may submit more than one play for consideration. Plays collaborated by two or more authors are acceptable; however, the prize money remains the same. A monetary prize of $300, a limited run of the play in the following year, and up to $200 in travel expenses are awarded annually. Established in 1977.

• 16621 •
Ohio Academy of History
Gary R. Hess, Pres.
Department of History
Kent State University
PO Box 5190
Kent, OH 44242-0001
Phone: (740)389-2361
Fax: (740)292-5817
E-mail: mheiss@kent.edu
Home Page: http://www2.uakron.edu/oah

• 16622 • **Dissertation Award**
For recognition of an outstanding historical doctorate granted by an Ohio institution in the preceding year. An engraved plaque is awarded annually. Established in 1994.

• 16623 • **Distinguished Service Award**
To recognize members for a specific achievement or a long-time contribution to the field of history. Nomination deadline is November 15. Engraved plaques are awarded annually. Established in 1946. Formerly: (1970) Historical Achievement Award.

• 16624 • **Distinguished Teaching Award**
To recognize excellence in teaching of history by an active member of the academy. Nomination deadline is November 15. An engraved plaque is awarded annually. Established in 1980.

• 16625 • **Outstanding Publication Award**
For recognition of an outstanding historical publication. Works published during the previous year by active members of the academy are eligible. Nomination deadline is November 15. An engraved plaque is awarded annually. Established in 1946. Formerly: (1970) Historical Achievement Award.

• 16626 • **Public History Award**
For recognition of an outstanding public history project in the preceding year. An engraved plaque is awarded annually. Established in 1996.

Awards are arranged in alphabetical order below their administering organizations

• 16627 •
Ohio Arts Council
Wayne P. Lawson, Exec.Dir.
727 E Main St.
Columbus, OH 43205-1796
Phone: (614)466-2613
Toll-Free: 800-TOGETOAC
Fax: (614)466-4494
E-mail: wayne.lawson@oac.state.oh.us
Home Page: http://www.oac.state.oh.us

• 16628 • **Individual Artist Fellowship**
To recognize outstanding artists living and working in Ohio. Professional artists who are residents of the State of Ohio are eligible. Students are not eligible. Fellowships of $5,000 or $10,000 based on the quality of work already created are awarded in the following categories: choreography, crafts, creative writing (fiction, poetry, and non-fiction), criticism, design arts, interdisciplinary and performance art, media arts, music composition, photography, playwriting, and visual arts. The annual deadline for this competition is September 1. Established in 1978 by the State of Ohio legislature and the Board of the Ohio Arts Council.

• 16629 •
Ohio Construction Suppliers Association
John C. Benson, Exec.V.Pres.
41 Croswell Rd.
Columbus, OH 43214
Phone: (614)267-7817
Phone: (614)267-7816
Toll-Free: 800-282-4632
Fax: (614)267-6448
E-mail: olaoffices@ohiolumber.org
Home Page: http://www.ohiolumber.org

• 16630 • **Charles E. and Marian Benson Scholarship Fund**
To provide financial assistance to forestry students at Ohio State University whose career interests include the distribution of lumber and building products. One or two scholarships are awarded annually. Established in 1978.

• 16631 •
Ohio Genealogical Society, Fairfield County Chapter
Karen S. Smith, Pres.
PO Box 1470
Lancaster, OH 43130-0570
Phone: (740)653-2745
E-mail: chapter@fairfieldgenealogy.org
Home Page: http://www.fairfieldgenealogy.org/

• 16632 • **4H-Genealogy Award**
For individual chosen by 4-H. Recognition award bestowed annually.

• 16633 •
Ohio Genealogical Society, Franklin County
PO Box 44309
Columbus, OH 43204-0309
E-mail: fcghs@yahoo.com
Home Page: http://www.rootsweb.com/~ohfcghs

• 16634 • **Pioneer Families of Franklin Co.**
For ancestors in Franklin County, Ohio by 1830. Recognition award bestowed annually.

• 16635 •
Ohio Genealogical Society, Mahoning County
Jocelyn Wilms, VP
PO Box 9333
Boardman, OH 44513-9333
E-mail: mccogs@zoominternet.net
Home Page: http://www.mahoningcountychapterogs.org

• 16636 • **Pioneer Families of Mahoning County Award**
For families with ancestors living in the county prior to 1851. Recognition award bestowed periodically.

• 16637 •
Ohio Genealogical Society, Seneca County
Steve Hartzell, Corresponding Sec.
PO Box 157
Tiffin, OH 44883-0157
E-mail: seneca09@senecasearchers.org
Home Page: http://www.senecasearchers.org/

• 16638 • **First Families of Seneca County Gold Award**
For people with ancestors who resided in Seneca County prior to 1841. Recognition award bestowed annually.

• 16639 • **First Families of Seneca County Silver Award**
For people with ancestors who resided in Seneca County during the period 1841-1860 Recognition award bestowed annually.

• 16640 •
Ohio Genealogical Society, Williams County
Pamela Pattison Lash, Pres.
PO Box 293
Bryan, OH 43506-0293
E-mail: lashpamela@cityofbryan.net
Home Page: http://www.wcgs-ogs.com

• 16641 • **Jennifer Lash Memorial Genealogical Award**
For 4-H award of A in genealogy field. Recognition award bestowed annually.

• 16642 •
Ohio Hospice and Palliative Care Organization
Jeff Lycan, Pres./CEO
1646 West Ln. Ave., Ste. 2
Columbus, OH 43221
Phone: (614)485-0021
Toll-Free: 800-776-9513
Fax: (614)485-0560
E-mail: hospiceoh@aol.com
Home Page: http://www.ohpco.org

• 16643 • **Stein Award**
For hospice excellence. Recognition award bestowed annually.

• 16644 •
Ohio Middle School Association
Philip Binkley, Exec.Dir.
PO Box 20363
Columbus, OH 43220
Phone: (614)457-3750
Fax: (614)457-5099
E-mail: pbinkley@hotmail.com
Home Page: http://www.ohiomsa.org

• 16645 • **OMSA Recognition and Component Awards**
For student/staff recognition, exemplary middle level programs. Recognition award bestowed annually.

• 16646 •
Ohio Recorders Association
Julia Scott, Contact
15 S. Court St.
Athens, OH 45701
Phone: (740)592-3228

• 16647 • **Recorder of the Year**
For service to public. Recognition award bestowed annually.

• 16648 •
Ohio State University Mershon Center
1501 Neil Ave.
Columbus, OH 43201
Phone: (614)292-1681
Fax: (614)292-2407
E-mail: mershoncenter@osu.edu
Home Page: http://www.mershon.ohio-state.edu

• 16649 • **Edgar S. Furniss Award**
For the best published book on national security. Awarded annually.

• 16650 •
Ohio State University Press
Malcolm Litchfield, Dir.
180 Pressey Hall
1070 Carmack Rd.
Columbus, OH 43210-1002
Phone: (614)292-6930
Fax: (614)292-2065
E-mail: ohiostatepress@osu.edu
Home Page: http://www.ohiostatepress.org

• 16651 • ***The Journal* Award in Poetry**
To recognize and publish an outstanding volume of poetry annually. *The Journal: The Literary Magazine of O.S.U.* makes the selection of one full-length manuscript of poetry. Previously unpublished manuscripts of at least 48 pages of original poetry must be submitted during the month of September. Some or all of the poems in the collection may have appeared in periodicals, chap-books, or anthologies, but must be identified. The Charles B. Wheeler Prize of $3,000 and publication of the winning manuscript are awarded to one recipient annually. Established in 1987 by David Citino.

• 16652 •
Ohio University Press and Swallow Press
David Sanders, Dir.
Ohio University Press
19 Circle Dr.
The Ridges
Athens, OH 45701-2979
Phone: (740)593-1157
Fax: (740)593-4536
E-mail: sandersd@ohio.edu
Home Page: http://www.ohio.edu/oupress

• 16653 • **Hollis Summers Poetry Prize**
To recognize the best collection of unpublished poems. A cash prize of $1,000 and publication are awarded annually.

• 16654 •
Ohio Women's Programs
Robin E. Rice, Contact
Ohio Department of Job & Family Services
145 S Front St.
Columbus, OH 43215
Phone: (614)466-4496
Fax: (614)466-7912

• 16655 • **Women Making History-Essay Contest**
For eighth grade students. Recognition award bestowed annually.

• 16656 •
Ohioana Library Association
Linda Hengst, Dir.
274 E 1st Ave.
Columbus, OH 43201
Phone: (614)466-3831
Fax: (614)728-6974
E-mail: ohioana@sloma.state.oh.us
Home Page: http://www.oplin.org/main.php?Id=66&msg=
Formerly: Martha Kinney Cooper Ohioana Library Association.

• 16657 • **James P. Barry Ohioana Award for Editorial Excellence**
For recognition of an Ohio-based serial (magazine, scholarly journal, newspaper, etc.) that covers subjects of interest to the Ohioana Library, namely literature, history, culture, or the general humanities. Nominations must be submitted by December 31. An original piece of glass sculpture by Robert Eickholt is awarded annually. The award honors James P. Barry, former editor and director. Established in 1979. Formerly: Ohioana Award for Editorial Excellence.

• 16658 • **Ohioana Award, Florence Roberts Head Memorial Award**
For recognition of an outstanding book written by an Ohio author (special attention to a woman author) during the preceding year. Persons born in Ohio or those who have lived in the state for at least five years are eligible. Nominations must be submitted by December 31. An original piece of glass sculpture by Robert Eickholt is awarded annually. Established in 1963 in honor of Florence Roberts Head, the first director of the Association. Formerly: .

• 16659 • **Ohioana Poetry Award, Helen and Laura Krout Memorial**
To recognize individuals whose body of work has made, and continues to make, a significant contribution to poetry and has developed interest in poetry through their work as writers, teachers, administrators, or in community service. Recipients must have been born in Ohio or lived in Ohio for a minimum of five years. Nominations must be submitted by December 31. A monetary award of $1,000 is presented annually. Established in 1985. Formerly: (2004) Helen and Laura Krout Ohioana Poetry Award.

• 16660 • **Walter Rumsey Marvin Grant**
To recognize an unpublished writer under 30 years of age who was born in Ohio or who has lived in Ohio for a minimum of five years. Up to six pieces of prose, a maximum of 60 pages for the total entry, may be submitted. Entries must be submitted by January 31. A monetary award of $1,000 is presented annually.

• 16661 • **Ohioana Book Awards**
For recognition of the best fiction, non-fiction, poetry, juvenile, and books about Ohio or an Ohioan. Authors born in Ohio or those who have lived in the state for at least five years are eligible for books published during the previous year. Nominations must be submitted by December 31. An original piece of glass sculpture by Robert Eickholt is awarded in each category annually. Established in 1942.

• 16662 • **Ohioana Career Award**
For recognition an outstanding native Ohioan who has attained national distinction in the arts and humanities. Nominations must be submitted by December 31. An original piece of glass sculpture by Robert Eickholt is awarded annually. Established in 1943.

• 16663 • **Ohioana Citation for Distinguished Service to Ohio**
For recognition of distinguished service to Ohio in the arts and humanities. Four citations may be given each year in various disciplines. Persons born in Ohio, or those who have lived in Ohio for five years, are eligible. An original piece of glass sculpture by Robert Eickholt is awarded to each recipient annually. Established in 1955.

• 16664 • **Ohioana Pegasus Award**
For recognition of an outstanding cultural contribution by an Ohioan. Native Ohioans or longtime residents of the state are eligible. Nominations must be received by December 31. An original piece of glass sculpture is awarded annually.

• 16665 • **Alice Louise Wood Memorial Ohioana Award for Children's Literature**
For recognition of an Ohio author whose body of work makes a significant contribution to literature for children and young adults. The recipient must, through their work as a writer, teacher, administrator, or through other community service, have encourage interest in children's literature and motivated children to read. Authors born in Ohio or those who have lived in the state for at least five years are eligible. A monetary prize of $1,000 is presented annually in the fall. Established in 1990. Formerly: .

• 16666 •
Oklahoma Archaeological Survey
Lois E. Albert, Contact
111 E Chesapeake
Norman, OK 73019
Phone: (405)325-7211
Fax: (405)325-7604
E-mail: archsurvey@ou.edu
Home Page: http://www.ou.edu/cas/archsur

• 16667 • **Bell Award**
Graduate students in anthropology are eligible. Inquire for application details.

• 16668 •
Oklahoma Association of School Library Media Specialists
Jeanie Johnson, Dir.
State Department of Education
2500 N Lincoln, Ste. 215
Oklahoma City, OK 73105-4599
Phone: (405)521-2956
Fax: (405)522-0611
E-mail: jeanie_johnson@sde.state.ok.us
Home Page: http://www.oklibs.org/oaslms/

• 16669 • **The Polly Clarke Award**
To honor an outstanding library media specialist who has exhibited professional involvement, curriculum support, integrated library/information skills instruction, and cooperative planning of instructional units incorporated into an exemplary library media program. A monetary prize of $500 and a plaque are awarded annually if merited.

• 16670 • **Oklahoma School Administrator Award**
To honor a school administrator who promotes library media services as an integral part of the public school's educational process, and to acknowledge the vital importance of the role of school administrators in the development and expansion of school library media programs. Oklahoma public school administrators actively employed in the school during the year covered by the nomination are eligible. A monetary award of $250 and a plaque are presented annually.

• 16671 • **The Barbara Spriestersbach Award for Excellence in Teaching**
To honor a teacher who has demonstrated resource-based teaching by cooperatively planning and teaching with a library media specialist colleague. Teachers are nominated by their library media specialist. A monetary prize of $250 and a plaque are awarded annually.

• 16672 •
Oklahoma Hemophilia Foundation
Karen Duncan, VP
PO Box 727
Edmond, OK 73083
Phone: (405)844-5850
Phone: (405)660-0874
Toll-Free: 800-735-3855
Fax: (405)524-7916
E-mail: ohf@domgp.com

• 16673 • **Jason Nelson Scholarship**
For high school senior or college student. Scholarship awarded annually.

• 16674 •
Oklahoma Library Association
Kay Boies, Exec.Dir.
300 Hardy Dr.
Edmond, OK 73013
Phone: (405)348-0506
Fax: (405)348-1629
E-mail: kboies@coxinet.net
Home Page: http://www.oklibs.org/

• 16675 • **Sequoyah Children's Book Award**
To encourage Oklahoma girls and boys in grades three through six to read books of literary quality. A master reading list of notable books, which represents the titles being considered for the award that year, is compiled by the Sequoyah Children's Book Award Committee. The author of the book must be a resident of the United States. A plaque depicting Sequoyah and his "talking leaves" is awarded annually to the author of the book receiving the most votes by students. Established in 1959 in honor of Sequoyah for his unique achievement in creating the Cherokee alphabet, the 85 symbols representing the different sounds in the Cherokee language.

• 16676 • **Sequoyah Young Adult Book Award**
To encourage young adults of Oklahoma in grades seven through nine to read books of literary quality. A master reading list of notable books, which represents the titles being considered for the award that year, is compiled by the Sequoyah Young Adult Book Award Committee. The author of the book must be a resident of the United States. A plaque depicting Sequoyah and his "talking leaves" is awarded annually to the author of the book receiving the most votes by students. Awarded at the spring conference. Established in 1988 in honor of Sequoyah for his unique achievement in creating the Cherokee alphabet, the 85 symbols representing the different sounds in the Cherokee language.

• 16677 •
Oklahoma Lupus Association
J. Mark Hedrik, Exec.Dir.
3131 N MacArthur, Ste. 106B
Oklahoma City, OK 73122
Phone: (405)495-8787
Phone: (405)495-8778
Toll-Free: 800-725-6445
Fax: (405)495-8778
E-mail: oklupus@flash.net
Home Page: http://www.oklupus.com

• 16678 • **Jane Bozart Research Grant**
For lupus research approved by nih. Grant awarded annually.

• 16679 •
Oklahoma Religious Coalition for Reproductive Choice
Rev. Linda K. Morgan-Clark, Exec. Officer
PO Box 35194
Tulsa, OK 74153-0194
Phone: (918)481-6444
Toll-Free: 800-214-3509
Fax: (918)481-6288

• 16680 • **Judy Halpern Religious Freedom Award**
For leadership in advocating reproductive choice as a religious freedom issue. Recognition award bestowed periodically.

• 16681 •
Old Dominion Kennel Club of Northern Virginia
D. Kay Tripp, Sec.
15209 Turkey Foot Rd.
Darnestown, MD 20878
Phone: (301)948-1919
Fax: (301)948-3931
E-mail: dktripp@aol.com
Home Page: http://www.olddominionkennelclub.com

• 16682 • **Scholarship to VPI-Veterinary College**
For interest in pure-bred dogs. Scholarship awarded annually.

• 16683 •
Old Timers Soccer Association of Maryland
Len Lewandowski, Contact
19 Northwood Dr.
Timonium, MD 21093
Home Page: http://www.marylandsoccer.com/oldtimers/form.htm

• 16684 • **Outstanding High School Player**
For achievement as a player and contribution to the team. Recognition award bestowed annually.

• 16685 • **John A. Schmid Service Award**
For contributions to the game of soccer. Recognition award bestowed annually.

• 16686 •
Oley Valley Combined Training Association
Nancy W. Peltier, Pres.
PO Box 497
Douglassville, PA 19518
Phone: (610)948-6787

• 16687 • **High-Score Award**
For high achievers from OVCTA competitions. Recognition award.

• 16688 • Year-end Achievement Award
For high achievers from OVCTA competitions. Recognition award bestowed annually.

• 16689 •
Olin Fine Arts Center Gallery
Washington and Jefferson College
60 S Lincoln St.
Washington, PA 15301
Phone: (412)223-6110
Toll-Free: 888-W-AND-JAY
Fax: (412)223-5271

• 16690 • W & J National Painting Show
For recognition of achievement in painting. Artists 18 years of age or over who are citizens of the United States must submit original art work on colored slides by January. Over $3,000 in cash and purchase awards, and the Grumbacher Gold Medal are presented annually at the Washington and Jefferson National Painting Show. Established in 1967 by Paul B. Edwards.

• 16691 •
Omaha Symphony Guild
Robert J. Hallam, Pres. and CEO
1605 Howard St.
Omaha, NE 68102
Phone: (402)342-3836
Fax: (402)342-3819
E-mail: info@omahasymphony.org
Home Page: http://www.omahasymphony.org

• 16692 • International New Music Competition
To recognize new composers and new music. All composers, age 25 and older are eligible. Works that are unpublished and have not been performed by a professional orchestra may be submitted by April 15. A monetary award of $3,000 and an optional premiere performance of the work are awarded annually. Established in 1976.

• 16693 •
Omicron Delta Epsilon
Dr. William D. Gunther, Exec.Sec.-Treas.
PO Box 1486
Hattiesburg, MS 39403
Phone: (601)264-3115
Fax: (601)264-3669
E-mail: odecf@aol.com
Formed by merger of: (1963) Omicron Delta Gamma; Omicron Chi Epsilon.

• 16694 • Irving Fisher Article Award
For recognition of the best article submitted by a graduate student or recent PhD in the field of economics. Members of the Society who are graduate students or have received their PhD or terminal M.A. not more than two years prior to entering the competition are eligible. Articles may be on any topic in economics; PhD dissertations are eligible. A monetary prize of $500, an invitation to present the paper at the next annual meeting of the American Economic Association, and publication of the article in *The American Economist* are awarded annually. Established in 1970 in memory of Irving Fisher.

• 16695 • Frank W. Taussig Article Award
For recognition of the best article submitted by an undergraduate or recent graduate in the field of economics. Any undergraduate student in a school with an ODE chapter who has received a bachelor's degree not more than two years prior to entering the competition is eligible. Articles may be on any topic in economics but must be based on work done as an undergraduate. Entries of up to 5,000 words are preferred, but up to 10,000 words are acceptable. A monetary prize of $500 to the winner, $200 to the winner's ODE chapter, and publication in *The American Economist* are awarded annually in the fall. Established in 1970 in memory of Frank W. Taussig.

• 16696 •
Omicron Delta Kappa
Dr. John D. Morgan, Exec.Dir.
456 Rose Ln.
Lexington, KY 40508
Phone: (859)455-8870
Fax: (859)455-8874
E-mail: odknhdq@odk.org
Home Page: http://www.odk.org

• 16697 • Distinguished Service Key
To recognize a member who has rendered an outstanding and conspicuous service to the Society. Awarded annually. Established in 1931.

• 16698 • Laurel Crowned Circle Award
This, ODK's highest honor, recognizes an outstanding American who has exemplified the ideals of the Omicron Delta Kappa Society. A certificate and an engrossed key are awarded. Established in 1980.

• 16699 • Leader of the Year Award
To recognize students who have made a qualitative difference in their institutions and in the lives of others. Each province elects the Province Leader of the Year from nominations submitted by the circles in the province. The province winners are transmitted to the national committee for the selection of the national winner. Awarded annually. Established in 1975.

• 16700 • Robert L. Morlan Faculty Secretary Award
For recognition of outstanding service to the Society and to the local circle by a faculty secretary. Awarded annually. A $500 honorarium accompanies the award.

• 16701 • Omicron Delta Kappa Scholarships
To provide scholarships for members of the Society who intend to take graduate work within three years at some recognized institution in the United States or some other country. Applicants must be active members of the Society and have a 3.5 grade point average. Eighteen $1,000 scholarships are awarded annually. Established in 1931.

• 16702 • Eldridge W. Roark Jr. Meritorious Service Certificate
To recognize members of the Society from time to time for their varied and meritorious service to the Society. Established in 1951.

• 16703 •
Omicron Kappa Upsilon
Jan John, Corr.Sec.
University of Nebraska Medical Center
College of Dentistry
40th & Holdgege St.
Lincoln, NE 68583-0740
Phone: (402)472-1339
Fax: (402)472-5290
E-mail: jkjohn@unmc.edu
Home Page: http://www.oku.org

• 16704 • William S. Kramer Award of Excellence
For recognition of the outstanding junior dental student in Chapter school who has demonstrated scholarship, character, and the potential promise for advancement of dentistry and service to humanity. Completion of two years of dental school is necessary for consideration. Certificates as well as monetary prizes at some chapters are awarded annually. Established in 1987 in honor of Dr. William S. Kramer, longtime secretary-treasurer of the Supreme Chapter.

• 16705 • Membership in Omicron Kappa Upsilon
To honor graduating seniors in dentistry in all of the 62 component chapters in dental schools in the United States and Canada. No more than 12 percent of the class may be elected, based upon scholarship and character. Certificates and keys or lapel pins are awarded annually. Established in 1914.

• 16706 •
Omohundro Institute of Early American History and Culture
Ronald Hoffman, Dir.
PO Box 8781
Williamsburg, VA 23187-8781
Phone: (757)221-1114
Phone: (757)221-1114
Fax: (757)221-1047
E-mail: ieahc1@wm.edu
Home Page: http://www.wm.edu/oieahc

Formerly: (1997) Institute of Early American History and Culture.

• 16707 • Jamestown Prize
To recognize the author of the best book-length, scholarly manuscript, usually based on a Ph.D. dissertation, on early American history or culture submitted to the Institute Prize Committee. The winning author receives $3,000, and the manuscript will be published by the University of North Carolina Press in conjunction with the Institute as part of the Institute's regular publication program. The prize competition is open only to au-

thors who have not previously published a book. The subject of the manuscript must pertain to North America between 1450 to 1820or to the related histories of the Caribbean, Latin America, the British Isles, Europe, or Africa. Manuscripts may be submitted for prize at any time. A separate letter of inquiry accompanied by a prospectus of the manuscript should be sent to the Institute, indicating interest in submission for the Jamestown prize. Correspondence and manuscripts should be mailed to the Editor of Publications, Omohundro Institute of Early American History and Culture, PO Box 8781, Williamsburg, VA 23187-8781. Formerly: (1974) Institute Manuscript Award; (1974) Jamestown Foundation Award.

• 16708 •
Oncology Nursing Society
Pearl Moore RN, CEO
125 Enterprise Dr.
125 Enterprise Dr.
Pittsburgh, PA 15275
Phone: (412)859-6100
Toll-Free: 877-369-5497
Fax: (412)859-6162
E-mail: customer.service@ons.org
Home Page: http://www.ons.org

• 16709 • **Advanced Oncology Certified Nurse of the Year Award**
To recognize outstanding achievement of an oncology certified nurse. The candidate must be an oncology certified nurse who has promoted oncology nursing certification and has demonstrated accomplishments in at least one area of oncology nursing such as clinical practice, education, research, and/or service. The application deadline is December 1. A monetary award of $1,000 and a crystal award are presented annually at the ONS Congress.

• 16710 • **Linda Arenth Excellence in Cancer Nursing Management Award**
To recognize and support excellence in cancer nursing management/administration. The candidate must be a RN and a Society member. A monetary award of $1,000, $1,000 toward ONS Congress expenses, and a plaque are presented annually at the ONS Congress. The application deadline is August 15. Established in memory of Linda Arenth, who was a leading nurse administrator and active in ONS and the Oncology Nursing Certification Corporation. Formerly: Roxane Laboratories Linda Arenth Excellence in Cancer Nursing Management Award.

• 16711 • **Susan Baird Oncology Excellence in Writing Award in Clinical Practice**
To recognize achievement and contributions to the oncology nursing literature, to promote the literary exchange of expertise and initiative to clinical practice, to stimulate the scholarly presentation of oncology nursing research, and to increase the visibility of oncology nursing as a specialty. All articles that have appeared in the appropriate volume of the *Oncology Nursing Forum* and meet the selection criteria are automatically considered for the award. A monetary award of $1,250 and a plaque are awarded annually. Formerly: Chiron Therapeutics Susan Baird Excellence in Writing Awards in Clinical Practice and Nursing Research.

• 16712 • **Ellyn Bushkin Friend of the Foundation Award**
To recognize persons who have provided continuous support of the mission of the Oncology Nursing Foundation. The Board of Trustees selects the recipient. To be eligible, the nominee must have demonstrated support of the Foundation by making major financial contributions, coordinating significant fund-raising events, or promoting/enhancing the image of the Foundation. Awarded annually.

• 16713 • **Chapter Excellence Award**
To recognize an ONS Chapter that has excelled in promoting the mission and goals of the Society. The chapter must have been chartered for at least two years and demonstrate how they have promoted the mission and goals of ONS. Three plaques and monetary awards of $1,500 are presented annually. Formerly: Chiron Therapeutics Chapter Excellence Award.

• 16714 • **Distinguished Researcher Award**
To recognize the contributions of a member who has conducted or promoted the research that has enhanced the science and practice of oncology nursing. The candidate must be an ONS member with an earned doctorate in nursing or a related field. A monetary award of $3,000 and a plaque are presented annually. The awardee must deliver an address at the ONS Congress and a reception is held in honor of the awardee. Sponsored by Bristol-Myers Squibb Oncology.

• 16715 • **Excellence in Breast Cancer Education Award**
To recognize and support excellence and dedication to educating the public or patients about breast cancer. The candidate must be a Registered nurse and an ONS member. The application deadline is August 15. A monetary award of $4,000 and a plaque are awarded annually. Sponsored by Susan G. Komen Breast Cancer Foundation. Formerly: Zeneca Pharmaceuticals/Komen Foundation Excellence in Breast Cancer Education Award.

• 16716 • **Excellence in Radiation Therapy Nursing Award**
To recognize and support excellence in radiation nursing. Nominees must be registered nurses and ONS members. The application deadline is August 15. A monetary award of $1,000 and a plaque are presented annually. Established in 1993. Sponsored by Varian Medical Systems.

• 16717 • **Excellence of Scholarship and Consistency of Contributions to the Oncology Nursing Literature Award**
To recognize an individual who has made consistent and excellent contributions to oncology nursing literature. The candidate must be an RN and a member of ONS. A monetary award of $4,000 and a plaque are presented annually. Sponsored by SuperGen Inc. Formerly: Chiron Therapeutics Award for Excellence of Scholarship and Consistency of Contribution to the Oncology Nursing Literature.

• 16718 • **FIRE Excellence Award**
To honor an oncology nurse who has made outstanding and significant contributions to cancer-related fatigue, clinical practice, education or research. Members who are registered nurses and have made significant contributions to research, education or clinical practice are eligible. A monetary award of $1,000 and a plaque are awarded annually at the ONS Congress. Established in 1996. Sponsored by Ortho Biotech Products LP.

• 16719 • **Mara Mogensen Flaherty Memorial Lectureship**
To support the presentation of an annual lecture on a topic related to the psychosocial aspects of cancer diagnosis, treatment, and care, presented by a health care professional who is involved in the field of psychosocial oncology, cancer care, education or research. The deadline for applications is August 15. The recipient delivers a lecture at the ONS Annual Congress and receives a $1,000 honorarium, airfare to ONS Congress, a two-day per diem, and a plaque. Sponsored by the Oncology Nursing Foundation and Sanofi-Synthelabo Inc.

• 16720 • **Purdue Frederick Quality of Life Lecture**
To recognize a registered nurse who is an active member of ONS who has demonstrated excellence in clinical practice, education, administration, or research related to quality of life issues. The recipient delivers a lecture at the ONS Annual Fall Institute, and receives a $2,000 honorarium, Fall Institute registration, a plaque, and possible publication of the lecture in the *Clinical Journal of Oncology Nursing (CJON)*.

• 16721 • **Honorary Membership**
To honor individuals (including non-members) who have made significant outstanding contributions to oncology nursing and have demonstrated a sustained interest and support of ONS at the national level. Honorary membership shall be at the national level only. The individual must be nominated by an ONS member, have received unanimous approval from the ONS Board of Directors, and three support letters, one of which comes from a non-ONS member, and a it1curriculum vitaeit2 must be submitted. The application deadline is January 1. A calligraphy certificate and an ONS gold pin are awarded annually.

• 16722 • **ONS/AMGEN Inc. Award for Excellence in Patient/Public Education**
To support and recognize excellence in patient/ public education. Oncology nurses must be members of the Society, be involved in creative public or patient education, and have at least two years experience in oncology nursing to be

eligible. A monetary award of $2,000 and a plaque are awarded annually at the ONS Congress. The application deadline is August 15. Established in 1990. Sponsored by Amgen Inc.

• 16723 • ONS/Pharmacia & Upjohn Excellence in Oncology Nursing Private Practice Award
To support and recognize excellence in private practice oncology nursing in the office setting. Nominee must be a member who has demonstrated initiative in developing creative programs that improve the quality of life for patients and families. A monetary award of $2,000 and a plaque are awarded annually at the ONS Congress. The application deadline is August 15. Established in 1990. Sponsored by Pharmacia & Upjohn.

• 16724 • ONS/Roche Distinguished Service Award
For recognition of an oncology nurse who has made outstanding contributions to ONS. Nominee must be a current member of the Society. A monetary award of $4,000 and a plaque are awarded annually at the Congress. The application deadline is August 15. Established in 1987. Sponsored by Roche.

• 16725 • ONS/Ross Products Division of Abbott Laboratories Award for Excellence in Cancer Nursing Education
To recognize and support excellence in cancer nursing education. An RN who is a member of the Society, and has at least two years experience in oncology education, is eligible. A monetary award of $2,000 and a plaque are awarded annually at the ONS Congress. The application deadline is August 15. Established in 1986. Sponsored by Ross Products Division of Abbott Laboratories.

• 16726 • ONS/Schering Excellence in Biotherapy Nursing Award
To recognize and support excellence in biotherapy nursing. Members who are registered nurses and have made significant contributions in the area of biotherapy nursing are eligible. A monetary award of $2,000 and a plaque are awarded annually at the ONS Congress. The application deadline is August 15. Established in 1990. Sponsored by Schering Oncology/Biotech.

• 16727 • ONS/Schering Excellence in Cancer Nursing Research Award
To recognize and support excellence in cancer nursing research likely to make a significant contribution to the body of nursing knowledge. A Society member(s) who has assumed major responsibility for a research study. A monetary award of $2,000 and a plaque are awarded annually at the Congress. The winning paper will be considered for publication in the *Oncology Nursing Forum*. Established in 1982. Sponsored by Schering Oncology/Biotech.

• 16728 • ONS/Upjohn Quality of Life Award
To recognize and support nursing excellence in the area of quality of life issues. All articles that have appeared in the appropriate volume of the 'Oncology Nursing Forum' and meet the selection criteria are automatically considered for the award. A monetary award of $1,000 and a plaque are awarded annually. Established in 1988. Sponsored by Pharmacia & Upjohn.

• 16729 • Public Service Award
To recognize and support persons who use their public prominence to have a positive impact on oncology services. To be eligible for the award, the nominee must be a publicly prominent individual who has created, delivered, or promoted an oncology service that influenced public perceptions, attitudes, and awareness. An acknowledgement gift, airfare to the ONS Congress, and a one-day per diem are awarded annually.

• 16730 • Schering Clinical Lecture
To recognize a member of ONS whose clinical practice exemplifies and is consistent with the ONS *Scope of Oncology Nursing Practice*. The applicant must have at least two years experience in oncology nursing. The deadline for applications is August 15. The recipient delivers a lecture at the ONS Annual Congress, and receives a $2,000 honorarium, Congress registration, a plaque, and publication of the lecture in the *Oncology Nursing Forum*. Sponsored by Schering Oncology/Biotech.

• 16731 •
One Club for Art & Copy
Mary Warlick, Exec.Dir.
21 E 26th St.
New York, NY 10010
Phone: (212)979-1900
Fax: (212)979-5006
E-mail: info@oneclub.com
Home Page: http://www.oneclub.com

• 16732 • One Show Awards
To recognize the joint effort of a copywriter and an art director in creating excellent advertising and to encourage higher standards of excellence in the advertising industry. Print, radio, and television work that was published or aired during the previous year may be submitted by copywriters, art directors, ad agencies or ad managers. The deadline is January 31. Double-pointed gold, silver, and bronze hexagonal pencils, which symbolize the contribution from the copy and art side, are presented to the winners. Approximately 100 awards are given annually at an awards dinner in the spring. Established in 1974.

• 16733 •
One Reel
Norman Langill, Pres. and CEO
PO Box 9750
Seattle, WA 98109
Phone: (206)281-7788
Fax: (206)281-7799
E-mail: info@onereel.org
Home Page: http://onereel.org

• 16734 • Bumbershoot, The Seattle Arts Festival
To recognize the best in the local, regional, and national literary arts field. The festival's multi-faceted Literary Arts program includes the Bookfair Pavilion featuring the largest small press bookfair on the west coast, publication panel discussions, hands-on projects and insightful exhibits; the finest international, national, and regional authors reading from their works in literary readings; and noteworthy programs like young writers and writers forums. The bookfair is open to literary writers, small presses, and independent publishing houses from all over the country. Awards include: best offset design, best letterpress book design, best cover design, best literary magazine, best children's publication, most significant contribution by a press or individual, and most adventurous publication or judges choice.

• 16735 •
Ontario Arts Council/Ontario Arts Council Foundation
(Conseil des arts de l'Ontario)
John Brotman, Exec.Dir.
151 Bloor St. W, 5th. Fl.
Toronto, ON, Canada M5S 1T6
Phone: (416)961-1660
Toll-Free: 800-387-0058
Fax: (416)961-7796
E-mail: info@arts.on.ca
Home Page: http://www.arts.on.ca

• 16736 • Louis Applebaum Composers Award
Established in 1998 by Canadian composer and champion of the arts, Louis Applebaum, the income generated funds an annual award recognizing excellence in composition. Awarded when merited.

• 16737 • Leslie Bell Prize for Choral Conducting
To advance the professional development of young Ontario choral conductors. The competition is juried and based on the candidate's ability to conduct a test choir. The conductor must be a resident of Ontario and a citizen or permanent resident of Canada. A monetary award of approximately $2,000 that is to be applied to further study is awarded biennially. Established in 1973 by the Leslie Bell Singers to honor the work of the Canadian choral conductor, Dr. Leslie Bell.

Awards are arranged in alphabetical order below their administering organizations

• 16738 • Canadian Music Centre John Adaskin Memorial Award

Established in memory of the Canadian Music Centre's first executive secretary, it supports projects that promote and develop Canadian music in schools. Income from the fund is given annually to a project approved by the Ontario Arts Council. Awarded annually. Established in 1981.

• 16739 • William and Mary Corcoran Craft Awards

To encourage excellence in crafts. Awards are given in the disciplines of glass, textiles, wood, and ceramics for students graduating from Sheridan College. Funded by arts patrons William and Mary Corcoran

• 16740 • John Hirsch Director's Award

To recognize a promising theatre director in Ontario. Nominees must be professional directors under the age of 36, residents of Ontario, and citizens or permanent residents of Canada. A monetary award of $5,000 is presented triennially. Established in 1989 by a bequest by the distinguished director, the late John Hirsch.

• 16741 • Paul de Hueck and Norman Walford Career Achievement Awards in the Performing Arts and in Visual Arts

To recognize the achievement of outstanding Canadian artists in singing, keyboard artistry, and art photography. Awarded biennially in odd-numbered years. Established in 1998.

• 16742 • K. M. Hunter Artists Awards

To support and encourage artists who have completed their professional training and have begun to establish themselves and make an impact on their chosen field. Every year, five awards of $8,000 are presented in the fields of dance, literature, music, theatre, and visual arts.

• 16743 • Fabian Lemieux Award

For recognition of outstanding contributions to arts education. Established in 1991 in memory of Fabian Lemieux, one of the pioneers of the Sudbury Arts Council and a supporter of the arts in education.

• 16744 • Pauline McGibbon Award

To recognize theatre artists of growing reputation by providing encouragement to further develop their professional skills through travel and study. The award is given in three-year cycles to a designer, a director, and production craftsperson. Nominees must be citizens or permanent residents of Canada. A monetary award of $7,000 and a medal designed by Dora de Pedery Hunt are presented annually. Established in 1981 to honor Pauline McGibbon, former Lieutenant Governor of Ontario.

• 16745 • Orford String Quartet Scholarship

To assist a Canadian string musician with studies, commissions, or performances related to work in chamber music. The Ontario Arts Council manages the selection process. The recipient is chosen by peer assessment from nominations submitted by Canadian universities and conservatories. A scholarship of $2,500 is awarded biennially in even-numbered years.

• 16746 • Ruth and Sylvia Schwartz Children's Book Awards

To recognize writers and illustrators creating literary work in English. Two awards are presented annually, one $5,000 award for picture books, and one $5,000 award for young adult/middle readers. The short list of books is selected by the Canadian Booksellers Association, and the winners are chosen by juries of school children. Candidates must be citizens or permanent residents of Canada. Established in 1976 by the Ruth Schwartz Foundation. Ruth Schwartz was a Toronto bookseller who had a special interest in and concern for children's books.

• 16747 • Tim Sims Encouragement Fund Award for Work in the Comedic Arts

The award is presented annually to support promising comedic performers or troupes in the early stages of their comedy careers. The winner is selected by a jury composed of members of the comedy community, from nominations.

• 16748 • Heinz Unger Award

To recognize the accomplishments of young to mid-career conductors employed in a professional capacity as an orchestral conductor. Nominees must be residents of Ontario and citizens or permanent residents of Canada. A monetary award of $7,000 is presented biennially. Established in 1968 by the York Concert Society in honor of Dr. Heinz Unger.

• 16749 •
Ontario County Historical Society
Ed Varno, Exec.Dir.
55 N Main St.
Canandaigua, NY 14424
Phone: (585)394-4975
Phone: (716)394-5065
Fax: (585)394-9351
E-mail: ochs@ochs.org
Home Page: http://www.ochs.org

• 16750 • Ellis Award

For significant contribution to mission of society. Recognition award bestowed periodically.

• 16751 •
Ontario Ministry of Citizenship and Immigration
Mike Colle, Min.
400 University Ave., 6th Fl.
Toronto, ON, Canada M7A 2R9
Phone: (416)327-2422
Toll-Free: 800-267-7329
Fax: (416)314-4965
E-mail: info@mczcr.gov.on.ca
Home Page: http://www.citizenship.gov.on.ca

• 16752 • Trillium Book Award (Prix Trillium)

To recognize excellence, support marketing, and foster increased public awareness of the quality and diversity of Ontario writers and writing. Books in English or French in any genre are eligible. Monetary awards of $20,000 are presented to the winning authors in both the English and French categories. In addition, the publishers of the winning books receive $2,500 for marketing and promotion. Established in 1987. Additionally, the Trillium Book Award for Poetry, established in 2003, grants $10,000 to a new or emerging poet and $2,500 to his or her publisher. Awarded annually.

• 16753 •
Ontario Ministry of Citizenship and Immigration
Ontario Honours and Awards Secretariat
Rick Beaver, Man.
400 University Ave.
Ground Floor-South Lobby
Toronto, ON, Canada M7A 2R9
Phone: (416)314-7526
Fax: (416)314-7743
E-mail: OntarioHonoursAndAwards@mci.gov.on.ca
Home Page: http://www.citizenship.gov.on.ca

• 16754 • Ontario Medal for Firefighter Bravery

To encourage the virtue of bravery, to recognize individuals whose actions exemplify courage without concern for personal safety, and to highlight the frequently dangerous duties performed by the firefighting force. Nominations are considered. A medal is awarded annually. Established in 1976.

• 16755 • Ontario Medal for Good Citizenship

To recognize personal sacrifice in all areas of society and to recognize the virtue that leads some citizens to act in a particularly generous, kind, or self-sacrificing way in the common good without expectation of reward. Nominations are considered. A medal is presented annually. Established in 1973 by Premier William G. Davis of Ontario.

• 16756 • Ontario Medal for Police Bravery

To encourage the virtue of bravery, to recognize individuals whose actions exemplify courage without concern for personal safety, and to highlight the frequently dangerous duties performed by the police force. Nominations are considered. A medal is awarded annually. Established in 1975 by Premier William G. Davis of Ontario.

• 16757 • Order of Ontario

This, the most prestigious official honor bestowed by the Province of Ontario, is given to recognize those persons who have rendered service of the greatest distinction and of singular excellence in any field of endeavor benefiting society in Ontario or elsewhere. Any resident of the province of Ontario who has demonstrated excellence and achievement of the highest degree in community leadership, business, labor, industry, volunteer service, the professions and other occupations, research, culture, the arts, sports, and other fields of endeavor is eligible for nomination. A medal is presented annually. Established in 1986 by Premier David Peterson of Ontario.

• 16758 •
Ontario Nature
Wendy Francis, Exec.Dir.
355 Lesmill Rd.
Toronto, ON, Canada M3B 2W8
Phone: (416)444-8419
Toll-Free: 800-440-2366
Fax: (416)444-9866
E-mail: info@ontarionature.org
Home Page: http://www.ontarionature.org

Formerly: Federation of Ontario Naturalists.

• 16759 • J. R. Dymond Public Service Award
To recognize an individual or a group for distinguished public service that resulted in an exceptional environmental achievement beyond the usual expectation. Awarded annually. Established in 1972. Formerly: (1960) FON Distinguished Service Award.

• 16760 • FON Achievement Award
To recognize achievement in the environmental field.

• 16761 • FON Corporate Award
To recognize outstanding leadership or sound action in the environmental field. Awarded to a corporation for protecting the natural environment either directly through corporate policies or through a major initiative, or indirectly through other undertakings that have stimulated significant environmental actions. Awarded annually. Established in 1993.

• 16762 • W. W. H. Gunn Conservation Award
This, the Federation's most prestigious award, is given to recognize an individual who has given outstanding personal service to a particular conservation initiative. Individuals working alone or as the leader of the group who, over a number of years, have not only demonstrated an unusual commitment to a particular goal but have achieved exceptional results, are considered. Awarded annually. Established in 1971. Formerly: (1986) FON Conservation Trophy.

• 16763 • Camp Scholarships Carl Nunn Award
To recognize an individual or organization (print, radio or TV media) representing any of the media for particularly effective communication of one or more conservation issues. Awarded annually. Established in 1971. Formerly: (1990) FON Conservation Award.

• 16764 • Richards Education and Medical Award
To recognize an individual who has made a very special contribution to natural history by motivating youth to gain a greater understanding of the natural world and to become enthusiastic supporters of environmental protection. The nominee may have been acting as a volunteer or been employed to do this kind of work. In the latter instance, the work must have been especially outstanding and more than normally successful. Nominees who acted as volunteers will receive preference. Awarded annually. Established in 1979.

• 16765 • W. E. Saunders Natural History Award
To recognize an individual or group that has achieved a significant goal related to some aspect of natural history. For example, it may be for raising public awareness, demonstrating local leadership, saving a natural area from destruction, successfully lobbying for important regulatory controls, generating funds, or creating a publication. Up to three awards are presented annually. Established in 1983. Formerly: (1990) FON Achievement Certificates.

• 16766 • Lee Symmes Community Award
For recognition of a town, city, region or municipality for outstanding leadership or sound planning in the environmental field. Achievements of any Ontario municipal government in protecting the natural environment within its jurisdiction directly (i.e. through the creation of parks, protection of wetlands) or indirectly (through planning measures which stimulate energy conservation) are considered. The municipality should have made either a large, important or pioneering step along with an acceptable general record, or have achieved an extended record of higher than average performance on a broad range of measures which protect the environment. Awarded annually. Established in 1981.

• 16767 •
Ontario Psychological Association
Dr. Douglas Saunders, Pres.
730 Yonge St., Ste. 221
Toronto, ON, Canada M4Y 2B7
Phone: (416)961-5552
Fax: (416)961-5516
E-mail: info@psych.on.ca
Home Page: http://www.psych.on.ca

• 16768 • Award of Merit
To honor an Ontario psychologist for his or her outstanding contribution to the application of psychology. Nominees must demonstrate evidence of outstanding contribution to psychology over a period of time relating to the profession of psychology, including administrative and organizational functions; science of psychology, including scholarly and editorial functions; or promotion of psychology in public service at the provincial level. Deadline for nomination is November 15. A plaque is awarded at the annual convention.

• 16769 •
Operation Clean Government
Mr. Robert P. Arruda, Chm.
PO Box 8683
Warwick, RI 02888-0595
Phone: (401)225-7965
Phone: (401)861-3900
Fax: (401)885-7241
E-mail: bobqbh@cox.net
Home Page: http://www.ocgri.org

• 16770 • Golden Broom Award
For promoting honest, responsible, and responsive state government. Recognition award bestowed annually.

• 16771 •
Operation Kindness Animal Shelter
Jeff Mahon, Pres.
3201 Earhart Dr.
Carrollton, TX 75006
Phone: (972)418-PAWS
Fax: (972)417-8956
E-mail: clientservices@operationkindness.org
Home Page: http://www.operationkindness.org

• 16772 • Kindness to Animals Award
For kindness and commitment to animals. Recognition award bestowed annually.

• 16773 •
Operation Oswego County
L. Michael Treadwell CEcD, Exec.Dir.
44 W Bridge St.
Oswego, NY 13126
Phone: (315)343-1545
Fax: (315)343-1546
E-mail: ooc@oswegocounty.org
Home Page: http://www.oswegocounty.org

• 16774 • Ally Award
For outstanding contributions to one area economy or special business activity. Recognition award bestowed annually.

• 16775 • Business Excellence Award
For outstanding contributions to one area economy or special business activity. Recognition award bestowed annually.

• 16776 • Economic Developer Award
For outstanding contributions to one area economy or special business activity. Recognition award bestowed annually.

• 16777 • Jobs Award
For outstanding contributions to one area economy or special business activity. Recognition award bestowed annually.

• 16778 •
Ophthalmic Photographers' Society
Barbara McCalley CRA, Contact
1869 W Ranch Rd.
Nixa, MO 65714-8262
Phone: (417)725-0181
Toll-Free: 800-403-1677
Fax: (417)724-8450
E-mail: ops@opsweb.org
Home Page: http://www.opsweb.org

• 16779 • **Outstanding Contribution to Ophthalmic Photography**
For recognition of prolonged active participation in the Ophthalmic Photographers' Society and notable contribution to the field of ophthalmic photography. Nominations by OPS active members may be submitted to the Board of Directors prior to January of the award year. A plaque is presented in October. Established in 1977.

• 16780 •
Optical Society of America
Elizabeth E. Rogan, Exec.Dir.
2010 Massachusetts Ave. NW
Washington, DC 20036-1023
Phone: (202)223-8130
Fax: (202)223-1096
E-mail: info@osa.org
Home Page: http://www.osa.org

• 16781 • **Esther Hoffman Beller Medal**
To recognize outstanding contributions to optical science and engineering education. Selection is based on outstanding teaching and/or original work in optics education that enhances the understanding of optics. A monetary prize of $2500, a silver medal, and a citation are awarded annually. Established in 1993 by a bequest from the estate of Esther Hoffman Beller.

• 16782 • **Max Born Award**
To recognize outstanding contributions to physical optics, either theoretical or experimental. The deadline for nominations is October 2. A certificate, a silver medal, and a monetary award of $1,500 are awarded annually. Established in 1982 in memory of Max Born, who made distinguished contributions to physics in general and to optics in particular. Endowed by the United Technologies Research Center.

• 16783 • **Distinguished Service Award**
For recognition of individuals who, over an extended period of time, have served the Society in an outstanding way, especially through volunteer participation in its management, operation, or planning. The deadline for nominations is October 2. A monetary prize of $1,500 and a glass sculpture are awarded when merited. Established in 1973 in cooperation with the American Optical Corporation in memory of Stephen M. MacNeille.

• 16784 • **Engineering Excellence Awards**
To recognize technical achievements in optical engineering by individuals or teams. Nominations are solicited in a number of areas: products, engineering publication, process, software, patents, engineering education, contributions to society, engineering management, and furthering public appreciation of optical engineering. The deadline for nominations is June 15. A certificate and a glass sculpture are awarded annually to one or more recipients. Established in 1989.

• 16785 • **Joseph Fraunhofer Award/ Robert M. Burley Prize**
For recognition of significant accomplishment in the field of optical engineering. A silver medal, a citation, and a monetary award of $1,500 are awarded annually. Established in 1982. Sponsored by the Baird Corporation.

• 16786 • **Frederic Ives Medal/Jarus W. Quinn Endowment**
This, the highest award of the Society, recognizes overall distinction in optics. A monetary award of $10,000, a silver medal, and a citation are awarded annually. The winner presents the Ives Medal Address at the OSA Annual Meeting. Established in 1928 to honor Frederic Ives for his pioneering contributions to color photography, photoengraving, three-color process printing, and other branches of applied optics. Formerly: (1997) Frederic Ives Medal.

• 16787 • **Nick Holonyak Jr. Award**
Presented to an individual who has made significant contributions to optics based on semiconductor materials, including basic science and technological applications. The award, made possible by a gift from students of Nick Holonyak consists of a citation and cash prize of $1,500. Established in 1997.

• 16788 • **Incubic/Milton Change Student Travel Grants**
To recognize outstanding papers presented by students at the Optics/OSA Annual Meeting and the Conference on Lasers and Electro-Optics (CLEO). Students must be the first author of the paper and be able to demonstrate need for the grant in order to attend the conferences. Twenty travel grants of $500 are awarded annually. Formerly: New Focus Student Travel Grants.

• 16789 • **Edwin H. Land Medal**
To recognize individuals who, from a base of scientific knowledge of optics in areas such mechanisms of vision; creation, manipulation, and communication of images; and the properties of light have demonstrated pioneering entrepreneurial activity that has had a major impact on the public. Activities may be performed in an industrial, business, academic, or government setting. A monetary prize of $3,000, a silver medal, and a citation are awarded. Established in 1992 in honor of Edwin H. Land. Co-sponsored by the Society for Imaging Science and Technology and funded by the Polaroid Foundation.

• 16790 • **Ellis R. Lippincott Award**
To recognize an individual who has made significant contributions to vibrational spectroscopy as judged by his or her influence on other scientists. A monetary award of $1,500 and a crystal box are awarded annually. Established in 1975 to honor the unique contributions of Ellis R. Lippincott to the field of vibrational spectroscopy. Cosponsored by the Coblentz Society and the Society for Applied Spectroscopy.

• 16791 • **Adolph Lomb Medal**
To recognize an individual under 35 years of age for noteworthy contributions to optics. A monetary award of $1,500, a silver medal, and a citation are awarded annually. Established in 1940 to recognize Adolph Lomb's devotion to the interests of the Society and to the advancement of optics.

• 16792 • **Acrhie Mahan Prize**
Recognizes the best feature article in Optics & Photonics News. The selection is based on accessibility of the material beyond the audience specialized in that field, clarity of text, use of figures and illustrations, topical interest, current relevance, and writing style. The prize consists of a certificate and $1,500.

• 16793 • **C. E .K. Mees Medal**
To recognize an individual who exemplifies the thought that "optics transcends all boundaries." A monetary award of $1,500, a silver medal, and a citation are awarded biennially in the odd-numbered years. Established in 1961 in memory of C. E. K. Mees, who contributed preeminently to the development of scientific photography.

• 16794 • **William F. Meggers Award**
For outstanding contributions to the field of spectroscopy. A monetary award of $1,500, a silver medal, and a citation are awarded annually. Established in 1970 to honor William F. Meggers for his notable contributions to the field of spectroscopy and metrology.

• 16795 • **OSA Leadership Award/New Focus Bookham Prize**
Intended to strengthen the link between the optics community and the public, the award recognizes an individual or group of optics professionals whose actions or policy outside the technology arena has made a significant contribution to society. The contribution may be social, economic, political, or humanitarian. The award may also be used to recognize a group whose action, policy, or support has made a significant impact on the field of optics. The recognition may be the result of one contribution or a record of contributions. The award grants a scroll, a commissioned optical art piece, and a lifetime OSA membership. Formerly: (2006) OSA Leadership Award/New Focus Prize.

• 16796 • **David Richardson Medal**
To recognize significant contributions to optical engineering, primarily in the commercial and industrial sector. A monetary award of $1,500, a silver medal, and a citation are awarded annu-

ally. Established in 1966 by an endowment of Howard Cary to honor the unique contributions to applied optics and spectroscopy made by David Richardson.

• 16797 • Edgar D. Tillyer Award
To recognize a person who has performed distinguished work in the field of vision, including, but not limited to, optics, physiology, anatomy, or psychology of the visual system. A monetary award of $1,500, a silver medal, and a citation are awarded biennially in even-numbered years. Established in 1953 by the American Optical Company.

• 16798 • Charles Hard Townes Award
To recognize an individual or a group for outstanding experimental or theoretical work, a discovery, or an invention in the field of quantum electronics. A monetary award of $1,500, a silver medal, and a citation are awarded annually. Established in 1980 to honor Charles Hard Townes, whose pioneering contributions to masers and lasers have led to the development of the field of quantum electronics.

• 16799 • John Tyndall Award
To recognize an individual for pioneering, highly significant, or continuing technical or leadership contributions to fiber optic technology. The deadline for nominations is August 10. A monetary prize of $3,200 and a citation are awarded annually. Established in 1986 to honor John Tyndall, the 19th century Irish scientist who was the first to demonstrate a phenomenon of internal reflection. Endowed by Corning Inc. and cosponsored by the Institute of Electrical and Electronics Engineers Laser and Electro-optics Society.

• 16800 • R. W. Wood Prize
To recognize an outstanding discovery, scientific or technological achievement, or invention in the field of optics. The accomplishment must open a new area of research or expand an established one. A monetary award of $1,500, a silver medal, and a citation are awarded annually. Established in 1975 in honor of the many contributions that R. W. Wood made to optics. Endowed by a grant from the Xerox Corporation.

• 16801 •
Optimist International
Dwaine R. Sievers, International Pres.
4494 Lindell Blvd.
St. Louis, MO 63108
Phone: (314)371-6000
Toll-Free: 800-500-8130
Fax: (314)371-6006
E-mail: headquarters@optimist.org
Home Page: http://www.optimist.org

• 16802 • Optimist International Awards
To recognize attainment of specific criteria relating to club growth and activities. Enrolled members of active clubs of Optimist International are eligible. Club, Lieutenant Governor, Governor, President's Special, and Activities Awards are presented annually.

• 16803 •
Oral and Maxillofacial Surgery Foundation
Frank J. Kurtz, Exec.Dir.
9700 W Bryn Mawr Ave.
Rosemont, IL 60018-5701
Phone: (847)233-4304
Toll-Free: (866)278-9221
Fax: (847)678-6254
E-mail: omsf@aaoms.org
Home Page: http://www.omsfoundation.org

• 16804 • Research Recognition Award
To emphasize the commitment of the AAOMS to foster programs of research and scientific investigation related to the specialty of oral and maxillofacial surgery and to recognize individuals who have made outstanding contributions to the specialty. Criteria considered include: the significance and impact of scientific achievement toward a better understanding of basic disease processes and improvement of care related to the disorders of the maxillofacial region; the originality and quality of the scientific accomplishments, including assessment by experts in the nominee's area of study; and the influence that the individual and/or contributions have had on the secondary scientific careers or contributions of his students, residents, or other colleagues. A plaque and travel expenses to the AAOMS annual meeting for the presentation are awarded when merited. Established in 1974.

• 16805 • Resident Research Award
To attract oral and maxillofacial surgery residents to biomedical and behavioral research applicable to oral and maxillofacial surgery; to increase the number and quality of investigators within the field of oral and maxillofacial surgery; and to provide additional support to institutions where there are active and productive programs of oral and maxillofacial surgery research. Institutions are eligible for the award. Institutions will be awarded $4,000 for each of up to three resident research trainees who must be matriculated as oral and maxillofacial surgery residents. Funds must be used to carry out the project (e.g., supplies, equipment, publication costs, etc.).

• 16806 • Student Research Training Award
To attract highly qualified health profession students to biomedical and behavioral research applicable to oral and maxillofacial surgery; to increase the number and quality of investigators within the field of oral and maxillofacial surgery; to interest dental students in the specialty of oral and maxillofacial surgery; and to provide additional support to institutions where there are active and productive programs of oral and maxillofacial surgery research. Both institutions and student trainees are eligible. Departments and/or divisions of oral and maxillofacial surgery within schools of dentistry and teaching hospitals must be accredited by the American Dental Association commission on Dental Accreditation. Students must be matriculated as full-time health professions students and must have completed at least one semester as such a student. An award of $12,500 will be used for five student stipends of $2,500 each.

• 16807 •
Oral Hearing-Impaired Section
K. Todd Houston PhD, Exec.Dir.
3417 Volta Pl. NW
Washington, DC 20007
Phone: (202)337-5220
Fax: (202)337-8314
E-mail: info@agbell.org
Home Page: http://www.agbell.org

• 16808 • OHIS Youth Achievement
Annual award of recognition. Only members are eligible.

• 16809 •
Orange Alumni Association
Laura Guentner, Dir.
32000 Chagrin Blvd.
Pepper Pike, OH 44124
Phone: (216)831-8601
Fax: (216)831-4209
E-mail: info@orangerec.com
Home Page: http://www.orangeschools.org

• 16810 • Alumni Scholarship
For graduating high school seniors (child of an Alumnus). Scholarship awarded annually.

• 16811 •
Oratorio Society of New York
Richard Pace, Pres.
881 7th Ave., Ste. 504
New York, NY 10019
Phone: (212)247-4199
Home Page: http://www.oratoriosocietyofny.org

• 16812 • Ruth Lopin Nash Award
For solo competition for oratorio singing only. Monetary award bestowed annually.

• 16813 • Solo Competition
To encourage the art of oratorio singing and give young singers an opportunity to advance their careers. Individuals, of any nationality, under 40 years of age may submit applications by February 15. The Competition is held in New York City during March or April of each year. Monetary awards total more than $15,000. The first prize winner receives the Ruth Lopin Nash Award, a monetary award of $7,000 and possible performance contracts with the Society; second place receives the $5,000 Herb Cohen Award; third place receives the $2,500 Stanley C. Meyerson Award; and other finalists each receive $500. Established in 1975.

• 16814 •
Orchard Lake Schools
3535 Indian Trl.
Orchard Lake, MI 48324
Phone: (248)683-1750
Fax: (248)738-6725
E-mail: dstearns@orchardlakeschools.com
Home Page: http://www.orchardlakeschools.com

• 16815 • Fidelitas Medal
For recognition of fidelity in serving God and country through the realization of the religious and cultural ideals of this country's forefathers. Outstanding American Catholics of Polish background are eligible. A medal and a citation are awarded annually. Established in 1949.

• 16816 •
Orchestras Canada
(Orchestres Canada)
56 The Esplanade, Ste. 203
Toronto, ON, Canada M5E 1A7
Phone: (416)366-8834
Fax: (416)366-1780
E-mail: info@oc.ca
Home Page: http://www.oc.ca

• 16817 • OC Award
Recognizes service to an orchestra. Awarded biennially. Inquire for application details.

• 16818 •
Order of Daedalians
Lt.Col. Dale Shaw, Sec.
PO Box 249
Randolph AFB, TX 78148-0249
Phone: (210)945-2111
Fax: (210)945-2112
E-mail: daedalus@daedalians.org
Home Page: http://www.daedalians.org

• 16819 • Lt. Gen. Allen M. Burdett, Jr. Army Aviation Flight Safety Award
To recognize the Army aviation training unit as judged by the Commanding General, TRADOC, to have the most effective aircraft accident prevention program. A Daedalian Trophy and an award are presented annually. Established in 1970.

• 16820 • Maj. Gen. Warren R. Carter Supply Effectiveness Award
To the United States Air Force Unit (Base Level) determined by the Chief of Staff, USAF, to have achieved the best supply effectiveness record during the preceding calendar year in support of mission aircraft and/or weapons. A Daedalian Trophy and an award are presented annually. Established in 1962. Formerly: Daedalian Supply Effectiveness Award.

• 16821 • Daedalian Distinguished Achievement Award
To recognize active Daedalians in good standing for outstanding feats of airmanship or other related and enduring achievements in the field of aeronautics. Established in 1984.

• 16822 • Daedalian Scholarship Awards
To provide scholarships for outstanding pilot and aerospace science candidates in the Navy, Army, and Air Force ROTC and the Civil Air Patrol.

• 16823 • Daedalian Weapon Systems Award
To recognize the individual, group or organization, military or civilian, judged to have contributed the most outstanding weapon system development currently utilized. The recipient(s) are selected by the Departments of the Army, the Navy, and the Air Force on a rotating basis. The Colonel Franklin C. Wolfe Memorial Trophy and Daedalian Award are presented annually. Established in 1969.

• 16824 • Maj. Gen. Eugene L. Eubank Morale, Welfare and Recreation Award
To recognize the USAF Unit (Base Level) judged by USAF Headquarters to have the best overall small base morale, welfare, and recreation program in the USAF. A Daedalian Trophy and award are presented annually. Established in 1990.

• 16825 • Gen. Muir S. Fairchild Education Achievement Award
To recognize individuals of the Air University responsible for significant contributions to Air University education or to Air Force education in general during the calendar year. A Daedalian Trophy and an award are presented annually. Established in 1964.

• 16826 • Maj. Gen. Benjamin D. Foulois Memorial Award
To recognize the Major Air Force Command determined by the USAF Chief of Staff to have achieved the best flying safety record during the preceding calendar year. A Daedalian Trophy and safety of flight award are presented annually. Established in 1938.

• 16827 • Lt. Gen. Harold L. George Civilian Airmanship Award
To recognize a pilot, co-pilot, and/or crew of a United States certified commercial airline that has, in the opinion of the Federal Aviation Agency, demonstrated the most outstanding ability, judgment, and/or heroism above and beyond normal operational requirements during the preceding calendar year. A Daedalian Trophy and an award are presented annually. Established in 1956. Formerly: Daedalian Civilian Air Safety Award.

• 16828 • Lt. Gens. Millard F. and Hubert R. Harmon Award
To recognize the outstanding cadet in the Order of Graduation at the United States Air Force Academy. A Daedalian Trophy and an award are presented annually. Established in 1959.

• 16829 • Brig. Gen. Carl I. Hutton Memorial Award
To reward the United States Army unit determined by the Department of the Army to have demonstrated outstanding professionalism and contributed immeasurably to the advancement of flight safety in Army aviation for the preceding calendar year. A Daedalian Trophy and an award are presented annually. Established in 1978.

• 16830 • Brig. Gen. Frank P. Lahm Memorial Award for Flight Safety
To recognize the flying training wing judged by the USAF Commander, Air Education and Training Command, to have the most effective flight safety program during the previous calendar year. A Daedalian Trophy and award are presented annually. Established in 1979.

• 16831 • Gen. Curtis E. LeMay Morale, Welfare, and Recreation Award
To recognize the Air Force Unit (Base Level) judged by USAF Headquarters to have the best overall morale, welfare, and recreation program in the Air Force for the preceding calendar year. A Daedalian Trophy and an award are presented annually. Established in 1965.

• 16832 • Maj. Gen. Clements McMullen Weapon System Maintenance Award
To recognize the USAF unit (Wing Level) determined by USAF Headquarters to have the best weapon system maintenance record for the preceding calendar year. Established in 1960.

• 16833 • Adm. James S. Russell Naval Aviation Flight Safety Award
To recognize the United States Navy flying unit determined by the USN Chief of Naval Operation to have the most effective flight safety accident prevention program for the preceding calendar year. A Daedalian Trophy and an award are presented annually. Established in 1978.

• 16834 • Adm. John H. Towers Flight Safety Award
To the training squadron of the Naval Air Training Command, judged by the Chief of Naval Air Training to have achieved the most outstanding record in its mission-orientated flight safety program. A Daedalian Trophy and an award are presented annually. Established in 1968.

• 16835 • Orville Wright Achievement Award
To recognize the outstanding United States graduates of the United States Army, United States Navy, and United States Air Force undergraduate pilot training programs. 10 Daedalian awards are presented annually. Established in the different services in 1973, 1973, and 1960 respectively.

• 16836 •
Order of Lafayette
Bruce A. Laue, Pres.Gen.
243 W. 70th St., Apt. 6f
New York, NY 10023-4321
Phone: (212)873-9162
E-mail: orderoflafayette@hotmail.com

• 16837 • Freedom Award
To recognize outstanding leadership in combating Communism. Distinguished individuals with a known record of helping to stop the spread of Communism and the promotion of better relations between France and the United States are eligible.

• 16838 •
Order of St. Lazarus
(Ordre de Saint-Lazare au Canada)
Jean Matheson, Exec.Dir.
1435 Caledon Pl., Ste. 100
Ottawa, ON, Canada K1G 3H3
Phone: (613)746-5280
Fax: (613)746-3982
E-mail: chancery@stlazarus.ca
Home Page: http://www.stlazarus.ca

• 16839 • **Meritorious Awards**
Recognizes individuals providing service to the order. Awarded annually.

• 16840 •
Order of the Coif
Sandy Jones, Admin.Asst.
Law Library, CB No. 3385
University of North Carolina
Chapel Hill, NC 27599-3385
Phone: (919)962-1321
Phone: (919)962-1322
Fax: (919)962-1193
E-mail: sjones2@email.unc.edu
Home Page: http://www.orderofthecoif.org

• 16841 • **Coif Book Award**
To recognize the author of preeminent legal scholarship as evidenced by a volume demonstrating creative talent of the highest order. Books of outstanding merit written during the previous two years are eligible. A monetary award and a specially engraved certificate are awarded biennially in even-numbered years. Established in 1964.

• 16842 •
Order of the Founders and Patriots of America
Alden Atwood, Governor Gen.
3892 College Ave.
Ellicott City, MD 21043
Phone: (410)461-9591
Fax: (410)461-9591
E-mail: info@founderspatriots.org
Home Page: http://www.founderspatriots.org

• 16843 • **Outstanding National Guard Unit Award**
To recognize the outstanding Army or Air National Guard unit in each state where the Order has a State Society (24 states). The criteria for the award are established by each State Society and the Adjutant General of each state, but usually include performance of mission assigned, grades received during unit inspections, and leadership qualities of officers and NCO's. A framed certificate is awarded annually. Established in 1984.

• 16844 • **Outstanding ROTC Cadet Award**
To encourage excellence in attainment by ROTC cadets in colleges and universities. The criteria are established by State Societies (24 states) and awards may be given at colleges and universities within the Society's borders or in nearby states where a Society does not exist. Outstanding Army, Air Force, or Navy ROTC cadets from each participating school are eligible. Recipients are selected by the Professor of Military, Air, or Naval Science. A certificate and a medal pendant with a ribbon in the colors of the Order are awarded. Established in 1986.

• 16845 • **Outstanding ROTC Unit Award**
For recognition of outstanding achievement in academic endeavors, military proficiency, and civic contributions by the top college or university ROTC battalion in each of the three U.S. Army ROTC Regions in the United States. The winner is chosen by criteria established by the Deputy Chief of Staff, ROTC Affairs, U.S. Army, and administered by the Commanding General of each of the three ROTC Regions. A certificate naming the school, reasons for the award and the U.S. Army ROTC Region is awarded annually. Established in 1984. Formerly: Award for Excellence.

• 16846 •
Order Sons of Italy in America
Philip R. Piccigallo Ph.D., Exec.Dir.
219 E St. NE
Washington, DC 20002
Phone: (202)547-2900
Toll-Free: 800-552-OSIA
Fax: (202)546-8168
E-mail: nationaloffice@osia.org
Home Page: http://www.osia.org

• 16847 • **Guglielmo Marconi Award**
Given to an American or global citizen whom the Order believes has contributed to the nation and its way of life in a manner that best exemplifies the ideals for which the Order stands. A plaque is awarded biennially in odd-numbered years. Established in 1955 in memory of Guglielmo Marconi, inventor of wireless telegraphy.

• 16848 •
Ordre des Psychologues du Quebec
Rose-Marie Charest, Pres.
1110 Ave. Beaumont, bureau 510
Mont-Royal, QC, Canada H3P 3H5
Phone: (514)738-1881
Toll-Free: 800-363-2644
Fax: (514)738-8838
E-mail: presidence@ordrepsy.qc.ca
Home Page: http://www.ordrepsy.qc.ca

Formerly: (1995) Corporation Professionnelle des Psychologues du Quebec.

• 16849 • **Noel Mailloux Award**
(Prix Noel-Mailloux)
To recognize a psychologist for demonstrated leadership in his or her field, for professional or scientific accomplishments, for universally recognized competency, for notorious services rendered to the population or to the profession, for an outstanding career, and for dedication or commitment on a regional or sectorial basis. OPQ members are eligible. Deadline for nomination is January 31. An original painting by a Quebec artist is awarded at the OPQ annual convention. Established in 1983 and named for its first recipient, Father Noel Mailloux.

• 16850 • **Prix de la Sante et du Bien-Etre Psychologique**
To honor a non-psychologist or non-psychological organization for a particular public contribution to the mental welfare of Quebecers. OPQ members are not eligible. The nomination deadline is February. A plaque is awarded annually. Established in 1989.

• 16851 • **Professional Award**
(Prix Professionel)
To honor a psychologist for a particular contribution during the past year to the development or promotion of the profession. OPQ members are eligible. Deadline for nomination is February. A plaque is awarded during the OPQ annual convention. Established in 1991.

• 16852 •
Oregon Blueberry Growers Association
Judy Ebert, Sec./Treas.
9751 SE Telford Rd.
Boring, OR 97009-7419
Phone: (503)663-6451
Fax: (503)663-1206
E-mail: obga@oregonblues.com
Home Page: http://www.oregonblues.com

• 16853 • **Outstanding Leader in Oregon Blueberry Industry**
For the person who has demonstrated outstanding leadership through years of dedicated effort toward advancing the growth of the blueberry industry. Recognition award bestowed annually.

• 16854 •
Oregon-California Trails Association
F. Travis Boley, Mgr.
524 S Osage St.
PO Box 1019
Independence, MO 64051-0519
Phone: (816)252-2276
Toll-Free: 888-811-6282
Fax: (816)836-0989
E-mail: contact@octa-trails.org
Home Page: http://www.octa-trails.org

• 16855 • **Education, Friend of the Trails Award**
For teachers on performance, trail preservation. Recognition award bestowed annually.

• 16856 •
Oregon Cattlemen's Association
Glenn Stonebrink, Exec.VP
3415 Commercial St. SE, Ste. 217
Salem, OR 97302-4668
Phone: (503)361-8941
Fax: (503)361-8947

• 16857 • **Voice of the Industry**
For agriculture student in Oregon. Scholarship awarded annually.

• 16858 •
Oregon Newspaper Publishers Association
J. LeRoy Yorgason, Exec.Dir.
7150 SW Hampton St., Ste. 111
Portland, OR 97223
Phone: (503)624-6397
Fax: (503)639-9009
E-mail: onpa@orenews.com
Home Page: http://www.orenews.com

• 16859 • **Amos E. Voorhies Award**
This, the highest award bestowed on an individual in the journalism profession in Oregon, is given to recognize outstanding journalistic achievement in the public welfare and honor of the journalism profession. Members may nominate individuals or newspapers by May 1. Recipients are chosen by a committee comprised of former winners. A plaque is awarded annually at the Summer Publishers' Convention. Established in 1938 to honor Amos E. Voorhies, former publisher of the *Grants Pass Daily Courier*.

• 16860 •
Oregon Society of Physician Assistants
PO Box 514
Oregon City, OR 97045-0029
Phone: (503)650-5864
Fax: (503)650-5864

• 16861 • **Award of Excellence**
For leadership qualities, and promotion of the profession. Recognition award bestowed annually.

• 16862 • **Physician Assistant of the Year**
For leadership qualities, and promotion of the profession. Recognition award bestowed annually.

• 16863 •
Oregon Thoroughbred Breeding Association
Ursula V. Gibbons, Exec.Sec. & Mgr.
PO Box 17248
Portland, OR 97217
Phone: (503)285-0658
Fax: (503)285-0659
E-mail: otba@qwest.net
Home Page: http://thoroughbredinfo.com/showcase/otba.htm

• 16864 • **Breeder Awards**
For thoroughbred race horse performance. Monetary award bestowed annually.

• 16865 •
Oregon Winegrowers Association
1200 NW Naito Pkwy., Ste. 400
Portland, OR 97209-2829
Phone: (503)228-8403
Fax: (503)228-8337
E-mail: info@oregonwinegrowers.org
Home Page: http://www.oregonwinegrowers.org

• 16866 • **OWA Founders Award/ President's Award**
For service to Oregon wine industry. Recognition award bestowed annually.

• 16867 •
Organ Historical Society
William T. VanPelt, Exec.Dir.
PO Box 26811
Richmond, VA 23261
Phone: (804)353-9226
Fax: (804)353-9266
E-mail: mail@organsociety.org
Home Page: http://www.organsociety.org

• 16868 • **E. Power Biggs Fellowship**
To introduce individuals to the Society and encourage appreciation for older American pipe organs. There is no age limit, but candidates aged 23 or older must not have previously attended the Society's annual convention. Financial assistance to attend the annual convention and an introductory membership in the Society are awarded annually. Established in 1978 in honor of E. Power Biggs, an organist and organ historian.

• 16869 • **Distinguished Service Award**
For recognition of significant contributions to the programs of the society. Society members may be nominated for contributions, such as research, writing, committee or council leadership roles, and convention programs. A plaque is awarded annually at the society's annual convention. Established in 1976.

• 16870 • **Honorary Member**
To recognize individuals who have made significant contributions to the study of the organ.

• 16871 • **Organ Historical Society Archival Fellowship**
To encourage scholarship on subjects dealing with the American pipe organ, its music, and its players. Individuals who have published previously in some area of research connected with the organ are eligible. Grants to fund research are awarded annually. Established in 1987. Additional information is available from Stephen L. Pinel, Archivist, Organ Historical Society, 629 Edison Drive, East Windsor, NJ 08520.

• 16872 •
Organization Development Institute
Dr. Donald W. Cole RODC, Pres.
11234 Walnut Ridge Rd.
Chesterland, OH 44026
Phone: (440)729-7419
Fax: (440)729-9319
E-mail: donwcole@aol.com
Home Page: http://www.odinstitute.org

• 16873 • **Award of Recognition**
Recognizes the best presentation at the Annual O.D Information Exchange. Awarded annually in May. Full time students working full time are eligible. Established in 1998.

• 16874 • **Jack Gibb Award**
Recognizes the best presentation at the National Conference by a full time student. Awarded annually.

• 16875 • **Outstanding Organization Development Article of the Year Award**
Annual award of recognition.

• 16876 • **Outstanding Organization Development Consultant of the Year Award**
Annual award of recognition.

• 16877 • **Outstanding Organization Development Project of the Year Award**
Annual award of recognition.

• 16878 • **Outstanding Presentation Award**
Recognizes the best presentation by full time student working full time. Awarded annually.

• 16879 •
Organization of American Historians
Lee W. Formwalt, Exec.Dir.
112 N. Bryan Ave.
Bloomington, IN 47408-4199
Phone: (812)855-7311
Fax: (812)855-0696
E-mail: oah@oah.org
Home Page: http://www.oah.org

Formerly: Mississippi Valley Historical Association.

• 16880 • **ABC-CLIO America: History and Life Award**
To encourage and recognize scholarship in American history in the journal literature advancing new perspectives on accepted interpretations or previously unconsidered topics. Individuals as well as editors may submit nominations by December 1. A monetary award of $750 and a certificate are presented biennially in odd-numbered years. Established in 1985.

• 16881 • **Willi Paul Adams Prize**
To recognize the best book on American history that has been published in languages other than English. Books concerned with the past (recent or distant), issues of continuity and change, or events or processes that began, developed, or ended in the United States are eligible. The deadline for nominations is May 1. A monetary prize of $1,000 is awarded biennially in odd-numbered years. Established in 1994.

• 16882 • **Erik Barnouw Award**
For recognition of outstanding programming on network or cable television, or in a documentary film dealing with American history, the study of American history, or the promotion of history. Entries must be submitted by December 1. A monetary award of $1,000 (or $500, if two recipients are selected) and a certificate are presented annually. Established in 1983 in honor of Erik Barnouw, a leading historian of mass media.

• 16883 • Ray Allen Billington Prize
To recognize the best book in American frontier history. The deadline for entry is October 1. A monetary award of $1,000 and a certificate are awarded biennially in odd-numbered years. Established in 1981 in honor of Ray Allen Billington, OAH President, 1962-63.

• 16884 • Binkley-Stephenson Award
To recognize the author of the best scholarly article published in the *Journal of American History* during the preceding calendar year. A monetary award of $500 and a certificate are presented annually. Established in 1967 in honor of William C. Binkley and Wendell H. Stephenson, former OAH presidents and editors of the *Journal of American History.*

• 16885 • Avery O. Craven Award
To recognize the most original book on the coming of the Civil War, the Civil War years, or the era of Reconstruction, with the exception of works of purely military history. This exception recognizes and reflects the Quaker convictions of Craven, president of the OAH (1963-64). Application deadline is October 1. A monetary award of $500 and a certificate are presented annually. Established in 1985.

• 16886 • Merle Curti Award
This award recognizes the best book in social, intellectual, and/or cultural history. The committee may decide to award two books, one in social and/or cultural history and one intellectual and/or cultural history. Works published during the preceding year are eligible. The deadline is October 1. A monetary award of $2,000 (or $1,000, if two books are awarded) and a certificate are awarded annually. Established in 1977 in honor of Merle Curti, president of OAH, 1951-52.

• 16887 • Ellis W. Hawley Prize
Awarded annually for the best book-length historical study of the political economy, politics, or institutions of the United States, in its domestic or international affairs, from the Civil War to the present. Eligible works include book-length historical studies, written in English, published during a given calendar year. The deadline for receipt of entries in October 1. Dissertations completed by October 1 are eligible. The winner of the prize will be presented with $500 and a certificate at the Annual meeting of the OAH. Given in honor of Ellis W. Hawley, Emeritus Professor of History, University of Iowa, an outstanding historian of these subjects. Established in 1997.

• 16888 • Huggins-Quarles Award
To recognize minority graduate students at the dissertation research stage of their Ph.D. programs for outstanding research proposals. The deadline for submissions is December 1. Two annual monetary awards of $1,000 are each given to facilitate completion of the dissertation research. Established in honor of the Benjamin Quarles and the late Nathan Huggins, two outstanding historians of the African American past.

• 16889 • Jamestown Scholars: New Dissertation Fellowships from the National Park Service and OAH
Awarded to support research that contributes to our understanding of the development and legacy of the 17th century Jamestown, where diverse peoples from three continents came together. Fellowship awards of $5,000 will be presented starting in 2007. Deadline will be June 30.

• 16890 • La Pietra Dissertation Travel Fellowship in Transnational History
Provides financial assistance to graduate students whose dissertation topics deal with aspects of American history that extend beyond U.S borders. One $1,250 fellowship will be granted annually. Deadline is December 1.

• 16891 • Richard W. Leopold Prize
To recognize the best book written by a historian connected with federal, state, or municipal government. The works considered may be in the areas of foreign policy, military affairs broadly construed, historical activities of the federal government, or biography in one of the above areas. The award recipient must have been employed in a government position for at least five years. The deadline for entry is October 1 of odd-numbered years. A monetary award of $1,500 and a certificate are presented biennially in even-numbered years. Established in 1984 in honor of Professor Richard W. Leopold, president of the Organization in 1976-77.

• 16892 • Lerner-Scott Dissertation Prize
To recognize the best doctoral dissertation in U.S. women's history. The deadline for submissions is October 1 for a dissertation completed during the previous academic year (July 1 through June 30). A monetary award of $1,000 and a certificate are presented annually. Established in 1992 to honor Gerda Lerner and Anne Firor Scott, both pioneers in women's history and past presidents of the Organization.

• 16893 • Liberty Legacy Foundation Award
Awarded for the best book on any aspect of the struggle for civil rights in the United States from the nation's founding to present. $2,000 and a certificate are awarded annually. Established in 2002.

• 16894 • Louis Pelzer Memorial Award
To recognize a graduate student for the best essay on American history, of any period or topic. Criteria include significance of the subject matter, literary craftsmanship, and competence in the handling of evidence. The deadline for entry is December 1. A monetary award of $500, a certificate, and publication of the essay in the *Journal of American History* are awarded annually. Established in 1949 in honor of Louis Pelzer, former president of the Mississippi Valley Historical Association.

• 16895 • James A. Rawley Prize
For recognition of a book dealing with the history of race relations in the United States. The deadline for entries is October 1. A monetary award of $1,000 and a certificate are awarded annually. Established in 1990 in honor of James A. Rawley, Carl Adolph Happold Professor of History Emeritus at the University of Nebraska-Lincoln.

• 16896 • Mary K. Bonsteel Tachau Teach of the Year Award
To recognize the contributions made by precollegiate or classroom teachers to improve history education. The deadline for nominations is December 1. The successful candidate will receive a certificate, a cash prize of $1,000, a one-year OAH membership, and a one-year subscription to the *OAH Magazine of History.* Awarded annually. Established in honor of Mary K. Bonsteel Tachau for her path-breaking efforts to build bridges between university and pre-collegiate teachers.

• 16897 • Frederick Jackson Turner Award
To recognize an author's first book on some significant phase of American history. Authors who have not previously published such a study and who have received a PhD degree no earlier than seven years before the manuscript is submitted are eligible. The deadline is October 1. The winning author receives $1,000 and a certificate; the winning press receives a complimentary ad in the *Journal of American History.* Awarded annually. Established in 1959 in honor of Frederick Jackson Turner, an American historian who formulated the renowned "frontier thesis."

• 16898 •
Organization of Military Museums of Canada
(L'Organisation des Musees Militaires du Canada)
Don Carrington Ret., Exec.Dir.
PO Box 323
Ottawa, ON, Canada K1C 1S7
Phone: (613)737-3223
Fax: (613)737-0821
E-mail: info@ommc.ca
Home Page: http://www.ommc.ca

• 16899 • Honorary Membership
Recognizes individuals providing service to Canadian military museology. Awarded periodically.

• 16900 •
Organization of Professional Employees of the United States Department of Agriculture
Otis N. Thompson, Exec.Dir.
PO Box 381
Washington, DC 20044
Phone: (202)720-4898
Fax: (202)720-6692
E-mail: opeda@usda.gov
Home Page: http://www.usda.gov/opeda

Awards are arranged in alphabetical order below their administering organizations

• 16901 • John W. Peterson Agricultural Scholarship Award

To encourage family members of employees of USDA to pursue careers in agriculture. Employees of the USDA and their children are eligible; applicants must have established a collegiate record of 2.5 or above; and the course of study must be at an accredited college or university. The minimum scholarship is $500 for one year. Applications must be received by August 1. Awarded annually.

• 16902 • Professional of the Year

To recognize the person who best exemplifies professional public service as described in the Code of Ethics. Candidates for the award must be employees of the United States Department of Agriculture and members of the Organization of Professional Employees of the United States Department of Agriculture. A plaque and an all-expense paid trip to the National Council Meeting are awarded annually. Established in 1979.

• 16903 • Unsung Hero Award

To recognize the valuable contributions made by USDA employees to the American public. It is preferable that the award be for something not previously recognized or awarded. The award must be in recognition for actual planning or performance of duties, tasks, or projects rather than for supervision or management functions. The recipient must have demonstrated overall dedication, a positive attitude, and service to the public directly related to those duties which the employee performs as a part of the mission of USDA. The deadline for nominations is March 31. Established in 1986 in observance of Public Employ Recognition Week. Co-sponsored by the Association of Technical & Supervisory Professionals, National Association of Federal Veterinarians, Senior Executives Association, and USDA's Employee Services and Recreation Association.

• 16904 •
Original Paper Doll Artists Guild
Judy M. Johnson, Managing Ed.
PO Box 14
Kingfield, ME 04947
Phone: (207)265-2500
Fax: (207)265-2500
E-mail: info@opdag.com
Home Page: http://www.opdag.com

• 16905 • Lifetime Achievement Award in Paper Doll Art

Recognizes the promotion, teaching, and production of paper doll art. Individuals in the industry for at least 20 years are eligible. Awarded periodically.

• 16906 •
Orphan Train Heritage Society of America
Becky Higgins, Pres.
PO Box 322
Concordia, KS 66901
Phone: (785)243-4471
Fax: (785)243-4471
E-mail: othsa@msn.com
Home Page: http://www.orphantrainriders.com

• 16907 • Charles Loring Brace Award

Recognizes a person or persons best preserving the history of Orphan Train Rides placed out by the Children's Kid Society. Awarded annually.

• 16908 • Sister Irene Award

Recognizes a person or persons best preserving the history of Orphan Train Rides placed out by the New York Foundling Hospital. Awarded annually.

• 16909 •
Orthodox Christian Association of Medicine, Psychology and Religion
Fr. Nicholas T. Graff PhD, Pres.
50 Goddard Ave.
Brookline, MA 02445
Phone: (617)850-1365
Fax: (904)399-1547
E-mail: srb1389@aol.com
Home Page: http://ocampr.org

• 16910 • S.S. Kosmos and Damian Award

Recognizes contributions to the development of the integration of medicine psychology and religion from an Orthodox Christian perspective. Awarded annually.

• 16911 •
Orthopaedic Research Society
Brenda Welborn, Exec.Dir.
6300 N River Rd., Ste. 727
Rosemont, IL 60018-4226
Phone: (847)698-1625
Fax: (847)384-4242
E-mail: ors@aaos.org
Home Page: http://www.ors.org

• 16912 • Marshall Urist Award

Annual award of recognition. A prize of $5,000 and commemorative plaque are awarded.

• 16913 • New Investigator Recognition Awards

Recognizes outstanding work in orthopedics. Awarded annuallly.

• 16914 • Shands Award

To recognize a United States or Canadian citizen who has made significant contributions to orthopaedics during the majority of his or her professional career. The person need not be a member of the Society, nor be an orthopaedic surgeon. The individual, usually a senior contributor, must have devoted a significant portion of his or her professional career to furthering knowledge in the fields of musculoskeletal disease. The award consists of a monetary prize of $1,000 and a scroll. The awardee is expected to give a presentation at the annual meeting of the society in combination with that of the academy. Awarded annually. Established in 1971.

• 16915 • Arthur Steindler Award

To recognize senior scientists, clinicians, and educators who, throughout their professional lifetime, have made significant contributions, both nationally and internationally, to the understanding of the musculoskeletal system and musculoskeletal diseases and injuries. The awardees must have started their professional careers outside the United States, and have advanced their specialty throughout the world. A monetary award of $2,000 is presented and the winner is invited to give a summary of his or her work at the annual meeting of the Research Society in conjunction with the academy. Awarded biennially in even-numbered years. Established in 1964 by the Iowa Medical School, Department of Orthopaedic Surgery.

• 16916 • William Harris Award

Annual award of recognition. A prize of $5,000 and commemorative plaque are awarded.

• 16917 •
Osborne Association
Elizabeth Gaynes, Exec.Dir.
36-31 38th St.
Long Island City, NY 11101-1621
Phone: (718)707-2600
Fax: (718)707-3103
E-mail: info@osborneny.org
Home Page: http://www.osborneny.org

• 16918 • Austin MacCormick Award

Recognizes work in the human services community. Awarded annually.

• 16919 • OA Medal

Recognizes service in criminal justice. Awarded annually.

• 16920 •
Osteopathic Physicians and Surgeons of California
Kathleen Creason, Exec.Dir.
1900 Point West Way, Ste. 188
Sacramento, CA 95815
Phone: (916)561-0724
Fax: (916)561-0728
E-mail: opsc@opsc.org
Home Page: http://www.opsc.org

• 16921 • Matt Weyuker Scholarship

For California students of osteopathic medicine. Scholarship awarded annually.

• 16922 •
Ostomy Association of Springfield Massachusetts
Jeri Bachli, Pres.
PO Box 80172
Forest Park Station
Springfield, MA 01138-0172
Phone: (413)567-1666
Phone: (413)781-2713

• 16923 • **Scholarship for Enterostomal Therapy Education**
For RN's enrolled in approved training centers. Scholarship awarded periodically.

• 16924 •
Oswego Heritage Council
Susan Headlee, Exec.Dir.
PO Box 1041
Lake Oswego, OR 97034-0118
Phone: (503)635-6373
Phone: (503)636-1730
E-mail: loheritagehouse@aol.com
Home Page: http://home.europa.com/~heritage/index2.html

• 16925 • **Historic Plaque**
For historically significant building or site in Lake Oswego. Recognition award bestowed annually.

• 16926 •
Ottawa Field-Naturalists' Club
Box 35069, Westgate Post Office
Ottawa, ON, Canada K1Z 1A2
Phone: (613)722-3050
E-mail: ofnc@ofnc.ca
Home Page: http://www.ofnc.ca

• 16927 • **Conservation Award**
To recognize an individual or a group for outstanding contribution in the cause of national history conservation in the Ottawa Valley, particularly in the Ottawa District. One certificate is awarded annually to a member and one to a non-member.

• 16928 • **Anne Hanes Natural History Award**
To recognize an amateur naturalist who, through independent study or investigation, has made a worthwhile contribution to the knowledge, understanding, and appreciation of the natural history of the Ottawa Valley. Only members are eligible. A certificate is awarded when merited. Established in 1981 in memory of Anne Hanes, an active naturalist and the founding editor of *Trail & Landscape*.

• 16929 • **Honorary Member**
To recognize an individual for outstanding contributions to Canadian natural history or Club operations. Members or non-members are eligible, though Honorary membership is limited to a total of 25 individuals. A certificate is awarded when merited. Established in 1879.

• 16930 • **George McGee Service Award**
To recognize members for outstanding service to the Club over several years. A certificate is awarded annually. Established in 1981 to honor George McGee, natural history teacher and Club President.

• 16931 • **Member of the Year**
To recognize a member for outstanding contributions to the Club during the previous year. A certificate is awarded annually.

• 16932 • **President's Prize**
To recognize a member for unusual support of the Club and its aims. The recipient is chosen by the President alone, based on knowledge of the year's accomplishments. Awarded when merited. Established in 1985.

• 16933 •
Ottawa International Animation Festival
Kelly Neal, Mng.Dir.
2 Daly Ave., Ste. 120
Ottawa, ON, Canada K1N 6E2
Phone: (613)232-8769
Fax: (613)232-6315
E-mail: info@animationfestival.ca
Home Page: http://www.awn.com/ottawa

• 16934 • **Frederick Back Award for Best Canadian Film**
No further information available for this edition.

• 16935 • **Best Animation Making Use of Unusual Techniques**
To recognize an animated film that uses unconventional and unusual methods of production.

• 16936 • **Best Animation Short Made for the Internet**
To recognize the best internet film. Awarded annually.

• 16937 • **Best Design**
No further information available this edition.

• 16938 • **Best Educational Production**
To give distinction to a well crafted film with educational content.

• 16939 • **Best Film Made for Children**
To recognize the best film intended for young audiences. Awarded annually.

• 16940 • **Best Graduate Film**
To recognize the best film by a graduate student. Awarded annually. Formerly: Crater Software Award for Best Graduate Film.

• 16941 • **Best Music Video**
For the best music video that makes use of animation. Awarded annually.

• 16942 • **Best Programme ID**
No further information available for this edition.

• 16943 • **Best Television Series for Adults**
For the best adult television series that makes use of animation. Awarded annually.

• 16944 • **Best Television Special**
No further information available this edition.

• 16945 • **Gordon Bruce Award for Humour**
To recognize the best film or video which not only makes us laugh, but which also demonstrates how humor is a combination of intelligence and anarchy. Awarded biennially in even-numbered years. Established in 1994.

• 16946 • **Cartoon Network Award for Best Animation**
No further information available this edition.

• 16947 • **Chromacolour Award for Best Use of Colour**
To give credit to the animated film that best uses colour.

• 16948 • **First Professional Work Award**
Awarded to encourage and recognize talented neophyte filmmakers. Awarded annually.

• 16949 • **Grand Prize for Commissioned Animation**
To recognize the best film made by commission. Awarded annually.

• 16950 • **Grand Prizes**
To recognize the best entries in the festival. Awarded in the following categories: Independent Short Animation, Commissioned Animation, Animated Feature, and Student Animation. A trophy and certificate is presented annually. Established in 1976.

• 16951 • **Norman McLaren Heritage Award**
To recognize the body of work by a filmmaker or group of filmmakers or an institution which ASIFA-Canada believes maintains the filmmaking heritage of Norman McLaren. Awarded biennially in even-numbered years. Established in 1988.

• 16952 • **Mike Gribble Peel of Laughter Award**
No further information available this edition.

• 16953 • **National Film Board of Canada Public Prize**
To honor the film from the official competition selected by the public as the best of the Festival. Awarded annually.

Awards are arranged in alphabetical order below their administering organizations

• 16954 • Nelvana Grand Prize for Independent Short Animation
To recognize the best film produced without major sponsorship. Awarded annually.

• 16955 • Object Animation
No further information available this edition.

• 16956 • Zack Schwartz Award for Best Story
To honor the animated film with the best story. Established in 1996.

• 16957 • Special Jury Prize
No further information available this edition.

• 16958 •
Ottawa Little Theatre
Beth Monaco, Gen.Mgr.
Canadian One-Act Playwriting Competition
400 King Edward Ave.
Ottawa, ON, Canada K1N 7M7
Phone: (613)233-8948
Fax: (613)233-8027
E-mail: olt-manager@on.aibn.com
Home Page: http://www.o-l-t.com

• 16959 • National Playwriting Competition
For recognition of outstanding one-act Canadian plays. Previously unproduced, original one-act plays in English (25-49 minutes) are eligible for submission. First place receives the President's Award ($1,000); second place receives the Dorothy White Award ($700); third place the Gladys Cameron Watt Award ($500); and the Sybil Cooke Memorial Award ($500) is given as a special award to encourage one-act plays for children. Awarded annually.

• 16960 •
Ouachita Council on Aging
Lynda McGehee, Exec.Dir.
PO Box 7418
Monroe, LA 71211
Phone: (318)387-0535
Fax: (318)322-0545
E-mail: ocoa@bayou.com
Home Page: http://www.monroe.k12.la.us/mcs/community/oca/

• 16961 • Volunteer of the Year Award
Awarded to the person who volunteers the most and does vital agency work. Recognition award bestowed annually.

• 16962 •
Outdoor Advertising Association of America
Ken Klein, Exec.VP
1850 M St. NW, Ste. 1040
Washington, DC 20036
Phone: (202)833-5566
Fax: (202)833-1522
E-mail: kklein@oaaa.org
Home Page: http://www.oaaa.org

• 16963 • Myles Standish Award
To recognize an individual who has made an outstanding and lasting contribution to the outdoor advertising industry. A framed medal is awarded biennially in odd-numbered years. Established in 1954 in honor of Myles Standish, an early pioneer in the standardized outdoor industry. Formerly: (1957) Chairman's Award.

• 16964 • L. Ray Vahue Memorial Award
To honor an individual who best embodies the marketing aims of the industry. The honoree must be active in outdoor advertising. A framed medal is presented biennially in odd-numbered years. Established in 1979 in memory of L. Ray Vahue, an industry leader.

• 16965 •
Outdoor Writers Association of America
Marty Malin, Pres.
121 Hickory St., Ste. 1
Missoula, MT 59801
Phone: (406)728-7434
Fax: (406)728-7445
E-mail: owaa@montana.com
Home Page: http://www.owaa.org

• 16966 • Ham Brown Award
To recognize outstanding continuous service to the Association. Members of OWAA are eligible. An inscribed plaque is awarded annually. Established in 1966. Formerly: J. Hammond Brown Memorial Award.

• 16967 • Conservation/Outdoor Recreation Film/Video Award Program
To recognize the eight most outstanding conservation and outdoor recreation feature films/videos produced during the preceding year. Monetary awards and plaques are presented annually. Established in the late 1950s in conjunction with the annual North American Wildlife and Natural Resources Conference of the Wildlife Management Institute.

• 16968 • Excellence in Craft Awards
To honor members for articles, photographs, and broadcasts that communicate the value of outdoor activities. Active members of the association are eligible. A plaque is awarded annually in each of 19 categories. Established in 1971.

• 16969 • Jade of Chiefs
This, OWAA's highest award, is given to recognize outstanding contributions to conservation. Though only OWAA members are eligible, the award is not actually presented by OWAA, but by members of the current Circle of Chiefs. Tenure and position in, or service to, OWAA are not criteria for the award. The Jade Award represents an affirmation of OWAA adherence to, and support of, the principles of conservation. A pewter belt buckle inlaid with jade and a scroll-design walnut plaque are awarded. Established in 1958.

• 16970 • Photography Awards
To recognize outstanding still photographs in five categories: Fauna, Action, People, Scenic, and Flora. Members of the association are eligible. These awards comprise one category of awards in the Excellence in Craft Contests. Plaques, citations, and monetary prizes are awarded annually. Established in 1972.

• 16971 •
Outdoor Writers of Canada
(Chroniqueurs de la Vie au Grand Air du Canada)
Bill Thompson, Exec.Dir.
PO Box 20008
Pioneer Park Postal Outlet
Kitchener, ON, Canada N2P 2B4
Phone: (403)932-3585
Fax: (905)743-7052
E-mail: bthompson@outdoorwritersofcanada.com
Home Page: http://www.outdoorwritersofcanada.com

• 16972 • Pete McGillen Award
To recognize members who, in their professional careers, have stimulated interest and appreciation of the outdoors, and have stimulated high standards of craftsmanship among professionals concerned with the portrayal of outdoor life. Individuals must be nominated by two members in good standing of OWC. A monetary prize of $300 and a plaque are awarded annually at the annual convention. Established in 1974 in memory of Pete McGillen, one of Canada's outstanding outdoor writers.

• 16973 • Outdoor Communications Awards
To promote improvement and reward excellence in the outdoor writing field. First-, second-, and third-place awards are given in eight categories: Newspaper Column; Newspaper Feature; Magazine Column; Magazine Feature (Hunting); Magazine Feature (Fishing); Television/Video; Photography; and Book. The Ron Miller Story Teller Award is presented for the best fiction or non-fiction storytelling effort with an outdoors theme. Awarded annually at the annual convention. Established in 1962 in memory of conservationist and author, Francis H. Kortright. Formerly: (1987) Outdoor Writing Awards.

• 16974 •
Outer Critics Circle
Marjorie Gunner, Pres.
101 W 57th St.
New York, NY 10019
Phone: (212)765-8557
Fax: (212)765-7979

• 16975 • Performance Awards
To recognize the best in theater of the season in New York, both on and off Broadway. Awards are given in the following categories: Outstanding Broadway Play, Performance Actor, Performance Actress, Featured Actor in a Play, Featured Actress in a Play, Featured Actor in a

Musical, Featured Actress in a Musical, Off-Broadway Play, Off-Broadway Musical, Design, Sets/Costume/Lights, Director of a Musical, Director of a Play, Broadway Musical, Music Revival, Play Revival, Special Awards, John Gassner Award for the most outstanding new playwright of an American Play, Actress Musical, Actor Musical, and Solo Awards (if season warrants). Presented annually.

• 16976 •
Outfest
Stephen Gutwillig, Exec.Dir.
3470 Wilshire Blvd., Ste. 1022
Los Angeles, CA 90010
Phone: (213)480-7088
Fax: (213)480-7099
E-mail: outfest@outfest.org
Home Page: http://www.outfest.org

• 16977 • **Audience and Juried Awards**
Honors those accepted in the Outfest Film Festival. A monetary award is given annually.

• 16978 •
Ovarian Cancer National Alliance
Sharon Flynn, Contact
910 17th St. NW, Ste. 413
Washington, DC 20006
Phone: (202)331-1332
Fax: (202)331-2292
E-mail: ocna@ovariancancer.org
Home Page: http://www.ovariancancer.org

Awards discontinued.

• 16979 • **Health Advocate of the Year**
To recognize outstanding achievement in public education, public policy, or scientific research to further prevention or early detection of ovarian cancer. A plaque and travel expenses to receive the award are presented biennially at an official OCPEDF event. Established in 1992.

• 16980 •
Overseas Press Club of America
Sonya Fry, Exec.Dir.
40 W 45 St.
New York, NY 10036
Phone: (212)626-9220
Fax: (212)626-9210
E-mail: sonya@opcofamerica.org
Home Page: http://www.opcofamerica.org/index.php

• 16981 • **Annual Awards in International News Coverage**
To recognize international coverage in newspapers, wire services, online sites, magazines, radio, television, cartoons, books, and photography. Work must be published in the U.S. or by a U.S.-based publication/broadcast during the calendar year. The entry deadline is January 27. The following prizes are awarded: (1) the Hal Boyle Award ($1,000) presented by AT&T for the best newspaper or wire service reporting from abroad; (2) the Bob Considine Award ($1,000) for the best newspaper or wire service interpretation of international affairs; (3) the Robert Capa Gold Medal (plus $1,000) presented by Time & Life Magazine for the best photographic reporting from abroad requiring exceptional courage and enterprise; (4) the Olivier Rebbot Award ($1,000) presented by Newsweek for best photography from abroad in magazines and books; (5) the John Faber Award ($1,000) presented by the Coca-Cola Company for the best photography from abroad in newspapers and wire services; (6) the Lowell Thomas Award ($1,000) presented by ABC for the best radio news or interpretation of foreign affairs; (7) the David Kaplan Award ($1,000) sponsored by Verizon for the best TV spot news reporting from abroad; (8) the Edward R. Murrow Award ($1,000) presented by CBS for the best TV interpretation or documentary on foreign affairs; (9) the Ed Cunningham Memorial Award ($1000) sponsored by Ford Motor Company for the best magazine reporting from abroad; (10) the Thomas Nast Award ($1,000) presented by *Newsday* for the best cartoon on foreign affairs; (11) the Morton Frank Award ($1,000) sponsored by Merrill Lynch for the best business reporting from abroad in magazines; (12) the Malcolm Forbes Award ($1,000) sponsored by Forbes Magazine for the best business reporting from abroad in newspapers or wire services; (13) the Carl Spielvogel Award for best broadcast showing a concern for the human condition; (14) the Cornelius Ryan Award ($1,000) sponsored by Morgan Stanley for the best non-fiction book on foreign affairs; (15) the Madeline Dane Ross Award ($1,000) for the best reporting in the print medium showing a concern for the human condition; (16) the Eric and Amy Burger Award ($1,000) for the best reporting in broadcast media dealing with human rights; (17) the Joe and Laurie Dine Award for the best reporting in a print medium dealing with human rights; (18) the Whitman Bassow Award sponsored by AT&T for the best reporting in any medium on international environmental issues; the (19) Robert Spiers Benjamin Award for the best reporting in any medium on Latin America; and (20) the Feature Photography Award for the best feature photography published in any medium on an international theme. Awarded annually.

• 16982 •
Owen M. Kupferschmid Holocaust and Human Rights Project
Wasana Punyasen, Pres.
140 Commonwealth Ave.
885 Centre St., 300 I EW
Chestnut Hill, MA 02467
Phone: (617)552-8550
E-mail: punyasen@bc.edu
Home Page: http://www.bc.edu/schools/law/services/studentorgs/hhrp

• 16983 • **Owen M. Kupferschmid Award**
Recognizes activity in areas of interest to HHRP.

• 16984 •
Owsley Family Historical Society
Ronny O. Bodine, Pres.
916 N Ridge Dr.
Columbus, GA 31904
Phone: (706)324-7237
E-mail: rbodine996@aol.com

• 16985 • **Certificate of Appreciation**
Recognizes special achievement, outstanding service, outstanding support. Awarded annually.

• 16986 • **Distinguished Service Award**
Recognizes special achievement, outstanding service, outstanding support. Awarded annually.

• 16987 • **Presidents's Award**
Recognizes special achievement, outstanding service, outstanding support. Awarded annually.

• 16988 •
OX5 Aviation Pioneers
Jim Ricklefs, Pres.
PO Box 7974
2961 W. Liberty Ave.
Pittsburgh, PA 15216-7974
Phone: (412)341-5650

• 16989 • **Hall of Fame**
To recognize the achievements of early aviation pioneers. A nameplate with brief description of achievements is attached to a master plaque that is housed in the Glen Curtiss Museum at Hammondsport, NY. Awarded annually. Established in 1971.

• 16990 • **National Awards Program**
To recognize members who further the educational and scientific purposes of the Society: to compile and record in detail the historical and educational history of the development of air transportation; to perpetuate the memory of pioneer airmen and their great sacrifices, their accomplishments and contributions to the development of civil aviation; to support projects and programs designed to increase safety and efficiency in the use of aircraft; to publish historical resumes and other information consistent with the educational objective; to encourage the establishment and operation of aviation museums and the collection of aviation memorabilia, particularly of the 1920-1940 era; and to establish and maintain suitable ways of recognizing and honoring the names and achievements of aviation pioneers. The following awards are presented: Mr. OX5, Outstanding Women's Award, Legion of Honor, Legion of Merit, Bronze Star, Distinguished Service, President's Award, and Clifford Ball Memorial Award.

• 16991 •
Ozark Society
Alice Barrett Andrews, Pres.
PO Box 2914
Little Rock, AR 72203
Phone: (501)847-3738
Phone: (501)219-4293
E-mail: alice209ok@yahoo.com
Home Page: http://www.ozarksociety.net

• 16992 • **Neil Compton Award**
To honor an individual for contributions and efforts toward the preservation of natural areas, particularly in the Ozark-Ouachita mountain region. Members of the Society are eligible. Established in 1970 to honor the founder of the Ozark Society.

• 16993 •
Pacific Arts Association
Carol Ivory, Pres.
PO Box 6061-120
Sherman Oaks, CA 91413
E-mail: ivorycs@wsu.edu
Home Page: http://www.pacificarts.org

• 16994 • **Manu Daula (Frigate Bird) Award**
To recognize an individual for outstanding achievement and dedication to the arts of the Pacific. A bronze medallion is awarded every two to four years at the International Symposium. Established in 1985. 170685

• 16995 •
Pacific Asia Travel Association
Mr. Peter de Jong, Pres./CEO
1611 Telegraph Ave., Ste. 550
Latham Sq. Bldg.
Oakland, CA 94612
Phone: (510)625-2055
Fax: (510)625-2044
E-mail: americas@pata.org
Home Page: http://www.pata.org

Formerly: (1986) Pacific Area Travel Association.

• 16996 • **Gold Awards**
To recognize creativity and achievement in the fields of environmental and cultural preservation, education, travel journalism, advertising, and marketing through an open competition. Members and nonmembers are eligible. Projects and creative efforts produced during the previous calendar year may be submitted by January 15. Forty-three awards are presented within the following categories: consumer travel brochures, travel advertisements, travel posters, digital travel videos, public relations campaign, CD-ROMs, websites, and E-newsletters. Additionally, four Grand Awards for "best of show" entries are awarded in four categories: marketing, environment, heritage and culture, and education and training. Awards are presented at PATA's Annual Conference.

• 16997 •
Pacific Center for Human Growth
Ralph Thomas, Board Pres.
2712 Telegraph Ave.
Berkeley, CA 94705
Phone: (510)548-8283
Phone: (510)548-2192
Fax: (510)548-2938
E-mail: info@pacificcenter.org
Home Page: http://www.pacificcenter.org

• 16998 • **Volunteer of the Year**
For outstanding service to the community. Trophy awarded annually.

• 16999 •
Pacific Coast Archaeological Society
PO Box 10926
Costa Mesa, CA 92627-0926
E-mail: quarterly@pcas.org
Home Page: http://www.pcas.org

• 17000 • **Soderberg Scholarship**
For local community college student. Scholarship awarded annually.

• 17001 •
Pacific Coast Paper Box Manufacturers' Association
D. Timothy Daze, Exec.VP
6360 Van Nuys Blvd., Ste. 220
Van Nuys, CA 91401
Phone: (818)781-3378
Fax: (818)787-6206
E-mail: pcpbma@aol.com

• 17002 • **Safety Award**
For safety record. Recognition award bestowed annually.

• 17003 • **Student Design-School Competition**
For the best boxes and cartons produced by class. Recognition award bestowed annually.

• 17004 •
Pacific Dermatologic Association
Kent Lindeman CMP, Exec.Dir.
2950 Buskirk Ave., Ste. 170
Walnut Creek, CA 94597
Phone: (925)472-5910
Fax: (925)472-5901
E-mail: pda@hp-assoc.com
Home Page: http://www.pacificderm.org

• 17005 • **Nelson Paul Anderson Award**
For the best essay relating to dermatology. Dermatology residents or dermatologists not more than 5 years out of residency are eligible. Awarded annually.

• 17006 •
Pacific Northwest Booksellers Association
Thom Chambliss, Exec.Dir.
317 W Broadway, Ste. 214
Eugene, OR 97401-2890
Phone: (541)683-4363
Fax: (541)683-3910
E-mail: info@pnba.org
Home Page: http://www.pnba.org

• 17007 • **PNBA Book Awards**
For authors who live in Alaska, Idaho, Montana, Oregon, or Washington states. Monetary award bestowed annually.

• 17008 •
Pacific Northwest Library Association
Montana State University - Bozeman
PO Box 173320
Bozeman, MT 59717-3320
Phone: (406)994-6554
Fax: (406)994-2851
E-mail: jzauha@montana.edu
Home Page: http://www.pnla.org

• 17009 • **Young Readers' Choice Award**
To promote reading as an enjoyable activity and to provide children with an opportunity to endorse a book they consider an excellent story. Readers in grades 4-12 vote for their favorite title from a list of books published three years previously. Books are arranged by division: Junior Division (grades 4-6), Middle Division (grades 7-9), and Senior Division (grades 10-12). Promoted by school and public libraries of the Northwest states of Idaho, Montana, Oregon, Washington, and Alaska, plus the Canadian provinces of British Columbia and Alberta. A silver medal is presented to the author of the books in each of the categories. Awarded annually at the Association's conference. Established in 1940.

• 17010 •
Pacific Northwest Writers Association
Sharyn Bolton, Pres.
PO Box 2016
23607 Hwy. 99, Ste. 2C
Edmonds, WA 98020-9516
Phone: (425)673-2665
Fax: (425)771-9588
E-mail: pnwa@pnwa.org
Home Page: http://www.pnwa.org

• 17011 • **PNWA Literary Contest**
To encourage professionalism in writing and to elicit and honor the best writing the Pacific Northwest has to offer. Cash awards are given in 11 categories. First, second, and third place awards are presented in each category. First place winners receive the Zola Award, a cash prize of $600, and a staged reading of the entry at the SecondStory repertory company in the Fall. Second place winners receive $300, and third place winners receive $150. Submission deadline is in February of each year. Awarded annually. Established in 1956.

• 17012 •
Pacific Science Association
Dr. John Burke Burnett, Exec.Sec.
1525 Bernice St.
Honolulu, HI 96817
Phone: (808)848-4124
Fax: (808)847-8252
E-mail: psa@bishopmuseum.org
Home Page: http://www.pacificscience.org

• 17013 • **Herbert E. Gregory Medal**
To recognize outstanding leaders in Pacific science. A medal is awarded every four years at the Pacific Science Congress of the PSA. Established in 1961 by the Bernice P. Bishop Museum in honor of Herbert E. Gregory, founder of the Association.

• 17014 • **Shinkishi Hatai Medal**
To recognize a scientist for a remarkable contribution to marine biology in the Pacific. A medal is awarded every four years at a Pacific Science Congress of the PSA. Established in 1966 by the Science Council of Japan in honor of Shinkishi Hatai, a leader in Pacific Marine Biology.

• 17015 • **Honorary Life Fellow**
To recognize a scientist either for distinguished service to the Association or for furthering the objectives for which the Association was founded. A certificate is awarded every two years. Established in 1961 by the Pacific Science Council.

• 17016 •
Pacific Sociological Association
Dean S. Dorn, Exec.Dir.
Dept. of Sociology
6000 J St.
California State University, Sacramento
Sacramento, CA 95819-6005
Phone: (916)278-5254
Fax: (916)278-6281
E-mail: psa@csus.edu
Home Page: http://www.csus.edu/psa

• 17017 • **Distinguished Contributions to Teaching**
To recognize sociologists from the Western region of the U.S. who have developed teaching programs, devices, or materials that have been effective in the promotion of student understanding and the appreciation of the sociology field. Producers of textbooks, teaching aids, laboratory designs, instructional computer packages, or innovative curricular that has made a special impact on students are eligible for nomination. Nominees must be members of the PSA at the time their work is submitted. A certificate is awarded at the annual meeting of the Association.

• 17018 • **Distinguished Practice Award**
To recognize sociological work in the Pacific region (whether by an academic or non-academic) that has an impact on government, business, health, or other settings not directly connected with academia. The grounds for nomination include (but are not limited to) any applied sociological activity that improves organizational performance, contributes to community betterment, and/or eases human suffering. Nomination deadline is February 1. The following awards are presented: a plaque; printed announcements in appropriate sociological outlets; letters describing the honor to the presiding executive officer of the institution, agency, or organization with which the nominee is affiliated; publication in the next available issue of *Sociological Perspectives* of an article-length version of the product with the stipulation that it meets normal journal standards for scholarship and style; and an entire meeting session allocated to presentations on the work being honored. Awarded biennially in odd-numbered years.

• 17019 • **Distinguished Scholarship Award**
To honor sociologists from the Pacific region in recognition of major intellectual contributions embodied in a recently published book or series of at least three articles on a common theme. Edited books are not eligible. Nominations are accepted from members of the PSA until December 1. A certificate is awarded at the annual meeting. Printed announcements are also included in major sociological outlets such as the PSA journal and ASA footnotes. Awarded annually.

• 17020 • **Distinguished Student Paper Awards**
To honor undergraduate and graduate students in the Pacific region who have produced scholarly papers of professional quality or promise, to encourage excellence in scholarship among students in the region, and to enhance the visibility of sociology as a desirable discipline worthy of pursuit by students and prospective students. Application deadline is February 1. A $200 honorarium is presented to the best undergraduate paper and to the best graduate paper. Awarded annually.

• 17021 •
Pacific Telecommunications Council
Sharon Nakama, Dir.
2454 S Beretania St., Ste. 302
Honolulu, HI 96826-1596
Phone: (808)941-3789
Fax: (808)944-4874
E-mail: info@ptc.org
Home Page: http://www.ptc.org

• 17022 • **PTC Essay Prize**
Annual award of recognition. Students and graduates within the last 5 years are eligible.

• 17023 •
Packaging Education Forum
Ben Miyares, Pres.
4350 N Fairfax Dr., Ste. 600
Arlington, VA 22203
Phone: (703)243-5717
Fax: (703)524-8691
E-mail: bmiyares@pmmi.org

• 17024 • **Packaging Hall of Fame**
To recognize individual contributions to the packaging industry and packaging education. Criteria for selection of members are: stature in the industry, organization, and community; contributions to the industry; and interest and activities in packaging education. The candidates must be 60 years of age or older. A trophy is presented annually to one or more recipients. Established in 1970 by the Packaging Education Forum.

• 17025 • **Packaging Leader of the Year**
To recognize corporate contributions to the packaging industry and packaging education. Criteria for selection of packaging leaders are: stature in the industry, the organization, and community; contribution to the industry; and interest and activities in packaging education. A trophy is presented annually at the Awards Dinner each Fall. Established in 1970. Formerly: (1982) Packaging Man of the Year.

• 17026 •
Painting and Decorating Contractors Association of the East Bay Counties
Suzy Schneider, Admin.
PO Box 2709
Fairfield, CA 94533
Phone: (707)864-9660
Fax: (707)864-9680
E-mail: ebaypdca@aol.com
Home Page: http://www.pdca.org

• 17027 • **C.C. Knight Award**
For membership service. Recognition award bestowed annually.

• 17028 •
Painting and Decorating Contractors of America
Dr. Richard Bright, Communications Dir.
11960 Westline Industrial Dr., Ste. 201
St. Louis, MO 63146-3209
Phone: (314)514-7322
Toll-Free: 800-332-PDCA
Fax: (314)514-9417
E-mail: rbright@pdca.org
Home Page: http://www.pdca.org

• 17029 • **"Picture It Painted Professionally" Awards**
To recognize professional painting contractors nationwide for their creative use of paint in residential, commercial, and industrial settings. Awards are given annually in 17 categories. Open to PDCA members only. Application deadline is November 25.

• 17030 •
Pajacam Friends of the Bella Vista Girls Home
Selwyn D. King, Pres.
PMB 1090
224-21 Merrick Blvd.
Laurelton, NY 11413-2024
Phone: (516)483-4694
Phone: (718)773-7562
E-mail: pajacam@hotmail.com

• 17031 • **Mother of the Humanitarian Scholarship**
For college-bound seniors. Scholarship awarded annually.

• 17032 •
Palatine Area Chamber of Commerce
Meg Bucaro Wojtas, Dir.
625 North Ct., Ste. 320
Palatine, IL 60067
Phone: (847)359-7200
Fax: (847)359-7246
E-mail: info@palatinechamber.com
Home Page: http://www.palatinechamber.com

• 17033 • **Ehlenfeldt Memorial Scholarship**
For community participation and school involvement. Scholarship awarded annually.

• 17034 •
Paleontological Research Institution
1259 Trumansburg Rd.
Ithaca, NY 14850
Phone: (607)273-6623
Fax: (607)273-6620
E-mail: allmon@museumoftheearth.org
Home Page: http://www.priweb.org

• 17035 • **Gilbert Harris Award**
Research scientists working in the centrality of systematics to paleontology are eligible. Awarded annuallly. Inquire for application details.

• 17036 • **Osgood Prize**
Recognizes an outstanding paper published in its monograph series. A cash prize is awarded.

• 17037 • **Katherine Palmer Award**
Annual award of recognition. Amateur paleontologists are eligible.

• 17038 • **Student Research Awards in Systematic Paleontology**
Graduate students are eligible. Cash prizes are awarded.

• 17039 •
Paleontological Society
Prof. Roger D.K. Thomas, Sec.
Dept. of Earth & Environment
Franklin & Marshall College
Box 870338
Lancaster, PA 17604-3003
Phone: (717)291-4135
Fax: (717)291-4186
E-mail: roger.thomas@fandm.edu
Home Page: http://paleosoc.org

• 17040 • **Paleontological Society Medal**
This, the most prestigious honor bestowed by the Society, recognizes an individual whose eminence is based on the advancement of knowledge in paleontology. A bronze medal is awarded annually. Established in 1963.

• 17041 • **Charles Schuchert Award**
To recognize young individuals whose work reflects excellence and promise in the science of paleontology. Members of the society under 40 years of age are eligible. A wood and metal plaque is awarded annually. Established in 1973.

• 17042 • **Strimple Award**
To recognize outstanding achievement in paleontology by an amateur. Individuals who do not derive their livelihood from the study of fossils are eligible. Contributions may be an outstanding record of research and publication, making outstanding collections, safeguarding unique paleontological materials through public service, teaching activities in the area of paleontology, and collaborations with others working in paleontology. Awarded annually. Established in 1983.

• 17043 •
Palm Springs International Festival of Short Films
Darryl Macdonald, Exec.Dir.
1700 E Tahquitz Canyon Way, Ste. 3
Palm Springs, CA 92262
Phone: (760)322-2930
Toll-Free: 800-898-7256
Fax: (760)322-4087
E-mail: info@psfilmfest.com
Home Page: http://www.psfilmfest.org

• 17044 • **Charles A. Crain Desert Palm Achievement Award**
To recognize lifetime achievement in film. Individuals are nominated by an awards committee. A trophy and an award dinner are given annually. Awards are presented in Palm Springs during the film festival. Established in 1989. Formerly: (1997) Desert Palm Achievement Award.

• 17045 •
Palomino Horse Breeders of America
Dr. Susan Bragg, Pres.
15253 E Skelly Dr.
Tulsa, OK 74116-2637
Phone: (918)438-1234
Fax: (918)438-1232
E-mail: yellahrses@aol.com
Home Page: http://www.palominohba.com

• 17046 • **Amateur Golden Horse**
To recognize the Amateur Palomino horse earning the most points at the PHBA World Championship Palomino Horse Show. A horse and rider team must compete in at least five amateur events at the World Show to be eligible for the Golden Horse Amateur title. An amateur may show more than one horse, but points earned by that amateur are compiled separately for each horse. The winner receives the use of a 4-Star Aluminum two-horse slant load trailer, estimated at over $11,000 in value, and a Trophy Tack Co. custom-made matching breast collar and headstall. The Reserve Golden Amateur Horse wins a Drysdales Western Wear belt buckle and $100. Established in 1983. Formerly: (1996) All-Around Amateur Golden Horse.

• 17047 • **Amateur Supreme Champion**
To recognize amateur exhibitors and their Palomino horses who have won a minimum of 325 amateur points. The amateur must have earned a PHBA Amateur Superior Award in one of the following events: Western Horsemanship, Hunt Seat Equitation, Saddle Seat Equitation, and Showmanship at Halter. They must have earned one APHBA Amateur Register of Merit in a fourth performance event. Awarded at the annual PHBA meeting. Established in 1984. In addition, the PHBA presents the following awards: the PHBA Amateur Champion, Top Ten Overall PHBA Amateurs, PHBA Amateur Register of Merit, PHBA Amateur Superior Award, and PHBA Honor Roll Award.

• 17048 • **Golden Horse Award**
To recognize the Palomino horse earning the most points at the PHBA World Championship Palomino Horse Show. To be eligible for the award, which rewards versatility, horses must be shown in a minimum of five open events. Total scores from placings in World Show classes determine the winner. The Golden Horse winner receives a Golden Horse saddle, a $1,000 gift certificate sponsored by Drysdales Western Wear in Tulsa, Oklahoma, and a bronze horse sculptured by Candice M. Libby, Excelsior, Minnesota. The Reserve Golden Horse wins a Trophy Tack Saddle and a $500 Drysdales Western Wear Gift Certificate. Established in 1983. Formerly: (1996) All-Around Golden Horse Award.

• 17049 • **Hall of Fame**
To recognize outstanding Palomino horses, and individuals who are exhibitors or who have served the organization. Awarded annually. Established in 1976.

• 17050 • Supreme Champion
To recognize outstanding Palomino horses. The title of PHBA Supreme Champion is awarded to any stallion, mare, or gelding registered with PHBA, providing the horse has earned a minimum of 150 points in halter, color, and performance classes at PHBA approved shows. A trophy is awarded at PHBA convention. Established in 1968.

• 17051 • Youth World Championship Horse Show Golden Horse
To recognize outstanding youth exhibitors and their Palomino horses. Young people come from all over the United States to compete for individual and team awards. The show awards multiple sets of national points and is a non-qualifying show. A saddle is awarded for first place and a belt buckle for second place. Established in 1972. In addition, the PHBA awards the following youth awards: PHBA Youth Honor Roll, PHBA Youth Register of Merit, PHBA Youth Champion, PHBA Youth Supreme Champion, and PHBA Top Ten Overall Youth. Formerly: PHBA National Youth Congress Horse Show High Point Youth.

• 17052 •
Pan-American Association of Ophthalmology
Teresa J. Bradshaw, Administrator
1301 S Bowen Rd., Ste. 365
Arlington, TX 76013
Phone: (817)275-7553
Fax: (817)275-3961
E-mail: info@paao.org
Home Page: http://www.paao.org

• 17053 • Benjamin F. Boyd Humanitarian Award
For ophthalmological service and blindness prevention activities. Awarded biennially.

• 17054 •
Pan American Development Foundation
John Sanbrailo, Exec.Dir.
2600 16th St. NW, 4th Fl.
Washington, DC 20009-4204
Phone: (202)458-3969
Fax: (202)458-6316
E-mail: padf-dc@padf.org
Home Page: http://www.padf.org

• 17055 • Leadership Award
Recognizes outstanding work by heads of state of OAS member nations. Awarded annually.

• 17056 •
Pan American Health and Education Foundation
Ms. Jess Gersky, Exec.Dir.
525 23rd St. NW
Washington, DC 20037
Phone: (202)974-3416
Fax: (202)974-3636
E-mail: info@pahef.org
Home Page: http://www.paho.org/foundation

• 17057 • Pedro N. Acha Award for Veterinary Public Health
To recognize outstanding research based on a thesis written by an undergraduate student in veterinary public health within the last three years, and to encourage dedication to the highest standards of study and professionalism. The research thesis should cover zoonoses, food protection, animal health and production, development of biomedical models, animal husbandry, biology, food animal technology, or environmental protection related to livestock or other domesticated animals. Nominations must be received by April 25. A monetary prize of $1,500 and a certificate are awarded annually. Established in 1990 in memory of Pedro Acha, long-time chief of the Pan American Health Organization's veterinary public health program.

• 17058 • Abraham Horwitz Award for Leadership in Inter-American Health
To honor creative public health leaders whose commitment to public health stimulates excellence among their peers, staff, and other public health professionals throughout the Americas. Nominees must be individuals whose professional achievement in any field of inter-American health stimulates excellence, and has impacted the health of populations across the borders of the Americas. A monetary prize of $5,000, a certificate, and a paid trip to attend the PAHO annual meeting in Washington DC are awarded annually. Established in 1975 by colleagues and friends of Dr. Abraham Horwitz, Director Emeritus of PAHO.

• 17059 • Clarence H. Moore Award for Voluntary Service
To recognize the benefits that the voluntary/nongovernmental sector contributes to the public health mission and to improving the lives of the peoples of the Americas. Nominees may be national or local non-governmental or private organizations operating in Latin America or the Caribbean. Nominations must be received by August 15. A monetary prize of $2,500 and a certificate are awarded annually. Established in 1988 in memory of Clarence H. Moore, a distinguished PAHO executive and executive secretary of PAHEF for over 20 years.

• 17060 • Fred L. Soper Award for Excellence in Health Literature
To encourage significant contributions to the literature on infectious diseases and other health problems in Latin America and the Caribbean. The award is limited to contributions by authors whose principal affiliation is with teaching, research, or service institutions located in the countries of Latin America and the Caribbean. Only articles published in scientific journals listed in the Index Medicus or in official PAHO journals are eligible for consideration. A monetary award of $2,500 and a certificate are awarded annually. Established in 1989 in memory of Dr. Fred Soper, Director of the Pan American Sanitary Bureau from 1947-1959.

• 17061 •
Pantone Color Institute
Leatrice Eiseman, Exec.Dir.
590 Commerce Blvd.
Carlstadt, NJ 07072-3098
Phone: (201)935-5500
Fax: (201)935-3338
Home Page: http://www.pantone.com/colorinstitute/consultation.html

• 17062 • Pantone Color Award
For innovative use of color by emerging designers in the areas of fashion, industrial, interior, and graphic design. Individuals must have been in the design industry for a minimum of three years, establishing themselves within a legitimate commercial enterprise, not merely an artistic endeavor. Submission must have been produced prior to December 31 of the preceding year. The design must be available in the United States. A trophy and a monetary award of $1,000 contributed to the design school or charity of choice are awarded annually in the autumn. Established in 1988.

• 17063 •
Paperboard Packaging Council
Jerome T. Van de Water, Pres.
201 N Union St., Ste. 220
Alexandria, VA 22314
Phone: (703)836-3300
Fax: (703)836-3290
E-mail: paperboardpackaging@ppcnet.org
Home Page: http://www.ppcnet.org

• 17064 • National Paperboard Packaging Competition
To recognize excellence achieved by the producers of the various packages. Entries are judged in 30 different categories against three criteria: members' internal production/converting excellence; consumer product company excellence; and end-user/retailer consumer excellence. Entries are also considered for technical achievement and innovation, craftsmanship, and overall appearance. Submissions must be received by December 16. The President's, Innovation, Gold, and Excellence Awards are presented at the Spring Meeting each year. Established in 1943.

• 17065 •
Parade
Lamar Graham, Gen.Mgr.
711 3rd Ave.
New York, NY 10017
Phone: (212)450-7000
Fax: (212)450-7284
E-mail: editor@parade.com
Home Page: http://www.parade.com

• 17066 • *Parade*/Kodak Photography Contest
To recognize outstanding photographs. Winners are selected on the basis of pictorial composition, originality, interest of subject matter, visual appeal and consistency with the contest theme. One hundred winning photographs are selected

for a permanent exhibit. Formerly: Young America Photography Contest.

• 17067 •
Paralyzed Veterans of America
Delatorro L. McNeal, Exec.Dir.
801 18th St. NW
Washington, DC 20006-3517
Phone: (202)872-1300
Toll-Free: 800-424-8200
Fax: (202)785-4452
E-mail: info@pva.org
Home Page: http://www.pva.org

• 17068 • **Patriot Award**
To recognize individuals and/or organizations that provide significant financial contribution toward advancing the missions and goals of PVA. Nomination deadline is June 1. A plaque is awarded annually at the Convention. Established in 1989. Formerly: PVA Donor Recognition Award.

• 17069 • **President Award**
No further information was provided for this edition.

• 17070 • **John M. Price Chapter Award**
No further information was provided for this edition.

• 17071 • **Harry A. Schweikert, Jr. Disability Awareness Award**
To recognize an individual or organization who, through their individual or collective efforts, increased the positive awareness of society to the needs and contributions of the disabled. Individuals or organizations must be nominated by PVA Chapters before April 1. A plaque is awarded. Established in 1977 to honor Harry A. Schweikert, Jr. Formerly: (1982) Disability Awareness Award.

• 17072 • **Speedy Award**
To recognize outstanding accomplishments of both members and non-members in the field of paraplegia. Nominations may be made by Chapters or individual members by April 1. A cast bronze shield on a walnut plaque is awarded annually at the national convention to a paraplegic and a non-paraplegic winner. Established in 1956.

• 17073 • **Sports and Recreation Award**
For recognition of outstanding chapters. A plaque is awarded annually. Established in 1988.

• 17074 • **Dwain Taylor Award for Voluntary Service**
To recognize the individual who has volunteered the highest number of hours for chapter programs that directly benefit members. All chapter volunteer records/reports are eligible for review. The deadline is September 30. A plaque is awarded annually at the mid-winter Board meeting. Established in 1981 in honor of Dwain Taylor.

• 17075 •
Parapsychology Institute of America
Roxanne S. Kaplan, Exec.Dir.
PO Box 5442
Babylon, NY 11707
Phone: (631)321-9362
Phone: (631)981-4270
Fax: (631)321-9362
E-mail: piavrc@go.com

• 17076 • **Award Certificates**
To recognize individuals who have made positive contributions to the field of parapsychology. Special award certificates are also presented to individuals who help expose false research and reports within the field of parapsychology. In addition, appreciation certificates are awarded to individuals who give evidence on the debunking CSICOP type. Established in 1991.

• 17077 • **Parapsychology Hall of Fame**
To recognize contributions to the field of parapsychology and to encourage professional development and pioneering work in the field of parapsychology. Teachers and researchers who participate in the field of parapsychology are eligible. Awarded annually. Established in 1977.

• 17078 •
Parent Cooperative Preschools International
Leta Mach, Pres.
1401 New York Ave. NW, Ste. 1100
Natl. Cooperative Business Ctr.
Washington, DC 20005-2102
Toll-Free: 800-636-6222
E-mail: inquiries@preschools.coop
Home Page: http://www.preschools.coop

• 17079 • **District Award**
To recognize outstanding service to the parent cooperative movement on a local, regional, and district level. Criteria include: effective leadership; dedicated cooperation with parents and teachers; tangible benefits to children; and dedicated commitment to the well-being of the local parent cooperative or council. Both the nominee and sponsor must be members of PCPI. Certificates are awarded annually. Established in 1965.

• 17080 • **Honorary Life Membership**
To recognize and individual for exceptional contribution to, or unique involvement in, the parent cooperative movement. The award is not based on years of service nor considered as part of an automatic progression to a higher award. The nominee need not be a member of PCPI, but the sponsor must. A certificate is awarded when merited. Established in 1965.

• 17081 • **International Award**
To recognize an individual for outstanding contributions to the parent co-operative movement on an international level. The nominee need not be a member of PCPI, but the sponsor must. Awarded annually. Established in 1972.

• 17082 • **National Award for Demonstrated Leadership**
To recognize an individual for demonstrated activity that has had a favorable impact on parent cooperatives at more than a local, Council, or regional level. This may include, but not be limited to, serving on the PCPI Board of Directors, liaison with other related national organizations, original research, writing or editorial work, or any unique contribution to the parent cooperative movement. Both nominee and sponsor must be members of PCPI. Certificates are awarded annually. Established in 1965.

• 17083 •
Parents' Choice Foundation
Claire S. Green, Contact
201 W Padonia Rd., Ste. 303
Timonium, MD 21093
Phone: (410)308-3858
Fax: (410)308-3877
E-mail: info@parents-choice.org
Home Page: http://www.parents-choice.org

• 17084 • ***Parents' Choice* Awards**
To identify choice materials for children of all ages and of diverse skills, backgrounds, and interests. Product categories include: audio recordings, books, toys, software, magazines, television programs, home videos, DVDs, and video games. Four award levels are presented each year: Gold Awards, Silver Honors, Recommended, and Approved, as well as the *Parents' Choice* Classic Award to products that have met the criteria of Gold Award for at least five years, and the *Parents' Choice* FunStuff Award for products that are well produced and enjoyable, yet not educational. Awarded annually. Established in 1980.

• 17085 •
Parents Without Partners
Ms. Kay Brewer, Intl. Website Liaison
1650 S Dixie Hwy., Ste. 510
Boca Raton, FL 33432
Phone: (561)391-8833
Toll-Free: 800-637-7974
Fax: (561)395-8557
E-mail: pwp@jti.net
Home Page: http://www.parentswithoutpartners.org
Formerly: Parents Without Partners.

• 17086 • **Annual Awards for Chapter Programming**
To recognize the presentation of an outstanding and balanced selection of programs and activities for the benefit of the membership, and for genuine efforts to serve the community. Special attention is paid to the attitude of the chapter in functioning as an educational and supportive organization. Local chapters are eligible. Many awards are presented annually based on membership size.

• 17087 • Distinguished Service to Children Award
To recognize the person or group considered to have made the greatest contribution to the welfare of children the world over. The following concerns are recognized: the contribution to the health, happiness, and well being of children; the extent of the influence of these efforts on children; and whether these efforts are non-discriminatory. A plaque and expenses to attend the International PWP Convention are awarded annually. Established in 1964.

• 17088 • Family International Talent Awards Program
To encourage and promote the cultural interests of PWP members, both adults and children. Members may display their talents in the competition in the area of arts, crafts, creative writing, science, and photography. Only amateurs are eligible. First, second, third, and fourth place certificates are awarded. Formerly: International Adult Talent Awards; International Youth Exhibit Awards.

• 17089 • Public Relations Awards
To recognize outstanding accomplishments in newsletters and publicity. Awards are given in the following divisions: Most Outstanding Chapter Newsletter, Most Outstanding Regional Council Newsletters, Most Outstanding Year - Long Program, and Most Outstanding Special - Event Program. Awards are presented in each division, corresponding with the size of the local chapters. Certificates are awarded annually at the International Convention of PWP.

• 17090 • Single Parent of the Year Award
To honor the PWP member who most typifies the single parent, with regard to fulfillment of responsibility to his or her child(ren), to his or her new life, to home, work, family, and community, as well as approach to the future; and to demonstrate appreciation and recognition of the difficulties involved in raising children in a one-parent family. Single parents with at least one child, without regard to sex or age, are eligible. An inscribed plaque and expenses to the International PWP Convention for the winner and children are awarded annually. Established in 1966.

• 17091 • Youth of the Year
To recognize youth who embody the aims and purposes of PWP concerning family, school, and community involvement. Children of members are eligible. A plaque and expenses to the international convention are awarded annually. Established in 1965.

• 17092 •
The Paris Review
62 White St.
New York, NY 10013
E-mail: foundation@theparisreview.org
Home Page: http://www.parisreview.com

• 17093 • Bernard F. Conners Prize for Poetry
To recognize the finest poem over 200 lines published in *The 1Paris Review* that year. A monetary prize of $1,000 is awarded annually.

• 17094 • Aga Khan Prize for Fiction
To recognize the author of the best short story published in *The Paris Review* that year. Manuscripts between 1,000 and 10,000 words may be submitted. A monetary prize of $1,000 is awarded annually. Established in 1955 by Prince Aga Khan.

• 17095 • Plimpton Prize
To recognize the best work of fiction or poetry published in *The Paris Review* that year by an emerging or previously unpublished writer. A monetary prize of $5,000 is awarded annually. Named in honor of the *Review*'s longtime editor, George Plimpton. Formerly: (2003) Discovery Prize.

• 17096 •
Parkinson's Disease Foundation
Dr. Lewis P. Rowland, Pres.
710 W 168th St.
3rd Fl.
New York, NY 10032
Phone: (212)923-4700
Toll-Free: 800-457-6676
Fax: (212)923-4778
E-mail: info@pdf.org
Home Page: http://www.pdf.org

• 17097 • Donna and Sidney Dorros Award
To recognize a Parkinson Disease support group that has an outstanding program. A support group that is truly self-help and not run by a health care professional receives a monetary award of $500. An outstanding program run by a professional is also recognized with a Certificate of Merit. Applications are accepted. Established in 1988 for recognition of Donna and Sidney Dorros' contributions to the self-help movement.

• 17098 •
Passaic River Coalition
Ella F. Filippone, Exec.Admin.
246 Madisonville Rd.
Basking Ridge, NJ 07920
Phone: (908)766-7550
Fax: (908)766-7550
E-mail: prc@passaicriver.org
Home Page: http://passaicriver.org

• 17099 • Award of Achievement
For outstanding contribution to the improvement of the Passaic River Watershed. Recognition award bestowed annually.

• 17100 •
The Passano Foundation
1122 Kenilworth Dr., Ste. 115
Baltimore, MD 21204
Phone: (410)825-0994
Fax: (410)825-0997
E-mail: passanofoundation@verizon.net
Home Page: http://passanofoundation.com

• 17101 • Passano Foundation Award
For recognition of a research physician who has made an exceptional contribution to the advancement of medical science. Prime consideration is given to work that has immediate clinical value or gives promise of practical application in the near future. Nomination deadline is November 30. A monetary prize of at least $25,000 is awarded annually. Established in 1943.

• 17102 •
Pastel Society of America
Barbara Fischman, Pres.
15 Gramercy Park S
New York, NY 10003
Phone: (212)533-6931
Fax: (212)353-8140
E-mail: pastelny@juno.com
Home Page: http://www.pastelsocietyofamerica.org

• 17103 • Annual Open Juried Exhibition
To recognize excellence achieved by pastel artists. Subjects include landscape, still-life, and portrait in various techniques. Awards totaling more than $20,000 are presented annually, including the Dianne B. Bernhard Gold Medal Award ($2,000); Andrew Giffuni Memorial Award ($1,000); and Dick Blick Art Materials Award ($2,995). Scholarships are also awarded. Held each September at the National Arts Club in New York City. Established in 1973 by Flora B. Giffuni.

• 17104 • Hall of Fame
To honor an outstanding artist for special achievement in pastel painting. The honoree's paintings are exhibited during the annual exhibition. Awarded to one recipient annually. Established in 1978.

• 17105 • Master Pastelist
To recognize individuals who win three or more awards in the Annual Open Juried Exhibition. Awarded to one or more recipients each September.

• 17106 • Signature Membership
To recognize individuals for outstanding work in pastel art. These select members may use "PSA" after their signature, and are entitled to other membership benefits. They are the premier members of the Society, and their membership dues are $60 per year. Bestowed by the Jury of Admissions when merited.

Awards are arranged in alphabetical order below their administering organizations

• 17107 •
Patriotic Order Sons of America
John B. Helms, Contact
PO Box 1847
Valley Forge, PA 19482
Phone: (610)783-0626
Fax: (610)783-0626

• 17108 • **American Citizenship Award**
For recognition of outstanding endeavors relating to patriotic activities toward America. A plaque is awarded annually. Established in 1977.

• 17109 • **Eagle Award**
For recognition of excellence in an educational endeavor that reflects a patriotic spirit. The award may be given to a school principal, superintendent, or teacher nominated from public schools, pre-school grades through 12th grade. Established in 1960.

• 17110 • **Open Bible Award**
For recognition of a sermon or art effort indicating how patriotism may be integrated and correlated with school, church, and personal lives. Established in 1960.

• 17111 • **Patriot's Award**
To recognize an individual for patriotic activity that impresses youth with the importance of loyalty to good causes. Established in 1960.

• 17112 • **Shield Award**
For recognition of outstanding civic leadership. Contributions may be through journalism, publicly distributed letters, an advertisement, witnessed activity, or a special communication effort in which civic leadership is evidenced. Established in 1960.

• 17113 •
PC World Communications Inc.
Harry McCracken, Editor-in-Chief
501 2nd St.
San Francisco, CA 94107
Phone: (415)243-0500
Fax: (415)442-1891
Home Page: http://www.pcworld.com

• 17114 • **Andrew Fluegelman Award**
To encourage personal computer software excellence and to recognize a software programmer or team of programmers. Innovative contributions by individuals to the personal computer community in commercial, shareware, or public-domain software including utilities, applications, and languages, are considered. Only individuals, not companies, may be nominated. A monetary award of $5,000 and a marble plaque are awarded at the annual Software Publishers Association Awards Dinner. Established in 1986 to honor Andrew Fluegelman. Sponsored by the Software Publishers Association.

• 17115 • **Macworld Editors' Choice Awards**
To recognize the best hardware, software, and computer services for Macintosh computers. Editors nominated products that they reviewed during the year, and selected winners in several categories, including Hardware of the Year, Digital Music Products of the Year, Design and Video Products of the Year, Productivity Applications and Games of the Year, Photo Products of the Year, and Reader Awards. Each year, the recipients are featured in the December issue of *Macworld* magazine. Established in 1985.

• 17116 • **PC World World Class Awards**
To recognize the best hardware, software, and computer services for personal computers. Criteria include design, features, performance, innovation, and price. Each year, the recipients, also known as the "100 Best Products," are ranked in the July issue of *PC World* magazine. Established in 1983.

• 17117 •
PCIA - The Wireless Infrastructure Association
Michael T.N. Fitch, Pres./CEO
500 Montgomery St., Ste. 700
Alexandria, VA 22314-1560
Phone: (703)739-0300
Toll-Free: 800-759-0300
Fax: (703)836-1608
E-mail: dentonj@pcia.com
Home Page: http://www.pcia.com

Formerly: (2003) Personal Communications Industry Association.

• 17118 • **Eugene C. Bowler Award**
No further information was provided for this edition.

• 17119 • **Industry Awards Program**
No further information was provided for this edition.

• 17120 • **Marketing Awards**
To recognize outstanding marketing efforts in the radio paging and cellular communications industries. Members are eligible for consideration by a deadline in August. A plaque is awarded annually. Established in 1979.

• 17121 • **Marketing Awards Program**
No further information was provided for this edition.

• 17122 •
Peabody Institute of Johns Hopkins University
Peter Landgren, Interim Dir.
1 E Mt. Vernon Pl.
Baltimore, MD 21202-2397
Phone: (410)659-8100
Fax: (410)659-8129
Home Page: http://www.peabody.jhu.edu

Formerly: (1977) The Peabody Institute of the City of Baltimore.

• 17123 • **George Peabody Medal**
For recognition of outstanding contributions to music in America. Contributions to music may be considered in one of the following areas: performance, composition, philanthropy, and musicology. A bronze medal is awarded annually at the Peabody Conservatory May Graduation Exercises. Established in 1980. Sponsored by the Peabody Conservatory of Music.

• 17124 •
Peace and Freedom Party
Paul Kangas, Contact
PO Box 24764
Oakland, CA 94623
Phone: (510)465-9414
Fax: (415)864-3389
E-mail: what_is@peaceandfreedom.org
Home Page: http://www.peaceandfreedom.org

• 17125 • **Emile Zola Award for Journalism**
To recognize journalists who do the most to expose secret news stories concerning: (1) Auto Urine Therapy for Curing Cancer & AIDS; (2) Vitamin C and Linus Pauling and Jay Patrick; (3) the Role of Selenium in stopping heart disease, breast cancer, and AIDS; (4) the John F. Kennedy assassination; Watergate co-conspirators; King assassination and role of U.S. Army; Robert F. Kennedy, etc. Awarded annually with a plaque. Established in 1991.

• 17126 •
Peace History Society
Mitchell K. Hall, Pres.
Dept. of History
Berry Coll.
5010 Mt. Berry Sta.
Mount Berry, GA 30149
Phone: (706)368-5652
E-mail: csnider@berry.edu
Home Page: http://www.berry.edu/phs

Formerly: Council on Peace Research in History.

• 17127 • **Charles DeBenedetti Prize in Peace History**
To recognize the author or authors of an outstanding article published in English. Articles reflecting new, cutting-edge research appearing either in edited works or journals may focus on the history of peace movements, the response of individuals to peace and war issues, the relationship between peace and other reform movements, gender issues in warfare and peacemaking, comparative analyses, and quantitative studies. The prize includes a cash award of $500. Awarded biennially in even-numbered years. Established in 1986.

• 17128 •
Pearl S. Buck International
Janet Mintzer, Pres./CEO
520 Dublin Rd.
Perkasie, PA 18944
Phone: (215)249-0100
Toll-Free: 800-220-BUCK
Fax: (215)249-9657
E-mail: info@pearl-s-buck.org
Home Page: http://www.pearlsbuck.org

• 17129 • **Pearl S. Buck International Woman of the Year Award**
Honors women who have distinguished themselves through their devotion to professional excellence, involvement and balance in their family lives, and compassion for those around them-whether in their immediate communities or around the world. These women embody the values Pearl Buck lived and promoted through her long influential life. The Woman of the Year Award was conceived in 1978 as a means to recognize the great literary and humanitarian contributions of Pearl S. Buck. Recipients have come from the surrounding community in eastern Pennsylvania, and from halfway around the world. They include activists and actresses, presidents and politicians, scholars and singers. PSBI Woman of the Year Award recipients are chosen in the Spring or Summer of each year. Nominees are accepted by the Board of Directors at any time.

• 17130 •
William T. Pecora Award Committee
U.S. Department of the Interior
Office of Personnel
MS-5203, MIB
Washington, DC 20240
Phone: (202)208-5284
E-mail: lpettinger@usgs.gov

Formerly: (1997) United States Department of Interior.

• 17131 • **William T. Pecora Award**
For recognition of outstanding contributions of individuals or groups toward the understanding of the earth by means of remote sensing. The award recognizes contributions of those in the scientific and technical community as well as those involved in the practical application of remote sensing. Consideration is given to sustained or single contributions of major importance to the art or science of the understanding of the earth through observations made from space. Individuals or groups working in the field of remote sensing of the Earth are eligible to apply. Individual award recognizes scientific and technical remote sensing community achievements and applications leading to related practical application development. Group award recognizes an organization or part of an organization that made major breakthroughs in remote sensing science or technology. The award is cosponsored by the Department of the Interior and the National Aeronautics and Space Administration. The award consists of a citation and a plaque. Established in 1974 in memory of Dr. William T. Pecora, former Director of the U.S. Geological Survey and later, Under Secretary of the Department of the Interior. Nominations may be made by an individual, organization, or professional society. A brief written statement in support of the nomination should be prepared using the format on the back of the application brochure (available on request). Actual deadline date varies annually, inquire for exact date.

• 17132 •
Pedal Steel Guitar Association
Bob Maickel, Pres.
PO Box 20248
Floral Park, NY 11002-0248
Phone: (516)616-9214
Fax: (516)616-9214
E-mail: bobpsga@optonline.net
Home Page: http://www.psga.org

• 17133 • **Appreciation Award**
For recognition of significant contributions to the art of playing the musical instrument known as the steel guitar. Nominations are by the membership of PSGA, and are confirmed by the nominating committee. A plaque is awarded annually. Established in 1974.

• 17134 •
Peerless Rockville Historic Preservation
Ms. Eileen McGuckian, Exec.Dir.
PO Box 4262
Rockville, MD 20849-4262
Phone: (301)762-0096
Fax: (301)762-0961
E-mail: info@peerlessrockville.org
Home Page: http://peerlessrockville.org

• 17135 • **Historic Preservation Award**
For excellence in restoration, compatible new construction, preservation. Recognition award bestowed annually.

• 17136 •
Pemiscot County Historical Society
Mary Belle Poteet, Contact
PO Box 604
Caruthersville, MO 63830

• 17137 • **Pioneer Heritage Award**
For individuals more than 75 years of age. Recognition award bestowed annually.

• 17138 •
PEN American Center
Michael Roberts, Exec.Dir.
588 Broadway
New York, NY 10012
Phone: (212)334-1660
Fax: (212)334-2181
E-mail: pen@pen.org
Home Page: http://www.pen.org

• 17139 • **PEN/Martha Albrand Award for First Nonfiction**
To recognize a first-published book of nonfiction by an American writer, distinguished by qualities of literary excellence. Authors must be American citizens or permanent residents. Publishers may submit books published in the calendar year under consideration by December 15. A monetary award of $1,000 is presented annually. Established in 1988.

• 17140 • **PEN/Martha Albrand Award for the Art of the Memoir**
To recognize an American author for his or her first published memoir, distinguished by qualities of literary and stylistic excellence. Authors must submit three copies of each eligible book which have been published in the current calendar year. Books submitted for this prize may not be submitted for the PEN/Martha Albrand Award for First Nonfiction. A monetary prize of $1,000 is awarded annually. Established in 1997.

• 17141 • **Gregory Kolovakos Award**
To recognize an American literary translator, editor, or critic whose work, in meeting the challenge of cultural difference, extends Gregory Kolovakos's commitment to the richness of Hispanic literature and to expanding its English-language audience. The award's primary purpose is to recognize works in Spanish, but distinguished contributions from the other languages of the Hispanic world are also considered. Nomination deadline is January 15. A $2,000 prize is awarded triennially. Established in 1992.

• 17142 • **PEN/Ralph Manheim Medal for Translation**
To recognize translators whose career has demonstrated an exceptional commitment to excellence through the body of their work. The PEN Translation Committee nominates the candidates. A medal is awarded triennially. Established in 1983.

• 17143 • **PEN/Phyllis Naylor Working Writer Fellowship**
Recognizes the fact that many writers' work is of high literary caliber but has not yet attracted a broad readership. Candidates must a writers of children or young adult fiction in financial need who has published at least two books, and no more than five, during the past ten years. Writers must be nominated by an editor or fellow writer. Application deadline is January 17. $5000 is offered annually. Established in 2001.

• 17144 • **PEN/Joyce Osterweil Award for Poetry**
Recognizes the high literary character of the published work to date of a new and emerging American poet of any age and the promise of further literary achievement. Poets nominated for the award may not have published more than one book of poetry. Nominations are accepted from PEN members only and should include one to two pages letter describing the literary character of the candidate's work, and summary of the candidate's publications to date. Emphasis should be placed on the degree of promise which the nominated poet's work indicates. Application deadline is January 7. $5000 is given in odd-numbered years and alternates with the PEN/Vocelcker Award for Poetry.

• 17145 • PEN/Laura Pels Foundation Awards for Drama
To honor two American playwrights. A medal will be presented to a master dramatist in recognition of his or her body of work, and a cash prize of $5,000 will be awarded to a playwright in mid-career whose literary achievements are apparent in the rich and striking language of his or her work. Letters of nomination and a list of the candidate's produced work must be received by January 7. Awarded annually. Established in 1998.

• 17146 • PEN Book-of-the-Month Club Translation Prize
For recognition of the best book-length translation into English of a work of prose, fiction, nonfiction, or poetry published in the United States during the previous calendar year. Technical, scientific, and reference books are not eligible. Publishers, agents, and authors may submit entries by December 15. A monetary prize of $3,000 is awarded annually in May. Established in 1963 and sponsored by the Book of the Month Club.

• 17147 • PEN/Jerard Fund Award
To recognize a work in progress of general nonfiction distinguished by high literary quality by a woman at the midpoint in her career. Applicants must have published at least one article in a national publication or a major literary magazine but must not have published more than one book in any field. Applicants should submit five copies of no more than 50 pages of an English-language, book-length nonfiction work-in-progress accompanied by a personal bibliography. Entry deadline is January 17. A monetary prize of $5,500 is awarded biennially in odd-numbered years. Established in 1987 in cooperation with the New York Community Trust.

• 17148 • PEN Prison Writing Awards
To recognize the best poetry, fiction, drama, and nonfiction received from prisoner-writers incarcerated in U.S. federal, state, or country prison. The deadline is September 1. Monetary prizes of $200 for first place, $100 for second, and $50 for third are awarded annually, and the pieces are published by the Fortune Society in *Fortune News*.

• 17149 • PEN Publisher Award
For recognition of publishers who have, throughout their careers, given distinctive and continuous service to international letters, to the freedom and dignity of writers, and to the free transmission of the printed word across the barriers of poverty, ignorance, censorship, and repression. The PEN Executive Board nominates the candidates. A citation is awarded periodically. Established in 1976.

• 17150 • PEN/Voelcker Award for Poetry
To recognize an American poet whose distinguished and growing body of work to date represents a notable and accomplished presence in American literature. A stipend of $5,000 is awarded biennially in even-numbered years. The deadline for nominations is January 1. Established in 1994 by a bequest from Hunce Voelcker.

• 17151 •
PEN Center U.S.A.
Adam Somers, Exec.Dir.
400 Corporate Pointe
Culver city, CA 90230
Phone: (310)862-1555
Fax: (310)862-1556
E-mail: pen@penusa.org
Home Page: http://penusa.org/go/home

• 17152 • Literary Awards
To recognize literary excellence in work produced or published by writers living west of the Mississippi River. Awards are presented in ten categories: fiction, creative nonfiction, research nonfiction, poetry, children⁄s literature, translation, journalism, drama, teleplay, and screenplay. Winners receive $1,000 cash prizes and are honored at the annual Literary Awards Festival in October in Los Angeles. Established in 1982.

• 17153 •
PEN/Faulkner Foundation
201 E Capitol St. SE
Washington, DC 20003
Phone: (202)675-0345
Fax: (202)608-1719
E-mail: penfaulkner@folger.edu
Home Page: http://www.penfaulkner.org

• 17154 • PEN/Faulkner Award for Fiction
To honor the best work of fiction published by an American writer in a calendar year. The deadline for submitting four copies of the published book is December 31. A monetary prize of $15,000 is awarded to the winner, and $5,000 to each of four other finalists. Awarded annually. Established in 1980.

• 17155 • PEN/Malamud Memorial Award
To recognize an individual for excellence in the art of short story writing. A monetary award of $1,000 is presented annually. This is a non-juried award given to an individual at the discretion of the foundation. Established in 1988 by the family of the late Bernard Malamud.

• 17156 •
PEN New England
Karen Wulf, Exec.Dir.
Emerson College
120 Boylston St.
Boston, MA 02116
Phone: (617)824-8820
Fax: (617)353-7134
E-mail: pen_ne@emerson.edu
Home Page: http://www.pen-ne.org

• 17157 • Hemingway Foundation/PEN Award
To recognize distinguished novels or books of short stories by an American author who has not previously published a book of fiction. Works written in English, excluding children's books, by an American author that were published in the calendar year of the award are eligible. The deadline is December 9. A monetary prize of $8,000 is awarded annually. Established in 1975 by Mary Hemingway in memory of her husband. Formerly: (1997) Ernest Hemingway Foundation Award.

• 17158 • Laurence L. Winship PEN New England Award
To recognize the author of the year's outstanding book project of New England origin: the book must be about New England or be by a New England Author. Books published in the calendar year of the award year may be submitted by the publishing company, agent, or author. The deadline is December 15th. A monetary prize of $3,000 is awarded annually. Established in 1975 in memory of Laurence L. Winship, the late editor of the *Boston Globe.*. Send a SASE to the above address for guidelines and an application form or download it from the above website.

• 17159 •
Pendleton District Historical, Recreational, and Tourism Commission
Donna K. Roper, Curator
125 E. Queen St.
PO Box 565
Pendleton, SC 29670
Phone: (864)646-3782
Toll-Free: 800-862-1795
Fax: (864)646-2506
E-mail: pendletontourism@bellsouth.net
Home Page: http://www.pendleton-district.org

• 17160 • Chairman's Award
For service to history/tourism of the tri-county area. Recognition award bestowed annually.

• 17161 •
Pennsylvania Association of Community Bankers
Frank A. Pinto, Pres./CEO
2405 N Front St.
PO Box 5319
Harrisburg, PA 17110
Phone: (717)231-7447
Toll-Free: 800-443-5076
Fax: (717)231-7445
E-mail: fap@pacb.org
Home Page: http://www.pacb.org

• 17162 • Community Service Awards
For members by asset size category who show an interest and commitment in reaching out to their respective communities. Recognition award bestowed annually.

• 17163 •
Pennsylvania Association of Environmental Professionals
PO Box 7602
Mechanicsburg, PA 17050
E-mail: paep@earthlink.net
Home Page: http://www.paep.org

• 17164 • Karl Mason Award
To recognize individuals or organizations for achievements in environmental protection in Pennsylvania. Professionals employed in the environmental field (administrative, management, technical) who are residents of Pennsylvania are eligible. The deadline for nominations is August 15. A trophy is awarded annually. Established in 1970 by the Pennsylvania Department of Health in memory of Karl Mason, Pennsylvania's first environmental administrator.

• 17165 •
Pennsylvania Association of Private School Administrators
Cynthia Reynolds, Contact
2090 Wexford Ct.
Harrisburg, PA 17112
Phone: (717)540-9010
Fax: (717)540-7121
E-mail: reynolds@pti-tec.com
Home Page: http://www.papsa.org

• 17166 • Outstanding Teacher Award
For evaluations students, peers, administrator. Grant awarded annually.

• 17167 •
Pennsylvania Council on the Arts
Philip Horn, Exec.Dir.
216 Finance Bldg.
Harrisburg, PA 17120
Phone: (717)787-6883
Fax: (717)783-2538
E-mail: keswartz@state.pa.us
Home Page: http://www.pacouncilonthearts.org

• 17168 • Fellowship Program
To support the work of Pennsylvania's creative artists. Pennsylvania artists who have had residency for 24 months are eligible to apply for support. Grants are awarded on a competitive basis based on the quality of work in the following arts disciplines: crafts, dance, folk and traditional arts, interdisciplinary arts, literature, media arts, music, theater, and visual arts. Fellowships are not offered in every discipline each year. Awards of $5,000 or $10,000 are awarded each year.

• 17169 •
Pennsylvania Cystic Fibrosis
Robert C. Derr, Sec.
PO Box 29
Mifflinburg, PA 17844
Phone: (570)374-2568
Phone: (570)966-2247
Toll-Free: 800-900-2790
Fax: (570)374-2612
E-mail: bobderr@sunlink.net
Home Page: http://www.pacfi.org

• 17170 • Nutritional Research Award
For most hopeful research as determined by board of directors. Monetary award bestowed annually.

• 17171 •
Pennsylvania Education of Children in the Arts Network
PO Box 99
Grantville, PA 17028-9142
Phone: (717)469-7517
Fax: (717)469-0537
E-mail: snolt@mindspring.com
Home Page: http://www.pecaninc.net

• 17172 • Allegro Award
For individual working with youth in the arts. Recognition award bestowed annually.

• 17173 • Crescendo Award
For individual working with youth in the arts. Recognition award bestowed annually.

• 17174 •
Pennsylvania Elks State Association
Paul Stanko, Office Mgr.
PO Box 1255
Somerset, PA 15501-1255
Phone: (814)444-1954
Fax: (814)444-1495
E-mail: paelks@wpia.net

• 17175 • State Allocated Scholarship Award
For scholastic and financial need. Scholarship awarded annually.

• 17176 •
Pennsylvania Library Association
220 Cumberland Pky., Ste. 10
Mechanicsburg, PA 17055
Phone: (717)766-7663
Toll-Free: 800-622-3308
Fax: (717)766-5440
E-mail: glenn@palibraries.org
Home Page: http://www.palibraries.org

• 17177 • Carolyn W. Field Award
To recognize outstanding children's books by authors and/or illustrators living in Pennsylvania. A medal is awarded annually at the conference. Established in 1983 by the Youth Services Division in honor of Carolyn W. Field, former Director of Children's Services, Free Library of Philadelphia.

• 17178 •
Pennsylvania Manufacturing Confectioners' Association
Mary D. Young, Admin.Dir.
2980 Linden St., Ste. E3
Bethlehem, PA 18017
Phone: (610)625-4655
Fax: (610)625-4657
E-mail: yvette.thomas@pmca.com
Home Page: http://www.pmca.com

• 17179 • Graduate Confectionery Fellowship - Penn State University
For BS in chemistry, biology, or engineering. Scholarship awarded biennially.

• 17180 •
Pennsylvania Music Educators Association
Margaret S. Bauer, Exec.Dir.
56 S Third St.
Hamburg, PA 19526
Phone: (610)562-9757
Toll-Free: 888-919-PMEA
Fax: (610)562-9760
E-mail: msbauer@comcast.net
Home Page: http://www.pmea.net

• 17181 • Irene R. Christman Scholarship
For outstanding graduating senior: music performance and high academic record. Scholarship awarded annually.

• 17182 • School Superintendents of the Year
For support of the arts, music in particular. Recognition award bestowed annually.

• 17183 •
Pennsylvania Newspaper Association
Tim Williams, Pres.
3899 N Front St.
Harrisburg, PA 17110
Phone: (717)703-3000
Fax: (717)703-3001
E-mail: info@pa-news.org
Home Page: http://www.pa-newspaper.org

• 17184 • G. Richard Dew Award
This, the Association's most prestigious honor for outstanding journalism, is given in recognition of an individual or organization that has made an outstanding contribution to the community or to journalism for material that exemplifies an improvement in the quality of community life; enhancement of public understanding of the role of the news media; or journalistic responsiveness to matters of public interest. A plaque is awarded annually in September. Established in 1983 in memory of G.R. Dew, the PNPA general manager from 1956-1980.

• 17185 • Distinguished Writing Award
For recognition of quality writing in the Keystone Press Awards Contest. Individual writers may submit any type of article without regard to circulation category. A plaque is awarded during the Pennsylvania Press Conference. Established in 1986.

• 17186 • Diversity Awards
No further information was available for this edition.

• 17187 • Keystone Press Awards
To recognize newspaper journalism that consistently provides relevance, integrity, and initiative in serving readers, and faithfully fulfills its First Amendment rights and responsibilities. Contestants compete in 20 categories: Editorial, Column, News Story, News Series, Sports Story, Sports Series, Sports Column, Feature Story, Feature Series, Investigative Reporting Series, News Photo, Feature Photo, Family Life/Living Section, Business and Economic News Story,

Awards are arranged in alphabetical order below their administering organizations

Front Page Makeup and Headlines, Photo Story, Sports Photo, Graphic Illustration, Layout/Design, and Health Care Story. The Student Division awards high school and collegiate journalism in 16 categories. Members of PNPA papers are eligible to submit entries by January 28. Plaques are awarded annually. Established in 1948. Co-sponsored by the Pennsylvania Society of Newspaper Editors.

• 17188 • Newspaper of the Year Contest
Recognizes outstanding newspaper work with the emphasis on overall excellence. Any PNA member newspapers in good standing can apply. A plaque will be given to all first and second place winners in each of six categories, and a certificate to honorable mention winners. Deadline is July 1. Awarded annually.

• 17189 •
Pennsylvania School Counselors Association
Dr. Judy Bookhamer, Exec.Dir.
2506 McCarrell St.
McKeesport, PA 15132
Phone: (717)243-6413
Fax: (717)243-6413
E-mail: jbookhamer@comcast.net
Home Page: http://www.psca-web.org

• 17190 • PSCA Graduate Student Scholarship
For graduate student studying counseling. Scholarship awarded annually.

• 17191 •
Pennsylvania School Librarians Association
Mrs. Anita Vance, Pres.
1413 Park Blvd
304 Timber Ridge Rd.
Altoona, PA 16601
Phone: (814)944-9688
Fax: (814)943-1439
E-mail: alv@lion.crsd.k12.pa.us
Home Page: http://www.psla.org

• 17192 • Outstanding Pennsylvania Author or Illustrator
To recognize an author or illustrator who is a present or former Pennsylvania resident, or whose work represents or reflects Pennsylvania, and who has made a notable contribution in the field of literature for youth. Nominee must have had at least two books published, at least one book in print, and must write or illustrate books of interest to children and/or young people up to grade 12. A certificate is awarded annually. Established in 1975.

• 17193 •
Pennsylvania Society for the Prevention of Cruelty to Animals
Erik Hendricks, Exec.Dir.
350 E Erie Ave.
Philadelphia, PA 19134
Phone: (215)426-6300
Phone: (215)426-6555
Fax: (215)425-5848
E-mail: getpspcainfo@aol.com
Home Page: http://www.pspca.org

• 17194 • Leroy J. Ellis Humane Educator of the Year
For best incorporation of kindness ethics in classroom programs. Monetary award bestowed annually.

• 17195 •
Pennsylvania Society of Anesthesiologists
Donald E. Martin MD, Sec.-Treas.
777 E Park Dr.
PO Box 8820
777 E. Park Dr.
PO Box 8820
Harrisburg, PA 17105-8820
Phone: (717)531-6140
Toll-Free: 888-633-5784
Fax: (717)558-7841
E-mail: melias@pamedsoc.org
Home Page: http://www.psanes.org

• 17196 • Distinguished Service Award
For recognition of service to specialty of anesthesiology. Recognition award bestowed annually.

• 17197 •
Pennsylvania Society of Newspaper Editors
Timothy M. Williams, Exec.Dir.
3899 N Front St.
Harrisburg, PA 17110
Phone: (717)703-3000
Phone: (717)703-3071
Fax: (717)703-3001
E-mail: info@pa-news.org
Home Page: http://www.pnpa.com

• 17198 • Keytone Press Awards
For excellence in newspaper journalism. Recognition award bestowed annually.

• 17199 •
Pennsylvania Society of Physician Assistants
PO Box 128
Greensburg, PA 15601-0128
Phone: (724)836-6411
Fax: (724)836-4449
E-mail: pspa@usaor.net

• 17200 • PSPA Student Scholarship
For one senior student from each accredited in-state physician assistant program. Scholarship awarded annually.

• 17201 •
Pennsylvania State Education Association
Carolyn C. Dumaresq, Exec.Dir.
400 N Third St.
PO Box 1724
Harrisburg, PA 17105-1724
Phone: (717)255-7000
Toll-Free: 800-944-7732
Fax: (717)255-7124
E-mail: cdumaresq@psea.org
Home Page: http://www.psea.org

• 17202 • Adler Award
For outstanding service to public education. Recognition award bestowed annually.

• 17203 •
Pennsylvania State Tax Collectors Association
Emiline I. Weiss, Pres.
PO Box 100
Telford, PA 18969
Phone: (215)723-5640
Fax: (215)721-4730
E-mail: emiweiss@hotmail.com

• 17204 • Legislator of the Year
For working towards training, certification to be better elected tax collectors and collection. Recognition award bestowed annually.

• 17205 •
Pennsylvania State University College of Communications
Doug Anderson, Dean
302 James Bldg.
University Park, PA 16801-3897
Phone: (814)865-8801
Fax: (814)863-6134
E-mail: sws102@psu.edu
Home Page: http://www.comm.psu.edu

• 17206 • Bart Richards Award for Media Criticism
To honor work that evaluates news media coverage of significant subjects or issues. Both individuals and media (or other organizations, enterprises, and groups) are eligible, including newspapers, periodicals, and broadcast/cable stations. It is intended to recognize constructively critical articles, books, and electronic media reports; academic and other research; and reports by media ombudsmen and journalism watchdog groups. Submission deadline is January 31. The winner receives $1,000 and is expected to present a lecture at the annual awards ceremony at the National Press Club in Washington DC. Renamed to honor Bart Richards, former editor of the *New Castle (PA) News.* Formerly: (1994) Lowell Mallett Award.

• 17207 •
Pennsylvania State University - Smeal College of Business Administration Institute for the Study of Business Markets
402 Business Administration Bldg.
University Park, PA 16802-3004
Phone: (814)863-2782
Fax: (814)863-0413
E-mail: isbm@psu.edu
Home Page: http://www.smeal.psu.edu/isbm/

• 17208 • **ISBM Business Marketing Doctoral Award Support Completion**
Provides research funding to doctoral students in business-to-business marketing. Awarded annually.

• 17209 •
Pensacola Historical Society
Tom Fitzsimmons, Exec.Dir.
110 E Church St.
Pensacola, FL 32501
Phone: (850)433-1559
Phone: (850)434-5455
Fax: (850)433-1559
E-mail: phstaff@pensacolahistory.org
Home Page: http://www.pensacolahistory.org

• 17210 • **Pensacola Heritage Award**
For contributors to Pensacola history. Recognition award bestowed annually.

• 17211 •
People for Animal Rights
PO Box 15358
Syracuse, NY 13215-0358
Phone: (315)488-7877
E-mail: linpar@acmgfcu.net
Home Page: http://www.geocities.com/parny/

• 17212 • **Humane Award**
For outstanding work for animal or environmental protection. Recognition award bestowed annually.

• 17213 •
People for the Ethical Treatment of Animals
Ingrid E. Newkirk, Pres.
501 Front St.
Norfolk, VA 23510
Phone: (757)622-7382
Fax: (757)622-0457
E-mail: info@peta.org
Home Page: http://www.peta.org

• 17214 • **Humanitarian Award**
To recognize celebrities, media people, members of Congress, and others who have made significant contributions in their field to benefit animals by bringing animal issues into the public eye. A plaque is awarded at a PETA Gala, or other special event. Established in 1987.

• 17215 •
People to People International
Mary Jean Eisenhower, Pres./CEO
501 E Armour Blvd.
Kansas City, MO 64109-2200
Phone: (816)531-4701
Fax: (816)561-7502
E-mail: ptpi@ptpi.org
Home Page: http://www.ptpi.org

• 17216 • **Eisenhower Medallion**
This, the highest honor bestowed by PPI, is given to recognize an individual known on the international level for an exceptional contribution to world peace and understanding over a period of at least five years. No more than one medallion may be given in any one year. Established in 1965.

• 17217 •
People With AIDS Coalition, Houston Chapter
N. Naomi Madrid, Exec.Dir.
3400 Montrose, Ste. 207
Houston, TX 77006
Phone: (713)522-5428
Toll-Free: 800-999-0325
Fax: (713)522-2674
E-mail: info@pwach.org
Home Page: http://www.PWACH.org

• 17218 • **Bill Napoli Award**
For volunteerism. Recognition award bestowed annually.

• 17219 •
Percussive Arts Society
Michael Kenyon, Exec.Dir.
701 NW Ferris Ave.
Lawton, OK 73507-5442
Phone: (580)353-1455
Fax: (580)353-1456
E-mail: percarts@pas.org
Home Page: http://www.pas.org

• 17220 • **Hall of Fame**
To recognize an individual who has influenced the percussion world as evidenced by his/her contributions in any performing excellence, inventions, and/or discoveries. A plaque and life membership in the Society are awarded annually. Established in 1973.

• 17221 •
Perfins Club
Ken Rehfeld, Sec.
PO Box 125
Greenacres, WA 99016-0125
Phone: (509)924-6375
E-mail: krehfeld@inwhealth.net

• 17222 • **Hallock Card Award**
For recognition of outstanding contributions to Perfins philately, the special field of perforated initials and insignia. Members of the Club are eligible. An engraved plaque or cup may be awarded annually. Established in 1967.

• 17223 •
Periodical Writers' Association of Canada
John Degen, Exec.Dir.
215 Spadina Ave., Ste. 123
Toronto, ON, Canada M5T 2C7
Phone: (416)504-1645
Fax: (416)913-2327
E-mail: info@pwac.ca
Home Page: http://www.pwac.ca

• 17224 • **Lawrence Jackson Award**
Recognizes outstanding contributions and exemplary commitment and service to the association. Only members are eligible. One year membership is awarded annually.

• 17225 •
Permanent International Altaistic Conference
Prof. Denis Sinor, Sec.Gen.
Indiana University
GoodBody Hall 157
Bloomington, IN 47405-7005
Phone: (812)855-0959
Fax: (812)855-7500
E-mail: sinord@indiana.edu

• 17226 • **Indiana University Prize for Altaic Studies**
For recognition of outstanding, lifelong contribution to Altaic (Inner Asian) studies. A gold medal is presented annually when merited. Established in 1962 by Indiana University.

• 17227 •
Pharmaceutical Research and Manufacturers of America
Billy Tauzin, Pres./CEO
1100 15th St. NW
Washington, DC 20005
Phone: (202)835-3400
Fax: (202)835-3414
Home Page: http://www.phrma.org

Formerly: (1995) Pharmaceutical Manufacturers Association.

• 17228 • **Discoverers Awards**
This, the pharmaceutical industry's highest scientific honor, is given to recognize scientists whose research and development of pharmaceuticals have greatly benefited mankind, and whose dedication and interest in improving the quality of life exemplify the best in the research industry today. Awarded annually. Established in 1987.

• 17229 •
Phelps-Stokes Fund
Dr. Badi Foster, Pres.
1420 K St. NW, Ste. 800
Washington, DC 20005
Phone: (202)371-9544
Fax: (202)371-9522
E-mail: bfoster@psfdc.org
Home Page: http://www.psfdc.org

• 17230 • Aggrey Medal
To recognize individuals who have made significant contributions in one of the charter areas of interest of the Phelps-Stokes Fund, i.e., education for Africans, African Americans, and American Indians. A silver medal is awarded from time to time by the Board of Trustees of the Phelps-Stokes Fund. Established in 1986 to honor Dr. J.E.K. Aggrey, the renowned African educator who was a member of the first Phelps-Stokes African Education Commission (1920-21), and one of the period's foremost proponents of racial equality.

• 17231 • Clarence L. Holte Literary Prize
To recognize a living writer for a significant contribution to the cultural heritage of Africa and the African diaspora made through published writings in the humanities. Nominations for this international prize are open to the public. A monetary prize of $7,500 is awarded biennially from the earnings of an endowment established anonymously in 1977 in honor of Clarence L. Holte, a writer, editor, and collector of books about the African heritage and diaspora. The prize was conceived by Cliff Lashley, scholar, book collector, and former Jamaican diplomat. Co-sponsored by the Schomburg Center for Research in Black Culture, the New York Public Library, and the Fund.

• 17232 •
Phi Alpha Theta
Graydon A. Tunstall Jr., Exec.Dir.
University of South Florida
4202 E Fowler Ave., SOC107
Tampa, FL 33620-8100
Phone: (813)974-8212
Toll-Free: 800-394-8195
Fax: (813)974-8215
E-mail: phialpha@phialphatheta.org
Home Page: http://www.phialphatheta.org

• 17233 • Best First Book Award
To recognize an outstanding first book by an author in the field of history. Members of the Society are eligible to submit books published in the previous year by July 1. A monetary prize of $500 is awarded annually. Established in 1965.

• 17234 • Best Subsequent Book Award
To recognize an author's second, or subsequent, book in the field of history. Members of the Society are eligible to submit books published in the previous year by July 1. A monetary prize of $500 is awarded annually. Established in 1965.

• 17235 • Manuscript Award
To recognize the author of a book length manuscript that makes a significant contribution to historical knowledge, either by offering a challenging new interpretation, by presenting important new material on subjects with the proper interpretation of primary sources utilized for the first time, or by providing new findings in heretofore neglected areas of history. Authors who have been members of Phi Alpha Theta for at least one year are eligible. Submission deadline is July 1. Awarded biennially in even-numbered years. Established in 1971.

• 17236 • Nash Student History Journal Prize
Prize of $100 awarded to the best electronic journal. $400 awarded to universities and colleges with history MA and/or Ph.D. programs. Other colleges and universities without history MA and/or Ph.D. are awarded $400. Majority of the papers and essays must be the work of presently matriculating or recently graduated students. Only publications that consist primarily of student research papers and other learned essays are eligible. Editorial staff must include students, and majority of those students must be members of Phi Alpha Theta. The journal must be associated with a recognized chapter of Phi Alpha Theta and must give notice of its affiliation. Journals will be judged on scholarly merit, variety, and overall literary merit of all printed material, artistry of cover and layout.

• 17237 • Paper Prize Awards
To recognize the authors of that combine original historical research on a significant subject, based on source material and manuscripts if possible, with good English composition and superior style. Graduate and undergraduate members of the Society may submit manuscripts by July 1. Six prizes are awarded annually: the Dr. George P. Hammond Prize of $300 is awarded for the best paper submitted by a graduate student member; the Dr. Lynn W. Turner Prize of $250 for the best paper submitted by an undergraduate student member; and the Nels Andrew Cleven Founder's Paper Prize Awards of $250 each for two undergraduate student and two graduate student members.

• 17238 • Phi Alpha Theta/Westerners International Award
To recognize a graduate student member of the Society for the best doctoral dissertation in Western history. All dissertations must have been completed during the preceding calendar year and submitted by June 15th of the following year. A monetary award of $1,000 is presented annually at the Phi Alpha Theta Luncheon at the Western History Association Annual Meeting. The award is funded by Westerners International Association. Established in 1987.

• 17239 •
Phi Beta Kappa
John Churchill, Sec.
1606 New Hampshire Ave. NW
Washington, DC 20009
Phone: (202)265-3808
Fax: (202)986-1601
E-mail: info@pbk.org
Home Page: http://www.pbk.org

• 17240 • Award in Science
To recognize outstanding contributions by scientists to the literature of science, and to encourage literate and scholarly interpretations of the physical and biological sciences and mathematics. Monographs and compendiums are not eligible. To be eligible, biographies of scientists must have a substantial critical emphasis on their scientific research. Authors must be U.S. citizens or residents. The deadline is April 30. A monetary prize of $2,500 is awarded annually. Established in 1959. Formerly: .

• 17241 • Ralph Waldo Emerson Award
To recognize outstanding scholarly studies that contribute significantly to interpretations of the intellectual and cultural condition of humanity. Work in the fields of history, philosophy, religion, and related subjects are eligible. Books entered must have been published in the United States during the preceding twelve months. Authors must be U.S. citizens or residents. Submission deadline is April 30. A monetary prize of $2,500 is awarded annually. Established in 1960 to honor Ralph Waldo Emerson, American intellectual, poet, and essayist, whose life, works, and interests exemplify the intellectual achievement the award is intended to honor.

• 17242 • Christian Gauss Award
To recognize the author of an outstanding book in the field of literary scholarship or criticism. Books entered must have been published in the United States during the preceding twelve months. Authors must be U.S. citizens or residents. Submission deadline is April 30. A monetary prize of $2,500 is awarded annually. Established in 1950 and named for Christian Gauss, distinguished Princeton University scholar, teacher, and dean who also served as president of the Phi Beta Kappa Society.

• 17243 • Sidney Hook Memorial Award
To recognize national distinction by a single scholar in scholarship, undergraduate teaching, and leadership in the cause of liberal arts education. Nomination is by members. A monetary award of $7,500 is presented triennially. Established in 1991 in memory of Sidney Hook, American philosopher.

• 17244 • Romanell - Phi Beta Kappa Professorship in Philosophy
For recognition of distinguished achievement by scholars in the field of philosophy, and for contributions and potential contributions to public understanding of philosophy. Although nominees need not be members of the Society, they must be on the faculty of an institution sheltering a chapter of the Society and must be nominated by that chapter. The deadline for nomination is in March each year. A stipend of $7,500 for a series of three lectures to be given at the home institution during the award year is awarded annually. Established in 1981 by an endowment from Patrick and Edna Romanell.

• 17245 • Mary Isabel Sibley Fellowship
To provide for advanced research in French language and literature, or Greek language, literature, history, or archaeology. Awards are given for French in even-numbered years and for Greek in odd-numbered years. Candidates must be unmarried women between 25 and 35 years of age who hold a doctorate or have fulfilled all of the requirements for the doctorate except the

dissertation. The deadline for applications is January 15. One fellowship of $20,000 is awarded annually in the spring for work beginning the following July. Established in 1934 by Isabelle Stone in honor of her mother, Mary Isabel Sibley.

• 17246 •
Phi Delta Chi
Thomas M. Ellington, Grand Pres.
618 Church St., Ste. 220
Nashville, TN 37219
Phone: (615)254-7047
Toll-Free: 800-PDC-1883
Fax: (615)254-7047
E-mail: pdc@walkermgt.com
Home Page: http://www.phideltachi.org

Formerly: (1909) Phi Chi Pharmacy Fraternity.

• 17247 • **Emory W. Thurston Grand President's Award**
To recognize the chapter that has promoted the profession of pharmacy and Phi Delta Chi to the fullest extent during the preceding year. To qualify, a chapter must have received an efficiency rating of at least 90 percent in the Achievement Award program. A trophy is presented annually. Established in 1974 in honor of the Past Grand President Emory W. Thurston.

• 17248 •
Phi Lambda Upsilon
Dr. Charles T. Campbell, Pres.
University of Washington
Box 351700
Chemistry Department
Seattle, WA 98195-1700
Phone: (206)616-6085
Phone: (206)616-9320
Fax: (206)616-6250
E-mail: campbell@chem.washington.edu
Home Page: http://www.cpac.washington.edu/~campbell/plu

• 17249 • **Honorary Member**
To recognize individuals for outstanding contributions to the science of chemistry. Awarded when merited to those who are at the height of or near the close of their careers.

• 17250 • **National Fresenius Award**
For recognition of an outstanding contribution in chemical research, education, and/or administration by a chemist under 35 years of age. A monetary award of $5,000, travel expenses, and a plaque are awarded annually. Established in 1965.

• 17251 •
Phi Theta Kappa, International Honor Society
Rod A. Risley, Exec.Dir.
Center For Excellence
1625 Eastover Dr.
Jackson, MS 39211-3729
Phone: (601)984-3504
Phone: 877-785-1918
Toll-Free: 800-946-9995
Fax: (601)984-3550
E-mail: member.services@ptk.org
Home Page: http://www.ptk.org

• 17252 • **Hallmark Award**
Annual awards of recognition for chapters, members, advisors, and regions.

• 17253 •
Phi Upsilon Omicron
Susan Rickards, Exec.Dir.
PO Box 329
Fairmont, WV 26555-0329
Phone: (304)368-0612
E-mail: rickards@mountain.net
Home Page: http://phiu.unl.edu

• 17254 • **Collegiate Advisor Award**
To recognize Phi U collegiate advisors who have demonstrated excellence as advisors. A certificate and an engraved piece of Phi U jewelry is awarded annually.

• 17255 • **Florence Faligatter Distinguished Service Award**
Recognizes a qualified alumni member for outstanding achievements in family and consumer sciences. Ten years of employment or volunteer activities is required. Nominations must be submitted by November 1 of odd-numbered years. A plaque and expenses to attend the Conclave are awarded biennially. Established in 1979.

• 17256 • **Frances Morton Holbrook Alumni Award**
To recognize an alumni member for fulfilling personal and professional goals that promote the purposes of family and consumer sciences. Criteria include demonstrated excellence in one of the areas of family and consumer sciences. Nominations must be submitted by November 1 of odd-numbered years. A plaque and expenses to attend the Conclave are awarded biennially. Established in 1983.

• 17257 • **Orinne Johnson Writing Award**
To recognize a collegiate member who submits the best creative writing related to the current professional project theme for publication in the Society's publication *The Candle.* Applications must be submitted by February 1. A monetary award of $300 is presented annually.

• 17258 • **Sarah Thorniley Phillips Leadership Award**
To recognize undergraduate members for outstanding leadership and participation in collegiate and community programs. Applications must be submitted by February 1. Three monetary awards of $300 are presented annually.

• 17259 •
Philadelphia County Medical Society
2100 Spring Garden St.
Philadelphia, PA 19103
Phone: (215)563-5343
Fax: (215)563-3627
Home Page: http://www.philamedsoc.org

• 17260 • **Benjamin Rush Award**
For community service. Recognition award bestowed annually.

• 17261 •
Philadelphia Home and School Council
Administration Bldg., Rm 310
21st St. and The Pkwy.
Philadelphia, PA 19103
Phone: (215)563-4114

• 17262 • **Annual Home and School Council Merit Awards**
For deeds that are considered exceptional, unusual, or heroic. Monetary award bestowed annually.

• 17263 •
Philalethes Society
Nelson King, Ed.
1670 River Rd.
Beaver, PA 15009
Phone: (724)775-6509
Fax: (804)328-2386
E-mail: psoc@freemasonry.org
Home Page: http://www.freemasonry.org/psoc

• 17264 • **Certificate of Literature**
To recognize the best article published in *The Philalethes* for a calendar year. A gold medallion is awarded to the winner. A silver medallion(s) may be given for Honorable Achievement when merited. Awarded annually.

• 17265 • **Fellow**
To recognize excellence in scholarly research on Freemasonry, service to the Society, service to Freemasonry, and service to the community. A certificate is awarded. There is a limit of 40 Fellows at any one time. Established in 1928.

• 17266 • **Philalethes Lecture**
To honor an individual by having him address the annual meeting. A pewter medallion is awarded annually.

• 17267 • **Special Achievement Award**
To recognize a non-member for furthering scholarship on Freemasonry. Selection is made by the Executive Board. A pewter medallion is awarded as merited.

• 17268 •
Philanthropic Service for Institutions
Ken Turpen, Dir.
Adventist World Headquarters
12501 Old Columbia Pke.
Silver Spring, MD 20904-6600
Phone: (301)680-6131
Fax: (301)680-6137
E-mail: chris.bearce@nad.adventist.org
Home Page: http://www.philanthropicservice.com

• 17269 • **Trailblazer in Philanthropy Award**
To recognize individuals for outstanding achievement through creativity, initiative, and consistent professional leadership on behalf of Adventist communication and philanthropy in its system of health and/or education. Nominations may be submitted by March 16. Awarded triennially. Established in 1981.

• 17270 •
Philatelic Foundation
George J. Kramer, Chm.
70 W 40th St., 15th Fl.
New York, NY 10018
Phone: (212)221-6555
Fax: (212)221-6208
E-mail: gjkk@optonline.net
Home Page: http://www.philatelicfoundation.org

• 17271 • **Mortimer L. Neinken Medal**
For recognition of meritorious service to philately. Selection is by nomination. A medal is awarded annually in October. Established in 1981 in memory of Mortimer L. Neinken, Chairman of the Foundation Expert Committee and member of the Board of Trustees. Formerly: (1985) Philatelic Foundation Medal.

• 17272 •
Philatelic Music Circle
Cathleen Osborne, Sec.
PO Box 1781
Sequim, WA 98382
Phone: (360)683-6373
E-mail: rickcath@olypen.com

• 17273 • **Robert Stolz Trophy for Music Philately**
To recognize the designer of the best music stamp each year. A panel of the worldwide membership makes the selection. A trophy is awarded annually at a special ceremony. Established in 1980 by Mrs. Einzi Stolz, widow of Robert Stolz (1880-1975), the last of the Viennese Waltz Kings.

• 17274 •
Phoenix Community Works Foundation
Larry Rooney, Exec.Dir.
344 Bloor St. W, Ste. 505
Toronto, ON, Canada M5S 3A7
Phone: (416)964-3380
Fax: (416)964-8516
E-mail: info@pcwf.ca
Home Page: http://www.pcwf.ca

• 17275 • **bp Nichol Chapbook Award**
To recognize the author of published chapbook (10-48 pp) of English language poetry published in Canada. Awarded annually with $1,000. Send 3 copies by March 30. Established in 1985.

• 17276 •
Phoenix House
Mitchell S. Rosenthal M.D., Pres.
164 W 74th St.
New York, NY 10023
Phone: (212)595-5810
Fax: (212)496-6035
E-mail: phcomm@phoenixhouse.org
Home Page: http://www.phoenixhouse.org

Formerly: (2000) Phoenix House Foundation.

• 17277 • **Phoenix House Award for Public Service**
To honor exceptional Americans, both men and women, whose achievements and service to society will inspire young people who are struggling to reclaim lives disordered by social deprivation, family disruption, or drug abuse. A crystal obelisk trophy is presented annually. Established in 1979.

• 17278 •
Phoenix Theatre
Sharon Gamble, Mng.Dir.
749 N Park Ave.
Indianapolis, IN 46202
Phone: (317)635-2381
Fax: (317)635-0010
E-mail: info@phoenixtheatre.org
Home Page: http://www.phoenixtheatre.org

• 17279 • **Festival of Emerging American Theatre New Plays Competition**
To recognize and produce new plays, both full-length and one-act. Plays must not have been previously professionally produced. The Phoenix has two intimate stages: 150-seat house and a 75-seat house. Sets and number of actors must be adaptable to the Phoenix environment. A $5 entry fee is required. Winners receive a $750 honorarium for full-length plays or $325 for one-acts. Established in 1984 by Bryan Fonseca, Artistic/Executive Director. Formerly: (1996) Resort Condominiums International (RCI) Festival of Emerging American Theatre Competition.

• 17280 •
Photographic Art and Science Foundation
Frederick Quellmalz, Chm.
2100 NE 52nd St.
Kirkpatrick Ctr.
Oklahoma City, OK 73111
Phone: (405)424-4055
Fax: (405)424-4058
E-mail: info@iphf.org
Home Page: http://www.iphf.org

• 17281 • **International Photography Hall of Fame and Museum**
To promote awareness and education of the history of photography, and to honor pioneers who have made significant contributions to the artistic and scientific progress of photography. A large plaque is awarded from selections by the Board of Trustees and election by the Foundation Electors. Usually awarded each year in the spring. Established in 1965.

• 17282 •
Photographic Society of America
Richard Frieders FPSA, Pres.
3000 United Founders Blvd., Ste. 103
Oklahoma City, OK 73112-3940
Phone: (405)843-1437
Fax: (405)843-1438
E-mail: hq@psa-photo.org
Home Page: http://www.psa-photo.org

• 17283 • **Amateur PSA/VMPD American International Film and Video Festival**
To promote interest in motion picture and video production by amateurs. The Festival is an open competition for individuals of all ages, nations and races in the following categories: (1) Class A - films made with no commercial or financial objective in mind, and films which have not been subject to any prior sale or rental agreement; (2) Class B - student films made by students enrolled in a school or department of cinematography (College level); (3) Class C - commercial films, covers all films that do not qualify in Class A, or Class B; (4) Class D - teenage competition for students in the 9th through 12th grades, both film and video, judged separately. Restricted to citizen residents of the United States or Canada; and (5) Class E - video productions produced with video equipment only. Entries may be submitted by May 20. Trophies, medals and certificates are awarded to the Ten Best Amateur Films and Honorable Mention entries. The film or video selected as the best overall entry, receives the Charles A. Kinsley Memorial Trophy, sponsored by the Eastman Kodak Company. Additional awards include: (1) VMPD Cinematography Award; (2) VMPD Nature Film Award; (3) The VMPD Golden Microphone Award; (4) The VMPD Scenario Award; (5) The VMPD Travel Film Award; (6) The VMPD Club Film Award; (7) The VMPD Humorous Film Award; (8) The VMPD Golden Scissors Award; (9) The VMPD Documentary Film Award; (10) The VMPD Foreign Film Award; (11) The VMPD Experimental Film Award; and (12) The VMPD Animation Film Award. Established in 1935 by the Video and Motion Picture Division of PSA.

• 17284 • Color Slide Division Awards
For recognition of the most outstanding color slides at the PSA International Exhibition. Awards are presented in two categories: North American Color Slides and Overseas Color Slides. The following prizes are awarded: (1) Charles A. Kinsley Memorial Trophy for the best three accepted entries showing diversification; (2) Gold Medal for Best of Show; (3) Douglas H. Wanzer, FPSA, Award for Best Portrait; (4) Gold Medal for Best of Show-Contemporary; (5) Best Animal Portrait Award in Memory of Marian Neill; and (6) four Silver Medals for Excellence. Awarded annually.

• 17285 • Editorial Awards
To recognize PSA members for articles or photographs published under their bylines during the previous year. A Merit Certificate is awarded.

• 17286 • Honorary Member
To recognize individuals for excellence in the art and science of photography and for service to the Society and to photography generally. In addition to Honorary Member, the Society also awards Society Associate, Fellow, and Honorary Fellow.

• 17287 • Nature Division Awards
For recognition of the most outstanding nature slides and prints at the PSA International Exhibition. The following prizes are awarded: (1) Charles A. Kinsley Memorial Trophy for the best three accepted entries showing diversification; (2) Gold Medal for Best of Show; (3) Silver Medal for Second Best of Show; (4) Bronze Medal for Third Best of Show; (5) Gold Medal for Best Wildlife; (6) Silver Medal for Second Best Wildlife; (7) Bronze Medal for Third Best Wildlife; (8) Best Botany Award in memory of Leslie B. Henney; (9) Lorena Medbery Nature Landscape/Seascape Award; (10) Geological Award in memory of Lloyd L. Reise; (11) Ornithological Wildlife Award in memory of Alice B. Kessler; and (12) Nature Division Best Insect Award. Awarded annually.

• 17288 • Photo Travel Division Awards
For recognition of the most outstanding photo travel slides at the PSA International Exhibition. The following prizes are awarded: (1) Charles A. Kinsley Memorial Trophy for the best three accepted entries showing diversification; (2) Joseph Van Gelder award for Best of Show; (3) Gold Medal for runner-up; (4) Gold Medal for runner-up; and (5) People at Work Award, in memory of Joe Seckendorf. Awarded annually.

• 17289 • Photojournalism Division Awards
For recognition of outstanding work in photojournalism at the PSA International Exhibition. Awards are given in the following categories: (1) Class "A" Large Prints; (2) Class "B" Small Prints; and (3) Color "C" Slides. The following prizes are awarded: (1) Gold Medal Award for Best of Show; (2) Silver Medal for Best Man in Action; and (3) Charles A. Kinsley Memorial Trophy - one for a print, large or small; and one for a slide. Awarded annually.

• 17290 • Pictorial Print Color Division Awards
For recognition of outstanding color prints at the PSA International Exhibition. The following prizes are awarded: (1) Charles A. Kinsley Memorial Trophy (note: The Kinsley Memorial Trophy is awarded by Eastman Kodak Company in honor of the late Charles A. Kinsley, a former director of Kodak's information department and member of PSA. It is given in ten of the Society's awards.) for the best three entries showing diversification; (2) Joe Kennedy-Clerk Maxwell Award for best color print; and (3) Wellington Lee Award for most creative and unusual use of color. Awarded annually.

• 17291 • Pictorial Print Monochrome Division Awards
For recognition of outstanding prints at the PSA International Exhibition. Awards are presented in two categories: North American Monochrome Prints and Overseas Monochrome Prints. The following prizes are awarded: (1) Charles A. Kinsley Memorial Trophy for the best three accepted entries showing diversification; (2) Gold Medal Award for Best of Show; and (3) John R. Hogan Memorial Award for the print judged most outstanding marine subject. Awarded annually.

• 17292 • Progress Award
To recognize individuals for contributions to development in the field of photography including film, camera, or technology.

• 17293 • Small and Commercial Print Division Awards
For recognition of the most outstanding small color, small monochrome, and commercial prints at the PSA International Exhibition. The Gold Medal Award for Best of Show is awarded annually.

• 17294 • Stereo Division Awards
For recognition of the most outstanding stereo electronic and slides/prints at the PSA International Exhibition. The following prizes are awarded: (1) Charles A. Kinsley Memorial Trophy for the best three accepted entries showing diversification; (2) Gold Medal for Best of Show; (3) Silver Medal for Best Contemporary Slide; (4) Paul J. Wolf Memorial Award for Best Portrait or Figure Study; (5) Stereo Division Best Landscape Award; and (6) Stereo Division Best Flower Award. Awarded annually.

• 17295 •
PhotoImaging Manufacturers and Distributors Association
Robert H. Nunn, Exec.Dir.
109 White Oak Ln., Ste. 72F
Old Bridge, NJ 08857
Phone: (732)679-3460
Fax: (732)679-2294
E-mail: Bnunn101@comcast.net
Home Page: http://www.pmda.com

• 17296 • Person of the Year
This, the highest award of the association, is given for recognition of achievement during the preceding year in the photographic industry in conjunction with life-time dedication. Nominations are made by voting members of the association. A plaque is generally awarded annually at the PMDA Awards Dinner preceding the United States industry convention. Established in 1965 to honor Phil Sperry.

• 17297 • Professional Photographer Award
For recognition of an outstanding world-class photographer. Presented at the PMDA Awards Dinner. Established in 1982. Formerly: PMDA Celebrity Photographer Award.

• 17298 • Scientific or Technical Achievement Award
For recognition of outstanding scientific or technical achievement in the photographic field. Presented annually at the PMDA Awards Dinner. Established in 1982.

• 17299 • Special Award
To recognize an individual for outstanding service to the association, the photographic industry, or both. Awarded when merited. Established in 1974. Formerly: Humanities Award.

• 17300 •
Phycological Society of America
Morgan L. Vis, VP/Pres.-Elect
Commerce Pl.
350 Main St.
Malden, MA 02148
Phone: (781)388-8250
Phone: (216)397-3077
Toll-Free: 888-661-5800
Fax: (781)388-8270
E-mail: psa@psaalgae.org
Home Page: http://www.psaalgae.org

• 17301 • Harold C. Bold Award
For recognition of the outstanding graduate student paper presented at the Annual Meeting. Established in 1973.

• 17302 • Gerald W. Prescott Award
To recognize the author(s) of a scholarly work devoted to phycology in the form of a book or monograph published in English during the previous two years. No edited volume, individual book chapter, or typical journal article is considered. Authors need not be members of the Society. A monetary prize is awarded biennially. Established in 1982 to honor Gerald W. Prescott.

• 17303 • Luigi Provasoli Award
To recognize outstanding papers published in the *Journal of Phycology* during the previous two years. Awarded biennially. Established in 1984 in honor of Luigi Provasoli, a past editor of the *Journal of Phycology*.

• 17304 •
Physician Insurers Association of America
Ann G. Horwich, Dir. of Bus.Devel. and Membership
2275 Research Blvd., Ste. 250
Rockville, MD 20850
Phone: (301)947-9000
Fax: (301)947-9090
E-mail: ahorwich@piaa.us
Home Page: http://www.thepiaa.org

• 17305 • **Peter Sweetland Award of Excellence**
To recognize an individual in the PIAA membership who epitomizes the high ideals and ethics for which Peter Sweetland stood. Awarded annually with a Waterford bowl. Established in 1993.

• 17306 •
Pi Gamma Mu
Sue Watters, Exec.Dir.
1001 Millington St., Ste. B
Winfield, KS 67156
Phone: (620)221-3128
Fax: (620)221-7124
E-mail: pgm@sckans.edu
Home Page: http://www.pigammamu.org

• 17307 • **Pi Gamma Mu Scholarships**
To encourage the most outstanding student members to seek graduate degrees in the social sciences. Eligible recipients will use the scholarships for their first- or second-year of graduate work in the areas of sociology, anthropology, political science, history, economics, international relations, public administration, criminal justice, law, social work, human geography, and psychology. No more than three awards will be awarded in a given discipline.Other interdisciplinary fields, excluding business administration, related to social sciences will be considered. Seven scholarships of $1,000 and three of $2,000 are awarded annually. Established in 1951.

• 17308 •
Pi Kappa Alpha
Raymond L. Orians, Exec.VP
8347 W Range Cove
Memphis, TN 38125
Phone: (901)748-1868
Fax: (901)748-3100
E-mail: pka@pikes.org
Home Page: http://www.pka.com

Formerly: Pi Kappa Alpha Memorial Foundation.

• 17309 • **Loyalty Award**
To recognize an alumnus for continuing involvement with and support of Fraternity programs through volunteer service. Awarded annually. Established in 1969.

• 17310 • **Order of West Range**
To recognize career achievement, service to society, and/or service to Pi Kappa Alpha. Presented annually by the Pi Kappa Alpha Educational Foundation to no more than six alumni members. Established in 1986.

• 17311 • **Pi Kappa Alpha Chapter and Alumni Awards**
To recognize chapters and alumni groups for outstanding contributions to the fraternity. The following awards are presented: Smythe Awards annually to 15 chapters for outstanding proficiency; Newell Award annually to the most improved chapter; Nester Award - annually to the most outstanding alumni association of Pi Kappa Alpha; and Programming Awards annually for all aspects of chapter operations. Presentations are made for top proficiency in publications, rush, intramurals, pledge education, alumni relations, scholarship, community service, and campus involvement.

• 17312 • **Robertson Most Outstanding Undergraduate Award**
To recognize the most outstanding undergraduate. Special consideration is given to graduating seniors, and the basic qualifications for nomination include academic excellence, leadership on the campus, commitment to the community, and involvement within his chapter of Pi Kappa Alpha. The Pi Kappa Alpha Educational Foundation solicits nominations from all chapters. A $2,500 scholarship is awarded to the winner and the four men who are runners-up each receive a $500 scholarship. A plaque is presented annually. Established in 1926.

• 17313 • **Judge Elbert P. Tuttle Distinguished Achievement Award**
This, the highest honor bestowed by the Society, is given to recognize an alumnus who has distinguished himself through achievement in his vocation, profession, or field of public service. Awarded annually. Established in 1936.

• 17314 •
Pi Kappa Phi
Mark E. Timmes, CEO
2102 Cambridge Beltway Dr., Ste. A
Charlotte, NC 28273
Phone: (704)504-0888
Toll-Free: 800-929-1905
Fax: (704)504-0880
E-mail: pikapphq@pikapp.org
Home Page: http://www.pikapp.org

• 17315 • **Hall of Fame**
To honor and recognize selected alumni members who have brought respect to the fraternity by distinguishing themselves in the fields of business, industry, the arts, sciences, sports, or professions. A plaque is presented at the discretion of the national council. Established in 1979.

• 17316 • **Merit Citation**
To recognize individuals making superior contributions to Pi Kappa Phi. A certificate is presented. No more than nine are awarded annually. Established in 1933.

• 17317 • **Mr. Pi Kappa Phi**
To recognize an individual who exemplifies the ideals of Pi Kappa Phi. The award is a resolution that may be presented annually. Established in 1964.

• 17318 • **Pi Kapp Scholar**
To recognize undergraduate students for outstanding scholarship and ability. A monetary prize and a plaque are presented to nine recipients annually.

• 17319 • **Student of the Year**
To an undergraduate student member whose abilities and accomplishments have had significant impact on the chapter and have brought credit to the Pi Kappa Phi Fraternity. A monetary prize and a plaque are awarded annually.

• 17320 •
Pi Lambda Theta
J. Ogden Hamilton, Exec.Dir.
4101 E 3rd St.
PO Box 6626
Bloomington, IN 47407-6626
Toll-Free: 800-487-3411
Fax: (812)339-3462
E-mail: office@pilambda.org
Home Page: http://www.pilambda.org

• 17321 • **Lillian and Henry Barry Award in Human Relations**
To recognize outstanding service to people with disabilities resulting in the development of their ability to lead useful, fulfilling lives, and/or in the promotion of better understanding of their needs by the general population. Members or chapters of Pi Lambda Theta are eligible. A monetary prize of $400 and a certificate are awarded biennially in odd-numbered years. Established in 1977 by Lillian Tracey Barry.

• 17322 • **Distinguished Pi Lambda Thetan Award**
To recognize contributions to Pi Lambda Theta and to the profession of education. Members who have demonstrated a professional spirit and leadership, have contributed to Pi Lambda Theta and to the field of education, and have exhibited commitment to excellence in professional endeavors are eligible. A plaque was awarded annually in 1979, 1980, and 1981, and has been awarded biennially in even-numbered years thereafter. Established in 1979.

• 17323 • **Distinguished Student Scholar Award**
To recognize an education major who has displayed leadership potential and a strong dedication to education. Nominees, whether member or non-member, must be at least second-semester sophomores with a grade point average of at least 3.5. Selection is based on leadership potential, dedication to the future of education, and contributions to local/national/international endeavors, including volunteer work, committee work, and leadership appointments or elections. Application deadline is February 10th of odd-numbered years. A $500 scholarship, an

unframed certificate, and one-year's paid membership in Pi Lambda Theta are awarded in odd-numbered years.

• 17324 • Ella Victoria Dobbs Award
To recognize unique or outstanding research conducted by a member and published within the two calendar years immediately preceding the biennial council. A monetary prize of $400 and a certificate are awarded biennially in odd-numbered years. Established in 1965.

• 17325 • Excellence in Education Award
To recognize a commitment to excellence in education and unique contributions to the field of education. Both members and non-members are eligible. A monetary prize of $1,000 and a plaque are awarded biennially in odd-numbered years. Established in 1979.

• 17326 • Graduate Student Scholar Award
To recognize an outstanding graduate student who is an education major. Selection is based on moral character, service at the local/regional/international level that enhances the educational community, including volunteer work, committee work, or positions of leadership, and unique performance for the betterment of the applicant's chosen discipline. Application deadline is February 10 of odd-numbered years. A $1,000 scholarship, a certificate, and one-year's paid membership in Pi Lambda Theta are awarded biennially in odd-numbered years. Established in 1993. Formerly: Outstanding Field Chapter.

• 17327 • Outstanding Faculty Adviser
To recognize an outstanding faculty adviser who demonstrates a cooperative, professional spirit within the chapter and educational community. Active members currently serving as a faculty adviser are eligible. The following criteria are considered: length and quality of service to the chapter; evidence of innovative support (e.g., enhances image of PLT on campus, has the ability to counsel/suggest, assists with programs and meetings); service as liaison to university officials and to other professional groups; and professional spirit of cooperation with members and with the national PLT organization. An engraved plaque is awarded biennially in odd-numbered years at the association's convention. Established in 1979.

• 17328 • Anna Tracey Memorial Award
To recognize producers of a communications medium that enhances the image of elderly persons. A monetary prize of $400 and a certificate are awarded biennially in odd-numbered years. Established in 1975 by Lillian Tracey Barry in honor of Anna M. Tracey, her mother.

• 17329 •
Piano Technicians Guild
Kent E. Swafford RPT, Pres.
444 Forest Ave.
Kansas City, KS 66106
Phone: (913)432-9975
Fax: (913)432-9986
E-mail: ptg@ptg.org
Home Page: http://www.ptg.org

• 17330 • Golden Hammer Award
To recognize an individual for exceptional personal service in and to the piano technological profession over many years. Members of PTG are eligible. A gold-plated tuning hammer displayed in a hand-made case in the shape of a grand piano is awarded annually. Established in 1969.

• 17331 • Hall of Fame
To perpetuate the memory of piano industry greats and to recognize a lifetime of very special services to the music industry. A framed certificate and pin are presented to the honoree, whose picture and resume are in the Hall of Fame book at the home office. Awarded annually. Established in 1976.

• 17332 • Honorary Member
To recognize individuals for outstanding service to the piano technological profession.

• 17333 • Member of Note
To recognize recent outstanding service to the piano tuning profession. Members of PTG are eligible. Up to four trophies are awarded annually. Established in 1969.

• 17334 •
Pickerington Area Chamber of Commerce
Kathy Lowrey, Pres.
13 W Columbus St.
Pickerington, OH 43147
Phone: (614)837-1958
Fax: (614)837-6420
E-mail:
partners@pickeringtonchamber.com
Home Page: http://
www.pickeringtonchamber.com

• 17335 • PACC Scholarship
For Pickerington School District students. Scholarship awarded annually.

• 17336 •
Pickle Packers International
Richard Hentschel, Exec.VP
1620 I St. NW, Ste. 925
One Pickle and Pepper Plz.
Washington, DC 20006
Phone: (202)331-2456
Fax: (630)584-0759
E-mail: bbursiek@therobertsgroup.net
Home Page: http://ilovepickles.org

• 17337 • Hall of Fame
To recognize an individual for contributions in leadership, technical services, machinery, and science to the industry. An engraved silver award is presented in odd-numbered years. Established in 1955.

• 17338 • Silver Shadow Award
To recognize outstanding individuals for contributions to the pickle industry. Engraved silver awards are presented as deemed appropriate. Established in 1970.

• 17339 •
Pierce-Arrow Society
Dr. Arnold Romberg, Pres.
PO Box 36637
Richmond, VA 23235-8013
Phone: (585)244-1664
E-mail: info@pierce-arrow.org
Home Page: http://www.pierce-arrow.org

• 17340 • Henry E. and Pauline S. Becker Award
To the owner of the Pierce-Arrow driven the longest distance to the annual meet, based on age of the vehicle and "straight line" map distance between home and meet location.

• 17341 • R. Vale Faro Trophy
To recognize the owner of the most original, unrestored Pierce-Arrow displayed at the Annual Meet. Established in memory of the founder of the Pierce-Arrow Society.

• 17342 • Otto Klausmeyer Distinguished Service Award
To recognize members who have provided outstanding service to the Pierce-Arrow Society. A plaque is awarded regularly in honor of Otto Klausmeyer, a Studebaker engineer who provided invaluable technical, mechanical, and historical assistance to the Society. Established in 1987.

• 17343 • Bernard J. Weis Trophy
Recognizes the owner of the most authentically restored Pierce-Arrow judged at the annual meet.

• 17344 •
Pierre Fauchard Academy
Dr. Richard A. Kozal, Sec.Gen.
PO Box 80330
Las Vegas, NV 89180-0330
Phone: (702)651-5013
Toll-Free: 800-232-0099
Fax: (702)651-5537
E-mail: rkozal@aol.com
Home Page: http://www.fauchard.org

• 17345 • Elmer S. Best Memorial Award
To recognize contributions of international significance to dentistry. Members of the dental profession outside the United States are eligible. A medal and a plaque are awarded annually.

Established in 1962 and named in memory of the founder of the Pierre Fauchard Academy.

• 17346 • Certificate of Merit
To recognize outstanding and dedicated service to the profession by a dentist. One certificate per section may be awarded annually.

• 17347 • Dental Trade and Industry Award of Recognition
To honor an outstanding leader in the field for contributions to dentistry. One plaque is awarded annually.

• 17348 • Distinguished Service Citation
For recognition of loyal and dedicated service to the academy. Candidates must be nominated by the Awards Committee and must have unanimous approval of the Board of Trustees.

• 17349 • Pierre Fauchard Academy Bronze Service Citation
To recognize members for loyal and dedicated service to the Academy. A bronze plaque is awarded occasionally when merited. In addition, a Distinguished Service Citation Certificate is awarded when merited.

• 17350 • Pierre Fauchard Academy Plaque
To recognize outstanding and dedicated services to the dental profession. Names and qualifications must be submitted to the secretary-treasurer six weeks prior to the presentation of the award. One plaque per section in any one year may be awarded annually.

• 17351 • Fauchard Gold Medal
To honor outstanding contributions to the dental profession. Members of the dental profession who are U.S. citizens are eligible to be nominated by the Committee of Past Recipients. A medal and a plaque are awarded annually. Established in 1928.

• 17352 • Honorary Member
To recognize all past recipients of the Fauchard Gold Medal and the Elmer S. Best Memorial Award and additional individuals elected by the Board of Trustees.

• 17353 • Undergraduate Certificate of Merit
To recognize outstanding and dedicated service to the profession by a dental student. Particular emphasis will be placed on the student's contribution to the dental literature. Awarded annually.

• 17354 •
Pipe Collectors Club of America
PO Box 5179
Woodbridge, VA 22194-5179
Phone: (703)878-7655
Fax: (703)878-7655
E-mail: rch@pipeguy.com

Formed by merger of: (1989) Pipe Collectors International.

• 17355 • Certified Kapnismologist Award
For recognition of contributions to pipe collecting. Individuals who are 18 years of age, members of PCCA, and recognized as experts in various fields of pipe collecting and tobacco are eligible. A kapnismologist is one who studies or who makes an art of the science of smoking, especially as applied to pipes. A certificate is awarded annually at the PCCA members' convention. Established in 1984 by C. Bruce Spencer.

• 17356 •
Pittsburgh History and Landmarks Foundation
Louise Sturgess, Exec.Dir.
100 West Sta. Sq. Dr., Ste. 450
Pittsburgh, PA 15219
Phone: (412)471-5808
Fax: (412)471-1633
E-mail: information@phlf.org
Home Page: http://www.phlf.org

• 17357 • Award of Merit
For exemplary architectural restoration. Recognition award bestowed annually.

• 17358 •
Pittsburgh New Music Ensemble
Jeffrey Nytch, Managing Dir.
PO Box 99476
Pittsburgh, PA 15233
Phone: (412)889-7231
Fax: (412)320-9913
E-mail: info@pnme.org
Home Page: http://www.pnme.org

• 17359 • Harvey Gaul Competition
To recognize an outstanding composer and to commission a new work for PNME. Contestants must be citizens of the United States and must submit a score and CD recording of the work. Entries must be submitted by September 30. A $6,000 monetary award is presented biennially in odd-numbered years, and the piece is premiered by the Pittsburg New Music Ensemble.

• 17360 •
Pittstown Historical Society
Constance Kheel, Contact
PO Box 252
Valley Falls, NY 12185-0252
Phone: (518)686-7514
Phone: (518)663-5601

• 17361 • Joyce Peckham Memorial Fund
For high school senior with highest grade average in social studies. Monetary award bestowed annually.

• 17362 •
Plainville Association for Retarded Citizens
Gary Willard, Pres.
28 E. Maple St.
PO Box 15
Plainville, CT 06062
Phone: (860)747-0316

• 17363 • Augur Scholarship
For college bound student who has a disability or plans a career in service to those with disabilities. Monetary award bestowed annually.

• 17364 •
Planet Drum Foundation
Peter Berg, Dir.
PO Box 31251
Shasta Bioregion USA
San Francisco, CA 94131
Phone: (415)285-6556
Fax: (415)285-6563
E-mail: planetdrum@igc.org
Home Page: http://www.planetdrum.org

• 17365 • Green City Hands-On Activist Award
Recognizes exemplary community service. Awarded occasionally.

• 17366 •
The Planetary Society
Dr. Louis Friedman, Exec.Dir.
65 N Catalina Ave.
Pasadena, CA 91106-2301
Phone: (626)793-5100
Toll-Free: 800-9-WORLDS
Fax: (626)793-5528
E-mail: tps@planetary.org
Home Page: http://www.planetary.org

• 17367 • Thomas O. Paine Memorial Award
Recognizes those who have advanced the goal of the human exploration of Mars. A monetary award is given annually.

• 17368 •
Planned Parenthood Federation of America
Karen Pearl, Interim Pres.
434 W 33rd St.
New York, NY 10001
Phone: (212)541-7800
Toll-Free: 800-230-7526
Fax: (212)245-1845
E-mail: communications@ppfa.org
Home Page: http://www.plannedparenthood.org

• 17369 • Maggie Awards
For recognition of outstanding achievement by the media and the arts and entertainment indus-

tries in support of reproductive rights and health care issues, including contraception, sexuality education, teenage pregnancy, abortion, and international family planning. Awards are given in the categories of television, radio, newspaper, music, magazine, book, new media, theater, film and video, and advertising categories. The deadline for nominations is January 1. A lucite pyramid sculpture is awarded annually at the meeting of the PPFA national membership. Established in 1978 in honor of Margaret Sanger, the founder of PPFA.

• 17370 • Margaret Sanger Award
This, the highest honor in the family planning movement, is given in recognition of excellence and leadership in the field. Individuals of national stature who have contributed to the family planning movement, whether in public advocacy, law, research, education, medicine, religion, or other specialty areas, are eligible. The deadline for nominations is in January. A bronze statuette titled Children of the World, by the American artist Stanley Bleifeld, is awarded each year at the meeting of the PPFA national membership. Established in 1966, the year of Margaret Sanger's death, as a memorial tribute to the founder of PPFA.

• 17371 •
Planned Parenthood Federation of Canada (Federation pour le planning des naissances du Canada)
Louise Harvey, Pres.
1 Nicholas St., Ste. 430
Ottawa, ON, Canada K1N 7B7
Phone: (613)241-4474
Fax: (613)241-7550
E-mail: admin@ppfc.ca
Home Page: http://www.ppfc.ca

• 17372 • Volunteer of the Year Award
To recognize outstanding contributions by a volunteer to the family planning movement in Canada. A monetary award of $1,000, a plaque, and travel expenses to PPFC's annual general meeting are awarded. Established in 1979. Sponsored by Janssen-Ortho Inc.

• 17373 •
Plant Growth Regulation Society of America
Mr. Charles Hall, Exec.Sec.
PO Box 2945
La Grange, GA 30241
Phone: (706)845-9085
Fax: (706)883-8215
E-mail: assocgroup@mindspring.com
Home Page: http://www.griffin.peachnet.edu/pgrsa

• 17374 • Bayer Crop Science Award
Recognizes the best paper presentation at annual meeting. Graduate students are eligible. Awarded annually.

• 17375 • Valent Biosciences- Best Paper Awards
Recognizes the best published manuscript in PGRSA Quarterly. Awarded annually.

• 17376 •
Plastic Surgery Educational Foundation
Brian M. Kinney MD, Pres.
444 E Algonquin Rd.
Arlington Heights, IL 60005
Phone: (847)228-9900
Toll-Free: 888-4-PLASTIC
Fax: (847)228-9131
E-mail: registration@plasticsurgery.org
Home Page: http://www.plasticsurgery.org

• 17377 • Award for Innovation and Excellence in Media Coverage of Plastic Surgery
To recognize excellence in media coverage in the field of plastic surgery. Accepts entries in the categories of newspapers and wire services, magazines, and radio and television.

• 17378 • Distinguished Service Award
To recognize a member or other individual who has devoted exceptional time and effort to the achievement of the Foundation's goals. Recipients are nominated by the PSEF President. Established in 1984.

• 17379 • Honorary Award
To recognize physicians who have contributed significantly to the advancement of maxillofacial surgery, and who have demonstrated leadership in the specialty. Recipients are chosen by the ASMS President. Awarded when merited. Established in 1953.

• 17380 • Honorary Citation
To recognize a senior member of ASPRS for his or her service to plastic surgery, including clinical contributions to the advancement of the specialty, demonstrated leadership skills within organized plastic surgery, and humanitarian actions. A silver plaque is awarded annually. Established in 1945.

• 17381 • Robert H. Ivy Society Award
To recognize excellence in the presentation of plastic surgery scientific information. Awarded annually to the presenter who demonstrates the greatest degree of skill in preparation, presentation, and illustration of scientific material at the annual meeting of the Society. Sponsored by the Robert H. Ivy Society, founded in Pennsylvania in 1954.

• 17382 • Presidential Award
To recognize an individual who has promoted the specialty of maxillofacial surgery by demonstrating leadership in the field and supporting ASMS programs. Recipients, who do not have to be maxillofacial surgeons, are selected by the ASMS President. Established in 1989.

• 17383 • Presidential Award (Presidential Citation)
To recognize an ASPRS member or consultant/manufacturer in the plastic surgery field for selflessly contributing extensive time and effort to an ASPRS activity. Established in 1985.

• 17384 • Public Education Award for Excellence in Plastic Surgery Journalism
To recognize and encourage those journalists who cover the specialty of plastic surgery comprehensively, accurately, and creatively. The award is given in the following categories: television/cable, radio, newspaper/wire, and magazine. Nominations may be made by American Society of Plastic and Reconstructive Surgeons' members, Society staff, or journalists themselves. Winners are selected by a panel of plastic surgeons, journalists, and public relations professionals. A monetary award of $500, a plaque, and announcement in a nationally distributed press release are awarded.

• 17385 • Research Fellowship Grants
To encourage research and academic career development in plastic and reconstructive surgery. Surgical residents or persons preparing for a plastic surgery residency, plastic surgery experience, or recent residency graduates wishing to supplement their clinical training with a research experience are eligible. Grants are $30,000 each, and are awarded for a minimum of one year.

• 17386 • Research Grants
To fund expenses in connection with studies by individuals based on originality, facilities, and merit of study. Approximately $160,000 is allocated to fund grants each year, averaging $5,000 each. Awarded annually in March.

• 17387 • Scholarship Contest
To stimulate research and expository expression among plastic surgeons, as well as to provide the journal of *Plastic and Reconstructive Surgery* with quality papers. Scholarships are provided in the following categories: Basic Science Scholarship and Clinical Research - to recognize a plastic surgery resident or plastic surgeon for less than five years prior to the submission of the manuscript. Basic Science and Clinical Research category - Junior Award $3,000 and Senior Award $3,000; Essay Scholarship Award - $2,000; Investigator Award - for an author who is not a plastic surgeon or a plastic surgery resident at the time of submission. A monetary award of $1,500 for first prize, $1,000 for second prize, and $500 for third prize is awarded. Established in 1948.

• 17388 • Special Achievement Award
To honor an outstanding physician who has brought credit and distinction to plastic surgery. Awarded at the discretion of the Board of Trustees of the Society. Established in 1976.

• 17389 •
Plastic Surgery Research Council
Jodie Ambrose, Membership Services Coor.
45 Lyme Rd., Ste. 304
Hanover, NH 03755
Phone: (603)643-2325
Fax: (603)643-1444
E-mail: psrc@sover.net
Home Page: http://www.ps-rc.org

• 17390 • **Crikelair, Snyder, Gingras, Hardesty, Shenaq**
Recognizes the best presentations and poster at the annual meeting. Awarded annually.

• 17391 •
Plastics Academy
Jay Gardiner, Pres.
210 Lancaster St.
Leominster, MA 01453
Phone: (978)537-9529
Fax: (978)537-3220
E-mail: halloffame@plasticsacademy.org
Home Page: http://www.plasticsacademy.org

• 17392 • **Plastics Hall of Fame**
To honor individuals who have contributed significantly to the development of plastics or the plastics industry in the United States. Criteria for nomination are: a significant scientific, engineering, or equipment invention or breakthrough; development of an outstanding product, market, or end-use niche or business endeavor; long and valuable service to a segment of the plastics industry; and/or a record of constructive, collaborative action with government, regulatory, academic, environmental, health, trade, or other industry-related groups. Inductees are admitted biennially. Established in 1972 by *Modern Plastics Magazine* in cooperation with The Society of the Plastics Industry, Inc.

• 17393 •
Playboy
Hugh M. Hefner, Editor-in-Chief
680 N Lake Shore Dr.
Chicago, IL 60611
Phone: (312)751-8000
Fax: (312)751-2818
Home Page: http://www.playboy.com

• 17394 • **College Fiction Contest**
To encourage the development of young talent. Registered graduate and undergraduate college students of any age are eligible to submit original works of fiction postmarked between September 1 and December 31. The following awards are presented: first prize of $3,000 and publication in the upcoming October issue of *Playboy*, second prize of $500 and a year's subscription to the magazine, and third prize of $200 of a year's subscription are awarded annually. Established in 1986.

• 17395 •
Playboy Foundation
Hugh M. Hefner, Editor-in-Chief
680 N Lake Shore Dr.
Chicago, IL 60611
Phone: (312)751-8000
Fax: (312)751-2818
E-mail: giving@playboy.com
Home Page: http://www.playboy.com/corporate/foundation

• 17396 • **Hugh M. Hefner First Amendment Award**
To recognize and honor individuals who have made significant contributions in the vital effort to protect and enhance First Amendment rights for Americans. Eligibility is not restricted by profession, but nominees traditionally have come from the areas of print journalism, education, book publishing, law, government, and entertainment (motion pictures, television, theater). Nominations open in Spring and close on June 27. A monetary award of $5,000 and a plaque are awarded annually. Established in 1979.

• 17397 •
Playwrights' Center
Polly K. Carl, Artistic Dir.
2301 Franklin Ave. E.
Minneapolis, MN 55406
Phone: (612)332-7481
Fax: (612)332-6037
E-mail: info@pwcenter.org
Home Page: http://www.pwcenter.org

• 17398 • **Jerome Fellowships**
To provide emerging playwrights throughout the United States with funds and services to aid them in the development of their craft. Applicants must be U.S. citizens or legal residents. Applicants may not have had more than two professionally produced plays. The deadline is mid-September. Five fellowships are awarded annually. Recipients receive an annual stipend of $9,000 and have access to additional development support and the Center's services, including classes, readings and workshops with professional theater artists. The twelve-month fellowship period must be spent in Minnesota at the Playwrights' Center. Established in 1976. Sponsored by the Jerome Foundation.

• 17399 • **McKnight Advancement Grants**
To recognize playwrights whose work demonstrates exceptional artistic merit and potential and whose primary residence is in the state of Minnesota. The grants are intended to significantly advance recipients' art and careers, and can be used to support a wide variety of expenses, including but not limited to writing time, artistic costs of residency at a theater or arts organization, travel/study, production or presentation. Applicants must have had a minimum of two different works fully produced by professional theaters and be a citizen of the U.S. and a legal resident of Minnesota. The deadline for application is the beginning of February. Three awards of $25,000 each plus additional development support are made annually. These grants are funded by the McKnight Foundation Arts Funding Plan.

• 17400 • **PlayLabs Festival**
To assist in the development of scripts by professionally-oriented playwrights during two-week workshops that culminate in a public reading performance. Applicants must be U.S. citizens or legal residents. Applications must be submitted by the beginning of December. Five to seven plays are selected annually. Workshop collaborators, travel expenses, housing, per diem, and a stipend are awarded annually. Established in 1981.

• 17401 •
Please Touch Museum
Nancy Kolb, Pres. and CEO
210 N 21st St.
Philadelphia, PA 19103
Phone: (215)963-0667
Fax: (215)963-0424
Home Page: http://www.pleasetouchmuseum.org

• 17402 • **Book Award**
To recognize and encourage the publication of books for young children that are of the highest quality and will aid them in enjoying the process of learning through books. One recipient is selected in each of two categories: Age 3 and Under, and Age 4 to 7. Awarded annually. Established in 1985.

• 17403 •
Plymouth Community Arts Council
Stella Greene, Exec.Dir.
774 N Sheldon Rd.
Plymouth, MI 48170-1047
Phone: (734)416-4278
Fax: (734)416-4267
E-mail: info@plymoutharts.com
Home Page: http://www.plymoutharts.com

• 17404 • **Student Scholarship**
For artistic or musical ability. Monetary award bestowed annually.

• 17405 •
Plymouth Owners Club
Jim Benjaminson, Membership Sec.-Treas.
PO Box 416
Cavalier, ND 58220-0416
Phone: (701)549-3746
Fax: (701)549-3744
E-mail: benji@utma.com
Home Page: http://www.plymouthbulletin.com

• 17406 • **Chrysler Cup**
Annual award of recognition.

• 17407 •
Plymouth Rock Foundation
Dr. Charles Wolfe, Exec.Dir./Pres.
1120 Long Pond Rd.
Plymouth, MA 02360
Phone: (508)833-1189
Phone: (603)876-4505
Toll-Free: 800-210-1620
Fax: (508)833-2481
E-mail: info@plymrock.org
Home Page: http://www.plymrock.org

• 17408 • **Pilgrim of the Year**
Recognizes outstanding service in community programs. Awarded annually.

• 17409 •
PNC Bank, Delaware
222 Delaware Ave., 18th Fl.
Wilmington, DE 19801
Phone: (302)428-1011
Toll-Free: 800-722-1172
Fax: (302)429-2825
Home Page: http://www.pncbank.com

Formerly: (1995) Bank of Delaware.

• 17410 • **Common Wealth Awards of Distinguished Service**
To recognize outstanding achievement and serve as an incentive for future contributions in diverse fields that enrich human life. The eight fields designated for awards are: Literature, Public Service, Science, Invention, Sociology, Government, Dramatic Arts, and Mass Communications. Award recipients are not necessarily U.S. citizens. Individuals and organizations meeting the primary criteria for outstanding past and potential contributions to the world community are eligible. Six organizations in the selected award field serve as the nominating organizations. Nominations from the public are not encouraged. Six monetary awards of $50,000 each are presented annually. In addition, each winner receives a certificate of commendation and a sculptured metal trophy symbolic of the honor. The Common Wealth Awards were conceived by Ralph Hayes who established the Common Wealth Trust under his will. Hayes combined a distinguished career in high executive office with lifelong commitment to public service. Bank of Delaware serves as Trustee and has administered the awards since Hayes's death in 1977.

• 17411 •
Podiatry Management
Barry H. Block, ed.
10 E Athens Ave., Ste. 208
Ardmore, PA 19003
Phone: (610)734-2420
Fax: (610)734-2423
E-mail: podiatrym@aol.com
Home Page: http://www.podiatrym.com

• 17412 • **Lifetime Achievement Award**
To recognize individuals who promote and advance the podiatry profession. Podiatrists vote for the winning candidate. A plaque and publicity are awarded annually. The Award has been recognized by the White House with letters from Presidents Reagan, Bush, and Clinton. It is the only award voted on by the entire podiatry profession. Established in 1984.

• 17413 •
Poet Lore
Gregory F. Robison, Exec.Dir.
The Writer's Center
4508 Walsh St.
Bethesda, MD 20815-6006
Phone: (301)654-8664
Fax: (301)654-8667
E-mail: postmaster@writer.org
Home Page: http://www.writer.org/pubs/poet-lore.asp

• 17414 • **Rose Lefcowitz Prize**
For recognition of the best poem to appear in a volume of the magazine. A monetary prize of $150 is awarded to each winner. All works published in the magazine are considered for the prizes.

• 17415 • **Narrative Poetry Prize**
To recognize previously unpublished work of an author that is not under consideration for publication elsewhere. All entries must be predominantly narrative and at least 100 lines. The deadline for submission to the contest is November 30. A monetary award of $350 and publication in *Poet Lore* are presented to the winner; honorable mentions may receive monetary prizes. Established in 1983.

• 17416 • **Sidney Sulkin Prize**
To recognize the best critical prose to appear in a volume of the magazine. A monetary prize of $150 is awarded to each winner. All works published in the magazine are considered for the prizes.

• 17417 •
Poetry
Christian Wiman, Ed.
Poetry Foundation
1030 N Clark St., Ste. 420
Chicago, IL 60610
Phone: (312)787-7070
Fax: (312)787-6650
E-mail: editors@poetrymagazine.org
Home Page: http://www.poetrymagazine.org

• 17418 • **Frederick Bock Prize**
To recognize the best verse published in the preceding two volumes (one year) of *Poetry* magazine. All verse published in *Poetry* is automatically considered, therefore there is no formal application procedure. A monetary award of $500 is given annually. Established in 1981 in memory of the former Associate Editor of *Poetry*.

• 17419 • **Bess Hokin Prize**
To recognize a poem or group of poems published in *Poetry* magazine by a young poet. A monetary prize of $500 is awarded annually. Established in 1947.

• 17420 • **Levinson Prize**
This, the oldest and most prestigious of *Poetry*'s prizes, is given for a poem or group of poems published in *Poetry* magazine. A monetary prize of $500 is awarded annually. Established in 1914.

• 17421 • **Ruth Lilly Poetry Fellowship**
To recognize and encourage young, emerging American poets. Eligible candidates are college or university students, who are then selected by a panel of judges. Two monetary awards of $15,000 are presented annually by the Poetry Foundation, publisher of *Poetry* magazine. Established in 1989 by Ruth Lilly, an Indianapolis philanthropist.

• 17422 • **Ruth Lilly Poetry Prize**
To recognize extraordinary artistic accomplishment by an American poet. Nominations are made solely by the Selection Panel, and no applications are accepted. A monetary award of $100,000 is presented annually in June by the Poetry Foundation, publisher of *Poetry* magazine. Established in 1986 by Ruth Lilly, an Indianapolis philanthropist.

• 17423 • **Union League Civic and Arts Foundation Poetry Prize**
To recognize an outstanding poem or group of poems published in the preceding two volumes (one year) of *Poetry* magazine. All verse published in *Poetry* is automatically considered, therefore there is no formal application procedure. A monetary award of $1,000 is given annually. Presented annually from 1951 through 1972 and re-established in 1993.

• 17424 • **J. Howard and Barbara M.J. Wood Prize**
To recognize the best verse published in the preceding two volumes (one year) of *Poetry* magazine. All verse published in *Poetry* is automatically considered. A monetary award of $5,000 is given annually. Established in 1994.

• 17425 •
The Poetry Center & American Poetry Archives
Steve Dickinson, Exec.Dir.
1600 Holloway Ave.
San Francisco State University
San Francisco, CA 94132
Phone: (415)338-2227
Fax: (415)338-0966
E-mail: poetry@sfsu.edu
Home Page: http://www.sfsu.edu/~poetry

Formerly: (1995) The Poetry Center.

• 17426 • **Book Award**
For recognition of the year's outstanding book of poetry. The book must have been copyrighted in the year of the current award, be the work of a living author, and be published in the year of the

award. Books may be submitted for consideration by January 31. A monetary prize of $500 and an invitation to read in the Poetry Center are awarded annually. Established in 1980.

• 17427 •
Poetry Society of America
Alice Quinn, Exec.Dir.
15 Gramercy Park
New York, NY 10003
Phone: (212)254-9628
Toll-Free: 888-USA-POEM
Fax: (212)673-2352
E-mail: brett@poetrysociety.org
Home Page: http://www.poetrysociety.org

• 17428 • **George Bogin Memorial Award**
To recognize a selection of four or five poems that reflects the encounter of the ordinary and the extraordinary, uses language in an original way, and takes a stand against oppression in any of its forms. There is no line limit. Members and non-members are eligible. A monetary award of $500 is awarded annually. Established in 1989.

• 17429 • **Alice Fay Di Castagnola Award**
To recognize a worthy work-in-progress, either poetry, prose, or verse-drama. Members of the Society are eligible. A monetary prize of $1,000 is awarded annually. Established in 1965.

• 17430 • **Norma Farber First Book Award**
To recognize an American author of a first book of original poetry published in either hard or soft cover in a standard edition during the calendar year. Publishers must submit entries. A monetary award of $500 is given annually. Established by the family and friends of Norma Farber, poet and author of children's books.

• 17431 • **The Frost Medal**
For distinguished lifetime service to American poetry. Awarded at the discretion of the PSA Board of Governors. A monetary prize of $2,500 and an invitation to deliver the Frost Medal Lecture at the annual awards ceremony are awarded when merited. Established in 1984 to honor Robert Frost.

• 17432 • **Cecil Hemley Memorial Award**
To recognize the best lyric poem under 100 lines that addresses a philosophical or epistemological concern. Members of the Society are eligible. A monetary prize of $500 is awarded annually. Established in 1969 by Jack Stadler, Treasurer of the Poetry Society of America, and his wife, Ralynn Stadler.

• 17433 • **Louise Louis/Emily F. Bourne Student Poetry Award**
To recognize the best unpublished poem, of any length, by a student in grades 9 through 12 in the United States. Members and non-members are eligible. A monetary prize of $250 is awarded annually. Formerly: (1996) Elias Lieberman Student Poetry Award.

• 17434 • **Lyric Poetry Award**
To recognize an unpublished lyric poem on any subject, not over 50 lines in length. Members of the Society were eligible. A monetary prize of $500 is awarded annually. Established in 1971 under the will of Mrs. Consuelo Ford and in memory of Mary Carolyn Davies.

• 17435 • **Lucille Medwick Memorial Award**
To honor an original, unpublished poem on a humanitarian theme, in any form, not over 100 lines. Poets who are members of the Society are eligible. A monetary prize of $500 is awarded annually. Established in 1973 by Maury Medwick in memory of his wife.

• 17436 • **Shelley Memorial Award**
To recognize a deserving, living American poet on the basis of published work and financial need. Applications are not accepted; publishers must submit nominations. A monetary prize between $6,000 and $9,000 is awarded annually. Established in 1929 by Mary P. Sears.

• 17437 • **William Carlos Williams Award**
To recognize the author of a book of poetry published by a small, non-profit, or university press. The author must be a permanent resident of the United States. Nominations must be submitted by publishers. A monetary purchase prize between $500 and $1,000 is awarded annually. Established in 1978.

• 17438 • **Robert H. Winner Memorial Award**
To recognize a poem or sequence of poems characterized by delight in language and the possibilities of discovery in ordinary life. Open to poets over 40 years old who have published no more than one book. Submissions are limited to 10 poems or 20 pages. A monetary award of $2,500 is given annually. Established by the family and friends of Robert H. Winner.

• 17439 • ***The Writer* Magazine/Emily Dickinson Award**
To recognize an unpublished poem, 30 lines or less, inspired by Emily Dickinson, though not necessarily in her style. Members of the Society are eligible. A monetary prize of $250 is awarded annually. Established in 1970.

• 17440 •
Point-of-Purchase Advertising International
Dick Blatt, Pres. and CEO
1660 L St. NW, 10th Fl.
Washington, DC 20036
Phone: (202)530-3000
Fax: (202)530-3030
E-mail: info@popai.com
Home Page: http://www.popai.com

• 17441 • **Outstanding Merchandising Achievement Awards Competition**
To recognize excellence in point-of-purchase advertising displays, signs, and programs. Members of the Institute and any manufacturers/marketers of consumer products that are part of the market place trade show are eligible. A statuette is awarded annually at the OMA Awards Gala. Established in 1959.

• 17442 •
Points of Light Foundation
Robert K. Goodwin, Pres./CEO
1400 I St. NW, Ste. 800
Washington, DC 20005-2208
Phone: (202)729-8000
Toll-Free: 800-750-7653
Fax: (202)729-8100
E-mail: info@pointsoflight.org
Home Page: http://www.pointsoflight.org

Formerly: (1991) Points of Light Volunteer Organization.

• 17443 • **Award for Excellence in Workplace Volunteer Programs**
To recognize companies of all sizes and all industries that have made employee and/or retiree volunteer efforts a central part of their operations. Community service projects and the corporate vision that supports those projects is considered by the judging committee, which includes the American Society of Association Executives, The Center for Corporate Community Relations at Boston College, the U.S. Chamber of Commerce, The Conference Board, Inc., The Drucker Foundation, Junior Achievement Inc., the National Alliance of Business, National Association of Women Business Owners, National Council of Negro Women, National Supplier Development Council, World Association of Women Entrepreneurs, the National Council of La Raza, and the Public Affairs Council. Deadline for nominations in typically in April; awards are presented in the fall. Approximately six winners are selected each year. Formerly: Award for Excellence in Corporate Community Service.

• 17444 • **Make a Difference Day Awards**
To honor the top ten projects completed on Make a Difference day in October during National Volunteer Week. Top projects receive $10,000 each to donate to a charity of their choice.

• 17445 • **President's Community Volunteer Award**
These awards, the most prestigious presented for volunteer service, are given by the President of the United States to individuals, groups, corporations, government agencies, and unions for their outstanding volunteer involvement. Nominations are accepted during the fall. The deadline varies but is usually in mid January. Awards are judged based on scope of activity, innovation, impact, and challenges overcome. Sterling silver medallions and certificates are traditionally presented by the President to approximately 20 awardees in a White House ceremony, during National Volunteer Week in April. Certificates are mailed to the finalists. The awards were established in 1982, and are co-sponsored by the Points of Light Foundation and the Corporation for National and Community Service. Formerly: (2006) President's Service Awards.

• 17446 • Lenore and George W. Romney Citizen Volunteer Award
Given to individuals who demonstrate the spirit of citizenship and volunteering that epitomized the lives of George and Lenore Romney. Presented annually in conjunction with the National Community Service Conference of the Points of Light Foundation in June.

• 17447 • Romney Volunteer Center Excellence Award
Recognizes member that have demonstrated deliberate and significant progress in implementing the organization's mission. $1000 is presented annually at the National Community Service Conference. Established in 1996 in honor of George W. Romney and his personal commitment to community service at all levels of society.

• 17448 •
Policy Studies Organization
% David Merchant
1527 New Hampshire Ave. NW
Washington, DC 20036
Phone: (202)483-2512
Fax: (202)483-2657
E-mail: dmerchant@ipsonet.org
Home Page: http://www.ipsonet.org

• 17449 • Donald Campbell Award
For innovation in public studies.

• 17450 • Hubert H. Humphrey Award
For outstanding public policy practitioners.

• 17451 • Theodore Lowi Award and Jeffrey Pressman Award
For best journal and review articles.

• 17452 • Miriam Mills Award
To an outstanding individual, under the age of 35, in the policy studies field.

• 17453 • PSO Book Award
For best policy studies book.

• 17454 •
Polish American Historical Association
Dr. Karen Majewski, Exec.Dir.
Central Connecticut States Univ.
New Britain, CT 06050
Phone: (860)832-2808
Fax: (248)738-6736
E-mail: paha@mail.ccsu.edu
Home Page: http://www.polishamericanstudies.org

• 17455 • Mieczyslaw Haiman Award
To recognize sustained scholarly effort in the field of Polish American Studies. A bronze medal is awarded annually at the Association's convention. Established in 1969 to honor Miecislas Haiman (1838-1949).

• 17456 • Oscar Halecki Award
To recognize an outstanding book or monograph written on Polish American history and culture. A monetary prize of $500 is awarded annually. Established in 1975; first awarded in 1981 to honor Oskar Halecki (1891-1973).

• 17457 • Rev. Joseph V. Swastek Award
To recognize the outstanding article on Polish American history published in the previous year's volume of *Polish American Studies.* A monetary award of $100 is presented annually. Established in 1980 to honor the Rev. Joseph V. Swastek (1913-1977).

• 17458 •
Polish Genealogical Society of America
Rosalie Lindberg, Pres.
984 N Milwaukee Ave.
Chicago, IL 60622
E-mail: pgsamerica@aol.com
Home Page: http://www.pgsa.org

• 17459 • Wigilia Medal
Recognizes contributions to Polish genealogy. Awarded annually.

• 17460 •
Pollock-Krasner Foundation
Eugene Victor Thaw, Pres. Emeritus
863 Park Ave.
New York, NY 10021
Phone: (212)517-5400
Fax: (212)288-2836
E-mail: grants@pkf.org
Home Page: http://www.pkf.org

• 17461 • Pollock-Krasner Foundation Grants
To provide assistance for professional artists of recognizable merit who are in need of financial assistance to pursue their careers. The foundation welcomes applications from painters, sculptors, and artists who work on paper, including printmakers. There is no age or geographic limitation. The foundation does not give grants to commercial artists, photographers, video artists, performance artists, filmmakers, or crafts-makers. Grants are not awarded to students as scholarships or for tuition. Grants ranging from $1,000 to $30,000 are awarded periodically throughout the year. Awarded when merited. Established in 1985 by Lee Krasner, an abstract expressionist painter and widow of Jackson Pollock.

• 17462 •
Polycystic Ovarian Syndrome Association
Kristin Rencher, Exec.Dir.
PO Box 3403
Englewood, CO 80111
Phone: (856)218-4815
Toll-Free: 877-775-PCOS
Fax: (413)751-4866
E-mail: info@pcosupport.org
Home Page: http://www.pcosupport.org

• 17463 • Chair's Award
Recognizes outstanding service of an individual volunteer. Awarded annually.

• 17464 • Director's Award
Recognizes outstanding service of an individual volunteer. Awarded annually.

• 17465 • Founder's Award
Recognizes outstanding service of an individual volunteer. Awarded annually.

• 17466 •
Polymer Alliance Zone of West Virginia
R.V. Buddy Graham, Pres.
104 Miller Dr.
Ripley, WV 25271
Phone: (304)372-1143
Toll-Free: 888-711-1143
Fax: (304)372-1167
E-mail: bgraham@pazwv.com
Home Page: http://www.pazwv.com

• 17467 • Award of Merit
For support and leadership role in WV's Polymer Alliance Zone. Monetary award bestowed annually.

• 17468 •
Population Institute
Hal Burdett, Dir.
107 2nd St. NE
Washington, DC 20002
Phone: (202)544-3300
Toll-Free: 800-787-0038
Fax: (202)544-0068
E-mail: web@populationinstitute.org
Home Page: http://www.populationinstitute.org

• 17469 • Global Media Awards for Excellence in Population Reporting
To draw attention to worldwide population issues and to honor those who have contributed, through their journalistic endeavors, to the education of the public in a meritorious manner. Entries may be submitted by any individual or organization and all entries must be accompanied by an exhibit as published, screened, or broadcast, including the name of the media and date of its use, as well as a justification for the entry and English translation, if necessary. The deadline varies each year. Awards are presented in the following categories: Best Columnist, Best Individual Reporting Effort, Most Conscientious News Service, Best Radio Program, Best Population Journal, Best Population/Environmental Reporting Effort, Best Team Reporting Effort, and Best Combined Media Effort. Additional awards include the Global Leaders Award, Country Award, and Gender Equity Award. Awarded annually. Established in 1981.

• 17470 •
Portland Opera
Christopher Mattaliano, Gen.Dir.
211 SE Caruthers St.
Portland, OR 97214
Phone: (503)241-1407
Toll-Free: (866)739-6737
Fax: (503)241-4212
E-mail: prmarketing@portlandopera.org
Home Page: http://www.portlandopera.org

• 17471 • **Eleanor Lieber Awards Competition**
To recognize outstanding young vocalists in the U.S. Northwest. Applicants must be: citizens of the U.S.; between 23 and 35 years of age; and residents or students enrolled in a college or university in Oregon, Washington, Idaho, Montana, Alaska, California, New Mexico, Arizona, Nevada, Wyoming, Utah, and Colorado. The following monetary awards are presented: first place - $10,000; second place - $5,000; third place - $2,500; audience favorite $1,000; and $500 for each of the 10 finalists. Awarded biennially in even-numbered years. Established in 1980 by Eleanor Lieber to honor Dean William Lieber. Formerly: Eleanor Lieber Awards for Young Singers; Portland Opera Lieber Awards.

• 17472 •
Portland State University
Research and Training Center on Family Support and Children's Mental Health
PO Box 751
Portland, OR 97201
Phone: (503)725-4040
Toll-Free: 800-628-1696
Fax: (503)725-4180
E-mail: gordon@pdx.edu
Home Page: http://www.rtc.pdx.edu

• 17473 • **Merit awards**
Certificate Students at Portland State University are eligible. Awarded annually. Inquire for application details.

• 17474 • **NIDRR Scholar**
Bestowed on a Portland State University student.

• 17475 •
Portuguese American Police Association
PO Box 51523
New Bedford, MA 02745-0045
Phone: (508)994-5390
E-mail: papal2@ici.net

• 17476 • **Sgt. Edward Neves Memorial Scholarship**
For individuals of Portuguese descent who are majoring in social service. Scholarship awarded annually.

• 17477 •
Post-Polio Health International
Joan L. Headley, Exec.Dir.
4207 Lindell Blvd., No. 110
St. Louis, MO 63108-2915
Phone: (314)534-0475
Fax: (314)534-5070
E-mail: info@post-polio.org
Home Page: http://www.post-polio.org

Formerly: (2003) Gazette International Networking Institute.

• 17478 • **Research Awards**
To promote scientific research leading to eventual amelioration of the consequences of poliomyelitis and/or neuromuscular respiratory diseases. Monetary awards of up to $25,000 are bestowed biennially in odd years, and a call for submissions is given in even years.

• 17479 •
Postal History Society
Kalman V. Illyefalvi, Sec.-Treas.
8207 Daren Ct.
Pikesville, MD 21208
Phone: (410)653-0665
E-mail: kalphyl@juno.com

• 17480 • **Edith M. Faulstich Grand Award**
To honor one of the Founders of the Society. Given to the Best Postal History Exhibit at the annual meeting. Gold, silver, and bronze medals are also given to the runner-up exhibitors.

• 17481 • ***Postal History Journal* Awards**
For recognition of the best long and short article appearing in *Postal History Journal* during the award year. A gold medal is presented in both categories annually.

• 17482 • **Postal History Society Medal**
To provide recognition for the best exhibit of postal history at stamp shows. Gold, silver, and bronze medals and/or certificates are awarded when merited.

• 17483 •
Postal History Society of Canada
Doug Murray, Pres.
Box 82055
Calgary, AB, Canada T3C 3W5
Phone: (613)257-5453
E-mail: doug@spicemerchants.ca
Home Page: http://postalhistory.tripod.com

• 17484 • **Frank W. Campbell Award**
To recognize major contributions to the study of postal history. Articles appearing in the *PHSC Journal* are not eligible. A plaque is awarded periodically. Established in 1982 to honor Frank W. Campbell, an outstanding contributor to the literature on Canadian postal history.

• 17485 • **Stan Shantz Award**
To recognize the best article or series in the *PHSC Journal* for the calendar year. Members of PHSC are eligible. A plaque is awarded periodically. Established in 1982 to honor Stan Shantz, founding member of the Society.

• 17486 •
Postmodern Culture
Eyal Ariman, Ed.
319 Alderman Library
Institute for Advanced Technology in the Humanities
University of Virginia
PO Box 400115
Charlottesville, VA 22904-4115
Phone: (919)515-4127
Fax: (919)515-8136
E-mail: pmc@jefferson.village.virginia.edu
Home Page: http://www3.iath.virginia.edu/pmc

• 17487 • **PMC Electronic Test Award**
To encourage new work in the field of postmodernism and to promote the use of electronic media in scholarly and literary publishing. Awarded annually with a monetary prize of $500.

• 17488 •
Postpartum Support, International
Mrs. Sherri Majors, Office Mgr.
927 N Kellogg Ave.
Santa Barbara, CA 93111
Phone: (805)967-7636
Fax: (805)967-0608
E-mail: psioffice@earthlink.net
Home Page: http://www.postpartum.net

• 17489 • **Susan Hickman Memorial Research Award**
Award of recognition. Members of PSI, graduate student, application process are eligible. A monetary prize is given annually.

• 17490 • **Jane Honikman Volunteer Award**
Award of recognition for outstanding contribution to mental health of mothers. Awarded annually.

• 17491 •
Poteet Strawberry Festival Association
Nita Harvey, Office Mgr.
PO Box 227
Poteet, TX 78065
Phone: (830)742-8144
Phone: (830)276-3323
Fax: (830)742-3608
E-mail: nitaharvey@sbcglobal.net
Home Page: http://www.strawberryfestival.com

• 17492 • **PSFA Scholarship Program**
For member of PSF Court. Scholarship awarded semiannually.

• 17493 •
Herman T. Pott National Inland Waterways Library
Bette Gorden, Curator
8001 Natural Bridge Rd.
University of Missouri, St. Louis
St. Louis, MO 63121-4401
Phone: (314)516-7244
Toll-Free: 800-766-6945
Fax: (314)621-1782
E-mail: bgorden@umsl.edu
Home Page: http://www.umsl.edu/pott

• 17494 • **Captain Donald T. Wright Award**
To recognize excellence in maritime journalism. Entries are invited from authors of articles on inland and intra-coastal waterways that have appeared in scholarly journals, books, magazines, and newspapers in the field of United States maritime journalism during the competition year. A monetary prize of $500 and a plaque are awarded annually. Editors of winning publications are also eligible for a co-award. Entry deadline is July 1. Established in memory of Captain Donald T. Wright, a riverboat pilot and editor and publisher of *Waterways Journal* for 43 years.

• 17495 •
Poultry Science Association
Mary Swenson, Admin.Asst.
1111 N Dunlap Ave.
Savoy, IL 61874
Phone: (217)356-5285
Fax: (217)398-4119
E-mail: marys@assochq.org
Home Page: http://www.poultryscience.org

• 17496 • **American Egg Board Research Award**
To increase the interest in research pertaining to egg science technology or marketing that has a bearing on egg or spent hen utilization. Manuscripts published in *Poultry Science* are automatically considered for the award. A monetary award of $1,000 and an engraved skillet are awarded annually. Administered by the American Egg Board Technical Committee.

• 17497 • **American Poultry Historical Society Award**
To recognize an individual who has made a contribution to the preservation and recording of historical information. A plaque and monetary prize of $200 are awarded in even-numbered years.

• 17498 • **Broiler Research Award**
Also known as the National Chicken Council Award, this award is presented for recognition of distinctive research that has had a strong economic impact on the broiler industry. Only research published in the preceding five calendar years and performed at public, nonprofit institutions, or similar organizations will be considered. A monetary award of $2,500 and an engraved plaque are awarded annually at the Association's awards banquet. Established in 1980 by the National Broiler Council.

• 17499 • **Merck Award for Achievement in Poultry Science**
For recognition of distinctive contributions to poultry science advancement. A framed scroll and monetary award of $1,500 are awarded annually.

• 17500 • **National Turkey Federation Research Award**
To recognize an outstanding record of turkey research in the United States published during the last six years. A plaque and monetary prize of $1,000 are awarded in even-numbered years.

• 17501 • **Philbro Extension Award**
To recognize a member for conducting an outstanding program of work in the area of poultry extension. Criteria include: preparation and publication of extension materials; usefulness and timeliness of materials in serving the needs of the poultry industry; improved practices as well as originality and stimulation of interest; use of mass media in dissemination of information; training programs for the industry and other extension workers; and implementation of new information and industry problem-solving programs. A monetary award of $1,500 and a plaque are awarded annually. Established in 1962. Formerly: Pfizer Extension Award.

• 17502 • **Poultry Products Research Award**
To recognize outstanding contributions in the field of poultry and/or egg technology. Individuals under the age of 40 are eligible. A plaque and monetary prize of $2,500 are awarded in odd-numbered years. Formerly: Continental Grain Company Poultry Products Research Award.

• 17503 • **Poultry Science Association Fellows**
To recognize activities, accomplishments, recognitions, and contributions to poultry science. Awarded annually.

• 17504 • **Poultry Science Association Research Award**
To recognize outstanding research published during the year. Members of the Association who are under 40 years of age are eligible. A monetary award of $1,000 and a certificate are awarded annually. Established in 1954.

• 17505 • **Poultry Welfare Research Award**
For recognition of outstanding turkey research in the United States published during the last six years. A monetary prize of $5,000 is awarded in even-numbered years. Established in 1992.

• 17506 • **Purina Mills Teaching Award**
To recognize a member who, over a period of years, has demonstrated outstanding success as a teacher. A monetary award of $1,500 and a plaque are awarded annually. Established in 1962 by the Ralston Purina Company.

• 17507 •
Poynter Institute for Media Studies
801 3rd. St. S
St. Petersburg, FL 33701
Phone: (727)821-9494
Toll-Free: 888-769-6837
Fax: (727)821-0583
Home Page: http://www.poynter.org

• 17508 • **ASNE Distinguished Writing Awards**
To recognize, foster and reward excellence in writing in American and Canadian daily newspapers. Awards of $2,500 are given annually to four individuals for non-deadline writing, editorial writing, commentary, and a revolving category. Established in 1979.

• 17509 • **Jesse Laventhol Prize for Deadline News Reporting**
To recognize excellence in deadline news writing in American and Canadian daily newspapers. Awarded annually to an individual winner and to a team with a monetary prize totaling $10,000. Established in 1979.

• 17510 •
Prairie Schooner
Hilda Raz, Editor-in-Chief
201 Andrews Hall
University of Nebraska
Lincoln, NE 68588-0334
Phone: (402)472-0911
Fax: (402)472-9771
E-mail: kgrey2@unlnotes.unl.edu
Home Page: http://prairieschooner.unl.edu

• 17511 • **Virginia Faulkner Award for Excellence in Writing**
For recognition of the best poem or group of poems published in *Prairie Schooner* during the preceding year. A monetary prize of $1,000 is awarded annually in the spring. Established in 1988 in honor of Virginia Faulkner, associate editor and fiction editor of *Prairie Schooner* and editor-in-chief for the University of Nebraska Press.

• 17512 • **Lawrence Foundation Award**
To recognize the best short story published in *Prairie Schooner* each year. A monetary award of $1,000 is presented annually. Established in 1977 by the Lawrence Foundation, a charitable trust in New York City.

• 17513 • **Larry Levis Prize for Poetry**
To recognize outstanding poetry published in the preceding year in *Prairie Schooner.* A monetary prize of $1,000 is awarded annually. Established in honor of the poet Larry Levis.

• 17514 • **Hugh J. Luke Award**
For recognition of creative and critical works in any genre published in *Prairie Schooner.* A mon-

etary prize of $250 is awarded annually. Established in 1988 in honor of Hugh J. Luke, editor of *Prairie Schooner* from 1980 through 1987.

• 17515 • Readers' Choice Awards
For recognition of the best work published during the year in the *Prairie Schooner*. Five to eight monetary prizes of $250 each are given annually.

• 17516 • Bernice Slote Award
To recognize the best work by a beginning writer published in *Prairie Schooner*. A monetary prize of $500 is awarded annually in the spring. Established in 1984 in honor of Bernice Slote, editor of *Prairie Schooner* from 1963-1980.

• 17517 • Edward Stanley Award
For recognition of poetry published in the *Prairie Schooner*. A monetary prize of $1,000 is awarded. Established in 1992 by the family and friends of Edward Stanley, a member of the committee that founded *Prairie Schooner* in 1927.

• 17518 • Strousse Award
To recognize the best poem or group of poems published in *Prairie Schooner*. A monetary prize of $500 is awarded annually in the spring. Established in 1975 in honor of Flora Strousse, a writer, editor, and teacher.

• 17519 •
Pratt Institute
Thomas F. Schutte, Pres.
200 Willoughby Ave.
Brooklyn, NY 11205
Phone: (718)636-3600
Home Page: http://www.pratt.edu

• 17520 • Founder's Award
To recognize philanthropic, community, and educational commitment. A scholarship is established in the name of the award recipient to benefit children of public service employees.

• 17521 •
Precast/Prestressed Concrete Institute
James G. Toscas, Pres.
209 W Jackson Blvd.
Chicago, IL 60606-6938
Phone: (312)786-0300
Phone: (312)360-3204
Fax: (312)786-0353
E-mail: info@pci.org
Home Page: http://www.pci.org

• 17522 • Certificate of Merit Award
For recognition of a PCI committee report judged to be technically outstanding and most worthy of special commendation for its merit as a contribution to the advancement of precast and/or prestressed concrete. Awarded annually. Established in 1984.

• 17523 • Harry H. Edwards Industry Advancement Award
For recognition of those ideas and concepts that hold the potential to move the precast and prestressed concrete industry to the next generation of technology. Awarded annually to one or more recipients. Established in 1985.

• 17524 • Fellow Award
To honor members for outstanding contributions to the precast/prestressed concrete industry and to PCI. Established in 1994.

• 17525 • Martin P. Korn Award
To recognize the best design/research paper appearing in the *PCI Journal* during a single year. A monetary award of $100 and a plaque are awarded annually at the convention. Established in 1960 in honor of the institute's first executive secretary.

• 17526 • Robert J. Lyman Award
To recognize the best construction/production/erection paper appearing in the *PCI Journal* during a single year. A monetary award of $100 and a plaque are awarded annually at the PCI Convention. Established in 1976 to honor Robert J. Lyman, the institute's eighth PCI President.

• 17527 • Medal of Honor Award
This, the highest honor bestowed by the PCI, is given to recognize a member who has made significant contributions to the prestressed concrete industry or the precast concrete industry and has demonstrated a sincere continuing interest in the institute. A plaque and lifetime membership are awarded when merited. Established in 1975.

• 17528 • Gale M. Spowers Marketing Award
For recognition of an outstanding overall marketing/advertising program or for an outstanding individual segment of a marketing/advertising program. Awarded annually. Established in 1986.

• 17529 • Charles C. Zollman Award
To recognize the best state of the art of precast and prestressed concrete paper appearing in the *PCI Journal* during a single year. A monetary award of $100 and a plaque are awarded annually at the convention. Established in 1981. Formerly: State of the Art Award.

• 17530 •
Precision Metalforming Association
William E. Gaskin CAE, Pres.
6363 Oak Tree Blvd.
Independence, OH 44131-2556
Phone: (216)901-8800
Fax: (216)901-9190
E-mail: pma@pma.org
Home Page: http://www.metalforming.com

• 17531 • Pitcher Insurance Agency Safety Award
Acknowledges either an effective comprehensive safety program or a specific innovative idea in the context of an effective safety program. Winners receive a $1,500 monetary award and a commemorative plaque. Sponsored by Pitcher Insurance Agency Inc. Formerly: (2004) Seastrom Safety Award.

• 17532 • R. D. Pritchard-Higgins Award for Design
Recognizes a metalforming company for creative and effective product design. Winners receive a $1,500 monetary award and a commemorative plaque. Created by the Worcester Pressed Steel Co. in 1955, and sponsored by Dave Pritchard, former chairman of PMA. Formerly: (2005) A.J. Rose-Higgins Design Award; (2004) Higgins Redesign Award.

• 17533 •
Preservation Maryland
Kristen Harbeson, Education & Outreach Dir.
24 W. Saratoga St.
Baltimore, MD 21201
Phone: (410)685-2886
Fax: (410)539-2182
E-mail: pm@preservationmaryland.org
Home Page: http://PreservationMaryland.org

• 17534 • Harrison Award
For volunteer service. Recognition award bestowed annually.

• 17535 •
Preservation Pennsylvania
Carol Bostian, Exec.Dir.
257 N St.
Harrisburg, PA 17101
Phone: (717)234-2310
Fax: (717)234-2522
E-mail: ppa@preservationpa.org
Home Page: http://www.preservationpa.org

• 17536 • Otto Haas Award
For excellence in preserving historic resources. Recognition award bestowed annually.

• 17537 • Initiative Awards
For excellence in preserving historic resources. Recognition award bestowed annually.

• 17538 •
President's Commission on White House Fellowships
Janet Slaughter Eissentat, Dir.
1900 E St. NW, Rm. B431
Washington, DC 20415
Phone: (202)395-4522
Fax: (202)395-6179
E-mail: almanac@ace.esusda.gov
Home Page: http://www.whitehouse.gov/fellows

• 17539 • **White House Fellows**
To recognize highly motivated individuals who have a desire to become involved personally in the process of national government. U.S. citizens who are in the early stages of their careers are eligible to apply. Employees of the Federal Government are not eligible, although members of the Armed Forces are an exception to this rule. There are no restrictions as to age, race, sex, creed, or national origin. Nearly all fellows have held college degrees and many have had professional or graduate training, though such training is not a prerequisite. Applicants must have excelled in their careers, have broad interests and knowledge, have participated in voluntary community service, and have demonstrated leadership ability. Applications may be submitted by February 1. Each year, the 11 to 19 individuals who are selected as White House Fellows become full-time Schedule A employees of the Federal Government and are assigned as special assistants in the Executive Office of the President, the Office of the Vice President, or to a Cabinet Member. There is a salary ceiling of approximately $66,000. Established in 1964 by President Lyndon Johnson.

• 17540 •
President's Council on Physical Fitness and Sports
Melissa Johnson, Exec.Dir.
200 Independence Ave. SW, Rm. 738 H
Washington, DC 20201
Phone: (202)690-9000
Fax: (202)690-5211
Home Page: http://www.fitness.gov

Formerly: (1961) President's Council on Youth Fitness.

• 17541 • **President's Challenge Physical Fitness Awards Program**
Motivates individuals six years and older to begin and continue an active lifestyle leading to enhanced physical fitness. The program focuses on three distinct program areas: physical fitness, health fitness, and active lifestlye. Four awards are given for different levels of accomplishment: the Presidential Active Lifestyle Award is presented to individuals who meet their daily activity goals for six weeks; the Presidential Champions Gold Award is for individuals who earn 80,000 points in the program; the Presidential Champions Silver Award for anyone who earns 45,000 points; and the Presidential Champions Bronze Award for anyone who earns 20,000 points. Awarded when merited.

• 17542 •
Prince Edward Island Council of the Arts
Darrin White, Exec.Dir.
115 Richmond St.
Charlottetown, PE, Canada C1A 1H7
Phone: (902)368-4410
Fax: (902)368-4418
E-mail: info@peiartscouncil.com
Home Page: http://www.peiartscouncil.com

• 17543 • **Milton Acorn Poetry Award**
To recognize Island writers by giving them the opportunity to submit work in one or more competitions. Awarded annually with money, and/or travel. Established in 1988.

• 17544 • **Father Adrien Arsenault Senior Arts Award**
To recognize the work of a senior Island Artist who has produced a significant body of work in the practice of visual arts, writing and publishing, music, dance, theater, film, or video. Awarded every two years with money and plaque. Established in 1990.

• 17545 • **Cavendish Area Tourist Association Creative Writing Award for Children**
To recognize Island writers by giving them the opportunity to submit work in one or more competitions. Awarded annually with money, and/or travel. Established in 1988.

• 17546 • **Feature Article Award**
To recognize Island writers by giving them the opportunity to submit work in one or more competitions. Awarded annually with money, and/or travel. Established in 1988.

• 17547 • **Lucy Maud Montgomery Children's Literature Award**
To recognize Island writers by giving them the opportunity to submit work in one or more competitions. Awarded annually with money, and/or travel. Established in 1988.

• 17548 • **Carl Sentner Short Story Award**
To recognize Island writers by giving them the opportunity to submit work in one or more competitions. Awarded annually with money, plaque, and travel. Established in 1988.

• 17549 • **Theater P.E.I. Playwriting Awards**
To recognize Island writers by giving them the opportunity to submit work in one or more competitions. Awarded annually with money, plaque, and travel. Established in 1988.

• 17550 •
Prince George's County Genealogical Society
Alice Nelson, Corr.Sec.
PO Box 819
Bowie, MD 20718-0819
Phone: (301)262-2063
E-mail: pgcgs@juno.com
Home Page: http://www.rootsweb.com/~mdpgcgs

• 17551 • **Jane Rousch McCafferty C.G. Award**
For excellence in genealogical research. Recognition award bestowed annually.

• 17552 •
Princess Grace Foundation - USA
Toby E. Boshak, Exec.Dir.
150 E 58th St., 25th Fl.
New York, NY 10155
Phone: (212)317-1470
Fax: (212)317-1473
E-mail: info@pgfusa.com
Home Page: http://www.pgfusa.com

• 17553 • **Dance Grants**
To provide funds for dancers. Nominations are accepted from the artistic directors of dance companies and the deans and department chairpersons of professional schools or university programs in dance. Grants are awarded to individuals through a school or company. All candidates must be United States citizens or have permanent resident status. The deadline is April 30. Scholarships for tuition for professional training at a non-profit school located in the United States and fellowship grants for salary assistance for an apprentice or a new member in a dance company are awarded. New members must have joined the company within the past five years. $15,000. Awarded annually. Established in 1984 to honor H. S. H. Princess Grace of Monaco.

• 17554 • **Film Grants**
To assist emergency filmmakers by providing film grants for senior and graduate thesis productions. Invited colleges and universities in the United States must submit applications by June 1. In the past, amounts for grants given were between $4,500 and $8,500 for senior and graduate thesis projects. Awarded annually. Established in 1984 to honor H. S. H. Princess Grace of Monaco.

• 17555 • **Theatre Grants**
To provide funds for actors, directors, and costume, scenic, lighting designers, and playwrights. Nominations are accepted from the artistic directors of theater companies and the deans and department chairpersons of professional schools in theater. Grants are awarded to individuals through a school or company. Playwrights may apply independently of an organization but require a letter of recommendation by a director or individual in the field. All candidates must be United States citizens or have permanent resident status. The deadline is March 31. Theater grants are made in the forms of scholarships, apprenticeships, and fellowships.

• 17556 •
Princeton University
MicroFluidic Research and Engineering Laboratory
A321 Engineering Quadrangle
Department of Chemical Engineering
Princeton, NJ 08544
Phone: (609)258-4574
Fax: (609)258-0211
E-mail: stroian@princeton.edu
Home Page: http://www.princeton.edu/~stroian/overview.html

• 17557 • **Kristine M. Layn Award**
Recognizes outstanding achievement in research by a 3rd-year chemical engineering student.

• 17558 •
Princeton University Alumni Council
Margaret Moore Miller, Dir.
PO Box 291
Princeton, NJ 08542-0291
Phone: (609)258-5814
Fax: (609)258-1281
E-mail: losborne@princeton.edu
Home Page: http://alumni.princeton.edu

• 17559 • **James Madison Medal**
To recognize an alumnus of the graduate school who has received distinction in his or her chosen profession, has advanced the cause of graduate education, or has achieved a record of outstanding public service. An engraved medal is awarded when merited. Established in 1973.

• 17560 • **Woodrow Wilson Award**
To recognize service to the public welfare, including governmental and non-governmental areas, in areas such as education through which Woodrow Wilson made such a significant contribution, religion, philanthropy, medicine, the arts, and others. A monetary award of $1,000 and a citation are presented annually to an alumnus of the undergraduate college for achievement in exemplifying Wilson's phrase, "Princeton in the nation's service." Established in 1956.

• 17561 •
The Print Center
Ashley Peel Pinkham, Asst.Dir.
1614 Latimer St.
Philadelphia, PA 19103
Phone: (215)735-6090
Fax: (215)735-5511
E-mail: info@printcenter.org
Home Page: http://www.printcenter.org

• 17562 • **Annual International Competition**
To recognize excellence in prints and photographs. Submission deadline is November 15. Awards are given in the following categories: (1) Purchase Awards - offered to the Philadelphia Museum of Art for their permanent collections; (2) Cash Prizes; (3) Patron Awards - prints and photographs selected either by the jurors or by the patron become part of the patron's collection; (4) Professional Prizes - art or paper supplies from the prize donors; and (5) Special Awards. Held annually in July or August. Established in 1924.

• 17563 •
PrintImage International
Steven D. Johnson, Pres./CEO
70 E Lake St., No. 333
Chicago, IL 60601-5907
Phone: (312)726-8015
Toll-Free: 800-234-0040
Fax: (312)726-8113
E-mail: info@printimage.org
Home Page: http://www.printimage.org

Formerly: (2003) National Association of Quick Printers.

• 17564 • **Honorary Lifetime Member**
To honor an individual who has contributed his/her time and effort over a number of years to the Association and the industry. Lifetime membership in the Association is awarded when merited. Established in 1980.

• 17565 • **Industry Award of Distinction**
To honor a non-printer (supplier, educator, author, media person, etc.) who has shown continuing support of the quick printing industry. A plaque is awarded as merited. Established in 1987.

• 17566 • **Printer of the Year**
This, the highest award the Association can bestow, is given to honor the quick printer who has done the most in the succeeding year to further the advancement of the industry and the Association. A plaque is awarded annually. Established in 1977.

• 17567 •
Printing Industries of America
Michael Makin, CEO
200 Deer Run Rd.
Sewickley, PA 15143
Phone: (412)741-6860
Toll-Free: 800-742-2666
Fax: (412)741-2311
E-mail: gain@printing.org
Home Page: http://www.gain.net

• 17568 • **Lewis Memorial Lifetime Achievement Award**
This, the highest honor awarded to an individual in the industry, is given to recognize long-term, outstanding contributions to the graphic arts industry. Nominations deadline is December 2. Awarded annually. Established in 1950 in honor of Abraham Lewis, founder of *Graphic Arts Monthly*. Formerly: (1997) Lewis Memorial Executive of the Year Award.

• 17569 • **Premier Print Awards**
Also known as the Benny, this award recognizes those companies that produce the best in print media and display a commitment to quality through their work. Entries may be submitted by printers, allied graphic arts firms, designers, advertising, marketing and public relations agencies, magazines, and other publications, clients, customers, writers, corporations, schools, associations, and other organizations. Material of any description produced during the previous year must be submitted by May 1. A Benjamin Franklin statuette, the "Benny" of the graphic arts industry, is presented at an Awards Recognition ceremony to the Best of Category winners. Certificates and plaques are also awarded. Presented annually. Established in 1950.

• 17570 •
Printing Industries of America
Non-Heatset Web Section
100 Daingerfield Rd.
Alexandria, VA 22314
Phone: (703)519-8100
Fax: (703)548-3227
E-mail: bparrott@printing.org
Home Page: http://www.gain.net

• 17571 • **Non-Heatset Web Printing Awards Competition**
To recognize excellence in pieces produced by non-heatset web press equipment to make the printing industry aware of its capabilities. Awards are given in ten categories. Any printing company that prints with non-heatset presses is eligible for pieces produced during the preceding year. The deadline for submissions is October 15. Complimentary hotel for two and registration for the meeting are awarded for first place in each category. In addition, all award winners receive two plaques: one to the printer for the category and placement and one for the customer whose piece won the award. Established in 1984. Formerly: Graphic Arts Awards Competition for Non-Heatset Printers.

• 17572 •
Pritzker Architecture Prize
Martha Thorne, Exec.Dir.
% Jensen and Walker, Inc.
8802 Ashcroft Ave.
Los Angeles, CA 90048-2402
Phone: (310)273-8696
Fax: (310)273-6134
E-mail: keithwalker@pritzkerprize.com
Home Page: http://www.pritzkerprize.com

• 17573 • **Pritzker Architecture Prize**
To recognize a living architect for his/her contributions to society through a substantial body of built work. The prize is also given for architecture as an art. Nominations may be submitted by others, excluding family, by January 31 of the award year. A monetary prize of $100,000, a citation, and since 1987, a bronze medallion are awarded annually. Established in 1979 by the Pritzker Family of Chicago of the Hyatt Foundation. The award has been sponsored by the Hyatt Foundation.

• 17574 •
Private Practice Section/American Physical Therapy Association
Stephen E. Anderson, Pres.
1055 N Fairfax St., Ste. 100
Alexandria, VA 22314
Phone: (703)299-2410
Toll-Free: 800-517-1167
Fax: (703)299-2411
E-mail: info@ppsapta.org
Home Page: http://www.ppsapta.org

• 17575 • **Robert G. Dicus Award**
To recognize significant and persistent achievement in the private practice of physical therapy in the following areas: clinical practice; education; delivery of new services; participation in the American Physical Therapy Association and the Private Practice Section; and commitment to private practice, public relations and community service. Members of the Section may be nominated. A plaque is awarded annually. Established in 1981 to honor Robert G. Dicus. Deadline is June 30. Formerly: (1981) Outstanding Service Award.

• 17576 •
Pro Football Hall of Fame
2121 George Halas Dr. NW
Canton, OH 44708
Phone: (330)456-8207
Fax: (330)456-8175
Home Page: http://www.profootballhof.com

• 17577 • **Photo Challenge**
To honor the outstanding amateur photographs of youth, middle school, high school football games. Entries may be submitted in two categories: action (any image that captures football action during a play) and feature (any imagery not including game action on the field, such as images of the sidelines, fans, and on-field images taken before or after a play). Submission deadline is December 9. The Grand Prize Winner receives a trip for four to the Super Bowl and to the Pro Football Hall of Fame. First, second, and third place winners in each category receive a camera, printer, and a gift certificate of $500, $250, and $100, respectively. Awarded annually. Sponsored by Canon USA Inc.

• 17578 • **Pro Football Hall of Fame**
To honor those players, coaches, and contributors who have enjoyed exceptional careers in the field of professional football. Elected players must have been retired for at least five years; coaches must be retired; and non-players are not subject to this limitation. Each inductee is honored in an individual niche in an enshrinement area in the Hall of Fame; each niche contains a bronze bust, a large mural, and a brief basic biography. Between three and six individuals are enshrined annually. First induction was in 1963.

• 17579 •
Pro Musicis
John E. Hagg, Exec.Dir.
140 W 79th St., Ste. 9F
New York, NY 10024-6428
Phone: (212)787-0993
Fax: (212)362-0352
E-mail: promusicis@.com
Home Page: http://www.promusicis.org

• 17580 • **International Award**
To recognize young concert soloists of great and proven talent, and to encourage the sharing of music through community service concerts to both concert and underserved audiences. Soloists must be aged 35 or younger. Eligible instruments vary by year. Submission deadline is April 21. Granted each year, the award includes sponsorship of community service and public recitals in major U.S. and European cities. Established in 1965 by Rev. Eugene Merlet.

• 17581 •
Professional Aviation Maintenance Association
Mr. Brian Finnegan, Pres.
717 Princess St.
Alexandria, VA 22314
Phone: (703)683-3171
Toll-Free: (866)865-PAMA
Fax: (703)683-0018
E-mail: hq@pama.org
Home Page: http://www.pama.org

• 17582 • **Aviation Maintenance Technician of the Year Award**
To recognize the general aviation mechanic who has made an outstanding contribution to air safety through maintenance practices. The selection of winners is based on: the suggestion of a design or improvement to an aircraft or powerplant; the suggestion or development of a maintenance and/or inspection procedure that contributed significantly to safety in aviation; or for the consistent demonstration of a high level of professionalism and excellence in the performance of duties as an aviation mechanic that led to, or resulted in, increased reliability and/or safety in aviation. Applications are accepted. The national winner is selected from the pool of regional winners. A trophy is presented annually in Washington, D.C. by the Federal Aviation Administration. Established in 1963. Formerly: (1983) Technician of the Year Award; (1983) Mechanic of the Year Award.

• 17583 • **Award of Excellence**
This, PAMA's highest award, is given to recognize individuals or companies that have promoted the tenets of professionalism and integrity on behalf of aviation maintenance technicians while exemplifying honor and diligence within the aviation community. Nomination deadline is November 30. The award must be approved by a majority vote of the Board of Directors and is presented during the annual symposium at the Awards Banquet. Awarded annually. Established in 1982.

• 17584 • **Award of Merit**
To recognize certified mechanics and avionics technicians who have demonstrated the precepts of safety and professionalism in their daily performance. Nomination deadline is November 30. Recipients are the winners of the Federal Aviation Administration's General Aviation Maintenance Technician Award and the Avionics Technician Award. A plaque or a certificate is awarded annually.

• 17585 • **Award of Special Merit**
In recognition of the efforts and achievements of non-certified persons or corporations whose actions on behalf of the aviation maintenance are distinguished. Nomination is by voice at the Board of Directors selection meeting.

• 17586 • **Chapter of the Year**
In recognition of the overall best PAMA Chapter in the categories of administration, membership growth and retention, scholarships awarded, and education. Awarded annually.

• 17587 • **Joe Chase Award**
To honor an individual who has shown outstanding personal achievement in improving the knowledge, safety, and dignity of the aircraft technician. Nominees must either be currently active or have presented a distinguished career in the aviation industry. The candidate must show dedication to learning and continuous education, and communicate the information to others in the aviation industry; show dedication to the improvement of communications between employer and employee in the aviation industry; and show dedication to a communications method that advances the knowledge of the aircraft mechanic. Nomination deadline is November 30. An honorarium of $1,000 and a citation are awarded. Established in 1973 in memory of Joe Chase for his integrity and devotion to the belief that a paramount need for safe flight is the upgrading of the aircraft mechanic. Awarded in cooperation with the Flight Safety Foundation.

• 17588 • **Company Appreciation Award**
To recognize PAMA company members whose continued support and assistance to PAMA has helped promote safety, knowledge, and dignity in the aviation maintenance profession. Awarded annually. Established in 1986.

• 17589 • **Member Service Award**
To honor members whose outstanding dedication and service has assisted in the growth of the association, as well as benefited the individuals and corporations that constitute PAMA's membership. The award must be approved by a majority vote of the Board of Directors and is presented during the annual symposium at the awards banquet. Awarded annually. Established in 1987.

• 17590 • **PAMA/ATP Award**
To honor a member of PAMA for outstanding performance in his or her profession. The nominee's daily actions must be dedicated to promoting a high degree of professionalism among avi-

ation maintenance personnel. The deadline for nominations is November 30. A monetary award of $1,000 and a plaque are awarded annually. Established in 1983. Co-sponsored by Aircraft Technical Publishers (ATP).

• 17591 •
Professional Bowlers Association of America
Ian Hamilton, Comm.
719 2nd Ave., Ste. 701
Seattle, WA 98104-1747
Phone: (206)332-9688
Fax: (206)332-9722
E-mail: info@pba.com
Home Page: http://www.pba.com

• 17592 • **Harry Golden Rookie of the Year**
To recognize the outstanding rookie bowler. Eligible nominees must have less than seven career PBA Tour appearances prior to the start of a season and earn an exemption for the following season. Awarded annually. Established in 1964.

• 17593 • **Hall of Fame**
To honor outstanding individuals of the world who, through their competitive skills and/or dedicated principles, have enriched and hastened the progress of the sport of bowling, particularly professional bowling. Induction depends upon the categories of performance, meritorious service, and other special categories that the Hall of Fame Board deems appropriate. Nominees are voted upon by the membership and the Board during the winter preceding the spring inductions. A ring and a portrait are awarded annually. Established in 1975.

• 17594 • **Chris Schenkel Player of the Year**
To designate and recognize the bowler who is voted by the PBA membership as the top player on the Tour that year. Only members are eligible. A crystal vase is awarded annually. Established in 1963. Named in honor of Chris Schenkel, PBA Hall of Fame inductee and long-time television play-by-play announcer.

• 17595 • **Senior Player of the Year**
To recognize the outstanding PBA senior bowler. Awarded annually. Established in 1990.

• 17596 • **Senior Rookie of the Year**
To recognize an outstanding senior rookie bowler. Awarded annually. Established in 1994.

• 17597 •
Professional Builder
Reed Business Information
2000 Clearwater Dr.
Oak Brook, IL 60523
Phone: (630)288-8180
Fax: (630)288-8179
E-mail: pbletters@cahners.com
Home Page: http://www.housingzone.com/pb

Formerly: *Practical Builder.*

• 17598 • **Best in American Living Awards**
To recognize the nation's most successful new housing designs for quality design and construction, energy efficiency, and successful market acceptance. Builders, architects, designers, developers, land planners, and interior designers nationwide are eligible. Entries must be submitted by July 1. Awards are presented in 17 categories each year at the annual convention of the National Association of Home Builders (NAHB), the awards' co-sponsor. Winning projects are featured in *Professional Builder*. Formerly: .

• 17599 • **Builder of the Year**
To recognize an outstanding home builder. Awarded annually.

• 17600 • **National Housing Quality Award**
To recognize builders split by size (large builders of more than 150 units per year and small builders of less than 150 units per year). Builders are judged in eight categories that evaluate their commitment to quality management. Awarded annually. Co-sponsored by the NAHB Research Center and *Professional Builder.*

• 17601 • **Professional Achievement Awards**
To recognize significant achievement in the home building industry. Awards are presented in several categories including, but not limited to: Infrastructure, Diversification, Remodeling, Planned Development, Adaptable Housing, Affordable Housing, Public/Private Partnerships, and Design Leadership.

• 17602 •
Professional Construction Estimators Association of America
Kim Lybrand, Exec.Mgr.
PO Box 680336
Charlotte, NC 28216
Phone: (704)987-9978
Toll-Free: 877-521-7232
Fax: (704)987-9979
E-mail: pcea@pcea.org
Home Page: http://www.pcea.org

• 17603 • **Rudolph John Barnes Award**
To recognize the most outstanding estimator on the national level. A traveling trophy with the names of all recipients inscribed is awarded annually at the PCEA National Convention. A permanent trophy or plaque is awarded to the winner at the end of the year. Established in 1976 to honor Rudolph J. Barnes, who helped in the original organization of PCEA in the mid 1950s.

• 17604 •
Professional Engineers Ontario
Kim Allen, CEO
25 Sheppard Ave. W, Ste. 1000
Toronto, ON, Canada M2N 6S9
Phone: (416)224-1100
Toll-Free: 800-339-3716
Fax: (416)224-8168
E-mail: webmaster@peo.on.ca
Home Page: http://www.peo.on.ca

Formerly: Association of Professional Engineers of Ontario.

• 17605 • **Engineering Medal**
To recognize a substantial contribution to the advancement of engineering in any of its branches. Contributions can be made in the areas of: new discoveries and developments; application of new technologies; solving of a unique problem; or excellence in the management of engineering projects. Members of the PEO are eligible. Awards are presented in five categories: Engineering Excellence, Management, Research and Development, Young Engineer (members under the age of 35), and Entrepreneurship. Silver medals and certificates are awarded annually. Established in 1964.

• 17606 • **Order of Honour Service Awards**
To recognize professional engineers and others who have rendered outstanding voluntary service to the engineering profession, primarily through participation in association affairs. Membership in the Order may be awarded to individuals who have served the profession diligently for many years and/or have made a substantial contribution to the operation of the profession or improvement in its status. A nonmember of the Association may be granted honorary membership in the Order for outstanding service to the engineering profession. Awarded annually when merited. Originally established as the Sons of Martha Medal in 1964.

• 17607 • **Professional Engineers Citizenship Award**
To recognize members of the Association who have made a substantial contribution to humanity as citizens and members of the community while maintaining their identify as professional engineers. This contribution may be in any milieu, and may encompass activities in such fields as education, the arts, medicine, law and social service. Gold medals and framed certificates are awarded annually. Established in 1970.

• 17608 • **Professional Engineers Gold Medal**
To recognize a professional engineer who has received wide recognition as a distinguished practitioner of his profession and, in addition, has rendered outstanding public service in other fields on a federal or provincial basis. The recipi-

ent should be recognized by the public as a professional engineer who has made significant sacrifices of time and effort for the benefit of society. A gold medal is awarded annually when merited. Established in 1947.

• 17609 •
Professional Fraternity Association
Andrew Sagan, Exec.Dir.
345 N Charles St., 3rd Fl.
Baltimore, MD 21201
Phone: (317)334-8743
Toll-Free: 888-771-4PFA
Fax: (410)347-3119
E-mail: info@profraternity.org
Home Page: http://www.profraternity.org

Formed by merger of: (1977) Professional Interfraternity Conference; Professional Panhellenic Association.

• 17610 • **Career Achievement Award**
To honor a member of a constituent fraternity who has achieved national or international renown in that fraternity's field, and who is actively participating on a regular or continuing basis in that fraternity. Members of a constituent fraternity, nominated by that fraternity are eligible. A plaque is awarded annually at the convention. Established in 1959 by the Professional Panhellenic Association, a predecessor organization.

• 17611 • **Faculty Award of Excellence**
To recognize an outstanding chapter advisor. Nominations may be made by member fraternities. A plaque is awarded annually at the convention. Established in 1992.

• 17612 •
Professional Golfers' Association of America
Jim Awtrey, CEO
100 Ave. of the Champions
Box 109601
Palm Beach Gardens, FL 33410
Phone: (561)624-8400
Fax: (561)624-8430
E-mail: info@pga.com
Home Page: http://www.pga.com

• 17613 • **Club Professional Player of the Year**
For recognition of the professional golfer who earns the most points in the following PGA of America events: PGA Championship, PGA Club Professional Championship, U.S. Open, Regional Club Professional Championships, PGA Stroke Play Championship, PGA Match Play Championship, regular PGA Tour events, Nationwide Tour events, PGA Tournament Series, Section Club Professional Championship, and Section Player of the Year standings. Awarded annually. Established in 1984.

• 17614 • **Distinguished Service Award**
This, the PGA's highest honor, is given to outstanding Americans who display leadership and humanitarian qualities, including integrity, sportsmanship, and enthusiasm for the game of golf. Awarded annually. Established in 1988.

• 17615 • **Golf Professional of the Year**
For recognition of the working golf professional whose total contributions to the game best exemplify the complete PGA professional. The annual award embraces a wide range of service executed by a golf professional and is based on overall performance, service to the PGA Section and the Association, leadership ability, image, ability to inspire fellow professionals, and the promotion of golf. Established in 1955.

• 17616 • **Junior Golf Leader**
To recognize the PGA professional who is a leader in junior golf and who reflects the ideals of those who work with youth. Work by nominees should include involvement in the promotion and development of junior golf programs at the club level and support for national junior golf programs. The interest, concern, and ability to provide opportunities and experience for juniors to learn and play golf are qualities of a successful junior golf leader. Awarded annually. Established in 1988.

• 17617 • **Merchandisers of the Year**
To recognize those PGA professionals who have excelled as businesspeople and merchandisers in the promotion of golf. The award is presented in three categories: private golf facility, public golf facility, and resort golf operations. Inaugurated in 1978 by *Sports Illustrated* magazine and the PGA of America.

• 17618 • **PGA Championship**
For recognition of the annual golf tournament winner. This tournament is one of the top four in the world. Held annually in August. Established in 1916.

• 17619 • **Player of the Year**
For recognition of the most outstanding professional golfer of the year on the PGA Tour. The winner is determined on the basis of tournament wins, official money standing, and scoring average. A plaque is awarded annually. Established in 1948.

• 17620 • **Horton Smith Award**
To recognize an individual PGA professional for outstanding and continuing contributions to golf professional education and the PGA's educational programs. Awarded annually. Established in 1965 to honor Horton Smith, the Association's president from 1952 to 1954 and an exponent of improving educational programs.

• 17621 • **Bill Strausbaugh Club Relations Award**
To recognize PGA professionals who, by their day-to-day efforts, have distinguished themselves by mentoring their fellow PGA professionals in improving their employment situations and through service to the community. Candidates should demonstrate a record of service to their Section or Association; leadership ability; involvement in civic activities and local charitable causes within their community; and be recognized as someone of outstanding character. Awarded annually. Established in 1979 to honor the late William Strausbaugh, Jr., former PGA golf professional at Columbia Country Club, Chevy Chase, MD.

• 17622 • **Teacher of the Year Award**
To recognize the outstanding teachers of golf among the ranks of the PGA of America membership. Based on overall performance in teaching; unusual, and innovative, and special teaching programs; articles published in books and magazines; and the outstanding golfers instructed. Awarded annually. Established in 1986.

• 17623 • **Vardon Trophy**
To honor the professional golfer with the lowest adjusted scoring average in 60 rounds of tournament play. A medallion is awarded annually in honor of the internationally renowned British golfer, Harry Vardon. Established in 1937. Formerly: Henry E. Radix Trophy.

• 17624 •
Professional Grounds Management Society
Thomas C. Shaner CAE, Exec.Dir.
720 Light St.
Baltimore, MD 21230
Phone: (410)223-2861
Phone: (410)752-3318
Toll-Free: 800-609-7467
Fax: (410)752-8295
E-mail: pgms@assnhqtrs.com
Home Page: http://www.pgms.org

Formerly: (1976) National Association of Professional Gardeners.

• 17625 • **Gold Medal Award**
For recognition of outstanding achievement in the field of professional grounds management. A gold medal and lifetime membership are presented as merited.

• 17626 • **Green Star Awards**
To recognize outstanding achievement in the grounds maintenance field. Awards are given for the best maintained areas in 17 categories, such as industrial or office park; condominium, apartment complex, or planned community; hotel, motel, or resort grounds; amusement or theme park; cemetery or memorial park; and recreation area or athletic field. Plaques are presented to the Grand Award winners and certificates are presented to Honor Winners in each category. Awarded annually at the awards banquet at the PGMS Annual Conference in the fall. Established in 1973. Formerly: Grounds Management Awards.

• 17627 • **President's Award**
To honor outstanding contributions to and support of grounds management and the PGMS. Candidates are chosen by the current president of PGMS. Plaques are presented by the presi-

dent at the Annual Conference of PGMS in the fall. Established in 1981.

• 17628 • Anne Seaman Memorial Scholarship

To provide financial aid to students currently studying landscape and grounds management, turf management, irrigation technology, or a closely related field. Applications are accepted from April 1 through July 1 every year. Scholarships of $500 and $1,000 are awarded each summer for the coming fall/spring academic year.

• 17629 •
Professional Institute of the Public Service of Canada
Michele Demers, Pres.
53 promenade Auriga Dr.
Nepean, ON, Canada K2E 8C3
Phone: (613)228-6310
Toll-Free: 800-267-0446
Fax: (613)228-9048
E-mail: pipscnet@pipsc.ca
Home Page: http://www.pipsc.ca

• 17630 • Gold Medal

To recognize individuals whose service in scientific and professional disciplines at the federal, provincial, municipal, or territorial level is deemed of outstanding importance to national or world advancement. In odd-numbered years, the award is for a field of pure or applied sciences, and in even-numbered years, the award is for some field outside of pure and applied sciences. Nominations must be submitted by April 15. A gold medal, inscribed with the crest of the Institute, is awarded yearly. Established in 1937.

• 17631 • Institute Service Awards

For recognition of outstanding service to the Institute. Only regular and retired members and employees of the Institute are eligible. Up to five bronze wall plaques are awarded annually. Established in 1970.

• 17632 •
Professional Insurance Marketing Association
Ralph M. Gill, Dir. of Communications
6300 Ridglea Pl., Ste. 1008
Fort Worth, TX 76116
Phone: (817)569-7462
Fax: (817)569-7461
E-mail: ralphgill@pima-assn.org
Home Page: http://www.pima-assn.org

Formerly: (1997) Professional Insurance Mass-Marketing Association.

• 17633 • Marketing Methods Competition

To recognize and help maintain the high standard of excellence in marketing materials. Awards are given in the following 11 categories: Mail solicitation for a guaranteed product, for a simplified-issue product, and for an underwritten product; multiple effort marketing campaign; conservation; retention; self-promotion/corporate continuity marketing; customer cross-sell and upgrade marketing; other media; non-insurance member benefits; and e-commerce websites. All PIMA members are eligible for one entry in each category. Category winners receive awards during the association's spring advertising and marketing seminar. The Best of PIMA Award for Excellence in Mass Marketing is awarded annually at the association's summer conference. Established in 1976.

• 17634 •
Professional Landcare Network
Dan Foley, Pres.
950 Herndon Pkwy., Ste. 450
Herndon, VA 20170
Phone: (703)736-9666
Toll-Free: 800-395-2522
Fax: (703)736-9668
E-mail: info@landcarenetwork.org
Home Page: http://www.landcarenetwork.org

• 17635 • ALCA Safety Award Contests

For recognition of outstanding safety records in two categories: (1) Employee Safety; and (2) Fleet Safety. Member companies may enter.

• 17636 • Environmental Improvement Awards Program

To recognize landscape contracting professionals who execute quality landscaping projects, and to recognize citizens who underwrite such work. Awards are given in the following categories: (1) Erosion Control/Revegetation; (2) Residential Landscape Maintenance; (3) Commercial Landscape Maintenance; (4) Interior Landscape Maintenance; (5) Interior Landscape Installation; (6) Interior Design/Build; (7) Residential Design/Build; (8) Commercial Design/Build; (9) Residential Landscape Contracting; (10) Commercial Landscape Contracting; (11) Special Event; (12)Artificial/Preserved Installation; (13) Artificial/Preserved Design/Build; (14) Natural Habitats; (15) Interior Containerized Plantings; (16) Interior Landscape Renovation; (17) Commercial Landscape Renovation; and (18) Ecological Restoration, Reclamation, and Creation. All commercial landscape firms which devote a major part of their business operation to landscape contracting, interior landscaping, erosion control and/or landscape maintenance are eligible to participate in the Awards Program. Work performed on entered projects must have been done by private industry. Membership in ALCA is required of entering firms. Grand, Merit and Distinction plaques are presented annually at the Convention.

• 17637 •
Professional Photographers of America
David P. Trust, CEO
229 Peachtree St. NE, Ste. 2200
Atlanta, GA 30303
Phone: (404)522-8600
Toll-Free: 800-786-6277
Fax: (404)614-6400
E-mail: csc@ppa.com
Home Page: http://ppa.com

• 17638 • Impact Through Applied Photography

To recognize the significant achievements of staff photographers who have created photographic images that display visual impact and technical excellence in the following categories: (1) technical/scientific/specialized; (2) public relations/advertising/promotion/publications; (3) people; and (4) electronic still images. Photographers employed by companies whose end product is not photography are eligible. Framed awards are presented for Best of Show, Best of Category, and Second and Third place winners. In addition, Best of Show and Best of Category winners receive cash awards and cameras. Certificates are awarded for honorable mention. Awarded annually. Co-sponsored by the Professional Photographers of America - Industrial Group, Eastman Kodak Company, and Photo Electronic Imaging.

• 17639 • International Exhibition of Professional Photography

To recognize outstanding professional photography in the following categories: (1) commercial/industrial; (2) portrait; (3) scientific/technical; (4) unclassified; (5) illustrative; (6) wedding; (7) wedding album; (8) electronic imaging; and (9) specialist (negative retoucher/color artist). Held annually. Established in 1891.

• 17640 •
Professional Photographers of Iowa
Mrs. Christy L. Brinkopf, Exec.Sec.
PO Box 108
Sumner, IA 50674
Phone: (563)578-1126
Fax: (563)578-0926
E-mail: ppichris@iowatelecom.net
Home Page: http://www.ppiowa.com

• 17641 • Medlar Award

For best photographer. Recognition award bestowed annually.

• 17642 •
Professional Picture Framers Association
Ted Fox, Exec.Dir./Sec.
3000 Picture Pl.
Jackson, MI 49201
Phone: (517)788-8100
Toll-Free: 800-556-6228
Fax: (517)788-8371
E-mail: ppfa@ppfa.com
Home Page: http://www.ppfa.com

• 17643 • Award of Distinction

For recognition of an outstanding contribution to the progress and continuing development of the Association. An engraved medallion is awarded as merited. Established in 1987.

• 17644 • Award of Recognition

For recognition of outstanding technical achievements that benefit the entire framing industry. The award varies. Awarded when merited. Established in 1980.

• 17645 • Exhibitors Competition
To encourage the design of a booth with the visual impact of the product being offered. Exhibitors of the annual trade show are eligible. Engraved plaques are awarded at each convention for first, second, and third place, and for Popular Choice. Established in 1974.

• 17646 • International Print Framing Competition
To encourage creativity of design and techniques in picture framing. Each participant uses identical prints. Entries are judged on the basis of overall impression, design and creative elements, technique, and critical assessment of skills. Retail members of the Association are eligible. Winning entries receive a monetary award of $1,000 and are hung in the PPFA Hall of Fame in Richmond, VA. Second and third place winners receive $500 and $200, respectively. Additional awards include honorable mentions, popular choice award, and judges' award. Held annually. Established in 1971.

• 17647 • New and Creative Framing Competition
To encourage creativity of new and unusual techniques and design in picture framing. Retail members of the Association are eligible. Purchase prizes are awarded at each convention. Winning entries are hung in the PPFA Hall of Fame in Richmond, VA. Established in 1975. Formerly: New and Creative Ideas Framing Competition.

• 17648 •
Professional Putters Association
Joe Aboid, Commissioner
5225 28th St.
Lubbock, TX 79407
Phone: (910)485-7131
Fax: (910)485-1122
E-mail: commissioner@proputters.com
Home Page: http://www.proputters.com

• 17649 • National Putting Championship
To recognize an outstanding putter from anywhere in the world. Individuals over 18 years of age who are members of the Association are eligible. Total monetary prizes of $25,000 and a variety of trophies are awarded annually. Established in 1960 by E. Don Clayton.

• 17650 •
Professional Rodeo Cowboys Association
Troy Ellerman, Commissioner
101 Pro Rodeo Dr.
Colorado Springs, CO 80919-2301
Phone: (719)593-8840
Fax: (719)548-4876
Home Page: http://www.prorodeo.com
Formerly: (1975) Rodeo Cowboys Association.

• 17651 • Clown of the Year
To recognize the PRCA clown (bullfighter or barrelman) who exemplifies the best image of the pro rodeo clown. Established in 1977. The Wrangler Jeans World Champion Bullfighter title goes to the PRCA bullfighter who wins the most points during the bullfight tour season and finals held in conjunction with the National Finals Rodeo; this program began in 1981. Also, the Coors "Man in the Can" title is given to the PRCA barrelman who scores highest in five categories of professionalism as judged by Wrangler Bullfight contestants, PRCA Wrangler Pro Officials, pro rodeo announcers, and top PRCA bull riders; this award was established in 1984. All are awarded annually.

• 17652 • Linderman Award
To recognize the PRCA contestant winning the most money in a combination of three events, including both rough stock and timed events. To qualify, a contestant must win at least $1,000 in each of his three events. Established in 1966 in memory of Bill Linderman, former PRCA President. Sponsored by *Prorodeo Sports News*.

• 17653 • Pro Rodeo Hall of Fame
For recognition of outstanding rodeo cowboys and stock. Honorees are selected by the Hall's board of directors according to achievement and overall contributions to professional rodeo. Established in 1979.

• 17654 • Resistol Rookie of the Year
To recognize a first-year competitor for outstanding performance and high earnings in the following rodeo events: all-around performance, bareback riding, bull riding, tie-down roping, saddle bronc riding, steer roping, steer wrestling, barrel racing, and team roping (heading and heeling). Awarded annually. Established in 1956. Sponsored by Resistol.

• 17655 • Stock of the Year
For recognition of outstanding rodeo stock. Three awards are given annually: Saddle Bronc of the Year, Bareback Horse of the Year, and Bull of the Year. Formerly: .

• 17656 • World Champions
To recognize the All-Around Cowboy and world champions in each of seven events: bareback riding, steer wrestling, team roping (heading and heeling), saddle bronc riding, tie-down roping, steer roping, barrel racing, and bull riding. Winners are determined by money won throughout the year and at the National Finals Rodeo in December. Saddles and belt buckles are awarded annually. Established in 1929. Formerly: .

• 17657 •
Professional Services Management Association
Ronald D. Worth CPSM, Exec.VP
99 Canal Center Plz., Ste. 330
Alexandria, VA 22314
Phone: (703)739-0277
Toll-Free: (866)739-0277
Fax: (703)549-2498
E-mail: info@psmanet.org
Home Page: http://www.psmanet.org

• 17658 • Management Achievement Awards
To recognize firms for achievement in the following fields: general management, financial management, marketing management, human resources management, operations management, and information technology management. A plaque is awarded annually in each category. Established in 1985.

• 17659 •
Professional Skaters Association
Carole K. Shulman, Exec.Dir.
3006 Allegro Park SW
Rochester, MN 55902
Phone: (507)281-5122
Fax: (507)281-5491
E-mail: office@skatepsa.com
Home Page: http://skatepsa.com

• 17660 • Edi Awards
To recognize and distinguish persons within the skating world including coaches, judges, producers, photographers, journalists, skaters, and patrons. The award deadline is March 15. Twenty-three awards are given out in the form of plaques and statues at the Annual International Conference. Named for Edi Scholdan, a World and Olympic Coach and first president of the Association.

• 17661 •
Progeria Research Foundation
(Asociacion Farmaceutica Mexicana)
Audrey Gordon Esq., Pres./Exec.Dir.
PO Box 3453
Col. Xaltocanxoch
Del. Xochimilco
Peabody, MA 01961-3453
Phone: (978)535-2594
Fax: (978)535-5849
E-mail: info@progeriaresearch.org
Home Page: http://www.progeriaresearch.org

• 17662 • Dr. Rio de La Loza Prize
To recognize an outstanding contribution to pharmaceutical sciences. A gold medal and a diploma are awarded annually.

• 17663 •
Project Censored
Peter Phillips, Dir.
Sonoma State University
1800 E Cotati Ave.
Rohnert Park, CA 94928
Phone: (707)664-2500
Fax: (707)664-2108
E-mail: censored@sonoma.edu
Home Page: http://www.projectcensored.org

• 17664 • Top 25 Censored Stories of the Year
To expose news stories of social significance that have been overlooked, under-reported, or self-censored by the U.S.'s major national news media, and to encourage investigative journal-

Awards are arranged in alphabetical order below their administering organizations

ists who cover those issues. The story must have appeared in the media during the current calendar year. Of the hundreds of stories submitted by journalists, scholars, librarians, and concerned citizens around the world, 25 are ranked in order of importance. Submission deadline is October 15. A certificate of recognition is awarded to the journalists and to the publications that printed their articles. Awarded annually in April.

• 17665 •
Project Management Institute
Gregory Balestrero, CEO
4 Campus Blvd.
Newtown Square, PA 19073-3299
Phone: (610)356-4600
Fax: (610)356-4647
E-mail: pmihq@pmi.org
Home Page: http://www.pmi.org

• 17666 • **Distinguished Contribution Award**
For recognition of a particularly significant achievement or sustained performance by an individual who contributes to the advancement of the project management profession and/or the Institute. The contribution may be academic in nature, such as the publication of an outstanding book, or of a business nature, such as successful completion of an extremely complex project. Nomination deadline is April 28. A plaque is awarded at the annual seminar/symposium. Established in 1980.

• 17667 • **Fellow Award**
This, the highest and most prestigious award of the Institute, is given to recognize and honor members who have, for 10 years or more, made sustained and outstanding contributions to the Institute and the project management profession. Candidates must be nominated by at least four members in good standing; deadline is April 26. A medal is awarded at the annual seminar/symposium. Established in 1975.

• 17668 • **Project of the Year Award**
To recognize and honor the accomplishments of a project team for superior performance and execution of exemplary project management. Projects from everywhere in the world are encouraged to participate, regardless of size, industry type, or location. PMI affiliation is not necessary. Submissions for the preliminary level of judging are due at the Chapter by January 27; finalists at the national level are selected by May 12. The winning project and its project team are featured in the *PMNETwork*. Awarded annually Established in 1992.

• 17669 • **Linn Stuckenbruck Person of the Year Award**
To recognize and honor a member for outstanding contributions to the development and advancement of the project management profession and the Institute. Candidates must be nominated by at least four individuals, one of which must be a member in good standing; deadline is April 28. A plaque is presented at the annual seminar/symposium. Established in 1976.

• 17670 • **Student Paper of the Year Awards**
To stimulate creative efforts directed toward advancing the concepts, tools, and techniques of managing project-oriented tasks. Students may submit any paper dealing with an original concept and related to any aspect of the management of projects. Papers must be written by a single author and not accepted for publication in any other journal. An $500 monetary prize is awarded to one undergraduate and one graduate student each year.

• 17671 •
ProLiteracy Worldwide
Robert Wedgeworth, Pres.
1320 Jamesville Ave.
Syracuse, NY 13210
Phone: (315)422-9121
Toll-Free: 888-528-2224
Fax: (315)422-6369
E-mail: info@proliteracy.org
Home Page: http://www.proliteracy.org

• 17672 • **Chairman's Award**
To recognize outstanding service to Literacy Volunteers of America over a long period of time. Individuals who have worked with Literacy Volunteers of America for a number of years are eligible. A gift is awarded and the honoree's name is inscribed on a plaque. Awarded annually at the conference. Established in 1978. Formerly: President's Award.

• 17673 • **Ruth J. Colvin Awards**
For recognition of achievement by an individual in each of the following categories: basic reading student, English as a second language student, administrative volunteer, basic reading volunteer tutor, and English as a second language volunteer tutor. Individuals must be affiliated with a Literacy Volunteers of America program to be considered. Established in 1985 in honor of Ruth J. Colvin, founder of Literacy Volunteers of America, Inc.

• 17674 • **Literacy Leadership Awards**
To recognize organizations and individuals for making a significant impact on the field of literacy nationwide. A plaque is awarded annually at the conference. Established in 1986.

• 17675 •
ProLiteracy Worldwide - Rochester New York Affiliate
Robert Mahar, Exec.Dir.
249 Highland Ave.
Rochester, NY 14620
Phone: (585)473-3030
Fax: (585)473-7478
E-mail: rmahar@literacyrochester.org
Home Page: http://www.literacyrochester.org

• 17676 • **Judy Dauphinee Volunteer of the Year**
For outstanding service to the field. Recognition award bestowed annually.

• 17677 • **Friend of Literacy Award**
For advocacy and innovation. Recognition award bestowed annually.

• 17678 •
PROMAX
Jim Chabin, CEO
9000 Sunset Blvd., Ste. 900
Los Angeles, CA 90069
Phone: (310)788-7600
Fax: (310)788-7616
E-mail: jim@promax.tv
Home Page: http://www.promax.tv

Formerly: (1985) Broadcasters Promotion Association.

• 17679 • **PROMAX Awards**
To recognize creative excellence in promotion and marketing of the electronic media. Submittals include audience promotion, sales/marketing presentations, and community involvement. Open to member and non-member radio stations, television stations, broadcast networks, cable networks and systems, and program distributors. A trophy for gold winners and a certificate for silver winners are awarded at the annual conference held each June. Deadline for entries is March of each year.

• 17680 •
Promoting Enduring Peace
Yael Martin, Exec.Dir.
23 Alden Rd.
West Haven, CT 06516
Phone: (203)387-0928
Fax: (203)387-0928
E-mail: office@pepeace.org
Home Page: http://www.pepeace.org

• 17681 • **Ghandi Peace Award**
To recognize individuals who have effectively and courageously worked for world peace and more harmonious international relations. A certificate describing the activities of the awardee and a bronze medal are awarded annually when merited. Established in 1959.

• 17682 •
Promotion Marketing Association
Claire Rosenzweig CAE, Pres./COO
257 Park Ave. S, Ste. 1102
New York, NY 10010-7304
Phone: (212)420-1100
Fax: (212)533-7622
E-mail: pma@pmalink.org
Home Page: http://www.pmalink.org

• 17683 • **Reggie Awards**
For recognition of the best promotion marketing programs of the year. All promotion marketers and advertising/promotion agencies, manufacturers, and suppliers, including PMA members

and non-members, are eligible. Entries are grouped into 14 categories, and are judged on the basis of overall originality of concept and execution, execution of promotion materials, and results in achieving marketing objectives. Gold, Silver, Bronze awards are presented in each category, with the Super Reggie Award selected from among the Gold winners. Submission deadline is January 4. Presented annually. Established in 1984.

• 17684 •
Promotional Products Association International
Steve Slagle CAE, Pres.
3125 Skyway Cir. N.
Irving, TX 75038-3526
Phone: (972)252-0404
Toll-Free: 888-IAM-PPAI
Fax: (972)258-3004
E-mail: info@ppa.org
Home Page: http://www.ppa.org

• 17685 • **Golden Pyramid Competition**
Recognizes outstanding use of promotional products in business promotions, individual contribution to industry. Awarded annually.

• 17686 • **Industry Hall of Fame**
Award of recognition. Inquire for application details.

• 17687 • **Suppliers Golden Achievement Award**
Award of recognition.

• 17688 •
Prospectors and Developers Association of Canada
Dr. Tony Andrews, Exec.Dir.
34 King St. E, Ste. 900
Toronto, ON, Canada M5C 2X8
Phone: (416)362-1969
Fax: (416)362-0101
E-mail: info@pdac.ca
Home Page: http://www.pdac.ca

• 17689 • **Bill Dennis Prospector of the Year Award**
To recognize an individual who has made a significant mineral discovery; provided outstanding service to the PDAC; been responsible for a technological invention or innovation with respect to improving Canadian prospecting and/or exploration techniques; or made an important contribution to the prospecting and/or exploration industry. Nominations must be submitted by November 30. The presentation is made annually at the March convention. Established in 1977 in memory of William W. Dennis, for his outstanding service to the Association and the industry.

• 17690 • **Distinguished Service Award**
To recognize an individual for a substantial contribution to mineral exploration and mining development over a number of years; contributions of time and effort to the Association; and/or outstanding contributions to the mineral industry in the fields of finance, geology, geophysics, geochemistry research, and related activities. Awarded annually at the March convention. Established in 1982.

• 17691 • **E3 Environmental Excellence in Exploration Award**
To recognize accomplishment in environmental protection or in developing good community relations during an exploration project or the operation of a mine. Awarded annually.

• 17692 • **Viola R. MacMillan Developer's Award**
To recognize an individual for leadership in management and financing for the exploration and development of mineral resources. Criteria include: long service to the financial aspect of the industry; ability to raise funds for a particular area, development, or project; use of new or innovative financing methods; and management skills, foresight, or persistence in successful projects. Awarded annually at the March convention. Established in 1985 and honors the memory of long time president Viola R. MacMillan.

• 17693 •
Psi Chi, National Honor Society in Psychology
Paula J. Miller, Exec. Officer
PO Box 709
825 Vine St.
Chattanooga, TN 37401-0709
Phone: (423)756-2044
Fax: (423)265-1529
E-mail: psichi@psichi.org
Home Page: http://www.psichi.org

• 17694 • **Allyn & Bacon Psychology Awards**
To recognize the best overall empirical study in psychology. The deadline for receipt of papers is a postmark of April 1. Cash awards will be presented to the winners as follows: first place, $1,000; second place, $650; and third place, $350. Awarded annually. Established in 1994. Sponsored by Allyn & Bacon Publishers.

• 17695 • **J. P. Guilford Undergraduate Research Awards**
To recognize scholarly endeavor relevant to psychology. Research papers submitted may cover experiments, correlational studies, historical studies, case histories, and evaluation studies. Only undergraduate members of the Society are eligible to submit papers. Entries must be postmarked by May 1. Cash awards will be presented to the winners as follows; first place, $1,000; second place, $650; third place, $350. Awarded annually. Established in 1979 to honor Prof. J. P. Guilford, an early Psi Chi member whose teaching career spanned 50 years.

• 17696 • **Psi Chi/APA Edwin B. Newman Graduate Research Award**
For recognition of significant graduate research in the field of psychology. To be eligible, an individual must be a graduate student at the time the research was carried out and the paper submitted for presentation. The paper must be the primary work of the graduate student who must also be the senior author. If the paper is published, the student senior author must be the first author. The paper must have been presented at a national, regional, or state psychological association meeting between January and December 30 of the previous calendar year. The deadline for receipt of papers February 1. Travel to the PSI Chi/APA national convention, hotel accommodations at the convention a plaque, a certificate, and a three-year subscription to the APA journal of the winner's choice are awarded annually. The award honors Edwin B. Newman, the cofounder and first president of Psi Chi. Cosponsored by the American Psychological Association (APA).

• 17697 • **Psi Chi/Florence L. Denmark National Faculty Advisor Award**
For recognition of an outstanding Psi Chi faculty advisor who has contributed to Psi Chi and psychology at the chapter level, as well as the state, regional, and/or national level. The nominee must have served as a Psi Chi advisor for a minimum of three years. The deadline for nomination is December 1. Travel to the Psi Chi/APA national convention, hotel accommodations at the convention, and a plaque are awarded annually. Established in 1987 in honor of Florence L. Denmark, Ph.D., former president of both Psi Chi and the American Psychological Association (APA).

• 17698 • **Psi Chi/Ruth Hubbard Cousins National Chapter Award**
To recognize the Psi Chi chapter that best fulfills the purpose of Psi Chi, which is to encourage, stimulate, and maintain excellence in scholarship of the individual members in all fields, particularly in psychology, and to advance the science of psychology. Any Psi Chi chapter that has not received the award in three years is eligible for nomination by February 1. A monetary prize of $3,500, a plaque, and trip for one to the Psi Chi/APA national convention are awarded annually. Established in 1992 in honor of Ruth Hubbard Cousins, Psi Chi Executive Director from 1958-1991.

• 17699 •
Psychologists for Social Responsibility
Anne Anderson MSW, Coord.
208 I St. NE No.B
Washington, DC 20002-4340
Phone: (202)745-7084
Fax: (202)745-0051
E-mail: psysrusa@cs.com
Home Page: http://www.psysr.org

• 17700 • **Distinguished Contribution Award**
To recognize individuals for outstanding contributions to the pursuit of peace. Members must be nominated. A certificate is awarded annually at the American Psychological Association convention. Established in 1984.

• 17701 • Distinguished Contribution to Building Cultures of Peace

Recognizes organizations that promote cultures of peace through programs that prevent or ameliorate direct or structural violence. Submit a description of work done. A plaque is awarded annually. Deadline in June 1. Established in 1999.

• 17702 • Psychological Dimensions of Peacework Award

To encourage students (future psychologists) to devote part of a career in psychology to peace research, education and development, practice, and public policy. Awarded annually. Established in 1989. Funded by the Psychological Dimensions of Peacework Fund and administered by the School of Professional Psychology at Wright State University.

• 17703 • Joel R. Seldin Award

For recognition of an analytical newspaper article that deals with psychology, war, and peace, and that significantly advances or illuminates the cause of peace. Writers must be nominated. A monetary prize is awarded annually. Established in 1987 in memory of Joel R. Seldin, newspaper reporter for the *New York Herald Tribune* who strongly supported the cause of peace.

• 17704 •
Public Broadcasting Service
Pat Mitchell, Pres./CEO
1320 Braddock Pl.
Alexandria, VA 22314
Phone: (703)739-5000
Fax: (703)739-0775
E-mail: viewer@pbs.org
Home Page: http://www.pbs.org

• 17705 • PBS Advertising and Promotion Awards

To recognize outstanding achievement in the promotion of all aspects of public television. All PBS member stations are eligible to enter. Regional networks and independent producers are eligible to enter a limited number of categories. A major portion of a campaign must have been executed during the calendar year. Awards are presented in 33 categories divided into three general áreas of competition: Campaigns, On-Air, and Print/Other. Areas of competition are further broken down into specific categories divided by market size. Trophies are awarded annually. In addition, each year PBS presents the Beryl Spector Award to honor one local advertising/promotion campaign that best exhibits ingenuity, creativity, and the most effective utilization of a small budget; and the Strategic Communications Award, which recognizes a public television station for integrating its communications function into its business plan. Judges select these winners from among the winners in various categories. Established in 1981. Currently under review. For more information contact Lisa Rosales at (703)739-5461.

• 17706 •
Public Choice Society
Steven J. Brams, Pres.
George Mason University
Buchanan House MSN 1E6
4400 University Blvd.
Fairfax, VA 22030-4444
Phone: (703)993-2337
Fax: (703)993-2334
E-mail: pubchsoc@gmu.edu
Home Page: http://www.pubchoicesoc.org

• 17707 • Duncan Black Prize

For recognition of the best article appearing in *Public Choice* during the preceding year. A monetary prize of $500 is awarded annually in March. Established in 1975 in honor of Duncan Black.

• 17708 •
Public Employees Roundtable
Adam Bratton, COO
PO Box 75248
500 N Capital St., Ste. 1204
Washington, DC 20001-5248
Phone: (202)927-4926
Fax: (202)927-4920
E-mail: info@theroundtable.org
Home Page: http://www.theroundtable.org

• 17709 • Chairman's Awards

To recognize outstanding service to individuals who have aided the Roundtable's mission. Board of Directors awards are also awarded.

• 17710 • Public Service Excellence Awards

For recognition of public organizations whose achievement exhibits the highest standard of dedication, excellence, and accomplishment. Federal, state, city, and county government organizational units whose outstanding contributions have either been on a sustained basis or performed as a single exceptional public service deed are considered. The awards are directed to the organizational unit as a whole and not merely one individual who may have made a significant contribution. Award winners are selected from within the federal, state, local government, and intergovernmental sectors. Nominees should have caused the accomplishment of significant programs or projects that have increased cost effectiveness, improved efficiency, and/or improved productivity in providing products or services to the American public. Nominations are solicited from the entire community - federal, state, and local, and are accepted from individuals, governmental units, professional groups, nonprofit organizations, and educational groups. The deadline is January 23. A plaque is awarded annually as part of Public Service Recognition Week. Established in 1985.

• 17711 •
Public Library Association
Clara Bohrer, Pres.
50 E Huron St.
Chicago, IL 60611
Phone: (312)280-5028
Toll-Free: 800-545-2433
Fax: (312)280-5029
E-mail: pla@ala.org
Home Page: http://www.pla.org

• 17712 • Advancement of Literacy Award

To honor a publisher, bookseller, hardware and/or software dealer, foundation, or similar group that has made a significant contribution to the advancement of adult literacy. The deadline for nominations is November 1. The Award is not for individuals. A plaque is awarded annually at the ALA Annual Conference. Established in 1984. Sponsored by *Library Journal.*

• 17713 • Baker & Taylor Entertainment Audio Music/VID Product Grant

Provides public libraries the opportunity to build or expand a collection of either or both formats in whatever proportion the library chooses. $2500 worth of Audio or Video Products is awarded. Established in 1997. Sponsored by Baker & Taylor Entertainment Co.

• 17714 • Demco New Leaders Travel Grant

To enhance the professional development and improve the expertise of public librarians new to the field by making their attendance at major professional development activities possible. The deadline for nominations is November 1. Plaques and travel grants of up to $1,500 are presented annually at the ALA Conference. Established in 1993. Sponsored by Demco Inc. Formerly: New Leaders Travel Grant.

• 17715 • Excellence in Small and/or Rural Public Library Service Award

To recognize a public library serving a population of 10,000 or less that demonstrates excellence of service to its community as exemplified by an overall service program or a special program of significant accomplishment. The deadline for nominations is November 1. A plaque and a $1,000 honorarium are presented annually at the ALA Conference. Established in 1991. Sponsored by EBSCO Information Services.

• 17716 • The Highsmith Library Innovation Award

Recognizes a public library's innovative achievement in planning and implementation of a creative program or service using technology. A plaque and $2000 are awarded annually at the ALA Annual Convention. Application deadline is November 1. Established in 1996. Sponsored by Highsmith, Inc.

• 17717 • Allie Beth Martin Award

To recognize a librarian who, in a public library setting, has demonstrated an extraordinary range and depth of knowledge about books or other library materials and has exhibited a distinguished ability to share that knowledge. Application deadline is November 1. A $3,000 honorarium and a plaque are presented annually at the ALA Annual Conference. Established in 1977 in honor of Allie Beth Martin. Sponsored by the Baker and Taylor.

• 17718 • Charlie Robinson Award
Recognizes a public library directory for change in the library. Applicants must have been directors for over a period of seven years. $1000 and a gift are awarded. Established in 19997. Sponsored by Baker & Taylor Co.

• 17719 •
Public Relations Society of America
Catherine A. Bolton, Exec.Dir./COO
33 Maiden Ln., 11th Fl.
New York, NY 10038-5150
Phone: (212)460-1400
Phone: (212)460-1401
Fax: (212)995-0757
E-mail: exec@prsa.org
Home Page: http://www.prsa.org

• 17720 • Bronze Anvil Awards
To recognize outstanding public relations tactics, the individual items or components of programs and campaigns. They are awarded in 50 categories and subcategories each year. Award consists of a bronze anvil trophy, symbolizing the anvil of public opinion on which public relations ideas and activities are shaped. Established in 1969. Formerly: Public Relations Flim/Video Competition.

• 17721 • Gold Anvil Award
This, the Society's highest individual award, is given for recognition of a public relations practitioner and member whose accomplishments have made major contributions to the public relations profession. Nomination deadline is July 25. A gold anvil trophy, symbolizing the anvil of public opinion on which public relations ideas and activities are shaped, is awarded annually. Established in 1948.

• 17722 • Paul M. Lund Public Service Award
To recognize a member whose participation as a volunteer in important public activities has increased the common good and reflected credit on the Society. Nomination deadline is July 26. A plaque is awarded annually when merited. Established in 1976 in memory of Paul Lund, former Vice President of public relations and employee information for AT&T, who devoted personal time to civic service.

• 17723 • Outstanding Educator Award
To recognize a member who has made a significant contribution to the advancement of public relations education through college or university teaching. Criteria include: teaching performance, research, involvement with students, and involvement in the profession. Nomination deadline is July 25. A copper anvil trophy, symbolizing the anvil of public opinion on which public relations ideas and activities are shaped, is awarded annually when merited in the fall. Established in 1970.

• 17724 • Silver Anvil Awards
To recognize organizations that have successfully addressed a contemporary issue with exemplary professional skill, creativity, and resourcefulness. Entries are considered in the following categories: (1) Community Relations; (2) Reputation Programs; (3) Special Events and Observances (seven days or less); (4) Special Events and Observances (extending more than seven days); (5) Public Service; (6) Public Affairs; (7) Marketing Consumer Products; (8) Marketing Consumer Services; (9) Marketing Business-to-Business; (10) Global Communications; (11) Crisis Communications; (12) Issues Management; (13) Internal Communications; (14) Investor Relations; (15) Multicultural Public Relations; (16) Integrated Communications; and (17) Brand Management. The deadline for entries is March 4. A silver anvil trophy, symbolizing the anvil of public opinion on which public relations ideas and activities are shaped, is awarded annually. Established in 1944.

• 17725 •
Public Relations Society of America
Health Academy
Catherine A. Bolton, Exec.Dir.
33 Maiden Ln.
New York, NY 10038-5150
Phone: (212)460-1400
Fax: (212)995-0757
E-mail: exec@prsa.org
Home Page: http://www.prsa.org

• 17726 • MacEachern Award
To recognize a health care chief executive who has used public relations in a particularly effective way to advance the goals of his or her organization. Awarded annually. Inspired by Malcolm MacEachern, M.D., who served as the Director of Hospital Activities for the American College of Surgeons.

• 17727 •
Public Risk Management Association
Jim Hirt, Exec.Dir.
500 Montgomery St., Ste. 750
Alexandria, VA 22314
Phone: (703)528-7701
Fax: (703)739-0200
E-mail: info@primacentral.org
Home Page: http://www.primacentral.org

Formerly: (1988) Public Risk Insurance Management Association.

• 17728 • Distinguished Service Award
To honor the lifetime achievements of individuals working within the field of risk management. Nominations are made by members of PRIMA's Board of Directors only, and selection is based on service to the Association, contributions to public sector risk management, and sustained involvement and leadership. Recipients of the award are recognized at a special ceremony during the PRIMA Annual Conference and in *Public Risk*, PRIMA's magazine.

• 17729 • PRIMA's Risk Management Achievement Awards
To allow the risk manager and the city to receive the recognition they both deserve, and to encourage professional development. PRIMA members may be nominated by February 15. A plaque is awarded annually at the conference in the spring. Established in 1987.

• 17730 • Public Risk Manager of the Year Award
To recognize and honor a public sector risk manager who has effectively coordinated and operated a risk management program for a public entity operating under adverse conditions. The recipient of the award will be recognized at a special ceremony during the PRIMA Annual Conference and in *Public Risk*, PRIMA's magazine, and will receive two complimentary conference registrations, hotel accommodations during the conference, and two round-trip airfares to the conference. The deadline for nominations is two months prior to the annual conference. Cosponsored by the Trident Insurance Services LLC.

• 17731 •
Publicity Club of New England
Amy Shanler, Exec.Dir.
PO Box 784
Bedford, MA 01730
Phone: (781)275-2866
Fax: (781)275-8228
E-mail: amy@pubclub.org
Home Page: http://www.pubclub.org

• 17732 • Bell Ringer Awards
For communications and public relations professionals. Recognition award bestowed annually.

• 17733 • William M. Cavanaugh Student Grant
For a New England public relations, marketing, or communications student who plans to enter the field of communications. Grant awarded annually.

• 17734 •
Publishers Association of the South
Pat Sabiston, Assn.Exec.
4412 Fletcher St.
Panama City, FL 32405-1017
Phone: (850)914-0766
Fax: (850)769-4348
E-mail: executive@pubsouth.org
Home Page: http://pubsouth.org

• 17735 • Robin Mays Award
For a person who advances book publishing in the South. Recognition award bestowed annually.

• 17736 •
Publishers Association of the West
Kalen Landow, Exec.Dir.
PO Box 18157
Denver, CO 80218
Phone: (303)447-2320
Fax: (303)279-7111
E-mail: kalen@pubwest.org
Home Page: http://www.pubwest.org

• 17737 • Western US Design & Production Awards Competition
To recognize excellence in design for book publishing in the following categories: Jacket/Cover, Trade Book (non-illustrated), Trade Book (illustrated), Art Book, Guide Book, Scholarly/Technical, How-to, and Children's titles. Any book published from July 1 of the previous year through June 30 of the award year is eligible. The deadline is August 15. Send SASE for brochure. Do not send books. A certificate, trade publicity, and display are awarded annually. Established in 1983.

• 17738 •
Publishers Marketing Association
Jan Nathan, Exec.Dir.
627 Aviation Way
Manhattan Beach, CA 90266
Phone: (310)372-2732
Fax: (310)374-3342
E-mail: info@pma-online.org
Home Page: http://www.pma-online.org

• 17739 • Benjamin Franklin Awards
To recognize excellence in independent book publishing. The following awards are given: Marketing Award; Combined Editorial and Design Awards for books and electronic media in thirty-two subject areas; and Design & Other Awards. All books, videos, and tapes published by independent book publishers and copyrighted in the year previous to the award are eligible. Titles entered for the Marketing Award may carry copyright dates earlier than the previous year. Deadlines are September 30 and January 31. Winners are announced at the annual PMA Benjamin Franklin Awards presentation held at the Book Expo America. Finalists receive certificates of excellence and winners receive the Benjamin Franklin trophy. Established in 1984.

• 17740 •
Pudding House Publications
Jennifer Bosveld, Pres.
Pudding House Innovative Writers Programs
81 Shadymere Lane
Columbus, OH 43213
Phone: (614)986-1881
E-mail: info@puddinghouse.com
Home Page: http://www.puddinghouse.com

• 17741 • Chapbook Competition
To recognize exceptional poetry; applicants should submit 10-30 pages of poetry. The poems may be previously published individually if author owns copyright and provides credits. Deadline is Sept. 30. First prize includes a $2,000 monetary prize ($1,000 to the poet; $1,000 to a charity in winner's name), publication, and 20 free books. Awarded annually. Established in 1980. Formerly: National Looking Glass Poetry Competition for a Single Poem.

• 17742 • Poets Greatest Hits National Archive
Honors poets and their twelve signature works. Poets and their publications will be published in an archive. Awarded annually. Established in 2000. INVITATION ONLY. Do not inquire. See website at www.puddinghouse.com for more information.

• 17743 •
Puerto Rico Manufacturers Association
William Riefkohl, Exec.VP
PO Box 195477
San Juan, PR 00919-5477
Phone: (787)759-9445
Fax: (787)756-7670
E-mail: prma@prma.com
Home Page: http://www.prma.com

• 17744 • Manufacturing Manager of the Year/Service Sector Manager of the Year
For members who fulfill their duties in the company that they represent. Recognition awards bestowed annually.

• 17745 • El Pitirre Award
For the company that excels in its support in purchasing to local capital industries. Recognition award bestowed annually.

• 17746 • Safety and Occupational Health Awards
For companies whose labor in the safety and occupational health field has been excellent and those companies that keep an accident record less than the annual average established by the National Safety Council. Recognition award bestowed annually.

• 17747 •
The Pulitzer Prizes
Columbia University
Lee C. Bollinger, Pres.
709 Journalism Bldg.
Columbia University
2950 Broadway
New York, NY 10027
Phone: (212)854-3841
Fax: (212)854-3342
E-mail: pulitzer@pulitzer.org
Home Page: http://www.pulitzer.org

• 17748 • Pulitzer Fellowships
On the recommendation of the faculty of the Graduate School of Journalism, three fellowships of $5,000 each are awarded to enable three of its outstanding graduates to travel, report, and study abroad. One fellowship for $5,000 is presented to an outstanding graduate who wishes to specialize in drama, music, literary, film, or television criticism. Awarded annually.

• 17749 • Pulitzer Prizes
To recognize outstanding accomplishments in journalism, letters, music, and drama. Awards are given in the following categories: Journalism Public Service, for meritorious public service by a newspaper through the use of its journalistic resources, which may include editorials, cartoons, photographs, reporting and an online presentation; breaking news reporting, for local reporting of breaking news; Investigative Reporting, for investigative reporting within a newspaper's area of circulation by an individual or team, presented as a single article or series; Explanatory Reporting, for explanatory reporting that illuminates significant and complex issues; Beat Reporting; National Reporting; International Reporting; Feature Writing, Commentary, Criticism, Feature Photography. For Books: Fiction, U.S. History, Biography/Autobiography, Poetry and General Nonfiction. Drama and Musical Composition.

• 17750 •
Pulmonary Hypertension Association
Rino Aldrighetti, Pres.
850 Sligo Ave., Ste. 800
Silver Spring, MD 20910
Phone: (301)565-3004
Phone: (301)565-3004
Toll-Free: 800-748-7274
Fax: (301)565-3994
E-mail: candibleifer@earthlink.net
Home Page: http://www.phassociation.org

• 17751 • Outstanding Physician Award
Biennial award of recognition.

• 17752 • Outstanding Volunteer Award
Biennial award of recognition.

• 17753 • Research Fellowships
For the best proposals relating to PH research. Two or three monetary awards are awarded annually to researchers at the front end of their careers.

• 17754 •
Pulp and Paper Safety Association
Pam Cordier, Exec.Dir.
1370 N Nealon Dr.
Portage, IN 46368
Phone: (219)764-4787
Fax: (219)764-4307
E-mail: ppsa.org@verizon.net
Home Page: http://www.ppsa.org

• 17755 • Award of Safety Excellence
This, the most prestigious award bestowed for operating excellence, is given to recognize the companies having the best safety record for the previous five years. Awards are given to companies in three following categories: (1) Pulp, Paper, Tissue, and Recycle Mills; (2) Bag Converting, Cartons, Corrugated, Sheeting, and Specialty; and (3) Woodlands, Sawmills, Wood Products, Plywood, and Particle Board. A cast metal on a wood plaque is awarded annually. Established in 1985.

• 17756 • Best One-Year Safety Record Award
To provide recognition for the company with the lowest OSHA total case incident rate for the preceding year. Members of the Association are eligible. A plaque is awarded annually. Established in 1950. Sponsored by *Pulp and Paper Magazine.*

• 17757 • Most Improved Award
To provide recognition for a company having the most improved safety record over the previous three years. Companies that are members of the Association for at least four years are eligible. A plaque is awarded annually. Established in 1960.

• 17758 •
Puppeteers of America
Paul Mesner, Pres.
1006 Linwood Blvd.
Kansas City, MO 64109
Phone: (816)756-3500
Toll-Free: 888-568-6235
Fax: (816)756-3045
E-mail: puppets@crn.org
Home Page: http://www.puppeteers.org

• 17759 • President's Award
To recognize an individual or group for a lifetime contributions to the art of puppetry and the goals of the organization, thus raising the standards of puppetry in America. Awarded to one or more recipients annually. Established in 1965.

• 17760 • Puppeteers of America Award
To recognize contributions to puppetry by individuals and/or groups not immediately involved in the field. A plaque is awarded annually.

• 17761 • Trustee's Award
To honor those members who have distinguished themselves in service to the Association. Awarded annually.

• 17762 •
Purchasing Management Association of Boston
Christiane Loup, Exec.Dir.
200 Baker Ave.
Concord, MA 01742
Phone: (978)371-2522
Fax: (978)369-9130
E-mail: info@pmaboston.org
Home Page: http://www.pmaboston.org

• 17763 • Harry J. Graham Award
For contribution to purchasing management. Recognition award bestowed annually.

• 17764 •
Purdue University
African American Studies and Research Center
1367 Beering Hall of Liberal Arts and Education
100 N University St.
West Lafayette, IN 47907-2067
Phone: (765)494-5680
Fax: (765)496-1581
E-mail: aasrc@sla.purdue.edu
Home Page: http://www.cla.purdue.edu/academic/idis/african-american/

• 17765 • African-American Culture and Philosophy Award
Inquire for application details.

• 17766 • H.H. Bemmers Award
MA and PhD students in Social Sciences are eligible. Inquire for application details.

• 17767 • Study Abroad Award
Inquire for application details.

• 17768 •
Pushcart Press
PO Box 380
Wainscott, NY 11975
Phone: (631)324-9300
Home Page: http://www.pushcartprize.com

• 17769 • Editors' Book Award
To encourage the writing of distinguished books of uncertain financial value and to support the enthusiasm of editors without regard to concerns other than literary merit. Fiction and nonfiction works by published and unpublished authors are eligible. Nominations by editors are accepted between May 15 and October 15 each year. The award consists of a monetary prize of $1,000 and publication by Pushcart Press. Awarded annually.

• 17770 • Pushcart Prize: Best of the Small Presses
To recognize works published by little magazine and small book presses. Nominations may be made by any small, non-commercial book press or literary journal in the world by December 1 of each year. Editors may submit up to six nominations in any combination of poetry, short fiction, or essays, as well as translations, reprints, or self-contained portions of books. Winning works are published in an anthology every summer. Established in 1976.

• 17771 •
Putnam County Historical Society
Karen Bailey, Pres.
PO Box 74
Hennepin, IL 61327
Phone: (815)925-7560
E-mail: pchs61327@yahoo.com

• 17772 • Whitaker Key History Award
For outstanding history student in District 535. Recognition award bestowed annually.

• 17773 •
PXE International
Patrick Terry, Pres.
4301 Connecticut Ave. NW, Ste. 404
Washington, DC 20008-2369
Phone: (202)362-9599
Fax: (202)966-8553
E-mail: info@pxe.org
Home Page: http://www.pxe.org

• 17774 • Excellence in PXE Research
Recognizes special contributions to PXE research. Awarded annually.

• 17775 •
Pyrotechnics Guild International
Frank Kuberry, Sec.-Treas.
304 W Main St.
Titusville, PA 16354
Phone: (814)827-0485
E-mail: kuberry@earthlink.net
Home Page: http://www.pgi.org

• 17776 • Pyrotechnics Guild International Competition
To recognize individuals for creating various pyrotechnic devices. Individuals who are at least 18 years of age and members of the Guild are eligible. The competition is divided into four divisions: aerial shell, rocket, ground, and commercially-produced items. Awards are presented in numerous categories within each division. Trophies awarded annually at the August convention. Established in 1976.

• 17777 •
Quality Digest
40 Declaration Dr., Ste. 100
Chico, CA 95973
Phone: (530)893-4095
Fax: (530)893-0395
Home Page: http://www.qualitydigest.com

• 17778 • *Quality Digest* Award
For recognition of the best in each major field of activity. The announcement of winners is made in the *Quality Digest* publication and through press releases to major media periodically. Established in 1969.

• 17779 •
Quality Paperback Book Club
PO Box 6375
Camp Hill, PA 17012-6375
Phone: (212)522-4200
Fax: (212)522-0303
Home Page: http://www.qpb.com

• 17780 • New Voices Award/New Vision Award
To recognize the author of the most distinctive and promising books published in a given year.

The New Voices Award recognizes the best work of fiction, and the New Vision Awards honors the best work of non-fiction. A monetary prize of $10,000 is awarded to the winner of each award annually. Established in 1984. Formerly: ; (1996) Joe Savago New Voice Award.

• 17781 • **QPB New Visions Award**
To recognize the author of the most distinctive nonfiction book published in a given year. The winner is chosen from a list of books already selected by the club. A monetary award of $5,000 is awarded annually. Established in 1994.

• 17782 •
Quarter Century Wireless Association, Southeast Wisconsin Chapter 162
Robert N. Jensen, Sec.-Treas.
5616 Cambridge Ln., No. 6
Racine, WI 53406-2870
Phone: (414)886-8551

• 17783 • **Olin Fox (Memorial) Award**
For significant contribution to an amateur radio community. Recognition award bestowed annually.

• 17784 •
Quarterly West
200 S Central Campus Dr., Rm. 317
University of Utah
Salt Lake City, UT 84112-0494
Phone: (801)581-3938
E-mail: quarterlywest@yahoo.com
Home Page: http://www.utah.edu/quarterlywest

• 17785 • **Novella Award**
To recognize and publish novellas, a neglected genre. Two monetary awards of $500 are presented biennially and winning works are published in *Quarterly West* magazine. Established in 1976.

• 17786 •
Quebec Federation of Historical Societies (Federation des Societes d'Histoire du Quebec)
Marc Beaudoin, Pres.
4545, ave. Pierre-De Coubertin
Case Postale 1000, succursale M
Montreal, QC, Canada H1V 3R2
Phone: (514)252-3031
Toll-Free: (866)691-7202
Fax: (514)251-8038
E-mail: fshq@histoirequebec.qc.ca
Home Page: http://www.histoirequebec.qc.ca

• 17787 • **Prix Honorius Provost**
Award of recognition. Only members are eligible. Awarded annually.

• 17788 • **Prix Leonidas-Belanger**
Award of recognition. Only members are eligible. A monetary prize is given annually.

• 17789 • **Prix Rodolphe-Fournier**
Award of recognition. A monetary prize is given annually.

• 17790 •
Quebec-Labrador Foundation/Atlantic Center for the Environment
Robert A. Bryan, Chm.
55 S Main St.
Ipswich, MA 01938
Phone: (978)356-0038
Fax: (978)356-7322
E-mail: atlantic@qlf.org
Home Page: http://www.qlf.org

• 17791 • **Caring for the Earth**
Annual award of recognition.

• 17792 •
Quebec Ministere de la Culture et des Communications
Prix du Quebec
225, Grande-Allee Est
Quebec, QC, Canada G1R 5G5
Phone: (418)380-2300
Fax: (418)380-2364
E-mail: dc@mcc.gouv.qc.ca
Home Page: http://www.mcc.gouv.qc.ca

• 17793 • **Prix Albert-Tessier**
This, one of the eleven Prix du Quebec, is the highest award given by the Quebec Government to a person who, through his/her career and work, has made a notable contribution to the reputation of Quebec cinema. Canadian citizens living in Quebec are eligible. A monetary prize of $30,000, a parchment scroll, and an original medal designed by a Quebec artist are awarded annually. Established in 1980.

• 17794 • **Prix Athanase-David**
This, one of the eleven Prix du Quebec, is the highest literary award given by the Quebec Government to honor an author's complete work. Canadian citizens living in Quebec are eligible. A monetary prize of $30,000, a parchment scroll, and an original medal designed by a Quebec artist are awarded annually. Established in 1968.

• 17795 • **Prix Denise-Pelletier**
This, one of the eleven Prix du Quebec, is the highest award given by the Quebec Government to honor a notable career in the field of music and/or song composition or interpretation, lyrical composition or interpretation, choreography or the interpretative arts, or the complete works of anyone who has made an outstanding contribution to the performing arts. Canadian citizens living in Quebec are eligible. A monetary prize of $30,000, a parchment scroll, and an original medal designed by a Quebec artist are awarded annually. Established in 1977.

• 17796 • **Prix Gerard-Morisset**
This, one of the eleven Prix du Quebec, is the highest award given by the Quebec government in the creation, production, education, preservation, or diffusion of patrimony, cultures, belongings, archives, museum affairs, and traditional folklore. Canadian citizens living in Quebec are eligible. A monetary prize of 30,000, a parchment scroll, and an original medal designed by a Quebec artist are awarded annually. Established in 1992.

• 17797 • **Prix Paul-Emile-Borduas**
This, one of the eleven Prix du Quebec, is the highest award given by the Quebec Government for the complete work of an artist or craftsperson in the field of the visual arts. Canadian citizens living in Quebec are eligible. A monetary prize of $30,000, a parchment scroll, and an original medal designed by a Quebec artist are awarded annually. Established in 1977.

• 17798 •
Quebec Writers' Federation
(Societe quebecoise pour la promotion de la litterature de langue anglaise)
Lori Schubert, Exec.Dir.
1200 Atwater Ave.
Montreal, QC, Canada H3Z 1X4
Phone: (514)933-0878
Fax: (514)933-0878
E-mail: admin@qwf.org
Home Page: http://www.qwf.org

• 17799 • **QSF Awards**
To honor excellence in writing by Quebec authors. Five awards are presented annually: Hugh MacLennan Prize for Fiction, Mavis Gallant Prize for Non-Fiction, A. M. Klein Prize for Poetry, McAuslan First Book Prize, QWF Translation Prize. Each winner receives a monetary prize of $2,000. Established in 1989. Formerly: (1998) QSPELL Book Awards.

• 17800 • **QSPELL Community Award**
To honor outstanding involvement in and contributions to Quebec's English-language literary life by an individual or group. Established in 1995.

• 17801 • **QWF Awards**
To encourage and support English language writing in Quebec. Awards are presented in five categories: Hugh MacLenan Prize for Fiction, Mavis Gallant Prize for Non-Fiction, A. M. Klein Prize for Poetry, McAuslan First Book Prize, and the QWF Translation Prize (French and English, with target audience alternating each year). Books published in the preceding year by authors who have resided in Quebec for three of the past five years may be submitted by May 31. Books must be written in English and have at least 48 pages. Edited collections, translations, and reprints are not eligible. A monetary award of $2,000 is presented to the winner in each category. Established in 1988. Formerly: (1998) QSPELL Awards.

• 17802 •
Queens Opera Association
% Messina
9707 4th Ave., Ste. 7-G
Brooklyn, NY 11209
Phone: (732)833-9607
E-mail: jmfgopera@aol.com

• 17803 • **Annual Vocal Competition**
To discover and assist artists. There is no age limit but the artists cannot qualify unless they have appeared in at least one full opera production (with piano or small orchestra). A workshop performance is acceptable. The following awards are offered annually: First Prize - a monetary award of $1,500; a concert performance with full orchestra (video and audio tapes for the artist) where other opera producers, agents, the media, etc., are invited; and a contract for a leading role in one of the Company's major opera productions. (First Prize Award values $5,000.) Second Prize - a monetary award of $300 (minimum), a concert recital (video and audio tapes for the artist), and a contract for a role in one of Queens Opera future productions. (Second Prize award values $3,000); Third Prize - a monetary award of $200 (minimum), a concert recital (with tapes), and an offer to sing in a future production of Queens Opera. (Third Prize Award values $1,500) and Fourth and Fifth Prizes - monetary awards of $100 and $50 (minimum), savings bonds and consideration for future roles with Queens Opera. (Fourth and Fifth Prize Awards value up to $1,000). Established in 1986 in memory of Denise Messina. The competition is partly sponsored by St. John's University and Consolidated Edison, in addition to many others.

• 17804 •
Queen's University
C. Baillie, Chancellor
Victoria School Bldg.
99 University Ave.
Kingston, ON, Canada K7L 3N6
Phone: (613)533-2000
Phone: (613)533-6000
Home Page: http://www.queensu.ca

• 17805 • **A. E. MacRae Award in Creative Leadership**
To promote the student who has developed and exhibited the greatest capacity for creative leadership. Awarded annually with a monetary prize of $500.

• 17806 • **Andrina McCulloch Prizes for Public Speaking**
To promote and encourage public speaking in the University. Awarded annually with a variable cash prize.

• 17807 • **Barbara Paul Prize**
To honor a graduating student with high academic standing who completed a degree on a full-time or part-time basis while combining family and/or employment responsibilities with academic studies. A medallion is awarded annually.

• 17808 • **Pride and Recognition**
To recognize achievements and contributions in the childbirth and preventing field. Awarded annually with a pin, plaque/certificate, and honorable mention. Established in 1995.

• 17809 • **Prince of Wales Prizes**
To honor two students who have the best academic records at Queen's. Scrolls are awarded annually. Established in 1860.

• 17810 • **Lilian Coleman Taylor Prize**
To honor the outstanding woman student from Leeds County registered in any faculty of Queen's University. Awarded annually with a prize of $440.

• 17811 •
Quilters Hall of Fame
Hazel Carter, Pres.
PO Box 681
Marion, IN 46952
Phone: (765)664-9333
Phone: (703)938-3246
Fax: (765)664-9333
E-mail: quilters@comteck.com
Home Page: http://www.quiltershalloffame.org

• 17812 • **Honoree of the Quilters Hall of Fame**
Recognizes outstanding contributions to Quilting. Awarded annually.

• 17813 •
R & D Magazine
Reed Business Information
Hal Avery, Publisher
100 Enterprise Dr., Ste. 600
Box 912
Rockaway, NJ 07866-0912
Phone: (973)920-7000
E-mail: havery@reedbusiness.com
Home Page: http://www.rdmag.com
Formerly: *Industrial Research and Development.*

• 17814 • **Executive of the Year**
To recognize outstanding leadership and job performance, both recent and throughout a career, as related to the administration of research and development in currently and potentially important disciplines. A trophy and a feature article in *Research & Development* magazine are awarded annually in the spring. Established in 1989.

• 17815 • **Innovator of the Year**
To recognize an individual for excellence and creativity in the design, development, and introduction into the marketplace of one or more technologically significant products over the past five years. A cash prize of $5,000 is awarded annually. Established in 2001.

• 17816 • **Laboratory of the Year**
To recognize the best new and renovated laboratories that combine all aspects of the building into a superior working environment. Consideration is given to esthetics, utility, and ease of maintenance. The deadline for entries is February 1. An engraved stainless steel on walnut plaque is presented to the winner in two categories: Laboratory of the Year and Renovated Laboratory of the Year. Awarded annually. Established in 1965.

• 17817 • **R & D 100 Awards**
To recognize innovators and organizations for outstanding technical developments by selecting the 100 most significant new technical products of the year. Technical products include any product, process, software program, or system of scientific or technical origin or use. Selection of winners is made by the editors and members of the Editorial Advisory Board of the magazine. The deadline for entries is March 1. Engraved stainless steel on walnut plaques are awarded annually at a formal banquet held at the Museum of Science and Industry in Chicago. Established in 1963. Formerly: IR-100 Competition.

• 17818 • **Scientist of the Year Award**
To recognize an individual for outstanding contributions to applied science and technology. An engraved stainless steel on walnut plaque is awarded annually. Established in 1966.

• 17819 •
The Radiance Technique International Association
Shoshana Shay, Asst.Dir.
PO Box 40570
St. Petersburg, FL 33743-0570
Phone: (727)347-2106
Fax: (727)347-2106
E-mail: trtia@aol.com
Home Page: http://www.trtia.org

• 17820 • **Peace Education Awards**
Recognizes elementary-school childrens' writing on a selected theme about peace. A monetary prize is awarded annually. Inquire for this years theme.

• 17821 • **Peace Profiles**
Recognizes a definite contribution towards peace locally or globally. Individuals and organizations are eligible.

• 17822 •
Radiation Research Society
Becky Noordsy, Exec.Dir.
810 E 10th St.
Lawrence, KS 66044
Phone: (703)757-4585
Toll-Free: 800-627-0629
Fax: (785)843-1274
E-mail: info@radres.org
Home Page: http://www.radres.org

Awards are arranged in alphabetical order below their administering organizations

• 17823 • RRS Research Award
Annual award of recognition.

• 17824 • RRS Young Investigator Travel Award
Award of recognition.

• 17825 •
Radio Advertising Bureau
Gary R. Fries, Pres./CEO
1320 Greenway Dr., No. 500
Irving, TX 75038
Phone: (212)681-7200
Toll-Free: 800-232-3131
Fax: (972)753-6727
E-mail: gfries@rab.com
Home Page: http://www.rab.com

• 17826 • Chassie Awards
To recognize the best auto dealer and auto dealer association radio advertisements during the preceding year. The RAB Chassie Awards were the top honors of the radio industry for ingenuity, creativity, and know-how that formed the backbone of an auto dealer's advertising program. Radio commercials produced by or for dealers or dealer associations that were creative, different, provocative, effective, or outstanding qualified. NADA-member dealers, dealer associations, ad agencies, production companies, and RAB member stations were eligible. Awarded annually. Established in 1976. Conducted in cooperation with the National Automotive Dealers Association.

• 17827 • Radio Mercury Awards
To honor the best radio advertising of the previous calendar year. Each spot entered must have aired for the first time between January 1 and December 31 of the previous year on a commercially licensed radio station in the United States. Spots must be predominantly in the English language and 30 to 60 seconds in length. The Radio Mercury Gold Award bestows $100,000 to the best radio commercial of the year. The $20,000 Mercury Gold Award and the $5,000 Mercury Silver Award are presented in each of four categories: humor, narrative, music/sound design, and radio station produced. A special Radio Mercury Public Service Award is presented to the best radio public service advertising; winners receive a Radio Mercury Gold trophy. Public Service Announcements could not be entered in any of the four cash prize categories. Entry deadline is in early March. Spots can be entered in more than one category; however, a single spot cannot win more than one cash prize. Awarded annually. Sponsored by the Radio Creative Fund.

• 17828 •
Radio Club of America
Lisa McCauley, Exec.Sec.
10 Drs. James Parker Blvd., Ste. 103
Red Bank, NJ 07701-1500
Phone: (732)842-5070
Fax: (732)219-1938
E-mail: exsec@radio-club-of-america.org
Home Page: http://www.radio-club-of-america.org

Formerly: (1911) Junior Wireless Club.

• 17829 • Armstrong Medal
To recognize a member of the Club who has made an important contribution to radio art and science. Selection is made by the Club's Board of Directors. A silver medal is awarded when merited. Established in 1935.

• 17830 • Ralph Batcher Memorial Award
To recognize a member who has assisted substantially in preserving the history of radio and electronic communications. A plaque is awarded annually. Established in 1975 in memory of Ralph Batcher.

• 17831 • Henri Busignies Memorial Award
To recognize individuals for contributions toward the advancement of electronics for the benefit of mankind. A plaque is awarded when merited. Established in 1981 in memory of Henri Busignies, a wartime inventor and developer of electronic navigation methods.

• 17832 • Centenarian Award
Awarded to any member attaining the age of 100 years. Established in 1989.

• 17833 • Lee DeForest Award
To recognize contributions to the radio communications industry. Awarded when merited. Established in 1983 in memory of Dr. Lee DeForest and his many contributions to the radio communications industry.

• 17834 • Allen B. DuMont Citation
To recognize an individual for important contributions in the field of electronics to the science of television. Candidates do not have to be members of the Club. Selection is made by the Board of Directors. A plaque is awarded when merited. Established in 1979 in honor of Allen B. DuMont, the man responsible for television.

• 17835 • Barry M. Goldwater Amateur Radio Award
Recognizes major contributions to the amateur radio service. Established in 1994.

• 17836 • Alfred H. Grebe Award
Recognizes those who have achieved outstanding quality in the design and manufacture of electronic components and equipment. Established in 1994.

• 17837 • Frank A. Gunther Award
For contributions to the advancement of military electronic communications systems. Established in 1996.

• 17838 • Edgar F. Johnson Pioneer Citation
Recognizes long-time members who have contributed substantially to the success and development of the Club or to the art of radio communications. Designated by the board of directors. Awarded when merited. Established in 1975. Formerly: Pioneer Citation.

• 17839 • Fred M. Link Award
For recognition of substantial contributions toward the advancement and development of landmobile radio and communications. A plaque is awarded annually. Established in 1986. Formerly: .

• 17840 • Jerry B. Minter Award
For significant contributions to the electronics art through innovation in instrumentation, avionics, and electronics. Established in 1996.

• 17841 • Jack Poppele Broadcast Award
Recognizes important and long-term contributions to the improvement of radio broadcasting. Awarded when merited. Established in 1989.

• 17842 • President's Award
To recognize unselfish dedication in support of the Club. A plaque is awarded at the discretion of the president. Established in 1974.

• 17843 • Sarnoff Citation
To recognize an individual or member for significant contributions to the advancement of electronic communications. A plaque is awarded when merited. Established in 1973.

• 17844 • Special Services Award
To recognize an individual for substantial contributions to the support and advancement of the Club. Members and non-members are eligible. Awarded annually if merited. Established in 1975.

• 17845 •
Radio-Television Correspondents Association
Michael J. Mastrian, Dir.
U.S. Capitol, Rm. S-325
Washington, DC 20510
Phone: (202)224-6421
Fax: (202)224-4882
E-mail: mike_mastrian@saa.senate.gov
Home Page: http://www.senate.gov/galleries/radiotv

• 17846 • Joan Shorenstein Barone Award
Recognizes excellence in Washington-based national affairs/public policy reporting. A monetary award is given annually.

• 17847 •
Radio-Television News Directors Association
Barbara Cochran, Pres.
1600 K St. NW, Ste. 700
Washington, DC 20006-2838
Phone: (202)659-6510
Toll-Free: 800-80-RTNDA
Fax: (202)223-4007
E-mail: rtnda@rtnda.org
Home Page: http://rtnda.org

• 17848 • **John F. Hogan Distinguished Service Award**
To recognize an individual for contributions to the journalism profession and the Freedom of the Press. Awarded when merited. Established in 1959.

• 17849 • **Edward R. Murrow Awards**
For recognition of outstanding achievements in electronic journalism. Awards are given in the following categories: Overall Excellence, Newscast, Spot News Coverage, Continuing Coverage, Investigative Reporting, Feature Reporting, Sports Reporting, News Series, News Documentary, Videography, Use of Sound, Writing, and Web Sites (both broadcast-affiliated and - nonaffiliated). Awards are given both on the regional and the national levels. Plaques are awarded annually to regional finalists. The winners of the 13 regions compete for the national Edward R. Murrow Trophy. Awarded annually. Established in 1974.

• 17850 • **Paul White Award**
This, the Association's highest honor, is given in recognition of an individual's lifetime contributions to electronic journalism. A trophy is awarded annually. Established in 1956 and named for the first news director of CBS. Formerly: (1995) Paul White Memorial Award for Electronic Journalism.

• 17851 •
Radiological Society of North America
Robert R. Hattery MD, Pres.
820 Jorie Blvd.
Oak Brook, IL 60523-2251
Phone: (630)571-2670
Toll-Free: 800-381-6660
Fax: (630)571-7837
E-mail: informat@rsna.org
Home Page: http://www.rsna.org

• 17852 • **Gold Medal**
This, the Society's highest honor, is given in recognition of those who have rendered unusual service to the science of radiology. Winners are selected by a unanimous vote of the Board of Directors. Gold medals are presented annually. No more than three medals are given in any one year. Established in 1919.

• 17853 • **Hans Langendorff Award**
Awarded to exhibits of exceptional scientific merit, the award is given at the Scientific Assembly and Annual Meeting of the Radiological Society of North America. Awards are given at the levels of Summa Cum Laude, Magna Cum Laude, Cum Laude, a Certificate of Merit, and Excellence in Design.

• 17854 • **Outstanding Educator Award**
To recognize and honor a senior individual who has made original and significant contributions to the field of radiology or radiological sciences throughout a career of teaching and education. The award is presented during the Opening Session of the RSNA Scientific Assembly, and is a monetary award of $25,000. The nominee must be from North America, and must demonstrate commitment to radiological education as a mentor for physicians and scientists, developing unique methods and materials for training, or publishing education-focused articles in scholarly peer-reviewed journals, textbooks or chapters of textbooks. It is expected that the winner will have devoted ten years to these activities. The deadline for nominations is June 15 of each year.

• 17855 • **Outstanding Researcher Award**
Established to recognize and honor an individual who has made significant research contributions to the field of radiology throughout his or her career. The award is a monetary sum of $25,000.

• 17856 • **Roentgen Resident/Fellow Research Award**
To promote radiology research to residents and fellows and recognize residents and fellows for completed research. Each residency program director nominates a member from their program who has participated meaningfully in scientific research during the academic year. The deadline is April 15. The winner will receive a clock plaque, and the program will receive a plaque which will allow winner's names to be added in subsequent years.

• 17857 •
Railway Tie Association
James C. Gauntt, Exec.Dir.
115 Commerce Dr., Ste. C
Fayetteville, GA 30214
Phone: (770)460-5553
Fax: (770)460-5573
E-mail: ties@rta.org
Home Page: http://www.rta.org

• 17858 • **Branding Hammer Award**
To recognize an associate member who is an employee of a railroad and participated over a period of years in the activities and programs of the Association. A crosstie branding hammer mounted on an inscribed plaque is awarded annually. Established in 1975.

• 17859 • **Broad Axe Award**
To recognize the producer members for outstanding service to the Association over a period of years. Owners or employees of a producer member of the Association are eligible. A miniaturized broad axe on an inscribed plaque is awarded annually. Established in 1974.

• 17860 •
Rainbow Resource Centre: Serving Manitoba's Gay, Lesbian, Bisexual, Transgendered, and Two-Spirited Communities
Donna Huen, Services Coor.
PO Box 1661 Stn. Main
Winnipeg, MB, Canada R3C 2Z6
Phone: (204)284-5208
Phone: (204)474-0212
Fax: (204)478-1160
E-mail: wglrc@mts.net

• 17861 • **Twinkie**
Given to homophobe of the year.

• 17862 •
Rainforest Action Network
Michael Brune, Exec.Dir.
221 Pine St., Ste. 500
San Francisco, CA 94104
Phone: (415)398-4404
Fax: (415)398-2732
E-mail: rainforest@ran.org
Home Page: http://www.ran.org

• 17863 • **World Rainforest Awards**
Annual award of recognition.

• 17864 •
Rainforest Alliance
Tensie Whelan, Exec.Dir.
665 Broadway, Ste. 500
New York, NY 10012
Phone: (212)677-1900
Toll-Free: 888-MY-EARTH
Fax: (212)677-2187
E-mail: canopy@ra.org
Home Page: http://www.rainforest-alliance.org

• 17865 • **Catalyst Grants**
For local initiatives in tropical forest conservation. A grant is given periodically.

• 17866 • **Kleinhans Fellowships**
For graduate research, particularly in tropical agriculture. A fellowship is awarded biennially.

• 17867 •
Raissa Tselentis Memorial Johann Sebastian Bach International Competitions
James Marra, Dir.
569 Legacy Pride Dr.
Herndon, VA 20170
Phone: (703)787-9652

• 17868 • **Bach Competitions**
To perpetuate the works of J.S. Bach and to honor the efforts of young instrumentalists (organ; piano; string instruments; fretted instruments) and vocalists willing to develop the necessary disciplines and artistry to perform the major solo compositions of J.S. Bach. Open to instrumentalists and vocalists from 20 to 40 years of age. The competitors must invariably

play or sing the required repertoire entirely from memory and to professional concert stage performance levels. Only Urtext editions of J.S. Bach's solo works may be used by the contestants. Monetary awards and concert engagements are presented. Established in 1958. Additional information is available from James Marra, Director.

• 17869 •
Raleigh Outlaw League
Karen Broderick, Sec.
504 N Clift Dr.
Raleigh, NC 27609
Phone: (919)518-1088
Fax: (919)518-1088
E-mail: tenpins@compuserve.com
Home Page: http://www.ncneighbors.com/202

• 17870 • **Most Improved Bowler**
For bowling scores. Monetary award bestowed annually.

• 17871 •
Ramsey County Historical Society
Priscilla Farnham, Contact
323 Landmark Center
75 W 5th St.
St. Paul, MN 55102
Phone: (651)222-0701
Fax: (651)223-8539
E-mail: info@rchs.com
Home Page: http://www.rchs.com

• 17872 • **AASLH Award**
For Ramsey County history. Recognition award.

• 17873 •
Randolph Chamber of Commerce
Marty Strange, Pres.
PO Box 9
PO Box 9
Randolph, VT 05060
Phone: (802)728-9027
Fax: (802)728-4705
E-mail: chamber@randolphvt.com
Home Page: http://www.randolphvt.com

• 17874 • **Business Executive of the Year**
For interest in the community and activity in the chamber. Recognition award bestowed annually.

• 17875 •
Raoul Wallenberg Committee of the United States
Rachel Oestreicher Bernheim, Chm./CEO
230 Park Ave., 7th Fl.
New York, NY 10169
Phone: (212)499-2695
Fax: (212)499-2671
E-mail: rachel@raoulwallenberg.org
Home Page: http://www.raoulwallenberg.org

• 17876 • **Raoul Wallenberg Awards**
To recognize service given in an exemplary manner. Two awards are presented annually: the A Hero for Our Time Award and the Civic Courage Award. Established in 1993.

• 17877 • **Raoul Wallenberg Civic Courage Award**
To recognize outstanding civic courage. The 2001 awards was given to the City of New York.

• 17878 • **Raoul Wallenberg Hero for Our Time Award**
To recognize heroic and humanitarian action on behalf of other human beings. Awarded only when actions merit the award. The 2001 award was given to the Prime Minister of Sweden, Goran Persson. Established in 1987. Formerly: Raoul Wallenberg World of Heroes Award.

• 17879 •
Ravenswood Community Council
Richard Hankett, Exec.Dir.
2348 W Irving Park Rd., Ste. 106
Chicago, IL 60618
Phone: (773)583-1600
Fax: (773)583-3243
E-mail: ravenswood@megsinet.net
Home Page: http://www.ravenswoodcommunity.org

• 17880 • **Raven Award**
For outstanding contributor to the Ravenswood community. Trophy awarded annually.

• 17881 •
Rawlings Sporting Goods Co.
Richard J. Heckmann, Pres. and CEO
% K2 Inc.
5818 El Camino Real
Carlsbad, CA 92008
Phone: (760)494-1000
Toll-Free: 888-5K2-SPRT
Fax: (760)494-1099
Home Page: http://www.rawlings.com

• 17882 • **Rawlings Big Stick Award**
To recognize the American Legion Baseball player who compiles the highest number of bases in regional and the national competition. Awarded annually. Established in 1972.

• 17883 • **Rawlings Bronze Glove Award**
To honor outstanding fielders in college or university play. A bronze leather baseball glove mounted on a wooden base is awarded annually.

• 17884 • **Rawlings Gold Glove Award**
To recognize major league baseball players for fielding performance. Managers of each team select a squad of the best defensemen in their league, excluding their own team. A gold-finished leather baseball glove mounted on a wooden base is awarded annually to each of the nine defense positions of both the American and National Leagues. Established in 1957.

• 17885 • **Rawlings Silver Glove Award**
To recognize minor league baseball players having the highest fielding percentage for the season at each position. A silver-finished leather glove mounted on a wooden base is awarded annually. Established in 1957.

• 17886 •
Reader's Digest Association
Thomas O. Ryder, Chm./CEO
Reader's Digest Rd.
Pleasantville, NY 10570-7000
Phone: (914)238-1000
Toll-Free: 800-846-2100
Fax: (914)238-4559
E-mail: thomas.ryder@rd.com
Home Page: http://www.readersdigest.com

• 17887 • **American Heroes in Education Awards**
To recognize teachers and principals who are making extraordinary contributions to our nation through their work with students in classrooms and schools throughout America. The American Heroes in Education are the teachers and principals who raise student aspirations, motivate students to learn under trying circumstances, and personify the vision of a better society through quality education. Ten educators or teams of up to six educators are selected. Individual winners or winning teams each receive a monetary award of $5,000. Each winner's school receives an incentive award of $10,000 to support the program or activities that earned the educator or team national recognition. Established in 1989. Awards are presented annually. The award is co-sponsored by the American Federation of Teachers, National Education Association, National Association of Elementary School Principals, National Association of Secondary School Principals and the National Catholic Education Association.

• 17888 •
Reading-Berks Democratic Socialists
Bob Millar, Chm.
19 Spring Ln.
Fleetwood, PA 19522
Phone: (610)944-0991
E-mail: lbrsmillar@earthlink.net

• 17889 • **Maurer-Stump Award**
For outstanding contributor to democratic socialism/trade unionism. Recognition award bestowed annually.

• 17890 •
Real Estate Educators Association
Jone Sienkiewicz, Exec.Dir.
19 Mantua Rd.
Mount Royal, NJ 08061
Phone: (856)423-3215
Fax: (856)423-3420
E-mail: info@reea.org
Home Page: http://www.reea.org

• 17891 • Award Emeritus
To honor an individual retired from active service who has devoted a lifetime to real estate education. Industry leaders who have been recognized as making notable contributions to the real estate profession on local and national levels are eligible for nomination. A plaque is awarded annually at the conference. Established in 1981.

• 17892 • Best Academic Paper
For recognition of the best academic paper in the field of real estate education among those presented at the annual conference. Peers make the selection. A plaque is awarded annually at the conference. Established in 1985.

• 17893 • Best Single Education Program
For recognition of the most successful real estate educational program (one day or less in duration) of the year. Selection is by nomination. A plaque is awarded annually at the conference. Established in 1984.

• 17894 • Consumer Education Award
For recognition of an outstanding example of real estate educational communications aimed at a consumer audience. Effectiveness in communication of interesting and understandable information, originality and creativity, and selection of strategically important subjects are considered. Selection is by nomination. A plaque is awarded annually at the conference. Established in 1984.

• 17895 • Distinguished Career Award
To recognize an individual for an outstanding contribution to the field of real estate education. Individuals who have devoted at least ten years to real estate education and who have notable careers that include the development of real estate programs, the authorship of articles and texts regarding real estate, and community and national promotion of real estate education are eligible for consideration. A plaque is awarded annually at the conference. Established in 1985.

• 17896 • Most Outstanding Educational Program
For recognition of the most successful real estate educational program of the year. Innovative use of technology, format and design of program, marketing/promotion of the program, and access to the program determined by cost and distribution are considered. Selection is by nomination. A plaque is awarded annually at the conference. Established in 1984.

• 17897 • Real Estate Educator of the Year
To recognize the individual who has made the single greatest contribution to the field of real estate education during the past year. Selection is by nomination. A plaque is awarded annually at the conference. Established in 1984.

• 17898 • Real Estate Regulator of the Year
To recognize the best overall agency program, with emphasis on educational aspects. Selection is by nomination. A plaque is awarded annually at the conference. Established in 1984.

• 17899 •
Real Estate Institute of Canada
(Institut Canadien de l'immeuble)
Maura Bella, Exec.VP
5407 Eglinton Ave. W, Ste. 208
Toronto, ON, Canada M9C 5K6
Phone: (416)695-9000
Toll-Free: 800-542-7342
Fax: (416)695-7230
E-mail: infocentral@reic.com
Home Page: http://www.reic.ca/

• 17900 • Morguard Literary Award
To recognize the outstanding articles which are relevant to the Canadian real estate industry. Awarded annually with a monetary prize of $2,000 for each category consisting of practicing industry writers and academic writers. Established in 1967.

• 17901 •
Rebecca Caudill Young Readers' Book Award Committee
Bonita Slovinski, Chm.
PO Box 6536
Naperville, IL 60567-6536
E-mail: bonitaslo@aol.com
Home Page: http://www.rcyrba.org

• 17902 • Rebecca Caudill Young Readers' Book Award
To recognize the author of the book voted most outstanding by students in grades 4 through 8 in participating Illinois schools. The purposes of the award are: to encourage children and young adults to read for personal satisfaction, to develop a statewide awareness of outstanding literature for children and young people, to promote a desire for literacy, and to encourage cooperation among Illinois agencies providing educational and library service to young people. The deadline for enrolling is November 30 each year. A plaque is awarded annually in the fall. Established in 1988 to honor Rebecca Caudill, a children's author who lived and wrote for 50 years in Urbana, Illinois. Sponsored by the Illinois Reading Council, the Illinois Association of Teachers of English, and the Illinois School Library Media Association.

• 17903 •
Recording for the Blind and Dyslexic
Mark Zustovich, Contact
20 Roszel Rd.
Princeton, NJ 08540
Phone: (609)452-0606
Phone: (866)732-3585
Toll-Free: 800-803-7201
Fax: (609)987-8116
E-mail: info@rfbd.org
Home Page: http://www.rfbd.org

Formerly: (1953) National Committee for Recording for the Blind.

• 17904 • Marion Huber Learning Through Listening Awards
To recognize outstanding high school seniors with learning disabilities who exhibit extraordinary scholarship, leadership, enterprise, and service to others. Candidates must be graduating high school seniors from U.S. public or private institutions, have a specific learning disability, maintain an overall grade point average of B or above during grades 10-12, plan to continue formal education beyond high school, and be registered RFB&D members for at least one year. Three $6,000 and three $2,000 awards with certificates are awarded annually. Established in 1990.

• 17905 • Mary P. Oenslager Scholastic Achievement Awards
To honor outstanding blind college seniors for the extraordinary scholarship, leadership, enterprise, and service to others displayed in earning their degrees. Applicants must be legally blind, be graduating or have graduated from an accredited four-year college in the United States, have at least a 3.0 grade-point average, and be registered RFB&D members for at least one year. Three top winners are awarded $6,000 each; three Special Honors winners receive $3,000 each; and three Honor winners receive $1,000 each. Awarded annually. Established in 1957. Formerly: (1991) Scholastic Achievement Awards.

• 17906 •
Recording Industry Association of America
Mitch Bainwol, Chair/CEO
1330 Connecticut Ave. NW, Ste. 300
Washington, DC 20036
Phone: (202)775-0101
Fax: (202)775-7253
E-mail: webmaster@riaa.com
Home Page: http://www.riaa.org

• 17907 • Cultural Award
For contributions to the advancement and protection of culture in America, and for efforts to make citizens more aware and appreciative of the many and diverse art forms that make up our civilized society. Individuals or groups in or associated with the Federal Government are given particular consideration. A Tiffany-designed silver trophy is awarded annually when merited. Established in 1969.

• 17908 • Gold Award
In recognition of the company that has produced single phonograph records that have sold in excess of 500,000 copies, and long-playing albums and their counterparts on pre-recorded tapes and compact discs that have sold more than 500,000 copies. A gilded record is awarded when sales criteria are audited, a minimum of 60 days after the release date. Established in 1958.

• 17909 • Gold Music Video Award
For recognition of pre-recorded videocassette or videodisc programs that have sold in excess of 50,000 copies. Companies that manufacture or are licensed to manufacture the video program in either or both formats are eligible. A gilded plaque is awarded when sales criteria are audited. Established in 1985.

• 17910 • Platinum Award
In recognition of companies that produced single phonograph records that have sold in excess of one million copies, and long-playing albums and their counterparts on pre-recorded tapes and compact discs that have sold more than one million copies. Platinum records are awarded when sales criteria are audited, a minimum of 60 days after the release date. Established in 1976.

• 17911 • Platinum Music Video Award
For recognition of pre-recorded videocassette or videodisc programs that have sold in excess of 100,000 units. Companies that manufacture or are licensed to manufacture the video program in either or both formats are eligible. A platinum plaque is awarded when sales criteria are audited. Established in 1985.

• 17912 •
Recreation Vehicle Industry Association
David J. Humphreys, Pres.
PO Box 2999
PO Box 2999
Reston, VA 20195-0999
Phone: (703)620-6003
Fax: (703)620-5071
Home Page: http://www.rvia.com

• 17913 • Distinguished Achievement in RV Journalism Award
To recognize a journalist whose work through the years has made significant contributions to the betterment of the recreation vehicle industry. Awarded annually when merited. Established in 1979 and renamed in 1980 in honor of J. Brown Hardison, a pioneer publisher in the RV industry. Formerly: (1980) J. Brown Hardison Award.

• 17914 • Distinguished Achievement in RV Standards Award
To recognize an individual for outstanding contributions toward the advancement of industry standards. Awarded annually when merited. Established in 1977 in honor of Walter D. Peck, the first Standards Director of RVIA. Formerly: Walter D. Peck Award.

• 17915 • Distinguished Service to the RV Industry Award
This, the highest honor of the Association, is bestowed as recognition to an individual within the recreation vehicle industry who has given outstanding service to the industry. Awarded annually when merited. Established in 1966 in honor of Paul Abel, a pioneer leader in the RV industry. Formerly: Paul Abel Award.

• 17916 • National Legislative Award
To recognize a public official for actions on behalf of the RV industry or outdoor recreation. Awarded annually when merited. Established in 1966.

• 17917 • National Scholastic Award
To recognize state or regional RV association directors who have contributed most to the advancement of the RV service industry in their area. Presented annually.

• 17918 • National Service Award
To recognize outstanding contributions to the recreation vehicle industry by an individual, corporation, or organization outside the RV industry. Awarded annually when merited. Established in 1979.

• 17919 • RV Automotive Achievement Award
To recognize those in the automotive industry who have made outstanding contributions to the RV industry. Awarded annually.

• 17920 •
Recycling Council of Alberta
Ms. Darryl Wolski, Pres.
PO Box 23
Bluffton, AB, Canada T0C 0M0
Phone: (403)843-6563
Fax: (403)843-4156
E-mail: info@recycle.ab.ca
Home Page: http://www.recycle.ab.ca

• 17921 • Rs of Excellence
Annual recognition of waste reduction innovation and recycling initiatives by individuals, municipalities and/or business.

• 17922 •
Recycling Council of Ontario
Joanne St. Goddard, Exec.Dir.
51 Wolseley St., 2nd Fl.
Toronto, ON, Canada M5T 1A4
Phone: (416)657-2797
Fax: (416)960-8053
E-mail: rco@rco.on.ca
Home Page: http://www.rco.on.ca

• 17923 • Ontario Waste Minimization Awards
To recognize individuals, businesses, municipal governments, and institutions whose efforts to minimize waste are contributing to a cleaner, more sustainable environment. Presented in 15 categories. Awarded annually with framed artwork. Established in 1984.

• 17924 •
Charles Redd Center for Western Studies
Brigham Young University
Provo, UT 84602
Phone: (801)422-4048
E-mail: Kn4@email.byu.edu

• 17925 • Annaley Naegle Redd Student Award in Women's History
Awarded to upper division or graduated students doing research on women in the American West. Awards of $1,500 may be used for a worthy project including preparation of seminar papers, theses, and dissertations. Deadline: March 15.

• 17926 • John Tropham and Susan Redd Butler Faculty Research Awards
Recognizes someone who has illuminated some aspect of the American experience in the Mountain West (defined as Idaho, Montana, Wyoming, Nevada, Utah, Colorado, Arizona, and New Mexico.) Applicants should be faculty members at an institution of higher Education. The amount of the award is a maximum of $3,000. Deadline: March 15.

• 17927 • Education Awards
Recognizes K-12 educators who would like to develop course curriculum, fund classroom projects, or research some aspect of the American experience in the Mountain West. An award of up to $1,000 is given. Deadline: March 15.

• 17928 • Independent Research and Creative Work Awards
Recognizes an individual not connected to a college or university as a faculty member or a student who is interested in researching or writing of some aspect of the American Experience in the Mountain West. A monetary award of up to $1,500 is given. Deadline: March 15.

• 17929 • Public Programming Awards
Award of recognition. A stipend of $3,000 is awarded to be used for research or the actual costs of presenting the individual program. The deadline is March 15.

• 17930 • Charles Redd Center Publication Grants
Awarded to publishers to help offset the costs of publishing books and to lower the book's selling price. Up to $3,000 is awarded to assist in the publication of studies on the Mountain West.

• 17931 • Summer Awards for Upper Division and Graduate Students
Recognizes research from upper division and graduate students for dealing with the Mountain West. A monetary award up to $1,500 is awarded for use in research. Deadline: March 15.

• 17932 •
Reebok Human Rights Foundation
Reebok International Ltd.
1895 JW Foster Blvd.
Canton, MA 02021
Phone: (781)401-7946
Fax: (781)401-4941
E-mail: rhrfoundation@reebok.com
Home Page: http://www.reebok.com/x/us/humanRights

• 17933 • **Reebok Human Rights Award**
An annual award which honors activists under the age of 30 who have significantly improved the human rights conditions in their communities. Grants are made to support the work of four Awardees each year. A monetary amount of $50,000 is given.

• 17934 •
Reference and USER Services Association of American Library Association
Cathleen J. Bourdon, Exec.Dir.
50 E Huron St.
Chicago, IL 60611
Phone: (312)280-4395
Toll-Free: 800-545-2433
Fax: (312)944-8085
E-mail: rusa@ala.org
Home Page: http://www.ala.org/rusa

Formerly: (1997) American Library Association - Reference and Adult Services Division.

• 17935 • **Virginia Boucher-OCLC Distinguished Interlibrary Loan Library Award**
An annual award consisting of $2,000 and a citation recognizing a librarian for outstanding professional achievement, leadership, and contributions to interlibrary loan and document delivery through publication, during the previous two years, of significant professional literature, participation in professional associations, and/or innovative approaches to practice in individual libraries that is administered by Sharing and Transforming Access to Resources (STARS) of the Reference and User Services Association (RUSA). Deadline for receiving submissions is December 15.

• 17936 • **BRASS Thomson Financial Student Travel Award**
To enable a student with an interest in a career as a business reference librarian to attend the American Library Association Annual Conference. Applicants must be enrolled in an ALA-accredited master's degree program and be making satisfactory progress toward that degree, have a demonstrated interest in pursuing a career as a business reference librarian, and have the potential to be a leader in the profession. The deadline is December 1. A monetary award of $1,000 and a one-year membership in ALA/RUSA/BRASS are awarded. Sponsored by Thomson Financial. Formerly: (2004) BRASS Primark Student Travel Award.

• 17937 • **Dartmouth Medal**
To honor achievement in creating reference works outstanding in quality and significance. Works published or otherwise made available for the first time during the calendar year preceding presentation of the award are eligible. Nominations should be submitted no later than December 15. A bronze medal donated by Dartmouth College, Hanover, New Hampshire, is awarded annually. For further information, contact the ALA-RUSA. Established in 1974.

• 17938 • **Dun & Bradstreet Award for Outstanding Service to Minority Business**
Annual award of $2,000 (up to half of which can be used to cover expense of attending ALA Annual Conference to receive award) that recognizes one librarian who, or library that has been recognized by that community as an outstanding service provider, presented by the Business and Reference Services Section (BRASS) of the Reference and User Services Association (RUSA). Deadline for receiving submissions is December 15.

• 17939 • **Dun & Bradstreet Public Librarian Support Award**
Annual award of $1,000 to support the attendance at Annual Conference of a public librarian who has performed outstanding business reference service and who requires financial assistance to attend the ALA Annual Conference. Presented by the Business Reference and Services Section (BRASS) of the Reference and User Services Association (RUSA). Deadline for receiving submissions is December 15.

• 17940 • **Thomson Gale Award for Excellence in Business Librarianship/ BRASS**
To honor individuals who have distinguished themselves in the field of business librarianship. Accomplishments may include: authoring a seminal book or article in business librarianship; developing an imaginative and successful program centered around business within a library; teaching business librarianship in a particularly creative and substantive manner; displaying unusually strong leadership in a professional association geared to business librarianship; or leadership in other activities that encourage librarians to excel in business librarianship. A monetary award of $3,000 and a citation are presented annually at the ALA Conference. Established in 1989 by Thomson Gale and the Business Reference and Services Section of the ALA Reference and User Services Association.

• 17941 • **Genealogical Publishing Company Award**
To recognize a librarian, library, or publisher for professional achievement in historical reference and research librarianship. Deadline for receiving submissions is December 15. A citation and $1,500 cash prize are awarded annually.

• 17942 • **Margaret E. Monroe Library Adult Services Award**
A citation to honor a librarian who has made significant contributions to library adult services, administered by the Reference and User Services Association (RUSA). Deadline for receiving submissions is December 15.

• 17943 • **Isadore Gilbert Mudge - R. R. Bowker Award**
An annual cash award of $5,000 and a citation to an individual who has made a distinguished contribution to reference librarianship, presented by the Reference and User Services Association (RUSA). Deadline for receiving submissions is December 15. Formerly: Isadore Gilbert Mudge Citation.

• 17944 • **Outstanding Reference Sources**
To recognize outstanding reference titles in the following areas: social sciences; psychology, religion, and mythology; science and technology; business and economics; genealogy and heraldry; and language, literature, and the arts. Reference works in print and in all nonprint and electronic formats are considered. Selected annually by the Reference Sources Committee. Established in 1959.

• 17945 • **Reference Service Press Award**
A plaque and $2,500 cash award (raised from $1,500 in 2001) presented to recognize the most outstanding article published in RUSQ (RQ) during the preceding two-volume year, presented by the Reference and User Services Association (RUSA). Deadline for receiving submissions is December 15.

• 17946 • **John Sessions Memorial Award**
A plaque given to a library or library system to honor significant work with the labor community and to recognize the history and contributions of the labor movement toward the development of this country, presented by the Reference and User Services Association (RUSA). Deadline for receiving submissions is December 15.

• 17947 • **Louis Shores - Greenwood Publishing Group Award**
A citation and $3,000 cash award to an individual reviewer, group, editor, review medium or organization to recognize excellence in book reviewing and other media for libraries. The award recipient is selected for significant achievement related to a reviewing process that helps librarians make selection decisions, administered by the Collection Development and Evaluation Section (CODES) of the Reference and User Services Association (RUSA). Deadline for receiving submissions is December 15.

• 17948 • **Thomson Gale Award for Excellence in Reference and Adult Services**
The Thomson Gale Award for Excellence in Reference and Adult Library Services is given to a library or library system for developing an imaginative and unique resource to meet patron's reference needs, administered by the Reference and User Services Association (RUSA). Dead-

line for receiving submissions is December 15. $3,000 and a citation are awarded.

• 17949 •
REFORMA: National Association to Promote Library Services to the Spanish-Speaking
Ana Elba Pavon, Pres.
PO Box 25963
Scottsdale, AZ 85255-0116
Phone: (480)471-7452
Fax: (480)471-7442
E-mail: reformaoffice@riosbalderrama.com
Home Page: http://www.reforma.org

• 17950 • **Pura Belpre Award**
To recognize a Latino/Latina writer and illustrator whose work best portrays, affirms, and celebrates the Latino cultural experience in an outstanding work of literature for children and youth. Books for children up to age 14 are considered, provided they were published in the U.S. or Puerto Rico by an author/illustrator who is a resident or citizen of the U.S. or Puerto Rico. Two awards are given biennially: one to an author for the most outstanding text, and one to an illustrator for outstanding picture book. Established in 1996 in honor of Pura Belpre, the first Latina librarian from the New York Public Library.

• 17951 • **REFORMA Scholarship**
To provide financial assistance and to encourage Spanish-speaking individuals to pursue a career in library or information science. Applicants must: qualify for graduate studies in library science; be citizens or permanent residents of the U.S.; and speak Spanish. Application deadline is March 15. The scholarship is not restricted as to age, sex, need, national origin, minority group, or association membership. The monetary awards of $1,500 are presented to one or more recipients annually. Established in 1983. Formerly: (1982) George I. Sanchez Memorial Award.

• 17952 •
The Refractories Institute
Robert W. Crolius, Pres.
650 Smithfield St., Ste. 1160
Centre City Tower
Pittsburgh, PA 15222-3907
Phone: (412)281-6787
Fax: (412)281-6881
E-mail: triassn@aol.com
Home Page: http://www.refractoriesinstitute.org

• 17953 • **Chairman's Safety Award**
To recognize the efforts of the refractory industry in promoting employee safety and health. All active member companies are eligible for one of four categories based on work hours: under 100,000 man hours; 100,000 to one million man hours; one million to two million man hours and, over two million man hours. A plaque is awarded annually. Established in 1986.

• 17954 •
Regional Business Partnership
Nikki Drake, Info.Spec.
744 Broad St., 26th Fl.
Newark, NJ 07102-3802
Phone: (973)522-0099
Fax: (973)824-6587
E-mail: rbp@rbp.org
Home Page: http://www.rbp.org

• 17955 • **Distinguished Service Award**
For regional contribution. Monetary award bestowed annually.

• 17956 • **Fast 50 Award**
For fastest 50 growing high-tech firms. Monetary award bestowed annually.

• 17957 •
Regional Plan Association
Robert D. Yaro, Pres.
4 Irving Pl., 7th Fl.
New York, NY 10003
Phone: (212)253-2727
Fax: (212)253-5666
Home Page: http://www.rpa.org

• 17958 • **Regional Plan Association Award**
To recognize distinguished service to the Tri-State New York Metropolitan Region. An inscribed gift is awarded annually. Established in 1971.

• 17959 •
Regular American Veterans
John Hearon, Natl. Commander
1309 Harrison Ln.
Austin, TX 78742-2871
Phone: (512)386-8387
Toll-Free: 800-981-8387
Fax: (512)385-1181
E-mail: rav@onr.com
Home Page: http://www.onr.com/user/rav/ravhome.htm

Formerly: (1934) U.S. Maimed Soldiers League.

• 17960 • **Order of the Compassionate Heart**
To recognize citizens who gave outstanding service and recognition to the combat and disabled veterans returning and adjusting to civilian life after severe wartime disabling injuries, and to recognize individuals who aided disabled veterans, in hospital programs and readjustment programs, to return to a normal lifestyle. Individuals who devote and dedicate their programs, time, money and energy to the cause of aiding the disabled veterans may be nominated at any time by members of the Order, members of the Regular Veterans Association, and individuals, fraternities, or groups. A medal, composed of four hearts edged with white enamel attached to a red heart with the official coat of arms of the Czar of Russia and the Russian eagle and shield, hung from a ribbon of white, maroon and gold, and a resolution and a certificate, with the seal of the Order, are awarded annually or when merited. Established in 1917 in memory of Czar Nicholas of Russia who established and bestowed the Order on individuals who aided the disabled war veterans of Russia and her World War I allies.

• 17961 • **Order of the Golden Eagle**
For recognition of outstanding service to veterans, Americans, the Armed Forces, and the Association. Any citizen, by nomination, who provides service on legislation aiding veterans/members of the Armed Forces, is eligible. A trophy, plaque, or citation is awarded upon selection by a Committee. Established in 1937.

• 17962 • **Silver Helmet Award**
To recognize police, fire, public safety officials, and members of the Armed Forces who demonstrate heroism on or off duty. A medal is awarded. Established in 1935 by Captain Walter Johnson, USN/RET. Formerly: (1995) Medal of Valor.

• 17963 •
Rehabilitation International
Michael Fox, Pres.
25 E. 21st St.
New York, NY 10010
Phone: (212)420-1500
Fax: (212)505-0871
E-mail: ri@riglobal.org
Home Page: http://www.rehab-international.org/

• 17964 • **Henry H. Kessler Awards**
To recognize three individuals or organizations whose achievements in a specified area of activity have contributed significantly to mankind's ability to overcome the occurrence and disadvantages of physical, mental, and/or sensory disability. Three monetary awards of $500 and bronze statuettes are awarded every four years at the Association's World Congress. Established in 1976. Formerly: Henry and Estelle Kessler Awards in International Rehabilitation.

• 17965 • **The Rehabilitation International Presidential Award**
Recognizes an individual whose work and accomplishments over an extended period of time have significantly contributed to the progress of international efforts to prevent or overcome physical, mental, and/or sensory disability. A statuette or plaque and $5,000 is awarded once every four years.

• 17966 • **Fenmore R. Seton Distinguished Volunteer Award**
To recognize a distinguished volunteer who has made a most special and meaningful contribution, nationally and/or internationally, to the improvement of the quality of life for persons with disabilities. Nominations are accepted from Member organizations. Selection is made by a committee composed of the President, the Past President, and the Secretary General. A monetary award of $1,000 and travel expenses to

attend the award ceremony are awarded every four years. Established in 1986.

• 17967 •
Relay and Switch Industry Association
Jeffrey Boyce, Exec.Dir.
2500 Wilson Blvd.
Arlington, VA 22201
Phone: (703)907-8025
Fax: (703)875-8908
E-mail: narm@ecaus.org
Home Page: http://www.ec-central.org/narm

• 17968 • **Distinguished Service Award**
For recognition of individual leadership that has enhanced the growth and vitality of the NARM. Established in 1983.

• 17969 • **Hall of Fame**
To recognize outstanding contributions to the relay industry consistent with the aims and purposes of the Association. Selection is by nomination of entire membership after criteria have been evaluated by the honors committee. A plaque is presented at the annual meeting. A master plaque listing names of all winners is held at headquarters office. Established in 1981.

• 17970 •
Religion Communicators Council
S. Struchen, Exec.Dir.
475 Riverside Dr., Rm. 1355
New York, NY 10115
Phone: (212)870-2985
Phone: (212)870-2402
Fax: (212)870-2171
E-mail: rccrprc@interport.net
Home Page: http://
www.religioncommunicators.org

• 17971 • **Wilbur Awards**
To recognize excellence in the communication of religious values, issues, and themes in the secular media. Criteria include content, creativity, execution, and results, with an emphasis on excellence in the communication of religious values. Awards are given in 18 categories. Entry deadline is February 1. Handcrafted, stained glass awards are presented annually in each category at the national convention in the spring. Established in 1949 and renamed in 1982 in honor of Dr. Marvin D. Wilbur, longtime leader in religious public relations. Formerly: (1982) Award of Merit in Broadcasting; (1959) Award of Merit in Journalism.

• 17972 •
Religion Newswriters Association
Debra Mason, Exec.Dir.
PO Box 2037
Westerville, OH 43086-2037
Phone: (614)891-9001
Fax: (614)891-9774
E-mail: info@rna.org
Home Page: http://www.rna.org

• 17973 • **Cassels Reporter of the Year Award**
For recognition of excellence in the reporting of news about religion in the secular press. Reporters employed by Canadian or United States secular newspapers with a circulation of 50,000 or less are eligible. The deadline is February 1. A monetary prize of $750 and a certificate are awarded annually.

• 17974 • **George Cornell Religion Reporter of the Year Award for Mid-Sized Papers**
For recognition of excellence in religion reporting in secular papers with circulations between 50,001 to 150,000. Any US or Canadian reporter whose entries were printed in secular newspapers, newsmagazines or news services is eligible. A monetary prize of $750 and a citation are awarded annually to the first place winner, with a second-place prize of $500 and a third place prize of $250.

• 17975 • **Harold J. Schachern Memorial Award Award**
For excellence in the religion pages or sections of the secular press. Any U.S. or Canadian secular newspaper or newsmagazine is eligible. Deadline is February 1. A citation is given to the first place winner in two categories: newspapers below 100,000 in circulation and newspapers about 100,000 in circulation. Awarded annually.

• 17976 • **Supple Religion Writer of the Year Award**
For recognition of excellence in the reporting of news about religion for secular newspapers in the United States and Canada. A monetary award of $1,000 is awarded at the Association's national meeting. Established in 1953 in honor of James O. Supple, a former officer of RNA.

• 17977 • **Templeton Religion Reporter of the Year Award**
For recognition of excellence in enterprise reporting and versatility in the field of religion in the secular press. Open to any reporter employed by a U.S. or Canadian secular newspaper, news magazine, or news service. Deadline is February 1. A monetary prize of $3,500 and a citation are awarded annually.

• 17978 •
Religious and Military Order of Knights of the Holy Sepulchre of Jerusalem
H.G. Duke Lloyd-Douglas S.G.M., Contact
3620 W 10th St., Ste. B-150
Greeley, CO 80634-1821
Fax: (419)793-6884
E-mail: ohs@maxalla.net
Home Page: http://www.greeleynet.com/~maxalla/OKHSSub/ohs.htm

• 17979 • **Order of Merit**
Recognizes outstanding contributions in religious and secular life, including arts and education. Awarded annually.

• 17980 •
Religious Communication Association
Thomas Lessl, Pres.
Dept. of Communication
3900 University Blvd.
University of Texas at Tyler
Tyler, TX 75799
Phone: (903)566-7093
Fax: (903)566-7287
E-mail: eiden@cox.net
Home Page: http://
www.americanrhetoric.com/rca

• 17981 • **Publication Awards**
For recognition of scholarly and academic publications. Candidates must be members. The following awards are presented: Article Award, Book Award, Dissertation Award, and Student Paper Award. Awarded annually at the convention. Established in 1975.

• 17982 •
Religious Freedom Council of Christian Minorities
Wesley H. Wakefield, Chm.
PO Box 223, Sta. A
Vancouver, BC, Canada V6C 2M3
Phone: (250)492-3376
Phone: (778)772-8014

• 17983 • **Religious Liberty Award**
Recognizes the best essay on religious freedom. Junior high student writers are eligible. Awarded annually. Inquire for application details.

• 17984 •
Renaissance Society of America
John Monfasani, Exec.Dir.
365 5th Ave., Rm. 5400
New York, NY 10016-4309
Phone: (212)817-2130
Fax: (212)817-1544
E-mail: rsa@rsa.org
Home Page: http://www.rsa.org

• 17985 • **Phyllis Goodhart Gordan Book Prize**
To recognize significant accomplishment in Renaissance Studies and to encourage Renaissance scholarship. Authors must be members of RSA, and books must be in English. A monetary prize of $1,000 is awarded to the author of the best book in Renaissance Studies. Established in memory of the late Phyllis Goodhart Gordan, a strong supporter of the RSA from its early days.

• 17986 • **William Nelson Prize**
For recognition of the best manuscript submitted to *Renaissance Quarterly* during the preceding year. A monetary prize of $600 is awarded annually in March. Established in 1984 in memory of William Nelson, former president of the Society.

• 17987 •
Renewable Natural Resources Foundation
Robert D. Day, Exec.Dir.
5430 Grosvenor Ln.
Bethesda, MD 20814
Phone: (301)493-9101
Fax: (301)493-6148
E-mail: info@rnrf.org
Home Page: http://www.rnrf.org

• 17988 • **Outstanding Achievement Award**
To recognize a project, publication, piece of legislation, or similar concrete accomplishment in the renewable natural resources fields that occurred during the three years prior to the nomination for the award. Nominations may be made by an individual or organization, and must be submitted by June 1. A crystal tower is awarded annually in November in Washington, D.C. The award is presented annually on behalf of 16 professional, scientific and educational organizations. The award was established in 1992.

• 17989 • **Sustained Achievement Award**
To recognize the long-term contribution and commitment by an individual to the advancement of the renewable natural resources sciences. Nominations may be made by any individual or organization. A crystal tower is awarded every November in Washington, D.C. The award is presented on behalf of 16 professional, scientific and educational organizations. The award was established in 1992.

• 17990 •
RenewAmerica
811 Virginia Ave. SE
Washington, DC 20003
Phone: (202)544-9555
Fax: (202)544-8775
E-mail: editor@renewamerica.us
Home Page: http://www.renewamerica.us

Formerly: Fund for Renewable Energy & Environment.

• 17991 • **National Awards for Environmental Sustainability - Searching for Success Program**
To recognize successful environmental programs that work to protect, restore, and enhance the environment. Programs in operation for at least six months are eligible. Winning programs are selected by the National Awards Council for Environmental Sustainability, made up of 60 environmental, government, community and business groups. 26 awards are presented annually in categories relating to natural resource protection, economic progress and human development. Established in 1990. Formerly: (1991) National Environmental Achievement Award - Searching for Success Program.

• 17992 •
REO Club of America
Karen A. Perkis, Sec.
7971 Vernon Rd.
Cicero, NY 13039-9314
Phone: (315)458-4721
E-mail: reoclub@yahoo.com
Home Page: http://clubs.hemmings.com/reo

• 17993 • **Fran Silky Award**
Established in 1980 in memory of Francis Silky of Lansing, Michigan, an early Reo Club of America member and longtime employee of the Reo Company. Fran was an active participant during the formative years of the Club, giving freely of his time and knowledge in support of other members. Annually, an award in his name is presented at the Convention to a member who has, through his or her contribution, given extraordinary service to the Club. Reo cars were manufactured by the Reo (Ransom E. Olds) Factory in Lansing, Michigan, from 1905 to 1936; trucks until 1976.

• 17994 • **Raymond M. Wood Award**
To recognize REO Club members who have contributed the most to the REO ECHO for the advancement of the Club and its purposes during the preceding twelve month period. Recipients announced at the annual banquet meeting of the club. In the event no suitable candidate is determined, there shall be no award for that year. The award perpetuates the memory of its esteemed late REO ECHO Editor, Raymond M. Wood.

• 17995 •
Research and Development Associates for Military Food and Packaging Systems
James F. Fagan, Exec.Dir.
16607 Blanco Rd., Ste. 1506
San Antonio, TX 78232
Phone: (210)493-8024
Phone: (210)493-8025
Fax: (210)493-8036
E-mail: hqs@militaryfood.org
Home Page: http://www.militaryfood.org

• 17996 • **Colonel Rohland A. Isker Award**
To recognize meritorious achievement to national preparedness in the areas of food and container research and development. Eligible contributions may be in the fields of basic research, applied research, developmental endeavor, or process improvement. Civilian employees, military personnel, personnel of the laboratories of other armed services and other federal governments are eligible. Nomination deadline is August 31. An engraved gold wrist watch and plaque are awarded annually. Established in 1958 to honor Col. Rohland A. Isker, who was the commanding officer of the U.S. Army Food and Container Institute in Chicago in World War II.

• 17997 • **Colonel Merton Singer Award**
To recognize outstanding contributions to the Association's mission in cooperation with agencies of the U.S. government related to supporting the needs of the government in the fields of foods, containers, food service, equipment, supply, or other related areas. An individual member, consultant member, or employee of a member company is eligible. A plaque and an engraved watch are awarded when merited. Established in 1989 to honor Merton Singer for his dedication to both military and industrial needs.

• 17998 •
Research Society for Victorian Periodicals
Laurel Brake, Pres.
Department of English
Boise State University
Boise, ID 83725
Phone: (208)426-1179
Fax: (208)426-4373
E-mail: secretary@rs4rp.org
Home Page: http://www.rs4vp.org

• 17999 • **VanArsdel Prize**
Recognizes an outstanding graduate student paper. Awarded annually.

• 18000 •
Resort and Commercial Recreation Association
Mike DiBenedetto, Pres.
PO Box 4327
Sunriver, OR 97707
Phone: (541)593-3711
Fax: (541)593-7833
E-mail: info@r-c-r-a.org
Home Page: http://www.r-c-r-a.org

• 18001 • **Achievement Award**
To recognize significant contribution to the Association and the profession of commercial recreation through dedicated service that is considered beyond average. Applicants must be RCRA members for at least five years and employed at least five years as a professional recreation and park executive, administrator, supervisor, director, leader, or specialist in the field of commercial recreation or employed in a university or college as educator for at least five years. Awarded annually.

• 18002 • **Excellence in Programming Award**
To recognize the professional(s) or student(s) who have created and implemented a special and unique program that has brought special recognition, significant increase in guest/student satisfaction, contributed to betterment of community, and/or increased profitability to the members' property university. Awarded annually.

• 18003 • **Fellow Award**
To recognize individual members who have consistently contributed to the well being of the Association and the industry of commercial recreation for a significant period of time, such

that they are considered to be one of the top professionals in the field. Applicants must be a member of RCRA for at least five years and employed at least 10 years as a professional recreation and park executive, administrator, supervisor, director, leader, or specialist in the field of commercial recreation or employed in a university or college as educator for at least 10 years. Applicants must also have served in an elected office of RCRA, and must have received the RCRA Achievement Award at least two years prior to consideration.

• 18004 • **Newcomer Award**
To reward the energies of a "new" professional's individual efforts and impact in a managerial/leadership position at their property. Applicants must be an RCRA member in good standing, hold a supervisory level job, and been hired or promoted to their current position within the past two years. Awarded annually.

• 18005 • **Outstanding Student Award**
To recognize the student/intern member who has worked to make a positive contribution to the Association, as well as their property or university. Awarded annually.

• 18006 • **Premier Recreation Operation Award**
To recognize those establishments that have displayed outstanding leadership in the development and promotion of quality recreation programs and services. Awarded annually. Formerly: Premier Property Award.

• 18007 • **Professional Recruitment Award**
To recognize the member who has recruited the most professional members to the benefit of the Association in the past year.

• 18008 • **Debbie Regnone Service Award**
To recognize contributions and achievements in the commercial recreation field. Achievements must be reflected in the field in general and also in the association. Candidates must have five years membership in RCRA, five years involvement in the field, be active on committees and board assignments, and demonstrate exemplary leadership and service to the association. A plaque is awarded at the annual conference. Established in 1987 in honor of Debbie Regnone. In addition, the association presents the following awards: Premier Property Award, Excellence in Programming Award, Meritorious Service Award, Outstanding Student Award, Achievement Award, and Fellow Award.

• 18009 •
Restaurant Hospitality
Penton Media, Inc.
Michael Sanson, Editor-in-Chief
1300 E 9th St.
Cleveland, OH 44114
Phone: (216)696-7000
Fax: (216)696-1752
E-mail: rheditors@aol.com
Home Page: http://www.restaurant-hospitality.com

• 18010 • **Best Kids Menu Competition**
To recognize creativity and innovation in marketing, presentation, and food. Awards are given after judging menus and marketing support material. Award categories are: Casual/Theme Restaurant; Quick Service Restaurant; Family Restaurant; Hotel/Resort/Club; Upscale Restaurant; and School.

• 18011 • **Best Wine Lists in America Awards**
To recognize U.S.-based restaurants and hotel companies offering spectacular wine lists. Each year, awards are given based on wine lists and menus in domestic and international categories.

• 18012 •
Results
Barbara Wallace, Exec.Dir.
440 First St. NW, Ste. 450
Washington, DC 20001
Phone: (202)783-7100
Fax: (202)783-2818
E-mail: results@results.org
Home Page: http://www.results.org

• 18013 • **Congressional Leadership Award**
Recognizes outstanding leadership in congress. Awarded annually.

• 18014 • **Cameron Duncan Media Award**
Recognizes the best print media on hunger/poverty issues. Awarded annually.

• 18015 •
Retail Advertising and Marketing Association
Peter Perweiler, Project Mgr.
325 7th St. NW, Ste. 1100
Washington, DC 20004-2802
Phone: (202)661-3052
Fax: (202)661-3049
E-mail: perweilerp@rama-nrf.com
Home Page: http://www.rama-nrf.com

Formerly: (1996) Retail Advertising Conference.

• 18016 • **Best of Show Award**
To recognize one entry as the very best of the industry for the year. The award is given annually at the RAC Conference Awards Dinner in February.

• 18017 • **Hall of Fame**
To recognize individuals who have contributed the most to the advancement of the retail advertising profession. Awarded annually as part of the RAC Awards event. Established in 1955.

• 18018 • **RAC Awards**
To select and reward exception advertising that accomplishes its stated objective. Ads or commercials may be entered in the following categories: billboards, new media, radio, television, TV campaign, direct mail, direct response, in-store, insert, international, magazine, online campaign, print campaign, and public relations. Any retail store is eligible to enter. Agencies, newspapers, broadcasters, producers, and freelancers are invited to enter for their clients. Any ad or commercial which appeared during the preceding year from September to September is eligible for entry. Entries are assessed on the basis of creativity, concept, merchandising, and execution (art, typography, copy, layout, music, production values, etc.) The Astar Award, awarded for the first time in 1988, is given to winners and finalists in every category when merited. The Heineman Trophy for Best of Show is awarded annually for extraordinary and exemplary advertising efforts, regardless of category, entry section, or store volume. Award certificates are presented in every category when merited. Established in 1976.

• 18019 •
Retail Merchants Association of New Hampshire
Nancy C. Kyle, Pres.
35A S Main St.
Concord, NH 03301-4942
Phone: (603)225-9748
Toll-Free: 800-336-3770
Fax: (603)229-0060
E-mail: rmanh@rmanh.com
Home Page: http://www.rmanh.org

• 18020 • **Mark E. Manus Scholarship**
For members, member employee, or child continuing in retailing, fashion merchandising, business management, or marketing. Scholarship awarded annually.

• 18021 •
Retirement Research Foundation
Edward J. Kelly, Chm.
8765 W Higgins Rd., Ste. 430
Chicago, IL 60631-4170
Phone: (773)714-8080
Fax: (773)714-8089
E-mail: info@rrf.org
Home Page: http://www.rrf.org

• 18022 • **Community Awards Program (Encore Awards)**
To recognize outstanding community efforts to serve the elderly and to encourage replication of these efforts in other parts of the Chicago metropolitan area. Social service, religious congregations, health organizations, hospitals, nursing homes, educational organizations, and community organizations in Cook, Lake, and DuPage

counties, IL, are eligible. Up to four monetary prizes of $25,000, in addition six prizes of $5,000 each are awarded annually. Established in 1987.

• 18023 •
Rhetoric Society of America
David Henry, Exec.Dir.
Univ. of Nevada, Las Vegas
4505 Maryland Pkwy.
Las Vegas, NV 89154
Phone: (702)895-4825
Fax: (702)895-4825
E-mail: rhetoric-society@byu.edu
Home Page: http://rhetoricsociety.org

• 18024 • Charles Kreupper Award
Recognizes the best piece published in RSQ. A monetary prize is given annually.

• 18025 •
Rhode Island Council of Community Mental Health Centers
Elizabeth V. Earls, Exec.Dir.
67 Cedar St., Ste. 1
Providence, RI 02903-1042
Phone: (401)273-0900
Fax: (401)273-0959
E-mail: info@riccmho.org
Home Page: http://www.riccmhc.org

• 18026 • Advocacy Award
For a family member and/or consumer whose advocacy has positively impacted upon people with mental illness and the services they receive. Recognition award bestowed annually.

• 18027 • Distinguished Service Award
For an individual working within the state public system who has had a positive influence on the mental health system. Recognition award bestowed annually.

• 18028 • A. Eric Palazzo Community Service Award
For outstanding volunteer record of sustained community contribution to the issues of mental health and mental illness. Recognition award bestowed annually.

• 18029 •
Rhode Island Health Center Association
Kerrie Jones Clark, Exec.Dir.
235 Promenade St., Ste. 2104
Providence, RI 02908
Phone: (401)274-1771
Fax: (401)274-1789
E-mail: info@rihca.org
Home Page: http://www.rihca.org

• 18030 • Cunningham Distinguished Citizen Award
For promotion of community health center mission. Recognition award bestowed annually.

• 18031 •
Rhode Island Turfgrass Foundation
Gary Sykes, Contact
28 Pelham St.
Newport, RI 02840
Phone: (401)841-5490
Fax: (401)846-5600
E-mail: director@nertf.org

• 18032 • RITF Noel Jackson Research Fellowship
For a URI turfgrass research graduate student. Scholarship awarded annually.

• 18033 •
Rhodes 19 Class Association
Kirk Williamson, Secretary
178 Main St.
Rockport, MA 01966
E-mail: krwphoto@adelphia.net
Home Page: http://rhodes19.org

• 18034 • National Championship
To recognize the first place winner of the National Championship Regatta of Rhodes 19 Class Sailboats. Members of the Rhodes 19 Class Association who are qualified per class rules to participate in the National Regatta are eligible. A large silver trophy is awarded annually at the completion of the Regatta. Established in 1962.

• 18035 •
Rhododendron Species Foundation
Rick Peterson, Co-Exec.Dir./Garden Dir.
2525 S 336th St.
PO Box 3798
Federal Way, WA 98063-3798
Phone: (253)838-4646
Phone: (253)927-6960
Fax: (253)838-4686
E-mail: rsf@rhodygarden.org
Home Page: http://www.rhodygarden.org

• 18036 • Northwest Flower & Garden Show Garden Award
Recognizes the best use of species rhododendron in an exhibit. Awarded annually.

• 18037 •
Richard III Society, American Branch
Carole M. Rike, Ed.
PO Box 13786
New Orleans, LA 70185
Phone: (504)827-0161
Fax: (504)822-7599
E-mail: info@r3.org
Home Page: http://www.r3.org

• 18038 • William B. and Maryloo Spooner Schallek Memorial Graduate Fellowship Awards
To assist students pursuing graduate education in a field or fields relating to the life and times of King Richard III (1452-1485) or, more generally, to late fifteenth-century England. Applications may be submitted by February 28. Successful candidates must be United States citizens or must have made application for first citizenship papers; further, they must be enrolled at a recognized educational institution, making normal progress toward an M.A. or more typically a Ph.D. Awards are for one year, although applications for an additional year or years are considered. Five dissertation awards of $2,000 each and a dissertation fellowship of $30,000 are awarded annually. Established in 1978. Administered by the Medieval Academy of America.

• 18039 •
Richard the III Foundation
Mary Kelly, Mgr.
47 Summit Ave.
Garfield, NJ 07026
Phone: (973)478-6466
Fax: (973)478-9096
E-mail: middleham@aol.com
Home Page: http://www.richard111.com

• 18040 • Richard III Scholarship for Medieval Studies
To pursue the studies of the medieval period with emphasis on the years between 1350 and 1500. Awarded annually. Established in 1994.

• 18041 •
Richards Free Library
58 N Main St.
Newport, NH 03773
Phone: (603)863-3430
Fax: (603)863-3022
E-mail: rfl@newport.lib.nh.us
Home Page: http://www.newport.lib.nh.us

• 18042 • Sarah Josepha Hale Award
For recognition of distinguished work in the field of literature and letters that reflects a New England atmosphere or influence based on the writer's whole body of work. Nominees are selected by a national board of judges; applications or submissions are not accepted. Candidates must be connected with New England by birth, residence, or work; should be a literary person (poet, dramatist, novelist, historian, journalist, writer, etc.); and must appear in Newport to give a speech. A monetary award of $500 and a bronze medal are awarded annually. Established in 1956 in honor of Sarah Josepha Hale, a 19th century feminist, author, editor, and crusader for women, women's rights, and social reform in general.

• 18043 •
RID - U.S.A.
Doris Aiken, Pres./Founder
PO Box 520
Schenectady, NY 12301
Phone: (518)372-0034
Phone: (518)393-4357
Fax: (518)370-4917
E-mail: dwi@rid-usa.org
Home Page: http://www.rid-usa.org

• 18044 • **National Humanitarian Award**
To recognize an individual who delivers lifesaving reforms in driving while intoxicated field. A plaque is awarded annually when merited. Established in 1983 by Doris Aiken, founder of RID.

• 18045 • **National Lifesaving Leadership Award**
To recognize individuals for leadership in effective deterrence of driving while intoxicated. Public figures who demonstrate outstanding track records and creative solutions may be nominated by the board. A plaque or framed certificate is awarded annually. Established in 1978 by Doris Aiken, founder. Awards are also presented to state officials for leadership in the fight against drunk driving.

• 18046 •
Rider University Student Government Association
Tracy Davison, Pres.
2083 Lawrenceville Rd.
Lawrenceville, NJ 08648
Phone: (609)896-5000
Phone: (609)257-9026
Toll-Free: 800-257-9026
Fax: (609)895-5497
E-mail: davisont@rider.edu
Home Page: http://www.rider.edu

• 18047 • **SGA Service Award**
For service to campus and community. Recognition award bestowed annually.

• 18048 •
Riders of the Wind, The Field Events Player's Association
Michael D. Conger, Dir.
PO Box 43
Wallops Island, VA 23337
Phone: (757)824-1642
Phone: (757)824-1642
Fax: (757)824-1768
E-mail: snapconger@earthlink.net

• 18049 • **Pegasus Award**
Bestowed to best U.S. player in field events play. Awarded annually.

• 18050 •
Ridgefield Chamber of Commerce
Penny S. Hoffman, Pres./CEO
9 Bailey Ave.
PO Box 191
Ridgefield, CT 06877
Phone: (203)438-5992
Fax: (203)438-9175
E-mail: chamberinfo@ridgefieldchamber.org
Home Page: http://www.ridgefieldchamber.org

• 18051 • **President's Eagle Award**
For outstanding contribution to the Chamber. Recognition award bestowed annually.

• 18052 •
Rin Tin Tin Fan Club
Ms. Daphne Hereford, VP/Founder
PO Box 27
Crockett, TX 75835
Phone: (936)545-0471
E-mail: info@rintintin.com
Home Page: http://www.RinTinTin.com

• 18053 • **Dog of the Year**
Annual award of recognition.

• 18054 •
Riot Relief Fund
Peter Megargee Brown, Pres.
1125 Park Ave., Ste. 6-A
New York, NY 10128
Phone: (212)427-6434
Fax: (212)996-4625

• 18055 • **Award of Recognition**
Recognizes a person who has demonstrated exceptional service to law enforcement. Awarded annually.

• 18056 •
Ripon Society
Hon. Richard Kessler, Pres.
1300 L St., NW, Ste. 900
Washington, DC 20005
Phone: (202)216-1008
Toll-Free: 800-98-RIPON
Fax: (202)547-6560
E-mail: info@riponsoc.org
Home Page: http://www.riponsoc.org

• 18057 • **Jacob K. Javits Excellence in Public Service Award**
To recognize an individual who serves the public through diligence, integrity, intellect, and leadership, setting the standard by which future public figures will be judged. Nominations are welcome. Selection is by the Society. A plaque is given annually at the award dinner. Established in 1987 in honor of Senator Javits' legacy of dedication to public service.

• 18058 • **Republican of the Year**
To honor outstanding Republicans. Awarded not more than once a year. Established in 1964.

• 18059 •
Risk and Insurance Management Society
Mary Roth, Exec.Dir.
1065 Avenue of the Americas, 13th Fl.
New York, NY 10018
Phone: (212)286-9292
Phone: (212)655-6032
Fax: (212)655-7423
E-mail: membership@rims.org
Home Page: http://www.rims.org

• 18060 • **The Arthur Quern Quality Award**
Honors professionalism, vision, ethics, and enthusiasm that Arthur Quern exhibited as Chairman and Chief Executive Officer. Contact Aurea Hernando: 212-655-6597

• 18061 • **The Cristy Award**
Recognized the individual who earned the highest marks on the three exams that make up the Associate of Risk Management designation. Contact Fran Jordan, 212-655-6221.

• 18062 • **The Fred H. Bossons Award**
Recognizes the individual who received the highest average score on the Canadian Risk Management exams. Contact Fran Jordan, 212-655-6221.

• 18063 •
Risk Management Association
Maurice H. Hartigan II, Pres. & CEO
1 Liberty Pl.
1650 Market St., Ste. 2300
Philadelphia, PA 19103-7398
Phone: (215)446-4000
Toll-Free: 800-677-7621
Fax: (215)446-4101
E-mail: member@rmahq.org
Home Page: http://www.rmahq.org

• 18064 • **Award for Journalistic Excellence**
Annual award of recognition. A monetary award is given annually.

• 18065 • **National Paper Writing Competition Award**
Recognizes an outstanding paper on commercial lending. RMA associates are eligible. Awarded annually.

• 18066 •
River City
Kristen Iversen, Editor-in-Chief
Dept. of English
University of Memphis
Memphis, TN 38152
Phone: (901)678-4591
Fax: (901)678-2226
E-mail: rivercity@memphis.edu
Home Page: http://www.people.memphis.edu/~rivercity

Formerly: (1989) *Memphis State Review*.

• 18067 • **Writing Awards**
To recognize excellence in short story and poetry writing. The Fiction Award honors a short story of 7,500 words or less. Monetary awards of $1,500 for first prize, $350 for second prize, and $150 for third prize plus publication of the story is awarded annually. The Poetry Award a poem with a maximum of two pages in length. A monetary prize of $1,000 and publication are awarded for first place; second and third place receive publication only. Submission deadline for both awards is March 15. Both are awarded annually.

• 18068 •
Road Runners Club of America
Jean Knaak, Exec.Dir.
8965 Guilford Rd., Ste. 150
Columbia, MD 21046
Phone: (410)290-3890
Fax: (410)290-3893
E-mail: office@rrca.org
Home Page: http://www.rrca.org

• 18069 • **Journalism Award**
Recognizes an outstanding contribution to running literature.

• 18070 • **Roadrunners of the Year Award**
Recognizes outstanding runners. Awards are given for male and female runners.

• 18071 •
Robert E. Lee Memorial Association
Col. Thomas C. Taylor, Exec.Dir.
485 Great House Rd.
Stratford, VA 22558-0001
Phone: (804)493-8038
Phone: (804)493-8371
Fax: (804)493-0333
E-mail: info@stratfordhall.org
Home Page: http://www.stratfordhall.org

• 18072 • **Lee Integrity Award**
Award of recognition.

• 18073 •
Robert F. Kennedy Memorial
Jennifer Jones, Coord.
1367 Connecticut Ave. NW, Ste. 200
Washington, DC 20036
Phone: (202)463-7575
Toll-Free: 800-558-1880
Fax: (202)463-6606
E-mail: jones@rfkmemorial.org
Home Page: http://www.rfkmemorial.org

• 18074 • **Robert F. Kennedy Book Awards**
To recognize authors whose books most faithfully and forcefully reflect Robert Kennedy's concerns: justice and equality for the poor, the minorities, and the young; and the responsible examination of major social issues. Fiction and nonfiction books published in the United States during the preceding year may be submitted the first week of January. A monetary award of $2,500 and a bust of Robert Kennedy are presented to the grand prize winner. Awarded annually at the Awards Ceremony in May. Established in 1980 by Professor Arthur Schlesinger, Jr., partially through proceeds from the sale of his biography, *Robert Kennedy and His Times*. The award is given in memory of the late U.S. Senator and Attorney General, Robert F. Kennedy.

• 18075 • **Robert F. Kennedy Human Rights Award**
To recognize a person or persons who, at great risk, stand up to opression in the nonviolent pursuit of respect of human rights. The award expresses Robert Kennedy's unequivocal opposition to tyranny and his belief in the power of moral courage to overcome injustice. Established in 1984, the RFK Human Rights Award brings national and international recognition to exemplary human rights activists and attention to their work and the issues they face. The award is presented annually at a ceremony in November in Washington D.C.

• 18076 • **Robert F. Kennedy Journalism Awards**
To recognize correspondents for outstanding coverage of the problems of the disadvantaged. Entries may include accounts of lifestyles, challenges, and potentials of the disadvantaged in the United States; insights into the causes, conditions, and remedies of their plights; critical analyses of public policies, programs, attitudes, and private endeavors relevant to their lives. Awards may be made in six categories of journalistic coverage: print, cartoon, television, radio, photojournalism, and international (honoring a correspondent reporting on foreign affairs in the American press). The competition is also open to college student print, broadcast, and photojournalism entries, although these entries will be judged separately. A cash prize of $1,000 may be awarded to the entry judged most outstanding in each group. At the discretion of the awards committee, a grand prize of $2,000 may be awarded to the most outstanding of the six categories. There is a $20 entry fee. Awarded annually at a ceremony in Washington D.C. Established in 1968 in memory of Robert F. Kennedy, the U.S. Senator and Attorney general.

• 18077 •
Robert Foster Cherry Awards Committee
Baylor University
1 Bear Pl.
PO Box 97412
Waco, TX 76798-7412
Phone: (254)710-2923
Fax: (254)710-2920
Home Page: http://www.baylor.edu/cherry%5Fawards/

• 18078 • **Robert Foster Cherry Award for Great Teachers**
To recognize great teachers and to expose Baylor University students to the world's greatest teachers. Eligible candidates include individuals who are extraordinary teachers with a record of positive, inspiring, and long-lasting effects on students. Candidates must be scholars with national and international achievements and residents of English-speaking countries. A monetary award of $25,000, split equally ($12,500) between two recipients is presented. Each recipient delivers a series of lectures at Baylor University during the fall or spring semester; travel expenses will be provided. The Award is given biennially, alternating years with the Robert Foster Cherry Chair for Distinguished Teaching. Established in 1991. The awards are made possible through the generosity of Mr. Robert Foster Cherry, a Baylor University alumnus.

• 18079 • **Robert Foster Cherry Chair for Distinguished Teaching**
To recognize great teachers and to expose Baylor University students to the world's greatest teachers. Eligible candidates include individuals who are extraordinary teachers with a record of positive, inspiring, and long-lasting effects on students. Candidates must be scholars with national and international achievements and residents of English-speaking countries. Winners receive a monetary award of $100,000, a furnished apartment, and travel expenses to present a lecture series at Baylor University in the fall and return in residence to teach for the spring semester. The Award is given biennially, alternating years with the Robert Foster Cherry Award for Great Teachers. Established in 1991. The awards are made possible through the generosity of Mr. Robert Foster Cherry, a Baylor University alumnus.

• 18080 •
Forest Roberts Theatre
James A. Panowski, Dir.
1401 Presque Isle Ave.
Northern Michigan University
Marquette, MI 49855
Phone: (906)227-2553
Fax: (906)227-2567
E-mail: bowersr1@chartermi.net
Home Page: http://www.nmu.edu/theatre

• 18081 • **Mildred and Albert Panowski Playwriting Award**
To encourage and stimulate artistic growth among educational and professional playwrights, and to afford students and faculty the chance to mount and produce an original work on the university stage. Any full-length, non-musical play that has not been previously produced or published may be entered. Plays that have been previously entered in this competition are not eligible. Submission deadline is November 18. A monetary prize of $2,000 and a fully mounted production of the play are awarded annually. Established in 1977 by Dr. James A. Panowski in cooperation with Northern Michigan University and the Shiras Institute. Formerly: (1991) Forest A. Roberts Playwriting Award; Shiras Institute/Mildred & Albert Panowski Playwriting Award.

• 18082 •
Robotic Industries Association
Donald A. Vincent, Exec.VP
PO Box 3724
900 Victors Way, Ste. 140
Ann Arbor, MI 48106
Phone: (734)994-6088
Fax: (734)994-3338
E-mail: ria@robotics.org
Home Page: http://www.robotics.org

Formerly: (1984) Robot Institute of America.

• 18083 • Joseph F. Engelberger Robotics Awards

To recognize individuals for achievement in robotics. Awards are presented in four categories: Technology Development - for work leading to the development of a new industrial robot or for robotics hardware such as hand tooling, sensors, or compliance devices; Application - for the development and execution of an outstanding primary robot application by an end-user; Education - for the enhancement of robot technology through the dissemination of robotics-related information; and Leadership - for outstanding individual contribution to the robotics industry. A monetary award $4,000 each and a commemorative medallion are awarded to the winner in each category annually. Established in 1977 in honor of Joseph F. Engelberger, the founding force behind industrial robotics. Formerly: (1989) Joseph F. Engelberger Awards.

• 18084 •
Rochester Institute of Technology
1 Lomb Memorial Dr.
Rochester, NY 14623-5603
Phone: (585)475-2411
Fax: (585)475-7029
Home Page: http://www.rit.edu

• 18085 • Byron G. Culver Award

For recognition of outstanding service to printing education. The recipient delivers a lecture and receives a handcrafted engraved silver bowl. Awarded annually during the Graphic Arts Industry Advisory Committee Meeting. Established in 1981 in honor of Byron G. Culver, the first director of the School of Printing Management and Sciences at Rochester Institute of Technology.

• 18086 • Frederic W. Goudy Distinguished Lecture

For recognition of outstanding contributions to the field of typography and printing. The recipient delivers a lecture and receives a handcrafted engraved silver cup. Awarded annually. Established in 1969 in honor of Frederic Goudy, a typedesigner who had designed more than 100 typefaces before his death in 1947. Sponsored by the Mary Flagler Cary Charitable Trust.

• 18087 • Isaiah Thomas Award

For recognition of outstanding service in newspaper management. Newspaper industry leaders are eligible. A handcrafted silver cup is awarded annually. Established in 1979 in honor of Isaiah Thomas, a patriot printer, who established the *Massachusetts Spy* in 1770 and the American Antiquarian Society in 1812.

• 18088 •
Rochester International Film Festival
PO Box 17746
Rochester, NY 14617
Phone: (716)288-5607
Fax: (716)473-4490
E-mail: moas@juno.com
Home Page: http://
www.rochesterfilmfest.org

Formerly: Rochester International Amateur Film Festival.

• 18089 • Rochester International Film Festival

For recognition of achievement in video and filmmaking. Films and videos of all genres are invited, but their duration must be no longer than 30 minutes. Submission deadline is 14. A shoestring trophy, designed and assembled by members, is awarded annually at the festival during the first weekend in May. Established in 1959 as Movies on a Shoestring.

• 18090 •
Rock and Roll Hall of Fame and Museum
Terry Stewart, Pres. and CEO
1 Key Plz.
Cleveland, OH 44144
Phone: (216)781-ROCK
E-mail: director@rockhall.org
Home Page: http://www.rockhall.com

• 18091 • Rock and Roll Hall of Fame

To honor legendary performers, producers, songwriters, disc jockeys, and other who have contributed to the enduring legacy of rock and roll music. Performers become eligible 25 years after the release of their first record; non-performers have no time requirement. Two other categories exist for induction: Early Influences (artists whose music predates, yet influenced, rock and roll) and Side Men (backup musicians who spend their career out of the spotlight). Awarded annually. Established in 1983.

• 18092 •
Rockefeller Brothers Fund
William F. McCalpin, Exec.VP/CEO
437 Madison Ave., 37th Fl.
New York, NY 10022-7001
Phone: (212)812-4200
Fax: (212)812-4299
E-mail: info@rbf.org
Home Page: http://www.rbf.org

• 18093 • Ramon Magsaysay Award

Awarded for up to five individuals and organizations in Asia whose civic contributions and leadership exemplify the greatness of spirit, integrity, and devotion to freedom of Ramon Magsaysay, former president of the Philippines who died tragically in an airplane crash. Often regarded as the Nobel Prizes of Asia, these awards are presented in five categories: government service, public service, community leadership, international understanding, and journalism, literature, and creative communication arts.

• 18094 •
Rockford College
Paul C. Pribbenow, Pres.
5050 E State St.
Rockford, IL 61108-2393
Phone: (815)226-4000
Toll-Free: 800-892-2984
Fax: (815)226-4119
E-mail: rockford_college_
information@rockford.edu
Home Page: http://www.rockford.edu

• 18095 • Jane Addams Medal

To recognize women who are pioneers in their professions, outstanding in character and vision, and widely recognized for their contributions to society. A large bronze medallion of Jane Addams, by Chicago artist Andrene Kauffman, is awarded as merited. Established in 1944 by Mr. George E. Frazer in honor of Jane Addams, a noted alumna, social reformer, winner of the 1931 Nobel Peace Prize, and founder of Hull House in Chicago.

• 18096 •
Rocky Mountain Coal Mining Institute
Karen L. Inzano, Exec.Dir.
8057 S Yukon Way
Littleton, CO 80128-5510
Phone: (303)948-3300
Fax: (303)948-1132
E-mail: mail@rmcmi.org
Home Page: http://www.rmcmi.org

• 18097 • Scholarship Program

To provide financial assistance to full-time students in their junior and senior year who are career-pathed in mining related industries. A resident from each of the RMCMI member states (AZ, CO, MT, NM, ND, TX, UT, and WY) is selected from among acceptable institutions. Awarded annually. Established in 1984.

• 18098 •
Rocky Mountain Elk Foundation
Buddy Smith, Chm.
5705 Grant Creek Rd.
PO Box 8249
Missoula, MT 59807
Phone: (406)523-4500
Toll-Free: 800-CALL-ELK
Fax: (406)523-4550
E-mail: info@rmef.org
Home Page: http://www.rmef.org

• 18099 • Wildlife Leadership Awards

To recognize, encourage, and promote leadership among future wildlife management professionals. Applicants must be an undergraduate student in a recognized wildlife program; have junior or senior standing; have at least one semester or two quarters remaining in their degree program; and be scheduled to be enrolled as a full-time student for the following fall semester or quarter. Ten awards, consisting of a scholarship of $2,000, a plaque, and a one-year membership to RMEF, are awarded annually in September.

Awards are arranged in alphabetical order below their administering organizations

• 18100 •
Rocky Mountain Masonry Institute
Laura Driver, Marketing Dir.
686 Mariposa St.
Denver, CO 80204
Phone: (303)893-3838
Fax: (303)893-3839
E-mail: laurad@rmmi.org
Home Page: http://www.rmmi.org

• 18101 • **Masterworks in Masonry Awards**
For overall design excellence, creative use of masonry, workmanship. Recognition award bestowed biennially.

• 18102 •
Rodeo Historical Society
Judy Dearing, Admin.Asst./Dir.
1700 NE 63rd St.
Oklahoma City, OK 73111
Phone: (405)478-6400
Fax: (405)478-2842
Home Page: http://www.nationalcowboymuseum.org

• 18103 • **Tad Lucas Memorial Award**
To recognize an outstanding woman for contributions to Western heritage. Women in any profession who epitomize what Tad Lucas stood for are eligible. Awarded annually. Established in 1991. Administered by the National Cowboy and Western Heritage Museum.

• 18104 • **Rodeo Hall of Fame**
To honor and memorialize the great performers in rodeo and its related profession, and to perpetuate the rich heritage of the American rodeo cowboy. Candidates must be at least 50 years old. Nomination deadline is December 31. A gold-plated medallion is presented annually at the Society's annual meeting. Established in 1968. Administered by the National Cowboy and Western Heritage Museum.

• 18105 •
Roll Call Inc.
Morton Kondracke, Exec.Dir.
50 F Street NW, Ste. 700
Washington, DC 20001
Phone: (202)824-6800
Fax: (202)824-0475
Home Page: http://www.rollcall.com

• 18106 • **Congressional Baseball Trophy**
To recognize the captain of the winning Democratic or Republican team that wins three games at the annual *Roll Call* Congressional Baseball Game. Established in 1960.

• 18107 • **Congressional Staff Award**
To recognize a Congressional aid for outstanding contributions in furthering a spirit of community in the Congress. A bronze plaque mounted on a mahogany base is awarded annually. Established in 1960 by Sidney Yudain, publisher of *Roll Call.*

• 18108 •
Rolling Stone
% Publicity Dept.
Wenner Media
1290 Avenue of the Americas, 2nd Fl.
New York, NY 10104
Phone: (212)484-1616
Fax: (212)484-1713
E-mail: letters@rollingstone.com
Home Page: http://www.rollingstone.com

• 18109 • **College Journalism Competition**
For recognition of excellence among college writers in the following categories: (1) Entertainment Reporting; (2) Essays and Criticism; and (3) Feature Writing. Entries must have been published in a university or college newspaper or magazine during the year prior to the award, and must be submitted by June 15. Entrants must have been actively enrolled as a full- or part-time student in an accredited college or university at the time of publication. A monetary award of $2,500 is awarded to the winner in each category. Awarded annually. Established in 1976.

• 18110 • **Readers' and Critics' Poll**
For recognition in the following categories: (1) Artist of the Year; (2) Best Album; (3) Best Single; (4) Best Band; (5) Best Male Singer; (6) Best Female Singer; (7) Worst Album; (8) Worst Single; (9) Worst Band; (10) Worst Male Singer; (11) Worst Female Singer; (12) Best American Band; (13) Best Foreign Band; (14) Best New Male Singer; (15) Best New Female Singer; (16) Best Producer; (17) Best Songwriter; (18) Best Heavy-Metal Band; (19) Best R&B Artist; (20) Best Country Artist; (21) Best Jazz Artist; (22) Best Rap Act; (23) Hype of the Year; (24) Best Radio Station - Large Market; (25) Best Radio Station - Medium market; (26) Best Radio Station - Small Market; (27) Best Song from a Movie; (28) Best Video; (29) Best Album Cover; (30) Best Live Performance; (31) Best Reissue Album; (32) Best Rock Movie; (33) Worst Video; (34) Worst Album Cover; (35) Worst Live Performance; (36) Best Guitarist; (37) Best Drummer; (38) Best Keyboard Player; (39) Best Bass Player; (40) Comeback of the Year; (41) Most Unwelcome Comeback; (42) Best Rock Couple; (43) Best-Dressed Male Rock Artist; (44) Best-Dressed Female Rock Artist; (45) Worst-Dressed Male Rock Artist; (46) Worst-Dressed Female Rock Artist; (47) Sexiest Male Rock Artist; and (48) Sexiest Female Rock Artist. Formerly: Critics' and Readers' Pick.

• 18111 •
Romance Writers of America
Allison Kelley, Exec.Dir.
16000 Stuebner Airline Rd., Ste. 140
Spring, TX 77379
Phone: (832)717-5200
Fax: (832)717-5201
E-mail: info@rwanational.org
Home Page: http://www.rwanational.com

• 18112 • **Janet Dailey Award**
To recognize the best romantic novel raising public consciousness about a social issue. A monetary prize is awarded annually at the Conference. Established in 1993. Sponsored by Janet Dailey/Harper Collins.

• 18113 • **Favorite Book of the Year Award**
To honor the favorite romance novel of the year. The annual award is eligible to any authors provided the copyright, first printing, or North American printing date of the book is from January 1 to December 31 of the year of the current contest. Winners are chosen by popular vote to receive the Gold RITA statuette. Editor winners receive a plaque.

• 18114 • **Golden Heart Award**
To recognize the best romance book in 12 categories by writers who have not published a romance book previously. Open both to members and to non-members. Application deadline is November 15. A 14k gold heart and a parchment certificate are presented to the winner in each category at the National Conference each year. Established in 1981.

• 18115 • **RITA Award**
To honor those books that have achieved the highest degree of excellence in the field of romantic fiction. Awards are presented for a specific novel that was submitted for judging. Open to members and non-members who have published a book between January 1 and December 31 of the year prior to the contest year. RITAs are awarded in 14 categories. A gold RITA statuette is presented to the winner in each category annually. Established in 1983.

• 18116 •
Ronald McDonald House Charities
Jackie Meara, Supervisor
1 Kroc Dr.
Oak Brook, IL 60523
Phone: (630)623-7048
Fax: (630)623-7488
Home Page: http://www.rmhc.org

• 18117 • **Ronald McDonald House Charities Awards of Excellence**
To recognize individuals whose efforts help children achieve their fullest potential. Two awards are given each year, one to a generalist in children's work and one to a physician or pediatrician. The awards come with a $100,000 grant to the children's charity of the recipient's choice. Established in 1986.

• 18118 • **Ronald McDonald House Charities Grants Program**
To assist children by creating, finding and supporting programs that directly improve the health and well being of children world wide. Grants ranging from $25,000 to $1 million are awarded to children's non profits.

• 18119 •
Roscoe Pound Institute
Dr. Lajuan H. Campbell, Membership and Education Coor.
1050 31st St. NW
Washington, DC 20007
Phone: (202)965-3500
Toll-Free: 800-424-2725
Fax: (202)965-0355
E-mail: pound@roscoepound.org
Home Page: http://www.roscoepound.org

Formerly: (2000) Roscoe Pound-American Trial Lawyers Foundation; Roscoe Pound Foundation.

• 18120 • **Roscoe Hogan Environmental Law Essay Contest**
To honor the writing ability of law students in the subject of environmental law. A cash award of $5,000 is presented annually, as well as an expense-paid trip to accept the award at the annual dinner. Established in 1970 in honor of the late Roscoe Hogan, an environmental advocate and lawyer.

• 18121 • **Elaine Osborne Jacobson Award for Women Working in Health Care Law**
To recognize women law students with an aptitude for, and commitment to, a career of advocacy for the health care needs of women, children, and elderly and disabled persons. Candidates may be nominated by a law school dean or a supervising law school faculty member. Awarded annually. Established in 1991 in honor of the late Elaine Jacobson, an advocate for health care needs of underserved populations.

• 18122 • **Richard S. Jacobson Award**
To recognize an outstanding law professor who exemplifies the best attributed of the trial lawyer as teacher, mentor, and advocate. A monetary prize of $5,000, a plaque, and expenses to attend the annual dinner to receive the award are presented annually. Established in 1984 to honor Richard S. Jacobson, first executive director of the Foundation.

• 18123 •
Rose Hybridizers Association
Larry D. Peterson, Treas.
21 S Wheaton Rd.
Horseheads, NY 14845-1077
Phone: (607)562-8592
E-mail: lpeterso@stny.rr.com
Home Page: http://www.rosehybridizers.org

• 18124 • **Best Seedling Award**
Recognizes the best seedling exhibited. Will be awarded at the Fall ARS National Convention. Established in 2001.

• 18125 •
Rosenstiel Basic Medical Sciences Research Center
Brandeis University
Rosenstiel Center (MS-029)
415 South St.
Waltham, MA 02454-9110
Phone: (781)736-2400
Fax: (781)736-2405
Home Page: http://www.rose.brandeis.edu

• 18126 • **Jacob Heskel Gabbay Award in Biotechnology and Medicine**
Recognizes, as early as possible in their careers, scientist in academica, medicine, or industry whose work had both outstanding scientific content and significant practical consequences in the biomedical sciences. Nominations are accepted from scientists in industry and academia. Selection is made by a panel of researchers representing the biotechnology and pharmaceutical industries as well as universities and schools of medicine. Medallions and a total cash prize of $15,000 (shared in the event of multiple winners) are presented annually. Recipients are asked to present seminars of their work. Established in 1998.

• 18127 • **Lewis S. Rosenstiel Award for Distinguished Work in Basic Medical Research**
Started as an expression of the conviction that educational institutions have an important role to play in the encouragement and development of basic science as it applies to medicine. Nominations are accepted from former Award winners, the life sciences research community, and by members of the Award Committee, which consists of distinguished scientists in the Boston area, and members of the Brandeis Faculty. Award recipients are selected based on the recommendations of the Award Committee. Members of Brandeis University are not eligible. Medallions and a total cash prize of $10,000 (shared in the event of multiple winners) are presented. Recipients are asked to present seminars of their work. Nominations, consisting of a short explanation of the contribution that merits the award and one or two key references, including reviews, must be submitted to the Award Committee no later than August 31 of each year. Established in 1971. 724465

• 18128 •
Rotary International
Ed Futa, Gen.Sec.
One Rotary Center
1560 Sherman Ave.
Evanston, IL 60201
Phone: (847)866-3000
Fax: (847)328-8554
E-mail: ers@rotaryintl.org
Home Page: http://www.rotary.org

• 18129 • **Rotary Award for World Understanding and Peace**
This, Rotary International's most prestigious honor, is given to recognize persons whose actions exemplify Rotary's objective of promoting international understanding, good will, and peace through selfless service to others. The prize of $100,000 may be donated by the winner to a charitable cause whose goals parallel Rotary's. The award, accompanied by a crystal flame that symbolizes the Rotary spirit of service, is usually presented at the annual Convention. Established in 1981.

• 18130 • **Significant Achievement Award**
To recognize a Rotary Club for a service project that helps satisfy a significant need in the local community. Nomination deadline is March 15. A certificate is awarded annually. Established in 1974.

• 18131 •
Rothko Chapel
K.C. Eynatten, Exec. Dir.
1409 Sul Ross St.
Houston, TX 77006
Phone: (713)524-9839
Fax: (713)524-7461
E-mail: info@rothkochapel.org
Home Page: http://www.rothkochapel.org

• 18132 • **Rothko Chapel Oscar Romero Award**
To recognize individuals who have risked or given their lives for the cause of freedom, peace, and justice. Individuals of any nationality, race, or creed, and organizations are eligible. A monetary award of $20,000 is presented every two years. Established in 1986 in memory of Oscar Arnulfo Romero, Archbishop of San Salvador, a man of integrity and courage who was murdered on March 24, 1980. Romero was an advocate of a just peace and openly opposed the forces of violence and oppression.

• 18133 •
Royal Architectural Institute of Canada (Institut Royal d'Architecture du Canada)
Jon F. Hobbs, Exec.Dir.
55 Murray St., Ste. 330
Ottawa, ON, Canada K1N 5M3
Phone: (613)241-3600
Fax: (613)241-5750
E-mail: info@raic.org
Home Page: http://www.raic.org

• 18134 • **Allied Arts Medal**
To recognize a Canadian artist/resident for outstanding creative achievement in the arts allied to architecture, such as mural painting, sculpture, decoration, stained glass, and industrial design. A silver medal is awarded at intervals of not less than one year and not more than three years. Established in 1953.

• 18135 • **Arthur Buckwell Memorial Scholarship**
To honor a student at the School of Architecture of the University of Manitoba who has, in the judgment of the faculty, demonstrated distinction in design. A monetary award of $1,500 is presented each year. Established in 1993.

Awards are arranged in alphabetical order below their administering organizations

• 18136 • Andre Francou Legacy
To assist graduates of the School of Architecture at the University of Montreal to go to France in order to study the characteristics of French architecture. A grant of $2,000 is awarded. Established in 1966 by Andre Francou, a French industrialist.

• 18137 • Gold Medal
This, the highest award the profession of architecture in Canada bestows, is given to recognize an individual for significant contribution to Canadian architecture. Eligible candidates are those whose personal work has demonstrated exceptional excellence in the design and practice or architecture, and/or whose work related to architecture has demonstrated exceptional excellence in research or education. A gold medal is awarded when merited. Established in 1930.

• 18138 • Student Medal
To recognize a student who has completed the course at a Canadian school of architecture for achieving the highest level of academic excellence and showing promise of being an architect of distinction after graduation. Selection is made by the head of the School and two other teachers associated with him or her in the work of the Architectural Department. Awarded annually. Established in 1935.

• 18139 • Ernest Wilby Memorial Scholarship
To provide assistance for students or graduate students of any recognized architectural school in Canada for the advancement of architecture and design in Canada, with special emphasis on outstanding achievement in design. Students entering the year before their final year architectural study, who show definite promise and talent, and who need financial assistance to continue are eligible. Selection is made by the school staff. A scholarship of $1,000 is awarded annually to schools across Canada on a rotating basis. Established in 1966.

• 18140 •
Royal Astronomical Society of Canada
Mr. Peter Jedicke, Pres.
136 Dupont St.
Toronto, ON, Canada M5R 1V2
Phone: (416)924-7973
Toll-Free: 888-924-7272
Fax: (416)924-2911
E-mail: nationaloffice@rasc.ca
Home Page: http://www.rasc.ca

• 18141 • C. A. Chant Medal
To recognize an amateur astronomer in Canada for valuable work in astronomy and closely allied fields of original investigation. Nomination deadline is December 31. A medal is awarded when merited. Established in 1940 in honor of Professor C.A. Chant who furthered the interest of astronomy in Canada.

• 18142 • Ken Chilton Prize
To recognize an amateur astronomer in Canada for a significant piece of astronomical work carried out or published during the year. Nomination deadline is December 31. Awarded when merited. Established in 1977 in memory of Ken E. Chilton, an active member of the Hamilton Centre.

• 18143 • Honorary Member
To provide recognition for contributions in the field of astronomy. Individuals from any country may be nominated.

• 18144 • Simon Newcomb Award
To recognize originality, scientific accuracy, and literary merit in articles relating to astronomy, astrophysics, or space science. Eligible entries must be written by non-professional members during the preceding year. Nomination deadline is December 31. A trophy and monetary award of $250 are awarded when merited. Established in 1978 in memory of Simon Newcomb, a native of Nova Scotia, who was an astronomer and a prominent scientist in America (1835-1909).

• 18145 • Plaskett Medal
To recognize the graduate from a Canadian university who submitted the most outstanding doctoral thesis in astronomy and astrophysics in the preceding two calendar years. A medal, monetary prize of $300, and invitation to contribute a paper to the Society's journal are awarded when merited. Established in 1987 by RASC and the Canadian Astronomical Society in recognition of the pivotal role played by John Stanley Plaskett in the establishment of astrophysical research in Canada.

• 18146 • Service Award
For recognition of outstanding service to a society centre or to the national Society over a period of at least ten years. Members who are recommended by a special committee are eligible. A bronze plaque is awarded when merited. Established in 1959.

• 18147 •
Royal Canadian Geographical Society
Louise Maffett, Exec.Dir.
39 McArthur Ave.
Ottawa, ON, Canada K1L 8L7
Phone: (613)745-4629
Toll-Free: 800-267-0824
Fax: (613)744-0947
E-mail: rcgs@rcgs.org
Home Page: http://www.rcgs.org

• 18148 • Gold Medal
To recognize a particular achievement in the general field of geography, or for recognition of a significant national or international event. Both individuals and groups of individuals are eligible. Awarded when merited. Established in 1972.

• 18149 • Massey Medal
For recognition of outstanding personal achievement in the exploration, development, or description of the geography of Canada. Eligibility is restricted to Canadian citizens, although the medal may be awarded to a non-Canadian under special circumstances. Awarded annually. Established in 1959 by the Massey Foundation, and named in honor of Canada's first native-born Governor General.

• 18150 •
Royal College of Physicians and Surgeons of Canada
Mrs. John W.D. McDonald MD, Pres.
774 Echo Dr.
Ottawa, ON, Canada K1S 5N8
Phone: (613)730-8177
Toll-Free: 800-668-3740
Fax: (613)730-8830
E-mail: publicaffairs@rcpsc.edu
Home Page: http://rcpsc.medical.org

• 18151 • Duncan Graham Award
To recognize an individual for an outstanding lifelong contribution to medical education. Nominations of any individual (whether physician or not) renowned in the field of medical education are solicited from the deans of the faculties of medicine. A monetary prize of $1,000 and an engraved memento are awarded annually. Established in 1969.

• 18152 • James H. Graham Award of Merit
To recognize an individual (whether physician or not) whose outstanding achievements reflect the aims and objectives of the Royal College. An engraved memento is awarded annually. Established in 1989.

• 18153 • Medal in Medicine
To recognize original work in clinical investigation or in the basic sciences relating to medicine. To qualify, a candidate must: be a fellow of the Royal College; have completed his/her training within the previous ten years; and have completed work mainly in Canada. The deadline for submission is November 30. A monetary award of $5,000 and a gold medal are awarded annually. Established in 1949.

• 18154 • Medal in Surgery
To recognize original work in clinical investigation or in the basic sciences relating to surgery. To qualify, a candidate must: be a fellow of the Royal College; have completed his/her training within the previous ten years; and have completed work mainly in Canada. The deadline for submission is November 30. A monetary award of $5,000 and a gold medal are awarded annually. Established in 1949.

• 18155 • National and Regional Continuing Education Award
Periodic award of recognition.

• 18156 •
Royal Neighbors of America
Ms. Rita Toalson FLMI, Mgr. of Public Relations
230 16th St.
Rock Island, IL 61201
Phone: (309)788-4561
Toll-Free: 800-627-4762
E-mail: contact@royalneighbors.org
Home Page: http://www.royalneighbors.org

• 18157 • **Fraternalist of the Year Award**
To recognize a deserving member of the Society. A plaque and an invitation to speak at the annual Field Managers' Meeting are awarded.

• 18158 • **Junior Director of the Year Award**
To recognize the Junior Director who best exemplifies the Society's fraternal principles and who has voluntarily contributed his or her services throughout the year. An invitation to speak at the Achievers' Conference is awarded.

• 18159 •
Royal Society of Canada
(Societe Royale Du Canada)
William Leiss, Pres.
283 Sparks St.
Ottawa, ON, Canada K1R 7X9
Phone: (613)991-6990
Fax: (613)991-6996
E-mail: adminrsc@rsc.ca
Home Page: http://www.rsc.ca

• 18160 • **Konrad Adenauer Research Award**
To recognize Canadian scholars whose research work in the humanities or in the social sciences has earned international recognition and who belong to the group of leading scholars in their area of specialization. Recipients are expected to carry out research work of their own choice at a German research institute for a period of up to one year. The deadline for nominations is January 31. A monetary award of up to 75,000 euros is presented annually. Established in 1988 by Dr. Helmut Kohl, Chancellor of the Federal Republic of Germany, and funded by the Alexander von Humboldt Foundation to promote academic relations between Canada and Germany.

• 18161 • **Bancroft Award**
(Bourse Bancroft)
For recognition of publication, instruction, and research in the earth sciences that have conspicuously contributed to public understanding and appreciation of the subject. Canadian citizens or persons who have been Canadian residents for the three years preceding the award are eligible. A monetary award of $2,500 and a scroll are awarded biennially in even-numbered years when merited. Established in 1968 to honor Joseph Austin Bancroft (1882-1957), Dawson Professor at McGill University, 1913-1929.

• 18162 • **Pierre Chauveau Medal**
(Medaille Pierre Chauveau)
For recognition of a distinguished contribution to knowledge in the humanities in Canada, other than Canadian literature and Canadian history. Canadian citizens or persons who have been Canadian residents for three years are eligible for nomination. A silver medal is awarded biennially in odd-numbered years when merited. Established in 1951 in memory of Pierre J.O. Chauveau, writer, orator, educator, and Canadian statesman.

• 18163 • **Sir John William Dawson Medal**
(Prix Sir John William Dawson)
To recognize an individual for important and sustained contributions in at least two different domains in the general areas of interest of the Society or in a broad domain that transcends the usual disciplinary boundaries. Canadian citizens or persons who have been Canadian residents for three years are eligible for nomination. A monetary prize of $2,500 and a silver medal are awarded biennially in odd-numbered years when merited. Established in 1985 to honor Sir William Dawson, the Society's first president (1882-83) and the foremost Canadian scientist and educator of his day. Dawson was a geologist, naturalist, teacher, author, man of religion, educational administrator, and promoter of learning.

• 18164 • **Thomas W. Eadie Medal**
(Medaille Thomas W. Eadie)
In recognition of major contributions to engineering or applied science, with preference given to those having an impact on communications, in particular the development of the Internet. Canadian citizens or persons who have been Canadian residents for the three years preceding the award are eligible. A monetary award of $3,000 and a bronze medal are awarded annually when merited. Established in 1975 and funded by Bell Canada to honor its past president, Thomas W. Eadie.

• 18165 • **Flavelle Medal**
(Medaille Flavelle)
For recognition of outstanding contributions to biological science during the preceding 10 years, or for significant additions to a previous outstanding contribution to biological science. Canadian citizens or persons who have been Canadian residents for the three years preceding the award are eligible. A gold-plated silver medal is awarded biennially in even-numbered years. Established in 1924 by Sir Joseph Wesley Flavelle, a financier and businessman.

• 18166 • **Jason A. Hannah Medal**
(Medaille Jason A. Hannah)
To recognize the author of an important Canadian publication in the history of medicine for works of high quality that have been published in the 10 years preceding the nomination. In this context, the word "Canadian" refers to the citizenship or residence of the author or to the content of the publication. A monetary award of $1,500 and a bronze medal are awarded annually when merited. Established in 1976. Cosponsored by the Associated Medical Services Inc. to honor Jason A. Hannah, their late president and managing director.

• 18167 • **Innis-Gerin Medal**
(Medaille Innis - Gerin)
For recognition of a distinguished and sustained contribution to the literature of the social sciences, including human geography and social psychology. Canadian citizens or persons who have been Canadian residents for the three years preceding the award are eligible. A bronze medal is awarded biennially in odd-numbered years when merited. Established in 1966 to honor economic historian H. A. Innis and sociologist Leon Gerin.

• 18168 • **McLaughlin Medal**
(Medaille McLaughlin)
To recognize important research of sustained excellence in any branch of the medical sciences. Canadian citizens or persons who have been Canadian residents for the three years preceding the award are eligible. A monetary award of $2,500 and a gold-plated silver medal are awarded annually. Established in 1978. Cosponsored by the R. Samuel McLaughlin Foundation.

• 18169 • **McNeil Medal for the Public Awareness of Science**
To recognize a candidate who has demonstrated outstanding ability to promote and communicate science to students and the public within Canada. Contributions can be made through public lectures, innovative programs and courses, and/or the media. The award consists of a medal plus a C$1,500 bursary. Candidates must be nominated by April 15. Awarded annually.

• 18170 • **Willet G. Miller Medal**
(Medaille Willet G. Miller)
For recognition of outstanding research in any branch of the earth sciences. Canadian citizens or persons who have been Canadian residents for the three years preceding the award are eligible. A gold-plated silver medal is awarded biennially in odd-numbered years. Established in 1941 by friends of Willet G. Miller, a distinguished geologist and a guiding force in the development of the Ontario mining industry.

• 18171 • **Lorne Pierce Medal**
(Medaille Lorne Pierce)
To recognize an achievement of special significance and conspicuous merit in imaginative or critical literature written in either English or French. Critical literature dealing with Canadian subjects has priority over critical literature of equal merit that does not deal with Canadian subjects. Canadian citizens or persons who have been Canadian residents for the three years preceding the award are eligible. A gold-plated silver medal is awarded biennially in even-numbered years when merited. Established in 1926 by Lorne Pierce (1890-1961), editor of Ryerson Press for 40 years.

• 18172 • Miroslaw Romanowski Medal
To recognize noteworthy contributions in the environmental sciences. The award is given to candidates who have made significant contributions to the resolution of scientific aspects of environmental problems or have brought about, by scientific means, important improvements to ecosystem quality. A medal, a cash award of $3000, and travel expenses to attend the Society's annual meeting are awarded each year, when merited. Established in 1993.

• 18173 • John L. Synge Award (Prix John L. Synge)
For recognition of outstanding research in any of the branches of the mathematical sciences. Some preference is given to candidates whose age is not over 40 in the year of the award. Canadian citizens or persons who have been Canadian residents for three years are eligible for nomination. A monetary prize of $2,500 and a diploma are awarded when merited. Established in 1986 to honor John Lighton Synge, one of the first mathematicians working in Canada to obtain international recognition by research in mathematics.

• 18174 • Henry Marshall Tory Medal (Medaille Henry Marshall Tory)
For recognition of outstanding research in a branch of astronomy, chemistry, mathematics, physics, or an allied science. Canadian citizens or persons who have been Canadian residents for three years are eligible for nomination. A medal is awarded biennially in odd-numbered years when merited. Established in 1941 by Henry Marshall Tory (1864-1947), founder of the Universities of British Columbia and Alberta, the National Research Council Laboratories, and Carleton University.

• 18175 • J. B. Tyrrell Historical Medal
For recognition of outstanding work in the history of Canada written in English or French. Canadian citizens or persons who have been Canadian residents for three years are eligible for nomination. A gold-plated silver medal is awarded biennially in even-numbered years when merited. Established in 1927 by Joseph Burr Tyrrell (1858-1957), a geologist, geographer, explorer, engineer, and amateur historian.

• 18176 •
R.R. Bowker LLC
Daryn Teague, Public Relations
630 Central Ave.
New Providence, NJ 07974
Phone: (908)286-1090
Toll-Free: 800-526-9537
Fax: (908)665-2898
E-mail: info@bowker.com
Home Page: http://www.bowker.com

• 18177 • The Annual LMP Awards
To honor individual, corporate, and supplier excellence and innovation in the book publishing industry. Books, loose-leaf products, and electronic editions must have been published from January through December of the preceding year. The following awards are presented: Individual Achievement Awards - design, production, editorial-trade, children's, professional, scholarly, reference, marketing and sales, and publicity; Corporate Awards - adult trade, children's, professional, scholarly, and reference; Outside Service Awards - graphic design, book manufacturing, and advertising/promotion/publicity; Technical Achievement/Innovation Award; and Person of the Year Award - to recognize an individual who has made permanent and significant contributions to the book publishing industry as demonstrated by specific accomplishments, actions, products, and philosophy during the eligibility period. A crystal sculpture of a book is awarded annually, and the winners' achievements are featured in a special section of the next edition of *Literary Market Place.* Established in 1989 by R. R. Bowker to celebrate the 50th anniversary of *Literary Market Place.*

• 18178 •
RTCA
Bill Jeffers, Chm.
1828 L St. NW, Ste. 805
Washington, DC 20036
Phone: (202)833-9339
Fax: (202)833-9434
E-mail: info@rtca.org
Home Page: http://www.rtca.org

Formerly: Radio Technical Commission for Aeronautics.

• 18179 • William E. Jackson Award
To recognize an outstanding graduate students in the field of aviation electronics and telecommunications. Candidates should submit a technical paper or thesis by September 30 of each year to be eligible. An honorarium of $2,000 and a plaque are presented annually at a special banquet during the RTCA Annual Symposium in the fall. Established in 1975 in honor of William E. Jackson, a pioneer in the development and implementation of the nation's air traffic control system. Formerly: Radio Technical Commission for Aeronatics.

• 18180 •
Rudolph E. Lee Gallery
College of Architecture, Arts, and Humanities
Denise Woodward-Dietrich, Dir.
Lee Hall, Rm. G-50
Clemson University
Clemson, SC 29634-0509
Phone: (864)656-3883
Fax: (864)656-7523
E-mail: woodwaw@clemson.edu
Home Page: http://www.clemson.edu/caah/leegallery/index.php

• 18181 • Clemson National Print and Drawing Exhibition
To recognize art works of high quality and to add to the collection of living American artists. Individuals 18 years of age or above may enter artworks in the Exhibition. Purchase awards are presented biennially. Established in 1983 by the Rudolph E. Lee Gallery. Co-sponsored by the Rudolph E. Lee Gallery and the College of Clemson Architectural Foundation.

• 18182 •
Rural Nurse Organization
Anna Mae Ericksen, Exec.Dir.
Capstone Coll. of Nursing
Univ. of Alabama
PO Box 870358
Tuscaloosa, AL 35487-0358
Phone: (509)363-3069
Fax: (509)623-7521
E-mail: rno@bama.ua.edu
Home Page: http://www.rno.org

• 18183 • Anna Mae Ericksen Award
For outstanding service to rural nursing. Monetary award bestowed annually.

• 18184 •
Rural Sociological Society
Edie Pigg, Business Mgr.
104 Gentry Hall
University of Missouri
Columbia, MO 65211-7040
Phone: (573)882-9065
Fax: (573)882-1473
E-mail: ruralsoc@missouri.edu
Home Page: http://www.ruralsociology.org

• 18185 • Awards for Excellence
To recognize a member for excellence in the general application and articulation of the discipline of rural sociology. Awards are given in four categories: extension and public outreach, research, instruction, and practice and application. A plaque is awarded annually in each category. Established in 1986.

• 18186 • Certificate of Appreciation
To recognize members for outstanding service to the Society in a singular area of effort. Awarded annually when merited. Established in 1982.

• 18187 • Distinguished Rural Sociologist Award
To recognize one or more member for superior career contributions to the field of rural sociology through research, teaching, extension, public service, and/or public policy. A plaque is awarded annually. Established in 1981.

• 18188 • Distinguished Service to Rural Life Award
To recognize an individual who has made continuous and long-term contributions to the enhancement of rural life and rural people. Members and non-members are eligible. A plaque and lifetime complementary membership in the Society are awarded annually. Established in 1981. Formerly: Outstanding Contribution to Rural Life Award.

• 18189 • Graduate Student Paper Award
To encourage graduate students in the development of their professional careers, to encourage

graduate student participation in annual meetings, and to provide a financial incentive for graduate student research. Papers by graduate students who are members of the Society are eligible. A monetary prize of $300 is awarded annually.

• 18190 •
Rutgers University
John J. Heldrich Center for Workforce Development
33 Livingston Ave., 5th Fl.
New Brunswick, NJ 08901
Phone: (732)932-4100
Fax: (732)932-3454
E-mail: hcwd@rci.rutgers.edu
Home Page: http://www.heldrich.rutgers.edu/

• 18191 • **Workforce Innovation Awards Program**
Recognizes private sector workplace improvements

• 18192 •
Rutland Region Chamber of Commerce
Thomas L. Donahue, Exec.VP/CEO
256 N Main St.
Rutland, VT 05701
Phone: (802)773-2747
Toll-Free: 800-756-8880
Fax: (802)773-2772
E-mail: info@rutlandvermont.com
Home Page: http://www.rutlandvermont.com

• 18193 • **Citizen of the Year**
For community involvement. Recognition award bestowed annually.

• 18194 •
Sacramento Convention and Visitors Bureau
Steve Hammond, Pres./CEO
1608 I St.
Sacramento, CA 95814
Phone: (916)808-7777
Toll-Free: 800-292-2334
Fax: (916)264-7788
E-mail: shammond@cityofsacramento.org
Home Page: http://www.sacramentocvb.org/sacramentocvb/

• 18195 • **Five Star Hospitality Awards**
For outstanding service. Recognition award bestowed annually.

• 18196 •
St. Bonaventure University
Russell J. Jandoli School of Journalism and Mass Communication
Margaret Carney, Pres.
3261 W State Rd.
PO Box J
St. Bonaventure, NY 14778
Phone: (716)375-2520
Fax: (716)375-2588
E-mail: lcoppola@sbu.edu
Home Page: http://www.sbu.edu

• 18197 • **Alumnus of the Year Award**
To recognize a journalism/mass communication major who has exemplified the highest professional standards and shared them unselfishly with the Jandoli School and the University in its educational mission. A certificate is awarded annually at the Media Excellence Awards Luncheon. Established in 1981.

• 18198 • **Bob Considine Award**
To recognize an individual in the print journalism profession for outstanding accomplishments and exemplary moral and ethical performance. A certificate is awarded annually at the Media Excellence Awards Luncheon. Established in 1978 in memory of Bob Considine, a columnist, writer, and newscaster.

• 18199 • **Douglas Edwards Award**
To honor a renowned broadcaster who has displayed exemplary moral and ethical performance in his or her profession. A certificate is awarded annually at the Media Excellence Awards Luncheon. Established in 1986 by Russell J. Jandoli to honor Douglas Edwards, pioneer CBS newscaster.

• 18200 • **Mark Hellinger Award**
This, the University's highest honor to a journalism/mass communication graduate, is given to recognize a graduate who demonstrates academic excellence and shows genuine promise in the communications arena. An award of $1,500 for the winner and $500 for runner-up, as well as a certificate are awarded annually at the Media Excellence Awards Luncheon. Established in 1960.

• 18201 • **Jandoli Award of Excellence**
To recognize a practicing journalist and/or journalism educator who has contributed meritoriously to the field and to the education of young journalists. Awarded on Communications Day at St. Bonaventure University by the School of Journalism and Mass Communication in memory of its founder, Russell J. Jandoli. Formerly: Distinguished Communicator Award.

• 18202 •
St. Cecilia Society
2302 Pierce St.
Flint, MI 48503
Phone: (810)239-6068
Fax: (810)239-6068
E-mail: almedahunter@netzero.com
Home Page: http://www.byrdartists.com

• 18203 • **William C. Byrd Young Artist Competition**
To encourage professional development in the field of music and to recognize outstanding musical performances. The focus of the competition rotates annually between piano, strings, winds and brass, and voice. The age limit is 30 years of age for contestants in piano, strings, and winds and brass, and 34 years of age for voice. The deadline for applications is January 15. A monetary prize of $5,000 and an appearance with the Flint Symphony Orchestra is awarded for first prize; $2,500 is awarded for second prize; and $1,000 is awarded to each of three finalists. Awarded annually. Established in 1975 in memory of William C. Byrd, artistic director of the Flint Institute of Music and conductor of the Flint Symphony Orchestra.

• 18204 •
St. David's Society of the State of New York
Lauranne Jones, Pres.
71 W 23rd St., Ste. 508
New York, NY 10010
Phone: (212)924-8415
Fax: (212)989-5159

• 18205 • **St. David's Society Scholarship**
For students who attend Welsh colleges and to students of Welsh descent.

• 18206 •
St. George's Society of New York
John Shannon, Exec.Dir.
216 E 45th St., Ste. 901
New York, NY 10017-3304
Phone: (212)682-6110
Fax: (212)682-3465
E-mail: info@stgeorgessociety.org
Home Page: http://www.stgeorgessociety.org

• 18207 • **Medal of Honor**
For distinguished service in British-American field. Recognition award bestowed annually.

• 18208 •
St. Joan's International Alliance U.S. Section
C. Virginia Finn, Pres.
1545 W. Armour Ave.
Milwaukee, WI 53221
Phone: (414)282-6943
E-mail: bala115@prodigy.net

• 18209 • **American Woman of the Year**
To recognize an American woman for extraordinary accomplishment that benefits the cause of security de jure and de facto equality between women and men in State, Society and Church. A letter of appreciation is awarded as merited. Established in 1979.

• 18210 •
St. Johns Area Chamber of Commerce
Brenda Terpening, Exec.Dir.
1013 S US 27
PO Box 61
St. Johns, MI 48879
Phone: (989)224-7248
Phone: (989)224-7209
Fax: (989)224-7667
E-mail: stjohnschamber@power-net.net
Home Page: http://www.stjohnschamber.org

• 18211 • **St. Johns Area Chamber of Commerce/Mint Festival Scholarship**
For education in business. Scholarship awarded annually.

• 18212 •
St. Louis Black Gay and Lesbian Pride Committee
Wil Strayhorn, Membership Chp.
6734 Myron
St. Louis, MO 63121-5348
E-mail: wstrayhorn@aol.com

• 18213 • **St. Louis Black Pride Scholarship**
For high school student in St. Louis area. Scholarship awarded annually.

• 18214 •
Saint Louis University
Rev. Lawrence Biondi, Pres.
221 N Grand Blvd., Rm. 206
Saint Louis, MO 63103
Phone: (314)977-2500
Toll-Free: 800-SLU-FORU
E-mail: admitme@slu.edu
Home Page: http://www.slu.edu

• 18215 • **Mary A. Bruemmer Award**
For recognition of outstanding contributions to student life outside the classroom at the University. Awarded annually. Established by the student government association in 1980.

• 18216 • **Jack and Julie Lally Distinguished Alumni Merit Award**
To recognize graduates of the School of Social Service who exemplify the school's mission through specific professional accomplishments. Awarded annually. Established in 1955.

• 18217 • **Nancy McNeir Ring Award**
To recognize student-teacher relations rather than strictly academic credentials. Awarded annually. Established in 1965 by Alpha Sigma Nu, the Jesuit Honor Society in memory of Nancy McNeir Ring, the first Dean of Women at Saint Louis University.

• 18218 • **Sword of Ignatius Loyola Award**
To recognize significant achievement of benefit to mankind. Nomination deadline is October 15. A Sword of Ignatius Loyola, handcrafted in Spain and employing symbols of Loyola, the founder of the Society of Jesus, is awarded when merited. Established in 1963. Formerly: (1988) Spirit of Saint Louis Award.

• 18219 •
St. Nicholas Society of the City of New York
Jill Spiller, Off.Mgr.
122 E 58th St., 2nd Fl.
New York, NY 10022-1909
Phone: (212)753-7175
Fax: (212)980-0769
E-mail: stnick@bestweb.net
Home Page: http://www.saintnicholassociety.org

• 18220 • **Washington Irving Medal of Literary Excellence**
To recognize the author of works about the city of New York. Awarded annually.

• 18221 • **Medal of Merit**
To recognize outstanding ability and service to the city of New York. Awarded annually. Established in 1937.

• 18222 •
Sales and Marketing Executives International
Willis Turner CSE, Pres.
PO Box 1390
Sumas, WA 98295-1390
Phone: (312)893-0751
Toll-Free: 800-999-1414
Fax: (604)855-0165
Home Page: http://www.smei.org

• 18223 • **International Marketing Executive of the Year**
Award of recognition for marketing business executives and educators. Awarded annually.

• 18224 • **International Sales Executive of the Year**
Annual award of recognitoin for sales business executives and educators.

• 18225 •
Sales Professionals USA
Steve Herbert, Pres.
PO Box 149
Arvada, CO 80001
Phone: (303)534-4937
Toll-Free: 888-763-7767
E-mail: info@salespros-usa.com
Home Page: http://www.salesprofessionals-usa.com

• 18226 • **SP USA Award**
For outstanding salesperson, sales manager, booster, or service person, outstanding entrepreneur. Awarded annually.

• 18227 •
Salina Arts and Humanities Commission
Martha Rhea, Exec.Dir.
PO Box 2181
Box 2181
Salina, KS 67402-2181
Phone: (785)826-7410
Fax: (785)826-7444
E-mail: sahc@salina.org
Home Page: http://www.salinaarts.com/sahc

• 18228 • **Horizons Grants Program**
For Saline County-arts organization and developing artists. Grant awarded annually.

• 18229 •
Salmon Unlimited
Jean Sliwa, Contact
4548 N Milwaukee Ave.
Chicago, IL 60630
Phone: (773)736-5757
Fax: (773)736-8900
E-mail: salmonunlimited@aol.com
Home Page: http://cdma95.tripod.com

• 18230 • **Fisherman of the Year**
For recognition of achievement of excellence in fishing. Members catching the most fish above the following weights from Lake Michigan are eligible: 20 lb. Chinook Salmon, 8 lb. Rainbow Trout, 9 lb. Lake Trout, 6 lb. Brown Trout; and 6 lb. CoHo Salmon. The award is determined as of December 31 each year. A plaque is awarded annually and only once to each winner. Established in 1971.

• 18231 •
Salon du Livre de l'Estrie
Sylvie L. Bergeron, Dir.Gen.
174, rue du Palais
Sherbrooke, QC, Canada J1H 4P9
Phone: (819)563-0744
Fax: (819)563-0962
E-mail: salonestrie@globetrotter.net
Home Page: http://www.salonlivredelestrie.net

• 18232 • **Grand Concours Litteraire**
To recognize amateur writing. Winners in each of five categories by age are awarded a monetary prize each year. Established in 1982.

• 18233 •
Salon du Livre de Montreal
300 rue du Saint-Sacrement, bur. 430
Montreal, QC, Canada H2Y 1X4
Phone: (514)845-2365
Fax: (514)845-7119
E-mail: slm.info@videotron.ca
Home Page: http://www.salondulivredemontreal.com

Awards are arranged in alphabetical order below their administering organizations

• 18234 • Fleury-Mesplet Literary Prize
For recognition of outstanding career in the industry.

• 18235 • Grand Prix du Livre de Montreal
To recognize outstanding Canadian authors of books. A monetary prize of $10,000 is presented. Administered by the Ville de Montreal since 1990.

• 18236 •
San Angelo Symphony
Jennifer Odom, Exec.Dir.
36 E Twohig Ave.
PO Box 5922
San Angelo, TX 76902
Phone: (325)658-5877
Fax: (325)653-1045
E-mail: receptionist@sanangelosymphony.org
Home Page: http://www.sanangelosymphony.org

• 18237 • Sorantin Young Artist Award
To recognize outstanding young artists in the areas of piano and strings (violin, viola, cello, bass, harp, and guitar). Candidates, who must be under the age of 28, are judged on technical proficiency, musicianship, rhythm, selection of repertoire, stage presence, and communication. A monetary award of $2,000 is awarded to the winner in each division; the runner-up in each division receives $1,000. Additionally, an overall competition winner may be selected to receive the Mayer Anderson Award, consisting of a $3,000 prize and an invitation to perform with the San Angelo Symphony. Awarded annually in November in San Angelo, TX. Established in 1959 and named after Dr. Eric Sorantin, the Orchestra's first conductor. Formerly: Hemphill-Wells Sorantin Award for Young Artists.

• 18238 •
San Antonio International Piano Competition
PO Box 39636
San Antonio, TX 78218
Phone: (210)270-3829
Fax: (210)824-5094
E-mail: info@saipc.org
Home Page: http://www.saipc.org

• 18239 • San Antonio International Piano Competition
To recognize and encourage young musicians of exceptional talent, and to provide an inspiring and educational music experience for the San Antonio and South Texas community. Pianists between 20 and 32 years of age are eligible. The following prizes are awarded: first prize - $15,000 and a gold medal; second prize - $10,000 and a silver medal; third prize - $5,000 and a bronze medal; fourth prize $1,500; fifth prize - $1,000; $1,000 for the best performance of the commissioned work; and $500 honorable mention awards for all semi-finalists. Additional prizes include the Michael J. Balint Memorial Award for best performance of a classical work ($1,000), and the Russell Hill Rogers Memorial Award for best performance of a romantic work $1,000. Awarded triennially. Established in 1984.

• 18240 •
San Antonio Rocks
PO Box 8056
San Antonio, TX 78208-0056
Phone: (210)228-9955
Home Page: http://www.rocksinc.org

• 18241 • San Antonio Chapter of Rocks Inc. Scholarship
For high school seniors planning on attending college. Scholarship awarded annually.

• 18242 •
San Diego County Fair
Exhibits Department
2260 Jimmy Durante Blvd.
Del Mar, CA 92014-2216
Phone: (858)755-1161
Phone: (858)793-5555
Fax: (858)755-7820
E-mail: info@sdfair.com
Home Page: http://www.sdfair.com

Formerly: (2003) Del Mar Fair.

• 18243 • Exhibition of Photography
To recognize outstanding photographic endeavors by professional and amateur still photographers in the black and white (monochrome) print, color print, digital imaging, photojournalism, and creative categories. The pre-registration deadline is May 2. There's over $ 17,000 awarded In six different catergories. Established in 1948. For more information, send a No. 10 SASE. Brochures and entry forms are available in early March.

• 18244 • Fine Art Show
To recognize outstanding achievement in art. Awards are given for two dimensional work, three dimensional work, and recycled art. Living artists and crafters must pre-register. Monetary prizes, including $200 awards for the best work in each class and two $250 awards for Best of Shows, are awarded annually. Established in 1880 by the 22nd District Agricultural Association of the State of California. For more information, send a No. 10 SASE. Brochures and entry forms are available in early March. The pre-registration deadline is May 2.

• 18245 •
San Francisco Film Festival
Graham Leggat, Exec.Dir.
39 Mesa St., Ste. 110
The Presidio
San Francisco, CA 94129
Phone: (415)561-5000
Fax: (415)561-5099
E-mail: info@sffs.org
Home Page: http://www.sffs.org

• 18246 • Golden Gate Awards
To honor the best in shorts, documentaries, animation, experimental, and youth-produced films/videos and work for television. The award program is the competitive section of the annual San Francisco International Film Festival, held each spring. Juries award cash prizes ranging up to $5,000 in ten of the 14 categories. Divisions include Film and Video, Television, New Visions, and Bay Area Film and Video. Established in 1959.

• 18247 •
The San Francisco Foundation
Sandra R. Hernandez, Exec.Dir.
225 Bush St., Ste. 500
San Francisco, CA 94104
Phone: (415)733-8500
Fax: (415)477-2783
E-mail: rec@sff.org
Home Page: http://www.sff.org

• 18248 • Community Leadership Awards
To recognize significant contributions to the quality of life in the Bay Area. Contributions may include work which improves, protects, or enhances Bay Area communities and their residents. Up to four awards of $10,000 for individuals and $20,000 for organizations are awarded annually.

• 18249 • Joseph Henry Jackson Literary Award
To recognize young authors of unpublished, work-in-progress in the form of fiction (novel or short stories), non-fictional prose, or poetry. Residents of Nevada or northern California for three consecutive years who are between 20 and 35 years of age are eligible. Entry deadline is January 31. A monetary prize of $2,000 is awarded annually. Established in 1955 to honor Joseph Henry Jackson, former literary editor of the San Francisco *Chronicle.*

• 18250 • James D. Phelan Art Awards
To recognize the achievements of California-born artists in a variety of disciplines. Up to six awards of $2,500-$7,500 each are made in printmaking and photography in odd-numbered years, and film and video in even-numbered years. Awarded annually.

• 18251 • James D. Phelan Literary Award
To recognize young, California-born authors of unpublished, work-in-progress in the form of fiction (novel or short stories), non-fictional prose, poetry, or drama. Individuals between 20 and 35 years of age who were born in the state of California, but are not necessarily current residents, are eligible. Entry deadline is January 31. A monetary prize of $2,000 is awarded annually. Established in 1935.

• 18252 •
San Francisco Planning and Urban Research Association
Jim Chappell, Pres.
312 Sutter St., Ste. 500
Ste. 500
San Francisco, CA 94108-4305
Phone: (415)781-8726
Fax: (415)781-7291
E-mail: info@spur.org
Home Page: http://www.spur.org

• 18253 • **Silver SPUR Awards**
Recognizes long-term contribution to the civic life of the city. Awarded annually.

• 18254 •
San Jose Astronomical Association
Jim Van Nuland, Sec.
3509 Calico Ave.
San Jose, CA 95124
Phone: (408)371-1307
E-mail: jvn@sjpc.org
Home Page: http://www.sjaa.net

• 18255 • **A.B. Gregory Award**
For generosity of time in helping others in astronomy. Recognition award bestowed annually.

• 18256 •
San Jose State University
Dept. of English
San Jose, CA 95192-0090
E-mail: srice@pacbell.net
Home Page: http://www.bulwer-lytton.com

• 18257 • **Bulwer-Lytton Fiction Contest**
To recognize the writer whose bad writing comes closest to the prose of the Victorian author, Edward George Earle Bulwer-Lytton, who opened his 1830 novel, *Paul Clifford*, with the now famous line, "It was a dark and stormy night. . ." One-sentence entries must be submitted by April 15. Winners and runners-up in each category are announced annually. Established in 1981 by Prof. Scott Rice of San Jose State University in memory of Edward George Earle Bulwer-Lytton, "a mediocre Victorian novelist."

• 18258 •
San Juan 21 Class Association
Ken Gurganus, Sec.-Treas.
211 Gloria St.
Greenville, NC 27858-8627
Phone: (252)355-6974
E-mail: kgurganus@cox.net
Home Page: http://www.sanjuan21.net/national

• 18259 • **National Champions**
To recognize the national sailing champions for the Eastern, Midwest, and Western divisions of Association. Awards are presented in two categories: Working Sails and All-Sails. Trophies are awarded annually. Established in 1971.

• 18260 •
San Martin Society of United States of America, Washington DC
Christian Garcia-Godoy, Pres.
19385 Cypress Ridge Ter., Unit 601
Leesburg, VA 20176-5166
Phone: (703)883-0950
Fax: (703)883-0950
E-mail: cggodoy@msn.com

• 18261 • **San Martin Bicentennial Medal**
For distinguished Samaritans. Medal awarded periodically.

• 18262 • **San Martin Palms**
For distinguished Samaritans. Recognition award bestowed periodically.

• 18263 •
Santa Fe Partners in Education
Valerie Ingram, Exec.Dir.
PO Box 23374
Santa Fe, NM 87502
Phone: (505)474-0240
Fax: (505)474-0240
E-mail: valingram@aol.com

• 18264 • **Teachers Who Inspire**
For outstanding educator in the Santa Fe public schools. Monetary award bestowed annually.

• 18265 •
SAS Institute Inc.
Dr. James Goodnight, CEO
100 SAS Campus Dr.
Cary, NC 27513-2414
Phone: (919)677-8000
Fax: (919)677-4444
E-mail: software@sas.sas.com
Home Page: http://www.sas.com

• 18266 • **Enterprise Computing Award**
To recognize organizations that have effectively used SAS software to achieve critical business objectives. Organizations must demonstrate productivity gains, cost or time savings, or a significant impact in achieving business goals. A plaque is presented annually at the SAS User's Group International Conference.

• 18267 • **User Feedback Award**
To recognize the user(s) of SAS software judged by the Institute to have contributed the most to the development and growth of the SAS System during the year. The SAS user may be in a company, university, government agency, or other institution where SAS software is installed. A plaque is presented annually at SUGI (SAS User's Group International) Conference. Established in 1979.

• 18268 •
Saskatchewan Library Association
Judith Silverthorne, Exec.Dir.
2010 7th Ave., Ste. 15
Regina, SK, Canada S4R 1C2
Phone: (306)780-9413
Fax: (306)780-9447
E-mail: slaexdir@sasktel.net
Home Page: http://www.lib.sk.ca/sla

• 18269 • **Mary Donaldson Award of Merit**
A bursary that has been given annually since 1977. It is awarded to a full-time or part-time Saskatchewan Institute of Applied Science and Technology.

• 18270 • **Francis Morrison Award**
To recognize an individual, organization, or group for outstanding contribution to librarians in the Province of Saskatchewan. Nomination deadline is March 15. A plaque is awarded annually. Established in 1985.

• 18271 •
Saskatchewan Music Festival Association
Doris Covey Lazecki, Exec.Dir.
62 Westfield Dr., Ste. 2
Regina, SK, Canada S4S 2S4
Phone: (306)757-1722
Toll-Free: 888-892-9929
Fax: (306)347-7789
E-mail: sask.music.festival@sasktel.net
Home Page: http://www.smfa.ca

• 18272 • **The Roy Aikenhead Memorial Choral Scholarship**
Recognizes the runner-up in the Saskatchewan Choral Federation Choral Competition. $200 is awarded.

• 18273 • **Mary Anderson Memorial Senior Woodwind Scholarship**
Recognizes the most outstanding Senior Woodwind competitor in Classes 500. 506. 518, 524, 530, 536, 542, 548, 5000, 5014, 5018, 5035, 5042, 5056, 5063, 5067, and 5071 in the Provincial Finals Competitions. A $300 scholarship is awarded. Formerly: (2006) The SMFA Senior Woodwind Scholarship.

• 18274 • **The Sister Boyle Award**
Recognizes an outstanding competitor of the Grand Awards Competition. $1,000 is awarded.

• 18275 • **The Boyle Memorial Senior French Music Scholarship**
Recognizes the winner of the Senior French Music Class 751 in the Provincial Finals Competitions. $300 is awarded.

• 18276 • **The Boyle Memorial Senior Hayden and Mozart Scholarship**
Recognizes the best performance in the Senior Hayden and Mozart Class 744 in the Provincial Finals Competitions. $300 is awarded.

Awards are arranged in alphabetical order below their administering organizations

• 18277 • The Ray Brookhart Memorial Intermediate Pipe Organ Scholarship
Recognizes the most outstanding Intermediate Pipe Organ competitor in Classes 804, 805, and 806 in the Provincial Finals Competitions. $200 is awarded.

• 18278 • L.I. Bryson Memorial Senior Speech Arts Scholarship
Recognizes the most promising competitor in the Senior Speech Arts Classes 1015, 1025, 1035, 1045, and 1075 in the Provincial Finals Competitions. $300 is awarded. Formerly: (2006) The SMFA Senior Speech Arts Scholarship.

• 18279 • The F. W. Chisholm Intermediate Woodwind Scholarship
Recognizes the best performance in the Intermediate Woodwind Classes 502, 508, 514, 520, 526, 532, 538, 544, 550, 5002, 5009, 5016, 5023, 5030, 5037, 5044, 5051, 5058, 5065, 5069, and 5073 in the Provincial Finals Competitions. A scholarship of $200 is awarded in honor of F. W. Chisholm, a founding member and the first Secretary/Treasurer of the SMFA.

• 18280 • Concerto Competition
To recognize outstanding musicians and vocalists. Individuals who are Saskatchewan residents or were born in Saskatchewan may submit applications. All instrumental and vocal categories are considered. Instrumentalists must be 30 years of age or younger; vocalists must be 35 years of age or younger. The first place winner appears as a guest artist with The Regina Symphony and receives an SMFA Scholarship of $1,000. Other scholarships are awarded for second and third place. Established in 1979. Sponsored by Yolande Hodges Fitzgerald.

• 18281 • The Covey Girls' Voice Scholarship
Recognizes the most promising competitor in the Girls' Voice Classes 416 and 417 in the Provincial Finals Competitions. A $200 scholarship is awarded in honor of Doris Covey Lazecki.

• 18282 • CTBI Intermediate Cello/Viola/ Double Bass Scholarship
Recognizes the best performance in the Intermediate Cello/Viola/Double Bass Classes 6002, 6010, 6016, 6024, 6030, 6037, 6044, 6602, 6610, 6618, 6627, 6634, 6642, 6649, 6802, 6807, 6809, 6818, and 6820 in the Provincial Finals Competitions. $200 is awarded. Donated by the Canadian Tenant Bureau, Inc. Established in 2000.

• 18283 • Janice Elliot-Drake Intermediate Chopin Scholarhip
Recognizes the winner of the Intermediate Chopin Class 749 in the Provincial Finals Competitions. $200 is awarded. Formerly: (2006) The Lyell Gustin Memorial Intermediate Chopin Scholarship.

• 18284 • The Frances England Intermediate Hayden and Mozart Scholarship
Recognizes the best performance in the Intermediate Hayden and Mozart Class 745 in the Provincial Finals Competitions. $200 is awarded.

• 18285 • The Goodfellow Memorial Award for Senior Vocal Concert Groups
Recognizes the male or female competitor presenting the finest performance in the Senior Vocal Concert Group Class 430 in the Provincial Finals Competitions. A $300 scholarship is awarded in memory of Ann Owen Goodfellow.

• 18286 • The Goodfellow Memorial Award in Voice/The Chief Justice J.T. Brown Shield
For the most outstanding vocal competitor of the Grand Awards Competitions. $400 scholarship is awarded.

• 18287 • The Goodfellow Memorial Canadian Vocal Music Scholarship
Recognizes the competitor presenting the best performance in the Senior Canadian Vocal Music Class 465 in the Provincial Finals Competitions. A $300 scholarship is awarded in memory of Mossie Hancock of Regina.

• 18288 • The Goodfellow Memorial Grade A Female Voce Scholarship
Recognizes the most accomplished singer in the Grade A Female Voice Glasses 401, 402, and 403 in the Provincial Finals Competition. $300 is awarded in memory of Anne Owen Goodfellow.

• 18289 • The Goodfellow Memorial Grade A Male Voice Scholarship
Recognizes the most accomplished singer in the Grade A Male Voice Classes 404, 4040, 405, and 406 in the Provincial Finals Competitions. $300 is awarded in honor of Madame Alicia Birkett.

• 18290 • The Goodfellow Memorial Lieder Scholarship
Recognizes the finest performance in the Senior Lieder Class 472 in the Provincial Finals Competitions. The award will be shared equally by the best male or female singer and pianist. A $600 scholarship is awarded in memory of Ann Owen Goodfellow.

• 18291 • The Goodfellow Memorial Operatic Scholarship
Recognizes the most accomplished singer in the Senior Operatic Classes 443 and 444 in the Provincial Final Competitions. A $300 scholarship is awarded in honor of Hazel Farnsworth.

• 18292 • The Goodfellow Memorial Oratorio Scholarship/ The Helen Davis Sherry Memorial Trophy
Recognizes the winner of the Senior Oratorio Classes 440, 441, and 442 in the Provincial Finals Competitions. A $300 scholarship is awarded in memory of Ann Owen Goodfellow and a Silver Rose Bowl is awarded in memory of Helen Davies Sherry.

• 18293 • The Hancock Memorial Award in Piano
Recognizes the most outstanding piano competitor of the Grand Awards Competitions. $300 is awarded.

• 18294 • The John and Judy Hrycak Award
Recognizes the runner-up in the string competition of the Grand Awards Competitions. $300 is awarded.

• 18295 • The Jackson Memorial Intermediate Piano Scholarship
Recognizes the best performance by well-known musicians in the Mainline area in the Intermediate Recital Class 722 in the Provincial Finals Competitions. $200 is awarded.

• 18296 • Kiwania of Wascana Senior Cello/Viola/Double Bass Scholarship
Recognizes the best performance in the Senior Cello/Viola/Double Bass Classes 6000, 6008, 6014, 6022, 6028, 6035, 6042, 6600, 6608, 6616, 6625, 6632, 6639, 6641, 6647, 6800, 6806, 6808, 6812, and 6818 in the Provincial Finals Competitions. $300 is awarded.

• 18297 • The Laxdal Memorial Grade B Female Voice Scholarship
Recognizes the most promising competitor in the Garde B Female Voice Classes 407. 408, and 409 in the Provincial Finals Competitions. $300 is awarded in honor of Heather Laxdal.

• 18298 • The Maude McGuire Memorial Intermediate Piano Scholarship
Recognizes outstanding performance in the Intermediate 20th Century/Canadian Music Classes 754 and 784 in the Provincial Finals Competitions. $200 is awarded.

• 18299 • The Maude McGuire Memorial Senior Piano Scholarship
Recognizes the best performance in the Senior 20th Century/Canadian Classes 753 and 782 in the Provincial Finals Competitions. $300 is awarded.

• 18300 • The Mildred Spence McPherson Memorial Piano Award
Recognizes the runner-up in the piano competition of the Grand Awards Competitions. $300 is awarded.

• 18301 • The Fred S. Mendal Memorial Award in Strings and Trophy
Recognizes an outstanding string competitor in the Grand Awards Competitions. A monetary prize of $500 and a trophy are awarded.

• 18302 • **Mrs. Clare K. Mendal Memorial Senior Violin Scholarship and Trophy**
Recognizes the finest performance in the Senior Violin Classes 621, 629, 638, 646, 654, 656, and 664 in the Provincial Finals Competitions. $300 is awarded.

• 18303 • **Robert C. Mitchell Memorial Intermediate Violin Scholarship and Trophy**
Recognizes the best performance in the Intermediate Violin Classes 603, 623, 631, 640, 648, 655, 658, and 666 in the Provincial Finals Competitions. $200 is awarded.

• 18304 • **The Dr. W.C. Murray Senior Brass Scholarship**
Recognizes the best performance in the Senior Brass Classes 554, 560, 566, 572, 578, 5540, 5547, 5554, 5561, 5568, 5575, 5579, and 5583 in the Provincial Finals Competitions. A scholarship of $300 is awarded in honor of Dr. W.C. Murray, the first President of the University of Saskatchewan and a founding member of the SMFA Executive.

• 18305 • **National Music Festival**
To help talented, young, amateur Canadian musicians progress toward professionalism. Instrumental contestants must be no older than 28 years; vocal contestants must be no more than 33 years. The competition is conducted at three progressive levels: Local Festival, Provincial Level, and National Festival. Monetary prizes are awarded annually. Sponsored and administered by the Federation of Canadian Music Festivals.

• 18306 • **Sask Power Award**
Recognizes the runner-up to the most outstanding competitor in the Grand Awards Competitions. $500 is awarded.

• 18307 • **The Regan Grant Memorial Musical Theatre Scholarship**
Recognizes a performance in the Senior Musical Theatre Classes 449 and 450 in the Provincial Final Competitions. A $300 scholarship is awarded in memory of Regan Grant.

• 18308 • **The Saskatchewan Choral Federation Choral Scholarship**
Recognizes the most outstanding performances by a Senior Choir in Classes 100, 101, 102, 103, 104, 120, 121, 122, 123, 126, 127, 140, 141, 146, 148, 160, and 161 in the Provincial Finals Competitions. $300 is awarded.

• 18309 • **The Minnie Schell Memorial Intermediate Piano Scholarship**
Recognizes the best Intermediate Piano Competition in the Provincial Finals Competitions. $400 is awarded.

• 18310 • **The SMFA Intermediate Brass Scholarship**
Recognizes the best performance in the Intermediate Brass Classes 556, 562, 568, 574, 580, 5542, 5549, 5556, 5563, 5570, 5577, 5581, and 5585 in the Provincial Finals Competitions. A scholarship of $200 is awarded.

• 18311 • **The SMFA Intermediate Percussion Scholarship**
Recognizes the best performance in the Intermediate Percussion Classes 586, 595, 596, 5882, 5888, and 5893 in the Provincial Final Competitions. A scholarship for $200 is awarded.

• 18312 • **SMFA Past President's Brass Scholarship**
Awarded to the runner-up in the brass competition of Grand Awards Competitions. A $300 scholarship is awarded. Formerly: (2006) SMFA Brass Award.

• 18313 • **The SMFA Senior Percussion Scholarship**
Recognizes the best performance in the Senior Percussion Classes 584, 590, 594, 5880, 5886, and 5891 in the Provincial Finals Competitions. A scholarship of $300 is awarded.

• 18314 • **Blanche Squires Memorial Senior Chopin Scholarhip**
Recognizes the winner of the Senior Chopin Class 748 in the Provincial Finals Competitions. $300 is awarded. Formerly: (2006) The Lyell Gustin Memorial Senior Chopin Scholarship.

• 18315 • **The Blanche Squires Memorial Senior Pipe Organ Scholarship**
Recognizes the best Senior Pipe Organ competitor in Classes 800, 801, and 802 in the Provincial Finals Competition. $600 is awarded.

• 18316 • **The Blanche Squires Memorial Woodwind Award**
Recognizes the most outstanding competitor in the woodwind competition of the Grand Awards Competition. A $400 scholarship is awarded in memory of Blanche Squires.

• 18317 • **The Thoms Hatton Memorial Grade B. Male Voice Scholarship**
Recognizes the most promising competitor in the Grade B Male Voce Classes 410, 4100, 411 and 412 in the Provincial Finals Competitions. A $300 scholarship is awarded in honor of Mr. Thomas Hatton.

• 18318 • **The Gordon C. Wallis Intermediate Beethoven Scholarship**
Recognizes the best performance in the Intermediate Beethoven Class 747 in the Provincial Finals Competitions. $300 is awarded.

• 18319 • **The Wallis Memorial Scholarship**
For the further study of piano or voice. Advanced students in the Grand Awards Competitions are eligible. Based on talent and industry. Selected by the adjudicators. $500 is awarded.

• 18320 • **The Gordon C. Wallis Senior Beethoven Scholarship**
Recognizes the Senior Beethoven Class 743 in the Provincial Finals Competitions. $300 is awarded.

• 18321 • **The Carla Ruth Webb Memorial Award in Woodwind**
Recognizes the runner-up in the woodwind competition at the Grand Awards Competitions. A scholarship of $300 is awarded.

• 18322 •
Save the Children Canada
Rita S. Karakas, CEO
4141 Yonge St., Ste. 300
Toronto, ON, Canada M2P 2A8
Phone: (416)221-5501
Toll-Free: 800-668-5036
Fax: (416)221-8214
E-mail: sccan@savethechildren.ca
Home Page: http://www.savethechildren.ca

• 18323 • **Save the Children - Canada Award**
To recognize significant contributions by an individual(s) to the goals inherent in the Declaration of the Rights of the Child. Both Canadians and non-Canadians are eligible. A framed scroll and a bronze plaque are awarded when merited. Established in 1971. Formerly: Cansave Children Award.

• 18324 •
Scandinavian Collectors Club
Donald Brent, Exec.Sec.
PO Box 13196
El Cajon, CA 92020
Phone: (619)447-8559
Fax: (619)447-8558
E-mail: dbrent47@sprynet.com
Home Page: http://www.scc-online.org

• 18325 • **Earl Grant Jacobsen Award**
For recognition of outstanding philatelic research serving to further advancement of Scandinavian philately. Philatelic research may be construed to be "material," such as in-depth research prepared for the collecting public, or "inspirational," wherein the recipient has lent his or her expertise and good fellowship to other students of Scandinavian philately. Members and non-members are eligible. Awarded when merited. Established in 1975 in memory of Dr. Earl Grant Jacobsen, a longtime member and past president of the Club, as well as a noted student of Norwegian and Scandinavian philately.

• 18326 • **Carl E. Pelander Award**
Recognizes outstanding work in furthering the aims of SCC and Scandinavian philately. The board of directors, on recommendation of members, makes the selection. A plaque is awarded when merited. Established in 1968 in memory of Carl E. Pelander, a founding member.

• 18327 • **SCC Award Medals**
To recognize outstanding exhibits of Scandinavian philately, and to act as an incentive to encourage the collection, study, and display of Scandinavian philatelic material. Membership in SCC is not required. The exhibit must contain 90 percent Scandinavian material; non-Scandinavian material must be directly related to the subject. Three awards are presented annually: Jed Richter Award for classic format exhibit; Paul Jensen Award for postal history format exhibit, and Victor Engstrom Award for exhibit research.

• 18328 • **Joanna Taylor Memorial Bowl**
For recognition of the best Scandinavian exhibit at the SCC National Convention each year. The award consists of a fine piece of Swedish crystal, a Corona Bowl made by Orrefors Glass Works in the province of Smaland, a glass-making center of Sweden. The nine-inch bowl has eight flat faces, and on one of these faces a detailed line-by-line reproduction of the SCC posthorn is engraved along with the year. The bowl for the SCC National Award is made available each year through the generosity of SCC members Scott and Joanna Taylor. Awarded annually.

• 18329 •
Scarab Club
Treena Flannery Ericson, Gallery Director
217 Farnsworth
Detroit, MI 48202
Phone: (313)831-1250
Phone: (313)831-1251
E-mail: scarabclub@aol.com

• 18330 • **Gold Medal Annual**
For artistic excellence. Recognition award bestowed annually.

• 18331 • **Silver Medal**
For artistic excellence. Recognition award bestowed annually.

• 18332 •
Schenectady Museum Association
15 Nott Ter. Heights
Schenectady, NY 12308
Phone: (518)382-7890
Fax: (518)382-7893
E-mail: schdymuse@schenectadymuseum.org
Home Page: http://www.schenectadymuseum.org

• 18333 • **Mohawk-Hudson Regional Art Exhibition Award**
To recognize artists in the Mohawk-Hudson region of New York. Several monetary awards are presented. The exhibition rotates annually between the Schenectady Museum, the Albany Institute of History and Art, and the University Art Museum of the University of Albany.

• 18334 •
School and Community Safety Society of America
% American Association for Active Lifestyles and Fitness
1900 Association Dr.
Reston, VA 20191
Phone: (703)476-3400
Toll-Free: 800-213-7193
Fax: (703)476-9527
E-mail: AAALF@aahperd.org
Home Page: http://www.aahperd.org/AAALF

Formerly: (1985) American School and Community Safety Association.

• 18335 • **Distinguished Service Award**
For recognition of an outstanding contribution to safety education, either by an individual or organization outside the safety education profession. Individuals/organizations outside the safety education profession making a significant contribution to safety education in any form, e.g., media development, legislation, creative arts, funding, or national impact are eligible. A commercial organization may only be nominated for a unique contribution to the profession which is over and above their normal realm of activity. A plaque is awarded annually at the national convention. Established in 1980. Formerly: Distinguished Service to Safety Education.

• 18336 • **Safety Society Presidential Citation**
To honor individuals or organizations for meritorious service or outstanding contributions to the Safety Society or the safety profession which resulted in improvement of the quality and/or quantity of programs in safety. To be considered, an individual or group must be in the areas of safety or related fields such as educators, government officials, lay leaders, business leaders, researchers, or inventors. A plaque is awarded annually at the national convention. Established about 1980.

• 18337 • **Charles Peter Yost Professional Service Award**
To recognize contributions to the profession and/or the Society by members/professionals. To be considered, an individual must have a minimum of ten years in the profession; be a member of TSS; have served the Society as officer, committee member, or other; and give evidence of service and leadership to the profession. A plaque is awarded annually at the national convention. Established in 1980. Formerly: (1992) Professional Service to Safety Education.

• 18338 •
School Library Media Specialists of Southeastern New York
Ellen Rubin, Pres.
% Library Media Ctr.
Scotchtown Ave. Elementary School
118 Scotchtown Ave.
Goshen, NY 10924
Phone: (914)342-3708
Fax: (914)343-3883
E-mail: secretary@slmsseny.org
Home Page: http://www.slmsseny.org

• 18339 • **Rip Van Winkle Award**
For recognition of outstanding contributions to children's and young adult literature. Authors and illustrators living or working in the seven-county region of New York that includes Dutchess, Ulster, Putnam, Westchester, Sullivan, Rockland, and Orange counties are eligible. An inscribed silver plate is awarded to an author and/or illustrator annually. Established in 1980.

• 18340 •
School Nurses Organization of Arizona
Shirley Rodriguez, Web Master
PO Box 25174
Phoenix, AZ 85002
Phone: (928)726-6715
Phone: (602)683-2400
Fax: (928)341-0097
E-mail: snoa@sprynet.com
Home Page: http://www.snoa.org

• 18341 • **School Nurse of the Year**
For member in good standing. Scholarship awarded annually.

• 18342 •
School Nutrition Association
Barbara S. Belmont CAE, Exec.Dir.
700 S Washington St., Ste. 300
Alexandria, VA 22314
Phone: (703)739-3900
Fax: (703)739-3915
E-mail: servicecenter@schoolnutrition.org
Home Page: http://www.asfsa.org

• 18343 • **Director of the Year Award**
Annual award of recognition. Inquire for additional details.

• 18344 • **Heart of the Program Award**
To recognize contributions made by persons who work with the school food and nutrition manager to prepare and serve appetizing meals in a pleasing atmosphere. The food and nutrition employees (excluding the manager) from a school select one person from the school food and nutrition staff to represent that school in the system competition. A certificate designed by the state association is presented to the winner from each school.

Awards are arranged in alphabetical order below their administering organizations

• 18345 • **Hubert Humphrey Research Grant**
To encourage active members to conduct academic, graduate-level research in child nutrition or school foodservice management. A minimum of $2,500 is awarded annually.

• 18346 • **Lincoln Foodservice Grant for Innovations in School Foodservice**
To encourage active members to conduct or supervise the conduct of academic or non-academic research that will advance the knowledge base of school foodservice and nutrition programs at the local or state levels. A minimum of $2,500 is awarded annually.

• 18347 • **President's Awards**
To recognize state affiliates for excellence achieved by planning their programs around ASFSA's Plan of Action. The Regional Director is responsible for determining if a State Association has followed the guidelines for earning one of the following awards: ASFSA President's Bronze Award, ASFSA President's Silver Award, and ASFSA Thelme Fienegan Gold Award. A framed certificate with a Gold, Silver or Bronze Seal is presented at the State President's Breakfast during the National Conference.

• 18348 • **Professional Development Awards**
To recognize states for attaining their certification and credentialing goals established by the SNA Education Committee, and for achieving the greatest increase in certified members. Awarded annually.

• 18349 • **John Stalker Award**
To recognize an individual who has made outstanding contributions to child nutrition programs in America. Awarded annually by the State of Massachusetts. Established in 1984 in honor of John Salker, former Massachusetts state director, ASFSA Board member and longtime legislative activist for ASFSA.

• 18350 • **Louise Sublette Award of Excellence**
To recognize an individual for contributions to the nutrition program in his or her school. The only persons who may apply are members of the single unit section. The project may extend over more than one year, but the major part of it must have been completed during the year of competition. Established in memory of Louise Sublette, a leader of food service programs in Tennessee and in ASFSA whose career of 43 years covered every area of the food service profession - public schools, colleges, hospitals, and elderly feeding programs.

• 18351 •
School of American Ballet
Marjorie Van Dercook, Exec.Dir.
70 Lincoln Ctr. Plz.
New York, NY 10023
Phone: (212)769-6600
Fax: (212)769-4897
E-mail: aschierman@sab.org
Home Page: http://www.sab.org

• 18352 • **Mae L. Wien Awards**
To honor outstanding faculty members and students who show exceptional promise. Students may receive the award for Outstanding Promise, while faculty may be eligible for the award for Distinguished Service. Monetary prizes are awarded annually. Established by the family of the late Mrs. Wien, an arts patron.

• 18353 •
School of American Research
Nancy Owen Lewis Ph.D, Director of Academic Programs
PO Box 2188
Santa Fe, NM 87504-2188
Phone: (505)954-7201
Phone: (505)954-7200
Fax: (505)954-7214
E-mail: scholar@sarsf.org
Home Page: http://www.sarweb.org

• 18354 • **J. I. Staley Prize**
To recognize a living author for a book that exemplifies outstanding scholarship and writing in anthropology. To be eligible for nomination, books must have been published as least two and not more than eight years before nomination. Edited volumes are not eligible for nomination and authors and publishers may not nominate their own books. Nominations received by October 1 will be considered for the next year's prize, as recommended by an outside review panel. A cash prize of $10,000 is awarded annually. Established in 1988.

• 18355 •
Science Fiction and Fantasy Writers of America
Jane Jewell, Exec.Dir.
PO Box 877
Chestertown, MD 21620
Phone: (410)778-3052
E-mail: execdir@sfwa.org
Home Page: http://www.sfwa.org

Formerly: Science Fiction Writers of America.

• 18356 • **Donal Knight Memorial Grand Master Award**
Recognizes a living author for a lifetime's achievement in science fiction and/or fantasy. Nominations are made by the president of SFWA. The award is given upon the approval of a majority of the officers. Established in 1974. Formerly: (2006) Grand Master Award.

• 18357 • **Nebula Awards**
To recognize excellence in science fiction and fantasy writing by honoring the authors of the best novel, novella, novelette, short story, and script published during the previous calendar year. In addition, the Damon Knight Memorial Grand Master Award is presented to recognize lifetime contributions to the field of science fiction, and the Andre Norton Award is given for an outstanding young adult science fiction or fantasy book. Engraved Lucite blocks with an embedded nebula formation are awarded annually. Established in 1965.

• 18358 • **SWFA Author Emeritus Award**
Recognizes and appreciates senior writers in the genres of science fiction and fantasy who have made significant contributions to the field. Applicants must no longer be active or their work may no longer be as widely known as it once was. Established in 1995.

• 18359 •
Science Fiction Writers of Earth
Gil Reis, Admin.
PO Box 121293
Fort Worth, TX 76121
Phone: (817)451-8674
E-mail: sfwoe@flash.net
Home Page: http://www.flash.net/~sfwoe

• 18360 • **Science Fiction/Fantasy Short Story Contest**
To promote the art of science fiction/fantasy short story writing. Unpublished members in good standing are eligible. Individuals who have never received money for a published piece of fiction writing may submit manuscripts of 2,000 to 7,500 words by October 30. Both members and nonmembers are eligible. (Nonmembers automatically become members when they submit a story for the contest.) Monetary prizes of $200 for first prize, $100 for second prize, and $50 for third prize are awarded annually. The first place winner is paid an additional $75 for placing their winning story on the SFWOE Website for 180 days. Established in 1980.

• 18361 •
Science Service
Donald R. Harless, Pres.
1719 N St. NW
Washington, DC 20036
Phone: (202)785-2255
Fax: (202)785-1243
E-mail: webmaster@sciserv.org
Home Page: http://www.sciserv.org

• 18362 • **Intel International Science and Engineering Fair**
Known as the "World's Series" of science fairs, the ISEF is the world's largest pre-college science competition. It is held annually with over 1,400 student contestants from affiliated fairs in the United States and 40 foreign nations. The fair culminates a selection process involving thousands of school and regional fairs, their student participants, and their judges from science, medicine, engineering, and education. Students in grades 9 to 12 compete for over $3 million in scholarships, tuition grants, scientific equipment, and scientific trips. Awards are presented

in the following 15 categories: Behavioral and Social Sciences, Biochemistry, Botany, Chemistry, Computer Science, Earth Science, Engineering, Environmental Science, Mathematics, Medicine & Health, Microbiology, Physics, Space Science, Team Projects, and Zoology. In each category, Grand Prizes are presented to the top four places: first place (cash award of $3,000), second ($1,500), third ($1,000), and fourth ($500). Numerous additional prizes are awarded, including the Intel Foundation Young Scientist Award, a $50,000 scholarship for the top three winners overall; Seaborg SIYSS Award, an expense-paid trip to the Stockholm International Youth Science Seminar; opportunities for the top teams at the ISEF to receive expense-paid trips to attend European Union Contest for Young Scientists and Intel Best of Category Awards, a $5,000 scholarship for the winner in each category; and Intel Achievement Awards, $5,000 cash prize for outstanding work in any field. Held annually in a different city each May. Established in 1949. Sponsored by Intel Corp.

• 18363 • Intel Science Talent Search

To discover youth whose scientific and engineering skill, talent, and ability indicate potential creative originality. High school seniors may submit a written report on an independent research project in science, mathematics, or engineering, along with a transcript, teacher recommendations, and standardized test scores. Three hundred semifinalists are selected, and their schools each receive an award of $1,000. From this group, 40 students are chosen as finalists and win a five-day all-expense-paid trip to Washington, DC to compete for scholarships. The following scholarships are awarded: first place ($100,000); second place ($75,000); third place ($50,000); fourth-sixth place ($25,000 each); and seventh-tenth place ($20,000 each). The remaining 30 finalists each receive a $5,000 scholarship. Held annually. Established in 1942. Sponsored by Intel Corp. Formerly: Westinghouse Science Talent Search.

• 18364 •
Scientific Equipment and Furniture Association
David J. Sutton, Exec.Dir.
1205 Franklin Ave., Ste. 320
Garden City, NY 11530
Phone: (516)294-5424
Fax: (516)294-2758
E-mail: sefalabs@aol.com
Home Page: http://www.sefalabs.com

• 18365 • Lab of the Year Award

Annual award of recognition. Judged and cosponsored with R&D magazine. Inquire for application details.

• 18366 •
Scleroderma Foundation
Elaine Furst, Chm.
300 Rosewood Dr., Ste. 105
Danvers, MA 01923
Phone: (978)463-5843
Toll-Free: 800-722-HOPE
Fax: (978)463-5809
E-mail: sfinfo@scleroderma.org
Home Page: http://www.scleroderma.com

• 18367 • USF Grant Awards

To provide for grants-in-aid to clinical and basic research projects concerning scleroderma, progressive systemic sclerosis, morphea, and linear scleroderma. Specific projects of young investigators are preferred, though new studies by established researchers are considered. Applications are due September 15. As many as seven grants up to $30,000 are awarded annually. Grant funding established in 1978.

• 18368 •
Scott Arboretum of Swarthmore College
Claire Swayers, Dir.
500 College Ave.
Swarthmore, PA 19081-1397
Phone: (610)328-8025
Fax: (610)328-7755
E-mail: scott@swarthmore.edu
Home Page: http://www.scottarboretum.org
Formerly: Scott Horticultural Foundation.

• 18369 • Scott Medal Award

To recognize an individual, organization, or corporate body for outstanding national contribution to the science and art of gardening. A medal and monetary prize are awarded annually. Established in 1929 by Owen Moon to honor Arthur Hoyt Scott, Swarthmore Class of 1895.

• 18370 •
Scott Joplin International Ragtime Foundation
Jo Ann Neher, Pres.
321 S Ohio Ave.
Sedalia, MO 65301
Phone: (660)826-2271
Phone: (660)827-5295
Toll-Free: (866)218-6258
Fax: (660)826-5054
E-mail: ragtimer@scottjoplin.org
Home Page: http://www.scottjoplin.org

• 18371 • Scott Joplin Foundation of Sedalia Lifetime Achievement Award

For research and achievements in ragtime. Awarded annually.

• 18372 •
Scottish Studies Program/Scottish Studies Foundation
Paul Thomson, Dir.
PO Box 45069
PO Box 45069
University of Guelph
Scottish Studies Program
Toronto, ON, Canada M4P 3E3
Phone: (905)274-1817
Fax: (905)274-1817
E-mail: info@scottishstudies.ca
Home Page: http://www.scottishstudies.ca

• 18373 • Frank Watson Prize

Recognizes the best new book on Scottish history. Awarded biennially.

• 18374 •
Screen Actors Guild
Greg Krizman, Managing Ed.
5757 Wilshire Blvd.
Los Angeles, CA 90036-3600
Phone: (323)954-1600
Toll-Free: 800-SAG-0767
Fax: (323)549-6603
Home Page: http://www.sag.org

• 18375 • Award for Outstanding Portrayal of the American Scene

To recognize a theatrical motion picture, television or cable program which best exemplifies the vision embodied by the American scene language found in the Screen Actors Guild contracts, where balanced representation involves seniors, performers of color, women and performers with disabilities in every social or occupational setting. Also, to encourage portrayals by performers in a balanced and realistic manner. Award may be given to a executive producer, writer, director, casting director or any combination thereof. Awarded periodically. Established in 1994.

• 18376 • Life Achievement Award

To recognize a member for fostering the finest ideals of the acting profession. The award recognizes outstanding career achievement as well as humanitarian contributions. A bronze representation of the actors' comedy and tragedy masks is awarded annually and presented at the Screen Actors Guild Awards. Established in 1962.

• 18377 • Outstanding Performance Awards

To recognize outstanding performances the following categories: Theatrical Motion Pictures (Male Actor in a Leading Role, Female Actor in a Leading Role, Male Actor in a Supporting Role, Female Actor in Supporting Roles and a cast of a motion picture); and Television or Cable Television Programs (Male Actor in a Television Movie or Miniseries, Female Actor in a Television Movie or Miniseries, Male Actor in a Drama Series, Female Actor in a Drama Series, An Ensemble in a Drama Series, Male Actor in a Comedy Series, Female Actor in a Comedy Series, and an Ensemble in a Comedy Series). The

Actor, a bronze representation of an actor holding comedy and tragedy masks, is awarded annually. Established in 1994.

• 18378 •
Scribes
Glen-Peter Ahlers Sr., Exec.Dir.
School of Law
6441 E Colonial Dr.
Barry University
Orlando, FL 32807-3650
Phone: (321)206-5701
Fax: (321)206-5730
E-mail: gahlers@mail.barry.edu
Home Page: http://www.scribes.org

• 18379 • **Book Award**
To recognize the best work of legal scholarship published during the preceding year. A citation is awarded annually at the American Bar Association Annual Meeting. Established in 1960.

• 18380 • **Brief-Writing Award**
To encourage the improvement in the writing of legal briefs among students. Nominees are submitted by a nationally recognized court competition. Selection is made by a panel of judges. The award is presented at the Annual American Bar Association meeting. Established in 1991.

• 18381 • **Law-Review Award**
To identify and recognize the best student-written article in a law review or journal. The award is intended to recognize that person who demonstrates the ability to understand, analyze, and coherently and accurately express very difficult and complex legal concepts. A plaque is awarded annually at the National Conference of Law Reviews annual meeting. Established in 1986.

• 18382 •
E. W. Scripps School of Journalism
Thomas Hodson, Dir.
Scripps Hall
Ohio University
Athens, OH 45701
Phone: (740)593-2590
Fax: (740)593-2592
E-mail: nohl@ohiou.edu
Home Page: http://www.scrippsjschool.org

• 18383 • **Honor Award**
To honor achievement in journalism and communication. Applications are not accepted. Nominations and selection are made by the faculty. Citations are awarded annually. Established in 1968.

• 18384 • **Carr Van Anda Award**
To honor enduring contributions to journalism. Applications are not accepted; nominations and selection are made by the faculty. A plaque and a citation are awarded annually. Established in 1968 in honor of Carr Van Anda, alumnus of Ohio University and managing editor of the *New York Times.*

• 18385 •
Sea Grant Association
Dr. Anders W. Andren, Dir.
1975 Willow Dr., 2nd Fl.
Goodnight Hall
Madison, WI 53706-1177
Phone: (608)262-0905
Fax: (608)262-0591
E-mail: awandren@aqua.wisc.edu
Home Page: http://www.sga.seagrant.org/

• 18386 • **Sea Grant Association Award**
To recognize an individual for direct demonstrable contributions through research, education/training, advisory, or public service activities that embody the Association's concepts or have been effective users of Sea Grant products. A monetary award, a framed certificate, and a plaque are awarded annually. Established in 1970.

• 18387 • **Student Awards**
To recognize students for outstanding ocean-related research. Students who have participated in Sea Grant projects and/or are conducting research at any member institution affiliated with the 29 Sea Grant Programs may be nominated. A monetary award and a certificate are awarded annually at the Sea Grant Week Conference. Established in 1976. Co-sponsored by the National Fisheries Institute.

• 18388 •
Seaplane Pilots Association
Michael E. Volk, Pres.
4315 Highland Park Blvd., Ste. C
Lakeland, FL 33813-1639
Phone: (863)701-7979
Toll-Free: 888-SPA-8923
Fax: (863)701-7588
E-mail: spa@seaplanes.org
Home Page: http://www.seaplanes.org

• 18389 • **Pilot of the Year**
To recognize an individual whose promotion and support of seaplane flying has been outstanding. Nominations may be submitted by July. A plaque is awarded annually. Established in 1983.

• 18390 •
Search for Common Ground
John Marks, Pres.
1601 Connecticut Ave. NW, Ste. 200
Washington, DC 20009-1077
Phone: (202)265-4300
Phone: (202)777-2227
Fax: (202)232-6718
E-mail: search@sfcg.org
Home Page: http://www.sfcg.org

• 18391 • **Common Ground Award for Journalism in the Middle East**
Awarded for one Arabic, one Hebrew, and one English-Language article, each of which surpasses the daily headlines to abolish myths and stereotypes, opens windows into other societies, provides insights into ongoing debates in the region, and exposes readers to new points of view in the Arab-Israeli context.

• 18392 •
Seattle Art Museum
1400 Prospect St.
PO Box 22000
Seattle, WA 98122-9700
Phone: (206)625-8900
Fax: (206)654-3135
E-mail: webmaster@seattleartmuseum.org
Home Page: http://www.seattleartmuseum.org

• 18393 • **Betty Bowen Memorial Award Competition**
To recognize and encourage visual artists in the Pacific Northwest. Residents of Oregon, Washington, and Idaho are eligible. A monetary award of $11,000 is presented to the winner, with PONCHO Special Recognition Awards of $1,500 presented on occasion. Awarded annually. Established in 1978 in memory of Betty Bowen (1918-1977), advocate of Northwest artists, historical preservation, civic improvement projects, and animal protection.

• 18394 •
Seattle International Film Festival
Deborah Person, Interim Exec.Dir.
400 9th Ave. N
Seattle, WA 98109
Phone: (206)464-5830
Fax: (206)464-7919
E-mail: helen@seattlefilm.org
Home Page: http://www.seattlefilm.com

• 18395 • **Golden Space Needle Audience Awards**
For recognition of films and filmmakers that are the favorites of the audience at the Seattle International Film Festival. Any film or filmmaker showcased at the Festival is eligible. Awards are given in six categories: Best Film, Best Documentary, Best Director, Best Actor, Best Actress, and Best Short Film. A certificate is awarded to winners each year. Established in 1985.

• 18396 • **New American Cinema Award**
To provide a spotlight for emerging American independent directors who have made exceptional films with smaller budgets and to recognize Washington as a State that supports their efforts. The prize package includes approximately $40,000 worth of donated goods and services from local vendors to encourage the winner to film future projects in Washington State. The winner is selected by a jury of local and national film industry representatives. Established in 1995. Formerly: (2000) American Independent Award.

• 18397 • **New Directors Showcase**
To recognize the best feature film by a new director. Each film must be a debut or a second feature by the selected director, and each is chosen on the basis of its original conception, striking style, and overall excellence. The winner

is selected by a jury of film industry professionals and journalists. A monetary prize of $5,000 is awarded annually. Established in 1991.

• 18398 •
Seattle Writers Association
Richard Gibbons, Pres.
PO Box 33265
Seattle, WA 98133
Phone: (206)860-5207
Phone: (425)747-5258
E-mail: publicity@seattlewriters.com
Home Page: http://members.tripod.com/seattlewriters_assoc/

• 18399 • Writers in Performance Literary Competition
For review of written works. Monetary award bestowed annually.

• 18400 •
Secondary School Admission Test Board
Regan Kenyon, Pres.
CN 5339
Princeton, NJ 08543
Phone: (609)683-4440
Fax: 800-442-SSAT
E-mail: info@ssat.org
Home Page: http://www.ssat.org

• 18401 • William B. Bretnall Award
For recognition of an educator who has contributed significantly to the field of independent school admission. Nominations are made by the award committee. A plaque is awarded annually at the annual meeting. Established in 1982 in honor of William B. Bretnall, the first Program Director of SSATB.

• 18402 •
Section for Women in Public Administration
Section for Women in Public Administration
Janet Hutchinson, Managing Ed.
1120 G St. NW, Ste. 700
Washington, DC 20005-3885
Phone: (202)393-7878
Fax: (202)638-4952
E-mail: jhutch@vcu.edu
Home Page: http://carbon.cudenver.edu/public/gspa/swpa

• 18403 • Joan Fiss Bishop Award
To recognize members who have contributed to increased involvement by women in the public sector and who have distinguished careers in public administration. Judging criteria include: contribution to increased involvement by women in the public sector; 2. innovative leadership and accomplished professionalism in a public sector career; and 3. commitment to the public administration profession. An engraved gift is awarded annually at the ASPA conference. Established in 1985 in honor of Joan Fiss Bishop, first female member of the Board of Governors of the Harvard Business School Association.

• 18404 • Distinguished Research Award
To recognize outstanding research contributions on gender-related issues. Members and non-members are eligible, and are judged on: research on an issue significant to the role of women in public administration; work that has made an impact on women's lives; or research that has brought forth other significant issues that could impact on women's lives. An engraved clock is awarded annually at the ASPA conference. Established in 1990.

• 18405 • Julia Henderson Service to the Section Award
To recognize outstanding members who have contributed to the success and functioning of the Section. A sculpture is awarded annually at the ASPA conference. The following year's chapter grants are given in the name of the award winner. Established in 1990 to honor Julia Henderson, the first woman admitted to the Graduate School of Public Administration at Harvard University and the first woman member of the ASPA National Council.

• 18406 •
Security Industry Association
Richard Chace, Exec.Dir.
635 Slaters Ln., Ste. 110
Alexandria, VA 22314
Phone: (703)683-2075
Toll-Free: (866)817-8888
Fax: (703)683-2469
E-mail: info@siaonline.org
Home Page: http://www.siaonline.org

Formerly: (1989) Security Equipment Industry Association.

• 18407 • George R. Lippert Memorial Award
To recognize contributions to the security industry. The candidate must be an active member of SIA who has worked in the industry for more than five years and is recognized and respected as a leader and viewed as a goodwill ambassador. A trophy is awarded annually in memory of George R. Lippert, a leader in the security industry for more than 20 years. Formerly: (1989) SIA Service Award.

• 18408 •
Self Storage Association
Michael R. Kidd, Exec.Dir.
6506 Loisdale Rd., Ste. 315
Springfield, VA 22150
Phone: (703)921-9123
Toll-Free: 888-SELF-STG
Fax: (703)921-9105
E-mail: info@selfstorage.org
Home Page: http://www.selfstorage.org

Formerly: (1989) Self-Service Storage Association.

• 18409 • Facility of the Year
To recognition outstanding characteristics and operations of a facility. A certificate is awarded annually at the convention.

• 18410 • Manager of the Year
To recognize achievements in the area of self storage facility management. The candidate must be an Association member and may apply or be nominated. A medal and a certificate are awarded annually at the convention.

• 18411 •
SEMI International
Stanley T. Myers, Pres./CEO
3081 Zanker Rd.
San Jose, CA 95134
Phone: (408)943-6900
Fax: (408)428-9600
E-mail: semihq@semi.org
Home Page: http://wps2a.semi.org/wps/portal

Formerly: (2002) Semiconductor Equipment and Materials Institute; Semiconductor Equipment and Materials International.

• 18412 • SEMI Award for North America
To recognize an outstanding technical achievement and meritorious contribution to the semiconductor industry. Eligible fields include semiconductor materials, wafer fabrication assembly and packaging, process control, test and inspection robotics and automation, and quality enhancement. Nominations of members, with the approval of the review board, may be made. A statuette and a certificate are presented at the Annual SEMI Dinner and Award Ceremony. Established in 1979.

• 18413 • Karel Urbanek Memorial Award
To recognize an outstanding contributor to the development of standards for the semiconductor and related industries. Awarded to one or more recipients each year.

• 18414 •
Seminar on the Acquisition of Latin American Library Materials
Laura Gutierrez-Witt, Exec.Sec.
Benson Latin Amer. Collection
Sid Richardson Hall 1.109
The Univ. of Texas at Austin
Austin, TX 78713-8916
Phone: (512)495-4471
Fax: (512)495-4488
E-mail: sandyl@mail.utexas.edu
Home Page: http://www.salalm.org

• 18415 • Jose Toribio Medina Award
For recognition of outstanding contributions by SALALM members to Latin American studies. An award is granted for a monograph or book-length manuscript that has been published or accepted for publication within the three years immediately preceding the closing date for nominations. Reprints, translations, or re-editions are not eligible. Nominations and applications may be made by members. The award consists of a certificate and honorarium of $250. Awarded annually, when merited, and presented at the opening general session of the annual conference. Established in 1982 in honor of Jose Toribio Medina, a well-known 19th century Chilean compiler of bibliographies.

• 18416 •
Senior Citizens Council of Bethlehem
Vicki Jackson, Exec.Dir.
720 Old York Rd.
Bethlehem, PA 18018
Phone: (610)867-4233
Phone: (610)865-2092
E-mail: bethsrs@ptd.net
Home Page: http://www.bethlehemseniors.org

• 18417 • **Slatter Memorial Volunteer of the Year Award**
For service to organization and community. Recognition award bestowed annually.

• 18418 •
Seventh Day Baptist Historical Society
Don A. Sanford, Historian
PO Box 1678
Janesville, WI 53547-1678
Phone: (608)752-5055
Fax: (608)752-7711
E-mail: sdbhist@seventhdaybaptist.org
Home Page: http://www.seventhdaybaptist.org

• 18419 • **Crystal Apple Award**
To recognize outstanding Sabbath School teachers who exhibit the qualities of faith and teaching found in the life and teachings of Christ. Awarded annually at the General Conference sessions. Established in 1986.

• 18420 • **Gold-Headed Cane**
To recognize individuals who have made an outstanding contribution to an appreciation of things past, the understanding or communication of our heritage and historic values. Seventh Day Baptists are eligible. Custodianship (for two years) of one of two gold-headed canes originally given in honor of another (Isaac D. Titsworth in 1881; Joseph W. Morton in 1884) is awarded when merited. Established in 1973.

• 18421 • **Robe of Achievement**
To recognize Seventh Day Baptist women who have made an outstanding contribution beyond the local church life and community. Nomination deadline is March 31. Custodianship of the traditional robe for one year and a plaque are awarded annually. Established in 1964.

• 18422 •
Severn River Association
Bob vom Saal, Pres.
PO Box 146
Annapolis, MD 21404-0146
Phone: (410)263-0435
Fax: (410)267-6106
E-mail: vomsaal@juno.com
Home Page: http://www.severnriver.org

• 18423 • **Blue Heron, Green Heron**
For service to the watershed. Recognition award bestowed annually.

• 18424 •
The Sewanee Review
The Univ. of the South
735 University Ave.
Sewanee, TN 37383
Phone: (931)598-1246
E-mail: rjones@sewanee.edu
Home Page: http://www.sewanee.edu/sreview/home.html

• 18425 • **Aiken Taylor Award in Modern American Poetry**
To recognize a contemporary American poet for the work of a substantial and distinguished career. The winner is selected by a small committee; applications or nominations are not accepted. A prize of $10,000 is awarded annually. Established in 1986 through a bequest by K.P.A. Taylor, a poet and the younger brother of Conrad Aiken.

• 18426 •
Seybold Publications
Chuck Lenatti, Ed.
999 Oakmont Plz. Dr.
Westmont, IL 60559
Phone: (630)986-0385
Toll-Free: 800-325-3830
Fax: (630)455-9529
E-mail: cynthia.wood@mlii.com
Home Page: http://www.seyboldreports.com

• 18427 • **Seybold Vision Award**
To recognize people and technologies that demonstrate a clear vision or direction in which the publishing industry should move. The awards are given in a three categories: Web/Internet, Print, and Media-Independent. Winners are selected by the Seybold Publications editorial staff based on their ability to impact the industry either by pioneering a new market, creating a new category of product technology, or actualizing a new product that will change the industry forever.

• 18428 •
The Shakespeare Theatre
Nicholas T. Goldsborough, Mng.Dir.
516 8th St. SE
Washington, DC 20003
Phone: (202)547-3230
Phone: (202)547-1122
Toll-Free: 877-487-8849
Fax: (202)547-0226
E-mail: webadmin@shakespearedc.org
Home Page: http://www.shakespearedc.org

Formerly: Shakespeare Theatre at the Folger.

• 18429 • **William Shakespeare Award for Classical Theatre (Will Award)**
To recognize individuals for extraordinary contributions "to the ongoing process of renewal and invigoration for the classics across America in regional and commercial theatres, the media, schools, and home." A statue designed by Phyllis Hammond is awarded annually at a gala benefit for the Theatre. Established in 1988.

• 18430 •
Shawnee Council of Camp Fire
Stephen Halbett, Exec.Dir.
4301 SW Huntoon
Topeka, KS 66604
Phone: (913)272-0601
Fax: (913)272-0602

• 18431 • **Evelyn Willis Award**
For exceptional service to Shawnee Council of Camp Fire. Recognition award bestowed annually.

• 18432 •
Shenandoah International Playwrights Retreat
717 Quick Mill Rd.
Staunton, VA 24401
Phone: (540)248-1868
Fax: (540)248-7728
E-mail: theatre@shenanarts.org
Home Page: http://www.shenanarts.org

Formerly: Shenan Arts.

• 18433 • **Fellowships for Playwrights**
To facilitate in-depth exploration and development of works-in-progress. Any playwright may apply. The deadline is February 1. Travel reimbursement, room and board are provided to playwrights who have been competitively selected for the retreat. Selections announced in June; Retreat meets last week in July through August. Established in 1977.

• 18434 • **Retreat Alumni Fellowship**
To honor a playwright for contributions to new American theatre, and to facilitate in-depth exploration and development of a current work-in-progress. Only alumni playwrights may apply. Travel reimbursement, room and board are provided to playwrights who have been competitively selected for the retreat. Selections announced in June; Retreat meets last week in July through August.

• 18435 •
Shenango Valley Chamber of Commerce
David Grande, Exec.Dir.
41 Chestnut St.
Sharon, PA 16146-2713
Phone: (724)981-5880
Fax: (724)981-5480
E-mail: david@svchamber.com
Home Page: http://www.svchamber.com

• 18436 • **Chamber Person of the Year**
Given to member who has made an outstanding contribution to the community. Recognition award bestowed annually.

• 18437 •
Joan Shorenstein Center on the Press, Politics and Public Policy
Goldsmith Awards
Nancy Palmer, Exec.Dir.
John F. Kennedy School of Government
Harvard University
79 JFK St., 2nd Fl. Taubman
Cambridge, MA 02138
Phone: (617)495-8269
Fax: (617)495-8696
Home Page: http://www.ksg.harvard.edu/presspol/goldsmith.shtml

• 18438 • **Goldsmith Book Prize**
To honor an author or authors of a book that best contributes to the improvement of the quality of government or politics through an examination of the press and government or the intersection of press and politics in the formation of public policy. The deadline for submissions is November 1. An award of $5,000 is presented each March to one recipient each in the trade and academic book categories. Established in 1991 by the Goldsmith-Greenfield Foundation.

• 18439 • **Goldsmith Prize for Investigative Reporting**
To honor the journalist or journalists whose investigative reporting best promotes more effective and ethical conduct of government, making of public policy, or practice of politics. The publication date must be within the twelve months preceding the submission deadline. The deadline for submissions is November 1. An award of $25,000 is presented each March. Established in 1991 by the Goldsmith-Greenfield Foundation.

• 18440 • **Goldsmith Research Awards**
To stimulate and assist research by scholars, graduate students, and journalists in the field of press/politics. There is no application deadline and grants of varying amounts, rarely exceeding $5,000, are made throughout the year. Established in 1991 by the Goldsmith-Greenfield Foundation.

• 18441 •
Shreveport Opera Company
Eric Dillner, Gen.Mgr.
212 Texas St., Ste. 101
Shreveport, LA 71101-3249
Phone: (318)227-9503
Fax: (318)227-9518
E-mail: hlross@bellsouth.net
Home Page: http://www.shreveopera.org

Formerly: (1980) Shreveport Civic Opera.

• 18442 • **Singer of the Year**
A competition to foster and showcase young operatic talent. To be eligible, the artist must be between ages 18 and 35 and have performed at least one role with a university, summer vocal program, or professional opera company. Application deadline is December 1. Eight finalists will present a concert open to the public at which prizes will be awarded. Prizes include the Grand Prize, the Charles Maggio Award of $2,500; second prize isthe Mary Jacobs Smith Award ($1,500); third Prize isthe Robert J. Murray Award ($1,000); and fourth Prize is the Alfred and Norma Lacy Award ($500). Also awarded are four Honorable Mention Awards of $100 each and one Audience Choice Award of $100. Awarded annually.

• 18443 •
Sidewise Awards for Alternate History
% Steven Silver
707 Sapling Ln.
Deerfield, IL 60015
E-mail: shsilver@sfsite.com
Home Page: http://www.uchronia.net/sidewise

• 18444 • **Sidewise Awards for Alternate History**
To honor the best genre publications of the year. Two awards are given annually: the Short-Form Award, presented for the best work of fewer than 60,000 words (for short stories, novelettes, novellas, and poems), and the Long-Form Award, presented for the best work longer than 60,000 words (novels and longer works). A Special Achievement Award may also be presented to honor a specific work or body of work published prior to the inception of this award. Awarded annually. Established in 1995.

• 18445 •
Sidney-Shelby County Young Men's Christian Association
Dennis E. Ruble, Exec.Dir.
300 East Parkwood St.
Sidney, OH 45365
Phone: (937)492-9622
Fax: (937)492-4705
E-mail: info@sidney-ymca.org
Home Page: http://www.sidney-ymca.org

• 18446 • **Lee E. Schauer Memorial Scholarship**
For graduating high school senior with minimum GPA of 2.5, heavy consideration given to volunteer activities and leadership abilities. The scholarship is only for graduating high school seniors who are members of the Sidney-Shelby County YMCA. Scholarship awarded annually.

• 18447 •
Siena College
Department of Creative Arts
Gary Maciag, Dir. of Theater
Theatre Program
515 Loudon Rd.
Loudonville, NY 12211-1462
Phone: (518)783-2381
Fax: (518)783-2381
E-mail: maciag@siena.edu
Home Page: http://www.siena.edu/theatre

• 18448 • **International Playwrights' Competition**
To encourage excellence in playwriting and to bring new plays to the Capital region of upstate New York and the Siena College community. Plays must be original, unpublished, and unproduced works with three to ten characters; musicals are ineligible. A monetary prize of $2,000, a living stipend for a four-to-six week residency, and production of the winning script are awarded biennially. Established in 1986.

• 18449 •
Sierra Club
Carl Pope, Exec.Dir.
85 2nd St., 2nd Fl.
San Francisco, CA 94105-3441
Phone: (415)977-5500
Fax: (415)977-5799
E-mail: information@sierraclub.org
Home Page: http://www.sierraclub.org

• 18450 • **Ansel Adams Award for Conservation Photography**
To honor superlative photography that has been used to further conservation causes. Selection is made by the Executive Committee of the Board of Directors upon the recommendation of the Honors and Awards Committee. Awarded annually. Established in 1971.

• 18451 • **Joseph Barbosa Earth Fund Award**
Honors club members under the age of 30 who are making a difference in protecting the environment. A monetary prize of $500 is awarded annually. Established in 1998.

• 18452 • **David R. Brower Environmental Journalism Award**
To recognize an outstanding journalism in the area of environmental reporting and for contributing a better public understanding of environmental issues. Selection is made by the Public Affairs Committee. Awarded annually. Established in 1989.

• 18453 • **Certificates of Appreciation, Citations, and Commendations**
To recognize individuals who seldom receive Club-wide acclaim, but whose efforts have been beneficial to the entire membership. Selection is made by the Honors and Awards Committee. Awarded as merited. Established in 1970. Formerly: (1997) Certificates of Appreciation, Citations, Commendations, First Class Award.

• 18454 • **William E. Colby Award**
This, the Sierra Club's highest award for service to the Club itself, honors an individual for outstanding leadership, dedication, and service to the Club as typified by Will Colby. Selection is made by the Executive Committee of the Board of Directors. Awarded annually. Established in 1966.

• 18455 • **Community Service Award**
To recognize the commitment to helping others through public service or community involvement in a non-Sierra Club cause. Awarded to employees of the Sierra Club. Awarded annually. Established in 1994.

• 18456 • Distinguished Service/ Achievement Awards
To recognize individuals who are or have been in public service. Distinguished Service recognition is for strong and consistent commitment to conservation over a considerable period of time, whereas Distinguished Achievement recognition is for some particular action of singular importance to conservation. Selection is made by the Executive Committee of the Board of Directors upon recommendation of the Honors and Awards Committee. Awarded annually to one, but no more than three, individuals. Established in 1971.

• 18457 • William O. Douglas Award
To recognize significant contributions in the field of environment law by those who have made outstanding use of the legal/judicial process to achieve environmental goals, particularly those with national significance. Selection is made by the decision of the Executive Committee of the Board of Directors. Awarded annually. Established in 1980.

• 18458 • Earthcare Award
To recognize an individual, organization, or agency distinguished by making a unique contribution to international environmental protection and conservation. Selection is made by the International Committee. Awarded from time to time. Established in 1975. The award may be co-sponsored in any given year by one or more environmental organizations sharing the same goals and interests as the Sierra Club.

• 18459 • Electronic Communication Award
Honors best web page or other use of electronic communications. Awarded annually. Established in 1999.

• 18460 • Francis P. Farquhar Mountaineering Award
To recognize an individual for major contributions to mountaineering and the enhancement of the Sierra Club's prestige in this field. Awarded annually. Established in 1970. Formerly: Francis P. Farquhar Award.

• 18461 • Virginia Ferguson Award
To honor an employee with at least three years of service, who has demonstrated consistent and exemplary service to the Sierra Club. Commitment to the organization is demonstrated not only through competence and longevity of employment, but also in the congenial attitude, spirit, and integrity. Awarded annually. Established in 1994.

• 18462 • Honorary Life Members
To recognize individuals for distinguished service to the cause of conservation or to the Club. Awardees are exempt from the payment of membership dues or fees. Selection is made by a unanimous vote of the Board of Directors. Awarded as merited. Established in 1892. In addition, an Honorary President and Honorary Vice Presidents Awards are designated as appropriate.

• 18463 • Oliver Kehrlein Award
To recognize an individual for long-time outstanding work in the outings program of the Sierra Club or a Chapter, or who has performed exceptionally well in a difficult situation on a Club outing. Selection is made by the Outing Committee. Awarded annually. Established in 1969.

• 18464 • Richard M. Leonard Award
To honor an outstanding record of leadership, dedication, and service to the cause of conservation and the Sierra Club through the work of the Sierra Club Foundation as typified by Dick Leonard. Selection is made by the Executive Committees of the Sierra Club and the Sierra Club Foundation. Awarded annually. Established in 1994.

• 18465 • Mike McCloskey Award
To recognize an employee, with at least three years of service, for work that reflects and strengthens the meaning, purpose, and mission of the Sierra Club, and has contributed to the prestige of the Club in the global community. Awarded annually. Established in 1994.

• 18466 • Chico Mendes Award
To recognize individuals or non-governmental organizations outside the United States who have exhibited extraordinary courage and leadership in the universal struggle to protect the environment. Awarded annually. Established in 1989.

• 18467 • Susan E. Miller Award/Chapter Service Awards
To recognize individual members for exceptional organizational or managerial contributions to chapters. Selection is made by the Council Honors and Awards Committee. Up to three Susan Miller Awards are presented annually; other nominees may receive Chapter Service Awards. Established in 1977.

• 18468 • John Muir Award
This, the Sierra Club's highest award, honors a distinguished record of achievement in national or international conservation causes, such as the continuation of John Muir's work of preservation and establishment of parks and wildernesses. A lifetime membership in the Club is awarded annually. Established in 1961.

• 18469 • One Club Award
Honors club members at any level who have used outings as a way to protect or improve public lands, instill an interest in conservation, increase Club membership, or increase awareness of the Sierra Club. Awarded annually. Established in 1999.

• 18470 • Raymond J. Sherwin Award
To recognize extraordinary volunteer service toward international conservation and the maintenance of global protection of what John Muir called "this grand show eternal." Selection is made by the International Committee. Awarded annually. Established in 1982.

• 18471 • Special Service/Achievement Awards
To recognize an individual member, committee, group, or chapter for special service. Special Service recognition is for strong and consistent commitment to conservation over a considerable period of time, whereas Special Achievement recognition is for some particular action of singular importance to conservation or the Club. Approximately three awards are presented annually. Established in 1966.

• 18472 • Walter A. Starr Award
To recognize the continuing active work and support of the Club by a former Director. Selection is made by the Executive Committee of the Board of Directors. Awarded annually. Established in 1970.

• 18473 • Edgar Wayburn Award
To recognize outstanding service to the cause of conservation and the environment by a government official, either executive or legislative. Selection is made by the Executive Committee of the Board of Directors. Awarded annually. Established in 1979.

• 18474 • Denny and Ida Wilcher Award
To recognize Sierra Club chapters and groups for outstanding work in either membership development or fund raising, particularly for specific conservation projects. Judging criteria include creativity, originality, and ratio of funds raised to expenses. A monetary award of $3,000 is awarded annually. Established in 1980. Sponsored by the Denny and Ida Wilcher Fund.

• 18475 •
Sigma Alpha Iota Philanthropies, Inc.
Ruth Sieber Johnson, Exec.Dir.
One Tunnel Rd.
Asheville, NC 28805
Phone: (828)251-0606
Fax: (828)251-0644
E-mail: nh@sai-national.org
Home Page: http://www.sai-national.org

Formerly: Sigma Alpha Iota Foundation.

• 18476 • Inter-American Music Awards
A music composition contest that is open to composers from North, Central, or South America regardless of nationality, age, race, creed, or sex. The particular combination of instruments and/or voices for which entries must be written, and the length of the work, varies each time the contest is held. Only previously unpublished and unperformed works are eligible. A monetary prize of $2,000, a world premiere, and publication by C. F. Peters Corp. are awarded. Held triennially. Established in 1948.

• 18477 • Scholarship/Grant Program of SAI Philanthropies Inc.
Up to 26 annual scholarships ranging from $1,000-$14,000 are awarded annually to both members and non-members of SAI Philanthropies. Inquire for application details.

• 18478 •
Sigma Delta Epsilon
Graduate Women in Science
Dr. Regina Vidaver, Pres.
Box 291
Avon, MA 02322
Phone: (858)573-1847
E-mail: kelleyk@ohio.edu
Home Page: http://www.gwis.org

• 18479 • Eloise Gerry Fellowships
To increase knowledge in the chemical and biological sciences, and to encourage research in science by women. Individuals who hold a degree in science from a recognized institution of higher learning, show evidence of outstanding ability and promise in research in the biological or chemical sciences, and are members of SDE/GWIS may submit applications by January 15. Two monetary fellowships of $4,000 and four fellowships of $2,000 are awarded annually. Established in 1975.

• 18480 • Honorary Member
To recognize women for outstanding achievement in all fields of scientific research or science education. Membership is not a requirement. A certificate and exemption from membership dues are awarded when merited. Established in 1926.

• 18481 • SDE Fellowships
To increase knowledge in all the natural sciences, and to encourage research by women. Individuals who hold a degree from a recognized institution of higher learning; give evidence of outstanding ability and promise in one of the mathematical, physical, environmental, computer, or life sciences; are currently involved in research, and are members of SDE/GWIS may submit applications by January 15. Three fellowships of $3,000; one fellowship of $1,000; and three fellowships of $500 are awarded annually. Established in 1921.

• 18482 •
Sigma Gamma Tau
Dr. Klaus Hoffmann, Pres.
Dept. of Aerospace Engineering
Wichita State University
Wichita, KS 67260-0044
Phone: (316)978-6327
Fax: (316)978-3307
E-mail: klaus.hoffmann@wichita.edu
Home Page: http://www.engr.wichita.edu/ae/sgt/sgthome.html

• 18483 • Undergraduate Award
To recognize undergraduate students in aerospace or aeronautical engineering for outstanding achievement at both the regional and national levels. Each chapter may nominate one student who is a senior Bachelor of Science degree candidate; nomination deadline is February 27. Regional winners each re ceive a plaque and a cash award of $100. The Ammon S. Andes National Award of $150 is presented to the national winner. Awarded annually. Established in 1976.

• 18484 •
Sigma Iota Epsilon
Dr. G. James Francis, Pres.
Colorado State Univ.
312 Rockwell Hall - Mgt. Dept.
Fort Collins, CO 80523-1275
Phone: (970)491-6265
Phone: (970)491-7200
Fax: (970)491-3522
E-mail: jimf@lamar.colostate.edu
Home Page: http://www.sienational.com

• 18485 • Sigma Iota Epsilon Scholarship Awards
To recognize scholarship and critical thinking in management. Active graduate student members of Sigma Iota Epsilon are eligible to submit a scholarly paper on an appropriate management theme. Application deadline is the last business day of the academic year. The Keith Davis Graduate Scholarship Award, which consists of a monetary prize of $1,250 and a plaque, is awarded annually for the best paper; two runners-up each receive $500. In addition, five undergraduate student members are annually awarded scholarships of $1,000 and two undergraduate student members are annually awarded scholarships of $500. Established in 1980.

• 18486 •
Sigma Phi Alpha
Donna Warren, Sec.
University of Texas, Health Science Center Houston, Dental Branch
6516 MD Anderson Blvd., Ste. 1.085
Houston, TX 77030
Phone: (713)500-4396
Fax: (713)500-0410

• 18487 • Honorary Member
To recognize an individual for outstanding contribution to the dental hygiene profession through educational or community services. Awarded when merited. Established in 1958.

• 18488 •
Sigma Phi Epsilon Fraternity
Craig Templeton, Exec.Dir.
Zollinger House
310 South Blvd.
PO Box 1901
Richmond, VA 23218-1901
Phone: (804)353-1901
Fax: (804)359-8160
E-mail: info@sigep.net
Home Page: http://www.sigep.org

• 18489 • Buchanan Outstanding Chapter Award
To recognize excellence in chapters across the country consistent with the Fraternity's strategic plan. The chapter must apply, be recognized by the District Governor of the School and Alumni Board, and be selected by the Buchanan Cup Selection Committee. Approximately 20 to 25 trophies are awarded biennially during the Grand Chapter Conclave. Established in 1961.

• 18490 •
Sigma Tau Delta, the International English Honor Society
Dr. William C. Johnson, Exec.Dir.
Department of English
Northern Illinois University
DeKalb, IL 60115
Phone: (815)753-1612
Fax: (815)753-6645
E-mail: sigmatd@niu.edu
Home Page: http://www.english.org

• 18491 • Scholarships, Writing Awards, Internships
Recognizes academic excellence. Awarded annually. Inquire for application details.

• 18492 •
Sigma Theta Tau International
Nancy Dickenson-Hazard, CEO
550 W North St.
Indianapolis, IN 46202
Phone: (317)634-8171
Toll-Free: 800-634-7575
Fax: (317)634-8188
E-mail: stti@stti.iupui.edu
Home Page: http://www.nursingsociety.org

• 18493 • Mildred Adams Chapter Heritage Award
To recognize and honor one or more chapters in a region that have an outstanding and comprehensive collection of materials that document the chapter's history, its association with the international organization, and its advancement of the mission of Sigma Theta Tau International.

• 18494 • Best of Image Awards
Recognizes superior contributions to nursing through *Image: Journal of Nursing Scholarship*

• 18495 • Best of the Online Journal Award
Recognizes an exceptional article that appeared in the *Online Journal of Knowledge Synthesis for Nursing*. Established in 1997.

• 18496 • Chapter Key Awards
Recognizes a chapter for overall excellence. Selection criteria is based on the resource development section of the organization's mission and goals developed in late 1989 and published in a pamphlet. Established in 1991.

Awards are arranged in alphabetical order below their administering organizations

• 18497 • **Chapter Newsletter Awards**
Encourages chapters to publish quality newsletters. Awards are given in the following six areas annually: Overall Excellence; Layout and Design Excellence; Special Edition Excellence; Editorial Excellence; Feature Article Excellence; and New Article Excellence.

• 18498 • **Chapter Research Advancement Award**
To recognize chapters for fostering the goals of the Society through significant research-related activities. Awarded annually. Formerly: Regional Chapter Research Advancement Award.

• 18499 • **Episteme Award**
Acknowledges a breakthrough in nursing research. A $15,000 stipend is awarded.

• 18500 • **Founders' Awards**
To recognize individuals and chapters for excellence of contemporary leaders in nursing. Awards are presented in the following seven categories: (1) Marie Hippenstell Lingeman Award for excellence in nursing practice; (2) Elizabeth McWilliams Miller Award for excellence in research; (3) Elizabeth Russell Belford Award for excellence in education; (4) Edith Moore Copeland Award for creativity; (5) Mary Tolle Wright Award for leadership; (6) Dorothy Garrigus Adams Award for fostering high professional standards; and (7) Ethel Palmer Clarke Award for excellence in chapter programming. Active members of the Society are eligible. The deadline for nominations is March 1. Plaques are awarded biennially in odd-numbered years at the convention. Established in 1977 in honor of the six founders and the director of the school in 1922 when Sigma Theta Tau was founded.

• 18501 • **Audrey Hepburn/Sigma Theta Tau International Award**
Recognizes a nurse who has made significant contributions to the health and wellbeing of children. Established in 1993 as a tribute to Ms. Hepburn's dedication and tireless work on behalf of children worldwide.

• 18502 • **Media Awards**
To recognize outstanding media coverage of nursing issues and outstanding efforts within nursing to communicate diverse images through the nursing press. Awards are presented in the categories of print, electronic, photography, and art media in both public media and nursing media. Nominations deadline is March 1. Engraved plaques are presented at the Biennial Convention. Established in 1982.

• 18503 • **Public Service Award**
To recognize and honor individuals in the public sector who have perceptively understood and communicated the increasingly vital role nurses play in the improvement of worldwide health care. Individuals outside the profession of nursing who have demonstrated excellence in: (1) interpreting nursing to the public; (2) promoting nursing's values to the public; (3) communicating nursing's positive impact and image to the public; and (4) supporting nursing's goals of improving the public's health. Established in 1986.

• 18504 • **Regional Information Technology Award**
To recognize and honor those who have successfully created and implemented the use of information technology to further the nursing profession and the health of the public.

• 18505 • **Regional Innovative Chapter Award**
To recognize one chapter in each region that has creatively implemented a successful project. A plaque is presented at an awards ceremony.

• 18506 • **Regional Multimedia Award**
To recognize communicators, information specialists, photo journalists, creative individuals, and groups who have pursued excellence in communicating nursing's rich and diverse stories and in sharing nursing's knowledge with the nursing field and the general public.

• 18507 • **Research Dissemination Award**
To recognize an individual or group who has made a major contribution to the dissemination of research to nurses for use in clinical nursing practice, education, administration and/or research. Awarded annually.

• 18508 • **Research Dissertation Award**
To recognize a nurse whose doctoral dissertation is exceptionally meritorious and exemplifies high standards of scholarship and knowledge development. Awarded annually.

• 18509 • **Research Utilization Award**
To recognize an individual or group who has either used research as a basis for a practice innovation or has provided the leadership for utilization of research in clinical nursing practice. Awarded to one or more recipients annually.

• 18510 •
Sigma Xi, The Scientific Research Society
Dr. Patrick D. Sculley, Exec.Dir.
PO Box 13975
PO Box 13975
Research Triangle Park, NC 27709
Phone: (919)549-4691
Toll-Free: 800-243-6534
Fax: (919)549-0090
E-mail: memberinfo@sigmaxi.org
Home Page: http://www.sigmaxi.org

Formed by merger of: (1974) Scientific Research Society of America; Sigma Xi.

• 18511 • **Monie A. Ferst Award**
To recognize a scientist for notable contributions to the motivation and encouragement of research through education. A medal and a $5,000 monetary prize are bestowed annually at the awards banquet. Established in 1975 by the Georgia Institute of Technology Chapter of Sigma Xi. The award honors Monie A. Ferst, an outstanding engineer and businessman who worked to establish the Georgia Tech Research Institute. Sponsored by Ferst Foundation of Atlanta.

• 18512 • **Grants-in-Aid of Research**
To provide support for scientific investigation in any field of science, engineering and math. Members and non-members from any country are eligible. Priority is usually given to applicants who are in an early stage of their scientific careers (undergraduate and graduate students in degree programs). Students use the funding to pay for travel expenses to and from a research site, or for purchase of non-standard laboratory equipment necessary to complete a specific research project. Awards are made in amounts up to $5,000 in astronomy, $2,500 in eye or vision research, and up to $1,000 in all other fields. Awarded annually.

• 18513 • **William Procter Prize for Scientific Achievement**
To recognize a scientist for outstanding or notable accomplishments in scientific research and demonstration of the ability to communicate this research to scientists in other disciplines. A Steuben glass sculpture, a monetary prize of $5,000, and the privilege of designating a younger scholar to receive a matching $5,000 grant-in-aid of research is awarded annually at the annual meeting of the society. Established in 1950 in honor of Dr. William Procter, a distinguished natural scientist, and co-founder of the Scientific Research Society of America.

• 18514 •
Sigma Zeta
Harold Wilkinson, Exec.Dir.
Millikin University
1184 W Main
Decatur, IL 62522
Phone: (217)424-6233
Fax: (217)362-6408
E-mail: hwilkinson@mail.millikin.edu
Home Page: http://www.sigmazeta.org

• 18515 • **Honor Award**
For recognition of academic achievement in science and mathematics, contributions of service to local chapters, and presentation of research results at the national meeting. Members of chapters may be nominated by the local chapters two weeks before the national meeting. A key is awarded annually.

• 18516 •
Silver Wings Fraternity
C.D. "Don" Fairbanks, Sec.
PO Box 44208
Cincinnati, OH 45244
Phone: (513)732-5852
Toll-Free: 800-554-1437
Fax: (513)732-5853
E-mail: cardinal5@msn.com
Home Page: http://www.silverwings.org

• 18517 • **National Man/Woman of the Year**

To recognize outstanding members for their aviation accomplishments and contributions toward advancement of the organization which is made up of men and women aviators who made first solo flights at least 25 years ago. Individuals must have flown powered aircraft as pilot in command at least 25 years before applying for membership. Only members are eligible. Plaques are awarded annually at the national convention. Each year the plaques are dedicated as a memorial to a departed member. Established in 1958 by Russ Brinkley, Founder.

• 18518 •
***Silverfish Review* Press**
Rodger Moody, Ed.
PO Box 3541
Eugene, OR 97403
Phone: (503)344-5060
E-mail: sfrpress@earthlink.net
Home Page: http://www.silverfishreviewpress.com

• 18519 • **Gerald Cable Book Award**

To recognize outstanding poetry. A monetary prize of $1,000, publication of a full-length book, and 100 copies of the book are awarded annually to a poet who has yet to publish a collection. Manuscripts should be at least 48 pages plus front matter (title, acknowledgment, dedication, contents and biographical pages). Previously published poems and simultaneous submissions are acceptable. Submit by October 15. Reading fee is $20. Send manuscripts with SASE for notification of winner. Manuscripts will not be returned. Entrants that include a SASE (7" x 10" w/$1.42 on it will receive two free copies selected from previous winners of the Gerald Cable Book Award or other SRP books). Established in 1995. Formerly: (1995) *Silverfish Review* Poetry Chapbook Award.

• 18520 •
Silvermine Guild Arts Center
Cynthia Clair, Exec.Dir.
1037 Silvermine Rd.
New Canaan, CT 06840-4398
Phone: (203)966-9700
Fax: (203)966-2763
E-mail: sgac@silvermineart.org
Home Page: http://www.silvermineart.org

• 18521 • **Art of the Northeast Competition**

To recognize outstanding works in the categories of oil painting, sculpture, watercolor, pastel, acrylic, or mixed media. Artists born or residing in nine New England states eligible for up to $10,000 in prizes. The exhibition is held annually in the spring. Established in 1949.

• 18522 • **Craft America Competition**

To recognize fine crafts by artists in the U.S. Selection is made by a jury. Three cash prizes are awarded. The competition is held biennially.

• 18523 • **International Prints Competition**

To recognize outstanding prints in several print media: intaglio, woodcut, lithography, and seriography. Selection is made by the exhibition juror. Purchase prizes are awarded biennially. Prints purchased become part of the Silvermine Print Collection. Established in 1956.

• 18524 •
Simba Information Inc.
Linda Kopp, Editorial Dir.
60 Long Ridge Rd., Ste. 300
Stamford, CT 06902
Phone: (203)325-8193
Fax: (203)325-8915
E-mail: info@simbanet.com
Home Page: http://www.simbanet.com

Formerly: Folio Educational Trust - % Hanson Publishing Group.

• 18525 • **Publishing Hall of Fame**

To recognize individuals who have made outstanding contributions to magazine and book publishing. Three individuals from magazine publishing and three from book publishing are honored. In addition, a special award is also given to the person who has contributed the most to fostering educational excellence in the publishing arts and sciences. Anyone in magazine publishing, book publishing and related fields may submit nomination ballots. The Selection Committee, an impartial group of industry leaders, makes its choices for the awards based upon past or present significant accomplishments and outstanding achievements in publishing. Awards are given in the following categories: (1) Magazine Publishing - consumer publishing; trade publishing; and magazine publishing that does not come under the heading of consumer or trade publishing; (2) Book Publishing - mass market publishing; trade publishing; and book publishing that does not come under the heading of mass market or trade publishing; and (3) Publishing Education - a Special Award for fostering publishing education. A plaque is awarded annually at the fall Magazine Publishing Congress. Established in 1984.

• 18526 •
Simon Fraser University
Office of Vice Preseident and Research Services
Ellen Loosley, Exec.Dir.
Kenneth Strand Hall, Rm. 2100
Burnaby, BC, Canada V5A 1S6
Phone: (604)291-3431
Fax: (604)291-3477
E-mail: ors@sfu.ca
Home Page: http://www.sfu.ca/vpresearch

• 18527 • **Frank Allison Linville's R. H. Wright Award in Olfactory Research**

To recognize and encourage outstanding and ongoing achievement in research in olfaction. Individuals must be nominated by February 14. A research grant of $25,000, a monetary prize of $5,000, a scroll, and an invitation to present a public lecture are awarded annually. Established in 1984 by Dr. Frank Allison Linville of General Monitors, to honor Dr. R. H. Wright. Formerly: (1989) R. H. Wright Award in Olfactory Research.

• 18528 •
Simon Wiesenthal Center
Rabbi Meyer May, Exec.Dir.
1399 S Roxbury Dr.
Los Angeles, CA 90035
Phone: (310)553-9036
Toll-Free: 800-900-9036
Fax: (310)553-4521
E-mail: information@wiesenthal.net
Home Page: http://www.wiesenthal.com

• 18529 • **International Leadership Award**

For recognition of excellence. Formerly: (1995) National Leadership; (2006) Simon Wiesenthal Center National Leadership Award.

• 18530 • **Simon Wiesenthal Center Humanitarian Award**

To recognize individuals for their efforts in working towards the betterment of humanity. Established in 1980 by Rabbi Marvin Hier, dean and founder of the Simon Wiesenthal Center.

• 18531 •
Sioux Empire Homeless Coalition
David Terrell, Pres.
413 N Main Ave.
Sioux Falls, SD 57104
Phone: (605)367-6012
Fax: (605)367-4235

• 18532 • **Friend of the Homeless Award**

For person who has made a difference in the lives of homeless people. Recognition award bestowed annually.

• 18533 •
Sister Cities International
Tim Honey, Exec.Dir.
1301 Pennsylvania Ave. NW, Ste. 850
Washington, DC 20004
Phone: (202)347-8630
Fax: (202)393-6524
E-mail: info@sister-cities.org
Home Page: http://www.sister-cities.org

• 18534 • **Young Artists Competition**

To engage youth from around the world with the sister city mission. Young artists between the ages of 13 and 18 are encouraged to express, through original artwork, their concept of the sister city mission to promote international peace through mutual respect, understanding, and cooperation. Only communities that are current members of Sister Cities International may submit entries. Each community may submit one entry created by a local young artist as well as an entry from each sister city abroad. Entries must be two-dimensional and no larger than 24 by 30 inches. Watercolor, oils, pastels, pen and ink, charcoal, photography, and mixed media are acceptable. Ten monetary prizes of $300 and certificates are awarded annually. Formerly:

Sister Cities Expressions of Peace Youth Art Contest.

• 18535 •
Sister Kenny Rehabilitation Institute
Public Relations Dept.
800 E 28th St.
Minneapolis, MN 55407
Phone: (612)863-4466
Fax: (612)863-4400
Home Page: http://www.allina.com/ahs/ski.nsf

• 18536 • **International Art Show by Artists with Disabilities**
To provide a forum for the creative talents of people with a physical or mental disability, to give them an outlet to sell their work, and to show that talent and disability are not mutually exclusive. Any artist with a disability that causes a physical or mental impairment that substantially limits one or more major life activities, such as caring for oneself, performing manual tasks, walking, seeing, hearing, breathing, learning, and working, may enter up to two works. Ribbons and monetary awards are given for first, second, and third place in the following categories: oils and acrylics, watercolor, graphic, mixed media, sculpture, and photography. Honorable mention awards for all categories are presented at the discretion of the judges. Held annually. Established in 1963 by Margaret Anderson, Sister Kenny Institute Auxiliary founder.

• 18537 •
Sitka Historical Society
Ms. Karen Meizner, Admin.
330 Harbor Dr.
Sitka, AK 99835
Phone: (907)747-6455
Fax: (907)747-6588
E-mail: sitkahis@ptialaska.net
Home Page: http://www.sitka.org/historicalmuseum

• 18538 • **Isabel Miller Service Award**
For largest number of hours annually donated to museum. Recognition award bestowed annually.

• 18539 •
Sixteenth Century Society and Conference
Department of History
211 Carlson Hall
380 South 1400 East
University of Utah
Salt Lake City, UT 84112
E-mail: megan.armstrong@utah.edu
Home Page: http://www.sixteenthcentury.org

• 18540 • **Roland H. Bainton Book Prize**
To honor the best books written in English in the field of early modern studies (1450-1660) dealing with three categories: Art and Music History, History/Theology, and Literature. A fourth prize for Reference works is awarded occasionally. Anthologies and collections of essays are not eligible, except in the reference category. The deadline for submission is April 1. A monetary prize of $500 is awarded to the winner in each category. Awarded annually. Established in 1990.

• 18541 • **Harold J. Grimm Prize**
To honor the best article that reflects and sustains Grimm's lifelong search for a broad understanding of the Reformation as a fundamentally religious phenomenon that permeated the whole civilization of Europe in the Reformation Era who write in the spirit and methodology of the late Professor Harold Grimm. Articles published in any journal qualify for the prize, but preference will be given to those published in the previous calendar year in *Sixteenth Century Journal, Archive for Reformation History, Church History,* and *Renaissance Quarterly*. A monetary prize of $500 is awarded annually. Established in 1985 in memory of Dr. Harold Grimm.

• 18542 • **Literature Paper Prize**
To recognize the best literature paper presented at the SCSC meeting. All presenters are eligible. A monetary prize of $500 is awarded annually. Established in 1993.

• 18543 • **Carl S. Meyer Prize**
For recognition of the best paper delivered at the yearly meeting by a scholar who is still in graduate school or has earned the PhD in the last five years. Criteria include quality and originality of research; methodological skill and/or innovation; development of fresh and stimulating interpretations or insights; and literary quality. A monetary prize of $500 plus the opportunity to have the paper published in *Sixteenth Century Journal* are awarded annually. Established in 1975 in honor of Carl S. Meyer, co-founder of the Society.

• 18544 • **Nancy Lyman Roelker Prize**
To recognize the best article published in English dealing with sixteenth-century French History. Articles that have appeared within the 12 months prior to September of the year of the award are eligible. Criteria include quality and originality of research; methodological skill and/or innovation; development of fresh and stimulating interpretations or insights; and literary quality. A monetary prize of $500 is awarded annually. Established in 1983 in honor of the contributions of Nancy Lyman Roelker to the study of 16th-century France.

• 18545 • ***Sixteenth Century Journal* Literature Prize**
To recognize the best paper in literature submitted to the *Sixteenth Century Journal* for publication during the calendar year. A monetary prize of $500 is awarded annually. Established in 1993.

• 18546 • **Sixteenth Century Society and Conference Medal**
To recognize a member for contributions to the promotion and advancement of early modern studies. Criteria may include: long-term commitment to the SCSC; continued participation in the various activities of the SCSC; and significant contributions to the field through publications, papers, leadership, and support of younger scholars. Awarded every five years. Established in 1990.

• 18547 •
Ski Racing
Inside Communications Inc.
Don Cameron, Editor-in-Chief
1830 N 55th St.
Boulder, CO 80301-2700
Phone: (303)440-0601
Fax: (303)444-6788
E-mail: info@insideinc.com
Home Page: http://www.skiracing.com

• 18548 • **Skier of the Year**
To recognize the American Alpine skiers who have done the best in world-wide competition in the previous ski season. Each year, one man and one woman is awarded the title. A plaque is presented at the close of the ski season. Established in 1975.

• 18549 •
Skills USA - VICA
Timothy W. Lawrence, Exec.Dir.
14001 James Monroe Hwy.
PO Box 3000
Leesburg, VA 20177-0300
Phone: (703)777-8810
Toll-Free: 800-321-8422
Fax: (703)777-8999
E-mail: anyinfo@skillsusa.org
Home Page: http://www.skillsusa.org

• 18550 • **Outstanding Vocational Educators**
For recognition of outstanding educators in the field of vocational education. Established in 1977.

• 18551 • **Professional Development Program Awards**
To provide individual recognition for a student's achievements in reaching various levels of competence in leadership and technical occupational skills. Members of the chapter are eligible. Awarded as merited. Established in 1970. Formerly: Vocational Initiative and Club Achievement Program Awards.

• 18552 • **SkillsUSA Championships**
To recognize and promote occupational and leadership skill excellence among students in technical, skilled, and service careers, including health occupations, and to improve the image and draw greater attention to the skills these students have. Active members of the chapter are eligible. Teams and individuals compete in leadership and occupational contests on the local, regional, district, and state levels. Once a year, SkillsUSA holds national competitions for state winners from across the country. Gold, silver, and bronze SkillsUSA Championships medallions are presented for first, second, and third place winners, respectively. National winners

are eligible for an international contest program. Scholarships and tools of various occupations are donated by industry, educational institutions, and trade associations. Awarded annually in 75 occupational and leadership skill contests. Established in 1973. Formerly: (1995) United States Skill Olympics.

• 18553 •
SLE Foundation
Margaret Graham Dowd, Exec.Dir.
149 Madison Ave., Ste. 205
New York, NY 10016
Phone: (212)685-4118
Toll-Free: 800-74-LUPUS
Fax: (212)545-1843
E-mail: lupus@lupusny.org
Home Page: http://www.lupusny.org

• 18554 • **Medical Research Grants**
For medical research. Monetary award bestowed annually.

• 18555 •
Slipstream
PO Box 2071
Dept. W-1
Niagara Falls, NY 14301
Phone: (716)282-2616
E-mail: editors@slipstreampress.org
Home Page: http://
www.slipstreampress.org

• 18556 • ***Slipstream*'s Annual Poetry Chapbook Contest**
To promote often ignored poets. Submissions of up to 40 pages of poetry, a S.A.S.E., and $ 10 reading fee must be received by December 1. The winner receives a cash award of $1,000, 50 copies of the Chapbook, and a one-issue subscription to *Slipstream*. All entrants receive a copy of the winning Chapbook and a one-issue subscription. Awarded annually. Established in 1987.

• 18557 •
Slovak Studies Association
Prof. Carol Skalnik Leff, Pres.
371 Lincoln Hall
University of Illinois
Department of Political Science
702 S. Wright St.
Urbana, IL 61801
Phone: (217)244-2270
Fax: (217)244-5712
E-mail: leffc@uiuc.edu
Home Page: http://faculty.luther.edu/
~lauersma/ssa

• 18558 • **Slovak Studies Association Prize**
To recognize an individual for outstanding scholarship on Slovakia, Slovaks, or related issues. Scholars outside of Czechoslovakia may submit work published within the previous three years, such as a book or an article in a scholarly journal. A monetary award of at least $150 and a plaque are presented every two years when merited at the convention. Established in 1989.

• 18559 •
Small Business Council of America
Paula Calimafde, Chair.
800 Delaware Ave., 7th Fl.
PO Box 1229
Wilmington, DE 19899
Phone: (302)691-7222
Toll-Free: 877-404-1329
Fax: 877-404-1329
E-mail: calimafd@paleyrothman.com
Home Page: http://www.sbca.net/

• 18560 • **Congressional Award**
To recognize a U.S. Congressman or Senator for efforts on behalf of small business in connection with federal tax matters. A plaque is awarded annually. Established in 1981.

• 18561 • **Connie Murdoch Award**
To recognize an SBCA member for outstanding leadership, dedication and work in SBCA. A plaque is awarded annually. Established in 1986 in memory of Converse Murdoch, the first SBCA president.

• 18562 • **Small Business Person of the Year**
To recognize an individual for outstanding efforts to promote small business through his or her own company or at large during the preceding year.

• 18563 •
Small Motor and Motion Association
Elizabeth B. Chalmers, Exec.Dir.
PO Box P182
South Dartmouth, MA 02748
Phone: (508)979-5935
Fax: (508)979-5845
E-mail: info@smma.org
Home Page: http://www.smma.org
Formerly: Small Motor Manufacturers Association.

• 18564 • **Distinguished Service Award**
To recognize an SMMA member who has made a significant contribution to the Association. The recipient is honored with a plaque at the spring meeting. Established in 1987. Formerly: (1995) President's Award.

• 18565 • **Hall of Fame Award**
To recognize an individual for a significant contribution to the electric motor industry. Eligibility is not limited to members of the Association. The recipient is honored with a plaque at the fall meeting. Established in 1985.

• 18566 •
Clarice Smith Performing Arts Center
Susie Farr, Exec.Dir.
Ste. 3800
University of Maryland
College Park, MD 20742-1625
Phone: (301)405-ARTS
Fax: (301)405-5977
E-mail: mertens@umd.edu
Home Page: http://
claricesmithcenter.umd.edu
Formerly: (1998) University of Maryland International Music Competitions, Rossborough Festival.

• 18567 • **University of Maryland International Music Competitions**
To recognize the most advanced pianists, singers, and cellists. Competition rounds examine solo repertoire and performance with symphony orchestra. The competitions are held in conjunction with a festival, featuring performances, lectures, and symposia by leading artists in the field. Each competition/festival is held quadrennially according to the following rotation: The Marian Anderson Vocal Arts Competition (1999); The Leonard Rose International Cello Competition and Festival (2001); and the William Kapell International Piano Competition and Festival (2002). Pianists between the ages of 18 and 33, vocalists between 21 and 39, and cellists between 18 and 30 are eligible. The application deadline is March 15 annually. Monetary awards exceeding $50,000 are awarded to competition finalists and semi-finalists. The first prize consists of $20,000, a New York recital, and other engagements. Formerly: (1991) University of Maryland International Piano Festival and William Kapell Piano Competition.

• 18568 •
James Smithson Society
Smithsonian Institution
900 Jefferson Dr. SW, Ste. 1130
PO Box 37012, MRC 410
Washington, DC 20013-7012
Phone: (202)357-1738
Toll-Free: 800-931-3226
Fax: (202)633-9816
E-mail: smithsoniansociety@si.edu
Home Page: http://
www.smithsonsociety.org

• 18569 • **James Smithson Society Founder Medal**
To recognize extraordinary contributions or services to the Smithsonian Institution. A medal, life membership, and name engraved on a plaque that hangs in the original Smithsonian building, now familiarly known as the Castle, are awarded when merited. Established in 1977 to honor James Smithson, the English scientist and benefactor who in 1826 bequeathed his fortune "to the United States of America, to found at Washington, under the name Smithsonian Institution, an establishment for the increase and diffusion of knowledge among men."

• 18570 • James Smithson Society Grants

To provide grants for various projects, including exhibitions, educational programs, research activities, and acquisitions within the Smithsonian Institution.

• 18571 •
Smithsonian Institution
Lawrence M. Small, Sec.
SI Bldg., Rm. 153, MRC 010
PO Box 37012
Washington, DC 20013-7012
Phone: (202)633-1000
Phone: (202)357-2020
Fax: (202)786-2377
E-mail: info@si.edu
Home Page: http://www.si.edu

• 18572 • Smithsonian Institution Fellowship Program

To support independent research in residence at the Smithsonian in association with the research staff and using the Institution's resources. Fellowships are awarded in the fields of history of science and technology, social and cultural history, history of art, anthropology, biological sciences, earth sciences, and materials analysis. Predoctoral and postdoctoral fellowship appointments for six to twelve months, senior postdoctoral appointments for three to twelve months, and graduate student appointments for ten weeks are awarded annually. Stipends range from $22,000 per year for predoctoral fellowships to $35,000 per year for senior and postdoctoral fellowships.

• 18573 •
Smithsonian Women's Committee
1000 Jefferson Dr. SW, Rm. 436
Smithsonian Institution
PO Box 37012
Washington, DC 20560-7012
Phone: (202)357-4000
Toll-Free: 888-832-9554
Fax: (202)786-2516
E-mail: craftshow@si.edu
Home Page: http://www.si.edu/giving/od/women.htm

Formerly: Washington Craft Show.

• 18574 • Smithsonian Craft Show

To provide a showcase and sales opportunity for craftspersons. Master artists and emerging talent exhibit and sell their work in 12 categories: basketry, ceramics, decorative fiber, furniture, glass, jewelry, leather, metal, paper, wearable art, wood, and mixed media combinations. One hundred twenty exhibitors are selected by a jury on the basis of originality, artistic conception, and quality of workmanship. Numerous awards are presented, including the Best of Show Award; gold, silver, and bronze awards; First-Time Exhibitor Award; Museum Acquisition Award, and Exhibitors' Choice Awards. Held annually at the National Building Museum in Washington DC. Established in 1966. Formerly: Washington Craft Show.

• 18575 •
Snipe Class International Racing Association
Jerelyn W. Biehl, Exec. Dir.
1833 Tustin St.
San Diego, CA 92106-1735
Phone: (619)224-6998
Fax: (619)224-6997
E-mail: scira@snipe.org
Home Page: http://www.snipe.org

• 18576 • Heinzerling Trophy

To recognize the highest placing finisher in the annual racing series organized by the Snipe Class Association in the United States. Membership in the Association is required, and entrants pre-qualify in local or regional competition. The U.S. championship is, itself, a qualifying event for the world championship trophy - the Issaccs Trophy or the Western Hemisphere Championship Trophy - the Hayward Trophy, held in alternate years. A perpetual trophy to be held for one year and a trophy to keep are awarded annually. Established in 1947 by Commodore Charles E. Heinzerling.

• 18577 •
Soaring Society of America
PO Box 2100
Jack Gornez Bldg., Ave. A
Hobbs, NM 88241-2100
Phone: (505)392-1177
Fax: (505)392-8154
E-mail: info@ssa.org
Home Page: http://www.ssa.org

• 18578 • Lewin B. Barringer Memorial Trophy

To recognize the greatest straight-line distance soaring flight during the previous year, other than at the U.S. National Championships. The pilot is awarded a perpetual trophy. Awarded when merited. Established in 1948.

• 18579 • Certificate of Appreciation

To recognize contributions by an individual or group to the Society that deem special recognition. An engraved certificate is awarded as merited. Established in 1964.

• 18580 • Marion C. Cruce Trophy

To recognize the 1-26 Soaring Champion, as determined at the annual 1-26 championships, at which pilots from any nation are invited to participate. The trophy is a large sterling silver punch bowl, which was donated to the 1-26 Association in 1966 by Mr. and Mrs. Cruce.

• 18581 • Richard C. du Pont Trophy

To recognize the U.S. National Unlimited Class Soaring Champion, as determined at the annual championships. A perpetual bronze trophy mounted on a mahogany base and a bronze medallion with bas-relief representation of the trophy are awarded annually. Established in 1947 by Mrs. Allaire du Pont in memory of her husband. This trophy succeeded the Edward S. Evans Trophy, which was the original national championship trophy presented from 1930 until 1946. Formerly: Edward S. Evans Trophy.

• 18582 • Warren E. Eaton Memorial Trophy

This, the Society's highest award, is given to recognize an individual for an outstanding contribution to the art, sport, or science of soaring flight in the United States. Members must be nominated in November. A monetary award of $325, a certificate, and a perpetual trophy are awarded annually. Established in 1939 by Mrs. Genevieve Eaton in memory of Warren E. Eaton, founder and first President of the Society.

• 18583 • Exceptional Achievement Award

To recognize achievement of importance by individuals or groups that merit recognition and are not covered by other awards of the Society. A certificate is awarded as merited. Established in 1964.

• 18584 • Exceptional Service Award

To recognize service to SSA by individuals or groups that has been of the utmost value to the Society. An engraved certificate is awarded as merited. Established in 1964.

• 18585 • Joe Giltner Memorial Trophy

To recognize the pilot scoring the fastest official speed on a task during the U.S. 15-Meter National Soaring Championships. A perpetual trophy and a certificate are awarded annually. Established in 1981 in memory of Joe Giltner, a dedicated soaring instructor and an outstanding competitor.

• 18586 • Kolstad Junior Soaring Awards

To recognize and encourage participation by youth in the soaring community. Individuals between the ages of 14 and 20 who have an FAI sporting license are eligible. Two types of awards are given, the Kolstad Youth Scholarship and the Century Awards. The Century Awards, consisting of a patch and pin, are presented in the following categories: Century I - awarded when a cross country flight of 100 km is completed; Century II - when a flight of 200 km is completed; and Century III - when a flight of 300 km is completed. Established in 1968 by the Kolstad family in memory of Paul Kenneth Kolstad.

• 18587 • Schreder 15-Meter Class Trophy

To recognize the United States 15-Meter Class National Champion, as determined by the annual championships. A trophy is presented annually. Established in 1977 by Richard and Angelike Schreder.

• 18588 • Soaring Hall of Fame

To recognize persons for outstanding achievements in soaring. The SSA Directors determine who is eligible for inclusion in this Hall of Fame. Two persons may be added annually. In general, it is intended that one position each year be awarded for a soaring achievement and the other for an outstanding contribution. Each person receives a certificate. Established in 1954.

• 18589 • Standard Class Trophy

To recognize the U.S. National Unlimited Class Soaring Champion, as determined at the annual championships. A perpetual trophy of free-form crystal is presented annually. Established in 1972.

• 18590 • Larissa Stroukoff Memorial Trophy

To recognize the U.S. citizen making the best speed around a triangular task during the Annual U.S. National Soaring Championships. A monetary prize of $5,000, a perpetual trophy, and a certificate are awarded annually. Established in 1955 by Larissa Stroukoff to assist young people in their aviation interests and education.

• 18591 • Paul E. Tuntland Memorial Award

To recognize important contributions to the science of soaring flight, as evidenced in a published paper or article discussing the results of a soaring flight made by the author. A certificate is awarded annually. Established in 1952 by the family of Paul Tuntland, whose work in the field of research, construction, and competition flying contributed to the science of soaring.

• 18592 •
The SOCAN Foundation
(Societe canadienne des auteurs, compositeurs, et editeurs de musique)
Rick MacMillan, Mgr.
41 Valleybrook Dr.
Toronto, ON, Canada M3B 2S6
Phone: (416)445-8700
Toll-Free: 800-557-6226
Fax: (416)442-3372
E-mail: macmillanr@socan.ca
Home Page: http://www.socanfoundation.ca

• 18593 • SOCAN Awards for Young Composers

For recognition of outstanding young composers. Composers who are under 30 years of age on the closing date of the competition, April 1, and who are Canadian citizens are eligible. Monetary prizes totaling $17,500 are available in five categories: The Sir Ernest MacMillan Awards for orchestral compositions; the Serge Garant Awards for chamber music compositions; the Pierre Mercure Awards for solo or duet compositions; the Hugh Le Caine Awards for live electronics or electroacoustic music; and the Godfrey Ridout Awards for choral compositions. Sponsored by The SOCAN Foundation.

• 18594 •
Soccer Association for Youth
Sheila A. Shay, Natl.Exec.Dir.
1 N Commerce Park Dr., No. 306-320
Cincinnati, OH 45215
Phone: (513)769-3800
Toll-Free: 800-233-7291
Fax: (513)769-0500
E-mail: sayusa@saysoccer.org
Home Page: http://www.saysoccer.org

• 18595 • Gold Ball Award

For recognition of significant achievements outside the normal channels of the Association. Nominations of individuals, corporations, or organizations are accepted. A plaque is presented at the annual meeting. Established in 1976 by Tom Stevens.

• 18596 • Silver Ball Award

For recognition of significant singular or long-range meritorious achievements and contributions to the National SAY program by an individual working within the organization. A plaque is presented at the annual meeting. Established in 1981 by James Gruenwald.

• 18597 •
Soccer Industry Council of America
Tom Cove, Exec.Dir.
200 Castlewood Dr.
North Palm Beach, FL 33408-5696
Phone: (561)842-4100
Fax: (202)296-7462
E-mail: info@sgma.com
Home Page: http://www.sgma.com

• 18598 • Simon Sherman Leadership Award

To recognize an individual who has made significant contributions to the advancement of soccer in the United States. Nominations may be submitted by July 1. A plaque is awarded annually at a testimonial dinner at the SICA convention in October. Established in 1988 in memory of Simon Sherman. Formerly: Simon Sherman Industry Service Award.

• 18599 •
Social Science Research Council
810 7th Ave, Fl 31
New York, NY 10019-5818
Phone: (212)377-2700
Home Page: http://www.ssrc.org

• 18600 • Louis Dupree Prize for Research on Central Asia

A prize of $2,500 will be awarded for the most promising dissertation involving field research in Central Asia, a region broadly defined to include Afghanistan, Azerbaijan, Kirghizia, Mongolia, Turkmenistan, Tajikistan, Uzbekistan, and culturally-related contiguous areas of Iran, Pakistan, Kazakhstan, and China. Only candidates who receive a dissertation research fellowship from an SSRC/ACLS program will be eligible to apply. The intent of the prize is to enrich the individual's field experience by making possible a longer stay or more extensive travel within the region.

• 18601 •
Socialist Party of Rhode Island
PO Box 2433
E Side Sta.
Providence, RI 02906
E-mail: sprhodeisland@hotmail.com
Home Page: http://www.sp-usa.org/spri

• 18602 • Dorr-Debs Award

For distinguished accomplishments in field of social change. Recognition award bestowed annually.

• 18603 •
Societe Saint-Jean-Baptiste de Montreal
Jean Dorion, Pres.
82, rue Sherbrooke Ouest
Montreal, QC, Canada H2X 1X3
Phone: (514)843-8851
Fax: (514)844-6369
E-mail: mbeaulieu@ssjb.com
Home Page: http://www.ssjb.com

• 18604 • Prix Andre-Guerin

To recognize an individual for outstanding contributions to film and video. Awarded periodically. Established in 1990.

• 18605 • Prix Bene Merenti de Patria

For recognition of individuals who have performed outstanding services for Canada. A silver medal is awarded when merited. Established in 1923.

• 18606 • Prix Calixa-Lavallee

To recognize a professional musician who is a resident of Quebec and whose activities are considered outstanding in the furtherance of French-Canadian culture. A monetary prize of $1,500 and the Bene Merenti de Patria Medal are awarded periodically. Established in 1959.

• 18607 • Prix Chomedey-de-Maisonneuve

To recognize a resident of Montreal whose efforts have contributed to the radiance of that city. A well-known resident of Montreal either by birth, work, or career is eligible. A silver medal is awarded when merited. Established in 1983.

• 18608 • Prix Esdras-Minville

To recognize an individual who is a resident of Quebec for contributions in the social sciences (history, sociology, economics, politics, etc.). A monetary prize of $1,500 and the Bene Merenti de Patria Medal are awarded periodically. Established in 1978. Formerly: Prix de Sciences Humaines Esdras-Minville.

• 18609 • Prix Leon-Lortie

For recognition of a scientist. Scientists living in Quebec are eligible. A monetary award of $1,500 Canadian dollars and a bronze medal

Awards are arranged in alphabetical order below their administering organizations

are awarded periodically. Established in 1987 in memory of Leon Lortie, a great teacher at the University of Montreal.

• 18610 • Prix Louis-Phillipe-Hebert
To recognize a professional artist who is a resident of Quebec and whose works are considered outstanding in the furtherance of Quebec's culture. A monetary prize of $1,500 and the Bene Merenti de Patria Medal are awarded periodically. Established in 1971.

• 18611 • Prix Ludger-Duvernay
To recognize an author who is a resident of Quebec and whose works are considered to be outstanding in the furtherance of Quebec's culture. A monetary prize of $1,500 and the Bene Merenti de Patria Medal are awarded periodically. Established in 1944.

• 18612 • Prix Maurice-Richard
To recognize residents of Quebec who have distinguished themselves in sports and in serving the higher interests of the Quebec's people. A monetary prize of $1,500 and the Bene Merenti de Patria Medal are awarded periodically. Established in 1979.

• 18613 • Prix Olivar-Asselin
To recognize a professional journalist who is a resident of Quebec and whose works are considered outstanding in the furtherance of French-Canadian culture. A monetary prize of $1,500 and the Bene Merenti de Patria Medal are awarded when merited. Established in 1955.

• 18614 • Prix Seraphin-Marion
To recognize a francophone outside of Quebec for exceptional dedication to the furtherance of the French cause. A monetary award of $1,500 and the Bene Merenti de Patria medal are awarded periodically. Established in 1984 in memory of Seraphin Marion, who worked for the rights of Quebec's people wherever they lived.

• 18615 • Prix Victor-Morin
To recognize an outstanding professional actor or actress whose activities serve to strengthen Quebec's culture. A monetary prize of $1,500 and the Bene Merenti de Patria Medal are awarded periodically. Established in 1962.

• 18616 •
Society for Adolescent Medicine
Eddie Moore, Communications Dir.
1916 NW Copper Oaks Circle
Blue Springs, MO 64015
Phone: (816)224-8010
Fax: (816)224-8009
Home Page: http://www.adolescenthealth.org

• 18617 • SAM/Adele D. Hofmann Visiting Professor in Adolescent Medicine and Health Award
To provide an educational experience in adolescent medicine for a group of health care providers who may not otherwise have the opportunity to benefit from the Professor's expertise. Awarded annually. Established in 1986. Formerly: (2003) Visiting Professor in Adolescent Medicine Award.

• 18618 • Hilary E. C. Millar Award for Innovative Approaches to Adolescent Health Care
To recognize any national or international individual, organization, or agency involved in adolescent health care, defined in its broadest sense. Nominations are made by peers. A plaque is awarded annually at the annual convention. Established in 1986 in honor of Dr. Hilary E. C. Millar, a member of the Society.

• 18619 • Outstanding Achievement in Adolescent Medicine Award
To recognize individuals national and internationally for their commitment to improving the health and health care resources for adolescents and young adults. Members and nonmembers are eligible for nomination. A monetary prize is awarded annually. Established in 1981.

• 18620 • Research Visiting Professor Award
To allocate monies to recognizing individuals within the Society for achievement in research, and to help a training program that is currently engaging in adolescent health research enhance its research program so that it will become better equipped to compete for resources and fund a research program. Awarded annually. Established in 1995. Sponsored by Organon Inc. Formerly: SAM/Organon Visiting Professor in Adolescent Research Award.

• 18621 • SAM/Mead Johnson Nutritionals New Investigator Award
To recognize professionals who, through excellence in research, have furthered the Society's goals: to promote the development, synthesis, and dissemination of scientific and scholarly knowledge unique to the development and health care needs of adolescents. Nominations must be made by SAM members. A monetary award is presented annually. Established in 1989. Sponsored by Mead Johnson Nutritionals.

• 18622 •
Society for Advancement of Management
Dr. Moustafa H. Abbelsamad, Pres./CEO
Texas A&M University- Corpus Christi
College of Business
6300 Ocean Dr.
Corpus Christi, TX 78412
Phone: (361)825-6045
Phone: (361)825-5574
Toll-Free: 888-827-6077
Fax: (361)825-2725
E-mail: moustafa@cob.tamucc.edu
Home Page: http://www.cob.tamucc.edu/sam/

• 18623 • Phil Carroll Advancement of Management Awards
To recognize a specific contribution as represented by a published article, and a case history of implementation of the new idea or technique. Awards are given in the following categories: (1) Operations Management; (2) Marketing Management; (3) Management of Product or Service Development; (4) Financial Management; (5) Personnel Management; and (6) General Management. Any key management person, whether a member or not, is eligible. A writeup of the contribution must have been published at least one year prior to the selection. Individuals of any nationality may be nominated. Awarded as merited.

• 18624 • Fellow
This grade of membership is open by invitation to all members of the Society who have achieved recognized competence in their respective areas and who have contributed in some manner in a major way to the operation of the Society at either the local, regional, or national level. Candidates should be members of the Society and have acknowledged significant attainments in the art and science of management and have had ten years of service in a managerial capacity. Academic status counts toward ten years of service.

• 18625 • Gilbreth Medal
To recognize noteworthy achievement in the field of motion, skill, and fatigue study. Individuals who have influenced the thinking of practitioners and have contributed to a public understanding of the role of motion economy are eligible. Established in 1931 in honor of the work of Frank B. and Lillian M. Gilbreth.

• 18626 • Human Relations Award
To recognize an individual for an outstanding accomplishment of permanent value to the field of human relations. Established in 1944.

• 18627 • Materials Handling Award
To recognize outstanding efforts leading to greater understanding, appreciation, and application of contributions to the materials handling field by management educators, management practitioners, and the general public. Established in 1956.

• 18628 • Taylor Key Award
This, one of the highest awards of the Society, is given for recognition of outstanding contributions to the art and science of management as conceived by Frederick W. Taylor. Individuals of any nationality are eligible. Established in 1937.

• 18629 •
Society for American Baseball Research
812 Huron Rd. E Ste. 719
Cleveland, OH 44115
Phone: (216)575-0500
Toll-Free: 800-969-7227
Fax: (216)575-0502
E-mail: info@sabr.org
Home Page: http://www.sabr.org

• 18630 • **Baseball Research Awards**
To honor individual researchers for research efforts and projects in baseball-related topics. Research carried out in such diverse baseball-related areas as statistics, literature, history, biography, art, music, poetry, architecture, equipment, sociology, economics, labor relations, advertising, collectibles, etc. is considered. A research effort covering several years' time could be recognized for up to two years following its completion. Research results need not have been published or presented as papers in order to be eligible. Nominees need not be members of SABR. Three monetary awards of $200 each are awarded annually at the SABR Annual Meeting. Established in 1976. Sponsored by *Sporting News* and MacFarland.

• 18631 • **Bob Davids Award**
For recognition of outstanding contributions to the Society's activities, particularly in the areas of voluntary administration and research. Members are eligible to be nominated by a committee by June 1. A trophy is awarded annually. Established in 1985 in honor of Bob Davids, founder of SABR.

• 18632 • **Hero of Baseball Award**
Honors a baseball personality whose career has been marked by heroism on the filed or off.

• 18633 • **Jack Kavanagh Memorial Youth Baseball Research Award**
Awarded for either a research presentation given at the SABR National Convention with an accompanying paper, or a research paper that is submitted to the awards committee between the end of one SABR Convention and no later than June 1 of the following year by a researcher under the age of 21. The winner will receive a plaque honoring their achievement and a $200 cash prize with a one-year SABR membership. The paper will be published on the SABR website and may be published in either The National Pastime or the Baseball Research Journal. Established in 1999.

• 18634 • **Lee Allen Award**
To honor the best baseball research project at the annual National History Day competition. Students compete on a regional basis followed by state competition, and national finals take place at the University of Maryland.

• 18635 • **Doug Pappas Research Award**
To recognize a member for the best research presentation at the SABR annual national convention. A monetary award of $250 is presented. Established in 1990. Sponsored by *USA Today Sports Weekly*. Formerly: (2004) *USA Today Sports Weekly* Award; John W. Cox Award.

• 18636 • **The SABR Salute**
To honor a member of the society for dedicated research efforts and other service to the organization. A full-page story about the individual honored appears in the *Membership Directory*. Awarded biennially in odd-numbered years. Established in 1976.

• 18637 • **SABR Special Achievement Award**
Honors extraordinary work that has facilitated the discussion of baseball research information and which has fostered the study of baseball as a significant American institution.

• 18638 • **Seymour Medal**
Honors the best book of baseball history or biography published during the preceding calendar year.

• 18639 •
Society for Applied Spectroscopy
201B Broadway St.
Frederick, MD 21701-6501
Phone: (301)694-8122
Fax: (301)694-6860
E-mail: sasoffice@aol.com
Home Page: http://www.s-a-s.org

• 18640 • **Distinguished Service Award**
To recognize individual members for their long service to the Society. An engraved plaque is awarded annually at the Federation of Analytical Chemistry and Spectroscopy (FACSS) Conference. Established in 1980.

• 18641 • **Graduate Student Award**
To recognize an outstanding graduate student in the field of spectroscopy. A scroll/plaque and travel expenses to receive the award at the national meeting are awarded annually at the Federation of Analytical Chemistry and Spectroscopy (FACSS) conference. Established in 1977.

• 18642 • **Honorary Membership Award**
To recognize individuals for outstanding contributions to the field of applied spectroscopy. Nominations may be made by any member of the Society by December 1. An engraved plaque and a lifetime membership in the Society are awarded annually.

• 18643 • **William F. Meggers Award**
To recognize an outstanding paper published in *Applied Spectroscopy* during the year. An honorarium of $500 and a scroll are awarded annually at the Federation of Analytical Chemistry and Spectroscopy (FACSS) Conference. Established in 1960. Formerly: Journal Award.

• 18644 • **William J. Poehlman Award**
To recognize a local section of the Society for outstanding programs and activities. A monetary award of $200 and a scroll are awarded annually at the Federation of Analytical Chemistry and Spectroscopy (FACSS) Conference. Established in 1975 to honor William J. Poehlman, the first president of the Society, and one of its founders.

• 18645 • **Lester W. Strock Award**
To recognize a selected publication of substantive research in/or application of analytical atomic spectrochemistry in the fields of earth, life, stellar, and cosmic sciences. Nomination deadline is February 15. A medal is awarded annually at the Federation of Analytical Chemistry and Spectroscopy (FACSS) Conference. Established in 1979. Sponsored by the New England Section of SAS.

• 18646 •
Society For Biomaterials
Steve Echard, Exec.Dir.
17000 Commerce Pky., Ste. C
Mount Laurel, NJ 08054
Phone: (856)439-0826
Fax: (856)439-0525
E-mail: info@biomaterials.org
Home Page: http://www.biomaterials.org

• 18647 • **Clemson Awards**
For recognition of outstanding achievement in the areas of basic research, applied research, and contributions to the literature of biomaterials. Separate awards are given for each category. Nominations and selections are made by the Ceremonies and Awards Committee with the approval of the Council of the Society for Biomaterials. A monetary award of $1,000 and partial travel expenses to the Annual Meeting are awarded to each of three winners. Presented annually. Established in 1973. Cosponsored by Clemson University.

• 18648 • **Founders Award**
For recognition of long-term, landmark contributions to the discipline of biomaterials. Applicants must be members of any of the world societies for biomaterials. A monetary award of $1,000, an invitation to submit a manuscript for publication in *Journal of Biomedical Materials Research,* and partial travel expenses to attend the Annual Meeting are presented annually. Established in 1981.

• 18649 • **Student Awards for Outstanding Research**
For recognition of promising student researchers. The award is presented to encourage superior students to pursue a professional career in the field of biomaterials science. Applicants must have approved student status (undergraduate; Master's or Health Science degree; or PhD candidate or equivalent). A certificate, an invitation to submit a manuscript for publication in *Journal of Biomedical Materials Research,* and partial travel expenses to attend the Annual Meeting are presented annually. Established in 1977.

• 18650 •
Society for Cinema and Media Studies
Stephen Prince, Pres.
Univ. of Oklahoma
640 Parrington Oval, Rm. 302
PO Box 7819
Norman, OK 73019
Phone: (405)325-8075
Fax: (405)325-7135
E-mail: office@cmstudies.org
Home Page: http://www.cmstudies.org

• 18651 • **Dissertation Award**
To recognize the author of an outstanding dissertation that deals with a cinema, television, or video studies topic. Candidates for the award must have completed the dissertation and have been awarded their degree during the year preceding the award. Members of SCS are eligible. Criteria for judging include clarity and strength of argumentation, quality and originality of scholarship and research, organization and coherence, prose style, and contribution to the understanding of the fields of film, television, or video studies. A monetary prize of $1,000 is awarded annually. Established in 1983.

• 18652 • **Student Award for Scholarly Writing**
To recognize students who show outstanding ability in the fields of film and television scholarship. Students enrolled in a recognized course of film and/or television study who are members of SCS may submit previously unpublished essays prepared for their courses. Monetary awards of $250, $150, and $100 are made to the winners, and the essay winning the first award is published in *Cinema Journal*. Awarded annually.

• 18653 •
Society for Clinical and Experimental Hypnosis
Dean Abby, Exec.Dir.
221 Rivermoor St.
Boston, MA 02132
Phone: (617)469-1981
Fax: (617)469-1889
E-mail: sceh@mspp.edu
Home Page: http://www.sceh.us

• 18654 • **Sherry K. and Harold B. Crasilneck Award**
For recognition of the best first paper on hypnosis by a young scientist that was presented at the last SCEH Scientific Meeting by a member. A plaque is awarded annually. Established in 1973.

• 18655 • **Roy M. Dorcus Award**
For recognition of the author(s) of the best clinical paper on hypnosis published during the year. A certificate is awarded annually. Established in 1962.

• 18656 • **Henry Guze Award**
For recognition of the author(s) of the best research paper on hypnosis published during the year. A certificate is awarded annually. Established in 1962.

• 18657 • **Ernest and Josephine Hilgard Award**
For recognition of the author(s) of the best theoretical paper on hypnosis published during the year. A certificate is awarded annually. Established in 1973. Formerly: Best Theoretical Paper on Hypnosis Award.

• 18658 • **Morton Prince Award**
For recognition of distinguished contributions to the development of hypnosis in the science and profession of psychology. Doctoral level psychologists and physicians are eligible. A certificate is awarded annually. Established in 1962 with the cooperation of the American Board of Psychological Hypnosis.

• 18659 • **Bernard B. Raginsky Award**
For recognition of leadership and achievement in the field of hypnosis by a physician, dentist, or licensed psychologist. A plaque is awarded annually. Established in 1960.

• 18660 • **Shirley R. Schneck Award**
To recognize a physician who has made significant contributions to the development of medical hypnosis. A certificate is awarded annually. Established in 1962.

• 18661 • **Arthur Shapiro Award**
For recognition of the author(s) of the best book on hypnosis published during the year. A certificate is awarded annually. Established in 1962.

• 18662 •
Society for Developmental and Behavioral Pediatrics
Nicolette Zuecca, Exec.Dir.
17000 Commerce Pkwy., Ste. C
Mount Laurel, NJ 08054
Phone: (856)439-0500
E-mail: nzuecca@ahint.com
Home Page: http://www.sdbp.org

Formerly: (1996) Society for Behavioral Pediatrics.

• 18663 • **Lectureship in Developmental and Behavioral Pediatrics**
To recognize lifetime achievements and contributions to the field of developmental-behavioral pediatrics. A $1,000 honorarium, plaque, and travel reimbursement are awarded each September at the SDBP annual scientific meeting. Established in 1983. Formerly: .

• 18664 •
Society for Economic Botany
Brian M. Boom, Pres.
PO Box 1897
Lawrence, KS 66044
Phone: (785)843-1235
Toll-Free: 800-627-0629
Fax: (785)843-1274
E-mail: info@econbot.org
Home Page: http://www.econbot.org

• 18665 • **Distinguished Economic Botanist**
To recognize an individual who has made outstanding contributions to the goals of the Society. Members and non-members are eligible. A certificate, paid travel to the annual meeting, lifetime membership in the Society, and an invitation to speak at the banquet of the annual meeting are conferred annually in June. Established in 1977.

• 18666 • **Edmund H. Fulling Award**
To honor the author of the best paper presented by a junior professional at the annual meeting. Investigators who are not more than five years beyond the doctorate are eligible. A monetary award of $500, a certificate, and an invitation to be published in *Economic Botany* are presented each year at the annual meeting. Established in 1980 to honor Edmund H. Fulling.

• 18667 •
Society for Environmental Graphic Design
Leslie Gallery Dilworth, Contact
1000 Vermont Ave., No. 400
Washington, DC 20005
Phone: (202)638-5555
Fax: (202)638-0891
E-mail: leslie@segd.org
Home Page: http://www.segd.org

Formerly: Society of Environmental Graphic Designers.

• 18668 • **Design Awards Competition**
To recognize excellence in environmental graphic design, to increase the visibility of environmental graphic design as a distinct profession, and to focus public attention on the most outstanding achievements of environmental graphic designers. Member or non-member designers may submit entries in 12 categories. Project types include sign programs, store fronts, displays, exhibits, showrooms, banners, maps, directories, identity systems, public art, sign guidelines and standards, and interactive displays. The deadline for entry is January. Honor and Merit Awards are presented at the SEGD annual conference in May. Established in 1986.

• 18669 •
Society for Epidemiologic Research
PO Box 990
Clearfield, UT 84089
Phone: (801)525-0231
E-mail: membership@epiresearch.org
Home Page: http://www.epiresearch.org

• 18670 • **Abraham Lilienfeld Student Prize Paper**
To recognize unpublished work done by a student in an epidemiology program. A monetary prize of $200 is awarded annually in June. Established in 1970.

• 18671 •
Society for Ethnomusicology
Alan Burdette, Exec. Dir.
Morrison Hall 005
1165 E 3rd St.
Bloomington, IN 47405-3700
Phone: (812)855-6672
Fax: (812)855-6673
E-mail: semexec@indiana.edu
Home Page: http://www.ethnomusicology.org

• 18672 • Jaap Kunst Prize
To recognize the best published paper written by a member on ethnomusicology. Nomination deadline is April 1. A monetary award of $200 is presented annually if merited. Established in 1969.

• 18673 • Charles Seeger Prize
To recognize an outstanding paper on ethnomusicology written and presented at the annual meeting of the Society by a student. A monetary award of $200 and consideration for publication in the Society's journal *Ethnomusicology* is presented annually if merited. Established in 1970.

• 18674 • Klaus P. Wachsmann Prize for Advanced and Critical Essays in Organology
To recognize a major publication that advances the field of organology through the presentation of new data and by using innovative methods in the study of musical instruments. The publication may be a monograph, an article, a unified series of articles, or a video/electronic media item. Eligibility is restricted to any organological publication regarding a specific instrument, set of instruments, class of instruments, instruments of a particular culture, instruments in general, or organology as a whole. A monetary award of $300 is awarded biennially in even-numbered years. Established in 1984.

• 18675 •
Society for French Historical Studies
Jeremy D. Popkin, Exec. Dir.
University of Kentucky
Department of History, 1725 POT
Lexington, KY 40506-0027
Phone: (859)335-6254
Fax: (804)924-7891
E-mail: popkin@uky.edu
Home Page: http://www.h-france.net/sfhs

• 18676 • Gilbert Chinard Prize
For recognition of distinguished scholarly books or manuscripts in the history of themes shared by France and North, Central, and South America. Books must be published in North America during the preceding year. Historical studies in any area or period are acceptable, including critical editions of significant source materials. The deadline for entry is December 15. A monetary prize of $1,000 is awarded annually. Co-sponsored by the Institut Francais de Washington.

• 18677 •
Society for Historians of American Foreign Relations
Dept. of History
Ohio State Univ.
106 Dulles Hall.
230 W. 17th Ave.
Columbus, OH 43210
Phone: (614)292-1951
Phone: (614)292-7200
Fax: (614)292-2282
E-mail: shafr@osu.edu
Home Page: http://www.shafr.org

• 18678 • Stuart L. Bernath Book Prize
To recognize and encourage distinguished research and writing on U.S. foreign relations. To be eligible, a book must be the author's first, and it must be a history of international relations. Biographies of statesmen and diplomats are eligible. General surveys, autobiographies, editions of essays and documents, and works that represent social science disciplines other than history are not eligible. Nomination deadline is December 1. A monetary prize of $2,500 is awarded at the Organization of American Historians luncheon each year. Established in 1972 by Dr. and Mrs. Gerald J. Bernath in memory of their son, Stuart L. Bernath.

• 18679 • Stuart L. Bernath Lecture Prize
To recognize and encourage excellence in teaching and research in the field of foreign relations by younger scholars. Candidates must be under 41 years of age or within 10 years of the receipt of a PhD. Nomination deadline is February 28. A cash prize of $500, travel expenses of $500, and publication in *Diplomatic History* are awarded annually. Established in 1977 by Dr. and Mrs. Gerald J. Bernath in memory of their son, Stuart L. Bernath.

• 18680 • Stuart L. Bernath Scholarly Article Prize
To recognize and encourage distinguished research and writing by young scholars in the field of diplomatic relations. Articles on any topic in U.S. foreign relations published during the previous year are eligible. The author must be under 41 years of age or within 10 years of receiving a PhD at the time of publication. Nominations should be submitted by February 1. A monetary prize of $1,000 is awarded at the Organization of American Historians meeting each year. Established in 1977 by Dr. and Mrs. Gerald J. Bernath in memory of their son, Stuart L. Bernath.

• 18681 • Arthur S. Link Prize/Warren F. Kuehl Prize for Documentary Editing
To recognize and encourage analytical scholarly editing of documents, in appropriate published form, relevant to the history of U.S. foreign relations, policy, and diplomacy. The term "analytical" refers to the inclusion (in headnotes, footnotes, essays, etc.) of both appropriate historical background needed to establish the content of the documents, and interpretive historical commentaries based on scholarly research. Nomination deadline is November 15. Awarded biennially in odd-numbered years. Established in 1991 as the Arthur S. Link Prize; combined with the Warren F. Kuehl Prize in 2003.

• 18682 •
Society for Historical Archaeology
Sara F. Mascia, Sec.-Treas.
15245 Shady Grove Rd., Ste. 130
Rockville, MD 20850
Phone: (301)990-2454
Fax: (301)990-9771
E-mail: hq@sha.org
Home Page: http://www.sha.org

• 18683 • Award of Merit
Annual award of recognition.

• 18684 • Carol Ruppe Distinguished Service Award
Periodic award of recognition.

• 18685 • Harrington Award
Periodic award of recognition.

• 18686 • John L. Cotter Award
Periodic award of recognition.

• 18687 •
Society for History in the Federal Government
Donald P. Steury, Pres.
Box 14139, Benjamin Franklin Sta.
Washington, DC 20044
Phone: (703)613-1790
E-mail: richard.mcculley@nara.gov
Home Page: http://www.shfg.org

• 18688 • Henry Adams Prize
To encourage and recognize excellence in book-length publications relating to the history of the United States federal government. The award is for a narrative history, documentary history, edited collection of papers, or any other historical work of comparable scope. Books must be published in the year preceding the granting of the award. Nomination deadline is November 15. A framed certificate is awarded each year at the Society's annual spring meeting. Established in 1983 in memory of Henry Adams, author of the classic multi-volume, *History of the United States.*

• 18689 • Thomas Jefferson Prize
For recognition of achievement and contributions to the understanding of the history of the United States federal government in the fields of documentary editing and reference materials. The award recognizes documentary editions (a documentary history project) and reference materials (an index, finding aid, bibliography, or bibliographic dictionary) on alternate years. A certificate is awarded at the Society's annual spring meeting. Established in 1986 in memory of the third president of the United States, who strongly believed in the study of history and preservation of historical records.

• 18690 • James Madison Prize
For recognition of outstanding quality in an article or essay dealing with any aspect of the history of the United States federal government. Eligible entries should have been published during the year preceding the granting of the award. Nomination deadline is November 15. A certificate is awarded at the Society's annual spring meeting. Established in 1983 in memory of James Madison, author of some of the most significant short works on the history of the federal government.

• 18691 • John Wesley Powell Prize
For recognition of achievement in historical preservation and historical display as an activity of the federal government. Awards are given in alternate years for historic preservation and historical display. The award for historic preservation includes achievement in the preservation of records, artifacts, buildings, historic sites, or other historical materials. The award for historical display includes achievement in a museum exhibit, a historical movie, an audiovisual display, or any other form of visual historical presentation. A framed certificate is awarded at the Society's annual spring meeting. Established in 1986 in memory of the explorer and federal administrator whose work very early demonstrated the importance of historic preservation.

• 18692 • Franklin Delano Roosevelt Award
This, the Society's most prestigious service award, is given for recognition of outstanding contributions to the study of the federal government's history. Individuals who have a demonstrated record of outstanding accomplishments in such areas as historical publication, preservation, display, administration, or education are eligible. A citation and a plaque are awarded triennially. Established in 1983 in memory of Franklin Delano Roosevelt, thirty-second President of the United States.

• 18693 •
Society for Human Resource Management
David B. Hutchins, SR.V. Pres./CAO
1800 Duke St.
Alexandria, VA 22314-3499
Phone: (703)548-3440
Phone: (703)535-6078
Toll-Free: 800-283-7476
Fax: (703)535-6490
E-mail: shrm@shrm.org
Home Page: http://www.shrm.org

Formerly: (1989) American Society for Personnel Administration.

• 18694 • Award for Professional Excellence
To recognize individuals for creative approaches and consistently high performances within the profession of human resource management that benefit their organization as well as the business and professional community. Nominees must have at least ten years of experience as human resource professionals and may not have been retired more than one year. The deadline for applications is March 31. Awards are presented in the following categories based on the size of the organization: small (1,000 or fewer employees), medium (1,001 to 5,000 employees), and large (more than 5,000 employees). A crystal award is presented each year at the annual conference. Established in 1981.

• 18695 • Awards for Educational Excellence
To recognize an SHRM Chapter/State Council and an educator/educational system that have designed effective teaching methodologies or programs to prepare students in grades K through twelve to be workforce ready. The deadline for entry is June 1. A monetary prize of $1,000 is awarded annually to the winner or winners of each category.

• 18696 • Book Award
To recognize and identify new publications that help human resource professionals maintain high standards for themselves, their employers, employees, and the profession. Nominations must be postmarked by November 30. Awards are presented at the Society's annual conference. Established in 1974.

• 18697 • Leonard R. Brice Outstanding Student Leadership Award
To recognize and encourage the development of leadership skills in undergraduate students pursuing a career in human resource management. Candidates must be student members of the Society, be full-time students that have completed their sophomore year, have a satisfactory grade point average. Applications must be postmarked by February 1. A monetary award of $1,000 and a commemorative plaque are awarded each year at the SHRM Annual Conference. Established in 1970.

• 18698 • Capital Leadership Award
To recognize an individual who has provided outstanding leadership, motivation, and organizational skills to the development of a chapter or state legislative affairs program. Nominees must be state council directors, state legislative affairs directors, chapter presidents, chapter legislative representatives, or national SHRM key contacts. The deadline for nominations is April 30. A plaque of accomplishment, public recognition, and complimentary registration to the SHRM Legislative Conference in Washington DC are awarded annually.

• 18699 • Chapter Merit Awards for Professional Chapters
To recognize professional chapters of SHRM for their exceptional ability in operations, the professional development of chapter members, promotion of the profession, and support of SHRM in partnership. Chapters must submit chapter activity plan by January 31 to be considered. Plaques and recognition in SHRM publications and at conferences are awarded annually.

• 18700 • Chapter Merit Awards for Students
To recognize student chapters of SHRM for their exceptional ability in operations, the professional development of chapter members, promotion of the profession, and support of SHRM. Submissions must be postmarked no later than March 31. Plaques and recognition in SHRM publications and at conferences are awarded annually.

• 18701 • Ted Henry Student Research Award
To recognize SHRM students for original research in the broad field of human resource management. Undergraduate national SHRM student members are eligible. Applications must be postmarked by February 1. A monetary prize of $1,000 and a commemorative plaque are awarded at the annual conference.

• 18702 • Pinnacle Awards
To recognize outstanding achievements in chapter development and contributions to the advancement of effective human resource management. All SHRM chapters are eligible. The deadline for entries is October 1. A $1,000 grant is presented annually. Established in 1991.

• 18703 • SHRM Foundation Award for Graduate Student Research
To encourage graduate research in the human resource management field. Student members of SHRM are eligible. Entries must be postmarked no later than February 1. A monetary prize of $1,000 and a commemorative plaque are awarded at the annual conference.

• 18704 • SHRM Foundation Outstanding Graduate Student Award
To recognize the outstanding graduate student preparing to work in the human resource management field. Student members of SHRM are eligible. Applications must be postmarked no later than February 1. A monetary prize of $1,000 and a commemorative plaque are awarded at the annual conference.

• 18705 • Yoder-Heneman Human Resource Management Creative Application Awards
To recognize successful efforts in applying creative management concepts to improve performance, advance the profession, and promote better understanding of human resource management. SHRM members are eligible. Submissions must be postmarked no later than December 31. Awards are presented in three categories: small organization, medium organization, and large organization. Monetary awards of $500 each and plaques are awarded at the annual conference. Established in 1964. Formerly: Yoder-Heneman Personnel Creative Application Awards.

• 18706 • Yoder-Heneman Human Resource Management Research Award
To recognize the finest empirical research in human resource management. Submissions must be postmarked no later than December 31. A monetary award of $1,000 and a plaque are awarded at the annual conference. Established in 1964 in memory of two prominent scholars in the human resources field. Formerly: Yoder-Heneman Personnel Research Award.

• 18707 •
Society for Humanistic Judaism
M. Bonnie Cousens, Exec.Dir.
28611 W 12 Mile Rd.
Farmington Hills, MI 48334
Phone: (248)478-7610
Fax: (248)478-3159
E-mail: info@shj.org
Home Page: http://www.shj.org

• 18708 • Jewish Humanist Leadership Award
To acknowledge leaders of merit. Leaders are chosen by the leadership of the Society, possibly the keynote speaker. A personal testimonial is awarded periodically. Established in 1979.

• 18709 •
Society for Imaging Science and Technology
7003 Kilworth Ln.
Springfield, VA 22151
Phone: (703)642-9090
Fax: (703)642-9094
E-mail: info@imaging.org
Home Page: http://www.imaging.org

• 18710 • Raymond C. Bowman Award
For recognition of an individual who has been instrumental in fostering, encouraging, helping, and otherwise facilitating individuals, either young or adult, to pursue a career beginning with an appropriate education in the technical-scientific aspects of photography or the imaging sciences. Nomination deadline is January 1. A plaque is awarded annually if merited. Established in 1982. Sponsored by the Tri-State Chapter of the Society.

• 18711 • Chester F. Carlson Award
To recognize outstanding contributions in the science or technology of electrophotography or related electrostatic imaging systems. Contributions in theoretical understanding of mechanisms fundamental to the improvement of xerographic processes or materials would qualify. Inventions, discoveries, or architectural innovations pivotal to advancing the technology would also warrant consideration. Both members and nonmembers are eligible. Nomination deadline is January 1. A plaque is awarded annually. Established in 1985. Sponsored by Xerox Corp.

• 18712 • Fellowship
To recognize a regular member for outstanding achievement in imaging science or engineering. Nomination deadline is January 1. Fellowships are awarded to one or more recipients annually. Established in 1954.

• 18713 • Honorary Membership
This, the highest award bestowed by the Society, is given to recognize an outstanding contribution to the advancement of photographic science or engineering. Nomination deadline is January 1. Awarded annually. Established in 1954.

• 18714 • Itek Award
To recognize an outstanding original student publication in the field of imaging science or engineering. Both members and nonmembers are eligible. Nomination deadline is January 1. A monetary prize of $500 and a certificate are awarded annually. Established in 1968.

• 18715 • Charles E. Ives Journal Award (Engineering)
To recognize an outstanding original contribution relating to engineering that was published in the *Journal of Imaging Science and Technology* in the previous year. The article should be in the general area of engineering, and should be concerned with the successful application engineering principles to an imaging problem or with a technical problem solved photographically. Both members and non-members are eligible. Nomination deadline is January 1. A plaque and a certificate are awarded annually. Established in 1963.

• 18716 • Journal Award (Science)
To recognize an outstanding original contribution relating to basic science that was published in the *Journal of Imaging Science and Technology* in the previous year. The article should be in the general area of basic science and should be concerned with the discovery of new principles or of improved understanding of imaging phenomena. Both members and non-members are eligible. Nomination deadline is January 1. A plaque and a certificate are awarded annually. Established in 1958.

• 18717 • Kosar Memorial Award
For recognition of significant contributions in the area of unconventional photography or imaging. Nomination deadline is January 1. A plaque is awarded annually. Established in 1967. Sponsored by the Tri-State Chapter of the Society.

• 18718 • Lieven Gevaert Medal
To recognize outstanding contributions in the field of silver halide photography. Both members and nonmembers are eligible. Nomination deadline is January 1. A medal is awarded annually. Established in 1976 to honor Lievan Gevaert, founder of the Agfa-Gev Corporation. Sponsored by Agfa-Gavaert.

• 18719 • President's Citation
To recognize an individual who has made major contributions to the Society over an extended period of time. The Citation is awarded at the discretion of the President with the approval of the Executive Committee. Awarded when merited. Established in 1977.

• 18720 • Senior Membership
For recognition of long-term outstanding service to the Society on the national level. Nomination deadline is January 1. Awarded to one or more recipients each year. Established in 1958.

• 18721 • Service Award
To recognize an individual for service to a Chapter or to the Society, usually for one or more outstanding services of relatively short duration. Nomination deadline is January 1. A certificate is awarded to one or more recipients annually. Established in 1960.

• 18722 •
Society for In Vitro Biology
David W. Altman, Pres.
13000-F York Rd., No. 304
Charlotte, NC 28278
Phone: (704)588-1923
Toll-Free: 800-741-7476
Fax: (704)588-5193
E-mail: sivb@sivb.org
Home Page: http://www.sivb.org

Formerly: (1995) Tissue Culture Association, Inc..

• 18723 • Cellular Toxicology Graduate Student Award
To recognize a student in the field of cellular toxicology presenting an oral presentation or poster at the annual meeting of the Society for In Vitro Biology. A travel grant of up to $500 to attend the meeting and a certificate are awarded.

• 18724 • Wilton R. Earle Award
To recognize the student-author of the best paper involving tissue culture work presented at the Association's annual meeting. The honoree must be enrolled in a pre-doctorate training program and sponsored by a supervisor or department head to be eligible. A monetary award of $300 is presented annually. Established in 1970 in memory of Dr. Wilton R. Earle, an early vice-president of the Association (1952-54). In addition, the Society for In Vitro Biology Student Travel Awards of up to $500 each are presented to two students to enable them to attend the annual meeting and present a paper.

• 18725 • Honor B. Fell Student Award
To recognize a graduate student doing research in the general field of animal organ culture, demonstrating by presentation of papers at the annual meeting. A monetary prize of $150 is awarded. Established in 1978 to honor the late Honor B. Fell.

• 18726 • Hope E. Hopps Award
To recognize a quality student presentation at the annual meeting. A monetary prize of $200 is awarded. Established in memory of Hope E. Hopps, a vital force in the expansion of the Society (1956-88).

• 18727 • Joseph F. Morgan Award
To provide travel funds for Canadian students to attend the annual meetings of the Society in the amount of $100. Established in memory of Joseph F. Morgan, a long-time member and Canadian scientist who contributed to the art and science of in vitro biology.

• 18728 • John S. Song Award
To promote and stimulate graduate student participation at the annual meeting. The student must be involved in plant cell biology-related research and submit an abstract to be presented via platform or poster. A monetary award to cover travel and a per diem to attend and present a paper at the annual meeting are awarded. Formerly: (2006) John S. Song Foundation Award for Plant Tissue Culture.

• 18729 • Philip R. White Memorial Award
To encourage professional development by supplementing expenses of qualified individuals to continue their education in plant tissue culture. Applicants must be able to demonstrate interest, scholastic achievement, and need. Applications must be submitted by January 1. A stipend of up to $650 is awarded annually for training at an institution of the awardee's choice. Established in 1980 to honor Dr. Philip R. White, an eminent teacher and researcher in plant cell and tissue culture techniques, and an early president of the Society for In Vitro Biology (1956-58).

• 18730 •
Society for Industrial and Applied Mathematics
James Crowley, Exec.Dir.
3600 University City Science Center
Philadelphia, PA 19104-2688
Phone: (215)382-9800
Toll-Free: 800-447-SIAM
Fax: (215)386-7999
E-mail: siam@siam.org
Home Page: http://www.siam.org

• 18731 • George David Birkhoff Prize
To recognize an outstanding contribution to applied mathematics in the highest and broadest sense. Members of the American Mathematical Society and/or SIAM who are residents of the United States, Canada, or Mexico are eligible. A monetary prize of $4,000 and a framed certificate are awarded triennially. Established in 1967. Co-sponsored by the American Mathematical Society in honor of Professor George David Birkhoff.

• 18732 • I. E. Block Community Lecture Series
To offer the opportunity for a mathematician to deliver a lecture at every annual meeting that deals with topics such as emerging areas of applied mathematics, opportunities for mathematical and computational analysis in the solution of important industrial and societal problems, strengthening the ties between mathematics and its applications, and the education of applied mathematics. The lecturer's travel expenses to the annual meeting will be paid by SIAM. Established in 1994 to honor I. Edward Block for his relentless efforts to promote and nourish mathematics and its applications.

• 18733 • Germund Dahlquist Prize
To recognize a young scientist (normally less than 45 years old) for original contributions to fields associated with Germund Dahlquist, especially the numerical solution of differential equations and numerical methods of scientific computing. The award includes a certificate containing the citation and a cash prize plus reasonable travel costs to the meeting at which the prize is awarded. Awarded biennially in odd-numbered years at one of the SciCADE conferences, ICIAM conference, or SIAM annual meeting. Established in 1995.

• 18734 • George B. Dantzig Prize
To recognize original work which, by its breadth and scope, constitutes an outstanding contribution to the field of mathematical programming. The contributions must be publicly available and may belong to any aspect of mathematical programming in its broadest sense. Preference is given to candidates under the age of 50. A monetary prize and a certificate are presented triennially. Established in 1979. Co-sponsored by the Mathematical Programming Society.

• 18735 • Richard C. DiPrima Prize
To recognize a young scientist who has done outstanding research in applied mathematics (defined as those topics covered by SIAM journals). Eligible candidates, who may or may not be members of SIAM, must have completed his or her doctoral dissertation and all other requirements for the doctorate during the period running from three years prior to the award date to one year prior to the award date. A monetary prize of $1,000 and framed certificate are awarded biennially in even-numbered years. Established in 1986 in memory of Richard C. DiPrima, a former president of SIAM.

• 18736 • Linear Algebra Prize
To recognize the author(s) of the most outstanding paper on a topic in applicable linear algebra published in English in a peer-reviewed journal. They must contain significant research contributions to the field of linear algebra, as commonly defined in the mathematical literature, with direct or potential applications. A plaque and certificate are awarded every three years at the SIAM Conference on Applied Linear Algebra. Established in 1987.

• 18737 • Mathematical Contest in Modeling
To recognize two teams judged best in the annual Mathematical Contest in Modeling (MCM). One winning team is chosen for each of two problems posed in the MCM. Teams competing in the MCM that are awarded the highest performance ranking (outstanding) by the official contest judges are eligible. Each of the three student members of the winning team receives a cash award of $300 and a one-year student membership in SIAM; up to $500 in travel expenses to attend the meeting is also awarded. A one-year membership in SIAM is awarded to non-winning teams judged outstanding in the official contest. Awarded annually. Established in 1988.

• 18738 • Frank and Brennie Morgan Prize for Outstanding Research in Mathematics by an Undergraduate Student
To recognize an undergraduate student (or students having submitted joint work) for outstanding research in mathematics. Any student who is an undergraduate in a college or university in Canada, Mexico, or the U.S. or its possessions is eligible. The annual award includes a $1,000 cash prize and a certificate. Established in 1995. Co-sponsored by the American Mathematical Society and the Mathematical Association of America.

• 18739 • George Polya Prize
To recognize (1) a notable application of combinatorial theory, or (2) a notable contribution in another area of interest to George Polya, such as approximation theory, complex analysis, number theory, orthogonal polynomials, probability theory, or mathematical discovery and learning. The prize alternates between the two categories. A monetary award of $20,000, an engraved bronze medal, and travel expenses are presented biennially in even-numbered years. Established in 1969.

• 18740 • Prize for Distinguished Service to the Profession
To recognize an applied mathematician who has made distinguished contributions to the furtherance of applied mathematics on the national level. Any member of the scientific community is eligible. A certificate and travel expenses to attend the award ceremony are awarded annually. Established in 1985.

• 18741 • W. T. and Idalia Reid Prize in Mathematics
To recognize research in, or other contributions to, the areas of differential equations and control theory. Notable achievement(s) by a member of the scientific community are the basis for selection. The award consists of a cash prize, an engraved medal, and travel expenses to attend the award ceremony at which the award is presented. Awarded annually. Established in 1994.

• 18742 • SIAM Activity Group on Optimization Prize
To recognize the author(s) of the most outstanding paper on a topic in optimization published in English in a peer-reviewed journal. Significant research contributions to the field of linear algebra, as commonly defined in the mathematical literature, with direct or potential applications published during the three years preceding the award are considered. A plaque and certificate are awarded every three years at SIAM Conference on Optimization. Established in 1992.

• 18743 • Student Paper Prize
To recognize the student authors of the three outstanding papers submitted to the SIAM Student Paper Competition. This award is based solely on the merit and content of the submitted papers, which must not have been previously published or submitted for publication. Eligibility is restricted to students in good standing who have not received their Ph.D. at the time of

submitting their entry. A framed certificate, cash award of $1,000, and travel expenses of $500 are presented to each winner. Awarded annually. Established in 1992.

• 18744 • Student Travel Awards
To encourage attendance at SIAM conferences/meeting by supporting travel and expenses incurred by students. Top priority is given to students presenting papers or receiving awards at the meeting. Second priority is given to students who are co-authors of papers given at the meeting. Any full-time student in good standing is eligible to receive an award. Awarded to one or more recipients annually. Established in 1992.

• 18745 • Theodore von Karman Prize
To recognize a notable application of mathematics to mechanics and/or the engineering sciences made during the five to ten years preceding the award. The award may be given either for a single notable achievement or for a collection of such achievements. The prize is normally awarded to a member of SIAM, but it may be awarded to a non-member. A monetary award of $1,000, a framed certificate, and travel expenses to the SIAM annual meeting are awarded every fifth year. The recipient presents a lecture at the award ceremony, and this lecture is then published in *SIAM Review*. Established in 1968.

• 18746 • John von Neumann Lecture
To recognize an individual for outstanding and distinguished contributions to the field of applied mathematical sciences and for the effective communication of these ideas to the community. Any member of the scientific community is eligible. An honorarium of $3,000 is awarded annually. The recipient presents the John von Neumann Lecture that surveys and evaluates a significant contribution to mathematics and its applications; a manuscript representing the lecture is required for publication in *SIAM Review*. Established in 1959.

• 18747 • Norbert Wiener Prize
To recognize outstanding contributions to applied mathematics in the highest and broadest sense. The recipient must be a member of SIAM and/or the American Mathematical Society and a resident of the United States, Mexico, or Canada. A monetary prize of $4,000 is awarded triennially. Established in 1967 with funds donated by the Department of Mathematics of the Massachusetts Institute of Technology in honor of Professor Norbert Wiener, the American mathematician and cyberneticist. Co-sponsored by the American Mathematical Society.

• 18748 • James H. Wilkinson Prize in Numerical Analysis and Scientific Computing
To stimulate younger contributors and to help them in their research. Selection is based on research in, or other contributions to, numerical analysis and scientific computing during the six years preceding the award. There are no eligibility restrictions. A monetary award of $1,000 and an engraved plaque are awarded every fourth year, normally at the SIAM annual meeting. Established in 1979. Formerly: (1987) SIAM Prize in Numerical Analysis and Scientific Computing.

• 18749 •
Society for Industrial and Organizational Psychology
Mr. David Nershi CAE, Exec.Dir.
PO Box 87
Bowling Green, OH 43402-0087
Phone: (419)353-0032
Fax: (419)352-2645
E-mail: siop@siop.org
Home Page: http://www.siop.org

• 18750 • Distinguished Early Career Contributions Award
This award is given to and individual who has made distinguished contributions to the science and/or practice of I-O psychology within seven (7) years of receiving the PhD degree. In order to be considered for the 2005 award, nominees must have defended their dissertation no earlier than 1998. The recipient of the award is given a plaque and a cash prize of $1000. In addition, the recipient is invited to give an address that relates to his or her contribution at the subsequent meeting of SIOP. Formerly: (2003) Earnest J. McCormick Award for Distinguished Early Career Contributions.

• 18751 • Distinguished Professional Contributions Award
To recognize an individual society member who has developed, refined, and implemented practices, procedures, and methods that have had a major impact on both people in organizational settings and the profession of industrial and organizational psychology. The contributions of the individual should have advanced the profession by increasing the effectiveness of industrial and organizational psychologists working in business, industry, government, and other organizational settings. Members are eligible. A monetary award of $1000 and a plaque are presented annually. Recipient is invited to make an address at the subsequent SIOP conference.

• 18752 • Distinguished Scientific Contributions Award
In recognition of outstanding contributions to the science of industrial and organizational psychology. This award is given to the individual society member who has made the most distinguished empirical and/or theoretical scientific contributions to the field of industrial and organizational psychology. The setting in which the nominee made the contribution (i.e. industry, academia, government) is not relevant. A monetary award of $1000 and a plaque are presented annually. Recipient is invited to make an address at the next SIOP conference.

• 18753 • Distinguished Service Contributions Award
In recognition of sustained, significant, and outstanding service to the Society. The Service contributions can be made in a variety of ways which include but are not limited to serving as 1. an elected officer of the Society, 2. a member of a standing or ad hoc committee, and 3. a formal representative of the Society to other organizations. A monetary award of $1000 and a plaque are presented annually.

• 18754 • John C. Flanagan Award
To recognize the best poster written solely or first authored by a student member. A $1,000 prize and a plaque are awarded annually.

• 18755 • M. Scott Myers Award for Applied Research in the Workplace
To recognize an individual practitioner or team of practitioners who have developed and conducted/applied a specific project or product representing an example of outstanding practice of I-O psychology in the workplace (e.g., business, industry, government). Projects must have been conducted in the workplace within the last 40 years and cover a time period of no more than 8 years. Products (e.g., tests, questionnaires, videos, software, but not books or articles) must be used in the workplace and developed within the last 40 years. Projects or products may be in any area of I-O psychology (e.g., compensation, employee relations, equal employment opportunity, human factors, job analysis, job design, organizational development, organizational behavior, leadership, position classification, safety, selection, training). Recipient(s) will receive a plaque, a cash prize of $1,500, and an invitation to make a presentation at the annual conference of SIOP. Awarded annually.

• 18756 • William A. Owens Scholarly Achievement Award
In recognition of the best publication in the field of industrial and organizational psychology during the past full year. This annual award, honoring William A. Owens, is given to the author(s) of the publication in a refereed journal judged to have the highest potential to significantly impact the field of I-O psychology. A plaque and monetary prize of $1,500 are awarded annually.

• 18757 • S. Rains Wallace Dissertation Award
In recognition of the best doctoral dissertation research in the field of industrial and organizational psychology. The winning dissertation should demonstrate the use of research methods that are both rigorous and creative. A monetary award of $1000 and a plaque are presented annually. Recipient is invited to present the research as a poster at the next SIOP conference.

• 18758 • Robert J. Wherry Award
To recognize an individual society member who presents the best research paper presented at the annual Industrial and Organizational Psychology and Organizational Behavior Graduate Student Convention. A monetary prize of $250 and a plaque are awarded at the annual meeting of the Society.

• 18759 •
Society for Industrial Microbiology
Demetra Pavlidis, Exec.Dir.
3929 Old Lee Hwy., Ste. 92A
Fairfax, VA 22030-2421
Phone: (703)691-3357
Fax: (703)691-7991
E-mail: info@simhq.org
Home Page: http://www.simhq.org

• 18760 • **Fellowship**
To recognize significant research and/or service contributions to the profession of applied microbiology. A sustained record of such contributions (nominee's excellence in microbial research and any contributions made in administrative, academic, industrial governmental, military, or public health positions) while a member of the society is the main criterion for fellowship. Nominee must have been an SIM member for five years and been employed professionally for at least 10 years. Awarded when merited. Established in 1984.

• 18761 • **Charles Porter Award**
For recognition of outstanding and sustained service to the Society. The nominee must be a member for at least 10 years and have an outstanding record of service to the society over a period of 7 years or more, including service as a SIM officer, chair of committee, or an outstanding record in a key assignment combined with other service to the Society. The deadline for nominations is March 1. Awarded annually. Established in 1960.

• 18762 • **Charles Thom Award**
For recognition of outstanding contribution(s) to research in industrial microbiology and/or biotechnology. These contributions should reflect independence of thought and add appreciably to scientific knowledge in either a basic or applied sense. Activities include journal editing, organizing and chairing conferences, and serving scientific societies in official capacities. Nominations by members are accepted by March 1. Awarded annually. Established in 1967.

• 18763 • **Waksman Outstanding Teaching Award**
To recognize an active full-time professor for excellence and dedication to teaching microbiology at a recognized institution of higher education for a minimum of 10 years. He or she shall have an active involvement in research in his or her teaching field and also be contributing to research that leads to advances in his or her career of industrial or applied microbiology or biotechnology. Individuals nominated by three previous students, graduate students, or postdoctoral students are eligible. A monetary award of $1,000, a plaque, and expenses paid to attend the annual meeting are awarded annually. Established in 1989.

• 18764 •
Society for Information Display
Jenny Needham, Data Mgr.
610 S 2nd St.
San Jose, CA 95112
Phone: (408)977-1013
Fax: (408)977-1531
E-mail: office@sid.org
Home Page: http://www.sid.org

• 18765 • **Karl Ferdinand Braun Prize**
To recognize outstanding technical achievement in, or contribution to, display technology. The award is made by the Board of Directors acting on the recommendation of the Honors and Awards Committee and carries a cash stipend of $2,000. Established in 1987.

• 18766 • **Fellow**
To recognize outstanding qualifications and experience of a scientist or engineer in the field of information display. Individuals who have been members of the Society for five years and have made widely recognized and significant contributions to the advancement of the field are eligible. Nominations by October 1 must be supported by five members in good standing. A citation is presented annually to one or more recipients. Established in 1963.

• 18767 • **Fellows of the SID**
Conferred by the Board of Directors, based on the recommendation of the Honors and Awards Committee, upon a SID member of outstanding qualifications and experience as a scientist or engineer in the field of information display. The candidate shall have been a member of the Society for five years and shall have made a widely recognized and significant contribution to the advancement of information display. The nomination must be supported and signed by at least five members in good standing.

• 18768 • **Johann Gutenberg Prize**
To recognize outstanding technical achievement in, or contribution to, printer technology. A stipend of $2,000 is awarded annually. Established in 1967.

• 18769 • ***JSID* Outstanding Student Paper of the Year Award**
To recognize the best manuscripts written by students and published in the *Jounal of the Society for Information Display (JSID)* during the year. Manuscripts are evaluated on the basis of originality, significance of results, organization, and clarity. A monetary award of $2,000 and a plaque are awarded annually. Established in 1986.

• 18770 • **Jan Rajchman Prize**
To recognize outstanding scientific or technical achievement in, or contribution to, research on flat-panel displays. The Award is made by the Board of Directors acting on the recommendation of the Honors and Awards Committee and carries a stipend of $2,000. Established in 1993. Sponsored by Sharp Corporation.

• 18771 • **Special Recognition Awards**
To recognize distinguished and valued contributions to the information display field by members of the technical, scientific, and business communities. Recipients need not be SID members. Awards may be made for contributions in one or more of the following categories: outstanding technical accomplishments, outstanding contributions to the literature, and outstanding service to the Society. Nomination deadline is October 1. A special citation is presented annually to one or more recipients. Established in 1972.

• 18772 • **Lewis and Beatrice Winner Award**
To recognize members for exceptional and sustained service to the Society. Nominations must be submitted by October 1. Awarded when merited. Established in 1983.

• 18773 •
Society for Integrative and Comparative Biology
Brett J. Burk, Exec.Dir.
1313 Dolley Madison Blvd., Ste. 402
McLean, VA 22101-3926
Phone: (703)790-1745
Toll-Free: 800-955-1236
Fax: (703)790-2672
E-mail: sicb@burkinc.com
Home Page: http://www.sicb.org

Formerly: American Society of Zoologists.

• 18774 • **Best Student Paper**
To recognize the best paper presented at the annual meeting. Reports based on work done by a graduate student that written within 12 months of completing the degree are eligible. Two awards will be given each year to students who have not yet been awarded a PH.D. Travel funds are awarded.

• 18775 •
Society for International Hockey Research
Len Kotylo, Pres.
415 Yonge St., Ste. 702
Toronto, ON, Canada M5B 2E7
Phone: (416)585-9373
Fax: (416)585-9376
E-mail: info@sihrhockey.org
Home Page: http://www.sihrhockey.org

• 18776 • **Brian MacFarlane Award**
Recognizes the writer of outstanding published work on the history of hockey. Awarded annually.

• 18777 •
Society for Investigative Dermatology
Angela Welsh, Exec.Dir.
820 W Superior Ave., 7th Fl.
Cleveland, OH 44113-1800
Phone: (216)579-9300
Fax: (216)579-9333
E-mail: welsh@sidnet.org
Home Page: http://www.sidnet.org

• 18778 • Stephen Rothman Memorial Award
This, the Society's highest honor, is given for recognition of distinguished service to investigative cutaneous medicine based on major achievements in the scientific field, contributions in teaching, and/or recruitment of outstanding people to dermatology. The recipient should be an individual who has distinctly altered the course and image of dermatology or its allied fields. A monetary award of $1,000 and a gold medal are presented annually when merited. Established in 1966 in honor of Stephen Rothman, M.D., Professor and Chairman of the Department of Dermatology, University of Chicago School of Medicine.

• 18779 •
Society for Italian Historical Studies
Prof. Alan J. Reinerman, Exec.Sec.-Treas.
Boston College
Dept. of History
Chestnut Hill, MA 02467
Phone: (617)552-3814
Fax: (617)552-2478
E-mail: pskclk@cfl.rr.com
Home Page: http://faculty.valenciacc.edu/ckillinger/sihs

• 18780 • Citation for Career Achievement
To recognize an individual for contributions to Italian history over the course of a career. Senior scholars who are citizens or permanent residents of the United States or Canada are eligible. A citation is awarded annually when merited. Established in 1963.

• 18781 • Helen and Howard R. Marraro Prize
For recognition of a distinguished and scholarly work, of book or essay length, dealing with Italian history on any epoch, Italian cultural history, or Italian-American relations. Authors must be resident citizens of the United States or Canada. A monetary prize of $500 is awarded annually. Established in 1973 by a bequest of the late Howard R. Marraro.

• 18782 •
Society for Judgement and Decision Making
Bud Fennema, Sec.-Treas.
Florida State University
College of Business
4202 E. Fowler Ave., PCD 4118G
Tallahassee, FL 32306-1110
Phone: (850)644-8231
Fax: (850)644-8234
E-mail: bfennema@garnet.acns.fsu.edu
Home Page: http://www.sjdm.org

• 18783 • Einhorn New Investigator Award
Recognizes a promising new research in the field. Awarded semiannually.

• 18784 •
Society for Leukocyte Biology
Debbie Weinstein PhD, Exec.Mgr.
9650 Rockville Pike
Bethesda, MD 20814
Phone: (301)634-7810
Toll-Free: 800-433-2732
Fax: (301)634-7813
E-mail: slb@faseb.org
Home Page: http://www.leukocytebiology.org

Formerly: (1988) Reticuloendothelial Society.

• 18785 • Marie T. Bonazinga Award
Recognizes excellence in research relating to the biology of the macrophage. A monetary prize of $3,000 and a plaque are awarded annually. Established in 1980.

• 18786 • Honorary Life Member
To recognize individuals for contributions to the knowledge of leukocyte biology.

• 18787 • Presidential Student/Post-Doctoral Award
Recognizes the best papers presented by students in training. Graduate or post-doctoral student presentations are eligible. A monetary prize and a plaque are awarded annually. Established in 1978. Formerly: Presidential Award of the RES - Annie R. Beasley Memorial Award.

• 18788 • Young Investigator Award
Recognizes the best paper by an investigator under the age of 36.

• 18789 •
Society for Marketing Professional Services
Ronald D. Worth, CEO
99 Canal Ctr. Plz., Ste. 330
Alexandria, VA 22314
Phone: (703)549-6117
Toll-Free: 800-292-7677
Fax: (703)549-2498
E-mail: info@smps.org
Home Page: http://www.smps.org

• 18790 • Chapter President Award
Annual award of recognition.

• 18791 • Design Awards
Annual award of recognition.

• 18792 • Marketing Achievement Award
Annual award of recognition.

• 18793 •
Society for Medical Decision Making
Aileen Cummings, Admin.Dir.
100 N 20th St.,4th Flr.
Philadelphia, PA 19103
Phone: (215)545-7697
Fax: (215)545-8107
E-mail: smdm-office@lists.smdm.org
Home Page: http://www.smdm.org

• 18794 • Career Achievement Award
Annual award of recognition.

• 18795 • Distinguished Service Award
Annual award of recognition.

• 18796 • Lee B. Lusted Student Prizes
For outstanding research presented at the SMDM annual meeting. A grant is awarded annually.

• 18797 • Outstanding Short Course
Award of recognition.

• 18798 • Young Investigator Award
Annual grant.

• 18799 •
Society for Military History
Dr. Robert H. Berlin, Dir.
3119 Lakeview Cir.
Leavenworth, KS 66048
Phone: (913)684-3365
Fax: (913)758-3309
E-mail: rhberlin@aol.com
Home Page: http://www.smh-hq.org

Formerly: American Military Institute.

• 18800 • Distinguished Book Award
To recognize the best book-length publication in English, copyrighted in the previous three calendar years in the field of military history. Two awards are presented annually: one in American military history and one in non-American military history. A monetary prize of $250 and a plaque accompanies each award. Occasionally, a third award will be made for an anthology reference work, or edition. Established in 1983.

• 18801 • Victor Gondos Memorial Service Award
To recognize long, distinguished, or particularly outstanding service to the Society for Military History. Members are eligible. A plaque is awarded annually. Established in 1983.

• 18802 • Moncado Prizes for Best Article
To recognize the authors of the four best articles in each volume of *The Journal of Military History*, formerly *Military Affairs*, during the previous calendar year. Monetary prizes of $100 and certificates are awarded annually. Established in 1958.

• 18803 • Samuel Eliot Morison Prize
To recognize a body of contributions in the field of military history extending over time and reflecting a spectrum of scholarly activity contributing significantly to the field. A monetary prize of $250 and a plaque are awarded annually. Established in 1983.

• 18804 •
Society for Mining, Metallurgy, and Exploration
Edith Yoder, Division and Local Section Coordinator
8307 Shaffer Pky.
Littleton, CO 80127-4102
Phone: (303)973-9550
Phone: (303)948-4210
Toll-Free: 800-763-3132
Fax: (303)973-3845
E-mail: sme@smenet.org
Home Page: http://www.smenet.org

• 18805 • A. Frank Alsobrook Industrial Minerals Distinguished Service Award
Recognizes members who have significantly contributed to the working of SME and the Industrial Minerals Division; and have an outstanding reputation for professionalism and accomplishments. A plaque is awarded annually by the Industrial Minerals Division. Established in 1995.

• 18806 • Coal and Energy Division Distinguished Service Award
To honor individuals for achievement in the coal mining industry. A plaque is awarded annually. Established in 1989.

• 18807 • Ben F. Dickerson Award
To recognize professionalism and contributions to the mining industry. A statuette is awarded annually by the Mining & Exploration Division. Established in 1987.

• 18808 • Distinguished Member Award
To recognize members who have demonstrated significant and sustained contributions to the minerals industry and to the Society. Outstanding service to SME may be to a section, a region, a technical division, committees, or as a representative of SME and the industry to the public. Outstanding contributions to the industry may be as a leader in exploration, production, manufacturing, environment, basic sciences, engineering applications, education, management, or public relations. Nomination deadline is December 1. An inscribed certificate in the form of a plaque is awarded to one or more recipients each year. Established in 1975.

• 18809 • Robert M. Dreyer Award in Applied Economic Geology
Recognizes outstanding achievements in applied economic geology. Achievements must have been accomplished through commercial exploration or development of metalliferous and/or non-metalliferous mineral deposits. A Baccarat Crystal on a base, a monetary award, and travel expenses to the annual meeting are awarded annually. Established in 1999.

• 18810 • Howard N. Eavenson Award
To recognize distinguished contributions to the advancement of coal mining whether by research, invention, publication, or advances in mining or development methods. Nominees must be U.S. citizens who may or may not be members of the Society. A monetary award and certificate are awarded annually. Established in 1968.

• 18811 • Antoine M. Gaudin Award
For recognition of specific engineering or scientific achievements that have furthered understanding of the technology of mineral processing. Eligible areas for contributions are agglomeration, classification, communication, electrical and magnetic separation, flocculation and sedimentation, froth flotation, hydrometallurgy, particulate behavior, and other related mineral processing operations. A plaque is awarded annually. Established in 1975.

• 18812 • GEM Awards
To recognize outstanding contributions to the SME GEM program by an individual, local section, or student chapter. An awarded is presented to a recipient in each category annually. Established in 1978.

• 18813 • Hal Williams Hardinge Award
To recognize outstanding achievement in the field of industrial minerals. A plaque and citation are awarded annually by the Industrial Minerals Division. Established in 1958.

• 18814 • Industrial Minerals Young Scientist Award
To bring recognition of scientific professionalism to young people working in the industrial minerals industry. Recipients must be under the age of 35, hold at least a baccalaureate degree, and be working in the industrial minerals industry. The award consists of an inscribed plaque, a stipend of $250 to help defray expenses while attending the Annual Meeting, and paid registration and tickets for the Meeting and IndMD Luncheon. Awarded annually by the Industrial Minerals Division. Established in 1985.

• 18815 • Daniel C. Jackling Award
For significant contributions to technical progress in mining, geology, and geophysics. A plaque and a citation are awarded annually. Established in 1953.

• 18816 • M & E Outstanding Young Professional Award
Recognizes the meritorious accomplishments of a young individual working in the mining and exploration industry, including related academic and governmental careers. A plaque is awarded annually by the Mining and Exploration Division. Established in 1996.

• 18817 • Mining and Exploration Division Distinguished Service Award
To recognize outstanding contributions to the Mining and Exploration Division. A plaque is awarded annually. Established in 1985.

• 18818 • MPD Outstanding Young Engineer Award
To recognize significant contributions of a young individual within the mineral processing/extractive discipline. Nominees must be graduate engineers working in the mineral processing/extractive industry; be under the age of 36; and be members of the Mineral and Metallurgical Processing Division (MPD) of the Society. A plaque is awarded annually. Established in 1984.

• 18819 • Percy W. Nicholls Award
To recognize notable scientific or industrial achievement in the field of solid fuels. Nominees must be members of SMME and/or the American Society of Mechanical Engineers. A certificate is awarded annually. Established in 1942.

• 18820 • Outstanding Student Chapter Award
For recognition of the Student Chapter that has brought together mineral engineering students to build a broad-based understanding of the industry and a sense of unity and identity with their peers. Selection is based on the Annual Report of the chapter. Entries must be postmarked by November 1. A monetary award of $500 is presented annually.

• 18821 • Robert Peele Memorial Award
For recognition of the most outstanding paper on a mining, geology, or geophysics subject by an SME member under the age of 35. A plaque and a citation are awarded annually. Established in 1953.

• 18822 • President's Citation
For recognition of a significant individual contribution culminating in the year of tenure of the selecting President of the Society. A framed certificate and citation are awarded when merited. Established in 1978.

• 18823 • Ivan B. Rahn Education Award
Recognizes distinguished contributions to the educational activities within SME. Open to members who have shown long term interest in and have significantly contributed to SME activities relating to ABET, student affairs, continuing education, professional registration, and/or the Council of Education. Applicants do not have to actually be educators. A statuette with an engraved inscription is awarded annually. Established in 1995.

• 18824 • Robert H. Richards Award
To recognize achievement in any form that unmistakably furthers the art of mineral beneficiation in any of its branches. A citation and sterling silver Vanning Dish are awarded annually by the Mineral and Metallurgical Processing Division. Established in 1950.

• 18825 • **Rock Mechanics Award**
For recognition of distinguished contributions to the advancement of the field of rock mechanics. Nominees may be of any age, nationality, or professional field, and need not be members of SME. A plaque and citation are awarded annually. Established in 1967.

• 18826 • **Stefanko Best Paper Award**
To recognize authors presenting papers in the Coal Division technical sessions at the SME Annual Meeting for contributions to the body of knowledge. A monetary award and certificate are awarded annually to one or more recipients.

• 18827 • **Arthur F. Taggart Award**
For recognition of the most notable paper or series of closely related papers with at least one common author in the area of minerals processing. Nominees must be members of SME. A plaque and a citation are awarded annually. Established in 1970.

• 18828 • **Milton E. Wadsworth Award**
To recognize distinguished contributions that advance the understanding of the science and technology of nonferrous chemical metallurgy. A plaque and citation are awarded annually by the Mineral and Metallurgical Processing Division. Established in 1992.

• 18829 • **J. W. Woomer Award**
For recognition of engineering professionalism of young people working in the coal industry. Nominees must be graduate engineers working in the coal industry; be under the age of 35; have prepared a technical report for presentation at any coal industry meeting or publication in any coal industry journal; and be members of SME. The deadline for nominations is July 1. Awarded annually. Established in 1976. Formerly: Young Engineer Award.

• 18830 •
Society for Pediatric Dermatology
Pat Fraser, Admin.
5422 N Bernard
Chicago, IL 60625
Phone: (773)583-9780
Fax: (773)583-9765
E-mail: patrici107@aol.com
Home Page: http://www.pedsderm.net

• 18831 • **Pediatric Dermatology Fellows/Residents Research Award**
To foster clinical or laboratory research projects relating to pediatric dermatology. Any resident or fellow in pediatrics or dermatology (M.D., D.O.) may apply. A $500 honorarium and expenses to attend the annual meeting are awarded annually. Established in 1984.

• 18832 • **Pediatric Dermatology Research Grant**
To provide for scholarly clinical or basic research in the field of pediatric dermatology. Any licensed physician (M.D., D.O.) is eligible. A monetary grant of up to $15,000 is awarded annually. Established in 1976.

• 18833 •
Society for Range Management
Samuel W. Albrecht, Exec.VP
445 Union Blvd., Ste. 230
Lakewood, CO 80228
Phone: (303)986-3309
Fax: (303)986-3892
E-mail: info@rangelands.org
Home Page: http://www.rangelands.org/

• 18834 • **W. R. Chapline Land Stewardship Award**
To recognize exceptional landowners, managers, administrators, and counselors in the field of range management and supporting disciplines. A plaque and honorarium are awarded annually.

• 18835 • **W. R. Chapline Research Award**
To encourage and maintain sustained research related to maintenance and restoration of rangeland. Open to SRM members. A plaque and honorarium are awarded annually.

• 18836 • **Distinguished Service Award**
To recognize outstanding accomplishment in any range-related area. Award is granted in special circumstances to recognize truly exemplary service to the profession of range management. Open to non-SRM members. Awarded to one or more recipients annually.

• 18837 • **Outstanding Young Range Professional Award**
To recognize outstanding potential and promise in their range management careers. Open to SRM members who have not reached their 35th birthday prior to January 1 of the next year. Awarded annually to one or more recipients.

• 18838 • **Sustained Lifetime Achievement Award**
To recognize SRM members for long-term contributions to SRM and range management. This is intended for "old-timers" who have never been previously recognized for their efforts. Awarded annually to one or more recipients.

• 18839 •
Society for Sedimentary Geology
Dr. Howard Harper, Exec.Dir.
6128 E 38th St., No. 308
Tulsa, OK 74135-5814
Phone: (918)610-3361
Toll-Free: 800-865-9765
Fax: (918)621-1685
E-mail: hharper@sepm.org
Home Page: http://www.sepm.org

Formerly: (1989) Society of Economic Paleontologists and Mineralogists.

• 18840 • **Best Paper in the *Journal of Sedimentary Research* Award**
To recognize an outstanding paper in the *Journal of Sedimentary Research* that stimulates interest in clearly presenting new ideas and techniques, gives support to conclusions, and contains superior illustrations. A plaque is awarded annually. Established in 1953.

• 18841 • **Distinguished Service Award**
For recognition of outstanding and sustained service to SEPM. Individuals promoting the objectives of SEPM through administration and overall dedication, in contrast to scientific achievements, are eligible. A free-form sculptured crystal mounted on an ebony base with silver plate inscription plate is awarded when merited. Established in 1974.

• 18842 • **Excellence of Poster Presentation Award**
To recognize an outstanding paper on the basis of originality, presentation, content, and quality of illustrations. A plaque is awarded annually. Established in 1958. Formerly: Outstanding Paper Presented at Convention.

• 18843 • **Honorary Membership**
To recognize persons of distinguished achievement in a scientific discipline of significance to SEPM. Candidates must be active members of the Society. A plaque and lifetime membership in SEPM are awarded annually. Established in 1930.

• 18844 • **Raymond C. Moore Medal for Paleontology**
To recognize a significant record of outstanding contributions in paleontology. Those aspects of paleontology that bear on a major objective of SEPM, such as promoting the science of stratigraphy through research in paleontology and evolution, are especially considered. Nominees can be of any nationality, and need not be members of SEPM. A bronze medal is awarded annually. Established in 1978. Formerly: .

• 18845 • **Outstanding Paper Award in *Palaios***
To recognize a paper appearing in *Palaios* that stimulates interest in clearly presenting new ideas and techniques, gives support to conclusions, and contains superior illustrations. A plaque is presented annually. Established in 1986.

• 18846 • **Francis J. Pettijohn Medal**
In recognition of excellence in the profession of sedimentary geology, including all aspects of sedimentology and stratigraphy. A medal is awarded annually. Established in 1990.

• 18847 • **Francis P. Shepard Medal for Marine Geology**
To recognize excellence in marine geology, especially in the fields of distribution and characteristics of the sediments, marine geomorphology, and structure at continental margins of the

world. The award is not limited to published work. A bronze medal is awarded annually. Established in 1966. Formerly: Francis P. Shepard Medal for Excellence in Marine Geology.

• 18848 • **Twenhofel Medal**
This, the highest award of SEPM, is given to recognize outstanding contributions to sedimentary geology, i.e., paleontology, sedimentology, stratigraphy, and/or allied disciplines. The contribution should include extensive personal research, but may involve a combination of research, teaching, administration, or other activities that have notably advanced scientific knowledge of sedimentary geology. Individuals with no restriction to society membership or nationality are eligible. A gold medal is awarded annually. Established in 1973 to honor William H. Twenhofel.

• 18849 • **James Lee Wilson Medal**
To recognize a significant record of research accomplishments in sedimentary geology, including all aspects of modern and ancient sedimentology, stratigraphy, and paleontology (fundamental and applied), by persons less than or equal to 40 years of age at the time of nomination. A medal is awarded annually. Established in 1994.

• 18850 •
Society for Sedimentary Geology, Great Lakes Section
615 E Peabody Dr.
Champaign, IL 61820
Phone: (217)333-5108
Fax: (217)333-2830
E-mail: weibel@isgs.uiuc.edu
Home Page: http://www.isgs.uiuc.edu/gls-sepm

• 18851 • **Best Paper Student Presentation**
For best paper by student at GSA-NC meeting on sedimentary geology. Monetary award bestowed annually.

• 18852 •
Society for Sex Therapy and Research
Blanche Freund PhD, Pres.
PO Box 96920
Washington, DC 20090-6920
Phone: (202)863-1644
E-mail: maurice@interchange.ubc.ca
Home Page: http://www.sstarnet.org

• 18853 • **Masters and Johnson Award**
For recognition of the lifetime achievement of excellence in clinical and/or research areas of sexual disorders. A trophy and the opportunity to present a lecture are awarded annually at the Society Convention. Established in 1985 in honor of William Masters and Virginia Johnson, sex therapists.

• 18854 •
Society for Social Studies of Science
Dr. Wesley Shrum, Sec.
Louisiana State University
Department of Sociology
126 Stubbs Hall
Baton Rouge, LA 70803
Phone: (225)578-1645
Fax: (225)578-5102
E-mail: shrum@lsu.edu
Home Page: http://www.4sonline.org

• 18855 • **John Desmond Bernal Prize**
For recognition of distinguished contributions to the field of social studies of science and technology. A monetary prize of $500 and a commemorative plaque are presented annually. Established in 1981 by the Institute for Scientific Information. Co-sponsored by Thomson Scientific.

• 18856 • **Rachel Carson Award**
To recognize the best book in science and technology studies with social or political relevance published in the preceding three years. A monetary award of $500 and a plaque are awarded annually. Established in 1996.

• 18857 • **Ludwik Fleck Prize**
To recognize the best book on science, technology, and society published in the preceding three years. Awarded annually. Monetary award of $500 and a plaque. Established in 1992.

• 18858 • **Nicholas C. Mullins Award**
To recognize outstanding work by a graduate student in the field of science and technology studies. Eligible papers include unpublished papers, published articles, and dissertation chapters. A monetary award of $1,000, a plaque, and partial travel expenses to the annual meeting are awarded each year. Established in 1990 to honor Nicholas C. Mullins.

• 18859 •
Society for Technical Communication
Peter Herbst, Exec.Dir.
901 N Stuart St., Ste. 904
Arlington, VA 22203-1822
Phone: (703)522-4114
Fax: (703)522-2075
E-mail: stc@stc.org
Home Page: http://www.stc.org

Formerly: (1970) Society of Technical Writers and Publishers.

• 18860 • **International Online Communication Competition**
For recognition of outstanding accomplishments and innovations of technical communicators who design and develop online information. Candidates much have won a chapter competition. Plaques are awarded annually for Best of Show, Distinguished Technical Communication, Excellence, Merit, and Achievement.

• 18861 • **International Technical Art Competition**
For recognition of creativity and expertise in visually communicating complex technical concepts. To be eligible, entries must first receive a Distinguished award in a chapter or regional competition. Each entry is then judged against criteria measuring the degree of technical content, achievement of purpose, and technical execution. Categories include mechanical and interpretative illustration and design graphics. Plaques are awarded annually for Best of Show, Distinguished Technical Communication, Excellence, Merit, and Achievement. Established in 1967.

• 18862 • **International Technical Publications Competition**
For recognition of excellence in published technical communication. To be eligible, entries must first have won a Chapter competition. Plaques are awarded annually for Best of Show, Distinguished Technical Communication, Excellence, Merit, and Achievement. Established in 1970.

• 18863 • **International Video Competition**
For recognition of excellence in the field of audiovisual communication. Slides and tape shows in VHS format may be submitted. Plaques are awarded annually for Best of Show, Distinguished Technical Communications, Excellence, Merit, and Achievement. Established in 1977. Formerly: (1991) Audiovisual Competition.

• 18864 •
Society for the Family of Man
% Council of Churches of the City of New York
475 Riverside Dr., Ste. 727
New York, NY 10115
Phone: (212)870-2120
Fax: (212)870-1025
Home Page: http://cccny.net

• 18865 • **Awards for Excellence**
To recognize individuals whose pursuit of excellence in a specific field helps to create guidelines for individual behavior. Awards have been given in the past in the following categories: The Arts, Business persons of the Year, Clergy of the Year, The Family, Communications, Education, Human Relations, Peace, Science, and Sports. A bronze medallion is awarded annually at a dinner. Established in 1963 by the Council of Churches of the City of New York.

• 18866 •
Society for the Historians of the Early American Republic
% The Library Co. of Philadelphia
1314 Locust St.
Philadelphia, PA 19107
Phone: (215)546-0754
Fax: (215)546-0755
E-mail: jer@shear.org
Home Page: http://jer.pennpress.org/strands/jer/home.htm

• 18867 • **Article Prize**
To recognize the best article published each year in the *Journal of the Early Republic.* A monetary prize of $250 and a certificate are presented annually at the Society's Summer Convention. Established in 1981.

• 18868 • **Book Prize**
To recognize an original monograph that deals with the period 1776-1861 in America. In order to qualify, the book or collection of essays must make its primary scholarly contribution to the history of the early American republic. Within that period, the book may treat virtually any aspect of history, including political, economic, social, or cultural history. A monetary prize of $500 and a certificate are awarded annually at the Society's Summer Conference. Established in 1981.

• 18869 • **First Book Prize**
To recognize the best published by a first-time author that deals with the period 1776-1861 in America. In order to qualify, the book or collection of essays must make its primary scholarly contribution to the history of the early American republic. Within that period, the book may treat virtually any aspect of history, including political, economic, social, or cultural history. A monetary prize of $500 and a certificate are awarded annually at the Society's Summer Conference. Established in 1998.

• 18870 •
Society for the History of Technology
Dr. Amy Bix, Sec.
603 Ross Hall
Dept. of History
Iowa State Univ.
Ames, IA 50011
Phone: (515)294-8469
Fax: (515)294-6390
E-mail: shot@iastate.edu
Home Page: http://www.shot.jhu.edu

• 18871 • **Leonardo Da Vinci Medal**
This, the highest recognition from the Society, is given to honor an individual for outstanding contributions to the history of technology through research, teaching, publication, or other activities. Individuals are eligible without regard to nationality, age, sex, or occupation. The deadline for nominations is April 15. A bronze medallion, designed by Andras Beck and cast by Arthus-Bertrand Cie., and a certificate are awarded annually. Established in 1962.

• 18872 • **Dibner Award for Excellence in Museum Exhibits**
To recognize excellence in museums and museum exhibits that interpret the history of technology, industry, and engineering to the general public. The winning exhibit, in addition to being well designed and produced, must raise pertinent historical issues. It must be based on scholarship that is solid, current, correct, and complete in its factual content and implication. Artifacts and images must be used in a manner that interests, teaches, and stimulates both the general public and historians. The deadline for nominations is February 15. A plaque and travel expenses up to $1,000 are awarded annually. Established in 1985. Sponsored by the Dibner Fund and the Charles Edison Fund.

• 18873 • **Edelstein Prize**
To recognize outstanding scholarly books in the history of technology and to promote their publication. Works published during the preceding three years are eligible. The deadline for nominations is April 1. A monetary award of $3,500 and a plaque are awarded annually. Established in 1968, and renamed in the memory of Sidney Edelstein, founder of the Dexter Chemical Corp. Formerly: Dexter Prize.

• 18874 • **Samuel Eleazar and Rose Tartakow Levinson Prize**
To recognize an original essay by an individual new to the profession on the history of technology. The essay, which must be the author's first work intended for publication, must explicitly examine in some detail a technology or technological device within the framework of social or intellectual history. The deadline for nominations is April 15. A monetary prize of $450 and a certificate are awarded annually. Established in 1985.

• 18875 • **IEEE Life Members' Prize in Electrical History**
To recognize the best paper in electrical history published in the previous year. Any historical paper published in a learned journal or magazine is eligible if it treats the art or engineering aspects of electrotechnology and its practitioners. Electrotechnology encompasses power, electronics, telecommunications, and computer science. The deadline for nominations is April 15. A monetary award of $500 and a certificate are awarded annually. Established in 1986 by the History Committee of the Institute of Electrical and Electronics Engineers (IEEE).

• 18876 • **Joan Cahalin Robinson Prize**
To recognize the best paper presented at the Society meeting by a young historian. Eligible candidates are graduate students who are presenting his/her first paper at the meeting, and those who received their PhD no more than one year previously. They are judged not only on the quality of the historical research and scholarship demonstrated in the written papers but also on the effectiveness of their oral presentations. The deadline for nominations is July 1. A monetary award of $350 and a certificate are awarded annually. Established in 1980 by Eric Robinson in memory of his wife, Joan Cahalin Robinson.

• 18877 • **Abbott Payson Usher Prize**
To encourage the publication of original research of the highest professional standard, and to recognize the author of the best scholarly work published during the preceding three years under the auspices of the Society (in the Society's journal *Technology and Culture*). A monetary award of $400 and a certificate are awarded annually. Established in 1961 in memory of the scholarly contributions of Dr. Usher.

• 18878 •
Society for the Preservation of Bluegrass Music of America
Chuck Stearman, Contact
PO Box 271
Kirksville, MO 63501
Phone: (660)665-7172
Fax: (660)665-7450
E-mail: spbgma@kvmo.net
Home Page: http://www.spbgma.com

• 18879 • **Bluegrass Music Awards**
To recognize Bluegrass Music bands, promoters, songwriters, radio stations, and publications. Nomination is through polls taken in national publications. A trophy is awarded in 25 categories annually. Established in 1974.

• 18880 •
Society for the Preservation of Old Mills
Esther A. Middlewood, Ed.
5667 Leisure South Dr. SE
Grand Rapids, MI 49548-6851
Phone: (616)455-0609
E-mail: eamedit@aol.com
Home Page: http://www.spoom.org

• 18881 • **Honorary Life Member**
To recognize an individual for devotion to molinology or to the Society. Members are eligible. A certificate is awarded annually, or at the discretion of the directors. Established in 1981.

• 18882 •
Society for the Psychological Study of Social Issues
Shari Miles PhD, Exec.Dir.
208 Eye St. NE
Washington, DC 20002-4340
Phone: (202)675-6956
Fax: (202)675-6902
E-mail: spssi@spssi.org
Home Page: http://www.spssi.org/ASIflyer.html

• 18883 • **Gordon Allport Intergroup Relations Prize**
To honor the author of the best paper or article of the year on intergroup relations. Originality of the contribution, whether theoretical or empirical, is given special consideration. The research area encompassing intergroup relations includes such dimensions as age, sex, socio-economic status, and race. A monetary prize of $1,000 is awarded annually. Established in 1969 in honor of Dr. Gordon W. Allport, a founder and past Resident of the Society. Sponsored by the Gordon W. Allport Memorial Fund of Harvard University. Please see http://spssi.org/Allport_flyer.html for more details.

• 18884 • **Applied Social Issues Internship**
To encourage intervention projects, non-partisan advocacy projects, applied research, and writing and implementing public policy. Proposals are invited for applying social science principles to social issues, in cooperation with a com-

munity, city, or state government organization, public interest group, or other not-for-profit entity. College seniors, graduate students, and first-year postdoctoral students in psychology, applied social science, and related disciplines are eligible. Awards ranging from $300 to $2,500 to cover research costs, community organizing, and summer stipends are awarded annually. The deadline for applications is May 1st.

• 18885 • Grants-in-Aid Program
To support scientific research in social problem areas related to the basic interests and goals of SPSSI and particularly those that are not likely to receive support from traditional sources. Grants of up to $2,000 each are presented. Grants of up to $1,000 each are available for graduate student research, with strong preference given to applications from students at the dissertation stage of the graduate career. Proposals for highly timely and event-oriented research may be submitted at any time during the year. The deadlines for all other applications are November 1st and May 1st. Awarded annually. Co-sponsored by the Sophie and Shirley Cohen Memorial Fund.

• 18886 • Louise Kidder Early Career Award
To recognize social issues researchers who have made substantial contributions to the field early in their career. Nominees should be investigators who have made substantial contributions to social issues research within five years of receiving a graduate degree and who have demonstrated the potential to continue such contributions. Nominees need not be current SPSSI members. A plaque and $500 are awarded annually.

• 18887 • Otto Klineberg Intercultural and International Relations Award
To recognize the best paper or article of the year on intercultural or international relations. Entries can be either papers published during the current year or unpublished manuscripts. Entries cannot be returned. Originality of the contribution, whether theoretical or empirical, will be given special weight. The competition is open to non-members, as well as members of SPSSI, and graduate students are especially urged to submit papers. Entries must be submitted in quintuplicate by February 15th. A monetary prize of $1,000 is awarded annually.

• 18888 • Social Issues Dissertation Award
To honor the author of the best doctoral dissertation in psychology or in a social science with psychological subject matter, accepted in the previous calendar year. (March to March) Selection is based on scientific excellence and application potential. Deadline for submissions is in April 1st. Monetary prizes of $750 for first place, and $500 for second place are awarded annually. Four copies of a 500-word summary; cover letter; a certification of dissertation acceptance date from the applicants advisor must be submitted. Please see http://spssi.org/Dissertationflyer.html for more details.

• 18889 •
Society for the Scientific Study of Sexuality
David L. Fleming, Exec.Dir.
PO Box 416
Allentown, PA 18105-0416
Phone: (610)530-2483
Fax: (610)530-2485
E-mail: thesociety@sexscience.org
Home Page: http://www.sexscience.org

• 18890 • Hugo G. Beigel Research Award
To recognize the author of the best article published in the *Journal of Sex Research* each year, and to promote and reward research excellence in sexual science. Selection is based on excellent original research reports, and includes theoretical papers, literature reviews, historical articles, and others. A monetary prize of $500, a certificate of research excellence, and a one-year honorary membership are awarded annually. Established in 1979 to honor Dr. Beigel, a founding member of the Society and the founding Editor of the *Journal of Sex Research.*

• 18891 •
Society for the Study of Amphibians and Reptiles
Donald Schmitt, Contact
PO Box 253
Marceline, MO 64658-0253
Phone: (660)256-3252
Fax: (660)256-3252
E-mail: ssar@mcmsys.com
Home Page: http://www.ssarherps.org

• 18892 • Grants in Herpetology
To provide financial support to deserving individuals or organizations engaged in herpetological research, education, or conservation. Preference is given to students, recent graduates, and others who might not have access to other funding sources. All applicants must be members of the Society. Grant proposals are considered in the following categories: International Research, Field Research, Laboratory Research, Conservation of Amphibians and/or Reptiles, Travel, and Educational projects. Deadline for submission is December 31. A monetary award of $500 is presented to one recipient in each category. Awarded annually.

• 18893 •
Society for the Study of Evolution
Evolution: International Journal of Organic Evolution
Jessica Gurevitch, Exec.VP
PO Box 7055
PO Box 1897
Lawrence, KS 66044-8897
Toll-Free: 800-627-0629
Fax: (913)843-1274
E-mail: evolution@asu.edu
Home Page: http://lsvl.la.asu.edu/evolution

• 18894 • Theodosius Dobzhansky Prize
To recognize the accomplishments and future promise of a young evolutionary biologist. Active researchers with a PhD (or equivalent degree) received within the past three years are eligible. A monetary award of $5,000 and an invitation to give a presentation at the annual meeting is awarded annually. Established in 1981 by friends and colleagues of Theodosius Dobzhansky, a great evolutionary biologists.

• 18895 •
Society for the Study of Lesbian, Gay and Bisexual Concerns (Division 44)
American Psychological Association
Public Interest Directorate
750 First St. NE
Washington, DC 20002-4242
Phone: (202)336-6050
E-mail: lgbc@apa.org
Home Page: http://www.apa.org/pi/lbgc/homepage.html

• 18896 • Dissertation Research Awards
Assists science-oriented doctoral students of psychology with research costs. Students must be student affiliates of APA and must be enrolled in graduate studies in a department listed in *Graduate Study in Psychology and Associated Fields.* Deadline for nominations is early February. Between 30 and 40 awards of $1,000 each, as well as several awards of $5,000 each, are presented annually by the Science Directorate.

• 18897 • Distinguished Career Contribution to Education and Training in Psychology
To recognize a psychologist who has consistently, over his or her career, provided significant contributions to education and training in psychology. Nominees must be current members of APA. Deadline for nominations is February 1. Awarded at the APA annual convention. Additional information is available from the Educational Programs Office.

• 18898 • Distinguished Contribution to Education and Training in Psychology
To recognize a psychologist for a major contribution to education and training at some time in his or her career. Nominees must be current members of APA. Deadline for nomination is February 1. Awards are presented at the APA annual convention. Additional information is available from the Education Programs Office.

• 18899 • Distinguished Contribution to Ethnic Minority Issues Award
To recognize individuals for distinguished contributions toward ethnic minority issues as related to lesbian and gay issues. APA members are eligible, and self-nominations are accepted. Deadline for nomination is February 1. A plaque or a certificate is presented at the APA annual convention.

• 18900 • Distinguished Contribution to Psychology and the Media
For recognition of a consistent contribution by a person(s) to advancing psychology and public awareness of psychological issues through work in any of the mass media. Recipients need not

be a member of the APA nor be a psychologist. Deadline for nomination is March 31. A plaque is awarded each year at the APA annual convention.

• 18901 • Distinguished Contribution to Psychology in the Public Interest

To recognize two individuals for single extraordinary achievements or lifetime contributions to advance psychology as a science and/or profession. These contributions might include the identification or solution of significant social problems, unusual initiative or dedication to activity in the public interest, or the integration of the science and/or profession of psychology with social action in a manner beneficial to all. One award is reserved to recognize an outstanding psychologist who has not held a Ph.D. for more than 15 years (Early Career). Deadline for nominations is March 1. A monetary prize of $1,000 and a certificate are presented. Additional information is available from the APA Public Interest Directorate.

• 18902 • Distinguished Contributions to Applied Psychology as a Professional Practice

To recognize outstanding service delivery by a psychologist who has provided leadership in changing the profession, its public image, and its public acceptance. Contribution in public and professional arenas involving legislative, political, and legal patterns of service delivery and reimbursement changes that contribute to the development of the profession are considered. Significant contributions of work done in professional or public organizations as psychologist at the national, state and local level, may be recognized. Deadline for nominations is February 1. A $1,000 honorarium and a plaque are presented at the APA annual convention. Additional information is available from the APA Practice Directorate.

• 18903 • Distinguished Contributions to Research in Public Policy

To recognize a psychologist who has made a distinguished empirical and/or theoretical contribution to research in public policy either through a single extraordinary achievement or a lifetime of work. This contribution may consist of such factors as research leading others to view specific national policies differently, research demonstrating the importance of the application of psychological methods and theory to public policy, and research clarifying the ways scientific knowledge of human behavior informs public policy. Deadline for nominations is March 1. A monetary prize of $1,000 and a certificate are awarded at the APA annual convention. Additional information is available from the APA Public Interest Directorate.

• 18904 • Distinguished Contributions to the International Advancement of Psychology

To recognize sustained and enduring contributions to international cooperations and advancement of knowledge in psychology. Deadline for nominations is February 1. A monetary award of $1,000 and a certificate are presented at the APA annual convention award ceremony. Sponsored by APA Committee on International Relations.

• 18905 • Distinguished Educational Contribution Award

To recognize individuals for distinguished contributions to the interests, goals, and purposes of the Society in the area of public or academic education. APA members are eligible, and self-nominations are accepted. Deadline for nomination is February 1. A plaque or a certificate is awarded at the APA annual convention.

• 18906 • Distinguished Professional Contributions to Knowledge

For recognition of the discovery and development of new information, empirical or otherwise, that contributes to the body of knowledge in applied psychology. The new information should permit innovative applications in a wide variety of situations. These should be in such areas as assessment, consultation, instruction, and direct or indirect intervention. The new theories, or original integration of existing theories or knowledge should provide direction so as to enable psychologists to better observe, define, predict, or control behavior. Also included in this category is actual research involving original development of procedures, methodologies, or technical skills that significantly improve the application of psychological knowledge in providing direct and immediate solutions to practical problem areas. Deadline for nominations is February 1. A $1,000 honorarium and a plaque are awarded at the APA annual convention. Additional information is available from the APA Practice Directorate.

• 18907 • Distinguished Professional Contributions to Public Service

To recognize psychologists who have made outstanding contributions in serving the public through their knowledge and practical skills. Such contributions must be seen as directed to and on behalf of the public. Consideration is given to psychologists whose professional involvement has resulted in a major benefit to the public as well as those who have made significant contributions to special populations, such as those who have disabilities, are disadvantaged or underprivileged, or are members of a minority group. Psychologists who are active in legislative, legal, political, organizational and other areas that are directed at providing benefits to the public are also considered. Deadline for nominations is February 1. A $1,000 honorarium and a plaque are presented at the APA annual convention. Additional information is available from the APA Practice Directorate.

• 18908 • Distinguished Scientific Award for an Early Career Contribution to Psychology

To recognize excellent young psychologists. Recipients of this award may not have held a PhD for more than nine years. For the purposes of this award, psychology has been divided into eight areas: cognition and human learning, psychopathology, health, developmental, applied research/psychometrics, social/personality, perception/motor performance, and biopsychology/animal behavior. Four areas are considered each year, with areas rotated in two-year cycles. Deadline for nominations is February 1. A citation is awarded at the annual APA convention. Established in 1974. Additional information is available from the APA Science Directorate.

• 18909 • Distinguished Scientific Award for the Applications of Psychology

To recognize an individual who has made distinguished theoretical or empirical advances in psychology leading to the understanding or amelioration of important practical problems. Deadline for nominations is February 1. A citation is presented at the APA convention. The award winner presents an address on some phase of his or her scientific work at the succeeding year's APA convention. Established in 1973. Additional information is available from the APA Science Directorate.

• 18910 • Distinguished Scientific Contribution Award

To recognize up to three persons who have made distinguished theoretical or empirical contributions to basic research in psychology. The award winners present addresses about some phase of their scientific work at the succeeding year's APA convention. Deadline for nominations is February 1. A citation is awarded at the annual APA convention. Established in 1956. Additional information is available from the APA Science Directorate.

• 18911 • Raymond D. Fowler Award

To recognize a psychologist for an outstanding contribution to the professional development of students. Deadline for nominations is December 15. A plaque is awarded each year at the APA annual convention. Sponsored by the American Psychological Association of Graduate Students.

• 18912 • Leadership Award

To recognize individuals who have made outstanding leadership contributions to women in psychology and share CWP's goal of ensuring that women achieve equality as members of the psychological community. Nominations are accepted in two categories: emerging leaders who have less than 10 years beyond their doctorate and established leaders who have 10 or more years of working experience beyond their doctorate. Current CWP members and APA staff are not eligible. Deadline for nominations is April 1. Up to three citations and a plaque are presented each year at the annual convention. Sponsored by APA Committee on Women in Psychology.

• 18913 • Media Psychology Graduate Student Research Award

To recognize a graduate student for his or her research work in the area of media psychology. Research papers must be on the effects of mass media on human behavior. Electronic products must use the media to advance psychology or Deadline for nomination is March 31. Graduate students need not be a psychology major. A monetary prize of $200 and a plaque are presented each year at the APA annual convention.

• 18914 • Meritorious Contributions to Psychology on the Part of Nonpsychologists

To recognize non-psychologists for contributions to psychology. Members may submit nominations. A plaque is awarded at the APA annual convention. Established in 1983 by Jacqueline C. Bouhoutsos, founder and past president. Formerly: (1990) Media Award.

• 18915 • National Psychology Awards for Excellence in the Media

To recognize writers who promote public understanding of psychology and psychologists through accurate and insightful reporting. Materials must be intended for the general public, deal with psychological issues and increase public understanding of psychology. Special consideration will be given to materials that include specific references to psychology and/or psychologists or application of psychological research. Deadline for receipt of entries is April 16. Awards are presented in the following categories: magazine, newspaper, radio, television (news/documentary), and television (drama/entertainment). Winners in each of the five categories receive a monetary prize of $1,000, a framed certificate, and an all-expense paid trip to attend the awards ceremony at the APA annual convention. Established in 1954 by the American Psychological Foundation. Since 1992, the award has been presented by the American Psychological Association. For further information, contact the APA Public Affairs Office.

• 18916 • Edwin B. Newman Award for Excellence in Research

To recognize a graduate student for the best paper presented at the APA or Psi Chi convention, any of the regional psychological association conventions, or any of the state psychological conventions between July 1 of the previous year and June 30 of the current year. For purposes of the award, research is broadly defined to include all forms of scholarly endeavor relevant to psychology, such as experiments, correlational studies, historical papers, case histories, and evaluation studies. The Edwin B. Newman Award Committee makes the final selection of a winner. An engraved plaque, a department certificate, and an expense-paid trip to the APA convention are awarded annually.

• 18917 • Outstanding Achievement Award

To recognize one female and one male individual for significant contributions to the mission of the Committee on Lesbian, Gay, and Bisexual Concerns. This mission is to study and evaluate on an ongoing basis how the issues and concerns of lesbian and gay psychologists can best be dealt with; encourage objective and unbiased research in area relevant to lesbians, gay men, and gay and lesbian youth in clinical practice; develop educational materials for distribution to psychologists and others; make recommendations regarding the integration of these issues into the APA's activities to further the cause of the civil and legal rights of lesbian and gay psychologists within the profession. APA members are eligible, and self-nominations are accepted. A plaque is presented at the APA Annual Convention by the Division of Lesbian, Gay and Bisexual Concerns.

• 18918 • Society for the Psychological Study of Lesbian and Gay Issues Distinguished Student Award

To recognize students who have made distinguished contributions to the Society through outstanding research and/or service. APA members are eligible, and self-nominations are also accepted. Deadline for nomination is February 1.

• 18919 • Student Travel Awards

Provide travel expenses for presentation of research at the annual convention. Applicants must be psychology graduate students enrolled full-time; student affiliates or associated members of the association; and have papers or posters that have already been accepted for presentation. Not more than three students per department can be nominated. Approximately 100 grants of $300 are awarded annually by the Science Directorate.

• 18920 • Jeffrey S. Tanaka Memorial Dissertation Award in Psychology

To recognize the most outstanding ethnic minority psychology dissertation. A contribution that enhances the understanding of ethnic minority communities; a contribution to the enhancement of service delivery systems in ethnic minority populations; the development of new and creative methodological paradigms that promote more effective ethnic minority research; or a creative approach in methodology sensitive to the unique character of the ethnic minority community. Deadline for entries is April 15. A monetary prize of $500, a travel grant of $300, and a certificate are presented at the APA annual convention. Sponsored by the APA Committee on Ethnic Minority Affairs.

• 18921 •
Society for the Study of Midwestern Literature
Mr. Roger Bresnahan PhD, Sec.-Treas.
Michigan State University
Bessey Hall
East Lansing, MI 48824-1033
Phone: (517)355-3507
Phone: (517)355-2400
Fax: (517)353-5250
E-mail: bresnaha@msu.edu

• 18922 • Mark Twain Award

For creative writing. Awarded annually.

• 18923 • Mid American Award

Recognizes outstanding scholarship. Awarded annually.

• 18924 •
Society for the Study of Social Problems
Thomas C. Hood, Exec.Off.
901 McClung Tower
Univ. of Tennessee
Knoxville, TN 37996-0490
Phone: (865)689-1531
Fax: (865)689-1534
E-mail: tomhood@utk.edu
Home Page: http://www.sssp1.org

• 18925 • Lee Founders Award

To recognize significant achievements that throughout a distinguished career have demonstrated continuing devotion to the ideals of the founders of the SSSP and especially to the humanist tradition of Alfred McClung Lee and Elizabeth Brant Lee. The nominee must have been an active member of the society for some years prior to receiving the award, and must have made significant achievements embodying the ideas of the founders of the Society. Entry deadline is April 15. Awarded annually. Established in 1981.

• 18926 • C. Wright Mills Award

To recognize the author of the book published during the past year that best exemplifies outstanding social science research and an understanding of the individual and society in the tradition of the distinguished sociologist C. Wright Mills. A stipend of $500 is awarded annually. Established in 1964.

• 18927 •
Society for the Study of Southern Literature
Jeff Abernathy, Dean/Sec.-Treas.
Augustana Coll.
639 38th St.
59 College Ave.
Rock Island, IL 61201
Phone: (504)865-2476
E-mail: abernathy@augustana.edu
Home Page: http://www.uark.edu/ua/sssl

• 18928 • C. Hugh Holman Award

To recognize the best book of literary scholarship or literary criticism in the field of Southern Literature published during the preceding calendar year. Eligible books may be literary criticism, literary history, scholarly editions, or bibliographies that show serious study of Southern literature and/or particular individual Southern writers (or groups of Southern writers). A plaque and a monetary award of $200 is awarded annually. Established in 1985 to honor C. Hugh Holman, who shared with Louis D. Rubin, Jr. the responsibilities for the *Southern Literary Journal.*

• 18929 •
Society for the Study of Symbolic Interaction
Michael Katovich, Pres.
%Rose M. Jensen Phd
Director of Gerontology, SSSI
Lynchburg College
Lynchburg, VA 24501
Phone: (804)544-8456
Fax: (804)544-8499
E-mail: lesliewasson@usa.net
Home Page: http://sun.soci.niu.edu/~ssi

• 18930 • **Herbert Blumer Award**
For recognition of the best graduate student paper in the tradition of symbolic interaction. The deadline for submission of papers is April 1. Awarded annually at the awards banquet.

• 18931 • **Charles Horton Cooley Award**
For recognition of an outstanding recent contribution to the study of symbolic interaction. The deadline for nominations is January 15. Awarded annually at the awards banquet.

• 18932 • **George Herbert Mead Award**
To recognize members for lifetime achievement in the field of symbolic interaction. Nomination deadline is May 1. Awarded annually at the awards banquet.

• 18933 •
Society for Utopian Studies
Kenneth M. Roemer, Contact
English-Box 19035
University of Texas at Arlington
Arlington, TX 76019-0035
Phone: (817)272-2729
Fax: (817)272-2718
E-mail: roemer@uta.edu
Home Page: http://www.utoronto.ca/utopia

• 18934 • **Eugenio Battisti Award**
To recognize the author of the best article appearing in the previous year's *Utopian Studies*. A monetary award is presented annually. Established in 1991.

• 18935 • **Arthur O. Lewis Award**
To recognize younger scholars for the best papers presented at the annual conference. Untenured members of the Society are eligible. Up to two monetary awards are presented annually. Established in 1986 to honor Arthur O. Lewis, one of the founders and long-time chair of the Society.

• 18936 •
Society for Women in Philosophy
Jo Triglio, Ed.
Dept. of Philosophy
Bloomsburg University
Bloomsburg, PA 17815
Fax: (570)389-2094
E-mail: jtriglio@bentley.edu
Home Page: http://www.uh.edu/~cfreelan/SWIP

• 18937 • **Distinguished Woman Philosopher Award**
To recognize and honor women who have been active and have made a significant contribution in the field of philosophy. An honorary award is given annually at the Eastern APA conference. Formerly: Woman of the Year Award.

• 18938 •
Society of Actuaries
Sarah Sandford, Exec.Dir.
475 N Martingale Rd., Ste. 800
Schaumburg, IL 60173-2226
Phone: (847)706-3500
Fax: (847)706-3599
E-mail: ssandford@soa.org
Home Page: http://www.soa.org

• 18939 • **AERF Practitioners Award**
In recognition of practical, innovative actuarial research done in a non-academic setting. Awarded annually. Established in 1988.

• 18940 • **Annual Prize**
For recognition of the best eligible paper published in the *North American Actuarial Journal* each year. A monetary prize of $500 and a plaque are awarded annually. Established in 1982.

• 18941 • **Halmstad Prize**
In recognition of the best published paper on actuarial research, as judged by the Society. Awarded annually. Established in 1978.

• 18942 • **Everett Curtis Huntington Prize**
In recognition of the best research paper submitted for Fellowship credit (under the Society's educational program for research papers). A monetary award of $1,000 and a plaque are awarded. Established in 1992 in honor of a Fellow of the Society who was a professional actuary from 1938 until his death in 1971.

• 18943 • **Triennial Prize**
For recognition of the best eligible paper published in the *North American Actuarial Journal*released to during each successive three-year period. The paper must have been submitted to the Director of Communications of the Society before the end of the fifth year succeeding the calendar year in which the author first qualified as an Associate of a recognized actuarial society. A monetary prize of $500 and a plaque are awarded triennially when merited. Established in 1912.

• 18944 •
Society of Allied Weight Engineers
Jerry L. Pierson, Pres.
204 Hubbard St.
Glastonbury, CT 06033-3063
Phone: (860)633-0850
Phone: (817)777-5171
Fax: (860)633-8971
E-mail: saweed@aol.com
Home Page: http://www.sawe.org

• 18945 • **Fellow Award**
To recognize an individual who has achieved distinction in the field of mass properties engineering, or who has materially contributed to the advancement of the Society. Election to Fellowship is by a three-fourths vote of the board of directors. A maximum of five fellows may be elected in one year. Awarded annually.

• 18946 • **L. R. Mike Hackney Award**
For recognition of the most outstanding technical paper presented at the international conference. Papers are judged for technical content, originality, usefulness, value, clarity, style, and form. A plaque is awarded annually.

• 18947 • **Honorary Fellow Award**
To recognize an individual who has achieved eminence in mass properties engineering or who has made outstanding contributions to the advancement of the Society. Election to Honorary Fellowship is by a three-fourths vote of the board of directors. Not more than two Honorary Fellows may be elected in any one year. Awarded annually.

• 18948 • **Ed Payne Award**
To recognize a young engineer, under the age of 35, who has contributed significantly to the Society or to the mass properties engineering profession. An inscribed plaque is awarded annually when merited.

• 18949 • **Student Award**
To recognize a student who shows interest in weight engineering and demonstrates a knowledge of mass properties engineering by writing papers, participating in seminars, or making outstanding contributions to the advancement of the Society. A monetary prize of $100 is awarded annually when merited.

• 18950 •
Society of American Archivists
Nancy Perkin Beaumont, Exec.Dir.
527 S Wells, 5th Fl.
Chicago, IL 60607
Phone: (312)922-0140
Fax: (312)347-1452
E-mail: info@archivists.org
Home Page: http://www.archivists.org

• 18951 • **C.F.W. Coker Award**
To recognize finding aids, finding aid systems, projects that involve innovative development in archival description, or descriptive tools that enable archivists to produce more effective finding aids. Eligible nominees must have, in some significant way, set national standards, represent a model for archival description, or otherwise have substantial impact on descriptive practices. Awarded annually. Established in 1983 in honor of SAA Fellow C.F.W. Coker.

• 18952 • **Colonial Dames of America Scholarship**
To enable two archivists each year to attend the National Archives' Modern Archives Institute. A

similar award, the Donna Cutts Scholarships, was instituted in 2002 to enable an additional archivist to visit the Institute. Each of these three scholarships consists of a monetary award of $1,200, and is awarded annually. Established in 1974. Co-sponsored by the Colonial Dames of America, Chapter III, Washington, D.C.

• 18953 • Distinguished Service Award

To recognize a North American archival institution, organization, education program, or nonprofit or governmental organization that has given outstanding service to its public and has made an exemplary contribution to the archival profession. Nominees must be supported by three SAA members, each representing a different institution. Awarded annually if merited. Established in 1964.

• 18954 • Philip M. Hamer and Elizabeth Hamer Kegan Award

To recognize an individual, organization, institution, or group of individuals, organizations, or institutions who have increased public awareness of manuscripts and archives through compilation, transcription, public presentation, exhibition, or publication. Awarded annually. Established in 1973 to honor SAA Fellows and former presidents, Philip M. Hamer and Elizabeth Hamer Kegan.

• 18955 • Oliver Wendell Holmes Travel Award

To enable overseas archivists who are already in the United States or Canada for training, to travel to or attend the SAA annual meeting. A certificate and monetary prize are awarded annually. Established in 1979 in honor of SAA Fellow and former president Oliver Wendell Holmes.

• 18956 • J. Franklin Jameson Archival Advocacy Award

To honor an individual, institution, or organization not directly involved in archival work that promotes greater public awareness, appreciation, or support of archival activities or programs. Contributions should have a direct or indirect national impact. Awarded annually. Established in 1989 in honor historian J. Franklin Jameson, who labored for more than 25 years to establish the United States National Archives.

• 18957 • Sister M. Claude Lane Award

To recognize individual archivists who have made a significant contribution to the field of religious archives. Awarded annually. Established in 1974 in honor of Sister M. Claude Lane. Co-sponsored by the Society of Southwest Archivists.

• 18958 • Waldo Gifford Leland Award

To encourage and reward writing excellence and usefulness in the field of archival history, theory, or practice. Authors of monographs, finding aids, or documentary publication published in North America during the previous calendar year are eligible. Periodicals are not eligible. A monetary prize is awarded annually. Established in 1959 in honor of Waldo Gifford Leland, second president of the Society. Formerly: Waldo Gifford Leland Memorial Prize.

• 18959 • Theodore Calvin Pease Award

To recognize superior writing achievements by students enrolled in archival administration classes or engaged in formal archival internship programs. Eligible manuscripts must be unpublished, 15 to 20 pages long, and conform to stylistic guidelines of the *American Archivist*. Papers examining major trends and issues in archival administration are preferred. A monetary prize of $100, a certificate, and publication in the *American Archivist* are awarded annually. Established in 1987 to honor Theodore Calvin Pease, first editor of the *American Archivist.*

• 18960 • Harold T. Pinkett Minority Student Award

To encourage minority students to consider careers in the archival profession and to promote minority participation in SAA. Nominees must have a minimum grade point average of 3.0 in the academic year preceding the award. Preference is given to full-time students. The award provides complimentary registration to the SAA Annual Meeting. Awarded annually. Established in 1993.

• 18961 • Fellows' Ernst Posner Prize

To recognize an outstanding essay dealing with some facet of archival administration, history, theory, and/or methodology that was published during the preceding year in the *American Archivist*. A certificate and cash prize is awarded annually. Established in 1982.

• 18962 • Preservation Publication Award

To honor the author(s) or editor(s) of an outstanding work published in North America that advances the theory of the practice of preservation in archival institutions. Eligible publications include articles, reports, chapters, and monographs in print, audio-visual, or electronic format. Awarded annually. Established in 1993.

• 18963 •
Society of American Business Editors and Writers
Carrie M. Paden, Exec.Dir.
134 Neff Annex
Columbia, MO 65211
Phone: (573)882-7862
Phone: (573)882-8985
Fax: (573)884-1372
E-mail: padenc@missouri.edu
Home Page: http://www.sabew.org

• 18964 • Best in Business Contest

Identifies the most outstanding daily business sections and business weeklies and honors outstanding news reports. Contestants compete against others at papers of similar size. In the section contest up to five awards are presented in each size category. Up to three awards are presented in each size category for news stories. Open to SBEW members only. Judges look for well-written, well coordinated section packages, and news reports and will select the best breaking new stories and, in a new part of the contest, the best timely enterprise stories. Awarded annually.

• 18965 •
Society of American Florists
Peter J. Moran, Exec.VP
1601 Duke St.
Alexandria, VA 22314-3406
Phone: (703)836-8700
Toll-Free: 800-336-4743
Fax: (703)836-8705
E-mail: info@safnow.org
Home Page: http://www.safnow.org

• 18966 • Floricultural Hall of Fame

To recognize outstanding members of the floral industry and the important role played by floriculture in the development of our country and our American way of life. Induction in the Hall of Fame is awarded annually and may be given posthumously.

• 18967 • Sylvia Cup Design Competition

For recognition of outstanding talent in floral design. Members of the floral industry are eligible. A silver engraved champagne bucket and cash prize of $1,000 are awarded annually. Established in 1967 to honor Sylvia MacGuffog Valencia.

• 18968 •
Society of American Foresters
Michael T. Goergen Jr., Exec.VP/CEO
5400 Grosvenor Ln.
Bethesda, MD 20814-2198
Phone: (301)897-8720
Fax: (301)897-3690
E-mail: safweb@safnet.org
Home Page: http://www.safnet.org

• 18969 • Award in Forest Science

To recognize distinguished individual research in any branch of the quantitative, managerial, and/or social sciences leading to the advancement of forestry. Evaluation will be based on (1) research quality, (2) research productivity, (3) research innovation, (4) research impact resulting in advances in forestry, and (5) overall evidence of distinguished individual research. The recipient need not be a member of the Society of American Foresters. Presented annually, the award includes a $1,000 honorarium.

• 18970 • John A. Beale Memorial Award

To recognize outstanding efforts over a sustained period of time by a member in the promotion of forestry through voluntary service to the Society. Each State Society may submit one nominee. The deadline for nominations is February 28. A $500 honorarium is awarded annually. Established in 1978.

• 18971 • Honorary Member

To recognize an individual who has rendered distinguished service to forestry. There are two alternate qualifications for Honorary member:

non-professional foresters who have made outstanding and well-known contributions to forestry in America or abroad. Conservationists and civic leaders, for example, are among those eligible for Honorary Member; and professional foresters from abroad, (or from countries other than the United States, its possessions, Canada, or Mexico) who have made professional contributions recognized as outstanding by their peers. Honorary Members receive a certificate and lifetime membership.

• 18972 • Barrington Moore Memorial Award
To recognize distinguished, individual research in any branch of the biological sciences that has resulted in substantial advances in forestry. The recipient need not be a member of SAF. The deadline for nominations is February 28. A $1,000 honorarium is awarded annually. Established in 1954.

• 18973 • Outstanding Forestry Journalism Award
The Outstanding Forestry Journalism Award recognizes high quality journalistic coverage of topics that increase the American public's understanding of forestry and natural resources. This award may be presented to an individual, a team, or a media organization involved in print (magazine, newspaper, book, etc.), television, or radio journalism. Eligible categories are: (a) a single story or series on a key forestry or natural resources topic, or (b) a documentary, special in-depth story, book, or (c) the best coverage of a single subject on a continuing basis. Evaluation will be based upon: (1) story-telling ability that builds public understanding, and, if present, visual elements that convey the same story as the narrative, and (2) the ability to break down a subject while maintaining the integrity of a topic, and (3) coverage that is useful to key leaders and leads to improved public understanding, and (4) the potential to advance forestry science, management, and/or education. Presented annually, the award includes cash honorarium of $500.

• 18974 • Gifford Pinchot Medal
To recognize outstanding contributions by forestry professionals to administration, practice, and professional development of North American forestry. Candidates need not be members of the Society. The deadline is February 28 of odd-numbered years. A $500 honorarium and medallion are awarded biennially in odd-numbered years at the national convention. Established in 1950.

• 18975 • Carl Alwin Schenck Award
To recognize devotion and demonstrated outstanding performance in the field of forestry education by individuals whose efforts exemplify those of Carl Alwin Schenck. Recipients must be actively employed in SAF-accredited forestry education programs in the United States. The deadline is February 28. Presented annually, the award includes a $500 honorarium. Established in 1988.

• 18976 • Sir William Schlich Memorial Award
To recognize broad and outstanding contributions to forestry with emphasis on, but not limited to, policy and national or international activities. The recipient need not be a member of the Society. The deadline for nominations is February 28 of even-numbered years. A $500 award and an engraved medallion are awarded biennially in even-numbered years at the SAF national convention. (First presented in 1935 to President Franklin D. Roosevelt.)

• 18977 • Technology Transfer Award
To recognize excellence in the areas of technology transfer, implementation, and extension by a member as evidenced in the recipient's career or involvement in SAF Working Group/Science Program Activities. The deadline is February 28. Presented annually, the award includes a $1,000 honorarium. Established in 1985.

• 18978 • Young Forester Leadership Award
To recognize a young forester for his or her development and promotion of an individual project or program, or a sustained leadership role benefiting the Society and the practice of forestry. Nominees should be SAF members under 40 years of age at the time of nomination. The deadline For nominations is February 28. Presented annually, the award includes a $500 honorarium. Established in 1984.

• 18979 •
Society of American Graphic Artists
Richard Sloat, Pres.
32 Union Sq., Rm. 1214
New York, NY 10003
E-mail: elind@astate.edu
Home Page: http://www.clt.astate.edu/elind/sagamain.htm

• 18980 • National Print Exhibition
To recognize the finest standards of creative expression in the print medium. Juror selection is made from submissions of both members and non-members. Prizes awarded include: Vera List Purchase Award - $150; Judith Lieber Purchase Award - $200; Associated American Artists Purchase Award - $150; Miriam Perlman Gallery Cash Award - $100; E. Weyhe Gallery Purchase Award - $150; Dick Blick Merchandise Award - $50; Joan Cohen Purchase Award - $200; Kathleen Caraccio Purchase Award - $200; and Ben and Beatrice Goldstein Foundation Purchase Award - $150. Additional cash and purchase awards are presented. Awarded annually. Established in 1924.

• 18981 •
Society of American Military Engineers
Dr. Robert D. Wolff, Exec.Dir.
607 Prince St.
Alexandria, VA 22314-0231
Phone: (703)549-3800
Toll-Free: 800-336-3097
Fax: (703)684-0231
E-mail: rwolff@same.org
Home Page: http://www.same.org

• 18982 • Walter O. Bachus Gold Medal
For recognition of outstanding leadership and accomplishment in support of the Society's mission. Individuals who have been members of the Society for at least 10 years are eligible. A gold medal is awarded annually; a gold eagle clasp is presented to a person who wins the medal more than once. Established in 1920, and named in honor the former Executive Director of the Society and two-time recipient of the Gold Medal. Formerly: (2005) Gold Medal for Distinguished Service.

• 18983 • Bliss Medal
To recognize the most outstanding contribution to military engineering education, or to promote recognition of the importance of technical leadership in the National Defense establishment. Eligible candidates are Society members and professors of architecture, engineering, construction, or related fields. Nominees should demonstrate excellence in educating, mentoring, and motivating students in architecture, engineering, and relateddisciplines, and partnering with the local SAME Post to allow Post members to mentor student members. A medal is awarded annually. A gold eagle clasp is presented in lieu of a medal to a person who wins the medal more than once. A silver plaque is presented if the winner is an institution. Established in 1958 in memory of the distinguished World War I Army Chief of Staff, General Tasker H. Bliss.

• 18984 • Colbert Medal
In recognition of the most outstanding contribution to military engineering through achievement in design, construction, administration, research, or development. Members of the National Ocean Service, officer or civilian, active or retired, are eligible. A silver medal is awarded annually. A gold eagle clasp is presented in lieu of a medal to a person who wins the medal more than once. Established in 1955 in memory of Rear Admiral Leo O. Colbert, former Director of the Coast and Geodetic Survey, and past president of the Society.

• 18985 • Cowart Plaque
To recognize an outstanding contribution to the U.S. Coast Guard civil engineering and shore facility management programs. One award is presented annually in each of two categories: civil engineering and facilities engineering. A plaque is awarded annually. Established in 1968 in honor of Vice Admiral Kenneth C. Cowart, former Chief of the Office of Engineering, U.S. Coast Guard, and a former director of the Society.

• 18986 • Curtin Plaque
To recognize the most outstanding U.S. Air Force unit in two categories: small and large. Eligible candidates are a unit of the U.S. Air Force Civil Engineer, Air Force Major Air Command, and other Air Force Civil Engineering. A plaque is awarded annually to a recipient in each category. Established in honor of the former director of Civil Engineering, U.S. Air Force, Major General Robert H. Curtin, president of the Society in 1964.

• 18987 • Goddard Medal
To recognize outstanding contributions to military engineering, including military troop construction, base maintenance, and contingency engineering. Active duty enlisted members of the U.S. Air Force, U.S. Air Force Reserve, and Air National Guard are eligible. Three silver medals are awarded annually, one to an individual from each of the three service components. A gold eagle clasp is presented in lieu of a medal to a person who wins the medal more than once. Established in 1973 in honor of Major General Guy H. Goddard, former Director of Civil Engineering, U.S. Air Force and past president of the Society.

• 18988 • George W. Goethals Medal
To recognize an engineer in civil or military practice for the most eminent and notable contribution in the field of engineering, particularly in design, construction, and methods. A silver medal is awarded annually. Established in 1956 in memory of George W. Goethals, the distinguished military engineer and builder of the Panama Canal.

• 18989 • Golden Eagle Award
To recognize annually a Fellow of The Society and an individual who is not a Fellow, who have made singularly distinctive contributions to the profession of military engineering and to America's defense establishment. Awardees are selected on the basis of having a national perspective and a vision for change; mentoring and sharing one's knowledge; continued professional development; contribution to national defense, readiness and/or emergency preparedness; and demonstrated high ethical standards. Established in 1995.

• 18990 • Itschner Plaque
For recognition of the most outstanding engineer company of the year. Silver plaques are awarded annually. From 1960, when it was first awarded, until 1973, it was offered annually by the Society to one engineer company of the Active Army selected as the most outstanding company during the year. Since 1974, three awards have been offered annually, one to an engineer company in the Active Army, Army Reserve, and Army National Guard. Named for the former Chief of Engineers, U.S. Army, Lieutenant General Emerson C. Itscher, president of the Society in 1958.

• 18991 • Karo Plaque
For recognition of an outstanding contribution in the engineering and scientific field by a field unit of the National Ocean Service. A silver plaque is awarded annually. Established in 1960 in honor of Rear Admiral H. Arnold Karo, former director of the U.S. Coast Guard and Geodetic Survey, and president of the Society in 1957.

• 18992 • J. W. Morris Sustaining Member of the Year Award
To recognize the Sustaining Member firm that has rendered the most eminent and notable contribution to the Society, on a voluntary basis, during the past year that materially assists the Society in reaching its objectives. A plaque is awarded annually. Established in 1981 in honor of Lieutenant General John W. Morris, former Chief of Engineers, U.S. Army, and past president of the Society.

• 18993 • Peltier Plaque
To recognize the Naval Mobile Construction Battalion selected as the most outstanding. A silver plaque is awarded annually. Established in 1960 in memory of Rear Admiral Eugene J. Peltier, CEC, USN, former Chief of Civil Engineers and Bureau of Yards and Docks, Department of the Navy, and president of the Society in 1960.

• 18994 • President's Medal
To recognize no more than three individuals per year for their accomplishments and contributions to the Society, the engineering profession, or the public. It is conferred to Society members on the initiative of the Society president. Established in 1992.

• 18995 • Sargent Medal
In recognition of the most outstanding contribution to Coast Guard Civil Engineering or Facilities Engineering. Active duty Coast Guard Warrant Officers, Chief Petty Officers, Petty Officers, or Coast Guard civilian employees of equivalent grade are eligible. A silver medal is awarded annually. Established in 1980 in honor of Vice Admiral Thomas R. Sargent, III, former Chief of Civil Engineering and Vice Commandant of the Coast Guard (1970-1974).

• 18996 • Shields Medal
To recognize outstanding contributions to facility construction and/or maintenance by demonstrated technical and leadership ability. Navy enlisted personnel in Occupational Field 13 ratings are eligible. A medal is awarded annually. A gold eagle clasp is presented in lieu of a medal to a person who wins the medal more than once. Established in 1974 in memory of Petty Officer Marvin G. Shields, USN, who was posthumously awarded the Congressional Medal of Honor for valor in combat while serving in Vietnam.

• 18997 • Sturgis Medal
To recognize outstanding contributions to military troop construction and/or base maintenance by demonstrated technical and leadership ability. Active duty enlisted members of the U.S. Army, U.S. Army Reserve, and Army National Guard within one of the following army career fields are eligible: combat engineering, construction and utilities, power production, heavy equipment and maintenance, drafting, surveying, printing, special electrical devices, instrument repairman, and reproduction repairman. Three silver medals are awarded annually, one to an individual from each of the three service components. A gold eagle clasp is presented in lieu of a medal to a person who wins the medal more than once. Established in 1974 in honor of Lieutenant General Samuel D. Sturgis, Jr., former Chief of Engineers of the U.S. Army.

• 18998 • Sverdrup Medal
For recognition of the most outstanding contribution to military engineering or similar achievement of significance to the Society, the military service, or the nation. Active duty military engineer members of the Society under 36 years of age at the time of nomination are eligible. A silver medal and a $500 travel stipend are awarded annually. A gold eagle clasp is presented in lieu of a medal to a person who wins the medal more than once. Established in 1980 in memory of Major General Leif J. Sverdrup, U.S. Army retired, a distinguished military engineer.

• 18999 • Toulmin Medal
To recognize the author of the article judged to be the best published in *The Military Engineer* for the year. Two silver medals are awarded annually, one to the best young writer and one to the best senior writer. A gold eagle clasp is presented in lieu of a medal to a person who wins the medal more than once. Established in 1932.

• 19000 • Tudor Medal
For recognition of the most outstanding contribution to engineering design, construction, research, development, or planning. Civilian members of the Society under 36 years of age in the year nominated are eligible. A medal and a travel stipend of $1,000 are awarded annually. A gold eagle clasp is presented in lieu of a medal to a person who wins the medal more than once. Established in 1966 in memory of Ralph A. Tudor, an eminent civil engineer and builder.

• 19001 • Urbahn Medal
To recognize on an annual basis an architect in civil or military practice for the most eminent and notable contribution to the profession of architecture. Society architects are eligible. Established in 1996 in honor of a distinguished architect and Fellow of The Society, Max O. Urbahn.

• 19002 •
Society of American Registered Architects
Richard C. Holden, Natl.Pres.
305 E 46th St.
New York, NY 10017
Phone: (218)728-4293
Fax: (218)728-5361
E-mail: rickhja@hotmail.com
Home Page: http://www.sara-national.org

• 19003 • Jean P. Boulanger Award
To recognize individuals who have given service to the Society in special ways. A certificate is awarded annually at the SARA Convention to one or more recipients. Established in 1976 in memory of Jean P. Boulanger, an outstanding former member.

• 19004 • Design Award
To recognize members for excellence and superior design of buildings. The following awards are given: Award of Excellence, Award of Merit, and Award of Honor. Gold, blue, and red ribbons are presented on submission. Two certificates are awarded: one for the member architect, and one for the building owner or developer. Awarded annually at the SARA Convention. The number of awards varies each year, depending on the number and quality of submissions. Established in 1957.

• 19005 • Distinguished Building Award
To recognize a significant structure in the city where the convention is held. Awarded when merited. Established in 1984.

• 19006 • Distinguished Presidential Citation
To recognize a past or present national elected officer who has earned distinguished recognition for dedication and contribution to the Society. Established in 1981.

• 19007 • Gold Medal
To recognize outstanding service and dedication to the profession of architecture by two members singled out by the Society. A ribboned gold medal and certificate are awarded annually. Established in 1956.

• 19008 • Gregson's Founder Award
To recognize contributions of service to the Society by members as judged by the Founder. A necktie in the plaid of the clan McGregor, to which the Founder belongs, is awarded annually. Established in 1960.

• 19009 • International Award
Presented to an architect, whether or not a SARA member, registered or licensed in any state, territory or possession of the United States or in any country in the North or South American continents and the Islands of the Western Hemisphere under the laws of that state, territory or possession or country who has distinguished himself or herself in the institutional, academic and/or professional fields and has generated a body of work and/or applied the Golden Rule materially, spiritually and intellectually towards the betterment of the profession of architecture and the unity of all architects of different cultures and countries.

• 19010 • Emily Munson Memorial Student Awards
To recognize superior architectural design projects submitted by students in architecture. Cash prizes are awarded to a student annually. Established in 1969 in honor of the past president, Thurston W. Munson, and in memory of Emily Munson.

• 19011 • Presidential Citation
To recognize exemplary service in special ways to the Society. A certificate is awarded annually. Established in 1968.

• 19012 • Special Service Awards (Citations)
To recognize members and nonmembers for outstanding service to the Society for Committee, State Council work, or other significant contributions. A certificate is awarded annually.

• 19013 • Synergy Award
To recognize an individual who has performed outstanding service to the architectural profession. A certificate is awarded annually when merited. Established in 1970.

• 19014 •
Society of American Travel Writers
Cathy Kerr, Exec.Dir.
1500 Sunday Dr., No. 102
Raleigh, NC 27607
Phone: (919)787-5181
Phone: (919)861-5586
Fax: (919)787-4916
E-mail: satw@satw.org
Home Page: http://www.satw.org

• 19015 • Phoenix Award
To recognize the important role played by individuals and organizations actively involved in the conservation, preservation, beautification, and anti-pollution campaigns that further the growth and appeal of North American travel areas. A Phoenix medallion, a symbol of new life, is awarded annually. Established in 1969.

• 19016 • Lowell Thomas Travel Journalism Awards
To recognize excellence in travel journalism. North American journalists are eligible to enter; membership in the Society is not necessary. Work published or broadcast in English during the preceding year. Judged by the faculty of outstanding university journalism schools throughout the nation. Awards are given in 27 categories, including a Grand Award and the title of Travel Journalist of the Year for the best portfolio by an individual journalist, Best Newspaper Travel Section awards in four circulation categories, Best Travel Magazine, Best Travel Coverage in General/Special Interest Magazines, Best Internet Travel Publication/Website, Best Guidebook and Best Travel Book (other than guidebook). There are 17 categories for travel-related articles and photography. The Grand Award, for the best portfolio of work by an individual journalist, is $1,500 Gold, $750 Silver, $500 Bronze; a plaque also is given for each of these awards. The 17 categories for individual articles and photography carry awards of $500 Gold, $250 Silver, $150 Bronze. Established in 1985.

• 19017 •
Society of Architectural Historians
Pauline Saliga, Exec.Dir.
1365 N Astor St.
Chicago, IL 60610-2144
Phone: (312)573-1365
Fax: (312)573-1141
E-mail: info@sah.org
Home Page: http://www.sah.org

• 19018 • Architectural Study Tour Scholarship
To enable an outstanding student to participate in the annual SAH tour of Eastern VA. The student must be engaged in graduate work in architecture or architectural history, city planning or urban history, landscape or the history of landscape design. The student must also be an SAH member. Awarded annually. Application (to be submitted with a curriculum vitae and at least two departmental recommendations) due July 1. Formerly: (1997) Annual Tour Scholarship.

• 19019 • Rosann S. Berry Fellowship
To defray the travel expenses an advanced graduate student who is delivering a paper at the annual meeting of the Society. Members of SAH for at least one year prior to the meeting who are currently engaged in advanced graduate study that involves some aspect of the history of architecture or of one of the fields closely allied to it may apply for the Fellowship by November 15. Travel expenses of up to $500 are awarded annually.

• 19020 • Antoinette Forrester Downing Award
To recognize an outstanding published work devoted to historical issues in the preservation field. Publications may include historic resource surveys, historical studies of the preservation movement, philosophical approaches to preservation, or historiographical methods. Only publishers may submit entries for consideration. Certificates and citation are given to both the sponsoring organization and the author. Awarded annually at the annual meeting.

• 19021 • Founder's Award
To recognize the best article on the history of architecture published each year in the *Journal of the Society of Architectural Historians* by a scholar 40 years of age or younger. Awarded annually. Established in 1970.

• 19022 • Alice Davis Hitchcock Award
To recognize the most distinguished work of scholarship in architectural history published by a North American scholar during the previous two years. Only publishers may submit entries. A citation and a framed photographic image are awarded annually. Established in 1949.

• 19023 • Philip Johnson Exhibition Catalogue Award
To recognize excellence in published exhibition catalogues in the realm of architectural history, including urbanism, landscape, interior architecture, and set design. The catalogue must be

Awards are arranged in alphabetical order below their administering organizations

written or edited by a North American scholar during the previous two years, or originate in an exhibition in a North American institution, or concern a North American subject. A certificate and a citation are awarded each year at the annual meeting.

• 19024 • Keepers Preservation Education Fund Fellowship
To enable a graduate student in historic preservation to attend the annual meeting. A stipend of $1,000 is awarded annually.

• 19025 • Edilia and Francois-Auguste de Montequin Fellowship
To fund travel for research on Iberian and Latin American architecture. The research to be supported must focus on Spanish, Portuguese, or Ibero-American architecture, including colonial architecture produced by the Spaniards in the Philippines and what is today the United States. A $2,000 stipend for a junior scholar and $6,000 for a senior scholar are awarded annually. Established in memory of Edilia and Francois-Auguste de Montequin. Formerly: (1997) Edilia de Montequin Fellowship in Iberian and Latin American Architecture.

• 19026 • Sally Kress Tompkins Fellowship
To enable an architectural history student to work as a summer intern on a 12-week Historic American Buildings Survey project. A stipend of $10,000 is awarded annually.

• 19027 •
Society of Arts and Crafts
Beth Ann Gerstein, Exec.Dir.
175 Newbury St.
Boston, MA 02116
Phone: (617)266-1810
Fax: (617)266-5654
E-mail: bgerstein@societyofcrafts.org
Home Page: http://www.societyofcrafts.org

• 19028 • Artist Awards
Encourages and supports Massachusetts artists who show a mastery of their craft media and create original innovative work. Limited to residents of Massachusetts. Three to four artists receive a $2,000 cash award and participate in a group exhibition. Awarded biennially in even-numbered years. Established in 1994.

• 19029 • Medal for Excellence in Craft Award
To honor nationally recognized master craftspeople and others who have made significant contributions to the decorative arts field. SAC was established in 1897 and this program was established in 1913.

• 19030 •
Society of Australasian Specialists/Oceania
Stuart Leven, Sec.
PO Box 24764
San Jose, CA 95154-4764
Phone: (408)978-0193
E-mail: stulev@ix.netcom.com
Home Page: http://members.aol.com/stampsho/saso.html

Formed by merger of: Society of Australasian Specialists; Oceania Philatelic Society.

• 19031 • Society of Australasian Specialists/Oceania Medals
To recognize superior exhibits in the field of Australasian philately that covers the area south the Equator, 90 degrees East and 90 degrees West. Philatelic organizations or exhibitors of Australasian materials are eligible. Gold, silver, and bronze medals accompanied by a certificate are awarded annually. Bronze medals are presented in conjunction with plaques for the Peter Kreisher Award for Literary Accomplishments and for Outstanding Service to the society.

• 19032 •
Society of Automotive Engineers
Raymond A. Morris, Sec.
400 Commonwealth Dr.
Warrendale, PA 15096-0001
Phone: (724)776-4841
Phone: (724)776-4970
Toll-Free: 800-TEAM-SAE
Fax: (724)776-0790
E-mail: sae@sae.org
Home Page: http://www.sae.org

• 19033 • Aerospace Engineering Leadership Award
To honor individuals at the corporate level for outstanding contributions to the field of aerospace engineering through his or her leadership skills, whether for a singular accomplishment or a lifetime achievement. An original sculpture of aluminum and marble is awarded annually. Established in 1992.

• 19034 • Award for Research on Automotive Lubricants
To recognize authors of the best papers relating to the adaptation of lubricants and lubricated automotive systems or components presented at a Society meeting, or to recognize an individual for distinguished accomplishments in research on automotive lubricants. A certificate and bronze medal are presented annually at the SAE Fuels & Lubricants Meeting. Established in 1986.

• 19035 • Vincent Bendix Automotive Electronics Engineering Award
To recognize the author(s) of the best paper relating to automotive electronics engineering that has been presented at a meeting of the Society or any of its Sections, or to recognize an individual for distinguished accomplishment in automotive electronics engineering. Material or development forming the subject matter of the paper must be based on personal work. In the event of recognition of individual achievement, the honoree is requested to present a lecture at a designated meeting of the Society. A certificate and a bronze medal are presented annually. Established in 1976 to honor Vincent Bendix, SAE's president in 1931, for his numerous engineering innovations.

• 19036 • L. Ray Buckendale Lecture
To provide for annual lectures that deal with automotive ground vehicles and to provide procedures and data useful in the formulation of solutions in commercial vehicle design, manufacture, operation, and maintenance. It is primarily directed to the needs of young engineers and students with emphasis on practical aspects of the topic. An honorarium and a certificate are awarded annually. Established in 1953 in honor of L. Ray Buckendale, former president of SAE.

• 19037 • Edward N. Cole Award for Automotive Engineering Innovation
To recognize an SAE member whose innovative design is described in an SAE paper or whose lifetime of accomplishment is judged to be a significant achievement in the engineering of automobiles, their components, systems, and accessories. Selection is based upon the value of the work as an original innovative contribution, not upon the application of some development or invention already known. Nomination deadline is August 1. A certificate and commemorative gift are presented annually. Established in 1978 to honor Edward N. Cole, automotive engineer and a retired president and chief operating officer of the General Motors Corporation.

• 19038 • Arch T. Colwell Cooperative Engineering Medal
To recognize a unique and outstanding contribution over a period of time to the work of the technical committees under the SAE Technical Standards Board in developing standards, specifications, technical reports, and data through cooperative research. A medal and a certificate are presented annually. Established in 1976 to honor Arch T. Colwell, former SAE president.

• 19039 • Arch T. Colwell Merit Award
To recognize the authors of papers of outstanding technical or professional merit that have been presented at a meeting of the Society or any of its sections during the calendar year. Papers are judged primarily for their value as new contributions to existing knowledge of mobility engineering. A certificate is presented annually. Established in 1965.

• 19040 • Distinguished Younger Member Award
To recognize the distinguished achievements and contribution to SAE on the local level by younger members. Recipients are selected from the candidates nominated each year by sections or groups for the Outstanding Younger Member Award. A certificate is presented at the annual SAE International Congress & Exposition; awardees also receive a gift from Mrs. Dollie Cole. Established in 1980 in memory of Edward

N. Cole, former President and Chief Operating Officer of General Motors Corporation.

• 19041 • Engineering Meetings Board Outstanding Oral Presentation Award
To recognize individuals who make outstanding presentations at SAE technical sessions. Selection is based on a random sampling of the audience that is asked to evaluate each individual making a presentation. A certificate is presented annually. Established in 1972. In addition, the SAE Lloyd L. Withrow Distinguished Speaker Award recognizes individuals who have received the Oral Presentation Award more than twice. A plaque is awarded when merited. Established in 1984.

• 19042 • Fellow Grade of Membership
To recognize and honor those members who have made a significant impact on the Society's mobility technology through research, innovation, or creative leadership. Nomination deadline is June 1. A Fellow pin and a certificate are awarded to approximately 20 recipients per year. Established in 1975.

• 19043 • Henry Ford II Distinguished Award for Excellence in Automotive Engineering
To recognize members who use their engineering skills to achieve product or manufacturing process contributions that are assessed to have had the greatest positive effect on the passenger car, truck, and bus industries. Nominations are due by August 1. A commemorative gift is awarded annually. Established in 1988 to honor Henry Ford II for his enormous impact on the automotive industry.

• 19044 • Cliff Garrett Turbomachinery Engineering Award
To promote engineering developments and the presentation of SAE papers on turbomachinery engineering. Nomination deadline is March 31. A plaque and Atmos Clock are awarded annually. Established in 1984 in honor of Cliff Garrett, an aerospace pioneer.

• 19045 • Honeywell SAE Outstanding Student Branch Award
To reward exemplary performance in the areas of technical meetings, projects, membership continuity, and recruitment. Branches compete in one of three classes based on size. The award consists of a plaque and a monetary prize and is presented in each class in May. Awarded annually. Established in 1963. Formerly: AlliedSignal Outstanding Student Branch Award.

• 19046 • Harry L. Horning Memorial Award
To recognize the author(s) of the best paper or combination of papers relating to the better mutual adaptation of fuels and internal combustion engines that are presented at a meeting of the Society or any of its sections, or to an individual for distinguished accomplishment in engine fuel relationships. In recognizing individual achievements, the awardee is requested to present a Horning Memorial Lecture at a designated meeting of the Society. A certificate and bronze medal are presented annually during the Fuels and Lubricants Meeting. Established in 1938 to honor Harry L. Horning, former SAE president.

• 19047 • International Leadership Citation
To provide public recognition to an individual well known internationally for continuous professional involvement and participation in SAE's meetings and conferences, and/or unique assistance and support in helping SAE achieve its goals and objectives, either in the broadest sense or related to one specific offshore conference. The recipient is presented with a bronze plaque annually. Established in 1988.

• 19048 • Ralph H. Isbrandt Automotive Safety Engineering Award
To recognize the author delivering the most outstanding paper at a Society or Section meeting on the subject of automotive safety engineering, or an individual who has contributed a distinguished accomplishment in automotive safety engineering. In the event of the latter, the individual is invited to present a Ralph H. Isbrandt Memorial Lecture on an appropriate subject at a designated meeting of the Society. A certificate and bronze medal are presented annually. Established in 1972 to honor Ralph H. Isbrandt, former SAE president.

• 19049 • Franklin W. Kolk Air Transportation Progress Award
To recognize an individual for unique and outstanding contributions to air transportation and/or the work of the aerospace technical committees in developing aerospace standards, specifications, technical reports, and data through cooperative research. Nominations are due May 1. A certificate and an honorarium are presented at the SAE World Aviation Congress each year. Established in 1978 in memory of Franklin W. Kolk for his advancement of civil air transportation and to the associated work of the Society.

• 19050 • William Littlewood Memorial Lecture
To advance air transport engineering and to recognize those who make personal contributions to the field. A certificate and an honorarium are presented at a national meeting of one of the sponsoring societies. Awarded annually. Established in 1971 in memory of William Littlewood's contributions to civil air transport. Co-sponsored by the American Institute of Aeronautics and Astronautics.

• 19051 • Charles M. Manly Memorial Medal
To recognize the author(s) of the best paper relating to theory or practice in the design or construction of, or research on, aerospace engines, their parts, components, or accessories that is presented at a meeting of the Society or its Sections during the calendar year. A certificate, bronze medal, and honorarium are presented annually. Established in 1928.

• 19052 • Forest R. McFarland Award
To recognize individuals for outstanding contributions toward the work of the SAE Engineering Meetings Board in the planning, development, and dissemination of technical information through technical meetings, conferences and professional development programs, or outstanding contributions to Engineering Meetings Board operations in facilitating or enhancing the interchanges of technical information. Up to 20 individuals are awarded certificates each year at the SAE Honors Convocation. Established in 1979 by the bequest of Forest McFarland, a session organizer, a chairman of the Passenger Car Activity, and a member of the Engineering Activity Board.

• 19053 • Medal of Honor
To recognize and honor a living SAE member for unique and significant contribution to the Society by strengthening or adding to its ability to further its purpose. The significance of such contribution shall have been tested over time, and shall be regarded as a major factor in SAE's success. A bronze medal is awarded annually. Established in 1986.

• 19054 • Outstanding Section/Student Chapter Partnership Award
To recognize SAE Sections and Student Chapters that engage in a high level of interaction with each other for the mutual benefit of their respective members. The award is designed to honor exceptional efforts by SAE Section and Student Chapter leaders for developing a comprehensive, year-round program of activities, events, services, and networking opportunities for the benefit of their local SAE professional members, SAE faculty advisors, and the student members of the local SAE collegiate chapters. Three awards are presented annually: President's Citation for Outstanding Section/Chapter Partnership, SAE Section/Chapter Partnerships of Distinction Awards, and Certificate of Recognition. Established in 1972.

• 19055 • Outstanding Younger Member Award
In recognition of younger members who have done an outstanding job in furthering the sections' contributions to the automotive arts and sciences. The award consists of a certificate and is presented at the recipient's last section meeting of the year. Awarded annually Established in 1976.

• 19056 • Thomas H. Speller Award
To recognize unusual achievements of an individual who, through dedicated service, tireless efforts, high ideals, and vision, contributed significantly to the implementation of manufacturing processes and methodologies in the dedicated discipline of automatic fastening machines and their applications. A certificate is presented annually at the AEROFAST Conference. Established in 1990.

• 19057 • Elmer A. Sperry Award
To recognize distinguished engineering contributions that, through application proven in ac-

tual service, have advanced the state-of-the-art of transportation whether by land, sea, or air. A bronze medal, a certificate, and a copy of the biography of Elmer A. Sperry are presented annually. Established in 1955 to honor Elmer A. Sperry, who was renowned for his navigational gyroscope and who coined the word "automotive," giving SAE its name. Co-sponsored by the American Society of Mechanical Engineers, the American Institute of Aeronautics and Astronautics, the Institute of Electrical and Electronics Engineers, American Society of Civil Engineers, and the Society of Naval Architects and Marine Engineers.

• 19058 • Russell S. Springer Award
For recognition of original and outstanding technical papers that are distinct contributions to the literature of the profession of mobility engineering, and for encouragement of the younger members. The award is made annually to a young member who authors a high quality paper that is presented at an SAE sponsored meeting and is published in SAE literature in the year for which the award is made. An honorarium and a certificate are presented to the recipient. Established in 1954.

• 19059 • Technical Standards Board Outstanding Contribution Award
To recognize individuals for outstanding service in the technical committee activities of the Society. Selection is based on outstanding contributions to the work of SAE technical committees, unusual leadership in the activities of an SAE technical committee, significant contributions as a representative of the Society to the accomplishments of technical committees of other organizations or of Government agencies, and outstanding contributions to SAE technical committee work in the form of research, test methods and procedures, and/or development of standards. A certificate is awarded annually. Established in 1953. Formerly: (2003) Technical Standards Board Certificate of Appreciation.

• 19060 • Ralph R. Teetor Educational Award
To honor Ralph R. Teetor's belief that engineering educators are the most effective link between engineering students and their future careers. This award provides for an exchange of views and technical information between outstanding engineering educators and practicing engineers in industry. Recipients are chosen on the basis of academic training, contributions to teaching and research, extracurricular student involvement, and benefits expected from the Teetor Award. Each recipient is awarded two years of SAE membership and a plaque. Awarded annually. Established in 1963 to honor Ralph R. Teetor, SAE's president in 1936.

• 19061 • Marvin Whitlock Award
To recognize an individual for outstanding technical contributions and/or innovation related to operational availability of aircraft in such areas as repair design, tooling, maintenance practices, logistics, inspection, modification, and safety. A bronze medal and an honorarium are awarded annually. Established in 1988 to acknowledge and commemorate the distinctive management contributions of the late Marvin Whitlock, Senior Vice President of maintenance and member of the Board of Directors of United Air Lines.

• 19062 • Wright Brothers Medal
To recognize the authors of the best papers relating to the invention, development, design, construction, or operation of an aircraft and/or spacecraft that has been presented at a meeting of the Society or any of its Sections. Consideration is given to the value of the author's contribution to the state-of-the-art in furthering flight technology, whether it pertains to aircraft or spacecraft systems or their parts, components, subsystems, or accessories. A bronze medal and certificate are awarded annually. Established in 1927 in honor of Orville and Wilbur Wright, the first successful constructors and operators of heavier-than-air flying equipment.

• 19063 •
Society of Automotive Historians
Kit Foster, Membership Sec.
1102 Long Cove Rd.
Gales Ferry, CT 06335-1812
Phone: (860)464-6466
Fax: (860)464-2614
E-mail: membership@autohistory.org
Home Page: http://www.autohistory.org

• 19064 • Carl Benz Award
To recognize the best periodical article on automotive history published during the previous calendar year. A framed award is presented each year at the Society's annual meeting. Awards of Distinction are also awarded to exceptional articles nominated for the award. Established as an element of the Cugnot Award in 1972. Renamed in 1982 to honor Carl Benz, regarded as the inventor of the first successful internal combustion engine in 1885 in Mannheim, Germany. Formerly: (1982) Cugnot Award.

• 19065 • James J. Bradley Distinguished Service Award
To recognize a library or archive, or an individual within an organization, for preservation of historic materials relating to motor vehicles of the world. Awarded each year at the Society's annual meeting. Established in 1982 to honor James J. Bradley, the late curator of the National Automotive History Collection at the Detroit Public Library.

• 19066 • Richard and Grace Brigham Award
To recognize outstanding coverage of automotive history by a periodical published during the previous calendar year. A framed award is presented each year at the Society's annual meeting in October. Established in 1989 to honor Richard and Grace Brigham, founding members of the Society and its first publications.

• 19067 • Nicholas-Joseph Cugnot Award
To recognize the best book that demonstrates original research and outstanding writing in the field of automotive history published during the previous calendar year. A framed award is presented each year at the annual meeting in October. Separate awards are presented to books published in a language other than English. Awards of Distinction are also awarded to exceptional books nominated for the award. Established in 1972 in honor of Nicholas-Joseph Cugnot, a French Army officer acknowledged to have built the first self-propelled vehicle.

• 19068 • Friend of Automotive History Award
To recognize an individual for outstanding service and contribution to the field of automotive history. Awarded to one or more recipients each year at the Society's annual meeting. Established in 1983.

• 19069 • E. P. Ingersoll Award
To recognize excellence in presentation of automotive history in forms other than print media. Awarded at the Society's annual meeting in October. Established in 1992 in honor of E. P. Ingersoll, editor and proprietor of *Horseless Age*, the first motoring magazine in the United States, and who was instrumental in organizing the first vehicle trade organization.

• 19070 •
Society of Biological Psychiatry
Maggie Peterson, Mgr.
Mayo Clinic of Jacksonville, Research-Birdsall 310
4500 San Pablo Rd.
Jacksonville, FL 32224
Phone: (904)953-2842
Fax: (904)953-7117
E-mail: peterson.maggie@mayo.edu
Home Page: http://www.sobp.org

• 19071 • A. E. Bennett Research Awards
To recognize the two best unpublished research papers, one in clinical science and the other in basic science, in the field of biological psychiatry. Investigators from any country who are under 45 years of age are eligible. The deadline for submissions is January 1. A monetary prize of $2,000 and a certificate are awarded in each category annually. Established in 1958. Funded by the A. E. Bennett Neuropsychiatric Research Foundation.

• 19072 • Eli Lilly Travel Fellowship Award
To provide monetary assistance to third-, fourth-, and fifth-year medical residents or fellowship trainees to attend the society's annual meeting. Awards are given based on past excellence and potential for professional growth in activities pertaining to academic psychiatry or clinical neuroscience. The deadline for submissions is January 31. Up to 15 fellowships of $1,500 in travel expenses are awarded annually. Established in 1991. Supported by Eli Lilly and Co.

• 19073 • Gold Medal Award
For recognition of pioneer contributions to the advancement and extension of knowledge in

biological psychiatry. Scientists working in the area of biological psychiatry including, but not limited to, individuals from academic institutions, foundations, governmental, industrial, and research organizations regardless of age, sex, or nationality are eligible. The deadline for nominations is January 1. An engraved gold medal and a plaque are awarded annually if merited. Established in 1967.

• 19074 • George N. Thompson Award for Distinguished Service

To honor members of the society who have given outstanding service to promote the welfare of the organization. Work in the areas of leadership, governance, development of publications, special projects, financial contributions, or other service recognized as distinguished by the council is considered. Nominations are accepted from society members by January 1. Awarded annually if merited. Established in 1982 to honor George N. Thompson, one of the founders of the society.

• 19075 • Ziskind-Somerfeld Research Award

To recognize the best research paper published in *Biological Psychiatry* during the year. Members involved in basic or clinical research who are at least 35 years of age are eligible. The deadline for submissions is January 1. A monetary prize of $2,500 and a certificate are awarded annually. Established in 1991. Supported by the Zisking-Somerfeld Research Foundation.

• 19076 •
Society of Cable Telecommunications Engineers
Tom Maguire, Sec.
140 Philips Rd.
Exton, PA 19341-1318
Phone: (610)363-6888
Toll-Free: 800-542-5040
Fax: (610)363-5898
E-mail: scte@scte.org
Home Page: http://www.scte.org

Formerly: (1996) Society of Cable Television Engineers.

• 19077 • Chairman's Award

To recognize an individual or organization for significant support of the Society. Awarded annually at the discretion of the Chairman of the Society. Established in 1980. Formerly: President's Award.

• 19078 • Member of the Year

To recognize a member who significantly contributed to the Society over the past year. Nomination deadline is March 1. Awarded annually. Established in 1974. Sponsored by Motorola Corp.

• 19079 •
Society of Canadian Ornithologists
(Societe des Ornithologistes du Canada)
Nancy Flood, Membership Sec.
8541 Esplanade
Montreal, QC, Canada H2P 2S1
Phone: (514)385-1917
Fax: (514)287-9687
E-mail: beaudet.lamothe@sympatico.ca
Home Page: http://www.sco-soc.ca/

• 19080 • Doris Huestis Speirs Award

This, the highest honor bestowed by the Society, is given to recognize an individual for outstanding lifetime contributions to Canadian ornithology. Awardees may include professionals who work at museums, government agencies, private companies, and universities, as well as amateur ornithologists and people who have contributed to ornithological infrastructure of Canada. Awarded annually. Established in 1986.

• 19081 •
Society of Cardiovascular Anesthesiologists
James G. Ramsay MD, Pres.
2209 Dickens Rd.
PO Box 11086
Richmond, VA 23230-1086
Phone: (804)282-0084
Fax: (804)282-0090
E-mail: sca@societyhq.com
Home Page: http://www.scahq.org

• 19082 • Research Starter Grant

To foster innovation and creativity by an individual researcher in the field of cardiac anesthesiology. Candidates must be members of the Society; possess an M.D. or PhD degree; and hold the rank of associate professor or less. One-year projects (for a total of $20,000) and two-year projects (for a total of $40,000) will be considered. Awarded annually. Formerly: (1995) Resident Research Competition.

• 19083 •
Society of Chemical Industry American Section
177 Terrace Dr.
Chatham, NJ 07928
Phone: (973)635-0189
Fax: (973)635-0958
E-mail: sciamerica@soci.info
Home Page: http://www.soci.org/SCI/sections/homepage.jsp?code=AME

• 19084 • Chemical Industry Medal

To recognize an individual for conspicuous contribution to the growth of the chemical industry. A gold medal and opportunity to speak at the formal awards dinner are awarded annually. Established in 1920. Formerly: (1932) Grasselli Medal.

• 19085 • Perkin Medal

To recognize innovation in applied chemistry resulting in outstanding commercial development. Individuals residing in the United States who are actively engaged in the chemical profession are eligible. Selection is made by representatives of the American Section of the Society of Chemical Industry, the American Chemical Society, the American Institute of Chemical Engineers, the American Institute of Chemists, the Electrochemical Society, and the American Section of the Societe de Chimie Industrielle. A medal and opportunity to speak at the awards presentation are awarded annually. Established in 1906 to honor Sir William Henry Perkin, who created the world's first synthetic aniline dye in 1856.

• 19086 •
Society of Children's Book Writers and Illustrators
Stephen Mooser, Pres.
8271 Beverly Blvd.
Los Angeles, CA 90048
Phone: (323)782-1010
Fax: (323)782-1892
E-mail: scbwi@scbwi.org
Home Page: http://www.scbwi.org

Formerly: (1992) Society of Children's Book Writers.

• 19087 • Golden Kite Awards

To give recognition to children/s book authors and artists by their fellow authors and artists. Statuettes and plaques are given in the following categories: fiction, nonfiction, picture book text, and picture book illustration. Presented annually. Established in 1973.

• 19088 • Magazine Merit Awards

To recognize outstanding original magazine work for young people published during the year by members of the society. Awards are presented in four categories: fiction, nonfiction, illustration, and poetry. Writers, artists, or photographer members must submit entries by December 15. Plaques are awarded annually. Established in 1988.

• 19089 • Society of Children's Book Writers and Illustrators Grants

To encourage continuing excellence in the creation of children's literature. Six grant programs are available: Work-in-Progress Grants (four grants of $1,500 each), Don Freeman Memorial Grant-in-Aid (one grant of $1,500; one grant of $500), Barbara Karlin Grant (one grant of $1,500; one grant of $500), Martha Weston Grant (one grant of $1,500), Kimberly Colen Memorial Grant (two grants of $2,500 each), and Amber Brown Grant ($250 and expenses-paid visit by a well-known author or illustrator). Awarded annually.

• 19090 •
Society of Cosmetic Chemists
Theresa Cesario, Exec.Dir.
120 Wall St., Ste. 2400
New York, NY 10005
Phone: (212)668-1500
Fax: (212)668-1504
E-mail: scc@scconline.org
Home Page: http://www.scconline.org

• 19091 • **Chapter Awards**
To recognize outstanding contributions by chapters of the Society. The Chapter Merit Award is presented for outstanding service, dedication, and voluntary services of a period of time. The Chapter Best Speaker Award is given for the best scientific paper presented at an SCC Chapter meeting. Sixteen awards are available, each consisting of a monetary award of $250 and a scroll. Awarded annually.

• 19092 • **Literature Award**
To recognize the author of scientific papers in basic research judged to be an outstanding contribution to cosmetic science and technology. A scroll and an honorarium are awarded annually. Established in 1955.

• 19093 • **Merit Award**
To recognize a member for outstanding service and distinguished leadership in the Society's actities. Awarded annually.

• 19094 • **Maison G. de Navarre Medal Award**
This, the Society's highest honor, is given to recognize an individual who has, over a period of many years, rendered significant technical contributions to cosmetic science. Awarded annually.

• 19095 • **Society of Cosmetic Chemists Awards**
To recognize outstanding achievement in cosmetic chemistry. Prizes are awarded in the following categories: for the best scientific paper presented before the membership and published in the *Journal of Cosmetic Science*; for the best scientific paper presented at the Society's Annual Scientific Seminar; and for the best paper presented at the Society's annual scientific meeting. Each consists of a scroll and an honorarium. Awarded annually. The awards are sponsored by the following organizations, respectively: International Flavors and Fragrances, Inc., Shaw Mudge & Co., and SYMRISE.

• 19096 •
Society of Decorative Painters
Cristy Keeton, Office Coord.
393 N McLean Blvd.
Wichita, KS 67203-9300
Phone: (316)269-9300
Fax: (316)269-9191
E-mail: sdp@decorativepainters.org
Home Page: http://www.decorativepainters.org

Formerly: National Society of Tole and Decorative Painters.

• 19097 • **Decorative Arts Collection Awards**
To recognize creative artists in decorative painting. Three monetary prizes and inscribed charms are awarded at the Annual Meeting and Convention. Established in 1984.

• 19098 • **Dedicated Service Award**
To recognize outstanding and dedicated service to the Society. A medal is awarded at the Annual Meeting and Convention. Established in 1984.

• 19099 • **Silver Palette Award**
To recognize noteworthy and exceptional contributions in furthering the purposes of the Society. A dated silver palette is awarded at the Annual Meeting and Convention. Established in 1977.

• 19100 •
Society of Design Administration, Hilton Head Chapter
Beth Wee, Contact
PO Box 6913
Hilton Head Island, SC 29938
Phone: (843)785-5171
Fax: (843)785-7471

• 19101 • **SDA Scholarship Award**
For outstanding architectural ability. Scholarship awarded annually.

• 19102 •
Society of Diagnostic Medical Sonography
Dawn Sanchez, Dir. Membership Marketing and Services
2745 N Dallas Pky., Ste. 350
Plano, TX 75093-4706
Phone: (214)473-8057
Toll-Free: 800-229-9506
Fax: (214)473-8563
E-mail: ccowser@sdms.org
Home Page: http://www.sdms.org

Formerly: (1980) American Society of Ultrasound Technical Specialists.

• 19103 • **Gottesfeld Award**
To recognize the authors of outstanding research, professional, technical, or review articles in the *Journal of Diagnostic Medical Sonography*. Sonographers who are or have been employed in the field and who are the primary authors of published articles are eligible. A monetary award of $1,000 is presented to each of three winners annually at the fall conference. Established in 1986 in memory of Kenneth R. Gottesfeld.

• 19104 • **W. Frederick Sample Student Excellence Award**
To acknowledge outstanding achievement in the field of diagnostic sonography. Awards are presented in two categories: Original Research and Literature Review. Students who are enrolled in or who have graduated within the past year from a formal education program (minimum 12 months), are members of the Society, and meet prerequisites to be eligible to take the ARDMS examinations are eligible. The following awards are presented: first place - a monetary award of $500 and a plaque; and second place - $150 and a plaque. Awarded annually at the yearly meeting. Established in 1979 in honor of W. Frederick Sample.

• 19105 •
Society of Economic Geologists
Brian G. Hoal, Exec.Dir.
7811 Shaffer Pkwy.
Littleton, CO 80127
Phone: (720)981-7882
Fax: (720)981-7874
E-mail: seg@segweb.org
Home Page: http://www.segweb.org

• 19106 • **Distinguished Lectureships**
Recognizes outstanding work in applied geology and geologic research. Awarded annually.

• 19107 • **Waldemar S. Lindgren Award**
To recognize a young scientist whose published research represents an outstanding contribution to economic geology. Members under the age of 37 are eligible. The award is given for contributions to economic geology from any subdiscipline of geology, including, among others, structural geology, mineralogy, environmental geology, hydrology, petrology, geochemistry, stratigraphy, geophysics, and mine geology. The award which consists of a citation, dues-free membership in the Society, and travel to the fall meeting for the presentation. Awarded annually. Established in 1960.

• 19108 • **Marsden Award**
Recognizes outstanding service to the association. Awarded annually.

• 19109 • **Penrose Medal**
Annual award of recognition.

• 19110 • **Silver Medal**
Annual award of recognition.

• 19111 •
Society of Experimental Test Pilots
Paula S. Smith, Exec.Dir.
PO Box 986
Lancaster, CA 93584-0986
Phone: (661)942-9574
Fax: (661)940-0398
E-mail: setp@setp.org
Home Page: http://www.setp.org/

• 19112 • **James H. Doolittle Award**
To recognize outstanding technical management or engineering achievement in aerospace technology. Living members of the Society are eligible. A trophy is awarded annually. Established in 1966. Sponsored by Boeing Co.

• 19113 • **Honorary Fellow**
To recognize an honorary fellow who has achieved particular distinction in the aerospace field and has been engaged as an experimental test pilot at some time during his career. He/she need not be a member of the Society. A certificate is awarded annually. Established in 1957.

• 19114 • Iven C. Kincheloe Award
To recognize outstanding professional accomplishment in the conduct of flight testing. Living members of the Society are eligible. A trophy is awarded annually. Established in 1958.

• 19115 • Ray E. Tenhoff Award
To recognize the author of the best technical paper presented at the Society's annual symposium. The individual need not be a member of the Society. Applications and nominations not accepted. A monetary award and a plaque are awarded annually. Established in 1962. Sponsored by BAE Systems.

• 19116 •
Society of Exploration Geo-physicists
Mary Fleming, Exec.Dir.
8801 S Yale
PO Box 702740
Tulsa, OK 74170
Phone: (918)497-5500
Fax: (918)497-5557
E-mail: web@seg.org
Home Page: http://www.seg.org

• 19117 • Best Paper in *Geophysics* Award
To recognize the author(s) of the outstanding technical papers(s) published in *Geophysics* each year. Awarded annually. Established in 1947.

• 19118 • Best Paper Presented at the Annual Meeting Award
To recognize an outstanding presentation of technical papers at the Annual Meeting. Awarded annually. Established in 1997.

• 19119 • Distinguished Achievement Award
To recognize company, institution, or other organization for a specific technical contribution or contributions that have substantially advanced the science of exploration geophysics. Awarded when merited. Established in 1986.

• 19120 • Maurice Ewing Medal
For special recognition of major contributions to the advancement of science and the profession of exploration geophysics. Awarded when merited. Established in 1978.

• 19121 • Reginald Fessenden Award
To recognize an individual for a specific technical contribution to exploration geophysics, such as an invention or a theoretical or conceptual advancement. Awarded when merited. Established in 1961. Formerly: Medal Award.

• 19122 • Honorary Membership
To recognize an individual for a distinguished contribution to exploration geophysics or a related field, or to the advancement of the profession of exploration geophysics through service to the Society. Awarded to one or more recipients when merited. Established in 1930.

• 19123 • Virgil Kauffman Gold Medal
To recognize an individual for outstanding contributions of a technical or professional nature to the advancement of the science of geophysical exploration, as manifested during the previous five years. Awarded annually. Established in 1966.

• 19124 • Life Membership
To recognize individuals who have voluntarily rendered exceptionally meritorious service to the Society. Awarded to one or more recipients each year. Established in 1954.

• 19125 • Outstanding OTC Geophysical Paper Award
To recognize the author(s) of the outstanding geophysical paper presented at the Society's sessions during each Offshore Technology Conference technical program. Awarded annually.

• 19126 •
Society of Fire Protection Engineers
Kathleen H. Almand, Exec.Dir.
7315 Wisconsin Ave., No. 1225W
Bethesda, MD 20814
Phone: (301)718-2910
Fax: (301)718-2242
E-mail: sfpehqtrs@sfpe.org
Home Page: http://www.sfpe.org

• 19127 • Jack Bono Engineering Communications Award
To recognize the author(s) of the technical paper that during the prior year most contributed to the advancement and application of professional fire protection engineering. Both technical content and usefulness to the Society in advancing competency are considered. Established in 1995 to recognize the first chairman of the SFPE Educational & Scientific Foundation Board of Governors.

• 19128 • Fire Protection Man/Woman of the Year
To recognize outstanding contributions toward the protection of life and property from the ravages of fire. Contributions must be broad in scope, at least of national importance. Individuals outside the Society are eligible. A certificate mounted on a walnut plaque is awarded annually if warranted. Established in 1973.

• 19129 • Arthur B. Guise Medal
This, the Society's highest honor, if given for outstanding contributions to the advancement of the science and technology of fire protection engineering. Such achievement may be in the areas of research, development, design, innovation, management, education, or literature. Individuals need not be members to be nominated, though at least one nominator must be a SFPE member. The deadline is June 1. A medal and honorarium are awarded annually. Established in 1983 in honor of Arthur B. Guise, noted engineer and scientist who was singularly responsible for the development of dry chemicals as fire extinguishing agents.

• 19130 • Harold E. Nelson Service Award
To recognize members who have rendered exceptional service to SFPE and to the profession. A trophy is awarded annually. Established in 1987.

• 19131 •
Society of Flight Test Engineers
Margaret Drury, Exec.Dir.
PO Box 4037
Lancaster, CA 93539-4037
Phone: (661)949-2095
Fax: (661)949-2096
E-mail: sfte@sfte.org
Home Page: http://www.sfte.org

• 19132 • Directors Award
To recognize individuals for significant and lasting contributions toward the welfare, stature, leadership, and membership of the Society. Awarded annually. Established in 1969.

• 19133 • Kelly Johnson Award
To recognize excellence in flight test engineering. Individuals, teams, or projects currently active in flight test engineering are eligible. An engraved plaque, bearing the society's emblem, is awarded annually. Established in 1973.

• 19134 •
Society of Forensic Toxicologists
Amanda J. Jenkins PhD, Pres.
PO Box 5543
Mesa, AZ 85211-5543
Phone: (480)839-9106
Fax: (480)839-9106
E-mail: disensch@co.wayne.mi.us
Home Page: http://www.soft-tox.org

• 19135 • Educational Research Award
To support education and research in the field of forensic toxicology. Students pursuing advanced degrees in the fields of chemistry, pharmacology, toxicology, or other related disciplines whose research is consistent with the needs of forensic toxicologists are eligible. Awards are considered on a continuing basis throughout the year. Monetary awards of $1,000 are presented to as many as six recipients each year. Established in 1978. Formerly: (1982) Education Award.

• 19136 •
Society of Illustrators
Terrence Brown, Dir.
128 E 63rd St.
New York, NY 10021-7303
Phone: (212)838-2560
Fax: (212)838-2561
E-mail: sil901@aol.com
Home Page: http://www.societyillustrators.org

• 19137 • Annual Exhibition Awards
To encourage the highest quality of illustration art in five categories: Sequential/Series, Edito-

Awards are arranged in alphabetical order below their administering organizations

rial, Book, Advertising, and Institutional. All commissioned work, whether published or not, is eligible. Gold and silver medals are awarded annually in each category. Held annually. Established in 1959.

• 19138 •

Society of Insurance Research
691 Crossfire Ridge
Marietta, GA 30064
Phone: (770)426-9270
Fax: (770)426-9298
E-mail: stanhopp@mindspring.com
Home Page: http://www.sirnet.org

• 19139 • President's Award
To recognize the individual who has contributed the most to furthering the purposes of the Society. Members of SIR are eligible for the award. A plaque is presented annually. Established in 1980.

• 19140 • Research Award
To recognize an individual for the best paper on a topic selected by SIR. Papers are judged by a panel of experts. Monetary awards are presented biennially for First and Second Prize. Established in 1989.

• 19141 •

Society of Manufacturing Engineers
Composites Manufacturing Association
Nancy S. Berg, Exec.Dir.
1 SME Dr.
PO Box 930
Dearborn, MI 48121-0930
Phone: (313)271-1500
Toll-Free: 800-733-4763
Fax: (313)425-3400
E-mail: service@sme.org
Home Page: http://www.sme.org

• 19142 • Award of Merit
To recognize outstanding members who have substantially contributed to the activity, growth, and prestige of their chapters or regions. As many as ten bronze plaques (medals mounted on engraved plaques) are awarded annually. Established in 1958.

• 19143 • Walt Bartram Memorial Education Award Fund
Provides a total of $1,200 for student scholarships and educational projects related to manufacturing engineering for high schools, trade schools, colleges or universities within Arizona, New Mexico, and Southern California. All applicants must be SME members unless they are a high school student with a minimum GPA of 3.5 or better.

• 19144 • Donald C. Burnham Manufacturing Management Award
For recognition of exceptional success in the integration of the infrastructure and process manufacturing through the innovative use of human, technical, and financial resources. A medal mounted on an engraved plaque is presented annually. Established in 1983.

• 19145 • Caterpillar Scholars Award Fund
Supports five scholarships of $2,000 each for students enrolled in manufacturing engineering programs. Minority applicants can apply as incoming freshman. A minimum GPA of 3.0 is required.

• 19146 • Arthur and Gladys Cervenka Scholarship Award
Supports one scholarship of $1,250 for a student enrolled in a manufacturing engineering or technology program. Preference is given, but not limited to, students attending a college or university in the state of Florida. Applicants must have a minimum overall GPA of 3.0.

• 19147 • Community College Scholarship Award
Provides at least three scholarships of $1,000 each to full-time entering freshmen or sophomore students with less than 60 college credit hours. Applicants must be enrolled in manufacturing or a closely related field at a community college, trade school, or other two-year degree granting institution. Applicants must also have an overall minimum GPA of 3.5.

• 19148 • Directors Scholarship Fund
Supports an undergraduate scholarship awarded annually to a full-time student enrolled in a degree program in manufacturing in the United States or Canada.

• 19149 • Roscoe Douglas Scholarship Award Fund
Supports one scholarship of $1,500 for a student enrolled in a manufacturing engineering or technology program, but the applicant must be attending one of the approved Michigan schools, and have a minimum GPA of 3.0.

• 19150 • Education Award
To recognize an individual for development of manufacturing-related curricula, fostering sound training methods, or inspiring students to enter the profession of manufacturing. A mounted gold medal and an engraved plaque are awarded annually when merited. Established in 1957.

• 19151 • Founding Chapter Scholarship Award
Supports three scholarships of at least $1000 each. One award will be available in each of the following academic levels to a student member of the SME Chapters sponsored by Detroit Chapter One. (1) Associate degree, (2) Baccalaureate degree, (3) Graduate degree programs. Applicants must be enrolled in manufacturing engineering, manufacturing engineering technology, or closely related degree or certificate programs at one of the five approved schools listed in the organization's announcement. An overall GPA of 3.0 or better is also required.

• 19152 • Gold Medal
To recognize outstanding service to the manufacturing engineering profession in technical communications through published literature, technical writings, and lectures. A mounted gold medal and an engraved plaque are awarded annually when merited. Established in 1955.

• 19153 • Connie and Robert T. Gunter Scholarship Award Fund
Supports one scholarship of $1,000 for a student enrolled in a manufacturing engineering or technology program. Applicants must attend one of the approved schools in Georgia and have a minimum GPA of 3.5.

• 19154 • J. H. "Jud" Hall Composites Manufacturing Award
To recognize an individual who has contributed to the composites manufacturing or tooling technology through leadership, technical developments, patents, or educational activities. Nominations may be submitted by August 1. Awarded annually. Established in 1991 to honor Jud Hall for his leadership and dedication to SME's composites technology.

• 19155 • Clinton J. Helton Manufacturing Scholarship Award Fund
Supports one scholarship of $3,500 for students enrolled in a manufacturing engineering or technology program. Applicants must attend one of the approved schools in Colorado and have an overall minimum GPA of 3.3.

• 19156 • Honorary Membership
This, the Society's highest honor, is given to recognize an individual for acknowledged professional eminence among manufacturing engineers. A gold medallion on a ribbon is awarded at the discretion of the Board of Directors. Established in 1935.

• 19157 • Lucille B. Kaufman Women's Scholarship Fund
Supports at least one scholarship of $1,000 for a female student enrolled in a manufacturing engineering or technology program. Applicants must have an overall minimum GPA of 3.5.

• 19158 • Wayne Kay Co-Op Scholarship Award
Provides two scholarships of $2,500 each for students enrolled in a manufacturing engineering or manufacturing engineering technology co-op program. Applicants must have a 3.5 minimum GPA.

• 19159 • Wayne Kay Graduate Fellowship
Provides fellowships of $4,000 to $12,000 each for (1) Graduate students seeking an advanced degree or (2) faculty seeking a doctorate degree. Applicants must be accepted in a graduate program for manufacturing engineering or industrial engineering. Graduate students will not be funded beyond the first post-master year.

Applicants must also have an overall minimum of a 3.5 GPA.

• 19160 • Wayne Kay High School Scholarship

Scholarship valued at up to $2,500, $1,000 the first year and $1,500 the second year if renewed, and academic excellence is continued. Applicants must have an overall GPA of 3.5.

• 19161 • Wayne Kay Scholarship Fund

Supports ten scholarships of $2,500 each for students enrolled in a manufacturing engineering or manufacturing engineering technology program. Applicants must have an overall minimum 3.5 GPA.

• 19162 • Guilliano Mazzetti Scholarship Award

Supports two scholarships of $1,500 for students enrolled in a manufacturing, engineering, or closely related field. Applicants must have an overall minimum of a 3.0 GPA.

• 19163 • Memphis Chapter High School Incentive Scholarship

Supports one scholarship of at least $600 for a high school student in senior year who intends to enroll in a manufacturing engineering or technology program at one of the approved institutions listed in the announcement. Applicants must live in the Memphis area and have an overall minimum of a 3.0 GPA.

• 19164 • Outstanding Young Manufacturing Engineer Award

For recognition of significant achievement and leadership in manufacturing engineering. Individuals under the age of 35 are eligible. As many as five gold medals mounted on engraved plaques are awarded annually. Established in 1979.

• 19165 • PACCAR Scholarship Award Fund

Supports three scholarships of $2,000 each for students enrolled in manufacturing engineering technology, or mechanical engineering technology at the University of North Texas. This is a one-time award. Applicants must have an overall GPA of at least 3.0, or, if working 30 hours a week while in school, a GPA of only 2.5 is required.

• 19166 • Edward S. Roth Manufacturing Engineering Scholarship

Will support one scholarship of $2,500 for a student enrolled in an accredited four-year degree program in manufacturing engineering in the United States at one of the qualified schools on a list accompanying the application information. All applicants must have and maintain a GPA of 3.0 or better and be a citizen of the United States. Preference will be given to students demonstrating financial need, minority status, and students participating in a co-op program.

• 19167 • S-B Power Tool Scholarship Award Fund

Supports one scholarship of $1,500 to students enrolled in a manufacturing engineering or technology program. Applicants must have an overall minimum of 3.5 as a GPA.

• 19168 • St. Louis Chapter 17 Scholarship Fund

Supports four scholarships of $1,000 each for students enrolled in manufacturing engineering, industrial technology, or other manufacturing related programs. Applicants must attend one of the approved schools with an SME Student Chapter sponsored by St. Louis Chapter 17 and have an overall minimum of 3.5 GPA.

• 19169 • Albert M. Sargent Progress Award

To recognize an individual for technical accomplishments in the field of manufacturing processes, methods, or systems. A mounted gold medal and an engraved plaque are awarded annually when merited. Established in 1955. Formerly: (1981) SME Progress Award.

• 19170 • Joseph A. Siegel Service Award

To recognize members for significant and unique contributions that benefit the Society. A gold medal on an engraved plaque is awarded annually when merited. Established in 1955. Formerly: (1987) Joseph A. Siegel Memorial Award.

• 19171 • SME Education Foundation Family Scholarship Award

Provides one scholarship valued at up to $20,000 annually for a child or grandchild of an SME member. The scholarship is renewable up to three times for a total of a four-year award based on continuing excellent academic performance. One-year scholarship awards are also awarded annually to two runners up. Applicants may be graduating high school students or undergraduate students with fewer than 30 credit hours. Applicants must have an overall GPA of 3.0, a minimum SAT score of 1000, or ACT score of 21.

• 19172 • SME Fellow

To honor members who have made an outstanding contribution to manufacturing on the social, technological, and educational aspects of manufacturing. Winners receive a lifetime membership to the SME. No more than 25 awards may be given in a year, and Fellows cannot exceed one percent of the senior membership.

• 19173 • Frederick W. Taylor Research Medal

To recognize an individual for significant published research leading to a better understanding of materials, facilities, principles, and operations, and their application to improve manufacturing processes. A mounted gold medal and an engraved plaque are awarded annually when merited. Established in 1957. Formerly: SME Research Medal.

• 19174 • Lawrence A. Walker Memorial Award

Supports two scholarships of $1,500 each for students enrolled in a degree program in manufacturing, mechanical, or industrial engineering in a college or university in the state of Wisconsin. Applicants must have a GPA of 3.0 or better.

• 19175 • Myrtle and Earl Walker Scholarship Fund

Supports 25 scholarships of $1,000 each for students of a manufacturing engineering or manufacturing engineering technology program. Applicants must have an overall minimum 3.5 GPA.

• 19176 • Eli Whitney Productivity Award

To recognize an individual for distinguished accomplishments in improving capability within the broad concept of orderly production. A mounted gold medal and an engraved plaque are awarded annually when merited. Established in 1957. Formerly: Eli Whitney Memorial Award.

• 19177 • William E. Weisel Scholarship Fund

Supports one scholarship of $1,000 for a student enrolled in a manufacturing engineering or technology program that is seeking a career in the robotics, automated systems used in manufacturing or robotics for use in the medical field. Applicants must have an overall minimum of a 3.5 GPA.

• 19178 • Albert E. Wischmeyer Memorial Scholarship Award

Supports two scholarships of at least $1,900 each. Applicants must be residents of Western New York State (west of Interstate 81), graduating high school seniors or current undergraduate students enrolled in an accredited degree program in manufacturing engineering, manufacturing engineering technology, or mechanical technology. Applicants must plan to attend a college or university in New York State, and have an overall GPA of 3.0 or better.

• 19179 •

Society of Medical-Dental Management Consultants

Patricia M. Salmon CPA, Exec.Sec.
125 Strafford Ave., Ste. 300
Wayne, PA 19087
Toll-Free: 800-826-2264
Fax: (602)759-3530
E-mail: patricia01@aol.com
Home Page: http://www.smdmc.org

• 19180 • President's Award

For recognition of outstanding contributions to the Society. An active voting member is selected by the President. A traveling trophy and a permanent plaque for each recipient are awarded annually. Established in 1981 by Leonard P. Schwartz, CPBC. Sponsored by Leonard P. Schawartz, CPBC.

• 19181 •
Society of Medical Friends of Wine
Susan Guerguy, Exec.Sec.
511 Jones Pl.
Walnut Creek, CA 94597-3141
Phone: (925)933-9691
Fax: (925)939-5224
E-mail: marq@inreach.com
Home Page: http://
medicalfriendsofwine.org

• 19182 • **Wine Research Award**
For recognition of outstanding original, published research in the area of the nutritive or therapeutic values of wine. A monetary prize of $1,500 is awarded biennially in odd-numbered years. Established in 1961.

• 19183 •
Society of Mexican American Engineers and Scientists
Rafaela Schwan, Exec.Dir.
711 W Bay Area Blvd., Ste. 206
Webster, TX 77598
Phone: (281)557-3677
Fax: (281)557-3757
E-mail: execdir@maes-natl.org
Home Page: http://www.maes-natl.org

Formerly: (1989) Mexican-American Engineering Society.

• 19184 • **Medalla de Oro**
This, the highest honor that MAES can bestow upon a member, is given to honor individuals who have distinguished themselves by demonstrating a dedication to service and to greatness, a dedication to humankind that carries with it responsibilities and strict disciplines. A solid gold medal and a plaque are awarded to the recipient. In addition, the winner will present the Madrina/Padrino Scholarship of $2,000 to a worthy MAES college student, thereby accepting a mentor role (Padrino-Godfather) with the student. In addition, the Medalla de Plata (Silver Award) is awarded to individuals who make personal contributions or outstanding achievement in limited areas. Awarded annually at the Society's Symposium. Established in 1983 by Oscar H. Cano.

• 19185 •
Society of Midland Authors
Thomas Frisbie, Pres.
PO Box 10419
Chicago, IL 60610
E-mail: tomfrisbie@aol.com
Home Page: http://
www.midlandauthors.com

• 19186 • **Society of Midland Authors Awards**
To create closer association among writers of the Middle West, stimulate creative literary effort, and encourage interest in reading and literature. Awards are given in the following categories: biography, children's fiction, children's nonfiction, adult fiction, adult nonfiction, and poetry. Works published or produced professionally for the first time during the previous year by authors from the 12 Midwestern states are eligible. A monetary award and a plaque are presented in each category. Awarded annually in May in Chicago. Established in 1915. Formerly: (1991) Summit Award.

• 19187 •
Society of Motion Picture and Television Engineers
Frederick Motts, Exec.Dir.
3 Barker Ave.
White Plains, NY 10607
Phone: (914)761-1100
Fax: (914)761-3115
E-mail: smpte@smpte.org
Home Page: http://www.smpte.org

• 19188 • **Agfa - Gevaert Gold Medal Award**
To recognize an individual for outstanding leadership, inventiveness and/or other achievement in the research, development, or engineering of new techniques and/or equipment that results in a significant improvement to the interface between motion picture film and television imaging systems, whereby the combined advantages both contribute to the further development of visual communications systems. The Award Committee comprises an equal number of members from both the motion picture and video technologies and considers mainly work completed over the past five years. It is implicit that motion picture film be used in some phase of the noted work, preferably as the input or output medium. Nominations by members are accepted. A gold medal is awarded annually. First presented in 1975.

• 19189 • **Citation of Outstanding Service to the Society**
To recognize individuals for dedicated service to the Society over a sustained period of time. Particular emphasis is to be placed on service performed at the Section level, including, but not limited to, services performed at Section meetings, special Section meetings, and national conferences. Nominations by members are accepted. A citation is awarded annually. Established in 1974.

• 19190 • **Eastman Kodak Gold Medal Award**
For recognition of notable contributions in the field of engineering development that lead to the introduction of new and unique educational techniques or programs utilizing motion pictures, television, high-speed, and instrumentation photography or other photographic science, the use of which advances the educational process itself at any or all levels. Nominations by members are accepted. A gold medal is awarded annually. Established in 1966.

• 19191 • **Fuji Gold Medal Award**
To recognize an individual for outstanding engineering achievements in the design and development of new or enhanced techniques and/or equipment that have contributed significantly to the advancement of photographic or electronic image origination. A development or invention in which a group has participated should be considered only if the individual to be honored has contributed the basic idea or has contributed substantially to the development of the idea. Preference is given to work completed within five years of the date of the award. A gold medal is awarded annually. Established in 1989 by Fuji Photo Film.

• 19192 • **John Grierson International Gold Medal Award**
For recognition of significant technical achievements related to the production of documentary motion picture films. The achievements may consist of a single outstanding development, preferably accomplished within the past five years, or an accumulation, over a period of years, of individual contributions to the art. Nominations by members are accepted. A gold medal is awarded annually. First presented in 1973.

• 19193 • **Honorary Member**
To honor individuals who have performed eminent service in the advancement of engineering in motion pictures, television, or in the allied arts and sciences. Such contributions shall represent substantially a lifetime's work. Upon the death of the Honorary Member, the name shall be added to the Society's Honor Roll. Awarded when merited.

• 19194 • **Journal Award**
To honor the author of the most outstanding paper originally published in the *Journal* of the Society during the preceding calendar year. In addition, up to two Journal Certificates may be presented to the runner-up. Nominations by members are accepted. Awarded annually. Established in 1934.

• 19195 • **Alexander M. Poniatoff Gold Medal Award**
To honor an individual by recognizing outstanding technical excellence of contributions in the research or development of new techniques and/or equipment that have contributed significantly to the advancement of audio or television magnetic recording and reproduction. A development or invention in which a group has participated will be considered only if the individual has contributed the basic idea, or has contributed substantially to the development of the idea. Preference is given to work which has reached completion within five years of the date of the award. A gold medal is awarded annually. Established in 1982.

• 19196 • **Presidential Proclamation**
To recognize individuals of established and outstanding status and reputation in the motion picture and television industries worldwide. Awarded annually. Established in 1982.

• 19197 • **Progress Medal Award**
This, the highest award the Society can bestow, is for recognition of an individual's distinguished technical contribution to the progress of the en-

Awards are arranged in alphabetical order below their administering organizations

gineering phases of the motion picture and/or television industries through an invention, or for research or development. Consideration is given to the awardee's continued technical contributions over a period of years. Honorary Members are not ordinarily considered. A medal is awarded annually. Established in 1935.

• 19198 • David Sarnoff Medal Award

For recognition of noteworthy contributions by an individual in the development of new techniques or equipment that have improved the engineering phases of television, including theater television. The Award Committee will judge work in the research, development, design, manufacture, operation, or other phase of television engineering. Preference is given for work completed during the past five years. Nominations by members are accepted. A medal is awarded annually. Established in 1951.

• 19199 • Technicolor/Herbert T. Kalmus Gold Medal Award

For recognition of outstanding contributions in the development of color films, processing techniques, or equipment useful in making color motion pictures for theater or television use. Since the award is to be made to an individual, a development or invention in which a group participates will be considered only if one person has contributed the basic idea, or has contributed substantially to the practical working out of the idea. Preferably, the work should have been done within five years of the date of the award. Nominations by members are accepted. A gold medal is awarded annually. Established in 1956.

• 19200 • Samuel L. Warner Memorial Medal Award

For recognition of outstanding contributions by an individual in the design and development of new and improved methods and/or apparatus for sound-on-film motion pictures, including any step in the process. The award is based on developments or inventions that are most likely to have the widest and most beneficial effect on the quality of the reproduced sound and picture. The work should have been done within five years of the award date. Nominations by members are accepted. A medal is awarded annually. Established in 1947 in memory of Samuel L. Warner (1888-1927).

• 19201 •
Society of Municipal Arborists
Jerri J. Lahaie CAE, Exec.Dir.
PO Box 641
Watkinsville, GA 30677
Phone: (706)769-7412
Fax: (706)769-7307
E-mail: urbanforestry@prodigy.net
Home Page: http://www.urban-forestry.com

• 19202 • Forestry Department Accreditation

To recognize the communities that meet the highest standards for municipal urban forestry set by a voluntary system of self regulation. A municipality must have an arborist, a master plan, a tree inventory, and meet several requirements in budget, time allocation, and employee standards to be eligible. A plaque is awarded annually at the SMA convention. Established in 1989.

• 19203 • Society of Municipal Arborists Awards

To recognize members for outstanding service to arboriculture or the society. The following awards are presented: Honorary Life Member, Award of Merit, Fellow, and Service to SMA Award. The awards program was established in 1965.

• 19204 •
Society of National Association Publications
Peter Banks, Pres.
8405 Greensboro Dr., No. 800
McLean, VA 22102
Phone: (703)506-3285
Fax: (703)506-3266
E-mail: snapinfo@snaponline.org
Home Page: http://www.snaponline.org

• 19205 • EXCEL Awards

To recognize excellence in the work of professionals in association publishing. Awards are presented in two competition categories: Editorial and Graphics Awards - established in 1980 to encourage society and association publishers to strive to achieve the highest standards in the editorial development and design of publications; and Advertising and Marketing Awards - established in 1989 to encourage excellence in the development of promotional material to sell advertising in publications. Entries published for the first time during the preceding calendar year are eligible. Awards for gold, silver, and bronze are presented in the following publication types: newsletters, newspapers, scholarly journals, magazines, special publications, online publishing, convention publications, media kits, direct mail, and advertising. Awarded annually. Formerly: Pinnacle Awards.

• 19206 •
Society of Naval Architects and Marine Engineers
Phillip Kimball, Exec.Dir.
601 Pavonia Ave.
Jersey City, NJ 07306
Phone: (201)798-4800
Toll-Free: 800-798-2188
Fax: (201)798-4975
E-mail: director@sname.org
Home Page: http://www.sname.org

• 19207 • Vice Admiral E. L. Cochrane Award

For recognition of the author(s) of the best paper published in *Marine Technology*. Members and non-members are eligible. An inscribed medallion is awarded annually. Established in 1961. Formerly: (1961) President's Award.

• 19208 • Davidson Medal

For outstanding scientific accomplishment in ship research. Members and non-members are eligible. An inscribed, gold plated medal is awarded biennially in even-numbered years. Established in 1959 and first awarded to Kenneth S. M. Davidson.

• 19209 • Distinguished Service Award

To recognize members for their dedicated personal service and/or technical contributions to the Society on the national and section levels. Personalized plaques are presented annually to up to five members. Established in 1988.

• 19210 • Elmer L. Hann Award

For recognition of the author or authors of the best paper on ship production delivered at the Ship Production Symposium. A personalized, framed certificate is awarded annually. Established in 1991.

• 19211 • William M. Kennedy Award

For outstanding service and contribution in the development of systems and planning applying to shipbuilding and ship repair. Members and non-members are eligible. A monetary award of $1,000 and a framed certificate are awarded annually when merited. Established in 1980.

• 19212 • American Bureau of Shipping - Captain Joseph H. Linnard Prize

For recognition of the author of the best paper contributed to the annual meeting and appearing in the *Transactions* of the Society. Members and non-members are eligible. An engrossed, illuminated certificate is awarded annually. Established in 1937. Sponsored by the American Bureau of Shipping. Formerly: (1993) Captain Joseph H. Linnard Prize.

• 19213 • Blakely Smith Medal

For outstanding accomplishment in ocean engineering. Members and non-members are eligible. An inscribed gold-plated medal is awarded biennially in odd-numbered years. Established in 1979 and first awarded to Blakely Smith.

• 19214 • Student Paper Awards

For recognition of papers by students of outstanding merit and originality contributed to a meeting of the Society or one of its sections. Members and non-members are eligible. The following prizes are awarded: Graduate Paper Honor Prize - $300 and a citation; Graduate Paper Award - $150 and a citation; Undergraduate Paper Honor Prize - $300 and a citation; and Undergraduate Paper Award - $150 and a citation. Awarded annually. Established in 1944. Formerly: (1950) Junior Paper Award.

• 19215 • David W. Taylor Medal

For notable achievement in naval architecture and/or marine engineering. Members and non-members are eligible. An inscribed gold plated medal is awarded annually. Established in 1935 and first awarded to David Watson Taylor.

• 19216 • Vice Admiral "Jerry" Land Medal
For outstanding accomplishment in the marine field. Members and non-members are eligible. A hexagonal, inscribed gold-plated medal is awarded annually. Established in 1952 and first awarded to Emery Scott "Jerry" Land.

• 19217 • William H. Webb Medal
To recognize an individual for outstanding contributions to education in naval architecture, marine engineering, or ocean engineering. Members and non-members are eligible. Awarded biennially in odd-numbered years. Established in 1987.

• 19218 •
Society of Nematologists
Andrew Nyczepir, Pres.
PO Box 311
Marceline, MO 64658
Phone: (660)256-3252
Fax: (660)256-3252
E-mail: son@mcmsys.com
Home Page: http://www.nematologists.org

• 19219 • Best Student Paper Award
To recognize outstanding student research. Students who are Society members may be nominated by January 15. A plaque is awarded annually at the Convention. Established in 1968.

• 19220 • Fellow of the Society
To recognize outstanding contributions to the science of nematology. Nominations of Society members may be made via letter and a dossier giving contributions. The deadline is January 15 each year. A plaque is presented annually to one or more recipients at the Convention. Established in 1981.

• 19221 • Honorary Member
To recognize scientists for meritorious and superlative contributions to the science of nematology. A plaque is awarded at the Society meeting. Established in 1968.

• 19222 • Meritorious Service Award
To recognize an individual for service to the Society. Awarded when merited. Established in 1986.

• 19223 • Syngenta Nematology Award
To recognize outstanding contributions to nematology. Members of the Society are eligible. A plaque is awarded annually. Established in 1979. Sponsored by Syngenta. Formerly: (2001) Novartis Nematology Award.

• 19224 •
Society of Nuclear Medicine
Virginia M. Pappas, Exec.Dir.
1850 Samuel Morse Dr.
Reston, VA 20190-5316
Phone: (703)708-9000
Fax: (703)708-9020
E-mail: vpappas@snm.org
Home Page: http://www.snm.org

• 19225 • Paul C. Aebersold Award
To recognize outstanding achievement in basic science applied to nuclear medicine. Awarded annually. Established in 1973.

• 19226 • Berson-Yalow Award
To recognize originality in, and contributions to, basic or clinical radioassay. Awarded annually when merited. Established in 1977.

• 19227 • Cardiovascular Young Investigator Award
To identify promising young investigators working in cardiovascular nuclear medicine, assist in furthering their professional careers, and strengthen the theory and practice of their subspecialty. All applicants must be currently enrolled in or within five years of completing a certified training program. All former prize winners are ineligible. Published in the September, October, November, and December issues of the *Journal of Nuclear Medicine*. Nominations should be sent to the attention of the Chairperson of the Standing Committee at the SNM Central Office. Plaques and cash prizes are awarded. Winners present their work at a special session of the SNM Annual Meeting.

• 19228 • Georg Charles de Hevesy Nuclear Pioneer Award
To recognize an individual for outstanding contributions to the field of nuclear medicine. Awarded annually. Established in 1960.

• 19229 • Honorary Member
To recognize individuals for outstanding contributions to the field of nuclear medicine.

• 19230 • Outstanding Technologist Award
To recognize the best original paper relating to a new technique or adaptation of an existing technique for a nuclear medicine procedure, submitted by a nuclear medicine technologist as a senior author. A cash award of $750 is presented annually. The winning manuscript is highlighted at the Technologist Section Scientific Program at the SNM Annual Meeting and published in the *Journal of Nuclear Medicine Technology*.

• 19231 • Presidential Distinguished Service Award
To recognize and honor SNM members for their dedicated service contributions. Selected solely by the SNM President when merited.

• 19232 • Scientific Exhibit Awards
To recognize the best scientific exhibits presented at the SNM Annual Meeting. Scientific judging takes place the day before the formal opening for the SNM Annual Meeting. Medals for first place (gold), second place (silver), third place (bronze), and certificates for honorable mentions are presented. Personalized letters of congratulations are sent to each awardee on behalf of the judges.

• 19233 •
Society of Petroleum Engineers
Mark Rubin, Exec.Dir.
222 Palisades Creek Dr.
PO Box 833836
Richardson, TX 75083-3836
Phone: (972)952-9393
Toll-Free: 800-456-6863
Fax: (972)952-9435
E-mail: spedal@spe.org
Home Page: http://www.spe.org
Formerly: Society of Petroleum Engineers of the American Institute of Mining, Metallurgical and Petroleum Engineers.

• 19234 • John Franklin Carll Award
Recognizes contributions of technical application and professionalism in petroleum development and recovery. Members and non-members are eligible. Nominations must be submitted by March 15. A bronze plaque, inscribed and mounted on walnut is awarded annually when merited. Established in 1956.

• 19235 • DeGolyer Distinguished Service Medal
To recognize distinguished and outstanding service to the Society, the professions of engineering and/or geology, and the petroleum industry. Individuals who are members of SPE and have at least 15 years of professional experience in the petroleum industry may be nominated by March 15. A silver medal is awarded when merited. Established in 1965.

• 19236 • Distinguished Achievement Award for Petroleum Engineering Faculty
Recognizes an individual for superior classroom teaching, excellence in research, significant contributions to the petroleum engineering profession, and/or special effectiveness in advising and guiding students. This award does not accept public nominations. Only SPE members who are faculty members in a petroleum engineering or technology school may be nominated by March 15. Awarded annually. Established in 1981.

• 19237 • Distinguished Member
To recognize members who achieve distinction worthy of special recognition. This classification of membership honors members who is outstanding in the petroleum industry or academic community and/or who have made unusual significant contributions to SPE. Nominations must be submitted by March 15. Awarded annually. Established in 1983.

• 19238 • **Distinguished Service Award**
To recognize contributions to the Society that exhibit such exceptional devotion of time, effort, thought, and action as to set them apart from other contributions to SPE. Members must be nominated by March 15. A walnut and silver-plated plaque is awarded when merited. Established in 1947. Formerly: Society of Petroleum Engineers of AIME Distinguished Service Award.

• 19239 • **Drilling and Completion Award**
To recognize outstanding technical achievements in or contributions to the advancement in the engineering discipline or field. Awarded annually. Established in 1983. Formerly: (2003) Drilling Engineering Award.

• 19240 • **Facilities and Construction Award**
Recognizes outstanding technical achievement in or contributions to the advancements of petroleum engineering in the field of facilities and construction.

• 19241 • **Cedric K. Ferguson Medal**
To recognize a young scholar for significant contributions to the permanent technical literature of the profession. This award does not accept public nominations. Only members of the Society under the age of 33 are eligible. Awarded annually. Established in 1954.

• 19242 • **Formation Evaluation Award**
To recognize outstanding technical achievement or contributions to the advancement of petroleum engineering in the area of formation evaluation (encompassing core analysis, well logging, and petrophysics). Nominations must be submitted by March 15. Awarded annually. Established in 1991.

• 19243 • **Health, Safety, and Environment Award**
To recognize outstanding achievement in or contributions to the advancement of the field of environmental protection or safety in oil and gas exploration, drilling, or production operations. Nominations must be submitted by March 15. Awarded annually. Established in 1990. Formerly: (1995) Environmental and Safety Distinguished Achievement Award; (2003) Environment, Health and Safety Award.

• 19244 • **Honorary Membership**
This, the highest honor conferred on an individual by the Society, recognizes distinguished scientific or engineering achievement in the fields encompassed by the Society's technical scope. Members must be nominated by March 15. Honorary membership is limited to 0.1 percent of the total membership. Awarded annually. Established in 1960.

• 19245 • **Management and Information Award**
To recognize outstanding technical achievements in, or contributions to, the advancement of petroleum engineering in the area of management and information. Nominations must be submitted by March 15. Awarded annually. Established in 1994. Formerly: (2003) Economics and Evaluation Award.

• 19246 • **Production and Operations Award**
To recognize an individual for outstanding technical achievements in or contributions to the advancement of petroleum engineering in the area of production and operations. Awarded annually. Established in 1983. Formerly: (2003) Production Engineering Award.

• 19247 • **Public Service Award**
To recognize distinguished public service to a country, state, community, or the public through excellence in leadership, service, or humanitarianism. Members must be nominated by March 15. The award is granted only to those individuals whose contributions have been exceptional and is awarded only on a periodic basis. Established in 1983.

• 19248 • **Reservoir Description and Dynamics Award**
To recognize an individual for outstanding technical achievements in or contributions to the advancement of petroleum engineering in the areas of reservoir description and dynamics. Awarded annually. Established in 1983. Formerly: (2003) Reservoir Engineering Award.

• 19249 • **Lester C. Uren Award**
To recognize distinguished achievements in petroleum engineering technology by a member who made the contribution before the age of 45. Nominations must be submitted by March 15. A bronze plaque, inscribed and mounted on walnut, is awarded annually. Established in 1963 to honor Lester C. Uren, an educator at the University of California for more than 40 years and the author of the first petroleum engineering textbook.

• 19250 • **Young Member Outstanding Service Award**
To recognize significant contributions to and leadership in public and community matters, as well as to the Society, the profession, and/or the industry by a member under the age of 36. Nominations must be submitted by March 15. Awarded annually. Established in 1983.

• 19251 •
Society of Petrophysicists and Well Log Analysts
Vicki King, Exec.Dir.
8866 Gulf Fwy., Ste. 320
Houston, TX 77017
Phone: (713)947-8727
Fax: (713)947-7181
E-mail: info@spwla.org
Home Page: http://www.spwla.org

• 19252 • **Best Paper Award**
To recognize the best paper published for a one-year period in the Society's technical magazine. Awarded annually.

• 19253 • **Best Paper Presentation Award**
To recognize merit in contents and oral presentation (with visual aids) of a technical paper at the Society's annual symposium. A bronze plaque mounted on a wooden base is awarded annually after the symposium. Established in 1975.

• 19254 • **Distinguished Service Award**
To recognize outstanding service to the corporation in the form of work on a specific project or projects during a period of several years. Up to three awards may be given in a calendar year. Awarded as merited. Established in 1980.

• 19255 • **Distinguished Technical Achievement Award**
To recognize exceptional contributions in one or more specific areas of formation evaluation technology. A gold medal is awarded annually. Established in 1989.

• 19256 • **Gold Medal Award for Technical Achievement**
This, the highest honor bestowed on any individual by the corporation is awarded for outstanding achievements in the science of formation evaluation that result in significant contributions to the technology of well logging. Award is accompanied by an award of Honorary Membership. Awarded as merited at a meeting of the Board of Directors by an affirmative vote of at least two-thirds of the board. No more than one award is given in a calendar year.

• 19257 • **Medal of Honor for Career Service**
To honor an individual of extraordinary and long-term service to the corporation. The service must further the purposes of the corporation as set forth in Article IV of the Amended Articles of Incorporation. The medal is accompanied by an award of Honorary Membership and is confirmed at a meeting of the Board of Directors by an affirmative vote of at least two-thirds of the board. No more than one award is given in a calendar year. Awarded as merited. Established in 1966.

• 19258 •
Society of Plastics Engineers
Michael R. Cappelletti, Exec.Dir.
14 Fairfield Dr.
PO Box 403
Brookfield, CT 06804-0403
Phone: (203)775-0471
Fax: (203)775-8490
E-mail: info@4spe.org
Home Page: http://www.4spe.org

• 19259 • **Business Management Award**
To encourage contributions and acknowledge outstanding achievement in the business man-

agement of a plastics firm. A $2,500 honorarium, a plaque, and a travel allowance to the presentation are awarded annually. Established in 1980.

• 19260 • Fred O. Conley Award
To stimulate fundamental contributions in plastics or processing technology and to acknowledge outstanding achievements. A $2,500 honorarium, a plaque, and a travel allowance to the presentation are awarded annually. Established in 1980 by the SPE Detroit Section in memory of the Society's first president, Fred O. Conley.

• 19261 • Consumer Plastics Product Design Award
To encourage the development of products for consumers that are fabricated of plastics and are outstanding in design and usefulness. A $2,500 honorarium, a plaque, and a travel allowance to the presentation are awarded annually in May. Established in 1980. Formerly known as the Unique and Useful Consumer Plastics Product Award, in honor of Glenn L. Beall.

• 19262 • Fellow of the Society
To recognize an SPE member for contributions in the field of plastics engineering, science, or technology. Nominees must be Senior Members of the Society for at least six years. A pin and a plaque are awarded to one or more recipients annually. Established in 1984.

• 19263 • Honored Service Member Award
To recognize a SPE member for long-term, outstanding service to, and support of, the Society and its objectives. Awarded to one or more recipients each year. Established in 1992.

• 19264 • John W. Hyatt Award
For recognition of an individual who has served humanity through plastics. The award consists of a $2,500 honorarium, a plaque, and a travel allowance to the award presentation. Established in honor of John Wesley Hyatt, who founded the plastics industry in 1868.

• 19265 • Industrial Plastics Product Design Award
To encourage the development of industrial products that are fabricated of plastics and are outstanding in design and usefulness. A $2,500 honorarium, a plaque, and a travel allowance to the presentation are awarded annually in May. Established in 1980. Formerly known as the Unique and Useful Industrial Plastics Product Award, in honor of Glenn L. Beall.

• 19266 • International Award
This, the Society's most distinguished award, is given to acknowledge outstanding and unique contributions to the field of plastics. A $5,000 honorarium, an inscribed gold medal, and a travel allowance to the presentation, where the winner delivers an award lecture, are awarded annually. Established in 1961. Sponsored by the South Texas Section of the Society.

• 19267 • President's Cup
To recognize a member for outstanding service to the Society. An engraved cup is awarded annually at the discretion of the President of the Society. Established in 1957.

• 19268 • Research Award
To stimulate fundamental contributions in plastics research and to acknowledge outstanding achievements. The award consists of a $2,500 honorarium, a plaque, and a travel allowance to the presentation. Awarded annually at the Annual Technical Conference in memory of John C. Moricoli. Established in 1980.

• 19269 • Fred E. Schwab Award
To recognize an individual who has made significant and enduring contributions to the advancement of education in the field of plastics science. A $2,500 honorarium, a plaque, and a travel allowance to the presentation are awarded annually. Established in 1968. Sponsored by the Detroit Section and the Automobile Division of SPE.

• 19270 •
Society of Professional Investigators
David E. Zeldin CFE, Pres.
PO Box 1128
Bellmore, NY 11710
Phone: (516)781-1000
Fax: (516)783-0000
E-mail: info@spionline.org
Home Page: http://www.spionline.org

• 19271 • Man of the Year in Law Enforcement
For recognition of outstanding service rendered in the crusade against crime, racketeering, and corruption in government. Individuals in the investigative area of law enforcement who are nominated by members of the Society are eligible. An engraved plaque is awarded annually. Established in 1957.

• 19272 • Irwin R. Rutman Award
Recognizes outstanding law enforcement achievement. Awarded annually.

• 19273 •
Society of Professional Journalists
Terrence G. Harper, Exec.Dir.
3909 N Meridian St.
Indianapolis, IN 46208-4011
Phone: (317)927-8000
Fax: (317)920-4789
E-mail: questions@spj.org
Home Page: http://www.spj.org

• 19274 • Distinguished Teaching in Journalism Award
To honor a journalism educator and recognize outstanding teaching ability, contributions to journalism, journalism education, and contributions toward maintaining the highest standards of the profession. Anyone teaching in the field of journalism is eligible; membership in the Society is not required. A plaque is awarded annually. Established in 1966.

• 19275 • Eugene C. Pulliam Fellowship for Editorial Writing
To encourage editorial writers to renew their personal resources and develop new or specialized interests. Individuals with at least three years full-time editorial writing experience are eligible. Application deadline is July 1. A monetary prize of $75,000 to cover the cost of study, research, and/or travel in any field is awarded annually. Established in 1978.

• 19276 • Sigma Delta Chi Awards
To stimulate and recognize outstanding accomplishment by journalists. Submissions must be aired on radio or television stations, or printed in newspapers or magazines, or books written or published during the calendar year. Nominations may be made by the nominee or the nominee's employer, individual journalists, or news organizations by February 6. Competition is open to both members and non-members of the Society. Awards are given in 49 categories within Newspapers and Wire Services; Magazines; Art and Graphics; Radio; Television; Newsletters; Research; and Online Reporting. Plaques and bronze medallions are awarded annually. Established in 1932 by Sigma Delta Chi. Formerly: (1932) Gold Key Awards.

• 19277 • Sunshine Award
To show appreciation for important contributions in the area of open government. Awarded to those who are working to keep our government open and are involved in Project Sunshine. Recipients need not be SPJ members. The deadline for nominations is August 1. Awarded annually.

• 19278 • Wells Memorial Key
To recognize a member for outstanding service to the Society over a period of years. The deadline for nominations is May 1. A jeweled key is awarded annually. Established in 1913 in memory of Chester Wells, an outstanding Sigma Delta Chi president who died while in office in 1913.

• 19279 •
Society of Publication Designers
Bride M. Whelan, Exec.Dir.
60 E 42nd St., Ste. 721
New York, NY 10165
Phone: (212)983-8585
Fax: (212)983-2308
E-mail: spdnyc@aol.com
Home Page: http://www.spd.org

• 19280 • Herb Lubalin Award
To recognize an individual for continuing excellence in the field of publication design. A medal/trophy is awarded annually. Established in 1979 to honor Herb Lubalin, a typographic innovator and designer.

• 19281 • **Publication Design Awards**
To promote and recognize the best in publication design for the calendar year. National and international publications may enter in 25 categories among the fields of Newsstand (magazines typically sold on newsstands); Non-newsstand (corporate, educational, institutional, controlled circulation, annual reports, trade, and business-to-business magazines); and New Media (web sites, CD-ROMs). A metal trophy in the shape of an open magazine is awarded in gold for the highest honor, and in silver for distinctive achievement. Up to 15 merit awards are given for the finalists for Magazine of the Year. The Members' Choice Award is also presented. All winning entries are included in the *Publication Design Annual.* Presented annually. Established in 1965.

• 19282 •
Society of Ration Token Collectors
Samuel M. Hevener, Dir.
3583 Everett Rd.
Richfield, OH 44286-9723
E-mail: samhevener@yahoo.com

• 19283 • **Executive Board Merit of Exhibit Award**
To recognize the showing of displays, exhibits, or talks at the State level related to rationing. A certificate is awarded when merited. Established in 1972.

• 19284 • **Roy Gates Memorial Award**
To recognize untiring efforts for the betterment of the Society, particularly in research into the history of rationing, which include tokens, methods, paper items, certificates and procedures, in the United States during World War II. Members of the Society are eligible. An inscribed wooden plaque is awarded only when merited. Established in 1966 in memory of Roy F. Gates, who, immediately following the conclusion of World War II, began to assemble and collect everything pertaining to United States rationing, in the hope of preserving this small bit of American heritage and history.

• 19285 • **National Merit of Exhibit Award**
To recognize displays and talks at the national level or conventions. Members of the Society are eligible. A certificate is awarded when merited. Established in 1972.

• 19286 • **President's Exhibit Award**
To recognize exhibiting, giving talks on and showing colored slides of rationing material for local club, show, or exhibition. A certificate is awarded when merited. Established in 1972. Sponsored by the late Jerry Bates, Chairman of Awards Committee.

• 19287 •
Society of Recreation Executives
K. W. Stephens, Pres.
Box 520
Gonzalez, FL 32560-0520
Phone: (850)937-8354
Toll-Free: 800-281-9186
Fax: (850)937-8356
E-mail: rltresoource@spydee.net

• 19288 • **Member of the Year Award**
To recognize an individual member or commercial member who has made the greatest contribution of time or talent to the field of recreation, leisure, and travel or has excelled within the industry with their efforts to promote the recreation lifestyle. Awards are presented in two categories: individual and commercial. A plaque is awarded annually when merited at the convention. Established in 1987.

• 19289 •
Society of Reliability Engineers
Henry Cook, Pres.
119 Sally Ln.
Madison, AL 35758
Phone: (256)876-2258
Fax: (201)945-0589
E-mail: henry.cook@rdec.redstone.army.mil
Home Page: http://www.sre.org

Formerly: International Society of Reliabilty Engineers.

• 19290 • **SRE Certificate of Excellence**
This, the highest award given by the SRE, recognizes individuals who have made truly outstanding contributions to the advancement of the philosophy and principles of reliability. Awarded periodically when merited. Established in 1975.

• 19291 • **SRE Certificate of Recognition**
For recognition of the promotion of professionalism among associates engaged in the reliability discipline. Nomination is by a Chapter Representative (other than candidate's own chapter). A certificate is awarded annually at the RAM Symposium.

• 19292 • **SRE Stan Ofsthun Award**
To recognize specific technical advancements in the field of reliability. Technical papers, presented at recognized International Reliability and Maintainability Symposia and authored or co-authored by SRE members are eligible. A monetary award of $1,000 and a plaque are presented annually in January. Established in 1989.

• 19293 •
Society of Research Administrators
Tamra K. Hackett, COO
1901 N Moore St., Ste. 1004
Arlington, VA 22209
Phone: (703)741-0140
Phone: (703)741-0158
Fax: (703)741-0142
E-mail: info@srainternational.org
Home Page: http://www.srainternational.org

• 19294 • **Distinguished Contribution to Research Administration Award**
To recognize distinguished contributions in the field of research administration. Members and non-members of the Society may be nominated by college and university presidents, as well as leaders in industry and government. The honoree is expected to give a lecture at the Society's meeting about his/her area of expertise. A plaque is awarded annually. Established in 1974.

• 19295 • **Excellence Award**
To recognize a member who has excelled in meeting SRA's purpose of expanding the knowledge and tools of research administration. A plaque is awarded annually. Established in 1977 in honor of the Society's tenth anniversary.

• 19296 • **Hartford-Nicholsen Award**
To recognize outstanding contributions to the Society by individual members over a period of years. A certificate is awarded annually. Established in 1968. Formerly: (1973) Distinguished Service Award.

• 19297 • **Rod Rose Award**
For recognition of the author of the best article published in each annual volume of the *Journal of the Society of Research Administrators.* A monetary prize of $200 and a certificate are awarded annually. Established in 1973.

• 19298 •
Society of Rheology
A. Jeffrey Giacomin, Sec.
Rheology Research Center
University of Wisconsin
Madison, WI 53706
Phone: (608)262-7473
Phone: (516)576-2404
Fax: (608)265-2316
E-mail: giacomin@wisc.edu
Home Page: http://www.rheology.org/sor/

• 19299 • **Bingham Medal**
For recognition of an outstanding contribution to the science of rheology or for meritorious service to the Society. Residents of North America are eligible. A medal is awarded annually. Established in 1948.

• 19300 •
Society of Surgical Oncology
Rick Slawny, Exec.Dir.
85 W Algonquin Rd., Ste. 550
Arlington Heights, IL 60005
Phone: (847)427-1400
Fax: (847)427-9656
E-mail: rickslawny@surgonc.org
Home Page: http://www.surgonc.org/

• 19301 • **James Ewing Layman Award**
To recognize a layman who has made an outstanding contribution in the broad field of cancer control. The awardee, man or woman, is selected from individuals in industry, labor, government, or other areas of endeavor, whose contri-

butions have been predominantly personal rather than financial. Awarded annually. Established in 1970.

• 19302 • James Ewing Lecturer
For recognition of outstanding contributions in the field of cancer. The awardee is asked to present a lecture as part of the Scientific Sessions at the Annual Meeting of the Society. Presented annually. Established in 1949 by the James Ewing Society, the predecessor of the Society of Surgical Oncology.

• 19303 • Resident Award
For recognition of the best manuscript dealing with some phase of the cancer problem. The author must be a Resident to be eligible. Awarded annually in two categories: (1) for a report of clinical studies of patients with cancer; and (2) for basic research in some aspect of cancer. Established in 1962.

• 19304 •
Society of Systematic Biologists
Keith A. Crandall, Exec.VP
325 Chestnut St., Ste. 800
Philadelphia, PA 19106
Phone: (801)422-3495
Toll-Free: 800-354-1420
Fax: (215)625-8914
E-mail: systbiol@uconn.edu
Home Page: http://systbiol.org
Formerly: (1991) Society of Systematic Zoology.

• 19305 • Ernst Mayr Award in Systematic Biology
To recognize an outstanding student paper in the field of systematic biology that was presented at the Society's annual meeting. Members of the Society who are students or have completed their PhD within the last 15 months are eligible. A monetary award of $500, a certificate, and a set of available back issues of *Systematic Zoology/Systematic Biology* are awarded annually. Established in 1975.

• 19306 •
Society of the Plastics Industry
Moldmakers Division
Thomas Rae Southall, Contact
1667 K St. NW, Ste. 1000
Washington, DC 20006
Phone: (202)974-5200
Fax: (202)296-7005
E-mail: feedback@socplas.org
Home Page: http://www.plasticsindustry.org

• 19307 • Annual Conference and EXPO Awards
To honor the plastics industry's best work. Awards of Excellence are presented in 13 categories. Best of Market Awards, sponsored by Amoco Chemical Company, are given to one product in each category. In addition, Ashland Chemicals Inc. sponsors the Walter A. Szymanski Award for best product in the corrosion-resistant equipment category; *Engineering News-Record* sponsors an award for the Infrastructure Category which recognizes an outstanding application of composites in building or updating the inner framework of transportation, water, power, and communications; and the Counterpoise Grand Design Award, sponsored by Owens-Corning, is bestowed annually to the product that most clearly demonstrates craftsmanship, design skill, market significance, and originality. Awarded at the Annual Conference and Exposition. Sponsored by the Composites Institute. Formerly: Exhibit Award.

• 19308 • Annual Conference Paper Awards
To recognize technical papers for excellence in the areas of design, applications, materials, processing, research/testing, and environmental/recycling. From these, *Modern Plastics* presents an award for the Best Overall Paper; the Composites Institute sponsors an award for the Best Paper in the category of Infrastructure/Construction; and *Plastics Compounding* sponsors an award for the Best Fillers and Additives Paper. Sponsored by the Composites Institute. Formerly: Best Paper Awards.

• 19309 • Awards for Outstanding Performance
To honor imaginative design, functionality, and workmanship. Awarded annually by the Vinyl Window and Door Institute.

• 19310 • Awards of Distinction
To recognize exceptional contributions to the moldmakers industry. Nominees are judged on achievements in the areas of product design, process and moldmaking technology, education and training, and division management. Awarded annually in honor of Ernest J. Csaszar.

• 19311 • Clare E. Bacon Person of the Year Award
To recognize outstanding contributions to the progress of the industry through effort and leadership in the Institute. The award is named for Clare E. Bacon, the late leader of the Institute who exemplified association participation. Sponsored by the Composites Institute.

• 19312 • Dow Award for Excellence in Composites Research
To recognize a graduate student whose research involves high performance, thermoset fiber reinforced composites that focuses on component materials, fabrication technology, or materials science. Selection is based on originality, creativity, commercial potential, and economic practicality of the candidate's research. A monetary prize of $2,000 plus sponsorship at the Annual Conference and EXPO are awarded.

• 19313 • Eastern Section Annual Achievement Award
To recognize contributions by an employee of an SPI member company in the Eastern Section to SPI other than to the Eastern Section; contributions to SPI or other plastics industry affiliated organizations; and achievements in the plastics industry including administration, sales or marketing, production record, technical record, and education contributions. A plaque is awarded. Established in 1976 by the Eastern Section of the Society.

• 19314 • Fred Ford Award
To honor exceptional members who have had a significant impact on the advancement of the industry. Established in memory of Fred Ford, a former SPI/EPS chairman. Sponsored by the Expanded Polystyrene Division.

• 19315 • Man of the Year
To recognize distinguished members of the extrusion industry. Leadership, technical achievement, marketing innovations, research and development initiatives, management achievement, and advances in production or machinery processes are considered in the selection process. Awarded annually. Sponsored by the Extrusion Division.

• 19316 • Midwest Section Founder's Award
To recognize the Midwest regional plastics industry executive who has exhibited exceptional effectiveness, service and support for SPI and SPI Midwest section activities. A plaque is awarded annually at the SPI Midwest Conference.

• 19317 • Polyurethane Division Awards
To recognize members who dedicate their time, energy, and expertise to committee projects and activities that help advance the science or promote the use of polyurethanes. The Division also has a Hall of Fame, which honors significant contributors to the industry.

• 19318 • Polyurethane Division Hall of Fame Awards
This, the Industry's highest honor, recognizes those few exceptional individuals whose contributions over a lifetime have propelled the industry's products, practices, and acceptance. Awarded during the international polyurethane technical and marketing conference.

• 19319 • Safety Award Program
To recognize outstanding occupational safety programs in the plastics industry. Winners are chosen from a confidential Safety Statistics Survey of SPI members conducted by the Occupational Health and Environmental Issues Committee. Three classes of awards are presented: the Distinguished Award, the Achievement Award, and the Merit Award. Established in 1969.

• 19320 • Structural Plastics Division Annual Recognition
To recognize an officer or employee of an SPI member company for outstanding contributions and significant service to the structural foam industry. A citation is awarded annually. Established in 1978. Formerly: SPI Structural Foam Division Annual Recognition Award.

• 19321 • Structural Plastics Division Awards

To recognize the best paper and the best new product design in several categories. These awards are given for excellence in functional application and innovative design and are awarded to molders, designers, moldmakers, and original equipment manufacturers. Formerly: Structural Foam Division Awards.

• 19322 • Thermoforming Institute National Awards

To recognize unique design and state-of-the-art thermoforming. A Best in Show award recognizes the best overall design, with additional awards presented to the winner in various categories among heavy and light gauge products in electronics, medical, consumer, and industrial fields. Awarded annually.

• 19323 • Vinyl Siding Institute Awards of Distinction

To recognize individuals or companies for outstanding projects using siding produced by manufacturers who are members of the Vinyl Siding Institute. Entries may be submitted by remodeling contractors, builders, architects, homeowners, and producer members of VSI. Entries are accepted in one or more of the following categories: residential re-siding, residential new construction, non-residential buildings (new construction and re-siding), historic buildings, and special applications. Each project is judged on the merits of the effective use of vinyl siding and vinyl accessories. Vinyl siding applications must clearly demonstrate excellence of workmanship and attention to detail. Entries should include photography documenting the project and must be received by January 31. Plaques are awarded annually in March. Established in 1983. Formerly: (1986) Homes of Distinction Awards.

• 19324 • Vinyl Window and Door Institute Awards for Outstanding Performance

To recognize individuals and companies for outstanding projects using vinyl windows and doors supplied by members of the Vinyl Window and Door Institute. Awards are presented in residential, non-residential, and multi-housing, including both new construction and replacement. Winners are selected on the basis of imaginative design, functionality, and quality of workmanship. All entries must be submitted on official VWD entry form. The deadline is September 30. A certificate is awarded annually in November. Established in 1987.

• 19325 • Hugh T. Warren Award

To recognize a block molder member who has made outstanding contributions to the organization and industry. Established in memory of Hugh T. Warren, a former SPI/EPS chairman. Sponsored by the Expanded Polystyrene Division.

• 19326 •
Society of the Silurians
PO Box 1195
Madison Square Station
New York, NY 10159
Phone: (212)532-0887
E-mail: silurians@aol.com
Home Page: http://www.silurians.com

• 19327 • Silurian Excellence in Journalism Awards

To recognize outstanding performance or quality of work in the following categories: spot news involving the New York metropolitan region; feature news involving the New York metropolitan region; humorous writing in the spirit of Frank Sullivan; editorial, interpretative or critical writing; investigative reporting; radio documentary; television documentary; news photo; and feature photo. Representatives of the media based in the metropolitan New York area are eligible for items published or aired in the year prior to the award. Awarded annually.

• 19328 • Twenty-Five Year News Achievement Award

To honor distinguished performance as a reporter, columnist, or commentator in a career that began at least 25 years before and is still current. Preference is given to a journalist whose base is or was New York City. An inscribed plaque is awarded annually in the fall. Established in 1969.

• 19329 •
Society of Toxicology
Dr. Shawn Lamb, Exec.Dir.
1821 Michael Faraday Dr., Ste. 300
Reston, VA 20190
Phone: (703)438-3115
Fax: (703)438-3113
E-mail: sothq@toxicology.org
Home Page: http://www.toxicology.org

• 19330 • Achievement Award

To recognize outstanding contributions to the science of toxicology. Members of the Society who have less than 15 years experience since obtaining his/her highest earned degree (in the year of the Annual Meeting of the Society of Toxicology) are eligible. Nominations may be submitted by October 9. A plaque and cash stipend are awarded annually. Established in 1967.

• 19331 • AstraZeneca Traveling Lectureship Award

Recognizes excellence in research and service in toxicology. Intended to enable North American toxicologists to undertake a three-to-four-week lecture tour of Europe, familiarize themselves with scientific issues in Europe, and bring North American perspective to European scientists. One or two awards are given annually by AstraZeneca Ltd.

• 19332 • Board of Publications Award for the Best Paper in *Toxicological Sciences*

For the best paper in *Toxicological Sciences* during a 12-month period, terminating with the June issue of the calendar year preceding the Annual Meeting at which the award is presented. Authors need not be Society members. A plaque and a cash stipend are awarded annually. Established in 1995.

• 19333 • Colgate-Palmolive Post-Doctoral Fellowship Award in In Vitro Toxicology

To provide funds for the development of in vitro alternatives to animal testing in toxicological research. Any post-doctoral trainee in the first year of study beyond the Ph.D., M.D., or D.V.M. degree and who is employed by an academic institution, federal/national laboratory, or research institute worldwide may apply. A stipend and research-related costs (up to $38,500) for one year are presented annually. Application deadline is October 9. Established in 1991. Sponsored by Colgate-Palmolive Company.

• 19334 • Colgate-Palmolive/SOT Awards for Student Research Training in Alternative Methods

To enhance student research training in alternative methods. Awards are presented to graduate students or to institutions providing undergraduate research internships. Graduate student awards are designed to defray expenses for students in toxicology to visit an off-site laboratory for the purpose of gaining knowledge about and developing in vitro toxicology techniques which will support student's dissertation research. Institution awards are awarded to institutions that propose a 10-week research experience for students involving in vitro toxicology or alternative methods to reduce, replace, or refine the use of animals in toxicology research. Up to six awards of $2500 each are available annually.

• 19335 • Contributions to Public Awareness of the Importance of Animals in Toxicology Research Award

Recognizes an individuals contributions to the public understanding of the role and importance of experimental animals in toxicological science. Made for either a single seminal piece of work or a longer-term contribution to public understanding of the necessity of the use of animals in toxicological research to ensure and enhance the quality of human and animal health and the environment. A plaque and cash stipend are awarded annually.

• 19336 • Education Award

To recognize an individual who is distinguished by the teaching and training of toxicologists and who has made significant contributions to education in the broad field of toxicology. Nominations may be submitted by October 9. A bronze plaque and a cash stipend are awarded annually.

• 19337 • Enhancement of Animal Welfare Award

Recognizes a society member for contributions made to the advancement of toxicological science through the development and application of methods that replace, refine, or reduce the need for experimental animals. The achievement may be either a seminal piece of work or a long-term contribution to toxicological science and animal welfare. A plaque and cash stipend are awarded annually.

• 19338 • Graduate Student Fellowship/ Novartis Award

To assist graduate students engaged in full-time study towards a PhD degree in toxicology. The major professor must be an SOT member and the applicant must be an SOT member or have applied for membership. Selection is primarily base on the Education Committee's of the originality of the dissertation research, research productivity, relevance to toxicology, scholastic achievement, and letters of recommendation. Finalists are interviewed at the Annual Meeting and receive travel support. A plaque and a $16,000 scholarship are awarded.

• 19339 • Arnold J. Lehman Award

To recognize an individual who has made major contribution(s) to risk assessment and/or the regulation of chemical agents, including pharmaceuticals. The contribution may have resulted from the application of sound scientific principles to regulation and/or from research activities that have significantly influenced the regulatory process. The nominee, who must be Society member, may be employed in academia, government, or industry. Nomination deadline is October 9. A plaque and a cash stipend are awarded annually. Established in 1978.

• 19340 • Merit Award

To recognize a career of outstanding merit in the profession of toxicology or noteworthy contributions to the science of toxicology. Members of the Society are eligible. Nominations may be submitted by October 9. A plaque and a cash stipend are awarded annually at the spring meeting. Established in 1966.

• 19341 • Public Communications Award

To recognize an individual who has made a major contribution to broadening the awareness of the general public on toxicological issues through any aspect of public communications. The award should reflect accomplishments made over a significant period of time. Examples of qualifying media in which the nominated communication may appear include books, brochures, continuing education courses, data bases, extension bulletins, magazines, newspapers (local or national), public presentations, public forums, radio and television scripts, and workshops. Awarded annually. Established in 1994.

• 19342 •
Society of Tribologists and Lubrication Engineers
Edward P. Salek CAE, Exec.Dir.
840 Busse Hwy.
Park Ridge, IL 60068-2376
Phone: (847)825-5536
Fax: (847)825-1456
E-mail: information@stle.org
Home Page: http://www.stle.org

• 19343 • Edmond E. Bisson Award

To recognize the best written contribution published by the Society during the period June 1 through May 31 preceding the annual meeting. The contribution must deal with tribology, lubrication engineering, or allied disciplines, and is not limited to technical papers. Any article or series of articles published by the Society in any of its technical journals or special publications is eligible for the award. A plaque or certificate is awarded annually when merited at the annual meeting. Established in 1991. The award is named for the former Editor-in-Chief of the Society who contributed, through the success of the publications, to fulfilling the Society's purpose.

• 19344 • Wilbur Deutsch Memorial Award

To recognize the author of the best paper on the practical aspects of lubrication of industrial equipment as published in the Society's official journals, *Lubrication Engineering* or *STLE Transactions,* between June 1st and May 31st preceding the annual meeting. The single author paper is limited to 5,000 words and must deal with those phases of lubrication of interest to plant personnel responsible for the lubrication of industrial equipment. Members of the Society are eligible. A plaque or certificate is awarded annually if merited. Established in 1958.

• 19345 • Walter D. Hodson Award

For recognition of the author of the best paper published in the Society's official journals by an STLE member aged 35 years or younger, and to stimulate the interest of young engineers in the science of lubrication engineering. The single-author paper, which is limited to the subject of lubrication engineering or an allied subject, must have been published by the Society between May 31st and June 1st preceding the annual meeting and may not exceed 5,000 words. A certificate or plaque is awarded annually if merited. Established in 1950. Sponsored by the Hodson Corporation.

• 19346 • Captain Alfred E. Hunt Memorial Award

For recognition of the best single-author paper in the field of lubrication or an allied field. The paper must be published in the Society's official journals and written by a member of the Society between June 1st and May 31st preceding the annual meeting. A plaque and medallion are awarded annually when merited. Established in 1948.

• 19347 • International Award

This, the Society's highest technical honor, is given for recognition of an outstanding contribution to the field of tribology, lubrication engineering, or allied fields. Awardees receive lifetime honorary membership in the Society. Candidates need not be members of the Society. As many as two certificates may be awarded at the annual meeting if merited. Established in 1948. Formerly: (1997) STLE National Award.

• 19348 • P. M. Ku Meritorious Award

For recognition of outstanding and selfless contributions to the Society. Members of the Society for at least 15 consecutive years who performed extensive, active, dedicated service for the Society are eligible. A medallion is awarded when merited. Established in 1978.

• 19349 • Al Sonntag Award

For recognition of the best paper on solid lubricants published in the Society's official journals, *Lubrication Engineering* and *Tribology Transactions,* between June 1st through May 31st preceding the annual meeting of the Society. Entrants must be members of the STLE. The previously unpublished single- or multi-author paper is limited to 5,000 words and not have been previously published. A plaque or certificate is awarded annually at the Society's meeting when merited. Established in 1983.

• 19350 •
Society of United States Air Force Flight Surgeons
Major Chris Borchardt, Exec.Off.
PO Box 35387
Brooks AFB, TX 78235-5387
Phone: (210)536-2844
Fax: (210)536-2017
E-mail: christopher.borchardt@brooks.af.mil
Home Page: http://www.sousaffs.org

• 19351 • Malcolm C. Grow Award

To advance the practice of aerospace medicine, and to recognize outstanding contributions and achievements in the aeromedical support of flyers. USAF flight surgeons may be nominated. An inscribed bronze plaque and an honorarium are awarded annually. Established in 1961.

• 19352 • George E. Schafer Award

To recognize a USAF medical corps officer who has made significant long-term contributions to the mission effectiveness of the United States Air Force, and to the vitality of the specialty of aerospace medicine. USAF physicians closely involved with aerospace medicine are eligible. A plaque is awarded annually. Established in 1978 to honor Lieutenant General George E. Schafer.

• 19353 •
Society of Vertebrate Paleontology
Sean Allen, Contact
60 Revere Dr., Ste. 500
Northbrook, IL 60062
Phone: (847)480-9282
Fax: (847)480-9282
E-mail: svp@vertpaleo.org
Home Page: http://www.vertpaleo.org/

• 19354 • **Joseph T. Gregory Award**
To recognize an individual member for contributions to the welfare of the Society. Awarded annually. Established in 1992.

• 19355 • **Bryan Patterson Memorial Grant**
To support student field work in vertebrate paleontology. Both undergraduate and graduate students are eligible to apply. Applicants and their sponsors must be Society members or pending members. One award of $2,000 or two awards of $1,000 are presented annually. Established in 1982.

• 19356 • **A. S. Romer - G. G. Simpson Medal**
This, the Society's highest honor, is given to recognize an individual member for sustained and outstanding scholarly excellence and service to the discipline of vertebrate paleontology. A medal is awarded annually. Established in 1987 in honor of A. S. Romer and George Gaylord Simpson.

• 19357 • **Alfred Sherwood Romer Prize**
To recognize an outstanding scientific contribution in vertebrate paleontology by a predoctoral student on the basis of the scientific value of the study and the quality of an oral presentation. Candidates who are enrolled in a Master}s program should be in her/his second or later year of enrollment; those enrolled in a Doctoral program should be in her/his third or later year of enrollment; or those who have completed the degree in question should have done so within the previous year. The deadline for applications is April 11. A monetary award of $250 is presented annually. Established in memory of the late Professor A. S. Romer.

• 19358 • **Morris F. Skinner Award**
To recognize an individual for outstanding and sustained contributions to scientific knowledge through the making of important collections of fossil vertebrates. Those who encourage, train, or teach others toward the same pursuits are eligible; membership in the Society is not mandatory. Awarded annually. Established in 1990.

• 19359 •
Society of Woman Geographers
Janet McGinn, Admin.
415 E Capitol St. SE
Washington, DC 20003
Phone: (202)546-9228
Fax: (202)546-5232
E-mail: swghq@verizon.net
Home Page: http://www.iswg.org

• 19360 • **Gold Medal Award**
To recognize a member of the society whose original, innovative, or pioneering contributions are of major significance to the world's knowledge and understanding of our universe. Only members of the society are eligible. A gold medal is awarded when merited. Established in 1933.

• 19361 • **Outstanding Achievement Award**
To recognize a member of the society for an outstanding contribution or service of lasting benefit to science, the arts, or humanity. Only members of the society are eligible. A certificate is awarded triennially. Established in 1978.

• 19362 •
Society of Women Engineers
Betty A. Shanahan, Exec.Dir./CEO
230 E Ohio St., Ste. 400
Chicago, IL 60611-3265
Phone: (312)596-5223
Toll-Free: 877-SWE-INFO
Fax: (312)596-5252
E-mail: hq@swe.org
Home Page: http://www.swe.org

• 19363 • **Achievement Award**
This, the highest honor of the SWE, is given to recognize a woman for significant contributions to engineering in the field of engineering practice, research, education, or administration over a long period of time. An engraved plaque, a gold pin, an engraved Steuben crystal bowl, and one year membership in the Society are awarded annually. Established in 1952.

• 19364 • **Rodney D. Chipp Memorial Award**
To recognize a man or corporation for significant contributions to the acceptance and advancement of women in the engineering profession. An engraved plaque, a citation, and a $1,000 honorarium are awarded when merited. Established in 1967 in memory of Dr. Chipp, a prominent engineer and the late husband of Dr. Beatrice A Hicks, first President of the Society.

• 19365 • **Distinguished Engineering Educator Award**
To recognize a female member who, as a full-time or emeriti engineering educator, has demonstrated excellence in teaching and the ability to inspire students to high levels of accomplishments, has shown evidence of scholarship through contributions to research and technical literature, and, through active involvement in professional engineering societies, has made significant contributions to the engineering profession. Candidates must have at least one earned engineering or engineering-related degree, be a full-time or emeriti faculty member in a school of engineering or engineering technology, have at least ten years teaching experience, hold the rank of at least associate professor, and be a member of SWE. An inscribed memento and plaque are awarded at the annual student award luncheon or banquet. Established in 1986.

• 19366 • **Distinguished New Engineer Award**
To honor those women who are members of the Society and who have demonstrated outstanding performance in both engineering and leadership, and who have no more than ten years of cumulative engineering experience. Technical achievements, Society participation, and community involvement are considered. Awarded annually to five members. Established in 1979.

• 19367 • **Fellows Awards**
To recognize continuous service to the public's advancement and awareness of engineering as a profession for women, and their contributions to the fields of engineering and/or engineering management. Applicants must senior members for at least eight years, or member for at least 20 years. Awarded annually. Established in 1980.

• 19368 • **Resnik Challenger Medal**
To recognize exceptional engineering contributions in broadening the frontiers of space exploration. Any woman engineer who has been practicing for ten or more years; who is an analytical visionary; and who has expanded the horizons of space exploration through an engineering breakthrough in aeronautics, astronautics, materials, electronics, structures, health, or other space-related engineering accomplishment may be nominated. A medal and a certificate are awarded as merited. Established in 1986 to honor Judith A. Resnik, mission specialist on the ill-fated Challenger space shuttle flight on January 28, 1986.

• 19369 • **Upward Mobility Award**
To recognize a woman who has made an outstanding contribution in the field of engineering and/or technical management such that she has, as a minimum, achieved the level of general manager or equivalent upper management position within her organization (industry, academia, or government service). Her academic training may be in either science or engineering, and she need not be a member of SWE. The qualifications are: an engineering degree from a recognized college or university, and not less than six years of increasingly important engineering/technical management experience, or a degree in science related to engineering from a recognized college or university, and not less than eight years of increasingly important engineering/technical management experience; and not less than eleven years of increasingly important engineering/technical management experience indicating outstanding competency and achievement. A citation and a Longines ATMOS

clock are awarded annually. Established in 1989. Underwritten by the Northrop Grumman Corp.

• 19370 •
Society of Wood Science and Technology
Vicki L. Herian, Exec.Dir.
1 Gifford Pinchot Dr.
Madison, WI 53726-2398
Phone: (608)231-9347
Fax: (608)231-9592
E-mail: vicki@swst.org
Home Page: http://www.swst.org

• 19371 • **Distinguished Service Award**
For recognition of significant contributions to the profession of wood science and technology. A lifetime honorary membership, citation, and plaque are awarded when merited. Established in 1980.

• 19372 • **George Marra Award**
To recognize an individual for excellence in writing and research. Articles published in *Wood and Fiber Science* are considered. First place recipient is presented with a monetary award of $1,000 and a plaque; second place winner receives a plaque. Awarded annually. Established in 1986 in memory of George G. Marra.

• 19373 •
Sociological Practice Association
Ross Koppel, Co-Pres.
Social Research Corpation
PO Box 15
901 S National Ave.
Wyncote, PA 19095
Phone: (215)576-8221
Fax: (215)576-8346
E-mail: rkoppel@sas.upenn.edu
Home Page: http://www.socpractice.org/

Formerly: (1986) Clinical Sociology Association.

• 19374 • **Distinguished Career in Clinical Sociology**
For recognition of a distinguished career in the practice of clinical sociology. Selection is by nomination. A plaque is awarded annually. Established in 1984.

• 19375 •
Sociologists for Women in Society
Nancy Miller, Exec.Off.
University of Akron
Dept. of Sociology
OLIN 251
Akron, OH 44325-1905
Phone: (330)972-7918
Fax: (330)972-5377
E-mail: sws@uakron.edu
Home Page: http://www.socwomen.org

• 19376 • **Feminist Activist Award**
Recognizes outstanding feminist activism. Awarded annually. Formerly: (2004) Pauline Bart Feminist Activist Award.

• 19377 • **Feminist Lecturer Award**
Presented annually to an SWS member whose work demonstrates outstanding feminist scholarship.

• 19378 • **Mentorship Award**
Award of recognition honoring an SWS member who is an outstanding feminist mentor. Inquire for application details.

• 19379 • **Cheryl Allyn Miller Scholarship**
Recognizes outstanding contribution to study of women and work. Inquire for application details.

• 19380 • **Minority Scholarship**
American Sociological Association Award to minority scholars and supported in part by SWS. Annual award of recognition.

• 19381 • **Barbara Rosenblum Dissertation Award**
Awarded biennially for the best cancer dissertation on women and cancer.

• 19382 •
Software and Information Industry Association
Ken Wasch, Pres.
1090 Vermont Ave., NW, 6th Fl.
Washington, DC 20005
Phone: (202)289-7442
Toll-Free: 800-388-7478
Fax: (202)289-7097
Home Page: http://www.siia.net

• 19383 • **Codie Awards**
To honor the best software products of the year as voted by peers in the industry. Judging is conducted by representatives from the software and information industry trade press, mainstream technology writers, analysts, consultants, and subject-matter experts. Awards are presented in various subcategories within the following broad categories: software, content, education, and corporate. Nomination deadline is October 14. Awards are presented annually at a gala dinner in early spring. Established in 1986. The name of the awards, Codie, is derived from the word "code" and alludes to the program's basis in the software industry. Formerly: (1993) Excellence in Software Awards.

• 19384 •
Soil and Water Conservation Society
Craig A. Cox, Exec.Dir.
945 SW Ankeny Rd.
Ankeny, IA 50021
Phone: (515)289-2331
Fax: (515)289-1227
E-mail: webmaster@swcs.org
Home Page: http://www.swcs.org

Formerly: (1989) Soil Conservation Society of America.

• 19385 • **Hugh Hammond Bennett Award**
This, the highest honor bestowed on an individual by the society, is given for superior and distinguished service in recognition of national and international accomplishments in the conservation of soil, water, and other natural resources. Society members or non-members are eligible. Nominations may be made by the society's board, society chapters, or individual society members. Awarded annually when merited.

• 19386 • **Commendation Award**
For national recognition of members for service to their own chapters or council of chapters and for professional achievement. Fellow award recipients are not eligible for at least five years after having been named a fellow. Each chapter, council of chapters, society officer, and council member may nominate one member each year. A certificate is awarded annually.

• 19387 • **Fellow**
The degree of fellow is conferred on society members who have performed exceptional service in advancing the science and art of good land use. It is given for professional excellence and for service to the organization. Service may be in practicing, investigating, administering, or teaching soil and water conservation or closely related fields. Society members with at least 10 years of membership who are also recognized outside the society for their expertise as professional conservationists are eligible. Nominations may be made by petition signed by at least 25 members of the society. Awarded annually when merited and permitted by the Society's bylaws, which cap the number of fellows at 0.1 percent of total membership.

• 19388 • **Honor Award**
To recognize individuals, usually non-members of the society or non-professional members of the society, for outstanding accomplishments compatible with the objectives of the society. Nomination may be made by society chapters only. No more than 10 awards are presented annually.

• 19389 • **Merit Award**
For recognition of an outstanding effort or activity by a group, business firm, corporation, or organization that promotes wise land use. Activities of industrial sustaining members of the society are eligible. Eligible organizations include press, radio, movies, television, industries, corporations, churches, societies, foundations, civic clubs, scout groups, and other organizations, public or private, that have carried out an outstanding conservation activity. Selection is based on the following criteria: the activity must be the result of an organized program and may include the activity of an agency or government; the activity must have an effect over a large area, at least a large part of a state or province, or parts of several states or provinces; the principle effect of the activity must have been directed to persons other than professional conservationists; and the activity must have clearly contributed to bringing about better land use and/or

better understanding of natural resource conservation. Nominations may be submitted by chapters and appropriate chapter committees, any three society members, society officers, council members, or committee and division chairmen. Awarded annually to one or more recipients.

• 19390 • Outstanding Service Award
In recognition of unusual efforts in helping the society develop and carry out its program over a long and sustained period of time. Any society member may be nominated. The nominee must have performed unusual service to the society on a sustained basis for at least 10 years. This service may have been performed at the chapter, regional, or international levels. Nomination must be by petition signed by at least 25 society members. Awarded annually when permitted by the Society's by-laws, which cap the number of awardees at 0.1 percent of total membership.

• 19391 •
Soil Science Society of America
Ellen Bergfeld, Exec.VP
677 S Segoe Rd.
Madison, WI 53711
Phone: (608)273-8080
Fax: (608)273-2021
E-mail: headquarters@agronomy.org
Home Page: http://www.soils.org

• 19392 • Fellow
This, the highest honor bestowed by the Society, is given for recognition of outstanding work in soil science over a period of time. Individuals who have been active members of the Society for at least ten years may be nominated. Awarded annually to one or more recipients. Established in 1976.

• 19393 • International Soil Science Award
To recognize outstanding contributions to soil science on the international scene. Members are eligible for nomination for contributions made within the past ten years. A certificate and monetary award of $1,000 are awarded annually. Established in 1986.

• 19394 • Soil Science Applied Research Award
For recognition of outstanding achievement in applying research principles to solve practical problems in soil science. Members are eligible for nomination for contributions made within the past ten years. A certificate and honorarium of $1,000 are awarded annually. Established in 1986.

• 19395 • Soil Science Distinguished Service Award
For recognition of outstanding service to soil science by distinguished members of the Society. Individuals who have 25 years or more of active membership in the Society and have ceased full-time professional employment are eligible for nomination for contributions during their career. A certificate and honorarium of $1,000 are awarded to up to three recipients annually. Established in 1984.

• 19396 • Soil Science Education Award
To recognize soil scientists who make outstanding educational contributions through such activities as resident, extension, or industrial education. Members are eligible for nomination for contributions made within the past ten years. A certificate and honorarium of $1,000 are awarded annually. Established in 1986.

• 19397 • Soil Science Professional Service Award
For recognition of outstanding service in promoting programs, practices, technology, or products that enhance soil service. Members are eligible for nomination for contributions made within the last ten years. A certificate and honorarium of $1,000 are awarded annually. Established in 1986.

• 19398 • Soil Science Research Award
To recognize an individual who has demonstrated unusual creativity, reasoning ability, and technical skill, and whose research contributions to basic and applied soil science are distinguished by originality and significance. Members are considered for contributions made within the past ten years. A certificate and honorarium of $1,000 are awarded annually. Established in 1957 by the American Society of Agronomy and administered by the SSSA since 1975.

• 19399 • Emil Truog Soil Science Award
To recognize a PhD recipient who has made an outstanding contribution to soil science as evidenced by his or her PhD thesis. Individuals who have received the PhD during the preceding calendar year are eligible. A certificate and honorarium of $500 are awarded annually. Established in 1971 in memory of Professor Emil Truog, chairman of the Soil Science Department at the University of Wisconsin (1939-1953) and one of the founding members of the SSSA.

• 19400 •
Somali International Cat Club
Monique Belton, Pres.
2210 21st St.
Lake Charles, LA 70601
Phone: (908)647-2275
E-mail: somali@prodigy.net
Home Page: http://somali.home.att.net

• 19401 • Merit Award for Somali
To recognize the achievements, contributions, development, and showing of Somali cats. To encourage friendship among Somali cat breeders and owners. Awarded annually with a certificate and rosettes. Established in 1994.

• 19402 •
Songtalk
6357 Primrose Ave
Hollywood, CA 90068-2887
Phone: (213)463-7178
E-mail: zollo@earthlink.net

Formerly: (1984) Songwriters' Resources and Services.

• 19403 • John Bettis Fellowship Award
To recognize an individual who has made a significant contribution to the songwriting community in the prior year. Awarded annually. Established in 1988.

• 19404 • Lifetime Achievement Award
To recognize a songwriter whose works have withstood the test of time and can be considered modern classics. Awarded annually as part of the National Academy of Songwriters' annual "Salute to the American Songwriter" concert. Established in 1986.

• 19405 •
Songwriters Guild of America
George Wurzbach, Natl.Proj.Dir.
1500 Harbor Blvd.
Weehawken, NJ 07086
Phone: (201)867-7603
Fax: (201)867-7535
E-mail: corporate@songwritersguild.com
Home Page: http://www.songwritersguild.com

Formerly: (1984) American Guild of Authors and Composers.

• 19406 • AGGIE Award
For recognition of achievement in, or contribution to the field of popular American music. A crystal trophy is awarded annually at the convention. Established in 1976.

• 19407 •
Sonia Shankman Orthogenic School
Henry J. Roth, Exec.Dir.
University of Chicago
1365 E 60th St.
Chicago, IL 60637
Phone: (773)834-2728
Fax: (773)702-1304
E-mail: pzimmerm@midway.uchicago.edu
Home Page: http://orthogenicschool.uchicago.edu

• 19408 • Graduate Internships
Recognizes 20 counselors and teaching assistants. Awarded annually.

Awards are arranged in alphabetical order below their administering organizations

• 19409 •
Sonoma County Culinary Guild
Christine Piccin, Pres.
PO Box 6191
Santa Rosa, CA 95406
E-mail:
sccg@sonomacountyculinaryguild.org
Home Page: http://
sonomacountyculinaryguild.org

• 19410 • **Jane G. Benet Culinary Scholarship**
For student with culinary arts/agribusiness major. Monetary award bestowed annually.

• 19411 •
Sons and Daughters of Oregon Pioneers
Merle Miller, Contact
PO Box 6685
Portland, OR 97228
Phone: (503)786-3677
Fax: (541)962-8417
E-mail: mpmiller@eoni.com
Home Page: http://www.webtrail.com/sdop

• 19412 • **Miss Pioneer Oregon Scholarship**
For pioneer descendant who shows appreciation of pioneer heritage and exhibits poise. Scholarship awarded annually.

• 19413 •
Sons of the Republic of Texas
Janet Hickl, Admin.
1717 8th St.
Bay City, TX 77414
Phone: (979)245-6644
Toll-Free: 800-624-5079
Fax: (979)244-3819
E-mail: srttexas@srttexas.org
Home Page: http://www.srttexas.org

• 19414 • **Presidio La Bahia Award**
To recognize writing that promotes the preservation of relics, appropriate dissemination of data, and research into Texas heritage, with particular attention to the Spanish Colonial period. Material may be submitted concerning the influence on Texas culture of Spanish Colonial heritage in laws, customs, language, religion, architecture, art, and other related fields. In 1993 a separate category was established with a prize for the best published paper, article published in a periodical, or project of a non-literary nature. A total of $2,000 is available annually for winning participants in the competition, with a minimum first place prize of $1,200 for the best published book. Established in 1968 by the Kathryn Stone O'Connor Foundation.

• 19415 • **Summerfield G. Roberts Award**
To encourage literary effort and research about historical events and personalities during the period of the Republic of Texas, 1836-1846. Authors of fiction or non-fiction, poems, essays, short stories, novels, or biographies may submit entries by January 15. Manuscripts must be written or published during the calendar year the award is given. A monetary prize of $2,500 is awarded annually. Established in 1951.

• 19416 •
Sons of the Revolution in the State of New York
Fraunces Tavern Museum
54 Pearl St.
New York, NY 10004
Phone: (212)425-1776
Phone: (212)425-1778
Fax: (212)509-3467
E-mail:
2director@fraucestavernmuseum.org
Home Page: http://
www.sonsoftherevolution.org

• 19417 • **Fraunces Tavern Museum Book Award**
For recognition of the best, newly published work that deals with American history and culture in the late 18th century, particularly the American Revolutionary War period, that combines original scholarship, insight, and good writing. The award is given in April for books published during the previous year. A plaque is presented annually at the commemoration of the Battles of Lexington and Concord. Established in 1972.

• 19418 •
Soroptimist International of the Americas
Leigh Wintz CAE, Exec.Dir.
1709 Spruce St.
Philadelphia, PA 19103-6103
Phone: (215)893-9000
Fax: (215)893-5200
E-mail: siahq@soroptimist.org
Home Page: http://www.soroptimist.org

• 19419 • **Violet Richardson Award**
To recognize and honor young women between the ages of 14 and 17 who make the community and world a better place through volunteer efforts such as fighting drugs, crime, and violence; cleaning up the environment; and working to end discrimination and poverty. Volunteer actions that benefit women and girls are of particular interest. Award amounts at the club level vary; club-level recipients become eligible for an additional award of $1,000, with a matching cash award for the charitable organization of the recipient's choosing. Additionally, the Organization grants one finalist an award of $2,500 to the recipient's volunteer organization. Established in 2000.

• 19420 • **The Venture Student Aid Awards**
Encourages and enhances the efforts of disabled individuals seeking further education to advance their status in life. Applicants should be between 15 and 40 years old at the time of application. Seven regional finalists receive $500 and compete for one first place award of $5,000 and on second place prize of $2,500.

• 19421 • **Women's Opportunity Awards**
To aid women who, as head of their household, must enter or return to the job market or further her skills and training in order to upgrade her employment status. Recipients are chosen on the basis of financial need as well as their statement of clear career goals. Only women entering vocational or technical training or completing an undergraduate degree are eligible. Approximately $800,000 is awarded through this program each year. Award amounts at the club level vary; club-level recipients become eligible for additional awards at other levels of the organization. Additionally, the Organization grants three $10,000 finalist awards each year. Established in 1972. Formerly: McCall Life Pattern Fund (Training Award).

• 19422 •
Soul Train Music Awards
Tribune Entertainment
Cushman Amberg Communications
180 N Michigan Ave.
Chicago, IL 60601
Phone: (312)263-2500
Fax: (312)263-1197
E-mail: tamberg@cushmanamberg.com

• 19423 • **Soul Train Music Awards**
To recognize the best recorded performance in the following categories: Best R&B/Urban Contemporary Single, Female; Best R&B/Urban Contemporary Single, Male; Best R&B/Urban Contemporary Single, Group or Band; Best R&B/Urban Contemporary Album of the Year, Female; Best R&B/Urban Contemporary Album of the Year, Male; Best R&B/Urban Contemporary Album of the Year, Group or Band; Best Rap Album; Best Jazz Album; Best Gospel Album; R&B/Urban Contemporary Song of the Year; Best New R&B/Urban Contemporary Artist; Best R&B/Urban Contemporary Music Video; Heritage Award for Outstanding Career Achievement; and Sammy Davis, Jr. Award for Entertainer of the Year. All recording artists on R&B/urban contemporary, rap, jazz, or gospel recordings that charted in either or all of the leading music trade publications during the previous year are eligible. Nominees are selected on voting ballots mailed to eligible recording artists, radio station music and program directors, and managers or representatives of appropriate retail outlets. Awarded annually. Established in 1987.

• 19424 •
Source Theatre Company
Joe Banno, Artistic Dir.
1835 14th St. NW
Washington, DC 20009
Phone: (202)462-1073
Fax: (202)462-2300
E-mail: info@sourcetheatre.com
Home Page: http://www.sourcetheatre.com

• 19425 • **Source Awards**
For recognition of achievement in the dramatic arts. Plays performed in Source Theatre Company's main season and late night scenes are eligible. Awards are given in the following cate-

gories: (1) Most Valuable Player; (2) Most Off-the-Wall Performance; (3) Outstanding Design; (4) Outstanding Director; (5) Outstanding Artistic Development; (6) Outstanding Graphics/Composition; (7) Creativity Award; (8) Board of Trustees award; and (9) Service Award.

• 19426 • Washington Theatre Festival Awards

For recognition of achievement in the dramatic arts. Plays produced in the festival are new plays that generally have never been performed. Awards are given in the following categories: (1) Best Actor; (2) Best Actress; (3) Best Supporting Actor; (4) Best Supporting Actress; (5) Best Director; (6) Judges Award - for exceptional contribution; (7) Best New Play; (8) Best Production; and (9) H.D. Lewis Award for new play development. The winners are selected by ballot from Festival judges (a group of leaders in the community) and the theatre. Certificates are awarded annually at an awards party. Established in 1982.

• 19427 •

John Philip Sousa Foundation
John R. Bourgeois, Pres. and CEO
℅ Prof. David Swanzy
Loyola University
New Orleans, LA 70118
E-mail: jrbourgeois@earthlink.net
Home Page: http://www.loyno.edu/sousafoundation

• 19428 • Colonel George S. Howard Citation of Musical Excellence for Military Concert Bands

To identify, recognize, and honor active duty and reserve military concert bands that have demonstrated particularly significant high standards of excellence in concert performances under the current conductor. Military band directors submit their nomination materials to the committee chairman. To be eligible, the band must perform standard band literature and the band's instrumentation must be suitable for selected band literature. A citation is awarded annually. Established in 1989 in honor of Colonel George S. Howard, United States Air Force, Retired, former commander and conductor of the United States Air Force Band and Symphony Orchestra.

• 19429 • Sousa Prize in Conducting

To recognize the highest standards of wind ensemble conducting musicianship at the international level of excellence through the medium of the wind ensemble. The competition is open to any conductor between the ages of 21 and 35 years. The winner will receive the Sousa Foundation Diploma of Honor and $2,500. The award is made biennially in even-numbered years. Established in 1994. Formerly: (1998) George Solti International Young Conductors Competition; Frederick Fennell International Young Conductor Competition.

• 19430 • Sudler Cup

To recognize and honor junior high school and middle school concert band programs throughout the United States that have demonstrated particularly significant high standards of excellence in concert activities over a period of several years. Nominations may be made from any source and at any time. The band should have performed at regional, state, national, and professional meetings of significance. These can include, but are not limited to, state music conventions, regional or national MENC meetings, and state or national band association conventions. The director must have been incumbent in his/her position for at least seven years, including the current year. A number of the students in the band should have participated in district and all-state honor bands or similar all-area groups. There is no specific number of schools to be honored each year. A silver cup with the name of the director and school engraved on the base is awarded annually. An engraved plaque is presented to the school and each member of the current concert band receives an individualized diploma.

• 19431 • Sudler Flag of Honor

To recognize and honor high school band programs throughout the United States that have demonstrated particularly significant high standards of excellence in concert activities over a period of several years. Nominations may be made from any source and at any time. The band program must offer to its participants a complete and balanced program of musical activities including the concert, solo-ensemble, and marching areas. The band should have performed at regional, state, national, or international professional meetings of significance. These can include, but are not limited to, state music conventions, regional or national MENC meetings, and state or national band association conventions. The director must have been incumbent in his/her position for at least seven years, including the present year. A number of the students in the band should have participated in district, all-state, and/or national honor bands. There is no specific number of schools to be honored each year. A nylon flag executed in red, white, and blue, and trimmed with gold fringe is awarded to the band, the director is given an engraved plaque, and each member of the band receives a handsome individualized diploma in color.

• 19432 • Louis Sudler International Wind Band Composition Competition

To encourage the composition and performance of superior wind band music at the international level and to further the wind band as a serious medium of performance. The contest is open to composers in any country regardless of age, sex, religious belief, or ethnic origin. The work must be composed for the wind band medium. This includes symphony band, wind orchestra, and wind ensemble. The instrumentation, form, and duration of the work are at the discretion of the composer, but the instrumentation should conform in general to the accepted wind band instrumentation of the composer's own country. The entry must be a recent original work by the contestant and prepared without collaboration. The prize includes $12,000 for the best new composition for the wind band, travel expenses of up to $500 to the international presentation, and the medal and ribbon of the Sudler Order of Merit of the Sousa Foundation. Awarded biennially. Established in 1983 and named for Louis Sudler of Chicago, a performing artist, businessman, and donor, and Sousa Foundation executive chairman.

• 19433 • Sudler Order of Merit

To recognize individuals who have made particularly outstanding contributions to bands and to band music through service and musicianship at the national and international levels. The Sudler Order of Merit has been established in four classes in keeping with international standards of laureate recognition. The order includes: (1) Star of the Order reserved for particularly outstanding contributions and service to bands and band music at the international level; (2) Medal of the Order awarded for outstanding service at the national level (This award is also made to the winner of the biennial Sudler Wind Band Composition Competition); (3) Badge of the Order - reserved for, but not limited to, recognition of student and staff membership in the Sousa International High School Honors Band which is organized biennially; and (4) Diploma of the Order - awarded to those making significant contributions to the activities and projects of the Sousa Foundation. Established in 1982. Sponsored by the Louis Sudler Foundation of Chicago.

• 19434 • Sudler Shield

To identify, recognize, and reward outstanding high school/youth marching bands at the international level of world class competition, and to establish national/international standards of excellence in musical performance, marching execution, and show design for high school/youth marching bands. The program is open to any high school/youth band, in any country. The adjudication is accomplished by means of a prestigious international jury evaluating marching band performances by viewing color-sound video tapes. All members of the competing band must be regularly enrolled students in the high school, or regular members of the organization the youth band represents. A miniature of the Sudler Shield is awarded to the director of each winning band. Established by Louis and Virginia Sudler. Formerly: Sudler International High School Marching Band Championship Video Competition.

• 19435 • Sudler Silver Scroll

To identify, recognize, and honor those community bands that have demonstrated particularly high standards of excellence in concert activities over a period of several years, and who have also played a leading role, year after year, in the cultural environment of their community. Nominations are received from any source and at any time by the Sousa Foundation, which in turn are processed and evaluated by the selection committee as they are received. There is no specific number of community bands to be honored each year. Awards are announced throughout the year as nominations are approved. Bands receive a diploma with the name of the director and the band inscribed. In addition, a plaque, with a scroll mounted on a walnut board, is presented to the director of the band. Established by Louis and Virginia Sudler. Sponsored by Louis Sudler.

• 19436 • Sudler Trophy
To identify and recognize collegiate marching bands of particular excellence that have made outstanding contributions to the American way of life. College or university marching bands that have demonstrated the highest of musical standards and innovative marching routines and ideas, and that have made important contributions to the advancement of the performance standards of college marching bands over a period of many years are eligible. A trophy designed by Ed Blackwell is awarded annually. Established in 1982. Sponsored by Louis Sudler Foundation of Chicago.

• 19437 •
South Atlantic Modern Language Association
Dr. Lynee Gaillet, Exec.Dir.
English Dept.
Georgia State University
38 Peachtree Ctr. Ave.
Atlanta, GA 30303
Phone: (404)651-2693
Fax: (404)651-2858
E-mail: samla@samla.org
Home Page: http://www.samla.org

• 19438 • *South Atlantic Review* Essay Prize
For recognition of scholarly achievement in modern languages and literatures by the selection of the outstanding article in the *South Atlantic Review*. Nominees must be members of the Association. A monetary prize of $500 and a citation are presented annually at the annual convention, usually held in November. Established in 1984.

• 19439 • Studies Book Award
For recognition of an outstanding scholarly book, written in English, in the field of literary criticism, theory, or history. Editions of work by other scholars (essay collections), editions, translations, and creative works are not eligible. Nominees must be members of the Association. A monetary prize of $1,000 is awarded annually. Established in 1967.

• 19440 •
South Carolina Arts Commission
Suzette M. Surkamer, Exec.Dir.
1800 Gervais St.
Columbia, SC 29201-3585
Phone: (803)734-8696
Fax: (803)734-8526
E-mail: burnette@arts.state.sc.us
Home Page: http://www.state.sc.us/arts

• 19441 • Elizabeth O'Neill Verner Awards
This, the highest honor South Carolina bestows in the arts, is given for recognition of outstanding contributions to the arts in South Carolina. Categories include education, organizations, government individuals and/or agencies, businesses or foundations, individuals, and artists. A bronze statue is awarded to one recipient in each category annually. Established in 1972 in honor of Elizabeth O'Neill Verner, noted South Carolina painter and printmaker.

• 19442 •
South Carolina Association of School Librarians
Lawren Hammond, Pres.
PO Box 2442
Columbia, SC 29202
Phone: (803)782-3956
Fax: (803)794-2585
E-mail: ksutusky@sc.rr.com
Home Page: http://www.scasl.net

• 19443 • Book Awards
To encourage students to read good quality contemporary literature and to honor the authors of the books annually chosen the favorites by student vote. Fiction or nonfiction books written by authors residing in the United States and published within the last three years are eligible. Participation in the program is open to all students who are attending public or private schools in grades K-12. Awards are presented in four categories: Picture Book Award (for grades K-3); Children's Book Award (grades 3-6); Junior Book Award (grades 6-9); and Young Adult Book Award (grades 9-12). Awarded annually. Established in 1976.

• 19444 •
South Carolina Poultry Federation
1921-A Pickens St.
Columbia, SC 29201
Phone: (803)779-4700
Fax: (803)779-5002
E-mail: egghouse@bellsouth.net

• 19445 • Legislator of the Year
For excellence in promoting the industry and the federation. Trophy awarded annually.

• 19446 • Lifetime Achievement Award
For excellence in promoting the industry and the federation. Trophy awarded annually.

• 19447 • Outstanding Service Award
For excellence in promoting the industry and the federation. Trophy awarded annually.

• 19448 •
South Dakota Broadcasters Association
Steve Willard, Exec.Dir.
106 W. Capitol Ave., No. 7
PO Box 1037
Pierre, SD 57501
Phone: (605)224-1034
Fax: (605)224-7426
Home Page: http://www.sdba.org

• 19449 • Tom Brokaw Award
For radio or TV broadcaster. Recognition award bestowed annually.

• 19450 • SD Broadcaster of the Year
For radio or TV broadcaster. Recognition award bestowed annually.

• 19451 •
South Dakota Library Association
Brenda Hemmelman, Exec.Sec.
PO Box 1212
Rapid City, SD 57709
Phone: (605)394-6139
E-mail: bkstand@rap.midco.net
Home Page: http://www.sdlibraryassociation.org

• 19452 • Prairie Pasque Children's Book Award
To encourage South Dakota students in fourth, fifth, and sixth grades to read books of literary quality and choose their favorite each year. The following books are eligible: fiction and nonfiction books, books written 2-3 years previous to the voting year, books must reflect children's reading choices, books may not include TV or movie tie-ins, books must meet library selection standards, books must be in print, books must be written by living American authors, and illustrations must be artistic and suitable. Students throughout South Dakota vote for their favorite book from the list of contest titles. Awarded annually at the Association's conference. Established in 1986.

• 19453 •
South Dakota State Historical Society
Jeff Mammenga, Program Asst.
900 Governors Dr.
Pierre, SD 57501-2217
Phone: (605)773-3458
Phone: (605)773-6000
Fax: (605)773-6041
E-mail: jeff.mammenga@state.sd.us
Home Page: http://www.sdhistory.org

• 19454 • Governor's Awards for History
For individual, teacher and group South Dakota historical accomplishments. Monetary award bestowed annually.

• 19455 •
South East Chicago Commission
Robert C. Mason, Exec.Dir
1511 E. 53rd St.
Chicago, IL 60615
Phone: (773)324-6926
Fax: (773)324-6685
E-mail: secc@forward.net
Home Page: http://www.hydeparksecc.com

• 19456 • Special Service Awards
For special service to community to persons in public or private sector. Recognition award bestowed annually.

Awards are arranged in alphabetical order below their administering organizations

• 19457 •
South Haven/Van Buren County Lakeshore Convention and Visitors Bureau
Bruce Barker, Exec.Dir.
546 Phoenix St.
South Haven, MI 49090
Phone: (269)637-5252
Toll-Free: 800-SO-HAVEN
Fax: (269)637-8710
E-mail: relax@southhaven.org
Home Page: http://www.southhaven.org

• 19458 • **Business of the Year**
For person or business active in tourism. Recognition award bestowed annually.

• 19459 •
South Metropolitan Planning Council
Jean Nielsen, Facilitator/Admin.
2300 S. Park St., Ste. 1
Madison, WI 53713-1997
Phone: (608)260-8078
Phone: (608)260-8098
Fax: (608)260-8133
E-mail: smpc@terracom.net

• 19460 • **"Hands Across South Madison" Community Services Initiative**
For youth development, human services and community building projects in southside Madison neighborhoods. Approximately $35,000 in grants awarded annually in the spring following a request-for-proposals process.

• 19461 •
South Monmouth Board of Realtors
Catherine Schwier-Mencer, Exec.V.Pres.
21 S St.
Manasquan, NJ 08736
Phone: (732)223-3100
Fax: (732)528-8566
E-mail: staff@smbr.org
Home Page: http://www.smbr.org

• 19462 • **Jim Hoag Scholarship**
For South Monmouth area resident. Scholarship awarded annually.

• 19463 •
Southeast Booksellers Association
2730 Devine St.
Columbia, SC 29205-2433
Phone: (803)779-0118
Fax: (803)779-0113
E-mail: info@sebaweb.org
Home Page: http://www.sebaweb.org

• 19464 • **Charles S. Haslam Award for Excellence in Bookselling**
To recognize a bookseller who exemplifies the highest standards of excellence in the profession. An employee, manager, or owner of a retail bookstore who shows excellence in buying and merchandising, store operations, advertising and promotion, and community service is eligible. Nominations must be submitted by December 31. A monetary award of $1,000 and a commemorative plaque are awarded annually at the American Booksellers Association Convention. Established in 1984 in honor of Charles S. Haslam "The Book Man" (1912-1983), a great bookman and owner of Haslam's Bookstore. Sponsored by Ingram Book Company.

• 19465 •
The Southeast Review
Florida State University
Julianna Baggott, Ed.
Dept. of English
Williams Bldg.
Tallahassee, FL 32306-1580
Phone: (850)644-2773
Fax: (850)644-0811
E-mail: southeastreview@english.fsu.edu
Home Page: http://southeastreview.org

• 19466 • **World's Best Short Short Story Contest**
Submissions must be typed, double-spaced, less than 500 words, and may include up to three previously-unpublished entries. Submissions must include a cover note listing the author's name, address, and telephone number; author names must not appear on the stories themselves. A fee of $10 ($25 for international entries) must also be included. Submissions must be postmarked by February 15 and will not be returned. Winner shall receive $500 and publication in *The Southeast Review*. Nine finalists will also be published. Established in 1986.

• 19467 •
Southeastern American Society for Eighteenth-Century Studies
Gary A. Richardson, Pres.
Academic Affairs
Barry University
11300 NE 2nd Ave.
Miami, FL 33161-6695
E-mail: seasecs@mail.barry.edu
Home Page: http://www.seasecs.org

• 19468 • **Percy G. Adams Article Prize**
To recognize the best article on an eighteenth-century subject published in a scholarly journal, annual, or collection during the previous year. Members of the Society who live or work in the SEASECS area (AL, FL, GA, KY, LA, MS, NC, SC, and TN) are eligible. A monetary prize of $500 and a certificate are awarded annually. Established in 1980. Formerly: SEASECS Article Prize.

• 19469 •
Southeastern Composers' League
Dr. Betty Wishart, Pres.
209 Maple Dr.
1100 College St., MUW-70
Erwin, NC 28339
Phone: (662)329-7203
E-mail: j.guthrie@charter.net
Home Page: http://www.radford.edu/~scl-web

• 19470 • **Arnold Sapop Memorial Award**
To recognize achievement in music composition by young composers the southeastern United States. Individuals must be sponsored by a member of the League. A monetary prize is awarded annually. Established in 1966.

• 19471 • **Philip Slates Memorial Award**
To recognize achievement in music composition by young composers in the southeastern United States. Individuals must be sponsored by a member of the League. A monetary prize is awarded annually. Established in 1970.

• 19472 •
Southeastern Conference
Mike Slive, Commissioner
2201 Richard Arrington Blvd. N
Birmingham, AL 35203
Phone: (205)458-3000
Fax: (205)458-3031
Home Page: http://www.secsports.com

• 19473 • **H. Boyd McWhorter Scholar-Athlete Award**
To recognize college athletes who have performed well in their sport and school. A male and female senior who are outstanding academically and in their sport are nominated by their school's athletic department. The nominations are voted on by the SEC member schools' faculty representatives (there are 12 schools in the SEC). Two $10,000 and eleven $5,000 scholarships for postgraduate work and a trophy are awarded annually at the all-conference spring meeting. Established in 1986.

• 19474 •
Southeastern Library Association
Bob Fox, Contact
P.O. Box 950
Rex, GA 30273
Phone: (678)466-4325
Fax: (678)466-4349
E-mail: sela-admin@jsu.edu
Home Page: http://sela.jsu.edu

• 19475 • **Honorary Membership Award**
To recognize an individual who has made an outstanding contribution to SELA or to a library development in the Southeast. Librarians or persons in related fields are eligible. Selection is based on regional rather than state or local contributions to the profession. Nominations must be made by members of SELA, but recipients need not be members. The deadline for nominations is April 1. Free life membership in SELA is awarded biennially when merited.

• 19476 • **Outstanding Southeastern Author Award**
To recognize authors in the states of the Southeastern Library Association for current works of literary merit. Works published within five years preceding December 31 of the year of the biennial conference may be nominated by member of SELA. Authors must be residents of a SELA state at the time the work was written or pub-

Awards are arranged in alphabetical order below their administering organizations

lished. The judges are guided by the significance and importance of the work to the general public. The deadline for nominations is August 31. A monetary award and a plaque are presented to one fiction winner and one non-fiction winner biennially when merited. Established in 1976.

• 19477 • Outstanding Southeastern Library Program Award
To recognize an outstanding program of service in any academic, public, or special library in any state of the Southeastern Library Association. Library programs of three months duration, including the development and evaluation stages of the program, must be nominated by members of SELA by January 10. Programs of service taking place at least two years prior to the award may include, but are not limited to, library activities, projects, or special outreach. A plaque is awarded biennially at the convention. Established in 1977.

• 19478 • President's Award
To honor an individual outside the library profession who has made a significant contribution to the development or promotion of libraries in the Southeast. The recipient does not need to be an SELA member, but the nominator must be a member. The deadline for nominations is December 31. A plaque is awarded biennially at the conference. Established in 1988.

• 19479 • Rothrock Award
This, the highest award bestowed by the Association, honors a librarian who has contributed substantially to the furtherance of librarianship in the Southeast during his or her career. Nominations must be made by SELA members. A monetary award and a plaque are awarded biennially at the convention. Established in 1976 by a bequest of Mary Utopia Rothrock.

• 19480 • *Southeastern Librarian* Wilson Award
To recognize the best article in the *Southeastern Librarian* during the preceding two years. The winner is chosen by the editor. A monetary prize and a certificate are awarded biennially at the conference. Established in 1982.

• 19481 • Southern Books Competition
To recognize outstanding books published in the Southeastern U.S. region during the preceding year. Selection is based on the design typography, materials, and quality of production. Content is considered only as to how the design and its execution have contributed in conveying the spirit of the book to the reader. Trade publishers, university presses, specialty publishers, and private presses are eligible to enter the competition. Hardbound books, paper-bound books, and pamphlets may be entered. Books must have been published in at least one of the following areas: Alabama, Arkansas, Florida, Georgia, Kentucky, Louisiana, Mississippi, North Carolina, South Carolina, Tennessee, Virginia, West Virginia, Puerto Rico, and the District of Columbia. Publishers of the winning books receive a certificate of recognition. For one year following the award, the winning books are exhibited at various libraries throughout the region. Awarded annually. Established in 1951.

• 19482 •
Southeastern Surgical Congress
R. Phillip Burns M.D., Sec.-Dir.
141 W Wieuca Rd., Ste. B100
Atlanta, GA 30342
Phone: (404)255-4549
Toll-Free: 800-558-8958
Fax: (404)255-5442
E-mail: sesc@sesc.org
Home Page: http://www.sesc.org

• 19483 • Gold Medal Forum
To recognize and encourage young doctors to present papers on their research. Residents in surgery may submit abstracts to a committee. Preference is given to papers that present investigative results of clinical significance. Monetary awards are given for best papers annually at the scientific meeting of the Congress. A grant from Ethicon provides the funds for the prizes. Formerly: (1991) Conrad Jobst Research Award.

• 19484 •
Southeastern Theatre Conference
Elizabeth N. Baun, Exec.Dir.
PO Box 9868
Greensboro, NC 27429
Phone: (336)272-3645
Fax: (336)272-8810
E-mail: setc@setc.org
Home Page: http://www.setc.org

• 19485 • Leighton M. Ballew Directing Award
To honor an undergraduate student with exceptional talent in directing. Nominees must be undergraduates enrolled in a graduate school in the southeast region of the United States. A monetary award of $3,200 is awarded annually.

• 19486 • Suzanne M. Davis Memorial Award
To honor distinguished achievement or service to theatre in the Southeast region of the United States or to the Conference. Candidates must reside in the Southeast and be member or past member of SETC. Awarded at the Annual Convention. Established in 1965 by Alvin Cohen.

• 19487 • Distinguished Career Award
To honor distinguished service to American theatre. Preference is given to individuals born in the South. Awarded annually at the Annual Convention. Established in 1960.

• 19488 • Charles M. Getchell Award
This, the award granted at the New Play Project, is dedicated to the discovery, development, and publicizing of worthy new plays and playwrights. This project will select one "winning script," which will be presented as a staged reading of that script at the annual Southeastern Theatre Conference. Eligible candidates are students and playwrights residing in or studying at an accredited college in the SETC member region are eligible for consideration. These states include Alabama, Florida, Georgia, Kentucky, Mississippi, North Carolina, South Carolina, Tennessee, Virginia, and West Virginia. The winning playwright will receive a $1,000 cash award. Awarded annually.

• 19489 • Polly Holliday Award
To recognize a qualifying high school student entering a College or University in the fall semester following the SETC Spring Convention. A monetary award of $850 is awarded annually.

• 19490 • Robert Porterfield Award
To recognize a graduate student for graduate study in theater. A monetary prize of $3,400 is awarded annually.

• 19491 • Student Design Competition
To recognize graduate and undergraduate school students in theatrical design. Awards are presented annually in four categories: Costume Design, Lighting Design, Scenic Design, and Crafts & Technology.

• 19492 •
Southern Appalachian Botanical Society
Dr. Charles Horn, Treas.
Biology Dept.
Newberry College
2100 College St.
Newberry, SC 29108
Phone: (803)321-5257
Fax: (803)321-5636
E-mail: chorn@newberry.edu
Home Page: http://www.newberrynet.com/sabs

• 19493 • Graduate Student Award
For research proposed in ecology and/or systematics of plants. Monetary award bestowed annually.

• 19494 •
Southern California Injury Prevention Research Center
UCLA School of Public Health
10911 Weyburn Ave., Ste. 200
Los Angeles, CA 90024
Phone: (310)794-2706
Fax: (310)794-0787
E-mail: sciprc@ucla.edu
Home Page: http://www.ph.ucla.edu/sciprc/

• 19495 • William Haddon Jr., M.D., Memorial Top Student Paper
To recognize student scientific contributions in the field of injury. Awarded annually with three prizes at $500, $250, and $150. Established in 1991.

• 19496 •
Southern Early Childhood Association
Glenda Bean, Exec.Dir.
PO Box 55930
Little Rock, AR 72215-5930
Phone: (501)221-1648
Toll-Free: 800-305-7322
Fax: (501)227-5297
E-mail: seca@aristotle.net
Home Page: http://www.SouthernEarlyChildhood.org

• 19497 • **Friend of Children**
For a strong advocate for children and families. Recognition award bestowed annually.

• 19498 •
Southern Economic Association
Joseph M. Jadlow, Sec.-Treas.
Oklahoma State University
Spears School of Business
Stillwater, OK 74078-4011
Phone: (405)744-7645
Fax: (405)744-5180
E-mail: jad1942@okstate.edu
Home Page: http://www.okstate.edu/economics/journal/south1.html

• 19499 • **Georgescu-Roegen Prize in Economics**
To encourage outstanding scholarly research in the field of economics. Non-mathematical articles published in the *Southern Economic Journal* during the preceding year are considered. A monetary award of about $3,000 and a plaque are presented annually at the convention. Established in 1986 by Professor and Mrs. Nicholas Georgescu-Roegen.

• 19500 •
Southern Historical Association
Dr. John C. Inscoe, Sec.-Treas.
University of Georgia
Dept. of History, Rm. 111A
LeConte Hall
Athens, GA 30602-1602
Phone: (706)542-8848
Fax: (706)542-2455
E-mail: jinscoe@uga.edu
Home Page: http://www.uga.edu/~sha

• 19501 • **Fletcher M. Green and Charles W. Ramsdell Award**
For recognition of the best article published in the *Journal of Southern History* during the two preceding years. A monetary prize is awarded biennially in even-numbered years. The Charles Ramsdell Award was established in 1957 and the Fletcher M. Green Award was established in 1967; they were combined in 1986.

• 19502 • **H. L. Mitchell Award**
For recognition of a distinguished book published during the two preceding years on the history of the southern working class, including industrial laborers and/or small farmers and agricultural laborers. Deadline is March 1. A monetary prize of $1,000 is awarded biennially in even-numbered years. Established in 1992.

• 19503 • **Frank L. and Harriet C. Owsley Award**
For recognition of a distinguished book in Southern history published in even-numbered years. Deadline is March 1. A monetary prize of $1,000 is awarded biennially in odd-numbered years. Established in 1984.

• 19504 • **Francis B. Simkins Award**
For recognition of an outstanding first book by an author(s) in the field of Southern history over a two-year period. Deadline is March 1. A monetary prize of $1,000 and a certificate are awarded biennially in odd-numbered years. Established in 1974 in connection with the Longwood College (Virginia) History Department.

• 19505 • **Charles S. Sydnor Award**
For recognition of an outstanding book in the field of Southern history published in odd-numbered years. Deadline is March 1. A monetary prize of $1,000 is awarded biennially in even-numbered years. Established in 1954.

• 19506 •
Southern Humanities Review
Dan Latimer, Co-Ed.
9088 Haley Ctr.
Auburn University
Auburn, AL 36849-5202
Phone: (334)844-9088
Fax: (334)844-9027
E-mail: shrengl@mail.auburn.edu
Home Page: http://www.auburn.edu/english/shr/home.htm

• 19507 • **Theodore Christian Hoepfner Awards**
For recognition of the best essay, story, and poem published in a volume (four issues per year) of *Southern Humanities Review*. In other words, the Hoepfner Awards are not a contest to be entered, but an award made for work already accepted and published through the regular submission process. Monetary prizes of $100 each for the best essay and short story, and $50 for the best poem are awarded annually after the fall issue is published. Established in 1968 in honor of Professor Theodore Christian Hoepfner of Auburn University, Alabama.

• 19508 •
Southern Illinois University at Carbondale
School of Journalism
North Wing
SIUC Communications Bldg.
Carbondale, IL 62901-6899
Phone: (618)536-3361
Fax: (618)453-5200
E-mail: jschool@siu.edu
Home Page: http://journal.siu.edu

• 19509 • **Elijah Parish Lovejoy Award**
To recognize courage in journalism by non-daily newspaper editors. A plaque is awarded as merited. Established in 1956.

• 19510 •
Southern Methodist University
Caruth Institute for Entrepreneurship
Edwin L. Cox School of Business
Fincher Bldg.
PO Box 750333
Dallas, TX 75275-0333
Phone: (214)768-3689
Fax: (214)768-3604
E-mail: caruth@mail.cox.smu.edu
Home Page: http://www.cox.smu.edu/corporate/centers/caruth/
Formerly: (2004) Southern Methodist University - Caruth Institute of Owner-Managed Business.

• 19511 • **Dallas 100 Award**
Recognizing the 100 fastest growing private companies in Dallas.

• 19512 •
Southern Methodist University
Meadows School of the Arts
Carole Brandt, Dean
Meadows School of the Arts
PO Box 750356
Dallas, TX 75275-0356
Phone: (214)768-2880
Fax: (214)768-2228
E-mail: meadows@smu.edu
Home Page: http://smu.edu/meadows

• 19513 • **Algur H. Meadows Award for Excellence in the Arts**
To honor the highest level of international achievement in the creative and performing arts. Recognizing that the arts are fundamental to any great civilization, the Meadows Award is designed to honor the accomplishments of one artist and to provide a forum for that artist to share ideas and aspirations with the students of the University who will become the professional artists and arts patrons of the future. Nominations are accepted. This award is international in scope and the recipient is selected by a specially appointed jury consisting of the dean of the Meadows School of the Arts and additional members who are distinguished in their various arts fields. The award consists of a monetary prize of $50,000 and a miniature of the sculpture, "Spirit's Flight" by Isamu Noguchi, which was commissioned to symbolize this award. Awarded annually. Established in 1978 as a permanent memorial to Algur H. Meadows (1899-1978), longtime trustee of the University, distinguished arts patron, and benefactor of the Meadows School of the Arts and the Meadows Museum and Sculpture Garden at Southern Methodist University. Sponsored by the Meadows Foundation, Inc.

• 19514 •
Southern Poetry Review
Robert Parham, Ed.
Department of Languages, Literature, & Philosophy
Armstrong Atlantic State University
11935 Abercorn St.
Savannah, GA 31419-1997
Phone: (704)330-6275
Fax: (704)330-6644
E-mail: rrparham@aug.edu
Home Page: http://www.spr.armstrong.edu

• 19515 • **Guy Owen Poetry Prize**
To recognize the best individual poem submitted during the competition. All poems submitted will be considered for publication in *Southern Poetry Review*. Entries must be postmarked by June 15. A monetary award of $1,000 and publication in the *Review* is presented annually. Established in 1983 as a memorial to Guy Owen, founder of *Southern Poetry Review*, novelist and poet.

• 19516 •
Southern Pressure Treaters Association
April James, Exec.Dir.
PO Box 2389
Gulf Shores, AL 36547-2389
Phone: (334)968-5726
Fax: (334)968-6008
E-mail: pbrvgge@awpi.org
Home Page: http://www.spta.org

• 19517 • **Safety and Service**
For OSHA standards. Recognition award bestowed annually.

• 19518 •
Southern Psychiatric Association
35 Lakeshore Dr.
PO Box 190088
Birmingham, AL 35219-0088
Phone: (205)945-8903
Fax: (205)945-1548
E-mail: spa@admin.sma.org
Home Page: http://www.smaservicesinc.com/spa

• 19519 • **Annual Award for Psychiatrists in Training**
For completed training after June 30 of that year. Monetary award bestowed annually.

• 19520 •
Southern Regional Council
Toni Fannin, Interim Exec.Dir.
133 Carnegie Way NW, Ste. 1030
Atlanta, GA 30303-1054
Phone: (404)522-8764
Fax: (404)522-8791
E-mail: info@southerncouncil.org
Home Page: http://www.southerncouncil.org

• 19521 • **Lillian Smith Book Awards**
To encourage outstanding writing about the American South. Seeks to honor fiction and nonfiction works of serious literary, artistic, or scholarly merit that enlarge public understanding of the diverse human experience in the South and illuminate the reform spirit of Lillian Smith and the progressive social values of the Southern Regional Council. Awarded annually. Established in 1968.

• 19522 •
The Southern Review
Louisiana State University
Bret Lott, Ed.
43 Allen Hall
Louisiana State University
Baton Rouge, LA 70803-5005
Phone: (225)578-5108
Fax: (225)578-5098
E-mail: southernreview@lsu.edu
Home Page: http://www.lsu.edu/thesouthernreview

• 19523 • **Eudora Welty Prize in Fiction**
For recognition of the best short story published in *The Southern Review* during the previous year. A monetary award of $1,500 is presented annually. Established in 1980.

• 19524 •
Southern States Communication Association
Dr. Hal W. Fulmer, Exec.Dir.
Dept. Communication Arts
Georgia Southern University
PO Box 8091-02
Statesboro, GA 30460
Phone: (912)681-5502
Fax: (912)681-0822
E-mail: ssca@georgiasouthern.edu
Home Page: http://www.ssca.net/

• 19525 • **John I. Sisco Excellence in Teaching Award**
To honor members who have consistently demonstrated excellence in teaching communication throughout their academic careers. Awarded annually.

• 19526 •
Southwest Review
William Spiegelman, Editor-in-Chief
Southern Methodist University
PO Box 750374
Dallas, TX 75275-0374
Phone: (214)768-1036
Fax: (214)768-1408
E-mail: swr@mail.smu.edu
Home Page: http://southwestreview.org

• 19527 • **McGinnis-Ritchie Award**
For recognition of the best works of fiction and nonfiction published in the *Southwest Review* during the previous year. Two to four monetary awards of $500 each are presented annually for fiction and nonfiction. Established in 1960 by Robert F. Ritchie in memory of John H. McGinnis, editor of the *Southwest Review;* renamed in 1998 as a posthumous tribute to Ritchie. Formerly: (1998) John H. McGinnis Memorial Award.

• 19528 • **Elizabeth Matchett Stover Memorial Award**
To recognize the author of the best poem or group of poems published in the *Southwest Review* during the previous year. A monetary award of $250 is presented annually. Established in 1978 by Jerry S. Stover in memory of his mother, a key member of the *Southwest Review* staff.

• 19529 •
Southwestern Association of Naturalists
Karen McBee, Pres.
Jacob Schaefer, Treas
The University of Southern Mississippi
118 College Dr., No. 5018
Hattiesburg, MS 39406-0001
Phone: (601)266-4928
Fax: (601)266-5797
E-mail: jake.schaefer@usm.edu
Home Page: http://www.biosurvey.ou.edu/swan/

• 19530 • **W. Frank Blair Eminent Naturalist Award**
To recognize an individual for excellence in a lifetime of commitment to outstanding study or conservation of the flora or fauna of the southwestern United States, Mexico, and Central America. Awarded annually. Established in 1986.

• 19531 • **Robert L. Packard Outstanding Educator Award**
To recognize a member of the society who has made significant contributions to the understanding of the biota of the Southwestern United States, Mexico, and Central America through teaching and/or presenting scientific information to the general public. Achievements in one or more of the following areas are considered for this award: number of graduate students, number of undergraduate and graduate courses taught, impact on the careers of students, public lectures, popular articles, public exhibitions, and field trips for the public. Awarded annually. Established in 1988.

• 19532 • **Donald W. Tinkle Research Excellence Award**
To recognize a member who, in the past 10 years, has made significant contributions to the knowledge and understanding of the biota of the Southwestern United States, Mexico, and Central America through scientific articles and books. Awarded when merited. Established in 1988.

• 19533 • **Wilks Award**
To recognize the best paper presented by a student at the Association's annual meeting. This honor is based on the student's submitted manuscript and presentation. A monetary award of $500 and all available past issues of *The Southwestern Naturalist* are presented annually. Established in 1996.

• 19534 •
Space Coast Writers' Guild
Joyce Henderson, Pres.
PO Box 362143
Melbourne, FL 32936-2143
Phone: (321)723-7345
Phone: (321)254-5631
E-mail: scwg02@aol.com
Home Page: http://www.scwg.org
Formerly: (1991) Florida Space Coast Writers Conference.

• 19535 • **Space Coast Writers Guild Conference Awards**
To recognize winning writers and authors for unpublished contest material submitted with conference registration activities. The following awards (monetary and plaque) are presented at the Guild's annual two-day writers conference in November: Best Novel, Best Play, Best Poetry, Best Short Story, Best Children's Story, Best Feature Article, and the 7th and 8th Grade Public School Essay Contest for students. Awards and plaques are also presented for the Distinguished Service Award and the prestigious Michael Shaara Outstanding Writer Award presented by the Guild at the conference. Established in 1981 by Betty and Andrew Melvin as an organization for professional and novice authors and writers in all media. Formerly: (1991) Florida Space Coast Writers Conference Awards.

• 19536 •
Spain-United States Chamber of Commerce
Lidia del Pozo, Exec.Dir.
350 5th Ave., Ste. 2029
New York, NY 10118
Phone: (212)967-2170
Fax: (212)564-1415
E-mail: info@spainuscc.org
Home Page: http://www.spainuscc.org

• 19537 • **Business Leader of the Year Award**
Recognizes business leadership between Spain and the US. Awarded annually.

• 19538 •
Spanish Institute
Dr. Fernando Aleu MD, Exec.Chm.
684 Park Ave.
New York, NY 10021
Phone: (212)628-0420
Fax: (212)734-4177
E-mail: information@spanishinstitute.org
Home Page: http://
www.spanishinstitute.org/

• 19539 • **Gold Medal Award**
Recognizes significant contributions towards the betterment of relations between Spain and the U.S. Americans and Spaniards are eligible. Awarded annually.

• 19540 •
Spanish Mustang Registry
Carol Dildine, Contact
681 County Rd. 229
Florence, TX 76527
Phone: (520)384-2886
Phone: (507)744-2704
E-mail: mat@vtc.net
Home Page: http://
www.spanishmustang.org

• 19541 • **Championship Awards**
To recognize registered Spanish Mustangs in various competitive fields. Championship points are cumulative throughout the life of the horse with no time limits in effect. The title Conquistador or Grande Conquistador is noted on the horse's registration record as merited. Established in 1974.

• 19542 • **Points and Awards Program**
For recognition of achievement of Spanish Mustangs. The awards program is based on an accumulation of points. The competitive categories awarded are Show, Games, Rodeo, Competitive Trail, and Endurance. Noncompetitive recognition includes the Compadre Award, La Parada Award, and El Caballo de Trabajo Award. The following awards are presented: Certificate of Achievement and Horse of the Year. Special achievement awards are made in addition to championship and noncompetitive categories. Awarded annually when merited. Established in 1979.

• 19543 •
Special Interest Group on Knowledge Discovery and Data Mining
Association for Computing Machinery
Gregory Piatesky-Shapiro, Chm.
% Rakesh Agrawal, Sec.
IBM Almaden Research Ctr.
650 Harry Rd.
San Jose, CA 95120
Phone: (408)927-1734
Toll-Free: 800-342-6626
Fax: (408)927-3215
E-mail: acmhelp@acm.org
Home Page: http://www.acm.org/sigs/
sigkdd

• 19544 • **Innovation Award**
To recognize an individual for outstanding and major technical contributions to the field of knowledge discovery in data and data mining that have had lasting impact in furthering the theory and/or development of commercial systems. Awarded annually.

• 19545 • **Service Award**
To recognize an individual for outstanding and major services contributions to the field of knowledge discovery in data and data mining that include such professional services as the running of professional societies and conferences, educating students and professionals, funding R&D activities, etc. Awarded annually.

• 19546 •
Special Libraries Association
Janice R. Lachance, Exec.Dir.
331 S Patrick St.
Alexandria, VA 22314-3501
Phone: (703)647-4900
Fax: (703)647-4901
E-mail: sla@sla.org
Home Page: http://www.sla.org/

• 19547 • **John Cotton Dana Award**
To recognize an SLA member or group of members for exceptional service to special librarianship. Awarded when merited. Established in 1979 to honor John Cotton Dana, the founder and first president of SLA.

• 19548 • **Fellow of the Special Libraries Association**
To recognize SLA members at or near the midpoint of an active professional career for outstanding leadership in the field of special librarianship and for their contributions and expected future service to the Association. No more than five members are selected as Fellows each year. Established in 1987.

• 19549 • **Hall of Fame**
To recognize a member for extended and sustained distinguished service to the Association in all spheres of its activities. Members at or near the end of an active professional career are eligible. Awarded annually. Established in 1959.

• 19550 • **Honorary Member**
To recognize the contributions of a nonmember to the advancement of special librarianship. Nominations by a member or membership unit and supporting documentation may be submitted in writing to the Board of Directors. Rights and privileges of an association membership are awarded annually. Maximum is 15 concurrent Honorary Members. Established in 1952.

• 19551 • **Innovations in Technology Award**
To honor SLA member(s) for innovative uses and applications of technology in a special library setting, and to raise visibility for the outstanding contributions members of the profession are making in developing and creatively using new information technologies and its applications. Candidates are evaluated on the following criteria: benefit of innovation or use of technology to clients served; benefit of innovation or use of technology to the information community; impact of innovation or use on library operations; marketability of innovation or use; and impact of innovation or use on perception of the library and librarian in the work setting and the specialized and/or general public. An honorarium of $1,000 is awarded annually. Established in 1991. Sponsored by LexisNexis. Formerly: SLA Meckler Award for Innovations in Technology.

• 19552 • International Special Librarians Day/National Library Week Award
To recognize the special public relations efforts made by an SLA member(s) during National Library Week and/or International Special Librarians Day. The recognition is reserved for any individual SLA member or group of members in good standing with the Association. Candidates may be nominated by any SLA member or Association staff. Self nominations are accepted. A Certificate of Recognition is presented to the recipient(s) during the Annual Conference. Formerly: Special Recognition for Excellence in Public Relations.

• 19553 • Media Award
To recognize journalists who published an outstanding feature on the special libraries profession, preferably in a general circulation publication or broadcast production. The award is intended to encourage writers to develop stories on the various aspects of special libraries and the information professionals who manage them. A monetary prize and travel expenses to attend the SLA Annual Conference are awarded during the Association's annual Business Meeting. Established in 1988.

• 19554 • Professional Award
To recognize an individual or group for a specific major achievement in, or a specific contribution to, the field of librarianship or information science that advances the objectives of the Association. Members and nonmembers are eligible. Awarded annually. Established in 1949.

• 19555 • Public Relations Member Achievement Award
To recognize the outstanding contributions made by members during the previous calendar year to the public relations goals of the profession, the Association unit, and/or the library/information center. The recognition is reserved for any SLA member in good standing with the Association. An award is given to individuals or groups from each of the three categories who: make a significant contribution to the public relations goals of the profession, make a significant contribution to the public relations goals of the Association unit (chapter, division, caucus, committee), and make a significant contribution to the public relations goals of the information center/library. A Certificate of Recognition is presented to each recipient during the SLA Annual Conference. Formerly: Member Recognition for Excellence in Public Relations.

• 19556 • Research Grant
To support a research project undertaken by a member of the profession. Research projects should focus on areas specified in SLA's research agenda, encompassing future technology in the special library, current user issues, measures of productivity and value, client user satisfaction measures, and staffing. Up to $15,000 is awarded to an applicant meeting SLA's Research Committee guidelines.

• 19557 • H. W. Wilson Company Award
To recognize the author of the best article that appears in the SLA's quarterly journal, *Special Libraries,* during the previous calendar year. A monetary award of $500 and a plaque are awarded annually at the conference. Established in 1977. Sponsored by the H. W. Wilson Company.

• 19558 •
Special Libraries Association
Museums, Arts and Humanities Division
Gerald F. Patout Jr., Chm.
℅ John Shea, Sec.
Union Bank of California
445 S Figueroa St., 14th Fl.
Los Angeles, CA 90071
Phone: (213)236-6873
Fax: (213)236-4268
E-mail: john.shea@uboc.com
Home Page: http://www.sla.org/division/dmah

• 19559 • Ron Coplen Roll of Honor Award
To honor a member of the division for exemplary service. A plaque is awarded annually. Established in 1980 and renamed in 1993. Formerly: (1993) Publishing Division Roll of Honor Award; Publishing Division Honor Roll.

• 19560 • Fannie Simon Award
To recognize a member of the Division for distinguished service to publishing librarianship or the field of publishing. The award consists of a cash stipend of $100 and a plaque. Established in 1980 in honor of Fannie Simon, founder of the SLA Publishing Division, and a 1962 SLA Hall of Fame Award winner.

• 19561 •
Special Libraries Association
News Division
Janice R. Lachance, Exec.Dir.
331 S Patrick St.
Wisconsin State Journal
PO Box 8056
Alexandria, VA 22314-3501
Phone: (703)647-4900
Fax: (703)647-4901
E-mail: sla@sla.org
Home Page: http://www.sla.org

• 19562 • Certificate of Appreciation and Recognition
To recognize an individual or institution for an outstanding contribution in the field of information science and/or news librarianship. Awarded when merited. Established in 1988.

• 19563 • Agnes Henebry Roll of Honor Award
For recognition of a member or former member for outstanding service to the Division. A certificate is awarded to one or more recipients annually. Established in 1978.

• 19564 • Joseph F. Kwapil Memorial Award
This, the highest recognition of the Division, is given for major achievement in the field of news librarianship and/or outstanding service to the Division. A $500 grant and a plaque are awarded annually. Established in 1978.

• 19565 • Ralph J. Shoemaker Award of Merit
For recognition of each Division Chairperson upon the completion of his/her term of office. A certificate is awarded annually. Established in 1978.

• 19566 •
Special Libraries Association
Transportation Division
Bob Sweet, Chair
℅ Bob Sweet, Chair
University of Michigan
Transportation Research Institute
2901 Baxter Rd.
Ann Arbor, MI 48109-2150
Phone: (734)936-1073
E-mail: bsweet@umich.edu
Home Page: http://www.library.northwestern.edu/transportation/slatran

• 19567 • Professional Achievement Award
To recognize outstanding contributions and service to transportation libraries and librarianship and to the Division. Past or present members are eligible. A plaque is awarded periodically at the SLA annual convention. Established in 1982.

• 19568 •
Special Olympics Canada
Jim Jordan, Pres.
60 St. Clair Ave. E, Ste. 700
Toronto, ON, Canada M4T 2N5
Phone: (416)927-9050
Toll-Free: 877-291-7404
Fax: (416)927-8475
E-mail: info@specialolympics.ca
Home Page: http://www.cso.on.ca

• 19569 • Athlete of the Year
To recognize outstanding male and female athletes. Awarded annually.

• 19570 • Chairman's Award
To recognize the volunteer making a significant contribution to a local Special Olympic movement. Awarded annually.

• 19571 • Coach of the Year
To recognize outstanding male and female coaches. Awarded annually.

• 19572 •
Special Recreation for Disabled International
Prof. John A. Nesbitt EdD, Pres./CEO
701 Oaknoll Dr.
Iowa City, IA 52246-5168
Phone: (319)466-3192
Phone: (319)351-1720
Fax: (319)351-6772
E-mail: john-nesbitt@uiowa.edu

Formerly: (1999) Special Recreation, Inc..

• 19573 • **Special Recreation for People with Disabilities Awards**
For recognition of a contribution to recreation of persons with disabilities. Individuals and organizations may be nominated by people with disabilities, professionals, parents and others. Nominations are reviewed by the Board of Directors of Special Recreation, Inc. Awards are presented in the following categories: Achievement in Recreation by a Disabled Person; Consumerism in Special Recreation; Congressional Leadership in Special Recreation; Corporate Innovation in Program or Service in Special Recreation; Foundation Innovation in Program or Service in Special Recreation; Public Innovation in Program or Service in Special Recreation; Voluntary Innovation in Program or Service Recreation; International Service in Special Recreation; Literature Award in Special Recreation; National Service in Special Recreation; Pioneer in Special Recreation; Professional Leadership in Special Recreation; Professional Organization in Special Organization; Publishing in Special Recreation; and Research and Scholarship in Special Recreation. Plaques are awarded annually. Established in 1978. Formerly: (1991) Special Recreation for Disabled Awards; Special Recreation Awards.

• 19574 •
Specialized Carriers and Rigging Association
Joel M. Dandrea, Exec.VP
2750 Prosperity Ave., Ste. 620
Fairfax, VA 22031-4312
Phone: (703)698-0291
Fax: (703)698-0297
E-mail: info@scranet.org
Home Page: http://www.scranet.org

Formerly: (1981) Heavy Specialized Carriers Conference.

• 19575 • **Crane and Rigging Safety/Safety Improvement Awards**
To recognize superior safety records in crane and rigging. First and second prize awards go to winners in five categories based on the amount of man-hours worked during the year: under 25,000 man-hours; 25,000 to 50,000 manhours; 50,000 to 100,000 man-hours; 100,000 to 250,000 man-hours; and over 250,000 manhours. Safety Improvement Awards are given to member companies that show an improved incidence rate, compared to the previous year's safety contest entry. Winners of the Safety Award are ineligible for the Safety Improvement Award. Awarded annually to multiple recipients.

• 19576 • **Distinguished Service Award**
Awarded to the chairpersons of SC&RA's four groups - Allied, Crane & Rigging, Ladies, and Transportation - upon completion of their terms. Each receives a personalized certificate printed in maroon and black on buff parchment.

• 19577 • **Driver of the Year Award**
To recognize a professional driver who has demonstrated outstanding performance through a deed of heroism, highway courtesy, or contribution to highway safety. To qualify, drivers must have a long record of safe and courteous driving. They also must be employed or contracted as a professional truck driver by the nominating SC&RA member company for at least the last five consecutive years. A belt buckle cast with white metal is awarded. Formerly: (1997) Truck Driver of the Year.

• 19578 • **Fleet Safety/Safety Improvement Awards**
To improve the safety record of motor carrier members. A winner with the lowest accident frequency rate will be selected for each of five mileage categories: 100,000 miles to 5 million miles; 5 million miles to 25 million miles; 25 million miles to 50 million miles; 50 million miles to 100 million miles; over 100 million miles. All entrants having zero accidents during the report period automatically receive an award. The entire operation of a participating company must be entered in the contest. Fleet Safety Improvement Awards go to contestants who can show a reduction in their accident frequency rate for miles traveled compared to their previous year accident frequency rate. Companies can receive both the Fleet Safety Award and the Fleet Safety Improvement Award. Winners receive personalized certificates. Awarded annually to multiple recipients.

• 19579 • **Golden Achievement Award**
To recognize the individual who has made an outstanding contribution to the specialized carriers and rigging industry. The honoree may be a member directly involved with specialized hauling, rigging, and millwrighting or an allied industry member serving the industry. Nonmembers such as government officials who have served the industry are also eligible. A porcelain eagle on a walnut base is awarded.

• 19580 • **Hauling Job of the Year Award**
To honor and give special recognition to transportation members who perform outstanding achievements in meeting professional challenges encountered in transporting commodities of unusual size or weight and unusual characteristics. Awards are given in the following categories: (1) Moving; (2) Hauling over 160,000 Pounds; and (3) Hauling under 160,000 Pounds. Selection is based on the following criteria: shipment routing; planning the job; physical elements; safety considerations; and execution. Members of the Association Transportation Group for a minimum of one year are eligible. The hauling job must have been completed during the calendar year immediately preceding the year's convention. A trophy is awarded annually to the winner in each category. Established in 1966.

• 19581 • **Longevity Awards**
To recognize loyal membership demonstrated by member companies at five-year intervals. A certificate, plaque, or trophy is awarded, depending on the number of years of membership.

• 19582 • **Million Miler Award for Safety Excellence**
To recognize the finest professional drivers in the specialized carriers industry. Professional drivers who have accumulated a minimum of one million miles of safe driving within the industry are eligible. An eleven inch pewter plate personalized with the winner's name is awarded.

• 19583 • **Pinnacle Award**
To recognize individuals who have served a full three-year term on the SC&RA Board of Directors or as a Governing Committee Member. An SC&RA medallion embedded in a crystal clear pyramid and mounted on an American black walnut base is awarded.

• 19584 • **Rigging Job of the Year Award**
To honor and give special recognition to members for outstanding achievement in meeting professional challenges encountered in rigging. Awards are given in the following categories: (1) jobs between $150,000 and $750,000; and (2) jobs under $150,000. Selection is based on the following criteria: safety; engineering and planning; limitations; and innovation and ingenuity. Members of the Crane and Rigging Group of the Specialized Carriers and Rigging Association are eligible and entries must be received in the Washington office four weeks before the start of the Convention. Winners of the contest are announced at the Annual Convention. A trophy is awarded annually to the winner in each category. Established in 1968.

• 19585 • **Transportation Safety Awards**
To recognize companies with outstanding safety records, and to encourage motor carrier members to transport, lift, and erect oversize/overweight items safely. Four awards are presented: Fleet Safety Award, for having the lowest accident frequency rate in four different mileage categories; Zero Accident Award, for having no recordable injuries during the year; Fleet Safety Improvement Award, for a reduction in the accident frequency rate for miles traveled; and Million Miler Award for Safety Excellence, to professional drivers in the specialized carrier industry who accumulated a minimum of one million consecutive miles of safe driving. Awarded annually. Established in 1985.

• 19586 • **Zero Accident Awards**
To recognize members who make it through an entire year without a single accident. Awarded annually to multiple recipients in the categories of transportation and crane/rigging.

• 19587 •
Specialty Equipment Market Association
Christopher Kersting CAE, Pres.
PO Box 4910
Diamond Bar, CA 91765-0910
Phone: (909)396-0289
Fax: (909)860-0184
E-mail: sema@sema.org
Home Page: http://www.sema.org
Formerly: Speed Equipment Market Association.

• 19588 • **Hall of Fame**
In recognition of outstanding contributions to the specialty automotive industry. Nominees are commonly involved in the industry for ten years or more (not necessarily currently) and are at least 40 years of age. A trophy is presented at the SEMA awards banquet in Las Vegas, Nevada, in conjunction with the annual SEMA Show. Established in 1972. Formerly: (1986) Paul Schiefer "Old Timer's" Memorial Award.

• 19589 •
Specialty Graphic Imaging Association
Michael E. Robertson, CEO/Pres.
10015 Main St.
Fairfax, VA 22031-3489
Phone: (703)385-1335
Toll-Free: 888-385-3588
Fax: (703)273-0456
E-mail: sgia@sgia.org
Home Page: http://www.sgia.org

• 19590 • **Booth Award**
Award of recognition for marketing effectiveness. Awarded annually.

• 19591 • **Certificate of Appreciation Award**
Annual award of recognition.

• 19592 • **Certificate of Merit**
Recognizes service to the association. Awarded annually.

• 19593 • **Distinguished Service Award**
Recognizes service to the association. Awarded annually.

• 19594 • **Golden Image Award**
Award of recognition for print quality. Awards are given in 44 categories. Awarded annually. Inquire for application details.

• 19595 • **Key Award**
Recognizes exceptional service to the association. Awarded annually.

• 19596 • **Magnus Award**
Recognizes outstanding service in membership development. Awarded annually.

• 19597 • **Mentor Award**
Recognizes an exceptional educational effort by a school and/or educator. Awarded annually.

• 19598 • **Outstanding Service Award**
Annual award of recognition.

• 19599 • **Parmele Award**
Recognizes an outstanding contribution to the industry. Awarded annually.

• 19600 • **Safety Recognition Award**
Recognizes outstanding achievement in plant safety. Awarded annually.

• 19601 • **Swormstedt Award**
Recognizes the author of the best technical paper on screen printing in the year. Awarded annually.

• 19602 •
Spectroscopy Society of Pittsburgh
Jennifer Cassidy, Asst.
300 Penn Center Blvd., STe. 332
Pittsburgh, PA 15235-5503
Toll-Free: 800-825-3221
Home Page: http://www.ssp-pgh.org

• 19603 • **Maurice F. Hasler Award**
To recognize and encourage notable achievements in spectroscopy that have resulted in significant applications of broad utility. Individuals of any nationality are eligible. A monetary award of $1,000 and a scroll are awarded biennially in odd-numbered years. Established in 1969. Sponsored by Thermo Electron Corp.

• 19604 •
SPIE: International Society for Optical Engineering
Dr. Eugene G. Arthurs, Exec.Dir.
1000 20th St.
PO Box 10
Bellingham, WA 98227-0010
Phone: (360)676-3290
Fax: (360)647-1445
E-mail: spie@spie.org
Home Page: http://spie.org

• 19605 • **A. E. Conrady Award**
To recognize individuals who have done outstanding work and have made a pronounced impact on the design and construction of optical instrumentation, representing that aspect of optical engineering now considered conventional, traditional, or classical, and yet essential for successful development in the broadly defined field of optics. A 2,000 honorarium is awarded. Established in 1990. Sponsored by Optical Research Associates.

• 19606 • **Harold E. Edgerton Award**
To recognize an individual who has made outstanding contributions to optical or photonic techniques in the application and understanding of high speed physical phenomena. Contribution may be a single specific event, device, invention, or system or a series of them. The field of high speed optics should be interpreted in the broadest sense, namely the application of high speed physical phenomena for capturing, imaging, and analyzing real or near-real time events in laboratory, industrial, and field settings. A $2,000 honorarium is awarded annually. Established in 1989.

• 19607 • **Dennis Gabor Award**
In recognition of outstanding accomplishments in diffractive wavefront technologies, especially those which further the development of holography and metrology applications. Both individuals and members of a team are eligible. A $2,000 honorarium is awarded annually when merited. Established in 1983.

• 19608 • **George W. Goddard Award**
To recognize exceptional achievement in the field of optical or photonic instrumentation for aerospace, atmospheric science, or astronomy. Selection is based on those developments, inventions, or techniques that have contributed significantly to an advance in the technology of photo-optical instrumentation. Since the award is to be made to an individual, a development, invention, or technique in which a group participates is considered for this award only if one person has contributed the basic idea or has made substantial contributions to the implementation of an idea. Preference is given to application work that has reached successful completion within five years of the date of the award. An honorarium of $2,000 is awarded annually when merited. Established in 1961.

• 19609 • **Gold Medal of the Society**
This, the principal award of the Society, is given in recognition of outstanding engineering or scientific accomplishments in optics, electro-optics, or photographic technologies or applications. The award strongly reflects the diversity of interests of SPIE in the fields of photography, optics, and electro-optics. Individuals or members of a team are eligible. Nominations are accepted. A gold medal and a $10,000 honorarium are awarded annually. Established in 1977.

• 19610 • **Rudolf Kingslake Medal and Prize**
To recognize the most noteworthy original paper to appear in the Society's official journal, *Optical Engineering,* on the theoretical or experimental aspects of optical engineering. All papers published in the journal are automatically eligible for consideration for this award. An honorarium of $2,000 and a silver plated bronze medal are awarded annually to one or more recipients. Established in 1974.

• 19611 • **SPIE Technology Achievement Award**
In recognition of outstanding accomplishment in optical, electro-optical, or photonic engineering technology, as demonstrated in a new system or application and its reduction to practice. The accomplishments may be made by individuals or

by members of a team. An honorarium of $2,000 is awarded annually when merited. Established in 1979. Sponsored by Loral Fairchild Systems.

• 19612 •
Spill Control Association of America
David Usher, Pres.
32500 Scenic Ln.
Franklin, MI 48025
Phone: (248)851-1936
Fax: (313)849-1623
E-mail: info@scaa-spill.org
Home Page: http://www.scaa-spill.org

• 19613 • **Howard E. Stanfield Distinguished Service Award**
To recognize distinguished achievements in, or contributions to, the technology of control of spills of oil and hazardous materials. Achievements may include contributions to the knowledge and literature of spill control; the design or invention of equipment or technical services; or outstanding service to government, companies, or organizations serving any field of spill control/cleanup technology. Candidates for the inscribed award need not be members, but must be recommended by an Award Committee. Established in 1983.

• 19614 •
Spina Bifida Association of Greater St. Louis
Chris Guzdial, Pres.
5609 Hampton Ave.
St. Louis, MO 63109
Phone: (314)353-7079
Toll-Free: 800-784-0983
Fax: (314)353-1446
E-mail: sbagstl2000@yahoo.com
Home Page: http://www.geocities.com/sbagstl2000/

• 19615 • **Education Training Scholarship**
For individual with spina bifida or neural tube defect. Scholarship awarded annually.

• 19616 •
Spiritual Science Fellowship
Dr. Marilyn Rossner PhD, Pres.
PO Box 1387, Sta. H
Montreal, QC, Canada H3G 2N3
Phone: (514)937-8359
Fax: (514)937-5380
E-mail: info@iiihs.org
Home Page: http://www.iiihs.com

• 19617 • **Meritorious Service Award**
Recognizes outstanding volunteer providing service to SSF. Awarded annually.

• 19618 •
Spiritualist Yoga Fellowship
Dr. Marilyn Zwaig Rossner, Pres.
PO Box 1445 Sta. H
Montreal, QC, Canada H3G 2N3
Phone: (514)937-8359
Fax: (514)937-5380
E-mail: mrossner@iiihs.org

• 19619 • **Meritorious Service**
Recognizes distinguished volunteer service to SSF. Awarded periodically.

• 19620 •
Spitball, the Literary Baseball Magazine
Mike Shannon, Editor-in-Chief
5560 Fox Rd.
Cincinnati, OH 45239
Home Page: http://www.angelfire.com/oh5/spitball

• 19621 • **Casey Award**
To recognize and honor the authors and publishers of the best books on the subject of baseball published during the preceding year. The Casey, a bronze plaque, is awarded annually by *Spitball: The Literary Baseball Magazine* at the CASEY Awards Banquet. Non-CASEY-winning nominees receive framed certificates. Established in 1983.

• 19622 •
B. J. Spoke Gallery
Marilyn Lavi, Mgr.
299 Main St.
Huntington, NY 11743
Phone: (631)549-5106
E-mail: managerbjs@verizon.net
Home Page: http://www.bjspokegallery.com
Formerly: (1995) Northport/B.J. Spoke Gallery.

• 19623 • **EXPO Juried Competition**
To recognize outstanding artists in oil, acrylics, mixed media, pastel, watercolor, drawings, graphics, photography, and sculpture. Deadline for entries is November 17. Six to eight artists will be invited to hold a one-month show at the B.J Spoke Gallery, including a reception, invitations, and press releases. Awarded annually. Established in 1980.

• 19624 •
Sport Canada
Daniel Bourdeau, Actg.Dir.
2197 Riverside Dr., Ste. 300
Ottawa, ON, Canada K1H 7X3
Phone: (613)521-3340
Fax: (613)521-3134
E-mail: info@truesport.ca
Home Page: http://www.canadianheritage.gc.ca/progs/sc/index_e.cfm
Formerly: Sports Federation of Canada.

• 19625 • **Johnny F. Bassett Memorial Award**
To recognize a Canadian amateur athlete who has displayed a combination of sporting excellence and community values. Awarded annually. Established in 1991.

• 19626 • **Corporate Excellence Award**
To recognize the President of the Canadian corporation selected by the Awards Committee for their most significant contribution to Canadian sport. Consideration is given to sustained support over a number of years and to more than one sport categories include: National Team Support, National Event Support, Program Development, and Individual Athlete Development. The trophy is awarded annually. Formerly: President's Shield; Corporate Award.

• 19627 • **Female Athlete of the Year**
To recognize Canada's most outstanding amateur female athlete of the year. Considerations are performance, sportsmanship, and good character.

• 19628 • **Junior Female Athlete of the Year**
To recognize Canada's most outstanding junior (under 20) amateur female athlete of the year. Established in 1972.

• 19629 • **Junior Male Athlete of the Year**
To recognize Canada's most outstanding junior (under 20) amateur male athlete of the year. Considerations include both performance and sportsmanship.

• 19630 • **Bruce Kidd Award**
This athlete leadership award is presented by the TSF and Athletes CAN to a retired national team athlete who has provided meaningful contributions to sport as a leader, advocate, change agent, or builder. This award is named in honor of Dr. Bruce Kidd who has made enormous contributions to Canada's sporting community as an athlete, advocate, author, historian, and academic.

• 19631 • **Leadership in Sport Award**
Presented to a male and female athlete who best exemplifies the qualities of leadership, excellence and team spirit at the most recent Canada Games. Awarded annually.

• 19632 • **Male Athlete of the Year**
To recognize Canada's most outstanding amateur male athlete of the year selected from nominations from sport governing bodies. Considerations are performance, sportsmanship, and good character.

• 19633 • **Male Team of the Year**
To recognize Canada's most outstanding national amateur team of the year. Consideration is given to a national championship winner and/or a national representative team. The Edmonton Grads Trophy is awarded to the female team

Awards are arranged in alphabetical order below their administering organizations

and the Tracy Wilson and Rob McCall Trophy is awarded to the pairs team.

• 19634 • Volunteer Achievement Award
This lifetime achievement award is presented to a volunteer who has made an overwhelming contribution to Canadian sport that is consistent with True Sport values in the areas of leadership, sport development, innovation, and growth. The award recognizes the significant contribution of Bryce Taylor who was a member of the board of Directors of the Sports Federation of Canada and the Canadian Olympic Committee, and was a founding director and professor of Physical Education at York University. Formerly: Donald King Memorial Award; (1997) All Sport Insurance Marketing Ltd. Volunteer of the Year Award.

• 19635 •
Sporting Goods Agents Association
Lois E. Halinton, COO
PO Box 998
Morton Grove, IL 60053
Phone: (847)296-3670
Fax: (847)827-0196
E-mail: sgaa998@aol.com
Home Page: http://www.r-sports.com/SGAA/

• 19636 • Lifetime Sales Achievement Award
Recognizes a member who serves as a role model to other agents. Awarded at a annual meeting. Established in 1984.

• 19637 • Manufacturers Appreciation Award
To recognize a company for contributions in the area of sporting goods manufacturing. Awarded at a annual meeting. Established in 1981.

• 19638 • Sporting Goods Agents Hall of Fame
This, the highest honor of the association, is given to recognize an individual for contribution to the association. Awarded at a annual meeting. Established in 1974.

• 19639 •
Sporting News
475 Park Ave. S, 27th Fl.
New York, NY 10016
Phone: (646)424-2227
Toll-Free: 800-777-6785
Fax: (646)424-2232
E-mail: pspina@sportingnews.com
Home Page: http://www.sportingnews.com

• 19640 • AL and NL Baseball Player Comeback of the Year
To recognize each baseball league's most outstanding comeback player of the year. Formerly: AL and NL Comeback Players of the Year.

• 19641 • AL and NL Hillerich and Bradsby/*The Sporting News* Silver Slugger Awards
Teams are chosen by a vote of coaches and managers to honor the best offensive players in each league. A silver bat mounted on a wooden base is presented to the awardees. Sponsored by Hillerich and Bradsby Co..

• 19642 • AL and NL Manager of the Year
Recognizes each baseball league's manager. AL and NL managers are polled for their selection. A Tiffany crystal award is given.

• 19643 • AL and NL Pitchers of the Year
To recognize each league's most outstanding pitcher.

• 19644 • AL and NL Relief Pitcher of the Year
To recognize each baseball league's leading relief pitcher of the year. Formerly: Fireman of the Year (Relief Pitcher).

• 19645 • AL and NL Rookie Pitchers of the Year
To recognize each league's most outstanding rookie pitcher of the year.

• 19646 • All-America Basketball Team
To recognize the full team named of the most outstanding collegiate athletes in basketball. A certificate with the TSN logo and their names are awarded annually.

• 19647 • All-America Football Team
To recognize the full team named of the most outstanding collegiate athletes in football. A certificate with the TSN logo and their names are awarded annually.

• 19648 • American and National League Managers of the Year
To recognize the most outstanding manager of the year in each league. A Tiffany crystal award is presented annually in each league.

• 19649 • American League All-Star Team
To recognize the most outstanding team players in the American League. Established in 1925 as the Major League All-Star Team. Since 1961, separate American League and National League teams have been selected.

• 19650 • American League Rookie of the Year
To recognize the most outstanding American League rookie of the year. Established in 1946.

• 19651 • College Basketball Coach of the Year
To recognize the nation's best collegiate basketball coach. A Tiffany crystal award is presented annually.

• 19652 • College Basketball Player of the Year
To recognize the nation's best collegiate athlete in basketball. A Tiffany crystal award is presented annually.

• 19653 • College Football Coach of the Year
To recognize the nation's best collegiate football coach. A Tiffany crystal award is presented annually.

• 19654 • College Football Player of the Year
To recognize the nation's best collegiate athlete in football. A Tiffany crystal award is presented annually.

• 19655 • Major League Baseball Player of the Year
This, the most prestigious baseball award, is given by TSN for the best player in major league baseball. The player receives a commemorative piece of Tiffany crystal. Established in 1936. The original trophy was called "the Sandlot Kid." Formerly: The Sandlot Kid.

• 19656 • Major League Executive of the Year
To recognize a major league baseball owner or executive each year. A Tiffany crystal award is presented annually. Established in 1936.

• 19657 • Minor League Executive of the Year
To recognize minor league's most outstanding executive of the year.

• 19658 • Minor League Manager of the Year
To recognize the outstanding minor league baseball manager. Established in 1936.

• 19659 • Minor League Player of the Year
To recognize the minor league player of the year. Established in 1936.

• 19660 • National League All-Star Team
To recognize the most outstanding team players in the National League. Certificates are awarded annually. Established in 1925 as the Major League All-Star Team. Since 1961, separate American League and National League teams have been selected.

• 19661 • National League Player of the Year
To recognize the National League player of the year.

• 19662 • National League Rookie of the Year
To recognize the most outstanding National League rookie of the year. Established in 1946.

• 19663 • NBA All-Star Team
To recognize the most outstanding players of the NBA teams. Established in 1946.

• 19664 • NBA Coach of the Year
To recognize the best NBA coach of the year. Established in 1983.

• 19665 • NBA Executive of the Year
To recognize the most outstanding NBA executive of the year. Established in 1972.

• 19666 • NBA Player of the Year
To recognize the best player in the NBA. Established in 1959.

• 19667 • NBA Rookie of the Year
To recognize the best NBA rookie of the year.

• 19668 • NFL All-Star Team
To recognize the outstanding NFL players of the year.

• 19669 • NFL Coach of the Year
To recognize the outstanding NFL coach of the year. Established in 1961.

• 19670 • NFL Executive of the Year
To recognize an NFL executive.

• 19671 • NHL All-Star Team
To recognize the most outstanding NHL players of the year. Selected by vote of the players.

• 19672 • NHL Coach of the Year
To recognize the most outstanding NHL coach of the year. Established in 1979.

• 19673 • NHL Executive of the Year
To recognize the most outstanding NHL executive of the year. Established in 1972.

• 19674 • NHL Player of the Year
To recognize the best player in the NHL. Selected by vote of the players. Established in 1967.

• 19675 • NHL Rookie of the Year
To recognize the best NHL rookie of the year. Selected by vote of the players.

• 19676 • Silver Slugger Team
To honor the eighteen foremost offensive players in the major leagues. Players were chosen by a vote of managers and coaches. Established in 1980. Sponsored by Hilerich and Bradsby Co..

• 19677 • *The Sporting News* NFL Player of the Year
To recognize the NFL's top player. A Tiffany crystal award is presented annually. Established in 1954.

• 19678 • *The Sporting News*/NFL Rookie of the Year
To recognize the NFL's top rookie.

• 19679 • *The Sporting News* Sportsman of the Year
This, the most prestigious award given by TSN, is awarded for the greatest contribution to sports during the year. A Tiffany Crystal engraved trophy is presented annually. Established in 1968. Formerly: *The Sporting News* Man of the Year.

• 19680 •
Sports Car Club of America
Aimee Quaney, Exec.Dir.
PO Box 19400
Topeka, KS 66619-0400
Phone: (785)357-7222
Toll-Free: 800-770-2055
Fax: (785)232-7728
E-mail: squaney@scca.com
Home Page: http://www.scca.org

• 19681 • American Continental Championship
To recognize the talents of young drivers in open wheel competition. Cars are based on formula Ford Format utilizing 2.0 liter Ford engines. A Driver's Championship award is given based on points. Established in 1992.

• 19682 • Woolf Barnato Trophy
This, the club's highest award, is given to recognize the member who has made the most outstanding long-term contribution. Nominations are made by the last three recipients of the award and must be approved by the Directors. Established in 1948 in honor of Woolf Barnato, famous English road racer, one of the "Bentley Boys," Bentley Club official, and Bentley Company Executive.

• 19683 • Best New National Rally Award
Recognizes the best new event on the National calendar. All new events are eligible with selection made by vote of the top 20 competitors in each National Series Class Competition.

• 19684 • Tom Burke Memorial Award
For recognition of the most improved membership from the previous year by an SCCA region. Presented by the SCCA Chairman of the Board and the National Membership Coordinator. Awarded annually. Established in 1983.

• 19685 • Course Rally Rookie of the Year
To recognize the Road Rallyist compiling the greatest number of championship points in the first season. SCCA Road rallyist members are eligible. Awarded annually. Established in 1968. Formerly: SCCA Road Rally Rookie of the Year; Heuer Timing Road Rally Rookie.

• 19686 • Divisional Achievement Award
To recognize a division's activities in Road Rally for a new or on-going program. This may include events, promotions, attendance, innovation in public relations, etc. Nominees can be made by any rally participant clearly indicating the qualifying details. Winners are selected by the Road Rally Board. Established in 1994.

• 19687 • Divisional Pro Rally of the Year Award
Selection is made from the seven best Divisional events on the basis of the following: results of competitor evaluation report; events must get 50% of their CER's returned to be eligible; evaluation of event Steward; evaluation of Division PRO Rally Steward; evaluation of the PRB. Awarded each season.

• 19688 • Divisional Pro Rally Program of the Year Award
Promotes the involvement of individual SCCA Regions and their members in the growth of the Divisional PRO Rally.

• 19689 • Divisional Pro Rally Region of the Year Award
Promotes the involvement of individual SCCA Regions and their members in the growth of the Divisional PRO Rally Programs. Selection is made by the PRO Rally Board to honor one SCCA Region which has conducted a balanced and successful program. Selections are made from recommendations submitted from the rally stewards, regional executives, PRO Rally board and members of the PRO Rally community at large. Awarded annually.

• 19690 • Mark Donohue Award
For recognition of outstanding performance, sportsmanship, and competitiveness in SCCA road racing. Awarded annually by the Road Racing Drivers Club. Established in 1971 and renamed in 1975 after the late race car driver Mark Donohue, who was killed in 1975 at a Formula One event in Austria.

• 19691 • Jim Fitzgerald Rookie of the Year
To recognize competition drivers showing great promise based on driving ability demonstrated during their first full year of national competition. Awarded annually. Established in 1964. Formerly: Nissan - Fitzgerald.

• 19692 • Arthur J. Gervais Award
In recognition of the outstanding National Course Rally of the Year. The top 20 Course Rally contestants may submit nominations. Awarded annually. Established in 1960.

• 19693 • Kimberly Cup
To recognize the SCCA race driver who has shown the greatest improvement in the past year. Awarded annually. Established in 1954 in honor of James H. Kimberly, former president and governor of SCCA and champion car owner and driver.

• 19694 • **John McGill Award**
For recognition of a member who has made significant contributions to the Club Racing program. Awarded annually. Established in 1975.

• 19695 • **Tom McKean Award**
Recognizes a member for a single, outstanding act of sportsmanship involving self-sacrifice. Awarded periodically. Established in 1949.

• 19696 • **David Morrell Memorial Award**
To encourage continued participation in the Steward's Program by recognition of an active National or National Chief Steward who has exhibited outstanding performance, dedication to the sport, and the highest principles. The winner is selected by the National Administrator of Stewards and the Executive Stewards. Awarded annually. Established in 1981.

• 19697 • **National Pro Rally of the Year Award**
For the best National PRO Rally of the year that best represents the intent of the National PRO Rally Series. Winners are selected by the SCCA PRO Rally Dept. Awarded annually.

• 19698 • **Novice Team Award**
Presented to a team showing the most promise in their first season of National Rallying. Nominees must be at their first event of the season and have participated in no more than four Rallies. Each organizing committee may nominate one team. Winners are selected by the Road Rally Board. Established in 1994.

• 19699 • **Outstanding National Touring Rally of the Year Award**
Recognizes an outstanding National Touring Rally. Selection is made by vote of the top 20 competitors in each class of the NTRC Series from all SCCA-sanctioned NTR's for the year. Awarded annually.

• 19700 • **President's Cup**
To recognize a driver demonstrating ability, competitiveness, and success at the National Runoffs. Winners are selected by the working Stewards of the Meeting and Chief Steward of the National Championship races. Established in 1954 by R.W. Woodruff, President of Coca-Cola Company.

• 19701 • **Public Relations Regional Achievement Award**
To recognize the outstanding Regional Public Relations Chairperson. Awarded annually. Established in 1975.

• 19702 • **Rally Awards**
For recognition of outstanding performance and contributions to PRO Rally, Touring Rally, and Road Rally. The following awards are presented: National PRO Rally of the Year (established in 1976), Divisional PRO Rally of the Year (established in 1984), PRO Rally Region of the Year (established in 1989), Divisional PRO Rally Program of the Year (established in 1989), National Touring Rally of the Year (established in 1989), National Touring Rally Manufacturer Champion (established in 1989), National Course Rally Manufacturer Champion (established in 1975), Best New Regional Road Rally Program (established in 1981), and Best New Divisional Road Rally (established in 1981).

• 19703 • **Regional Achievement Award**
For recognition of achievement by racing regions. Awards are given according to member size category. Awarded annually. Established in 1954.

• 19704 • **Regional Publication Awards**
For recognition of regional publications in the field of road racing. Awards are given according to member size category. Awarded annually. Established in 1967.

• 19705 • **Robert V. Ridges Memorial Award**
In recognition of outstanding sportsmanship in rallying. Awarded annually, when merited. Established in 1965.

• 19706 • **SCCA/CASCT North American Rally Cup**
For recognition of outstanding contributions to sports car racing and to stimulate international competition between Canada and the United States. Awards are given in the following categories: driver, co-driver, and manufacturer. Awarded annually. Established in 1975.

• 19707 • **SCCA Mechanic of the Year**
To recognize a mechanic for outstanding contributions to sports car racing. Awarded annually. Established in 1983. Formerly: "Mac Tools" SCCA Mechanic of the Year.

• 19708 • **SCCA Pro Rally Cup**
Presented in recognition of the outstanding Pro Rally of the Year. Awarded annually. Established in 1976.

• 19709 • **SCCA Pro Rally Manufacturer's Award**
For recognition of outstanding contributions in the field of manufacturing. Awarded annually. Established in 1975.

• 19710 • **Val D. Scroggie, M.D. Memorial Award**
To recognize the race physician who has made the greatest contribution to racing during the preceding year. Awarded annually. Established in 1962.

• 19711 • **Gordon Smiley Memorial Award**
For recognition of outstanding promotion of motor sports on a national and international level. The winner is chosen by a panel put together by the SCCA. Awarded annually. Established in 1983 in honor of Gordon Smiley.

• 19712 • **Dr. George G. Snively Memorial Award**
Recognizes outstanding contributions to safety in motorsports.

• 19713 • **Solo Driver of Eminence Award**
Recognizes the Solo I or Solo II driver who has consistently demonstrated excellence behind the wheel, and an exemplary degree of sportsmanship, dedication, and unselfishness. Nominees are made by the membership at large. Winners are selected by the Solo Events Board. Previous winners may not be nominated again.

• 19714 • **Solo I Event of the Year Award**
Recognizes the host region of an event of singular high quality, including inventive and enjoyable concept, smooth organization and execution, and consideration for the competitor. Nominees are made by the membership at large. Winners are selected by the Solo Events Board.

• 19715 • **Solo II Cup**
For recognition of outstanding contributions to the SCCA Solo Events Program. A trophy is awarded annually. Established in 1978.

• 19716 • **Solo II Divisional of the Year Award**
Recognizes the host region of an event of singular high quality, including inventive and enjoyable concept, smooth organization and execution, and consideration for the competitor. Nominees are made by the membership at large. Winners are selected by the Solo Events Board.

• 19717 • **Solo II Driver of the Year**
For recognition of outstanding driving performance at the Solo II Nationals. Awarded annually. In addition, the Solo II Driver of Eminence Award is presented. Established in 1984.

• 19718 • **Solo II Rookie of the Year**
For recognition of outstanding driving performance at Solo II Nationals in the first year of the National Solo competition. Awarded annually. Established in 1984.

• 19719 • ***SportsCar* Awards**
To recognize individuals for journalistic achievement in the field of sports cars. Awards are given in the following categories: photography, rally article, technical article, Pro racing article, feature article, solo article, and cover. Awarded annually. Established in 1954.

• 19720 • **Martin W. Tanner Award**
To recognize an SCCA corner worker who displays unusual courage while exposed to danger. Awarded when merited. Established in 1963 in honor of Martin W. Tanner of Saginaw, MI, former SCCA Governor, and well-known race car designer.

• 19721 • Trans-Am Tour
For recognition of outstanding performance in the professional sedan-based road racing series. The following awards are given: Driver Champion determined by points; Rookie of the Year - Pro Racing Staff makes the selection based on points; Most Improved Driver - Entrant's Poll makes the selection; and Manufacturer of the Year - determined by points. Established in 1966 as the Trans-American Sedan Championship. Formerly: Liquid Tide Trans-Am Tour.

• 19722 • Vic and Jessie Wallder Award
To recognize the highest-placing husband and wife road rally team. Established in 1983.

• 19723 • Wimberly Cup
To recognize drivers over the age of 50 for outstanding achievement at the National Champions Runoffs. Presented annually by Les Chevaliers. Established in 1993.

• 19724 • World Challenge
To provide an opportunity for manufacturers and competitors to showcase the vehicles and products they sell to the general public through a Championship series of closed-circuit speed events. In keeping with this purpose, vehicles and products used in the series are both intended and suitable for use on public roads and available to the public at large through a manufacturer's normal distribution channels. The following awards are given: Manufacturer Champion - awarded by points; Driver Champion - awarded by points; and Jim Cook Memorial Trophy determined by Pro Staff. An annual award honoring the memory of James Edwin Cook (1939-1985) is also presented to an entrant/driver who has made significant contributions to the overall success of the Endurance Racing Championship series through promotional activities and a consistent display of good character and sportsmanship. Established in 1990.

• 19725 •
Sports Foundation
National Sporting Goods Association
James L. Faltinek, Pres. and CEO
1601 Feehanville Dr., Ste. 300
Mt. Prospect, IL 60056-6035
Phone: (847)296-6742
Toll-Free: 800-815-5422
Fax: (847)391-9827
E-mail: info@nsga.org
Home Page: http://www.nsga.org

• 19726 • National Gold Medal Awards
For excellence in the field of park and recreation management. Nominations may be made by a sporting goods retailer who is a member of the National Sporting Goods Association. Each entrant is categorized according to population size. Park District and Recreation Department Award Finalists and winners are named in the following population size classes: (1) Class I - cities over 250,000; (2) Class II - 100,000 to 250,000; (3) Class III - 50,000 to 100,000; (4) Class IV - 25,000 to 50,000; and (5) Class V less than 25,000. Winners in each category receive the Grand Award Winner Plaque. Finalists receive a plaque. Awarded annually in the fall at NRPA Convention. Established in 1966.

• 19727 • State Park Awards
To acknowledge the achievements of state park systems and their contributions in providing park, recreation and leisure services to the citizens of their state. Finalists receive a plaque. State Park programs are presented in odd numbered years. Established in 1997.

• 19728 •
Sports Illustrated
Time and Life Bldg., Rm. 21-40
Rockefeller Center
1271 Avenue of the Americas
New York, NY 10020
Phone: (212)522-1212
E-mail: cnnsi@cnnsi.com
Home Page: http://
sportsillustrated.cnn.com

• 19729 • Face in the Crowd
To recognize unheralded amateur competitors who may never get, but richly deserve, national recognition. Six engraved silver Paul Revere bowls are awarded per week. Established in the 1950s.

• 19730 • *Sports Illustrated* Sportsman/ Sportswoman of the Year
To honor a sportsman/sportswoman, a team, or a group for "Symbolizing in Character and Performance The Ideals of Sportsmanship". The trophy is a reproduction of a Grecian amphora with decorations that portray discus and javelin throwers, a sprinter, and a trainer. Awarded annually. Established in 1954.

• 19731 •
Sports Philatelists International
Mark Maestrone, Pres.
5310 Lindenwood Ave.
St. Louis, MO 63109
E-mail: doj3@sportstamps.org
Home Page: http://www.sportstamps.org

• 19732 • Sports Philatelists International Awards
For recognition of the best sport or Olympic philatelic exhibits at the exhibition. Awards are given at both the adult and youth levels. The adult exhibit must have received at least a silver or bronze medal from the American Philatelic Society or the American Topical Association accredited judges. The youth level award is made at the discretion of the judge regardless of medal obtained. A certificate is presented as merited. Established in 1962.

• 19733 •
Springfield Art Museum
Jerry Berger, Dir.
1111 E. Brookside Dr.
Springfield, MO 65807-1899
Phone: (417)837-5700
Fax: (417)837-5704
E-mail: artmuseum@ci.springfield.mo.us
Home Page: http://
www.ci.springfield.mo.us/egov/art

• 19734 • Watercolor U.S.A.
To recognize and encourage aqua media painting. Open to any artist , 18 years of age or older, living in the United States. A maximum of one slide each of two entries, per artist, must be submitted for consideration. Paintings must have been executed using a water-soluble pigment on paper or a paper derivative. All paintings must be original, executed after January 1, 2004 and not previously shown at the Springfield Art Museum. All entries submitted must be available for purchase at the time of exhibition. Approximately $40,000 in cash, patron purchases, and Springfield Art Museum purchase, awards are presented. For entry form, please contact the Museum or find it online in late January.

• 19735 •
Springfield Association for Retarded Citizens
Carlissa Puckett, Exec.Dir.
One SPARCenter Plz.
232 Bruns Ln.
Springfield, IL 62702
Phone: (217)793-2100
Phone: (217)793-2206
Toll-Free: 800-800-6401
Fax: (217)793-2127
E-mail: inquire@spfldsparc.org
Home Page: http://
www.springfieldsparc.org/

• 19736 • Adele Karlson Lifetime Achievement Award
For lifelong support of and/or advocacy for individuals with developmental disabilities. Recognition award bestowed annually.

• 19737 •
Springfield Labor Council, AFL-CIO
Russell Strunk, Pres.
PO Box 5805
Springfield, MO 65801
Phone: (417)866-2236
Fax: (417)869-1814

• 19738 • SPFD, MO Labor Council, AFL-CIO Endowment Fund
For Southwest Missouri State University student involved in 15-page thesis on organized labor. Scholarship awarded annually.

Awards are arranged in alphabetical order below their administering organizations

• 19739 •
Stamford Community Arts Council
46 Sound View Ave.
Stamford, CT 06902
Phone: (203)348-ARTS
Phone: (203)856-7803
E-mail: stamarts@aol.com

• 19740 • **Maxwell Anderson Playwrights Series Prize**
To recognize the best new play included in the October-June staged reading series. Scripts of previously unproduced full-length plays or related one-act plays may be submitted year-round for the reading series. A monetary award of $500 is presented annually in the fall.

• 19741 • **Stamford Radio Theater Competition**
For recognition of outstanding scripts suitable for radio. Entries may be submitted at any time. Winning scripts are featured on a regional radio production. Co-sponsored by WSTC-AM radio. Established in 1991.

• 19742 •
Standards Council of Canada
Monica Pantusa, Marketing Commun.Off.
270 Albert St., Ste. 200
Ottawa, ON, Canada K1P 6N7
Phone: (613)238-3222
Fax: (613)569-7808
E-mail: info@scc.ca
Home Page: http://www.scc.ca

• 19743 • **Jean P. Carriere Award**
Recognizes outstanding contribution to standards and standardization. Awarded annually.

• 19744 •
Standards Engineering Society
H. Glenn Ziegenfuss, Exec.Dir.
13340 SW 96th Ave.
Miami, FL 33176
Phone: (305)971-4798
Fax: (305)971-4799
E-mail: director@ses-standards.org
Home Page: http://www.ses-standards.org

• 19745 • **Fellow Award**
Recognizes and individual for professional distinction and accomplishment in the field of standardization to an individual. Only individuals who have been members of SES for the past 10 years are eligible for nomination. Established in 1958.

• 19746 • **Honorary Life Member**
To recognize an individual for unusual professional distinction and outstanding accomplishment in the field of standardization. Only individuals who are not current members or who have not been members for the previous five years are eligible for nomination.

• 19747 • **Leo B. Moore Medal**
This, the highest honor of the Society, is presented for highest achievement, extraordinary contribution, and distinguished service in the field of standardization, and its advancement through original research and writing, creative application and development of service. Any individual is eligible.

• 19748 • **SES/ASTM Robert J. Painter Memorial Award**
To recognize an individual for special service in the field of standardization through a company program, managerial support, or educational research. Any individual is eligible.

• 19749 • **SES/CSA Lorne K. Wagner Memorial Award**
Awarded to an SES member who has made an outstanding contribution to SES. Only SES individuals who are current members are eligible for nomination.

• 19750 • **World Standards Day Paper Awards**
Awarded to an author for a paper prepared on the theme of World Standards Day.

• 19751 •
Standing Committee of Correspondents
Julie Hirschfield Davis, Chm.
U.S. Senate Press Gallery
Capitol Bldg., S 316
Washington, DC 20510-9042
Phone: (202)224-0241
Fax: (202)228-1142
E-mail: chuck.mccutchen@newhouse.com
Home Page: http://www.senate.gov/galleries/daily/standing.htm

• 19752 • **Raymond Clapper Memorial Awards**
To recognize meritorious local, national, or international news coverage. Washington-based daily newspaper writers, or a writing team of not more than two individuals, whose work during the previous year approximates the ideals of fair and painstaking reporting and good craftsmanship characteristic of Raymond Clapper are considered for the award. Subjects can be local, national, or international. The deadline is April 7. A monetary award of $1,500 for First Prize and $500 for Second Prize are awarded annually at the White House Correspondents' Association Dinner in April. Established in 1944.

• 19753 • **Barnet Nover Memorial Awards**
To recognize excellence in reporting. Any Washington-based Capitol Hill or White House daily newspaper reporter or pair of reporters is eligible to submit either a single story or a series of articles from the previous year. Subjects can be local, national, or international. The only standard is excellence in the tradition of Barnet Nover. The deadline is April 7. Monetary awards of $1,500 for First Prize and $500 for Second Prize are presented annually. Established in 1982 by friends of Barnet Nover.

• 19754 •
Stanford University
Center for Integrated Facility Engineering
Terman Engineering Center
MC: 4020
380 Panama Mall
Stanford, CA 94305-4020
Phone: (650)723-4945
Fax: (650)723-4806
E-mail: cife-email@lists.stanford.edu
Home Page: http://cife.stanford.edu

• 19755 • **Seed Research Awards**
Recognizes outstanding contribution to architecture. Faculty on campus is eligible.

• 19756 •
Stanford University
Stanford Center on Conflict and Negotiation
Stanford Law School
Crown Quadrangle
Stanford, CA 94305
Phone: (650)724-3996
Fax: (650)723-9421
E-mail: bland@stanford.edu
Home Page: http://www.stanford.edu/group/sccn/

• 19757 • **Richard S. Goldsmith Award**
For the best paper on conflict resolution by Stanford University student. Awarded annually.

• 19758 •
State Bar of California
180 Howard St.
San Francisco, CA 94105
Phone: (415)538-2000
Fax: (415)538-2361
Home Page: http://www.calbar.org

• 19759 • **Golden Medallion Media Awards**
To recognize and encourage outstanding reporting by editorial writers and news reporters that educates the public about the administration of justice, law, lawyers, and the courts. Awards are given in three categories: print (California general circulation and legal newspapers); television (all commercial, educational, and public broadcasting television stations in California); and radio (all AM and FM radio stations in California). Judging is based on each entry's accuracy, skill, thoroughness, public service, significance of the topic or event, difficulty, and originality. Golden medallions are awarded annually. Established in 1954 by Berton Ballard, the State Bar's first public information officer. Additional information is available from Anne Charles (415) 561-8283.

• 19760 • **Loren Miller Legal Services Award**
To recognize an individual who has personally done significant work in extending legal services to the poor. Selection of the recipient is based on the following criteria: demonstrated dedication to the development and delivery of legal ser-

vices to the poor; significant work toward developing innovative approaches to delivery of legal services; activity which resulted in satisfying previously unmet needs or in extending services to underserved segments of the population; the successful litigation of cases that favorably affected the delivery of legal and other necessary services to the poor; legislative achievements that contributed substantially to legal services for the poor; effective community organization and facilitation of legal services programs; and significant involvement with the client community in development of legal services for the poor. Nominations are accepted. A monetary prize of $1,000 and a plaque are awarded annually at the Bar's Annual Meeting. Established in 1977 in memory of Loren Miller, a California lawyer and judge who was a leader in civil rights litigation. Additional information is available from Susan Mattox, (415) 561-8243.

• 19761 • **President's Pro Bono Service Award**
To encourage and recognize California lawyers or law firms for contributions of time and expertise in providing legal services to people and charitable organizations in their community who could not otherwise afford those services. Selection of lawyers is based on the following criteria: those who practice in California; those who are not employed on a full-time basis by an organization that has as its primary purpose the provision of free legal services to the poor; those who have provided direct delivery of legal services in civil or criminal matters, with no expectation of receiving a fee, to a client or client group that does not have the resource to employ compensated counsel; those who have made a voluntary contribution of a significant portion of time to providing legal services to poor people without charge; those who have made such contributions through organized pro bono programs, including legal services programs, legal aid societies, local bar association pro bono programs, lawyer referral service no-fee panels, etc.; and those whose voluntary contributions have resulted in the increased access to legal services on the part of low and moderate-income persons. One recipient will be selected from each State Bar District for a total of nine winners each year. The nominee must be admitted to practice in California. Nominations are solicited from March to May. A plaque and recognition at the Annual Meeting are awarded annually. Winners also receive a legal volume of their choice from California Continuing Education of the Bar. Established in 1983 by the State Bar Board of Governors. Additional information is available from Lyle Wing; telephone: (415) 561-8297.

• 19762 •
State Bar of Michigan
306 Townsend
Lansing, MI 48933-2083
Phone: (517)346-6300
Toll-Free: 800-968-1442
Fax: (517)482-6248
Home Page: http://www.michbar.org

• 19763 • **Wade H. McCree, Jr. Awards for the Advancement of Justice**
For statewide recognition of published material and radio and television broadcasts that: foster greater public understanding of the inherent values of our legal and judicial system; inform and educate citizens as to the role of the law, the courts, law enforcement agencies, and the legal profession in today's society; disclose practices and procedures in need of correction or improvement; and encourage and promote local and state legislative efforts to update and modernize our laws, courts, and law enforcement agencies. The entry deadline is January 2. Only work published between July 1 and December 31 will be considered. Judges consider entries on a basis of originality, effectiveness, thoroughness, and newsworthiness. Any newspaper, wire service, news syndicate, magazine, radio station, television station, legal publication, or network in Michigan - or any of their employees - is eligible to enter the awards competition. Freelance writers and producers are eligible if their Michigan-created work has been published or produced on the air for the people of that State. Awards are given in the following categories: Newspapers and Magazines - newspaper, wire service, news syndicate, or magazine entries may consist of feature articles, news articles, interpretive analyses, editorials, or combinations of these; and Broadcast - documentary, educational, or editorial programs. The following prizes are awarded in each category: First Prize - a bronze medal, and a $2,000 Communication or Journalism Scholarship in the name of the recipient is awarded by the Michigan College or University of the recipient's choice; Second Prize - a bronze plaque; Third Prize - a bronze plaque; and Fourth Prize - a bronze plaque. Awarded annually at the Michigan Journalism Hall of Fame Awards. Established in 1973. Renamed in 1988 to honor the late Wade H. McCree, Jr., former judge, law professor, U.S. Solicitor General, and early supporter of the Advancement of Justice Awards.

• 19764 •
State Capital Global Law Firm Group
J. Phil Carlton Esq., CEO
1747 Pennsylvania Ave. NW, Ste. 1200
8 Amber Business Village, Amber Close
Washington, DC 20006
Phone: (202)659-6601
Fax: (202)659-6641
E-mail: inquiry@statecapitallaw.org
Home Page: http://www.statecapitallaw.org

• 19765 • **Gold Medal**
Annual award of recognition for members.

• 19766 • **Silver Medal**
Annual award of recognition for members.

• 19767 •
State Debt Management Network
Robin Reedy, Chm.
2760 Research Park Dr.
PO Box 11910
Lexington, KY 40578-1910
Phone: (859)244-8175
Fax: (859)244-8053
E-mail: nast@csg.org
Home Page: http://www.nast.net/debtnet/index.htm

• 19768 • **Distinguished Service Award**
Recognizes an individual for continued professionalism, support and commitment.

• 19769 • **Tanya Gritz Award for Excellence in Public Finance**
For individual or group demonstrating excellence in authorization, planning, issuance and management of public debt. Recognition is given.

• 19770 •
State Farm Insurance
Edward B. Rust Jr., Chm. and CEO
1 State Farm Plz.
Bloomington, IL 61701
Phone: (309)766-2311
Home Page: http://www.statefarm.com

• 19771 • **Good Neighbor Teacher Award**
To recognize innovative primary and secondary teachers. The award consists of a $10,000 check payable to the educational institution of the recipient's choice, a commemorative plaque and recognition in selected national publications. Established in 1990.

• 19772 •
State Historical Society of Missouri
Gary Kremer, Exec.Dir.
1020 Lowry St.
Columbia, MO 65201-7298
Phone: (573)882-7083
Toll-Free: 800-747-6366
Fax: (573)884-4950
E-mail: kremerg@umsystem.edu
Home Page: http://www.umsystem.edu/shs/

• 19773 • **Richard S. Brownlee Fund**
For individuals who have proposal to publish, or make other tangible contributions to, the history of Missouri and its citizens. Monetary award bestowed annually.

• 19774 •
Status of Women Canada
Liza Frulla, Min.
MacDonald Bldg., 10th Fl.
123 Slater St.
Ottawa, ON, Canada K1P 1H9
Phone: (613)995-7835
Fax: (613)957-3359
E-mail: information@swc-cfc.gc.ca
Home Page: http://www.swc-cfc.gc.ca

• 19775 • Governor General's Awards in Commemoration of the Persons Case
To recognize outstanding contributions towards promoting the equality of women in Canada. Canadian citizens who have worked most of their lives to promote equality for women in Canada are eligible. Medals are awarded annually. Established in 1979 to celebrate the 50th anniversary of the Persons Case that constitutionally recognized women as "persons" under the British North America Act. Formerly: Persons Awards.

• 19776 •
E. W. R. Steacie Memorial Fund
(Fondation E.W.R. Steacie)
A.R.W. McKellar, Sec.
100 Sussex Dr.
Ottawa, ON, Canada K1A 0R6
Phone: (613)990-0736
Fax: (613)954-5242
E-mail: robert.mckellar@nrc-cnrc.gc.ca
Home Page: http://www.steacieprize.ca

• 19777 • Steacie Prize
(Prix Steacie)
For recognition of outstanding scientific work in a Canadian context. This is generally regarded as Canada's highest honor for young scientists and engineers. The nominee must be under 40 years of age. The deadline is October 1. A monetary award of $8,000 and a certificate are presented annually. Established in 1963 in memory of Edgar W. R. Steacie, a physical chemist and former President of the National Research Council of Canada, who did much to encourage young people in research in the natural sciences.

• 19778 •
Stedman Art Gallery
Prof. Martin Rosenberg, Chm.
Department of Fine Arts
Rutgers, the State University of New Jersey
Camden, NJ 08102
Phone: (856)225-6251
Fax: (856)225-6330
E-mail: mrosenbe@camden.rutgers.edu
Home Page: http://
finearts.camden.rutgers.edu/art

• 19779 • Rutgers National/Works on and of Paper Competition
To encourage artists working with paper using traditional and/or experimental techniques. Professional artists residing in the United States are eligible. Works must be submitted by October. Purchase awards totaling $5,000 are awarded biennially, and the works become part of the Rutgers-Camden Collection of Art. Established in 1975.

• 19780 •
Steel Founders' Society of America
Raymond W. Monroe, Exec.VP
780 McArdle Dr., Unit G
Crystal Lake, IL 60014
Phone: (815)455-8240
Fax: (815)455-8241
E-mail: monroe@sfsa.org
Home Page: http://www.sfsa.org

• 19781 • Thomas E. Barlow Award of Honor
To recognize distinguished contributions to the steel castings industry. Individuals and groups are eligible. An engraved Steuben glass bowl and certificate are awarded periodically. Established in 1961.

• 19782 • Charles W. Briggs Memorial Technical and Operating Medal
To recognize an outstanding scientific or engineering contribution that has furthered the technical or operating aspect of the steel castings industry. Employees of member companies of the society are eligible. The award consists of a bronze medal, a gold charm, and a certificate. A scholarship in the recipient's name is also presented to the school of his or her choice. Awarded periodically. Established in 1944.

• 19783 • Frederick A. Lorenz Memorial Medal
To recognize outstanding service to the steel castings industry. Employees of member companies of the society are eligible. The award consists of a bronze medal, a gold charm, and a certificate. A scholarship in the recipient's name is also presented to the school of his or her choice. Awarded periodically. Established in 1938.

• 19784 •
Steely Library
Northern Kentucky University
Nunn Dr.
Highland Heights, KY 41099
Phone: (859)572-5456
Phone: (859)572-5457
Toll-Free: 800-637-9948
Fax: (859)572-5390
E-mail: smithjen@nku.edu
Home Page: http://library.nku.edu

• 19785 • Kentucky Bluegrass Awards
To encourage Kentucky students in grades K-12 to read quality literature. Children read from a list of recently published books and then vote for the best books. There are four divisions: K-2, 3-5, 6-8, and 9-12. A plaque is awarded annually in each division at the Kentucky Bluegrass Award Luncheon. Established in 1982. Co-sponsored by Kentucky Reading Association and Kentucky School Media Association.

• 19786 •
Stein Collectors International
Steven Steigerwald, Exec.Dir.
PO Box 380592
Birmingham, AL 35238-0592
E-mail: sassteins@aol.com
Home Page: http://www.steincollectors.org

• 19787 • Jack Heimann Service Award
To recognize continued service to Stein Collectors International and beneficial activity in the organization. Nominations may be made by a chapter or a member for selection by the Board of Trustees. A hand-illuminated plaque is awarded at the General Membership Meeting. Established in 1980 in memory of Jack Heimann, former Executive Secretary. Awarded when merited.

• 19788 • Master Steinologist
To recognize expertise in the area of beer steins and other antique drinking vessels, and to recognize efforts in research, publications and other information dissemination. Members may be nominated, and are chosen by a committee. A hand-illuminated plaque is awarded annually at the General Membership Meeting. Established in 1973.

• 19789 •
Stephen Leacock Association
Maureen Harris, Past Pres.
PO Box 854
Orillia, ON, Canada L3V 6K8
Phone: (705)835-7061
Fax: (705)835-7062
E-mail: info@leacock.ca
Home Page: http://www.leacock.ca

• 19790 • Stephen Leacock Medal for Humour
To recognize a book of humor published in the previous calendar year, written by a Canadian, in verse, prose, drama, or any other form. Books published during the award year may be submitted either by the author or the publisher. The entry deadline is December 31. The T.D Financial Group of $10,000 and the silver Leacock Medal, designed by Emanual Hahn, are presented at a dinner held in Orillia in June. Awarded annually. Established in 1946 in memory of Stephen Leacock (1869-1944), a renowned humorist, author, and lecturer. Additional information is available from Judith Rapson Line 12, RR2 Coldwater, ON, Canada L0K 1EO.

• 19791 • Order of Mariposa
For recognition of non-literary fields of humor. Canadians whose efforts in expressing or encouraging humor have made some mark on the nation are eligible. Awarded when merited, the award consists of a caricature of the recipient. Sponsored by T.D Financial Group. Established in 1946.

• 19792 •
Strafford County Wind Symphony
Eleanor Taylor, Pres.
PO Box 7041
Gonic, NH 03839-7041
Phone: (603)749-9246

• 19793 • **Stanley Hettinger Memorial Scholarship**
For high school student attending summer music camp. Scholarship awarded annually.

• 19794 •
Strategic Account Management Association
Lisa Napolitano, Pres/CEO
150 N. Wacker Dr., Ste. 2222
Chicago, IL 60606
Phone: (312)251-3131
Fax: (312)251-3132
E-mail: sama@strategicaccounts.org
Home Page: http://www.strategicaccounts.org

• 19795 • **Executive of the Year Award**
For recognition of outstanding executive ability. Top management executives with a proven record in organizational development who support their company's strategic Accounts Program, and are known in the sales and marketing function may be nominated by any SAMA member. Awarded each year at SAMA's annual conference. Established in 1965. Formerly: (1980) Marketing Man of the Year.

• 19796 •
Stratton Mountain and Valley Community Benefit Foundation
Barbara McCarty, Exec.Dir.
Box 523
Stratton Mountain, VT 05155
Phone: (802)297-4425
Phone: (802)362-2056
Fax: (802)362-2217
E-mail: info@strattonfoundation.org
Home Page: http://strattonfoundation.org

• 19797 • **Emo Henrich Award**
For community service. Recognition award bestowed annually.

• 19798 •
Structural Board Association
Mark Angelini, Pres./CEO
25 Valleywood Dr., Unit 27
Markham, ON, Canada L3R 5L9
Phone: (905)475-1100
Fax: (905)475-1101
E-mail: info@osbguide.com
Home Page: http://www.osbguide.com

• 19799 • **Ron Baker Award**
Recognizes excellence in OSB manufacturing. Awarded annually.

• 19800 •
Studebaker Driver's Club
Jan Lockmon, Sec.
PO Box 1715
Maple Grove, MN 55311
Phone: (763)420-7829
Fax: (763)420-7849
E-mail: mark@cornerstonereg.com
Home Page: http://www.studebakerdriversclub.com

• 19801 • **Minnie Barnes Award**
To recognize a subgroup of the Club that has helped less fortunate individuals, such as in children's homes, hospitals, the deaf and blind, or veterans. A trophy is awarded when merited at the Club's international meet. Established in 1970 by Harry Barnes, founder of SDC, in memory of his mother as a tribute to her ideals.

• 19802 • **Harold E. Churchill Award**
For recognition of the best article contributed to the monthly magazine *Turning Wheels.* awarded annually. Established in 1981 in memory of Harold E. Churchill who had risen through the Engineering Department of the Studebaker Corporation to become its president.

• 19803 • **SDC Concours Awards**
To honor excellence in the restoration and preservation of Studebaker and Studebaker-related vehicles. Forty-two classes (three trophies per class) cover the years that Studebaker built vehicles (1952-1966), and seven classes (three trophies per class) are awarded in the senior division. The awards vary from year to year. Awarded annually. Established in 1966.

• 19804 • **SDC Publication Committee Awards**
To recognize excellence in newsletters of local chapters. A wall plaque is awarded annually to a number of local chapters. Established in 1970.

• 19805 •
Student American Veterinary Medical Association
Travis McDermott, Pres.
1931 N Meacham Rd., Ste. 100
Schaumburg, IL 60173
Toll-Free: 800-248-2862
E-mail: savma@cvm.tamu.edu
Home Page: http://www.avma.org/savma/about.htm

• 19806 • **AVMA Student Chapter Certificates**
Recognition is given annually to SAVMA member graduates from the AVMA..

• 19807 •
Student Film & Video Festival
1432 de Bleury St.
Montreal, QC, Canada H3A 2J1
Phone: (514)848-7186
Fax: (514)848-3886
E-mail: info@ffm-montreal.org

• 19808 • **Young Canadian Filmmakers**
To recognize creative film talent. Awarded annually in four categories.

• 19809 •
Student Press Law Center
1815 N. Fort Myer Dr. Ste. 900
Arlington, VA 22209
Phone: (703)807-1904
E-mail: splc@splc.org
Home Page: http://www.splc.org

• 19810 • **Champion of the Student Press Award**
To recognize persons and organizations that have aggressively protected First Amendment freedom for students. Awarded with a plaque. Established in 1995.

• 19811 • **College Press Freedom Award**
To recognize outstanding support for the free press rights of students by individual student journalists or student media. Nomination of any individual student, student newspaper, magazine, yearbook or broadcast station will be accepted. Nominees should illustrate a responsible representation of press freedom through writing and actions and the ability to raise difficult and necessary issues in news coverage. Nominations should clearly explain why the nominee deserves the Scholastic Press Freedom Award and should include supporting materials when available. Awarded annually with a plaque. Entry deadline is August 1. Established in 1984. Given jointly by National Scholastic Press Association/Associated Collegiate Press and the Student Press Law Center. Formerly: (2001) Scholastic Press Freedom Award.

• 19812 •
Studio Museum in Harlem
144 W 125th St.
New York, NY 10027
Phone: (212)864-4500
Fax: (212)864-4800
Home Page: http://www.studiomuseuminharlem.org

• 19813 • **Artist Award**
To recognize an individual artist for achievement in and/or contribution to the arts. A plaque is awarded annually at the spring fundraising dinner. Established in 1984.

• 19814 • **Artists-in-Residence Program**
To serve emerging African American artists and other emerging artists from African derived cultures (e.g., African, Puerto Rican, Caribbean, etc.). Awards are presented in the following categories: sculpture, painting, printmaking, fiber arts, or assemblage. A fellowship and studio space for a period of 12 months are awarded annually. An exhibition in the Museum's gallery is also held. Established in 1968.

• 19815 •
Stulberg International String Competition
359 S Kalamazoo Mall, Ste. 14
Kalamazoo, MI 49007
Phone: (269)343-2776
Fax: (269)343-2797
E-mail: stulbergcomp@yahoo.com
Home Page: http://www.stulberg.org

• 19816 • **Stulberg International String Competition**
For recognition of talented young string players studying the violin, viola, cello, and string bass. Applicants who are 19 years of age or younger as of January 1 of the year of audition may submit applications, signed by a teacher, and audiocassettes by mid December. First place is a monetary prize of $4,000 and a performance as soloist with the Kalamazoo Symphony Orchestra. Second place is $3,000 and a solo recital performance At the Fontana Chamber Arts summer Festival. Third place is $2,000 and a Performance with Kalamazoo Junior Symphony Orchestra. Established in 1975 by colleagues, friends and former students as a suitable memorial for Julius Stulberg, artist violinist, conductor of the Youth Symphony for 32 years, and a teacher who imparted his love for music to his students through 37 years of university teaching. Additional information is available from Elizabeth Rohn, Office Manager. Formerly: Julius Stulberg Auditions.

• 19817 •
Suburban Newspapers of America
Nancy Lane, Exec.Dir.
PO Box 1219
North Myrtle Beach, SC 29582
Phone: (843)390-1531
Toll-Free: 888-486-2466
Fax: (231)932-2985
E-mail: nancylanesna@aol.com
Home Page: http://www.suburban-news.org

• 19818 • **Advertising/Promotion Awards**
To recognize the best advertising and marketing efforts of suburban newspapers. Awards are given in the following categories: (1) Best Publication Promotion - In Paper; (2) Best Sales Promotional Materials; (3) Best Regular Advertising Section; (4) Best Special General Interest Promotion Section; (5) Best Special Shopping Area Promotion Section; (6) Best Single Ad (Black and White); (7) Best Single Ad (Color; 1 or 2 colors plus black); (8) Best Single Ad Using Process Color; (9) Best Cover Design; (10) Best Ad Series; (11) Best Signature Page or Signature Section; and (12) Best Graphically Designed Classified Section. Members and non-members of SNA are eligible. Plaques are presented to first, second, and third place awardees. Awarded annually.

• 19819 • **Editorial Awards**
To recognize outstanding editorial achievements of SNA member and non-member newspapers. Awards are given in the following categories: (1) Suburban Journalist of the Year; (2) Community Service Award; (3) In-Depth Reporting; (4) Best Breaking News Story; (5) Best Editorial Writing; (6) Best Column Writing; (7) Best Editorial Page Cartoon; (8) Best Editorial Pages; (9) Lifestyle Feature; (10) Best Lifestyle Section; (11) Best Feature; (12) Best Coverage of Local Business and Economic News; (13) Sports Writing; (14) Sports Photojournalism; (15) Best Sports Section; (16) Best Feature Photography; (17) Best Spot News Photojournalism; and (18) Best Special Issue or Special Section. Full or part-time staff members of member newspapers are eligible. A plaque is awarded to the first, second and third place winners. Awarded annually.

• 19820 •
Successful Meetings Magazine
April I. Torrisi, Mng. Editor
770 Broadway
New York, NY 10003
Phone: (646)654-5049
Fax: (646)654-7365
E-mail: info@successmtgs.com
Home Page: http://www.mimegasite.com

• 19821 • **Ace Award**
For recognition of the top 50 United States and Caribbean golf resorts that host meetings. Also recognizes the highest vote-getter in each of five regions (Northeast, Southeast, Midwest, Southwest, and the West). The nominees list is put together by a panel of golf and meeting industry leaders. Established in 1991.

• 19822 • **Convention Service Manager of the Year**
To recognize hotel and resort convention service managers who excel in helping meeting planners. Individuals who have worked as a convention service manager for a hotel or resort for a minimum of one year are eligible. A winner is chosen from each of the following categories: hotels, convention and visitor bureaus, and convention centers. A plaque is awarded annually.

• 19823 • **Pinnacle Awards for Convention and Visitor Bureaus**
For recognition of the top meeting destination support organizations, such as convention and visitor bureaus and national tourist/tourism offices, that have done an outstanding job in servicing meetings, incentive travel programs, and conventions in the meetings industry. Selection is by nomination and application. Plaques are awarded annually in August. Established in 1991.

• 19824 • **Pinnacle Awards for Hotels/ Resorts**
For recognition of the top 210 hotels/resorts in the United States, Canada, Mexico, and Offshore. Nominated by the readers of the *Successful Meetings Magazine*. The top 30 winners are recognized in each of the following categories: Northeast, Southeast, Midwest, Southwest, West, Mexico/Canada, and International. Plaques are awarded annually in August. Established in 1985.

• 19825 •
Sudden Infant Death Syndrome Alliance-Greater Houston Chapter
Anita Carmona, Pres.
Beechnut Professional Bldg.
7500 Beechnut, Rm. 378
Houston, TX 77074
Phone: (713)271-5460
Fax: (713)271-5385
E-mail: acarmona@us.rhodia.com

• 19826 • **The M'4s Brewer Memorial Scholarship**
For SIDS siblings at Texas A & M. Scholarship awarded annually.

• 19827 •
Sugar Industry Technologists
L. Anhaiser, Exec.Dir.
164 N Hall Dr.
Sugar Land, TX 77478
Phone: (281)494-2046
Fax: (281)494-2304
E-mail: sit@sucrose.com
Home Page: http://sucrose.com/sit/

• 19828 • **Crystal Award**
For recognition of outstanding contributions to the progress of sugar refining technology. Individuals in a sugar-related industry are eligible. An engraved, clear crystal of lucite is awarded annually. Established in 1961.

• 19829 • **George and Eleanore Meade Award**
For recognition of an outstanding paper(s) presented at the annual meeting. Individuals in a sugar-related industry who present papers to the general membership at the annual meeting are eligible. Cash awards and plaques are awarded annually. Established in 1965 by Dr. and Mrs. George P. Meade from the royalties of *Cane Sugar Handbook*, by Dr. Meade.

• 19830 •
Sumi-e Society of America
Norene Spencer, Membership Sec.
510 Heather Dr.
Virginia Beach, VA 23462
Phone: (410)730-7597
E-mail: blueiris2k@earthlink.net
Home Page: http://www.sumiesociety.org

• 19831 • **Annual Art Competition & Exhibition**
For recognition of excellence in Oriental brush painting and calligraphy, and to encourage Oriental painting in the West. The competition is open to all artists. Entries must be the original creation of the artist. Work must be brush painting or calligraphy in oriental ink, or ink and watercolor on rice paper or silk. Only works not previously exhibited by the Society, and painted in the previous two years are accepted. A combination of cash, purchase, and merchandise awards, exceeding $4,000 in value, are presented annually. Established in 1964. Additional information is available from president Cecil H.

Uyehara, 7914 Arnet Ln., Bethesda, MD 20817-5502; telephone: (301)229-3184; Fax: (301)320-9029.

• 19832 •
Summer and Casual Furniture Manufacturer Association
Joseph P. Logan, Exec.Dir.
PO Box HP-7
High Point, NC 27261
Phone: (336)884-5000
Fax: (336)884-5303
E-mail: info@afma4u.org
Home Page: http://www.afma4u.org

• 19833 • **Apollo Award**
To recognize excellence in the merchandising of summer/casual furniture. Retailers in good standing are considered for the award. An Apollo sun-god statuette is awarded to winners in three categories - Single Store, Multi-Store, and International. Awarded annually. Established in 1959.

• 19834 •
Suncoast Waldorf Association
Kelista Sanders, Admin.
2476 Nursery Rd.
Clearwater, FL 33764
Phone: (727)532-0696
Fax: (727)532-0608

• 19835 • **Honorary Lifetime Membership**
For outstanding contribution to Suncoast Waldorf Association. Recognition award.

• 19836 •
Sunset Center
Jack Globenfelt, Exec.Dir.
PO Box 1950
Carmel, CA 93921-1950
Phone: (831)624-3996
Fax: (831)624-0147
E-mail: execdir@sunsetcenter.org
Home Page: http://www.sunsetcenter.org

• 19837 • **Festival of Firsts Playwriting Competition**
To recognize an original, unproduced, full-length stage play. Scripts must be submitted between June 15 and August 31. Musicals and operas are not eligible. A monetary award of up to $1,000 and possible production may be awarded annually. Please include SASE.

• 19838 •
Sunset Magazine
% Awards Programs Coordinator
80 Willow Rd.
Menlo Park, CA 94025
Phone: (650)324-5471
Fax: (650)327-8994
E-mail: corporate@sunset.com
Home Page: http://www.sunset.com

Formerly: American Institute of Architects - *Sunset Magazine.*

• 19839 • **Interior Design Awards**
To recognize achievement in residential interior design. This program is open to both amateur and professional designers. The built project must be in one of the thirteen western United States. Entry information is presented in the February issue of the magazine. Deadlines vary but applications are usually due in April. The award includes a certificate and publication in a fall issue of *Sunset Magazine.* Presented biennially in even-numbered years.

• 19840 • **Western Garden Design Awards**
To recognize achievement in residential garden design. This program is open to professional landscape architects. The garden must be in one of the thirteen western United States. Awards are presented in five categories: Small-space gardens; gardens for outdoor living and entertaining; regional gardens; renovated gardens; and garden details. The award includes a certificate and publication in a spring issue of *Sunset Magazine.* Presented biennially in even-numbered years.

• 19841 • **Western Home Awards**
To recognize achievement in residential architecture. Entrance is based on the following criteria: the project must be in the 13 western United States; a registered architect must have been involved in the project; and a project may be submitted by a homeowner with the architect's permission. Entry information is presented in the February issue of *Sunset Magazine.* Deadlines vary, but applications are usually due in May. The award includes a certificate and publication in the October issue of *Sunset Magazine.* Presented biennially in odd-numbered years. Established in 1957. Co-sponsored by the western regional branches of the American Institute of Architects.

• 19842 •
Surface Design Journal
Surface Design Association
Jason Pollen, Pres.
PO Box 360
Sebastopol, CA 95472-0360
Phone: (707)829-3110
Fax: (707)829-3285
E-mail: surfacedesign@mail.com
Home Page: http://www.surfacedesign.org

• 19843 • **Betty Park Award in Critical Writing**
To recognize an appropriate essay that deals with the development of critical vocabulary in the field of contemporary textiles, in particular surface design, and its application. Theoretical essays or an original piece of scholarship that illustrates a practical application of critical language may be submitted by February 15. A monetary award of $1,000 and publication of the essay in the *Surface Design Journal* are awarded annually. Additional awards of merit of $500 each are presented. Established in 1989. Additional information is available from *Surface Design Journal,* PO Box 360, Sebastopol, CA 95472. Formerly: Critical Writing Awards Competition.

• 19844 •
Surfrider Foundation
Michelle Kremer Esq., Deputy Exec.Dir.
PO Box 6010
San Clemente, CA 92674-6010
Phone: (949)492-8170
Toll-Free: 800-743-7873
Fax: (949)492-8142
E-mail: info@surfrider.org
Home Page: http://www.surfrider.org

• 19845 • **Pratte Scholarship**
For students in environmental education attending Humboldt State University. Awarded annually.

• 19846 •
Susan G. Komen Breast Cancer Foundation
Susan Braun, CEO/Pres.
5005 LBJ Freeway, Ste. 250
Dallas, TX 75244
Phone: (972)855-1600
Toll-Free: 800-IM-AWARE
Fax: (972)855-1605
E-mail: info@komen.org
Home Page: http://www.komen.org

• 19847 • **Awards for Excellence in Community Service, Philanthropy, and Media**
To recognize individuals for contributions in the following categories: Philanthropy - for generating funds to support The Komen Foundation or other breast cancer programs; Volunteerism - for a volunteer effort on behalf of the work of the Foundation; Media - for work in print, television, or radio that communicates an important message about breast cancer concerns; Community Service - for assisting the Foundation in its efforts to reach the community at large; and Corporate Philanthropy - for generating significant funds with a corporate sponsored program. Not every award is bestowed every year.

• 19848 • **Brinker International Award for Breast Cancer Research**
To honor outstanding achievements in the field of breast cancer research. Two awards are given, one for basic research and one for clinical research. A $10,000 honorarium and a statuette are awarded annually. Established in 1992.

• 19849 • **Betty Ford Award**
The most prestigious award the Foundation bestows is given to recognize significant impact on the research, education, or treatment of breast disease.

• 19850 • **Komen Award of Scientific Distinction**
To recognize an individual who has demonstrated leadership in either basic or clinical breast cancer research. The award carries a $20,000 honorarium, a citation and statuette.

• 19851 • Population-Specific Research Project Award
To address the special needs of a diverse range of populations at risk for breast cancer. Awards are presented to model programs that can be implemented in communities throughout the country. All grant recipients are selected through a peer review process recognized by the National Cancer Institute. Awarded annually.

• 19852 • Research Fellowships
To provide funds for scientists who are working with an expert in the area of breast cancer research. These can be in the basic science or in the clinical area. Applications are accepted annually, usually in March, and are peer reviewed.

• 19853 •
Susan Smith Blackburn Prize
3239 Avalon Pl.
Houston, TX 77019
Phone: (713)308-2842
Fax: (713)654-8184
Home Page: http://www.blackburnprize.org

• 19854 • Susan Smith Blackburn Prize
To recognize women who have written full-length plays of outstanding quality for the English-speaking theatre. Prominent theatre professionals are invited to submit scripts in September. Send SASE ($.60 stamp for brochure and list of theaters asked to submit. Deadline is Sept. 20 each year.) The winner received $ 10,000, along with a signed and numbered lithograph by Willem de Kooning, and honorable mention (at the discretion of the judges receives $1000) presented annually in February. Each of the other 8-10 finalists receives $500. Established in 1978 by the family and friends of Susan Smith Blackburn, the noted American actress and writer who lived in London the last 15 years of her life.

• 19855 •
Swedish-American Chambers of Commerce, USA
Gunilla Girardo, Pres.
1403 King St.
Alexandria, VA 22314
Phone: (703)836-6560
Fax: (703)836-6561
E-mail: gunilla@sacc-usa.org
Home Page: http://sacc-usa.org

• 19856 • Lucia Trade Award
Recognizes outstanding work. World leaders are eligible. Awarded annually.

• 19857 •
Swedish Council of America
2600 Park Ave.
Minneapolis, MN 55407
Phone: (612)871-0593
Toll-Free: 800-981-4SCA
Fax: (612)871-0687
E-mail: swedcoun@swedishcouncil.org
Home Page: http://www.swedishcouncil.org/

• 19858 • Award of Merit
To recognize deserving individuals who make meaningful contributions to Swedish America at the local organization level. A plaque is awarded biennially by nominations. Established in 1997.

• 19859 • Great Swedish Heritage Award
To recognize Swedish-Americans who have made a significant contribution in their chosen field. U.S. citizens who are not members of the Council Board of Directors are eligible. A glass eagle created by Orrefors is awarded biennially. Established in 1980.

• 19860 •
Sheldon Swope Art Museum
David Vollmer, Dir.
25 S 7th St.
Terre Haute, IN 47807-3692
Phone: (812)238-1676
Fax: (812)238-1677
E-mail: finley@swope.org
Home Page: http://www.swope.org

• 19861 • Wabash Valley Juried Exhibition
To recognize outstanding art in the annual exhibition. Purchase Prizes, and Awards of Merit are presented annually. Established in 1944.

• 19862 •
Symphony of the Mountains
Ann L. Myers, Exec.Dir.
Kingsport Renaissance Center, Box 13
1200 E Center St.
Kingsport, TN 37660
Phone: (423)392-8423
Fax: (423)392-8428
E-mail: info@symphonyofthemountains.org
Home Page: http://www.symphonyofthemountains.org

• 19863 • Elizabeth Harper Vaughn Concerto Competition
For recognition of outstanding performance in piano, strings, winds, and percussion. The competition rotates annually between piano, winds and brass, and strings. Winner will receive a monetary prize of $1,000 and will perform with the Kingsport Symphony Orchestra during the regular concert series. To enter, a performance tape, $20 entry fee, and recommendation from a private instructor must accompany the application. Deadline is December 31. Established in 1971 as the Concerto Competition, it was renamed The Elizabeth Harper Vaughn Concerto Competition in 1985. Formerly: (1985) KSO Young People's Concerto Competition Award.
27332 Athcongress

• 19864 •
Synchro Swimming U.S.A.
Mr. Terry Harper, Exec.Dir.
201 S Capitol, Ste. 901
Indianapolis, IN 46225
Phone: (317)237-5700
Fax: (317)237-5705
Fax: (317)237-5705
E-mail: webmaster@usasynchro.org
Home Page: http://www.usasynchro.org

Formerly: (2002) United States Synchronized Swimming.

• 19865 • Collegiate Athlete of the Year
To recognize the outstanding collegiate athlete, selected by vote of coaches and regional athlete representatives based on the principles of sportsmanship and academic and athletic achievement. Established in 1984.

• 19866 • Hall of Fame - Contributor
To recognize outstanding contributors to the sport of synchronized swimming from a local to a national level. Awarded annually. Established in 1959.

• 19867 • Lillian MacKeller Distinguished Service Award
To recognize a person who has given unselfishly of herself for synchronized swimming without thought of personal gain, and with a particular emphasis on working for the benefit of the athlete. Awarded annually. Established in 1971.

• 19868 • May McEwan Memorial Award (Masters Athlete of the Year)
To recognize the person who best represents the ideals of Masters Synchronized Swimming. Established in 1984. Formerly: Masters Award.

• 19869 • USSS Athlete of the Year
To recognize the outstanding athlete of the year, one who has made the most significant, positive impact on the sport during the most recent competitive season. Established in 1984.

• 19870 • USSS Coach of the Year
To recognize the coach who has made the most significant impact on athletes' performances at the highest levels of competition within the twelve previous months. In Olympic years, coaching performance related to the Games will be a primary consideration. Although active coaching should be the main reason for receiving the award, supporting consideration may be given for the following contributions in the field of coaching: distinguished career in coaching, educating, or mentoring other coaches, development of coaching materials, promotion of character development, service to the community, and pioneering new training or competition methods.

• 19871 •
Syngenta
1800 Concord Pke
Wilmington, DE 19850
Phone: (910)632-6000
Fax: (910)632-2290
Home Page: http://www.syngenta-us.com

Formerly: CIBA Plant Protection.

• 19872 • Novartis Corp Protection American Phytopathological Society Award
To recognize significant recent contributions to the advancement of knowledge of plant diseases or their control. Members of the American Phytopathological Society are eligible. A trophy and an all-expense paid trip to Switzerland are awarded annually. Established in 1975.

• 19873 • Novartis Crop Protection Agricultural Writing Award
To recognize outstanding contributions to agriculture through journalism. Members of the American Agricultural Editors Association are eligible. A trophy and an all-expense paid trip to Switzerland are presented to the top winner. Awarded annually. Established in 1970. Formerly: CIBA-GEIGY Corporation; CIBA Crop Protection and Sandoz Agro.

• 19874 • Novartis Crop Protection Award in Agronomy
To recognize outstanding work in agronomy by a member of the American Society of Agronomy. A trophy and an all-expense paid trip to Switzerland are awarded annually. Established in 1970.

• 19875 • Novartis Crop Protection Entomological Society of America Award
To recognize outstanding work in entomology by a member of the Entomological Society of America. A trophy and an all-expense paid trip to Switzerland are awarded annually. Established in 1970.

• 19876 • Novartis Crop Protection NAFB Farm Broadcasting Award
To recognize creativity, effectiveness, and contributions to the profession of farm broadcasting. Voting members of the National Association of Farm Broadcasters are eligible. A trophy and an all-expense paid trip to Switzerland are awarded annually. Established in 1970.

• 19877 • Novartis Crop Protection Weed Science Society of America Award
To recognize outstanding achievement in research, teaching, and extension work. Members of the WSSA are eligible. A trophy and an all-expense paid trip to Switzerland are awarded annually. Established in 1973.

• 19878 •
Syracuse University
S. I. Newhouse School of Public Communications
215 University Pl.
Syracuse, NY 13244-2100
Phone: (315)443-2301
Fax: (315)443-3946
E-mail: newhouse@syr.edu
Home Page: http://newhouse.syr.edu

• 19879 • Distinguished Service Medal Awards
For recognition of long and distinguished service in any area of communications. Awarded irregularly on the basis of recommendations from members of the University's faculty and by a faculty vote. Established in 1936.

• 19880 • Newhouse Citation
To recognize men and women in photography for significant contributions to the field of visual communications. Nominees are selected by the faculty of the Newhouse School of Public Communications. A certificate is awarded periodically. Established in 1961.

• 19881 •
Syracuse University Press
Peter Webber, Dir.
621 Skytop Rd., Ste. 110
Syracuse, NY 13244-5290
Phone: (315)443-5534
Fax: (315)443-5545
E-mail: supress@syr.edu
Home Page: http://www.syracuseuniversitypress.syr.edu

• 19882 • John Ben Snow Prize
To encourage the writing of nonfiction books of genuine significance and literary distinction that will augment knowledge of New York State and appreciation for its unique physical, historical, and cultural characteristics. Authors of nonfiction, unpublished, book-length manuscripts dealing with some aspect of New York State, with emphasis on central New York, are eligible. The deadline for submission is December 31. A monetary prize of $1,500 advance against royalties to the author, and publication by the Syracuse University Press are awarded annually if merited. Established in 1978.

• 19883 •
System Safety Society
Cathy Carter, Contact
PO Box 70
Unionville, VA 22567-0070
Phone: (540)854-8630
E-mail: syssafe@ns.gemlink.com
Home Page: http://www.system-safety.org

• 19884 • Chapter of the Year
To recognize exceptional effort on the part of a Chapter's membership to promote system safety and the Society. Nominations may be submitted from February 1 through May 1. Annual report must be included. Awarded annually. Established in 1975.

• 19885 • Educator of the Year Award
To recognize an individual for outstanding achievement in system safety education. Nominations may be submitted from February 1 through May 1. A suitably engraved plaque is awarded annually. Established in 1981.

• 19886 • Engineer of the Year
To recognize an individual member of the Society who has made significant engineering contributions in the field of system safety. Nominations may be submitted from February 1 through May 1. A suitably engraved plaque is awarded annually. Established in 1981. Formerly: Safety Engineer of the Year.

• 19887 • International Award
To recognize persons or organizations for outstanding achievement in promoting the discipline of systems safety in a country other than the United States. Nominations may be submitted from February 1 through May 1. A suitably engraved plaque is awarded annually when merited.

• 19888 • Manager of the Year
To recognize an individual member of the Society who made significant contributions to the development and implementation of effective system safety management programs. Nominations may be submitted from February 1 through May 1. A suitably engraved plaque is awarded annually. Established in 1981. Formerly: Safety Manager of the Year.

• 19889 • Presidents Achievement Award
To recognize persons and/or organizations for outstanding achievement in performing service for the System Safety Society. A trophy and citation (organizations) or a plaque (individuals) are awarded annually when merited. Established in 1988.

• 19890 • Professional Development Award
This, the highest award presented by the Society, recognizes a member for sustained professional achievement that significantly enhances system safety as a profession. Senior/Fellow members of the Society are eligible. Nominations may be submitted from February 1 through May 1. A plaque and desk set are awarded annually. Established in 1976.

• 19891 • Scientific Achievement Award
To recognize an individual, group, or corporation who has made contributions and advancements to system safety through research or testing programs. Nominations must be submitted from February 1 to May 1. A suitably inscribed plaque is presented annually. Established in 1985. Formerly: (2006) Scientific Research and Development Award.

• 19892 • System Safety Technology Innovation Award

To encourage and recognize individuals who advance the state of the art of system safety. Individuals whose technological innovations constitute a substantial contribution to system safety technology are eligible for consideration. A contribution must be described and documented in a published paper, book, or other medium and communicated to SSS members and others. The contribution must be current (originated within the past five years) but need not originate or be completed in the year the award is made. Nominations may be submitted from February 1 through May 1. A monetary award of $1,000 is presented when merited. Established in 1985. Sponsored by Events Analysis, Inc.

• 19893 •
T-Town Paws
Sherry Romain, Pres.
1911 8th Place E
PO Box 861403
Tuscaloosa, AL 35486-0012
Phone: (205)633-1002
Fax: (205)556-0052
E-mail: ttownpaws@hotmail.com
Home Page: http://www.t-townpaws.org

• 19894 • Alabama Pet Hall of Fame

Based upon a set of guidelines. Recognition award bestowed annually.

• 19895 •
Tacoma-Pierce County Sports Commission
Tim Waer, Exec.Dir.
1119 Pacific Ave., 5th Fl.
Tacoma, WA 98402
Phone: (253)284-3260
Toll-Free: 800-272-2662
Fax: (253)627-8783
E-mail: timw@tacomasports.com
Home Page: http://www.tacomasports.com

• 19896 • Amateur Athletic Fund

For amateur athletic events hosted in Tacoma-Pierce County. Grant awarded quarterly.

• 19897 •
The Taft Group
27500 Drake Rd.
Farmington Hills, MI 48331-3535
Phone: (248)699-4253
Fax: (248)699-8035
E-mail: gale.galeord@thomson.com
Home Page: http://www.gale.com/taft.htm

• 19898 • Taft Awards Program for Non-Profit Resource Centers

To recognize and encourage the development of nonprofit fund-raising resource centers. Four recipients will receive $2,500 in TAFT print and/or electronic products. Two awards will be given to libraries or not for profit organizations seeking to enhance their existing fund-raising resource centers. Two additional awards will go to libraries, not-for-profit organizations, or development offices preparing to launch new fund raising resource centers.

• 19899 •
Talbot County Arts Council
Gerald H. Early, Exec.Dir.
PO Box 6
Easton, MD 21601
Phone: (410)745-0222
Fax: (410)770-4879
E-mail: gearly@talbotarts.org
Home Page: http://www.talbotarts.org

• 19900 • Outstanding Arts Educator Award

For arts educator in Talbot County, MD. Recognition award bestowed annually.

• 19901 • TCAC Grants

For schools and nonprofit organizations. Grant awarded semiannually.

• 19902 •
Talented Youth Development
Kimberly Thomas, Contact
147 S Oxford St., No. 1B
Brooklyn, NY 11217
Phone: (313)492-0946
Phone: (718)788-4350
Fax: (718)788-4350
E-mail: tydinc2000@aol.com
Home Page: http://www.hometown.aol.com/mitalenteens

• 19903 • Hal Jackson's Michigan Talented Teens Scholarship

For girls in the performing arts. Scholarship awarded annually.

• 19904 •
Talk Show Hosts.com
Carol Nashe, Pres.
2791 S Buffalo Dr.
Las Vegas, NV 89117
Phone: (702)248-4884
Fax: (702)889-1474
E-mail: carolnashe@mindspring.com
Home Page: http://www.talkshowhosts.com

Formerly: (2003) Radio Talk Show Hosts Association.

• 19905 • Freedom of Speech Award

Annual award of recognition.

• 19906 • Talk Show Host of the Year

Annual award of recognition.

• 19907 •
Tall Clubs International
Oliver Gruter, Pres.
741 Winterside Cir.
San Ramon, CA 94583
Toll-Free: 888-IMT-ALL2
E-mail: tci-president@tall.org
Home Page: http://www.tall.org

• 19908 • Man of the Year

Annual award of recognition. Awarded to tall males.

• 19909 • Miss Tall International

Annual award of recognition.

• 19910 • Woman of the Year

Award of recognition. Awarded to tall females.

• 19911 •
Tallahassee Soccer Association
Ms. Danielle Galvin, Pres.
PO Box 13026
Tallahassee, FL 32317-3026
Phone: (850)847-3821
E-mail: tsasoccer@yahoo.com
Home Page: http://www.tallahasseesoccer.net

• 19912 • Goslin Award - Man of the Year

For greatest contribution to soccer group and soccer community. Trophy awarded annually.

• 19913 • Malchow Award - Woman of the Year

For greatest contribution to soccer group and soccer community. Trophy awarded annually.

• 19914 •
Tampa Bay Business Committee for the Arts
Franci G. Rudolph, Exec.Dir.
PO Box 559
Tampa, FL 33601-0559
Phone: (813)221-2787
Fax: (813)221-1679
E-mail: tbbca@tbbca.org
Home Page: http://www.tbbca.org

• 19915 • Business in the Arts Award

For support of the arts by businesses. Recognition award bestowed annually.

• 19916 •
Tampa Builders Exchange
Gerald D. Hansen, Exec.Dir.
605 S Fremont Ave.
Tampa, FL 33606
Phone: (813)253-5733
Fax: (813)251-5082
E-mail: tbe@tampabx.com
Home Page: http://www.tampabx.com

• 19917 • TBE Scholarship Fund

For architecture student at the University of South Florida. Scholarship awarded annually.

• 19918 •
TAPPI - Technical Association of the Pulp and Paper Industry
Kathleen M. Bennett, Pres.
15 Technology Pkwy. S
Norcross, GA 30092
Phone: (770)446-1400
Toll-Free: 800-332-8686
Fax: (770)446-6947
E-mail: memberconnection@tappi.org
Home Page: http://www.tappi.org

• 19919 • **Division Leadership and Service Award**
To recognize an individual for outstanding leadership and exceptional service to the awarding Division which have resulted in significant and demonstrable benefits to the Division's members. A lapel pin and a suitable plaque bearing the individual's name and the awarding Division's name is awarded along with a cash honorarium. The winning division may choose to name its award after the individual or organization for whom the honorarium was established.

• 19920 • **Division Technical Awards**
To recognize outstanding accomplishments or contributions which have advanced the industry's technology in the awarding division's field of interest. A suitable medal and a lapel pin, both of special design, and a plaque bearing the individual's name and the awarding Division's name is awarded along with a cash honorarium. The winning division may choose to name its award after the individual or organization for whom the honorarium was established.

• 19921 • **TAPPI Herman L. Joachim Distinguished Service Award**
To recognize an individual for voluntary leadership and service which have significantly and demonstrably contributed to the advancement of the Association. The Board of Directors may, by a vote of two-thirds of the members present, give award to individuals who have performed outstanding service to the Association, including its councils, committees, divisions, sections, chapters, and programs. Established in 1983.

• 19922 • **Gunnar Nicholson Gold Medal Award**
This, the highest honor of the Association, is given for scientific and engineering achievements of proven commercial benefit to the world's pulp, paper, board, and forest product industries. The forest product industries include forestry, derived products, their process technology, and their applications. Recipients become TAPPI Fellows. Awarded annually. Awardees received the TAPPI Gold Medal from 1928 through 1984. The award was re-named in 1985. Formerly: (1984) TAPPI Gold Medal.

• 19923 • **Outstanding Local Section Member Award**
To recognize outstanding leadership and exceptional service to one or more Local Sections and which have resulted in significant and demonstrable benefits to Local Section members. The nominee must be an individual whose outstanding leadership and exceptional service in Local Section activities have resulted in significant and measurable benefits to Section members. The contributions may be through a single activity or through an accruement of longtime efforts. A lapel pin and a suitable plaque bearing the individual's name is awarded.

• 19924 • **TAPPI Fellow Award**
To recognize meritorious service to the pulp and paper industry or the Association. Individuals who have been members of TAPPI for not less than ten years are eligible. One or more Fellow designations are awarded annually. Established in 1968.

• 19925 •
TASH
Nancy Weiss, Exec.Dir.
29 W Susquehanna Ave., Ste. 210
Baltimore, MD 21204
Phone: (410)828-8274
Fax: (410)828-6706
E-mail: nweiss@tash.org
Home Page: http://www.tash.org

• 19926 • **Alice H. Hayden Award**
An award granted to a qualified applicant who is currently enrolled in a doctoral program in special education or a related field of education. Applicants must show the potential for leadership in teaching, scholarship, and service for people with significant disabilities. $500 is awarded annually at the Fall Conference. A curriculum vitae, including information on higher education, employment, and research and publications, a 500 1000 word essay on current work and objectives; and three letters of support must be submitted. Application deadline is July 1st. Established in 1978 in honor of Alice Hayden. Formerly: (1997) Alice H. Hayden Fellowship.

• 19927 • **Positive Images Award**
Recognize print, film, and the other media form presentations. Eligible works must show positive images of people with disabilities in community-related situations. Selection criteria include quality, accuracy of information, meaningfulness, degree of impact, and the promotion of positive images of people with disabilities. A description of the project, including medium used: length of piece (if in video), format; and at least one copy of the work must be submitted. Application deadline is July 1st.

• 19928 •
Tatry Housing Organization
Mrs. Ivanna Zhyzko, Dir.
603 S Ann St.
Baltimore, MD 21231
Phone: (410)342-7200
Phone: (410)276-8681
Fax: (410)276-1233
E-mail: lemkoinc@aol.com

• 19929 • **Annual Recognition Award**
No additional information available at this time.

• 19930 •
Tau Beta Pi Association
James D. Froula, Exec.Dir.
PO Box 2697
Knoxville, TN 37901-2697
Phone: (865)546-4578
Fax: (865)546-4579
E-mail: tbp@tbp.org
Home Page: http://www.tbp.org

• 19931 • **Chapter Awards**
The following awards are presented: (1) R.C. Matthews Outstanding Chapter Award - established in 1956; re-named in 1978; and (2) R.H. Nagel Most Improved Chapter Award - established in 1971, re-named in 1983.

• 19932 • **Distinguished Alumnus Award**
To recognize alumni who have demonstrated outstanding adherence to the ideals of Tau Beta Pi in fostering a spirit of liberal culture in our society, and to honor members who have made exceptional efforts to foster a spirit of liberal culture on local, national and international scales. Each winner receives a recognition plaque, awarded at the convention, and a $2,000 scholarship named in the winner's honor is given to a student. Established in 1993.

• 19933 • **National Outstanding Advisor Award**
To recognize outstanding performance by an advisor. The award includes a plaque, a $1,000 prize to the winner, and $1,000 in the name of the winner to the dean's discretionary fund. Established in 1994.

• 19934 • **Tau Beta Pi Laureate**
To recognize collegiate student members who outstandingly exemplify the spirit of liberal culture in engineering colleges. Student members may be nominated by their local chapter by March 15. A monetary award of $2,500, a plaque and travel to the Convention are awarded annually at the Convention. Established in 1982.

• 19935 •
Tau Beta Sigma
Alan Bonner, Natl.Exec.Dir.
PO Box 849
Stillwater, OK 74076-0849
Phone: (405)372-2333
Toll-Free: 800-543-6505
Fax: (405)372-2363
E-mail: kkytbs@kkytbs.org
Home Page: http://www.kkytbs.org

• 19936 • **Outstanding Women in Music Award**
To honor a woman who has made a distinct or unique contribution to the field of band music in some way. The candidate must be out of college, and have at least five years experience in her particular area. Nominations are accepted before December 1 and should include a letter of nomination, a resume, and letters of recommendation from individuals who know the nominee

well. A trophy is awarded biennially. Established in 1969.

• 19937 • Scroll of Honor

To honor the top band member in each summer session band camp. The award is designed and offered by bands women to a young musician, in recognition of outstanding performance, attendance, diligence and proficiency. A certificate is awarded to one female camper per session. Established in 1974.

• 19938 • Wava Banes Turner Award

To honor individuals who have made outstanding contributions to the sorority through continued support of chapter activities and national programs. Nominees must be a life, honorary or alumnae member of the sorority. National officers are not eligible until out of office for five years. Awarded biennially. Established in 1977.

• 19939 •

Tau Sigma Delta
John P. White, Pres.
Texas Tech University
College of Architecture
PO Box 42091
Lubbock, TX 79409-2091
Phone: (806)742-3136
Home Page: http://www.ttu.edu/~tsd/

• 19940 • Bronze Medal

To recognize students for distinction in design in the field of architecture, landscape architecture, or the allied arts. A brass medal is awarded at the discretion of students in each chapter. Awarded annually if merited. Established in 1969.

• 19941 • Gold Medal

To recognize a professional for distinction in design in the field of architecture, landscape, or the allied arts. A gold medal is awarded annually by the Grand Chapter of the Society. Established in 1969.

• 19942 • Silver Medal

To recognize a professional for distinction in design in the field of architecture, landscape architecture, or the allied arts. A silver medal is awarded at the discretion of students in individual chapters. Awarded annually if merited. Established 1969.

• 19943 •

Tax Foundation
William Ahern, Comm.Dir.
2001 L St., Ste. 1050
Washington, DC 20036
Phone: (202)464-6200
Fax: (202)464-6201
E-mail: tf@taxfoundation.org
Home Page: http://www.taxfoundation.org

• 19944 • Distinguished Service Award

To honor an individual for distinguished service for contribution in realm of excellence in tax policy in the United States. The award is presented in two categories: public sector and private sector. Nominations are made by the Policy Council. An award is presented at the Annual Dinner held in the fall. Established in 1941.

• 19945 •

Teachers Association of Baltimore County
Bob Anzelc, Exec.Dir.
305 E. Joppa Rd.
Towson, MD 21286-3252
Phone: (410)828-6403
Fax: (410)337-7081

• 19946 • TABCO Recognition Award

For outstanding contributions to education. Recognition award bestowed annually.

• 19947 •

Teachers of English to Speakers of Other Languages
Elliot Judd, Pres.
700 S Washington St., Ste. 200
Alexandria, VA 22314-4287
Phone: (703)836-0774
Toll-Free: 888-547-3369
Fax: (703)836-7864
E-mail: info@tesol.org
Home Page: http://www.tesol.org

• 19948 • TESOL Virginia French Allen Award for Scholarhip and Service

To honor a ESOL teacher who has shared scholarship and provided service at the ESOL affiliate level. The nomination deadline is October 20. Established in 1990 by Dr. Allen's former students to honor her many years of contributions to the field. A three-year membership is awarded.

• 19949 • Ryan Crymes TESOL Fellowship for Graduate Study

To support graduate studies in the teaching of English to speakers of other languages. TESOL members who are presently enrolled or have been enrolled within the calendar year in a TESL or TEFL graduate program that prepares teachers to teach English to speakers of other languages are eligible. The deadline for application is October 20. A monetary prize of $1,500 is awarded annually. Formerly: TESOL/Regents Publishing Company Fellowship; (2006) TESOL Fellowship for Graduate Study.

• 19950 • Mary Finocchiaro Award for Excellence in the Development of Pedagogical Materials

To recognize an individual who has achieved excellence through the development of practical pedagogical materials. Applicants must apply by October 20. A monetary award of $500 is presented annually.

• 19951 • Albert H. Marckwardt Travel Grants

To enable graduate students who are TESOL members to attend a TESOL convention. The deadline is October 20. A monetary prize of $500 and convention registration are awarded.

• 19952 • TESOL Research Interest Section/Thomson Heinle Distinguished Research Award

To recognize excellence in any area of research on language teaching and learning. The deadline for submission of unpublished manuscripts is October 23. A monetary prize of $1,000 is awarded. Sponsored by Newbury House, Division of Heinle and Heinle Publishers. Formerly: (2006) TESOL Research Interest Section/ Newbury House Distinguished Research Award.

• 19953 • TESOL Thomson Heinle Award for Excellence in Teaching

To honor a teacher who is considered by his or her colleagues to be an excellent teacher. Any member of TESOL who has at least 5 years experience in the EFL classroom is eligible. The nominator must be a TESOL member who has seen the nominee (another TESOL member) teach. The deadline is October 23. A monetary prize of $1,000 is awarded. Sponsored by the Newbury House, Division of Heinle and Heinle Publishers. Formerly: (2006) TESOL/Newbury House Award for Excellence in Teaching.

• 19954 • TESOL Travel Grant

To support an ESL/EFL professional who wants to attend a TESOL convention. Any TESOL member who is a teacher, teacher trainer, supervisor, or who is otherwise engaged in some aspect of teaching English as a foreign language for a minimum of 5 years is eligible and must apply by October 20. A monetary award not to exceed $2,500 is awarded. Formerly: (1996) Robert Maple/Longman Memorial Travel Grant.

• 19955 •

Technical Association of the Graphic Arts
Karen E. Lawrence, Managing Dir.
200 Deer Run Rd.
Sewickley, PA 15143
Phone: (412)259-1813
Fax: (412)741-2311
E-mail: tagaofc@aol.com
Home Page: http://www.taga.org

• 19956 • TAGA Honors Award

For recognition of outstanding contributions to the progress of printing technology and graphic science in the association and throughout the world. Members are eligible. The TAGA Honors symbol is awarded annually at the conference. This was designed in 1976 by R.E. Maurer, former president of TAGA, and consists of a spire with three transparent side panels in the subtractive primary colors - yellow, magenta, and cyan - which are the colors of the three dye layers in transparencies and the colorants used in printing inks for process-color reproduction. The overlap color of red, green, and blue (violet) are generated by the colored panels. The black base represents the black printer and the white base of the pyramid the printing paper. Established in 1976.

• 19957 •
Technology Student Association
Dr. Rosanne T. White, Exec.Dir.
1914 Association Dr.
Reston, VA 20191-1540
Phone: (703)860-9000
Fax: (703)758-4852
E-mail: general@tsaweb.org
Home Page: http://www.tsaweb.org

Formerly: (1988) American Industrial Arts Student Association.

• 19958 • **Gold Level Achievement Awards**
To promote active participation at the local, community, state, and national level; to provide information for future career and education choices; to assist in leadership development; and to recognize participation in TSA activities. Total points during the year determine the type of award received. Silver and bronze awards are presented.

• 19959 • **Technology Honor Society**
To recognize those students who excel in academics, leadership, and service towards their school and community. Two levels exist: middle school and high school. Certificates and pins are awarded to one or more recipients annually.

• 19960 • **TSA Star Recognition Program**
To recognize the highest level of service performed on TSA's behalf by students and technology/industrial arts professionals. Recipients are nominated by TSA state advisors and corporate members, and selected by the TSA Board of Directors. Awards are given in the following areas: Honorary Life Membership, Outstanding Recognition, Distinguished Student, and Distinguished Service. Formerly: AIASA Recognition Awards.

• 19961 •
Teen Court of Huerfano County
Michele L. George, Coord.
401 Main St., Ste. 304
Walsenburg, CO 81089-2045
Phone: (719)742-0240
Fax: (719)738-1267
E-mail: hcteencourt@yahoo.com

• 19962 • **Professionalism Award**
For outstanding service. Recognition award bestowed annually.

• 19963 •
Telly Awards
41 Union Sq. W, Ste. 1131
New York, NY 10003
Phone: (212)675-3555
Home Page: http://www.tellyawards.com

• 19964 • **Telly Awards**
To honor creativity in local and regional TV commercials, cable TV spots, and non-Broadcast videos such as corporate training films. Awards are given in more than 200 categories, including local spots, regional spots, non-broadcast films and videos, work produced for less than 500, autos, banks, clothing and furniture stores, corporate image, dairy products, hospitals, political issues, real estate companies, and utilities. The judging criteria are based on the Clios and other awards programs. Six to 12 previous Telly winners review commercials and rate them on a point system. Silver and bronze statuettes are awarded annually. Established in 1980 by David E. Carter.

• 19965 •
Tennessee Council of Teachers of English
331 Park Manor Lane
Collierville, TN 38017
Phone: (901)754-3923

• 19966 • **Tennessee Teacher of Excellence**
For an English teacher in Tennessee. Recognition award bestowed annually.

• 19967 •
Tennessee Library Association
Annelle Huggins, Exec.Dir.
PO Box 241074
Memphis, TN 38124-1074
Phone: (901)485-6952
E-mail: ahuggins@midsouth.rr.com
Home Page: http://www.tnla.org

• 19968 • **Frances Neel Cheney Award**
To recognize a member of the Tennessee Library Association who has made a significant contribution to the world of books and librarianship through encouraging the love of books and reading. A significant contribution includes but need not be limited to: notable professional/bibliographical writing or editing that deals with books, the book arts, and reading; a program in a library (academic, public, school, special) that encourages reading and/or appreciation of books; creative teaching with books; and promotion of books and reading by media. A monetary award of $100 and a plaque are awarded annually at the convention. Established about 1982 to honor Frances Neel Cheney, an outstanding Tennessee librarian who wrote well-known books on reference sources and was a teacher and professor at Peabody/Vanderbilt.

• 19969 • **Honor Award**
To recognize any person or group who has made a significant contribution to Tennessee library and information services. Nominations must be made by a TLA member and may include librarians, trustees, or groups who have contributed to the furtherance of librarianship on a statewide or national level. A plaque is awarded annually at the convention. Established in 1978.

• 19970 • **Tennessee History Book Award**
To recognize excellence in historical writing. Content and theme should be centered on Tennessee history and the publication imprint must be during the previous year. The following categories are not eligible for this award: children]s books, fiction, poetry, and individual volumes in an uncompleted set or series. A cash award of $200 and a plaque are awarded annually.

• 19971 • **Tennessee Resource Sharing Award**
To recognize any person, institution, or organization in Tennessee who has done outstanding work in promoting resource sharing within and among Tennessee libraries. Recipient selected by TENN-SHARE. The award consists of a plaque and $100. The cash award is given to a library or other institution of the recipient's choice that provides resource sharing among Tennessee libraries, with the money being earmarked for resource sharing services. Awarded annually.

• 19972 • **TLA/SIRS Freedom of Information Award**
To recognize the contribution of an individual or group who has actively promoted intellectual freedom in Tennessee. $500 and a plaque are awarded annually. The recipient is selected by the Intellectual Freedom Committee in conjunction with the Honors and Awards Committee of the Tennessee Library Association. Sponsored by Social Issues Resources Series, Inc. Established in 1988.

• 19973 • **Trustee Award**
To recognize a trustee who has made a significant contribution to library and information services in the State of Tennessee. Members of the Association are eligible. A plaque is awarded annually at the convention.

• 19974 • **Volunteer State Book Award**
To recognizes the contribution of an individual or group who has actively promoted intellectual freedom in Tennessee. Winners are selected by school children in grades K-12 in the State of Tennessee. Awarded annually. Formerly: Tennessee Children's Choice Book Award.

• 19975 • **James E. Ward Library Instruction Award**
To recognizes a member of TLA who participates in the planning, execution, or evaluation of a continuing program or special project of library instruction for an academic, school, public, or special library. Where the significant contributions of more than one person are involved, the award may be shared. Winner(s) is selected by the TLA Library Instruction Roundtable. Awarded annually.

• 19976 •
***Tennis* Magazine**
Miller Sports Group LLC
79 Madison Ave., 8th Fl.
New York, NY 10016
Phone: (212)636-2700
Fax: (212)636-2730
E-mail: editors@tennis.com
Home Page: http://www.tennis.com

• 19977 • 50 Greatest U.S. Tennis Resorts
To recognize the best tennis resorts in America based on *Tennis* Magazine's reader survey. Winners are featured in the November issue of the magazine. Awarded every two years. Established in 1982.

• 19978 • Comeback Player of the Year
To recognize the professional player who has returned successfully to the pro tour after a protracted layoff due to injury, illness, or other circumstance. Selection is made by the editors of *Tennis* magazine, and the player is featured in the January issue. Awarded annually. Established in 1978.

• 19979 • Junior Players of the Year
To recognize the outstanding junior male and female players. Selection is made by the editors of *Tennis* magazine. Players age 18 and under are eligible and are featured in the November issue. Awarded annually. Established in 1980.

• 19980 • Most Improved Pros
To recognize the male and female professional tennis players who have shown the most progress in their tennis game. Selection is made by the editors of *Tennis* magazine and the players are featured in the January issue of the magazine. Awarded annually. Established in 1973.

• 19981 • Rolex Watch/*Tennis* Magazine Rookies of the Year
To recognize two outstanding first-year professional tennis players, male and female, as selected by the editors of *Tennis* magazine. They are featured in the January issue of the magazine. Awarded annually. Established in 1972.

• 19982 • *Tennis* Magazine /ITA College Players of the Year
To recognize the outstanding male and female college players. Selection is made by the editors of *Tennis* magazine. Players are featured in the August issue. Awarded annually. Established in 1980. Formerly: Volvo College Players of the Year.

• 19983 •
Tennis Week
Eugene L. Scott, Editor-in-Chief
15 Elm Pl.
Rye, NY 10580-2918
Phone: (914)967-4890
Fax: (914)967-8178
E-mail: tennisweek@tennisweek.com
Home Page: http://www.sportsmediainc.com/tennisweek

• 19984 • *Tennis Week* Great American Tennis Writing Awards
To encourage tennis journalism. Awards are given in the following categories: Aspiring Journalist - for writers with no previous by-line in a national publication; Non-Tennis Journalist - for writers who do not cover the tennis beat regularly (to expand the game's overall body of high quality journalism); Tennis Journalist - for writers who specialize in tennis; Tennis Journalism - three categories to cover a tennis related article, essay, or feature story that has appeared in any publication worldwide (English only); one award to journalists who write to a daily deadline; and one award to the best book or screenplay. Submissions must be original works for publication in *Tennis Week*. There is no age limit, and submissions may come from the United States, Canada, and abroad. The six yearly winners are presented awards in New York City. Awarded annually. Established in 1986.

• 19985 •
Texas Association of Bank Counsel
John Brigance, Exec.Dir.
203 W 10th St.
Austin, TX 78701
Phone: (512)472-8388
Fax: (512)473-2560
E-mail: tabc@texasbankers.com
Home Page: http://www.texasbankers.com

• 19986 • Texas Tech Law School Foundation
For student editor of the Texas Bank Lawyer. Scholarship awarded annually.

• 19987 •
Texas Association of Sports Officials - Baseball, Houston Chapter
Bob Charmo, Pres.
PO Box 812
Cypress, TX 77410
Phone: (281)370-4765
E-mail: bcsc11@sbcglobal.net
Home Page: http://www.sbua.com

• 19988 • Baseball Players Scholarship Award
For athletics, academics, community service. Scholarship awarded annually.

• 19989 •
Texas Cable and Telecommunications Association
Dale Laine, Pres./COO
PO Box 13518
Austin, TX 78711-3518
Phone: (512)474-2082
Toll-Free: 800-666-2082
Fax: (512)474-0966
E-mail: txcable@txcable.com
Home Page: http://www.txcable.com

• 19990 • John E. Mankin Award
For individual who has demonstrated great commitment and leadership in the cable television industry. Recognition award bestowed annually.

• 19991 • Project Community Award
For cable operators who have sponsored projects that have enhanced the quality of life for the citizens in the operator's service area. Medal awarded annually.

• 19992 •
Texas Council for the Social Studies
PO Box 8207
Fort Worth, TX 76124
Phone: (817)534-3440
E-mail: aa102@rgfn.epcc.edu

• 19993 • Outstanding Elementary, Middle Level and Secondary Teachers
For service to social studies. Monetary award bestowed annually.

• 19994 •
Texas Daily Newspaper Association
718 W Fifth St., Ste. 200
Austin, TX 78701-2796
Phone: (512)476-4351
Fax: (512)476-0515
E-mail: info@tdna.org
Home Page: http://www.tdna.org

• 19995 • Bright Idea Awards
To recognize the best newspaper self-promotion during the previous year. Entries may promote any department (advertising, circulation, editorial) or the entire newspaper. All TDNA newspapers are eligible. Awards are given for papers with circulation under 10,000, 10,000 to 35,000, 35,000 to 100,000 and over 100,000. The deadline for submission is January 15. Plaques are awarded for separate circulation categories at the annual meeting.

• 19996 • H. M. Fentress Memorial Award for Editorial Excellence
To recognize an outstanding reporting or feature writing intern participating in the TDNA Student Intern Summer Program. A plaque and a monetary prize of $250 is awarded to the first-place winner and a monetary prize of $100 is awarded to the second-place winner. The deadline for nominations is September 15. Sponsored by Cox Newspapers.

• 19997 • Fred Hartman Excellence in Sportswriting Award
To recognize an outstanding sportswriter or sports editor on a TDNA member paper. The annual competition alternates between circulation categories of less than 100,000 in odd years and more than 100,000 in even years. Nomination deadline is January 15. A plaque and a $1,000 award are presented at the annual meeting.

• 19998 • Frank Mayborn Award for Community Leadership
To recognize an outstanding publisher or newspaper executive who has provided significant community leadership during the year. A plaque is awarded at the annual meeting and a $3,000 scholarship is presented to the Texas college or university of the winner's choice. Nomination deadline is January 15. Awarded annually. The award was established in memory of Frank W. Mayborn.

• 19999 • John Murphy Award for Excellence in Copy Editing

For recognition of an outstanding copy editor on a TDNA member paper. Only work appearing in TDNA member papers between January 1 and December 31st are eligible. The annual competition alternates between circulation categories of less than and more than 100,000. Nominations must be received before January 15. A plaque and a monetary prize of $1,000 is awarded at the TDNA Annual Meeting.

• 20000 • Pat Taggart Award for Texas Newspaper Leader of the Year

To recognize a publisher or newspaper executive who has provided exceptional service to his or her newspaper, the newspaper business, and to the community. Biographical background information and supporting documents must be submitted. The deadline for submissions is January 15. A plaque is awarded at the annual meeting. Established in 1977.

• 20001 •
Texas Engineering Experiment Station
G. Kemble Bennett, Dir.
301 Wisenbaker Engineering Research Ctr.
Texas A&M University
College Station, TX 77843-3577
Phone: (979)845-7203
Fax: (979)845-8986
E-mail: teesweb@tamu.edu
Home Page: http://tees.tamu.edu

• 20002 • Chairs and Professorships Awards

Inquire for application details.

• 20003 • Outstanding Achievement Awards

Women and minorities are eligible. Inquire for application details.

• 20004 •
Texas Fine Arts Association, The Jones Center for Contemporary Art
Sue Graze, Exec.Dir.
700 Congress Ave.
Austin, TX 78701
Phone: (512)453-5312
Fax: (512)459-4830
E-mail: info@tfaa.org

• 20005 • Disaster Relief Fund

For full-time artists from Texas who are members of TFAA and have experienced an unforeseen health or property disaster that prevents their normal production of art. Grant awarded annually.

• 20006 •
Texas Heart Institute
PO Box 20345
MC 3-117
Houston, TX 77225-0345
Phone: (832)355-3089
Toll-Free: 800-292-2221
E-mail: mmattsson@hcart.thitmc
Home Page: http://www.texasheartinstitute.org

• 20007 • Denton A. Cooley Leadership Award

To recognize an individual for exceptional leadership and meritorious contributions to society. Awarded annually with a monetary prize, medallion, and travel. Established in 1992.

• 20008 •
Texas Independent Producers and Royalty Owners Association
Martin V. Fleming, VP of Pub.Aff.
515 Congress, Ste. 1910
Austin, TX 78701
Phone: (512)477-4452
Fax: (512)476-8070
E-mail: kathie@tipro.org
Home Page: http://www.tipro.org

• 20009 • Hat's Off Award

For special service to the oil and gas industry. Recognition award bestowed annually.

• 20010 •
Texas Institute of Letters
Dave Hamrick, Pres.
4703 Fieldstone Dr.
Austin, TX 78735
Phone: (817)689-4123
Fax: (817)689-4042
E-mail: franvick@aol.com
Home Page: http://www.wtamu.edu/til

• 20011 • Book Publishers of Texas Children's/Young People's Award

To recognize the best book for children written by a Texas author or about Texas. Entries may be submitted by publishers or authors by January 8. A monetary prize of $250 is awarded annually. Established in 1949. Formerly: Steck - Vaughn Award.

• 20012 • Brazos Bookstore Short Story Award

To recognize the best single story published during the award year in book form or in a periodical. Stories by Texas authors or about Texas may be submitted by January 2. A Texas author may be one who was born in Texas, presently resides in Texas, or has spent formative years in Texas. A monetary prize of $750 is awarded annually. Funded by the Brazos Bookstore in Houston.

• 20013 • Carr P. Collins Award

To recognize the best nonfiction book. Texas authors or authors of nonfiction books on a Texas subject are eligible. Entries may be submitted by publishers, editors, and writers by January 8. A monetary prize of $5,000 is awarded annually. Established in 1946.

• 20014 • Dobie-Paisano Writing Fellowships

To provide for two six-month grants to writers every year. Entries may be submitted by publishers or authors by January 1. Applicants must have a connection with Texas by birth, or by having lived in the state for two years at some time, or by having written about the state. Free residence and monthly stipends (currently $1,200 a month) are provided, at J. Frank Dobie's old ranch near Austin. Co-sponsored by the Texas Institute of Letters and the University of Texas at Austin. Additional information is available from Dr. Audrey Slate, Dobie-Paisano Project, Office of Graduate Studies, Main Building 101, UT-Austin, Austin, TX 78712.

• 20015 • Soeurette Diehl Fraser Award for Best Book of Translation

To recognize the best literary translation into English by a translator associated with Texas. A monetary award of $1,000 is presented. Established in 1990. Formerly: (2006) Soeurette Diehl Fraser Award.

• 20016 • Friends of the Dallas Public Library Award

To recognize the most useful and informative book in the field of general knowledge. Texas authors or authors of books on a Texas subject are eligible. Entries may be submitted by publishers, editors, and writers by January 8. A monetary prize of $1,000 is awarded annually. Established in 1960.

• 20017 • O. Henry Award

To recognize the best nonfiction writing appearing in a magazine, journal, or other periodical, or in a newspaper Sunday supplement. Articles by Texas writers may be submitted by January 8. A monetary award of $1,000 is presented.

• 20018 • Jesse Jones Award for Best Work of Fiction

To recognize the best book of fiction, either a novel or story collection. Texas authors or authors of books on Texas subjects are eligible. Entries may be submitted by publishers or authors by January 8. A monetary prize of $6,000 is awarded annually. Established in 1960 by Houston Endowment, Inc. Formerly: (2006) Jesse H. Jones Award.

• 20019 • Stanley Marcus Award for Book Design

To recognize the best book design. Typography and general appearance of the book are both considered. Designers must have a connection with Texas by birth or by having lived in the state for two consecutive years at some time to be eligible. Entries may be submitted by publishers by January 8. A monetary prize of $350 is awarded annually. Established in 1966. Formerly: Texas Collector's Institute Award.

Awards are arranged in alphabetical order below their administering organizations

• 20020 • Natalie Ornish Award

To recognize the best volume of poetry. Texas poets or poems on a Texas subject are eligible. Entries may be submitted by publishers by January 8. A monetary prize of $1,000 is awarded annually. Established in 1965.

• 20021 • Lon Tinkle Award

To recognize an individual with Texas association for continuing excellence in letters. TIL membership is not required. A monetary award of $1,500 is awarded.

• 20022 • Stanley Walker Award

To recognize the best work of journalism appearing in a daily newspaper or Sunday supplement. Texas authors or authors of work on Texas subjects are eligible. Entries may be submitted by publishers or writers by January 8. A monetary prize of $1,000 is awarded annually.

• 20023 • Fred Whitehead Award

To recognize the best design of a trade book. Texas designers are eligible. Entries may be submitted by publishers or designers by January 2. A monetary prize of $750 is awarded annually. Established in 1996.

• 20024 •

Texas League for Nursing
Box 80110
Austin, TX 78708-0110
Phone: (512)453-8199
Fax: (512)465-1090

• 20025 • Nursing Research Award

For research contributing to excellence in nursing and health care practice in Texas. Recognition award bestowed annually.

• 20026 • Teaching Excellence Award

For quality teaching in schools in nursing. Recognition award bestowed annually.

• 20027 •

Texas Library Association
Patricia H. Smith, Exec.Dir.
3355 Bee Cave Rd., Ste. 401
Austin, TX 78746
Phone: (512)328-1518
Toll-Free: 800-580-2852
Fax: (512)328-8852
E-mail: tla@txla.org
Home Page: http://www.txla.org

• 20028 • Texas Bluebonnet Award

To encourage Texas children in grades 3 to 6 to read more books, explore a variety of current books, and identify their favorite books. Books selected for the TBA master reading list must be written by U.S. citizens and have been published in the United States and copyrighted within three years of selection for the master reading list. Both fiction and non-fiction are eligible. A medallion is presented annually at the Texas Library Association conference. Established in 1979.

• 20029 •

Texas Medical Association
Louis J. Goodman PHD, Exec.VP/CEO
401 W 15th St.
Austin, TX 78701
Phone: (512)370-1300
Toll-Free: 800-880-1300
Fax: (512)370-1632
E-mail: knowledge@texmed.org
Home Page: http://www.texmed.org

• 20030 • Excellence in Science Teaching Awards

To honor dedicated science teachers of Texas who inspire future physicians and scientists and foster appreciation of science among their students. Teachers must have at least five years teaching experience. First place and merit awards are presented at three levels: elementary, middle/junior high, and high school. The deadline for nominations is December 31. The first place winner receives a plaque, a monetary prize of $2,500, and a $2,500 resource grant for his/her school; three merit winners each receive a plaque and a cash award of $2,000. Awarded annually. Established in 1990.

• 20031 • Golden Apple Awards for Service in Health Promotion and Disease Prevention

To recognize the health promotion and disease prevention achievements of both a physician and a non-physician in Texas. Examples that merit award include innovative community outreach programs, health promotion advocacy, voluntarily providing preventive services to the economically disadvantaged or other special populations, or implementing a tracking system for preventive services. To be eligible for the physician award, the nominee must be a member in good standing with a Texas health organization. A candidate for either award must be nominated by a Texas county medical society, specialty society, or medical section. Nominations should describe the individual's activities. These activities should address a need in disease prevention or health promotion based on needs assessment data, reach target audience(s) with appropriate objectives and intervention strategies, reflect sensitivity to special populations, and demonstrate achievement of objectives for improved health outcomes. The nomination packet must include the full name, title, address, and phone number of the nominee, a letter of nomination no more than three double-spaced typed pages addressing each criterion for election, and one additional letter of endorsement. Winners will be recognized with a commemorative award at TMA's Interim Session in November.

• 20032 • Anson Jones, M.D., Award

To recognize the media of Texas for excellence in communicating health information to the public. The two major categories are: Science of Medicine and Socioeconomics of Medicine. Material published or broadcast during the year may be submitted. For the Science of Medicine category, awards are given for: (1) Newspapers - daily newspapers with circulation (excluding Sunday) of 100,000 or more; daily newspapers with circulation (excluding Sunday) between 24,000 and 99,999; daily newspapers with circulation (excluding Sunday) below 24,000; and weekly, bi-weekly, or semi-weekly newspapers; (2) Magazines/Newsletters - company, employee, association, chamber, or trade publications; and consumer-oriented, general interest publications; (3) Radio - stations in Dallas, Forth Worth, Houston, San Antonio, and Austin; and all other stations; and (4) Television - stations in Dallas, Forth Worth, Houston, San Antonio, Austin; and all other stations. For the Socioeconomics of Medicine category, awards are given for any medicine, by market size only, in the following locations: Dallas, Fort Worth, Houston, San Antonio, and Austin; and all other locations. Entries must be received by January 15. Entries are limited to one article or series. A monetary prize of $1000 and a plaque are awarded annually. Citations of Merit winners receive a certificate and a $250 cash award. Established in 1957 in honor of Anson Jones, M.D., a pioneer Texas physician, who served the Republic of Texas as a member of Congress, as Secretary of State and as its last President. He established the first regulations concerning the practice of medicine in Texas, and was a prolific writer.

• 20033 •

Texas Nonprofit Theatres
Linda M. Lee, Exec.Dir.
1300 Gendy St.
Fort Worth, TX 76107-4036
Phone: (817)731-2238
Fax: (817)731-2239
E-mail: tnt@texastheatres.org
Home Page: http://www.texastheatres.org

• 20034 • Steadfast Service Award

For support of theatre. Recognition award bestowed annually.

• 20035 •

Texas Oral History Association
Lois E. Myers, Sec.-Treas.
1 Bear Pl., No. 97271
Baylor University
Waco, TX 76798-7271
Phone: (254)710-3437
Fax: (254)710-1571
E-mail: lois_myers@baylor.edu
Home Page: http://www3.baylor.edu/TOHA/

• 20036 • Mary Faye Barnes Award for Excellence for Community History Projects

For an oral history project exemplifying distinguished preservation of community history. Recognition award bestowed annually.

• 20037 • W. Stewart Caffey Award for Excellence for Pre-Collegiate Teaching

For an elementary or secondary classroom teacher who led students in a research project involving oral history methods in an exemplary way. Recognition award bestowed annually.

• 20038 • Thomas L. Charlton Lifetime Achievement Award

For individuals exemplifying outstanding and continuing contributions to oral history. Recognition award bestowed annually.

• 20039 •
Texas Sign Association
Marcie Funchess CAE, Contact
8200 Northeast Pkwy., Ste. 101
North Richland Hills, TX 76180
Phone: (817)498-8601
Toll-Free: 800-588-8762

• 20040 • Dewayne Billingsley Memorial Scholarship

For high school senior or continuing education student. Scholarship awarded annually.

• 20041 •
Texas Society of Architects/ AIA
David Lancaster, Exec.VP
816 Cong. Ave., Ste. 970
Austin, TX 78701-2443
Phone: (512)478-7386
Fax: (512)478-0528
E-mail: info@texasarchitect.org
Home Page: http://www.texasarchitect.org

• 20042 • Design Award

For excellence in design - judged by national jury. Recognition award bestowed annually.

• 20043 • Firm of the Year

For service and design. Recognition award bestowed annually.

• 20044 •
Texas Tech University
College of Mass Communications
Jerry Hudson, Dean
PO Box 43082
Lubbock, TX 79409-3082
Phone: (806)742-3385
Fax: (806)742-1085
E-mail: jerry.hudson@ttu.edu
Home Page: http://www.depts.ttu.edu/mcom

• 20045 • Mass Communications Hall of Fame

To recognize alumni who have distinguished themselves in the field of mass communications, or persons who have distinguished themselves in mass communications and have specifically aided the educational programs in mass communications at Texas Tech University. A colored picture is hung in the Hall of Fame. Awarded annually. Established in 1973.

• 20046 • Mass Communications Outstanding Alumni Awards

To recognize Alumni of Texas Tech University who have attained outstanding accomplishments in the field of mass communications. Any individual, organization, media group, or company may submit nominations. A laser-etched photo is presented to the recipient and a recognition breakfast at Homecoming are awarded. Established in 1981.

• 20047 •
Texas Western Press
500 W University Ave.
University of Texas at El Paso
El Paso, TX 79968-0633
Phone: (915)747-5688
Toll-Free: 800-488-3789
Fax: (915)747-7515
E-mail: jbristol@utep.edu
Home Page: http://www.utep.edu/twp

• 20048 • C. L. Sonnichsen Book Award

To recognize the best original, unpublished nonfiction manuscript dealing with the history, literature, or cultures of the Southwest. Academic and non-academic authors may submit manuscripts of at least 100 typed pages by March 1. A monetary award of $1,000 and publication of the award-winning book are presented annually. Those planning to submit work must first notify the Press of intention to submit a manuscript. Established in 1977 by Texas Western Press to honor Dr. Charles Leland Sonnichsen, professor emeritus of the University of Texas at El Paso.

• 20049 •
Textile Study Group of New York
Nancy Koenigsberg, Pres.
A.I.R. Gallery II
511 W 25th St., No. 301
New York, NY 10001
Phone: (212)753-0749
E-mail: info@tsgny.org
Home Page: http://www.tsgny.org

• 20050 • Nancy and Harry Koenigsberg Award

For artist. Monetary award bestowed periodically.

• 20051 •
Theatre Communications Group
Ben Cameron, Exec.Dir.
520 8th Ave., 24th Fl.
New York, NY 10018-4156
Phone: (212)609-5900
Fax: (212)609-5901
E-mail: tcg@tcg.org
Home Page: http://www.tcg.org

• 20052 • NEA/TCG Career Development Program for Designers

Provides financial support and creative opportunities to exceptional early-career scenic-lighting, costume and sound designers who seek a career in America's not-for-profit professional theatre. The program offers recipients the opportunity to spend six months over a two-year period developing their design skills and expanding their knowledge of the field. Under a cooperative agreement with the National Endowment for the Arts, recipients receive stipends of $17,500 each, plus a small travel stipend. Formerly: (1996) TCG/NEA Designer Fellows.

• 20053 • NEA/TCG Career Development Program for Directors

Provides financial support and creative opportunities to exceptional early-career stage directors who seek a career in America's not-for-profit professional theatre. The program offers recipients the opportunity to spend six months over a two-year period developing their directing skills and increasing their knowledge of the field. Under a cooperative agreement with the National Endowment for the Arts, recipients receive stipends of $17,500 each, plus a small travel stipend.

• 20054 • Alan Schneider Director Award

To assist mid-career directors who have exhibited exceptional talent and established local or regional reputations, but who have not yet achieved national visibility. Individual directors may not apply directly. Selection for the award is by nomination only; nominations may be submitted by artistic directors of TCG member theatres. Given in tribute to the late director's lifelong concern for nurturing new generations of theatre artists, the cash award of $10,000 provides support for activities specifically tied to the development of the directing craft, such as travel to observe master directors, research aimed at specific directing projects, and travel for artistic directors to see productions directed by the recipient.

• 20055 • TCG/MetLife Foundation Extended Collaboration Grants for Artists

To enable playwrights to work collaboratively with other artists for an extended period beyond that which a sponsoring theatre normally supports. Artistic directors of TCG member theatres must apply on behalf of the artists. The deadline for applications is the early spring and late fall. $5500 grants are awarded semiannually. Established in 1989 by TCG and the MetLife Foundation. Sponsored by MetLife Foundation.

• 20056 •
Theatre Historical Society of America
Richard J. Sklenar, Exec.Dir.
York Theatre Bldg.
152 N York, 2nd Fl.
Elmhurst, IL 60126-2806
Phone: (630)782-1800
Fax: (630)782-1802
E-mail: thrhistsoc@aol.com
Home Page: http://www.historictheatres.org

• 20057 • *Marquee* Award

For recognition of theatre preservation or research into the history of theatres. Nominations must be submitted by March 1. Two types of awards are presented: Honorary Member - to recognize an individual who is not a member of the organization and who has contributed to the ideals of organization, and Member of the Year - to recognize an active member who has contributed to the ideals of the organization. A plaque is awarded annually at the yearly Conclave. Established in 1970 by B. Andrew Corsini and named for *Marquee,* the quarterly theatre publication of the organization.

• 20058 •
Theatre Library Association
Martha S. LoMonaco, Pres.
40 Lincoln Ctr. Plz.
New York, NY 10023
Phone: (212)944-3895
Fax: (212)944-4139
E-mail: martilomonaco@optonline.net
Home Page: http://tla.library.unt.edu

• 20059 • **George Freedley Memorial Award**
To recognize the author of an outstanding book in the field of live theater performance including vaudeville, puppetry, pantomime, and the circus. Such publications may include biography, history, criticism, reference, or related fields. Books published during the preceding year must be nominated by early February. A monetary prize of $500 and a certificate are presented to the winner; $250 and a certificate are awarded for Special Jury Prize. Awarded annually. Established in 1968 in memory of George Freedley, first curator of the New York Public Library Theatre Collection and a founder of the Association. Additional information is available from Richard Wall, TLA, % Shubert Archive 149 W. 45th Street, New York, NY 10036.

• 20060 • **Theatre Library Association Award**
To recognize the author of a notable book in the areas of motion pictures, television and radio. Books published during the preceding year must be nominated by early February. A monetary prize of $500 and a certificate are awarded annually to the winner; and $250 and a certificate are awarded for Special Jury Prize. Established in 1973. Additional information is available from Richard Wall, TLA, % Shubert Archive 149 W. 45th Street New York, NY 10036.

• 20061 •
Theatre World
190 Riverside Dr.
New York, NY 10024
Phone: (646)221-8078
Fax: (212)337-8024
E-mail: ben@fatchanceproductions.org

• 20062 • ***Theatre World* Awards**
This, the oldest awards for debuting actors in the New York theatre, is given to recognize, reward, and encourage promising new talent in the legitimate theatre. Six actors and six actresses are selected for an outstanding performance in a theatrical debut (on or off Broadway/NYC), for a first appearance in an outstanding small or featured role, or for lead in a play or musical. A Special Theatre World Award is also presented. The award is a bronze sculpture by Harry Marinsky, an internationally recognized artist, with masks of comedy and tragedy back to back mounted on a black marble base with gold name plate is awarded annually at the end of each theatre season. Established in 1944 the current award is named for the mythical Janus, god of entrances and exits and all beginnings. Formerly: (1963) Promising Personality.

• 20063 •
Theodore Roethke Memorial Foundation
Patricia Shek, Pres.
11 W. Hannum Blvd.
Saginaw, MI 48602
Phone: (989)792-5567
Fax: (989)792-5567
E-mail: patriciashek2004@yahoo.com

• 20064 • **Theodore Roethke Memorial Foundation Poetry Prize**
For recognition of an individual published book of poems within the preceding three years. Living American poets are eligible. A monetary award of $3,000 is awarded triennially. Established in 1968.

• 20065 •
Theodore Roosevelt Association
Mr. Edward J. Renehan Jr., Exec.Dir.
PO Box 719
Oyster Bay, NY 11771
Phone: (516)921-6319
Fax: (516)921-6481
E-mail: trinfo@cs.com
Home Page: http://www.theodoreroosevelt.org
Formerly: (1955) Roosevelt Memorial Association.

• 20066 • **Theodore Roosevelt Distinguished Service Medal**
To recognize in contemporary life those who have rendered distinguished service in fields that Theodore Roosevelt worked in his lifetime. The medal is given in the following fields: public and international law, industrial peace, science, American literature, outdoor life, national defense, international affairs, administration of public office, conservation of natural resources, advancement of social justice, expression of pioneer virtues, distinguished public service by a private citizen, and leadership of youth and development of American character. U.S. citizens may be nominated. Selection is made by the executive committee. A medal is awarded annually.

• 20067 •
Theta Alpha Phi
Kitty Laurich, Sec.-Treas.
PO Box 14773
Columbus, OH 43214
Phone: (614)447-8045

• 20068 • **Medallion of Honor**
To honor an individual for long-term, outstanding, and distinguished service to the theater profession on the national level. Members of the National Council make the nominations. A wooden shield-shaped plaque with a theater mask in raised gold-finish metal is awarded annually. Established in 1956.

• 20069 •
Third Reich Study Group
Myron Fox, Dir.
PO Box 283
Needham Heights, MA 02494-0904
E-mail: myronfox1@aol.com
Home Page: http://gps.nu/studygroup/thirdreich/

• 20070 • **Bob Houston Memorial Award**
For the best III Reich Exhibit in National Exposition.

• 20071 •
Third Street Music School Settlement
Barbara E. Field, Exec.Dir.
235 E 11th St.
New York, NY 10003
Phone: (212)777-3240
Fax: (212)477-1808
E-mail: info@thirdstreetmusicschool.org
Home Page: http://www.thirdstreetmusicschool.org

• 20072 • **Award for Distinguished Achievement in the Arts**
To recognize an outstanding performing artist. Individuals who have provided original and lasting achievement in music or the performing arts are considered. A plaque is presented annually at the School's Anniversary Luncheon in New York City. Established in 1975. Formerly: Award for Distinguished Achievement in Music.

• 20073 • **Award for Distinguished Service to the Arts**
To recognize significant contributions to the world of music or the performing arts. Those who have provided leadership in promoting the musical and/or performing arts and providing financial support are considered for the award. A plaque is presented annually at the School's Anniversary Luncheon in New York City. Established in 1975. Formerly: Award for Distinguished Service to Music.

• 20074 •
Thistle Class Association
Patty Lawrence, Sec.-Treas.
154 Back Acres Rd.
Chapin, SC 29036-8539
Phone: (803)732-9648
E-mail: secretary@thistleclass.com
Home Page: http://www.thistleclass.com/

• 20075 • **Carron Keeper**
To recognize an individual who achieves first place in a national sailboat racing championship. Membership in the association and qualification through a district or regional championship are required. A trophy is presented annually at the August National Championship Regatta. Established in 1946 in honor of I. Louis Carron, a former member and officer of the association. Formerly: (2006) I. Louis Carron Award.

Awards are arranged in alphabetical order below their administering organizations

• 20076 • Growth and Promotion Award

To recognize fleets that have done an outstanding recruiting job. Established fleets within national requirements are eligible. A plaque is awarded annually. Established in 1986 by North Cape (Toledo) Thistle Fleet 37.

• 20077 •

Thomas Paine National Historical Association
Marvin Edelman, Contact
983 North Ave.
New Rochelle, NY 10804-3609
Phone: (609)298-3980
E-mail: info@thomaspaine.org
Home Page: http://www.thomaspaine.org

• 20078 • Thomas Paine Journalism Award

To recognize lifelong achievement in the field of journalism by those whose professional lives reflect Thomas Paine's ideals as embodied by his observation: "When opinions are free...Truth will prevail." A monetary award and a medal are awarded annually at the annual Thomas Paine Dinner in January at Iona College or the College of New Rochelle. Established in 1990.

• 20079 •

Thomas Wolfe Society
David Strange, Membership
TWS Membership
PO Box 1146
Bloomington, IN 47402-1146
E-mail: twostrange2000@yahoo.com
Home Page: http://www.thomaswolfe.org

• 20080 • Zelda & Paul Gitlin Literary Prize

To recognize the best scholarly article on Thomas Wolfe. Articles published during that year are eligible. A monetary award is presented annually when merited at the Annual Meeting of the Thomas Wolfe Society. Established in 1982 by Paul Gitlin in honor of Zelda Gitlin. Formerly: (2004) Zelda Gitlin Literary Prize.

• 20081 • Richard S. Kennedy Student Essay Prize

To foster and recognize scholarship about Thomas Wolfe by undergraduate and graduate students. Individuals enrolled in undergraduate or graduate schools may make submissions by January 15. A monetary prize of $500 and publication of the essay in the Society's *Thomas Wolfe Review* are presented. Winner also receives a year's membership in the Thomas Wolfe Society and is invited to deliver the essay at the Society's annual meeting. Established in 1987 in memory of Thomas Wolfe. The prize was renamed in 2004 in honor of Dr. Richard S. Kennedy. Formerly: (2004) Thomas Wolfe Society Literary Prize.

• 20082 • William B. Wisdom Grant in Aid of Research

Designed for travel and living expenses for scholars and students working out of the William B. Wisdom Collection in the Houghton Library, Harvard University. Established by the Society in 1990 through the generosity of Adelaide Wisdom Benjamin. Deadline for submission is April 1. Consideration will also be given to applicants who wish to use the Thomas Wolfe Collection in the University of North Carolina at Chapel Hill. Candidates at work on Ph.D. dissertations are especially encouraged.

• 20083 •

Thoroughbred Racing Associations
Christopher Scherf, Exec.VP
420 Fair Hill Dr., Ste. 1
Elkton, MD 21921-2573
Phone: (410)392-9200
Fax: (410)398-1366
E-mail: info@tra-online.com
Home Page: http://www.tra-online.com

• 20084 • Eclipse Awards

To recognize outstanding performances by horses and humans in Thoroughbred Racing. The 11 Eclipse Award categories are: Two-Year Old Colt or Gelding; Two-Year Old Filly; Three-Year-Old Colt or Gelding; Three-Year-Old Filly; Older Colt, Horse or Gelding; Older Filly or Mare; Male Turf Horse; Female Turf Horse; Sprinter; Stepplechase Horse and Horse of the Year. The human categories are: Owner, Trainer; Jockey; Apprentice Jockey; and Breeder. Eclipse Awards are presented at an annual dinner. The Eclipse Awards are named after the great 18th-century racehorse and sire Eclipse and are presented by the National Thoroughbred Racing Association; National Turf Writers Association; and the *Daily Racing Form.*

• 20085 • Eclipse Awards for Media

To recognize outstanding coverage of the sport of Thoroughbred horseracing. Awards are presented for Writing Features; Writing News/Commentary; Television Features; Television Live Racing; Local Television; Audio/Multi-Media Internet; and Photography. Deadline for entries is November 13. Awards are presented at an annual dinner and are named after the great 18th-century racehorse and sire Eclipse. Sponsored by the National Thoroughbred Racing Association; the National Turf Writers Association and the *Daily Racing For.*

• 20086 •

Thurber House
Susanne Jaffe, Exec.Dir.
77 Jefferson Ave.
Columbus, OH 43215
Phone: (614)464-1032
Fax: (614)280-3645
E-mail: thurberhouse@thurberhouse.org
Home Page: http://www.thurberhouse.org

• 20087 • Thurber Prize for American Humor

To recognize the author who best illustrates American humor. The award honors James Thurber, a humorist and cartoonist who gained recognition for his work through the New Yorker magazine. Any trade, university, or commercial publishing house may submit books, which must be received (not postmarked) with all accompanying material by the April 1. Books published between January 1 and December 31 of the previous year are acceptable. A monetary prize of $5,000 for the winner is awarded annually. To submit a book or manuscript for consideration, the publisher should provide the following: four copies of each submitted title, a $50 application fee, and a complete application, as provided online at www.thurberhouse.org.

• 20088 •

Tile Contractors' Association of America
Patty Nolte, Exec.Dir.
4 E 113th Terrace
Kansas City, MO 64114
Phone: (816)941-7063
Toll-Free: 800-655-8453
Fax: (816)767-0194
E-mail: info@tcaainc.org
Home Page: http://www.tcaainc.org

• 20089 • Cesery Award

For recognition of achievement in the ceramic tile industry including those who produce ceramic tile, those who contract for the installation of ceramic tile, and those who set ceramic tile. Selection is by nomination from within the ceramic tile industry. A medal is awarded annually at the convention. Established in 1964 in memory of Carl V. Cesery.

• 20090 •

Time Inc.
1271 Avenue of the Americas
New York, NY 10020
Phone: (212)522-1212
Fax: (212)522-0602
Home Page: http://www.time.com

• 20091 • Andrew Heiskell Awards

To recognize individuals for outstanding personal leadership and accomplishment in the area of public service, human rights and/or equal opportunity in their workplace and communities. Full-time employees of Time Warner and its operating businesses may be nominated for the award. A monetary prize of $1,000 and a scroll are presented to the awardee, and an additional $1,000 is presented to charity. Awarded annually in July. Established in 1982. The award honors Andrew Heiskell, former chairman of Time Incorporated.

• 20092 • *Time* Magazine Quality Dealer Award

To recognize individuals for outstanding performance as automobile dealers and as citizens of their communities. Established in 1970. Cosponsored by the National Automobile Dealers Association and Time Inc. Magazine Company.

• 20093 • *Time* Man of the Year

A designation on the part of the editors of *TIME* of the person, people, or thing that, for better or worse, has most significantly influenced the course of world events in the preceding twelve months. It is a news judgment, not an accolade nor a moral judgment. Established in 1927 by Time Inc. Magazine Company.

• 20094 •
Toastmasters International
Donna H. Groh, Exec.Dir.
23182 Arroyo Vista
PO Box 9052
Mission Viejo, CA 92690
Phone: (949)858-8255
Toll-Free: 800-993-7732
Fax: (949)858-1207
E-mail: tminfo@toastmasters.org
Home Page: http://www.toastmasters.org

• 20095 • Golden Gavel Award
To pay tribute to persons for outstanding achievements in and contributions to the fields of communications and leadership. Selection of recipient is made one to one and a half years prior to presentation. A trophy is presented annually at the International Convention held in August. Established in 1959.

• 20096 •
Tonga and Tin Can Mail Study Circle
Society of Australasian Specialists/Oceania
% Stuart Leven
PO Box 24764
San Jose, CA 95154-4764
Phone: (513)625-8543
E-mail: stulev@ix.netcom.com
Home Page: http://members.aol.com/TongaJan/ttcmsc.html

• 20097 • Clyde Carriker, Jr. Memorial Award
To recognize the writer of the best article appearing in *Tin Canner,* the Study Circle's journal. Members of the Circle are eligible. An engraved plaque is awarded annually. Established in memory of Clyde H. Carriker, Jr. philatelic journalist.

• 20098 • Writers Contest
To recognize Circle members for literary contributions to the *Tin Canner*. Manuscripts may be submitted by August 30. Established in 1985.

• 20099 •
Toni Morrison Society
Carolyn Denard, Chm., Advisory Bd.
PO Box 54401
Georgia State University
Atlanta, GA 30308
Phone: (404)378-6410
Fax: (404)378-7262
E-mail: tmsociety@aol.com
Home Page: http://www.gsu.edu/tms

• 20100 • Morrison Book Prize
For the best book on Morrison's fiction. Recognition award bestowed biennially.

• 20101 •
Topps Company, Inc.
Arthur T. Shorin, Chm. and CEO
1 Whitehall St.
New York, NY 10004
Phone: (212)376-0300
Fax: (212)376-0573
Home Page: http://www.topps.com

Formerly: Topps Chewing Gum.

• 20102 • Topps - J. G. Taylor Spink Minor League Player-of-the-Year
For recognition of the player of the year in all of the minor leagues. Awarded annually. Established in 1960.

• 20103 • Topps All-Star Scout Award
For recognition of the scout(s) who signed the winners of the Topps Major League Rookie All-Star Team to their professional baseball contracts. An engraved trophy is awarded annually. Established in 1959.

• 20104 • Topps Major League Rookie All-Star Team
For recognition of outstanding major league baseball rookies. Major league managers vote for ten outstanding first-year players for the All-Star Team. Each of the ten selected receives a trophy. Awarded annually. Established in 1959.

• 20105 • Topps Minor League Player-of-the-Month
For recognition of outstanding minor league players, in each of the 17 National Association Leagues, during each month of the baseball season. Selection is made by the Minor League managers in official balloting supervised by the National Association of Professional Baseball Leagues. Each winner receives a Topps Engraved Watch Award and a certificate. Established in 1960.

• 20106 • Topps National Association All-Star Teams
To recognize an All-Star Team for each Minor League Classification. Awards are presented in the following categories: Class AAA, Class AA, Class A, and Class A/Rookie. Selection is made by the National Association of Baseball Writers. An engraved Paul Revere Bowl is awarded to each of the 48 top Minor Leaguers. Awarded annually. Established in 1960.

• 20107 • Topps Organization Trophy
For recognition of the major league baseball club whose organization has won the most Topps awards. A trophy is awarded at the Annual Baseball Winter Convention. Established in 1966.

• 20108 • Topps Scout-of-the-Month Awards
For recognition of the scout(s) who signed winners to their professional baseball contracts. Candidates for the award are the scouts of the winners of the Topps Player-of-the-Month awards. A personalized citation and memento are awarded. Presented monthly, May through August. Established in 1960.

• 20109 • Topps - George M. Trautman Minor League Player-of-the-Year
For recognition of the top player in each of 17 National Association Leagues. Winners are elected by the National Association of Baseball Writers, and each receives an engraved plaque. Awarded annually. Established in 1960.

• 20110 •
Toronto Arts Council Foundation
Claire Hopkinson, Exec.Dir.
141 Bathurst St., Ste. 101
Toronto, ON, Canada M5V 2R2
Phone: (416)392-6800
Fax: (416)392-6920
E-mail: mail@torontoartscouncil.org
Home Page: http://www.torontoartscouncil.org/foundation.htm

• 20111 • Protege Awards
To provide Toronto Arts Award recipients with a personal memento of their award and to provide exposure and encouragement to an up-and-coming artist. Each recipient of a Toronto Arts Award has the opportunity to purchase or commission the work, valued at $2,500, of a younger artist. Formerly known as the Commemorative Arts Awards.

• 20112 • Toronto Arts Awards
To recognize achievement and excellence of artists from the various artistic disciplines who have contributed significantly to the arts and culture of greater metropolitan Toronto. Living Canadian citizens, landed immigrants, or long-term residents of Canada who have demonstrated an ongoing association with Toronto are eligible. Eight awards are presented in the following categories: Visual Arts; Performing Arts; Music; Writing and Publishing; Media Arts Award; and Architecture and Design. In addition, two Lifetime Achievement Awards are presented. Awarded annually. Established in 1985.

• 20113 •
Toronto International Film Festival Group
2 Carlton St., Ste. 1600
Toronto, ON, Canada M5B 1J3
Phone: (416)968-3456
Phone: (416)967-7371
Fax: (416)967-9477
E-mail: tiffg@torfilmfest.ca
Home Page: http://www.tiffg.ca

• 20114 • Air Canada People's Choice Award
For recognition of the most popular film in the festival. The festival public votes on all films, excluding retrospectives, that are shown at the festival. A trophy is awarded annually. Established in 1978. Formerly: (1991) John Labatt Classic Film Award; Labatt's Award for the Most Popular Film; Carlsberg Light People's Choice Award.

• 20115 • CITYN Award for Best Canadian First Feature Film

To honor a Canadian filmmaker whose first feature film is considered exemplary. The award carries a cash prize of $15,000.

• 20116 • Rottimans World Film International Critics' Award as Selected by Fipresci

For recognition of the best film of the Festival selected by a jury formed from accredited international press attending the Festival. Established in 1992. Formerly: (1991) Four Seasons Critics Awards; International Critics Award.

• 20117 • NFB - John Spotton Award for Best Canadian Short Film

For recognition of the best short film in the Perspective Canada program. Jurors from the Canadian film community make the selection. A monetary prize of $2,500 is awarded annually. Established in 1989. Sponsored by the National Film Board of Canada. Formerly: National Film Board Award for Best Short Film.

• 20118 • Toronto-City Award for Best Canadian Feature Film

For recognition of the best Canadian feature film voted by the international jury. All Canadian films shown in the Festival are eligible. A monetary prize of $30,000 is awarded. Established in 1984. Sponsored by the City of Toronto and CITY-TV. Formerly: (1991) Toronto City Award for Excellence in Canadian Production.

• 20119 •
Toronto International Salon of Photography
Betty Roots, Pres.
% Toronto Camera Club
587 Mt. Pleasant Rd.
Toronto, ON, Canada M4S 2M5
Phone: (416)480-0720
E-mail: camera@torontocameraclub.com
Home Page: http://www.torontocameraclub.com/salon.htm

• 20120 • Toronto International Salon of Photography

To recognize creative photo and slides talent. Awarded annually. Established in 1892.

• 20121 •
Toronto Press Club
Commerce Ct. S
Box 262
Toronto, ON, Canada M4L 1E8
E-mail: b.somerville@rogers.com

• 20122 • Canadian News Hall of Fame

To recognize individuals for outstanding contributions to journalism in Canada.

• 20123 •
Torrey Botanical Society
John Gillen, Pres.
% Gregory Cheplick, Sec.
Bldg. 6S, Rm. 319
2800 Victory Blvd.
College of Staten Island/CUNY
Staten Island, NY 10314
Phone: (718)982-3931
Fax: (718)982-3852
E-mail: cheplick@mail.csi.cuny.edu
Home Page: http://www.torreybotanical.org

Formerly: Torrey Botanical Club; Metropolitan Botanical Club.

• 20124 • Andrew Award

To recognize graduate student research. Theses projects by members in botany or topics related to botany that are published in the Club's *Bulletin* are eligible. A monetary prize of $250 is awarded annually. Funds may be used for research-related travel, field work, or laboratory supplies. Established in 1981.

• 20125 • Annette Hervey - Torrey Botanical Club Award

To recognize the best student paper published in the *Bulletin* of the Torrey Botanical Club. A monetary prize of $250 is awarded annually when merited. Established in 1981 in honor of Annette Hervey, Senior Research Associate of the New York Botanical Garden. Additional information is available from the above address.

• 20126 • William J. Robbins Award

For recognition of the best research paper published in the *Bulletin* of the Torrey Botanical Club in the fields of plant tissue culture, microbial metabolism, and biochemical control of growth. A monetary prize is awarded occasionally. Established in 1980 in memory of Dr. William J. Robbins, former director of the New York Botanical Garden. (Through 1987, no awards have been presented.)

• 20127 •
Touchdown Club Charities of Washington, D.C.
Pat Carrol, Contact
1749 Old Meadow Rd., Ste. 500
McLean, VA 22102
Phone: (202)624-9766
Fax: (202)624-9769
E-mail: tdclub@webdesigners.net
Home Page: http://www.touchdownclubcharities.com

• 20128 • Gene Brito Award

To recognize an individual who recovered from a serious illness and subsequently achieved success in sports. Established in 1983 in memory of Gene Brito, a former Redskin football player, who continued to play football after being struck with a crippling bone disease that eventually killed him at the age of 39.

• 20129 • Dial Award

To recognize the outstanding male and female high school athlete-scholars. Awarded annually. Established in 1979.

• 20130 • Clark C. Griffith Memorial Award

For recognition of an outstanding contribution to baseball. Presented at the Touchdown Club's Annual Awards dinner in January. The award was first presented in 1953. Re-named in 1955 to honor Clark C. Griffith, owner of the Senators.

• 20131 • Sam Ormes Trophy

To recognize the Prognosticator of the Year for super selection ability. Established in 1941.

• 20132 • Timmie Awards

For recognition of outstanding contributions to football by teams and individuals. Awards are given in the following categories: Local Schoolboy Player of the year, presented annually since 1955 in memory of Peter S. Haley, Sr.; Prep School Player of the Year, presented annually since 1948 in memory of J. O'Connor Roberts; Suburban Maryland High School Player of the Year, presented annually since 1957 in memory of Joseph S. Sanford; Suburban Virginia High School Player of the Year, presented annually since 1956; Washington, D.C. High School Player of the Year, presented annually since 1944 in memory of Ben Zola; Local Athlete Makes Good award, presented annually since 1960 in memory of Arch McDonald; High School Coach of the Year, presented annually since 1979 in memory of Tuffy Leemans; NCAA Division 1A Team of the Year; winner of the National Collegiate Athletics Association Division III each year; winner of the NCAA Division II; major college football team of the year, presented annually since 1955; College Football Coach of the Year, presented annually since 1946; local college player of the year, presented annually since 1948 in memory of Robert B. Smith; College Lineman of the Year, presented annually since 1939 in memory of Knute Rockue; College Back of the Year, presented annually since 1937 in memory of Walter Camp; College Quarterback of the Year; College All-Purpose Back of the Year; National Football League Rookie of the Year; National Football League Coach of the Year; National Football League Player of the Year - American Conference, presented annually since 1966 in memory of Wayne Millner; and National Football League Player of the Year - National Conference, presented annually since 1946 in memory of Dick McCann; and Outstanding Redskin Offensive Player of the Year, presented annually since 1975 in memory of Clifford (Cliff) Battles, rate NFL greatest halfback in the 1930's; and Outstanding Redskin Defensive Player of the Year, presented annually since 1975 in memory of Cliff Battles. In 1987, the Golden Timmie award was established to honor the Outstanding National Football League Player of the Year. In addition, Special Timmie Awards are presented. In 1989 and 1990, the following were awarded: Lifetime Achievement Award in Professional Basketball; Lifetime Achievement Award in Entertainment; Lifetime Achievement Award in Broadcasting and Com-

Awards are arranged in alphabetical order below their administering organizations

munity Service; George Allen Leadership and Achievement Award; Lifetime Achievement Award for Outstanding Performance National Football League; and Lifetime Achievement Award in College Coaching; Outstanding Achievement in Broadcasting Award; and Lifetime Achievement Award for Outstanding Performance in College Football. A silver statue of a young boy, either going to or returning from a sandlot game of football, mounted on a pedestal with an engraved plaque is awarded at the annual awards dinner.

• 20133 • Touchdown Club Arch McDonald Achievement Award
To recognize an individual for long and devoted service to sports and to the community. Established in 1960.

• 20134 • Touchdown Club Hubert H. Humphrey Award
To recognize an individual for achievements and unselfish generosity for the betterment of mankind. Awarded annually. Established in 1978.

• 20135 • Touchdown Club Local Personality Makes Good Award
To recognize an outstanding sportscaster from the Washington Metropolitan area. Established in 1988.

• 20136 • Touchdown Club Mr. Sam Award
To recognize a government figure who has fostered and contributed to sports through example and leadership. Awarded annually. Established in 1961 in memory of Sam Rayburn.

• 20137 • Touchdown Club's Board of Governors Award
To recognize a sports contributor for demonstrated excellence over a period of years rather than for the accomplishments of a single season. Awarded annually. Established in 1969.

• 20138 • U.S. Military Male and Female Athletes
No further information was available for this edition.

• 20139 •
Towing and Recovery Association of America
Harriet S. Cooley, Exec.Dir.
2121 Eisenhower Ave., Ste. 200
Alexandria, VA 22314
Phone: (703)684-7734
Phone: (703)684-7713
Toll-Free: 800-728-0136
Fax: (703)684-6720
E-mail: execdir@traasite.com
Home Page: http://www.traasite.com

• 20140 • Citizenship Award
To recognize an individual for good citizenship qualities demonstrated in business, community activities, and state and national association participation. Individuals are nominated and selected by an awards committee. Plaques are awarded annually. Established in 1982.

• 20141 • Distinguished Service Award
For recognition of an individual's outstanding contribution, untiring devotion, and dedicated sacrifice to the towing-recovery-storage industry. Individuals who are actively engaged in the towing industry and members of TRAA are eligible. A plaque is awarded annually at the national convention. Established in 1982.

• 20142 •
Town of New Scotland Historical Association
Joseph Hogan, Pres.
PO Box 541
Voorheesville, NY 12186-0541
Home Page: http://www.voorheesvillelibrary.org

• 20143 • Joslin Essay Award
For best essay in contest (three separate awards). Monetary award bestowed annually.

• 20144 •
Towson University
College of Liberal Arts
Rita D. Marinho, Dean
8000 York Rd.
Towson, MD 21252
Phone: (410)704-2128
E-mail: rmarinho@towson.edu
Home Page: http://www.towson.edu/cla

• 20145 • Towson University Prize for Literature
For recognition of a book or book-length manuscript of fiction, poetry, drama, or imaginative non-fiction published within the previous three years or scheduled for publication within the nomination year. Maryland authors under 40 years of age who have resided in the state for at least three years are eligible. The deadline for submissions is May 15. A monetary prize of $1,500 is awarded annually. Established in 1979 by the Franklin and Alice Cooley Endowment.

• 20146 •
Trade Show Exhibitors Association
Michael Bandy, Pres.
2301 S Lake Shore Dr., Ste. 1005
Chicago, IL 60616
Phone: (312)842-8732
Fax: (312)842-8744
E-mail: tsea@tsea.org
Home Page: http://www.tsea.org

Formerly: (1997) International Exhibitors Association.

• 20147 • Exhibit Focus Awards
To recognize companies which achieve specific marketing goals through their exhibit programs. In 1996, a design category was added to the competition; awards are presented in six categories. In addition, a Best of Show Award is presented.

• 20148 •
Transcultural Nursing Society
Beverly Horn PhD, Exec.Dir.
Madonna University, College of Nursing
36600 Schoolcraft Rd.
Livonia, MI 48150
Phone: (734)432-5470
Toll-Free: 888-432-5470
Fax: (734)432-5463
E-mail: executive.director@tcns.org
Home Page: http://www.tcns.org

• 20149 • Career Development Award
For research by professional nurses. A grant is awarded annually.

• 20150 • Leininger Transcultural Nursing Award
Annual financial award for outstanding and creative leadership in transcultural nursing.

• 20151 •
Transplant Recipients International Organization
Elizabeth Rubin, Pres.
2100 M St. NW, No. 170-353
Washington, DC 20037-1233
Phone: (202)293-0980
Toll-Free: 800-TRIO-386
Fax: (703)820-3948
E-mail: info@trioweb.org
Home Page: http://www.trioweb.org

• 20152 • Thomas Starzl Humanitarian Award
Recognizes a person who has greatly influenced the field of transplantation. Awarded annually.

• 20153 • Transplant Recipients International Organization Scholarship
Annual scholarship.

• 20154 •
Transportation and Logistics Council
John L. Burke, Sec.-Treas.
120 Main St.
Huntington, NY 11743
Phone: (631)549-8988
Phone: (631)549-8962
Fax: (631)549-8962
E-mail: tcpc@transportlaw.com
Home Page: http://www.tlcouncil.org

• 20155 • Transportation Professional of the Year
Annual award of recognition.

• 20156 •
Transportation Lawyers Association
Stephanie Newman, Exec.Dir.
PO Box 15122
Lenexa, KS 66285-5122
Phone: (913)541-9077
Fax: (913)599-5340
E-mail: tla-info@goamp.com
Home Page: http://www.translaw.org

• 20157 • **Distinguished Service Award**
Award of recognition. 248664 NASWUR

• 20158 •
Transportation Research Board
Robert E. Skinner Jr., Exec.Dir.
500 Fifth St. NW
Washington, DC 20001
Phone: (202)334-2934
Fax: (202)334-2003
E-mail: jrichardson@nas.edu
Home Page: http://www.trb.org

• 20159 • **Fred Burggraf Award**
To honor and encourage young researchers for papers selected for publication by TRB in the field of transportation. Researchers who are 35 years of age or younger and graduates of an accredited college or university are eligible. A monetary prize and a citation may be awarded annually. Established in 1966 in honor of Fred Burggraf, who served as the Board's director.

• 20160 • **W. N. Carey, Jr. Distinguished Service Award**
For recognition of leadership and distinguished service to the Board by an individual who has not necessarily been personally active in transportation research. A bronze plaque is awarded annually. Established in 1972. Formerly: (1988) Transportation Research Board Distinguished Service Award.

• 20161 • **Roy W. Crum Distinguished Service Award**
For recognition of outstanding achievement in the field of transportation research. A bronze plaque is awarded annually. Established in 1948 as the Highway Research Board Distinguished Service Award and redesignated the Roy W. Crum Distinguished Service Award in 1952 in memory of Roy W. Crum, the Board's director. Formerly: (1952) Highway Research Board Distinguished Service Award.

• 20162 • **Thomas B. Deen Distinguished Lectureship**
To recognize the career contributions and achievements of an individual in one of five areas covered by TRB's Technical Activities Division. Those honored are given the opportunity to present overviews of their technical areas, including evolution, present status, and prospects for the future. Each lecture is also published. Awarded annually. First awarded in 1992. Formerly: (2002) Distinguished Lectureship.

• 20163 • **Pyke Johnson Award**
For recognition of an outstanding paper selected for publication by TRB in the field of transportation systems planning and administration. A certificate may be awarded annually. Established in 1971 in honor of Pyke Johnson, the 23rd chairman of the Highway Research Board.

• 20164 • **D. Grant Mickle Award**
For recognition of an outstanding paper selected for publication by TRB in the field of operation, safety, and maintenance of transportation facilities. A certificate may be awarded annually. Established in 1976 in honor of D. Grant Mickle, the fifth executive director who became the 33rd chairman.

• 20165 • **John C. Vance Award**
For recognition of an outstanding paper selected for publication by TRB in the field of transportation law. A certificate may be awarded annually. Established in 1979 in honor of John C. Vance, who served with distinction as the Board's Counsel for Legal Research.

• 20166 • **K. B. Woods Award**
For recognition of an outstanding paper selected for publication by TRB in the field of design and construction of transportation facilities. A certificate may be awarded annually. Established in 1971 in honor of K.B. Woods, the 19th Chairman of the Highway Research Board.

• 20167 •
Travel Air Club
R. L. Taylor, Contact
PO Box 127
Blakesburg, IA 52536
Phone: (641)938-2773
Fax: (641)938-2093
E-mail: antiqueairfield@sirisonline.com

• 20168 • **Best Travel Air**
Annual award of recognition. Selection is based on votes by members.

• 20169 •
Travel and Tourism Research Association
P O Box 2133
Boise, ID 83701
Phone: (208)429-9511
Fax: (208)429-9512
E-mail: info@ttra.com
Home Page: http://www.ttra.com

Formerly: (1980) Travel Research Association.

• 20170 • **Boeing Student Research Award**
For recognition of a paper submitted by a graduate student for the Travel Research Contest. All university students at the graduate or undergraduate level may submit papers by February 1. (Doctoral dissertations are not eligible.) Judging is based upon its relationship to tourism, quality of research, creative approach, usefulness and applicability, quality of presentation, and level of research. The following monetary awards are presented: $1,000 and travel expenses to the TTRA Conference for the winner; Merit Award - $250 and conference registration; and three Honorable Mention Awards. Awarded annually. Established in 1965 in honor of Dr. Wesley Ballaine, University of Oregon. Sponsored by Boeing Commercial Airplanes Group. Formerly: (1988) Travel Research Contest.

• 20171 • **William B. Keeling Dissertation Award**
For recognition of the best doctoral dissertation on a subject directly related to the travel/tourism field. To be eligible, an individual must have: a Ph.D. or DBA being earned, or a dissertation completed during the previous three years. A travel/tourism subject, in any related field business, parks and recreation, geography, hospitality, transportation, economics, sociology, etc., is considered. Entries must be submitted by December 1. A monetary award of $1,000 and travel expenses for the winner, and meritorious achievement awards in the form of a certificate to the two runner-up candidates are awarded triennially at the annual conference. Established in 1975 in memory of William B. Keeling, president of TTRA, and a professor at the University of Georgia.

• 20172 • **J. Desmond Slattery Marketing Awards**
For recognition of achievement in the travel marketing field. Entries must be submitted by February 1. Awards are presented in two categories: Educational Category - to recognize a university student enrolled in a degree granting program. The educational institution selects a paper or project to submit. The student whose entry is selected as the winner receives a monetary award of $1,000, a plaque, and a one-year complimentary student TTRA membership. The university or college receives a plaque. Professional Category - to recognize a travel marketing professional for any travel marketing-related program, project, or activity that demonstrates an innovative and significant contribution to travel and tourism marketing. The winning company or individual receives a plaque. Established in 1987 by The Travel and Tourism Association in honor of J. Desmond Slattery, past president.

• 20173 • **TTRA Achievement Award**
To recognize an individual or organization who has made a significant contribution to the TTR organization or to the travel/tourism industry. Nominations from TTRA members are solicited on an annual basis. All nominations must be received on or before February 1. An engraved plaque, a TTRA life membership, and lifetime complimentary annual conference registration are awarded.

• 20174 • **TTRA Travel Research Award**
To recognize an individual or organization responsible for the development of a research technique, the production of significant benefits to the travel/tourism industry, or the application of a research method in a particularly creative manner. Individuals or organizations that developed, produced, or applied such a research ef-

fort during the preceding year are eligible. Documentation of the research effort must be submitted by February 1. A monetary award of $1,000, an engraved plaque, a travel allowance, and registration for the TTRA Annual Conference are awarded.

• 20175 •
Travel Industry Association of America
Susan Cook, VP, Research
1100 New York Ave. NW, Ste. 450
Washington, DC 20005-3934
Phone: (202)408-8422
Fax: (202)408-1255
E-mail: feedback@tia.org
Home Page: http://www.tia.org/Travel/default.asp

• 20176 • **Travel Industry Hall of Leaders**
For recognition of outstanding accomplishment in the travel industry field. To be selected, individuals must have made sustained and distinguished contributions that have had a positive impact on the overall travel and tourism industry. The only individuals ineligible to receive the award are those who have in the past received TIA's Man and Woman of the Year in Travel Award, or the Myron Glazer Award. A framed certificate is presented annually at the TIA Awards Banquet held in October. Established in 1969. Formerly: Man of the Year in Travel; Woman of the Year in Travel.

• 20177 • **Travel Industry Odyssey Awards**
To recognize excellence in travel promotion and public and community service activities in the following categories: Cultural Heritage, Travel Advertising (domestic and international); Travel Marketing (domestic and international); Tourism Awareness; Environment; Travel Facilitation; Education Training; and Employment. Candidates must be members of TIA. The deadline for applications is mid-June. A framed certificate is presented annually at the TIA Awards Banquet held in October. Established in 1967. Formerly: (1991) National Travel Marketing Awards; Discover America National Travel Marketing Awards; (2006) Travel Industry Awards for Excellence.

• 20178 •
Treasure Coast Builders Association
Gail Kavanagh, Exec.VP
6560 S Federal Hwy.
Port St. Lucie, FL 34952
Phone: (561)464-8222
Fax: (561)461-4054
E-mail: info@treasurecoastba.com
Home Page: http://www.tcbuilders.org

• 20179 • **Builder and Associate of the Year**
For association and community service. Recognition award bestowed annually.

• 20180 •
Treasury Board of Canada Secretariat Awards, Recognition and Special Events Dept.
The Leadership Network
Jackson Bldg., 3rd Fl.
122 Bank St.
Ottawa, ON, Canada K1A 0R5
Phone: (613)996-1353
Fax: (613)996-2228
E-mail: tlnweb@hrma-agrh.gc.ca
Home Page: http://www.tbs-sct.gc.ca

• 20181 • **Awards of Excellence**
To recognize individuals and teams within the federal public service for their exceptional performance over an extended period of time or under extraordinary circumstances. A maximum of 12 awards are granted annually. Two awards are allocated specifically to small departments and agencies. The awards consist of an inscribed plaque and represent one of the highest expressions of official tribute beyond departmental award program recognition.

• 20182 • **Head of Public Service Award**
No further information was provided for this edition.

• 20183 • **Outstanding Achievement Award**
(Prix de la Fonction Publique du Canada pour Services Insignes)
To recognize Canadian government employees for exceptional accomplishments that have been in the national interest and for the public good, bringing distinction to the public service. Any career public servant occupying a full-time executive position at the senior management or equivalent level in a federal government organization is eligible for nomination. A citation signed by the Prime Minister of Canada and a work of Canadian art are presented by the Governor General of Canada in the presence of the Prime Minister. A maximum of five awards are presented annually. Established in 1966.

• 20184 •
Tree Care Industry Association
Cynthia Mills CAE, Pres.
The Meeting Place Mall
3 Perimeter Rd., Unit 1
Manchester, NH 03103
Phone: (603)314-5380
Toll-Free: 800-733-2622
Fax: (603)314-5386
E-mail: tcia@treecareindustry.org
Home Page: http://www.treecareindustry.org

• 20185 • **Award of Merit**
To recognize an individual or a firm that has made a unique contribution to the field of commercial arboriculture. Any individual or firm that has a relationship with commercial arboriculture is eligible. A plaque is awarded annually. Established in 1978.

• 20186 •
Trees for Tomorrow
Jim Holperin, Dir.
Natural Resources Specialty School
519 Sheridan St. E
PO Box 609
Eagle River, WI 54521
Phone: (715)479-6456
Phone: (715)479-6457
Toll-Free: 800-838-9472
Fax: (715)479-2318
E-mail: learning@treesfortomorrow.com
Home Page: http://www.treesfortomorrow.com

• 20187 • **M. N. "Mully" Taylor Award**
To recognize individual contributions of service to Trees for Tomorrow for a period of five or more years. A plaque is awarded annually. Established in 1984 to honor M. N. Taylor, the founder of Trees for Tomorrow.

• 20188 • **Trees for Tomorrow Award**
To recognize corporate or organizational contributions of service and financial support over a period of five or more years. A plaque is awarded annually. Established in 1978.

• 20189 •
Tri-City Gang Prevention Task Force
Lucy Mason, Ch.
PO Box 4072
Prescott, AZ 86302-4072
Phone: (928)759-2772
Phone: (928)445-6674

• 20190 • **Gang Prevention Scholarship**
For civics or law enforcement student. Scholarship awarded annually.

• 20191 •
Tri-County Arts Council Gallery
54 Main St.
PO Box 730
Cobleskill, NY 12043
Phone: (518)234-7380
Fax: (518)234-6180
E-mail: schoart@aol.com

• 20192 • **National Small Works Exhibition**
For recognition of achievement in the field of small works. Artwork previously selected for exhibition by juror is not eligible. Works may be submitted in five categories: drawing, painting, prints, mixed media, and sculpture. Artists residing in the United States, Canada, and Mexico may submit slides by April 1. Winners receive cash awards. Awarded annually. Established in 1978.

• 20193 •
Tri-County Specialty Contractors Association
G. Daniel Carson, Exec.Dir.
PO Box 7142
Fort Myers, FL 33911-7142
Phone: (239)945-7142
Fax: (239)949-2764
E-mail: tcsca@comcast.net

• 20194 • **Apprenticeship Awards**
For apprentice performance. Recognition award bestowed annually.

• 20195 •
TRI-M Music Honor Society
Pierre Beelendorf, Dir. Student Programs
1806 Robert Fulton Dr.
Reston, VA 20191
Phone: (703)860-4000
Toll-Free: 800-336-3768
Fax: (703)860-9143
E-mail: pierreb@menc.org
Home Page: http://www.menc.org/tri-m

• 20196 • **Master Musician Award**
Recognizes outstanding musicianship. A certificate is awarded annually. Application deadline is April 30. Established in 1971. All applicants must be members of Tri-M.

• 20197 • **National Chapter of the Year**
Awarded for outstanding Tri-M chapter participation. A trophy is awarded. Application deadline is April 30. All applicants must be members of Tri-M.

• 20198 • **State Chapter of the Year Award**
Awarded for outstanding Tri-M chapter participation at the state level. A certificate is awarded annually. Application deadline is April 30. All applicants must be members of Tri-M. Established in 2002.

• 20199 • **Tri-M Leadership Award**
Awarded for outstanding leadership. A certificate is awarded annually. Application deadline is April 30. The award was established in 1954. All applicants must be members of Tri-M.

• 20200 • **Tri-M Service Award**
Recognizes outstanding service. A certificate is awarded annually. Application deadline is April 30. Established in 2003. All applicants must be members of Tri-M.

• 20201 •
Tri-State Bird Rescue and Research
110 Possum Hollow Rd.
Newark, DE 19711
Phone: (302)737-9543
Fax: (302)737-9562
E-mail: giftsandmembership@tristatebird.org
Home Page: http://www.tristatebird.org

• 20202 • **Summer Study Grants**
Veterinary medicine students are eligible. Inquire for application details.

• 20203 •
Trial Lawyers for Public Justice
Jonathan Hutson, Communications Dir.
1717 Massachusetts Ave. NW, Ste. 800
Washington, DC 20036
Phone: (202)797-8600
Fax: (202)232-7203
E-mail: tlpj@tlpj.org
Home Page: http://www.tlpj.org

• 20204 • **Trial Lawyer of the Year Award**
The award is best owned annually upon the trial lawyer(s) who made the greatest contribution to the public interest by trying or settling a precedent-setting case in the past year. It is the single most prestigious honor given to trial lawyers. The deadline for nominations is April 1 for cases that were tried or settled in the preceding 12 months. Established in 1983.

• 20205 •
Triple Crown Productions, Inc.
Steve Sexton, Pres.
Churchill Downs
700 Central Ave.
Louisville, KY 40208-1200
Phone: (502)636-4405
Fax: (502)636-4439
E-mail: triplecrown@kyderby.com
Home Page: http://www.churchilldowns.com

• 20206 • **Triple Crown Trophy**
The Triple Crown stands unchallenged as the pinnacle of success in Thoroughbred racing. The task of winning the Kentucky Derby at Churchill Downs, Louisville, Kentucky; The Preakness Stakes at Pimlico, Baltimore, Maryland; and The Belmont Stakes at Belmont Park, New York within a five-week span is sufficiently testing to bestow the accolade of greatness upon any 3-year-old able to accomplish the feat. The Belmont Stakes, the oldest of the Triple Crown events, was inaugurated in 1867, just two years after the end of the Civil War. The Preakness came into being in 1873 and the Kentucky Derby in 1875; since then, only 11 horses have been able to win the three races. Sir Barton became the first to sweep the three races in 1919. In 1950, the Thoroughbred Racing Association commissioned a special Triple Crown trophy, which also was presented retroactively to previous winners of the three races.

• 20207 • **VISA Triple Crown Challenge**
To guarantee a total of $5 million in prize money to a Triple Crown Champion. An entry fee of $600 by the first deadline January 18, or $6,000 by the second deadline, March 29 is required. Triple Crown Productions, Inc. pays to the owner of a horse winning all of the races the amount necessary to bring total earnings for the Triple Crown winner to $5 million. The total includes the winner's purse distributed by each racing association and a further bonus guaranteed by Triple Crown Productions to reach the $5 million total. Officials of VISA USA are on hand for a special presentation to the VISA Triple Crown Challenge winner following the running of the Belmont Stakes. Established in 1987. Formerly: (1996) Chrysler Triple Crown Challenge.

• 20208 •
Trout Unlimited
Charles F. Gauvin, Pres./CEO
1300 N 17th St., Ste. 500
Arlington, VA 22209
Phone: (703)522-0200
Phone: (703)284-9401
Toll-Free: 800-834-2419
Fax: (703)284-9400
E-mail: trout@tu.org
Home Page: http://www.tu.org

• 20209 • **Distinguished Service Award**
To recognize individuals for outstanding service to Trout Unlimited.

• 20210 • **Gold Trout Award**
To recognize a chapter for the most outstanding conservation activities of the year. In addition, a Silver Trout is awarded to a chapter in each region for conservation activities.

• 20211 • **Trout Conservationist of the Year**
To honor distinguished and dedicated service to the cause of the cold water fishery resource and the improvement and perpetuation of the recreational qualities of fishing on the American continent. Individuals are eligible in three categories: professional; communications; layman or nonprofessional. Wooden plaques with a medal plate showing fisherman on water are awarded annually. Established in 1963.

• 20212 •
Trout Unlimited Canada
Doug Cressman, CEO
PO Box 6270, Sta. D
Calgary, AB, Canada T2P 2C8
Phone: (403)221-8360
Toll-Free: 800-909-6040
Fax: (403)221-8368
E-mail: tuc@tucanada.org
Home Page: http://www.tucanada.org

• 20213 • **Bill Griffiths Memorial Conservation Award**
Recognizes outstanding contribution to fisheries conservation. Awarded annually.

• 20214 •
Trout Unlimited, Naugatuck Valley
Daniel Kenny, Contact
17 Galpin St.
Naugatuck, CT 06770
Phone: (203)723-4837
Phone: (203)574-5587
E-mail: djkenny@msn.com
Home Page: http://www.tu.org/

• 20215 • **Kathern Mathies Grant**
For past performance on local scale. Monetary award bestowed biennially.

• 20216 •
Troy Rotary Club
Margaret Poupard, Pres.
3001 W Big Beaver, Ste. 610
Troy, MI 48084-3107
Phone: (248)528-3400
Phone: (810)268-9440

• 20217 • **Paul Harris Award**
For community service. Recognition award.

• 20218 • **Troy Rotary Scholarship Awards**
For academic achievement. Scholarship awarded annually.

• 20219 •
Truck Renting and Leasing Association
Peter Vroom, Pres. & CEO
675 N Washington St., Ste. 410
Alexandria, VA 22314-1939
Phone: (703)299-9120
Fax: (703)299-9115
E-mail: pvroom@trala.org
Home Page: http://www.trala.org

• 20220 • **Driver of the Year**
To encourage professional development of all drivers and to promote safe, professional truck driving. Selection is by nomination and application. A plaque and a check are awarded annually. Established in 1987.

• 20221 •
Trudeau Institute
Susan L. Swain, Pres. and Dir.
154 Algonquin Ave.
Saranac Lake, NY 12983
Phone: (518)891-3080
Fax: (518)891-5126
E-mail: info@trudeauinstitute.org
Home Page: http://www.trudeauinstitute.org

• 20222 • **Local Community College Award**
Inquire for application details.

• 20223 • **Science Award**
Recognizes an outstanding local high school. Inquire for application details.

• 20224 •
Harry S. Truman Good Neighbor Award Foundation
PO Box 26746
Shawnee Mission, KS 66225-6746
Phone: (913)722-1211
Fax: (913)722-1211
E-mail: pfarrell@trumanaward.org
Home Page: http://www.trumanaward.org

• 20225 • **Scholarships**
Five scholarships are awarded annually to underwrite the exchange of students between the United States and other countries for educational purposes. Established in 1985 in memory of deceased officers of the Foundation.

• 20226 • **Harry S. Truman Good Neighbor Award**
To honor a distinguished individual for contributions to promoting goodwill, not only in this country, but also throughout the world. The honoree is selected by the Awards' Advisory Board. In 1985, the International Good Neighbor Award was presented to a citizen of another country. A bronze bust of President Truman mounted on a Missouri marble base, a leather bound Truman photo album with 50 historical photos of Mr. Truman, and a framed plaque done in gold-leaf calligraphy with the name of the honoree and award-winning attributes are awarded annually on May 8, the birthday of former President Truman. Established in 1973.

• 20227 • **Truman Silver Veteran's Medal**
To recognize a veteran. Selection is made by the Foundation's Veterans Committee. Awarded annually on May 8th, the birthday of former President Truman. Established in 1973.

• 20228 •
Richard Tucker Music Foundation
Peter H. Carwell, Exec.Dir.
1790 Broadway, Ste. 715
New York, NY 10019
Phone: (212)757-2218
Fax: (212)757-2347
Home Page: http://www.richardtucker.org

• 20229 • **Career Grants**
To encourage professional vocal music development. The candidate must be an American born and recommended by a professional, such as a conductor or a director. Applications are not accepted. Four monetary grants of $7,500 each are awarded annually. Established in 1981. The grant honors the late Richard Tucker, a famous Metropolitan Opera tenor, and his interest in young singing talent.

• 20230 • **Richard Tucker Award**
To recognize a vocal artist on the brink of a world-class career. The candidate must be American born and nominated by a professional, such as a conductor or a director. A singer may not apply. A monetary award of $30,000 is conferred annually. Established in 1978. The award honors the late Richard Tucker, a famous Metropolitan Opera tenor, and his interest in young singing talent.

• 20231 • **Sarah Tucker Study Grants**
To assist singers at the start of their careers, having just completed a conservatory or graduate school program. Singers may be at the apprentice level in a company. Four study grants of $5,000 each are awarded.

• 20232 •
Tucson Arts Brigade
Michael Schwartz, Dir.
PO Box 545
Tucson, AZ 85702-0545
Phone: (215)935-4289
E-mail: artbrigade@aol.com
Home Page: http://www.tucsonartsbrigade.org

• 20233 • **Youth Arts Awards**
For youth ages 4-17. Recognition award bestowed annually.

• 20234 •
Tulsa Library Trust
400 Civic Ctr.
Tulsa, OK 74103
Phone: (918)596-7977
Fax: (918)596-7990
E-mail: trust@tulsalibrary.org
Home Page: http://www.tulsalibrary.org

• 20235 • **American Indian Festival of Words Author Award**
To recognize nationally acclaimed American Indian authors, for their vision and contribution to contemporary American Indian Writing. A monetary prize of $5000 and a bronze medallion are awarded every second year. Established in 2001. Sponsored by the Tulsa Library Trust and Tulsa City-County Library System.

• 20236 • **Peggy V. Helmerich Distinguished Author Award**
To recognize nationally acclaimed authors who have written a distinguished body of work and made a major contribution to the field of literature and letters. A monetary prize of $25,000 and an engraved crystal book are awarded annually. Established in 1985 by the Tulsa Library Trust. Sponsored by the Tulsa Library Trust and the Tulsa City - County Library System.

• 20237 • **Anne V. Zarrow Award for Young Readers' Literature**
To recognize nationally acclaimed authors who have made a significant contribution to the field of literature for children and young adults. A monetary prize of $5,000 and an engraved crystal book are awarded annually. Established in 1991. Sponsored by the Tulsa Library Trust and Tulsa City - County Library System. Formerly: Tulsa Library Trust Award for Young Readers' Literature.

• 20238 •
Turkish Studies Association
Jenny B. White, Contact
Dept. of Anthropology
Boston University
232 Bay State Rd.
Boston, MA 02215
Phone: (617)353-7709
E-mail: jbwhite@acs.bu.edu
Home Page: http://www.h-net.org/~thetsa

• 20239 • Omer Lutfi Barkan Article Prize
To recognize the best article in the area of Turkish and Ottoman studies published in a two-year period. A $300 monetary prize is awarded biennially in odd-numbered years.

• 20240 • Halide Edib Adivar Scholarship Citation
Intended to introduce undergraduate students who have not had extensive experience to Turkey and Turkish studies. The value of the scholarship is $750.

• 20241 • Sydney N. Fisher Graduate Student Paper Prize
To recognize the best paper written by a graduate student in Turkish or Ottoman studies during the academic year. A $200 monetary prize is awarded annually.

• 20242 • M. Fuat Koprulu Book Prize
To recognize the best book in the area of Turkish and Ottoman studies published in a two-year period. A $500 monetary prize is awarded biennially in odd-numbered years.

• 20243 • James W. Redhouse Student Prize
To recognize students in each of four regions of the United States and Canada who have made the best progress in Turkish in the academic year. Any student (graduate or undergraduate) who has completed a full one-year course at any level of modern or Ottoman Turkish at a university offering such courses in its regular program may be nominated. Four prizes of $100 each are awarded annually.

• 20244 •
Tuskegee United Women's League
Amelia W. Peterson, Sec./Treas.
PO Box 830097
Tuskegee, AL 36083-0097
Phone: (334)727-4840
Fax: (334)727-4482

• 20245 • Thomas Reed Memorial Scholarship
For a student with at least a C average (2.0-2.9 GPA). Scholarship awarded annually.

• 20246 •
TVR Car Club North America
Marshall Moore, Pres.
3559 Overbrook Dr.
Roanoke, VA 24018
Phone: (540)772-0952
E-mail: tvrccna@cox.net
Home Page: http://www.tvrccna.org

Formerly: (1989) TVR Car Club of England.

• 20247 • Trevor Award
For recognition of a TVR automobile that has been maintained as close to original factory condition as possible, regardless of the original year of manufacture. TVR Car Club members who are present at the annual national meet, "Woodwork" (the full name of the meet is "Out of the Woodwork") are eligible. An engraved silver cup is awarded annually at the national meet. Established in 1990 by the ruling committee of the TVR Car Club North America. Formerly: David - Gerald Award.

• 20248 •
Twin Cities Musicians Union, Local 30-73
Thomas W. Baskerville, Sec.-Treas.
Itasca Building
708 First St. North, Ste. 243
Minneapolis, MN 55401-1145
Phone: (612)338-5013
Fax: (612)338-5018
E-mail: tcmu@mn.rr.com
Home Page: http://www.tcmu.com

• 20249 • Amy L. Bloom Memorial Scholarship Fund
For less than college age music students who are recommended by music teachers and who have been accepted to summer music camp programs. Scholarship awarded annually.

• 20250 •
Two/Ten International Footwear Foundation
Peggy Kim Meill, Pres.
1466 Main St.
Waltham, MA 02451
Phone: (781)736-1500
Toll-Free: 800-FIND-210
Fax: (781)736-1555
E-mail: pmeill@twoten.org
Home Page: http://www.twoten.org

Formerly: (1990) Two/Ten Foundation.

• 20251 • A. A. Bloom Memorial Award
For recognition of service to the Two/Ten Foundation and commitment in the spirit of the late A.A. Bloom. A shoeperson active within the Two/Ten Foundation may be nominated. A crystal trophy is awarded at the annual dinner meeting. Established in 1969 in memory of A.A. Bloom, a founder of the Two/Ten Foundation.

• 20252 • T. Kenyon Holly Memorial Award
To recognize an individual in the footwear industry who exemplifies humanitarian characteristics similar to the late Ken Holly. Members of the footwear industry and allied industries who have demonstrated outstanding involvement, charitable giving, and commitment to civic, regional, and national community needs and concerns are eligible. A bronze trophy is awarded annually. Established in 1949 to honor T. Kenyon Holly, a former Two/Ten president and charter member.

• 20253 •
UCLA Alumni Association
James West Alumni Center
Box 951397
Los Angeles, CA 90095-1397
Phone: (310)825-4321
Toll-Free: 800-UCL-ALUM
Fax: (310)825-8678
E-mail: alumni@uclalumni.net
Home Page: http://www.uclalumni.net

• 20254 • Ralph Bunche Memorial Award
To honor an individual whose demonstrated altruism reflects the humanity of Ralph Bunche. Consideration for this award is based on how the individual's life has affected a community, however large or small, without regard to personal wealth or fame. The honoree does not have to be an alumnus of UCLA. A plaque containing the names and brief statement of the achievement recognized is displayed near the Ralph Bunche Memorial. Awarded as merited. The award may be given posthumously. Established in 1971 upon the death of Ralph Bunche '27, Nobel Peace Laureate and Alumnus of the Year for 1949.

• 20255 • Community Service Award
To honor those who have a record of distinguished volunteer service to their communities. Alumni must be nominated. A maximum of two awards are bestowed annually at the special ceremony. Established in 1967.

• 20256 • Edward A. Dickson Alumnus of the Year Achievement Award
To honor an individual who has rendered a special and outstanding service to UCLA or who, by his or her personal achievement, has brought honor and distinction to the University. Alumni of UCLA are eligible. Awarded annually at a special ceremony. Established in 1946.

• 20257 • Distinguished Teaching Award
To honor distinguished teachers. Five awards are presented. At least one is to be presented to a non-tenured faculty member; one is for distinction in graduate teaching; and one is designated the Harvey L. Eby Memorial Award for the Art of Teaching. Each recipient of the award receives a $6,000 honorarium. Established in 1961. Sponsored by the UCLA Alumni Association.

• 20258 • Honorary Alumnus Award
For recognition of individuals whose unique contributions singularly qualify them for special recognition as members of the UCLA community and family. The award entitles the recipient to all the benefits of Alumni Association membership except the holding of office in The Alumni Association. This award, first presented in 1954, is bestowed only on the rare occasion when deemed appropriate.

• 20259 • Outstanding Graduate Student Award
To honor general achievement and service, thus offering recognition to graduate students whose talents and contributions might not otherwise be

Awards are arranged in alphabetical order below their administering organizations

noted. General criteria for the award are: scholastic achievement, exceptional initiative and service, evidence of significant creative academic contribution, and evidence of exceptional initiative and interest in community/public service. Each recipient receives a life membership to the Alumni Association and a $500 honoraria. A maximum of two awards are presented annually. Established in 1983.

• 20260 • Outstanding Senior Award
To recognize and honor achievements of distinguished graduating seniors. Awards are granted based on academic excellence, creativity within academic department and outstanding service to the University and fellow students. All recipients of the Outstanding Senior Award receive the Chancellor's Service Award. Each recipient is presented with a Life Membership in the UCLA Alumni Association and a senior class ring. Established in 1966 and instituted by the Alumni Association.

• 20261 • Professional Achievement Awards
To honor individuals for a distinguished record of achievement in their professional fields. Alumni of UCLA must be nominated. Several awards are presented annually at a special ceremony. Established in 1962.

• 20262 • Public Service Award
To recognize alumni who have distinguished themselves or the University while being elected, appointed, commissioned, charged, or otherwise involved in addressing public sector or governmental needs. Alumni of UCLA must be nominated. One award is presented annually at a special ceremony. Established in 1982.

• 20263 • University Service Awards
To honor those who have a record of outstanding service to the University. Alumni, members of the staff or faculty, or friends of the University may be nominated. Awards are bestowed annually at a special ceremony. Established in 1962.

• 20264 •
Ucross Foundation
Chip Lawrence, Chm.
30 Big Red Ln.
Clearmont, WY 82835-9712
Phone: (307)737-2291
Fax: (307)737-2322
E-mail: info@ucross.org
Home Page: http://www.ucrossfoundation.org

• 20265 • Ucross Foundation Artists-in-Residence Program
To encourage professional development and provide time and space to pursue individual work or collaborative projects. Applications are accepted by March 1 for fall sessions and October 1 for spring sessions. Up to 60 awards of room, board, and studio space for two weeks to two months are awarded annually. Established in 1983.

• 20266 •
Uglies Unlimited
Danny McCoy, Founder
1906 Juniper Ln.
Lufkin, TX 75904
Phone: (936)634-1429
Fax: (936)675-5169
E-mail: dannymccoy@cox-internet.com

• 20267 • Ugly Stick
To recognize an individual for outstanding programs that enhance ugly awareness and lead to less discrimination. Individuals who are 18 years of age and older are eligible. Nominations must be submitted by September 15 of each year. A plaque is awarded annually at the convention. Established in 1973.

• 20268 •
Ukrainian Congress Committee of America
Michael Sawkiw Jr., Pres.
203 2nd Ave.
New York, NY 10003
Phone: (212)228-6840
Phone: (212)228-6841
Fax: (212)254-4721
E-mail: info@ucca.org
Home Page: http://www.ucca.org

• 20269 • Shevchenko Freedom Award
Recognizes supporters of Ukrainian independence. Awarded quadrennially.

• 20270 •
Ukrainian Institute of America
Walter Nazarewicz, Pres.
2 E 79th St.
New York, NY 10021
Phone: (212)288-8660
Fax: (212)288-2918
E-mail: mail@ukrainianinstitute.org
Home Page: http://www.ukrainianinstitute.org

• 20271 • Ukrainian of the Year Award
Annual award of recognition.

• 20272 •
Ukrainian National Women's League of America
Iryna Kurowyckyj, Pres.
203 2nd Ave.
New York, NY 10003
Phone: (212)533-4646
Phone: (212)477-0039
Fax: (212)533-5237
E-mail: unwla@unwla.org
Home Page: http://www.unwla.org

• 20273 • Award of Recognition
Recognizes literary works dealing with Ukrainian history and historical fiction. Awarded annually.

• 20274 • UNWL Scholarship
For needy student in South America and Europe.

• 20275 •
Ukrainian Philatelic and Numismatic Society
Dr. Ingert Kuzych-Berezovsky, Pres.
PO Box 3
Springfield, VA 22150-0003
Fax: (703)569-0223
E-mail: ingert@starpower.net
Home Page: http://www.upns.org

• 20276 • Best UKRAINPEX Show Theme Exhibit
To recognize the best exhibit featuring the UKRAINPEX convention-exhibit theme. Exhibits entered in UKRAINPEX are eligible. A monetary award of $25 is awarded annually at the UKRAINPEX convention-exhibit. Established in 1982.

• 20277 • Wes Capar Award
To encourage Ukrainian-related philatelic and numismatic exhibiting. Exhibits that have received an award in a United States or foreign philatelic or numismatic exhibition are eligible. Photocopies of the exhibit must be submitted to the Ukrainian Philatelic and Numismatic Society one month prior to the convention. A plaque for first prize and certificates for all entries are awarded annually at the UKRAINPEX convention. Established in 1985 and renamed in 1988 to honor the society's foremost exhibit promoter. Formerly: Golden Trident.

• 20278 • Eugene Kotyk Award
To recognize the best articles in the *Ukrainian Philatelist* journal. Balloting is open to all society members. A certificate is awarded annually. Established in 1987 in honor of Eugene Kotyk, the first editor of the journal.

• 20279 • Julian Maksymczuk Award
To recognize individuals or societies for a contribution to Ukrainian philately and numismatics. Nominations may be submitted by anyone. The decision is made by the Ukrainian Philatelic and Numismatic Society Executive Board. A certificate is awarded annually at the UKRAINPEX convention. Established in 1984 in memory of Julian Maksymczuk, a society founder, author, and a promoter of Ukrainian philately and numismatics.

• 20280 •
Ultimate Players Association
Sandie Hammerly, Exec.Dir.
741 Pearl St., Side Ste.
Boulder, CO 80302
Phone: (303)447-3472
Toll-Free: 800-872-4384
Fax: (719)447-3483
E-mail: ed@upa.org
Home Page: http://www.upa.org

• 20281 • UPA National Championships
Award of recognition. Given for sectional regional competition annually.

• 20282 • UPA Spirit of the Game Awards
Recognizes sectional regional national competition and sportsmanship. Awarded annually.

• 20283 •
Ultrasonic Industry Association
Fran Rickenbach CAE, Exec.Dir.
PO Box 2307
Dayton, OH 45401-2307
Phone: (937)586-3725
Fax: (937)586-3699
E-mail: uia@ultrasonics.org
Home Page: http://www.ultrasonics.org

• 20284 • Award of Recognition
Recognizes significant contribution to the ultrasonic industry. Individuals are eligible.

• 20285 •
Underfashion Club
Janet A. Malecki, Pres.
326 Field Rd.
Clinton Corners, NY 12514
Phone: (845)758-6405
Fax: (845)758-2546
E-mail: underfashionclub@aol.com
Home Page: http://www.underfashionclub.org

• 20286 • Femmy
Recognizes leaders of the intimate apparel industry. Awarded annually.

• 20287 • Underfashion Club Scholarship Program
Awarded to graduating high school and/or current college students who have committed themselves to courses of study progressing toward careers in or peripheral to the Initimate Apparel industry.

• 20288 •
Undersea and Hyperbaric Medical Society
Donald R. Chandler, Exec.Dir.
PO Box 1020
Dunkirk, MD 20754
Phone: (410)257-6606
Fax: (410)257-6617
E-mail: uhms@uhms.org
Home Page: http://www.uhms.org

Formerly: Undersea Medical Society, Inc..

• 20289 • Albert R. Behnke, Award
To recognize outstanding contributions toward advancement in the undersea or hyperbaric biomedical field. Members of the society are eligible. A plaque, citation, and honorarium are awarded annually when merited. Established in 1969.

• 20290 • Craig Hoffman Memorial Award
To recognize a significant contribution to diving safety. An honorarium and a plaque are awarded at the annual meeting when merited. Established in 1978.

• 20291 • Oceaneering International Award
For recognition of outstanding contributions to the commercial diving industry in the areas of increased productivity or performance of the working diver. Specific consideration is given to the practical application of biomedical knowledge to the solution of problems encountered in diving operations. Members of the society are eligible. A plaque and honorarium are awarded annually when merited. Established in 1975.

• 20292 • Charles W. Shilling Award
To recognize outstanding contributions to the goals of the society. Teachers who educate the diving community and the public about the science and practice of diving medicine and related fields, research managers who support diving science, and patrons who lend financial and emotional support to the diving community are eligible. An honorarium and a plaque are presented at the annual meeting. Established in 1982.

• 20293 •
Underwater Society of America
Carol Rose, Pres.
PO Box 628
Daly City, CA 94017
Phone: (650)583-8492
Phone: (408)286-8840
Fax: (650)583-0614
E-mail: croseusoa@aol.com
Home Page: http://www.underwater-society.org

• 20294 • All American Dive Team
To promote national competitions annually in free diving spearfishing, scuba skill and spearfishing, underwater hockey, underwater photography, fin swimming, and underwater rugby. Each discipline has a method to determine their top competitors, and all these men and women comprise the All American Dive Team each year. From each All American Dive Team, each sports director chooses one man and one woman athlete of the year; selection is based on performance for the year and service to their sport. Selections are submitted to the Executive Committee by October 1 annually. The initial selection year was 1989. The Executive Committee selects from the nominated Men and Women Athletes of the Year, one man and one woman athlete; selection is based on performance and service to their sport and to the society. These athletes are then nominated to the United States Olympic Committee as the Underwater Society of America Underwater Athletes of the Year. The first Underwater Athletes were selected in 1989.

• 20295 • NOGI Awards
To recognize outstanding individuals who have exemplified themselves as leaders and contributors in the areas of Arts, Science, Sports/Education, and Distinguished Service to the world underwater. The nominations and the voting are made by the previous recipients of the NOGI. Statues are awarded annually in each of the four categories. Established in 1960 by the founder of the awards system, Mr. Jay Albanese, Jr. Additional information is available from NOGI USA, 4545 Holmes, Kansas City, MO 64100.

• 20296 • Regional Diver of the Year Award
To encourage and give local recognition to divers in the eight Society regions who have demonstrated leadership in the field of the underwater Arts, Science, Sports or Education, and Distinguished Service. A plaque is awarded annually. Established in 1981 by Armand Zigahn.

• 20297 •
Unicycling Society of America
Tom Daniels, Pres.
PO Box 790
North Bend, WA 98045
Phone: (425)831-4906
Phone: (425)830-6951
Fax: (425)831-4906
E-mail: thomasdaniels@earthlink.net
Home Page: http://www.unicycling.org/usa

• 20298 • National Unicycle Meet Top Point Winners
Event winners are recognized at the annual North American Unicycling Championships. Only members in good standing of the Unicycling Society of America, Inc. who register for the events are eligible to compete. Individuals are awarded medals for winning their age group in the following events: 100 meter, 400 meter, 800 meter, and 1500 meter track races; slow forward and slow backward races; 50 meter one foot track race; 30 meter walk-the-wheel track races; obstacle course; individual freestyle; pairs freestyle; group freestyle; standard skill. Medals and trophies are also presented to the overall winners in these categories: North American racing champions, North American Individual Freestyle champions, North American Standard Skill champions, North American Group champions, North American Junior Group champions, North American Club Show champions, and North American Parade Champions. Awards are bestowed to the best male and the best female athlete in each category.

• 20299 •
UNIMA-U.S.A., American Center of the Union Internationale de la Marionnette
Marianne Tucker, Pres.
1404 Spring St. NW
1404 Spring St., NW
Atlanta, GA 30309-2820
Phone: (404)873-3089
Fax: (404)873-9907
E-mail: unima@mindspring.com
Home Page: http://www.unima-usa.org

• 20300 • UNIMA Citation for Excellence in the Art of Puppetry
To acknowledge excellence in puppetry and, in this way, to list and honor the best shows in the country. Puppet shows done by a solo performer, group, child or adult are eligible. UNIMA citations designed by Brad Williams are awarded annually. Established in 1975.

• 20301 • UNIMA-USA Scholarships
To encourage professional development in the art of puppetry. U.S. puppeteers of professional level who are accepted for study abroad may submit applications by December 15. A monetary award is paid to the accepting school of puppetry. Awarded annually. Must be an UNIMA-USA member to be eligible. Established in 1981.

• 20302 •
Union des Ecrivaines et Ecrivains Quebecois
Stanley Pean, Pres.
3492 rue Laval
Montreal, QC, Canada H2X 3C8
Phone: (514)849-8540
Toll-Free: 888-849-8540
Fax: (514)849-6239
E-mail: ecrivez@uneq.qc.ca
Home Page: http://www.uneq.qc.ca

• 20303 • Prix Emile-Nelligan
For recognition of poetry published for the first time during the preceding year. Works of poetry, written in French by a North American poet who is 35 years of age or less, are eligible. A monetary prize of $5,000 and a medal are awarded annually. Established in 1979. Sponsored by Fondation Emile-Nelligan.

• 20304 • Prix Gilles - Corbeil
For recognition of the total literary work of a living writer from Canada or the United States. Works considered must be written in French. A monetary prize of $100,000 is awarded triennially. Established in 1990 to honor Gilles Corbeil, a prominent Montreal gallery-owner. Administered by La Fondation Emile-Nelligan, 261, rue Bloomfield, Quebec, Canada, H2V 3R6; telephone (514)522-0652.

• 20305 •
Union of Councils for Jews in the Former Soviet Union
Micah H. Naftalin, Dir./Sec.
Cleveland Park
PO Box 11676
Washington, DC 20008
Phone: (202)237-8262
Fax: (202)237-2236
E-mail: mnaftalin@ucsj.com
Home Page: http://www.fsumonitor.com
Formerly: (1993) Union of Councils for Soviet Jews.

• 20306 • Anatoly Scharansky Freedom Award
To recognize individuals for their commitment to and participation in the fight for freedom of Soviet Jews. Individuals with outstanding dedication and achievement in support of freedom of emigration and human rights for Soviet Jews are eligible. A plaque is awarded at the UCSJ Annual Meeting. Established in 1982 in honor of Anatoly Scharansky, Soviet Jewish Prisoner of Conscience, who was released in 1986.

• 20307 •
Unitarian Universalist Association of Congregations
Janet Hayes, Information Officer
25 Beacon St.
Boston, MA 02108
Phone: (617)742-2100
Fax: (617)637-3237
E-mail: info@uua.org
Home Page: http://www.uua.org

• 20308 • Distinguished Service to the Cause of Unitarian Universalism
To recognize a Unitarian Universalist who, over a considerable period of time, has strengthened the denomination. Awarded annually. Established in 1949. Formerly: (1991) Distinguished Service to the Cause of Liberal Religion.

• 20309 • Holmes - Weatherly Award
For recognition of that person or group whose pursuit of social justice best exemplifies the liberal religious, activist spirit and societal impact of John Haynes Holmes and Arthur L. Weatherly. A monetary prize of $500 is awarded annually. Established in 1951 in honor of two ministers who were the founders in 1908 of the Unitarian Fellowship for Social Justice: Rev. John Haynes Holmes and Rev. Arthur L. Weatherly.

• 20310 • Angus H. MacLean Award
For recognition of excellence and outstanding achievement in the field of religious education within the past year. The deadline is April 1. A monetary prize of $250 is awarded annually. Established in 1971 to honor Angus H. MacLean.

• 20311 • Frederic G. Melcher Book Award
For recognition of excellence and outstanding career achievement in the field of liberal religious education. A monetary award of $2000 and a citation are awarded annually. The deadline is March 15. Established in 1964 to honor Frederic G. Melcher, dean of American publishers.

• 20312 • Skinner Sermon Award
To recognize a minister, religious educator or a lay person for a sermon best expressing Unitarian Universalist's social principles. Criteria employed in judging include: grasp for the subject, religious depth, originality, conviction, and understanding of other perspectives. Also considered are prophecy and timeliness, courage, personal involvement, orientation and inspiration. The deadline is March 1. A monetary prize of $250 is awarded annually. Established in 1958. Formerly: (2006) Clarence R. Skinner Award.

• 20313 • Unsung Unitarian Universalist Award
To recognize a person or group whose actions express and inspire Unitarian Universalist ideals, and who is not generally eligible for recognition within the framework of other awards. The degree of service and prior recognition is important. The deadline is April 15. Established in 1973.

• 20314 •
Unitarian Universalist Service Committee
Kim McDonald, Senior Assoc. for Programs
130 Prospect St.
Cambridge, MA 02139-1845
Phone: (617)868-6600
Fax: (617)868-7102
E-mail: programs@uusc.org
Home Page: http://www.uusc.org

• 20315 • James Luther Adams Award
Award of recognition. Inquire for application details.

• 20316 • Banner Award
Annual award of recognition. Open only to membership.

• 20317 • Social Action Leadership Award
Awarded annually for UUSC volunteer work on human rights issues.

• 20318 • Vision of Justice Sermon Award
Recognizes a sermon that exemplifies UUSC's commitment to justice issues worldwide.

• 20319 •
United Cerebral Palsy Association of Central Minnesota
Judy Moening, Exec.Dir.
510B 25th Ave. N
St. Cloud, MN 56303
Phone: (320)253-0765
Toll-Free: 888-616-3726
Fax: (320)253-6753
E-mail: info@ucpcentralmn.org
Home Page: http://www.ucpcentralmn.org

• 20320 • Post-Secondary Scholarship
For persons diagnosed with cerebral palsy, resident of Benton, Sherburne, or Stearns county, for post-secondary education. Scholarship awarded annually.

• 20321 •
United Cerebral Palsy Association of Metropolitan Detroit
23077 Greenfield, Ste. 205
Southfield, MI 48075
Phone: (248)557-5070
Fax: (248)557-4456

• 20322 • Empowerment Award
Given by random drawing to eligible individuals. Monetary award bestowed annually.

• 20323 •
United Church of Christ Coordinating Center for Women in Church and Society
700 Prospect Ave.
Cleveland, OH 44115
Phone: (866)822-8224
Fax: (216)736-2156
Home Page: http://www.ucc.org

• 20324 • Antoinette Brown Award
To lift up the gifts and the ministries of ordained women. A medal is presented biennially at the General Synod. Established in 1975 by the Task Force on Women to honor Antoinette Brown, the first woman in the United States to be ordained.

• 20325 •
United Citizens and Neighborhoods
R.J. Williams, Pres.
5311 E Idlewood Ct.
New Orleans, LA 70128-2951

• 20326 • Community Service Leadership Award
For individual demonstrating active participation in local community work. Monetary award bestowed annually.

• 20327 •
United Commercial Travelers of America, Butler Council 465
Marilyn K. Stephenson, Secretary-Treasurer
303 Old Plank Rd.
Butler, PA 16002
Phone: (724)287-7938
E-mail: mks303@zbzoom.net

• 20328 • Butler Council No. 465, UCT Scholarship Award
For a student entering the field of special education. Scholarship awarded annually.

• 20329 •
United Daughters of the Confederacy
Mrs. Winfred D. Cope, Pres.Gen.
UDC Business Office
328 North Blvd.
Richmond, VA 23220-4009
Phone: (804)355-1636
Fax: (804)353-1396
E-mail: hqudc@rcn.com
Home Page: http://www.hqudc.org

• 20330 • Mrs. Simon Baruch University Award
Awarded for the best unpublished book or monograph of high merit in the field of Southern history in or near to the period of the Confederacy, or bearing upon the causes that led to secession and the War Between the States. Anyone who has received a Master's, Doctor's, or other advanced degree within the past fifteen years from a university or college in the United States, or any graduate student whose thesis or dissertation has been accepted by such an institution is eligible. Manuscripts must be received by May 1 in odd-numbered years. thought, accuracy of statement, and excellence of style. Studies must be presented in scholarly form and based, at least in part, upon primary sources, with the usual documentation and bibliography. Manuscripts are judged by three outstanding historians, drawn from different sections of the country, who make recommendations to the Chairman of the Committee. A monetary prize of $2,000 and $500 author's award are awarded biennially, in even-numbered years. Established in 1927. Additional information is available from UDC Business Office, 328 North Blvd. Richmond VA 23220-4057.

• 20331 •
United Engineering Foundation
Dr. David L. Belden, Exec.Dir.
PO Box 70
Mount Vernon, VA 22121-0070
Phone: (973)244-2328
Fax: (973)882-5155
E-mail: engfnd@aol.com
Home Page: http://www.uefoundation.org

• 20332 • AAES-EF Engineering Journalism Awards
To recognize outstanding reporting of an event or issue furthering the public's understanding of engineering. Awards of $5,000 are given in each of the following categories: daily newspapers, other general circulation print media, and broadcast or television. Applications deadline January 31.

• 20333 •
United Hellenic Voters of America
Dr. Dimitrios Kyriazopoulos, Supreme Chm.
525 W Lake St.
Addison, IL 60101
Phone: (630)628-0820
Phone: (630)686-0600
Fax: (708)543-7001
E-mail: uhva@smartbiz.net
Home Page: http://www.smartbiz.net/uhva

• 20334 • UHVA Awards
Awards are issued in the following categories: Legislator of the Year, Man of the Year, and Most Distinguished Greek American. Five plaques are awarded annually in October. Established in 1974. For more information, contact Dr. D. Kyriazopoulos.

• 20335 •
United in Group Harmony Association
Ronald Italiano, Founder/Pres.
PO Box 185
Clifton, NJ 07015-0185
Phone: (973)365-0049
Phone: (973)470-UGHA
Fax: (201)365-2665
E-mail: ugha@verizon.net
Home Page: http://www.ugha.org

• 20336 • Hall of Fame Awards
To recognize achievements in American vocal group musical history. Categories include: honorary, industry, literary, and humanitarian. Awarded annually with a plaque. Established in 1990.

• 20337 •
United Israel World Union
James D. Tabor, Pres.
PO Box 561476
Charlotte, NC 28256
Phone: (704)841-3689
E-mail: info@unitedisrael.org
Home Page: http://www.unitedisrael.org

• 20338 • Humanitarian-Brotherhood Award
Recognizes activity in human rights. Awarded annually.

• 20339 •
United Jewish Appeal - Federation of Jewish Philanthropies of New York
Dr. John S. Ruskay, Exec.VP/CEO
130 E 59th St.
New York, NY 10022
Phone: (212)980-1000
Phone: (212)836-1486
Fax: (212)836-1778
E-mail: contact@ujafedny.org
Home Page: http://www.ujafedny.org

• 20340 • Hurowitz Award
To recognize outstanding cooperative programming involving social work and the religious community. Rabbis and professional social workers who have initiated and implemented major programs involving cooperation and new dimensions of communal relationships are eligible. Citations are awarded annually. Established in 1950.

• 20341 • Joseph Reiss Memorial Judaica Library Awards
To recognize one professional librarian and one volunteer for efforts to foster and encourage interest in and appreciation of Jewish literature. The award consists of a plaque and is presented annually by the Task Force on Art and Literature in Jewish life of the UJA-Federation Commission on Synagogue Relations. Established in 1986.

Awards are arranged in alphabetical order below their administering organizations

• 20342 • Tzedakah Award
For outstanding communal service on behalf of the city's religious Jewish community. Lay or professional leaders affiliated with UJA - Federation's Commission on Synagogue Relations who have achieved a significant breakthrough in Commission programming and furthered its efforts city-wide are eligible. Plaques are awarded annually. Established in 1955.

• 20343 • UJA - Federation Distinguished Communal Service Award
To recognize significant communal service by a lay leader or in one or more of the UJA - Federation's fields of service city-wide. A scroll is awarded annually. Established in 1950.

• 20344 •
United Kennel Club
Wayne R. Cavanaugh, Pres.
100 E Kilgore Rd.
Kalamazoo, MI 49002-5584
Phone: (269)343-9020
Fax: (269)343-7037
E-mail: stickley@ukcdogs.com
Home Page: http://www.ukcdogs.com

• 20345 • Distinguished Service Award
To recognize individuals who by word, deed, exemplary conduct, public communication and professional excellence promote the best interest of the sport of dogs. A monetary prize of $500 and a plaque are awarded annually. Established in 1985.

• 20346 • Hunting Retriever Champion
To recognize the natural and trained qualities of a Hunting Retriever and to provide a gene pool for future generations for the improvement of these breeds. Dogs compete against a recognized, established standard. Points are awarded in three categories: started, seasoned, finished. These points are accumulated toward the title of Champion. A Championship Certificate is awarded upon completion of the required hunt tests. Established in 1984. Co-sponsored by United Kennel Club and Hunting Retriever Club.

• 20347 •
United Methodist Association of Health and Welfare Ministries
Rev.Dr. Mearle L. Griffith CAE, CEO/Pres.
407 Corporate Center Dr., Ste. B
Vandalia, OH 45377
Phone: (937)415-3624
Toll-Free: 800-411-9901
Fax: (937)222-7364
E-mail: info@umassociation.org
Home Page: http://www.umassociation.org

Formerly: (1983) National Association of Health and Welfare Ministries of the United Methodist Church.

• 20348 • Administrator of the Year
To give recognition to four administrators of United Methodist-related agencies that have exhibited outstanding leadership abilities in the field of service that their agencies represent. Nominations may be made by any peer administrator, a board of directors, or chairperson of the nominee's institution or agency; conference leadership chairperson of the nominee's annual conference; or staff from a general agency of the UMC. The nominee must come from an organization that is a member of the Association. The following administrative categories are awarded annually at the National Convention Awards Assembly: older adult ministries; children, youth and family services section; community-based ministries; and hospitals and hospitals section. A wooden plaque with an inscribed metal plate is awarded annually. Established in 1970.

• 20349 • Chaplain of the Year
To give recognition to United Methodist Chaplains who have discharged their responsibilities with exemplary skill and dedication. The organization of the nominee must be a current member of the United Methodist Association. A wooden plaque is awarded annually at the National Convention Awards Assembly. Established in 1970.

• 20350 • Hall of Fame in Philanthropy
To recognize a member of a United Methodist-related organization's governing board, auxiliary, volunteer group or an interested individual who has made significant financial or personal service contributions to a United Methodist-related organization. Employees of a United Methodist organization are not eligible. Awarded annually at the Association's national convention.

• 20351 • Organization of the Year
To honor organizations that have provided outstanding community service programs. Applications nominating an organization must contain evidence of these programs, the need for this kind of new and/or continuing service, and of acceptance of these services by the community and the clients. Programs must have begun within the last 10 years and have a two-year operational record. Awarded annually at the Association's national convention.

• 20352 • Public Relations/Development/ Marketing/Director of the Year Award
To recognize those directing and administering public relations/development/marketing departments of institutions which are current members of the United Methodist Association of Health and Welfare Ministries. Eligible candidates include those who have worked for at least three years in the public relations/development/marketing field, view their position as a Christian vocation, and are recognized for their accomplishments to the institution in public relations/ development/marketing. Nominations may be made by the chairperson of the Board of Trustees, the administrator of the institution submitting the recommendation, or a peer public relations worker. Established in 1981. Formerly: Public Relations Award.

• 20353 • Trustee of the Year
To recognize trustees and boards of directors members at an Association member organization that has given at least six years of service and views such service as part of a Christian ministry. Nominee's contribution to the organization must have been in "service" rather than "finance." They must have shown consistent evidence of personal dedication of time and talent and must understand the concept of the organization's broadened service to the community. Awarded annually at the Association's national convention.

• 20354 • United Methodist Association Award of Distinguished Service
For recognition of distinguished service. The Association gives an award recognizing Distinguished Service by a Local Church Congregation and the Special Recognition Award. Nominations may be made by current members or individuals who are part of an institution, or annual conference leadership that is an Association member. Awarded annually at the National Convention Awards Assembly. Established in 1983.

• 20355 • Volunteer of the Year/Volunteer Group of the Year
To give national recognition to an individual and/ or group of persons for voluntary contributions in the direct service of others through a United Methodist related organization. Any person or group of persons (regardless of denominational affiliation) is eligible for nomination who: engages in regular unpaid volunteer service within an organization that is a current member of the Association rendering service to staff or persons being served by the institution; works on a regular voluntary basis outside the agency for the benefit of the organization; or has given a minimum of 1,000 hours in service to the organization. Awarded annually at the National Convention Awards Assembly. Established in 1975.

• 20356 •
United Methodist Church, Board of Global Ministries
Health and Welfare Ministries Division
475 Riverside Dr., Ste. 330
New York, NY 10115
Phone: (212)870-3871
Toll-Free: 800-UMC-GB6M
Fax: (212)870-3624
E-mail: hwmin@gbgm-umc.org
Home Page: http://gbgm-umc.org/health

• 20357 • Conference Chairperson of the Year
To give national recognition to the diligent work of leaders at the conference level of church organization for their efforts in support of United Methodist Health and Welfare Ministries. A wooden plaque is awarded annually. Formerly: Conference Division Chairman Award.

• 20358 • Institution of the Year
To give national recognition to an outstanding United Methodist institution which exemplifies high quality of professional service under the auspices of the Conferences. A wooden plaque with an engraved metal plate is awarded annually at the National Convention. Established in 1970.

• 20359 •
United Nations
Kofi Annan, Sec.Gen.
First Ave., 46th St.
New York, NY 10017
Phone: (212)963-4475
Fax: (212)963-0071
E-mail: inquiries@un.org
Home Page: http://www.un.org

• 20360 • **United Nations Prize in the Field of Human Rights (Prix pour les Droits de l'Homme)**
To recognize individuals and organizations who have made outstanding contributions to the promotion of the protection of human rights and fundamental freedoms. Nominations obtained from member states of the United Nations, specialized agencies, international non-governmental organizations, in consultative status with the Economic and Social Council, are presented to the selection committee composed of the President of the United Nations General Assembly, the President of the Economic and Social Council, the Chairman of the Commission on Human Rights, the Chairman of the Sub-Commission on Prevention of Discrimination and Protection of Minorities, and the Chairman of the Commission on the Status of Women. A citation on a plaque is awarded at intervals of not less than every five years. Established in 1966. Formerly: Human Rights Prize.

• 20361 •
United Nations Association of Rochester
Margaret Corbin, Pres.
494 East Ave.
Rochester, NY 14607
Phone: (585)473-7286
Fax: (585)473-7296
E-mail: unar@frontiernet.net
Home Page: http://www.unar.org

Formerly: (1998) Rochester Association for the United Nations.

• 20362 • **Media Award**
To recognize a local news writer, producer, publisher, broadcaster, reporter, or news organization that has increased the understanding of international affairs. Any person or organization that, at the time of publication or broadcast, was a resident of or had a place of business within Monroe County or one of its contiguous counties is eligible. The deadline for nominations is February 1.

• 20363 •
United Nations Association of the United States of America
Ambassador William H. Luers, Pres./CEO
801 2nd Ave., 2nd Fl.
New York, NY 10017
Phone: (212)907-1300
Fax: (212)682-9185
E-mail: unahq@unausa.org
Home Page: http://www.unausa.org

• 20364 • **U Thant Peace Award**
To acknowledge, appreciate and admire distinguished accomplishments toward the attainment of world peace, one of the major goals of the United Nations. Nominated individuals or organizations must reflect the lofty spiritual ideals of U Thant, the late Secretary-General of the United Nations. Presented by Sri Chinmoy: the Peace Mediation at the United Nations, a group whose members work for the international community in various capacities and have made an additional personal commitment by holding regular meditations for world peace. Nominations are offered by members of the Peace Meditation Group. Established in 1982. Awarded when merited. Some previous recipients include Dr. Jorge Illueca, President of the 38th Session of the United Nations General Assembly and the President of Panama; Mr. James Grant, the late Executive Director of UNICEF; Mother Teresa; President Mikhail Gorbachev; Archbishop Desmond Tutu and President Nelson Mandela of South Africa. Additional information is available from Nilima Silver, Programme Coordinator, Sri Chinmoy: The Peace Meditation at the United Nations, PO Box 20, Rm. DN-1406, New York, NT 10163.

• 20365 •
United Nations Association of the U.S.A.
Ambassador William H. Luers, Pres./CEO
801 2nd Ave., 2nd Fl.
New York, NY 10017
Phone: (212)907-1300
Fax: (212)682-9185
E-mail: unahq@unausa.org
Home Page: http://www.unausa.org

• 20366 • **Arnold Goodman Award**
For recognition of outstanding leadership among chapters and divisions of UNA-USA. Nomination is by peers. A framed certificate and gift are awarded annually. The winner's name is added to a permanent plaque located at the national headquarters. Established in 1981 by the Council of Chapter and Division Presidents of UNA-USA in memory of Arnold Goodman.

• 20367 •
United Nations Population Fund
Thoraya Obaid, Exec.Dir.
Committee of the UN/Population Award
220 E 42nd St.
New York, NY 10017
Phone: (212)297-5000
Fax: (212)370-0201
E-mail: dungus@unfpa.org
Home Page: http://www.unfpa.org

• 20368 • **United Nations Population Award**
For recognition of the most outstanding contributions to the awareness of population questions or to their solutions by an individual, individuals or an institution. Each nominator may submit no more than one nomination, either for an individual or an institution, by December 31. The award consists of a monetary prize, a gold medal, and a diploma. Presented annually in June by the United Nations Secretary-General at a ceremony at the United Nations Headquarters. Established in 1981 by the United Nations General Assembly.

• 20369 •
United Press International
Dr. Chung Hwan Kwak, Pres./Chm.
1510 H St. NW
Washington, DC 20005
Phone: (202)898-8000
Toll-Free: 800-796-4874
Fax: (202)898-8057
E-mail: sales@upi.com
Home Page: http://www.upi.com

• 20370 • **Helen Thomas Unipresser Award**
For recognition of excellence in reporting by UPI staff members and stringer-correspondents. A monetary prize of $1,500 is awarded annually. Established in 1991.

• 20371 • **UPI National Broadcast Awards**
To recognize excellence in broadcast journalism. Awards are given to both small and large television and radio stations in the following categories: (1) Outstanding Spot News; (2) Outstanding Newscast; (3) Outstanding Sports Coverage; (4) Outstanding Feature; (5) Outstanding Documentary; (6) Outstanding Videography; and (7) Outstanding Reporting/Individual Achievement. UPI clients are eligible. Judging is carried out by broadcasters from different regions of the country. Engraved UPI statues are awarded annually. Established in 1980.

• 20372 •
United Seamen's Service
Talmage E. Simpkins, Pres.
125 Maiden Ln., 14th Fl.
New York, NY 10038
Phone: (212)269-0711
Fax: (212)269-5721
E-mail: ussammla@ix.netcom.com
Home Page: http://www.uss-ammla.com

• 20373 • **Admiral of the Ocean Sea**
For recognition of distinguished service to American Flag shipping. A silver statue of Columbus is awarded annually. Established in 1970.

• 20374 • **AOTOS Mariner's Plaque**
For outstanding seamanship in rescue operations at sea by officers and crews. An engraved plaque is awarded. Established in 1971. Formerly: Andrew Furuseth Award.

• 20375 • **Benjamin Castleman Award**
For a pathologist or pathologist-in-training under 40 years old who has written an outstanding paper on human pathology in English. A monetary award is given annually.

• 20376 • **Council's Distinguished Pathologist Award**
Recognizes an individual who has made a major contribution to pathology over the years.

• 20377 • F. K. Mostofi Distinguished Service Award
Recognizes outstanding service to the Academy and the International Academy of Pathology. Only members are eligible. Awarded annually.

• 20378 • Mariner's Rosette
For recognition of conspicuous bravery and outstanding seamanship. Individuals who have been cited for bravery by the Maritime Administration or by ships' companies are eligible. A lapel button or tie tack and certificates are awarded annually. Established in 1971.

• 20379 • Ocean Crew and Great Lake Crew Award of Merit
Recognizes contributions to AMMLA.

• 20380 • Stowell-Orbison Awards for Pathologists-in-Training
For authors of outstanding papers. A monetary prize is given.

• 20381 •
United States Air Force Academy
Lt. Gen. John F. Regni, Supt.
2304 Cadet Dr.
USAF Academy, CO 80840
Phone: (719)333-1110
Toll-Free: 800-443-9266
Fax: (719)333-3647
E-mail: webmaster@usafa.af.mil
Home Page: http://www.usafa.af.mil

• 20382 • Thomas D. White National Defense Award
To recognize an individual who has contributed significantly to the national defense and security of the United States. Any specific field of endeavor such as science, technology, management, national affairs, international affairs, or a combination thereof will be considered. Only under special circumstances will government employees (active military, civil service, or statutory appointees) currently on the Federal payroll are not eligible for nomination. Former military, civil service, and statutory appointees are eligible upon termination from government service. Qualifying contributions made both in and out of government service will be considered. A deceased citizen may be nominated and, if selected, posthumously presented the award if death occurred during the period since nominations were made for the last annual award (normally the end of the previous calendar year). A trophy and a citation are presented, and the name of the recipient is inscribed on a plaque in Arnold Hall at the USAF Academy. Awarded annually. Established in 1962.

• 20383 •
United States Amateur Boxing, Inc.
Lamont Jones, Exec.Dir.
One Olympic Plz.
Colorado Springs, CO 80909
Phone: (719)866-4506
Fax: (719)632-3426
E-mail: astampley@usaboxing.org
Home Page: http://www.usaboxing.org

Formerly: (1991) United States of America Amateur Boxing Federation.

• 20384 • Boxer of the Year
To recognize the outstanding boxer of the year. Amateur boxers who are registered with USA Boxing are eligible. A plaque is awarded at the annual meeting. Established in 1978.

• 20385 • Coach of the Year
To recognize an outstanding achievement in coaching. Registered members of USA Boxing are eligible. A plaque is awarded at the annual meeting. Established in 1969.

• 20386 • Official of the Year
To recognize outstanding achievement/contributions by an official. USA Boxing members are eligible. A plaque is awarded at the annual meeting. Established in 1978.

• 20387 • Outstanding Progress Award
To recognize outstanding progress in amateur boxing. Local Boxing Committees who have shown growth in membership and events in their local area are eligible. A plaque is awarded when merited at the annual meeting. Established in 1985.

• 20388 • United States Boxing Hall of Fame
For recognition of achievement/contributions to the sport of boxing. Members of USA Boxing are eligible. A plaque is awarded at the annual meeting. Established in 1967.

• 20389 • Dr. Ray Wesson Memorial Physician of the Year Award
To recognize the contributions and efforts of a physician within the amateur boxing community. Physicians who are members of USA Boxing and who work within or contribute to amateur boxing are eligible. A plaque is awarded at the annual convention. Established in 1980 in memory of Dr. Ray Wesson of Ocean Springs, MS, who was killed in the plane crash on March 14, 1980, that claimed the lives of a 22-member USA delegation to Warsaw, Poland. Formerly: (1981) Physician of the Year.

• 20390 •
United States Amateur Confederation of Roller Skating
Richard Hawkins, Exec.Dir.
4730 South St.
Lincoln, NE 68506
Phone: (402)483-7551
Fax: (402)483-1465
E-mail: rhawkins@usarollersports.org
Home Page: http://www.usarollersports.org

• 20391 • United States National Roller Skating Championships
Amateur competitions for men, women, and children held in various cities and venues on regional, and national levels. The competition is held in the following major categories: Artistic skating - dance, figures, pairs, and singles; Conventional and In-Line Speed skating; and In-Line Roller Hockey skating - ball hockey and puck hockey. Awarded annually.

• 20392 •
U.S. Aquatic Sports
Chuck Wielgus, Exec.Dir.
1 Olympic Plz.
Colorado Springs, CO 80909
Phone: (719)866-4578
Fax: (719)866-4669
Home Page: http://www.usaquatic.org

• 20393 • Athlete of the Year Award
Recognizes the athlete who has made the most significant contribution to the sport during the year.

• 20394 • Coach of the Year Award
Awarded annually. Selection is made by the Coach of the Year Sub-committee.

• 20395 • Lillian MacKeller Distinguished Service Award
Recognizes an individual who has given unselfishly to synchronized swimming without thought of personal gain, and with a particular emphasis on working for the benefit of the athlete.

• 20396 • Glenn McCormick Memorial Diving Award
Recognizes outstanding contributions to the sport of Diving. Awarded annually. Established in 1969.

• 20397 • Moose Moss Age Group Diving Coach of the Year Award
Recognizes the outstanding Age Group Diving Coach in the United States. Awarded annually.

• 20398 • Outstanding Women in Swimming Award
Recognizes years of outstanding service to swimming. Women involved in the sport are eligible. Established in 1979.

• 20399 • Mike Peppe Award
Recognizes an outstanding Senior Diving Coach in the United States. Awarded annually. Established in 1979.

• 20400 • David Yorzyk Memorial Award
Recognizes the swimmer who performs the most outstanding 400 yard Individual Medley at Short Course.

• 20401 •
United States Arms Control and Disarmament Agency
Foster Fellow Visiting Scholars Program
Office of the Chief Science Advisor
320 21st St. NW
Washington, DC 20451
Phone: (202)647-4153
Home Page: http://dosfan.lib.uic.edu/acda/aboutacd/foster1.htm

• 20402 • William C. Foster Fellows Visiting Scholars Program
To give specialists in the physical sciences and other disciplines relevant to the Agency's activities an opportunity for active participation in the arms control and disarmament activities of the Agency and to gain for the agency the perspective and expertise such scholars can offer. The emphasis is on the expertise and service that the visiting scholars can provide rather than on general interest in arms control and the pursuit of the scholars' own research. Visiting scholars must be citizens or nationals of the United States and on the faculty of a recognized institution of higher learning. Desirable attributes for a candidate would include an understanding of the role of arms control in national security planning, familiarity with weapons characteristics and capabilities, knowledge of political-military conditions in developing regions, a highly-developed analytical ability, and facility in written and oral communications. Candidates must obtain a top secret security clearance before entering on duty. The deadline is January 31. Awarded annually. Established in 1984 to honor the first Director of ACDA, William C. Foster, who served from the inception of ACDA in 1961 to 1969.

• 20403 • Hubert H. Humphrey Doctoral Fellowships in Arms Control and Disarmament
To encourage specialized training and research in the arms control field. The fellowships are intended for the support of advanced graduate students who have completed all of their Ph.D. requirements, except for the doctoral dissertation. Candidates for the J.D. degree (law) are also eligible for fellowships during their third year. The program is open only to applicants who are citizens or nationals of the United States at the time of application. Students across the range of academic disciplines including, but not limited to, political science, economics, law, sociology, psychology, physics, chemistry, biology, engineering, philosophy, public policy, operations research, and area studies may apply. Research proposals should be designed to contribute to a better understanding of current and future arms control and disarmament issues. Although special attention will be paid to research with direct policy or technical implications, innovative theoretical or empirical efforts will also be considered. Historical, quantitative, and policy analyses are all appropriate for this program. The relevance of the research to arms control issues and policy is an essential criterion. The application deadline is March 15. Awards are for the 12-month period beginning September 1 or January 1. For these fellowships, each fellow receives a stipend of $8,000. In addition, ACD pays any applicable tuition and fees for one year, up to a maximum of $6,000, to the institution in which the fellow is enrolled. For J.D. candidates, who, unlike Ph.D. candidates, do not devote a full year to research, the fellowship stipend of $8,000 and the tuition grant of up to $6,00 will be prorated by dividing the number of credits assigned to the writing of the J.D. paper by the total number of credits required to be taken by the fellow's law school; in no case, however, shall the tuition be less than 20 percent of the tuition charged by the law school. Established in 1979 and named in honor of the late Senator Humphrey, who fostered the Agency and its goals throughout his career in the U.S. Senate.

• 20404 •
United States Army Corps of Engineers
441 G St. NW
Washington, DC 20314
Phone: (202)761-0011
Phone: (202)761-0001
Fax: (202)761-1683
Home Page: http://www.usace.army.mil

• 20405 • Chief of Engineers Design and Environmental Awards Program
To recognize excellence in the design of, or environmental achievement related to, recently completed structures or area developments by the Corps of Engineers Field Operating Agencies and their professional design contract firms. To provide an incentive for design and environmental professionals to develop new projects which will exhibit excellence in function, economy, resource conservation, aesthetics and creativity, while being in harmony with the environment. Recognition is given to the Corps of Engineers District which is responsible for design, and to the private sector design firm, if one has been retained by the District. Both civil works and military construction projects are eligible, as long as they have been completed within three years of the date of the award. The awards are presented in two major categories: civil works, and military programs; and on three levels: Chief of Engineers Award of Excellence, Award of Merit and Honor Award. Plaques are awarded to the District Engineer and to the designing firm in each category. Awarded annually. Established in 1965.

• 20406 •
U.S. Association for Blind Athletes
Mark Lucas, Exec.Dir.
33 N Institute St.
Colorado Springs, CO 80903
Phone: (719)630-0422
Phone: (719)630-0610
Fax: (719)630-0616
E-mail: mlucas@usaba.org
Home Page: http://www.usaba.org/

• 20407 • Arthur E. Copeland Award
To recognize a person(s) or organization that has done the most to promote sports for the blind and visually impaired. Member athletes may be nominated. A plaque is awarded annually at the national games. Established in 1985 in honor of Arthur E. Copeland.

• 20408 • Arthur E. Copeland Scholarship
To provide financial assistance to a male USABA member based on athletic participation and academic achievement. Legally blind scholar/athletes, active with the association during the current year, and entering or already in an academic, vocational, technical, professional, or certification program at the postsecondary level may submit applications by October 1. A monetary award of $500 is presented annually. Established in 1988 to honor Arthur and Helen Copeland, who founded USABA in 1976 and are instrumental in blind sports.

• 20409 • Helen Copeland Scholarship
To provide financial assistance to a female USABA member based on athletic participation and academic achievement. Legally blind scholar/athletes, active with the association during the current year, and entering or already in an academic, vocational, technical, professional, or certification program at the postsecondary level may submit applications by October 1. A monetary award of $500 is presented annually. Established in 1988 to honor Arthur and Helen Copeland, who founded USABA in 1976 and are instrumental in blind sports.

• 20410 • Disabled Athletes of the Year
To recognize and honor disabled athletes for athletic and community achievement. Two awards are presented: Male Athlete of Year and Female Athlete of Year. Members of USABA may be nominated by the USABA Executive Committee. A plaque, travel, and housing expenses to attend the banquet are awarded annually. Established in 1988 by the Colorado Amateur Sports Corporation.

• 20411 •
United States Association of Former Members of Congress
Peter M. Weichlein, Exec.Dir.
233 Pennsylvania Ave. SE, Ste. 200
Washington, DC 20003-1121
Phone: (202)543-8676
Fax: (202)543-7145
E-mail: admin@usafmc.org
Home Page: http://www.usafmc.org

• 20412 • **Distinguished Service Award**
To recognize an individual for distinguished public service to the United States. The selection is made by the Board of Directors and is rotated annually between Democratic and Republican recipients. Established in 1974.

• 20413 •
United States Auto Club
Rollie Helmling, Pres.
4910 W 16th St.
Speedway, IN 46224
Phone: (317)247-5151
Fax: (317)247-0123
E-mail: johnny@usaracing.com
Home Page: http://www.usacracing.com

• 20414 • **Jim Blunk Memorial Award**
For recognition of contributions to the sport of USAC Midget racing. Established in 1971 in memory of Jim Blunk, USAC Midget Series Steward.

• 20415 • **Bob Stroud Memorial Rookie of the Year Award National Midget Car Div.**
For the series' top rookie driver basedon performance participation, and professionalism. Awarded annually. Established in 1969. Sponsored by the USAC Motoring Div.

• 20416 • **Jimmy Caruthers Memorial Award**
To recognize the USAC Championship Series driver who, in the past season, has exhibited the spirit and determination of the late Jimmy Caruthers. This award was previously presented to the USAC Championship Division Rookie of the Year. Formerly: Jimmy Caruthers Memorial Championship Rookie Driver of the Year Award.

• 20417 • **Eddie Edenburn Trophy**
To honor individuals for contribution to racing, not for the year of the award but throughout their lives. A trophy is awarded annually. Established in 1939 by Mrs. E.D. Edenburn in memory of her husband, Eddie Edenburn, Chief Steward of the Indianapolis 500 from 1919 until his death in 1935.

• 20418 • **Diana Fell Gilmore - Woman Behind the Scenes Award**
To recognize the woman behind the scenes in the sport of auto racing who best exemplifies the dedication, support, and undying spirit of Diana Fell Gilmore. Established in 1980.

• 20419 • **Ross Hadley Memorial Achievement Award**
To recognize an individual for contributions to the United States Auto Club, and the sport of auto racing. Presented by the USAC Winners Circle Club. Established in 1985.

• 20420 • **Jostens Most Improved National Midget Championship Series Driver Award**
To recognize the National Midget Championship Series driver demonstrating the most improvement over previous years' performances. Established in 1976.

• 20421 • **Roger McCluskey Award of Excellence**
To recognize the individual who best represents standards of excellence in the sport of auto racing. Presented annually. Established in 1993 in memory of USAC executive and former champion driver, Roger McCluskey.

• 20422 • **Mechanic of the Year Award**
Recognizes a USAC mechanic as selected by USAC officials. Based on performance and professionalism. Awarded annually. Established in 1999. Sponsored by Weld Racing.

• 20423 • **Most Improved Championship Driver Award**
To recognize the licensed Silver Crown championship division driver demonstrating the most improvement over the previous year's performances. A monetary prize of $1,000 and a replica trophy are awarded annually. Established in 1976. Formerly: Shaler Company's Rislone Most Improved Championship Driver Award; (1998) STP Most Improved Championship Driver Award.

• 20424 • **Most Improved Driver Award**
To recognize the licensed Sprint Car Championship Series driver demonstrating the most improvement over previous years' performances. Established in 1993. Formerly: (1998) Most Improved Sprint Car Driver Award; (1998) Water Solutions Unlimited Most Improved Sprint Car Driver.

• 20425 • **Jack O'Neal Safety Award**
To recognize outstanding contributions to auto racing safety by an individual or a company. Awarded when merited. Established in 1956. Formerly: Continental Casualty Award.

• 20426 • **Race Organizer of the Year**
For recognition of the outstanding race organizer of the year. Established in 1983. Formerly: Promoter of the Year.

• 20427 • **Rookie of the Year Award National Sprint Care Div.**
Recognizes a rookie diver basn on performance, participation and professionalism. Awarded annually by the USAC. Established in 1981. Sponsored by True Value Hardware Stores.

• 20428 • **Rookie of the Year Award Silver Crown Div.**
Presented to the series' top rookie driver based on performance, participation and professionalism. Awarded annually. Established in 1981. Sponsored by Oliver Trucking.

• 20429 • **USAC Special Recognition Awards**
To recognize a company or individuals who have demonstrated their interest in USAC racing by significant contributions to the overall racing fraternity rather than selected racing teams, and through five or more years of active participation and dedication to the betterment of the sport of USAC auto racing. Awarded when merited. Established in 1974.

• 20430 •
United States BASE Association
Jean Boenish, Dir.
12619 Manor Dr.
Hawthorne, CA 90250-4313
Phone: (310)676-1935

• 20431 • **BASE Award**
For recognition of an individual's achievement in the sport of BASE jumping (jumping off fixed objects with parachutes). To qualify, an individual must dive off a building, a (antenna) tower, a span, and an earth formation, hence the acronym BASE. All jumps must involve the use of a parachute as a life-saving device that is not inflated prior to the jump. The award consists of the assignment of an officially-recorded BASE jumper number. BASE patches and certificates are offered. Established in 1981.

• 20432 •
U.S. Bicycling Hall of Fame
941 E Main St.
Bridgewater, NJ 08807
Phone: (732)356-7016
E-mail: usbhof@optonline.net
Home Page: http://www.usbhof.com

• 20433 • **U.S. Bicycling Hall of Fame**
To recognize an individual for achievement as a competitor and contributor to the national cycling scene. A competitor must be retired for five years or eligible for age group competitions. Contributors must have been active on the national scene for a minimum of ten years. A plaque is awarded annually on Memorial Day weekend. Established in 1986 as a permanent institution devoted to the past, present, and future of bicycling in America.

• 20434 •
United States Billiard Association
Jerome Karsh, Pres.
650 Cherry St.
Denver, CO 80246-5016
Phone: (303)433-6000
Phone: (303)433-6000
Fax: (303)825-8800
E-mail: jkarsh@karshcpa.com
Home Page: http://www.usbilliardassn.org

Formed by merger of: Billiard Federation of the United States of America; American Billiard Association.

• 20435 • U S Open Three Cushion Billiard Championships

To recognize outstanding billiard players. The field is open but limited to the first 32 qualified entries. Players must be current members of USBA. Awards totaling $30,000 and trophies are presented annually at local and national tournaments.

• 20436 •
U.S. Boomerang Association
Clay Dawson, Pres.
3351 236th St., SW
Brier, WA 98036-8421
Phone: (425)643-6298
Toll-Free: (740)363-8332
E-mail: clayton.dawson@honeywell.com
Home Page: http://www.usba.org

• 20437 • Competition Honors

To recognize U.S. National Champions in various competitive events and overall titles. Computer rankings determine the top throwers in competitions. Awarded annually. Established in 1982.

• 20438 • President's Award

For recognition of distinguished service. A plaque is awarded when merited. Established in 1985.

• 20439 •
U.S. Cancellation Club
Roger Rhoads, Sec.-Treas.
6160 Brownstone Ct.
Mentor, OH 44060
E-mail: rrrhoads@aol.com
Home Page: http://www.geocities.com/Athens/2088/uscchome.htm

• 20440 • Charles D. Root Memorial Award

For recognition of contributions to philately, particularly cancellations. A plaque and certificate are awarded. Established in 1981 in honor of Charles D. Root.

• 20441 •
U.S. Catholic
Claretians Ministries
Rev. John Molyneux, Ed.
205 W Monroe St.
Chicago, IL 60606
Phone: (312)236-7782
Toll-Free: 800-328-6515
Fax: (312)236-8207
E-mail: editors@uscatholic.org
Home Page: http://www.uscatholic.org

• 20442 • *U.S. Catholic* Award

To recognize individuals for furthering the cause of women in the church. Nominations may be submitted to the editors of the national magazine, *U.S. Catholic* by December 31. Awarded annually at a special luncheon. Established in 1978.

• 20443 •
U.S. Census Bureau
4700 Silver Hill Rd.
Washington, DC 20233-0001
E-mail: pio@census.gov
Home Page: http://www.census.gov

• 20444 • Census Award of Excellence

To recognize the extra efforts, exceptional contributions, and/or innovative ideas that have substantially advanced the goals of the Bureau of the Census through the employee's exceptional performance. Employees in grades 10 and below who have a minimum of two years service at the Bureau of the Census and have a current performance rating of meets expectations are eligible. A monetary award of $5000 and a certificate are awarded annually. Established in 1986.

• 20445 •
United States Chess Federation
Beatriz Marinello, Pres.
PO Box 3967
Crossville, TN 38557
Phone: (931)787-1234
Toll-Free: 800-903-8723
Fax: (931)787-1200
E-mail: beatchess@aol.com
Home Page: http://www.uschess.org

• 20446 • U.S. Chess Championship

For recognition of the winner of the U.S. Chess Championship. The competition is held annually. Monetary prizes are awarded. Established in 1845.

• 20447 •
U.S. Committee for Scientific Cooperation With Vietnam
Dr. Judith L. Ladinsky, Pres.
1760 Medical Science Center
1300 University Ave.
Madison, WI 53706
Phone: (608)263-4150
Phone: (608)262-0895
Fax: (608)262-2327
E-mail: jlladins@facstaff.wisc.edu

• 20448 • Kovaleskaia Award

Recognizes the best woman scientist and female research group in Vietnam. Awarded annually.

• 20449 • Vietnam Educational Exchange Program

For graduate students from Vietnam and Laos. Awarded annually.

• 20450 • Women in Science Award

Annual award of recognition. Inquire for application details.

• 20451 •
United States Committee of the International Council on Monuments and Sites
Gustavo F. Araoz AIA, Exec.Dir.
401 F St. NW, Rm. 331
Washington, DC 20001-2728
Phone: (202)842-1866
Fax: (202)842-1861
E-mail: info@usicomos.org
Home Page: http://www.icomos.org/usicomos

• 20452 • US/ICOMOS Fellows

For recognition of achievement in international preservation. American scholars, professionals, and civic volunteers who have made notable long-term contributions to the enhancement of the quality of life are eligible. Outstanding accomplishments are recognized in one or more areas of activity, including but not limited to architecture, architectural history, conservation, history, landscape architecture and urban planning. Nominees must be members of US/ICOMOS. Board of Trustee members of US/ICOMOS are not eligible for the designation until three years after the initiation of the Fellow program. Fellows shall serve US/ICOMOS in an advisory capacity as preservation experts, cultural ambassadors, mentors, critics, and friends, and as hosts to other American and foreign preservationists. The Fellow honor is bestowed for life. The designation, "Fellow, US/ICOMOS," following a Fellow's name may be used on correspondence and as an identification as appropriate. A certificate is presented. Fellows are inducted officially at annual meetings. Established in 1983.

• 20453 •
United States Conference of Mayors
J. Thomas Cochran, Exec.Dir.
1620 Eye St. NW
Washington, DC 20006
Phone: (202)293-7330
Fax: (202)293-2352
E-mail: info@usmayors.org
Home Page: http://www.usmayors.org

• 20454 • Award for Distinguished Public Service

To recognize outstanding and meritorious public service at any level of government: federal, state, or local. A bronze medallion is awarded as merited. Established in 1949.

• 20455 • "Buy Recycled" Campaign Awards Program

To recognize mayors who have implemented wide-ranging and creative programs to buy recycled goods. The deadline for applications is May 20. Awards are presented for first place to one city with a population of more than 100,000, one city with a population of less than 100,000, and one city for outstanding achievement. Awarded at the Annual Meeting of the Conference.

Awards are arranged in alphabetical order below their administering organizations

• 20456 • City Livability Awards Program
For recognition of exemplary mayoral leadership in support of any and all city programs that encourage greater quality of life and urban livability. Any Mayor may submit an application based upon guidelines provided by the Conference of Mayors. Plaques and media recognition are awarded annually at the Annual Conference of Mayors Meeting in June. Established in 1979 by U.S. Conference of Mayors and supported by WMX Technologies, Inc. (Waste Management, Inc.).

• 20457 • National City Challenge to Stop Drunk Driving
To challenge cities to implement activities and programs that deter drunk driving and nationally recognize those cities with exemplary anti-DUI efforts. A monetary award of $20,000 is presented to the Grand Prize winners in two categories: cities over 100,000 in population and cities under 100,000 in population. All cities over 30,000 are eligible.

• 20458 •
United States Congress
Committee on Banking, Finance, and Urban Affairs
Domestic and International Monetary Policy
U.S. House of Representatives
Washington, DC 20515
Phone: (202)224-3121
Home Page: http://www.house.gov

• 20459 • Congressional Gold Medal
To recognize individuals for outstanding contributions to society. Nominees must be approved by a vote of the full House and Senate and the resolution must be signed into law by the President. A gold medal, designed for the recipient, is awarded irregularly when merited. First awarded in 1776 to George Washington. Co-sponsored by United States Executive Office of the President.

• 20460 •
United States Council for International Business
Thomas M. T. Niles, Vice Chm.
1212 Ave. of the Americas
New York, NY 10036
Phone: (212)354-4480
Fax: (212)575-0327
E-mail: info@uscib.org
Home Page: http://www.uscib.org

Formerly: (1981) United States Council of the International Chamber of Commerce.

• 20461 • International Leadership Award
To recognize a business leader for outstanding contributions to international trade and investment. A Kaiser porcelain eagle figurine is awarded annually. Established in 1980 at the annual dinner.

• 20462 •
United States Curling Association
David Garber, Exec.Dir.
1100 Center Point Dr.
PO Box 866
Stevens Point, WI 54481
Phone: (715)344-1199
Toll-Free: 888-CUR-LERS
Fax: (715)344-2279
E-mail: info@usacurl.org
Home Page: http://www.usacurl.org

• 20463 • Hall of Fame
To recognize outstanding individuals in the sport of curling. Awarded when merited. Established in 1984.

• 20464 • National Championships
To recognize the national champion team in the following categories: Men, Women, Mixed, Junior Men, and Junior Women. Members of the Association are eligible. A team trophy, individual medals, and patches are awarded in each category annually. The Men's Championship was established in 1957, the Junior Men's in 1974, the Mixed in 1975, the Junior Women's in 1987, and the Women's Championship in 1977.

• 20465 •
United States Department of Army
Civilian Marksmanship Program
Gary Anderson, Dir.
Camp Perry Training Site, Bldg. 3
PO Box 576
Port Clinton, OH 43452
Phone: (419)635-2141
Toll-Free: 888-267-0796
Fax: (419)635-2802
E-mail: custserve@odcmp.com
Home Page: http://www.odcmp.com

• 20466 • National Rifle and Pistol Championship Trophy Match
To recognize excellence in the use of firearms. All U.S. citizens 16 years of age or older, any other persons subject to induction in the U.S. Armed Forces, and all members of the U.S. Armed Forces, Regular and Reserve Components are eligible. Competitors designated distinguished with the arm concerned may enter in only one of the following categories: Regular Service, Reserve, National Guard, Service Academy and Reserve Office Training Corps, Police, Civilian, and Junior, on the basis of individuals or teams. National Trophy Matches are listed as follows: President's Pistol Match, National Trophy Individual Pistol Match, National Trophy Pistol Team Match, President's Rifle Match, National Trophy Individual Rifle Match, National Trophy Rifle Team Match, and National Trophy Infantry Team Match. Fifty-three trophies are awarded annually in the seven Match categories.

• 20467 •
United States Department of Commerce
Carlos Gutierrez, Sec.
Office of Human Resources Management
1401 Constitution Ave. NW
Washington, DC 20230
Phone: (202)482-3919
Fax: (202)482-3160
E-mail: cgutierrez@doc.gov
Home Page: http://www.commerce.gov

• 20468 • Cash-In-A-Flash Award Program
To provide supervisors with a means of recognizing employees for going the extra mile in getting the job done. This small monetary award program provides immediate recognition with minimal documentation. Awards may be granted to employees for noteworthy contributions which have benefited the employing office, the employee's bureau, or the Department. All Commerce employees, except employees in the Senior Executive Service, are eligible for consideration for awards under this program. Individuals and groups are eligible for awards under this program.

• 20469 • Honor Awards Program
To recognize deserving employees for their contributions to the Department. The following awards are given: Gold Medal this award, the highest honorary award given by the Department, is granted by the Secretary for rare and distinguished contributions of major significance to the Department, the Nation, or the world; Silver Medal this award, the second highest honorary award given by the Department, is granted by the Secretary for meritorious contributions of unusual value to the Department or the Nation; and Bronze Medal - this award, the highest award given by an operating unit, is granted by the Secretarial Officer, for significant contributions to that operating unit. Each honor award consists of a medal, lapel emblem, and certificate. Awarded annually. Established in 1948.

• 20470 • On-the-Spot Awards
To recognize accomplishments that represent steps toward achievement of organizational goals or purposes, but for which higher levels of recognition such as honor awards, performance awards, or superior accomplishment awards are not appropriate. Under this program, merchandise items may be granted to employees for noteworthy contributions which have benefited the employing office, the employee's bureau, or the Department. Operating units may implement instant award programs which meet their specific needs and are compatible with their organizational climate. This program is not meant to replace other traditional methods of recognition, but rather to increase supervisors' options in rewarding and reinforcing employee excellence.

• 20471 •
United States Department of Commerce
International Trade Administration
U.S. & Foreign Commercial Service
14th St. & Constitution Ave. NW, Rm. H3128
Washington, DC 20230
Phone: (202)482-6228
Toll-Free: 800-USA-TRADE
Fax: (202)482-3159
E-mail: tic@ita.doc.gov
Home Page: http://www.ita.doc.gov

• 20472 • **President's "E" Award for Exports Program**
To recognize persons, firms, or organizations for significant contributions to increasing U.S. exports, based on the following criteria: efforts that produced a substantial increase in volume of exports over a four-year period and/or produced a breakthrough in particularly competitive markets; efforts that introduced a new product into U.S. export trade; or efforts that opened a trade area previously closed to American products. Exports should constitute a significant portion of total product sales and/or be materially in excess of the industry's average percentage. An "E" flag, a presidential certificate signed by the Secretary of Commerce, and lapel pins are awarded when merited. In addition, the "E" Certificate for export service may be awarded to persons, firms, and organizations that may or may not export directly, but assist or facilitate export efforts through financing, transportation, market promotion, or other export-related services. Nonmanufacturers such as banks, utilities, export firms, chambers of commerce, trade associations, and individuals that promote and assist exporting may receive this award. Established by an Executive Order of the President in 1961.

• 20473 • **President's "E Star" Award**
To recognize noteworthy export promotion efforts by "E" Award winners. The level of performance must exceed that for which the "E" Award was given. An "E Star" flag, a presidential certificate signed by the Secretary of Commerce, and "E Star" lapel pins are awarded when merited. Established in 1969.

• 20474 •
United States Department of Commerce
National Institute of Standards and Technology
Office of Personnel & Civil Rights
100 Bureau Dr., Stop 3460
Gaithersburg, MD 20899-3460
Phone: (301)975-NIST
Toll-Free: 800-437-4385
Fax: (301)948-6107
Home Page: http://www.nist.gov

Formerly: (1988) National Bureau of Standards.

• 20475 • **Applied Research Award**
To recognize superior achievement in the practical application of the results of scientific or engineering research. Any qualified NIST employee or group of employees is eligible. A monetary award of $3,000 and a plaque are awarded annually. Established in 1975 in honor of Dr. Milton Harris, former research associate who funded the original award.

• 20476 • **Allen V. Astin Measurement Science Award**
To recognize outstanding achievement in the advancement of measurement science or in the delivery of measurement services. Any qualified NIST employee or group of employees is eligible. A monetary award of $3,000 and a bronze plaque are presented annually. Established in 1984 to honor Allen V. Astin, the fifth director of the National Bureau of Standards.

• 20477 • **Edward Uhler Condon Award**
To recognize distinguished achievement in effective written exposition in science or technology. Work published by a qualified NIST employee or group of employees, within the twelve-month period ending June 30 each year, is considered. A monetary award of $3,000, and a plaque are presented annually. Established in 1974 in honor of Dr. Edward Uhler Condon, fourth director of the National Bureau of Standards.

• 20478 • **Eugene Casson Crittenden Award**
To recognize superior achievement by permanent employees, who perform supporting services that have a significant impact on technical programs beyond their own offices. Any full-time, or part-time (with at least a 32-hour tour) permanent employee of NIST in announced pay plan and level, with at least five years' creditable service at NIST is eligible. Up to eight awards consisting of $1,500 , and a certificate are presented annually. Established in 1967 in honor of Eugene Casson Crittenden, former NBS executive.

• 20479 • **Equal Employment Opportunity Award**
For recognition of exceptionally significant accomplishments and contributions to Equal Employment Opportunity and Affirmative Action goals. Any qualified NIST employee or group of employees is eligible. An engraved plaque, and $1,000 are awarded annually. Established in 1977.

• 20480 • **Edward Bennett Rosa Award**
To recognize outstanding achievements in the development of engineering or related standards, either within the Institute or in cooperation with other Government agencies or private groups. Any qualified NIST employee or group of employees is eligible. A monetary award of $3,000, and a plaque are presented annually. Established in 1964 in honor of Dr. Edward Bennett Rosa, first Chief Physicist of the original National Bureau of Standards.

• 20481 • **Safety Award for Superior Accomplishment**
To recognize unusually significant contributions to the NIST Occupational Safety and Health program activities. Any qualified and deserving NIST employee (supervisory or non-supervisory categories) is eligible. A framed certificate and $500 are awarded annually. Established in 1977.

• 20482 • **William P. Slichter Award**
For recognition of outstanding achievements by NIST staff in building or strengthening ties between NIST and industry. Any qualified NIST employee or group of employees may be nominated. A framed certificate and a $3,000 honorarium are awarded each year at the NIST Annual Awards Ceremony. Established in 1992 in memory of Dr. William P. Slichter, who played a major role in building ties between NIST (NBS) and industry.

• 20483 • **Samuel Wesley Stratton Award**
To recognize outstanding scientific or engineering achievements in support of NIST objectives with distinguished publications and professional journals. Any qualified NIST employee or group of employees is eligible. A monetary award of $3,000, and a plaque are presented annually. Established in 1962 in honor of Dr. Samuel Wesley Stratton, first Director of the National Bureau of Standards.

• 20484 •
United States Department of Defense
Defense Logistics Agency
Attn: DASC-HPR
8725 John J. Kingman Rd., Rm. 2545
Ft. Belvoir, VA 22060-6220
Phone: (703)767-6200
Fax: (703)767-6187
Home Page: http://www.dla.mil

• 20485 • **Honorary Awards to Private Citizens and Organizations**
To recognize private citizens, groups, or organizations for significant assistance or support to Agency functions, service, or operations as a public service. A plaque and/or certificate is awarded when merited. Established in 1971.

• 20486 •
United States Department of Defense
Office of the Secretary of Defense
1000 Defense Pentagon, Rm. 3A750
Washington, DC 20301-1400
Home Page: http://www.defenselink.mil

• 20487 • **Commander-in-Chief's Annual Award for Installation Excellence**
To recognize the outstanding efforts of individuals within each Service and the Defense Logistics Agency (DLA) who operate and maintain the defense installations. The primary focus of the award is to identify an installation in each Service and DLA where the command has done the best job with its available resources to support the mission, concentrating on imaginative and

innovative management actions that have increased the productivity of the work force and enhanced the quality of life of all the people. The award is designed to: (1) Encourage competition to increase readiness through emphasis on efficiency of installation management; (2) Recognize creative opportunities for economies and efficiencies in installation management without impairing mission effectiveness of the military unit; (3) Promote ways to improve upon present organization, procedures, functions and policies; (4) Motivate people to advance new ideas for management improvements and innovation; and (5) Generate interest and recognize conscious leadership in improving the quality of life of all the people. Each Service DLA installation, regardless of location or size, is eligible and encouraged to compete for this award. A trophy with the name of the winning installation is presented for permanent retention. Awarded annually. Established in 1985. Co-sponsored by the United States Executive Office of the President.

• 20488 •
United States Department of Education
Office of Intergovernmental and Interagency Affairs
400 Maryland Ave. SW
Washington, DC 20202
Phone: (202)401-0404
Toll-Free: 800-438-7232
Fax: (202)401-8607
Home Page: http://www.ed.gov/about/offices/list/oiia/index.html?src=oc

• 20489 • **The President's Education Award Program**
To honor students for outstanding academic achievement. The President's Award for Educational Excellence is presented at three levels to students graduating from elementary, middle or junior high, and senior high school. Eligible students must have an A- average, meet the standards established by their school, and have either received a battery score at the 85th percentile or higher in a reading or mathematics standardized achievement test, or have the recommendation from a teacher plus one other school staff member. The President's Award for Educational Improvement recognizes all students, including those with special needs, who are making an outstanding effort to learn and improve in their academic subjects. Eligible students must meet the standards established by their school. Suggested criteria, presented in the past, could include, illness, personal crisis, or special need that could not maintain such high standards during the year or unusual behavior change that produced a notable improvement in learning and achievement. Colored pins and certificates are awarded annually. Established in 1983. Awarded in cooperation with the National Association of Elementary School Principals and the National Association of Secondary School Principals. Formerly: (1996) Presidential Academic Fitness Awards.

• 20490 •
United States Department of Education
White House Commission on Presidential Scholars
400 Maryland Ave. SW
Washington, DC 20202
Phone: (202)401-0961
Fax: (202)205-0676
E-mail: presidential_scholars@ed.gov
Home Page: http://www.ed.gov/programs/psp/commission.html?exp=0

• 20491 • **United States Presidential Scholars Program**
To recognize and honor outstanding achievement of high school seniors. This award is the nation's highest honor bestowed upon graduating high school seniors for exceptional talent in the visual, creative and performing arts. Each year up to 141 students are named as Presidential Scholars. Established in 1964.

• 20492 •
United States Department of Energy
Samuel W. Bodman, Sec.
1000 Independence Ave. SW
Washington, DC 20585
Phone: (202)586-5575
Toll-Free: 800-DIAL-DOE
Fax: (202)586-4403
Home Page: http://www.energy.gov

• 20493 • **Sadi Carnot Award in Energy Conservation**
For recognition of outstanding achievement in research, development, or application of energy conservation technologies. Candidates may be at any stage in their careers. The award may recognize a single noteworthy achievement or a sustained level of accomplishment throughout a lifetime. Nominations are judged primarily on the basis of scientific and technical merit and achievement, with secondary weight given to managerial ability or innovative talents. Deadline varies each year. A monetary award of $10,000, a gold medal, and a citation are awarded. Additional information is available from the Office of Energy Efficiency and Renewable Energy, E-541, Department of Energy, 1000 Independence Ave. SW, Washington, DC 20585; telephone: (202) 586-9114.

• 20494 • **John Ericsson Award in Renewable Energy**
For recognition of outstanding achievement in research, development, or application of renewable energy technologies. Candidates may be at any stage in their careers. The award may recognize a single noteworthy achievement or a sustained level of accomplishment throughout a lifetime. Nominations are judged primarily on the basis of scientific and technical merit and achievement, with secondary weight given to managerial ability or innovative talents. Deadline varies each year. A monetary award of $10,000, a gold medal, and a citation are awarded. Established in 1987. Additional information is available from the Office of Conservation and Renewable Energy, EE-541, Department of Energy, 1000 Independence Ave. SW, Washington, DC 20585; telephone: (202) 586-9114.

• 20495 • **Enrico Fermi Award**
To recognize exceptional achievements throughout a lifetime in the development, use, or control of energy (broadly interpreted to include science, engineering, and scientific management in nuclear, atomic, molecular, and particle interactions and their effects). The Award is not limited to U.S. citizens and is usually given annually. The Award consists of a gold medal(s), a citation(s), and a monetary prize of $200,000, but not to exceed $100,000, to any one individual. Established in 1956 to honor Enrico Fermi, whose brilliant contributions to the science and engineering of nuclear energy opened new scientific and technological realms. Awarded by the Secretary of Energy on behalf of the Department and the President of the United States. For more information, contact the Office of Science, JC-5, U.S. Department of Energy, 1000 Independence Ave. SW, Washington, DC 20585. Telephone: (202)586-5767.

• 20496 •
United States Department of Health and Human Services
HHH Bldg., Rm. 536 E
200 Independence Ave. SW
Washington, DC 20201
Phone: (202)619-0257
Toll-Free: 877-696-6775
Home Page: http://www.hhs.gov

• 20497 • **HHS Distinguished Public Service Award**
To recognize individuals for outstanding contributions to the betterment of health and welfare throughout the nation and the world. Any individual of national or international reputation is eligible, as are contributions made by organizations locally or regionally. The Under Secretary, Assistant Secretaries, General Counsel, Division Heads, Directors of Staff Offices and Regional Directors may initiate nominations at any time. A plaque is awarded by the Secretary.

• 20498 •
United States Department of Health and Human Services
National Institutes of Health
Natl. Inst. of Neurological Disorders and Stroke
Financial Management Branch
Neuroscience Center, Rm. 309
6001 Executive Bldg. MSC 9531
Bethesda, MD 20892
Phone: (301)496-9248
Fax: (301)402-4370
E-mail: ca23c@nih.gov
Home Page: http://www.ninds.nih.gov

• 20499 • **NINDS Javits Neuroscience Investigator Award**
To provide a unique opportunity for research aimed at understanding the biology of neurological disorders and the functioning of the brain and nervous system. The award is given to distin-

guished investigators with a record of substantial contributions on the "cutting edge" in some field of neurological science who are expected to be highly productive for the next seven years. These scientists must have demonstrated scientific excellence and exceptional productivity, be pursuing research of strategic scientific importance, and have proposals of the highest scientific merit with a high probability of continued accomplishment. No solicitation or announcement is made; applications specifically for this award cannot be submitted. Selection is by the institute, on the favorable recommendation by the National Advisory Council. Established in 1983 by the U.S. Congress to honor former Senator Jacob Javits (R-NY), a victim of amyotrophic lateral sclerosis (ALS), a degenerative neurological disorder that is also known as Lou Gehrig's disease. Senator Javits championed research support for a wide range of disorders of the brain and central nervous system.

• 20500 •
United States Department of Health and Human Services, Public Health Service Centers for Disease Control and Prevention (CDC)
1600 Clifton Rd., NE
Mailstop K-17
Atlanta, GA 30333
Phone: (404)639-3311
Fax: (404)639-3534
Home Page: http://www.cdc.gov/

• 20501 • **Charles C. Shepard Science Award**
To recognize an outstanding contribution to the scientific literature by CDC scientists. Awarded annually. Established in 1986. The Science Award was named in honor of the ideals, goals, and accomplishments of Charles C. Shepard, a CDC scientist from 1953-85. It was created to help foster a CDC spirit of scientific excellence for the benefit of the health of the nation and the world.

• 20502 • **William C. Watson, Jr. Medal of Excellence**
To recognize exceptional employees whose services and achievements deserve special recognition of a high order. The award was created to honor those whose specific accomplishment, scientific or administrative, and/or careers have significantly contributed to the advancement of public health. Established in 1977 as the CDC Medal of Excellence, the name was changed to the William C. Watson, Jr. Medal of Excellence in 1985 in honor of the former CDC Deputy Director. Formerly: (1985) CDC Medal of Excellence.

• 20503 •
United States Department of Justice
Federal Bureau of Investigation
Robert Mueller, Dir.
Personnel Div.
935 Pennsylvania Ave. NW, Rm. 7350
Washington, DC 20535
Phone: (202)324-3000
Fax: (202)324-8021
Home Page: http://www.fbi.gov

• 20504 • **FBI Honorary Medals**
To acknowledge FBI employees for their acts of heroism, valor, and meritorious achievements. The five medals are: FBI Medal of Valor presented for exceptional acts of heroism or voluntary risk of personal safety and life when act occurs in direct line of duty and/or within the scope of FBI employment and in the face of criminal adversary(ies); FBI Shield of Bravery - presented for brave and courageous acts occurring in the direct line of duty and/or within the scope of FBI employment; FBI Medal for Meritorious Achievement - presented for extraordinary and exceptional meritorious service in a duty of extreme challenge and great responsibility or for an exemplary act that results in the protection of life; FBI Star - presented for serious injuries sustained in the direct line of duty from physical confrontation with criminal adversary(ies); and FBI Memorial Star - presented to primary next-of-kin when an employee's death occurs in the line of duty as the direct result of an adversarial action, in the performance of a law enforcement duty, or in the scope of FBI employment in the face of criminal adversary(ies). Established in 1989.

• 20505 •
United States Department of Justice
Office of Justice Programs
Alberto R. Gonzales, Atty.Gen.
Office of Congressional & Public Affairs
810 7th St. NW
Washington, DC 20531
Phone: (202)307-5933
Fax: (202)514-5958
E-mail: ASKOPC@ojp.usdoj.gov
Home Page: http://www.ojp.gov

• 20506 • **Young American Medal for Bravery**
For recognition of exceptional courage, decision, presence of mind, and unusual swiftness of action, regardless of personal safety, in an effort to save the life of any person or persons in actual imminent danger. Youths 18 years old or younger who reside in the United States, its territories, or possessions and the Panama Canal Zone are eligible. A certificate, a medal, and travel to Washington, DC for the recipient and two guests are awarded annually at the discretion of the President of the United States. Established in 1950 by an Act of Congress. Co-sponsored by United States Executive Office of the President.

• 20507 • **Young American Medal for Service**
For recognition of outstanding or unusual commendation for character and community service worthy of public report and beneficial to the public in nature. It must have been acknowledged by the chief executive officer or officers of a state, county, municipality, or other political subdivision, or by a civic, educational, or religious institution, group, or society, and must have been prominently mentioned in the public press, or on radio or television in the community where the service was accomplished or where the candidate resides. Citizens of the United States under the age of 19 are eligible. A certificate, a medal, and travel to Washington DC for the recipient and two guests are awarded annually at the discretion of the President of the United States. Established in 1950 by an Act of Congress. Co-sponsored by the United States Executive Office of the President.

• 20508 •
United States Department of Labor
Elaine L. Chao, Sec.
Secretary's Honor Awards Committee
Frances Perkins Bldg.
200 Constitution Ave. NW
Washington, DC 20210
Phone: (202)219-6741
Toll-Free: (866)4US-ADOL
Fax: (202)219-8127
Home Page: http://www.dol.gov

• 20509 • **Philip Arnow Award**
For recognition of consistently outstanding performance and service to the Department over a period of 15 years or more. Nominations are made through an Agency Committee with selection by the Secretary's Honor Awards Committee. A monetary prize of $1,000 and an engraved plaque are awarded annually to no more than two employees. Established in 1972 in honor of Philip Arnow.

• 20510 • **Distinguished Career Service Awards**
For recognition of career service marked by sustained high quality and efficiency over a period of at least 10 years in the Department of Labor. Nominations must be submitted by October 15. Awarded annually in March.

• 20511 • **Equal Employment Opportunity Awards**
To recognize employees for actively contributing to DOL's EEO goals through effective leadership, imagination, or innovation in extending equal employment opportunity within the Department. Categories of award recipients are: managers and supervisors, employees whose primary work does not specifically involve EEO, and employees having specific full-time or collateral duty EEO responsibilities. All employees are eligible. Nominations must be submitted by October 15. Awarded annually in March.

• 20512 • Safety and Health Awards
To recognize and demonstrate management's high regard for DOL employees who have made unusual and significant contributions toward the achievement of positive results in the advancement of safety and health in DOL. The three categories of award recipients are: managers and supervisors who have implemented the Department's safety and health program in their jurisdictions in an outstanding manner, developing appropriate written and oral policies, plans, and programs; employees whose primary work is not in safety and health, but whose superior accomplishments have advanced the cause of safety and health; and employees with full-time or collateral duty safety and health responsibilities who have achieved outstanding results in furthering safety and health. All employees are eligible. Nominations may be made any time during the year. Awards are given at the end of the fiscal year.

• 20513 • Secretary's Exceptional Achievement Awards
To recognize and honor individual employees and groups of employees who have achieved an unusually significant work product. Annual awards are presented for three categories of employees: professional, supervisor/managerial, and clerical/secretarial. All employees are eligible. The following are criteria for: Professional - the project or program should be national or otherwise broad in scope and demonstrate exceptional skill, excellence, creativity, or constitute a significant productivity or quality improvement; Supervisory/Managerial - the outstanding creative and productive results of the staff, including quality and productivity improvements, should be the direct result of successful supervisory or managerial practices such as planning, scheduling, directing, and motivating personnel; and Clerical/Secretarial - the highly significant accomplishments are directly related to the skills and diligence of the employee. Accomplishments could be the development of new or improved methods of operations or procedures, excellence in communications within or outside the Agency, significant productivity or quality improvements, or another contribution that demonstrates notable creativity. The nominations must be submitted by October 15. Awarded annually in March.

• 20514 • Valor Awards
To recognize DOL employees who demonstrate unusual courage involving a high degree of personal risk in the face of danger. All employees are eligible. Nominations may be submitted at any time. In order to be considered for presentation at the annual awards ceremony in March, the nominations must be submitted by October 15 of the prior year.

• 20515 • Veterans Employment Awards
To recognize employees who have made unusual and significant contributions to increase employment opportunities for veterans within DOL. All employees except those having primary job responsibility for veterans programs are eligible. The nominations must be submitted by October 15. Awarded annually in March.

• 20516 •
United States Department of Labor
Bureau of Labor Statistics
Kathleen P. Utgoff, Commissioner
Postal Square Bldg.
2 Massachusetts Ave. NE
Washington, DC 20212
Phone: (202)691-5200
Fax: (202)691-6325
E-mail: feedback@bls.gov
Home Page: http://www.bls.gov

• 20517 • Lawrence R. Klein Award
To recognize the best articles in labor economics or related subjects appearing in the *Monthly Labor Review* during the year. The award is made on the basis of originality of ideas or method of analysis, adherence to principles of scientific inquiry, and adherence to principles of good writing. Two monetary prizes are awarded annually; one to a Bureau of Labor Statistics author, and one to an author outside the Bureau. Established in 1969 in honor of Lawrence R. Klein, editor-in-chief of the *Monthly Labor Review* for 22 years until his retirement in 1968.

• 20518 •
U.S. Department of Labor
Office of Job Corps
Grace A. Kilbane, Admin.
Frances Perkins Bldg.
200 Constitution Ave. NW
Washington, DC 20210
Phone: (202)693-3000
Toll-Free: 877-US-2JOBS
Fax: (202)693-2767
E-mail: webmaster@jobcorps.org
Home Page: http://jobcorps.doleta.gov

• 20519 • Donald A. Buchannon Scholarship
Recognizes a deserving current or former Job Corps student who has displayed exemplary performance while in Job Corps and has the aptitude and ability to benefit from further education. Applicants must be currently enrolled in the Job Corps Advanced Career Training Program (ACT), desire to continue their academic training, and be nearing the three-year enrollment limitation, or have been enrolled in Job Corps within the past two years and be currently enrolled in a college program, or planning to enter an institute of higher learning. In addition, the scholarship may be available to students pursing graduate or post graduate degrees. Candidates must also have maintained a 2.0 or better grade point average (out of a possible 4.0) for college level courses. The deadline for applications is announced annually. A scholarship of $1000 is awarded annually. Established in 1991 in memory of Don Buchannon who died suddenly on January 21, 1989, after 25 years of dedicated service to the Job Corps program and its students. Additional information is available at the above address.

• 20520 • Harpers Ferry Memorial Scholarship
Recognizes four deserving current or former Job Corps students who have displayed exemplary performance while in Job Corps and have the ability and motivation to benefit from further education. Applicants must be enrolled or accepted for enrollment in a college, university, or trade school. The deadline for applicantions is announced annually. Four scholarships of $1000 each is awarded annually. Established in 1996 to commemorate the lives of eight Harper Ferr Job Corps students who perished in a MARC/AMTRAK train collision on February 16, 1996, in Silver Spring, Maryland, while traveling home from a holiday weekend from Job Corps.

• 20521 • Information Technology Scholarship
Intended to provide Job Corps students and graduates the opportunity to pursue careers in the Information Technology industry. All candidates must have participated for a minimum of 6 months in a Job Corps computer related field, possess a high school diploma or a GED. One scholarship is awarded to a current or former Job Corps student in each of the Department of Labor Job Corps regions to pursue a certificate or degree in the information technology field. A $4000 scholarship is awarded to each regional winner on an annual basis. The deadline for nominations is announced annuallly. Established in 1999 as a result of interest express by the FGIPC/IAC to establish a closer pertnership with the Department of Labor Job Corps program. Additional information available at the above address.

• 20522 • Job Corps Hall of Fame
Recognizes former Job Corps students who have distinguished themselves by significant or outstanding achievements that merit national recognition. Must have participated in the Job Corps program for at least 90 days; must have been acceptable personal conduct, progress, and performance while in Job Corps; and have accomplished significant achievements in such areas as public service, personal achievement, human interest, social action, community achievement, and educational development are eligible. A monetary prize, a certificate of admission to the Hall of Fame, and a plaque are awarded annually. Established in 1979.

• 20523 •
United States Department of Navy
U.S. Naval Observatory
% Public Affairs Office
3450 Massachusetts Ave. NW
Washington, DC 20392
Phone: (202)762-1438
Fax: (202)762-1489
E-mail: grc@usno.navy.mil
Home Page: http://www.usno.navy.mil/pao

• 20524 • Captain James M. Gilliss Award for Outstanding Service
To recognize individuals, military or civilian, employed at the USNO sat the time of nomination for outstanding achievement during the previous two-year period. General criteria for consideration include: extraordinary dedication to one's duty, positive and enthusiastic performance of one's job, or a creative and resourceful ap-

proach to problems leading to an improvement in the USNO or its mission. The Gilliss Award is intended to be a general award and is not restricted to scientific personnel. Awarded annually when merited in January. Established in 1982.

• 20525 • Simon Newcomb Award for Research Achievement

To recognize employees of the USNO at the time of nomination who have made a significant and identifiable contribution to a specific USNO research effort of considerable consequence during the previous two-year period. Nominees must have exercised a leading role in the project and be recognized in the relevant community as having contributed to the betterment of that field. To this end, the nominee should have published at least one major paper of merit on the project in a referred journal associated with the field of endeavor. Awarded annually when merited. Established in 1982.

• 20526 • Superintendent's Award for Distinguished Service

To recognize distinguished and dedicated service by an individual employed by, or closely associated with, the USNO. Consideration for this award may include, but is not restricted to volunteerism in connection with jobs, special assignments, special tours, public relations, and community affairs for which the USNO and the Department of the Navy gain recognition; the adoption of beneficial suggestions that improve the USNO environment or cost effectiveness in operation; or special work of an emergency nature.

• 20527 •
United States Department of State
2201 C St. NW
Washington, DC 20520
Phone: (202)647-4000
Toll-Free: 800-877-8339
Fax: (202)647-0150
Home Page: http://www.state.gov

• 20528 • Award for Excellence in Labor Diplomacy

To recognize outstanding contributions in reporting labor developments and issues. This award is granted to State Department employees serving in Labor Counselor, Labor Attache, or Labor Reporting Officer positions. The annual award consists of $5,000 and a certificate signed by the Deputy Secretary.

• 20529 • Award for Heroism

To recognize employees of State, AID, USIA, and Marine Guards assigned to U.S. Embassies who, without concern for personal safety, exhibit unusual heroism in an emergency, whether or not in connection with performance of assigned duties, which reflects credit on the Federal Service. The award consists of a silver medal, a lapel emblem, and a certificate signed by the Secretary of State. One or more recipients may be honored each year.

• 20530 • Baker-Wilkins Award for Outstanding Deputy Chief of Mission

To honor a Deputy Chief of Missions who demonstrates the proficiency, creativity, and overall capacity to serve effectively for ambassadors and as charge d'affaires in their absence. The recipient receives $2,000 and a certificate signed by the Secretary; two runners-up are selected to receive $1,000 and an honor award. Awarded annually.

• 20531 • Cash Award

To reward a special act or service by all U.S. citizen direct hire and all Foreign Service National Personnel. Criteria for nomination include: original development of major improvements in methods, organization procedures, or products that result in substantial savings; exemplary or courageous handling of an emergency situation; creative effort that makes an important contribution to the Federal Service; one-time or nonrecurring contributions that are clearly deserving of special recognition; or handling of a special project or assuming the duties of a temporarily vacant position in addition to the employee's own responsibilities. The Department Awards Committee reviews, analyzes, and evaluates the effectiveness of the program and approves or disapproves awards in amounts from $2,000 to $10,000.

• 20532 • Chief Financial Officers Award for Distinction in Public Finance

To honor Foreign Service (including Foreign Service Nationals) and Civil Service employees of the Department serving in financial management positions. The annual award consists of $5,000 and a certificate signed by the Secretary.

• 20533 • Charles E. Cobb, Jr. Award for Initiative and Success in Trade Development

To recognize outstanding contributions by a Department Foreign Service Officer serving abroad who is the most innovative and successful in developing trade and promoting exports for the United States. Two recipients each year receive a monetary award of $5,000 and a certificate signed by the Secretary.

• 20534 • Diplomatic Security Employee of the Year Award

To honor Foreign and Civil Service employees in the security field serving domestically or overseas. The annual award consists of a $5,000 and a certificate signed by the Secretary; one runner-up receives $2,000. Formerly: (1998) Security Officer of the Year Award.

• 20535 • Director General's Award for Excellence in Human Resource Management

To recognize FS-01/GS-15 and below ranked Foreign Service (Foreign Service Nationals included) and Civil Service full-time direct hire employees of the Department serving in a personnel position. A monetary prize of $5,000 and a certificate signed by the Secretary are awarded to one or more recipients each year.

• 20536 • Director General's Award for Reporting and Analysis

To recognize Foreign Service employees irrespective of pay plan or rank. Nominations must include three examples of excellence in reporting. The annual award consists of an engraved desk pen set, $5,000, and a certificate signed by the Secretary.

• 20537 • Distinguished Honor Award

To recognize achievement upon which nominations should be comparable to the following: exceptionally outstanding service to the Department or the Government for achievements of marked national or international significance; exceptionally outstanding service and/or leadership in the administration of one or more agency programs that results in highly successful accomplishment of mission, or in a major attainment of objectives or specific accomplishment to meet unique or emergency situations; outstanding accomplishments over a prolonged period that involve the exercise of authority or judgment in the public interest. The award consists of a gold medal, a lapel emblem, and a certificate signed, as appropriate, by the Secretary of State, the Administrator of AID, or the Director of USIA.

• 20538 • James Clement Dunn Award for Excellence

To recognize FO-01 Foreign Service Officers whose record of leadership, intellectual skills, managerial ability, and personal qualities most fully exemplifies standards of excellence desired of Foreign Service Officers. The annual award consists of $5,000 and a certificate signed by the Secretary.

• 20539 • Eleanor Roosevelt Award for Outstanding Contributions to the Cause of Human Rights

Given to up to five individual Americans by the President of the United States for outstanding contributions to the promotion of human rights, either in the United States or overseas. Nominations are coordinated by the Bureau of Democracy, Human Rights and Labor in the Department of State. The Secretary of State submits recommendations to the President, who makes the final determination. Awardees are honored at a White House ceremony on or around December 10 each year.

• 20540 • Equal Employment Opportunity Award

To honor employees of the Department who have made significant achievement in the furtherance of affirmative action and equal employment opportunity. The annual award consists of a certificate signed by the Secretary and $5,000.

• 20541 • Foreign Service Award

To honor departing non-career employees who, during their association with the Department, have performed with exceptional dedication and distinction. Recipients receive a certificate signed by the Secretary. Awarded annually.

• 20542 • Foreign Service National of the Year Award

In recognition of high standards of performance and the value to the U.S. Government of the special contributions made by foreign national employees. The annual award consists of $5,000 and a certificate signed by the Secretary. There are five runners-up representing each of the Bureaus not represented by the winner. Each runner-up receives $2,500 and a certificate signed by the Bureau Assistant Secretary.

• 20543 • Foreign Service Office Management Specialist of the Year/Civil Service Secretary of the Year

To recognize employees of State, including Foreign Service Nationals. A certificate and monetary award of $5,000 are awarded annually to one recipient from Civil Service and Foreign Service.

• 20544 • General Services Achievement Award

To recognize FS-01/GS-15 and below ranked Foreign Service (Foreign Service Nationals included) or Civil Service employees of the Department serving in general services, building maintenance, and construction engineering positions overseas in a mission or a regional center. The annual award consists of $5,000 and a certificate signed by the Secretary.

• 20545 • Leamon R. Hunt Award for Administrative Excellence

To honor Foreign Service employees (mid-level or below) in an administrative position overseas who have made notable contributions to the efficiency and quality of service in fulfilling the objectives of the Mission. The annual award consists of a certificate signed by the Secretary and $5,000.

• 20546 • Meritorious Honor Award

To recognize achievement upon which nominations should be comparable to the following: outstanding service in the conduct or improvement of the programs or operations of State, AID, or USICA; accomplishment of assigned responsibilities in an exemplary manner and establishment of a record of achievement; or the demonstration of unusual initiative in contributing to efficiency, improved management, or outstanding executive or technical ability. The award consists of a bronze medal, a lapel emblem, and a certificate signed, as appropriate, by an Assistant Secretary of State or an official of equivalent rank or the chief of mission, by the Mission Director for AID, or the Director of USIS.

• 20547 • Thomas Morrison Information Management Award

To recognize State government employees of the Foreign Service (except Senior Foreign Service) including Foreign Service Nationals in the communications field serving at Headquarters and in the Communications Program Unit or Regional Communications Program Office of an overseas post. The annual award consists of a certificate signed by the Secretary and $5,000. Formerly: (1998) Thomas Morrison Communicator Award.

• 20548 • Arnold L. Raphel Memorial Award

To recognize international affairs employees who embody the special human qualities and extra effort put forth to promote and develop the people around them, especially junior officers. The annual award consists of $5,000 and a certificate signed by the Secretary. The award is named in honor of the late Ambassador Raphel to recognize the qualities that he brought to U.S. diplomacy and to the work of the Foreign Service.

• 20549 • Luther I. Replogle Award for Management Improvement

To honor employees of State, AID, or USIA who have made outstanding contributions to management improvement. The annual award consists of $5,000 and a certificate signed by the Secretary.

• 20550 • Safe Driving Award

To recognize full-time chauffeurs for outstanding driving care and ability. Employees who have driven one or more years without a preventable accident and whose other performance is highly satisfactory are eligible for consideration. The amount of the cash award given depends on the number of years of safe driving and the availability of post funds. A congratulatory letter or a certificate or lapel emblem will accompany the cash award.

• 20551 • Herbert Salzman Award for Excellence in International Economic Performance

To recognize employees serving abroad in FS-1 through FS-6 or equivalent (GS-15 and below) in the field of international economic policy. The annual award consists of $5,000 and a certificate signed by the Secretary.

• 20552 • Secretary of State's Distinguished Service Award

To honor senior members of the foreign affairs community in recognition of exceptionally outstanding leadership, professional competence, and significant accomplishment over a sustained period of time in the field of foreign affairs. Achievements must of notable national or international significance and have made an important contribution to the advancement of U.S. national interests. Any member of the foreign affairs community is eligible for the award. The award is made directly by the Secretary of State.

• 20553 • Secretary's Award

To recognize sacrifice of personal health, including life, in the performance of official duties by employees of State, AID, USIA, and Marine Guards assigned to U.S. Embassies. The award consists of a gold medal, a lapel emblem, and a certificate signed by the Secretary of State.

• 20554 • Superior Honor Award

In recognition of achievement upon which nominations should be comparable to the following: outstanding service to the agencies or the Government, service of significance where the interests of the United States are involved or that has aided the agencies in furthering objectives; outstanding results in increased productivity, increased efficiency, and economy of operations resulting in a substantial contribution to the accomplishment of an agency's goals; or a superior creative service or contribution such as the development of a new and highly effective product, program, or method for accomplishment of an agency objective. The award consists of a silver medal, a lapel emblem, and a certificate signed, as appropriate, by an Assistant Secretary of State or the Chief of Mission, an Administrator of AID, or by the Director of USIS.

• 20555 • Barbara M. Watson Award for Consular Excellence

To recognize Foreign Service members (classes FS-1 through FS-6) serving in a consular position overseas who have made notable contributions to the efficiency and quality of service in fulfilling the objectives of the Mission. A monetary award of $5,000 and a certificate signed by the Secretary are awarded to one or more recipients each year. Formerly: (1998) Consular Service Award.

• 20556 •

United States Department of the Treasury
Financial Management Service
Richard Gregg, Commissioner
401 14 St. SW
Washington, DC 20227
Phone: (202)874-6950
Home Page: http://fms.treas.gov

• 20557 • Annual Awards for Distinction in Financial Management

These awards, the highest honors granted by the Federal government for specific achievement in the areas of collections, payments, and credit/debt management, are given to encourage and recognize exemplary leadership and excellence in endeavors directly or indirectly associated with the collection of Federal government funds, cash position management, and optimum use of excess Federal government funds. Individuals or groups in an Executive Branch, department or agency are eligible. Employees of the Department of the Treasury are not eligible. Nominations may be submitted by November 9. Monetary awards up to $10,000 for each individual or group and/or certificates are awarded annually. Established in 1985.

• 20558 •
United States Department of Transportation
Federal Highway Administration
Frederick G. Wright, Exec.Dir.
400 7th St. SW
Washington, DC 20590
Phone: (202)366-0660
Fax: (202)366-3988
E-mail: hrentz@fhwa.dot.gov
Home Page: http://www.fhwa.dot.gov

• 20559 • **Excellence in Highway Design Awards**
To recognize excellence in the design of highways and highway-related facilities and to recognize programs that contribute effectively to a more pleasing highway experience. Awards are presented in nine categories and are judged on the basis of five general criteria: compatibility with/or adaption to the environment, visual appeal, safety and traffic operation factors, functional efficiency, and pleasing user experience. The nine categories include: urban highway; rural highway; major highway structures; highway-related projects; intermodal transportation facilities; historic preservation; public/private participation; highway improvements on federal, state, or other publicly owned lands; and environmental enhancement. Any project completed in the past four years by a state, county, or local agency or a design or engineering firm, and not previously a winner may be nominated. The deadline is July 1. Awards consisting of a photo of the winning project and a bronze tone plaque in a hardwood frame are awarded biennially at the annual meeting of American Association of State Highway and Transportation Officials. Awarded annually from 1966-1977, and renewed in 1980 as a biennial award.

• 20560 •
United States Department of Veterans Affairs
Regional Office
R. James Nicholson, Sec.
Research & Development Office 12A3
1722 I St. NW
Washington, DC 20421
Phone: (202)273-8292
Toll-Free: 800-827-1000
Home Page: http://www.va.gov

• 20561 • **William S. Middleton Award**
This, the highest award given by the Department of Veterans Affairs, recognizes scientists for outstanding achievement in biomedical research. Individuals who have had a career in research in the Department of Veterans Affairs, with recent scientific contributions of an outstanding nature may be nominated by their medical center director by January 15. A monetary award of $5,000, a plaque for the recipient and the medical center, and the opportunity to give the Middleton Address at an appropriate professional annual meeting of the Senior Management Conference are awarded annually. Established in 1960 to honor William S. Middleton, Chief Medical Director of the Veterans Administration from 1955-1963.

• 20562 •
United States Dressage Federation
Stephan Hienzsch, Exec.Dir.
220 Lexington Green Cir., Ste. 510
Lexington, KY 40503
Phone: (859)971-2277
Fax: (859)971-7722
E-mail: shienzsch@usdf.org
Home Page: http://www.usdf.org

• 20563 • **Adult Amateur Award**
To be eligible for award rider must be a participating member of USDF at the time the scores are earned; rider must meet the AHSA dressage definition of adult at the time the score are earned; a competitor must be an adult from the beginning of the year in which they reach the age of 22; submit a current copy of AHSA amateur card to USDF prior to the end of the year; owner must be a participating or business member at the time the scores are earned; horse must be registered with USDF at the time the scores are earned; horse and rider are considered a team for each level of competition; and memberships and horse registrations shall begin upon receipt of the application form and all necessary fees. Six awards will be presented at each level for Training, First, Second, Third, Fourth and Prix St. Georges. Three awards will be given at each level for Intermediate I, Intermediate II, and Grand Prix.

• 20564 • **All-Breeds Awards**
To recognize outstanding horses. The following awards are presented: (1) Training Level Champion; (2) First Level Champion; (3) Second Level Champion; (4) Third Level Champion; (5) Fourth Level Champion; (6) Prix St. Georges Champion; (7) Grand Prix Champion; (8) Intermediate I Champion; (9) Intermediate II Champion; (10) Fourth Level Musical Freestyle; and (11) Intermediate I Musical Freestyle. A USDF Award and a diploma are presented annually. Established in 1984.

• 20565 • **Footing of the Year Award**
To be eligible nominees must have served as manager or secretary for at least five USDF/AHSA recognized competitions; must be a current USDF member; and be nominated up to one year following competition. Nominations must be made by a member of the competitions management committee, a member of a USDF Group Member Organization, or a USDF member competing in competition. Up to three certificates per region will be presented at the Annual Convention.

• 20566 • **Horse of the Year Awards**
For recognition of outstanding horses. The horse must be registered with USDF and owned by a USDF participating member or business member at the time the scores are earned. Scores are recorded directly from the official competition results submitted by competition management. Scores must be from open or AB-IG qualifying classes: (1) Open class: a class which is open to all. There are no restrictions based on the horse (e.g., age, breed, sex, size, previous performance, residence or membership of owner) or rider (e.g., age, experience, qualification, sex, residence, or membership). The award year is October 1 through September 30. Horse of the Year Awards are presented at the Annual Convention. Awards are presented as follows: 20 at each level for Training Level, First Level, Second Level, Third Level, Fourth Level, 15 at each level for Prix St. Georges; Intermediate I, Intermediate II, and Grand Prix.

• 20567 • **Junior/Young Rider Awards**
To recognize outstanding horsemanship of young riders. A junior/young rider is a competitor who has not reached his/her 21st birthday by December 1 of the previous calendar year. Birthdate must be on file at USDF. The horse must be registered with USDF and owned by a USDF participating member or business member at the time the scores are earned. The rider and horse are considered a team for each level of competition. The award year is October 1 through September 30. Junior/Young Rider Awards will be presented at the Annual Convention. Awards will be presented as follows: six at each level for Training Level, First Level, Second Level, Third Level, and Fourth Level; and three at each level for Prix St. Georges, Intermediate I, Intermediate II, and Grand Prix.

• 20568 • **Musical Freestyle Awards**
For recognition of outstanding horses. The horse must be registered with USDF and owned by a USDF participating member or business member at the time the scores were earned. Scores are recorded directly from the official competition results submitted by competition management. Scores must be from open or AB-IG qualifying classes: (1) Open class: a class which is open to all. There are no restrictions based on the horse (e.g., age, breed, sex, size, previous performance, residence or membership of owner) or rider (e.g., age, experience, qualification, sex, residence, or membership). The award year is October 1 through September 30. The USDF Freestyle Awards are presented at the Annual Meeting. Three awards are presented at each level: First Level, Second Level, Third Level, Fourth Level. Six awards are represented at Intermediate I and Grand Prix.

• 20569 • **Outstanding Competition Management Awards**
For recognition of individuals who manage the competitions. Individuals must be nominated to be eligible for this award. The nominee must serve as competition manager or competition secretary for at least 5 USDF/AHSA recognized competitions and be identified in the official prize list as officers in this capacity.

• 20570 • **Rider Award Program**
For recognition of outstanding horsemanship. All USDF individual and participating members are eligible. Riders must be members of USDF at the time the scores are earned. The rider is personally responsible for submitting scores to USDF using official Rider Award Report forms. Any score earned at a USDF Recognized Competition in a regular AHSA or FEI test may be used (freestyle scores do not count). All scores must be reported to USDF by September 30 in

order to be awarded in that year. The following levels and qualification are awarded: (1) Qualified Rider Award - a certificate and the USDF Qualified Rider patch; (2) Bronze Medal Rider Award - a certificate and the USDF Bronze Medal; (3) Silver Medal Rider Award - a certificate and the USDF Silver Medal; and (4) Gold Medal Rider Award - a certificate and the USDF Gold Medal. Rider Award Medals are presented at the Annual Convention. Qualified Rider Awards are issued as soon as the final score is reported.

• 20571 • Vintage Cup Awards

To recognize outstanding horsemanship of older riders. To qualify for the Vintage Cup Award the rider must be 50 years of age or older as of December 1 of the previous calendar year. The rider must be a participating member of USDF at the time the scores are earned and his/her birthdate must be submitted to USDF prior to the end of the award year. The horse must be registered with USDF and owned by a USDF participating member or business member at the time scores are earned. The rider and horse are considered a team for each level of competition. Scores are recorded directly from the official competition results submitted by competition management. The award year is October 1 through September 30. Vintage Cup Awards are presented at the Annual Convention. Awards are presented as follows: three at each level for Training Level, First Level, Second Level, Third Level, Fourth Level, Prix St. Georges, Intermediate I, Intermediate II, and Grand Prix.

• 20572 •

U.S. Energy Association
Barry K. Worthington, Exec.Dir.
1300 Pennsylvania Ave. NW, Ste. 550
Mailbox 142
Washington, DC 20004-3022
Phone: (202)312-1230
Fax: (202)682-1682
Home Page: http://www.usea.org/

• 20573 • U.S. Energy Award

Recognizes lifetime achievement in energy sector. Awarded annually.

• 20574 •

United States Environmental Protection Agency
Steve Johnson, Admin.
Ariel Rios Bldg.
1200 Pennsylvania Ave. NW
Washington, DC 20460
Phone: (202)272-0167
Fax: (202)564-2754
Home Page: http://www.epa.gov

• 20575 • President's Environmental Youth Awards (PEYA)

To recognize young people, as individuals or in groups, for promoting environmental awareness and channeling this awareness into positive community involvement. Activities range from developing recycling programs to protecting sensitive wetlands. To be eligible, a young person, or group of young persons, must have completed an environmental project while in grades Kindergarten through 12, and the project must be sponsored by at least one adult representative of their school, camp, youth group, or public interest group. All participants of completed projects receive certificates signed by the President of the United States, honoring them for their efforts in environmental protection. One outstanding project from each of the ten EPA Regions is selected for regional recognition. Regional project winners, or one representative from a regional award winning group project, along with one project sponsor, will be honored by EPA with a presidential plaque - presented at an EPA sponsored ceremony. Established in 1971. Sponsored by the United States Executive Office of the President. Formerly: President's Environmental Merit Awards Program.

• 20576 •

U.S. Environmental Protection Agency
Office of Research and Development
1200 Pennsylvania Ave. NW, MC 8722R
Washington, DC 20460
Phone: (202)564-6825
E-mail: webmaster.ord@epa.gov
Home Page: http://www.epa.gov/ord

• 20577 • STAR Program

Funds research grants and graduate fellowships. Inquire for application details.

• 20578 •

U.S. Federation for Culture Collections
Mary Meeker, Treas.
1519 Little Farms Rd.
Oxnard, CA 93030-4738
Phone: (805)984-6947
Fax: (503)725-8570
E-mail: booned@pdx.edu
Home Page: http://usfcc.us

• 20579 • J. Roger Porter Award

To recognize individuals who have contributed in an outstanding way to the objectives of the USFCC. Some general objectives are: to establish and maintain liaison between persons interested in culture collections; to encourage and assist in training personnel to operate culture collections; to encourage research on procedures for culture isolation, maintenance, characterization, identification, preservation, distribution, and microbial systematics; and to aid members in solving problems related to culture collections. Nominations by members of the American Society for Microbiology or members of the United States Federation for Culture Collections are accepted. The deadline for nominations is October 1. A monetary award of $1,000 a certificate and travel expenses are conferred each year at the Annual Meeting of the American Society for Microbiology. Established in 1982 in honor of J. Roger Porter. Administered by the American Society for Microbiology. Additional information is available from Helen Bishop, Director, Office of Education and Professional Recognition, American Society for Microbiology, 1913 I Street, N.W., Washington, DC 20006.

• 20580 •

United States Fencing Coaches Association
Arnold Mercado Jr., Pres.
138 E Racine Pl.
Mundelein, IL 60060
Phone: (847)444-7811
E-mail: donq@totheescrime.org
Home Page: http://www.usfca.org/usfca

• 20581 • Certificate of Merit

To recognize outstanding contributions to the development of fencing. Individuals, groups, or organizations are eligible.

• 20582 • Collegiate Coach of the Year

To recognize a coach for professionalism and service to the sport of fencing. The selection is made by the Awards and Recognition Committee. Awards are made at the NCAA championships, as well as at various local conference championships (I.F.A., M.A.C., N.I.W.F.A., etc.).

• 20583 • Fencer of the Year (Men and Women)

To recognize the outstanding qualities of a fencer in each weapon at the National Collegiate Athletic Association Championships. All finalists are eligible to be nominated by all participating fencers at the competition. A plaque is presented annually. Established in the 1950s.

• 20584 • Regional Coach of the Year

To recognize the many coaches throughout the United States who work tirelessly year after year and produce most of the fencers who later vie for honors at the collegiate level. Coaches from clubs, high schools, or universities may be nominated. Awarded annually. Established in 1986.

• 20585 • USFCA All-America Certificates (Men)

To recognize the individual finalists of the NCAA Championships in each weapon. Certificates are presented annually to the fencer and to his coach at the close of the NCAA Championships.

• 20586 • USFCA All-America Certificates (Women)

To recognize the individual finalists in the NCAA Championships. Established in 1981.

• 20587 • USFCA Honorable Mention

To recognize the semi-final finishers in the NCAA Championships in all three weapons. Certificates are presented to the fencer and his/her coach at the close of the NCAA Championships. Established in 1986.

• 20588 •
United States Figure Skating Association
Laura Fawcett, Dir. Online Services
20 1st St.
Colorado Springs, CO 80906
Phone: (719)635-5200
Fax: (719)635-9548
E-mail: info@usfigureskating.org
Home Page: http://www.usfsa.org

• 20589 • **United States Figure Skating Champions**
To recognize outstanding figure skaters in the following categories: Men, Ladies, Pair, Dance, Junior Men, Junior Ladies, Junior Pair, Junior Dance, Novice Men, and Novice Ladies. United States citizens over the age of 13 are eligible to compete. Skaters enter categories according to a proficiency test, rather than age. Perpetual trophies are on permanent display at the USFSA Museum. These trophies are inscribed annually with the names of winners: Champion of the United States - George H. Browne Memorial Bowl; Ladies' Champion of the United States - Owen Memorial Trophy; Pair Champions of the United States - Henry Wainwright Howe Memorial Trophy; Dance. Champions of the United States - Radix Trophy; Junior Men's Champion - Irving Brokaw Memorial Trophy; Junior Ladies' Champion - Tower Trophy; Junior Pair Champions Trophies presented by The Skating Club of New York; Junior Dance Champions - Hartshorne Trophies; Novice Men's Champion - Jean-Pierre Brunet Memorial Trophy; and Novice Ladies' Champion - Heaton R. Robertson Memorial Trophy. Champions receive a token silver trophy bowl and a gold Harry E. Radix Pin with a diamond. Established in 1914.

• 20590 • **World Figure Skating Hall of Fame**
To honor the achievements and to preserve the records in the sport of figure skating of persons in the following categories: skaters from throughout the world who have compiled an outstanding competitive record or who have made a noteworthy contribution in style or technique and have been retired from competitive skating for at least ten years; and persons who have made a noteworthy contribution in a non-amateur capacity. Non-teaching professionals must have been retired at least five years, while teaching professionals must have at least twenty-five years of experience as such. Nominees are selected by the general public, are not limited to living persons, and need not be either U.S. citizens or members of the USFSA. A plaque and a medal are awarded annually in May. The name, picture, and record of each new member is added to the Hall of Fame display in the World Figure Skating Museum in Colorado Springs. Established in 1975. Additional information is available from the World Figure Skating Museum, % Beth E. Davis, Curator, 20 First St., Colorado Springs, Colorado 80906.

• 20591 •
United States Fish and Wildlife Service
Federal Duck Stamp Program
Pat Fisher, ch.
4401 N Fairfax Dr.
Mail Stop MBSP-4070
Arlington, VA 22203
Phone: (703)358-2000
Fax: (703)358-2009
E-mail: duckstamps@fws.gov
Home Page: http://duckstamps.fws.gov

• 20592 • **Federal Duck Stamp Contest**
To select the design for the following year's Migratory Bird Hunting and Conservation Stamp. (Proceeds from the sale of Duck Stamps purchase wetlands & wildlife habitat for the National Wildlife Refuge System). Any U.S. Citizen, national, or resident alien may submit a design between July 1 and September 15. A live portrayal of any bird(s) of the five or fewer identified eligible species must be the dominant feature of the design. The design may depict more than one of the eligible species. The design must be the contestant's original creation and may not be copied or duplicated from previously published art, including photographs. Entries are judged on the basis of anatomical accuracy, artistic composition, and suitability for engraving in the production of a stamp. The Winning Artist receives: (1) publicity and media recognition; (2) a pane of Duck Stamps signed by the Secretary of the Interior: (3) limited edition "artist's" souvenir card; (4) select travel to prestigious national waterfowl and wildlife ceremonies; (5) special recognition as guest speaker at special events: and (6) the opportunity to enter a contract with publisher of their choice. Winning artists also sell prints of their prize entries, which are eagerly sought by collectors. Awarded annually. From 1934 to 1948, a nationally recognized wildlife artist was commissioned to produce the design. Since 1949, an open competition has been held. Formerly: (2006) Federal Migratory Bird Hunting and Conservation Stamp Contest.

• 20593 •
U.S. Forest Service
Northeastern Research Station
PO Box 267
Irvine, PA 16329
Phone: (814)563-1040
Fax: (814)563-1048
E-mail: cweldon@fs.fed.us
Home Page: http://www.fs.fed.us/ne/warren

• 20594 • **Summer Paid Internships**
For biological and ecological data collection. 7607848

• 20595 •
U.S. Fund for UNICEF
U.S. Committee
Carol Bellamy, Exec.Dir.
333 E 38th St.
New York, NY 10016
Phone: (212)686-5522
Phone: 800-FOR-KIDS
Toll-Free: 800-553-1200
Fax: (212)779-1670
Fax: (212)779-1670
E-mail: information@unicefusa.org
Home Page: http://www.unicefusa.org

• 20596 • **Goodwill Ambassadors for UNICEF**
To recognize individuals who have made outstanding contributions over a long period of time. A silver statuette is awarded on rare occasions at the discretion of UNICEF's Executive Director.

• 20597 • **Maurice Pate Memorial Award**
To recognize an institution for its contributions in fields benefiting children. The selected institution is given assistance to strengthen its services to other developing countries. In addition, fellowships are awarded which enable people from outside the country to study at the chosen institution. A monetary award is presented for a variety of purposes such as having a faculty member teach in other regions or travel to become more familiar with requirements of students outside the institution. Awarded annually. Established in 1965 in memory of Maurice Pate, the first Executive Director of UNICEF.

• 20598 • **UNICEF Award for Distinguished Service**
For outstanding services at the international level to UNICEF. A UNICEF medallion is awarded as appropriate.

• 20599 • **UNICEF Award for Films**
To recognize films that put special emphasis on children in developing countries. A UNICEF statuette is awarded at international film festivals when the occasion arises.

• 20600 •
United States General Services Administration
David L. Bibb, Actg.Dir.
1800 F St. NW
Washington, DC 20405
Phone: (202)501-0100
Home Page: http://www.gsa.gov

• 20601 • **Excellence in Administration Award**
To recognize outstanding achievements in administration by Federal managers. Achievements that may be recognized are restricted to the areas of supply, procurement, automatic data processing, information management, traffic and travel management, telecommunications, building management, real estate, design and construction management, fleet manage-

ment, general administrative management, and health and safety contributions to these areas. Only agency heads may nominate employees who have demonstrated outstanding leadership resulting in effective administrative management improvements within the last two years. Established in 1986.

• 20602 •
United States Golf Association
James T. Snow, Natl.Dir.
PO Box 708
Far Hills, NJ 07931
Phone: (908)234-2300
Fax: (908)234-9687
E-mail: usga@usga.org
Home Page: http://www.usga.org

• 20603 • **Curtis Cup**
To recognize the winning team of a match between two amateur women's teams representing the United States and the British Isles. The American team (eight players) is selected by the USGA. The match is held every other year, with the site alternating between the two countries. The match was inaugurated in 1930 as a vehicle of international friendship and understanding. The Cup was donated by the Misses Harriot and Margaret Curtis who, between them, won four USGA Women's Amateur championships between the years 1906 and 1912.

• 20604 • **Joseph Dey Award**
Recognizes meritorious service to the game as a volunteer. Awarded annually. Established in 1995 in honor of Joe Dey, United States Golf Association Executive Director from 1934 to 1969.

• 20605 • **Green Section Award**
To recognize distinguished service to golf through work with turf grass. Individuals in the field of agronomy are eligible. A bronze plaque is awarded annually at the Golf Course Superintendents Association of America Annual Banquet and Show. Established in 1961.

• 20606 • **Bob Jones Award**
This, the highest USGA honor, is given for distinguished sportsmanship in golf, and for the demonstration of the following personal qualities esteemed in sport: fair play; self-control and, perhaps, self-denial; generosity of spirit; respect for the game and individuals involved; and unselfishness. A bronze plaque is awarded annually. Established in 1955 in honor of Bob Jones and his vast contributions toward the cause of fair play.

• 20607 • **USGA Championships**
Thirteen golf championships are held each year in various places: the U.S. Open (players may be professional or amateur); the U.S. Amateur (players must be amateur); the U.S. Women's Open (players may be professional or amateur); the U.S. Women's Amateur (players must be amateur); the U.S. Senior Open (players may be professional or amateur but all players must be 50 years or older); the U.S. Amateur Public Links (must be amateur public course players); the U.S. Women's Amateur Public Links (must be amateur public course players); the U.S. Junior Amateur (players must be amateurs under 18 years of age); the U.S. Girls' Junior (players must be amateurs under 18 years of age); the U.S.G.A. Senior Amateur (players must be amateurs over 55 years of age); the U.S.G.A.Senior Women's Amateur (players must be amateurs over 50 years of age); the U.S. Mid-Amateur (players must be amateurs over 25 years of age); and U.S. Women's Mid-Amateur (players must be amateurs over 25 years of age). Three of these tournaments were first played in 1895; the Women's Open began in 1946.

• 20608 • **Walker Cup**
Presented to the winning team of a match between amateur teams representing the United States and Great Britain. The American team (ten players) is selected by the USGA. The match is held every other year, with the site alternating between the two countries. The Walker Cup competition was inaugurated in 1922. The Cup was given by George Herbert Walker, president of the United States Golf Association in 1920.

• 20609 •
United States Handball Association
Vern Roberts, Exec.Dir.
2333 N Tucson Blvd.
Tucson, AZ 85716
Phone: (520)795-0434
Fax: (520)795-0455
E-mail: handball@ushandball.org
Home Page: http://ushandball.org

• 20610 • **USHA National Championships**
To recognize the winners of the one-wall, three-wall and four-wall national championships. The competition is held in various events amateurs, junior, pro, singles, doubles, etc., in age categories from 11 and under to 80 and over. Conducted annually. Cash awards of $30,000 are given to pro entrants in the Pro Singles event. Established in 1951.

• 20611 •
U.S. Hang Gliding Association
Jayne Depanfilis, Exec.Dir.
PO Box 1330
Colorado Springs, CO 80901-1330
Phone: (719)632-8300
Toll-Free: 800-616-6888
Fax: (719)632-6417
E-mail: ushga@ushga.org
Home Page: http://www.ushga.org

• 20612 • **Chapter of the Year**
For recognition of the USHGA chapter that has conducted during the current year the most outstanding programs in various activities which reflect in a positive manner upon the Chapter and the sport. Consideration is given to beginner and novice programs, site procurement, safety, membership development and retention, USHGA membership development, and civic service. A USHGA Chapter may be nominated by a member by December 1. A plaque is presented annually at the spring meeting of the board of directors. Established in 1983.

• 20613 • **Exceptional Service**
To recognize the Association member who has provided the most outstanding volunteer service to USHGA at the national, regional or local level during the current year. Members of Association may be nominated by December 1. A plaque is presented annually at the spring meeting of the board of directors. Established in 1983.

• 20614 • **Newsletter of the Year**
For recognition of the most outstanding hang gliding and/or parasailing newsletter series in the current year that has been supportive of the sport and the sponsoring Chapter's activities. Consideration is given to member service, layout, article variety, safety promotion, and pictures. A USHGA newsletter may be nominated by an Association member by December 1. A plaque is presented annually at the spring meeting of the board of directors. Established in 1983.

• 20615 • **Presidential Citation**
This, the Association's highest award, is given to recognize an individual, group, or organization that has made a significant contribution to the advancement of the sport of hang gliding and/or parasailing. Members of the Association may make nominations by December 1. A plaque is presented annually at the spring meeting of the board of directors. Established in 1972. Formerly: (1985) Ed Guardia Memorial Trophy.

• 20616 • **United States Hang Gliding Association Commendation**
To recognize a member who has in the current year exhibited volunteer service to USHGA that is of excellent quality and of significant importance to the Association. The volunteer work may have begun prior to the current year, but must be ongoing or have been completed in the current year. A USHGA member may be nominated by a member by December 1. A plaque is presented annually at the spring meeting of the board of directors. Established in 1985.

• 20617 •
United States Harness Writers' Association
Jerry Connors Jr., Sec.
Box 1314
Mechanicsburg, PA 17055
Phone: (717)651-5889
Fax: (716)344-1187
E-mail: ushwa@paonline.com
Home Page: http://www.ustrotting.com/absolutenm/anmviewer.asp?a=6793&z=30

• 20618 • **Ed Binneweg Trophy**
To recognize the leading money-winning driver of North America. Awarded annually. Established in 1979.

• 20619 • Glen Garnsey Trainers Award
To recognize an outstanding harness horse trainer. Awarded annually. Established in 1985.

• 20620 • E. Roland Harriman Memorial Trophy Horse of the Year Award
To recognize the horse of the year as determined through voting by members of the Association. Awarded annually. Established in 1949.

• 20621 • Bill Haughton Good Guy Award
To honor an individual and/or an organization for cooperation with the press, and to honor those whose personality and character best exemplify the late Clem McCarthy. Race tracks, horses, publicity men, and newspapermen are not eligible. A plaque is awarded annually. Established in 1964. Formerly: Clem McCarthy Good Guy Award.

• 20622 • Headliner Award
To recognize the owner of the horse of the opposite gait of the Horse of the Year. Established in 1949.

• 20623 • Honorary Member
To recognize outstanding achievement. Awarded annually. Established in 1950.

• 20624 • Mike Lee Trophy
To recognize the driver winning the most races in North America. Awarded annually. Established in 1949.

• 20625 • Living Hall of Fame
To honor an individual whose contributions and achievements in the sport of harness racing are truly outstanding. Trainers, drivers, race secretaries, administrators, breeders, owners, etc., are eligible. A lifelike, full color statuette is placed on permanent exhibit in the Hall of Fame of the Trotter in the Trotting Horse Museum in Goshen, New York, and a Hall of Fame ring is given to the honoree. Awarded annually. Established in 1958. Co-sponsored by the Harness Racing Museum and Hall of Fame, P.O. Box 590, 240 Main St., Goshen, NY 10924, telephone: (914) 294-6330.

• 20626 • National Breeders Trophy
To recognize the breeder of the Horse of the Year. Awarded annually. Established in 1961.

• 20627 • Dan Patch Awards
To recognize eight two- and three-year-old top trotters and pacers of the previous year.

• 20628 • Proximity Achievement Award
To honor an individual or organization for outstanding contributions to the sport of harness racing over a long period of time. A plaque and membership pin are awarded annually. Established in 1951.

• 20629 • Rising Star Award
To recognize an outstanding young harness trainer and/or driver for exceptional early career accomplishments. Awarded annually. Established in 1986.

• 20630 • Jack Schultz Perpetual Memorial Trophy
To recognize the national dash-winning driver with the highest in-the-money percentages for 500 or more starts. Awarded annually. Established in 1969.

• 20631 • Special Awards
To recognize outstanding achievement. Awarded annually. Established in 1972.

• 20632 • USHWAn-of-the-Year
To recognize a member for outstanding service and dedication to the Association. Awarded annually. Established in 1979.

• 20633 • Writers Corner Hall of Fame
To recognize outstanding media coverage of harness racing. Association members, living or deceased, are eligible.

• 20634 •
United States Harness Writers' Association, Vernon Chapter
James J. Moran, Sec.-Treas.
Vernon Downs
PO Box 860
Vernon, NY 13476-0860
Phone: (315)829-2201
Toll-Free: 877-777-8559
Fax: (315)829-2931
E-mail: vdowns@tds.net
Home Page: http://www.vernondowns.com

• 20635 • Dick Mumpton Memorial Award
For most promising driver. Recognition award bestowed annually.

• 20636 •
United States Hockey Hall of Fame
801 Hat Trick Ave.
PO Box 657
Eveleth, MN 55734
Phone: (218)744-5167
Toll-Free: 800-443-7825
Fax: (218)744-2590
Home Page: http://www.ushockeyhall.com

• 20637 • United States Hockey Hall of Fame
To honor American developed hockey personnel in the categories of player, coach, referee, administrator, and support personnel who have performed in the areas of high school, college, amateur, international, and professional hockey; and who have distinguished themselves by an outstanding level of performance and character, reflecting favorably on the game. Enshrinees are honored within the Hall of Fame by individual plaques which contain their biography and photograph. The enshrinees are presented with individual plaques showing their likeness during the time of active participation in the sport. Awarded annually. Established in 1973.

• 20638 •
U.S. Holocaust Memorial Council
Sara J. Bloomfield, Dir.
100 Raoul Wallenberg Pl. SW
Washington, DC 20024-2126
Phone: (202)488-0400
Phone: (202)488-0406
Fax: (202)314-7881
Home Page: http://www.ushmm.org

• 20639 • Eisenhower Liberation Medal
To honor those individuals who played a significant role in the fight against Nazism and the liberation of Nazi death camps. A medal is awarded annually. Established in 1986 in memory of President Dwight D. Eisenhower and his role as the Supreme Commander of the Allied Forces in the European Theater.

• 20640 • U.S. Medal of Remembrance
To recognize extraordinary service to remembrance and to the U.S. Holocaust Memorial Council. A medal is awarded when merited. Established in 1990.

• 20641 •
United States Institute for Theatre Technology
John S. Uthoff, Pres.
6443 Ridings Rd.
Syracuse, NY 13206-1111
Phone: (315)463-6463
Toll-Free: 800-938-7488
Fax: (866)398-7488
E-mail: info@office.usitt.org
Home Page: http://www.usitt.org

• 20642 • Award for Scene Design
Awarded to an individual who has demonstrated skill in the area of scene design in the performing arts while pursuing a graduate degree, provision has been made to allow nominations of individuals who have completed an advanced degree in the previous two years. A sample portfolio with five to ten slides, showing the nominee's work, must accompany a nomination. The award, founded in 1997, is co-sponsored by Rose Brand.

• 20643 • Barbizon Award for Lighting Design
Awarded to an individual who has demonstrated skill in the area of lighting in the performing arts while pursuing a graduate degree. The nominee may also have completed an advanced degree in within the previous two years. A portfolio and five to ten slides must accompany the nomination, showing the nominee's work. Established in 1997, the award is co-sponsored by Barbizon.

• 20644 • Clear-Com Intercom Systems Sound Achievement Award
Awarded to an individual who has demonstrated tallent or great potential in the area of sound in

Awards are arranged in alphabetical order below their administering organizations

the performing arts while pursuing a graduate degree. Nominees must be in an advanced degree program or have completed an advanced program no longer than two years earlier. Nomination should be accompanied by a portfolio and cassette, CD-ROM, or VHS recording of the nominee's work. Established in 1996 the award is co-sponsored by Clear-Com.

• 20645 • Golden Hammer Scenic Technology Award
Annual award of recognition.

• 20646 • The KM Fabrics Technical Production Award
Awarded to an individual who has demonstrated excellence or outstanding potential in the area of technical direction or production management in the performing arts while pursuing a graduate degree or have completed an advanced degree in the last two years. Nominations must cite examples of work and include a portfolio of 5 to 10 slides of the nominee's work. Co-sponsored by KM Fabrics, Inc. The award was established in 1994.

• 20647 • Kryolon Makeup Design Award
Awarded to recognize skill in makeup design in the performing arts while pursuing a graduate degree, the nominee may have completed an advanced degree in the previous two years. A portfolio with slides must accompany nominations to show the nominee's work. Established in 1998, the award is co-sponsored by Kryolan.

• 20648 • Rose Brand Award for Scenic Lighting
Annual award of recognition.

• 20649 • Scenic Technology Award
Awarded to an individual who has demonstrated skill as a scenic technitian in stage engineering, shop management, scene painting, scenery or properties construction and craft while pursuing a graduate degree, the nominee may also have completed an advanced degree in the preceding two years. A portfolio must be sent, with five to ten slides of the nominee's work, for each nomination. The award was established in 1998 by Bernhard R. Works to honor Frederick A. Buerki.

• 20650 • Stage Management Award
Awarded to an individual who has demonstrated skill in stage management while completing a graduate degree, the nominee may have also finished the advanced degree in the previous two years. A sample script with cues and blocking, all schedules, lists, plots and running sheets used for one show should be included with the nomination, as well as a playbill or program for the show. Established in 2000.

• 20651 • USITT Architecture Design Award
Annual award of recognition.

• 20652 • USITT/Edward Kook Endowment Fund
Annual award of recognition.

• 20653 • Zelma H. Weisfeld Costume Design & Technology Award
Awarded to an individual who has demonstrated skill in costume design in the performing arts while pursuing a graduate degree, nominees may have completed an advanced degree in the previous two years. A portfolio with slides must accompany the nomination to show the nominee's work. Established in 1997 by Zelma H. Weisfield, she is co-sponsor of this award.

• 20654 •
U.S. Institute of Peace
Richard H. Solomon, Pres.
1200 17th St. NW
Washington, DC 20036-3011
Phone: (202)457-1700
Fax: (202)429-6063
E-mail: usiprequests@usip.org
Home Page: http://www.usip.org

• 20655 • Grant Program
To provide financial support for research, education, and training, and the dissemination of information on international peace and conflict resolution. Unsolicited grants are provided for any topics that fall within the Institute's broad mandate. Deadlines are April 1 and October 1. In addition, the Institute conducts an annual solicited grants competition on themes and topics of special interest. The deadline for application is January 1.

• 20656 • National Peace Essay Contest
To provoke serious thought and careful writing on a subject regarding peace or the resolution of international conflict. A new topic is announced each year. State first-place winners receive expense-paid trips to Washington, DC for a week-long awards program and the announcement of national winners. Both state and national high school winners receive college scholarships. Awarded annually. Established in 1988.

• 20657 • Jennings Randolph Program for International Peace
To enable outstanding professionals and scholars to undertake research and education projects that will increase knowledge and spread awareness among the public and policymakers regarding the nature of violent international conflict and the full range of ways to deal with it peacefully. Individuals from a broad spectrum of backgrounds - higher education, government, diplomacy, international affairs, military service, law, the media, business, labor, religion, humanitarian affairs, and others - may submit proposals. Open to individuals from any country who have specific interest or experience in international peace and conflict management. Two types of awards are presented: Senior Fellows - statesmen, scholars, or other professionals with national or international stature by virtue of widely recognized scholarly or practical accomplishments in international peace and conflict management or other relevant fields, or professionals or scholars who demonstrate substantial accomplishment or promise of exceptional leadership in various career fields; and Peace Scholars outstanding students in recognized doctoral programs in American universities who have demonstrated a clear interest in issues of international peace and conflict management and have completed all required work toward their doctoral degrees except their dissertations. Applications are due October 5 for Senior Fellows and November 15 for Peace Scholars. Stipends and other support are ordinarily provided for a one-year period.

• 20658 •
United States Intercollegiate Lacrosse Association
John Spring, Exec.Dir.
3738 West Lake Rd.
Perry, NY 14530
Phone: (585)237-5886
Fax: (585)237-5886
E-mail: usilajspring@aol.com
Home Page: http://www.usila.org/

• 20659 • W. H. Brine Awards
To recognize the outstanding player in the Division I and Division III Championship games.

• 20660 • Edward A. Devine Memorial Award
To recognize the most outstanding lacrosse player in a community college.

• 20661 • Lt. Raymond J. Enners Award
To recognize the most outstanding lacrosse player of the year in Division I.

• 20662 • C. Markland Kelly Trophy
To recognize the best goalie among team members of the Association. Awarded annually.

• 20663 • Francis L. (Babe) Kraus Award
To recognize the most outstanding Coach of the Year in Division II, and III.

• 20664 • Lt. Donald McLaughlin, Jr. Memorial Award
To recognize the most outstanding midfielder of the year in Division I.

• 20665 • Howdy Myers Man of the Year Award
To recognize the most outstanding lacrosse player of the year.

• 20666 • William Schmeisser Award
To recognize the most outstanding defense lacrosse player of the year. Formerly: (2006) William Schmeisser Memorial Trophy.

• 20667 • William C. Stiles Memorial Award
To recognize the most outstanding lacrosse defenseman of the year in Division III.

• 20668 • Jason G. (Stranny) Stranahan Award
To recognize the most valuable lacrosse player of the year in the North-South All-Star Game.

• 20669 • F. Morris Touchstone Award
To recognize the most outstanding Coach of the Year in Division I.

• 20670 • Lt. Col. J.L. (Jack) Turnbull Award
To recognize the best attack player among team members of the Association. Awarded annually. Formerly: (2006) Jack Turnbull Trophy.

• 20671 • USILA Awards
To recognize the outstanding midfield player and the outstanding player in Division III.

• 20672 • USILA Trophy
To recognize the Championship Team for Division III.

• 20673 • Wilson Wingate Trophy
To recognize the championship team of Division I. The team is selected by a committee of the Association, based on club records. Awarded annually. Established in 1936.

• 20674 •
U.S. International Film and Video Festival
Lee W. Gluckman Jr., Chm.
713 S Pacific Coast Hwy., Ste. A
Redondo Beach, CA 90277-4233
Phone: (310)540-0959
Fax: (310)316-8905
E-mail: filmfestinfo@filmfestawards.com
Home Page: http://www.filmfestawards.com

• 20675 • U.S. International Film and Video Festival
To honor business, television, documentary, industrial and informational productions with a broad array of both subject and production technique categories. International producers may submit their production prior to the annual March 1st entry deadline. Productions produced or released in the 18 months prior to the deadline are eligible. Various awards are presented, including the Gold Camera Award, Silver Screen Award, Grand Prix, and the One World Award. Awarded annually. Established in 1968.

• 20676 •
U.S. Junior Chamber of Commerce
John Shiroma, Exec.VP
PO Box 7
Tulsa, OK 74102-0007
Phone: (918)584-2481
Toll-Free: 800-JAY-CEES
Fax: (918)584-4422
E-mail: directorcommunications@usjaycees.org
Home Page: http://www.usjaycees.org
Formerly: (1991) United States Jaycees.

• 20677 • Outstanding Young Farmer Awards
To foster better urban-rural relations by creating an understanding and interest in today's farmers, their professional abilities, and problems as a world food supplier. Individuals between the ages of 21 and 39 who are actual farm operators, deriving a minimum of two-thirds of their income from farming are eligible. Selection is based on progress in agricultural career, extent of soil and water conservation practices, and contributions to well-being of the community, state, and nation. Each state participating in the awards program selects one state winner; the national organization then selects four national winners. Awarded annually in February. Established in 1954. Sponsored by John Deere and Company. Supported by the Outstanding Farmers of America (OFA) Fraternity.

• 20678 • Ten Outstanding Young Americans
To recognize young American citizens between the ages of 18 through 40 who have made significant contributions to their community, state, or nation. Selection is based on outstanding involvement exhibited in three of the following areas: personal improvement, financial success and economic innovation, social improvement as regards major social problems, philanthropic contribution or charitable service, politics and governmental service, scientific or technological contribution, legal reform, cultural achievement, academic leadership, athletic accomplishment, moral and religious leadership, success in the influence of public opinion, and other important contributions. The TOYA "Touching Hands" trophy and a sterling silver medallion are awarded annually to ten individuals in January. Established in 1938 as the Ten Outstanding Young Men of America by Durward Howes, 1930-31 president of the national Junior Chamber organization, and changed names in 1984 in concordance with the admittance of women as members. Nomination deadline August 1. Formerly: America's Ten Outstanding Young Men.

• 20679 •
U.S. Lacrosse and The Lacrosse Museum and National Hall of Fame
Steven B. Stenersen, Exec.Dir.
113 W University Pkwy.
Baltimore, MD 21210
Phone: (410)235-6882
Fax: (410)366-6735
E-mail: info@uslacrosse.org
Home Page: http://www.uslacrosse.org

• 20680 • National Lacrosse Hall of Fame
To honor those men and women, past and present, who by their deeds as players and coaches, and other contributors to the sport of lacrosse, and by the example of their lives, personify the great contribution to our way of life. Applicants must be 15 years removed from college, if they attended college, or 15 years from high school. Plaques are also awarded. Established in 1959.

• 20681 •
United States Lighthouse Society
Wayne C. Wheeler, Pres. & Exec.Dir.
244 Kearny St., 5th Fl.
San Francisco, CA 94108
Phone: (415)362-7255
Fax: (415)362-7464
Home Page: http://www.uslhs.org

• 20682 • Annual Photography Contest
To recognize the best color photographs and 35mm slides and prints of lighthouses. Members of the Society are eligible. Certificate and cash prizes are awarded annually in November and announced in the January magazine. All photos become property of USLHS Established in 1985.

• 20683 •
U.S. Marine Corps Combat Correspondents Association
Don H. Gee, Exec.Dir.
238 Cornwall Circle
Chalfont, PA 18914-2318
Phone: (215)822-6898
Phone: (215)822-6723
Fax: (215)822-0163
E-mail: usmccca@aol.com
Home Page: http://www.usmccca.org

• 20684 • Brig. Gen. Robert L. Denig Distinguished Service Award
This, the Association's highest award, was established to recognize civilian media personnel for their contributions in presenting a true picture of the United States Marine Corps and the ideals and traditions for which it stands to the American public. A person, or persons, whose primary employment is as a journalist, writer, photographer, photojournalist, radio or television broadcaster, artist or illustrator, cinematographer, author or director working in print, film or electronic media; or a person or persons employed in a management and/or supervisory position for a newspaper, magazine, radio or television broadcasting outlet, motion picture firm, art gallery or graphic arts business may be nominated by April 30. Awarded when merited at the Association's Annual conference. Established in 1968.

• 20685 • Donald L. Dickson Memorial Award
To recognize a member of the USMCCCA for notable achievement in support of the Association. Nominations may be submitted by April 30. Presented annually when merited. Established in 1975.

• 20686 • Distinguished Performance Award
To recognize material prepared and published, broadcast or publicly exhibited during the previous award year which documents Marine Corps history or activities by Marine Corps units, organizations or individual Marines. Material is considered in the following categories: news story; news feature story; feature story; picture story; news photograph; feature photograph; photojournalism; radio news; radio feature; tele-

vision/motion picture news; television/motion picture feature; illustration; marine corps art; sports writing for print media; TV sports show; sports photography; radio sports show; and an open category. Journalists, broadcasters, photographers and artists responsible for the work who are active duty Marines, members of the Marine Corps Reserve on active duty, or members of the Marine Corps Reserve attending regular drill periods are eligible. The deadline for entries is April 22. Monetary awards of $50 to $100, engraved plaques, and certificates are awarded annually. Established in 1967 at the request of General Wallace M. Greene, Jr., then Commandant of the Marine Corps.

• 20687 • Louis R. Lowery Memorial Award

To recognize an active duty marine for best photography appearing in *Leatherneck* magazine. Established in 1987 in memory of Louis R. Lowery, an active member of USMCCCA since its founding and Director of Photography for *Leatherneck* for many years.

• 20688 • Ronald D. Lyons Memorial Award

To recognize an active duty marine for the best article appearing in *Leatherneck* magazine. Awarded annually. Established in 1986 in memory of Ronald D. Lyons, an active member of USMCCCA since its founding, and the editor of *Leatherneck* magazine at the time of his death in 1985.

• 20689 •

United States Masters Swimming
Tracy Grilli, Admin.
PO Box 185
Londonderry, NH 03053-0185
Toll-Free: 800-550-SWIM
Fax: (603)537-0204
E-mail: info@usms.org
Home Page: http://www.usms.org

• 20690 • Capt. Ransom J. Arthur, M.D. Award

To recognize the person who has done the most to further the objectives of Masters Swimming. An engraved plaque is awarded annually. A permanent trophy resides at the International Hall of Fame in Ft. Lauderdale, Florida. Established in 1973 in honor of Captain Ransom J. Arthur, M.D. who, by his sacrifice, perseverance, and dedication to improving the health of the adults of this nation through swimming, established the Masters Swimming Program.

• 20691 • Dawn Musselman Award

To honor the fighting spirit, moral and physical courage, and outstanding performances in setting world records in five events through three age groups of Masters Swimming. The woman who wins the Long Course 100 meter USMS Championship in the 60-64 age group is eligible. An engraved plaque is awarded annually at the Long Course Championship. Established in 1986 by Pacific Northwest Masters Swimming Committee and Bob Musselman, husband of Dawn Musselman who was 72 when she died, and set her last world record three months before her death. Additional information is available from Kathy Casey, 11114 111th Street, SW, Tacoma, Washington 98498.

• 20692 • Speedo/USMS Coach of the Year Award

To honor a Masters Swimming Coach for club and individual accomplishments, publications and articles, contributions on the local and national level, and long-term contributions to Masters Swimming. Nominations must be submitted by July 1. Presented annually at the USMS/USAS Convention. Established in 1986.

• 20693 • David Yorzyk Memorial Award

To recognize the male or female who performs the most outstanding 400 yard Individual Medley at the USMS National Short Course Championships. A plaque embedded with a collector's Olympic bronze medal is awarded annually. Established in 1986 by Dr. Manuel Sanquily in memory of David Yorzyk, a brilliant age group and college swimmer, killed in a highway mishap. Additional information is available from Dr. Manuel Sanquily, Country Club Rd., Scarboro, NY 10591; telephone: (914) 631-7553.

• 20694 •

U.S. Metric Association
Valerie Antoine, Exec.Dir.
10245 Andasol Ave.
Northridge, CA 91325-1504
Phone: (818)363-5606
Fax: (818)363-5606
E-mail: hillger@cira.colostate.edu
Home Page: http://lamar.colostate.edu/~hillger

Awards discontinued.

• 20695 • Science Fair Award

To recognize students who exemplify the best use of the metric system in a science entry at each fair hosted by the Regional Science Service of the International Science & Engineering Fair. Awarded annually.

• 20696 •

U.S.-Mexico Border Health Association
Dr. Manuel Robles Linares, Exec.Dir.
5400 Suncrest Dr., Ste. C-5
El Paso, TX 79912-5615
Phone: (915)833-6450
Fax: (915)833-7840
E-mail: mail@usmbha.org
Home Page: http://www.usmbha.org

• 20697 • Outstanding Health Worker (Trabajador del Ano en Salud)

For recognition of contributions to the health field. Nominations must be submitted by March 15. A plaque is awarded annually at the convention. Established in 1965 by Dr. Stella B. Soroker.

• 20698 •

United States-Mexico Chamber of Commerce
Albert Zapanta, Pres./CEO
1300 Pennsylvania Ave. NW, Ste. 270
Washington, DC 20004-3021
Phone: (202)312-1520
Toll-Free: 800-USM-COC1
Fax: (202)312-1530
E-mail: news-hq@usmcoc.org
Home Page: http://www.usmcoc.org

• 20699 • Good Neighbor Award

Recognizes for contributions to improved US-Mexico relations. Awarded annually.

• 20700 •

United States Military Academy Association of Graduates
Seth Hudgins, Pres.
698 Mills Rd.
Herbert Alumni Center
West Point, NY 10996
Phone: (845)446-1569
Toll-Free: 800-BE-A-GRAD
Fax: (914)446-5325
E-mail: aog@aogusma.org
Home Page: http://www.aogusma.org

• 20701 • Sylvanus Thayer Award

For recognition of citizens of the United States whose records of service to their country, accomplishments in the national interest, and manner of achievement exemplify outstanding devotion to the principles expressed in the motto of the United States Military Academy - "Duty, Honor, Country." Graduates of the United States Military Academy are not eligible. A citation and inscribed gold medal are presented annually, usually in September. Established in 1958 in honor of the legendary graduate of 1808, Sylvanus Thayer, known as the Father of the Military Academy.

• 20702 •

U.S. Mirror Class Association
John M. Borthwick, Sec.
5305 Marian Dr.
Lyndhurst, OH 44124
Phone: (440)461-7231
E-mail: jmbrbb@aol.com

• 20703 • Honorary Member

To recognize individuals who have made a significant contribution to the United States Mirror Class Association activities, and those who have furthered the skills of others in sailing mirror dinghy boats. A plaque and a free lifetime membership are awarded when merited at the annual meeting. Established in 1972.

• 20704 •
United States Modern Pentathlon Association
Charlene Loeffler, Exec.Asst.
5415 Bandera Rd., Ste. 512
San Antonio, TX 78238
Phone: (210)229-2008
Phone: (210)229-2004
Fax: (210)647-7194
E-mail: loefflercharlene@aol.com
Home Page: http://www.usapentathlon.org

• 20705 • **General George S. Patton, Jr. Memorial Trophy**
For recognition of the overall winner of the Seniors Division of the U.S. National Championships, an annual competition. The pentathlon events consist of riding, fencing, shooting, swimming, and running. A rotating trophy and permanent plaque are awarded annually. Established in 1955 and renewed in 1971 in memory of General George S. Patton, Jr., the first Olympic athlete of the United States in the Modern Pentathlon in 1912, and a military leader. In addition, a women's champion and a junior champion have been presented since 1977 and 1973, respectively.

• 20706 •
United States Naval Institute
Thomas L. Wilkerson, CEO/Publisher
291 Wood Rd.
Annapolis, MD 21402
Phone: (410)268-6110
Toll-Free: 800-233-8764
Fax: (410)269-7940
E-mail: twilkerson@usni.org
Home Page: http://www.navalinstitute.org

• 20707 • **Armed Forces Joint Warfighting Essay Contest**
To recognize outstanding essays on combat readiness. Essays must include uni-service detail, but must focus on joint application in terms of tactics, strategy, weaponry, combat training, force structure, doctrine, operations, organization for combat, or interoperability of hardware, software, and procedures. Military professionals and civilians are eligible. The deadline for entries is April 1. Monetary prizes of $2,500, $2,000, and $1,000, as well as publication in the July *Proceedings,* are awarded annually. Formerly: Colin L. Powell Joint Warfighting Essay Contest.

• 20708 • **Vincent Astor Memorial Leadership Essay Contest**
To promote research, thinking, and writing on the topic of leadership in the U.S. Navy, Marine Corps, and Coast Guard. The contest is open to commissioned officers, regular and reserve, in the U.S. Navy, Marine Corps, and Coast Guard in pay grades 0-1, 0-2, and 0-3 (ensign/2nd lieutenant; lieutenant (junior grade)/first lieutenant; and lieutenant/captain) at the time the essay is submitted; and U.S. Navy, Marine Corps, and Coast Guard officer trainees within one year of receiving their commissions. Essays must be original and must not exceed 3,500 words. The deadline for entry is February 15. Essays are judged by the Naval Institute's Editorial Board for depth of research, analytical and interpretive qualities, and original thinking on the topic of leadership. Essays should not be merely expositions or personal narratives. The following prizes are awarded: First Prize - $1,500, a Naval Institute Gold Medal, and a Life Membership in the Naval Institute; Second Prize - $1,000, a silver medal, and a one-year membership in the Naval Institute; two Third Prizes - $500 each, a bronze medal and a oneyear membership in the Naval Institute. Established in 1973 in memory of Vincent Astor.

• 20709 • **Arleigh Burke Essay Contest**
For recognition of an essay relating to the objective of the U.S. Naval Institute: "The advancement of professional, literary, and scientific knowledge in the naval and maritime services, and the advancement of the knowledge of sea power." Essays must be original, must not exceed 3,500 words, and must not have been previously published. Essays must be received on or before December 1. An essay entered in this contest should be analytical and/or interpretive, not merely an exposition, a personal narrative, or a report. The following prizes are awarded: First prize $3,000, a Gold Medal, and a Life Membership in the Naval Institute; Second Prize - $2,000, a Silver Medal, and a one-year membership in the Naval Institute; and Third Prize - $1,000, a Bronze Medal, and a one-year membership in the Naval Institute. Awarded annually. Established in honor of Admiral Arleigh A. Burke, USN (Ret.).

• 20710 • **Coast Guard Essay Contest**
To recognize outstanding essays that discuss current issues and new directions for the Coast Guard. The deadline for entries is June 1. Monetary prizes of $2,000, $1,500, and $750, as well as publication of the essays in the December issue of *Proceedings,* are awarded annually.

• 20711 • **Enlisted Essay Contest**
To recognize outstanding essays written by enlisted personnel (active duty, reserve and retired). Essay must speak to the mission of the Naval Institute: The advancement of professional, literary and scientific knowledge in the naval and maritime services, and the advancement of the knowledge of sea power. Prizes are $1,500 for First Place, $1,000 for Second Place, and $500 for Third Place. Held annually.

• 20712 • **International Navies Essay Contest**
To recognize outstanding essays that discuss strategic, geographic, and cultural influences on individual or regional navies, their commitments and capabilities, and relationships with other navies. The deadline for entry is August 1. Monetary prizes of $1,000, $750, and $500 are awarded.

• 20713 • **International Navies Photo Contest**
To recognize the best photos of international and maritime subjects from countries other than the United States. Up to five photos may be submitted by amateur or professional photographers. The deadline for entries is August 1. Monetary prizes of $200, $100, and $50, as well as publication of the photos in the annual March International Navies issue of *Proceedings,* are awarded for the top three entries.

• 20714 • **Marine Corps Essay Contest**
To recognize outstanding essays on current issues and new directions for the Marine Corps. The deadline for entries is May 1. Monetary prizes of $2,000, $1,500, and $750, as well as publication of the essays in the November issue of *Proceedings,* are awarded annually.

• 20715 • **Naval and Maritime Photo Contest**
For recognition of outstanding photos of a naval or maritime subject. Individuals must submit up to five photos by December 31. Entries must be either black and white prints, color prints, or color transparencies. The following monetary prizes are awarded: first prize - $500, second prize $350, third prize - $250, and 15 Honorable mentions - $100 each. The winning photos are published in an issue of *Proceedings.* Established in 1961. Co-sponsored by Eastman Kodak Company.

• 20716 •
United States Office of Personnel Management
Linda M. Springer, Dir.
Performance Management & Incentive Awards Division
1900 E St. NW
Washington, DC 20415
Phone: (202)606-1800
Fax: (202)606-2532
Home Page: http://www.opm.gov

Formerly: (1978) United States Civil Service Commission.

• 20717 • **Presidential Rank Awards**
To recognize members of the Senior Executive Service for sustained distinguished performance. Career SES members may be granted one of two Presidential ranks: Distinguished Executive and Meritorious Executive. An executive may earn each award only once in any five-year period. Neither non-career nor limited appointees are eligible. SES executives who receive the rank of Distinguished Executive are awarded 35% of their base salary; those who receive the rank of Meritorious Executive are awarded 20% of their base salary. Each recipient receives a framed certificate signed by the President.

• 20718 • **President's Award for Distinguished Federal Civilian Service**
This award stands at the pinnacle of the government's system of granting honorary recognition to its career employees for special efforts significantly above and beyond the requirements of their position. Individuals whose outstanding achievements have current impact on improved government or the public interest, and that exemplify to an exceptional degree, imagination, courage, and high ability in carrying out the mis-

sion of the government are eligible. The heads of federal departments and agencies make nominations. The director of the Office of Personnel Management advises the President on the selection of persons to receive the award. Recipients are selected by the President. A gold medal, a rosette, and a citation signed by the President are awarded. Established in 1957. Co-sponsored by the United States Executive Office of the President. 187258 USOC UT

• 20719 •
United States Olympic Committee
Darryl Seibel, CCO
1 Olympic Plz.
Colorado Springs, CO 80909-5760
Phone: (719)632-5551
Fax: (719)578-4654
E-mail: media@usoc.org
Home Page: http://www.olympic-usa.org

• 20720 • **Robert J. Kane Award**
To recognize athletes who have distinguished themselves in Olympic Festival competition, who have continued to give something back to sport, and who has exemplified the spirit and ideals fostered by Bob Kane as a lifetime devotee of both the Olympic Movement and American athletes. Established in 1993 to honor the late USOC President Robert J. Kane, creator of the U.S. Olympic Festival.

• 20721 • **Jack Kelly Fair Play Award**
To recognize an athlete, coach, or official for an outstanding act of fair play and sportsmanship displayed during the past year. A trophy is awarded annually at USOC's House of Delegates Meeting. Established in 1985 to honor former USOC President John B. "Jack" Kelly, Jr.

• 20722 • **Olympic Spirit Award**
To recognize America's greatest Olympic heroes. Criteria for the award include: displaying the ideals of Olympism, overcoming adversity, demonstrating extraordinary performance that exceeds expectation, demonstrating a never-give-up attitude, being committed to the challenge of training to compete in the Games, and being dedicated to furthering the sport through the training of others. Winners are selected by a ballot among the members of the U.S. print and broadcast media covering the Games. Awarded every four years at the Olympic Games. Established in 1988.

• 20723 • **SportsMan and SportsWoman of the Year**
To honor athletic accomplishments and contributions to sport during the year. Nominations may be made by the athlete's national sport governing body (NGB). A trophy, specially selected each year, is awarded annually at the House of Delegates meeting. Established in 1974 by *The Olympian* magazine. Sponsored by the United States Olympic Committee.

• 20724 • **U.S. Olympic Hall of Fame**
To honor, in perpetuity, the outstanding U.S. gold medal winners in the Olympic Games and other special contributors, such as USOC and IOC Presidents and Directors, coaches, and sportscasters. "Classes" were elected from 1983 to 1992 by a vote among members of the National Sportscasters and Sportswriters Association. Established in 1982.

• 20725 • **USOC Sports Equipment Student Design Contest**
To recognize students for outstanding design of sports equipment. The Committee wishes to see the results of student and school endeavors in actual use in the quadrennial Olympic Games. Open to students attending U.S. four-year colleges or universities. The project must relate to equipment used in an Olympic or Pan Am sport. The deadline for entries is June 1. The five winning teams and their faculty advisors are invited to give a presentation at a sports symposium on equipment and apparatus. The USOC will provide transportation and room and board for each team's Project Leader, and room and board only for other attendees. The top three winners receive $1,000, $500, and $300 (with equivalent amounts going to the respective schools). The other two teams received $100 as an honorable mention. Established in 1991.

• 20726 •
United States Orienteering Federation
Robin Shannonhouse, Exec.Dir.
PO Box 1444
Forest Park, GA 30298-1444
Phone: (404)363-2110
E-mail: usof@comcast.net
Home Page: http://www.us.orienteering.org

• 20727 • **Silva Service Award**
For recognition of service to the Federation over the past five years. Members of the Federation are eligible. A trophy is awarded annually at the USOF Convention. Established in 1985 by Silva, a Division of Johnson Camping.

• 20728 •
U.S. Pan Asian American Chamber of Commerce
Susan Au Allen, Pres./CEO
1329 18th St. NW
Washington, DC 20036
Phone: (202)296-5221
Fax: (202)296-5225
E-mail: administrator@uspaacc.com
Home Page: http://www.uspaacc.com

• 20729 • **Excellence 200 Awards**
For students and achievers in business, science, education, arts, sports, public and private community service. Awarded annually.

• 20730 •
U.S. Particle Accelerator School
Prof. Helmut Wiedemann, Dir.
Fermilab, MS 125
Kirk Rd. and Wilson St.
PO Box 500
Batavia, IL 60510
Phone: (630)840-3896
Fax: (630)840-8500
E-mail: uspas@fnal.gov
Home Page: http://uspas.fnal.gov

• 20731 • **Prize for Meritorious Achievement**
To recognize individuals for achievement in accelerator physics and technology. Two monetary awards of $3,000 each and certificates are presented annually. Established in 1981. Sponsored by the United States Department of Energy, The National Science Foundation, and major U.S. High Energy Physics Laboratories. Formerly: Prize for Achievement in Accelerator Physics and Technology.

• 20732 •
United States Patent and Trademark Office
USPTO Contact Center (UCC)
Plz. 3, Rm. 2C02
PO Box 1450
Alexandria, VA 22313-1450
Phone: (703)308-4357
Toll-Free: 800-786-9199
E-mail: usptoinfo@uspto.gov
Home Page: http://www.uspto.gov

• 20733 • **National Inventor's Hall of Fame**
The Hall of Fame is dedicated to the individuals who conceived the great technological advances that this nation fosters through its patent system. It honors inventors who have made significant contributions to the nation's welfare. The invention under consideration must have been patented in the United States. It must be demonstrated that the invention is important in terms of its effects on the public welfare and its consequent advancement of science and technology. Nominations are accepted from any responsible source. Applications are available from the National Inventor's Hall of Fame Foundation, Inc. at the above address. The Selection Committee is composed of representatives from national scientific and technical organizations. A certificate is presented to the inventor or descendants, and a medallion, designed by Dr. Howard I. Forman who was elected Chairman of the National Council of Patent Law Associations, is also awarded. Induction ceremonies are held annually in April in Akron, Ohio, the new home of the National Inventors Hall of Fame (1993). Thomas A. Edison, holder of 1,093 patents, was the first inductee into the National Inventors Hall of Fame. Established in 1973.

• 20734 •
United States Police Canine Association
Russell Hess, National Exec.Dir.
PO Box 80
Springboro, OH 45066
Phone: 800-531-1614
Fax: 800-531-1614
E-mail: uspcadir@aol.com
Home Page: http://www.uspcak9.com/

• 20735 • **John "Sonny" Burke Memorial Award**
For recognition of the Top Canine Team (four handlers/four dogs). This award goes to the team that receives the highest combined score at the National USPCA Field Trials. A plaque is awarded annually at the National Field Trials. Established in 1971 in memory of John "Sonny" Burke.

• 20736 • **Top Case of the Year**
For recognition of the top police case of the year involving the use of a police service dog. Members of the Association and police officers are eligible. A plaque and trip to the National Police Dog Trials are awarded annually. Established in 1980.

• 20737 •
U.S. Powerlifting Federation
Dave Jeffrey, Pres.
PO Box 231
Parkersburg, WV 26102
Phone: (304)489-2428
Toll-Free: 800-835-5826
E-mail: uspf@netassoc.net
Home Page: http://www.uspf.com

Formerly: (1983) United States Powerlifting Federation of the AAU.

• 20738 • **Powerlifting National Hall of Fame**
To honor the greatest achievers in powerlifting - a sport which consists of three lifts performed with a standard barbell: squat, bench press and deadlift. Awards are given in the categories of sport; administration and pioneer. A lifter nominee must be retired for at least three years. No athlete or administrator who was active in powerlifting only prior to 1962 is eligible for nomination. No person is eligible for nomination to the National Hall of Fame in the category of pioneer who has been active in powerlifting since 1962. Selection of new members to the Hall of Fame in any one year does not exceed one administrator, two athletes, and one pioneer. Inductees receive a large certificate signed by the previous winners. A plaque goes into the Hall of Fame. Voted upon annually at the National Convention and given at the next important meet. Established in 1976 by the Powerlifting Committee of the AAU.

• 20739 •
United States Professional Tennis Association
Tim Heckler, CEO
3535 Briarpark Dr., Ste. 1
Houston, TX 77042
Phone: (713)978-7782
Toll-Free: 800-USPTA-4U
Fax: (713)978-7780
E-mail: uspta@uspta.org
Home Page: http://www.uspta.com

• 20740 • **Coach of the Year**
To recognize individuals for achievements as tennis team coaches. Consideration is given to coaches who have done an outstanding job with individuals. Applicants must be actively coaching a school team from August 1 to July 31 of the assigned award year. A plaque is awarded annually at the USPTA National convention. Established in 1976. In addition, the High School Coach of the Year and the Touring Coach of the Year are also recognized.

• 20741 • **Division of the Year**
To provide recognition for USPTA tennis divisions based on participation and activities. Activities are judged from August 1 to July 31 of the designated year. A plaque is awarded annually at the convention. Established in 1976.

• 20742 • **Newsletter of the Year**
To provide recognition for the best USPTA tennis division newsletter of the year. Newsletters are judged in areas including: frequency of publication, content, and originality. A plaque is awarded annually at the convention. A Most Improved Newsletter award is also presented. Established in 1976.

• 20743 • **Player of the Year**
To recognize an individual as the best tennis player of the year. The tournament results must be listed in the order of priority - the USPTA tournament is most important. Dues paying members are eligible. The tournament results calendar year is from August 1 to July 31 (twelve months prior to convention). Awards are given in six categories: Men's Open Division; Men's 35 and Over; Men's 45 and Over; Women's Open; Women's 35 and Over; Women's 45 and Over; and Player of the Year. Plaques are awarded annually at the convention. Established in 1976.

• 20744 • **Professional of the Year**
To recognize an individual as the top tennis teaching professional of the year. Consideration is given based on contributions and accomplishments in seven categories: Contributions to USPTA; Contributions to USTA; As a Teaching Pro; As a Player; As a Coach; Education, Research, and Publications; and Organization, Affiliation, Special Achievement, and Contributions to Community. Established in 1976.

• 20745 •
United States Rowing Association
Glenn Merry, Exec.Dir.
201 S Capitol Ave., Ste. 400
Indianapolis, IN 46225
Phone: (317)237-5656
Toll-Free: 800-314-4769
Fax: (317)237-5646
E-mail: members@usrowing.org
Home Page: http://www.usrowing.org

Formerly: (1982) National Association of Amateur Oarsmen.

• 20746 • **John Carlin Service Award**
To honor an individual whose personal commitment to support rowing is significant and outstanding. Awarded periodically. Further information is available from Jack Franklin, P.O. Box 6030, Arlington, Virginia 22206.

• 20747 • **Female Athlete of the Year**
To recognize the outstanding female athlete in U.S. rowing. Individuals who participate on the U.S. National Rowing Team are eligible. Awarded annually. Established in 1985.

• 20748 • **Jack Franklin Service Award**
For recognition of lifetime achievement as a rowing official. USRowing registered judges and referees are eligible. A clock and a plaque are awarded annually. Established in 1986 to honor Jack Franklin, Chairman Emeritus of the USRowing Judge/Referee Committee.

• 20749 • **Jack Kelly Award**
To recognize outstanding individuals who represent the ideals which Jack Kelly exemplified - superior achievements in rowing service to amateur athletes and success in their chosen profession, thereby serving as an inspiration to American rowers. A Philadelphia bowl is awarded annually. Established in 1986 to honor Jack Kelly, Olympic oarsman, businessman, former USRowing Director and President of the United States Olympic Committee.

• 20750 • **Male Athlete of the Year**
To recognize the outstanding male athlete in U.S. rowing. Individuals who participate on the U.S. National Rowing Team are eligible. Awarded annually. Established in 1985.

• 20751 • **Rowing Hall of Fame**
This, the highest accolade in American rowing, is given to recognize outstanding rowing achievements of a person whose contribution to the respective business, social and civic activities have demonstrated the value of the discipline which rowing excellence requires. Selection is made by the Rowing Hall of Fame Committee. Awarded annually at the USRowing banquet. Established in 1936.

• 20752 • **USAT Girls' Sportsmanship Trophy Award**
To recognize outstanding achievement as a rowing official. Registered USRowing judges

and referees are eligible. A trophy is awarded annually. Established in 1986 to honor Julian Wolf, a rowing official. Formerly: (2006) Julian Wolf Officiating Award.

• 20753 • USRowing Medal
To recognize individuals for contributions to the sport of rowing. Awarded annually.

• 20754 • Vesper Cup
To honor the individual or crew whose outstanding international achievement serves as an inspiration to American rowing. Selection is made by the members of the 1964 Olympic Gold Medal eight oared crew (from the Vesper Boat Club). Awarded annually. Established in 1965. The honor is given by USRowing, though it is selected by the 1964 crew members.

• 20755 • Women of the Year
To honor the woman who has made the greatest contribution to the advancement of women's rowing in the past year. Women active in the sport of rowing are eligible. A Revere bowl is awarded annually at the convention. Established in 1982 by the National Women's Rowing Association which merged with USRowing in 1986. Formerly: NWRA Woman of the Year.

• 20756 •
United States Rugby Football Union
Dan Lyle, Mgr. of Operations
1033 Walnut St., Ste. 200
Boulder, CO 80302
Phone: (303)539-0300
Fax: (303)539-0311
E-mail: info@usarugby.org
Home Page: http://www.usarugby.org
Formerly: (1996) United States of America Rugby Football Union Ltd..

• 20757 • Ed Lee Scholarship Award
To assist a rugby player who best exemplifies Ed Lee's qualities of character as a student and sportsman. Full-time college students who are members of a college rugby football club in the United States are eligible. Funding is awarded for assistance with academic expenses.

• 20758 • National Club Championship Award (Men)
To recognize the winner of the National Rugby Club Championship. The team must be a non-college club and a member of a rugby union recognized and approved by the United States of America Rugby Football Union. The winner of the national tournament is awarded a large cup annually. Established in 1979.

• 20759 • National Club Championship Award (Women)
To recognize the winner of the National Rugby Women's Club Championships. The team must be a non-college club and a member of a rugby union recognized and approved by the United States of American Rugby Football Union. The winner of the national tournament is awarded a large cup annually. Established in 1981.

• 20760 • National Club Sevens Championship Award (Men)
To recognize the winner of the National Rugby Club Sevens Championship. To receive the award, the team must be a member of a rugby union recognized and approved by the United States of America Rugby Football Union. The winner of the national tournament is awarded a large cup annually. Established in 1985.

• 20761 • National College Championship Award
To recognize the winner of the National College Rugby Club Championship. The team must be a college rugby club and a member of a rugby union recognized and approved by the United States of America Rugby Football Union. The winner of the national tournament is awarded a large cup annually. Established in 1980.

• 20762 • National College Championship Award (Women)
To recognize the winner of the National College Women's Rugby Club Championship. The team must be a college rugby club and a member of a rugby union recognized and approved by the United States of America Rugby Football Union. The winner of the national tournament is awarded a large cup annually. Established in 1991.

• 20763 • National Collegiate All Conference Championships Award
To recognize the winner of the National Collegiate All Conference Championships. Competitors must be members of a college rugby club recognized by a rugby union and approved by the United States of America Rugby Football Union in order to represent their territory in this championship. The winner of the national tournament is awarded a large cup annually. Established in 1989.

• 20764 • National High School Championships Award
To recognize the winner of the National High School Championship. The team must be a high school rugby club and a member of a rugby union recognized and approved by the United States of America Rugby Football Union. The winner of the national tournament is awarded a large cup annually. Established in 1985.

• 20765 • National Military Championships Award
To recognize the winner of the National Military Championships. The team must be a military rugby club and a member of a rugby union recognized and approved by the United States of America Rugby Football Union. The winner of the national tournament is awarded a large cup annually. Established in 1981.

• 20766 • National Territorial Union Championship Award
To recognize the winner of the Territorial Union Championship. Competitors must be one of the USARFU Member Territorial Unions and be the winner of the national tournament to be eligible. A large cup is awarded annually. Established in 1976.

• 20767 • President's Award
In recognition of outstanding contributions to the sport of rugby in the United States. Established in 1976.

• 20768 • Craig Sweeney Award
To honor an athlete who is an outstanding leader as a rugby football player and who best exemplifies Craig Sweeney's qualities of character as a gentleman and sportsman. Members of a rugby football club in the United States are eligible. A large cup is awarded annually. Established in 1978. 704592 USYRU NORT UD

• 20769 •
United States Sailing Association
Janet Baxter, Pres.
PO Box 1260
Portsmouth, RI 02871-0907
Phone: (401)683-0800
Toll-Free: 800-US-SAIL1
Fax: (401)683-0840
E-mail: info@ussailing.org
Home Page: http://www.ussailing.org
Formerly: (1980) U.S. Yacht Racing Union.

• 20770 • Jack Brown Trophy
The Championship of Champions is an invitational regatta that brings together 20 current titlists from a variety of one-design classes. Current U.S. Sailing Association member one-design class champions may apply through their class associations. Medals are awarded annually. Established in 1976. Formerly: Championship of Champions.

• 20771 • U.S. Sailing/Rolex Junior Women's Championship - Nancy Leiter Clagett Trophy
To recognize the U.S. Junior Women's Champion. The annual competition is open to female sailors from 13 to 18 years of age. The original Nancy Leiter Clagett Memorial Trophy was given to Ida Lewis Yacht Club by C. Thomas Clagett, Jr. in memory of his wife. Ida Lewis and Clagett donated the Trophy to U.S. SAILING in 1985, making the event national. Formerly: U.S. Junior Women's Sailing Championship - Nancy Leiter Clagett Trophy.

• 20772 • Founder's Trophy
To award the winner of the St. Francis International Masters Regatta. The regatta is open to skippers (men or women) who have reached their 55th birthday on or before October 22, 1993. Other crew members must have reached their 45th birthday on or before October 22, 1993. In the case of a borrowed boat with the owner aboard, the owner shall have no age limit

but cannot serve as either helmsman or foredeck crew. If a borrowed boat has an owner's representative aboard, he or she can serve in any crew position, but must be over 45 years old. All competitors must be members in good standing of U.S. SAILING. Registration deadline is September 30.

• 20773 • Nathaniel G. Herreshoff Trophy
This, the U.S. Sailing Association's most prestigious award, is presented to an individual who has made an outstanding contribution to the sport of sailing in the United States - whether as skipper, crew, designer, builder, writer, or in any other activity associated with the sport. A trophy is awarded annually. The trophy was donated to the U.S. Sailing Association in 1957 by the National Marine Manufacturers Association. Established in 1957.

• 20774 • Chandler Hovey Trophy
To provide an opportunity for sailors with disabilities to compete in a national sailing championship. The U.S. Independence Cup is open, by invitation, to crews (men and women) of two sailors with disabilities. In instances where either the nature or severity of a particular disability requires assistance, the owner's representative may assist the skipper or crew in transfers from leeward to windward, sheeting of main and jib, and at any point where personal safety of crew and/or safety of vessel is in question. The helmsman must be a disabled competitor. All skippers and crews must be members of U.S. SAILING. The regatta is held at the Chicago Yacht Club in July. A perpetual trophy will be awarded to the winning crew. U.S. SAILING medals for permanent possession will be awarded to the first, second, and third place skippers and crews. A sportsmanship trophy is also awarded to the skipper or crew who best exemplifies the ideals of good sportsmanship both on and off the water during the regatta. Awarded annually.

• 20775 • National Multihull Championship - Alter Cup
To recognize the National Multihull Champion. Open Area competitions qualify two skippers in each area. Awarded annually. Established in 1987 in honor of Hobie Alter, Sr.'s contribution to multihull sailing.

• 20776 • National Offshore Championship - Lloyd Phoenix Trophy
To recognize the National Offshore Championship Crew. Ten Area qualified crews are selected from sailing resumes. Awarded annually. The Phoenix Trophy was donated by the U.S. Naval Academy. Established in 1986.

• 20777 • National Sportsmanship Award
To recognize the American sailor who best exemplifies the ideals and traditions of good sportsmanship. Awarded annually. Established in 1987. Formerly: (2006) W. Van Alan Clark, Jr. Trophy.

• 20778 • One Ton Championship - Hawk Trophy
For recognition of the One Ton Champion. Offshore yachts in IOR level One Ton class, with maximum 30.5' rating are eligible. A trophy is awarded annually. Established in 1922.

• 20779 • Rolex International Women's Keelboat Championship
To provide women keelboat and offshore sailors with high quality racing competition in keelboats against the top women sailors in the world. The race is open to all women sailors (skippers and crews) who are members of a yacht club, class association, or national federation. Entry deadline is August 1. Winner receives the Bengt Julin Trophy. Held annually.

• 20780 • St. Petersburg Yacht Club Trophy
To recognize excellence in race management. The trophy was originally awarded by St. Petersburg Yacht Club in the late 1960s to recognize the club responsible for running the best regatta. The trophy was retired for several years, then was donated to the U.S. Sailing Association in 1977.

• 20781 • U.S. Match Racing Championship - Prince of Wales Bowl
For recognition of the U.S. Match Racing Champion. The two-boat matches are between yacht club teams for YRA/Area eliminations. A silver bowl is awarded annually. Established in 1931 at the Acadia Yacht Club under the sponsorship of the Royal Nova Scotia Yacht Squadron. Competition was held among clubs on the Eastern Seaboard for crews under 19 years of age. The trophy was permanently retired by the Vineyard Haven Yacht Club in 1937, but in 1965, the same club restored the Prince of Wales Bowl to active competition as a perpetual trophy for interclub match racing in North America.

• 20782 • U.S. Men's Sailing Championship - Clifford D. Mallory Cup
For recognition of the U.S. Men's Sailing Champion. The skipper must be male and the crew can be either sex. The minimum age is 18. All crew members must belong to clubs within the same YRA. A trophy is awarded annually. Established in 1952 by the family of the late Mr. Mallory, who was the first president of the North American Yacht Racing Union.

• 20783 • U.S. Sailing One-Design Awards
To recognize, and create as role models, the outstanding individual and organizational initiatives of the year in one-design yacht racing. The following awards are presented: U.S. SAILING One-Design Leadership Award in recognition of individual initiative, enthusiasm, organizing ability, and leadership in creating the one-design fleet building program of the year; U.S. SAILING One-Design Club Award - to recognize administrative excellence, fleet growth, creative programming, regatta support, and member contribution at regional, national, and international levels of the One-Design Yacht Club of the Year; U.S. SAILING One-Design Regatta Award to recognize excellence in development, promotion, and management by the organizers and sponsors of the Year's Outstanding Multi-Class Regional Regatta; U.S. SAILING One-Design Creativity Award - to recognize outstanding individual creativity and contribution in the year's most innovative one-design event of national or international significance; and U.S. SAILING One-Design Class Award - in recognition of commitment to the goals of the United States Yacht Racing Union by members of the One-Design Class of the Year. The names of the winners are engraved on perpetual trophies. Entry deadline is December 1. Established in 1986.

• 20784 • U.S. Sailing/Rolex Junior Championships
To recognize the crews of the Junior Sailing Championships. All crew members must be between the ages of 13 and 18 and belong to the same yacht club; and skipper and crew can be male or female. The Sears Cup is awarded to the U.S. Junior Sailing Champion Crew. Established in 1921 by Commodore Herbert M. Sears of the Eastern Yacht Club in Marblehead, Massachusetts. In addition, The F. Gregg Bemis Trophy is awarded to the U.S. Junior Doublehanded Sailing Champion. Established in 1975 by the sailors who served as regatta officials with Mr. Bemis for junior and intercollegiate competitions. It was presented in recognition of his many contributions to yacht racing among young sailors in North America. The D. Verner Smythe Trophy is awarded annually to the U.S. Junior Singlehanded Sailing Champion. Donated in 1974 by friends of the National Junior Sailing program and dedicated to Mr. Smythe in appreciation of his many years of support to junior sailing activities. The Massachusetts Bay Trophy is awarded to the U.S. Junior Boardsailing Champion. Established in 1982 by the Yacht Racing Union of Massachusetts Bay. Formerly: U.S. Junior Sailing Championships.

• 20785 • U.S. Singlehanded Sailing Championship - George D. O'Day Trophy
For recognition of the U.S. Singlehanded Sailing Champion. The minimum age is 16. The competition is open to one representative each from Area A-H (YRA/Area eliminations); one each intercollegiate, Nautica/U.S. SAILING Youth Championship, and U.S. Women's Open Championship; and one from the All Services Championship. A trophy is awarded annually. Established in 1962 by George D. O'Day.

• 20786 • U.S. Team Race Championship - George R. Hinman Trophy
For recognition of the U.S. Sailing Association's team race champion. The race is an open competition. The Hinman Committee selects 18 teams on the basis of applications or winners of selected events. A trophy is awarded annually. The trophy was donated in 1981 in recognition of George R. Hinman's many years of service and contributions to yachting.

• 20787 • **U.S. Women's Open Championships**
To serve the interests of female sailors who wish to compete against other women at the national level in double and singlehanded boats. The regattas are organized along traditional one-design racing lines where boat preparation is a factor and no eliminations are required. Women must be U.S. citizens. The Mrs. Charles Francis Adams Memorial Trophy (Doublehanded), The Allegra Knapp Mertz Trophy (Singlehanded), and The Gardner Trophy (Boardsailing) are awarded annually. Established in 1974. A boardsailing championship was added in 1982.

• 20788 • **U.S. Women's Sailing Championship - Mrs. Charles Francis Adams Trophy**
For recognition of the U.S. Women's Sailing Champion. Women over the age of 18 are eligible (one crew member 15 years of age or older is allowed). All crew members must belong to clubs within the same YRA. A trophy is awarded annually. The original Women's Sailing Championship trophy, the Hodder Cup, was placed in competition by Commodore James R. Hodder of Boston Yacht Club in 1924. Established in 1925 by William Upham Swan in honor of Mrs. Charles Francis Adams.

• 20789 • **U.S. Youth Sailing Championship**
To serve the interests of sailors under the age of 20 who wish to compete at the national level. The Robert L. Johnstone III Trophy (Singlehanded), the Manton D. Scott Memorial Trophy (Doublehanded), and the Major Hall Trophy (Boardsailing) are awarded annually. The winners of each division become the U.S. Youth Sailing Team for the World Youth Sailing Championship, organized by the International Yacht Racing Union. Established in 1973. Formerly: Nautica/U.S. SAILING Youth Championship.

• 20790 •
United States Ski and Snowboard Association
Bill Marolt, Sec.-Treas.
PO Box 100
1500 Kearns Blvd.
Park City, UT 84060
Phone: (435)649-9090
Fax: (435)649-3613
E-mail: info@ussa.org
Home Page: http://www.usskiteam.com

Formerly: (1991) United States Ski Association.

• 20791 • **Alaska Cup Award**
To recognize the outstanding divisional team performance in cross country skiing at the USSA Junior Olympics. Established in 1987.

• 20792 • **Paul Bacon Award**
To recognize an individual or a group for the greatest contributions to USSA in the field of race organization. Established in 1969 in memory of Paul Bacon, an outstanding contributor in the area of race organization, by the Bacon family and the Rocky Mountain Division.

• 20793 • **Dan Bean Award**
To recognize the men's combined winner at the U.S. Alpine Championships. Awarded annually. Previously, this award was part of the White Stag Award. Now the White Stag award is given to recognize the women's combined winner at the U.S. Alpine Championships. Formerly: (1990) White Stag Award.

• 20794 • **Beck International Award**
To recognize a competitor based on outstanding performance in international competition during the past season. This highest athletic award of the USSA draws from alpine, cross country, freestyle, disables, ski jumping, nordic combined, and snowboard sport committees, with selection by the USSA Board of Directors. Established in 1931.

• 20795 • **Paul Bietila Award**
To recognize an American born skier scoring highest in the 70-meter competition at the U.S. Ski Jumping Championships. Awarded annually. Established in 1940 by Dr. and Mrs. H.C. Bradley of Madison, WI, in memory of Paul Bietila, an outstanding ski jumper.

• 20796 • **Julius Blegen Award**
This, the Association's highest volunteer honor, is given in recognition of the USSA member who contributed his/her outstanding service to the sports of skiing or snowboarding in the United States during the year. Awarded annually. Established in 1946 in memory of Julius Blegen, an outstanding contributor to the sport of skiing.

• 20797 • **Fred Braun Award**
To recognize dedicated volunteers who have contributed greatly to the USSA Recreation Program and recreational skiing. Nominees do not need to be members of the Recreation Program. Established in 1986.

• 20798 • **Burkett-Dodge Award**
For recognition of outstanding contribution to alpine race officiating. Awarded by the USSA Eastern Alpine Official's Committee. Members of the Committee are not eligible. Established in 1987. The award is named for Douglas Burkett and Joe Dodge, two pioneer officials, particularly in race timing.

• 20799 • **Gale Cotton Burton Award**
To recognize the winner of the National 15 km race at the U.S. Cross Country Championships. A trophy is awarded. Established in 1907 by the Burton family of Wayzata, Minnesota, in memory of their son.

• 20800 • **John J. Clair Jr. Award**
To recognize outstanding service to the benefit of the United States Ski or Snowboard Teams. Awarded when merited. Established in 1971 by the Long Island Ski Club in memory of John Clair.

• 20801 • **Cross Country Coach of the Year**
To recognize a USSA staff or club coach based on outstanding performance of his or her athletes in international or domestic competition during the past season.

• 20802 • **Sally Deaver Award**
To recognize the winner of the National Women's Slalom competition. Awarded annually. Established in 1965 by the Deaver family in memory of Sally Deaver, an outstanding slalom champion.

• 20803 • **Domestic Alpine Coach of the Year**
To recognize a coach's outstanding contribution to a domestic program resulting in high-level performance of his or her athletes in domestic or international competition. Established in 1986.

• 20804 • **Finlandia Award**
To recognize the outstanding cross-country skier in the United States. Awarded annually. Established in 1964 and sponsored by the Finnish Ski Club.

• 20805 • **Mike Gallagher Award**
To recognize the Senior men's overall winner at the U.S. Cross Country Championships. The athlete must compete in all U.S. championship events. It is based on results. Established in 1987 in honor of Mike Gallagher, an outstanding international competitor on the U.S. Ski Team in the 1960s and 1970s. He is also a former U.S. Ski Team coach.

• 20806 • **Ann Hansen Award**
To recognize the top U.S. female and male acro and mogul skiers by virtue of their World Cup finishes. Awarded annually. Established in memory of Ann Hansen and her dedication to the Freestyle Ski Team.

• 20807 • **Hart Cup Award**
To recognize the male and female senior combined champions from the U.S. Freestyle Championships. Beginning in 1992, the award is given to the inverted combined champions; prior to that, it was awarded to the upright combined champions.

• 20808 • **Erik Judeen Memorial Award**
To recognize the woman who scores the highest at the U.S. Cross Country Championships. The athlete must compete in all U.S. Championship events. Ranking is established on the basis of the World Cup point scoring system. Established in 1986.

• 20809 • **Paul Nash Layman Award**
To recognize the winner of the National Nordic Combined Championship. Established in 1941.

• 20810 • Bud and Mary Little Award
To recognize an individual who has contributed significantly to USSA skiing or snowboard interests in the United States through a long-term involvement with the FIS or Olympic sports communities, internationally or domestically. This award is not automatically awarded each year.

• 20811 • Meeker Award
To recognize the top seeded U.S. freestyle aerialist each year. The Award is presented by the International Judges Association. Established in 1980 in memory of Don Meek who, in the latter years of his life, gave his all to freestyle skiing.

• 20812 • Al Merrill Nordic Award
To recognize the individual or group involved with any aspect of nordic skiing, i.e., cross country, nordic combined and ski jumping, who or which demonstrates an exceptional level of commitment, leadership and devotion to excellence. Each of the nordic discipline committees submits a nominee with the final selection being made by the discipline committee chairpersons.

• 20813 • Mittelstadt Ski Jumping Officials Award
To recognize the USSA ski jumping official who contributed outstanding service to ski jumping officiating and to the sport of ski jumping in the United States during the year. Awarded annually. Established in 1987 by Mr. and Mrs. Fritz Mittelstadt.

• 20814 • National Ski Hall of Fame
To recognize individuals who have been outstanding in the sport of skiing. Individuals are inducted in the following categories: (1) athlete - living and posthumous; (2) skisport builder - living and posthumous; (3) skisport builder - athlete (living and posthumous); and (4) foreign skiers - living and posthumous (this is the only category not requiring United States citizenship). Athletes older than 40 years of age or out of competitive skiing for ten years at the time of nomination are eligible. A skisport builder older than 50 years of age at the time of nomination who made a major, national contribution of time and effort to the Association is eligible. Inductions usually coincide with the annual ski tourney of the Ishpeming Ski Club. Awarded annually. Additional information is available from the National Ski Hall of Fame, P.O. Box 191, Ishpeming, MI 49849.

• 20815 • Nordic Award
To recognize outstanding divisional participation and competence in the National Nordic Championships. Selection is made from the results of the Senior and Junior National Championships. Established in 1971.

• 20816 • Martha Rockwell Award
To recognize the fastest woman in the 5-km at the U.S. Cross Country Championships. It is based on results. Established in 1986 in honor of Martha Rockwell, an outstanding international competitor in the early days of the U.S. Women's Cross Country Team in the 1960's and 70's. She retired in 1976.

• 20817 • Willy Schaeffler Award
To recognize the alpine combined winners, man and woman, at the USSA Junior I Olympics. Established in 1974 and named in 1988 in memory of Willy Schaeffler, a skiing pioneer and former U.S. Olympic alpine coach.

• 20818 • Al Sise Outstanding Alpine Masters Award
To recognize the outstanding man and woman Alpine Masters racers, based on results at the annual USSA Masters National Championships. Selections are made by the USSA National Alpine Masters Committee. Established in 1987. Formerly: (1996) USSA Outstanding Alpine Masters Award.

• 20819 • Ski Jumping/Nordic Combined Coach of the Year
To recognize the most deserving USSA staff or club coach based on outstanding performance of his or her athletes in international or domestic competition during the past season. Established in 1986.

• 20820 • *Ski Magazine* Cup
To recognize the female and male junior combined champions of the U.S. Junior Freestyle Championships.

• 20821 • *Skiing Magazine* Development Cup
To recognize the combined female and male champions, age 16 (JII) or younger, at the Junior Freestyle Championships.

• 20822 • Sons of Norway Jumping Award
To recognize the best junior at the U.S. Ski Jumping Championships. Established in 1950 by the Supreme Lodge of the Sons of Norway.

• 20823 • Torger Tokle Award
To recognize the USSA large hill national ski jumping Champion. Established in 1948 by the Norway Club of New York.

• 20824 • Wallace "Buddy" Werner Award
To recognize the outstanding competitor in the USSA who showed leadership and good sportsmanship in national or international competition. Awarded only when merited. Established in 1965 in memory of Buddy Werner, an outstanding U.S. Alpine racer who was killed in 1965 at the height of his ski career.

• 20825 • Russell Wilder Award
To recognize the year's most outstanding effort in focusing the interests of America's youth on the sport of skiing or snowboard. Presented annually when merited. Established in 1955 in memory of Russell Wilder.

• 20826 • Willauer Cup Award
To recognize the USSA geographic division whose racers score the most points, using the World Cup scoring system, in the giant slalom and slalom races at the USSA National Citizens' Championships. Established in 1988 in honor of Whiting "Whitey" Willauer, former USSA President, who initiated the planning for a national championship for recreational skiers.

• 20827 • Dick Zue Award
To recognize the United States Junior Alpine combined champions, both male and female. Selection of awardees is from the United States Alpine Championship results. Established in 1977 in memory of Dick Zue by his friends.

• 20828 •
U.S. Small Business Administration
Hector V. Barreto, Admin.
409 3rd St. SW
Washington, DC 20416
Phone: (202)606-4000
Toll-Free: 800-UASK-SBA
Fax: (202)205-6901
Home Page: http://www.sba.gov

• 20829 • Entrepreneurial Success Award
To honor businesses that started small and after receiving SBA assistance, have grown into large businesses. To be eligible for the award, businesses must be considered "large" by SBA size standards. The award serves as an example for small businesses on the fast-track, honors businesses that have had extraordinary success, and shows the dramatic impact that SBA has had on American business. The deadline is November 15. Awarded during Small Business Week.

• 20830 • National Small Business Person of the Year
To recognize outstanding small business owners and operators for their personal achievements and contributions to the nation. Criteria considered for the award are: (1) staying power; (2) growth in number of employees; (3) increase in sales and/or unit volume; (4) current and past financial reports; (5) innovativeness of product or service; (6) response to adversity; and (7) evidence of contributions to aid community-oriented projects. Nominations of entrepreneurs who are recognized in each state, the District of Columbia, and Puerto Rico as State Small Business Persons of the Year are accepted by November 15. A certificate, national recognition, and a plaque are presented annually during Small Business Week. During this time, ten finalists representing the ten Federal regions are announced. On the recommendation of the SBA Administrator, the President then announces the National Small Business Person of the Year. Established in 1964.

• 20831 • Phoenix Award for Outstanding Contributions to Disaster Recovery
To recognize individuals whose efforts and contributions have enabled their businesses or

communities to recover successfully from disaster.

• 20832 • Phoenix Award for Small Business Disaster Recovery
To recognize individuals whose efforts and contributions have enabled their businesses or communities to recover successfully from disaster.

• 20833 • Procurement Awards
A Small Business Prime contractor of the Year and a Subcontractor of the Year will be recognized in each of the 10 SBA regions for their performance under federal contract. Federal agencies nominate small businesses for Prime Contractor of the Year while federal large business prime contractors nominate small businesses for Subcontractor of the Year. The deadline is December 22. Each nominee is evaluated on the following basis: (1) Management - ability to organize resources to ensure accomplishment of business objectives; (2) Financial Stamina and Control financial condition, ability to assume risk, and adequacy of accounting system; (3) Labor Relations - management-employee relations, including equal employment opportunity compliance; (4) Customer Interface - ability to understand contractual work tasks, make timely progress reports, and willingness to function as a member of the team; (5) Technical Capability - ability to resolve complex problems; (6) Resource Utilization - use of capital assets and cash flow; (7) Cost Performance - competitive posture and ability to estimate and to control costs to yield profitable results; (8) Delivery Performance - ability to meet time schedules; and (9) Quality Performance - quality control mechanisms and ability to provide a reliable product or service. Regional winners are considered for the national award.

• 20834 • Small Business Advocates of the Year
To recognize individuals in various professions who have significantly increased awareness of small business concerns or created opportunities for small business to succeed. Advocates of the Year are recognized in each of the 50 states, the District of Columbia, and Puerto Rico for their efforts in the following areas of importance to small businesses: (1) accountant advocate; (2) banker advocate; (3) media advocate; (4) minority advocate; (5) veteran advocate, home-based business advocate, research advocate; and (6) women in business advocate. State winners are then eligible for national recognition. The criteria for selection are: engaging in civic and community activities that promote small business; volunteering services to assist small firms experiencing management, financial, or legal problems; sponsoring or participating in legislative or regulatory initiatives; communicating publicly through speech or the written word; actively participating in small business organizations; or pursuing initiatives that will help a large number of small businesses. Nominations are accepted. Awards are presented during Small Business Week. Established in 1978.

• 20835 • Small Business Exporter of the Year
To recognize owners of small business firms who have substantially increased sales through exporting. Exporters that have developed creative overseas marketing strategies, cooperated with other firms in the creation of export trading companies, and/or introduced unique trading relationships, products, or services that have enhanced the Nation's role in exporting are deemed worthy of recognition. Selection is based on increased export sales and profits or growth in employment due to exports. Increases in exports as a percentage of total sales are noted as well as examples of export-related programs faced by the business and the solutions taken to resolve them. Evidence that the nominee has assisted other small businesses in entering the export market are described when appropriate. Nominations are accepted. Awarded during Small Business Week.

• 20836 • Young Entrepreneur Award
To recognize an outstanding young American who is the owner of a small business. A young entrepreneur is defined as the majority owner of a successful small business who will not have attained the age of 30 prior to June 1 of the award year. Nominees may be students or full-time owner/managers who have successfully entered the business world. Candidates must show evidence of success as measured by sales, profits, or employment growth. Awarded during Small Business Week.

• 20837 •
United States Soccer Federation
Dr. S. Robert Contiguglia, Pres.
1801 S Prairie Ave.
Chicago, IL 60616
Phone: (312)808-1300
Fax: (312)808-1301
Home Page: http://www.ussoccer.com

• 20838 • Hall of Fame Meritorious Award
To recognize soccer players who have completed a successful playing career and have remained active in the game of soccer in various capacities on the national, state, league or club level, or in coaching or soccer journalism. Established in 1970.

• 20839 • National Soccer Hall of Fame Award
To recognize soccer players of high standard and achievement who have played top grade soccer for a minimum of seven years and were chosen to represent the United States in international competition, such as the World Cup, Olympic, or Pan American Games. Established in 1950.

• 20840 •
United States Space Foundation
Elliot G. Pulham, Pres. and CEO
310 S 14th St.
Colorado Springs, CO 80904
Phone: (719)576-8000
Fax: (719)576-8801
Home Page: http://www.ussf.org

• 20841 • Education Achievement Award
To recognize organizations that demonstrate involvement in exemplary education initiatives for the purpose of motivating young people to excel in space-based education. Awarded annually. Established in 1991.

• 20842 • Douglas S. Morrow Public Outreach Award
Presented to an individual or organization for outstanding achievement in the promotion of America's space endeavors. Awarded annually. Established in memory of Douglas S. Morrow, renowned writer, film producer, space advocate, and former U.S. Space Foundation Director.

• 20843 • Space Achievement Award
To recognize individuals or organizations that have demonstrated space achievement, breakthrough space technology, or program or product success deemed to represent a critical milestone in the evolution of space exploration and development. Awarded annually to one or more recipients. Established in 1995.

• 20844 • Space Technology Hall of Fame
To honor those individuals and organizations who have made a significant contribution to the utilization of space technology for the benefit of all people. A plaque and induction into the Space Technology Hall of Fame are awarded annually at the National Space Symposium. Established in 1988 by the United States Space Foundation and the National Aeronautics and Space Administration (NASA).

• 20845 •
U.S. Speedskating
Katie Marquard, Exec.Dir.
PO Box 450639
Westlake, OH 44145
Phone: (440)899-0128
Fax: (440)899-0109
E-mail: kmarquard@usspeedskating.org
Home Page: http://www.usspeedskating.org

• 20846 • Hall of Fame
To recognize an individual for achievement in speedskating on ice or in the promotion and development of the sport. Skaters must have competed in the senior class and must have achieved at least one of the following distinctions as a minimum for eligibility: won National or North American Championships - at least two in the senior class; set National or North American Records - at least three in the senior class; or won at least one Olympic or World medal. Spe-

cial consideration is given to those who qualify on the basis of the above criteria who in addition have contributed to the advancement and promotion of the sport during or after their active participation as competitors for at least a period of five years. Noncompetitors may be nominated for a major advance or lasting contribution to the sport on a national or international level for a period of at least fifteen years. A plaque, certificate, and enshrinement in the Speedskating Hall of Fame of the Amateur Speedskating Union in Newburgh, NY, are awarded annually. Established in 1960. The Speedskating Hall of Fame is being relocated and is closed until further notice.

• 20847 •
U.S. Sports Acrobatics
Carisa Laughon, Dir.
201 S Capitol Ave.
Indianapolis, IN 46225
Phone: (317)829-5667
Fax: (317)237-5069
E-mail: claughon@usa-gymnastics.org
Home Page: http://www.ussportsacrobatics.com

• 20848 • **National Champion**
To recognize the winning participant in the annual USSAF Championships. Awards are given in the following categories: (1) Men's Platform Tumbling; (2) Women's Platform Tumbling; (3) Men's Pair; (4) Women's Pair; (5) Mixed Pair; (6) Women's Trio; (7) Men's Fours; and (8) Elite Team. Medals are awarded in each of the eight events. Presented annually. Established in 1976.

• 20849 •
United States Stamp Society
Larry Ballantyne, Exec.Sec.
PO Box 6634
Katy, TX 77491-6634
E-mail: stampsjoann@prodigy.net
Home Page: http://www.usstamps.org

• 20850 • **Hopkinson Award**
Recognizes the best exhibit at national, regional, and local exhibitions. Awarded annually.

• 20851 • **Southgate Award**
For recognition for the best article in the monthly magazine. Awarded annually.

• 20852 •
United States Tennis Association
D. Lee Hamilton, Exec.Dir./COO
70 W Red Oak Ln.
White Plains, NY 10604
Phone: (914)696-7000
Phone: (914)696-7262
Toll-Free: 800-990-8782
Fax: (914)696-7167
Home Page: http://www.usta.com

Formerly: United States Lawn Tennis Association.

• 20853 • **Maureen Connolly Brinker Award**
To recognize the girl player considered by the selection committee to have had the most outstanding full season performance. Selection is based on exceptional ability, sportsmanship, and competitive spirit. The winner's name is inscribed on a large silver bowl kept at the Philadelphia Cricket Club; each recipient receives a silver tray and lifetime enrollment in the USTA. Awarded annually at the USTA's Girls' 18 National Championships. Established in 1969 by the Maureen Connolly Brinker Foundation. Formerly: Maureen Connolly Brinker Outstanding Junior Girl Award.

• 20854 • **Sarah Palfrey Danzig Award**
To recognize a female player who by character, sportsmanship, manners, spirit of cooperation, and contribution to the growth of the game ranks first in the opinion of the Selection Committee. Presented annually at the International Club Dinner during the U.S. Open. Nominations must be submitted before August 1 of each year. The name of the winner is engraved on the trophy and silver tray suitably inscribed is given to the recipient as a memento of the award. Established in 1986 in honor of Sarah Palfrey Danzig as an award comparable to the William M. Johnston Award for men.

• 20855 • **Davis Cup**
An annual tennis competition open to men's teams throughout the world. From 1961-1971, the annual challenge round matches were played in the country of the defending champion. Since 1971, however, the challenge round has been abolished and the defending nation must play through from the start of the tournament. Established in 1900.

• 20856 • **Girls' 18 National Championships Sportsmanship Award**
To recognize a girl who exemplifies outstanding sportsmanship, conduct, and character. Awarded annually based on the selection of the committee of judges. Awarded annually. Established in 1936.

• 20857 • **William M. Johnston Award**
To recognize a male player who by character, sportsmanship, manners, spirit of cooperation, and contribution to the growth of the game ranks first in the opinion of the Selection Committee. Awarded annually at the International Club Dinner during the U.S. Open. This includes help which the player renders not only the players in the recipient's own class, but to Junior players as well. The name of the winner is engraved on the trophy, and a small silver inscribed tray is given to the recipient as a memento of the award. Established in 1947 as the result of a suggestion by the late "Little Bill" Johnston, who gave one of his championship cups to the International Lawn Tennis Club of the United States to be used for this purpose.

• 20858 • **Bobby Kaplan Sportsmanship Award**
To recognize a boy who combines sportsmanship and tennis ability. Awarded annually at the USTA Boys' 16 National Championships. Established in 1978 by the Eastern Tennis Association in honor of Bobby Kaplan, a prominent teaching professional on Long Island, who devoted his career to junior tennis.

• 20859 • **John T. McGovern Umpires' Award**
To recognize valuable contributions to the cause of tennis officiating by an umpire or linesman. A gold perpetual trophy and medalettes are awarded. A silver medalette is awarded to a junior official. Presented annually at the U.S. Open. Established in 1949 by John T. (Terry) McGovern, a well-known leader in amateur sports.

• 20860 • **Member Organization of the Year**
To recognize the services rendered to the USTA by its Member Organizations. Selection is made on the basis of service to the tennis community, to the organization's members, and to the game of tennis. The format of the competition is three tiered, in which the Sections select their winners, four Regional winners are selected from these, and the National winner is then selected from the four Regional winners. Appropriate presentations are made to the Sectional winners and the Regional winners, and, at the annual meeting, the President presents to the selected National Organization a crystal urn engraved with the USTA seal on a lighted wood and glass pedestal bearing an engraved plate. Awarded annually. Established in 1981.

• 20861 • **Seniors' Service Award**
To recognize notable efforts, cooperation and participation in play or organizational work for the betterment and furtherance of seniors' competition. A perpetual trophy is engraved with the honoree's name, and the awardee receives a replica. Awarded annually at the USTA Annual Meeting and Conference. Established in 1958, the trophy is named after its first winner, W. Dickson Cunningham of Rahway, New Jersey.

• 20862 • **Service Bowl Award**
To recognize the player who most notably contributes to the sportsmanship, fellowship, and service of tennis. A Service Bowl trophy is awarded annually at the USTA Semiannual Meeting and Conference. Established in 1940 by Mrs. Lyman H.B. Olmstead and a group of 30 New England women in honor of Mrs. Hazel H. Wightman.

• 20863 • **Jack Stahr Award**
To recognize an umpire, age 21 or over, who in one of his or her first three years at the U.S. Open, is recognized for hard work, professionalism, technical ability, and cooperative attitude. It recognizes his or her outstanding work primarily as a line umpire. Awarded annually at the U.S. Open. Established in 1984.

• 20864 • Dr. Allen B. Stowe Sportsmanship Award
To recognize a junior player for the qualities of outstanding sportsmanship and distinguished tennis ability. Selection is made by the National Junior and Boys' Championships Committee. A trophy, with the name and hometown of its recipients inscribed upon it, is awarded annually. Established in 1957 in memory of Dr. Allen B. Stowe, longtime director of the National Junior and Boys Tennis Championships. Formerly: Allen B. Stowe Award; (2006) USTA Junior and Boys' Sportsmanship Award.

• 20865 • Super Senior Service Award
To recognize the person who, in the opinion of the SST Board of Directors, has made a notable contribution to the promotion of tennis for the 55 thru 80 USTA-recognized age divisions. This contribution may be made by a player, a tennis enthusiast, a Tournament Director, or a non-player who has helped to promote tennis for the young at heart. Awarded annually during the USTA Men's 55 & 65 Clay Court Championships. Established in 1975.

• 20866 • Bill Talbert Junior Sportsmanship Awards
To recognize one junior player from each of the four USTA regions who exemplify the finest qualities of sportsmanship in tournament play and the finest traditions of the great sportsmen of tennis past and present. The junior players are nominated by the USTA Regional Vice President serving the region. The awards consist of being guests of the International Tennis Hall of Fame for the annual Enshrinement Ceremonies in Newport, Rhode Island. Established in 1988.

• 20867 • Tennis Facility Awards
To recognize outstanding tennis facilities and encourage excellence in future construction and/or renovation. Facilities must be under the jurisdiction of a parks and recreation department, an educational institution, or an industrial complex. All facilities are judged in one of five categories, depending upon the number of courts and spectators accommodated. Nominations must be submitted by July 1. Awarded annually. Recipients receive an inscribed plaque. Established in 1981.

• 20868 • United States Open Tennis Championships
To recognize the winners of the annual tennis tournament held at Flushing Meadow, New York. The competition is held in the following categories: men's singles; women's singles; men's doubles; women's doubles; and mixed doubles. Awarded annually. Established in 1881 as a tournament for amateurs. In 1968, it became "open" and both amateurs and professionals could compete.

• 20869 • USTA Community Service Award
To honor persons for outstanding field work in recreational tennis. The award is given for significant contributions made by individuals actively involved in tennis development through community tennis associations, park and recreation departments, schools or community centers. Established in 1974.

• 20870 • USTA Girls' Sportsmanship Award
To recognize an outstanding display by a girl player of sportsmanship, appearance, court manners, and tactics. A sterling silver plate engraved with the names of each of its recipients is awarded annually at the close of the USTA 18 International Grass Court Championship, along with a small silver replica. Established in 1936.

• 20871 • USTA Tennis NJTL Chapter of the Year Award
To honor an outstanding USTA National Junior Tennis League chapter that has demonstrated continued excellence in recreational tennis programming. Awarded annually. Established in 1978. Formerly: National Junior Tennis League Chapter of the Year Award.

• 20872 • USTA/USPTA Public Service Award
To recognize a tennis professional who has contributed to community development by working with programs for underprivileged youth or volunteering time in community centers, schools, parks, or public programs. The candidate must have at least three consecutive seasons of field work. Nominations may be submitted by August 1. Awarded at the United States Professional Tennis Association's national convention. Additional information is available from the USTA Center for Education & Recreational Tennis, Princeton, NJ.

• 20873 • Volunteer Service Award
To recognize USTA volunteers for 10, 25, or 50 years or more of national service to the Association. A gold lapel pin with a diamond chip in the laureate signifies 50 years or more of service. A silver lapel pin signifies 25 years or more of service. A gold pin signifies 10 years or more of service.

• 20874 • Ralph W. Westcott USTA Family of the Year Award
To recognize a family for noteworthy efforts to promote amateur tennis, primarily on a volunteer basis. All members of the family should participate in some way, either as players or by offering their services in running programs, tournaments and junior development. A large silver tray, which was bestowed upon Ralph W. Westcott at his retirement as President of the Western Tennis Association and Secretary of the USTA and later donated to the Association, is given as the Perpetual Award. The names of each winner is engraved on the tray and a replica is presented to the honorees. Awarded annually. Established in 1965 by Martin L. Tressel to emphasize that "Tennis is a Family Game". Formerly: Ralph W. Westcott Award.

• 20875 •
United States Trotting Association
Eric Sharbaugh, Exec.VP
750 Michigan Ave.
Columbus, OH 43215
Phone: (614)224-2291
Toll-Free: 877-800-USTA
Fax: (614)224-4575
E-mail: customerservice@ustrotting.com
Home Page: http://www.ustrotting.com

• 20876 • Harness Horse of the Year
To honor the trotter or pacer voted the best in North America. Selection is made by a vote of harness writers and radio/TV sportscasters interested in the sport. Awarded annually. Established in 1947. Co-sponsored by the U.S. Harness Writers' Association.

• 20877 • John Hervey Broadcasters' Awards George Smallreed Award
To recognize newspaper and magazine writers for excellence in the reporting of harness racing. The award consists of a monetary prize of $500 for the first prize winner, and $250 and $100 for the second and third place winners, respectively. Awarded annually. Established in 1962 in honor of the noted sports journalist, John Hervey. Awards to recognize television journalists were begun in 1984. The Smallsreed Award was begun in 2000. Formerly: John Hervey Journalism Award.

• 20878 • Pacing Triple Crown
To win the Triple Crown, a three-year-old must score victories in three harness races: the Little Brown Jug classic at Delaware, Ohio; the Cane Pace (originally called the Cane Futurity) at Freehold Raceway, New Jersey; and the Messenger Stake at The Meadows, Pennsylvania. All three events have purses approaching $500,000. The Little Brown Jug began in 1946, the Cane Pace in 1955, and the Messenger Stake in 1956.

• 20879 • Trotting Triple Crown
To win the Triple Crown, a three-year-old trotter must score victories in a series of three harness races: the $1 million Hambletonian at the Meadowlands in New Jersey; the Kentucky Futurity, a feature of the Lexington Trots meeting at Lexington, Kentucky; and the Yonkers Trot at Yonkers Raceway, New York. Awarded as merited. Established in 1955.

• 20880 •
United States Water Polo
Rich Foster, Pres.
1631 Mesa Ave., Ste. A-1
Colorado Springs, CO 80906
Phone: (719)634-0699
Fax: (719)634-0866
E-mail: tseitz@usawaterpolo.org
Home Page: http://www.usawaterpolo.com

• 20881 • Curren Award
To recognize the outstanding player in the Men's Senior National Indoor Water Polo Champion-

ships. Awarded annually. Established in 1962 in memory of John J. Curren by the New York Athletic Club.

• 20882 • John R. Felix Memorial Award
To recognize the outstanding player in the National Women's Outdoor Water Polo Championships. Established in 1989 in memory of John R. Felix, an outstanding national and international referee, and contributor to the sport of Water Polo.

• 20883 • Hall of Fame
For recognition of outstanding contributions in the sport of water polo.

• 20884 • James W. Lee Memorial Award
To recognize the outstanding player in the National Men's Outdoor Water Polo Championships. Awarded annually. Established in 1963 by Mrs. Frederick Mintz in memory of Mr. Lee, a member of the San Francisco Olympic Club Water Polo Team from 1954 until his untimely death in April 1963. (This award is being re-named.)

• 20885 • James R. "Jimmy" Smith - U.S. Water Polo Award
This, the most prestigious award presented by the Association, recognizes outstanding contributions to United States Water Polo. A trophy donated by Kalos Kagathos Foundation remains at USWP headquarters. Winners receive a replica of the original sculpture. Awarded annually at the convention. Established in 1984. Additional information is available from Frank Moorman, 310 East 55th Street, New York, NY 10022. Formerly: (1990) Peter V. Ueberroth - U.S. Water Polo Award.

• 20886 • United States Water Polo Award
To recognize an individual, group, or corporate entity for outstanding contributions to the sport of water polo. The award was conceived, commissioned, and funded by the Kalos Kagathos Foundation in 1990. A representational sculpture in the tradition of the Greek classics, designed by the distinguished artist, Joe Slockbower, is awarded annually. Established in memory of James R. "Jimmy" Smith.

• 20887 •
United States Women's Curling Association
Florence Springstead, Pres.
4006 Heartstone Dr.
Janesville, WI 53545
Phone: (608)752-8799
E-mail: president@uswca.org
Home Page: http://www.uswca.org

• 20888 • USWCA Senior Ladies Trophy
To recognize the winner of the Senior Ladies Bonspiel. Members of local clubs affiliated with USWCA are eligible. A traveling trophy (a silver teapot) is awarded. Team members receive a pin. Established in 1983.

• 20889 • Wauwatosa Event
To recognize the first place winners in a 32-game competition. Members of local clubs affiliated with the USWCA are eligible. A traveling trophy (the Wauwatosa Trophy - a large silver punch bowl) is awarded annually. Each of four team members receives a pin. Established in 1947 by the Wauwatosa Club of Wisconsin. The trophy was donated by the Wauwatosa Club, one of the charter members of the National Association.

• 20890 •
United States Youth Soccer Association
Jim Cosgrove, Exec.Dir.
1717 Firman Dr., Ste. 900
Richardson, TX 75081
Phone: (972)235-4499
Toll-Free: 800-4SO-CCER
Fax: (972)235-4480
E-mail: troby@usyouthsoccer.org
Home Page: http://www.usyouthsoccer.org

• 20891 • Don Greer Cup
For recognition of the best under-17 boys soccer team in the United States. The team must have won a state championship and regional championship (four regions in the United States) to participate in the National Finals; and they must win a semi-final and a final game in the Snickers US Youth Soccer National Championship. A trophy is awarded annually. Established in 1991.

• 20892 • Patricia L. Masotto Cup
For recognition of the best under-16 girls soccer team in the United States. The team must have won its state championship and regional championship (four regions in the United States) to participate in the National Cup finals, and it must win a semi-final and a final game in the Snickers US Youth Soccer National Championship. A trophy is awarded annually. Established in 1985 in honor of Patricia Masotto.

• 20893 • James P. McGuire Cup
For recognition of the best under-19 boys soccer team in the United States. The team must have won its state championship and regional championship (four regions in the United States) to participate in the National Cup Finals, and it must win a semi-final and a final game in the Snickers US Youth National Championship. A trophy is awarded annually. Established in 1935 in honor of James P. McGuire.

• 20894 • Laura Moynihan Cup
For recognition of the best under-17 girls' soccer team in the United States. The team must have won a state championship and regional championship (four regions in the United States) to participate in the National Finals; and they must win a semi-final and a final game in the Snickers US Youth Soccer National Championship. A trophy is awarded annually. Established in 1991. Formerly: (1998) National Cup Girls Under 17 Cup.

• 20895 • National Cup Boys Under 18 (Boys National Championship)
For recognition of the best under-18 boys soccer team in the United States. The team must have won a state championship and regional championship (four regions in the United States) to participate in the Snickers US Youth Soccer National Championship; and they must win a semi-final and a final game in the National Tournament. A trophy is awarded annually. Established in 1994.

• 20896 • National Cup Girls Under 18 (Girls National Championship)
For recognition of the best under-18 girls soccer team in the United States. The team must have won a state championship and regional championship (four regions in the United States) to participate in the Snickers US Youth Soccer National Championship; and they must win a semi-final and a final game in the National Tournament. A trophy is awarded annually. Established in 1994.

• 20897 • D. J. Niotis Cup
For recognition of the best under-16 boys soccer team in the United States. The team must have won its state championship and regional championship (four regions in the United States) to participate in the National Cup Finals, and it must win a semi-final and a final game in the Snickers US Youth Soccer National Championship. A trophy is awarded annually. Established in 1976 in honor of Niotis. Formerly: National Youth Cup Boys.

• 20898 • Ross Stewart Cup
For recognition of the best under-19 girls soccer team in the United States. The team must have won its state championship and regional championship (four regions in the United States) to participate in the National Cup Finals, and the team must win a semi-final and a final game in the Snickers US Youth Soccer National Championship. A trophy is awarded annually. Established in 1980. Formerly: Athena Cup.

• 20899 • United States Youth Soccer Association Coach of the Year for Boys and Girls
To recognize youth coaches of boys and girls in the United States based upon nominations from member state youth soccer associations. One regional winner's each for boys and girls coaches are selected in each of the four regions of USYSA. The eight regional winners are invited to the USYSA National Workshop where the two winners are announced. Awarded annually. Established in 1987.

• 20900 • United States Youth Soccer Association Youth Referee of the Year
For recognition of youth referees in the United States based upon nominations from member state youth soccer associations. A boy and girl youth referee are selected in each of the four regions that comprise USYSA. The eight regional winners are invited to attend the Snickers/US Youth Soccer National Championship as part of the referee delegation. The two winners

Awards are arranged in alphabetical order below their administering organizations

are announced during the Championship. Awarded annually. Established in 1969.

• 20901 •
United Synagogue of Conservative Judaism
Rabbi Lois Goldrich, Dir. of Pub.Aff.
155 5th Ave.
New York, NY 10010
Phone: (212)533-7800
Fax: (212)353-9439
E-mail: info@uscj.org
Home Page: http://www.uscj.org

• 20902 • **Solomon Schechter Award**
Recognizes excellence in synagogue programming. Awarded biennially.

• 20903 •
United Way of America
Brian A. Gallagher, Pres./CEO
701 N Fairfax St.
Alexandria, VA 22314
Phone: (703)836-7112
Fax: (703)683-7840
Home Page: http://national.unitedway.org

• 20904 • **Spirit of America Award**
For recognition of corporate community involvement by a company for sustaining company wide support for the United Way. Participation is limited to companies involved in the National Corporate Leadership Program. Companies and corporations are first nominated by their local United Way, and after completing entry packages, are selected by a panel of judges. A glass trophy featuring five stars is bestowed annually.

• 20905 • **Summit Awards**
For recognition of companies with the best programs for the strengthening of communities. Program categories include: employee education - for giving employees an opportunity to learn about the United Way's role in building communities; company wide campaign - for providing employees an opportunity to contribute without being coerced; corporate contributions for making generous corporate contributions of dollars and resources as investments in community; volunteer programs - for encouraging and recognizing individual volunteer involvement. A glass trophy featuring four stars is presented to awardees. Up to three awards are presented annually for each category.

• 20906 •
United Way of Chester County
Stephen J. Dillon, Pres.
2 W Market St.
West Chester, PA 19382
Phone: (610)429-9400
Fax: (610)738-8990
E-mail: claudia.hellebush@unitedwaychestercounty.org
Home Page: http://www.unitedwaychestercounty.org

• 20907 • **Chester County Community Hero**
For exceptional volunteer in community service. Recognition award bestowed annually.

• 20908 • **Chester County Youth Community Hero**
For exceptional volunteer in community service. Recognition award bestowed annually.

• 20909 •
United Way of Illinois Valley
Dixie M. Reed, Exec.Dir.
126 1/2 Marquette St.
PO Box 1285
La Salle, IL 61301-2413
Phone: (815)223-8339
Fax: (815)224-4956
E-mail: uwayiv@ivnet.com

• 20910 • **Venture Grants**
For new initiatives and not-for-profit organizations in La Salle, Buriace, and Putnam Counties. Monetary award bestowed annually.

• 20911 •
United Way of Jay County
Susan D. Reichard, Exec.Dir.
PO Box 204
PO Box 204
Portland, IN 47371-0204
Phone: (260)726-7010
Fax: (260)726-4434
E-mail: uwjay@jayco.net

• 20912 • **Lee G. Hall Memorial Award**
For leadership contributing. Trophy awarded annually.

• 20913 •
United Way of South Central Nebraska
Kiersten Hill, Exec.Dir.
421 N. Kansas Ave.
Hastings, NE 68901
Phone: (402)462-6600
Fax: (402)462-6670
E-mail: unitedway@inebraska.com

• 20914 • **Inez C. Peterson Citizenship Award**
For United Way donor. Recognition award bestowed annually.

• 20915 •
United Way of the Berwick Area
Cynthia Lombard, Exec.Dir.
139R E St.
Berwick, PA 18603
Phone: (570)759-8203
Fax: (570)759-8512
E-mail: bauw@bwkip.com
Home Page: http://www.berwickareaunitedway.org

• 20916 • **Senior High Youth Voluntarism Award**
For graduating senior, demonstrates volunteer commitment through written essay describing volunteer experiences. Monetary award bestowed annually.

• 20917 •
United Way of the Valley Area
John J. Walsh, Pres./COO
75 Liberty St.
72 Liberty St.
Ansonia, CT 06401
Phone: (203)735-9331
Fax: (203)732-8831
E-mail: valleyuw@snet.net
Home Page: http://www.valleyunitedway.org/

• 20918 • **Charles H. Flynn Humanitarian Award**
For community service. Recognition award bestowed annually.

• 20919 •
Unity-and-Diversity World Council
Leland P. Stewart, Founder/Central Coord.
PO Box 661401
Los Angeles, CA 90066-9201
Phone: (310)391-5735
Fax: (310)827-9187
E-mail: udcworld@gte.net
Home Page: http://www.udcworld.org

• 20920 • **Heart of Humanity Award**
Recognizes one outstanding individual. Suggestions are welcome, but selection is made by the steering committee. A trophy is awarded annually. Established in 2000. Sponsored by Unity-and-Diversity World Council.

• 20921 • **Unity-and-Diversity Service Award**
Recognizes individuals and groups for effective use of diversity programs. Awarded annually.

• 20922 •
Universal Pantheist Society
Harold W. Wood Jr., Dir.
PO Box 3499
Visalia, CA 93278
E-mail: ups@pantheist.net
Home Page: http://www.pantheist.net/society

• 20923 • **Spinoza Award**
To recognize any scholar, writer, activist, or other outstanding individual, who has made a significant contribution toward the establishment of a Pantheist world-view. Established in 1986 in honor of Baruch Spinoza, the leading philosopher of Pantheism in the Western world.

• 20924 •
Universal Ship Cancellation Society
Richard Jones, Ed.
137 Putnam Ave.
Ormond Beach, FL 32174
Phone: (860)667-1400
Phone: (386)672-2112
E-mail: bmcmjones@yahoo.com
Home Page: http://www.uscs.org

• 20925 • **Best of the Rest Award**
For the best gold or silver level exhibit which has not received another Named Award. Established in 1994.

• 20926 • **Championship Award**
To recognize the best exhibit in the Championship Class (which is limited to Fernandez Award winners). A plaque is awarded every five years. Established in 1982.

• 20927 • **Franklin Erwin Memorial Trophy**
To recognize the best exhibit of steel hulled battleship covers at the annual USCS National Convention by USCS members and gold or silver medal winners at the same show. A plaque is awarded annually when merited. Established in 1971 in honor of Franklin Erwin, USCS Number Eight.

• 20928 • **USCU Fernandez Award**
To recognize the best exhibit of maritime covers at the annual USCS National Convention by USCS members and gold or silver medal winners at the same show. Awarded annually. Established in 1967. Formerly: (2006) Anthony Fernandez Trophy.

• 20929 • **Guardians of the Seas Award**
For recognition of the best exhibit of covers from Coast Guard ships or stations, exhibited at the National Convention. USCS members and gold or silver medal winners at the same show are eligible. A plaque is awarded annually. Established in 1985. Formerly: (1987) Smokies of the Seas Award.

• 20930 • **Admiral Lockwood Award**
To recognize the best exhibit of submarine related covers at the annual USCS National Convention by USCS members and gold or silver medal winners at the same show. A trophy is awarded annually. Established in 1968 in memory of of VADM Charles A. Lockwood.

• 20931 • **Francis E. Locy Award**
To recognize the best exhibit of maritime postmarks classified by the Locy system at the annual USCS National Convention. USCS members and gold or silver medal winners at the same show are eligible. Awarded annually when merited. Established in 1965.

• 20932 • **Novice Award**
For recognition of the best exhibit of naval/maritime covers by an exhibitor who has never shown maritime covers in competition before, exhibited at the National Convention. Members are eligible. A plaque is awarded annually. Established in 1973.

• 20933 • **Nuclear Ships Trophy**
To recognize the best exhibit of nuclear ship related covers at the annual USCS National Convention. USCS members and gold or silver medal winners at the same show are eligible. An engraved plaque is awarded annually when merited. Established in 1965.

• 20934 • **Reserve Grand Award**
To recognize runner-up exhibits of maritime covers at the annual USCS National Convention. USCS members and gold or silver medal winners at the same show are eligible. Awarded annually. Established in 1979.

• 20935 • **Sixteen One Frame Exhibit**
To recognize the best one frame (16 page) exhibit at a national convention. Established in 1995.

• 20936 • **Jesse Burgess Thomas Memorial Award**
To recognize the best exhibit of maritime covers or covers pertaining to a naval historical event by USCS members and gold or silver medal winners at the annual USCS National Convention. Awarded annually. Established in 1974 in honor of J. Burgess Thomas, long time member of the Admiral Byrd Chapter and a Naval Historian.

• 20937 • **Graf von Spee Chapter Award**
To recognize the best non-navy or foreign navy exhibit by an American exhibitor at the annual USCS National Convention. USCS members and winners of the gold or silver medal at the same show are eligible. A plaque is awarded annually. Established in 1975.

• 20938 • **Albert O. Wickard Award**
To recognize the best exhibit of destroyer covers at the annual USCS National Convention by USCS members and gold or silver medal winners at the same show. A plaque is awarded annually. Established in 1975 in honor of A.O. Wickard by Mrs. Laura Wickard.

• 20939 • **Wings of Gold Award**
To recognize the best exhibit relative to the history or operations of U.S. Naval Aviation at the annual USCS National Convention. USCS members and gold or silver medal winners at the same show are eligible. A plaque is awarded annually when merited. Established in 1980.

• 20940 • **Workhorses of the Fleet Award**
For recognition of the best exhibit of covers of auxiliary ships (naval vessels with a hull designation starting with "A") exhibited at the National Convention. USCS members and gold or silver medal winners at the exhibit are eligible. A plaque is awarded annually when merited. Established in 1984.

• 20941 •
University Aviation Association
Carolyn Williamson, Exec.Dir.
3410 Skyway Dr.
Auburn, AL 36830
Phone: (334)844-2434
Fax: (334)844-2432
E-mail: uaa@auburn.edu
Home Page: http://uaa.auburn.edu

• 20942 • **Capt. W. W. Estridge, Jr. Award**
For recognition of dedicated service to collegiate aviation education. Nominations must be submitted by the UAA Membership by May 31. Final approval must be made by the awards committee. A plaque is presented annually at the UAA fall meeting. Established in 1991 by American Airlines in honor of Captain W. W. Estridge, Jr., long-time pilot and Director of Training for American Airlines.

• 20943 • **Capt. V. L. Laursen Award**
For recognition of teaching excellence in collegiate aviation. Nominations must be submitted by the UAA membership by May 31. Final approval must be made by the awards committee. A plaque is presented annually at the UAA fall meeting. Established in 1991 by TransWorld Airlines in honor of retired Captain V. L. Laursen, who made significant contributions in the areas of flight training, equipment, and procedures.

• 20944 • **William A. Wheatley Award**
For recognition of contributions made to the field of aviation education by a university educator. Nominations must be submitted by the UAA membership by May 31. Final approval must be made by the awards committee. A plaque is presented annually at the UAA fall meeting. Established in 1955 by United Airlines in memory of William A. Wheatley, United Airlines, who established a relationship between educational institutions and the aviation industry.

• 20945 •
University Continuing Education Association
Kay J. Kohl, Exec.Dir./CEO
1 Dupont Cir., Ste. 615
Washington, DC 20036
Phone: (202)659-3130
Fax: (202)785-0374
E-mail: kjkohl@ucea.edu
Home Page: http://www.ucea.edu

Formerly: (1980) National University Extension Association.

• 20946 • **Walton S. Bittner Service Citation for Outstanding Service in UCEA**
To recognize an individual for outstanding service to continuing education at his/her institution, and service of major significance to UCEA. Nominees must be members of the UCEA institution and have contributed to the development of his/her institution and UCEA over a period of

years. Nomination deadline is December 6. A plaque is awarded annually when merited at the national conference. Established in 1968 in honor of Walton S. Bittner, who served as a NUEA secretary-treasurer from 1927 to 1956.

• 20947 • Gayke B. Childs Award
Recognizes an individual who has distinguished himself or herself through outstanding contributions to the field of distance learning through a combination of sustained research, writing, and leadership activities. Candidates must have demonstrated significant contributions in one or both of the following areas: Research and writing that have been recognized as making a clear contribution to the field of distance learning and Significant leadership activities such as national and international presentations and speeches and recognition by the service to other organizations. Appropriate activities may also include those that have contributed to a better understanding of distributed learning, have resulted in cooperative efforts with other organizations, or have brought about specific improvements in distributed learning methods. Nominations need not be restricted to person with whom the nominator is directly associated.

• 20948 • Devoted Service Award
Recognizes professional members who have made a long-term contributions to the field of distance learning and who are leaving it because of retirement or career changes. Submission deadline is January 15. For additional information see the website listed above.

• 20949 • Distance Learning Course Awards
Recognizes new and innovative courses that utilize one or more forms of instruction at a distance in three categories; college, K-12, and non-credit. One course may be submitted in each category. Courses submitted must have been completed and opened to enrollment since December 1, 1998. Revised courses may be submitted for an award if they have undergone major revision and have not been submitted for an award during the past 3 years. The following criteria are used for judging: Introductory Materials: Introduction, overview, and general objectives of the course, course mechanics, structure, special instructions, and performance standards; Lesson/Units: Stated instructional objectives, commentary, discussion, and help, including possible audio and video components; submitted assignments and assessment. Communication Variants: Writing style, writing mechanics and editorial consistency; page organization, layout, cover, appropriateness and quality of graphics and illustrations and General Quality. For complete details on the nomination procedure, consult the UCEA website above.

• 20950 • Distinguished Service Key and Certificate for Retiring Continuing Educators
To honor retiring continuing educators who have been active in UCEA during their career. Members who fit the criteria are retroactively eligible up to and including one year after retirement. Nomination deadline is February 10. Presented at the Association's annual conference.

• 20951 • Exemplary Program Award
Recognizes short-term continuing education programs that are exemplary, including professional education and youth activities. Awarded to large and small institutions for large and small programs. Nominees or applicants must be members of UCEA. The program should not span more than one year, should have been held within the last two years, and should be completed by the date of the nomination.

• 20952 • Faculty Service Award
Recognizes faculty for outstanding contributions to conference and professional programs or other continuing education programs. Awarded to individual faculty members with a long-term commitment to conference and professional programs, including one or more areas in program development, teaching, research, administration, publishing, or student involvement. Individuals nominated for this award cannot be a staff member of an extension or continuing education unit and do not have to be university faculty members. For additional nomination information, see the website listed above.

• 20953 • Phillip E. Frandson Award for Innovative Programming
To recognize original, exemplary programming in the humanities, arts, or sciences and provide an opportunity for national recognition of outstanding contributions to continuing education. Nominees' projects must address issues in the humanities, arts, or sciences; reflect originality in approach, content, format, mode of delivery, or in reaching new audiences; have been offered no earlier than 1995; and demonstrate potential duplication by other institutions. Inquire for additional nomination details.

• 20954 • Phillip E. Frandson Award for Sustained Excellence
Recognizes original, exemplary programming in the humanities, arts, or sciences and provides an opportunity for national recognition of outstanding contributions to continuing education. Nominees' projects must address issues in the humanities, arts, or sciences; demonstrate long-term success, having been offered on an ongoing basis for at least six terms; exemplify outstanding quality; exhibit ease of duplication by other institutions. Inquire for additional nomination information.

• 20955 • Independent Study Catalog Awards
Recognizes the best independent study catalog produced in the previous year. Categories include: those listing high school programs only; those listing college programs only; and those listing both high school and college programs. Criteria for judging includes: Information - Program features and benefits, procedures and policies, enrollment form, governance, etc.; Course Listings - Course descriptions; Communication Variants Written and Organizational - Writing style, writing mechanics and editorial consistency, and page organization and layout; Communication Variants Visual - Front and back cover design and graphics and pictures; General Quality - All elements. Application deadline is January 15. Visit the above website for additional information.

• 20956 • International Futures Award for Exceptional and Innovative Leadership in Continuing Higher Education
For the most valued professionals in continuing higher education who is leading peers and the profession successfully into the future. Nominees must have a professional history of at least five years in continuing education; be currently engaged in a leadership role; be engaged beyond the boundaries of a single institution when thinking about and shaping continuing higher education; and be the kind of leader that would be pointed to as the best in the field. A framed certificate and a small sculptural piece are presented at the UCEA Annual Conference. For complete details on the nomination procedure, consult the UCEA website above.

• 20957 • Marketing and Publications Awards
Recognizes excellence in marketing publications; promotion and publicity; and advertising and communications. Application deadline is January 15. Visit the above website for additional information.

• 20958 • Memorial Awards
Honors deceased continuing education professionals who gave long and sustained service to UCEA. Nominations are made by continuing education units wishing to honor recently deceased colleagues. A complete nomination form, including appropriate biographical information must be submitted by February 10. Awarded when merited.

• 20959 • Nofflet William Up-and-Coming Leadership Award
Recognizes an individual who has made strong contributions to UCEA's Distance Learning Community of Practice through elected or committee service in the Community or its predecessor UCEA division. Candidates must have demonstrated service to the Distance Learning Community of Practice or its predecessors through strong leadership activities. Submission deadline is in January.

• 20960 • Julius M. Nolte Award for Extraordinary Leadership
This, the most prestigious UCEA award, is given for recognition of unusual and extraordinary contributions to the cause of university continuing education on the regional, national, and/or international level. Affiliation with the UCEA is not necessary. Nomination deadline is December 6. A plaque and professional recognition by peers are awarded when merited at the national conference. Established in 1965 in memory of Julius M. Nolte, a pioneer in the field of continuing education and president of NUCEA in 1950-51.

• 20961 • Outstanding Continuing Education Student Awards
To honor continuing education students who are either credit or non-credit students at UCEA member institutions for achievement of excellence in pursuit of their educational goals. Eligible credit students must be 25 years of age or older and enrolled in an undergraduate or graduate program at a UCEA member institution within the past 12 months. Eligible non-credit students must be enrolled in a non-credit program at a UCEA member institution within the past 12 months. One award is presented in each category annually.

• 20962 • Outstanding Program Awards
To recognize credit and non-credit continuing education programs at UCEA member institutions for excellence in achieving their educational objectives. Qualified programs are those that have been offered within the last two years, be original in substantive ways, demonstrate a contribution to the field of continuing education that can be replicated by other higher education institutions, and be cost effective. Nomination deadline is December 6. Awarded when merited. Formerly: ACT-NUCEA Innovations in Continuing Education Awards.

• 20963 • Outstanding Program Awards for Credit and Non-Credit Programs
Honors credit and non-credit continuing education programs at UCEA member institutions for excellence in achieving their educational objectives. Programs must have been offered within the last two years; have completed at least one cycle; be original in a substantive way(s); and demonstrate a contribution to the field of continuing education, which can be replicated by other higher education institutions. A complete nomination form, including a description of the program explaining how the program objectives were met and a summary of the program evaluations must be submitted. This award is not necessarily given annually.

• 20964 • Elizabeth Powell Award
Recognizes publications of merit that make significant contributions to research in the field of distance education. Eligible publications must have been published during the previous year. Exceptions will be made for publications in overseas journals dated two year previously, journals with a two year span covering the previous two years, and books copyrighted in the previous year but released late the year before. Qualifying publications are published articles or written versions of papers presented at professional meetings or conferences.

• 20965 • Adelle F. Robertson Continuing Professional Educator Award
To recognize scholarship, leadership, and contributions to the profession of a person who has entered the profession in the past five to ten years. Nominees must be UCEA members. Awarded when merited. Established in memory of Adelle Frances Robertson, whose career in continuing education spanned 30 years and who served as President of the Association.

• 20966 • Stanley C. Robinson Distinguished Service Award
Recognizes outstanding long-term leaders in continuing education for commitment and contributions to the field of conferences and professional programs. Nominees must be or have engaged in full-time conferences and professional programs work for a period of at least 10 years and is or has been a member of the Conferences and Professional Programs Community of Practice of UCEA. Nominees must have made substantial contributions to the development and operation of conferences and professional programs, not only at his/her institution, but also through active participation and demonstrated leadership within the Conferences and Professional Programs Community of Practice of UCEA.

• 20967 • Signature of Excellence Award
To recognize a chief executive officer of a higher education institution who has demonstrated exemplary service to the field of continuing higher education. Service may include leadership concerning federal legislation, a major research project, or policies in higher education. Awarded when merited. Established in 1985.

• 20968 • Special Award or Citation to Institutions and Individuals
Recognizes outstanding service at the regional or national level by individuals or institutions that is not otherwise recognized by the Association's awards program. Nomination deadline is December 6. Awarded when merited.

• 20969 • Charles A. Wedemeyer Award
Recognizes publications of merit that make significant contributions to research in the field of distance education. Eligible publications must have been published during the previous year. Exceptions will be made for publications in overseas journals for two years; journals with a two-year span of the previous two years, and books copyrighted in the previous year that appeared late in the year before. Entries must be books, theses, and dissertations. For additional information on the nomination procedure, see the above web site.

• 20970 •
University Council for Educational Administration
Michelle D. Young, Exec.Dir.
Univ. of MO/Columbia
205 Hill Hall
Columbia, MO 65211-2185
Phone: (573)884-8300
Fax: (573)884-8302
E-mail: execucea@missouri.edu
Home Page: http://www.ucea.org

• 20971 • Roald Campbell Award
Rewards senior professors in the field of educational administration whose professional lives have been characterized by extraordinary commitment, excellence, leadership, productivity, generosity, and service. It celebrates the pioneering life of Roald F. Campbell. Awarded annually.

• 20972 • Jack A. Culbertson Award
To recognize individuals for accomplishments in the early years of their professional careers in educational administration. The contribution can be in the form of an innovation in training, a published book, instructional materials produced, a new course or program developed, a completed research project, and/or other related products. Individuals are judged for innovativeness, originality, ability to generalize, potential impact, relation to UCEA goals, significance with respect to the training mission at the individual's institution, degree of effort required to produce the contribution, and extent of support for the effort provided by the candidate's employing institution. Young or beginning professors from member universities may be nominated by May 15. A monetary award and a plaque are presented annually at the Plenary Session Representatives meeting in October. Established in 1982 in honor of Jack A. Culbertson, UCEA's first full-time Executive Director.

• 20973 • William J. Davis Memorial Award
To recognize the individuals for the most outstanding article published in the *Educational Administration Quarterly* during the preceding year. A monetary award and a certificate of recognition are awarded annually. Established in 1979 in honor of William J. Davis, a former Associate Director of UCEA and assistant professor of educational administration at the University of Wisconsin-Madison.

• 20974 •
University Musical Society
Kenneth C. Fischer, Pres.
Burton Memorial Tower
881 N Univ. Ave.
Ann Arbor, MI 48109-1011
Phone: (734)764-2538
Toll-Free: 800-221-1229
Fax: (734)647-1171
E-mail: umstix@umich.edu
Home Page: http://www.ums.org

• 20975 • UMS Distinguished Artist Award
For internationally recognized performer. Recognition award bestowed annually.

• 20976 •
University of Alabama at Birmingham
Department of Theatre
1530 3rd Ave. S
ASC 255
Birmingham, AL 35294-1263
Phone: (205)934-3236
Fax: (205)934-8076
Home Page: http://theatre.hum.uab.edu

• 20977 • Ruby Lloyd Apsey Playwriting Award
To recognize original works by non-American playwrights living anywhere in the world but ei-

ther writing in English or with translated into English are eligible. Seeking thought provoking full length plays or Related one-acts that relate experience and points of view originating in Other parts of the world. A script, character/ scene breakdown and a SASE Must be submitted.

• 20978 •
University of Alberta
Perinatal Research Centre
220 HMRC
Edmonton, AB, Canada T6G 2S2
Phone: (780)492-2765
Fax: (780)492-1308
E-mail: eileen.marco@nalberta.ca
Home Page: http://www.ualberta.ca/ PERINATAL/

• 20979 • **Travel Awards**
For graduate students and fellows to attend national or international meetings to present their work. Awarded annually.

• 20980 •
University of Arizona
Department of Journalism
Marshall Bldg.
PO Box 210158B
Tucson, AZ 85721-0158
Phone: (520)621-7556
Fax: (520)621-7557
E-mail: journal@email.arizona.edu
Home Page: http://journalism.arizona.edu

• 20981 • **John Peter and Anna Catherine Zenger for Freedom of the Press and the Peoples Right to Know**
To recognize an individual or organization that has given distinguished service on behalf of freedom of information. A plaque is awarded annually. Established in 1954 to honor John Peter and Anna Catherine Zenger.

• 20982 •
University of Arizona
Udall Center for Studies in Public Policy
803 E 1st St.
Tucson, AZ 85719
Phone: (520)884-4393
Fax: (520)884-4702
E-mail: udallctr@u.arizona.edu
Home Page: http://udallcenter.arizona.edu

• 20983 • **Lillian S. 3Fisher Prize in Environmental Law and Public Policy**
for UA College of Law students

• 20984 • **Udall Center Prize in American Indian Public Policy**
For UA American Indian studies program students.

• 20985 •
University of British Columbia
Wine Research Centre
Faculty of Agricultural Sciences
2205 East Mall
Vancouver, BC, Canada V6T 1Z4
Phone: (604)822-0005
Fax: (604)822-5143
E-mail: hjjvv@interchange.ubc.ca
Home Page: http://www.agsci.ubc.ca/wine/

• 20986 • **Chardonnay Challenge**
Wine competition. Inquire for application details.

• 20987 •
University of California, Davis
Davis Arboretum
1 Shields Ave.
Davis, CA 95616-8526
Phone: (530)752-4880
Fax: (530)752-5796
E-mail: arboretum@ucdavis.edu
Home Page: http://arboretum.ucdavis.edu

• 20988 • **Pinkerton Prize**
Recognizes an outstanding student employee. Inquire for application details.

• 20989 •
University of California, Los Angeles
Anderson School of Management
Mary Ann Lowe, Program Man.
Gerald Loeb Awards
110 Westwood Plaza
Mullin Mgmt. Commons, Ste. F321B
Los Angeles, CA 90095-1481
Phone: (310)206-1877
Fax: (310)825-4479
E-mail: loeb@anderson.ucla.edu
Home Page: http:// www.loeb.anderson.ucla.edu

• 20990 • **Gerald Loeb Awards**
To recognize writers who have made significant contributions to the public's understanding of business, finance, and the economy, thus encouraging excellent writing on these subjects and protecting the private investor and general public. Distinguished journalists throughout the nation may participate. Any writer or commercial publication may submit an entry on a subject related to business, economics, and/or finance under any of the following categories: large newspapers - daily circulation of more than 400,000; medium-sized newspapers - daily circulation of between 150,000 and 400,000; small newspapers - daily circulation of less than 150,000; magazines; commentary; deadline writing; beat writing; news services or online content; television short form; television long form.

• 20991 •
University of Chicago
Cancer Research Center
5841 S Maryland Ave.
Duchossois Center for Advanced Medicine, 1st Fl.
Chicago, IL 60637-1470
Phone: (773)702-6180
Fax: (773)702-9311
E-mail: judith.romaine@cancer.org
Home Page: http://www-uccrc.bsd.uchicago.edu

• 20992 • **Shubitz Award**
Recognizes outstanding research.

• 20993 •
University of Chicago
Department of Music
Kathy Holmes, Admin.
Administrator, Chicago Folklore Prize
1010 E 59th St.
Chicago, IL 60637
Phone: (773)702-8484
Fax: (773)753-0558
E-mail: cullinan@uchicago.edu
Home Page: http://music.uchicago.edu

• 20994 • **Chicago Folklore Prize**
To further research and recognize outstanding monographs in folklore and related disciplines. Three copies of entries, submitted by publishers or individual authors, must be received by April 1. To be considered a book must bear an imprint from the previous year or have appeared prior to April 1. Articles, dissertations, and works in progress are not considered. Folklore is interpreted in its broadest sense, and entries in any major language are welcome. Prize winners receive a modest monetary award. Honorable mentions may also be awarded. Announcement of the prize occurs in October. Established by the International Folklore Association and awarded annually since 1928.

• 20995 •
University of Chicago Alumni Association
Stephanie Rada Zocco, Pres.
5555 S Woodlawn Ave.
Chicago, IL 60637
Phone: (773)702-2150
Toll-Free: 800-955-0065
Fax: (773)702-2166
Home Page: http:// www.alumni.uchicago.edu/aa.html

• 20996 • **Alumni Medal**
To recognize an individual for achievement of an exceptional nature in any field, vocational or voluntary, covering an entire career. Traditionally, the medal has not been given in recognition of some single remarkable achievement but has been reserved for those few persons who have attained and maintained extremely high stations in their chosen fields of endeavor and in their service to society. A medal is awarded to no more than one person each year and need not be awarded on an annual basis. Established in 1941.

• 20997 • **Alumni Service Citations**
To recognize an individual for outstanding service to the University. The citations recognize the achievements of individuals working on behalf of the University through service in alumni programs, on advisory committees, and through efforts made to ensure the welfare of the institution. Established in 1983.

• 20998 • **Alumni Service Medal**
To recognize an individual for extended, extraordinary service to the University. The medal is awarded to no more than one person each year and need not be awarded on an annual basis. Established in 1983.

• 20999 • **Professional Achievement Citations**
To recognize an individual for outstanding achievement in any professional field, including but not limited to the arts and letters, industry and commerce, and the academic professions. The citations honor those alumni whose achievements in their vocational fields have brought distinction to themselves, credit to the University, and real benefit to their communities. Established in 1967.

• 21000 • **Public Service Citations**
To recognize an individual for voluntary service. The awards honor individuals who have fulfilled the obligations of their education through creative and exemplary leadership in voluntary service that has benefited society and reflected credit on the University. Established in 1941.

• 21001 • **Young Alumni Service Citations**
To acknowledge and encourage service to the University by individuals aged 35 and younger. The citations recognize outstanding achievements in promoting the University through volunteer support for the Alumni Association, alumni clubs, class reunions, fund-raising, and student recruitment. Established in 1991 to be awarded for the first time during the University Centennial celebration.

• 21002 •
University of Chicago Medical and Biological Sciences Alumni Association
David H. Whitney, Pres.
5632 S Maryland Ave.
Chicago, IL 60637
Phone: (773)702-0655
Toll-Free: 888-303-0030
Fax: (773)834-9160
E-mail: alumni@mcdmail.uchicago.edu
Home Page: http://bsdalumni.uchicago.edu

Formerly: University of Chicago Medical Alumni Association.

• 21003 • **Distinguished Service Awards**
To recognize alumni who, through outstanding leadership and contributions to the health field through basic research, clinical care, health service administration, or public service/civic duties, have brought honor and distinction to the University of Chicago. Candidates must be graduates of the University of Chicago Biological Sciences Division, Medical School, Rush Medical College (through 1942), former faculty or house staff. Current University faculty and house staff are not eligible. A certificate, a gift from the Association, and guest status while in Chicago for the Annual Reunion are awarded. Established in 1952.

• 21004 • **Gold Key Awards**
For recognition of faculty members of the Division of Biological Sciences and to the University of Chicago. Traditionally presented to Divisional faculty members who are at or near retirement. A gold key and a gift are given as recognition from the Alumni Association. Awarded as merited. Established in 1951.

• 21005 •
University of Chicago Press
1427 E 60th St.
Chicago, IL 60637
Phone: (773)702-7700
Fax: (773)702-9756
Home Page: http://www.press.uchicago.edu

• 21006 • **Gordon J. Laing Prize**
For recognition of a book published during the preceding three years by the University of Chicago Press that added the greatest distinction to the press list. Authors, editors, or translators of the selected book who are members of the faculty of the University of Chicago at the time of publication are eligible. A monetary award of $1,000 and a certificate are awarded annually. Established in 1962 to honor Gordon J. Laing, general editor of the University of Chicago Press from 1909 to 1940.

• 21007 •
University of Colorado
School of Journalism and Mass Communication
478 UCB
Armory Bldg.
1511 University Ave.
Boulder, CO 80309-0478
Phone: (303)492-5007
Fax: (303)392-0969
E-mail: elizabeth.gaeddert@colorado.edu
Home Page: http://www.colorado.edu/journalism/alumni/nakkula.html

• 21008 • **Al Nakkula Award for Police Reporting**
To recognize newspaper police and crime reporting. Open to individual reporters working at daily United States newspapers or news services that regularly cover police and crime stories. Works submitted can be in the form of a single article or a series of no more than six stories. A $2,000 prize and a trip to Boulder, Colorado, are awarded. Deadline is February 1. Established in honor of Al Nakkula, a reporter covering cops and crooks for The *Denver Rocky Mountain News* for 46 years.

• 21009 •
University of Colorado at Boulder
Center of the American West
Macky 229, 282 UCB
Boulder, CO 80309-0282
Phone: (303)492-4879
Fax: (303)492-1671
E-mail: info@centerwest.org
Home Page: http://www.centerwest.org

• 21010 • **Wallace Stegner Award**
Recognizes a Westerner who displays dedication to the public perception of the West.

• 21011 •
University of Dayton
Office of Provost
Fred P. Pestello, Provost
St. Mary's Hall 212
300 College Park
Dayton, OH 45469-1634
Phone: (937)229-2245
Fax: (937)229-3400
E-mail: info@udayton.edu
Home Page: http://provost.udayton.edu

• 21012 • **Marian Library Award**
To recognize significant contributions to the advancement of Marian studies. Established in 1953, the award originally recognized the author of a specific book. Beginning in 1971, the award was conferred every four years at the time of the International Mariological Congress to individuals in recognition of their scholarly accomplishments. Administered by the Marian Library at the University of Dayton.

• 21013 • **Marianist Award**
To recognize a Catholic distinguished for achievement in scholarship and the intellectual life. Selection is by the President upon the recommendation of a committee of university faculty. A monetary prize of $5,000 and a work of art are awarded annually. Established in 1950.

• 21014 •
University of Denver
Daniels College of Business
Karen L. Newman, Dean
2101 S University Blvd.
Denver, CO 80208
Phone: (303)871-3411
Toll-Free: 800-662-4723
Fax: (303)871-2156
E-mail: daniels@du.edu
Home Page: http://www.daniels.du.edu

• 21015 • **Morton Margolin Prize for Distinguished Business Reporting**
To recognize and reward outstanding reporting about business and the economy of Colorado. The award recognizes noteworthy reporting that is timely, accurate, skillfully researched, and written in such a way as to bring new insight and understanding to the subject. The degree to which an article reflects high standards, competency, and integrity is considered, as is the manner in which the entry illuminates the topic or

topics of significance or opens up new concerns and provides greater understanding of them. Articles published during the preceding year in local publications about Colorado business or economy are considered. All entries must be received by August 8. A plaque and one monetary award of $1,000 is presented annually to a local article published in a Colorado publications. Established in 1980 by friends of the late Morton Margolin, a widely known and highly respected reporter and editor.

• 21016 •
University of Georgia
Artificial Intelligence Center
Boyd Graduate Studies Research Center, Rm. 111
Athens, GA 30602-7415
Phone: (706)542-0358
Fax: (706)542-8864
E-mail: mc@uga.edu
Home Page: http://www.ai.uga.edu

• 21017 • Graduate Assistantships
Provides stipends of $8400 plus tuition waiver during a nine-month school year.

• 21018 •
University of Georgia
Grady College of Journalism and Mass Communication
Dr. Horace Newcomb, Dir.
Sanford Dr. at Baldwin St.
Athens, GA 30602
Phone: (706)542-3787
Fax: (706)542-4785
E-mail: peabody@uga.edu
Home Page: http://www.peabody.uga.edu

• 21019 • Atrium Award
To recognize excellence in reporting on the American garment industry by staff reporters and freelance journalists. Entries may be submitted by February 1 in the following categories: (1) Editorial, Column, Opinion Piece, Comment or Criticism; (2) Reporting on the Apparel Industry from a Business or Economic Standpoint; (3) Reporting of a Specific Event; (4) Feature Stories and Special Pages or Sections; (5) Graphic Design, Artwork and Photojournalism; and (6) Special Pages or Sections. A plaque is awarded annually in April. Established in 1980. Additional information is available from Atrium Award Program director John W. English.

• 21020 • Peabody Awards Collection
For recognition of distinguished achievement and the most meritorious public service rendered by electronically-delivered programming (radio, television and cable). Programs, stations, networks, and individuals are considered for the award. Entries may be submitted by radio and television stations producers and networks worldwide. Statuettes are awarded annually in May. Established in 1940 to honor George Foster Peabody, a Columbus, Georgia, native who was a successful New York banker and philanthropist. Call (706)542-3787 or Fax (706)542-9273 for additional information. Formerly: (2006) George Foster Peabody Awards.

• 21021 •
University of Georgia
Language Education Office
125 Aderhold Hall
University of Georgia
Athens, GA 30602
Phone: (706)583-8130
Fax: (706)542-4509
E-mail: lle@uga.edu
Home Page: http://www.coe.uga.edu/language

• 21022 • Georgia Children's Book Award
To encourage the reading of good books as a part of the curriculum for elementary level children in the state of Georgia. The winning author and book are chosen by a vote of school children; K-4 for the picture book category and grades 4-8 for the novel category. A plaque and an honorarium for appearing at the University of Georgia Conference on Children's Literature are awarded annually. Established in 1968.

• 21023 • Georgia Children's Picture Storybook Award
To encourage the reading of good books as a part of the curriculum for children in the primary grades of kindergarten through fourth. The winning authors/illustrators are chosen by a vote of children in grades K-4 from a list of 20 nominees selected by a committee of teachers and librarians and chaired by a faculty member at the University of Georgia. A plaque and an honorarium are awarded annually. Established in 1976.

• 21024 •
University of Georgia Press
Nicole Mitchell, Dir.
330 Research Dr.
Athens, GA 30602
Phone: (706)369-6130
Toll-Free: 800-266-5842
Fax: (706)369-6131
E-mail: books@ugapress.uga.edu
Home Page: http://www.ugapress.uga.edu

• 21025 • Contemporary Poetry Series
To recognize outstanding poetry collections by published and unpublished poets. Collections must be written in English. Poets who have never published a full-length collection of poetry must submit manuscripts of at least 50 pages during September. Poets who have published one or more books of poetry should submit during January. Send SASE for guidelines. Two winners are selected biannually and are published by UGA Press.

• 21026 • Flannery O'Connor Award for Short Fiction
To recognize outstanding writers of short fiction by publishing a collection of their work. Published and unpublished writers may submit manuscripts ranging in length from 200 to 275 pages between April 1 and May 31. Send SASE for guidelines and for notification of winners. Manuscripts will not be returned. Two monetary prizes of $1,000 each and publication of the winning manuscripts are awarded annually. Established in 1981 in memory of Flannery O'Connor (1925-1964), novelist, short-story writer, and native Georgian.

• 21027 •
University of Hawaii at Manoa
School of Communications
Gerald Kato, Chm.
Journalism Dept.
Crawford Hall 320
2250 Campus Rd.
Honolulu, HI 96822-2217
Phone: (808)956-8881
Fax: (808)956-5396
E-mail: gkato@hawaii.edu
Home Page: http://www.communications.hawaii.edu/journ

• 21028 • UH Journalism Carol Burnett Prizes in Journalism Ethics
To recognize an outstanding research paper on ethical issues in journalism. Two monetary awards are presented: one to an undergraduate student and one to a graduate student. Funded by a $100,000 endowment from the Carol Burnett Fund.

• 21029 •
University of Illinois
Agricultural Communications and Education
263 Bevier Hall
905 S Goodwin
Urbana, IL 61801
Phone: (217)333-3790
Fax: (217)244-7877
E-mail: dahl@cesadmin.ag.uluc.edu
Home Page: http://www.uiuc.edu

• 21030 • Oscars in Agriculture
To recognize excellence in media reporting about agriculture, food, natural resources, and rural affairs. Awards are presented in four categories: magazine, newspaper, radio, and television. Eligible candidates include any writer, editor, or broadcaster employed as a staff member of or freelance reporter for a commercial (for-profit) magazine, newspaper, radio or television station, or broadcast or news wire service. Entries are also accepted from public broadcasting services. Materials published or broadcast during the preceding 12 months may be submitted by July 1. Each year, $1,000 cash awards and certificates are awarded. Established in 1961. Administered by the University of Illinois with financial support from DeKalb Genetics Corporation, New Holland, Inc., and Pfizer Agricultural Division.

• 21031 •
University of Illinois
College of Fine & Applied Arts
Dr. Kathleen F. Conlin, Dean
Kate Neal Kinley Memorial Fellowship
100 Architecture Bldg.
608 E Lorado Taft Dr.
Champaign, IL 61820
Phone: (217)333-1661
Fax: (217)244-8381
E-mail: nacox3@uiuc.edu
Home Page: http://www.faa.uiuc.edu

• 21032 • **Kate Neal Kinley Memorial Fellowship**
To promote advanced study in the fine arts. The Fellowship is open to graduates of the College of Fine and Applied Arts of the University of Illinois at Urbana-Champaign and graduates of similar institutions of equal educational standing whose principal or major studies have been in one of the following: architecture design or history, art (all branches), and music (all branches). The Fellowship is based on the following criteria: high attainment in the applicant's major field of study as witnessed by academic marks and quality of work; high attainment in related cultural fields as witnessed by academic marks; the character, merit, and suitability of the program proposed by the applicant; and excellence of personality, seriousness of purpose, and good moral character. Preference will be given to applicants who have not reached their 25th birthday. Applications may be submitted by February 15. Two fellowships of $7,500 each are awarded annually to defray the expenses of advanced study of the arts architecture, or music in America or abroad and an additional one will be given in music for $15,000. Two or three additional annual Fellowships of a lesser amount may also be granted upon committee recommendations. Established in 1931 by the late President-Emeritus David Kinley in memory of his wife and in recognition of her influence in promoting the fine arts and similar interests upon the Urbana-Champaign campus. Partially funded by the John Robert Gregg Fund at Community Funds, Inc.

• 21033 •
University of Illinois
Graduate School of Library and Information Science
John Unsworth, Dean
501 E Daniel St.
MC-493
Champaign, IL 61820
Phone: (217)333-3280
Fax: (217)244-3302
E-mail: gslis@alexia.lis.uiuc.edu
Home Page: http://alexia.lis.uiuc.edu

• 21034 • **Robert B. Downs Intellectual Freedom Award**
To recognize a contribution that is directly related to the furtherance of the cause of intellectual freedom particularly as it has an impact on libraries and information centers and the dissemination of ideas. Granted to those who have resisted censorship, the award may be in recognition of a particular action or for long term interest in and dedication to the cause of intellectual freedom, either by individuals or groups. A monetary award and certificate are presented annually. Established in 1969 to honor Dean Robert B. Downs for his defense of intellectual freedom and to mark his 25 years at the University of Illinois. Greenwood Publishing Group, Inc., Westport, Connecticut, provides the honorarium.

• 21035 •
University of Illinois at Chicago
Center for Urban Economic Development
MC 345
322 S Green St., Ste. 108
College of Urban Planning and Public Affairs
Chicago, IL 60607-3555
Phone: (312)996-6336
Fax: (312)996-5766
E-mail: theodore@uic.edu
Home Page: http://www.uic.edu/cuppa/uicued/

• 21036 • **Research Assistantships**
For graduate students. Inquire for application details.

• 21037 •
University of Illinois at Urbana-Champaign
Agricultural Bioprocess Laboratory
1302 W Pennsylvania Ave.
Urbana, IL 61801
Phone: (217)333-9332
Fax: (217)333-9592
E-mail: mcheryan@uiuc.edu
Home Page: http://www.cheryan.com

• 21038 • **Agricultural Bioprocess Laboratory Awards**
Recognizes outstanding membrane technology. Awarded annually.

• 21039 •
University of Kentucky
Lucille Parker Markey Cancer Center
800 Rose St.
Lexington, KY 40536-0093
Phone: (859)257-4500
Fax: (859)323-2074
E-mail: acohen@email.uky.edu
Home Page: http://www.mc.uky.edu/markey

• 21040 • **Pilot Project Research Awards**
Recognizes outstanding research in cancer-related areas.

• 21041 •
University of Louisville
College of Education and Human Development
Robert Felner, Dean
Rm. 292
Louisville, KY 40292
Phone: (502)852-6411
Fax: (502)852-1464
E-mail: allan@louisville.edu
Home Page: http://www.louisville.edu/edu

• 21042 • **University of Louisville Grawemeyer Award for Ideas Improving World Order**
To recognize the best idea promoting improved relations between nations published or presented in the last five years. The purpose of the award is to stimulate the recognition, dissemination, and critical analysis of outstanding proposals for the improvement of relations between nations. Submissions for the award may address a wide range of international concerns, such as foreign policy and its formation, the conduct of international relations, global economic issues, international trade and investment, resolving regional conflicts, addressing ethnic and racial disputes, halting the proliferation of destructive technologies, international cooperation in environmental protection and other global issues, international law and organization, any combination or particular aspects of these, or any idea that could at least incrementally lead to a more just and peaceful international order. Submissions are judged according to originality, feasibility, and potential impact. The University committee overseeing the award invites nominations from throughout the world by individual political scientists expert in the area, by professional associations of political scientists or related disciplines in international relations, by university presidents, or by publishers and editors of journals and books in political science and international affairs. Self-nominations are accepted and considered. Entries may be submitted through October 15. A monetary award of up to $200,000 (5 installments of $ 40,000) is awarded annually. Established in 1988 by H. Charles Grawemeyer, a University graduate and retired industrialist.

• 21043 •
University of Louisville
Labor-Management Center
College of Business & Public Administration
Patterson Hall, Rm. 105
Louisville, KY 40292
Phone: (502)852-6482
Fax: (502)852-6453
E-mail: lmcenter@gwise.louisville.edu
Home Page: http://www.louisville.edu/cbpa/lmc/

• 21044 • **Labor-Management Annual Award**
Honors a workplace where management and the union(s) have promoted and demonstrated positive labor-management relations..

• 21045 •
University of Louisville
Louisville Presbyterian Theological Seminary
K. Thompson, Dean
1044 Alta Vista Rd.
Louisville, KY 40205-1798
Phone: (502)895-3411
Toll-Free: 800-264-1839
Fax: (502)895-3411
E-mail: lpts@lpts.edu
Home Page: http://www.lpts.edu

• 21046 • **Louisville Grawemeyer Award in Religion**
To recognize the most significant contributions to religious and spiritual understanding. The purpose of the award is to honor and publicize creative insights into the relationship between human beings and the divine (or what some may prefer to call the spiritual ground of being), and ways this relationship may inspire or empower human beings to attain wholeness, integrity, or meaning, either individually or in community. Open to persons of all religious and cultural worldviews and traditions for a wide variety of concerns and issues. Nominated works must be accessible to nonspecialists. Such issues may include, but are not limited to: the experience of divine or ultimate reality; the origin and purpose of human existence; authority and freedom in religious understanding; pluralism and religious truth; evil, suffering, and death; compassion, joy, and hope; religion and science; and divine involvement in human history. Any work presented or published in the eight years preceding the year of the award is eligible. Nominations are invited from religious organizations, appropriate academic associations, religious leaders and scholars, presidents of universities or schools of religion, and publishers and editors of scholarly journals. Self-nominations are not accepted or considered. There is no discrimination based on religious affiliation or belief. Nominations must be submitted by November 1. A monetary award of $150,000 is presented annually. The winner is expected to come to Louisville to make a formal presentation based on the winning idea and receive the award. Established in 1988 by H. Charles Grawemeyer, a University of Louisville graduate and retired industrialist.

• 21047 •
University of Louisville
School of Education
Dean's Office
Louisville, KY 40292
Phone: (502)852-4023
Fax: (502)852-1464
E-mail: anita.russell@louisville.edu
Home Page: http://www.louisville.edu/ur/onpi/grawemeyer

• 21048 • **University of Louisville Grawemeyer Award in Education**
To recognize the author(s) of the theory, policy proposal, technological advance, program initiative, or research study published in the recent past that is judged to have the most potential for educational improvement. The purpose of this award is to stimulate worldwide the dissemination, public scrutiny, and implementation of ideas that have potential to contribute to improvement in educational practice and attainment. The award is intended not only to recognize the individual(s) responsible, but also to draw critical attention to the award-winning ideas, proposals, or achievements. The criteria for judging the quality of submissions are originality, creativity, feasibility, and scope of potential applicability. Professional educators, educational institutions and organizations, and editors and publishers of journals and books worldwide are eligible. Self-nominations are not considered. Submissions written in a language other than English need to be accompanied by an English translation. Nominations must be submitted by November 1. A monetary award of $200,000 is awarded annually. Acceptance of the award requires personal delivery of a public address setting out the winning concept or idea at the University of Louisville. Established in 1987 by the late H. Charles Grawemeyer.

• 21049 •
University of Louisville
School of Music
Christopher Doane, Dean
University of Louisville
Louisville, KY 40292
Phone: (502)852-1623
Fax: (502)852-0520
E-mail: marc.satterwhite@louisville.edu
Home Page: http://www.louisville.edu/music/

• 21050 • **University of Louisville Grawemeyer Award for Music Composition**
For recognition of outstanding achievement by a composer in a large musical genre: choral, orchestral, chamber, song-cycle, dance, opera, musical theater, extended solo work, etc. Works premiered during the preceding five-year period are considered. The award is based on the single work submitted for the competition. The deadline for entries is late January. Each entry must be sponsored by a professional musical organization or individual (performer or performing group, conductor, critic, publisher, or head of a professional music school or department). A composer may not submit his or her own work, and no more than one work of any composer may be submitted. A monetary prize of $200,000 is awarded annually. Established in 1985 by the late H. Charles Grawemeyer, a University of Louisville graduate.

• 21051 •
University of Maryland
College of Library and Information Services
R. Lee Hornbake Bldg., Ste. 4105
College Park, MD 20742
Phone: (301)405-2033
Fax: (301)314-9145
E-mail: dbarlow@umd.edu
Home Page: http://www.clis.umd.edu

• 21052 • **Distinguished Alumnus Award**
To recognize and honor an outstanding alumnus. A plaque and engraved book-ends are awarded at the annual Alumni Day Luncheon. Established in 1983.

• 21053 •
University of Maryland Center for Quality and Productivity
Mary Stephens, Prog.Mgr.
3114 Potomac Bldg. 092
University of Maryland
College Park, MD 20742-3415
Phone: (301)403-7173
Fax: (301)403-4105
E-mail: jsahni@umcqp.umd.edu
Home Page: http://www.umcqp.umd.edu

• 21054 • **Maryland Quality Awards**
To honor Maryland organizations that have made significant progress in quality and productivity improvement within the categories of manufacturing, service, public/nonprofit sector, small business, and education. All organizations with five or more full-time employees are eligible. Awards are presented at the gold, silver, and bronze levels. Awarded annually as part of the Maryland Performance Excellence Award program. Established in 1997.

• 21055 • **U.S. Senate Productivity Award for Maryland**
To promote awareness of productivity and quality as vital elements of competitiveness in the categories of manufacturing, service, and public sector. Awarded annually with a plaque. Established in 1983.

• 21056 •
University of Massachusetts Press
Bruce Wilcox, Dir.
PO Box 429
Amherst, MA 01004
Phone: (413)545-2217
Fax: (413)545-1226
E-mail: info@umpress.umass.edu
Home Page: http://www.umass.edu/umpress

• 21057 • **Juniper Prize**
To recognize the author of an original, book-length manuscript of poems, alternately for first and subsequent books. Submissions must be postmarked by September 30. Recipients receive publication of the book by the University of Massachusetts Press, a cash award of $1,500 and an invitation to read in University's Visiting Writers Series. Awarded annually. Established in 1975 in honor of the poet, Robert Francis, who for many years had made his home at Fort Juniper in Amherst, Massachusetts.

Awards are arranged in alphabetical order below their administering organizations

• 21058 •
University of Miami
School of International Studies
Richard L. Williamson, Interim Chm.
1531 Brescia Ave.
PO Box 248123
Coral Gables, FL 33124-3010
Phone: (305)284-4303
Fax: (305)284-5637
Home Page: http://www.as.miami.edu/international%2Dstudies/

• 21059 • **Letras de Oro Literary Prizes**
For yearly recognition of unpublished literary works written in Spanish by any person who resides in the United States. Awards are given in five categories: Novel, Short Story, Theater, Essay, and Poetry. Winners in each category receive a $2,500 cash prize, an honorary diploma, and the publication of the winning entries in the Letras de Oro collection. Entry deadline is October 12. Established in 1986 by the University of Miami (Iberian Studies Institute/North-South Center), it has been sponsored by American Express, Spain's '92 Foundation, and the Directorate for Cultural Relations with Iberoamerica of the Foreign Affairs Department of the Spanish Government. Formerly: (1986) Pluma de Oro.

• 21060 •
University of Michigan
Wallace House
620 Oxford Rd.
Ann Arbor, MI 48109
Phone: (734)764-1817
Fax: (734)998-7979
E-mail: info@umich.edu
Home Page: http://www.umich.edu

• 21061 • **Livingston Awards for Young Journalists**
To recognize the best examples of print or broadcast news reporting in three categories: local, national, and international reporting. Each applicant may submit only one entry. The Livingston Awards do not include still photography. Journalists 34 years of age or younger employed or paid by United States-controlled print or broadcast media are eligible. Submissions must consist of materials prepared in the ordinary course of the journalist's professional production. Organizations may apply on behalf of individuals, or individuals may submit their own work. Competition is limited to work done during the calendar year ending December 31. Three $10,000 awards are presented annually. Established in 1980 by the Mollie Parnis Livingston Foundation, New York, NY in memory of Robert Livingston, one-time publisher of *More*, who died in 1979.

• 21062 •
University of Michigan
Matthaei Botanical Gardens and Nichols Arboretum
1610 Washington Heights
Ann Arbor, MI 48104-1700
Phone: (734)998-9540
Fax: (734)998-9536
E-mail: arb@umich.edu
Home Page: http://www.umich.edu/~wwwarb/

• 21063 • **Nanette LaCross Memorial Prize**
Given in conjunction with School of Natural Resources and Environment. Inquire for application details.

• 21064 •
University of Michigan
Stephen M. Ross School of Business
701 Tappan St.
Ann Arbor, MI 48109
Phone: (734)936-2150
Fax: (734)647-2401
Home Page: http://www.bus.umich.edu

• 21065 • **Business Leadership Award**
To honor a distinguished American business executive who has shown an understanding of the role of business in our society, the responsibility of business to society, and an interest in business and management education. A bronze medallion and scroll are awarded annually. Established in 1958.

• 21066 •
University of Michigan Press
Phil Pochoda, Dir.
839 Greene St.
Ann Arbor, MI 48104-3209
Phone: (734)764-4388
Fax: (734)615-1540
E-mail: ump.webmaster@umich.edu
Home Page: http://www.press.umich.edu

• 21067 • **University of Michigan Press Book Award**
To recognize work, written or edited by a University of Michigan faculty member, that has added the greatest distinction to the Press's list. Books published by the Press within the two preceding calendar years are eligible. Established in 1965.

• 21068 •
University of Minnesota
Center for Advanced Feminist Studies
425 Ford Hall
224 Church St. SE
Minneapolis, MN 55455
Phone: (612)624-6310
Fax: (612)624-3573
E-mail: cafs@tc.umn.edu
Home Page: http://womenstudy.cla.umn.edu/

• 21069 • **Personal Narratives Award**
Recognizes research on a woman's memoir and life history. CAFS minor students conducting research are eligible.

• 21070 •
University of Minnesota
Center for Labor Policy
301 19th Ave. S
260 Hubert H. Humphrey Center
Minneapolis, MN 55455
Phone: (612)624-5592
Fax: (612)625-3513
E-mail: mkleiner@hhh.umn.edu

• 21071 • **Minnesota Award**
Recognizes the best labor paper published during the past two years.

• 21072 •
University of Minnesota
Children's Literature Research Collection
Prof. Karen Nelson Hoyle, Curator
Kerlan Collection
113 Andersen Library
222-21st Ave. S
Minneapolis, MN 55455
Phone: (612)624-4576
Fax: (612)626-0377
E-mail: clrc@umn.edu
Home Page: http://special.lib.umn.edu/clrc

• 21073 • **Ezra Jack Keats/Kerlan Collection Fellowship**
To recognize a talented writer and/or illustrator of children's books who wishes to use the Kerlan Collection at the University of Minnesota for the furtherance of his or her artistic development. Special consideration is given to someone who would find it difficult to finance the visit to the Kerlan Collection. Applications must be submitted by May 31. A monetary award of $1,500, transportation, and per diem expenses are awarded. The award honors Ezra Jack Keats (1916-1983), a world-famous writer and illustrator of children's books. When he died in 1983, he had written and illustrated over 25 books; many were translated into 16 languages, and several are already recognized as classics. Formerly: (1991) Ezra Jack Keats Memorial Fellowship.

• 21074 • **Kerlan Award**
To recognize singular attainments in the creation of children's literature, and in appreciation for a generous donation of unique resources to the Kerlan Collection for the study of children's literature. A plaque is awarded annually in the spring. Established in 1975 by the Twenty-Fifth Kerlan Anniversary Committee.

• 21075 •
University of Minnesota
Office of the Sencor Vice President for Academic Affairs and Provost
Tom Sullivan, Provost
234 Morrill Hall
1000 Church St. SE
University of Minnesota
Minneapolis, MN 55455
Phone: (612)625-0051
E-mail: provost@umn.edu
Home Page: http://www.academic.umn.edu/provost

• 21076 • **John Tate Award for Undergraduate Academic Advising**
To recognize and reward high-quality academic advising, namely advising makes to helping students formulate and achieve intellectual, career, and personal goals. Three or four recipients are typically awarded each year. Established in 1986 in honor of John Tate, Professor of Physics and first Dean of University College (1930-41).

• 21077 •
University of Missouri-Columbia
School of Journalism
120 Neff Hall
Columbia, MO 65211-1200
Phone: (573)882-4821
Fax: (573)884-5400
E-mail: journalism@missouri.edu
Home Page: http://www.journalism.missouri.edu

• 21078 • **Missouri Honor Awards**
To recognize a journalist for distinguished performance and services in the field of journalism. A medallion is awarded annually. Established in 1930.

• 21079 • **Missouri Lifestyle Journalism Award**
To recognize excellence in lifestyle and feature writing and editing. The deadline is October 31 for entries published between September 1 and August 31. Prizes are awarded in the following categories: (1) Pages or Sections: $1,000 for first place, $500 for second place and $250 for third place in each of the following daily circulation ranges: Class I - less than 25,000; Class II - 25,001 to 50,000; Class III - 50,001 to 100,000; Class IV - 100,001 to 300,000; Class V - more than 300,000; (2) Reporting categories: $1,000 to the winner in each of seven categories: Single Story General Reporting, Series or Special Section General Reporting, Fashion and Clothing Reporting, Consumer Affairs Reporting, Health and Nutrition Reporting, Health and Fitness Reporting, and Arts and Entertainment Reporting. (The Paul Myhre Awards are presented to the Single Story General Reporting and the Series or Special Section General Reporting Category winners.) Established in 1960 by the JCPenney Company Inc. and the School of Journalism, University of Missouri. Formerly: JCPenney - University of Missouri Awards in Lifestyle Journalism; (2006) JCPenney - University of Missouri Newspaper Awards.

• 21080 • **Frank Luther Mott-Kappa Tau Alpha Research Award**
For a research book on journalism or mass communication published the previous year. A monetary prize of $1,000 is awarded annually.

• 21081 • **University of Missouri Television Awards for Community Leadership**
To encourage local television stations to spot community problems and do something about them; and to recognize those stations already providing such community leadership. Each of the following criteria will be given equal weight: (1) significance of the project or activity: appropriateness, need, depth, originality, and public interest; (2) total station involvement; (3) use of community resources; and (4) demonstrable achievements. Videotapes no longer than 30 minutes, written documents detailing the project or activity, and support materials demonstrating the effectiveness of the project should be submitted by February 15. Trophies for the noted station and individual plaques are awarded in each of the following categories: (1) Project according to market size: (a) large market stations, 1-30, and group broadcasters; (b) medium market stations, 31-100; and (c) small market stations, 101 plus; and (2) PSA for all market sizes. An additional award of $1,000 is given to a community organization or project of each winner's choice. Established in 1983. Formerly: (1991) JCPenney - University of Missouri Television Awards for Community Leadership.

• 21082 •
University of Missouri—St. Louis
Center for International Studies
8001 Natural Bridge Rd.
St. Louis, MO 63121-4499
Phone: (314)516-5753
Fax: (314)516-6757
E-mail: jglassman@umsl.edu
Home Page: http://www.center-for-international-studies.org

• 21083 • **Global Citizenship Award**
Recognizes outstanding public service.

• 21084 •
University of Missouri—St. Louis
Center for Trauma Recovery
Weinman Bldg., Lower Level
Department of Psychology
8001 Natural Bridge Rd.
St. Louis, MO 63121
Phone: (314)516-6738
Fax: (314)516-7233
E-mail: resick@umsl.edu
Home Page: http://www.umsl.edu/divisions/artscience/psychology/ctr/colloquium.html

• 21085 • **Paid Research Appointments**
First and second year graduate clinical psychology students are eligible. Inquire for application details.

• 21086 •
University of New Orleans Eisenhower Center for American Studies
923 Magazine St.
New Orleans, LA 70130
Phone: (504)539-9560
Fax: (504)539-9563
E-mail: kwilley@uno.edu

• 21087 • **Forrest C. Poque Prize**
For the best book on U.S. Army History.

• 21088 •
University of Notre Dame
News and Information
Matthew V. Storin, Asoc. VP
317 Main Bldg.
Notre Dame, IN 46556-5614
Phone: (574)631-7367
Fax: (574)631-8212
E-mail: newsinfo@nd.edu
Home Page: http://www.nd.edu/~prinfo

• 21089 • **Laetare Medal**
This, the most prestigious award conferred on American Catholics, is given to honor an American Catholic man or woman whose genius has ennobled the arts and sciences, illustrated the ideals of the Church, and enriched the heritage of humanity. Catholic men and women are eligible. An inscribed gold medal is awarded annually. Established in 1883 and so named because the honoree is announced on Laetare Sunday, the fourth Sunday in the season of heart.

• 21090 • **Notre Dame Award**
To recognize international humanitarian service. Awarded when merited. The award was established in 1992 in celebration of the University's Sesquicentennial to honor persons "within and without the Catholic Church, citizens of every nation whose religious faith has quickened learning, whose learning has engendered deeds, and whose deeds give witness to God's kingdom among us."

• 21091 •
University of Oregon
Institute for a Sustainable Environment
130 Hendricks Hall
5247 University of Oregon
Eugene, OR 97403-5247
Phone: (541)346-0675
Fax: (541)346-2040
E-mail: rribe@darkwing.uoregon.edu
Home Page: http://gladstone.uoregon.edu/~enviro

• 21092 • **Sustainable Business Award**
Recognizes an Oregon "green" businesses under development.

• 21093 •
University of Pennsylvania
David Mahoney Institute of Neurological Sciences
215 Stemmler Hall
Philadelphia, PA 19104-6074
Phone: (215)898-8048
Fax: (215)573-2248
E-mail: fiona@mail.med.upenn.edu
Home Page: http://www.uphs.upenn.edu/ins/

• 21094 • **Internal Recognition Awards**
Recognizes outstanding faculty and student accomplishments.

• 21095 •
University of Pennsylvania Museum of Archaeology and Anthropology
Dr. Richard M. Leventhal, Dir.
3260 South St.
Philadelphia, PA 19104-6324
Phone: (215)898-4000
Fax: (215)898-0657
E-mail: websiters@museum.upenn.edu
Home Page: http://www.museum.upenn.edu

Formerly: (1995) The University Museum.

• 21096 • **Marian Angell Godfrey Boyer Medal**
To recognize an outstanding contribution to the museum by a non-academic. Established in 1987, the centennial year of the museum, in honor of Marian Angell Godfrey Boyer, an acting director of the museum, and longtime volunteer and supporter.

• 21097 • **Lucy Wharton Drexel Medal**
To recognize the most outstanding archaeological work. A gold medal is awarded as merited. Established in 1898 by Lucy Wharton Drexel.

• 21098 •
University of Pittsburgh Press
Cynthia Miller, Dir.
Eureka Bldg., 5th Fl.
3400 Forbes Ave.
Pittsburgh, PA 15260
Phone: (412)383-2456
Fax: (412)383-2466
E-mail: press@pitt.edu
Home Page: http://www.pitt.edu/~press

• 21099 • **Drue Heinz Literature Prize**
For recognition of a collection of short fiction to be published by the Press. The award is open to writers who have published a book-length collection of fiction or a minimum of three short stories or novellas in commercial magazines or literary journals of national distribution. The award is open to writers in English, whether or not they are citizens of the United States. Translations are not eligible, unless they are translations into English done by the author. Eligible submissions include a manuscript of short stories, one or more novellas. For the purpose of this award, a novella is defined as a longer piece of fiction, no more than 150 double-spaced typed pages or a combination of the two. Manuscripts must be received during May and June. A monetary award of $15,000 and publication by the University of Pittsburgh Press under its standard contract. Established in 1980.

• 21100 • **Agnes Lynch Starrett Poetry Prize Competition**
To provide recognition for and publication of first full-length books of poetry. The competition is open to any poet who has not had a full-length book published previously. Manuscripts must be postmarked during March and April only. The winner is announced in the late fall. A "full-length book" is a volume of 48 or more pages published in an edition of 750 or more copies, but books whose publication costs have been borne by their authors are not excluded by this definition. Manuscripts should be between 48 and 100 typed pages in length. A monetary prize of $5,000 and publication of the book by the University of Pittsburgh Press in the Pitt Poetry Series. Submissions must be postmarked between March 1 and April 30, and must include a check for $20.00 made out to the University of Pittsburgh Press. Poets must request complete guidelines by sending a self-addressed stamped envelope to: University of Pittsburgh Press at the above address.

• 21101 •
University of Rochester
Prof. Randall Curren, Chr.
Philosophy Dept.
Box 270078
Rochester, NY 14627-0078
Phone: (585)275-4105
Fax: (585)273-2964
E-mail: phladmin@philosophy.rochester.edu
Home Page: http://www.rochester.edu/College/PHL/prize.html

• 21102 • **Colin and Ailsa Turbayne International Berkeley Essay Prize Competition**
A biennial essay competition to honor new and unpublished essays. Submissions on any aspect of Berkeley's philosophy are welcome. Essays should be new and unpublished and should be written in English and not exceed 5,000 words in length. All references to Berkeley should be to Luce/Jessop, and a MLA or similar standard for notes should be followed. Submissions are due November 1, and will be judged by members of a review board selected by the Department of Philosophy at the University of Rochester. The winner will be announced March 1, and will receive a prize of $2,000. Copies of the winning essays are to be sent to the George Berkeley Library Study Center located in Berkeley's home in Whitehall, Newport, RI. Established by Professor and the late Mrs. Colin Turbayne in conjunction with the Philosophy Department at the University of Rochester.

• 21103 •
University of San Diego - School of Law Children's Advocacy Institute
5998 Alcala Park
San Diego, CA 92110
Phone: (858)260-4806
Fax: (858)260-4753
E-mail: childrensissues@acusd.edu
Home Page: http://www.caichildlaw.org

• 21104 • **Price Journalist and Scholar of the Year Awards**
Recognizes those advancing understanding of child problems in California.

• 21105 •
University of Toronto
Faculty of Law
84 Queen's Park
Toronto, ON, Canada M5S 2C5
Phone: (416)978-0210
Fax: (416)978-7899
Home Page: http://www.law.utoronto.ca

• 21106 • **Law Alumni Association's Distinguished Alumnus Award**
To recognize the faculty's most distinguished graduates for excellence and outstanding service to the University, the profession, and the law. The award was established in 1982 and is made by the University of Toronto Law Alumni Association when merited. Previous winners include Chief Justice Charles Dubin, Mr. Justice Arthur Martin, John Robinette, Lionel Schipper, James M. Tory, The Hon. Madam Justice Rosalie Silberman Abella, Prof. J. Bruce Dunlop, and The Hon. Edwin Goodman.

• 21107 •
University of Toronto
Pulp and Paper Centre
Department of Chemical Engineering & Applied Chemistry
200 College St.
Toronto, ON, Canada M5S 3E5
Phone: (416)978-3062
Fax: (416)971-2106
E-mail: paper@chem-eng.utoronto.ca
Home Page: http://www.chem-eng.utoronto.ca/%7Epphome/

• 21108 • **D.A.I. Goring Award**
For the best presentations. Inquire for application details.

• 21109 • **The Leadership Award**
Inquire for application details.

• 21110 • **John Peter Reeve Memorial Award**
For the best poster. Inquire for application details.

• 21111 •
University of Toronto
University College
The Registrar
15 King's College Cir.
Toronto, ON, Canada M5S 3H7
Phone: (416)978-3160
Fax: (416)978-8854
E-mail: uc.regoffice@utoronto.ca
Home Page: http://www.utoronto.ca/uc

• 21112 • **Norma Epstein Foundation Awards**
To recognize and encourage promise, talent, and achievement in creative writing in the categories of drama, poetry, novel, short story or other prose. All manuscripts must be submitted in duplicate under a pseudonym to the college registrar. Each entry must be covered by a separate entry form and a different pseudonym. Two competitions are held: the National Literary Contest for College and University Students, which is held biennially and is open to undergraduates and graduate students of all Canadian universities and colleges. The deadline is May 15; and College Competition which is held annually and is open to undergraduates of University College only. The entry date is January 15. Awards and honorable mentions of $100 to $1,000 are presented. Established in 1962 in memory of Norma Epstein, daughter of Mr. and Mrs. Milton Epstein, of the class of 1945.

• 21113 •
University of Toronto Innovations Foundation
Roy Venter, Interim Exec.Dir.
243 College St., Ste. 100
Toronto, ON, Canada M5T 1R5
Phone: (416)978-5117
Fax: (416)978-6052
E-mail: info@innovationsfoundation.com
Home Page: http://www.innovationsfoundation.com

• 21114 • **Innovations Challenge**
Business plan competition. Inquire for application details.

• 21115 •
University of Virginia
Center for Russian and East European Studies
223 Minor Hall
Charlottesville, VA 22903
Phone: (434)924-3033
Fax: (434)924-7867
E-mail: crees@virginia.edu
Home Page: http://www.virginia.edu/~crees/

• 21116 • **Vladimar A. Pertzoff Prize**
Inquire for application details.

• 21117 • **Thomas T. Hammond Award**
Award of recognition for Russian studies for graduate students

• 21118 •
University of Virginia
Center for South Asian Studies
110 Minor Hall
PO Box 400169
University of Virginia
Charlottesville, VA 22904-4169
Phone: (434)924-8815
Fax: (434)982-3011
E-mail: southasia@virginia.edu
Home Page: http://www.virginia.edu/soasia/

• 21119 • **South Asia Foreign Language and Area Studies Fellowships**
University students are eligible. Inquire for application details.

• 21120 •
University of Wisconsin—Madison
Center for South Asia
203 Ingraham Hall
1155 Observatory Dr.
Madison, WI 53706
Phone: (608)262-4884
Fax: (608)265-3062
E-mail: info@southasia.wisc.edu
Home Page: http://www.wisc.edu/southasia/

• 21121 • **Foreign Language and Area Studies Awards**
Graduate students are eligible. Inquire for application details.

• 21122 •
University of Wisconsin—Madison
Institute on Aging
2245 Medical Science Center
1300 University Ave.
Madison, WI 53706
Phone: (608)262-1818
Fax: (608)263-6211
E-mail: aging@ssc.wisc.edu
Home Page: http://www.wisc.edu

• 21123 • **New Investigator Awards**
Recognizes biomedical and social/behavioral research. Awarded annually.

• 21124 •
University of Wisconsin Press
Department of English
Sheila Leary, Interim Dir.
600 N. Park St.
Madison, WI 53706
Phone: (608)263-1110
Fax: (608)263-1120
E-mail: rwallace@wisc.edu
Home Page: http://www.wisc.edu/wisconsinpress

• 21125 • **The Brittingham Prize in Poetry and Felix Pollak Prize in Poetry**
For recognition of the two best collections of original poetry submitted in an open competition. Book length manuscripts may be submitted in September. Send SASE for required guidelines. Two monetary prizes of $1,000 each and publication by the Press are awarded annually.

• 21126 •
University Photographers Association of America
Jim Dusen, Pres.
SUNY Brockport
350 New Campus Dr.
Brockport, NY 14420-2931
Phone: (585)395-2133
Fax: (585)395-2733
E-mail: jdusen@brockport.edu
Home Page: http://www.upaa.org

• 21127 • **Roland Barrett Award**
To recognize the author of the best article published in the *UPAA Journal*. Members of the Association are eligible. A plaque is awarded annually. Established in 1962.

• 21128 • **Fellowship Award**
To recognize outstanding service and contributions to the advancement of photography. Members of the Association are eligible. A plaque on a walnut base is awarded when merited. Established in 1961.

• 21129 • **Honor Awards**
To recognize outstanding photographs and to encourage better photography among members of the Association. A bi-colored certificate is awarded annually. Established in 1962.

• 21130 •
Upper Cumberland Funeral Directors Association
Jerry Claiborne, Pres.
205 E. Cleveland Ave.
Monterey, TN 38574
Phone: (931)839-2311
Fax: (931)839-2311

• 21131 • **U.C.F.D.A. Scholarship**
For a mortuary student who lives or works in upper Cumberland area. Scholarship awarded annually.

• 21132 •
Upsilon Pi Epsilon Association
Orlando S. Madrigal PhD, Sec.
California State University, Chico
Department of Computer Science
Chico, CA 95929-0410
Phone: (530)898-6442
Phone: (530)898-4415
Fax: (530)898-5995
E-mail: omadrigal@csuchico.edu
Home Page: http://www.acm.org/upe

• 21133 • **UPE Scholarship Awards**
To recognize outstanding academic achievements of computer science students. Full-time students in computer science who are recommended by their home chapters are eligible. Sixteen monetary awards of $500-$1000 each and

Awards are arranged in alphabetical order below their administering organizations

certificates are presented annually on October 1. Established in 1967.

• 21134 •
Uptown Chamber of Commerce
Wally Rozak, Interim Exec.Dir.
4753 N Broadway, Ste. 822
Chicago, IL 60640
Phone: (773)878-1184
Fax: (773)878-3678
E-mail: info@uptownchamber.com
Home Page: http://www.uptownchamber.com

• 21135 • **Stone Award**
For outstanding businessperson. Recognition award bestowed annually.

• 21136 •
Urban Affairs Association
Margaret Wilder, Exec.Dir.
297 Graham Hall
University of Delaware
Newark, DE 19716
Phone: (302)831-1681
Fax: (302)831-4225
E-mail: uaa@udel.edu
Home Page: http://www.udel.edu/uaa

• 21137 • **Annual Meeting Best Paper Award**
To recognize the best paper presented at the Annual Meeting of the Association. A plaque plus complimentary registration at the next year's annual meeting are awarded annually at the succeeding year's convention. Established in 1985. Formerly: (2006) Governing Board's Award for the Best Paper.

• 21138 • **Alma H. Young Emerging Scholars Award**
To recognize and encourage outstanding scholarship in urban affairs. Students pursuing doctoral research in urban affairs, regardless of academic discipline, are eligible. A plaque and honorarium of $1,000 are awarded annually. Formerly: (2004) Emerging Scholars Award.

• 21139 •
Urban Land Institute
Marilyn J. Taylor, Chair
1025 Thomas Jefferson St. NW, Ste. 500W
Washington, DC 20007
Phone: (202)624-7000
Toll-Free: 800-321-5011
Fax: (202)624-7140
E-mail: customerservice@uli.org
Home Page: http://www.uli.org

• 21140 • **ULI Awards for Excellence**
To honor innovative land development projects in both the public and private sectors that exemplify superior design, relevance to contemporary issues and needs, and a resourceful use of land while also improving the quality of the living environment. The following requirements must be met: the developer must submit the project; the project must be economically viable; the project must be located in the United States or Canada; and the project must demonstrate relevance to issues and needs of the community. An engraved cube is awarded annually at the institute's fall meeting. Established in 1979.

• 21141 •
US International Film and Video Festival
Kristen Gluckman, Exec.Dir.
713 S Pacific Coast Hwy., Ste. A
Redondo Beach, CA 90277-4233
Phone: (310)540-0959
Fax: (310)316-8905
E-mail: filmfestinfo@filmfestawards.com
Home Page: http://www.filmfestawards.com

• 21142 • **Mobius Advertising Awards**
To recognize outstanding creativity in television and radio commercials, print advertising, and package design. Advertising produced, screened, aired, published or marketed anywhere in the world within the year preceding the annual October 1st entry deadline is eligible. Entries may be in any of 88 subject categories and may also be entered in any of 16 production technique categories (not all apply for each medium). Entries are eligible for recognition in each category entered. The Mobius statuette is presented annually to winners of first place recognition in the various categories. A Best of Show award is also presented to the television, radio commercial, and print advertisement that best exemplify the production talents of the industry. Certificates are presented to selected runners-up. Awards held in Los Angeles. Formerly: Mobius Broadcasting Awards; U.S. Television & Radio Commercials Festival.

• 21143 • **U.S. International Film and Video Festival**
To select and recognize outstanding business, television, documentary, industrial and informational productions. Entries are invited from throughout the world prior to the festival's yearly March 1st deadline. There are 68 subject categories and 11 production technique categories. First place Gold Camera Awards and Silver Screen Awards may be presented within each category of subject matter and production technique. Engraved plaques are presented to gold and silver winners. Certificates are presented to selected runners-up. Several special awards are presented each year, including the Chairman's Special Award for the Best of Festival. Additional awards are sponsored by various segments of the industry. Awards held in Los Angeles early June. For more information, visit www.filmfestawards.com. Established in 1968. Formerly: U.S. Industrial Film and Video Festival.

• 21144 •
USA Badminton
Dan Cloppas, Exec.Dir.
1 Olympic Plz.
Colorado Springs, CO 80909
Phone: (719)866-4808
Fax: (719)866-4507
E-mail: usab@usabadminton.org
Home Page: http://www.usabadminton.org
Formerly: (1998) American Badminton Association; United States Badminton Association.

• 21145 • **Badminton Hall of Fame**
To recognize an outstanding badminton personality. Selection is based on excellence of playing and sportsmanship, or exceptional contributions to the advancement of badminton. Individuals who have represented the United States in international competitions or who have made outstanding administrative contributions to the game of badminton are eligible. A plaque is awarded annually. Established in 1956.

• 21146 • **Kenneth R. Davidson Memorial Award for Sportsmanship**
To recognize outstanding contributions to the game of badminton through sportsmanship, attitude, and achievement. Individual contestants in the U.S. Championships are eligible. Awards are presented in two categories: Adult Award; and Junior Award - for individuals under 19 years of age. A silver bowl is awarded annually. Established in 1955 in memory of Ken R. Davidson.

• 21147 • **High School All-American Awards**
To honor high school badminton players in the United States for their outstanding accomplishments on the badminton court and in the classroom. Plaques are presented annually to recipients. Established in 1995.

• 21148 • **IBF Distinguished Service Award**
For recognition of service in the field of badminton. Established in 1985.

• 21149 • **IBF Meritorious Service Award**
For recognition of outstanding service in the field of badminton. Established in 1986.

• 21150 • **National Championships**
To recognize the annual U.S. Badminton Champions in the following manner: to juniors in five age categories (under 21, under 18, under 16, under 14, under 12) in the five areas of boys' singles, girls' singles, boys' doubles, girls' doubles, and mixed doubles. Similar awards are made for adult champions as well as the older players in the over 35 (junior-senior) over 40 years (Senior), over 50 years (Master), over 60 years (Grand Master), and over 70 years (Golden Master) categories. Medals are awarded annually.

• 21151 • **Players Appreciation Award**
To honor an outstanding behind the scenes worker by recognizing outstanding service on the national level to the game of badminton as well as dedication to the sport. A sterling silver cup is awarded annually when merited. Established in 1966. Formerly: Players Appreciation Cup.

• 21152 •
U.S.A. Baseball
Paul V. Seiler, Exec.Dir. & CEO
PO Box 1131
Durham, NC 27702
Phone: (919)474-8721
Fax: (919)474-8822
E-mail: info@usabaseball.com
Home Page: http://www.usabaseball.com/

• 21153 • **Achievement Award**
To honor an individual who has excelled in a career outside of sports after participating in amateur baseball.

• 21154 • **William P. "Dutch" Fehring Award of Merit**
To honor individuals for life-long dedication to promoting amateur baseball nationwide.

• 21155 • **Golden Diamond Awards**
To honor select amateur players and members of the baseball community who display outstanding involvement with organized youth baseball at both the state and national level. Any amateur junior baseball player, volunteer amateur baseball coach, or woman who has demonstrated exceptional involvement with youth baseball may be nominated. Anyone may nominate a candidate for the Golden Diamond Awards. Awards are given in the following categories: Amateur Junior Baseball Player of the Year - to recognize one player 18 years and under in every state; Amateur Baseball Woman of the Year - to recognize a woman in every state who has made an outstanding contribution on any level to amateur baseball in any capacity; and Volunteer Amateur Baseball Coach of the Year - to recognize an outstanding non-paid coach in every state for exceptional contribution to the development of amateur baseball in his or her community. There is one winner from each state in the three Golden Diamond categories. All state winners are selected by USA Baseball appointed state committee. The committee uses the same criteria for nominations as stated above. State winners then become candidates for the national awards. The national Golden Diamond Award winners are chosen by the USA Baseball National Awards Committee. The awards are presented at USA Baseball's annual honors banquet.

• 21156 • **Golden Field Award**
This award is given automatically to the institution fielding the Golden Spikes Award Winner.

• 21157 • **Golden Spikes Award**
To recognize the outstanding amateur baseball player in the United States. Athletic ability, sportsmanship, character, and overall contributions to the sport are considered. All exceptional collegiate, high school, youth program, and independent amateur baseball players in America may be nominated for this award. Anyone may nominate a candidate for the Golden Spikes Award. A trophy is awarded annually at USA Baseball's annual honors banquet. Each winner of the Golden Spikes Award is automatically enshrined in The USA Baseball Amateur Baseball Hall of Fame and becomes USA Baseball's nominee for the U.S. Olympic Committee's Sportsman of the Year, the AAU's Sullivan Award (Amateur Athlete of the Year) and the Olympia Award. Established in 1978.

• 21158 • **Media Award**
To honor a media representative who has helped promote greater awareness of amateur baseball throughout the United States.

• 21159 • **Service Awards**
To recognize five individuals for their dedication and contributions to amateur baseball in their community.

• 21160 • **Umpire Award**
To honor an umpire who has helped advance and improve amateur baseball throughout the United States.

• 21161 •
USA Cycling
1 Olympic Plz.
Colorado Springs, CO 80909
Phone: (719)866-4581
Fax: (719)866-4628
E-mail: usac@usacycling.org
Home Page: http://www.usacycling.org

• 21162 • **National Championships**
To recognize the winners of national championship cycling competitions. The championship events are: (1) Road race; (2) Time Trial; (3) Criterium; (4) Cyclocross; (5) Track; (6) Mountain Biking; (7) Masters Track; (8) National Madison; (9) Masters Road and TT; (10) Master Criterium; and (11) Senior Men Team Pursuit. The various National Championships rotate from year to year between Eastern, Central and Western sections of the country. Championship medals are awarded for the first three places in each of the championships conducted which are held at various times during the year. Established in 1920. In addition, Junior National Championships are scheduled for mountain biking, track events, road races, and velodrome events.

• 21163 •
USA Deaf Sports Federation
Bobbie Beth Scoggins, Pres.
102 N Krohn Pl.
Sioux Falls, SD 57103-1800
Phone: (605)367-5760
Phone: (605)367-5761
Fax: (605)367-4979
E-mail: homeoffice@usdeafsports.org
Home Page: http://www.usdeafsports.org

• 21164 • **Athlete of the Year**
To recognize the deaf person who has brought the most national or international acclaim to deaf athletes. A wall plaque is awarded annually. Established in 1965. Additional information is available from (801) 393-7916 TTY.

• 21165 • **Hall of Fame**
To recognize outstanding athletic accomplishments by coaches and leaders who have given their time unselfishly and without compensation, and to honor those who have contributed over the years in the field of sports writing covering events for the deaf. Players must have been retired from active play for at least one year, coaches must have been coaching for at least ten years, and leaders must have contributed at least ten years of service to sports. Nominations are accepted. A wall plaque is presented annually at a banquet. Established in 1965. Additional information is available from Cole Zulauf, Hall of Fame Chairman, 1313 Tanforan Dr., Lexington, KY 40517-2826. Selbyville, DE 19975.

• 21166 •
USA Diving
Todd B. Smith, Administrator
Pan American Plz.
201 S Capitol Ave., Ste. 430
Indianapolis, IN 46225
Phone: (317)237-5252
Fax: (317)237-5257
E-mail: todd.smith@usadiving.org
Home Page: http://www.usadiving.org

• 21167 • **Age Group Diving Coach of the Year**
To recognize the outstanding Age Group Diving Coach in the United States. Presented annually. Formerly: Pennsylvania Diving Association Award.

• 21168 • **Athlete Service Award**
To recognize an individual who volunteers many hours of behind the scenes work to ensure successful competitions. Initiated and voted upon by athletes only. Established in 1987.

• 21169 • **Phil Boggs Award**
To recognize an individual who has excelled in diving and has contributed to the sport's continuation and success. Established in 1990 in memory of Phil Boggs, the 1976 Olympic gold medalist.

• 21170 • **Mike Malone Memorial Diving Award**
For recognition of outstanding contributions to the sport of diving. Presented annually. Established in 1969.

• 21171 • **Mike Peppe Award**
To recognize the outstanding Senior Diving Coach in the United States. Awarded annually. Established in 1979.

• 21172 • **Phillips Performance Award**
To recognize the outstanding U.S. Diver of the Year. Selection is made by vote of United States Diving's Board of Directors. Established in 1990. (910)920-4946

• 21173 •
USA Hockey
Doug Palazzari, Exec.Dir.
1775 Bob Johnson Dr.
Colorado Springs, CO 80906-4090
Phone: (719)576-8724
Toll-Free: 800-566-3288
Fax: (719)538-1160
Fax: (719)538-1160
E-mail: usah@usahockey.org
Home Page: http://www.usahockey.com/

Formerly: (1991) Amateur Hockey Association of the United States.

• 21174 • **Citation Award**
To recognize an individual's contributions to amateur hockey. A maximum of two awards are made annually.

• 21175 • **College Player of the Year**
To recognize the accomplishments of the top American-born player in college hockey. Awarded each season.

• 21176 • **Distinguished Achievement Award**
To recognize a United States citizen who has made hockey his or her profession and who has made outstanding contributions, on or off the ice, to the sport in America. Awarded annually. Formerly: Jofa-Titan/USA Hockey Distinguished Achievement Award.

• 21177 • **Bob Johnson Award**
To recognize excellence in international hockey competition during a specific season. Awarded annually.

• 21178 • **Junior Player of the Year**
To recognize the outstanding American-born player in junior hockey. Awarded annually.

• 21179 • **Service Awards**
To recognize National and District level volunteers who have served at least five years with USA Hockey in the positions of Board Member, District Registrar, Coach-in-Chief, Referee-in-Chief, or Risk Manager. Sponsored by Itech.

• 21180 • **Wm. Thayer Tutt Award**
For recognition of achievement over an extended period, and to honor an outstanding volunteer, who, in the spirit of Wm. Thayer Tutt, has done much for the benefit of others in amateur hockey. The recipient must have been affiliated with the Association and must currently be a U.S. citizen. Members of USA Hockey may make nominations. A bronze statuette is awarded annually. Established in 1986 in honor of Wm. Thayer Tutt, former president of the Association and a longtime devotee to amateur sports specifically amateur hockey in this country.

• 21181 • **Women's Player of the Year**
To recognize the accomplishments of an outstanding American-born women's ice hockey player. Awarded annually.

• 21182 • **Walter Yaciuk Award**
To recognize an individual who has made an outstanding contribution to the Coaching Education Program during many years of service as a volunteer. Awarded annually.

• 21183 •
USA International Ballet Competition
Sue Lobrano, Exec.Dir.
PO Box 3696
Jackson, MS 39207-3696
Phone: (601)355-9853
Fax: (601)355-5253
E-mail: usaibc@netdoor.com
Home Page: http://www.usaibc.com

• 21184 • **USA International Ballet Competition**
For recognition of the best male and female dancers. Competitions are held in the senior division (ages 19-26) and the junior division (ages 15-18). Gold, Silver, and Bronze Medals, cash awards, and scholarships are awarded in each division. The competition is held every four years. Established in 1978 and sponsored by Mississippi Ballet International, Inc.

• 21185 •
USA International Harp Competition
David Green, Pres.
PO Box 5157
Bloomington, IN 47407-5157
Phone: (812)856-5715
Fax: (812)856-5715
E-mail: harpcomp@indiana.edu
Home Page: http://www.indiana.edu/~harpcomp

• 21186 • **USA International Harp Competition**
To recognize young professional harpists. The competition is open to any young professional harpist from any nation between 16 and 32 years of age. A Lyon & Healy Concert Grand Harp is awarded. Other prizes to be announced. Awarded triennially. Next competition will take place July 2007.

• 21187 •
USA Swimming
Chuck Wielgus, Exec.Dir.
1 Olympic Plz.
Colorado Springs, CO 80909
Phone: (719)866-4578
Fax: (719)578-4669
E-mail: cwielgus@usa-swimming.org
Home Page: http://www.usswim.org

• 21188 • **Adapted Committee Award**
No additional information available for this edition. Inquire for details

• 21189 • **Athletes Appreciation Award**
Recognizes the individual or organization perceived by the committee to have contributed most significantly to the Athletes' Movement. Awarded annually. Established in 1983.

• 21190 • **Counsilman Coach of the Year Award**
Chosen based on the performance of an athlete at the Nationals and any International meets since the last voting. Coaches in attendance at the Summer National Meet will vote for the award.

• 21191 • **Developmental Coach of the Year**
Recognizes coaches who develop athletes a step or two away from jacor national or international success. The winner of the award will be the coach who places themost swimmers on the National Junior Team. Established in 1997.

• 21192 • **Glen S. Hummer Award**
Recognizes the person or group making the greatest contributions to open water (long distance) swimming. Awarded annually. Established in 1978 and named for an Olympian and Coach.

• 21193 • **John B. Kelly Memorial Award**
To recognize the outgoing president of USA Swimming. The award is the "Philadelphia Bowl," produced by Wedgewood and named in honor of John B. Kelly, Jr., the late president of the USOC and a friend of swimming. A permanent award is housed at the national headquarters and a replica award is presented to the honoree. Established in 1986.

• 21194 • **Kiphuth Award**
For recognition of the high point scorers. Male and female awards are presented at the Phillips 66 National Swimming Championships. Named after Robert J. Kiphuth, the great swimming coach from Yale University. Established in 1968.

• 21195 • **William A. Lippman Jr. USA Swimming Combined Team Traveling Trophy**
This award is presented at the Phillips 66 National Swimming Championships to the team achieving the highest combined point total.

• 21196 • **Neilson-Bell Comeback Award**
Given for an outstanding performance by a U.S. citizen competing in their first national championships after a hiatus from competitive swimming of two or more years, or since recovering from a career-threatening illness or injury. A 16th place finish or better is required to be considered and may not be presented at every championship.

• 21197 • Open Water Swimmer of the Year
Recognizes the most outstanding open water swimmer of the previous year. A silver bowl is presented annually. Established in 1984.

• 21198 • Kenneth J. Pettigrew Award
To recognize an official of United States Swimming who has contributed much time and work on behalf of the sport of swimming. A silver trophy/bowl is presented annually. Established in 1977 in honor of Ken Pettigrew, who devoted over 30 years of his life to swimming.

• 21199 • Phillips Performance Award
For recognition of the single most outstanding performance during the year. The award is voted upon by selected coaches and members of the swimming media. A crystal trophy is presented at the annual USAS convention. Established in 1981. Sponsored by Phillips Petroleum Company.

• 21200 • Phillips Performance of the Meet Award
Presented to the swimmer who achieves the single most outstanding performance of the meet. It is voted on by the attending media. Sponsored by USA Swimming and Phillips Petroleum Company.

• 21201 • R. Max Ritter Award
Recognizes the organization or individual of a FINA member country who has contributed the most to the advancement of understanding and good will among nations through international participation in amateur aquatic sports. Awarded annually. Donated by the Ritter Family. Presented by the United State Aquatic Sports. Established in 1976.

• 21202 • Rookies of the Meet Award
For recognition of a male and female swimmer participating in their first Senior National Championship felt to be the United States Swimming Senior National Rookies of the meet. Awards are presented at each Senior National Championship.

• 21203 • Safety Commendation Award
Recognizes outstanding commitment to aquatic safety. Individuals and organizations are eligible. Recipient is selected by the USA Swimming Safety Education Committee. Not necessarily awarded every year. Established in 1989.

• 21204 • Swimmer of the Year Award
To recognize the athlete with the best overall performance of the year. The award is a bronze statue of a male and female swimmer, which is permanently located at the National Headquarters. A bronze replica is presented to the winner annually. Established in 1981.

• 21205 • Team Awards
Team awards are given in the following categories: Women's Top Ten; Women's Team Champion; Women's Team Runner-up; Men's Team Champion; Men's Team Runner-up; Men's Team Top Ten; Men's and Women's Combined Team Champion; Men's and Women's Combined Team Runner-up Champion; Men's and Women's Combined Team Top Ten; Men's and Women's Combined Team; and Men's and Women's 18-Under Combined Team Champion. Inquire for more details.

• 21206 • United States Swimming Award
Recognizes exceptional contributions to the sport of swimming. Individuals and organizations are eligible. Selection is based on financial, material or service contributions to USA Swimming. A two thirds, life-size bronze sculpture of a swimmer mounted over a wave of marble is awarded annually. Established in 1981.

• 21207 • United States Swimming Life Members
Life membership is recognized annually. Established in 1979.

• 21208 • Trish L Zorn Award
Presented for the outstanding performance of the year by a USA Swimming adapted swimmer. Voted upon by the Adapted Swimming Committee. Named after the most accomplished USA athlete, with a disability, in any sport. Established in 1999.

• 21209 •
U.S.A. Table Tennis
Doru Gheorghe, Exec.Dir.
1 Olympic Plz.
Colorado Springs, CO 80909
Phone: (719)866-4583
Fax: (719)632-6071
E-mail: usatt@usatt.org
Home Page: http://www.usatt.org

Formerly: (1994) U.S. Table Tennis Association.

• 21210 • USA Table Tennis National Championships
The Championship winners are determined in the following categories: men's singles, women's singles, men's doubles, women's doubles, mixed doubles, senior men, senior women, senior doubles, veterans, men's team, women's team, championship age events, wheelchair events, and special events. The competition is held annually. 27332

• 21211 •
U.S.A. Track and Field
Bill Roe, Pres.
1 RCA Dome, Ste. 140
Indianapolis, IN 46225
Phone: (317)261-0500
Fax: (317)261-0514
E-mail: bill.roe@usatf.org
Home Page: http://www.usatf.org
Formerly: The Athletics Congress of the USA.

• 21212 • Association-of-the-Year Award
To recognize the most improved of 56 member associations in each of the four regions - north, south, east, and west. Awarded annually. Established in 1989.

• 21213 • Andy Bakjian Award
For recognition of outstanding effort and achievement. Awarded annual. Established in 1982 and renamed in 1985 in memory of Andy Bakjian, the Award's first recipient and long-time USATF official and former chairman of USATF's Officials Committee. Formerly: (1985) National Officials Outstanding Service Award.

• 21214 • John Bennett Award
To recognize the athlete and individual who best exemplify the qualities of leadership, integrity, and dedication to the support and promotion of the decathlete. Awarded annually.

• 21215 • Gwilym Brown Award
To recognize outstanding male and female track and field athletes in the Masters Program. A plaque is awarded annually at the national convention. Established in 1978.

• 21216 • Ted Corbitt Ultra Runner-of-the-Year Award
To honor the outstanding male ultra distance runner. Awarded annually.

• 21217 • Cross Country Contributor Award
Presented for outstanding contributions and service to Women's Long Distance Running. Established in 1990.

• 21218 • Horace Crow Award
To recognize an outstanding field event official. Established in 1992 in memory of the late Horace Crow.

• 21219 • Glenn Cunningham Award
To recognize the outstanding male athlete in the distance events of 800 or more meters. Awarded annually. Established in 1983.

• 21220 • Robert E. DeCelle Award
To honor the outstanding male long distance runner. A trophy is awarded annually at the national convention. Established in 1978.

• 21221 • Harrison Dillard Award
To recognize the outstanding male athlete in the sprint and hurdle category. Awarded annually. Established in 1983.

• 21222 • Otto Essig Award
For recognition of meritorious service to Masters Long Distance Running. Consideration is given to both men and women. A plaque is awarded annually at the national convention. Established in 1977.

• 21223 • Robert Giegengack Award
To recognize a person who excels in contributing to the excellence and high standards of the amateur sport of athletics. It is USATF's only accolade for contributions to athletics not limited to one of the sport's three disciplines (track and field, long distance running, and race walking), or to any one of the three areas of consideration (Official, Coach, administrator). Presented annually. Established in 1982 in recognition of the former Yale University track and field coach's half-century of superior and outstanding contributions as an official, as a coach, as an administrator, to the sport, and to the organization.

• 21224 • H. Browning Ross Long Distance Running Merit Award
To recognize outstanding contribution and service to the sport of long distance running. Awarded annually. Established in 1969.

• 21225 • Scott Hamilton Award
To recognize outstanding male long distance runners. A plaque is awarded annually at the national convention. Established in 1976 by Scott Hamilton.

• 21226 • Bill Hargrove Award
To recognize the association that has best promoted youth athletics in the United States. Awarded annually. Established in 1983. Renamed in 1989 to honor Father Patrick O'Byrne, the first chairman of USATF's Youth Athletics Committee. Formerly: (1989) Father Patrick O'Byrne Award; Youth Athletics Outstanding Association Award.

• 21227 • Doris Heritage Award
In recognition of outstanding contributions to the sport of women's cross country. Awarded annually. Established in 1989.

• 21228 • C. C. Jackson Awards
To recognize outstanding women in track and field. A plaque is awarded annually at the national convention. Established in 1978 in memory of C. C. Jackson, one of the foremost promoters of women's track and field.

• 21229 • Male Thrower of the Year
Awarded annually to the outstanding male thrower of the year.

• 21230 • Masters Administrator of the Year
To recognize outstanding men and women Masters administrators. A plaque is awarded annually at the national convention. Established in 1978.

• 21231 • Masters Long Distance Running Awards (Age Group)
To recognize outstanding men and women Master Long Distance Runners in the following age categories: 40-49, 50-59, 60-69, and 70 years of age or older. Plaques are awarded annually at the national convention. Established in 1977.

• 21232 • Masters Race Walking Award
To recognize the outstanding men and women walkers in the Masters classification. A plaque is awarded annually at the national convention. Established in 1978.

• 21233 • National Track and Field Hall of Fame
To recognize outstanding achievement in track and field. U.S. citizens may be nominated in the following categories: athletics, coaches, and contributors. A ring with the Hall of Fame insignia and a plaque are awarded annually at the national convention. In addition, a picture of the inductee is placed in the Track and Field Museum. Four or five men and women are selected each year. Established in 1974 by Dr. Donald P. Cohen. In 1983, the Hall of Fame moved to Indianapolis under the aegis of USA Track and Field.

• 21234 • Outstanding Disabled Athlete of the Year
To recognize four sports groups for the disabled that are affiliated with the Congress - U.S. Cerebral Palsy Athletic Association, National Wheelchair Athletic Association, Special Olympics, and U.S. Association for Blind Athletes. Awarded annually in rotation. Established in 1987 by USATF's Athletes for the Disabled Committee.

• 21235 • Jesse Owens Award
For recognition of the outstanding American performer of the year in athletics as a whole. Nominations are accepted. The permanent commemorative is maintained at the USATF National Headquarters, and a replica is presented to the recipient. Awarded at the annually banquet. Established in 1981 as a tribute to Jesse Owens whose accomplishments are enshrined in athletics history. Sponsored by the Atlantic Richfield Company.

• 21236 • President's Award
To honor those individuals whose dedication and support have been an inspiration and whose leadership have played a vital role in the fruition of the Congress' purposes and programs. Nominations are accepted. A plaque is presented at the annual banquet. Established in 1980.

• 21237 • Joseph Robichaux Award
To recognize outstanding contribution to the Women's Track and Field program in the United States. Awarded annually. Established in 1972 in remembrance of the many years of dedicated service Joseph Robichaux contributed to Women's Track and Field and to the youth of our country.

• 21238 • Runner of the Year
To honor the woman long-distance runner of the year. Consideration is based upon the runner's performances and/or achievements in competitions. A plaque is awarded annually at the national convention. Established in 1981.

• 21239 • Frank Sevigne Award
To recognize outstanding contribution to youth athletics. Awarded annually. Established in 1983. Renamed in 1989 to honor the late Frank Sevigne, head track and field coach at the University of Nebraska. Formerly: Youth Athletics Outstanding Individual Award.

• 21240 • Jim Thorpe Award
To recognize the outstanding male athlete in the field events and decathlon category. Awarded annually. Established in 1983.

• 21241 • *Track & Field News* Award
To recognize the outstanding male athlete-of-the-year. A plaque is awarded annually at the national convention. Established in 1978 by *Track & Field News*.

• 21242 • Ultra Distance Athlete-of-the-Year
To recognize an outstanding distance runner. An award is presented to a female and to a male runner. Established in 1990.

• 21243 • USATF Heptathlon Award
To recognize the most outstanding woman in the seven track and field events of the Heptathlon. A special trophy is presented as merited. Established in 1982. Formerly: Multi-Event Outstanding Women Award; TAC Heptathlon Award.

• 21244 • Women's Development Athletes-of-the-Year
The following awards are given annually. Sprinter of the Year, Hurdler of the Year, Thrower of the Year, Runner of the Year, and Jumper of the Year.

• 21245 • Captain Ron Zinn Memorial Awards
To recognize outstanding contributions in race walking. Awards are presented in the following categories: Outstanding Athlete, Outstanding Contributor, and Outstanding Association. A plaque is awarded annually at the national convention. Established in 1975. The awards commemorate Captain Ron Zinn, a 1964 U.S. Olympic Team race walker who lost his life in combat during the Vietnam War.

• 21246 •
USA Triathlon
B.J. Evans, Communications and Media Rel. Man.
1365 Garden of the Gods Rd., Ste. 250
Colorado Springs, CO 80907-3425
Phone: (719)597-9090
Fax: (719)597-2121
E-mail: info@usatriathlon.org
Home Page: http://www.usatriathlon.org

Formerly: (1997) Triathlon Federation.

• 21247 • Events of the Year
To honor race directors for achievements in the following categories: sprint distance and long course distance. Events are based on quality of

service, challenge of the course, community involvement, amenities to athletes, and stability of race organization. Awarded annually. Established in 1992.

• 21248 • **Official of the Year Award**
To recognize an official who has continually demonstrated the ability to uphold the philosophy and mission of the Officials Program, and who has substantially contributed to the Officials Program through volunteering time, ideas, suggestions, special projects and/or any other self-initiated input. Nominations are made by the Board of Officials. A plaque or trophy is awarded annually. Established in 1989 by Sean Phelps, Officials Coordinator, to honor Ed Roberts.

• 21249 • **Triathletes of the Year**
To honor males and females in the following categories: Overall Triathletes of the Year, Master Triathletes of the Year; and Junior Triathletes of the Year. Awarded annually. Established in 1992.

• 21250 • **USA Triathlon Appreciation Award**
For recognition of outstanding contributions to the development and growth of the sport of triathlon. The award is given to outgoing board members and other volunteers of the Federation. A plaque was awarded annually at the meeting of the Federation. Established in 1984. Formerly: (1997) Triathlon Federation USA Appreciation Award.

• 21251 •
USA Water Ski
Steve McDermeit, Exec.Dir.
1251 Holy Cow Rd.
Polk City, FL 33868
Phone: (863)324-4341
Toll-Free: 800-533-AWSA
Fax: (863)325-8259
E-mail: usawaterski@usawaterski.org
Home Page: http://www.usawaterski.org

• 21252 • **Open Division Overall**
To recognize excellence in tournament waterskiing. The tournament features three events, slalom, trick, and jump, for men and women. A gold medal is awarded annually to the overall male and female winners based on performance in all three events. Established in 1942.

• 21253 •
USC Canada
Ms. Susan Walsh, Exec.Dir.
56 Sparks St., Ste. 705
Ottawa, ON, Canada K1P 5B1
Phone: (613)234-6827
Toll-Free: 800-565-6USC
Fax: (613)234-6842
E-mail: info@usc-canada.org
Home Page: http://www.usc-canada.org

• 21254 • **Harry Bolster Memorial Award**
Recognizes outstanding volunteerism. Awarded annually. Inquire for application details.

• 21255 •
USF Faculty Association, California Federation of Teachers (AFL-CIO), Local 4269
Alan Heineman, Pres.
University of San Francisco
San Francisco, CA 94117
Phone: (415)422-6454
Phone: (415)422-6485
Fax: (415)665-2414
E-mail: heinemana@usfca.edu

• 21256 • **Distinguished Teaching, Distinguished Research**
For full-time faculty member selected by committee. Monetary award bestowed annually.

• 21257 •
USO of Metropolitan New York
Rosemarie Dackerman, Exec.Dir.
625 8th Ave.
North Wing, 2nd Level
New York, NY 10018
Phone: (212)695-5590
Fax: (212)695-5734
E-mail: usonyc16@aol.com
Home Page: http://www.usony.org

• 21258 • **Gold Medal Award for Distinguished Service**
To recognize a man who has contributed significantly to help support active duty military personnel and their families. Financial, entertainment, or volunteer contributions by residents of the New York metropolitan area are considered. A medal is awarded annually at the Fall Fund Raiser Dinner. Established in 1961.

• 21259 • **USO Woman of the Year**
To recognize a woman who has contributed significantly to help support active duty military personnel and their families. Financial, entertainment, or volunteer contributions by residents of the New York metropolitan area are considered. Awarded annually at the Spring Fund Raiser Luncheon. Established in 1961.

• 21260 •
USS Nevada Association (BB-36/SSBN-733)
Woodrow W. Derby, Pres.
16401 Rhone Ln.
Huntington Beach, CA 92647
Phone: (714)848-2039

• 21261 • **Sailors of the Year on SSBN-733**
Annual award of recognition. Winners are determined by C.O.

• 21262 •
Utah Professional Videographers Association
Michael W. Nelson, Pres.
4227 S Highland Dr., Ste. 1
Salt Lake City, UT 84124
Phone: (801)278-4322
E-mail: president@upva.org
Home Page: http://www.upva.org

• 21263 • **Creative Video Productions Awards**
For video quality. Recognition award bestowed annually.

• 21264 •
Utility Communicators International
Elliot Boardman, Exec.Dir.
229 E Ridgewood Rd.
Georgetown, TX 78628
Phone: (512)869-1313
Fax: (512)864-7203
E-mail: eboardman@att.net
Home Page: http://www.uci-online.com

Formerly: (1989) Public Utilities Communicators Association.

• 21265 • **Better Communications Contest**
For recognition of outstanding advertising by public utilities companies in the following categories: (1) Complete Campaign Public Relations; (2) Complete Campaign Marketing; (3) Single Newspaper Ad: Image or Public Relations; (4) Single Newspaper Ad: Marketing; (5) Series of Newspaper Ads: Image or Public Relations; (6) Series of Newspaper Ads: Marketing; (7) Single Magazine Ad; (8) Radio; (9) Single Television Ad: Image or Public Relations; (10) Single Television Ad: Marketing; (11) Billboard; (12) Bill Insert; (13) Direct Mail; (14) Special Booklet or Pamphlet; (15) Annual Report; (16) Employee Communications; (17) Internet Sites. The Communicator of the Year Award is presented annually, as well as plaques and prizes in each category. Established in 1923.

• 21266 •
Valley Industrial Development Corp.
Brian Fazio, Exec.Dir.
112 S Riverfront Dr.
PO Box 999
Mankato, MN 56002-1269
Phone: (507)345-4519
Toll-Free: 800-657-4733
Fax: (507)345-4451
E-mail: info@greatermankato.com
Home Page: http://www.greatermankato.com

• 21267 • **Business-Education Partnership Award**
For commitment to the community. Recognition award bestowed annually.

• 21268 •
Valley Players
Kathy Anderson, Sec.
PO Box 441
Waitsfield, VT 05673
Phone: (802)496-5208
E-mail: valleyplayers@madriver.com
Home Page: http://www.valleyplayers.com

• 21269 • **Vermont Playwrights Award**
To recognize full-length non-musical plays. Vermont, Maine, and New Hampshire residents may submit unproduced, unpublished plays suitable for a community group and for the theatre's facilities. A monetary award of $1,000 and possible production are awarded annually. Funding for the award is provided by the Audrey Mixer Endowment Fund. Deadline is Feb 1. Formerly: Northern New England Playwrights Award.

• 21270 •
Van Alen Institute
30 W 22nd St.
New York, NY 10010
Phone: (212)924-7000
Fax: (212)366-5836
E-mail: vanalen@vanalen.org
Home Page: http://www.vanalen.org

• 21271 • **Dinkeloo Fellowship**
For recognition in the field of architecture. The competition is open to U.S. citizens who have or anticipate receiving their first professional degree in architecture during the preceding 30 months. The submission consists of a portfolio illustrating work and a brief written description of the proposed project. Each fellowship consists of complimentary two months room, board, and design studio space at the American Academy in Rome and an additional $4,000 for travel expenses. Established in 1978 in honor of John Dinkeloo, longtime partner in Kevin Roche John Dinkeloo & Associates.

• 21272 •
Vancouver International Film Festival
Alan Franey, Festival Dir.
1181 Seymour St.
Vancouver, BC, Canada V6B 3M7
Phone: (604)685-0260
Fax: (604)688-8221
E-mail: viff@viff.org
Home Page: http://www.viff.org

• 21273 • **Vancouver International Film Festival**
To recognize those films deemed the festival-going public's favorites. Patrons at the Festival vote in two categories: Air Canada People's Choice Award for Most Popular film - open to any film participating in the Festival and Federal Express Award for Most Popular Canadian Film - open to any Canadian film participating in the Festival. There are five adjudicated award - Rogers Awards for Best Canadian Screenplay - includes the prize of a high-end personal computer system; The National Film Board of Canada Awards for Best Documentary Feature (seventy minutes and longer) $1,500 (Canadian) cash prize, The Telefilm Canada Awards for Best Emerging Western Canadian Feature & Short or Mid-length films- $5,000 & $ 4,000 cash prizes respectively, The Dragons and Tigers Award for Young Cinema$5,000 cash prize.

• 21274 •
Vanderbilt University Press
Michael Ames, Dir.
112 21st Av. S
Box 1813, Sta. B
Nashville, TN 37235-1813
Phone: (615)322-3585
Toll-Free: 800-627-7377
Fax: (615)343-8823
E-mail: vupress@vanderbilt.edu
Home Page: http://www.vanderbiltuniversitypress.com

• 21275 • **Norman L. and Roselea J. Goldberg Prize for Manuscripts in American Philosophy**
To recognize outstanding manuscripts in Art and medicine. Manuscripts must be original book-length works. A monetary award of $1,000 and publication by the Vanderbilt University Press may be awarded annually. Established in 1994 by Roselea J. Goldberg in honor of her husband, Norman Lewis Goldberg, a Vanderbilt alumnus, surgeon, and an art historian.

• 21276 •
Vanguard Youth Services
Kathy Belge, Program Mgr.
2100 SE Belmont St.
Portland, OR 97214
Phone: (503)872-9664
Fax: (503)231-3051
E-mail: info@smyrc.org
Home Page: http://smyrc.org/blog/?page_id=10

• 21277 • **Jack Abele Award**
For contribution as a volunteer to the gay, lesbian, bi-trans communities. Recognition award bestowed annually.

• 21278 •
Variety International - The Children's Charity
Jane Brody, Exec.Dir.
350 5th Ave., Ste. 1233
New York, NY 10118
Phone: (212)695-3818
Fax: (212)695-3857
E-mail: info@varietychildrenscharity.org
Home Page: http://www.varietychildrenscharity.org

• 21279 • **Communications Media Award**
To recognize an individual for the best newspaper, magazine, radio or television coverage pertaining to a local Variety Club project or to the overall objectives of Variety Clubs International. Three plaques are awarded annually for a radio, television, and newspaper winner. Established in 1965.

• 21280 • **Great Heart Award**
To recognize the local organization (called a "Tent") for the most outstanding collective efforts and contributions to community welfare in accordance with the aims and objectives of Variety Clubs International. The amount of money the Tent raises or spends is not the deciding factor for the award. Awarded annually.

• 21281 • **Humanitarian Award**
To honor and recognize distinguished citizens of the world whose good deeds have won world recognition. A gold heart-shaped emblem is awarded annually. Established in 1938.

• 21282 •
Vegetarian Awareness Network
Lige Weill, Exec.Dir.
PO Box 321
Knoxville, TN 37901
Phone: (865)558-8343
Toll-Free: 800-872-8343
Fax: (865)693-8329

• 21283 • **Vegetarian Awareness Month Awards**
Recognizes an event promotion achievement. Awarded annually.

• 21284 •
Vegetarian Resource Group
Charles Stahler, Co-Dir.
PO Box 1463
Baltimore, MD 21203
Phone: (410)366-8343
Fax: (410)366-8804
E-mail: vrg@vrg.org
Home Page: http://www.vrg.org

• 21285 • **Vegetarian Essay Contest**
For an essay on vegetarianism. Writers age 18 or younger are eligible. A $50 savings bond is given annually.

• 21286 •
Veitch Historical Society
Patricia A. McConnell, VP/Membership
134 Rhonda Dr.
Universal City, TX 78148-3420
Phone: (210)659-6813
E-mail: jmcconn529@aol.com
Home Page: http://veitchhistoricalsociety.org

• 21287 • **Veitch Historical Society Scholarship**
Annual monetary award. Given to a descendant of a Veitch, Veach, Veatch, Veech

Awards are arranged in alphabetical order below their administering organizations

• 21288 •
Velo-Cardio-Facial Syndrome
Dr. Karen J. Golding-Kushner PhD, Exec.Dir.
PO Box 874
University Hospital
708 Jacobsen Hall (CDU)
750 E Adams St.
Milltown, NJ 08850
Phone: (732)238-8803
Toll-Free: (866)VCF-SEF5
Fax: (732)238-8803
E-mail: info@vcfsef.org
Home Page: http://www.vcfsef.org

• 21289 • **Caitlin Lynch Memorial Fund Award**
Annual scholarship. Inquire for additional information.

• 21290 • **Tony Lipson Memorial Fund Award**
Helps members from Australia attend annual meetings. A monetary award is given annually.

• 21291 •
Venezuelan American Association of the United States
Montserrat Hernandez, Program Dir.
30 Vesey St., Rm. 506
New York, NY 10007
Phone: (212)233-7776
Fax: (212)233-7779
E-mail: andean@nyct.net
Home Page: http://venezuelanamerican.org

• 21292 • **Amistad Award**
Recognizes the promotion of friendship and understanding between both countries. Awarded periodically.

• 21293 •
Venture Clubs
1709 Spruce St.
Philadelphia, PA 19103-6103
Phone: (215)893-9000
Fax: (215)893-5200
E-mail: siahq@soroptimist.org
Home Page: http://www.soroptimistnwr.com/venture.htm

• 21294 • **Student Aid Award**
Bestowed to physically disabled individuals between ages 15-40. A monetary award is given. Applications are available from local participating venture clubs, or send a self-addressed envelope to the main office.

• 21295 •
Vermont Business Round Table
Lisa Ventriss, Pres.
69 Swift St., Ste. 300
South Burlington, VT 05403
Phone: (802)865-0410
Fax: (802)865-0662
E-mail: contact@vtroundtable.org
Home Page: http://www.vtroundtable.org

• 21296 • **Annual Public Medallion Award**
For public school that best demonstrates leadership in supporting and implementing systemic changes that significantly enhance the educational experience of US students. Grant awarded annually.

• 21297 •
Vermont Chamber of Commerce
Duane Marsh, Pres.
PO Box 37
Montpelier, VT 05601
Phone: (802)223-3443
Fax: (802)223-4257
E-mail: info@vtchamber.com
Home Page: http://www.vtchamber.com

• 21298 • **Citizen of the Year**
For outstanding citizenship in Vermont. Recognition award bestowed annually.

• 21299 • **Diane C. Davis Business of the Year**
For outstanding business practices. Recognition award bestowed annually.

• 21300 •
Vermont Historical Society
J. Kevin Graffagnino Ph.D., Dir.
Vermont History Center
60 Washington St.
Barre, VT 05641-4209
Phone: (802)479-8500
Fax: (802)479-8510
E-mail: vhs@vhs.state.vt.us
Home Page: http://www.vermonthistory.org

• 21301 • **Ben B. Lane Award**
For recognition of the best article on Vermont history published in the previous year's edition of our journal, *Vermont History.* A monetary award of $200 is presented annually. Established in 1982 by Lane Press in memory of Ben B. Lane.

• 21302 • **Local Society Awards**
To recognize the achievements of local historical societies in Vermont. Societies that have ongoing projects that deserve more than local recognition are eligible for nomination. Nominations may be made by the group seeking the award or by another group or individual. The nominations deadline is April 1. Activities in the following categories are eligible: history - including publications, oral history, education, programming, and similar projects; society operations - including publicity, membership development, fundraising projects, and similar efforts; and collecting, interpretation, and display - including exhibitions, historic preservation, and museum techniques. Awards are presented at the Annual Local Societies Meeting. In addition, honorable mentions may be awarded.

• 21303 •
Vermont Parent Teacher Association
Linda Hodge, Pres.
PO Box 284
Richmond, VT 05477
Phone: (802)434-4078
E-mail: info@vermontpta.org
Home Page: http://www.vermontpta.org

• 21304 • **Dorothy Canfield Fisher Children's Book Award**
To encourage Vermont school children to read more and better books and to discriminate in choosing worthwhile books to read. Living authors who are residents of the United States are eligible for original works published during the previous year. Selection is made by Vermont school children in the fourth through eighth grades. An illuminated scroll is awarded annually. Established in 1956 by the Vermont State PTA and the Vermont State Department of Libraries. The award honors the memory of Dorothy Canfield Fisher, who felt that reading from the earliest years on was one of the greatest influences on character development.

• 21305 •
Vermont Society of Land Surveyors
Margaret A. Shields, Adm.Sec.
Capitol Plz., Ste. 250
100 State St.
Montpelier, VT 05602
Phone: (802)239-6358
Fax: (802)239-6358
E-mail: vsls@sover.net
Home Page: http://www.vsls.org

• 21306 • **VSLS Education Foundation Scholarships**
For senior in accredited surveying school demonstrating financial need. Scholarship awarded annually.

• 21307 •
Vermont Superintendents Association
Jeffrey D. Francis, Exec.Dir.
2 Prospect St., Ste. No. 2
Montpelier, VT 05602
Phone: (802)229-5834
Fax: (802)229-4739
E-mail: jfrancis@vsa.k12.vt.us
Home Page: http://vt-vsa.org

• 21308 • **Frederick H. Tuttle Award**
For exceptional leadership in the district, community, state or professional association for the benefit of public education and/or students. Recognition award bestowed annually.

• 21309 •
Vernacular Architecture Forum
Gabrielle M. Lanier, Sec.
PO Box 1511
Harrisonburg, VA 22803-1511
E-mail: rginsbur@uiuc.edu
Home Page: http://www.vernaculararchitectureforum.org

• 21310 • **Abbott Lowell Cummings Award**
Recognizes an outstanding scholarly book about North American vernacular architecture. Awarded annually.

• 21311 • **Paul Buchanan Award**
Recognizes an outstanding non-published field-based work about North American vernacular architecture. Awarded annually.

• 21312 •
Vernon County Historical Society
Gary Marquardt, Pres.
231 N Main St.
Nevada, MO 64772
Phone: (417)667-9602
Phone: (417)667-8425
Fax: (417)667-4571
E-mail: bushwhackerjail@sbcglobal.net
Home Page: http://www.bushwhacker.org

• 21313 • **Richard S. Brownlee Fund**
For historical publication. Monetary award bestowed periodically.

• 21314 • **State History Society of Missouri**
For historical publication. Monetary award bestowed periodically.

• 21315 •
Vesterheim Norwegian-American Museum
Janet Pultz, Exec.Dir.
523 W Water St.
PO Box 379
Decorah, IA 52101-0379
Phone: (563)382-9681
Fax: (563)382-8828
E-mail: vesterheim@vesterheim.org
Home Page: http://vesterheim.org/index.php

• 21316 • **National Exhibition of Rosemaling in the Norwegian Tradition**
To provide for a juried showing of recent decorative painting in the style of Norwegian folk painting of the late-eighteenth and early-nineteenth centuries. Any painter who has been a resident of the United States or Canada for the past five years is eligible to exhibit in the competition. The exhibit is confined to work executed by the exhibitor within the past five years. Ribbon awards and a limited number of monetary awards are presented. After an artist has accumulated eight points at these exhibitions, a Medal of Honor is awarded. Held annually. Established in 1967.

• 21317 • **National Exhibition of Weaving in the Norwegian Tradition**
To provide for a judged showing of handwoven objects in the tradition of Norwegian folk weaving. The intrinsic technical and artistic qualities of the works are considered. Pieces directly adapted from old designs are considered as well as pieces in which early designs and techniques are creatively used. Weavings should be executed in techniques and/or with stylistic characteristics common to or adapted from Norwegian folk weaving. Monetary awards and ribbons for first place, second place, and honorable mention are awarded in each of two categories: Traditional and Contemporary. After a weaver has accumulated a total of eight points, he or she receives a Medal of Honor. Held annually. Established in 1982.

• 21318 • **National Exhibition of Woodworking in the Norwegian Tradition**
To provide for a judged showing of woodworking in types and styles traditional to the rural areas of Norway. Carvers may enter up to two pieces total in the following four categories: Acanthus, Chip carving, Figure carving, or Other. The intrinsic technical and artistic qualities of the works are considered regardless of the styles or techniques they represent. Monetary awards and ribbons are awarded. After a woodworker has accumulated a total of eight points, he or she receives a Medal of Honor. Held annually. Established in 1982.

• 21319 •
Veteran Corps of Artillery, State of New York
BG David J. Ramsay, Commandant
7th Regiment Armory
643 Park Ave.
New York, NY 10021
Phone: (212)249-3919
Fax: (212)249-3919
E-mail: information@vcall790.org
Home Page: http://www.vca1790.org

• 21320 • **Marksmanship**
For proficiency in small arms. Recognition award bestowed annually.

• 21321 •
Veteran Corps of Artillery, State of New York, Constituting the Military Society of the War of 1812
BG David J. Ramsay, Commandant
7th Regiment Armory
643 Park Ave.
New York, NY 10021
Phone: (212)249-3919
Fax: (212)249-3919
E-mail: info@vca1790.org
Home Page: http://www.vca1790.org

• 21322 • **Marksmanship Award**
Recognizes proficiency in small arms. Awarded annually.

• 21323 •
Veteran Wireless Operators Association
Dr. Raymond J. Mullin, Sec.
575 Jefferson Blvd.
Staten Island, NY 10312-2225
Phone: (718)967-9763
E-mail: wenben@nyc.rr.com
Home Page: http://www.vwoa.org

• 21324 • **DeForest Audion Gold Medal Award**
To recognize an outstanding contribution in the field of communications. A gold medal is awarded annually. Established in 1962. Formerly: (2006) DeForest Audion Award.

• 21325 • **Marconi Memorial Gold Medal of Service**
To recognize an individual for outstanding advancement in the communications field. A gold medal is awarded annually. Established in 1938.

• 21326 • **Marconi Memorial Scroll of Honor**
To recognize outstanding service in the line of duty. A scroll is awarded irregularly. Established in 1938.

• 21327 •
Veterans Bedside Network
Douglas Lutz, Pres.
10 Fiske Place, Rm. 301
Mount Vernon, NY 10550-3205
Phone: (914)699-6069
Fax: (914)667-0405

• 21328 • **Helping Hand Award**
Recognzes the person who did the most in preceding year to advance VBN's mission. Awarded annually.

• 21329 •
Veterans for Peace
Mr. Michael T. McPhearson, Exec.Dir.
216 S Meramec Ave.
438 N Skinker
St. Louis, MO 63105
Phone: (314)725-6005
Fax: (314)725-7103
E-mail: vfp@igc.org
Home Page: http://www.veteransforpeace.org

• 21330 • **VFP Medal**
Recognizes courage and personal sacrifice in peacework. Awarded annually.

• 21331 •
Veterans of Foreign Wars of the United States
Raymond C. Sisk, Commander-in-Chief
406 W 34th St.
Kansas City, MO 64111
Phone: (816)756-3390
Fax: (816)968-1149
E-mail: info@vfw.org
Home Page: http://www.vfw.org

• 21332 • **Outstanding Post Service Officer Award**
To recognize individuals for outstanding service to VFW members and their families. A citation, lapel pin, cap, and plaque are awarded annually at the National Convention. Established in 1991.

• 21333 • VFW Americanism Award
To recognize an individual for outstanding contributions to Americanism principles. Awarded on recommendation of the National Committee on Awards and Citations and authorized by the National Council of Administration. A medal and citation are awarded annually at the National Convention. Established in 1959.

• 21334 • VFW Armed Forces Award
To recognize active or retired members of the Armed Forces for outstanding contributions to national security. Awarded on recommendation of the National Committee on Awards and Citations and authorized by the National Council of Administration. A medal and citation are awarded annually at the National Convention. Established in 1964.

• 21335 • VFW Aviation and Space Award
To recognize an individual for outstanding contributions in the field of aviation/space. Awarded on recommendation of the National Committee on Awards and Citations and authorized by the National Council of Administration. An honorarium, medal, and citation are awarded annually at the National Convention. Established in 1964.

• 21336 • VFW Congressional Award
To recognize a sitting member of the Congress for outstanding service to the nation. Awarded on recommendation of the National Committee on Awards and Citations and authorized by the National Council of Administration. An honorarium and a scroll plaque are awarded annually in March. Established in 1964.

• 21337 • VFW Dwight David Eisenhower Distinguished Service Award
To recognize an individual for contributions to the cause of American security, unity, and world peace. Awarded on recommendation of the National Committee on Awards and Citations and authorized by the National Council of Administration. An honorarium, medal, and citation are awarded annually at the National Convention. Established in 1952.

• 21338 • VFW Emergency Services Award
Awarded to an individual for outstanding service in the field of emergency service. To recognize an individual(s) who provide emergency medical treatment, provides rescue service or civil disaster assistance as a member of a public or volunteer company organized for those purposes. Formerly: VFW Emergency Medical Technician Award.

• 21339 • VFW Firefighter Award
For outstanding service in the field of emergency service. Recognizes an individual(s) who acrively fights fires gives emergency medical treatment, provides rescue service or civil disaster assistance as a member of a public or volunteer company organized for those purposes.

• 21340 • VFW Hall of Fame Award
To recognize an individual for distinguished service rendered through outstanding contributions in the field of entertainment. Awarded on recommendation of the National Committee on Awards and Citations and authorized by the National Council of Administration. An honorarium, medal, and citation are awarded annually at the National Convention. Established in 1952.

• 21341 • VFW J. Edgar Hoover Award
To recognize an individual for outstanding service in the field of law enforcement. Awarded on recommendation of the National Committee on Awards and Citations and authorized by the National Council of Administration. An honorarium, medal, and citation are awarded annually at the National Convention. Established in 1966.

• 21342 • VFW James E. Van Zandt Citizenship Award
To recognize outstanding service contributing to American citizenship. Awarded on recommendation of the National Committee on Awards and Citations and authorized by the National Council of Administration. An honorarium, medal, and citation are awarded annually at the National Convention. Established in 1946.

• 21343 • VFW News Media Award
To recognize an individual or organization for outstanding contributions to a better understanding of the American way of life and its institutions and interests by honest and forthright reporting. Awarded on recommendation of the National Committee on Awards and Citations and authorized by the National Council of Administration. An honorarium, medal, and citation are awarded annually at the National Convention. Established in 1978.

• 21344 •
Veterans of Foreign Wars of the U.S., Department of Alabama
Travis Whaley, Adjutant
PO Box 231177
Montgomery, AL 36123-1177
Phone: (334)270-8399
Fax: (334)270-9056
E-mail: adjqm@alvfw.org
Home Page: http://www.alvfw.org

• 21345 • Voice of Democracy Scholarship
For winner of essay contest. Monetary award bestowed annually.

• 21346 •
Veterans of Foreign Wars Post 5850
William Willsey, Quartermaster
PO Box 513
Eufaula, AL 36072-0513
Phone: (334)687-8522
Phone: (334)687-6986
Fax: (334)687-8545

• 21347 • ROTC (Junior) Scholarship
For outstanding Jr. ROTC student - nominated by Sr. ROTC instructor. Recognition award bestowed annually.

• 21348 •
Veterans of Safety
Dr. Robert L. Baldwin, Exec.Dir.
Central Missouri State University Safety Center
Humphreys Bldg., No. 201
Warrensburg, MO 64093
Phone: (660)543-4281
Fax: (660)543-4482
E-mail: info@veteransofsafety.org

• 21349 • Award of Recognition
Recognizes the best published technical safety papers. Awarded annually.

• 21350 •
Via Christi Research, Inc.
1100 N St. Francis, Ste. 200
Wichita, KS 67214-2878
Phone: (316)291-4900
Fax: (316)291-7704
E-mail: inquiry@viamtec.org
Home Page: http://www.via-christi.org

• 21351 • Marsh and Henning Awards
Recognizes outstanding research by orthopedic surgery residents.

• 21352 •
Video Data Bank
School of the Art Institute of Chicago
Kate Horsfield, Exec.Dir.
112 S Michigan Ave.
Chicago, IL 60603
Phone: (312)345-3550
Fax: (312)541-8073
E-mail: info@vdb.org
Home Page: http://www.vdb.org

• 21353 • Barbara Aronofsky Latham Memorial Grants
To recognize the work of emerging talent and to foster the excellence, diversity, vitality, and appreciation of experimental video and electronic visualization art. The award is given for any form of experimental video or electronic visualization art and original writing on the history, theory, or criticism of video or electronic visualization art. Monetary awards ranging from $300 to $1,500 are awarded biannually. Established in 1987 by Julius Aronofsky in memory of Barbara Aronofsky Latham.

• 21354 •
Video Software Dealers Association
Crossan R. Andersen, Pres.
16530 Ventura Blvd., Ste. 400
Encino, CA 91436-4551
Phone: (818)385-1500
Toll-Free: 800-955-8732
Fax: (818)385-0567
E-mail: vsdaoffice@vsda.org
Home Page: http://www.vsda.org

• 21355 • **VSDA Home Entertainment Awards**
To honor the year's top movies and programs on video and DVD. Nominations are determined by a committee comprised of key retailers, distributors and members of the press. The winners are determined by a vote of the retailer and distributor members of the association. Key award categories include: Archival Title of the Year(motion picture), Archival Television Program of the Year, Direct To Video/Limited Release of the Year, Documentary Title of the Year, Family Title of the Year, Foreign Language Title of the Year, Marketing Campaign of the Year, Music DVD of the Year, Sell-through Title of the Year, Rental Title of the Year, TV Series of the Year, Video Game of the Year.

• 21356 • **VSDA Presidential Award**
To recognize an individual for sustained creative achievement in the entertainment industry. Individuals whose achievements in theater and film have been translated successfully into home video are eligible. Established in 1985.

• 21357 •
Vietnam Combat Veterans
John Devitt, Chm./Founder
PO Box 10
L'Anse, MI 49946
Phone: (906)885-5599
E-mail: johndv8@aol.com
Home Page: http://www.themovingwall.org

• 21358 • **Veteran's Community Service Award**
For recognition of services dedicated and rendered to the veteran's community, to the families of veterans, or to the dependents of veterans. Services provided without fee or compensation are considered. Nominations may be submitted by April 15. A certificate and an article in the national newsletter are awarded annually in June in the city of the recipient. Established in 1982 in memory of the 2,500 Missing in Action abandoned in Indochina.

• 21359 •
Vietnam Veterans of America
Thomas Corey, Pres.
8605 Cameron St., Ste. 400
Silver Spring, MD 20910
Phone: (301)585-4000
Toll-Free: 800-882-1316
Fax: (301)585-0519
E-mail: communications@vva.org
Home Page: http://www.vva.org

• 21360 • **Excellence in the Arts Award**
To recognize Vietnam veterans for contributions to American culture. A plaque is awarded. Established in 1987.

• 21361 • **Excellence in the Media Award**
To recognize the media for thorough and detailed coverage of veterans issues. A plaque is awarded. Established in 1987.

• 21362 • **Legislator of the Year**
To recognize a legislator for outstanding advocacy of positive veteran legislation. A plaque is awarded annually. Established in 1984.

• 21363 •
Vietnamese Culture and Science Association
Anhlan Nguyen, Pres.
PO Box 741301
Houston, TX 77274
Phone: (713)406-3030
Phone: (281)847-3396
Fax: (281)847-4264
E-mail: vhkh@vhkhvn.org
Home Page: http://www.vhkhvn.org

• 21364 • **Vietnamese Youth Excellence Award**
For valedictorian or salutatorian high school graduate who is of Vietnamese descent. Scholarship awarded annually.

• 21365 •
Vietnamese Medical Association in the U.S.A.
Dr. B.S. Nguyenlehieu MD, Contact
Shelton Medical Clinic
302 C St.
PO Box 476
Shelton, NE 68876
Phone: (308)647-6828
Fax: (308)647-5219
E-mail: bshieu@nctc.net

• 21366 • **Pham bieu Tam MD Award**
For contribution to advancing medical knowledge for Vietnamese. A monetary award is given biennially.

• 21367 •
The Village Voice
36 Cooper Sq.
New York, NY 10003
Phone: (212)475-3300
Fax: (212)475-8947
Home Page: http://www.villagevoice.com

• 21368 • **The Village Voice OBIE Awards**
To recognize achievement in Off and Off-Off Broadway theatre. Awards are given in the following categories: Best New American Play, Sustained Achievement, Sustained Excellence of Perfection, Performance, Direction, Sustained Excellence of Design, Lighting Design, and Set and Costume Design. All Off and Off-Off Broadway theatres are eligible. Monetary prizes, certificates, and cash grants are presented annually at the OBIE awards ceremony. Established in 1955 by the Plumsock Fund and *The Village Voice*.

• 21369 •
Vinegar Connoisseurs International
Lawrence Diggs, Contact
PO Box 41
104 W Carlton Ave.
Roslyn, SD 57261
Phone: (605)486-4536
Phone: (605)486-0075
Toll-Free: 800-342-4519
Fax: (605)486-4536
E-mail: vinegar@vinegarman.com
Home Page: http://www.vinegarman.com

• 21370 • **Mother of All Vinegar Contest**
To recognize excellence and innovation in vinegar making and use. Three prizes (a plaque and two trophies) are awarded annually in September. Established 1996.

• 21371 •
Vinifera Wine Growers Association
Gordon W. Murchie, Pres.
PO Box 10045
Alexandria, VA 22310
Phone: (703)922-7049
Fax: (703)922-0617
E-mail: thewinexchange@aol.com

• 21372 • **Vinifera Perpetual Monteith Trophy Award**
To honor superior contributions to the progressive growth and development of the wine industry. Recipients can come from any sector of the industry, allied businesses, media, government, educational or health communities within the U.S. or abroad. The awardee retains possession of the Silver Trophy for one year. The Tiffany trophy, the most expensive in the industry (insured for $12,000), is a sterling silver replica of an ancient wine service bowl. Presented annually, usually at the Virginia Wine Festival in August. Established in 1980.

• 21373 • **Virginia Wine Competition**
The Competition is open to all Virginia vineyards and is held annually in July. The following awards are presented: Best-of-Show - the Jefferson Grape-wine Loving Cup Trophy; and Gold, Silver, and Bronze Medals; for Chardonnay, White Vinefera, Red Vinifera, White French Hybrid, Red French Hybrid, Sparkling Wine, Blush Wine, Dessert, and specialty brands. Awarded annually. Established in 1982. Awards are presented at annual August Wine Festival.

• 21374 • **Winegrape Productivity Trophy**
To recognize individuals or groups that make outstanding contributions in the field of viticulture and enology or to public wine appreciation and education. A large silver "champagne" tray, heavily embossed with vines and grapes, is presented at the annual August wine festival.

Established in 1982. Formerly: (2006) Vinifera Perpetual Wine-Grape Productivity Trophy.

• 21375 •
Vintage Sailplane Association
Linn Buell, Sec.
1709 Baron Ct.
Port Orange, FL 32128
Phone: (770)446-5533
Fax: (770)446-5533
E-mail: lbuell@cfl.rr.com
Home Page: http://www.vintagesailplane.org

• 21376 • **Frank Gross Restoration Award**
To recognize the owner of the best vintage sailplane restored in the previous year. A monetary award of up to $500 and a trophy are presented annually. Established in 1990.

• 21377 • **Harland Ross Award**
For recognition of the best flight in a vintage sailplane. Members in a sailplane more than 30 years old are eligible. A trophy is awarded annually. Established in 1979 in honor of Harland Ross, sailplane designer.

• 21378 • **Robert Stanley Award**
To recognize outstanding administrative or flying performance at a VSA regatta. A trophy is awarded annually. Established in 1979.

• 21379 •
Vintage Thunderbird Club International
Mr. Lou Paliani, Pres.
1304 Greenwood
Schertz, TX 78154-2808
Phone: (210)566-2118
E-mail: lpaliani@satx.rr.com
Home Page: http://www.vintagethunderbirdclub.org/welcome.htm
Formerly: Vintage Thunderbird Club of America.

• 21380 • **Concours Awards**
To recognize the highest scoring show cars for 1958 through today's Thunderbird. Photo engraved plaques are awarded annually. Established in 1968.

• 21381 •
Violin Society of America
Barbara Van Itallie, Exec.Dir.
48 Academy St.
Poughkeepsie, NY 12601
Phone: (845)452-7557
Fax: (845)452-7618
E-mail: info@vsa.to
Home Page: http://www.vsa.to

• 21382 • **International Competitions for New Instruments and Bows**
To recognize excellence in workmanship and tone quality by contemporary makers of bowed stringed instruments and bows. Members of the VSA may enter the competitions. Gold Medals and certificates are awarded biennially. Established in 1973.

• 21383 •
Virginia Association of Chiefs of Police
Dana G. Schrad, Exec.Dir.
1606 Santa Rosa Rd., Ste. 134
Richmond, VA 23288
Phone: (804)285-8227
Fax: (804)285-3363
E-mail: dana@vachiefs.org
Home Page: http://www.vachiefs.org

• 21384 • **NHTSA**
For traffic safety activities. Monetary award.

• 21385 •
Virginia Association of Independent Specialized Education Facilities
Debbie Pell, Board Pres.
118 N. 8th St.
Richmond, VA 23219
Phone: (804)780-2776
Fax: (804)648-8036
E-mail: belwood@erols.com

• 21386 • **Margaret Shepherd Teaching Award**
For outstanding teacher of children with special needs. Recognition award bestowed annually.

• 21387 •
Virginia Film Office
Rita McClenny, Contact
901 E Byrd St.
Richmond, VA 23219-4048
Phone: (804)545-5530
Toll-Free: 800-854-6233
Fax: (804)545-5531
E-mail: vafilm@virginia.org
Home Page: http://www.film.virginia.org

• 21388 • **Governor's Screenwriting Competition**
To support and encourage Virginia screenwriters and to provide them an opportunity to present their work to professionals in the motion picture and television industry. Full-length scripts for a feature film or television movie may be submitted by Virginia residents. At least 75 percent of the script must be set in Virginia or in a place that could reassembly be expected to be found in Virginia Screenplays currently in production are ineligible. Three monetary awards of $1,000 each are announced at the Virginia Film Festival. Established in 1988. Sponsored by the Virginia Film Office.

• 21389 •
Virginia Interscholastic Athletic Administrators Association
Jerry Carter, Pres.
Liberty High School
6300 Independence Ave.
Bealeton, VA 22712-6843
Phone: (540)439-4202
Fax: (540)439-3397
E-mail: jcarter@fcpsl.org

• 21390 • **John Youngblood Scholarships**
For character, leadership, scholarship, athletic participation. Scholarship awarded annually.

• 21391 •
Virginia Library Association
Linda Hahne, Exec.Dir.
PO Box 8277
Norfolk, VA 23503
Phone: (757)583-0041
Fax: (757)583-5041
E-mail: lhahne@coastalnet.com
Home Page: http://www.vla.org

• 21392 • **Jefferson Cup Award**
To honor books written for young people in the areas of U.S. history, historical fiction, and biography and promotes the reading of books about America's past. Awarded annually. Established in 1984.

• 21393 •
Virginia Peninsula Chamber of Commerce
Clyde R. Hoey II, Pres./CEO
1919 Commerce Dr., Ste. 320
PO Box 7269
Hampton, VA 23666-0269
Phone: (757)262-2000
Toll-Free: 800-556-1822
Fax: (757)262-2009
E-mail: vpcc@vpcc.org
Home Page: http://www.vpcc.org

• 21394 • **Distinguished Citizen**
Recognizes an individual who has made an outstanding and distinguished ongoing contribution to the well-being and quality of life in the Virginia Peninsula. Recognition award bestowed annually.

• 21395 •
Virginia Quarterly Review
Ted Genoways, Ed.
1 W Range
PO Box 400223
Charlottesville, VA 22904-4223
Phone: (804)924-3124
Fax: (804)924-1397
E-mail: vqreview@virginia.edu
Home Page: http://www.virginia.edu/vqr

• 21396 • **Emily Clark Balch Prize**
To stimulate the appreciation and creation of American literature by recognizing the best story and best poem published in a calendar year in the *Virginia Quarterly Review*. A monetary prize

of $500 for Best Short Story and $500 for Best Poem are awarded annually. Established in 1956.

• 21397 •
Virginia Recreation and Park Society
James C. Stutts, Exec.Dir.
6038 Cold Harbor Rd.
Mechanicsville, VA 23111
Phone: (804)730-9447
Fax: (804)730-9455
E-mail: vrps@vrps.com
Home Page: http://www.vwc.edu/vrps/home.htm

• 21398 • Fellows Award
For recognition of exceptional service to the society and the profession. A candidate must be a current member of the society for a minimum of the past five years and have at least 10 years of experience in the general field of parks and/or recreation. Candidates may be nominated by May 1. An engraved sculpture is awarded annually at the conference of the society. Established in 1963.

• 21399 •
Virginia Volkssport Association
Nancy C. Stenger, President
14402 William Carr Ln.
Centreville, VA 20120-2813
Phone: (703)631-8512
Fax: (703)631-8512
E-mail: walkvirginia@erols.com
Home Page: http://walkvirginia.com

• 21400 • VVA Achievement Award
For service in promoting volkssporting within the commonwealth of Virginia. Recognition award bestowed annually.

• 21401 •
Virginia Waring International Piano Competition
College of the Desert
43-500 Monterey Ave.
Palm Desert, CA 92260
Phone: (760)773-2575
Fax: (760)776-0168
E-mail: info@vwipc.com
Home Page: http://www.vwipc.com

• 21402 • Joanna Hodges International Piano Competition/Virginia Waring International Piano Competition
To recognize outstanding young pianists from all over the world. Competitions are held in the following categories: Master Class Competition - for ages 18-25, 13-17, 10-12, and 9 and under; Solo Competition - for junior and intermediate divisions; Concerto Competition - for junior and intermediate divisions; senior division features solo and orchestral categories; Senior Master Classes in Solo Works, Piano with Orchestra and Conductors. Plaques and certificates are awarded to all winners. Numerous performance awards including international debuts are presented. All prize performance expenses are paid.

• 21403 •
Virginians Opposing Drunk Driving - State Headquarters
Lillian N. DeVenny, State Pres.
Chapter R.I.D., USA
PO Box 62302
Virginia Beach, VA 23462
Phone: (757)497-2494
Phone: (757)466-1777
Fax: (757)466-1777

• 21404 • Bob Bowers Scholarship
For outstanding S.A.D.D. high school student or students. Monetary award bestowed annually.

• 21405 •
Visions in Action
Shaun Skelton PhD, Dir.
2710 Ontario Rd. NW
Washington, DC 20009
Phone: (202)625-7402
Fax: (202)588-9344
E-mail: visions@visionsinaction.org
Home Page: http://www.visionsinaction.org

• 21406 • Global Justice Award
Annual award of recognition.

• 21407 •
VMI Cadet Investment Group
Robert McLean, Chm.
Drawer JH
Williamsburg, VA 23187-3632
Phone: (757)220-3838
Toll-Free: 800-451-4504
Fax: (757)220-0294
E-mail: westct@mail.vmi.edu
Home Page: http://academics.vmi.edu/econ/cig.htm

• 21408 • VMI (Virginia Military Institute) Future Captain of Industry Award
For recognition of a cadet member of the VMI Cadet Investment Group which is sponsored by The Department of Economics and Business at VMI who illustrates the character and qualities characteristic of a future captain of industry. Members of the Cadet Investment Group who are graduating in the year of the award are eligible. A framed antique stock certificate signed by a famous businessman, for example, J. P. Morgan, is awarded annually. Established in 1986 by Haley and Hannelore Garrison of Antique Stocks and Bonds, Williamsburg, Virginia and presented in the name of the Society for the Preservation of American Business History.

• 21409 •
VMI Research Laboratories
Virginia Military Institute
Lexington, VA 24450-0304
Phone: (540)464-7434
Fax: (540)464-7761
E-mail: rowera@vmi.edu
Home Page: http://vmirl.vmi.edu/

• 21410 • Maury and Hinman research awards
Awarded to VMI faculty and students. Inquire for application details.

• 21411 • Research Performance Awards
Awarded to VMI faculty and students. Inquire for application details.

• 21412 •
VSA Arts
Soula Antoniou, Pres.
Progran Development Department
818 Connecticut Ave. NW, Ste. 600
Washington, DC 20006
Phone: (202)628-2800
Toll-Free: 800-933-8721
Fax: (202)737-0725
E-mail: info@vsarts.org
Home Page: http://www.vsarts.org

• 21413 • Very Special Arts Playwright Discovery Program
Very Special Arts sponsors an annual call for entries, inviting individuals with a disability, to submit original scripts addressing some aspect of disability in their themes. The final scripts are read by a distinguished Artists Selection Committee which selects two scripts for professional production at The John F. Kennedy Center for the Performing Arts. A scholarship is also provided. Formerly: (1989) Henry Fonda Young Playwrights Project; (1985) Integrated Young Playwrights Project; (1997) Very Special Arts Young Playwrights Program.

• 21414 • Young Soloists Award
To recognize and encourage further professional development of an outstanding performing artist who resides inside the United States, age 25 and under with a physical or mental disability. Recipients receive a $5,000 cash award and the opportunity to perform at the John F. Kennedy Center for Performing Arts in Washington DC. Formerly: Itzhak Perlman Award.

• 21415 •
Wagner Society of Dallas
Virginia R. Abdo, Co-Founder
PO Box 25201
Dallas, TX 75225-0201
Phone: (214)363-6070
Fax: (214)363-6070
E-mail: wsd@wagnerdallas.com
Home Page: http://www.WagnerDallas.com

• 21416 • Dallas Opera Young Artist Competition
For young musicians and operatic singers. Recognition award bestowed annually.

• 21417 •
Wagner Society of New York
Nathalie D. Wagner, Pres.
PO Box 230949 Ansonia Sta.
New York, NY 10023-0949
Phone: (212)749-4561
Fax: (212)749-1542
E-mail: wagnerring@aol.com
Home Page: http://www.wagnersocietyny.org

• 21418 • Robert Lauch Memorial Grant
For outstanding promising Wagner singer. Grant awarded annually.

• 21419 • Student and Young Professional Grant
For potential in singing Wagner repertoire. Grant awarded semiannually.

• 21420 •
Wahpeton Area Chamber of Commerce and CVB
Jim Oliver, Exec.VP
118 6th St. N
Wahpeton, ND 58075-4327
Phone: (701)642-8744
Toll-Free: 800-892-6673
Fax: (701)642-8745
E-mail: wahpetonchamber@702com.net
Home Page: http://www.wahpchamber.com

• 21421 • Extra Mile Award
For community service. Recognition award bestowed quarterly.

• 21422 •
WAIF
Gerald H. Cornez, Exec.Dir.
300 E 40th St., Ste. 25-K
New York, NY 10016-2148
Fax: (212)986-4402

• 21423 • National Humanitarian Award
For recognition of service, fund raising, or other activities that enhance WAIF's goal of a permanent and loving family for every child. Candidates are approved by the National Board. Awarded when merited. Established in 1979. Has been presented to Julie Andrews and Blake Edwards, Helen Hayes, Gary Nardino (then head of Paramount Pictures, TV Division) and Ralph Barnett (Chairman of Gestetener Corp.) A Founder's Award was presented in 1980 to Jane Russell as founder of WAIF on WAIF's 25th anniversary. Outstanding Service Awards are presented from time to time as merited for furthering the adoption of special needs children.

• 21424 • Outstanding Service Award
Awarded from time to time as merited for furthering the adoption of special needs children.

• 21425 •
Walkaloosa Horse Association
Lee Waddle, Registrar
PO Box 3170
Carefree, AZ 85377
Phone: (480)488-7169
Fax: (805)528-3128
E-mail: contact@walkaloosaregistry.com
Home Page: http://walkaloosaregistry.com

• 21426 • National Most Colorful Contest
To recognize the breeding of the most colorful and desirable Walkaloosa. Horses must be registered with the Walkaloosa Horse Association during the year that the contest is taking place. Registration pictures are used for judging. A monetary prize of 80 per cent of the application fees to the contest is awarded annually. Established in 1985. Formerly: Most Colorful Walkaloosa.

• 21427 •
Walking Horse Trainers Association
David Landrum, Pres.
PO Box 61
Shelbyville, TN 37162
Phone: (931)684-5866
Fax: (931)684-5895
E-mail: whta@walkinghorsetrainers.com
Home Page: http://www.walkinghorsetrainers.com

• 21428 • Trainer of the Year
To recognize the trainer who has contributed the most to the Walking Horse industry. Any member of the Association is eligible. A monetary prize and a 14K gold ring are awarded annually. Established in 1968.

• 21429 •
Lila Wallace Reader's Digest Fund
M. Christine De Vita, Pres.
2 Park Ave., 23rd Fl.
New York, NY 10016
Phone: (212)251-9700
Fax: (212)679-6990
Home Page: http://www.wallacefunds.org

• 21430 • Lila Wallace-Reader's Digest Writers' Awards
To provide financial support for experienced, outstanding writers. Poets, fiction writers, playwrights, essayists, and other writers of literary non-fiction are eligible for the award. Nominees are proposed by a body composed of writers, editors, scholars, and critics. Direct applications are not accepted. Candidates must propose an affiliation with a nonprofit organization that will be maintained throughout the duration of the award. Affiliations should be based on their potential to foster an exchange of ideas and experiences between the writer, the participating organization, and the constituency served by the organization. Consideration is also given to the potential impact of the award on the candidate's ability to devote significant amounts of time to his or her craft during the period of the award. A selection committee evaluates nominations based on quality of each writer's work, the promise of continued writing, and evidence of firm commitment to writing as a career. A monetary grant of $35,000 per year for up to three years is awarded.

• 21431 •
WAMSO Young Artist Competition
Teri E. Popp, Pres.
1111 Nicollet Mall
Minneapolis, MN 55403-2477
Phone: (612)371-5654
Fax: (612)371-7176
E-mail: wamso@mnorch.org
Home Page: http://wamso.org

• 21432 • Vincent R. Bastien Memorial Cello Award
$500 is awarded. Inquire for application details.

• 21433 • Mary Winston Smail Memorial Piano Award
$500 is awarded to a pianist in the final round.

• 21434 • Twin Cities Musicians Union AFM Award
A $1000 award is given. Inquire for application details.

• 21435 • WAMSO Young Artist Competition
To recognize outstanding piano and orchestral instrument performance and to provide performance, scholarship and cash opportunities for young musicians. Performers of instruments which have permanent chairs in the Minnesota Orchestra who are legal residents of Illinois, Indiana, Iowa, Kansas, Michigan, Minnesota, Missouri, Nebraska, North Dakota, South Dakota, Wisconsin, Manitoba, and Ontario, or students registered in schools in these states and provinces are eligible. Entrants must be 25 years of age or younger. The deadline for entry varies. Preliminary submissions are made by CD/tape. Application and fee due in September. CD/tape due in October. Only finalists and semi-finalists receive awards. The following prizes are awarded: (1) Grand Award - $1,000 from the Minnesota Orchestral Association and a performance with the Orchestra under the direction of the music director; (2) First Prize - $3,000 WAMSO Young Artist Award, Ehrma Strachauer Medal, and a performance with the Minnesota Orchestra; (3) Second Prize - $2,500 WAMSO Award; (4) Third Prize - $1,000 WAMSO Award; (5) Mathilda Heck Prize - $1000 Award to an outstanding wind player; (6) Performances; (7) Summer Opportunities scholarships for several summer programs; and (8) Scholarships - full tuition and partial to a number of colleges. Established in 1955.

• 21436 •
Washington Academy of Sciences
Doug Witherspoon, Pres.
1200 New York Ave. NW, Ste. 637
Washington, DC 20005
Phone: (202)326-8975
E-mail: was@washacadsci.org
Home Page: http://www.washacadsci.org

• 21437 • **Awards for Scientific Achievement**

To recognize achievement by young scientists in the behavioral and social sciences, biological sciences, engineering sciences, physical sciences, mathematics and computer science, for the teaching of science, and for distinguished careers in science. For the teaching of science, the Bernice G. Lamberton Award for Teaching High School Science and the Leo Schubert Award for Teaching College Science are presented. Scientists who are working in the Washington, D.C., area are eligible. Awarded annually. Established in 1940.

• 21438 •
Washington-Baltimore Newspaper Guild
1100 15th St. NW, Ste. 350
Washington, DC 20005
Phone: (202)785-3650
Fax: (202)785-3659
E-mail: local32035@wbng.org
Home Page: http://www.wbng.org

• 21439 • **Front Page Awards**

To recognize and reward excellence in stories, pictures, design, and layout. The contest is open to employees covered by contracts negotiated by the Washington-Baltimore Newspaper Guild as well as "at-large" WBNG members, those who do not have a Guild contract but belong to the union anyway. It is not necessary to be a member of the Guild to enter. Entries must be for work performed in the preceding calendar year. Free-lance work is not accepted. Awards are given in three main categories: writing, photography, and design. In the writing category, awards are given for: national news; non-daily specialized or technical reporting; the Frank C. Porter Memorial Award for labor and business reporting; public service; the Morton Mintz Award for investigative reporting; sports; local news; the Bernie Harrison Memorial Award for commentary; criticism; headline writing; and features. In the design category awards are given for: advertising design; bargaining unit publication; illustration design; page design; covers; and graphics. In the photo category, awards are given for: features; local news; national news; picture story; black and white picture; portrait; and sports. Guild members who win in individual categories are eligible for the Bill Pryor Memorial Award grand prize for writing or photography or the John Albano Memorial Award grand prize for design. Guild activists are also eligible to win four Guild Service Awards: The Dan de Souza Memorial Award for Member of the Year, named after the first president of the old Washington Newspaper Guild, and the Nadine Grinder Memorial Award for Shop Steward of the Year, named after a legendary rank and file activist. Awarded annually. Established around 1942.

• 21440 •
Washington College
Baird Tipson, Pres.
College Relations Office
300 Washington Ave.
Chestertown, MD 21620-1197
Phone: (410)778-2800
Toll-Free: 800-422-1782
Fax: (410)778-7802
E-mail: meredith.davies@washcoll.edu
Home Page: http://www.washcoll.edu

• 21441 • **Sophie Kerr Prize**

To recognize a member of the senior class for excellence in creative writing and promise for future fulfillment in the field of literary endeavor. A monetary prize of approximately $60,000 is awarded annually at commencement. Established in 1968 in honor of Sophie Kerr, a writer and Eastern Shore native. One-half of the annual income from her bequest to the college is awarded each year to a graduating senior demonstrating the best potential for writing. The other half is used to support the English program, bringing visitors of literary merit to campus each year.

• 21442 •
Washington County Historical Society
Charles W. Stewart, Contact
118 E. Dickson St.
Fayetteville, AR 72701
Phone: (501)521-2970
Phone: (501)521-2020

• 21443 • **Distinguished Citizen's Award**

For significant contribution to the community. Recognition award bestowed periodically.

• 21444 •
Washington Crossing Foundation
Eugene C. Fish Esq., Contact
PO Box 503
Levittown, PA 19058
Phone: (215)949-8841
Phone: (215)949-8842
Fax: (215)949-8843
E-mail: info@gwcf.org
Home Page: http://www.gwcf.org

• 21445 • **Washington Crossing Foundation Scholarship**

For high school seniors planning government service careers. Scholarship awarded annually.

• 21446 •
Washington Independent Writers
Donald O. Graul Jr., Exec.Dir.
220 Woodward Bldg.
733 15th St. NW
Washington, DC 20005
Phone: (202)737-9500
Fax: (202)638-7800
E-mail: info@washwriter.org
Home Page: http://www.washwriter.org

• 21447 • **Philip M. Stern Award**

To recognize a member who has made a significant contribution(s) to the writing profession in general or to writers in particular. A certificate is awarded annually at the spring conference reception. Established in 1986 by the WIW Board of Directors to honor Philip M. Stern.

• 21448 •
Washington International Trade Association
James Wilkinson, Exec.Dir.
1300 Pennsylvania Ave. NW, Ste. 350
Washington, DC 20004
Phone: (202)312-1600
Fax: (202)312-1601
E-mail: wita@wita.org
Home Page: http://www.wita.org

• 21449 • **Distinguished Service Award**

For contributions to international trade. Recognition award bestowed annually.

• 21450 • **Lifetime Achievement Award**

For contributions to international trade. Recognition award bestowed annually.

• 21451 •
The Washington Monthly
Paul Glastris, Editor-in-Chief
733 15th St. NW, Ste. 520
Washington, DC 20005
Phone: (202)393-5155
Fax: (202)393-2444
E-mail: cristina@washingtonmonthly.com
Home Page: http://www.washingtonmonthly.com

• 21452 • **Annual Political Book Award**

To recognize the best books that explore the processes and values of the institutions that govern America, the books that share *The Washington Monthly*'s purpose of identifying where the system breaks down, why it breaks down, and what can be done to make it work. Authors of books that were published during the calendar year for which the award is given are eligible. The review and announcement are made in the March "Political Book Award Issue" of the magazine. Awarded annually. Established in 1969.

• 21453 • ***The Washington Monthly* Journalism Award**

To recognize the best newspaper, magazine, television, or radio story (or series of stories) on our political system. Nominations for any newspaper, magazine, or radio or television station in the country are welcome. Mention/description in the magazine is awarded monthly.

Awards are arranged in alphabetical order below their administering organizations

• 21454 •
Washington National Opera
Michael R. Sonnenreich, Pres.
John F. Kennedy Center for the Performing Arts
2600 Virginia Ave. NW, Ste. 104
Washington, DC 20037
Phone: (202)295-2420
Toll-Free: 800-US-OPERA
Fax: (202)295-2479
E-mail: info@dc-opera.org
Home Page: http://www.dc-opera.org

• 21455 • **The Martin and Bernice Feinstein Award**
To recognize a young American singer who has displayed exceptional artistic merit during the season with The Washington Opera. Young American conductors, singers, or costume and set designers are selected by the artistic staff of The Washington Opera in conjunction with the Board of The Washington Opera Guild. A monetary prize of $2,500 plus an engraved bowl are awarded at the annual luncheon. A fund to support the award was established in 1977 by Mrs. Rosalind Shifrin in memory of her sister, Beatrice Vaccara, a former member of The Washington Opera Guild. Formerly known as the Artist of the Year, the award was renamed in 1995 in honor of retiring general director, Martin Feinstein and his late wife, Bernice.

• 21456 •
The Washington Post
Children's Book Guild of Washington, D.C.
Maria Salvadore, Pres.
2602 Valey Dr.
Alexandria, VA 22302
Phone: (703)549-0753
Fax: (703)836-5949
E-mail: theguild@childrensbookguild.org
Home Page: http://www.childrensbookguild.org

• 21457 • ***The Washington Post*/ Children's Book Guild Award for Nonfiction**
To honor an author or author-illustrator whose total work has contributed significantly to the quality of nonfiction for children, that is, for creatively produced books that make a difference. Any living American author or author-illustrator is eligible. Illustrators are eligible only if they have written as well as illustrated their books. Recipients are selected by a committee. A monetary award of $2,000 and an inscribed Baccarat crystal cube are awarded annually at the Children's Book Week Luncheon in November. Established in 1977.

• 21458 •
The Washington Post Company Educational Foundation
1150 15th St. NW
Washington, DC 20071
Phone: (202)334-6834
Fax: (202)334-5609

• 21459 • **Agnes Meyer Outstanding Teacher Awards**
To recognize and reward excellence in education by teachers in the Washington, D.C., area. Teachers who motivate students to appreciate and seek learning and to attain their maximum potential may be nominated. Nominees must be professional, full-time classroom teachers in grades pre-kindergarten through 12 and must have three years of successful teaching experience. A monetary award of $3,000 is presented annually. Established in 1983. The award is named for Agnes Meyer, wife of Eugene Meyer, who purchased the *Washington Post* in 1933. Mrs. Meyer was greatly concerned with public education.

• 21460 •
Washington State Bar Association
2101 Fourth Ave., Ste. 400
Seattle, WA 98121-2330
Phone: (206)443-9722
Phone: (206)727-8244
Toll-Free: 800-945-9722
Fax: (206)727-8319
E-mail: questions@wsba.org
Home Page: http://www.wsba.org

• 21461 • **Ralph Bunche Award**
To recognize an individual or an orgranization for an outstanding contribution to world peace through law. A plaque and travel expenses are awarded annually. Established in 1973 by the Sea-King County Bar, WPTL Committee to commemorate Dr. Ralph Bunche.

• 21462 •
Washington Theatre Awards Society
Elizabeth Brown, Exec.Dir.
2233 Wisconsin Ave. NW, Ste. 300
Washington, DC 20007
Phone: (202)337-4572
Fax: (202)625-1238
E-mail: lgrossman@helenhayes.org
Home Page: http://www.helenhayes.org

• 21463 • **Helen Hayes Awards**
For recognition of outstanding achievement in the professional theatre. The award celebrate and promote excellence in the professional theatre and, by doing so, have brought national and international attention to one of our greatest cultural resource. The presentation of the awards pay tribute to outstanding achievement in profession theatre. Twenty-one awards are given for artistic excellence as well as three special corporate awards: The American Express Tribute for lifetime achievement in the professional theatre, the KPMG Award for Distinguished Service to the Theatre Community, and The Washington Post Award for Distinguished Community Service. Resident Musical; Outstanding Lead Actor/Resident Musical; Outstanding Lead Actress/Resident Musical; Outstanding Supporting Actor/Resident Musical; Outstanding Supporting Actress/Resident Musical; Outstanding Non-Resident Production; Outstanding Lead Actor/Non-Resident Production; Outstanding Lead Actress/Non-Resident Production; Outstanding Supporting Performer/Non-Resident Production; American Express Tribute; KPMG Peat Marwick Award for Distinguished Service to the Washington Theatre Community; *The Washington Post* Award for Distinguished Community Service; Outstanding Musical Direction/Resident Musical; and Outstanding Choreography/Resident Production. A production must be presented a minimum of 16 times and artists must be paid to be considered. A trophy with a medallion is awarded in each category annually in May. Established in 1983 to honor Helen Hayes, a native of Washington and the first lady of the American theatre.

• 21464 •
Washington University in St. Louis
Diabetes Research and Training Center
660 S Euclid Ave., Box 8127
St. Louis, MO 63110
Phone: (314)362-8680
Fax: (314)747-2692
E-mail: gskolnic@im.wustl.edu
Home Page: http://www.medicine.wustl.edu/drtc

• 21465 • **Pilot and Feasibility Awards**
Inquire for application details.

• 21466 •
Washington Writers' Publishing House
PO Box 15271
Washington, DC 20003
Phone: (301)652-5636
E-mail: moirae333@earthlink.net
Home Page: http://www.wwph.org

• 21467 • **Poetry Books Award**
For recognition of excellence in poetry by a poet living in the greater Washington DC area. Manuscripts of 50-60 pages may be submitted from July 1 through September 30. Writers within a 60-mile radius of Washington, D.C., (including Baltimore) are eligible. Send self-addressed, stamped envelope for guidelines. Publication of the book is awarded annually. Established in 1975.

• 21468 •
Washingtonian Magazine
John Limpert, Ed.
1828 L St. NW, Ste. 200
Washington, DC 20036
Phone: (202)296-3600
E-mail: washmag@dc.infi.net
Home Page: http://www.washingtonian.com

• 21469 • **Washingtonians of the Year**
For recognition of individuals who have improved the quality of life in the Washington area. Nominations are open to the public. The deadline is September 30. A plaque is presented annually at a special event. Established in 1971.

• 21470 •
Washtenaw Contractors Association
Gretchen A. Waters, Exec.Dir.
3135 S State St., Ste. 210
Ann Arbor, MI 48108
Phone: (734)662-2570
Phone: (734)662-2755
Fax: (734)662-1695
E-mail: info@wcaonline.org
Home Page: http://www.wcaonline.org

• 21471 • **Pyramid Awards**
For outstanding project teams, for safety, for innovation, for outstanding subcontractors. Recognition award bestowed annually.

• 21472 • **Nelson VanderHyden Award**
For contractor exemplifying high standards of professionalism and community involvement. Recognition award bestowed annually.

• 21473 •
Washtenaw Literacy
Pat Kessler, Sec.
5577 Whittaker Rd.
Ypsilanti, MI 48197
Phone: (734)879-1320
Phone: (734)769-0099
Fax: (734)879-1319
E-mail: washtenawliteracy@ypsilibrary.org
Home Page: http://washtenawliteracy.org

• 21474 • **Scholar Award**
For outstanding performance as literacy student. Recognition award bestowed annually.

• 21475 •
Water Environment Federation
William Bertera, Exec.Dir.
601 Wythe St.
Alexandria, VA 22314-1994
Phone: (703)684-2400
Phone: (703)684-2452
Toll-Free: 800-666-0206
Fax: (703)684-2492
E-mail: csc@wef.org
Home Page: http://www.wef.org

• 21476 • **Arthur Sidney Bedell Award**
Recognizes personal service to a Member Association. Applicants must be members of the Federation. A plaque is awarded.

• 21477 • **Canham Graduate Studies Scholarship**
To provide funding for a post-baccalaureate student in the water environment field. Application deadline is March 1. A monetary award of $2,500 is awarded annually. Recipients of the scholarship are expected to make a commitment to work in the environmental field for two years after completion of the degree.

• 21478 • **Charles Alvin Emerson Medal**
This award is presented to an individual whose contributions to the wastewater collection and treatment industry most deserves recognition. Nominees must be a members of a Federation Member Association. Particular emphasis is given to the nominee's involvement in the problems and activities of the Water Environment Federation, including the stimulation of membership, improving standards of techniques of wastewater treatment, water resource protection, and fostering fundamental research. Eight copies of the nomination Form; one page biography of the nominee; specific reasons for nomination (one page maximum) ; and any other supporting material required under criteria or that you feel would be helpful in the selection process must be submitted by April 1. Established in 1943.

• 21479 • **Citation of Excellence in Advertising**
Recognizes outstanding contribution to the water environment field through the effective and original presentation of equipment and services in a Federation periodical. Selection is based on the attention getting, information, reliability, simplicity, aesthetics, and recall. All advertisements appearing in Water Environment Federation periodicals are automatically eligible and considered for this award

• 21480 • **Collection System Award**
Recognizes contributions to the advancement of the state of the art wastewater collection. Water Environment Federation members in the areas of service must have been in any of the following areas: management, overall planning, operation and maintenance, facility design, education, training, or research are eligible. Six copies of nomination form; one page biography of the nominee; specific reasons for nomination (one page maximum); and any other supporting material required under criteria or that you feel would be helpful in the selection process must be submitted by April 1.

• 21481 • **George Bradley Gascoigne Medal**
To recognize outstanding contributions to the art of wastewater treatment plant operation through the successful solution of important and complicated operational problems, as described in a paper published in a Federation periodical or any member association publication. Members of the Federation are eligible. Established in 1943 in memory of George Bradley Gascoigne, a consultant from 1922-1940.

• 21482 • **George J. Schroepfer Medal**
Engineering consultants, municipal engineers, or industrial engineers who are professional engineers in responsible charge of the design of facilities for the conveyance, treatment or disposal of wastewater and/or treatment residues are eligible. Eight copies of the nomination form; one page biography of the nominee; specific reasons for nomination (one page maximum); and any other supporting material required under Criteria or that you feel would be helpful in the selection process must be submitted by April 1. See the above web site for additional information.

• 21483 • **George W. Burke, Jr. Award**
Encourages an active and effective safety program in municipal and industrial wastewater facilities. Applicants must meet criteria. See the above web site for additional details. A plaque is awarded annually. Member Associations should submit the name and a one-page biography of their selection. Nominations deadline is four months prior to the MA Annual Meeting Established in 1982 in honor of George W. Burke, Jr.

• 21484 • **Gordon Maskew Fair Medal**
Recognizes worthy accomplishments in the training and development of future engineers. Federation members are eligible. Nominations are accepted from Member Associations only. Eight copies of the nomination form; one page biography of the nominee; specific reasons for nomination (one page maximum); and any other supporting material required under Criteria or that you feel would be helpful in the selection process must be submitted by April 1. A medal is awarded annually. Established in 1967.

• 21485 • **Harrison Prescott Eddy Medal**
Recognizes research that makes a vital contribution to the existing knowledge of the fundamental principles or process of wastewater treatment, as comprehensively described and published in a federation periodical. Federation member engineers are eligible. Selection is based on articles published in a Federation periodical during any stated calendar year. A nomination form; specific reasons for nomination (one page maximum); and any other supporting material required under criteria or that you feel would be helpful in the selection process must be submitted. Established in 1943.

• 21486 • **Harry E. Schlenz Medal**
Recognizes an individual who takes up the banner of water environment public education and presents it to the public in a productive process. The contribution should be in the area of journalism, film or video production, or any other communication endeavor. Individuals whose principal employment are outside the water environment profession are eligible. Members of the Federation are not eligible. Eight copies of the nomination form; one page biography of the nominee; specific reasons for nomination (one page maximum); and any other supporting material required under criteria or that you feel would be helpful in the selection process must be submitted by April 1. Nominations are only accepted from Member Associations. Established in 1970 memory of Harry E. Schlenz, who served as Federation President in 1961-1962.

• 21487 • **Hazardous Waste Management Award**
Recognizes an individual for their efforts in promoting quality technical and/or management performance in activities and professionalism within and on behalf of the field of hazardous waste management. Members of the Water Environment Federation. Eight copies of nomination form; one page biography of the nominee; specific reasons for nomination (one page maximum); and any other supporting material re-

Awards are arranged in alphabetical order below their administering organizations

quired under criteria or that you feel would be helpful in the selection process must be submitted by April 1.

• 21488 • High School Science Fair National Award
Annual award of recognition.

• 21489 • Honorary Membership
Honorary membership is extended to persons who have proven their preeminence in the fields of activity encompassed by Federation objectives. The recipient of this honor shall be elected for life, be awarded a plaque by the Federation, pay no Federation dues, and receive, without cost, those publications of the Federation that the Board designates. Applicants shall be a person of acknowledged eminence in one or more fields of activity within the scope of the stated objectives of the Federation. A nomination form; one page biography of the nominee; specific reasons for nomination (one page maximum); and any other supporting material required under criteria or that you feel would be helpful in the selection process must be submitted. Nominations are accepted from member associations and the nominating committee. Eight copies of nomination material should reach the Water Environment Federation Awards Department by March 1.

• 21490 • Industrial Water Quality Achievement Award
Recognizes significant, lasting, and measurable excellence in water quality improvement or in the prevention of water quality degradation as demonstrated by innovative design and operation of an industrial wastewater, pretreatment or source prevention program. Corporations and, if applicable, their engineering firms are eligible. Visit the above web site for program criteria. Six copies of the nomination form; letter of nomination originating from an officer of the Member Association; letter of acknowledgment of nomination from a responsible member of the potential award recipient must be submitted by April 1.

• 21491 • Innovative Technology Awards
Recognizes associate members who have introduced new, innovative products or services related to the construction, operation, or maintenance of water pollution control facilities. Awards are presented annually in the following categories: instrumentation, process equipment, collection systems, and solids handling/disposal. Selection is based on the products or services demonstration of an n innovative aspect utilizing new ideas, methods, alterations and/or unique changes from existing systems. Six copies of nomination form; documentation stating specific reasons for nomination; supporting documentation required under criteria; and detailed summary data showing significant reduction in micro pollutants, chlorinated hydrocarbons, pesticides, metals, or hazardous compounds by the products or services, method of wastewater treatment or sludge handling/disposal that maintains efficiency and results in lower capital, operating or maintenance costs as a result of using the products or services must be submitted by April 1.

• 21492 • Jack Edward McKee Medal
Recognizes a publication that demonstrates a significant contribution to groundwater science or engineering in the context of an applied problem or basic scientific inquiry, as described in a paper presented in a WEF publication. A nomination form; specific reasons for nomination (one page maximum); and any other supporting material required under criteria or that you feel would be helpful in the selection process must be submitted. Established in honor of Jack Edward McKee, the 1962-63 president of the Water Environment Federation.

• 21493 • Laboratory Analyst Excellence Award
To recognize individuals for outstanding performance, professionalism, and contributions to the water quality analysis profession. Candidates must be members of the Federation who are employed at an educational facility laboratory, industrial, commercial, or municipal laboratory that performs wastewater-related analysis, and must have direct analytical responsibilities. The award consists of a plaque suitably inscribed with the recipient's name and is presented by a Federation representative at the Member Association annual meeting. Established by the Board of Control in 1993.

• 21494 • Member Association Safety Awards
Recognizes the success of a safety program in local wastewater works. Awards are presented annually to Member Associations in the following categories: Member Associations with membership of less than 400; Member Associations with membership of 400 to 1000; and Member Associations with membership of 1,000 or more. Six copies of the nomination form; one page biography of the nominee; specific reasons for the nomination (one page maximum); and any other supporting material required under criteria or that you feel would be helpful in the selection process must be submitted by April 1.

• 21495 • Outstanding Achievement in Water Quality Improvement Award
Recognizes the water quality improvement program that best demonstrates significant, lasting, and measurable excellence in water quality improvement or in prevention of water quality degradation in a region, basin, or water body. The program must lie within the boundaries of one or more Member Associations sponsoring the nomination. A program is eligible during a three-year period immediately after documented results become a matter of public record. Renomination is permitted at any time during this three-year period. Nominations must be submitted by a sponsor to a Member Association within whose boundary the head office of the sponsor is located. The sponsor should be the entity with the greatest and most direct responsibility for successful completion of the program. Awarded annually. Nomination form; one page biography of the nominee; specific reasons for nomination (one page maximum) ; and any other supporting material required under criteria or that you feel would be helpful in the selection process must be submitted by April 1.

• 21496 • Philip F. Morgan Medal
Recognizes valuable contributions to the in-plant study and solution of an operational problem. A medal is given in two categories: (1) work accomplished in plants serving more than 5,000 people, and (2) work accomplished in plants serving less than 5,000 people. Nominees must be members of a Federation Member Association. Nominations must demonstrate originality, significance, comprehensiveness, effort, and the verification of an idea. The solution should involve the use of innovative technological methods, be generally applicable, and increase plant efficiency. Publication of a paper is not required, but supporting evidence must accompany each nomination. Eight copies of the nomination form; one page biography of the nominee; specific reasons for nomination (one page maximum); and any other supporting material required under criteria or that you feel would be helpful in the selection process must be submitted by April 1. Established in1963 in honor of Philip F. Morgan, who served with distinction as professor of sanitary engineering at the State University of Iowa from 1948 to 1961.

• 21497 • Public Education Award
Recognizes significant accomplishments in promoting awareness and understanding of water environment issues among the general public, through the development and implementation of public education programs. Only Federation members are eligible. Awards are given in the categories of Individual, Member Association, and Other. Individual Recognizes an individual Federation member. Member Association - Recognizes a Member Association. Other - Recognizes organizations, groups of individuals, events, campaigns, or other persons or efforts that make a significant contribution to the public education effort, but that do not fit one of the other categories. The criteria is the same for each category. Which is documented achievements of public education activities in the water environment field; identification and description of exceptional efforts to educate the public on water environment issues; the activity or effort must have been implemented within the two years immediately prior to nomination. Specific programs are eligible for nomination only once. A detailed narrative description of the activities or efforts, including the objective and results; ten copies of associated program materials; documented evidence of the program's accomplishment must be submitted by April 1. Associated program materials include nomination form; one page biography of the nominee specific reasons for nomination (one page maximum); and any other supporting material required under criteria or that you feel would be helpful in the selection process. Established in 1990.

• 21498 • Richard S. Engelbrecht International Activities Service Award
Recognizes sustained and significant contributions to the furtherance and improvement of the activities of the Water Environment Federation in the international field. Applicants must be members of the Water Environment Federation (the award is not restricted to members outside North America); must demonstrate sustained and ongoing contributions, over a period of not

less than 5 years, towards the furtherance and improvement of the activities of the Federation in the international field. Service should primarily reflect Federation activities outside North America. Nomination Form, eight copies of a one page biography of the nominee to include membership history and general details of their participation in committee and other Federation activities; specific details concerning the nominee's activities in the international field and the benefits derived or to be derived by the Federation as a whole from these activities must be submitted by April 1. Nominations are accepted from Federation Members with the endorsement of the appropriate Member Association and by Member Associations. The award consists of a plaque suitably inscribed with the recipient's name.

• 21499 • **Thomas R. Camp Medal**
Recognizes a unique application of basic research or fundamental principles through the design or development of a wastewater collection or treatment system. Members of Federation Member Association are eligible. Nominations must demonstrate a unique application of basic research or fundamental principles through the design or development of a wastewater collection or treatment system. Eight copies of complete project description; nomination form; one page biography of the nominee; specific reasons for nomination (one page maximum); and any other supporting material required under criteria or that you feel would be helpful in the selection process must be submitted before April 1. A medal is awarded annually. Established in 1964 in honor of Thomas R. Camp, an outstanding educator, consultant, and writer.

• 21500 • **Willem Rudolfs Medal**
Recognizes noteworthy accomplishments in any aspect of industrial waste control. Members of a Federation Member Association are eligible. Article published in a Federation periodical in the calendar year immediately preceding consideration are eligible. A nomination form; specific reasons for nomination (one page maximum); and any other supporting material required under criteria or that you feel would be helpful in the selection process must be submitted. Established in 1966.

• 21501 • **William D. Hatfield Award**
Recognizes outstanding performance and professionalism. Member associations control the selection process. Nominees must be members of the Federation falling within the general criteria as described to each member association. A plaque is awarded. Established in honor of Dr. William D. Hatfield.

• 21502 • **William J. Orchard Medal**
Established in 1961 to honor William J. Orchard. Nominations are made by the Executive Committee. Awarded when merited.

• 21503 •
Water Environment Research Foundation
635 Slaters Ln., Ste. 300
Alexandria, VA 22314-1994
Phone: (703)684-2470
Fax: (703)299-0742
E-mail: werf@werf.org
Home Page: http://www.werf.org

• 21504 • **Paul L. Busch Award**
For innovation in applied water quality research. Awarded annually.

• 21505 •
Wayne State University
Merrill-Palmer Institute
71 E Ferry Ave.
Detroit, MI 48202
Phone: (313)872-1790
Fax: (313)875-0947
E-mail: mpi@wayne.edu
Home Page: http://www.mpi.wayne.edu

• 21506 • **Merrill-Palmer Citation Award**
Recognizes distinction in the field of child development.

• 21507 •
Wedding and Portrait Photographers International
Valerie Stever, Dir.
1312 Lincoln Blvd.
PO Box 2003
Santa Monica, CA 90406-2003
Phone: (310)451-0090
Fax: (310)395-9058
E-mail: jobrien@rfpublishing.com
Home Page: http://www.wppinow.com/index2.tml

Formerly: (1998) Wedding Photographers of America; Wedding Photographers International.

• 21508 • **World of Wedding Photography and Portrait Of Excellence**
To recognize outstanding wedding photographers and to advance the art of wedding and portrait photography. The competition is open to members and non-members. Awards of Excellence are given in two competitions: 16x20 Print Competition - the deadline for six entries per entrant is January 31. Monetary and other prizes are awarded to first through third place in eleven wedding and portrait categories: Bride or Groom Together, Bride or Groom Alone, Bridal Party, Engagement, Special Effects, Wedding Photojournalism, and Special Event; child, high school senior. individual; group; animal/pets; and Wedding Album Competition - judging is based on storytelling excellence. Up to two albums per wedding story may be entered with a limit of two wedding stories (up to four albums) by February 15. Monetary and other prizes are awarded to first through third place in two categories: Intermediate and Advanced. Awarded annually at the convention. Established in 1981.

• 21509 •
Weiser Chamber of Commerce
Mrs. Sheri Shoemaker, Chamber Coor.
309 State St.
Weiser, ID 83672-2530
Phone: (208)414-0452
Fax: (208)414-1909
E-mail: weisercc@ruralnetwork.net
Home Page: http://www.ruralnetwork.net/~weisercc

• 21510 • **Nick Speropolus Sportsmanship Award**
For a graduating senior. Scholarship awarded annually.

• 21511 •
The Welch Foundation
Norbert Dittrich, Pres.
5555 San Felipe St., Ste. 1900
Houston, TX 77056-2730
Phone: (713)961-9884
Fax: (713)961-5168
Home Page: http://www.welch1.org

Formerly: (1996) Robert A. Welch Foundation.

• 21512 • **Welch Award in Chemistry**
To encourage basic chemical research and to recognize the value of chemical research contributions for the benefit of mankind. Nominations are solicited from appropriate scientific organizations, and nominations received from appropriate organizations and individuals are considered (no self nominations). Nominations due February 1. A monetary prize of $300,000, a gold medal, and a certificate are awarded annually at a dinner in honor of the recipient. Established in 1972 under the terms of the will of Robert Alonzo Welch.

• 21513 •
Welsh Pony and Cob Society of America
Lisa L. Landis, Exec.Sec.-Treas.
PO Box 2977
Winchester, VA 22604
Phone: (540)667-6195
Fax: (540)667-3766
E-mail: info@welshpony.org
Home Page: http://www.welshpony.org

Formerly: (1986) Welsh Pony Society of America.

• 21514 • **National High Score Awards**
To recognize outstanding ponies and cobs, and encourage show participation. Some categories include: fillies - two and under; colts two and under; mares - three and over; stallions - three and over; geldings; English pleasure; Western pleasure; pleasure driving; roadster; and hunter. Members of the WPCSA are eligible. High Score Ribbons are awarded annually.

Awards are arranged in alphabetical order below their administering organizations

• 21515 •
Welsh Society of Philadelphia
PO Box 7287
St. Davids, PA 19087-7287
Phone: (215)656-3870
Home Page: http://members.macconnect.com/users/d/dalex

Formerly: (1980) Welsh Society of Philadelphia.

• 21516 • **Robert Morris Award**
For recognition of a person of Welsh descent who, by outstanding achievements, has brought public recognition of the Welsh heritage. Candidates are nominated by the acting committee of the society. A gold medal and a plaque are presented annually on the Saturday nearest March 1, St. David's Day, where the honoree is a speaker at the annual banquet. Established in 1954 in memory of Robert Morris, the financier of the American Revolution and one of the early members of the society. Formerly: (1976) Welsh Society Medallion.

• 21517 •
West Coast Book Prize Society
Sherry McGarvie, Project Coordinator
207 W Hastings St., No. 902
Vancouver, BC, Canada V6B 1H7
Phone: (604)687-2405
Fax: (604)669-3701
E-mail: info@bcbookprizes.ca
Home Page: http://www.bcbookprizes.ca

• 21518 • **Bill Duthie Booksellers' Choice**
For recognition of the best book published in British Columbia. Entries are judged on initiative, content, presentation, and quality. A monetary prize of $2,000 is awarded annually to the publisher. Established in 1985.

• 21519 • **Sheila A. Egoff Children's Prize**
For recognition of the best children's book by an author and/or illustrator who has lived in British Columbia for three of the last five years. The book may have been published anywhere in the world. A monetary prize of $2,000 is awarded annually. Established in 1985. Formerly: Children's Book Prize.

• 21520 • **Hubert Evans Nonfiction Prize**
To recognize the author of the best original work of nonfiction, including philosophy, belles lettres, biography, and history. The writer must have lived in British Columbia for three of the last five years, although the book may have been published anywhere in the world. A monetary prize of $2,000 is awarded annually. Established in 1985.

• 21521 • **Dorothy Livesay Poetry Prize**
For recognition of the best book of poetry by a writer who has lived in British Columbia for three of the last five years. The book may have been published anywhere in the world. A monetary prize of $2,000 is awarded annually. Established in 1985. Formerly: BC Prize for Poetry.

• 21522 • **Roderick Haig-Brown Regional Prize**
To recognize the author of the book that contributes most to the enjoyment and understanding of British Columbia. Eligible books may deal with any aspect of the province, including the people, history, geography, and oceanography. The writer must have lived in British Columbia for three of the last five years. The book may have been published anywhere in the world. A monetary prize of $2,000 is awarded annually. Established in 1985.

• 21523 • **Ethel Wilson Fiction Prize**
For recognition of the best work of fiction by an author who has lived in British Columbia for three of the last five years. The book can be published anywhere in the world. A monetary prize of $2,000 is awarded annually. Established in 1985.

• 21524 •
West Coast Classical Ballet Society
Golden Koscuik, VP
1365 Westwood Blvd.
Los Angeles, CA 90024
Phone: (310)477-6414
Phone: (310)386-3407
Fax: (310)265-0938

• 21525 • **Legends of Dance Awards**
For community leadership in dance specific work. Scholarship awarded annually.

• 21526 •
West Michigan Tourist Association
Linda Singer, Pres.
950 28th St. SE, Ste. E-200
Grand Rapids, MI 49508
Phone: (616)245-2217
Toll-Free: 800-442-2084
Fax: (616)245-2760
E-mail: travel@wmta.org
Home Page: http://www.wmta.org

• 21527 • **Hospitality Award**
For outstanding service/contribution to industry. Recognition award bestowed annually.

• 21528 •
West Texas Press Association
Barbara Craig Kelly, Sec.-Treas.
W Texas Press Assn.
706 SW Tenth
Perryton, TX 79070
Phone: (806)435-9770
Phone: (806)435-3631
Fax: (806)435-2420
E-mail: secretary@wtpa.org
Home Page: http://www.wtpa.org

• 21529 • **Bob Craig Memorial Scholarship**
For print media majors. Scholarship awarded annually.

• 21530 •
West Virginia Children's Book Award
Jeanne Goodman, Chairperson
% West Virginia University
PO Box 6122
Morgantown, WV 26506-6122
Phone: (304)293-4769
Phone: (304)291-3608
Fax: (304)293-3802
E-mail: chair@wvcba.org
Home Page: http://www.wvcba.org

Formerly: West Virginia University Reading Center.

• 21531 • **West Virginia Children's Book Award**
To recognize outstanding current fiction for children in grades 3 through 6 and to enrich their lives by encouraging reading. After reading and/or listening to at least three books from the master list, children in registered schools vote for their favorite book from a master reading list. The WVCBA Committee is responsible for selecting books to appear on an annual master list. Only fiction books in print, published within the last three years in the United States, are considered. A certificate and an invitation to come to Morgantown are awarded annually. Established in 1984.

• 21532 •
Westchester Library Association
Srivalli Rao, Sec.
% Srivalli Rao, Sec.
Mercy College, White Plains
277 Martine Ave.
White Plains, NY 10601
Phone: (914)948-3666
Fax: (914)948-6732
E-mail: srao@mercy.edu
Home Page: http://www.wliba.org

• 21533 • **Washington Irving Children's Book Choice Award**
To honor Westchester authors of children's books, and to encourage reading and reading aloud throughout the county. Candidates for the awards are selected by a committee of school and public librarians based on a combination of literary quality and appeal to a range of ages. All titles published during the qualifying years by an author living in Westchester County are eligible. A medal is awarded to the author and a sticker is placed on the book biennially. Established in 1982. For more information contact Jane Marino, Scarsdale Public Library, Scarsdale, NY 10583.

• 21534 •
Western Associated Modelers
Doug Barton, Pres.
160 Park Ave.
Woodland, CA 95695
Phone: (530)662-6469
E-mail: yoloflo@aol.com
Home Page: http://www.wamsite.com

Awards are arranged in alphabetical order below their administering organizations

• 21535 • **Overall Control Line Flyers Champion**
To recognize the member who has placed in at least three of the events and has the most place points. Entrants in Control Line Events are eligible. A trophy is awarded annually at the end of a year's flying. Established in 1957. Affiliated with NAMBA International.

• 21536 •
Western Association of Map Libraries
Julie Hoff, Business Mgr.
Arizona State Library & Archives
1700 W Washington
Phoenix, AZ 85007
Phone: (602)542-4343
Fax: (602)542-4400
E-mail: jhoff@lib.az.us
Home Page: http://www.waml.org

• 21537 • **Executive Committee Award**
To recognize outstanding achievements in map librarianship. Members are eligible. Winners are determined by the Executive Committee. A plaque is awarded on a special occasion. Established in 1982.

• 21538 • **Honorary Lifetime Membership**
To recognize outstanding achievements in map librarianship. Members are eligible. Winners are determined by the Executive Committee. A plaque is awarded on a special occasion. Established in 1982.

• 21539 •
Western Building Material Association
Casey Voorhees, Exec.Dir.
PO Box 1699
Olympia, WA 98507
Phone: (360)943-3054
Fax: (360)943-1219
E-mail: casey@wbma.org
Home Page: http://www.wbma.org

• 21540 • **Distinguished Dealer of the Year**
For service to community, state, federal, industry. Recognition award bestowed annually.

• 21541 •
Western Canada Wilderness Committee
Sue Fox, Communications Dir.
227 Abbott St.
Vancouver, BC, Canada V6B 2K7
Phone: (604)683-8220
Toll-Free: 800-661-9453
Fax: (604)683-8229
E-mail: info@wildernesscommittee.org
Home Page: http://
www.wildernesscommittee.org

• 21542 • **Eugene Rogers Award**
Recognizes a wilderness defender. Awarded annually.

• 21543 •
Western Economic Association International
Robert Barro, Pres.
7400 Center Ave., Ste. 109
Huntington Beach, CA 92647-3039
Phone: (714)898-3222
Fax: (714)891-6715
E-mail: info@weainternational.org
Home Page: http://
www.weainternational.org

• 21544 • ***Economic Inquiry* Article Award**
Annual award of recognition. Winners are chosen by *Economic Inquiry* editors.

• 21545 •
Western-English Trade Association
Glenda Chipps, Exec.Dir.
451 E 58th Ave., No. 4323
Denver, CO 80216-8468
Phone: (303)295-2001
Fax: (303)295-6108
E-mail: weta@netway.net
Home Page: http://www.wetaonline.com

Formerly: (2003) Western and English Manufacturers Association.

• 21546 • **In the Tradition of the American West Award**
For recognition of a company or individual that has made an impact on or outstanding contribution to the Western/English apparel and tack industry. Nominees from outside the industry are considered for the award. The winner must attend the award ceremonies. A plaque is presented annually at the conference in July. Established in 1980. Formerly: In the Tradition of the American Cowboy Award.

• 21547 • **Special Recognition Award**
To honor individuals or organizations whose efforts have benefited the Western and English apparel and tack industry. Nominees from outside the industry are considered for the award. The winner must attend the award ceremonies. A plaque is presented annually at the conference in July. Established in 1981.

• 21548 •
Western Forestry and Conservation Association
Richard A. Zabel, Exec.Dir.
4033 SW Canyon Rd.
Portland, OR 97221
Phone: (503)226-4562
Fax: (503)226-2515
E-mail: richard@westernforestry.org
Home Page: http://www.westernforestry.org

• 21549 • **Western Forestry Award for Current Achievement**
To recognize individuals for significant service to western North American forestry and to inspire others to greater performance. A plaque is awarded annually when merited. Established in 1961.

• 21550 • **Western Forestry Award for Lifetime Service**
To recognize individuals for significant service to western North American forestry through a lifetime of service and to inspire others to greater performance. A plaque is awarded annually when merited. Established in 1951.

• 21551 •
Western Kentucky Construction Association
Michael B. Gerescher, Exec.VP
PO Box 1059
2201 McCracken Blvd.
Paducah, KY 42002-1059
Phone: (270)744-6261
Fax: (270)744-9522
E-mail: information@wkca.org
Home Page: http://www.wkca.org

• 21552 • **Construction Person of the Year**
For individual making significant contribution to construction industry. Recognition award bestowed annually.

• 21553 •
Western North Carolina Historical Association
Rebecca Lamb, Exec.Dir.
283 Victoria Rd.
Asheville, NC 28801
Phone: (828)253-9231
Fax: (828)253-5518
E-mail: smh@wnchistory.org
Home Page: http://www.wnchistory.org

• 21554 • **Western North Carolina Historical Association Achievement Award**
For general services deemed outstanding. Recognition award bestowed annually.

• 21555 • **Thomas Wolfe Literary Award**
For outstanding publication about western North Carolina. Monetary award bestowed annually.

• 21556 •
Western Political Science Association
Ron Schmidt Jr., Pres.
6000 J St.
Sacramento, CA 95819-6016
Phone: (916)278-7418
Fax: (916)278-6959
E-mail: rschmidt@csulb.edu
Home Page: http://www.csus.edu/org/wpsa

• 21557 • **Western Political Science Association Awards**
To recognize outstanding unpublished papers in the field of political science. The following awards are presented: Dissertation Award - $250 for the best doctoral dissertation completed at a university within the regional groupings of the WPSA between July 1 and June 30 of the previous academic year; Pi Sigma Alpha Award - $250 for the best paper presented at the last WPSA annual meeting; WPSA Women and

Politics Awards - $250 for an outstanding paper on women and politics; WPSA Best Paper Award on Latino/Latina Politics - $250 for an outstanding paper on Latino/Latina politics and its relative aspects; and Award by Committee on the Status of Blacks - $250 for an outstanding paper discussing issues and problems that concern most Black Americans; Political Research Quarterly Best Article Award - $1000 for the best article published; Charles Redd Award - $250 for best paper on the politics of the American West.

• 21558 •
Western Reserve Historical Society
Tamera Brown, Dir. of External Affairs
10825 E Blvd.
Cleveland, OH 44106
Phone: (216)721-5722
Fax: (216)721-8934
E-mail: preymann@wrhs.org
Home Page: http://www.wrhs.org

• 21559 • **Affirmative Action and Equal Employment Opportunity Award**
To recognize individuals and organizations that have distinguished themselves in the area of affirmative action. A plaque is awarded annually at the Martin Luther King, Jr. Celebration Program. Established in 1991 in memory of Dr. Martin Luther King, Jr. Administered by the African American Archives Auxiliary of the Society.

• 21560 • **Corporate Leadership Award**
For recognition of outstanding corporate leadership in Cleveland. A plaque is awarded annually at the Martin Luther King, Jr. Celebration Program. Established in 1991 in memory of Dr. Martin Luther King, Jr. Administered by the African American Archives Auxiliary of the Society.

• 21561 • **Social Justice Award**
To recognize individuals and organizations that have distinguished themselves in the area of social justice as promulgated by Dr. Martin Luther King, Jr. A plaque is awarded annually at the Martin Luther King, Jr. Celebration Program. Established in 1991 in memory of Dr. Martin Luther King, Jr. Administered by the African American Archives Auxiliary of the Society.

• 21562 • **Youth Leadership Award**
For recognition of outstanding youth in Cleveland. A plaque is awarded annually at the Martin Luther King, Jr. Celebration Program. Established in 1991 in memory of Dr. Martin Luther King, Jr. Administered by the African American Archives Auxiliary of the Society.

• 21563 •
Western Snow Conference
Randall Osterhuber, Documents Mgr.
PO Box 810
Soda Springs, CA 95728
Phone: (530)426-0318
E-mail: randall@sierra.net
Home Page: http://www.westernsnowconference.org/WSC.htm

• 21564 • **JE Church Award**
For research in snow or hydrologic sciences at the university level within conference area. Recognition award bestowed annually.

• 21565 •
Western Society of Engineers
Dennis Lamont, Pres.
4513 Lincoln Ave., Ste. 213
Lisle, IL 60532-1290
Phone: (630)724-9770
Fax: (630)241-0142
E-mail: wse@wsechicago.org
Home Page: http://www.wsechicago.org

• 21566 • **Octave Chanute Medal**
To recognize the author of the best paper published on any aspect of engineering by a member of WSE. Papers may be submitted by March 1. A bronze medal with the likeness of Octave Chanute, an engineer who experimented with gliders, and a certificate are awarded annually. Established in 1901 by Octave Chanute, former president of the society.

• 21567 • **Charles Ellet Award**
To recognize an individual who has made outstanding progress in his professional development. Members of the society who are under 35 years of age are eligible. The deadline for nominations is March 1. The award consists of a monetary prize of $50, a certificate, and the name of the recipient is inscribed on a silver loving cup. Awarded annually. Established in 1929 by E.C. Shuman in memory of Charles Ellet, a young engineer of Civil War days.

• 21568 • **President's Club**
To honor members who help to strengthen the Society through the sponsorship of new members. A personal engraved President's Club Plaque and a permanent plate on the master WSE plaque hung in WSE's headquarters are awarded annually. Established in 1974.

• 21569 • **Service Awards**
To recognize those members who have given their personal time, service, and cooperation to the various activities of the society. Awarded at the society's annual Installation Award dinner. Established in 1951.

• 21570 •
Western States Arts Federation
Anthony Radich, Exec.Dir.
1743 Wazee St., Ste. 300
Denver, CO 80202
Phone: (303)629-1166
Toll-Free: 888-562-7232
Fax: (303)629-9717
E-mail: staff@westaf.org
Home Page: http://www.westaf.org

• 21571 • **Western States Book Awards**
To recognize and promote writers of exceptional merit living in the West; to encourage effective production, marketing and distribution of quality books published in the West; and to increase sales and critical attention for quality literary works from the West. Unpublished works of fiction, creative nonfiction, and poetry are considered. Works must be written by authors living in the member states of Alaska, Arizona, California, Colorado, Idaho, Montana, Nevada, New Mexico, Oregon, Utah, Washington, or Wyoming and must be accepted for publication by publishers located in those states. Manuscripts must be submitted by the publisher and must be scheduled for publication in fall of the award year Monetary awards of $5,000 for authors and $5,000 for their respective publishers are presented annually. Technical assistance in production, marketing, distribution, and promotion of the winning titles are included. Established in 1984. Supported by the Crane Duplicating Service, Inc., and the National Endowment for the Arts.

• 21572 •
Western Women Professional Bowlers
Mrs. Laura Hardeman, Sec.
938 Redbud Rd.
Chula Vista, CA 91910
E-mail: wwpb@wwpb.com
Home Page: http://www.wwpb.com

• 21573 • **Bowler of the Year**
To recognize the bowling achievements during the tournament year. Awarded annually with a plaque and free membership the following year. Established in 1976.

• 21574 • **Rookie of the Year**
To recognize the bowling achievements during the tournament year. Awarded annually with a plaque and free membership the following year. Established in 1976.

• 21575 •
Western Writers of America
James A. Cratchfield, Sec.-Treas.
1012 Fair St.
Franklin, TN 37064-2718
Phone: (615)791-1444
Phone: (307)327-5465
Fax: (615)791-1444
E-mail: tncratch@aol.com
Home Page: http://www.westernwriters.org

• 21576 • **Spur Awards**
For recognition of excellence in western fiction and nonfiction and poetry. Awards are given in the following categories: Best Western Novel, Best Novel of the West, Best Original Paperback Novel, Best Western Nonfiction Book Historical (to 1900), Best Western Nonfiction Book Contemporary (1900 to present), Beat Western Nonfiction - Biography, Best Western Juvenile Fiction, Best Western Juvenile Nonfiction, Best Western Short Fiction, Best Western Short Nonfiction, Best Western Poetry, Best Western TV/Movie Script (fiction),Best Western TV/Movie Documentary (nonfiction), Story Teller Award and the Medicine Pipe Bearer's Award - for the best first novel. Any author or publishing house may submit only one entry per category of work that was published during the year with the ex-

ception of the Medicine Pipe Bearer's Award. The entry deadline is December 31. Nonmembers of WWA may also enter. Plaques with bronze spurs are awarded annually. The Medicine Pipe Bearers honoree receives a medicine pipe. Established in 1953. Formerly: (1983) Golden Spur Awards.

• 21577 • Owen Wister Award
For recognition of outstanding contributions to the legends and history of the West. A statuette of an American Bison and a monetary prize of $500 are awarded annually. Established in 1961. Formerly known as the Levi Strauss Saddleman Award. Formerly: (1983) Golden Saddleman Award.

• 21578 •
Westerners International
Donald W. Reeves, Sec.
1700 NE 63rd St.
Oklahoma City, OK 73111
Toll-Free: 800-541-4650
E-mail: wihomeranch@aol.com
Home Page: http://www.westerners-intl.org

• 21579 • Co-Founders Book Award
For recognition of Westerner members who author books about the American West. Authors of nonfiction that is not self-published, is a minimum of 96 pages, and copyrighted during the year of entry are eligible. Entries must be submitted by April 30. A monetary prize of $250, a plaque, and a certificate are awarded for the best book in regular format. Awarded annually at the Western History Association Conference. Formerly: Ray A. Billington Book Award.

• 21580 • Philip A. Danielson Award
To encourage Westerner members to write their talks given to Westerner Corrals. Any talk, published or not published, given by a Westerner member at a Westerner Corral during the year it is entered is eligible. Entries must be submitted by April 30. Monetary prizes of $100, "Old Joe" plaques, and certificates are awarded annually at the Western History Association Conference. Sponsored by Philip A. Danielson, who set up a fund at the University of Pacific.

• 21581 • Heads Up Award
To recognize Westerners' Corrals for active programs that promote preservation of knowledge of the American West. Entries must be submitted by April 30. Three Corrals are honored annually at the Western History Association Conference. Two US Corrals and one foreign (overseas)corrals are Honored. Established in 1973.

• 21582 • Coke Wood Award
For recognition of the best monograph or journal article on the topic of the American West. Active or corresponding members of a Westerner Corral are eligible. Entries must be submitted by May 31. A monetary prize of $100, a "Little Old Joe" plaque, and a certificate are awarded annually at the Western History Association Conference. Established in 1986 by E Clampus Vitus chapters in the San Francisco bay area in honor of Coke Wood, a former member of Stockton and San Francisco Westerner Corrals and also a member of E Clampus Vitus.

• 21583 •
Westerville Area Chamber of Commerce
Janet Tressler-Davis, Pres./CEO
99 Commerce Park Dr.
Westerville, OH 43082
Phone: (614)882-8917
Fax: (614)882-2085
E-mail: info@westervillechamber.com
Home Page: http://www.westervillechamber.com

• 21584 • Outstanding Business Person of the Year
For involvement in business and the community. Recognition award bestowed annually.

• 21585 •
Westminster Kennel Club
Peter R. Van Brunt, Pres.
149 Madison Ave., Ste. 803
New York, NY 10016-6713
Phone: (212)213-3165
Fax: (212)213-3270
E-mail: write@wkcpr.org
Home Page: http://www.westminsterkennelclub.org

• 21586 • Best in Show
To recognize the best dog or bitch in the Westminster Kennel Club's Annual All Breed Dog Show. Entries are based on the following: each dog must have one U.S. championship point, or be a Champion of record (under American Kennel Club rules). A silver plated engraved Revere Bowl is awarded annually. Established in 1907.

• 21587 • Best of Breed or Best of Variety of Breed
For each Breed or Variety of Breed, dogs must have AKC approval as purebreds and fulfill other requirements of eligibility under WKC/AKC rules. A sterling silver medal is awarded annually for each breed or variety entered and present. Established in 1877.

• 21588 • Group Trophies
To recognize excellence by groups. A silver-plated trophy is given for each of the following groups: Sporting, Hound, Working, Terrier, Toy, Non-Sporting, and Herding. In addition, the McGivern Challenge Bowl is given for the Sporting Group; The St. Hubert's Giralda Trophy for the Hound Group; The Louis F. Bishop, III Memorial Trophy for the Working Group; The William A. Rockefeller Trophy for the Terrier Group; The Walter M. Jeffords, Jr. Trophy for the Toy Group; The James F. Stebbins Trophy for the Non-Sporting Group; and the Strathglass Trophy for the Herding Group.

• 21589 • James Mortimer Memorial Silver Plated Trophy
To encourage American breeders to breed their own dogs rather than import them from elsewhere. A sterling silver trophy is awarded for Best in Show, if American-bred. For permanent possession, the honor must be won five times by the same owner. A sterling silver plaque is awarded for each win. Established in 1942.

• 21590 •
Westport Historical Society
Sheila C. O'Neill, Exec.Dir.
25 Avery Pl.
Westport, CT 06880
Phone: (203)222-1424
Fax: (203)221-0981
E-mail: info@westporthistory.org
Home Page: http://westporthistory.org

• 21591 • Orpherians
For high school choir member. Monetary award bestowed annually.

• 21592 •
Wexner Center for the Arts
Ohio State University
1871 N. High St.
Columbus, OH 43210-1393
Phone: (614)292-3535
Fax: (614)292-3369
E-mail: jmzimmer@magnus.acs.ohio-state.edu
Home Page: http://www.wexarts.org

• 21593 • Wexner Graduate Fellows
Awards are given to up to 20 individuals annually who plan to enter graduate programs in the rabbinate, Jewish communal service, Jewish education, Jewish studies, or the cantorate in preparation for professional leadership careers in the North American Jewish community. Only North Americans who have not yet entered qualifying graduate programs are eligible to apply. Fellows must engage in full-time graduate study without outside employment and exhibit leadership achievement and Jewish commitment. Fellowships cover full tuition and academic fees plus generous living stipends and annual leadership institutes. Applications are due February 15. Awarded annually. Established in 1987 by Leslie H. Wexner and his mother, Bella Wexner.

• 21594 • Wexner Prize
To recognize an individual in any artistic field whose highly original and influential work has consistently challenged convention. An engraved sculpture and monetary prize of $50,000 are awarded annually. Established in 1991.

• 21595 •
Wheelchair Sports, USA
Dennis Runyan, COO
1668 320th Way
Earlham, IA 50072
Phone: (515)833-2450
Fax: (515)833-2450
E-mail: wsusa@aol.com
Home Page: http://www.wsusa.org

Formerly: (1995) National Wheelchair Athletic Association.

• 21596 • **Athletes of the Year**
To recognize outstanding athletes in wheelchair sports. Awarded annually. Formerly: NWAA Athletes of the Year.

• 21597 • **Hall of Fame**
For recognition of a wheelchair athlete. The Hall of Fame is located on the campus of the Roosevelt Sports Center in Warm Springs, Georgia. The following criteria are considered: consistency - the athlete must demonstrate a high degree of skill in National Games competition by virtue of consistent winnings or high places in one or more events throughout his or her life; excellence the athlete's record must demonstrate excellence by record-producing performances in a particular class event; versatility - because of the nature of wheelchair sports, which permits athletes to specialize in a variety of events, the athlete's skills must be demonstrated by excellent performance in more than one area of athletic endeavor and regarded as concrete evidence of his or her versatility; and the athlete's durability is regarded as a significant factor in selection. The nominee whose record meets any of the foregoing criteria and who has also demonstrated a concern and commitment to advancing the wheelchair sports movement in the form of unselfish service to it should receive additional weight for selection. Awarded annually. Established in 1970. Formerly: NWAA Hall of Fame.

• 21598 •
Whirly-Girls - International Women Helicopter Pilots
Teen Corey, Pres.
PO Box 7446
Menlo Park, CA 94026
Phone: (650)462-1441
Fax: (650)323-3840
E-mail: whirlygirls@aol.com
Home Page: http://www.whirlygirls.org

• 21599 • **Doris Muellen Whirly-Girls Scholarship**
To assist a financially deserving woman to further her career in the helicopter industry through add-on ratings to her helicopter license. Members of the Whirly-Girls who show financial need and commitment to aviation are eligible. A scholarship of $6,000 is awarded annually. Established in 1967 in memory of Doris Muellen, No. 84, who was fatally injured in an airplane accident in 1967. Doris personified the high standards and ideals of women in aviation.

• 21600 • **Whirly-Girls Helicopter Flight Training Scholarship**
To assist a deserving woman to acquire her initial helicopter rating. A woman who currently has an airplane, balloon, or glider pilot license, and shows financial need and commitment to aviation is eligible. A scholarship of $6,000 is awarded annually. Established in 1978 by the Whirly-Girls Men's Auxiliary in memory of different individuals each year who have contributed to the Whirly-Girls and the Helicopter Industry. Formerly: (1995) Memorial Scholarship.

• 21601 •
White House Correspondents' Association
Julia Whiston, Exec.Dir.
1920 N St. NW, Ste. 300
Washington, DC 20036
Phone: (202)452-4836
E-mail: whca@starpower.net
Home Page: http://www.whca.net

• 21602 • **Aldo Beckman Award**
Recognizes repeated excellence in White House coverage, with a single award for either a print or broadcast journalist. Entries may be made in the form of clippings, original material, wire service printouts, photocopies, or broadcast scripts. A monetary prize of $1,000 is awarded annually. Established to recognize Aldo Beckman, the award winning correspondent for the Chicago Tribune.

• 21603 • **Edgar A. Poe Award**
Recognizes excellence in coverage of news of national or regional significance, with a single award for either a print or broadcast journalist. Entries may be in the form of clippings, original material, wire service printouts, photocopies or broadcast scripts. Broadcast tapes may also be submitted with scripts. A monetary prize of $2,500 is awarded annually. Funded by New Orleans Time-Picayune and Newhouse Newspapers. In honor of their former correspondent Edgar A. Poe.

• 21604 • **Merriam Smith Award**
Recognizes presidential news coverage under deadline pressure, with separate awards for print and broadcast journalists. A monetary prize of $1,000 funded by Merriman Smith Memorial Fund is presented annually.

• 21605 •
White House News Photographers Association
Susan Walsh, Pres.
7119 Ben Franklin Sta.
Washington, DC 20044-7119
Phone: (202)785-5230
E-mail: info@whnpa.org
Home Page: http://www.whnpa.org

• 21606 • **White House News Photographers' Association Awards**
To recognize outstanding photojournalists who daily cover the Office of the President of the United States and major events in Washington, DC, as well as other parts of the world. Awards are presented in categories in the following classes: Still Division: Presidential; Insiders' Washington; News; Sports/Action; Sports/Feature; Personalities/Color; Personalities/Black & White; Feature/Color; Feature Black & White; Pictorial; Picture Story/News; Picture Story/Feature; and Tape/Film Division: News Feature; Presidential; Spot News; General News; Day Feature; Feature; Series; Sports; Editing; Sound; Magazine Feature; and Lighting. First, second, third place, and often honorable mention winners are selected in each class. Prizes vary from year to year depending on sponsors, and are often camera equipment and monetary prizes. Fuji and Nikon and the American University are major sponsors. The Still Photographer of the Year Award is presented. Awarded annually. Established in 1921. All winning photographs are displayed at photo exhibitions that travel around the United States and abroad.

• 21607 •
William Allen White Library
Alaine Martaus, Assistant Professor, Children's Lit.
Children's Book Award Program
1200 Commercial
Box 4051
Emporia, KS 66801
Phone: (620)341-5207
Toll-Free: 877-613-7323
Fax: (620)341-5997
E-mail: martausa@emporia.edu

• 21608 • **William Allen White Children's Book Award**
To encourage the boys and girls of Kansas to read and enjoy good books. Books chosen for the White Award Master List must have been first published in the English language in the United States, Canada or Mexico during the year preceding the year of selection. Authors must reside in the United States, Canada or Mexico. Children in Kansas schools in grades three through eight vote to select the winners. There is one award for grades 3-5 and one for grades 6-8. A bronze medal is awarded annually. Established in 1952 by Ruth Garver Gagliardo, a specialist in children's literature. The award honors William Allen White, a noted American newspaper editor and distinguished citizen from Emporia, Kansas.

• 21609 •
Mrs. Giles Whiting Foundation
1133 Avenue of the Americas, 22nd Fl.
New York, NY 10036-6710
Phone: (212)336-2138
Home Page: http://
www.whitingfoundation.org

• 21610 • **Whiting Writers' Award**
To identify and support deserving writers of exceptional promise. The program places special emphasis on exceptionally promising emerging talent. To qualify, writers need not be "young," given that new talent may emerge at any age. Recipients of the award are selected by a selection committee from nominations made by writ-

ers, educators, and editors from communities across the country whose experience and vocations bring them in contact with individuals of unusual talent. The nominators and selectors are appointed by the foundation and serve anonymously. Direct applications and informal nominations are not accepted by the foundation. Nominated candidates may be writers of fiction, poetry, or nonfiction; they may be essayists, literary scholars, playwrights, novelists, poets, or critics. Selections are based on the quality of writing and the likelihood of outstanding future work. Monetary awards of $35,000 each are awarded annually to ten candidates. Established in 1985.

• 21611 •
Whooping Crane Conservation Association
Walter Sturgeon, Pres.
1475 Regal Ct.
Kissimmee, FL 34744
Phone: (407)348-3009
Phone: (337)233-8817
Fax: (337)228-7424
E-mail: webadmin@whoopingcrane.com
Home Page: http://www.whoopingcrane.com

• 21612 • Honor Award
To recognize substantial contributions to the preservation of endangered wildlife in North America. Members are eligible. A parchment on a plaque is awarded annually. Established in 1976.

• 21613 •
Wichita Falls Board of Commerce and Industry
Tim Chase, Pres. CEO
900 8th St. No. 218
PO Box 1860
Wichita Falls, TX 76307
Phone: (940)723-2741
Fax: (940)723-8773
E-mail: ewaite@wf.net
Home Page: http://www.wichitafallscommerce.com

• 21614 • Small Business Person of Year
For stability, growth, creativity in business. Recognition award bestowed annually.

• 21615 •
Wichita State University Center for Entrepreneurship
Devlin Hall
1845 Fairmount
Wichita, KS 67260-0147
Phone: (316)978-3000
Fax: (316)978-3687
Home Page: http://www.cfe.wichita.edu

• 21616 • Metro Awards
Honoring the fastest-growing privately-held companies in greater Wichita.

• 21617 •
Wider Opportunities for Women
Joan A. Kuriansky Esq., Exec.Dir.
1001 Connecticut Ave. NW, No. 930
Washington, DC 20036
Phone: (202)464-1596
Fax: (202)464-1660
E-mail: info@wowonline.org
Home Page: http://www.wowonline.org

Absorbed: (1987) National Commission on Working Women.

• 21618 • Women at Work Awards
To recognize those who have made outstanding contributions to working women's issues. Categories include broadcast journalism, entertainment, workplace initiatives, public policy, and individual leadership. All winners receive an "Alice," a Tiffany crystal awards named after the waitress portrayed by Linda Lavin in the CBS television series. In addition, the Commissioners' Award may be presented. Awarded annually at a gala awards ceremony in Washington, D.C., in the fall. Established in 1979.

• 21619 •
Elie Wiesel Foundation for Humanity
Alexandrea J. Ravenelle, Dir.
529 5th Ave., Ste. 1802
New York, NY 10017
Phone: (212)490-7777
Fax: (212)490-6006
E-mail: alexandrea@eliewieselfoundation.org
Home Page: http://www.eliewieselfoundation.org

• 21620 • Humanitarian Award
To recognize an individual for outstanding contributions to progress and humanity. Tzedaka Boxes are awarded annually.

• 21621 • Elie Wiesel Prize in Ethics
To challenge students to examine and analyze urgent ethical issues confronting them in today's complex world. Undergraduate juniors and seniors nationwide who are enrolled full-time in an accredited college or university may submit 3,000 to 4,000 word essays. Monetary prizes of $5,000 for first prize, $2,500 for second prize, $1,500 for third prize and two prizes of $500 for honorable mention are awarded annually. Established in 1989. Must send self addressed stamped envelope to Foundation to receive guidelines and application. Deadlines are announced in early December.

• 21622 •
Wilderness Medical Society
Mr. Jason Gilbert, Mgr.
PO Box 1897
Lawrence, KS 66044
Phone: (785)843-1235
Fax: (785)843-1274
E-mail: wms@wms.org
Home Page: http://www.wms.org

• 21623 • Charles S. Houston Research Award
To promote research in the field of wilderness and environmental medicine. Students at accredited American or Canadian medical schools are eligible. Proposals must be submitted by November 15. A research grant of up to $5,000 is awarded annually. Established in 1987 to honor Charles S. Houston, M.D.

• 21624 •
The Wilderness Society
William H. Meadows III, Pres.
1615 M St. NW
Washington, DC 20036
Phone: (202)833-2300
Toll-Free: 800-843-9453
Fax: (202)429-8443
E-mail: member@tws.org
Home Page: http://www.wilderness.org

• 21625 • Ansel Adams Conservation Award
Presented to a current or former Federal official who has shown exceptional commitment to the cause of conservation and the fostering of an American land ethic. A plaque is awarded annually at the spring meeting of the Governing Council. Established in 1980 to honor Ansel Adams, a landscape photographer.

• 21626 • Robert Marshall Award
To recognize a private citizen who has devoted exceptional time, thought and energy to preserving America's wilderness, prime forests, parks, rivers and shore lands. Awarded annually at the fall meeting of the Governing Council. Established in 1981.

• 21627 • Olaus and Margaret Murie Award
To recognize exceptional dedication to the principles of natural resource protection by a frontline employee of a federal or state land management agency. Awarded annually. Established in 1988 to honor Olaus Murie, a renowned federal wildlife biologist who served as executive director of The Wilderness Society, and his wife Margaret (Mardy), an author and leading conservationist who has been on The Society's Governing Council since 1976.

• 21628 •
The Wildlife Society
Thomas M. Franklin, Exec.Dir.
5410 Grosvenor Ln., Ste. 200
Bethesda, MD 20814-2144
Phone: (301)897-9770
Fax: (301)530-2471
E-mail: tws@wildlife.org
Home Page: http://www.wildlife.org

• 21629 • Emeritus Award
To recognize a retired member of the Association who, in the opinion of the Council, has contributed significantly to the study of wildlife diseases.

• 21630 • **Aldo Leopold Memorial Award**
This, the highest award of the Association, honors a long-standing member who, through outstanding accomplishments in research, teaching, or other activities, including participation in WDA affairs, has made a noteworthy contribution to furthering the aims of the Association. Recipients receive a medal, plaque, and honorary membership to the Association. Awarded when merited. Formerly: (2006) Distinguished Service Award.

• 21631 • **Student Awards**
To recognize students doing graduate studies on wildlife diseases. Two awards are presented: Terry Amundson Student Presentation Award, and Student Research Recognition Travel Award. A monetary award and a plaque are presented at the annual banquet. The student awards program was established about 1972. In 1987, the Student Presentation Award was renamed to honor Terry Amundson, a former recipient of the award and an employee of the Wisconsin Department of Natural Resources.

• 21632 •
William T. Grant Foundation
Robert Granger EdD, Pres.
570 Lexington Ave., 18th Fl.
New York, NY 10022-1398
Phone: (212)752-0071
Fax: (212)752-1398
E-mail: info@wtgrantfdn.org
Home Page: http://www.wtgrantfoundation.org

• 21633 • **William T. Grant Faculty Scholars**
To promote the research development of promising junior scholars who investigate topics relevant to understanding and promoting the well-being and healthy development of children, adolescents, and youth. Scholars in any discipline are eligible. Nominations must be submitted by July 1. Every year, four to six William T. Grant Scholars are selected and each receives $300,000 distributed over a five-year period.. Awarded annually. Established in 1982.

• 21634 •
H.W. Wilson Co.
Roseward Sky, Press Off.
950 University Ave.
Bronx, NY 10452
Phone: (718)588-8400
Toll-Free: 800-367-6770
Fax: 800-590-1617
E-mail: rsky@hwwilson.com
Home Page: http://www.hwwilson.com

• 21635 • **John Cotton Dana Award**
To honor a library's annual coordinated public relations program, including publicity, programs advertising, publications, exhibits, special events, promotions, and audio-visual presentations. Awarded annually. Co-sponsored by The American Library Association.

• 21636 •
Wilson Ornithological Society
Dr. Doris J. Watt, Pres.
Museum of Zoology
University of Michigan
1109 Geddes Ave.
Ann Arbor, MI 48109-1079
Phone: (734)764-0457
E-mail: dwatt@jade.saintmarys.edu
Home Page: http://www.ummz.lsa.umich.edu/birds/wos.html

• 21637 • **Louis Agassiz Fuertes Award**
Open to all ornithologists. Graduate students and young professionals are preferred. Any avian research is eligible. One award of $2500 is given.

• 21638 • **George A. Hall/Harold F. Mayfield Award**
For independent researchers without access to funds and facilities available at colleges, universities, or governmental agencies and is restricted to non-professionals, including high school students. Any kind of avian research is eligible. One $1000 award is given.

• 21639 • **Paul A. Stewart Awards**
Preference will be given to proposals for studies of bird movements based on banding, analysis of recoveries, and returns of banded birds, with an emphasis on economic ornithology. Up to four awards of $500 each are given annually.

• 21640 • **Alexander Wilson Prize**
To recognize the best student paper at the annual meeting. To be eligible, the student must be the first author and presenter.

• 21641 •
Windsor Chamber of Commerce
Michal Connors, Ofc.Mgr.
421 Main St.
Windsor, CO 80550
Phone: (970)686-7189
Fax: (970)686-0352
E-mail: michal@windsorchamber.net
Home Page: http://www.windsorchamber.net

• 21642 • **Windsor Chamber/Harvest Festival Scholarship Award**
For senior at Windsor High School with 3.0 GPA or better.

• 21643 •
Wine Country Film Festival
12000 Henno Rd.
PO Box 303
Glen Ellen, CA 95442
Phone: (707)935-FILM
Fax: (707)996-6964
E-mail: wcfilmfest@aol.com
Home Page: http://www.winecountryfilmfest.com

• 21644 • **Best First Feature Award**
To recognize the director of the best first feature film for use of creativity, imagination, and excellence. Directors from any country whose films are accepted in the Wine Country Film Festival are eligible. A plaque is awarded annually at Festival. Established in 1992. Sponsored by the Society for the Advancement of the Arts and Film.

• 21645 • **Short Film Award**
Short films from any country are eligible. A plaque is awarded to one or more recipients each year. Established in 1994.

• 21646 • **David L. Wolper Best Documentary Award**
Documentaries from any country are eligible. A plaque is awarded to one or more recipients each year. Established in 1994.

• 21647 •
Wine Spectator
387 Park Ave. S
New York, NY 10016
Phone: (212)684-4224
Toll-Free: 800-395-3364
Fax: (212)684-5424
Home Page: http://www.winespectator.com

• 21648 • **Distinguished Service Award**
For recognition of dedication and contribution to the wine industry. A plaque is awarded annually at the Grand Award Banquet in October. Established in 1982 by M. Shanken Communications Inc. Sponsored by the Wine Spectator Scholarship Foundation.

• 21649 • **Grand Award**
For recognition of those restaurants having the finest wine lists in the world. Wine lists submitted are judged on the basis of depth, breadth, value, and selection of wines. A plaque, to be displayed in the restaurant, is awarded annually. Awarded at the Grand Award Banquet in October. Established in 1981 by M. Shanken Communications, Inc. Sponsored by the Wine Spectator Scholarship Foundation.

• 21650 •
Wines of France
80 Main Ln., Ste. 310
New York, NY 10038
E-mail: alice.louhaton@sopexa.com
Home Page: http://www.frenchwinesfood.com

• 21651 • **French Wine and Spirits Sommelier Competition**
To recognize the best sommelier of French wine and spirits in America. The winning contestants are selected on the basis of their knowledge and expertise in recommending and serving French wines, as demonstrated by written tests, and theoretical and practical exams. The competition is open to all persons, American or foreign, employed by a hotel, restaurant or club in the United States, and age 21 or over. The contest

has three rounds: (1) Quarter final; (2) Semi-final; and (3) The Grand Final held in New York. The winning contestant is named "The Best Sommelier of French Wine and Spirits in America" and represents the United States at the next International Competition in France; and the winners of the semi-finals are named "The Best French Wine Sommelier in (name of region)." These trips are designed to enhance the winners' skill and knowledge of French wines through meetings, organized tours and related industry activities. Winners are inducted into the International Association of Maitres-Conseils in French Gastronomy. Established in 1984.

• 21652 •
Wings Club
T. Allan McArtor, Pres.
PO Box 4464
New York, NY 10163
Phone: (212)867-1770
Fax: (212)480-3641
E-mail: wingsclub@aol.com
Home Page: http://www.wingsclub.org

• 21653 • **Distinguished Achievement Award**
For recognition of significant accomplishments in the field of aviation and astronautics by an individual, and for significant public service of enduring value to aviation. Awarded annually. Established in 1975.

• 21654 • **Distinguished Scholar Award**
Recognizes outstanding academic achievement in the field of aviation. Awarded annually. Established in 2000.

• 21655 •
Winston Churchill Foundation
Harold Epstein, Exec.Dir.
PO Box 1240
Gracie Sta.
New York, NY 10028
Phone: (212)879-3480
Fax: (212)879-3480
E-mail: churchillf@aol.com
Home Page: http://thechurchillscholarships.com

• 21656 • **Winston Churchill Award**
To recognize exceptional accomplishments which reflect the qualities Winston Churchill exemplified. The foundation seeks to encourage a spirit of British-American cooperation. A medal and a citation are awarded occasionally. Established in 1981 in memory of Winston Churchill.

• 21657 •
Wire Association International
Steven J. Fetterolf, Exec.Dir.
PO Box 578
PO Box 578
Guilford, CT 06437
Phone: (203)453-2777
Fax: (203)453-8384
E-mail: ljacobs@wirenet.org
Home Page: http://www.wirenet.org

• 21658 • **J. Edward Donnellan Award**
To recognize a WAI member who has made an outstanding contribution to the Wire Association and the wire industry. A plaque is awarded annually. Established in 1969 as a tribute to T. Edward Donnellan, former Executive Director and Executive Secretary of the Association.

• 21659 • **Mordica Memorial Award**
To recognize outstanding contributions that have benefited and advanced the wire and cable industry. A medal is awarded annually. Established in 1940 as a tribute to John Mordica and to memorialize him as the Founding President of the Association.

• 21660 • **Technical Paper Awards**
To recognize the author of the most meritorious paper on wire manufacture or fabrication during the year. The following awards are presented: Urbain J.H. Malo Medal Award (electrical division); Horace Pops Medal Award (general division); Allan B. Dove Medal Award (ferrous division); and Marshall V. Yokelson Medal Award (nonferrous divisions). A bronze medal is presented to the winners. Honorable mentions are also awarded annually. Established in 1934.

• 21661 •
Wireless Communications Association International
Andrew Kreig, Pres.
1333 H St. NW, Ste. 700W
Washington, DC 20005-4754
Phone: (202)452-7823
Fax: (202)452-0041
E-mail: president@wcai.com
Home Page: http://www.wcai.com

• 21662 • **Golden Eagle Award**
Annual award of recognition.

• 21663 •
Wisconsin Agri-Service Association
John Petty, Exec.Dir.
6000 Gisholt Dr., Ste. 208
Madison, WI 53713-4816
Phone: (608)223-1111
Fax: (608)223-1147
E-mail: info@wasa.org
Home Page: http://www.wasa.org

• 21664 • **Eldon Roesler Scholarship**
For an individual with a GPA of 3.0 or greater who has completed 1 year of college and is studying an agricultural related field. Scholarship awarded annually.

• 21665 •
Wisconsin Arts Board
George Tzougros, Exec.Dir.
101 E Wilson St., Fl. 1
Madison, WI 53702
Phone: (608)266-0190
Fax: (608)267-0380
E-mail: artsboard@arts.state.wi.us
Home Page: http://www.arts.state.wi.us

• 21666 • **Wisconsin Arts Board Fellowships**
To assist artists in the creation of works and activities aimed towards professional growth in visual arts, literature, music composition, performance art, choreography, and media arts. Candidates may not be degree credit students at the time of application and must be Wisconsin residents. Established in 1973. The fellowship program is created with funds provided by the National Endowment for the Arts and the Wisconsin State Legislature and is intended to assist outstanding Wisconsin artists in their continued development.

• 21667 •
Wisconsin Cheese Makers' Association
John Umhoefer, Exec.Dir.
8030 Excelsior Dr., Ste. 305
Madison, WI 53717-1950
Phone: (608)828-4550
Fax: (608)828-4551
E-mail: office@wischeesemakersassn.org
Home Page: http://www.wischeesemakersassn.org

• 21668 • **World Champion Cheesemaker**
To encourage excellence in the art of cheese making. The highest scoring natural cheese entered in the WCMA's World Natural Cheese Championship Contest is honored. The contest is open to any cheese maker or manufacturer of natural cheese in the world. Any style natural cheese, colored or uncolored, having its own characteristic shape may be entered in the appropriate contest class: Class I - Cheddar; Class II Cheddar-Aged; Class III - Colby, Monterey Jack; Class IV - Swiss Style; Class V Brick, Muenster, Limburger; Class VI - Mozzarella; Class VII Provolone; Class VIII - Blue-Veined; Class IX - Edam, Gouda; Class X Brie, Camembert; Class XI - Baby Swiss Style; Class XII - Feta; Class XIII Flavored Soft Cheeses; Class XIV - Flavored Semi-soft Cheeses; Class XV Flavored Hard Cheeses; Class XVI - Open Class Soft Cheeses; Class XVII Open Class Semi-soft Cheeses; Class XVIII - Open Class Hard Cheeses; Class XIX - Reduced Fat Cheese; Class XX - Cold Pack Cheese/ Cheesefood Class XXI - Pasteurized Processed Cheese/Cheese Food/Cheese Spread; Class XXII Fresh Goat's Milk Cheese; Class XXIII - Aged Goat's Milk Cheese; Class XXIV - Sheep's Milk Cheese; Class XXV - Salted Butter; Class XXVI Unsalted Butter; Class XXVII - Flavored Butter; Class XXVIII - Retail Packages of Cheese and Butter. A monetary award of $1,000, a ribbon, a plaque, and the title World Champion Cheese Maker are awarded in even-numbered years at the convention.

• 21669 •
Wisconsin Educational Media Association
Kate Bugher, Pres.
PO Box 206
Boscobel, WI 53805
Phone: (608)375-6020
Fax: (608)822-6884
E-mail: wema@centurytel.net
Home Page: http://www.wemaonline.org

• 21670 • **Golden Archer Award**
To honor a living American author for a juvenile book published within the past five years and selected by the school children of Wisconsin in grades four through eight. Established in 1974 by Marion Archer and Sally Teresinski at the EMC Polk Library, University of Wisconsin-Oskosh. The award honored the author whose book, like the arrow of the medieval bowman who appears on the award medal, struck the target - the young reader's heart.

• 21671 •
Wisconsin Farm Bureau Federation
Bill Bruins, Pres.
1212 Deming Way
PO Box 5550
Madison, WI 53705-0550
Phone: (608)828-5701
Phone: (608)836-5575
Toll-Free: 800-261-FARM
E-mail: info.demingway@wfbf.com
Home Page: http://www.wfbf.com

• 21672 • **Scholarship Program**
For students in agriculture related fields. Scholarship awarded annually.

• 21673 •
Wisconsin Fertilizer and Chemical Association
Elizabeth Ahner, Contact
2317 Intl. Ln., Ste. 115
Madison, WI 53704-3154
Phone: (608)249-4070
Fax: (608)249-5311
E-mail: wfca@aol.com
Home Page: http://www.wfca.biz

• 21674 • **Member Scholarship**
For incoming college freshman in agriculture-related field; members, children only. Scholarship awarded annually.

• 21675 •
Wisconsin Historical Society
George L. Vogt, Dir.
816 State St.
Madison, WI 53706-1482
Phone: (608)264-6400
Phone: (608)264-6587
Toll-Free: 888-748-7479
Fax: (608)264-6545
E-mail: info@whs.wisc.edu
Home Page: http://www.wisconsinhistory.org

• 21676 • **John C. Geilfuss Fellowship**
For graduate research on Wisconsin business or economic history. Grant of $1,000 to $2,000 is awarded annually.

• 21677 • **Amy Louise Hunter Fellowship**
For graduate research on the history of women and public policy. Grant of $1,000 to $2,000 is awarded biennially.

• 21678 • **Alice E. Smith Fellowship**
For woman conducting graduate research on the history of Wisconsin or the Midwest. Grant of $1,000 to $2,000 is awarded annually.

• 21679 •
Wisconsin Labor History Society
Kenneth Germanson, Pres.
6333 W Blue Mound Rd.
Milwaukee, WI 53213
Phone: (414)771-0700
Phone: (414)483-1754
Fax: (608)771-1715
E-mail: info@wisconsinlaborhistory.org

• 21680 • **Labor History High School Essay Contest**
For high school students who complete 750 word essay on contributions of unions. Monetary award bestowed annually.

• 21681 • **Solidarity Award for Lifetime Contribution to the Labor Movement**
For long time and significant participation in worker organization by a rank and file individual. Recognition award bestowed annually.

• 21682 •
Wisconsin Library Association
5250 E Terr. Dr., Ste. A-1
Madison, WI 53718
Phone: (608)245-3640
Fax: (608)245-3646
E-mail: strand@scls.lib.wi.us
Home Page: http://www.wla.lib.wi.us

• 21683 • **Banta Awards**
To recognize a book by a Wisconsin author that contributes to the world of literature and ideas. Authors born in Wisconsin, currently residing in the state, or who have lived in Wisconsin for a significant period are eligible for single works published during the preceding year. A bronze medallion is awarded at the annual conference. Established in 1974. Sponsored by the George Banta Company, Inc. of Menasha, WI.

• 21684 • **Elizabeth Burr/Worzalla Award**
To honor a Wisconsin author/illustrator for distinguished achievement in children's literature. Nominations are accepted by the Children's Book Award Committee, which selects authors/illustrators based on the following criteria: books must be published in the calendar year preceding the presentation of the award; award given for a single publication, not for the body of an author/illustrator's work; work must be written or illustrated by a person who was born in Wisconsin, or is currently living in Wisconsin or who lived in Wisconsin for a significant length of time; work must be notable and contribute to the world of children's literature; only original works written or illustrated for children or young adults will be considered (books that are traditional in origin will be eligible if they are the result of original research and if the retelling or interpretation is that of the author or illustrator); textbooks will not be considered. Awarded at annual conference. Established in 1992.

• 21685 • **Notable Wisconsin Authors**
To honor Wisconsin authors, past and present, for their literary contributions and to promote a greater awareness of the state's literary heritage. Nominations are accepted by the Literary Awards Committee which selects authors based on the following criteria: authors, must have had residence in Wisconsin; works must be contributions to the world of literature and ideas; texts or works of specialized or technical content are not ordinarily considered for an award. No more than three living authors are recognized each year. Awarded annually. Established in 1973.

• 21686 •
Wisconsin Park and Recreation Association
Steven J. Thompson CPRP, Exec.Dir.
6601-C Northway
Greendale, WI 53129
Phone: (414)423-1210
Fax: (414)423-1296
E-mail: sthompson@wpraweb.org
Home Page: http://www.wpraweb.org

• 21687 • **WPRA Foundation**
For professional development. Scholarship awarded annually.

• 21688 •
Wisconsin Parkinson Association
Jackie Hoeft, Contact
945 N. 12th St., Ste. 4602
Milwaukee, WI 53233
Phone: (414)447-2563
Toll-Free: 800-972-5455
Fax: (414)871-7942
E-mail: jackiehoeft@aurora.org

• 21689 • **Clinical Center of Excellence**
For advocacy, education, clinical expertise. Grant awarded annually.

• 21690 •
Wisconsin State Genealogical Society
J.A. Brissee, Pres.
PO Box 5106
Madison, WI 53705-0106
Phone: (608)325-2609
E-mail: wsgs@chorus.net
Home Page: http://www.wsgs.org

• 21691 • **Book Award**
For Wisconsin family history. Recognition award bestowed annually.

• 21692 • **Pioneer Family Certificates and Century Family Certificates**
For descendants of pioneer families. Recognition award bestowed annually.

• 21693 •
W.K. Kellogg Foundation
William C. Richardson, CEO & Pres.
1 Michigan Ave. E
Battle Creek, MI 49017-4012
Phone: (269)968-1611
Fax: (269)968-0413
Home Page: http://www.wkkf.org

• 21694 • **Kellogg National Leadership Program**
Approximately 40 three-year leadership development fellowships are awarded to American professionals in the early years of their professional careers. Individuals with proven leadership potential are selected for this non-degree program, which includes Foundation-sponsored leadership laboratories where Fellows explore domestic and global social issues that impact organizations and communities.

• 21695 •
Wolfe Pack
Ellen E. Krieger, Exec. Officer
PO Box 822, Ansonia Sta.
New York, NY 10023
E-mail: webmaster@nerowolfe.org
Home Page: http://www.nerowolfe.org

• 21696 • **Nero Award**
For recognition of the best detective novel published during the current year. A work of detective fiction first published in the United States during the preceding year, September to September, is eligible. A trophy AND a bust of Nero Wolfe is awarded annually at the Wolfe Pack's Black Orchid Banquet the first Saturday in December. Established in 1979 in honor of Rex Stout's Nero Wolfe mystery series.

• 21697 •
Woman's Building
Slide Archive
9045 Lincoln Blvd.
Los Angeles, CA 90045
E-mail: maberry@otis.edu
Home Page: http://
www.womansbuilding.org

• 21698 • **Vesta Award**
To honor women who have made significant contributions to the arts in Southern California. Individuals may be nominated by members of the Board or Advisory Council, or by a former award winner. A plaque is awarded annually in October at a ceremony. Established in 1982 and named after Vesta, the Roman goddess, keeper of the flame of inspiration who symbolizes women's dedication to their creative work.

• 21699 •
Women for Faith and Family
Mrs. Helen Hull Hitchcock, Exec.Dir.
PO Box 300411
St. Louis, MO 63130-0261
Phone: (314)863-8385
Fax: (314)863-5858
E-mail: info@wf-f.org
Home Page: http://www.wf-f.org

• 21700 • **Women for Faith and Family Award**
Recognizes an outstanding Roman Catholic religious or lay person. Awarded annually.

• 21701 •
Women Health Executives Network
Nancy A. Peterman, Pres.
PO Box 350
Kenilworth, IL 60043
Phone: (847)251-1400
Phone: (847)292-6716
Fax: (847)256-5601
E-mail: lgibbons@phcs.com
Home Page: http://www.whenchicago.org

• 21702 • **Achievement in Health Care Management**
For contribution to health care management and promotion of women executives. Recognition award bestowed annually.

• 21703 •
Women in Agribusiness
Dolores Hamelin, Pres.
PO Box 986
Kearney, MO 64060

• 21704 • **CERES**
Recognizes outstanding women in agribusiness. Awarded annually.

• 21705 •
Women in Cable and Telecommunications
Benita Fitzgerald Mosley, Pres./CEO
14555 Avion Pkwy., Ste. 250
Chantilly, VA 20151
Phone: (703)234-9810
Phone: (703)234-9801
Fax: (703)817-1595
E-mail: bfmosley@wict.org
Home Page: http://www.wict.org

• 21706 • **Accolades Award**
Annual award of recognition.

• 21707 •
Women in Direct Marketing International
Berenice Ladden, Pres.
285 Madison Ave., 14th Fl.
New York, NY 10017
Phone: (732)469-5900
Fax: (732)469-8414
E-mail: bladden@directmaildepot.com
Home Page: http://www.wdmi.org

• 21708 • **Direct Marketing Woman of the Year Award**
Recognizes significant professional and personal contributions to the industry. Applicants must have 10 years in the industry. Awarded annually.

• 21709 •
Women in Endocrinology
Carolyn L. Smith PhD, Communications Committee Chair
Department of Molecular and Cellular Biology
Baylor College of Medicine
One Baylor Plz.
Houston, TX 77030-3411
Phone: (713)798-6235
Fax: (713)790-1275
E-mail: carolyns@bcm.tmc.edu
Home Page: http://www.women-in-endo.org/Pages/index.shtml

• 21710 • **WE Mentor Award**
Recognizes outstanding scientists who have encouraged and promoted female endocrinologists who have been instrumental in changing institutional policy toward professional women. An honorarium and $1000 and travel expenses to the Annual WE Meeting is presented. Deadline is January 8.

• 21711 •
Women in Film
Iris Grossman, Pres.
8857 W. Olympic Blvd., Ste. 201
Beverly Hills, CA 90211-3605
Phone: (310)657-5144
Fax: (310)657-5154
E-mail: info@wif.com
Home Page: http://www.wif.org

• 21712 • **Creative Caf Sound Completion & Design Grant**
To aid filmmakers in post-production sound editing and design services, awarded by the Women In Film Foundation as part of the Film Finishing Fund.

• 21713 • **Crystal Awards**
To honor outstanding individuals who, through their endurance and the excellence of their work, have helped to expand the role of women within the entertainment industry. Women and men are eligible. The recipients are chosen for both the diversity of their accomplishments and their contributions to the support and advancement of women within the entertainment industry. A Crystal is awarded annually. Established in 1977.

• 21714 • **Dockers Khakis for Women of Independent Vision Grant**
For excellence by a woman filmmaker. Completion funds of up to $5000 are awarded annually. Awarded by the Women In Film Foundation as part of the Film Finishing Fund.

• 21715 • "Focus on Disability" Grant
To recognize an exceptional film or video depicting issues of disability or providing opportunities for disabled performers. A monetary prize up to $5,000 is awarded annually by the Women In Film Foundation's Film Finishing Fund. Established by Loren Arbus.

• 21716 • "Focus on Discrimination" Grant
To recognize an exceptional film or television program that explores or depicts discrimination of any kind. Awarded by the Women in Film Foundation as part of the annual Film Finishing Fund. A monetary prize up to $5,000 is awarded annually. Established by Loren Arbus.

• 21717 • International Award
To recognize a woman working internationally who represents the highest ideals of the film industry. Established in 1987.

• 21718 • Liberty Live Wire Grant
For post production services. Awarded by the Women in Film Foundation as part of the Film Finishing Fund.

• 21719 • Jose L. Nazar Grant for Latino Projects and/or Latina Filmmakers
Recognizes a project for or about Latinos. Completion funds of up to $5000 are awarded. Awarded by the Women in Film Foundation as prt of the Film Finishing Fund.

• 21720 • New York Women in Film and Television Post Production Completion Grants
For post production services for New York area filmmakers. Awarded by New York Women in Film and Television in conjunction with the Women in Film Foundation Film Finishing Fund.

• 21721 • Women in Film and Television Florida Independent Filmmaker Grant
For post production services for filmmakers in the south eastern United States. Awarded by Women in Film and Television-Florida in conjunction with the Women in Film Foundation Film Finishing Fund.

• 21722 • Women in Film Foundation Cash Grant
For completion of film or videotape on a subject that meets the dated guidelines of Women in Film. Awarded by the Women in Film Foundation as part of the Film Finishing Fund. A cash award of up to $5000 is presented.

• 21723 • Norma Zarky Humanitarian Award
To recognize an individual for outstanding support for the advancement of equal opportunities and unending devotion to the improvement of the human condition. Established in 1979 to honor Norma Zarky, renowned entertainment attorney, advocate of human rights and women's issues, President of the Beverly Hills Bar Association, and founding member of Women In Film.

• 21724 •
Women in Film and Video
Melissa Houghton, Exec.Dir.
1233 20th St. NW, Ste. 401
Washington, DC 20036
Phone: (202)429-9438
Phone: (202)333-1557
Fax: (202)429-9440
E-mail: membership@wifv.org
Home Page: http://www.wifv.org

• 21725 • Certificate of Appreciation
To honor a non-member or firm for outstanding contributions or service to WBDNA. One to three certificates are awarded annually. Established in 1971.

• 21726 • Citation of Merit Award
To honor outstanding members of WBDNA. Candidates must consistently produce bands of high performance level, consistently perform programs of high musical quality, have made an outstanding contribution to the community through music, and must be active members of WBDNA. At least one and no more than three certificates are given annually. Established in 1976.

• 21727 • International Golden Rose Award
To honor women of outstanding achievement and/or international reputation in the field of instrumental music. A trophy with a baton and a certificate are awarded biennially. Established in 1971.

• 21728 • Pioneer Women of the Podium
To recognize women pioneers in directing bands.

• 21729 • Scroll of Excellence
To honor outstanding women band directors, preferably not members of WBDNA. Candidates must consistently produce bands of high performance level with programs of high musical quality, and/or has contribute significantly in other ways to instrumental music education; must actively participate in regional and/or state events; and must be sponsored by one WBDNA member with the endorsement of two other WBDNA members. Only one award per state is given annually and no more than ten nationally each year. A scroll signed by the president is presented at a public concert or other public event whenever possible. Established in 1985.

• 21730 • Silver Baton Award
To honor outstanding women in the field of instrumental music. Candidates must consistently produce bands of high performance level, consistently perform program of high musical quality, have made an outstanding contribution to the community and the country through music, have made an outstanding contribution to the improvement of bands in America through participation and leadership in professional organizations, be an active member of WBDNA, and have made an outstanding contribution to the association through participation. A certificate and plaque are awarded annually. Established in 1972.

• 21731 • WBDNA Achievement Award
To recognize outstanding women graduating from high school for their work in instrumental music. A certificate is awarded. Established in 1971.

• 21732 • WBDNA Performing Artists Award
To identify talented young female soloists in their junior year and to enhance their profile in the community, state, and universities of their choice. Any outstanding young woman soloist who is enrolled in a high school band program is eligible for recommendation. A certificate with a gold seal and a lapel pin are awarded. Established in 1986 in honor of Dorothy Stewart Jones for her outstanding work with young soloists.

• 21733 •
Women in Film and Video/New England
Cristina Cacioppo, Membership Coor.
50 Hunt St.
Watertown, MA 02138
Phone: (617)617-0091
Phone: (202)333-1557
Fax: (617)923-9292
E-mail: info@womeninfilmvideo.org
Home Page: http://www.womeninfilmvideo.org

• 21734 • Bi-Annual Image Awards
Honors New England women media-makers who have demonstrated remarkable achievements in their respective fields.

• 21735 •
Women in Government Relations and WGR LEADER Foundation
PO Box 66812
Washington, DC 20035-6812
Phone: (202)347-0437
Fax: (202)508-6083
E-mail: leaderfoundation@hotmail.com
Home Page: http://www.leaderfoundation.org/

• 21736 • Distinghished Member
Annual award of recognition.

• 21737 •
Women in Government Relations LEADER Foundation
Tiffany N. Adams, Pres./Chair
PO Box 66812
Washington, DC 20035-6812
Phone: (202)347-0437
Fax: (202)508-6083
E-mail: leaderfoundation@hotmail.com
Home Page: http://www.leaderfoundation.org

• 21738 • **Distinguished Member Award**
For recognition of special leadership, service, and contributions to the ideals and goals of Women in Government Relations. Members may be nominated by January of each year. A plaque is presented at the annual meeting in March. Established in 1977.

• 21739 •
Women in Insurance and Financial Services
Diane M. Dixon CLU, Pres.
6748 Wauconda Dr.
Larkspur, CO 80118
Phone: (303)681-9777
Toll-Free: (866)264-9437
Fax: (303)681-3221
E-mail: wifsmanagement@aol.com
Home Page: http://www.w-wifs.org

• 21740 • **Chapter Achievement Award**
Annual award of recognition.

• 21741 • **Leaders Recognition Society Award**
Annual award of recognition.

• 21742 • **Woman of the Year Award**
Annual award of recognition.

• 21743 •
Women in Livestock Development
Jo Luck, Pres.
PO Box 8058
Little Rock, AR 72203
Phone: (501)907-2600
Phone: (501)907-2644
Toll-Free: 800-422-0474
E-mail: info@heifer.org
Home Page: http://www.heifer.org

• 21744 • **Wild Award**
For outstanding achievement in livestock community development. A monetary award is given annually.

• 21745 •
Women in Management
Trish Peters, Pres.
PO Box 1032
Dundee, IL 60118
Toll-Free: 877-946-6285
Fax: (847)683-3751
E-mail: nationalwim@wimonline.org
Home Page: http://www.wimonline.org

• 21746 • **Charlotte Danstrom Award**
To recognize women of outstanding achievement in each of the following categories: Corporate, Academia, Entrepreneur, and Government/Not For Profit/Social Services. Members may be nominated by their individual chapter. They must have professional leader experiences, community contributions/activities and have helped others develop professionally. A plaque is awarded annually. Established in 1982 in honor of Charlotte Danstrom, for her dedication to the leadership skills and unflagging support.

• 21747 •
Women in Production
David Luke, Pres.
276 Bowery
New York, NY 10012
Phone: (212)334-2108
Phone: (212)334-2106
Fax: (212)431-5786
E-mail: admin@p3-ny.org
Home Page: http://www.p3-ny.org

• 21748 • **Luminaire**
Recognizes members of the print and production industry. Five awards are given annually.

• 21749 • **Women in Production Scholarship**
For high school and college students of the graphic arts. Awarded annually.

• 21750 •
Women in Scholarly Publishing
Maria Coughlin, Pres.
1070 Beacon St., Apt. 6D
Brookline, MA 02446-3951
E-mail: sworst@comcast.net
Home Page: http://www.womeninscholarlypublishing.org

• 21751 • **Career Development Fund**
Gives members funds to attend workshops and seminars for professional development.

• 21752 •
Women in Science and Engineering
Tenecia Brown, Chair
500 5th St. NW
Washington, DC 20001
Phone: (202)334-2063
E-mail: tbrown@nas.edu
Home Page: http://www7.nationalacademies.org/wise
Formerly: Interagency Committee for Women in Science and Engineering.

• 21753 • **WISE Award for Engineering Achievement**
To recognize a specific or special engineering/technical contribution by a woman engineer in the federal service; and to recognize a specific contribution made by a woman engineer in the federal service in promoting the entry of girls and/or the advancement of women in engineering. Factors included in evaluating the nominations include: a significant engineering achievement which has led to an advancement in the state of the art in a particular field; an invention, patent, or design of equipment which has significantly enhanced a field of work or opened up new fields; an exceptionally innovative and/or creative research paper or project which has either significantly improved or led to a new field of research, or the results of which are considered by that discipline as having made a major breakthrough in relation to that particular field of engineering; and an unusual act which facilitated the entry of girls and/or the advancement of women in science or engineering. Nominations must be submitted by January 15. A plaque and an honorary citation are awarded annually at the annual awards luncheon at the WISE National Training Conference. Established in 1978.

• 21754 • **WISE Award for Scientific Achievement**
To recognize a specific or special scientific or technical contribution by a woman scientist in the federal service; and to recognize a specific contribution made by a woman scientist in the federal service in promoting the entry of girls and/or the advancement of women in science. All women scientists employed by the Federal Government in either a civilian or non-civilian status are eligible. Factors included in evaluating the nominations include: a significant scientific achievement which has led to an advancement in the state of the art in a particular field; an invention, patent, or design of equipment which has significantly enhanced a field of work or opened up new fields; an exceptionally innovative and/or creative research paper or project which has either significantly improved or led to a new field of research, or the results of which are considered by that discipline as having made a major breakthrough in relation to that particular field of science; and an unusual act which facilitated the entry of girls and/or advancement of women in science or engineering. Nominations must be submitted by January 15. A plaque is awarded annually at the annual awards luncheon at the WISE National Training Conference. Established in 1978.

• 21755 • **WISE Lifetime Achievement Award**
To recognize the sustained scientific and technical contributions by a woman scientist or engineer in the federal service; and to recognize the contributions made by a woman scientist or engineer in the federal service in promoting the entry of girls and/or in facilitating the advancement of women in science or engineering. All women scientists or engineers with 20 years service in the Federal Government in either a civilian or non-civilian status are eligible. Factors included in evaluating the nominations include: exceptional scientific or engineering achievements as evidenced by publications, inventions, patents or awards; recognition as a scientist or engineer at national and international levels; unusual degree of imagination, innovation, and initiative in the pursuit of science/engineering; and unusual dedication to facilitating the entry of girls and/or the advancement of women in science and engineering. Nominations must be submitted by January 15. A plaque and an honorary citation are awarded annually at the annual awards luncheon at the WISE National Training Conference. Established in 1978.

• 21756 •
Women in Show Business for Children
Scherr Lillico, Pres.
PO Box 2535
Toluca Lake, CA 91610
Phone: (310)271-3415

Formerly: (1981) Girls Friday of Show Business.

• 21757 • **Angel of the Year**
To recognize a member of the entertainment community who has given time, energy, and support to WISB. Members of the organization make the selection through ballot. A crystal angel is awarded annually at the Installation of New Officers and Awards luncheon each June. Established in 1970.

• 21758 • **Bella Rackoff Humanitarian Award**
To recognize an individual who has unselfishly donated both time and energy to humanitarian causes, especially those involving children. Members of the organization make the selection through ballot. A crystal bell is awarded annually at the Tribute Gala fundraiser. Established in 1981 in memory of Bella Rackoff, one of the founders of the organization.

• 21759 •
Women in Technology International
Carolyn Leighton, Founder/Chair
PMB 441
13351-D Riverside Dr., No. 441
Sherman Oaks, CA 91423
Phone: (818)788-9484
Toll-Free: 800-334-WITI
Fax: (818)788-9410
E-mail: member-info@corp.witi.com
Home Page: http://www.witi.com

• 21760 • **CEO Recognition Award**
Recognizes leaders for their support in advancing highly talented and well qualified women within their companies.

• 21761 • **WITI Hall of Fame**
Recognizes, honors, and promotes outstanding contribution to the scientific and technological communities that improve and evolve society. Industry related women are eligible. Awarded annually. Established in 1996.

• 21762 •
Women in the Wind
Becky Brown, Founder/Treas.
PO Box 8392
Toledo, OH 43605
E-mail: becky@womeninthewind.org
Home Page: http://www.womeninthewind.org

• 21763 • **Safe Mileage Award**
Recognizes a person for riding motorcycles safely with the highest mileage. Awarded annually.

• 21764 •
Women Marines Association
Lucille Teixeira, Pres.
PO Box 8405
Falls Church, VA 22041-8405
Toll-Free: 888-525-1943
E-mail: wma@womenmarines.org
Home Page: http://www.womenmarines.org

• 21765 • **WMA National Service Award**
For recognition of outstanding service in keeping with the purposes and objectives of the Association. Members may nominate members, who must be approved by the Board. Established in 1974.

• 21766 •
Women on Stamps Study Unit
Davida Kristy, Pres.
515 Ocean Ave., No. 608S
Santa Monica, CA 90402
Phone: (310)394-5587
Fax: (310)899-3927
E-mail: dkristy@sprintmail.com

• 21767 • **Award of Recognition**
Rrecognizes topical exhibiting involving women.

• 21768 •
Women's Action for New Directions
Susan Shaer, Exec.Dir.
691 Massachusetts Ave.
Arlington, MA 02476
Phone: (781)643-6740
Fax: (781)643-6744
E-mail: info@wand.org
Home Page: http://www.wand.org

Formerly: (1982) Action for Nuclear Disarmament.

• 21769 • **Helen Caldicott Leadership Award**
For recognition of a contribution to the Women's Action for New Directions and the cause of nuclear disarmament, and for recognition of leadership on behalf of women in society. A hand blown piece of glass created especially for the recipients is awarded. Established in 1982 in honor of Helen Caldicott, founder of WAND, disarmament spokesperson, and woman leader. Formerly: Women's Action for Nuclear Disarmament Education Fund.

• 21770 • **WAND Family Award**
To recognize members of Women's Action for New Directions Advisory Board for their contributions to the WAND family, as well as their distinguished years of service to the global family. A hand blown piece of glass created especially for the recipients is awarded. Established in 1990.

• 21771 •
Women's All-Star Association
Sharon Nasta, Exec.Dir.
16 Ward Ave.
Toms River, NJ 08753
Phone: (732)367-0257
Fax: (732)367-3949
E-mail: mcwba@aol.com
Home Page: http://www.wasabowling.com

• 21772 • **Hall of Fame**
To recognize achievements as a member of WASA over the years. Awarded annually with a plaque. Established in 1987.

• 21773 • **Jean-Fish-Pearl Keller High Average Award**
To recognize achievements for bowling skill. Awarded annually with a plaque. Established in 1988.

• 21774 • **Barbara Leicht-Bowers Bowler of the Year**
To recognize achievements as the most outstanding bowler of the year. Awarded annually with a plaque. Established in 1974.

• 21775 • **Lisa Maurice Rookie of the Year**
To recognize achievements as the rookie of the year. Awarded annually with a plaque. Established in 1974.

• 21776 • **Senior Bowler of the Year**
To recognize the achievements as the most outstanding senior bowler of the year. Awarded annually with a plaque. Established in 1997.

• 21777 • **Sportswoman of the Year Award**
To recognize the WASA member who best exemplifies an ideal WASA member on and off the lanes. Awarded annually with a plaque. Established in 1987.

• 21778 •
Women's Art Association of Canada
Lynn Whiteley, Sec.
23 Prince Arthur Ave.
Toronto, ON, Canada M5R 1B2
Phone: (416)922-2060
Fax: (416)922-4657
E-mail: womensart@bellnet.ca

• 21779 • **Derazy Violin Award**
Presented to Violin student selected by the Royal Conservatory of Music. Awarded annually.

• 21780 • **National Ballet of Canada School Scholarship**
Presented to two young Canadian dancers. Awarded annually.

• 21781 • Ontario College of Art & Design Scholarship
Presented to two young Canadian artists. Awarded annually.

• 21782 • Royal Conservatory of Music Scholarship
Presented to three young Canadian musicians. Awarded annually.

• 21783 • University of Toronto Faculty of Music Scholarship
Presented to two young Canadian musicians. Awarded annually.

• 21784 •
Women's Bar Association of the District of Columbia
Karen Lockwood, Pres.
1717 K St. NW, Ste. 503
Washington, DC 20006
Phone: (202)639-8880
Fax: (202)639-8889
E-mail: wba@wbadc.org
Home Page: http://www.wbadc.org

• 21785 • Woman Lawyer of the Year
For recognition of achievement in and significant contributions to the legal profession, and dedication to the advancement of justice in the District of Columbia. Nominations are accepted. A plaque is presented at the annual membership meeting in May. Established in 1964.

• 21786 •
Women's Business Enterprise National Council
Susan Phillips Bari, Pres.
1120 Connecticut Ave. NW, Ste. 1000
Washington, DC 20036
Phone: (202)872-5515
Fax: (202)872-5505
E-mail: admin@wbenc.org
Home Page: http://www.wbenc.org

• 21787 • Applause Award
Recognizes barrier breakers who expand opportunities for women business owners with a significant first-time contribution.

• 21788 •
Women's Caucus for Art
Dena Muller, Pres.
Canal Street Sta.
PO Box 1498
New York, NY 10013
Phone: (212)634-0007
E-mail: info@nationalwca.com
Home Page: http://www.nationalwca.com

• 21789 • WCA Honors
For recognition of contributions to the visual arts by women artists. Nominations are made by the Honors Committee. A plaque and lifetime membership in the Women's Caucus for Art are presented annually at the conference along with a retrospective exhibition with catalogue that includes monograph, chronology, and reproductions. Established in 1979.

• 21790 •
Women's Center of Fayetteville
Sylvia G. Ray, Exec.Dir.
230 Hay St.
Fayetteville, NC 28301
Phone: (910)323-3377
Fax: (910)323-8828
Home Page: http://www.wcof.org

• 21791 • Celebrating Women Awards
For women who work to make a difference in the lives of others in the community. Recognition award bestowed annually.

• 21792 •
Women's Economic Club
Terry A. Barclay, Pres. and CEO
3663 Woodward Ave., Ste. 4-1610
Detroit, MI 48201-2403
Phone: (313)578-3230
Fax: (313)578-3245
E-mail: info@womenseconomicclub.org
Home Page: http://www.womenseconomicclub.org

• 21793 • Today's Workplace of Tomorrow
For innovation in the workplace. Recognition award bestowed biennially.

• 21794 •
Women's International League for Peace and Freedom, U.S. Section
Mary Day Kent, Exec.Dir.
1213 Race St.
Philadelphia, PA 19107-1691
Phone: (215)563-7110
Fax: (215)563-5527
E-mail: wilpf@wilpf.org
Home Page: http://www.wilpf.org

• 21795 • Jane Addams Children's Book Award
For a youth oriented book that best promotes ideals of international friendship and understanding geared towards youth. Awarded annually.

• 21796 •
Women's International Network of Utility Professionals
Vickey Setters, Exec.Dir.
PO Box 335
30 Flatbush Ave., Rm. 613
Whites Creek, TN 37189
Phone: (512)473-3200
Fax: (718)802-5554
E-mail: winup@aol.com
Home Page: http://www.winup.org

• 21797 • Professional Development
For research in electric related fields. Scholarship awarded annually.

• 21798 •
Women's National Book Association
Susannah Greenberg, Public Relations Mgr.
2166 Broadway, Apt. 9E
New York, NY 10024-6671
Phone: (212)208-4629
Fax: (212)208-4629
E-mail: publicity@bookbuzz.com
Home Page: http://www.wnba-books.org

• 21799 • Lucile Micheels Pannell Award
To recognize creativity by booksellers that bring children and books together. Applications must be submitted by February 15. Two monetary awards of $1,000 each and original pieces of art by children's book illustrators are given annually at the American Booksellers Association annual convention. Established in 1982 in honor of Lucile Micheels Pannell, manager of Hobby Horse Book Shop at Carson Pirie Scott from 1943 to 1953.

• 21800 • Women's National Book Association Award
To recognize a distinguished bookwoman for outstanding contributions to the world of books and, through books, to society. The nominee must be a living American and derive her income from books and the allied arts. A citation is awarded biennially in even-numbered years. Established in 1940 in memory of Constance Lindsay Skinner, author/editor and founder of the WNBA publication, *The Bookwoman*. Formerly: (1983) Constance Lindsay Skinner Award.

• 21801 •
Women's National Book Association - New York Chapter
Jenine Bockman, Pres.
PO Box 237
FDR Station
New York, NY 10150
Phone: (212)208-4629
Fax: (212)989-7542
E-mail: publicity@bookbuzz.com
Home Page: http://bookbuzz.com

• 21802 • WNBA Award
For a bookwoman who has made an outstanding contribution. Recognition award bestowed biennially.

• 21803 •
Women's Services Worldwide
Dr. Kate Alexander, CEO & Pres.
PO Box 136
Frazier Park, CA 93225
Phone: (661)361-1177
Fax: (818)727-7992
E-mail: anodyne911@hotmail.com

• 21804 • Glenayre Award
Recognizes individuals and organizations helping women. Awarded periodically.

• 21805 •
Women's Sports Foundation
Dr. Donna Lopiano PhD, CEO
Eisenhower Park
East Meadow, NY 11554
Phone: (516)542-4700
Toll-Free: 800-227-3988
Fax: (516)542-4716
E-mail: wosport@aol.com
Home Page: http://www.womenssportsfoundation.org

• 21806 • **CAR Coach of the Year Award**
To recognize female coaches working with youth, school, and college athletes. These are the less visible unsung heroines who work to broaden the base of the girls and women's sports pyramid. NCAA Division III, NAIA, NJCAA, High School, or grass root coach is eligible. National level coaches, NCAA I and II are not eligible. Established in 1986.

• 21807 • **Flo Hyman Memorial Award**
To recognize a woman athlete who captures the dignity, spirit, and commitment to excellence of the late Flo Hyman. It honors an athlete who recognizes the far-reaching benefits of sport and who is determined to share these values with others. Awarded on National Girls and Women in Sports Day, celebrated the second Thursday in February. Established in 1987. Formerly: (2006) Women's Sports Foundation Flo Hyman Award.

• 21808 • **International Women's Sports Hall of Fame**
For recognition of great female athletes of the world. Becoming a member of the Women's Sports Hall of Fame requires international recognition of an athlete's sports performance and of her continuing commitment to the development of women's sports. Athletes whose major accomplishments were achieved prior to 1960 are inducted as Pioneers, while the Contemporary category recognizes athletes whose greatest success has been since 1960. Nominations for both categories are received from sport historians, international and national sport organizations, and the public. In 1990 the Hall of Fame added a coach category. Criteria for nomination states that the candidate must be a U.S. female coach with at least ten years of coaching experience. Other considerations include a majority of the following: win/loss record, impact on style of game or sport, contribution to sport, community service, outstanding athletes produced, number of years coaching, and record of mentoring. A selection committee, comprised of current Hall of Fame members, selects the new inductees. Only one person from a specific sport may be nominated in each category each year. Awarded annually at the award dinner. Established in 1980.

• 21809 • **Billie Jean King Contribution Award**
To recognize an individual, organization, or corporation for significant contributions to the development of women's sports. Demonstration of a continuing, lasting commitment and dedication to the growth of sports for women is necessary. Recipients are selected by the Awards Committee of the Women's Sports Foundation.

• 21810 • **President's Award**
For recognition of advisory board members for their work for the Foundation and their contributions toward the development of women's sports. Established in 1985 by Donna de Varona. Originally given by the Foundation president to honor someone who has made a major contribution to the development of women's sports. It is not given on an annual basis. Formerly: Donna de Varona Award.

• 21811 • **Sportswomen of the Year Awards**
To recognize the outstanding individual and team amateur and professional female athletes whose performances over a twelve-month span have been exceptional. Criteria for these awards are new records and world championships won. Nominations are received from sport organizations and the public, and the winners are selected by voting members of the Foundation. Established in 1980.

• 21812 • **Women's Sports Journalism Awards**
To recognize a journalist for articles or publications in which women in sports are portrayed in a positive manner. Categories include newspaper (daily/weekly) magazine, column (newspaper/magazine), series (newspaper/magazine), local television, network television, radio and documentaries. Awarded annually. Established in 1987. Formerly: (2006) Miller Lite Women's Sports Journalism Awards.

• 21813 •
Women's Transportation Seminar
Sunnie House, Pres.
1666 K St. NW, Ste. 1100
Washington, DC 20006
Phone: (202)496-4340
Fax: (202)496-4349
E-mail: wts@wtsinternational.org
Home Page: http://wtsinternational.org

• 21814 • **Helene Overly Scholarship**
To encourage and assist women who are beginning professional careers or advancing their existing transportation careers to consider the field of transportation. Students in the top quarter of their class, who are in a program related to transportation, and plan to remain in the field following completion of studies are eligible. A monetary award of $1,200 is awarded annually.

• 21815 • **WTS National Member of the Year**
To recognize achievement and contribution by a WTS member who has demonstrated outstanding support of the organization. Selection is based on the following criteria: a member of WTS; supports the ideas and has demonstrated an interest in WTS; has demonstrated a willingness to work with the Chapter structure and promote intra-Chapter communication and development; and has enhanced the reputation of WTS within the transportation industry. Nominations must be submitted through local WTS Chapters. A crystal obelisk is awarded each year at the annual conference in May. In addition, the winner's name is added to a plaque honoring all recipients. Established in 1981.

• 21816 • **WTS National Woman of the Year**
To recognize a woman for achievement and contribution to the transportation industry. Selection is based on the following criteria: outstanding contributions to the transportation industry, significant contributions toward the advancement of women in developing a career in transportation and/or enhancing their career paths, overcoming substantial obstacles in order to achieve career successes in the transportation field, and support of the ideas of and a demonstrated interest in WTS. A crystal obelisk is awarded each year at the annual conference in May. Established in 1980.

• 21817 •
Wood County Historical Society
Christie Raber, Dir.
13660 County Home Rd.
Bowling Green, OH 43402-9563
Phone: (419)352-0967
Fax: (419)352-6220
E-mail: museum@woodcountyhistory.org
Home Page: http://www.woodcountyhistory.org

• 21818 • **Internship**
For graduate and undergraduate students interested in museums. Monetary award bestowed annually.

• 21819 •
Wood Design and Building Magazine
Janam Publications Inc.
Don Griffith, Ed.
26 St. Raymond Blvd. Ste 206
Gatineau, QC, Canada J8Y 1R4
Phone: (819)778-5040
Toll-Free: 800-520-6281
Fax: (819)595-8553
E-mail: dgriffith@janam.net
Home Page: http://www.woodmags.com

• 21820 • **American Wood Council Wood Design Award**
Recognizes outstanding examples of wood construction exemplifying the practical environmental benefits of wood as well as wood's versatility. Awarded annually.

• 21821 • **Wood Design Awards**
To recognize excellence in the design of buildings in which wood has a significant role. Various Honor Awards, Merit Awards, and Citation Awards are presented annually.

• 21822 •
Woodmen of the World/Omaha Woodmen Life Insurance Society
James L. Mounce, Chm./Pres./CEO
Woodmen Tower
1700 Farnam St.
Omaha, NE 68102-2002
Toll-Free: 800-225-3108
Fax: (402)271-7269
E-mail: wow@woodmen.com
Home Page: http://www.woodmen.com

• 21823 • **Howard Christensen Award**
Recognizes dedicated DBIA members. Awarded annually.

• 21824 •
Woodrow Wilson National Fellowship Foundation
Beverly Sanford, Sec./Dir.
5 Vaughn Dr., Ste. 300
Princeton, NJ 08543-5281
Phone: (609)452-7007
Fax: (609)452-0066
E-mail: communications@woodrow.org
Home Page: http://www.woodrow.org

• 21825 • **Doctoral Dissertation Grants in Women's Studies**
To encourage original and significant research about women that crosses disciplinary, regional, or cultural boundaries. Each winner receives $3,000 to be used for travel and research expenses connected to their dissertation. Established in 1974 by the Ford Foundation.

• 21826 • **Charlotte W. Newcombe Doctoral Dissertation Fellowship**
To encourage original and significant study of ethical or religious values in all fields of the humanities and social sciences. Individuals who are enrolled in graduate school in the United States who have completed all requirements for the doctorate except the dissertation may apply by November 7. Fellowships of $18,500 are awarded annually. Established in 1981 by the Charlotte Newcombe Foundation.

• 21827 •
Leigh Yawkey Woodson Art Museum
700 N 12th St. Franklin & 12th St.
Wausau, WI 54403-5007
Phone: (715)845-7010
Fax: (715)845-7103
E-mail: museum@lywam.org
Home Page: http://www.lywam.org

• 21828 • **Master Wildlife Artist**
To recognize and encourage achievements and contributions to the field of wildlife art. Past Master Wildlife Artist honorees, Museum staff, and Board of Directors may submit nominations. A medallion is awarded annually at the opening of the Birds in Art exhibition. Established in 1976.

• 21829 •
Woodstock School of Art
2470 Rte. 212
PO Box 338
Woodstock, NY 12498
Phone: (845)679-2388
Fax: (914)679-2388
E-mail: wsart@earthlink.net
Home Page: http://www.woodstockschoolofart.com

• 21830 • **Woodstock National Exhibition**
For recognition of artistic excellence in various media. Monetary awards of $200 were awarded annually. Established in 1983.

• 21831 •
Woolknit Associates
267 5th Ave.
New York, NY 10016
Phone: (212)683-7785
Fax: (212)683-2682

• 21832 • **Woolknit Design Awards**
To recognize American designers of men's and women's wool knitwear who have stimulated new creative efforts in knitted wool fabrics and have contributed styling innovations. Nominees are selected by a jury of retail executives represented by ready-to-wear sportswear buyers and merchandising managers. Two Design Award Citations, one for the men's category and one for the women's category, are awarded annually. Established in 1952.

• 21833 •
The Word Works
Miles David Moore, Admin. of the Washington Prize
PO Box 42164
Washington, DC 20015
E-mail: editor@wordworksdc.com
Home Page: http://www.wordworksdc.com

• 21834 • **Washington Prize**
To recognize a living American poet for an outstanding volume of original poetry. Poets may submit manuscripts of 48 to 64 pages. Manuscripts must not have been published, and must be submitted between January 15 and March 1 inclusive. Send self-addressed, stamped envelope for complete rules. A monetary prize of $1,500 and book publication for a volume of original poetry are awarded annually. Established in 1981.

• 21835 •
Workers' Defense League
Jon Bloom, Exec.Dir.
275 7th Ave.
New York, NY 10001
Phone: (212)627-1931
Fax: (212)627-4628

• 21836 • **David L. Clendenin Award**
To recognize distinguished service by prominent labor, religious or political figures to the labor movement and civil rights. A plaque is awarded annually in memory of David L. Clendenin, cofounder of the League and a strong advocate of democratic trade unionism. Established in 1941.

• 21837 •
Workforce Management
Crain Communications Inc.
John Hollon, Ed.
4 Executive Cir., Ste. 185
Irvine, CA 92614
Phone: (949)255-5340
Fax: (949)221-8964
E-mail: mailroom@workforce.com
Home Page: http://www.workforceonline.com

• 21838 • **Optimas Awards**
To recognize human resources programs that challenge traditional assumptions about human resources management and prove that human resources leaders are playing a more active role in business success. Awarded in 10 categories annually. Established in 1991.

• 21839 •
World Affairs Council of Pittsburgh
Dr. Schuyler Foerster, Pres.
501 Grant St., Ste. 1175
Pittsburgh, PA 15219-4406
Phone: (412)281-7970
Fax: (412)281-1795
E-mail: welcome@worldaffairspittsburgh.org
Home Page: http://www.worldaffairspittsburgh.org/

• 21840 • **Donald E. Farr Award**
For outstanding student. Recognition award bestowed annually.

• 21841 • **David Glick Award**
For individuals who have made significant contributions towards better understanding world affairs. Recognition award bestowed annually.

• 21842 • **George C. Oehmler Award**
For outstanding teacher involved in the international affairs program for high schools. Recognition award bestowed annually.

• 21843 •
World Airlines Clubs Association
Mr. Keith Miller, Mgr.
PO Box 113
PO Box 113
Montreal, QC, Canada H4Z 1M1
Phone: (514)874-0202
Phone: (514)697-8374
Fax: (514)874-1753
E-mail: millerk@iata.org
Home Page: http://www.waca.org

• 21844 • **Certifications of Appreciation**
Presented to individuals for outstanding contributions. Awarded periodically.

• 21845 • **Regional Clubs of the Year**
For recognition of the best regional club of the year. Clubs are judged by such factors as the number of members in good standing, communication, active participation, attendance at meetings, ideas, and overall involvement. Plaques are awarded annually at the general assembly. Established in 1982.

• 21846 • **Emile Tocze Memorial Trophy**
For recognition of the best overall member club in the world (all five regions). Clubs are judged by such factors as the number of members in good standing, communication, active participation, attendance at meetings, ideas, and overall involvement. A trophy is awarded annually at the general assembly. Established in 1982 in honor of Emile Tocze, founder.

• 21847 •
World Archaeological Society
Ron Miller, Dir.
120 Lakewood Dr.
Hollister, MO 65672
Phone: (417)334-2377
E-mail: ronwriterartist@aol.com
Home Page: http://www.worldarchaeologicalsociety.com

• 21848 • **WAS Special Commendations**
Recognizes publishers and individual artists of publications, photographs, graphic art, and film. Awarded periodically.

• 21849 •
World Association for Public Opinion Research
Dr. Salma Ghanem, Sec./Treas.
University of Nebraska-Lincoln
UNL Gallup Research Center
200 N 11th St.
Lincoln, NE 68588-0242
Phone: (402)458-2030
Fax: (402)458-2038
E-mail: ghanem@panam.edu
Home Page: http://www.unl.edu/WAPOR/

• 21850 • **Helen Dinerman Award**
For outstanding contributions and published articles. Awarded annually.

• 21851 • **Worcester, Nelson and Turner Prizes**
Award of recognition.

• 21852 •
World Association for the Advancement of Veterinary Parasitology
Dr. Ann R. Donoghue DVM, Sec.-Treas.
PO Box 8
North Aurora, IL 60542
Phone: (630)262-1997
Phone: (630)892-2321
Fax: (630)892-0818
E-mail: isvma@aol.com

• 21853 • **Excellence in Teaching Veterinary Parasitology**
Recognizes merit for research, publications, service. Awarded biennially.

• 21854 • **Outstanding Contributions to Research in Veterinary Parasitology**
Recognizes merit for research, publications, service. Awarded biennially.

• 21855 • **Peter Nancen Award for Young Scientists**
Recognizes merit for research, publications, service. Awarded biennially.

• 21856 • **Research Award**
For outstanding contributions to Research in Veterinary Parasitology; for excellence in teaching veterinary parasitology.

• 21857 •
World Association of Community Radio Broadcasters
(Association Mondial de Radios Communautarias)
Steve Buckley, Pres.
705 Bourget St., Ste. 100
Montreal, QC, Canada H4C 2M6
Phone: (514)982-0351
Fax: (514)849-7129
E-mail: amarc@amarc.org
Home Page: http://www.amarc.org

• 21858 • **Solidarity Prize**
Recognizes a defender of the right to communicate of community based broadcasters. Awarded quadrennially.

• 21859 •
World Association of Industrial and Technological Research Organizations
(Association Mondiale des Organisations de Recherche Industrielle et Technologique)
Frank Bean, Pres.
PO Box 79
Scranton, PA 18504
Fax: (717)342-1368
E-mail: armsport@uslt.net
Home Page: http://www.armsport.com/waf.htm

• 21860 • **Hall of Champions**
To recognize contributions to and excellence in arm wrestling and service to the organization. Ten awards are awarded per year.

• 21861 •
World Atlatl Association
Leni Clubb, Sec.
PO Box 56
Ocotillo, CA 92259
Phone: (760)358-7835
E-mail: waaleni@earthlink.net
Home Page: http://www.worldatlatl.org

• 21862 • **Fellowship Award**
Recognizes outstanding service to the association through organizational, educational and leadership skills. A certificate granting all of the entitlements and rights of this organization is awarded.

• 21863 • **Grand Champion Primitive and Modern Equipment - U.S. and Europe**
Annual award of recognition. Inquire for details.

• 21864 • **International Standard Accurracy ATLATL Contest-U.S and Europe**
Annual contest of skill.

• 21865 • **President's Award**
Recognizes accomplishments of members. Awarded annually.

• 21866 •
World Bank Group
Paul Wolfowitz, Pres.
1818 H St. NW
Washington, DC 20433
Phone: (202)473-1000
Phone: (202)477-1234
Fax: (202)477-6391
E-mail: newsbureau@worldbank.org
Home Page: http://www.worldbank.org

• 21867 • **Robert S. McNamara Fellowships Program**
To provide for full-time work research at the post-graduate level in fields related to economic development and institution building. The innovative or imaginative character of the work research to be undertaken is a major factor in selection. Individuals who meet the following basic criteria are considered: (1) must be a national of a Bank member country that is eligible to borrow (i.e. a developing country); (2) normally 35 years of age or under; (3) holder of a minimum Master's degree or equivalent; and (4) research must be carried out in the national's home country. The award amount is fixed at $7,500 to cover research costs through the twelve months fellowship period. The Fellowships program is not intended to support work leading to an advanced degree. Established in 1982 in honor of Robert McNamara, a former president of the World Bank.

• 21868 •
World Bowling Writers
Bob Johnson, Administrator
122 S Michigan Ave., Ste. 1506
Chicago, IL 60603
Phone: (312)341-1110
Fax: (312)341-1469
E-mail: bobj@bowlersjournal.com
Home Page: http://www.bowlersjournal.com

• 21869 • **International Bowling Hall of Fame**
To honor amateur bowlers whose achievements have caused them to be recognized as premier

performers and standard-setters of the game of tenpin bowling. Enshrinees are selected by annual ballot by the current officers and past presidents of the WBW and are announced in September. One or more people are enshrined each year. Established in 1993.

• 21870 • Male and Female Bowler of the Year Award
For performance in international competitions. Awarded annually.

• 21871 • WBW Bowlers of the Year
To recognize superior performance in international amateur competition. Individual must be an amateur athlete (hold no memberships in professional bowling organizations) to be eligible. A plaque is awarded to one male and one female bowler each year Established in 1980.

• 21872 • WBW Distinguished Service Award
To recognize outstanding and continued efforts of individuals in furthering the development and expansion of international amateur bowling competition. Individual must be actively involved in the promotion of international amateur bowling competition in the capacity of tournament organizer or director, bowling industry spokesperson, or communicator. A plaque is awarded at the annual meeting in conjunction with the AMF Bowling World Cup or quadrennially, in conjunction with the FIQ (Federation Internationale des Quillieurs) World Championships. Established in 1977.

• 21873 • WBW Gosta Zellen Golden Quill Award
To recognize outstanding and continued excellence in writing about, reporting on, and publicizing or promoting international amateur bowling competition. Individual must be an active bowling journalist, which can include written, spoken or photographic delivery of the message. A plaque is awarded at the annual meeting in conjunction with the AMF Bowling World Cup or quadrennially, in conjunction with the FIQ (Federation International des Quillieurs) World Championships. Established in 1977.

• 21874 •
World Communication Association
Barbara S. Monfils, Pres.
Communication Dept.
University of Wisconsin-Whitewater
800 W Main St.
Whitewater, WI 53190-1790
Phone: (262)472-1055
Fax: (262)472-1670
E-mail: monfilsb@uww.edu
Home Page: http://facstaff.uww.edu/wca

Formerly: (1983) Communication Association of the Pacific.

• 21875 • Distinguished Service Award
For recognition of extraordinary professional service toward achievement of the purposes of the Association. A plaque was awarded biennially at the Convention. Established in 1985.

• 21876 •
World Confederation of Productivity Science
Linda Carbone, Exec.Dir.
500 Sherbrooke St. W, Ste. 900
Montreal, QC, Canada H3A 3C6
Phone: (514)282-3838
Fax: (514)844-7556
E-mail: secretariat@wcps.info
Home Page: http://www.wcps.info

• 21877 • Recognizes outstanding performance in the field of productivity. New chapters and academy fellows are eligible.

• 21878 •
World Council for Curriculum and Instruction
Dr. Estela C. Matriano, Exec.Dir.
Cross Cultural Studies Institute
Graduate School of Education
Alliant International University
10455 Pomerado Rd.
San Diego, CA 92131-1799
Phone: (858)635-4719
Phone: (858)635-4718
Fax: (858)635-4714
E-mail: wcci@alliant.edu
Home Page: http://www.wcci-international.org

• 21879 • Masako Shoji Scholarship
For research on early childhood development. Awarded annually.

• 21880 • Shigeka Talumura Scholarship
For research on global education. Awarded annually.

• 21881 • Yoneji Ebitani Scholarship
For research on curriculum and instruction. Awarded annually.

• 21882 •
World Council of Credit Unions
Arthur Arnold, Pres./CEO
5710 Mineral Point Rd.
PO Box 2982
Madison, WI 53705
Phone: (608)231-7130
Fax: (608)238-8020
E-mail: mail@woccu.org
Home Page: http://www.woccu.org

• 21883 • Distinguised Service Award
For contributions to credit union development. Awarded annually.

• 21884 •
World Council of Optometry
Dr. Anthony F. Di Stefano, Exec.Dir.
8360 Old York Rd., 4th Fl. W
Elkins Park, PA 19027
Phone: (215)780-1320
Fax: (215)780-1325
E-mail: wco@pco.edu
Home Page: http://www.worldoptometry.org

Formerly: International Optometric and Optic League.

• 21885 • International Optometrist of the Year
For recognition of achievement in the field of international optometry. Nomination is made by the executive committee of the League. A plaque is awarded annually. Established in 1988.

• 21886 • WCO Emeritus
To recognize past delegates and officers who have served the League and world optometry with distinction. Holders of the title are eligible to attend meetings of the League. The title of Emeritus (e.g., Delegate Emeritus, President Emeritus, etc.) is awarded. Established in 1978. Formerly: IOOL Emeritus.

• 21887 • WCO Medal
For recognition of service to the League and to international optometry. Contributions by optometrists, ophthalmologists, and others to the advancement of the science or profession of optometry or ophthalmic optics are considered. A medal is awarded when merited. Established in 1965. Formerly: IOOL Medal.

• 21888 •
World Development Federation
Laura Lyne, Prog.Dir.
35 Technology Pkwy., Ste. 150
Norcross, GA 30092
Phone: (770)446-6996
Fax: (770)263-8825
E-mail: wdf@conway.com
Home Page: http://www.wdf.org

• 21889 • Distinguished Service Award
Recognition service to WDF. Selected by WDF Board. Awarded annually.

• 21890 •
World Diving Coaches Association
Judy Estes, Sec.Treas.
5810 N 59th Ave.
Glendale, AZ 85301-5810
Phone: (623)930-8115
Fax: (623)930-8118
Home Page: http://www.biorgen.com

• 21891 • Sammy Lee Award
Recognizes the person who has done the most for the sport of diving throughout the world during his life time. Awarded quadrennially.

• 21892 •
World Environment Center
Mr. John Mizroch, Pres./CEO
1300 Pennsylvania Ave. NW, Ste. 550
Mailbox 142
Washington, DC 20004
Phone: (202)312-1210
Fax: (202)682-1682
E-mail: john@wec.org
Home Page: http://www.wec.org

• 21893 • **WEC Gold Medal for International Corporate Achievement in Sustainable Development**
To recognize a corporation that demonstrates preeminent industry leadership, worldwide environmental quality, and global sustainable development. Nominations are judged by an independent international jury of environmentalists from academia, government, and industry on the following broad criteria: environmental policy and commitment, innovative implementation and application of said policy, and international environmental leadership. More specific criteria changes annually. Awarded annually. Established in 1985. Formerly: (2006) WEC Gold Medal for International Corporate Environmental Achievement.

• 21894 •
World Evangelical Alliance
Gary Edmonds, Sec.Gen.
PO Box 1839
Edmonds, WA 98020
Phone: (425)778-5513
Fax: (425)640-3671
E-mail: info@worldevangelical.org
Home Page: http://
www.worldevangelical.org

• 21895 • **Religious Liberty Award**
Recognizes leadership during persecution. Awarded during the WEA General Assembly which meets at least every six years. Formerly: (2003) World Evangelical Fellowship.

• 21896 •
World Federalist Association
John B. Anderson, Pres./CEO
418 7th St. SE
Washington, DC 20003
Phone: (202)546-3950
Toll-Free: 800-WFA-0123
Fax: (202)546-3749
E-mail: information@wfa.org
Home Page: http://www.wfa.org

• 21897 • **Norman Cousins Global Governance Award**
For best contribution in media piece to public understanding of need for global governance. Awarded annually.

• 21898 •
World Federalist Association, Minnesota Chapter
Verlyn O. Smith, Pres.
5145 16th Ave. S.
Minneapolis, MN 55417
Phone: (651)636-6544
E-mail: vosjh@aol.com

• 21899 • **Builders of a Better World Prize**
For students and young people up to age 30. Monetary award bestowed annually.

• 21900 •
World Federalist Association of Pittsburgh
Roseann Rife, Exec.Dir.
239 Fourth Ave., Ste. 1607
Pittsburgh, PA 15222
Phone: (412)471-7852

• 21901 • **Norman Cousins Award**
Given to individual or group in west PA on the basis of an outstanding contribution to the peace, security, and well-being of the world community. Recognition award bestowed annually.

• 21902 •
World Federation for Mental Health
Preston Garrison, CEO
PO Box 16810
Alexandria, VA 22302-0810
Phone: (703)838-7543
Phone: (703)838-7525
Fax: (703)519-7648
E-mail: info@wfmh.com
Home Page: http://www.wfmh.org

• 21903 • **Distinguished Citizen Award**
For outstanding contribution to international mental health. Awarded annually.

• 21904 •
World Federation of Direct Selling Associations
Neil H. Offen, Sec.
1275 Pennsylvania Ave., NW, Ste. 800
Washington, DC 20004
Phone: (202)347-8866
Fax: (202)347-0055
E-mail: info@wfdsa.org
Home Page: http://www.wfdsa.org

• 21905 • **Outstanding Service Award**
Triennial award of recognition.

• 21906 •
World Federation of Estonian Women's Clubs
Mrs. Juta Kurman, Pres.
68-50 Juno St.
Forest Hills, NY 11375
Phone: (718)261-9618
Fax: (718)261-9618

• 21907 • **Honorary Member**
Recognizes outstanding achievements and services. Awarded annually.

• 21908 •
World Federation of Hemophilia (Federation Mondiale de l'Hemophilie)
Miklos Fulop, CEO/Exec.Dir.
1425 Rene-Levesque West
Ste. 1010
Montreal, QC, Canada H3G 1T7
Phone: (514)875-7944
Fax: (514)875-8916
E-mail: wfh@wfh.org
Home Page: http://wfh.org

• 21909 • **International Hemophilia Training Centres Fellowships**
Annual monetary award.

• 21910 •
World Federation of Neurosurgical Societies
Dr. Edward R. Laws, Pres.
University of Virginia
Department of Neurosurgery
PO Box 800212
Charlottesville, VA 22908
Phone: (434)924-2650
Toll-Free: 800-650-2650
Fax: (434)924-5894
E-mail: el5g@virginia.edu
Home Page: http://www.wfns.org

• 21911 • **Gold Medal of Honor**
For excellence in neurosurgery. A monetary award is given quadrennially.

• 21912 • **Scoville Award**
For excellence in neurosurgery. A monetary award is given quadrennially.

• 21913 • **Young Neurosurgeons Award**
For excellence in neurosurgery. A monetary award is given quadrennially.

• 21914 •
World Federation of Personnel Management Associations
Sue R. Meisinger, Sec.Gen.
1800 Duke St.
CIPD House
Camp Rd.
Wimbledon
Alexandria, VA 22314-3499
Phone: (703)548-3440
Fax: (703)258-6035
E-mail: smeisinger@shrm.org
Home Page: http://www.wfpma.com

• 21915 • **Georges Petitpas Memorial Award**
To recognize exemplary contributions to the human resource management field. Awarded biennially in even-numbered years at the Federation Congress. Established in 1986.

• 21916 •
World Folk Music Association
Richard A. Cerri, Pres.
PO Box 40553
Washington, DC 20016
Phone: (202)362-2225
Toll-Free: 800-779-2226
Fax: (301)589-2037
E-mail: webmaster@wfma.net
Home Page: http://www.wfma.net

• 21917 • **Kate Wolf Memorial Award**
Award of recognition. Bestowed to singer/songwriter who best represents qualities of Kate Wolf. Awarded annually.

• 21918 •
The World Food Prize Foundation
Kenneth Quinn, Pres.
666 Grand Ave., Ste. 1700
Des Moines, IA 50309
Phone: (515)245-3783
Fax: (515)245-3785
E-mail: wfp@worldfoodprize.org
Home Page: http://www.worldfoodprize.org

• 21919 • **The World Food Prize**
To recognize, encourage, and reward outstanding individual achievement in improving the quality, quantity and availability of the world's food supply. Beyond the recognition component, the World Food Prize conducts an annual International Symposium and a Youth Institute, at the same time the award is presented. The award is made without regard to race, color, religion, national origin, sex, or political persuasion of nominees. Candidates may be nominated by any private or public organization in the world. Nominations remain valid for three years. A monetary award of $250,000 and a commemorative sculpture are presented annually at a ceremony held each October in Des Moines, Iowa. Established in 1986 by Nobel Peace Prize Laureate, Dr. Norman E. Borlawg, the award is sponsored by The World Food Prize Foundation, of which Mr. John Ruan is the chairman. Ambassador Kenneth M. Quinn serves as the president.

• 21920 •
World Footbag Association
Bruce Guettich, Pres.
PO Box 775208
Steamboat Springs, CO 80477
Phone: (970)870-9898
Toll-Free: 800-878-8797
Fax: (970)870-2846
E-mail: wfa@worldfootbag.com
Home Page: http://www.worldfootbag.com

Formerly: (1977) National Hacky Sack Footbag Players Association.

• 21921 • **World Footbag Championships**
For recognition of achievement in and contribution to the sport of footbag. Players must have professional status to be eligible for world awards. Awards are given in the following categories: Women's Footbag Golf, Open Footbag Golf, Women's Singles Footbag Freestyle, Women's Doubles Footbag Freestyle, Open Singles Footbag Freestyle, Open Doubles Footbag Freestyle, Mixed Doubles Footbag Net, Women's Singles Footbag Net, Women's Doubles Footbag Net, Open Singles Footbag Net, and Open Doubles Footbag Net. The most prestigious prize is the Men's and Women's World "Overall" Award. Awards are given to the top three finishing competitors in the combined six events. Monetary prizes totaling $7,000 and trophies are awarded annually. Established in 1979 by the National Hacky Sack Footbag Players Association. Sponsored by Mattel Sports, SIPA Footbags and Adidas Footbags. Formerly: National Footbag Championships.

• 21922 •
World Golf Hall of Fame
One World Golf Place
St. Augustine, FL 32092
Phone: 800-WGV-GOLF
E-mail: sam@resortgolf.com
Home Page: http://www.wgv.com

• 21923 • **World Golf Hall of Fame**
To broaden interest in the game of golf by recognizing the achievements of its greatest individuals (both players and contributors to the game) and providing an entertaining, interactive, and educational experience. Established in 1974 in Pinehurst, NC, it reopened in 1998 as a part of the World Golf Village in St. Augustine, FL. Individuals are inducted annually. Affiliated with the American Junior Golf Association, American Society of Golf Course Architects, Asian PGA, Augusta National Golf Club, Club Managers Association of America, Golf Course Builders Association of America, Golf Course Superintendents Association of America, Golf Writers Association of America, International Association of Golf Administrators, Japan Golf Tour, Ladies Professional Golf Association, National Golf Course Owners Association, National Golf Foundation, Professional Golf Tournaments Association, Professional Golfers' Association of America, PGA Tour of Australasia, PGA European Tour, PGA Tour, Sunshine Tour, Royal and Ancient Golf Club of St. Andrews, Royal Canadian Golf Association, United States Golf Association, and World Golf Championships. Formerly: .

• 21924 •
World Hunger Year
Bill Avres, Exec.Dir.
505 8th Ave., 21st Fl.
New York, NY 10018
Phone: (212)629-8850
Toll-Free: 800-5HU-NGRY
Fax: (212)465-9274
E-mail: why@worldhungeryear.org
Home Page: http://www.worldhungeryear.org

• 21925 • **Harry Chapin Media Awards**
To encourage, honor, and reward print and electronic media for their outstanding coverage that positively impacts hunger, poverty, development, and self-reliance. Nominees are considered in the following categories: best newspaper coverage, best periodical coverage, best broadcast (television, radio, or film) best photojournalism, and best book. Work appearing in the United States during the preceding year must be submitted by February 15. A monetary award of up to $2,500 is awarded annually in each category. Established in 1982 by Kenny and Marianne Rogers. The HCMA have been administered and financed since 1988 by World Hunger Year, and the Washington-based group, RESULTS, funds the newspaper category in memory of late activist Cameron R. Duncan. Formerly: World Hunger Media Awards.

• 21926 • **Harry Chapin Self-Reliance Award**
Grants to grassroots organizations judged outstanding for their innovative and creative approaches to fighting domestic hunger and poverty by empowering poor people and building self-reliance. Monetary grants of $5,000 are awarded annually. Established in 1985. Cosponsored by the Harry Chapin Foundation. 629 4840

• 21927 •
World International Nail and Beauty Association
David Kellenberger, VP
1221 N. Lake View Ave.
Anaheim, CA 92807
Phone: (714)779-9892
Toll-Free: 800-541-9838
Fax: (714)779-9971
E-mail: dkellenberger@inmnails.com

• 21928 • **WINBA Championship Title**
For recognition of achievement and field activity in cosmetology. World Championship Titles are given in the following categories: Student, Nails, Nail Arts, U.S. Championship Nails, and Nail Wrapping. Monetary awards, medallions, and jewelry, annually in each category. Awards are also given in the following categories: Professional Haircutting Two Phase, Student Haircutting Two Phase, Student Mannequin Two Phase Comb Out, Student Styling Contest, and Evening Corrective Make-up. First, second, and third prizes include trophies, cash, and gift packages. A 14 carat gold ring and 8 foot trophy are given for Professional Sculptured Acrylic Nails, Professional Hairstyling, and Fantasy Make-up categories. Established in 1980 by James George.

• 21929 •
World Learning
James A. Cramer, Pres.
U.S. Headquarters, Kipling Rd.
PO Box 676
Brattleboro, VT 05302-0676
Phone: (802)258-3400
Toll-Free: 800-257-7752
Fax: (802)258-3470
E-mail: business@worldlearning.org
Home Page: http://www.worldlearning.org

Awards are arranged in alphabetical order below their administering organizations

• 21930 • Experiment Citation Award
Recognizes distinguished service in international education and exchange. Awarded annually.

• 21931 •
World Leisure and Recreation Association
Gerald S. Kenyon, Sec.Gen.
World Leisure Secretariat
Site 81 C, Comp 0
Okanagan Falls, BC, Canada V0H 1R0
Phone: (250)497-6578
Fax: (250)497-6578
E-mail: secretariat@worldleisure.org
Home Page: http://www.worldleisure.org

Formerly: (1973) International Recreation Association.

• 21932 • World Leisure International Scholarship
Intended to provide opportunities for senior graduate students who are studying recreation, leisure studies, leisure resources or tourism studies in college programs, the scholarship allows the students to attend and participate in the international congress. The scholarship includes the congress registration fee, accommodations, and transportation by air from a suitably located departure airport. Meals are not included. The winner must be a final year graduate or undergraduate student, have a GPA of 3.2 or above if an undergraduate and 3.5 if a graduate, be recommended by the faculty members at the college, have exhibited interest, have worked in a recreation or tourist field, and submit an acceptable abstract.

• 21933 •
World Literature Today
Robert Davis-Undiano, Exec.Dir.
Univ. of Oklahoma
630 Parrington Oval, Ste. 110
Norman, OK 73019-4033
Phone: (405)325-4531
Fax: (405)325-7495
E-mail: vav@ou.edu
Home Page: http://www.ou.edu/worldlit

Formerly: (1977) *Books Abroad.*

• 21934 • Neustadt International Prize for Literature
For recognition of outstanding achievement in poetry, fiction, or drama that is conferred solely on the basis of literary merit. Any living author writing in any language is eligible, provided that at least a representative portion of his or her work is available in English, Spanish, and/or French - the three languages used in the jury deliberations. The prize may serve to crown a lifetime of achievement or to direct attention to an important body of work that is still developing. Applications are not accepted. Nominations of a poet, a novelist, or a playwright are made by each of the 12 jurors on the International Jury. The following prizes are awarded: $50,000; a Silver Eagle Feather; an award certificate; and a special issue of WLT devoted to his or her work. Award biennially. Established in 1969. Formerly: (1978) *Books Abroad*/Neustadt International Prize.

• 21935 •
World Methodist Council
Dr. George Freeman, Gen.Sec.
545 N Lakeshore Dr.
PO Box 518
Lake Junaluska, NC 28745
Phone: (828)456-9432
Fax: (828)456-9433
E-mail: wmc6@juno.com
Home Page: http://www.worldmethodistcouncil.org

• 21936 • World Methodist Peace Award
To recognize the exercise of courage, creativity, and consistency on the part of individuals pursuing peace and reconciliation between people and nations. Nominations may be submitted to the chairman of the executive committee or general secretary of the World Methodist Council. A monetary award of $1,000 and an inscribed medallion in gilded silver are awarded when merited. Established in 1976.

• 21937 •
World Ocean and Cruise Liner Society
George C. Devol, Pres.
PO Box 4850
Stamford, CT 06907-0850
Phone: (203)329-2787
Fax: (203)329-2787
E-mail: membership@wocls.org
Home Page: http://www.wocls.org

• 21938 • Ship of the Year
To provide recognition for the cruise ship that receives the highest degree of passenger satisfaction during the year. After completing a cruise, members fill out and return a report form to the organization. At the end of each year, the ship with the highest overall score is designated "Ship of the Year." A plaque is awarded annually. Established in 1981 by George C. Devol.

• 21939 •
World Organization for Human Potential
Glenn Domann, Founder
8801 Stenton Ave.
Wyndmoor, PA 19038
Phone: (215)233-2050
Toll-Free: 800-736-4663
Fax: (215)233-3940
E-mail: institutes@iahp.org
Home Page: http://www.iahp.org

• 21940 • Spectrum Award
Annual award of recognition for unique contributions to human potential.

• 21941 •
World Organization of Building Officials
Omkar Nath Channan, Founding World Pres.
155 Bearspaw Meadows
Calgary, AB, Canada T3L 2M3
Phone: (403)239-2889
Fax: (403)547-4546

• 21942 • Research Award
Award of recognition given for outstanding contribution. Awarded periodically.

• 21943 • Service Award
Award of recognition given for outstanding contribution. Awarded periodically.

• 21944 •
World Pan African Movement - Canada
(Mouvement Pan Africain du Canada)
Charley Roach, Pres.
688 St. Clair Ave. W
Toronto, ON, Canada M6C 1B1
Phone: (416)657-1472
Phone: (416)657-1465
Fax: (416)657-1511
E-mail: charoa@sympatico.ca

• 21945 • Naiwu Osahon Award
Recognizes Pan African work in many countries. A trophy is awarded semiannually.

• 21946 •
World Relief
Mr. Christopher Pettit, Marketing and Media Mgr.
7 E Baltimore St.
Baltimore, MD 21202
Phone: (443)451-1900
Toll-Free: 800-535-5433
E-mail: worldrelief@wr.org
Home Page: http://www.worldrelief.org

Formerly: (1944) World Relief Commission.

• 21947 • Helping Hands Award
To recognize an individual's contribution to alleviate suffering consistently in Jesus' name. Nominee should be evangelical in theology with unquestionable integrity in spiritual living and ministry. Nominations must be made by WRC staff, board of directors, and denominational partners. The award is given annually at the National Association of Evangelicals convention in March. Established in 1979.

• 21948 •
World Research Foundation
41 Bell Rock Plz.
Sedona, AZ 86351-8804
Phone: (928)284-3300
Fax: (928)284-3530
E-mail: info@wrf.org
Home Page: http://www.wrf.org

• 21949 • **Annual Awards Program**
For public recognition of significant contributions to the field of holistic health.

• 21950 •
World Science Fiction Society
Carl G. Brandon, Exec.Sec.
PO Box 426159, Kendall Sq. Sta.
Cambridge, MA 02142
Phone: (818)366-3827
Fax: (818)366-7987
E-mail: worldcons@worldcon.org
Home Page: http://www.wsfs.org

• 21951 • **Hugo Awards**
To recognize outstanding achievement in science fiction or fantasy in the following categories: (1) novel; (2) novella; (3) novelette; (4) short story; (5) non-fiction book; (6) dramatic presentation; (7) professional artist; (8) professional editor; (9) semi-prozine; (10) fanzine; (11) fan writer; (12) fan artist; and (13) original artwork. Selection is made by members of each year's World Science Fiction Convention. A metal rocket ship designed by Jack McKnight and Ben Jason mounted on a base is awarded annually. In addition to the category awards, the John W. Campbell Memorial Award for the best new writer, and the Special Award are presented when merited at the annual convention. Established in 1953 in honor of Hugo Gernsback who founded the first science fiction magazine and invented the term "science fiction." The John W. Campbell Memorial Award is sponsored by Davis Publications.

• 21952 •
World Sidesaddle Federation
Linda A. Bowlby, Pres.
PO Box 1104
Bucyrus, OH 44820
Phone: (419)284-3176
Fax: (419)284-3176
E-mail: worldsfi@aol.com
Home Page: http://www.sidesaddle.org

• 21953 • **Member of the Year**
To recognize contributions to WSFI and efforts to promote the use of the sidesaddle. Awarded annually with a plaque or gift.

• 21954 • **Participation Awards**
An award for participating in equestrian events and competitions while riding sidesaddle or for promoting the use of the sidesaddle via demonstrations, clinics, talks, etc. Awarded annually with a trophy, plaque, or gift.

• 21955 • **Year-End High Point Awards**
Various awards (including the High Point Youth) for use of the sidesaddle in equestrian events and competitions. Awarded annually with a trophy, plaque, or gift except for $50 savings bond for High Point Youth.

• 21956 •
World Teleport Association
Robert Bell, Exec.Dir.
55 Broad St. 14th Fl.
New York, NY 10004
Phone: (212)825-0218
Fax: (212)825-0075
E-mail: wta@worldteleport.org
Home Page: http://www.worldteleport.org

• 21957 • **Intelligent Community Awards**
For outstanding examples of teleport development and operation, executive leadership, intelligent cities and intelligent buildings. Awarded annually.

• 21958 • **Teleport Awards for Excellence**
For outstanding examples of teleport development and operation, executive leadership, intelligent cities and intelligent buildings. Awarded annually.

• 21959 •
World Trade Center for North Carolina
Pamela Davison, Sr. Staff Advisor
World Trade Park
10900 World Trade Blvd., Ste. 202
Raleigh, NC 27617
Phone: (919)281-2740
Phone: (919)743-0178
Fax: (919)281-2741
E-mail: wtcnc@wtcnc.org
Home Page: http://www.wtcnc.org

• 21960 • **Avery Upchurch Award**
For a board member who exhibits outstanding dedication to the furthering of the center's mission. Recognition award bestowed annually.

• 21961 •
World Trade Center of New Orleans
Natalie Rideau, Membership Dir.
2 Canal St., Ste. 2900
New Orleans, LA 70130
Phone: (504)529-1601
Fax: (504)529-1691
E-mail: wtc-info@wtcno.org
Home Page: http://www.wtcno.org

Formed by merger of: (1985) International House - World Trade Center; International Trade Mart.

• 21962 • **Award for Outstanding Achievement in International Business**
To recognize the head of a foreign corporation that has made major investments in Louisiana resulting in the creation of new jobs and an increase in international trade. A plaque is awarded when merited. Established in 1978.

• 21963 • **Thomas F. Cunningham Award**
For recognition of outstanding service toward better understanding and cooperation among the peoples of the Western Hemisphere, and to stimulate and inspire continued understanding and friendship among all Americans. A plaque is awarded when merited. Established in 1945 in memory of Thomas F. Cunningham, founder of the Mississippi Steamship Co. in 1919 which primarily served Latin America. Formerly: (1986) Thomas F. Cunningham Inter-American Award.

• 21964 •
World Wide Pet Industry Association
Doug Poindexter CAE, Exec.VP
406 S 1st Ave.
Arcadia, CA 91006-3829
Phone: (626)447-2222
Toll-Free: 800-999-7295
Fax: (626)447-8350
E-mail: info@wwpsa.com
Home Page: http://www.wwpia.org

• 21965 • **Jiro Matsui Award**
To recognize significant contributions of personal effort to the pet industry. An engraved plaque is awarded annually. Established in 1963 and named for Jiro Matsui, former Board Member and Industry Visionary.

• 21966 •
World Wildlife Fund
Carter Roberts, Pres./CEO
1250 24th St. NW
PO Box 97180
Washington, DC 20037
Phone: (202)293-4800
Toll-Free: 800-225-5993
Fax: (202)293-9211
Home Page: http://www.worldwildlife.org

• 21967 • **J. Paul Getty Wildlife Conservation Prize**
For recognition of an outstanding achievement of direct or indirect international impact on the conservation of wildlife. Individuals or organizations are chosen by an international jury based on a diversity of accomplishments such as the conservation of rare or endangered species and habitats, the increase in public awareness of the importance of wildlife and nature by scientific, educational, or aesthetic contributions, or the establishment of legislation or of an organization or society of unusual importance to wildlife conservation. In all cases the achievement must be pioneering and substantial so that the recognition accorded by the award will bring public attention to the winning achievement and will increase public appreciation of the significance of wildlife and its conservation. A monetary prize of $100,000 is awarded annually. Established in 1974 by J. Paul Getty and now funded by his son, Gordon P. Getty.

• 21968 •
WORLDFEST - Houston International Film and Video Festival
Kathleen Haney, Program Dir.
PO Box 56566
Houston, TX 77256-6566
Phone: (713)965-9955
Toll-Free: 800-501-0111
Fax: (713)965-9960
E-mail: mail@worldfest.org
Home Page: http://www.worldfest.org

Formerly: (1991) Houston International Film Festival.

• 21969 • **WORLDFEST - Houston International Film and Video Festival**
To recognize outstanding achievement in the art of film and television. Films produced or released during the preceding two years may be submitted by December 15 each year. Remi Awards are given in the following categories: Best Feature Film, Best Documentary Film, Best Short Subject, Best TV Commercial, Best Television Production, Best Experimental Film, Best Screenplay, Best Student Film - $2,500, Best Music Video, Best Print Advertising, and Best Radio Advertising. The Gold Grand Award, the Remi Lone Star Statuette, is awarded to the best film in each of the major categories. Platinum, Gold, Silver, and Bronze awards are presented for the best film in a sub-category. Gold Special Jury Awards are given to the entries of special excellence. The $2,500 Eastman Kodak Award and the Hewlett Packard Crystal Vision Award are also bestowed. Formerly: (1991) Festival of the Americas.

• 21970 •
Worldpress.org
All Media Inc.
Teri Schure, Founder
735 N. Mulberry Pl.
North Woodmere, NY 11581
Phone: (516)791-6788
E-mail: tschure@worldpress.org
Home Page: http://www.worldpress.org
Formerly: *Atlas World Press Review*.

• 21971 • **International Editor of the Year**
To honor courage, enterprise, and leadership on an international level in advancing press freedom and responsibility, enhancing world understanding, defending human rights, and fostering journalistic excellence. Editors of publications outside the United States are eligible. A plaque is awarded annually. Established in 1974.

• 21972 •
WorldRadio
2120 28th St.
Sacramento, CA 95818
Phone: (916)457-3655
Fax: (916)457-7339
E-mail: info@wr6wr.com
Home Page: http://www.wr6wr.com

• 21973 • **Worked 100 Nations Award**
For recognition of making contact via amateur wave radio with licensed amateur radio operators in 100 of the world's nations. Operators must furnish a log showing date, time, and frequency band and call sign of station in the other countries to be considered. A certificate is awarded when earned. Established in 1971 by Armond Noble, N6WR.

• 21974 •
WPC Club
Richard Bowman, Pres.
PO Box 3504
Kalamazoo, MI 49003-3504
Phone: (269)375-5535
Fax: (269)375-5535
E-mail: clubinfo@chryslerclub.org
Home Page: http://www.chryslerclub.org

• 21975 • **Chrysler Corporation Cup**
For recognition of the finest original or restored Chrysler-produced vehicle at the National Meet Car Show. Candidates must be members and must participate in the Annual National Meet Car Show. A trophy cup is presented annually. Established in 1976 by the Chrysler Corporation.

• 21976 • **President's Award**
To recognize the best original Chrysler-built vehicle at the annual meeting.

• 21977 •
Writer's Digest
F & W Publications, Inc.
4700 Gailbraith Rd.
Cincinnati, OH 45236
Phone: (513)531-2690
E-mail: writersdig@fwpubs.com

• 21978 • **Writers Digest Short Story Competition**
Recognizes the authors of the best entries submitted. Submissions must be 1500 words or less. Awards are presented to 25 winning entries. The Grand-Prize winner receives $1500. Entries must be postmarked by December 3.

• 21979 • ***Writer's Digest* Writing Competition**
To recognize the authors of the best entry in the annual *Writer's Digest* Writing Competition. Awards are presented in the following 10 categories: article - memoir, personal essay and feature articles; short story - mainstream, and genre; poetry - rhyming and non-rhyming poems; script - stage play and television/movie script; children fiction and inspirational writing. Entries must be postmarked by May 31. The following awards are presented: grand prize - $1,500 and either (1) a trip to New York to meet with editors and or (2) a trip to the 2002 Maui writers conference. More than $25,000 in prizes.

• 21980 •
Writers' Federation of Nova Scotia
Jane BUss, Exec.Dir.
1113 Marginal Rd.
Halifax, NS, Canada B3H 4P7
Phone: (902)423-8116
Fax: (902)422-0881
E-mail: talk@writers.ns.ca
Home Page: http://www.writers.ns.ca

• 21981 • **Thomas Raddall Atlantic Fiction Award**
To recognize the outstanding book of fiction published by a native or resident Atlantic Canadian in the previous year. Must be a native of Atlantic Canada (Newfoundland, Prince Edward Island, New Brunswick, or Nova Scotia) or must have lived there for the past two years. A monetary award of $4,000 Canadian is awarded annually. Established in 1990 by the Writers' Federation of Nova Scotia and the Writers' Development Trust to honor Thomas Raddall.

• 21982 • **Evelyn Richardson Memorial Literary Trust**
To recognize the outstanding book of non-fiction prose by a Nova Scotian published in the previous year. Residents or natives of Nova Scotia are eligible. Entries may be submitted by April 15. A monetary award of $1000 is presented. The trust was established in 1977 in memory of Evelyn Richardson, the 1945 Governor General's award winner for *We Keep a Light*. Awarded annually.

• 21983 •
Writers Guild of Alberta
Liz Grieve, Exec.Dir.
11759 Groat Rd.
Edmonton, AB, Canada T5M 3K6
Phone: (780)422-8174
Toll-Free: 800-665-5354
Fax: (780)422-2663
E-mail: mail@writersguild.ab.ca
Home Page: http://www.writersguild.ab.ca

• 21984 • **Edmonton Book Prize**
Honors books which contribute to the appreciation and understanding of the City of Edmonton. Emphasis should be on special characters and/or achievement of its residents and should deal with some aspect of the City of Edmonton, including history, geography, current affairs, its arts or its people or be written by an Edmonton author. Entries can be fiction, nonfiction, poetry or drama written for adults or children. Authors must be 18 years of age or older. Works must be produced between March 16 of the previous year and March 15 of the current year. $2000 is awarded. Submission deadline is March 19. Established in 1995.

• 21985 • **Jon Whyte Memorial Essay Prize**
Recognizes writers of the best essays submitted to the province-wide competition. Applicants must be 18 years or older and have resided in Alberta at least 12 of the last 18 months. $1000 is awarded for the winning entry and $500 each

is awarded for the runners-up. Applicants can submit one original (not previously published) essay written in English. Essays may be of any topic and can be no longer than 2800 words. Each submission must be typed or printed on plain 8.5 X 11 inch paper. The manuscript should not contain the author's name. Name, address, telephone number, number of pages and approximate number of words must be submitted on a separate cover page sent with the manuscript. Manuscripts will not be returned and inclusion of each essay is determined by the Banff Centre for the Arts. A $10 processing fee must also be submitted. Application deadline is late February. Co-sponsored by the Banff Centre for the Arts. Established in 1992.

• 21986 • W.O. Mitchell City of Calgary Book Prize
Recognizes literary achievement by Calgary authors. Submissions must be works of fiction, poetry, non-fiction, children's literature, or drama published in the previous year. Authors must be Calgary residents on December 31 of the event year and for a minimum of two years prior. Submission deadline is February 28. Established in honor of W.O. Mitchell, an acclaimed Calgary writer.

• 21987 • Writers Guild of Alberta Awards for Excellence
To recognize excellence in writing by Alberta authors. Entrants must reside in Alberta for at least 12 of the 18 months prior to the December 31 submission deadline. Unpublished manuscripts, except in the drama category, are not eligible. The following awards are presented: Georges Bugnet Award for Novel, Howard O'Hagan Award for Short Fiction, R. Ross Annett Award for Children's Literature, Stephan G. Stephansson Award for Poetry, Wilfrid Eggleston Award for Non-fiction, Gwen Pharis Ringwood Award for Drama and Henry Kreisel Award for Best First Book. A monetary award and a leather-bound copy of the winning book are presented annually at the annual conference. Established in 1982.

• 21988 •
Writers Guild of America, West
John McLean, Exec.Dir.
7000 W Third St.
Los Angeles, CA 90048
Phone: (323)951-4000
Toll-Free: 800-548-4532
Fax: (323)782-4800
E-mail: website@wga.org
Home Page: http://www.wga.org

• 21989 • Paddy Chayefsky Laurel Award for Television
To recognize a member who has advanced the literature of television through the years, and has made outstanding contributions to the profession of the television writer. Selection is made by the Board of Directors. Awarded annually. Established in 1976.

• 21990 • Morgan Cox Award
To recognize vital ideas, continuing efforts and personal sacrifice which exemplify the ideal of service to the Guild which the life of Morgan Cox represented. Members or a group of members are eligible. A silver medallion is awarded annually. Established in 1970.

• 21991 • Valentine Davies Award
To recognize a member whose contributions to the entertainment industry and the community at-large have brought dignity and honor to writers everywhere. A silver medallion is awarded annually. Established in 1962.

• 21992 • Laurel Award for Screen
To recognize outstanding contributions to the profession of the screen writer and of notable work which has advanced the literature of the motion picture. Members of the Guild are eligible. Selection is made by the Board of Directors. A silver medallion is awarded annually. Established in 1953.

• 21993 • Screen Awards
To honor the best written screenplays in the categories of screenplays written directly for the screen or based on material from another medium. Members of the Guild are eligible. Bronze plaques are awarded annually. Established in 1948. Awarded jointly with the Writers Guild of America, east, Inc.

• 21994 • Television-Radio Awards
To honor the best written television or radio scripts. Awards are given in the following categories: (1) Television - (A) Long Form - over one hour one part, one airing time: (a) Original; and (b) Adaptation; (B) Anthology Episode/Single Program - one hour or less - one part, one airing time; (C) Episodic - Drama - limit of one hour - one airing time, no longer than its normal length; (D) Episodic - Comedy - limit of one hour - one airing time, no longer than its normal length; (E) Variety - Musical, Award, Tribute, Special Event - any length; (F) Documentary Script - current events/other than current events - any length; (G) Spot News Script; (H) Daytime Serial; and (I) Children's Script - meant primarily for children, any type, any length. (2) Radio - (A) Documentary - any length; (B) Radio Drama/Comedy - any length; and (C) Spot News Script. Members of the Guild are eligible. Bronze plaques are awarded annually. Established in 1956. Awarded jointly with the Writers Guild of America, east, Inc.

• 21995 •
Writers' Journal
PO Box 394
Perham, MN 56573
Phone: (218)346-7921
Fax: (218)346-7924
E-mail: writersjournal@writersjournal.com
Home Page: http://www.writersjournal.com

• 21996 • Fiction Contest
To recognize outstanding works of fiction. Entries must not exceed 5,000 words. The deadline for entries is January 30. The following awards are presented: first prize - $500; second prize - $200; third prize - $100; and Honorable Mentions. Winners and selected honorable mentions will be published in the future issues of *Writers' Journal*. Awarded annually.

• 21997 • Horror/Ghost Contest
To recognize outstanding works of horror/ghost stories. Entries must not exceed 2000 words. Deadline for entries is March 30 annually. A reading fee of $5.00 per entry must also be submitted. The following awards are presented: First prize $50.00; Second Prize $25.00; and Third Prize $15.00; and honorable mentions. First, second, and third prizes and selected honorable mention winners will be published in future issues of the *writers' Journal*. Send SASE at the above address for guidelines.

• 21998 • Photo Contest
Open to amateur or aspiring photographers of any age. Entries may not have been previously published and can be in color or black and white. Entries will be judged originality, composition, color, contrast, and quality. The following awards are presented: first place $25, second place $15, and third place $10. First, second, and third prize winners and some honorable mention will be published in future issues of the Writers Journal. Awarded annually.

• 21999 • Poetry Contest
To recognize outstanding poetry. Up to six poems less than 25 lines may be submitted by each entrant. The deadlines are April 30, August 30, and December 30. The following awards are presented: first prize - $50; second prize - $25; and third prize - $15. Winning entries will be published in future issues of the *Writers' Journal*. Held three times per year.

• 22000 • Romance Contest
To recognize outstanding romance stories. Entries must not exceed 2000 words. The deadline for entries is July 30, annually. A reading fee of $5.00 per entry must also be submitted. The following awards are presented: First Prize $50.00; Second Prize $25.00; Third Prize $15.00; and honorable mentions. First, second, and third prize and selected honorable mention winners will be published in future issues of the *Writers' Journal*. Send SASE for guidelines.

• 22001 • Short Story Contest
To recognize outstanding short stories. Previously unpublished stories that do not exceed 2,000 words may be submitted. The deadline for entries is May 30. The reading/entry fee is $ 7.00. The following awards are presented: first prize - $300; second prize - $100; third prize - $50; and Honorable Mention. First, second and third prize are selected honorable Mention winners will be published in the future issues of *WRITERS' Journal*. Awarded annually. Send SASE for guidelines.

• 22002 • **Travel Writing Award**
To recognize outstanding travel writing. Entries must not exceed 2000 words. The deadline for entries is November 30, annually. A reading fee of $5.00 per entry must also be submitted. The following awards are presented: First Prize $50.00; Second Prize $25.00; Third Prize $15.00; and honorable mentions. First, second, and third prizes and selected honorable mention winners will be published in future issues of the *Writers' Journal*. Send a SASE for guidelines.

• 22003 •
Writers' Trust of Canada
Janet Wright, Chair
90 Richmond St. E
Ste. 200
Toronto, ON, Canada M5E 1P1
Phone: (416)504-8222
Fax: (416)504-9090
E-mail: info@writerstrust.com
Home Page: http://www.writerstrust.com

Formerly: (1998) Writers' Development Trust.

• 22004 • **Marian Engel Award**
For recognition of outstanding prose writing by a Canadian woman in mid-career. A monetary prize of $10,000 is awarded annually. Established in 1986 by Margaret Atwood in memory of Marian Engel.

• 22005 •
Xavier University
Joseph Ventura, Exec.Dir.
% Alumni Relations
3800 Victory Pky.
Cincinnati, OH 45207-1096
Phone: (513)745-2078
Toll-Free: 800-344-4698
Fax: (513)745-2083
E-mail: alumni@xu.edu
Home Page: http://
www.xu.onlinecommunity.com

• 22006 • **St. Francis Xavier Medal**
For recognition of persons in contemporary society who exemplify the qualities of mind and heart of Saint Francis Xavier. Persons of action, of courage, and of imagination who have had a direct impact on their fellow man are eligible for consideration. An embossed medallion is awarded annually on Xavier Communion Sunday (the Sunday closest to December 3, the feast of St. Francis Xavier). Established in 1952 in memory of St. Francis Xavier, the school patron.

• 22007 •
Xplor International
Jeanne Mowlds, Exec.Dir.
24238 Hawthorne Blvd.
Torrance, CA 90505-6505
Phone: (310)373-3633
Toll-Free: 800-669-7567
Fax: (310)375-4240
E-mail: info@xplor.org
Home Page: http://www.xplor.org

• 22008 • **Innovator of the Year Award**
Annual award of recognition.

• 22009 • **Xplorer of the Year Award**
Annual award of recognition.

• 22010 •
Yale Series of Younger Poets
Yale University Press
PO Box 209040
New Haven, CT 06520-9040
Phone: (203)432-0900
Fax: (203)432-2394
E-mail: yyp@yalepress3.unipress.yale.edu

• 22011 • **Yale Series of Younger Poets**
Series of first books of poetry selected by an annual competition open to all writers under the age of 40 who have not previously published a book of poetry. Manuscripts should be 48-64 pages in length. Submissions must be postmarked in the month of January. Entry fee $15 made payable to Yale University Press. Publication by Yale University Press and royalties. Established 1919. Past winners include Adrienne Rich, John Hollander, Robert Hass, Carolyn Forche, and Richard Kenney.

• 22012 •
Yale University
Beinecke Rare Book and Manuscript Library
Frank Turner, Dir.
121 Wall St.
PO Box 208240
New Haven, CT 06520-2840
Phone: (203)432-2972
Fax: (203)432-4047
E-mail: beinecke.library@yale.edu
Home Page: http://www.library.yale.edu/beinecke

• 22013 • **Bollingen Prize in Poetry**
To recognize an American poet for the best collection published in a two year period, or for a body of poetry written over several years. A monetary prize of $50,000 is awarded biennially in odd-numbered years. Established in 1948 by the Bollingen Foundation, financed by Paul Mellon for support of learning in the humanities, and named for the Swiss home of Carl Jung. In 1973, the prize received a permanent endowment from the Andrew F. Mellon Foundation.

• 22014 •
Yale University
Yale Center for International and Area Studies
Henry R. Luce Hall, Box 208206
34 Hillhouse Ave.
New Haven, CT 06520-8206
Phone: (203)432-3410
Fax: (203)432-9383
E-mail: ycias@yale.edu
Home Page: http://www.yale.edu/ycias/

• 22015 • **Yale Center for International and Area Studies Awards**
Awarded to approximately 300 Yale students for research and travel.

• 22016 •
Yankee Magazine
1121 Main St.
PO Box 520
Dublin, NH 03444
Phone: (603)563-8111
Fax: (603)563-8252
E-mail: queries@yankeepub.com
Home Page: http://
www.yankeemagazine.com

• 22017 • ***Yankee* Awards**
To recognize excellence in printmaking, and art. The following awards are presented annually: Robb Sagendorph Memorial Prize for Art - to the winners of three annual exhibits held by the Copley Society of Boston. In addition to monetary awards, winners receive publicity in *Yankee Magazine*.

• 22018 •
Yasme Foundation
Wayne Mills, Pres.
PO Box 2025
Castro Valley, CA 94546
E-mail: wrights@worldnet.attnet
Home Page: http://www.yasme.org

• 22019 • **Yasme Award**
To recognize anyone who submits QSL cards showing contact with 30 YASME different officers, directors and/or operators. For proof of 60 contacts, a trophy in the shape of the sailboat 'Yasme' is given.

• 22020 •
Yellow Pages Association
Kimberly Enik, Exec.Asst.
2 Connell Dr., 1st Fl.
Berkeley Heights, NJ 07922-2747
Phone: (908)286-2380
Fax: (908)286-0620
E-mail: kimberly.enik@ypassociation.org
Home Page: http://
www.yellowpagesima.org

Formerly: (2002) Yellow Pages Publishers Association.

• 22021 • **Industry Excellence Awards**
Annual award of recognition.

• 22022 •
Yeshiva University
Richard M. Joel, Pres.
500 W 185th St.
New York, NY 10033-3201
Phone: (212)960-5400
Fax: (212)960-0043
Home Page: http://www.yu.edu

• 22023 • Mordecai Ben David Award
To recognize outstanding achievement in promotion of self-respect, independence, and courage among members of the Jewish faith. Monetary prize. Awarded when merited. Established in 1940 by Enrico Garda, Ambassador of San Marino to France.

• 22024 • Canadian Friends of Yeshiva University Bora Laskin Distinguished Service Award
To recognize steadfast commitment to the democratic principles of the Canadian heritage, the value of higher education, and the promise of its accessibility to all-exemplifying the ideals of the late Chief Justice of Canada, Bora Laskin. Scroll awarded on occasion by the Canadian Friends of Yeshiva University. Established in 1987.

• 22025 • Benjamin N. Cardozo School of Law Distinguished Public Service Award
To recognize outstanding achievement in the area of public service. Plaque awarded on occasion by the Benjamin N. Cardozo School of Law of Yeshiva University. Established in 1983.

• 22026 • Albert Einstein Commemorative Award
To recognize outstanding achievement in various fields of arts, sciences, and humanities, thus honoring the ideals for which Albert Einstein stood. Medallion awarded annually by the Albert Einstein College of Medicine of Yeshiva University.

• 22027 • Wurzweiler School of Social Work Community Service Award
To recognize outstanding professional leadership and exemplary service in national and international Jewish affairs. Scroll awarded on occasion by the Wurzweiler School of Social Work of Yeshiva University.

• 22028 • Wurzweiler School of Social Work Distinguished Professor Award
To recognize innovative contributions to the Wurzweiler School and the field of social work by a faculty member held in rare esteem and affection by students and colleagues. Scroll awarded on occasion by the Wurzweiler School of Social Work of Yeshiva University.

• 22029 • Yeshiva University Award
To recognize outstanding leadership in support of higher education and the cultural advancement of the community. Plaque awarded annually.

• 22030 • Yeshiva University Citation
To recognize outstanding leadership in support of higher education and the cultural advancement of the community. Plaque awarded annually.

• 22031 • Yeshiva University Distinguished Service Award
To recognize outstanding leadership in support of higher education and the cultural advancement of the community. Plaque awarded annually.

• 22032 • Yeshiva University Heritage Award
To recognize outstanding leadership in support of higher education and the cultural advancement of the community. Plaque awarded annually.

• 22033 • Yeshiva University Sephardic Heritage Award
To recognize outstanding leadership in support of higher education and the cultural advancement of the Sephardic community. Plaque awarded on occasion.

• 22034 •
YMCA of Greater New York
Jack Lund, Pres. and CEO
333 7th Ave., 15th Fl.
New York, NY 10001
Phone: (212)630-9600
Fax: (212)630-9604
Home Page: http://www.ymcanyc.org

• 22035 • Dodge Award
For recognition of humanitarian service over a long period of time. Individuals who exemplify the tradition of concern of the Dodge family are eligible. A medallion is awarded annually at a dinner in the fall or spring. Established in 1974 in honor of the Dodge family, a family who, for more than a century and a half, helped found, support and guide institutions and causes beneficial to all people.

• 22036 • Order of Red Triangle
This, the highest award given by the Association for volunteer service, recognizes service of singular distinction in support of the ideals of the Association. A medallion is awarded annually when merited. Established in 1966.

• 22037 • YMCA Men, Women and Youth of the Year
To honor individuals who exemplify, in personal and professional life, qualities which personify the best in responsible leadership, volunteer service, compassion for others, and commitment to the community. Established in 1973. Formerly: (1991) Service to Youth Award.

• 22038 •
YMCA of the United States of America
Dr. Kenneth Gladish, CEO
101 N Wacker Dr.
Chicago, IL 60606
Phone: (312)977-0031
Toll-Free: 800-872-9622
Fax: (312)977-9063
E-mail: webmaster@ymca.net
Home Page: http://www.ymca.net

• 22039 • National Treasure Award
To honor volunteer leaders who have given long and selfless service to the YMCA. It is given in profound appreciation of their exemplary volunteer service. Life-long service to the YMCA, including the National YMCA, is considered. A gold medallion is awarded biennially at the National Assembly of YMCAs. Established in 1983.

• 22040 • Volunteerism Award
Recognizes YMCA program volunteers who provide direct service as leaders and assistants in delivering programs. Selection based on meaningful service through the YMCA; extraordinary dedication; and the demonstration of initiative, effectiveness, and innovation in meeting the needs of the YMCA and the community. Awarded twice a year at the YMCA's National Board Meeting. Established in 1990.

• 22041 •
York County Astronomical Society
Jeri Jones, Asst.Sec.
400 Mundis Race Rd.
York, PA 17402-9721
Phone: (717)840-7440
Phone: (717)854-1527

• 22042 • Messier Observing Certificate
For observing a designated list of objects in a telescope. Recognition award bestowed periodically.

• 22043 •
Yorkshire Terrier Club of America
Janet Jackson, Pres.
3738 E Hwy. 47
3738 E Highway 47
Winfield, MO 63389
Phone: (636)668-6332
E-mail: ytca_sec@ytca.org
Home Page: http://www.ytca.org

• 22044 • Merit Award for Breeders and Yorkshire Terrier
Annual award of recognition.

• 22045 • Top-Producing Dogs
To encourage more thoughtful breeding among members. The male Yorkshire Terrier siring the most champions as listed in the AKC Gazette, January through December, and the female Yorkshire Terrier producing the most champions are eligible. A silverplated serving tray is awarded annually. Established in 1978.

• 22046 • Top-Winning Yorkshire Terrier in the United States Award
To encourage and promote competition in the conformation classes at dog shows. The dog with the most Best in Show and Toy Group awards as listed in the AKC Gazette, January through December issues, is eligible. A wine cooler is awarded annually. Established in 1978.

• 22047 •
Yorkton Short Film & Video Festival
49 Smith St. E
Yorkton, SK, Canada S3N 0H4
Phone: (306)782-7077
Fax: (306)782-1550
E-mail: info@yorktonshortfilm.org
Home Page: http://www.yorktonshortfilm.org

Formerly: Yorkton International Short Film & Video Festival 1981.

• 22048 • **Golden Sheaf Awards**
To recognize the best short films and videos produced in Canada during the preceding year, both in terms of the categories, and in terms of craftsmanship. Awards are given in the following categories for both film and video productions 60 minutes or under: Animation, Arts/Entertainment, Children's Production, Community Cable, Comedy, Commercials (under two minutes), Documentary by a Broadcaster, Documentary Over 30 Minutes, Documentary Under 30 Minutes, Drama Over 30 Minutes, Drama Under 30 Minutes, Educational/Instructional, Experimental, Industrial/Promotional, Multicultural/Race Relations, Music Video, Public Affairs, Science/Nature, and Multimedia. All entries are eligible for the following Golden Sheaf Craft Awards: Art Direction, Cinematography, Direction, Editing, Original Music Score, Performance, Script, Sound, and Videography. Also presented is the Best of Saskatchewan Award, for which all Saskatchewan entries are eligible. Additional awards include: Superchannel Award — $1,000 for the most outstanding script; Antoinette (Nettie) Kryski Canadian Heritage Award — $500 cash award and plaque for an outstanding production exemplifying historical Canadian people or events; National Film Board Kathleen Shannon Award — $1,000 to an independent film maker whose production provided an opportunity for people outside the dominant culture to speak for themselves; SCN Elizabeth Lowry Award — $500 for the most outstanding educational/instructional production; and Jury Awards — presented at the discretion of the adjudicator. The awards consist of a bronze golden sheaf; other awards include monetary prizes, plaques, and certificates. Awarded annually. Established in 1947 by the Yorkton Film Council. Sponsored by Telefilm Canada, the Saskatchewan Motion Picture Association, Saskatchewan Lotteries, and the City of Yorkton.

• 22049 •
Young Adult Library Services Association
Ms. Beth Yoke, Exec.Dir.
50 E Huron St.
Chicago, IL 60611
Phone: (312)664-7459
Toll-Free: 800-545-2433
Fax: (312)664-7459
E-mail: yalsa@ala.org
Home Page: http://www.ala.org/yalsa.html

Formerly: (1990) American Library Association - Young Adult Services Division.

• 22050 • **Alex Awards**
Given to ten books written for adults that have special appeal to young adults, ages 12 through 18. Books are selected from the previous year's publications. Nominations are accepted until December 1st. This award is sponsored by the Margaret A. Edwards Trust.

• 22051 • **Baker and Taylor Conference Grants**
To enable librarians who work directly with young adults in public or school libraries to attend the ALA Annual Conference for the first time. Members with one to ten years experience working with teenagers are eligible to apply by December 1. Two grants of $1,000 each are awarded to attend the ALA Annual Conference. Sponsored by Baker and Taylor Company.

• 22052 • **BWI/YALSA Collection Development Grant**
To provide money for collection development and YALSA members who represent a public library and work directly with young adults ages 12 to 18. Each application is judged on the following: the degree of need for additional materials for young adults; the degree of the current collection's use and the specificity of examples used; the soundness of the rationale for the selection of the materials; the quality of the description of the benefits the grant will bring to young adults; and the degree to which the applicant's philosophy reflects the concepts identified in *Directions for Library Service to Young Adults*. Applications and a description statement are due no later than December 1. Up to two $1,000 grants are awarded annually.

• 22053 • **Margaret A. Edwards Award**
To recognize an author whose book or books, over a period of time, have been accepted by young adults and teenagers as an authentic voice that continues to illuminate their experiences and emotions, giving insight into their lives and their role in society. A monetary award of $2,000 and a citation are awarded annually. Established in 1988. Sponsored by *School Library Journal*. Formerly: YASD/*School Library Journal* Young Adult Author Award; YASD/*School Library Journal* Author Achievement Award.

• 22054 • **Frances Henne YALSA/VOYA (Voice of Youth Advocates) Research Grant**
To provide seed money to an individual, institution, or group for a project to encourage research on library service to young adults. Proposals due December 1. A monetary award of $500 is presented. Sponsored by Voice of Youth Advocates. Formerly: Frances Henne Research Grant.

• 22055 • **YALSA Sagebrush Award**
To honor a member of the Young Adult Library Services Association who has developed an outstanding reading or literature program for young adults. The following criteria are considered: the purpose of the reading or literature program must be to bring young adults and books together and to encourage the development of life-long reading habits; the program must be specifically designed for and targeted at reaching young adults; all or part of the program must have taken place during the preceding year; and the applicant must work directly with young adults and be a personal member of the Young Adult Services Division. Applications are due December 1. Co-sponsored by Sagebrush. Established in 1990. Formerly: ALSA/Econo-Clad Award for Outstanding Young Adult Reading or Literature Program.

• 22056 •
Young Audiences of Greater Cleveland
13110 Shaker Sq., Ste. C203
Cleveland, OH 44120-2313
Phone: (216)561-5005
Fax: (216)561-3444
E-mail: yagc@yagc.org
Home Page: http://www.yagc.org

• 22057 • **Sunshine Award**
For community service in arts education. Recognition award bestowed annually.

• 22058 •
Young Concert Artists
Susan Wadsworth, Dir.
250 W 57th St., Ste. 1222
New York, NY 10107
Phone: (212)307-6655
Fax: (212)581-8894
E-mail: yca@yca.org
Home Page: http://www.yca.org

• 22059 • **Young Concert Artists International Auditions**
To discover and develop the careers of exceptionally gifted solo classical musicians and quartets. Winners are selected by a jury of distinguished musicians on the basis of extraordinary talent, virtuosity, artistic individuality, projection as a performer, and promise. There is no limit to the number of winners each year. Applicants who are at the beginning of professional concert careers are eligible to apply. Winners are presented in recital in the Young Concert Artists Series in New York and Washington, DC, and are added to the Roster of Young Concert Artists which provides all management services, including booking of concert engagements and publicity. Established in 1961.

• 22060 •
Young Entomologists' Society
Dianna K. Dunn, Exec.Dir./Acting Chair
6907 W Grand River Ave.
Lansing, MI 48906-9131
Phone: (517)886-0630
Fax: (517)886-0630
E-mail: yesbugs@aol.com
Home Page: http://members.aol.com/yesbugs/bugclub.html

Formerly: (1983) Teen International Entomology Group.

• 22061 • Entomology Writing Competition Award

For recognition of excellence in entomology scientific writing. Members may be selected by a panel of judges. A certificate, a prize, and publication of the winning article are awarded biennially in September. Established in 1985.

• 22062 • Sustaining Member Recognition Award

For recognition of exceptional support of youth entomology programs. Members who have made a contribution/donation are eligible. A certificate is awarded annually. Established in 1984.

• 22063 •
Young Israel Youth
Brad Karasak, Dir.
3 W. 16th St.
New York, NY 10011
Phone: (212)929-1525
Fax: (212)727-9526
E-mail: ncyi@youngisrael.org
Home Page: http://www.yiyouth.org

• 22064 • Herbert S. Schweitzer Memorial Youth Services Award

Recognizes long-term involvement on leadership level in area of youth activities. Awarded annually.

• 22065 • Shofar Award

Recognizes leadership and dedication. Awarded annually.

• 22066 •
Young Menswear Association
Joseph Rivers, Sec.-Treas.
47 W 34th St., No. 534
New York, NY 10001
Phone: (212)594-6422
Fax: (212)594-9349
E-mail: the-yma@att.net
Home Page: http://the-yma.com

Formerly: (1966) Young Menswear Association of the Men's Apparel Industry.

• 22067 • AMY Awards

To recognize achievement, good citizenship, and leadership in the men's apparel, textile/fiber industries over a sustained period of time. Members of the association are eligible. An individually sculptured abstract art form is awarded annually at the group's dinner dance held in January. In addition, four-year undergraduate scholarships are granted to students enrolled in men's apparel/textile career courses in honor of the recipients. Established in 1967.

• 22068 •
Young Playwrights Inc.
Julia Belozersky Asst., Contact
306 W 38th St., Ste. 300
New York, NY 10018
Phone: (212)594-5440
Fax: (212)594-5441
E-mail: writeaplay@aol.com
Home Page: http://www.youngplaywrights.org

• 22069 • Young Playwrights Festival

To identify and encourage young playwrights. Plays written entirely by one or more U.S. citizens or permanent residents age 18 or younger on December 1 may be submitted. Annual deadline is December 1. Musicals and screenplay adaptations are not eligible. Royalties and a professional production Off-Broadway are awarded annually. Established in 1982.

• 22070 •
Young Republican National Federation
April Canter, Exec.Dir.
525 G St. SE, Ste. 17
Washington, DC 20003
Phone: (202)608-1417
Fax: (202)608-1430
E-mail: aprilcanter@yahoo.com

• 22071 • Outstanding Local Chapter

Biennial award of recognition.

• 22072 • Outstanding YR State Chapter

Biennial award of recognition

• 22073 • Young Republican Man of the Year

Biennial award of recognition.

• 22074 • Young Republican Woman of the Year

Biennial award of recognition.

• 22075 •
Young Women's Christian Association of Elmira and the Twin Tiers
Judith H. Clovsky, CEO
211 Lake St.
Elmira, NY 14901
Phone: (607)733-5575
Toll-Free: 800-933-1185
Fax: (607)733-9524
E-mail: info@ywcaelmira.org
Home Page: http://www.ywcaelmira.org

• 22076 • Tribute to Women Award

For business women. Recognition award bestowed annually.

• 22077 •
Young Women's Christian Association of Lubbock
Betty E. Wheeler, Exec.Dir.
3101 35th St.
Lubbock, TX 79413
Phone: (806)792-2723
Fax: (806)792-0556
E-mail: moreinfo@ywclubbock.org
Home Page: http://www.ywcalubbock.org

• 22078 • Women of Excellence

For professional women. Recognition award bestowed annually.

• 22079 •
Young Women's Christian Association of San Diego County
Judith Case, Exec.Dir.
1012 C St.
San Diego, CA 92101
Phone: (619)239-0355
Fax: (619)233-8545
E-mail: ywca@ywcasandiego.org
Home Page: http://www.ywcasandiego.org

• 22080 • Twin Tribute to Women and Industry

For outstanding women managers and professionals. Recognition award bestowed annually.

• 22081 •
Young Women's Christian Association of the United States of America YWCA of the U.S.A.
Peggy Sanchez Mills PhD, CEO
1015 18th St. NW, Ste. 1100
Washington, DC 20036-5271
Phone: (202)467-0801
Fax: (202)467-0802
E-mail: info@ywca.org
Home Page: http://www.ywca.org

• 22082 • Tribute to Women in Industry Award

Award of recognition.

• 22083 •
Youth Assisting Youth
Jennifer Morris, Dir. of Public Affairs
5734 Yonge St., Ste. 401
Toronto, ON, Canada M2M 4E7
Phone: (416)932-1919
Toll-Free: 877-932-1919
Fax: (416)932-1924
E-mail: mail@yay.org
Home Page: http://www.yay.org

• 22084 • Barry Moffatt Award

Presented to individuals for outstanding community service to youth assisting youth.

• 22085 • Shawn Barnett Memorial Award

Presented to a child in the program who best exemplifies the qualities of courage.

• 22086 • **Youth Recognition Award**
Award of recognition. For an individual providing outstanding service as a volunteer friend to a child. Awarded annually.

• 22087 •
Yuki Teikei Haiku Society
Jean Hale, Sec.
5135 Cribari Pl.
San Jose, CA 95135
E-mail: jeanhale@redshift.com
Home Page: http://www.youngleaves.org

• 22088 • **Kiyoshi Tokutomi Memorial Haiku Contest**
Award of recognition.

• 22089 •
YWCA El Paso del Norte Region
Myrna J. Deckert, CEO
1918 Texas
El Paso, TX 79901
Phone: (915)577-YWCA
Fax: (915)533-7921
E-mail: au238@rgfn.epcc.edu

• 22090 • **REACH Racial Justice Corporate Award**
For an area business that has made a significant effort to eliminate institutionalized racism in the workplace and in the community. Recognition award bestowed annually.

• 22091 • **REcognized ACHievement-REACH Awards for Women**
Awards in seven categories are given to women who exhibit qualities of leadership, promote positive attitudes, make significant contributions in their work and serve as role models. Recognition awards bestowed annually.

• 22092 •
YWCA of Houston
3621 Willia St.
Houston, TX 77007
Phone: (713)868-9922
Fax: (713)868-5235
E-mail: vicki@ws13.fpl.fs.fed.us/swst

• 22093 • **Carroll Sterling Masterson Award & Outstanding Women's Awards**
To recognize the outstanding achievements and superlative contributions of Houston area women in the areas of business, arts, public service, media, education, science and technology, community service, and medicine. Any woman 21 years of age and over who lives in the Houston area and has made important contributions to her field of expertise is eligible. Awards are presented annually at the Outstanding Women's Luncheon. Established in 1976.

• 22094 • **Texas Star Award**
To recognize the Agency's and a community's outstanding volunteers of the year. Nominees are judged based on their community service, demonstration of leadership, identification as a role model, and involvement in the YWCA. Awards are presented at the annual meeting. Established in 1992.

• 22095 •
YWCA of the City of New York
Communications/Development Department
610 Lexington Ave.
New York, NY 10022
Phone: (212)755-4500
Fax: (212)838-1279
E-mail: info@ywcanyc.org

• 22096 • **Elizabeth Cutter Morrow Award**
For recognition of women who make a difference in the quality of life in New York and who, by their leadership and ability, elevate the status of women everywhere. The award, which varies, is an item designed by a craft student league instructor. Presented annually. Established in 1977 by Polly Gordon to honor Elizabeth Cutter Morrow.

• 22097 • **William I. Spencer Award**
For the provision of educational support to disadvantaged women. Established in 1991 to honor William I. Spencer, former president and chief administrative officer of Citicorp/Citibank.

• 22098 •
YWCA of Vermont
Janet R. Francis, Exec.Dir.
64 North St.
Burlington, VT 05401
Phone: (802)862-7520
Fax: (802)862-0926

• 22099 • **Susan B. Anthony Award**
For Vermont women who have made a significant contribution to the community. Recognition award bestowed annually.

• 22100 •
Zelienople-Harmony Chamber of Commerce
Marnie Repasky, Exec.Dir.
111 W Newcastle St.
PO Box 464
Zelienople, PA 16063
Phone: (724)452-5232
Fax: (724)452-5712
E-mail: zhcc@zoominternet.net

• 22101 • **Distinguished Service Award**
For community service. Recognition award bestowed annually.

• 22102 •
Zelienople Historical Society
Joyce M. Bessor, Admin.
243 S Main St.
PO Box 45
Zelienople, PA 16063
Phone: (724)452-9457
E-mail: zeliehistory@fyi.net
Home Page: http://www.fyi.net/~zhs

• 22103 • **Angel Award**
For person(s) or groups for contributions to historical preservation. Recognition award bestowed annually.

• 22104 •
Zen-do Kai Martial Arts
Michael J. Campos, Dir.
PO Box 186
Johnstown, NY 12095
Phone: (518)762-4723
Fax: (518)762-4723
E-mail: zendokai@superior.net
Home Page: http://www.superior.net/~zendokai

• 22105 • **Hall of Fame**
For recognition of and contributions to the martial arts. Nomination is by a committee. A plaque is awarded annually. Established in 1984 by John Izzo.

• 22106 • **Instructor of the Year**
For recognition of achievement in karate. Members of ZDK who have a black belt and are voted upon by the membership in January are eligible. A plaque is presented annually. Established in 1980 by Michael Campos, Director.

• 22107 • **Bill Wallace Competitor of the Year Award**
For recognition of achievement in competition karate. Competitors with black belts are eligible. A plaque is awarded annually. Established in 1987.

• 22108 •
Zero to Three: National Center for Infants, Toddlers and Families
Matthew E. Melmed JD, Exec.Dir.
2000 M St. NW, Ste. 200
Washington, DC 20036
Phone: (202)638-1144
Toll-Free: 800-899-4301
Fax: (202)638-0851
E-mail: oto3@presswarehouse.com
Home Page: http://www.zerotothree.org

Formerly: National Center for Clinical Infant Programs..

• 22109 • **Dolley Madison Award**
For recognition of achievement and contributions to the field of infant health, mental health, and development. Applications for this award are not accepted. The honoree is chosen by the Board of Directors. A certificate and expenses to participate in the national meeting are awarded biennially. Established in 1979 in honor of Dolley Madison, wife of President James Madison. As first lady, she established one of the first public programs for children. Formerly: .

• 22110 •
Zeta Beta Tau
Jonathan I. Yulish, Exec.Dir.
3905 Vincennes Rd., Ste. 300
Indianapolis, IN 46268
Phone: (317)334-1898
Fax: (317)334-1899
E-mail: zbt@zbtnational.org
Home Page: http://www.zbt.org

• 22111 • **Richard J. H. Gottheil Award**
To honor a person or group for fostering better human understanding and relationships among people. The award is not limited to members of the fraternity. A medal is awarded annually. Established in 1925.

• 22112 • **National President's Trophy - Man of the Year**
To recognize an alumnus who has been outstanding as a result of his personal deeds and accomplishments. A plaque is awarded annually. Established in 1930.

• 22113 •
Zionist Organization of America
Morton Klein, Pres.
4 E 34th St.
New York, NY 10016
Phone: (212)481-1500
Fax: (212)481-1515
E-mail: info@zoa.org
Home Page: http://www.zoa.org

• 22114 • **Theodore Herzl Award**
To recognize an individual for distinguished contributions to the cause of Zion ism and to the safeguarding of Israel. A gold medallion is awarded.

Subject Index of Awards

The Subject Index of Awards classifies all awards described in this volume by their principal areas of interest. The index contains some 400 subject headings, and each award is indexed under all relevant headings. The index also contains *see* and *see also* references. Awards are arranged alphabetically under each subject heading. Identically named awards are followed by an indented alphabetical list of the organizations administering an award by that name. The numbers following award and organization names are book entry numbers, not page numbers.

Academic achievement (*See also* Professional and personal achievement)
Acacia Leadership Scholarship 74
Academic Achievement Award 4837
Academic Scholarships 10408
Achieving Chapter Excellence (ACE) 12509
ADA Foundation Scholarships 2146
Adam Hirschfeld Creativity Scholarship 9847
All-America Scholar-Athlete Awards 14281
Allwork Grants 2725
Alpha Beta Kappa Award 8904
American Society of Swedish Engineers Award 4615
AMSUS Medical Student Award 5764
Annual Manuscript Award 6319
Appreciation Award 5043
ASF Awards for Scandinavians 3878
Award for Best Exam 4619
Award for Distinguished Service to N4A 14061
Award for Outstanding Performance in Third World Studies 5897
Award of Merit 6897
AZO Undergraduate Award 498
Balfour Scholarship 11720
Myer Barr Award 8905
Belgian American Educational Foundation Fellowships 6304
Best Transaction Paper 10654
Big East Conference Academic Awards 6369
Book-of-the-Year Award 12510
Book Prize 7440
Boys State Scholarship 2954
Frank G. Brooks Award for Excellence in Student Research 6324
Donald A. Buchannon Scholarship 20519
Career Awareness Award 6336
Career Development Grants 1471
CCCC Exemplar Award 8376
Co-Op Student of the Year Award 8502
CPhA Centennial Award 7334
Developmental Disabilities Awareness Award 6337
Developmental Disabilities Scholastic Achievement Scholarship 6338
Distinguished Dissertation Award 12511
Distinguished Women's Awards 16572
A. O. Duer Scholarship Award 14286
Eagle Scholarship 9750
Fellowship Program 1472
Fischer Scholarship 8894
Fraternal Order of Eagles Education Scholarship 9748
Galvin Scholarship 8895
President Garfield Humanitarian Award 13141
Gay, Lesbian, Bisexual and Transgender Community Leader Scholarship 12621
George R. Mach Distinguished Service Award 12517
Graduate and Undergraduate Scholarships 12512
Graduate Fellowships 10533
Dr. Randy Gregg Award 7217
GTE Academic All-America Hall of Fame 8190
GTE Academic All-American of the Year 8191
Hall of Fame 17315
Charles Harris Award 8918
Rev. Theodore M. Hesburgh, C.S.C., Award 5591
Frank Hesselroth Leadership Award 14288
High School Essay Contest 6396
Sidney Hook Memorial Award 17243
Marion Huber Learning Through Listening Awards 17904
Rewey Belle Inglis Award 14834
International Inn of the Year 11721
ION Navigation Award (California Maritime Academy) 11013
ION Navigation Award (U.S. Air Force Academy) 11014
JETS National TEAMS Awards 12466
Martin Luther King, Jr. Scholarship Award 2026
Legion of Valor Bronze Cross for Achievement 12772
Legislator of the Year Award 6397
Life Membership Award 6898
Emil S. Liston Award 14289
Mahomet Chamber of Commerce Scholarship 13021
Marianist Award 21013
Thomas F. Marshall Travel Fellowship 4202
Minerva Awards 16255
Mortar Board Chapter Citation Award 13612
Mortar Board Honorary Member 13613
Mr. Pi Kappa Phi 17317
Mustang Spirit Award 13103
N4A National Academic Achievement Award 14062
National Access Awareness Week Student Awards Program 5906
National Association of University Women National Fellowship 14453
National Citation 13614
National Honor Society Scholarship Program 14385
National Scholar-Athlete Awards 15073
National Student Teacher of the Year 12513
NSPS Scholarship 15760
Outstanding Accountant of the Year Award 6320
Outstanding Achievement Award 6899
Outstanding Alumni Achievement Award 16579
Outstanding Electrical Engineering Junior Award 9343
Outstanding Electrical Engineering Student Award 9344
Outstanding Faculty Development Award 6321
Outstanding Graduate Student Award 20259
Outstanding Senior Award 20260
Barbara Paul Prize 17807
Personal or Academic Achievement Award 6407
Pi Kapp Scholar 17318
J. Will Pless International Graduate of the Year 11722
Presidential Award for Outstanding Contributions to the Promotion of Scholarship in the Third World 5899
The President's Education Award Program 20489
Prince of Wales Prizes 17809
Regional Recognition Award 6900
Robertson Most Outstanding Undergraduate Award 17312
Rotary Scholarship 10130
Lee E. Schauer Memorial Scholarship 18446
Dave Schultz High School Excellence Award 15990
The Spirit of America Award 4925
Student of the Year 17319
Student Paper Award 3927
Student Science Project Contest 6398
John Tate Award for Undergraduate Academic Advising 21076
Lilian Coleman Taylor Prize 17810
Ten Outstanding Young Americans 20678
Thomas Reed Memorial Scholarship 20245
Troy Rotary Scholarship Awards 20218
Undergraduate Research Paper Awards 6334
United States Presidential Scholars Program 20491
University Medal for Excellence 8245
Vender Heide Award 6404

Academic (continued)

Volunteer Recognition Award 6901
John Wiley & Sons Award 11530
Windsor Chamber/Harvest Festival Scholarship Award 21642
Lightner Witmer Award 3712

Academic freedom
Alex P. Alain Intellectual Freedom Award 12935
Defense of Academic Freedom Award 14778
Barry R. Gross Memorial Award 14370
Sidney Hook Memorial Award 14371
Beatrice G. Konheim Award 1465
Alexander Meiklejohn Award 1466
Peter Shaw Memorial Award 14372
Noel Ross Strader Memorial Award 8176
TLA/SIRS Freedom of Information Award 19972

Accounting
Achievement of the Year Award 5708
AICPA Accredited in Business Valuation (ABV) Hall of Fame Award 2745
AICPA Business and Industry Hall of Fame 2746
AICPA Distinguished Achievement in Accounting Education Award 2747
AICPA Gold Medal Award for Distinguished Service 2748
AICPA Medal of Honor 2749
AICPA Outstanding CPA in Government Award 2750
AICPA PFP Distinguished Service Award 2751
AICPA Public Service Award 2752
AICPA Special Recognition Award 2753
Andy Barr Award 5710
Robert Beyer Award 10985
Bower Award for Business Leadership 9742
Victor Z. Brink Award for Distinguished Service 10969
Rawn Brinkley Award 10986
Carter Trophy 10987
Chapter Competition 10988
Chapter Service Award 5711
Chartered Accountants/Beta Alpha Psi Scholarships 5597
Davis Productivity Awards Program 9635
J. Frank Dickson Award 4766
Distinguished Graduate Award in Premium Auditing 15739
Doctoral Fellowship 8856
Education and Training Awards 5713
Financial Executive of the Year 11004
Betty Gerdes Distinguished Service Award 15740
Frank Greathouse Distinguished Leadership Award 5715
Arthur B. Gunnarson Award 10989
Independent Accountants Scholarship Award 10711
International Chartered Accountants Education Award 5598
Joint AICPA/AAA Accounting Literature Award 2754
Junior Scholarship 13590
Keller Trophy 10990
Robert W. King Memorial Award 5716
Lybrand Medals 10991
Neil Magruder Scholarship 13504
Stuart Cameron McLeod Society Trophy 10992
Meritorious Accountant of the Americas 11131
National President's Awards 5717
Newsletter Competition 10993
J. Lee Nicholson Award 10994
S. Alden Pendleton Award 10995
Presidents' Award 10996
Public Relations Competition 10997
Remington Rand Trophy 10998
Research Achievement Awards 5720
James E. Roelker Award 4767
Small Business Advocates of the Year 20834
Special Achievement Award 5721
Special Innovation Award 10999
Elmer Staats Award 5722
Stevenson Trophy 11000
Vice Presidents' Award 11001
Jeanne Vost Celebration of Leadership 133
Warner Trophy 11002
Wildman Medal 8857

Acoustics (*See also* Audio engineering)
Aeroacoustics Award 2630
AES Publications Award 6051
Autosound Grand Prix Awards 6057
Per Bruel Noise Control and Acoustics Medal 4504
Degelleke Award 7690
Directors' Awards 6850
Distinguished Service Citation 137
Eckel Student Prize in Noise Control 6851
Fessenden Student Prize in Underwater Acoustics 6852
Gold Medal 138
Helmholtz-Rayleigh Interdisciplinary Silver Medal 139
Hi-Fi Grand Prix Awards 6058
Honorary Fellow 140
R. Bruce Lindsay Award 141
Pioneers of Underwater Acoustics Medal 142
Wallace Clement Sabine Medal 143
Edgar and Millicent Shaw Postdoctoral Prize in Acoustics 6853
Silver Medal 144
Student Presentation Award 6854
Trent - Crede Medal 145
Dr. Irwin Vigness Memorial Award 10931
von Bekesy Medal 146
Wallace Waterfall Award 5997

Acquired immune deficiency syndrome
Awards for Action on HIV/AIDS and Human Rights 7157
Bill Napoli Award 17218
Developmental Awards 12847
National Leadership Awards 305
Thomas Parran Award 7899
Seed and Pilot Programs 9074

Actuary *See* Insurance

Addiction *See* Drug addiction; Alcoholism treatment

Administration *See* Management

Adoption *See* Family relations

Adult and continuing education
AASL Information Plus Continuing Education Scholarship 1412
Walton S. Bittner Service Citation for Outstanding Service in UCEA 20946
Gayke B. Childs Award 20947
Devoted Service Award 20948
Distance Learning Course Awards 20949
Distinguished Service Key and Certificate for Retiring Continuing Educators 20950
Tom C. Drewes Scholarship 2973
Exemplary Program Award 20951
Faculty Service Award 20952
Phillip E. Frandson Award for Innovative Programming 20953
Phillip E. Frandson Award for Sustained Excellence 20954
Mary V. Gaver Scholarship 2978
Cyril O. Houle World Award for Literature in Adult Education 947
Independent Study Catalog Awards 20955
International Futures Award for Exceptional and Innovative Leadership in Continuing Higher Education 20956
Malcolm Knowles Award for Outstanding Adult Education Program Leadership 948
Marketing and Publications Awards 20957
Harold W. McGraw, Jr. Prize in Education 13221
Membership Award 949
Memorial Awards 20958
National Leadership Award 14753
Nofflet William Up-and-Coming Leadership Award 20959
Julius M. Nolte Award for Extraordinary Leadership 20960
Imogene Okes Award 950
Outstanding Adult Learner 951
Outstanding Continuing Education Student Awards 20961
Outstanding Program Awards for Credit and Non-Credit Programs 20963
Outstanding Service Medallion 952
Elizabeth Powell Award 20964
President's Award for Exceptional and Innovative Leadership in Adult and Continuing Education 953
President's Leadership Award 14754
Regional Leadership Award 14755
Adelle F. Robertson Continuing Professional Educator Award 20965
Stanley C. Robinson Distinguished Service Award 20966
Signature of Excellence Award 20967
Charles A. Wedemeyer Award 20969

Advertising (*See also* Marketing; Public relations; Publicity)
AAF Best in the West Creative Competition 854
ACA Gold Medal Award 5589
Achieving Excellence Award 11536
Advertising Age Awards 202
Advertising and Marketing Awards 14357
Advertising Awards
- ABA Marketing Network 55
- National Auctioneers Association 14464

Advertising Design Club of Canada Awards 204
Advertising Executive of the Year 10515
Advertising Hall of Achievement 855
Advertising Hall of Fame 856
Advertising Leader of the Year Award 12923

Advertising (continued)

Advertising/Promotion Awards 19818
Advertising Woman of the Year 214
Aid to Advertising Education Award 857
The American Advertising Awards 858
American Advertising Awards 6023
AMOA Cigarette Vending Machine Promotion Award 4943
ANDY Awards 206
Annie Award for Best Animated Television Commercial 11187
Annual Exhibitions 5115
Aqua Awards 11430
ATME Atlas Awards 5902
ATME Awards 5903
Awards for Excellence in Cable Marketing and Advertising 8684
Al Bard Award 10551
Batchy, Hickey, and Powers Award 16389
Leo G. Bill Bernheimer, Jr. Award 13027
Best in Business Award 6342
Best in Media Awards 7915
Best of Show Award 18016
Better Communications Contest 21265
Better Newspapers Competition 7034
Bright Idea Awards 19995
CA Advertising Annual 8308
Chassie Awards 17826
Clarion Awards 5522
Classified Federation Awards 16329
Clio Awards 8112
Communications Graphics 2810
Corporate Leadership Award 2811
G. D. Crain Jr. Award 6712
Cresta International Advertising Awards 11171
Crystal Prism Award 215
DANDY Awards 16331
Direct Marketing Woman of the Year Award 21708
Display Contest 14360
Distinguished Advertising Educator Award 859
Distinguished Service Award 610
Doctoral Dissertation Competition 611
Editor & Publisher/INMA Marketing Awards 9163
Effie Awards 16206
EMA Creative Excellence Awards 9255
EXCEL Awards 19205
Excellence in Advertising Awards 14431
Fragrance Foundation Recognition Awards (FIFI Awards) 9720
Ben Franklin Award 7950
Gold Awards 16996
Golden Pyramid Competition 17685
Hall of Fame 18017
Harold Hammerman Spirit of Education Award 14434
Harrison Awards 11172
Peggy Hereford Excellence in Communications Award 403
Henry Hoke, Sr. Award 13028
HSMAI Adrian Advertising Awards 10554
Harlan Page Hubbard Lemon Award 7745
Industry Excellence Awards 22021
Industry Hall of Fame 17686
InterAd 11173
International ANDY Awards 11184
International Best Newspaper Online Services Award 9164
International Broadcasting Awards 10516
International Design, Print and Outdoor Advertising Awards 16221
International Pro-Comm Awards Competition 6713
International Radio Programming and Promotion Awards 16222
Journal of Advertising Best Article Award 612
L. U. "Luke" Kaiser Educational Award 13029
Miles Kimball Medallion 13030
Albert E. Koehl Award 10557
Mailing Industry Ingenuity Award 13031
MASA President's Plaque 13032
Matrix Award 16312
MAXI Awards Program 11517
McGovern Award 16333
Mobius Advertising Awards
  The Mobius Awards 13551
  US International Film and Video Festival 21142
MPA Kelly Awards 13015
National Club Achievement Competition 860
National Council Awards 16334
National Mature Media Awards Program 13207
National Student Advertising Competition (NSAC) 861
Network Affiliate Sales Achievement Award 6723
One Show Awards 16732
O'Toole Agency Award 1076
O'Toole Multicultural Advertising Award 1077
O'Toole Public Service Award 1078
Outstanding Contribution to Research Award 613
PBS Advertising and Promotion Awards 17705
Pollie Awards 1385
President's Award 216
RAC Awards 18018
Radio Mercury Awards 17827
Reggie Awards 17683
Silver Medal Award
  Advertising Women of New York 217
  American Advertising Federation 862
Gale M. Spowers Marketing Award 17528
Staffing Industry Communications Awards 4689
Myles Standish Award 16963
Suppliers Golden Achievement Award 17687
Telly Awards 19964
Tennessee Big "I" Advertising Award 10740
Travel Industry Odyssey Awards 20177
L. Ray Vahue Memorial Award 16964
Wilbur Awards 17971
John Howie Wright Cup 13033

Aeronautical engineering

Aerospace Design Engineering Award 2635
AIAA Aerospace Software Engineering Award 2638
AIAA Air Breathing Propulsion Award 2639
AIAA Aircraft Design Award 2640
AIAA Command, Control, Communication & Intelligence Award 2643
AIAA Computer-Aided Engineering and Manufacturing Award 2644
AIAA Engineer of the Year Award 2648
AIAA Propellants and Combustion Award 2664
AIAA Reed Aeronautics Award 2666
John Leland Atwood Award 3997
Walter J. and Angeline H. Crichlow Trust Prize 2678
Delta Air Lines Puffer Award 13904
Directors Award 19132
James H. Doolittle Award 19112
Exceptional Engineering Achievement Medal 13891
Exceptional Service Medal 13893
Robert Horonjeff Award of the Air Transport Division 4330
Kelly Johnson Award 19133
Franklin W. Kolk Air Transportation Progress Award 19049
William Littlewood Memorial Lecture 19050
Charles M. Manly Memorial Medal 19051
Multidisciplinary Design Optimization Award 2689
NAS Award in Aeronautical Engineering 13840
AIAA F. E. Newbold V/STOL Award 2690
Resnik Challenger Medal 19368
Elmer A. Sperry Award 19057
Spirit of St. Louis Medal 4547
John Paul Stapp Award 240
Theodore von Karman Award 364

Aeronautics and aviation (*See also* Aeronautical engineering; Aviation safety; Flying; Helicopters)

AAS Distinguished Service Medallions 5100
AAS Flight Achievement Award 1497
AAS Honorary National Commander 5101
AAS Individual Awards 5102
AAS National Commander Awards 5103
AAS National Medal and Ribbon 5104
AAS Squadron Awards 5107
Achievement Award 12849
Aeroacoustics Award 2630
Aerodynamics Award 2632
AFAA Airmanship Award 2235
AFAA Honorees 2236
AFRES Outstanding Unit Award 332
Agrinaut Award 13902
AHS Fellows 2425
AIAA Career Enhancement Award 2641
AIAA Certificate of Merit Awards 2642
AIAA Digital Avionics Award 2645
AIAA Distinguished Service Award 2646
AIAA Foundation National Student Conference Awards 2650
AIAA Ground Testing Award 2651
AIAA International Cooperation Award 2656
AIAA Losey Atmospheric Science Award 2657
AIAA National Faculty Advisor Award 2659
AIAA Outstanding Section Awards 2660
AIAA Pre-College Outreach Award 2663
AIAA Reed Aeronautics Award 2666
AIAA Support Systems Award 2672
Air Force Association Special Presidential Citations 5108
Air Force Test Team of the Year Award 333
Air National Guard Outstanding Unit Award 334
Air Transport World Awards 395
Airman of the Year 9640

Aeronautics (continued)

Airport Commissioners Roundtable Congressional Leadership Award 401
Allied Industry Individual Award 13903
The Alouette Award 6866
J. Leland Atwood Award 2675
Aviation Education Certificates of Merit 6125
Aviation Environment Award 9426
Aviation Hall of Fame and Museum of New Jersey 6128
Aviation Journalism Award 13917
Award for Distinguished Service 9427
Award for Extraordinary Service 9428
Award of Special Merit 17585
Award of Valor 1080
F. W. (Casey) Baldwin Award 6867
CMSAF Thomas N. Barnes Award 337
Belt of Orion Award 6834
Best Space Operations Crew Award 338
Best Travel Air 20168
Frank G. Brewer Trophy 13876
Business Aviation Meritorious Award 9580
Milton Caniff Spirit of Flight Award 14473
Maj. Gen. Warren R. Carter Supply Effectiveness Award 16820
CAS Award for Accomplishment on Aerophilately 6874
Certificate of Appreciation
  Federal Aviation Administration 9429
  National Aeronautics and Space Administration 13883
Certificate of Commendation 9430
Certifications of Appreciation 21844
Chairman's Award 14513
Chanute Flight Award 2676
Chapter of the Year 17586
Jim Charlson Award 5546
Lt. General Claire Lee Chennault Award 339
Citation of Honor 340
Civilian Awards 342
Robert J. Collier Trophy 13877
Commandant's Aviation Trophy 13069
Communications Award 2677
Congressional Space Medal of Honor 13884
Alfred A. Cunningham Award (Marine Aviator of the Year) 13070
Daedalian Distinguished Achievement Award 16821
Daedalian Scholarship Awards 16822
Distinguished Achievement Award 21653
Distinguished Public Service Medal 13885
Distinguished Scholar Award 21654
Distinguished Service Award
  Flying Physicians Association 9641
  National Air Transportation Association 13918
Distinguished Service Medal (NASA Medal) 13886
Distinguished Service Medals 6129
John P. "Jack" Doswell Award 14565
William E. Downes Jr. Memorial Award 402
AIAA Dryden Lectureship in Research 2680
Durand Lectureship for Public Service 2681
Janice Marie Dyer Award 6126
Elder Statesman of Aviation Award 13878
Maj. Gen. Eugene L. Eubank Morale, Welfare and Recreation Award 16824
Excellence in Pilot Training Award 13919
Exceptional Achievement Medal 13888
Exceptional Administrative Achievement Medal (EAAM) 13889
Exceptional Bravery Medal 13890
Exceptional Engineering Achievement Medal 13891
Exceptional Scientific Achievement Medal 13892
Exceptional Service Medal 13893
Exceptional Technology Achievement Medal (ETAM) 13894
Gen. Muir S. Fairchild Education Achievement Award 16825
Fellowship in Aviation History 373
Fixed Wing Scholarship 5547
Joseph J. Foss Award 2237
Edward S. Fris Award (Command and Control Unit of the Year) 13074
Francis S. Gabreski Award 2238
GAMA Excellence in Aviation Education Award 9911
Geiger Award 13097
General Aviation Service Technician Award 13920
Robert F. Gibson Award (Marine Air Command and Control Officer of the Year) 13075
Glen A. Gilbert Memorial Award 386
Dr. Robert H. Goddard Scholarship 15789
Gold Medal of Honor and Achievement 14474
Gold Wing Award for Excellence In Journalism 14566
Grand Champion 14514
Frank Gross Restoration Award 21376
Group Achievement Award 13895
Hall of Fame 16989
Hall of Fame Award 14475
Robert M. Hanson Award (Fighter/Attack Squadron of the Year) 13078
Lt. Gens. Millard F. and Hubert R. Harmon Award 16828
Joseph B. Hartranft Award 397
Earle Hattaway Award (Marine Aviation Ground Officer of the Year) 13080
Paul E. Haueter Award 2430
Peggy Hereford Excellence in Communications Award 403
Barbara A. Hess Award 5548
Honorary Fellow 19113
Honorary Member
  Arnold Air Society 5109
  Flying Physicians Association 9642
C. D. Howe Award 6868
The Kenneth A. Innis Award (Aviation Command and Control Marine of the Year) 13081
William E. Jackson Award 18179
Max Karant Award for Excellence in Aviation Journalism 398
Iven C. Kincheloe Award 19114
Dr. Alexander Klemin Award 2434
Theodor W. Knacke Aerodynamic Decelerator Systems Award 2684
Captain William J. Kossler, USCG Award 2435
Larsen-Miller Community Service Award 13906
Capt. V. L. Laursen Award 20943
General Curtis E. LeMay Bomber Aircrew Award 345
Gen. Curtis E. LeMay Morale, Welfare, and Recreation Award 16831
William Littlewood Memorial Lecture 2685
Ivan D. Livi Outstanding Aviation Maintenance Technology Instructor 6134
Mackay Trophy 13879
James MaGuire Award (Exceptional Achievement) 13082
Maintenance/Avionics Technician Safety Award 14567
Marriott-Carlson Award 5549
Lieutenant Theodore C. Marrs Plaques 5110
David McCampbell Award 2239
McCurdy Award 6869
Keith B. McCutcheon Award (Marine Heavy Helicopter Squadron of the Year) 13083
Medal of Honor 19053
Medical Crew/Crew Member of the Year Award 5550
Membership Award 2687
Meritorious Service to Aviation Award 14568
General Billy Mitchell Award for C4 Excellence 346
Robert P. Moore Memorial Award 14515
Douglas S. Morrow Public Outreach Award 20842
Most Active Woman Award 13908
NAAA Falcon Club 13909
National Awards Program 16990
National Chief of Protocol 5111
National Man/Woman of the Year 18517
AIAA F. E. Newbold V/STOL Award 2690
James E. Nicholson Award (Marine Non-Commissioned Officer Leadership Award) 13085
Ninety-Nines NIFA Awards 16365
General Jerome F. O'Malley Award 348
William A. "Bill" Ong Memorial Award 13921
Joan Orr Award 349
Outstanding Leadership Medal 13897
Outstanding Service Awards 13910
Pilot of the Year 18389
Robert L. Pinckney Award 2438
Plasmadynamics and Lasers Award 2691
General Thomas S. Power Missile Crew Award 351
President's Award 12599
Public Service Group Achievement Award 13898
Public Service Medal 13899
Danny Radish Award (Marine Enlisted Aircrew of the Year) 13086
Chief Master Sergeant Dick Red Award for ANG Aerospace Maintenance 354
Related Industry Award 13911
Reserve Grand Champion 14516
Earl T. Ricks Award 357
Robert Guy Robinson Award (Marine Naval Flight Officer of the Year) 13087
Harland Ross Award 21377
Pete Ross Safety Award 13088
Lawson H. M. Sanderson Award (Attack Squadron of the Year) 13089
Laurence P. Sharples Perpetual Award 399
Shields-Trauger Award 6225
David C. Shilling Award 358
Silver Dart Aviation History Award 6960
Silver Hawk Award 13090
Silver Medal of Outstanding Service 14476
Silver Wings Individual Awards 5112
Silver Wings Unit Award 5113
Space Achievement Award 20843
Space Flight Medal 13900

Aeronautics (continued)
Space Operations and Support Award 2692
AIAA Jay Hollingsworth Speas Airport Award 2693
Special Service Citation 2694
AIAA Lawrence Sperry Award 2695
Willie D. Sproule Award (Aviation Maintenance Marine of the Year) 13092
Robert Stanley Award 21378
Teaching Excellence Awards 2705
Ray E. Tenhoff Award 19115
Trans-Canada (McKee) Trophy 6870
Lt. General William H. Tunner Aircrew Award 360
W. Rupert Turnbull Award 6871
Undergraduate Award 18483
United States Air Force Twelve Outstanding Airmen of the Year 361
Romeo Vachon Award 6872
Paul G. Vess Award (Avionics Marine of the Year) 13093
VFW Aviation and Space Award 21335
Dolly Vinsant Flight Nurse of the Year Award 8284
Edward Warner Award 11483
Fred L. Wehran Aviation Achievement Award 6130
William A. Wheatley Award 20944
Marvin Whitlock Award 19061
Henry Wildfang Award 13094
Otto C. Winzen Lifetime Achievement Award 2699
Orville Wright Achievement Award 16835
Wright Brothers Lectureship in Aeronautics 2700
Wright Brothers Medal 19062
Wright Brothers Memorial Trophy 13880
Katharine Wright Memorial Award 13881
Writing Awards 378
Young Professional Activity Award 2702
Abe M. Zarem Award for Distinguished Achievement 2703

Aerospace (*See also* Aerospace medicine)
AAS Space Flight Award 1498
Aerodynamic Measurement Technology Award 2631
Aerospace Communications Award 2633
Aerospace Contribution to Society Award 2634
Aerospace Engineering Leadership Award 19033
Aerospace Maintenance Award 2636
Aerospace Power Systems Award 2637
AIAA Digital Avionics Award 2645
AIAA Ground Testing Award 2651
AIAA Haley Space Flight Award 2652
AIAA HAP Arnold Award for Excellence in Aeronautical Program Management 2653
AIAA History Manuscript Award 2654
AIAA International Cooperation Award 2656
AIAA Mechanics and Control of Flight Award 2658
AIAA Pendray Aerospace Literature Award 2661
AIAA Public Service Award 2665
AIAA Section Public Policy Award 2667
AIAA Space Processing Award 2668
AIAA Space Science Award 2669
AIAA Space Systems Award 2670
AIAA Structures, Structural Dynamics, and Materials Award 2671
AIAA Support Systems Award 2672
The Alouette Award 6866
H. H. Arnold Award 336
F. W. (Casey) Baldwin Award 6867
Lloyd V. Berkner Award 1499
Burka Award 11011
Civil Air Patrol Aerospace Education Cadet of the Year 341
Congressional Space Medal of Honor 13884
Walter J. and Angeline H. Crichlow Trust Prize 2678
De Florez Award for Flight Simulation 2679
Distinguished Achievement Award 21653
AIAA Dryden Lectureship in Research 2680
Durand Lectureship for Public Service 2681
Eugene M. Emme Astronautical Literature Award 1501
Capt. W. W. Estridge, Jr. Award 20942
Goddard Astronautics Award 2682
George W. Goddard Award 19608
C. D. Howe Award 6868
IFATCA Award of Merit 11578
Industrial Leadership Award 1502
International Space Hall of Fame 16196
John F. Kennedy Astronautics Award 1503
Theodor W. Knacke Aerodynamic Decelerator Systems Award 2684
Laurels/Laureates Awards 6136
Lifetime Achievement Award 6137
W. Randolph Lovelace II Award 1504
George M. Low Award 13896
AIAA George M. Low Space Transportation Award 2686
Christa McAuliffe Memorial Award 228
McCurdy Award 6869
Membership Award 2687
Military Astronautics Award 1505
Missile Systems Award 2688
Multidisciplinary Design Optimization Award 2689
Simon Newcomb Award 18144
William T. Pecora Award 17131
Victor A. Prather Award 1506
Judith A. Resnik Award 10879
Space Simulation Award 10930
Space Technology Hall of Fame 20844
Special Achievement Award 6138
Special Service Citation 2694
AIAA Lawrence Sperry Award 2695
Survivability Award 2696
W. Rupert Turnbull Award 6871
Romeo Vachon Award 6872
Hoyt S. Vandenberg Award 363
von Braun Award for Excellence in Space Program Management 2697
Theodore von Karman Award 364
von Karman Lectureship in Astronautics 2698
White Space Trophy 15162
Wyld Propulsion Award 2701
Young Professional Activity Award 2702

Aerospace medicine
Louis H. Bauer Founders Award 230
Melbourne W. Boynton Award 1500
Kent K. Gillingham Award 232
Gold Medal 11162
Malcolm C. Grow Award 19351
Jeffries Aerospace Medicine and Life Sciences Research Award 2683
Won Chuel Kay Award 233
Mary T. Klinker Award 234
Sidney D. Leverett, Jr. Environmental Science Award 235
Eric Liljencrantz Award 236
Raymond F. Longacre Award 237
Theodore C. Lyster Award 238
Paul W. Myers Award 347
George E. Schafer Award 19352
John Paul Stapp Award 240
John A. Tamisiea Award 241
Arnold D. Tuttle Award 242
Julian E. Ward Memorial Award 243

African American culture
AABE Scholarship 1098
Affirmative Action and Equal Employment Opportunity Award 21559
African-American Culture and Philosophy Award 17765
Aggrey Medal 17230
Kelly M. Alexander, Sr., NAACP State Conference President's Award 14047
ASALH/DLAMC African American History Essay Contest 5509
H.H. Bemmers Award 17766
Black Caucus Certificate of Appreciation 6412
Black Caucus of the American Library Association Literary Awards 6413
Black Caucus Special Recognition Plaques 6415
Black Engineer of the Year Awards 7585
Black History Month Contest 12912
Alice C. Browning Award 11420
Candace Award 14678
Coretta Scott King Award 6416
Corporate Leadership Award 21560
DEMCO/ALA Black Caucus Award for Excellence in Librarianship 6417
Distinguished Officer of the Year 6442
Du Bois-Mandela-Rodney Fellowship 7699
S. Randolph Edmonds Playwriting Award 14200
S. Randolph Edmonds Young Scholars Competition 6436
Ford Foundation Postdoctoral Diversity Fellowships 15622
Solomon Carter Fuller Award 3618
Lorraine Hansberry Playwriting Award 12545
Clarence L. Holte Literary Prize 17231
Image Awards 14049
Jazz Masters Fellowships 14931
Harry Jerome Award 6409
Harry Jerome Scholarship 6410
E. J. Josey Scholarship Award 6419
Coretta Scott King Book Award 3004
McKnight Doctoral Fellowship Program in Arts and Sciences, Mathematics, Business and Engineering 9599
New Talent Award 3005
Office of Civilian Radioactive Waste Management Historically Black Colleges and Universities Undergraduate Scholarship Program 16599
"Prized Pieces" International Film and Video Festival 14526
Rhythm and Blues Award Show 6260
Paul Robeson Awards 16314
Salute to Excellence Awards 14101
Social Justice Award 21561

Subject Index

African (continued)

Spingarn Medal 14050
Rosina Tucker Award 30
Samuel Z. Westerfield Award 14920
Western Political Science Association Awards 21557
Carter G. Woodson Award 4997
Youth Leadership Award 21562

African art (*See also* African studies)
Artists-in-Residence Program 19814
Du Bois-Mandela-Rodney Fellowship 7699

African studies (*See also* African art)
Aggrey Medal 17230
Claude Ake Memorial Award 259
Annual Meeting International Visitors Award 260
Children's Africana Book Awards 261
Conover-Porter Award 262
Distinguished Africanist Award 263
Du Bois-Mandela-Rodney Fellowship 7699
Paul Hair Prize 264
Herskovits Award 265
Clarence L. Holte Literary Prize 17231
Study Abroad Award 17767
Bishop John T. Walker Humanitarian Award 269
Wesley-Logan Prize 2482
Yale Center for International and Area Studies Awards 22015

Aging (*See also* Geriatrics; Gerontology; Nursing homes)
Age Diversity in the Workplace Award 1396
The ASA Award 4635
ASA-Metlife Foundation MindAlert Awards 4636
ASA Undergraduate Student Award 4637
Award for Best Practices in Human Resources and Aging 4638
Business and Aging Awards 4639
Jean Camper Cahn Award 14633
The Gloria Cavanaugh Award for Excellence in Training and Education in Aging 4640
Golden Age Award 12713
Graduate Student Research Award 4641
Hall of Fame Award 4642
Healthcare and Aging Awards 4643
M. Powell Lawton Distinguished Contribution Award for Applied Gerontology 3644
Media Awards 4645
National Community Service Awards 1399
National Mature Media Awards Program 13207
New Investigator Awards 21123
Outstanding Leadership and Research in Physical Activity and Aging Award 7747
Student Research Awards 3645
Volunteer of the Year Award 16961

Agricultural economics
Animal Management Award 4254
Awards for Research and Outstanding Publications in Agricultural Economics 868
CERES 21704
Neiland Award 279
Outstanding Article in *American Journal of Agricultural Economics* Award 872
Outstanding Doctoral Thesis Award 873
Outstanding Master's Thesis Award 874
World Food Policy Award 277

Agricultural education
AAAE Outstanding Young Member Award 960
Achievement Award 14170
Agronomic Extension Education Award 4239
Agronomic Resident Education Award 4241
Broome County Farm Bureau Scholarship 6653
Distinguished Achievement in Agriculture Award 9867
Distinguished Educator Award 16402
Distinguished Extension Programs 869
Distinguished Service Award
American Association for Agricultural Education 961
National Association of County Agricultural Agents 14171
Distinguished Teacher Award 16403
Distinguished Teaching Awards 871
Educational Aids Competition Blue Ribbon Awards 4219
Fellow Designation 962
Georgia Peanut Research and Education Award 9965
Graduate Student Teaching Award 16404
International Service in Agronomy Award 4246
E. B. Knight *NACTA Journal* Award 16405
Land O'Lakes/Purina Teaching Award in Dairy Production 2106
Massey-Ferguson Educational Award 4227
Milk Industry Foundation and Kraft General Foods Teaching Award in Dairy Science 2109
NACTA John Deere Awards 16406
Outstanding Teacher Award 16407
Outstanding Young Farmer Advisor 16004
Eldon Roesler Scholarship 21664
Shurgain Award for Excellence in Nutrition and MeatScience 7445
Soil Science Education Award 19396
Spokesperson for Agriculture 16005
Teacher Fellow Award 16408
Tressler - VNR/AVI Teacher Award 16409
Young Scientist's Award 7446

Agricultural engineering
AE 50 Company Recognition Program 4212
ASABE Fellows 4213
ASABE Paper Awards 4214
ASAE Past Presidents Award 4215
ASAE Student Paper Awards 4216
Jim Beamish Award 7398
John Clark Award 7399
CSAE Fellow 7400
CSAE Maple Leaf Award 7401
John Deere Medal 4218
Glenn Downing Award 7402
Engineering Achievement Awards Program 4220
A. W. Farrall Young Educator Award 4221
G. B. Gunlogson Countryside Engineering Award 4223
Hancor Soil and Water Engineering Award 4224
Dalton S. Harrison/Florida Irrigation Society Scholarship 9608
C. A. Hogentogler Award 5955
Kishida International Award 4226
Massey-Ferguson Educational Award 4227
Mayfield Cotton Engineering Award 4228
Cyrus Hall McCormick - Jerome Increase Case Medal 4229
NAMIC Engineering Safety Award 4231
National Food and Energy Council Electric Technology Award 4232
National Student Design Competition 4233
New Holland Young Researcher Award 4234
Rain Bird Engineering Concept of the Year Award 4235
Robert E. Stewart Engineering-Humanities Award 4236
John Turnbull Award 7403
Young Agricultural Engineer of the Year Award 7404

Agricultural history
Vernon Carstensen Memorial Award 281
Everett Eugene Edwards Memorial Award 282
Theodore Saloutos Memorial Book Award 283

Agriculture (*See also* Agricultural economics; Agricultural education; Agricultural engineering; Agricultural history; Agronomy; Animal husbandry; Dairy industry; Forestry; Irrigation; Poultry science; Rural economics)
Agricultural Hall of Fame 13913
Agricultural Institute of Canada Fellow 285
Agricultural Institute of Canada Honorary Member Award 286
Agricultural Leadership Award 16090
Agricultural Organization of the Year Public Sector 16091
Agrinaut Award 13902
American Agri-Women Awards 864
American Farm Bureau Federation's Award for Distinguished Service 2220
Andrew Rutherford Scholarship 10745
ASAS Extension Award 4256
ASAS Fellow 4257
Award of Honor 6735
Forrest Bassford Student Award 12896
Beekeeper of the Year 6763
Jane G. Benet Culinary Scholarship 19410
Best Paper Award 12131
Bouffault Memorial Award in International Animal Agriculture 4258
Reuben Brigham Award 5292
Charles A. Black Award 8533
Conservation Tillage Awards 14150
Cooperative Month Awards 14800
Zur Craine Award 11907
Delta Air Lines Puffer Award 13904
Distinguished Achievement in Agriculture Award 9867
Distinguished Grasslander Award 2273
Distinguished Policy Contribution 870
Distinguished Service Award
California Walnut Commission 6769
Georgia Agricultural Commodity Commission for Peanuts 9962
Distinguished Service to Agriculture 4405
District Newsletter Contest 14152
DiVelbiss Award 9095
D. Howard Doane Award 4406
Farm and Ranch Management Award 16003
Farm-City Award 14961

Agriculture (continued)

Farm Management Conservation Award 14154
FFA Award 9096
Front Range Young Farmers Scholarship 9821
Georgia Media Award 9963
Georgia Peanut Export Award 9964
Gold Quill Award 4407
Golden ARC Awards 292
Governors Award 16501
Graduate Awards 14801
Graduate Student Award 9097
Graduate Student Plant Breeding Award 14793
Grindley Medal 287
Hall of Fame Outstanding Service 13525
Dennis Robert Hoagland Award 4589
Honorary Beekeeper of the Year 6764
Honorary Life Member 7388
Honorary Member 11908
Institute Recognition Award 288
International Recognition Award 289
International Service Award 9316
J. I. Hambleton Award 9098
Kansas Premier Seed Grower 12491
KCFB Scholarship 12595
Leaven Award 865
LGFF Scholarship Award 12933
Meats Research Award 4261
Medallion Award 2274
Member Scholarship 21674
Merit Award
  American Forage and Grassland Council 2275
  Association of Official Seed Analysts 5801
Meritorious Service in Communications Award 4408
Nolan Mitchell Young Extension Worker Award 4230
Most Active Woman Award 13908
NAAA Falcon Club 13909
NAMO Marketing Award 16508
Nathaniel Dwings Award 6767
National Corn Yield Contest 14736
National Distinguished Service Ruby Award 9317
National Friend of Extension Award 9318
Clark - Newman Award 7389
Northern Rockies Sustainable Agriculture Award 511
Novartis Crop Protection Agricultural Writing Award 19873
Novartis Crop Protection NAFB Farm Broadcasting Award 19876
Novartis Crop Protection Weed Science Society of America Award 19877
Oberly Award for Bibliography in the Agricultural Sciences 5616
Oscars in Agriculture 21030
Outstanding Grassland Farmer or Rancher Award 2276
Outstanding Service Awards 13910
Outstanding Young Agrologist Award 290
Outstanding Young Farmer Awards 20677
Peanut Hall of Fame 9966
Pioneer Award 5293
Pioneer Hi-Bred Forage Award 2113
Private Plant Breeding Award 14794
Production Award 7002
Professional Award 5294
Public Plant Breeding Award 14795
Regional Distinguished Service Award 9319
Regional Mid-Career Award 9320
Regional Team Award 9321
Related Industry Award 13911
Research and Education Award 16079
Robertson Associate 7390
Roger A. Morse Teaching/Extension/Regulatory Award 9099
Scholarship Program 21672
Seedsman of the Year, Honorary Member 6045
Show Award 7003
Special Awards 9967
Special Recognition Awards 13914
Spokesperson for Agriculture 16005
Stewardship Award 16080
Undergraduate Awards 14802
Veritas Award 866
Voice of the Industry 16857
Volunteer of the Year Award 13915
The World Food Prize 21919
Young Beekeeper of the Year 6765

Agronomy
Agricultural Initiative Award 16089
Agronomic Extension Education Award 4239
Agronomic Industry Award 4240
Agronomic Resident Education Award 4241
Agronomic Service Award 4242
Crop Science Award 8659
Crop Science International Activity Award 8660
Crop Science Teaching Award 8661
Fellow 19392
Fellow of the American Society of Agronomy 4244
Fellow of the Crop Science Society of America 8662
Fred V. Grau Turfgrass Science Award 8663
Honorary Member
  American Society of Agronomy 4245
  Crop Science Society of America 8664
International Service in Agronomy Award 4246
International Soil Science Award 19393
Frank N. Meyer Memorial Medal 8665
Monsanto Crop Science Distinguished Career Award 8666
Gerald O. Mott Scholarship 8667
NCCPB Genetics and Plant Breeding Award for Industry 8668
Werner L. Nelson Award for Diagnosis of Yield Limiting Factors 4247
Novartis Crop Protection Award in Agronomy 19874
Leo Parizeau Prize in Biology 5540
Seed Science Award 8669
Soil Science Applied Research Award 19394
Soil Science Distinguished Service Award 19395
Soil Science Education Award 19396
Soil Science Professional Service Award 19397
Soil Science Research Award 19398
Carl Sprengel Agronomic Research Award 4248
Syngenta Crop Protection Recognition Award 4249
Emil Truog Soil Science Award 19399
Young Crop Scientist Award 8670

AIDS *See* Acquired immune deficiency syndrome

Air pollution *See* Environmental conservation

Alcoholism treatment
Bob Bowers Scholarship 21404
Bronze Key Award 14848
Community Service Award 12900
Gold Key Award 14849
Humanitarian Award 14850
Impact Award 12736
E. M. Jellinek Memorial Award 12314
Lamplighter of the Year 14855
Marty Mann Founder's Award 14851
Medical Student and Resident Travel Stipend 608
National City Challenge to Stop Drunk Driving 20457
Silver Key Award 14852
R. Brinkley Smithers Award 14853

Alumni activities
125th Anniversary Medals 8028
Alumni Achievement Awards 7664
Alumni Career Achievement Award 8179
Alumni Scholarship 16810
Alumni Service Award 515
Alumni Service Citations 20997
Alumni Service Medal 20998
Alumni Volunteer Leadership Award 8180
Alumnus of the Year 8496
Award for Distinguished Achievement 8237
Brown Bear Award 6661
Buchanan Outstanding Chapter Award 18489
Centennial Medal 516
DeMello School Scholarships 8877
Edward A. Dickson Alumnus of the Year Achievement Award 20256
Distinguished Alumni Citation of the Year 14005
Distinguished Alumnus Award 21052
Effective Use of Retirement Award 12579
Founder's Day Alumni/Alumnae Citations 12969
Hall of Fame Award 7666
Townsend Harris Medal 519
Harvard Alumni Association Award 10270
William M. Henderson Alumni Award 8865
John Hope Award 6662
Law Alumni Association's Distinguished Alumnus Award 21106
Loyalty Award 17309
Mass Communications Hall of Fame 20045
Mass Communications Outstanding Alumni Awards 20046
Sister Mary Lea Mueller Human Services Award 8181
Outstanding Alumnus Award 16540
Outstanding Young Alumnus 9857
Professional Achievement 12580
Pupin Medal 8230
George J. Quinn, Class of '50 Distinguished Service Award 7668
Recent Graduate Award 12581
William Rogers Award 6663
Service to Keuka 12582
Young Alumni Merit Award 7669
Young Alumni Service Citations 21001

American history (*See also* Historic preservation; Native Americans)

ABC-CLIO America: History and Life Award 16880
Willi Paul Adams Prize 16881
Administrative Committee Prize 2900
American Revolution Round Table Book Award 3845
Annual Achievement Award 62
Appreciation Award 12800
Article Prize 18867
Award of Distinction 1039
Award of Merit 1040
Award of Meritorious Achievement 12801
Homer D. Babbidge, Jr. Award 5511
Caroline Bancroft History Prize 8887
Bancroft Prizes 8238
Erik Barnouw Award 16882
Annette K. Baxter Awards 4705
Albert J. Beveridge Award 2465
Ray Allen Billington Prize 16883
Binkley-Stephenson Award 16884
Bode - Pearson Prize 4706
Book Prize 18868
James Henry Breasted Prize 2467
John M. Carroll Literary Award 12878
Certificate of Commendation 1041
Chuck and Linda Pratt Essay Award of the Lincoln Forum 12858
Co-Founders Book Award 21579
Commonwealth Club of California Book Awards 8306
Conductor of the Year 9790
Robert D. W. Connor Award 16517
Constance M. Rourke Prize 4707
Albert B. Corey Award 1042
Albert B. Corey Prize in Canadian-American Relations
American Historical Association 2468
Canadian Historical Association 7151
Christopher Crittenden Memorial Award 16518
Merle Curti Award 16886
Philip A. Danielson Award 21580
Jefferson Davis Award 8351
The Jack Detwiler Memorial Service Award 8058
Distinguished Service Award 12802
Alfred E. Driscoll Prize 16169
John H. Dunning Prize in United States History 2469
Executive Board Merit of Exhibit Award 19283
Ruth B. Fein Prize 2901
Fellowship for Creative and Performing Arts and Writers 914
First Book Prize 18869
First Families Award 9825
Founders Award 8352
John Hope Franklin Publication Prize 4708
Fraunces Tavern Museum Book Award 19417
Lee Max Friedman Award Medal 2902
Dr. Lawrence A. Frost Award 12879
Ralph Henry Gabriel Dissertation Prize 4709
Roy Gates Memorial Award 19284
Governor's Awards for History 19454
Fletcher M. Green and Charles W. Ramsdell Award 19501
Littleton - Griswold Prize in American Law and Society 2474
Willie D. Halsell Prize 13506
Ellis W. Hawley Prize 16887
Logan Hay Medal 63
Heads Up Award 21581
History Prize 12781
Herbert Hoover Book Award 10416
Huggins-Quarles Award 16888
J. Franklin Jameson Fellowship in American History 12833
Jamestown Prize 16707
Jamestown Scholars: New Dissertation Fellowships from the National Park Service and OAH 16889
Jewish Historical Society of New York Fellowships 2903
Kerr History Prize 16289
La Pietra Dissertation Travel Fellowship in Transnational History 16890
Leadership Award 17055
Richard W. Leopold Prize 16891
Lerner-Scott Dissertation Prize 16892
Liberty Legacy Foundation Award 16893
Lincoln the Lawyer Award 64
Arthur S. Link Prize/Warren F. Kuehl Prize for Documentary Editing 18681
Betty M. Linsley Award 5512
Literary Awards Program 8059
Lora Romero First Book Publication Prize 4710
Tad Lucas Memorial Award 18103
John Lyman Book Awards 16469
Mary C. Turpie Award 4711
Richard P. McCormick Prize 16170
McLemore Prize 13507
Mellon Post-Dissertation Fellowship 915
Miss Pioneer Oregon Scholarship 19412
H. L. Mitchell Award 19502
Glover Moore Prize 13508
Gerald E. Morris Prize Article Contest 13734
National Award of Achievement 12860
National Merit of Exhibit Award 19285
Outstanding Junior Member Contest 15712
Outstanding Teacher of American History 15713
Frank L. and Harriet C. Owsley Award 19503
Louis Pelzer Memorial Award 16894
Pioneer Certificate 9033
Pioneer Families of Franklin Co. 16634
Pioneer Families of Mahoning County Award 16636
Pioneer Family Certificates and Century Family Certificates 21692
President's Exhibit Award 19286
Presidio La Bahia Award 19414
Susy Pryor Award 5083
Pulitzer Prizes 17749
James A. Rawley Prize 16895
Franklin L. Riley Prize 13509
Summerfield G. Roberts Award 19415
Dunbar Rowland Award 13510
Francis B. Simkins Award 19504
Anne D. Snyder Award 8056
Wallace Stegner Award 21010
Charles S. Sydnor Award 19505
Mary K. Bonsteel Tachau Teach of the Year Award 16896
Harry S Truman Book Award 10266
Frederick Jackson Turner Award 16897
U.S. History Award 10439
Saul Viener Prize 2904
A.G Vietor Maritime Research Award 13735
Visiting Research Fellowships 916
B. L. C. Wailes Award 13511
Leo Wasserman Foundation Prizes 2905
Western Heritage Awards (Wrangler Award) 14887
Walter Muir Whitehill Prize 8207
Kemper and Leila Williams Prize in Louisiana History 10460
Gene Wise - Warren Susman Prize 4712
Coke Wood Award 21582
Yasuo Sakakibara Prize 4713
Youth Achievement Award 12803

American Indians *See* Native Americans

American literature

Ambassador Book Awards 9277
American Book Awards 6302
ASJA Outstanding Author Award 4468
Family History Writing Contest Award of Excellence 15146
Fellowship for Creative and Performing Arts and Writers 914
Sarah Josepha Hale Award 18042
Heartland Prizes 7893
C. Hugh Holman Award 18928
Louisiana Literary Award 12941
Mark Twain Award 18922
Mid American Award 18923
H. L. Mitchell Award 19502
National Book Critics Circle Awards 14530
Frank L. and Harriet C. Owsley Award 19503
PEN/Voelcker Award for Poetry 17150
Pulitzer Prizes 17749
Theodore Roosevelt Distinguished Service Medal 20066
Francis B. Simkins Award 19504
Lillian Smith Book Awards 19521
Spur Awards 21576
Charles S. Sydnor Award 19505
Thurber Prize for American Humor 20087
W. D. Weatherford Award Competition 4996
Western States Book Awards 21571
Owen Wister Award 21577

Animated films

Annie Award for Best Animated Feature 11186
Annie Award for Best Animated Television Commercial 11187
Annie Award for Best Animated Television Production 11188
Annie Award for Outstanding Individual Achievement in the Field of Animation 11189
Atlanta Film and Video Festival 6025
Frederick Back Award for Best Canadian Film 16934
Best Animation Making Use of Unusual Techniques 16935
Best Animation Short Made for the Internet 16936
Best Design 16937
Best Educational Production 16938
Best Film Made for Children 16939
Best Graduate Film 16940
Best Music Video 16941
Best Programme ID 16942
Best Television Series for Adults 16943
Best Television Special 16944
Best Use of Music or Sound 6848
Gordon Bruce Award for Humour 16945
Cartoon Network Award for Best Animation 16946

Animated (continued)

Certificate of Merit 11190
Chicago International Children's Film Festival 7888
Chicago International Film Festival 8001
Chromacolour Award for Best Use of Colour 16947
Computer Animation 6849
First Professional Work Award 16948
June Foray Award 11191
Golden Sheaf Awards 22048
Grand Prize for Commissioned Animation 16949
Grand Prizes 16950
Humboldt International Film Festival 10610
Windsor McCay Award 11192
Norman McLaren Heritage Award 16951
Mike Gribble Peel of Laughter Award 16952
Nashville Film Festival 13758
National Film Board of Canada Public Prize 16953
Nelvana Grand Prize for Independent Short Animation 16954
Object Animation 16955
OSU Photography and Cinema Alumni Society Award 7951
Philadelphia International Film Festival (Philafilm Awards) 468
Zack Schwartz Award for Best Story 16956
Special Jury Prize 16957

Anatomy
Cajal Medal 6725
Certificate of Recognition 6726
Henry Gray Award 1082
C. Judson Herrick Award 1083
Krieg Cortical Kudos 6727

Anesthesiology
Awards of Appreciation 1291
Certificate of Honor 3908
Clinical Instructor of the Year Award 1292
Didactic Instructor of the Year Award 1293
Distinguished Service Award 17196
John J. Downes Resident Research Award 769
Hillel Feldman Award 3909
Agatha Hodgins Award for Outstanding Accomplishment 1294
Honorary Member 1295
Helen Lamb Outstanding Educator Award 1296
Alice Magaw Outstanding Clinical Practitioner Award 1297
Program Director of the Year Award 1298
Public Relations Recognition Award 1299
Research in Action Award 1300
Research Starter Grant 19082
Resident Research Award 6757
Robert M. Smith Award 798

Animal care and training (*See also* Animal husbandry; Animal rights; Horsemanship; Poultry science; Veterinary medicine)
AATA Animal Welfare Award 4961
African Wildlife Leadership Award 267
AKC Licensed Field Trail for Championship Points 16531
Alabama Pet Hall of Fame 19894
American Association of Cat Enthusiasts Annual Awards 1130
Animal Control Employee of the Year 13936
Animal Welfare Award 4811
Annual Writing Competition 8979
AVMA Humane Award 4813
Award of Merit 4658
Henry Bergh Medal of Honor 4195
Best American Mouse Award 12881
Best English Mouse Award 12882
Best in Show 21586
Best In Show Award 12883
Best of Breed 8722
Best of Breed or Best of Variety of Breed 21587
Best Pet Mouse Award 12884
Beagle Brace Consistency Award 6198
Breeder of Top Ten Winning Bichon Frises, Owner of Top Ten Winning Bichon Frises 6363
John Brill Trophy 13179
Dr. Robert Campbell Memorial Award 4962
Canadian Federation of Humane Societies Media Award 7091
Certificate of Excellence in Exhibit Renovation 1486
Certificate of Merit for Zookeeper Education 1487
Challenge Trophies 2218
Waco F. Childers, Jr., Award 2572
Chow Chow Club Annual Awards 7945
George R. Collins Award 1024
Director of the Year 11375
Distinguished Service Award 20345
Doberman Pinscher Club of America Awards Program 8969
Dog of the Year
American Brittany Club, Heart of Illinois 1592
Loveland Beagle Club 12965
Rin Tin Tin Fan Club 18053
FFC Award of Recognition 9535
Raymond Figeroa Keeper Scholarship 1492
Founder's Award for Humane Excellence 4196
Friend of the Rottweiler 3874
Friskies Canine Frisbee Disc World Championships 13058
Gaines Medal for Good Sportsmanship 16320
Joseph J. Garvey Award 1025
Giant of the Year (The Gaines Award) 10017
Giant Schnauzer of the Year, Dog 10018
Gift of Sight Award 10194
Good Sportsmanship Award 3875
Charles A. Griffin Award 1026
Group Trophies 21588
Hall of Fame 6659
James Herriot Award 10597
Jean M. Hromadka Excellence in Zookeeping Award 1488
Humanitarian Award 17214
Hunting Retriever Champion 20346
Iditarod Trail International Sled Dog Race 10649
Inter-American Awards 1651
International Award 4963
Jiro Matsui Award 21965
Judge of the Year 11453
K-9 Dog Award 3571
Kal Kan Volunteer of the Year 2575
Kindness to Animals Award 16772
L/M Award 1820
Diane Lane Memorial Award 13937
Bill Lehman Memorial Award 13938
Lifetime Achievement Award 1489
May McCommon Memorial Trophy 13673
Merit Award for Somali 19401
Meritorious Achievement Award 1490
James Mortimer Memorial Silver Plated Trophy 21589
National Champion Donkey, National Champion Mule 2150
National Convention Awards Program 3812
National Kind Teacher Award 14016
Old Timers 16283
Outstanding Animal Control Agency of the Year 13939
Outstanding Giant Schnauzer Award 10019
Outstanding Sate Association Award 13940
Rutherford T. Phillips Award 2576
President's Award
American Humane Association 2577
International Association of Pet Cemeteries 11376
Prinz Wilhelm Obedience Award (The Willie Award) 10020
Public Service Award 4964
Recognition of achievement 9976
Register of Merit Award 6364
Research Grant 1202
Riding Hours and Riding Miles Awards 2151
Scholarship to VPI-Veterinary College 16682
Albert Schweitzer Medal 4966
Shetland People Hall of Fame 3897
Show a Little Heart 13351
Show Awards 10361
Small Animal Practitioner Award 7536
William O. Stillman Award 2578
Technician of the Year Award 1027
Technician Publication Award 1028
Top Archite 3876
Top Case of the Year 20736
Top-Producing Dogs 22045
Top-Winning Yorkshire Terrier in the United States Award 22046
Trial and Show Trophies 8705
United States Dressage Federation All Breed Award 12872
Versatility Hall of Fame 2152
R.D. 'Bob' Ward Memorial Posthumous Award 13941
Year-End Achievement Award 8122

Animal husbandry
ABC Breed Promotion 1549
American Beefalo World Registry's National Beefalo Show & Sale 1555
American Beefalo World Registry's Regional Beefalo Shows 1556
American Feed Industry Association Award
American Dairy Science Association 2097
American Society of Animal Science 4251
American North Country Cheviot Hall of Fame 3194
Animal Industry Service Award 4253
Animal Management Award 4254
ASAS Extension Award 4256
ASAS Fellow 4257
Award for Technical Innovation in Enhancing Production of Safe Affordable Food 7439
Bealer Award 5135
Book Prize 7440

Animal (continued)
Bouffault Memorial Award in International Animal Agriculture 4258
Breeder Awards 16864
Harry T. Burn Award 6310
CSAS Fellowship Award 7441
Dairy Progressive Breeder Awards 3113
Distinguished Dairy Cattle Breeder Award 14891
Distinguished Scholar Award 11364
Distinguished Service Award
Ayrshire Breeders' Association 6176
National Association of Animal Breeders 14068
National Swine Improvement Federation 15831
Distinguished Teacher Award 4260
Distinguished Young Couple 13478
Graduate Student 15832
Graduate Student Paper Competition Awards 7442
Grand Champion and Reserve Grand Champion Boar and Gilt 15216
Hall of Fame Award 12897
Headliner Award 12898
Hog Promoter of the Year 15217
Honorary Knights of the Golden Fleece 7032
Honorary Life Membership 7443
Joe Humble Award 5136
International Show and Sale 3195
Junior Showmanship 15218
King Contest 15219
La Reine Pittman Memorial Award 1594
Longtime Meritorious Service 13479
J. L. Lush Award 2107
Member Director Award 14069
Merit Award 9838
Merit Award for Breeders and Yorkshire Terrier 22044
Merit of Breeding Award 2149
Michigan Hall of Fame 13348
Morrison Award 4262
Most Registrations 15220
NAAB Research Award 14070
National Breeders Trophy 20626
National Most Colorful Contest 21426
Old Timers 16283
Outstanding Junior Shorthorn Breeder Award 2915
Past-President's Certificate 7444
Person of the Year 13480
Pets in Cities Award 11365
Pfizer Animal Health Physiology Award 2112
Premier Breeder at the North American International Livestock Exposition 2031
Queen Contest 15221
Scholarship Award 10761
Shetland People Hall of Fame 3897
Shurgain Award for Excellence in Nutrition and MeatScience 7445
Southwest Regional Beefalo Show 1557
Top Ranking Cotswold Breeder's Young Flock at the Illinois State Fair 2032
Voice of the Industry 16857
West Agro, Inc. Award 2114
Wild Award 21744
Young Scientist's Award 7446

Animal rights
Animal Welfare Award 4811
Bill Rosenberg Award 9416
Certificate of Appreciation 12667
Humane Award 17212
Leroy J. Ellis Humane Educator of the Year 17194
Russell and Burch Award 10599
Sabina Fund 9417
Albert Schweitzer Medal 4966
Shaw-Worth Memorial Scholarship 10601

Anthropology
Claude C. Albritton, Jr. Award 10844
Anthropology in Media Award 909
Samuel W. Brown, Jr. Root Cutter Award 10842
Juan Comas Prize 1355
Charles R. Darwin Lifetime Achievement Award 1356
Distinguished Lecture Award 910
Gungywamp Society Scholarship 10208
Robert F. Heizer Prize 4070
Honorary Fellow 5471
Howard Fellows 10571
Ales Hrdlicka Prize 1357
Margaret Mead Award 912
Outstanding Contribution Award 7502
Outstanding Service Award 7503
John Porter Tradition of Excellence Book Award 7504
Presidents Citation 10210
President's Excellence in Presentation Award 1358
Benjamin Rush Lectureship Award 3637
Smithsonian Institution Fellowship Program 18572
South Asia Foreign Language and Area Studies Fellowships 21119
J. I. Staley Prize 18354
Student Prize Paper Award 1359
Mildred Trotter Prize 1360
Trustees Award 10211
Sherwood L. Washburn Award 1361

Antiquity
Bliss Prize Fellowship in Byzantine Studies 9049
Dumbarton Oaks Fellowships 9050
Foreign Language and Area Studies Awards 21121

Apparel *See* Fashion

Appraisement *See* Assessment

Archaeology
Claude C. Albritton, Jr. Award 10844
Award of Merit 18683
Bell Award 16667
Carol Ruppe Distinguished Service Award 18684
Conservation and Heritage Management Award 5030
Lucy Wharton Drexel Medal 21097
Excellence in Undergraduate Teaching Award 5031
John Glaser Award 9779
Gold Medal Award for Distinguished Archaeological Achievement 5032
Graduate and Undergraduate Essay Awards 10828
Gungywamp Society Scholarship 10208
Harrington Award 18685
Honorary Member 13521
Howard Fellows 10571
John L. Cotter Award 18686
Martha and Arlenis Joukowsky Distinguished Service Award 5033
Alfred Vincent Kidder Award for Eminence in the Field of American Archaeology 911
Erwin T. Koch Award 13522
Stephen Tyng Mather Award 15490
National Endowment for the Humanities Grant Programs 14938
Outstanding Public Service Award 5034
Pomerance Award for Scientific Contributions to Archaeology 5035
Presidents Citation 10210
Rip Rapp Archaeological Geology Award 9955
Soderberg Scholarship 17000
Trustees Award 10211
Undergraduate Research Assistantships 13515
Charles Doolittle Walcott Medal 13852
WAS Special Commendations 21848
James R. Wiseman Book Award 5036
Jesse Wrench Scholarship 13523

Archery
National Field Archery Championship 15045
National Target Championships 13952
Shenk Award 13953
Thompson Award 13954

Architectural history
Architectural Study Tour Scholarship 19018
Award of Merit 17357
Rosann S. Berry Fellowship 19019
Antoinette Forrester Downing Award 19020
Founder's Award 19021
Alice Davis Hitchcock Award 19022
Philip Johnson Exhibition Catalogue Award 19023
Kate Neal Kinley Memorial Fellowship 21032
Edilia and Francois-Auguste de Montequin Fellowship 19025
Charles E. Peterson Fellowships/ Internships 6016
Sally Kress Tompkins Fellowship 19026
US/ICOMOS Fellows 20452

Architecture (*See also* Architectural history; Construction; Historic preservation; Housing; Landscape architecture; Library design; Monument restoration; Park planning; Planning)
Abbott Lowell Cummings Award 21310
ACSA Honors and Awards Program 5632
AIA/ACSA Topaz Medallion for Excellence in Architectural Education 2707
AIA/ALA Library Buildings Award 2708
AIANYS Educator Award 294
AIANYS Student Award 295
AIASAC Design Award 2732
AIBD Design Competition 2743
Allwork Grants 2725
American Architecture Awards 7872
American School and University Annual Architectural Portfolio 3883
Arango Design Award 5023
Architectural Awards of Excellence 2848
Architectural Study Tour Scholarship 19018
Architecture Firm Award 2709
Artists' Fellowships 16229
Associate Remodeler of the Year Award 14257
The Austin Chronicle Best of Austin 6093

Architecture (continued)

Award of Merit - Earth Shelter and Architecture 4777
Bard Awards for Excellence in Architecture and Urban Design 8026
Best in American Living Awards
National Association of Home Builders 14258
Professional Builder - Reed Business Information 17598
Best of Home Architectural Design Award 5229
Jean P. Boulanger Award 19003
Robert Brady Award 2737
Bronze Medal 19940
Rudy Bruner Award for Urban Excellence 6668
Arnold W. Brunner Grant 2726
Arthur Buckwell Memorial Scholarship 18135
Builder's Choice Design and Planning Awards 6676
Daniel Burnham Award 3548
Canadian Architect Magazine Awards of Excellence 6879
CCA Competition 7025
Chapter President Award 18790
Chief of Engineers Design and Environmental Awards Program 20405
Cintas Foundation Fellowships 10981
City of Ottawa Heritage Day Prize 8041
College of Fellows Grants 2710
Community Development Award 296
Shirley Cooper Architecture Award 1404
CRSI Design Awards Program 8346
Matthew W. Del Gaudio Award 297
Design Award
Society of American Registered Architects 19004
Texas Society of Architects/ AIA 20042
Design Awards
American Institute of Architects, Arizona Chapter 2730
Society for Marketing Professional Services 18791
Design Awards Competition 18668
Developer of the Year 14276
Dinkeloo Fellowship 21271
Distinguished Building Award 19005
Distinguished Contribution Award 3551
Distinguished Presidential Citation 19006
Distinguished Service Award 5909
EDRA Career Award 9300
EDRA Student Award 9301
EDRA Student Design Competition 9302
El Angel Award - Distinguished Hispanic-American Artist 6374
European Awards Program 11515
Fellowship 2711
Firm of the Year 20043
Andre Francou Legacy 18136
Ruth Freeman Award 2738
Gold Medal
American Institute of Architects 2712
Royal Architectural Institute of Canada 18137
Society of American Registered Architects 19007
Tau Sigma Delta 19941
GOOD DESIGN Competition and Exhibition 7873
Graham Foundation Grant 10126
Gregson's Founder Award 19008
Haskell Awards 2727
Hawaiian Architectural Arts Award 10296
Henry Hering Medal 15700
Honor Award 14549
Honor Awards 5910
Honorary Fellowship 2713
Honorary Member 2714
Honorary Member of AUA New York State Award 298
IALD International Lighting Design Awards 11369
ICSC International Design and Development Awards 11516
Institute Honor Awards for Architecture 2715
Institute Honor Awards for Interiors 2716
Institute Honor Awards for Regional and Urban Design 2717
Institute Honors for Collaborative Achievements 2718
Interior Design Awards 19839
International Award 19009
International Excellence in Masonry Award 13139
Thomas Jefferson Awards for Public Architecture 2719
Thomas Jefferson Memorial Foundation Medal in Architecture 13596
Edward C. Kemper Award 2720
James William Kideney Gold Medal Award 299
Kate Neal Kinley Memorial Fellowship 21032
William A. Klinger Memorial Award 274
Legislator of the Year Award 300
Fred L. Liebmann Book Award 16266
Lifetime Achievement Award 16267
Literature and Video Awards 14277
Loeb Fellowship 10281
Marketing Achievement Award 18792
Masterworks in Masonry Awards 18101
Eckert - Mauchly Award 5303
Medal of Honor 2734
Most Beautiful House in America Competition 7874
Emily Munson Memorial Student Awards 19010
National Federation of the Blind Scholarship Program 15039
Ottawa Architectural Conservation Awards 8042
Paul Buchanan Award 21311
Presidential Citation 19011
President's Award 301
Pritzker Architecture Prize 17573
Prix de Rome in Architecture 6806
Pullara Award 2735
Record Houses of the Year 5040
Record Interiors of the Year 5041
Restaurant Design and Graphics Awards 12289
Rome Prize Fellowships 605
Ronald J. Thom Award for Early Design Achievement 6807
Arthur Ross Awards 10853
Augustus St. Gaudens Medal 8498
SDA Scholarship Award 19101
Seed Research Awards 19755
Silver Medal 19942
Special Service Awards (Citations) 19012
Sidney L. Strauss Award 16268
Student Medal 18138
Synergy Award 19013
TBE Scholarship Fund 19917
Toronto Arts Awards 20112
Travel Grants 2728
Tucker Architectural Awards Competition 6687
Twenty-Five Year Award 2721
US/ICOMOS Fellows 20452
William H. Webb Medal 19217
Martin Eli Weil Prize 6447
Western Home Awards 19841
Ernest Wilby Memorial Scholarship 18139
Wood Design Award 2292
Young Architects Award 2722
Young Architects Forum 5038
Whitney M. Young, Jr., Award 2723

Archival science *See* Library and information services

Art (*See also* African art; Art education; Art history; Design; Exhibiting; Photography; specific disciplines, e.g. Ceramics)
Alice Abel Cultural and Creative Arts Program 3141
Achievement in the Arts Award 16575
Gladys Agell Award for Excellence in Research 927
Allegro Award 17172
American Romanian Academy Awards 3869
Americas 2000 Paper Works Competition 13491
ANA Numismatic Art Award for Excellence in Medallic Sculpture 3197
Annual Art Show 16163
Annual Chautauqua National Exhibition of American Art 7819
Annual National Art Exhibition 3504
Annual Open Exhibition 5121
Annual Spring Show Award 9325
Arrowhead Biennial Exhibition 9047
Father Adrien Arsenault Senior Arts Award 17544
Art Competition 5145
Art in the Park Awards 9855
Artist Award 19813
Artist Award for a Distinguished Body of Work, Exhibition, Presentation or Performance 8142
Artist Awards 19028
Artist of the Year 10753
Artistic Capacity-Building Program 11083
Artists' Fellowships 16229
Artists in Residence Program 11084
The Artist's Magazine Art Competition 5146
Arts for the Parks Competition 15477
Arts Management Award for Arts Administrator of the Year 5155
Arts Management Award for Career Service 5156
Arts Management Special Award 5157
Arts Recognition and Talent Search (ARTS) 15117
ASFA Web Awards 5847
The Austin Chronicle Best of Austin 6093
Awards for Excellence 18865
Awards of Merit 15478
Banner Competition 7773
Alfred H. Barr, Jr. Award 8143
Basic Subvention to the Arts and Cultural Work 11085
Bell Canada Award in Video Art 6785
Paul and Margaret Bertelsen Prize 13779

Art (continued)

Betty Bowen Memorial Award Competition 18393
Boynton's G.A.L.A. Artist Awards 6594
Brand Annual Art Competition 5261
Breakfast of Champions 16558
Bush Artist Fellows Program 6700
Business in the Arts 8209
Business in the Arts Award 19915
Business Volunteers for the Arts Awards 6715
Estelle Campbell Award 15730
Career Advancement of Visual Artists (CAVA) 15118
Carnegie Prize 7607
Certificate of Appreciation 4264
Certificates of Merit 13675
Chesley Awards 5848
Citations of Merit 13984
City Livability Awards Program 20456
Clemson National Print and Drawing Exhibition 18181
Benjamin West Clinedinst Memorial Medal 5138
College Art Association/National Institute for Conservation Award 8144
Conservation Guest Scholars 10003
Craft America Competition 18522
Charlotte Crawford Art Award 8917
Crescendo Award 17173
Cultural Development Fund 5151
Cultural Medal 11086
Curatorial Research Fellowships 10004
Elisha Darlin Arts Award 9031
Manu Daula (Frigate Bird) Award 16994
Clare Hart DeGolyer Memorial Fund Award 8716
Brig. Gen. Robert L. Denig Distinguished Service Award 20684
Dillman's Creative Arts Scholarship Award 8922
Disaster Relief Fund 20005
Distant Accords Awards 11593
Distinguished Artist Award for Lifetime Achievement 8145
Distinguished Performance Award 20686
Distinguished Service Awards 15170
Distinguished Teaching of Art Award 8146
Don Fox Memorial Scholarship 414
Otis and Velma Davis Dozier Travel Grant 8717
Excellence in Communication Award 13978
EXPO Juried Competition 19623
Fellowship for Creative and Performing Arts and Writers 914
Fellowship Program 17168
Fine Art Show 18244
Fine Arts Work Center Fellowships 9553
John P. Fisher Award for Media Support of the Arts 8544
Florida Artists Hall of Fame 9587
Florida Arts Recognition Awards 9588
Fondo Puertorriqueno para el Financiamiento del Quehacer Cultural 11087
Founder's Favorite Winner Award 15479
Freedom of Expression Award 12294
Brendan Gill Prize 13677
Gold Medal Annual 18330
Gold Medal of Honor for Visual Arts 13991
Governor General's Awards in Visual and Media Arts 6796
Gradiva Awards 14052
Grand Prize Winner Award 15480
Grants for Arts Projects 14930
Great Plains National Exhibition 13616
Greater Haverhill Arts Association Annual Exhibition 10147
Greater Midwest International Exhibition 7771
John Simon Guggenheim Memorial Foundation Fellowships 10192
Harness Track of America's Art Competition/ Auction 10258
Honorary Life Member 928
Honorary Member
American Bugatti Club 1596
American Society of Artists 4265
Horizons Grants Program 18228
Hoyt Mid Atlantic Art Show 10573
Paul de Hueck and Norman Walford Career Achievement Awards in the Performing Arts and in Visual Arts 16741
K. M. Hunter Artists Awards 16742
Hunterdon Museum of Art National Print Exhibition Purchase Awards 10618
Images Competition 7775
Indiana Governor's Arts Awards 10755
Individual Artist Fellowship
Montana Arts Council 13586
Ohio Arts Council 16628
Individual Artists Fellowships 10297
International Juried Show 16164
International Society for Education through Art Awards 11930
International Technical Art Competition 18861
Judges Award of Merit 15481
Kaleidoscope - A Fair of the Arts 7816
Arch and Anne Giles Kimbrough Fund Award 8718
Kate Neal Kinley Memorial Fellowship 21032
LaGrange National 7817
Barbara Aronofsky Latham Memorial Grants 21353
Laureates 900
Leo Award 10718
Leonardo Award for Excellence 11957
Lifetime Achievement Award in Paper Doll Art 16905
Lifetime Achievement Awards 10196
Victor Martyn Lynch-Staunton Awards 6802
Frank J. Malina - Leonardo Prize for Lifetime Achievement 11958
Marie-Paule Nolin Award 13213
Master Wildlife Artist 21828
Carroll Sterling Masterson Award & Outstanding Women's Awards 22093
Frank Jewett Mather Award 8148
Mature Women Scholarship Grant 15334
Ronald McDonald House Charities Grants Program 18118
Medal for Excellence in Craft Award 19029
Medal for Peace and Friendship through Music and Arts 11595
Gari Melchers Memorial Medal 5139
Mesa Contemporary Arts 13305
Mohawk-Hudson Regional Art Exhibition Award 18333
Money for Women/Barbara Deming Memorial Fund Grants 13582
Montreal International Festival of Films on Art 11613
NAMTA Hall of Fame Award 13979
National Jewish Book Award - Visual Arts 12332
National Medal of Arts 14933
National Post Awards for Business in the Arts 8541
National Small Works Exhibition 20192
National Society of Arts and Letters First Place Award 15733
National Women's Hall of Fame 15960
New American Talent Show 5123
New Horizons Award for Innovation 11959
Mollie Davis Nicholson Award 15734
NLAG Regrant Program 16542
O'Malley Art Award 12201
Jacqueline Kennedy Onassis Medal 13680
Ontario College of Art & Design Scholarship 21781
Order of Ontario 16757
Outstanding Booth Awards 13980
Outstanding Reference Sources 17944
Past President Scholarship 10231
Petro-Canada Award in New Media 6805
Pollock-Krasner Foundation Grants 17461
Arthur Kingsley Porter Prize 8150
Prints, Drawings and Photographs Exhibition 5071
Prix Louis-Phillipe-Hebert 18610
Prix Paul-Emile-Borduas 17797
Project Funding Program 5161
Red Cloud Indian Art Show 10424
Regifting Grants Program 8686
Regional Awards 15482
Irene Rosenzweig Biennial Competition 5149
Arthur Ross Awards 10853
Rutgers National/Works on and of Paper Competition 19779
Augustus St. Gaudens Medal 8498
Scholarship Award 8507
Secondary Art Achievement Award 13972
Richard Seyffert Memorial Award 13995
Sidewalk Sale and Exhibition 7776
Silver Medal 18331
Sister Kenny Institute International Art Show for Artists with Disabilities 13485
State of Florida Fellowship 9589
Joseph S. Stauffer Prizes 6809
Ann G. Stein Memorial Arts Person of the Year Award 16165
Dorothy and Bruce Strong Award 15735
Student Scholarship 17404
TCAC Grants 19901
Colonel John W. Thomason, Jr. Award 13101
Travel to Artists Grant 11088
Tributary Awards 9127
Makepeace Tsao Leonardo Award 11960
Ucross Foundation Artists-in-Residence Program 20265
U.S. Art Magazine Award of Merit 15483
United States Presidential Scholars Program 20491
Elizabeth O'Neill Verner Awards 19441
Voice of the Dispora, Founders Achievement Award, UCLA Extension Scholarships 11421
Wabash Valley Juried Exhibition 19861
J. B. C. Watkins Award 6810
WCA Honors 21789
Western States Book Awards 21571
Wildlife Category Award of Merit 15484
Oscar Williams and Gene Derwood Award 16219
Wisconsin Arts Board Fellowships 21666
Women's Artist Award 12864
Woodstock National Exhibition 21830

Art (continued)

Yankee Awards 22017
Young American Creative Patriotic Art Competition 12648
Young Artists Competition 18534
Youth Arts Awards 20233

Art education
Art Scholarship 5141
Manuel Barkan Memorial Award 13956
James M. Brahney Grant 11836
Committee on Multiethnic Concerns J. Eugene Grisby, Jr. Award 13957
Creative Ticket National Schools of Distinction Award 12536
Design Standards Award 13958
Distinguished Service Award (Outside the Profession) 13959
Distinguished Service Award (Within the Profession) 13960
Marion Quin Dix Leadership Award 13961
Dorothy's 60 Award 12486
Mahmoud El-Bassioury Award 11929
Focus on Education 8694
Galva Arts Council Scholarship 9863
GATF Awards of Excellence in Education for an Individual in Industry and in Education 10133
Gold Medal of Honor for Education 13988
Higher Education Student Achievement Award 13962
Frederick D. Kagy Education Award of Excellence 10135
Kennedy Center Alliance for Arts Education Network/National School Boards Association Award 12554
Kennedy Center Alliance for the Arts Education Network and National School Board Association Award 12537
W. David Kingery Award 1687
Fabian Lemieux Award 16743
Lowenfeld Award 13963
Jean Mantz Best of Show Student Award 10306
National Art Educator Award 13964
National Art Honor Society Sponsor Award 13965
National Division Art Educator Award 13966
National Junior Art Honor Society Sponsor Award 13967
Outstanding Arts Educator Award 19900
Presidential Citation Award 13968
President's Award 15179
Program Standards Award 13969
Sir Herbert Read Award 11931
Regional Division Art Educator Award 13970
Retired Art Educator Award 13971
Colonel Samuel Rosenbaum Memorial Award 15180
State/Province Art Educator Award 13973
State/Province Association Newsletter Award 13974
Ann G. Stein Memorial Arts Person of the Year Award 16165
Student Chapter Sponsor Award of Excellence 13975
Sunshine Award 22057
Youth Art Month Award 13976
Youth Art Month State Report Awards 8535

Art history
Albion Book Prize/NACBS Book Prize 16411
American Council of Learned Societies Fellowships 2037
College Art Association/National Institute for Conservation Award 8144
Distinguished Teaching of Art History Award 8147
J. Paul Getty Postdoctoral Fellowships in the History of Art and the Humanities 10005
Howard Fellows 10571
Henry Allen Moe Prize for Catalogs of Distinction in the Arts 16290
Charles Rufus Morey Book Award 8149
Rome Prize Fellowships 605
Senior Collaborative Research Grants 10008
Smithsonian Institution Fellowship Program 18572

Arts and humanities (*See also* Antiquity; Archaeology; Ethics; Humanities research; Museums; Philosophy; Philosophy of science; Religion)
American Council of Learned Societies Fellowships 2037
Annaley Naegle Redd Student Award in Women's History 17925
Gustave O. Arlt Award in the Humanities 8578
Arts and Letters Award 7029
Edmund C. Bovey Award 8543
Bravo Award 8987
Business in the Arts Awards 6702
John Tropham and Susan Redd Butler Faculty Research Awards 17926
Canada Council Molson Prizes 6787
Charles Frankel Prize 14935
Pierre Chauveau Medal 18162
Ron Coplen Roll of Honor Award 19559
Creative Arts Award 12159
Sir John William Dawson Medal 18163
Dickinson College Arts Award 8911
Diplome d'honneur 7036
Distinguished Humanities Educator 8317
Distinguished Individual of Foreign Birth Award 11460
Distinguished Women's Awards 16572
Alden B. Dow Creativity Center Summer Residency Fellowships 16578
Education Awards 17927
Albert Einstein Commemorative Award 22026
El Angel Award - For Corporate Contribution to the Development of Hispanic-American Arts 6375
Ralph Waldo Emerson Award 17241
Fellow 7697
Fellow or Foreign Honorary Member 620
Fellowship 15250
John Fisher Memorial Prize 12444
Founders Award 6703
Norman L. and Roselea J. Goldberg Prize for Manuscripts in American Philosophy 21275
Governor's Arts Awards 16276
Governor's Award for Distinguished Achievement in the Arts 10294
John Simon Guggenheim Memorial Foundation Fellowships 10192
John Whitney Hall Book Prize 5276
Hall of Fame
American Indian Lore Association 2605
Pi Kappa Phi 17315
Hall of Outstanding Americans 15986
Heinz Award in the Arts and Humanities 10380
HSSFC Scholarly Book Prizes 7084
Humanist Arts Award 2585
Independent Research and Creative Work Awards 17928
International Hall of Fame World Award 12162
The Jefferson Lecture Award 14936
Jefferson Lecture in the Humanities 14937
Thomas Jefferson Medal for Distinguished Achievement in the Arts, Humanities, or Social Sciences 3435
Keith Kelly Award for Cultural Leadership 7037
Laetare Medal 21089
Leadership Award 6704
Edward MacDowell Medal 13008
Mayor's Arts Awards 8771
McKnight Doctoral Fellowship Program in Arts and Sciences, Mathematics, Business and Engineering 9599
Algur H. Meadows Award for Excellence in the Arts 19513
Merit Award 8784
Henry Allen Moe Prize in the Humanities 3440
Dorothy Mullen National Arts and Humanities Award 15576
National Endowment for the Humanities Grant Programs 14938
National Federation of the Blind Scholarship Program 15039
National Humanities Medal 14939
Ohioana Career Award 16662
Ohioana Citation for Distinguished Service to Ohio 16663
Outstanding Achievement Award 19361
Outstanding Business Leader Awards 16573
Prize in Humanities 5541
Protege Awards 20111
Public Programming Awards 17929
Charles Redd Center Publication Grants 17930
Rome Prize Fellowships 605
Benjamin Rush Award 8913
Aldo and Jeanne Scaglione Prize for Comparative Literary Studies 13571
Sower Award 16066
Robert E. Stewart Engineering-Humanities Award 4236
Student Paper Award 3927
Summer Awards for Upper Division and Graduate Students 17931
Toronto Arts Awards 20112
University Medal 16304
Vesta Award 21698
Marcel Vincent Prize in Human Sciences 5542
Wexner Prize 21594
Elie Wiesel Award for Jewish Art and Culture 10433
Gill Robb Wilson Award 365

Asian American culture
Asian American Journalists Association National Awards 5165
Chinese-American Librarians Association Distinguished Service Award 7927
Kun-Po Soo Award 3624
Ernest M. Pon Memorial Award 14010

Asian (continued)

Special Recognition Award 5167
Vietnamese Youth Excellence Award 21364

Asian history
James Henry Breasted Prize 2467
John K. Fairbank Prize in East Asian History 2470

Asian studies (*See also* Japanese culture)
Acupuncture Patient of the Year 1314
Acupuncturist of the Year 1315
American Council of Learned Societies Fellowships 2037
APALA Distinguished Service Award 5171
Harry J. Benda Prize 5273
Anada Kentish Coomaraswamy Book Prize 5274
Distinguished Contributions to Asian Studies 5275
Louis Dupree Prize for Research on Central Asia 18600
John Whitney Hall Book Prize 5276
Indiana University Prize for Altaic Studies 17226
Legislator of the Year 1316
Joseph Levenson Prizes in Chinese Studies 5277
Mike Mansfield Award 12302
Ernest M. Pon Memorial Award 14010
Student Scholarships 12300

Asphalt paving
Board of Directors Award of Recognition 5574
Brochure Award 13997
Ecological Award 13998
Emmons Award 5575
Hall of Fame Award 5202
Honorary Member 5576
Hot Mix Asphalt Hall of Fame 13999
Tom Nonnenmacher Industry Service Award 14274
President's Award 5205
Quality in Construction Award 14000
Recognition of Achievement Award 5203
Special Recognition Award 5206

Assessment
Appraiser of the Year Award 14271
Robert H. Armstrong Award 5006
Bernard L. Barnard Award 11267
CAAO Scholarship 8410
Distinguished Assessment Jurisdiction Award 11268
Distinguished Research and Development Award 11269
D. Howard Doane Award 4406
Donehoo Essay Award 11270
Robert L. Foreman Award 5007
Harry Galkin Award 11271
IAAO Global Award 11272
IAAO Journalism Citation 11273
International Award 11274
International Property Tax Achievement Award 11275
Journalism Citation 11276
S. Edwin Kazdin Memorial Fund Award 5009
Dr. William Kinnard, Jr. Academic Award 5010
Louise and Y. T. Lum Award 5011
Arthur A. May Award 5012
McCarren Award 11277
Media Award 11976
Member of the Year Award 11278
Most Valuable Member Award 11279
Outstanding Chapter Award 11280
Outstanding Contribution Award 14295
Person of the Year Award 14296
Verne W. Potorff Professional Designee of the Year Award 11281
Public Information Program Award 11282
Alfred E. Reinman, Jr. Award 5013
George L. Schmutz Award 5014
Charles B. Shattuck Award 5015
H. Grady Stebbins, Jr. Distinguished Service Award 5016
Percy and Betty Wagner Award 5017
Zangerle Award 11283

Astronautics *See* Aerospace

Astronomy
A.B. Gregory Award 18255
AIAA Space Science Award 2669
AIP Science Writing Awards 2831
Amateur Achievement Award 6006
Amateur Astronomers Medal 521
Arctowski Medal 13826
Astronomical League Award 6001
Astronomical League Observing Awards 6251
George Van Biesbroeck Prize 1508
Priscilla and Bart Bok Award 1509
Bower Award and Prize for Achievement in Science 9741
Thomas J. Brennan Award 6007
Dirk Brouwer Award 1510
Catherine Wolfe Bruce Medal 6008
BSAS Science Fair Prize 6252
Annie Jump Cannon Award in Astronomy
American Association of University Women Educational Foundation 1470
American Astronomical Society 1511
C. A. Chant Medal 18141
Ken Chilton Prize 18142
Comstock Prize in Physics 13829
Henry Draper Medal 13831
Education Awards 9335
Ernest F. Fullum Award 9039
Gungywamp Society Scholarship 10208
Walter H. Haas Award 5751
George Ellery Hale Prize 1512
Dannie N. Heineman Prize for Astrophysics 2834
Harry H. Hess Medal 2351
Honorary Member 18143
Klumpke-Roberts Award 6009
Gerard P. Kuiper Prize 1513
La Cumbres Ameteur Outreach Award 6010
Richard D. Lines Award in Astronomy 11182
Magellanic Premium Award 3439
Harold Masursky Award for Meritorious Service 1514
Messier Observing Certificate 22042
Maria and Eric Muhlmann Prize 6011
National Young Astronomer Award 6002
Simon Newcomb Award 18144
Thomas O. Paine Memorial Award 17367
Leslie C. Peltier Award 6003
Newton Lacy Pierce Prize in Astronomy 1515
Plaskett Medal 18145
Herbert C. Pollock Award 9040
Presidents Citation 10210
Research Associateship Programs 15623
Bruno Rossi Prize 1516
Henry Norris Russell Lectureship 1517
Service Award 18146
Lester W. Strock Award 18645
Beatrice M. Tinsley Prize 1518
Robert J. Trumpler Award 6012
Trustees Award 10211
Harold C. Urey Prize 1519
Helen B. Warner Prize for Astronomy 1520
James Craig Watson Medal 13854
Charles A. Whitten Medal 2359
Bob Wright Al Service Award 6004

Athletics *See* Physical education; Sports; Track and field

Atmospheric science *See* Meteorology

Atomic energy (*See also* Nuclear engineering)
Davisson-Germer Prize in Atomic or Surface Physics 3454
Distinguished Service Award 11019
Industry Award 11020
Meritorious Service Award 11021
Henry DeWolf Smyth Statesman Award 16594

Auctions
Advertising Awards 14464
Hall of Fame 14471
Hall of Fame Award 14465
International Auctioneers Championship 14466

Audio engineering (*See also* Acoustics)
AES Publications Award 6051
Audio Engineering Society Medal Award 6052
Autosound Grand Prix Awards 6057
Board of Governors Award 6053
Gold Medal Award 6054
Hi-Fi Grand Prix Awards 6058
Alexander M. Poniatoff Gold Medal Award 19195
Silver Medal Award 6055
Video Grand Prix Awards 6059
Samuel L. Warner Memorial Medal Award 19200
Wallace Waterfall Award 5997

Audiology *See* Speech and hearing

Audiovisuals
Gold Screen Awards 14243
International Television Programming and Promotions Awards 16223
International Video Competition 18863
Carl F. and Viola V. Mahnke Film Production Award 5359
National Student Production Awards Competition 14539
Northwest Film and Video Festival 16560

Auto racing
AARWBA All-America Auto Racing Teams 1522
AARWBA Hall of Fame Award (Legends of Racing) 1523
All-American Soap Box Derby 11914

Auto (continued)
American Continental Championship 19681
"Cannonball" Baker Award 8764
Woolf Barnato Trophy 19682
Best New National Rally Award 19683
Jim Blunk Memorial Award 20414
Bob McLaughlin Vintage Spirit Award 8516
Bob Stroud Memorial Rookie of the Year Award National Midget Car Div. 20415
Bracket World Finals Team Championship 11676
Tom Burke Memorial Award 19684
Jimmy Caruthers Memorial Award 20416
Championship Awards 14912
Concours 7973
Course Rally Rookie of the Year 19685
Daytona Gatorade Victory Lane Award 8765
Divisional Achievement Award 19686
Divisional Pro Rally of the Year Award 19687
Divisional Pro Rally Program of the Year Award 19688
Divisional Pro Rally Region of the Year Award 19689
Mark Donohue Award 19690
Drivers World Champions 2565
Harley J. Earl Trophy (Daytona 500) 8766
Eddie Edenburn Trophy 20417
ESPY Awards 9337
Exxon Supreme GT 11754
Exxon World Sports Car Championship 11755
Ferrari Challenge 11756
Jim Fitzgerald Rookie of the Year 19691
Arthur J. Gervais Award 19692
Diana Fell Gilmore - Woman Behind the Scenes Award 20418
Ross Hadley Memorial Achievement Award 20419
IHRA Pro Alcohol Funny Car World Champion 11677
IHRA Pro Stock World Championship 11678
IHRA Pro Top Fuel Dragster World Champion 11679
Indianapolis 500 Mile Race 10779
Indianapolis Motor Speedway Hall of Fame 10780
International Motorsports Hall of Fame 11760
Jostens Most Improved National Midget Championship Series Driver Award 20420
Kimberly Cup 19693
Roger McCluskey Award of Excellence 20421
John McGill Award 19694
Tom McKean Award 19695
Mechanic of the Year Award 20422
David Morrell Memorial Award 19696
Most Improved Championship Driver Award 20423
Most Improved Driver Award 20424
NASCAR Championships 14045
National Pro Rally of the Year Award 19697
Novice Team Award 19698
Jack O'Neal Safety Award 20425
Outstanding National Touring Rally of the Year Award 19699
Pepsi 400 Trophy 8767
President's Cup 19700
Pro Modified World Champion 11680
Public Relations Regional Achievement Award 19701
Race Organizer of the Year 20426
Rally Awards 19702
Regional Achievement Award 19703
Regional Publication Awards 19704
Robert V. Ridges Memorial Award 19705
Rolex Trophy 8768
Rookie of the Year Award National Sprint Care Div. 20427
Rookie of the Year Award Silver Crown Div. 20428
SCCA/CASCT North American Rally Cup 19706
SCCA Mechanic of the Year 19707
SCCA Pro Rally Cup 19708
SCCA Pro Rally Manufacturer's Award 19709
Val D. Scroggie, M.D. Memorial Award 19710
Slick 50 Pro Series 11757
Gordon Smiley Memorial Award 19711
Dr. George G. Snively Memorial Award 19712
Solo Driver of Eminence Award 19713
Solo I Event of the Year Award 19714
Solo II Cup 19715
Solo II Divisional of the Year Award 19716
Solo II Driver of the Year 19717
Solo II Rookie of the Year 19718
SportsCar Awards 19719
Street Stock Endurance Championship 11758
Martin W. Tanner Award 19720
Trans-Am Tour 19721
USAC Special Recognition Awards 20429
Vic and Jessie Wallder Award 19722
Wimberly Cup 19723
Winston Cup (Winston Cup Series) 8769
World Challenge 19724

Automobile industry
10Best Cars 7581
Automotive Aftermarket Education Award 16576
Induction into the Automotive Hall of Fame 6110
Automotive Industry Leader of the Year 6111
Automotive Leader of the Year 6123
Award for Young Leadership and Excellence 6112
Customer Service Excellence Award 1274
Dealer Education Award 16577
Distinguished Service Citation 6113
Distinguished Service to the RV Industry Award 17915
Hall of Fame 19588
Al Hines Award 9595
Member of the Year 6119
Motor Trend Car of the Year 13626
Motor Trend Import Car of the Year 13627
National Quality Dealer Award 15254
Outstanding Achievement Award 6115
Outstanding Younger Member Award 19055
Pathfinder Award 6117
Promotional Achievement Awards 6108
Public Affairs Competition 1276
Ken W. Purdy Award 11752
RV Automotive Achievement Award 17919
Time Magazine Quality Dealer Award 20092
Triangle Award 13624

Automobiles
Annual Meeting Best Of Show Founders Award 12236
Automotive Achievement Award 13309
Automotive Innovation Award 13310
Autosound Grand Prix Awards 6057
Henry E. and Pauline S. Becker Award 17340
Carl Benz Award 19064
Best Cars 3107
Best Indy 500 Camaro Award 11444
Best Stock Z28 Award 11445
Bigelow Trophy 8079
James J. Bradley Distinguished Service Award 19065
Ken Brady Award 13553
Richard and Grace Brigham Award 19066
Cecil Kimber Enthusiasts Award 13323
Chassie Awards 17826
Chrysler Corporation Cup 21975
Harold E. Churchill Award 19802
Citation for Distinguished Service 8080
Concours Awards 21380
Coons Achievement Award 8081
Crawford Award 9117
Nicholas-Joseph Cugnot Award 19067
George De Angelis Award 13554
William Dendinger Driver of the Year 13362
Hernando DeSoto Award 14914
Deutsch Memorial Trophy 8082
Dietrich Trophy 8083
Duntov Mark of Excellence Award 14738
R. Vale Faro Trophy 17341
Folz Memorial Award 14739
Friend of Automotive History Award 19068
Jack Gehrt Memorial Award 8084
Ed Grace Memorial Award 4988
Hall of Fame 14471
IAMA Award 11970
E. P. Ingersoll Award 19069
Thomas B. Jeffery Award 13756
Otto Klausmeyer Distinguished Service Award 17342
Member of the Year Award 11446
Most Popular Convention Award 3105
Motor Trend Truck of the Year 13628
The Order of NSU 16587
Presidential Award 11447
President's Award 21976
Walter Rosenthal Award 13557
SDC Concours Awards 19803
SDC Publication Committee Awards 19804
Fran Silky Award 17993
Steiner Trophy 8085
Tarnopol Trophy 8086
Trevor Award 20247
Turnquist Trophy 8087
Bernard J. Weis Trophy 17343
Winner's Circle National Winners 13555
Raymond M. Wood Award 17994
Don Yenko Memorial Award 11448

Automotive engineering
Automotive Training Awards 6121
Vincent Bendix Automotive Electronics Engineering Award 19035
L. Ray Buckendale Lecture 19036
Edward N. Cole Award for Automotive Engineering Innovation 19037
Arch T. Colwell Cooperative Engineering Medal 19038
Arch T. Colwell Merit Award 19039

Automotive (continued)

Engineering Meetings Board Outstanding Oral Presentation Award 19041
Fellow Grade of Membership 19042
Henry Ford II Distinguished Award for Excellence in Automotive Engineering 19043
Cliff Garrett Turbomachinery Engineering Award 19044
Harry L. Horning Memorial Award 19046
International Leadership Citation 19047
Ralph H. Isbrandt Automotive Safety Engineering Award 19048
Forest R. McFarland Award 19052
Medal of Honor 19053
Elmer A. Sperry Award 19057
Russell S. Springer Award 19058
Technical Standards Board Outstanding Contribution Award 19059

Automotive safety
Distinguished Service Award 1275
Catherine "Cathy" Hensel Award 9026
National Law Enforcement Saved by the Belt/Air Bag Awards Program 11309
Safe Mileage Award 21763
H. B. Vinson Award 9027

Aviation *See* Aeronautics and aviation

Aviation safety
ACTA Special Medallion Award 380
AIAA Piper General Aviation Award 2662
Air Traffic Control Specialist of the Year Award 381
Airport Crash/Fire/Rescue/Medical Preparedness Award 6132
Airway Transportation Systems Specialist of the Year 382
Annual Aviation Mechanic Safety Award 9425
ATCA Industrial Award 383
ATCA Life Cycle Management Award 384
Aviation Education Award 7704
Aviation Maintenance Department Safety Award 14562
Aviation Maintenance Technician of the Year Award 17582
Aviation Support Services Safety Award 14563
Aviation Week & Space Technology Distinguished Service Award 9577
Award for Distinguished Service 9427
Award for Extraordinary Service 9428
Award of Excellence 17583
Award of Merit 17584
Laura Taber Barbour Award 9578
Cecil Brownlow Publications Award 9579
Lt. Gen. Allen M. Burdett, Jr. Army Aviation Flight Safety Award 16819
Certificate of Appreciation 9429
Certificate of Commendation 9430
Chairman's Citation of Merit Awards 385
Joe Chase Award 17587
Joe M. Chase Award 9581
Company Appreciation Award 17588
Corporate/Commercial Business Flying Safety Awards 14564
Admiral Luis de Florez Flight Safety Award 9582
Flight Instructor of the Year Award Program 9432
Maj. Gen. Benjamin D. Foulois Memorial Award 16826
Lt. Gen. Harold L. George Civilian Airmanship Award 16827
Glen A. Gilbert Memorial Award 386
Helicopter Maintenance Award 10398
Heroism Award 9583
John Robert Horne Memorial Award 13905
Brig. Gen. Carl I. Hutton Memorial Award 16829
Harry T. Jensen Award 2433
George W. Kriske Memorial Award 387
Brig. Gen. Frank P. Lahm Memorial Award for Flight Safety 16830
William O. Marsh Safety Award 13907
Joe Mashman Safety Award 10400
Member Service Award 17589
Meritorious Service to Aviation Award 14568
Harry G. Moseley Award 239
National Awards Program 16990
PAMA/ATP Award 17590
William A. Parenteau Memorial Award 388
Pilot Safety Award
Helicopter Association International 10404
National Business Aviation Association 14569
General E. R. Quesada Memorial Award 389
Adm. James S. Russell Naval Aviation Flight Safety Award 16833
Shields-Trauger Award 6225
Small and Disadvantaged Business Award 390
John Paul Stapp Award 240
Technical Writing Awards 391
Adm. John H. Towers Flight Safety Award 16834
Charles E. Varnell Memorial Award for Small Business 392
Earl F. Ward Memorial Award 393

Aviculture *See* Ornithology

Bacteriology *See* Microbiology

Badminton
Badminton Hall of Fame 21145
Kenneth R. Davidson Memorial Award for Sportsmanship 21146
High School All-American Awards 21147
IBF Distinguished Service Award 21148
IBF Meritorious Service Award 21149
National Championships 21150
Players Appreciation Award 21151

Ballet
American Ballet Competition 1525
Erik Bruhn Prize 14478
Legends of Dance Awards 21525
New York International Ballet Competition 16235
USA International Ballet Competition 21184
Mae L. Wien Awards 18352

Banking
Advertising Awards 55
Community Service Awards 17162
John Hughes Scholarship 12181
Innovation Showcase Award 14222
NAFCU Awards Program 14223
Quarter-Century Honor Roll 14224
Robert A. Mooney Distinguished Service Award 9208
Small Business Advocates of the Year 20834

Baseball
ABCA Twenty-Five Year Awards 1539
Achievement Award 21153
AL and NL Baseball Player Comeback of the Year 19640
AL and NL Hillerich and Bradsby/*The Sporting News* Silver Slugger Awards 19641
AL and NL Manager of the Year 19642
AL and NL Pitchers of the Year 19643
AL and NL Relief Pitcher of the Year 19644
AL and NL Rookie Pitchers of the Year 19645
All-American Awards 15307
Amateur Baseball Hall of Fame 10161
American and National League Managers of the Year 19648
American League All-Star Team 19649
American League Rookie of the Year 19650
Baseball Outstanding Volunteer Award 543
Baseball Players Scholarship Award 19988
Baseball Research Awards 18630
Big East Conference Academic Awards 6369
Casey Award 19621
Century Club Award 1540
Coach of the Year
Baseball Canada 6262
Canadian Federation of Amateur Baseball 7086
Coach of the Year Award 1541
Coaches Association Awards 15309
Congressional Baseball Trophy 18106
Joe Cronin Award 2939
Bob Davids Award 18631
ESPY Awards 9337
William P. "Dutch" Fehring Award of Merit 21154
Field Maintenance Award 1542
Ford C. Frick Award 14494
Golden Diamond Awards 21155
Golden Field Award 21156
Golden Spikes Award 21157
Lefty Gomez Award 1543
Tom Gorman Memorial Award 10162
Clark C. Griffith Memorial Award 20130
Hall of Fame
American Baseball Coaches Association 1544
National Baseball Hall of Fame and Museum 14495
Hero of Baseball Award 18632
Honor Awards 1545
Jack Kavanagh Memorial Youth Baseball Research Award 18633
Jimmy Rattlesnake Award 7087
John H. Johnson President's Trophy 14339
Kenesaw M. Landis Award (Most Valuable Player) 6266
League Executive of the Year Awards 14340
Lee Allen Award 18634
Louisville Slugger 14659
Larry MacPhail Trophy 14341
Major League Baseball Player of the Year 19655
Major League Executive of the Year 19656

Baseball (continued)

Manager of the Year Award 6267
Media Award 21158
Meritorious Service Award 1546
Minor League Executive of the Year 19657
Minor League Manager of the Year 19658
Minor League Player of the Year 19659
National Championship 1547
National League All-Star Team 19660
National League Player of the Year 19661
National League Rookie of the Year 19662
NCAA National Championships 14687
Doug Pappas Research Award 18635
Jim Quinn Award 14511
Jimmy Rattlesnake Award 6263
Rawlings Big Stick Award 17882
Rawlings Bronze Glove Award 17883
Rawlings Gold Glove Award 17884
Rawlings Silver Glove Award 17885
The SABR Salute 18636
SABR Special Achievement Award 18637
Senior Team Canada Junior MVP 6264
Service Awards 21159
Seymour Medal 18638
Silver Slugger Team 19676
Special NJCAA Awards 15316
J. G. Taylor Spink Award 14496
Topps - J. G. Taylor Spink Minor League Player-of-the-Year 20102
Topps All-Star Scout Award 20103
Topps Major League Rookie All-Star Team 20104
Topps Minor League Player-of-the-Month 20105
Topps National Association All-Star Teams 20106
Topps Organization Trophy 20107
Topps Scout-of-the-Month Awards 20108
Topps - George M. Trautman Minor League Player-of-the-Year 20109
Umpire Award 21160
Cy Young Award 6268

Basketball

Stuart W. Aberdeen Memorial Trophy 7208
Arnie Aizstrauts Team Sportsmanship 537
All-America Basketball Team 19646
All-American Awards 15307
All-Defensive Team 14498
All-NBA Team 14499
All-Star Game Most Valuable Player 8479
Big East Conference Academic Awards 6369
Boys' Basketball Past Chair Recognition 545
Boys' Basketball Vision Award 546
The Bronze Baby 7211
John W. Bunn Award 13750
Canadian Basketball Hall of Fame 8971
Coach of the Year
  Continental Basketball Association 8480
  National Association of Basketball Coaches 14081
Coach of the Year - Red Auerbach Trophy 14500
Coaches Association Awards 15309
College Basketball Coach of the Year 19651
College Basketball Player of the Year 19652
Nan Copp Award 7212
Defensive Player of the Year
  Continental Basketball Association 8481
  National Association of Basketball Coaches 14082
  National Basketball Association 14501
Division I Player of the Year 14083
Division II Player of the Year 14084
Division III Player of the Year 14085
Peter Ennis Award 7215
ESPY Awards 9337
Executive of the Year 14502
Girls' Basketball National Volunteer of the Year 552
Golden Anniversary Award 14086
got milk? All-Rookie Team 14503
got milk? Rookie of the Year - Eddie Gottlieb Trophy 14504
Curt Gowdy Media Award 13751
Willard Greim Award 553
Hall of Fame 15943
Colonel Harry D. Henshel Award 555
Frank Hesselroth Leadership Award 14288
J. Walter Kennedy Citizenship Award 14505
Emil S. Liston Award 14289
Pete Maravich Memorial Award 14660
W. P. McGee Trophy 7224
Metropolitan Award 14087
Herbert Joseph Mols Award 559
Mike Moser Memorial Trophy 7228
Most Improved Player 14506
Most Valuable Player
  Continental Basketball Association 8482
  National Wheelchair Basketball Association 15944
Most Valuable Player Award - Maurice Podoloff Trophy 14507
Frances Pomeroy Naismith Award 13752
Naismith College Coach of the Year 6027
Naismith College Officials of the Year 6028
Naismith Collegiate Awards (Naismith Trophy) 6029
Naismith High School Awards 6030
Naismith Outstanding Contribution to Basketball Award 6031
NBA All-Star Team 19663
NBA Coach of the Year 19664
NBA Executive of the Year 19665
NBA Player of the Year 19666
NBA Rookie of the Year 19667
NCAA National Championships 14687
Newcomer of the Year 8483
Playoff Most Valuable Player 8484
Rookie of the Year 8485
Sixth Man Award 14508
Special NJCAA Awards 15316
Captain James S. Ure Award for Sportsmanship 15945
Wade Trophy 14014
Cliff Wells Appreciation Award 14088
Louis G. Wilke Memorial Award 582
John R. Wooden Award 12925
World Championship - Larry O'Brien Trophy 14509

Beauty contests

America's Junior Miss 4927
Miss America 13495
Miss Galaxy 9853
Miss Indian World 9900
Miss Teen USA 13498
Miss Universe 13499
Miss USA 13500

Bibliography

Joseph L. Andrews Bibliographic Award 1248
Instruction Publication of the Year Award 5610
Marta Lange/CQ Press Award 5612
Jose Toribio Medina Award 18415
Oberly Award for Bibliography in the Agricultural Sciences 5616
Quadrennial Prize for Bibliography 11718
Tremaine Fellowship 6360
Marie Tremaine Medal 6361

Bicycling

National Championships 21162
NEMBA Trail Grant 16103
U.S. Bicycling Hall of Fame 20433

Biochemistry

ASBMB/Amgen Award 3917
ASBMB/Avanti Award in Lipids 3918
ASBMB - Merck Award 3919
ASBMB/Schering Plough Institute Award 3920
Boehringer Mannheim Award 7452
Bower Award and Prize for Achievement in Science 9741
Melvin Calvin Award 11694
Louisa Gross Horwitz Prize 8243
IIS Award 11695
Intel International Science and Engineering Fair 18362
ISCE Silver Medal 11986
Walter J. Johnson Annual Prize 10235
Ralph D. Lillie Award 10446
Fritz Lipmann Lectureship 3921
Merck Frosst Centre for Therapeutic Research Lecture Award 7845
NAS Award in Molecular Biology 13843
William C. Rose Award 3922
Silverstein-Simeone Award Lecture 11987
Herbert Sober Award 3923
Student Travel Awards 11988

Biography

Anisfield-Wolf Book Awards 8097
Bancroft Prizes 8238
Evans Biography Award 13641
Evans Handcart Award 13642
Hubert Evans Nonfiction Prize 21520
Zelda & Paul Gitlin Literary Prize 20080
Los Angeles Times Book Prizes 12931
James Russell Lowell Prize 13561
National Book Critics Circle Awards 14530
National Jewish Book Award - Autobiography/Memoir 12321
National Jewish Book Award - Yiddish Literature 12333
Ohioana Book Awards 16661
Personal Narratives Award 21069
Prix Maxime-Raymond 10820
Prize for a First Book 13566
Pulitzer Prizes 17749
Richard S. Kennedy Student Essay Prize 20081
Summerfield G. Roberts Award 19415
Society of Midland Authors Awards 19186
William B. Wisdom Grant in Aid of Research 20082

Biology (*See also* Anatomy; Biochemistry; Biophysics; Biomedical engineering; Biotechnology; Botany; Genetics; Marine biology; Microbiology; Mycology; Nature; Ornithology; Physiology; Zoology)
ACS Award in Separations Science and Technology 1721
Adhesion Society Award for Excellence in Adhesion Science 184
AIBS Distinguished Service Award 2740
ASCB/Bruce Alberts Award for Distinguished Contributions to Science Education 3940
ASBMB/Amgen Award 3917
ASBMB/Avanti Award in Lipids 3918
ASBMB - Merck Award 3919
ASBMB/Schering Plough Institute Award 3920
ASCB/Promega Early Career Life Scientist Award 3941
ASGSB Founder's Award 4077
ASGSB President's Award 4078
Award for Excellence in Encouraging Equity 14090
Award in Science 17240
Alfred Bader Award in Bioinorganic or Bioorganic Chemistry 1736
BD Biosciences Investigator Award 1242
Lloyd M. Bertholf Award for Chapter Excellence 6323
Biometeorological Research Foundation Award 11978
Bower Award and Prize for Achievement in Science 9741
Frank G. Brooks Award for Excellence in Student Research 6324
Burgdorf Award 16208
Capranica Foundation Award in Neuroethology 7579
Caroline tum Suden/France Hellebrandt Professional Opportunity Awards 3512
Frank M. Chapman Memorial Fund Award 3155
Chapter History Award 6325
Creativity Awards 10612
Cytotechnologist Award for Outstanding Achievement 4389
Cytotechnologist Scientific Presentation Award 4390
Distinguished Service Award 14092
Theodosius Dobzhansky Prize 18894
Mac V. Edds Memorial Lecture in Developmental Biology 6665
Established Investigator Award 2406
Excellence in Education Award 4391
FASEB Excellence in Science Award 9462
Fellow or Foreign Honorary Member 620
Flavelle Medal 18165
Ford Foundation Postdoctoral Diversity Fellowships 15622
Four-Year College Biology Teaching Award 14093
Geno Saccamanno, M.D. New Frontiers in Cytology award 4392
Geraldine Colby Zeiler Award 4393
Graduate Confectionery Fellowship - Penn State University 17179
Guest Lectureship Award on Basic Cell Research in Cytology 4394
Melody Hall Memorial Award 14094
Dalton S. Harrison/Florida Irrigation Society Scholarship 9608
Honorary Life Member 18786
Honorary Member 6326
Honorary Membership 14095
Louisa Gross Horwitz Prize 8243
Impact of Workload on Diagnostic Accuracy Award 4395
Internal Recognition Awards 21094
International Society of Biometeorology Honorary Member 11979
ISDP Dissertation Prize 11926
Walter J. Johnson Annual Prize 10235
E.E. Just Lecture Award 3942
Gordin Kaplan Award 7089
Louis N. Katz Basic Science Research Prize for Young Investigators 2412
David Kucharski Young Investigator Award for Research in Developmental Psychobiology 11927
Jeffery P. LaFage Graduate Student Research Award 9282
Warren R. Lang Resident Physician Award 4396
Karl Spencer Lashley Award 3437
Lerner-Gray Fund for Marine Research Award 3156
Linda D. Barber Award 4079
Fritz Lipmann Lectureship 3921
Richard Lounsbery Award 13835
MAC Poster Awards 3943
Ernst Mayr Award in Systematic Biology 19305
MBC Paper of the Year Award 3944
McClung Award 6328
Media Awards 2741
The Merton Bernfield Memorial Award 3945
Middle School Teaching Award 14096
NAS Award in Molecular Biology 13843
NAS Award in the Neurosciences 13844
New Frontiers in Cytology Award 4397
NSF-REV 13634
Katherine Ordway Stewardship Award 16036
Orr E. Reynolds Distinguished Service Award 4080
Outstanding Biology Teacher Award 14097
Outstanding New Biology Teacher Achievement Award 14098
Papanicolaou Award of the American Society of Cytology 4398
William F. Peterson Foundation Awards 11980
Potamkin Prize for Research in Pick's, Alzheimer's, and Related Diseases 704
President's Award
American Society of Cytopathology 4399
American Society of Naturalists 4562
Public Service Award 3946
Pulp Biology Research Award 11209
Research Associateship Programs 15623
Henry and Sylvia Richardson Research Grant 9284
Theodore Roosevelt Memorial Fund Award 3158
William C. Rose Award 3922
Rosen Prize 12921
Smithsonian Institution Fellowship Program 18572
Snodgrass Memorial Research Award 9285
Herbert Sober Award 3923
Special Distinguished & Outstanding Service Award 4081
Thora W. Halstead Young Investigator's Award 4082
Two-Year College Biology Teaching Award 14099
Robert W. Vance Award 8680
E. B. Wilson Medal 3947
Women in Cell Biology 3948
Sewall Wright Award 4563
Young Investigators' Prizes 4564
Young UK Cell Biologist of the Year Award 3949

Biomedical engineering
AAMI Annual Meeting Manuscript Awards 5486
AAMI Foundation Laufman - Greatbatch Prize 5487
AAMI/GE Healthcare BMET of the Year Award 5488
Biomedical Instrumentation & Technology Outstanding Paper Awards 5489
Roger W. Boom Award 8679
Clinical/Biomedical Engineering Achievement Award 5490
Becton Dickinson Career Achievement Award 5491
Distinguished Lecturer Award 6388
Graduate Student Awards 6389
H. R. Lissner Award 4527
AAMI Foundation/ACCE Robert L. Morris Humanitarian Award 5495
Theo C. Pilkington Outstanding Educator Award 4039
Johnny Roland Grant 7786
SBET/Renshaw-Heilman BMET of the Year Award 15737
Rita Schaffer Young Investigator Award 6390
Visionary Award 6743
Whitaker Senior Student Bioengineering Design Awards 6391

Biophysics
Biological Physics Prize 3449
Walter J. Johnson Annual Prize 10235

Biotechnology
Biotechnology Research Award 4132
Biotechnology Teaching Award 14091
Sheldon K. Friedlander Award 955
H. R. Lissner Award 4527
Visionary Award 6743

Black culture *See* African American culture

Blindness
Access Awards 2300
Alfred Allen Award 5337
E.A. Baker Foundation for the Prevention of Blindness Fellowships 7301
Mary K. Bauman Award 5338
C. Warren Bledsoe Award 5339
Blind Service Association Scholarships 6453
Robert S. Bray Award 2039
Francis Joseph Campbell Award 5856
George Card Award 2040
The Carroll Society 7613
Certificate of Appreciation 6455
Arthur E. Copeland Award 20407
Arthur E. Copeland Scholarship 20408
Helen Copeland Scholarship 20409
Irving Diener Award 6456
Distinguished Service Award 13868
Ned E. Freeman Writing Award 2041

Blindness (continued)

William F. and Catherine T. Gallagher Award 2301
Winston Gordon Award 7302
Wayne and Walter Gretzky Scholarship Foundation 7303
Kitty Carlisle Hart Award of Merit for Lifetime Achievement 10035
Vernon Henley Media Award 2042
International Blindness Prevention Award 712
Robert B. Irwin Award 15258
Helen Keller Achievement Awards 2302
Spirit of Helen Keller Award 10388
Lions SightFirst Diabetic Retinopathy Research Program 2139
Wilburn H. Long Employment Award 6457
Major General Melvin J. Maas Achievement Award 6458
Douglas MacFarland Award 5340
Arthur Napier Magill Distinguished Service Award 7304
Man/Woman of Vision 9385
Anna Marklund Scholarship 15043
John H. McAulay Award 5341
Durward K. McDaniel Ambassador Award 2043
Medal Awards 1568
Migel Medal for Outstanding Service to Blind Persons 2303
NAC Award 13869
National Federation of the Blind Scholarship Program 15039
Mary P. Oenslager Scholastic Achievement Awards 17905
Newel Perry Award 15040
Ross C. Purse Doctoral Fellowship 7305
Peter J. Salmon Award - Blind Worker of the Year 15259
Alexander Scourby Narrator of the Year Award 2304
Service Award 13870
Ambrose M. Shotwell Memorial Award 5342
Jacobus TenBroek Award 15041
Torgi Talking Book of the Year 7306
Grace Worts Staff Service Award 7307

Boating (*See also* Rowing)
All American Inter-Collegiate Sailor 11123
America's Cup 4923
APBA Gold Cup 3587
APBA Honor Squadron 3588
Mel Barr Award 15366
F. Gregg Bemis President's Trophy 11157
Boating Writers International Annual Writing Contest 6494
Broad Axe Award 7629
Jack Brown Trophy 20770
Carron Keeper 20075
Charles F. Chapman Memorial Award 15363
U.S. Sailing/Rolex Junior Women's Championship - Nancy Leiter Clagett Trophy 20771
Director's Award 15364
Dolphin Award 7630
Edith Oliver Dusmet World Championship Cup 11727
Founder's Trophy 20772
Gar Wood of the Year Award 9872
Geary 18 International Yacht Racing Association Championship Regatta 9905
Colonel Green Round Hill Trophy 3589
Growth and Promotion Award 20076
Hall of Champions 3590
Heinzerling Trophy 18576
Nathaniel G. Herreshoff Trophy 20773
Honorary Member 20703
Chandler Hovey Trophy 20774
Inter-Collegiate Sailing Hall of Fame 11124
Inter-Collegiate Sailor of the Year 11125
Junior, Intermediate, and Senior Championship Awards 9197
MC National Championship Regatta 13209
John Killam Murphy Award 7631
National Champions 18259
National Championship 18034
National Multihull Championship - Alter Cup 20775
National Offshore Championship - Lloyd Phoenix Trophy 20776
National Sportsmanship Award 20777
North American Championship Trophy 11728
Ocean Crew and Great Lake Crew Award of Merit 20379
One Ton Championship - Hawk Trophy 20778
Rolex International Women's Keelboat Championship 20779
St. Petersburg Yacht Club Trophy 20780
Mark Thornton Gold Challenge Award 11682
Randy Tilton Memorial Award 3591
U.S. Match Racing Championship - Prince of Wales Bowl 20781
U.S. Men's Sailing Championship - Clifford D. Mallory Cup 20782
U.S. Sailing One-Design Awards 20783
U.S. Sailing/Rolex Junior Championships 20784
U.S. Singlehanded Sailing Championship - George D. O'Day Trophy 20785
U.S. Team Race Championship - George R. Hinman Trophy 20786
U.S. Women's Open Championships 20787
U.S. Women's Sailing Championship - Mrs. Charles Francis Adams Trophy 20788
U.S. Youth Sailing Championship 20789
Vice-President's Trophy 11158
World Champion Award 12050

Bobsledding *See* Sledding

Book and newspaper design
AAUP Design Show 5567
Alcuin Book Design Awards 430
Bumbershoot, The Seattle Arts Festival 16734
Canada Awards for Excellence 15568
Certificate of Merit 6514
Distinguished Service Award 6515
ILCA Media Awards Contest 11700
Herb Lubalin Award 19280
Stanley Marcus Award for Book Design 20019
Lucile Micheels Pannell Award 21799
Publication Design Awards 19281
Western US Design & Production Awards Competition 17737
Fred Whitehead Award 20023
Women's National Book Association Award 21800

Book collecting
Sir Thomas More Medal for Book Collecting 10037

Book illustration *See* Illustration

Books *See* Publishing

Botany
Ruth Allen Award 3533
Ralph E. Alston Award 6536
Glenn Anderson Lectureship on World Food Security 7336
Andrew Award 20124
APS Fellow 3534
Award for Outstanding Research 7337
Award of Distinction 3535
Charles Reid Barnes Life Membership Award 4586
Bayer Crop Science Award 17374
Bernard Lowy Fund 12952
Charles Edwin Bessey Award 6537
Best Student Presentation Award 7338
Harold C. Bold Award 17301
William Boright Hewitt and Maybelle E. Ball Hewitt Award 3536
BSA Merit Awards 6538
Michael Cichan Award 6539
Isabel C. Cookson Paleobotanical Award 6540
George R. Cooley Award
American Society of Plant Taxonomists 4593
Botanical Society of America 6541
Corresponding Members 6542
Darbaker Prize 6543
Distinguished Economic Botanist 18665
Distinguished Paper in Phychology Award 6544
Distinguished Service Award 3537
Ecological Section Award 6545
Katherine Esau Award 6546
Excellence in Extension Award 3538
Excellence in Teaching Award 3539
Fellow 7339
Edmund H. Fulling Award 18666
Henry Gleason Award 16214
Henry Allan Gleason Award 6547
Glen Helen Ecology Institute Awards 4986
Gold, Silver, and Bronze Medals 8692
Graduate Student Award 19493
Graduate Student Plant Breeding Award 14793
Graduate Student Research Grant 4594
Asa Gray Award 4595
Gordon J. Green Outstanding Young Scientist Award 7340
Stanley Greene Award in Bryology 11290
Jesse M. Greenman Award 6548
D. Todd Gresham Award 13019
Adolph E. Gude, Jr. Award 4587
Stephen Hales Prize 4588
S. Hattori Prize 11291
Hedwig Medal 11292
Herbert Medal 11440
Annette Hervey - Torrey Botanical Club Award 20125
Dennis Robert Hoagland Award 4589
Honorary Member 7341
Lee M. Hutchins Award 3540
Intel International Science and Engineering Fair 18362
International Organization of Plant Biosystematists Life Membership 11781

Botany (continued)

J. S. Karling Graduate Student Research Award 6549
Charles F. Kettering Award 4590
Lawrence Memorial Award 10616
Mary Bancroft Memorial Scholarship 12502
Margaret Menzel Award 6550
Northwest Flower & Garden Show Garden Award 18036
Novartis Corp Protection American Phytopathological Society Award 19872
Leo Parizeau Prize in Biology 5540
Jeanette Siron Pelton Award 6551
Physiological Section Award 6552
Pinkerton Prize 20988
Frances Jones Poetker Award 2534
Samuel Noel Postlethwait Award 6553
Gerald W. Prescott Award 17302
Private Plant Breeding Award 14794
Professional Award 2535
Luigi Provasoli Award 17303
Public Plant Breeding Award 14795
Peter Raven Award 4596
William J. Robbins Award 20126
A.J. Sharp Award 6554
Charles Albert Shull Award 4591
Richard Spruce Award 11293
Syngenta Award 3541
Valent Biosciences- Best Paper Awards 17375
Edgar T. Wherry Award 6555

Bowling
All-American Awards 15307
Amateur Bowler of the Year 6561
Annual Championship Prizes 9523
Bowler of the Month 6562
Bowler of the Year
  Bowling Writers Association of America 6563
  Western Women Professional Bowlers 21573
Bowling Hall of Fame and Museum 11432
Bowling Magazine Writing Competition 1585
Coaches Association Awards 15309
Collegiate Bowlers of the Year 6564
Harry Golden Rookie of the Year 17592
Hall of Fame
  Professional Bowlers Association of America 17593
  Women's All-Star Association 21772
Industry Service Award 6380
International Bowling Hall of Fame 21869
Jean-Fish-Pearl Keller High Average Award 21773
Barbara Leicht-Bowers Bowler of the Year 21774
Victor Lerner Memorial Medal 6557
Local Association Public Relations Contest 1586
Local Association Service Award 1587
Mort Luby Senior Hall of Fame Award 6565
John O. Martino Award 6566
Lisa Maurice Rookie of the Year 21775
Medal Awards 1568
Most Improved Bowler 17870
National Trophy 14918
President's Medal 6558
Rookie of the Year 21574
Chris Schenkel Player of the Year 17594
Senior Bowler of the Year
  Bowling Writers Association of America 6567
  Women's All-Star Association 21776
Senior Player of the Year 17595
Senior Rookie of the Year 17596
Sportswoman of the Year Award 21777
VA Wapensky Award 6559
Rip Van Winkle Award 6568
WBW Bowlers of the Year 21871
WBW Distinguished Service Award 21872
WBW Gosta Zellen Golden Quill Award 21873

Boxing
Steve Belloise Award 12112
Boxer of the Year 20384
Boxing Hall of Fame Award 12113
Coach of the Year 20385
ESPY Awards 9337
Freddie Fiducia Award 12114
Fighter of the Year 12115
Humanitarian Award 12116
Manager of the Year 12117
Official of the Year 20386
Babe Orlando Award 12118
Outstanding Progress Award 20387
Joe Poodles, Sr. Award 12119
Irving Silverman Award 12120
Special Award 12121
Trainer of the Year 12122
United States Boxing Hall of Fame 20388
Dr. Ray Wesson Memorial Physician of the Year Award 20389

Bravery *See* Heroism

Bridal consulting
"Miss Dorothy" Heart 5586
Outstanding Educator Award 5520
Wedding Professional of the Year 5587

Bridge
$1000 King of Bridge Award 2016
Bridge Book of the Year 1589
Homer Shoop $5000 Preteen 10-Year Maturity Bond Certificate 2017
Honorary Member 1590
Youth Flight 2018

Broadcast journalism
American Legion Fourth Estate Award 2946
Annual Awards in International News Coverage 16981
Art Award 16241
Nellie Bly Cub Reporter Award 16242
Business/Economic Writing Award 8170
Byline Awards 16244
Canadian Federation of Humane Societies Media Award 7091
Cover Plaque Award 47
Niles Davis Award 14066
Deadline Club Awards 8773
EDI Awards (Equality/Dignity/Independence) 9088
Editor & Publisher/INMA Marketing Awards 9163
Feature Stories Awards 16246
Goldsmith Prize for Investigative Reporting 18439
Charles E. Green Journalism Awards 10308
Harold S. Hirsch Award for Excellence in Broadcasting 16461
John F. Hogan Distinguished Service Award 17848
Edwin M. Hood Award for Diplomatic Correspondence 15517
Humanitas Prize 10608
IAAO Journalism Citation 11273
ILCA Film and Broadcast Competition 11699
IRE Awards 12170
Journalism Award 9029
Journalism Awards Program 10354
Rev. Mychal Judge Heart of New York Awards 16249
Max Karant Award for Excellence in Aviation Journalism 398
Katz Award for Excellence in the Coverage of Immigration 7729
John S. Knight Fellowships 12605
Louis M. Lyons Award 16357
MDA Broadcast Journalism Awards 13683
Edward R. Murrow Awards 17849
Nieman Fellowships for Journalists 16358
Peabody Awards Collection 21020
George Polk Awards 12915
Public Service Award 15324
Radiology News Awards Competition 1943
Residential Fellowships 9758
Bart Richards Award for Media Criticism 17206
Science-in-Society Journalism Awards 14380
Sigma Delta Chi Awards 19276
Silurian Excellence in Journalism Awards 19327
Sol Taishoff Award for Excellence in Broadcast Journalism 15529
Technical Excellence Award 52
Lowell Thomas Award 11813
Lowell Thomas Travel Journalism Awards 19016
Twenty-Five Year News Achievement Award 19328
Unity Awards in Media 12866
UPI National Broadcast Awards 20371
Washington Correspondence Award 15524
Paul White Award 17850

Broadcasting (*See also* Broadcast journalism; Cable television; Media; Radio; Sports broadcasting; Television; Video)
Academy & Achievement Awards 80
Accolades Award 21706
Advisory Board Member of the Year 14535
BDA International Design Award 6296
Hugh Malcolm Beville, Jr. Award 14106
Belva B. Brissett Award 14107
Broadcast Excellence Award 6890
Broadcasting Hall of Fame 14108
Elizabeth Campbell Outstanding Public Broadcasting Award 15127
Chairman's Award 15612
Chapter of the Year 14536
Chassie Awards 17826
Clarion Awards 5522
Grover C. Cobb Memorial Award 14109
CPB Public Radio Program Awards 8523
CPB Public Television Local Program Awards 8524
Creative Achievement Award 14413
Brig. Gen. Robert L. Denig Distinguished Service Award 20684
Distinguished Service Award

Broadcasting (continued)
National Association of Broadcasters 14111
National Religious Broadcasters 15613
Ben East Prize 13364
Douglas Edwards Award 18199
Engineering Achievement Awards 14112
Foundation Award 11847
Gavel Awards 1533
Golden Mike Awards 16151
Grassroots Award 5570
Charlotte Hill Volunteers in Fund-Raising Award 15128
International Broadcasting Awards 10516
International Broadcasting Excellence Award 14113
International Emmy Award 11519
Joan Shorenstein Barone Award 17846
Anson Jones, M.D., Award 20032
Wally Jorgenson Award 14114
Ralph Lowell Award 8525
Matrix Award 16312
Member of the Year 14537
Milestone Award 15614
Jan Mitchell Community Development Award 15129
Most Improved Chapter of the Year 14538
National Headliner Awards 15194
National Student Production Awards Competition 14539
Novartis Crop Protection NAFB Farm Broadcasting Award 19876
Peabody Awards Collection 21020
Elaine Peterson Distinguished Service Award 15130
Professional Development Coordinator of the Year 14540
Professional Member of the Year 14541
Region of the Year 14543
Regional Representative of the Year 14544
Religious Broadcasting Hall of Fame Award 15617
Rookie Chapter of the Year 14545
Rookie Member of the Year 14546
Spirit of Broadcasting Award 14118
State Coordinator 14547
Theatre Library Association Award 20060
Women at Work Awards 21618

Brotherhood
Aim Quarterly Magazine Short Story Award 316
Big Brother of the Year 6366
Big Sister of the Year 6367
Fraternalist of the Year Award 18157
Junior Director of the Year Award 18158
Scholarships 20225
Harry S. Truman Good Neighbor Award 20226

Bureaucracy
INATAPROBU Rejection Scroll 11388
INATAPROBU Spirometric Citation 11389
Naiwu Osahon Award 21945
Order of the Bird 11390
Order of the Egg 11391

Burglar and fire alarms *See* Security

Business (*See also* Accounting; Advertising; Business education; Business history; Business journalism; Consumer affairs; Conventions; Economics; Management; Manufacturing; Marketing)
Academy of Distinguished Entrepreneurs 6178
ACFAS/Caisse de Depot et Placement du Quebec Prize (in Finance) 5536
Amistad Award 21292
Applause Award 21787
Athena Award
Kankakee River Valley Chamber of Commerce 12481
North San Antonio Chamber of Commerce 16533
Award for Achievement in Business Growth 8290
Awards for Distinguished Service in Environmental Planning 8513
Awards for Excellence 18865
Malcolm Baldrige National Quality Award 6202
Lloyd V. Berkner Award 1499
Best in Business Award 6342
Better Business Bureau Integrity Award 6340
Robert Bosch Foundation Fellowship Program 7687
Edmund C. Bovey Award 8543
BRASS Thomson Financial Student Travel Award 17936
Warren Brookes Award for Excellence in Journalism 2958
Business and Aging Awards 4639
Business-Education Partnership Award 21267
Business Excellence Award 16775
Business Executive of the Year 17874
Business in the Arts Awards 6702
Business Leader of the Year Award 19537
Business Leadership Award 21065
Business Speaks Award 16210
Canada Awards for Excellence 15568
Canadian Business Hall of Fame 12464
Chairman's Leadership Award 1702
Charles Alvin Emerson Medal 21478
Citation of Excellence in Advertising 21479
Codie Awards 19383
Collection System Award 21480
Congressional Award 18560
Corporate Advocate Leadership Award 12707
Corporate Conscience Award 8591
Corporate Leadership Award 21560
Coulee Region Entrepreneurial Award 12623
G. D. Crain Jr. Award 6712
Francis X. Crowley Scholarship 16133
Cruickshank Alumni Leadership Award 6179
Crystal Award 14311
ACTFL Edwin Cudecki International Business Award 2057
Dallas 100 Award 19511
Diane C. Davis Business of the Year 21299
Distinghished Member 21736
Distinguised Service Award 21883
Distinguished Individual of Foreign Birth Award 11460
Distinguished Recent Alumnus Award 6180
Distinguished Service Award
Defense Credit Union Council 8795
Regional Business Partnership 17955
Distinguished Service to College Award 6181
Distinguished Women's Awards 16572
The Douglass Foundation Graduate Business Plan Competition 6182
EDI Award for Corporate Leadership 9087
Emerging Company Award 5331
Entrepreneur of the Year
Ernst & Young 9331
International Franchise Association 11636
Entrepreneurial Success Award 20829
Benjamin F. Fairless Memorial Award 2874
Financial Post Design Effectiveness Awards 8538
Financial Post Environment Awards for Business 8539
Financial Post Outstanding CEO of the Year Award 8540
Founders Award 6703
Free Enterprise Award 11637
French-American Chamber of Commerce Person of the Year Award 9768
Future Business Executive 9843
Future Business Leaders 9844
Thomson Gale Award for Excellence in Business Librarianship/BRASS 17940
George J. Schroepfer Medal 21482
George W. Burke, Jr. Award 21483
Golden Torch Award 6344
Good Neighbor Award 20699
Gordon Maskew Fair Medal 21484
Government Advocate Leadership Award 12709
Warren Green Free Enterprise Scholarship 5085
Hall of Fame 17315
Hall of Outstanding Americans 15986
Harrison Prescott Eddy Medal 21485
Harry E. Schlenz Medal 21486
Haynes Prize for Best Paper 103
Hazardous Waste Management Award 21487
Hispanic Leadership Award 12710
Historic New York City Business Award 13695
Honorary Membership 21489
Idaho Quality Award 10638
IFA Hall of Fame Award 11638
Industrial Water Quality Achievement Award 21490
Innovations Challenge 21114
Innovative Technology Awards 21491
INTERCOM: International Communication Film and Video Festival 8003
International Honorees 6331
International Pro-Comm Awards Competition 6713
Jack Edward McKee Medal 21492
Jerry Jacob Scholarship 13295
John Guice Award 13618
Junior Achievement National Business Hall of Fame 12462
Herman Lay Memorial Award 5817
Leadership Award 6704
IFA Bonny LeVine Award 11639
Elizabeth Lewin Award 14649
Lifetime Membership Award 13619
Gerald Loeb Awards 20990
Lucia Trade Award 19856
Manufacturer Member of the Year 8975
Carroll Sterling Masterson Award & Outstanding Women's Awards 22093

Business (continued)

Harold W. McGraw, Jr. Prize in Education 13221
McKinsey Awards 10273
McKnight Doctoral Fellowship Program in Arts and Sciences, Mathematics, Business and Engineering 9599
Medallion for Entrepreneurship 6332
Member Association Safety Awards 21494
Member of the Year 8976
Metro Awards 21616
Minority Business Leadership Awards 15389
John H. Muller Jr. Undergraduate Business Plan Competition 6183
Connie Murdoch Award 18561
National Achievement Award 14312
National Appreciation Award 14313
National Minority Supplier Development Council Awards 15390
National Post Awards for Business in the Arts 8541
National Small Business Person of the Year 20830
National Women's Hall of Fame 15960
National Youth Award 14315
Optimas Awards 21838
Order of Ontario 16757
Outstanding Achievement in Water Quality Improvement Award 21495
Outstanding Associate Business Member of the Year 13375
Outstanding Business Leader Awards 16573
Outstanding Business Person of the Year 21584
Outstanding Corporate Growth Award 5332
Outstanding Reference Sources 17944
Outstanding Service Award 21905
Frank Pace Award 11558
Philip F. Morgan Medal 21496
Phoenix Award for Outstanding Contributions to Disaster Recovery 20831
Phoenix Award for Small Business Disaster Recovery 20832
President's Award 8977
Procurement Awards 20833
Public Education Award 21497
Recognizes outstanding performance in the field of productivity. New chapters and academy fellows are eligible. 21877
Research Awards 17478
Richard S. Engelbrecht International Activities Service Award 21498
Rising Star Leadership Award 12711
Robert E. Graham Development Entrepreneur of the Year Award 12521
Rebecca Sand Volunteer of the Year Award 7806
Small Business Advocates of the Year 20834
Small Business Exporter of the Year 20835
Small Business Person of the Year 18562
Small Business Person of Year 21614
Adam Smith Award 5818
Adam Smith Free Enterprise Award 2960
SP USA Award 18226
Student Business Initiative Award 6184
Student Prize Essay/Project 13620
Thomas R. Camp Medal 21499
Tribute to Women Award 22076
Tribute to Women in Industry Award 22082
Arthur E. Turner Entrepreneur Award 16580
Venture Grants 20910
WEC Gold Medal for International Corporate Achievement in Sustainable Development 21893
Wilford L. White Fellow 11513
Lawrence A. Wien Prize for Social Responsibility 8252
Willem Rudolfs Medal 21500
William J. Orchard Medal 21502
Women of Enterprise Awards 6145
Lee Wulff Award 9490
Young Entrepreneur Award 20836

Business administration *See* Management

Business education
AMA/Irwin Distinguished Marketing Educator Award 3025
George Hay Brown/AMA Marketing Scholar of the Year 3026
Business Leadership Award 21065
Chamber Scholarship Award 10233
Robert B. Clarke Outstanding Educator Award 8931
Collegiate or University Teacher of the Year 14571
Delta Pi Epsilon Research Award 8874
Distinguished Service Award 14572
Distinguished Service Award for an Administrator or Supervisor 14573
Distinguished Service Award in Investment Education 12175
Einhorn New Investigator Award 18783
Future Business Teacher 9845
John Robert Gregg Award in Business Education 10042
HSMAI Hall of Fame 10556
Independent Research Award 8875
Instructional Innovation Award 8786
International Honorees 6331
Dr. William Kinnard, Jr. Academic Award 5010
Leavey Awards for Excellence in Private Enterprise Education 9765
Edward N. Mayer Award for Educational Leadership 8932
National Club Achievement Competition 860
National Temporary Employee of the Year Award 4687
Packaging Hall of Fame 17024
Packaging Leader of the Year 17025
Postsecondary Teacher of the Year 14574
St. Johns Area Chamber of Commerce/Mint Festival Scholarship 18211
Secondary Teacher of the Year 14575
H. Grady Stebbins, Jr. Distinguished Service Award 5016
Touch of Knowledge Award 4690

Business history
Award of Merit - Preservation 8367
John C. Geilfuss Fellowship 21676
Harvard-Newcomen Postdoctoral Fellowship 16318
Krooss Prize 6710

Business journalism
Robert H. Armstrong Award 5006
Atrium Award 21019
Author's Award 5709
Award for Excellence in Corporate Reporting 5393
Bernard L. Barnard Award 11267
Forrest Bassford Student Award 12896
Elliott V. Bell Award 16225
Business/Economic Writing Award 8170
Chapter Publications Contest 10971
American Business Media G. D. Crain Award 1607
Distinguished Achievement in RV Journalism Award 17913
Editorial and Design Awards 5572
Editorial and Design Excellence Awards 4270
Excellence in Financial Journalism 16292
Graham and Dodd Award 5396
Charles E. Green Journalism Awards 10308
Hall of Fame Award 12897
Headliner Award 12898
Journalism Citation 11276
Sanders A. Kahn Award 5008
Lawrence R. Klein Award 20517
Gerald Loeb Awards 20990
Lybrand Medals 10991
Magazine of the Year Award 4271
Morton Margolin Prize for Distinguished Business Reporting 21015
Harold H. Maynard Award 3033
National Magazine Awards 15355
Jesse H. Neal National Business Journalism Awards 1608
Newsletter Awards 5718
William O'Dell Award 3034
Outstanding Contributor Awards 10973
H. Paul Root Award 3036
Round Table Award 10975
John B. Thurston Award 10976

Cable television (*See also* Television)
Accolades Award 21706
American Center for Children's Television - Ollie Awards 1664
Avatar Award 6641
Award for Local Sales Achievement 6721
Awards for Excellence in Cable Marketing and Advertising 8684
Broadcast Media Awards for Television 11853
Chairman's Award 19077
Creative Commercial Production Awards 6722
Distinguished Vanguard Awards for Leadership 14577
Hometown Video Festival 458
John E. Mankin Award 19990
Member of the Year 19078
Network Affiliate Sales Achievement Award 6723
Peabody Awards Collection 21020
Project Community Award 19991
PROMAX Awards 17679
Publications and Electronic Media Awards 15669
Vanguard Award for Associates and Affiliates 14578
Vanguard Award for Marketing 14579
Vanguard Award for Programmers 14580
Vanguard Award for Public Relations 14581
Vanguard Award for Science and Technology 14582
Vanguard Award for Young Leadership 14583

Cable (continued)

Calligraphy *See* Graphic arts

Camping *See* Recreation

Canadian history
Bernt Carlesson Memorial Award 8606
Best Article Award 6633
Albert J. Beveridge Award 2465
John Bullen Prize 7149
Canadian Friends of Yeshiva University Bora Laskin Distinguished Service Award 22024
Certificates of Merit Awards - Regional History 7150
City of Toronto Book Awards 8048
Albert B. Corey Prize in Canadian-American Relations
American Historical Association 2468
Canadian Historical Association 7151
Distinguished Dissertation Award 5281
Donner Medal in Canadian Studies 5282
Francois-Xavier Garneau Medal 7153
Green Mountain Power 7749
Heritage Award 7147
Heritage Canada Achievement Awards 10420
Heritage Toronto Awards of Merit 10426
Gabrielle Leger Medal 10421
Lieutenant-Governor's Medal 10422
Lieutenant-Governor's Medal for Historical Writing 6634
Sir John A. Macdonald Prize 7154
Hilda Neatby Prize 7155
Northern Science Award 10751
Prix du Quebec 7750
Prix Maxime-Raymond 10820
Silver Dart Aviation History Award 6960
Rufus Z. Smith Prize 5283
J. B. Tyrrell Historical Medal 18175

Canadian journalism
Canadian News Hall of Fame 20122
National Newspaper Awards 7309
Science in Society Journalism Awards 7384

Canadian literature
Alcuin Book Design Awards 430
bp Nichol Chapbook Award 17275
CAA Awards for Adult Literature 6953
CAA Jubilee Award for Short Stories 6954
CAA MOSAID Technologies, Inc. Award for Fiction 6956
Canada - Australia Literary Prize 6786
Canada - Japan Literary Awards 6788
CBC Literary Awards 6789
CAA Jack Chalmers Award for Poetry 6957
City of Toronto Book Awards 8048
Edmonton Book Prize 21984
Marian Engel Award 22004
Fleury-Mesplet Literary Prize 18234
Governor General's Literary Awards 6797
Journey Prize 13211
Stephen Leacock Medal for Humour 19790
Municipal Chapter of Toronto IODE Children's Book Award 12177
Lorne Pierce Medal 18171
Prix Athanase-David 17794
Prix Ludger-Duvernay 18611
QSF Awards 17799
QSPELL Community Award 17800
QWF Awards 17801
Thomas Raddall Atlantic Fiction Award 21981
Evelyn Richardson Memorial Literary Trust 21982
Allan Sangster Memorial Award 6958
Ruth and Sylvia Schwartz Children's Book Awards 16746
Toronto Arts Awards 20112
Trillium Book Award 16752
Jon Whyte Memorial Essay Prize 21985
W.O. Mitchell City of Calgary Book Prize 21986
Writers Guild of Alberta Awards for Excellence 21987
Young Adult Canadian Book Award 7252

Cancer (*See also* Radiology)
ACS Medal of Honor 1634
Advanced Oncology Certified Nurse of the Year Award 16709
Linda Arenth Excellence in Cancer Nursing Management Award 16710
Awards for Excellence in Community Service, Philanthropy, and Media 19847
Susan Baird Oncology Excellence in Writing Award in Clinical Practice 16711
Brinker International Award for Breast Cancer Research 19848
Ellyn Bushkin Friend of the Foundation Award 16712
Bruce F. Cain Memorial Award 964
Cancer Control Society Awards 7551
Cancer Research Award Program 12498
Career Development Awards 965
Chapter Excellence Award 16713
Clinical Investigator Awards 7560
Clinical Research Award 5634
Clinician Scientist Awards 7549
G. H. A Clowes Memorial Award 966
Community Partnership Grant 1641
Courage Award 1635
CRFA Fellowship Grants 7555
Marie Curie Award 1072
Distinguished Researcher Award 16714
Distinguished Service Award 1636
Gertrude Elion Cancer Research Award 967
James Ewing Layman Award 19301
James Ewing Lecturer 19302
Excellence in Breast Cancer Education Award 16715
Excellence in Radiation Therapy Nursing Award 16716
Excellence of Scholarship and Consistency of Contributions to the Oncology Nursing Literature Award 16717
Fellowship Award 8728
Fellowship Awards of the Jane Coffin Childs Memorial Fund for Medical Research 7921
Fellowship for Cancer Research 968
FIRE Excellence Award 16718
Mara Mogensen Flaherty Memorial Lectureship 16719
Flame of Courage Award 7553
Fletcher Scholar Awards 7557
Betty Ford Award 19849
Cecille Gould Memorial Fund for Cancer Research 2298
Oliver R. Grace Award 7562
Great Lakes Division Foundation 1643
Lila Gruber Memorial Cancer Research Award and Lectureship 638
Health Advocate of the Year 16979
Hippocratic Oath Award 11302
Cecile Pollack Hoffman Memorial Award 11303
Honorary Membership 16721
Humanitarian Award
American Cancer Society 1637
International Association of Cancer Victors and Friends 11304
Journalism Awards 12788
Charles F. Kettering Medal 9920
Komen Award of Scientific Distinction 19850
Leadership Award 11305
Leadership in Oncology Social Work Award 5803
Agnes K. Mackey Assistance Fund 8688
Media Awards 12791
Eleanor Montague Distinguished Resident Award in Radiation Oncology 1073
Charles S. Mott Medal 9921
National Volunteer Leadership Award 1638
NCCC Focus Award 14647
NCIC Awards for Excellence in Cancer Research 14585
Oncology Social Worker of the Year 5804
ONS/AMGEN Inc. Award for Excellence in Patient/Public Education 16722
ONS/Pharmacia & Upjohn Excellence in Oncology Nursing Private Practice Award 16723
ONS/Roche Distinguished Service Award 16724
ONS/Ross Products Division of Abbott Laboratories Award for Excellence in Cancer Nursing Education 16725
ONS/Schering Excellence in Biotherapy Nursing Award 16726
ONS/Schering Excellence in Cancer Nursing Research Award 16727
ONS/Upjohn Quality of Life Award 16728
Pilot Project Research Awards 21040
Population-Specific Research Project Award 19851
Public Service Award 16729
Research Awards 9744
Research Fellowships 19852
Resident Award 19303
Rubinstein Award 1288
St. George National Award 1639
Michael Schoenbrun Award 12794
Shubitz Award 20992
Alfred P. Sloan, Jr. Medal 9922
Travel Grants 969
Young Investigator Award 18788
Young Investigator Awards 7558
Young Oncologist Essay Awards 3815
Young Oncologist Travel Grants 3816

Canoeing *See* Boating

Cardiology
Alfred Soffer Research Awards 1843
Award of Recognition 466
C. R. Bard Foundation Prize 15368
Basic Research Prize 2403
Howard W. Blaskeslee Awards 2404
Cardiovascular Section Young Investigator Award 3511
Philip K. Caves Award 11933
Clinician - Scientist Award 2405
Michael E. DeBakey Award 13327
Distinguished Fellow 1836
Distinguished Scientist 1837
Distinguished Scientist Award 10365

Cardiology (continued)

Distinguished Service 1838
Distinguished Service Award 10366
Gifted Teacher 1839
Gold Heart Award 2407
Heart of the Year Award 2408
James B. Herrick Award 2409
Martha N. Hill New Investigator Award 2410
Honorary Fellow 1840
Melvin Judkins Young Clinical Investigator Award 2411
Katharine A. Lembright Award 2413
Samuel A. Levine Young Clinical Investigator Award 2414
Melvin L. Marcus Young Investigator Awards in Cardiovascular Sciences 2415
Cecile Lehman Mayer Research Award 1844
Minority Scientist Development Award 2416
Pioneer Award 10368
Presidential Citation 1841
Research Achievement Award 2418
Paul Dudley White Award 5790
Young Investigator Awards 1845
Cournand and Comroe Young Investigator Prize 2420
Young Investigator Prizes in Thrombosis 2421
Young Investigators Awards 10369

Career achievement *See* Academic achievement; Professional and personal achievement

Cars *See* Automobiles

Cartography (*See also* Geography)
ACA Honors Award 1991
ACA Outstanding Achievement Award 1992
ACSM Map Design Competition Awards 1993
American Cartographic Association Scholarship Award 1994
Awards for Outstanding Achievements in Cartographic Design 1995
Bill McFaden Cartography Award 14003
Andrew McNally Award 2000
O. M. Miller Cartographic Medal 2333
National Geographic Society Award 2001
Time Magazine Award for Outstanding Map Design on Current Events 2006

Cartoons (*See also* Animated films; Drawing; Humor)
ACE Award 14589
Annual Awards in International News Coverage 16981
Atlantic Journalism Awards 6035
Clifford K. and James T. Berryman Award for Editorial Cartoons 15526
Better Newspapers Competition 7034
Cartoon Award 11106
Category Awards 14590
Distinguished Service Award 15414
Editorial and Cartoon Strip Contest 8172
John Fischetti Editorial Cartoon Competition 9564
Global Media Awards for Excellence in Population Reporting 17469
Golden Toonie Award 7615
ILCA Media Awards Contest 11700
Robert F. Kennedy Journalism Awards 18076
John Locher Memorial Award 5554
National Newspaper Awards 7309
Pulitzer Prizes 17749
Reuben Award 14591
Sigma Delta Chi Awards 19276
Silver T-Square 14592

Catholic literature
Catholic Book Awards 7658
John Tracy Ellis Dissertation Award 1653
St. Francis de Sales Award 7660

Cats *See* Animal care and training

Ceramic engineering
Arthur Frederick Greaves-Walker Award 1683
John Jeppson Medal 1686
John E. Marquis Memorial Award 1689
Schwartzwalder - PACE Award 1697
Roland B. Snow Award 1698

Ceramics (*See also* Glass)
Advanced Ceramic Award 5927
Affaire in the Gardens 8035
Alfred W. Allen Award 1666
Albert Victor Bleininger Award 1667
S. Brunauer Award 1668
Cesery Award 20089
Robert L. Coble Award for Young Scholars 1669
Copeland Award 1670
Corporate Environmental Achievement Award 1671
Corporate Technical Achievement Award 1672
W. E. Cramer Award 1673
Distinguished Ceramist Award 1674
Distinguished Life Member 1675
Distinguished Speaker Award 1676
Harry E. Ebright Service Award 1677
Fellow 1678
Fine Art Show 18244
Friedberg Lecture 1679
Frontiers of Science and Society - Rustum Roy Lecture 1680
Richard M. Fulrath Award 1681
Samuel Geijsbeek Award 1682
Greaves-Walker Roll of Honor Award 12572
Edward C. Henry Award 1684
Honorary Member 1685
W. David Kingery Award 1687
James I. Mueller Lecture Award 1691
F. H. Norton Distinguished Ceramist Award 1692
Edward Orton, Jr., Memorial Lecturer 1693
Outstanding Educator Award 1694
Ross Coffin Purdy Award 1695
St. Louis Refractories Award 1696
Smithsonian Craft Show 18574
Sosman Memorial Lecture Award 1699
Hewitt Wilson Memorial Award 1700

Charity activities *See* Philanthropy; Volunteerism

Chemical engineering
ACS Award for Creative Invention 1705
ACS Award in Separations Science and Technology 1721
Award for Chemical Engineering Research 477
Award for Service to Society 2757
Award in Chemical Engineering Practice 2758
Award in Industrial Practice 7406
Thomas Baron Award in Fluid-Particle Systems 2759
Richard E. Bellman Control Heritage Award 2760
Best Paper Published in the *Canadian Journal of Chemical Engineering* 7832
Canadian Society for Chemical Engineering Award in Industrial Practice 7835
Emmitt B. Carmichael Members and Fellows Lecture Award 2799
Lawrence K. Cecil Award 2761
Chemical Institute of Canada Medal 7836
Chemical Pioneer Awards 2800
CIC Fellowship 7837
Allan P. Colburn Award for Excellence in Publications by a Young Member of the Institute 2762
Community Outreach Award 2763
Computing in Chemical Engineering Award 2764
Computing Practice Award 2765
William H. Corcoran Award 4008
William H. Doyle Award 2767
Paul J. Flory Polymer Education Award 1754
Fluidized Processes Recognition Award 2769
Food, Pharmaceutical and Bioengineering Division Award in Chemical Engineering 2770
Forest Products Division Award in Chemical Engineering 2771
Fuels and Petrochemical Division Award 2773
Gold Medal 2801
HTEC Division Award 2778
Institute Award for Excellence in Industrial Gases Technology 2779
R. S. Jane Memorial Lecture Award 7839
R.S. Jane Memorial Lecture Award 7407
Donald Q. Kern Award 2781
Kirkpatrick Chemical Engineering Achievement Award 7823
Warren K. Lewis Award for Contributions in Chemical Engineering Education 2782
Arthur Dehon Little Award for Chemical Engineering Innovation 2783
Herman F. Mark Division of Polymer Chemistry Award 1769
J. J. Martin Award 4026
Carl S. Marvel Creative Polymer Chemistry Award 1770
Montreal Medal 7846
E. V. Murphree Award in Industrial and Engineering Chemistry 1773
North American Mixing Forum Award 2785
Personal Achievement in Chemical Engineering Awards 7824
Professional Progress Award for Outstanding Progress in Chemical Engineering 2786
SNC-Lavalin Plant Design Competition 7848
Charles M. A. Stine Award in Materials Engineering and Science 2789
Student Awards 2790
Syncrude Canada Innovation Award 7408

Chemical (continued)

John A. Tallmadge Award for Contributions to Coating Technology 2791
Union Carbide Award for Chemical Education 7850
Union Carbide Lectureship Award 4046
William H. Walker Award for Excellence in Contributions to Chemical Engineering Literature 2793
Norton H. Walton/Russell L. Miller Award 2794
R. H. Wilhelm Award in Chemical Reaction Engineering 2795
Robert E. Wilson Award in Nuclear Chemical Engineering 2796

Chemical industry

ACS Award in Applied Polymer Science 1713
Chemical Industry Medal 19084
Perkin Medal 19085

Chemistry (*See also* Biochemistry; Chemical engineering; Chemical industry; Color technology; Fiber science; Geochemistry; Industrial chemistry)

AACC International Travel Fellowship Award 971
AACC Lectureship Award 972
AACC Past President's Award 973
ACS Award for Computers in Chemical and Pharmaceutical Research 1704
ACS Award for Creative Invention 1705
ACS Award for Creative Work in Fluorine Chemistry 1706
ACS Award for Creative Work in Synthetic Organic Chemistry 1707
ACS Award for Distinguished Service in the Advancement of Inorganic Chemistry 1708
ACS Award for Outstanding Performance by Divisions 1709
ACS Award for Outstanding Performance by Local Sections 1710
ACS Award for Research at an Undergraduate Institution 1711
ACS Award in Analytical Chemistry 1712
ACS Award in Chromatography 1714
ACS Award in Colloid and Surface Chemistry 1715
ACS Award in Inorganic Chemistry 1717
ACS Award in Organometallic Chemistry 1718
ACS Award in Polymer Chemistry 1719
ACS Award in Pure Chemistry 1720
ACS Award in the Chemistry of Materials 1722
ACS Award in Theoretical Chemistry 1723
Roger Adams Award in Organic Chemistry 1724
Arthur W. Adamson Award for Distinguished Service in the Advancement of Surface Chemistry 1725
Adhesion Society Award for Excellence in Adhesion Science 184
AIC Ethics Award 2798
Alcan Lecture Award 7826
Alpha Chi Sigma Pure Chemistry Award 475
Alpha Chi Sigma Scholarship Award 476
Alsop Award 2941
AOCS/Supelco Research Award 3305
AORC Award 5799
Urgel Archambault Prize in Physical Sciences and Mathematics 5537
Award for Cooperative Research in Polymer Science and Engineering 1726
Award for Creative Advances in Environmental Science and Technology 1727
Award for Creative Work in Synthetic Organic Chemistry 1728
Award for Encouraging Disadvantaged Students into Careers in the Chemical Sciences 1729
Award for Encouraging Women into Careers in the Chemical Sciences 1730
Award for Excellence in Teaching 1731
Award for Outstanding Scholastic Achievement 2756
Award for Pure or Applied Inorganic Chemistry 7827
Award for Team Innovation 1732
Award in Chemical Instrumentation 1733
Award in Electrochemistry 1734
Award in Spectrochemical Analysis 1735
Award of Merit 3306
Alfred Bader Award in Bioinorganic or Bioorganic Chemistry 1736
Alfred Bader Award in Organic Chemistry 7828
Alton E. Bailey Award 3307
A. Richard Baldwin Distinguished Service Award 3308
Fred Beamish Award 7829
Clara Benson Award 7831
Board of Directors Distinguished Service Award for Senior ACS Administrators 1740
Boehringer Ingelheim Award for Organic or Bioorganic Chemistry 7833
Bower Award and Prize for Achievement in Science 9741
Brasted Memorial Lecture 1741
Norman and Marion Bright Memorial Award 7834
Robert Burwell Lectureship in Catalysis 16397
Emmitt B. Carmichael Members and Fellows Lecture Award 2799
Herbert O. Carne Service Award 975
Certificate of Honor 976
Chaney Award 977
Stephen S. Chang Award 3309
Chapter Awards 19091
Chemical Health and Safety Award 1743
Chemical Institute of Canada Medal 7836
Chemical Pioneer Awards 2800
Max E. Chilcote Young Investigator Award 978
F. G. Ciapetta Lectureship in Catalysis 16398
CIC Fellowship 7837
James Bryant Conant Award in High School Chemistry Teaching 1744
Arthur C. Cope Award 1745
Arthur C. Cope Scholar Award 1746
Peter Debye Award in Physical Chemistry 1747
Dexter Award in the History of Chemistry 1748
Albert A. Dietz Service Award 980
Distinguished Service Award
American Association for Clinical Chemistry 981
American Institute of Chemical Engineers 2766
DivCHAS College Health and Safety Award 1750
Dr. Robert M. Lollar Prize Paper Award 2942
Arthur K. Doolitte Award 1751
Education Award 982
Paul H. Emmett Award in Fundamental Catalysis 16399
ExxonMobil Solid State Chemistry Faculty Fellowship 1752
FACSS Student Award 9464
Frank H. Field and Joe L. Franklin Award for Outstanding Achievement in Mass Spectrometry 1753
Founders Award for Outstanding Contributions to the Field of Chemical Engineering 2772
Bernard J. Garulat Award 984
Francis P. Garvan-John M. Olin Medal 1755
Clarence (Larry) G. Gerhold Award 2774
Gold Medal 2801
V. M. Goldschmidt Medal 9939
Graduate Confectionery Fellowship - Penn State University 17179
James T. Grady - James H. Stack Award for Interpreting Chemistry for the Public 1757
William W. Grimes Award for Excellence in Chemical Engineering 2775
Ernest Guenther Award in the Chemistry of Natural Products 1758
Heat Transfer & Energy Conversion Division Award 2776
John C. Heiman Impact Award for Excellence in Educational Support 2777
E. B. Hershberg Award for Important Discoveries in Medicinally Active Substances 1759
Joel Henry Hildebrand Award in the Theoretical and Experimental Chemistry of Liquids 1760
Hirschfeld Scholar Award 9465
Ralph F. Hirschmann Award in Peptide Chemistry 1761
Honorary Fellow 7838
Honorary Fellow Award 2802
Honorary Member 17249
Honored Student Award 3310
Eugene J. Houdry Award in Applied Catalysis 16400
Claude S. Hudson Award in Carbohydrate Chemistry 1762
Intel International Science and Engineering Fair 18362
International Organization for Chemical Sciences in Development Awards 11779
Ipatieff Prize 1763
Marx Isaacs Awards for Outstanding Newsletter 2780
Frederic Stanley Kipping Award in Silicon Chemistry 1765
Norman Kubasik Award 985
John R. Kuebler Award 478
Laidler Award 7840
Irving Langmuir Award in Chemical Physics 1767
Irving Langmuir Prize in Chemical Physics 3460
R. U. Lemieux Award for Organic Chemistry 7842
Eli Lilly Award in Biological Chemistry 1768
Management Division Award 2784

Chemistry (continued)

Richard Marshall Education Award 986
W. A. E. McBryde Medal 7844
Medicinal Chemistry Award 1771
Member Scholarship 21674
Merck Frosst Centre for Therapeutic Research Lecture Award 7845
Merit Award 19093
Montreal Medal 7846
Nakanishi Prize 1774
NAS Award for Chemistry in Service to Society 13836
NAS Award in Chemical Sciences 13841
Samuel Natelson Senior Investigation Award 987
National Fresenius Award 17250
Maison G. de Navarre Medal Award 19094
Albert L. Nichols Innovation Award 988
Nobel Laureate Signature Award for Graduate Education in Chemistry 1775
James Flack Norris Award in Physical Organic Chemistry 1776
Fred O'Flaherty Service Award 2943
George A. Olah Award in Hydrocarbon or Petroleum Chemistry 1777
Outstanding Contributions in Education 990
Outstanding Contributions Through Service to the Profession of Clinical Chemistry 991
Outstanding Contributions to Clinical Chemistry 992
Outstanding Contributions to Clinical Chemistry in a Selected Area of Research 993
Outstanding Contributions to Clinical Chemistry Through Science or Technology 994
Outstanding Contributions to Education 995
Outstanding Scientific Achievements by a Young Investigator 996
Anselme Payen Award 1779
Pfizer Award in Enzyme Chemistry 1780
Philadelphia Section Award 1796
Philadelphia Section Awards for Excellence in Science Teaching 1797
George C. Pimentel Award in Chemical Education 1781
John C. Polanyi Lecture Award 7847
Ralph H. Potts Memorial Fellowship Award 3311
Priestley Medal 1782
Procter & Gamble Award in Physical Chemistry 1783
Miriam Reiner Award 998
Repligen Corporation Award in Chemistry of Biological Processes 1784
Research Achievement Awards in the Pharmaceutical Services 3397
Research Associateship Programs 15623
Roe Award 999
Glenn T. Seaborg Award for Nuclear Chemistry 1785
Seligson/Golden Award 1000
Randall D. Sheeline Award for Excellence in Public Relations 2788
Sherwin-Williams Student Award in Applied Polymer Science 1786
Herman Skolnik Award 1787
Tillmanns-Skolnok Award 1788
Smissman-Bristol-Myers-Squibb Award 1789
Society of Cosmetic Chemists Awards 19095
Somogyi-Sendroy Award 1001
Jules Stachiewicz Medal 7849
Statistics in Chemistry Award 4696
Henry H. Storch Award in Fuel Chemistry 1791
Student Research Awards 1002
Roy W. Tess Award in Coatings 1792
Texas Service Award for Outstanding Contributions to Clinical Chemistry 1003
Henry Marshall Tory Medal 18174
Travel Grant 1004
Union Carbide Award for Chemical Education 7850
F. J. & Dorothy Van Antwerpen Award for Service to the Institute 2792
Harold Van Remortel Service Award 1006
Van Slyke Award 1007
Robert W. Vance Award 8680
Welch Award in Chemistry 21512
Harvey W. Wiley Award 4992
E. Bright Wilson Award in Spectroscopy 1794
John Arthur Wilson Memorial Lecture Award 2944
Young Clinical Chemist Award 1008

Chess
Chess Journalism Merit Awards Competition 7862
Koshnitsky Award 11378
Purdy Award 11379
Steiner Award 11380
U.S. Chess Championship 20446

Child welfare (*See also* Youth work)
Adoption Activist Awards 16417
Award for Outstanding Service to Maltreated Children 761
Best in Media Awards 7915
G. F. Bettineski Child Advocate of the Year Award 14874
Chief Justice Warren E. Burger Healer Awards 7916
Child Advocate of the Year
 Children's Watch International 7919
 North American Council on Adoptable Children 16418
Complete Single Mother Award 15456
Vincent De Francis Award 2573
Distinguished Contribution to Child Advocacy Award 3715
Distinguished Service to Children Award 17087
Easter Seals Canada Award 7374
Friend of Adoption 14749
Friend of Children 19497
Friend of Children Award 16419
Ray E. Helfer Award 775
Nicholas Hobbs Award 3719
Judge of the Year Award 14875
Kappa Alpha Theta Program Director of the Year Award 14876
Norman Kretchmer Memorial Award in Nutrition and Development 3959
La Leche League International Award of Achievement 12628
La Leche League International Award of Appreciation 12629
La Leche League International Award of Excellence 12630
La Leche League International Award of Recognition 12631
La Leche League International Founders' Award 12632
Dolley Madison Award 22109
Ronald McDonald House Charities Awards of Excellence 18117
Ronald McDonald House Charities Grants Program 18118
National Humanitarian Award 21423
Outstanding Service Award 21424
Parenting Awards 7917
Price Journalist and Scholar of the Year Awards 21104
Henrietta Szold Award 10215
Albert E. Trieschman Award 1136

Children and youth
AATE Research Award 884
Alliance Award 885
ALSC/Book Wholesalers Summer Reading Program Grant 5430
ALSC/Sagebrush Education Resources Literature Grant 5431
American Center for Children's Television - Fran Allison Award 1663
American Center for Children's Television - Ollie Awards 1664
The Austin Chronicle Best of Austin 6093
Awards of Excellence 453
Campton Bell Lifetime Achievement Award 887
Andrew Carnegie Medal 5437
CBC Honors Program 7904
CEC Research Award 8548
Children's Choice Award 454
Charlotte B. Chorpenning Playwright Award 888
James Comer Minority Research Fellowship for Medical Students 625
Community Service Grant 13062
Distinguished Service Award
 American Psychological Association - Society of Clinical Psychology (Division 12) 3747
 Association for Library Service to Children 5438
FAMY Awards 12351
Father of the Year Award 8714
Ann Flagg Multicultural Award 891
Selma Fraiberg Award 13332
Susan Phillips Gorin Award 8549
William T. Grant Faculty Scholars 21633
Great Friend to Kids Award 5600
Florence Halpern Award for Distinguished Professional Contributions 3748
HTCNE Service Award 10310
Clarissa Hug Teacher of the Year Award 8551
Langston Hughes Award 6717
Blanche F. Ittleson Research in Child Psychiatry Award 3621
Jane Addams Children's Book Award 21795
Lifetime Achievement Award 455
Mark Twain Award 6718
Agnes Purcell McGavin Award 3628
Monte Meacham Award 892
Outstanding Achievement Award 456
Outstanding Student CEC Undergraduate Member of the Year Award 8554
Parents' Choice Awards 17084
Penguin Putnam Books for Young Readers Group Award 5442
Service to Children Television Awards 14117

Children (continued)

Spectrum Award 21940
Sara Spencer Artistic Achievement Award 893
StoryTeller of the Year Award 6719
Betty Tableman Award 13333
J. E. Wallace Wallin Lifetime Achievement Award 8555
Winifred Ward & Award for Outstanding New Children's Theatre & Company 894
Zeta Phi Eta Winifred Ward Prize for Outstanding New Children's Theatre Company 895
F. Loren Winship Secondary School Theatre Award 896
Logan Wright Distinguished Service Award 3757
AATE Lin Wright Special Recognition Award 897
Youth Theatre Director of the Year Award 898

Children's literature
Jane Addams Children's Book Award 12296
Alabama Authors Award 405
ALAN Award 14846
American Association of University Women Award in Juvenile Literature 16516
Americas Book Award for Children's and Young Adult Literature 7733
Marguerite de Angeli Prize 8845
Annual Awards Competition 8565
Arbuthnot Award 11851
Arizona Author Award 5052
Arizona Young Readers Award 5054
Award for Excellence in Poetry for Children 14827
Mildred L. Batchelder Award 5432
L. Frank Baum Memorial Award 12143
Pura Belpre Award 5434
Best Illustrated Children's Books of the Year 16297
Beverly Hills Theatre Guild Play Competition for Children's Theatre 6349
Irma S. and James H. Black Award for Excellence in Children's Literature 6241
Book Award 17402
Book Awards
Children's Literature Council of Southern California 7913
South Carolina Association of School Librarians 19443
Book of the Year for Children Award 7259
Book Publishers of Texas Children's/Young People's Award 20011
Boston Globe - Horn Book Awards 6526
Buckeye Children's Book Award/Teen Buckeye 6670
Elizabeth Burr/Worzalla Award 21684
BWI/YALSA Collection Development Grant 22052
Randolph Caldecott Medal 5436
California Young Reader Medal 6745
Canadian Library Association Book of the Year for Children Award 7254
Rebecca Caudill Young Readers' Book Award 17902
Cavendish Area Tourist Association Creative Writing Award for Children 17545
Children's Literature Association Article Award 7908
Children's Literature Association Book Award 7909
Children's Literature Association Research Fellowship 7910
Children's Literature Festival Award 12528
Christopher Awards 7971
Commonwealth Club of California Book Awards 8306
Delacorte Press Prize for a First Young Adult Novel 8846
Margaret A. Edwards Award 22053
Sheila A. Egoff Children's Prize 21519
Carolyn W. Field Award 17177
Dorothy Canfield Fisher Children's Book Award 21304
FOCAL Award 12929
Josette Frank Award 7901
Garden State Children's Book Awards 16179
Garden State Teen Book Awards 16180
Georgia Author of the Year Awards 9972
Georgia Children's Book Award 21022
Georgia Children's Picture Storybook Award 21023
Golden Archer Award 21670
Golden Kite Awards 19087
Golden Sower Awards 16068
Eva L. Gordon Award 3188
Governor General's Literary Awards 6797
Great Stone Face Book Award 7906
Grolier Foundation Award 2979
May Hill Arbuthnot Honor Lecture Award 5439
Amelia Frances Howard-Gibbon Illustrator's Award 7260
IRA Children's Book Award 11862
Washington Irving Children's Book Choice Award 21533
Jefferson Cup Award 21392
Ezra Jack Keats/Kerlan Collection Fellowship 21073
Kentucky Bluegrass Awards 19785
Kerlan Award 21074
Coretta Scott King Book Award 3004
Janusz Korczak Literary Competition 4983
FIT Astrid Lindgren Translation Prize 11608
Magazine Merit Awards 19088
Lucy Maud Montgomery Children's Literature Award 17547
Milkweed Prize for Children's Literature 13422
Milner Award 9804
Municipal Chapter of Toronto IODE Children's Book Award 12177
National Jewish Book Award - Children's Literature 12322
National Jewish Book Award - Children's Picture Book 12323
Nene Award 10292
John Newbery Medal 5441
Ohioana Book Awards 16661
Orbis Pictus Nonfiction Award 14835
Helen Keating Ott Award for Outstanding Contribution to Children's Literature 7976
Outstanding Pennsylvania Author or Illustrator 17192
Lucile Micheels Pannell Award 21799
Phoenix Award 7911
PNWA Literary Contest 17011
Prairie Pasque Children's Book Award 19452
Prix Alvine-Belisle 5920
Regina Medal 7654
Rising Moon Outstanding Youth Services Librarian Award 5064
Carl Sandburg Literary Arts Award 9806
Ruth and Sylvia Schwartz Children's Book Awards 16746
Sequoyah Children's Book Award 16675
Sequoyah Young Adult Book Award 16676
Show Me Award 13527
Charlie May Simon Children's Book Award 5073
Society of Children's Book Writers and Illustrators Grants 19089
Society of Midland Authors Awards 19186
Space Coast Writers Guild Conference Awards 19535
Flora Stieglitz Straus Award 7902
Sydney Taylor Body of Work Award 5743
Sydney Taylor Children's Book Awards 5744
Sydney Taylor Manuscript Competition 5745
Texas Bluebonnet Award 20028
Mark Twain Award 13528
University of Southern Mississippi Medallion 13517
The Washington Post/Children's Book Guild Award for Nonfiction 21457
West Virginia Children's Book Award 21531
Western Heritage Awards (Wrangler Award) 14887
William Allen White Children's Book Award 21608
Wilbur Awards 17971
Laura Ingalls Wilder Award 5444
Rip Van Winkle Award 18339
Paul A. Witty Short Story Award 11880
Alice Louise Wood Memorial Ohioana Award for Children's Literature 16665
Carter G. Woodson Book Award 14791
YALSA Sagebrush Award 22055
Young Adult Canadian Book Award 7252
Young Hoosier Book Award 5388
Young Hoosier Picture Book Award 5389
Young Readers' Choice Award 17009
Anne V. Zarrow Award for Young Readers' Literature 20237

Chiropractic
Chiropractor of the Year 11466
Lee - Homewood Chiropractic Heritage Award 5505
Scientific Researcher of the Year 11467
Silver Member Medal 11165

Choral music
Accord Award 10243
Marshall Bartholomew Award 11133
Leslie Bell Prize for Choral Conducting 16737
Bulletin Contest 10244
CBC Radio National Competition for Amateur Choirs 6997
Chorus America/ASCAP Awards for Adventurous Programming 7941
Jerry Dunlop Memorial Award 10245
Findlay Plaque 10246
G. Ruth Geils Memorial Award 10247
Harmony Queens 10248
Margaret Hillis Achievement Award for Choral Excellence 7942
International Championship Chorus 10250
The Michael Korn Founder's Award 7943
LABBS Trophy 10251

Choral (continued)

MacIntosh Award 10252
Alfred Nash Patterson Grants 7939
National College Band and Choral Directors Hall of Fame Band of the Year 15228
National College Band Director of the Year 15229
National College Choral Director of the Year 15230
National College Choral Directors Hall of Fame Choir of the Year 15231
National Music Festival 18305
Orpherians 21591
Chris Scott Quartette Service Award 10253
Tait Trophy 10254
Robert Turcotte Memorial Award 10255
University of Louisville Grawemeyer Award for Music Composition 21050
Sandi White Membership Award 10256
Healey Willan Prize 6811

Choreography
Artists' Fellowships 16229
Bush Artist Fellows Program 6700
Choreography and Flamenco Dance Competition 9227
Dance Magazine Annual Awards 8736
Dance/USA National Honors 8747
Distinguished Service Award 8742
El Angel Award - Distinguished Hispanic-American Artist 6374
Emmy Awards for Primetime Programming 127
Fellowship Program 17168
Heritage Award 14895
Individual Artist Fellowship 16628
Kennedy Center Honors 12552
Kentucky Artists Fellowships 12562
New York Dance and Performance Awards (Bessie Awards) 8745
Antoinette Perry Awards (Tony Awards) 12742
Prix Denise-Pelletier 17795
Samuel H. Scripps/American Dance Festival Award 2117
Ben Sommers Award 8743
USA International Ballet Competition 21184
Wisconsin Arts Board Fellowships 21666

Christianity (*See also* Catholic literature; Gospel music)
ACPA Young Scholars Award 1660
Anton Boisen Professional Service Award 5820
Aquinas Medal 1661
Athletic Competition 1138
Beasley Award 8713
Board of Directors' Award 15611
Board of Directors Awards 14606
Polly Bond Award 9310
Book of the Year Award 119
Bross Prize 6655
Saint Edmund Campion Award 7635
Catholic Pharmacist of the Year 14628
Catholic Secondary Education Award 14607
CCL Book of the Year Award 8373
Certificate of Achievement of Focused Studies 120
Chaplain Emeritus Award 5821
Chaplain of the Year 20349
Chapter President of the Year Award 7964
Christian Management Award 7965
Christian Stewardship Award 11455
Christian Unity Award 9152
Christus Magister Award 12989
College Awards 2034
Bishop William G. Connare Award for Distinguished Service 11456
Contender's Award 2035
Crystal Apple Award 18419
Emmanuel d'Alzon Medal 6091
O'Neil D'Amour Award 14608
Distinguish Service to Social Work 16382
Distinguished Principal Awards 14609
Distinguished Service Award
Association of Professional Chaplains 5822
Catholic Kolping Society of America 7644
Christian Holiness Partnership 7959
Distinguished Service to Social Welfare 16383
Elementary Departmental Award in Recognition of Commitment to Catholic Elementary Education 14610
Exhibitor Awards 14611
Miriam Joseph Farrell Distinguished Teacher Award 14612
Father of the Year Award 8714
Father Washington Award 7673
Fidelitas Medal 16815
James Fitzgerald Award 14194
For Church and Profession (of Pharmacy) Award 14629
Charles Forsyth Award 7637
Franciscan International Award 9728
Gabriel Award 7633
Cardinal Gibbons Medal 7665
Good Samaritan Award 14603
Hall of Fame
Council for Health and Human Services Ministries, United Church of Christ 8557
National Christian College Athletic Association 14657
Hall of Fame in Philanthropy 20350
Archbishop Paul Hallinan Award 7638
Susan R. Hellings Award 14658
Edgar J. Helms Award for Staff and Graduate Staff 10089
Helping Hands Award 21947
Rev. Theodore M. Hesburgh, C.S.C., Award 5591
Holiness Exponent of the Year 7960
Honorary Founder of the Guild 14630
John Paul II Religious Freedom Award 7647
Julia Hull Schilling Award 9153
Kolping Award 7645
C. Albert Koob Award 14613
Laetare Medal 21089
Bishop Loris Lane Award 14614
Layman of the Year 13177
Local Ecumenical Award for Christian Unity and Mission 10671
Louisville Slugger 14659
Lumen Christi Award 7640
Pete Maravich Memorial Award 14660
Marian Library Award 21012
Marianist Award 21013
Maryknoll Student Essay Contest 13129
Father McKenna Award 14419
John F. Meyers Award 14615
Ministry Support Award 6270
Robert F. Morneau Distinguished Service Award 14604
David Morsey Award 11469
Sister Mary Lea Mueller Human Services Award 8181
Mustard Seed Awards 14616
NABE Board Member of the Year 14617
NABE Executive Officer of the Year 14618
NABE Honor Roll of Outstanding Members 14619
National Competition 1139
NCEA Presidential Award 14620
Notre Dame Award 21090
Outstanding Contribution to Campus Ministry Award 5850
Outstanding Lithuanian Woman Award 12876
Outstanding Local Leadership Award 5823
Parent Organization Recognition Awards 14621
Parent Partnership Awards 14622
Parish Pastor of the Year 121
Performance Citation Award 7642
Ben Peterson Christian Sportsmanship Award 14663
Janette Pierce Award 9311
Poverello Medal 9730
Presidential Award 14421
Religious Broadcasting Hall of Fame Award 15617
Religious Education Excellence Awards 14623
Loretta Richards Distinguished Alumni Award 8182
Role of Law Award 7566
St. Francis de Sales Award 7660
St. Michael Religious Freedom Award 7648
Elizabeth Ann Seton Award 14624
Saint Elizabeth Ann Seton Award 14625
Shield of Blessed Gregory X Crusader 14422
Student-Athlete of the Week 14666
Teen Scholarship 7962
Tekakwitha Award 6451
Trustee of the Year 20353
United Methodist Association Award of Distinguished Service 20354
U.S. Catholic Award 20442
University Founders Award 9731
Vercelli Medal 14423
Ellen Waldschmidt Award 12990
Warren Weaver Service Award 7967
Wheeler Cross Country Award 14667
Wheeler Track and Field Awards 14668
Wittnauer NCCAA Player of the Year 14670
St. Francis Xavier Medal 22006
Oleg Zinam Award 11470

Church history
Award of Commendation 8340
Best First Article Award 16452
Frank S. and Elizabeth D. Brewer Prize 4284
Distinguished Service Award
Baptist History and Heritage Society 6244
Concordia Historical Institute 8341
Lutheran Historical Conference 12992
Jane Dempsey Douglass Prize 4285
Fagley Awards Competition 8387
Peter Guilday Prize 1654
Jesse Lee Prize 9913
Sidney E. Mead Prize 4286
John Harrison Ness Memorial Seminary Award 9914
Albert C. Outler Prize in Ecumenical Church History 4287

Church (continued)

John Gilmary Shea Prize 1656
Davis C. Woolley Award 6245

Cinema *See* Films

Citizenship and patriotism
Advancement and Preservation of Civilization Award 15900
American Citizenship Award 17108
Americanism Award 2950
Americanism News Media Award 7671
AMVETS National Awards Program 4947
AMVETS Silver Helmet Awards 4949
Barry Award 1658
Bronze Good Citizenship Medal 15764
CBC Medal 8011
Celtic Cross Award 7672
Certificate of Appreciation
American Police Hall of Fame 3565
National Society, Sons of the American Revolution 15765
Certificate of Distinguished Service 15766
Chai Award 6483
Citizen of the Year
Center for Philosophy, Law, Citizenship 7741
Darien Chamber of Commerce 8752
Greater Mount Airy Chamber of Commerce 10151
Greater Quitman Area Chamber of Commerce 10159
Kankakee River Valley Chamber of Commerce 12482
Minnewaukan Community Club 13487
Rutland Region Chamber of Commerce 18193
Vermont Chamber of Commerce 21298
Civic Scholarship 6460
Daughters of Liberty Medal 15767
Distinguished Awards 9764
Distinguished Citizen 21394
Distinguished Citizen Award 8401
Distinguished Patriot Award 15768
Distinguished Service Award 13419
Distinguished Service Medal 2947
Captain William Driver Award 15049
Eagle Award 17109
Ellis Island Medals of Honor 14955
Excellence Awards 12424
Father Washington Award 7673
Flag Certificate 15769
Flags of America Award 15050
Freedom Award 7609
Global Citizen Award 7731
Gold Good Citizenship Medal 15770
Great American Artificer Award 15051
Hatikvah Award 12365
Heroism Medal 15771
Honor et Veritas Award 7674
International Medal 15772
John Charnley Award 10441
J. Walter Kennedy Citizenship Award 14505
Law Enforcement and Fire Safety Commendation Medal 15773
Leadership Award 3981
Liberty Medal 15775
Medal of Appreciation 15776
Meritorious Service Medal 15777
Minuteman Medal 15778
Most Outstanding Catholic War Veteran 7675
Most Outstanding Post of the Year Award 7676
National Awards Program 9766
National Citizen of the Year 13404
National Public Citizen of the Year 14389
New Constellation Award 15052
Open Bible Award 17110
Optimist International Awards 16802
Order of Canada 6827
Otto Aufranc Award 10442
Outstanding Citizenship Award 15779
Outstanding Junior Member Contest 15712
Patriot Award 8402
Patriot Medal 15780
Patriot of the Nation 16007
Patriots Award 3575
Patriot's Award 17111
Philip Crosby Award 3982
Presidential Citizens Medal 9363
Presidential Medal of Freedom 9364
Presidential Rank Awards 20717
Quality Award 3983
Reach for the Stars Award 15901
Republican of the Year 18058
Violet Richardson Award 19419
ROTC Medals 15781
Dave Schultz High School Excellence Award 15990
Shield Award 17112
Silver Good Citizenship Medal 15783
Sojourners ROTC Awards 15787
Sylvanus Thayer Award 20701
VFW Americanism Award 21333
VFW James E. Van Zandt Citizenship Award 21342
Voice of Democracy Scholarship 21345
Martha Washington Medal 15785
Whitney Award 16497
Wilkinson Award 13303
Young American Creative Patriotic Art Competition 12648

City management
All-Star Community Awards 12187
C.C. Ludwig Award 12749
City Achievement Award 12750
National Gold Medal Awards 19726
Dr. Jackson R. E. Phillips Award 5830
Service Awards 5831
Township Leader of the Year 13467

City planning (*See also* Park planning; Planning)
Annual Meeting Best Paper Award 21137
Architectural Study Tour Scholarship 19018
Bard Awards for Excellence in Architecture and Urban Design 8026
Harland Bartholomew Award 4298
Stephen D. Bechtel Pipeline Engineering Award 4300
Rudy Bruner Award for Urban Excellence 6668
Charles Eliot II Award 13316
Honor Award 14549
IDA Downtown Achievement Awards 11547
Institute Honor Awards for Regional and Urban Design 2717
International Parking Awards Competition 11788
Loeb Fellowship 10281
Jim Marvin Award 12685
Ralph C. Menapace Fellowship in Urban Land Use Law 13678
Regional Service Award 13636
ULI Awards for Excellence 21140
US/ICOMOS Fellows 20452
Van Cleef Memorial Medal 2335
Elliot Willensky Fund 13681
Alma H. Young Emerging Scholars Award 21138

Civil engineering (*See also* Construction)
O. H. Ammann Research Fellowship in Structural Engineering 4290
Arid Lands Hydraulic Engineering Award 4291
ASCE Presidents' Award 4293
ASCE State-of-the-Art of Civil Engineering Award 4295
Award for Service To People 4296
Award of Excellence of the Pipeline Division 4297
Award of Merit - Earth Shelter and Architecture 4777
Award of Merit - Planning and Development 4778
Award of Merit - Tunnels and Deep Space 4779
Harland Bartholomew Award 4298
Stephen D. Bechtel, Jr. Energy Award 4299
Stephen D. Bechtel Pipeline Engineering Award 4300
Albert E. Berry Medal 7410
Best Paper Award 4001
John O. Bickel Award 4301
Arthur J. Boase Award of the Reinforced Concrete Research Council 4302
Roger J. E. Brown Award 7122
CAN-AM Amity Award 7411
Can-AM Civil Engineering Amity Award 4303
Canadian Geotechnical Colloquium 7123
Arthur Casagrande Professional Development Award 4304
Civil Engineering History and Heritage Award 4306
Collingwood Prize 4308
J. James R. Croes Medal 4310
Francis X. Crowley Scholarship 16133
Camille A. Dagenais Award 7412
Charles Martin Duke Lifeline Earthquake Engineering Award 4311
Hans Albert Einstein Award 4312
Fellow 7413
Freeman Fellowship 4313
Simon W. Freese Environmental Engineering Award and Lecture 4314
Alfred M. Freudenthal Medal 4315
Edmund Friedman Young Engineer Award for Professional Achievement 4317
John Fritz Medal 4318
Fulton Awards 108
Government Civil Engineer of the Year Award 4319
Gzowski Medal 7414
Shortridge Hardesty Award 4321
R.M. Hardy Keynote Address 7126
Julian Hinds Award 4324
Phillip R. Hoffman Award 4325
Honorary Fellow 4326
Honorary Member 4327
Walter L. Huber Civil Engineering Research Prizes 4332
Hydraulic Structures Medal 4333
Innovation in Civil Engineering Award 4334

Civil (continued)

International Coastal Engineering Award 4335
Donald Jamieson Fellowship 7415
Keefer Medal 7416
Elson T. Killam Memorial Scholarship 16138
Kenneth S. Lane Award 4780
James Laurie Prize 4337
R.F. Legget Award 7127
Leipholz Medal 7417
Burton W. Marsh Graduate Fellowship 11051
Frank M. Masters Transportation Engineering Award 4339
Daniel W. Mead Prizes 4340
Geofrey G. Meyerhof Award 7128
Thomas A. Middlebrooks Award 4341
John G. Moffat - Frank E. Nichol Harbor and Coastal Engineering Award 4342
Moisseiff Award 4343
Nathan M. Newmark Medal 4344
Norman Medal 4346
Outstanding Civil Engineering Achievement 4347
John I. Parcel - Leif J. Sverdrup Civil Engineering Management Award 4348
Peurifoy Construction Research Award 4349
Harold R. Peyton Award for Cold Regions Engineering 4350
P. L. Pratley Award 7418
Prize Bridge Award 2850
R.M. Quigley Award 7129
Raymond C. Reese Research Prize 4351
Robert Ridgway Student Chapter Award 4353
Roebling Award 4354
Thomas Roy Award 7130
A. B. Sanderson Award 7419
Wilbur S. Smith Award 4357
J. Waldo Smith Hydraulic Fellowship 4358
Karl Terzaghi Lecture 4361
Royce J. Tipton Award 4362
Francis C. Turner Lecture 4364
Urban Traffic Engineering Achievement Awards 11059
James A. Vance Award 7420
Theodore von Karman Medal 4365
George K. Wadlin Distinguished Service Award 4047
George Winter Award 4368
William H. Wisely American Civil Engineer Award 4369
E. Whitman Wright Award 7421
Young Government Civil Engineer of the Year Award 4370
Younger Member Group Award 4371

Civil rights and liberties (*See also* Academic freedom; Brotherhood; Child welfare; Citizenship and patriotism; Freedom; Heroism; Human relations; Human rights; Humanitarianism; Intellectual freedom; Women's rights)

Jane Addams Children's Book Award 12296
Affirmative Action and Equal Employment Opportunity Award 21559
Anisfield-Wolf Book Awards 8097
Alan Barth Service Award 1811
Hon. William J. Brennan Award for Outstanding Jurist 16272
Goler T. Butcher Medal 4462
Joe Callaway Prize for the Defense of the Right to Privacy 16216
Civil Liberties Award
American Civil Liberties Union of Vermont 1814
American Civil Liberties Union, Ohio Affiliate 1818
Jacob Clayman Award 14815
David L. Clendenin Award 21836
Cooperating Atty Award 1815
Frederick Douglass Award 16309
William Edward Burghardt Du Bois Medal 14048
Henry W. Edgerton Civil Liberties Award 1812
Equal Justice Award 14490
Equal Opportunity/Affirmative Action Exemplary Practices Award 4183
Equal Opportunity Day Award 15925
Freedom Award 9760
Mary Ellen Hamilton Award 15338
Andrew Heiskell Awards 20091
The Sidney Hillman Foundation Prize Awards 10435
William P. Hubbard Race Relations Award 8050
Human Rights Award 10591
Humanitarian Award 14966
Hubert H. Humphrey Civil Rights Award 12738
Robert F. Kennedy Book Awards 18074
Robert F. Kennedy Journalism Awards 18076
Coretta Scott King Book Award 3004
Martin Luther King, Jr. - Abraham Joshua Heschel Award 6490
Martin Luther King, Jr. Achievement Award 8394
Beatrice G. Konheim Award 1465
Labor Affairs Award 15926
Florina Lasker Civil Liberties Award 16217
Living Legends Award 15927
Medal of Liberty 1809
Mary D. Pinkard Leader in Federal Equity Award 9455
Professionalism Award 19962
A. Philip Randolph/Bayard Rustin Freedom Award 28
Robie Award for Achievement in Industry 12275
Robie Humanitarianism Award 12276
Renault Robinson Award 14523
Gertrude E. Rush Award 14491
Sexual Orientation and Gender Identity Conference Awards 6974
Dr. Phillip Sigal Peace and Justice Scholarship 9187
Reginald Heber Smith Award 15339
Social Justice Award 21561
Felipa da Souza Award 11647
C. Francis Stradford Award 14492
Ann Tanneyhill Award 15928
Unity Awards in Media 12866
Victory Awards 15609
Volunteer of the Year 1816
Ida B. Wells Award 14102
Wimps, Grumblers, and Grousers Award 15438
Whitney M. Young, Jr. Memorial Scholarship 16310

Coaching

ABCA Twenty-Five Year Awards 1539
Academic Athletes of the Year (All Academic Team) 14691
AFCA Coach of the Year 2267
Age Group Diving Coach of the Year 21167
All-America Awards 15707
All American Awards 14692
All American Team 2268
ASCA Awards of Excellence 4719
ASCA Chapter Age Group Coaches of the Year 4720
ASCA Coaches Hall of Fame 4721
Canada's Sports Hall of Fame 6842
CAR Coach of the Year Award 21806
Century Club Award 1540
Citations of Merit 9672
Coach of the Year
American Football Coaches Association 2269
Canadian Federation of Amateur Baseball 7086
College Gymnastics Association 8158
Continental Basketball Association 8480
Ladies Professional Golf Association 12652
National Association of Basketball Coaches 14081
National Christian College Athletic Association 14656
United States Amateur Boxing, Inc. 20385
United States Professional Tennis Association 20740
Coach of the Year Award
American Baseball Coaches Association 1541
American Swimming Coaches Association 4722
National Association of Intercollegiate Athletics 14284
National Soccer Coaches Association of America 15708
Coach of the Year Awards 15983
Coach of the Year - Red Auerbach Trophy 14500
Coaches of the Year 15223
College Basketball Coach of the Year 19651
College Football Coach of the Year 19653
College Football Hall of Fame 15067
Collegiate Coach of the Year 20582
Councilman Creative Coaching Awards 4723
Cross Country Coach of the Year 20801
Diamond Key Award 15099
Distinguished Service Award (Coaching) 14982
Distinguished Service Key 15100
District Coach of the Year 14693
Domestic Alpine Coach of the Year 20803
ESPY Awards 9337
First Interstate Athletic Foundation Gymnastics Hall of Fame Award 8159
Jim Fullerton Award 2489
Robert Giegengack Award 21223
Golden Diamond Awards 21155
Lefty Gomez Award 1543
Hall of Fame 1544
Hall of Fame Award 15282
Honor Award 15709
Honor Awards 1545
Honor Coach Award 8160
Honor Coach Certificate 8161

Coaching (continued)
Honorary Membership (Outstanding Contributors) 14694
International Women's Sports Hall of Fame 21808
Edward Jeremiah Award/College Division Coach of the Year 2490
Jimmy Rattlesnake Award 7087
Francis L. (Babe) Kraus Award 20663
Letter of Commendation 15710
Lincoln Financial Group Awards of Excellence 15104
Louisville Slugger 14659
Meritorious Service Award 1546
Naismith College Coach of the Year 6027
National Coach of the Year 14695
National Collegiate and Scholastic Swimming Trophy 8196
National Collegiate and Scholastic Swimming Trophy 15283
National Federation Interscholastic Coaches Association Annual Awards 14984
National High School Sports Hall of Fame Awards 14979
National Lacrosse Hall of Fame 20680
National Merit Award 15278
NBA Coach of the Year 19664
NFICA Certificates for Each State 14985
NFL Coach of the Year 19669
NHL Coach of the Year 19672
Outstanding Football Official Award 15075
Outstanding Male and Female Athlete of the Year 14696
Outstanding Service Awards 15284
Spencer Penrose Award/University Division Coach of the Year 2496
Pro Football Hall of Fame 17578
Regional Coach of the Year 20584
Eddie Robinson Coach of the Year 9676
Schlueter Stroke Awards National Winners 4725
Ski Jumping/Nordic Combined Coach of the Year 20819
Speedo/USMS Coach of the Year Award 20692
F. Morris Touchstone Award 20669
United States Youth Soccer Association Coach of the Year for Boys and Girls 20899
USSS Coach of the Year 19870

Coin collecting *See* Numismatics

Collectibles *See* Hobbies and clubs

Collegiate journalism
John A. Boyd Hall of Fame Award 8169
Business/Economic Writing Award 8170
College Journalism Competition 18109
Distinguished Adviser Award 8171
Editorial and Cartoon Strip Contest 8172
John R. Emens Award for Support of a Free Student Press 6205
Honor Roll Adviser Award 8173
Martin Luther King Award 12914
Reid H. Montgomery Distinguished Service Award 8175
NAA Foundation - Associated Collegiate Press Pacemakers Awards 16337
Noel Ross Strader Memorial Award 8176
Student Article Contest 7251

Color technology
Godlove Award 11127
Macbeth Award 11128
Dorothy Nickerson-ISCC Award 11129
Pantone Color Award 17062

Combustion (*See also* Energy conservation)
Sir Alfred Egerton Medal 8264
Gas Turbine Award 4512
Internal Combustion Engine Award 4521
James N. Landis Medal 4524
Bernard Lewis Medal 8265
R. Tom Sawyer Award 4545
Silver Combustion Medal 8266
Ya B. Zeldovich Gold Medal 8267

Comedy *See* Entertainment; Humor

Commerce *See* Business; Finance

Communications (*See also* Audiovisuals; Broadcasting; Communications technology; Cybernetics; Human relations; Linguistics; Office technology; Public relations; Public speaking)
$500,000 Lemelson-MIT Prize 12777
AAU Association Communications Award 526
Achievement Awards 10323
Advertising Executive of the Year 10515
Aerospace Communications Award 2633
Alfred N. Goldsmith Award 10664
Alumnus of the Year Award 18197
APEX - Awards for Publication Excellence 4994
ASJMC Distinguished Service Award 5845
Awards for Excellence 18865
Awards for Excellence in Distance Learning 11090
Stuart Ballantine Medal 9739
Ralph Batcher Memorial Award 17830
Samuel L. Becker Distinguished Service Award 14706
Bell Ringer Awards 17732
Best Subscriber Communication Program 15859
Better Communications Contest 21265
Blue Pencil Awards 14242
Polly Bond Award 9310
Robert Bosch Foundation Fellowship Program 7687
James M. Brahney Grant 11836
Bridge School International Award 11918
Reuben Brigham Award 5292
Ham Brown Award 16966
Carol Burnett/University of Hawaii/AEJMC Ethics Prize 5344
Henri Busignies Memorial Award 17831
William M. Cavanaugh Student Grant 17733
CCCC Outstanding Book Award 8378
Certificate of Commendation 673
Charles Kreupper Award 18024
Christopher Awards 7971
Clarion Awards 5522
Common Wealth Awards of Distinguished Service 17410
Communication and Marketing Awards 11035
Communication Award 7714
Communication Policy Research Award 13217
Communications Award 2891
Communications Awards 10084
Communicator of Achievement Award 14972
Cooperative Month Awards 14800
Walter Cronkite Award for Excellence in Journalism and Mass Communication 8657
DeForest Audion Gold Medal Award 21324
Brig. Gen. Robert L. Denig Distinguished Service Award 20684
Design Award 12150
Design for Humanity Award 4460
Donald L. Dickson Memorial Award 20685
Director's Award 15364
Distinguished Service Award
Internet Alliance 12151
World Communication Association 21875
Distinguished Service Medal Awards 19879
Distinguished Women's Awards 16572
Donald H. Ecroyd Award for Outstanding Teaching in Higher Education 14707
Douglas W. Ehninger Distinguished Rhetorical Scholar Award 14708
Excellence in Communication Leadership (EXCEL) 11295
Excellence in Communications Award 10394
Excellence in Communications Awards 14153
Excellence in Training 5825
The F.L. "Gus" Cooper Award for Meritorous Service 11093
Gold Screen Awards 14243
Golden Anniversary Monograph Awards 14709
Golden Eagle Award 21662
Golden Gavel Award 20095
Golden Raster Award 10325
Golden Torch Award 11095
Government Communicator of the Year 14244
Alfred H. Grebe Award 17836
Frank A. Gunther Award 17837
Franklyn S. Haiman Award for Distinguished Scholarship in Freedom of Expression 14710
James E. Hatch Award 13079
Headliner Award 5523
HeSCA Interactive Materials Festival 10327
Lilla A. Heston Award for Outstanding Scholarship in Interpretation and Performance Studies 14711
Hoar Award 7499
Honor Award 18383
Honor Roll of Excellence in Communication 5826
Honorary Member 14973
Horticultural Communication Award 2528
IABC Chairman's Award 11296
IABC Fellow 11297
Icko Iben Award 4831
ICIA Distinguished Achievement Award 11498
IDA Downtown Achievement Awards 11547
IEEE Award in International Communication 10867
Innovation Award 12152
Intelligent Community Awards 21957
International Online Communication Competition 18860
International Pro-Comm Awards Competition 6713

Communications (continued)

International Technical Art Competition 18861
International Technical Publications Competition 18862
International Video Competition 18863
William E. Jackson Award 18179
JCC Biennial Communications Awards Competition 12339
Robert J. Kibler Memorial Award 14712
Koji Kobayashi Computers and Communications Award 10873
Krieghbaum Under-40 Award 5345
La Salle Collegian Award 12634
Fred M. Link Award 17839
Ramon Magsaysay Award 18093
Marconi Memorial Gold Medal of Service 21325
Marconi Memorial Scroll of Honor 21326
The Marconi Prize 13064
Mass Communications Hall of Fame 20045
Mass Communications Outstanding Alumni Awards 20046
Matrix Award 16312
Shirley McNaughton Exemplary Communication Award 11919
Gerald R. Miller Outstanding Doctoral Dissertation Award 14713
Jerry B. Minter Award 17840
National Club Achievement Competition 860
National Commander's Public Relations Award 2948
Newhouse Citation 19880
Marcella E. Oberle Award for Outstanding Teaching in Grades K-12 14714
Outstanding Achievement Award 12153
Janette Pierce Award 9311
Pioneer Award 5293
Alexander M. Poniatoff Gold Medal Award 19195
Pat Porter Memorial Award - "Friend of the Satellite Dealer" Award 9220
President's Award 14974
Product and Service Awards 12154
Professional Award 5294
PTC Essay Prize 17022
Rogers Communications Inc. Media Award for Coverage of the Arts 7038
Rookie Newsletter Award 573
Sarnoff Citation 17843
Service Award 5295
Service Awards 10331
John I. Sisco Excellence in Teaching Award 19525
Solidarity Prize 21858
Special Awards 10333
Special Services Award 17844
Sweepstakes Winner 14975
Telecommunications Award 10350
Teleport Awards for Excellence 21958
Anna Tracey Memorial Award 17328
Karl R. Wallace Memorial Award 14715
James A. Winans/Herbert A. Wichelns Memorial Award for Distinguished Scholarship in Rhetoric and Public Address 14716
Charles H. Woolbert Research Award 14717
Words+ Outstanding Consumer Lecture Award 11922
Worked 100 Nations Award 21973

Communications technology

AECT Leadership Development Grants 5349
AECT Memorial Scholarship Award 5350
AECT National Convention Internship Program 5351
Agfa - Gevaert Gold Medal Award 19188
Armstrong Memorial Research Foundation Awards 5098
ARRL Herb S. Brier Instructor of the Year Award 45
ARRL Professional Educator of the Year Award 46
Robert S. Bray Award 2039
James W. Brown Publication Award 5354
Citation of Outstanding Service to the Society 19189
Robert de Kieffer International Fellowship Award 5355
Eastman Kodak Gold Medal Award 19190
Engineering Achievement Awards 14112
ETR&D Young Scholar Award 5356
Fuji Gold Medal Award 19191
Robert M. Gagne Instructional Development Research Award 5357
John Grierson International Gold Medal Award 19192
Honorary Member 19193
IEEE Life Members' Prize in Electrical History 18875
Innovation Award 19544
International Humanitarian Award 48
Jules Leger Prize for New Chamber Music 6799
Dean and Sybil McClusky Research Award 5360
Progress Medal Award 19197
Don Rennie Memorial Award for Excellence in Government Public Relations 7363
David Sarnoff Medal Award 19198
Service Award 19545
Technical Engineering Achievement Awards 13866
Technical Excellence Award 52
Samuel L. Warner Memorial Medal Award 19200

Community affairs (*See also* Citizenship and patriotism; Community service; Heroism; Humanitarianism; Organizational service; Public affairs)

Rudy Bruner Award for Urban Excellence 6668
Certificates of Merit 13675
Citizen Activist Award 10039
Community Association Board Member of the Year 8315
Community-Constable Partnership Award 14727
Community of the Year 8313
Community Partnership Program Accessible America Award 15458
Community Relations Award (Labor) 2892
Distinguished Member Award 11568
Distinguished Service Award 9398
Scott Goodnight Award for Outstanding Performance as a Dean 14403
Hometown Video Festival 458
Major General Melvin J. Maas Achievement Award 6458
Outstanding Service to the Constable System by a Non-Constable Award 14731
Outstanding Society Awards 12845
Gertrude E. Rush Award 14491
Shared Vision Award 16082
STAR Events - Students Taking Action with Recognition 9399
Stir-the-Pot Award 15460

Community service (*See also* Public service; Social service; Volunteerism)

Accountants, Bankers and Factors Division Award 2890
Achievement Awards 14165
Advertising Leader of the Year Award 12923
Affiliated Chapter Awards 10342
S. Y. Agnon Gold Medal 2306
Alec and Mora Dickson Scholarship 11790
Horatio Alger Awards 10539
All-America City Awards 14674
Ambassador of the Month 9223
AMVETS National Awards Program 4947
AMVETS National Employer of the Year Award 4948
Annual Awards for Chapter Programming 17086
Brooke Russell Astor Award 16253
Atlantic High School Scholarship 8861
Award for Community Service 15164
Award for Service to Society 2757
Award of Gratitude 13493
Award of Merit
B'nai Brith Canada 6487
City of Toronto 8045
Awards for Excellence in Community Service, Philanthropy, and Media 19847
Malcolm Baldrige Community Award 10168
Beasley Award 8713
Alexander Graham Bell Volta Award 435
Benjamin Rush Award 17260
Best in Business Award 6342
Big Chief Award 10097
Big Oscars 6280
Bridge Awards 6620
James Brown IV Annual Award of Excellence for Outstanding Community Service 7883
Bruck Award 10363
Business Executive of the Year 17874
Business of the Year
Evergreen Area Chamber of Commerce 9359
Galt District Chamber of Commerce 9860
Fred M. Butzel Memorial Award for Distinguished Community Service 12353
"Buy Recycled" Campaign Awards Program 20455
Ralph D. Casey Minnesota Award 10811
Celebrating Women Awards 21791
Chai Award 6483
Chamber of Commerce 13428
Chamber Person of the Year 18436
Pedro Joaquin Chamorro Inter-American Relations Award 11107
Chester County Community Hero 20907
Chester County Youth Community Hero 20908
Citizen of the Year
Darien Chamber of Commerce 8752
Greater Mount Airy Chamber of Commerce 10151
Greater Quitman Area Chamber of Commerce 10159
Kankakee River Valley Chamber of Commerce 12482
Minnewaukan Community Club 13487

Community (continued)

Rutland Region Chamber of Commerce 18193
Vermont Chamber of Commerce 21298
Civic Award Citation 12967
Civic Leadership Award 8022
Civic Service Award 8018
Civitan International Honor Keys 8061
Allen W. Clark Award 15467
Community Awards Program (Encore Awards) 18022
Community-Constable Partnership Award 14727
Community Leadership Award 10812
Community Leadership Awards 18248
Community Service Award
American Academy of Facial Plastic and Reconstructive Surgery 668
American Association of Homes and Services for the Aging 1224
American Correctional Association 2023
Black Archives of Mid-America 6406
East Mount Airy Neighbors 9076
Essex Community Heritage Organization 9339
Florida State Grange 9631
Keuka College Alumni Association 12578
Latrobe Area Chamber of Commerce 12715
National Council of Social Security Management Associations 14821
National Grange 15172
UCLA Alumni Association 20255
Community Service Award/Certificate of Merit 14816
Community Service Awards 17162
Community Service Fellowship 7884
Community Service Leadership Award 20326
Congressman of the Year 15395
Coordinator Award 8520
Corporate Conscience Award 8591
Crystal Radio Awards 14110
Valentine Davies Award 21991
Davison Chamber of Commerce Service Scholarship 8758
G. Richard Dew Award 17184
Distinguished Alumni Award 13632
Distinguished Citizen 21394
Distinguished Service Award
Association of Professional Chaplains 5822
National Parkinson Foundation 15486
Zelienople-Harmony Chamber of Commerce 22101
Dolly Award 6622
Rhea Eckle Clark Citizenship Award 9644
Editorial Awards 19819
Ehlenfeldt Memorial Scholarship 17033
Enterprise Spirit Award 12576
Extra Mile Award 21421
Fabulous Fashion Independents 13654
Fifty-Year Award 9525
Fighter Against Drug Abuse 14730
John H. Finley Award 518
Elaine R. "Boots" Fisher Award 9436
Charles H. Flynn Humanitarian Award 20918
Founder's Award
Civitan International 8063
Pratt Institute 17520
Gold Cup of Industry Award 9078
Gold Medal Award 4953
Gold Ribbon for Community Service (Radio) 6891
Gold Ribbon for Community Service (Specialty/Pay/PPV) 6892
Gold Ribbon for Community Service (Television) 6893
Gold Ribbon for Outstanding Community Service by an Individual Broadcaster 6894
Golden Youth Awards 6598
Good Servant Medal 7047
Government Affairs Award of Recognition 6683
Governor of the Year 15397
Green City Hands-On Activist Award 17365
Dr. Randy Gregg Award 7217
Grocers Care Awards 15174
James L. Guinn Awards 12292
Hall of Fame 13488
Hall of Fame Award 4642
"Hands Across South Madison" Community Services Initiative 19460
Paul Harris Award 20217
Hatikvah Award 12365
Emo Henrich Award 19797
T. Kenyon Holly Memorial Award 20252
Sylvia Holmes Scholarship 10030
Honor Awards for Program Excellence 6599
Honor Club of Distinction 8064
The Howard A. Berry Scholarship 11791
Humanitarian Award
B'nai Brith Canada 6488
National Parkinson Foundation 15487
IDA Downtown Achievement Awards 11547
Industry Achievement Award 15470
Horace M. Kallen Award 2896
Knights of Justice Award 3572
Kolping Award 7645
Sidney G. Kusworm Award 6484
Fiorello H. La Guardia Award 16200
Larsen-Miller Community Service Award 13906
Leadership Award
Camp Fire USA El Dorado Council 6778
Corona Norco United Way 8521
Leadership in Human Services Award 3782
Legion of Honor 12366
Lifetime Achievement 6281
Local Chapter Community Project Award 14436
Local Chapter Excellence Award 14437
Local Council Community Service Award 11866
Diego Lopez Community Service Award in New York 10592
Lou Gordon Humanitarian Award 13593
Loyola Camellia 12970
Ramon Magsaysay Award 18093
Jim Marvin Award 12685
Harry Mattin Award 9123
Durward K. McDaniel Ambassador Award 2043
Medal of Merit 18221
Meritorious Service Award 3363
Loren Miller Legal Services Award 19760
Mitch Trubitt Community Asthma Champion Award 7870
MSMA Community Service Award 13513
Murray-Green-Meany-Kirkland Award for Community Service 2227
NALPA Past President Award 13929
National Community Service Award
Jewish Theological Seminary 12379
National Association of Negro Business and Professional Women's Clubs 14314
National Leadership Award 14753
National Quality Dealer Award 15254
National Recognition Award 601
National Youth of the Year Award 6601
New Englander of the Year Awards 16099
New Yorker for New York Awards 8013
Colonel Elliott A. Niles Award 6485
Order of Ontario 16757
Organization of the Year 20351
Outstanding Business Leader Awards 16573
Outstanding Citizen Award 8509
Outstanding Civitan Awareness Project 8065
Outstanding Community Service Project 8067
Outstanding Junior Member Contest 15712
Outstanding Lithuanian Woman Award 12876
Outstanding Service to the Constable System by a Non-Constable Award 14731
Outstanding Service to the Mentally and/or Physically Handicapped 8068
Outstanding Sponsor Award 6905
Outstanding Young Electrical Engineer Award 9346
S. Alden Pendleton Award 10995
Claude Pepper Award 14818
Personal Contribution Award 6906
Pilgrim of the Year 17408
Pioneer Award 8593
President of Chamber Award 9861
President's Eagle Award 18051
President's Environmental Youth Awards (PEYA) 20575
President's Medallion 12971
President's Pro Bono Service Award 19761
Pride and Progress 13580
Professional Engineers Citizenship Award 17607
Professional of the Year Award 5738
Program Excellence Awards 11477
Public and Community Service Emmy Awards 13864
Sidney R. Rabb Award 9663
Raven Award 17880
Recognition of Service 8051
Remodeler of the Month/Year Awards 14260
Violet Richardson Award 19419
Robe of Achievement 18421
Robertson Most Outstanding Undergraduate Award 17312
Romney Volunteer Center Excellence Award 17447
Melvin J. Schneidermeyer Regional Leadership Award 7767
Scopus Award 2309
The Seymour Eskow Scholarship 11792
Silver Good Citizenship Medal 15783
Slatter Memorial Volunteer of the Year Award 18417
Carroll Sledz - Lou Wener Community Service Award in Washington, DC 10593
Small Town America Hall of Fame 14445
Adam Smith Award 5818
Special Innovation Award 10999
Special Service Awards 19456
Bart Starr Award 6019
Steel Oleander Award 9865
Stone Award 21135
Susan B. Anthony Award 22099

Community (continued)

The Sven Groennings Scholarship 11793
Sword of Loyola 12974
Henrietta Szold Award 10215
Texas Star Award 22094
Textile Citizen of the Year 410
Time Magazine Quality Dealer Award 20092
Torch Award 9511
Trustee of the Year 20353
Twenty-Four Dollar Award 13696
Tzedakah Award 20342
UJA - Federation Distinguished Communal Service Award 20343
University of Missouri Television Awards for Community Leadership 21081
USTA/USPTA Public Service Award 20872
Veteran's Community Service Award 21358
Vision for Tomorrow Award 8937
Volunteer of the Year 16998
Washingtonians of the Year 21469
Wilkinson Award 13303
Jay Worrall Public Official Award 16612
YMCA Men, Women and Youth of the Year 22037
Young American Medal for Service 20507
Youth as Resources 12740

Company publications
Communications Program Awards 9658
Corporate Leadership Award 2811
Editorial and Design Excellence Awards 4270
Financial Post Annual Report Awards 8537
HSMAI Adrian Advertising Awards 10554

Composing *See* Music composition

Computer programming
Edgar F. Codd Innovations Award 5313
Codie Awards 19383
Dantzig Prize 13199
Enterprise Computing Award 18266
Johann Gutenberg Prize 18768
Loebner Prize Turing Test Award 6773
Macworld Editors' Choice Awards 17115
Management Information Systems Annual Professional Award (MISAPA) 10118
W. Wallace McDowell Award 10898
Byron B. Oberst Award 784
Orchard-Hays Prize 13201
PC World World Class Awards 17116
SIGCOMM Award 5323
SIGMOD Contributions Award 5314
Software Process Achievement Award 10900
Software System Award 5307
User Feedback Award 18267

Computer science (*See also* Communications; Computer programming; Computers; Information management; Library and information services)
$100,000 Lemelson-MIT Lifetime Achievement Award 12776
ACM Doctoral Dissertation Award 5297
ACM Eugene Lawler Award for Humanitarian Contributions within Computer Science and Informatics 5298
ACM Fellows 5299
AIAA Aerospace Software Engineering Award 2638
AIAA Command, Control, Communication & Intelligence Award 2643
AIAA Computer-Aided Engineering and Manufacturing Award 2644
Award for Lifetime Service 5320
Gordon Bell Prize 10885
Taylor Booth Award 10886
Karl Ferdinand Braun Prize 18765
Canadian Architect Magazine Art of CAD Competition 6878
Canadian Software Systems Award 7164
CASA/SME Industry and University LEAD Awards 8326
Edgar F. Codd Innovations Award 5313
Computer Educator of the Year 11201
Computer Pioneer Award 10888
Computing in Chemical Engineering Award 2764
Computing Practice Award 2765
Diana Award 5310
Eckert - Mauchly Award 10891
Douglas Engelbart Best Paper Award 5325
Fellow 18766
Sidney Fernbach Memorial Award 10892
Andrew Fluegelman Award 17114
Godel Prize 5316
Harry M. Good Memorial Award 10893
Richard W. Hamming Medal 10864
Grace Murray Hopper Award 5300
Innovation Award 19544
Intel International Science and Engineering Fair 18362
JSID Outstanding Student Paper of the Year Award 18769
Tsutomu Kanai Award 10896
Paris Kanellakis Theory and Practice Award 5301
Hans Karlsson Award for Leadership and Achievement through Collaboration 10897
Karl V. Karlstrom Outstanding Educator Award 5302
Donald E. Knuth Prize 5317
Koji Kobayashi Computers and Communications Award 10873
Eckert - Mauchly Award 5303
Richard E. Merwin Award for Distinguished Service 10899
Allen Newell Award 5304
NSF-Funded Paid Internships 7727
Outstanding Contribution to ACM Award 5305
Emanuel R. Piore Award 10876
Jan Rajchman Prize 18770
Research Associateship Programs 15623
Joseph T. Rigo Award 5311
SDE Fellowships 18481
Service Award 19545
SIGACT Distinguished Service Prize 5318
SIGCOMM Award 5323
SIGCSE Award 5321
SIGMOD Contributions Award 5314
SIGPLAN Distinguished Service Award 5306
Software Process Achievement Award 10900
Special Recognition Awards 18771
Technical Achievement Award 10901
A. M. Turing Award 5308
UPE Scholarship Awards 21133
Norbert Wiener Award for Social and Professional Responsibility 8331
Lewis and Beatrice Winner Award 18772

Computers
$500,000 Lemelson-MIT Prize 12777
A.A. Michelson Award 8328
ACS Award for Computers in Chemical and Pharmaceutical Research 1704
Best Student Paper Award 13366
Computer Entrepreneur Award 10887
Computer Science and Engineering Undergraduate Teaching Award 10889
Conference Contribution Award 10890
CRA Distinguished Service 8333
Crave the Dave Award 8760
Creative Arts Award 12159
Design Award 12150
Distinguished Service Award 12151
EAI Award 4016
Woody Everett Award 4017
Golden Screen Award 8336
Harlan D. Mills Award 10894
Harry Hayman Award for Distinguished Staff Service 10895
Information Technology Pathfinder Award 1416
Innovation Award 12152
Augusta Ada Lovelace Award 5525
Macworld Editors' Choice Awards 17115
W. Wallace McDowell Award 10898
Merl K. Miller Award 4030
Nico Haberman 8334
Outstanding Achievement Award 12153
PC World World Class Awards 17116
Product and Service Awards 12154
Service Award 10478
Seymour Cray Computer Science and Engineering Award 10479
Harden-Simons Prize 4043
Ray H. Speiss Award 4044
Student Fellowship Award 8329

Concrete
ACI Commemorative Lecture Series 1957
ACI Construction Award 1958
ACI Design Award 1959
ACI Fellows 1960
Arthur R. Anderson Award 1961
Award of Merit 1978
Delmar L. Bloem Distinguished Service Award 1962
Certificate of Merit Award 17522
Chapter Activities Award 1963
Chester Paul Siess Award for Excellence in Structural Research 1964
Concrete Paving Awards 13341
Roger H. Corbetta Concrete Constructor Award 1965
CRSI Design Awards Program 8346
Harry H. Edwards Industry Advancement Award 17523
Fellow Award 17524
Fulton Awards 108
Honorary Member 1966
Joe W. Kelly Award 1967
Henry L. Kennedy Award 1968
Martin P. Korn Award 17525
Alfred E. Lindau Award 1969
Richard C. Longfellow Award 1980
Robert J. Lyman Award 17526
Medal of Honor Award 17527
Minnesota Masonry Project Awards 13469
NJACI Merit Award 1976
Outstanding Service Award 1981
REACH Award 5813
Henry C. Turner Medal 1970
Wason Medal for Materials Research 1971

Concrete (continued)

Wason Medal for the Most Meritorious Paper 1972
Charles S. Whitney Medal 1973
Cedric Willson Award 1974
Charles C. Zollman Award 17529

Conducting
Jean-Marie Beaudet Award in Orchestra Conducting 6784
Leslie Bell Prize for Choral Conducting 16737
Certificate of Appreciation 21725
Citation of Merit Award 21726
Hall of Fame of Distinguished Band Conductors 14484
International Golden Rose Award 21727
Kennedy Center Honors 12552
Virginia Parker Award 6804
Antoinette Perry Awards (Tony Awards) 12742
Pioneer Women of the Podium 21728
Thelma A. Robinson Scholarship/Award in Conducting 8348
Scroll of Excellence 21729
Silver Baton Award 21730
Sousa Prize in Conducting 19429
Theodore Thomas Award 8349
Heinz Unger Award 16748
Charles R. Winking Award 14600

Conservation (*See also* Ecology; Energy; Energy conservation; Environmental conservation; Environmental health; Forestry; Nature; Planning; Recycling; Sanitary engineering; Water conservation; Water resources; Wildlife conservation)
ACI Annual Awards 5327
Adirondack Council Annual Awards 186
Affiliate Award 16027
Audubon Medal 14468
Eugene Baker Memorial Award 5636
Paul Bartsch Award 6063
Alfred D. Bell, Jr. Visiting Scholars Program 9694
Theodore C. Blegen Award 9695
John Brooks' Memorial Award 6072
Ham Brown Award 16966
Charles H. Callison Award 14469
Canadian Conservation Achievement Award 7538
Catalyst Grants 17865
CEN-IP 7082
Certificate of Merit 15795
Certificate of Recognition 6073
Cetacean Citation 7788
Chapter of the Year 6074
ChevronTexaco Conservation Awards Program 7864
James Lawton Childs Award 12264
Doug Clarke Conservation Award 7539
College Art Association/National Institute for Conservation Award 8144
Collier Award 9696
Connecticut River Watershed Council Conservation Award 8420
Conservation Award
Joshua's Tract Conservation and Historic Trust 12440
Nature Saskatchewan 16038
Ottawa Field-Naturalists' Club 16927
Conservation Award - Private Citizen 6064
Conservation Award - Public Official 6065
Conservation Guest Scholars 10003
Conservation/Outdoor Recreation Film/Video Award Program 16967
Conservation Tillage Awards 14150
Conservationist of the Year
Chesapeake Bay Foundation 7859
Minnesota Conservation Federation 13471
Contractor of the Year 12689
Corporate Award 6066
Coupes Merites Aux Individus 7780
Robert W. Crawford Young Professional Award 15575
Allan D. Cruickshank Memorial Award 6077
District Newsletter Contest 14152
John and Harriet Dunning Award 16031
Ben East Prize 13364
Environmental Educator of the Year 7860
Eugene Rogers Award 21542
Excellence in Craft Awards 16968
Fellow of the Society 15796
Fellows Award 16039
Group and Grotto Conservation Award 15797
W. W. H. Gunn Conservation Award 16762
J. B. Harkin Conservation Award 7330
Stan Hodgkiss Canadian Outdoorsman Award 7540
Carl L. Hubbs Award 8897
IWLA Conservation Award 12265
IWLA Hall of Fame Award 12266
Jade of Chiefs 16969
Kleinhans Fellowships 17866
Legislative Excellence Award 6078
Roland Michener Conservation Award 7541
Frances Hubbs Miller Award 8898
Larry Morgotch Memorial Award 16040
NACD - ICI Americas Conservation District Awards 14156
NACD - ICI Americas Conservation Teacher Awards 14157
National Award for Media Excellence 15577
National Congressional Award 15578
National Corporate Humanitarian Award 15579
National Distinguished Professional Award 15580
National Literary Award 15582
National Voluntary Service Award 15583
National Wildlife Week Awards 7542
North American Conservation Award 4918
Camp Scholarships Carl Nunn Award 16763
Oak Leaf Award 16032
Olin Fellowships 6043
Outdoor Ethics Awards 12269
Outstanding Achievement Award 17988
Outstanding Journalist Award 6079
Past Presidents' Canadian Legislator Award 7543
Phoenix Award 19015
Douglas H. Pimlott Conservation Award 16028
President's Award 5637
President's Conservation Achievement Award 16033
President's Fishery Conservation Award 2256
President's Stewardship Award 16034
Joan Hodges Queneau Palladium Medal 1199
Polly Redford Memorial Award 6080
Tudor Richards Award 6084
William E. Ricker Resource Conservation Award 2257
Rs of Excellence 17921
Cliff Shaw Award 16041
Special Commendation Award 6081
Carl R. Sullivan Fishery Conservation Award 2260
Summer Fellowship 6674
Sustained Achievement Award 17989
M. N. "Mully" Taylor Award 20187
Arthur R. Thompson Memorial Award 12271
Trees for Tomorrow Award 20188
US/ICOMOS Fellows 20452
Volunteer Award 16029
Volunteer of the Year Award 16042
C. W. Watson Award 2262
Charles A. Weyerhaeuser Award 9697
Ralph C. Wilson Award 15585
World Rainforest Awards 17863

Construction (*See also* Architecture; Asphalt paving; Civil engineering; Concrete)
ABC Excellence in Construction Awards 5233
ACI Commemorative Lecture Series 1957
ACI Construction Award 1958
ACI Design Award 1959
ACI Fellows 1960
Arthur R. Anderson Award 1961
Apprenticeship Awards 20194
Associate Remodeler of the Year Award 14257
Award of Excellence 9279
Award of Merit 8996
Ron Baker Award 19799
Rudolph John Barnes Award 17603
Albert H. Baum Award 6678
Best Builder Award 5245
Best in American Living Awards 17598
Delmar L. Bloem Distinguished Service Award 1962
Bob Sawyer Award 8343
Robert F. Boger Award 8446
Robert P. Brosseau Memorial Award 8433
Builder and Associate of the Year 20179
Builder of the Year 17599
Builder's Choice Design and Planning Awards 6676
Building with Trees Awards of Excellence 13950
Carl E. Darrow Student Wood Design Competition 2855
Cesery Award 20089
Chainlink Fence Design Award 7790
Chapter Achievement Award 8997
Chapter Activities Award 1963
Chester Paul Siess Award for Excellence in Structural Research 1964
Concrete Achiever of the Year 107
Construction Excellence Award 7689
Construction Management Award 4309
Construction Person of the Year 21552
Continuing Publication Commendation 8434
Contractor of the Year Award
American Public Works Association 3800
Concrete Foundations Association 8344

Construction (continued)

Contractor of the Year Awards (CotY Awards) 14429
Roger H. Corbetta Concrete Constructor Award 1965
Joseph M. Corwin Award 5255
DCA Scholarship 8850
Degelleke Award 7690
Distinguished Chapter Award 5885
Distinguished Dealer of the Year 21540
Distinguished Service Award
Construction Specifications Institute 8435
Deep Foundations Institute 8792
Distributor of the Year Award 14430
Ernest Dobbelsteyn Memorial Trophy 7040
Electronic Innovation Commendation 8436
Engineering and Construction Contracting Division Award 2768
Engineering Excellence Awards 2009
Environmental Achievement Award 7041
Excellence in EIFS Construction 9189
Fellowship 8437
Henry Fenderbosch Leadership Award 14432
John Fies Award 11502
Fred Ford Award 19314
Founders' Memorial Award 8998
General Services Achievement Award 20544
Goddard Medal 18987
Gold Star Award 15468
Golden Trowel Award 11742
Government Affairs Award 14433
Gzowski Medal 7414
Harold Hammerman Spirit of Education Award 14434
George Baugh Heckel Award 15469
Honorary Member 1966
Honorary Membership 8438
J. Norman Hunter Memorial Award 8439
Industry Statesman Awards 15471
Peter H. Johnson Image Award 14435
Joe W. Kelly Award 1967
Henry L. Kennedy Award 1968
Walker S. Lee Award 6679
Lifetime Achievement 10520
Wilbur H. Lind Award 6680
Alfred E. Lindau Award 1969
Local Chapter Community Project Award 14436
Local Chapter Excellence Award 14437
A. J. (Jack) Lund Award 11503
Robert J. Lyman Award 17526
Frank M. Masters Transportation Engineering Award 4339
MCA Annual Merit Awards Program 13307
J. D. McNulty Award 5886
Merit Shop Award of Excellence in Construction 5236
Dale C. Moll Memorial Quality Management Award 8440
Montgomery Memorial Award 7042
MRCA Foundation Scholarship Grants 13398
National Housing Quality Award 17600
NOVA Award 8427
Organizational Certificate of Appreciation 8441
Outstanding Association Executive Award 5887
Outstanding Committee Chairman Award 5888
Outstanding Project Award 8793
Outstanding Regional Chairman Award 5889
Outstanding Regional Director 8999
Peltier Plaque 18993
Pinnacle Award 5890
Pollution Prevention Award 15472
President's Award 11910
President's Plaques 8442
Professional Achievement Awards 17601
Professional Development Awards 15754
Pyramid Awards 21471
Recognition of Service and Involvement 9000
Remodeler of the Month/Year Awards 14260
Renaissance Awards 14261
Research Award 21942
Frank E. Richart Award 5980
Phil Roberts Award 11504
Thomas Fitch Rowland Prize 4356
Robert G. Ryan Memorial Award 9001
Safety Award 16523
Safety Awards 15473
Robert G. Saunders Memorial Award 7043
Service Award 21943
Shields Medal 18996
Silver Hardhat Award 8450
Ben John Small Memorial Award 8443
Robert Stollery Award 7044
Student Liaison Award 8444
Superintendent of the Year Award 7691
Supplier Member of the Year Award 5891
Surveying and Mapping Award 4360
Sanford E. Thompson Award 5992
Jake Thygesen Membership Award 7045
John Trimmer Merit Shop Teaching Award of Excellence 5234
Henry C. Turner Medal 1970
Unsung Hero Award 5892
Nelson VanderHyden Award 21472
M. C. Vaughan Scholarship Fund 4715
Vinyl Siding Institute Awards of Distinction 19323
Vinyl Window and Door Institute Awards for Outstanding Performance 19324
Walter C. Voss Award 5996
Hugh T. Warren Award 19325
Wason Medal for Materials Research 1971
Wason Medal for the Most Meritorious Paper 1972
Gordon M. Waters Distinguished Service Award 7611
Charles S. Whitney Medal 1973
Cedric Willson Award 1974
Winning Spirit Award 5893
Women's Advocate Award 9521
Wood Design Awards 21821
Young Member Achievement Award 5894

Consulting

ACF Public Service Award 5645
Awards of Excellence 5639
Beaubien Award 5640
Engineering Excellence Awards 2009
Fellows Distinguished Award of Merit 2010
Green Award 9667
Manuscript Award 11708
Merit Award 5641
Niles Newton Memorial Award for Outstanding Achievement in Human Lactation 11709
PEPP Chairman's Award 15751
Public Service Award 5642
QBS Award 15755
Schreyer Award 5643
Service Award 9668
Trendsetter Award 9669

Consumer affairs

ACCI Thesis/Dissertation Award 2045
Achievement in Consumer Education Awards 14162
Agency of the Year Award 14163
Applied Consumer Economics Award 2046
Best Subscriber Communication Program 15859
Commemorative Lecture Award 939
Consumer Involvement Award 7267
Consumer Journalism Award 15515
Samuel J. Crumbine Consumer Protection Award 9665
Customer Service Excellence Award 1274
Margaret Dana Award 5942
Design and Engineering Exhibition Award 9211
Distinguished Fellows Award 2047
Russell A. Dixon Award 2048
Excellence in Extension Award 940
Florence Faligatter Distinguished Service Award 17255
Robert Ferber Award for Consumer Research 12446
Friend of Consumers Award 2049
Betty Furness Consumer Media Service Award 8460
Philip Hart Public Service Award 8461
ICSA Award of Excellence 11534
Florence Kelley Consumer Leadership Award 14733
Stewart M. Lee Consumer Education Award 2050
Mid Career Award 2051
Esther Peterson Consumer Service Award
Consumer Federation of America 8462
Food Marketing Institute 9662
Public Affairs Competition 1276
Teacher of the Year Award 944
Trumpeter Award 14734
Harvey W. Wiley Award 4992
Wiley-Berger Award for Volunteer Service 945
WORDS/ISAAC Outstanding Consumer User Lecture Award 11921

Conventions

Best Trade Show Product and Best Booth Display 6167
Lloyb Bobby Chapter of the Year Award 8429
Convention Service Manager of the Year 19822
Meeting Facility of the Year 12005
Meeting Planner of the Year 5329
National Award of Merit 8430
New Product Showcase Award 3372
Outstanding Regional Chairman Award 5889
Pinnacle Awards for Convention and Visitor Bureaus 19823
Pinnacle Awards for Hotels/Resorts 19824
Program Directors' Award 8431

Cookbook writing

The James Beard Foundation Book Awards 12285
The James Beard Foundation/Cervena Council/D'Artagnan Who's Who of Food and Beverage in America 12286

Cookbook (continued)

Cooking *See* Food

Copyright
Nathan Burkan Memorial Competition 4379

Corrosion engineering
R. A. Brannon Award 13742
A. B. Campbell Award 13743
Distinguished Service Award 13744
T. J. Hull Award 13745
Francis L. LaQue Memorial Award 5965
Frank Newman Speller Award 13746
Technical Achievement Award 13747
Sam Tour Award 5994
Willis Rodney Whitney Award 13748

Cosmetology
American Image Enhancement Award 14741
Best Black/Gray Back Piece 15836
Best Black/Gray Tattoo 15837
Best Black/White Design Sheet 15838
Best Colored Back Piece 15839
Best Colored Design Sheet 15840
Best Cover-Up Tattoo 15841
Best Large Tatoo/Female 15842
Best Large Tattoo/Male 15843
Best Portrait Tattoo 15844
Best Sleeve 15845
Best Tattooed Female 15846
Best Tattooed Male 15847
Best Tattooist 15848
Best Traditional Tattoo 15849
Best Unique Tattoo 15850
Bob Show Golden Age Award 15851
Conference Coordinator Award 11663
District Representatives Award 11664
Emmy Awards for Primetime Programming 127
Female Style Maker of the Year 14742
Fifth Sense Commendation 9719
Fine Art Award 15852
Founder and First President Award 11665
Fragrance Foundation Recognition Awards (FIFI Awards) 9720
Make-Up Competition 245
Male Style Maker of the Year 14743
Medal of Honor 9721
Dr. Michel Award 11666
Most Realistic Tattoo 15853
Nicest Studio Award 15854
Officers Medallion 11667
Olfactory Research Fund Sense of Smell Award 9722
Outgoing Officer Award 11668
Saturn Awards 123
Jack Stein Make-up Award 16129
Elizabeth Weinzirl Award 15855
WINBA Championship Title 21928

Costume design
Emmy Awards for Primetime Programming 127
American Theatre Wing's Henry Hewes Design Awards 4741
Antoinette Perry Awards (Tony Awards) 12742
Saturn Awards 123
Theatre Grants 17555

Counseling
AASECT Award 1423
ACA Extended Research Award 2064
ACA Legislative Service Award 2065
ACA Professional Development Award 2066
ACA Research Award 2067
AFA Perspectives Award 5691
Jack L. Anson Award 5692
Ralph F. Berdie Memorial Research Award 2068
John D. Black Award for Outstanding Achievement in the Practice of Counseling Psychology 3661
Kitty Cole Human Rights Award 2069
Collegiate Advisor Award 17254
Counselor Educator of the Year 3087
Counselor of the Year 3088
Counselor of the Year Award 15603
Distinguished Service Award 5693
Arthur A. Hitchcock Distinguished Professional Service Award 2070
Glen E. Hubele National Graduate Student Award 2071
Fritz and Linn Kuder Early Career Scientist/Practitioner Award 3664
Local, State Branch, and Regional Award 2072
NACADA Student Research Award 13768
National Citation Awards 15604
National Distinguished Service Award 15605
NRCA Fellow 15606
Outstanding Advising Awards 13769
Outstanding Advising Program Awards 13770
Outstanding School Psychological Services in Public Schools Award 3711
Pacesetter Award 13771
PSCA Graduate Student Scholarship 17190
Harley B. Reger Memorial Award 15607
Researcher of the Year 3089
Service to NACADA Award 13772
Robert H. Shaffer Award 5694
Leona Tyler Award 3666

Country music
Academy of Country Music Awards 86
American Heritage Award 15895
America's Old-Time Country Music Hall of Fame 15896
America's Old-Time Fiddler's Hall of Fame 15897
AMOA Jukebox Awards 4945
Bluegrass Music Awards 18879
Canadian Country Music Association's Citation Awards 7064
Country Music Association Awards 8620
Country Music Hall of Fame 8621
Grammy Awards 13822
Hall of Fame 8623
IFCO Tex Ritter Award 11576
Juno Awards 6846
Life-Time Membership Award 8624
Nashville Songwriters Association International Awards 13760
National Traditional Music Performer Award 15898

Crafts
American Craft Council Fellows 2076
American Needlepoint Guild Literary Award 3190
Artists' Fellowships 16229
Aurora Award 8981
Awards of Distinction 2077
Beck Scholarship Fund 7890
Best of Show 9597
Boynton's G.A.L.A. Artist Awards 6594
Saidye Bronfman Award for Excellence in the Crafts 6647
Helen Bullard Scholarship 15261
Cake Show Competition Plaques 7494
Certificates of Excellence 10228
William and Mary Corcoran Craft Awards 16739
Crafts National Exhibition 7774
Decorative Arts Collection Awards 19097
Dedicated Service Award 19098
Rolf Ericson's Award for Outstanding Doll Sculpture 8982
Eva's Choice Award 8983
Excellence in Craft Awards 16968
Family International Talent Awards Program 17088
Robert Fleming Prize 6793
Florida Folk Heritage Awards 9626
Folk Heritage Award 16503
Gilpin County Arts Association Annual Exhibition 10028
Gold Medal 2078
HGA Award 10229
Hoyt Mid Atlantic Art Show 10573
Individual Artist Fellowship
Montana Arts Council 13586
Ohio Arts Council 16628
International Juried Show 16164
International Old Lacers Contest 11773
Kaleidoscope - A Fair of the Arts 7816
Lee Kirschner-Lewis Study Grant 16564
Magge Award 8984
Pauline McGibbon Award 16744
Medal for Excellence in Craft Award 19029
Millie Award 8985
National Exhibition of Weaving in the Norwegian Tradition 21317
National Exhibition of Woodworking in the Norwegian Tradition 21318
National Heritage Fellowships 14932
Patron Honor Award 15262
Saidye Bronfman Award 6808
Silver Palette Award 19099
Smithsonian Craft Show 18574
Pat Stall Memorial Award 15263
Aileen Osborn Webb Award 2079

Craftsmanship
Certificate of Craftsmanship 13175

Creative writing
Arts Recognition and Talent Search (ARTS) 15117
Omer Lutfi Barkan Article Prize 20239
Black Caucus of the American Library Association Literary Awards 6413
Richard Braddock Award 8375
Alice C. Browning Award 11420
Cavendish Area Tourist Association Creative Writing Award for Children 17545
CCCC Exemplar Award 8376
CCCC Outstanding Book Award 8378
William L. Crawford Fantasy Award 11259
Edgar Dale Award 7949
Dobie-Paisano Writing Fellowships 20014
Family International Talent Awards Program 17088
Virginia Faulkner Award for Excellence in Writing 17511

Creative (continued)
Sydney N. Fisher Graduate Student Paper Prize 20241
Gaston-Gouin, Alfred-DesRochers et Alphonse-Desjardins 5263
Grand Concours Litteraire 18232
Howard Fellows 10571
Implications of Research for Educational Practice 5500
Individual Artist Fellowship 16628
Orinne Johnson Writing Award 17257
M. Fuat Koprulu Book Prize 20242
Herb Lampert Student Writing Award 7382
Lesbian Caucus Prize 15968
Literary Awards 17152
Loft Creative Nonfiction Award 12904
Hugh J. Luke Award 17514
Pete McGillen Award 16972
McKnight Artist Fellowships for Writers 12906
Jenny McKean Moore Writer-in-Washington 13610
Morguard Literary Award 17900
National Magazine Awards 15355
National Outdoor Book Awards 15465
Outdoor Communications Awards 16973
Readers' Choice Awards 17515
James W. Redhouse Student Prize 20243
Eliot Rosewater Indiana High School Book Award 5387
Philip Shehadi New Writers Award 13379
Sidewise Awards for Alternate History 18444
Bernice Slote Award 17516
Wallace E. Stegner Fellowships in Creative Writing 8647
Bram Stoker Awards 10549
Robert W. Wagner Narrative Screenwriting Award 7953
Writing Awards 378

Crime prevention
Donald R. Cressey Memorial Award 5594
DEA Explorer Drug Abuse Prevention Service Award 6574
Gang Prevention Scholarship 20190
Gold and Silver Shield Awards 12318
G.O.O.D. for You Award 9869
G.O.O.D. Friendship Award 9870
ISCPP National Law Enforcement Explorer Community Crime Prevention Award 6583
James B. White JSA Award 12319
Margaret Mead Award 11500
OA Medal 16919
Shared Vision Award 16082
Morris R. Walker Memorial Award 5595

Crime writing *See* Mystery writing

Criminology (*See also* Law enforcement; Crime prevention; Prisons; Victims)
Academy Fellow 88
Anderson Student Paper Award 89
Herbert Bloch Award 4384
E. R. Cass Correctional Achievement Award 2022
Corrections Film Festival 2024
Exemplary Offender Program Award 2025
Founder's Award 90
Sellin - Glueck Award 4385
Robert C. Heeney Memorial Award 14185
Peter P. Lejins Research Award 2027
Man of the Year in Law Enforcement 19271
Herman Mannheim Award 11458
Medal of Valor Award 2028
Outstanding Book Award 91
Presidential Commendation 14186
Irwin R. Rutman Award 19272
William L. Simon/Anderson Publishing Outstanding Paper Award 92
Bruce Smith Sr. Award 93
Edwin H. Sutherland Award 4386
August Vollmer Award 4387

Culinary arts *See* Food

Culture (*See also* African studies; Asian studies; Ethnic affairs; Folklore; Islamic culture; Mythology; Native Americans; specific cultural groups, e.g. African American culture)
Academy & Achievement Awards 80
Dr. Tajuddin Ahmed Book Publication Award 12230
Annual Caribbean Review Award 7594
Brooke Russell Astor Award 16253
Bet Nahrain National Awards 6317
Bode - Pearson Prize 4706
Breakfast of Champions 16558
Cultural Award 17907
Cultural Development Fund 5151
Cultural Diversity Outreach Award 3823
Distinguished Contribution to Social Justice Award 2216
Halide Edib Adivar Scholarship Citation 20240
Ehrenstein Award 9980
Essay Competition 12231
Excellence in the Arts Award 21360
Ann Flagg Multicultural Award 891
John Hope Franklin Publication Prize 4708
Ralph Henry Gabriel Dissertation Prize 4709
Gale/EMIERT Multicultural Award 2962
Global Citizenship Award 21083
Gold Awards 16996
Gold Medal 2871
Governor's Award for Distinguished Achievement in the Arts 10294
Honorary Service Awards 4955
Howard Christensen Award 21823
Lifetime Achievement Award 3900
Abraham Lincoln Award 2594
National Magazine Awards 15355
Ohioana Pegasus Award 16664
Jacqueline Kennedy Onassis Medal 13680
Order of Ontario 16757
Outstanding Lithuanian Woman Award 12876
Outstanding Promotion Award 9518
Parmalee Scholarship 11688
Presidential Medal of Freedom 9364
Prix Gerard-Morisset 17796
Quran Recitation 12228
Carl A. Ross Student Paper Award 5001
Salvatori Teaching Award 10437
Travel Grants to Students Coming to USA from Developing Countries 12232
Vilis Vitols Award 5481
Cratis D. Williams/James S. Brown Service Award 5002
Gene Wise - Warren Susman Prize 4712
World Citizen 11692

Cybernetics
ASC Recognition Award 3985
Warren Sturgis McCulloch Award 3986
Norbert Wiener Medal 3987

Cycling *See* Bicycling

Dairy industry
American Feed Industry Association Award 2097
Award of Honor 2098
Sam Beadleston Memorial Award 3111
Donald H. Cande Memorial Trophy 3112
Cargill Animal Nutrition Young Scientist Award 2099
DeLaval, Inc. Dairy Extension Award 2100
Distinguished Service Award 2101
Distinguished Young Couple 13478
Gain Program Awards 3114
Guest of Honor Award 14892
W. J. Hardy Awards 3115
National Milk Producers Federation - Richard M. Hoyt Award 2102
International Dairy Foods Association Research Award 2103
International Dairy Production Award 2104
Land O'Lakes, Inc. 2105
Land O'Lakes/Purina Teaching Award in Dairy Production 2106
Longtime Meritorious Service 13479
Marschall Rhodia Award 2108
Irving Meyer Memorial Award 3116
Milk Industry Foundation and Kraft General Foods Teaching Award in Dairy Science 2109
National Milk Producers Federation Graduate Student Paper Presentation Contest 2110
Nutrition Professionals, Inc. Applied Dairy Nutrition Award 2111
Person of the Year 13480
Pioneer Award 14893
Pioneer Hi-Bred Forage Award 2113
Protein Awards 3117
Lillian B. Wood Rowe & John O. Rowe Citizen of the Year Award 3118
Scholarship Award 10761
W. Arthur Simpson Memorial Award 3119
West Agro, Inc. Award 2114
W. C. Wood Memorial Trophy 3120

Dance (*See also* Ballet; Choreography)
ADG Award for Outstanding Achievement in Dance 2119
William G. Anderson Merit Award 876
Arts Recognition and Talent Search (ARTS) 15117
Award of Artistry 2120
Balasaraswati/Joy Ann Dewey Beinecke Chair for Distinguished Teaching 2116
CALLERLAB Milestone Award 6771
Estelle Campbell Award 15730
Capezio Dance Award 7575
Choreography and Flamenco Dance Competition 9227
Dance Grants 17553
Dance Magazine Annual Awards 8736
Dance/USA National Honors 8747
Distinguished Service Award 8742
DMA Annual Award 8738
DMA President's Award 8739
Peter Dwyer Scholarships 6792
El Angel Award - Distinguished Hispanic-American Artist 6374

Dance (continued)

Emmy Awards for Primetime Programming 127
Fanny Award 9373
Fellowship Program 17168
Mary Perry Fife Memorial Award 15732
Gold Medal of Honor for Dance 13986
Grants for Arts Projects 14930
Luther Halsey Gulick Award 877
Heritage Award 14895
Honor Award 879
K. M. Hunter Artists Awards 16742
Individual Artist Fellowship 13586
Juno Awards 6846
Jury Prize for the Dance on Camera Festival 8734
K-12 Dance Educator of the Year 14896
Kennedy Center Honors 12552
Mabel Lee Award 880
Jacqueline Lemieux Prize 6801
Member of the Year Award 8740
Music Center Spotlight Awards 13698
National Ballet of Canada School Scholarship 21780
National Society of Arts and Letters First Place Award 15733
New York Dance and Performance Awards (Bessie Awards) 8745
Mollie Davis Nicholson Award 15734
Outstanding Student Recognition Awards 14897
Scholar/Artist Award 14898
Ben Sommers Award 8743
State of Florida Fellowship 9589
Dorothy and Bruce Strong Award 15735
Student Literary Award 14899

Data base management *See* Information management

Data processing *See* Computer science

Deafness (*See also* Speech and hearing)

Able ALDA Award 5747
ALDA Angel Award 5748
Athlete of the Year 21164
Award of Merit
Deafness Research Foundation 8777
Jewish Deaf Congress 12344
Alexander Graham Bell Award 432
Alexander Graham Bell DHHS Youth Achievement Award (Deaf and Hard of Hearing Section) 433
Alexander Graham Bell Honors 434
Alexander Graham Bell Volta Award 435
Bellfasher Award 179
Glen Bollinger Humanitarian Award 10352
Laura Bridgman Memorial Award 1459
CISS Medallions of Honor 11494
Deaf/Hard of Hearing Entrepreneur of the Year 8775
Deafness Research Foundation Otological Research Fellowship for Medical Students 8778
Grants for Otologic and Related Science Research Projects 8779
Hall of Fame 21165
Phillip Hanover Memorial Recognition Award 12345
Bob Hawley Fearless Leader Award 5749
Outstanding Article Award 180
Henry and Anna Papinger Endowment Award 12346
Rubens-Alcais Challenge 11495
Frederick C. Schreiber Award 181
Celia Warshawsky Award 12347
Boyce R. Williams Award 182
Youth Achievement Awards 436

Democracy *See* Freedom

Demography

Global Media Awards for Excellence in Population Reporting 17469
John Brinckerhoff Jackson Prize 5556
Statistics New Zealand/Jacoby Prize 12841
United Nations Population Award 20368

Dental research

Award in Geriatric Oral Research 11203
Behavioral Science and Health Service Research Award 11204
Biological Mineralization Research Award 11205
Clinical Research Award in Periodontology 802
Craniofacial Biology Research Award 11206
H. Trendley Dean Memorial Award 11207
William J. Gies Foundation Award in Memory of Arthur Hastings Merritt 804
Gold Medal Award 805
Louis I. Grossman Award 1192
Edward H. Hatton Awards Competition for Junior Investigators 11208
Pulp Biology Research Award 11209
Research in Dental Caries Award 11210
Research in Oral Biology Award 11211
Research in Periodontal Disease Award 11212
Research in Prosthodontics and Implants Award 11213
R. Earl Robinson Periodontal Regeneration Award 810
Roerig Fellow in Hospital Dental Practice 1237
Salivary Research Award 11214
Bernard G. Sarnat Award in Craniofacial Biology 11215
Bernard G. Sarnat Prize 11220
Carl A. Schlack Award 5782
David B. Scott Student Research Fellowship 11216
Wilmer Souder Award 11217
Student Awards 1478
Stanley D. Tylman Research Grant Program 678
Young Investigators Award 11218

Dentistry (*See also* Dental research; History of dentistry; Orthodontistry)

Achievement Award
Alpha Omega International Dental Fraternity 486
American Equilibration Society 2199
American Academy of Periodontology Student Award 801
Award for Special Service to Hospital Dentistry 1235
The Award of Distinction 95
Award of Excellence 115
Award of Merit 1853
Elmer S. Best Memorial Award 17345
Buonocore Memorial Lecturer 116
Lester Burket Award 734
Certificate of Honor 3908
Certificate of Merit 17346
Lawrence J. Chasko Award 1236
Citizen of the Year 1182
Clinical Research Award in Periodontology 802
Colgate-Palmolive Research Scholarship Award 1482
Committee Man of the Year 1309
Community Preventive Dentistry Award 2127
Edgar D. Coolidge Award 1191
Dannon Institute Award for Excellence in Medical/Dental Nutrition Education 3957
Dental Student Award 726
Dental Trade and Industry Award of Recognition 17347
Dentist of the Year 13532
Distinguished Fellowship 96
Distinguished Service 13533
Distinguished Service Award
American Association of Oral and Maxillofacial Surgeons 1310
American College of Dentists 1854
Distinguished Service Citation 17348
F. Gene Dixon, DDS Leadership Award 8863
Pierre Fauchard Academy Bronze Service Citation 17349
Pierre Fauchard Academy Plaque 17350
Fauchard Gold Medal 17351
Hillel Feldman Award 3909
Fellow 803
Alfred C. Fones Award 2130
Foundation Clinical Surgery Fellowship 1311
Foundation Research Award 1312
Geriatric Oral Health Care Award 2128
William John Gies Award 1855
Herschfus Memorial Award 735
The Hillenbrand Award 97
Hirsh Award 1878
Hollenback Memorial Prize 117
Honorary Fellow 736
Honorary Fellowship
Academy of Dentistry International 98
American College of Dentists 1856
Honorary Member
American Academy of Periodontology 806
Pierre Fauchard Academy 17352
Sigma Phi Alpha 18487
The Humanitarian Award 99
International Dentist of the Year 100
William S. Kramer Award of Excellence 16704
Leverett Graduate Student Merit Award for Outstanding Achievement in Dental Public Health 1392
Master Clinician Award 807
Membership in Omicron Kappa Upsilon 16705
Meritorious Service Award 487
Samuel Charles Miller Memorial Lecture Award 737
Dr. Richard L. Moore Distinguished Service Award 3348
Thelma J. Neff Distinguished Service Award 470
Balint Orban Prize 808
Edward M. Osetek Educator Award 1193
Outstanding Student Award 3068
Presidential Award 809
Abraham Reiner Diamond Pin Award 738
Research Recognition Award 16804
Resident Research Award 16805

Dentistry (continued)

Scientific Award 1238
Scientific Investigation and Research Award 2200
David B. Scott Student Research Fellowship 11216
Ralph F. Sommer Award 1194
Wilmer Souder Award 11217
Special Citations 811
Beulah K. Spencer Award 471
Student Awards 1478
Student Research Training Award 16806
Undergraduate Certificate of Merit 17353

Dermatology
ACDS Mentoring Award 2012
Mohamed Amer Award 8187
Nelson Paul Anderson Award 17005
Award for Young Investigators 636
Award of Merit 7073
Career Development Award in Skin Research 8891
Castellani - Reiss Medal and Award 11990
Fellowship and Grant Award Program 8892
Alexander A. Fisher Resident Award 2013
Everett C. Fox, M.D. Memorial Lectureship 637
Lila Gruber Memorial Cancer Research Award and Lectureship 638
Howard Maibach Travel Award 2014
Alvin H. Jacobs Award 778
Clarence S. Livingood Lectureship 639
Pediatric Dermatology Fellows/Residents Research Award 18831
Pediatric Dermatology Research Grant 18832
President's Cup 7074
Marion B. Sulzberger Memorial Award and Lectureship 640
Barney Usher Award 7075
Young Dermatologists' Volunteer Award 7076
Samuel J. Zakon Lectureship 10474
Samuel J. Zakon Prize 10475

Design (*See also* Art; Architecture; Book and newspaper design; Costume design; Fiber science; Fashion; Graphic arts; Industrial design; Interior design; Jewelry design; Lighting design; Set design; Textile design)
William C. Ackermann Medal for Excellence in Water Management 4822
ACTF Awards for Theatrical Design Excellence 12539
AIBD Design Competition 2743
Walter C. Alvarez Memorial Award 3081
American Graphic Design Awards 10139
Annual Exhibitions 5115
Art Directors Awards 5116
ASFD Life-Time Achievement Award 4410
Awards for Achievement in Arc Welded Design, and Engineering and Fabrication 12851
Awards Program 2132
Best in American Living Awards 14258
Best Kids Menu Competition 18010
Best of Collegiate Design 8168
Brewster Award for Creative Ingenuity 6616
CA Design Annual 8309
Citations of Merit 13984
Design Award 303
Design for Humanity Award 4460
Distinguished Designer Award 4411
Excellence in Highway Design Awards 20559
Financial Post Design Effectiveness Awards 8538
Gold Medal of Honor for Design 13987
Good Poster Award 11583
Grand International Trophy for Excellence of Design and Fabric 14745
Grants for Arts Projects 14930
Harold Hammerman Spirit of Education Award 14434
Major Harrelson Service Award 14746
American Theatre Wing's Henry Hewes Design Awards 4741
Honorary Member 4412
Ice Carving Classic 15628
ID Annual Design Review 10636
Individual Artist Fellowship 16628
Institute Honors for Collaborative Achievements 2718
International Achievement Awards Competition 10784
International Aluminum Extrusion Design Competition 513
International Awards of Excellence 5815
International Designer Awards 11314
International Greeting Card Awards (Louie Awards) 10174
International Society for Education through Art Awards 11930
Martin P. Korn Award 17525
Loeb Fellowship 10281
Management Award 5118
Pauline McGibbon Award 16744
Fred Merryfield Design Award 4029
Mobius Advertising Awards 21142
National, City and Regional Magazine Editorial and Design Awards 8024
National Magazine Awards 4492
National Paperboard Packaging Competition 17064
NEA/TCG Career Development Program for Designers 20052
New York Dance and Performance Awards (Bessie Awards) 8745
Antoinette Perry Awards (Tony Awards) 12742
Pinnacle Design Achievement Award 4413
Quilt National Awards 8709
Rome Prize Fellowships 605
Sign Design Competition 11905
Spur Awards 21576
Sunkist Young Designer Award 4237
Toronto Arts Awards 20112
USOC Sports Equipment Student Design Contest 20725
The Village Voice OBIE Awards 21368
Vision Award 5119
Philip L. Walker Jr. Award 1649
Whitaker Senior Student Bioengineering Design Awards 6391
Woolknit Design Awards 21832
Henry R. Worthington Medal 4554

Dietetics *See* Nutrition

Diplomacy *See* International relations

Diving
Age Group Diving Coach of the Year 21167
All American Dive Team 20294
Athlete Service Award 21168
Phil Boggs Award 21169
Dr. Charlie Brown Memorial Award 14449
Steve Gerrad Outstanding Service Award 14002
Leonard Greenstone Diving Safety Award 14450
Mike Malone Memorial Diving Award 21170
Charles McCaffree Award 8195
Mike Peppe Award 21171
Phillips Performance Award 21172
Reaching Out Award - Diving Hall of Fame 8967
Regional Diver of the Year Award 20296
Service Awards 14451
Richard Steadman Award 8197

Diving safety *See* Water safety

Divorce *See* Family relations

Documentary films
ACE Eddie Award 1804
Atlanta Film and Video Festival 6025
Chicago International Film Festival 8001
Christopher Columbus Award 7947
Columbus International Film and Video Festival 7948
Fellowship for Creative and Performing Arts and Writers 914
Golden Sheaf Awards 22048
Golden Space Needle Audience Awards 18395
Humboldt International Film Festival 10610
International Documentary Association Achievement Awards 11541
International Emmy Award 11519
Nashville Film Festival 13758
News and Documentary Emmy Awards 13863
OSU Photography and Cinema Alumni Society Award 7951
Philadelphia International Film Festival (Philafilm Awards) 468
President's Award 7952
SHINE (Sexual Health in Entertainment) Awards 13238
Spur Awards 21576
Western Heritage Awards (Wrangler Award) 14887
David L. Wolper Student Documentary Achievement Award 11542
WORLDFEST - Houston International Film and Video Festival 21969

Dogs *See* Animal care and training

Drama (*See also* Drama criticism; Theater)
AATE Distinguished Book Award 883
AATE Research Award 884
ACTF Musical Theatre Award 12540
Maxwell Anderson Playwrights Series Prize 19740
Anisfield-Wolf Book Awards 8097
Annual Awards Competition 8565
Ruby Lloyd Apsey Playwriting Award 20977
Artists' Fellowships 16229
St. Clair Bayfield Award 165
Campton Bell Lifetime Achievement Award 887

Drama (continued)

Beverly Hills Theatre Guild Play Competition for Children's Theatre 6349
Susan Smith Blackburn Prize 19854
Elmer Holmes Bobst Literary Awards 16301
CAA Carol Bolt Award 6952
Waldo M. and Grace C. Bonderman IUPUI Youth Theatre Playwriting Competition and Workshop 10777
Bush Artist Fellows Program 6700
Butler Literary Award 12194
Joe A. Callaway Award 166
Estelle Campbell Award 15730
John Cauble Short Play Award 12541
Charlotte Festival/New Plays in America 7812
Charlotte B. Chorpenning Playwright Award 888
Columbia Pictures Television Playwriting Award 12542
Creative Drama Award 889
David Library of the American Revolution Award for Playwriting on American Freedom 12543
Dayton Playhouse Future Fest 8762
Clarence Derwent Award 167
DFAP National One-Act Playwriting Contest 9035
Distinguished Play Awards 890
Drama Desk Awards 9018
Drama League's Distinguished Performance Award 9020
S. Randolph Edmonds Playwriting Award 14200
Emmy Awards for Primetime Programming 127
Norma Epstein Foundation Awards 21112
Fellowship for Creative and Performing Arts and Writers 914
Fellowship Program 17168
Fellowships for Playwrights 18433
Festival of Emerging American Theatre New Plays Competition 17279
Festival of Firsts Playwriting Competition 19837
Ann Flagg Multicultural Award 891
FMCT Playwrights Competition 9414
Freedom Forum Playwriting Award 12544
Fund for New American Plays 12550
Gold Medal of Honor for Theater/Drama 13990
Gold Ribbon for Promotion of Canadian Talent (Radio) 6895
Golden Globe Awards 10513
H. W. Nelson Award 10209
James K. Hackett Award 8031
Lorraine Hansberry Playwriting Award 12545
Julie Harris Playwright Award Competition 6350
Elizabeth Hull - Kate Warriner Award 9024
International Playwrights' Competition 18448
Jerome Fellowships 17398
Kennedy Center Honors 12552
Kentucky Artists Fellowships 12562
Kesselring Prize 13992
Eric Kocher Playwrights Award 15507
Letras de Oro Literary Prizes 21059
Lifetime Achievement Award 14201
Little Theatre of Alexandria National One-Act Playwriting Competition 12888
Love Creek Mini Festival 12962
Love Creek Short Play Festival 12963
Pauline McGibbon Award 16744
McKnight Advancement Grants 17399
Mixed Blood versus America 13545
NADSA Outstanding Service Award 14202
NADSA Research Award 14203
NADSA Scholar Award 14204
National Federation Citations 14978
National Playwrights Conference and New Drama for Media Project 15508
National Playwriting Competition 16959
National Society of Arts and Letters First Place Award 15733
National Student Playwriting Award 12546
National Ten-Minute Play Contest 172
Neustadt International Prize for Literature 21934
Mollie Davis Nicholson Award 15734
O'Neill Awards 15509
George Oppenheimer/*Newsday* Playwriting Award 16322
Outstanding Playwright for Year 9907
Mildred and Albert Panowski Playwriting Award 18081
Peace Play Contest 10095
PEN/Laura Pels Foundation Awards for Drama 17145
James D. Phelan Literary Award 18251
Robert J. Pickering Award for Playwriting Excellence 8128
PlayLabs Festival 17400
PNWA Literary Contest 17011
Promising Playwright Award 8205
Pulitzer Fellowships 17748
Pulitzer Prizes 17749
Sir Walter Raleigh Award for Fiction 16520
Retreat Alumni Fellowship 18434
Paul Robeson Citation Award 168
Ruby Yoshino Schaar Biennium Playwright Award 12306
Screen Awards 21993
Screenplay Contest 15995
Dorothy Silver Playwriting Competition 10226
Dorothy Silver Playwriting Competition Prize 12336
Jean Kennedy Smith Playwriting Award 12548
Space Coast Writers Guild Conference Awards 19535
Harold and Mimi Steinberg Prize 15510
Dorothy and Bruce Strong Award 15735
Theater P.E.I. Playwriting Awards 17549
Theatre Grants 17555
Tilden Canadian Literary Awards 7000
Towngate Theatre National Playwriting Contest 16620
Vermont Playwrights Award 21269
Very Special Arts Playwright Discovery Program 21413
The Village Voice OBIE Awards 21368
Lila Wallace-Reader's Digest Writers' Awards 21430
Winifred Ward & Award for Outstanding New Children's Theatre & Company 894
Theodore Ward Prize for Playwriting 8227
L. Arnold Weissberger Playwriting Award 16097
Whiting Writers' Award 21610
WORLDFEST - Houston International Film and Video Festival 21969
AATE Lin Wright Special Recognition Award 897
Writer's Digest Writing Competition 21979
Year End Series Festival of New Plays 16554
Young Playwrights Festival 22069
Youth Theatre Director of the Year Award 898

Drama criticism
George Jean Nathan Award for Dramatic Criticism 13764

Drawing (*See also* Cartoons; Graphic arts; Illustration)
Affaire in the Gardens 8035
Annual Open Exhibition 5121
Annual Open Juried Exhibition 17103
Artists' Fellowships 16229
The Artist's Magazine Art Competition 5146
Boynton's G.A.L.A. Artist Awards 6594
Bush Artist Fellows Program 6700
Cape Cod Art Association Awards 7571
Gladys Emerson Cook Prize 13785
Hall of Fame 17104
International Art Show by Artists with Disabilities 18536
Kentucky Artists Fellowships 12562
LaGrange National 7817
Master Pastelist 17105
National Society of Artists Awards 15728
New Mexico Juried Exhibition 13689
Prints, Drawings and Photographs Exhibition 5071
Prix de West Invitational Exhibition 14886
Signature Membership 17106
Southwest Juried Exhibition 13690

Drug addiction
Janssen Research Award 607
Lamplighter of the Year 14855
Medical Student and Resident Travel Stipend 608
National Recognition Award 14959
Wyeth Young Psychopharmacologist Award 3766

Early childhood education
District Award 17079
Abigail Eliot Award 6517
Dina Feitelson Research Award 11855
Honorary Life Membership 17080
International Award 17081
National Award for Demonstrated Leadership 17082

Earth science *See* Geology and paleontology; Seismology

East European culture
Academic Year Grant Program 11062
American Council of Learned Societies Fellowships 2037
Baltic Freedom Award
Baltic American Freedom League 6228
Joint Baltic American National Committee 12426
Distinguished Contributions to Slavic Studies Award 1054
Freedom Award 157
Ed A. Hewett Prize 1055
Barbara Jelavich Prize 1056
Orbis Books Prize for Polish Studies 1057
Research Assistantships 21036
Marshall Shulman Book Prize 1058

East (continued)

Slovak Studies Association Prize 18558
Wayne S. Vucinich Prize 1059

Ecology (*See also* Nature; Recycling)
$500,000 Lemelson-MIT Prize 12777
Rupert Barneby Award 16213
Blue Heron, Green Heron 18423
E. Lucy Braun Award 9131
Murray F. Buell Award 9132
Chief of Engineers Design and Environmental Awards Program 20405
W. S. Cooper Award 9133
Corporate Award 9134
Distinguished Service Citation 9135
Ecological Award 13998
Ecological Section Award 6545
Eminent Ecologist 9136
Anne Hanes Natural History Award 16928
Honorary Member
Ecological Society of America 9137
Ottawa Field-Naturalists' Club 16929
Robert H. MacArthur Award 9138
George McGee Service Award 16930
Member of the Year 16931
George Mercer Award 9139
James R. Mildon Award 10924
Nanette LaCross Memorial Prize 21063
National Kind Teacher Award 14016
Leo Parizeau Prize in Biology 5540
President's Prize 16932
Stoye Awards 4455
Summer Paid Internships 20594
Tyler Prize for Environmental Achievement 4975

Economic development
Achievement Awards 14165
Ally Award 16774
Award for Academic Excellence in Global Awareness 5896
Business Excellence Award 16775
Harry Chapin Self-Reliance Award 21926
CIDA Awards for Professionals 7006
City Livability Awards Program 20456
Collaborative Community Award 16546
Cecil B. Currey Book-Length Publications Award 5898
Director's Award 12624
Distinguished Service Award 12625
Economic Developer Award 16776
Economic Development Volunteer 12762
German Marshall Fund of the United States Fellowships and Awards 9974
Jefferson Award 8016
Jobs Award 16777
Robert S. McNamara Fellowships Program 21867
Outstanding Business Leader Awards 16573
President's Award 12626
Dr. Lawrence Dunbar Reddick Memorial Scholarship Award 5900
Richard A. Snelling Economic Development Award 5246
Ten Outstanding Young Americans 20678
Udall Center Prize in American Indian Public Policy 20984

Economic education
Certificate for Outstanding Service 15675
Education and Training Awards 5713
Heinz Award in Technology, the Economy and Employment 10379
Herman Lay Memorial Award 5817
NCEE/Nasdaq National Teaching Awards 14857
Michael Smith Awards for Science Promotion 16024

Economic history
Arthur H. Cole Grants-in-Aid 9143
Arthur H. Cole Prize 9144
Fellow Membership 7931
Alexander Gerschenkron Prize 9145
Alice Hanson Jones Prize 9146
Allan Nevins Prize 9147
Ranki Prize in Economic History 9148

Economics (*See also* Agricultural economics; Economic development; Economic education; Finance; International trade; Medical economics; Rural economics; Social science research)
American Romanian Academy Awards 3869
Award for Outstanding Paper *The Energy Journal* 11222
Best Article - *Journal of Parametrics* Award 12007
Robert Bosch Foundation Fellowship Program 7687
Bower Award for Business Leadership 9742
John Bates Clark Medal 2154
Conference Speaker Award and Best Workshop Speaker Awards 12009
Distinguished Contribution to Social Justice Award 2216
Distinguished Economic Botanist 18665
Distinguished Fellow 2155
Distinguished Fellow Award 10477
Thomas F. Divine Award 5473
Economic Award 11828
Economic Inquiry Article Award 21544
Richard T. Ely Lecture 2156
Emerging Company Award 5331
Essay Contest for College Students 4921
Irving Fisher Article Award 16694
Foreign Honorary Member 2157
Frank Freiman Award 12010
Frisch Medal Award 9141
Edmund H. Fulling Award 18666
Georgescu-Roegen Prize in Economics 19499
Eugene L. Grant Award 4021
IAEE Journalism Award 11223
Institutionalist Prize 5362
Harry G. Johnson Prize 7078
Anson Jones, M.D., Award 20032
Lawrence R. Klein Award 20517
Gerald Loeb Awards 20990
Ludwig Mai Service Award 5474
Management and Information Award 19245
Erwin Plein Nemmers Prize in Economics 16569
Outstanding Contributions to the IAEE 11224
Outstanding Contributions to the Profession Award 11225
Outstanding Corporate Growth Award 5332
Outstanding Reference Sources 17944
Outstanding Service Award 10143
Parametrician of the Year 12011
Paul E. Tsongas Economic Patriot Award 8338
Helen Potter Award of Special Recognition 5475
Herbert Salzman Award for Excellence in International Economic Performance 20551
Sir Antony Fisher International Memorial Award 6047
Smith Breeden Prizes 2244
Frank W. Taussig Article Award 16695
University of Louisville Grawemeyer Award for Ideas Improving World Order 21042
Veblen - Commons Award 5363
Samuel Z. Westerfield Award 14920

Editing
ACE Eddie Award 1804
AESE Award for Outstanding Editorial or Publishing Contributions 5660
Editor of the Year Award 15527
Jim Gordon Editor of the Year Award 15535
J. Franklin Jameson Prize for Editorial Achievement 2476
Thomas Jefferson Prize 18689
Arthur S. Link Prize/Warren F. Kuehl Prize for Documentary Editing 18681
John Murphy Award for Excellence in Copy Editing 19999
Picture Editor of the Year 15543
Silver Quill Editorial Achievement Award 4895
Texas Tech Law School Foundation 19986

Editorial writing
Advertising Design Club of Canada Awards 204
ASNE Distinguished Writing Awards 17508
Atlantic Journalism Awards 6035
James P. Barry Ohioana Award for Editorial Excellence 16657
Better Newspapers Competition 7034
Robert F. Boger Award 8446
American Business Media G. D. Crain Award 1607
Editorial and Cartoon Strip Contest 8172
Editorial Awards 19819
Editorial Excellence Award 10813
EXCEL Awards 19205
John Fischetti Editorial Cartoon Competition 9564
Kneeland Godfrey Award 8447
Golden Quill Award 12028
IAFF Media Awards Contest 11355
ILCA Media Awards Contest 11700
International Editor of the Year 21971
Laurence B. Johnson Award 5668
Journalism Awards 16326
Jesse Laventhol Prize for Deadline News Reporting 17509
Marketing Communications Award 8448
National, City and Regional Magazine Editorial and Design Awards 8024
National Magazine Awards 15355
Jesse H. Neal National Business Journalism Awards 1608
Pulitzer Prizes 17749
Eugene C. Pulliam Fellowship for Editorial Writing 19275
T. Randolph Russell Award 8449
Sigma Delta Chi Awards 19276
Silurian Excellence in Journalism Awards 19327

Editorial (continued)

Website Award 8451

Education (*See also* Academic achievement; Academic freedom; Alumni activities; Educational research; Intellectual freedom; Learning disabled; Literacy; Reading skills; Scholarly works; School publications; Teaching; Training and development)

AAIE Hall of Fame 5483
AASECT Award 1423
AATE Distinguished Book Award 883
ACE Education Program Award 5649
Achievement Award 8645
Adler Award 17202
Administrator of the Year 8500
Advisor of the Year 6189
Advocates for Children Award 15562
Advocates for Justice Award 1143
AECT Annual Achievement Award 5347
AECT Distinguished Service Award 5348
AECT Leadership Development Grants 5349
AECT Memorial Scholarship Award 5350
AECT National Convention Internship Program 5351
AECT/SIRS Intellectual Freedom Award 5352
AECT Special Service Award 5353
AFS Award for Excellence in Fisheries Education 2250
AIA/ACSA Topaz Medallion for Excellence in Architectural Education 2707
ALISE Award for Professional Contribution to Library and Information Science Education 5418
The American College of Psychiatrists Award for Creativity in Psychiatric Education 1937
American Education Award 1403
American Heroes in Education Awards 17887
American School and University Annual Architectural Portfolio 3883
Annual Merit (Professional Librarian) 8528
Annual Public Medallion Award 21296
Jack L. Anson Award 5692
Brooke Russell Astor Award 16253
Athletic Competition 1138
Aviation Education Certificates of Merit 6125
Award for Comprehensive Services in Education 1144
Award for Distinguished Contributions to Education and Training in Psychology 7346
Award for the Innovative Use of Technology 1145
Awards for Educational Excellence 18695
Awards for Excellence 18865
Best Practice Award for Gender Equality 1146
Best Practice Award for Global and International Teacher Education 1147
Bowker/Ulrich's Serials Librarianship Award 5424
Boyd-Orr International Award 12504
Chef Herman Breithaupt Award 11523
James W. Brown Publication Award 5354
Esther V. Burrin Award 5383
Business-Education Partnership Award 21267
Butler Medal 8240
Bradford Cadmus Memorial Award 10970
Roald Campbell Award 20971
Career Development Fund 21751
CCID Faculty Fellowship Award 8319
CCID Presidents' Award 8320
James Centorino Award 15357
Chapter Award for Excellence in Educational Programming 11562
Chapter of the Year 6190
CHRIE Industry Recognition Award 11524
Christus Magister Award 12989
Civil Air Patrol Aerospace Education Cadet of the Year 341
Miriam Clubok Award 15432
Co-Op Student of the Year Award 8502
Codie Awards 19383
Computer Educator of the Year 11201
James Bryant Conant Award 9168
Cooperative Month Awards 14800
Reginald J. Cressman ACE Award Recognizing Commitment to Staff Development 5650
Jack A. Culbertson Award 20972
Byron G. Culver Award 18085
Edgar Dale Award 5384
O'Neil D'Amour Award 14608
Charles A. Dana Awards for Pioneering Achievements in Higher Education 8730
DASA Scholarship 8848
David G. Imig Award for Distinguished Achievement in Teacher Education 1148
William J. Davis Memorial Award 20973
Robert de Kieffer International Fellowship Award 5355
Dealer Education Award 16577
Eugene V. Debs Award 9350
Distinguished Athletic Therapy Educator Award 6949
Distinguished Career Contribution to Education and Training in Psychology 18897
Distinguished Contribution to Education and Training in Psychology 18898
Distinguished Educational Contribution Award 18905
Distinguished Fellow Award 11521
Distinguished Pi Lambda Thetan Award 17322
Distinguished Programs in Teacher Education 5879
Distinguished School Administrators Award 1413
Distinguished Service Award
American Association of School Administrators 1405
American Association of School Librarians 1414
American Association of Teachers of Italian 1450
Council of Chief State School Officers 8570
National School Transportation Association 15671
Nevada Association of School Boards 16084
Distinguished Teacher Award 10367
Distinguished Teaching Award 3052
Downtown Jaycees Teachers Grant Awards 9014
Janice Marie Dyer Award 6126
Eagle Award 17109
EdPress Distinguished Achievement Awards for Excellence in Educational Journalism 5663
EdPress Honor Awards - Best Newsletter 5664
EdPress Honor Awards - Golden Lamp Award 5665
EdPress Honor Awards - Most Improved Publication 5667
Education Achievement Award 20841
Education Award
American Zoo and Aquarium Association 4915
Audubon Naturalist Society of the Central Atlantic States 6067
Education Training Scholarship 19615
Educational Assistance Award 6468
Educational Interiors Showcase 3884
Educational Sponsorship Award 14018
Capt. W. W. Estridge, Jr. Award 20942
ETR&D Young Scholar Award 5356
ETS Award for Distinguished Service to Measurement 9177
Alvin C. Eurich Award 76
Excellence 200 Awards 20729
Excellence in Education Award 17325
Excellence in Education Awards 9205
Faculty Award of Excellence 17611
Faculty Service Award 517
Gen. Muir S. Fairchild Education Achievement Award 16825
Paul and Kate Farmer Award 14833
Foundation Research Award 1312
Founder's Award 17520
Friend of Education Award 9387
Fund for the Advancement of Social Studies Education (FASSE) Grant 14780
Robert M. Gagne Instructional Development Research Award 5357
Betty Garlick Lifetime Achievement Award 13335
Gender Equity Architects Award 1149
Glenn Gilbert National Leadership Award 14824
Golden Key Scholar Awards 10062
Golden Merit Award 15672
Good Neighbor Teacher Award 19771
Gordon Maskew Fair Medal 21484
Government Affairs Award of Recognition 6683
William S. Gray Citation of Merit 11856
Deborah and Franklin Tepper Haimo Award for Distinguished College or University Teaching of Mathematics 13193
Hall of Fame Award 15673
Hallmark Award 17252
Phoebe Aperson Hearst/National PTA Excellence in Education Partnership Award 15563
Hugh M. Hefner First Amendment Award 17396
Justice J.A. Higgins Award 7020
The William Hlushko Award to Young Co-operative Educators 5651
Honor Roll for Education in a Free Society 12406
Honorary Fellow of the Genesis Academy 9924
Honorary Fellow of the Photographic Society 9925
Honorary Lifetime Membership 19835
Honorary Member 15358
Honorary Service Awards 4955
Human Rights Award 2233

Education (continued)

J. Norman Hunter Memorial Award 8439
IEEE Process Improvement Award 7605
Imagineer Awards 13430
IMCC National Annual Minerals Education Awards 12157
Innovation in Higher Education 9206
Innovative Educational Theatre Award 9182
International Superintendent of the Year 5484
Jeske Award 16371
Jewish Prize 15967
Laurence B. Johnson Award 5668
K-12 Dance Educator of the Year 14896
Joseph Katz Award 5371
Joe W. Kelly Award 1967
Charles F. Kettering Award 8503
Kilby International Awards 12586
C. Albert Koob Award 14613
Mandayam Chakravarthi Krishnan Award for Educational Excellence 9926
Kuhmerker Award 5451
Helen Lamb Outstanding Educator Award 1296
Bishop Loris Lane Award 14614
Leadership Award 10537
Leadership for Learning Award 1406
Stewart M. Lee Consumer Education Award 2050
Richard B. Lewis Memorial Award 5358
Lifetime Achievement Award
  American Association of Colleges for Teacher Education 1150
  IES, Institute for the International Education of Students 10666
Margaret B. Lindsey Award for Distinguished Research in Teacher Education 1151
Management Effectiveness Awards 3885
Marine Education Award 15359
Masako Shoji Scholarship 21879
Carroll Sterling Masterson Award & Outstanding Women's Awards 22093
Harold Masursky Award for Meritorious Service 1514
Ronald McDonald House Charities Grants Program 18118
W. Wallace McDowell Award 10898
Harold W. McGraw, Jr. Prize in Education 13221
R. Tait McKenzie Award 881
Lenore McNeer Award 15433
Medal for Distinction in Engineering Education 7058
Media and Methods Magazine Awards Portfolio Competition 13233
Howard B. Meek Award 11526
Membership Awards 15564
John F. Meyers Award 14615
Missouri Teacher of the Year Program 13535
Grover E. Murray Distinguished Educator Award 1344
NABE Board Member of the Year 14617
NABE Executive Officer of the Year 14618
NABE Honor Roll of Outstanding Members 14619
NACD - ICI Americas Conservation District Awards 14156
NAE/Spencer Postdoctoral Fellowship Program 13803
NAPT Distinguished Service Award 14026
National and Regional Continuing Education Award 18155
National Awards for Education Reporting 9170
National Awards Program 9766
National Competition 1139
National Leadership Award 14753
National School Library Media Program of the Year Award 1418
National School Plant Manager of the Year Award 3886
National Superintendent of the Year Award 1407
National Women's Hall of Fame 15960
NAWL Trust for Research & Education - Essay Competition 14455
NCEA Presidential Award 14620
Newspaper in Education Award 11113
Notable Achievements 5334
OMSA Recognition and Component Awards 16645
Outstanding Affiliate Award 16372
Outstanding Business Leader Awards 16573
Outstanding Chapter Award 12505
Outstanding Contribution by an Individual for Educational/Training Activities 5267
Outstanding Contribution by an Organization 15434
Outstanding Contribution to ACE by an Organization 5652
Outstanding Contribution to Co-operative Education and Training 5653
Outstanding Dissertation Award 1152
Outstanding Educator Award 1694
Outstanding Human Service Student 15435
Outstanding Individual at the Local Level 16373
Outstanding Individual at the National/International Level 16374
Outstanding Junior Member Contest 15712
Outstanding Organization at the Local Level 16375
Outstanding Organization at the National/International Level 16376
Outstanding Paper Awards 11527
Outstanding School Award 9183
Outstanding Service to Environmental Education Award 16377
Outstanding Teacher Award
  Council for Learning Disabilities 8561
  National Marine Educators Association 15360
  Pennsylvania Association of Private School Administrators 17166
Outstanding Training Programs 5268
Outstanding Writing Award 1153
ACTFL Anthony Papalia Award for Excellence in Teacher Education 2058
Parent Organization Recognition Awards 14621
Person of the Year in Education 9172
Peggy Leach Pfeiffer Service Award 5386
Paul R. Pintrich Outstanding Dissertation Award 3678
Plummer Memorial Educational Lecture Award 4892
Edward C. Pomeroy Award 1154
President's Award
  Association for Counselors and Educators in Government 5335
  Massachusetts Association of School Business Officials 13147
  National Marine Educators Association 15361
  National Organization for Human Service Education 15436
  North American Association for Environmental Education 16378
President's Leadership Award 14754
Professional Contribution by an ACE Member 5654
Professional Development Award 10667
Professional Development Awards 15754
Leon R. Radde - Educator of the Year Award 10974
John R. Ragazzini Award 2787
Reading/Literacy Award 15565
Regional Leadership Award 14755
J.H. Stewart Reid Memorial Fellowship 6943
Eleanor Roosevelt Fund Award 1474
The Rose of Sharon Award 9927
St. David's Society Scholarship 18205
Dean Herman Schneider Achievement Award 8504
Priscilla A. Scotlan Award for Distinguished Service 1011
Margaret B. Scott Award of Merit 7262
Scrapbook Award 12506
Section Achievement Award 1857
Elizabeth Ann Seton Award 14624
Saint Elizabeth Ann Seton Award 14625
Henry L. Shattuck Public Service Awards 6524
Shigeka Talumura Scholarship 21880
SHIP Citation 9173
Sarah Shorten Award 6944
Showcase for Excellence Awards 1429
Richard E. Snow Early Career Award in Educational Psychology 3679
Social Studies Programs of Excellence 14789
South California Educator of the Year Award 7955
Space Imaging Award for Application of High Resolution Digital Satellite Imagery 5225
Special Achievement Award 15866
Special Award or Citation to Institutions and Individuals 20968
The Barbara Spriestersbach Award for Excellence in Teaching 16671
James R. Squire Award 14841
Stevenson Fletcher Achievement Award 11529
Donald C. Stone Award 3807
Student Involvement Award 15566
Support of Diversity Award 1155
Support of Teacher Education Accreditation Award 1156
Sustainable Development Award of Excellence 10120
Henrietta Szold Award 10215
TABCO Recognition Award 19946
Teachers Quest Awards 9633
Teaching Award 2538
Tutorial Citation Award 4153
Frederick H. Tuttle Award 21308
Dr. Ralph W. Tyler Research Award 8505
U.S. International Film and Video Festival 20675
University of Louisville Grawemeyer Award in Education 21048
Utilization Award 14019
Hoyt S. Vandenberg Award 363
Ellen Waldschmidt Award 12990
William H. Webb Medal 19217

Education (continued)
Leslie A. Whittington Excellence in Teaching Award 14377
F. Loren Winship Secondary School Theatre Award 896
Writing Award 12507
Yoneji Ebitani Scholarship 21881

Education, adult and continuing *See* Adult and continuing education

Education, agricultural *See* Agricultural education

Education, art *See* Art education

Education, business *See* Business education

Education, early childhood *See* Early childhood education

Education, economic *See* Economic education

Education, elementary *See* Elementary education

Education, engineering *See* Engineering education

Education, geographic *See* Geographic education

Education, health *See* Health education

Education, higher *See* Higher education

Education, journalism *See* Journalism education

Education, legal *See* Legal education

Education, medical *See* Medical education

Education, music *See* Music education

Education, physical *See* Physical education

Education, science *See* Science education

Education, secondary *See* Secondary education

Education, special *See* Special education

Education, vocational *See* Vocational education

Educational films
"Focus on Disability" Grant 21715
Carl F. and Viola V. Mahnke Film Production Award 5359

Educational research
James L. Allhands Essay Competition 273
Award of Distinction 12064
Award of Merit - Scholastic/Authorship 8368
Henry Barnard Prize 10481
Raymond B. Cattell Early Career Award for Programmatic Research 2159
CEA Whitworth Award for Educational Research 7080
CEC Research Award 8548
CEE James N. Britton Award for Inquiry within the English Language Arts 14829
CEE Richard A. Meade Award 14830
Chapter of Excellence Award 11939
Delta Pi Epsilon Research Award 8874
Distinguished Chapter Award 11940
Distinguished Contributions to Education Research 2160
Distinguished Dissertation in Teacher Education 5878
Distinguished Research in Teacher Education 5880
Ella Victoria Dobbs Award 17324
ETR&D Young Scholar Award 5356
Graduate Student Awards 11260
History of Education Society Award 10482
Implications of Research for Educational Practice 5500
Palmer O. Johnson Memorial Award 2161
Kappa Delta Pi National Student Teacher/Intern of the Year Award 5881
E. F. Lindquist Award 2162
Dean and Sybil McClusky Research Award 5360
NAE/Spencer Postdoctoral Fellowship Program 13803
Imogene Okes Award 950
Outstanding Book Award
American Educational Research Association 2163
History of Education Society 10483
Outstanding Chapter Communication Products Award 11941
Outstanding Human Performance Intervention Award 11942
Outstanding Instructional Communication Award 11943
Outstanding Instructional Product or Intervention Award 11944
Outstanding Performance Aid Award 11945
Outstanding Research Award 11946
Outstanding Student Research Award 11947
ACTFL - MLJ Paul Pimsleur Award for Research in Foreign Language Education 2059
Promising Researcher Award 14838
Relating Research to Practice Awards 2164
Review of Research Award 2165
ACTFL - MLJ Emma Marie Steiner Award for Leadership in Foreign Language Research in Foreign Language Education 2062
Teacher-Researcher Grants 14842
University of Louisville Grawemeyer Award in Education 21048
Waddingham/Doctor Award 8371
William A. Wheatley Award 20944

Electrical engineering (*See also* Electronics)
Award for Excellence in Power Distribution Engineering 10903
W. R. G. Baker Prize Award 10855
Chapters Council Award 10904
Control Systems Award 10857
Edison Medal 10858
Richard M. Emberson Award 10859
Walter Fee Outstanding Young Engineer Award 10905
Donald G. Fink Prize Award 10860
Charles LeGeyt Fortescue Fellowship 10861
Founders Medal 10862
T. Burke Hayes Student Prize Paper Award 10906
IEEE Corporate Innovation Recogniton Award 10868
IEEE Engineering Leadership Recognition 10870
IEEE Life Members' Prize in Electrical History 18875
IEEE Medal of Honor 10871
Charles A. Johnson Award 5961
Morris E. Leeds Award 10874
Meritorious Service Award 10907
Richard E. Merwin Award for Distinguished Service 10899
Outstanding Chapter Award 9342
Outstanding Chapter Awards 10908
Outstanding Electrical Engineering Junior Award 9343
Outstanding Electrical Engineering Student Award 9344
Outstanding Engineer Award 10909
Outstanding Power Engineering Educator Award 10910
Outstanding Teacher Award 9345
Outstanding Young Electrical Engineer Award 9346
Power-Life Award 10911
Haraden Pratt Award 10877
Prize Paper Award 10912
Simon Ramo Medal 10878
Judith A. Resnik Award 10879
Arnold H. Scott Award 5982
Charles Proteus Steinmetz Award 10882
Technical Committee Prize Paper Awards 10913
Technical Council Distinguished Individual Service Award 10914
Frederick Emmons Terman Award 4045
Uno Lamm High Voltage Direct Current Award 10915
Working Group Recognition Award 10916

Electrical industry
Leroy H. Carpenter Award 9203
Dakin Award 10651
James D. Donovan Individual Achievement Award 3789
EASA Exceptional Achievement and Service Award 9199
Edison Award 9159
EERA Scholarships 9201
Energy Innovator Award 3790
Forster Award 10652
Man of the Year 11553
Mittlemann Achievement Award 10656
National Lighting Awards Program 14922
Frederik Philips Award 10875
Thomas F. Preston Manufacturer of the Year Award 14924
Professional Development 21797
Nikola Tesla Award 10883

Electronics
Autosound Grand Prix Awards 6057
Awards 7721
John Bardeen Award 13441
Cledo Brunetti Award 10856

Electronics (continued)
Chairman's Award 11982
Clinton S. Lee Market Services and Engineering Award of Excellence 9210
Corporate Achievement Award 11747
Design and Engineering Exhibition Award 9211
Distinguished Service Award
Electronic Industries Alliance 9212
Small Motor and Motion Association 18564
Edison Medal 10858
Electronic Innovation Commendation 8436
Engineering Award of Excellence 9213
Fellow of the Society 11748
Charles LeGeyt Fortescue Fellowship 10861
Governor's Award 11983
Hall of Fame 17969
Hall of Fame Award 18565
Hall of Fame Awards 8458
Herman Halperin Electric Transmission and Distribution Award 10863
Helicopter Electrical/Electronics Technician Award 10397
Heinrich Hertz Medal 10865
Hi-Fi Grand Prix Awards 6058
Daniel C. Hughes, Jr., Memorial Award 11749
Masaru Ibuka Consumer Electronics Award 10866
Individual Award 9215
Innovator of the Year Award 22008
Morris E. Leeds Award 10874
Legislator of the Year Award 225
Medal of Achievement 226
Medal of Honor 9216
Richard E. Merwin Award for Distinguished Service 10899
NESDA Awards 14926
Outstanding Teacher of the Year Awards 1453
PMC Electronic Test Award 17487
Pat Porter Memorial Award - "Friend of the Satellite Dealer" Award 9220
Quantum Electronics Award 10662
David Sarnoff Award 10880
SEMI Award for North America 18412
Solid-State Circuits Award 10881
Charles Proteus Steinmetz Award 10882
Technical Achievement Award 11750
Technician of the Year 9221
Technician of the Year Award 11984
Charles Hard Townes Award 16798
Karel Urbanek Memorial Award 18413
Paul G. Vess Award (Avionics Marine of the Year) 13093
Video Grand Prix Awards 6059
Xplorer of the Year Award 22009

Elementary education
Board of Directors Awards 14606
CIBA Specialty Chemicals Exemplary Middle Level and High School Science Teaching Awards 15685
Distinguished Informal Science Education Award 15687
Distinguished Principal Awards 14609
Distinguished Service Awards 14206
Distinguished Teaching Award 15689
Elementary Departmental Award in Recognition of Commitment to Catholic Elementary Education 14610
Exhibitor Awards 14611
Miriam Joseph Farrell Distinguished Teacher Award 14612
Sue Hefley Educator of the Year Award 12939
Eleanor M. Johnson Award 11864
Mustard Seed Awards 14616
National Distinguished Principal Award 14207
National Teacher of the Year 8571
Parent Partnership Awards 14622
Religious Education Excellence Awards 14623
Regie Routman Teacher Recognition Award 11874
Nila Banton Smith Award 11875
Toshiba/NSTA ExploraVision Awards 15693

Emergency medicine
American Eurocopter Golden Hour Award 10390
Award for Outstanding Contributions in Research and Education 1859
Council Meritorious Service Award 1860
Dedication Award 9235
Distinguished Service Award 767
Augustine D'Orta Award 9236
EMRA Academic Excellence Award 9237
EMRA Award for Excellence in Teaching 9238
EMRA Clinical Excellence Award 9239
EMRA Leadership Award 9240
EMT-Paramedic Emergency Medical Service of the Year Award (ALS Service of the Year Award) 14209
J. D. Farrington Award of Excellence 14210
A. Roger Fox Founder's Award 14211
Gold Medal 11119
Governor's National Leadership Award 14212
Jeffrey S. Harris State Leadership Award 14213
Jean Hollister Award 9241
William Klingensmith EMS Administrator of the Year Award 14214
Asmund S. Laerdal Award for Excellence (EMT-Paramedic of the Year Award) 14215
James D. Mills Outstanding Contribution to Emergency Medicine 1861
Rocco V. Morando Lifetime Achievement Award 14216
Robert E. Motley EMT of the Year Award 14217
National Association of First Responders Awards 14232
Presidential Leadership Award 14218
Public Safety Recognition 6287
Leo R. Schwartz Emergency Medical Service of the Year Award (BLS Service of the Year Award) 14219
Mary Ann Talley EMS Instructor/Coordinator of the Year Award 14220
VFW Emergency Services Award 21338
Joseph F. Waeckerle Founder's Award 9242
John G. Wiegenstein Leadership Award 1862

Emergency services
MVP of Year 5647

Employment practices (*See also* Labor; Occupational health; Occupational safety; Office technology; Personnel management; Training and development)
Achievement Awards 14165
AMVETS National Employer of the Year Award 4948
Award of Merit 11413
Chapter Merit Awards 4685
Citation of Merit 11414
Community Relations Award (Labor) 2892
Joe Cooney Award 14166
Epilepsy Foundation of America Awards 9308
Equal Employment Opportunity Award 20479
Equal Employment Opportunity Awards 20511
Equal Employment Opportunity Medal 13887
Freedom of the Human Spirit Award 10629
Heinz Award in Technology, the Economy and Employment 10379
Industry Leader Hall of Fame Award 4686
Robert B. Irwin Award 15258
JTPA Awards for Excellence 14168
Wilburn H. Long Employment Award 6457
Major General Melvin J. Maas Achievement Award 6458
Mary Mahoney Award 3281
Mental Health in the Workplace Award 7270
Outstanding Disabled Veteran of the Year 8955
Outstanding Disabled Veteran Outreach Coordinator 8956
Outstanding Large and Small Employer Award 8957
Outstanding Local Veterans' Employment Representative 8958
President's Award 11367
Professional Development Awards 15754
Recognition Award 1421
Cedric A. Richner, Jr. Scholarship Award 4688
Robie Award for Achievement in Industry 12275
Peter J. Salmon Award - Blind Worker of the Year 15259
Priscilla A. Scotlan Award for Distinguished Service 1011
Georgina Smith Award 1467
Ugly Stick 20267
Assistant Excellence in Leadership Award in Memory of Buford M. Watson, Jr. 11480
Workplace Diversity Professional Development Award 11481

Endocrinology
Edwin B. Astwood Lecture Award 9258
Gerald D. Aurbach Lecture Award 9259
Clinical Investigator Lecture Award 9260
Sidney H. Ingbar Distinguished Service Award 9261
Fred Conrad Koch Award 9262
Ernst Oppenheimer Memorial Award 9263
WE Mentor Award 21710
Richard E. Weitzman Award 9264
Robert H. Williams Distinguished Leadership Award 9265

Energy
$500,000 Lemelson-MIT Prize 12777
AABE Scholarship 1098

Energy (continued)

Charles Greeley Abbot Award 4656
Aerospace Power Systems Award 2637
AIAA Energy Systems Award 2647
Award for Excellence in Fusion Engineering 9840
Award for Outstanding Paper *The Energy Journal* 11222
Stephen D. Bechtel, Jr. Energy Award 4299
The Chairman's Cup 1095
Champlin Research Award 10845
Comstock Prize in Physics 13829
John Ericsson Award in Renewable Energy 20494
Peter F. Heaney Memorial Scholarship 16239
Hollis D. Hedberg Award in Energy 10846
HTEC Division Award 2778
IAEE Journalism Award 11223
International Awards 5670
Donald Q. Kern Award 2781
Leadership Awards 9841
Link Foundation Energy Fellowship Program 12870
Outstanding Contributions to the IAEE 11224
Outstanding Contributions to the Profession Award 11225
James E. Stewart Award 1096
Tyler Prize for Environmental Achievement 4975
U.S. Energy Award 20573

Energy, atomic *See* Atomic energy

Energy conservation
Best in American Living Awards 17598
Sadi Carnot Award in Energy Conservation 20493
Design for Humanity Award 4460
William T. Hornaday Bronze and Silver Medals 6579
William T. Hornaday Gold Certificate 6580
William T. Hornaday Gold Medal 6581
William T. Hornaday Unit Award 6582
National Awards for Environmental Sustainability - Searching for Success Program 17991
National Water and Energy Conservation Award 12205

Engineering (*See also* Combustion; Communications technology; Cybernetics; Electronics; Energy; Engineering education; Materials science; Mining and metallurgy; Photogrammetry; Robotics; Standards; Surveying; Testing; Water resources)
AAAS Award for Public Understanding of Science and Technology 1045
AAAS Mentor Award 1046
AAAS Science Journalism Awards 1047
AAAS Scientific Freedom and Responsibility Award 1048
Academic Excellence for Leadership of Engineering and Technical Management for Undergraduate Programs 4051
Achievement Award 19363
Adhesion Society Award for Excellence in Adhesion Science 184
Advanced Manufacturing Technology Engineering Certification 6352
AEG Publication Award 5672
Aerospace Engineering Leadership Award 19033
AES Awards of Excellence 66
AIAA Energy Systems Award 2647
The Alouette Award 6866
American Society of Safety Engineers Fellow 4602
American Society of Swedish Engineers Award 4615
F. Paul Anderson Award 4418
ASCE Presidents' Medal 4294
ASEM Fellows 4052
ASHRAE - Alco Medal for Distinguished Public Service 4419
ASHRAE Fellows 4420
ASHRAE Journal Paper Award 4421
ASHRAE Symposium Paper Award 4422
ASHRAE Technical Paper Award 4423
ASM International and The Minerals, Metals and Materials Society Distinguished Lectureship in Materials and Society 5173
Award for Excellence in Fusion Engineering 9840
Award for the Advancement of Surface Irrigation 4217
Award of Merit
AACE International 35
Society of Manufacturing Engineers - Composites Manufacturing Association 19142
Awards for Achievement in Arc Welded Design, and Engineering and Fabrication 12851
Awards for Scientific Achievement 21437
AWIS Educational Foundation Predoctoral Award 5530
Eugene Baker Memorial Award 5636
Bernard R. Sarchet Award 4053
Homer I. Bernhardt Distinguished Service Award 4000
Best Paper Award 11532
Black Engineer of the Year Awards 7585
Blasters Leadership Award 11992
Andrew T. Boggs Service Award 4424
Lincoln Bouillon Award 4425
Bower Award and Prize for Achievement in Science 9741
Raymond C. Bowman Award 18710
George E. Briggs Dissertation Award 3651
Donald C. Burnham Manufacturing Management Award 19144
Edward DeMille Campbell Memorial Lecture 5174
Canadian Engineers' Award-Gold Medal Award 7051
Canadian Engineers' Awards-Award for the Support of Women in the Engineering Profession 7052
Canadian Engineers' Awards-Gold Medal Student Award 7053
Canadian Engineers' Awards-Meritorious Service Award for Community Service 7054
Canadian Engineers' Awards-Meritorious Service Award for Professional Service 7055
Canadian Engineers' Awards-National Award for Engineering Achievement 7056
Canadian Engineers' Awards-Young Engineer Achievement Award 7057
Canadian Pacific Railway Medal 9269
Chester F. Carlson Award 18711
ASHRAE - Willis H. Carrier Award 4427
Chairman's Award
American Association of Engineering Societies 1196
Machine Vision Association of the Society of Manufacturing Engineers 13010
Chairman's Award for Career Achievement 6289
Chairs and Professorships Awards 20002
Octave Chanute Medal 21566
Chapter Awards 11995
Chapter of the Year Award 4276
Chief of Engineers Design and Environmental Awards Program 20405
Rodney D. Chipp Memorial Award 19364
Ven Te Chow Award 4305
Samuel C. Collins Award 8677
W. Leighton Collins Award 4007
William J. Collins, Jr. Research Promotion Award 4428
Fred O. Conley Award 19260
A. E. Conrady Award 19605
County Engineer of the Year Awards 14179
CRSI Design Awards Program 8346
DeGolyer Distinguished Service Medal 19235
Design and Engineering Exhibition Award 9211
Distinguished 50-Year Member Award 4429
Distinguished New Engineer Award 19366
Distinguished Service Award
American Society for Engineering Education 4012
American Society of Heating, Refrigerating and Air-Conditioning Engineers 4430
Illuminating Engineering Society of North America 10692
International Society of Logistics 11996
National Council of Examiners for Engineering and Surveying 14797
National Society of Professional Engineers 15746
Doctoral Prizes 16022
Charles Stark Draper Prize 13806
Gano Dunn Award 8497
Thomas W. Eadie Medal 18164
Eccles Medal 11997
ECMA Awards 9267
Education Award 19150
Egleston Medal 8229
William Hunt Eisenman Award 5176
Charles Ellet Award 21567
Emmy Awards for Primetime Programming 127
Employer of the Month Award 4277
Employer of the Year Award 4278
Engineer of the Year 19886
Engineering and Construction Contracting Division Award 2768
Engineering Award of Excellence 9213
Engineering Excellence Award 8453
Engineering Excellence Awards
American Consulting Engineers Council 2009
Optical Society of America 16784
Engineering Manager of the Year Award 4054
Engineering Materials Achievement Award 5177
Engineering Medal 17605
John Ericsson Medal Award 4616

Engineering (continued)

Excellence in Highway Design Awards 20559
Facilities Management Excellence Awards (FAME Awards) 5366
Federal Engineer of the Year Award 15747
Fellow
AACE International 36
ASM International 5178
Engineering Institute of Canada 9270
International Society of Logistics 11998
Fellow Designation 10693
Fellow Grade of Membership 19042
Fellow of the Society 19262
Fellows Awards 19367
Fellows Distinguished Award of Merit 2010
Fellowship 18712
Enrico Fermi Award 20495
Crosby Field Award 4431
Field Awards 11999
Ford Foundation Postdoctoral Diversity Fellowships 15622
Founders Award
American Society for Engineering Management 4055
National Academy of Engineering 13807
Founders Medal 12000
Franklin B.W. Woodbury Award for Special Achievement 4056
Joseph Fraunhofer Award/Robert M. Burley Prize 16785
Sheldon K. Friedlander Award 955
Edmund Friedman Professional Recognition Award 4316
Milton W. Garland Refrigeration Award 4432
Gold Medal
ASM International 5179
Society of Manufacturing Engineers - Composites Manufacturing Association 19152
Gold Medal Awards 6290
Gold Medal of the Society 19609
Government Affairs Award 4433
Graduate Confectionery Fellowship - Penn State University 17179
Eugene L. Grant Award 4021
Samuel Arnold Greeley Award 4320
J. H. "Jud" Hall Composites Manufacturing Award 19154
Hall of Fame 4434
Gerhard Herzberg Canada Gold Medal for Science and Engineering 16023
Hispanic Engineer National Achievement Awards 7586
Claire P. Holdredge Award 5673
Louise and Bill Holladay Distinguished Fellow Award 4435
Holley Medal 4517
Honorary Life Member 37
Honorary Member
American Society for Engineering Education 4023
American Society of Civil Engineers 4327
American Society of Heating, Refrigerating and Air-Conditioning Engineers 4436
American Society of Swedish Engineers 4617
ASM International 5182
Engineering Institute of Canada 9271
Honorary Membership
Society for Imaging Science and Technology 18713
Society of Manufacturing Engineers - Composites Manufacturing Association 19156
Hoover Medal 4520
Wesley W. Horner Award 4329
Ernest E. Howard Award 4331
C.D. Howe Memorial Foundation Engineering Awards Program 5905
IES Medal 10694
Industrial Appreciation Award 38
Intel International Science and Engineering Fair 18362
International Awards 5670
International Graduate Student Paper Contest 5184
International Illumination Design Awards Program 10695
International Student Paper Contest 5185
ISA Fellow 12219
Itek Award 18714
Charles E. Ives Journal Award (Engineering) 18715
Richard H. Jahns Distinguished Lecturer in Engineering Geology Award 5674
John F. James International Award 4437
JETS National TEAMS Awards 12466
Alfred E. Johnson Achievement Award 1432
Floyd T. Johnston Service Award 5675
Reginald H. Jones Distinguished Service Award 13874
Journal Award (Science) 18716
Martin S. Kapp Foundation Engineering Award 4336
Charles V. Keane Distinguished Service Award 39
Sir John Kennedy Medal 9272
Izaak Walton Killam Memorial Prizes 6800
Rudolf Kingslake Medal and Prize 19610
Kosar Memorial Award 18717
James N. Landis Medal 4524
Lieven Gevaert Medal 18718
K.Y. Lo Medal 9273
Thomas H. MacDonald Memorial Award 1433
Macromolecular Science and Engineering Lecture Award 7843
The Marconi Prize 13064
McKnight Doctoral Fellowship Program in Arts and Sciences, Mathematics, Business and Engineering 9599
Medal for Distinction in Engineering Education 7058
Medal for the Advancement of Research 5187
Medalla de Oro 19184
Member of the Year Award 4279
Meritorious Service Award 14798
Merl Baker Best Conference Paper Award 4057
Merrit Williamson Best Student Paper Award 4058
Michelson - Morley Award 7619
Chandler - Misener Award 11241
National Engineering Award 1197
National Federation of the Blind Scholarship Program 15039
Carl E. Nelson Engineering Award 312
New Product Award 15748
Alexander A. Nikolsky Honorary Lectureship 2437
Alfred Noble Prize 4345
NSPE Award 15749
Office of Civilian Radioactive Waste Management Graduate Fellowship Program 16598
Office of Civilian Radioactive Waste Management Historically Black Colleges and Universities Undergraduate Scholarship Program 16599
Oppenheimer Award 4033
Order of Honour Service Awards 17606
Outstanding Achievement Awards 20003
Outstanding Environmental and Engineering Geologic Project Award 5676
Outstanding Section and Region Award 40
Outstanding Service Award 6739
Outstanding Young Manufacturing Engineer Award 19164
Ely ("Eli") S. Parker Award 2607
PEI Distinguished Service Award 15750
PEPP Chairman's Award 15751
PEPP Merit Award 15752
Douglas R. Piteau Outstanding Young Member Award 5677
Presidental Award 4059
President's Award
Association of Conservation Engineers 5637
International Society of Explosives Engineers 11993
President's Award for Merit 12001
President's Citation 18719
President's Club 21568
President's Cup 19267
Private Practice Professional Development Award 15753
Professional Development Awards 15754
Professional Engineers Citizenship Award 17607
Professional Engineers Gold Medal 17608
Public Service Award 5642
Public Service Medal 13899
Pupin Medal 8230
Allan Ray Putnam Service Award 5189
QBS Award 15755
Joan Hodges Queneau Palladium Medal 1199
Research Associateship Programs 15623
Rickey Medal 4352
Kenneth Andrew Roe Award 1200
Ralph Coats Roe Medal 4543
Hunter Rouse Hydraulic Engineering Lecture 4355
Albert M. Sargent Progress Award 19169
Albert Sauveur Achievement Award 5190
Senior Membership 18720
Service Award 18721
Service Awards 21569
SES - ASTM Robert J. Painter Memorial Award 5985
Joseph A. Siegel Service Award 19170
Julian C. Smith Medal 9274
Special Awards 5678
Elmer A. Sperry Award 19057
SPIE Technology Achievement Award 19611
SRE Certificate of Excellence 19290
SRE Certificate of Recognition 19291
SRE Stan Ofsthun Award 19292
Standards Achievement Award 4439
Steacie Memorial Fellowships 16025
Steacie Prize 19777
J. C. Stevens Award 4359
John B. Stirling Medal 9275
Bradley Stoughton Award for Young Teachers 5191

Engineering (continued)
Student Chapter of the Year Award 4280
Student Design Project Competition 4440
Student Professional Paper 5679
Franklin V. Taylor Award 3652
Frederick W. Taylor Research Medal 19173
Technical Engineering Achievement Awards 13866
Technician of the Month Award 4281
Technician/Technologist of the Year Award 4282
Technology Award/Award of Engineering Excellence 4441
Ted Eschenbach Best EMJ Journal Paper Award 4060
Richard R. Torrens Award 4363
Undergraduate Award 18483
Upward Mobility Award 19369
Vanguard Award for Science and Technology 14582
Worcester Reed Warner Medal 4551
Washington Award 4366
Albert Easton White Distinguished Teacher Award 5192
Eli Whitney Productivity Award 19176
Jack L. Williams Space Logistics Medal 12002
WISE Award for Engineering Achievement 21753
WISE Lifetime Achievement Award 21755
Young Engineer of the Year Award 15756
Young Engineers of the Year 13169
Young Logistician Award 12003
O. T. Zimmerman Founder's Award 41

Engineering, aeronautical *See* Aeronautical engineering

Engineering, agricultural *See* Agricultural engineering

Engineering, audio *See* Audio engineering

Engineering, automotive *See* Automotive engineering

Engineering, biomedical *See* Biomedical engineering

Engineering, ceramic *See* Ceramic engineering

Engineering, chemical *See* Chemical engineering

Engineering, civil *See* Civil engineering

Engineering, corrosion *See* Corrosion engineering

Engineering education
ABET Honor Roll 59
Achievement Award 19363
Homer Addams Award 4417
AES Man of the Year Award 67
Aglient Technologies Award for Excellence in Laboratory Instruction 3994
ASEE Minorities in Engineering Award 3995
ASEE Section Outstanding Teaching Award 3996
John Leland Atwood Award 3997
Ferdinand P. Beer and E. Russell Johnston Jr. Outstanding New Mechanics Educator Award 3998
Esther Hoffman Beller Medal 16781
Frederick J. Berger Award 3999
Best Paper Award 4001
Joseph M. Biedenbach Distinguished Service Award 4002
Bliss Medal 18983
Taylor Booth Award 10886
Alvah K. Borman Award 4003
Jim Bottorf Award 68
Chester F. Carlson Award for Innovation in Engineering Education 4004
Certificate of Merit 4005
Chapter Awards 19931
Willard D. Cheek Exemplary Service Award 4006
Edwin F. Church Medal 4505
W. Leighton Collins Award 4007
William H. Corcoran Award 4008
John A. Curtis Lecture Award 4009
Benjamin J. Dasher Best Paper Award 4010
Distinguished Alumnus Award 19932
Distinguished Educator and Service Award 4011
Distinguished Engineering Educator Award 19365
Distinguished Service Citation 4013
Distinguished Teaching Award 4014
Dow Outstanding New Faculty Award 4015
EAI Award 4016
Educational Aids Competition Blue Ribbon Awards 4219
Woody Everett Award 4017
Fellow Grade Membership 4018
Fellows Distinguished Award of Merit 2010
Fluids Engineering Award 4509
Clement J. Freund Award 4019
General Electric Senior Research Award 4020
Linton E. Grinter Distinguished Service Award 60
Hancor Soil and Water Engineering Award 4224
Archie Higdon Distinguished Educator Award 4022
Albert G. Holzman Distinguished Educator Award 10956
Honorary Member
American Society for Engineering Education 4023
American Society of Civil Engineers 4327
IEEE Education Medal 10869
Karl V. Karlstrom Outstanding Educator Award 5302
Kishida International Award 4226
Victor K. LaMer Award 1766
Benjamin Garver Lamme Award 4024
Warren K. Lewis Award for Contributions in Chemical Engineering Education 2782
Donald E. Marlowe Award 4025
J. J. Martin Award 4026
Massey-Ferguson Educational Award 4227
James H. McGraw Award 4027
Curtis W. McGraw Research Award 4028
Fred Merryfield Design Award 4029
Merl K. Miller Award 4030
Glenn Murphy Award 4031
NAMIC Engineering Safety Award 4231
National Outstanding Advisor Award 19933
Olmsted Liberal Education Award for Innovation 4032
Oppenheimer Award 4033
Outstanding Community College Educator Award 4034
Outstanding Educator Award 4035
Outstanding Paper Award 4036
Outstanding Section Campus Representative Award 4037
Outstanding Zone Campus Representative Award 4038
Theo C. Pilkington Outstanding Educator Award 4039
Helen L. Plants Award for Special Events 4040
Ralph Coats Roe Award 4041
Ronald J. Schmitz Award for Outstanding Contributions to the Frontiers in Education Conference 4042
Fred E. Schwab Award 19269
Harden-Simons Prize 4043
Wilbur S. Smith Distinguished Transportation Educator Award 11055
Ben C. Sparks Medal 4546
Ray H. Speiss Award 4044
Student Section Advisor Award 4548
Tau Beta Pi Laureate 19934
Ralph R. Teetor Educational Award 19060
Frederick Emmons Terman Award 4045
Union Carbide Lectureship Award 4046
George K. Wadlin Distinguished Service Award 4047
George Westinghouse Award 4048
Meriam/Wiley Distinguished Author Award 4049
George Winter Award 4368
WISE Award for Engineering Achievement 21753

Engineering, electrical *See* Electrical engineering

Engineering, human *See* Human engineering

Engineering, industrial *See* Industrial engineering

Engineering, lubrication *See* Lubrication engineering

Engineering, marine *See* Naval engineering

Engineering, mechanical *See* Mechanical engineering

Engineering, military *See* Military engineering

Engineering, naval *See* Naval engineering

Engineering, nuclear *See* Nuclear engineering

Engineering, petroleum *See* Petroleum engineering

Engineering, sanitary *See* Sanitary engineering

English history
Albion Book Prize/NACBS Book Prize 16411
Dissertation Year Fellowship 16412
Morris D. Forkosch Prize 2472
Walter D. Love Prize in History 16413
NACBS-Huntington Library Fellowship 16414
John Ben Snow Foundation Prize 16415
Donald M. Sutherland Prize 4126

English literature
ADE Francis Andrew March Award 5656
Albion Book Prize/NACBS Book Prize 16411
Distinguished Scholar Award 12523
Distinguished Service Award 14831
Keats - Shelley Association Annual Prize 12524
Tennessee Teacher of Excellence 19966
Calvert, Woodall, and McMillan Writing Awards 5627

Entertainment (*See also* Animated films; Humor)
Academy & Achievement Awards 80
Academy of Country Music Awards 86
Angel of the Year 21757
The Austin Chronicle Best of Austin 6093
Award of Excellence 9541
Circus Fans Association of American Award 8009
Country Music Association Awards 8620
Crystal Awards 21713
Cecil B. De Mille Award 10512
Emmy Awards for Primetime Programming 127
"Focus on Disability" Grant 21715
GIAA Entertainment Achievement Awards 10202
Gold Ribbon for Promotion of Canadian Talent (Radio) 6895
Golden Globe Awards 10513
Hugh M. Hefner First Amendment Award 17396
Helping Hand Award 21328
Humanitas Prize 10608
ILDA Award 11713
Juno Awards 6846
Lefthanders of the Year Awards 12764
Lifetime Achievement 200
SHINE (Sexual Health in Entertainment) Awards 13238
VFW Hall of Fame Award 21340

Entomology *See* Zoology

Entrepreneurship *See* Business

Environmental conservation
"54" Founders Award 12263
Achievement Awards 14165
Ansel Adams Award for Conservation Photography 18450
Ansel Adams Conservation Award 21625
Alice Hamilton Prize 4065
AMAS Scholarship 5163
American Wood Council Wood Design Award 21820
Annual Essay Contest Award 9003
Archie Carr Lifetime Achievement Award 7590
Arthur Sidney Bedell Award 21476
Aviation Environment Award 9426
Award for Environmental Achievement 9572
Award for Excellence in Environmental Conservation 15419
Awards for Distinguished Service in Environmental Planning 8513
Awards for Science and Ethics in Transportation Research 460
Banff Mountain Film Festival 6236
Joseph Barbosa Earth Fund Award 18451
BBC Environment Award 7723
Hugh Hammond Bennett Award 19385
Albert E. Berry Medal 7410
David R. Brower Environmental Journalism Award 18452
Business Conservation Leadership Award 14149
CAEAL Appreciation Award 6881
CBI International Environmental Award 2877
Lawrence K. Cecil Award 2761
Certificates of Appreciation, Citations, and Commendations 18453
Frank A. Chambers Award 318
ChevronTexaco Conservation Awards Program 7864
Citizens for Alternatives to Chemical Contamination Award 8015
Edward J. Cleary Award 645
Climatics Award 10918
William E. Colby Award 18454
Commendation Award 19386
Community Service Award
American Society of Landscape Architects 4475
Sierra Club 18455
Neil Compton Award 16992
Conservation Award 16145
Conservation Teacher of the Year 13150
Conservationist of the Year 6075
Corporate Award 6076
Corporate Environmental Achievement Award 1671
Distinguished Service/Achievement Awards 18456
Distinguished Service Award 14151
DiVelbiss Award 9095
Marjory Stoneman Douglas Award 15489
William O. Douglas Award 18457
Mark Dubois Award 9817
J. R. Dymond Public Service Award 16759
Earthcare Award 18458
Education Award 16146
Environment and Energy Achievement Awards Program 2288
Environmental Achievement Award 5795
Environmental Award 16020
Environmental Conservation Distinguished Service Award 2818
Environmental Education Award 14950
Environmental Issues Council Corporate Award 9214
Environmental Personality of the Year in Africa 255
Environmental Quality Research Award 4243
Park W. Espenschade Award 10919
Excellence in Communications Awards 14153
Excellence in Environmental Engineering 646
Gordon Maskew Fair Memorial Award 647
Farm Management Conservation Award 14154
Francis P. Farquhar Mountaineering Award 18460
Fellow
Institute of Environmental Sciences and Technology 10920
Soil and Water Conservation Society 19387
Fellow Grade of Membership 319
Virginia Ferguson Award 18461
FFA Award 9096
Financial Post Environment Awards for Business 8539
FON Achievement Award 16760
FON Corporate Award 16761
Founders Award 9296
Simon W. Freese Environmental Engineering Award and Lecture 4314
George Perkins Marsh Prize 4066
German Marshall Fund of the United States Fellowships and Awards 9974
GGAS Service Awards 10059
Henry Giese Structures and Environment Award 4222
Goldman Environmental Prize 10064
Goodyear Conservation Awards 14155
Graduate Student Award 9097
Great Lakes Commission - Sea Grant Fellowship 13357
Samuel Arnold Greeley Award 4320
S. Smith Griswold Award 320
The GWIC Award 10055
Health, Safety, and Environment Award 19243
Heinz Award in the Environment 10381
Fred Hermann Memorial Award 10921
High School Science Fair National Award 21488
Honor Award 19388
Honorary Fellow 10922
Honorary Life Members 18462
Honorary Member
Air and Waste Management Association 321
American Academy of Environmental Engineers 648
William T. Hornaday Bronze and Silver Medals 6579
William T. Hornaday Gold Certificate 6580
William T. Hornaday Gold Medal 6581
William T. Hornaday Unit Award 6582
Wesley W. Horner Award 4329
IAEWP Diploma of Honour 11344
IAEWP Membership in Good Standing 11345
Iron Eyes Cody Award 12530
J. I. Hambleton Award 9098
Jeske Award 16371
Mrs. Lyndon B. Johnson Award 12531
Fraser Johnstone Award 1764
Stanley E. Kappe Award 649
Keep America Beautiful National Awards 12532
Oliver Kehrlein Award 18463
George A. Kinias Service Award 14951
Knauss Marine Policy Fellowship 13358
Robert L. Kozik Award for Environmental Reporting 15519
Alfred B. LaGasse Medal 4478
John Lambert, Jr. Forest Stewardship Award 13159
Richard M. Leonard Award 18464
Leopold-Hidy Prize 4067
Lindbergh Grants 7808
Loeb Fellowship 10281

Environmental (continued)
Robert Marshall Award 21626
John Martin Outstanding Younger Member Award 10923
Karl Mason Award 17164
Stephen Tyng Mather Award 15490
Mike McCloskey Award 18465
Robert Earll McConnell Award 2821
Euan P. McFarlane Environmental Award 12234
Richard Beatty Mellon Award 322
Chico Mendes Award 18466
Merit Award 19389
Susan E. Miller Award/Chapter Service Awards 18467
George T. Minasian Award 323
Chandler - Misener Award 11241
William Penn Mott Jr. Park Leadership Award 15491
John Muir Award 18468
Olaus and Margaret Murie Award 21627
National Awards for Environmental Sustainability - Searching for Success Program 17991
National Medal of Technology 15678
Newsletter Award 10925
Frederick Law Olmsted Medal 4483
One Club Award 18469
Outstanding Affiliate Award 16372
Outstanding Environmental and Engineering Geologic Project Award 5676
Outstanding Individual at the Local Level 16373
Outstanding Individual at the National/ International Level 16374
Outstanding Organization at the Local Level 16375
Outstanding Organization at the National/ International Level 16376
Outstanding Service Award
Colorado River Watch Network 8221
Great Lakes Commission 10143
Soil and Water Conservation Society 19390
Outstanding Service to Environmental Education Award 16377
Palladium Medal 1198
Pollution Prevention Award 15472
President's Award
Institute of Environmental Sciences and Technology 10926
North American Association for Environmental Education 16378
President's Award for the Outstanding Conference Paper 14952
President's Environment and Conservation Challenge Awards 9365
President's Environmental Youth Awards (PEYA) 20575
Professional Service Award 14158
Rachel Carson Prize 4068
General Edwin W. Rawlings Award for Environmental Achievement (Manager and Technician) 353
Reliability Test and Evaluation Award 10927
Lyman A. Ripperton Award 324
Elsie Roemer Conservation Awards 10060
Roger A. Morse Teaching/Extension/ Regulatory Award 9099
Miroslaw Romanowski Medal 18172
Theodore Roosevelt Distinguished Service Medal 20066
Rosner/Johnson Memorial Scholarships 9004
Albert Schweitzer Prize for Humanitarianism 12417
Monroe Seligman Award 10928
J. Deane Sensenbaugh Environmental Technology Award 325
Raymond J. Sherwin Award 18470
Silver Anchor Award 9819
Space Simulation Award 10930
Special Recognition Award 14159
Special Service/Achievement Awards 18471
Special Service Award 14160
Harold and Margaret Sprout Award 12048
Howard E. Stanfield Distinguished Service Award 19613
STAR Program 20577
Walter A. Starr Award 18472
Sustainable Business Award 21092
Lee Symmes Community Award 16766
Freeman Tilden Award 15492
Trainer of the Year Award 14953
Trophee Environment 7782
Tyler Prize for Environmental Achievement 4975
University of Louisville Grawemeyer Award for Ideas Improving World Order 21042
Waste Management Award 326
Edgar Wayburn Award 18473
WEC Gold Medal for International Corporate Achievement in Sustainable Development 21893
Willis J. Whitfield Award 10932
Denny and Ida Wilcher Award 18474
Harvey W. Wiley Award 4992
William D. Hatfield Award 21501

Environmental health
Annual Essay Contest Award 9003
Arizona Heritage Grant 13215
Audubon A Award 13149
Award for Excellence in Environmental Health 14173
Awards for Courage 15947
A. Harry Bliss Editors' Award 14941
Bouquet of the Month 16535
Caring for the Earth 17791
Certificate of Merit 14942
Earth Keeper of the Year 13056
EBEE Award 9298
Environmental Excellence Award 8412
ETEBA Scholarship 9080
Jonathan Forman Award 651
Friend of Casco Bay Award 9788
Honorary Member 14944
Joseph Wood Krutch Medal 10598
Carlton Lee Award 652
Sidney D. Leverett, Jr. Environmental Science Award 235
Walter S. Mangold Award 14945
National Medal of Technology 15678
Past Presidents' Award 14946
Power-Life Award 10911
Presidential Citation 14947
President's Award 11426
Herbert J. Rinkel Award 653
Rosner/Johnson Memorial Scholarships 9004
Sabbatical Exchange Program 14948
William D. Schaeffer Environmental Award 10137
Walter F. Snyder Award 16584
Fred L. Soper Lecture 4633
Spes Hominum Award 16585

Equestrian *See* Horsemanship

Essays
Alice Abel Cultural and Creative Arts Program 3141
Anthem Essay Contest 6173
Arizona Authors' Association Annual National Literary Contest 5048
Armed Forces Joint Warfighting Essay Contest 20707
Vincent Astor Memorial Leadership Essay Contest 20708
Award for Research on Automotive Lubricants 19034
Arleigh Burke Essay Contest 20709
L. J. Cartwright Award 6917
Coast Guard Essay Contest 20710
Arch T. Colwell Merit Award 19039
Dissertation Competition 15427
Enlisted Essay Contest 20711
Essay Contest in Progress in Religion Through the Sciences 12403
The Fountainhead Essay Contest 6174
Dr. Robert H. Goddard Scholarship 15789
Theodore Christian Hoepfner Awards 19507
Roscoe Hogan Environmental Law Essay Contest 18120
E. I. Hood Award 6918
Harry L. Horning Memorial Award 19046
Institutionalist Prize 5362
International Navies Essay Contest 20712
The W. Turrentine Jackson Prize 2484
Laureates 900
Letras de Oro Literary Prizes 21059
Light Metals Division *JOM* Best Paper Award 13454
Charles M. Manly Memorial Medal 19051
Marine Corps Essay Contest 20714
Maryknoll Student Essay Contest 13129
McGinnis-Ritchie Award 19527
Robert A. Miller Memorial Prize 8155
National Jewish Book Award - Yiddish Literature 12333
National Magazine Awards 15355
New Letters Writing Awards 16190
Nonfiction Contest 15992
Richard O'Connor Essay Award 5132
William Osler Medal 1061
Outstanding Technologist Award 19230
PACS Technology Award 6920
Robert Peele Memorial Award 18821
Dr. Petrie Memorial Award 6921
Fellows' Ernst Posner Prize 18961
Publications Awards 10348
Pushcart Prize: Best of the Small Presses 17770
Summerfield G. Roberts Award 19415
Scholarly Paper Competition 15429
Scholarship Contests 15782
Richard H. Shryock Medal 1062
Sister Mary Arthur "Sharing the Light" Award 6924
Space Coast Writers Guild Conference Awards 19535
Russell S. Springer Award 19058
Stefanko Best Paper Award 18826
Student Essay Competition in Healthcare Management 1876
Colin and Ailsa Turbayne International Berkeley Essay Prize Competition 21102

Essays (continued)

Lila Wallace-Reader's Digest Writers' Awards 21430
WORDS/ISAAC AAC Consumer User Scholarship 11920
Wright Brothers Medal 19062
Writer's Digest Writing Competition 21979

Ethics
AIC Ethics Award 2798
Award of Recognition 20273
William G. Bartholome Award for Ethical Excellence 763
Bird Dog Award 8302
Elliott - Black Award 2202
Bower Award for Business Leadership 9742
Carol Burnett/University of Hawaii/AEJMC Ethics Prize 5344
Business Ethics Award 6314
COGEL Award 8603
Conscience In Media Award 4469
Ethical Culture School Book Award 9348
Executive Scholar and Research Fellow Programs 6315
Golden Broom Award 16770
Henry Knowles Beecher Award 10286
Herbert H. Lehman Ethics Award 12377
Master of the Game Award 15809
Daniel W. Mead Prizes 4340
National Endowment for the Humanities Grant Programs 14938
Charlotte W. Newcombe Doctoral Dissertation Fellowship 21826
ONS/Upjohn Quality of Life Award 16728
Outstanding Service Award 8604
Shevchenko Freedom Award 20269
Ukrainian of the Year Award 20271
UNWL Scholarship 20274
Elie Wiesel Prize in Ethics 21621

Ethnic affairs (*See also* Culture)
ARA Annual Award 3870
Award for Excellence in Multicultural Health 14174
Award for Outstanding Scholastic Achievement 2756
Pura Belpre Award 17950
The Byzantine-Patristic Medal and Certificate 2626
Chapter Award for Minority Enhancement 3487
James Comer Minority Research Fellowship for Medical Students 625
DAAD Prize for Distinguished Scholarship in German Studies 2623
Distinguished Contribution to Ethnic Minority Issues Award 18899
Distinguished Service Award 2766
Ethnic Minorities Screenwriting Competition 16000
Founders Award 10757
Freedom Award 10758
Global Leadership Award 2624
Gold Awards 16996
William W. Grimes Award for Excellence in Chemical Engineering 2775
HateBuster Hero Award 10290
Charles D. Henry Award 878
Huggins-Quarles Award 16888
Indiana State Senator Carolyn Mosby Above and Beyond Award 10759
Charles C. Irby Distinguished Service Award 14009
Reginald H. Jones Distinguished Service Award 13874
Jaap Kunst Prize 18672
Rosetta LeNoire Award 162
LITA-LSSI Minority Scholarship in Library and Information Technology 12829
LITA/OCLC Minority Scholarship in Library and Information Technology 12830
Literary Awards 9982
Mary Mahoney Award 3281
Minority Achievement Award 3495
Minority Business Leadership Awards 15389
Minority Initiatives Award 3496
Robert Morris Award 21516
National Minority Supplier Development Council Awards 15390
Outstanding Women of Color 11265
Ernest M. Pon Memorial Award 14010
George E. Pozzetta Dissertation Research Award 10705
Carlton C. Qualey Article Award 10706
REACH Racial Justice Corporate Award 22090
REFORMA Scholarship 17951
Robie Award for Achievement in Industry 12275
Theodore Saloutos Memorial Book Award in Immigration History 10707
Charles Seeger Prize 18673
Kalman Silvert Award 12701
Skanderbeg Medal 416
Small Business Advocates of the Year 20834
Student Awards 8700
Jeffrey S. Tanaka Memorial Dissertation Award in Psychology 18920
University of Louisville Grawemeyer Award for Ideas Improving World Order 21042
World Citizen 11692

European culture (*See also* East European culture)
Awards for Excellence in Teaching of the Classics 3418
Blenheim Award 7984
Farrow Award 7985
Charles J. Goodwin Award of Merit 3419
Honorary Member 7986
WESS Coutts Nijhoff International West European Specialist Study Grant 5615
Research Contracts 14757
Emery Reves Award 7987

European history
Herbert Baxter Adams Prize 2463
George Louis Beer Prize 2464
James Henry Breasted Prize 2467
Gilbert Chinard Prize 18676
Vladimar A. Pertzoff Prize 21116
Leo Gershoy Award 2473
Phyllis Goodhart Gordan Book Prize 17985
Thomas T. Hammond Award 21117
Jerzy Lojek Award 12458
WESS Coutts Nijhoff International West European Specialist Study Grant 5615
Premio del Rey Prize 2480

European literature (*See also* English literature; French literature; Irish literature; Italian literature; Spanish literature)
ASF Translation Prize 3879
Aldo and Jeanne Scaglione Prize for Studies in Germanic Languages and Literatures 13574
Aldo and Jeanne Scaglione Prize for Studies in Slavic Languages and Literatures 13575
Weiss/Brown Publication Subvention Award 16316

Exhibiting
Americas 2000: All Media Competition 13490
Americas 2000 Paper Works Competition 13491
Best Booth in Show 4806
Charles L. Towle Award 13549
Distinguished Service Award 10335
E-Cubed Awards 9370
Exhibit Focus Awards 20147
Fifth Sense Commendation 9719
Hazel Hays Award 9371
Philip Johnson Exhibition Catalogue Award 19023
Kohlstedt Exhibit Award 2965
Merit Award 5188
Sidewalk Sale and Exhibition 7776
James Smithson Society Grants 18570

Exploration (*See also* Geography)
Lew Bicking Award 15794
Certificate of Merit 15795
George Davidson Medal 2330
Explorers Medal 9375
Fellow of the Society 15796
National Geographic Society Centennial Award 15160
Research Grant 15801
Edward C. Sweeney Medal 9376

Export *See* International trade

Family planning
Celebrate Life Essay and Poster Contest 8106
Rosa Cisneros Award 11797
Judy Halpern Religious Freedom Award 16680
Jean Garton Award 16527
Maggie Awards 17369
Red Rose-White Rose Award 12568
Margaret Sanger Award 17370
SHINE (Sexual Health in Entertainment) Awards 13238
Volunteer of the Year Award 17372

Family relations (*See also* Child welfare; Counseling)
Adoption Hall of Fame Award 14748
AFT Foster Scholarship 196
Helen Allen Award 191
American Family Therapy Academy Awards 2215
Annual Awards for Chapter Programming 17086
Awards for Excellence 18865
Best in Media Awards 7915
Biennial Communications Award 447
H. Barksdale Brown Voluntarism Award 448

Subject Index

Family (continued)

BUDDY Award (Bringing Up Daughters Differently) 12768
Chief Justice Warren E. Burger Healer Awards 7916
Ernest W. Burgess Award 14859
Certificate of Appreciation 3670
Champions for Children 9705
Distinguished Contribution to Child Advocacy Award 3715
Distinguished Service to Children Award 17087
Distinguished Service to Families Award 14860
Family Faith & Freedom 9412
Family International Talent Awards Program 17088
Family Psychologist of the Year 3671
Father of the Year 9421
Heart of America 2952
Susan Hickman Memorial Research Award 17489
Reuben Hill Award 14861
Nicholas Hobbs Award 3719
Honorary Lifetime Membership 851
Jane Honikman Volunteer Award 17490
Judith Grove Adoption Activist Award 192
David Kirk Award 193
Victoria Leach Award 194
Phyllis B. Marriott President's Award 3142
Media Awards Competition 14862
Mother of the Year 3143
Jack Nicklaus Golf Family of the Year Award 15168
Ernest Osborne Award 14863
Outstanding Contribution to the Adoption Community 9396
Parenting Awards 7917
Ethel Parham Memorial Award 3144
Robert Rice Innovative Program Award 450
Margaret Elden Rich Memorial Award 451
Silver Ribbon Award to Outstanding Volunteer 10001
Single Parent of the Year Award 17090
STAR Awards 9401
Student Award 14864
Student Research Award 3673
Jan Trost Award 11899
Emma May Vilardi Humanitarian Award 852
Wimps, Grumblers, and Grousers Award 15438
Young Mother Representative 3145

Fashion (*See also* Beauty contests; Cosmetology; Design; Hairstyling; Modeling)

AMY Awards 22067
Atrium Award 21019
Black Tie Award 11633
CFDA Fashion Awards 8575
City of Toronto Awards for Excellence in Fashion Design 8047
Fabulous Fashion Independents 13654
Femmy 20286
FGF Awards 9419
In the Tradition of the American West Award 21546
International Designer Awards 11314
Lifetime Achievement Award 8576
Motion Picture Academy Awards/Television Emmy Awards: Black Tie Award 11634
Pantone Color Award 17062
Special Recognition Award 21547
Underfashion Club Scholarship Program 20287
Woolknit Design Awards 21832
Worst-Dressed Women 13655

Fashion modeling *See* Modeling

Feminism *See* Women

Fencing

Certificate of Merit 20581
Collegiate Coach of the Year 20582
Fencer of the Year (Men and Women) 20583
NCAA National Championships 14687
General George S. Patton, Jr. Memorial Trophy 20705
Regional Coach of the Year 20584
USFCA All-America Certificates (Men) 20585
USFCA All-America Certificates (Women) 20586
USFCA Honorable Mention 20587

Fiber science (*See also* Textile design; Textile industry)

Harold C. Chapin Award 1455
Distinguished Achievement in Basic or Applied Fiber Science 9539
International Achievement Awards Competition 10784
Henry E. Millson Award for Invention 1456
Olney Medal 1457
Howard DeWitt Smith Memorial Award 5988

Fiction (*See also* Science fiction; Short stories)

Alabama Authors Award 405
Ambassador Book Awards 9277
Marguerite de Angeli Prize 8845
Anisfield-Wolf Book Awards 8097
Annual Awards Competition 8565
Artists' Fellowships 16229
Aspen Gold Award 10358
AWP Award Series 5259
Elmer Holmes Bobst Literary Awards 16301
Bulwer-Lytton Fiction Contest 18257
Bumbershoot, The Seattle Arts Festival 16734
Butler Literary Award 12194
CAA Awards for Adult Literature 6953
Citations of Merit 13984
Matt Clark Prize 16095
College Fiction Contest 17394
Commonwealth Club of California Book Awards 8306
William L. Crawford Fantasy Award 11259
Delacorte Press Prize for a First Young Adult Novel 8846
Eaton Literary Awards Program 9125
Norma Epstein Foundation Awards 21112
ERB Life Achievement Award 6697
Ethical Culture School Book Award 9348
Favorite Book of the Year Award 18113
Fellowship for Creative and Performing Arts and Writers 914
Fellowship Program 17168
Fiction Contest 21996
Fine Arts Work Center Fellowships 9553
Gaston-Gouin, Alfred-DesRochers et Alphonse-Desjardins 5263
Georgia Author of the Year Awards 9972
Golden Heart Award 18114
Golden Lion Award 6698
The Greensboro Review Literary Awards 10170
Hackney Literary Awards 6402
Hall of Fame 12805
Heartland Prizes 7893
Drue Heinz Literature Prize 21099
Hemingway Foundation/PEN Award 17157
Horror/Ghost Contest 21997
Iowa Short Fiction Award 12190
Joseph Henry Jackson Literary Award 18249
Jesse Jones Award for Best Work of Fiction 20018
Kentucky Artists Fellowships 12562
Aga Khan Prize for Fiction 17094
Lannan Literary Awards 12691
Laureates 900
Letras de Oro Literary Prizes 21059
Literary Writers Competition 9467
Loft Mentor Series Award 12905
Los Angeles Times Book Prizes 12931
Matrix Award 16312
Michael Shaara Award 12957
James A. Michener - Paul Engle Fellowship 12191
Milkweed National Fiction Prize 13421
Milkweed Prize for Children's Literature 13422
Molly Award 10359
Morrison Book Prize 20100
Mythopoeic Fantasy Awards 13739
National Book Awards 14532
National Book Critics Circle Awards 14530
National Jewish Book Award - Fiction 12325
National Jewish Book Award - Yiddish Literature 12333
National Magazine Awards 4492
National Magazine Awards 15355
PEN/Phyllis Naylor Working Writer Fellowship 17143
Neustadt International Prize for Literature 21934
New Letters Writing Awards 16190
New Writers Awards 10141
Novel Manuscript Award 15993
Novella Award 17785
Ohioana Book Awards 16661
Outstanding Southeastern Author Award 19476
PEN Book-of-the-Month Club Translation Prize 17146
PEN/Faulkner Award for Fiction 17154
PEN Prison Writing Awards 17148
James D. Phelan Literary Award 18251
Plimpton Prize 17095
PNWA Literary Contest 17011
Poetry, Fiction and Nonfiction Contest 8225
Katherine Anne Porter Prize for Fiction 16361
Prometheus Award 12806
Pulitzer Prizes 17749
Pushcart Prize: Best of the Small Presses 17770
QWF Awards 17801
Sir Walter Raleigh Award for Fiction 16520
Harold U. Ribalow Prize 10213
RITA Award 18115

Fiction (continued)

Summerfield G. Roberts Award 19415
Romance Contest 22000
Carl Sandburg Literary Arts Award 9806
John Simmons Short Fiction Award 12192
Lillian Smith Book Awards 19521
Society of Midland Authors Awards 19186
Space Coast Writers Guild Conference Awards 19535
Spur Awards 21576
Three-Day Novel Contest 4990
TNR Awards in Fiction and Poetry 16075
Torgi Talking Book of the Year 7306
Towson University Prize for Literature 20145
Travel Writing Award 22002
Lila Wallace-Reader's Digest Writers' Awards 21430
Western States Book Awards 21571
Edith Wharton Citation of Merit for State Author 16294
Whiting Writers' Award 21610
Wilbur Awards 17971
Ethel Wilson Fiction Prize 21523
Young Hoosier Book Award 5388

Field hockey *See* Hockey

Film competitions *See* Film festivals

Film criticism
Pulitzer Fellowships 17748

Film festivals
Air Canada People's Choice Award 20114
Alberta Film and Television Awards 422
Amateur PSA/VMPD American International Film and Video Festival 17283
American International Film/Video Festival 3147
Animal Behavior Society Film Festival Awards 4959
Ann Arbor Film Co-op Award 4968
Aspen Filmfest 5196
Aspen Shortsfest 5197
Atlanta Film and Video Festival 6025
Atlantic Film Festival 6033
Audience and Juried Awards 16977
Audience Awards 9603
Banff Mountain Film Festival 6236
Banff Television Festival 6239
Best First Feature Award 21644
Between the Lines Award Best Gay/Lesbian Film 4969
Bi-Annual Image Awards 21734
Big Muddy Film Festival Awards 6372
Stan Brakhage Award for Best Short Subject 8881
Gordon Bruce Award for Humour 16945
Ken Burns Best of the Festival Award 4970
Canadian International Annual Film/Video Festival 7206
John Cassavetes Award 8882
Chicago International Children's Film Festival 7888
Chicago International Film Festival 8001
Cin(E)-Poetry Festival 15512
CITYN Award for Best Canadian First Feature Film 20115
Christopher Columbus Award 7947
Columbus International Film and Video Festival 7948
Charles A. Crain Desert Palm Achievement Award 17044
Edgar Dale Award 7949
EARTHWATCH Film Awards 9065
Edition International Film Festival 9230
Ben Franklin Award 7950
Golden Gate Awards 18246
Golden Sheaf Awards 22048
Golden Space Needle Audience Awards 18395
Grand Jury Awards 9604
Grand Prizes 16950
HeSCA Film Festival 10326
Honorable Mentions 4971
Humboldt International Film Festival 10610
INTERCOM: International Communication Film and Video Festival 8003
International Wildlife Film Festival 12141
Lawrence Kasdan Award Best Narrative Film 4972
Krzysztof Kieslowski Award for Best Foreign Feature 8883
Mayor's Lifetime Achievement Award 8884
Norman McLaren Heritage Award 16951
Montreal International Festival of Films on Art 11613
Montreal International Festival of New Cinema and Video 13598
Montreal World Film Festival 13607
Mountainfilm in Telluride 13647
Nashville Film Festival 13758
National Film Board of Canada Public Prize 16953
New American Cinema Award 18396
New Directors Showcase 18397
Northwest Film and Video Festival 16560
Portland International Film Festival 16561
Pratt & Whitney Canada Grand Prix 11614
President's Award 7952
Paul Robeson Awards 16314
Rochester International Film Festival 18089
Rottimans World Film International Critics' Award as Selected by Fipresci 20116
San Antonio Cine Festival 10188
Short Film Award 21645
Special Awards 10333
Starz People's Choice Award 8885
Ten Best of the West Film Festival 3148
Toronto-City Award for Best Canadian Feature Film 20118
UNICEF Award for Films 20599
U.S. International Film and Video Festival 21143
U.S. Outdoor Travel Film Festival 13355
Vancouver International Film Festival 21273
Robert W. Wagner Narrative Screenwriting Award 7953
David L. Wolper Best Documentary Award 21646
WORLDFEST - Houston International Film and Video Festival 21969
Young Canadian Filmmakers 19808
Young People's Film and Video Festival 16562

Films (*See also* Animated films; Audiovisuals; Cable television; Documentary films; Educational films; Entertainment; Film criticism; Film festivals; Television; Video)
Academy Honorary Awards 111
Academy of Country Music Awards 86
ACE Eddie Award 1804
Agfa - Gevaert Gold Medal Award 19188
Robert B. Aldrich Service Award 8939
Father Adrien Arsenault Senior Arts Award 17544
Artists' Fellowships 16229
Award of Excellence 9541
Baltimore Independent Film/Video Makers Competition 6230
Erik Barnouw Award 16882
Barometer Star Poll 6570
Big Muddy Film Festival Awards 6372
Blue Ribbon Awards 6571
Breakthrough Director Award 10720
Bronze Anvil Awards 17720
Bush Artist Fellows Program 6700
Frank Capra Achievement Award 8940
Career Achievement Award 9543
Central Florida Film and Video Awards 9724
Harry Chapin Media Awards 21925
Chetwynd Award for Entrepreneurial Excellence 7093
Chicago Film Critics Awards - Chicago Flame 7886
Chicago International Film Festival 8001
Jack Chisholm Award for Lifetime Achievement 7094
Christopher Awards 7971
CINE Eagle Award 8608
CINE Golden Eagle Award 8609
CINE Master's Series Award 8610
City of Toronto Apprenticeship Screen Award 8046
Christopher Columbus Award 7947
Columbus International Film and Video Festival 7948
Conservation/Outdoor Recreation Film/Video Award Program 16967
Corporate Leadership Award 2811
Corrections Film Festival 2024
Creative Arts Award 12159
Creative Caf Sound Completion & Design Grant 21712
Valentine Davies Award 21991
Brig. Gen. Robert L. Denig Distinguished Service Award 20684
Dissertation Award 18651
Distinguished Performance Award 20686
Dockers Khakis for Women of Independent Vision Grant 21714
Eastman Kodak Gold Medal Award 19190
Thomas A. Edison Black Maria Film and Video Festival 9161
The Epiphany Prizes 12402
Ethnic Minorities Screenwriting Competition 16000
Mrs. Inez M. Fauria Award 8614
Fellowship for Creative and Performing Arts and Writers 914
Film Grants 17554
"Focus on Discrimination" Grant 21716
Fuji Gold Medal Award 19191
Gavel Awards 1533
Geminis 82
Genies 83
Global Media Awards for Excellence in Population Reporting 17469
Gold Awards 16996
Gold Medal of Honor for Film/Video 13989
Golden Globe Awards 10513
Golden Sheaf Awards 22048
Gotham Awards 10721
Governor's Screenwriting Competition 21388

Films (continued)

Grants for Arts Projects 14930
John Grierson International Gold Medal Award 19192
D. W. Griffith Award 8942
Heart of America 2952
Jean Hersholt Humanitarian Award 112
HeSCA Film Festival 10326
Honorary Life Member 8943
Dutch Horton Award 5683
Howard Fellows 10571
Humanitas Prize 10608
ILCA Film and Broadcast Competition 11699
Image Awards 14049
INTERCOM: International Communication Film and Video Festival 8003
International Award 21717
International Competition Cinema in Industry (CINDY) 11287
International Documentary Association Achievement Awards 11541
International Television Programming and Promotions Awards 16223
Journal Award 19194
Jury Prize for the Dance on Camera Festival 8734
Kennedy Center Honors 12552
Kentucky Artists Fellowships 12562
Laurel Award for Screen 21992
Liberty Live Wire Grant 21718
Lifetime Achievement Award 8944
Arthur Loew Jr. Crystal Vision Award 5684
Mangled Skyscraper Award 10057
MBFS 13325
Media Awards Competition 14862
Movie Worsts Awards 10276
National Student Production Awards Competition 14539
NATO Awards 14441
Jose L. Nazar Grant for Latino Projects and/or Latina Filmmakers 21719
New York Women in Film and Television Post Production Completion Grants 21720
Northwest Film and Video Festival 16560
OSU Photography and Cinema Alumni Society Award 7951
Outstanding American Films of the Year Awards 2241
Outstanding Directorial Achievement Award for Feature Films 8947
James D. Phelan Art Awards 18250
Philadelphia International Film Festival (Philafilm Awards) 468
Presidential Proclamation 19196
Prix Albert-Tessier 17793
Prix Andre-Guerin 18604
Prix de la Critique Internationale 5922
Prix des Montreal 13608
Prix Gemeaux 84
Mrs. Ann Radcliffe Awards 8615
President Dr. Donald A. Reed Award 8616
Ruben Salazar Award for Communications 14808
Saturn Awards 123
Franklin J. Schaffner Achievement Award 8949
Dore Schary Awards 4984
Science Screen Report Award 15691
Screen Awards 21993
Screenwriter's Contest Award and Promotion 16001
SHINE (Sexual Health in Entertainment) Awards 13238
Show Canada Showmanship Awards 13622
Sidney Poitier Fellowship 6425
Special Achievement Awards 113
NFB - John Spotton Award for Best Canadian Short Film 20117
Spur Awards 21576
Student Award for Scholarly Writing 18652
Rev. Dr. Montague Summers Memorial Award 8617
Technicolor/Herbert T. Kalmus Gold Medal Award 19199
Telly Awards 19964
Theatre Library Association Award 20060
Tribute of the Film Society of Lincoln Center 9545
UNICEF Award for Films 20599
Vancouver International Film Festival 21273
Visual Communicators Department of the Year Awards 11288
Horace Walpole Gold Medal 8618
Samuel L. Warner Memorial Medal Award 19200
John Wayne Award 11815
Western Heritage Awards (Wrangler Award) 14887
Wilbur Awards 17971
Women in Film and Television Florida Independent Filmmaker Grant 21721
Women in Film Foundation Cash Grant 21722
Young People's Film and Video Festival 16562

Finance (*See also* Accounting; Banking; Business; Economics; Financial planning; Insurance; Public finance)
Accountants, Bankers and Factors Division Award 2890
ACFAS/Caisse de Depot et Placement du Quebec Prize (in Finance) 5536
Affiliated Chapter Awards 10342
AIMR Distinguished Service Award 5391
AIMR Special Service Award 5392
Annual Awards for Distinction in Financial Management 20557
Avatar Award 6641
Award for Achievement in Business Growth 8290
Award for Excellence in Corporate Reporting 5393
Award for Professional Excellence 5394
Award of Distinction 12173
Award of Merit 35
Awards for Excellence 10110
Board of Directors' Award 10337
Bower Award for Business Leadership 9742
Brattle Prizes in Corporate Finance 2243
Paul Bunyan Award 70
Canadian Award for Financial Reporting 10111
Certificate of Achievement for Excellence in Financial Reporting 10112
Certified International Financier 11685
Chapter Achievement Award 21740
Competitive Papers Award 9549
Continuous Service Award 71
Graham L. Davis Awards of Excellence 10338
Distinguised Service Award 21883
Distinguished Budget Presentation Award 10113
Distinguished Service Award
Defense Credit Union Council 8795
Prospectors and Developers Association of Canada 17690
Distinguished Service Award 19768
Distinguished Service Award in Investment Education 12175
Loren Dunton Memorial Award 11395
Excellence in Financial Journalism 16292
Fellow 36
Financial Post Annual Report Awards 8537
Daniel J. Forrestal III, Leadership Award for Professional Ethics and Standards of Investment Practice 5395
Good Grant Award 8994
Graham and Dodd Award 5396
Harold Hammerman Spirit of Education Award 14434
Thomas L. Hansberger Leadership in Global Investing Award 5397
Honorary Life Member 37
Industrial Appreciation Award 38
International Fellowship of Certified Collectors 72
International Leadership Award 20461
Charles V. Keane Distinguished Service Award 39
Justin Ford Kimball Award 2546
Leaders Recognition Society Award 21741
Gerald Loeb Awards 20990
Viola R. MacMillan Developer's Award 17692
Nicholas Molodovsky Award 5398
Frederick C. Morgan Award 10339
Outstanding Section and Region Award 40
Policymaker of the Year 11551
Popular Annual Financial Reporting Award Program 10114
President's Award 11396
Nancy Ruggles Travel Awards 11255
Donald L. Scantlebury Memorial Award 12428
Robert M. Shelton Award 10340
C. Stewart Sheppard Award 5399
Smith Breeden Prizes 2244
Tanya Gritz Award for Excellence in Public Finance 19769
James R. Vertin Award 5400
VMI (Virginia Military Institute) Future Captain of Industry Award 21408
Woman of the Year Award 21742
O. T. Zimmerman Founder's Award 41

Financial journalism *See* Business journalism

Financial law *See* Law

Financial planning
Chief Financial Officers Award for Distinction in Public Finance 20532
Competitive Papers Award 9549
Distinguished Service Award 14325
P. Kemp Fain, Jr. Award 9551
Gale Financial Development Award 2977
Government Affairs Award of Recognition 6683

Fine arts *See* Art; Arts and humanities; Music

Fire fighting
Award of Valor 1080
Director's Franklin Award 9555
Fire Explorer Post Award 11352
Fire Fighter of the Quarter 6286
Fire Fighter of the Year 14554
Fireman of the Year 11616
Franklin Award for Federal Excess Personal Property 9557
Franklin Award for State Fire Assistance 9558
Franklin Award for Volunteer Fire Assistance 9559
Everett E. Hudiburg Award 11623
IAFF Media Awards Contest 11355
International Benjamin Franklin Fire Service Award 11353
Law Enforcement and Fire Safety Commendation Medal 15773
Man of the Year
International Fire Photographers Association 11619
National Association of Fire Investigators 14230
Master Fire Photographer 11620
William G. Nolan Service Award 11621
Ontario Medal for Firefighter Bravery 16754
Public Safety Recognition 6287
VFW Emergency Services Award 21338
VFW Firefighter Award 21339
Henry N. Wilwers Fire Buff of the Year 11617

Fire prevention
Jack Bono Engineering Communications Award 19127
Burn Prevention Award 1600
Design for Humanity Award 4460
Fire Management Award 9556
Fire Protection Man/Woman of the Year 19128
Arthur B. Guise Medal 19129
S. H. Ingberg Award 5958
National Smokey Bear Awards 9560
Harold E. Nelson Service Award 19130
Poster Contest 9777

Firearms
Award of Merit 14228
Intercollegiate Pistol Championships 15645
Marksmanship Award 21322
National Championships 15646
National Police Shooting Championships 15647

Fireworks
Montreal International Fireworks Competition 13600
Pyrotechnics Guild International Competition 17776

Fishing
Ambassador Award 9471
Andrew J. Boehm Graduate Fellowship in the Fisheries Sciences 4671
Charles E. Brooks Memorial Award 9472
Buz Buszek Memorial Award 9473
Council Award of Excellence 9474
Distinguished Service Award 20209
Fisherman of the Year 18230
Arnold Gingrich Memorial Award 9476
Gold Trout Award 20210
Roderick Haig-Brown Award 9477
Don Harger Memorial Award 9478
Dr. James Henshall Award 9479
Honorary Membership Award 15047
International Game Fish Association Awards 11645
Lew Jewett Memorial Award 9480
Kathern Mathies Grant 20215
Stanley Lloyd Conservation Award 9481
Man of the Year 9482
McKenzie Cup 9483
Memorial Life Membership Awards 9484
Dick Nelson Fly Tying Teaching Award 9485
NRA Club Achievement Award 10264
Order of the Lapis Lazuli 9486
President's Pin Award 9487
Trout Conservationist of the Year 20211
Warmwater Management Award 9488
Woman of the Year 9489
Lee Wulff Award 9490

Fishing industry
AFS Award for Excellence in Fisheries Education 2250
AFS Award of Excellence 2251
AFS Distinguished Service Award 2252
AFS Meritorious Service Award 2253
Dr. J. Frances Allen Scholarship Award 2254
Atlantic Offshore Fishermen's Association Annual Award 6041
Best Student Paper Award 11684
Distinguished Service Award 11686
Honorary Membership 2255
National Recreational Fisheries Awards 9568
Olin Fellowships 6043
President's Fishery Conservation Award 2256
Skinner Memorial Fund Award 2258
Student Writing Contest 2259
Carl R. Sullivan Fishery Conservation Award 2260
Carl R. Sullivan Memorial Membership Award 2261
David Wallace Award 15705

Fitness *See* **Health and fitness**

Fluid power industry
Distinguished Achievement Award to Fluid Power Educator 11627
Fluid Power Achievement Award 15054
Outstanding Chapter Award 11628
Outstanding Industry Leader 11629
Standards Development Awards 15055

Flying
Airport Safety Award 9576
Lewin B. Barringer Memorial Trophy 18578
BFA President's Award 6215
Certificate of Appreciation 18579
Chairman of the Board Awards 6216
Championship Director Awards, Competition Division 6217
Chapter of the Year 20612
Marion C. Cruce Trophy 18580
CSPA Service Award 7508
Albert Desmond Memorial Award, Competition Division 6218
Richard C. du Pont Trophy 18581
Warren E. Eaton Memorial Trophy 18582
Exceptional Achievement Award 18583
Exceptional Service 20613
Exceptional Service Award 18584
Farmer Appreciation Award 6219
Gas Balloon Championships 6220
Joe Giltner Memorial Trophy 18585
Kolstad Junior Soaring Awards 18586
Glenn R. Masterson Memorial Trophy 7509
National Championships 7510
National Point Leader Award, Competition Division 6221
National Soaring Hall of Fame 9735
Newsletter of the Year 20614
Presidential Citation 20615
Annie Pryne Memorial Award, Competition Division 6222
Regional Directors Award 6223
Rookie of the Year 6224
Schreder 15-Meter Class Trophy 18587
Shields-Trauger Award 6225
Soaring Hall of Fame 18588
Standard Class Trophy 18589
Larissa Stroukoff Memorial Trophy 18590
Paul E. Tuntland Memorial Award 18591
United States Hang Gliding Association Commendation 20616
U.S. National Hot Air Balloon Champion 6226

Folklore
Chicago Folklore Prize 20994
Folk Heritage Award 16503
Wayland D. Hand Award for Academic Achievement in Folklore and Mythology Studies 8889
W. W. Newell Prize 2264
Peter and Iona Opie Prize 2265
Prix Gerard-Morisset 17796

Food (*See also* Cookbook writing; Dairy industry; Food processing; Nutrition; Restaurants; Wine)
Achievement Award 3049
Achieving Excellence Award 11536
AFJ Awards Competition 5686
Amis d'Escoffier Society Awards 12783
The Austin Chronicle Best of Austin 6093
The Austin Chronicle Hot Sauce Contest 6094
The James Beard Foundation/Cervena Council/D'Artagnan Who's Who of Food and Beverage in America 12286
The James Beard Foundation Restaurant Awards 12287
Jane G. Benet Culinary Scholarship 19410
Best Paper Award 12131
Borden Award 938
Cake Show Competition Plaques 7494
Caterer Award 11324
Chef Award 11325
Julia Child Cookbook Awards 11326
Culinary Educator Award 11327
Distinguished Extension-Industry Service Award 3050
Distinguished Research Award 3051
Distinguished Teaching Award 3052
Doctorate of Bananistry Medal 11417
Electronic Media Award 11328
Entrepreneur Award 11329
Food Industry Award 14943
Gold Show Award 6844
Golden & Silver Penguin Awards 10145
Bert Greene Memorial Awards 11330
Hall of Flame 12488
Hubert Humphrey Research Grant 18345

Food (continued)
IFT Food Science Journalism Awards 10940
Industry Advancement Award 3045
Intercollegiate Meat Judging Meritorious Service Award 3053
International Chili Cook-off 4667
International Leadership Award 11233
Edward C. Jones Community Service Award 3046
Journalism Awards 12288
La Leche League International Award of Achievement 12628
La Leche League International Award of Appreciation 12629
La Leche League International Award of Excellence 12630
La Leche League International Award of Recognition 12631
La Leche League International Founders' Award 12632
Lincoln Foodservice Grant for Innovations in School Foodservice 18346
Marketing Publicist Award 11331
Master of Bananistry Medal 11418
Mother of All Vinegar Contest 21370
National Chef of the Year 7066
Peanut Hall of Fame 3367
Peanut Research and Education Award 3368
Pillsbury Bake-Off (R) Contest 9918
Presidential Award 9654
President's Award 7067
Professional Development Awards 18348
Edward T. Sajous Achievement Award 14054
Sandy Sanderson Award 7068
Ronald C. Schmitz Silver Spoon Award 14055
Supplier of the Year Award 3047
Team of the Year 12489
Vegetarian Awareness Month Awards 21283
Vegetarian Essay Contest 21285
Viking Range Awards for Broadcast Media 12290
The World Food Prize 21919

Food processing
Accomplishment Award 1259
Achievement Award
American Association of Meat Processors 1260
American Meat Science Association 3049
AHA National Homebrew Competition Awards 2522
American Cured Meat Championships 1261
Andrew Rutherford Scholarship 10745
Nicholas Appert Award 10934
Babcock-Hart Award 10935
Best Booth Award 1262
Brewer of the Year 10535
Stephen S. Chang Award for Lipid or Flavor Science 10936
William V. Cruess Award 10937
Samuel J. Crumbine Consumer Protection Award 11229
Cured Meat Awards 10669
Cured Meats Hall of Fame 1263
DFISA-ASAE Food Engineering Award 11362
Endowment Fund 32
Excellence in Teaching Award 33
Carl R. Fellers Award 10938
Food, Pharmaceutical and Bioengineering Division Award in Chemical Engineering 2770
Food Technology Industrial Achievement Award 10939
Golden Cleaver Award 1264
Hall of Fame Outstanding Service 13525
IAFIS-FPEI Food Engineering Award 4225
IFT International Award 10941
Industrial Scientist Award 10942
Intercollegiate Meat Judging Meritorious Service Award 3053
International Award 3054
Colonel Rohland A. Isker Award 17996
Clarence Knebel Best of Show Memorial Award 1265
Marcel Loncin Research Prize 10943
Meat Processing Award 3055
Outstanding Service Award 1266
R. C. Pollock Award 3056
Samuel Cate Prescott Award 10944
Quality Award 6737
Research and Development Award 10945
Sharpest Knife in North America Award 1267
Shogren Award 11235
Signal Service Award 3057
Colonel Merton Singer Award 17997
Special Recognition Award 3058
Elizabeth Fleming Stier Award 10946
Harvey W. Wiley Award 4992
Calvert L. Willey Distinguished Service Award 10947
F. W. Witt Supplier of the Year Award 1268
World Champion Cheesemaker 21668

Food service (*See also* Restaurants)
ACUHO-I Award 5622
William H. Albers Award 9660
William Applebaum Award 9653
Chef Herman Breithaupt Award 11523
William W. Carpenter Award 16385
CHRIE Industry Recognition Award 11524
Communications Program Awards 9658
Samuel J. Crumbine Consumer Protection Award 9665
Horst G. Denk Congressional Award 10713
Director of the Year Award 18343
Doctorate of Food Service Award 16386
FMI - *Woman's Day* Advertising Merit Awards 9661
Foodservice Operator of the Year 11631
Golden Chain Award 16010
Golden Penguin Awards 15132
Heart of the Program Award 18344
Daryl Van Hook Industry Award 14128
Loyal E. Horton Dining Awards 14129
Hot Concepts! Awards 16011
Richard Lichtenfelt Award 14130
Market Manager of the Year 14337
Howard B. Meek Award 11526
Theodore W. Minah Distinguished Service Award 14131
MUFSO Innovator Award 16012
Operator of the Year 16013
Outstanding Paper Awards 11527
John W. Peterson Agricultural Scholarship Award 16901
Esther Peterson Consumer Service Award 9662
Pioneer of the Year 16014
President's Award 16387
President's Awards 18347
Sidney R. Rabb Award 9663
Regional Presidents Award 14132
Van Nostrand Reinhold Research Award 11528
Restaurant Award of Excellence 14519
Silver Service/Silver Cup Awards 14680
Colonel Merton Singer Award 17997
Stevenson Fletcher Achievement Award 11529
Louise Sublette Award of Excellence 18350
S. Earl Thompson Award 5625
John Wiley & Sons Award 11530

Food technology *See* Food processing

Football (*See also* Soccer)
AFCA Coach of the Year 2267
All-America Football Team 19647
All America Team 9671
All-American Awards 15307
All American Team 2268
DeMarco - Becket Memorial Trophy 7100
Asa S. Bushnell Trophy 15066
Canadian Football Hall of Fame and Museum 7101
CFL Outstanding Player Awards 7102
Citations of Merit 9672
Coach of the Year 2269
College Football Coach of the Year 19653
College Football Hall of Fame 15067
College Football Player of the Year 19654
Commissioner's Award 7103
Hec Crighton Trophy 7213
Leo Dandurand Trophy 7104
Distinguished American Award 15068
Distinguished Arizonan Award 15079
Dave Dryburgh Memorial Trophy 7105
Dwight D. Eisenhower Trophy 15069
ESPY Awards 9337
Terry Evanshen Trophy 7106
Norm Fieldgate Trophy 7107
First Data Corp. Outland Trophy Dinner Award 10155
Frank M. Gibson Trophy 7108
Gold Medal 15070
Peter Gorman Trophy 7216
Grey Cup 7109
George S. Halas Trophy 15084
Lew Hayman Trophy 7110
Heisman Memorial Trophy 10386
Lamar Hunt Trophy 15085
Eddie James Memorial Trophy 7111
JB Awards 15091
John F. Kennedy Trophy 15071
Don Loney Trophy 7221
MacArthur Trophy 15072
Dr. Beattie Martin Trophy 7112
James P. McCaffrey Trophy 7113
Tuss McLaughry Award 2270
J. P. Metras Trophy 7226
Middletown Pee Wee Football Scholarship Award 13388
Ted Morris Memorial Trophy 7227
Bronko Nagurski Award 9673
National College Football Champions 14686
National Scholar-Athlete Awards 15073
NCAA National Championships 14687
NFL All-Star Team 19668
NFL Coach of the Year 19669
NFL Executive of the Year 19670

Football (continued)

Jeff Nicklin Memorial Trophy 7114
Offensive and Defensive Linemen of the Year 15086
Sam Ormes Trophy 20131
Outland Trophy 9674
Outstanding Coach's Award 15080
Outstanding Contribution to Amateur Football Award 15074
Outstanding Football Official Award 15075
Outstanding Offensive and Defensive Linemen of the Year Awards 15092
Jackie Parker Trophy 7115
Tom Pate Award 7116
Photo Challenge 17577
President's Trophy (Football) 7230
Pro Football Hall of Fame 17578
Grantland Rice National Championship Trophy 9675
Eddie Robinson Coach of the Year 9676
Theodore Roosevelt Trophy 15076
Rose Bowl Player in the Game 524
Pete Rozelle Trophy 15087
Scholar-Athlete Awards 15081
The Sporting News NFL Player of the Year 19677
The Sporting News/NFL Rookie of the Year 19678
Amos Alonzo Stagg Award 2271
Amos Alonzo Stagg Trophy 15077
Robert L. Stanfield Trophy 7233
Jack Stewart Award 15082
Annis Stukus Trophy - Coach of the Year 7117
Super Bowl 15088
Timmie Awards 20132
Frank Tindall Trophy 7237
Uteck Bowl 7239
M. L. Van Vliet Trophy 7240
Vanier Cup Trophy 7241
Byron "Whizzer" White Humanitarian Award 15093

Foreign policy
Stuart L. Bernath Book Prize 18678
Stuart L. Bernath Lecture Prize 18679
Avis Bohlen Award 2278
Winston Churchill Award 11802
Delavan Award 2279
W. Averell Harriman Award 2280
Christian A. Herter Award 2282
Edwin M. Hood Award for Diplomatic Correspondence 15517
Leadership in the Americas Award 11046
Arthur S. Link Prize/Warren F. Kuehl Prize for Documentary Editing 18681
Helen and Howard R. Marraro Prize 18781
Minister's Award for Consular Excellence 9688
Minister's Award for Foreign Policy Excellence 9689
Hans J. Morgenthau Award 14704
William R. Rivkin Award 2283
Herbert Salzman Award for Excellence in International Economic Performance 20551
Secretary of State's Distinguished Service Award 20552
University of Louisville Grawemeyer Award for Ideas Improving World Order 21042

Forestry (*See also* Paper industry; Wood and wood products)
ACF Public Service Award 5645
Award for Outstanding Forestry Legislation 15976
Award for Outstanding Forestry Magazine of an Affiliated State Woodland Owner Association 15977
Award in Forest Science 18969
John A. Beale Memorial Award 18970
Alfred D. Bell, Jr. Visiting Scholars Program 9694
Charles E. and Marian Benson Scholarship Fund 16630
Theodore C. Blegen Award 9695
Canadian Forestry Achievement Award 7172
Canadian Forestry Group Achievement Award 7173
Canadian Forestry Scientific Achievement Award 7174
Collier Award 9696
Forest Capital of Canada Award 7119
Forest Landowner Award 9699
Forest Products Division Award in Chemical Engineering 2771
Forest Stewardship State of the Year 15978
Forestry Department Accreditation 19202
Gold Medal 7175
Hall of Fame and Distinguished Service 12148
Honorary Member 18971
International Forestry Achievement Award 7176
James L. Goodwin Memorial Scholarship 8416
James M. Kitz Award 7177
John Lambert, Jr. Forest Stewardship Award 13159
Massachusetts Tree Farmer of the Year 13160
McColl Family Fellowship 2332
Barrington Moore Memorial Award 18972
National Poster Challenge Award 7120
National Woodland Owners Award of Merit 15979
Northeastern Loggers' Association Awards Program 16548
Outstanding Forest Steward of the Year 16167
Outstanding Forestry Extension Publication Award 15980
Outstanding Forestry Extension Video Award 15981
Outstanding Forestry Journalism Award 18973
Leo Parizeau Prize in Biology 5540
Gifford Pinchot Medal 18974
Safety Award 11408
Carl Alwin Schenck Award 18975
Sir William Schlich Memorial Award 18976
Silver Ring 7178
Society of Municipal Arborists Awards 19203
M. N. "Mully" Taylor Award 20187
Technology Transfer Award 18977
Tree of Life Award 7179
Trees for Tomorrow Award 20188
Urban and Community Forestry Award 13519
Western Forestry Award for Current Achievement 21549
Western Forestry Award for Lifetime Service 21550
Charles A. Weyerhaeuser Award 9697
Wood Design Awards 7545
Wrigley-Fairchild Prize 2337
Young Forester Leadership Award 18978

Franco-American relations
Gilbert Chinard Prize 18676
Freedom Award 16837

Freedom
Jane Addams Children's Book Award 12296
American Experiment Award 7760
American Liberties Medallion 2884
America's Democratic Legacy Award 4979
Appeal of Conscience Award 5004
Aspen Institute Corporate Award for Excellence in Leadership 5199
Aspen Institute Public Service Award for Excellence in Leadership 5200
John Aubuchon Freedom of the Press Award 15514
Baltic Freedom Award 12426
Joseph L. Brechner Freedom of Information Award 6614
Colin M. Brown Freedom Medal 14672
Emery A. Brownell Media Award 15336
Calihan Fellowships 159
Champion of the Student Press Award 19810
Civil Courage Prize 16537
College Press Freedom Award 19811
David Library of the American Revolution Award for Playwriting on American Freedom 12543
Distinguished Awards 9764
William J. Donovan Award 16614
Ellis Island Medals of Honor 14955
Benjamin F. Fairless Memorial Award 2874
First Amendment Defender Award 10823
Freedom Award
Carolina's Citizens Freedom Foundation 7609
Freedom House 9760
International Rescue Committee - USA 11888
Freedom of Information Award 5251
Freedom Torch 11935
Harold Friedman Memorial Award 10371
Friends of Patrick Henry Awards 9799
Franklyn S. Haiman Award for Distinguished Scholarship in Freedom of Expression 14710
Hall of Fame 12805
Herbert Harley Award 2911
W. Averell Harriman Democracy Award 14910
Hugh M. Hefner First Amendment Award 17396
Hellman-Hammet Award 10595
Holmes - Weatherly Award 20309
Horizon Award 12752
Human Rights Award 12361
Hubert H. Humphrey First Amendment Freedoms Prize 4981
John Humphrey Freedom Award 11464
Louis E. Inglehart First Amendment Award 8174
International Press Freedom Award 7245
Henry M. Jackson Distinguished Service Award 12359
Thomas Jefferson Freedom Award 2959

Freedom (continued)

Journalists in Distress 7246
Justice Award 2912
Justice Award/Fund for Religious Liberty Award 2895
Robert F. Kennedy Book Awards 18074
Robert F. Kennedy Journalism Awards 18076
Martin Luther King, Jr. Award 9528
Liberty Award 10372
Life and Freedom Award 12890
Elijah Parish Lovejoy Award 8126
Zvi Hirsch Masliansky Award 10373
National Awards Program 9766
A.l Neuharth Free Spirit of the Year Award 9756
Novak Award 160
PEN Publisher Award 17149
Philadelphia Liberty Medal 10157
Prometheus Award 12806
Religious Liberty Award 11064
Theodore Roosevelt Distinguished Service Medal 20066
Franklin D. Roosevelt Four Freedoms Awards 9737
Rothko Chapel Oscar Romero Award 18132
Anatoly Scharansky Freedom Award 20306
Special Merit Citation 2913
Struggle for Liberation of Bulgaria Award 6689
United Nations Prize in the Field of Human Rights 20360
Voice of Democracy Scholarship 21345
Louise Waterman Wise Award 2897
Stephen S. Wise Award 2898
Young Artists Competition 18534
John Peter and Anna Catherine Zenger for Freedom of the Press and the Peoples Right to Know 20981

French-Canadian culture
Ordre du Conseil de la Vie Francaise en Amerique 8422
Prix Calixa-Lavallee 18606
Prix Chomedey-de-Maisonneuve 18607
Prix Lionel-Groulx-Foundation Yves-Saint-Germain 10819
Prix Louis-Phillipe-Hebert 18610
Prix Ludger-Duvernay 18611
Prix Maxime-Raymond 10820
Prix Michel-Brunet 10821
Prix Olivar-Asselin 18613
Prix Seraphin-Marion 18614
Prix Victor-Morin 18615

French culture
Prix Champlain 8423

French history
Nancy Lyman Roelker Prize 18544

French literature
Governor General's Literary Awards 6797
Aldo and Jeanne Scaglione Prize for French and Francophone Studies 13572
Mary Isabel Sibley Fellowship 17245

Friendship *See* Brotherhood

Funerals
Award of Recognition 11506
Periwinkle Award 8120

Robert C. Slater 13473
U.C.F.D.A. Scholarship 21131

Furniture (*See also* Interior design; Industrial design)
Apollo Award 19833
ASFD Life-Time Achievement Award 4410
Distinguished Designer Award 4411
Honorary Member 4412
Pinnacle Design Achievement Award 4413

Games (*See also* Recreation)
National Scrabble Championship 15696
U S Open Three Cushion Billiard Championships 20435
George Zammit Award 13049

Gardening *See* Horticulture

Gastronomy *See* Food; Restaurants

Genealogy
4H-Genealogy Award 16632
Award for Achievement: Individual 15138
Award for Achievement: Organization 15139
Award for Excellence: Genealogical Methods and Sources 15140
Award for Excellence: Genealogy and Family History 15141
Award for Excellence: *National Genealogical Society Quarterly* 15142
Award of Merit
Federation of Genealogical Societies 9494
National Genealogical Society 15143
Book Award
New York Genealogical and Biographical Society 16231
Wisconsin State Genealogical Society 21691
Certificate of Appreciation
Federation of Genealogical Societies 9495
National Genealogical Society 15144
Certificate of Merit 13639
Coddington Award of Merit 16101
Delegate Award 9496
Director's Award 9497
Distinguished Service Award
Federation of Genealogical Societies 9498
National Genealogical Society 15145
Endowment Fund 3881
Family History Writing Contest Award of Excellence 15146
Fellow of the National Genealogical Society 15147
Fellowship of the Augustan Society 6089
First Families Award 9825
First Families of Seneca County Gold Award 16638
First Families of Seneca County Silver Award 16639
Genealogical Research Award 177
Honorary Member (Individual) 15148
Honorary Member (Institutional) 15149
Donald Lines Jacobus Award 4415
Jennifer Lash Memorial Genealogical Award 16641
Life Membership 9909
Rabbi Malcolm H. Stern Award 12357
National Genealogy Hall of Fame 15150
Newsletter Competition 15151

Outstanding Genealogists 16077
Outstanding Reference Sources 17944
Pioneer Families of Mahoning County Award 16636
President's Citation 9499
Prix Archange-Godbout 9770
Prix Percy-W.-Foy 9771
Jane Rousch McCafferty C.G. Award 17551
Rubincam Youth Award 15152
Rabbi Malcolm H. Stern Humanitarian Award 9500
Edythe Stevens Family History Award 9155
Veitch Historical Society Scholarship 21287
David S. Vogels, Jr. Award 9501
Wigilia Medal 17459
George E. Williams Award 9502

Genetics
William Allan Award 4449
Art of Listening Award 9929
Art of Reporting Award 9930
Award of Excellence 9935
Allen Crocker Award 16121
Genetics Society of America Medal 9932
Graduate Student Plant Breeding Award 14793
Thomas Hunt Morgan Medal 9933
Pilot Project Research Awards 21040
Presidential Citation 9936
Private Plant Breeding Award 14794
Public Plant Breeding Award 14795
Young Scientist Award 9937

Geochemistry
N.L. Bowen Award 2343
Distinguished Service Award 17690
V. M. Goldschmidt Medal 9939

Geographic education
College/University Excellence of Scholarship Award 14761
Cram Scholarships 14762
Distinguished Mentor Award 14763
Distinguished Teaching Achievement Awards 14764
Geographic Education Dissertation Award 14765
Journal of Geography Awards 14766
George J. Miller Distinguished Service Award 14767
Publication Award 14768
Women in Geography Education Scholarship 14769

Geography (*See also* Cartography; Exploration; Geographic education)
Australian Geography Competition 11253
Award for Excellence in Teaching Geography 6908
Award for Geography in the Service of Government or Business 6909
Alexander Graham Bell Medal 15154
Henry Grier Bryant Gold Medal 9941
Franklin L. Burr Award 15155
CAG Award for Scholarly Distinction in Geography 6910
CAG Award for Service to the Profession of Geography 6911
Cullum Geographical Medal 2328
Charles P. Daly Medal 2329
Foreign Language and Area Studies Awards 8256
Gold Medal 18148

Geography (continued)

Gold Medal Award 19360
Grant for Geographic Literacy 14782
Grosvenor Medal 15156
Angelo Heilprin Literary Award Medal 9942
Hubbard Medal 15158
John Brinckerhoff Jackson Prize 5556
Elisha Kent Kane Medal 9943
John Oliver La Gorce Medal 15159
Laureat d'Honneur of the International Geographical Union 11649
David Livingstone Centenary Medal 2331
Massey Medal 18149
Samuel Finley Breese Morse Medal 2334
National Geographic Society Centennial Award 15160
J. Warren Nystrom Award 5557
Starkey Robinson Award 6912
Van Cleef Memorial Medal 2335
Paul P. Vouras Medal 2336

Geology and paleontology (*See also* Geochemistry; Geophysics; Photogrammetry; Seismology)
ACS Award in Separations Science and Technology 1721
AEG Publication Award 5672
AESE Award for Outstanding Editorial or Publishing Contributions 5660
AFMS Scholarship Foundation Honorary Award 2229
Claude C. Albritton, Jr. Award 10844
Award for Outstanding Contribution to Public Understanding of the Geosciences 2339
Andrew D. Baillie Award 7481
Bancroft Award 18161
Barlow Memorial Award 7181
Mel W. Bartley Award 7182
Best Paper Award 1326
Best Paper in the *Journal of Sedimentary Research* Award 18840
Best Paper Student Presentation 18851
Best Student Paper Award 1327
Best Student Poster Award 1328
Ziad Beydoun Memorial Award for Best International Poster 1329
Lew Bicking Award 15794
Selwyn G. Blaylock Medal 7183
Julian Boldy Memorial Award 7184
Jules Braunstein Memorial Award 1330
Roger J. E. Brown Award 7122
Kirk Bryan Award 9945
E. B. Burwell, Jr., Award 9946
Gilbert H. Cady Award 9947
Medal in Memory of Ian Campbell 2340
Carlos Walter M. Campos Memorial Award for Best International Student Paper 1331
Canadian Geotechnical Colloquium 7123
CANMET Technology Transfer Award 7185
Certificate of Merit 15795
Certificates of Merit 1332
CFMS Scholarship 6741
CIM Distinguished Lecturers 7186
CIM Fellowship 7187
CIM/NRCan Journalism Awards 7188
CIM Student Essay Competition 7189
Coal Award 7190
Isabel C. Cookson Paleobotanical Award 6540
CSPG Graduate Students Thesis Awards 7482
Arthur L. Day Medal 9948
DeGolyer Distinguished Service Medal 19235
Gabriel Dengo Memorial Award for Best International Paper 1333
Distinguished Lectureships 19106
Distinguished Service Award
Prospectors and Developers Association of Canada 17690
Society for Sedimentary Geology 18841
Distinguished Service Awards 1335
District Distinguished Service Awards 7191
District Proficiency Medals 7192
Robert H. Dott, Sr., Memorial Award 1336
R. J. W. Douglas Memorial Medal 7483
A.O. Dufresne Award 7193
Daniel Giraud Elliot Medal 13832
Robert Elver Mineral Economics Award 7194
Excellence of Poster Presentation Award 18842
Fellow of the Society 15796
Fifty Year Club 7195
Foundation Grants-in-Aid 1337
John A. Franklin Award 7124
John T. Galey, Sr. Memorial Public Service Award 2843
G. K. Gilbert Award 9949
Gold Medal Award 13463
Graduate Student Paper Award 7125
Joseph T. Gregory Award 19354
Group and Grotto Conservation Award 15797
GSA Distinguished Service Award 9950
Gungywamp Society Scholarship 10208
Arnold Guyot Memorial Award 15157
Michel T. Halbouty Human Needs Award 1338
R.M. Hardy Keynote Address 7126
Gilbert Harris Award 17035
Peter M. Hauer Spelean History Award 15798
William B. Heroy, Jr. Award for Distinguished Service to AGI 2341
History of Geology Award 9951
Claire P. Holdredge Award 5673
Honorary Fellow 9952
Honorary Member
American Institute of Professional Geologists 2844
Canadian Society of Petroleum Geologists 7484
National Speleological Society 15799
Honorary Membership
American Association of Petroleum Geologists 1339
Society for Sedimentary Geology 18843
INCO Medal 7196
Institute Medal for Distinguished Service 7197
ISEM Seed Grants 10847
Daniel C. Jackling Award 18815
Richard H. Jahns Distinguished Lecturer in Engineering Geology Award 5674
Floyd T. Johnston Service Award 5675
Journalism Award 1340
R.F. Legget Award 7127
A. I. Levorsen Memorial Award 1341
Life Membership Award 1342
Waldemar S. Lindgren Award 19107
Link Award 7485
Marsden Award 19108
George C. Matson Memorial Award 1343
McParland Memorial Award 7198
Medal of Merit 7486
O. E. Meinzer Award 9953
Members Award 7199
Metal Mining Division Award 7200
Willet G. Miller Medal 18170
Neil A. Miner Award 14238
James G. Mitchell Award 15800
Raymond C. Moore Medal for Paleontology 18844
Grover E. Murray Distinguished Educator Award 1344
Northern Science Award 10751
Order of Sancta Barbara 7201
Osgood Prize 17036
Outstanding Earth Science Teacher Award 14239
Outstanding Environmental and Engineering Geologic Project Award 5676
Outstanding Explorer Award 1345
Outstanding Paper Award in *Palaios* 18845
Paleontological Society Medal 17040
Katherine Palmer Award 17037
Ben H. Parker Memorial Medal 2845
Past Presidents' Award 1346
Past Presidents' Memorial Medal 7202
Bryan Patterson Memorial Grant 19355
Robert Peele Memorial Award 18821
Penrose Medal 19109
Penrose Medal Award 9954
Francis J. Pettijohn Medal 18846
Douglas R. Piteau Outstanding Young Member Award 5677
Sidney Powers Memorial Award 1348
Wallace E. Pratt Memorial Award 1349
President's Award 7487
Presidents Citation 10210
Public Service Awards 1350
R.M. Quigley Award 7129
Regional Graduate Scholarships 7488
Research Associateship Programs 15623
Rip Rapp Archaeological Geology Award 9955
A. S. Romer - G. G. Simpson Medal 19356
Alfred Sherwood Romer Prize 19357
Thomas Roy Award 7130
John T. Ryan Trophies 7203
Charles Schuchert Award 17041
Service Awards 7489
James H. Shea Award 14240
Francis P. Shepard Medal for Marine Geology 18847
Silver Medal 19110
Morris F. Skinner Award 19358
Stanley Slipper Gold Medal 7490
Smithsonian Institution Fellowship Program 18572
Special Awards 1351
Frank H. Spedding Award 16601
J. C. "CAM" Sproule Memorial Award 1352
J.C. Sproule Memorial Plaque 7204
William J. Stephenson Award for Outstanding Service 15802
Ralph W. Stone Graduate Fellowship 15803
Strimple Award 17042
Structural Geology and Tectonics Division Career Contribution Award 9956
Student Professional Paper 5679
Student Research Awards in Systematic Paleontology 17038
Ozan Sungurlu Memorial Award for Best International Student Poster 1353
Mary Clark Thompson Medal 13849
Tracks Award 7491
Trustees Award 10211

Geology (continued)
Twenhofel Medal 18848
Undergraduate Student Thesis and Report Awards 7131
Martin C. Van Couvering Memorial Award 2846
Volunteer Awards 7492
G. K. Warren Prize 13853
James Lee Wilson Medal 18849
George P. Woollard Award 9957
Young Scientist Award (Donath Medal) 9958

Geophysics (*See also* Physics; Geology and paleontology)
Bancroft Award 18161
Best Paper in *Geophysics* Award 19117
Best Paper Presented at the Annual Meeting Award 19118
N.L. Bowen Award 2343
Bower Award and Prize for Achievement in Science 9741
William Bowie Medal 2344
Frank C. Brautigam Award 5932
Walter H. Bucher Medal 2345
Committee E-8 Fracture Mechanics Medal 5939
Committee E-8 on Fatigue and Fracture Best Student Paper Award 5940
Anthony DeBellis Award 5943
Distinguished Achievement Award 19119
Distinguished Service Award 17690
Maurice Ewing Medal
American Geophysical Union 2346
Society of Exploration Geophysicists 19120
Excellence in Geophysical Education Award 2347
Fellow 2348
Reginald Fessenden Award 19121
John Adam Fleming Award 2349
Edward A. Flinn III Award 2350
G. K. Gilbert Award 9949
Honorary Membership 19122
Robert E. Horton Medal 2352
Hydrology Section Award 2353
Daniel C. Jackling Award 18815
Virgil Kauffman Gold Medal 19123
Inge Lehmann Medal 2354
Life Membership 19124
James B. Macelwane Medal 2355
Ocean Sciences Award 2356
Outstanding OTC Geophysical Paper Award 19125
Robert Peele Memorial Award 18821
Roger Revelle Medal 2357
Waldo E. Smith Medal 2358
Lester W. Strock Award 18645
George P. Woollard Award 9957

Geriatrics (*See also* Gerontology; Nursing homes)
Paul B. Beeson Career Development Awards in Aging Research 2222
Carl I. Brahce Gerontology Award 12558
Community Awards Program (Encore Awards) 18022
Geriatric Oral Health Care Award 2128
Geriatrician of the Year 5050
Edward Henderson Memorial Student Award 2361
New Investigator Awards 2362
Annual National Press Club Joseph D. Ryle Award for Excellence in Writing on the Problems of Geriatrics 15523
Jack Weinberg Memorial Award for Geriatric Psychiatry 3642

Gerontology (*See also* Geriatrics; Nursing homes)
Allied Signal Award for Research on Aging 10526
Andrus Award 1397
ASA-Metlife Foundation MindAlert Awards 4636
ASA Undergraduate Student Award 4637
Award of Honor 1222
Award of Merit/Distinguished Service Award 14814
BSS Student Research Award 9987
The Gloria Cavanaugh Award for Excellence in Training and Education in Aging 4640
Chair's Citation 1223
Chapter or Unit Anniversary Awards 1398
Clinical Medicine Person-in-Training Award 9988
Clinical Medicine Research Award 9989
Community Service Award/Certificate of Merit 14816
Nelson Cruikshank Award 14817
Distinguished Creative Contribution to Gerontology Award 9990
Distinguished Mentorship in Gerontology Award 9991
Distinguished Service Award 1225
Distinguished Service in Aging Award 1226
Excellence in Media Award 1227
Excellence in Practice Award 1228
Joseph T. Freeman Award 9992
Louise B. Gerrard Award 14399
Geron Corporation - Samuel Goldstein Distinguished Publication Award 9993
Healthcare and Aging Awards 4643
Innovation of the Year Awards 1229
Hobart Jackson Social Responsibility Award 1230
Richard Kalish Innovative Publication Award 9994
Donald P. Kent Award 9995
Robert W. Kleemeier Award 9996
Leadership Award 4644
Jeanne Manco Award 7311
Geneva Mathiasen Award 14869
Media Award 7312
Merit awards 17473
Meritorious Service Award 1231
Claude Pepper Award 14818
Ollie A. Randall Award 14870
Royal Canadian Legion Fellowships in Gerontological Nursing 7313
George Sacher Student Award 9997
Mildred M. Seltzer Distinguished Service Recognition 5373
Nathan Shock New Investigator Award 9998
Social Research, Policy & Practice Student Research Award 9999
State Public Official Award for Significant Legislative Achievement 1400
Clark Tibbitts Award 5374
Anna Tracey Memorial Award 17328
Trustee of the Year Award 1233
Widowed Persons Service Award 1401
Irving S. Wright Award of Distinction 2223

Glass (*See also* Ceramics)
J. Allen Alexander Award 3894
Helmet Drechsel Achievement Award 3895
Fellowship 8643
Honorary Lifetime Membership Award 10032
Lifetime Achievement Award 10033
George W. Morey Award 1690

Golf
Ace Award 19821
All-American Awards 15307
Charlie Bartlett Award 10077
Patty Berg Award 12650
Big East Conference Academic Awards 6369
Board of Governors Trophy 14298
Budget Service Award 12651
Certificate of Appreciation 13931
Clarence Camp Award 9628
Club Championship President's Cup 13649
Club Professional Player of the Year 17613
Coach of the Year 12652
Coaches Association Awards 15309
Commissioner's Award 12653
Curtis Cup 20603
Joseph Dey Award 20604
Distinguished Service Award
Golf Course Superintendents Association of America 10066
Professional Golfers' Association of America 17614
Eisenhower Trophy 11651
Espirito Santo Trophy 11652
ESPY Awards 9337
Leo Feser Award 10067
Golf Digest - LPGA Founders Cup 12654
Golf Professional of the Year 17615
The Graffis Award 15167
Green Section Award 20605
Ellen Griffin Rolex Award 12655
Hall of Fame 14299
Ben Hogan Award 10078
Bob Jones Award 20606
The Junior Golf Association of Mobile Scholarship 12468
Junior Golf Grant 9629
Junior Golf Leader 17616
Low Gross 13650
Low Net 13651
LPGA Hall of Fame 12656
Masters Golf Tournament 6087
Merchandisers of the Year 17617
Old Tom Morris Award 10068
Most Improved Golfer 13932
Most Improved Golfer Men/Women Pros 10071
National Amputee Golf Champion (Men and Women) 13933
National Putting Championship 17649
NCAA National Championships 14687
Byron Nelson Award 10072
Jack Nicklaus Golf Family of the Year Award 15168
Harvey Penick Award for Excellence in the Game of Life 7599
PGA Championship 17618
Player of the Year 17619
Player of Year 16153
William and Mousie Powell Award 12657
President's Award for Environmental Stewardship 10069
Professional of the Year 12658
William D. Richardson Award 10079

Golf (continued)

Rolex Player of the Year 12659
Rolex Rookie of the Year 12660
Rolex Rookie of the Year Men/Women Pros 10073
Rookie of the Year 13652
Samaritan Award 12661
Horton Smith Award 17620
Bill Strausbaugh Club Relations Award 17621
Teacher of the Year 12662
Teacher of the Year Award 17622
USGA Championships 20607
Vardon Trophy 17623
Vare Trophy 12663
Walker Cup 20608
Waltke Trophy 14300
World Golf Hall of Fame 21923
World Player of the Year 10074
Mickey Wright Award 10075

Gospel music
Covenant Awards 7133
Dove Awards 10101
Gospel Music Hall of Fame 10102
Grammy Awards 13822

Government service (*See also* Bureaucracy; Public service)
Achievement of the Year Award 5708
AFGE Local 3523 Education Award 10106
American Community Leadership Award 14443
Annual Awards for Distinction in Financial Management 20557
Philip Arnow Award 20509
Award for Excellence in Labor Diplomacy 20528
Award for Heroism 20529
Baker-Wilkins Award for Outstanding Deputy Chief of Mission 20530
Andy Barr Award 5710
BGA Tribute Award 6346
Bird Dog Award 8302
Ray E. Brown Award 5766
Buyer of the Year Award 15265
Capital Leadership Award 18698
Cash Award 20531
Census Award of Excellence 20444
Chapter of the Year Award 15266
Chapter Service Award 5711
Chief Financial Officers Award for Distinction in Public Finance 20532
Civic Achievement Award 6347
Civil Government Award 4307
Justice Tom C. Clark Award 9435
Charles E. Cobb, Jr. Award for Initiative and Success in Trade Development 20533
COGEL Award 8603
Glenn J. Cook Regional Services Award 6612
Diplomatic Security Employee of the Year Award 20534
Director General's Award for Excellence in Human Resource Management 20535
Director General's Award for Reporting and Analysis 20536
Distinguished Career Service Awards 20510
Distinguished Honor Award 20537
Distinguished Local Government Leadership Award 5712
Distinguished Member Award 21738
Distinguished Service Award
Defense Credit Union Council 8795
United States Association of Former Members of Congress 20412
Distinguished Service Awards
National Governors Association 15170
National Institute of Governmental Purchasing 15267
Distinguished Women's Awards 16572
James Clement Dunn Award for Excellence 20538
E. Benjamin Nelson Government Service Award 10180
Edith Stevens Groundwater Hero Award 10181
Epilepsy Foundation of America Awards 9308
Equal Employment Opportunity Award 20540
Excellence in Administration Award 20601
Excellence in Government Leadership Award 5714
Exemplary State and Local Awards Program 14637
Federal Engineer of the Year Award 15747
Federal Health Care Executive Special Achievement Award 2544
Foreign Service Award 20541
Foreign Service National of the Year Award 20542
Foreign Service Office Management Specialist of the Year/Civil Service Secretary of the Year 20543
General Services Achievement Award 20544
Golden Broom Award 16770
Goldsmith Prize for Investigative Reporting 18439
Government Civil Engineer of the Year Award 4319
Government Technology Leadership Award 10108
Governor of the Year Award 6395
Frank Greathouse Distinguished Leadership Award 5715
Albert H. Hall Memorial Award 15268
Joseph B. Hartranft Award 397
H. John Heinz Award 15446
Honorary Awards to Private Citizens and Organizations 20485
Horizon Award 16278
Hubert H. Humphrey Award 3392
Leamon R. Hunt Award for Administrative Excellence 20545
Innovations in American Government Awards Program 10116
Roger W. Jones Award for Executive Leadership 4784
Robert W. King Memorial Award 5716
Richard W. Leopold Prize 16891
Ramon Magsaysay Award 18093
Manager of the Year Award 15269
Harold W. McGraw, Jr. Prize in Education 13221
R. Tait McKenzie Award 881
Meritorious Honor Award 20546
Thomas Morrison Information Management Award 20547
Myrdal Award for Government Service 2207
National President's Awards 5717
National Women's Hall of Fame 15960
New Jersey Exemplary State and Local Awards 14638
Outstanding Achievement Award 20183
Outstanding County Program Awards 16506
Outstanding Government Service Award 1535
Outstanding Service Award 8604
Mary D. Pinkard Leader in Federal Equity Award 9455
Pioneer Award 5231
Presidential Rank Awards 20717
President's Award for Distinguished Federal Civilian Service 20718
Private Sector Financial Excellence Award 5719
Program Excellence Awards 11477
Public Policy Award 4207
Arnold L. Raphel Memorial Award 20548
Regional Leadership Award 13370
Luther I. Replogle Award for Management Improvement 20549
Safety and Health Awards 20512
Dr. Daniel E. Salmon Award 14226
Herbert Salzman Award for Excellence in International Economic Performance 20551
Secretary of State's Distinguished Service Award 20552
Secretary's Award 20553
Secretary's Exceptional Achievement Awards 20513
Ernest Thompson Seton Award 11360
Special Achievement Award 5721
Elmer Staats Award 5722
Superior Honor Award 20554
Henrietta Szold Award 10215
Taxpayer's Friend Award 15857
Ten Outstanding Young Americans 20678
Touchdown Club Mr. Sam Award 20136
University Medal 16304
Vern Haverstick Groundwater Hero Award 10182
Veterans Employment Awards 20515
Washington Crossing Foundation Scholarship 21445
Barbara M. Watson Award for Consular Excellence 20555
White House Fellows 17539
Young Government Civil Engineer of the Year Award 4370

Graphic arts
50 Books/50 Covers Competition 2808
Advertising Design Club of Canada Awards 204
Affaire in the Gardens 8035
AIGA Medal 2809
American Graphic Design Awards 10139
Annual Art Competition & Exhibition 19831
Annual Exhibition 6061
Annual Exhibitions 5115
Annual International Competition 17562
Annual Open Exhibition 5121
Anonymous Prize 13777
Art Directors Club Hall of Fame 5117
Artists' Fellowships 16229
Naomi Berber Memorial Award 10132
Booth Award 19590
James M. Brahney Grant 11836
Brewster Award for Creative Ingenuity 6616
Cape Cod Art Association Awards 7571
Certificate of Appreciation Award 19591
Certificate of Merit 19592
Certificates of Merit 13783

Graphic (continued)

Thomas Cochrane Sr. Scholarship Award 212
Communication and Marketing Awards 11035
Communications Graphics 2810
Corporate Leadership Award 2811
Design Awards Competition 18668
Distinguished Service Award 19593
EXCEL Awards 19205
Exhibit and Poster Award 748
Ralph Fabri Prize 13786
Fellowship for Creative and Performing Arts and Writers 914
Fine Art Show 18244
GATF Awards of Excellence in Education for an Individual in Industry and in Education 10133
Gold Awards 16996
Golden Image Award 19594
Grand National Exhibition 930
Great Menu Contest 15626
Greening of Design 2812
Honorary Membership 1211
Hunterdon Museum of Art National Print Exhibition Purchase Awards 10618
In-Print Award 11838
Information Graphics: Design of Understanding 2813
Institute Honors for Collaborative Achievements 2718
International Art Show by Artists with Disabilities 18536
International Prints Competition 18523
InterTech Technology Awards 10134
Frederick D. Kagy Education Award of Excellence 10135
Key Award 19595
Lewis Memorial Lifetime Achievement Award 17568
Herb Lubalin Award 19280
Luminaire 21748
Magnus Award 19596
Management Award 11843
Leo Meissner Prize 13791
Mentor Award 19597
Henry Allen Moe Prize for Catalogs of Distinction in the Arts 16290
National Print Exhibition 18980
National Small Painting Exhibition 16192
Ewell L. Newman Award 2486
Non-Heatset Web Printing Awards Competition 17571
Outstanding Service Award 19598
Pantone Color Award 17062
Parmele Award 19599
James D. Phelan Art Awards 18250
Pollock-Krasner Foundation Grants 17461
Premier Print Awards 17569
Publication Design Awards 19281
Red Cloud Indian Art Show 10424
Robert F. Reed Technology Medal 10136
Restaurant Design and Graphics Awards 12289
Safety Recognition Award 19600
Augustus St. Gaudens Medal 8498
William D. Schaeffer Environmental Award 10137
Sign Design Competition 11905
Source Awards 19425
Swormstedt Award 19601
TAGA Honors Award 19956
Visionary Art Show Awards 10502
Kenneth Wilson Awards 7012
Women in Production Scholarship 21749
Yankee Awards 22017

Greek culture
Homeric Award 7866
Mary Isabel Sibley Fellowship 17245
UHVA Awards 20334

Guidance counseling *See* Counseling

Gymnastics
All-American Awards 15307
Coach of the Year 8158
Frank J. Cumiskey Hall of Fame 15182
First Interstate Athletic Foundation Gymnastics Hall of Fame Award 8159
Gymnastics National Volunteer of the Year 554
Honor Coach Award 8160
Honor Coach Certificate 8161
National Champion 20848
NCAA National Championships 14687
Nissen-Emery Award 8162
Regional Judge of the Year Award 15183
Research Award 8163
Service Award 15184
Special Service Award 8164
Trampoline and Tumbling National Leadership Award 579

Hairstyling
American Image Enhancement Award 14741
Bald is Beautiful 6200
Female Style Maker of the Year 14742
Male Style Maker of the Year 14743
North American Hairstyling Awards 6298

Handball
USHA National Championships 20610

Handicapped (*See also* Blindness; Deafness; Mentally disabled; Rehabilitation and therapy; Speech and hearing)
AAAS Mentor Award 1046
Ability Fund/ March of Dimes Canada 7372
Achiever of the Year 10081
Advocacy for the Disabled Award 2931
American Therapeutic Recreation Association Awards 4743
AMVETS National Awards Program 4947
Athletes of the Year 21596
Award for Outstanding Achievement 9084
Award for Outstanding Service 9085
Lillian and Henry Barry Award in Human Relations 17321
Elmer C. Bartels Leadership Recognition Award 15805
Boston Marathon 6519
Gene Brito Award 20128
Business Award 8546
Cal Haworth Leadership Award 8953
Francis Joseph Campbell Award 5856
CEC Leadership Award 8547
CEC Research Award 8548
Century Scholarship 5857
Certificate of Appreciation 13931
Certificate of Merit 14425
Community Partnership Program Accessible America Award 15458
Congressman of the Year 15395
CRCD Award 7373
Date Able Image Award 8754
Design for Humanity Award 4460
Disabled Athletes of the Year 20410
Distinguished Service Award 9086
Donna and Sidney Dorros Award 17097
John Dystel Prize 15396
Easter Seals Canada Award 7374
EDI Award for Corporate Leadership 9087
EDI Awards (Equality/Dignity/ Independence) 9088
Empowerment Award 20322
Epilepsy Foundation of America Awards 9308
Everest and Jennings Player of the Year 508
Freedom of the Human Spirit Award 10629
Gardening From the Heart Award 9886
Susan Phillips Gorin Award 8549
Governor of the Year 15397
Graduate of the Year 10088
Graduation Awards 8550
Hall of Fame
National Wheelchair Basketball Association 15943
Wheelchair Sports, USA 21597
Edgar J. Helms Award for Staff and Graduate Staff 10089
Ben Hogan Award 10078
Chandler Hovey Trophy 20774
Individual Citation 15873
International Art Show by Artists with Disabilities 18536
The Jackie Award 5028
Henry H. Kessler Awards 17964
MDA Broadcast Journalism Awards 13683
Most Improved Golfer 13932
Most Valuable Player 15944
Mother/Father of the Year Award 15398
MS Achievement Award 15399
NAPH Medallion 14426
National Access Awareness Week Student Awards Program 5906
National Amputee Golf Champion (Men and Women) 13933
National Organization on Disability Award 1232
NFWT Service Award 509
Organization and Institution Citations 15876
Outstanding Advocate Award 9089
Outstanding Disabled Athlete of the Year 21234
Outstanding Disabled Veteran of the Year 8955
Outstanding Disabled Veteran Outreach Coordinator 8956
Outstanding Graduate Student Member of the Year Award 8552
Outstanding Large and Small Employer Award 8957
Outstanding Local Veterans' Employment Representative 8958
Outstanding Public Service Award 8553
Outstanding Service to the Mentally and/or Physically Handicapped 8068
Outstanding Student CEC Undergraduate Member of the Year Award 8554
Outstanding Total Service to the Mentally and/or Physically Handicapped 8069
Patriot Award 17068
Perseverance Award 13934
Pike Prize for Service to People with Disabilities 6532

Handicapped (continued)

Johanna Cooke Plaut Community Leadership Award 9090
Post-Secondary Scholarship 20320
President Award 17069
Presidential Citations and Awards 15877
John M. Price Chapter Award 17070
Professional Recognition Award 5918
Public Service Award 15342
Regional Service Award for the Disabled 13637
The Rehabilitation International Presidential Award 17965
Harry A. Schweikert, Jr. Disability Awareness Award 17071
George H. Seal Memorial Trophy Award 8959
Fenmore R. Seton Distinguished Volunteer Award 17966
Sister Kenny Institute International Art Show for Artists with Disabilities 13485
Special Recreation for People with Disabilities Awards 19573
Speedy Award 17072
Sports and Recreation Award 17073
Student Aid Award 21294
Dwain Taylor Award for Voluntary Service 17074
Captain James S. Ure Award for Sportsmanship 15945
Very Special Arts Playwright Discovery Program 21413
J. E. Wallace Wallin Lifetime Achievement Award 8555
Young Soloists Award 21414

Health and fitness
Business and Industry Awards 148
Community Service Grant 13062
Cunningham Distinguished Citizen Award 18030
Abraham Horwitz Award for Leadership in Inter-American Health 17058
IDEA Fitness Inspiration Award 10642
IDEA Fitness Instructor of the Year 10643
IDEA Personal Trainer of the Year Award 10644
IDEA Program Director of the Year 10645
International Health Advocacy Award 10046
International Health Service Award for Individuals 10047
International Health Service Award for Organizations 10048
Lifetime Achievement Award 149
Melpomene Outstanding Achievement Award 13289
Merit Award 150
Dean Meyerson Award 4782
Clarence H. Moore Award for Voluntary Service 17059
President's Challenge Physical Fitness Awards Program 17541
Professional Preparation Award 151
Research Associateship Programs 15623
Steven Royce, Jr. Award 3060
School & Community Award for Youth in Health & Safety 3837
Spirit of Caring Award 7762

Health care (*See also* Health and fitness; Health education; Health care administration; Hospital administration; Medicine; Preventive medicine)
$100,000 Lemelson-MIT Lifetime Achievement Award 12776
$500,000 Lemelson-MIT Prize 12777
AAMI Annual Meeting Manuscript Awards 5486
AAPA Rural Physician Assistant of the Year 816
Achievement Awards
Health Science Communications Association 10323
National Association of Counties 14165
AGPAM National Recognition Award 1213
AHA Hospital Awards for Volunteer Excellence 2541
Art of Listening Award 9929
Curtis P. Artz Distinguished Service Award 1599
Lewis Barbato Award 1822
Baxter Allegiance Prize Health Services Research 5912
The Becky Award 3062
Better Life Award 2394
Board Awards 5835
Ruth E. Boynton Award 1823
Canadian Healthcare Association Award for Distinguished Service 7145
Caregiver Appreciation Certificate 506
Certificates of Merit for Excellence in Writing - *Journal of Allied Health* 5836
Certification Excellence Award 1214
Consumer Conference Awards 15256
CSIH Lifetime Achievement Award for International Health 7423
Cultural Pluralism Award 5837
Damien - Dutton Award 8726
Distinguished Achievement Awards 3064
Distinguished Educator Award 15649
Distinguished Researcher Award 15650
Distinguished Service 13249
Distinguished Service Award
American Association of Public Health Physicians 1394
Association of Schools of Allied Health Professions 5838
Health Science Communications Association 10324
Healthcare Convention and Exhibitors Association 10335
Distinguished Service Awards 21003
Donna and Sidney Dorros Award 17097
Joseph D. Early Advocate of the Year Award 15204
Editor's Award - *Journal of Allied Health* 5839
Exceptional Merit Awards 3065
Fellows Program Award 5840
Friend of the Maine Hospice Council 13035
Golden Raster Award 10325
Hall of Fame 8557
Bernard P. Harrison Award of Merit 14698
Donald Hawryliuk Rural and Remote Opportunities Grant 7140
Health Advocate Award 3296
Heinz Award in the Human Condition 10382
HeSCA Film Festival 10326
HeSCA Interactive Materials Festival 10327
HeSCA Print Media Festival 10329
HeSCA Video Festivals 10330
Hirsh Award 1878
Edward Hitchcock Award 1825
Honorary Life Membership 2545
Honorary Member 18487
Hospice Team Awards 16172
HTCNE Service Award 10310
Individual of the Year Award 9459
Industry Award of Distinction 10312
Robert Wood Johnson Health Policy Fellowships 13856
Jonathatn Mann Award for Global Health and Human Rights 10049
Justin Ford Kimball Award 2546
J. Leon Lascoff Memorial Award 1833
Gustav O. Lienhard Award 13857
Edward R. Loveland Memorial Award 1922
E. Dean Lovett Memorial Award 1826
MacEachern Award 17726
Ronald McDonald House Charities Grants Program 18118
Mary McMillan Lecture Award 3493
Mitch Trubitt Community Asthma Champion Award 7870
MLA Award for Distinguished Public Service 13262
Ollie B. Moten Award 1827
National Association of Community Health Centers Awards 14138
National Editors Award 1217
National Health Information Awards 10315
National Journal Award 1218
Nebraska Hospice Volunteer of the Year 16064
New Member Sponsor Award 1220
Outstanding Health Worker 20697
Outstanding Member Award 5841
PA Service to the Underserved Award 817
Parent-Patient Leadership Award 8094
Performance Citation Award 7642
J. Warren Perry Distinguished Authors Award 5842
The Pillar Award 3069
President's Achievement Award 9460
President's Award
Accreditation Association for Ambulatory Health Care 135
Association of Schools of Allied Health Professions 5843
President's Continuing Education Grant 1604
Donna Pruzansky Memorial Fund for Maternal and Child Health Nursing 8095
Frank M. Rhatigan Award 10313
Richard and Hinda Rosenthal Foundation Awards 1927
Service Award 152
Service Awards 10331
The Silver Service Award 3072
Sister Mary Arthur "Sharing the Light" Award 6924
Fred L. Soper Award for Excellence in Health Literature 17060
Special Achievement Award 10332
Special Awards 10333
Spirit of Hospice Award 12185
Spirit of Hospice Awards 16173
Stein Award 16643
Teen Health Leadership Award 219
Trustees Award 2548
Martin C. Ushkow Community Service Award 799
Volunteer Leader 4401

Health care administration

AACC Lectureship Award 972
Achievement in Health Care Management 21702
Administrator of the Year 20348
Administrator of the Year Award 1882
Affiliated Group Award 1866
Linda Arenth Excellence in Cancer Nursing Management Award 16710
Baxter Allegiance Prize Health Services Research 5912
Board of Directors' Award 10337
Bower Award for Business Leadership 9742
Ray E. Brown Award 5766
Chairman's Award 684
Chapter Excellence 1215
Dean Conley Award 1867
Graham L. Davis Awards of Excellence 10338
Distinguished Service 1838
Distinguished Service Award 685
Faculty Publication of the Year 686
Federal Health Care Executive Special Achievement Award 2544
Fred Graham Award for Innovation in Improving Community Health 1883
Gold Award 2400
Gold Medal Award 1868
James A. Hamilton Award 1869
Leslie A. Hampel Award 1216
Harry J. Harwick Lifetime Achievement Award 1884
Edgar C. Hayhow Award 1870
Health Management Research Award 1871
Bernice Hemphill Memorial Award 1111
HIMSS John E. Gall Jr./CIO Award 10344
Hirsh Award 1878
Honorary Fellowship 1872
Honorary Fellowships 687
Robert S. Hudgens Memorial Award - Young Healthcare Executive of the Year 1873
Marriott Corporation Health Care Services Charles U. Letourneau Student Research Paper of the Year Award 688
Management Innovation Poster Session Award 1874
Mary McMillan Lecture Award 3493
Frederick C. Morgan Award 10339
National President's Award 1219
William Newcomer Health Care Executive of the Year Award 689
Outstanding Federal Services Health Administrator Award 5778
Parke-Davis Award 7469
Physician Executive Award 1885
Harold C. Piepenbrink Award for Outstanding Service to the Field of Mental Health Administration 5580
President's Award 19180
Publications Awards 10348
Regional Director of the Year Award 690
Robert M. Shelton Award 10340
State Director of the Year Award 691
Student Chapter Awards 1875
Student Essay Competition in Healthcare Management 1876
Volunteers of the Year 16286
Young Federal Healthcare Administrator Award 5791

Health education

AAHE Distinguished Service Award 1016
AAHE Scholar Award 1017
William G. Anderson Merit Award 876
Awards of Distinction in Programs 15201
Awards of Merit 1101
Black Lung Association Award 6429
Burn Prevention Award 1600
George Crile Award 11803
Damien - Dutton Award 8726
Charles A. Dana Awards for Pioneering Achievements in Higher Education 8730
The John Dieckman Distinguished Educational Award of Honor 15642
Epilepsy Foundation of America Awards 9308
Golden Raster Award 10325
Morten Grove-Rasmussen Memorial Award 1109
Luther Halsey Gulick Award 877
Harry J. Harwick Lifetime Achievement Award 1884
Health Advancement Award 15321
Health Education Professional of the Year Awards 1018
Health Information Management Scholarship 2398
Health Journalism Awards 1802
Vernon Henley Media Award 2042
HeSCA Film Festival 10326
HeSCA Interactive Materials Festival 10327
HeSCA JBC Literary Award 10328
HeSCA Print Media Festival 10329
HeSCA Video Festivals 10330
Honor Award 879
Horizon Award 1019
Anson Jones, M.D., Award 20032
Mabel Lee Award 880
Media Awards 11349
ONS/AMGEN Inc. Award for Excellence in Patient/Public Education 16722
ONS/Ross Products Division of Abbott Laboratories Award for Excellence in Cancer Nursing Education 16725
Outstanding School Health Educator Award 3890
Presidential Citation 1020
Professional Service to Health Education Award 1021
Public Service Award 15324
Service Awards 10331
Special Awards 10333
Ryan White and Loras Goedken Meritorious Service Awards 15214

Health physics

Distinguished Scientific Achievement Award 10318
Fellow Awards 10319
Founders Award 10320
Student Awards 10321

Hearing *See* Speech and hearing

Helicopters

AHS Fellows 2425
American Eurocopter Golden Hour Award 10390
Gruppo Augusta International Helicopter Fellowship Award 2426
Francois Xavier Bagnoud Award 2427
Grover E. Bell Award 2428
Lawrence D. Bell Memorial Award 10391
Community Service Award 10392
Crew of the Year Award 10393
Edward C. Dyer Award 13073
Excellence in Communications Award 10394
Frederick L. Feinberg Award 2429
John P. Giguere Award 13076
Helicopter Airframe Technician Award 10395
Helicopter Avionics Technician Award 10396
Helicopter Electrical/Electronics Technician Award 10397
Helicopter Maintenance Award 10398
Helicopter Powerplant Technician Award 10399
Honorary Fellows 2431
Howard Hughes Award 2432
Harry T. Jensen Award 2433
Dr. Alexander Klemin Award 2434
Captain William J. Kossler, USCG Award 2435
Robert L. Lichten Award 2436
Joe Mashman Safety Award 10400
Keith B. McCutcheon Award (Marine Heavy Helicopter Squadron of the Year) 13083
McDonnell Douglas Law Enforcement Award 10401
Doris Muellen Whirly-Girls Scholarship 21599
Alexander A. Nikolsky Honorary Lectureship 2437
Outstanding Certified Flight Instructor Award 10402
Pilot of the Year Award 10403
Pilot Safety Award 10404
Robert L. Pinckney Award 2438
Igor I. Sikorsky Award for Humanitarian Service 10405
Igor I. Sikorsky International Trophy 2439
Supplier Excellence Award 2440
Robert E. Trimble Memorial Award 10406
Whirly-Girls Helicopter Flight Training Scholarship 21600

Heroism

Airman's Award 8269
American Hero Award 12335
Annual Home and School Council Merit Awards 17262
AOTOS Mariner's Plaque 20374
Award for Heroism 20529
Award of Valor
National Collegiate Athletic Association 14685
National Transportation Week 15905
Carnegie Medal 7603
Lois Clark McCoy Service Award 14037
Robert P. Connelly Heroism Award 12601
Courage Award 1635
Cross of Valour 6818
Department of Transportation Award for Heroism 9431
Disabled Athletes of the Year 20410
Exceptional Bravery Medal 13890
Extraordinary Service/Hero Award 14729
Father Washington Award 7673
FBI Honorary Medals 20504
Hal Foss Award 14038
Gold Lifesaving Medal 8816
Gold Medal 11119
Hero of the Year 4676
Heroism Award
Flight Safety Foundation 9583
National Telecommunications Cooperative Association 15860
Humanitarian Award 15536

Subject Index

Heroism (continued)

INEOA Medal of Valor 11764
Knights of Justice Award 3572
Legion of Valor Silver Cross for Valor 12773
Lifesaving and Meritorious Action Awards of the National Court of Honor 6585
Mariner's Rosette 20378
Glenn R. Masterson Memorial Trophy 7509
Medal of Bravery 6821
Medal of Military Valour 6822
Medal of Valor Award 2028
National Association of First Responders Awards 14232
National Volunteer Disaster Services Award 3834
Ontario Medal for Firefighter Bravery 16754
Ontario Medal for Police Bravery 16756
Police Medal of Honor 3576
Police Posthumous Medal of Honor 3578
Prisoner of War Medal 8835
Secretary's Award 20553
Silver Helmet Award 17962
Silver Lifesaving Medal 8838
Silver Star for Bravery 3579
Star of Courage 6831
Star of Military Valour 6832
State/Canadian Province SAR Award 14039
William O. Stillman Award 2578
Valor Award 14040
Valor Awards 20514
Raoul Wallenberg Civic Courage Award 17877
Raoul Wallenberg Hero for Our Time Award 17878
Young American Medal for Bravery 20506

Higher education (*See also* Academic freedom; Alumni activities)

125th Anniversary Medals 8028
AASCU Distinguished Alumnus Award 1428
AAUP Award for Excellence in Coverage of Higher Education 1464
ACE Distinguished Service Award for Lifetime Achievement 2053
ACE Fellows Program 2054
Achieving Professional Excellence in Education Administration 1158
ACUHO-I Award 5622
ADE Francis Andrew March Award 5656
Gustave O. Arlt Award in the Humanities 8578
Award of Recognition: State/Regional Professional Activity 1159
Award of Recognition: Workshop Grant 1160
Lewis Barbato Award 1822
Baytown Chamber of Commerce Scholarship 6285
Chester A. Berry Scholar Award for Excellence in Writing 5629
Biotechnology Teaching Award 14091
Ruth E. Boynton Award 1823
Mary A. Bruemmer Award 18215
Mildred Bulpitt Woman of the Year Award 1068
Butts - Whiting Award 5630
Canadian Friends of Yeshiva University Bora Laskin Distinguished Service Award 22024
CCCC Richard Braddock Award 14828
CEA Honorary Life Membership 8152
CEA Professional Achievement Award 8153
Chamber of Commerce Scholarship Award 7803
Champions of Higher Independent Education in Florida (C.H.I.E.F.) Awards 10715
Gayke B. Childs Award 20947
College Fiction Contest 17394
Communicator of the Year Award 14773
Creative and Innovative Awards 16391
William V. Cruess Award 10937
John Dennis Scholarship 13541
Carolyn Desjardins President of the Year Award 1069
Devoted Service Award 20948
Dissertation of the Year Award 14012
Distance Learning Course Awards 20949
Distinguished Advertising Educator Award 859
Distinguished Faculty Award 14682
Distinguished Service Award
American Association of Collegiate Registrars and Admissions Officers 1161
American Association of University Administrators 1461
Florida Association of Colleges and Universities 9591
Distinguished Service Citation 1371
Distinguished Service Key and Certificate for Retiring Continuing Educators 20950
Distinguished Student Scholar Award 17323
Distinguished Teaching Award 15689
Distinguished Women's Awards 16572
Doctoral Awards Program 14326
Donald H. Ecroyd Award for Outstanding Teaching in Higher Education 14707
Excellence in Pre-College Physics Teaching Award 1372
Excellence in Undergraduate Physics Teaching Award 1373
Exemplary Program Award 20951
Faculty Service Award 20952
Feminist Theory and Gender Studies Graduate Paper Award 12047
Charles Forsyth Award 7637
Four-Year College Biology Teaching Award 14093
Phillip E. Frandson Award for Innovative Programming 20953
Phillip E. Frandson Award for Sustained Excellence 20954
Golden Award 14134
Golden Eagle Award 18989
Richard S. Goldsmith Award 19757
Scott Goodnight Award for Outstanding Performance as a Dean 14403
Graduate Assistantships 21017
Graduate Student Awards 6389
Graduate Student Scholar Award 17326
James C. Grimm Leadership and Service Award 5623
William Haber Award 10432
Robert Hacke Scholar-Teacher Award 8154
Archbishop Paul Hallinan Award 7638
Melvene D. Hardee Dissertation of the Year Award 14404
Harkness Fellowships 10239
Rev. Theodore M. Hesburgh, C.S.C., Award 5591
Edward Hitchcock Award 1825
Roscoe Hogan Environmental Law Essay Contest 18120
Honorary Alumnus Award 20258
James A. Hurd Award 5624
Independent Study Catalog Awards 20955
Interamerica Prize 11104
International Futures Award for Exceptional and Innovative Leadership in Continuing Higher Education 20956
Frederick D. Kagy Education Award of Excellence 10135
Klopsteg Memorial Lecture 1375
Frank A. Kuntz '07 Award 7667
Lecturer of Merit 14683
Liberty Bell Award 10716
Local Community College Award 20222
The M'4s Brewer Memorial Scholarship 19826
Management Achievement Award 14124
Marketing and Publications Awards 20957
Mathematics Excellence Award 3038
Memorial Awards 20958
Robert A. Miller Memorial Prize 8155
Robert A. Millikan Medal 1376
Neil A. Miner Award 14238
Margaret L. Moore Award for Outstanding New Academic Faculty Member 3497
Ollie B. Moten Award 1827
Mother Evelyn Murphy Excellence in Teaching Award 8991
National Student Competition 4482
Jason Nelson Scholarship 16673
Frederic W. Ness Book Award 5552
Nofflet William Up-and-Coming Leadership Award 20959
Julius M. Nolte Award for Extraordinary Leadership 20960
Oersted Medal 1377
Gustav Ohaus Award for Innovations in Science Teaching 15690
Outstanding Continuing Education Student Awards 20961
Outstanding Contribution to Higher Education Award 14405
Outstanding Contribution to Literature or Research Award 14406
Outstanding Contributions to the Orientation Profession Award 15462
Outstanding Educator Award 275
Outstanding Faculty Adviser 17327
Outstanding Program Awards 20962
Outstanding Program Awards for Credit and Non-Credit Programs 20963
Outstanding Service Award 14135
Outstanding Teacher Educator in Reading Award 11870
Outstanding Undergraduate Educator Award 4094
PACC Scholarship 17335
Pacesetter of the Year Award 14774
Paragon Awards 14775
D. Richard Petrizzo Award for Career Achievement 14776
Elizabeth Powell Award 20964
Presidents' Distinguished Service Award 5592
President's Medal 18994
Pride of the 20th Century Award 6639
Process Improvement Award 14125
Regional Awards 14407
Resource Enhancement Award 14126
Richtmyer Memorial Lecture 1379
Nancy McNeir Ring Award 18217

Higher (continued)

Adelle F. Robertson Continuing Professional Educator Award 20965
Stanley C. Robinson Distinguished Service Award 20966
Norman K. Russell Scholarship 15463
San Antonio Chapter of Rocks Inc. Scholarship 18241
SGA Service Award 18047
Robert H. Shaffer Award for Academic Excellence as a Graduate Faculty Member 14408
James H. Shea Award 14240
Signature of Excellence Award 20967
Silver Torch Award 14136
Special Student Awards 1495
Academic Award in Memory of Stephen B. Sweeney 11479
Joe D. Thomas CEA Distinguished Service Award 8156
S. Earl Thompson Award 5625
Torch of Learning Award 2310
Eileen M. Tosney AAUA Award for Excellence in the Practice of Higher Education Administration 1462
Trustee of the Year Award 1070
Fred Turner Award for Outstanding Service to NASPA 14409
University Medal 7617
University Service Awards 20263
Urbahn Medal 19001
Charles A. Wedemeyer Award 20969
Calvert, Woodall, and McMillan Writing Awards 5627
WORDS/ISAAC AAC Consumer User Scholarship 11920
Yeshiva University Award 22029
Yeshiva University Citation 22030
Yeshiva University Distinguished Service Award 22031
Yeshiva University Heritage Award 22032
Yeshiva University Sephardic Heritage Award 22033

Highway safety (*See also* Asphalt paving)
Award of Merit 5477
J. Stannard Baker Award for Highway Safety 11308
George S. Bartlett Award 1431
Driver of the Year Award 4770
Excellence in Highway Design Awards 20559
John C. "Jake" Landen ARTBA Annual Highway Safety Award 3863
Thomas H. MacDonald Memorial Award 1433
Man of the Year 11890
Theodore M. Matson Memorial Award 11052
A. J. Mirkin Service Award 5478
National Police Award for Traffic Safety 6813
NHTSA 21384
Past Presidents' Award for Merit in Transportation 11053
President's Modal Awards 1434
Safe and Courteous Driver of the Year 13377
Section Activities Award 11054
John D. States Award 5479
Student Chapter Award 11056
Student Paper Award 11057
Truck Safety Contest 4775

Hiking *See* Recreation

Hispanic culture
Affiliate of the Year Award 14804
Maclovio Barraza Leadership Award 14805
Simon Bolivar Award 3615
El Angel Award - Distinguished Hispanic-American Artist 6374
El Angel Award - For Corporate Contribution to the Development of Hispanic-American Arts 6375
Hispanic Council Scholarship 10444
Hispanic Engineer National Achievement Awards 7586
Judges Award of Merit 15481
Gregory Kolovakos Award 17141
Medallion of Excellence for Distinguished Service 8398
Medallion of Excellence for Role Model 8399
Jose Toribio Medina Award 18415
National Conference of Puerto Rican Women Award 14721
Graciela Olivarez La Raza Award 14806
President's Award 14807
Ruben Salazar Award for Communications 14808
Western Political Science Association Awards 21557

Historic preservation (*See also* Monument restoration)
A. Lewis Smith Award 8852
AICP National Historic Planning Landmarks and Pioneers Program 3545
Angel Award 22103
Architectural Awards 10458
Article Award 7367
Award of Merit 17357
Awards of Merit 10464
Book Award 7368
James J. Bradley Distinguished Service Award 19065
Certificate of Achievement 7854
Certificate of Appreciation
Chesapeake and Ohio Historical Society 7855
National Carousel Association 14587
Owsley Family Historical Society 16985
Charles Loring Brace Award 16907
Louise du Pont Crowninshield Award 15917
Distinguished Service Award 16986
Harriette Merrifield Forbes Award 5376
Friend of History 10504
Oliver Torry Fuller Award 5453
Government Affairs Award of Recognition 6683
Great American Main Street Award 15918
Otto Haas Award 17536
Harrison Award 17534
Heritage Award 7147
Heritage Canada Achievement Awards 10420
Heritage Toronto Awards of Merit 10426
Historic Harmony Heritage Award 10454
Historic Plaque 16925
Historic Preservation Award
Billings Preservation Society 6384
Fairfield Historical Society 9394
Historic Augusta 10450
Peerless Rockville Historic Preservation 17135
Historic Preservation Awards 8114
Honorary Life Member 18881
Honorary Member 7856
Honorary Society Membership 13225
Initiative Awards 17537
Keepers Preservation Education Fund Fellowship 19024
Landmarks 10418
Gabrielle Leger Medal 10421
Lauri W. Leskinen Memorial Award 12584
Lieutenant-Governor's Medal 10422
Lifetime Achievement 7369
Local Society Awards 21302
LPA Honor Awards 12946
Marquee Award 20057
Mary Mason Anderson Williams Award 5507
Harley J. McKee Award 5454
Merit Award 13000
National Preservation Honor Awards 15919
New York Preservation Awards 13679
Oakley Certificate of Merit 5377
Periwinkle Award 8120
Charles E. Peterson Fellowships/ Internships 6016
John Wesley Powell Prize 18691
Preservation Award
Birmingham Historical Society 6400
Canadian Railroad Historical Association 7370
Historical Society of Frederick County 10462
Los Angeles Conservancy 12927
Preservation Awards
Essex Community Heritage Organization 9340
Historical Society of Princeton 10470
Preservation Merit Awards 10448
Preservationist of the Year 13001
President's Awards 7857
Presidents's Award 16987
Prix Honorius Provost 17787
Prix Leonidas-Belanger 17788
Prix Rodolphe-Fournier 17789
Renchard Prize 10472
Franklin Delano Roosevelt Award 18692
Servaas Award 10456
Sister Irene Award 16908
James Smithson Society Founder Medal 18569
James Smithson Society Grants 18570
Anne D. Snyder Award 8056
Village Award 10172
Irving Weber Award 12419
Winner's Circle National Winners 13555
Youth Achievement Award 12803

History (*See also* Antiquity; Biography; Culture; Genealogy; Historic preservation; History of dentistry; History of medicine; History of science; History of technology; Medieval studies; Monument restoration; Social science research)
AASLH Award 17872
Achievement Award 10452
Percy G. Adams Article Prize 19468
Henry Adams Prize 18688
J.H. Atkinson Award for Excellence in Arkansas Teaching 5075
Helen August Memorial Award 3404
Award of Appreciation 16086

History (continued)

Award of Merit
Kenosha History Center 12556
New Baltimore Historical Society 16087
Society for Historical Archaeology 18683
Award of Merit - Commercial 8364
Award of Merit - Governmental 8365
Award of Merit - Individual 8366
Award of Merit - Scholastic/ Authorship 8368
Awards of Merit 10464
Roland H. Bainton Book Prize 18540
Mary Faye Barnes Award for Excellence for Community History Projects 20036
Mrs. Simon Baruch University Award 20330
Bath County Historical Society Scholarship 6272
Evelyn Bauer Prize 11826
Bayles Award 16093
Emilio Bernabei Prize 11827
Pierre Berton Award 6836
Best First Book Award 17233
Best Subsequent Book Award 17234
Dr. Phyllis R. Blakeley Lifetime Achievement Award 9516
Theodore C. Blegen Award 13475
Richard S. Brownlee Fund 21313
Solon J. Buck Award 13476
John Bullen Prize 7149
CAA Lela Common Award for Canadian History 6955
W. Stewart Caffey Award for Excellence for Pre-Collegiate Teaching 20037
California History Day Award 8369
Carol Ruppe Distinguished Service Award 18684
Jonathan Carter Award 10237
Certificate of Appreciation 12400
Chairman's Award
Friends of the Pendleton District 9812
Pendleton District Historical, Recreational, and Tourism Commission 17160
Howard I. Chapelle Award for Nautical Research 16047
Chapter History Award 6325
Thomas L. Charlton Lifetime Achievement Award 20038
The Gilbert Chinard Prize 7925
James L. Clifford Prize 3991
Norman W. Cox Award 6243
Avery O. Craven Award 16885
CT History Day Awards 10262
Dissertation Award 16622
Distinguished Citizen's Award 21443
Distinguished Service Award 16623
Distinguished Teaching Award 16624
Economic Award 11828
Ellis Award 16750
Rose and Michael David Elovitz Prize 11829
Emeritus Membership 13392
Ralph Waldo Emerson Award 17241
Endowment Fund 3881
Hubert Evans Nonfiction Prize 21520
Herbert Feis Award 2471
Fellow of The Athenaeum 6015
Fellowship of the Augustan Society 6089
Wallace K. Ferguson Prize 7152
First Families of Seneca County Gold Award 16638
First Families of Seneca County Silver Award 16639
Four Masters Award 12195
Dixon Ryan Fox Manuscript Prize 16288
Friends of Historical Museum Awards 9808
Genealogical Publishing Company Award 17941
Gilmanton Historic Essay Competition 10026
Violet B. Gingles Award 5076
Gold-Headed Cane 18420
Louis Gottschalk Prize 3992
Governor General's Award 6837
Harold J. Grimm Prize 18541
Gungywamp Society Scholarship 10208
H. W. Nelson Award 10209
Harrington Award 18685
Peter M. Hauer Spelean History Award 15798
Henry Chapman Mercer Award 6672
Historian of the Year
Fulton County Historical Society 9827
Goshen Historical Society 10099
History Book Contest 10249
History of Macon Award 13386
Historymaker Award 16233
Howard Fellows 10571
Rockwell D. Hunt Young Historian Award 8370
Amy Louise Hunter Fellowship 21677
Jan Ilavsky Memorial Scholarship 10468
Individual Award 3595
Institutional Award 3596
The W. Turrentine Jackson Prize 2484
J. Franklin Jameson Prize for Editorial Achievement 2476
Jefferson Cup Award 21392
Thomas Jefferson Prize 18689
John L. Cotter Award 18686
G. Wesley Johnson Award 14866
Joslin Essay Award 20143
Azar Kalbache and Zahara Ben Mamou Award 11830
Robert Kelly Memorial Award 14867
Joan Kelly Memorial Prize 2477
Whitaker Key History Award 17772
Judge R. Knott Award 10466
Ben B. Lane Award 21301
Helen H. Lane History Award 8919
William L. Langer Award 10184
Laureate of the Federation 11610
Waldo Gifford Leland Award 18958
Waldo G. Leland Prize 2478
Local History Award 9327
Local Society Awards 21302
Ottis Lock Award 9082
Los Angeles Times Book Prizes 12931
James Madison Prize 18690
Manuscript Award 17235
Carl S. Meyer Prize 18543
Myrtle Butts Fleming Award 6496
Nash Student History Journal Prize 17236
NASSH Book Award 16471
National Endowment for the Humanities Grant Programs 14938
National Federation of the Blind Scholarship Program 15039
Natural History Award 6069
William Nelson Prize 17986
Margaret Cross Norton Award 13393
Otto A. Rothert Award 9547
Outstanding Exhibit Award 9517
Outstanding Promotion Award 9518
Outstanding Publication Award 16625
Paper Prize Awards 17237
Pensacola Heritage Award 17210
Phi Alpha Theta/Westerners International Award 17238
Pioneer Heritage Award 17137
John Wesley Powell Prize 18691
Burtram J. Pratt Memorial Award 8124
President's Award 13394
President's Awards 9519
Presidents Citation 10210
Prix Guy-Fregault 10818
Prix Lionel-Groulx-Foundation Yves-Saint-Germain 10819
Prix Michel-Brunet 10821
Public History Award 16626
Joanne T. Rainsford Memorial Scholarship 9157
Richard S. Brownlee Fund 19773
James Harvey Robinson Prize 2481
Franklin Delano Roosevelt Award 18692
William B. and Maryloo Spooner Schallek Memorial Graduate Fellowship Awards 18038
Sidewise Awards for Alternate History 18444
Sixteenth Century Society and Conference Medal 18546
Alice E. Smith Fellowship 21678
C. L. Sonnichsen Book Award 20048
Special Citation in Honor of Rudy and Hertha Benjamin 3443
State History Society of Missouri 21314
Student Achievement Award 6731
Studies Book Award 19439
Erwin C. Surrency Prize 4125
Maude C. Trimble History Award 6691
Trustees Award 10211
US/ICOMOS Fellows 20452
VanArsdel Prize 17999
Vexillon 11611
Waddingham/Doctor Award 8371
Wesley-Logan Prize 2482
Lucille Westbrook Local History Award 5077
Western North Carolina Historical Association Achievement Award 21554
Thomas Wolfe Literary Award 21555
Writers' Award Contest 12312

History, agricultural *See* Agricultural history

History, American *See* American history

History, architectural *See* Architectural history

History, art *See* Art history

History, Asian *See* Asian history

History, business *See* Business history

History, Canadian *See* Canadian history

History, church *See* Church history

History, English *See* English history

History, European *See* European history

History, French *See* French history

History, Italian *See* Italian history

History, Jewish *See* Jewish history

History (continued)

History, Latin American *See* Latin American history

History, library *See* Library history

History, military *See* Military history

History of art *See* Art history

History of dentistry
M. D. K. Bremner Awards 844
Hayden-Harris Award 845

History of medicine
Murray Gottlieb Prize 13257
Jason A. Hannah Medal 18166
New York Chapter History of Military Medicine Essay Award 5777
William Osler Medal 1061
Benjamin Rush Lectureship Award 3637
Richard H. Shryock Medal 1062
William H. Welch Medal 1063

History of science
AIAA History Manuscript Award 2654
Watson Davis and Helen Miles Davis Prize 10485
Derek Price-Rod Webster Award 10486
Dexter Award in the History of Chemistry 1748
Joseph H. Hazen Education Prize 10487
Howard Fellows 10571
Margaret W. Rossiter History of Women in Science Prize 10488
Pfizer Award 10489
Sarton Medal 10490
Henry and Ida Schuman Prize 10491
Smithsonian Institution Fellowship Program 18572

History of technology
AIAA History Manuscript Award 2654
Carl Benz Award 19064
Richard and Grace Brigham Award 19066
Nicholas-Joseph Cugnot Award 19067
Leonardo Da Vinci Medal 18871
Dibner Award for Excellence in Museum Exhibits 18872
Edelstein Prize 18873
Samuel Eleazar and Rose Tartakow Levinson Prize 18874
Friend of Automotive History Award 19068
E. P. Ingersoll Award 19069
Joan Cahalin Robinson Prize 18876
Smithsonian Institution Fellowship Program 18572
Abbott Payson Usher Prize 18877

Hobbies and clubs (*See also* Animal care and training; Automobiles; Book collecting; Crafts; Genealogy; Horticulture; Numismatics; Philately; Photography; Recreation)
American Crossword Puzzle Champion 2081
Annual Meeting Best Of Show Founders Award 12236
Belleek Hall of Fame Award 6308
Best of Show Award 12479
Certified Kapnismologist Award 17355
Chrysler Cup 17406
Commendation and Promotion 12603
Cutlery Hall of Fame 6445
Duffy Award 11697
DXer of the Year 5797
Executive Board Merit of Exhibit Award 19283
Family International Talent Awards Program 17088
H. Galloway Spacemodeling Service Award 14368
Roy Gates Memorial Award 19284
GI Joe Fan Award 10015
Globe International Gold Award 16618
Golden Pen 9105
Hal Rogers Endowment Fund 12597
Hall of Foam 9106
Jack Heimann Service Award 19787
Honoree of the Quilters Hall of Fame 17812
Elmer Lester Award 9504
Man of the Year 19908
Robert E. Manning Award 9333
Master Steinologist 19788
Member of the Year Award 15500
Miss Tall International 19909
MPEC Award 13461
NAMBA Hall of Fame 16446
National Merit of Exhibit Award 19285
Newsletter Contest 9505
Overall Control Line Flyers Champion 21535
Pipe Smoker of the Year 11386
President's Exhibit Award 19286
Walter Rosenthal Award 13557
Show Flyer/Poster Contest 9506
Steven Edeiken Memorial Kiteflier of the Year Award 2922
Andrew Whyte Award 12283
Woman of the Year 19910
Writers Contest 9507

Hockey
All-American Awards 15307
Larry Ashley Award 6946
Hobey Baker Memorial Award 10493
Aldege Baz Bastien Memorial Trophy (Outstanding Goaltender) 2498
Jack A. Butterfield Trophy 2499
Calder Cup (Playoff Champion) 2500
Canadian Chrysler Cup 2501
Richard F. Canning Trophy 2502
John Chick Trophy (Empire Division Champion) 2503
Citation Award 21174
Robert W. Clarke Trophy (Western Conference Trophy) 2504
Coach of the Year Award 2488
Coaches Association Awards 15309
College Player of the Year 21175
Les Cunningham Award (Most Valuable Player) 2505
Distinguished Achievement Award 21176
James H. Ellery Memorial Award (Outstanding Media) 2506
ESPY Awards 9337
Elmer Ferguson Memorial Award 10495
Jim Fullerton Award 2489
Dudley (Red) Garrett Memorial Award (Rookie of the Year) 2507
Dr. Randy Gregg Award 7217
James C. Hendy Memorial Award (Outstanding Executive) 2508
Foster Hewitt Memorial Award 10496
Hockey Hall of Fame and Museum Honored Member 10497
Hockey Hall of Fame Builder Category 6859
Hockey Hall of Fame International Friends 6860
Hockey Hall of Fame John Sergnese Category (Friends of CARHA) 6861
Hockey Hall of Fame Media Category 6862
Hockey Hall of Fame Player Category 6863
Hockey Hall of Fame Team Category 6864
Harry (Hap) Holmes Memorial Award (Outstanding Goaltender) 2509
Fred T. Hunt Memorial Award (Sportsmanship, Determination, and Dedication to Hockey) 2510
Edward Jeremiah Award/College Division Coach of the Year 2490
Jofa All American Hockey Squad (East and West) for Colleges 2491
Jofan All-American Hockey Squad (East and West) for Universities 2492
Bob Johnson Award 21177
Junior Player of the Year 21178
Fr. George Kehoe Memorial Award 7220
John Snooks Kelly - Founder's Award 2493
Kilpatrick Trophy 2511
Brian MacFarlane Award 18776
John MacInnes Award 2494
John Mariucci Award 2495
Frank Mathers Trophy 2512
McCrae Cup 7223
Ken McKenzie Award (Outstanding Executive - PR and Marketing) 2513
Marina Van Der Merwe Award 7225
NCAA National Championships 14687
NHL All-Star Team 19671
NHL Coach of the Year 19672
NHL Executive of the Year 19673
NHL Player of the Year 19674
NHL Rookie of the Year 19675
F. G. (Teddy) Oke Trophy (New England Division Champion) 2514
Lester B. Pearson Award 15235
Spencer Penrose Award/University Division Coach of the Year 2496
Louis A. R. Pieri Memorial Award (Coach of the Year) 2515
Sam Pollock Trophy 2516
Service Awards 21179
Eddie Shore Plaque (Outstanding Defenseman) 2517
John B. Sollenberger Trophy (Leading Scorer - Regular Season) 2518
Senator Joseph A. Sullivan Trophy 7234
Wm. Thayer Tutt Award 21180
United States Hockey Hall of Fame 20637
United States National Roller Skating Championships 20391
University Cup 7238
Women's Player of the Year 21181
Walter Yaciuk Award 21182

Home economics (*See also* Consumer affairs)
AAFCS Leaders Award 936
AAFCS New Achievers Awards 937
Reuben Brigham Award 5292
Frances Morton Holbrook Alumni Award 17256
Orinne Johnson Writing Award 17257
KCFB Scholarship 12595
Massachusetts Avenue Building Assets Fund Grants Program 941

Home (continued)

National Family and Consumer Sciences Teacher of the Year Award - Home Economics Teacher of the Year Award 942
Ruth O'Brien Project Grants 943
Sarah Thorniley Phillips Leadership Award 17258

Home inspection
Stephen Greenford Award 6914
President's Award 6915

Homosexuality
Jack Abele Award 21277
AGLBIC Service Award 5368
Angel Award 12994
Gay, Lesbian, Bisexual and Transgender Community Leader Scholarship 12621
Gay/Lesbian Book Award 3003
GSBA Scholarships 10164
Kameny Award 9451
Joseph Norton Award 5369
St. Louis Black Pride Scholarship 18213
Sexual Orientation and Gender Identity Conference Awards 6974
Twinkie 17861

Horse racing
Adult Amateur Award 20563
Award of Excellence 9323
Belmont Stakes 16257
Ed Binneweg Trophy 20618
F. Ambrose Clark Memorial Award 15818
Eclipse Awards 20084
Eclipse Awards for Media 20085
Eugene (Butch) Eseman Award 13133
ESPY Awards 9337
Mr. Fitz Award 15921
Glen Garnsey Trainers Award 20619
Walter Haight Award 15922
Hall of Fame 15404
Harness Horse of the Year 20876
Harness Track of America's Art Competition/ Auction 10258
E. Roland Harriman Memorial Trophy Horse of the Year Award 20620
Bill Haughton Good Guy Award 20621
Headliner Award 20622
John Hervey Broadcasters' Awards George Smallreed Award 20877
Honorary Member 20623
HTA/Hanover Show Farms Caretaker of the Year Award 10259
Kentucky Derby 7989
Kentucky Oaks 7990
Mike Lee Trophy 20624
Living Hall of Fame 20625
National Breeders Trophy 20626
Nova Awards 10260
Pacing Triple Crown 20878
Joe Palmer Award 15923
Dan Patch Awards 20627
Preakness Stakes 13136
Proximity Achievement Award 20628
Rising Star Award 20629
Jack Schultz Perpetual Memorial Trophy 20630
Sovereign Award 12396
Special Awards 20631
Triple Crown Trophy 20206
Trotting Triple Crown 20879
USHWAn-of-the-Year 20632
VISA Triple Crown Challenge 20207
Writers Corner Hall of Fame 20633

Horsemanship
500 Mile Limited Distance Horse Program 2174
1000 Mile Horse Program 2175
AAEA Founders Award for Painting 655
AAEA Founders Award for Sculpture 656
AAEA Museum Directors Award 657
AAEA Sporting Art Award 658
ABC Champion Performance Horse 1550
ABC Champion Trail Horse 1551
Adult Amateur Award 20563
AERC Hall of Fame 2176
All Around NAMAR Mustang 16448
All-Breeds Awards 20564
Amateur Golden Horse 17046
Amateur Supreme Champion 17047
AMHA Man of the Year Award/AMHA Woman of the Year Award 3122
AMHA Medal Class Awards 3123
AMHA Open Competition Awards 3124
AMHA Trail Ride Award 3125
AMHA Youth of the Year Award 3126
AMHA Youth Person of the Year Award 3127
AMHAY Horsemastership Awards 3128
Annual High Point Awards 16454
Appreciation Certificates for Service to NATRC 16479
Awards Program
American Hanoverian Society 2386
American Holsteiner Horse Association 2520
Harry Bennett Award 1324
Jean Bowman Memorial Award for Painting 659
Breed Awards 16480
Breeder Awards 16864
Polly Bridges Memorial Award 16481
Cecil J. Brown Memorial Sportsmanship Award 3129
Championship Awards 19541
Competition and Achievement Awards 4804
Counting Coup Award 2599
CTHS Annual Award 7520
Cumulative Mileage Awards 16482
Peter L. Damele Memorial Award 1552
Distance Award and Best-Conditioned & Trail Class Award 10634
Distinguished Founders Award 1334
Footing of the Year Award 20565
Golden Horse Award 17048
Golden Reins Award 3130
Hall of Fame
American Morgan Horse Association 3131
Brotherhood of Working Farriers Association 6659
Palomino Horse Breeders of America 17049
High Point Honors 6449
High Point Horsemenship Award 16483
High Point Performance Horse Awards 16455
High-Score Award 16687
Honor Roll 11436
Horse and Rider Awards 16062
Horse Awards 14140
Horse Hall of Fame 14889
Horse of the Year Awards
National Spotted Saddle Horse Association 15815
United States Dressage Federation 20566
Horseback Hours Award 2600
Horseback Miles Award 2601
Husband/Wife Team Award 2177
Eleonora Hydar Memorial Award 7521
IHIC Scholarship 12183
Indian Horse Hall of Fame Award 2602
Jim Jones Award - Most Miles Stallion Award 2178
Judges Award 3132
Junior Division Award 2179
Junior Grand Champion 16484
Junior High Average Horsemanship 16485
Junior National Championship 16486
Junior/Young Rider Awards 20567
Limited Distance Program 2180
Medallion de Bronce 16456
Medallion de Oro 16457
Medallion de Plata 16458
Leonard J. Meiselman Memorial Award for Painting 660
Leonard J. Meiselman Memorial Award for Sculpture 661
Member of the Year 21953
Jim Menefee Memorial Award 16487
Jane Miller Memoriam 8216
Most Versatile Horse Award 8217
Dick Mumpton Memorial Award 20635
Musical Freestyle Awards 20568
National 100 Mile Award 2181
National and International High Points Competition 4904
National Best Condition Award 2182
National Champion Bronze Statue 11903
National High School Finals Rodeo 15233
National High Score Awards 21514
National Jockeys Hall of Fame 13134
National Limited Distance Mileage Award 2183
National Mileage Championship 2184
National Series Championship 2185
NATRC Honorary Lifetime Membership 16488
NATRC National Champions 16489
NATRC Ride Awards 16490
North American Warmblood Association Awards 16499
Kimbel E. Oelke Memorial Award for Painting 662
Elke Otremba Memorial Award 7522
Outstanding Competition Management Awards 20569
Outstanding Promoter Award 15816
Eugene Palmer Memorial Trophy 13349
Pard'ners Award 2186
Participation Awards 21954
General George S. Patton, Jr. Memorial Trophy 20705
Perfect Ten (Equine Only) Award 2187
Pioneer Award 2188
Points and Awards Program 19542
Popular Choice Award 663
Presidents Cup 16491
Regional Best Conditions Award 2189
Regional Horse Awards 16492
Regional Medallions 16459
Ride Managers 14142
Rider Award Program 20570
Rider Awards 14143
Rider Mileage Championship 2190
Rider Mileage Program 2191

Horsemanship (continued)

Mike Ruby Honorarium 8218
Hanna Schmocker Memorial Award 7523
State Awards and National Awards 14144
Bill Stuckey Award 2192
Supreme Champion 17050
Herbert N. Swecker Award 8219
Therapy Horse of the Year Award 3133
Bill Thornburgh Family Award 2193
Bev Tibbitts Grand Champion Horse Award 16493
Trainer of the Year 21428
Else Tuckerman Memorial Award for Painting 664
Vintage Cup Awards 20571
Hans Wulff Memorial Award 7524
Year-end Achievement Award 16688
Year End Awards 5021
Year-End High Point Awards 21955
Year End High Score Awards 10575
Young Competitor Award 7525
Youth Award 1553
Youth World Championship Horse Show Golden Horse 17051

Horticulture

Evelyn A. Abendroth Award 1612
Achievement Award
  American Fuchsia Society 2312
  National Peach Council 15494
AHS Best Variegated Hosta in a Tour Garden Award 2550
All-America Rose Selections Award of Excellence 438
All-America Rose Selections Certificate of Merit 439
American Iris Society Gold Medal 2866
AOS Show Trophy 3320
Johnny Appleseed Award 9882
Arbor Day Awards 13949
Artistic Certificate (for Artistic Display of Orchids in Use) 3321
ASHS Hall of Fame 4084
Association and Industry Awards 9610
Australian Camellia Research Society Trophy 1613
Award for Outstanding Service to the Society 16144
Award of Distinction 3322
Award of Merit
  American Association of Botanical Gardens and Arboreta 1120
  American Orchid Society 3323
  Tree Care Industry Association 20185
Award of Quality 3324
Liberty Hyde Bailey Medal 2524
Best Gesneriad 2364
Best Hosta in a Tour Garden Award 2551
Best Hosta Seedling or Sport in a Tour Garden Award 2552
Best Seedling Award 18124
Big Bucks Award 2553
Bonsai and Orchid Association Award 6500
Building with Trees Awards of Excellence 13950
Luther Burbank Award 2525
Butterworth Prize 3325
Celia Carr Flower Arranging Award 8915
Harold Cawood Award 1614
Arminta Cawood Japonica Award 1615
Certificate of Achievement 10410
Certificate of Appreciation
  The Gardeners of America/Men's Garden Clubs of America 9883
  Herb Society of America 10411
Certificate of Botanical Recognition 3326
Certificate of Cultural Merit 3327
Certificate of Meritorious Arrangement 3328
Certificate of Recognition 9884
Commercial Horticulture Distinguished Achievement Award 4085
Conservation Award 16145
Consumer Horticulture Distinguished Achievement Award 4086
Cut Leaf Show Awards 2554
Helen de Conway Little Medal of Honor 10412
Dorothy Stredicke Dickson Memorial Award 3593
Distinguished Recognition Award 11730
Distinguished Service Award 2867
Ray Dittus Award 16436
Herbert P. Dyckman Award for Service 1559
Dykes Medal Award 2868
Paul Ecke Jr. Commercial Award 2526
Education Award 16146
Educational Exhibit 3329
Educational Materials Award 4087
Exemplary Journalism Award 15136
Bertrand Farr Medal 2444
Fellow
  American Camellia Society 1616
  Garden Writers Association 9878
First Class Certificate 3330
Helen Field Fischer Medal 2445
Eunice Fisher Award 2555
Floricultural Hall of Fame 18966
FM Foundation Downtown Beautification Grant 16556
Foliage Hall of Fame 9611
Foliage Writer of the Year Contest 9612
French Wine and Spirits Sommelier Competition 21651
Garden Club of America Medals and Awards 9876
Gardeners of America/Men's Garden Clubs of America Scholarship 9885
Gardening From the Heart Award 9886
Milo Gibson Award 16434
Gold Certificate 3331
Gold Honor Medal 3872
Gold Medal
  American Rhododendron Society 3851
  The Gardeners of America/Men's Garden Clubs of America 9887
  State Capital Global Law Firm Group 19765
Gold Medal Awards 16437
Gold Medal of Achievement 3332
Eva Kenworthy Gray Award 1560
G. B. Gunlogson Medal 2527
GWAA Hall of Fame 9879
GWAA Honorary Member 9880
Harris Hybrid Award 1617
Harshbarger Landscape Design Plaque 2556
U. P. Hedrick Awards 3583
Herb Society of America Grant 10413
Hibiscus of the Year Award 2450
Highly Commended Certificate 3333
Honorary Life Membership 2557
Honors and Achievement Award 11731
Horticultural Communication Award 2528
Horticultural Therapy Award 2529
Horticultural Writing Citation 2530
Nancy Putnam Howard Award for Horticulture 10414
Hybridizer's Medal 2869
Illges Seedling Japonica Award 1618
Industry Division ASHS President's Corporate Council Award 4088
RITF Noel Jackson Research Fellowship 18032
Ann and Phil Jessup Botanical Trophy 3334
Judges' Commendation 3335
Charlotte C. Knox Reticulata Award 1619
William F. Kosar Award 10508
Landscape Design Award 2531
Keith Laver Award 7316
Local Horticulture Award 2532
Longevity Award 2313
Homer Lucas Landscape Award 16147
Arch McKean Award 11732
Medallion of Honor 442
Median Iris Awards 13240
Meritorious Service Award 2533
MGCA Beautification Certificate 9888
MGCA Golden Quill Award 9889
Carroll R. Miller Award 15495
Minnesota Blue Award 2558
Minnesota Gold Award 2559
William Mohr Medal 5045
National Camellia Hall of Fame 1620
Neighborhood Greening Project 9898
Outstanding Extension Educator Award 4089
Outstanding Graduate Educator Award 4090
Outstanding Industry Scientist Award 4091
Outstanding International Horticulturist ASHS Career Awards 4092
Outstanding Leader in Oregon Blueberry Industry 16853
Outstanding Researcher Award 4093
Outstanding Undergraduate Educator Award 4094
Peer Sasanqua Award 1621
Photography Awards 2446
Frances Jones Poetker Award 2534
President's Award
  International Lilac Society 11733
  Professional Grounds Management Society 17627
President's Exhibitor Trophy 2560
Professional Award 2535
PSFA Scholarship Program 17492
Public Plant Breeding Award 14795
Public Rose Garden Achievement Award 440
Alfred D. Robinson Memorial Medal for Begonia Hybrid 1561
Jack F. Schneider Award 9874
Schutt Silver Cup 2561
Scientific Award 2536
Scott Medal Award 18369
Sewell Mutant Award 1622
Paul Shepard Award 3584
Shiu-Ying Hu Award 10509
Silver Medal
  American Rhododendron Society 3852
  The Gardeners of America/Men's Garden Clubs of America 9890
  State Capital Global Law Firm Group 19766
Silver Medal of Merit 3336
Lucille Simpers Award 2562
Slate - MacDaniels Award 16441

Subject Index

Horticulture (continued)
State Awards 16148
Sturdy Oaks Award 5079
Alex J. Summers Distinguished Merit Award 2563
Catherine H. Sweeney Award 2537
Sylvia Cup Design Competition 18967
Kathryn S. Taylor Award for Private Gardens 16149
Teaching Award 2538
Tri-Color Trophy 2447
Turf Research 12959
Turf Scholarship 12960
John A. Tyler, Jr. Miniature Award 1623
Undergraduate Student Awards for an Outstanding Horticulture Student 4095
Urban Beautification Award 2539
Varietal Awards 2448
Western Garden Design Awards 19840
Clarence G. White Medal 5046
Wilder Medal 3585
E. H. Wilson Award 16442
W. W. Wilson Cypridedioideae Award 3337
Wolf-Fenton Award 10510
Working Group Vegetable Breeding Working Group Award of Excellence 4096
Working Groups Distinguished Achievement Award for Nursery Crops 4097
Working Groups Outstanding Fruit Cultivar Award 4098
Youth Gardening Award 9891

Hospital administration (*See also* Nursing homes)
Apotex Award 7459
Distinguished Service Award 2543
Robert S. Hudgens Memorial Award - Young Healthcare Executive of the Year 1873
Leadership Award 2547
Merit Award 1529
Seymour Award 5379

Hotels *See* Travel

Houseware
Hall of Fame 7135

Housing (*See also* Real estate)
ACUHO-I Award 5622
Tessie Agan Award 1240
Annual Distinction Award 11243
Ronald B. Atlas Award 16188
Builder's Choice Design and Planning Awards 6676
Carl A.S. Coan, Sr. Award 15246
James C. Grimm Leadership and Service Award 5623
M. Justin Herman Memorial Award 14263
Housing Person of the Year Award 15247
James A. Hurd Award 5624
Nathaniel S. Keith Award 15248
John D. Lange International Award 14264
C. F. "Buzz" Meadows Memorial Award 14265
Medallion Award 8584
NAHRO Agency Awards of Excellence in Housing and Community Development 14266
NAHRO Agency Awards of Merit in Housing and Community Development 14267
National Housing Hall of Fame 14259
Sand Dollar 8203
S. Earl Thompson Award 5625

Frederic M. Vogelsang Memorial Manuscript Award 14268
Elizabeth Wells Memorial Award 14269

Human engineering
Alphonse Chapanis Best Student Paper Award 10577
Distinguished International Colleague Award 10578
Jerome H. Ely *Human Factors* Article Award 10579
Fellow Award 13657
Paul M. Fitts Education Award 10580
Jack A. Kraft Innovator Award 10581
A. R. Lauer Safety Award 10582
President's Award 13658
Today's Workplace of Tomorrow 21793
Alexander C. Williams, Jr., Design Award 10583

Human relations
Awards for Excellence 18865
Avis Bohlen Award 2278
Distinguished Service Award 12886
Richard J. H. Gottheil Award 22111
Percy Grainger Medallion 12146
Heinz Award in the Human Condition 10382
The Sidney Hillman Foundation Prize Awards 10435
Honorary Fellow of the College of Human Sciences 11690
Human Relations Award 18626
Humanitarian Award 6631
Joseph Prize for Human Rights 4982
Robert F. Kennedy Journalism Awards 18076
Theodore W. Kheel Award of the Institute for Mediation and Conflict Resolution 10825
Herbert H. Lehman Human Relations Award 2886
National Human Relations Award 2887
National Mass Media Award 2888
James A. Rawley Prize 16895
Carter G. Woodson Award 4997

Human resource management *See* Personnel management

Human rights (*See also* Civil rights and liberties)
ACI Founders Award 4977
Appeal of Conscience Award 5004
Baltic Freedom Award 6228
Heywood Broun Award 16343
Builders of a Better World Prize 21899
Goler T. Butcher Award for Lifetime Achievement 10051
Civil Courage Prize 16537
Kitty Cole Human Rights Award 2069
Vincent De Francis Award 2573
William Edward Burghardt Du Bois Medal 14048
Eleanor Roosevelt Award for Outstanding Contributions to the Cause of Human Rights 20539
Freedom Award 9760
Hala-Negri Award 10603
Judge Learned Hand Award 2885
W. Averell Harriman Democracy Award 14910
Moss Hart Memorial Award 16125
Andrew Heiskell Awards 20091
Homeric Award 7866

Honorary Human Rights Award 3278
Human Rights Award
American Federation of Teachers, AFL-CIO 2233
American Psychiatric Association 3620
International Association of Official Human Rights Agencies 11371
Jewish Labor Committee 12361
National Committee on American Foreign Policy 14702
Humanist of the Year 10606
Humanitarian Award 14966
Hubert H. Humphrey First Amendment Freedoms Prize 4981
John Humphrey Freedom Award 11464
IAEWP Diploma of Honour 11344
IAEWP Membership in Good Standing 11345
International Editor of the Year 21971
International Human Rights Law Award 10052
International Human Rights Partners Award 10053
Jonathatn Mann Award for Global Health and Human Rights 10049
Joseph Prize for Human Rights 4982
Robert F. Kennedy Human Rights Award 18075
Martin Luther King, Jr. - Abraham Joshua Heschel Award 6490
Owen M. Kupferschmid Award 16983
Letelier - Moffitt Memorial Human Rights Awards 10830
Manhattan College Pacem in Terris Medal 13052
Media Awards for Excellence 4941
Loren Miller Legal Services Award 19760
Minnesota Awards for Human Rights 13465
Ashley Montagu Human Nurturance Award 10604
NED Democracy Award 14928
Norman Cousins Award 21901
Outstanding Achievement Award 18917
Outstanding Lithuanian Woman Award 12876
Heinz R. Pagels Human Rights of Scientists Award 16204
Perlman Award for Human Advancement 12392
Philadelphia Liberty Medal 10157
A. Philip Randolph/Bayard Rustin Freedom Award 28
Red Rose-White Rose Award 12568
Reebok Human Rights Award 17933
Rothko Chapel Oscar Romero Award 18132
Gertrude E. Rush Award 14491
Bayard Rustin Humanitarian Award 29
Save the Children - Canada Award 18323
Anatoly Scharansky Freedom Award 20306
Soviet Jewry Freedom Awards 16060
Struggle for Liberation of Bulgaria Award 6689
The Honourable Walter S. Tarnopolsky Human Rights Award 6977
Hon. Walter S. Tarnopolsky Medal 11490
United Nations Prize in the Field of Human Rights 20360
Raoul Wallenberg Civic Courage Award 17877
Simon Wiesenthal Center Humanitarian Award 18530
Stephen S. Wise Award 2898

Humanitarianism (*See also* Hunger)
AAPA National and International Humanitarian Physician Assistant of the Year 813
Acacia Leadership Scholarship 74
Appeal of Conscience Award 5004
Austin MacCormick Award 16918
Award of Merit/Distinguished Service Award 14814
Awards for Excellence 18865
Bellarmine Medal 6306
Glen Bollinger Humanitarian Award 10352
Harry Bolster Memorial Award 21254
Jim Bottorf Award 68
Bronze Medal Award 15826
Pearl S. Buck International Woman of the Year Award 17129
Builders of a Better World Prize 21899
Ralph Bunche Memorial Award 20254
George Card Award 2040
Caring Award 7597
Caritas Medal 16349
Certificate of Literature 17264
Chai Award 6483
Chalice Award 9656
Harry Chapin Memorial Humanitarian Award 14359
Chapter of the Year Award 2583
Waco F. Childers, Jr., Award 2572
Citizenship Award 20140
Jacob Clayman Award 14815
Corporate Conscience Award 8591
The Leonardo da Vinci Award 11066
The John Dieckman Distinguished Educational Award of Honor 15642
Distinguished Alumnus Award 14285
Distinguished Service Award 4936
Dodge Award 22035
Dunleavy Award 16350
Eisenhower Liberation Medal 20639
Ethical Humanist Award 16264
Exemplar of Humanics Award 2580
Explorers Medal 9375
Fellow 17265
Fighter Against Drug Abuse 14730
Freedom Award 10758
Friend of the Homeless Award 18532
Miguel Garcia-Tunon Memorial Award in Human Dignity 1824
Gold Medal Award 15827
Golden Scorpion Award for Outstanding Service 57
Good Neighbor Award 3828
Good Samaritan Award 3569
Mary M. Gooley Humanitarian of the Year Award 15205
Great Heart Award 21280
Hala-Negri Award 10603
Michel T. Halbouty Human Needs Award 1338
Lawton S. Heart Award 9593
The Dr. Bernard Heller Prize 10375
Helping Hands Award 21947
Herbert A. Rothman Award 12238
Heroism Award 15860
Jean Hersholt Humanitarian Award 112
T. Kenyon Holly Memorial Award 20252
Human Rights Award
American Psychiatric Association 3620
Council on Economic Priorities 8592
Humane Award 2574
Humanist Arts Award 2585
Humanist Contributions to Science Award 2586
Humanist Distinguished Service Award 2587
Humanist Hero Award 2588
Humanist Heroine Award 2589
Humanist Media Award 2590
Humanist Music Award 16175
Humanist of the Year 10606
Humanist of the Year Award 2591
Humanist Pioneer Award 2592
Humanitarian Award
American Cancer Society 1637
American College of Oral and Maxillofacial Surgeons 1911
American Sportscasters Association 4677
AMIT USA 4937
Doctors to the World 8973
International Veteran Boxers Association 12116
Inventors Clubs of America 12161
National Federation of Democratic Women 14966
National Parkinson Foundation 15487
Variety International - The Children's Charity 21281
Elie Wiesel Foundation for Humanity 21620
Humanitarian-Brotherhood Award 20338
Humanitarian of the Year 13301
Humanitas Prize 10608
Interamerica Prize 11104
International Humanitarian Award
AARL Foundation 48
American Red Magen David for Israel - American Friends of Magen David 3843
La Sertoma International 12637
International Humanitarian Service Award 3831
Roger E. Joseph Prize 10376
Joseph Jozwiak Memorial Special Achievement Award 11818
Kal Kan Volunteer of the Year 2575
Martin Luther King, Jr. Medal 8033
Joseph Wood Krutch Medal 10598
Elaine J. Lasky Humanitarian Service Award 15643
Legion of Honor 12366
Lifetime Achievement Award 7096
Magna Charta Day Award 6258
Colonel Mickey Marcus Award 12388
Louis Marshall Award 12378
Zvi Hirsch Masliansky Award 10373
Master of the Game Award 15809
Medallion for Entrepreneurship 6332
Lucille Medwick Memorial Award 17435
Merit Award 8784
Ministry Support Award 6270
Ashley Montagu Human Nurturance Award 10604
Mother of the Humanitarian Scholarship 17031
National Humanitarian Award
National Recreation and Park Association 15581
WAIF 21423
National Women's Hall of Fame 15960
Norman Cousins Award 21901
Notre Dame Award 21090
Ontario Medal for Good Citizenship 16755
Outstanding Humanitarian Service Award 714
Outstanding Service Award 21424
Maurice Pate Memorial Award 20597
Philalethes Lecture 17266
Pioneer Award 8593
Poverello Medal 9730
President's Award
American Humane Association 2577
Institution for Operations Research and the Management Sciences 11079
Pro Bono Publico Awards 1536
Public Service Award 19247
Bella Rackoff Humanitarian Award 21758
RHR International Award for Excellence in Consultation 3753
Paul Robeson Award 163
Robie Humanitarianism Award 12276
William Rogers Award 6663
Rookie of the Year 15828
Bayard Rustin Humanitarian Award 29
Samaritan Award 12661
Albert Schweitzer Prize for Humanitarianism 12417
Service to Others 9858
Signum Fidei Medal 12635
Silver Medal Award 15829
Irving Silverman Award 12120
Special Achievement Award 17267
The Statuette with Pedestal 11160
Henrietta Szold Award 10215
Temple Award for Creative Altruism 12179
Ten Outstanding Young Americans 20678
Touchdown Club Hubert H. Humphrey Award 20134
UNICEF Award for Distinguished Service 20598
University Founders Award 9731
Bishop John T. Walker Humanitarian Award 269
Raoul Wallenberg Hero for Our Time Award 17878
Washington Award 4366
Byron "Whizzer" White Humanitarian Award 15093
World Citizen Humanitarian 9802
World Citizenship Award 16592
Gilbert and Kathleen Wrenn Award for a Humanitarian and Caring Person 2074
Norma Zarky Humanitarian Award 21723

Humanities *See* Arts and humanities

Humanities research
Honorary Life Membership 2581

Humor (*See also* Cartoons; Entertainment)
Banana Club (R) Man/Woman of the Year 11416
The Buster 8724
Clown of the Year 17651
Columbia Pictures Television Playwriting Award 12542
Elmer Award 10275
Golden Toonie Award 7615
Grammy Awards 13822
IPA Top Discovery in the Field of Humor 11807
Stephen Leacock Medal for Humour 19790
Movie Worsts Awards 10276
Order of Mariposa 19791
Performance Awards 16975
Punster of the Year 11892
The Elsa Shaine Memorial Award 10278
Silurian Excellence in Journalism Awards 19327
Thurber Prize for American Humor 20087
Mark Twain Award 11814

Subject Index

Hunger
Africa Prize for Leadership for the Sustainable End of Hunger 10614
Bronze Medal Award 15826
Harry Chapin Media Awards 21925
Congressional Leadership Award 18013
Cameron Duncan Media Award 18014
Gold Medal Award 15827
Pearl Soil Hunger Fighter of the Year 7868
Rookie of the Year 15828
Silver Medal Award 15829

Hunting
ACHA World Champion Coonhound 2020
Johnson Medal 7365
NRA Club Achievement Award 10264

Hydrography (*See also* Oceanography)
G. Evelyn Hutchinson Award 4489
R. Lindeman Award 4490

Hypnosis
Best Research Paper 3759
Best Theoretical Paper Award 3760
Sherry K. and Harold B. Crasilneck Award 18654
Roy M. Dorcus Award 18655
Henry Guze Award 18656
Ernest and Josephine Hilgard Award 18657
E. R. Hilgard Best Graduate Level Academic Thesis Award 3761
Dr. Marco Marchesan Award 10835
Morton Prince Award 18658
Morton Prince, M.D. Award 10836
Bernard B. Raginsky Award 18659
Shirley R. Schneck Award 18660
Arthur Shapiro Award 18661
Nicholas P. Spanos Best Graduate Student Paper Award 3762
Therapist of the Year 11320

Ice hockey *See* Hockey

Ice skating
Edi Awards 17660
Hall of Fame 20846
Ice Skating Hall of Fame 10631
Ice Skating Man and Woman of the Year 10632
United States Figure Skating Champions 20589
World Figure Skating Hall of Fame 20590

Illustration
Walter C. Alvarez Memorial Award 3081
Annual Awards Competition 8565
Annual Exhibition Awards 19137
Annual Exhibitions 5115
Art Award 16241
Pura Belpre Award 17950
Best Illustrated Children's Books of the Year 16297
Irma S. and James H. Black Award for Excellence in Children's Literature 6241
Book Award 17402
Book Awards 7913
Boston Globe - Horn Book Awards 6526
CA Advertising Annual 8308
CA Design Annual 8309
Randolph Caldecott Medal 5436
Children's Literature Festival Award 12528
Fellowship for Creative and Performing Arts and Writers 914
Carolyn W. Field Award 17177
FOCAL Award 12929
Georgia Children's Picture Storybook Award 21023
Golden Kite Awards 19087
Golden Sower Awards 16068
Golden Toonie Award 7615
Governor General's Literary Awards 6797
Amelia Frances Howard-Gibbon Illustrator's Award 7260
Illustration Annual 8310
Ezra Jack Keats/Kerlan Collection Fellowship 21073
Coretta Scott King Book Award 3004
Magazine Merit Awards 19088
Management Innovation Poster Session Award 1874
Municipal Chapter of Toronto IODE Children's Book Award 12177
National Jewish Book Award - Children's Picture Book 12323
National Magazine Awards 15355
Outstanding Pennsylvania Author or Illustrator 17192
Ruth and Sylvia Schwartz Children's Book Awards 16746
University of Southern Mississippi Medallion 13517
The Washington Post/Children's Book Guild Award for Nonfiction 21457
Laura Ingalls Wilder Award 5444
Rip Van Winkle Award 18339
Young Hoosier Picture Book Award 5389

Illustration, medical *See* Medical illustration

Imaging
Award of Excellence 10699
Image Consultant of the Year 10700

Indians *See* Native Americans

Individual rights *See* Civil rights and liberties

Industrial arts
Award of Distinction 12064
D.A.I. Goring Award 21108
Gold Level Achievement Awards 19958
The Leadership Award 21109
John Peter Reeve Memorial Award 21110
Teacher Recognition Awards 12072
Technology Honor Society 19959
TSA Star Recognition Program 19960

Industrial chemistry
ACS Award in Industrial Chemistry 1716
Canadian Society for Chemical Engineering Award in Industrial Practice 7835
Victor K. LaMer Award 1766

Industrial design
$100,000 Lemelson-MIT Lifetime Achievement Award 12776
Allied Arts Medal 18134
AmeriStar Package Awards 11023
Design Award 11738
Design Awards Competition 18668
Gifts and Decorative Accessories Merchandising Achievement Awards 10011
ID Annual Design Review 10636
Industrial Design Excellence Awards (IDEA) 10782
ISA Fellow 12219
Laboratory of the Year 17816
New Product Award 15748
Pantone Color Award 17062
Playthings Merchandising Achievement Awards 10013
Student Paper Award for Four and Five Year Students 12224
Student Paper Award for Two and Three Year Students 12225
Technical Division Executive Committee Award 2320

Industrial engineering
Award for Outstanding Achievement in Management 10949
Award for Technical Innovation in Industrial Engineering 10950
Dr. David F. Baker Distinguished Research Award 10951
Consumer Plastics Product Design Award 19261
Fred C. Crane Distinguished Service Award 10952
Fellow Award
Institute of Industrial Engineers 10953
MTM Association for Standards and Research 13657
Frank and Lillian Gilbreth Industrial Engineering Award 10954
Graduate Research Award 10955
Albert G. Holzman Distinguished Educator Award 10956
Honorary Member Award 10957
Honored Service Member Award 19263
IIE Award for Excellence in Productivity Improvement 10958
IIE Excellence Award for Minority Advancement 10959
IIE - Joint Publishers Book of the Year Award 10960
IIE Transactions Award 10961
Industrial Plastics Product Design Award 19265
R. S. Jane Memorial Lecture Award 7839
Richard Harold Kaufmann Award 10872
Lifetime Achievement Award 11336
S. Ray Miller International Award 11337
Outstanding IIE Publication Award 10962
Outstanding Young Industrial Engineer Award 10963
Package Printing and Converting's Diecutter/Diemaker of the Year Award 11338
Presidential Award 11339
President's Award 13658
Pritsker Doctoral Dissertation Award 10964
Safety Award 11340
Student Award for Excellence 10965
Systems Modeling Student Competition - Student 10966
Undergraduate Student Paper Competition 10967
J. W. Woomer Award 18829

Industries and trades (*See also* Business; Craftsmanship; specific industries and trades, e.g. Dairy industry)
$500,000 Lemelson-MIT Prize 12777
AESF Charles Henry Proctor Leadership Award 2167

Industries (continued)

AESF Franklane Industrial Achievement Award 2168
AESF Gold Medal 2169
AESF Kergan Wells Service Award 2170
AESF Scientific Achievement Award 2171
AESF Silver Medal 2172
Al Padur Scholarship Fund 8116
Associate Remodeler of the Year Award 14257
Automated Imaging Achievement Award 6098
Award for Community Service 15164
Award of Distinction 17643
Award of Merit 14304
Award of Recognition 17644
Award of Special Recognition 14305
A. A. Bloom Memorial Award 20251
Candle Artisan of the Year 11658
Cesery Award 20089
Connie Award 8472
Joseph M. Corwin Award 5255
Crystal Award 19828
Cutlery Hall of Fame 6445
Distinguished Life Member 16422
Doehler Award 16423
J. Edward Donnellan Award 21658
EDI Award for Corporate Leadership 9087
Edison Awards 3028
Educational Sponsorship Award 14018
Exhibitors Competition 17645
Glass Professional of the Year 15165
Graduate Student Plant Breeding Award 14793
Grocers Care Awards 15174
Gullo and Treiber Award 16424
Hall of Fame 17315
Hall of Fame Award
 International Federation of Leather Guilds 11597
 National Association of Pipe Coating Applicators 14330
Maurice Holland Award 10786
Honorary Member 14306
Industrial Research Institute Achievement Award 10787
Industrial Research Institute Medal 10788
Industry Leadership Award 13700
International Award 16425
International Graphoanalyst of the Year 11656
International Print Framing Competition 17646
Judges Choice Award 11659
Edward A. Kruszynski Achievement Award 16426
David Laine Memorial Scholarship Program 16427
Life Member 14307
Austin T. Lillegren Award 16428
Marketer of the Year 3031
James McAnsh Award 7564
George and Eleanore Meade Award 19829
Members Choice Award 11660
Membership Enrichment Award 16429
Merit Award 16430
Mordica Memorial Award 21659
MRCA Foundation Scholarship Grants 13398
NASSTRAC Awards Program 13762
New and Creative Framing Competition 17647
Nyselius Award 16431
Order of Ontario 16757
Outstanding Achievement Award 14308
El Pitirre Award 17745
Private Plant Breeding Award 14794
Professional Development 21797
Professional Development Awards 15754
Pursuit of Excellence Award 15134
Pyramid Awards 21471
Safety in Seas Award 15420
William P. Slichter Award 20482
Special Service Award 16432
Taguchi Award 4717
Silvio C. Taormina Memorial Award 14309
Technical Paper Awards 21660
Lois Tollefsen Award 11661
U.S. International Film and Video Festival 21143
Utilization Award 14019
M. C. Vaughan Scholarship Fund 4715
VMI (Virginia Military Institute) Future Captain of Industry Award 21408

Information management (*See also* Records management)

AIAA Information Systems Award 2655
AIIM Company of Fellows 307
Thomas P. Anderson Sr. Micrographics Awards 308
Annual Award for Excellence in Writing on an Information Topic 10798
Annual Award to Regular Columnists 10799
ASIS Research Award 4100
Award of Merit
 AIIM - The Enterprise Content Management Association 309
 American Society for Information Science and Technology 4101
Best Chapter Event Award 4102
Best Information Science Book Award 4103
Best *JASIS* Paper Award 4104
Best SIG Publication Award 4105
Bower Award for Business Leadership 9742
Canadian Information Productivity Awards 10796
Canadian Information Technology Innovation Award 7163
Chapter Member-of-The-Year Award 4106
Chapter of the Year Award 4107
Chapter Publication of the Year Award 4108
Clinical Systems Award 10343
Company of Fellows 5090
James M. Cretsos Leadership Award 4109
Customer Service Award 7165
Watson Davis Award 4110
Design Award 12150
Distinguished Education and Behavioral Sciences Librarian Award 5605
Distinguished Information Sciences Award 5731
Distinguished Service Award 12151
Distinguished Service Citation 310
EBSCO Community College Learning Resources and Library Achievement Awards 5608
Electronic Imaging Management Award 311
Fellows of the SID 18767
LITA/Gaylord Award for Achievement in Library and Information Technology 12823
Government Computer News Awards Program 10104
Paul F. Greene Telecommunications Research Fund Award 6186
HIMSS John E. Gall Jr./CIO Award 10344
Industry Specific Group of the Year Award 5091
Information Processing Public Service Award 5732
Information Systems Award
 Babson College - Center for Information Management Studies 6187
 Healthcare Information and Management Systems Society 10345
Innovation Award 12152
Instruction Section Innovation Award 5611
Margaret T. Lane Award 12940
Samuel Lazerow Fellowship for Research in Collections and Technical Services in Academic and Research Libraries 5613
LITA/OCLC Minority Scholarship in Library and Information Technology 12830
George McKinney Award 9585
NASIRE Recognition Awards for Outstanding Achievement in the Field of Information Technology 14395
National Iway Awards 7547
Rolf Nevanlinna Prize 11745
WESS Coutts Nijhoff International West European Specialist Study Grant 5615
Outstanding Achievement Award 12153
Outstanding Information Science Teacher Award 4111
Pioneer Award 313
Pratt-Severn Best Student Research Paper Award 4112
Product and Service Awards 12154
Publications Awards 10348
SIG Member-of-The-Year Award 4113
SIG-of-the-Year Award 4114
Fannie Simon Award 19560
Special Award
 AIIM - The Enterprise Content Management Association 314
 American Society for Information Science and Technology 4115
Student Chapter of the Year Award 4116
H. W. Wilson Company Indexing Award 4457
Christine Zanotti Award for Excellence in Non-Serial Publications 5092

Innovation *See* Inventions

Instructional films *See* Audiovisuals; Educational films

Insurance

Achievement Award 1257
AERF Practitioners Award 18939
Annual Prize 18940
The Arthur Quern Quality Award 18060
Walter H. Bennett Memorial Award 10727
Harold S. Bowen Public Relations Award 10728
Bernard J. Burns Award 10729
CCIA Gavel Award 8455
Chapter Achievement Award 21740
Company Award of Excellence 14343
Company Representative of the Year 14344
Connecticut Association Membership Award 10730
The Cristy Award 18061

Insurance (continued)

Dach InVEST Award 10731
Distinguished Graduate Award in Premium Auditing 15739
Dorweiler Prize 7621
Excellence in Education Award 12843
Federation of Insurance and Corporate Counsel Annual Award 9469
Financial Security Nest Egg Award 11092
FLMI Insurance Education Award 12844
Woodward - Fondiller Prize 7622
The Fred H. Bossons Award 18062
Betty Gerdes Distinguished Service Award 15740
Golden Torch Award 11095
Harold R. Gordon Memorial Award 14246
Charles A. Hachemeister Prize 7623
Halmstad Prize 18941
Maurice G. Herndon National Legislative Award 10732
Everett Curtis Huntington Prize 18942
IIAA Publications Award 10733
InVEST Award 10734
Kulp Wright Award 3854
Leaders Recognition Society Award 21741
Leading Producer Round Table Awards 14247
Legal Writing Contest 11333
Marketing Methods Competition 17633
L. P. McCord Education Award 10735
Robert I Mehr Award 3855
Membership Service Award 10736
Michelbacher Prize 7624
Arthur J. Morris Award 8456
Outstanding Society Awards 12845
Outstanding Young Agents Committee Award 10737
President's Award 19139
PRIMA's Risk Management Achievement Awards 17729
Professional Agent of the Year 14345
Public Risk Manager of the Year Award 17730
Research Award 19140
Matthew Rodermund Service Award 7625
Emmett Russell, Jr. Award 5724
Sidney O. Smith National Award 10738
Ezra M Sparlin Award 10739
Les B. Strickler Innovation in Instruction Award 3856
Tennessee Big "I" Advertising Award 10740
Triennial Prize 18943
Witt Award 3857
Woman of the Year Award 21742
Woodworth Memorial Award 10741
Yancey Memorial Award 11334

Intellectual freedom (*See also* Academic freedom)
AzLA/SIRS Intellectual Freedom Award 5055
Joseph L. Brechner Freedom of Information Award 6614
Robert B. Downs Intellectual Freedom Award 21034
Freedom to Read Roll of Honor 9762
Danny Gunnells Intellectual Freedom Award 10765
Hoosier Intellectual Freedom Award 10766
John Phillip Immroth Memorial Award for Intellectual Freedom 2986
Intellectual Freedom Award
American Association of School Librarians 1417
Illinois Library Association 10678
Intellectual Freedom Round Table State and Regional Achievement Award 2987
NCLA/SIRS Intellectual Freedom Award 16513
Eli M. Oboler Memorial Award 2988
Open Book Awards 4470

Intellectual property *See* Copyright; Inventions

Intelligence *See* National security

Interior design
ASID Designer of Distinction Award 4459
Builder's Choice Design and Planning Awards 6676
C.C. Knight Award 17027
Design Awards Competition 18668
Educational Interiors Showcase 3884
Fellow Recognition 11641
Honorary Recognition 11642
ID Annual Design Review 10636
Institute Honor Awards for Interiors 2716
ISP Student Competition 11043
ISP/*VM & SD* International Design Competition 11044
Louis B. Marks Award 10697
National Lighting Awards Program 14922
Pantone Color Award 17062
Record Interiors of the Year 5041
Restaurant Design and Graphics Awards 12289
Retail Design Awards 14401
Trailblazer Award 11643
Louis S. Tregre Award 14771

International law
Certificate of Merit 4463
Francis Deak Award 11715
Francis O. Deak Award 4464
Manley O. Hudson Medal 4465
Pan American Gold Insigne of the Americas Society 4929
Pan American Gold Medal of the Americas Society 4930
Dean Rusk Award 11716
Robert G. Storey International Award 7702
University of Louisville Grawemeyer Award for Ideas Improving World Order 21042

International relations (*See also* Franco-American relations; United States-Latin American relations; World peace)
AACC International Travel Fellowship Award 971
AIAA International Cooperation Award 2656
Albert Hourani Book Award Competition 13381
America/Israel Friendship Award 4934
Baker-Wilkins Award for Outstanding Deputy Chief of Mission 20530
Carl Beck Award 12045
Stuart L. Bernath Book Prize 18678
Stuart L. Bernath Lecture Prize 18679
Stuart L. Bernath Scholarly Article Prize 18680
Robert Bosch Foundation Fellowship Program 7687
CICS Graduate Research Awards 16566
CIDA Awards for Canadians 7005
CIDA Awards for Professionals 7006
Gerald R. Clore International Award 10083
Paul W. Conner Memorial Scholarship 11154
Cultural Cooperation Award 9229
Karl Deutsch Award 12046
Distinguished Contributions to the International Advancement of Psychology 18904
William Edward Burghardt Du Bois Medal 14048
Foreign Service National of the Year Award 20542
Friendship Award 4727
Galatti Award for Outstanding Volunteer Service 271
GEI Award 10186
German Marshall Fund of the United States Fellowships and Awards 9974
Ghandi Peace Award 17681
Good Neighbor Award 11654
Governor General's International Award in International Studies 11510
Grant Program 20655
Harold Guetzkow Prize 16567
Harkness Fellowships 10239
W. Averell Harriman Democracy Award 14910
Honor Award 5726
Honorary Member 21907
ICCS Certificate of Merit 11511
International Affairs Fellowship Program 8595
International Mediation Medal 921
International Service Award 5497
George F. Kennan Award for Distinguished Public Service 14703
Malcolm H. Kerr Dissertation Award competition 13382
John Oliver La Gorce Medal 15159
Mike Mansfield Award 12302
R. Tait McKenzie Award 881
Medal of Honor 18207
Mentoring Award 13383
National Peace Essay Contest 20656
Order of Magellan 8007
Parmalee Scholarship 11688
Planetary Award/Crystal Helmet 5852
Pomerance Award 16347
Jennings Randolph Program for International Peace 20657
Arnold L. Raphel Memorial Award 20548
Herbert Roback Scholarship 13820
Theodore Roosevelt Distinguished Service Medal 20066
Herbert Salzman Award for Excellence in International Economic Performance 20551
Service Award 13384
Hugh H. and Mable M. Smythe International Service Citation 11155
Harold and Margaret Sprout Award 12048
Student Scholarships 12300
U Thant Peace Award 20364
University Medal 16304
University of Louisville Grawemeyer Award for Ideas Improving World Order 21042
Frank Watson Prize 18373
Edward Weintal Prize for Diplomatic Reporting 9960

International trade
Award for Outstanding Achievement in International Business 21962

International (continued)
Canada Export Award 9686
Charles E. Cobb, Jr. Award for Initiative and Success in Trade Development 20533
CWT Award 8467
Distinguished Service Award
Defense Credit Union Council 8795
Washington International Trade Association 21449
Distinguished Service in the Cause of Open and Competitive World Trade Award 8468
Experiment Citation Award 21930
Exporter of the Year 12091
Richard N. Farmer International Business Dissertation Award 102
Sylvan Gotshal World Trade Arbitration Medal 920
International Leadership Award 20461
Kovaleskaia Award 20448
Lifetime Achievement Award 21450
Minister for International Trade Challenge Cup 9687
Person of the Year 14236
Person of the Year Award 6610
President's "E" Award for Exports Program 20472
President's "E Star" Award 20473
Small Business Exporter of the Year 20835
University of Louisville Grawemeyer Award for Ideas Improving World Order 21042
Avery Upchurch Award 21960
Harriet VanMeter Humanitarian Award for International Relations 11428
Vietnam Educational Exchange Program 20449
Women in Science Award 20450

International understanding (*See also* Brotherhood; Human relations; Humanitarianism)
Award for Outstanding Performance in Third World Studies 5897
Builders of a Better World Prize 21899
Citizen Diplomat Award 12124
Cultural Cooperation Award 9229
Dharmaraja - King of Dharma 11342
Donald E. Farr Award 21840
German Summer Study Award 1445
David Glick Award 21841
IAEWP Diploma of Honour 11344
IAEWP Membership in Good Standing 11345
International Cooperation Awards 8859
Laureat d'Honneur of the International Geographical Union 11649
Ramon Magsaysay Award 18093
Jerry Mische Global Service Award 10044
National Testing and Awards Program for Secondary Students 1446
Norman Cousins Award 21901
George C. Oehmler Award 21842
Presidential Award for Outstanding Contributions to the Promotion of Scholarship in the Third World 5899

Inventions (*See also* Technology)
$30,000 Lemelson-MIT Student Prize 12775
$100,000 Lemelson-MIT Lifetime Achievement Award 12776
$500,000 Lemelson-MIT Prize 12777
ACS Award for Creative Invention 1705
Canada Awards for Excellence 15568
Edward N. Cole Award for Automotive Engineering Innovation 19037
Common Wealth Awards of Distinguished Service 17410
Howard N. Eavenson Award 18810
Gaede-Langmuir Award 6148
Great Idea Contest 12166
Honorary Title of Inventor 12160
Imagination Fair Great Idea Contest 12167
Imagineer Awards 13430
Industrial Research Institute Achievement Award 10787
International Science and Engineering Fair 2862
Kilby International Awards 12586
Magellanic Premium Award 3439
Manning Awards 9329
The Marconi Prize 13064
Henry E. Millson Award for Invention 1456
National Inventor of the Year 11097
National Inventor's Hall of Fame 20733
New Product Award 12163
John Scott Award 6492
Space Technology Hall of Fame 20844
Special Recognition Award 12164
Thurlow Award 11016
Young Eco Inventors Contest With Eco Expo 12168

Investment *See* Finance

Irish culture
William C. Dunlop Piping Scholarship 16552
Four Masters Award 12195
Heritage Award 12196
Irish American Cultural Institute Awards 12197
Irish Research Funds 12199
Irish Way Scholarships 12200
O'Malley Art Award 12201
Visiting Fellowship in Irish Studies at University College Galway 12202

Irish literature
Butler Literary Award 12194
Irish American Cultural Institute Poetry Award 12198

Iron and steel industry
American Iron and Steel Institute Medal 2873
Thomas E. Barlow Award of Honor 19781
Joseph Becker Award 5402
Kenneth J. Boedecker Jr. Distinguished Service Award 5931
Charles W. Briggs Award 5403
Charles W. Briggs Memorial Technical and Operating Medal 19782
John Chipman Award 5404
Distinguished Member Award 5405
Ductile Iron Society Annual Award 9037
Electric Furnace Honorable Mention 5406
Benjamin F. Fairless Award 2819
Gary Medal 2875
Charles W. Herty, Jr., Award 5407
T. R. Higgins Lectureship Award 2849
Howe Memorial Lecture 5408
Robert W. Hunt Award 5409
J. E. Johnson, Jr., Award 5410
Thomas L. Joseph Award 5411
Josef S. Kapitan Award 5412
Frederick A. Lorenz Memorial Medal 19783
Frank B. McKune Memorial Award 5413
MWSP Meritorious Award 5414
Presidents Award of Merit 5868
Prize Bridge Award 2850
Science Award 20223
Space Grant Fellowship Program 9622
Special Citation Award 2851
Steel Distributor of the Year Award 5869
Steelmaking Conference Award 5415
Michael Tenenbaum Award 5416

Irrigation
Bronze Irrigation Award 418
Gold Irrigation Award 419
Industry Achievement Award 12204
National Water and Energy Conservation Award 12205
Partner of the Year 12206
Person of the Year Award 12207
Crawford Reid Memorial Award 12208
Silver Irrigation Award 420

Islamic culture
Joseph J. Malone Fellowship in Arab and Islamic Studies 14872

Israeli culture
ARA Pacis Award (Altar of Peace) 12259
Solomon Bublick Hebrew University Awards 2307
Hatikvah Award 12365
Theodore Herzl Award 22114
Legion of Honor 12366
National Jewish Book Award - Israel 12327
Tree of Life Award 12368

Italian culture
Business and Culture Award 12261
Distinguished Service Award 1450
IFAFA Award 12247
Leonardo da Vinci Award 12252
Man of the Year 12242
Man of the Year Award 12253
Helen and Howard R. Marraro Prize 18781
Memorial Fellowships 2882
Michaelangelo Award 12254
Renaissance Award 12255
Special Achievement - Man/Woman of the Year 12257
Women of the Year 12243

Italian history
Citation for Career Achievement 18780
Helen and Howard R. Marraro Prize 18781
Howard R. Marraro Prize 1655
Howard R. Marraro Prizes in Italian History 2479
Meucci Award 12249
Varrazano Award 12250

Italian literature
Campana Translation Prize 12245
Howard R. Marraro Prize 13562

Japanese culture (*See also* Asian studies)
Hiromi Arisawa Awards 5568
Canada - Japan Literary Awards 6788
CBC Literary Awards 6789
John Whitney Hall Book Prize 5276
Japan Society Award 12304

Jewelry design
Affaire in the Gardens 8035
Boynton's G.A.L.A. Artist Awards 6594

Subject Index

Jewelry (continued)

Cutting Edge Gemstone Competition 2324
Fashion Forward Awards 2325
Robert M. Shipley Award 2322
Smithsonian Craft Show 18574
Spectrum Awards Design Competition 2326

Jewelry industry
Myer Barr Award 8905
Melvin B. Foer Memorial Award 8906
Barnett Helzberg Scholarship 8907
Outstanding Contribution Award 14295
Person of the Year Award 14296
Paul Storm Award 8908
Lode Van Bercken Award 8909

Jewish culture
The AJL Scholarship for Library School Students 5740
Aleph Award 15297
America/Israel Friendship Award 4934
American ORT Chapter of the Year 3342
Rabbi Max Arzt Distinguished Rabbinic Service Award 12374
Association of Jewish Libraries Reference Book Award 5741
Association of Orthodox Jewish Teachers Awards 5806
Mordecai Ben David Award 22023
Paul Bennick New Leadership Award 3343
Fred M. Butzel Memorial Award for Distinguished Community Service 12353
Courage to Care Award 4980
Deborah Award 2894
Distinguished Achievement Award 4935
David Dornstein Memorial Creative Writing Contest for Young Adult Writers 8118
Eternal Light Medal 12375
Etz Chaim (Tree of Life) Award 15298
Gold Medal of Merit 12386
Rabbi Simon Greenberg Rabbinic Achievement Award 12376
Guardian of Liberty 2295
William Haber Award 10432
William Haber Prize 3344
Florence G. Heller Award 12338
Herbert S. Schweitzer Memorial Youth Services Award 22064
Hurowitz Award 20340
International Doctoral Scholarship for Studies Specializing in Jewish Fields 13291
International Fellowships in Jewish Studies 13292
JCC Biennial Communications Awards Competition 12339
JCC Program Awards 12340
JEA Research and Development Fund Award 12349
Jewish Humanist Leadership Award 18708
Leadership Development Awards 12341
Commodore Uriah P. Levy Citizen's Award 12387
Liberty Award 10372
Lifetime Achievement Award 4938
Maccabee Award 15299
Judah L. Magnes Award 2308
Man of the Year Award 3345
Colonel Mickey Marcus Award 12388
Louis Marshall Award 12378
Zvi Hirsch Masliansky Award 10373
National Jewish Book Award - Autobiography/Memoir 12321
National Jewish Book Award - Children's Literature 12322
National Jewish Book Award - Children's Picture Book 12323
National Jewish Book Award - Contemporary Jewish Life 12324
National Jewish Book Award - Fiction 12325
National Jewish Book Award - Jewish Thought 12329
National Jewish Book Award - Scholarship 12330
National Jewish Book Award - Sephardic Studies 12331
National Jewish Book Award - Visual Arts 12332
National Jewish Book Award - Yiddish Literature 12333
New Generations Award 12380
Ora Award 15303
Doris Orenstein Memorial Fund 5742
Joseph Polakoff Award 2907
Presidential Award 9510
Professional of the Year Award 5738
Rabbinical Service Award of Appreciation 12381
Recognition of Goodness Award 12355
Joseph Reiss Memorial Judaica Library Awards 20341
Religious Freedom Award 2296
Harold U. Ribalow Prize 10213
Simon Rockower Awards for Excellence in Jewish Journalism 2908
Anna Davidson Rosenberg Award for Poems on the Jewish Experience 13017
Anatoly Scharansky Freedom Award 20306
Solomon Schechter Medal 12382
Second Century Award 12383
Shin Award 12384
Shofar Award 22065
Shofar Award (Ram's Horn) 15300
Silver Medallion Award 4939
Dorothy Silver Playwriting Competition 10226
Dorothy Silver Playwriting Competition Prize 12336
Boris Smolar Award for Excellence in North American Jewish Journalism 2909
King Solomon Award 599
Soviet Jewry Freedom Awards 16060
Mayer Sulzberger Award 12363
Henrietta Szold Award 10215
Ner Tamid Award 15301
Sydney Taylor Body of Work Award 5743
Sydney Taylor Children's Book Awards 5744
Sydney Taylor Manuscript Competition 5745
Torch Award 9511
Torch of Learning Award 2310
Tzedakah Award 20342
UJA - Federation Distinguished Communal Service Award 20343
Frank L. Weil Awards 12342
Wexner Graduate Fellows 21593
Elie Wiesel Award for Jewish Art and Culture 10433
Louise Waterman Wise Award 2897
Stephen S. Wise Award 2898
Wurzweiler School of Social Work Community Service Award 22027
Yeshiva University Award 22029
Yeshiva University Citation 22030
Yeshiva University Distinguished Service Award 22031
Yeshiva University Heritage Award 22032
Yeshiva University Sephardic Heritage Award 22033
Yitzah Rabin Award 3346
Youth Medallion 9512

Jewish history
Administrative Committee Prize 2900
Eisenhower Liberation Medal 20639
Ruth B. Fein Prize 2901
Lee Max Friedman Award Medal 2902
International Doctoral Scholarship for Studies Specializing in Jewish Fields 13291
International Fellowships in Jewish Studies 13292
Jewish Historical Society of New York Fellowships 2903
Rabbi Malcolm H. Stern Award 12357
National Jewish Book Award - Holocaust 12326
National Jewish Book Award - Jewish History 12328
U.S. Medal of Remembrance 20640
Saul Viener Prize 2904
Leo Wasserman Foundation Prizes 2905

Journalism (*See also* Literature; Cartoons; Editing; Editorial writing; Journalism education; Media; Publications; Radio; School publications; Television; Travel literature; specific types of journalism, e.g. Broadcast journalism)
AAES-EF Engineering Journalism Awards 20332
AAUP Award for Excellence in Coverage of Higher Education 1464
AFJ Awards Competition 5686
Alumnus of the Year Award 18197
The American Advertising Awards 858
American Legion Fourth Estate Award 2946
Amos Award 15410
Jack Anderson Award 11799
Annual Award for Excellence in Writing on an Information Topic 10798
Annual Award to Regular Columnists 10799
Annual Awards in International News Coverage 16981
Annual Writing Competition 8979
APA Journalism Awards 3547
Art Award 16241
Art of the Automobile Competition 6100
ASCAP - Deems Taylor Awards 4376
ASCE News Correspondent Award 4292
ASHA Media Awards for Journalists 4662
Asian American Journalists Association National Awards 5165
ASJMC Distinguished Service Award 5845
ASNE Distinguished Writing Awards 17508
Atlantic Journalism Awards 6035
John Aubuchon Freedom of the Press Award 15514
Santo J. Aurelio Award for Altruism 14882
Aviation Journalism Award 13917
Award for Innovation and Excellence in Media Coverage of Plastic Surgery 17377
Award for Journalistic Excellence 18064

Journalism (continued)

Award for Outstanding International Investigative Reporting 11508
Roland Barrett Award 21127
Batten Awards for Innovations in Journalism 12273
Aldo Beckman Award 21602
Burton Benjamin Memorial Award 8297
Meyer Berger Award 8248
Helen B. Bernstein Book Award for Excellence in Journalism 16254
Best in Business Contest 18964
Best New Design 6101
Best New Technology 6102
Best Publication Awards 13927
Better Newspaper Contest 15411
Better Newspapers Competition 7034
Worth Bingham Prize 6386
Theodore C. Blegen Award 9695
Nellie Bly Cub Reporter Award 16242
Robert Bosch Foundation Fellowship Program 7687
Brock Awards 6645
Warren Brookes Award for Excellence in Journalism 2958
Heywood Broun Award 16343
David R. Brower Environmental Journalism Award 18452
UH Journalism Carol Burnett Prizes in Journalism Ethics 21028
Carol Burnett/University of Hawaii/AEJMC Ethics Prize 5344
Business Award 16243
By-Line Award 13124
Byline Awards 16244
Maria Moors Cabot Prizes 8249
Canadian Federation of Humane Societies Media Award 7091
Car of the Year Awards 6103
Car of the Year (COTY) 6104
Cartoon Award 11106
Ralph D. Casey Minnesota Award 10811
Cassels Reporter of the Year Award 17973
Russell L. Cecil Arthritis Medical Journalism Awards 5125
Eugene Cervi Award 12027
Champion of the Student Press Award 19810
Harry Chapin Media Awards 21925
Christopher J. Georges Fellowship 16355
CIM/NRCan Journalism Awards 7188
Circulation Federation Awards 16328
Rosa Cisneros Award 11797
Raymond Clapper Memorial Awards 19752
Classified Federation Awards 16329
College Press Freedom Award 19811
Collier Award 9696
Columbia Journalism Award 8241
Column Writing Contest 15742
Common Ground Award for Journalism in the Middle East 18391
Community Leadership Award 10812
Conscience In Media Award 4469
Bob Considine Award 18198
Consumer Journalism Award 15515
Cooperative Marketing and Sales Council Awards 16330
Courage in Journalism Award 12145
Jane Cunningham Croly/GFWC Print Journalism Award 9916
Walter Cronkite Award for Excellence in Journalism and Mass Communication 8657
Crossroads Market/NLGJA Print Awards 15344
Deadline Club Awards 8773
Brig. Gen. Robert L. Denig Distinguished Service Award 20684
G. Richard Dew Award 17184
Director General's Award for Reporting and Analysis 20536
Distinguished Journalism Award 9446
Distinguished Performance Award 20686
Distinguished Service Award
- Association of Free Community Papers 5696
- Independent Free Papers of America 10723
- National Court Reporters Association 14879

Distinguished Writing Award 17185
Distinguished Writing Award in Commentary/Column Writing 4576
Distinguished Writing Award in Editorial Writing 4577
Distinguished Writing Award in Non-Deadline Writing 4579
District Bulletin Award 8062
District/Section Newsletter Award 11048
Diversity Awards 17186
John L. Dougherty Award 5250
Ben East Prize 13364
EDI Awards (Equality/Dignity/Independence) 9088
Editor & Publisher/INMA Marketing Awards 9163
Editor of the Year Award 15527
Editorial Awards 19819
EdPress Distinguished Achievement Awards for Excellence in Educational Journalism 5663
EdPress Honor Awards - Golden Lamp Award 5665
EdPress Honor Awards - Golden Shoestring 5666
Excellence in Craft Awards 16968
Excellence in Documentation Award 12215
Excellence in Professional Journalism 15758
Feature Stories Awards 16246
Features Award 11108
Fellow of the Academy of Professional Reporters 14880
H. M. Fentress Memorial Award for Editorial Excellence 19996
Benjamin Fine Awards 14384
John P. Fisher Award for Media Support of the Arts 8544
Gerald R. Ford Prize for Distinguished Reporting on National Defense 9681
Gerald R. Ford Prize for Distinguished Reporting on the Presidency 9682
Freedom of Information Award 5251
Front Page Awards 21439
Gavel Awards 1533
German Marshall Fund of the United States Fellowships and Awards 9974
Global Media Awards for Excellence in Population Reporting 17469
Gold Typewriter Award 16248
Gold Wing Award for Excellence In Journalism 14566
Golden Achievement Award 12217
Golden Medallion Media Awards 19759
Goldsmith Prize for Investigative Reporting 18439
Goldsmith Research Awards 18440
Robin Goldstein Award for Washington Regional Reporting 15516
Horace Greeley Award 16119
Fletcher M. Green and Charles W. Ramsdell Award 19501
Charles E. Green Journalism Awards 10308
H. W. Nelson Award 10209
Hearst Newspapers Writing and Photography Contests 10356
Heart of America 2952
Mark Hellinger Award 18200
O. Henry Award 20017
The Sidney Hillman Foundation Prize Awards 10435
Honor Award 18383
Honorary Member 12218
Edwin M. Hood Award for Diplomatic Correspondence 15517
Annual National Press Club Sandy Hume Memorial Award for Excellence in Political Journalism 15518
IAAO Journalism Citation 11273
IAEE Journalism Award 11223
IAFF Media Awards Contest 11355
IAPA-Pedro Joaquin Chamorro Inter-American Relations Award 11109
ILCA Media Awards Contest 11700
Imperial Oil Prize for Excellence 6037
In-Depth Reporting Award 11110
Indiana Journalism Award 6206
Indiana Scholastic Journalism Award 6207
Infographics Award 11111
Louis E. Inglehart First Amendment Award 8174
International Best Newspaper Online Services Award 9164
International Press Freedom Awards 8298
IRE Awards 12170
Jandoli Award of Excellence 18201
Vic Jose Award for General Excellence 10724
Journalism Alumni Award 6208
Journalism Award
- American Association of Petroleum Geologists 1340
- American Podiatric Medical Association 3562
- Road Runners Club of America 18069

Journalism Awards 16326
Journalism Awards Program 10354
Journalism Hall of Fame 6209
Journalist of the Year 6105
Journalistic Achievement Award 6038
Rev. Mychal Judge Heart of New York Awards 16249
Max Karant Award for Excellence in Aviation Journalism 398
Robert F. Kennedy Journalism Awards 18076
Donald E. Keyhoe Journalism Award 9836
Keystone Press Awards 17187
Keytone Press Awards 17198
Kiplinger Distinguished Contributions to Journalism Award 15528
Knight-Bagehot Fellowships 8250
John S. Knight Fellowships 12605
Robert L. Kozik Award for Environmental Reporting 15519
Krieghbaum Under-40 Award 5345
Jesse Laventhol Prize for Deadline News Reporting 17509
Jesse Laventhol Prizes for Deadline News Reporting 4580

Journalism (continued)

Dick Leary Award 10564
Lefthanders of the Year Awards 12764
Lifetime Achievement Award 5166
Lifetime Achievement Award in News Direction 8945
Literary Award 8790
Literary Awards Program 8059
Livingston Awards for Young Journalists 21061
Local News Writing Awards 10815
Elijah Parish Lovejoy Award
Colby College 8126
Southern Illinois University at Carbondale - School of Journalism 19509
Louis M. Lyons Award 16357
Ronald D. Lyons Memorial Award 20688
Magazine Merit Awards 19088
Ramon Magsaysay Award 18093
Market Development and Promotion Federation Awards 16332
Guillermo Martinez-Marquez Journalism Award 14249
Matrix Award 16312
Wade H. McCree, Jr. Awards for the Advancement of Justice 19763
McKinney Award 15412
Media Award 20362
Member Awards 16465
Meritorious Service in Communications Award 4408
MGCA Golden Quill Award 9889
Michener-Deacon Fellowship 13329
Michener Four-Month Fellowships 13330
Missouri Honor Awards 21078
Missouri Lifestyle Journalism Award 21079
Mitford Memorial Scholarship 13231
Clark Mollenhoff Award for Excellence in Investigative Reporting 9829
Frank Luther Mott-Kappa Tau Alpha Research Award 21080
Frank Luther Mott - Kappa Tau Alpha Research/Book Award 12519
NAA Foundation - International Circulation Managers Association C. K. Jefferson Award 16338
NAA Foundation - National Scholastic Press Association Pacemaker Awards 16339
NAA Foundation - Newspaper in Education Program Excellence Award 16340
Al Nakkula Award for Police Reporting 21008
National Council Awards 16334
National Court Reporters Foundation Scholarships 14883
National Headliner Awards 15194
National Literary Award 15582
National Magazine Awards 4492
National Magazine Awards 15355
National Media Awards 4373
National Newspaper Association - Quill and Scroll Award 16341
National Paper Writing Competition Award 18065
National Psychology Awards for Excellence in the Media 18915
New Professional Reporter Grant 14884
News Coverage Award 11112
Newsletter Award 10925
Newsletter Journalism Award 15520
Newspaper in Education Award 11113
Newspaper of the Year Contest 17188
Nieman Fellowships for Journalists 16358
Novartis Crop Protection Agricultural Writing Award 19873
Barnet Nover Memorial Awards 19753
Online Journalism Award 15521
Opinion Award 11114
Outstanding Article in *American Journal of Agricultural Economics* Award 872
Outstanding Club Bulletin 8066
Outstanding Forestry Journalism Award 18973
Outstanding Journalism Award 2029
Outstanding Media Coverage of Child Maltreatment Award 3608
Thomas Paine Journalism Award 20078
PMC Electronic Test Award 17487
Edgar A. Poe Award 21603
Joseph Polakoff Award 2907
George Polk Awards 12915
Print Media Award 11871
Prix Olivar-Asselin 18613
Professional Excellence in Religious Communication Award 13125
Public Service Award 5252
Publisher of the Year 5697
Pulitzer Fellowships 17748
Pulitzer Prizes 17749
Eugene S Pulliam National Journalism Writing Award 6212
Ken W. Purdy Award 11752
Reference Service Press Award 17945
Region Newsletter of the Year Award 5223
Regional Multimedia Award 18506
Thomas Renner Crime Reporting Award 12171
Research Council Awards 16335
Residential Fellowships 9758
Bart Richards Award for Media Criticism 17206
Selden Ring Award for Investigative Reporting 4974
Simon Rockower Awards for Excellence in Jewish Journalism 2908
Rogers Communications Inc. Media Award for Coverage of the Arts 7038
Annual Arthur Rose Award for Press Criticism 15522
T. Randolph Russell Award 8449
Annual National Press Club Joseph D. Ryle Award for Excellence in Writing on the Problems of Geriatrics 15523
Ruben Salazar Award for Communications 14808
Salute to Excellence Awards 14101
Harold J. Schachern Memorial Award Award 17975
Section Performance Award 12221
Joel R. Seldin Award 17703
Sigma Delta Chi Awards 19276
Silurian Excellence in Journalism Awards 19327
Joe Skelnar Award 10725
Merriam Smith Award 21604
Boris Smolar Award for Excellence in North American Jewish Journalism 2909
Southern Journalism Award 10838
Special Citation in Journalism 6213
Special Recognition Award 5167
Sports and Recreation Award 17073
Standards and Practices Award 12223
I. F. Stone Award 13766
Sunshine Award 19277
Supple Religion Writer of the Year Award 17976
Pat Taggart Award for Texas Newspaper Leader of the Year 20000
Templeton Religion Reporter of the Year Award 17977
Lowell Thomas Travel Journalism Awards 19016
Helen Thomas Unipresser Award 20370
Thurgood Marshall Journalism Award 8781
Top 25 Censored Stories of the Year 17664
Top Performance Awards 5253
Toulmin Medal 18999
Truck of the Year 6106
Twenty-Five Year News Achievement Award 19328
Unity Awards in Media 12866
Carr Van Anda Award 18384
Vaughan and Bushnell Awards (Golden Hammer Awards) 14255
Veritas Award 866
Amos E. Voorhies Award 16859
Stanley Walker Award 20022
Washington Correspondence Award 15524
The Washington Monthly Journalism Award 21453
Edward Weintal Prize for Diplomatic Reporting 9960
Ida B. Wells Award 14102
Wells Memorial Key 19278
Charles A. Weyerhaeuser Award 9697
Wilbur Awards 17971
Captain Donald T. Wright Award 17494
Writers Digest Annual Writing Competition 5147
Yearbook Marketing Award 8177
John Peter and Anna Catherine Zenger for Freedom of the Press and the Peoples Right to Know 20981
Emile Zola Award for Journalism 17125

Journalism education

All American Hall of Fame 15664
Atlantic Lottery Corporation Achievement Award 6036
Distinguished Teaching in Journalism Award 19274
Robin F. Garland Educator Award 15534
Jandoli Award of Excellence 18201
Journalism Awards Program 10354
Le Prix D' Excellence Aliant 6039
Lifetime Achievement Award 12448
Medal of Merit 12449
Media Citation 12450
National High School Journalism Teacher of the Year 9008
National High School Journalist of the Year 12451
National Yearbook Adviser of the Year 12452
Pacemaker Award 15665
James Frederick Paschal Award 8235
Student Impact Award 12453
Carl Towley Award 12454

Judaism

Distinguished Service Award 9509
Kaplan Medal 12372
Kavod Award 7568
Herbert H. Lehman Ethics Award 12377
National Community Service Award 12379
Ramah Leadership Award 15573
Solomon Schechter Award 20902
Wexner Graduate Fellows 21593
Yuval Award 7569

Judaism (continued)

Judo *See* Martial arts

Justice *See* Civil rights and liberties

Juvenile literature *See* Children's literature

Karate *See* Martial arts

Kayak *See* Boating

Labor (*See also* Occupational health; Occupational safety)
AFGE Local 3523 Education Award 10106
Philip Arnow Award 20509
Award for Excellence in Labor Diplomacy 20528
David L. Clendenin Award 21836
Eugene V. Debs Award 9350
Ernest DeMaio Award for Trade Union Activism 12641
Distinguished Career Service Awards 20510
Distinguished Service Award 918
Distinguished Teaching, Distinguished Research 21256
Equal Employment Opportunity Awards 20511
Benjamin F. Fairless Memorial Award 2874
Samuel Gompers American Red Cross National Labor Award 3827
Harpers Ferry Memorial Scholarship 20520
The Sidney Hillman Foundation Prize Awards 10435
Human Rights Award 12361
ILCA Film and Broadcast Competition 11699
ILCA Media Awards Contest 11700
ILHA Book of the Year 11702
Information Technology Scholarship 20521
International Labor Rights Advocate Award 11704
Job Corps Hall of Fame 20522
Lawrence R. Klein Award 20517
Labor Affairs Award 15926
Labor History High School Essay Contest 21680
Labor-Management Annual Award 21044
Labor Participation Citation for Services 3832
Lewis Hine Awards 14652
LRA Labor Award 12642
Maurer-Stump Award 17889
Billy Mayo/Rubin Jones Scholarship 9649
Murray-Green-Meany-Kirkland Award for Community Service 2227
Order of Ontario 16757
A. Philip Randolph Achievement Award 27
B. Douglas Sawtelle Scholarship 13716
Scholarship Fund CBMC Area Local 7881
Scholarships and Research Grants, Behavioral Studies 14650
Secretary's Exceptional Achievement Awards 20513
John Sessions Memorial Award 17946
Solidarity Award for Lifetime Contribution to the Labor Movement 21681
SPFD, MO Labor Council, AFL-CIO Endowment Fund 19738
Troublemaker Awards 12639
Rosina Tucker Award 30
Veterans Employment Awards 20515
Workforce Innovation Awards Program 18191

Laboratory technology
Aglient Technologies Award for Excellence in Laboratory Instruction 3994
George R. Collins Award 1024
Joseph J. Garvey Award 1025
Charles A. Griffin Award 1026
Order of the Golden Microscope 3067
Outstanding Student Award 3068
Technician of the Year Award 1027
Technician Publication Award 1028

Lacrosse
All-American Awards 15307
W. H. Brine Awards 20659
Edward A. Devine Memorial Award 20660
Lt. Raymond J. Enners Award 20661
C. Markland Kelly Trophy 20662
Francis L. (Babe) Kraus Award 20663
Lt. Donald McLaughlin, Jr. Memorial Award 20664
Howdy Myers Man of the Year Award 20665
National Lacrosse Hall of Fame 20680
NCAA National Championships 14687
Outstanding Service Award 7503
William Schmeisser Award 20666
William C. Stiles Memorial Award 20667
Jason G. (Stranny) Stranahan Award 20668
F. Morris Touchstone Award 20669
Turnbill Trophy 11706
Lt. Col. J.L. (Jack) Turnbull Award 20670
USILA Awards 20671
USILA Trophy 20672
Wilson Wingate Trophy 20673

Landscape architecture (*See also* Horticulture)
Architectural Study Tour Scholarship 19018
The ASLA Design Medal 4472
ASLA Medal 4473
ASLA President's Medal 4474
Bronze Medal 19940
Chief of Engineers Design and Environmental Awards Program 20405
Community Service Award 4475
CSLA Awards of Excellence 7476
Dumbarton Oaks Fellowships 9050
Environmental Improvement Awards Program 17636
Excellence in Landscape 5248
Fellows Medal 4476
Field Maintenance Award 1542
Gold Medal 19941
Gold Medal Award 17625
Green Star Awards 17626
Honorary Member 4477
Alfred B. LaGasse Medal 4478
The Landmark Award 4479
The Landscape Architecture Film Award 4480
Landscape Architecture Medal of Excellence 4481
Landscape Awards 9613
Landscape Design Award 2531
Loeb Fellowship 10281
Homer Lucas Landscape Award 16147
National Student Competition 4482
Neighborhood Greening Project 9898
Frederick Law Olmsted Medal 4483
Professional Awards Program 4484
Rome Prize Fellowships 605
Arthur Ross Awards 10853
Anne Seaman Memorial Scholarship 17628
Silver Medal 19942
US/ICOMOS Fellows 20452

Language *See* Linguistics; Translations

Latin American history (*See also* United States-Latin American relations)
Albert J. Beveridge Award 2465
Herbert Eugene Bolton Memorial Prize 8380
James Henry Breasted Prize 2467
Howard Francis Cline Memorial Prize 8381
Conference on Latin American History Prize 8382
Distinguished Service Award 8383
Clarence H. Haring Prize 2475
Edilia and Francois-Auguste de Montequin Fellowship 19025
James Alexander Robertson Memorial Prize 8384
James R. Scobie Memorial Award for Preliminary Ph.D. Research 8385

Latin American Literature
Domus Dei 12704
Katherine Singer Kovacs Prize 13560

Latin American Studies
Katherine Singer Kovacs Prize 13560
Premio Iberoamericano Book Award 12700
Bryce Wood Book Award 12702

Law (*See also* Civil rights and liberties; Consumer affairs; Copyright; Crime prevention; Criminology; Firearms; International law; Inventions; Law enforcement; Legal education; Legal literature; Legislative improvement; Prisons; Victims)
AALL Lexis Nexis Call for Papers Awards Program 1244
AALL Public Access to Government Information Award 1245
AALL Spectrum Article of the Year Award 1246
AALL/West Excellence in Marketing Award 1247
James C. Adkins Award 6049
Advocacy for the Disabled Award 2931
American Bar Association Medal 1531
Joseph L. Andrews Bibliographic Award 1248
Article Prize 12719
Balfour Scholarship 11720
Viscount Bennett Fellowship 6964
BESLA Award 6421
Best New Product Award 1249
James H. Bocking Memorial Award 6965
Bolton Award for Professional Excellence 14079
Book Award 18379
Robert Bosch Foundation Fellowship Program 7687
Bower Award for Business Leadership 9742
Hon. William J. Brennan Award for Outstanding Jurist 16272
Brief-Writing Award 18380
Emery A. Brownell Media Award 15336
Warren E. Burger Award 14640

Law (continued)

Chief Justice Warren E. Burger Healer Awards 7916
Goler T. Butcher Medal 4462
CBA President's Award 6966
Renee D. Chapman Memorial Award for Outstanding Contributions to Technical Services Law Librarianship 1250
Chapter Activity Award Contest 9434
Charles Carroll Award 10200
Justice Tom C. Clark Award 9435
Coif Book Award 16841
Corporate Award 6422
CPR Institute for Dispute Resolution Awards for Excellence and Innovation in Alternative Dispute Resolution 8626
Clarence Darrow Award 11804
Niles Davis Award 14066
Department of Justice - CBA University Law School Essay Contest 6967
L. Harold DeWolf Award 16611
Dissertation Award 3647
Distinguished Contribution to Psychology and Law 3648
Distinguished Faculty Award 14682
Distinguished Officer of the Year 6442
Distinguished Public Service 15294
Distinguished Service Award 918
Distinguished Service Awards 14641
Samuel J. Duboff Award 9831
Educational Research Award 19135
Equal Justice Award 14490
Equity Award 1476
Fifty-Year Award 9525
Judge Edward R. Finch Law Day U.S.A. Speech Award 1532
Elaine R. "Boots" Fisher Award 9436
Clara Shortridge Foltz Award 15337
Fordham - Stein Prize 9684
Friend of the Legal Profession Award 12590
Elizabeth Fry Memorial Award 6903
Marian Gould Gallagher Distinguished Service Award 1251
Gavel Award 919
Gavel Awards 1533
Helen M. Geisness Outstanding Lawyer or Non-Lawyer Award 12591
Golden Medallion Media Awards 19759
Sylvan Gotshal World Trade Arbitration Medal 920
Littleton - Griswold Prize in American Law and Society 2474
Manfred S. Guttmacher Award 3619
R. C. Hakanson Award 9361
Mary Ellen Hamilton Award 15338
Judge Learned Hand Award 2885
Learned Hand Medal 9442
The Jay Healey Award 4486
Robert C. Heeney Memorial Award 14185
Hugh M. Hefner First Amendment Award 17396
Frederick Charles Hicks Award for Outstanding Contributions to Academic Law Librarianship 1252
Hirsh Award 1878
Ramon John Hnatyshyn Award for Law 6968
Roscoe Hogan Environmental Law Essay Contest 18120
Honoree of the Year Award 14459
Hurst Prize 12720
International Inn of the Year 11721
International Mediation Medal 921
International Science and Engineering Fair 2862
Intra-Society Merit Award 8783
Herbert Jacob Book Prize 12721
Elaine Osborne Jacobson Award for Women Working in Health Care Law 18121
Jefferson Medal 16177
Thomas Jefferson Memorial Foundation Award in Law 13595
Richard B. Johnson Memorial Award 13152
Justica Awards 6969
Justice Award 7170
Kalven Prize 12722
Kelley - Wyman Award 14076
Earl Kintner Award for Distinguished Service 9437
Rufus C. Kuykendall 13116
Marta Lange/CQ Press Award 5612
Law Alumni Association's Distinguished Alumnus Award 21106
Law Day U.S.A. 2934
Law Day U.S.A. Public Service Awards 1534
Law Library Journal Article of the Year Award 1253
Law Library Publications Award 1254
Law-Review Award 18381
Lecturer of Merit 14683
Legal Writing Contest 11333
Legends Award 6423
Letourneau Award 1879
Lillian S. 3Fisher Prize in Environmental Law and Public Policy 20983
Lincoln the Lawyer Award 64
March Fong Eu Achievement Award 15416
C. Raymond Marvin Award 14077
John J. McCloy Memorial Award 9832
Wade H. McCree, Jr. Awards for the Advancement of Justice 19763
Ralph C. Menapace Fellowship in Urban Land Use Law 13678
Douglas Miller Award 6970
Loren Miller Legal Services Award 19760
National Federation of the Blind Scholarship Program 15039
National Health Law Moot Court Competition 7725
Cynthia Northrop Distinguished Service Award 1302
Notary of the Year Award 15417
Bethany J. Ochal Award for Distinguished Service to the Profession 1255
Joseph E. O'Neill Award 15810
Outstanding Advocate Award 1303
Outstanding Individual Volunteer Award 2936
Outstanding Judge Award 12592
Outstanding Lawyer Award 12593
Outstanding Paralegal Award
  Central Pennsylvania Paralegal Association 7778
  Massachusetts Paralegal Association 13164
Walter Owen Book Prize 6971
PAJLO Award 6972
Paralegal of the Year 8711
Henry M. Philips Prize in Jurisprudence 3441
J. Will Pless International Graduate of the Year 11722
Presidential Commendation 14186
Presidents Award 4487
President's Award 14916
President's Pro Bono Service Award 19761
Pro Bono Award
  Massachusetts Paralegal Association 13165
  National Italian American Bar Association 15295
Pro Bono Publico Awards 1536
Pro Bono Service Awards 12766
Public Service Award 14723
Publications Board's Newsletter Competition 9438
Isaac Ray Award in Memory of Margaret Sutermeister 3634
Paul C. Reardon Award 14642
Recognition for Legal Achievement 8414
Red Apple Award 828
William H. Rehnquist Award for Judicial Excellence 14643
Stuart Reichart Award 356
Research Award 9526
Giles Sutherland Rich Moot Court Competition 2863
Role of Law Award 7566
Theodore Roosevelt Distinguished Service Medal 20066
Edward K. Rowan-Legg Award 6973
Gertrude E. Rush Award 14491
Schwartz Award 1880
Sexual Orientation and Gender Identity Conference Awards 6974
Whitney North Seymour Award 9443
Whitney North Seymour, Sr. Award 922
Reginald Heber Smith Award 15339
Louis St-Laurent Award of Excellence 6975
C. Francis Stradford Award 14492
Student Advocacy Award 11167
Erwin C. Surrency Prize 4125
Donald M. Sutherland Prize 4126
John Tait Award of Excellence 6976
The Honourable Walter S. Tarnopolsky Human Rights Award 6977
Touchstone Award 6978
Trial Lawyer of the Year Award 20204
Harrison Tweed Award 1537
John C. Vance Award 20165
A. Frank Vick Outstanding Province President Award 11723
James "Tick" Vickrey Award 5544
Volunteer Service Award 2937
Arthur von Briesen Award 15340
Robert C. Watson Award 2864
Woman Lawyer of the Year 21785
Jay Worrall Public Official Award 16612
Max Yost Distinguished Services Award 5257
Young Lawyers' Pro Bono Award 6979
Younger Federal Lawyer Award 9439

Law enforcement

3M Vehicle Theft Investigators Award 11194
AAPL Outstanding Service Award 824
Achievement Award 14521
AGC/IAATI Award 11195
Alabama Sheriffs Association Scholarship 407
Amicus Award 825
Annual National Chief's Challenge 11307
Anslinger Award 11762
APPA Awards for Excellence in Community Crime Prevention 3598
APPA Community Awareness Through Media Award 3599

Law (continued)

APPA Member of the Year Award 3600
Award of Recognition 18055
Awards for Valor 12484
J. Stannard Baker Award for Highway Safety 11308
Albert H. Baum Award 6678
John "Sonny" Burke Memorial Award 20735
Civilian of the Year Award 13343
Commendation Awards 11763
Correctional Officer of the Year 11318
Criminal Investigation Award 3566
DEA Explorer Drug Abuse Prevention Service Award 6574
Distinguished Faculty Award 14682
Distinguished Service Award
American Association of Motor Vehicle Administrators 1275
American Police Hall of Fame 3567
Raymond H. Dreher Memorial Award 11196
Walter Dunbar Memorial Award 3601
Enforcement Officer of the Year 1141
Explorer Award 5688
FOP86 Scholarship Fund 9752
Gang Prevention Scholarship 20190
General Commendation 3568
Carl A. Gerstacker Trooper of the Year Award 13344
Golden Apple Award 826
G.O.O.D. for You Award 9869
Hall of Fame 8102
John Edgar Hoover Police Service Award 3570
Sam Houston State University Award 3602
Human Rights Award 11371
IAATI Award of Merit 11197
IAATI Lo-Jack Award 11198
INEOA Medal of Valor 11764
International Recognition and Scholarship Award 11410
K-9 Dog Award 3571
Joe Kegans Award for Victim Services in Probation and Parole 3603
Scotia Knouff Line Officer of the Year Award 3604
Law Enforcement Assistance Explorer Award 6584
Law Enforcement Award
Association of Former Agents of the U.S. Secret Service 5689
National Black Police Association 14522
Law Enforcement Commendation Medal 15774
Walker S. Lee Award 6679
Donald S. Leonard Award 13345
Wilbur H. Lind Award 6680
London Club Award 12910
Man of the Year in Law Enforcement 19271
McDonnell Douglas Law Enforcement Award 10401
Merit Award for Excellent Arrest 3573
Motor Carrier Officer of the Year 13346
Sgt. Edward Neves Memorial Scholarship 17476
NHTSA 21384
NOBLE Central Virginia Chapter 15454
Officer of the Year Awards 11411
Vincent O'Leary Award 5808
Ontario Medal for Police Bravery 16756
Outstanding Law Enforcement Achievement Award 11359
A.T. Phillips Award 11199
Police Exemplary Service Medal 6828
Police Medal of Honor 3576
Police Officer of the Year
American Police Hall of Fame 3577
National Burglar and Fire Alarm Association 14556
Police Officer of the Year Award 11310
Police Posthumous Medal of Honor 3578
Seymour Pollack Distinguished Achievement Award 827
President's Award 3605
Public Safety Recognition 6287
Recognition Award 11299
Renault Robinson Award 14523
Royal Canadian Mounted Police Long Service Medal 6830
Irwin R. Rutman Award 19272
Webber Seavey Quality in Law Enforcement Award Program 11311
Silver Star for Bravery 3579
Willie Smoot Organizational Meritorious Award 14524
Special Agency Awards 11765
Special Awards of Honor 11766
Survivors' Club 11312
UN/INEOA Law Enforcement Medal 11767
University of Cincinnati Award 3606
Alan J. Vargo Memorial 12724
VFW J. Edgar Hoover Award 21341
Volunteer Service Award for Law Enforcement Explorers 6591

Leadership (*See also* Academic achievement; Professional and personal achievement)

AASL ABC/CLIO Leadership Grant 1409
Ability Fund/ March of Dimes Canada 7372
Acacia Leadership Scholarship 74
Achievement Award 1260
Advisor of the Year 14534
AECT Leadership Development Grants 5349
AESF Charles Henry Proctor Leadership Award 2167
Africa Prize for Leadership for the Sustainable End of Hunger 10614
The American College of Psychiatrists Distinguished Service Award in Psychiatry 1938
Aspen Institute Corporate Award for Excellence in Leadership 5199
Aspen Institute Public Service Award for Excellence in Leadership 5200
Vincent Astor Memorial Leadership Essay Contest 20708
Automated Imaging Achievement Award 6098
Award for Excellence in Association Leadership 7448
Award of Merit 6487
bioMerieux Sonnenwirth Award for Leadership in Clinical Microbiology 4131
BLG Awards 7210
Boys State Scholarship 2954
Branch Leadership Award 6168
Emil Breitkreutz Leadership Award - Volleyball 547
Canadian Healthcare Association Award for Distinguished Service 7145
Chapter President of the Year Award 7964
Chinese Martial Arts Leadership Award 549
Kenneth E. Clark Research Award 7718
CLTA Merit Award 7265
Club of Champions Award 7678
Art Cole Award 1166
Commission Matching Grants 9902
Paul W. Conner Memorial Scholarship 11154
Council of the Year Award 11566
CRCD Award 7373
Dedicated Service Award 4507
Department of Defense Distinguished Service Award 14904
Distinguished Honor Award 20537
Distinguished Leadership Award for a Citizen Planner 3552
Distinguished Leadership Award for a Student Planner 3554
Distinguished Leadership Award for an Elected Official 3555
Distinguished Member Award 11568
Distinguished Membership Award 3277
Distinguished Service Award
American Association of School Administrators 1405
Public Risk Management Association 17728
Relay and Switch Industry Association 17968
Distinguished Service Key 16697
James Clement Dunn Award for Excellence 20538
Easter Seals Canada Award 7374
EBSCO Community College Learning Resources and Library Achievement Awards 5608
Engineering and Construction Contracting Division Award 2768
Henry Fenderbosch Leadership Award 14432
FEW Distinguished Service Award 9453
Fountain of Universal Peace Award 11343
Future Business Executive 9843
Future Business Leaders 9844
John W. Gardner Leadership Award 10747
GATF Awards of Excellence in Education for an Individual in Industry and in Education 10133
Gay, Lesbian, Bisexual and Transgender Community Leader Scholarship 12621
LITA/Gaylord Award for Achievement in Library and Information Technology 12823
Mandy Goetze 21st Century Award 11177
Golden Gavel Award 20095
Golden Raster Award 10325
Arnold Goodman Award 20366
Scott Goodnight Award for Outstanding Performance as a Dean 14403
Government Affairs Award of Recognition 6683
Government Technology Leadership Award 10108
John Griner Award 7449
Lee G. Hall Memorial Award 20912
Hall of Fame 17337
Harvard Medal 10271
Andrew Heiskell Awards 20091
Frances Henne Award 1415
Honorary Member 11625
C. D. Howe Award 6868
Marion Huber Learning Through Listening Awards 17904
Humanitarian Award 6488

Leadership (continued)

Industrial Research Institute Medal 10788
Information Processing Public Service Award 5732
International Leadership Citation 19047
International Member of the Year Award 11839
International Superintendent of the Year 5484
Sara E. Jackson Memorial Award 14555
Jewish Humanist Leadership Award 18708
Donald P. Kent Award 9995
Leader of the Year Award 16699
Leadership Award
Association of Surgical Technologists 5874
Camp Fire USA El Dorado Council 6778
Corona Norco United Way 8521
International Association of Cancer Victors and Friends 11305
National Association for Equal Opportunity in Higher Education 14006
National Trappers Association 15911
Leadership Award for Residents 627
Leadership Development Awards 12341
Leadership for Learning Award 1406
Legacy Award 9903
Legion of Valor Bronze Cross for Achievement 12772
Richard M. Leonard Award 18464
Commodore Uriah P. Levy Citizen's Award 12387
Local Chapter President Award 14438
A. E. MacRae Award in Creative Leadership 17805
B. Charles Malloy Leadership Award 5969
Marks of Excellence Award 15111
Lieutenant Theodore C. Marrs Plaques 5110
Chico Mendes Award 18466
Robert L. Morlan Faculty Secretary Award 16700
Elizabeth Cutter Morrow Award 22096
Mortar Board Chapter Citation Award 13612
Mortar Board Honorary Member 13613
NADD Award 14188
National Citation 13614
National Honor Society Scholarship Program 14385
National Leadership 12394
National Scholar-Athlete Awards 15073
Werner L. Nelson Award for Diagnosis of Yield Limiting Factors 4247
New Englander of the Year Awards 16099
James E. Nicholson Award (Marine Non-Commissioned Officer Leadership Award) 13085
Omicron Delta Kappa Scholarships 16701
Order of Ontario 16757
Outstanding Human Service Student 15435
Outstanding Leadership Award 249
Outstanding Leadership Medal 13897
Outstanding Local Leadership Award 5823
Outstanding Member Award 5841
Outstanding Mentor Award 489
Outstanding Young Range Professional Award 18837
Pace Award 563
Sarah Thorniley Phillips Leadership Award 17258
Esther J. Piercy Award 5427
Pinnacle Award 7450
President's National Leadership 565
Principal's Leadership Award 14386
Professional Development Program Awards 18551
Professionalism Award 14439
Public Recreation Man and Woman of the Year 568
Public Recreation Volunteer of the Year Award 569
Public Service Award
American Public Power Association 3793
Society of Petroleum Engineers 19247
Alex Radin Distinguished Service Award 3794
Recognition Award 14191
REcognized ACHievement-REACH Awards for Women 22091
Regional Leadership Award 13370
Eldridge W. Roark Jr. Meritorious Service Certificate 16702
Robertson Most Outstanding Undergraduate Award 17312
Robie Award for Achievement in Industry 12275
Eleanor Roosevelt Award 11809
Gertrude E. Rush Award 14491
Lee E. Schauer Memorial Scholarship 18446
Service Award 5859
Shield Award 17112
Ambrose M. Shotwell Memorial Award 5342
SkillsUSA Championships 18552
Georgina Smith Award 1467
Edward A. Smith Awards 13396
Hugh H. and Mable M. Smythe International Service Citation 11155
Special Award 14192
William I. Spencer Award 22097
Ten Outstanding Young Americans 20678
Texas Star Award 22094
Torch Award 4208
Fred Turner Award for Outstanding Service to NASPA 14409
Walter F. Ulmer, Jr. Applied Research Award 7719
United Methodist Association Award of Distinguished Service 20354
United States Presidential Scholars Program 20491
U.S. Sailing One-Design Awards 20783
University Medal 7617
Volunteer Fund Raiser of the Year 3839
Jeanne Vost Celebration of Leadership 133
Cynthia Wedel Award 3840
Bob Wright Award 14041
YMCA Men, Women and Youth of the Year 22037
Young Forester Leadership Award 18978
Whitney M. Young, Jr. Memorial Scholarship 16310
Young Optometrist of the Year 3318
Youth Leadership Awards 6780

Learning disabled
John Arena Memorial Scholarship 12760
Experimental Analysis of Behavior Dissertation Award 3654
Marion Huber Learning Through Listening Awards 17904
Floyd G. Hudson Service Award 8559
Samuel Kirk Award 13145
Norman Scholarship 12758
Samuel T. Orton Award 11549
Outstanding Researcher Award 8560
Outstanding Teacher Award 8561

Legal education
Academy Fellow 88
H. Thomas Austern Memorial Writing Competition 9651
Auxiliary Excellence Award 2932
James H. Bocking Memorial Award 6965
Alice Carr Award 2933
Don Eppler Memorial Scholarship 12564
Founder's Award 90
Richard S. Jacobson Award 18122
Law-Related Education Teacher of the Year Award 2935
Rochelle Scholarship 12950
Gertrude E. Rush Award 14491
Cristine Swanson Wilson Memorial Scholarship 12726

Legal literature
H. Thomas Austern Memorial Writing Competition 9651
Editor-Publisher Award 14302
Outstanding Book Award 91
Walter Owen Book Prize 6971
William L. Simon/Anderson Publishing Outstanding Paper Award 92
Texas Tech Law School Foundation 19986

Legislative improvement
ACA Legislative Service Award 2065
AMVETS Silver Helmet Awards 4949
Applied Social Issues Internship 18884
Award of Merit/Distinguished Service Award 14814
Barbed Wire Award 2210
Lindy Boggs Award 3292
Congressional Award 18560
Congressman of the Year 15395
Conservationist of the Year 6075
CQ Press Award 8404
Distinguished Service Award 15932
William O. Douglas Award 18457
Epilepsy Foundation of America Awards 9308
Global Statesman Award 6782
Goldsmith Book Prize 18438
Government Achievement Award 15206
Government Affairs Award 14433
Governor of the Year 15397
Harold Hammerman Spirit of Education Award 14434
Maurice G. Herndon National Legislative Award 10732
Peter H. Johnson Image Award 14435
Dr. L. Michael Kuhn Advocate of the Year Award 15208
Leadership in Human Services Award 3782
Legislation Award 5875
Legislative Excellence Award 6078
Legislator of the Year
Pennsylvania State Tax Collectors Association 17204
Vietnam Veterans of America 21362
Richard Beatty Mellon Award 322
Connie Murdoch Award 18561
National Congressional Award 15578
National Legislative Award 17916
National Lifesaving Leadership Award 18045
Outstanding Advocate Award 9089
Past Presidents' Canadian Legislator Award 7543

Legislative (continued)

Carl D. Perkins Government Relations Award 2073
Esther Peterson Consumer Service Award 8462
Johanna Cooke Plaut Community Leadership Award 9090
President's Award 15594
Public Service Award 15596
Giles Sutherland Rich Moot Court Competition 2863
Special Award 4115
State Public Official Award for Significant Legislative Achievement 1400
Ten Outstanding Young Americans 20678
Water Statesman of the Year 15933
Edgar Wayburn Award 18473
E. B. Whitten Silver Medallion Award 15597
Max Yost Distinguished Services Award 5257

Library and information services (*See also* Bibliography; Information management; Library design; Library history; Literacy; Medical librarianship; Reference)

AALL Lexis Nexis Call for Papers Awards Program 1244
AALL Public Access to Government Information Award 1245
AALL Spectrum Article of the Year Award 1246
AALL/West Excellence in Marketing Award 1247
AASL ABC/CLIO Leadership Grant 1409
AASL Collaborative School Library Media Award 1410
AASL/Highsmith Research Grant 1411
AASL Information Plus Continuing Education Scholarship 1412
Academic Librarians' Distinguished Service Award 6942
Academic/Research Librarian of the Year Award 5602
Elmer Adler Prize 9814
Aggiornamento Award 7650
The AJL Scholarship for Library School Students 5740
ALA Equality Award 2967
ALA/Information Today Library of the Future Award 2968
Alex P. Alain Intellectual Freedom Award 12935
Alex Awards 22050
ALISE Award for Professional Contribution to Library and Information Science Education 5418
ALISE Service Award 5419
ALSC/Book Wholesalers Summer Reading Program Grant 5430
ALSC/Sagebrush Education Resources Literature Grant 5431
ALTA/Gale Outstanding Trustee Conference Grant 5446
ALTA Major Benefactor Honor Award 5448
American Library Association Trustee Citation 5449
Joseph L. Andrews Bibliographic Award 1248
Annual Merit (Professional Librarian) 8528
Arizona Author Award 5052
Arizona Highways Adult Nonfiction Book Award 5053
ASCLA Exceptional Service Award 5854
ASCLA Leadership Achievement Award 5855
Association of Jewish Libraries Reference Book Award 5741
Hugh C. Atkinson Memorial Award
Association of College and Research Libraries 5603
Illinois Library Association 10673
Award for Achievement in Technical Services 7248
Award for Special Librarianship in Canada 6939
Award for Teaching Excellence in the Field of Library and Information Science Education 5420
Award of Outstanding Achievement 7137
AzLA/SIRS Intellectual Freedom Award 5055
Carrol Preston Baber Research Grant 2998
Baker and Taylor Conference Grants 22051
Baker & Taylor Entertainment Audio Music/VID Product Grant 17713
Mildred L. Batchelder Award 5432
Louise Seaman Bechtel Fellowship 5433
Anthony H. Benoit Mid-Career Award 12936
Homer I. Bernhardt Distinguished Service Award 4000
Best New Product Award 1249
Best of LRTS Award 5422
Best of Show Awards 12814
Beta Phi Mu Award 2969
Black Caucus Certificate of Appreciation 6412
Black Caucus of the American Library Association Trailblazer's Award 6414
Black Caucus Special Recognition Plaques 6415
Blackwell's Scholarship Award 5423
BMC Research Paper Prize 7138
Virginia Boucher-OCLC Distinguished Interlibrary Loan Library Award 17935
Bound to Stay Bound Books Scholarship 5435
Rev. Andrew L. Bouwhuis Memorial Scholarship 7651
Bowker/Ulrich's Serials Librarianship Award 5424
W.Y. Boyd Literary Award 2970
BRASS Thomson Financial Student Travel Award 17936
Robert S. Bray Award 2039
John Brubaker Memorial Award 7652
BWI/YALSA Collection Development Grant 22052
Francis Joseph Campbell Award 5856
Canadian Hospital Librarian of the Year Award 7139
CAPL Public Library Services Award 7256
Andrew Carnegie Medal 5437
Marshall Cavendish Excellence in Library Programming Award 2971
Century Scholarship 5857
Certificate of Achievement 12815
Certificate of Appreciation and Recognition 19562
Renee D. Chapman Memorial Award for Outstanding Contributions to Technical Services Law Librarianship 1250
Frances Neel Cheney Award 19968
Chinese-American Librarians Association Distinguished Service Award 7927
Choice Outstanding Academic Books and Nonprint Materials 7935
CIPPS Distinguished Service Awards 7159
Citizen's Award 10763
CLA/Information Today Award for Innovative Technology 7249
The Polly Clarke Award 16669
CLTA Achievement in Literacy Award 7264
CLTA Merit Award 7265
C.F.W. Coker Award 18951
Colonial Dames of America Scholarship 18952
Community College Learning Resources Library Achievement Awards 5604
Miles Conrad Award/Lecturer 14963
Crosman Memorial Award 10674
Essae M. Culver Distinguished Service Award 12937
Ann Marie Cunningham Memorial Award 14964
Phyllis Dain Library History Dissertation Award 2993
John Cotton Dana Award
Special Libraries Association 19547
H.W. Wilson Co. 21635
John Cotton Dana Library Public Relations Awards 12816
Donald G. Davis Article Award 2994
Davis Cup Award 10675
DEMCO/ALA Black Caucus Award for Excellence in Librarianship 6417
Demco New Leaders Travel Grant 17714
Melvil Dewey Medal 2972
Distinguished Alumnus Award 21052
Distinguished Education and Behavioral Sciences Librarian Award 5605
Distinguished School Administrators Award 1413
Distinguished Service Award
American Association of School Librarians 1414
Association for Library Service to Children 5438
Black Caucus of the American Library Association 6418
Society of American Archivists 18953
Doctoral Dissertation Fellowship 5606
Mary Donaldson Award of Merit 18269
Robert B. Downs Intellectual Freedom Award 21034
Tom C. Drewes Scholarship 2973
Miriam Dudley Instruction Librarian Award 5607
Dun & Bradstreet Award for Outstanding Service to Minority Business 17938
Dun & Bradstreet Public Librarian Support Award 17939
EBSCO ALA Conference Sponsorship 2974
EBSCO Community College Learning Resources and Library Achievement Awards 5608
Margaret A. Edwards Award 22053
Jackie Eubanks Award 3002
Excellence in Academic Libraries Award 5609
Excellence in Small and/or Rural Public Library Service Award 17715
Executive Committee Award 21537
Federation Leadership Award 10764
Fellow of the Special Libraries Association 19548

Library (continued)

Follett School Librarian of the Year Award 5056
FOLUSA/Baker & Taylor Books Award 9792
Lucy B. Foote Award 12938
Friend of Libraries U.S.A. Award (Friend of the Year) 9793
Friends of Libraries U.S.A. Public Service Award 9794
Elizabeth Futas Catalyst for Change Award 2975
Loleta D. Fvan Public Library Research Grant 2976
Thomson Gale Award for Excellence in Business Librarianship/BRASS 17940
Gale/EMIERT Multicultural Award 2962
Gale Financial Development Award 2977
Marian Gould Gallagher Distinguished Service Award 1251
Garden State Children's Book Awards 16179
Mary V. Gaver Scholarship 2978
Gay/Lesbian Book Award 3003
LITA/Gaylord Award for Achievement in Library and Information Technology 12823
Genealogical Publishing Company Award 17941
Eliza Atkins Gleason Book Award 2995
Great Lakes Crew Award of Merit 3091
Grolier Foundation Award 2979
Grolier National Library Week Grant 3000
Danny Gunnells Intellectual Freedom Award 10765
Hall of Fame 19549
Philip M. Hamer and Elizabeth Hamer Kegan Award 18954
Sue Hefley Educator of the Year Award 12939
Agnes Henebry Roll of Honor Award 19563
Frances Henne Award 1415
Frances Henne YALSA/VOYA (Voice of Youth Advocates) Research Grant 22054
Frederick Charles Hicks Award for Outstanding Contributions to Academic Law Librarianship 1252
The Highsmith Library Innovation Award 17716
Highsmith Library Innovative Award 10676
Highsmith Library Literature Award 2980
Oliver Wendell Holmes Travel Award 18955
Honor Award 19969
Honorable Mention Award 3092
Honorary Life Member 7975
Honorary Life Membership 7141
Honorary Lifetime Membership 21538
Honorary Member 19550
Honorary Membership Award 19475
Hoosier Intellectual Freedom Award 10766
Paul Howard Award for Courage 2981
Christopher J. Hoy/ERT Scholarship 2964
John Ames Humphrey/OCLC/Forest Press Award 2990
Donald F. Hyde Award 9815
IASL/SIRS International Commendation Award 11398
Illinois Academic Librarian of the Year Award 10677
John Phillip Immroth Memorial Award for Intellectual Freedom 2986
Information Technology Pathfinder Award 1416
Innovation Award 6747
Innovations in Technology Award 19551
Instruction Section Innovation Award 5611
Intellectual Freedom Award
  American Association of School Librarians 1417
  Illinois Library Association 10678
Intellectual Freedom Round Table State and Regional Achievement Award 2987
International Special Librarians Day/National Library Week Award 19552
IREAD Awards 10679
J. Franklin Jameson Archival Advocacy Award 18956
Thomas Jefferson Prize 18689
Jerome Award 7653
E. J. Josey Scholarship Award 6419
Frederick G. Kilgour Award for Research in Library and Information Technology 12824
Martin Luther King, Jr. Leadership Awards 8965
Barbara Kingsolver Award 9795
Joseph F. Kwapil Memorial Award 19564
"L. PeRCy" Awards 12836
Lake Placid Education Foundation / NYLA Scholarship 16237
LAMA Cultural Diversity Grant 12817
LAMA President's Award 12818
Sister M. Claude Lane Award 18957
Marta Lange/CQ Press Award 5612
LATA Scholarship Award 5058
Law Library Journal Article of the Year Award 1253
Law Library Publications Award 1254
Samuel Lazerow Fellowship for Research in Collections and Technical Services in Academic and Research Libraries 5613
LDA Award for Excellence in Library Achievement 12732
Leadership in Library Acquisitions Award 5425
Legislator Award 10767
Librarian of the Year 10680
Library Leadership Award 5059
Library Research and Development Grants 6940
Library Research Grants 10007
Library Service Awards 16181
Joseph W. Lippincott Award 2982
LITA/Christian Larew Memorial Scholarship in Library and Information Technology 12825
LITA/Endeavor Student Writing Award 12826
LITA/GEAC Scholarship in Library and Information Technology 12827
LITA/Library Hi Tech Award 12828
LITA-LSSI Minority Scholarship in Library and Information Technology 12829
LITA/OCLC Minority Scholarship in Library and Information Technology 12830
Jean Lowrie Leadership Development Grant 11399
Margaret Mann Citation 5426
Allie Beth Martin Award 17717
Robert R. McClarren Legislative Development Award 10681
Media Award 19553
Frederic G. Melcher Scholarship 5440
Meritorious Service Award 16069
Modisette Award 12942
Margaret E. Monroe Library Adult Services Award 17942
Velma Moore Award 16274
Francis Morrison Award 18270
Takeshi Murofushi Research Award 11400
National Book Service Teacher-Librarian of the Year Award 7261
National School Library Media Program of the Year Award 1418
NCLA Distinguished Library Service Award 16512
WESS Coutts Nijhoff International West European Specialist Study Grant 5615
Oberly Award for Bibliography in the Agricultural Sciences 5616
Oberman and Rich Award 10682
Eli M. Oboler Memorial Award 2988
Jane O'Brien Award 10683
Ocean Crew and Great Lakes Awards of Merit 3093
Ocean Crew Award of Merit 3094
Bethany J. Ochal Award for Distinguished Service to the Profession 1255
Oklahoma School Administrator Award 16670
Doris Orenstein Memorial Fund 5742
Outreach Services Award 5060
Outstanding Academic Librarian Award 12943
Outstanding Congregational Librarian 7977
Outstanding Congregational Library 7978
Outstanding Contribution to Congregational Libraries 7979
Outstanding Decision Maker Award 5061
Outstanding Librarian Award 10768
Outstanding Library Award 10769
Outstanding Library Board Award 5062
Outstanding Library Service Award 5063
Outstanding New Librarian Award 10770
Outstanding Pennsylvania Author or Illustrator 17192
Outstanding Reference Sources 17944
Outstanding Service to Librarianship Award 7250
Outstanding Southeastern Library Program Award 19477
Outstanding Support Staff Award 10771
Outstanding Trustee Award 10772
Partnership Award 10773
Theodore Calvin Pease Award 18959
Penguin Putnam Books for Young Readers Group Award 5442
Esther J. Piercy Award 5427
Harold T. Pinkett Minority Student Award 18960
Fellows' Ernst Posner Prize 18961
Bogle/Pratt International Library Travel Fund 2991
Preservation Publication Award 18962
President's Award 19478
Professional Achievement Award
  Association of Specialized and Cooperative Library Agencies 5858
  Special Libraries Association - Transportation Division 19567
Professional Award 19554
Public Person 8529
Public Relations Member Achievement Award 19555
Rare Books and Manuscripts Librarianship Award 5617
Ray Moore Award 16514
Recognition of Group Achievement Award 12820
Reference Service Press Award 17945
Reference Services Award 10684
REFORMA Scholarship 17951

Library (continued)

Regina Medal 7654
Joseph Reiss Memorial Judaica Library Awards 20341
Research Grant 19556
Rising Moon Outstanding Youth Services Librarian Award 5064
Charlie Robinson Award 17718
Rosenzweig Distinguished Service Award 5065
Rothrock Award 19479
Rowe Marketing Award 7257
St. Katharine Drexel Award 7655
Mari Sandoz Award 16070
K. G. Saur Award for Best Article in *College and Research Libraries* 5618
School Librarian's Workshop Scholarshp 1419
School Library Media Specialist Award 12944
Margaret B. Scott Award of Merit 7262
Service Award 5859
John Sessions Memorial Award 17946
Share the Wealth Packets 12837
Ralph J. Shoemaker Award of Merit 19565
Louis Shores - Greenwood Publishing Group Award 17947
Fannie Simon Award 19560
Alexander J. Skrzypek Award 10685
Southeastern Librarian Wilson Award 19480
Student Article Contest 7251
Student Loan 8963
Student Writing and Development Award 12821
Pat Tabler Memorial Award 7980
Taft Awards Program for Non-Profit Resource Centers 19898
TBS, INC. Technical Services Award 10686
Tennessee History Book Award 19970
Tennessee Resource Sharing Award 19971
Tenth Anniversary Commemorative Award 7142
Texas Bluebonnet Award 20028
Thomson Gale Award for Excellence in Reference and Adult Services 17948
TLA/SIRS Freedom of Information Award 19972
Trustee Award 19973
Trustee Citation 10687
Trustee Citation Award 16071
Trustee Recognition Award 16182
Twentieth Anniversary Professional Development Award 7143
Volunteer State Book Award 19974
Volunteerism Award 10688
James E. Ward Library Instruction Award 19975
First Step Award - Wiley Professional Development Grant 5428
H. W. Wilson Company Award 19557
H. W. Wilson Library Staff Development Grant 2983
The Sharon G. Womack Outstanding Library Technician Award 5066
Davis C. Woolley Award 6245
World Book - ALA Goal Grant 2984
World Book Award 7656
WSS Achievement in Women's Studies Librarianship Awards - Career Achievement Award 5620
YALSA Sagebrush Award 22055

Library design
AIA/ALA Library Buildings Award 2708
Innovation Award 6747
Library Buildings Award Program 12819

Library history
Phyllis Dain Library History Dissertation Award 2993
Justin Winsor Prize Essay 2996

Library services *See* Library and information services

Lighting design
Distinguished Service Award 10692
Fellow Designation 10693
IALD International Lighting Design Awards 11369
IES Medal 10694
International Illumination Design Awards Program 10695
Lumen Award Program 10696
Louis B. Marks Award 10697

Limnology *See* Hydrography

Linguistics
TESOL Virginia French Allen Award for Scholarhip and Service 19948
ASHA Media Awards for Journalists 4662
Awards for Excellence in Teaching of the Classics 3418
ACTFL Nelson Brooks Award for Excellence in the Teaching of Culture 2056
CEE James N. Britton Award for Inquiry within the English Language Arts 14829
Certificate of Merit 1444
CLA Award Scholarship 8166
Ryan Crymes TESOL Fellowship for Graduate Study 19949
ACTFL Edwin Cudecki International Business Award 2057
Delavan Award 2279
Distinguished Service Award 1452
Doublespeak Award 14832
Mary Finocchiaro Award for Excellence in the Development of Pedagogical Materials 19950
German Summer Study Award 1445
Charles J. Goodwin Award of Merit 3419
Heritage Award 16444
Honors of the Association 12013
Kay Elemetrics Award for Research in Phonetics 12014
Language Proficiency Award 9978
James Russell Lowell Prize 13561
Albert H. Marckwardt Travel Grants 19951
Kenneth W. Mildenberger Prize 13563
National Endowment for the Humanities Grant Programs 14938
National Testing and Awards Program for Secondary Students 1446
George Orwell Award for Distinguished Contribution to Honesty and Clarity in Public Language 14836
Outstanding German Educator Award 1447
Outstanding Reference Sources 17944
ACTFL Anthony Papalia Award for Excellence in Teacher Education 2058
Parmalee Scholarship 11688
ACTFL - MLJ Paul Pimsleur Award for Research in Foreign Language Education 2059
Presidents' Prize 12868
Prize for a First Book 13566
Prize for Independent Scholars 13567
Pro Lingua Award 9691
Queen Elizabeth Silver Jubilee Endowment Fund for Study in a Second Official Language Award Program 5907
Aldo and Jeanne Scaglione Prize for Studies in Germanic Languages and Literatures 13574
Aldo and Jeanne Scaglione Prize for Studies in Slavic Languages and Literatures 13575
Scholarships, Writing Awards, Internships 18491
Mina P. Shaughnessy Prize 13576
Mary Isabel Sibley Fellowship 17245
Matilda W. Sinclaire Award 2284
Smith Memorial 12015
South Atlantic Review Essay Prize 19438
Spring Conference Scholarships 8211
ACTFL Florence Steiner Award for Leadership in Foreign Language Education, K-12 2060
ACTFL Florence Steiner Award for Leadership in Foreign Language Education, Postsecondary 2061
ACTFL - MLJ Emma Marie Steiner Award for Leadership in Foreign Language Research in Foreign Language Education 2062
Teacher Award 8214
TESOL Research Interest Section/Thomson Heinle Distinguished Research Award 19952
TESOL Thomson Heinle Award for Excellence in Teaching 19953
TESOL Travel Grant 19954
Virginia Literacy Foundation 6462
Alec Vitarius Memorial Scholarship 9754
Ronald W. Walker Memorial Grant 8212
A. Ronald Walton Award 14810
Graciela Wilborn Foreign Language Teacher of the Year in North Dakota 9692

Literacy (*See also* Reading skills)
Advancement of Literacy Award 17712
ALTA Literacy Award 5447
Beverly Buntin Volunteer of the Year 7695
Celebrate Literacy 10809
Chairman's Award 17672
CLTA Achievement in Literacy Award 7264
Ruth J. Colvin Awards 17673
Judy Dauphinee Volunteer of the Year 17676
Edith Stager Memorial Award 8075
Ethel Minter Award 12998
Extra Mile Award 6464
Friend of Literacy Award 17677
General Laubach Award 9423
International Citation of Merit 11861
Literacy Leadership Awards 17674
Local Council Community Service Award 11866
Maynard Jensen Award 10288
Member of the United Way 7769
Lisa Morrill Volunteer Award 6465
Scholar Award 21474
G'anne Sparks Tutoring Award 6466
Student/Tutor Recognition Certificates 6300
Tennessee Teacher of Excellence 19966

Literacy (continued)

Tutor Appreciation Awards 12278
Women's National Book Association Award 21800

Literary criticism
Albion Book Prize/NACBS Book Prize 16411
The Ben Shuster Memorial Award 666
Best Information Science Book Award 4103
Elmer Holmes Bobst Literary Awards 16301
Truman Capote Award for Literary Criticism in Memory of Newton Arvin 12189
Children's Literature Association Article Award 7908
Children's Literature Association Book Award 7909
Christian Gauss Award 17242
Roma Gill Prize 13122
Zelda & Paul Gitlin Literary Prize 20080
Honorary Member 10627
Howard Fellows 10571
Rose Lefcowitz Prize 17414
Harry Levin Prize 1952
James Russell Lowell Prize 13561
Mythopoeic Scholarship Awards 13740
National Book Critics Circle Awards 14530
Lorne Pierce Medal 18171
Prize for a First Book 13566
Richard S. Kennedy Student Essay Prize 20081
Aldo and Jeanne Scaglione Prize for Comparative Literary Studies 13571
Aldo and Jeanne Scaglione Prize for French and Francophone Studies 13572
Aldo and Jeanne Scaglione Prize for Studies in Germanic Languages and Literatures 13574
Aldo and Jeanne Scaglione Prize for Studies in Slavic Languages and Literatures 13575
Studies Book Award 19439
Rene Wellek Prize 1953
William B. Wisdom Grant in Aid of Research 20082

Literature (*See also* Creative writing; Drama criticism; Editing; Essays; Editorial writing; Humor; Illustration; Linguistics; Literacy; Literary criticism; Mystery writing; Scholarly works; Translations; specific literary genres, e.g. Biography)
Milton Acorn Poetry Award 17543
Agatha Awards 13046
AIAA Pendray Aerospace Literature Award 2661
American Indian Festival of Words Author Award 20235
Brooke Russell Astor Award 16253
Athenaeum Literary Award 6014
Atlantic Journalism Awards 6035
Banff Mountain Book Festival 6235
Banta Awards 21683
Omer Lutfi Barkan Article Prize 20239
Bellwether Prize for Social Justice Fiction 15998
Pura Belpre Award 17950
Black Caucus of the American Library Association Literary Awards 6413
Book Sense Book of the Year Award 1582
James Henry Breasted Prize 2467
Bross Prize 6655
Bumbershoot, The Seattle Arts Festival 16734
Bush Artist Fellows Program 6700
Bradford Cadmus Memorial Award 10970
Estelle Campbell Award 15730
Canada - Australia Literary Prize 6786
Casey Award 19621
Catherine A. M. Cavanaugh Award 15731
Christopher Awards 7971
Cintas Foundation Fellowships 10981
Citations of Merit 13984
CLA Award Scholarship 8166
Common Wealth Awards of Distinguished Service 17410
Conover-Porter Award 262
William L. Crawford Fantasy Award 11259
Janet Dailey Award 18112
Dante Prize 8749
Director's Award 11775
Distinguished Career Awards 6142
Distinguished Service Citation 11776
Bill Duthie Booksellers' Choice 21518
Howard N. Eavenson Award 18810
Editors' Book Award 17769
El Angel Award - Distinguished Hispanic-American Artist 6374
Ralph Waldo Emerson Award 11805
Norma Epstein Foundation Awards 21112
Mrs. Inez M. Fauria Award 8614
Feature Article Award 17546
Richard F. Fenno, Jr. Book Prize 3581
Sydney N. Fisher Graduate Student Paper Prize 20241
Florida Artists Hall of Fame 9587
Folger Shakespeare Library Fellowships and National Endowment for the Humanities Senior Fellowships 9646
Gaston-Gouin, Alfred-DesRochers et Alphonse-Desjardins 5263
Grand Prix du Livre de Montreal 18235
Charles Hall Grandgent Award 8750
Grants for Arts Projects 14930
Paul Hair Prize 264
Hall of Outstanding Americans 15986
Harbourfront Festival Prize 11882
Haskell Awards 2727
Hawaii Award for Literature 10295
Ohioana Award, Florence Roberts Head Memorial Award 16658
Hellman-Hammet Award 10595
Peggy V. Helmerich Distinguished Author Award 20236
Clarence L. Holte Literary Prize 17231
Howard Fellows 10571
Image Awards 14049
Individual Artist Fellowship 13586
Innis-Gerin Medal 18167
Washington Irving Medal of Literary Excellence 18220
Jane Addams Children's Book Award 21795
Juvenile Awards 9783
Robert F. Kennedy Book Awards 18074
Sophie Kerr Prize 21441
Coretta Scott King Book Award 3004
KODAK International Educational Literature Award 5216
M. Fuat Koprulu Book Prize 20242
Gordon J. Laing Prize 21006
Lambda Literary Awards 12683
Land of Enchantment Book Awards 16194
Dorothea Lange - Paul Taylor Prize 9045
Lesbian Caucus Prize 15968
Letras de Oro Literary Prizes 21059
Lifetime Achievement Awards 10196
Literary Awards
Boston Book Review 6521
Friends of American Writers 9784
PEN Center U.S.A. 17152
Literature Paper Prize 18542
James Russell Lowell Prize 13561
Ramon Magsaysay Award 18093
Walter Rumsey Marvin Grant 16660
Mature Women Scholarship Grant 15334
Medal of Honor for Literature 13993
The Michael 16184
Kenneth W. Mildenberger Prize 13563
Minnesota Voices Project 16198
Money for Women/Barbara Deming Memorial Fund Grants 13582
National Jewish Book Award - Scholarship 12330
National Outdoor Book Awards 15465
National Society of Arts and Letters First Place Award 15733
NEMLA Book Prize 16544
New Talent Award 3005
New Voices Award/New Vision Award 17780
Mollie Davis Nicholson Award 15734
Notable Wisconsin Authors 21685
Novella Prize 13044
Outstanding Reference Sources 17944
R. Hunt Parker Memorial Award 16519
Pegasus Prize for Literature 9379
Prix Champlain 8423
Prix Gilles - Corbeil 20304
Prize for a First Book 13566
Prize for Independent Scholars 13567
Publishers Award 9785
Pulitzer Fellowships 17748
QPB New Visions Award 17781
Mrs. Ann Radcliffe Awards 8615
James W. Redhouse Student Prize 20243
President Dr. Donald A. Reed Award 8616
Joseph Reiss Memorial Judaica Library Awards 20341
Andrew E. Robin Memorial Award 10277
Roderick Haig-Brown Regional Prize 21522
Rome Prize Fellowships 605
Mari Sandoz Award 16070
Aldo and Jeanne Scaglione Prize for Comparative Literary Studies 13571
Aldo and Jeanne Scaglione Prize for Italian Literary Studies 13573
Philip Schaff Prize 4288
Carl Sentner Short Story Award 17548
Mina P. Shaughnessy Prize 13576
Philip Shehadi New Writers Award 13379
Sixteenth Century Journal Literature Prize 18545
South Atlantic Review Essay Prize 19438
Special Awards 6143
State of Florida Fellowship 9589
Joseph S. Stauffer Prizes 6809
Philip M. Stern Award 21447
Charles Wharton Stork Fellow 6017
Dorothy and Bruce Strong Award 15735
Student Literary Award 14899
Sidney Sulkin Prize 17416
Rev. Dr. Montague Summers Memorial Award 8617
Arthur F. Taggart Award 18827
Emerson - Thoreau Medal 623
Lon Tinkle Award 20021
University Medal 16304

Literature (continued)

Volunteer of the Year 11777
William H. Walker Award for Excellence in Contributions to Chemical Engineering Literature 2793
Lila Wallace-Reader's Digest Writers' Awards 21430
Horace Walpole Gold Medal 8618
Philip H. Ward, Jr. Memorial Award 2248
Western Heritage Awards (Wrangler Award) 14887
Thomas J. Wilson Award 10284
Laurence L. Winship PEN New England Award 17158
Wisconsin Arts Board Fellowships 21666
Abel Wolman Award 3810
Women's National Book Association Award 21800
Writers Digest Short Story Competition 21978
Young People's Literature Awards 9786

Literature, American *See* American literature

Literature, Canadian *See* Canadian literature

Literature, Catholic *See* Catholic literature

Literature, Children's *See* Children's literature

Literature, English *See* English literature

Literature, European *See* European literature

Literature, French *See* French literature

Literature, Irish *See* Irish literature

Literature, Italian *See* Italian literature

Literature, legal *See* Legal literature

Literature, religion *See* Religion literature

Literature, Spanish *See* Spanish literature

Literature, travel *See* Travel literature

Lubrication engineering
Award for Research on Automotive Lubricants 19034
Edmond E. Bisson Award 19343
Committee D-2 Award 5936
Wilbur Deutsch Memorial Award 19344
Mayo D. Hersey Award 4515
Walter D. Hodson Award 19345
Captain Alfred E. Hunt Memorial Award 19346
International Award 19347
P. M. Ku Meritorious Award 19348
Lowrie B. Sargent, Jr. Award 5981
Al Sonntag Award 19349

Luge *See* Sledding

Magazines *See* Journalism; Publications

Management (*See also* Employment practices; Health care administration; Hospital administration; Human relations; Information management; Leadership; Operations research; Planning; Public administration; Records management; Research administration)
AAS Individual Awards 5102
ACE Fellows Program 2054
Achievement Award 1257
Achievement Awards 14165
William C. Ackermann Medal for Excellence in Water Management 4822
Administrative Division Executive Committee Award 2317
Administrative Psychiatry Award 3610
Administrator of the Year 14279
Administrator of the Year Award 1882
Advertising Credit Executive of the Year 210
AES Man of the Year Award 67
Affiliate Corporation Award 11560
AFMC Junior Management Award 329
AFMC Logistics Executive Management Award 330
AFMC Middle Management Award 331
AIAA HAP Arnold Award for Excellence in Aeronautical Program Management 2653
Allied Corporation Award 11561
American and National League Managers of the Year 19648
Animal Management Award 4254
ARM of the Year 11032
Arts Management Award for Arts Administrator of the Year 5155
Arts Management Award for Career Service 5156
ASAE Fellow 4267
ASAS Fellow 4257
Association Executive of the Year 5924
Automotive Training Awards 6121
Award for Innovative Management 11028
Award for Outstanding Achievement in Management 10949
Award of Excellence 8223
Paul Bacon Award 20792
Malcolm Baldrige National Quality Award 6202
Bernard L. Barnard Award 11267
Board of Directors' Award 10337
Bonder Scholarship for Applied Operations Research in Military Applications 11068
Bonder Scholarship in Health Care 11069
Bower Award for Business Leadership 9742
Box Office of the Year Award 12084
George M. Brooker Collegiate Scholarship for Minorities 11033
Warren E. Burger Award 14640
Business Leadership Award 21065
Business Management Award 19259
Businessperson of the Year 12706
Butts - Whiting Award 5630
Roald Campbell Award 20971
Phil Carroll Advancement of Management Awards 18623
Certified Property Manager (CPM) of the Year Award 11034
Chairman's Award 684
Chapter of the Year 15558
Chapter of the Year Award
International Facility Management Association 11565
Mail Systems Management Association 13023
Chapter President of the Year Award 7964
W. Howard Chase Award for Excellence in Issue Management 12240
Christian Management Award 7965
Civilian Awards 342
Gerald R. Clore International Award 10083
Joseph P. Collins Award 14820
Communicator of the Year Award 14773
Community Counselling Service Award for Outstanding Fundraising Professional 5700
Community Service Award 14821
Computer Entrepreneur Award 10887
Construction Management Award 4309
Convention Service Manager of the Year 19822
Corporate and Professional Firm Leadership Award 7627
Council of the Year Award 11566
County Engineer of the Year Awards 14179
Jack A. Culbertson Award 20972
Charlotte Danstrom Award 21746
George B. Dantzig Dissertation Award 11070
Graham L. Davis Awards of Excellence 10338
William J. Davis Memorial Award 20973
Dawson Awards 5810
Distinguished Author Award 11567
Distinguished Contribution Award 17666
Distinguished Leadership Award for a Professional Planner 3553
Distinguished Member Award
International Facility Management Association 11568
Society for Mining, Metallurgy, and Exploration 18808
Distinguished School Administrators Award 1413
Distinguished Service Award
American Academy of Medical Administrators 685
American Arbitration Association 918
Council of Logistics Management 8580
National Association of Fleet Administrators 14234
Public Risk Management Association 17728
D. Howard Doane Award 4406
Doctoral Dissertation Award 8581
Donehoo Essay Award 11270
James Clement Dunn Award for Excellence 20538
Earth Award 6682
Franz Edelman Award for Achievement in Management Science and Operations Research 11071
Education and Training Awards 5713
Educator Award 11569
Emerging Company Award 5331
Engineering and Construction Contracting Division Award 2768
Engineering Medal 17605
Entrepreneur of the Year 12708
Excellence in Administration Award 20601
Executive of the Year
Federal Executive Institute Alumni Association 9449
National Basketball Association 14502
R & D Magazine - Reed Business Information 17814

Management (continued)

Executive of the Year Award 19795
Facility Management Achievement Award 11570
Facility of the Year 18409
Faculty Publication of the Year 686
Benjamin F. Fairless Memorial Award 2874
Farm and Ranch Management Award 16003
Federal Property Person of the Year 15559
Fellow 18624
Fellow Award 17667
Financial Post Outstanding CEO of the Year Award 8540
Founders Medal 10862
Future Business Executive 9843
Future Business Teacher 9845
Henry Laurence Gantt Medal 4511
Gilbreth Medal 18625
Gold Medal Award 17625
Golden Circles Award 11571
Scott Goodnight Award for Outstanding Performance as a Dean 14403
Goodyear Conservation Awards 14155
Seth Gordon Award 11358
Government Affairs Award of Recognition 6683
Harry J. Graham Award 17763
Great Menu Contest 15626
Jack Griffiths Property Person of the Year 15560
Hall of Fame Award 15110
Harold Hammerman Spirit of Education Award 14434
Lloyd D. Hanford Sr. Distinguished Faculty Award 11036
Melvene D. Hardee Dissertation of the Year Award 14404
Harvard Medal 10271
Harry J. Harwick Lifetime Achievement Award 1884
Bernice Hemphill Memorial Award 1111
Hennessy Awards 15627
Larry Hobart Seven Hats Award 3791
IDA Downtown Achievement Awards 11547
IEEE Engineering Leadership Recognition 10870
INFORMS Fellow Award 11073
INFORMS Prize 11074
International Awards 5670
International Honorees 6331
International Property Tax Achievement Award 11275
Alfred E. Johnson Achievement Award 1432
John H. Johnson President's Trophy 14339
Roger W. Jones Award for Executive Leadership 4784
Henry L. Kennedy Award 1968
Key Award 4268
Kenneth K. King Management Award 10090
James N. Landis Medal 4524
League Executive of the Year Awards 14340
Marriott Corporation Health Care Services Charles U. Letourneau Student Research Paper of the Year Award 688
Lifetime Achievement Award
- International Ticketing Association 12085
- National Telecommunications Cooperative Association 15862

Louise L. and Y. T. Lum Award 11038
Major League Executive of the Year 19656
Management Achievement Award
- National Association of College and University Business Officers 14124
- National Telecommunications Cooperative Association 15863

Management Achievement Awards 17658
Management Award
- Art Directors Club 5118
- International Publishing Management Association 11843

Management Engineering Award 10346
Manager of the Year
- Self Storage Association 18410
- System Safety Society 19888

Manager of the Year Award 13024
Market Manager of the Year 14337
Marks of Excellence Award 15111
Donald E. Marlowe Award 4025
Masters Administrator of the Year 21230
Materials Handling Award 18627
W. Wallace McDowell Award 10898
McKinsey Awards 10273
Meeting Planner of the Year 5329
Merit Award 5188
Susan E. Miller Award/Chapter Service Awards 18467
Frederick C. Morgan Award 10339
MSMA Distinguished Service Award 13025
MTS Special Commendation 13112
National Credit Executive of the Year 14183
NBA Executive of the Year 19665
Carl E. Nelson Engineering Award 312
William Newcomer Health Care Executive of the Year Award 689
NFL Executive of the Year 19670
NHL Executive of the Year 19673
The Office Building of the Year (TOBY) 6685
Operations-Services Awards 10091
Organizing Excellence Award 14347
Outstanding Association Executive Award 5887
Outstanding Competition Management Awards 20569
Outstanding Contribution to Higher Education Award 14405
Outstanding Corporate Growth Award 5332
Outstanding Scientific Materials Managers Award 14382
Pacesetter of the Year Award 14774
J. Wallace Paletou Award 11039
John I. Parcel - Leif J. Sverdrup Civil Engineering Management Award 4348
Dan Patrick Award 11438
Ike Pearson Award 14292
Physician Executive Award 1885
President's Award
- American Society for Nondestructive Testing 4151
- Society of Medical-Dental Management Consultants 19180

President's Environment and Conservation Challenge Awards 9365
Prize for the Teaching of OR/MS Practice 11080
Process Improvement Award 14125
Professional Achievement Award 11040
Professional Award 2535
Professional of the Year 12658
Project of the Year Award 17668
Quality Management Award 10349

Charles F. Rand Memorial Gold Medal 2825
Regional Awards 14407
Regional Director of the Year Award 690
Luther I. Replogle Award for Management Improvement 20549
Research Awards 12280
Resource Enhancement Award 14126
Paul H. Rittle, Sr. Memorial Scholarship Award 11041
St. Petersburg Yacht Club Trophy 20780
Scholarships and Research Grants, Behavioral Studies 14650
Secretary of the Year, Executive of the Year 11169
Service and Performance Award 12442
Robert M. Shelton Award 10340
J. Shipman Gold Medal Award 10840
Sigma Iota Epsilon Scholarship Awards 18485
Special Achievement Award 14822
Spirit Award 12086
State Director of the Year Award
- American Academy of Medical Administrators 691
- National Propane Gas Association 15556

Linn Stuckenbruck Person of the Year Award 17669
Student Chapter of the Year Award 11572
Student Paper of the Year Awards 17670
The Summit Award 11245
Surveying and Mapping Award 4360
Fannie Taylor Distinguished Service Award 5811
Taylor Key Award 18628
Isaiah Thomas Award 18087
Helen M. Thompson Award 4732
Ticketing Professional of the Year Award 12087
Top Ten Business Women of ABWA 1610
Paul F. Truran, Jr., Medical Materiel and Logistics Management Award 5788
Fred Turner Award for Outstanding Service to NASPA 14409
Twin Tribute to Women and Industry 22080
U.S. Military Academy General Management Award 13414
U.S. Sailing One-Design Awards 20783
Volunteer Achievement Award 19634
The Washington Post Award for Excellence in Nonprofit Management 7739
Marvin Whitlock Award 19061
Donald B. Woodbridge Award 14676
Young Member Achievement Award 5894
Earle F. Zeigler Lecture Award 16473

Manufacturing (*See also* Industries and trades)

Charles Allderdice Award 8465
ARA Hall of Fame Award 6166
Associate Remodeler of the Year Award 14257
Award of Merit 19142
Malcolm Baldrige National Quality Award 6202
Walt Bartram Memorial Education Award Fund 19143
Best Trade Show Product and Best Booth Display 6167
The Blade Magazine Manufacturers Awards 6444
Board of Directors' Award 2318
Donald C. Burnham Manufacturing Management Award 19144

Manufacturing (continued)

Caterpillar Scholars Award Fund 19145
Arthur and Gladys Cervenka Scholarship Award 19146
Chairman's Award 13010
Chassis Inspectors Award 10978
Community College Scholarship Award 19147
Company of the Year Award 11951
Edward P. Connell Award 2319
Container Inspectors Award 10979
DeLaval, Inc. Dairy Extension Award 2100
Directors Scholarship Fund 19148
Distinguished Service Award 18564
Roscoe Douglas Scholarship Award Fund 19149
H. A. B. Dunning Award 3385
Education Award 19150
The Founders Award 6169
Founding Chapter Scholarship Award 19151
Gold Key Award 10709
Gold Medal 19152
Connie and Robert T. Gunter Scholarship Award Fund 19153
J. H. "Jud" Hall Composites Manufacturing Award 19154
Hall of Fame Award
  Asphalt Emulsion Manufacturer Association 5202
  Small Motor and Motion Association 18565
Clinton J. Helton Manufacturing Scholarship Award Fund 19155
Honorary Membership 19156
ICIA Distinguished Achievement Award 11498
J.H. Hall Composites Manufacturing Award 8324
Lucille B. Kaufman Women's Scholarship Fund 19157
Wayne Kay Co-Op Scholarship Award 19158
Wayne Kay Graduate Fellowship 19159
Wayne Kay High School Scholarship 19160
Wayne Kay Scholarship Fund 19161
Manufacturer Member of the Year 8975
Manufacturers Appreciation Award 19637
Manufacturing Manager of the Year/Service Sector Manager of the Year 17744
Guilliano Mazzetti Scholarship Award 19162
Memphis Chapter High School Incentive Scholarship 19163
M. Eugene Merchant Manufacturing Medal 4531
National Medal of Technology 15678
New Product Showcase Award 3372
Outstanding Young Manufacturing Engineer Award 19164
PACCAR Scholarship Award Fund 19165
Thomas F. Preston Manufacturer of the Year Award 14924
R. D. Pritchard-Higgins Award for Design 17532
Process Award 11739
Rally Awards 19702
Edward S. Roth Manufacturing Engineering Scholarship 19166
S-B Power Tool Scholarship Award Fund 19167
St. Louis Chapter 17 Scholarship Fund 19168
Albert M. Sargent Progress Award 19169
SCCA Pro Rally Manufacturer's Award 19709
Joseph A. Siegel Service Award 19170
SME Education Foundation Family Scholarship Award 19171
SME Fellow 19172
Frederick W. Taylor Research Medal 19173
Technical Division Executive Committee Award 2320
U.S. Senate Productivity Award for Maryland 21055
Lawrence A. Walker Memorial Award 19174
Myrtle and Earl Walker Scholarship Fund 19175
Eli Whitney Productivity Award 19176
William E. Weisel Scholarship Fund 19177
Albert E. Wischmeyer Memorial Scholarship Award 19178
World Challenge 19724

Marine biology
AFS Award of Excellence 2251
Aylesworth Foundation Advancement Award 9617
Best Student Paper/Poster Award 8674
James Centorino Award 15357
Joseph A. Cushman Award 8690
Dean John A. Knauss Marine Policy Fellowship 9618
Maurice Ewing Medal 2346
Excellence in Research 8675
Herbert E. Gregory Medal 17013
Shinkishi Hatai Medal 17014
Honorary Life Fellow 17015
Honorary Member 15358
Marine Education Award 15359
Outstanding Achievement Award-Group 2804
Outstanding Achievement Award-Individual 2805
Outstanding Teacher Award 15360
President's Award 15361
Gilbert Morgan Smith Medal 13847
W. F. Thompson Award 2806

Marine engineering *See* Naval engineering

Marketing (*See also* Advertising; Public relations; Merchandising)
AALL/West Excellence in Marketing Award 1247
Advertising Awards 55
William H. Albers Award 9660
AMA/Irwin Distinguished Marketing Educator Award 3025
American Egg Board Research Award 17496
Author of the Year Award 6981
Automotive Leader of the Year 6123
Award for Executive Excellence 8286
Award for Local Sales Achievement 6721
Awards for Excellence in Cable Marketing and Advertising 8684
C.H. Barnes Award 7343
Frank W. Berkman Chapter of the Year Award 10552
Best Doctoral Dissertation of the Year Award 105
Best Paper of the Year Award 8287
Best Student Paper of the Year Award 106
Dewayne Billingsley Memorial Scholarship 20040
Bower Award for Business Leadership 9742
Eugene C. Bowler Award 17118
George Hay Brown/AMA Marketing Scholar of the Year 3026
Canada Awards for Excellence 15568
Candy Salesman of the Year 13592
Certificate of Merit - Commercial Wool Production in Canada 7031
Chapter Award for Excellence in Membership Marketing 11563
Chapter Excellence Awards and Chapter of the Year Award 3027
Chapter President Award 18790
Chevron U.S.A. Marketing Award 15348
Circulation Hall of Fame 8005
Robert B. Clarke Outstanding Educator Award 8931
Alden G. Clayton Doctoral Dissertation Proposal Award 13120
Clinton S. Lee Market Services and Engineering Award of Excellence 9210
Communication and Marketing Awards 11035
Communicator of the Year Award 14773
Cooperative Marketing and Sales Council Awards 16330
Creative Commercial Production Awards 6722
Dealer Education Award 16577
DeLaval, Inc. Dairy Extension Award 2100
Design Awards 18791
Direct Marketing International ECHO Awards 8924
Direct Marketing Woman of the Year Award 21708
Distinguished Service Award 8288
Distributor of the Year Award 13664
DMA Hall of Fame 8925
Edison Awards 3028
Editor & Publisher/INMA Marketing Awards 9163
EXCEL Awards 19205
Excellence in Communication Award 13978
Executive of the Year Award 19795
Georgia Media Award 9963
Gold and Platinum Video Awards 11884
Gold Awards 16996
Gold Key Award 10709
Golden Penguin Awards 15132
Hall of Fame 13665
Hall of Fame Award 8934
Peggy Hereford Excellence in Communications Award 403
HSMAI Adrian Advertising Awards 10554
HSMAI Hall of Fame 10556
ICIA Distinguished Achievement Award 11498
IDA Downtown Achievement Awards 11547
Indie Awards Competition 13118
Industry Awards Program 17119
Industry Innovation Award 8935
International Company Award 13666
International Marketing Executive of the Year 18223
International Sales Executive of the Year 18224
ISBM Business Marketing Doctoral Award Support Completion 17208

Marketing (continued)

Key Employee Award 15861
The Philip Kotler Award for Excellence in Healthcare Marketing 3029
Wayne A. Lemburg Award for Distinguished Service 3030
Lifetime Sales Achievement Award 19636
Jeremiah Ludington Memorial Award 9175
MacEachern Award 17726
Market Development and Promotion Federation Awards 16332
Marketer of the Year 3031
Marketing Achievement 15864
Marketing Achievement Award 18792
Marketing Achievement Awards 15554
Marketing Awards 17120
Marketing Awards Program 17121
Marketing Methods Competition 17633
Marketing Person of the Year and Marketing Firm of the Year 3032
Marketing Practitioner of the Year Award 109
Edward N. Mayer Award for Educational Leadership 8932
Harold H. Maynard Award 3033
Carroll R. Miller Award 15495
MLM Company of the Year 13667
NAMO Marketing Award 16508
NAMTA Hall of Fame Award 13979
National Mature Media Awards Program 13207
Network Affiliate Sales Achievement Award 6723
New Product Award 12163
New Product Showcase Award 3372
William O'Dell Award 3034
Outstanding Booth Awards 13980
Outstanding Business Leader Awards 16573
Pacesetter of the Year Award 14774
Paragon Awards 14775
Parlin Award 3035
Partnership Award 8936
Esther Peterson Consumer Service Award 9662
D. Richard Petrizzo Award for Career Achievement 14776
PROMAX Awards 17679
Promotion Retailer of the Year Award 5833
Public Relations/Development/Marketing/ Director of the Year Award 20352
Sidney R. Rabb Award 9663
Reggie Awards 17683
Frank M. Rhatigan Award 10313
H. Paul Root Award 3036
Silver Apple 8929
Silver Shovel Award 11771
Gale M. Spowers Marketing Award 17528
Supplier of the Year 13668
Support Company of the Year 13669
Target Award 8927
Technology Marketing ICON Awards 223
TELO Award 4735
Vanguard Award for Marketing 14579
Yearbook Marketing Award 8177

Martial arts

Centurion Award 548
Chinese Martial Arts Leadership Award 549
Chinese Martial Arts Outstanding Service Award 550
Bud Estes Memorial Pioneer Jujitsu Award 551
Hall of Fame 22105
Instructor of the Year 22106
Jujitsu Outstanding Competitor 557
KKI Black Belt Certification 2917
Outstanding Service Award - Karate 562
Pioneer Man-of-the-Year Chinese Martial Arts Award 564
Professor Regennitter AAU Jujitsu Service Award 571
David G. Rivenes Award - Taekwondo 572
Bill Wallace Competitor of the Year Award 22107

Materials science (*See also* Ceramic engineering; Mining and metallurgy; Plastics and rubber)

Adhesion Society Award for Excellence in Adhesion Science 184
Adhesives Award 5926
AES Awards of Excellence 66
AIAA Structures, Structural Dynamics, and Materials Award 2671
ASM International and The Minerals, Metals and Materials Society Distinguished Lectureship in Materials and Society 5173
P. H. Bates Memorial Award 5930
Roger W. Boom Award 8679
Bower Award and Prize for Achievement in Science 9741
Chairman's Award 426
Chester Paul Siess Award for Excellence in Structural Research 1964
Committee D-12 Award 5937
Copper Club Award/Committee B-5 Award 5941
Distinguished Life Member 5175
Distinguished Service Award 11019
Doctoral Dissertation Award 8581
Dow Award for Excellence in Composites Research 19312
Charles B. Dudley Medal 5945
William Hunt Eisenman Award 5176
Engineering Materials Achievement Award 5177
Fatigue Achievement Award 5948
Fellow 5178
Gold Medal
  Acta Materialia, Inc. 154
  ASM International 5179
Graduate Student Award 13181
Daniel H. Green Award 5952
Historical Landmarks Designation 5181
J. Herbert Hollomon Award 155
Honorary Member 5182
Prevost Hubbard Award 5956
International Graduate Student Paper Contest 5184
International Student Paper Contest 5185
IMS and ASM Jacquet-Lucas Award for Excellence in Metallography 5186
T. Y. Lin Award 4338
Robert R. Litehiser Memorial Award 5966
Lundell-Bright Memorial Award 5968
Medal for the Advancement of Research 5187
MRS Medalist Program 13182
John Nachtsheim 5972
Nadai Medal 4532
National Materials Advancement Award 9514
Mary R. Norton Memorial Scholarship Award for Women 5973
Outstanding Young Investigator Award 13183
William T. Pearce Award 5975
David R. Peryam Award 5976
Allan Ray Putnam Service Award 5189
Frank W. Reinhart and Henry "Butch" Kuhlmann Award 5978
Albert Sauveur Achievement Award 5190
Sealants Hall of Fame Award 5984
Tilton E. Shelburne Award 5986
Smithsonian Institution Fellowship Program 18572
Charles M. A. Stine Award in Materials Engineering and Science 2789
Bradley Stoughton Award for Young Teachers 5191
Structural Materials Distinguished Materials Scientist/Engineer Award 13457
Structural Materials Distinguished Service Award 13458
The David Turnbull Lectureship 13184
Von Hippel Award 13185
Wason Medal for Materials Research 1971
Albert Easton White Distinguished Teacher Award 5192
Alan H. Yorkdale Memorial Award 5999

Mathematics (*See also* Statistics; Surveying)

ACP-CRM/CAP-CRM Prize in Theoretical and Mathematical Physics 13203
Andre Aisenstadt Prize 13204
Carl B. Allendoerfer Awards 13187
Urgel Archambault Prize in Physical Sciences and Mathematics 5537
Award for Distinguished Public Service 3040
Award in Science 17240
Awards for Scientific Achievement 21437
Ralph H. Beard Memorial Award 9016
Beckenback Book Prize 13188
George David Birkhoff Prize 18731
George David Birkhoff Prize in Applied Mathematics 3041
I. E. Block Community Lecture Series 18732
Bocher Memorial Prize 3042
Bower Award and Prize for Achievement in Science 9741
Vannevar Bush Award 15677
Certificate of Merit 13189
Chauvenet Prize 13190
Frank Nelson Cole Prizes in Algebra and Number Theory 3043
CRM-Fields-PIMS Prize 13205
Germund Dahlquist Prize 18733
Dantzig Prize 13199
George B. Dantzig Prize 18734
Richard C. DiPrima Prize 18735
Fields Medal 11744
Lester R. Ford Awards 13191
Ford Foundation Postdoctoral Diversity Fellowships 15622
Fulkerson Prize 13200
Glenn Gilbert National Leadership Award 14824
Yueh-Gin Gung and Dr. Charles Y. Hu Award for Distinguished Service to Mathematics 13192
Deborah and Franklin Tepper Haimo Award for Distinguished College or University Teaching of Mathematics 13193

Mathematics (continued)
Hans Schneider Prize in Linear Algebra 11735
Merten Hasse Prize 13194
Louise Hay Award 5527
Hedrick Lectureship 13195
Honor Award 18515
Intel International Science and Engineering Fair 18362
Linear Algebra Prize 18736
Mathematical Contest in Modeling 18737
Mathematics Excellence Award 3038
McKnight Doctoral Fellowship Program in Arts and Sciences, Mathematics, Business and Engineering 9599
Frank and Brennie Morgan Prize for Outstanding Research in Mathematics by an Undergraduate Student 18738
NAS Award in Mathematics 13842
Frederic Esser Nemmers Prize in Mathematics 16570
Rolf Nevanlinna Prize 11745
Office of Civilian Radioactive Waste Management Graduate Fellowship Program 16598
Office of Civilian Radioactive Waste Management Historically Black Colleges and Universities Undergraduate Scholarship Program 16599
Orchard-Hays Prize 13201
George Polya Award 13196
George Polya Prize 18739
President's National Medal of Science 15679
Prize for Distinguished Service to the Profession 18740
W. T. and Idalia Reid Prize in Mathematics 18741
Research Associateship Programs 15623
Alice T. Schafer Prize 5528
SDE Fellowships 18481
SIAM Activity Group on Optimization Prize 18742
Edyth May Sliffe Awards for Distinguished Junior High and High School Mathematics Teaching 13197
Student Paper Prize 18743
Student Travel Awards 18744
John L. Synge Award 18173
Henry Marshall Tory Medal 18174
U.S. Naval Academy Mathematics Award 13415
Theodore von Karman Prize 18745
John von Neumann Lecture 18746
Alan T. Waterman Award 15681
Norbert Wiener Prize 18747
James H. Wilkinson Prize in Numerical Analysis and Scientific Computing 18748

Mechanical engineering (*See also* Combustion)
Robert W. Angus Medal 7425
Joe Asali Scholarship Award 13037
ASME Medal 4502
The Atomic Energy of Canada Ltd. Award 7426
Blackall Machine Tool and Gage Award 4503
Certificate of Service 7427
Edwin F. Church Medal 4505
John P. Davis Award 4506
Dedicated Service Award 4507
C. N. Downing Award 7428
G. H. Duggan Medal 7429
Charles Martin Duke Lifeline Earthquake Engineering Award 4311
William T. Ennor Manufacturing Technology Award 4508
Fellow Award 18945
Fellow of the CSME 7430
Fluids Engineering Award 4509
Freeman Scholar Award 4510
Gas Turbine Award 4512
Melvin R. Green Codes and Standards Medal 4513
L. R. Mike Hackney Award 18946
Heat Transfer Memorial Award 4514
Henry Hess Award 4516
Archie Higdon Distinguished Educator Award 4022
Soichiro Honda Medal 4518
Honorary Fellow Award 18947
Honorary Member 4519
Internal Combustion Engine Award 4521
International Gas Turbine Institute Scholar Award 4522
George R. Irwin Medal 5960
Thomas A. Jaeger Prize 11257
Max Jakob Memorial Award 4523
Gustus L. Larson Award 4526
Machine Design Award 4528
Charles T. Main Awards 4529
Melville Medal 4530
M. Eugene Merchant Manufacturing Medal 4531
National Research Council Canada, Division of Mechanical Engineering Award 7431
Burt L. Newkirk Award 4533
Percy Nicholls Award 4534
Old Guard Prizes 4535
Rufus Oldenburger Medal 4536
Ed Payne Award 18948
Performance Test Codes Medal 4537
Pi Tau Sigma Gold Medal 4538
James Harry Potter Gold Medal 4539
Pressure Vessel and Piping Award 4540
Prime Movers Committee Award 4541
Charles Russ Richards Memorial Award 4542
R. Tom Sawyer Award 4545
I. W. Smith Award 7432
Ben C. Sparks Medal 4546
Elmer A. Sperry Award 19057
Jules Stachiewicz Medal 7433
Student Award 18949
Student Section Advisor Award 4548
Timoshenko Medal 4550
Theodore von Karman Prize 18745
Richard P. Walsh Scholarship 13229
George Westinghouse Medals 4552
Arthur L. Williston Medal 4553
George Winter Award 4368
Henry R. Worthington Medal 4554

Media (*See also* Cable television; Communications; Journalism; Radio; Television)
AAN Media Award 708
Americanism News Media Award 7671
Anthropology in Media Award 909
Arbor Day Awards 13949
ASHA Media Awards for Journalists 4662
ASJMC Distinguished Service Award 5845
The Austin Chronicle Best of Austin 6093
Awards for Excellence in Community Service, Philanthropy, and Media 19847
Awards of Excellence 5291
Best in Media Awards 7915
Biennial Communications Award 447
Howard W. Blakeslee Awards 2404
John D. Blodger Diversity Award 13235
Emery A. Brownell Media Award 15336
Esther V. Burrin Award 5383
Communications Media Award 21279
Conscience In Media Award 4469
Courage in Journalism Award 12145
Walter Cronkite Award for Excellence in Journalism and Mass Communication 8657
Edgar Dale Award 5384
Distinguished Contribution to Psychology and the Media 18900
Distinguished Women's Awards 16572
EDI Awards (Equality/Dignity/Independence) 9088
Excellence in the Media Award 21361
Exceptional Media Merit Award 15963
Betty Furness Consumer Media Service Award 8460
Gavel Awards 1533
Golden Medallion Media Awards 19759
Grants for Arts Projects 14930
Vernon Henley Media Award 2042
IAFF Media Awards Contest 11355
Individual Artist Fellowship 16628
Institute Honors for Collaborative Achievements 2718
Anson Jones, M.D., Award 20032
Sena Kautz Merit Award 5385
Richard B. Lewis Memorial Award 5358
Carroll Sterling Masterson Award & Outstanding Women's Awards 22093
Jessie McCanse Award 15868
Media Award
American Association of Critical-Care Nurses 1178
Emergency Nurses Association 9247
Special Libraries Association 19553
United Nations Association of Rochester 20362
Media Awards 18502
Media Medal 12699
Media Psychology Graduate Student Research Award 18913
Mediaweek's Media All-Stars 221
Mediaweek's Media Plan of the Year 222
Mental Health Media Awards 15378
Meritorious Contributions to Psychology on the Part of Nonpsychologists 18914
National Award for Media Excellence 15577
National Mass Media Award 2888
National Media Award 7272
National Psychology Awards for Excellence in the Media 18915
New Mexico Juried Exhibition 13689
News Media Award for Community Service 3574
Oscars in Agriculture 21030
Peggy Leach Pfeiffer Service Award 5386
Pollie Awards 1385
Residential Fellowships 9758
Rogers Communications Inc. Media Award for Coverage of the Arts 7038
Al Schoenfield Media Award 12060
Fred Sgambati Award 7231
SHINE (Sexual Health in Entertainment) Awards 13238
Small Business Advocates of the Year 20834
Southwest Juried Exhibition 13690

Media (continued)

Toronto Arts Awards 20112
VFW News Media Award 21343
Jake Wade Memorial Award and Honorary Membership 8192

Medical economics
Elmer Award 13242
Robert T. Hellrung Award 13243
Lifetime Achievement Award 13244
Pinnacle Award 13245

Medical education
Alpha Omega Alpha Distinguished Teacher Awards 482
American College of Physicians Distinguished Teacher Award 1916
APA Teaching Award 593
ASCP Associate Member Lifetime Achievement Award 3963
ASCP Associate Member Section Distinguished Service Award 3964
Oswald Avery Award 10790
Award for Outstanding Contributions in Research and Education 1859
Baxter Healthcare, Scientific Products Division Graduate Scholarship 3951
The Ben Shuster Memorial Award 666
Elisabeth Bing Award 12669
Bristol-Myers Squibb Award for Excellence in Medical Teaching 6625
Irwin Chabon Award 12670
Chapter of the Year 12671
Chapter Program of the Year 12672
Clinical Instructor of the Year Award 1292
Dannon Institute Award for Excellence in Medical/Dental Nutrition Education 3957
Diabetes Camp Educator Award 1184
Diabetes Educator of the Year Award 1185
John Dickinson Teacher Award 669
Didactic Instructor of the Year Award 1293
Distinguished Educator Award 4072
Distinguished Service Award 1186
East Baton Rouge Parish Medical Society Premedical Scholarship Award 9069
Education Award 5873
Fellows Program Award 5840
Alexander Fleming Award 10791
Fleur-de-Lis Awards 12980
Abraham Flexner Award for Distinguished Service to Medical Education 5560
Fresno-Madera Medical Society Scholarship 9773
Harry L. Gardner Award 3021
Gifted Teacher 1839
Gold Key Awards 21004
Duncan Graham Award 18151
Ruth I. Heinemann Memorial Trustee Award for Educational Development 3953
David M. Hume Memorial Award 15322
Thomas W. Johnson Award 675
Marjorie Karmel Award 12674
Lay Education Project Award 780
Linn Chapter Scholarship 1270
Mary McMillan Lecture Award 3493
Medical Education Lifetime Achievement Awards 782
Robin H. Mendelson Memorial Awards 3955
Samuel Charles Miller Memorial Lecture Award 737
Minneapolis Foundation 13588
MS Public Education Awards 15400
National Research Awards 5127
New Hanover-Pender Co. Medical Society Premedical Scholarship 16161
Thomas L. Northup Lecturer Award 741
Nutrition Education Award 1187
Ortho Pharmaceutical Corporation and McNeil Pharmaceutical Young Investigator Award in Infectious Diseases 10792
Outstanding Chapter of the Year Award 1188
Outstanding Contributions in Education 990
Pfizer Minority Summer Fellowship Award 1898
Professional Education Project Award 790
Program Director of the Year Award 1298
Research in Action Award 1300
Nancy C. A. Roeske Certificate of Recognition for Excellence in Medical Student Education 3636
ASCP Distinguished Pathology Educator Award Honoring H. P. Smith 3970
Society Citation 10793
Allene Von Son Diabetes Educator Award 1189
Special Awards 10333
Special Recognition Award 12678
Traveling Fellowship Award 1605
Seymour D. Vestermark Award for Psychiatric Education 3641
Robert Wartenberg Lecture 706
Marian Williams Award for Research in Physical Therapy 3499
Catherine Worthingham Fellows of APTA 3500
Wyeth Young Investigator Award in Vaccine Development 10794

Medical illustration
AMI Salon Awards 5756
William P. Didusch Award 4787
Lifetime Achievement Award 5757
Literary Award 5758
Outstanding Service Award 5759

Medical journalism (*See also* Science journalism)
AAAS Mass Media Science and Engineering Fellowship 3506
AAN Media Award 708
Walter C. Alvarez Memorial Award 3081
AMWA Medical Book Awards 3082
Art of Reporting Award 9930
ASCP Associate Member Section Distinguished Service Award 3964
Susan Baird Oncology Excellence in Writing Award in Clinical Practice 16711
Biomedical Instrumentation & Technology Outstanding Paper Awards 5489
Howard W. Blaskeslee Awards 2404
Cardiovascular Young Investigator Award 19227
McKeen Cattell Memorial Award 1847
Russell L. Cecil Arthritis Medical Journalism Awards 5125
Clinical Research Award in Periodontology 802
ECRI Medical Technology Media Awards Program 9150
Excellence of Scholarship and Consistency of Contributions to the Oncology Nursing Literature Award 16717
Edgar C. Hayhow Award 1870
Health Journalism Awards 1802
JNMA Awards for Medical Journalism 15370
Anson Jones, M.D., Award 20032
Journalism Awards 12788
Manuscript Award 11708
Eric W. Martin Memorial Award 3083
John P. McGovern Award 3084
Moore Award 1287
Robert T. Morse Writer's Award 3630
Cordelia Myers Writers Award 3297
National Media Awards 1829
Newsletter of the Year Award 15720
Outstanding Chapter Newsletter Award 15211
George Polk Awards 12915
Public Education Award for Excellence in Plastic Surgery Journalism 17384
Radiology News Awards Competition 1943
Fred L. Soper Award for Excellence in Health Literature 17060
State Society Publications Awards 3073
Harold Swanberg Distinguished Service Award 3085
Rennie Taylor/Alton Blakeslee Fellowship in Science Writing 8563
Weil Award 1289

Medical librarianship
Estelle Brodman Award for the Academic Medical Librarian of the Year 13251
Lois Ann Colaianni Award for Excellence and Achievement in Hospital Librarianship 13252
Cunningham Memorial International Fellowship 13253
Louise Darling Medal for Distinguished Achievement in Collection Development in the Health Sciences 13254
Janet Doe Lectureship 13255
Fellows and Honorary Members 13256
ISI Frank Bradway Rogers Information Advancement Award 13258
Joseph Leiter Lectureship 13259
Majors/MLA Chapter Project of the Year Award 13260
John P. McGovern Award Lectureship 13261
MLA Research, Development and Demonstration Projects Awards 13263
MLA Scholarships and Fellowships 13264
Marcia C. Noyes Award 13265
President's Award 13266
Rittenhouse Award 13267

Medical research (*See also* Scientific research)
AACP Clinical Research Award 631
AAP Nutrition Award 757
ABOHN Research Award 1570
The (ACP) American College of Psychiatrists Dean Award 1936
ACS Medal of Honor 1634
ADA Career Development Awards 2134
Ada-EASD Trans-Atlantic Fellowship Award 2135
ADA Research Awards 2136
AFUD Ph.D. Research Scholar Program 4799
AFUD Research Scholars 4800
AHS/Merck US Human Health Migraine and Women's Health Research Award 2388
Alfred Soffer Research Awards 1843
Harvey Stuart Allen Distinguished Service Award 1598

Medical (continued)

Alpha Omega Alpha Student Research Fellowships 484
Nicolas Andry Award 5584
Annual Central Prize Award, President's Certificate of Merit Award, and Central Poster Award 7764
APA Award for Research in Psychiatry 3612
APA Research Award 592
APIC New Investigator Research Award 5456
Apotex Award 7459
Arthroscopy Research Grants 5131
ASCP Sheard - Sanford Medical Student Award 3967
ASH Scholar Awards 4443
Edwin B. Astwood Lecture Award 9258
Gerald D. Aurbach Lecture Award 9259
Louis Avioli Founders Award 3930
Award for Distinguished Research in the Biomedical Sciences 5559
Award for Outstanding Contributions in Research and Education 1859
Award for Outstanding Research in the Pathophysiology of Osteoporosis 3931
Award of Merit 2402
Bard UTI Research Award 5457
Barringer Medal 1204
Frederic C. Bartter Award 3932
Baxter Allegiance Prize Health Services Research 5912
BD Biosciences Investigator Award 1242
Paul B. Beeson Career Development Awards in Aging Research 2222
A. E. Bennett Research Awards 19071
Bernstein Grant 667
Albion O. Bernstein, M.D. Award 13272
Pravin N. Bhatt Young Investigator Award 1023
Bio-Medical Research 5129
Marie T. Bonazinga Award 18785
Boothby - Edwards Award 231
Jane Bozart Research Grant 16678
M. D. K. Bremner Awards 844
Bristol-Myers Squibb Award 7461
Dr. Gordon D. Brown Memorial Training Award in Diabetes 13718
Bruce F. Cain Memorial Award 964
Camps For Kids 7577
Canadian Cardiovascular Society Research Achievement Award 6627
Career Development Awards 965
Philip K. Caves Award 11933
CFF/NIH Funding Award 8696
Chairman's Citation 12785
J.D. Chastain Renal Research Award 15330
Clemson Awards 18647
Clinical Center of Excellence 21689
Clinical Investigator Lecture Award 9260
Clinical Medicine Research Award 9989
Clinical Research Grants 2137
Clinician - Scientist Award 2405
G. H. A Clowes Memorial Award 966
Cogan Award 5464
William B. Coley Award 7561
Collaborative Research Award 9071
J.B. Collip Diabetes Studentship 13719
Community Hospital Award 7765
Community Service Award 668
Community Service Grant 13062
Continuing Education Achievement Awards 746
Cooper Award 979
Mary Jo Cosio, RN Award 15332
Dr. Maurice H. Cottle Honor Award 3848
Dr. James W. Cruickshank Award 694
Cystic Fibrosis Foundation Special Research Awards 8697
William Dameshek Award 12786
Dameshek Prize 4444
Damien - Dutton Award 8726
Chaim Danieli Young Professional Award 11965
DeVilliers Award 12787
Diabetes Research Grants 12473
Seymour Diamond Clinical Fellowship in Headache Education 15188
John Dickinson Teacher Award 669
Distinguished Investigator Award 13923
Distinguished Physician Award 1282
Distinguished Researcher Award 1283
Distinguished Scientist Award 10365
Distinguished Service Award
American Cancer Society 1636
American Society for Bioethics and Humanities 3925
American Society of Abdominal Surgeons 4210
Distinguished Service Awards 21003
Ivor Dunsford Memorial Award 1104
John Dystel Prize for Multiple Sclerosis Research 697
John Dystel Prize 15396
Eagle Award 1864
Wilton R. Earle Award 18724
Marie H. Eldredge Award 3617
Eli Lilly Travel Fellowship Award 19072
Gertrude Elion Cancer Research Award 967
Elsevier Research Initiative Award 9708
EMS Award 9304
Epilepsy Research Award for Outstanding Contributions to the Pharmacology of Antiepileptic Drugs 4171
Shelia Essey Award 698
Established Investigator Award 2406
Everett Idris Evans Memorial Lecture 1601
Faculty Research Award 9072
Honor B. Fell Student Award 18725
Fellowship and Grant Award Program 8892
Fellowship Award 8728
Fellowship for Cancer Research 968
Miles and Shirley Fiterman Foundation Basic Research Awards 9709
Five Year Research Support Program 12979
Fletcher Scholar Awards 7557
Fleur-de-Lis Awards 12980
Founders Award 18648
Glenn A. Fry Lecture Award 720
Jacob Heskel Gabbay Award in Biotechnology and Medicine 18126
Garry/Labbe Award 983
Goodman and Gilman Award in Drug Receptor Pharmacology 4172
William D. Godbey Award 5734
Golseth Young Investigator Award 1284
William T. Grant Faculty Scholars 21633
Morten Grove-Rasmussen Memorial Award 1109
Lila Gruber Memorial Cancer Research Award and Lectureship 638
William Haddon Jr., M.D., Memorial Top Student Paper 19495
Sarah Haley Memorial Award for Clinical Excellence 11966
Ham-Wasserman Lecture 4445
Health Science Award 4794
Heiser Program for Research in Leprosy and Tuberculosis 10384
Lucien Dean Hertert Memorial Award 1092
Martha N. Hill New Investigator Award 2410
Hoechst Marion Roussel Postdoctoral Fellowship in Nosocomial Infection Research and Training 15120
Alexander Hollaender Award 9305
Honorary Fellow Award 2859
Honorary Member 1285
Hope E. Hopps Award 18726
Charles S. Houston Research Award 21623
Lee C. Howley, Sr. Prize for Research in Arthritis 5126
Humanitarian Efforts Award 751
David M. Hume Memorial Award 15322
Charles A. Hunter, Jr. Award Thesis 2379
Sidney H. Ingbar Distinguished Service Award 9261
Jaffe Family Foundation Food Allergy Research Award 615
Dr. Paul Janssen Schizophrenia Research Award 8200
Louise Ada Jarabak Memorial International Teachers and Research Award 1321
Junior Faculty Award 2138
Kaplan Award for Chronic Daily Headache 2389
Louis N. Katz Basic Science Research Prize for Young Investigators 2412
APA/Kempf Fund Award for Research Development in Psychobiological Psychiatry 3623
Dr. John J. Kenny Award 12789
Charles F. Kettering Medal 9920
Fred Conrad Koch Award 9262
Jessie Stevenson Kovalenko Medal 13834
Kupfer Award 5466
Mary Woodard Lasker Award for Public Service in Behalf of Medical Research 12695
Albert Lasker Award for Special Achievement in Medical Research 12696
Albert Lasker Basic Medical Research Award 12697
Robert S. Laufer PhD Memorial Award for Outstanding Scientific Achievement 11967
Katharine A. Lembright Award 2413
Leo Award 14957
Samuel A. Levine Young Clinical Investigator Award 2414
Lifetime Achievement Award
American Society for Bioethics and Humanities 3926
International Society for Traumatic Stress Studies 11968
Lupus Foundation of America, Arizona Area Coordinator 12983
Eric Liljencrantz Award 236
APA/Lilly Products Resident Research Award 3625
APA/Lilly Psychiatric Research Fellowship 3626
Frank Allison Linville's R. H. Wright Award in Olfactory Research 18527
Lions SightFirst Diabetic Retinopathy Research Program 2139
Walter Lorenz Research Award 1912

Medical (continued)

Richard Lounsbery Award 13835
Ludwig-Seidel Award 597
Man/Woman of the Year 12475
Melvin L. Marcus Young Investigator Awards in Cardiovascular Sciences 2415
Marsh and Henning Awards 21351
Masters 1923
Maury and Hinman research awards 21410
Cecile Lehman Mayer Research Award 1844
William R. McAlpin, Jr. Mental Health Research Achievement Award 15377
Kenneth B. McCredie 12790
Ronald McDonald House Charities Grants Program 18118
Walter P. McHugh Award 5776
William M. McKinney Award 4573
McLaughlin Medal 18168
Medal of Honour 6839
Media Awards 12791
Medical Research Grants 18554
Medical Student Diabetes Research Fellowship Program 2140
Medical Student Essay Awards 702
Memorial Hall of Fame Award 2860
Robin H. Mendelson Memorial Awards 3955
Mentor-Based Minority Fellowship 2141
Mentor-Based Postdoctoral Fellowships 2142
William S. Middleton Award 20561
Miles and Shirley Fisherman Foundation Awards for Clinical Research 9711
Minority Scientist Development Award 2416
S. Weir Mitchell Award 703
Moore Award 1287
Joseph F. Morgan Award 18727
Most Outstanding Abstract Award 3934
Charles S. Mott Medal 9921
Dr. John Nardini Award 2211
National Hypertension Association Recognition Award 15252
National Leadership Award 12792
National Lupus Hall of Fame 12981
National Research Awards 5127
National Research Service Awards 15272
William F. Neuman Award 3935
NINDS Javits Neuroscience Investigator Award 20499
Thomas L. Northup Lecturer Award 741
Nursing Research Award 20025
Nutritional Research Award 17170
Oceaneering International Award 20291
Alton Ochsner Award Relating Smoking and Health 16609
William H. Oldendorf Award 4574
Ernst Oppenheimer Memorial Award 9263
Irvine H. Page Award for Young Investigators 2417
Paid Research Appointments 21085
Passano Foundation Award 17101
Patient Aid 12798
Pediatric Dermatology Fellows/Residents Research Award 18831
Pediatric Dermatology Research Grant 18832
Pediatric Resident Research Award 787
Pfizer Mycology Postdoctoral Fellowship/ John P. Utz Award 15121
Physician Scientist Training Award 2143
Pilot and Feasibility Awards 8698
Pioneer Award for Milestones 11555
Judith Graham Pool Postgraduate Research Fellowships in Hemophilia 15212
Population-Specific Research Project Award 19851
Postdoctoral Fellowship in Emerging Infectious Diseases 15122
Postdoctoral Fellowship in Infectious Disease Training and Herpes Virus Research 15123
Postdoctoral Fellowships in Infectious Diseases 15124
Practicing Urologist Research Awards 4801
Practitioner Research Award 789
Charles F. Prentice Medal 724
Presidential Student/Post-Doctoral Award 18787
Professional Organization Awards 9073
Donette Rachelle White Memorial Award 6608
Bret Ratner Award 791
Rawls-Palmer Progress in Medicine Lecture and Award 3976
Research Achievement Award 2418
Research Award
  Lamaze International 12677
  Lupus Foundation of Minnesota 12987
Research Awards
  American Heart Association, Talbot County Branch 2423
  Fraternal Order of Eagles, Havre No. 166 9744
Research Awards in Otolaryngology 754
Research Fellowship Grants 17385
Research Grants
  American Lung Association of Eastern Missouri 3017
  Plastic Surgery Educational Foundation 17386
Research in Action Award 1300
Research Performance Awards 21411
Research Recognition Award 16804
Research Scholar Award 9712
Resident Award 19303
Resident/Fellow Travel Award Program - Annual Scientific Meeting 2390
Resident Research Award 16805
Resident Research Grants 670
Respiratory Diseases Research Award 616
Return of the Child Award 12793
Gideon A. Rodan Excellence in Mentorship Award 3937
Lewis S. Rosenstiel Award for Distinguished Work in Basic Medical Research 18127
Stephen Rothman Memorial Award 18778
Rubinstein Award 1288
Bruce S. Schoenberg International Award in Neuroepidemiology 705
Michael Schoenbrun Award 12794
Science Recognition Award for New Investigators 8110
Donald W. Seldin Award 15325
Shands Award 16914
Charles W. Shilling Award 20292
Edwin Shneidman Award 1438
Alfred P. Sloan, Jr. Medal 9922
Small Research Grants Program 10585
John S. Song Award 18728
Special Recognition Award 12795
Spiral of Life Award 12796
Fred Springer Award 3365
Arthur Steindler Award 16915
Henry M. Stratton Medal 4446
Ralph I. Straus Award 15402
Stritch Medal 12973
Student and New Investigator Travel Awards 9306
Student Awards for Outstanding Research 18649
Student Competition 11556
Student Research Fellowships 9713
Student Research Training Award 16806
Summer Student Fellowships 4802
Sustaining Membership Lecture Award 5787
Tanner-Vandeput-Boswick Prize for Burn Research 11442
Dr. Murray Thelin Researcher of the Year Award 15213
E. Donnall Thomas Lecture and Prize 4447
Travel Grant 1004
Travel Grants 969
Trudeau Award 3015
Arnold D. Tuttle Award 242
USF Grant Awards 18367
Weil Award 1289
Richard E. Weitzman Award 9264
Edward J. Welsh M.D. Memorial Research Fund 3019
Paul Dudley White Award 5790
Philip R. White Memorial Award 18729
Wightman Special Achievement Award 9851
Marian Williams Award for Research in Physical Therapy 3499
Robert H. Williams Distinguished Leadership Award 9265
Harold G. Wolff Lecture Award 2391
Irving S. Wright Award of Distinction 2223
Young Investigator Award 13925
Young Investigator Awards
  American College of Chest Physicians 1845
  Cancer Research Foundation 7558
  National Foundation for Infectious Diseases 15125
Cournand and Comroe Young Investigator Prize 2420
Young Investigator Prizes in Thrombosis 2421
Young Investigators Award 1831
Young Investigators Awards 10369
Zak Award 1009
Ziskind-Somerfeld Research Award 19075

Medical technology (*See also* Biomedical engineering; Biotechnology)

$100,000 Lemelson-MIT Lifetime Achievement Award 12776
AABB Scholarship Awards 1100
Abbott Award 7457
ASCP Associate Member Lifetime Achievement Award 3963
Baxter Award 7460
Baxter Healthcare, Scientific Products Division Graduate Scholarship 3951
The Becky Award 3062
Becton Dickinson Career Achievement Award 5494
Maureen Berkeley Memorial Award 4403
bioMerieux Award 11580
Leona Lyons Carter Award 3063
L. J. Cartwright Award 6917
Emily Cooley Memorial Award
  American Association of Blood Banks 1103
  American Association of Blood Banks 1102

Medical (continued)

Dade International Award 11581
Distinguished Achievement Awards 3064
Charles R. Drew Award 3825
ECRI Medical Technology Media Awards Program 9150
Education Award 5873
Educational Scholarships 15715
Addine Erskine Outstanding Achievement Award 1091
Evergreen Latex Award 11582
Exceptional Merit Awards 3065
Sally Frank Memorial Lecturer Award 1107
William J. Fry Memorial Lecture 2857
Gloria F. "Mike" Gilbert Memorial Trustee Award 3952
Golseth Young Investigator Award 1284
Good Poster Award 11583
Morten Grove-Rasmussen Memorial Award 1109
William J. Hacker Memorial Award 15716
Ruth I. Heinemann Memorial Trustee Award for Educational Development 3953
Hemphill-Jordan Leadership Award 1110
Histotechnologist of the Year Award 15717
Joseph H. Holmes Pioneer Award 2858
Honorary Fellow Award 2859
E. I. Hood Award 6918
IAMLT Award for Outstanding Services to Medical Laboratory Technology 11584
IAMLT General Award 11585
IAMLT Scholarship 11586
Joseph J. Kleiner Memorial Awards 3954
Legislation Award 5875
Lee G. Luna Foreign Travel Scholarship 15718
Dr. M. Mallett Student Award 6919
Marriott-Carlson Award 5549
J. B. McCormick, M.D. Award 15719
Medallion of Merit 3066
Medical Crew/Crew Member of the Year Award 5550
Memorial Hall of Fame Award 2860
Robin H. Mendelson Memorial Awards 3955
Nordic Award 11587
Order of the Golden Microscope 3067
Rosemary and Donald Ostermeier Memorial Award 15721
Outstanding Achievement Award 1113
PACS Technology Award 6920
Past President's Award 11588
Dr. Petrie Memorial Award 6921
Philips Rose Bowl 6922
The Pillar Award 3069
President's Award 3070
Public Relations Award 5876
George Reason Memorial Cup 6923
Stanley S. Reitman Memorial Award 1093
RMA of the Year 3071
SBET/Renshaw-Heilman BMET of the Year Award 15737
The Silver Service Award 3072
Student Scholarships 15722
Sysmex Award 11589
Technical and Feature Writing Awards 3074
Technologist of the Year 3075
Paul F. Truran, Jr., Medical Materiel and Logistics Management Award 5788
Visionary Award 6743
Young Investigator Award 5492

Medicine (*See also* Biomedical engineering; Biotechnology; Health care; History of medicine; Occupational health; Rehabilitation and therapy; Toxicology; specific fields of medicine, e.g. Anesthesiology)
$500,000 Lemelson-MIT Prize 12777
AACC International Travel Fellowship Award 971
AACC Past President's Award 973
AAFP Award of Merit 672
AAPA National and International Humanitarian Physician Assistant of the Year 813
AAPA Outstanding Physician Assistant of the Year Award 814
AAPA PA Awareness Achievement Award 815
AAPA Rural Physician Assistant of the Year 816
Achievement 7008
ACS Award in Separations Science and Technology 1721
Acupuncture Patient of the Year 1314
Acupuncturist of the Year 1315
Airman of the Year 9640
Fuller Albright Award 3929
Alfred Soffer Research Awards 1843
Alpha Omega Alpha Student Essay Award 483
American College of Physicians Award 1915
American Laryngological Association Award 2924
AMSUS Medical Student Award 5764
Annual Awards Program 21949
Annual National Art Exhibition 3504
Leonard Apt Lecture 760
Harry Archer Award 1910
Bailey K. Ashford Medal 4629
Australia/New Zealand Chapter Traveling Fellowship 1946
Award for Outstanding Service to Maltreated Children 761
Award for Service 13247
Award of Excellence 16861
Award of Merit
  American Otological Society 3359
  Association for the Advancement of Automotive Medicine 5477
Award of Outstanding Achievement 7137
Award of Recognition 20284
Awards of Distinction in Programs 15201
Awards of Merit 1101
William G. Bartholome Award for Ethical Excellence 763
Benjamin Castleman Award 20375
Albion O. Bernstein, M.D. Award 13272
Carroll L. Birch Award 3077
Trish Blair Leadership Services Awards 1484
BMC Research Paper Prize 7138
BMMA Awards 6393
Joel T. Boone Award 5765
Dr. Kenneth Brinkhous Physician of the Year Award 15202
Caitlin Lynch Memorial Fund Award 21289
John R. Cameron Young Investigator Award 1366
Canadian Hospital Librarian of the Year Award 7139
Career Achievement Award 18794
Casselberry Fund 2925
Castellani - Reiss Medal and Award 11990
William Fields Caveness, M.D. Memorial Award 6605
CCFC Book Prize 8653
CCFC/CAG Student Research Award 8654
Certificate of Achievement 4786
Certificate of Appreciation 10622
Certificate of Commendation 673
Certificate of Merit
  Canadian Society of Diagnostic Medical Sonographers 7454
  Huntington Society of Canada 10623
Chairman's Award 15319
Chair's Award 17463
Philip Champney Prize 12644
John D. Chase Award for Physician Executive Excellence 5767
Chinese American Medical Society Scientific Achievement Award 7929
CIPPS Distinguished Service Awards 7159
Ralph O. Claypoole, Sr. Memorial Award 1918
Clinical Scientist in Nephrology Fellowship Award 2919
Co-Sponsor Award 7009
Coder of the Year Award 820
Riva Cohen Award 444
Colposcopy Recognition Award 3978
Denton A. Cooley Leadership Award 20007
William D. Coolidge Award 1367
Council's Distinguished Pathologist Award 20376
Dag Hammarksjold Award 11382
Farrington Daniels Award 1368
Nicholas E. Davies Memorial Scholar Award for Scholarly Activities in Humanities and History of Medicine 1919
William C. Dement Academic Achievement Award 837
deRoaldes Award 2927
William P. Didusch Award 4787
Director's Award 17464
Distinguished Achievement Award 9707
Distinguished Contribution Award 4788
Distinguished Service Award
  American Liver Foundation 3011
  American Society for Gastrointestinal Endoscopy 4073
  American Urological Association 4789
  Flying Physicians Association 9641
  National Kidney Foundation 15320
  Society for Medical Decision Making 18795
Distinguished Volunteer Service Award 445
John Elliott Memorial Award 1105
Ralph W. Ellison Memorial Prize 15369
Essay Contest for Professionals in Rehabilitation 1986
Etta Nathan Award 6283
Excellence in Ultrasound 7455
F. K. Mostofi Distinguished Service Award 20377
Bernard Fantus, M.D., Medal 1106
Fellow
  American Academy of Somnology 842
  Center for Advanced Study in the Behavioral Sciences 7697
Giles F. Filley Memorial Awards for Excellence in Respiratory Physiology and Medicine 3517
Finkelstein Award 8655
John Fisher Memorial Prize 3913
Fleischner Society Memorial Award 9570
Jonathan Forman Award 651
Founders Award 6606

Medicine (continued)

Founder's Award 17465
Founder's Medal 5771
Founders of Adolescent Health Award 771
Chapman-Franzmeier Memorial Award 1108
Eugene Fuller Triennial Prostate Award 4790
G. Trombetta Teaching Award 3979
Stephen L. Gans Distinguished Overseas Lectureship 772
Janet M. Glasgow Achievement Award 3078
Glasgow-Rubin Student Achievement 3079
Gold Cane Award 4791
Gold Cystoscope Award 4792
Gold Medal Awards 6290
Gold Medal of Honor 21911
Gold Member 11164
Golden Hysteroscope Award 1207
Golden Laparoscope Award 1208
Gottesfeld Award 19103
Gradiva Awards 14052
James H. Graham Award of Merit 18152
Sylvia Sorkin Greenfield Award 1369
Ramon Guiteras Award 4793
Hall of Outstanding Americans 15986
Mark O. Hatfield Public Policy Award 838
The Jay Healey Award 4486
Health Science Award 4794
Donald O. Hebb Distinguished Contribution 5381
Philip Hench Award 5773
Georg Charles de Hevesy Nuclear Pioneer Award 19228
Hirsh Award 1878
Jerome J. Hoffman Award for the Best Postgraduate Paper 1209
Honorary Fellow 1920
Honorary Life Membership
  Canadian Health Libraries Association 7141
  International Association of Astacology 11285
Honorary Member
  American Academy of Family Physicians 674
  American Otological Society 3360
  Flying Physicians Association 9642
  Society of Nuclear Medicine 19229
Humanitarian Award
  American College of Oral and Maxillofacial Surgeons 1911
  Doctors to the World 8973
Oscar B. Hunter Memorial Award in Therapeutics of the ASCPT 3975
IAPAC Hero In Medicine 11383
Sidney H. Ingbar Distinguished Lectureship Award 4745
Intel International Science and Engineering Fair 18362
International Guest Scholarships 1949
International Hemophilia Training Centres Fellowships 21909
International Oxidative Therapists Award 11251
International Travel Fellowship Awards 9710
JA Campbell Research Award 7022
Alvin H. Jacobs Award 778
Annual Conrad Jobst Foundation Award 1988
John Alexander Media Award 13671
Joseph F. Boyle Award for Distinguished Public Service 1921
Robert A. Kehoe Award of Merit 1906
Richard A. Kern Lecture Award 5774
Izaak Walton Killam Memorial Prizes 6800
John W. Kirklin MD Award 1442
Nathaniel Kleitman Distinguished Service Award 839
Lamaze Childbirth Educator Program Scholarship 12675
Karl Landsteiner Memorial Award 1112
Robert Lapham Outstanding Service Award 9010
Lay Education Project Award 780
Layman Support Award 15189
Carlton Lee Award 652
Lee B. Lusted Student Prizes 18796
Legislator of the Year 1316
Joseph Augustin LePrince Medal 4631
Letourneau Award 1879
Lifetime Achievement Award 4669
Abraham Lilienfeld Student Prize Paper 18670
Local Chapeter of the Year 821
Walter Lorenz Research Award 1912
Magida Award 9392
Jonathan Mann Health & Human Rights Award 11384
E. O. Martin Medallion 1363
Master Endoscopist Award 4074
Masters 1923
Carroll Sterling Masterson Award & Outstanding Women's Awards 22093
Cecile Lehman Mayer Research Award 1844
Medal in Medicine 18153
Media Support Award 15190
Medical Education Lifetime Achievement Awards 782
Medicinal Chemistry Award 1771
Thomas T. Mercer Joint Prize 956
Meritorious Service Award 16605
A. J. Mirkin Service Award 5478
Carl A. Moyer Resident Award 1603
MSMA Community Service Award 13513
National Federation of the Blind Scholarship Program 15039
National Headache Foundation Lectureship Award 15191
National Health Law Moot Court Competition 7725
National Hypertension Association Recognition Award 15252
National Torchbearer Award 2920
Neonatal Education Award 783
Networker of the Year Award 822
James E. Newcomb Award 2928
Outstanding Achievement Award 1113
Outstanding Chapter Leadership Award 15210
Outstanding Community Service Award 5561
Outstanding Contributions for a Publication in the *Journal of Clinical Chemistry* Award 989
Outstanding Contributions Through Service to the Profession of Clinical Chemistry 991
Outstanding Contributions to Clinical Chemistry 992
Outstanding Medical Information Management Executive Award 5779
Outstanding Rural PA Award 9011
Outstanding Short Course 18797
Outstanding Statistical Application Awards 4694
Outstanding Student Award 3068
Outstanding Volunteer Clinical Teacher Award 1925
Pham bieu Tam MD Award 21366
John Phillips Memorial Award 1926
Physician Assistant Award 5780
Physician Assistant of the Year 16862
Physician of the Year 1364
Pilot and Feasibility Awards 21465
Presidential Citations 4795
Presidents Award 4487
President's Award
  Lamaze International 12676
  National Kidney Foundation 15323
Joseph Price Oration 2380
Professional Education Project Award 790
Professional Support Award 15192
PSPA Student Scholarship 17200
Recognition Awards 1383
Walter Reed Medal 4632
Research Presentation Award 11393
Resident Award 1931
Resident/Fellow Essay Award 5133
Resident Research Award 3849
Richmond Cerebral Palsy Center Award 603
David E. Rogers Award 5562
Richard and Hinda Rosenthal Foundation Awards 1927
Arnold M. Salzberg Mentorship Award 794
W. Frederick Sample Student Excellence Award 19104
Schindler Award 4075
Shirley R. Schneck Award 18660
Schwartz Award 1880
Scientific Poster Awards 1913
Scoville Award 21912
Lewis L. Seaman Awards for Oustanding Operational Support 5783
Thomas E. Shaffer Award 796
Smissman-Bristol-Myers-Squibb Award 1789
Dale Smith Memorial Award 1114
Special Certificate of Appreciation 4796
Specialists in Blood Banking Scholarship Awards 1116
Colonel Thomas L. Spruiell Medical Field Training Excersize Planner Award 5784
Paul Starr Clinical Day Lectureship Prize 4746
John D. States Award 5479
Alfred Stengel Memorial Award 1928
Stowell-Orbison Awards for Pathologists-in-Training 20380
Stritch Medal 12973
Charles A. Stuart Memorial Lectureship 6666
Peter Sweetland Award of Excellence 17305
Henrietta Szold Award 10215
Tanner-Vandeput-Boswick Prize for Burn Research 11442
Tanner-Vandeput Prize for Burn Research 11924
Tenth Anniversary Commemorative Award 7142
Tibor Greenwalt Scientific Lectureship 1117
Tony Lipson Memorial Fund Award 21290
Transfusion Medicine Fellowship Awards 1118
Trustees' Award 15326

Medicine (continued)
Gabriel F. Tucker Award 2929
Twentieth Anniversary Professional Development Award 7143
Edwin F. Ullman Award 1005
Susan Vincent Memorial Scholarship 9012
Volunteer of Year Award 7010
Martin Wagner Memorial Award 15328
John G. Walsh Award 676
Sir Henry Wellcome Medal and Prize 5789
Wightman Special Achievement Award 9851
Clifford G. Woolfe Award 174
Hugh Hampton Young Award 4797
Young Investigator Award
Association for the Advancement of Medical Instrumentation 5492
International College of Angiology 11488
Society for Medical Decision Making 18798
Young Investigator Awards 1845
Young Investigator's Award 840
Young Investigators Award 7023
Young Neurosurgeons Award 21913

Medicine, aerospace *See* Aerospace medicine

Medicine, emergency *See* Emergency medicine

Medicine, preventive *See* Preventive medicine

Medicine, sports *See* Sports medicine

Medicine, veterinary *See* Veterinary medicine

Medieval studies
John Nicholas Brown Prize 13274
Van Courtlandt Elliott Prize 13275
Haskins Medal 13276
Richard III Scholarship for Medieval Studies 18040

Meetings *See* Conventions

Membership organizations
CFA Totem 7098
Irregular Shillings 6195
Morley/Montgomery Award 6196
Outstanding Program 6191

Mental health (*See also* Counseling; Psychiatry)
Addison Pope, MD Award 6431
Advocacy Award 18026
Award for Exemplary State/University Collaboration 3613
Award for Patient Advocacy 3614
Award of Special Recognition 6432
Awards of Excellence 14751
Clifford W. Beers Award 15372
Sandy Brandt Volunteer Service Award 15373
Ruth P. Brudney Award 15374
The Compassionate Friends Award 8322
Consumer Involvement Award 7267
Counselor Educator of the Year 3087
Counselor of the Year 3088
Davenport Distinguished Service Award 13297
Bea Decker Memorial Outreach Award 12080
Distinguished Citizen Award 21903
Distinguished Public Service Award 3769
Distinguished Service Award 18027
Faculty Psychiatric Technician of the Year 1387
Robert O. Gilbert Foundation Research Award 12023
Tipper Gore "Remember the Children" Award 15375
William T. Grant Faculty Scholars 21633
Katherine Hamilton Volunteer of the Year Award 15376
C. M. Hincks Award 7268
Independent Investigator Award 13924
Jacob K. Javits Public Service Award 3622
Dolley Madison Award 22109
Maxie T. Collier, MD Award 6433
William R. McAlpin, Jr. Mental Health Research Achievement Award 15377
William C. Menninger Memorial Award 1924
Mental Health Media Awards 15378
Minneapolis Foundation 13588
National Psychiatric Technician of the Year 1388
NIDRR Scholar 17474
A. Eric Palazzo Community Service Award 18028
Harold C. Piepenbrink Award for Outstanding Service to the Field of Mental Health Administration 5580
Positive Images Award 19927
Presidential Award 1272
Prix de la Sante et du Bien-Etre Psychologique 16850
Regional Psychiatric Technician of the Year 1389
Researcher of the Year 3089
Robert L. Robinson Awards 3635
Lela Rowland Prevention Award 15379
Silver Ribbon Award to Outstanding Volunteer 10001
Special Recognition Award 7273
State Psychiatric Technician of the Year 1390
Volunteer of the Year 6434

Mentally disabled
AAMR Awards 1494
Augur Scholarship 17363
Distinguished Investigator Award 13923
Edgar A. Doll Award 3691
Marie H. Eldredge Award 3617
Gardening From the Heart Award 9886
Adele Karlson Lifetime Achievement Award 19736
Henry H. Kessler Awards 17964
Marjorie Hiscott Keyes Award 7269
Leadership Award 13944
Agnes Purcell McGavin Award 3628
Mental Health in the Workplace Award 7270
NAMI Kansas Award of Appreciation 13754
National Distinguished Service Awards 7271
National Media Award 7272
Outstanding Service to the Mentally and/or Physically Handicapped 8068
Outstanding Total Service to the Mentally and/or Physically Handicapped 8069
Program Award 13945
The Rehabilitation International Presidential Award 17965
Service Award 13946
Special Recognition Award 7273
Special Student Awards 1495
Young Investigator Award 13925
Youth Award 13947

Merchandising (*See also* Store planning)
American Spirit Award 15633
Annual Display Award 14196
Apollo Award 19833
ARA Hall of Fame Award 6166
Best of Show Award 18016
Bookseller of the Year Award 6982
Candy Hall of Fame 14719
Candy Salesman of the Year 13592
Chain Bookseller of the Year Award 6984
Children's Illustrator of the Year Award 6985
Distinguished Service Award 15634
Distributor of the Year Award 6986
Editor of the Year Award 6987
ERA Awards 9218
Fiction Book of the Year Award 6988
First-Time Author of the Year Award 6989
The Founders Award 6169
Founders Award 14197
Fragrance Foundation Recognition Awards (FIFI Awards) 9720
Gifts and Decorative Accessories Merchandising Achievement Awards 10011
Gold Medal Award 15635
Golden Penguin Awards 15132
Hall of Fame 14198
Hall of Fame Award 8934
Charles S. Haslam Award for Excellence in Bookselling 19464
Industry Innovation Award 8935
International Retailer of the Year 15636
Leadership in Public Service Award 15637
Lifetime Achievement Award (Author) 6990
Mark E. Manus Scholarship 18020
MAXI Awards Program 11517
McAllister Editorial Fellowship Award 10012
Merchandise Mart Hall of Fame 13299
Merchandisers of the Year 17617
Non-Fiction Book of the Year Award 6991
Outstanding Merchandising Achievement Awards Competition 17441
Partnership Award 8936
Playthings Merchandising Achievement Awards 10013
Publisher of the Year Award 6992
Retailer of the Year 10640
Retailer of the Year Award 14365
Retailer of the Year Awards 6170
Sales Representative of the Year Award 6993
J. Shipman Gold Medal Award 10840
Silver Plaque Award 15638
Small Retailer of the Year Award 15639
Specialty Book of the Year 6994
Specialty Bookseller of the Year Award 6995
Sporting Goods Agents Hall of Fame 19638
Supplier of the Year Award 6171
J. Thomas Weyent Lifetime Achievement Award 15640
Wholesaler of the Year Award 14366
Willis Award of Merit 15237

Merchandising (continued)

Metallurgy *See* Mining and metallurgy

Meteorology
AIAA Losey Atmospheric Science Award 2657
Biometeorological Research Foundation Award 11978
Citation for Outstanding Radio and Television Weather Presentation 7275
Environmental Citation 7276
Fellow 3096
Howard H. Hanks, Jr., Scholarship in Meteorology 3097
Honorary Life Membership 1425
Industry/Government Graduate Fellowships 3098
Industry Undergraduate Scholarships 3099
International Society of Biometeorology Honorary Member 11979
Helmut Landberg Award for Excellence in Applied Climatology 1426
Father James B. Macelwane Annual Awards in Meteorology 3100
Howard T. Orville Scholarship in Meteorology 3101
William F. Peterson Foundation Awards 11980
Postgraduate Scholarship 7277
Rube Hornstein Prize in Operational Meteorology 7280
Science Fair 3103
J. Lawrence Smith Medal 13848
Tertia M.C. Hughes Memorial Prize 7281
Moyer D. Thomas Award 5991
Dr. Andrew Thomson Prize in Applied Meteorology 7282
Undergraduate Scholarships 7284

Microbiology
Abbott Laboratories Award in Clinical and Diagnostic Immunology 4128
ASM Founders Distinguished Service Award 4129
Becton Dickinson and Company Award in Clinical Microbiology 4130
bioMerieux Sonnenwirth Award for Leadership in Clinical Microbiology 4131
Biotechnology Research Award 4132
Canadian Society of Microbiologists Award 7478
Carski Foundation Distinguished Teaching Award 4133
Fellowship 18760
Honorary Member 4135
Intel International Science and Engineering Fair 18362
Eli Lilly and Company Research Award 4136
Merck ICAAC Young Investigator Awards 4137
Pasteur Award 10690
Charles Porter Award 18761
J. Roger Porter Award 20579
Procter & Gamble Award in Applied and Environmental Microbiology 4138
Charles A. Stuart Memorial Lectureship 6666
Student Award 7479
Charles Thom Award 18762
Travel Grant 4141
USFCC/J. Roger Porter Award 4139
Selman A. Waksman Award in Microbiology 13851
Waksman Outstanding Teaching Award 18763

Microfilms *See* Information management

Military engineering
Armed Forces Joint Warfighting Essay Contest 20707
Walter O. Bachus Gold Medal 18982
Bliss Medal 18983
Colbert Medal 18984
Cowart Plaque 18985
Curtin Plaque 18986
Daedalian Weapon Systems Award 16823
Gaines G. Gilbert Award 13077
George W. Goethals Medal 18988
James E. Hatch Award 13079
Itschner Plaque 18990
Karo Plaque 18991
Maj. Gen. Clements McMullen Weapon System Maintenance Award 16832
J. W. Morris Sustaining Member of the Year Award 18992
Sargent Medal 18995
Sverdrup Medal 18998
Toulmin Medal 18999
Tudor Medal 19000

Military history
Award of Merit 3846
Paul Birdsall Prize in European Military and Strategic History 2466
Daedalian Foundation Award of Recognition 8707
Sgt. Maj. Dan Daly Award 13096
Daughters of Union Veterans of the Civil War, 1861-1865 Award 8756
Distinguished Book Award 18800
Fellowship in Aviation History 373
Victor Gondos Memorial Service Award 18801
General Wallace M. Greene, Jr., Award 13098
Colonel Robert D. Heinl, Jr., Memorial Award in Marine Corps History 13099
John Lyman Book Awards 16469
Magruder Award for Museology (Museum Displays) 13100
Moncado Prizes for Best Article 18802
Samuel Eliot Morison Prize 18803
New York Chapter History of Military Medicine Essay Award 5777
Forrest C. Poque Prize 21087
Voice of Democracy Scholarship 21345
Writing Awards 378

Military service
369th Veterans' Association Service Award 25
AAS Distinguished Service Medallions 5100
AAS Honorary National Commander 5101
AAS Individual Awards 5102
AAS National Commander Awards 5103
AAS National Medal and Ribbon 5104
AAS Outstanding Area Advisor 5105
AAS Outstanding Squadron Advisor 5106
AAS Squadron Awards 5107
Academic Excellence Awards - Joint Military Intelligence College 15383
Achievement Medal: Air Force 8797
Achievement Medal: Army 8798
Achievement Medal: Coast Guard 8799
Achievement Medal: Navy - Marine Corps 8800
Active Duty Literary Prize 16052
Aerial Achievement Medal 8801
AF ROTC Cadet of the Year Award 328
AFAA Airmanship Award 2235
AFAA Honorees 2236
AFMC Junior Management Award 329
AFMC Logistics Executive Management Award 330
AFMC Middle Management Award 331
Air Force Academy Award 369
Air Force Association Special Presidential Citations 5108
Air Force Institute of Technology Award 370
Air Force ROTC Scholarship 371
Air Force Test Team of the Year Award 333
Air Reserve Forces Meritorious Service Medal - Air Force 8802
Air War College Award for Research and Writing 372
Airman's Award 8269
AMCSUS President's Medal 5761
Americanism Award 2956
Americanism News Media Award 7671
AMVETS National Awards Program 4947
AMVETS Silver Helmet Awards 4949
Antarctica Service Medal 8803
Armed Forces Expeditionary Medal 8804
Armed Forces Reserve Medal 8805
Army of Occupation Medal - Army-Air Force 8806
Army Reserve Components Achievement Medal 8807
Association of the United States Army Awards 5883
Vincent Astor Memorial Leadership Essay Contest 20708
Aviation Awards 367
Award of Merit 13418
Award of the Order of the Brass Jackass 8270
Awards of Recognition 13105
Barbed Wire Award 2210
Richard H. Barchi Prize 13406
CMSAF Thomas N. Barnes Award 337
Blackhorse Scholarship 6
Bolling Cross 15
Arleigh Burke Essay Contest 20709
CAF Unit Letter of Commendation 8271
Canadian Coast Guard Exemplary Service Medal 6816
Canadian Forces Decoration 6817
Celtic Cross Award 7672
Certificate of Appreciation 6455
Lt. General Claire Lee Chennault Award 339
China Service Medal - Navy, Marine Corps, Coast Guard 8808
CID Hall of Fame 7992
CID Soldier of the Year 7993
Coast Guard Arctic Service Medal 8809
Coast Guard Essay Contest 20710
Coast Guard Reserve Good Conduct Medal 8810
Combat Readiness Medal 8811
Commandant's Aviation Trophy 13069
Commander-in-Chief's Annual Award for Installation Excellence 20487
Commendation Medal: Navy 8812

Military (continued)

Alfred A. Cunningham Award (Marine Aviator of the Year) 13070
Jack N. Darby Award for Inspirational Leadership and Excellence of Command 16053
Donald E. Davis Award 13071
Defense Distinguished Service Medal 8813
Defense Meritorious Service Medal 8814
Defense Superior Service Medal 8815
Jack W. Demmond Award 13072
Brig. Gen. Robert L. Denig Distinguished Service Award 20684
Department of Veteran's Affairs Employee of the Year Award 343
Donald L. Dickson Memorial Award 20685
Irving Diener Award 6456
Distinguished Flying Medal 8272
Distinguished Maintenance Award 8273
Distinguished Performance Award 20686
Distinguished Service Award
303rd Bomb Group (H) Association 23
Military Chaplains Association of the U.S.A. 13403
Distinguished Service Medal 8274
Distinguished Service Star 12609
Distinguished Unit Citation 8275
Distinguished Unit Maintenance Award 8276
Douglas R. Drum Memorial Scholarship Award 3109
Edward C. Dyer Award 13073
Eisenhower Liberation Medal 20639
Enlisted Essay Contest 20711
Excellence in the Arts Award 21360
Excellence in the Media Award 21361
Joseph J. Foss Award 2237
Founder's Medal 5771
Frederick Award for Outstanding Soldier - Major General Robert F. Frederick Award 9562
Edward S. Fris Award (Command and Control Unit of the Year) 13074
Francis S. Gabreski Award 2238
Charles S. Gersoni Military Psychology Award 3722
Robert F. Gibson Award (Marine Air Command and Control Officer of the Year) 13075
John P. Giguere Award 13076
Gaines G. Gilbert Award 13077
Captain James M. Gilliss Award for Outstanding Service 20524
Goddard Medal 18987
Gold Lifesaving Medal 8816
Gold Medal Award for Distinguished Service 21258
Gold Medal of Merit 12386
Good Conduct Medal 8817
Hall of Outstanding Americans 15986
Robert M. Hanson Award (Fighter/Attack Squadron of the Year) 13078
James E. Hatch Award 13079
Earle Hattaway Award (Marine Aviation Ground Officer of the Year) 13080
Hennessy Awards 15627
Honor et Veritas Award 7674
Honorary Member 5109
Colonel George S. Howard Citation of Musical Excellence for Military Concert Bands 19428
Humanitarian Service Medal 8818
Humanity Award 12390
Individual Maintenance Award 8277
The Kenneth A. Innis Award (Aviation Command and Control Marine of the Year) 13081
Insignia for Mention in Dispatches 6820
International Navies Essay Contest 20712
International Navies Photo Contest 20713
Jack Quilter Award 7
Joint Service Achievement Medal 8819
Joint Service Commendation Medal 8820
Jonah E. Kelley Award 13
Korean Service Medal 8821
Lee Integrity Award 18072
Legion of Merit 8822
Legion of Valor Bronze Cross for Achievement 12772
Legislator of the Year 21362
General Curtis E. LeMay Bomber Aircrew Award 345
Letter of Commendation 8278
Letter of Commendation (Non-CAF Member) 8279
Commodore Uriah P. Levy Citizen's Award 12387
Literary Honorarium Award 16054
Logistics Lessons Learned Award 374
Wilburn H. Long Employment Award 6457
Louis R. Lowery Memorial Award 20687
Ronald D. Lyons Memorial Award 20688
Major General Melvin J. Maas Achievement Award 6458
James MaGuire Award (Exceptional Achievement) 13082
Colonel Mickey Marcus Award 12388
Marine Corps Essay Contest 20714
Marine Corps Expeditionary Medal 8823
Lieutenant Theodore C. Marrs Plaques 5110
David McCampbell Award 2239
Keith B. McCutcheon Award (Marine Heavy Helicopter Squadron of the Year) 13083
MCJROTC Awards 13106
Medal of Military Valour 6822
Memorial Plaques 4
Meritorious Service Cross - Military Division 6824
Meritorious Service Medal 8824
Meritorious Service Medal - Military Division 6826
Military Astronautics Award 1505
Military Photographer of the Year 15540
Mission Award 8280
General Billy Mitchell Award for C4 Excellence 346
Royal N. Moore Award 13084
Most Outstanding Catholic War Veteran 7675
Most Outstanding Post of the Year Award 7676
Multinational Force and Observers Medal 8825
Paul W. Myers Award 347
Dr. John Nardini Award 2211
National Chief of Protocol 5111
National Defense Service Medal 8826
National Guard Association of the United States Awards Program 15176
National Military Intelligence Association Annual Awards 15384
Naval and Maritime Photo Contest 20715
Naval Reserve Medal 8827
Navy Expeditionary Medal 8828
Navy Occupation Service Medal - Navy-Marine Corps-Coast Guard 8829
Simon Newcomb Award for Research Achievement 20525
James E. Nicholson Award (Marine Non-Commissioned Officer Leadership Award) 13085
Notable Achievements 5334
NROTC Essay Contest 16055
General Jerome F. O'Malley Award 348
Order of the Compassionate Heart 17960
Order of the Eagle 16
Order of the Golden Eagle 17961
Order of the Golden Lion 21
Orders of the U.S. Air Force 8830
Orders of the U.S. Army 8831
Orders of the U.S. Coast Guard 8832
Orders of the U.S. Marine Corps 8833
Orders of the U.S. Navy 8834
Joan Orr Award 349
Verne Orr Award 350
Outstanding Disabled Veteran of the Year 8955
Outstanding Disabled Veteran Outreach Coordinator 8956
Outstanding Federal Services Health Administrator Award 5778
Outstanding Large and Small Employer Award 8957
Outstanding Local Veterans' Employment Representative 8958
Outstanding National Guard Unit Award 16843
Outstanding ROTC Cadet Award 16844
Outstanding ROTC Unit Award 16845
Outstanding Service Award for Military Pediatrics 786
Outstanding Trailblazer Award 11
Patriot Award 17068
Peltier Plaque 18993
P.O.W. of the Year 2213
General Thomas S. Power Missile Crew Award 351
President Award 17069
President's Award 5335
Presidents' Award for the AFRES 352
John M. Price Chapter Award 17070
Prisoner of War Medal 8835
Danny Radish Award (Marine Enlisted Aircrew of the Year) 13086
Railsplitter of the Year 17
General Edwin W. Rawlings Award for Environmental Achievement (Manager and Technician) 353
Stuart Reichart Award 356
Republic of Vietnam Campaign Medal 8836
David Rist Prize 13407
Robert Guy Robinson Award (Marine Naval Flight Officer of the Year) 13087
Pete Ross Safety Award 13088
ROTC (Junior) Scholarship 21347
Royal Canadian Mounted Police Long Service Medal 6830
Sailors of the Year on SSBN-733 21261
Lawson H. M. Sanderson Award (Attack Squadron of the Year) 13089
Sargent Medal 18995
School of Advanced Airpower Studies Thesis Award 375
Harry A. Schweikert, Jr. Disability Awareness Award 17071
George H. Seal Memorial Trophy Award 8959
Selected Marine Corps Reserve Medal 8837

Military (continued)

Service Award (Non-CAF Member) 8281
Seventeen Seventy-Six Award ("1776 Award") 16050
Shields Medal 18996
Silver Hawk Award 13090
Silver Helmet Award 17962
Silver Lifesaving Medal 8838
Silver Magnolia Blossom Award 8282
Silver Star: Navy 8839
Silver Wings Individual Awards 5112
Silver Wings Unit Award 5113
Small Business Advocates of the Year 20834
Levering Smith Award for Submarine Support Achievement 16056
Sojourners ROTC Awards 15787
Kenneth W. Southcomb Award 13091
Southwest Asia Service Medal 8840
Speedy Award 17072
Sports and Recreation Award 17073
Willie D. Sproule Award (Aviation Maintenance Marine of the Year) 13092
Star of Military Valour 6832
Edward Rhodes Stitt Lecture Award 5785
Sturgis Medal 18997
Submarine/ASW Writing Award 16057
Superintendent's Award for Distinguished Service 20526
Richard E. Szepski Award 8283
Dwain Taylor Award for Voluntary Service 17074
Clayton J. Thomas Award 13408
Colonel John W. Thomason, Jr. Award 13101
Harry S. Truman Award 15177
Truman Silver Veteran's Medal 20227
Lt. General William H. Tunner Aircrew Award 360
Two Air Forces Award USAF/RAF 376
United Nations Medal 8841
United Nations Service Medal (Korea) 8842
U.S. Air Force Academy Physics Award 13412
United States Air Force Twelve Outstanding Airmen of the Year 361
U.S. Coast Guard Academy Most Proficient Cadet in Handling a Sailing Vessel 13413
U.S. Military Academy General Management Award 13414
U.S. Military Male and Female Athletes 20138
US Merchant Marine Academy Award 13416
USAF Personnel Manager of the Year 362
USO Woman of the Year 21259
Paul G. Vess Award (Avionics Marine of the Year) 13093
Veteran's Community Service Award 21358
Veterans Employment Awards 20515
Vietnam Service Medal 8843
W. Averell Harriman Award 12728
John K. Walker, Jr. Award 13409
Vance R. Wanner Award 13410
War Service Medal 15784
Frederick B. Warder Award for Outstanding Achievement 16058
Joe and Josephine Warth Air Force Historical Foundation Award 377
Frank L. Weil Awards 12342
Sir Henry Wellcome Medal and Prize 5789
Henry Wildfang Award 13094
Gill Robb Wilson Award 365
Witherspoon Memorial Chaplain's Award 6357
WMA National Service Award 21765
Robert M. Yerkes Award 3724

Mineralogy

AFMS Scholarship Foundation Honorary Award 2229
American Mineralogist Undergraduate Award 13432
Marilyn and Sturges W. Bailey Distinguished Member Award 8089
George W. Brindley Lecture 8090
CFMS Scholarship 6741
Crystallographic Research Grant 13433
Distinguished Public Service Medal 13434
G. K. Gilbert Award 9949
Grant for Student Research in Mineralogy and Petrology 13435
Marion L. and Chrystie M. Jackson Mid-Career Clay Scientist Award 8091
Mineral Economics Award 2822
Mineral Industry Education Award 2823
Mineralogical Society of America Award 13436
Ambrose Monell Medal and the Ambrose Monell Prize for Distinguished Service in Mineral Technology 8244
MPD Outstanding Young Engineer Award 18818
Pioneer in Clay Science Lecture 8092
Roebling Medal 13437
Undergraduate Award for Outstanding Students in Mineralogy 13438

Mining and metallurgy (*See also* Materials science)

AIME Distinguished Service Award 2815
Henry J. Albert Award 11822
A. Frank Alsobrook Industrial Minerals Distinguished Service Award 18805
Frank F. Aplan Award 2816
Application Award 11737
Application to Practice Award 13440
Automotive Achievement Award 13309
Automotive Innovation Award 13310
Award of Merit 13337
Barlow Memorial Award 7181
Mel W. Bartley Award 7182
Selwyn G. Blaylock Medal 7183
Julian Boldy Memorial Award 7184
Kenes C. Bowling National Mine Reclamation Awards 12156
CANMET Technology Transfer Award 7185
CIM Distinguished Lecturers 7186
CIM Fellowship 7187
CIM/NRCan Journalism Awards 7188
CIM Student Essay Competition 7189
Coal and Energy Division Distinguished Service Award 18806
Coal Award 7190
Bill Dennis Prospector of the Year Award 17689
Design Award 11738
Ben F. Dickerson Award 18807
Distinguished Member Award 18808
Distinguished Service Award
  Minerals, Metals, and Materials Society 13442
  National Mining Association 15386
  Prospectors and Developers Association of Canada 17690
Distinguished Service to Powder Metallurgy Award 13311
District Distinguished Service Awards 7191
District Proficiency Medals 7192
James Douglas Gold Medal 2817
Robert M. Dreyer Award in Applied Economic Geology 18809
A.O. Dufresne Award 7193
E3 Environmental Excellence in Exploration Award 17691
Howard N. Eavenson Award 18810
Educator Award 13443
Robert Elver Mineral Economics Award 7194
Environmental Conservation Distinguished Service Award 2818
Excellence in Hot-Dip Galvanizing Awards 2315
Extraction and Processing Distinguished Lecture Award 13444
Extraction and Processing Science Award 13445
Extraction and Processing Technology Award 13446
Benjamin F. Fairless Award 2819
Fellow Award 13447
Fifty Year Club 7195
Antoine M. Gaudin Award 18811
GEM Awards 18812
Gold Medal Award 13463
Marcus A. Grossmann Young Author Award 5180
John L. Hague Award 5953
Hal Williams Hardinge Award 18813
Robert Lansing Hardy Medal Award 13448
Henry Marion Howe Medal 5183
Howe Memorial Lecture 5408
William Hume-Rothery Award 13449
IMCC National Annual Minerals Education Awards 12157
INCO Medal 7196
Industrial Minerals Young Scientist Award 18814
Institute Medal for Distinguished Service 7197
Institute of Metals Lecturer and Robert Franklin Mehl Award 13450
IPMI Distinguished Achievement Award 11823
IPMI Student Award 11824
Daniel C. Jackling Award 18815
IMS and ASM Jacquet-Lucas Award for Excellence in Metallography 5186
J. E. Johnson, Jr., Award 5410
Noah A. Kahn Award 5963
Gary M. Kralik Distinguished Service Award 5964
Leadership Award 13451
Light Metals Award 13452
Light Metals Distinguished Service Award 13453
Light Metals Division *JOM* Best Paper Award 13454
Light Metals Technology Award 13455
Frederick A. Lowenheim Memorial Award 5967
M & E Outstanding Young Professional Award 18816
Viola R. MacMillan Developer's Award 17692
Champion H. Mathewson Award 13456
Robert Earll McConnell Award 2821
McParland Memorial Award 7198
Members Award 7199

Mining (continued)

Mining and Exploration Division Distinguished Service Award 18817
John Nachtsheim 5972
Percy W. Nicholls Award 18819
Mary R. Norton Memorial Scholarship Award for Women 5973
H. R. "Russ" Ogden Award 5974
Order of Sancta Barbara 7201
Outstanding Student Chapter Award 18820
Outstanding Technical Paper Award 13312
Past Presidents' Memorial Medal 7202
Robert Peele Memorial Award 18821
William T. Plass Award 4556
Powder Metallurgy Design Competition 13313
Powder Metallurgy Pioneer Award 13314
President's Citation 18822
Allan Ray Putnam Service Award 5189
Ivan B. Rahn Education Award 18823
Erskine Ramsay Medal 2824
Charles F. Rand Memorial Gold Medal 2825
W. Raymond Award 2826
Reclamation Researcher of the Year 4557
Reclamationist of the Year 4558
Robert H. Richards Award
American Institute of Mining, Metallurgical, and Petroleum Engineers 2827
Society for Mining, Metallurgy, and Exploration 18824
Rock Mechanics Award 18825
John T. Ryan Trophies 7203
William Lawrence Saunders Gold Medal 2828
Scholarship Program 18097
Sentinels of Safety 15387
Special Award 11740
J.C. Sproule Memorial Plaque 7204
Steelmaking Conference Award 5415
Stefanko Best Paper Award 18826
Arthur F. Taggart Award 18827
TMS/ASM Joint Distinguished Lectureship in Materials and Society Award 13459
Joseph R. Vilella Award 5995
Milton E. Wadsworth Award 18828
Hal Williams Hardinge Award 2829
L. L. Wyman Memorial Award 5998

Minority groups *See* Ethnic affairs

Modeling
Barbara Rosenblum Dissertation Award 19381

Monument restoration
Award of Merit 17357
Harriette Merrifield Forbes Award 5376
Oakley Certificate of Merit 5377

Motion pictures *See* Films

Motorcycle racing
Ambassadors Award 7288
Award of Merit 7289
Fulvio Callimaci Memorial Supporters Award 7290
Daytona 200 3150
Bert Irwin Memorial Cup 7291
Billy Matthews Memorial Fair Play Award 7292
Media Award 7293
Dud Perkins Award 3151
Schoolboy Motorcross Award 7294
White Trophy 7295

Moving
Distinguished Service Award 3153

Museums
Alfred H. Barr, Jr. Award 8143
Marian Angell Godfrey Boyer Medal 21096
CMA Awards for Outstanding Achievement 7297
Ron Coplen Roll of Honor Award 19559
Curatorial Research Fellowships 10004
Distinguished Service Award 1278
Grants for Arts Projects 14930
Nancy Hanks Memorial Award for Professional Excellence 1279
Honorary Membership 16899
Internship 21818
Medal for Distinguished Philanthropy 1280
Isabel Miller Service Award 18538
Postdoctoral Fellowship Program 3157
James Smithson Society Founder Medal 18569
James Smithson Society Grants 18570
Thoreau Award 7573

Music (*See also* Conducting; Music competitions; Music composition; Music education; Musical instruments; Musicology; Opera; Performing arts; Piano technology; Recording industry; specific types of music, e.g. Choral music)
Alice Abel Cultural and Creative Arts Program 3141
Achievement and Hall of Fame Award 3164
Achievement in the Arts Award 16575
AGGIE Award 19406
AGO Examination Prize 2369
Albion Book Prize/NACBS Book Prize 16411
All Sonatina, All Sonata, All Bach Programs 1887
American Eagle Award 15406
American Jazz Hall of Fame 10983
American Music Awards 3160
Annual Achievement Awards 3899
Appreciation Award 17133
Archbishop Iakovos' Years of Service Award 15113
ARS Distinguished Achievement Award 3820
Father Adrien Arsenault Senior Arts Award 17544
Arts Recognition and Talent Search (ARTS) 15117
ASCAP - Deems Taylor Awards 4376
ASCAP - Richard Rodgers Award 4377
The Austin Chronicle Readers' Poll Music Awards 6095
AWAPA (Academy of Wind and Percussion Arts) Award 14480
Award for Distinguished Achievement in the Arts 20072
Award for Distinguished Service to Historical Recordings 5460
Award for Distinguished Service to the Arts 20073
Awards 176
Awards for School Bands Youth Groups 9357
Audrey Baird Gold Ribbon Audience Development Awards 4729
Band Booster Award 14481
Frank Huntington Beebe Award 9733
E. Power Biggs Fellowship 16868
Billboard Music Awards 6377
Thomas Binkley Award 9058
Blues Hall of Fame 6473
Blues Music Awards (W. C. Handy Awards) 6474
Richard J. Bogomolny National Service Award 7792
Howard Mayer Brown Award 9059
Estelle Campbell Award 15730
Canadian Music Centre John Adaskin Memorial Award 16738
Celia Carr Music Award 8916
CBA National Music Award 6962
Certificate of Appreciation 21725
Certificate of Merit for Marching Excellence 14482
Irene R. Christman Scholarship 17181
Citation of Excellence 14483
Citation of Merit Award 21726
Citations of Merit 13984
CMA/ASCAP Awards for Adventuresome Programming 7795
Creative Arts Award 12159
Cultural Achievement Award 2893
Derazy Violin Award 21779
Distant Accords Awards 11593
Distinguished Service Award 16869
Alice M. Ditson Conductor's Award 8242
Drama League's Musical Achievement Award 9021
Early Music Brings History Alive Award 9060
El Angel Award - Distinguished Hispanic-American Artist 6374
Emmy Awards for Primetime Programming 127
Fellowship for Creative and Performing Arts and Writers 914
Avery Fisher Career Grants 12854
Avery Fisher Prize 12855
Folk Heritage Award 16503
Frank Munro Memorial Trophy 8073
Sylva Gelber Foundation Award 6794
Ralph J. Gleason Music Book Awards 16302
Gold Baton Award 4730
Gold Music Video Award 17909
Golden Score Award 4560
Glenn Gould Prize 6795
Grammy Awards 13822
Grand Prize 7601
Felix Grant/Stan Getz Award 6470
Grants for Arts Projects 14930
Hall of Fame
American Theatre Organ Society 4737
Percussive Arts Society 17220
Hall of Outstanding Americans 15986
Stanley Hettinger Memorial Scholarship 19793
High School Jazz Student Award 14485
Honorary Life Member
Canadian Society for Traditional Music 7437
International Double Reed Society 11545
Honorary Member
American Theatre Organ Society 4738
Guild of Carillonneurs in North America 10198
Organ Historical Society 16870

Music (continued)

Honorary Recognition Awards 12096
Colonel George S. Howard Citation of Musical Excellence for Military Concert Bands 19428
Howlin' Wolf Award 6475
K. M. Hunter Artists Awards 16742
IAJE Hall of Fame 11249
IBMA Award of Merit 11423
Image Awards 14049
Individual Artist Fellowship 13586
Industry Leadership Award 13700
International Golden Rose Award 21727
Jazz Contribution Awards 6471
Jazz Masters Fellowships 14931
Jules Leger Prize for New Chamber Music 6799
Juno Awards 6846
Keeping the Blues Alive Awards 6476
Kennedy Center Honors 12552
Key to the Highway Award 6477
Kate Neal Kinley Memorial Fellowship 21032
Laurel Leaf Award 1955
Lefthanders of the Year Awards 12764
Leo Award for Technical Innovation 10206
Adam P. Lesinsky Award 14596
Lifetime Achievement Award 6478
Lifetime Achievement Awards 8260
Liszt Medal 3007
Master Musician Award 20196
Mature Women Scholarship Grant 15334
Medal for Peace and Friendship through Music and Arts 11595
Medal of Honor for Music 13994
Mu Phi Epsilon Annual Grants and Scholarships 13662
Music Arts and Flowers History Award 8920
Music Campers Citation 14486
National Chapter of the Year 20197
National Federation Citations 14978
National High School Band Director of the Year 15226
The National Music Festival 15408
National Society of Arts and Letters First Place Award 15733
National Student Playwriting Award 12546
National Young Performers Competition 6803
NCBA Service Award 14597
Mollie Davis Nicholson Award 15734
Robert F. O'Brien Award 14598
OC Award 16817
Ohioana Citation for Distinguished Service to Ohio 16663
Orford String Quartet Scholarship 16745
Outstanding Band Musician Award 14487
Outstanding Jazz Educator Award 14488
Outstanding Women in Music Award 19936
Virginia Parker Award 6804
Sally Parker Education Gold Ribbon Awards 4731
Patriach Athenagoras Diocesan Service Award 15114
George Peabody Medal 17123
Performance Scholarships 11674
Antoinette Perry Awards (Tony Awards) 12742
Pied Piper Award 4382
Pioneer Women of the Podium 21728
Platinum Music Video Award 17911
Polka Music Awards 11819
Polka Music Hall of Fame 11820
Presidential Award 14364
President's Award 14599
Prix Calixa-Lavallee 18606
George Proctor Prize 7529
Pulitzer Fellowships 17748
Pulitzer Prizes 17749
Q107 Homegrown Contest 7997
Readers' and Critics' Poll 18110
Rock and Roll Hall of Fame 18091
Royal Conservatory of Music Scholarship 21782
St. Romanos the Melodist Medallion 15115
Saturn Awards 123
B. Douglas Sawtelle Scholarship 13716
Scott Joplin Foundation of Sedalia Lifetime Achievement Award 18371
Scroll of Excellence 21729
Scroll of Honor 19937
Norma Sharpe Award 6888
Silver Baton Award 21730
Songwriters Hall of Fame 13816
Soul Train Music Awards 19423
State Chapter of the Year Award 20198
State of Florida Fellowship 9589
Joseph S. Stauffer Prizes 6809
Steel Guitar Hall of Fame 12043
Dorothy and Bruce Strong Award 15735
Sudler Cup 19430
Sudler Flag of Honor 19431
Sudler Order of Merit 19433
Sudler Shield 19434
Sudler Silver Scroll 19435
Sudler Trophy 19436
Theatre Organist of the Year 4739
Helen M. Thompson Award 4732
Toronto Arts Awards 20112
Tri-M Leadership Award 20199
Tri-M Service Award 20200
Trustees' Honor Roll 3901
Wava Banes Turner Award 19938
UMS Distinguished Artist Award 20975
University of Toronto Faculty of Music Scholarship 21783
University Women's Association-Schaible-Strohmaier 9390
Irvin Warwick Memorial Award 11175
WBDNA Achievement Award 21731
WBDNA Performing Artists Award 21732
Western Heritage Awards (Wrangler Award) 14887
Reverend George C. Wiskirchen Jazz Award 14601
Andrew Wolf Chamber Music Award 6278
Kate Wolf Memorial Award 21917
W.S. Gwynn Williams Award 11402
Young Concert Artists International Auditions 22059

Music competitions (*See also* Opera; Piano competitions; Violin competitions; Vocal music)

American Accordionists' Association Contest and Festival 849
Mary Anderson Memorial Senior Woodwind Scholarship 18273
Artists International New York Debut Award Auditions 5143
ASCAP Chamber Music Awards 4375
Bach Competitions 17868
Banff International String Quartet Competition 6234
Vincent R. Bastien Memorial Cello Award 21432
Joseph H. Bearns Prizes in Music 8239
The Sister Boyle Award 18274
The Boyle Memorial Senior French Music Scholarship 18275
The Boyle Memorial Senior Hayden and Mozart Scholarship 18276
The Ray Brookhart Memorial Intermediate Pipe Organ Scholarship 18277
Bursary Competition 13982
William C. Byrd Young Artist Competition 18203
Canadian Music Competitions 7299
Carmel Chamber Music Competition 7797
Carmine Caruso International Jazz Trumpet Solo Competition 12095
CBC Radio National Competition for Young Performers 6999
Chamber Music Competition 13702
Chamber Music Yellow Springs Competition 7801
The F. W. Chisholm Intermediate Woodwind Scholarship 18279
Coleman Chamber Ensemble Competition 8130
Competitive Awards 14970
Concerto Competition 18280
Concours OSM 13605
Convention Performers Competition 15057
CTBI Intermediate Cello/Viola/Double Bass Scholarship 18282
Discovery Artist Award 16202
East & West Artists International Auditions 9067
Eckhardt-Gramatte National Competition for the Performance of Canadian Music 9129
The Frances England Intermediate Hayden and Mozart Scholarship 18284
European Young Jazz Artists 12310
Fischoff National Chamber Music Competition 9566
For Peace and Friendship International Song Contest 11594
Fernand Gillet Performance Competition 11544
The Goodfellow Memorial Oratorio Scholarship/ The Helen Davis Sherry Memorial Trophy 18292
Guelph Spring Festival Music Competition 10190
Haddonfield Symphony Solo Competition for Young Instrumentalists 10217
Hall of Fame and Band of the Year Award 15225
Heida Hermanns International Competition 8408
High School Flute Choir Competition 15058
High School Solo Competition 11485
High School Soloist Competition 15059
Houston Symphony Ima Hogg Young Artist Competition 10499
Houston Symphony League Concerto Competition 10500
The John and Judy Hrycak Award 18294
International Award 17580
International Bluegrass Music Awards 11424
ITG Student Performance Competitions 12098
The Jackson Memorial Intermediate Piano Scholarship 18295
Jazz Flute Masterclass 15060
Jazz Prize 9537
Joseph/Wilson Study Grant 10153

Music (continued)

Kiwania of Wascana Senior Cello/Viola/ Double Bass Scholarship 18296
Masterclass Performers Competition 15061
The Maude McGuire Memorial Intermediate Piano Scholarship 18298
The Maude McGuire Memorial Senior Piano Scholarship 18299
The Fred S. Mendal Memorial Award in Strings and Trophy 18301
Thelonious Monk International Jazz Competition 13584
MTNA Collegiate Artist Competition 13703
MTNA Junior Performance Competitions 13705
MTNA Senior Performance Competition 13706
Mu Phi Epsilon International Competition 13660
The Dr. W.C. Murray Senior Brass Scholarship 18304
Music Center Spotlight Awards 13698
MUSICA SACRA Bach Vocal Competition 13710
National Chopin Piano Competition 12613
The National Music Festival 15408
National Music Festival 18305
National Young Artist Competition 13390
National Young Artists Competition in Organ Performance 2372
Naumburg Chamber Music Award 16044
Naumburg International Competition 16045
New York International Competition for Solo Oboists 16603
Orchestral Audition and Masterclass Competition 15062
Sask Power Award 18306
Professional Flute Choir Competition 15063
RYOC 2375
Mary Winston Smail Memorial Piano Award 21433
The SMFA Intermediate Brass Scholarship 18310
The SMFA Intermediate Percussion Scholarship 18311
SMFA Past President's Brass Scholarship 18312
The SMFA Senior Percussion Scholarship 18313
Ellsworth Smith Solo Performance Competition 12099
Sorantin Young Artist Award 18237
Blanche Squires Memorial Senior Chopin Scholarhip 18314
The Blanche Squires Memorial Senior Pipe Organ Scholarship 18315
The Blanche Squires Memorial Woodwind Award 18316
Stulberg International String Competition 19816
Twin Cities Musicians Union AFM Award 21434
University of Maryland International Music Competitions 18567
USA International Harp Competition 21186
Elizabeth Harper Vaughn Concerto Competition 19863
The Gordon C. Wallis Intermediate Beethoven Scholarship 18318
The Gordon C. Wallis Senior Beethoven Scholarship 18320
WAMSO Young Artist Competition 21435
Washington International Competition 9775
The Carla Ruth Webb Memorial Award in Woodwind 18321
Young Artist Competition
Fort Collins Symphony Association 9701
National Flute Association 15064
New York Flute Club 16227
Young Artists Auditions Competition 16186
Young Artists Competition 11486
Young Composers' Competition 14147
Young Soloists' Competition 15834

Music composition
ABA Ostwald Band Composition Award 1527
ACTF Musical Theatre Award 12540
AGO/ECS Publishing Award in Choral Composition 2368
ALEA International Composition Prize 6534
Louis Applebaum Composers Award 16736
Artists' Fellowships 16229
ASCAP - Deems Taylor Awards 4376
ASCAP Triple Play Award 4378
Barlow Prize 6249
John Bettis Fellowship Award 19403
Biennial Composers Competition 847
BMI Student Composer Awards 6643
Bush Artist Fellows Program 6700
Career Achievement Award 9543
CBC Radio National Competition for Young Composers 6998
CBC Young Composers Competition 6790
Chamber Opera Competition 15426
Cintas Foundation Fellowships 10981
Citations 14146
El Angel Award - Distinguished Hispanic-American Artist 6374
Emmy Awards for Primetime Programming 127
Fellowship Program 17168
Gaston Writing Award 3168
Harvey Gaul Competition 17359
Golden Globe Awards 10513
Golden Score Award 4560
Grammy Awards 13822
Grants to Young Composers 4380
John Simon Guggenheim Memorial Foundation Fellowships 10192
Guitar Foundation of America Solo Guitar Competition 10204
Holtkamp/AGO Award in Organ Composition 2370
Howard Fellows 10571
Humanist Music Award 16175
Individual Artist Fellowship 16628
Inter-American Music Awards 18476
International New Music Competition 16692
International Trumpet Guild Composition Contest 12097
Merle J. Isaac Composition Contest 4703
Juno Awards 6846
Kennedy Center Friedheim Awards for New Music 12551
Kennedy Center Honors 12552
Kentucky Artists Fellowships 12562
Koussevitzky Commissions 12616
Laurel Leaf Award 1955
Letter of Distinction 3162
Lifetime Achievement Award 19404
Edward MacDowell Medal 13008
MTNA-Shepherd Distinguished Composer of the Year Award 13707
MTNA Student Composition Competition 13708
Music Award 15013
National Competition for Composers Recording 8477
National Competition in Organ Improvisation 2371
National Composers' Competition 12747
New York Dance and Performance Awards (Bessie Awards) 8745
Rudolf Nissim Award 4381
George Peabody Medal 17123
Antoinette Perry Awards (Tony Awards) 12742
Prix Denise-Pelletier 17795
Quimby Regional Competitions for Young Organists 2373
Rome Prize Fellowships 605
Arnold Sapop Memorial Award 19470
Scholarship/Grant Program of SAI Philanthropies Inc. 18477
William Schuman Award 8254
Search for New Music 11179
Philip Slates Memorial Award 19471
SOCAN Awards for Young Composers 18593
Songwriter of the Year 8720
Elise L. Stoeger Prize 7799
Louis Sudler International Wind Band Composition Competition 19432
Triennial Composition Competition 8872
University of Louisville Grawemeyer Award for Music Composition 21050
Van de Vate Prize for Orchestral Music 11180
Wisconsin Arts Board Fellowships 21666
Young Composers' Competition 14147

Music education
AGO Scholarship 2377
Artist-Teacher Award 4700
Amy L. Bloom Memorial Scholarship Fund 20249
Joseph M. Bryan, Jr. Scholarships 9113
Castleman Award for Excellence in Chamber Music Teaching 7793
Chamber Music America Commissioning Program 7794
Elizabeth A.H. Green School Educator Award 4701
International Scholarship Program 9114
JAMS Scholarship 12308
Wynton Marsalis Scholarship 9115
MCBA Scholarship 13339
Music Educator of the Year Award 14363
NPM Scholarships 14320
Colonel Samuel Rosenbaum Memorial Award 15180
School Superintendents of the Year 17182
Evelyn Bonar Storrs Memorial Piano Scholarships 13714
Young Musician Scholarship 10024

Musical instruments
Nicolas Bessaraboff Prize 3170
Frances Densmore Prize 3171
Avery Fisher Career Grants 12854
International Competitions for New Instruments and Bows 21382
Wynton Marsalis Scholarship 9115
Curt Sachs Award 3172

Musicology
Philip Brett Award 3174
Einstein Award 3175
Fellow 10625

Musicology (continued)
Noah Greenberg Award 3176
Howard Fellows 10571
Alvin H. Johnson AMS 50 Dissertation Fellowships 3177
Otto Kinkeldey Award 3178
Jaap Kunst Prize 18672
Organ Historical Society Archival Fellowship 16871
George Peabody Medal 17123
Paul A. Pisk Prize 3179
Charles Seeger Prize 18673
Klaus P. Wachsmann Prize for Advanced and Critical Essays in Organology 18674

Mycology
C.J. Alexopoulos Prize 13721
Annual Lecturer Award 13722
Award for Contributions to Amateur Mycology 16450
Rhoda Benham Award 13269
Billy H. Cooper Memorial Meridian Award 13270
Distinguished Mycologist Award 13723
Graduate Fellowships in Mycology 13724
Graduate Research Prizes 13725
William H. Weston Award for Teaching Excellence 13726

Mystery writing
The Dilys Award 10743
Arthur Ellis Award 8649
Robert L. Fish Memorial Award 13730
Grandmaster Award 13731
Hammett Prize 11322
Macavity Awards 13728
Nero Award 21696
Edgar Allan Poe Awards (Edgars) 13732

Mythology
Wayland D. Hand Award for Academic Achievement in Folklore and Mythology Studies 8889
Outstanding Reference Sources 17944

National security
Academic Excellence Awards - Joint Military Intelligence College 15383
John R. Alison Award 335
American Hero Award 12335
American Preparedness Award 1806
AMVETS Silver Helmet Awards 4949
Association of the United States Army Awards 5883
Defense Industry Award 14901
Department of Defense Distinguished Service Award 14905
Gerald R. Ford Prize for Distinguished Reporting on National Defense 9681
William C. Foster Fellows Visiting Scholars Program 20402
Edgar S. Furniss Award 16649
Thomas P. Gerrity Award 344
Gold Medal of Merit 12386
Lorne Greene Homeland Defense Award 1807
Honorary Citations 11348
Henry M. Jackson Distinguished Service Award 12359
Media Awards 11349
Military Psychology Student Paper Award 3723
National Guard Association of the United States Awards Program 15176
National Military Intelligence Association Annual Awards 15384
National Security Medal 15703
National Transportation Award 14906
NDTA Distinguished Service Award 14907
Outstanding Leadership Award 2125
Presidential Citation 11350
Presidential Medal of Freedom 9364
Theodore Roosevelt Distinguished Service Medal 20066
ROTC Award 14902
W. Stuart Symington Award 359
Harry S. Truman Award 15177
Hoyt S. Vandenberg Award 363
VFW Armed Forces Award 21334
VFW Dwight David Eisenhower Distinguished Service Award 21337
Thomas D. White National Defense Award 20382

Native Americans
Aggrey Medal 17230
Artist of the Year 10753
Samuel W. Brown, Jr. Root Cutter Award 10842
Catlin Peace Pipe Award
Continental Confederation of Adopted Indians 8487
American Indian Lore Association 2604
Cherokee National Hall of Fame 7852
Consumer Conference Awards 15256
Ford Foundation Postdoctoral Diversity Fellowships 15622
Friend of the American Indian 2596
Hall of Fame 2605
Miss Indian World 9900
Outstanding American Indian Awards 2597
Ely ("Eli") S. Parker Award 2607
Red Cloud Indian Art Show 10424

Natural history *See* Science

Natural science *See* Science

Nature
Arts for the Parks Competition 15477
Awards of Merit 15478
Paul Bartsch Award 6063
Coupes Merites Aux Individus 7780
Arnold Davis Prairie Restoration Award 16016
E.J. Dyksterhuis Memorial Award 16017
Earth Day Award 9062
Earthwatch Education Awards 9064
Ernst Mayr Grants 13687
Founder's Favorite Winner Award 15479
Goodhue-Elkins Award 6083
Grand Prize Winner Award 15480
IWLA Honor Roll Award 12267
Lindbergh Grants 7808
R.C. Mauldin Award 16018
National Outdoor Book Awards 15465
Naturalistes de l'Annee 7781
Katherine Ordway Stewardship Award 16036
Paid Internships 16607
Regional Awards 15482
Trophees Desjardins 7783
U.S. Art Magazine Award of Merit 15483
Volunteer of the Year Award 6085
Wildlife Category Award of Merit 15484

Nature photography
Ansel Adams Award for Conservation Photography 18450
Nature Division Awards 17287
Photography Awards 16970

Naval architecture *See* Naval engineering

Naval engineering
Vice Admiral E. L. Cochrane Award 19207
Davidson Medal 19208
Distinguished Service Award 19209
Maurice Ewing Medal 2346
Gibbs Brothers Medal 13833
Gold Medal Award 4566
Jimmy Hamilton Award 4567
Elmer L. Hann Award 19210
Claud A. Jones Fleet Engineer Award 4568
William M. Kennedy Award 19211
Frank G. Law Award 4569
American Bureau of Shipping - Captain Joseph H. Linnard Prize 19212
Lockheed/Martin Ocean Engineering Award 13111
John Lyman Book Awards 16469
Mississippi-Alabama Sea Gran Consortium Grants 13502
Harold E. Saunders Award 4570
Blakely Smith Medal 19213
Solberg Award 4571
Elmer A. Sperry Award 19057
Student Paper Awards 19214
David W. Taylor Medal 19215
Vice Admiral "Jerry" Land Medal 19216
William H. Webb Medal 19217

Navigation
Admiral of the Ocean Sea 20373
AOTOS Mariner's Plaque 20374
Burka Award 11011
J. B. Charcot Award 12430
Hakluyt Award 12431
Hays Award 11012
Honorary Member Award 12432
ION Navigation Award (California Maritime Academy) 11013
ION Navigation Award (U.S. Air Force Academy) 11014
Joshua Trophy 12433
Magellanic Premium Award 3439
Mariner's Rosette 20378
Northern Light Award 12434
Jack A. Pierce Award 11769
Slocum Award 12435
Spray Trophy 12436
Superior Achievement Award 11015
Thurlow Award 11016
Carl H. Vilas Literary Award 12437
Voss Award 12438
Weems Award 11017
Captain Donald T. Wright Award 17494

Neurology
Central Nervous System Section Van Harrevold Memorial Award 3513
Central Neuropsychiatric Association Resident Award 3192
Jeanne Timmins Costello Fellowships 13602
George Cotzias Lecture 696
Distinguished Neuropsychologist Award 13809
Distinguished Service Award 8389

Neurology (continued)

Shelia Essey Award 698
Founder's Award 699
Galbraith Award 8390
C. Judson Herrick Award 1083
Honorary Distinguished Physicians Award 1891
Honorary Distinguished Service Award 1892
International Affairs Committee Foreign Scholarship Award 700
Sydney M. Kanev Memorial Award 1893
Mayfield Award 8391
Lawrence C. McHenry Award 701
Medical Student Essay Awards 702
S. Weir Mitchell Award 703
Moore Award 1287
NAS Award in the Neurosciences 13844
Potamkin Prize for Research in Pick's, Alzheimer's, and Related Diseases 704
Resident Award 8392
Resident's Award 4191
Preston Robb Fellowship 13603
Rubinstein Award 1288
Bruce S. Schoenberg International Award in Neuroepidemiology 705
Robert Wartenberg Lecture 706
Weil Award 1289

Newspapers *See* Journalism

Non-destructive testing *See* Testing

Nonfiction
Alabama Authors Award 405
PEN/Martha Albrand Award for First Nonfiction 17139
PEN/Martha Albrand Award for the Art of the Memoir 17140
Ambassador Book Awards 9277
Annual Awards Competition 8565
ASJA Outstanding Article Award 4467
ASJA Outstanding Author Award 4468
AWP Award Series 5259
C. Warren Bledsoe Award 5339
Elmer Holmes Bobst Literary Awards 16301
Boston Globe - Horn Book Awards 6526
CAA Awards for Adult Literature 6953
Harry Chapin Media Awards 21925
Julia Child Cookbook Awards 11326
Co-Founders Book Award 21579
Carr P. Collins Award 20013
Commonwealth Club of California Book Awards 8306
Avery O. Craven Award 16885
Eaton Literary Awards Program 9125
Hubert Evans Nonfiction Prize 21520
Fine Arts Work Center Fellowships 9553
Fraunces Tavern Museum Book Award 19417
Friends of the Dallas Public Library Award 20016
Gavel Awards 1533
Georgia Author of the Year Awards 9972
Heartland Prizes 7893
O. Henry Award 20017
The Sidney Hillman Foundation Prize Awards 10435
Joseph Henry Jackson Literary Award 18249
Lannan Literary Awards 12691
Gordon K. Lewis Book Award 7595
Literary Writers Competition 9467
Matrix Award 16312
Milkweed Prize for Children's Literature 13422
National Book Awards 14532
National Book Critics Circle Awards 14530
National Jewish Book Award - Holocaust 12326
National Outdoor Book Awards 15465
Nonfiction Contest 15992
Ohioana Book Awards 16661
Orbis Pictus Nonfiction Award 14835
Outstanding Book Award 10483
Outstanding Southeastern Author Award 19476
Robert Troup Paine Prize 10283
PEN Book-of-the-Month Club Translation Prize 17146
PEN/Jerard Fund Award 17147
PEN Prison Writing Awards 17148
James D. Phelan Literary Award 18251
PNWA Literary Contest 17011
Pulitzer Prizes 17749
QWF Awards 17801
Evelyn Richardson Memorial Literary Trust 21982
Summerfield G. Roberts Award 19415
Carl Sandburg Literary Arts Award 9806
Barbara Savage "Miles From Nowhere" Memorial Award 13645
Lillian Smith Book Awards 19521
John Ben Snow Prize 19882
Society of Midland Authors Awards 19186
Spur Awards 21576
Student Writing Contest 2259
Technical and Scientific Communication Award 14843
Towson University Prize for Literature 20145
Lila Wallace-Reader's Digest Writers' Awards 21430
The Washington Post/Children's Book Guild Award for Nonfiction 21457
Western Heritage Awards (Wrangler Award) 14887
Western States Book Awards 21571
Whiting Writers' Award 21610
Wilbur Awards 17971
Yearbook Marketing Award 8177

Nuclear disarmament *See* World peace

Nuclear engineering (*See also* Atomic energy)
Harlan J. Anderson Award 5928
Bernard F. Langer Nuclear Codes and Standards Award 4525
Glenn Murphy Award 4031
Glenn T. Seaborg Award for Nuclear Chemistry 1785
Robert E. Wilson Award in Nuclear Chemical Engineering 2796

Numismatic journalism
Ray Byrne Memorial Literary Award 3204
Gould Memorial Literary Award 3223
Heath Literary Award 3224
Outstanding Club Publication Award 3246
Catherine Sheehan Award for U.S. Paper Money Studies 3256

Numismatics
Kamal M. Ahwash Literary Award 12812
American Numismatic Society Graduate Fellowship 3271
ANA Numismatic Art Award for Excellence in Medallic Sculpture 3197
Annual Medal Design Award 2879
Armenian Numismatic Memorial Award 5096
Terry Armstrong Memorial Award for Outstanding Regional Coordinator 3198
Award for Private Mint Issues 3199
Al Baber Member Booster Award 3200
George Bauer Memorial Exhibit Award 3201
Best Radio Script for "Money Talks" Award 3202
Best UKRAINPEX Show Theme Exhibit 20276
Best Written and Researched Article 8651
James L. Betton Youth Exhibit Award 3203
Wes Capar Award 20277
Helen Carmody-Lebo Memorial Award for Outstanding District Delegate 3205
Century Award 3206
Menachem Chaim and Simcha Tova Mizel Memorial Exhibit Award 3207
Henry Christensen Memorial Exhibit Award 3208
Fred Cihon Exhibit Award 3209
Coin of the Year Award 12618
Dr. Charles W. Crowe Memorial Exhibit Award 3210
John S. Davenport Memorial Exhibit Award 3211
Dealer Booster Award 3212
Gaston DiBello Memorial Exhibit Award 3213
William Donlan Memorial Exhibit Award 3214
R.R. Donnelley & Sons Co. Exhibit Award 3215
Edgerton-Lenker Memorial Youth Exhibit Award 3216
Exemplary Service Award 3217
Aaron Feldman Memorial Exhibit Award 3218
Fifty Year Club Member Certificate 3219
Fifty Year Membership Medal and Pin 3220
Forty Year Membership Pin 3221
Goodfellowship Award 3222
Donald Groves Fund 3272
Robert Hendershott Award 3225
William C. Henderson Memorial Exhibit Award 3226
Alan Herbert Youth Exhibit Award 3227
Archer M. Huntington Medal Award 3273
Incoming President Award 3228
Judges Appreciation Award 3229
Kagin Family Paper Money Youth Exhibit Award 3230
Dr. Lyndon King Award 8262
Melvin and Leona Kohl Memorial Exhibit Award 3231
Abe Kosoff Memorial Literary Award 3232
Robert J. Leuver Exhibit Award 3233
Lifetime Achievement Award 3234
Literary Award 7321
Charles "Cheech" Litman Memorial Youth Exhibit Award 3235
Local Committee Appreciation 3236
Love Token Society Exhibit Award 3237
Julian Maksymczuk Award 20279
Master of Ceremonies - ANA Banquet 3238

Numismatics (continued)
Medal of Merit 3239
Merit of Exhibits 3240
National Coin Week 3241
Numismatic Ambassador Award 12619
Numismatic Error Collectors Exhibit Award 3242
Ben and Sylvia Odesser Judaic Literary Award 2880
Outgoing Governor Award 3243
Outgoing President Award 3244
Outstanding Adult Advisor Award 3245
Outstanding Club Representative Award 3247
Outstanding Government Service Award 3248
Outstanding Young Numismatist of the Year 3249
People's Choice Award 3250
John Jay Pittman, Sr. Memorial Exhibit Award 3251
Wayte and Olga Raymond Literary Award 3252
Lelan G. Rogers Memorial Exhibit Award 3253
J. Sanford Saltus Medal Award 3274
Burton Saxton Memorial Exhibit Award 3254
Seventy-Five Year Club Member Certificate 3255
M. Vernon Sheldon Audio-Visual Award 3257
Sixty Year Membership Medal 3258
Glenn Smedley Memorial Award 3259
Sidney W. Smith Memorial Exhibit Award 3260
Twenty-Five Year Club Member Certificate 3261
Twenty-Five Year Membership Medals 3262
Melissa Van Grover Youth Exhibit Award 3263
Louis S. Werner Host Club Award 3264
Charles H. Wolfe Sr. Youth Best of Show Exhibit Award 3265
Charles H. Wolfe Sr. Youth Exhibit Award 3266
Howland Wood Memorial Award for Best of Show Exhibit 3267
B. P. Wright Memorial Exhibit Award 3268
Farran Zerbe Award 3269

Nursing
AAN Media Award 708
ABOHN Research Award 1570
Mildred Adams Chapter Heritage Award 18493
Advanced Oncology Certified Nurse of the Year Award 16709
Allen Ergen Scholarship 16525
Alumni PRN Grant 491
Linda Arenth Excellence in Cancer Nursing Management Award 16710
Awards of Appreciation 1291
Susan Baird Oncology Excellence in Writing Award in Clinical Practice 16711
Best of Image Awards 18494
Best of the Online Journal Award 18495
Mary Louise Brown Research Recognition Award 1305
Ellyn Bushkin Friend of the Foundation Award 16712
Business Recognition Award 1306
Career Development Award 20149
Career Development Awards 15271
Chapter Excellence Award 16713
Chapter Key Awards 18496
Chapter Newsletter Awards 18497
Chapter Presidents Trophy Award 10801
Chapter Research Advancement Award 18498
Luther Christman Award 934
Teresa E. Christy Award 1065
Clinical Instructor of the Year Award 1292
Clinical Nursing Excellence Award 5768
CMA Affirmative Action Award 3276
Community Service Award 1171
Constituent Association Award 1307
Dale Medical Products Excellent Clinical Nurse Specialist Award 1172
Datascope Excellence in Collaboration Award - Multidisciplinary Teams 1173
Datascope Excellence in Collaboration Award - Nurse to Family 1174
Jane A. Delano Award 3824
Distinguished Contribution to Nursing Science Award 3287
Distinguished Researcher Award 16714
Distinguished Scholar Program 3288
Lavinia L. Dock Award 1066
Employer Recognition Award 1571
ENA Micromedex Best Original Research Award 9244
Episteme Award 18499
Anna Mae Ericksen Award 18183
Ethics Award 9245
Excellence in Breast Cancer Education Award 16715
Excellence in Caring Practices Award 1175
Excellence in Education Award 1176
Excellence in Radiation Therapy Nursing Award 16716
Excellence of Scholarship and Consistency of Contributions to the Oncology Nursing Literature Award 16717
Excellent Nurse Manager Award 1177
Federal Nursing Service Award 5770
Mara Mogensen Flaherty Memorial Lectureship 16719
Loretta C. Ford Distinguished Fellow Award 14322
Founders' Awards 18500
Purdue Frederick Quality of Life Lecture 16720
Miriam Fay Furlong Grant 492
Margarite Ahern Graff Excellence Award 1572
Hattie Hemschemeyer Award 1902
Audrey Hepburn/Sigma Theta Tau International Award 18501
Martha N. Hill New Investigator Award 2410
Hirsh Award 1878
Agatha Hodgins Award for Outstanding Accomplishment 1294
Honorary Human Rights Award 3278
Honorary Member 1295
Honorary Membership 16721
Honorary Nursing Practice Award 3279
Honorary Recognition Award 3280
Judith C. Kelleher Award 9246
Marjorie Hiscott Keyes Award 7269
Mary T. Klinker Award 234
Helen Lamb Outstanding Educator Award 1296
Leininger Transcultural Nursing Award 20150
Katharine A. Lembright Award 2413
Alice Magaw Outstanding Clinical Practitioner Award 1297
Ann Magnussen Award 3833
Mary Mahoney Award 3281
Robyn Main Excellence in Clinical Practice Award 14317
Pearl McIver Public Health Nurse Award 3282
Media Award
- American Association of Critical-Care Nurses 1178
- Emergency Nurses Association 9247

Media Awards 18502
Member of the Year Award 10802
Mentoring Award 1179
National Advisor of the Year Award 493
National Member of the Year Award 494
Diane Norkool Award 6256
Cynthia Northrop Distinguished Service Award 1302
Nurse Manager Award 9248
Nurse of the Year
- National Association of Traveling Nurses 14447
- New York State Health Facilities Association 16285

Nurse of the Year Award 15209
Nurse Practitioner of the Year 16155
Nursing Education Award 9249
Nursing Practice Award 9250
Nursing Professionalism Award 9251
Nursing Research Award
- Emergency Nurses Association 9252
- Texas League for Nursing 20025

Nursing Scholarship 8418
ONS/AMGEN Inc. Award for Excellence in Patient/Public Education 16722
ONS/Pharmacia & Upjohn Excellence in Oncology Nursing Private Practice Award 16723
ONS/Roche Distinguished Service Award 16724
ONS/Ross Products Division of Abbott Laboratories Award for Excellence in Cancer Nursing Education 16725
ONS/Schering Excellence in Biotherapy Nursing Award 16726
ONS/Schering Excellence in Cancer Nursing Research Award 16727
ONS/Upjohn Quality of Life Award 16728
Outstanding Advocate Award 1303
Outstanding Performance Award 10803
Outstanding School Nurse of the Year Award 3891
Hildegard Peplau Award 3283
Pride and Recognition 17808
Program Director of the Year Award 1298
Donna Pruzansky Memorial Fund for Maternal and Child Health Nursing 8095
Public Relations Recognition Award 1299
Public Service Award
- Oncology Nursing Society 16729
- Sigma Theta Tau International 18503

Juanita Redmond Award for Nursing 355
Regional Information Technology Award 18504
Regional Innovative Chapter Award 18505
Regional Multimedia Award 18506
Research Awards 15273
Research Dissemination Award 18507
Research Dissertation Award 18508
Research in Action Award 1300
Research Utilization Award 18509

Nursing (continued)

RNR Chapter Community Service Award 9620
Royal Canadian Legion Fellowships in Gerontological Nursing 7313
Schering Clinical Lecture 16730
Scholarship for Enterostomal Therapy Education 16923
School Nurse of the Year 18341
Jessie M. Scott Award 3284
SIG Leadership Award 14318
Henry K. Silver Memorial Award 14323
Special Board Recognition Award 9253
Special Contributor Award 1180
Ada Mayo Stewart Awards 1573
Study Awards Program 7314
Mayrose Synder Excellence Award 1574
Teaching Excellence Award 20026
Shirley Titus Award 3285
Henrietta Villaescusa Community Service Award 14252
Dolly Vinsant Flight Nurse of the Year Award 8284
Janie Menchaca Wilson Leadership Award 14253

Nursing homes

Adult Volunteer of the Year 2393
Group Volunteer of the Year Award 2395
Teen Volunteer of the Year 2396

Nutrition

AAP Nutrition Award 757
ADA Foundation Awards for Excellence 2145
ADA Foundation Scholarships 2146
ANAD Award 14072
ANAD Service Awards 14073
Babcock-Hart Award 10935
Bio-Serv Award in Experimental Animal Nutrition 4156
Borden Award 938
Borden Award in Nutrition 7435
Lenna F. Cooper Memorial Lecturer 2147
Dannon Institute Award for Excellence in Medical/Dental Nutrition Education 3957
Murray Davidson Award 765
Director of the Year Award 18343
Distinguished Dietitian of the Year 12493
Stanley J. Dudrick Research Scholar Award 4165
Conrad A. Elvehjem Award for Public Service in Nutrition 4157
Fellow 4158
Future Leader Awards 11725
Garry/Labbe Award 983
Heart of the Program Award 18344
Robert H. Herman Memorial Award 3958
Hubert Humphrey Research Grant 18345
IFT Food Science Journalism Awards 10940
International Dairy Foods Association Research Award 2103
Norman Kretchmer Memorial Award in Nutrition and Development 3959
La Leche League International Award of Achievement 12628
La Leche League International Award of Appreciation 12629
La Leche League International Award of Excellence 12630
La Leche League International Award of Recognition 12631
La Leche League International Founders' Award 12632
Lederle Award in Human Nutrition 4159
Lincoln Foodservice Grant for Innovations in School Foodservice 18346
Manuscript Award 11708
The McCollum Award 3960
E. V. McCollum International Lectureship in Nutrition 4160
Mead Johnson Award 4161
Osborne and Mendel Award 4162
Niles Newton Memorial Award for Outstanding Achievement in Human Lactation 11709
Nutrition Education Award 1187
Nutrition Professionals, Inc. Applied Dairy Nutrition Award 2111
Nutritional Research Award 17170
Professional Development Awards 18348
Research and Development Award 10945
Jonathan E. Rhoads Lecture 4166
Shurgain Award for Excellence in Nutrition and MeatScience 7445
John Stalker Award 18349
E.L.R. Stokstad Award 4163
Louise Sublette Award of Excellence 18350
Harry M. Vars Award 4167
Harvey W. Wiley Award 4992
Wine Research Award 19182
Women Helping Women Awards 14074
Young Dietitian of the Year 12494
Young Investigator Award Competition 3961

Occupational health

ABOHN Research Award 1570
Edward J. Baier Technical Achievement Award 2609
John J. Bloomfield Award 2610
Mary Louise Brown Research Recognition Award 1305
Chemical Health and Safety Award 1743
Corporate Health Achievement Award 1904
Donald E. Cummings Memorial Award 2611
Distinguished Service Award 2612
DivCHAS College Health and Safety Award 1750
Employer Recognition Award 1571
Gold Medal Award 13463
Margarite Ahern Graff Excellence Award 1572
Alice Hamilton Award 2613
Honorary Member 2614
Adoph G. Kammer Merit in Authorship Award 1905
Ben Kean Medal 4630
Robert A. Kehoe Award of Merit 1906
Knudsen Award 1907
Kusnetz Award 2615
Mental Health in the Workplace Award 7270
Meritorious Achievement Award 2616
Meritorious Service Award 1908
Michigan Industrial Hygiene Society Award for Authorship 2617
Occupational Safety/Health Award Program 15658
Occupational Safety/Health Contests 15659
Poster Session Awards 2618
Tillmanns-Skolnok Award 1788
William Steiger Award 2619
Herbert E. Stokinger Award 2620
Mayrose Synder Excellence Award 1574
William B. Yant Award 2621

Occupational safety

Annual Contest 11117
APPA Safety Contest Awards 3787
Award of Safety Excellence 17755
Awards for Courage 15947
Best One-Year Safety Record Award 17756
Chairman's Safety Award 17953
Chemical Health and Safety Award 1743
Company Safety Awards 16421
DivCHAS College Health and Safety Award 1750
Extraordinary Plaque 11118
Gold Medal Award 13463
Industrial Safety Contest 4771
Letter of Recognition 11120
Most Improved Award 17757
NAMIC Engineering Safety Award 4231
Occupational Safety/Health Award Program 15658
Occupational Safety/Health Contests 15659
Pitcher Insurance Agency Safety Award 17531
President's Award 11367
President's Trophy 4772
Edgar Monsanto Queeny Safety Professional of the Year Award 4607
Safe Worker Award 4773
Safety Achievement 409
Safety and Health Awards 20512
Safety and Occupational Health Awards 17746
Safety and Service 19517
Safety Award 17002
Safety Award Program 19319
Safety Awards 15473
Sentinels of Safety 15387
Tillmanns-Skolnok Award 1788
Special Certificate 11121

Occupational therapy *See* Rehabilitation and therapy

Oceanography (*See also* Hydrography)

Alexander Agassiz Medal 13825
Albert R. Behnke, Award 20289
Behrens Award 9606
Bower Award and Prize for Achievement in Science 9741
Compass Distinguished Achievement Award 13108
Compass Industrial Award 13109
Compass International Award 13110
G. Evelyn Hutchinson Award 4489
R. Lindeman Award 4490
Lockheed/Martin Ocean Engineering Award 13111
MTS Special Commendation 13112
Ocean Sciences Award 2356
Oceaneering International Award 20291
President's Prize 7278
Prize in Applied Oceanography 7279
Safety in Seas Award 15420
Sea Grant Association Award 18386
Student Awards 18387
J.P. Tully Medal in Oceanography 7283

Office technology

Award of Excellence 6706
Member of the Year - Regional 6707
Today's Workplace of Tomorrow 21793

Office (continued)

Jo Warner Award 6708

Oil painting *See* Painting

Oncology *See* Cancer

Opera (*See also* Vocal music)
Annual Vocal Competition 17803
Belmont Medal 13321
Chamber Opera Competition 15426
Cincinnati Opera Education Program 7999
Concerto Competition 18280
Dallas Opera Young Artist Competition 21416
Dissertation Competition 15427
The Martin and Bernice Feinstein Award 21455
Grants for Arts Projects 14930
Houston Opera Studio Member 10569
Individual Artist Fellowship 13586
International Opera Singers Competition 7716
Kennedy Center Honors 12552
MacAllister Awards for Opera Singers 10775
Metropolitan Opera National Council Auditions 13318
Opera Production Competition 15428
Rose Palmai-Tenser Scholarship 13547
Scholarly Paper Competition 15429
Singer of the Year 18442
Richard Tucker Award 20230
Sarah Tucker Study Grants 20231
University of Louisville Grawemeyer Award for Music Composition 21050
Verdi Medal of Achievement 13319
Vocal Competition 15430

Operations research
EURO Golden Medal 11599
George E. Kimball Medal 11075
Frederick W. Lanchester Prize 11076
Local Society Awards 21302
Philip McCord Morse Lectureship Award 11077
George Nicholson Student Paper Competition 11078
John von Neumann Theory Prize 11081

Ophthalmology
Achievement Award 710
Leonard Apt Lecture 760
E.A. Baker Foundation for the Prevention of Blindness Fellowships 7301
Binkhorst Medal Lecture 4273
Benjamin F. Boyd Humanitarian Award 17053
Cogan Award 5464
Duke-Elder Award 11602
Education Achievement Award 13811
Jules Francois Award 11603
Friedenwald Memorial Award 5465
Gift of Sight Award 9381
Gonin Award 11604
Guest of Honor 711
Heise Award 9382
Howe Medal 3313
Edward Jackson Memorial Lecture Award 713
Charles D. Kelman Innovator's Lecture 4274
Kupfer Award 5466
Lifetime Achievement Award 1799
Beverly Myers Nelson Achievement Awards 13812
Beverly Myers Nelson Student Awards 13813
The National Academy Hall of Fame Award Program 13814
Outline of Sanity Award 1800
Outstanding Contribution to Ophthalmic Photography 16779
Outstanding Humanitarian Service Award 714
Paton Award 9383
Proctor Medal 5467
Scobee Lecturer 1134
Special Recognition Award 5468
Edgar D. Tillyer Award 16797
WCO Medal 21887
Mildred Weisenfeld Award for Excellence in Ophthalmology 5469

Optics
Esther Hoffman Beller Medal 16781
Max Born Award 16782
A. E. Conrady Award 19605
Distinguished Service Award 16783
Harold E. Edgerton Award 19606
Education Achievement Award 13811
Engineering Excellence Awards 16784
Joseph Fraunhofer Award/Robert M. Burley Prize 16785
Frederic Ives Medal/Jarus W. Quinn Endowment 16786
Dennis Gabor Award 19607
George W. Goddard Award 19608
Gold Medal of the Society 19609
Nick Holonyak Jr. Award 16787
Honor Certificate 1132
ICO Prize 12105
Incubic/Milton Change Student Travel Grants 16788
John Tyndall Award 10658
Rudolf Kingslake Medal and Prize 19610
Lancaster Award 1133
Edwin H. Land Medal 16789
LEOS Distinguished Service Award 10659
LEOS Engineering Achievement Award 10660
LEOS William Streifer Award 10661
Ellis R. Lippincott Award 16790
Adolph Lomb Medal 16791
Acrhie Mahan Prize 16792
C. E .K. Mees Medal 16793
William F. Meggers Award 16794
Beverly Myers Nelson Achievement Awards 13812
Beverly Myers Nelson Student Awards 13813
OSA Leadership Award/New Focus Bookham Prize 16795
David Richardson Medal 16796
Scobee Lecturer 1134
SPIE Technology Achievement Award 19611
Edgar D. Tillyer Award 16797
John Tyndall Award 16799
R. W. Wood Prize 16800

Optometry
Apollo Award 3315
Garland W. Clay Award 716
Joseph Dallos Award 8470
Distinguished Service Award 3316
Eminent Service Award 717
William Feinbloom Award 718
Founder's Award 719
Glenn A. Fry Lecture Award 720
G. N. Getman Award 8184
Honorary and Life Fellowships 721
International Optometrist of the Year 21885
Carel C. Koch Memorial Medal Award 722
National Optometrist of the Year Award 3317
Julius F. Neumueller Award in Optics 723
Charles F. Prentice Medal 724
A. M. Skeffington Award 8185
W. David Sullins Award for Outstanding Service in Optometry 5786
WCO Emeritus 21886
WCO Medal 21887
Young Optometrist of the Year 3318

Orchestral conducting *See* Conducting

Organizational service
Achievement Award 1260
Association of the United States Army Awards 5883
Award of Recognition 16873
Chapter of the Year Award 5365
Corps d'Elite Award 8258
Morgan Cox Award 21990
Enterprise Spirit Award 12576
Forty Year Plaque 8030
Jack Gibb Award 16874
Shirley Hohl Service Award 3933
Honorary Life Membership 2557
Lion Trophy 8866
Member of the Year Award 13048
Outstanding Organization Development Article of the Year Award 16875
Outstanding Organization Development Consultant of the Year Award 16876
Outstanding Organization Development Project of the Year Award 16877
Outstanding Presentation Award 16878
Partnership Award 3835
Pi Kappa Alpha Chapter and Alumni Awards 17311
Pioneer Award 1347
Helen L. Plants Award for Special Events 4040
Regional Clubs of the Year 21845
Kenneth Andrew Roe Award 1200
Stone Award 21135
Tiffany Awards for Employee Excellence 3838
Emile Tocze Memorial Trophy 21846

Oriental culture *See* Asian studies; Japanese culture

Ornithology
Arthur A. Allen Award 8518
Kathleen S. Anderson Research Grant 13060
Avy Award 2225
Bergstrom Research Award 5681
Best Bird of the Christmas Count 8511
Board of Directors Student Paper Awards 8489
William Brewster Memorial Award 3339
Maurice Broun Award 10299
Conservation Award 12133
Elliott Coues Award 3340
First Breeding Award
Avicultural Advancement Council of Canada 6140

Ornithology (continued)

International Wild Waterfowl Association 12134
Louis Agassiz Fuertes Award 21637
George A. Hall/Harold F. Mayfield Award 21638
Ludlow Griscom Award 1566
Hall of Fame 15502
Hawk Migration Association of North America Research Award 10300
Hawk Mountain Sanctuary Award 10304
Hawk Mountain - Student Research Award 10302
A. Brazier Howell Award 8490
L/M Award 1820
P.P. Levine Award 1087
Lifetime of Service to Aviculture Award 12135
Loye and Alden Miller Research Award 8491
Willetta Lueshen Harris' Sparrow Endowment 10805
Willetta Lueshen Student Membership Award 10806
Master Breeder Award 15503
Master Judge Award 15504
Gerard McQuade Memorial Fund Award 12136
Memorial Grants 9103
Mewaldt-King Student Research Award 8492
NABS Research Grants 16395
Sigurd T. Olson Common Loon Research Award 12917
Outstanding Achievement Awards 12137
Outstanding Service Award 15505
Harry R. Painton Award 8493
Phibro Animal Health Excellence in Poultry Research Award 1088
Frances Roberts Award 8494
Justin A. Southwick Memorial Award in Aviculture 12138
Special Service Award 1089
Doris Huestis Speirs Award 19080
Paul A. Stewart Awards 21639
Paul Stewart Endowment 10807
Waterfowl Breeders Hall of Fame 12139
Alexander Wilson Prize 21640

Orthodontistry
James E. Brophy AAO Distinguished Service Award 1318
Thomas M. Graber Award of Special Merit 1319
Milo Hellman Research Award 1320
Louise Ada Jarabak Memorial International Teachers and Research Award 1321
Albert H. Ketcham Memorial Award 1576
Leon J. Pinsker Merit Award 11373
Harry Sicher First Research Essay Award 1322

Orthopedics
Fuller Albright Award 3929
Nicolas Andry Award 5584
Frederic C. Bartter Award 3932
Marshall Urist Award 16912
William F. Neuman Award 3935
New Investigator Recognition Awards 16913
O'Donoghue Sports Injury Research Award 3352
Orthopedic Allied Professional of the Year 4582
Wiebrecht Award 680
William Harris Award 16916

Osteopathy
The Academy Award 740
Award of Fellow 3354
Exceptional Service Award 8638
Fellow of The Cranial Academy Award 8639
Honorary Life Member 8640
Matt Weyuker Scholarship 16921
Thomas L. Northup Lecturer Award 741
President's Appreciative Award 3355
Andrew Taylor Still Medallion of Honor 742
Sutherland Memorial Lecture 8641
Yearbook Dedication Award 743

Packaging
Aerosol Package Design Award 8464
AmeriStar Package Awards 11023
Award for Environmental Achievement 9572
Fellow Member 11024
Hall of Fame 17337
Honorary Member 11025
Member of the Year 11026
National Paperboard Packaging Competition 17064
Packaging Competition Awards 15475
Packaging Hall of Fame 17024
Packaging Leader of the Year 17025
President's Award 9573
Silver Shadow Award 17338
Top Packaging Awards 9574

Painting (*See also* Watercolor painting)
AAEA Founders Award for Painting 655
Alice Abel Cultural and Creative Arts Program 3141
Affaire in the Gardens 8035
Allied Arts Medal 18134
Benjamin Altman (Figure) Prize 13775
Benjamin Altman (Landscape) Prize 13776
Annual Art Competition & Exhibition 19831
Annual Exhibition
  Allied Artists of America 473
  Audubon Artists 6061
Annual Exhibition Awards 14457
Annual Open Exhibition 5121
Art of the Northeast Competition 18521
Artists' Fellowships 16229
Artists-in-Residence Program 19814
The Artist's Magazine Art Competition 5146
Jean Bowman Memorial Award for Painting 659
Boynton's G.A.L.A. Artist Awards 6594
Bush Artist Fellows Program 6700
Cape Cod Art Association Awards 7571
Emil and Dines Carlsen Award 13781
Andrew Carnegie Prize 13782
Certificates of Merit 13783
Cintas Foundation Fellowships 10981
Thomas B. Clarke Prize 13784
Decorative Arts Collection Awards 19097
Dedicated Service Award 19098
Delta Art Exhibition 5070
El Angel Award - Distinguished Hispanic-American Artist 6374
Fine Art Show 18244
Gilpin County Arts Association Annual Exhibition 10028
Grand National Exhibition 930
Greater Haverhill Arts Association Annual Exhibition 10147
George Hitchcock Landscape in Sunlight Prize 13787
Howard Fellows 10571
International Art Show by Artists with Disabilities 18536
Joseph S. Isidor Memorial Medal 13789
Kentucky Artists Fellowships 12562
LaGrange National 7817
Isaac N. Maynard Prize 13790
Leonard J. Meiselman Memorial Award for Painting 660
National Exhibition of Rosemaling in the Norwegian Tradition 21316
National Small Painting Exhibition 16192
National Society of Artists Awards 15728
New American Talent Show 5123
New Mexico Juried Exhibition 13689
NSPCA Annual Exhibition 15744
Adolph and Clara Obrig Prize for Painting in Oil 13793
Kimbel E. Oelke Memorial Award for Painting 662
Edwin Palmer Memorial Prize 13794
"Picture It Painted Professionally" Awards 17029
Pollock-Krasner Foundation Grants 17461
Prix de West Invitational Exhibition 14886
Thomas R. Proctor Prize 13796
Red Cloud Indian Art Show 10424
Rome Prize Fellowships 605
Arthur Ross Awards 10853
Mikhail and Ekateryna Shatalov Award 13798
Silver Palette Award 19099
Southwest Juried Exhibition 13690
Ellin P. Speyer Memorial Prize 13799
S. J. Wallace Truman Prize 13800
Visionary Art Show Awards 10502
W & J National Painting Show 16690

Paleontology *See* Geology and paleontology

Paper industry (*See also* Forestry; Wood and wood products)
American Wood Council Wood Design Award 21820
Award of Safety Excellence 17755
Best One-Year Safety Record Award 17756
Environment and Energy Achievement Awards Program 2288
TAPPI Herman L. Joachim Distinguished Service Award 19921
Most Improved Award 17757
Gunnar Nicholson Gold Medal Award 19922
George Olmsted Award 2289
Student Design-School Competition 17003
TAPPI Fellow Award 19924

Parachuting *See* Flying

Parenting *See* Family relations

Park planning (*See also* City planning)
Award of Merit 7323
Harry Boothman Bursary 7324
W. Allison and Elizabeth Stubbs Davis Award 13676
Fellows Award 21398

Park (continued)
J. B. Harkin Conservation Award 7330
National Corporate Humanitarian Award 15579
National Gold Medal Awards 19726
Theodore and Franklin Roosevelt Award for Excellence in Recreation and Park Research 15584
State Park Awards 19727
Young Professional Award 7328

Parks *See* Recreation

Patents *See* Inventions

Pathology
Amgen Outstanding Investigator Award 4118
ASCP Associate Member Lifetime Achievement Award 3963
ASCP Associate Member Section Distinguished Service Award 3964
ASCP - CAP Joint Distinguished Service Award 3965
ASCP Medical Photography Competition 3966
ASCP Sheard - Sanford Medical Student Award 3967
William Boyd Lectureship 6928
ASCP Distinguished Service to Clinical Pathology Award Honoring Ward Burdick 3968
Chugai Award for Meritorious Mentoring and Scholarship 4119
Experimental Pathologist-in-Training Award 4120
Fellow 3357
The Gold-Headed Cane Award 4121
Leica Canada Scientific Award 6929
ASCP Outstanding Research Award Honoring Philip Levine 3969
Donald W. Penner Prize 6930
Rous-Whipple Award 4122
ASCP Distinguished Pathology Educator Award Honoring H. P. Smith 3970
Edward Rhodes Stitt Lecture Award 5785
Trainee Travel Awards 4123

Patriotism *See* Citizenship and patriotism

Peace *See* World peace

Pediatrics
AAP Excellence in Public Service Award 756
AAP Nutrition Award 757
C. Anderson Aldrich Award 758
APA Public Policy and Advocacy Award 591
APA Research Award 592
APA Teaching Award 593
Virginia Apgar Award 759
Leonard Apt Lecture 760
Award for Outstanding Service to Maltreated Children 761
Henry L. Barnett Award 762
William G. Bartholome Award for Ethical Excellence 763
Canadian Pediatric Society Research Award 7318
E. H. Christopherson Lectureship Award 764
Seymour R. Cohen Award 2926
Murray Davidson Award 765
Distinguished Career Award
Ambulatory Pediatric Association 594
American Academy of Pediatrics 766
Distinguished Service Award
American Academy of Pediatrics 768
American Academy of Pediatrics 767
Loretta C. Ford Distinguished Fellow Award 14322
Founders Award 770
Stephen L. Gans Distinguished Overseas Lectureship 772
Jerome Glaser Distinguished Service Award 773
Clifford G. Grulee Award 774
Health Care Delivery Award 595
Ray E. Helfer Award 596
Adele Dellenbaugh Hofmann Award 776
SAM/Adele D. Hofmann Visiting Professor in Adolescent Medicine and Health Award 18617
John Howland Award 3370
Abraham Jacobi Award 777
Alvin H. Jacobs Award 778
William E. Ladd Award 779
Lay Education Project Award 780
Lectureship in Developmental and Behavioral Pediatrics 18663
Ludwig-Seidel Award 597
Dolley Madison Award 22109
Ronald McDonald House Charities Awards of Excellence 18117
Medical Education Awards 781
Medical Education Lifetime Achievement Awards 782
Hilary E. C. Millar Award for Innovative Approaches to Adolescent Health Care 18618
Neonatal Education Award 783
Byron B. Oberst Award 784
Outstanding Achievement in Adolescent Medicine Award 18619
Outstanding Chapter Awards 785
Outstanding Service Award for Military Pediatrics 786
Pediatric Dermatology Fellows/Residents Research Award 18831
Pediatric Dermatology Research Grant 18832
Pediatric Division Award for Outstanding Contributions to Pediatric Clinical Chemestry 997
Pediatric Resident Research Award 787
Pediatric Urology Medal 788
Practitioner Research Award 789
Professional Education Project Award 790
Bret Ratner Award 791
Research Visiting Professor Award 18620
Resident and Fellow Achievement Awards 792
Dale Richmond Lectureship 793
Ross Award 7319
Routh Student Research Grant 3755
Arnold M. Salzberg Mentorship Award 794
SAM/Mead Johnson Nutritionals New Investigator Award 18621
Milton J. E. Senn Lectureship and Award 795
Thomas E. Shaffer Award 796
Henry K. Silver Memorial Award 14323
Job Lewis Smith Award 797
Robert M. Smith Award 798
Student Research Award Competition 3756

Pentathlon
General George S. Patton, Jr. Memorial Trophy 20705

Performing arts (*See also* Ballet; Choreography; Costume design; Dance; Drama; Entertainment; Music; Puppetry; Theater)
Achievement in the Arts Award 16575
Actors' Fund Medal 170
Artists' Fellowships 16229
Arts and Letters Award 7029
Arts Management Award for Arts Administrator of the Year 5155
Arts Management Award for Career Service 5156
Arts Management Special Award 5157
Arts Recognition and Talent Search (ARTS) 15117
Award for Distinguished Achievement in the Arts 20072
Award for Distinguished Service to the Arts 20073
Award for Outstanding Portrayal of the American Scene 18375
Awards 176
Harry Blackstone Award 11801
Dawson Awards 5810
DEA Award 8732
Distant Accords Awards 11593
El Angel Award - Distinguished Hispanic-American Artist 6374
Gold Baton Award 4730
Hal Jackson's Michigan Talented Teens Scholarship 19903
Heartland Arts Fund 5159
Honorary Member 6856
Paul de Hueck and Norman Walford Career Achievement Awards in the Performing Arts and in Visual Arts 16741
Image Award 9195
Individual Artist Fellowship 16628
Kennedy Center Honors 12552
Life Achievement Award 18376
Life Member 6857
Lifetime Achievement Awards 10196
Algur H. Meadows Award for Excellence in the Arts 19513
Medal for Peace and Friendship through Music and Arts 11595
Music Center Spotlight Awards 13698
National Student Playwriting Award 12546
New York Dance and Performance Awards (Bessie Awards) 8745
Outstanding Performance Awards 18377
Performance Awards 16975
Antoinette Perry Awards (Tony Awards) 12742
Paul Robeson Award 163
Irene Ryan Winners Circle Evening of Scenes 12547
Martin E. Segal Award 12856
Tim Sims Encouragement Fund Award for Work in the Comedic Arts 16747
Fannie Taylor Distinguished Service Award 5811
Theatre Grants 17555
Toronto Arts Awards 20112
Young Soloists Award 21414

Perfumes *See* Cosmetology

Personal achievement *See* Professional and personal achievement

Performing (continued)

Personal finance *See* Financial planning

Personnel management (*See also* Employment practices; Training and development)
Achievement Awards 14165
Award for Professional Excellence 18694
Awards for Educational Excellence 18695
Book Award 18696
Booster Award 1979
Leonard R. Brice Outstanding Student Leadership Award 18697
Capital Leadership Award 18698
Catalyst Award 13236
Chapter Merit Awards for Professional Chapters 18699
Chapter Merit Awards for Students 18700
Director General's Award for Excellence in Human Resource Management 20535
EMA Foundation School/Business Partnership Award 9256
Excellence in Education Award 12843
Georges Petitpas Memorial Award 21915
Ted Henry Student Research Award 18701
IPMA Award for Excellence 11832
IPMA Honorary Life Membership 11833
National Medal of Technology 15678
Verne Orr Award 350
Pinnacle Awards 18702
Harris F. Seidel Award 5582
SHRM Foundation Award for Graduate Student Research 18703
SHRM Foundation Outstanding Graduate Student Award 18704
Warner W. Stockberger Achievement Award 11834
USAF Personnel Manager of the Year 362
Volunteer Awards 7332
Yoder-Heneman Human Resource Management Creative Application Awards 18705
Yoder-Heneman Human Resource Management Research Award 18706

Pest control *See* Public health

Petroleum engineering
Fernley H. Banbury Award 1737
Best Paper Award
American Association of Petroleum Geologists 1326
Society of Petrophysicists and Well Log Analysts 19252
Best Paper Presentation Award 19253
Best Student Paper Award 1327
Best Student Poster Award 1328
Ziad Beydoun Memorial Award for Best International Poster 1329
Carlos Walter M. Campos Memorial Award for Best International Student Paper 1331
John Franklin Carll Award 19234
Certificates of Merit 1332
DeGolyer Distinguished Service Medal 19235
Gabriel Dengo Memorial Award for Best International Paper 1333
Distinguished Achievement Award for Petroleum Engineering Faculty 19236
Distinguished Member 19237
Distinguished Service Award
American Chemical Society 1749
Society of Petroleum Engineers 19238
Society of Petrophysicists and Well Log Analysts 19254
Distinguished Technical Achievement Award 19255
Drilling and Completion Award 19239
Clarence E. Earle Memorial Award 15349
Facilities and Construction Award 19240
Fellows Award 15350
Cedric K. Ferguson Medal 19241
Formation Evaluation Award 19242
Gold Medal Award for Technical Achievement 19256
Charles Goodyear Medal 1756
Health, Safety, and Environment Award 19243
Honorary Membership 19244
Journalism Award 1340
Donald L. Katz Award 9896
A. I. Levorsen Memorial Award 1341
Life Membership Award 1342
Anthony F. Lucas Gold Medal 2820
Management and Information Award 19245
Medal of Honor for Career Service 19257
Melvin Mooney Distinguished Technology Award 1772
George A. Olah Award in Hydrocarbon or Petroleum Chemistry 1777
Outstanding Explorer Award 1345
Past Presidents' Award 1346
Pioneer Trophy 15353
Production and Operations Award 19246
Public Service Award 19247
W. Raymond Award 2826
Reservoir Description and Dynamics Award 19248
Sparks-Thomas Award 1790
Ozan Sungurlu Memorial Award for Best International Student Poster 1353
Lester C. Uren Award 19249
George Stafford Whitby Award for Distinguished Teaching and Research 1793
Young Member Outstanding Service Award 19250

Petroleum industry
Authors' Award 15346
Award for Achievement 15347
Andrew D. Baillie Award 7481
Chevron U.S.A. Marketing Award 15348
CSPG Graduate Students Thesis Awards 7482
Distinguished Service Award 15552
R. J. W. Douglas Memorial Medal 7483
FPGA Scholarship Program 9615
Fuels and Petrochemical Division Award 2773
Gold Medal 3374
GPA Citation for Service 9893
GPA Recognition Award 9894
Hanlon Award 9895
Hat's Off Award 20009
Bill Hill Memorial Award 15553
Honorary Member 7484
Honorary Membership
American Association of Petroleum Geologists 1339
National Lubricating Grease Institute 15351
Link Award 7485
Marketing Achievement Awards 15554
George C. Matson Memorial Award 1343
Medal of Merit 7486
Meritorious Service Trophy 15352
Percy W. Nicholls Award 18819
Sidney Powers Memorial Award 1348
President's Award 7487
Regional Graduate Scholarships 7488
John Rogers Award 7701
Safety Award 15555
Safety Awards 6926
Sanford-Springvale Rotary Club Scholarship Fund 13039
Service Awards 7489
Stanley Slipper Gold Medal 7490
J. C. "CAM" Sproule Memorial Award 1352
State Director of the Year Award 15556
Tracks Award 7491
Volunteer Awards 7492

Pets *See* Animal care and training

Pharmacology
Abbott Award 7457
William B. Abrams Award in Geriatric Clinical Pharmacology 3972
Academy of Pharmaceutical Research and Science Fellow 3376
Academy of Pharmacy Practice and Management Fellow 3377
Affiliate of the Year Award 11949
American Pharmacists Association Fellows 3378
American Society of Pharmacognosy Awards and Grants 4584
AMGEN Award 7458
AMSUS Award for Excellence in Clinical Pharmacy Practice 5763
APHA - APPM Merit Awards 3379
Apotex Award 7459
ASPET Award for Experimental Therapeutics 4169
Association of Faculties of Pharmacy of Canada Excellence in Teaching Award 6624
Award of Merit 12680
Award of Merit Certificate 14627
AZO Achievement Medal 496
AZO Meritorious Award 497
AZO Undergraduate Award 498
Baxter Award 7460
James Hartley Beal Award 4177
Bernard Belleau Award 7830
Brady/Schuster Award 3764
William H. Briner Nuclear Pharmacy Practice Award 3380
Bristol-Myers Squibb Award 7461
Bristol-Myers Squibb Award for Excellence in Pharmaceutical Teaching 6626
Bernard B. Brodie Award in Drug Metabolism 4170
Alfred Burger Award in Medicinal Chemistry 1742
Canadian Cardiovascular Society Research Achievement Award 6627
Catholic Pharmacist of the Year 14628
McKeen Cattell Memorial Award 1847
Chapter Excellence Awards 11950
Company of the Year Award 11951
CPhA Centennial Award 7334
Andrew Craigie Award 5769
Discoverers Awards 17228
Distinguished Achievement Award in Clinical/Pharmacotherapeutic Practice 3381
Distinguished Achievement Award in Community and Ambulatory Practice 3382

Subject Index

Pharmacology (continued)

Distinguished Achievement Award in Hospital and Institutional Practice 3383
Distinguished Achievement Award in Specialized Pharmaceutical Services 3384
Distinguished Investigator Award 1848
Distinguished Service Award by Ortho-McNeil 7462
Distinguished Service Citation 12681
H. A. B. Dunning Award 3385
Ebert Prize 3386
Daniel H. Efron Research Award 1895
Joel Elkes International Award 1896
Henry W. Elliott Distinguished Service Award 3973
Epilepsy Research Award for Outstanding Contributions to the Pharmacology of Antiepileptic Drugs 4171
Food, Pharmaceutical and Bioengineering Division Award in Chemical Engineering 2770
For Church and Profession (of Pharmacy) Award 14629
Gloria Niemeyer Francke Leadership Mentor Award 3387
Goodman and Gilman Award in Drug Receptor Pharmacology 4172
Glaxco Award 7463
Leon I. Goldberg Young Investigator Award of the ASCPT 3974
Good Government Pharmacist of the Year Award 3388
Max Hamilton Memorial Prize 8199
Takeru Higuchi Research Prize 3389
Hirsh Award 1878
Paul Hoch Distinguished Award 1897
Honorary Fellowship Award 1849
Honorary Founder of the Guild 14630
Honorary Member 3390
Honorary President 3391
Honorary President of the Guild 14631
Horner Travel Award 7464
Lester E. Hosto Distinguished Service Award 14104
Oscar B. Hunter Memorial Award in Therapeutics of the ASCPT 3975
ISPE Distinguished Achievement Award 11952
Janssen Award 7465
Kilmer Prize 3393
Nathaniel T. Kwit Distinguished Service Award 1850
J. Leon Lascoff Memorial Award 1833
Eric W. Martin Memorial Award 3083
Medicinal Chemistry Award 1771
Merck Frosst Award 7466
NHPA Scholarship Trust Fund 16157
NovoPharm Award 7467
Organon Award 7468
Outstanding Chapter Advisor Award 3394
Outstanding Dissertation Award 3765
Past President's Award 6628
P.B. Dews Award 4173
Pfizer Minority Summer Fellowship Award 1898
Pharmacia-ASPET Award 4174
K.M. Piafsky Award of the Canadian Society for Clinical Pharmacology 6629
PMAC Health Research Foundation 6840
Postdoctoral Fellowship Awards for Minorities 1899
Postgraduate Best Paper Award 3395
President's Award 4178
Rafaelsen Fellowship Award 8201
Rawls-Palmer Progress in Medicine Lecture and Award 3976
Remington Honor Medal 3396
Research Achievement Awards in the Pharmaceutical Services 3397
Dr. Rio de La Loza Prize 17662
Roche Award 7470
Sidney R. Rome Memorial Award 499
Albert E. Rosica, Jr. Memorial Award 1834
Sabex Award 7471
Sandoz Award 7472
Hugo H. Schaefer Award 3398
Schering Award 7473
Shering Award 7474
Smissman-Bristol-Myers-Squibb Award 1789
Daniel B. Smith Practice Excellence Award 3399
Torald Sollmann Award in Pharmacology 4175
Student Leadership Awards 3400
Tanabe Young Investigator Award 1851
Emory W. Thurston Grand President's Award 17247
Linwood F. Tice Friend of the AphA-ASP Award 3401
Tyler Prize for Stimulation of Research 3402
Warren Weaver Service Award 7967
Wyeth Young Psychopharmacologist Award 3766
Young Investigator Memorial Travel Awards 1900

Philanthropy

S. Y. Agnon Gold Medal 2306
ALTA Major Benefactor Honor Award 5448
Awards for Excellence in Community Service, Philanthropy, and Media 19847
Minnie Barnes Award 19801
Camp Hemlocks Camperships 9093
Campbell & Company Award for Excellence in Fundraising 5699
Community Counselling Service Award for Outstanding Fundraising Professional 5700
Damien - Dutton Award 8726
Distinguished Grant Maker Award 8597
Founder's Award 17520
Founders' Award for Public Service 5701
John W. Gardner Leadership Award 10747
Gold Medal Award for Distinguished Service 21258
Good Grant Award 8994
John Grenzebach Awards 43
Hall of Outstanding Americans 15986
Harvard Medal 10271
Lawton S. Heart Award 9593
Henry Hampton Award for Excellence in Film and Digital Media 8598
Imagine Mutual Fund Industry Corporate Citizenship Award 10702
Inez C. Peterson Citizenship Award 20914
Institution of the Year 20358
Ketchum Award for Outstanding Volunteer Fundraiser 5703
Medal for Distinguished Philanthropy 1280
Medal of Honor 9721
Robert F. Morneau Distinguished Service Award 14604
Paschal Murray Award for Outstanding Philanthropist 5704
National Women's Hall of Fame 15960
New Spirit of Community Partnership Awards Program 10703
No Small Change Award 12588
Northern Science Award 10751
Outstanding Business Leader Awards 16573
Outstanding Corporation Award 5705
Outstanding Foundation Award 5706
Patriot Award 17068
Paul Ylvisaker Award for Public Policy Engagement 8599
George Peabody Medal 17123
Philos Award - Philanthropist of the Year 3836
Wilmer Shields Rich Awards for Excellence in Communications 8600
Scopus Award 2309
Robert W. Scrivner Award for Creative Grantmaking 8601
Seymour Award 5379
SFORZA Medal 5619
Edward A. Smith Awards 13396
Spirit of America Award 20904
Summit Awards 20905
Henrietta Szold Award 10215
Trailblazer in Philanthropy Award 17269
USO Woman of the Year 21259
Venture Grants 20910
Volunteer Council Fundraising Gold Ribbon Awards 4733
Volunteer Fund Raiser of the Year 3839
Lawrence A. Wien Prize for Social Responsibility 8252

Philatelic journalism

Bob Houston Memorial Award 20070
Clyde Carriker, Jr. Memorial Award 20097
Gerard Gilbert Memorial Award 9726
Eugene Kotyk Award 20278
Postal History Journal Awards 17481
Writers Contest 20098

Philately

AFDCS Distinguished Service Award 2246
Annual Competition - Grand Award (One-Frame Competition) 8134
Helen August Memorial Award 3404
Award of Recognition 21767
Jere. Hess Barr Award 3405
Best in Topical Awards 4748
Best of the Rest Award 20925
Best UKRAINPEX Show Theme Exhibit 20276
Best Written and Researched Article 8651
George A. Blizil Memorial Literature Award 9984
Frank W. Campbell Award 17484
Wes Capar Award 20277
Champion of Champions 3414
Championship Award 20926
Clark Award 9191
Dorothy Colby Memorial Award 3406
Collectors Club Medal for Best Program Presented to the Collectors Club 8135
Collectors Club Medal for Outstanding Article in *The Collectors Club Philatelist* 8136
COROS Ribbon 8140
CP Writers Award 8355
CSA Trophy 8356
Dealer and Exhibit Awards 8357
August Dietz Award 8358
Distinguished Topical Philatelist Award 4749

Philately (continued)

Erani P. Drossos Award 3407
Franklin Erwin Memorial Trophy 20927
Edith M. Faulstich Grand Award 17480
James Waldo Fawcett Award 3408
Federal Duck Stamp Contest 20592
USCU Fernandez Award 20928
Grand Award 2247
Guardians of the Seas Award 20929
Herman L. Halle Research Award 9985
Hallock Card Award 17222
JPA H. E. Harris Ribbon 12470
Honorary Life Member
American Helvetia Philatelic Society 2442
Confederate Stamp Alliance 8359
Hopkinson Award 20850
India Study Circle Award 10749
Philip W. Ireland Special Award 7923
Earl Grant Jacobsen Award 18325
JPA Blue Ribbon and Certificate 12471
Eugene Klein Award 3409
Alfred F. Lichtenstein Medal 8137
Admiral Lockwood Award 20930
Francis E. Locy Award 20931
Luff Awards 3415
Julian Maksymczuk Award 20279
Walter R. McCoy Award 3410
Meritorious Service Award 3411
Haydn Myer Award 8360
Mortimer L. Neinken Medal 17271
Novice Award 20932
Nuclear Ships Trophy 20933
Carl E. Pelander Award 18326
Philatelic Hall of Fame 3416
Postal History Society Medal 17482
President's Medal for Merit 8138
President's Trophy 8361
Reserve Grand Award 20934
Charles D. Root Memorial Award 20440
SCC Award Medals 18327
Stan Shantz Award 17485
Sixteen One Frame Exhibit 20935
Society of Australasian Specialists/Oceania Medals 19031
Southgate Award 20851
Sports Philatelists International Awards 19732
Robert Stolz Trophy for Music Philately 17273
Joanna Taylor Memorial Bowl 18328
Jesse Burgess Thomas Memorial Award 20936
Trustees Trophy 8362
Graf von Spee Chapter Award 20937
C. Corwith Wagner Award 3412
Philip H. Ward, Jr. Memorial Award 2248
Albert O. Wickard Award 20938
Wings of Gold Award 20939
Workhorses of the Fleet Award 20940

Philology ***See*** **Linguistics**

Philosophy
ACPA Young Scholars Award 1660
Anthem Essay Contest 6173
APA/PDC Prize for Excellence and Innovation in Philosophy Programs 3421
Aquinas Medal 1661
Article Prize 3422
David Baumgardt Memorial Fellowship 3423
Fred Berger Memorial Prize 3424
Book Prize 3425
Butler Medal 8240
Carus Lectures 3426
John Dewey Humanist Award 2584
Distinguished Woman Philosopher Award 18937
Ralph Waldo Emerson Award 17241
Hubert Evans Nonfiction Prize 21520
Fellow for Research in Esoteric Areas of Knowledge 5025
John Fisher Memorial Prize 12444
The Fountainhead Essay Contest 6174
Hala-Negri Award 10603
Howard Fellows 10571
Humanist of the Year 10606
"Kimble" - Fugitive of the Year 9823
John F. Lewis Award 3438
Mentor 11954
John William Miller Essay Prizes and Research Fellowships 13426
Ashley Montagu Human Nurturance Award 10604
National Endowment for the Humanities Grant Programs 14938
National Federation of the Blind Scholarship Program 15039
C. S. Peirce Essay Contest Award 7810
Pessimist of the Year 6312
Realia Honors 10849
Rockefeller Prize 3427
Patrick Romanell Lecture 3428
Romanell - Phi Beta Kappa Professorship in Philosophy 17244
Royce Lectures in the Philosophy of the Mind 3429
Schutz Lecture 3430
Second Intellectual List of Leaders Yearbook 5026
Frank Chapman Sharp Memorial Prize 3431
Sisyphus Award 14759
Spinoza Award 20923
URAM Award for Excellence in Creative Endeavors for Research and Scholarship 11962
URAM Award for Excellence in Creative Scholarly Writing 11963
Whiting Memorial Fund Award 11955

Philosophy of science
Magellanic Premium Award 3439

Photogrammetry
Talbert Abrams Award 5208
Ford Bartlett Award 5209
Boeing Award 5210
John I. Davidson ASPRS President's Award for Practical Papers 5211
ESRI Award for Best Scientific Paper in Geographic Information Systems 5212
Fellow 5213
Honor Award 5214
Honorary Member 5215
KODAK International Educational Literature Award 5216
LEICA Geosystems Award for Best Scientific Paper in Remote Sensing 5217
Leica Geosystems Internship 5218
Ta Liang Memorial Award 5219
Outstanding Service Award 5220
Photogrammetric (Fairchild) Award 5221
Presidential Citations for Meritorious Service 5222
Region Newsletter of the Year Award 5223
Region of the Year Award 5224
Space Imaging Award for Application of High Resolution Digital Satellite Imagery 5225

Photographic prints
Annual International Competition 17562
New Mexico Juried Exhibition 13689
Pictorial Print Color Division Awards 17290
Pictorial Print Monochrome Division Awards 17291
Small and Commercial Print Division Awards 17293
Southwest Juried Exhibition 13690

Photography (*See also* Nature photography; Photogrammetry; Photographic prints; Photojournalism; Slide photography)
Academy & Achievement Awards 80
Affaire in the Gardens 8035
Annual Exhibitions 5115
Annual Photography Contest 20682
Arrowhead Biennial Exhibition 9047
Artists' Fellowships 16229
ASCP Medical Photography Competition 3966
Association Fellowship Award 15531
Banff Mountain Photography Competition 6237
Roland Barrett Award 21127
Edward B. Berkowitz Memorial Award 15820
Blue Pencil Awards 14242
Raymond C. Bowman Award 18710
Boynton's G.A.L.A. Artist Awards 6594
Bush Artist Fellows Program 6700
CA Advertising Annual 8308
Chester F. Carlson Award 18711
The CDS/Honickmand First Book Prize in Photography 9044
Cintas Foundation Fellowships 10981
Clarion Awards 5522
Color Slide Division Awards 17284
Joseph Costa Courtroom Photography Award 6204
Courage in Journalism Award 12145
Brig. Gen. Robert L. Denig Distinguished Service Award 20684
Distinguished Performance Award 20686
Duke and Duchess of York Prize in Photography 6791
Eastman Kodak Gold Medal Award 19190
Editorial Awards 17285
Emmy Awards for Primetime Programming 127
Exhibition of Photography 18243
Family International Talent Awards Program 17088
Fellowship 18712
Fellowship Award 21128
Fine Arts Work Center Fellowships 9553
Front Page Awards 21439
Gilpin County Arts Association Annual Exhibition 10028
George W. Goddard Award 19608
Gold Awards 16996
Gold Medal of Excellence for Photography 13985
Gold Medal of the Society 19609
R. C. Hakanson Award 9361
Hearst Newspapers Writing and Photography Contests 10356
Harold S. Hirsch Award for Excellence in Ski Photography 16462
Honor Awards 21129

Subject Index

Photography (continued)

Honorary Fellow of the Photographic Society 9925
Honorary Member 17286
Honorary Membership 18713
Howard Fellows 10571
Hoyt Mid Atlantic Art Show 10573
IAFF Media Awards Contest 11355
Impact Through Applied Photography 17638
Individual Artist Fellowship
  Montana Arts Council 13586
  Ohio Arts Council 16628
Infinity Awards 11462
International Art Show by Artists with Disabilities 18536
International Exhibition of Professional Photography 17639
International Navies Photo Contest 20713
International Photography Hall of Fame and Museum 17281
Itek Award 18714
Charles E. Ives Journal Award (Engineering) 18715
Journal Award (Science) 18716
Kentucky Artists Fellowships 12562
Kodak International Newspaper Snapshot Awards 9121
Kosar Memorial Award 18717
La Croix Award 14328
LaGrange National 7817
Dorothea Lange - Paul Taylor Prize 9045
J. Winton Lemen Award 15537
Lenehan Log Cabin Photography Competition 12908
Lieven Gevaert Medal 18718
Louis R. Lowery Memorial Award 20687
Anthony Majeri Jr. Award for Innovation and Leadership in Graphic Journalism 6210
Man of the Year 11619
Master Fire Photographer 11620
Medlar Award 17641
National Magazine Awards 4492
National Magazine Awards 15355
National Newspaper Awards 7309
National Society of Artists Awards 15728
National Wildlife Photo Contest 15952
Nature Division Awards 17287
Naval and Maritime Photo Contest 20715
New Mexico Juried Exhibition 13689
Newhouse Citation 19880
William G. Nolan Service Award 11621
Outstanding Contribution to Ophthalmic Photography 16779
Parade/Kodak Photography Contest 17066
Gordon Parks Commemorative Photography Competition 9703
Person of the Year 17296
James D. Phelan Art Awards 18250
Photo Challenge 17577
Photo Contest 21998
Photo Travel Division Awards 17288
Photographers Fellowship Fund 7743
Photography Annual 8311
Photography Awards 2446
Photojournalism Division Awards 17289
Pictorial Print Color Division Awards 17290
President's Award 7952
President's Citation 18719
Prints, Drawings and Photographs Exhibition 5071
Professional Photographer Award 17297
Progress Award 17292
Pulitzer Prizes 17749
Railroad Calendar Color Slide Contest 13737
Scientific or Technical Achievement Award 17298
Senior Membership 18720
Service Award 18721
Small and Commercial Print Division Awards 17293
Southwest Juried Exhibition 13690
Special Award 17299
Special Citation in Honor of Rudy and Hertha Benjamin 3443
Joseph A. Sprague Memorial Award 15548
Stereo Division Awards 17294
Colonel John W. Thomason, Jr. Award 13101
Toronto International Salon of Photography 20120
World of Wedding Photography and Portrait Of Excellence 21508

Photojournalism

Annual Awards in International News Coverage 16981
Asian American Journalists Association National Awards 5165
Association Fellowship Award 15531
Atlantic Journalism Awards 6035
Atrium Award 21019
Better Newspapers Competition 7034
Book Awards 7913
Harry Chapin Media Awards 21925
Joseph Costa Award 15532
Ernie Crisp Television News Photographer of the Year 15533
Niles Davis Award 14066
Deadline Club Awards 8773
Brig. Gen. Robert L. Denig Distinguished Service Award 20684
Distinguished Performance Award 20686
Eclipse Awards for Media 20085
Editorial Awards
  Photographic Society of America 17285
  Suburban Newspapers of America 19819
Exhibition of Photography 18243
Feature Photo Award 16245
Robin F. Garland Educator Award 15534
Jim Gordon Editor of the Year Award 15535
Charles E. Green Journalism Awards 10308
Humanitarian Award 15536
ILCA Media Awards Contest 11700
Infinity Awards 11462
International Exhibition of Professional Photography 17639
Journalism Awards Program 10354
Robert F. Kennedy Journalism Awards 18076
Keystone Press Awards 17187
J. Winton Lemen Award 15537
Kenneth P. McLaughlin Award of Merit 15538
Sam Mellor Award 15539
Military Photographer of the Year 15540
Missouri Lifestyle Journalism Award 21079
National Magazine Awards 15355
News Picture Contest 10816
NPPA Citations 15541
Outstanding Publication Award 15542
Peabody Awards Collection 21020
Photography Award 11115
Photojournalism Award 14250
Photojournalism Division Awards 17289
Picture Editor of the Year 15543
Pictures of the Year Competition 15544
George Polk Awards 12915
President's Award 15545
Pulitzer Prizes 17749
Regional Television Photographer of the Year 15546
Salute to Excellence Awards 14101
Sigma Delta Chi Awards 19276
Silurian Excellence in Journalism Awards 19327
Special Citations 15547
Spot News Photo Award 16250
Joseph A. Sprague Memorial Award 15548
Television Newsfilm Awards 15549
Lowell Thomas Travel Journalism Awards 19016
Top Performance Awards 5253
White House News Photographers' Association Awards 21606
Burt Williams Award 15550
Captain Donald T. Wright Award 17494

Physical education

William G. Anderson Merit Award 876
Award for Distinguished Service to N4A 14061
Luther Halsey Gulick Award 877
Hall of Fame Award 7666
Hetherington Award 682
Honor Award 879
Mabel Lee Award 880
N4A National Academic Achievement Award 14062
Physical Education School Recognition Award 6883
The R. Tait McKenzie Award of Honour 6884
The Spirit of America Award 4925
Student Award 6885
Teacher of the Year Awards 14043
Tennis Educational Merit Award for Men 12077
Tennis Educational Merit Award for Women 12078
Young Professional Award 6886

Physical fitness *See* Health and fitness

Physical medicine *See* Rehabilitation and therapy

Physical science

Award in Science 17240
The Benjamin Franklin Medals 9740
Canadian Mineral Analysts Scholarships 7286
Fellow or Foreign Honorary Member 620
William C. Foster Fellows Visiting Scholars Program 20402
Henry Marshall Tory Medal 18174
Vetlesen Prize 8246

Physical therapy *See* Rehabilitation and therapy

Physics

ACA Public Service Award 2083
ACP-CRM/CAP-CRM Prize in Theoretical and Mathematical Physics 13203
Adhesion Society Award for Excellence in Adhesion Science 184

Physics (continued)

David Adler Lectureship Award in the Field of Materials Physics 3445
AIAA Fluid Dynamics Award 2649
AIAA Thermophysics Award 2674
AIP Science Writing Awards 2831
Will Allis Prize for Study of Ionized Gases 3446
Leroy Apker Award 3447
Urgel Archambault Prize in Physical Sciences and Mathematics 5537
Award for Excellence in Plasma Physics Research 3448
Award in Magnetism 12103
AWIS Educational Foundation Predoctoral Award 5530
Best Paper Award 11532
Bingham Medal 19299
Biological Physics Prize 3449
Boltzmann Medal 12104
Tom Bonner Prize in Nuclear Physics 3450
Edward A. Bouchet Award 3451
Bower Award and Prize for Achievement in Science 9741
Herbert P. Broida Prize 3452
Oliver E. Buckley Prize in Condensed Matter Physics 3453
Martin J. Buerger Award 2084
John R. Cameron Young Investigator Award 1366
CAP Medal for Achievement in Physics 6932
Charles E. Szper Memorial Fund 2085
Samuel C. Collins Award 8677
Karl Taylor Compton Award 2832
Comstock Prize in Physics 13829
William D. Coolidge Award 1367
Farrington Daniels Award 1368
Davisson-Germer Prize in Atomic or Surface Physics 3454
Arthur L. Day Prize and Lectureship 13830
John H. Dillon Medal for Research in Polymer Physics 3455
Dissertation in Nuclear Physics Award 3456
Distinguished Service Award 18640
Distinguished Service Citation 1371
Henry Draper Medal 13831
Elizabeth A. Wood Science Writing Award 2086
Excellence in Pre-College Physics Teaching Award 1372
Excellence in Undergraduate Physics Teaching Award 1373
Fluid Dynamics Prize 3457
Ford Foundation Postdoctoral Diversity Fellowships 15622
Andrew Gemant Award 2833
Graduate Student Award 18641
Sylvia Sorkin Greenfield Award 1369
Maurice F. Hasler Award 19603
Dannie N. Heineman Prize for Astrophysics 2834
Dannie N. Heineman Prize for Mathematical Physics 2835
Honorary Membership Award 18642
ICPE Medal for Physics Teaching 12106
Innovative Teaching of Secondary School Physics Award 1374
Intel International Science and Engineering Fair 18362
Frank Isakson Prize for Optical Effects in Solids 3458
Isidor Fankuchen Award 2088
Joseph F. Keithley for Advances in Measuresment Sciences 3459
Kenneth N. Trueblood Awards 2089
Peter Kirby Memorial Medal for Outstanding Service to Canadian Physics 6934
Klopsteg Memorial Lecture 1375
Irving Langmuir Prize in Chemical Physics 3460
Langmuir Prize in Chemical Physics
Langmuir Prize in Chemical Physics 3461
Otto Laporte Award for Research in Fluid Dynamics 3462
London Award 12107
Fritz London Memorial Award 9042
Margaret C. Etter Early Career Award 2090
James Clerk Maxwell Prize for Plasma Physics 3463
James C. McGroddy Prize in New Materials 3464
Medal for Excellence in Teaching 6935
Medal for Outstanding Achievement in Industrial and Applied Physics 6936
William F. Meggers Award 18643
William F. and Edith R. Meggers Project Award 2836
Robert A. Millikan Medal 1376
Oersted Medal 1377
Lars Onsager Prize 3465
Outstanding Doctoral Thesis Research in Atomic, Molecular, or Optical Physics Award 3466
Outstanding Doctoral Thesis Research in Beam Physics Award 3467
Outstanding SPS Chapter Advisor Award 2837
George E. Pake Prize 3468
W. K. H. Panofsky Prize in Experimental Particle Physics 3469
A. Lindo Patterson Award 2091
Pauling Prize 2092
Penning Award Excellence in Low-Temperature Plasma Physics 12108
Melba Newell Phillips Award 1378
Earle K. Plyler Prize for Molecular Spectroscopy 3470
William J. Poehlman Award 18644
Polymer Physics Prize 3471
Prize for Industrial Applications of Physics 2838
Prize for Meritorious Achievement 20731
Prize in Theoretical and Mathematical Physics 6937
Prize to a Faculty Member for Research in an Undergraduate Institution 3472
Public Service Award 2093
I. I. Rabi Prize in Atomic, Molecular and Optical Physics 3473
Aneesur Rahman Prize for Computational Physics 3474
Research Associateship Programs 15623
Richtmyer Memorial Lecture 1379
Rumford Prize 622
J. J. Sakurai Prize for Theoretical Particle Physics 3475
Arthur L. Schawlow Prize in Laser Science 3476
Shock Compression Science Award 3477
Sigma Pi Sigma Undergraduate Research Award 2839
SunAmco Medal 12109
Leo Szilard Lectureship Award 3478
John T. Tate International Award 2840
George E. Valley Prize 3479
Bertram E. Warren Diffraction Physics Award 2095
John Wheatley Award 3480
Marsh W. White Award 2841
Robert R. Wilson Prize for Achievement in the Physics of Particle Accelerators 3481
Young Author Best Paper Award 12110

Physiology

Abbott Laboratories Distinguished Research Award 3507
Francis Amory Prize 619
Charles Reid Barnes Life Membership Award 4586
Bowditch Award Lecture 3508
Physiology in Perspective: Walter B. Cannon Lecture 3510
Cardiovascular Section Young Investigator Award 3511
Caroline tum Suden/France Hellebrandt Professional Opportunity Awards 3512
Comparative Physiology Section Scholander Award 3514
Ray G. Daggs Award 3515
William C. Dement Academic Achievement Award 837
Environmental and Exercise Physiology Section Gatorade Young Investigator Award 3516
Giles F. Filley Memorial Awards for Excellence in Respiratory Physiology and Medicine 3517
Adolph E. Gude, Jr. Award 4587
Arthur C. Guyton Awards for Excellence in Integrative Physiology 3518
Mark O. Hatfield Public Policy Award 838
Nathaniel Kleitman Distinguished Service Award 839
Liaison with Industry Committee Novel Disease Model Award 3519
Lazaro J. Mandel Young Investigator Award 3520
Minority Travel Fellowship Awards 3522
Ralph G. Nevins Physiology and Human Environment Award 4438
Oceaneering International Award 20291
John F. Perkins, Jr. Memorial Award 3523
Pfizer Animal Health Physiology Award 2112
Porter Physiology Fellowships for Minorities 3524
Postdoctoral Fellowship in Physiological Genomics 3525
Procter & Gamble Professional Opportunity Awards 3526
Renal Section Pfizer Predoctoral Excellence in Renal Research Award 3527
Orr E. Reynolds Award 3528
Teaching Career Enhancement Awards 3529
Shih-Chun Wang Young Investigator Award 3530
Young Investigator Award in Regulatory and Integrative Physiology 3531
Young Investigator's Award 840

Piano competitions

American National Chopin Piano Competition 7937
American Pianists Association Classical Fellowship Awards 3543
Art Song Festival 8099
Bach Competitions 17868

Piano (continued)

Gina Bachauer International Piano Competition 6193
William C. Byrd Young Artist Competition 18203
CBC Radio National Competition for Young Performers 6999
Cleveland International Piano Competition 8100
Van Cliburn International Piano Competition 8108
Concours OSM 13605
Contemporary Music Award 9228
Eckhardt-Gramatte National Competition for the Performance of Canadian Music 9129
Janice Elliot-Drake Intermediate Chopin Scholarhip 18283
Guelph Spring Festival Music Competition 10190
The Hancock Memorial Award in Piano 18293
Heida Hermanns International Competition 8408
Joanna Hodges International Piano Competition/Virginia Waring International Piano Competition 21402
Esther Honens International Piano Competition 10524
International Piano Competition Prize 9231
The Mildred Spence McPherson Memorial Piano Award 18300
Missouri Southern International Piano Competition 13543
Thelonious Monk International Jazz Competition 13584
MPEC Award 13461
MTNA Junior High School Piano Competition 13704
Naumburg International Competition 16045
New Orleans International Piano Competition 13712
San Antonio International Piano Competition 18239
The Minnie Schell Memorial Intermediate Piano Scholarship 18309
Sorantin Young Artist Award 18237
Evelyn Bonar Storrs Memorial Piano Scholarships 13714
University of Maryland International Music Competitions 18567
The Wallis Memorial Scholarship 18319
Andrew Wolf Chamber Music Award 6278
World Piano Competition 3166
Young Artist Competition 9701
Young Soloists' Competition 15834

Piano technology

Golden Hammer Award 17330
Hall of Fame 17331
Honorary Member 17332
Member of Note 17333

Ping pong *See* Table tennis

Placement *See* Employment practices

Planning (*See also* City planning; Park planning)

AICP National Historic Planning Landmarks and Pioneers Program 3545
AICP Student Project and Outstanding Student Awards 3546
APA Journalism Awards 3547
Awards for Outstanding Area Research 8514
Daniel Burnham Award 3548
Chapters of the Year 13278
Current Topic Award 3549
Paul Davidoff Award 3550
Distinguished Contribution Award 3551
Distinguished Leadership Award for a Citizen Planner 3552
Distinguished Leadership Award for a Professional Planner 3553
Distinguished Leadership Award for a Student Planner 3554
Distinguished Leadership Award for an Elected Official 3555
Divisions' Council Awards 3556
Diana Donald Award 3557
Global Paragon Awards 13279
Ernest E. Howard Award 4331
Industry Award 13280
International Coastal Engineering Award 4335
Marion Kershner Memorial Chapter Leader Award 13281
Loeb Fellowship 10281
Frank M. Masters Transportation Engineering Award 4339
MPI Planner of the Year 13282
MPI Supplier of the Year 13283
Outstanding Planning Awards 3558
Planner of the Year 8573
President's Award 13284
Regional Plan Association Award 17958
Secretary's Opportunity and Empowerment Award 3559
Student Planner Award 3560
Surveying and Mapping Award 4360
Tomorrow's Leaders of MPI Award 13285

Plastics and rubber

Annual Conference and EXPO Awards 19307
Annual Conference Paper Awards 19308
Award of Merit 17467
Awards for Outstanding Performance 19309
Awards of Distinction 19310
Clare E. Bacon Person of the Year Award 19311
Fernley H. Banbury Award 1737
Best of Conference Paper Award 13578
Business Management Award 19259
Committee D-20 Award of Excellence 5938
Fred O. Conley Award 19260
Consumer Plastics Product Design Award 19261
Dow Award for Excellence in Composites Research 19312
Eastern Section Annual Achievement Award 19313
Elan Awards 11450
Fellow of the Society 19262
Paul J. Flory Polymer Education Award 1754
Charles Goodyear Medal 1756
Honored Service Member Award 19263
John W. Hyatt Award 19264
Industrial Plastics Product Design Award 19265
International Award 19266
Man of the Year 19315
Herman F. Mark Division of Polymer Chemistry Award 1769
Carl S. Marvel Creative Polymer Chemistry Award 1770
Midwest Section Founder's Award 19316
Melvin Mooney Distinguished Technology Award 1772
Plastics Hall of Fame 17392
Polyurethane Division Awards 19317
Polyurethane Division Hall of Fame Awards 19318
President's Cup 19267
Research Award 19268
Safety Award Program 19319
Fred E. Schwab Award 19269
Sparks-Thomas Award 1790
Spiritus Awards 11451
Structural Plastics Division Annual Recognition 19320
Structural Plastics Division Awards 19321
Thermoforming Institute National Awards 19322
George Stafford Whitby Award for Distinguished Teaching and Research 1793

Plays *See* Drama; Theater

Playwriting *See* Drama

Podiatry

Hirsh Award 1878
Lifetime Achievement Award 17412
William J. Stickel Awards 3563

Poetry

The Abafazi-Africana Women's Studies Essay Award 15965
Alice Abel Cultural and Creative Arts Program 3141
Milton Acorn Poetry Award 17543
Alabama State Poetry Society Award 14987
All Poets Award 14988
Anhinga Poetry Prize 8425
Anisfield-Wolf Book Awards 8097
Annual Awards Competition 8565
Annual Contests 14989
Arizona Authors' Association Annual National Literary Contest 5048
Arizona State Poetry Society Award 14990
Artists' Fellowships 16229
Award for Excellence in Poetry for Children 14827
Awards 176
AWP Award Series 5259
Emily Clark Balch Prize 21396
Rebekah Johnson Bobbitt National Prize for Poetry 12832
Elmer Holmes Bobst Literary Awards 16301
Frederick Bock Prize 17418
George Bogin Memorial Award 17428
Bollingen Prize in Poetry 22013
Book Award 17426
Rosalie Boyle/Norma Farber Award 16108
bp Nichol Chapbook Award 17275
Barbara Bradley Award 16109
Gerald Brady Memorial Awards 10219
The Brittingham Prize in Poetry and Felix Pollak Prize in Poetry 21125
Bumbershoot, The Seattle Arts Festival 16734
Butler Literary Award 12194
CAA Awards for Adult Literature 6953
Gerald Cable Book Award 18519

Poetry (continued)

Chapbook Competition 17741
Chelsea Award 7821
Cin(E)-Poetry Festival 15512
Matt Clark Prize 16095
Cleveland State University Poetry Center Prize 8104
Columbine Poets of Colorado Award 14991
Commonwealth Club of California Book Awards 8306
Connecticut Poetry Society Award 14992
Bernard F. Conners Prize for Poetry 17093
Contemporary Poetry Series 21025
Alice Fay Di Castagnola Award 17429
"Discovery"/*The Nation* Contest 19
Bernard Lionel Einbond Renku Competition 10220
Norma Epstein Foundation Awards 21112
Norma Farber First Book Award 17430
Fellowship Program 17168
Fine Arts Work Center Fellowships 9553
Florida State Poets Association, Inc. Award 14993
Founders Award 14994
Ruth Berrien Fox Award 16110
The Frost Medal 17431
Futuristic Award 14995
Georgia Author of the Year Awards 9972
Georgia Poetry Society Award 14996
Golden Rose Award 16111
Dorman John Grace Memorial Award 14997
Gradiva Awards 14052
The Greensboro Review Literary Awards 10170
Griffin Poetry Prize 10176
Grolier Poetry Prize 10178
Hackney Literary Awards 6402
O. B. Hardison Jr. Poetry Prize 9647
Cecil Hemley Memorial Award 17432
Harold G. Henderson Memorial Award 10221
Joseph V. Hickey Memorial Award 14998
Theodore Christian Hoepfner Awards 19507
Bess Hokin Prize 17419
John Holmes Award 16112
Lee Bennett Hopkins Promising Poet Award 11859
Firman Houghton Award 16113
Humorous Poetry Award 14999
Indiana State Federation of Poetry Clubs Award 15000
Iowa Poetry Association Award 15001
Irish American Cultural Institute Poetry Award 12198
Joseph Henry Jackson Literary Award 18249
The Journal Award in Poetry 16651
Juniper Prize 21057
Barbara Mandigo Kelly Peace Poetry Awards 16590
Kentucky Artists Fellowships 12562
Kentucky State Poetry Society Award 15002
Kiyoshi Tokutomi Memorial Haiku Contest 22088
Ohioana Poetry Award, Helen and Laura Krout Memorial 16659
Gerald Lampert Memorial Award 12744
Lannan Literary Awards 12691
Laureates 900
League of Minnesota Poets Award 15003
Rose Lefcowitz Prize 17414
Letras de Oro Literary Prizes 21059
Levinson Prize 17420
Larry Levis Prize for Poetry 17513
Lighten Your Life Award 15004
Ruth Lilly Poetry Fellowship 17421
Ruth Lilly Poetry Prize 17422
Literary Awards 6521
Literary Writers Competition 9467
Dorothy Livesay Poetry Prize 21521
Loft Mentor Series Award 12905
Ben Lomond Poets Award 15005
Amelia Reynolds Long Memorial Award 15006
Long Poem Prize 13043
Los Angeles Times Book Prizes 12931
Louise Louis/Emily F. Bourne Student Poetry Award 17433
Louisiana State Poetry Society Award 15007
Amy Lowell Poetry Traveling Scholarship 7933
Pat Lowther Memorial Award 12745
The Lyric Annual Awards 13003
Lyric Poetry Award 17434
Massachusetts State Poetry Society Award 15008
Lucille Medwick Memorial Award 17435
Merit Book Awards 10222
James A. Michener - Paul Engle Fellowship 12191
Minute Award 15009
Mississippi Poetry Society Award 15010
Missouri State Poetry Society Award 15011
Money for Women/Barbara Deming Memorial Fund Grants 13582
Erika Mumford Prize 16114
Jack Murphy Memorial Award 15012
Museum of Haiku Literature Awards 10223
Music Award 15013
Narrative Poetry Prize 17415
National Book Awards 14532
National Book Critics Circle Awards 14530
National Jewish Book Award - Yiddish Literature 12333
National Magazine Awards 15355
Nebraska State Poetry Society Award 15014
Pablo Neruda Prize for Poetry 16360
Neustadt International Prize for Literature 21934
Nevada Poetry Society Award 15015
New Jersey Poetry Society Award 15016
New Letters Writing Awards 16190
New Writers Awards 10141
New York Poetry Forum Award 15017
Ohio Award 15018
Ohioana Book Awards 16661
Natalie Ornish Award 20020
PEN/Joyce Osterweil Award for Poetry 17144
Our American Indian Heritage Award 15019
Guy Owen Poetry Prize 19515
PEN Book-of-the-Month Club Translation Prize 17146
PEN Prison Writing Awards 17148
PEN/Voelcker Award for Poetry 17150
James D. Phelan Literary Award 18251
Plains Poets Award 15020
Plimpton Prize 17095
PNWA Literary Contest 17011
Poet Laureate, Consultant in Poetry 12834
Poetry Award 15994
Poetry Books Award 21467
Poetry Chapbook Competition, Artist Residency Program 7710
Poetry Contest 21999
Poetry, Fiction and Nonfiction Contest 8225
Poetry Society of Michigan Award 15021
Poetry Society of Oklahoma Award 15022
Poetry Society of Tennessee Pirouette Award 15023
Poetry Society of Texas Award 15024
Poets Greatest Hits National Archive 17742
Poets' Roundtable of Arkansas Award 15025
Power of Woman Award 15026
Prix Emile-Nelligan 20303
Morton D. Prouty and Elsie S. Prouty Memorial Award 15027
Pulitzer Prizes 17749
Pushcart Prize: Best of the Small Presses 17770
Quarterly Awards 13004
QWF Awards 17801
Roanoke-Chowan Award for Poetry 16521
Summerfield G. Roberts Award 19415
Theodore Roethke Memorial Foundation Poetry Prize 20064
Anna Davidson Rosenberg Award for Poems on the Jewish Experience 13017
Carl Sandburg Award 11811
Carl Sandburg Literary Arts Award 9806
May Sarton Award 16115
Save Our Earth Award 15028
Delmore Schwartz Memorial Poetry Award 16303
Shelley Memorial Award 17436
Slipstream's Annual Poetry Chapbook Contest 18556
Society of Midland Authors Awards 19186
Space Coast Writers Guild Conference Awards 19535
William Stafford Memorial Award 15029
Ann Stanford Poetry Prize 13173
Edward Stanley Award 17517
Agnes Lynch Starrett Poetry Prize Competition 21100
Barbara Stevens Memorial Award 15030
Don R. Stodghill Award 15031
Elizabeth Matchett Stover Memorial Award 19528
Strousse Award 17518
Student Award 15032
Hollis Summers Poetry Prize 16653
Aiken Taylor Award in Modern American Poetry 18425
Tilden Canadian Literary Awards 7000
TNR Awards in Fiction and Poetry 16075
Towson University Prize for Literature 20145
Two Ladies from Texas Award 15033
Union League Civic and Arts Foundation Poetry Prize 17423
Utah State Poetry Society Award 15034
Daniel Varoujan Award 16116
Nicholas A. Virgilio Memorial Haiku Competition 10224
Lila Wallace-Reader's Digest Writers' Awards 21430
Gretchen Warren Award 16117
Washington Prize 21834
West Virginia Poetry Society Award 15035
Western States Book Awards 21571
Whiting Writers' Award 21610

Poetry (continued)
Walt Whitman Award 78
Walt Whitman Citation of Merit Award for State Poet 16295
Oscar Williams and Gene Derwood Award 16219
William Carlos Williams Award 17437
Robert H. Winner Memorial Award 17438
Winners' Circle Award 15036
J. Howard and Barbara M.J. Wood Prize 17424
The Writer Magazine/Emily Dickinson Award 17439
Writer's Digest Writing Competition 21979
Writing Awards 18067
WYOpoets Award 15037
Yale Series of Younger Poets 22011
Yankee Awards 22017

Police *See* Law enforcement

Polish culture
Mieczyslaw Haiman Award 17455
Oscar Halecki Award 17456
Kosciuszko Foundation Doctoral Dissertation Award 12611
Kosciuszko Foundation Exchange Program with Poland 12612
Rev. Joseph V. Swastek Award 17457

Political science (*See also* Foreign policy; Franco-American relations; Human relations; International relations; Legislative improvement; National security; Social science research; United States-Latin American relations; World peace)
Annual Political Book Award 21452
Award of Merit - Governmental 8365
Bird Dog Award 8302
Robert Bosch Foundation Fellowship Program 7687
Boston College Student Paper Competition 6523
Bread and Roses Award 8879
Karl Brey Award 12808
Congressional Research Grant Program 8951
CQ Press Award 8404
Dorr-Debs Award 18602
Richard F. Fenno, Jr. Book Prize 3581
Gerald R. Ford Prize for Distinguished Reporting on the Presidency 9682
Freedom Award 9969
Georgia No Excuses Awards 9970
Goldsmith Research Awards 18440
Good Neighbor Award 20699
Hall of Outstanding Americans 15986
D. B. Hardeman Prize 12422
Howard Fellows 10571
Annual National Press Club Sandy Hume Memorial Award for Excellence in Political Journalism 15518
Wally Jorgenson Award 14114
Kahlil Gibran Spirit of Humanity Award 5019
Marta Lange/CQ Press Award 5612
Maurer-Stump Award 17889
Outstanding Local Chapter 22071
Outstanding YR State Chapter 22072
Pollie Awards 1385
Herbert Roback Scholarship 13820
University of Louisville Grawemeyer Award for Ideas Improving World Order 21042
The Washington Monthly Journalism Award 21453
Western Political Science Association Awards 21557
Young Republican Man of the Year 22073
Young Republican Woman of the Year 22074

Pollution control *See* Environmental conservation; Water conservation

Population *See* Demography; Family planning

Portuguese culture
The Goodfellow Memorial Award for Senior Vocal Concert Groups 18285
Outstanding Teacher of the Year Awards 1453

Poultry science
American Egg Board Research Award 17496
American Poultry Historical Society Award 17497
Book Prize 7440
Broiler Research Award 17498
Sarah Louise Gruver Memorial Scholarship 16073
Legislator of the Year 19445
Lifetime Achievement Award 19446
Merck Award for Achievement in Poultry Science 17499
National Turkey Federation Research Award 17500
Outstanding Service Award 19447
Philbro Extension Award 17501
Poultry Products Research Award 17502
Poultry Science Association Fellows 17503
Poultry Science Association Research Award 17504
Poultry Welfare Research Award 17505
Purina Mills Teaching Award 17506
Young Scientist's Award 7446

Poverty *See* Humanitarianism

Preventive medicine
AACC Lectureship Award 972
Boothby - Edwards Award 231
James D. Bruce Memorial Award 1917
Chapter of the Year 5458
Charles A. Dana Awards for Pioneering Achievements in Higher Education 8730
Distinguished Service Award 1930
Gorgas Medal 5772
Melvin Judkins Young Clinical Investigator Award 2411
William R. McAlpin, Jr. Mental Health Research Achievement Award 15377
MSD AGVET AABP Award for Excellence in Preventive Veterinary Medicine Dairy Cattle 1127
Research Grants 3017
Rising Star Award 1932
Lela Rowland Prevention Award 15379
Fred L. Soper Lecture 4633
Special Recognition Award 1933

Printed materials *See* Publications

Printing industry
Ault Award 14332
Bob Craig Memorial Scholarship 21529
R. C. Cann Plaque 13928
Certificate of Craftsmanship 13175
Byron G. Culver Award 18085
Frederic W. Goudy Distinguished Lecture 18086
Honorary Lifetime Member 17564
In-House Promotional Excellence Award 11837
In-Print Award 11838
Individual Award 3595
Industry Award of Distinction 17565
Institutional Award 3596
International Member of the Year Award 11839
International Retired Member of the Year Award 11840
International Thermographers Association Product Excellence Contest 12082
IPMA Fellow Member 11841
IPMA International Vendor/Associate Member of the Year Award 11842
Management Award 11843
Non-Heatset Web Printing Awards Competition 17571
Print on Demand Applications Award 11844
Print on Demand Award 11845
Printer of the Year 17566
Printing Ink Pioneer Award 14333
TAGA Honors Award 19956
Technical Achievement Award 14334
Technical Associate Member Service Award 14335

Prints *See* Graphic arts; Photographic prints

Prisons
Correctional Officer of the Year 11318
Bernard P. Harrison Award of Merit 14698
Poetry and Poster Contest 14699
Presidential Award 1272
Warden of the Year 16393

Professional and personal achievement (*See also* Academic achievement; Leadership)
Achievement Award
American Association of University Women Educational Foundation 1469
Foundation of American Women in Radio and Television 9715
Achievement of the Year Award 5708
Jane Addams Medal 18095
Advertising Hall of Fame 856
Horatio Alger Awards 10539
Alumni Medal 20996
AMI Salon Awards 5756
Annual Achievement Award 62
Anton Boisen Professional Service Award 5820
Award for Distinguished Achievement 8237
Award of Merit 19858
Woolf Barnato Trophy 19682
Bolton Award for Professional Excellence 14079
John A. Boyd Hall of Fame Award 8169
Bernard B. Brodie Award in Drug Metabolism 4170
Pearl S. Buck International Woman of the Year Award 17129

Professional (continued)

Can-AM Civil Engineering Amity Award 4303
Candace Award 14678
CAP Medal for Achievement in Physics 6932
Career Achievement Award 17610
Career Development Resource Award 7588
Career/Lifetime Achievement Award 5265
William W. Carpenter Award 16385
Cash Award 20531
CEA Honorary Life Membership 8152
CEA Professional Achievement Award 8153
Certified Remodeler (CR) "Superstar" Award 14428
Chaplain Emeritus Award 5821
Chapters Council Award 10904
Winston Churchill Award 21656
Committee D-2 Award 5936
Congressional Gold Medal 20459
Constable of the Year 14728
CPRS Awards of Excellence Program 7360
CRCD Award 7373
The Leonardo da Vinci Award 11066
Damen Award 12968
Charlotte Danstrom Award 21746
Dawson Awards 5810
John Deere Medal 4218
Directors Emeriti Award 12853
Distinguished Eagle Scout Award 6575
Distinguished Friend to Behavior Therapy 5266
Distinguished Honor Award 20537
Distinguished Service 13249
Distinguished Service Award
American Society for Bioethics and Humanities 3925
Association of Fraternity Advisors 5693
National Association of the Holy Name Society 14415
Society for Range Management 18836
Distinguished Younger Member Award 19040
Division Leadership and Service Award 19919
Mark Donohue Award 19690
Dunleavy Award 16350
James Clement Dunn Award for Excellence 20538
Engineering Achievement Awards Program 4220
ERB Life Achievement Award 6697
Executive Committee Award 21537
Fellow 5213
Henry Fenderbosch Leadership Award 14432
Louis C. Fink Literary Award 14416
Foreign Service Award 20541
Alfred M. Freudenthal Medal 4315
Harold Friedman Memorial Award 10371
GALA (Got a Lot Accomplished) Award 7166
Albert Gallatin Medal 16299
President Garfield Humanitarian Award 13141
Gold Medal for Distinguished Achievement 10506
C. C. Gotlieb Contribution Award 7167
Great Swedish Heritage Award 19859
Townsend Harris Medal 519
Harry J. Harwick Lifetime Achievement Award 1884
Heart of the Year Award 2408
Nathaniel G. Herreshoff Trophy 20773
Honeywell SAE Outstanding Student Branch Award 19045
Honorary Fellow
American College of Cardiology 1840
Association for Social Anthropology in Oceania 5471
Honorary Lifetime Membership 21538
Honorary Member 4135
Robert Horonjeff Award of the Air Transport Division 4330
Humanitarian Award 14417
Interamerica Prize 11104
IPMA Fellow Member 11841
Larry Kadis Memorial Scholarship 16345
Keystone Award 14418
Martin Luther King, Jr. Scholarship Award 2026
Jack and Julie Lally Distinguished Alumni Merit Award 18216
Laurel Crowned Circle Award 16698
Lefthanders of the Year Awards 12764
Lifetime Achievement Award 3926
Eli Lilly and Company Research Award 4136
Living Legends Award 15927
Luck and Pluck Award 10541
MacArthur Fellows 13006
James Madison Medal 17559
Ann Magnussen Award 3833
Margaret Mann Citation 5426
E. O. Martin Medallion 1363
Medallion Circle Award 14420
Member of the Year 14537
Merit Citation 17316
Meritorious Honor Award 20546
Miss Teen USA 13498
Miss Universe 13499
Miss USA 13500
National Book Service Teacher-Librarian of the Year Award 7261
National Food and Energy Council Electric Technology Award 4232
National President's Trophy - Man of the Year 22112
Newsboy Award 10542
Bart O'Leary Award 14189
Olympic Spirit Award 20722
Order of Canada 6827
Order of West Range 17310
Outstanding Achievement Award 16539
Outstanding Faculty Adviser 17327
Outstanding Local Section Member Award 19923
Outstanding Section/Student Chapter Partnership Award 19054
Outstanding Young Range Professional Award 18837
L. B. "Mike" Pearson Award 7229
Personal Achievement Award 13685
Philbin Award 14190
Physician Assistant Award 5780
Pied Piper Award 4382
Pioneer of the Year 16014
Presidential Distinguished Service Award 19231
President's Award 16387
President's Awards 10543
Professional Achievement Awards 20261
Professional Achievement Citations 20999
Professional Development Coordinator of the Year 14540
Professional Member of the Year 14541
Quality Digest Award 17778
Elise Ramos Awards 5270
Realtor of the Year 14355
Regional Representative of the Year 14544
Rous-Whipple Award 4122
Secretary of State's Distinguished Service Award 20552
Secretary's Award 20553
Richard Seddon Award 10544
Senior Bowler of the Year 21776
Small Town America Hall of Fame 14445
Special Achievement Award 15866
Thomas H. Speller Award 19056
Spingarn Medal 14050
State Coordinator 14547
Statesman of the Year 692
Strive and Succeed Award 10545
Student Dissertation Award 5271
Student of the Year 17319
Superior Honor Award 20554
Surveying Excellence Award 15762
Sustained Lifetime Achievement Award 18838
Sword of Ignatius Loyola Award 18218
Sword of Loyola 12974
Technician of the Month Award 4281
Joe D. Thomas CEA Distinguished Service Award 8156
Emerson - Thoreau Medal 623
Trans-Canada (McKee) Trophy 6870
Trustee of the Year 20353
Judge Elbert P. Tuttle Distinguished Achievement Award 17313
TV Hall of Fame 128
United Methodist Association Award of Distinguished Service 20354
U.S. Sailing One-Design Awards 20783
University Medal for Excellence 8245
Theodore von Karman Medal 4365
Morris F. Weinstock Award 14557
Young NDT Professional Award 4154

Psychiatry (*See also* Mental health)
AACP Clinical Research Award 631
AAPL Outstanding Service Award 824
The (ACP) American College of Psychiatrists Bowis Award 1935
The (ACP) American College of Psychiatrists Dean Award 1936
Administrative Psychiatry Award 3610
The American College of Psychiatrists Award for Creativity in Psychiatric Education 1937
The American College of Psychiatrists Distinguished Service Award in Psychiatry 1938
Amicus Award 825
Annual Award for Psychiatrists in Training 19519
APA Assembly Warren Williams Awards 3611
APA Award for Research in Psychiatry 3612
ASAP - Gralnick Foundation Research Award 3903
Award for Exemplary State/University Collaboration 3613
Award for Patient Advocacy 3614
A. E. Bennett Research Awards 19071
Bick Award 12948
Barry Bingham Media Award 12566

Subject Index

Psychiatry (continued)

Simon Bolivar Award 3615
Central Neuropsychiatric Association Resident Award 3192
James Comer Minority Research Fellowship for Medical Students 625
Robinson/Cunningham Award 626
Distinguished Fellow Award 1889
Distinguished Service Award
American College of Neuropsychiatrists 1890
American Society for Adolescent Psychiatry 3904
Distinguished Service Awards 3616
Louis I. Dublin Award 1437
Early Career Award 13943
Daniel H. Efron Research Award 1895
Marie H. Eldredge Award 3617
Eli Lilly Travel Fellowship Award 19072
Joel Elkes International Award 1896
Faculty Psychiatric Technician of the Year 1387
Fellow 3905
Fellowship in the Association 2366
Sigmund Freud Award 4598
Solomon Carter Fuller Award 3618
Gold Medal Award 19073
Golden Apple Award 826
Gradiva Awards 14052
Graduate Internships 19408
Manfred S. Guttmacher Award 3619
Samuel Hamilton Award 3772
Max Hamilton Memorial Prize 8199
Paul Hoch Distinguished Award 1897
Honorary Distinguished Physicians Award 1891
Honorary Distinguished Service Award 1892
Human Rights Award 3620
Blanche F. Ittleson Research in Child Psychiatry Award 3621
Janssen Research Award 607
Sydney M. Kanev Memorial Award 1893
APA/Kempf Fund Award for Research Development in Psychobiological Psychiatry 3623
Kun-Po Soo Award 3624
Leadership Award for Residents 627
APA/Lilly Products Resident Research Award 3625
APA/Lilly Psychiatric Research Fellowship 3626
Bruno Lima Award for Excellence in Disaster Psychiatry 3627
Raymond F. Longacre Award 237
Agnes Purcell McGavin Award 3628
Medical Student and Resident Travel Stipend 608
Adolf Meyer Lectureship 3629
Robert T. Morse Writer's Award 3630
Oskar Pfister Award 3631
Pfizer Minority Summer Fellowship Award 1898
Pilot Research Award for Junior Faculty and Child Psychiatry Fellows 628
Seymour Pollack Distinguished Achievement Award 827
William C. Porter Lecture Award 5781
Postdoctoral Fellowship Awards for Minorities 1899
Presidential Commendations 3632
Presidential Scholar Award 629
Public Affairs Network Awards 3633
Rafaelsen Fellowship Award 8201
Isaac Ray Award in Memory of Margaret Sutermeister 3634
Red Apple Award 828
Robert L. Robinson Awards 3635
Benjamin Rush Lectureship Award 3637
William A. Schonfeld Award (Honorary Members) 3906
Edwin Shneidman Award 1438
Assembly William Sorum Awards 3638
George Tarjan Award 3639
George N. Thompson Award for Distinguished Service 19074
Arnold L. van Ameringen Award in Psychiatric Rehabilitation 3640
Seymour D. Vestermark Award for Psychiatric Education 3641
Jack Weinberg Memorial Award for Geriatric Psychiatry 3642
Young Investigator Memorial Travel Awards 1900
Ziskind-Somerfeld Research Award 19075
Joseph Zubin Award 3773

Psychology

Gordon Allport Intergroup Relations Prize 18883
Earl A. Alluisi Award 3650
Allyn & Bacon Psychology Awards 17694
American Family Therapy Academy Awards 2215
Annaley Naegle Redd Student Award in Women's History 17925
Applied Social Issues Internship 18884
Award Certificates 17076
Award for Distinguished Contributions in the Application of Psychology 7345
Award for Distinguished Contributions to Education and Training in Psychology 7346
Award for Distinguished Contributions to Psychology as a Profession 7347
Award for Distinguished Contributions to Public or Community Service 7348
Award for Distinguished Contributions to the International Advancement of Psychology 7349
Award for Exemplary State/University Collaboration 3613
Award of Merit 16768
Evelyn Bauer Prize 11826
Emilio Bernabei Prize 11827
Eric Berne Memorial Award 12093
Best Paper Published in History of Psychology 3729
Best Research Paper 3759
Best Theoretical Paper Award 3760
William C. Bier Award 3701
John D. Black Award for Outstanding Achievement in the Practice of Counseling Psychology 3661
George E. Briggs Dissertation Award 3651
John Tropham and Susan Redd Butler Faculty Research Awards 17926
Donald T. Campbell Award for Distinguished Research in Social Psychology 3726
Certificate of Appreciation 3670
Community Psychology Dissertation Award 3714
Park O. Davidson Practice of the Profession Award 6636
Developmental Psychology Awards 3668
Diplomate of the American Board of Psychological Hypnosis 1580
Dissertation Award 3647
Dissertation Research Awards 18896
Distinguished Awards for the Contributions to the Science and Professional of Clinical Psychology 3744
Distinguished Career Contribution to Education and Training in Psychology 18897
Distinguished Contribution Award 17700
Distinguished Contribution to Child Advocacy Award 3715
Distinguished Contribution to Education and Training in Psychology 18898
Distinguished Contribution to Practice in Community Psychology Award 3716
Distinguished Contribution to Psychology and Law 3648
Distinguished Contribution to Psychology in the Public Interest 18901
Distinguished Contribution to Theory and Research in Community Psychology Award 3717
Distinguished Contributions to Applied Psychology as a Professional Practice 18902
Distinguished Contributions to Research in Public Policy 18903
Distinguished Contributions to the International Advancement of Psychology 18904
Distinguished Early Career Contributions Award 18750
Distinguished Neuropsychologist Award 13809
Distinguished Professional Achievement in Psychology 1578
Distinguished Professional Contributions Award 18751
Distinguished Professional Contributions to Knowledge 18906
Distinguished Professional Contributions to Public Service 18907
Distinguished Psychologist Award 3704
Distinguished Psychologist of the Year 3768
Distinguished Scholar Award 16475
Distinguished Scientific Award for an Early Career Contribution to Psychology 18908
Distinguished Scientific Award for the Applications of Psychology 18909
Distinguished Scientific Contribution Award
American Psychological Association - Society of Clinical Psychology (Division 12) 3745
Society for the Study of Lesbian, Gay and Bisexual Concerns (Division 44) 18910
Distinguished Scientific Contributions Award 18752
Distinguished Scientist Award 3746
Distinguished Service Award 3747
Distinguished Service Contributions Award 18753
Barbara Dohrenwend Lecture in Social and Community Epidemiology 3718
Edgar A. Doll Award 3691
Early Career Distinguished Scholar Award 16476
Economic Award 11828
Education Awards 17927
Rose and Michael David Elovitz Prize 11829
Erik H. Erikson Award 12017
ETS Award for Distinguished Service to Measurement 9177

Psychology (continued)

Experimental Analysis of Behavior Dissertation Award 3654
Family Psychologist of the Year 3671
Fellow Award 13657
Fellows Awards 3672
Ming Fisher Award 5861
John C. Flanagan Award 18754
Flandrin/Michon Life Achievement Award 2382
Ford Foundation Postdoctoral Diversity Fellowships 15622
Raymond D. Fowler Award 18911
Alfred M. Freedman Award 12018
Geis Memorial Award 3731
Charles S. Gersoni Military Psychology Award 3722
Gold Medal Award for Distinguished Lifetime Contributions to Canadian Psychology 7350
Graduate Student Awards 3705
Graduate Student Research Competition in Population and Environmental Psychology 3693
J. P. Guilford Undergraduate Research Awards 17695
Don F. Hake Basic/Applied Research Award 3655
Florence Halpern Award for Distinguished Professional Contributions 3748
Donald O. Hebb Award for Distinguished Contributions to Psychology as a Science 7351
D. O. Hebb Distinguished Scientific Contribution Award 3659
Heritage Award 3732
Harold M. Hildreth Award 3698
Ernest R. Hilgard Award for Distinguished Contributions to General Psychology 3684
E. R. Hilgard Best Graduate Level Academic Thesis Award 3761
Nicholas Hobbs Award 3719
John Holland Award for Outstanding Achievement in Career or Personality Research 3662
Humanitarian Award 7352
Hyde Graduate Student Research Award 3733
Hyde Graduate Student Research Grant 3734
Imagineer Awards 13430
Independent Research and Creative Work Awards 17928
ISDP Dissertation Prize 11926
William James Award 3702
William James Book Award 3685
Azar Kalbache and Zahara Ben Mamou Award 11830
Fred S. Keller Behavioral Education Award 3656
Louise Kidder Early Career Award 18886
Barbara A. Kirk Award for Outstanding Graduate Student Research 3663
Otto Klineberg Intercultural and International Relations Award 18887
Jeanne N. Knutson Award 12019
Jack D. Krasner Memorial Award 3706
Ernst Kris Prize 4600
David Kucharski Young Investigator Award for Research in Developmental Psychobiology 11927
Fritz and Linn Kuder Early Career Scientist/Practitioner Award 3664
William L. Langer Award 10184
Harold D. Lasswell Award 12020
M. Powell Lawton Distinguished Contribution Award for Applied Gerontology 3644
Leadership Award 18912
Harry and Miriam Levinson Award 3752
Lifetime Mentor Award 1050
Gardner Lindzey Dissertation Award 3686
Loebner Prize Turing Test Award 6773
Raymond F. Longacre Award 237
Noel Mailloux Award 16849
Masters and Johnson Award 18853
John P. McGovern Award Lecture in the Behavioral Sciences 1051
Media Psychology Graduate Student Research Award 18913
Meritorious Contributions to Psychology on the Part of Nonpsychologists 18914
Military Psychology Student Paper Award 3723
George A. Miller Award 3687
Walter D. Mink Award 13482
Henry A. Murray Award 3727
M. Scott Myers Award for Applied Research in the Workplace 18755
National Psychology Awards for Excellence in the Media 18915
Edwin B. Newman Award for Excellence in Research 18916
Outstanding Achievement Award 18917
Outstanding Contributions to Health Psychology 3689
Outstanding Dissertation Award
American Psychological Association - Exercise and Sport Psychology Division (Division 47) 3682
American Psychological Association - Society of Clinical Psychology (Division 12) 3749
Outstanding Executive Director of a State, Provincial, and Territorial Association (SPTA) Award 3675
Outstanding Psychologist Award 3676
Outstanding Reference Sources 17944
Outstanding School Psychological Services in Public Schools Award 3711
Outstanding Student Research Award 11947
William A. Owens Scholarly Achievement Award 18756
Parapsychology Hall of Fame 17077
Donald G. Paterson Award 13483
Paul R. Pintrich Outstanding Dissertation Award 3678
Presidential Award for Outstanding Contribution to Peace Psychology 3740
President's Award
American Handwriting Analysis Foundation 2383
Association of Psychologists of Nova Scotia 5828
MTM Association for Standards and Research 13658
North American Society for the Psychology of Sport and Physical Activity 16477
President's New Researcher Awards 7353
President's New Researcher's Award 5269
Morton Prince Award 18658
Prix de la Sante et du Bien-Etre Psychologique 16850
Professional Award 16851
Psi Chi/APA Edwin B. Newman Graduate Research Award 17696
Psi Chi/Florence L. Denmark National Faculty Advisor Award 17697
Psi Chi/Ruth Hubbard Cousins National Chapter Award 17698
Psychoanalysis Doctoral Award 3695
Psychoanalysis Post-Doctoral Award 3696
Psychological Dimensions of Peacework Award 17702
Psychology Association Award 5194
Charles Redd Center Publication Grants 17930
Research Associateship Programs 15623
Research Award on Psychotherapy with Women 3735
RHR International Award for Excellence in Consultation 3753
Clifford J. Robson Award 13054
Donald K. Sampson Excellence in Teaching Award 6637
Nevitt Sanford Award 12021
Section on the Psychology of Black Women Award 3736
Joel R. Seldin Award 17703
Senior Recognition Award for Distinguished Contributors to the Division of Counseling Psychology 3665
Carolyn Wood Sherif Award 3737
Norma P. Simon Award 5862
B. F. Skinner New Researcher Award 3657
Roger C. Smith Award 5863
Richard E. Snow Early Career Award in Educational Psychology 3679
Social Issues Dissertation Award 18888
Society for the Psychological Study of Lesbian and Gay Issues Distinguished Student Award 18918
Nicholas P. Spanos Best Graduate Student Paper Award 3762
Special Achievement Awards 3699
Special Award 3720
Student Research Award 3673
Student Research Award Competition 3756
Student Research Award for Clinical Child Psychology 3750
Student Research Awards 3645
Student Travel Awards 18919
The Geri Stuparich "Heart of Gold" Award 2384
Summer Awards for Upper Division and Graduate Students 17931
Jeffrey S. Tanaka Memorial Dissertation Award in Psychology 18920
Franklin V. Taylor Award 3652
Teaching Awards Program 3742
Edward L. Thorndike Award for Career Achievement in Educational Psychology 3680
Troland Research Awards 13850
Leona Tyler Award 3666
S. Rains Wallace Dissertation Award 18757
Barbara Strudler Wallston Award 3738
Rosalee G. Weiss Award 3770
Robert J. Wherry Award 18758
Lightner Witmer Award 3712
Logan Wright Distinguished Service Award 3757
Wyeth Young Psychopharmacologist Award 3766
Robert M. Yerkes Award 3724

Public administration (*See also* Bureaucracy; City management; Government service; Historic preservation; Planning; Public finance; Public works)
Achievement Awards 14165
Administrator of the Year 2231
Award for Innovative Management 11028
Award for Local Government Education 11472
Award for Skill in Intergovernmental Relations 11473
Awards for Excellence 10110
Joan Fiss Bishop Award 18403
Louis Brownlow Award 4180
Louis Brownlow Book Award 13818
Laverne Burchfield Award 4181
Canadian Award for Financial Reporting 10111
CAPAM International Innovations Award 8304
Award for Career Development in Memory of L.P. Cookingham 11474
Cronin Club Award 14397
Marshall E. Dimock Award 4182
Distinguished Budget Presentation Award 10113
Distinguished Research Award 18404
Distinguished Service Award
American Association of School Administrators 1405
American Association of University Administrators 1461
Doctoral Awards Program 14326
Equal Opportunity/Affirmative Action Exemplary Practices Award 4183
Benjamin F. Fairless Memorial Award 2874
Heinz Award in Public Policy 10378
Julia Henderson Service to the Section Award 18405
Roger W. Jones Award for Executive Leadership 4784
JTPA Awards for Excellence 14168
William A. Jump Award 12460
Award for Excellence in Honor of Mark E. Keane 11475
Leadership for Learning Award 1406
Charles E. Levine Memorial Award for Excellence in Public Service 4184
Management Effectiveness Awards 3885
McCormack Award 5865
Harold W. McGraw, Jr. Prize in Education 13221
Richard Beatty Mellon Award 322
William E. Mosher and Frederick C. Mosher Award 4185
NASPAA/ASPA Distinguished Research Award 4186
National Public Service Awards 13819
National Superintendent of the Year Award 1407
International Award in Honor of Orin F. Nolting 11476
Outstanding Elected Democratic Woman Holding Public Office 14967
Program Excellence Awards 11477
Public Risk Manager of the Year Award 17730
In-Service Training Award in Memory of Clarence E. Ridley 11478
Herbert Roback Scholarship 13820
Theodore Roosevelt Distinguished Service Medal 20066
Donald L. Scantlebury Memorial Award 12428
Sloan Public Service Awards of the Fund for the City of New York 9834
Donald C. Stone Award 4187
Noble G. Swearingen Award 5866
Academic Award in Memory of Stephen B. Sweeney 11479
Top Ten Public Works Leaders of the Year 3809
Eileen M. Tosney AAUA Award for Excellence in the Practice of Higher Education Administration 1462
The Lent D. Upson-Loren B. Miller Fellowship 8020
Vanier Medal 11029
Dwight Waldo Award 4188
Assistant Excellence in Leadership Award in Memory of Buford M. Watson, Jr. 11480
James E. Webb Award 4189
Abel Wolman Award 3810
Workplace Diversity Professional Development Award 11481

Public affairs (*See also* Community affairs; Consumer affairs; Housing; Leadership; Legislative improvement; Military service)
Africa Prize for Leadership for the Sustainable End of Hunger 10614
ASPA/NASPAA Distinguished Research Award 14374
Robert Bosch Foundation Fellowship Program 7687
Donald Campbell Award 17449
Distinguished Contributions to Research in Public Policy 18903
Dr. Eisenhower Medal 9193
Moses Leo Gitelson Memorial Essay Awards 7758
Good Government Pharmacist of the Year Award 3388
Grolier National Library Week Grant 3000
Guardian of Seniors' Rights 9
Bryce Harlow Business-Government Relations Award 10241
Hubert H. Humphrey Award 17450
International Activist Award 10040
Robert F. Kennedy Book Awards 18074
Irving Kristol Lecture on Public Policy 2195
Theodore Lowi Award and Jeffrey Pressman Award 17451
Miriam Mills Award 17452
NASPAA Annual Dissertation Award 14375
National Magazine Awards 15355
Outstanding NFDW Member of the Year 14968
PSO Book Award 17453
Public Affairs Competition 1276
Service to Democracy Award 932
Elmer B. Staats Public Service Career Awards 14376
Time Man of the Year 20093
Daniel Webster Award 11816
Leslie A. Whittington Excellence in Teaching Award 14377
Whitney M. Young, Jr., Award 2723
Alfred M. Zuck Public Courage Award 14378

Public finance
ACFAS/Caisse de Depot et Placement du Quebec Prize (in Finance) 5536
Achievement Awards 14165
Achievement of the Year Award 5708
Andy Barr Award 5710
Chapter Service Award 5711
Education and Training Awards 5713
Frank Greathouse Distinguished Leadership Award 5715
Ketner Productivity Awards 16505
Robert W. King Memorial Award 5716
National President's Awards 5717
Dr. Jackson R. E. Phillips Award 5830
Service Awards 5831
Special Achievement Award 5721
Elmer Staats Award 5722

Public health
Elda E. Anderson Award 10317
APHA Award for Excellence 3778
Award for Excellence in Multicultural Health 14174
Award of Honor 2542
Babcock-Hart Award 10935
Harold Barnum Industry Award 11227
J. Howard Beard Award 14175
Certificate of Merit 7355
Committee of the Year Award 15497
Committee Person of the Year Award 15498
Community Preventive Dentistry Award 2127
H. Trendley Dean Memorial Award 11207
R. D. Defries Award 7356
Distinguished Service Awards 3888
Jay S. Drotman Memorial Award 3779
Educator Award 11231
Bart Eldredge Award 16105
Golden Apple Awards for Service in Health Promotion and Disease Prevention 20031
Louis Gorin Award for Outstanding Achievement in Rural Health Care 15651
Health Advocate of the Year 16979
Honorary Life Member 7357
William A. Howe Award 3889
Janssen-Ortho Award 7358
Anson Jones, M.D., Award 20032
Leverett Graduate Student Merit Award for Outstanding Achievement in Dental Public Health 1392
Abraham Lilienfeld Student Prize Paper 18670
McCormack Award 5865
Pearl McIver Public Health Nurse Award 3282
R. Tait McKenzie Award 881
MMCA Annual Scholarship 13353
National Essay Contest on "The Role of Public Health in Healthcare Reform" 8870
National Organization for Rare Disorders Awards 15440
Alton Ochsner Award Relating Smoking and Health 16609
Outstanding Chapter Awards 785
Outstanding Rural Health Practice 15652
Outstanding Rural Health Program 15653
Outstanding School Health Educator Award 3890
Jim Parker Memorial Award 14176
President's Award 3013
Primary Care Award 14177
Public Service Award 4819
Research Council Award 3892
Will Ross Medal 3014
Rural Health Practitioner of the Year 15654
Louis B. Russell, Jr., Memorial Award 2419
Sanitarian's Award 11234

Public (continued)

Sedgwick Memorial Medal 3780
Noble G. Swearingen Award 5866
William C. Watson, Jr. Medal of Excellence 20502
Mark Weintraub Scholarship 16106

Public opinion research
AAPOR Award 1036
AIAA Section Public Policy Award 2667
Duncan Black Prize 17707
Student Paper Competition 1037

Public relations (*See also* Advertising; Publicity)
AALL/West Excellence in Marketing Award 1247
AH&MA Achievement Awards 2567
AMVETS National Awards Program 4947
Aqua Awards 11430
Awards of Excellence 14181
Al Bard Award 10551
Bell Ringer Awards 17732
Harold S. Bowen Public Relations Award 10728
Bronze Anvil Awards 17720
William M. Cavanaugh Student Grant 17733
Certified Residential Specialist Designation 8583
Clarion Awards 5522
Communicator of the Year Award 14773
Community Outreach Award 2763
Company Award of Excellence 14343
CPRS Awards of Excellence Program 7360
CPRS Major Awards Program 7361
John Cotton Dana Library Public Relations Awards 12816
Epilepsy Foundation of America Awards 9308
Gold Anvil Award 17721
Gold Key Laureates 130
Gold Medallion Award 15667
Golden Achievement Award 15668
Golden ARC Awards 292
Winthrop W. Grice Award 10553
Harold Hammerman Spirit of Education Award 14434
Abel Hanson Awards Program 5702
Helen Dinerman Award 21850
Peggy Hereford Excellence in Communications Award 403
HSMAI Golden Bell Public Relations Awards 10555
International Special Librarians Day/National Library Week Award 19552
Peter H. Johnson Image Award 14435
"L. PeRCy" Awards 12836
MacEachern Award 17726
Larry MacPhail Trophy 14341
Master's Thesis Award 10832
Matrix Award 16312
National Golden Target Award 13066
National Public Relations Achievement Award 6211
Philip A. Novikoff Memorial Award 7362
Outstanding Educator Award 17723
Pacesetter of the Year Award 14774
Paragon Awards 14775
Pathfinder Award 10833
D. Richard Petrizzo Award for Career Achievement 14776
PR Professional of the Year 131
Professional Development Coordinator of the Year 14540
Professionalism Award 14439
Public Affairs Competition 1276
Public Affairs Network Awards 3633
Public Relations Achievement 15865
Public Relations Award
- Amateur Athletic Union 570
- National Association of Independent Fee Appraisers 14272

Public Relations Awards 17089
Public Relations Competition 10997
Public Relations Coordinator of the Year 14542
Public Relations/Development/Marketing/Director of the Year Award 20352
Public Relations Member Achievement Award 19555
Public Relations Regional Achievement Award 19701
Public Service Award 18503
Don Rennie Memorial Award for Excellence in Government Public Relations 7363
Rowe Marketing Award 7257
Louis B. Russell, Jr., Memorial Award 2419
Save Our Streams Award 12270
Share the Wealth Packets 12837
Silver Anvil Awards 17724
Sidney O. Smith National Award 10738
Staffing Industry Communications Awards 4689
State Award for Excellence 13067
Vanguard Award for Public Relations 14581
Volunteer Service Award 15327
Worcester, Nelson and Turner Prizes 21851

Public sanitation *See* Sanitary engineering

Public service (*See also* Community service; Government service)
AAAS Scientific Freedom and Responsibility Award 1048
AAP Excellence in Public Service Award 756
AASCU Distinguished Alumnus Award 1428
AAAS Philip Hauge Abelson Prize 1049
Access Award 8044
Pedro N. Acha Award for Veterinary Public Health 17057
Additional Honours 6815
Advertising Council Award for Public Service 208
Advertising Leader of the Year Award 12923
AHS Business Partner Award 2452
Alumni Medal 20996
APWA Distinguished Service Award 3798
ASCE Presidents' Award 4293
ASHRAE - Alco Medal for Distinguished Public Service 4419
Association of the United States Army Awards 5883
Award for Distinguished Public Service
- American Mathematical Society 3040
- United States Conference of Mayors 20454

Award for Patient Advocacy 3614
Awards of Excellence 20181
Barry Award 1658
Charlie Bartlett Award 10077
Broadcast Excellence Award 6890
Emory Buckner Medal 9441
Butch Henley Award 2453
Benjamin N. Cardozo School of Law Distinguished Public Service Award 22025
Cash-In-A-Flash Award Program 20468
Census Award of Excellence 20444
Certificate of Merit 3822
Chairman's Awards 17709
Citizen of the Year 1182
Common Wealth Awards of Distinguished Service 17410
Congressional Staff Award 18107
Cooperative Month Awards 14800
Cultural Diversity Outreach Award 3823
Deadline Club Awards 8773
Eugene V. Debs Award 9350
Distinguished Achievement Award for Petroleum Engineering Faculty 19236
Distinguished Contribution to Psychology in the Public Interest 18901
Distinguished Diplomatic Award 9445
Distinguished Professional Contributions to Public Service 18907
Distinguished Public Service Medal 13885
Distinguished Service/Achievement Awards 18456
Distinguished Service Award
- American Public Gas Association 3775
- National Association of Realtors 14354
- Tax Foundation 19944
- United States Association of Former Members of Congress 20412

Distinguished Service Award for Elected County Official 14167
Distinguished Service Awards
- National Governors Association 15170
- University of Chicago Medical and Biological Sciences Alumni Association 21003

Richard Douthit Public Service Award 2454
J. R. Dymond Public Service Award 16759
EDI Awards (Equality/Dignity/Independence) 9088
Edmund S. Muskie Distinguished Public Service Award 7737
Electronic Communication Award 18459
Conrad A. Elvehjem Award for Public Service in Nutrition 4157
Emergency Medical Services Exemplary Service Medal 6819
Equal Employment Opportunity Award 20479
Exceptional Achievement Medal 13888
FBI Honorary Medals 20504
Federal City Club Award for Very Distinguished Public Service 9447
Founders Award 16351
Benjamin Franklin Medal for Distinguished Public Service 3434
Friend of Libraries U.S.A. Award (Friend of the Year) 9793
Friends of Libraries U.S.A. Public Service Award 9794
John T. Galey, Sr. Memorial Public Service Award 2843
Cardinal Gibbons Medal 7665
Gold Medal
- American Irish Historical Society 2871
- American Petroleum Institute 3374
- National Football Foundation and College Hall of Fame 15070

Gold Typewriter Award 16248
Golf Digest - LPGA Founders Cup 12654

Subject Index

Public (continued)

Samuel Gompers American Red Cross National Labor Award 3827
Goodwill Ambassadors for UNICEF 20596
Horace Greeley Award 16119
Hall of Fame Award 15110
W. Averell Harriman Award 2280
Philip Hart Public Service Award 8461
Head of Public Service Award 20182
Heart of Humanity Award 20920
Andrew Heiskell Awards 20091
Christian A. Herter Award 2282
HHS Distinguished Public Service Award 20497
Harold M. Hildreth Award 3698
Honor Award 14549
Honor Awards Program 20469
Hoover Medal 4328
John W. Hyatt Award 19264
Information Processing Public Service Award 5732
Innovations in American Government Awards Program 10116
Institute Service Awards 17631
International Certificate of Appreciation 3830
International Leadership Award 18529
International Platform Association Award 11806
Jacob K. Javits Excellence in Public Service Award 18057
Jacob K. Javits Public Service Award 3622
Jefferson Awards 2628
George F. Kennan Award for Distinguished Public Service 14703
John F. Kennedy Profile in Courage Award 12398
Eugene J. Keogh Award for Distinguished Public Service 16307
Martin Luther King, Jr. Leadership Awards 8965
Barbara Kingsolver Award 9795
Krieghbaum Under-40 Award 5345
John Oliver La Gorce Medal 15159
Labor Participation Citation for Services 3832
Helmut Landberg Award for Excellence in Applied Climatology 1426
Paul M. Lund Public Service Award 17722
James Madison Award for Distinguished Public Service 4902
James Madison Medal 17559
Making Democracy Work Award 12754
Manhattan College De La Salle Medal 13051
Guglielmo Marconi Award 16847
Marks of Excellence Award 15111
Carroll Sterling Masterson Award & Outstanding Women's Awards 22093
Hiram Percy Maxim Memorial Award 49
Medal of Honor 16352
Mental Health Media Awards 15378
Meritorious Service Cross - Civil Division 6823
Meritorious Service Medal - Civil Division 6825
Michener-Deacon Fellowship 13329
Miss America Women's Achievement Award 13496
MLA Award for Distinguished Public Service 13262
National Association of Community Health Centers Awards 14138
National Club Achievement Competition 860
National Commander's Public Relations Award 2948
National Public Service Awards 13819
National Smokey Bear Awards 9560
New Englander of the Year Awards 16099
On-the-Spot Awards 20470
Order of West Range 17310
Outstanding Achievement Award 20183
Outstanding County Program Awards 16506
Outstanding Post Service Officer Award 21332
Outstanding Public Service Award 8553
Charles Lathrop Parsons Award 1778
Phoenix House Award for Public Service 17277
President's Award for Distinguished Federal Civilian Service 20718
President's Medal 16353
Prix Bene Merenti de Patria 18605
Professional Engineers Gold Medal 17608
Professional of the Year 16902
Public Policy Award 4207
Public Service Achievement Awards 8300
Public Service Award
 American Public Power Association 3793
 American Veterinary Medical Association 4819
 Associated Press Managing Editors - Managing Editors Association 5252
 Association of Consulting Engineers of Canada 5642
 National Kidney Foundation 15324
 Society of Petroleum Engineers 19247
 UCLA Alumni Association 20262
Public Service Awards 1350
Public Service Excellence Awards 17710
Public Service Medal 13899
Public Service National Leadership Award 2456
Public Welfare Medal 13845
Pulitzer Prizes 17749
Recorder of the Year 16647
William R. Rivkin Award 2283
Eleanor Roosevelt Award 11809
Theodore Roosevelt Award 11810
Theodore Roosevelt Distinguished Service Medal 20066
Safe Driving Award 20550
Scholarship Fund CBMC Area Local 7881
Section Achievement Award 1857
Whitney North Seymour Award 9443
Sigma Delta Chi Awards 19276
Special Achievement Award 15866
Special Achievement Awards 3699
Special Awards Established by the President 9366
Statesman of the Year 692
Sunshine Award 19277
Tall Man Water Freezer Award 10279
Ten Outstanding Young Americans 20678
Locksin Thompson Memorial Public Service Award 6761
Trail Development Award 2458
Harry S. Truman Public Service Award 8037
Unity-and-Diversity Service Award 20921
University Medal for Excellence 8245
Unsung Hero Award 16903
Spence Vanderlinden Public Official Award 3796
Veblen - Commons Award 5363
VFW Congressional Award 21336
Martin Wagner Memorial Award 15328
Raoul Wallenberg Awards 17876
Simon Wiesenthal Center Humanitarian Award 18530
Bill Wilcox Award 2459
Woodrow Wilson Award 17560
Wright Brothers Memorial Trophy 13880
Young Member Outstanding Service Award 19250

Public speaking

Phyllis Flory Barton Top Debate Speaker Award 15097
Best Conference Program Award 11800
Best Paper Presented at the Annual Meeting Award 19118
George W. Brindley Lecture 8090
Ralph E. Carey Distinguished District Chair Awards 15098
Cavett Award 15791
Council of Peers Award for Excellence/ Speaker Hall of Fame 15792
Diamond Key Award 15099
Distinguished Service Award
 American Association of Collegiate Registrars and Admissions Officers 1161
 American Forensic Association 2286
 Association of Schools of Allied Health Professions 5838
Distinguished Service Key 15100
Engineering Meetings Board Outstanding Oral Presentation Award 19041
Golden Gavel Award 20095
Hall of Fame 15101
Pi Kappa Delta/Bruno E. Jacob Trophy 15102
Erwin T. Koch Award 13522
Leading Chapter Award 15103
Lifetime Achievement Award 14201
Howard Lillie Memorial Award 1688
Lincoln Financial Group Awards of Excellence 15104
William Littlewood Memorial Lecture 19050
Andrina McCulloch Prizes for Public Speaking 17806
Memorial Lecturer Award and Honoree(s) 3137
Harland B. Mitchell National Debate Trophy 15105
Stanislaw W. Mrozowski Award 1646
Senator Karl E. Mundt Trophy 15106
NADSA Outstanding Service Award 14202
NADSA Research Award 14203
NADSA Scholar Award 14204
National Awards 15107
National Federation Citations 14978
National Forensic Association Awards 15095
Orators Hall of Fame 11808
Outstanding Lecture Award 15198
Scholarship Contests 15782
Spokesperson for Agriculture 16005
John C. Stennis Student Congress Awards 15108
Voice of Democracy Scholarship Program 12647
James A. Winans/Herbert A. Wichelns Memorial Award for Distinguished Scholarship in Rhetoric and Public Address 14716
WORDS/ISAAC Outstanding Consumer User Lecture Award 11921

Public utilities
Academic Achievement Award 4837
Annual Report Award 3784
APPA Century Award 3785
APPA Honor Roll 3786
APPA Safety Contest Awards 3787
Community Service Award 3788
Distinguished Service Award 3775
James D. Donovan Individual Achievement Award 3789
Education Award 4838
Energy Innovator Award 3790
Larry Hobart Seven Hats Award 3791
Harold Kramer - John Preston Personal Service Award 3792
Personal Service Award 3776
Professional Development 21797
Public Service Award 3793
Alex Radin Distinguished Service Award 3794
Safety Award 16523
E. F. Scattergood System Achievement Award 3795
Spence Vanderlinden Public Official Award 3796

Public works
Award of Merit 3799
Contractor of the Year Award 3800
Rodney R. Fleming Award 3801
Samuel A. Greeley Local Government Service Award 3802
Heritage Award 3803
Honorary Member 3804
Meritorious Service Award 3805
Donald C. Stone Award 3807
Harry S. Swearingen Award 3808
Top Ten Public Works Leaders of the Year 3809
Abel Wolman Award 3810

Publications (*See also* Company publications; School publications; Travel literature)
AACP Clinical Research Award 631
AAN Media Award 708
AESF Gold Medal 2169
Affiliated Chapter Awards 10342
Walter C. Alvarez Memorial Award 3081
Annual Writing Competition 8979
Award for Outstanding Forestry Magazine of an Affiliated State Woodland Owner Association 15977
Award for Outstanding Publication 5661
F. W. (Casey) Baldwin Award 6867
James P. Barry Ohioana Award for Editorial Excellence 16657
Blue Pencil Awards 14242
Book Award 18696
Richard and Grace Brigham Award 19066
Britt Literary Award 5087
Vernon Carstensen Memorial Award 281
Russell L. Cecil Arthritis Medical Journalism Awards 5125
Certificates of Merit Awards - Regional History 7150
Chapter Newsletter of the Year Award 5088
Chester Paul Siess Award for Excellence in Structural Research 1964
Clarion Awards 5522
Allan P. Colburn Award for Excellence in Publications by a Young Member of the Institute 2762
Consumer Journalism Award 15515
Continuing Publication Commendation 8434
Discover Award 6254
Distinguished Scholarship Award 17019
Russell A. Dixon Award 2048
Robert H. Dott, Sr., Memorial Award 1336
ECRI Medical Technology Media Awards Program 9150
Editor of the Year Award 15527
Editorial and Design Awards 5572
EdPress Honor Awards - Best Newsletter 5664
EdPress Honor Awards - Most Improved Publication 5667
Everett Eugene Edwards Memorial Award 282
John Hope Franklin Publication Prize 4708
Henry Allan Gleason Award 6547
Louis I. Grossman Award 1192
Roderick Haig-Brown Award 9477
Dorothy E. Hansell Publication Award 1121
Ed A. Hewett Prize 1055
Hopkinson Award 20850
T. J. Hull Award 13745
IIAA Publications Award 10733
Instruction Publication of the Year Award 5610
International ANDY Awards 11184
Lawrence Jackson Award 17224
Barbara Jelavich Prize 1056
Philip Johnson Exhibition Catalogue Award 19023
Palmer O. Johnson Memorial Award 2161
Harry G. Johnson Prize 7078
Journey Prize 13211
Adoph G. Kammer Merit in Authorship Award 1905
Kenneth S. Lane Award 4780
Marta Lange/CQ Press Award 5612
Law Library Journal Article of the Year Award 1253
John F. Lewis Award 3438
Matrix Award 16312
Mobius Advertising Awards 21142
National Magazine Awards 4492
Frederic W. Ness Book Award 5552
Newsletter Competition 15151
Margaret Cross Norton Award 13393
Outstanding Book Award 2163
Outstanding Forestry Extension Publication Award 15980
Outstanding Paper in Surveying 2002
Outstanding Publication Award 15542
Outstanding Writing Award 1153
Pollie Awards 1385
Wallace E. Pratt Memorial Award 1349
Prize for a Distinguished Bibliography 13564
Prize for a Distinguished Scholarly Edition 13565
Prize Paper Award 10912
Public Affairs Competition 1276
Publications and Electronic Media Awards 15669
Regional Publication Awards 19704
Wilmer Shields Rich Awards for Excellence in Communications 8600
Lois Roth Award for a Translation of a Literary Work 13568
Theodore Saloutos Memorial Book Award 283
Science in Society Journalism Awards 7384
Marshall Shulman Book Prize 1058
Maurice Simpson Technical Editor's Award 10929
George W. Snedecor Award 4695
Ralph F. Sommer Award 1194
J. C. "CAM" Sproule Memorial Award 1352
Technical Committee Prize Paper Awards 10913
Wayne S. Vucinich Prize 1059
Barbara Strudler Wallston Award 3738

Publicity (*See also* Advertising; Public relations)
Audrey Baird Gold Ribbon Audience Development Awards 4729
Chapter Award for Excellence in Newsletter Publishing 11564
Chapter of Excellence Award 11939
Communications Awards 10084
Distinguished Chapter Award 11940
Health Advancement Award 15321
Public Relations Awards 17089
Robert F. Sibert Informational Book Award 5443
Gordon Smiley Memorial Award 19711
World Challenge 19724

Publishing (*See also* Bibliography; Book and newspaper design; Book collecting; Editing; Illustration; Printing industry; Publications; Reference; Typography)
AAUP Design Show 5567
AESE Award for Outstanding Editorial or Publishing Contributions 5660
Alberta Book Design Awards 6502
Alberta Children's Book of the Year 6503
Alberta Educational Book of the Year 6504
Alberta Emerging Publisher of the Year 6505
Alberta Publisher of the Year Award 6506
Alberta Scholarly Book of the Year 6507
Alcuin Book Design Awards 430
Mary Alexander Award 7876
Amtmann Fellowship 6359
The Annual LMP Awards 18177
APEX - Awards for Publication Excellence 4994
Hiromi Arisawa Awards 5568
Father Adrien Arsenault Senior Arts Award 17544
Award for Excellence: Genealogical Methods and Sources 15140
Award for Excellence: Genealogy and Family History 15141
Award for Excellence: *National Genealogical Society Quarterly* 15142
Mildred L. Batchelder Award 5432
Elmer Holmes Bobst Literary Awards 16301
Bookbuilders West Book Show 6513
Cecil Brownlow Publications Award 9579
Campus Bookseller of the Year Award 6983
Catalog of the Year Awards 14594
Catalyst Award 13236
Certificate of Merit 6514
Clarion Awards 5522
Commonwealth Club of California Book Awards 8306
J. Gordon Coogler Award 4660
Curtis G. Benjamin Award for Creative Publishing 5564
Distinguished Scholar Award 12523
Distinguished Service Award

Subject Index

Publishing (continued)

Association of Free Community Papers 5696
Chicago Book Clinic 7877
National Newspaper Publishers Association 15414
Bill Duthie Booksellers' Choice 21518
William A. Dwiggins Award 6510
Economic Inquiry Article Award 21544
EXCEL Awards 19205
Tom Fairley Award for Editorial Excellence 9166
Henry Johnson Fisher Award 13014
Benjamin Franklin Awards 17739
Front Page Award 10814
Gold Book Awards 5658
Gradiva Awards 14052
Charley Haslam International Scholarship 1583
Hugh M. Hefner First Amendment Award 17396
Honorary Member 7878
Industry Excellence Awards 22021
Jefferson Cup Award 21392
Laurence B. Johnson Award 5668
Journalism Award 7659
Journalism Awards 16326
Katharine Kyes Leab and Daniel J. Leab *American Book Prices Current* Exhibition Catalogue Awards 5614
Jeremiah Ludington Memorial Award 9175
Jack Mason Award 6274
Robin Mays Award 17735
McGovern Award 16333
Harold W. McGraw, Jr. Prize in Education 13221
Mid-America Publishers Association (MAPA) Awards Program 13368
National, City and Regional Magazine Editorial and Design Awards 8024
New England Book Show Juried Selection 6511
Newsletter Journalism Awards 16324
Robert Troup Paine Prize 10283
PEN Publisher Award 17149
PNBA Book Awards 17007
Publisher of the Year 5697
Publishing Hall of Fame 18525
Pushcart Prize: Best of the Small Presses 17770
School Division Education Research Award 5565
Science in Society Book Awards 7383
Seybold Vision Award 18427
Silurian Excellence in Journalism Awards 19327
Silver Quill Editorial Achievement Award 4895
Fannie Simon Award 19560
Southern Books Competition 19481
Gary Spitler Memorial Award 14293
Top Honor Books, Chicago Book Clinic Annual Exhibit 7879
Toronto Arts Awards 20112
Trade Book of the Year 6508
Weiss/Brown Publication Subvention Award 16316
Western US Design & Production Awards Competition 17737
Thomas J. Wilson Award 10284
James R. Wiseman Book Award 5036
WNBA Award 21802
World and National Calendar Awards 6729

Puppetry
President's Award 17759
Puppeteers of America Award 17760
Trustee's Award 17761
UNIMA Citation for Excellence in the Art of Puppetry 20300
UNIMA-USA Scholarships 20301

Quality control *See* Standards

Race relations *See* Ethnic affairs

Radio (*See also* Broadcasting; Cable television; Media; Television)
5 Band WAZ Award 8628
AAAS Science Journalism Awards 1047
Academy of Country Music Awards 86
Achievement Award 9715
Advertising Design Club of Canada Awards 204
The Gracie Allen Awards 9716
The American Advertising Awards 858
Annual Awards in International News Coverage 16981
Armstrong Medal 17829
Armstrong Memorial Research Foundation Awards 5098
ARRL Herb S. Brier Instructor of the Year Award 45
ARRL Professional Educator of the Year Award 46
ASHA Media Awards for Journalists 4662
Asian American Journalists Association National Awards 5165
Ralph Batcher Memorial Award 17830
Billboard Radio Awards 6378
Howard W. Blakeslee Awards 2404
Broadcast Excellence Award 6890
Tom Brokaw Award 19449
Russell L. Cecil Arthritis Medical Journalism Awards 5125
Centenarian Award 17832
Harry Chapin Media Awards 21925
Chassie Awards 17826
Consumer Journalism Award 15515
CPB Public Radio Program Awards 8523
CQ DX Awards 8629
CQ DX Honor Roll 8630
Crystal Radio Awards 14110
Deadline Club Awards 8773
Lee DeForest Award 17833
Distinguished Performance Award 20686
DX Hall of Fame 8631
DXer of the Year 5797
Eclipse Awards for Media 20085
Freedom of Speech Award 19905
Friends of Old-Time Radio Award 9797
Gabriel Award 7633
Gavel Awards 1533
Global Media Awards for Excellence in Population Reporting 17469
Gold Medal Award 11848
Gold Ribbon for Community Service (Radio) 6891
Gold Ribbon for Outstanding Community Service by an Individual Broadcaster 6894
Gold Ribbon for Promotion of Canadian Talent (Radio) 6895
Golden Medallion Media Awards 19759
Barry M. Goldwater Amateur Radio Award 17835
Grants for Arts Projects 14930
Alfred H. Grebe Award 17836
Heart of America 2952
The Sidney Hillman Foundation Prize Awards 10435
HSMAI Adrian Advertising Awards 10554
IAFF Media Awards Contest 11355
ILCA Film and Broadcast Competition 11699
International ANDY Awards 11184
International Broadcasting Awards 10516
International Humanitarian Award 48
International Radio Programming and Promotion Awards 16222
IRE Awards 12170
Edgar F. Johnson Pioneer Citation 17838
Robert F. Kennedy Journalism Awards 18076
Robert L. Kozik Award for Environmental Reporting 15519
Mort Luby Senior Hall of Fame Award 6565
Marconi Radio Awards 14115
Hiram Percy Maxim Memorial Award 49
Wade H. McCree, Jr. Awards for the Advancement of Justice 19763
Philip J. McGan Silver Antenna Award 50
Mental Health Media Awards 15378
Michener-Deacon Fellowship 13329
Mobius Advertising Awards 21142
Edward R. Murrow Award 8526
National Headliner Awards 15194
National Media Awards 1829
National Psychology Awards for Excellence in the Media 18915
National Radio Award 14116
Olin Fox (Memorial) Award 17783
One Show Awards 16732
Peabody Awards Collection 21020
Polka Music Hall of Fame 11820
Jack Poppele Broadcast Award 17841
President's Award 17842
Professional Instructor of the Year Award 51
PROMAX Awards 17679
Publications and Electronic Media Awards 15669
Radio Mercury Awards 17827
Radio Program Producer of the Year 15615
Radio Station of the Year 15616
Robert L. Robinson Awards 3635
Ruben Salazar Award for Communications 14808
Salute to Excellence Awards 14101
Science in Society Journalism Awards 7384
SD Broadcaster of the Year 19450
Sigma Delta Chi Awards 19276
Silurian Excellence in Journalism Awards 19327
Silver Satellite Award 9717
Stamford Radio Theater Competition 19741
Talk Show Host of the Year 19906
Television-Radio Awards 21994
Tilden Canadian Literary Awards 7000
UPI National Broadcast Awards 20371
USA-CA Award 8632
Wilbur Awards 17971
Women at Work Awards 21618
Worked All Zones Award 8633
WORLDFEST - Houston International Film and Video Festival 21969
WPX Award 8634
WPX Award of Excellence 8635
WPX Honor Roll 8636

Radio (continued)

Yasme Award 22019
You've Got a Friend in Pennsylvania Award 53

Radiology
Berson-Yalow Award 19226
L. J. Cartwright Award 6917
Certificates of Honor and Appreciation 1940
Marie Curie Award 1072
Fleischner Society Memorial Award 9570
Gold Award 2400
Gold Medal
American College of Radiology 1941
Radiological Society of North America 17852
Georg Charles de Hevesy Nuclear Pioneer Award 19228
Honorary Fellow 1942
E. I. Hood Award 6918
ICRU - Gray Medal 11492
Janeway Medal 3814
Hans Langendorff Award 17853
Dr. M. Mallett Student Award 6919
Eleanor Montague Distinguished Resident Award in Radiation Oncology 1073
Charles R. Morris Student Research Award 728
Outstanding Educator Award 17854
Outstanding Researcher Award 17855
Dr. Petrie Memorial Award 6921
Philips Rose Bowl 6922
Radiology News Awards Competition 1943
Howard R. Raper Oral and Maxillofacial Radiology Award 729
George Reason Memorial Cup 6923
Albert G. Richards Graduate Student Research Grant 730
Roentgen Resident/Fellow Research Award 17856
William H. Rollins Graduate Student Research Grant 731
Sister Mary Arthur "Sharing the Light" Award 6924
Lucy Frank Squire Distinguished Resident Award in Diagnostic Radiology 1074
Student Award 732
Young Oncologist Essay Awards 3815
Young Oncologist Travel Grants 3816

Radiotherapy *See* Cancer

Railway transportation
Branding Hammer Award 17858
Broad Axe Award 17859
Dr. Gary Burch Memorial Safety Award 14349
Distinguished Service Award 3818
George Falcon Golden Spike Award 14350
Member of the Year 15570
Railroad Calendar Color Slide Contest 13737
Safe Contractor of the Year Awards 15571

Reading skills (*See also* Literacy)
Advocacy Award 11850
Award of Excellence 11852
Broadcast Media Awards for Television 11853
Developing Country Grants 11854
Dina Feitelson Research Award 11855
William S. Gray Citation of Merit 11856
Albert J. Harris Award 11857
Honor Council Program 11858
Institute for Reading Research Fellowship 11860
International Citation of Merit 11861
IRA Presidential Award for Reading and Technology 11863
Eleanor M. Johnson Award 11864
Elva Knight Research Grant 11865
Constance M. McCullough Award 11867
Ronald W. Mitchell Convention Travel Grant 11868
Outstanding Dissertation of the Year Award 11869
Outstanding Teacher Educator in Reading Award 11870
Print Media Award 11871
Reading/Literacy Research Fellowship 11872
Helen M. Robinson Grant 11873
Nila Banton Smith Award 11875
Special Service Award 11876
Teacher as Researcher Grant 11877
Travel Grants for Educators 11878
Gertrude Whipple Professional Development Grant 11879

Real estate (*See also* Assessment; Construction; Housing; Real estate journalism)
Aloha Aina Award 10528
ARM of the Year 11032
Robert H. Armstrong Award 5006
Award Emeritus 17891
Best Academic Paper 17892
Best Single Education Program 17893
George M. Brooker Collegiate Scholarship for Minorities 11033
Certified Property Manager (CPM) of the Year Award 11034
Certified Residential Specialist Designation 8583
W. R. Chapline Land Stewardship Award 18834
W. R. Chapline Research Award 18835
Chapter of the Year 15558
Consumer Education Award 17894
Distinguished Career Award 17895
Distinguished Service Award
National Association of Realtors 14354
Society for Range Management 18836
Earth Award 6682
Federal Property Person of the Year 15559
Robert L. Foreman Award 5007
Jack Griffiths Property Person of the Year 15560
Lloyd D. Hanford Sr. Distinguished Faculty Award 11036
Jim Hoag Scholarship 19462
S. Edwin Kazdin Memorial Fund Award 5009
Dr. William Kinnard, Jr. Academic Award 5010
Louise and Y. T. Lum Award 5011
Louise L. and Y. T. Lum Award 11038
Arthur A. May Award 5012
Most Outstanding Educational Program 17896
Outstanding Young Range Professional Award 18837
J. Wallace Paletou Award 11039
Professional Achievement Award 11040
Real Estate Educator of the Year 17897
Real Estate Regulator of the Year 17898
Realtor of the Year 14355
Realtor of the Year (ROTY) 10529
Alfred E. Reinman, Jr. Award 5013
Paul H. Rittle, Sr. Memorial Scholarship Award 11041
George L. Schmutz Award 5014
Charles B. Shattuck Award 5015
H. Grady Stebbins, Jr. Distinguished Service Award 5016
Sustained Lifetime Achievement Award 18838
Percy and Betty Wagner Award 5017

Real estate journalism
Academy of Authors 11031
Communication and Marketing Awards 11035
Journal of Property Management Article of the Year Awards 11037
Real Estate Journalism Competition 14352

Recording industry
Advertising and Marketing Awards 14357
American Music Awards 3160
Award for Distinguished Service to Historical Recordings 5460
Best Seller Awards 14358
Harry Chapin Memorial Humanitarian Award 14359
Competition for Performing Artists 8476
Display Contest 14360
Felix Awards, Artistic 188
Felix Awards, Industrial 189
Gold Award 17908
Grammy Awards 13822
Mickey Granberg Award 14361
Hall of Fame Awards 13823
Independent Distributors Best Seller Awards - Indie Best Sellers 14362
Juno Awards 6846
Platinum Award 17910
Readers' and Critics' Poll 18110
Retailer of the Year Award 14365
Wholesaler of the Year Award 14366

Records management (*See also* Information management)
Britt Literary Award 5087
Chapter of the Year 5089
Company of Fellows 5090
Industry Specific Group of the Year Award 5091
Emmett Leahy Award 10851
Phyllis B. Marriott President's Award 3142
Recorder of the Year 16647

Recreation (*See also* Hobbies and clubs)
Achievement Award 18001
Achievement Awards 14165
Achievement of Excellence 7014
Acorn Award 1632
AHS Business Partner Award 2452
American Therapeutic Recreation Association Awards 4743
William G. Anderson Merit Award 876
Arial Anaker Award 14028
Athlete of the Year 19569
The Austin Chronicle Best of Austin 6093
Award of Honour 7015
Award of Merit 7323
Best of *Grist* Awards 15724
Harry Boothman Bursary 7324
Ham Brown Award 16966
Butch Henley Award 2453

Subject Index

Recreation (continued)

Certificate of Appreciation 7016
Chairman's Award 19570
Champion of the Trail Award 9637
Citation of Outstanding Achievement 7325
Coach of the Year
Canadian Federation of Amateur Baseball 7086
Special Olympics Canada 19571
Robert W. Crawford Young Professional Award 15575
Hedley S. Dimock Award 1625
Directors Award of The Friends of Algonquin Park 9781
Distinguished Fellow 3362
Distinguished Service Award
Alpine Club of Canada 501
American Camping Association 1626
National Therapeutic Recreation Society 15872
Richard Douthit Public Service Award 2454
Ben East Prize 13364
Education, Friend of the Trails Award 16855
Eleanor P. Eells Award for Program Excellence 1627
Maj. Gen. Eugene L. Eubank Morale, Welfare and Recreation Award 16824
Excellence for Innovation Award 7326
Excellence in Programming Award 18002
Francis P. Farquhar Mountaineering Award 18460
Fellow Award 18003
Fellows Award 21398
George Fletcher Award 7062
Friend of Recreation 1030
Friend of the Florida Trail Award 9638
Luther Halsey Gulick Award 877
Honor Award
American Alliance for Health, Physical Education, Recreation and Dance 879
American Association for Leisure and Recreation 1031
American Camping Association 1628
Honorary Life Member 7327
Honourary Membership 502
Individual Citation 15873
Jimmy Rattlesnake Award 7087
Jim Kern Award 2455
Mabel Lee Award 880
Gen. Curtis E. LeMay Morale, Welfare, and Recreation Award 16831
Letter from the CCA/ACC President 7017
Member of the Year 15874
Member of the Year Award
International Family Recreation Association 11574
Society of Recreation Executives 19288
Meritorious Service Award
American Association for Leisure and Recreation 1032
American Park and Recreation Society 3363
National Therapeutic Recreation Society 15875
William Penn Mott, Jr. Awards Program 15725
National Award for Media Excellence 15577
National Congressional Award 15578
National Corporate Humanitarian Award 15579
National Distinguished Professional Award 15580
National Gold Medal Awards 19726
National Legislative Award 17916
National Literary Award 15582
National Student Award for Excellence 15726
National Voluntary Service Award 15583
NEMBA Trail Grant 16103
Newcomer Award 18004
Organization and Institution Citations 15876
Outstanding Council Award 1033
Outstanding Student Award 18005
Premier Recreation Operation Award 18006
Presidential Citations and Awards 15877
Professional Recruitment Award 18007
Public Recreation Department of the Year 567
Public Recreation Man and Woman of the Year 568
Public Recreation Volunteer of the Year Award 569
Public Service National Leadership Award 2456
Debbie Regnone Service Award 18008
Research Awards 15878
Theodore and Franklin Roosevelt Award for Excellence in Recreation and Park Research 15584
Michael Sansone Award 8052
Glenn T. Seaborg Award 2457
Service Award 1629
Silva Service Award 20727
Silver Rope Award for Leadership 503
Snowmobile Excellence Award 7060
Special Recognition Award 1630
Special Recreation for People with Disabilities Awards 19573
State Park Awards 19727
Locksin Thompson Memorial Public Service Award 6761
Trail Development Award 2458
USTA Community Service Award 20869
Volunteer Award 7018
VVA Achievement Award 21400
A. O. Wheeler Legacy Award 504
Bill Wilcox Award 2459
Ralph C. Wilson Award 15585
Tommy Wilson Award 1034
World Leisure International Scholarship 21932
WPRA Foundation 21687
Young Professional Award 7328

Recreation industry
Distinguished Service to the RV Industry Award 17915
Eleanor P. Eells Award for Program Excellence 1627
International Award of Merit 11912
Member of the Year Award 15587
National Scholastic Award 17917
National Service Award 17918
RV Automotive Achievement Award 17919
World Leisure International Scholarship 21932

Recycling
"Buy Recycled" Campaign Awards Program 20455
Grand Challenge Award 15422
William T. Hornaday Bronze and Silver Medals 6579
William T. Hornaday Gold Certificate 6580
William T. Hornaday Gold Medal 6581
William T. Hornaday Unit Award 6582
Industry Recycler of the Year Award 12534
National Awards for Environmental Sustainability - Searching for Success Program 17991
National Leadership Awards 15423
National Recycling Coalition Annual Awards 15589
Ontario Waste Minimization Awards 17923
Recycler of the Year Award 15424

Reference
Association of Jewish Libraries Reference Book Award 5741
BRASS Thomson Financial Student Travel Award 17936
Dartmouth Medal 17937
Genealogical Publishing Company Award 17941
Waldo G. Leland Prize 2478
Jose Toribio Medina Award 18415
Isadore Gilbert Mudge - R. R. Bowker Award 17943
Outstanding Reference Sources 17944
Thomson Gale Award for Excellence in Reference and Adult Services 17948

Refugees *See* Humanitarianism

Rehabilitation and therapy
Academy of Research Honorary Member 3290
Gladys Agell Award for Excellence in Research 927
American Occupational Therapy Foundation Awards 3303
American Therapeutic Recreation Association Awards 4743
AMVETS Silver Helmet Awards 4949
Award of Merit 3291
Dorothy E. Baethke - Eleanor J. Carlin Award for Excellence in Academic Teaching 3483
Roger Barker Distinguished Research Contribution Award 3708
Elmer C. Bartels Leadership Recognition Award 15805
Bernard M. Baruch Essay Award For Students 1983
Lucy Blair Service Award 3484
Lindy Boggs Award 3292
Dorothy Briggs Memorial Scientific Inquiry Award 3485
Terry Brittell COTA/OTR Partnership Award 3293
Rosemary Brown Award 5227
Signe Brunnstrom Award for Excellence in Clinical Teaching 3486
Certificate of Appreciation 3294
Chapter Award for Minority Enhancement 3487
Chattanooga Research Award 3488
COTA Award of Excellence 3295
John Stanley Coulter Memorial Lecturer 1984
Counselor of the Year Award 15603
Damien - Dutton Award 8726
Robert G. Dicus Award 17575
Distinguished Member Award 1985
Distinguished Service Award 15872

Rehabilitation (continued)

Employers of the Year 10085
Essay Contest for Professionals in Rehabilitation 1986
W. F. Faulkes Award 15591
Gaston Writing Award 3168
Gold Key Award 1987
Golden Pen Award 3489
Graduate of the Year 10088
Belle Greve Memorial Award 15592
Ada Gruber Grant 7785
Health Advocate Award 3296
Helen J. Hislop Award for Outstanding Contributions to Professional Literature 3490
Paul R. Hoffman Award 15599
Honorary Life Member 928
Honorary Member 3491
Individual Citation 15873
Henry O. Kendall and Florence P. Kendall Award for Outstanding Achievement in Clinical Practice 3492
Henry H. Kessler Awards 17964
Lifetime Achievement Award 4669
Edward W. Lowman Award 1989
Mary McMillan Lecture Award 3493
Member of the Year 15874
Meritorious Service Award 15875
Eugene Michels New Investigator Award 3494
Minority Achievement Award 3495
Minority Initiatives Award 3496
Margaret L. Moore Award for Outstanding New Academic Faculty Member 3497
Cordelia Myers Writers Award 3297
National Citation Awards 15604
National Distinguished Service Award 15605
NRCA Fellow 15606
Order of the Compassionate Heart 17960
Organization and Institution Citations 15876
Organizational Award 15593
Outstanding Contribution to Rehabilitation Award 3709
Outstanding Physician Award 17751
Outstanding Volunteer Award 17752
Past President's Best Practices Award 15600
Presidential Citations and Awards 15877
President's Award 15594
Max T. Prince Meritorious Service Award 15595
Public Service Award
National Legislative Council for the Handicapped 15342
National Rehabilitation Association 15596
Harley B. Reger Memorial Award 15607
The Rehabilitation International Presidential Award 17965
Research Awards 15878
Research Fellowships 17753
Roster of Fellows 3298
Roster of Honor 3299
Service Award 3300
Ambrose M. Shotwell Memorial Award 5342
Sister Mary Arthur "Sharing the Light" Award 6924
Eleanor Clarke Slagle Lectureship 3301
Mary Stanton Scholarships 3502
VEWAA Service Award 15601
Jack Walker Award 3498
E. B. Whitten Silver Medallion Award 15597
Catherine Worthingham Fellows of APTA 3500

Religion (*See also* Catholic literature; Christianity; Church history; Gospel music; Judaism; Religion journalism; Religion literature; Theology)

James Luther Adams Award 20315
Albion Book Prize/NACBS Book Prize 16411
American Bible Society Award 1563
American Statesman Award 2294
Angel Award 12994
Banner Award 20316
Berakah Award 16369
William C. Bier Award 3701
Bomm/Presidential Citation 5578
Antoinette Brown Award 20324
Calihan Fellowships 159
Celebrate Life Essay and Poster Contest 8106
Certificate of Appreciation Award 12730
Chairman's Award 15612
Conference Chairperson of the Year 20357
Distinguished Service Award
Military Chaplains Association of the U.S.A. 13403
National Association of Catholic Chaplains 14120
National Religious Broadcasters 15613
Distinguished Service to the Cause of Unitarian Universalism 20308
Ecumenical Leadership Award 7027
Ralph Waldo Emerson Award 17241
The Epiphany Prizes 12402
Essay Contest in Progress in Religion Through the Sciences 12403
Excellence in Baha'i Studies 5279
Exemplary Papers in Humility Theology 12404
Gold-Headed Cane 18420
Guardian of Liberty 2295
Judy Halpern Religious Freedom Award 16680
Harvest Award 15620
The Dr. Bernard Heller Prize 10375
Justice J.A. Higgins Award 7020
Honor Roll for Education in a Free Society 12406
Honorary Life Member 7975
Howard Fellows 10571
Institution of the Year 20358
IRLA Award 11886
Isaacs Lifetime Achievement Award 6355
William James Award 3702
Jean Garton Award 16527
Roger E. Joseph Prize 10376
Justice Award/Fund for Religious Liberty Award 2895
Kupferman Award 6356
Laws of Life Essay Contest - Christian Education Movement/BT Campus World 12407
Laws of Life Essay Contest - Franklin County, Tennessee 12408
Laws of Life Essay Contest - Nassau, Bahamas 12409
Laws of Life Essay Contest - Peale Center for Christian Living 12410
Louisville Grawemeyer Award in Religion 21046
Angus H. MacLean Award 20310
Man/Woman of the Year 257
Martin E. Marty Public Understanding of Religion Award 833
Maryknoll Mission Award 13127
Frederic G. Melcher Book Award 20311
Merit Award 1529
Meritorious Awards 16839
Meritorious Service Award
National Christian College Athletic Association 14661
Spiritual Science Fellowship 19617
Milestone Award 15614
National Citizen of the Year 13404
National Federation of the Blind Scholarship Program 15039
Charlotte W. Newcombe Doctoral Dissertation Fellowship 21826
Nostra Aetate Award 7712
Novak Award 160
Open Bible Award 17110
Order of Merit 17979
Helen Keating Ott Award for Outstanding Contribution to Children's Literature 7976
Outstanding Colleague Award 14121
Outstanding Congregational Librarian 7977
Outstanding Congregational Library 7978
Outstanding Contribution to Congregational Libraries 7979
Outstanding Reference Sources 17944
Oskar Pfister Award 3631
Pioneer Woman Award 6528
Prestigious Award 14122
Radio Program Producer of the Year 15615
Radio Station of the Year 15616
Religious Freedom Award 2296
Religious Liberty Award
Institute on Religion and Democracy 11064
Religious Freedom Council of Christian Minorities 17983
World Evangelical Alliance 21895
Robe of Achievement 18421
St. Stephen Recognition of Diaconal Ministry 16380
Scholarship Award 1564
Science and Religion Course Program 12413
Service Pin Award 6247
Jim Siefkes Justice Maker Award 12996
Skinner Sermon Award 20312
Social Action Leadership Award 20317
Social Activist of the Year Award 253
Special Recognition Award 7969
Sports Ministries Award 14665
S.S. Kosmos and Damian Award 16910
Pat Tabler Memorial Award 7980
Television Program Producer of the Year 15618
Templeton Prize for Progress toward Research or Discoveries about Spiritual Realities 12414
Templeton United Kingdom Project Trust Award 12415
Ten Outstanding Young Americans 20678
Unsung Unitarian Universalist Award 20313
URAM Award for Excellence in Creative Endeavors for Research and Scholarship 11962
URAM Award for Excellence in Creative Scholarly Writing 11963
Vision of Justice Sermon Award 20318
Wilbur Awards 17971

Religion (continued)

Wilhelmi-Haskell Stewardship Award 14669
Witherspoon Memorial Chaplain's Award 6357
Will Wittkamper Peace Award 8961
Women for Faith and Family Award 21700

Religion journalism
Alpha Sigma Nu National Jesuit Book Award 5736
Award of Merit 5238
Best First Article Award 16452
Polly Bond Award 9310
Citation of Honor 5239
George Cornell Religion Reporter of the Year Award for Mid-Sized Papers 17974
Norman W. Cox Award 6243
Dialogue Writing Awards 8902
Distinguished Writing Award in Local Watchdog Reporting 4578
Journalism Award 7659
William B. Lipphard Award for Distinguished Service to Religious Journalism 5240
Janette Pierce Award 9311
Publication Awards 17981
St. Francis de Sales Award 7660
St. Michael Religious Freedom Award 7648
Writing and Design Award 5241

Religion literature
Amy Writing Awards 4951
Award for Excellence in Teaching 830
Best First Book in the History of Religions 831
Saint Edmund Campion Award 7635
CCL Book of the Year Award 8373
Citation of Appreciation 6354
Gold Medallion Book Awards 9354
Ray L. Hart Service Award 832
Jordan Christian Book of the Year Award 9355

Research (*See also* Dental research; Educational research; Humanities research; Medical research; Research administration; Scientific research; Social science research)
AATE Research Award 884
ACA Extended Research Award 2064
ACA Research Award 2067
ACCI Thesis/Dissertation Award 2045
AES Man of the Year Award 67
Allied Signal Award for Research on Aging 10526
American Feed Industry Association Award 2097
Award for Distinguished Service to Historical Recordings 5460
Award for Outstanding Research Paper 4620
Dr. David F. Baker Distinguished Research Award 10951
Barbara Hollander Award 9403
Best Doctoral Dissertation 9404
Best Unpublished Research Paper 9405
William Bowie Medal 2344
Bradford Cadmus Memorial Award 10970
Chapter Research Award 10972
Kenneth E. Clark Research Award 7718
Communication Policy Research Award 13217
Conservation Guest Scholars 10003
CRM-Fields-PIMS Prize 13205
Debra Research Grants 9054
Distinguished Service Award 5822
Doctoral Dissertation Grants in Women's Studies 21825
AIAA Dryden Lectureship in Research 2680
Editor's Choice Award 16048
ESRA Award 9368
Excellence in PXE Research 17774
Fellow for Research in Esoteric Areas of Knowledge 5025
First Encounters Award 10827
John Adam Fleming Award 2349
Edward A. Flinn III Award 2350
Folger Shakespeare Library Fellowships and National Endowment for the Humanities Senior Fellowships 9646
William C. Foster Fellows Visiting Scholars Program 20402
Getty Scholars 10006
Robert O. Gilbert Foundation Research Award 12023
Violet B. Gingles Award 5076
GRA Annual Awards 10122
Grants for Otologic and Related Science Research Projects 8779
Grants-in-Aid Program 12421
Shortridge Hardesty Award 4321
Robert H. Herman Memorial Award 3958
Hoffman LaRoche-American Association of Bovine Practitioners Award for Excellence 1125
Honorary Emeritus Membership 5499
B. Elizabeth Horner Award 4495
Ernest E. Howard Award 4331
Hubert H. Humphrey Doctoral Fellowships in Arms Control and Disarmament 20403
Hydrolab/IAGLR Best Student Paper and Poster Competition 11239
IAFIS-FPEI Food Engineering Award 4225
Interdisciplinary Award 9406
International Award 9407
J. W. Hook Memorial Award 9225
Jack Kavanagh Memorial Youth Baseball Research Award 18633
Kellogg National Leadership Program 21694
Barbara A. Kirk Award for Outstanding Graduate Student Research 3663
Krieghbaum Under-40 Award 5345
Jeffery P. LaFage Graduate Student Research Award 9282
Lee Allen Award 18634
Library Research and Development Grants 6940
Library Research Grants 10007
Marcel Loncin Research Prize 10943
J. L. Lush Award 2107
The McCollum Award 3960
Samuel Finley Breese Morse Medal 2334
National Milk Producers Federation Graduate Student Paper Presentation Contest 2110
Order of Ontario 16757
Peurifoy Construction Research Award 4349
Phibro Animal Health Excellence in Poultry Research Award 1088
President's Book Award 3936
Prize for Independent Scholars 13567
Leon R. Radde - Educator of the Year Award 10974
Recognition Award for Young Scholars 1473
Van Nostrand Reinhold Research Award 11528
Research Achievement Award 14007
Research Award 7805
Research Grant 19556
Research Visiting Professor Award 18620
Richard Beckhard Practice Award 9408
Henry and Sylvia Richardson Research Grant 9284
RRS Research Award 17823
SABR Special Achievement Award 18637
Scientific Investigation and Research Award 2200
Silver Dart Aviation History Award 6960
Silver SPUR Awards 18253
Snodgrass Memorial Research Award 9285
Surveying and Mapping Award 4360
Henrietta Villaescusa Community Service Award 14252
Virginius Dabney Award 8353
Visiting Research Fellowships 916
Visiting Scholars 10009
Lucille Westbrook Local History Award 5077
John Wiley & Sons Award 11530
Young Investigator Award Competition 3961
Young Investigator Awards 3938
Young Scientist's Award 7446
Emile Zola Award for Journalism 17125

Research administration
Earle B. Barnes Award for Leadership in Chemical Research Management 1738
Distinguished Contribution to Research Administration Award 19294
Excellence Award 19295
Hartford-Nicholsen Award 19296
Maurice Holland Award 10786
Industrial Research Institute Achievement Award 10787
Industrial Research Institute Medal 10788
Charles E. Levine Memorial Award for Excellence in Public Service 4184
Myrdal Award for Government Service 2207
NASPAA/ASPA Distinguished Research Award 4186
Frederik Philips Award 10875
Rod Rose Award 19297

Restaurants
Ambassador of Hospitality Award 15630
American Culinary Classic 15625
The Austin Chronicle Readers' Restaurant Poll 6096
The James Beard Foundation Restaurant Awards 12287
Best Kids Menu Competition 18010
Best Wine Lists in America Awards 18011
College of Diplomats Award 15631
Fine Dining Hall of Fame 16009
Great Menu Contest 15626
Hennessy Awards 15627
Hot Concepts! Awards 16011
Ice Carving Classic 15628
Operator of the Year 16013
Restaurateur of the Year 8854

Retailing *See* Merchandising

Rhetoric *See* Public speaking

Restaurants (continued)

Riflery *See* Firearms; Hunting; Shooting; Skeet shooting

Robotics
Joseph F. Engelberger Robotics Awards 18083

Rodeo
Clown of the Year 17651
Linderman Award 17652
Tad Lucas Memorial Award 18103
National High School Finals Rodeo 15233
Pro Rodeo Hall of Fame 17653
Resistol Rookie of the Year 17654
Rodeo Hall of Fame 18104
Stock of the Year 17655
World Champions 17656

Rowing
Russell S. Callow Memorial Award 9101
John Carlin Service Award 20746
Female Athlete of the Year 20747
Jack Franklin Service Award 20748
Jack Kelly Award 20749
Male Athlete of the Year 20750
National Championship Regatta 11135
Rowing Hall of Fame 20751
USAT Girls' Sportsmanship Trophy Award 20752
USRowing Medal 20753
Vesper Cup 20754
Women of the Year 20755

Rubber *See* Plastics and rubber

Rugby
Ed Lee Scholarship Award 20757
National Club Championship Award (Men) 20758
National Club Championship Award (Women) 20759
National Club Sevens Championship Award (Men) 20760
National College Championship Award 20761
National College Championship Award (Women) 20762
National Collegiate All Conference Championships Award 20763
National High School Championships Award 20764
National Military Championships Award 20765
National Territorial Union Championship Award 20766
President's Award 20767
Craig Sweeney Award 20768

Rural economics
George Atkins Communications Award 8900
Farm-City Award 14961
Louise B. Gerrard Award 14399
Missouri Rural Foundation Awards 13539

Safety (*See also* Crime prevention; Environmental health; Fire fighting; Fire prevention; Sanitary engineering; Security; Victims; specific types of safety, e.g. Automotive safety)
Academy Fellow 125
AIAA System Effectiveness and Safety Award 2673
ALCA Safety Award Contests 17635
American Society of Safety Engineers Fellow 4602
William G. Anderson Merit Award 876
Award for Outstanding Achievement 16363
Award of Recognition 21349
Awards for Courage 15947
Dr. Gary Burch Memorial Safety Award 14349
Chapter of the Year 19884
Crane and Rigging Safety/Safety Improvement Awards 19575
Charles V. Culbertson Outstanding Volunteer Service Award 4603
Design for Humanity Award 4460
Distinguished Service Award
National School Transportation Association 15671
School and Community Safety Society of America 18335
Educator of the Year Award 19885
Engineer of the Year 19886
Fleet Safety/Safety Improvement Awards 19578
Alfred M. Freudenthal Medal 4315
Golden Merit Award 15672
Luther Halsey Gulick Award 877
Hall of Fame Award 15673
Honor Award 879
Honorary Member 4604
William F. Hulse Memorial Award 5957
International Award 19887
Ralph H. Isbrandt Automotive Safety Engineering Award 19048
Jerome F. Lederer Award 11972
Mabel Lee Award 880
Manager of the Year 19888
Medallion Award 15662
Media Awards 11349
Million Mile Club Award 15656
Mine Safety Appliance Company Student Section Scholarship Award 4605
Motorcycle Safety Foundation Awards Program 13630
MVP of Year 5647
National Fleet Safety Contests 15657
National Humanitarian Award 18044
National Lifesaving Leadership Award 18045
Presidents Achievement Award 19889
Professional Development Award 19890
Professional Safety Paper Awards 4606
Edgar Monsanto Queeny Safety Professional of the Year Award 4607
Safe Driver Award Program 15660
Safe Driving Award 20550
Safety award 6693
Safety Award 15555
Safety Award for Superior Accomplishment 20481
Safety Codes and Standards Medal 4544
Safety Director of the Year Award 4774
Safety Professionals of the Year 4609
Safety Society Presidential Citation 18336
School & Community Award for Youth in Health & Safety 3837
Scientific Achievement Award 19891
William Steiger Award 2619
System Safety Technology Innovation Award 19892
Transportation Safety Awards 19585
Norton H. Walton/Russell L. Miller Award 2794
Charles Peter Yost Professional Service Award 18337
Zero Accident Awards 19586

Salesmanship *See* Marketing; Merchandising

Sanitary engineering (*See also* Public works)
3-A Bronze Plaque 2
AIDIS Prize 11099
Harold Barnum Industry Award 11227
Edward Bartow Award 1739
Biennial AIDIS Prize 11100
Citation Award 11228
Samuel J. Crumbine Consumer Protection Award 11229
Henry B. Davis Award 4611
Dewey R. Dedrick, Jr. Award 4612
Developing Scientist Awards 11230
Educator Award 11231
Fellow of the A.S.S.E. 4613
George Bradley Gascoigne Medal 21481
Hemisphere Award 11101
Rudolph Hering Medal 4322
Honorary Life Membership Award 11232
Charles Walter Nichols Award 3806
Sanitarian's Award 11234
Shogren Award 11235
Walter F. Snyder Award 16584
Solid Waste Manager of the Year 16270
Spes Hominum Award 16585
Davis Calvin Wagner Sanitarian Award 835
Abel Wolman Award 11102

Scholarly works
AAHE Scholar Award 1017
Gordon Allport Intergroup Relations Prize 18883
American Academy Award for Humanistic Studies 618
Annual Awards Competition 8565
Gustave O. Arlt Award in the Humanities 8578
ASABE Paper Awards 4214
ASAE Student Paper Awards 4216
Best Student Paper 18774
Harold C. Bold Award 17301
CAG Award for Scholarly Distinction in Geography 6910
T. W. N. Cameron Award 7497
Arthur Casagrande Professional Development Award 4304
CCCC James Berlin Memorial Outstanding Dissertation Award 8377
Certificate of Merit 4463
Choice Outstanding Academic Books and Nonprint Materials 7935
Morton N. Cohen Award for a Distinguished Edition of Letters 13559
Computer Educator of the Year 11201
Continuum Women's Studies Award 8672
Anada Kentish Coomaraswamy Book Prize 5274
Robinson/Cunningham Award 626
Dante Prize 8749
John I. Davidson ASPRS President's Award for Practical Papers 5211
Dissertation Award 4650
Distinguished Educator Award 4072
Charles B. Dudley Medal 5945

Scholarly (continued)

ESRI Award for Best Scientific Paper in Geographic Information Systems 5212
Expository Writing Award 11072
Richard N. Farmer International Business Dissertation Award 102
Federal Nursing Service Award 5770
Christian Gauss Award 17242
Louis Gottschalk Prize 3992
Charles Hall Grandgent Award 8750
John Simon Guggenheim Memorial Foundation Fellowships 10192
D. B. Hardeman Prize 12422
Herskovits Award 265
Herbert Hoover Book Award 10416
Cyril O. Houle World Award for Literature in Adult Education 947
Philip Johnson Exhibition Catalogue Award 19023
Journal of Research in Science Teaching Award JRST Award 14032
Gerald Kahan Scholars Prize 4201
Joseph Levenson Prizes in Chinese Studies 5277
T. Y. Lin Award 4338
R. Lindeman Award 4490
Jeremiah Ludington Memorial Award 9175
Thomas J. Lyon Book Award 13643
L. J. Markwardt Award 5970
Daniel W. Mead Prizes 4340
New York Chapter History of Military Medicine Essay Award 5777
Operational Research Development Prize 11600
Outstanding Dissertation Award 14033
Outstanding Paper Award
American Society for Engineering Education 4036
National Association for Research in Science Teaching 14035
William T. Pearce Award 5975
J. Warren Perry Distinguished Authors Award 5842
Pratt-Severn Best Student Research Paper Award 4112
Gerald W. Prescott Award 17302
Prix Champlain 8423
Prize for a Distinguished Scholarly Edition 13565
Luigi Provasoli Award 17303
Aldo and Jeanne Scaglione Prize for a Translation of a Literary Work 13569
Aldo and Jeanne Scaglione Prize for a Translation of a Scholarly Study of Literature 13570
Aldo and Jeanne Scaglione Prize for French and Francophone Studies 13572
Student Project of the Year Award 15761
Studies Book Award 19439
Technical and Scientific Communication Award 14843
Richard L. Templin Award 5990
Sanford E. Thompson Award 5992
Sam Tour Award 5994
University of Michigan Press Book Award 21067
URAM Award for Excellence in Creative Scholarly Writing 11963
Joseph R. Vilella Award 5995
William H. Welch Medal 1063
Sir Henry Wellcome Medal and Prize 5789

School publications
All American Hall of Fame 15664
Crown Awards 8232
ECMA Awards 9267
Gold Circle Awards 8233
Gold Key Award 8234
Pacemaker Award 15665
Program to Recognize Excellence in Student Literary Magazines 14837
Publications and Electronic Media Awards 15669

Science (*See also* History of science; Research administration; Science education; Scientific research; Technology; specific fields of science, e.g. Astronomy)
AAAS Award for Public Understanding of Science and Technology 1045
AAAS Mentor Award 1046
AAAS Scientific Freedom and Responsibility Award 1048
AAAS Philip Hauge Abelson Prize 1049
Paul C. Aebersold Award 19225
Agricultural Bioprocess Laboratory Awards 21038
The Alouette Award 6866
American College of Physicians Award 1915
American Romanian Academy Awards 3869
Astrobiology Award 4932
Award for Excellence in Integrated Pest Management 9281
Award in Science 17240
Awards for Excellence 18865
Awards for Scientific Achievement 21437
AWIS Educational Foundation Predoctoral Award 5530
AWIS Educational Foundation Undergraduate Award 5531
Benjamin Franklin Medal for Distinguished Achievement in Science 3433
John Desmond Bernal Prize 18855
W. Frank Blair Eminent Naturalist Award 19530
W. Frank Blair Memorial Award 7895
Arthur M. Bueche Award 13805
ISPA Keith Bulbridge Award 12008
Vannevar Bush Award 15677
John J. Carty Award for the Advancement of Science 13828
Chairman's Award for Career Achievement 6289
Renate W. Chasman Scholarship for Women 6649
Common Wealth Awards of Distinguished Service 17410
Dade Behring MicroScan Young Investigator Award 4134
Sir John William Dawson Medal 18163
Distinguished Individual of Foreign Birth Award 11460
Distinguished Leadership for Landslide Research 11711
Distinguished Service Award 14064
Doctoral Prizes 16022
Alden B. Dow Creativity Center Summer Residency Fellowships 16578
Gano Dunn Award 8497
E.J. Dyksterhuis Memorial Award 16017
Thomas W. Eadie Medal 18164
Albert Einstein Commemorative Award 22026
Anderson - Everett Award 11238
Exceptional Scientific Achievement Medal 13892
Family International Talent Awards Program 17088
Fellow 7697
Fellow Award 14021
Fellows' Medal 6733
Enrico Fermi Award 20495
Kermit Fischer Environmental Award 12216
Ludwik Fleck Prize 18857
The Forensic Sciences Award 5949
John Fritz Medal 4318
Frontiers of Science and Society - Rustum Roy Lecture 1680
Gold Medal 17630
Gold Medal Awards 6290
Eva L. Gordon Award 3188
Loran L. Goulden Memorial Award 9457
Gradiva Awards 14052
Grants for Astrological Research 11916
Hall of Fame 17315
Hall of Outstanding Americans 15986
Gerhard Herzberg Canada Gold Medal for Science and Engineering 16023
Honor Award 18515
Honorary Member 14022
Honorary Title of Inventor 12160
Humanist Contributions to Science Award 2586
Hydrolab/IAGLR Best Student Paper and Poster Competition 11239
IAIA - Rose Hulman Award 11247
ICRU - Gray Medal 11492
Intel International Science and Engineering Fair 18362
Intel Science Talent Search 18363
ISA Fellow 12219
Isaacs Scholarship 6753
ISEM Seed Grants 10847
JE Church Award 21564
Judson Daland Prize 3436
Michel Jurdant Prize in Environmental Science 5539
Karo Plaque 18991
Kilby International Awards 12586
Izaak Walton Killam Memorial Prizes 6800
W. David Kingery Award 1687
Knauss National Marine Policy Fellowship 6754
Knowles Kousin 12607
John Oliver La Gorce Medal 15159
Lab of the Year Award 18365
Laetare Medal 21089
Jeffery P. LaFage Graduate Student Research Award 9282
Herb Lampert Student Writing Award 7382
Leonardo Award for Excellence 11957
Los Angeles Times Book Prizes 12931
Magellanic Premium Award 3439
Maine Space Grant Consortium Internships 13041
Frank J. Malina - Leonardo Prize for Lifetime Achievement 11958
Manning Awards 9329
Carroll Sterling Masterson Award & Outstanding Women's Awards 22093
Mayor's Awards for Excellence in Science and Technology 8039
Medal of Honour 6839
Medalla de Oro 19184
Meritorious Service Award 14023
Chandler - Misener Award 11241
Nicholas C. Mullins Award 18858

Science (continued)

National Federation of the Blind Scholarship Program 15039
National Geographic Society Centennial Award 15160
National Women's Hall of Fame 15960
New Horizons Award for Innovation 11959
Newcomb Cleveland Prize 1052
Nininger Meteorite Award 7735
Office of Civilian Radioactive Waste Management Historically Black Colleges and Universities Undergraduate Scholarship Program 16599
Outstanding Achievement Award
Armenian Behavioral Science Association 5094
Renewable Natural Resources Foundation 17988
Society of Woman Geographers 19361
Outstanding Division Award 12220
Outstanding Professional Service Award 5753
Outstanding Reference Sources 17944
Outstanding Scientific Materials Managers Award 14382
Outstanding Statistical Application Awards 4694
Heinz R. Pagels Human Rights of Scientists Award 16204
Ely ("Eli") S. Parker Award 2607
Postdoctoral Fellowship Program 3157
President's National Medal of Science 15679
Prix Leon-Lortie 18609
Prize for Outstanding Books in Theology and the Natural Sciences 12411
Public Service Award 15680
Public Welfare Medal 13845
Pupin Medal 8230
The Ram Award 5754
Research Seed Grant Program 13360
Robertson Memorial Lecture 13846
Theodore Roosevelt Distinguished Service Medal 20066
Science and Religion Course Program 12413
Science Fair Award 20695
Science in Society Book Awards 7383
Science in Society Journalism Awards 7384
Sea Grant State Fellowship 6755
Glenn Seaborg Award 11812
Special Award 14024
Special National Geographic Society Award 15161
Steacie Memorial Fellowships 16025
Steacie Prize 19777
Charles M. A. Stine Award in Materials Engineering and Science 2789
Summer Stipends 13219
Sustained Achievement Award 17989
Henrietta Szold Award 10215
Ten Outstanding Young Americans 20678
Thoreau Award 7573
Toshiba/NSTA ExploraVision Awards 15693
Makepeace Tsao Leonardo Award 11960
United States Presidential Scholars Program 20491
University Medal 16304
Volunteer of the Year 6293
Walker Prize 13692
Bradford Washburn Award 13693
Alan T. Waterman Award 15681
Wilks Award 19533
Young Innovator Award 6294

Science education

Arizona Heritage Grant 13215
J. Leland Atwood Award 2675
Awards for Scientific Achievement 21437
Charles Edwin Bessey Award 6537
Biotechnology Teaching Award 14091
Brasted Memorial Lecture 1741
Bradley Brooks Moore Scholarship 13530
Robert H. Carleton Award 15683
Herbert O. Carne Service Award 975
Chaney Award 977
CIBA Specialty Chemicals Exemplary Middle Level and High School Principal Awards 15684
CIBA Specialty Chemicals Exemplary Middle Level and High School Science Teaching Awards 15685
James Bryant Conant Award in High School Chemistry Teaching 1744
Craftsman/NSTA Young Inventors Awards 15686
CSSP Educational Research Award 8586
Distinguished Contributions to Science Education Through Research Award 14030
Distinguished Informal Science Education Award 15687
Distinguished Informal Science Educator Award 6749
Distinguished Service Award 14092
Distinguished Service to Science Education Award 15688
Distinguished Teaching Award 15689
Early Career Research Award 14031
Education Achievement Award 20841
Education Award 982
Educator Award 13443
Excellence in Science Teaching Awards 20030
Earle J. Fennell Award 1997
Four-Year College Biology Teaching Award 14093
Future Science Teacher Awards 6750
GAMA Excellence in Aviation Education Award 9911
Bernard J. Garulat Award 984
Honorary Emeritus Membership 5499
Honorary Member 18480
Honorary Membership 14095
ICPE Medal for Physics Teaching 12106
Ignatian Educator 12316
Implications of Research for Educational Practice 5500
Innovation in Teaching Science Teachers 5501
Journal of Research in Science Teaching Award JRST Award 14032
Kilby International Awards 12586
Norman Kubasik Award 985
Lanxess Inc. Award for High School Chemistry Teachers 7841
Leadership Citation 8587
Warren K. Lewis Award for Contributions in Chemical Engineering Education 2782
Christa McAuliffe Memorial Award 228
McNeil Medal for the Public Awareness of Science 18169
Mentor Award 5502
Neil A. Miner Award 14238
MMCA Annual Scholarship 13353
Margaret Nicholson Distinguished Service Award 6751
Gustav Ohaus Award for Innovations in Science Teaching 15690
Outstanding Biology Teacher Award 14097
Outstanding Contributions to Education 995
Outstanding Dissertation Award 14033
Outstanding Earth Science Teacher Award 14239
Outstanding Masters Thesis Award 14034
Outstanding New Biology Teacher Achievement Award 14098
Outstanding Paper Award 14035
Outstanding Science Educator of the Year 5503
Robert L. Packard Outstanding Educator Award 19531
George C. Pimentel Award in Chemical Education 1781
President's Prizes for Outstanding Achievement in Primary and Secondary Education 9283
Richards Education and Medical Award 16764
Albert E. Rosica, Jr. Memorial Award 1834
Sagan Award for Public Understanding of Science 8588
Donald K. Sampson Excellence in Teaching Award 6637
W. E. Saunders Natural History Award 16765
Eve Savory Award for Science Communication 6292
Science Educator's Hall of Fame 13167
Science Screen Report Award 15691
Science Teaching Award 15692
James H. Shea Award 14240
Support of Science Award 8589
Toshiba/NSTA ExploraVision Awards 15693
Toyota Tapestry Grant 15694
Union Carbide Award for Chemical Education 7850
Waksman Outstanding Teaching Award 18763
Waste Management Award 326
WISE Award for Scientific Achievement 21754
WISE Lifetime Achievement Award 21755

Science fiction

ASCB/Bruce Alberts Award for Distinguished Contributions to Science Education 3940
John W. Campbell Memorial Award 7752
Donal Knight Memorial Grand Master Award 18356
L. Ron Hubbard's Writers of the Future Contest 6618
Hugo Awards 21951
Locus Awards 12902
Nebula Awards 18357
Mrs. Ann Radcliffe Awards 8615
Saturn Awards 123
Science Fiction/Fantasy Short Story Contest 18360
Theodore Sturgeon Memorial Award 7753
SWFA Author Emeritus Award 18358
Horace Walpole Gold Medal 8618

Science journalism (*See also* Medical journalism)

AAAS Science Journalism Awards 1047
AEG Publication Award 5672

Science (continued)

AIP Science Writing Awards 2831
Roger J. E. Brown Award 7122
Clemson Awards 18647
Communications Award 2677
District Newsletter Contest 14152
ECMA Awards 9267
Graduate Student Awards 6389
James T. Grady - James H. Stack Award for Interpreting Chemistry for the Public 1757
Claire P. Holdredge Award 5673
IFT Food Science Journalism Awards 10940
P.P. Levine Award 1087
Robert A. Lindberg Award 1602
James H. McGraw Award 4027
NAS Award for Scientific Reviewing 13838
National Magazine Awards 15355
Newcomb Cleveland Prize 1052
Camp Scholarships Carl Nunn Award 16763
Oscars in Agriculture 21030
Outstanding Journalist Award 6079
Outstanding Paper Awards 4150
R.M. Quigley Award 7129
Thomas Roy Award 7130
Rita Schaffer Young Investigator Award 6390
Science in Society Journalism Awards 7384
Science-in-Society Journalism Awards 14380
Special Awards 5678
Student Professional Paper 5679

Scientific research

AAAS Academy Research Grants 1044
Aaron Allan Awards 7706
Achievement Award 3049
Konrad Adenauer Research Award 18160
Claude C. Albritton, Jr. Award 10844
American Feed Industry Association Award 4251
American Society of Mammalogists Award 4494
Animal Clinical Chemistry 974
Animal Growth and Development Award 4252
Animal Management Award 4254
Animal Physiology and Endocrinology Award 4255
AOCS/Supelco Research Award 3305
Arctowski Medal 13826
ASAS Fellow 4257
ASNT Fellowship Award 4144
Alfred Bader Award in Organic Chemistry 7828
Alton E. Bailey Award 3307
Becton Dickinson and Company Award in Clinical Microbiology 4130
Hugo G. Beigel Research Award 18890
A. E. Bennett Research Awards 19071
Albion O. Bernstein, M.D. Award 13272
Lloyd M. Bertholf Award for Chapter Excellence 6323
Best Student Paper Award 19219
Biotechnology Research Award 4132
Boehringer Mannheim Award 7452
George W. Brindley Lecture 8090
Michael J. Brody Young Investigator Award 3509
Frank G. Brooks Award for Excellence in Student Research 6324
Brown-Hazen Lectureship for Research Excellence in Life Sciences 16280
Burgdorf Award 16208
Cargill Animal Nutrition Young Scientist Award 2099
Herbert O. Carne Service Award 975
Sadi Carnot Award in Energy Conservation 20493
L. E. Casida Award 4259
CBR Scholar Awards 7707
Certificate of Honor 976
Chaney Award 977
Stephen S. Chang Award 3309
Renate W. Chasman Scholarship for Women 6649
Max E. Chilcote Young Investigator Award 978
Seymour R. Cohen Award 2926
Cooper Award 979
CRFA Fellowship Grants 7555
Crystallographic Research Grant 13433
CSSP Educational Research Award 8586
George Davidson Medal 2330
Developing Scientist Awards 11230
Developmental Psychology Awards 3668
Herbert W. Dickerman Lectureship 16281
Albert A. Dietz Service Award 980
Dissertation Research Awards 18896
Distinguished Achievement Award for Petroleum Engineering Faculty 19236
Distinguished Education and Behavioral Sciences Librarian Award 5605
Distinguished Extension-Industry Service Award 3050
Distinguished Public Service Medal 13434
Distinguished Research Award 3051
Distinguished Scientific Award for an Early Career Contribution to Psychology 18908
Distinguished Scientific Award for the Applications of Psychology 18909
Distinguished Scientific Contribution Award
American Psychological Association - Society of Clinical Psychology (Division 12) 3745
Society for the Study of Lesbian, Gay and Bisexual Concerns (Division 44) 18910
Distinguished Service Awards 21003
Distinguished Teaching Award 3052
Doctoral Prizes 16022
Ronald Dubner Research Prize 11262
Howard N. Eavenson Award 18810
Ebert Prize 3386
Editor's Award 11237
Epilepsy Research Awards Program 2197
John Ericsson Award in Renewable Energy 20494
Explorers Medal 9375
FASEB Excellence in Science Award 9462
Monie A. Ferst Award 18511
Founder's Award 699
Friedenwald Memorial Award 5465
Future Leader Awards 11725
Jacob Heskel Gabbay Award in Biotechnology and Medicine 18126
Garry/Labbe Award 983
Eloise Gerry Fellowships 18479
Captain James M. Gilliss Award for Outstanding Service 20524
Graduate Research Prizes 13725
Grant for Student Research in Mineralogy and Petrology 13435
Grants-in-Aid of Research 18512
Herbert E. Gregory Medal 17013
Prix Hallopeau 11783
Health Advocate of the Year 16979
Herzberg Medal 6933
Hoar Award 7499
Louise and Bill Holladay Distinguished Fellow Award 4435
Maurice Holland Award 10786
Honorary Member 18480
Honorary President and Honorary Member 11784
Honored Student Award 3310
Louisa Gross Horwitz Prize 8243
Brazier Howell Award 4496
National Milk Producers Federation - Richard M. Hoyt Award 2102
IAE/AIE Best Papers Award 11974
IAGLR Scholarship 11240
Intercollegiate Meat Judging Meritorious Service Award 3053
International Award 3054
International Dairy Foods Association Research Award 2103
International Dairy Production Award 2104
Isidor Fankuchen Award 2088
Anna M. Jackson Award 4497
John C. Johnson Award 6327
A. Ivan Johnson Outstanding Achievement Award 5962
Morton J. Klein Award 11785
Kristine M. Layn Award 17557
Leadership Citation 8587
L. S. B. Leakey Foundation Prize for Multidisciplinary Research on Ape and Human Evolution 12756
Liaison with Industry Committee Novel Disease Model Award 3519
Eli Lilly and Company Research Award 4136
Literature Award 19092
Macromolecular Science and Engineering Lecture Award 7843
Lazaro J. Mandel Young Investigator Award 3520
Marschall Rhodia Award 2108
McCurdy Award 6869
Curtis W. McGraw Research Award 4028
Mead Johnson Award 4161
Mead Johnson Research Award in Endocrinology and Metabolism 3521
Meat Processing Award 3055
Meats Research Award 4261
Medal for the Advancement of Research 5187
Mehl Honor Lecture 4149
Osborne and Mendel Award 4162
Merck ICAAC Young Investigator Awards 4137
C. Hart Merriam Award 4499
Michelson - Morley Award 7619
Willet G. Miller Medal 18170
Mineralogical Society of America Award 13436
James G. Mitchell Award 15800
Barrington Moore Memorial Award 18972
Morrison Award 4262
NAS Award for Initiatives in Research 13837
NAS Award for the Industrial Application of Science 13839
Samuel Natelson Senior Investigation Award 987
Einar Naumann - August Thienemann Medal 11406
Simon Newcomb Award for Research Achievement 20525

Scientific (continued)
Edwin B. Newman Award for Excellence in Research 18916
Albert L. Nichols Innovation Award 988
NINDS Javits Neuroscience Investigator Award 20499
Alton Ochsner Award Relating Smoking and Health 16609
Olfactory Research Fund Sense of Smell Award 9722
Outstanding Contributions to Clinical Chemistry in a Selected Area of Research 993
Outstanding Contributions to Clinical Chemistry Through Science or Technology 994
Outstanding Contributions to Education 995
Outstanding Scientific Achievements by a Young Investigator 996
Passano Foundation Award 17101
A. Lindo Patterson Award 2091
Pediatric Division Award for Outstanding Contributions to Pediatric Clinical Chemestry 997
R. C. Pollock Award 3056
Pomerance Award for Scientific Contributions to Archaeology 5035
Ralph H. Potts Memorial Fellowship Award 3311
Samuel Cate Prescott Award 10944
President's New Researcher's Award 5269
Joseph Priestley Award 8912
Procter & Gamble Award in Applied and Environmental Microbiology 4138
William Procter Prize for Scientific Achievement 18513
Proctor Medal 5467
Miriam Reiner Award 998
Research Achievement Awards in the Pharmaceutical Services 3397
Research Award 19268
Research Scholarships 6329
Roe Award 999
Roebling Medal 13437
Miroslaw Romanowski Medal 18172
Harvey M. Rosen Memorial Award 11786
Lewis S. Rosenstiel Award for Distinguished Work in Basic Medical Research 18127
Henry Norris Russell Lectureship 1517
Sagan Award for Public Understanding of Science 8588
Charles Schuchert Award 17041
Scientific Achievement Award 19891
Scientific Award 2536
Scientific Exhibit Awards 19232
SDE Fellowships 18481
Hans Selye Award 2853
Charles C. Shepard Science Award 20501
Signal Service Award 3057
David Sinclair Award 957
Small Research Grants Program 10585
Somogyi-Sendroy Award 1001
Space Achievement Award 20843
Special Recognition Award 3058
SPRITE undergraduate summer research 7708
Jules Stachiewicz Medal 7849
Steacie Memorial Fellowships 16025
William J. Stephenson Award for Outstanding Service 15802
Wayne W. Stinchcomb Memorial Lecture and Award 5989
Ralph W. Stone Graduate Fellowship 15803
Summer Fellowship 6674
Superintendent's Award for Distinguished Service 20526
Support of Science Award 8589
Texas Service Award for Outstanding Contributions to Clinical Chemistry 1003
Donald W. Tinkle Research Excellence Award 19532
Henry Marshall Tory Medal 18174
Travel Awards 20979
Travel Grant 1004
Troland Research Awards 13850
W. Rupert Turnbull Award 6871
Van Slyke Award 1007
Robert W. Vance Award 8680
Patrick D. Wall Young Investigator Award 11263
Shih-Chun Wang Young Investigator Award 3530
Kenneth T. Whitby Award 958
Wine Research Award 19182
WISE Award for Engineering Achievement 21753
WISE Award for Scientific Achievement 21754
WISE Lifetime Achievement Award 21755
William B. Yant Award 2621
Young Clinical Chemist Award 1008
Young Investigator Award in Regulatory and Integrative Physiology 3531
Zak Award 1009

Sculpture
Alice Abel Cultural and Creative Arts Program 3141
Affaire in the Gardens 8035
Agop Agopoff Award 13774
Allied Arts Medal 18134
Annual Exhibition
Allied Artists of America 473
Audubon Artists 6061
Annual Exhibition Awards
National Association of Women Artists 14457
National Sculpture Society 15698
Annual Open Exhibition 5121
Arrowhead Biennial Exhibition 9047
Art of the Northeast Competition 18521
Artists' Fellowships 16229
Artists-in-Residence Program 19814
The Artist's Magazine Art Competition 5146
Helen Foster Barnett Prize 13778
Boynton's G.A.L.A. Artist Awards 6594
Bush Artist Fellows Program 6700
Cape Cod Art Association Awards 7571
Certificates of Merit 13783
Cintas Foundation Fellowships 10981
Delta Art Exhibition 5070
El Angel Award - Distinguished Hispanic-American Artist 6374
Alex J. Ettl Grant 15699
Fine Art Show 18244
Fine Arts Work Center Fellowships 9553
Gilpin County Arts Association Annual Exhibition 10028
Grand National Exhibition 930
Henry Hering Medal 15700
Artists Fund Malvina Hoffman Prize 13788
Howard Fellows 10571
Hoyt Mid Atlantic Art Show 10573
Images Competition 7775
Institute Honors for Collaborative Achievements 2718
Kentucky Artists Fellowships 12562
LaGrange National 7817
Lifetime Achievement in Contemporary Sculpture 11894
National Society of Artists Awards 15728
New Mexico Juried Exhibition 13689
North American Sculpture Exhibition Awards 9678
Outstanding Sculpture Educator 11895
Outstanding Student Achievement in Contemporary Sculpture 11896
Patron's Recognition Award 11897
Pollock-Krasner Foundation Grants 17461
Prix de West Invitational Exhibition 14886
Thomas R. Proctor Prize 13796
Rome Prize Fellowships 605
Arthur Ross Awards 10853
Augustus St. Gaudens Medal 8498
J. Sanford Saltus Medal Award 3274
Southwest Juried Exhibition 13690
Ellin P. Speyer Memorial Prize 13799
Harry Watrous Award 13801
Young Sculptor Awards 15701

Secondary education
Achievement Awards in Writing 14826
Administrators' Award 9180
Athletic Director of the Year Award 14812
Awards for Scientific Achievement 21437
Biotechnology Teaching Award 14091
William B. Bretnall Award 18401
Catholic Secondary Education Award 14607
CIBA Specialty Chemicals Exemplary Middle Level and High School Principal Awards 15684
James Bryant Conant Award in High School Chemistry Teaching 1744
Distinguished Informal Science Education Award 15687
Distinguished Teaching Award 15689
Education Award 4838
Benjamin Fine Awards 14384
Sue Hefley Educator of the Year Award 12939
High School Jazz Student Award 14485
Marion Huber Learning Through Listening Awards 17904
Innovative Teaching of Secondary School Physics Award 1374
Lanxess Inc. Award for High School Chemistry Teachers 7841
Louise Louis/Emily F. Bourne Student Poetry Award 17433
NAA Foundation - National Scholastic Press Association Pacemaker Awards 16339
National Honor Society Scholarship Program 14385
National Newspaper Association - Quill and Scroll Award 16341
National Teacher of the Year 8571
Outstanding Biology Teacher Award 14097
Outstanding Earth Science Teacher Award 14239
Principal's Leadership Award 14386
Program to Recognize Excellence in Student Literary Magazines 14837
Promising Young Writers Program 14839
Edyth May Sliffe Awards for Distinguished Junior High and High School Mathematics Teaching 13197
Nila Banton Smith Award 11875

Secondary (continued)

Toshiba/NSTA ExploraVision Awards 15693
United States Presidential Scholars Program 20491

Security (*See also* National security)
Chartered State Association Executive Director of the Year 14551
Chartered State Association of the Year 14552
Chartered State Association President of the Year 14553
Diplomatic Security Employee of the Year Award 20534
R.A. Henderson Award 7386
Instructor of the Year 14559
Sara E. Jackson Memorial Award 14555
George R. Lippert Memorial Award 18407
National Lighting Awards Program 14922
Professional Alarm Technician of the Year 14560
Morris F. Weinstock Award 14557

Seismology
Charles Martin Duke Lifeline Earthquake Engineering Award 4311

Service
Chancellor's Medal 8029
Golden Eagle Grant 9746
Robert J. Kibbee Award for Public Service and Achievement 8032
State Allocated Scholarship Award 17175

Set design
Source Awards 19425
The Village Voice OBIE Awards 21368

Shooting (*See also* Skeet shooting)
Canadian Championship Trophies 7527
Intercollegiate Pistol Championships 15645
Marksmanship 21320
National Championships 15646
National Police Shooting Championships 15647
NCAA National Championships 14687
Outstanding Service 11670
General George S. Patton, Jr. Memorial Trophy 20705
Queen's Medal for Champion Shot 6829

Short stories
Alice Abel Cultural and Creative Arts Program 3141
Nick Adams Short Story Contest 5243
Aim Quarterly Magazine Short Story Award 316
Nelson Algren Awards for Short Fiction 7892
Arizona Authors' Association Annual National Literary Contest 5048
AWP Award Series 5259
Emily Clark Balch Prize 21396
Brazos Bookstore Short Story Award 20012
Chelsea Award 7821
David Dornstein Memorial Creative Writing Contest for Young Adult Writers 8118
Eaton Literary Awards Program 9125
Norma Epstein Foundation Awards 21112
Hackney Literary Awards 6402
Drue Heinz Literature Prize 21099
Hemingway Foundation/PEN Award 17157
Theodore Christian Hoepfner Awards 19507
HONOLULU Magazine/Borders Books and Music Fiction Contest 10531
Joseph Henry Jackson Literary Award 18249
Journey Prize 13211
Lawrence Foundation Award 17512
Letras de Oro Literary Prizes 21059
McGinnis-Ritchie Award 19527
James A. Michener - Paul Engle Fellowship 12191
Milkweed National Fiction Prize 13421
Milkweed Prize for Children's Literature 13422
National Jewish Book Award - Fiction 12325
Flannery O'Connor Award for Short Fiction 21026
O'Henry Awards 9006
PEN/Malamud Memorial Award 17155
James D. Phelan Literary Award 18251
PNWA Literary Contest 17011
Edgar Allan Poe Awards (Edgars) 13732
Sir Walter Raleigh Award for Fiction 16520
Rea Award for the Short Story 9052
Harold U. Ribalow Prize 10213
Summerfield G. Roberts Award 19415
Carl Sentner Short Story Award 17548
Short Story Award 15996
Short Story Contest
Affaire de Coeur Magazine 247
Writers' Journal 22001
Space Coast Writers Guild Conference Awards 19535
Tilden Canadian Literary Awards 7000
Eudora Welty Prize in Fiction 19523
World's Best Short Short Story Contest 19466
Writer's Digest Writing Competition 21979
Writing Awards 18067

Skeet shooting
World Skeet Shooting Championships 15807

Skiing
Alaska Cup Award 20791
All-American Awards 15307
Paul Bacon Award 20792
Dan Bean Award 20793
Beck International Award 20794
Paul Bietila Award 20795
Julius Blegen Award 20796
Fred Braun Award 20797
Burkett-Dodge Award 20798
Gale Cotton Burton Award 20799
John J. Clair Jr. Award 20800
Cross Country Coach of the Year 20801
Sally Deaver Award 20802
Domestic Alpine Coach of the Year 20803
Finlandia Award 20804
Mike Gallagher Award 20805
Ann Hansen Award 20806
Hart Cup Award 20807
Harold S. Hirsch Award for Excellence in Broadcasting 16461
Harold S. Hirsch Award for Excellence in Ski Photography 16462
Erik Judeen Memorial Award 20808
Judith Kilbourne Award 7392
Paul Nash Layman Award 20809
Lifetime Achievement Award 16464
Bud and Mary Little Award 20810
Meeker Award 20811
Member Awards 16465
Al Merrill Nordic Award 20812
Mittelstadt Ski Jumping Officials Award 20813
National Ski and Snowboard Week Best Event 7393
National Ski Hall of Fame 20814
National Ski Safety Award 7394
National Snow Industries Association Recognition Award 7395
NCAA National Championships 14687
Nordic Award 20815
Outstanding Competitor Award 16466
Martha Rockwell Award 20816
Willy Schaeffler Award 20817
Silver Rope Award for Leadership 503
Al Sise Outstanding Alpine Masters Award 20818
Ski Jumping/Nordic Combined Coach of the Year 20819
Ski Magazine Cup 20820
Skier of the Year 18548
Skier/Snowboarding Development Recognition Award 7396
Skiing Magazine Development Cup 20821
Sons of Norway Jumping Award 20822
Torger Tokle Award 20823
Water Ski Days Queen 12665
Wallace "Buddy" Werner Award 20824
The Carson White Golden Quill Award 16467
Russell Wilder Award 20825
Willauer Cup Award 20826
Dick Zue Award 20827

Sledding
Iditarod Trail International Sled Dog Race 10649

Slide photography
Color Slide Division Awards 17284
Greater Lynn International Color Slide Salon 10149
Larry Morgotch Memorial Award 16040
Photo Travel Division Awards 17288
Photojournalism Division Awards 17289
Stereo Division Awards 17294
Toronto International Salon of Photography 20120

Soccer
All-America Awards 15707
All-American Awards 15307
Gladys Bean Memorial Trophy 7209
Dr. Raymond Bernabei Honor Award 15275
Big East Conference Academic Awards 6369
Coach of the Year Award 15708
Coaches Association Awards 15309
Sam Davidson Memorial Trophy 7214
Gold Ball Award 18595
Goslin Award - Man of the Year 19912
Don Greer Cup 20891
Hall of Fame Award 15276
Hall of Fame Meritorious Award 20838
Honor Award 15709
Interscholastic Member Recognition Award 15277
Joe Johnson Memorial Trophy 7219
Letter of Commendation 15710

Soccer (continued)

Malchow Award - Woman of the Year 19913
Patricia L. Masotto Cup 20892
James P. McGuire Cup 20893
Laura Moynihan Cup 20894
National Cup Boys Under 18 (Boys National Championship) 20895
National Cup Girls Under 18 (Girls National Championship) 20896
National Merit Award 15278
National Soccer Hall of Fame Award 20839
NCAA National Championships 14687
D. J. Niotis Cup 20897
OLSC Youth Grant 16596
Outstanding High School Player 16684
Recognition Award 15279
John A. Schmid Service Award 16685
Simon Sherman Leadership Award 18598
Silver Ball Award 18596
Soccer Coach of the Year 7232
Soccer Outstanding Service Award 575
Special NJCAA Awards 15316
Ross Stewart Cup 20898
Robert Sumpter Excellence in Teaching Award 15280
United States Youth Soccer Association Coach of the Year for Boys and Girls 20899
United States Youth Soccer Association Youth Referee of the Year 20900
Wittnauer NCCAA Player of the Year 14670

Social science (*See also* Anthropology; Archaeology; Criminology; Demography; Economics; Genealogy; Geography; History; Political science; Psychology; Public opinion research; Social science research; Sociology)

American Romanian Academy Awards 3869
Annaley Naegle Redd Student Award in Women's History 17925
Applied Social Issues Internship 18884
AWIS Educational Foundation Predoctoral Award 5530
Eugenio Battisti Award 18934
Brooklyn School Scholarship 6651
John Tropham and Susan Redd Butler Faculty Research Awards 17926
Canada Council Molson Prizes 6787
Defense of Academic Freedom Award 14778
Education Awards 17927
Elementary Teachers of Excellence in Social Studies 13154
Employment Equity Gold Medals 10587
Fellow 7697
Fellow or Foreign Honorary Member 620
Ford Foundation Postdoctoral Diversity Fellowships 15622
Fund for the Advancement of Social Studies Education (FASSE) Grant 14780
Grant for Geographic Literacy 14782
High School Teachers of Excellence in Social Studies 13155
HSSFC Scholarly Book Prizes 7084
Independent Research and Creative Work Awards 17928
Individual and Organizational 7957
Innis-Gerin Medal 18167
Intel International Science and Engineering Fair 18362
Thomas Jefferson Medal for Distinguished Achievement in the Arts, Humanities, or Social Sciences 3435
Louise Keysa Scholarship 12687
Arthur O. Lewis Award 18935
Christa McAuliffe Reach for the Stars Award 14783
Middle School Teachers of Excellence in Social Studies 13156
Office of Civilian Radioactive Waste Management Historically Black Colleges and Universities Undergraduate Scholarship Program 16599
Outstanding Elementary, Middle Level and Secondary Teachers 19993
Outstanding Elementary Social Studies Teacher of the Year Award 14786
Outstanding Middle Level Social Studies Teacher of the Year 14787
Outstanding Reference Sources 17944
Outstanding Secondary Social Studies Teacher of the Year 14788
Talcott Parsons Prize for Social Science 621
Joyce Peckham Memorial Fund 17361
Pi Gamma Mu Scholarships 17307
Prix Esdras-Minville 18608
Race Relations Gold Medal 10588
Race Relations Trophy 10589
Charles Redd Center Publication Grants 17930
John Ben Snow Foundation Prize 16415
Social Studies Programs of Excellence 14789
Spirit of America Award 14790
Summer Awards for Upper Division and Graduate Students 17931
Supervisor of Excellence in Social Studies 13157
Marcel Vincent Prize in Human Sciences 5542
Carter G. Woodson Book Award 14791

Social science research (*See also* Public opinion research)

American Council of Learned Societies Fellowships 2037
Applied Social Issues Internship 18884
Award for Behavioral Research Relevant to the Prevention of Nuclear War 13827
Stuart L. Bernath Lecture Prize 18679
Ernest W. Burgess Award 14859
Exemplary Research in Social Studies Award 14779
Jean Dresden Grambs Distinguished Career Research in Social Studies Award 14781
William T. Grant Faculty Scholars 21633
Grants-in-Aid Program 18885
Marcia Guttentag Award 2204
Reuben Hill Award 14861
Howard Fellows 10571
Robert Ingle Service Award 2205
APA/Kempf Fund Award for Research Development in Psychobiological Psychiatry 3623
Lazarsfeld Award for Evaluation Theory 2206
Lee Founders Award 18925
Peter P. Lejins Research Award 2027
Larry Metcalf Exemplary Dissertation Award 14784
James Michener Prize in Writing Award 14785
C. Wright Mills Award 18926
Alva and Gunnar Myrdal Practice Award 2208
Research Award 9526
David H. Russell Award for Distinguished Research in the Teaching of English 14840
Scholarships and Research Grants, Behavioral Studies 14650
Social Issues Dissertation Award 18888
Edwin H. Sutherland Award 4386
Veblen - Commons Award 5363
Seymour D. Vestermark Award for Psychiatric Education 3641

Social service (*See also* Community affairs; Public affairs; Child welfare; Counseling; Family relations; Handicapped; Social work; Victims; Youth work)

AFDCS Distinguished Service Award 2246
AFS Meritorious Service Award 2253
Annual Recognition Award 19929
Awards of Recognition 9410
Citizen Activist Award 10039
Cooperman-Boque Awards 12477
Deborah Award 2894
Distinguished Service Award 21889
Global Justice Award 21406
The Sidney Hillman Foundation Prize Awards 10435
International Activist Award 10040
Laubach Literacy of Canada Award 12717
Ronald McDonald House Charities Grants Program 18118
Murray-Green-Meany-Kirkland Award for Community Service 2227
Sgt. Edward Neves Memorial Scholarship 17476
Norman Cousins Global Governance Award 21897
Ordo Honorium Award 12515
Phoenix House Award for Public Service 17277
Ray of Light 12574
San Martin Bicentennial Medal 18261
San Martin Palms 18262
Michael Smith Awards for Science Promotion 16024
Henrietta Szold Award 10215

Social work

Award for Exemplary State/University Collaboration 3613
Ruth P. Brudney Award 15374
Citizen Activist Award 10039
Hurowitz Award 20340
International Activist Award 10040
Knee/Whitman Lifetime Achievement Award 14388
Minnesota Award 21071
National Social Worker of the Year 14390
President's Award 14391
Social Worker of the Year; Public Citizen of the Year 14393
Wurzweiler School of Social Work Distinguished Professor Award 22028

Sociology

Gordon Allport Intergroup Relations Prize 18883

Sociology (continued)

Award for the Public Understanding of Sociology 4647
Awards for Excellence 18185
John Desmond Bernal Prize 18855
Jessie Bernard Award 4648
Herbert Blumer Award 18930
Career of Distinguished Scholarship Award 4649
Rachel Carson Award 18856
Certificate of Appreciation 18186
Common Wealth Awards of Distinguished Service 17410
Charles Horton Cooley Award 18931
Dissertation Award 4650
Distinguished Career Award for the Practice of Sociology 4651
Distinguished Career in Clinical Sociology 19374
Distinguished Contributions to Teaching 17017
Distinguished Contributions to Teaching Award 4652
Distinguished Practice Award 17018
Distinguished Rural Sociologist Award 18187
Distinguished Scholarly Publication Award 4653
Distinguished Scholarship Award 17019
Distinguished Service to Rural Life Award 18188
Distinguished Student Paper Awards 17020
DuBois-Johnson-Frazier Award 4654
Ludwik Fleck Prize 18857
Graduate Student Paper Award 18189
George Herbert Mead Award 18932
Nicholas C. Mullins Award 18858
Outstanding Contribution Award 7502
John Porter Tradition of Excellence Book Award 7504
Benjamin Rush Lectureship Award 3637
Undergraduate Student Paper Competition 480

Softball

All-American Award 585
All-American Awards 15307
ASA National Championships 586
Bob Welby Memorial Recognition of Service Award 12037
Marvin Casteel Memorial Award 12038
Carrol Forbes Memorial Award 12039
ISC Hall of Fame 12040
Erv Lind Award 587
National Softball Hall of Fame 588
NCAA National Championships 14687
Rawlings Sporting Goods Company ISC All-World Awards 12041
Bertha Tickey Award 589
Youth Softball Volunteer of the Year 583

Spanish culture

Choreography and Flamenco Dance Competition 9227
Cultural Cooperation Award 9229
Gold Medal Award 19539
Katherine Singer Kovacs Prize 13560
Outstanding Teacher of the Year Awards 1453

Spanish literature

Katherine Singer Kovacs Prize 13560

Special education

Mary K. Bauman Award 5338
Butler Council No. 465, UCT Scholarship Award 20328
CASE Outstanding Administrator Award 8567
CEC Leadership Award 8547
CEC Research Award 8548
Certificate of Merit 10124
Direct Vocational Special Needs Support Person of the Year 14057
Susan Phillips Gorin Award 8549
Graduation Awards 8550
Albert J. Harris Award 11857
Alice H. Hayden Award 19926
Clarissa Hug Teacher of the Year Award 8551
Indirect Provider of Major Support Services and Contributions to the Field of Vocational Special Needs Education Award 14058
Outstanding Graduate Student Member of the Year Award 8552
Outstanding Public Service Award 8553
Outstanding Student CEC Undergraduate Member of the Year Award 8554
Outstanding Vocational Special Needs Teacher of the Year 14059
Harrie M. Selenick - CASE Distinguished Service Award 8568
Margaret Shepherd Teaching Award 21386
J. E. Wallace Wallin Lifetime Achievement Award 8555

Special Olympics

Athlete of the Year 19569
Chairman's Award 19570
Coach of the Year 19571

Spectroscopy *See* Optics

Speech and hearing (*See also* Deafness)

Annual Prize for Hearing Research 12954
ASHA Media Awards for Journalists 4662
Award of Merit 5462
Alexander Graham Bell Student Prize in Speech Communication and Behavioral Acoustics 14645
Glen Bollinger Humanitarian Award 10352
Laura Bridgman Memorial Award 1459
L.I. Bryson Memorial Senior Speech Arts Scholarship 18278
Certificate of Merit 10124
Deaf/Hard of Hearing Entrepreneur of the Year 8775
Distinguished Service Awards 4663
Elizabeth Guild Award 13400
Fellows of the Association 4664
Founder's Award 13401
Marylene Freshley Award 14528
Honors of the Association 4665
Media Award 15196
Marcella E. Oberle Award for Outstanding Teaching in Grades K-12 14714
OHIS Youth Achievement 16808
Outstanding Hearing Conservationist Award 15197
Pioneer Award 12496
Special Ad Hoc Awards 12955
Michael Beall Threadgill Award 15199
Leland A. Watson Award 11672

Speleology *See* Geology and paleontology

Sporting goods

Jack Cooper Lifetime Achievement Award 7512

Sports (*See also* Coaching; Physical education; Sports broadcasting; Sports journalism; Sports medicine; Sportsmanship; Water sports; specific sports, e.g. Auto racing)

AAU Promotions Award 530
Academic Team-of-the-Year 15305
Academy Award of Sports 13859
Achievement Award 15306
Achievement Awards 15239
Administrator of the Year 14279
ADO National Champions 2122
ADO Points Champions 2123
Aerobics Athlete of the Year 533
Aerobics Contributor of the Year 534
Aerobics Man and Woman of the Year 535
Aerobics Official of the Year 536
All-America Awards 14280
All-America Scholar-Athlete Awards 14281
All-American Association Award 538
All-American Awards 15307
All-Tournament Team 14654
All-Tournament Teams/Outstanding Athlete Award 14282
Amateur Athletic Fund 19896
William G. Anderson Merit Award 876
Appreciation Award 15308
Armwrestler of the Year (Male and Female) 924
Association Silver Pin Awards 539
Association Youth Sport Membership Award 541
Association Youth Sport Programming Award 542
Athlete of the Year 21164
Athletes of the Year 21596
Athletes United for Peace Award 6021
Athletic Director of the Year Award 14812
Award of Merit 14981
Award of Valor 14685
Awards for Excellence 18865
Awards of Merit 14283
Banff Mountain Film Festival 6236
BASE Award 20431
Johnny F. Bassett Memorial Award 19625
Baton Twirling Achievement 544
BLG Awards 7210
Boston Marathon 6519
Gene Brito Award 20128
Canada's Sports Hall of Fame 6842
CATA Writing Award 6948
Championship Banners 14655
CISS Medallions of Honor 11494
Coach of the Year Award 14284
Commissioner's Trophy Awards 6370
Competition Honors 20437
Arthur E. Copeland Award 20407
Arthur E. Copeland Scholarship 20408
Helen Copeland Scholarship 20409
Corporate Excellence Award 19626
CoSIDA Backbone Award 8189
Creative Arts Award 12159
Dial Award 20129
Disabled Athletes of the Year 20410
Distinguished Alumnus Award 14285
Distinguished Athletic Therapy Educator Award 6949
Distinguished Service Award (Coaching) 14982
Distinguished Service Awards

Sports (continued)

National Federation of State High School Associations 14977
National Federation of State High School Associations - National Federation Interscholastic Coaches Association 14983
A. O. Duer Scholarship Award 14286
ECAC Distinguished Achievement Award 9108
ECAC Merit Medal 9109
ESPY Awards 9337
Events of the Year 21247
Face in the Crowd 19729
Fellowship Award 21862
Female Athlete of the Year 19627
Four Wheel Drive Truck Puller of the Year 15882
Betty Jo Graber Female Student-Athlete-of-the-Year 15310
Grand Champion Primitive and Modern Equipment - U.S. and Europe 21863
Grand National Pulling Circuit Rookie of the Year 15883
Grants for Girls 13171
GTE Academic All-America Hall of Fame 8190
GTE Academic All-American of the Year 8191
Luther Halsey Gulick Award 877
Hall of Champions 21860
Hall of Fame
Billiard Congress of America 6382
National Christian College Athletic Association 14657
Pi Kappa Phi 17315
United States Curling Association 20463
USA Deaf Sports Federation 21165
Wheelchair Sports, USA 21597
Hall of Fame Program 14287
High School Awards Program 523
Honor Award 879
Honorary Member 12089
Hooker of the Year 15884
Horseshoe Hall of Fame 15240
William F. Hulse Memorial Award 5957
Humanitarian Award 4677
The Ira Hurley Association Officers Award for Outstanding Achievement 556
Flo Hyman Memorial Award 21807
ING New York City Marathon 16260
International Standard Accurracy ATLATL Contest-U.S and Europe 21864
International Women's Sports Hall of Fame 21808
John Youngblood Scholarships 21390
Junior Female Athlete of the Year 19628
Junior Male Athlete of the Year 19629
Robert J. Kane Award 20720
Jack Kelly Fair Play Award 20721
Jim Kern Award 2455
Bruce Kidd Award 19630
Billie Jean King Contribution Award 21809
Leadership in Sport Award 19631
Mabel Lee Award 880
Lefthanders of the Year Awards 12764
Lifetime Achievement Award in Sports Direction 8946
Lifetime Sales Achievement Award 19636
Loyalty Award 15311
Male and Female Bowler of the Year Award 21870
Male Athlete of the Year 19632
Male Team of the Year 19633
John V. Mara Memorial CYO Sportsman of the Year Award 7679
Master of the Game Award 15809
Austin-Matthews Award 7222
H. Boyd McWhorter Scholar-Athlete Award 19473
Merit Award 15312
Meritorious Service 19619
Meritorious Service Award 14661
Mini Rod Puller of the Year 15885
Mini Sled of the Year 15886
Monthly Most Valuable Player Award 6438
Most Valuable Player Award 6439
NAIA - SIDA All-Sports Championship Awards 14290
NASSH Book Award 16471
National Championship Awards 925
National Championships 20464
National Federation Citations 14978
National Federation Interscholastic Coaches Association Annual Awards 14984
National Gold Pin Awards 560
National High Point Awards 14141
National High School Sports Hall of Fame Awards 14979
National Rifle and Pistol Championship Trophy Match 20466
National Snow Industries Association Recognition Award 7395
National Unicycle Meet Top Point Winners 20298
National Women's Hall of Fame 15960
NCAA National Championships 14687
NFICA Certificates for Each State 14985
Official of the Year Award 21248
Olympic Spirit Award 20722
Joseph E. O'Neill Award 15810
Order of Ontario 16757
Outstanding Disabled Athlete of the Year 21234
Outstanding Dissertation Award 3682
Outstanding Player 14662
Jesse Owens Award 21235
Pace Award 563
Ike Pearson Award 14292
L. B. "Mike" Pearson Award 7229
Pegasus Award 18049
Lea Plarski Award 15313
Player of the Year Award 6440
President's Award
U.S. Boomerang Association 20438
U.S.A. Track and Field 21236
Women's Sports Foundation 21810
World Atlatl Association 21865
President's National Leadership 565
Prix Maurice-Richard 18612
Pro Stock Puller of the Year 15887
Progress Award 566
Public Relations Award 570
Pull of the Year 15888
Pulling Family of the Year 15889
Pulling Hall of Fame 15890
Regional and Major Sports Grants 9624
Regional Director of the Year 15241
Theodore Roosevelt Award 14688
David Rowlands Male Student-Athlete-Of-The-Year 15314
Rubens-Alcais Challenge 11495
Sammy Lee Award 21891
Scholar-Athlete 14664
Bill Schroeder Distinguished Service Award 11404
Senior Scholarships 5068
Service Award 15315
Mel Allen Service Award 4681
Fred Sgambati Award 7231
George L. Shiebler Award 9111
Silver Anniversary Award 14689
Special Recognition and Presidential Awards 15242
Spirit Award 576
Sport in Society Hall of Fame 7756
Sporting Goods Agents Hall of Fame 19638
The Sporting News Sportsman of the Year 19679
Sports and Recreation Award 17073
Sports Emmy Awards 13865
Sports Illustrated Sportsman/Sportswoman of the Year 19730
Sports Legend of the Year Award 4682
Sports Ministries Award 14665
SportsMan and SportsWoman of the Year 20723
Sportsman/Sportswoman of the Year 11496
Sportswomen of the Year Awards 21811
Bart Starr Award 6019
Stokes Memorial Award 15243
Student-Athlete of the Week 14666
Super Stock Puller of the Year 15891
Reed K. Swenson Leadership Award 15317
Team Awards 11901
Ten Outstanding Young Americans 20678
Arthur Carling Toner, Jr. Memorial Award 578
Touchdown Club Arch McDonald Achievement Award 20133
Touchdown Club Local Personality Makes Good Award 20135
Touchdown Club Mr. Sam Award 20136
Touchdown Club's Board of Governors Award 20137
Trail Development Award 2458
Triathletes of the Year 21249
True Value Man of the Year 15089
Twenty-Five Year Award 14462
Two Wheel Drive Puller of the Year 15892
U.S. Olympic Hall of Fame 20724
Unlimited Modified Puller of the Year 15893
UPA National Championships 20281
UPA Spirit of the Game Awards 20282
USA Triathlon Appreciation Award 21250
USOC Sports Equipment Student Design Contest 20725
USWCA Senior Ladies Trophy 20888
Veterans Award 581
Volunteer Achievement Award 19634
Tom Waddell Award 9492
Jake Wade Memorial Award and Honorary Membership 8192
Arch Ward Memorial Award 8193
Wauwatosa Event 20889
Western Heritage Awards (Wrangler Award) 14887
Wilhelmi-Haskell Stewardship Award 14669
World Footbag Championships 21921
World Horseshoe Tournament 15244
World Unicycling Championships 12101
Earle F. Zeigler Lecture Award 16473

Sports broadcasting

Academy & Achievement Awards 80
Bowling Magazine Writing Competition 1585

Sports (continued)

Distinguished Performance Award 20686
Ford C. Frick Award 14494
Curt Gowdy Media Award 13751
Hall of Fame 15812
Hall of Fame Award 4675
International Sportscasters of The Year 4678
Graham McNamee Award 4679
National Sportscaster and Sportswriter of Year 15813
National Sportscaster of the Year/Play by Play/Studio Host/Color Analyst/Reporter Award 4680
Sports Legend of the Year Award 4682
Sports Personality of the Year Award 4683
UPI National Broadcast Awards 20371
Women's Sports Journalism Awards 21812

Sports journalism
AAU Media Award 528
Better Newspapers Competition 7034
Boating Writers International Annual Writing Contest 6494
Bowling Magazine Writing Competition 1585
Niles Davis Award 14066
Distinguished Performance Award 20686
ECAC - SIDA Media Award 9110
Eclipse Awards for Media 20085
Editorial Awards 19819
Excellence in Sports Journalism Award 7755
Curt Gowdy Media Award 13751
Charles E. Green Journalism Awards 10308
Walter Haight Award 15922
Hall of Fame 15812
Fred Hartman Excellence in Sportswriting Award 19997
Bill Haughton Good Guy Award 20621
John Hervey Broadcasters' Awards George Smallreed Award 20877
Harold S. Hirsch Award 16463
Murray Kramer 6530
Local Association Public Relations Contest 1586
Mort Luby Senior Hall of Fame Award 6565
Frank Mayborn Award for Community Leadership 19998
National Sportscaster and Sportswriter of Year 15813
Newsletter of the Year
U.S. Hang Gliding Association 20614
United States Professional Tennis Association 20742
Old Hilltop Award 13135
Babe Orlando Award 12118
Outstanding Newsletter Award 561
Sovereign Award 12396
SportsCar Awards 19719
Tennis Week Great American Tennis Writing Awards 19984
Touchdown Club Local Personality Makes Good Award 20135
Carl H. Vilas Literary Award 12437
Women's Sports Journalism Awards 21812
David F. Woods Memorial Award 13137
Writers Corner Hall of Fame 20633

Sports medicine
Award of Excellence 7506
Cabaud Memorial Award 3350
CATA Merit Award 6947
Niles Davis Award 14066
Distinguished Scholar Award 16475
Early Career Distinguished Scholar Award 16476
Excellence in Research Awards 3351
Honorary Membership Award 14461
James R. Andrews Award for Excellence in Baseball Sports Medicine 4673
O'Donoghue Sports Injury Research Award 3352
President's Award 16477
Val D. Scroggie, M.D. Memorial Award 19710
Thomas E. Shaffer Award 796
Special Recognition Award 6950
Dr. Ray Wesson Memorial Physician of the Year Award 20389

Sportsmanship
AAU James E. Sullivan Memorial Award 527
Arnie Aizstrauts Team Sportsmanship 537
Maureen Connolly Brinker Award 20853
Mark Donohue Award 19690
Founder's Trophy 20772
Gaines Medal for Good Sportsmanship 16320
Girls' 18 National Championships Sportsmanship Award 20856
Frederic S. Horner Sportsmanship Award 12282
William M. Johnston Award 20857
Bobby Kaplan Sportsmanship Award 20858
Jack Kelly Fair Play Award 20721
Tom McKean Award 19695
National Sportsmanship Award 20777
Tom Pate Award 7116
Robert V. Ridges Memorial Award 19705
Solo Driver of Eminence Award 19713
Nick Speropolus Sportsmanship Award 21510
SportsMan and SportsWoman of the Year 20723
Dr. Allen B. Stowe Sportsmanship Award 20864
Captain James S. Ure Award for Sportsmanship 15945
USTA Girls' Sportsmanship Award 20870
Wallace "Buddy" Werner Award 20824
World Challenge 19724
Whitney M. Young, Jr. Memorial Scholarship 16310

Stamp collecting *See* Philately

Standards
AIAA HAP Arnold Award for Excellence in Aeronautical Program Management 2653
Applied Research Award 20475
Allen V. Astin Measurement Science Award 20476
Astin - Polk International Standards Medal 3181
ASTM Award of Merit 5929
Malcolm Baldrige National Quality Award 6202
Robert P. Brosseau Memorial Award 8433
Jean P. Carriere Award 19743
W. T. Cavanaugh Memorial Award 5934
H. V. Churchill Award 5935
Edward Uhler Condon Award 20477
Howard Coonley Medal 3182
Eugene Casson Crittenden Award 20478
Earl Curl Award 12030
Margaret Dana Award 5942
Distinguished Achievement in RV Standards Award 17914
Wayne P. Ellis Award 5946
Equal Employment Opportunity Award 20479
Euverard Innovation Award 5947
Fellow Award
MTM Association for Standards and Research 13657
Standards Engineering Society 19745
Finegan Standards Medal 3183
Kermit Fischer Environmental Award 12216
Miles D. Fishman Memorial Award 12031
Henry A. Gardner Award 5950
R. A. Glenn Award 5951
Melvin R. Green Codes and Standards Medal 4513
John L. Hague Award 5953
Honorary Life Member 19746
S. H. Ingberg Award 5958
Charles H. Irvine Memorial Award 5959
ISA Fellow 12219
ISWM Woody Woodland Memorial Award 12032
Lady of the Year Award 12033
Bernard F. Langer Nuclear Codes and Standards Award 4525
Edward Lohse Information Technology Medal 3184
George M. Low Award 13896
Maryland Quality Awards 21054
Katharine and Bryant Mather Award 5971
Meritorious Service Award 3185
Dale C. Moll Memorial Quality Management Award 8440
Leo B. Moore Medal 19747
SES/ASTM Robert J. Painter Memorial Award 19748
William T. Pearce Award 5975
Mark Pickell Award 12034
Cedric Powell Award 5977
President's Award 13658
Frank W. Reinhart and Henry "Butch" Kuhlmann Award 5978
Frank W. Reinhart Award 5979
Frank E. Richart Award 5980
Edward Bennett Rosa Award 20480
Safety Award for Superior Accomplishment 20481
Safety Codes and Standards Medal 4544
B. F. Scribner Award 5983
SES - ASTM Robert J. Painter Memorial Award 5985
Woodland G. Shockley Memorial Award 5987
William P. Slichter Award 20482
Charles Proteus Steinmetz Award 10882
Samuel Wesley Stratton Award 20483
J. Hall Taylor Medal 4549
Technical Excellence Award 12035
Technology Award/Award of Engineering Excellence 4441
Richard L. Templin Award 5990
Moyer D. Thomas Award 5991
Sanford E. Thompson Award 5992
Robert D. Thompson Memorial Award 5993
SES/CSA Lorne K. Wagner Memorial Award 19749
George S. Wham Leadership Medal 3186

Standards (continued)
World Standards Day Paper Awards 19750

Statistics
AERF Practitioners Award 18939
Harold F. Dodge Award 5944
Dorweiler Prize 7621
Fellows of the American Statistical Association 4692
R. A. Fisher Award 8292
Fisher Memorial Lecture 11006
Woodward - Fondiller Prize 7622
Founders Award 4693
Charles A. Hachemeister Prize 7623
Halmstad Prize 18941
Everett Curtis Huntington Prize 18942
Michelbacher Prize 7624
Neyman Lecture 11007
Outstanding Statistical Application Awards 4694
Presidents' Award 8293
Rietz Lecture 11008
Matthew Rodermund Service Award 7625
Elizabeth L. Scott Award 8294
George W. Snedecor Award
American Statistical Association 4695
Committee of Presidents of Statistical Societies 8295
Statistics in Chemistry Award 4696
Wald Memorial Lecture 11009
Wilks Memorial Award 4697
W. J. Youden Award in Interlaboratory Testing 4698

Steel industry *See* Iron and steel industry

Store planning (*See also* Merchandising)
ISP Student Competition 11043
ISP/*VM & SD* International Design Competition 11044
Retail Design Awards 14401

Stroke
Award of Hope and Courage 15822
Community Education Award 15823
Research Fellowship Award in Cerebrovascular Disease 15824
Sister Kenny Institute International Art Show for Artists with Disabilities 13485

Surfing
ASP World Title 5871
Dr. Colin J. Couture Award for Outstanding Volunteer Service to Eastern Surfing 9119
Kahuna Award 12052
Pratte Scholarship 19845

Surgery
American College of Surgeons Faculty Fellowship 1945
Harry Archer Award 1910
Arthroscopy Research Grants 5131
Award for Distinguished Service 3989
Barringer Medal 1204
Bernstein Grant 667
Board of Governors Service Award—Model State/Regional Society Program 745
James Barrett Brown Award 1381
Champlain Award 7049
George H. A. Clowes, Jr., M.D., F.A.C.S. Memorial Research Career Development Award 1947
Committee Man of the Year 1309
Community Service Award 668
Crikelair, Snyder, Gingras, Hardesty, Shenaq 17390
Michael E. DeBakey Award 13327
John Dickinson Teacher Award 669
Distinguished Member Award 5914
Distinguished Service Award
American Academy of Otolaryngology - Head and Neck Surgery 747
American Association of Oral and Maxillofacial Surgeons 1310
American Society of Abdominal Surgeons 4210
Plastic Surgery Educational Foundation 17378
Education Award 5873
Exhibit and Poster Award 748
Faculty Career Development Award for Toncology of the Head and Neck 1948
Foundation Clinical Surgery Fellowship 1311
Stephen L. Gans Distinguished Overseas Lectureship 772
Gold Medal Forum 19483
Jerome C. Goldstein Public Service Award 749
Honor Awards 750
Honorary Award 17379
Honorary Citation 17380
Honorary Member Award 5915
Humanitarian Award 1911
Robert H. Ivy Society Award 17381
Journalism Achievement on Aesthetic Surgery Award 3911
Keyes Medal 1205
John W. Kirklin M.D. Award for Professional Excellence 1440
William E. Ladd Award 779
Leadership Award 5874
Legislation Award 5875
Walter Lorenz Research Award 1912
Medal in Surgery 18154
Practitioner Excellence Award 752
Presidential Award 17382
Presidential Award (Presidential Citation) 17383
Presidential Citation 753
Public Education Award for Excellence in Plastic Surgery Journalism 17384
Public Relations Award 5876
Research Fellowship Grants 17385
Research Grants 17386
Research Recognition Award 16804
Resident Research Award 16805
Resident Research Grants 670
Resident Research Scholarship 1950
Resident/Trainee Award 3915
Royal Canin Award 4820
Arnold M. Salzberg Mentorship Award 794
Scholarship Contest 17387
Scientific Poster Awards 1913
Special Achievement Award 17388
Student Research Training Award 16806
Thomas Starzl Humanitarian Award 20152
Transplant Recipients International Organization Scholarship 20153
Nina Starr Braun Wald Award 5916
Young Investigators Award 1831
Young Oncologist Essay Awards 3815
Young Oncologist Travel Grants 3816

Surveying
American Association for Geodetic Surveying Graduate Fellowship Award 1013
Berntsen Scholarship in Surveying 1996
Joseph F. Dracup Scholarship Award 1014
Excellence in Professional Journalism 15758
Earle J. Fennell Award 1997
Gzowski Medal 7414
Honorary Member 1998
Leica Surveying Scholarships 1999
Most Interesting Surveying Project of the Year Award 15759
NSPS Scholarship 15760
Outstanding Paper in Surveying 2002
Presidential Citations for Exceptional Service 2003
Schonstedt Scholarship in Surveying 2004
Student Project of the Year Award 15761
Surveying and Mapping Award 4360
Surveying Excellence Award 15762
Sustaining Members Twenty-Year Awards 2005
VSLS Education Foundation Scholarships 21306
Wild Heerbrugg Geodetic Fellowship 2007

Swimming (*See also* Diving; Surfing; Water polo)
25 Year Award 15286
Adapted Committee Award 21188
All-American Awards 15307
Appreciation Award 15287
Capt. Ransom J. Arthur, M.D. Award 20690
ASCA Awards of Excellence 4719
ASCA Chapter Age Group Coaches of the Year 4720
ASCA Coaches Hall of Fame 4721
Athlete of the Year Award 20393
Athletes Appreciation Award 21189
Big East Conference Academic Awards 6369
Coach of the Year Award 4722
Collegiate Athlete of the Year 19865
Completion of Service Award 15288
Councilman Creative Coaching Awards 4723
Counsilman Coach of the Year Award 21190
Developmental Coach of the Year 21191
Hall of Fame Award 15282
Hall of Fame - Contributor 19866
Nelson C. Hart Trophy 7218
Honorary Membership Award 15289
Glen S. Hummer Award 21192
International Marathon Swimming Hall of Fame Award 12054
International Swimming Hall of Fame Gold Medallion Award 12055
International Swimming Hall of Fame Honoree 12056
ISHOF Service Award 12057
John B. Kelly Memorial Award 21193
Kiphuth Award 21194
Life Membership Award 15290
Lillian MacKeller Distinguished Service Award 20395
William A. Lippman Jr. USA Swimming Combined Team Traveling Trophy 21195
Lillian MacKeller Distinguished Service Award 19867
G. Harold Martin Award 12058

Swimming (continued)

Charles McCaffree Award 8195
Glenn McCormick Memorial Diving Award 20396
May McEwan Memorial Award (Masters Athlete of the Year) 19868
Moose Moss Age Group Diving Coach of the Year Award 20397
Dawn Musselman Award 20691
National Collegiate and Scholastic Swimming Trophy 8196
National Collegiate and Scholastic Swimming Trophy 15283
NCAA National Championships 14687
Neilson-Bell Comeback Award 21196
Open Water Swimmer of the Year 21197
Robert Ousley Special Service Award 4724
Outstanding Service Awards 15284
Outstanding Women in Swimming Award 20398
General George S. Patton, Jr. Memorial Trophy 20705
Mike Peppe Award 20399
Kenneth J. Pettigrew Award 21198
Phillips Performance Award 21199
Phillips Performance of the Meet Award 21200
Power Point Rankings Award 15291
Presidential Honor Award 12059
R. Max Ritter Award 21201
Rookies of the Meet Award 21202
Safety Commendation Award 21203
Schlueter Stroke Awards National Winners 4725
Al Schoenfield Media Award 12060
Special NJCAA Awards 15316
Special Service Award 15292
Speedo/USMS Coach of the Year Award 20692
Richard Steadman Award 8197
Swimmer of the Year Award 21204
Swimming Coach of the Year 7235
Team Awards 21205
Locksin Thompson Memorial Public Service Award 6761
United States Swimming Award 21206
United States Swimming Life Members 21207
USSS Athlete of the Year 19869
USSS Coach of the Year 19870
John K. Williams Jr. International Adaptive Aquatic Award 12061
David Yorzyk Memorial Award
U.S. Aquatic Sports 20400
United States Masters Swimming 20693
Trish L Zorn Award 21208

Systems management *See* Information management; Operations research

Table tennis
USA Table Tennis National Championships 21210

Tapestry *See* Textile design

Tattooing *See* Cosmetology

Teaching (*See also* Education)
Academy Fellow 88
Adams Memorial Membership Award 4876
ADE Francis Andrew March Award 5656
Howard E. Adkins Memorial Instructor Membership Award 4877
AICPA Distinguished Achievement in Accounting Education Award 2747
TESOL Virginia French Allen Award for Scholarhip and Service 19948
Alpha Omega Alpha Distinguished Teacher Awards 482
American Heroes in Education Awards 17887
APA Teaching Award 593
Arbuthnot Award 11851
ARRL Herb S. Brier Instructor of the Year Award 45
ARRL Professional Educator of the Year Award 46
ASAS Fellow 4257
ASCP Associate Member Lifetime Achievement Award 3963
ASCP Associate Member Section Distinguished Service Award 3964
ASEE Section Outstanding Teaching Award 3996
Association of Orthodox Jewish Teachers Awards 5806
Auxiliary Excellence Award 2932
Award for Excellence in Encouraging Equity 14090
Award for Excellence in Teaching 1731
Award for Teaching Excellence in the Field of Library and Information Science Education 5420
Award of Distinction 12064
Award of Excellence 9935
Awards for Excellence in Teaching of the Classics 3418
Awards for Scientific Achievement 21437
Dorothy E. Baethke - Eleanor J. Carlin Award for Excellence in Academic Teaching 3483
John C. Barner Teacher of the Year Award 886
Stuart L. Bernath Lecture Prize 18679
Biotechnology Teaching Award 14091
Taylor Booth Award 10886
Richard Braddock Award 8375
Thomas J. Brennan Award 6007
ACTFL Nelson Brooks Award for Excellence in the Teaching of Culture 2056
Signe Brunnstrom Award for Excellence in Clinical Teaching 3486
E. K. Campbell Award of Merit 4426
Alice Carr Award 2933
Carski Foundation Distinguished Teaching Award 4133
L. E. Casida Award 4259
Castleman Award for Excellence in Chamber Music Teaching 7793
CCCC Exemplar Award 8376
CEA Professional Achievement Award 8153
CEE James N. Britton Award for Inquiry within the English Language Arts 14829
CEE Richard A. Meade Award 14830
Certificate of Merit 1444
Robert Foster Cherry Award for Great Teachers 18078
Robert Foster Cherry Chair for Distinguished Teaching 18079
CIBA Specialty Chemicals Exemplary Middle Level and High School Principal Awards 15684
CIBA Specialty Chemicals Exemplary Middle Level and High School Science Teaching Awards 15685
Leta Clark Elementary Teacher Scholarship 13223
Clinical Instructor of the Year Award 1292
Coach of the Year 12652
Collegiate or University Teacher of the Year 14571
James Bryant Conant Award in High School Chemistry Teaching 1744
Emily Cooley Memorial Award 1103
Ryan Crymes TESOL Fellowship for Graduate Study 19949
Dance Magazine Annual Awards 8736
DASA Scholarship 8848
Decades of Excellence Crystal Bell Teacher Award 12734
DeMello School Scholarships 8877
Distinguished Achievement Award for Petroleum Engineering Faculty 19236
Distinguished Achievement Award to Fluid Power Educator 11627
Distinguished Advertising Educator Award 859
Distinguished Adviser Award 8171
Distinguished Career Award 594
Distinguished Contributions to Teaching 17017
Distinguished Contributions to Teaching Award 4652
Distinguished Dissertation in Teacher Education 5878
Distinguished Educator Award 16402
Distinguished Fellow Award 11521
Distinguished Member Award 18808
Distinguished Programs in Teacher Education 5879
Distinguished Research in Teacher Education 5880
Distinguished Service Award
American Association of Teachers of Spanish and Portuguese 1452
American Society of Abdominal Surgeons 4210
Association of Professional Chaplains 5822
Distinguished Service to Science Education Award 15688
Distinguished Teacher Award
American Society of Animal Science 4260
North American Colleges and Teachers of Agriculture 16403
Distinguished Teaching Achievement Awards 14764
Distinguished Teaching Award 15689
Distinguished Teaching Award
Ohio Academy of History 16624
UCLA Alumni Association 20257
Distinguished Teaching Awards
American Agricultural Economics Association 871
Kent State University Alumni Association 12560
Distinguished Teaching, Distinguished Research 21256
Distinguished Teaching of Art Award 8146
Distinguished Teaching of Art History Award 8147
Meneve Dunham Award for Excellence in Teaching 8077
Donald H. Ecroyd Award for Outstanding Teaching in Higher Education 14707

Teaching (continued)

Education Award 19336
EMRA Award for Excellence in Teaching 9238
Excellence in Pre-College Physics Teaching Award 1372
Excellence in Teaching Award
American Phytopathological Society 3539
Dominican University 8988
Miriam Joseph Farrell Distinguished Teacher Award 14612
Mary Finocchiaro Award for Excellence in the Development of Pedagogical Materials 19950
Follett Library Resources & Software Companies Excellence in Teaching Award (Graduate School of Library and Information Science) 8989
Four-Year College Biology Teaching Award 14093
Future Business Teacher 9845
Robin F. Garland Educator Award 15534
Gifted Teacher 1839
Great Teachers Award 16306
Ellen Griffin Rolex Award 12655
Arthur C. Guyton Awards for Excellence in Integrative Physiology 3518
Melody Hall Memorial Award 14094
Harvard Medal 10271
Rev. Theodore M. Hesburgh, C.S.C., Award 5591
Hoffman LaRoche-American Association of Bovine Practitioners Award for Excellence 1125
Home Baking Association Educator Award 10518
Honorary Emeritus Membership 5499
Honorary Membership 14095
Clarissa Hug Teacher of the Year Award 8551
Oscar B. Hunter Memorial Award in Therapeutics of the ASCPT 3975
ICPE Medal for Physics Teaching 12106
IMCC National Annual Minerals Education Awards 12157
Rewey Belle Inglis Award 14834
Innovative Teaching of Secondary School Physics Award 1374
Instructor of the Year 14559
International Citation of Merit 11861
International Dairy Production Award 2104
John Wiley & Sons Award for Innovation in Teaching 11525
Eleanor M. Johnson Award 11864
Kappa Delta Pi National Student Teacher/Intern of the Year Award 5881
Donald P. Kent Award 9995
Krieghbaum Under-40 Award 5345
Benjamin Garver Lamme Award 4024
Land O'Lakes/Purina Teaching Award in Dairy Production 2106
Capt. V. L. Laursen Award 20943
Law-Related Education Teacher of the Year Award 2935
Leavey Awards for Excellence in Private Enterprise Education 9765
Charles E. Levine Memorial Award for Excellence in Public Service 4184
Margaret B. Lindsey Award for Distinguished Research in Teacher Education 1151
Ottis Lock Award 9082
Albert H. Marckwardt Travel Grants 19951
Harold Masursky Award for Meritorious Service 1514
Christa McAuliffe Memorial Award 228
Medal for Excellence in Teaching 6935
Mentor Award 5502
C. Hart Merriam Award 4499
Fred Merryfield Design Award 4029
Agnes Meyer Outstanding Teacher Awards 21459
Middle School Teaching Award 14096
Midwest Bank Excellence in Teaching Award (School of Education) 8990
Kenneth W. Mildenberger Prize 13563
Milk Industry Foundation and Kraft General Foods Teaching Award in Dairy Science 2109
Merl K. Miller Award 4030
Robert A. Millikan Medal 1376
Missouri Teacher of the Year Program 13535
Mother Evelyn Murphy Excellence in Teaching Award 8991
NACD - ICI Americas Conservation Teacher Awards 14157
NACTA John Deere Awards 16406
National Book Service Teacher-Librarian of the Year Award 7261
National Family and Consumer Sciences Teacher of the Year Award - Home Economics Teacher of the Year Award 942
National High School Journalism Teacher of the Year 9008
National Kind Teacher Award 14016
National Teacher of the Year 8571
NCEE/Nasdaq National Teaching Awards 14857
Nutrition Professionals, Inc. Applied Dairy Nutrition Award 2111
Marcella E. Oberle Award for Outstanding Teaching in Grades K-12 14714
Oersted Medal 1377
Gustav Ohaus Award for Innovations in Science Teaching 15690
Ernest Osborne Award 14863
Outstanding Biology Teacher Award 14097
Outstanding Community College Educator Award 4034
Outstanding Educator Award 17723
Outstanding Elementary Social Studies Teacher of the Year Award 14786
Outstanding Extension Educator Award 4089
Outstanding German Educator Award 1447
Outstanding Graduate Educator Award 4090
Outstanding High School Senior in German 1448
Outstanding Information Science Teacher Award 4111
Outstanding Jazz Educator Award 14488
Outstanding Middle Level Social Studies Teacher of the Year 14787
Outstanding New Biology Teacher Achievement Award 14098
Outstanding Science Educator of the Year 5503
Outstanding Secondary Social Studies Teacher of the Year 14788
Outstanding Teacher Educator in Reading Award 11870
Outstanding Teacher of American History 15713
Outstanding Teacher of Theatre in Higher Education Award 5516
Outstanding Vocational Special Needs Teacher of the Year 14059
Robert L. Packard Outstanding Educator Award 19531
ACTFL Anthony Papalia Award for Excellence in Teacher Education 2058
Philadelphia Section Awards for Excellence in Science Teaching 1797
Philbro Extension Award 17501
Melba Newell Phillips Award 1378
Physician Assistant Educator of the Year Award 818
William T. Plass Award 4556
Postsecondary Teacher of the Year 14574
President's National Medal of Science 15679
President's Prizes for Outstanding Achievement in Primary and Secondary Education 9283
Professional Instructor of the Year Award 51
Purina Mills Teaching Award 17506
Leon R. Radde - Educator of the Year Award 10974
Recognition Award for Young Scholars 1473
Herbert J. Rinkel Award 653
Lyman A. Ripperton Award 324
James Harvey Robinson Prize 2481
David H. Russell Award for Distinguished Research in the Teaching of English 14840
St. Paul Federal Bank for Savings Excellence in Teaching Award (Graduate School of Business) 8992
Schindler Award 4075
Charles Schuchert Award 17041
Secondary Teacher of the Year 14575
Robert H. Shaffer Award for Academic Excellence as a Graduate Faculty Member 14408
Mina P. Shaughnessy Prize 13576
Shurgain Award for Excellence in Nutrition and MeatScience 7445
Nila Banton Smith Award 11875
James R. Squire Award 14841
Jules Stachiewicz Medal 7849
Steacie Memorial Fellowships 16025
ACTFL Florence Steiner Award for Leadership in Foreign Language Education, K-12 2060
ACTFL Florence Steiner Award for Leadership in Foreign Language Education, Postsecondary 2061
Wayne W. Stinchcomb Memorial Lecture and Award 5989
Bradley Stoughton Award for Young Teachers 5191
Noel Ross Strader Memorial Award 8176
Mary K. Bonsteel Tachau Teach of the Year Award 16896
Teacher Educational Mini-Grant 7693
Teacher Fellow Award 16408
Teacher of the Year
Correctional Education Association - Region III 8531
Ladies Professional Golf Association 12662
Teacher of the Year Award
Fairbanks Education Association 9388
Professional Golfers' Association of America 17622

Teaching (continued)

Teacher of the Year Awards 14043
Teachers Who Inspire 18264
Teaching Awards Program 3742
Technology Teacher Educator of the Year 8612
Tennessee Teacher of Excellence 19966
Frederick Emmons Terman Award 4045
TESOL Research Interest Section/Thomson Heinle Distinguished Research Award 19952
TESOL Thomson Heinle Award for Excellence in Teaching 19953
TESOL Travel Grant 19954
TETYC Best Article of the Year Award 14844
Tressler - VNR/AVI Teacher Award 16409
John Trimmer Merit Shop Teaching Award of Excellence 5234
Two-Year College Biology Teaching Award 14099
Utilization Award 14019
Veblen - Commons Award 5363
Waksman Outstanding Teaching Award 18763
William H. Weston Award for Teaching Excellence 13726
Albert Easton White Distinguished Teacher Award 5192
Leslie A. Whittington Excellence in Teaching Award 14377
Calvert, Woodall, and McMillan Writing Awards 5627

Technology (*See also* Biotechnology; Computer science; Engineering; History of technology; Industrial arts; Inventions; Robotics; Science; Standards; Testing)

Academic Achievement Award 4837
Academy of Fellows 12063
Achievement Awards 14165
American Egg Board Research Award 17496
Thomas P. Anderson Sr. Micrographics Awards 308
Douglas H. Annin Award 12210
Award for Achievement in Technical Services 7248
Award of Distinction 12064
E.G. Bailey Award 12211
Arnold O. Beckman Founder Award 12212
J. Armand Bombardier Prize in Technological Innovation 5538
Arthur M. Bueche Award 13805
Canada Awards for Excellence 15568
Canadian Information Technology Innovation Award 7163
Rachel Carson Award 18856
CEO Recognition Award 21760
Renate W. Chasman Scholarship for Women 6649
CLA/Information Today Award for Innovative Technology 7249
Compass Distinguished Achievement Award 13108
Compass Industrial Award 13109
Compass International Award 13110
Fred O. Conley Award 19260
Creative Arts Award 12159
Customer Service Award 7165
Arthur Vining Davis Award 427
Distinguished EEA - SHIP Member Award 12065
Distinguished Society Service Award 12213
Distinguished Technology Educator Award 12066
Division Technical Awards 19920
Charles Stark Draper Prize 13806
Donald P. Eckman Education Award 12214
Albert Einstein Award 4193
Electronic Imaging Management Award 311
Engineering and Construction Contracting Division Award 2768
Excellence in Manufacturing Technology Achievement Awards 3023
Extraction and Processing Technology Award 13446
Fast 50 Award 17956
Ludwik Fleck Prize 18857
Francis C. Frary Award 428
Sheldon K. Friedlander Award 955
George W. Goddard Award 19608
Gold Medal Awards 6290
Golden Hammer Scenic Technology Award 20645
Graffin Lectureship Award 1645
Cecil Green Award for Technology Entrepreneurship 6291
Gary Hadford Professional Achievement Award 7168
Hall of Outstanding Americans 15986
Heinz Award in Technology, the Economy and Employment 10379
Paul T. Hiser Exemplary Publication Award 9313
Maurice Holland Award 10786
IAIA - Rose Hulman Award 11247
Innovations in Technology Award 19551
Innovator of the Year 17815
International Achievement Awards Competition 10784
International ANDY Awards 11184
International Award 3054
International Hall of Fame World Award 12162
InterTech Technology Awards 10134
Kilby International Awards 12586
Leonardo Award for Excellence 11957
John F. Limmer Award for Best Restored Steam Engine 15880
Lindbergh Grants 7808
Rutherford B. Lockette Humanitarian Award 12067
Lockheed/Martin Ocean Engineering Award 13111
Los Angeles Times Book Prizes 12931
Frank J. Malina - Leonardo Prize for Lifetime Achievement 11958
Manning Awards 9329
The Marconi Prize 13064
Carroll Sterling Masterson Award & Outstanding Women's Awards 22093
Meritorious Service Award 12068
Metallized Package/Label of the Year 5728
Stanislaw W. Mrozowski Award 1646
Nicholas C. Mullins Award 18858
NAIA-SIDA Top Web Sites of the Year 14291
New Horizons Award for Innovation 11959
Outstanding Division Award 12220
Outstanding Reference Sources 17944
Outstanding Technical Paper Award 13312
Ely ("Eli") S. Parker Award 2607
Petinos Foundation Award 1647
Pioneer Award 313
Prakken Professional Cooperation Award 12069
Program Excellence Award 12070
Progress Award 17292
Pupin Medal 8230
R & D 100 Awards 17817
Recognition of Achievement Award 5203
Robert F. Reed Technology Medal 10136
Rose Brand Award for Scenic Lighting 20648
Arthur L. Schawlow Award 12693
Science in Society Journalism Awards 7384
Scientist of the Year Award 17818
SGL Carbon Award 1648
Maurice Simpson Technical Editor's Award 10929
Smithsonian Institution Fellowship Program 18572
Space Technology Hall of Fame 20844
Special Award 4115
Special Recognition Citation 12071
Albert F. Sperry Founder Award 12222
SPIE Technology Achievement Award 19611
Standards Achievement Award 4439
Howard E. Stanfield Distinguished Service Award 19613
Technical Excellence Award 12035
Technology Award/Award of Engineering Excellence 4441
Technology of the Year 5729
Technology Teacher Educator of the Year 8612
Technology Transfer Award
Arkansas Technology Transfer Society 5081
Society of American Foresters 18977
Ten Outstanding Young Americans 20678
Toshiba/NSTA ExploraVision Awards 15693
Makepeace Tsao Leonardo Award 11960
John Tyndall Award 16799
UOP Technology Award 12226
USITT Architecture Design Award 20651
USITT/Edward Kook Endowment Fund 20652
Volunteer of the Year 6293
Philip L. Walker Jr. Award 1649
William E. Warner Awards Program 9314
Norbert Wiener Award for Social and Professional Responsibility 8331
George E. Willis Award 4900
WITI Hall of Fame 21761
R. W. Wood Prize 16800
Young Innovator Award 6294

Technology, color *See* Color technology

Technology, medical *See* Medical technology

Technology, office *See* Office technology

Technology, piano *See* Piano technology

Technology, vacuum *See* Vacuum technology

Telecommunications *See* Communications

Television (*See also* Broadcasting; Cable television; Media; Radio; Video)
AAAS Science Journalism Awards 1047
Academy & Achievement Awards 80
ACE Eddie Award 1804
Achievement Award 9715
Advertising Design Club of Canada Awards 204
The Gracie Allen Awards 9716
The American Advertising Awards 858
American Center for Children's Television - Fran Allison Award 1663
American Center for Children's Television - Ollie Awards 1664
Annual Awards in International News Coverage 16981
Annual Exhibitions 5115
ASHA Media Awards for Journalists 4662
Asian American Journalists Association National Awards 5165
Atlantic Journalism Awards 6035
Award of Excellence 9541
Awards of Excellence 453
Banff Television Festival 6239
Erik Barnouw Award 16882
Howard W. Blakeslee Awards 2404
Broadcast Excellence Award 6890
Broadcast Media Awards for Television 11853
Tom Brokaw Award 19449
Russell L. Cecil Arthritis Medical Journalism Awards 5125
Harry Chapin Media Awards 21925
Paddy Chayefsky Laurel Award for Television 21989
Chetwynd Award for Entrepreneurial Excellence 7093
Chicago International Children's Film Festival 7888
Chicago International Film Festival 8001
Children's Choice Award 454
Jack Chisholm Award for Lifetime Achievement 7094
Christopher Awards 7971
CINE Eagle Award 8608
CINE Golden Eagle Award 8609
CINE Master's Series Award 8610
Commercial Director Award 8941
Consumer Journalism Award 15515
CPB Public Television Local Program Awards 8524
Creative Achievement Award 14413
Ernie Crisp Television News Photographer of the Year 15533
Daytime Emmy Awards 13861
Deadline Club Awards 8773
Dissertation Award 18651
Distinguished Performance Award 20686
Distinguished Service Award 7683
Allen B. DuMont Citation 17834
Eastman Kodak Gold Medal Award 19190
Eclipse Awards for Media 20085
ECRI Medical Technology Media Awards Program 9150
Emmy Awards 13862
Emmy Awards for Primetime Programming 127
Executive of the Year 7684
Feature Video Photo Award 16247
Gabriel Award 7633
Gavel Awards 1533
Gemeaux Awards 81
Global Media Awards for Excellence in Population Reporting 17469
Gold Medal Award 11848
Gold Ribbon for Community Service (Radio) 6891
Gold Ribbon for Community Service (Specialty/Pay/PPV) 6892
Gold Ribbon for Community Service (Television) 6893
Gold Ribbon for Outstanding Community Service by an Individual Broadcaster 6894
Gold Ribbon for Promotion of Canadian Talent (Radio) 6895
Golden Gate Awards 18246
Golden Globe Awards 10513
Golden Medallion Media Awards 19759
Grants for Arts Projects 14930
Grassroots Award 5570
Heart of America 2952
The Sidney Hillman Foundation Prize Awards 10435
HSMAI Adrian Advertising Awards 10554
The Hugos: The Chicago International Television Awards 8002
Humanitas Prize 10608
IAFF Media Awards Contest 11355
ILCA Film and Broadcast Competition 11699
Image Awards 14049
International ANDY Awards 11184
International Broadcasting Awards 10516
International Emmy Award 11519
International Television Programming and Promotions Awards 16223
IRE Awards 12170
Journal Award 19194
Kennedy Center Honors 12552
Robert F. Kennedy Journalism Awards 18076
Robert L. Kozik Award for Environmental Reporting 15519
Lefthanders of the Year Awards 12764
Lifetime Achievement Award 455
Ralph Lowell Award 8525
Mort Luby Senior Hall of Fame Award 6565
Wade H. McCree, Jr. Awards for the Advancement of Justice 19763
Member of the Year 7685
Mental Health Media Awards 15378
Michener-Deacon Fellowship 13329
Mobius Advertising Awards 21142
National Headliner Awards 15194
National Media Awards 1829
National Playwrights Conference and New Drama for Media Project 15508
National Psychology Awards for Excellence in the Media 18915
News and Documentary Emmy Awards 13863
One Show Awards 16732
Outstanding Achievement Award 456
Outstanding American Films of the Year Awards 2241
Outstanding Directorial Achievement Award for Television 8948
PBS Advertising and Promotion Awards 17705
Peabody Awards Collection 21020
Edgar Allan Poe Awards (Edgars) 13732
Polka Music Hall of Fame 11820
Presidential Proclamation 19196
PROMAX Awards 17679
Public and Community Service Emmy Awards 13864
Mrs. Ann Radcliffe Awards 8615
Regional Television Photographer of the Year 15546
Robert L. Robinson Awards 3635
Ruben Salazar Award for Communications 14808
Salute to Excellence Awards 14101
David Sarnoff Medal Award 19198
Science in Society Journalism Awards 7384
SD Broadcaster of the Year 19450
Service to Children Television Awards 14117
SHINE (Sexual Health in Entertainment) Awards 13238
Sigma Delta Chi Awards 19276
Silurian Excellence in Journalism Awards 19327
Silver Satellite Award 9717
Sports Emmy Awards 13865
Spot News Video Award 16251
Spur Awards 21576
Student Award for Scholarly Writing 18652
Technical Engineering Achievement Awards 13866
Technicolor/Herbert T. Kalmus Gold Medal Award 19199
Television Newsfilm Awards 15549
Television Program Producer of the Year 15618
Television-Radio Awards 21994
Telly Awards 19964
Lowell Thomas Travel Journalism Awards 19016
TV Hall of Fame 128
U.S. International Film and Video Festival 21143
University of Missouri Television Awards for Community Leadership 21081
UPI National Broadcast Awards 20371
Western Heritage Awards (Wrangler Award) 14887
White House News Photographers' Association Awards 21606
Wilbur Awards 17971
Women at Work Awards 21618
WORLDFEST - Houston International Film and Video Festival 21969
Young People's Film and Video Festival 16562

Tennis (*See also* Table tennis)
50 Greatest U.S. Tennis Resorts 19977
All-American Awards 15307
Arthur Ashe Award 16582
Tennis Magazine/Arthur Ashe Collegiate Awards for Leadership and Sportsmanship 11137
Assistant Coach of the Year Award 11138
Big East Conference Academic Awards 6369
Maureen Connolly Brinker Award 20853
Coach of the Year 20740
Coaches Association Awards 15309
Comeback Player of the Year 19978
Sarah Palfrey Danzig Award 20854
Davis Cup 20855
Division of the Year 20741
ESPY Awards 9337
Everest and Jennings Player of the Year 508
Ted Farnsworth Senior Player of the Year Award 11139
Girls' 18 National Championships Sportsmanship Award 20856

Subject Index

Tennis (continued)

Samuel Hardy Award 12074
International Tennis Hall of Fame Enshrinement 12075
ITA All America Team 11140
ITA/Osuna Sportsmanship Award 11141
ITA Rookie Player of the Year 11142
ITA Scholar-Athlete All-American 11143
ITA Senior Player of the Year 11144
William M. Johnston Award 20857
Junior Players of the Year 19979
Bobby Kaplan Sportsmanship Award 20858
Cissie Leary Sportsmanship Award 11145
John T. McGovern Umpires' Award 20859
Member Organization of the Year 20860
Most Improved Pros 19980
NCAA National Championships 14687
Newsletter of the Year 20742
NFWT Service Award 509
Penn/ITA Player to Watch 11146
Player of the Year 20743
Professional of the Year 20744
Rolex Collegiate All-Star Team 11147
Rolex/Tennis Magazine College Player of the Year 11148
Rolex Watch/*Tennis* Magazine Rookies of the Year 19981
Seniors' Service Award 20861
Service Bowl Award 20862
Jack Stahr Award 20863
Dr. Allen B. Stowe Sportsmanship Award 20864
Super Senior Service Award 20865
Bill Talbert Junior Sportsmanship Award 12076
Bill Talbert Junior Sportsmanship Awards 20866
Tennis Educational Merit Award for Men 12077
Tennis Educational Merit Award for Women 12078
Tennis Facility Awards 20867
Tennis Magazine Collegiate Journalism Award 11149
Tennis Magazine /ITA College Players of the Year 19982
Tennis Magazine/ITA Player of the Year 11150
Tennis Week Great American Tennis Writing Awards 19984
United States Open Tennis Championships 20868
USTA Community Service Award 20869
USTA Girls' Sportsmanship Award 20870
USTA Tennis NJTL Chapter of the Year Award 20871
USTA/USPTA Public Service Award 20872
John Van Nostrand Memorial Award 11151
Volunteer Service Award 20873
Ralph W. Westcott USTA Family of the Year Award 20874
Wilson Coach of the Year Award 11152

Testing
ASNT Fellows 4143
ASNT Fellowship Award 4144
Charles W. Briggs Award 5933
Lou Di Valerio Technician of the Year Award 4145
John L. Hague Award 5953
Philip D. Johnson Honorary Member Award 4146
Lester Honor Lecture 4147
Robert C. McMaster Gold Medal 4148
Mehl Honor Lecture 4149
Outstanding Paper Awards 4150
Performance Test Codes Medal 4537
President's Award 4151
Frank W. Reinhart and Henry "Butch" Kuhlmann Award 5978
Charles N. Sherlock Meritorious Service Award 4152
Moyer D. Thomas Award 5991
Tutorial Citation Award 4153
Young NDT Professional Award 4154

Textile design
Artists-in-Residence Program 19814
Nancy and Harry Koenigsberg Award 20050
National Exhibition of Weaving in the Norwegian Tradition 21317
Betty Park Award in Critical Writing 19843
Prints, Drawings and Photographs Exhibition 5071

Textile industry (*See also* Fiber science)
Textile Citizen of the Year 410
Textile Section Award 16211

Theater
AACT Corporate Award 1163
AATE Distinguished Book Award 883
AATE Research Award 884
ACTF Awards for Theatrical Design Excellence 12539
Administrators' Award 9180
Alliance Award 885
American Association of Community Theatre Festival Award 1164
Father Adrien Arsenault Senior Arts Award 17544
Arts Recognition and Talent Search (ARTS) 15117
ASCAP - Richard Rodgers Award 4377
Award for Outstanding Creative Achievement in the American Theatre 16123
Award for Scene Design 20642
Leighton M. Ballew Directing Award 19485
Barbizon Award for Lighting Design 20643
John C. Barner Teacher of the Year Award 886
St. Clair Bayfield Award 165
Beverly Hills Theatre Guild Play Competition for Children's Theatre 6349
Edwin Booth Award 8054
Bravo Award 10547
Elston Brook Lifetime Achievement Award 12892
David C. Bryant Outstanding Service Award 1165
Joe A. Callaway Award 166
Career Achievement Award - Professional Theatre 5514
Career Achievement Award - Teacher in Higher Education 5515
Clear-Com Intercom Systems Sound Achievement Award 20644
Harry and Martha Cohen Award 424
Nathan Cohen Award 7514
Art Cole Award 1166
Common Wealth Awards of Distinguished Service 17410
Corporate Award 12893
Creative Drama Award 889
Cultural Achievement Award 2893
Suzanne M. Davis Memorial Award 19486
Dissertation Award 4198
Distinguished Career Award 19487
Distinguished Merit Award 1167
Drama Desk Awards 9018
Drama League's Distinguished Performance Award 9020
Drama League's Musical Achievement Award 9021
Drama League's Unique Contribution to the Theatre Award 9022
Peter Dwyer Scholarships 6792
S. Randolph Edmonds Young Scholars Competition 6436
El Angel Award - Distinguished Hispanic-American Artist 6374
Fellows of the American Association of Community Theatre 1168
Fellowship Program 17168
Ann Flagg Multicultural Award 891
Founders' Award 9181
George Freedley Memorial Award 20059
Fund for New American Plays 12550
Robert E. Gard Superior Volunteer Award 1169
John Gassner Memorial Playwriting Award 16124
Gavel Awards 1533
Charles M. Getchell Award 19488
Jean-Cleo Godin Award 5285
Grants for Arts Projects 14930
Ruby Griffith Award 9233
Hall of Outstanding Americans 15986
Moss Hart Memorial Award 16125
Helen Hayes Awards 21463
American Theatre Wing's Henry Hewes Design Awards 4741
Barnard Hewitt Award 4199
Errol Hill Award 4200
John Hirsch Director's Award 16740
John Hirsch Prize 6798
Polly Holliday Award 19489
Host Awards 16126
K. M. Hunter Artists Awards 16742
Individual Artist Fellowship 13586
Innovative Educational Theatre Award 9182
Charles Jehlinger Award 642
Gerald Kahan Scholars Prize 4201
The KM Fabrics Technical Production Award 20646
Eric Kocher Playwrights Award 15507
Kryolon Makeup Design Award 20647
Robert G. Lawrence Prize 5286
Rosetta LeNoire Award 162
Lucille Lortel Award 12919
Marquee Award 20057
Thomas F. Marshall Travel Fellowship 4202
Heather McCallum Scholarship 5287
Monte Meacham Award 892
Medallion of Honor 20068
NATO Awards 14441
NEA/TCG Career Development Program for Designers 20052
NEA/TCG Career Development Program for Directors 20053
Norwood Cultural Council 9810
NTC Citation 15870
Outstanding School Award 9183
Outstanding Teacher of Theatre in Higher Education Award 5516
Outstanding Theatre Education 9184

Theater (continued)

Patron of the Year Award 12894
Performance Awards 16975
Antoinette Perry Awards (Tony Awards) 12742
Richard Plant Award 5288
Robert Porterfield Award 19490
President's Award 9185
Prix Denise-Pelletier 17795
Prix Victor-Morin 18615
Promising Playwright Award 8205
Regional Awards 16127
Research Award for Outstanding Booklength Study 5517
Research Award for Outstanding Journal Article 5518
Jessie Richardson Theatre Awards (Jessies) 10166
Ann Saddlemyer Award 5289
Ruben Salazar Award for Communications 14808
Sargent Award 643
Scenic Technology Award 20649
Alan Schneider Director Award 20054
Screenplay Contest 15995
William Shakespeare Award for Classical Theatre (Will Award) 18429
Source Awards 19425
Special Awards 16128
George Spelvin Award 13143
Sara Spencer Artistic Achievement Award 893
Stage Management Award 20650
State of Florida Fellowship 9589
Steadfast Service Award 20034
Jack Stein Make-up Award 16129
Harold and Mimi Steinberg Prize 15510
Student Design Competition 19491
TCG/MetLife Foundation Extended Collaboration Grants for Artists 20055
Theatre Grants 17555
Theatre Library Association Award 20060
Theatre World Awards 20062
The Village Voice OBIE Awards 21368
Winifred Ward & Award for Outstanding New Children's Theatre & Company 894
Zeta Phi Eta Winifred Ward Prize for Outstanding New Children's Theatre Company 895
Washington Theatre Festival Awards 19426
F. Loren Winship Secondary School Theatre Award 896
AATE Lin Wright Special Recognition Award 897
Zelma H. Weisfeld Costume Design & Technology Award 20653

Theology
ACP-CRM/CAP-CRM Prize in Theoretical and Mathematical Physics 13203
Exemplary Papers in Humility Theology 12404
Faith & Medicine Competitive Grant Award 12405
James K. Mathews Service Award 7982
John Courtney Murray Award 7662
Prize for Outstanding Books in Theology and the Natural Sciences 12411
Religion Reporter of the Year Award 12412
Science and Religion Course Program 12413

Cardinal John J. Wright Mariological Award 13114

Therapy *See* Rehabilitation and therapy

Third world *See* Economic development

Tourism *See* Travel

Town planning *See* City planning

Toxicology
AACT Research Award 633
Achievement Award 19330
AstraZeneca Traveling Lectureship Award 19331
Board of Publications Award for the Best Paper in *Toxicological Sciences* 19332
Cellular Toxicology Graduate Student Award 18723
Colgate-Palmolive Post-Doctoral Fellowship Award in In Vitro Toxicology 19333
Colgate-Palmolive/SOT Awards for Student Research Training in Alternative Methods 19334
Contributions to Public Awareness of the Importance of Animals in Toxicology Research Award 19335
Education Award 19336
Educational Research Award 19135
Enhancement of Animal Welfare Award 19337
Founders' Award 7995
Graduate Student Fellowship/Novartis Award 19338
Lampe-Kunkle Memorial Award 634
Arnold J. Lehman Award 19339
Thomas T. Mercer Joint Prize 956
Merit Award 19340
PMAC Health Research Foundation 6840
Public Communications Award 19341
Herbert E. Stokinger Award 2620

Toys
Award of Excellence 7516
Best Bet Awards 7517
Children's Choice Award 7518

Track and field
Academic Athletes of the Year (All Academic Team) 14691
Achievement Award 12810
All American Awards 14692
Association-of-the-Year Award 21212
Andy Bakjian Award 21213
John Bennett Award 21214
Big East Conference Academic Awards 6369
Abebe Bikila Award 16259
Gwilym Brown Award 21215
Coaches Association Awards 15309
Ted Corbitt Ultra Runner-of-the-Year Award 21216
Cross Country Contributor Award 21217
Horace Crow Award 21218
Glenn Cunningham Award 21219
Robert E. DeCelle Award 21220
Harrison Dillard Award 21221
District Coach of the Year 14693
ESPY Awards 9337
Otto Essig Award 21222
Robert Giegengack Award 21223
H. Browning Ross Long Distance Running Merit Award 21224

Scott Hamilton Award 21225
Bill Hargrove Award 21226
Doris Heritage Award 21227
Honorary Membership (Outstanding Contributors) 14694
C. C. Jackson Awards 21228
Male Thrower of the Year 21229
Masters Administrator of the Year 21230
Masters Long Distance Running Awards (Age Group) 21231
Masters Race Walking Award 21232
Jack Milne Memorial Award 558
National Coach of the Year 14695
National Track and Field Hall of Fame 21233
NCAA National Championships 14687
Outstanding Male and Female Athlete of the Year 14696
General George S. Patton, Jr. Memorial Trophy 20705
Roadrunners of the Year Award 18070
Joseph Robichaux Award 21237
Runner of the Year 21238
Frank Sevigne Award 21239
Special NJCAA Awards 15316
Jim Thorpe Award 21240
Track & Field News Award 21241
Ultra Distance Athlete-of-the-Year 21242
USATF Heptathlon Award 21243
Wheeler Cross Country Award 14667
Wheeler Track and Field Awards 14668
Women's Development Athletes-of-the-Year 21244
Captain Ron Zinn Memorial Awards 21245

Trade *See* Business; Finance; International trade

Trade shows *See* Conventions

Trade unions *See* Labor

Trades *See* Industries and trades

Training and development
AAS Distinguished Service Medallions 5100
Academy Fellow 125
Automotive Training Awards 6121
Awards for Excellence in Distance Learning 11090
Gordon M. Bliss Memorial Award 4204
Donald A. Buchannon Scholarship 20519
CAG Award for Service to the Profession of Geography 6911
Career Development Resource Award 7588
De Florez Award for Flight Simulation 2679
Dissertation Award 4205
Distinguished Contribution to Workplace Learning and Performance 4206
Education and Training Awards 5713
EMA Foundation School/Business Partnership Award 9256
Employers of the Year 10085
Environmental Education Award 14950
Harold Hammerman Spirit of Education Award 14434
HSMAI Hall of Fame 10556
George A. Kinias Service Award 14951
Mustang Spirit Award 13103
Outstanding Disabled Veteran Outreach Coordinator 8956

Training (continued)

President's Award for the Outstanding Conference Paper 14952
Public Policy Award 4207
In-Service Training Award in Memory of Clarence E. Ridley 11478
Torch Award 4208
Trainer of the Year Award 14953
P. J. Trevethan Award 10093
Twenty-Five Year Award 14462
The Venture Student Aid Awards 19420
Percy and Betty Wagner Award 5017
Women's Opportunity Awards 19421

Translations

Hiromi Arisawa Awards 5568
ASF Translation Prize 3879
Mildred L. Batchelder Award 5432
Pierre Francois Caille Memorial Medal 11606
Campana Translation Prize 12245
Canada - Japan Literary Awards 6788
CBC Literary Awards 6789
FIT - Translation Prize 11607
Soeurette Diehl Fraser Award for Best Book of Translation 20015
Lewis Galantiere Literary Translation Prize 4751
German Translation Award 4752
John Glassco Translation Prize 12874
Alexander Gode Medal 4753
Governor General's Literary Awards 6797
Japan-U.S. Friendship Commission Prize for the Translation of Japanese Literature 12526
Gregory Kolovakos Award 17141
FIT Astrid Lindgren Translation Prize 11608
PEN/Ralph Manheim Medal for Translation 17142
National Translation Award 3009
PEN Book-of-the-Month Club Translation Prize 17146
Pfizer Award 10489
Jacqueline A. Ross Dissertation Award 9178
Lois Roth Award for a Translation of a Literary Work 13568
Student Translation Award 4754

Transportation (*See also* Aeronautics and aviation; Automobiles; Automotive engineering; Automotive safety; Aviation safety; Helicopters; Highway safety; Navigation; Railway transportation; Trucking)

Achievement Awards 14165
ARTBA Award 3859
Award for Outstanding Research Paper 4620
Award of Achievement 15903
Award of Excellence 15904
Award of Valor 15905
Awards for Science and Ethics in Transportation Research 460
Bartelsmeyer Award 3860
George S. Bartlett Award 1431
Fred Burggraf Award 20159
Business and Industry Award 461
W. N. Carey, Jr. Distinguished Service Award 20160
Citizenship Award 20140
Connie Award 8472
Crane and Rigging Safety/Safety Improvement Awards 19575
Roy W. Crum Distinguished Service Award 20161
CSL Gold Medal 7814
Thomas B. Deen Distinguished Lectureship 20162
Department of Defense Distinguished Service Award 14905
Department of Transportation Award for Heroism 9431
Design for Humanity Award 4460
Distinguished Service Award
National School Transportation Association 15671
Specialized Carriers and Rigging Association 19576
Towing and Recovery Association of America 20141
Transportation Lawyers Association 20157
Distribution Executive of the Year 7161
Driver of the Year 16159
Driver of the Year Award 19577
Fleet Safety/Safety Improvement Awards 19578
Golden Achievement Award 19579
Golden Merit Award 15672
Golden Wheel Society Awards 3861
Hall of Fame Award 15673
Bill Harmer Award 6480
James E. Hatch Award 13079
Hauling Job of the Year Award 19580
Soichiro Honda Medal 4518
Innovative Intermodal Solutions for Urban Transportation Award 11049
International Award 462
Alfred E. Johnson Achievement Award 1432
Pyke Johnson Award 20163
Guy Kelsey Award 3862
Walt Klein Award 6481
John C. "Jake" Landen ARTBA Annual Highway Safety Award 3863
James Laurie Prize 4337
Life Membership Award 3864
Longevity Awards 19581
AIAA George M. Low Space Transportation Award 2686
Thomas H. MacDonald Memorial Award 1433
Man of the Year 11890
Maritime Heritage Award 10647
Marriott-Carlson Award 5549
Burton W. Marsh Distinguished Service Award 11050
Burton W. Marsh Graduate Fellowship 11051
Frank M. Masters Transportation Engineering Award 4339
Theodore M. Matson Memorial Award 11052
Medical Crew/Crew Member of the Year Award 5550
D. Grant Mickle Award 20164
Million Miler Award for Safety Excellence 19582
NAPT Distinguished Service Award 14026
National Award 463
National Fleet Safety Contests 15657
National Transportation Award 14906
NDTA Distinguished Service Award 14907
Outstanding Transportation & Logistics Executive in North America 4621
Helene Overly Scholarship 21814
The Partnership Award 4622
Past Presidents' Award for Merit in Transportation 11053
Paul F. Phelan Memorial Award 3865
Pinnacle Award 19583
President's Award 14908
President's Modal Awards 1434
Public Service Award 464
Rigging Job of the Year Award 19584
Safety Awards 16262
Section Activities Award 11054
Wilbur S. Smith Distinguished Transportation Educator Award 11055
Special President's Award of Merit 1435
S. S. Steinberg Award 3866
Student Chapter Award 11056
Student Paper Award 11057
Nello L. Teer, Jr. Award 3867
Toll Innovation Awards 11434
Transportation Achievement Award 11058
Transportation Man of the Year 8868
Transportation Person of the Year 15906
Transportation Professional of the Year 20155
Transportation Safety Awards 19585
John C. Vance Award 20165
Arthur M. Wellington Prize 4367
K. B. Woods Award 20166
WTS National Member of the Year 21815
WTS National Woman of the Year 21816
Young Consultants Award 11060
Zero Accident Awards 19586

Trapshooting *See* Skeet shooting

Travel

Ace Award 19821
Achievement Award 10452
AH&MA Achievement Awards 2567
Allied Member Award 4624
Arts and Tourism Grants Program 10430
ATME Atlas Awards 5902
ATME Awards 5903
Boeing Student Research Award 20170
John K. Bryan Scholarship 13537
Business of the Year 19458
Caribbean Hotel Association Awards 7592
Chairman's Award
Friends of the Pendleton District 9812
Pendleton District Historical, Recreational, and Tourism Commission 17160
Convention Service Manager of the Year 19822
Europa Award 9352
Five Star Hospitality Awards 18195
Friend of Tourism 9849
Gold Awards
Meetings and Conventions 13287
Pacific Asia Travel Association 16996
Hospitality Award 21527
HSMAI Golden Bell Public Relations Awards 10555
HSMAI Hall of Fame 10556
JTTM Award for Excellence in Travel and Tourism Education 12025
William B. Keeling Dissertation Award 20171
Albert E. Koehl Award 10557
Member of the Year Award
National Recreational Vehicle Owners Club 15587
Society of Recreation Executives 19288
Mobil Five-Star Award 9378

Travel (continued)

National Magazine Awards 15355
NATJA Awards Competition 16495
Francois L. Nivaud Award 13162
Outstanding Achievement Award 2461
Outstanding General Manager 2568
Outstanding Leadership Award 249
Outstanding Lodging Employee of the Year 2569
Outstanding Lodging Manager 2570
Outstanding Promotional Service Award 250
Outstanding Service Award 251
Peak Award 16367
Phoenix Award 19015
Pinnacle Awards for Convention and Visitor Bureaus 19823
Pinnacle Awards for Hotels/Resorts 19824
RRS Young Investigator Travel Award 17824
Ship of the Year 21938
J. Desmond Slattery Marketing Awards 20172
Student Intern Scholarship Award 13012
Tech-Savvy Hotels Award 8406
Lowell Thomas Travel Journalism Awards 19016
Tourism Award 16529
Tourism Employee Excellence Award 10128
Tourism Promotion Grant 10620
Travel Agent of the Year Award 4626
Travel Hall of Fame 4627
Travel Industry Hall of Leaders 20176
Travel Industry Odyssey Awards 20177
TTRA Achievement Award 20173
TTRA Travel Research Award 20174
U.S. Outdoor Travel Film Festival 13355
Frank M. Washburn Award 11316

Travel literature
HSMAI Adrian Advertising Awards 10554
Melva C. Pederson, CTC Award 4625
Lowell Thomas Travel Journalism Awards 19016

Trucking
Achievement Award 4765
ATA National Truck Driving Championships 4769
J. Frank Dickson Award 4766
Driver of the Year 20220
Driver of the Year Award 4770
Founder Award 4756
Founders Award
American Truck Historical Society, Arizona Chapter 4759
American Truck Historical Society, Metro Jersey Chapter 4763
Founders Award of American Truck Historical Society 4761
Industrial Safety Contest 4771
Motor Trend Truck of the Year 13628
Outstanding Associate Business Member of the Year 13375
Outstanding Member of the Year 13376
President's Trophy 4772
James E. Roelker Award 4767
Safe and Courteous Driver of the Year 13377
Safety Director of the Year Award 4774
Harris Saunders Sr. Award 4757
Truck Safety Contest 4775

Typography
Front Page Award 10814
National, City and Regional Magazine Editorial and Design Awards 8024
Quadrennial Prize for Bibliography 11718

Uniforms *See* Fashion

Unions *See* Labor

United States-Latin American relations (*See also* Hispanic culture)
Thomas F. Cunningham Award 21963
Pan American Gold Insigne of the Americas Society 4929
Pan American Gold Medal of the Americas Society 4930

Urban development *See* City planning

Vacuum technology
Fellow of the Society 6147
Gaede-Langmuir Award 6148
Graduate Research Award 6149
George T. Hanyo Award 6150
Dorothy M. and Earl S. Hoffman Award 6151
Dorothy M. and Earl S. Hoffman Scholarship 6152
Honorary Member 6153
Peter Mark Memorial Award 6154
Albert Nerken Award 6155
John A. Thornton Memorial Award and Lecture 6156
Russell and Sigurd Varian Fellowship 6157
John L. Vossen Memorial Award 6158
Medard W. Welch Award in Vacuum Science 6159
Nellie Yeoh Whetten Award 6160

Veterans *See* Military service

Veterinary medicine
AAHA Award 902
Pedro N. Acha Award for Veterinary Public Health 17057
American Feed Industry Association Award (AFIA) 4808
American Kennel Club Career Achievement Award in Canine Research 4809
American Kennel Club Excellence in Research Awards 4810
American Veterinary Medical Association Explorer Award 6573
Amstutz-Williams Award 1123
Animal Clinical Chemistry 974
Animal Growth and Development Award 4252
Animal Physiology and Endocrinology Award 4255
AVMA Award 4812
AVMA Student Chapter Certificates 19806
Bayer-Snoeyenbos New Investigator Award 1085
Best Booth in Show 4806
Pravin N. Bhatt Young Investigator Award 1023
Lasher-Bottorff Award 1086
Bustad Companion Animal Veterinarian Award 4814
L. E. Casida Award 4259
Charles River Prize 4815
CVMA Humane Award 7531
CVMA Plaque 7532
Distinguished Service Award 5533
Emeritus Award 21629
Excellence in Teaching Veterinary Parasitology 21853
Fort Dodge Animal Health - Bovine Practitioner of the Year Award 1124
Hill's Animal Welfare and Humane Ethics Award 903
Hoffman LaRoche-American Association of Bovine Practitioners Award for Excellence 1125
Industry Leadership Award 6876
Innovative Veterinary Diets Award 904
International Veterinary Congress Prize 4816
Aldo Leopold Memorial Award 21630
P.P. Levine Award 1087
James A. McCallam Award 5775
MSD AGVET AABP Award for Excellence in Preventive Veterinary Medicine Beef Cattle 1126
MSD AGVET AABP Award for Excellence in Preventive Veterinary Medicine Dairy Cattle 1127
Outstanding Contributions to Research in Veterinary Parasitology 21854
Outstanding Woman Veterinarian Award 5534
Peter Nancen Award for Young Scientists 21855
Pfizer Animal Health-AABP Distinguished Service Award 1128
Phibro Animal Health Excellence in Poultry Research Award 1088
E. P. Pope Award 1480
Practitioner of the Year Award 905
Practitioner Research Award 4817
President's Award
American Veterinary Medical Association 4818
Canadian Veterinary Medical Association 7533
Public Service Award 4819
Research Award 21856
Research Grant 1202
Royal Canin Award
American Animal Hospital Association 906
American Veterinary Medical Association 4820
RVL Walker Award 7534
Dr. Daniel E. Salmon Award 14226
Schering Veterinary Award 7535
Pamela Slack Award for Excellence 13372
Small Animal Practitioner Award 7536
Special Awards 10333
Special Service Award 1089
E. L. Stubbs Research Grant 13373
Student Achievement Award 907
Student Awards 21631
Summer Study Grants 20202

Victims
Tadini Bacigalupi Program of Distinction Awards 15442
Morton Bard Allied Professional Award 15443
John J. P. Dussich Founder's Award 15444
Margery Fry Award 15445
H. John Heinz Award 15446
Donald E. Santarelli Award for Public Policy 15447
Stephen Shafer Award 15448
Edith Surgan Award 15449

Victims (continued)

Volunteer of the Year Award 15450

Video
Academy & Achievement Awards 80
Academy of Country Music Awards 86
Agfa - Gevaert Gold Medal Award 19188
Amateur PSA/VMPD American International Film and Video Festival 17283
American Music Awards 3160
AMOA Games Awards 4944
Father Adrien Arsenault Senior Arts Award 17544
Artist Equipment Access Awards 6276
Artists' Fellowships 16229
Atlanta Film and Video Festival 6025
Atlantic Film Festival 6033
Award of Excellence 9541
Baltimore Independent Film/Video Makers Competition 6230
Bell Canada Award in Video Art 6785
Bi-Annual Image Awards 21734
Big Muddy Film Festival Awards 6372
Bronze Anvil Awards 17720
Bush Artist Fellows Program 6700
Canadian International Annual Film/Video Festival 7206
Andrew Carnegie Medal 5437
Central Florida Film and Video Awards 9724
Chicago International Children's Film Festival 7888
CINE Eagle Award 8608
CINE Golden Eagle Award 8609
CINE Master's Series Award 8610
Cin(E)-Poetry Festival 15512
Citations of Merit 13984
Christopher Columbus Award 7947
Columbus International Film and Video Festival 7948
Conservation/Outdoor Recreation Film/Video Award Program 16967
Country Music Association Awards 8620
Creative Video Productions Awards 21263
Dissertation Award 18651
Thomas A. Edison Black Maria Film and Video Festival 9161
Educational Aids Competition Blue Ribbon Awards 4219
Emmy Awards for Primetime Programming 127
Feature Video Photo Award 16247
Felix Awards, Artistic 188
Felix Awards, Industrial 189
Ben Franklin Award 7950
Gold and Platinum Video Awards 11884
Gold Medal of Honor for Film/Video 13989
Gold Music Video Award 17909
Gold Screen Awards 14243
Golden Gate Awards 18246
Golden Sheaf Awards 22048
Governor General's Awards in Visual and Media Arts 6796
HeSCA Video Festivals 10330
Hometown Video Festival 458
Humboldt International Film Festival 10610
ICIA Distinguished Achievement Award 11498
ILCA Film and Broadcast Competition 11699
INTERCOM: International Communication Film and Video Festival 8003
International ANDY Awards 11184
International Documentary Association Achievement Awards 11541
International Video Competition 18863
Juno Awards 6846
Jury Prize for the Dance on Camera Festival 8734
Kentucky Artists Fellowships 12562
Law Library Publications Award 1254
Literature and Video Awards 14277
Media Awards Competition 14862
Montreal International Festival of Films on Art 11613
Montreal International Festival of New Cinema and Video 13598
National Student Production Awards Competition 14539
New Mexico Juried Exhibition 13689
Northwest Film and Video Festival 16560
Outstanding Forestry Extension Video Award 15981
Petro-Canada Award in New Media 6805
James D. Phelan Art Awards 18250
Philadelphia International Film Festival (Philafilm Awards) 468
Platinum Music Video Award 17911
President's Award 7952
Public Affairs Competition 1276
Publications and Electronic Media Awards 15669
Readers' and Critics' Poll 18110
Rochester International Film Festival 18089
San Antonio Cine Festival 10188
Dore Schary Awards 4984
Science Screen Report Award 15691
SHINE (Sexual Health in Entertainment) Awards 13238
Southwest Juried Exhibition 13690
Spot News Video Award 16251
Telly Awards 19964
Lowell Thomas Travel Journalism Awards 19016
U.S. International Film and Video Festival 21143
Video Grand Prix Awards 6059
VSDA Home Entertainment Awards 21355
VSDA Presidential Award 21356
Young People's Film and Video Festival 16562

Visually impaired *See* Blindness

Violin competitions
CBC Radio National Competition for Young Performers 6999
Eckhardt-Gramatte National Competition for the Performance of Canadian Music 9129
International Competitions for New Instruments and Bows 21382
Mrs. Clare K. Mendal Memorial Senior Violin Scholarship and Trophy 18302
Robert C. Mitchell Memorial Intermediate Violin Scholarship and Trophy 18303
Naumburg International Competition 16045

Vocal music (*See also* Choral music; Opera)
Academy of Country Music Awards 86
The Roy Aikenhead Memorial Choral Scholarship 18272
AMOA Jukebox Awards 4945
Art Song Festival 8099
Artist Awards 14411
Artists International New York Debut Award Auditions 5143
Bach Competitions 17868
John Bettis Fellowship Award 19403
BMI Student Composer Awards 6643
William C. Byrd Young Artist Competition 18203
The Canticum Dominum Vocal Competition 6232
Career Grants 20229
CBC Radio National Competition for Amateur Choirs 6997
CBC Radio National Competition for Young Performers 6999
Competitive Awards 14970
Concerto Competition 18280
Contemporary A Cappella Recording Awards ("CARAs") 8474
Country Music Association Awards 8620
The Covey Girls' Voice Scholarship 18281
East & West Artists International Auditions 9067
Eckhardt-Gramatte National Competition for the Performance of Canadian Music 9129
The Goodfellow Memorial Award in Voice/ The Chief Justice J.T. Brown Shield 18286
The Goodfellow Memorial Canadian Vocal Music Scholarship 18287
The Goodfellow Memorial Grade A Female Voce Scholarship 18288
The Goodfellow Memorial Grade A Male Voice Scholarship 18289
The Goodfellow Memorial Lieder Scholarship 18290
The Goodfellow Memorial Operatic Scholarship 18291
Grammy Awards 13822
Grand Prize 7601
Guelph Spring Festival Music Competition 10190
Hall of Fame Awards 20336
The Heather Laxdal Memorial Vocal Award/ The Golan E. Hoole Memorial Shield 2281
Heida Hermanns International Competition 8408
Houston Opera Studio Member 10569
"Jeanie" Musical Scholarship Winner 9601
Joy In Singing Award Recital 12456
Juno Awards 6846
Kennedy Center Honors 12552
Robert Lauch Memorial Grant 21418
The Laxdal Memorial Grade B Female Voice Scholarship 18297
Eleanor Lieber Awards Competition 17471
Liederkranz Scholarship Awards Competitions 12839
Lifetime Achievement Award 19404
Ruth Lopin Nash Award 16812
MTNA Collegiate Artist Competition 13703
MTNA Senior Performance Competition 13706
Mu Phi Epsilon International Competition 13660
Music Center Spotlight Awards 13698
MUSICA SACRA Bach Vocal Competition 13710
Naumburg International Competition 16045
Rose Palmai-Tenser Scholarship 13547
Virginia Parker Award 6804
Polka Music Awards 11819
Readers' and Critics' Poll 18110
The Regan Grant Memorial Musical Theatre Scholarship 18307
Rhythm and Blues Award Show 6260

Vocal (continued)

The Saskatchewan Choral Federation Choral Scholarship 18308
Marcella Sembrich Scholarship in Voice 12614
Solo Competition 16813
Student and Young Professional Grant 21419
The Thoms Hatton Memorial Grade B. Male Voice Scholarship 18317
Richard Tucker Award 20230
University of Louisville Grawemeyer Award for Music Composition 21050
University of Maryland International Music Competitions 18567
The Wallis Memorial Scholarship 18319
Washington International Competition 9775
Young Soloists' Competition 15834

Vocational education (*See also* Industrial arts)
Automotive Aftermarket Education Award 16576
Award of Distinction 12064
Myer Barr Award 8905
CASE Award of Excellence 14878
Direct Vocational Special Needs Support Person of the Year 14057
Hefty Scholarship 6695
Barnett Helzberg Scholarship 8907
Paul R. Hoffman Award 15599
Indirect Provider of Major Support Services and Contributions to the Field of Vocational Special Needs Education Award 14058
MAPCS Scholarship Program 13131
National Court Reporters Foundation Scholarships 14883
NATTS Hall of Fame 7583
Outstanding Business, Industry, Organization, or Individual Contribution Award 15930
Outstanding Student Research Award 11947
Outstanding Vocational Educators 18550
Outstanding Vocational Special Needs Teacher of the Year 14059
Past President's Best Practices Award 15600
Professional Development Program Awards 18551
SkillsUSA Championships 18552
Special Recognition Citation 12071
Paul Storm Award 8908
Student Liaison Award 8444
Lode Van Bercken Award 8909
VEWAA Service Award 15601

Volleyball
All-American Awards 15307
Big East Conference Academic Awards 6369
Emil Breitkreutz Leadership Award - Volleyball 547
Coaches Association Awards 15309
Susan R. Hellings Award 14658
Metal Mining Division Award 7200
NCAA National Championships 14687
Jack Schatz Award 574
Tantramar Trophy 7236
Volleyball Coach of the Year 7242
Youth Softball Volunteer of the Year 583

Volunteerism
AAU Promotions Award 530
AAU Volunteer Hall of Fame 531
Ability Fund/ March of Dimes Canada 7372
Access Awards 2300
Achievement Awards 14165
Adult Volunteer of the Year 2393
AHA Hospital Awards for Volunteer Excellence 2541
ANAD Service Awards 14073
Award for Excellence in Workplace Volunteer Programs 17443
Awards for Excellence in Community Service, Philanthropy, and Media 19847
Awards of Distinction in Programs 15201
George Barco Volunteer of the Year 13227
Alan Barth Service Award 1811
Baseball Outstanding Volunteer Award 543
G. F. Bettineski Child Advocate of the Year Award 14874
Big Brother of the Year 6366
Big Chief Award 10097
Big Sister of the Year 6367
Bill Napoli Award 17218
Boys & Girls Club Medallion 6596
Sandy Brandt Volunteer Service Award 15373
H. Barksdale Brown Voluntarism Award 448
H. Barksdale Brown Volunteer/Community Service Award 449
Butch Henley Award 2453
Elizabeth Campbell Outstanding Public Broadcasting Award 15127
Chairman's Award 10082
Chapter Volunteer of the Year 12673
The Norman Cohn Hope Award 15394
Community Service Award 20255
The Congressional Award 8396
Corporate Leadership Award 15203
Davison Chamber of Commerce Service Scholarship 8758
Dedicated Service Award 19098
Directors Emeriti Award 12853
Distinguished Service Award 11301
Distinguished Women's Awards 16572
Charles R. Drew Award 3825
Eagle Awards for Volunteer Service 9056
Easter Seals Canada Award 7374
Epilepsy Foundation of America Awards 9308
Peggy Etter Student Travel Award Fund 2087
Exemplar of Humanics Award 2580
Clara Shortridge Foltz Award 15337
Founders Award 6606
Franklin Award for Volunteer Fire Assistance 9559
William F. and Catherine T. Gallagher Award 2301
John W. Gardner Leadership Award 10747
Girls' Basketball National Volunteer of the Year 552
Golden Acorn Award 13294
Samuel Gompers American Red Cross National Labor Award 3827
Goodwill Industries Volunteer Services (GIVS) Volunteer Group of the Year 10086
Goodwill Industries Volunteer Services (GIVS) Volunteer of the Year 10087
Mary M. Gooley Humanitarian of the Year Award 15205
Governor General's Awards in Commemoration of the Persons Case 19775
Group Volunteer of the Year Award 2395
Gymnastics National Volunteer of the Year 554
Hall of Fame 8623
Hall of Fame in Philanthropy 20350
Mary Ellen Hamilton Award 15338
Katherine Hamilton Volunteer of the Year Award 15376
Harriman Award for Distinguished Volunteer Service 3829
Robert Lee Henry Volunteer of the Year Award 15207
Hero Awards 5230
Charlotte Hill Volunteers in Fund-Raising Award 15128
Imagine Mutual Fund Industry Corporate Citizenship Award 10702
International Certificate of Appreciation 3830
Martha and Arlenis Joukowsky Distinguished Service Award 5033
Kal Kan Volunteer of the Year 2575
Helen Keller Achievement Awards 2302
Jim Kern Award 2455
Ketchum Award for Outstanding Volunteer Fundraiser 5703
Key Award 4268
Lewis Hine Awards 14652
Ann Magnussen Award 3833
Make a Difference Day Awards 17444
Carroll Sterling Masterson Award & Outstanding Women's Awards 22093
Merit Award
American Baptist Homes and Hospitals Association 1529
Gift from the Heart Foundation 10022
Migel Medal for Outstanding Service to Blind Persons 2303
Millbrook-Proctor and Gamble Student Service 13424
Jack Milne Memorial Award 558
Jan Mitchell Community Development Award 15129
National Club Achievement Competition 860
National Distinguished Service Awards 7271
National Recognition Award 601
National Treasure Award 22039
National Voluntary Service Award 15583
National Volunteer Disaster Services Award 3834
National Volunteer Leadership Award 1638
New Spirit of Community Partnership Awards Program 10703
Order of Honour Service Awards 17606
Order of Ontario 16757
Outstanding Individual Volunteer Award 2936
Outstanding International Service Award 10092
Outstanding Volunteer Clinical Teacher Award 1925
Outstanding Volunteer Service Award 15401
Outstanding Young Volunteer of the Year Award 12646
John A. Page Outstanding Service Award 10347
Parish Volunteer Award 7680
Partnership Award 3835

Volunteerism (continued)

Elaine Peterson Distinguished Service Award 15130
President's Award 3013
President's Community Volunteer Award 17445
President's Pro Bono Service Award 19761
Pro Bono Publico Awards 1536
Public Recreation Volunteer of the Year Award 569
Public Service Citations 21000
Public Service National Leadership Award 2456
Margaret Elden Rich Memorial Award 451
Lenore and George W. Romney Citizen Volunteer Award 17446
Will Ross Medal 3014
St. George National Award 1639
Lee E. Schauer Memorial Scholarship 18446
Alexander Scourby Narrator of the Year Award 2304
George H. Seal Memorial Trophy Award 8959
Senior High Youth Voluntarism Award 20916
Service Awards 2094
Service to Youth Award 6602
Fenmore R. Seton Distinguished Volunteer Award 17966
SFORZA Medal 5619
Raymond J. Sherwin Award 18470
Siedenburg Award 12972
Silver Antelope 6586
Silver Beaver 6587
Silver Buffalo Award 6588
Silver Medallion 6603
Joel Solomon Memorial Award 1115
Special Recognition Award 7273
Special Service Citation 2694
Spirit of America Award 20904
Sports and Recreation Award 17073
Summit Awards 20905
Dwain Taylor Award for Voluntary Service 17074
Teen Volunteer of the Year 2396
Trail Development Award 2458
Louis S. Tregre Award 14771
Trustee of the Year Award 1233
Volunteer Achievement Award 19634
Volunteer Award
- Audubon Naturalist Society of the Central Atlantic States 6070
- Nature Canada 16029

Volunteer Fund Raiser of the Year 3839
Volunteer of the Year
- Lupus Foundation of America, Arkansas Chapter 12985
- Pacific Center for Human Growth 16998

Volunteer of the Year Award
- Audubon Society of New Hampshire 6085
- Easter Seals 9091
- National Organization for Victim Assistance 15450
- Ouachita Council on Aging 16961
- Planned Parenthood Federation of Canada 17372

Volunteer of the Year/Volunteer Group of the Year 20355
Volunteer Service Award
- American Lawyers Auxiliary 2937
- National Kidney Foundation 15327

Volunteerism Award
- Illinois Library Association 10688
- YMCA of the United States of America 22040

Volunteers of the Year 16286
Arthur von Briesen Award 15340
Martin Wagner Memorial Award 15328
Cynthia Wedel Award 3840
Bill Wilcox Award 2459
Evelyn Willis Award 18431
Woodrow Wilson Award 3841
Wohelo Order 6776
YMCA Men, Women and Youth of the Year 22037
Youth Softball Volunteer of the Year 583

Walking *See* Track and field

Water conservation

Award for Excellence in Environmental Conservation 15419
Business Conservation Leadership Award 14149
Distinguished Service Award 15932
Excellence in Communications Awards 14153
Farm Management Conservation Award 14154
National Water and Energy Conservation Award 12205
Paul L. Busch Award 21504
Special Recognition Award 14159
Special Service Award 14160

Water pollution control

AMRC P&E Awards 5793
William T. Hornaday Bronze and Silver Medals 6579
William T. Hornaday Gold Certificate 6580
William T. Hornaday Gold Medal 6581
William T. Hornaday Unit Award 6582

Water polo

Curren Award 20881
United States Water Polo Award 20886

Water resources (*See also* Sanitary engineering)

William C. Ackermann Medal for Excellence in Water Management 4822
Inge Anderson Award 7070
Award of Achievement 17099
Award of Merit 16131
AWRA Board of Directors Service Awards 4823
AWRA Outstanding State Section Award 4824
The Best Paper Award 12126
William R. Boggess Award 4825
Dexter Brackett Memorial Award 16132
Business Conservation Leadership Award 14149
Canham Graduate Studies Scholarship 21477
Henry P. Caulfield, Jr. Medal for Exemplary Contributions to National Water Policy 4826
Chow Memorial Endowed Lecturer 12127
Francis X. Crowley Scholarship 16133
Crystal Drop Award 12128
Sandor C. Csallany Institutional Award for Exemplary Contributions to Water Resources Management 4827
Distinguished Drinking Water Public Involvement Award 16134
Drinking Water Protection Business Awards Program 16135
Farm Management Conservation Award 14154
Fellow Member 4828
Max Hecht Award 5954
Richard A. Herbert Memorial Scholarships 4829
Karl Emil Hilgard Hydraulic Prize 4323
Kenneth O. Hodgson Distinguished Service Award 16136
Honorary Member
- American Water Resources Association 4830
- New England Water Works Association 16137

William T. Hornaday Bronze and Silver Medals 6579
William T. Hornaday Gold Certificate 6580
William T. Hornaday Gold Medal 6581
William T. Hornaday Unit Award 6582
Icko Iben Award 4831
IWRA Distinguished Lecturer 12129
Elson T. Killam Memorial Scholarship 16138
Laboratory Analyst Excellence Award 21493
Mary H. Marsh Medal for Exemplary Contributions to the Protection and Wise Use of the Nation's Water Resources 4832
National Awards for Environmental Sustainability - Searching for Success Program 17991
NEWWA Scholarships 16139
Outstanding Student Chapter Award 4833
Past Presidents' Award 16140
President's Award for Outstanding Service 4834
Pyramid Award 4835
Save Our Streams Award 12270
Student Award 7071
Trans Atlantic Reciprocal Award 16141
Dr. Robert O. Vernon Memorial Lecture Award 11538
Water Quality Improvement Man of the Year Award 11539
Water Statesman of the Year 15933
Water Works State Leadership Award 16142

Water safety

Award of Merit 15935
Dr. Charlie Brown Memorial Award 14449
Certificate of Merit 3822
Leonard Greenstone Diving Safety Award 14450
Craig Hoffman Memorial Award 20290
National Award 15936
NOGI Awards 20295
Oceaneering International Award 20291
President's Award 15937
Regional Awards 15938
Regional Diver of the Year Award 20296
Safety in Seas Award 15420
Service Awards 14451
Charles W. Shilling Award 20292

Water sports (*See also* Boating; Diving; Fishing; Rowing; Surfing; Swimming; Water polo)

Coach of the Year Award 20394

Water (continued)

Director's Award 15364
John R. Felix Memorial Award 20882
Hall of Fame 20883
James W. Lee Memorial Award 20884
Moose Moss Age Group Diving Coach of the Year Award 20397
NOGI Awards 20295
Open Division Overall 21252
Mike Peppe Award 20399
James R. "Jimmy" Smith - U.S. Water Polo Award 20885
David Yorzyk Memorial Award 20400

Watercolor painting (*See also* Painting)
Adirondacks National Exhibition of American Watercolors 5153
Annual Exhibition
Allied Artists of America 473
National Watercolor Society 15940
Aqueous USA Exhibition 12570
Arjomaria/Arches/Rivers Award 4840
Art of the Northeast Competition 18521
The Artist's Magazine Award 4841
AWS Bronze Medal of Honor 4842
AWS Gold Medal of Honor 4843
AWS Silver Medal of Honor 4844
Boynton's G.A.L.A. Artist Awards 6594
Harrison Cady Award 4845
Elizabeth Callan Memorial Medal 4846
Cannon Prize 13780
Cape Cod Art Association Awards 7571
Certificates of Merit 13783
CFS Medal 4847
Mario Cooper Award 4848
Dolphin Medal 4849
Ann Williams Glushien Award 4850
Emily Goldsmith Award 4851
Hardie Gramatky Memorial Award 4852
Grand National Exhibition 930
Walser S. Greathouse Medal 4853
High Winds Medal 4854
Honorary Member 4855
International Art Show by Artists with Disabilities 18536
KWS Great 8 Exhibition 12500
Samuel Leitman Memorial Award 4856
Mary S. Litt Medal 4857
Emily Lowe Memorial Award 4858
Marthe T. McKinnon Award 4859
Barse Miller Memorial Award 4860
Lucy B. Moore Memorial Award 4861
National Small Painting Exhibition 16192
National Watercolor Society Arts and Humanities Award 15941
Lena Newcastle Award 4862
Adolph and Clara Obrig Prize 13792
William A. Paton Prize 13795
Mary Pleissner Memorial Award 4863
Ogden Pleissner Memorial Award 4864
Prix de West Invitational Exhibition 14886
Nicholas Reale Memorial Award 4865
Red Cloud Indian Art Show 10424
Paul B. Remmey AWS Memorial Award 4866
Rocky Mountain National Watermedia Exhibition Awards 9679
Paul Schwartz Memorial Award 4867
William P. and Gertrude Schweitzer Prizes 13797
Clara Stroud Memorial Award 4868
Ida Wells Stroud Memorial Award 4869
Traveling Show Appreciation Award 4870
Watercolor U.S.A. 19734
Edgar A. Whitney Award 4871
Winsor and Newton Award 4872
John Young - Hunter Memorial Award 4873

Waterfowl management *See* Wildlife conservation

Weather *See* Meteorology

Weightlifting
Powerlifting National Hall of Fame 20738
Special Medals for Fitness Achievement 11591

Welding
Comfort A. Adams Lecture Award 4875
Adams Memorial Membership Award 4876
Howard E. Adkins Memorial Instructor Membership Award 4877
Arsham Amirikian Memorial Maritime Welding Award 4878
Awards for Achievement in Arc Welded Design, and Engineering and Fabrication 12851
Robert J. Conkling Memorial Award 4879
A. F. Davis Silver Medal Award 4880
Dalton E. Hamilton Memorial CWI of the Year Award 4881
McKay - Helm Award 4882
W. H. Hobart Memorial Medal Award 4883
Honorary Membership Award 4884
William Irrgang Memorial Award 4885
Charles H. Jennings Memorial Award 4886
James F. Lincoln Gold Medal Award 4887
Professor Koichi Masubuchi Award 4888
Samuel Wylie Miller Memorial Medal Award 4889
National Meritorious Award 4890
Robert L. Peaslee Brazing Award 4891
Plummer Memorial Educational Lecture Award 4892
Safety and Health Award 4893
Warren F Savage Memorial Award 4894
Silver Quill Editorial Achievement Award 4895
William Spraragen Memorial Membership Award 4896
R. D. Thomas Memorial Award 4897
Elihu Thomson Resistance Welding Award 4898
Prof. Dr. Rene D. Wasserman Memorial Award 4899
George E. Willis Award 4900

Welfare *See* Child welfare; Social service

Wildlife conservation (*See also* Environmental conservation)
Ambassador Award 9471
Edward H. Bean Award 4913
Benefactor Award 15908
Bill Griffiths Memorial Conservation Award 20213
Andrew J. Boehm Graduate Fellowship in the Fisheries Sciences 4671
Boone and Crockett Award 11357
Buffalo Hall of Fame 14518
Certificate of Appreciation 15909
Doug Clarke Conservation Award 7539
Conservation Awards 4914
Director of the Year 15910
Distinguished Service Award 20209
Education Award 4915
Exhibit Award 4916
FFF Conservation Award 9475
J. Paul Getty Wildlife Conservation Prize 21967
Gold Trout Award 20210
Seth Gordon Award 11358
Stan Hodgkiss Canadian Outdoorsman Award 7540
Honor Award 21612
William T. Hornaday Bronze and Silver Medals 6579
William T. Hornaday Gold Certificate 6580
William T. Hornaday Gold Medal 6581
William T. Hornaday Unit Award 6582
International Wildlife Film Festival 12141
Roger M. Latham Sportsman Service Award 15949
Leadership Award 15911
Lifetime Achievement Award 15954
Roland Michener Conservation Award 7541
Henry S. Mosby Award 15950
National Awards for Environmental Sustainability - Searching for Success Program 17991
NWRA Grants 15955
Sigurd T. Olson Common Loon Research Award 12917
Outstanding Law Enforcement Achievement Award 11359
Past Presidents' Canadian Legislator Award 7543
President's Award 15912
Dave Reed Memorial Award 15913
Restaurant Award of Excellence 14519
Ernest Thompson Seton Award 11360
Significant Achievement Award 15956
Special Act Award 15381
Trapper/Conservationist Award 15914
Trapper of the Year 15915
Trout Conservationist of the Year 20211
C. W. Watson Award 2262
Wildlife Leadership Awards 18099

Wine
Award of Merit - Life Member 4906
The James Beard Foundation Restaurant Awards 12287
Best Wine Lists in America Awards 18011
Chardonnay Challenge 20986
Commercial Wine Competition Awards 4907
Distinguished Service Award 21648
French Wine and Spirits Sommelier Competition 21651
Gold Vine Award 6657
Grand Award 21649
Honorary Life Members 4908
Honorary Research Lecture 4062
HWBTA Service Award 10522
Journal Contributor Awards 4909
Merit Award 4063
National Amateur Wine Competition Awards 4910
Outstanding Member 4911
OWA Founders Award/President's Award 16866
Vinifera Perpetual Monteith Trophy Award 21372
Virginia Wine Competition 21373
Wine Research Award 19182
Winegrape Productivity Trophy 21374

Women
The Abafazi-Africana Women's Studies Essay Award 15965
Alice Abel Cultural and Creative Arts Program 3141
Achievement Award
American Association of University Women Educational Foundation 1469
Foundation of American Women in Radio and Television 9715
Society of Women Engineers 19363
Jane Addams Medal 18095
Advertising Woman of the Year 214
Affiliated Group Award 1866
The Gracie Allen Awards 9716
Dr. J. Frances Allen Scholarship Award 2254
American Agri-Women Awards 864
Angel of the Year 21757
Annual Exhibition Awards 14457
Annual Open Exhibition 5121
Athena Award
Kankakee River Valley Chamber of Commerce 12481
North San Antonio Chamber of Commerce 16533
Award for Encouraging Women into Careers in the Chemical Sciences 1730
Award of Recognition 21767
AWIS Educational Foundation Predoctoral Award 5530
AWIS Educational Foundation Undergraduate Award 5531
Robertine Barry Prize 7376
Evelyn Bauer Prize 11826
Gladys Bean Memorial Trophy 7209
Naomi Berber Memorial Award 10132
Patty Berg Award 12650
Jessie Bernard Award 4648
Carroll L. Birch Award 3077
Joan Fiss Bishop Award 18403
Susan Smith Blackburn Prize 19854
Barbara Bradley Award 16109
Maureen Connolly Brinker Award 20853
The Bronze Baby 7211
Antoinette Brown Award 20324
Pearl S. Buck International Woman of the Year Award 17129
Budget Service Award 12651
Mildred Bulpitt Woman of the Year Award 1068
Helen Caldicott Leadership Award 21769
Candace Award 14678
Annie Jump Cannon Award in Astronomy
American Association of University Women Educational Foundation 1470
American Astronomical Society 1511
CAR Coach of the Year Award 21806
Career Development Grants 1471
Celebrating Women Awards 21791
CEO Recognition Award 21760
Renate W. Chasman Scholarship for Women 6649
Rodney D. Chipp Memorial Award 19364
Citation of Merit Award 21726
U.S. Sailing/Rolex Junior Women's Championship - Nancy Leiter Clagett Trophy 20771
Clarion Awards 5522
Coach of the Year 12652
Commissioner's Award 12653
Communicator of Achievement Award 14972
Continuum Women's Studies Award 8672
Helen Copeland Scholarship 20409
Nan Copp Award 7212
Corporate and Professional Firm Leadership Award 7627
Creative Caf Sound Completion & Design Grant 21712
Jane Cunningham Croly/GFWC Print Journalism Award 9916
Crystal Award 14311
Crystal Awards 21713
Crystal Prism Award 215
Charlotte Danstrom Award 21746
Sarah Palfrey Danzig Award 20854
Sally Deaver Award 20802
Deborah Award 2894
Carolyn Desjardins President of the Year Award 1069
Distinguished Engineering Educator Award 19365
Distinguished Member Award 21738
Distinguished New Engineer Award 19366
Distinguished Research Award 18404
Distinguished Service Award 5533
Distinguished Woman Philosopher Award 18937
Distinguished Women's Awards 16572
Doctoral Dissertation Grants in Women's Studies 21825
Muriel Duckworth Award 7377
Marian Engel Award 22004
Peter Ennis Award 7215
Essay Contest 15452
FASEB Excellence in Science Award 9462
Fellowship Program 1472
Female Athlete of the Year
Sport Canada 19627
United States Rowing Association 20747
Feminist Activist Award 19376
Feminist Lecturer Award 19377
The Femmy Awards 9531
FEW Distinguished Service Award 9453
Geis Memorial Award 3731
Eloise Gerry Fellowships 18479
Diana Fell Gilmore - Woman Behind the Scenes Award 20418
Janet M. Glasgow Achievement Award 3078
Glasgow-Rubin Student Achievement 3079
Gold Medal Award 19360
Golden Pig Award 9533
Governor General's Awards in Commemoration of the Persons Case 19775
Headliner Award 5523
Heart of America 2952
Susan R. Hellings Award 14658
Julia Henderson Service to the Section Award 18405
Catherine "Cathy" Hensel Award 9026
Heritage Award 3732
Doris Heritage Award 21227
Honorary Fellow of the Genesis Academy 9924
Honorary Member
National Federation of Press Women 14973
Sigma Delta Epsilon - Graduate Women in Science 18480
Honorary memberships 7378
Honoree of the Year Award 14459
Humanist Heroine Award 2589
Hyde Graduate Student Research Award 3733
Hyde Graduate Student Research Grant 3734
Flo Hyman Memorial Award 21807
Illinois - NWSA Graduate Scholarship Award 15966
Rewey Belle Inglis Award 14834
International Award 21717
International Golden Rose Award 21727
International Recognition and Scholarship Award 11410
International Women's Sports Hall of Fame 21808
C. C. Jackson Awards 21228
Elaine Osborne Jacobson Award for Women Working in Health Care Law 18121
Laura Jamieson Prize 7379
"Jeanie" Musical Scholarship Winner 9601
Jewish Prize 15967
Mrs. Lyndon B. Johnson Award 12531
Erik Judeen Memorial Award 20808
Junior Female Athlete of the Year 19628
Joan Kelly Memorial Prize 2477
Billie Jean King Contribution Award 21809
Mandayam Chakravarthi Krishnan Award for Educational Excellence 9926
Leadership Award 18912
Leaven Award 865
Rosetta LeNoire Award 162
Lerner-Scott Dissertation Prize 16892
IFA Bonny LeVine Award 11639
Elizabeth Lewin Award 14649
Erv Lind Award 587
Augusta Ada Lovelace Award 5525
Pat Lowther Memorial Award 12745
Loyola Camellia 12970
LPGA Hall of Fame 12656
Tad Lucas Memorial Award 18103
Margaret W. Rossiter History of Women in Science Prize 10488
Phyllis B. Marriott President's Award 3142
Carroll Sterling Masterson Award & Outstanding Women's Awards 22093
Matrix Award 16312
Mature Women Scholarship Grant 15334
McKinney Award 15412
Medal of Appreciation 15776
Melpomene Outstanding Achievement Award 13289
Mentorship Award 19378
Marina Van Der Merwe Award 7225
Cheryl Allyn Miller Scholarship 19379
Minority Scholarship 19380
Miss America 13495
Miss America Women's Achievement Award 13496
Money for Women/Barbara Deming Memorial Fund Grants 13582
Elizabeth Cutter Morrow Award 22096
Most Active Woman Award 13908
Mother of the Year 3143
Doris Muellen Whirly-Girls Scholarship 21599
Frances Pomeroy Naismith Award 13752
National Achievement Award 14312
National Appreciation Award 14313
National Citation 13614
National Club Championship Award (Women) 20759
National College Championship Award (Women) 20762
National Community Service Award 14314
National Conference of Puerto Rican Women Award 14721
National Women's Hall of Fame 15960

Women (continued)

National Youth Award 14315
NCAA National Championships 14687
Hilda Neatby Prize 7155
Ninety-Nines NIFA Awards 16365
Officer of the Year Awards 11411
Outstanding Achievement Award 19361
Outstanding Elected Democratic Woman Holding Public Office 14967
Outstanding Lithuanian Woman Award 12876
Outstanding Mother Award 15392
Outstanding NFDW Member of the Year 14968
Outstanding Woman Veterinarian Award 5534
Outstanding Women in Music Award 19936
Outstanding Women of Color 11265
Helene Overly Scholarship 21814
Ethel Parham Memorial Award 3144
PEN/Jerard Fund Award 17147
Pioneer Women of the Podium 21728
Marion Porter Prize 7380
William and Mousie Powell Award 12657
President's Award
Advertising Women of New York 216
Women's Sports Foundation 21810
Professional of the Year 12658
Susy Pryor Award 5083
Public Service Award 14723
Recognition Award for Young Scholars 1473
REcognized ACHievement-REACH Awards for Women 22091
Research Award on Psychotherapy with Women 3735
Resnik Challenger Medal 19368
Loretta Richards Distinguished Alumni Award 8182
Robe of Achievement 18421
Joseph Robichaux Award 21237
Rolex International Women's Keelboat Championship 20779
Rolex Player of the Year 12659
Rolex Rookie of the Year 12660
Eleanor Roosevelt Fund Award 1474
The Rose of Sharon Award 9927
Runner of the Year 21238
Safe Mileage Award 21763
Samaritan Award 12661
Scholarships and Research Grants, Behavioral Studies 14650
Elizabeth L. Scott Award 8294
Scroll of Excellence 21729
Scroll of Honor 19937
SDE Fellowships 18481
Search for New Music 11179
Section on the Psychology of Black Women Award 3736
Carolyn Wood Sherif Award 3737
Mary Isabel Sibley Fellowship 17245
Silver Baton Award 21730
Silver Medal Award 217
Silver Medallion Award 4939
Silver Satellite Award 9717
Small Business Advocates of the Year 20834
Georgina Smith Award 1467
William I. Spencer Award 22097
Sportswomen of the Year Awards 21811
Susan B. Anthony Award 22099
Sweepstakes Winner 14975
Teacher of the Year 12662
Tennis Educational Merit Award for Women 12078
Bertha Tickey Award 589
Top Ten Business Women of ABWA 1610
Tribute to Women Award 22076
Wava Banes Turner Award 19938
Twin Tribute to Women and Industry 22080
U.S. Catholic Award 20442
U.S. Women's Open Championships 20787
U.S. Women's Sailing Championship - Mrs. Charles Francis Adams Trophy 20788
Upward Mobility Award 19369
USATF Heptathlon Award 21243
USO Woman of the Year 21259
USWCA Senior Ladies Trophy 20888
Van de Vate Prize for Orchestral Music 11180
Vare Trophy 12663
Wade Trophy 14014
WAND Family Award 21770
Martha Washington Medal 15785
Wauwatosa Event 20889
WBDNA Achievement Award 21731
WBDNA Performing Artists Award 21732
WCA Honors 21789
Western Political Science Association Awards 21557
Nellie Yeoh Whetten Award 6160
Whirly-Girls Helicopter Flight Training Scholarship 21600
WISE Award for Engineering Achievement 21753
WISE Award for Scientific Achievement 21754
WISE Lifetime Achievement Award 21755
WITI Hall of Fame 21761
WMA National Service Award 21765
Woman Lawyer of the Year 21785
Woman of the Year 9489
Women at Work Awards 21618
Women Helping Women Awards 14074
Women Making History-Essay Contest 16655
Women of Color Recognition Award 6427
Women of Enterprise Awards 6145
Women of Excellence 22078
Women of the Year 20755
Women's Advocate Award 9521
Women's National Book Association Award 21800
Women's Opportunity Awards 19421
Mickey Wright Award 10075
Katharine Wright Memorial Award 13881
WSS Achievement in Women's Studies Librarianship Awards - Career Achievement Award 5620
WTS National Member of the Year 21815
WTS National Woman of the Year 21816
Young Mother Representative 3145

Women's rights

Martin Abzug Memorial Award 15962
ALA Equality Award 2967
Alice Award 15958
American Woman of the Year 18209
BUDDY Award (Bringing Up Daughters Differently) 12768
Diana Donald Award 3557
Equal Opportunity Award 12769
Erasmus Correll Award 12862
Exceptional Media Merit Award 15963
Muriel Fox Communications Award 12770
Glenayre Award 21804
Constance E. Hamilton Award 8049
Alice Paul Award 12863
Catherine Roraback Award 8682
Woman of Courage 13872

Wood and wood products (*See also* Forestry; Paper industry)

Associate of the Year 12976
Craftsman Degree 15970
Design Award 8788
Distinguished Service Award 19371
Environmental and Energy Achievement Award 2291
Floor of the Year Contest 15971
Harold Butner Award 8789
Honorary Life Member 16550
Honorary Vanguard Degree 15972
Lumberman of the Year 12977
L. J. Markwardt Award 5970
George Marra Award 19372
Master Craftsman Degree 15973
National Exhibition of Woodworking in the Norwegian Tradition 21318
Northeastern Loggers' Association Awards Program 16548
Outstanding Research Award 15186
Prints, Drawings and Photographs Exhibition 5071
Smithsonian Craft Show 18574
Vanguard Degree 15974
Wood Design Award 2292

Work safety *See* Occupational safety

World peace

Jane Addams Children's Book Award 12296
AMVETS Silver Helmet Awards 4949
Appalachian Ohio Peace Prize 4999
Athletes United for Peace Award 6021
Awards for Excellence 18865
Builders of a Better World Prize 21899
Ralph Bunche Award 21461
Goler T. Butcher Award for Lifetime Achievement 10051
Helen Caldicott Leadership Award 21769
Winston Churchill Memorial Award 14635
Charles DeBenedetti Prize in Peace History 17127
Dharmaraja - King of Dharma 11342
Distinguished Contribution Award 17700
Distinguished Contribution to Building Cultures of Peace 17701
Distinguished Peace Leadership Award 16589
Distinguished Peacekeeper Award 11795
Distinguished World Citizen 9801
Eisenhower Medallion 17216
William J. Flynn Initiative for Peace Award 14701
William C. Foster Fellows Visiting Scholars Program 20402
Fountain of Universal Peace Award 11343
Friend of the Legal Profession Award 12590
Ghandi Peace Award 17681
Grant Program 20655
W. Averell Harriman Democracy Award 14910
Margaret S. Herrman Founder's Award 14725
Abraham Joshua Heschel Peace Award 12370

World (continued)
Hubert H. Humphrey Doctoral Fellowships in Arms Control and Disarmament 20403
IAEWP Diploma of Honour 11344
International Children's Peace Prize 7897
Barbara Mandigo Kelly Peace Poetry Awards 16590
Martin Luther King, Jr. Award 9528
Lentz International Peace Research Award 12779
Liberty Award 10372
Manhattan College Pacem in Terris Medal 13052
National Peace Essay Contest 20656
Norman Cousins Award 21901
Office of the Americas Peace & Justice Award 16616
Peace Education Awards 17820
Peace Play Contest 10095
Peace Profiles 17821
Peace Quilt Awards 6498
Pfeffer Peace Prize 9529
Presidential Medal of Freedom 9364
Psychological Dimensions of Peacework Award 17702
Jennings Randolph Program for International Peace 20657
Theodore Roosevelt Distinguished Service Medal 20066
Rotary Award for World Understanding and Peace 18129
Rothko Chapel Oscar Romero Award 18132
Joel R. Seldin Award 17703
Shalom Peace Award 12367
Frank Chapman Sharp Memorial Prize 3431
Dr. Phillip Sigal Peace and Justice Scholarship 9187
Significant Achievement Award 18130
Swackhamer Peace Essay Contest 16591
U Thant Peace Award 20364
Harry S. Truman Good Neighbor Award 20226
University of Louisville Grawemeyer Award for Ideas Improving World Order 21042
VFP Medal 21330
VFW Dwight David Eisenhower Distinguished Service Award 21337
WAND Family Award 21770
Will Wittkamper Peace Award 8961
World Citizen Humanitarian 9802
World Food Policy Award 277
World Methodist Peace Award 21936
World Peace Academy Diploma 11346

Wrestling
AAU Outstanding Wrestling Official of the Year 529
AAU Wrestling Person of the Year 532
All-American Awards 15307
Association Wrestling Award 540
Coach of the Year Awards 15983
Coaches Association Awards 15309
Hall of Outstanding Americans 15986
Medal of Courage 15987
Most Outstanding Wrestler 15984
National Wrestling Hall of Fame Distinguished Member 15988
NCAA National Championships 14687
Order of Merit 15989
Ben Peterson Christian Sportsmanship Award 14663
Dave Schultz High School Excellence Award 15990
Sustained Superior Performance Award 577
Willard T. (Billy) Vandiver Award 580
Wrestling Coach of the Year 7243

Writing
Asian American Literary Awards 5169
Aspen Gold Award 10358
Award for Notable Endeavor ("The Jane") 12298
High School Literary Arts Award 412
Imitate Keeler Contest 10268
Judy Goddard/Libraries Limited Awards 5057
Molly Award 10359
Harry T. Moore Award 8702
Morrison Book Prize 20100
New Scholar Award 8703
Saidi-Sirjani Memorial Book Prize 11937
Writers in Performance Literary Competition 18399

Yachting *See* Boating

Youth achievement
AMHA Youth of the Year Award 3126
AMHAY Horsemastership Awards 3128
Arts Recognition and Talent Search (ARTS) 15117
Barry Moffatt Award 22084
Chester County Youth Community Hero 20908
U.S. Sailing/Rolex Junior Women's Championship - Nancy Leiter Clagett Trophy 20771
Club of Champions Award 7678
The Congressional Award 8396
Dial Award 20129
Eagle Scout 6577
Explorer Leadership Award 6578
Fire Explorer Post Award 11352
Lifesaving and Meritorious Action Awards of the National Court of Honor 6585
Miss Galaxy 9853
National Youth of the Year Award 6601
Naturalistes de l'Annee 7781
Outstanding Young Volunteer of the Year Award 12646
Parish Volunteer Award 7680
President's Challenge Physical Fitness Awards Program 17541
Scholarship Contests 15782
School & Community Award for Youth in Health & Safety 3837
Shawn Barnett Memorial Award 22085
Sudler Shield 19434
Teen Volunteer of the Year 2396
Teenage Youth Award 7681
Trophee Environment 7782
Trophees Desjardins 7783
U.S. Sailing/Rolex Junior Championships 20784
Voice of Democracy Scholarship Program 12647
Woodrow Wilson Award 3841
J. W. Woomer Award 18829
Young American Awards 6592
Young American Creative Patriotic Art Competition 12648
Young American Medal for Bravery 20506
Young American Medal for Service 20507
Young People's Film and Video Festival 16562
Youth Arts Awards 20233
Youth as Resources 12740
Youth Leadership Award 21562
Youth of the Year 17091
Youth Recognition Award 22086
Youth World Championship Horse Show Golden Horse 17051

Youth work
Achievement Awards 14165
Achievement in the Arts Award 16575
Aleph Award 15297
Allegro Award 17172
American Center for Children's Television - Fran Allison Award 1663
AMVETS National Awards Program 4947
AYH Pioneer Leader Award 10559
Chester A. Berry Scholar Award for Excellence in Writing 5629
G. F. Bettineski Child Advocate of the Year Award 14874
Book Awards 7913
Boys & Girls Club Medallion 6596
Citation Award 6162
Crescendo Award 17173
DeLaval, Inc. Dairy Extension Award 2100
Distinguished Service to Children Award 17087
District Award of Merit 6576
George M. Elsey Award for Outstanding Involvement of Youth 3826
Etz Chaim (Tree of Life) Award 15298
Fellow 3905
Gold and Silver Medals 16439
Gold Medallion 6597
Golden Triangle Award 10560
Golden Youth Awards 6598
Honor Awards for Program Excellence 6599
Herbert Hoover Humanitarian Award 6600
William T. Hornaday Bronze and Silver Medals 6579
Houseparents Length of Service Awards 10561
Interpret America Award 10562
Robert B. Johnson Award 10563
Judge of the Year Award 14875
Junior Golf Leader 17616
Kappa Alpha Theta Program Director of the Year Award 14876
Lewis Hine Awards 14652
Maccabee Award 15299
Ronald McDonald House Charities Awards of Excellence 18117
Meritorious Trophy 6163
Merrill-Palmer Citation Award 21506
Ruth and Bill Nelson Award 10565
Robert C. O'Hair Memorial Award 12268
On Behalf of Youth Award 6775
Open Door Award 10566
Ora Award 15303
Order of Red Triangle 22036
Outstanding Total Youth 8070
Outstanding Youth Project 8071
Maurice Pate Memorial Award 20597
Professionalism Award 19962
Psi Chi/Florence L. Denmark National Faculty Advisor Award 17697
Theodore Roosevelt Distinguished Service Medal 20066
Save the Children - Canada Award 18323
Service to Youth Award 6602

Youth (continued)

Shofar Award (Ram's Horn) 15300
Silver Antelope 6586
Silver Beaver 6587
Silver Buffalo Award 6588
Silver Medallion 6603
Silver World Award 6589
Isabel and Monroe Smith Award 10567
William H. Spurgeon III Award 6590
Ner Tamid Award 15301
Timothy Trophy 6164
Albert E. Trieschman Award 1136
UNICEF Award for Films 20599
U.S. Youth Sailing Championship 20789
USTA/USPTA Public Service Award 20872
Louise Waterman Wise Award 2897
YMCA Men, Women and Youth of the Year 22037
Youth Gardening Award 9891
Youth Leadership Awards 6780
Youth Medallion 9512
Youth of the Year 198

Zoology (*See also* Ornithology)
ABS Founders' Memorial Award 4957
Warder Clyde Allee Best Student Paper Award of the Animal Behavior Society 4958
American Society of Mammalogists Award 4494
Animal Behavior Society Film Festival Awards 4959
Helen I. Battle Award 7496
John N. Belkin Memorial Award 3135
Best Student Paper 18774
Best Student Paper Award 19219
T. W. N. Cameron Award 7497
Coleopterists Society Youth Award 8132
Daniel Giraud Elliot Medal 13832
Entomological Society of Canada Gold Medal Award 9293
Entomology Writing Competition Award 22061
ESA Distinguished Achievement Award in Extension 9287
ESA Distinguished Achievement Award in Regulatory Entomology 9288
ESA Distinguished Achievement Award in Teaching 9289
ESA Founder's Memorial Award 9290
Fellow of ESA 9291
Fellow of the Society 19220
Fry Medal 7498
Gaige Fund Award 4451
Robert H. Gibbs, Jr. Memorial Award 4452
Grants in Herpetology 18892
Herpetologists' League Award for Graduate Research 10428
C. Gordon Hewitt Award 9294
Hoar Award 7499
Honorary Member 19221
B. Elizabeth Horner Award 4495
Brazier Howell Award 4496
Intel International Science and Engineering Fair 18362
Anna M. Jackson Award 4497
Hartley H. T. Jackson Award 4498
L. S. B. Leakey Foundation Prize for Multidisciplinary Research on Ape and Human Evolution 12756
Lerner-Gray Fund for Marine Research Award 3156
Ernst Mayr Award in Systematic Biology 19305
Medal of Honor Award 3136
Memorial Lecturer Award and Honoree(s) 3137
Meritorious Service Award
  American Mosquito Control Association 3138
  Society of Nematologists 19222
C. Hart Merriam Award 4499
Munson Aquatic Conservation Exhibitory Award 4917
NCHS Grants in Herpetology 16510
Novartis Crop Protection Entomological Society of America Award 19875
Leo Parizeau Prize in Biology 5540
R. Marlin Perkins Award for Professional Excellence 4919
Presidential Citation 3139
Raney Fund Award 4453
Albert R. and Alma Shadle Fellowship 4500
Storer Award 4454
Stoye Awards 4455
Sustaining Member Recognition Award 22062
Syngenta Nematology Award 19223
R. A. Wardle Award 7500

Organization Index

The alphabetical Organization Index provides access to all sponsoring and administering organizations listed in both volumes, as well as to organization acronyms and alternate-language and former names. In the case of a sponsoring organization, the citation is to the specific award it sponsors. Each organization name is followed by the volume in which it appears. The numbers following the volume references are book entry numbers, not page numbers.

3-A Sanitary Standards Committees Vol 1: 1
3M Canada Vol 1: 7248
3M Company Vol 1: 184
6th Bomb Group Association Vol 1: 3
11th Armored Cavalry's Veterans of Vietnam and Cambodia Vol 1: 5
60 Plus Association Vol 1: 8
70th Infantry Division Association Vol 1: 10
76 Corporation Vol 1: 11760
78th Division Veterans Association Vol 1: 12
84th Infantry Division, Railsplitter Society Vol 1: 14
The 92nd Street Y Vol 1: 18
106th Infantry Division Association Vol 1: 20
303rd Bomb Group (H) Association Vol 1: 22
369th Veterans' Association Vol 1: 24
A. Philip Randolph Institute Vol 1: 26
AACC International Vol 1: 31
AACE International Vol 1: 34
AAFRC Trust for Philanthropy Vol 1: 42
AAMR Vol 2: 461
AAR Cadillac Manufacturing, Inc. Vol 1: 13091
AARL Foundation Vol 1: 44
ABA Marketing Network Vol 1: 54
Abalekwa Development Organization Vol 2: 4343
Abandoned Babies Committee Vol 2: 9332
Abarth Register, U.S.A. Vol 1: 56
ABB Kent - Taylor Ltd. Vol 2: 8773
Abbott Diagnostics Vol 2: 5621
Abbott Laboratories Vol 1: 4128
ABC Vol 1: 16981
ABC - CLIO Vol 1: 1409
The Abdus Salam International Centre for Theoretical Physics Vol 2: 3788
ABET Vol 1: 58
Abraham Lincoln Association Vol 1: 61
Abrasive Engineering Society Vol 1: 65
ACA International Vol 1: 69
Acacia Fraternity Vol 1: 73
Acadamh Rioga na Heireann Vol 2: 3700
Academia Argentina de Letras Vol 2: 15
Academia Brasileira de Letras Vol 2: 1151, 5412
Academia Colombiana de Ciencias Exactas, Fisicas y Naturales Vol 2: 1266
Academia das Ciencias de Lisboa Vol 2: 5404
Academia de la Investigacion Cientifica Vol 2: 4554
Academia Europaea Vol 2: 6662
Academia Ludoviciana Gissensis Vol 2: 2995
Academia Mexicana de Ciencias Vol 2: 4554
Academia Mexicana de Dermatologia Vol 2: 4552
Academia Musicale Chigiana Vol 2: 3792
Academia Nacional de Agronomia y Veterinaria Vol 2: 1
Academia Nacional de Ciencias de Bolivia Vol 2: 1132
Academia Nacional de Geografia Vol 2: 43
Academia Nacional de la Historia de la Republica Argentina Vol 2: 11
Academia Nacional de Medicina Vol 2: 1320
Academia Portuguese da Historia Vol 2: 5480
Academia Romana Vol 2: 5809
Academic Press Vol 2: 7513
Academie Canadienne du Cinema et de la Television Vol 1: 79
Academie d'Agriculture de France Vol 2: 1667
Academie des Beaux-Arts Vol 2: 1671
Academie des Inscriptions et Belles-Lettres Vol 2: 1744
Academie des Sciences Vol 2: 1781
Academie des Sciences Morales et Politiques Vol 2: 2008
Academie Francaise Vol 2: 2093
Academie Internationale d'Astronautique Vol 2: 2434
Academie Internationale de Medecine Aeronautique et Spatiale Vol 1: 11161
Academie Royale des Sciences, des Lettres at des Beaux-Arts de Belgique Vol 2: 1072
Academy for Educational Development Vol 1: 75
Academy for Ethics in Medicine Vol 2: 2638
Academy of American Poets Vol 1: 77
Academy of Applied Osteopathy Vol 1: 739
Academy of Athens Vol 2: 3160
Academy of Canadian Cinema and Television Vol 1: 79
Academy of Country Music Vol 1: 85
Academy of Country Music Entertainment Vol 1: 7063
Academy of Criminal Justice Sciences Vol 1: 87
Academy of Dentistry International Vol 1: 94
Academy of International Business Vol 1: 101
Academy of Marketing Science Vol 1: 104
Academy of Motion Picture Arts and Sciences Vol 1: 110
Academy of Operative Dentistry Vol 1: 114
Academy of Parish Clergy Vol 1: 118
Academy of Parish Clergy Vol 1: 118
Academy of Science Fiction, Fantasy, and Horror Films Vol 1: 122
Academy of Sciences for the Developing World Vol 2: 3794
Academy of Sciences, Lithuania Vol 2: 4383
Academy of Sciences of the Czech Republic Vol 2: 1412
Academy of Scientific Research Vol 2: 4554
Academy of Scientific Research and Technology Vol 2: 1550
Academy of Security Educators and Trainers Vol 1: 124
Academy of Television Arts and Sciences Vol 1: 126
Academy of Television Arts and Sciences Vol 1: 13862
Academy of the Social Sciences in Australia Vol 2: 47
Academy of Wind and Percussion Arts Vol 1: 14480
Accademia Agraria Vol 2: 3800
Accademia d'Arte e Design - Leonetto Cappiello Vol 2: 3802
Accademia delle Scienze di Torino Vol 2: 3804
Accademia di Medicina di Torino Vol 2: 3808
Accademia di Studi Storici Aldo Moro Vol 2: 3810
Accademia Internazionale Medicea Vol 2: 3812
Accademia Nazionale dei Lincei Vol 2: 3814
Accademia Pontaniana Vol 2: 3835
Access Intelligence LLC Vol 1: 129
Accordion Society of Australia Vol 2: 49
Accounting Aid Society Vol 1: 132
Accreditation Association for Ambulatory Health Care Vol 1: 134
ACM SIGCOMM Vol 1: 5323
Acoustical Society of America Vol 1: 136
Acoustical Society of America Vol 2: 7643
ACS Committee on Corporation Associates Vol 1: 1705
ACSM Health Promotion Vol 1: 147
Acta Materialia, Inc. Vol 1: 153
Action for Nuclear Disarmament Vol 1: 21768
Action for Post-Soviet Jewry Vol 1: 156
Action Health - Nigeria Vol 2: 5100
Action Medical Research Vol 2: 6665
Action Research for the Crippled Child Vol 2: 6665
Activ Foundation Vol 2: 51
Acton Institute for the Study of Religion and Liberty Vol 1: 158
Actors' Equity Association Vol 1: 161
Actors' Equity Foundation Vol 1: 164
Actors' Fund of America Vol 1: 169
Actors Theatre of Louisville Vol 1: 171
ACTRA Vol 1: 6033

Acupuncture Foundation of Canada Institute Vol 1: 173
A.D. Johnson Family Association Vol 1: 175
ADA Health Foundation Vol 1: 2127, 2128
Adapted Physical Activity Council Vol 1: 1034
Adapted Swimming Committee Vol 1: 21208
ADARA: Professionals Networking for Excellence in Service Delivery with Individuals who are Deaf or Hard of Hearing Vol 1: 178
Adelaide Philosophical Society Vol 2: 545
Ademe Vol 2: 2532
Adhesion Society Vol 1: 183
Adidas Vol 1: 15708
The Adirondack Council Vol 1: 185
ADISQ (Association Quebecoise de L'Industrie du Disque, du Spectacle et de la Video) Vol 1: 187
Adoption Council of Canada Vol 1: 190
Adoptive Families Today Vol 1: 195
Adriaticocinema Festival Vol 2: 3838
Adrich Chemical Company, Inc. Vol 1: 1728
Adult Education of the U.S.A. Vol 1: 946
Adult Friends for Youth Vol 1: 197
Adult Learning Australia Vol 2: 57
Adult Video Association Vol 1: 199
Adventist World Headquarters Vol 1: 17268
Adventure Foundation Pakistan Vol 2: 5185
Advertising Age - Crain Communications Inc. Vol 1: 201
Advertising and Design Club of Canada Vol 1: 203
Advertising Association of the West Vol 1: 854
Advertising Club of New York Vol 1: 205
Advertising Council Vol 1: 207
Advertising Media Credit Executives Association Vol 1: 209
Advertising Production Club of New York Vol 1: 211
Advertising Women of New York Vol 1: 213
Advocates for Animals Vol 2: 8046
Advocates for Youth Vol 1: 218
ADWEEK, East Edition - VNU Business Publications, USA, Inc. Vol 1: 220
AeA Vol 1: 224
AECI Limited Vol 2: 5689
AEG Hausgerate GmbH Vol 2: 2640
Aero Club of America Vol 1: 13875
Aero Club of Egypt Vol 2: 6346
Aero Club of Poland Vol 2: 6343
Aeronautical Research Laboratories Vol 2: 380
Aeronautical Society of India Vol 2: 3328
Aerospace Education Foundation Vol 1: 227
Aerospace Medical Association Vol 1: 229
Aestheticians International Association Headquarters Vol 1: 244
Aesthetics International Association Vol 1: 244
Affaire de Coeur Magazine Vol 1: 246
Affiliation of Honourable Photographers Vol 2: 6668
Africa Rice Center Vol 2: 1367
Africa Travel Association Vol 1: 248
African-American Women's Clergy Association Vol 1: 252
African Environmental Research and Consulting Group Vol 1: 254
African Insurance Organisation Vol 2: 1247
African Organization of Supreme Audit Institutions Vol 2: 6624
African Peoples' Christian Organization Vol 1: 256
African Reinsurance Corp. Vol 2: 5102
African Studies Association Vol 1: 258
African Studies Association of the United Kingdom Vol 2: 6670
African Wildlife Foundation Vol 1: 266
Africare Vol 1: 268
Afro-Asian Book Council Vol 2: 3337
AFS Intercultural Programs Vol 1: 270
Aga Khan Trust for Culture Vol 2: 6301
AGC Education and Research Foundation Vol 1: 272
AGCO Vol 1: 4233
The Age Vol 2: 59
AGFA Vol 2: 290
Agfa-Gavaert Vol 1: 18718
AGFA Medical Systems Vol 1: 6920
Agri-Energy Roundtable Vol 1: 276
Agrichemical Age Vol 1: 14150
Agricultural and Forestry Experiment Station Vol 1: 278
Agricultural History Society Vol 1: 280
Agricultural Institute of Canada Vol 1: 284
Agricultural Relations Council Vol 1: 291
Agriservices Foundation Vol 1: 16403
Aguda l'Haanakat Prasim Sifrutiim Al Shem Mordechai Bernstein Vol 2: 3726
Agudat Achsaniot Noar Beisrael Vol 2: 3760
Agudat Hametargmim Beyisrael Vol 2: 3758
Ahrend Groep N.V. Vol 2: 4919
AIA New York State, Inc. Vol 1: 293
AIA Pennsylvania Vol 1: 302
AICHE Vol 1: 477
AIDS Action Council Vol 1: 304
AIIM - The Enterprise Content Management Association Vol 1: 306
AIM Magazine - AIM Publication Association Vol 1: 315
AIP Task Force Vol 1: 3002
Air and Waste Management Association Vol 1: 317
Air-Britain Historians Vol 2: 6672
Air Force Association Vol 1: 327
Air Force Association - Aerospace Education Foundation Vol 1: 227
Air Force Association of Canada Vol 1: 366
Air Force Historical Foundation Vol 1: 368
Air League Vol 2: 6675
Air Products and Chemicals, Inc. Vol 1: 1727, 2786
Air Traffic Control Association Vol 1: 379
Air Transport World Vol 1: 394
Aircraft Owners and Pilots Association Vol 1: 396
Aircraft Owners and Pilots Association of the United Kingdom Vol 2: 6681
Aircraft Technical Publishers Vol 1: 13920, 17590
Airey Neave Trust Vol 2: 6683
Airports Council International - North America Vol 1: 400
Airtour International Vol 2: 7604
Airts Cooncil o Norlin Airlann Vol 2: 6760
Airways Corporation Vol 2: 5051
Akademie fur Ethik in der Medizin Vol 2: 2638
Akademie Ved Ceske Republiky Vol 2: 1412
Akademiet for de tekniske Videnskaber Vol 2: 1445
Akashvani Vol 2: 3342
AKM Vol 2: 705
Akzo Chemical America Vol 1: 3311
Alabama Library Association Vol 1: 404
Alabama Sheriffs Association Vol 1: 406
Alabama State Poetry Society Vol 1: 14987
Alabama Textile Manufacturers Association Vol 1: 408
Alabama Writers' Forum Vol 1: 411
Alamogordo Music Theatre Vol 1: 413
Alarm and Security Association; Canadian Vol 1: 7385
Albanian Catholic Institute Vol 1: 415
Albany Institute of History and Art Vol 1: 18333
Albany Trustee Co., Ltd. Vol 2: 7354
Albany; University of Vol 1: 18333
Albemarle Corporation Vol 1: 1744
Alberta Irrigation Projects Association Vol 1: 417
Alberta Motion Picture Industries Association Vol 1: 421
Alberta Publishers Association Vol 1: 6501
Alberta Theatre Projects Vol 1: 423
Albright and Wilson Ltd. Vol 2: 8773
Alcaldia Municipal Vol 2: 1122
ALCAN Vol 1: 9537
Alcan Canada Limited Vol 1: 7826
Alco Control Company Vol 1: 4419
Alcoa Company Vol 1: 4508
Alcoa Inc. Vol 1: 425
Alcohol Awareness and Family Recovery Vol 2: 61
Alcuin Society Vol 1: 429
Aldeburgh Bookshop Vol 2: 6686
Aldeburgh Poetry Trust Vol 2: 6685
Aldrich Chemical Co., Inc Vol 1: 1717
Aldrich Chemical Company, Inc. Vol 1: 1707
Alexander Graham Bell Association for the Deaf and Hard of Hearing Vol 1: 431
Alfa Laval Agri, Inc. Vol 1: 2100
Alfred Heineken Fondsen Foundation Vol 2: 4886, 4888, 4889, 4890
Algemeen Nederlands Verbond Vol 2: 4679, 4735
All-America Rose Selections Vol 1: 437
All-America Selections Vol 1: 441
All England Lawn Tennis and Croquet Club Vol 2: 6687
All India Primary Teachers Federation Vol 2: 3339
All India Radio Vol 2: 3342
All India Stainless Steel Industries Association Vol 2: 3346
All Island Jamaica Cane Farmers Association Vol 2: 4072
All Russia Association of the Blind Vol 2: 5884
All-Russian Public Veterans of War and Military Service Organization Vol 2: 5888
Allard Charitable Foundation; Peter Vol 2: 8376
Allegiance Healthcare Corporation Vol 1: 973
Allen & Unwin Pty. Ltd. Vol 2: 63
Allergie Asthme Association d'information Vol 1: 443
Allergy/Asthma Information Association Vol 1: 443
Alliance for Aging Research Vol 1: 10526
Alliance for Children and Families Vol 1: 446
Alliance for Children and Television Vol 1: 452
Alliance for Community Media Vol 1: 457
Alliance for Transportation Research Institute - University of New Mexico Vol 1: 459
Alliance Francais Vol 2: 2534
Alliance of Cardiovascular Professionals Vol 1: 465

Alliance of Independent Retailers Vol 2: 6689
Alliance of Motion Picture and Television Producers Vol 1: 467
Alliance of the American Dental Association Vol 1: 469
L'Alliance pour l'Enfant et la Television Vol 1: 452
Allianz Cornhill Musical Insurance Vol 2: 8165
Allied Artists of America Vol 1: 472
Allis Chalmers Corporation Vol 1: 14156, 14157
Allport Memorial Fund of Harvard University; Gordon W. Vol 1: 18883
Allyn & Bacon Publishers Vol 1: 17694
Alpert Foundation; Herb Vol 1: 12095
Alpha Chi Sigma Vol 1: 474
Alpha Chi Sigma Fraternity Vol 1: 1720
Alpha Epsilon Rho; National Broadcasting Society - Vol 1: 14533
Alpha Kappa Delta Vol 1: 479
Alpha Omega Alpha Honor Medical Society Vol 1: 481
Alpha Omega Dental Fraternity Vol 1: 485
Alpha Omega International Dental Fraternity Vol 1: 485
Alpha Sigma Lambda, Pennsylvania State University-University Park Vol 1: 488
Alpha Sigma Nu Vol 1: 5736
Alpha Tau Delta Vol 1: 490
Alpha Zeta Omega Vol 1: 495
Alpine Club of Canada Vol 1: 500
Alpine Garden Society Vol 2: 6694
ALS Association, West Michigan Chapter Vol 1: 505
ALTA Foundation Vol 1: 507
Alternative Energy Resources Organization Vol 1: 510
Altran Engineering Academy Vol 2: 7836
Aluminum Association Inc. - Extruded Products Division Vol 1: 512
Alumni Association Vol 1: 1869
Alumni Association of the City College of New York Vol 1: 514
Alumni Federation of New York University Vol 1: 16305
Alvis Owner Club Vol 2: 6701
Amado Foundation; Maurice Vol 1: 12331
Amanah Al Ammah Li Jaezat Al Malik Faisal Al Alamiyyah; Al Vol 2: 5921
Amateur Astronomers Association Vol 1: 520
Amateur Athletic Association of England Vol 2: 6703
Amateur Athletic Foundation of Los Angeles Vol 1: 522
Amateur Athletic Union Vol 1: 525
Amateur Boxing Federation; United States of America Vol 1: 20383
Amateur Cinema League Vol 1: 3147
Amateur Hockey Association of the United States Vol 1: 21173
Amateur Softball Association of America Vol 1: 584
Amateur Swimming Association Vol 2: 6705
Amaury Sport Organisation Vol 2: 2223
Ambulatory Pediatric Association Vol 1: 590
Amelia Reynolds Long Memorial Fund Vol 1: 15006
America-Israel Cultural Foundation Vol 1: 598
America the Beautiful Fund Vol 1: 600
American Academy for Cerebral Palsy Vol 1: 602
American Academy for Cerebral Palsy and Developmental Medicine Vol 1: 602
American Academy in Rome Vol 1: 604, 21271
American Academy of Addiction Psychiatry Vol 1: 606
American Academy of Advertising Vol 1: 609
American Academy of Allergy, Asthma and Immunology Vol 1: 614
American Academy of Arts and Sciences Vol 1: 617
American Academy of Child and Adolescent Psychiatry Vol 1: 624
American Academy of Child Psychiatry Vol 1: 624
American Academy of Clinical Psychiatrists Vol 1: 630
American Academy of Clinical Toxicology Vol 1: 632
American Academy of Crown and Bridge Prosthodontics Vol 1: 677
American Academy of Dermatology Vol 1: 635
American Academy of Dramatic Arts Vol 1: 641
American Academy of Environmental Engineers Vol 1: 644
American Academy of Environmental Medicine Vol 1: 650
American Academy of Equine Art Vol 1: 654
American Academy of Facial Plastic and Reconstructive Surgery Vol 1: 665
American Academy of Family Physicians Vol 1: 671
American Academy of Fixed Prosthodontics Vol 1: 677
American Academy of Gnathologic Orthopedics Vol 1: 679
American Academy of Kinesiology and Physical Education Vol 1: 681
American Academy of Medical Administrators Vol 1: 683
American Academy of Neurological and Orthopaedic Surgeons Vol 1: 693
American Academy of Neurology Vol 1: 695
American Academy of Neurology Vol 1: 15396
American Academy of Nursing Vol 1: 707
American Academy of Occupational Medicine Vol 1: 1903
American Academy of Ophthalmology Vol 1: 709
American Academy of Ophthalmology and Otolaryngology Vol 1: 709
American Academy of Optometry Vol 1: 715
American Academy of Optometry - British Chapter Vol 2: 6724
American Academy of Oral and Maxillofacial Pathology Vol 1: 725
American Academy of Oral and Maxillofacial Radiology Vol 1: 727
American Academy of Oral Medicine Vol 1: 733
American Academy of Osteopathic Surgeons Vol 1: 1362
American Academy of Osteopathy Vol 1: 739
American Academy of Otolaryngology - Head and Neck Surgery Vol 1: 744
American Academy of Pediatrics Vol 1: 755
American Academy of Periodontology Vol 1: 800
American Academy of Physician Assistants Vol 1: 812
American Academy of Professional Coders Vol 1: 819
American Academy of Psychiatrists in Alcoholism and Addiction Vol 1: 606
American Academy of Psychiatry and the Law Vol 1: 823
American Academy of Religion Vol 1: 829
American Academy of Sanitarians Vol 1: 834
American Academy of Sleep Medicine Vol 1: 836
American Academy of Somnology Vol 1: 841
American Academy of the History of Dentistry Vol 1: 843
American Accordion Musicological Society Vol 1: 846
American Accordionists' Association Vol 1: 848
American Action Fund for Blind Children and Adults Vol 1: 15039
American Adoption Congress Vol 1: 850
American Advertising Federation Vol 1: 853
American Agri-Women Vol 1: 863
American Agricultural Economics Association Vol 1: 867
American Agricultural Editors Association Vol 1: 19873
American Alliance for Health, Physical Education, Recreation and Dance Vol 1: 875
American Alliance for Theatre and Education Vol 1: 882
American Amateur Press Association Vol 1: 899
American Animal Hospital Association Vol 1: 901
American Anthropological Association Vol 1: 908
American Antiquarian Society Vol 1: 913
American Arbitration Association Vol 1: 917
American Armsport Association Vol 1: 923
American Armwrestling Association Vol 1: 923
American Art Therapy Association Vol 1: 926
American Artists Professional League Vol 1: 929
American Assembly Vol 1: 931
American Assembly for Men in Nursing Vol 1: 933
American Association Family Consumer Sciences Vol 1: 935
American Association for Adult and Continuing Education Vol 1: 946
American Association for Aerosol Research Vol 1: 954
American Association for Agricultural Education Vol 1: 959
American Association for Artificial Intelligence Vol 1: 5304
American Association for Automotive Medicine Vol 1: 5476
American Association for Cancer Research Vol 1: 963
American Association for Cancer Research Vol 2: 4033
American Association for Clinical Chemistry Vol 1: 970
American Association for Conservation Information Vol 1: 5326
American Association for Counseling and Development Vol 1: 2063
American Association for Counseling and Development Vol 1: 5333
American Association for Employment in Education Vol 1: 1010

Organization Index

American Association for Geodetic Surveying Vol 1: 1012
American Association for Health Education Vol 1: 1015
American Association for Laboratory Animal Science Vol 1: 1022
American Association for Leisure and Recreation Vol 1: 1029
American Association for Public Opinion Research Vol 1: 1035
American Association for State and Local History Vol 1: 1038
American Association for the Advancement of Science Vol 1: 1043
American Association for the Advancement of Sciences Vol 1: 3506
American Association for the Advancement of Slavic Studies Vol 1: 1053
American Association for the History of Medicine Vol 1: 1060
American Association for the History of Nursing Vol 1: 1064
American Association for Theatre in Secondary Education Vol 1: 882
American Association for Women in Community Colleges Vol 1: 1067
American Association for Women Radiologists Vol 1: 1071
American Association of Advertising Agencies Vol 1: 1075
American Association of Agricultural College Editors Vol 1: 5290
American Association of Airport Executives, Great Lakes Chapter Vol 1: 1079
American Association of Anatomists Vol 1: 1081
American Association of Avian Pathologists Vol 1: 1084
American Association of Bioanalysts Vol 1: 1090
American Association of Blacks in Energy Vol 1: 1094
American Association of Blacks in Energy, Arkansas Vol 1: 1097
American Association of Blood Banks Vol 1: 1099
American Association of Botanical Gardens and Arboreta Vol 1: 1119
American Association of Bovine Practitioners Vol 1: 1122
American Association of Cat Enthusiasts Vol 1: 1129
American Association of Cereal Chemists Vol 1: 31
American Association of Certified Orthoptists Vol 1: 1131
American Association of Children's Residential Centers Vol 1: 1135
American Association of Christian Schools Vol 1: 1137
American Association of Code Enforcement Vol 1: 1140
American Association of College Baseball Coaches Vol 1: 1538
American Association of Colleges for Teacher Education Vol 1: 1142
American Association of Collegiate Registrars and Admissions Officers Vol 1: 1157
American Association of Community Colleges Vol 1: 14753, 14755
American Association of Community Theatre Vol 1: 1162
American Association of Cost Engineers Vol 1: 34
American Association of Critical-Care Nurses Vol 1: 1170
American Association of Dental Examiners Vol 1: 1181
American Association of Diabetes Educators Vol 1: 1183
American Association of Electromyography and Electrodiagnosis Vol 1: 1281
American Association of Endodontists Vol 1: 1190
American Association of Engineering Societies Vol 1: 1195
American Association of Feline Practitioners Vol 1: 1201
American Association of Fitness Directors in Business and Industry Vol 1: 147
American Association of Genito-Urinary Surgeons Vol 1: 1203
American Association of Gynecologic Laparoscopists Vol 1: 1206
American Association of Handwriting Analysts Vol 1: 1210
American Association of Healthcare Administrative Management Vol 1: 1212
American Association of Homes and Services for the Aging Vol 1: 1221
American Association of Hospital Dental Chiefs Vol 1: 1234
American Association of Hospital Dentists Vol 1: 1234
American Association of Housing Educators Vol 1: 1239
American Association of Immunologists Vol 1: 1241
American Association of Industrial Physicians and Surgeons Vol 1: 1903
American Association of Law Libraries Vol 1: 1243
American Association of Managing General Agents Vol 1: 1256
American Association of Meat Processors Vol 1: 1258
American Association of Medical Assistants, Linn Chapter Vol 1: 1269
American Association of Mental Health Professionals in Corrections Vol 1: 1271
American Association of Motor Vehicle Administrators Vol 1: 1273
American Association of Museums Vol 1: 1277
American Association of Neuromuscular and Electrodiagnostic Medicine Vol 1: 1281
American Association of Neuropathologists Vol 1: 1286
American Association of Nurse Anesthetists Vol 1: 1290
American Association of Nurse Attorneys Vol 1: 1301
American Association of Occupational Health Nurses Vol 1: 1304
American Association of Oral and Maxillofacial Surgeons Vol 1: 1308
American Association of Oriental Medicine Vol 1: 1313
American Association of Orthodontists Vol 1: 1317
American Association of Osteopathic Specialists Vol 1: 1362
American Association of Owners and Breeders of Peruvian Paso Horses Vol 1: 1323
American Association of Pathologists and Bacteriologists Vol 1: 4117
American Association of Petroleum Geologists Vol 1: 1325
American Association of Physical Anthropologists Vol 1: 1354
American Association of Physician Specialists Vol 1: 1362
American Association of Physicists in Medicine Vol 1: 1365
American Association of Physics Teachers Vol 1: 1370
American Association of Plastic Surgeons Vol 1: 1380
American Association of Poison Control Centers Vol 1: 1382
American Association of Political Consultants Vol 1: 1384
American Association of Psychiatric Administators Vol 1: 3610
American Association of Psychiatric Technicians Vol 1: 1386
American Association of Public Health Dentistry Vol 1: 1391
American Association of Public Health Physicians Vol 1: 1393
American Association of Retired Persons Vol 1: 1395
American Association of School Administrators Vol 1: 1402
American Association of School Librarians Vol 1: 1408
American Association of School Personnel Administrators Vol 1: 1420
American Association of Sex Educators, Counselors and Therapists Vol 1: 1422
American Association of State Climatologists Vol 1: 1424
American Association of State Colleges and Universities Vol 1: 1427
American Association of State Highway and Transportation Officials Vol 1: 1430
American Association of Suicidology Vol 1: 1436
American Association of Surgeon Assistants Vol 1: 1439
American Association of Surgical Physician Assistants Vol 1: 1441
American Association of Teacher Educators in Agriculture Vol 1: 959
American Association of Teachers of German Vol 1: 1443
American Association of Teachers of Italian Vol 1: 1449
American Association of Teachers of Spanish and Portuguese Vol 1: 1451
American Association of Textile Chemists and Colorists Vol 1: 1454
American Association of the Deaf-Blind Vol 1: 1458
American Association of University Administrators Vol 1: 1460
American Association of University Professors Vol 1: 1463
American Association of University Women Educational Foundation Vol 1: 1468
American Association of University Women Legal Advocacy Fund Vol 1: 1475
American Association of Veterinary Immunologists Vol 1: 1477
American Association of Veterinary Laboratory Diagnosticians Vol 1: 1479
American Association of Wardens and Superintendents Vol 1: 16392
American Association of Women Dentists Vol 1: 1481

American Association of Women Emergency Physicians Vol 1: 1483
American Association of Zoo Keepers Vol 1: 1485
American Association of Zoo Keepers - San Antonio Chapter Vol 1: 1491
American Association of Zoological Parks and Aquariums Vol 1: 4912
American Association on Mental Deficiency Vol 1: 1493
American Association on Mental Retardation Vol 1: 1493
American Astronautical Society Vol 1: 1496
American Astronomical Society Vol 1: 1470
American Astronomical Society Vol 1: 1507
American Auto Racing Writers and Broadcasters Association Vol 1: 1521
American Automatic Control Council Vol 1: 2760, 2787
American Award Manufacturers Association Vol 1: 6165
American Badminton Association Vol 1: 21144
American Ballet Competition Vol 1: 1524
American Bandmasters Association Vol 1: 1526
American Baptist Homes and Hospitals Association Vol 1: 1528
American Bar Association Vol 1: 1530
American Bar Association Vol 1: 15337
American Baseball Coaches Association Vol 1: 1538
American Baseball Coaches Association Vol 1: 14659
American Bashkir Curly Registry Vol 1: 1548
American Basketball Association Vol 1: 14497
American Beefalo Association Vol 1: 1554
American Beefalo World Registry Vol 1: 1554
American Begonia Society Vol 1: 1558
American Bible Society Vol 1: 1562
American Billiard Association Vol 1: 20434
American Birding Association Vol 1: 1565
American Blade Collectors Association and *The Blade Magazine* Vol 1: 6443
American Blind Bowling Association Vol 1: 1567
American Board for Occupational Health Nurses, Inc. Vol 1: 1569
American Board of Orthodontics Vol 1: 1575
American Board of Professional Psychology Vol 1: 1577
American Board of Psychological Hypnosis Vol 1: 1579
American Board of Psychological Hypnosis Vol 1: 18658
American Booksellers Association Vol 1: 1581
American Bottled Water Association Vol 1: 11429
American Bowling Congress Vol 1: 1584
American Bowling Congress Vol 1: 11432
American Breeders Service Vol 1: 2107
American Bridge Teachers' Association Vol 1: 1588
American Brittany Club, Heart of Illinois Vol 1: 1591
American Brittany Club, Missouri Vol 1: 1593
American Bugatti Club Vol 1: 1595
American Bureau of Shipping Vol 1: 19212
American Burn Association Vol 1: 1597
American Business Media Vol 1: 1606
American Business Women's Association Vol 1: 1609
American Businessmen of Jeddah Vol 2: 5917
American Camellia Society Vol 1: 1611
American Camping Association Vol 1: 1624
American Camping Association, Wisconsin Section Vol 1: 1631
American Cancer Society Vol 1: 1633
American Cancer Society Vol 1: 5803
American Cancer Society, Capital Region Unit Vol 1: 1640
American Cancer Society, Porter County Unit Vol 1: 1642
American Carbon Committee Vol 1: 1644
American Carbon Society Vol 1: 1644
American Cat Fanciers Association Vol 1: 1650
American Catholic Historical Association Vol 1: 1652
American Catholic Historical Society Vol 1: 1657
American Catholic Historical Society Vol 1: 2479
American Catholic Philosophical Association Vol 1: 1659
American Center for Children's Television - % Central Educational Network Vol 1: 1662
American Ceramic Society Vol 1: 1665
American Chamber of Commerce Executives Vol 1: 1701
American Chamber of Commerce for Brazil - Rio de Janeiro Vol 2: 1136
American Chamber of Commerce in Azerbaijan Vol 2: 808
American Chamber of Commerce of Brazil - Sao Paulo Vol 2: 1138
American Chamber of Commerce of Guatemala Vol 2: 3201
American Chemical Society Vol 1: 1703
American Chemical Society Vol 1: 3460
American Chemical Society, Philadelphia Section Vol 1: 1795
American Chesterton Society Vol 1: 1798
American Children's Television Festival Vol 1: 1662
American Chinese Medical Society Vol 1: 7928
American Chiropractic Association Vol 1: 1801
American Cinema Editors Vol 1: 1803
American Citizens Abroad Vol 2: 6303
The American Civil Defense Association Vol 1: 1805
American Civil Liberties Union Vol 1: 1808
American Civil Liberties Union of the National Capital Area Vol 1: 1810
American Civil Liberties Union of Vermont Vol 1: 1813
American Civil Liberties Union, Ohio Affiliate Vol 1: 1817
American Cleft Palate Education Foundation Vol 1: 8093
American Cockatiel Society Vol 1: 1819
American College Health Association Vol 1: 1821
American College of Allergy, Asthma and Immunology Vol 1: 1828
American College of Angiology Vol 1: 1830
American College of Apothecaries Vol 1: 1832
American College of Cardiology Vol 1: 1835
American College of Chest Physicians Vol 1: 1842
American College of Clinical Pharmacology Vol 1: 1846
American College of Dentists Vol 1: 1852
American College of Emergency Physicians Vol 1: 1858
American College of Forensic Examiners International Vol 1: 1863
American College of Healthcare Executives Vol 1: 1865
American College of Hospital Administrators Vol 1: 1865
American College of Legal Medicine Vol 1: 1877
American College of Legal Medicine Vol 1: 7725
American College of Medical Practice Executives Vol 1: 1881
American College of Musicians Vol 1: 1886
American College of Neuropsychiatrists Vol 1: 1888
American College of Neuropsychopharmacology Vol 1: 1894
American College of Nurse-Midwives Vol 1: 1901
American College of Occupational and Environmental Medicine Vol 1: 1903
American College of Occupational Medicine Vol 1: 1903
American College of Oral and Maxillofacial Surgeons Vol 1: 1909
American College of Physicians Vol 1: 1914
American College of Preventive Medicine Vol 1: 1929
The American College of Psychiatrists Vol 1: 1934
American College of Radiology Vol 1: 1939
American College of Surgeons Vol 1: 1944
American Community Theatre Association Vol 1: 1162
American Comparative Literature Association Vol 1: 1951
American Composers Alliance Vol 1: 1954
American Concrete Institute Vol 1: 1956
American Concrete Institute - New Jersey Chapter Vol 1: 1975
American Concrete Pipe Association Vol 1: 1977
American Congress of Rehabilitation Medicine Vol 1: 1982
American Congress on Surveying and Mapping Vol 1: 1990
American Congress on Surveying and Mapping Vol 1: 15758, 15762
American Consular Association Vol 1: 2277
American Consulting Engineers Council Vol 1: 2008
American Contact Dermatitis Society Vol 1: 2011
American Contract Bridge League Vol 1: 2015
American Coon Hunters Association Vol 1: 2019
American Correctional Association Vol 1: 2021
American Cotswold Record Association Vol 1: 2030
American Council for Better Broadcasts Vol 1: 15867
American Council of Christian Churches Vol 1: 2033
American Council of Learned Societies Vol 1: 2036
American Council of the Blind Vol 1: 2038

American Council on Consumer Interests Vol 1: 2044
American Council on Education Vol 1: 2052
American Council on Industrial Arts Teacher Education Vol 1: 8611
American Council on the Teaching of Foreign Languages Vol 1: 2055
American Counseling Association Vol 1: 2063
American Craft Council Vol 1: 2075
American Crossword Puzzle Tournament Vol 1: 2080
American Crystallographic Association Vol 1: 2082
American Dairy Science Association Vol 1: 2096
American Dance Festival Vol 1: 2115
American Dance Guild Vol 1: 2118
American Darts Organization Vol 1: 2121
American Deafness and Rehabilitation Association Vol 1: 178
American Defense Institute Vol 1: 2124
American Dental Association Vol 1: 2126
American Dental Hygienists' Association Vol 1: 2129
American Design Drafting Association Vol 1: 2131
American Diabetes Association Vol 1: 2133
American Die Casting Institute Vol 1: 16420
American Dietetic Association Foundation Vol 1: 2144
American Documentation Institute Vol 1: 4099
American Donkey and Mule Society Vol 1: 2148
American Economic Association Vol 1: 2153
American Educational Research Association Vol 1: 2158
American Egg Board Technical Committee Vol 1: 17496
American Electroplaters and Surface Finishers Society Vol 1: 2166
American Electroplaters' Society Vol 1: 2166
American Endurance Ride Conference Vol 1: 2173
American Enterprise Institute for Public Policy Research Vol 1: 2194
American Epilepsy Society Vol 1: 2196
American Equilibration Society Vol 1: 2198
American Ethical Union Vol 1: 2201
American Evaluation Association Vol 1: 2203
American Ex-Prisoners of War Vol 1: 2209
American Ex-Prisoners of War, East Tennessee Chapter Vol 1: 2212
American Express Vol 1: 21059
American Express Company Vol 1: 12550
American Family Therapy Academy Vol 1: 2214
American Family Therapy Association Vol 1: 2214
American Fancy Rat and Mouse Association Vol 1: 2217
American Farm Bureau Federation Vol 1: 2219
American Farm Economics Association Vol 1: 867
American Federation for Aging Research Vol 1: 2221
American Federation of Aviculture Vol 1: 2224
American Federation of Labor - Congress of Industrial Organizations Vol 1: 2226
American Federation of Mineralogical Societies Vol 1: 2228
American Federation of Police Vol 1: 3564
American Federation of School Administrators Vol 1: 2230
American Federation of Teachers Vol 1: 17887
American Federation of Teachers, AFL-CIO Vol 1: 2232
American Fighter Aces Association Vol 1: 2234
American Film Institute Vol 1: 2240
American Film Institute Alumni Association Writers Workshop Vol 1: 15999
American Finance Association Vol 1: 2242
American First Day Cover Society Vol 1: 2245
American Fisheries Society Vol 1: 2249
American Folklore Society Vol 1: 2263
American Football Coaches Association Vol 1: 2266
American Forage and Grassland Council Vol 1: 2272
American Foreign Service Association Vol 1: 2277
American Forensic Association Vol 1: 2285
American Forest and Paper Association Vol 1: 2287
American Forest and Paper Association - American Wood Council Vol 1: 2290
American Forum for Jewish-Christian Cooperation Vol 1: 2293
American Foundation for Aging Research Vol 1: 2297
American Foundation for the Blind Vol 1: 2299
American Friends of The Hebrew University Vol 1: 2305
American Fuchsia Society Vol 1: 2311
American Galvanizers Association Vol 1: 2314
American Gastroenterological Association Foundation Vol 1: 9706
American Gear Manufacturer Association Vol 1: 2316
American Gem Society Vol 1: 2321
American Gem Trade Association Vol 1: 2323
American Geographical Society Vol 1: 2327
American Geological Institute Vol 1: 2338
American Geophysical Union Vol 1: 2342
American Geriatrics Society Vol 1: 2360
American Gloxinia and Gesneriad Society, Grow and Study Chapter Vol 1: 2363
American Greetings Vol 1: 15565
American Group Psychotherapy Association Vol 1: 2365
American Guild of Authors and Composers Vol 1: 19405
American Guild of Organists Vol 1: 2367
American Guild of Organists, Region II Vol 1: 2374
American Guild of Organists, Wyoming (606) Vol 1: 2376
American Gynecological and Obstetrical Society Vol 1: 2378
American Gynecological Club Vol 2: 8441
American Gynecological Society Vol 1: 2378
American Handwriting Analysis Foundation Vol 1: 2381
American Hanoverian Society Vol 1: 2385
American Headache Society Vol 1: 2387
American Health Care Association Vol 1: 2392
American Health Information Management - Wisconsin Chapter Vol 1: 2397
American Healthcare Radiology Administrators Vol 1: 2399
American Heart Association Vol 1: 2401
American Heart Association, Talbot County Branch Vol 1: 2422
American Helicopter Society Vol 1: 2424
American Helvetia Philatelic Society Vol 1: 2441
American Hemerocallis Society Vol 1: 2443
American Hibiscus Society Vol 1: 2449
American Hiking Society Vol 1: 2451
American Historic Inns Vol 1: 2460
American Historical Association Vol 1: 2462
American Historical Association Vol 1: 7151, 12833
American Historical Association, Pacific Coast Branch Vol 1: 2483
American Historical Print Collectors Society Vol 1: 2485
American Hockey Coaches Association Vol 1: 2487
American Hockey League Vol 1: 2497
American Holsteiner Horse Association Vol 1: 2519
American Home Economics Association Foundation Vol 1: 935
American Homebrewers Association Vol 1: 2521
American Horticultural Society Vol 1: 2523
American Hospital Association Vol 1: 2540
American Hospital Radiology Administrators Vol 1: 2399
American Hosta Society Vol 1: 2549
American Hot Rod Association Vol 1: 2564
American Hotel and Lodging Association Vol 1: 2566
American Hotel & Motel Association Vol 1: 2566
American Humane Association Vol 1: 2571
American Humanics Vol 1: 2579
American Humanist Association Vol 1: 2582
American Hungarian Foundation Vol 1: 2593
American Indian Ethnohistoric Conference Vol 1: 4069
American Indian Heritage Foundation Vol 1: 2595
American Indian Horse Registry Vol 1: 2598
American Indian Lore Association Vol 1: 2603
American Indian Science and Engineering Society Vol 1: 2606
American Industrial Arts Student Association Vol 1: 19957
American Industrial Hygiene Association Vol 1: 2608
American Institute for Contemporary German Studies Vol 1: 2622
American Institute for Decision Sciences Vol 1: 8785
American Institute for Design and Drafting Vol 1: 2131
American Institute for Patristic and Byzantine Studies Vol 1: 2625
American Institute for Public Service Vol 1: 2627
American Institute of Aeronautics and Astronautics Vol 1: 2629
American Institute of Aeronautics and Astronautics Vol 1: 19050, 19057
American Institute of Aeronautics and Astronautics - Stanford University Branch Vol 1: 2704
American Institute of Architects Vol 1: 2706

American Institute of Architects Vol 1: 8346, 12819, 19841
American Institute of Architects - New York Chapter Vol 1: 2724
American Institute of Architects, Arizona Chapter Vol 1: 2729
American Institute of Architects, Southern Arizona Vol 1: 2731
American Institute of Architects - *Sunset Magazine* Vol 1: 19838
American Institute of Architects, Tampa Bay Vol 1: 2733
American Institute of Architects Vermont Vol 1: 2736
American Institute of Biological Sciences Vol 1: 2739
American Institute of Building Design Vol 1: 2742
American Institute of Certified Planners Vol 1: 3545, 3546
American Institute of Certified Public Accountants Vol 1: 2744
American Institute of Chemical Engineers Vol 1: 2755
American Institute of Chemical Engineers Vol 1: 4318, 4328, 4523
American Institute of Chemists Vol 1: 2797
American Institute of Cooperation Vol 1: 14799
American Institute of Fishery Research Biologists Vol 1: 2803
American Institute of Graphic Arts Vol 1: 2807
American Institute of Industrial Engineers Vol 1: 10948
American Institute of Mechanical Engineers Vol 1: 4534
American Institute of Mining, Metallurgical, and Petroleum Engineers Vol 1: 2814
American Institute of Mining, Metallurgical and Petroleum Engineers Vol 1: 4318
American Institute of Mining, Metallurgical, and Petroleum Engineers Vol 1: 4328
American Institute of Mining, Metallurgical and Petroleum Engineers Vol 1: 4520
American Institute of Mining, Metallurgical and Petroleum Engineers; Iron and Steel Society of the Vol 1: 5401
American Institute of Mining, Metallurgical and Petroleum Engineers; Society of Petroleum Engineers of the Vol 1: 19233
American Institute of Musical Studies Vol 1: 15430
American Institute of Park Executives Vol 1: 4478
American Institute of Physics Vol 1: 2830
American Institute of Planners Vol 1: 3544
American Institute of Plant Engineers Vol 1: 5364
American Institute of Professional Geologists Vol 1: 2842
American Institute of Real Estate Appraisers Vol 1: 5005
American Institute of Steel Construction Vol 1: 2847
American Institute of Stress Vol 1: 2852
American Institute of Timber Construction Vol 1: 2854
American Institute of Ultrasound in Medicine Vol 1: 2856
American Intellectual Property Law Association Vol 1: 2861
American Interior Designers Vol 1: 4458
American Intraocular Implant Society Vol 1: 4272
American Iris Society Vol 1: 2865
American Irish Historical Society Vol 1: 2870
American Iron and Steel Institute Vol 1: 2872
American-Israel Environmental Council Vol 1: 2876
American-Israel Numismatic Association Vol 1: 2878
American Italian Historical Association Vol 1: 2881
American Jewish Committee Vol 1: 2883
American Jewish Congress Vol 1: 2889
American Jewish Historical Society Vol 1: 2899
American Jewish Press Association Vol 1: 2906
American Journal of International Law Vol 1: 4464
American Judicature Society Vol 1: 2910
American Junior Golf Association Vol 1: 21923
American Junior Shorthorn Association Vol 1: 2914
American Kenpo Karate International Vol 1: 2916
American Kidney Fund Vol 1: 2918
American Kitefliers Association Vol 1: 2921
American Laryngological Association Vol 1: 2923
American Lawyers Auxiliary Vol 1: 2930
American League of Professional Baseball Clubs Vol 1: 2938
American Leather Chemists Association Vol 1: 2940
American Legion Vol 1: 2945
American Legion A.J. Jurek Post 1672 Vol 1: 2949
American Legion Auxiliary Vol 1: 2951
American Legion Baseball Vol 1: 17882
American Legion, Sumner Vol 1: 2953
American Legion Virginia Vol 1: 2955
American Legislative Exchange Council Vol 1: 2957
American Library Association Vol 1: 3000
American Library Association - Children's Services Division Vol 1: 5429
American Library Association - Ethnic and Multicultural Information Exchange Round Table Vol 1: 2961
American Library Association - Exhibits Round Table Vol 1: 2963
American Library Association - Governance Office Vol 1: 2966
American Library Association - Intellectual Freedom Round Table Vol 1: 2985
American Library Association - International Relations Committee Vol 1: 2989
American Library Association - Library History Round Table Vol 1: 2992
American Library Association - Office for Research and Statistics Vol 1: 2997
American Library Association - Public Information Office Vol 1: 2999
American Library Association - Reference and Adult Services Division Vol 1: 17934
American Library Association - Resources and Technical Services Division Vol 1: 5421
American Library Association - Social Responsibilities Round Table Vol 1: 3001
American Library Association - Young Adult Services Division Vol 1: 22049
American Library Association/Library Administration & Management Association Vol 1: 2708
American Liszt Society Vol 1: 3006
American Literary Translators Association Vol 1: 3008
American Liver Foundation Vol 1: 3010
American Lung Association Vol 1: 3012
American Lung Association of Eastern Missouri Vol 1: 3016
American Lung Association of Massachusetts Vol 1: 3018
American Lung Association of Rhode Island Vol 1: 3020
American Machinist Vol 1: 3022
American Marketing Association Vol 1: 3024
American Mathematical Association of Two-Year Colleges Vol 1: 3037
American Mathematical Society Vol 1: 3039
American Mathematical Society Vol 1: 13200, 13842, 18731
American Mathematical Society Vol 1: 18738
American Mathematical Society Vol 1: 18747
American Meat Institute Vol 1: 3044
American Meat Science Association Vol 1: 3048
American Medical Association Vol 1: 777
American Medical Athletic Association Vol 1: 3059
American Medical Technologists Vol 1: 3061
American Medical Women's Association Vol 1: 3076
American Medical Writers Association Vol 1: 3080
American Mental Health Clergy Vol 1: 3631
American Mental Health Counselors Association Vol 1: 3086
American Merchant Marine Library Association Vol 1: 3090
American Meteorological Society Vol 1: 3095
American Meteorological Society - National Weather Association, Aloha Chapter Vol 1: 3102
American MGB Association Vol 1: 3104
American MGC Register Vol 1: 3106
American Military Institute Vol 1: 18799
American Military Retirees Association Vol 1: 3108
American Milking Shorthorn Society Vol 1: 3110
American Mining Congress Vol 1: 15385
American Mizrachi Women Vol 1: 4933
American Morgan Horse Association Vol 1: 3121
American Mosquito Control Association Vol 1: 3134
American Mothers Committee Vol 1: 3140
American Mothers, Inc. Vol 1: 3140
American Motion Picture Society Vol 1: 3146
American Motorcyclist Association Vol 1: 3149
American Moving and Storage Association Vol 1: 3152
American Museum of Natural History Vol 1: 3154
American Music Awards Vol 1: 3159
American Music Center Vol 1: 3161
American Music Festival Association Vol 1: 3163
American Music Scholarship Association Vol 1: 3165
American Music Therapy Association Vol 1: 3167

American Musical Instrument Society Vol 1: 3169
American Musicological Society Vol 1: 3173
American National Standards Institute Vol 1: 3180
American Nature Study Society Vol 1: 3187
American Needlepoint Guild Vol 1: 3189
American Neuropsychiatric Association Vol 1: 3191
American Newspaper Publishers Association Foundation Vol 1: 16336
American North Country Cheviot Sheep Association Vol 1: 3193
American Nuclear Society Vol 1: 16594
American Numismatic Association Vol 1: 3196
American Numismatic Society Vol 1: 3270
American Nursery and Landscape Association Vol 1: 9288
American Nurses Association Vol 1: 3275
American Nurses Foundation Vol 1: 3286
American Occupational Medical Association Vol 1: 1903
American Occupational Therapy Association Vol 1: 3289
American Occupational Therapy Foundation Vol 1: 3302
American Oil Chemists' Society Vol 1: 3304
American Ophthalmological Society Vol 1: 3312
American Optical Company Vol 1: 16797
American Optical Corporation Vol 1: 16783
American Optometric Association Vol 1: 3314
American Optometric Foundation Vol 1: 720
American Orchid Society Vol 1: 3319
American Ornithologists' Union Vol 1: 3338
American ORT Vol 1: 3341
American Orthodontic Society Vol 1: 3347
American Orthopaedic Society for Sports Medicine Vol 1: 3349
American Osteopathic Academy of Orthopedics Vol 1: 3353
American Osteopathic College of Pathologists Vol 1: 3356
American Otological Society Vol 1: 3358
American Park and Recreation Society Vol 1: 3361
American Parkinson Disease Association Vol 1: 3364
American Patent Law Association Vol 1: 2861
American Peanut Council Vol 1: 3366
American Pediatric Society Vol 1: 3369
American Pet Products Manufacturer Association Vol 1: 3371
American Petanque Association U.S.A. Vol 1: 9522
American Petroleum Institute Vol 1: 3373
American Pharmacists Association Vol 1: 3375
American Philatelic Association Vol 1: 3413
American Philatelic Congress Vol 1: 3403
American Philatelic Society Vol 1: 3413
American Philatelic Society Writers Unit Junior Division Vol 1: 12469
American Philological Association Vol 1: 3417
American Philosophical Association Vol 1: 3420
American Philosophical Society Vol 1: 3432
American Photographic Historical Society Vol 1: 3442
American Physical Society Vol 1: 3444
American Physical Therapy Association Vol 1: 3482
American Physical Therapy Association, New Hampshire Chapter Vol 1: 3501
American Physicians Art Association Vol 1: 3503
American Physiological Society Vol 1: 3505
American Phytopathological Society Vol 1: 3532
American Phytopathological Society Vol 1: 7336, 19872
American Pianists Association Vol 1: 3542
American Planning Association Vol 1: 3544
American Plant Life Society Vol 1: 11439
American Podiatric Medical Association Vol 1: 3561
American Podiatry Association Vol 1: 3561
American Police Hall of Fame Vol 1: 3564
American Political Science Association Vol 1: 3580
American Pomological Society Vol 1: 3582
American Power Boat Association Vol 1: 3586
American Primrose Society Vol 1: 3592
American Printing History Association Vol 1: 3594
American Probation and Parole Association Vol 1: 3597
American Professional Society on the Abuse of Children Vol 1: 3607
American Protestant Health Association; College of Chaplains of the Vol 1: 5819
American Psychiatric Association Vol 1: 3609
American Psychological Association Vol 1: 17696, 17697
American Psychological Association - Adult Development and Aging Division (Division 20) Vol 1: 3643
American Psychological Association - American Psychology-Law Society (Division 41) Vol 1: 3646
American Psychological Association - Applied Experimental and Engineering Psychology Division (Division 21) Vol 1: 3649
American Psychological Association - Behavior Analysis Division (Division 25) Vol 1: 3653
American Psychological Association - Behavioral Neuroscience and Comparative Psychology Division (Division 6) Vol 1: 3658
American Psychological Association - Counseling Psychology Division (Division 17) Vol 1: 3660
American Psychological Association - Developmental Psychology Division (Division 7) Vol 1: 3667
American Psychological Association - Division of Family Psychology (Division 43) Vol 1: 3669
American Psychological Association - Division of State, Provincial, and Territorial Psychological Association Affairs (Division 31) Vol 1: 3674
American Psychological Association - Educational Psychology Division (Division 15) Vol 1: 3677
American Psychological Association - Exercise and Sport Psychology Division (Division 47) Vol 1: 3681
American Psychological Association - General Psychology Division (Division 1) Vol 1: 3683
American Psychological Association - Health Psychology Division (Division 38) Vol 1: 3688
American Psychological Association - Mental Retardation and Developmental Disabilities Division (Division 33) Vol 1: 3690
American Psychological Association - Population and Environmental Psychology Division (Division 34) Vol 1: 3692
American Psychological Association - Psychoanalysis Division (Division 39) Vol 1: 3694
American Psychological Association - Psychologists in Public Service Division (Division 18) Vol 1: 3697
American Psychological Association - Psychology of Religion (Division 36) Vol 1: 3700
American Psychological Association - Psychotherapy Division (Division 29) Vol 1: 3703
American Psychological Association - Rehabilitation Psychology Division (Division 22) Vol 1: 3707
American Psychological Association - School Psychology Division (Division 16) Vol 1: 3710
American Psychological Association - Society for Community Research and Action: Division of Community Psychology (Division 27) Vol 1: 3713
American Psychological Association - Society for Military Psychology (Division 19) Vol 1: 3721
American Psychological Association - Society for Personality and Social Psychology (Division 8) Vol 1: 3725
American Psychological Association - Society for the History of Psychology (Division 26) Vol 1: 3728
American Psychological Association - Society for the Psychology of Women (Division 35) Vol 1: 3730
American Psychological Association - Society for the Study of Peace, Conflict, and Violence (Division 48) Vol 1: 3739
American Psychological Association - Society for the Teaching of Psychology (Division 2) Vol 1: 3741
American Psychological Association - Society of Clinical Psychology (Division 12) Vol 1: 3743
American Psychological Association - Society of Consulting Psychology (Division 13) Vol 1: 3751
American Psychological Association - Society of Pediatric Psychology (Division 54) Vol 1: 3754
American Psychological Association - Society of Psychological Hypnosis (Division 30) Vol 1: 3758
American Psychological Association (Division 28) Vol 1: 3763
American Psychological Association Division of Independent Practice - Division of Independent Practice Vol 1: 3767
American Psychological Association of Graduate Students Vol 1: 18911
American Psychological Foundation Vol 1: 18915
American Psychopathological Association Vol 1: 3771
American Public Gas Association Vol 1: 3774

American Public Health Association Vol 1: 3777
American Public Human Services Association Vol 1: 3781
American Public Power Association Vol 1: 3783
American Public Works Association Vol 1: 3797
American Rabbit Breeders Association Vol 1: 3811
American Radium Society Vol 1: 3813
American Railway Development Association Vol 1: 3817
American Recorder Society Vol 1: 3819
American Red Cross National Headquarters Vol 1: 3821
American Red Magen David for Israel - American Friends of Magen David Vol 1: 3842
American Revolution Round Table Vol 1: 3844
American Rhinologic Society Vol 1: 3847
American Rhododendron Society Vol 1: 3850
American Risk and Insurance Association Vol 1: 3853
American Road and Transportation Builders Association Vol 1: 3858
American Road Builders Association Vol 1: 3858
American Roentgen Ray Society Vol 1: 1943
American Romanian Academy of Arts and Sciences Vol 1: 3868
American Rose Society Vol 1: 3871
American Rottweiler Club Vol 1: 3873
American Rural Health Association Vol 1: 15648
American-Scandinavian Foundation Vol 1: 3877
American Schleswing-Holstein Heritage Society Vol 1: 3880
American School and Community Safety Association Vol 1: 18334
American School and University Vol 1: 3882
American School Health Association Vol 1: 3887
American Scientific Glassblowers Society Vol 1: 3893
American Shetland Pony Club/American Miniature Horse Registry Vol 1: 3896
American-Slovenian Polka Foundation Vol 1: 3898
American Society for Adolescent Psychiatry Vol 1: 3902
American Society for Advancement of Anesthesia and Sedation in Dentistry Vol 1: 3907
American Society for Aesthetic Plastic Surgery Vol 1: 3910
American Society for Aesthetics Vol 1: 3912
American Society for Aesthetics Vol 1: 12444
American Society for Bariatric Surgery Vol 1: 3914
American Society for Biochemistry and Molecular Biology Vol 1: 3916
American Society for Bioethics and Humanities Vol 1: 3924
American Society for Bone and Mineral Research Vol 1: 3928
American Society for Cell Biology Vol 1: 3939
American Society for Clinical Laboratory Science Vol 1: 3950
American Society for Clinical Nutrition Vol 1: 3956
American Society for Clinical Pathology Vol 1: 3962
American Society for Clinical Pharmacology and Therapeutics Vol 1: 3971
American Society for Colposcopy and Cervical Pathology Vol 1: 3977
American Society for Competitiveness Vol 1: 3980
American Society for Cybernetics Vol 1: 3984
American Society for Dermatologic Surgery Vol 1: 3988
American Society for Eighteenth-Century Studies Vol 1: 916
American Society for Eighteenth-Century Studies Vol 1: 3990
American Society for Engineering Education Vol 1: 3993
American Society for Engineering Management Vol 1: 4050
American Society for Enology and Viticulture Vol 1: 4061
American Society for Environmental History Vol 1: 4064
American Society for Ethnohistory Vol 1: 4069
American Society for Experimental Pathology Vol 1: 4117
American Society for Gastrointestinal Endoscopy Vol 1: 4071
American Society for Gravitational and Space Biology Vol 1: 4076
American Society for Horticultural Science Vol 1: 4083
American Society for Information Science and Technology Vol 1: 4099
American Society for Investigative Pathology Vol 1: 4117
American Society for Legal History Vol 1: 4124
American Society for Metals Vol 1: 5172
American Society for Microbiology Vol 1: 4127
American Society for Microbiology Vol 1: 20579
American Society for Microbiology, Arizona Chapter Vol 1: 4140
American Society for Nondestructive Testing Vol 1: 4142
American Society for Nutritional Sciences Vol 1: 4155
American Society for Parenteral and Enteral Nutrition Vol 1: 4164
American Society for Personnel Administration Vol 1: 18693
American Society for Pharmacology and Experimental Therapeutics Vol 1: 4168
American Society for Pharmacy Law Vol 1: 4176
American Society for Photogrammetry and Remote Sensing Vol 2: 6636
American Society for Public Administration Vol 1: 4179
American Society for Public Administration Vol 1: 10108, 14374
American Society for Public Administration (ASPA) Vol 1: 13819
American Society for Quality Control Vol 1: 6202
American Society for Stereotactic and Functional Neurosurgery Vol 1: 4190
American Society for Technion-Israel Institute of Technology Vol 1: 4192
American Society for Testing and Materials Vol 1: 5925
American Society for the Prevention of Cruelty to Animals Vol 1: 4194
American Society for Theatre Research Vol 1: 4197
American Society for Therapeutic Radiology and Oncology Vol 1: 1943
American Society for Training and Development Vol 1: 4203
American Society of Abdominal Surgeons Vol 1: 4209
American Society of Agricultural and Biological Engineers Vol 1: 4211
American Society of Agricultural Engineers Vol 1: 11362
American Society of Agronomy Vol 1: 4238
American Society of Agronomy Vol 1: 19398, 19874
American Society of Animal Science Vol 1: 4250
American Society of Artists Vol 1: 4263
American Society of Association Executives Vol 1: 4266
American Society of Biological Chemists Vol 1: 3916
American Society of Business Press Editors Vol 1: 4269
American Society of Business Publication Editors Vol 1: 4269
American Society of Cataract and Refractive Surgery Vol 1: 4272
American Society of Certified Engineering Technicians Vol 1: 4275
American Society of Church History Vol 1: 4283
American Society of Civil Engineering Vol 1: 4289
American Society of Civil Engineers Vol 1: 4289, 19057
American Society of Clinical Pathologists Vol 1: 3962
American Society of Colon and Rectal Surgeons Vol 1: 4372
American Society of Composers, Authors and Publishers Vol 1: 4374
American Society of Composers, Authors and Publishers Vol 1: 7941
American Society of Criminology Vol 1: 4383
American Society of Cytopathology Vol 1: 4388
American Society of Directors of Volunteer Services Vol 1: 4400
American Society of Electroencephalographic Technologists Vol 1: 4402
American Society of Electroneurodiagnostic Technologists Vol 1: 4402
American Society of Enologists Vol 1: 4061
American Society of Farm Managers and Rural Appraisers Vol 1: 4404
The American Society of Farm Managers and Rural Appraisers Vol 1: 14154
American Society of Furniture Designers Vol 1: 4409
American Society of Genealogists Vol 1: 4414
American Society of Golf Course Architects Vol 1: 21923
American Society of Heating, Refrigerating and Air-Conditioning Engineers Vol 1: 4416
American Society of Hematology Vol 1: 4442

American Society of Human Genetics Vol 1: 4448
American Society of Ichthyologists and Herpetologists Vol 1: 4450
American Society of Indexers Vol 1: 4456
American Society of Interior Designers Vol 1: 4458
American Society of International Law Vol 1: 4461
American Society of Journalism School Administrators Vol 1: 5844
American Society of Journalists and Authors Vol 1: 4466
American Society of Landscape Architects Vol 1: 4471
American Society of Law, Medicine and Ethics Vol 1: 4485
American Society of Limnology and Oceanography Vol 1: 4488
American Society of Magazine Editors Vol 1: 4491
American Society of Mammalogists Vol 1: 4493
American Society of Mechanical Engineers Vol 1: 4318, 4328
American Society of Mechanical Engineers Vol 1: 4501
American Society of Mechanical Engineers Vol 1: 4511, 19057
American Society of Mining & Reclamation Vol 1: 4555
American Society of Music Arrangers and Composers Vol 1: 4559
American Society of Naturalists Vol 1: 4561
American Society of Naval Engineers Vol 1: 4565
American Society of Neuroimaging Vol 1: 4572
American Society of Newspaper Editors Vol 1: 4575
American Society of Oral Surgeons Vol 1: 1308
American Society of Orthopedic Professionals Vol 1: 4581
American Society of Pharmacognosy Vol 1: 3393
American Society of Pharmacognosy Vol 1: 4583
American Society of Photogrammetry Vol 1: 5207
American Society of Physician Analysts Vol 1: 4597
American Society of Planning Officials Vol 1: 3544
American Society of Plant Biologists Vol 1: 4585
American Society of Plant Taxonomists Vol 1: 4592
American Society of Plant Taxonomists Vol 1: 6541
American Society of Psychoanalytic Physicians Vol 1: 4597
American Society of Psychopathology of Expression Vol 1: 4599
American Society of Safety Engineers Vol 1: 4601
American Society of Safety Engineers, Arkansas/Louisiana/Texas Chapter Vol 1: 4608
American Society of Sanitary Engineering Vol 1: 4610
American Society of Swedish Engineers Vol 1: 4614
American Society of Traffic and Transportation Vol 1: 4618
American Society of Transportation and Logistics Vol 1: 4618
American Society of Travel Agents Vol 1: 4623
American Society of Tropical Medicine and Hygiene Vol 1: 4628
American Society of Tropical Medicine and Hygiene Vol 2: 8846
American Society of Ultrasound Technical Specialists Vol 1: 19102
American Society of Zoologists Vol 1: 18773
American Society on Aging Vol 1: 4634
American Society on Aging Vol 1: 4637
American Sociological Association Vol 1: 4646
American Solar Energy Society Vol 1: 4655
American Spaniel Club Vol 1: 4657
The American Spectator Vol 1: 4659
American Speech and Hearing Association Vol 1: 4661
American Speech Language Hearing Association Vol 1: 4661
American Spelean Historical Association Vol 1: 15798
American Spice Trade Association Vol 1: 4666
American Spinal Injury Association Vol 1: 4668
American Sportfishing Association Vol 1: 4670
American Sports Medicine Institute Vol 1: 4672
American Sportscasters Association Vol 1: 4674
American Staffing Association Vol 1: 4684
American Statistical Association Vol 1: 4691
American Steamship and Tourist Agents Association Vol 1: 4623
American String Teachers Association Vol 1: 4699
American String Teachers Association/ National School Orchestra Association Vol 1: 4702
American Studies Association Vol 1: 4704
American Subcontractors Association of Mississippi Vol 1: 4714
American Supplier Institute Vol 1: 4716
American Swimming Coaches Association Vol 1: 4718
American-Swiss Foundation Vol 1: 4726
American Symphony Orchestra League Vol 1: 4728
American Telephone and Telegraph Company Vol 1: 13828
American Teleservices Association Vol 1: 4734
American Theatre Organ Society Vol 1: 4736
American Theatre Wing Vol 1: 4740, 12742
American Therapeutic Recreation Association Vol 1: 4742
American Thyroid Association Vol 1: 4744
American Topical Association Vol 1: 4747
American Translators Association Vol 1: 4750
American Truck Historical Society Vol 1: 4755
American Truck Historical Society, Arizona Chapter Vol 1: 4758
American Truck Historical Society, Gateway Chapter Vol 1: 4760
American Truck Historical Society, Metro Jersey Chapter Vol 1: 4762
American Trucking Associations Vol 1: 4764
American Trucking Associations - Safety Management Council Vol 1: 4768
American TV Commercials Festival Vol 1: 8111
American Underground Association Vol 1: 4776
American Underground Construction Association Vol 1: 4776
American Underground-Space Association Vol 1: 4776
American University - National Center for Health Fitness Vol 1: 4781
American University - School of Public Affairs Vol 1: 4783
American Urological Association Vol 1: 4785
American Urological Association Foundation Vol 1: 4798
American Vaulting Association Vol 1: 4803
American Veterinary Exhibitors Association Vol 1: 4805
American Veterinary Medical Association Vol 1: 4807
American Water Resources Association Vol 1: 4821
American Water Works Association Vol 1: 4836
American Watercolor Society Vol 1: 4839
American Welding Society Vol 1: 4874
American Whig-Cliosophic Society Vol 1: 4901
American White American Creme Horse Registry Vol 1: 4903
American Wine Society Vol 1: 4905
American Zoo and Aquarium Association Vol 1: 4912
Americanism Educational League Vol 1: 4920
America's Cup Global Information Service Vol 1: 4922
America's Foundation Vol 1: 4924
America's Junior Miss Foundation Vol 1: 4926
Americas Society Vol 1: 4928
America's Young Woman of the Year Vol 1: 4926
Ames Research Center - Astrobiology Institute Vol 1: 4931
AMF Vol 1: 8163
Amgen Vol 1: 16722
Amiens International Film Festival Vol 2: 2225
Amis de la Reliure d'Art Vol 2: 4399
Amis de la Reliure d'art Vol 2: 4399
AMIT USA Vol 1: 4933
Amnesty International - Canadian Section Vol 1: 4940
Amoco Chemical Company Vol 1: 19307
Amsterdams Fonds voor de Kunst Vol 2: 4682
Amt der o.o. Landesregierung Vol 2: 795
Amt der Salzburger Landesregierung - Kulturabteilung Vol 2: 667
Amt der Tiroler Landesregierung, Kulturabteilung Vol 2: 670
Amusement and Music Operators Association Vol 1: 4942
AMVETS - American Veterans Vol 1: 4946
Amy Foundation Vol 1: 4950
Anaren Microwave, Inc. Vol 1: 4035
Anchor Bay Chamber of Commerce Vol 1: 4952
Ancient & Medieval History Book Club Vol 2: 6915

Ancient Mediterranean Research Association Vol 1: 4954
Anda Foundation; Geza Vol 2: 6365
Anderson Poetry Club Vol 1: 15000
Anglo-Austrian Music Society Vol 2: 6726
Animal Air Transportation Association Vol 1: 4960
Animal Behavior Society Vol 1: 4956
Animal Feed Manufacturers Association Vol 2: 5514
Animal Health Distributors Association Vol 2: 6728
Animal Transportation Association Vol 1: 4960
Animal Transportation Association - European Office Vol 2: 6730
Animal Welfare Institute Vol 1: 4965
Animalia - Federation for the Protection of Animals Vol 2: 1570
Animals Australia Vol 2: 65
Ann Arbor Film Festival Vol 1: 4967
Anna Bijns-Stichting Vol 2: 4702
Annenberg School for Communication Vol 1: 4973
Annual Reviews Inc. Vol 1: 13838
Anti-Communist International Vol 1: 4976
Anti-Defamation League Vol 1: 4978
Anti-Slavery International Vol 2: 6735
Antioch College - Glen Helen Ecology Institute Vol 1: 4985
Antiquarian Field Club Vol 2: 7388
Antique Automobile Club of America, Northwestern Michigan Region Vol 1: 4987
Antwerp Diamond High Council Vol 2: 834
Anuvibha - Anuvrat Global Organization Vol 2: 3350
Anuvrat Vishva Bharati (Anuvibha) Vol 2: 3350
Anvil Press Vol 1: 4989
ANZIAM-Australian and New Zealand Industrial and Applied Mathematics - Australian Mathematical Society Vol 2: 67
AOAC International Vol 1: 4991
Aontas Teilgin Agus Amais na h'Eireann Vol 2: 3678
APA Committee on Ethnic Minority Affairs Vol 1: 18920
APA Committee on International Relations Vol 1: 18904
APA Committee on Women in Psychology Vol 1: 18912
Apalachee Poetry Center Vol 1: 8424
Apex Awards Vol 1: 4993
APMI International Vol 1: 13312
Apotekarsocieteten Vol 2: 6274
Apotex/PACE Vol 1: 7334
APPA Public Relations Committee Vol 1: 3599
Appalachian Center Vol 1: 4995, 4996
Appalachian Peace and Justice Network Vol 1: 4998
Appalachian Studies Association Vol 1: 5000
Appeal of Conscience Foundation Vol 1: 5003
Appita - Technical Association for the Australian and New Zealand Pulp and Paper Industry Vol 2: 71
Appraisal Institute Vol 1: 5005
APPROTECH ASIA Vol 2: 5288
ARA International Vol 2: 4399
Arab American Institute Vol 1: 5018
Arab Institute of Navigation Vol 2: 1552
Arab Towns Organization Vol 2: 4373
Arabian Sport Horse Association, Inc. Vol 1: 5020
Arango Design Foundation Vol 1: 5022
Arbeitsgemeinschaft Schweizer Grafiker Vol 2: 6530
Arboricultural Association Vol 2: 6737
The Arc of the US Vol 1: 5024
Arc of Tucson Vol 1: 5027
Archaeological Geology Division Vol 1: 9955
Archaeological Institute of America Vol 1: 5029
Archimage International Festival of Urban Architecture, Town Planning, and Environment Films of Bordeaux Vol 2: 2227
Architectural Association Vol 2: 6739
Architectural Institute of the Republic of China Vol 2: 6587
Architectural League of New York Vol 1: 5037
Architectural Record Vol 1: 5039
Archival Issues Vol 1: 13393
Archivio Disarmo Vol 2: 3842
Arcos Corporation Vol 1: 4897
Arctowski Fund; Henryk Vol 1: 13826
Arden Terrace Neighborhood Association Vol 1: 5042
Argentine Academy of Letters Vol 2: 15
Argentine Paleontological Association Vol 2: 18
Argentine Society of Botany Vol 2: 23
Argentine Society of Geographical Studies Vol 2: 25
Argentinian Association of Dermatology Vol 2: 29
Ari Stiftelsen; Carina Vol 2: 6141
Aril Society International Vol 1: 5044
Arisawa Memorial Fund; Hiroma Vol 1: 5568
Arizona Authors' Association Vol 1: 5047
Arizona Geriatrics Society Vol 1: 5049
Arizona Library Association Vol 1: 5051
Arizona State Poetry Society Vol 1: 14990
Arizona Twirling Athletes Vol 1: 5067
Arkansas Arts Center Vol 1: 5069
Arkansas Elementary School Council - Arkansas Department of Education Vol 1: 5072
Arkansas Historical Association Vol 1: 5074
Arkansas Nurserymen's Association Vol 1: 5078
Arkansas Technology Transfer Society Vol 1: 5080
Arkansas Women's History Institute Vol 1: 5082
Arlen Memorial Fund; Stephen Vol 2: 6743
Arlington Chamber of Commerce Vol 1: 5084
ARMA International - The Association of Information Management Professionals Vol 1: 5086
Armenian Behavioral Science Association Vol 1: 5093
Armenian Numismatic Society Vol 1: 5095
Armstrong Memorial Research Foundation Vol 1: 5097
Army Families Federation Vol 2: 6745
Arnold Air Society Vol 1: 5099
Art Directors Club Vol 1: 5114
Art Directors Club of Toronto Vol 1: 203
Art Gallery of New South Wales Vol 2: 73
Art Niche New York Vol 1: 5120
Arthouse at the Jones Center Vol 1: 5122
Arthritis Foundation Vol 1: 5124
Arthritis Foundation, Rocky Mountain Chapter Vol 1: 5128
Arthroscopy Association of North America Vol 1: 5130
Arthur Rubinstein International Music Society Vol 2: 3719
Artisjus, Hungarian Organization for Defence of Copyright Vol 2: 3272
Artist-Blacksmith's Association of North America Vol 1: 5134
Artists and Educators Serving Young People Vol 1: 882
Artists' Association of Finland Vol 2: 1573
Artists' Fellowship Vol 1: 5137
Artists Guild of the Santa Ynez Valley Vol 1: 5140
Artists International Presentations, Inc. Vol 1: 5142
The Artist's Magazine Vol 1: 5144
Arts and Business Vol 2: 6748
Arts & Crafts Exhibition Society Vol 2: 9026
Arts & Science Center for Southeast Arkansas Vol 1: 5148
Arts Council England Vol 2: 6752
Arts Council of Ireland Vol 2: 3611
Arts Council of Northern Ireland Vol 2: 6760
Arts Council of Northwest Florida Vol 1: 5150
Arts Council of Wales Vol 2: 6763
The Arts Guild of Old Forge Vol 1: 5152
Arts Management Vol 1: 5154
Arts Midwest Vol 1: 5158
The ARTS of the Southern Finger Lakes Vol 1: 5160
Arvon Foundation Vol 2: 6765
Asahi Broadcasting Corporation Vol 2: 4114
The Asahi Glass Foundation Vol 2: 4089
Asamblea de Directores-Realizadores Cinematograficos y Audiovisuales Espanoles (ADIRCAE) Vol 2: 5996
Asbury Graphite Mills Vol 1: 1645
ASCAP Foundation Vol 1: 4380
Ascutney Mountain Audubon Society Vol 1: 5162
ASEAN Federation of Electrical Engineering Contractors Vol 2: 4414
ASEE/ERM Vol 1: 4042
ASHBEAMS Vol 1: 5545
Ashland Chemicals Inc. Vol 1: 19307
Asia-Pacific Association of Forestry Research Institutions Vol 2: 4416
Asia-Pacific Broadcasting Union Vol 2: 4418
Asia-Pacific Council of American Chambers of Commerce Vol 2: 5249
Asia/Pacific Cultural Centre for UNESCO Vol 2: 4091
Asian American Journalists Association Vol 1: 5164
Asian American Writers' Workshop Vol 1: 5168
Asian Association of Agricultural Engineering Vol 2: 6606
Asian Association of Management Organisations Vol 2: 4422
Asian Confederation of Credit Unions Vol 2: 6608
Asian Cultural Centre for UNESCO Vol 2: 4091
Asian Football Confederation Vol 2: 4424
Asian Institute of Technology Vol 2: 6610
Asian Medical Student's Associaton-Philippines Vol 2: 5251
Asian NGO Coalition for Agrarian Reform and Rural Development Vol 2: 5253

Organization Index

Asian/Pacific American Librarians Association Vol 1: 5170
Asian PGA Vol 1: 21923
Asian Productivity Organization Vol 2: 4093
ASM International Vol 1: 5172
ASM International Vol 1: 13459
Asociacion Argentina de Dermatologia Vol 2: 29
Asociacion Colombiana de Universidades ASCUN Vol 2: 1347
Asociacion Colombiana para el Avance de la Ciencia Vol 2: 1305
Asociacion de Industriales Metalurgico y Mineria de Venezuela Vol 2: 9326
Asociacion de Psicologia de Puerto Rico Vol 1: 5193
Asociacion Demografica Salvadorena Vol 2: 1560
Asociacion Farmaceutica Mexicana Vol 1: 17661
Asociacion Interamericana de Contabilidad Vol 1: 11130
Asociacion International de Escritores Policiacos Vol 2: 1393
Asociacion Latinoamericana de Fitopatologia Vol 2: 5243
Asociacion Latinoamericana de Instituciones Financieras Para el Desarrollo Vol 2: 5241
Asociacion Mundial de las Guias Scouts Vol 2: 9237
Asociacion Mundial Veterinaria de Avicola Vol 2: 3146
Asociacion Nacional Contra el Cancer Vol 2: 5208
Asociacion Nacional de Actores Vol 2: 4459
Asociacion Nacional de la Publicidad Vol 2: 4461
Asociacion Odontologica Argentina Vol 2: 31
Asociacion Paleontologica Argentina Vol 2: 18
Asociacion Panamericana de Instituciones de Credito Educativo Vol 2: 1330
Asociacion Peruana para la Conservacion de la Naturaleza Vol 2: 5245
Asociacion Quimica Colombiana Vol 2: 1339
Asociacion Universitaria Iberoamericana de Postgrado Vol 2: 6040
Asociata Pentru Protectia Consumatorilor Din Romania Vol 2: 5803
Asociatia Femeilor din Romania Vol 2: 5882
Aspen Filmfest Vol 1: 5195
Aspen Institute Vol 1: 5198
Aspen Technology, Inc. Vol 1: 2765
Asphalt Emulsion Manufacturer Association Vol 1: 5201
Asphalt Recycling and Reclaiming Association Vol 1: 5204
ASPRS - The Imaging and Geospatial Information Society Vol 1: 5207
Assaulted Women's Helpline Vol 1: 5226
Assisted Living Federation of America Vol 1: 5228
Associacao Brasileira de Embalagem Vol 2: 1163
Associacao Brasileira de Metalurgia e Materiais Vol 2: 1160
Associacao do Comercio Automovel de Portugal Vol 2: 5388
Associacao Portuguesa de Educacao Musical Vol 2: 5487
Associacion Internacional de la Seguridad Social Vol 2: 6448
Associated Builders and Contractors Vol 1: 5232
Associated Builders and Contractors, Southeast Pennsylvania Chapter Vol 1: 5235
Associated Church Press Vol 1: 5237
Associated Colleges of the Midwest Vol 1: 5242
Associated General Contractors of Vermont Vol 1: 5244
Associated Landscape Contractors of Colorado Vol 1: 5247
Associated Medical Services Inc. Vol 1: 18166
Associated Press Managing Editors - Managing Editors Association Vol 1: 5249
Associated Subcontractors of Massachusetts Vol 1: 5254
Associated Taxpayers of Idaho Vol 1: 5256
Associated Writing Programs Vol 1: 5258
Associates of Brand Library and Art Center Vol 1: 5260
Association Aeronautique et Astronautique de France Vol 2: 2229
Association canadianne de la mececine du travail et de l'environnement Vol 1: 16604
Association canadienne de dermatologie Vol 1: 7072
Association Canadienne de la Construction Vol 1: 7039
L'Association Canadienne de la Maladie Coeliaque Vol 1: 7021
Association canadienne de la paie Vol 1: 7331
L'Association Canadienne de la Securite Vol 1: 7385
Association canadienne de la technologie de l'information Vol 1: 10795
Association canadienne de l'informatique Vol 1: 7162
Association Canadienne de Production de Film et de Television Vol 1: 7092
Association Canadienne De Sante Publique Vol 1: 7354
Association Canadienne de Traitement d'Images et de Reconnaissance des Formes Vol 1: 7158
Association Canadienne de Transport Industriel Vol 1: 7160
Association Canadienne de Vexillologie Vol 1: 7097
Association Canadienne d'Economique Vol 1: 7077
Association Canadienne d'Education Vol 1: 7079
Association Canadienne Des Annonceurs Vol 1: 5588
Association Canadienne des Artistes de la Scene Vol 1: 6855
Association Canadienne des Banques Alimentaires Vol 1: 6904
Association Canadienne Des Barrages Vol 1: 7069
Association Canadienne Des Commissaires D'Ecoles Catholiques Vol 1: 7019
Association Canadienne des Courtiers en Valeurs Mobilieres Vol 1: 12172
Association Canadienne des Fabricants de Produits de Quincaillerie et d'Articles Menagers Vol 1: 7134
Association Canadienne des Harmonies Vol 1: 6961
Association Canadienne des Inspecteurs de Biens Immobiliers Vol 1: 6913
Association Canadienne des Journaux Vol 1: 7308
Association Canadienne des laboratories d'analyses environmentale Vol 1: 6880
Association Canadienne des Massotherapeutes du Sport Vol 1: 7505
Association Canadienne des Medecins Veterinaires Vol 1: 7530
Association Canadienne des Parcs et Loisirs Vol 1: 7322
Association Canadienne des Pathologistes Vol 1: 6927
Association canadienne des physiciens et physiciennes Vol 1: 6931
Association Canadienne des Producteurs de Semences Vol 1: 7387
Association canadienne des professeures et professeurs d'universite Vol 1: 6941
L'association Canadienne des Professionnels de la Vente Vol 1: 7342
Association Canadienne des Radiodiffuseurs Vol 1: 6889
Association canadienne des redacteurs scientifiques Vol 1: 7381
Association canadienne des reviseurs Vol 1: 9165
Association Canadienne des Societes Elizabeth Fry Vol 1: 6902
Association Canadienne des Technologues en Radiation Medicale Vol 1: 6916
Association Canadienne des Therapeutes du Sport Vol 1: 6945
Association Canadienne des Veterans de la Coree Vol 1: 12608
Association Canadienne D'Histoire Ferroviaire Vol 1: 7366
Association Canadienne pour la Sante Mentale Vol 1: 7266
Association Canadienne pour l'Etude du Quarternaire Vol 1: 7364
Association Cartographique Internationale Vol 2: 4802
Association catholique canadienne de la sante Vol 1: 7641
Association de la Recherche Theatrale au Canada Vol 1: 5284
Association de Musicotherapie du Canada Vol 1: 6887
L'Association des architects paysagistes du Canada Vol 1: 7475
Association des auteurs des Cantons de l'Est Vol 1: 5262
Association des Bibliotheques de la Sante du Canada Vol 1: 7136
Association des Camps du Canada Vol 1: 7013
Association des Chimistes de l'Industrie Textile Vol 2: 2241
Association des Comites Nationaux Olympiques Vol 2: 2245
Association des Congres Belges de la Route Vol 2: 2633
Association des critiques de theatre du Canada Vol 1: 7513
Association des Ecoles de Sante Publique de la Regional Europeenne Vol 2: 2247
L'Association des Forces aeriennes du Canada Vol 1: 366
Association des Ingenieurs-Conseils du Canada Vol 1: 5638
Association des Journalistes Automobile du Canada Vol 1: 6099
Association des Musees Canadiens Vol 1: 7296
Association des Pharmaciens du Canada Vol 1: 7333

Association des Traducteurs et Traductrices Litteraires du Canada Vol 1: 12873
Association des universites et colleges du Canada Vol 1: 5904
Association d'Etudes Baha'ies Vol 1: 5278
L'Association du Barreau Canadien Vol 1: 6963
Association du Prix Albert Londres Vol 2: 2234
Association Europeene des Galvanisateurs Vol 2: 7471
Association Europeenne d'Athletisme Vol 2: 2744
Association Europeenne de Traitement de Signaux Vol 2: 5397
Association Europeenne des Vehicules Electriques Routiers Vol 2: 852
Association Europeenne pour la Promotion de la Poesie Vol 2: 854
Association Europeenne Thyroide Vol 2: 1485
Association Fiscale Internationale Vol 2: 4822
Association for Advancement of Behavior Therapy Vol 1: 5264
Association for Asian Studies Vol 1: 5272
Association for Baha'i Studies Vol 1: 5278
Association for Canadian Studies in the United States Vol 1: 5280
Association for Canadian Theatre Research Vol 1: 5284
Association for Civil Rights in Israel Vol 2: 3721
Association for Clinical Biochemists Vol 2: 6767
Association for Communication Excellence in Agriculture, Natural Resources, and Life and Human Sciences Vol 1: 5290
Association for Computer Educators Vol 1: 11200
Association for Computing Machinery Vol 1: 5296
Association for Computing Machinery Vol 1: 10891
Association for Computing Machinery - Special Interest Group for Design of Communications Vol 1: 5309
Association for Computing Machinery - Special Interest Group for Management of Data Vol 1: 5312
Association for Computing Machinery - Special Interest Group on Algorithm and Computation Theory Vol 1: 5315
Association for Computing Machinery - Special Interest Group on Computer Science Education Vol 1: 5319
Association for Computing Machinery - Special Interest Group on Data Communications Vol 1: 5322
Association for Computing Machinery - Special Interest Group on Hypertext, Hypermedia and the Web Vol 1: 5324
Association for Conferences and Events Vol 2: 6773
Association for Conservation Information Vol 1: 5326
Association for Consumer Research Vol 1: 12446
Association for Convention Operations Management Vol 1: 5328
Association for Corporate Growth Vol 1: 5330
Association for Counselors and Educators in Government Vol 1: 5333
Association for Education and Rehabilitation of the Blind and Visually Impaired Vol 1: 5336
Association for Education in Journalism Vol 1: 5343
Association for Education in Journalism and Mass Communication Vol 1: 5343
Association for Educational Communications and Technology and the ECT Foundation Vol 1: 5346
Association for Electrical, Electronic and Information Technologies Vol 2: 2642
Association for Environmental Education, Russia Vol 2: 5890
Association for Evolutionary Economics Vol 1: 5361
Association for Facilities Engineering Vol 1: 5364
Association for Film and Television in the Celtic Countries Vol 2: 7243
Association for Fitness in Business Vol 1: 147
Association for Gay, Lesbian, and Bisexual Issues in Counseling Vol 1: 5367
Association for General and Liberal Studies Vol 1: 5370
Association for Gerontology in Higher Education Vol 1: 5372
Association for Gravestone Studies Vol 1: 5375
Association for Healthcare Philanthropy Vol 1: 5378
Association for Heritage Interpretation Vol 2: 6775
Association for Holotropic Breathwork International Vol 1: 5380
Association for Indiana Media Educators Vol 1: 5382
Association for Industrial Archaeology Vol 2: 6777, 6916
Association for Investment Management and Research Vol 1: 5390
Association for Iron and Steel Technology Vol 1: 5401
Association for Library and Information Science Education Vol 1: 5417
Association for Library Collections and Technical Services Vol 1: 5421
Association for Library Service to Children Vol 1: 5429
Association for Library Trustees and Advocates Vol 1: 5445
Association for Moral Education Vol 1: 5450
Association for Preservation Technology International Vol 1: 5452
Association for Professionals in Infection Control and Epidemiology Vol 1: 5455
Association for Promotion of Skiing Vol 2: 5116
Association for Recorded Sound Collections Vol 1: 5459
Association for Research in Ophthalmology Vol 1: 5463
Association for Research in Otolaryngology, Inc. Vol 1: 5461
Association for Research in Vision and Ophthalmology Vol 1: 5463
Association for Social Anthropology in Oceania Vol 1: 5470
Association for Social Economics Vol 1: 5472
Association for Tertiary Education Management Vol 2: 78
Association for the Advancement of Automotive Medicine Vol 1: 5476
Association for the Advancement of Baltic Studies Vol 1: 5480
Association for the Advancement of Health Education Vol 1: 1015
Association for the Advancement of International Education Vol 1: 5482
Association for the Advancement of Medical Instrumentation Vol 1: 5485
Association for the Advancement of Medical Instrumentation (AAMI) Foundation Vol 1: 5493
Association for the Advancement of Policy, Research and Development in the Third World Vol 1: 5496
Association for the Diffusion of Japanese Films Abroad Vol 2: 4311
Association for the Education of Teachers in Science Vol 1: 5498
Association for the History of Chiropractic Vol 1: 5504
Association for the Preservation of Virginia Antiquities Vol 1: 5506
Association for the Protection of Consumers Vol 2: 5803
Association for the Study of African American Life and History Vol 1: 2482
Association for the Study of African American Life and History, Dayton Branch Vol 1: 5508
Association for the Study of Australian Literature Vol 2: 80
Association for the Study of Connecticut History Vol 1: 5510
Association for Theatre in Higher Education Vol 1: 5513, 12546
Association for Women Geoscientists Vol 1: 5519
Association for Women in Communications Vol 1: 5521
Association for Women in Computing Vol 1: 5524
Association for Women in Mathematics Vol 1: 5526
Association for Women in Science Vol 1: 5529
Association for Women Veterinarians Vol 1: 5532
Association Forestiere Canadienne Vol 1: 7118
Association Francaise du Froid Vol 2: 2236
Association Francaise pour l'Etude des Sols Vol 2: 2238
Association Francophone pour le Savoir Vol 1: 5535
Association in Scotland to Research Into Astronautics Vol 2: 6784
Association International du Tube Vol 2: 7997
Association International pour l'Etude de l'Economie de l'Assurance Vol 2: 6383
Association Internationale de Droit Penal Vol 2: 2441
Association Internationale de Geodesie Vol 2: 1499
Association Internationale de Geologie de l'Ingenieur Vol 2: 4792
Association Internationale de la Couleur Vol 2: 2941
Association Internationale de la Presse Sportive Vol 2: 3296
Association Internationale de la Securite Sociale Vol 2: 6448

Association Internationale de Navigation Vol 2: 929
Association Internationale de Sedimentologistes Vol 2: 907
Association Internationale de Sociologie Asociacion Internacional de Sociologia Vol 2: 6064
Association Internationale de Volcanologie et de Chimie de l'Interieur de la Terre Vol 2: 443
Association Internationale des Cordeliers Vol 2: 3642
Association Internationale des Echecs en Braille Vol 2: 6155
Association Internationale des Ecoles de Travail Social Vol 2: 7902
Association Internationale des Ecoles Superieures d'Education Physique Vol 2: 899
Association Internationale des Educateurs pour la paix Vol 1: 11341
Association Internationale des Etudes Hongroises Vol 2: 3291
Association Internationale des Experts en Philatelie Vol 2: 3958
Association Internationale des Federations di Athletisme Vol 2: 4661
Association Internationale des Instituts de Navigation Vol 2: 8593
Association Internationale des Numismates Professionnels Vol 2: 904
Association Internationale des Registres du Cancer Vol 2: 2443
Association Internationale des Sciences Hydrologiques Vol 2: 2445
Association Internationale des Technologistes de Laboratoire Medical Vol 1: 11579
Association Internationale d'Esthetique Experimentale - Associazione Internationale Di Estetica Empirica Vol 2: 2935
Association Internationale du Barreau Vol 2: 7908
Association Internationale du Film d'Animation Vol 2: 1381
Association Internationale du Film d'Animation Vol 1: 11185
Association Internationale du Theatre pour l'Enfance et la Jeunesse Vol 2: 6153
Association Internationale pour la Taxonomie Vegetale Vol 2: 733
Association Internationale pour les Voiles Minces en Beton Vol 2: 6045
Association Internationale pour l'Etude des Argiles Vol 2: 901
Association Internationale Pour l'Etude Scientifique de la Deficience Intellectuelle Vol 2: 7896
Association Internationale pour l'Evaluation du Rendement Scolaire Vol 2: 4794
Association Mondial de Radios Communautarias Vol 1: 21857
Association Mondiale de la Route Vol 2: 2631
Association Mondiale des Agences de Voyages Vol 2: 6546
Association Mondiale des Journaux Vol 2: 2622
Association Mondiale des Organisations de Recherche Industrielle et Technologique Vol 2: 4445
Association Mondiale des Organisations de Recherche Industrielle et Technologique Vol 1: 21859
Association Mondiale des Radio-Amateurs et des Radioclubs Chretiens Vol 2: 9230
L'Association Motocycliste Canadienne Vol 1: 7287
Association Nationale de la Femme et du Droit Vol 1: 14454
Association of Administrative Law Judges Vol 1: 5543
Association of Air Medical Services Vol 1: 5545
Association of American Colleges and Universities Vol 1: 5551
Association of American Editorial Cartoonists Vol 1: 5553
Association of American Geographers Vol 1: 5555, 14761
Association of American Library Schools Vol 1: 5417
Association of American Medical Colleges Vol 1: 482, 5558, 5562
Association of American Publishers Vol 1: 5563
Association of American Schools in Central America, Colombia, Caribbean and Mexico Vol 2: 1548
Association of American University Presses Vol 1: 5566
Association of Americans and Canadians in Israel Vol 2: 3724
Association of America's Public Television Stations Vol 1: 5569
Association of Area Business Publications Vol 1: 5571
Association of Asphalt Paving Technologists Vol 1: 5573
Association of Austrian Librarians Vol 2: 682
Association of Baptists for World Evangelism Vol 1: 5577
Association of Behavioral Healthcare Management Vol 1: 5579
Association of Boards of Certification Vol 1: 5581
Association of Bone and Joint Surgeons Vol 1: 5583
Association of Bridal Consultants Vol 1: 5585
Association of British Correspondence Colleges Vol 2: 6789
Association of British Philatelic Societies Vol 2: 6791
Association of British Sailmakers Vol 2: 6795
Association of British Travel Agents Vol 2: 6797
Association of Building Engineers Vol 2: 6799
Association of Business Publishers Vol 1: 1606
Association of Canadian Advertisers Vol 1: 5588
Association of Catholic Colleges and Universities Vol 1: 5590
Association of Certified Accountants Vol 2: 6803
Association of Certified Fraud Examiners Vol 1: 5593
Association of Chartered Accountants in the United States Vol 1: 5596
Association of Chartered Certified Accountants - United Kingdom Vol 2: 6803
Association of Chemists of the Textile Industry Vol 2: 2241
Association of Chief Police Officers of England, Wales and Northern Ireland Vol 2: 6805
Association of Children's Museums Vol 1: 5599
Association of College and Research Libraries Vol 1: 5601
Association of College and University Housing Officers International Vol 1: 5621
Association of College English Teachers of Alabama Vol 1: 5626
Association of College Unions International Vol 1: 5628
Association of Collegiate Schools of Architecture Vol 1: 2707
Association of Collegiate Schools of Architecture Vol 1: 5631
Association of Commonwealth Universities Vol 2: 6807, 7334
Association of Community Cancer Centers Vol 1: 5633
Association of Conservation Engineers Vol 1: 5635
Association of Consulting Engineers New Zealand Vol 2: 4950
Association of Consulting Engineers, Norway Vol 2: 5119
Association of Consulting Engineers of Australia Vol 2: 85
Association of Consulting Engineers of Canada Vol 1: 5638
Association of Consulting Foresters of America Vol 1: 5644
Association of Contingency Planners- Capital of Texas Chapter Vol 1: 5646
Association of Cooperative Educators Vol 1: 5648
Association of Cricket Statisticians and Historians Vol 2: 6814
Association of Cricket Umpires and Scorers Vol 2: 6816
Association of Cycle Traders Vol 2: 6820
Association of Departments of English Vol 1: 5655
Association of Development Financing Institutions in Asia and the Pacific Vol 2: 5255
Association of Directory Publishers Vol 1: 5657
Association of Earth Science Editors Vol 1: 5659
Association of Educational Publishers Vol 1: 5662
Association of Energy Engineers Vol 1: 5669
Association of Engineering Geologists Vol 1: 5671
Association of Equipment Manufacturers Vol 1: 14153
Association of European Chambers of Commerce and Industry Vol 2: 836
Association of European Operational Research Societies Vol 1: 11599
Association of European Toxicologists and European Societies of Toxicology Vol 2: 1437
Association of Fashion Advertising and Editorial Photographers Vol 2: 6834
Association of Field Ornithologists Vol 1: 5680
Association of Film Commissioners International Vol 1: 5682
Association of Food Journalists Vol 1: 5685
Association of Former Agents of the U.S. Secret Service Vol 1: 5687
Association of Fraternity Advisors Vol 1: 5690

Association of Free Community Papers Vol 1: 5695
Association of Fundraising Professionals Vol 1: 5698
Association of German Pharmacists Vol 2: 2683
Association of Golf Club Secretaries Vol 2: 6822
Association of Golf Writers Vol 2: 6824
Association of Government Accountants Vol 1: 5707
Association of Home Office Underwriters Vol 1: 5723
Association of Hungarian Geophysicists Vol 2: 3222
Association of Hungarian Journalists Vol 2: 3229
Association of Hungarian Librarians Vol 2: 3231
Association of Hungarian Medical Societies Vol 2: 3233
Association of Indians in America Vol 1: 5725
Association of Industrial Metallizers, Coaters and Laminators Vol 1: 5727
Association of Information Technology Professionals Vol 1: 5730
Association of Interior Specialists Vol 2: 6826
Association of International Health Researchers Vol 1: 5733
Association of Interpretive Naturalists Vol 1: 14020
Association of Irish Musical Societies Vol 2: 3620
Association of Jesuit Colleges and Universities Vol 1: 5735
Association of Jewish Center Professionals Vol 1: 5737
Association of Jewish Ex-Servicemen and Women Vol 2: 6828
Association of Jewish Libraries Vol 1: 5739
Association of Late-Deafened Adults Vol 1: 5746
Association of Lunar and Planetary Observers Vol 1: 5750
Association of Management/International Association of Management Vol 1: 5752
Association of Medical Illustrators Vol 1: 5755
Association of Merchants and Manufacturing of Textile Stores and Machinery Vol 2: 3352
Association of Microbiologists of India Vol 2: 3503
Association of Military Colleges and Schools of the United States Vol 1: 5760
Association of Military Surgeons of the United States Vol 1: 5762
Association of Municipal Recycling Coordinators Vol 1: 5792
Association of National Olympic Committees Vol 2: 2245
Association of National Park Authorities Vol 2: 6830
Association of Natural Burial Grounds Vol 2: 6832
Association of New Jersey Environmental Commissions Vol 1: 5794
Association of North American Radio Clubs Vol 1: 5796
Association of Official Analytical Chemists Vol 1: 4991
Association of Official Racing Chemists Vol 1: 5798
Association of Official Seed Analysts Vol 1: 5800
Association of Oncology Social Work Vol 1: 5802
Association of Organizations of Slovak Writers Vol 2: 5956
Association of Orthodox Jewish Teachers Vol 1: 5805
Association of Paroling Authorities International Vol 1: 5807
Association of Performing Arts Presenters Vol 1: 5809
Association of Personal Computer User Groups Vol 1: 5812
Association of Photographers Vol 2: 6834
The Association of Pool and Spa Professionals Vol 1: 5814
Association of Private Enterprise Education Vol 1: 5816
Association of Professional Chaplains Vol 1: 5819
Association of Professional Communication Consultants Vol 1: 5824
Association of Professional Engineers of Ontario Vol 1: 17604
Association of Professors of Higher Education Vol 1: 14011
Association of Psychologists of Nova Scotia Vol 1: 5827
Association of Public Treasurers of the United States and Canada Vol 1: 5829
Association of Pulp and Paper Chemists and Engineers in Germany Vol 2: 2644
Association of Records Managers and Administrators Vol 1: 5086
Association of Retail Marketing Services Vol 1: 5832
Association of Schools of Allied Health Professions Vol 1: 5834
Association of Schools of Journalism and Mass Communication Vol 1: 5844
Association of Schools of Public Health in the European Region Vol 2: 2247
Association of Science Fiction and Fantasy Artists Vol 1: 5846
Association of Sleep Disorders Centers Vol 1: 836
Association of South African Quantity Surveyors Vol 2: 5517
Association of Southeast Asian Institutions of Higher Learning Vol 2: 5258
Association of Southern Baptist Campus Ministries Vol 1: 5849
Association of Space Explorers - U.S.A. Vol 1: 5851
Association of Specialized and Cooperative Library Agencies Vol 1: 5853
Association of Sports Museums and Halls of Fame Vol 1: 11403
Association of State and Provincial Psychology Boards Vol 1: 5860
Association of State and Territorial Health Officials Vol 1: 5864
Association of State and Territorial Local Liaison Officials Vol 1: 14176
Association of State Territorial and Health Officials Vol 1: 14176
Association of Steel Distributors Vol 1: 5867
Association of Surfing Professionals Vol 1: 5870
Association of Surgical Technologists Vol 1: 5872
Association of Teacher Educators Vol 1: 5877
Association of the United States Army Vol 1: 5882
Association of the Wall and Ceiling Industries - International Vol 1: 5884
Association of Third World Studies Vol 1: 5895
Association of Track and Field Statisticians Vol 2: 87
Association of Travel Marketing Executives Vol 1: 5901
Association of Universities and Colleges of Canada Vol 1: 5904
Association of University Architects Vol 1: 5908
Association of University Programs in Health Administration Vol 1: 5911
Association of Veterinary Anaesthetists Vol 2: 6839
Association of Women Surgeons Vol 1: 5913
Association of Writers' Organizations in Slovakia Vol 2: 5956
Association on Handicapped Student Service Programs in Postsecondary Education Vol 1: 5917
Association on Higher Education and Disability Vol 1: 5917
Association Paul Neumann Vol 2: 2569
Association pour l'Avancement des Sciences et des Techniques de la Documentation Vol 1: 5919
Association Quebecoise des Critiques de Cinema Vol 1: 5921
Association Trends Newsweekly Vol 1: 5923
Associations des proprietaires de cinemas du Canada Vol 1: 13621
Associazione Compagnia Jazz Ballet Vol 2: 3844
Associazione Culturale Antonio Pedrotti Vol 2: 3846
Associazione Culturale Ennio Flaiano e *Oggi E Domani* Vol 2: 3848
Associazione Culturale "Rodolfo Lipizer" Vol 2: 3892
Associazione Elettrotecnica ed Elettronica Italiana Vol 2: 4004
Associazione Internazionale Guido Dorso Vol 2: 3850
Associazione Italiana Amici del Cinema d'Essai Vol 2: 3852
Associazione Italiana Biblioteche Vol 2: 3854
Associazione Italiana di Metallurgia Vol 2: 3991
Associazione Musicale di Monza Vol 2: 3857
Associazione Napoletana Amici di Malta Vol 2: 3859
Associazione per il Disegno Industriale Vol 2: 3862
Associazione Premio Grinzane Cavour Vol 2: 3880
ASTM International Vol 1: 5925
Astra Chernwood Vol 2: 8773
AstraZeneca Ltd. Vol 1: 19331
AstraZeneca Pharmaceuticals Vol 2: 6861
AstraZeneca plc Vol 2: 8774
Astrological Association of Great Britain Vol 2: 6843
Astronomical League Vol 1: 6000
Astronomical Society of Australia Vol 2: 90
Astronomical Society of France Vol 2: 2249
Astronomical Society of Japan Vol 2: 4096
Astronomical Society of Southern Africa Vol 2: 5519

Astronomical Society of the Pacific Vol 1: 6005
Astronomical Society of Western Australia Vol 2: 96
Asundi Endowment Fund Vol 2: 3470
AT&T Vol 2: 8328
AT&T Bell Laboratories Vol 1: 3453, 3454
AT&T Labs Vol 1: 10864
Ataturk Kultur, Dil ve Tarih Yuksek Kurumu Vol 2: 6626
Ataturk Supreme Council for Culture, Language and History Vol 2: 6626
ATEGRUS: Asociacion Tecnica para la gestion de Residues y Medio Vol 2: 6104
L'Atelier Imaginaire Vol 2: 2251
Athenaeum International Cultural Center Vol 2: 3164
Athenaeum of Philadelphia Vol 1: 6013
Athletes in Action Vol 1: 6018
Athletes United for Peace Vol 1: 6020
The Athletics Congress of the USA Vol 1: 21211
Atlanta Advertising Club Vol 1: 6022
Atlanta Film Festival - IMAGE Film and Video Center Vol 1: 6024
Atlanta Independent Film and Video Festival Vol 1: 6024
Atlanta Tipoff Club Vol 1: 6026
Atlantic Film Festival Association Vol 1: 6032
Atlantic Journalism Awards Vol 1: 6034
Atlantic Offshore Lobstermen's Association Vol 1: 6040
Atlantic Richfield Company Vol 1: 21235
Atlantic Salmon Federation Vol 1: 6042
Atlantic Seed Association Vol 1: 6044
Atlantis Films Vol 1: 7093
Atlas Economic Research Foundation Vol 1: 6046
Atlas World Press Review Vol 1: 21970
Atomic Industrial Forum Vol 1: 16593
Attorneys Bar Association of Florida Vol 1: 6048
Audio Engineering Society Vol 1: 6050
AudioVideo International Vol 1: 6056
Audubon Artists Vol 1: 6060
Audubon Naturalist Society of the Central Atlantic States Vol 1: 6062
Audubon of Florida Vol 1: 6071
Audubon Society of New Hampshire Vol 1: 6082
Augusta National Golf Club Vol 1: 6086
Augusta National Golf Club Vol 1: 21923
Augustan Society Vol 1: 6088
Augustinians of the Assumption Vol 1: 6090
The Austin Chronicle Vol 1: 6092
Austin Ten Drivers Club Ltd. Vol 2: 6845
Australasian Corrosion Association Vol 2: 98
Australasian Federation of Family History Organisations Vol 2: 100
Australasian Institute of Metals Vol 2: 361
Australasian Institute of Mining and Metallurgy Vol 2: 403
Australasian Political Studies Association Vol 2: 102
Australia Arts Victoria Vol 2: 607
Australia Council Vol 2: 105
Australia Council - Literature Board Vol 2: 107
Australia Council for the Arts - Visual Arts/ Craft Board Vol 2: 109
Australia Department of Veterans' Affairs Vol 2: 115
Australia-Japan Research Centre Vol 2: 246
Australian Academy of Science Vol 2: 117
Australian Academy of the Humanities Vol 2: 134
Australian Acoustical Society Vol 2: 136
Australian-American Fulbright Commission Vol 2: 138
Australian and New Zealand Association for the Advancement of Science Vol 2: 141
Australian Association of the Deaf Vol 2: 145
Australian Beef Association Vol 2: 147
Australian Broadcasting Commission Vol 2: 618
Australian Catholic Social Justice Council Vol 2: 149
Australian Cinematographers Society Vol 2: 151
Australian College of Educators Vol 2: 153
Australian College of Veterinary Scientists Vol 2: 282
Australian Council for Educational Leaders Vol 2: 156
Australian Council for International Development Vol 2: 159
Australian Entertainment Industry Association Vol 2: 161
Australian Federation of University Women Vol 2: 163
Australian Federation of University Women - South Australia Vol 2: 163
Australian Film Institute Vol 2: 174
Australian Honours Secretariat Vol 2: 179
Australian Institute of Agricultural Science and Technology Vol 2: 206
Australian Institute of Energy Vol 2: 208
Australian Institute of Genealogical Studies Vol 2: 210
Australian Institute of Physics Vol 2: 212
Australian Institute of Physics (NSW Branch) Vol 2: 638
Australian Institute of Quantity Surveyors Vol 2: 218
Australian Institute of Radiography Vol 2: 220
Australian Library and Information Association Vol 2: 222
Australian Literature Society Vol 2: 80
Australian Maritime College Vol 2: 427
Australian Mathematical Society Vol 2: 234
Australian Music Centre Vol 2: 237
Australian National Sportfishing Association Vol 2: 240
Australian National University Vol 2: 245
Australian Nuclear Association Vol 2: 247
Australian Numismatic Society Vol 2: 250
Australian Publishers' Association Vol 2: 254
Australian Secondary Principals Association Vol 2: 256
Australian Sesquicentennial Gift Trust for Oral History Vol 2: 4970
Australian Singing Competition Vol 2: 258
Australian Skeptics - NSW Branch Vol 2: 260
Australian Society for Medical Research Vol 2: 263
Australian Society for Parasitology Vol 2: 266
Australian Society of Archivists Vol 2: 269
Australian Teachers of Media Vol 2: 276
Australian Veterinary Association Vol 2: 278
Australian Water Association Vol 2: 284
Australian Widescreen Association Vol 2: 289
Australian Writers' Guild Vol 2: 291
Australlian Federal Ministry Science Vol 2: 769
Austria Ministry of Economic Affairs Vol 2: 684
Austrian Booksellers' and Publishers' Association Vol 2: 700
Austrian Broadcasting Corporation Vol 2: 702
Austrian Composers Association Vol 2: 704
Austrian Computer Society Vol 2: 706
Austrian Golf Association Vol 2: 708
Austrian P.E.N. Centre Vol 2: 710
Austrian Radion-Studio Carinthia Vol 2: 716
Austrian Statistical Society Vol 2: 712
Austro Mechana Vol 2: 705
Austro-Merck Vienna (Austria) Vol 2: 779
Auto-Alloys Ltd Vol 2: 7605
Autodesk Canada Vol 1: 6878
Automated Imaging Association Vol 1: 6097
Automated Vision Association Vol 1: 6097
Automobilclub von Deutschland Vol 2: 2654
Automobile Club de l'Ouest Vol 2: 2254
Automobile Club; Royal Scottish Vol 2: 8875
Automobile Journalists Association of Canada Vol 1: 6099
Automotive Communications Council Vol 1: 6107
Automotive Hall of Fame Vol 1: 6109
Automotive Industry Action Group Vol 1: 6114
Automotive Occupant Restraints Council Vol 1: 6116
Automotive Oil Change Association Vol 1: 6118
Automotive Organization Team Vol 1: 6109
Automotive Training Managers Council Vol 1: 6120
Automotive Warehouse Distributors Association Vol 1: 6122
Aventis Foundation Vol 2: 8691
AVI Publishing Company Vol 1: 16409
Aviation Distributors and Manufacturer Association Vol 1: 6124
Aviation Hall of Fame` Vol 1: 14472
Aviation Hall of Fame and Museum of New Jersey Vol 1: 6127
Aviation Safety Institute Vol 1: 6131
Aviation Technician Education Council Vol 1: 6133
Aviation Week & Space Technology Vol 1: 6135, 9577
Avicultural Advancement Council of Canada Vol 1: 6139
Avon Books - HarperCollins Publishers Inc. Vol 1: 6141
Avon Products, Inc. Vol 1: 6144
AVS Vol 1: 6146
Awana Clubs International Vol 1: 6161
Awards and Recognition Association Vol 1: 6165
AXA Dublin International Piano Competition Vol 2: 3622
Ayn Rand Institute Vol 1: 6172
Ayrshire Breeders' Association Vol 1: 6175
Ayuntamiento de Benicasim Vol 2: 5998
Azienda Autonoma di Soggiorno e Turismo Vol 2: 3864
Azienda di Promozione Turistica di Varese Vol 2: 3980
Babcock and Wilcox Company Vol 2: 7606
Babson College Vol 1: 6177
Babson College - Center for Information Management Studies Vol 1: 6185
BACCHUS Network Vol 1: 6188
Bach Competition; International Johann Sebastian Vol 2: 2656

Bachauer International Piano Foundation; Gina Vol 1: 6192
Back Pain Association Vol 2: 6847
BackCare - The Charity for Healthier Backs Vol 2: 6847
Bactlab Systems (Pty.) Ltd. Vol 2: 5624, 5625
Badminton Association of England Vol 2: 6849
BAE Systems Vol 1: 19115
Bagutta Restaurant Vol 2: 3866
Bahamas Chamber of Commerce - Nassau Vol 2: 811
Bahamas Red Cross Society Vol 2: 814
Baird Corporation Vol 1: 16785
Baker and Taylor Vol 1: 17717
Baker and Taylor Books Vol 1: 1414, 5602
Baker and Taylor Company Vol 1: 9792
Baker & Taylor Co. Vol 1: 17718
Baker and Taylor Company Vol 1: 22051
Baker & Taylor Entertainment Co. Vol 1: 17713
Baker Street Irregulars Vol 1: 6194
Bakerstown Beagle Club Vol 1: 6197
Bald-Headed Men of America Vol 1: 6199
Baldridge National Quality Program - National Institute of Standards and Technology Vol 1: 6201
Baldwin Piano and Organ Company Vol 1: 13704
Balfour Beatty Ltd. Vol 2: 7774
Balgarska Akademija na Naukite Vol 2: 1205
Balint Society Vol 2: 6852
Ball State University - Department of Journalism Vol 1: 6203
Ballarat University College Vol 2: 430
Ballet Makers Dance Foundation Vol 1: 7574
Balloon Federation of America Vol 1: 6214
Baltic American Freedom League Vol 1: 6227
Baltimore Film Forum Vol 1: 6229
Baltimore Opera Company Vol 1: 6231
Banco de la Republica Colombia Vol 2: 1269
The Banff Centre Vol 1: 6233
Banff Centre for the Arts Vol 1: 6233, 21985
Banff School of Fine Arts Vol 1: 6233
Banff World Television Festival Vol 1: 6238
Bangkok Bank Public Co. Ltd. Vol 2: 6613
Bank Marketing Association Vol 1: 54
Bank of Delaware Vol 1: 17409
Bank of Ireland Vol 2: 3656
Bank Street College Vol 1: 7900
Bank Street College of Education Vol 1: 6240
Banque Nationale de Paris Vol 2: 2526
Banta Company, Inc.; George Vol 1: 21683
Baptist History and Heritage Society Vol 1: 6242
Baptist Mid-Missions Vol 1: 6246
Barbados Association of Medical Practitioners Vol 2: 816
Barbados Dental Association Vol 2: 818
Barbados National Trust Vol 2: 820
Barbados Union of Teachers Vol 2: 822
Barbizon Vol 1: 20643
Barcelona Theatre Institute Vol 2: 6000
Bard; C.R. Vol 1: 4793
Bard International; C. R. Vol 2: 6946
Bard Urological Division Vol 1: 5457
Barlow Endowment for Music Composition Vol 1: 6248
Barnard-Seyfert Astronomical Society Vol 1: 6250
Barnes and Noble Bookstores, Inc. Vol 1: 14124, 14126
Barnes & Noble Inc. Vol 1: 6253
Baromedical Nurses Association Vol 1: 6255
Baronial Order of Magna Charta and the Military Order of Crusades Vol 1: 6257
Baruch Entertainment Vol 1: 6259
Baseball Canada Vol 1: 6261
Baseball Writers Association of America Vol 1: 6265
Baseball Writers Association of America Vol 1: 14495, 14496
BASF Aktiengesellschaft Vol 2: 2914
BASICS in Milwaukee Vol 1: 6269
Bataan Relief Organization Vol 1: 2209
Bath County Historical Society Vol 1: 6271
Bavarian Academy of Fine Arts Vol 2: 2658
Bavarian Academy of Sciences and Humanities Vol 2: 2663
Baxter Healthcare Vol 2: 3632
Baxter Healthcare Corporation Vol 1: 3951
Bay Area Independent Publishers Association Vol 1: 6273
Bay Area Video Coalition Vol 1: 6275
Bay Chamber Concerts Vol 1: 6277
Bay Improvement Group Vol 1: 6279
Bayer Corporation Vol 1: 1189
Bayer Corporation Diagnostics Group Vol 1: 972
Bayer Inc. Vol 1: 7841
Bayer SA Vol 2: 5626, 5627
Bayerische Akademie der Schonen Kunste Vol 2: 2658
Bayerische Akademie der Wissenschaften Vol 2: 2663
Baylor College of Medicine - Roy M. and Phyllis Gough Huffington Center on Aging Vol 1: 6282
Baytown Chamber of Commerce Vol 1: 6284
Baywood Publishing Company Vol 1: 9994
BBC Wildlife Magazine Vol 2: 8204
BBR Auctions Vol 2: 6854
B.B.R. Publishing; Old Bottle Club of Great Britain/ Vol 2: 6854
BC Innovation Council Vol 1: 6288
BD Biosciences Vol 1: 1242
BDA Vol 1: 6295
Beauty and Barber Supply Institute Vol 1: 6297
Beaver Lake Literacy Council Vol 1: 6299
Bechtel Fund Vol 1: 5433
Becton Dickinson Consumer Products Vol 1: 1186, 1188
Beecham Pharmaceuticals Vol 2: 8773
Before Columbus Foundation Vol 1: 6301
Belgian American Educational Foundation Vol 1: 6303
Belgian Centre for Music Documentation Vol 2: 838
Belgrade International Film Festival Vol 2: 9330
Bell Canada Vol 1: 18164
Bell Helicopter Textron Vol 1: 13076
Bell Laboratories; AT&T Vol 1: 3453, 3454
Bellarmine University Vol 1: 6305
Belleek Collectors' International Society Vol 1: 6307
Bellona Publishing House Vol 2: 5293
Belted Galloway Society Vol 1: 6309
Benevolent and Loyal Order of Pessimists Vol 1: 6311
Benjamin/Cummings Publishing Company Vol 1: 14093
Benn Brothers plc Vol 2: 8240
Bennett Neuropsychiatric Research Foundation; A. E. Vol 1: 19071
Benoist Foundation; Marcel Vol 2: 6307
Benoist Stiftung; Marcel Vol 2: 6307
Bentley College - Center for Business Ethics Vol 1: 6313
Bergamo Film Meeting Vol 2: 3868
Bergen International Festival Vol 2: 5121
Berkeley Enthusiasts Club Vol 2: 6856
Berlin International Film Festival Vol 2: 2669
Bernstein; Aguda l'Haanakat Prasim Sifrutiim Al Shem Mordechai Vol 2: 3726
Bernstein Literary Prizes Association; Mordechai Vol 2: 3726
Berntsen International Vol 1: 1996
Bertelsmann Stiftung Vol 2: 2671
Bet Nahrain Vol 1: 6316
Beta Alpha Psi Vol 1: 6318
Beta Beta Beta National Biological Honor Society Vol 1: 6322
Beta Gamma Sigma Vol 1: 6330
Beta Kappa Chi Vol 1: 6333
Beta Phi Mu International Library Science Honorary Society Vol 1: 2969
Bethesda Lutheran Homes and Services Vol 1: 6335
Better Business Bureau Vol 1: 6339
Better Business Bureau of Western Michigan Vol 1: 6341
Better Business Bureau Serving Upstate South Carolina Vol 1: 6343
Better Government Association Vol 1: 6345
Beverly Hills Theatre Guild Vol 1: 6348
Bevill Manufacturing Technology Center Vol 1: 6351
Bibby Scientific Products; J. Vol 2: 7195
Bibiana, International House of Art for Children Vol 2: 5959
Bibiana, Medzinarodny dom umenia pre deti Vol 2: 5959
Biblenets Vol 1: 6353
Bibliographic Institute of Mannheim Vol 2: 3070
Bibliographical Society of Canada Vol 1: 6358
Bibliographical Society - United Kingdom Vol 2: 6858
Biblioteca Nacional de Mexico Vol 2: 4619
Bibliotheque Publique d'Information Vol 2: 2261
Bichon Frise Club of America Vol 1: 6362
Bienek Stiftung; Horst Vol 2: 2659
Biennales Internationales de Poesie Vol 2: 911
Big Brothers Big Sisters of America Vol 1: 6365
Big Brothers of America Vol 1: 6365
Big East Conference Vol 1: 6368
Big Muddy Film Festival Vol 1: 6371
Big Sisters International Vol 1: 6365
Bilingual Foundation of the Arts Vol 1: 6373
Billboard - VNU Business Publications USA Vol 1: 6376
Billiard and Bowling Institute of America Vol 1: 6379
Billiard Congress of America Vol 1: 6381
Billiard Federation of the United States of America Vol 1: 20434
Billings Preservation Society Vol 1: 6383
Bingham Memorial Fund; Worth Vol 1: 6385
Bio-Serv Company Vol 1: 4156
Biochemical, Biophysical and Microbiological Society of Finland Vol 2: 1575
Biochemical Society - England Vol 2: 6860

Organization Index

Bioelectrochemical Society Vol 2: 6006
Biomedical Engineering Society Vol 1: 6387
bioMerieux Inc. Vol 1: 4131
Biometric Society Vol 1: 8293
Biophysical Society Vol 1: 3918
Biotech Medical Management Association Vol 1: 6392
Biotechnology Industry Organization Vol 1: 6394
Bird Life International - United Kingdom Vol 2: 6873
Birkebeiner-Rennet Vol 2: 5125
Birkenhead Photographic Association Vol 2: 6875
Birmingham Historical Society Vol 1: 6399
Birmingham-Southern College Vol 1: 6401
Biscuit and Cracker Manufacturer Association Vol 1: 6403
Black Archives of Mid-America Vol 1: 6405
Black Business and Professional Association Vol 1: 6408
Black Caucus of the American Library Association Vol 1: 6411
Black Entertainment and Sports Lawyers Association Vol 1: 6420
Black Filmmakers Hall of Fame Vol 1: 6424
Black, Indian, Hispanic, and Asian Women in Action Vol 1: 6426
Black Lung Association Vol 1: 6428
Black Mental Health Alliance Vol 1: 6430
Black Theatre Network Vol 1: 6435
Black Women's House of Culture Vol 2: 1140
Blackhawk Standbys Vol 1: 6437
Blacks in Law Enforcement Vol 1: 6441
Blackwell Vol 1: 5423
Blackwell North America, Inc. Vol 1: 13254
Blackwell's Book Services Vol 1: 5609
Blade Magazine Vol 1: 6443
Blair Society for Genealogical Research Vol 1: 6446
Blazer Horse Association Vol 1: 6448
Blekinge County Council Vol 2: 6138
Blessed Kateri Tekakwitha League Vol 1: 6450
Blind Service Association Vol 1: 6452
Blinded Veterans Association Vol 1: 6454
Blue Hill Peninsula Chamber of Commerce Vol 1: 6459
Blue Ridge English as a Second Language Council Vol 1: 6461
Blue Ridge Literacy Council Vol 1: 6463
Blue Star Mothers of America Vol 1: 6467
Blues Alley Music Society Vol 1: 6469
The Blues Foundation Vol 1: 6472
BMW Riders Association International Vol 1: 6479
B'nai B'rith Vol 1: 6482
B'nai Brith Canada Vol 1: 6486
B'nai B'rith Hillel Foundations Vol 1: 10431
B'nai B'rith International Vol 1: 6489
B'nai B'rith Women Vol 1: 12391
Board of Directors of City Trusts acting for the City of Philadelphia Vol 1: 6491
Boardman Tasker Charitable Trust Vol 2: 6877
Boating Industry Vol 1: 15366
Boating Writers International Vol 1: 6493
Bob und Schlittenverband fur Deutschland e.V. Vol 2: 2673
Boca Raton Historical Society Vol 1: 6495
Boehringer-Mannheim Canada Vol 1: 7452
Boehringer Mannheim Corporation Vol 1: 996
Boeing Commercial Airplanes Group Vol 1: 20170
Boeing Co. Vol 1: 13090, 19112
Boeing Defense & Space Group Vol 1: 13073
Boersenverein des Deutschen Buchhandels e.V. Vol 2: 2864
Boesendorfer GmbH; L. Vol 2: 805
Bogle Memorial Fund Vol 1: 2991
Boise Peace Quilt Project Vol 1: 6497
Boito Conservatory of Music Parma; A. Vol 2: 3870
Bonsai and Orchid Association Vol 1: 6499
Book of the Month Club Vol 1: 17146
Book Publishers Association of Alberta Vol 1: 6501
Book Publishers Association of Israel Vol 2: 3726
Book Publishers Association of New Zealand Vol 2: 4956
Book Publishers Representatives Association Vol 2: 4956
Book Trust Vol 2: 7331
Book Trust (England) Vol 2: 6879
Book Wholesalers Vol 1: 5430
Bookbuilders of Boston Vol 1: 6509
Bookbuilders West Vol 1: 6512
Booker PLC Vol 2: 6880
Books Abroad Vol 1: 21933
Booksellers Association of the United Kingdom and Ireland Vol 2: 6884
Booksellers New Zealand Vol 2: 4958
Boosey and Hawkes Ltd., Music Publishers Vol 2: 8166
Borden Foundation Vol 1: 7435
Borden Ladner Gervais LLP Vol 1: 7210
Borders Books and Music Vol 1: 10531
The Boris Christoff International Competition for Young Opera Singers Foundation Vol 2: 1203
Boston Association for the Education of Young Children Vol 1: 6516
Boston Athletic Association Vol 1: 6518
Boston Book Review Vol 1: 6520
Boston College - Center for Corporate Citizenship Vol 1: 6522
The Boston Globe Vol 1: 6525
Boston University - Anna Howard Shaw Center Vol 1: 6527
Boston University - Department of Athletics Vol 1: 6529
Boston University - Pike Institute on Law and Disability Vol 1: 6531
Boston University - School of Music Vol 1: 6533
Botanical Society of America Vol 1: 6535
Bottle Club of Great Britain/B.B.R. Publishing; Old Vol 2: 6854
Bound to Stay Bound Books, Inc Vol 1: 5435
Bound to Stay Bound Books Inc. Vol 1: 5443
Bowker; R. R. Vol 1: 1415, 5424
Bowling Proprietors' Association of America Vol 1: 6556
Bowling Proprietors' Association of America Vol 1: 11432
Bowling Writers Association of America Vol 1: 6560
Box Office Management International Vol 1: 12083
Boxoffice Magazine Vol 1: 6569
Boy Scouts Association of Zimbabwe Vol 2: 9336
Boy Scouts of America Vol 1: 6572, 15050
Boynton Beach Recreation & Park Department Vol 1: 6593
Boys and Girls Clubs of America Vol 1: 6595
Boys Clubs of America Vol 1: 6595
BP America, Inc. Vol 1: 2761
BP Research and Engineering Centre Vol 2: 8773
Brain Injury Association of America Vol 1: 6604
Brain Injury Association of Utah Vol 1: 6607
Bralco Metal Industries Vol 2: 3450
Brandon University Vol 1: 9128
Brasserie Lipp Vol 2: 2537
Bratislava City Hall Vol 2: 5961
The Brattle Group, Inc. Vol 1: 2243
Braun GmbH Vol 2: 2675
Braunschweig City Cultural Office Vol 2: 2677
Brazil Office of the President Vol 2: 1142
Brazilian Academy of Letters Vol 2: 1151, 5412
Brazilian Agricultural Research Corporation Vol 2: 1158
Brazilian-American Chamber of Commerce Vol 1: 6609
Brazilian Chamber of Commerce in Great Britain Vol 2: 6887
Brazilian Metallurgy and Materials Association Vol 2: 1160
Brazilian Packaging Association Vol 2: 1163
Brazilian Society for the Advancement of Science Vol 2: 1165
Brazos Valley Council of Governments Vol 1: 6611
Brechner Center for Freedom of Information; Joseph L. Vol 1: 6613
Brewster Society Vol 1: 6615
Brick Development Association Vol 2: 6889
Bridge Publications Inc. Vol 1: 6617
Bridge School Foundation Vol 1: 11918
Bridge Syndicate Vol 1: 6619
Bridport Arts Centre Vol 2: 6891
Brigantine Beach Chamber of Commerce Vol 1: 6621
Brigitte Vol 2: 2679
Brisbane Warana Festival Ltd. Vol 2: 293
Brisbane Writers Festival Vol 2: 293
Bristol Myers Vol 1: 1893
Bristol-Myers-Squibb Vol 1: 629
Bristol-Myers Squibb Vol 1: 816
Bristol-Myers Squibb Canada Co. Vol 1: 6623
Bristol-Myers Squibb Oncology Vol 1: 16714
Brith Sholom Vol 1: 6630
British Academy Vol 2: 6893
British Academy of Film and Television Arts Vol 2: 6904
British Aerospace Vol 2: 7382
British Agricultural and Garden Machinery Association Vol 2: 6907
British Aikido Association Vol 2: 6909
British Appaloosa Society Vol 2: 6911
British Archaeological Awards Vol 2: 6914
British Association for Applied Linguistics Vol 2: 6927
British Association of Aviation Consultants Vol 2: 6931
British Association of Barbershop Singers Vol 2: 6933
British Association of Communicators in Business Vol 2: 6936
British Association of Dermatologists Vol 2: 6939

British Association of Industrial Editors Vol 2: 6936
British Association of Landscape Industries Vol 2: 6941
British Association of Paediatric Surgeons Vol 2: 6943
British Association of Rheumatology and Rehabilitation Vol 2: 7172
British Association of Urological Surgeons Vol 2: 6945
British Astronomical Association Vol 2: 6948
British Balneological and Climatological Society Vol 2: 8818
British Birds Vol 2: 6953
British Broadcasting Corp. Vol 2: 6960
British Broadcasting Corporation and Welsh National Opera Vol 2: 6962
British Business Press Vol 2: 7187
British Canoe Union Vol 2: 6964
British Cartographic Society Vol 2: 6969
British Chess Federation Vol 2: 6976
British Christmas Tree Growers Association Vol 2: 6981
British Coatings Federation Vol 2: 6983
British Columbia Historical Federation Vol 1: 6632
British Columbia Psychological Association Vol 1: 6635
British Comparative Literature Association Vol 2: 6985
British Computer Society Vol 2: 6987
British Concrete Masonry Association Vol 2: 6992
British Cycle Speedway Commission Vol 2: 6994
British Cycle Speedway Federation Vol 2: 6994
British Cycling Federation Vol 2: 6996
British Deaf Association Vol 2: 6998
British Design and Art Direction Vol 2: 7000
British Direct Marketing Association Vol 2: 7384
British Drilling Association Vol 2: 7002
British Ecological Society Vol 2: 7004
British Federation of Film Societies Vol 2: 7013
British Fertility Society Vol 2: 7015
British Film Institute Vol 2: 7014, 7018
British Geotechnical Association Vol 2: 7021
British Grassland Society Vol 2: 7024
British Guild of Travel Writers Vol 2: 7026
British Gypsom Vol 2: 7515
British Health Care Association Vol 2: 7028
British Helicopter Advisory Board Vol 2: 7607
British Industrial and Scientific Association Vol 2: 8011
British Infection Society Vol 2: 7030
British Institute of Architectural Technicians Vol 2: 7032
British Institute of Architectural Technologists Vol 2: 7032
British Institute of Non-Destructive Testing Vol 2: 7036
British Institute of Radiology Vol 2: 7042
British International Freight Association Vol 2: 7050
British Interplanetary Society Vol 2: 7052
British Italian Society Vol 2: 8971
British Lichen Society Vol 2: 7056
British Medical Association Vol 2: 7058
British Menswear Guild Vol 2: 7082
British Mexican Society Vol 2: 7084
British Music Society Vol 2: 7086
British Nuclear Energy Society Vol 2: 7088
British Numismatic Society Vol 2: 7091
British Origami Society Vol 2: 7093
British Ornithologists' Union Vol 2: 7095
British Orthodontic Society Vol 2: 7098, 7101
British Paper and Board Industry Federation Vol 2: 8239
British Paper and Board Makers' Association Vol 2: 8239
British Pelargonium and Geranium Society Vol 2: 7105
British Petroleum Vol 2: 6874, 8188, 8781
British Phonographic Industry Vol 2: 7107
British Poultry Council Vol 2: 7110
British Printing Industries Federation Vol 2: 7112
British Psychological Society Vol 2: 7119
British Puppet and Model Theatre Guild Vol 2: 7127
British Reserve Insurance Vol 2: 8167
British Resorts Association Vol 2: 8128
The British School at Rome Vol 2: 7129
British Schools and Universities Club of New York Vol 1: 6638
British Science Fiction Association Vol 2: 7145
British Security Industry Association Vol 2: 7147
British Show Pony Society Vol 2: 7149
British Slot Car Racing Association Vol 2: 7154
British Small Animal Veterinary Association Vol 2: 7156
British Society for Antimicrobial Chemotherapy Vol 2: 7166
British Society for Cell Biology Vol 1: 3949
British Society for Clinical Neurophysiology Vol 2: 7168
British Society for Research on Ageing Vol 2: 7170
British Society for Rheumatology Vol 2: 7172
British Society for the History of Science Vol 2: 7176
British Society of Animal Production Vol 2: 7180
British Society of Animal Science Vol 2: 7180
British Society of Hearing Aid Audiologists Vol 2: 7182
British Society of Magazine Editors Vol 2: 7185
British Society of Rheology Vol 2: 7190
British Society of Scientific Glassblowers Vol 2: 7194
British Sound Recording Association Vol 2: 7203
British Thematic Association Vol 2: 7205
British Trust for Ornithology Vol 2: 7207
British Union for the Abolition of Vivisection Vol 2: 8046
British Universities Film and Video Council Vol 2: 7211
British Vehicle Rental and Leasing Association Vol 2: 7213
British Veterinary Association Vol 2: 7215
British Vintage Wireless Society Vol 2: 7217
British Wrestling Association Vol 2: 7219
Britten-Pears Foundation Vol 2: 7221
Broadcast Cable Financial Management Association Vol 1: 6640
Broadcast Education Association Vol 1: 14106
Broadcast Financial Management Association Vol 1: 6640
Broadcast Music, Inc. Vol 1: 6642
Broadcast Promotion and Marketing Executives Vol 1: 17678
Broadcasters Promotion Association Vol 1: 17678
Brock Center for Agricultural Communication Vol 1: 6644
Bronfman Family Foundation; Samuel and Saidye Vol 1: 6646
Brookdale Center on Aging Vol 1: 4638
Brookhaven Women in Science Vol 1: 6648
Brookhaven Women in Science Scholarship Program Vol 1: 6648
Brooklyn Historical Society Vol 1: 6650
Brooks/Cole Vol 1: 5301
Broome County Farm Bureau Vol 1: 6652
Broquette-Gonin; Fondation Vol 2: 2097, 2100, 2129
Bross Foundation Vol 1: 6654
Brotherhood of the Knights of the Vine Vol 1: 6656
Brotherhood of Working Farriers Association Vol 1: 6658
Brothers of Charity Vol 2: 3872
Brown Alumni Association Vol 1: 6660
Brown Foundation; James Barrett Vol 1: 1381
Brown; James Vol 1: 15091
Brown University - Department of Biology Vol 1: 6664
Bruner Foundation Vol 1: 6667
Brussels International Festival of Fantastic Film Vol 2: 840
Buchhandlung Ziemann & Ziemann, Buxtehude Vol 2: 3065
Buckeye Children's Book Award Council Vol 1: 6669
Bucks County Historical Society Vol 1: 6671
Budapest City Council Vol 2: 3235
Buddle Findlay New Zealand Lawyers Vol 2: 5089
Budget Rent a Car Vol 1: 12651
Buffalo Audubon Society Vol 1: 6673
Builder Vol 1: 6675
Building Officials and Code Administrators International Vol 1: 6677
Building Owners and Managers Association International Vol 1: 6681
Building Owners and Managers Association International, San Antonio Federation Vol 1: 6684
Building Stone Institute Vol 1: 6686
Bulgarian Academy of Sciences Vol 2: 1205
Bulgarian Academy of Sciences Institute of Physical Chemistry Vol 2: 1210
Bulgarian Bookpublishers Association Vol 2: 1212
Bulgarian National Front Vol 1: 6688
Bulgarian National Television Vol 2: 1214
Bulgarian Orienteering Federation Vol 2: 1218
Bulgarian Red Cross Vol 2: 1220
Bulgarian Television and Radio Vol 2: 1214
Bulgarian Tourism Administration Vol 2: 1235
Bulgarian Youth Red Cross Vol 2: 1222
Bulgarska Natcionalna Televiziya Vol 2: 1214
Bund der Steuerzahler Europa Vol 2: 3108
Bund Deutscher Innenarchitekten Vol 2: 2840
Bundesarztekammer Vol 2: 2845
Bundesvereinigung Deutscher Apothekerverbande Vol 2: 2681

Organization Index

Bundesvereinigung Lebenshilfe fur Menschen mit geistiger Behinderung Vol 2: 3037
BundeszahnArztekammer-BZAK Vol 2: 2821
Bungei Shunju Ltd. Vol 2: 4114
Bureau County Historical Society Vol 1: 6690
Bureau de Controle Technique pour la Construction Vol 2: 1098
Bureau de la Coordination des Affaires Humanitaires Vol 2: 6489
Bureau International de la Paix Vol 2: 6433
Bureau International de la Recuperation Vol 2: 842
Bureau International du Beton Manufacture Vol 2: 913
Bureau International pour l'Epilepsie Vol 2: 3639
Bureau of International Recycling Vol 2: 842
Bureau of Security Control of Construction Vol 2: 1098
Burke County Chamber of Commerce Vol 1: 6692
Burlesque Historical Society Vol 1: 9373
Burlington Lions Club Vol 1: 6694
Burnett Fund; Carol Vol 1: 21028
Burns and Roe, Inc. Vol 1: 4041
Burroughs Bibliophiles Vol 1: 6696
Bush Artist Fellows Program - Bush Foundation Vol 1: 6699
Business Archives Council Vol 2: 7223
Business Committee for the Arts Vol 1: 6701
Business Forms Management Association Vol 1: 6705
Business Forum on Aging Vol 1: 4639
Business History Conference Vol 1: 6709
Business Marketing Association Vol 1: 6711
Business Press Editors; American Society of Vol 1: 4269
Business/Professional Advertising Association Vol 1: 6711
Business Roundtable Vol 1: 9365
Business Volunteers for the Arts/ Washington Vol 1: 6714
Business Week Vol 1: 10782
Busoni International Piano Competition Foundation Vol 2: 3874
Butsuri Tansa Gakkai Vol 2: 4297
By Word of Mouth Storytelling Guild Vol 1: 6716
Bydale Foundation Vol 1: 8254
C. F. Peters Corp. Vol 1: 18476
Cabletelevision Advertising Bureau Vol 1: 6720
CableVision Vol 1: 8684
Cafe des Deux Magots Vol 2: 2256
Cairo Regional Centre for International Commercial Arbitration Vol 2: 1554
Caisse de depot et placement du Quebec Vol 1: 5536
Caisses Populaires Desjardins Vol 1: 7783
Cajal Club Vol 1: 6724
Caldwell AMROP Partners International Vol 1: 8540
Caledonian Research Foundation Vol 2: 8785
Calendar Marketing Association Vol 1: 6728
Califon Historical Society Vol 1: 6730
California Academy of Sciences Vol 1: 6732
California Association of Teachers of English Vol 1: 6745
California Avocado Society Vol 1: 6734
California Canning Peach Association Vol 1: 6736
California Engineering Foundation Vol 1: 6738
California Federation of Mineralogical Societies Vol 1: 6740
California Healthcare Institute Vol 1: 6742
California Library Assoc. Vol 1: 6745
California National Watercolor Society Vol 1: 15939
California Notary Association Vol 1: 15415
California Reading Association Vol 1: 6744
California School Library Association Vol 1: 6745
California School Library Association Vol 1: 6746
California Science Teachers Association Vol 1: 6748
California Sea Grant College Program Vol 1: 6752
California Society of Anesthesiologists Vol 1: 6756
California Society of Printmakers Vol 1: 6758
California Spa and Pool Industry Education Council Vol 1: 6760
California State Beekeepers Association Vol 1: 6762
California State Polytechnic University, Pomona - John T. Lyle Center for Regenerative Studies Vol 1: 6766
California Walnut Commission Vol 1: 6768
Call Centre Association Vol 2: 7225
Callerlab - International Association of Square Dance Callers Vol 1: 6770
Calouste Gulbenkian Foundation Vol 2: 7227
Camanachd Association Vol 2: 7229
Camara de Comercio Guatemalteco-Americana Vol 2: 3201
Camara de Diputados Vol 2: 4564
Camara Municipal de Coimbra Vol 2: 5390
Camara Municipal de Lisboa Vol 2: 5422
Cambodian Human Rights and Development Association Vol 2: 1243
Cambodian People's Party Vol 2: 1245
Cambridge Center for Behavioral Studies Vol 1: 6772
Cambridge Philosophical Society Vol 2: 7232
Camcorder User Vol 2: 9195
Camerata Musicale Barese Vol 2: 3876
Camif Group Vol 2: 2532
Camp Fire Vol 1: 6774
Camp Fire USA Vol 1: 6774
Camp Fire USA El Dorado Council Vol 1: 6777
Camp Fire USA, Minnesota Council Vol 1: 6779
Campaign for the Protection of Rural Wales Vol 2: 7235
Campaign for United Nations Reform Vol 1: 6781
Campiello Foundation Vol 2: 3878
Canada Council for the Arts Vol 1: 6783
Canada Safety Council Vol 1: 6812
Canada - The Chancellery Vol 1: 6814
Canada's Aviation Hall of Fame Vol 1: 6833
Canada's National History Society Vol 1: 6835
Canada's Research-Based Pharmaceutical Companies Vol 1: 6838
Canada's Sports Hall of Fame Vol 1: 6841
Canadian Aberdeen Angus Association Vol 1: 6843
Canadian Academy of Recording Arts and Sciences Vol 1: 6845
Canadian Acoustical Association Vol 1: 6847
Canadian Actors' Equity Association Vol 1: 6855
Canadian Adult Recreational Hockey Association Vol 1: 6858
Canadian Aeronautics and Space Institute Vol 1: 6865
Canadian Aerophilatelic Society Vol 1: 6873
Canadian Alarm and Security Association Vol 1: 7385
Canadian Animal Health Institute Vol 1: 6875
Canadian Architect Vol 1: 6877
Canadian Association for Environmental Analytical Laboratories Vol 1: 6880
Canadian Association for Health, Physical Education, Recreation and Dance Vol 1: 6882
Canadian Association for Music Therapy Vol 1: 6887
Canadian Association of Broadcasters Vol 1: 6889
Canadian Association of Career Educators and Employers Vol 1: 6896
Canadian Association of Elizabeth Fry Societies Vol 1: 6902
Canadian Association of Food Banks Vol 1: 6904
Canadian Association of Geographers Vol 1: 6907
Canadian Association of Home and Property Inspectors Vol 1: 6913
Canadian Association of Home Inspectors Vol 1: 6913
Canadian Association of Medical Radiation Technologists Vol 1: 6916
Canadian Association of Oilwell Drilling Contractors Vol 1: 6925
Canadian Association of Pathologists Vol 1: 6927
Canadian Association of Physicists Vol 1: 6931
Canadian Association of Special Libraries and Information Services Vol 1: 6938
Canadian Association of University Teachers Vol 1: 6941
Canadian Astronomical Society Vol 1: 18145
Canadian Athletic Therapists Association Vol 1: 6945
Canadian Authors Association Vol 1: 6951
Canadian Aviation Historical Society Vol 1: 6959
Canadian Band Association Vol 1: 6961
Canadian Bar Association Vol 1: 6963
Canadian Booksellers Association Vol 1: 6980
Canadian Broadcasting Corp. Vol 1: 6996
Canadian Brown Swiss and Braunvieh Association Vol 1: 7001
Canadian Bureau for International Education Vol 1: 7004
Canadian Burn Survivors Association Vol 1: 7007
Canadian Business Press Vol 1: 7011
Canadian Camping Association Vol 1: 7013
Canadian Catholic School Trustees Association Vol 1: 7019
Canadian Celiac Association Vol 1: 7021
Canadian Centre for Architecture Vol 1: 7024
Canadian Centre for Ecumenism Vol 1: 7026
Canadian Club of New York Vol 1: 7028
Canadian Co-Operative Wool Growers Vol 1: 7030
Canadian Committee on Women's History Vol 1: 7155

Canadian Community Newspapers Association Vol 1: 7033
Canadian Conference of the Arts Vol 1: 7035
Canadian Construction Association Vol 1: 7039
Canadian Council of Christians and Jews Vol 1: 7046
Canadian Council of Land Surveyors Vol 1: 7048
Canadian Council of Professional Engineers Vol 1: 7050
Canadian Council of Snowmobile Organizations Vol 1: 7059
Canadian Council of Technicians and Technologists Vol 1: 7061
Canadian Country Music Association Vol 1: 7063
Canadian Culinary Federation Vol 1: 7065
Canadian Daily Newspaper Publishers Association Vol 1: 7308
Canadian Dam Association Vol 1: 7069
Canadian Dermatology Association Vol 1: 7072
Canadian Economics Association Vol 1: 7077
Canadian Education Association Vol 1: 7079
Canadian Environmental Network Vol 1: 7081
Canadian Federation for the Humanities and Social Sciences Vol 1: 7083
Canadian Federation of Amateur Baseball Vol 1: 7085
Canadian Federation of Biological Societies Vol 1: 7088
Canadian Federation of Chefs and Cooks Vol 1: 7065
Canadian Federation of Humane Societies Vol 1: 7090
Canadian Film and Television Association Vol 1: 7092
Canadian Film and Television Production Association Vol 1: 7092
Canadian Film Centre Vol 1: 7095
Canadian Flag Association Vol 1: 7097
Canadian Folk Music Society Vol 1: 7436
Canadian Football Council Vol 1: 7099
Canadian Football League Vol 1: 7099
Canadian Forestry Association Vol 1: 7118
Canadian Foundation for Ileitis and Colitis Vol 1: 8652
Canadian Geotechnical Society Vol 1: 7121
Canadian Gospel Music Association Vol 1: 7132
Canadian Hardware and Housewares Manufacturers Association Vol 1: 7134
Canadian Health Libraries Association Vol 1: 7136
Canadian Healthcare Association Vol 1: 7144
Canadian Heritage Vol 1: 7146
Canadian Historical Association Vol 1: 2468, 7148
Canadian HIV/AIDS Legal Network Vol 1: 7156
Canadian Hospital Association Vol 1: 7144
Canadian Image Processing and Pattern Recognition Society Vol 1: 7158
Canadian Industrial Transportation Association Vol 1: 7160
Canadian Information Processing Society Vol 1: 7162
Canadian Institute for the Administration of Justice Vol 1: 7169
Canadian Institute of Forestry Vol 1: 7171
Canadian Institute of Mining, Metallurgy, and Petroleum Vol 1: 7180
Canadian Institute of Public Health Inspectors Vol 1: 14948
Canadian Institute of Surveying Vol 2: 6637
Canadian International Amateur Film Festival Vol 1: 7205
Canadian International Annual Film/Video Festival Vol 1: 7205
Canadian Interuniversity Sport Vol 1: 7207
Canadian Journalists for Free Expression Vol 1: 7244
Canadian Legal Conference Vol 1: 6973
Canadian Library Association Vol 1: 7247
Canadian Library Association - Canadian Association of Children's Librarians Vol 1: 7253
Canadian Library Association - Canadian Association of Public Libraries Vol 1: 7255
Canadian Library Association - Canadian School Library Association Vol 1: 7258
Canadian Library Trustees' Association Vol 1: 7263
Canadian Mental Health Association Vol 1: 7266
Canadian Meteorological and Oceanographic Society Vol 1: 7274
Canadian Mineral Analysts Vol 1: 7285
Canadian Motorcycle Association Vol 1: 7287
Canadian Museum of Civilization Vol 1: 6647
Canadian Museums Association Vol 1: 7296
Canadian Music Competition Vol 1: 7298
Canadian National Institute for the Blind Vol 1: 7300
Canadian Newspaper Association Vol 1: 7308
Canadian Numismatic Association Vol 1: 7321
Canadian Nurses Foundation Vol 1: 7310
Canadian Organization of Medical Physicists Vol 1: 6934
Canadian Ornamental Plant Foundation Vol 1: 7315
Canadian Paediatric Society Vol 1: 7317
Canadian Paper Money Society Vol 1: 7320
Canadian Parks and Recreation Association Vol 1: 7322
Canadian Parks and Wilderness Society Vol 1: 7329
Canadian Payroll Association Vol 1: 7331
Canadian Pharmacists Association Vol 1: 7333
Canadian Phytopathological Society Vol 1: 7335
Canadian Professional Sales Association Vol 1: 7342
Canadian Psychological Association Vol 1: 7344
Canadian Public Health Association Vol 1: 7354
Canadian Public Relations Society Vol 1: 7359
Canadian Quaternary Association Vol 1: 7364
Canadian Railroad Historical Association Vol 1: 7366
Canadian Rehabilitation Council for the Disabled Vol 1: 7371
Canadian Research Institute for the Advancement of Women Vol 1: 7375
Canadian Science Writers' Association Vol 1: 7381
Canadian Security Association Vol 1: 7385
Canadian Seed Growers' Association Vol 1: 7387
Canadian Ski Council Vol 1: 7391
Canadian Society for Bioengineering Vol 1: 7397
Canadian Society for Chemical Engineering Vol 1: 7405, 7433
Canadian Society for Civil Engineering Vol 1: 7409
Canadian Society for International Health Vol 1: 7422
Canadian Society for Mechanical Engineering Vol 1: 7424, 7849
Canadian Society for Nutritional Sciences Vol 1: 7434
Canadian Society for Traditional Music Vol 1: 7436
Canadian Society of Animal Science - Agricultural Institute of Canada Vol 1: 7438
Canadian Society of Association Executives Vol 1: 7447
Canadian Society of Biochemistry, Molecular and Cellular Biology Vol 1: 7451
Canadian Society of Diagnostic Medical Sonographers Vol 1: 7453
Canadian Society of Hospital Pharmacists Vol 1: 7456
Canadian Society of Landscape Architects Vol 1: 7475
Canadian Society of Microbiologists Vol 1: 7477
Canadian Society of Petroleum Geologists Vol 1: 7480
Canadian Society of Sugar Artistry Vol 1: 7493
Canadian Society of Zoologists Vol 1: 7495
Canadian Sociology and Anthropology Association Vol 1: 7501
Canadian Sport Council Vol 1: 19624
Canadian Sport Massage Therapists Association Vol 1: 7505
Canadian Sport Parachuting Association Vol 1: 7507
Canadian Sporting Goods Association Vol 1: 7511
Canadian Tenant Bureau, Inc. Vol 1: 18282
Canadian Theatre Critics Association Vol 1: 7513
Canadian Toy Testing Council Vol 1: 7515
Canadian Trakehner Horse Society Vol 1: 7519
Canadian Trapshooting Association Vol 1: 7526
Canadian University Music Society Vol 1: 7528
Canadian Veterinary Medical Association Vol 1: 7530
Canadian Weekly Newspapers Association Vol 1: 7033
Canadian Wildlife Federation Vol 1: 7537
Canadian Wood Council Vol 1: 7544
Canarias Mediafest - International Canary Islands Video and Multimedia Festival Vol 2: 6008
CANARIE Vol 1: 7546
Cancer Association of South Africa Vol 2: 5523
Cancer Care Ontario Vol 1: 7548
Cancer Control Society Vol 1: 7550
Cancer Hope Network Vol 1: 7552
Cancer Research & Prevention Foundation Vol 1: 7554
Cancer Research Foundation Vol 1: 7556

Cancer Research Institute, Inc. Vol 1: 7559
Cancer Research U.K. Beatson Laboratories Vol 2: 7237
Cancer Society of Finland Vol 2: 1577
Canda Council for the Arts Vol 1: 6647
C&G Software Systems, Inc. Vol 1: 15761
Cannes International Film Festival Vol 2: 2258
Canola Council of Canada Vol 1: 7563
Canon Law Society of America Vol 1: 7565
Canon USA Inc. Vol 1: 17577
Canterbury Historical Association Vol 2: 4960, 4961
Cantors Assembly Vol 1: 7567
Cape Cod Art Association Vol 1: 7570
Cape Cod Museum of Natural History Vol 1: 7572
Cape Tercentenary Foundation Vol 2: 5525
Capezio Ballet Makers Dance Foundation Vol 1: 7574
Capezio Foundation Vol 1: 7575
Capitol Association of Diabetes Educators Vol 1: 7576
Capote Literary Trust; Truman Vol 1: 12189
Capranica Foundation Vol 1: 7578
Car and Driver Vol 1: 7580
Cardiac Society of Australia and New Zealand Vol 2: 295
Cardinal Health Vol 1: 15715
CARE Guatemala Vol 2: 3203
Career College Association Vol 1: 7582
Career Communications Group Vol 1: 7584
Career Planning and Adult Development Network Vol 1: 7587
Cargill Vol 1: 3308
Caribbean Conference of Churches Vol 2: 824
Caribbean Conservation Corporation and Sea Turtle Survival League Vol 1: 7589
Caribbean Culinary Federation Vol 1: 7592
Caribbean Hotel Association Vol 1: 7591
Caribbean Hotel Council of the Caribbean Travel Association Vol 1: 7591
Caribbean Studies Association Vol 1: 7593
Carina Ari Foundation Vol 2: 6141
The Caring Institute Vol 1: 7596
Caritas of Austin Vol 1: 7598
Carlsberg Laboratorium Vol 2: 1441
Carlsberg Laboratory Vol 2: 1441
Carmel Music Society Vol 1: 7600
Carnegie Corporation of New York Vol 1: 5437
Carnegie Foundation Vol 2: 4704
Carnegie Hero Fund Commission Vol 1: 7602
Carnegie Mellon University - Software Engineering Institute Vol 1: 7604
Carnegie Museum of Art Vol 1: 7606
Carnegie Stichting Vol 2: 4704
Carolina Biological Supply Company Vol 1: 5500, 5503
Carolina's Citizens Freedom Foundation Vol 1: 7608
Carolinas Roofing and Sheet Metal Contractors Association Vol 1: 7610
Carrier Corporation Vol 1: 4427
Carroll Center for the Blind Vol 1: 7612
Cartier Vol 2: 7362
Cartoonists' Club of Great Britain Vol 2: 7239
Cartoonists Northwest Vol 1: 7614
Cary Charitable Trust; Mary Flagler Vol 1: 18086
CASA Association; National Vol 1: 14874
Casa de Cultura da Mulher Negra Vol 2: 1140
Casablanca Sound & Picture Vol 1: 6033
Case IH Vol 1: 4229
Case Western Reserve University Vol 1: 7616
Case Western Reserve University - Michelson Morley Award Committee Vol 1: 7618
Cassa di Risparmio di Parma Vol 2: 3871
Casualty Actuarial Society Vol 1: 7620
Catalyst Vol 1: 7626
Catboat Association Vol 1: 7628
Catering Equipment Distributors Association of Great Britain Vol 2: 7241
Caterpillar Tractor Company Vol 1: 4019
Catholic Academy for Communication Arts Professionals Vol 1: 7632
Catholic Book Club Vol 1: 7634
Catholic Broadcasting Association Vol 1: 7632
Catholic Campus Ministry Association Vol 1: 7636
Catholic Church Extension Society of the U.S.A. Vol 1: 7639
Catholic Health Association of Canada Vol 1: 7641
Catholic Hospital Association of Canada Vol 1: 7641
Catholic Kolping Society of America Vol 1: 7643
Catholic League for Religious and Civil Rights Vol 1: 7646
Catholic Library Association Vol 1: 7649
Catholic Press Association Vol 1: 7657
Catholic Theological Society of America Vol 1: 7661
Catholic University of America Alumni Association Vol 1: 7663
Catholic War Veterans of the United States of America Vol 1: 7670
Catholic Women's League of New Zealand Vol 2: 4962
Catholic Youth Organization of the Archdiocese of New York Vol 1: 7677
Catskill Center for Photography Vol 1: 7742
Caucus for Television Producers, Writers and Directors Vol 1: 7682
Cavour Prize Association; Grinzane Vol 2: 3880
CBS Vol 1: 16981
CDS International Vol 1: 7686
Ceilings and Interior Systems Construction Association Vol 1: 7688
Ceilings and Interior Systems Contractors Association Vol 1: 7688
Celanese Mexicana S.A. de C.V. Vol 2: 4463
Celette (Industrial Housings) Ltd. Vol 2: 7843
Celtic Film and Television Festival Vol 2: 7243
Cement and Concrete Association of New Zealand Vol 2: 4981
Centennial Education Foundation Vol 1: 7692
Center for Adult Reading and Enrichment Vol 1: 7694
Center for Advanced Study in the Behavioral Sciences Vol 1: 7696
Center for Afroamerican and African Studies Vol 1: 7698
The Center for American and International Law Vol 1: 7700
Center for Aviation Research and Education Vol 1: 7703
Center for Bioenvironmental Research Vol 1: 7705
Center for Book Arts Vol 1: 7709
Center for Career Management Professionals Vol 2: 357
Center for Chinese Studies Vol 2: 6591
Center for Christian/Jewish Understanding of Sacred Heart University Vol 1: 7711
Center for Communication Vol 1: 7713
Center for Contemporary Opera Vol 1: 7715
Center for Creative Leadership Vol 1: 7717
Center for Democratic Policy Vol 1: 7736
Center for Design of Analog-Digital Integrated Circuits Vol 1: 7720
Center for Ecoliteracy Vol 1: 7722
Center for Entrepreneurial Leadership Vol 1: 9331
Center for Health Law and Policy at Southern Illinois University School of Law Vol 1: 7724
Center for Human-Computer Communication - OGI School of Science and Engineering Vol 1: 7726
Center for Immigration Studies Vol 1: 7728
Center for International Studies Vol 1: 7730
Center for Latin America and Caribbean Studies Vol 1: 7732
Center for Meteorite Studies Vol 1: 7734
Center for National Policy Vol 1: 7736
Center for Nonprofit Management Vol 1: 7738
Center for Philosophy, Law, Citizenship Vol 1: 7740
Center for Photography at Woodstock Vol 1: 7742
Center for Population Options (California) Vol 1: 13237
Center for Public Resources - CPR Legal Program Vol 1: 8625
Center for Public Safety Vol 1: 11308
Center for Science in the Public Interest Vol 1: 7744
Center for the Protection of Children's Rights Foundation Vol 2: 6616
Center for the Study of Aging, Inc. Vol 1: 7746
Center for the Study of Canada Vol 1: 7748
Center for the Study of Comparative Folklore and Mythology Vol 1: 8888
Center for the Study of Science Fiction Vol 1: 7751
Center for the Study of Sport in Society Vol 1: 7754
Center for the Study of the Presidency Vol 1: 7757
Center of the American Experiment Vol 1: 7759
Centers for Disease Control and Prevention Vol 1: 14176
Centracare Health Foundation Vol 1: 7761
Central Association of Obstetricians and Gynecologists Vol 1: 7763
Central Chancery of the Orders of Knighthood Vol 2: 7245
Central Connecticut Regional Planning Agency Vol 1: 7766
Central Engineering Consultancy Bureau of Sri Lanka Vol 2: 6125
Central Institute for Labour Protection - National Research Institute Vol 2: 5297
Central Louisiana Partners in Literacy Vol 1: 7768
Central Missouri State University - Art Center Gallery Vol 1: 7770

Central Pennsylvania Festival of the Arts Vol 1: 7772
Central Pennsylvania Paralegal Association Vol 1: 7777
Centre Belge de Documentation Musicale Vol 2: 838
Centre Canadien d'Architecture Vol 1: 7024
Centre Canadien d'Oecumenisme Vol 1: 7026
Centre Canadien du Film Vol 1: 7095
Centre de Cooperation pour les Recherches Scientifiques Relatives au Tabac Vol 2: 2284
Centre de Recherches Mathematiques Vol 1: 6937
Centre de recherches mathematiques, Universite de Montreal Vol 1: 13202
Centre de Recherches sur l'histoire, l'art et la Culture Islamiques Vol 2: 6645
Centre du Cinema Grec Vol 2: 3189
Centre du riz pour l'Afrique de l'Ouest Vol 2: 1367
Centre for Latin American Monetary Studies Vol 2: 4466
Centre International de Criminologie Comparee Vol 1: 11457
Centre International de Recherche sur le Cancer - International Mondiale de la Sante Vol 2: 6568
Centre National de la Cinematographie Vol 2: 2335
Centre National de la Recherche Scientifique Vol 2: 2394
Centre national de la Recherche Scientifique et Technologique Vol 2: 2636
Centre of Films for Children and Young People in Germany Vol 2: 2687
Centre Universitaire du Film Scientifique Vol 2: 844
Centro de Estudios Monetarios Latinoamericanos Vol 2: 4466
Centro de Medios Audiovisuales Vol 2: 9296
Centro Gerontologico Latino Vol 1: 12712
Centro Regional de Sismologia para America del Sur Vol 2: 5247
Centro Studi Nuovo Mezzogiorno Vol 2: 3850
Century Productions Vol 1: 9565
Ceramic Society of Japan Vol 2: 4101
Cercles des Jeunes Naturalistes Vol 1: 7779
Cerebral Palsy of Louisiana Vol 1: 7784
Certamen Internacional de Cine Amateur Ciutat d'Igualada Vol 2: 6010
Certamen Internacional de Cine para la Infancia y la Juventud de Gijon Vol 2: 6036
Certamen Internacional de Films Cortos, Ciudad de Huesca Vol 2: 6029
Ceska Radiologicka Spolecnost Vol 2: 1421
Ceska Spolecnost Chemicka Vol 2: 1416
Cesky Rozhlas, Praga Vol 2: 1419
Cetacean Society International Vol 1: 7787
Ceylon Development Engineering Company, Ltd. Vol 2: 6118
Ceylon Electricity Board Vol 2: 6125
CH2M Hill Vol 1: 3866, 4029
Chain Link Fence Manufacturer Institute Vol 1: 7789
Challenger Society Vol 2: 7268
Challenger Society for Marine Science Vol 2: 7268
Chamber Music America Vol 1: 4375
Chamber Music America Vol 1: 7791
Chamber Music Monterey Bay Vol 1: 7796
Chamber Music Society of Lincoln Center Vol 1: 7798
Chamber Music Yellow Springs Vol 1: 7800
Chamber of Commerce and Industry of Slovenia Vol 2: 5972
Chamber of Commerce of Harrison County Vol 1: 7802
Chamber of Geological Engineers of Turkey Vol 2: 6628
Chamber of Mines of South Africa Vol 2: 5527
Chamber Week Coordinating Committee Vol 2: 812
Champagne d'Argent Federation Vol 1: 3811
Champlin Refining and Chemicals, Inc. Vol 1: 10845
Chancery of Netherlands Orders Vol 2: 4706
Channel Four Television Vol 2: 6917
Chapin Foundation; Harry Vol 1: 21926
Chapman and Hall Journals Division Vol 2: 8773
Chapman and Hall, Scientific Data Division Vol 2: 8773
Charcot-Marie-Tooth Association Vol 1: 7804
Charities Aid Foundation Vol 2: 7662
Charity Forum Vol 2: 7662
Charles A. and Anne Morrow Lindbergh Foundation Vol 1: 7807
Charles Darwin University Vol 2: 298
Charles Nypels Foundation Vol 2: 4711
Charles S. Peirce Society Vol 1: 7809
Charlotte Repertory Theatre Vol 1: 7811
Charta 77 Foundation Vol 2: 6143
Charter Behavioral Health Systems Vol 1: 627
Chartered Institute of Arbitrators Vol 2: 7271
Chartered Institute of Building Vol 2: 7273
Chartered Institute of Environmental Health Vol 1: 14948
Chartered Institute of Journalists Vol 2: 7275
Chartered Institute of Library and Information Professionals Vol 2: 7277
Chartered Institute of Logistics and Transport in Australia Vol 2: 300
Chartered Institute of Logistics and Transport in North America Vol 1: 7813
Chartered Institute of Management Accountants - Hong Kong Division Vol 2: 5210
Chartered Institute of Public Relations Vol 2: 7279
Chartered Institution of Building Services Engineers - England Vol 2: 7281
Chartered Insurance Institute Vol 2: 7294
Chartered Society of Designers Vol 2: 7298
Chattahoochee Valley Art Museum Vol 1: 7815
Chautauqua Center for the Visual Arts - Chautauqua Institution Vol 1: 7818
Chefs and Cooks Circle Vol 2: 7302
Chelsea Vol 1: 7820
Chemical Dynamics - B. P. Chemicals Ltd. Vol 2: 8773
Chemical Engineering - Chemical Week Publishing Vol 1: 7822
Chemical Industry Institute of Toxicology Vol 1: 7994
The Chemical Institute of Canada Vol 1: 7825
Chemical Marketing Research Association Vol 1: 8285
Chemical Organization of Mexico Vol 2: 4468
Chemical Society Vol 2: 8737
Chemical Society of Japan Vol 2: 4103
Chemical Specialties Manufacturers Association Vol 1: 8463
Cherokee National Historical Society Vol 1: 7851
Chesapeake and Ohio Historical Society Vol 1: 7853
Chesapeake Bay Foundation Vol 1: 7858
Chess Journalists of America Vol 1: 7861
Chevron Chemical Company Vol 1: 14150
Chevron USA Vol 1: 7863
ChevronTexaco Conservation Awards Program Vol 1: 7863
Chia Hsin Cement Corporation Vol 2: 6594
Chia Hsin Foundation Vol 2: 6593
Chian Federation of America Vol 1: 7865
Chicago Anti-Hunger Federation Vol 1: 7867
Chicago Asthma Consortium Vol 1: 7869
The Chicago Athenaeum: Museum of Architecture and Design Vol 1: 7871
Chicago Book Clinic Vol 1: 7875
Chicago Bulk Mail Center Area Local, American Postal Workers Union, AFL-CIO, LU 7033 Vol 1: 7880
The Chicago Community Trust Vol 1: 7882
Chicago Film Critics Awards - Chicago Film Critics Association Vol 1: 7885
Chicago International Children's Film Festival Vol 1: 7887
Chicago International Festival of Children's Films Vol 1: 7887
Chicago Midwest Bead Society Vol 1: 7889
Chicago Tribune Vol 1: 7891, 7892
Chihuahuan Desert Research Institute Vol 1: 7894
Children as Teachers of Peace Vol 1: 7896
Children as the Peacemakers Vol 1: 7896
Children's AIDS Fund Vol 1: 7898
Children's Book Committee Vol 1: 7900
Children's Book Council Vol 1: 7903
Children's Book Council of Australia Vol 2: 302
Children's Book Council of Iran Vol 2: 3607
Children's Film Society, India Vol 2: 3354
Children's Librarians of New Hampshire Vol 1: 7905
Children's Literature Association Vol 1: 7907
Children's Literature Council of Southern California Vol 1: 7912
Children's Rights Council Vol 1: 7914
Children's Watch International Vol 1: 7918
Childs Memorial Fund for Medical Research; Jane Coffin Vol 1: 7920
Chile Ministerio de Educacion Vol 2: 1249
China Stamp Society Vol 1: 7922
Chinard Prize Committee; Gilbert Vol 1: 7924
Chinese American Librarians Association Vol 1: 7926
Chinese American Medical Society Vol 1: 7928
Chinese Association on Smoking and Health Vol 2: 5212
Chinese Chemical Society Vol 2: 6595
Chinese Economists Society Vol 1: 7930
Chiropractic Association of South Africa Vol 2: 5529
Chiropraktiese Vereniging van Suid-Afrika Vol 2: 5529
Chivers Press Vol 2: 7363
Choate, Hall & Stewart LLP Vol 1: 7932
Choice - American Library Association Vol 1: 7934

Chopin Foundation of the United States Vol 1: 7936
Chopin-Gesellschaft in der Bundesrepublik Deutschland Vol 2: 2690
Chopin Society Vol 2: 1414
Choral Arts New England Vol 1: 7938
Chorus America Vol 1: 7940
Chow Chow Club, Inc. Vol 1: 7944
The Chris Awards Vol 1: 7946
Christian Educators Association International Vol 1: 7954
Christian Foundation for Children and Aging Vol 1: 7956
Christian Health Association of Kenya Vol 2: 4345
Christian Holiness Partnership Vol 1: 7958
Christian Home Educators Association of California Vol 1: 7961
Christian Management Association Vol 1: 7963
Christian Ministries Management Association Vol 1: 7963
Christian Pharmacists Fellowship International Vol 1: 7966
Christians Concerned for Racial Equality Vol 1: 7968
The Christophers Vol 1: 7970
Chroniqueurs de la Vie au Grand Air du Canada Vol 1: 16971
Chrysler 300 Club International Vol 1: 7972
Chrysler Canada Vol 1: 2501
Chung Nip Hwe Gwan Vol 2: 5499
Church & Dwight Company Vol 1: 11211
Church and Synagogue Library Association Vol 1: 7974
Churches' Center for Theology and Public Policy Vol 1: 7981
Churchill Center Vol 1: 7983
Churchill Downs Inc. Vol 1: 7988
Churchill Study Unit Vol 1: 7983
CIBA - GEIGY Plc Vol 2: 8773
CIBA Plant Protection Vol 1: 19871
CIBA Specialty Chemicals Education Foundation Vol 1: 15684, 15685
CID Agents Association Vol 1: 7991
CIGNA Corporation Vol 1: 8626
CIIT Centers for Health Research Vol 1: 7994
CILQ-FM (Q107 Radio) Vol 1: 7996
CINANIMA - Festival Internacional de Cinema de Animacao Vol 2: 5392
CINANIMA - International Animated Film Festival Portugal Vol 2: 5392
Cincinnati Opera Association Vol 1: 7998
Cincinnati Scholarship Association Vol 1: 3165
Cinema/Chicago Vol 1: 8000
Cinema du Reel Vol 2: 2260
Cinema Giovani- Torino Film Festival Vol 2: 3882
Cinema Novo Fantasporto Vol 2: 5394
Cinematheque Royale Vol 2: 1092
Cineteca Nacional Vol 2: 4470
Cintas Foundation, Inc. Vol 1: 10981
Circle of the Greek Children's Book Vol 2: 3167
Circo Acmi Vol 1: 4792
Circulation Council of DMA Vol 1: 8004
Circumnavigators Club Vol 1: 8006
Circus Fans Association of America Vol 1: 8008
Citizens Budget Commission Vol 1: 8010
Citizens Committee for New York City Vol 1: 8012
Citizens for Alternatives to Chemical Contamination Vol 1: 8014
Citizens League of Greater Cleveland/Citizens League Research Institute Vol 1: 8017
Citizens Research Council of Michigan Vol 1: 8019
Citizens Union of the City of New York Vol 1: 8021
City and Guilds of London Institute Vol 2: 7304
City and Regional Magazine Association Vol 1: 8023
City Club of New York Vol 1: 8025
City College of New York Vol 1: 8027
City Council of Pforzheim Vol 2: 3073
City of Beverly Hills Vol 1: 8034
City of Boynton Beach Vol 1: 6594
City of Greater Dandenong Vol 2: 309
City of Independence, Missouri Vol 1: 8036
City of Linz Vol 2: 703
City of New York Department of Cultural Affairs Vol 1: 8038
City of Ottawa Vol 1: 8040
City of Paris Vol 2: 2615
City of Philadelphia - Greater Philadelphia First Corporation Vol 1: 10156
City of Sydney Cultural Council Vol 2: 311
City of Sydney Eisteddfod Vol 2: 311
City of Toronto Vol 1: 8043, 20118
City of Yorkton Vol 1: 22048
CITY-TV Vol 1: 20118
City University of New York Graduate Center - Doctoral Theater Students Association Vol 1: 8053
Civic Trust Vol 2: 7312
Civil Aviation Medical Association Vol 1: 241
Civil War Society Vol 1: 8055
Civil War Token Society Vol 1: 8057
Civitan International Vol 1: 8060
Cladan Cultural Exchange Institute of Australia Vol 2: 316
Clan Hunter Association Vol 2: 7314
Clan Munro Association of Canada Vol 1: 8072
Clarinet International Vol 1: 11484
Clarinetwork International Vol 1: 11484
Clark County Literacy Coalition Vol 1: 8074
Clarke College Vol 1: 8076
Classic Car Club of America Vol 1: 8078
Clay Minerals Society Vol 1: 8088
Clayton Environmental Vol 1: 2609
Clear-Com Vol 1: 20644
Clear Communications Vol 2: 4953
Cleft Palate Foundation Vol 1: 8093
Clemens & Associates Insurance Agency Vol 1: 13377
Clemson Architectural Foundation Vol 1: 18181
Clemson University Vol 1: 18647
The Cleveland Foundation Vol 1: 8096
Cleveland Institute of Music Vol 1: 8098
Cleveland Police Historical Society and Museum Vol 1: 8101
Cleveland State University Poetry Center Vol 1: 8103
Cleveland West Lutherans for Life Vol 1: 8105
Cliburn Foundation; Van Vol 1: 8107
Clinical Immunology Society Vol 1: 8109
Clinical Sociology Association Vol 1: 19373
Clio Awards Inc. Vol 1: 8111
Closter Historical Society Vol 1: 8113
Clowes Fund Vol 1: 1947
Club Managers Association of America Vol 1: 21923
Club Partir Vol 2: 2262
Club Tenco Vol 2: 3884
CMP Educational Foundation of the Cincinnati Master Plumbers' Association Vol 1: 8115
Co-op Subscriptions Vol 2: 229
Coal Preparation Society Vol 2: 8123
Coalition for Alternatives in Jewish Education Vol 1: 8117
Coalition for the Advancement of Jewish Education Vol 1: 8117
Coalition to Protect Maryland Burial Sites Vol 1: 8119
Coastal Emergency Services Vol 1: 9241
Coblentz Society Vol 1: 16790
Coca-Cola Company Vol 1: 16981
Cocker Spaniel Club of Western Pennsylvania Vol 1: 8121
Codus: Wales Historic Monuments Vol 2: 6919
Coffee Growers Association Vol 2: 9340
COGEDIM Vol 2: 2264
Cohasset Historical Society Vol 1: 8123
Cohen Memorial Fund; Sophie and Shirley Vol 1: 18885
Colby College Vol 1: 8125
Coldwater Community Theater Vol 1: 8127
Colegio de Arquitectos del Peru Vol 2: 5237
Colegio de Contadores Publicos de Mexico Vol 2: 4472
Coleman Chamber Music Association Vol 1: 8129
Coleopterists' Society Vol 1: 8131
Colgate-Palmolive Vol 1: 11207
Colgate-Palmolive Company Vol 1: 11212, 19333
Collective Promotion of the Dutch Book Vol 2: 4713
Collectors Club Vol 1: 8133
Collectors of Religion on Stamps Vol 1: 8139
College Art Association Vol 1: 8141
College English Association Vol 1: 8151
College Gymnastics Association Vol 1: 8157
College Language Association Vol 1: 8165
College Media Advisers Vol 1: 8167
College of Chaplains of the American Protestant Health Association Vol 1: 5819
College of Chemical Engineers Vol 2: 428
College of Mount Saint Joseph Vol 1: 8178
College of Mount Saint Joseph on the Ohio Vol 1: 8178
College of Optometrists in Vision Development Vol 1: 8183
College of Physicians of Philadelphia - Section on Dermatology Vol 1: 8186
College of Piping Vol 2: 7316
College of Psychologists of British Columbia Vol 1: 6635
College Ouest Africain des Chirurgiens Vol 2: 5108
College Sports Information Directors of America Vol 1: 8188
College Swimming Coaches Association Vol 1: 15283
College Swimming Coaches Association of America Vol 1: 8194
Collegium Internationale Neuro-Psychopharmacologicum Vol 1: 8198
Collier Building Industry Association Vol 1: 8202
Cologne International Pianoforte Competition - Foundation Tomassoni Vol 2: 2692

Cologne International Singing Competition Vol 2: 2696
Cologne International Violin Competition Vol 2: 2694
Cologne International Vocal Competition Vol 2: 2696
Colombia Ministry of Agriculture and Rural Development Vol 2: 1271
Colombia Ministry of Foreign Affairs Vol 2: 1274
Colombia Ministry of National Defence Vol 2: 1279
Colombia Ministry of the Interior and Justice Vol 2: 1296
Colombia Ministry of Transportation Vol 2: 1303
Colombian Association for the Advancement of Science Vol 2: 1305
Colombian Oceanographic Commission Vol 2: 1307
Colombian Society of Economists Vol 2: 1270
Colonial Dames of America Vol 1: 18952
Colonial Players, Inc. Vol 1: 8204
Colonial Society of Massachusetts Vol 1: 8206
Colorado Business Committee for the Arts Vol 1: 8208
Colorado Congress of Foreign Language Teachers Vol 1: 8210
Colorado Language Arts Society Vol 1: 8213
Colorado Ranger Horse Association Vol 1: 8215
Colorado River Watch Network Vol 1: 8220
Colorado Society of Association Executives Vol 1: 8222
Columbia: A Journal of Literature and Art Vol 1: 8224
Columbia: A Magazine of Poetry and Art Vol 1: 8224
Columbia College Chicago - Theater/Music Center Vol 1: 8226
Columbia Engineering School Alumni Association Vol 1: 8228
Columbia Pictures Television Vol 1: 12542
Columbia Scholastic Press Association Vol 1: 8231
Columbia University Vol 1: 8236
Columbia University Vol 1: 12245
Columbia University - Gannett Center for Media Studies Vol 1: 9757
Columbia University - Graduate School of Journalism Vol 1: 4492
Columbia University - Graduate School of Journalism Vol 1: 8247
Columbia University - School of Law Vol 1: 8251
Columbia University - School of the Arts Vol 1: 8253
Columbia University - Southern Asian Institute Vol 1: 8255
Columbian Squires Vol 1: 8257
Columbine Poets of Colorado Vol 1: 14991
Columbus Blues Alliance Vol 1: 8259
Columbus Foundation of Columbus, Ohio Vol 1: 12099
Colworth Laboratory Vol 2: 8932
Combined Organizations of Numismatic Error Collectors of America Vol 1: 8261
Combustion Institute Vol 1: 8263
Comhaltas Ceoltoiri Eireann Vol 2: 3713
Comision Colombiana de Oceanografia Vol 2: 1307
Comision Federal de Electricidad Vol 2: 4561
Comision Nacional Bancaria y de Valores Vol 2: 4474
Comision para la Defensa de los Derechos Humanos en Centroamerica Vol 2: 1348
Comite Canadien d'Action sur le Statut de la Femme Vol 1: 13871
Comite des Associations Europeennes de Fonderie Vol 2: 2266
Comite International de la Croix-Rouge Vol 2: 6394
Comite International des Sports des Sourds Vol 1: 11493
Comite International Olympique Vol 2: 6424
Comite Olympique Hongrois Vol 2: 3265
Comite pour la Recherche Spatiale Vol 2: 2268
Commemorative Air Force Vol 1: 8268
Commercial Development and Marketing Association Vol 1: 8285
Commercial Finance Association Vol 1: 8289
Commission des Pares Nationaux et Vol 2: 6553
Commission for the Defense of Human Rights in Central America Vol 2: 1348
Commission Geographical Education Vol 2: 1632
Commission Internationale de Juristes - Section Canadienne Vol 1: 11489
Commission Internationale des Oeufs Vol 2: 7919
Commission Internationale d'Optique Vol 2: 6057
Commission Internationale du Genie Rural Vol 2: 2943
Commitment Recognition Award Vol 1: 10638
Committee for Accreditation of Canadian Medical School in Canada Vol 1: 1948
Committee of 100 in Finland Vol 2: 1580
Committee of European Foundry Associations Vol 2: 2266
Committee of Presidents of Statistical Societies Vol 1: 8291
Committee on Space Research Vol 2: 2268
Committee to Protect Journalists Vol 1: 8296
Common Cause Vol 1: 8299
Common Cause/Tennessee Vol 1: 8301
Commonwealth Association for Public Administration and Management Vol 1: 8303
Commonwealth Association of Architects Vol 2: 7319
Commonwealth Association of Science and Mathematics Educators Vol 2: 7321
Commonwealth Association of Science, Technology and Mathematics Educators Vol 2: 7321
Commonwealth Association of Tax Administrators Vol 2: 7323
Commonwealth Bank of Australia Vol 2: 103
Commonwealth Broadcasting Association Vol 2: 7330
Commonwealth Club of California Vol 1: 8305
Commonwealth Council for Educational Administration and Management Vol 2: 1396, 1397
Commonwealth Forestry Association Vol 2: 7325
Commonwealth Foundation Vol 2: 7322, 7329
Commonwealth Games Federation Vol 2: 7335
Commonwealth Magistrates and Judges' Association Vol 2: 7337
Commonwealth Magistrates' Association Vol 2: 7337
Commonwealth Pharmaceutical Association Vol 2: 7339
Commonwealth Press Union - United Kingdom Vol 2: 7341
Commonwealth Youth Programme Vol 2: 7344
Communication Arts Vol 1: 8307
Communication Association of the Pacific Vol 1: 21874
Communications Industry Association; Personal Vol 1: 17117
Community Associations Institute - Greater Houston Chapter Vol 1: 8312
Community Associations Institute - Orange County Regional Chapter Vol 1: 8314
Community College Humanities Association Vol 1: 8316
Community Colleges for International Development Vol 1: 8318
Community Counselling Service Vol 1: 5700
Community Funds, Inc. Vol 1: 21032
Community Relations Commission for a Multicultural New South Wales Vol 2: 614
Compact Holding Vol 2: 1238
Compass Publications Inc. Vol 1: 13108, 15420
The Compassionate Friends Vol 1: 8321
Composers and Authors Society of Hong Kong Vol 2: 5216
Composites Institute Vol 1: 19307, 19308
Composites Manufacturing Association of the Society of Manufacturing Engineers Vol 1: 8323
Computer and Automated Systems Association of Society of Manufacturing Engineers Vol 1: 8325
Computer Measurement Group Vol 1: 8327
Computer Professionals for Social Responsibility Vol 1: 8330
Computer Society of South Africa Vol 2: 5544
Computer Society of Zimbabwe Vol 2: 9342
Computing Research Association Vol 1: 8332
Computing Technology Industry Association Vol 1: 8335
Comune di Sondrio Mostra Internazionale dei Documentari sui Parchi Vol 2: 3969
Conamus Vol 2: 4720
Conamus; Stichting Vol 2: 4720
Concord Coalition Vol 1: 8337
Concordia Historical Institute Vol 1: 8339
Concorso Ettore Pozzoli Vol 2: 3886
Concorso Pianistico Internazionale Alessandro Casagrande Vol 2: 3888
Concorso Pianistico Internazionale Ferrucio Busoni Vol 2: 3874
Concours de Geneve Vol 2: 6309
Concours de musique du Canada Vol 1: 7298
Concours International de Ballet, Varna Vol 2: 1239
Concours International de Harpe en Israel Vol 2: 3737
Concours International de Violoncelle Rostropovitch Vol 2: 2276
Concours International d'Execution Musicale - Geneve Vol 2: 6309

Concours International J. S. Bach Vol 2: 2656
Concours International Robert Schumann Vol 2: 2972
Concours Internationaux de la Ville de Paris Vol 2: 2276
Concours Musical International Reine Elisabeth de Belgique Vol 2: 949
Concrete Foundations Association Vol 1: 8342
Concrete Reinforcing Steel Institute Vol 1: 8345
Concrete Society Vol 2: 7346
Concrete Society of Southern Africa Vol 2: 5532
Concurs Internacional de Cant Francesc Vinas Vol 2: 6113
Concurso Internacional de Ejecucion Musical Dr. Luis Sigall Vol 2: 1261
Concurso Internacional de Piano de Santander Paloma O'Shea Vol 2: 6097
Concurso Internacional de Piano Premio Jaen Vol 2: 6068
Conductors Guild Vol 1: 8347
Confederate Air Force Vol 1: 8268
Confederate Memorial Literary Society Vol 1: 8350
Confederate Stamp Alliance Vol 1: 8354
Confederation Europeenne de Baseball Vol 2: 856
Confederation Internationale d'Analyse Thermique Vol 2: 5584
Confederation Internationale des Accordeonistes Vol 2: 735
Confederation Internationale des Negociants en Oeuvres d'Art Vol 2: 917
Confederation Internationale des Societes d'Auteurs et Compositeurs Vol 2: 2459
Confederation Mondiale pour la Therapie Physique Vol 2: 9242
Conference Canadienne des arts Vol 1: 7035
Conference Internationale de la Mutualite et des Assurances Sociales Vol 2: 6448
Conference of California Historical Societies Vol 1: 8363
Conference of European Churches Vol 2: 6311
Conference on British Studies Vol 1: 16410
Conference on Christianity and Literature Vol 1: 8372
Conference on College Composition and Communication Vol 1: 8374
Conference on College Composition and Communication Vol 1: 14828
Conference on English Education Vol 1: 14829, 14830
Conference on Latin American History Vol 1: 8379
Conferences and Professional Programs Community of Practice Vol 1: 20966
Conferencia de Iglesias del Caribe Vol 2: 824
Congregational Christian Historical Society Vol 1: 8386
Congres Mondiaux du Petrole Vol 2: 9256
Congress of Neurological Surgeons Vol 1: 8388
Congress of Racial Equality Vol 1: 8393
Congress of Women of the Kyrgyz Republic Vol 2: 4371
The Congressional Award Foundation Vol 1: 8395
Congressional Hispanic Caucus Institute Vol 1: 8397
Congressional Medal of Honor Society Vol 1: 8400
Congressional Quarterly Vol 1: 8403
Conjunto Universitario Candido Mendes of Brazil Vol 2: 2505
Connected International Meeting Professionals Association Vol 1: 8405
Connecticut Alliance for Music Vol 1: 8407
Connecticut Association of Assessing Officers Vol 1: 8409
Connecticut Audubon Center at Glastonbury Vol 1: 8411
Connecticut Bar Association Vol 1: 8413
Connecticut Forest and Park Association Vol 1: 8415
Connecticut League for Nursing Vol 1: 8417
Connecticut Poetry Society Vol 1: 14992
Connecticut River Watershed Council Vol 1: 8419
Conseil canadien de la securite Vol 1: 6812
Conseil Canadien des Ingenieurs Vol 1: 7050
Conseil Canadien des Organismes de la Motoneige Vol 1: 7059
Conseil Canadien des Techniciens et Technologues Vol 1: 7061
Conseil canadien du ski Vol 1: 7391
Conseil d'adoption du Canada Vol 1: 190
Conseil de Canola du Canada Vol 1: 7563
Conseil de la Vie Francaise en Amerique Vol 1: 8421
Conseil de l'Europe Vol 2: 2288
Conseil de recherches en sciences naturelles et en genie du Canada Vol 1: 16021
Conseil des arts de l'Ontario Vol 1: 16735
Conseil Europeen des Urbanistes Vol 2: 7467
Conseil General des Hauts de Seine Vol 2: 2528
Conseil International d Etudes Canadiennes Vol 1: 11509
Conseil International de la Langue Francaise Vol 2: 2463
Conseil International de l'Enseignement a Distance Vol 2: 5127
Conseil International d'Education des Adultes Vol 2: 9299
Conseil International des Associations Graphiques Vol 2: 919
Conseil International des Monuments et des Sites Vol 2: 2465
Conseil International des Sciences Sociales Vol 2: 2504
Conseil International du Batiment Vol 2: 4804
Conseil International du Droit de l'Environnement Vol 2: 2947
Conseil Mondiale pour la Danse de Salon et la Danse Sportive Vol 2: 9246
Consejo Cultural Mundial Vol 2: 4651
Consejo Interamericano de Seguridad Vol 1: 11116
Consejo Internacional de Buena Vecindad Vol 1: 11653
Consejo Mundial de Boxeo Vol 2: 4649
Consejo Nacional de Ciencia y Tecnologia Vol 2: 4476, 4561
Consejo Nacional de Investigaciones Cientificas y Tecnologicas - CONICIT Vol 2: 9320
Consejo Nacional de Poblacion Vol 2: 4478
Conservation and Research Foundation Vol 1: 6551
Conservation Foundation Vol 2: 7348
Conservation Southeast Inc. Vol 1: 8424
Conservatorio di Musica A. Boito di Parma Vol 2: 3870
consilting Engineer Magazine Vol 1: 5642
Consolidated Edison Vol 1: 17803
Consortium of Manufacturing Engineering Heads Vol 2: 7823
Construction Industry Computing Association Vol 2: 7350
Construction Innovation Forum Vol 1: 8426
Construction Specifications Canada Vol 1: 8428
Construction Specifications Institute Vol 1: 8432
Construction Writers Association Vol 1: 8445
Consulting Engineers Council of Metropolitan Washington Vol 1: 8452
Consulting Psychologists Press Vol 1: 3661, 3663
Consumer Credit Insurance Association Vol 1: 8454
Consumer Electronics Association Vol 1: 8457
Consumer Electronics Group Vol 1: 9211
Consumer Federation of America Vol 1: 8459
Consumer Specialty Products Association Vol 1: 8463
Consumers for World Trade Vol 1: 8466
Contact Lens Manufacturer Association Vol 1: 8469
Containerization and Intermodal Institute Vol 1: 8471
Contemporary A Cappella Society of America Vol 1: 8473
Contemporary Record Society Vol 1: 8475
Continental Basketball Association Vol 1: 8478
Continental Confederation of Adopted Indians Vol 1: 8486
Conway Data Vol 1: 8513, 8514
Cook Europe; William Vol 2: 6947
Cook Publishing; Thomas Vol 2: 7352
Cookson Group plc. Vol 2: 8773
Cooper Memorial Prize; Duff Vol 2: 7398
Cooper Ohioana Library Association; Martha Kinney Vol 1: 16656
Cooper Ornithological Society Vol 1: 8488
Cooper Union for the Advancement of Science and Art Vol 1: 8495
Cooperation Centre for Scientific Research Relative to Tobacco Vol 2: 2284
Cooperative Council for Oklahoma School Administration Vol 1: 8499
Cooperative Education and Internship Association Vol 1: 8501
The Cooperative Foundation Vol 1: 5648
Cooperative Research Centre for Polymers Vol 2: 319
Coopers Hill Society Vol 2: 7760
Cooperstown Art Association Vol 1: 8506
Coordinating Committee for International Voluntary Service Vol 2: 2286
Coos County Historical Society Museum Vol 1: 8508
Copley Society of Boston Vol 1: 22017
Copper Country Audubon Club Vol 1: 8510
CoreNet Global Inc. Vol 1: 8512
Corinthian Vintage Auto Racing Corporation Vol 1: 8515
Cork Film Festival Vol 2: 3624

Cork International Choral Festival Vol 2: 3626
Cork International Film Festival Vol 2: 3624
Cornell Laboratory of Ornithology Vol 1: 8517
Corning, Inc. Vol 1: 3995
Corning Inc. Vol 1: 16799
Corona Norco United Way Vol 1: 8519
The Corporation Associates Vol 1: 1732
Corporation for National and Community Service Vol 1: 17445
Corporation for Public Broadcasting Vol 1: 8522
Corporation of Professional Librarians of Quebec Vol 1: 8527
Corporation Professionnelle des Psychologues du Quebec Vol 1: 16848
Correctional Education Association - Region III Vol 1: 8530
Costa Rica Ministry of Culture, Youth and Sport Vol 2: 1350
Cotton Foundation; Dr. M. Aylwin Vol 2: 7354
Council for Agricultural Science and Technology Vol 1: 8532
Council for Art Education Vol 1: 8534
Council for Art Education, Inc. Vol 1: 13976
Council for Business and Arts in Canada Vol 1: 8536
Council for Business and the Arts in Canada Vol 1: 8542
Council for Education in World Citizenship Vol 2: 7357
Council for Exceptional Children Vol 1: 8545
Council for Health and Human Services Ministries, United Church of Christ Vol 1: 8556
Council for Learning Disabilities Vol 1: 8558
Council for the Advancement of Science Writing Vol 1: 8562
Council for the Order of Australia Vol 2: 179
Council for the Protection of Rural Wales Vol 2: 7235
Council for Wisconsin Writers Vol 1: 8564
Council of Administrators of Special Education Vol 1: 8566
Council of Authors and Journalists Vol 1: 9971
Council of Chief State School Officers Vol 1: 8569
Council of Commercial Plant Breeders Vol 1: 8668
Council of Education Vol 1: 18823
Council of Educational Facility Planners, International Vol 1: 8572
Council of Engineering Deans of the Historically Black Colleges and Universities Vol 1: 7585
Council of EU Chambers of Commerce in India Vol 2: 3356
Council of Europe Vol 2: 2288
Council of Fashion Designers of America Vol 1: 8574
Council of Graduate Schools Vol 1: 8577
Council of Graduate Schools in the United States Vol 1: 8577
Council of Jewish Women of New Zealand Vol 2: 4964
Council of Logistics Management Vol 1: 8579
Council of Natural Waters Vol 1: 11429
Council of Residential Specialists Vol 1: 8582
Council of Scientific Society Presidents Vol 1: 8585
Council on Approved Student Education Vol 1: 14878
Council on Arteriosclerosis Vol 1: 2417
Council on Arteriosclerosis, Thrombosis and Vascular Biology Vol 1: 2421
Council on Basic Cardiovascular Sciences Vol 1: 2415
Council on Basic Science Vol 1: 2412
Council on Cardiopulmonary, Perioperative and Critical Care Vol 1: 2420
Council on Cardiovascular Nursing Vol 1: 2410, 2413
Council on Cardiovascular Radiology and Intervention Vol 1: 2411
Council on Clinical Cardiology Vol 1: 2414
Council on Economic Priorities Vol 1: 8590
Council on Environmental Quality Vol 1: 9365
Council on Foreign Relations Vol 1: 8594
Council on Foundations Vol 1: 8596
Council on Governmental Ethics Laws Vol 1: 8602
Council on Hemispheric Affairs Vol 1: 8605
Council on International Nontheatrical Events Vol 1: 8607
Council on Peace Research in History Vol 1: 17126
Council on Technology Teacher Education Vol 1: 8611
Count Dracula Society Vol 1: 8613
Country Land & Business Association Vol 2: 7359
Country Landowners Association Vol 2: 7359
Country Markets Ltd. Vol 2: 3695
Country Music Association Vol 1: 8619
Country Music Showcase International Vol 1: 8622
Cour permanente d'arbitrage Vol 2: 4868
Courmayeur Noir in Festival Vol 2: 3890
Courtaulds plc. Vol 2: 8773
Cox Newspapers Vol 1: 19996
CPhA Vol 1: 7334
CPR Institute for Dispute Resolution Vol 1: 8625
CQ Press Vol 1: 5612
CQ, The Radio Amateur's Journal Vol 1: 8627
Cracow International Festival of Short Films Vol 2: 5300
Crain Communications, Inc. Vol 1: 6712
Cram Co.; George F. Vol 1: 14782
Crane Duplicating Service, Inc. Vol 1: 21571
Cranial Academy Vol 1: 8637
Craniofacial Biology Group Vol 1: 11215
Crate and Barrel Vol 2: 3744
Crawford Productions Vol 2: 290
Cray Research France Vol 2: 2325
Creative Glass Center of America Vol 1: 8642
Creative Standards International Vol 1: 11171
Creative Studies Alumni Foundation Vol 1: 8644
Creative Writing Program Vol 1: 8646
Crime Writers' Association Vol 2: 7361
Crime Writers of Canada Vol 1: 8648
Critikon Vol 1: 1300
Croatian Chess Federation Vol 2: 1369
Croatian Library Association Vol 2: 1371
Croatian Managers' and Entrepreneurs Association Vol 2: 1374
Croatian National Theatre Split Vol 2: 1376
Croatian Pharmaceutical Society Vol 2: 1379
Croatian Philatelic Society Vol 1: 8650
Crohn's and Colitis Foundation of Canada Vol 1: 8652
Cromwell Association Vol 2: 7371
Cronkite Endowment for Journalism and Telecommunication; Walter Vol 1: 8656
Crop Science Society of America Vol 1: 8658
Crossroad Publishing Co. Vol 1: 8671
Crouch Foundation; George E. Vol 1: 3470
Crown Princess Sonja International Music Competition Vol 2: 5179
The Crustacean Society Vol 1: 8673
Cryogenic Engineering Conference Vol 1: 8676
Cryogenic Society of America Vol 1: 8678
CT NARAL, the Connecticut Affiliate of NARAL Pro-Choice America Vol 1: 8681
CTAM - Cable and Telecommunications Association for Marketing Vol 1: 8683
Cuban Government Vol 2: 2595
Cultural Arts Council of Estes Park Vol 1: 8685
Cultural Association "Rodolfo Lipizer" Vol 2: 3892
Cultural Department of the Municipality of Spittal and the Singkreis Porcia Vol 2: 715
Cumann Corpoideachais na hEireann Vol 2: 3675
Cumhuriyet Matbaacilik ve Gazetecilik T.A.S. Vol 2: 6630
Cumhuriyet Newspaper Vol 2: 6630
Cumunn na Camanachd Vol 2: 7229
CURE Childhood Cancer Association Vol 1: 8687
Curtin University of Technology Vol 2: 408
Curtins Consulting Engineers Vol 2: 7762
Cushman Foundation for Foraminiferal Research Vol 1: 8689
Cutty Sark Maritime Trust Vol 2: 8112
Cymbidium Society of America Vol 1: 8691
Cymdeithas Ddrama Cymru Vol 2: 7392
Cyngor Celfyddydau Cymru Vol 2: 6763
Cyngor Llyfrau Cymru Vol 2: 9201
Cypress Creek Foundation for the Arts and Community Enrichment Vol 1: 8693
Cyprus Foote Mineral Company Vol 1: 15349
Cyprus Sport Organization Vol 2: 1400
Cyprus Tennis Federation Vol 2: 1403
Cyprus Veterans Association World War II Vol 2: 1405
Cystic Fibrosis Foundation Vol 1: 8695
Cystic Fibrosis Trust Vol 2: 7373
Czech Chemical Society Vol 2: 1416
Czech Radio, Prague Vol 2: 1419
Czech Radiological Society Vol 2: 1421
Czech Television Vol 2: 1423
Czechoslovak Society of Arts and Sciences Vol 1: 8699
Czechoslovak Television, Prague Vol 2: 1423
D. H. Lawrence Society of North America Vol 1: 8701
Dachshund Club of the Great Lakes Vol 1: 8704
Dade Behring Inc. Vol 1: 1008, 4134
Daedalian Foundation Vol 1: 8706
Dagens Nyheter Vol 2: 1518
Daily Racing For Vol 1: 20085
Daily Racing Form Vol 1: 20084
Dairy and Food Industries Supply Association Vol 1: 4225, 11361

The Dairy Barn: Southeastern Ohio Arts Center Vol 1: 8708
Dairy Shrine Vol 1: 14890
Daiwa Anglo-Japanese Foundation Vol 2: 7376
Dakshinayan Vol 2: 3358
Dale Medical Products Vol 1: 1172
Dallas Area Paralegal Association Vol 1: 8710
Dallas Metropolitan Young Men's Christian Association Vol 1: 8712
Dallas Museum of Art Vol 1: 8715
Dallas Songwriters Association Vol 1: 8719
Dalmatian Club of America Vol 1: 8721
Damfinos: The International Buster Keaton Society Vol 1: 8723
Damien-Dutton Society for Leprosy Aid Vol 1: 8725
Damon Runyon Cancer Research Foundation Vol 1: 8727
Dana Foundation; Charles A. Vol 1: 8729
Dance Division Vol 1: 14894
Dance Educators of America Vol 1: 8731
Dance Films Association Vol 1: 8733
Dance Magazine Vol 1: 8735
Dance Masters of America Vol 1: 8737
Dance Notation Bureau Vol 1: 8741
Dance Theater Workshop Vol 1: 8744
Dance/U.S.A. Vol 1: 8746
Danish Academy Vol 2: 1443
Danish Academy of Technical Sciences Vol 2: 1445
Danish Association for International Cooperation - Denmark Vol 2: 1447
Danish Association of the Specialist Press Vol 2: 1449
Danish Broadcasting Corp. Vol 2: 1451
Danish Dental Association Vol 2: 1456
Danish Jazz Association Vol 2: 1458
Danish Jazz Center Vol 2: 1458
Danish Jazz Federation Vol 2: 1458
Danish Library Association Vol 2: 1460
Danish Samoyed Club Vol 2: 1463
Danish Terrier Club Vol 2: 1465
Danish Women's Society Vol 2: 1467
Danish Writers Association Vol 2: 1469
Danly Machine Corporation Vol 1: 4019
Danmarks Biblioteksforening Vol 2: 1460
Danmarks Radio Vol 2: 1451, 1505
Dansk Fagpresse Vol 2: 1449
Dansk Forfatterforening Vol 2: 1469
Dansk Geologisk Forening Vol 2: 1493
Dansk Husflidsselskab Vol 2: 1476
Dansk Jazzforbund Vol 2: 1458
Dansk Journalistforbund Vol 2: 1478
Dansk Kvindesamfund Vol 2: 1467
Dansk Tandlaegeforening Vol 2: 1456
Dansk Terrier Klub Vol 2: 1465
Danske Akademi Vol 2: 1443
Danske Arkitekters Landsforbund/Akademisk Arkitektforening Vol 2: 1487
Dante Society of America Vol 1: 8748
Danube Prize Vol 2: 5969
Darien Chamber of Commerce Vol 1: 8751
Data Processing Management Association Vol 1: 5730
DateAble, Inc. Vol 1: 8753
Daughters of the American Revolution Vol 1: 15776
Daughters of Union Veterans of the Civil War, 1861-1865 Vol 1: 8755
David; Pierre - Weill Foundation Vol 2: 1740
Davis Publications Vol 1: 21951
Davison Area Chamber of Commerce Vol 1: 8757
Davison Chemical Division Vol 1: 16398
Davy Devotees - The Official Fan Club for Davy Jones Vol 1: 8759
The Dayton Playhouse Vol 1: 8761
Dayton Repertory Theatre Vol 1: 8761
Daytona International Speedway Vol 1: 8763
D.C. Commission on the Arts and Humanities Vol 1: 8770
Deadline Club Vol 1: 8772
Deaf and Hard of Hearing Entrepreneurs Council Vol 1: 8774
Deafness Research Foundation Vol 1: 8776
Death Penalty Information Center Vol 1: 8780
Decalogue Society of Lawyers Vol 1: 8782
DECHEMA Vol 2: 2748, 9005
Dechema - Society for Chemical Engineering and Biotechnology Vol 2: 2698
DECHEMA Subject Group Catalysis Vol 2: 2909
Decision Sciences Institute Vol 1: 8785
Decorative Lighting Association Vol 2: 8064
Dedicated Wooden Money Collectors Vol 1: 8787
Deep Foundations Institute Vol 1: 8791
Defense Credit Union Council Vol 1: 8794
Defense Logistics Agency - United States Air Force Vol 1: 8796
DeKalb Genetics Corporation Vol 1: 21030
Del Mar Fair Vol 1: 18242
Delacorte Press Vol 1: 8844
Delaware Association of School Administrators Vol 1: 8847
Delaware Contractors Association Vol 1: 8849
Delaware County Historical Society Vol 1: 8851
Delaware Restaurant Association Vol 1: 8853
Delhi Management Association Vol 2: 3362
Deloitte Touche Tohmatsu Vol 1: 8855
Delphi International Program of World Learning Vol 1: 8858
Delphinium Society Vol 2: 7378
Delray Beach Lions Club Vol 1: 8860
Delta Air Lines Vol 1: 13904
Delta Dental Plans Association Vol 1: 8862
Delta Education Vol 1: 5501
Delta Kappa Epsilon Fraternity Vol 1: 8864
Delta Nu Alpha Transportation Fraternity Vol 1: 8867
Delta Omega National Honorary Society, Pi Chapter Vol 1: 8869
Delta Omicron Vol 1: 8871
Delta Pi Epsilon Vol 1: 8873
Delta Society Vol 1: 4814
Delta Society Australia Vol 2: 321
DEMCO Vol 1: 10673
Demco Inc. Vol 1: 17714
Demello School Parent Teacher Organization Vol 1: 8876
Demeure Historique Vol 2: 2294
Democratic Socialists of America, Pittsburgh Vol 1: 8878
Den norske Forfatterforening Vol 2: 5148
Denmark - Ministry of Cultural Affairs Vol 2: 1471
Denmark Ministry of Cultural Affairs Vol 2: 1481
Denstu Inc. Vol 2: 4112
Dentists Association of Argentina Vol 2: 31
Dentsply International Vol 1: 11209
Denver Film Society Vol 1: 8880
Denver Public Library - Western History/ Genealogy Department Vol 1: 8886
Denver Rocky Mountain News Vol 1: 21008
Department of Education, Culture, and Sports Vol 2: 5292
Department of the Interior Vol 1: 17131
Department of Trade and Industry Vol 2: 7187
Department of Veterans Affairs Leadership/ Volunteer of the Year Award Vol 1: 4947
Department of World Arts and Culture - University of California, Los Angeles Vol 1: 8888
Derechos Iguales para la Mujer Argentina Vol 2: 34
Dermatology Foundation Vol 1: 8890
Des Moines Education Association Vol 1: 8893
Desert Fishes Council Vol 1: 8896
Design Council Vol 2: 7380
Design Office Consortium Vol 2: 7350
Designers Institute of New Zealand Vol 2: 4966
Det Kongelige Norske Videnskabers Selskabs Akademi Vol 2: 5183
Deutsche Akademie der Naturforscher Leopoldina Vol 2: 2701
Deutsche Akademie fur Sprache und Dichtung Vol 2: 2772
Deutsche Elektrochemische Gesellschaft Vol 2: 2792
Deutsche Forschungs fur Luft - und Raumfahrt E.V. Vol 2: 2781
Deutsche Gemmologische Gesellschaft e.V. Vol 2: 2831
Deutsche Geologische Gesellschaft Vol 2: 2833
Deutsche Gesellschaft fur Amerikastudien Vol 2: 2785
Deutsche Gesellschaft fur Dokumentation Vol 2: 2870
Deutsche Gesellschaft fur Endokrinologie Vol 2: 2849
Deutsche Gesellschaft fur Ernahrung Vol 2: 2893
Deutsche Gesellschaft fur Fettwissenschaft e.V. Vol 2: 2872
Deutsche Gesellschaft fur Kinderheilkunde und Jugendmedizin e.V Vol 2: 2898
Deutsche Gesellschaft fur Parasitologie Vol 2: 2709
Deutsche Gesellschaft fur Physikalische Medizin und Rehabilitation Vol 2: 2883
Deutsche Gesellschaft fur Plastische und Wiederherstellungschirurgie e.V. Vol 2: 2901
Deutsche Gesellschaft fur Sozialwissenschaftliche Sexualforschung e.V. Vol 2: 2887
Deutsche Gesellschaft fur Zerstorungsfreie Prufung e.V. Vol 2: 2880
Deutsche Glastechnische Gesellschaft Vol 2: 2889
Deutsche Landwirtschafts-Gesellschaft Vol 2: 2783
Deutsche Meteorologische Gesellschaft Vol 2: 2711
Deutsche Mineralogische Gesellschaft Vol 2: 2716
Deutsche Ornithologen-Gesellschaft Vol 2: 2854
Deutsche Physikalische Gesellschaft Vol 2: 2721

Deutsche Phytomedizinische Gesellschaft Vol 2: 2860
Deutscher Anwaltverein Vol 2: 2790
Deutscher Verband fur Fotografie DVF, Vol 2: 3122
Deutscher Volkshochschul-Verband Vol 2: 2779
Deutscher Zentralausschuss fur Chemie Vol 2: 2723
Deutsches Filmmuseum Vol 2: 2689
Deutsches Forum fur Figurentheater und Puppenspielkunst e.V. Vol 2: 2731
Developing Countries Farm Radio Network Vol 1: 8899
DeVilliers Foundation Vol 1: 12784
Dexter Chemical Corporation Vol 1: 1748
Dextra Laboratories Vol 2: 8746
Dialogue: A Journal of Mormon Thought Vol 1: 8901
Diamond Council of America Vol 1: 8903
Diamond Shamrock Corporation Vol 1: 4019
Diario Monitor Vol 2: 4480
Dibner Fund Vol 1: 18872
Dickinson College Vol 1: 8910
Die Misstofvereniging van Suid-Afrika Vol 2: 5556
Die Suid-Afrikaanse Vereniging van Musiekonderwysers Vol 2: 5761
Dierkundige Vereniging van Suidelike Afrika Vol 2: 5799
Dighton Historical Society Vol 1: 8914
Digital Equipment Corporation Europe Vol 2: 2325
Dillmans Creative Arts Foundation Vol 1: 8921
Direct Mail/Marketing Educational Foundation Vol 1: 8930
Direct Marketing Association Vol 2: 7384
Direct Marketing Association Vol 1: 8923
Direct Marketing Association of Detroit Vol 1: 8926
Direct Marketing Club of New York Vol 1: 8928
Direct Marketing Educational Foundation Vol 1: 8930
Direct Selling Association Vol 1: 8933
Direct Selling Association - United Kingdom Vol 2: 7386
Directorate for Cultural Relations with Iberoamerica Vol 1: 21059
Directors Guild of America Vol 1: 8938
Directors Guild of Canada Vol 1: 6033
Dirksen Congressional Center Vol 1: 8950
Disability Awareness Council of West Michigan Vol 1: 8952
Disabled American Veterans Vol 1: 8954
Disciples Peace Fellowship Vol 1: 8960
Discovering Skiing/Snowboarding Program Vol 1: 7395
Dista Products Co. Vol 1: 3629
Distribution Magazine Vol 1: 4622
Distribution Magazine Vol 1: 13762
District of Columbia Library Association Vol 1: 8962
District of Columbia Public Library Vol 1: 8964
Diversity World Council; Unity-and- Vol 1: 20920
Diving Equipment and Marketing Association Vol 1: 8966
Dixie Council of Authors and Journalists Vol 1: 9971
Doberman Pinscher Club of America Vol 1: 8968
Dr. Declan Millett Vol 2: 7100
Dr. H.P. Heineken Foundation Vol 2: 4887
Dr. James Naismith Basketball Foundation Vol 1: 8970
Doctors to the World Vol 1: 8972
Document Management Industries Association Vol 1: 8974
Documentary Film Festival - Amsterdam Vol 2: 4806
Dodge Foundation; Geraldine R. Vol 1: 9161
Dog Writers Association of America Vol 1: 8978
Dohne Merino Breed Society of South Africa Vol 2: 5536
Doll Artisan Guild Vol 1: 8980
Dominican University Vol 1: 8986
Dominion Council of Canada Vol 1: 7050
Dominion Salt Limited Vol 2: 4994
Donnelley and Sons Company; R. R. Vol 1: 1993
Donors Forum of Wisconsin Vol 1: 8993
Donovan Memorial Foundation; William J. Vol 1: 16614
Door and Hardware Institute Vol 1: 8995
Door County Environmental Council Vol 1: 9002
Dorper Sheep Breeders' Society of South Africa Vol 2: 5538
Dorpers Skaaptelersgenootskap van Suid-Afrika Vol 2: 5538
Dorset Natural History Vol 2: 7388
Dorset Natural History and Archaeological Society Vol 2: 7388
Doubleday Vol 1: 9005
Dow Chemical Company; The Vol 1: 1738
Dow Chemical Company Vol 1: 1769, 1770, 2764, 2792, 4015
Dow Chemical Co. Vol 1: 15683
Dow Chemical Company Foundation Vol 1: 1718, 1733, 2769
Dow Chemical U.S.A. Vol 1: 4019
Dow Corning Corporation Vol 1: 1765
Dow Jones Newspaper Fund Vol 1: 9007
Downeast Association of Physician Assistants Vol 1: 9009
Downtown Jaycees of Washington, D.C. Vol 1: 9013
Dozenal Society of America Vol 1: 9015
Dracula Society Vol 2: 7390
Drama Association of Wales Vol 2: 7392
Drama Desk Vol 1: 9017
The Drama League Vol 1: 9019
Drama Theatre Sica Alexandrescu Vol 2: 5805
Dramatists Guild of America Vol 1: 9023
Dreyfus Foundation, Inc; Camille and Henry Vol 1: 1729
Dreyfus Foundation, Inc.; Camille and Henry Vol 1: 1730
Driving School Association of the Americas Vol 1: 9025
Drug Enforcement Administration Vol 1: 6574
Drug Strategies Vol 1: 9028
Drustvo Slovenskih Pisateljev Vol 2: 5986
Dry Stone Walling Association of Great Britain Vol 2: 7396
Drysdales Western Wear Vol 1: 17048
du Pont de Nemours and Company; E. I. Vol 1: 1731, 1754, 2762, 2789, 13836
Du Pont KEVLAR Vol 1: 11312
Dubuque County Fine Arts Society Vol 1: 9030
Dubuque County-Key City Genealogical Society Vol 1: 9032
Dubuque Fine Arts Players Vol 1: 9034
Dubuque Fine Arts Society Vol 1: 9035
Ductile Iron Society Vol 1: 9036
Dudley Observatory Vol 1: 9038
Duff Cooper Prize Vol 2: 7398
Duke University Vol 1: 9041
Duke University - Center for Documentary Studies Vol 1: 9043
Duluth Art Institute Vol 1: 9046
Dumbarton Oaks Vol 1: 9048
Duncan Guthrie Memorial Fund Vol 2: 6666
Duncan Lawrie Limited Vol 2: 6766
Dungannon Foundation - Rea Award for the Short Story Vol 1: 9051
Duodecimal Society of America Vol 1: 9015
duPont de Nemours and Co.; E. I. Vol 1: 1722
duPont de Nemours and Company Inc.; E. I. Vol 1: 1744
duPont deNemours and Co.; E.I. Vol 1: 1747
Durban Camera Club Vol 2: 5540
Durban International Film Festival Vol 2: 5542
Dutch Cancer Society Vol 2: 4726
Dutch Film Festival Foundation Vol 2: 4861
Dutch International Vocal Competition - Hertogenbosch Vol 2: 4729
Dykes Medal Vol 1: 13240
Dystrophic Epidermolysis Bullosa Research Association of America Vol 1: 9053
Eagle Forum Vol 1: 9055
Eaglehawk Dahlia and Arts Festival Vol 2: 323
Early Music America Vol 1: 9057
Earth Society Foundation Vol 1: 9061
Earthwatch Institute Vol 1: 9063
East African Wild Life Society Vol 2: 4347
East & West Artists Vol 1: 9066
East Baton Rouge Parish Medical Society Vol 1: 9068
East Carolina University - Office of Research and Scholarship Vol 1: 9070
East Mount Airy Neighbors Vol 1: 9075
East Polk County Committee of 100 Vol 1: 9077
East Tennessee Environmental Business Association Vol 1: 9079
East Texas Historical Association Vol 1: 9081
East-West News Bureau Vol 1: 16494
Easter Seals Vol 1: 9083
Easter Seals of Connecticut Vol 1: 9092
Eastern Apicultural Society of North America Vol 1: 9094
Eastern Association of Mosquito Control Workers Vol 1: 3134
Eastern Association of Rowing Colleges Vol 1: 9100
Eastern Bird Banding Association Vol 1: 9102
Eastern Coast Breweriana Association Vol 1: 9104
Eastern College Athletic Conference Vol 1: 9107
Eastern College Athletic Conference Sports Information Directors Association Vol 1: 9110
Eastern Music Festival Vol 1: 9112
Eastern Packard Club Vol 1: 9116
Eastern Surfing Association Vol 1: 9118
Eastman Kodak Company Vol 1: 1726, 9161, 11541, 17290, 17638, 20715

Organization Index

Eastman Kodak Company - Consumer Imaging Vol 1: 9120
Eastman Kodak Company Aerial Systems Division Vol 1: 5216
Eastport Area Chamber of Commerce Vol 1: 9122
Eaton Literary Associates Vol 1: 9124
Eau Claire Regional Arts Council Vol 1: 9126
EBSCO Information Services Vol 1: 17715
EBSCO Subscription Services Vol 1: 2974, 5608
Eckhardt Gramatte National Music Competition Vol 1: 9128
Ecological Society of America Vol 1: 9130
Econometric Society Vol 1: 9140
Economic History Association Vol 1: 9142
ECRI Vol 1: 9149
Ecumenical Council of San Diego County Vol 1: 9151
Edgar County Genealogical Society Vol 1: 9154
Edgefield County Historical Society Vol 1: 9156
Edinburgh Festival Fringe Vol 2: 7400
Edinburgh International Film Festival Vol 2: 7406
Edison Awards Vol 2: 4731
Edison Electric Institute Vol 1: 4031
Edison Electric Institute Vol 1: 9158
Edison Fund; Charles Vol 1: 18872
Edison Media Arts Consortium Vol 1: 9160
Edison National Historic Site Vol 1: 9161
Edison Stichting Vol 2: 4731
Editor & Publisher Vol 1: 9162
Editorial Costa Rica Vol 2: 1357
Editorial *El Porvenir* Vol 2: 4484
Editorial Planeta Vol 2: 6018
Editorial Planeta SA Vol 2: 6012
Editors; American Society of Business Press Vol 1: 4269
Editors Association Vol 2: 5160
Editors' Association of Canada Vol 1: 9165
Edmond Hustinx Foundation Vol 2: 4734
Education Commission of the States Vol 1: 9167
Education Forum; Packaging Vol 1: 17024
Education; U.S. Department of Vol 1: 14207
Education Writers Association Vol 1: 9169
Educational Building Society Vol 2: 3695
Educational Communications Inc. Vol 1: 14812
Educational Exhibitors Association Vol 1: 9171
Educational Paperback Association Vol 1: 9174
Educational Publishers Council Vol 2: 9147
Educational Testing Service Vol 1: 9176
Educational Theatre Association Vol 1: 9179
Educational Trust Fund Vol 2: 7863
Educators for Social Responsibility, Grand Rapids Chapter Vol 1: 9186
Eesti Haridustootajate Liit Vol 2: 1566
Eesti Teaduste Akadeemia Vol 2: 1562
EG&G Princeton Applied Research Vol 1: 1734
Egypt Exploration Society Vol 2: 7408
Egyptian Ophthalmological Society Vol 2: 1556
Egyptian Red Crescent Society Vol 2: 1558
E.I. du Pont de Nemours and Company Vol 1: 2770
Eidgenossische Technische Hochschule Zurich Vol 2: 6516
EIFS Industry Members Association Vol 1: 9188
Eighteen-twenty Foundation Vol 2: 5571
Eire Philatelic Association Vol 1: 9190
Eisenhower Fellowships Vol 1: 9192
Eisteddfod Genedlaethol Frenhinol Cymr Vol 2: 8172
Ekotopfilm: International Festival of Professional Films, TV and Videoprogrammes Vol 2: 5964
El Nacional Vol 2: 4487
El Paso Association for the Performing Arts Vol 1: 9194
El Toro International Yacht Racing Association Vol 1: 9196
Elanco Vol 1: 7439
Elanco Animal Health Vol 1: 4261
Electric Car Racing Association Vol 2: 7154
Electric Power Society - Association of German Electrical Engineers Vol 2: 2733
Electric Road Vehicle Association; European Vol 2: 852
Electrical Apparatus Service Association Vol 1: 9198
Electrical Equipment Representatives Association Vol 1: 9200
Electrical Generating Systems Association Vol 1: 9202
Electricite de France Vol 2: 2532
Electricity Association Vol 2: 7410
Electricorp Production Vol 2: 4990
Electronic Associates, Inc. Vol 1: 4016
Electronic Document Systems Foundation Vol 1: 9204
Electronic Funds Transfer Association Vol 1: 9207
Electronic Industries Alliance Vol 1: 9209
Electronic Retailing Association Vol 1: 9217
Electronics Industries Federation Vol 2: 5544
Electronics Technicians Association, International Vol 1: 9219
Eli Lilly Vol 1: 7829
Eli Lilly & Co. Vol 1: 628
Eli Lilly and Company Vol 1: 4629, 9462
Elizabeth Futas Memorial Fund Vol 1: 2975
Elkader Development Corp. Vol 1: 9222
Elkins; Kimball Vol 1: 6083
Ellen La Forge Memorial Poetry Foundation Vol 1: 10178
Eller Family Association Vol 1: 9224
Elsevier/JAI Press Vol 1: 5607
Elsevier Science Ltd. Vol 2: 8773
Elsevier Science Publishers Vol 2: 7936, 7937
Elsevier Scientific Publishing Company Vol 1: 9708
Embassy of Spain in the United States - Cultural Office Vol 1: 9226
Embassy Players Vol 1: 9232
EmCare, Inc. Vol 1: 9237
Emergency Department Nurses Association Vol 1: 9243
Emergency Medicine Residents' Association Vol 1: 9234
Emergency Nurses Association Vol 1: 9243
Employment Management Association Vol 1: 9254
Empresa Brasileira de Pesquisa Agropecuaria Vol 2: 1158
Emprise Bank of Wichita Vol 1: 12500
EMSA Limited Partnership Vol 1: 9240
ENCAMS: Keep Britain Tidy Vol 2: 7412
Encyclopaedia Universalis Vol 2: 2296
Encylcopedia Britannica Vol 1: 3004
Endocrine Society Vol 1: 9257
Engelhard Vol 2: 8773
Engelhard Corporation Vol 1: 11822
Engineering College Magazines Associated Vol 1: 9266
Engineering Geology Division Vol 1: 9946
Engineering Industries Association - England Vol 2: 7414
Engineering Institute of Canada Vol 1: 7414, 7416, 9268
Engineering News-Record Vol 1: 9278, 19307
Engineering Research Council Vol 1: 4028
Engineers' Association of Chile Vol 2: 1255
Engineers' Council for Professional Development Vol 1: 58
England and Wales Cricket Board Vol 2: 7416
England Basketball Vol 2: 7418
English Academy of Southern Africa Vol 2: 5546
English Association Sydney Vol 2: 325
English Centre of International PEN Vol 2: 7424
English China Clays Vol 2: 7557
English Draughts Association Vol 2: 7427
English Folk Dance and Song Society Vol 2: 7430
English Heritage Vol 2: 6919
English; National Council of Teachers of Vol 1: 14834
English-Speaking Union of the United States Vol 1: 9276
ENR: Engineering News-Record - The McGraw-Hill Cos., Inc. Vol 1: 9278
Ente David di Donatello Vol 2: 3894
Entertainment and Leisure Software Publishers Association Vol 2: 7432
Entomological Foundation Vol 1: 9280
Entomological Society of America Vol 1: 9286
Entomological Society of America Vol 1: 19875
Entomological Society of Canada Vol 1: 9292
Environment Canada Vol 1: 7146
Environmental and Conservation Organization Vol 1: 9295
Environmental Business Council of New England Vol 1: 9297
Environmental Camps for Conservation Awareness Vol 2: 4674
Environmental Design Research Association Vol 1: 9299
Environmental Mutagen Society Vol 1: 9303
Environmental Systems Research Institute Vol 1: 5212
Environmental Tectonics Corporation Vol 1: 240
Environmental Transport Association Vol 2: 7434
Ephemera Society Vol 2: 7436
Epilepsy Foundation Vol 1: 9307
Episcopal Communicators Vol 1: 9309
Epitestudomanyi Egyesulet Vol 2: 3278
Epsilon Pi Tau Vol 1: 9312
Epsilon Sigma Phi Vol 1: 9315
Epson Vol 2: 6838
Equal Rights for Argentine Women Vol 2: 34
Equine Guelph Vol 1: 9322
Equine Research Centre Vol 1: 9322
Equity, the British Actors' Union Vol 2: 7438
Erasmus Prize Foundation Vol 2: 4736
Ergonomics Society - England Vol 2: 7440

The Eric Hosking Trust Vol 2: 6958
Erie Art Museum Vol 1: 9324
Erie County Historical Society Vol 1: 9326
Ernest C. Manning Awards Foundation Vol 1: 9328
Ernst & Young Vol 1: 9330
Errors, Freaks and Oddities Collector's Club Vol 1: 9332
Errors, Freaks, Oddities Collectors Association Vol 1: 9332
Escambia Amateur Astronomer's Association Vol 1: 9334
Escobar Foundation; Alejandro Angel Vol 2: 1309
ESOMAR: World Association of Opinion and Marketing Research Professionals Vol 2: 4738
ESPN Inc. Vol 1: 9336
Espoir Sans Frontieres Vol 2: 5929
Essex Community Heritage Organization Vol 1: 9338
Esso Petroleum Company Ltd. Vol 2: 8773
Estate of Ellis Peters Vol 2: 7369
Estee Corporation Vol 1: 1187
Estonian Academy of Sciences Vol 2: 1562
Estonian Education Personnel Union Vol 2: 1566
Estonian Society for Nature Conservation Vol 2: 1568
Eta Kappa Nu Vol 1: 9341
Eta Verde Vol 2: 3896
Ethical Culture Fieldston School Vol 1: 9347
Ethicon Vol 1: 19483
Eugene V. Debs Foundation Vol 1: 9349
Eurail Group Vol 2: 4741
Eureka Vol 2: 846
Eureka Secretariat Vol 2: 846
Euroavia - European Association of Aerospace Students Vol 2: 5302
Europa Nostra Pan European Federation for Heritage Vol 2: 4743
Europa Nostra Pan European Federation for Heritage Vol 2: 4744
Europaische Gesellschaft fur Herbologie Vol 2: 4770
Europaische Kernenergie-Gesellschaft Vol 2: 868
Europaische Union der Musikwettbewerbe fur die Jugend Vol 2: 2759
Europaische Union Judischer Studenten Vol 2: 880
Europaischer Verband der Veranstaltungs-Centren Vol 2: 2742
European Academy of Facial Plastic Surgery Vol 2: 3898
European Aerosol Federation Vol 2: 848
European and Mediterranean Plant Protection Organization Vol 2: 2298
European Aquaculture Society Vol 2: 850
European Association for Animal Production Vol 2: 3900
European Association for Battery, Hybrid and Fuel Cell Electric Vehicles Vol 2: 852
European Association for Cancer Research Vol 2: 7450
European Association for Computer Assisted Language Learning Vol 2: 3629
European Association for Distance Learning Vol 2: 4749
European Association for Lexicography Vol 2: 7459
European Association for Signal Processing Vol 2: 5397
European Association for Signal, Speech and Image Processing Vol 2: 5397
European Association for the Promotion of Poetry Vol 2: 854
European Association for the Study of Diabetes Vol 2: 2736
European Association for Theoretical Computer Science Vol 1: 5316
European Association of Event Centers Vol 2: 2742
European Association of Geoscientists and Engineers Vol 2: 4751
European Association of Organic Geochemists Vol 2: 2300
European Association of Programmes in Health Services Studies Vol 2: 3631
European Association of Radiology Vol 2: 2302
European Athletic Association Vol 2: 2744
European Baseball Confederation Vol 2: 856
European Bridge League Vol 2: 3904
European Broadcasting Union Vol 2: 6314
European Cancer Conference Vol 2: 4032
European Chemical Industry Council Vol 2: 860
European Coordinating Committee for Artificial Intelligence Vol 2: 717
European Council for the Village and Small Town Vol 2: 7461
European Council of International Schools Vol 2: 7463
European Council of Town Planners Vol 2: 7467
European Disposables and Nonwovens Association Vol 2: 862
European Electric Road Vehicle Association Vol 2: 852
European Environmental Mutagen Society Vol 2: 2304
European Express Association Vol 2: 864
European Federation of Clean Air and Environmental Protection Associations Vol 2: 4754
European Federation of Corrosion Vol 2: 2746
European Federation of Food Science and Technology Vol 2: 4756
European Federation of National Engineering Associations Vol 2: 866
European Federation of Societies for Ultrasound in Medicine and Biology Vol 2: 7469
European Federation of the Contact Lens Industry Vol 2: 4758
European General Galvanizers Association Vol 2: 7471
European Geosciences Union Vol 2: 2307
European Health Management Association Vol 2: 3631
European Herpetological Society Vol 2: 3906
European Hotel Managers Association Vol 2: 3908
European Institute of Public Administration Vol 2: 4762
European Mariculture Society Vol 2: 850
European Molecular Biology Organization Vol 2: 2750
European Money and Finance Forum Vol 2: 719
European Network of Policewomen Vol 2: 4764
European Nuclear Society Vol 2: 868
European Optical Society Vol 2: 2752
European Organization for Caries Research Vol 2: 4767
European Organization for Testing New Flower Seeds Vol 2: 4772
European Orthodontic Society Vol 2: 7475
European Packaging Federation Vol 2: 2320
European Parliament - London Information Office Vol 2: 7483
European Perforators Association Vol 2: 4401
European Physical Society Vol 2: 2322
European Piano Teachers Association Vol 2: 7485
European Process Safety Centre Vol 2: 7487
European Rhinologic Society Vol 2: 1582
European Society for Ballistocardiography and Cardiovascular Dynamics Vol 2: 5974
European Society for Cardiovascular Surgery Vol 2: 3911
European Society for Cognitive Psychology Vol 2: 6025
European Society for Engineering Education Vol 2: 870
European Society for Microcirculation Vol 2: 2754
European Society for Neurochemistry Vol 2: 3240
European Society for Noninvasive Cardiovascular Dynamics Vol 2: 5974
European Society for Therapeutic Radiology and Oncology Vol 2: 872
European Society of Anaesthesiology Vol 2: 874
European Society of Biomechanics Vol 2: 3913
European Society of Comparative Physiology and Biochemistry Vol 2: 876
European Society of Culture Vol 2: 3918
European Society of Intensive Care Medicine Vol 2: 878
European Society of Paediatric Radiology Vol 2: 7489
European Sports Press Union Vol 2: 6146
European Surfing Federation Vol 2: 7491
European Table Tennis Union Vol 2: 4403
European Thyroid Association Vol 2: 1485
European Travel Commission Vol 1: 9351
European Union Vol 2: 3625
European Union of Geosciences Vol 2: 2327
European Union of Jewish Students Vol 2: 880
European Union of Music Competition for Youth Vol 2: 2759
European Water Pollution Control Association Vol 2: 2761
European Weed Research Society Vol 2: 4770
European Wound Management Association Vol 2: 7493
Eutectic Castolin Corporation Vol 1: 4899
Evaluation Network Vol 1: 2203
Evaluation Research Society Vol 1: 2203
Evangelical Christian Publishers Association Vol 1: 9353
Events Analysis, Inc. Vol 1: 19892
Ever-Reddy Packing Ltd. Vol 1: 6846
Everest and Jennings Vol 1: 508
Everett Salty Sea Days Association Vol 1: 9356
Evergreen Area Chamber of Commerce Vol 1: 9358
Evidence Photographers International Council Vol 1: 9360

Executive Office of the President Vol 1: 9362
Executive Search Roundtable Vol 1: 9367
Exhibit Designers and Producers Association Vol 1: 9369
Exhibition Association of Southern Africa Vol 2: 5551
Exotic Dancers League of America Vol 1: 9372
Experimental Psychology Society Vol 2: 7495
The Explorers Club Vol 1: 9374
Exxon Chemical Company Vol 1: 1760, 1773, 1790
Exxon Co. Vol 1: 11754
Exxon Company, U.S.A. Vol 1: 11755
Exxon Research and Engineering Company Vol 1: 1760, 1773
ExxonMobil Chemical Company Vol 1: 2765
ExxonMobil Corporation - Downstream Operations Vol 1: 9377
ExxonMobil Foundation Vol 1: 1752
ExxonMobil Research and Engineering Company Vol 1: 2782
ExxonMobil Research & Engineering Company Vol 1: 2795
Eye Bank Association of America Vol 1: 9380
Eye-Bank for Sight Restoration Vol 1: 9384
Facets Multi-Media, Inc. Vol 1: 7888
Fachverband Messe-und Ausstellungsbau Vol 2: 2763
Faculty of Astrological Studies Vol 2: 7498
Faculty of Building Vol 2: 7500
Faculty of Journalism and Mass Communications - Sofia University St. Kliment Ohridski Vol 2: 1215
Fair and Exhibition Association Vol 2: 2763
Fairbanks Education Association Vol 1: 9386
Fairbanks Symphony Association Vol 1: 9389
Fairfield County Medical Association Vol 1: 9391
Fairfield Historical Society Vol 1: 9393
Fairleigh Dickinson University Press Vol 1: 16544
Families with Children from China - New England Vol 1: 9395
Family, Career and Community Leaders of America Vol 1: 9397
Family, Career, and Community Leaders of America, Arkansas Chapter Vol 1: 9400
Family Education Trust Vol 2: 7502
Family Federation of Finland Vol 2: 1584
Family Firm Institute Vol 1: 9402
Family Mart Co., Ltd. Vol 2: 4309
Family Mediation Canada Vol 1: 9409
Family Planning Association of Sri Lanka Vol 2: 6115
Family Planning Association of WA Vol 2: 346
Family Research Council Vol 1: 9411
Family Service Association of America Vol 1: 446
Famous Players Vol 1: 6033
Fan Circle International Vol 2: 7504
Fargo-Moorhead Community Theatre Vol 1: 9413
Farm and Industrial Equipment Institute Vol 1: 14152
FARM (Farm Animal Reform Movement) Vol 1: 9415
Farm Machinery Dealer's Association of Western Australia Vol 2: 327
Farmaceutsko drustvo Hrvatske Vol 2: 1379
Farrel Corporation Vol 1: 1737
Farrer Memorial Trust Vol 2: 330
Fashion Group Foundation of Houston Vol 1: 9418
Father's Day/Mother's Day Council - National Father's Day Committee Vol 1: 9420
Faulding and Company, Ltd.; F. H. Vol 2: 523
Faulkner County Literacy Council Vol 1: 9422
Fauna and Flora International Vol 2: 7506
Fauna and Flora Preservation Society Vol 2: 7506
Federacion Internacional de Asociaciones de Profesores de Ciencias Vol 2: 7912
Federacion Latinoamericana de Bancos Vol 2: 1318
Federacion Nacional de Cafeteros de Colombia Vol 2: 1327
Federacion Nacional de Cultivadores de Cereales y de Leguminosas Vol 2: 1311
Federal Aviation Administration Vol 1: 9424, 17582, 17584
Federal Bar Association Vol 1: 9433
Federal Bar Council Vol 1: 9440
Federal Chamber of Pharmacists Vol 2: 2684
Federal City Club Vol 1: 9444
Federal Executive Institute Alumni Association Vol 1: 9448
Federal Globe: Gay, Lesbian, Bisexual and Transgender Federal Employees Vol 1: 9450
Federal Ministry of Education and Arts Vol 2: 716
Federally Employed Women Vol 1: 9452
Federally Employed Women - Legal & Education Fund Vol 1: 9454
Federasie van Afrikaanse Kultuurvereniginge Vol 2: 5554
Federation Aeronautique Internationale Vol 2: 6320
Federation Canadienne de la Faune Vol 1: 7537
Federation Canadienne de la Nature Vol 1: 16026
Federation canadienne des societes de biologie Vol 1: 7088
Federation Culinaire Canadienne Vol 1: 7065
Federation des Jeux du Commonwealth Vol 2: 7335
Federation des Societes d'Histoire du Quebec Vol 1: 17786
Federation Europeenne d'Associations Nationales d'Ingenieurs Vol 2: 866
Federation Europeenne de la Corrosion Vol 2: 2746
Federation Europeenne de l'Emballage Vol 2: 2320
Federation Europeenne de Zootechnie Vol 2: 3900
Federation Europeenne des Aerosols Vol 2: 848
Federation International des Societes de Recherche Operationnelle Vol 1: 11598
Federation Internationale d'Astronautique Vol 2: 2451
Federation internationale de associations vexillologiques Vol 1: 11609
Federation Internationale de Basketball Vol 2: 6385
Federation Internationale de Canoe Vol 2: 6055
Federation Internationale de Football Association Vol 2: 6355
Federation Internationale de Handball Vol 2: 6409
Federation Internationale de Judo Vol 2: 5497
Federation Internationale de l'Approvisionnement et de l'Achat Vol 2: 742
Federation Internationale de l'Art Photographique Vol 2: 3122, 4405
Federation Internationale de l'art Photographique Vol 2: 8919
Federation Internationale de l'Automobile Vol 2: 2453
Federation Internationale de Luge de Course Vol 2: 2968
Federation Internationale de Medecine du Sport Vol 2: 1409
Federation Internationale de Motocyclisme Vol 2: 6418
Federation Internationale de Natation Amateur Vol 2: 6362
Federation Internationale de Navigabilite Aerospatiale Vol 2: 7927
Federation Internationale de Neurophysiologie Clinique Vol 2: 7935
Federation Internationale de Ski Vol 2: 6446
Federation Internationale de Tennis Vol 2: 7993
Federation Internationale de Tennis de Table Vol 2: 6466
Federation Internationale des Architectes d'Inter Vol 2: 5589
Federation Internationale des Architectes Paysagistes Vol 2: 2467
Federation Internationale des Associations d'Apiculture Vol 2: 3967
Federation Internationale des Associations de Controleurs du Trafic Aerien Vol 1: 11577
Federation Internationale des Associations de Patrons de Navires Vol 2: 7945
Federation Internationale des Associations de Pilotes de Ligne Vol 2: 7923
Federation Internationale des Associations Medicales Catholiques Vol 2: 9305, 9318
Federation Internationale des Auberges de Jeunesse Vol 2: 8018
Federation Internationale des Bureaux de Justification de la Diffusion Vol 2: 5587
Federation Internationale des Chasseurs de Son Vol 2: 6401
Federation Internationale des Culturistes Vol 1: 11590
Federation Internationale des Echecs Vol 2: 3191
Federation Internationale des Femmes Diplomees des Universites Vol 2: 6405
Federation Internationale des Ingenieurs Conseils Vol 2: 6399
Federation Internationale des Journalistes Vol 2: 924
Federation Internationale des Organisations de Festivals; F.I.D.O.F. - Vol 1: 11592
Federation Internationale des Personnes Handicapees Physiques Vol 2: 2960
Federation Internationale des Professions Immobilieres Vol 2: 2502
Federation Internationale des Quilleurs Vol 2: 5260
Federation Internationale des Societes Oto-Rhino-Laryngologiques Vol 2: 4819
Federation Internationale des Traducteurs Vol 1: 11605

Federation Internationale du Diabete Vol 2: 922
Federation Internationale Pharmaceutique Vol 2: 4827
Federation Internationale pour la Recherche Theatrale Vol 2: 7921
Federation Internationale pour le Traitement de l'Information Vol 2: 737
Federation Internationale pour l'Habitation, l'Urbanisme et l'Amenagement des Territoires Vol 2: 4808
Federation Luxembourgeoise de Tennis Vol 2: 4410
Federation Mondiale de l'Hemophilie Vol 1: 21908
Federation Mondiale des Anciens Combattants Vol 2: 2634
Federation Mondiale des Organisations d'Ingenieurs Vol 2: 2624
Federation nationale des Entrepreneurs routiers Vol 2: 2633
Federation Naturiste Internationale Vol 2: 928
Federation of Afrikaans Cultural Societies Vol 2: 5554
Federation of Alberta Naturalists Vol 1: 9456
Federation of American Hospitals Vol 1: 9458
Federation of American Hospitals Vol 1: 9458
Federation of American Societies for Experimental Biology Vol 1: 9461
Federation of Analytical Chemistry and Spectroscopy Societies Vol 1: 9463
Federation of BC Writers Vol 1: 9466
Federation of British Artists Vol 2: 7508
Federation of British Tape Recordists Vol 2: 7203
Federation of Canadian Music Festivals Vol 1: 15407, 18305
Federation of Children's Book Groups Vol 2: 7510
Federation of Danish Architects Vol 2: 1487
Federation of Defense and Corporate Counsel Vol 1: 9468
Federation of European Cancer Societies Vol 2: 4032
Federation of European Direct Marketing Vol 2: 882
Federation of European Societies of Plant Physiology Vol 2: 7512
Federation of Fly Fishers Vol 1: 9470
Federation of Gay Games Vol 1: 9491
Federation of Genealogical Societies Vol 1: 9493
Federation of Historical Bottle Clubs Vol 1: 9503
Federation of Historical Bottle Collectors Vol 1: 9503
Federation of Hong Kong Industries Vol 2: 5218
Federation of Insurance and Corporate Counsel Vol 1: 9468
Federation of Insurance Counsel Vol 1: 9468
Federation of International Bandy Vol 2: 6148
Federation of Jewish Men's Clubs Vol 1: 9508
Federation of Materials Societies Vol 1: 9513
Federation of Museums, Heritage & Historical Societies of Nova Scotia Vol 1: 9515
Federation of Nova Scotia Historical and Heritage Societies Vol 1: 9515
Federation of Nova Scotian Heritage Vol 1: 9515
Federation of Ontario Naturalists Vol 1: 16758
Federation of Plastering and Drywall Contractors Vol 2: 7514
Federation of Reconstructionist Congregations and Havurot Vol 1: 12371
Federation of Women Contractors Vol 1: 9520
Federation Petanque U.S.A. Vol 1: 9522
Federation Polonaise de Football Vol 2: 5345
Federation pour le planning des naissances du Canada Vol 1: 17371
Federazione Italiana Badminton Vol 2: 3920
Federazione Ordini Farmacisti Italiani Vol 2: 3922
Felag bokasafns-og upplysingafraeda Vol 2: 3322
Feline Control Council of Western Australia Vol 2: 332
Fell Pony Society Vol 2: 7516
Fellows of the American Bar Foundation Vol 1: 9524
Fellowship of Australian Writers NSW Vol 2: 334
Fellowship of Engineering Vol 2: 8365
Fellowship of Reconciliation - USA Vol 1: 9527
The Feminist Press at the City University of New York Vol 1: 9530
Feministas en Marcha Vol 1: 9532
Feminists on the March Vol 1: 9532
Ferenc Liszt Society, Budapest Vol 2: 3242
Ferrari North America Vol 1: 11756
Ferreira de Castro High School Vol 2: 5446
Ferret Fanciers Club Vol 1: 9534
Ferst Foundation of Atlanta Vol 1: 18511
Fertiliser Association of India Vol 2: 3364
Fertiliser Association of Ireland Vol 2: 3633
Fertilizer Society of South Africa Vol 2: 5556
Festa Musicale Vol 2: 1425
Festival Cinema d'Ales Vol 2: 2517
Festival de Cine de Alcala de Henares Vol 2: 6027
Festival de Television de Monte Carlo Vol 2: 4667
Festival dei Popoli - International Review of Social Documentary Film Vol 2: 3924
Festival dei Popoli - Rassegna Internazionale del Film di Documentazione Sociale Vol 2: 3924
Festival der Nationen Vol 2: 721
Festival des Films du Monde - Montreal Vol 1: 13606
Festival du Court Metrage en Plein Air Vol 2: 2332
Festival du Film Court de Villeurbanne Vol 2: 2334
Festival Internacional de Cine de Bilbao Documental y Cortometraje Vol 2: 6060
Festival Internacional de Cine Iberoamericano de Huelva Vol 2: 6043
Festival Internacional de Cine para la Juventud de Gijon Vol 2: 6036
Festival Internacional de Video de Canarias Vol 2: 6008
Festival International de Films de Femmes de Creteil et du Val de Marne Vol 2: 2515
Festival International de Films et Video Amateurs a Hiroshima Vol 2: 4119
Festival International de Jazz de Montreal Vol 1: 9536
Festival International de Musique de Besancon et de Franche-Comte Vol 2: 2336
Festival International du Cinema d'Animation - Annecy Vol 2: 2439
Festival International du Film Vol 2: 2258
Festival International du Film Alpin et de l'Environment de Montagne, Les Diablerets, Suisse Vol 2: 6407
Festival International du Film d'Amiens Vol 2: 2225
Festival International du Film d'Architecture d'Urbanisme et d'Environnement Urbain de Bordeaux Vol 2: 2227
Festival International du Film de Berlin Vol 2: 2669
Festival International du Film de Vol Libre Vol 2: 2339
Festival International du Film Maritime et d'Exploration Vol 2: 2469
Festival International du Film sur l'Art Montreal Vol 1: 11612
Festival International du Nouveau Cinema et de la Video Montreal Vol 1: 13597
Festival Internationale del Cinema di Salerno Vol 2: 4045
Festival Internazionale Cinema Giovani Vol 2: 3882
Festival Internazionale del Film Locarno Vol 2: 6481
Festival Internazionale del Film Turistico Vol 2: 3979
Festival Mondial de l'Image Sous-Marine Vol 2: 2341
Festival of Kerry, Ltd. Vol 2: 3685, 3686
Festival of Nations, Ebensee Vol 2: 721
Festival of Underwater Images Vol 2: 2341
Festival Panafricain du Cinema et de la Television de Ouagadougou Vol 2: 1241
Festival van Mechelen Vol 2: 943
Festspillene I Bergen Vol 2: 5121
Ffederasiwn Cerddoriaeth Amatur Cymru Vol 1: 11401
FIBA Oceana Vol 2: 341
Fiber Society Vol 1: 9538
Fideicomiso Vol 2: 4620
FIDIA Research Foundation Vol 1: 13844
Fidia S.p.a. Vol 2: 3241
F.I.D.O.F. - Federation Internationale des Organisations de Festivals Vol 1: 11592
Field Naturalists Club of Victoria Vol 2: 343
Filharmonia Narodowa w Warszawie Vol 2: 5386
Film Advisory Board Vol 1: 9540
Film and Television Institute of Western Australia Vol 2: 345
Film Festival of Huesca Vol 2: 6029
Film Finishing Fund Vol 1: 21722
Film Music Society Vol 1: 9542
Film Safety Awards Committee Vol 1: 15655
Film Victoria Vol 2: 460
Filmfest Munchen Vol 2: 2766
Filmfestival Alpinale Vol 2: 723
Filmfestival of Nations Vol 2: 725
FilmLinc: Film Society of Lincoln Center Vol 1: 9544
Filson Historical Society Vol 1: 9546
Filtration Society Vol 2: 7518
Financial Analysts Federation Vol 1: 5390
Financial Management Association International Vol 1: 9548
Financial Planning Association Vol 1: 9550
Fine Arts Club of Arkansas Vol 1: 5069

Organization Index

Fine Arts Work Center in Provincetown Vol 1: 9552
Fingerprint Society Vol 2: 7522
Finland Ministry of Defense Vol 2: 1587
Finnish Academies of Technology Vol 2: 1591
Finnish Art Society Vol 2: 1594
Finnish Broadcasting Company Vol 2: 1596
Finnish Chemical Society Vol 2: 1576
Finnish Cultural Foundation Vol 2: 1598
Finnish Dramatists' Union Vol 2: 1601
Finnish Foundation for Cancer Research Vol 2: 1579
Finnish Historical Society Vol 2: 1603
Finnish Library Association Vol 2: 1605
Finnish Museums Association Vol 2: 1607
Finnish Ski Club Vol 1: 20804
Finnish Society of Sciences and Letters Vol 2: 1612
Finska Vetenskaps-Societeten-Societas Scientiarum Fennica Vol 2: 1612
Fire & Aviation Management - United States Forest Service Vol 1: 9554
Fire Protection Association - England Vol 2: 7524
Fireball International Vol 2: 7526
First Marine Aviation Force Veterans' Association Vol 1: 13068
First Special Service Force Association Vol 1: 9561
Fischetti Editorial Cartoon Competition; John Vol 1: 9563
Fischoff National Chamber Music Association Vol 1: 9565
Fisher Scientific Company, Inc. Vol 1: 1712
Fisheries and Oceans Canada Vol 1: 9567
Fiterman Foundation; Miles and Shirley Vol 1: 9709, 9711
Fitness Industry Association Vol 2: 7528
Flag Plaza Foundation Vol 1: 15048
Flanders International Film Festival - Ghent Vol 2: 885
Fleischner Society Vol 1: 9569
Fleuroselect Vol 2: 4772
Flexible Packaging Association Vol 1: 9571
Flight Safety Foundation Vol 1: 9575
Flight Safety Foundation Vol 1: 17587
Flint Symphony Orchestra Vol 1: 18203
Florida Alliance of Information and Referral Services Vol 1: 9584
Florida Arts Council Vol 1: 9586
Florida Association of Colleges and Universities Vol 1: 9590
Florida Association of Nonprofit Organizations Vol 1: 9592
Florida Automotive Industry Association Vol 1: 9594
Florida Craftsmen Vol 1: 9596
Florida Education Fund Vol 1: 9598
Florida Federation of Music Clubs Vol 1: 9600, 9601
Florida Film Festival Vol 1: 9602
Florida Freedom of Information Clearinghouse Vol 1: 6613
Florida Institute of Oceanography Vol 1: 9605
Florida Irrigation Society Vol 1: 9607
Florida Nurserymen and Growers Association Vol 1: 9609
Florida Park Service Vol 1: 9601
Florida Propane Gas Association Vol 1: 9614
Florida Sea Grant College Program Vol 1: 9616
Florida Society of Registered Nurses Retired Vol 1: 9619
Florida Space Coast Writers Conference Vol 1: 19534
Florida Space Grant Consortium Vol 1: 9621
Florida Sports Foundation Vol 1: 9623
Florida State Archives Vol 1: 9625
Florida State Golf Association Vol 1: 9627
Florida State Grange Vol 1: 9630
Florida State Poets Association Vol 1: 14993
Florida State University - Center for Performance Technology Vol 1: 9632
Florida TaxWatch Vol 1: 9634
Florida Trail Association Vol 1: 9636
Florilege Vocal de Tours Vol 2: 2343
Fluckiger Foundation Vol 2: 2683
The Fluke Corporation Vol 1: 3994
Fluor Daniel, Inc. Vol 1: 2757
Flygtekniska Foreningen Vol 2: 6294
Flying Fifteen International Vol 2: 7531
Flying Physicians Association Vol 1: 9639
Focolare Movement - Italy Vol 2: 3926
FOCUS Greater Syracuse Vol 1: 9643
Foerderkreis Deutscher Schriftsteller in Baden-Wuerttemberg Vol 2: 2768
Folger Shakespeare Library Vol 1: 9645
Folio Educational Trust - % Hanson Publishing Group Vol 1: 18524
Folklore Society Vol 2: 7533
Follett Library Resources Vol 1: 1418
Follett Software Company Vol 1: 1416
Fondation Agathon De Potter Vol 2: 1042
Fondation Bonderjnstichting Vol 2: 939
Fondation Broquette-Gonin Vol 2: 2097, 2100, 2129
Fondation Cousin de Mandet Vol 2: 2201
Fondation de la Maison de la Chimie Vol 2: 2346
Fondation des Infirmieres et Infirmiers du Canada Vol 1: 7310
Fondation des Prix Michener Vol 1: 13328
Fondation du Basket-Ball Dr. James Naismith Vol 1: 8970
Fondation du Festival des Films du Monde Vol 1: 13608
Fondation Emile-Nelligan Vol 1: 20303
Fondation E.W.R. Steacie Vol 1: 19776
Fondation Feneon Vol 2: 2348
Fondation France-Libertes Vol 2: 2351
Fondation Francqui Vol 2: 892
Fondation International Vol 2: 2095
Fondation le Metais-Larlviere Fils Vol 2: 2096
Fondation Napoleon Vol 2: 2353
Fondation Paul Guggenheim Vol 2: 6493
Fondation pour la Recherche Medicale Vol 2: 2363
Fondation Prince Pierre de Monaco Vol 2: 4657
Fondation Roucoules Vol 2: 2098
Fondation Universitaire Vol 2: 1114
Fondazione Arturo Toscanini Vol 2: 3928
Fondazione Cassa di Risparmio di Torino Vol 2: 3881
Fondazione Francesco Somaini Vol 2: 3931
Fondazione Franco Michele Napolitano Vol 2: 3933
Fondazione I Teatri Vol 2: 4053
Fondazione Il Campiello Vol 2: 3878
Fondazione Internazionale Balzan Vol 2: 3960
Fondazione Medikinale International Parma Vol 2: 3935
Fondazione Pezcoller Vol 2: 4031
Fondazione Premio Napoli Vol 2: 3937
Fondazione Prof. Domenico Ganassini Vol 2: 3940
Fondazione Russolo-Pratella Vol 2: 3942
Fondazione Valentino Bucchi Vol 2: 3944
Fonds National de la Recherche Scientifique Vol 2: 888
Food and Agriculture Organization of the United Nations Vol 2: 3946
Food and Commercial Workers AFL-CIO, LU 513 T Vol 1: 9648
Food and Drug Law Institute Vol 1: 9650
Food Distribution Research Society Vol 1: 9652
Food for the Poor Vol 1: 9655
Food Industry Association Executives Vol 1: 9657
Food Marketing Institute Vol 1: 9659
Foodservice and Packaging Institute Vol 1: 9664
Foodservice Consultants Society International Vol 1: 9666
Football Association of Moldova Vol 2: 4655
Football Writers Association of America Vol 1: 9670
Foothills Art Center Vol 1: 9677
An Foras um Cheannacht agus Bainistocht Abhar Vol 2: 3661
FORATOM: Association of European Atomic Forums Vol 2: 890
Forbes Vol 1: 6702, 6704
Forbes Magazine Vol 1: 16981
Ford Foundation and Harvard University - Innovations Program Vol 1: 10115
Ford Library; Gerald R. Vol 1: 9680
Ford Motor Co, Vol 2: 578
Ford Motor Company Vol 1: 3471, 7586
Ford Motor Co. Vol 1: 14804
Ford Motor Company Vol 1: 16981
Fordham University - School of Law Vol 1: 9683
Foreign Affairs Canada Vol 1: 9685
Foreign Language Association of North Dakota Vol 1: 9690
Foreign Language Learning Today Vol 1: 2062
Foreign Press Association in London Vol 2: 7536
Foreningen Svensk Form Vol 2: 6297
Foreningen til Ski-Idrettens Fremme Vol 2: 5116
Forensic Science Society Vol 2: 7538
Forest History Society Vol 1: 9693
Forest Landowners Association Vol 1: 9698
Forest Press, Inc.; OCLC/ Vol 1: 2972
Fork Lift Truck Association Vol 2: 7540
Forsyth County Defense League Vol 1: 16006
Fort Collins Symphony Association Vol 1: 9700
Fort Scott Community College Vol 1: 9702
Forum Atomique Europeen Vol 2: 890
Foster Care Association of Oklahoma Vol 1: 9704
Foto Cine Clube Bandeirante Vol 2: 1167
Foundation for Australian Literary Studies Vol 2: 347
Foundation for Digestive Health and Nutrition Vol 1: 9706
Foundation for Microbiology Vol 1: 13851
Foundation for Nutrition Research Vol 2: 1576
Foundation for the Promotion of Finnish Music Vol 2: 1617

Foundation of American Women in Radio and Television Vol 1: 9714
Foundation of Lower Saxony Vol 2: 2770
Foundation of the Wall and Ceiling Industry Vol 1: 5886
Foundation "Open Society" Vol 2: 1237
Foundry Educational Foundation Vol 1: 16427
Four Freedoms Foundation Vol 1: 9736
Fragrance Foundation Vol 1: 9718
Fragrance Foundation and Fragrance Research Fund Vol 1: 9718
Frameworks Alliance Vol 1: 9723
France - Ministry of Culture and Communication Vol 2: 2615
France and Colonies Philatelic Society Vol 1: 9725
France Ministry of Culture Vol 2: 2526
France Ministry of Defense Vol 2: 2355
Franciscan Retreats Vol 1: 9727
Franciscan University of Steubenville Vol 1: 9729
Franck Organ Competition Committee; Cesar Vol 2: 4775
Franco-British Society Vol 2: 7542
Francqui Foundation Vol 2: 892
Frank Huntington Beebe Fund Vol 1: 9732
Frankfort-Elberta National Soaring Hall of Fame Vol 1: 9734
Franklin and Eleanor Roosevelt Institute Vol 1: 9736
Franklin Institute Vol 1: 9738
Franklin National Memorial; Benjamin Vol 1: 9741
Frans Hals Museum Vol 2: 4777
Fraternal Order of Eagles, Havre No. 166 Vol 1: 9743
Fraternal Order of Eagles, Lisbon No. 2968 Vol 1: 9745
Fraternal Order of Eagles, Marshfield No. 624 Vol 1: 9747
Fraternal Order of Eagles, Stevenson No. 1744 Vol 1: 9749
Fraternal Order of Police Lodge 86 Vol 1: 9751
Frederick Chopin Society Vol 2: 5304
Fredericksburg Sister City Association Vol 1: 9753
Free Market Foundation of Southern Africa Vol 2: 5560
Freedom Forum Vol 1: 9755
Freedom Forum - Media Studies Center Vol 1: 9757
Freedom House Vol 1: 9759
Freedom to Read Foundation Vol 1: 9761
Freedoms Foundation at Valley Forge Vol 1: 9763
Freixenet Group Vol 2: 6024
French-American Chamber of Commerce Vol 1: 9767
French-Canadian Genealogical Society Vol 1: 9769
French Chemical Society Vol 2: 2359
French Embassy in the Netherlands Vol 2: 4779
French Foundation for Medical Research Vol 2: 2363
French, Inc.; Samuel Vol 1: 12546
French League for Animal Rights Vol 2: 2368
French Ministry of Culture and Communication Vol 2: 2370
French Ministry of Environment Vol 2: 2532
French National Center for Scientific Research Vol 2: 2394
Freres de la Charite Vol 2: 3872
Fresno-Madera Medical Society Vol 1: 9772
Friday Morning Music Club Foundation Vol 1: 9775
The Friday Morning Music Club, Inc. Vol 1: 9774
Friedheim Foundation; Eric Vol 1: 12551
Friends in Residential Emergency Fire Vol 1: 9776
Friends of Alexandria Archaeology Vol 1: 9778
Friends of Algonquin Park Vol 1: 9780
Friends of American Writers Vol 1: 9782
Friends of Casco Bay Vol 1: 9787
Friends of Freedom Society Vol 1: 9789
Friends of Libraries U.S.A. Vol 1: 9791
Friends of Old-Time Radio Vol 1: 9796
Friends of Patrick Henry Vol 1: 9798
Friends of Radio for Peace International Vol 1: 9800
Friends of the Atlanta-Fulton Public Library System Vol 1: 9803
Friends of the Chicago Public Library Vol 1: 9805
Friends of the Earth - Cyprus Vol 2: 1407
Friends of the Historical Museum Vol 1: 9807
Friends of the Morrill Memorial Library Vol 1: 9809
Friends of the Pendleton District Vol 1: 9811
Friends of the Princeton University Library Vol 1: 9813
Friends of the River Vol 1: 9816
Friends of the Waterfront Vol 1: 9818
Friestelersvereniging van Suid-Afrika Vol 2: 5618
Friskies Vol 1: 13058
Fritzsche-Dodge and Olcott Inc. Vol 1: 1758
Front Range Young Farmers Chapter of the Colorado Young Farmer Educational Association Vol 1: 9820
F.U.G.I.T.I.V.E.S. Vol 1: 9822
Fuji Photo Film Vol 1: 19191
Fujihara Foundation of Science Vol 2: 4115
Fujisankei Communications International Vol 2: 2526
Fuller Foundation Vol 1: 8108
Fulton Chapter, Ohio Genealogical Society Vol 1: 9824
Fulton County Historical Society Vol 1: 9826
Funarte Fundacao Nacional De Arte Vol 2: 1169
The Fund for American Studies Vol 1: 9828
Fund for Modern Courts Vol 1: 9830
Fund for Renewable Energy & Environment Vol 1: 17990
Fund for the City of New York Vol 1: 9833
Fund for UFO Research Vol 1: 9835
Fundacao Nacional de Arte Vol 2: 1169
Fundacion Alejandro Angel Escobar Vol 2: 1309
Fundacion Miguel Aleman Vol 2: 4489
Fundacion Nexos Vol 2: 4491
Fundacion Pablo Neruda Vol 2: 1257
Fundacion Pedro Barrie de la Maza, Conde de Fenosa Vol 2: 6031
Fundacion Principe de Asturias Vol 2: 6034
Fundacion Unicaja Vol 2: 9298
Fundacion Unicaja Ronda Vol 2: 9297
Fur Commission U.S.A. Vol 1: 9837
Fusion Power Associates Vol 1: 9839
Future Business Leaders of America - Phi Beta Lambda Vol 1: 9842
Future Problem Solving Program of New Jersey Vol 1: 9846
G. W. Blunt White Library Vol 1: 13734
Gadjah Mada University - Center for Population and Policy Studies Vol 2: 3597
Gage County Convention and Visitors Bureau Vol 1: 9848
Gaines Dog Research Center Vol 1: 16320
Gairdner Foundation Vol 1: 9850
Galaxy International Pageants Vol 1: 9852
Gale Vol 1: 2977
Gale Group Vol 1: 2962
The Gale Group Vol 1: 5446
Galesburg Civic Art Center Vol 1: 9854
Gallaudet University Alumni Association Vol 1: 9856
Galpin Society Vol 2: 7546
Galt District Chamber of Commerce Vol 1: 9859
Galva Arts Council Vol 1: 9862
Galveston Historical Foundation Vol 1: 9864
Gamma Sigma Delta Vol 1: 9866
Gangs Out of Downey Vol 1: 9868
Gannett Center for Media Studies - Columbia University Vol 1: 9757
Gar Wood Society Vol 1: 9871
Garden Centers of America Vol 1: 9873
Garden Club of America Vol 1: 9875
Garden Writers Association Vol 1: 9877
The Gardeners of America/Men's Garden Clubs of America Vol 1: 9881
GARDENEX: Federation of Garden and Leisure Manufacturers Vol 2: 7548
Gas Processors Association Vol 1: 9892
Gateway Greening Vol 1: 9897
Gathering of Nations Vol 1: 9899
Gaudeamus Foundation Vol 2: 4782
Gay and Lesbian Association of Choruses Vol 1: 9901
Gaylord Brothers, Inc. Vol 1: 12823
Gazette International Networking Institute Vol 1: 17477
GE Fund Vol 1: 10747
Geary 18 International Yacht Racing Association Vol 1: 9904
GEC Marconi Avionics Vol 1: 13086
Geijutsu-in Vol 2: 4156
Gem State Award Recognition Vol 1: 10638
Gemini Industries, Inc. Vol 1: 11824
Gemini Theater Company Vol 1: 9906
Gemmological Association and Gem Testing Laboratory of Great Britain Vol 2: 7550
Gemmological Association of Great Britain Vol 2: 7550
Genealogical Association of Nova Scotia Vol 1: 9908
Genealogical Society of South Africa Vol 2: 5562
General Association of Engineers in Romania Vol 2: 5807
General Aviation Manufacturer Association Vol 1: 9910
General Commission on Archives and History of the United Methodist Church Vol 1: 9912
General Electric Company Vol 1: 4020
General Electric Foundation Vol 1: 1767, 3460
General Federation of Women's Clubs Vol 1: 9915
General Mills, Inc. Vol 1: 9917
General Monitors Vol 1: 18527

General Motors Cancer Research Foundation Vol 1: 9919
Genesis Academy Vol 1: 9923
Genetic Alliance Vol 1: 9928
Genetics Society of America Vol 1: 9931
Genetics Society of Canada Vol 1: 9934
Genetics Society of Japan Vol 2: 4117
Geneva Association Vol 2: 6384
Geneva Initiative on Psychiatry Vol 2: 4786
Geochemical Society Vol 1: 9938
Geografiska Sallskapet i Finland Vol 2: 1619
Geographic Society of Lima Vol 2: 5239
Geographical Organization of Finland Vol 2: 1619
Geographical Society of Philadelphia Vol 1: 9940
Geologica Belgica Vol 2: 894
Geological Society of America Vol 1: 5674
Geological Society of America Vol 1: 9944
Geological Society of Denmark Vol 2: 1493
Geological Society of France Vol 2: 2399
Geological Society of London Vol 2: 7556
Geological Society of South Africa Vol 2: 5564
Geological Society of Sweden Vol 2: 6151
Geological Society of Turkey Vol 2: 6628
Geological Society of Zimbabwe Vol 2: 9347
Geological Survey of Finland Vol 2: 1624
Geologiska Foreningen Vol 2: 6151
Geologiska Foreningen i Stockholm Vol 2: 6151
George F. Cram Co. Vol 1: 14762
George Montefiore Foundation Vol 2: 897
Georgetown University - Institute for the Study of Diplomacy Vol 1: 9959
Georgia Agricultural Commodity Commission for Peanuts Vol 1: 9961
Georgia Peanut Commission Vol 1: 9961
Georgia Public Policy Foundation Vol 1: 9968
Georgia Writers Association and Young Georgia Writers Vol 1: 9971
Gepipari Tudomanyos Egyesulet Vol 2: 3309
Geranium Society Vol 2: 7105
German Academy of Language and Poetry Vol 2: 2772
German Adult Education Association Vol 2: 2779
German Aerospace Center Vol 2: 2781
German Agricultural Society Vol 2: 2783
German Association for American Studies Vol 2: 2785
German Association for Water, Wastewater and Waste Vol 2: 2787
German Bar Association Vol 2: 2790
German Booksellers Association Vol 2: 2864
German Bunsen Society for Physical Chemistry Vol 2: 2792
German Chemical Society Vol 2: 2801
German Dental Association Vol 2: 2821
German Design Council Vol 2: 2828
German Gemmological Association Vol 2: 2831
German Geological Society Vol 2: 2833
German Informatics Society Vol 2: 2838
German Interior Architects Association Vol 2: 2840
German Language Society Vol 2: 2842
German Marshall Fund of the United States Vol 1: 9973
German Medical Association Vol 2: 2845
German Ministry of Economic Affairs Vol 2: 2829
German Nutrition Foundation Vol 2: 2897
German Organization of Endocrinology Vol 2: 2849
German Ornithologists] Society Vol 2: 2854
German Physical Society Vol 2: 7723
German Phytomedical Society Vol 2: 2860
German Publishers and Booksellers Association Vol 2: 2864
German Shoe Industry Association Vol 2: 2866
German Shorthaired Pointer Club of Orange County Vol 1: 9975
German Society for Biochemistry and Molecular Biology Vol 2: 2868
German Society for Documentation Vol 2: 2870
German Society for Fat Science Vol 2: 2872
German Society for Medicinal Plant Research Vol 2: 3055
German Society for Mining, Metallurgy, Resource and Environmental Technology Vol 2: 2876
German Society for Non-Destructive Testing Vol 2: 2880
German Society for Physical Medicine and Rehabilitation Vol 2: 2883
German Society for Social Scientific Sexuality Research Vol 2: 2887
German Society of Glass Technology Vol 2: 2889
German Society of Metallurgical and Mining Engineers Vol 2: 2876
German Society of Nutrition Vol 2: 2893
German Society of Pediatrics and Adolescent Medicine Vol 2: 2898
German Society of Pennsylvania Vol 1: 9977
German Society of Plastic and Reconstructive Surgery Vol 2: 2901
German Society of School Music Educators Vol 2: 2903
German Texan Heritage Society Vol 1: 9979
Germans From Russia Heritage Society Vol 1: 9981
Germany Philatelic Society Vol 1: 9983
Gerontological Society of America Vol 1: 9986
Gerontological Society of the Russian Academy of Sciences Vol 2: 5892
Gesellschaft Deutscher Chemiker Vol 2: 2794, 2796, 2801
Gesellschaft Deutscher Naturforscher und Arzte Vol 2: 2905
Gesellschaft fuer Informatik Vol 2: 2838
Gesellschaft fur Arzneipflanzenforschung Vol 2: 3055
Gesellschaft fur Biochemie und Molekularbiologie Vol 2: 2868
Gesellschaft fur Chemische Technik und Biotechnologie Vol 2: 2907
Gesellschaft fur Deutsche Sprache Vol 2: 2842
Gesellschaft fur Wirbelsaulenforschung Vol 2: 3057
Gesellschaft zur Forderung des Instituts fur Weltwirtschaft Vol 2: 3006
Gesellschaft zur Wissenschaftlichen Untersuchung von Parawissenschaften Vol 2: 3059
Get Involved for Mental Health Vol 1: 10000
Getty Grant Program Vol 1: 10002
Geyer - McAllister Publications Vol 1: 10010
Geza Anda Foundation Vol 2: 6364
Ghana Institution of Engineers Vol 2: 3149
Ghana Red Cross Society Vol 2: 3151
GI Joe Collectors Club Vol 1: 10014
Giant Schnauzer Club of America Vol 1: 10016
Gibson Musical Rasturants Vol 1: 13703
Gift from the Heart Foundation Vol 1: 10021
Gijon; Festival Internacional de Cine para la Juventud de Vol 2: 6036
Gijon International Film Festival for Young People Vol 2: 6036
Gilbert and Sullivan Society of Austin Vol 1: 10023
Gilmanton Historical Society Vol 1: 10025
Gilpin County Arts Association Vol 1: 10027
Girl Scouts of the Pioneer Council Vol 1: 10029
Girls' Brigade International Council Vol 2: 7569
Girls Friday of Show Business Vol 1: 21756
Givaudan-Roure Vol 1: 1758
Glasgow Development Agency Vol 2: 8890
Glass Art Society Vol 1: 10031
The Glaucoma Foundation Vol 1: 10034
Glaxo Vol 1: 3388
Glaxo Group Research Ltd. Vol 2: 8773
GlaxoSmithKline plc Vol 2: 8698
GlaxoWellcome Vol 1: 616
Gleeson Library Associates Vol 1: 10036
Gleitsman Foundation Vol 1: 10038
Glencoe Vol 1: 942
Glencoe/McGraw Hill - The McGraw Hill Companies Vol 1: 10041
Gloag and Son Ltd.; Matthew Vol 2: 7609
Global Education Associates Vol 1: 10043
Global Harmony Foundation Vol 2: 6366
Global Health Council Vol 1: 10045
Global Rights Vol 1: 10050
Global Warming International Center Vol 1: 10054
Globe and Horn Book, Inc. Vol 1: 6526
Go Kart Club of America Vol 1: 11696
Gobierno del Estado de Morelos Vol 2: 4493
Gobierno del Estado de Puebla Vol 2: 4495
Gobierno del Estado de Sinaloa Vol 2: 4501
Gobierno del Estado de Veracruz Vol 2: 4499
Godzilla Society of North America Vol 1: 10056
Goethe Institut Vol 2: 2917
Goethe Institute Vol 2: 2917
Goethe Institute Inter Nationes Vol 1: 1444
Golden Gate Audubon Society Vol 1: 10058
Golden Key International Honour Society Vol 1: 10061
Golden Key National Honor Society Vol 1: 10061
Goldman Environmental Foundation Vol 1: 10063
Goldsmith-Greenfield Foundation Vol 1: 18438, 18439
Goldsmiths' Company Vol 2: 7572
Golf Course Builders Association of America Vol 1: 21923
Golf Course Superintendents Association of America Vol 1: 10065
Golf Course Superintendents Association of America Vol 1: 21923
Golf Digest Vol 1: 10070
Golf Writers Association of America Vol 1: 10076, 21923
Goodhue; Charles Vol 1: 6083
Goodwill Industries International Vol 1: 10080
Goodyear Tire and Rubber Company Vol 1: 14155

Gordon and Breach Publishing Group Vol 1: 1785
Gorgas Memorial Institute Vol 1: 4633
Gorsedd Board Vol 2: 8173
Goshen College Vol 1: 10094
Goshen County Chamber of Commerce Vol 1: 10096
Goshen Historical Society Vol 1: 10098
Gospel Music Association Vol 1: 10100
Goto Optics Vol 2: 4099
Gottlieb Duttweiler Institut Vol 2: 6368
Government Computer News Vol 1: 10103
Government Employees AFGE AFL-CIO, USDA, LU 3523 Vol 1: 10105
Government Executive - National Journal Group Vol 1: 10107
Government Finance Officers Association of United States and Canada Vol 1: 10109
Government Innovators Network Vol 1: 10115
Government Management Information Sciences Vol 1: 10117
Government of India Vol 2: 3399
Government of Manitoba - Sustainable Development Coordination Unit Vol 1: 10119
Government of the State of Sinaloa Vol 2: 4501
Governmental Research Association Vol 1: 10121
Governor Baxter School for the Deaf Vol 1: 10123
Governors of Dromkeen Vol 2: 350
GPA Dublin International Piano Competition - Guradian Dublin International Piano Competition Vol 2: 3622
Grace and Company; W. R. Vol 1: 16398, 16399
Grace Leven Prize for Poetry Trust Vol 2: 353
Grafia - Graafisen Suunnittelun Jarjesto Vol 2: 1626
GRAFIA - The Finnish Association of Graphic Design Vol 2: 1626
Graham Foundation Vol 1: 10125
Grahamstown Foundation Vol 2: 5571
Grand American Road Racing Association Vol 1: 8768
Grand Haven-Spring Lake Convention and Visitors Bureau Vol 1: 10127
Grandview Rotary Club Vol 1: 10129
Graphic Arts Technical Foundation Vol 1: 10131
Graphic Design USA Vol 1: 10138
Graphic Design: USA Vol 1: 10139
Grassland Society of Southern Africa Vol 2: 5573
Graviner, Ltd. Vol 1: 9583
Great Britain/B.B.R. Publishing; Old Bottle Club of Vol 2: 6854
Great Lakes Carbon Corporation Vol 1: 1648
Great Lakes Colleges Association Vol 1: 10140
Great Lakes Commission Vol 1: 10142
Greater Detroit Frozen Food Association Vol 1: 10144
Greater Haverhill Arts Association Vol 1: 10146
Greater Lynn Photographic Association Vol 1: 10148
Greater Mount Airy Chamber of Commerce Vol 1: 10150
Greater Muskegon Music Teachers Association Vol 1: 10152
Greater Omaha Sports Committee Vol 1: 10154
Greater Philadelphia Chamber of Commerce Vol 1: 10156
Greater Pittsburgh Council Vol 1: 15050
Greater Quitman Area Chamber of Commerce Vol 1: 10158
Greater St. Louis Amateur Baseball Hall of Fame Vol 1: 10160
Greater Seattle Business Association Vol 1: 10163
Greater Vancouver Professional Theatre Alliance Vol 1: 10165
Greater Waterbury Chamber of Commerce Vol 1: 10167
Greek Alzheimer's Association Vol 2: 3171
Green Earth Organisation Vol 2: 3153
Green Meadow Foundation Vol 2: 6368
Green Organisation Vol 2: 7574
Greenland Society Vol 2: 1495
The Greensboro Review Vol 1: 10169
Greenwich Village Society for Historic Preservation Vol 1: 10171
Greenwood Publishing Group, Inc. Vol 1: 5620
Greeting Card Association Vol 1: 10173
Gregg Fund; John Robert Vol 1: 21032
Griffin Trust for Excellence in Poetry Vol 1: 10175
Grolier Educational Corp. Vol 1: 2979
Grolier Educational Corporation Vol 1: 3000
The Grolier Poetry Book Shop Vol 1: 10177
Grolier Poetry Book Shop, Inc. Vol 1: 10178
Gronlandske Selskab Vol 2: 1495
Groundwater Foundation Vol 1: 10179
Group for Design in Business Vol 1: 8538
Group for the Use of Psychology in History Vol 1: 10183
Groupe Consultatif International de Recherche sur le Colza Vol 2: 2461
Groupe International de Recherches sur la Preservation du Bois Vol 2: 6162
Groupement Latin et Mediterraneen de Medecine du Sport Vol 2: 2523
Groupement Regional d'Action Cinematographique Vol 2: 2335
Grune & Statton Vol 1: 4446
Grupo Aluminio, S.A. de C.V. Vol 2: 4507
Grupo Prisa: Promotora de Informaciones SA Vol 2: 6038
Gruppo Esponenti Italiani Vol 1: 10185
Guadalupe Cultural Arts Center Vol 1: 10187
Guelph Spring Festival Vol 1: 10189
Guggenheim; Fondation Paul Vol 2: 6493
Guggenheim Memorial Foundation; John Simon Vol 1: 10191
Guide Dogs of America Vol 1: 10193
Guild Hall Vol 1: 10195
Guild of Agricultural Journalists Vol 2: 7576
Guild of Air Pilots and Air Navigators Vol 2: 7578
Guild of Air Traffic Control Officers Vol 2: 7580
Guild of Carillonneurs in North America Vol 1: 10197
Guild of Catholic Lawyers Vol 1: 10199
Guild of Food Writers Vol 2: 7582
Guild of International Professional Toastmasters Vol 2: 7584
Guild of Italian American Actors Vol 1: 10201
Guild of Motoring Writers Vol 2: 7586
Guild of Registered Tourist Guides Vol 2: 7590
Guild of Taxidermists Vol 2: 7592
Guild of Television Cameramen Vol 2: 7594
Guild of Yachting Writers Vol 2: 9271
Guilde Europeenne du Raid Vol 2: 2415
Guildhall School of Music and Drama Vol 2: 7596
Guitar Foundation of America Vol 1: 10203
Guitar Player Magazine Vol 1: 10205
Gujarat Vidyapith Vol 2: 3370
Gulbenkian Foundation; Calouste Vol 2: 5485
Gulf Coast Association of Geological Societies Vol 1: 1330
Gungywamp Society Vol 1: 10207
Gutenberg-Gesellschaft Vol 2: 2919
Gutenberg Society Vol 2: 2919, 2920
Guyana Office of the President Vol 2: 3205
Gyldendaal Vol 2: 1497
Gym Master Vol 1: 8163
Gynaecological Visiting Society of Great Britain and Ireland Vol 2: 8441
Haagudah Lezechuyot Haezrach Beyisrael Vol 2: 3721
Hacker Instruments, Inc. Vol 1: 15716
Hadassah Magazine Vol 1: 10212
Hadassah, The Women's Zionist Organization of America Vol 1: 10214
Haddonfield Symphony Vol 1: 10216
Hague Academy of International Law Vol 2: 4788
Haiku Society of America Vol 1: 10218
Hall and Company; G. K. Vol 1: 2980
Hall Memorial Fund; Melody Vol 1: 14094
Halle Theatre Vol 1: 10225
Handweavers Guild of America Vol 1: 10227
Hannibal Arts Council Vol 1: 10230
Hanover Chamber of Commerce Vol 1: 10232
Happold Trust Vol 2: 7286
Harcourt Brace Jovanovich Vol 1: 2056, 10234
Harcourt, Inc. Vol 1: 10234
Harcros Chemical Group Vol 2: 8773
Hardin County Historical Museums Vol 1: 10236
Harding Foundation Vol 1: 3631
Hardwood Research Council Vol 1: 15185
Harkness Fellowships of the Commonwealth Fund Vol 1: 10238
Harlow Foundation; Bryce Vol 1: 10240
Harmony, Inc. Vol 1: 10242
Harness Racing Museum and Hall of Fame Vol 1: 20625
Harness Tracks of America Vol 1: 10257
Harper Collins Vol 1: 18112
HarperCollins Publishers Vol 2: 6958
Harrassowitz Co. Vol 1: 5425
Harriet Beecher Stowe Center Vol 1: 10261
Harrisburg Hunters' and Anglers' Association Vol 1: 10263
Harrogate International Festival Vol 2: 7598
Harry S. Truman Library Institute for National and International Affairs Vol 1: 10265
Harry Stephen Keeler Society Vol 1: 10267
Hartley Fund; Marcellus Vol 1: 13845
Harvard Alumni Association Vol 1: 10269
Harvard Business Review Vol 1: 10272
Harvard Business School Vol 1: 16318
Harvard Lampoon Vol 1: 10274
Harvard University - Graduate School of Design Vol 1: 10280
Harvard University Center for Italian Renaissance Studies Vol 2: 4068
Harvard University Press Vol 1: 10282

Organization Index

Harvey W. Watt & Co. Vol 1: 231
Harveys Leeds International Pianoforte Competition Vol 2: 8049
Haskil Association; Clara Vol 2: 6370
The Hastings Center Vol 1: 10285
Hastings Literacy Program Vol 1: 10287
Hastings Writers' Group Vol 2: 7601
Hatebusters Incorporated Vol 1: 10289
Hauptverband der Deutschen Schuhindustrie Vol 2: 2866
Hauptverband des Osterreichischen Buchhandels Vol 2: 700
Hawaii Association of School Librarians Vol 1: 10291
Hawaii Literary Arts Council Vol 1: 10295
Hawaii Society - American Institute of Architects Vol 1: 10296
Hawaii State Foundation on Culture and the Arts Vol 1: 10293
Hawk Migration Association of North America Vol 1: 10298
Hawk Mountain Sanctuary Vol 1: 10301
Hawk Mountain Sanctuary Association Vol 1: 10303
Hawley Russell & Baker Ltd. UK Vol 2: 7100
Hazleton Art League Vol 1: 10305
Headline Book Publishing Vol 2: 7369
Headliners Club Vol 1: 10307
Headliners Foundation Vol 1: 10307
Healing the Children, Northeast Chapter Vol 1: 10309
Health & Hygiene and Society of Public Health; Royal Institute of Public Vol 2: 8604
Health Care Exhibitors Association Vol 1: 10334
Health Education Division Vol 1: 1015
Health Industry Distributors Association Vol 1: 10311
Health Information Resource Center Vol 1: 10314
Health Physics Society Vol 1: 10316
Health Science Communications Association Vol 1: 10322
Healthcare Convention and Exhibitors Association Vol 1: 10334
Healthcare Financial Management Association Vol 1: 10336
Healthcare Information and Management Systems Society Vol 1: 10341
HEAR Center Vol 1: 10351
HEAR Foundation Vol 1: 10351
Hearst Corporation Vol 1: 9365
Hearst Foundation; William Randolph Vol 1: 10353, 15563
Hearst Newspapers Vol 1: 10355
Heart of Denver Romance Writers Vol 1: 10357
Heart of New England Chihuahua Club Vol 1: 10360
Heart of Tyler-Main Street Vol 1: 10362
Heart Rhythm Association Vol 1: 10364
Heat Transfer Research, Inc. Vol 1: 2781
Heavy Specialized Carriers Conference Vol 1: 19574
Heberden Society Vol 2: 7172
Hebrew Immigrant Aid Society Vol 1: 10370
Hebrew Union College - Jewish Institute of Religion Vol 1: 10374
Hebrew University of Jerusalem - Center for Research on the History and Culture of Polish Jews Vol 2: 3733
Hebrew Writers Association in Israel Vol 2: 3735
Heinrich-Tessenow-Gesellschaft Vol 2: 3093
The Heinz Family Foundation Vol 1: 10377
Heiser Program for Research in Leprosy and Tuberculosis Vol 1: 10383
Heisman Trophy Trust Vol 1: 10385
Helen Keller International Vol 1: 10387
Helen Keller Worldwide Vol 1: 10387
Helicopter Association International Vol 1: 10389
Helicopter Association of America Vol 1: 10389
Helicopter Club of Great Britain Vol 2: 7603
Helmholtz Fonds Vol 2: 2921
HelpAge International - Latin America Regional Development Centre Vol 2: 1125
Helsinki International Ballet Competition Vol 2: 1628
Hemophilia Foundation of Michigan Vol 1: 10407
Henley - Management College Vol 2: 8707
Herb Society of America Vol 1: 10409
Herbert Hoover Presidential Library Association Vol 1: 10415
Herff Jones, Inc. Vol 1: 14386
Heritage Association of San Marcos Vol 1: 10417
Heritage Canada Foundation Vol 1: 10419
Heritage Center Vol 1: 10423
Heritage Railway Association Vol 2: 7614
Heritage Toronto Vol 1: 10425
Herpetologists' League Vol 1: 10427
Hewlett-Packard Company Vol 1: 4045
High Point Convention and Visitors Bureau Vol 1: 10429
Highsmith Inc. Vol 1: 6747
Highsmith, Inc. Vol 1: 17716
Hiking Federation of Southern Africa Vol 2: 5575
Hiking South Africa Vol 2: 5575
Hildegard Doerenkamp and Gerhard Zbinden Foundation for Realistic Animal Protection in Bio-Medical Research Vol 2: 2923
Hill and Knowlton U.K. Vol 2: 7616
Hillel Vol 1: 10431
Hillerich and Bradsby Co. Vol 1: 19641
Hillman Foundation, Inc.; The Sidney Vol 1: 10434
Hills Pet Nutrition Vol 2: 1546
Hill's Pet Nutrition, Inc. Vol 1: 4814
Hillsdale College - Center for Constructive Alternatives/The Shavano Institute Vol 1: 10436
Hillside Historical Society Vol 1: 10438
The Hip Society Vol 1: 10440
Hiradastechnikai Tudomanyos Egyesulet Vol 2: 3306
Hiroshima International Amateur Film and Video Festival Vol 2: 4119
Hiroshima International Animation Festival Vol 2: 4121
Hispanic Council of St. Clair County Vol 1: 10443
Hispanic Engineer Vol 1: 7586
Histochemical Society Vol 1: 10445
Historic Albany Foundation Vol 1: 10447
Historic American Buildings Survey Vol 1: 19026
Historic Augusta Vol 1: 10449
Historic Chattahoochee Commission Vol 1: 10451
Historic Harmony Vol 1: 10453
Historic Landmarks Foundation of Indiana Vol 1: 10455
Historic Mobile Preservation Society Vol 1: 10457
Historic New Orleans Collection - Williams Prize Committee Vol 1: 10459
Historic Scotland Vol 2: 6919
Historical and Ethnological Society of Greece Vol 2: 3173
Historical Association Vol 2: 7618
Historical Branch Advisory Committee Vol 2: 4968
Historical Metallurgy Society Vol 2: 7620
Historical Radio Society of Australia Vol 2: 355
Historical Society of Frederick County Vol 1: 10461
Historical Society of Michigan Vol 1: 10463
Historical Society of Palm Beach County Vol 1: 10465
Historical Society of Pennsylvania Vol 1: 10467
Historical Society of Princeton Vol 1: 10469
Historical Society of Washington, DC Vol 1: 10471
History of Dermatology Society Vol 1: 10473
History of Economics Society Vol 1: 10476
History of Education Society Vol 1: 10480
History of Science Society Vol 1: 10484
Hitachi, Ltd., Vol 1: 8595
Hobey Baker Memorial Award Vol 1: 10492
Hochschule fur Grafik und Buchkunst Leipzig Vol 2: 3019
Hochschule fur Musik und Darstellende Kunst, Graz Vol 2: 793
Hochschule fur Musik und Darstellende Kunst, Wien Vol 2: 804
Hockey Hall of Fame Vol 1: 10494
Hodder and Stoughton Publishers Vol 2: 8063
Hodson Corporation Vol 1: 19345
Hoechst AG Vol 2: 2915
Hoechst Marion Roussel Vol 1: 15120
Hoffman LaRoche Vol 1: 3637
Hoge Raad voor Diamant Vol 2: 834
Hogg Young Artist Competition; Houston Symphony Ima Vol 1: 10498
Hoi Chur thap do Viet Nam Vol 2: 9328
Holistic Arts Fair Association Vol 1: 10501
Holland Animation Film Festival Vol 2: 4790
Holland Historical Trust Vol 1: 10503
Holland Society of New York Vol 1: 10505
Holly Society of America Vol 1: 10507
Hollywood Chapter of the National Academy of Television Arts and Sciences Vol 1: 126
Hollywood Foreign Press Association Vol 1: 10511
Hollywood Radio and Television Society Vol 1: 10514
Home Baking Association Vol 1: 10517
Home Builders Association of Western Massachusetts Vol 1: 10519
Home Diagnostics, Inc. Vol 1: 1184
Home Inspectors; Canadian Association of Vol 1: 6913
Home Wine and Beer Trade Association Vol 1: 10521
HomeStyles Publishing Vol 1: 2743
Honda Foundation Vol 2: 4123
Honda Motor Company. Vol 1: 4518
Honens Calgary International Piano Competition; Esther Vol 1: 10523
Honeywell International Foundation Vol 1: 10525
Hong Kong Film Awards Association Ltd. Vol 2: 5220
Hong Kong International Film Festival Vol 2: 5220

Hong Kong Medical Association Vol 2: 5223
Hong Kong Productivity Council Vol 2: 5225
Honolulu Board of Realtors Vol 1: 10527
Honolulu Publishing Co. Ltd. Vol 1: 10530
Honor Society of Phi Kappa Phi Vol 1: 10532
Hop Barley and the Alers Vol 1: 10534
Hope Unlimited Vol 2: 5929
Horace Mann League of the U.S.A. Vol 1: 10536
Horatio Alger Association of Distinguished Americans Vol 1: 10538
Horatio Alger Society Vol 1: 10540
Horizons Theatre Vol 1: 10546
Horror Writers Association Vol 1: 10548
Hosei Daigaku Kokusaikouryu Center Vol 2: 4125
Hosei University - International Center Vol 2: 4125
Hospital Financial Management Association Vol 1: 10336
Hospital General Dr. Manuel Gea Gonzalez Vol 2: 4509
Hospital Management Systems Society Vol 1: 10341
Hospitality Sales and Marketing Association International Vol 1: 10550
Hostelling International-American Youth Hostels Vol 1: 10558
Hotel Rotorua Vol 2: 5026
Hotel Sales and Marketing Association International Vol 1: 10550
Hotel Sales Management Association Vol 1: 10550
Houston Grand Opera Vol 1: 10568, 10569
Houston International Film Festival Vol 1: 21968
Howard Foundation; George A. and Eliza Gardner Vol 1: 10570
Hoyt Institute of Fine Arts Vol 1: 10572
HR Alliance Vol 2: 357
HR Society Vol 2: 7622
Hrvatski Sahovski Savez Vol 2: 1369
Hrvatsko Bibliotekarsko Drustvo Vol 2: 1371
Hrvatsko Farmaceutsko Drustvo Vol 2: 1379
Hrvatsko narodno kazaliste Split Vol 2: 1376
HTV Cymru/Wales Vol 2: 6764
Huddersfield Contemporary Music Festival Vol 2: 7624
Hudson Valley Arabian Horse Association Vol 1: 10574
Hughes Aircraft Company Vol 1: 13085
Human and Ergonomics Factors Society Vol 1: 10576
Human Factors and Ergonomics Society Vol 1: 10576
Human Growth Foundation Vol 1: 10584
Human Rights and Race Relations Centre Vol 1: 10586
Human Rights Campaign Vol 1: 10590
Human Rights Institute of the Bar of Bordeaux Vol 2: 2417
Human Rights Watch Vol 1: 10594
Humane Slaughter Association and Council of Justice to Animals Vol 2: 7626
Humane Society of the United States Vol 1: 10596
Humane Society of the United States, New England Regional Office Vol 1: 10600
Humanist Association of Los Angeles Vol 1: 10602
Humanist Association of Salem Vol 1: 10605
The Humanitas Prize Vol 1: 10607
Humble Oil and Refining Company Vol 1: 1747
Humboldt International Short Film Festival Vol 1: 10609
Humboldt State University - Office for Research and Graduate Studies Vol 1: 10611
Hungarian Academy of Sciences Vol 2: 3244
Hungarian Chemical Society Vol 2: 3248
Hungarian Mining and Metallurgical Society Vol 2: 3253
Hungarian Olympic Committee Vol 2: 3265
Hungarian Organization of Textile Technology and Science Vol 2: 3267
Hungarian Publishers and Booksellers Association Vol 2: 3271
Hungarian Real Estate Association Vol 2: 3274
Hungarian Scientific Society for Building Vol 2: 3278
Hungarian Society for Surveying, Mapping and Remote Sensing Vol 2: 3290
Hungarian Society of Cardiology Vol 2: 3282
Hungarofest Vol 2: 3284
Hungary Ministry of Agriculture and Rural Development Vol 2: 3288
The Hunger Project Vol 1: 10613
Hunt Institute for Botanical Documentation Vol 1: 10615
Hunterdon Museum of Art Vol 1: 10617
Hunterian Society Vol 2: 7628
Hunting Vol 2: 8245
Hunting Retriever Club Vol 1: 20346
Huntington County Visitor and Convention Bureau Vol 1: 10619
Huntington Library Vol 1: 16414
Huntington Society of Canada Vol 1: 10621
Hustinx Foundation; Edmond Vol 2: 1118
Hutchins Library Vol 1: 4996
Huysmans Stichting; Camille Vol 2: 839
Hyatt Foundation Vol 1: 17573
Hygiene and Society of Public Health; Royal Institute of Public Health & Vol 2: 8604
Hymn Society in the United States and Canada Vol 1: 10624
Hymn Society of America Vol 1: 10624
IADR Dental Materials Group Vol 1: 11217
Ian Fleming (Glidrose) Publications Ltd. Vol 2: 7367
IBC Advanced Technologies and Millipore Corporation Vol 1: 1721
IBC Award Vol 2: 7910
Ibero-American Association of Postgraduate Universities Vol 2: 6040
Iberoamerican Film Festival - Huelva Vol 2: 6043
IBM Vol 1: 3464, 5307, 11028
IBM Corporation Vol 1: 1723
Ibsen Society of America Vol 1: 10626
ICD - International Center for the Disabled Vol 1: 10628
Ice Skating Institute Vol 1: 10630
Icelandic Center for Research Vol 2: 3319
Icelandic Horse Trekkers Vol 1: 10633
Icelandic Library and Information Science Association Vol 2: 3322
Icelandic Pony Trekkers Vol 1: 10633
Icelandic Publishers' Association Vol 2: 3326
ICI plc Vol 2: 8773
ICOGRADA Vol 2: 1238
I.D., The International Design Magazine - F+ Publications Inc. Vol 1: 10635
Idaho Quality Award, Inc. - Idaho Department of Commerce Vol 1: 10637
Idaho Quality Award Recognition Vol 1: 10638
Idaho Retailers Association Vol 1: 10639
IDEA Health and Fitness Association Vol 1: 10641
Idea Innovative Directions an Educational Alliance Vol 1: 10646
Iditarod Trail Committee Vol 1: 10648
IEE Scotland Vol 2: 7805
IEEE Vol 1: 4042
IEEE Aerospace and Electronic Systems Society, IEEE Control Systems Society, and IEEE Engineering in Medicine and Biology Society Vol 1: 10879
IEEE Computer Society Vol 1: 5303
IEEE Dielectrics and Electrical Insulation Society Vol 1: 10650
IEEE Education Society Vol 1: 10653
IEEE Industrial Electronics Society Vol 1: 10655
IEEE Industry Applications Society Vol 1: 10872
IEEE Lasers and Electro-Optics Society Vol 1: 10657
IEEE Professional Communication Society Vol 1: 10663
IES, Institute for the International Education of Students Vol 1: 10665
IFA International Aviation Scholarship Vol 2: 7927
IFRA Vol 2: 2925
Ikatan Dokter Indonesia Vol 2: 3599
Il Tempo Vol 2: 3952
Illinois Association of Meat Processors Vol 1: 10668
Illinois Association of Teachers of English Vol 1: 17902
Illinois Conference of Churches Vol 1: 10670
Illinois Ethnic Consultation Vol 1: 2057
Illinois Foreign Language Teachers Association Vol 1: 2057
Illinois Library Association Vol 1: 10672
Illinois Reading Council Vol 1: 17902
Illinois School Library Media Association Vol 1: 17902
Illinois Society for Microbiology Vol 1: 10689
Illuminating Engineering Society of North America Vol 1: 10691
ILSI-North America Vol 1: 4162
Ima Hogg National Young Artist Audition Vol 1: 10498
Image Industry Council International/Institute for Image Management Vol 1: 10698
Imagine Canada Vol 1: 10701
Imaging Geospatial Information Society Vol 1: 5207
Imaging Science and Technology Group Vol 2: 8668
Immigration and Ethnic History Society Vol 1: 10704
Imperial Chemical Industries Vol 2: 8765
Imperial Tobacco Company Vol 2: 7611
In-Plant Graphics Vol 1: 11838
In-Plant Management Association Vol 1: 11835
In-Plant Printing Management Association Vol 1: 11835
The Inamori Foundation Vol 2: 4127
Incentive Manufacturer and Representatives Alliance Vol 1: 10708
Inco Europe Ltd. Vol 2: 8773
Incorporated Society of Musicians Vol 2: 7630

Incorporating Professional Association of Nursery Nurses Vol 2: 8291
Independent Accountants Association of Illinois Vol 1: 10710
Independent Bakers Association Vol 1: 10712
Independent Colleges and Universities of Florida Vol 1: 10714
Independent Curators International Vol 1: 10717
Independent Feature Project Vol 1: 10719
Independent Free Papers of America Vol 1: 10722
Independent Insurance Agents and Brokers of America Vol 1: 10726
Independent Mystery Booksellers Association Vol 1: 10742
Independent Organic Inspectors Association Vol 1: 10744
Independent Sector Vol 1: 10746
India Ministry of Science and Technology Vol 2: 3372
India Office of the Prime Minister Vol 2: 3374
India Study Circle for Philately Vol 1: 10748
Indian Adult Education Association Vol 2: 3393
Indian and Northern Affairs Canada Vol 1: 10750
Indian Arts and Crafts Association Vol 1: 10752
Indian Books Centre Vol 2: 3396
Indian Council for Cultural Relations Vol 2: 3398
Indian Council of Agricultural Research Vol 2: 3400
Indian Council of Medical Research Vol 2: 3402
Indian Dairy Association Vol 2: 3440
Indian Institute of Metals Vol 2: 3444
Indian Law Institute Vol 2: 3465
Indian National Science Academy Vol 2: 3467
Indian Physics Association Vol 2: 3526
Indian Science Congress Association Vol 2: 3528
Indian Society of Advertisers Vol 2: 3545
Indian Society of Agricultural Economics Vol 2: 3547
Indian Space Research Organization Vol 2: 2274
Indiana Arts Commission Vol 1: 10754
Indiana Black Expo Vol 1: 10756
Indiana Holstein Association Vol 1: 10760
Indiana Library Federation Vol 1: 10762
Indiana Mental Health Memorial Foundation Vol 1: 15376
Indiana Opera Theatre Vol 1: 10774
Indiana Repertory Theatre Vol 1: 10776
Indiana State Federation of Poetry Clubs Vol 1: 15000
Indianapolis Motor Speedway Vol 1: 10778
India's National Academy of Letters Vol 2: 3550
Indo-French Chamber of Commerce and Industry Vol 2: 3555
Indonesian Medical Association Vol 2: 3599
Indonesian Planned Parenthood Association Vol 2: 3605
Industrial Designers Society of America Vol 1: 10781
Industrial Fabrics Association International Vol 1: 10783
Industrial Research and Development Vol 1: 17813
Industrial Research Institute Vol 1: 10785
Industry Canada Vol 1: 15568
Infectious Diseases Society of America Vol 1: 10789
Information Access Company Vol 1: 10798, 10799
Information Technology Association of Canada Vol 1: 10795
Information Technology Society Vol 2: 2927
Information Today Inc. Vol 1: 2968, 7249
Information Today, Inc. Vol 1: 10797
Informationstechnische Gesellschaft im Verband der Elektrotechnik Elektronik Informationstechnik Vol 2: 2927
Infusion Nurses Society Vol 1: 10800
ING Foundation. Vol 1: 8571
Ingenjorsvetenskapsakademien Vol 2: 6197
Ingram Book Company Vol 1: 19464
Inhlangano Yezokusakaza Eningizimu Afrika Vol 2: 5681
Inland Bird Banding Association Vol 1: 10804
Inland Empire Reading Council Vol 1: 10808
Inland Press Association Vol 1: 10810
Insititute of Metal and Materials Australasia Vol 2: 361
Insolvency Practitioners Association of Australia Vol 2: 359
Institut Aeronautique et Spatial du Canada Vol 1: 6865
Institut agree de la logistique et des transports Amerique du Nord Vol 1: 7813
Institut Canadien d Administration de la Justice Vol 1: 7169
Institut Canadien de l'immeuble Vol 1: 17899
Institut Canadien des Ingenieurs Vol 1: 9268
Institut canadien des mines, Metallurgie et Petrole Vol 1: 7180
L'Institut d'administration publique du Canada Vol 1: 11027
Institut de Biologie Physico-Chimique Vol 2: 2419
Institut de Chimie du Canada Vol 1: 7825
Institut de Droit International Vol 2: 6372
Institut de France Vol 2: 2421
Institut del Teatre de la Diputacio de Barcelona Vol 2: 6000
Institut d'Histoire de l'Amerique Francaise Vol 1: 10817
Institut et Hospital Neurologiques de Montreal Vol 1: 13601
Institut Europeen d'Administration Publique Vol 2: 4762
Institut Forestier du Canada Vol 1: 7171
The Institut Francais de Washington Vol 1: 7925
Institut fur Weltwirtschaft an der Universitat Kiel Vol 2: 3005
Institut International d'Aluminium Vol 2: 7892
Institut International de Droit Humanitaire Vol 2: 3973
Institut International de Droit Spatial Vol 2: 2485
Institut International de Finances Publiques Vol 2: 2964
Institut International de la Potasse Vol 2: 6435
Institut International de la Soudure Vol 2: 2488
Institut International de Promotion et de Prestige Vol 2: 6414
Institut International de Statistique Vol 2: 4841
Institut International des Droits de l'Homme Vol 2: 2479
Institut International des Sciences Humaines Integrales Vol 1: 11689
Institut International du Froid Vol 2: 2481
Institut International pour l'Analyse des Systemes Appliques Vol 2: 753
Institut Mondial du Phosphate Vol 2: 4670
L'Institut National Canadien pour les Aveugles Vol 1: 7300
Institut national de la qualite Vol 1: 15567
Institut National du Cancer du Canada Vol 1: 14584
Institut Royal d'Architecture du Canada Vol 1: 18133
Institut Tal-Gurnalisti Maltin Vol 2: 4447
Institut Valencia de la Juventut Vol 1: 9230
Institute de la Fondation D'Acupuncture du Canada Vol 1: 173
Institute for Communications Law Studies Vol 1: 10822
Institute for Complementary Medicine Vol 2: 7633
Institute for Energy Law Vol 1: 7701
Institute for Financial Crime Prevention Vol 1: 5593
Institute for Integration of Latin America and the Caribbean Vol 2: 36
Institute for International Economics Vol 2: 5495
Institute for Latin American Cooperation Vol 2: 6081
Institute for Manufacturing Vol 2: 7635
Institute for Media Analysis Vol 2: 5548
Institute for Mediation and Conflict Resolution Vol 1: 10824
Institute for Mesoamerican Studies Vol 1: 10826
Institute for Numerical Computation and Analysis Vol 2: 3635
Institute for Policy Studies Vol 1: 10829
Institute for Public Relations Vol 1: 10831
Institute for Research in Hypnosis and Psychotherapy Vol 1: 10834
Institute for Scientific Information Vol 1: 4111, 5606, 13838, 18855
Institute for Social Inventions Vol 2: 7637
Institute for Southern Studies Vol 1: 10837
Institute for Supply Management Vol 1: 10839
Institute for the Study of American Cultures Vol 1: 10841
Institute for the Study of Earth and Man Vol 1: 10843
Institute for University Cooperation Vol 2: 3954
Institute of Acoustics Vol 2: 7639
Institute of Actuaries - United Kingdom Vol 2: 7644
Institute of Administrative Accountants Vol 2: 7691
Institute of Administrative Management Vol 2: 7647
Institute of Advanced Legal Studies Vol 2: 7649
Institute of Advanced Philosophic Research Vol 1: 10848
Institute of African Studies Vol 2: 3155
Institute of British Geographers Vol 2: 8517, 8521
Institute of Cast Metal Engineers Vol 2: 7652

Institute of Certified Management Accountants Vol 1: 10985
Institute of Certified Records Managers Vol 1: 10850
Institute of Chartered Accountants in England and Wales Vol 2: 7660
Institute of Chartered Accountants in Ireland Vol 2: 7661
Institute of Chartered Accountants of New Zealand Vol 2: 4971
Institute of Chartered Accountants of Scotland Vol 2: 7661, 7664
Institute of Chartered Financial Analysts Vol 1: 5390
Institute of Civil Defence and Disaster Studies Vol 2: 7683
Institute of Civil Engineers Vol 2: 8889
The Institute of Classical Architecture and Classical America Vol 1: 10852
Institute of Contemporary History and Wiener Library Vol 2: 7685
Institute of Early American History and Culture Vol 1: 16706
Institute of Electrical and Electronics Engineers Vol 1: 4318, 4328, 4520
Institute of Electrical and Electronics Engineers Vol 1: 10854
Institute of Electrical and Electronics Engineers Vol 1: 18875, 19057
Institute of Electrical and Electronics Engineers - Computer Society Vol 1: 10884
Institute of Electrical and Electronics Engineers - Power Engineering Society Vol 1: 10902
Institute of Electrical and Electronics Engineers Laser and Electro-optics Society Vol 1: 16799
Institute of Entertainment and Arts Management Vol 2: 7687
Institute of Environmental Sciences Vol 1: 10917
Institute of Environmental Sciences and Technology Vol 1: 10917
Institute of Export Vol 2: 7689
Institute of Field Archaeologists Vol 2: 6920
Institute of Financial Accountants Vol 2: 7691
Institute of Food Science and Technology - UK Vol 2: 7693
Institute of Food Technologists Vol 1: 10933
Institute of Heraldic and Genealogical Studies Vol 2: 7697
Institute of Industrial Engineers Vol 1: 10948
Institute of Information Scientists Vol 2: 7277
Institute of Internal Auditors Vol 1: 10968
Institute of International Container Lessors Vol 1: 10977
Institute of International Education Vol 1: 10980
Institute of International Law Vol 2: 6372
Institute of Jamaica Vol 2: 4076
Institute of Jazz Studies Vol 1: 10982
Institute of Journalists Vol 2: 7275
Institute of Landscape Architects of South Africa Vol 2: 5577
Institute of Language and Literature Vol 2: 4426
Institute of Legal Cashiers and Administrators Vol 2: 7700
Institute of Maltese Journalists Vol 2: 4447
Institute of Management Vol 2: 7702
Institute of Management Accountants Vol 1: 10984
Institute of Management Accountants, Rochester Vol 1: 11003
Institute of Management Sciences Vol 1: 11067
Institute of Marine Engineering, Science and Technology Vol 2: 7705
Institute of Marine Engineers Vol 2: 7705
Institute of Marketing Management Graduate School of Marketing Vol 2: 5579
Institute of Materials Vol 2: 8741
Institute of Materials Engineering Australasia Vol 2: 361
Institute of Mathematical Statistics Vol 1: 8293
Institute of Mathematical Statistics Vol 1: 11005
Institute of Measurement and Control Vol 2: 7713
Institute of Mechanical Engineering Vol 2: 567
Institute of Mechanical Engineers Vol 2: 569, 7763
Institute of Navigation Vol 2: 8593
Institute of Navigation Vol 1: 11010
Institute of Nuclear Materials Management Vol 1: 11018
Institute of Packaging Professionals Vol 1: 11022
Institute of Pharmacology - Polish Academy of Sciences Vol 2: 5307
Institute of Physics Vol 2: 7722
Institute of Physics (England) Vol 2: 216
Institute of Practitioners in Advertising Vol 2: 7738
Institute of Professional Engineering Technologists Vol 2: 5582
Institute of Public Administration of Canada Vol 1: 11027
Institute of Quarrying - England Vol 2: 7740
Institute of Real Estate Management Vol 1: 11030
Institute of Road Transport Engineers Vol 2: 9061
Institute of Store Planners Vol 1: 11042
Institute of Technology and Higher Studies of Monterrey Vol 2: 4511
Institute of the Americas Vol 1: 11045
Institute of Transportation Engineers Vol 1: 11047
Institute of Turkish Studies Vol 1: 11061
Institute on Political Journalism Vol 1: 9829
Institute on Religion and Democracy Vol 1: 11063
Institutes for the Achievement of Human Potential Vol 1: 11065
Institution for Operations Research and the Management Sciences Vol 1: 11067
Institution of Chemical Engineers Vol 2: 377, 378, 428, 7742
Institution of Civil Engineers Vol 2: 7755, 7797
Institution of Diagnostic Engineers Vol 2: 7788
Institution of Electrical Engineers Vol 2: 7763
Institution of Electrical Engineers - England Vol 2: 7790
Institution of Engineers Australia/Engineers Australia Vol 2: 364
Institution of Engineers, Pakistan Vol 2: 5187
The Institution of Engineers, Sri Lanka Vol 2: 6117
Institution of Gas Engineers and Managers Vol 2: 7840
Institution of Mechanical Engineers Vol 2: 7856
Institution of Nuclear Engineers Vol 2: 7859
Institution of Occupational Safety and Health Vol 2: 7872
Institution of Plant Engineers Vol 2: 7882
Institution of Professional Engineers New Zealand Vol 2: 4974
Institution of Structural Engineers Vol 2: 7885
Institutional and Municipal Parking Congress Vol 1: 11787
Instituto Caro y Cuervo Vol 2: 1313
Instituto Cultural Domecq, A.C. Vol 2: 4514
Instituto de Cultura Puertorriquena Vol 1: 11082
Instituto de Investigaciones Electricas Vol 2: 4560
Instituto Geografico Agustin Codazzi Vol 2: 1315
Instituto Interamericano de Cooperacion para la Agricultura Vol 2: 1361
Instituto Interamericano de Direitos Humanos Vol 2: 1365
Instituto Mexicano de Contadores Publicos, A.C. Vol 2: 4517
Instituto Mexicano de Ejecutivos de Finanzas Vol 2: 4520
Instituto Mexicano de Recursos Naturales Renovables Vol 2: 4522
Instituto Mexicano del Seguro Social Vol 2: 4524
Instituto Mexiquense de Cultura Fisica y Deporte Vol 2: 4526
Instituto Nacional de Administracion Publica Vol 2: 4531
Instituto Nacional de Antropologia e Historia Vol 2: 4533
Instituto Nacional de Neurologia y Neurocirugia Vol 2: 4545
Instituto para la Integracion de America Latina y el Caribe Vol 2: 36
Instituto Politecnico Nacional Vol 2: 4547
Instituto Technologico y de Estudios Superiores de Monterrey Vol 2: 4511
Instituto Torcuato di Tella Vol 2: 38
Instituut van Landskapargitekte van Suid Afrika Vol 2: 5577
Instructional Technology Council Vol 1: 11089
Instructional Telecommunications Council Vol 1: 11089
Instrument and Measurement Topical Group Vol 1: 3459
Instrumentation Laboratories Vol 1: 987
Instytut Historii Vol 2: 5334
Insurance and Financial Communicators Association Vol 1: 11091
Insurance Institute of America Vol 1: 15739
Insurance Marketing Communications Association Vol 1: 11094
Intel Corp. Vol 1: 18362, 18363
Intellectual Property Law Association Vol 1: 16176
Intellectual Property Owners Vol 1: 11096
Intellectual Property Owners Association Vol 1: 11096
Inter-American Association of Sanitary and Environmental Engineering Vol 1: 11098
Inter-American Institute for Cooperation on Agriculture Vol 2: 1361
Inter-American Institute of Human Rights Vol 2: 1365

Inter-American Organization for Higher Education Vol 1: 11103
Inter American Press Association Vol 1: 11105
Inter-American Safety Council Vol 1: 11116
Inter-American Society of Cardiology Vol 2: 4550
Inter-Collegiate Sailing Association of North America Vol 1: 11122
Inter-Collegiate Yacht Racing Association of North America Vol 1: 11122
Inter Press Service International Association Vol 2: 3956
Inter-Society Color Council Vol 1: 11126
Interactive Publishing Vol 2: 6374
Interagency Committee for Women in Science and Engineering Vol 1: 21752
Interamerican Accounting Association Vol 1: 11130
Interart Festivalkozpont Vol 2: 3284
Interatom Vol 2: 2325
Intercollegiate Men's Chorus, An International Association of Male Choruses Vol 1: 11132
Intercollegiate Musical Council Vol 1: 11132
Intercollegiate Rowing Association Vol 1: 11134
Intercollegiate Tennis Association Vol 1: 11136
Interconcert Festival Bureau Vol 2: 3284
Interfest: Moscow International Film Festival Vol 2: 5894
InterFuture Vol 1: 11153
Internationaal Filmfestival van Vlaanderen - Gent Vol 2: 885
Internationaal Vocalisten Concours 's-Hertogenbosch Vol 2: 4729
International 5.5 Class Association Vol 2: 6376
International 210 Association Vol 1: 11156
International Academy for Child Brain Development Vol 1: 11159
International Academy of Architecture - Bulgaria Vol 2: 1224
International Academy of Astronautics Vol 2: 2434
International Academy of Aviation and Space Medicine Vol 1: 11161
International Academy of Cytology Vol 2: 2930
International Academy of Olympic Chiropractic Officers Vol 1: 11163
International Academy of Television Arts and Sciences Vol 1: 13862
International Academy of Trial Lawyers Vol 1: 11166
International Administration of Administrative Professionals Razorback Chapter Vol 1: 11168
International Advertising Association Vol 1: 11170
International Advertising Festival Vol 2: 7888
International Agency for the Prevention of Blindness Vol 2: 3557
International Al Jolson Society Vol 1: 11174
The International Alliance, An Association of Executive and Profession - al Women Vol 1: 11176
The International Alliance for Women Vol 1: 11176
International Alliance for Women in Music Vol 1: 11178
International Aluminium Institute Vol 2: 7892
International Amateur-Professional Photoelectric Photometry Vol 1: 11181
International American Albino Association and White Horse Ranch National Foundation Vol 1: 4903
International ANDY Awards Vol 1: 11183
International Animated Film Association Vol 2: 1381
International Animated Film Festival Vol 2: 2439
International Animated Film Society, ASIFA - Hollywood Vol 1: 11185
International Association Auto Theft Investigators Vol 1: 11193
International Association for Bridge and Structural Engineering Vol 2: 6378
International Association for Cereal Science and Technology Vol 2: 727
International Association for Computer Information Systems Vol 1: 11200
International Association for Dental Research Vol 1: 11202
International Association for Dental Research Craniofacial Biology Group Vol 1: 11219
International Association for Energy Economics Vol 1: 11221
International Association for Engineering Geology and the Environment Vol 2: 4792
International Association for Food Protection Vol 1: 11226
International Association for Great Lakes Research Vol 1: 11236
International Association for Housing Science Vol 1: 11242
International Association for Human Resource Information Management Vol 1: 11244
International Association for Impact Assessment Vol 1: 11246
International Association for Insurance Law - Portuguesa Section Vol 2: 5494
International Association for Jazz Education Vol 1: 11248
International Association for Oxygen Therapy Vol 1: 11250
International Association for Pattern Recognition Vol 2: 731
International Association for Penal Law Vol 2: 2441
International Association for Physical Education in Higher Education Vol 2: 899
International Association for Plant Taxonomy Vol 2: 733
International Association for Professional Art Advisors Vol 1: 11252
International Association for Religious Freedom Vol 2: 7894
International Association for Research in Income and Wealth Vol 1: 11254
International Association for Shell and Spatial Structures Vol 2: 6045
International Association for Sports and Leisure Facilities Vol 2: 2933
International Association for Structural Mechanics in Reactor Technology Vol 1: 11256
International Association for the Evaluation of Educational Achievement Vol 2: 4794
International Association for the Exchange of Students for Technical Experience Vol 2: 3637
International Association for the Fantastic in the Arts Vol 1: 11258
International Association for the Prevention of Blindness Vol 2: 3557
International Association for the Scientific Study of Intellectual Disabilities Vol 2: 7896
International Association for the Scientific Study of Mental Deficiency Vol 2: 7896
International Association for the Study of Clays Vol 2: 901
International Association for the Study of Insurance Economics Vol 2: 6383
International Association for the Study of Pain Vol 1: 11261
International Association for Vehicle System Dynamics Vol 2: 1427
International Association for Women of Color Day Vol 1: 11264
International Association of Assessing Officers Vol 1: 11266
International Association of Astacology Vol 1: 11284
International Association of Athletics Federations Vol 2: 4661
International Association of Audio Visual Communicators Vol 1: 11286
International Association of Broadcasting Manufacturers Vol 2: 7898
International Association of Bryologists Vol 1: 11289
International Association of Business Communicators Vol 1: 11294
International Association of Campus Law Enforcement Administrators Vol 1: 11298
International Association of Cancer Registries Vol 2: 2443
International Association of Cancer Victims and Friends Vol 1: 11300
International Association of Cancer Victors and Friends Vol 1: 11300
International Association of Chiefs of Police Vol 1: 11306
International Association of Clothing Designers and Executives Vol 1: 11313
International Association of Conference Center Administrators Vol 1: 11315
International Association of Cooking Professionals Vol 1: 11323
International Association of Correctional Officers Vol 1: 11317
International Association of Counselors and Therapists Vol 1: 11319
International Association of Crime Writers Vol 2: 1393
International Association of Crime Writers - North American Branch Vol 1: 11321
International Association of Culinary Professionals Vol 1: 11323
International Association of Defense Counsel Vol 1: 11332
International Association of Diecutting and Diemaking Vol 1: 11335
International Association of Educators for World Peace - USA Vol 1: 11341
International Association of Emergency Managers Vol 1: 11347
International Association of Empirical Aesthetics - Internationale Gesellschaft Fuer Empirische Aesthetik Vol 2: 2935
International Association of Energy Economists Vol 1: 11221
International Association of Fire Chiefs Vol 1: 11351
International Association of Fire Fighters Vol 1: 11354
International Association of Fish and Wildlife Agencies Vol 1: 11356
International Association of Food Industry Suppliers Vol 1: 11361

International Association of Geodesy Vol 2: 1499
International Association of Gerontology Vol 2: 1186
International Association of Golf Administrators Vol 1: 21923
International Association of Horticultural Producers Vol 2: 4796
International Association of Human-Animal Interaction Organizations Vol 1: 11363
International Association of Hungarian Studies Vol 2: 3291
International Association of Hydraulic Engineering and Research Vol 2: 6048
International Association of Hydrological Sciences Vol 2: 2445
International Association of Industrial Accident Boards and Commissions Vol 1: 11366
International Association of Insurance Counsel Vol 1: 11332
International Association of Jazz Educators Vol 1: 11248
International Association of Lighting Designers Vol 1: 11368
International Association of Music Libraries, Archives and Documentation Centres - United Kingdom and Ireland Vol 2: 7900
International Association of Official Human Rights Agencies Vol 1: 11370
International Association of Orthodontics Vol 1: 11372
International Association of Paediatric Dentistry Vol 2: 2448
International Association of Personnel in Employment Services Vol 1: 11412
International Association of Pet Cemeteries Vol 1: 11374
International Association of Philatelic Experts Vol 2: 3958
International Association of Physicians and Health Care Professionals Vol 1: 11377
International Association of Physicians in AIDS Care Vol 1: 11381
International Association of Pipe Smokers Clubs Vol 1: 11385
International Association of Political Consultants Vol 2: 2939
International Association of Ports and Harbors Vol 2: 4129
International Association of Professional Bureaucrats Vol 1: 11387
International Association of Professional Numismatists Vol 2: 904
International Association of Radiopharmacology Vol 1: 11392
International Association of Registered Financial Consultants Vol 1: 11394
International Association of School Librarianship Vol 1: 11397
International Association of Schools of Social Work Vol 2: 7902
International Association of Sedimentologists Vol 2: 907
International Association of Special Investigation Units Vol 1: 11401
International Association of Sports Museums and Halls of Fame Vol 1: 11403
International Association of Technological University Libraries Vol 2: 7905
International Association of Theatre for Children and Young People Vol 2: 6153
International Association of Theoretical and Applied Limnology Vol 1: 11405
International Association of Traffic and Safety Sciences Vol 2: 4131
International Association of Trichologists Vol 2: 441
International Association of Volcanology and Chemistry of the Earth's Interior Vol 2: 443
International Association of Wall and Ceiling Contractors Vol 1: 5884
International Association of Wildland Fire Vol 1: 11407
International Association of Women in Radio and Television Vol 2: 3559
International Association of Women Police Vol 1: 11409
International Association of Workforce Professionals Vol 1: 11412
International Astronautical Federation Vol 2: 2451
International Atlantic Salmon Federation Vol 1: 6042
International Automobile Federation Vol 2: 2453
International Badminton Federation Vol 2: 4431
International Balzan Foundation Vol 2: 3960
International Banana Club Vol 1: 11415
International Bar Association Vol 2: 7908
International Basketball Federation Vol 2: 6385
International Beefalo Association Vol 1: 1554
International Biennials of Poetry Vol 2: 911
International Bird Strike Committee Vol 2: 4798
International Black Writers and Artists Vol 1: 11419
International Bluegrass Music Association Vol 1: 11422
International Board of Environmental Medicine Vol 1: 11425
International Board on Books for Young People Vol 2: 6388
International Board on Books for Young People - Dutch Section Vol 2: 4800
International Board on Books for Young People (IBBY) - Canadian Section Vol 2: 6388
International Book Project Vol 1: 11427
International Bottled Water Association Vol 1: 11429
International Bowling Federation Vol 2: 5260
International Bowling Museum and Hall of Fame Vol 1: 11431
International Braille Chess Association Vol 2: 6155
International Bridge, Tunnel and Turnpike Association Vol 1: 11433
International Broadcasting Convention Vol 2: 7910
International Buckskin Horse Association Vol 1: 11435
International Builders Exchange Executives Vol 1: 11437
International Bulb Society Vol 1: 11439
International Bureau for Epilepsy Vol 2: 3639
International Bureau for Precast Concrete Vol 2: 913
International Burn Foundation Vol 1: 11441
International Business Council MidAmerica Vol 1: 2057
International Business Machines Corporation Vol 1: 13839
International Camaro Club Vol 1: 11443
International Canoe Federation Vol 2: 6055
International Card Manufacturers Association Vol 1: 11449
International Cartographic Association Vol 2: 4802
The International Cat Association Vol 1: 11452
International Catholic Organization for Cinema and Audiovisual Vol 2: 1101
International Catholic Stewardship Council Vol 1: 11454
International Center for Comparative Criminology Vol 1: 11457
International Center in New York Vol 1: 11459
International Center of Photography Vol 1: 11461
International Centre for Heat and Mass Transfer Vol 2: 6632
International Centre for Human Rights and Democratic Development Vol 1: 11463
International Centre for the Study of the Preservation and Restoration of Cultural Property Vol 2: 3962
International Centre of Graphic Arts Vol 2: 5977
International Centre of Insect Physiology and Ecology Vol 2: 4349
International Chiropractors Association Vol 1: 11465
International Christian Studies Association Vol 1: 11468
International Circulation Managers Association Vol 1: 16338
International City/County Management Association Vol 1: 11471
International Civil Aviation Organization Vol 1: 11482
International Civil Defence Organization Vol 2: 6392
International Clarinet Association Vol 1: 11484
International Clarinet Society Vol 1: 11484
International Classical Guitar Competition Vol 2: 915
International College of Angiology Vol 1: 11487
International Colour Association Vol 2: 2941
International Commission for Optics Vol 2: 3790, 6057
International Commission for the Eriksson Prize Fund Vol 2: 6158
International Commission for the Preservation of Islamic Cultural Heri - tage (ICPICH) Vol 2: 6645
International Commission of Agricultural Engineering Vol 2: 2943
International Commission of Jurists - Canadian Section Vol 1: 11489
International Commission on Physics Education Vol 2: 6160
International Commission on Radiation Units and Measurements Vol 1: 11491
International Committee for Shell Structures Vol 2: 6045
International Committee of Sports for the Deaf/DEAFLYMPICS Vol 1: 11493
International Committee of Systematic Bacteriology Vol 2: 454
International Committee of the Red Cross Vol 2: 1228, 6394
International Communications Industries Association Vol 1: 11497
International Community Corrections Association Vol 1: 11499

Organization Index

International Competition of Ceramic Arts: "Premio Faenza" Vol 2: 3965
International Confederation for Thermal Analysis Vol 2: 5584
International Confederation for Thermal Analysis and Calorimetry Vol 2: 5584
International Confederation of Accordionists Vol 2: 735
International Confederation of Art Dealers Vol 2: 917
International Confederation of Societies of Authors and Composers Vol 2: 2459
International Conference of Building Officials Vol 1: 11501
International Conference of Funeral Service Examining Boards Vol 1: 11505
International Consortium of Investigative Journalists Vol 1: 11507
International Consultative Research Group on Rapeseed Vol 2: 2461
International Cost Engineering Council Vol 2: 446
International Council for Adult Education Vol 2: 9299
International Council for Bird Preservation Vol 2: 6873
International Council for Canadian Studies Vol 1: 11509
International Council for Open and Distance Education Vol 2: 5127
International Council for Research and Innovation in Building and Construction Vol 2: 4804
International Council for Small Business Vol 1: 11512
International Council for the Improvement of Reading Vol 1: 11849
International Council of Associations for Science Education Vol 2: 7912
International Council of Ballroom Dancing Vol 2: 9246
International Council of Christians and Jews Vol 2: 2945
International Council of Environmental Law Vol 2: 2947
International Council of Graphic Design Associations Vol 2: 919
International Council of Shopping Centers Vol 1: 11514
International Council of Societies of Industrial Design Vol 2: 2619
International Council of Sport and Physical Education Vol 2: 2950
International Council of Sport Science and Physical Education Vol 2: 2950
International Council of the French Language Vol 2: 2463
International Council of the National Academy of Television Arts and Sciences Vol 1: 11518
International Council on Education for Teaching Vol 1: 11520
International Council on Hotel, Restaurant and Institutional Education Vol 1: 11522
International Council on Monuments and Sites Vol 2: 2465
International Cryogenic Engineering Committee Vol 2: 2953
International Cryogenic Materials Conference Vol 1: 11531
International Customer Service Association Vol 1: 11533
International Dairy Foods Association Vol 1: 2103
International Dairy Foods Association Vol 1: 11535
International Dance Teachers' Association Vol 2: 7914
International Desalination Association Vol 1: 11537
International Diabetes Federation Vol 2: 922
International Documentary Association Vol 1: 11540
International Documentary Film Festival - Amsterdam Vol 2: 4806
International Double Reed Society Vol 1: 11543
International Downtown Association Vol 1: 11546
International Downtown Executive Association Vol 1: 11546
International Dyslexia Association Vol 1: 11548
International Ecology Institute Vol 2: 2955
The International Economy Vol 1: 11550
International Egg Commission Vol 2: 7919
International Electrical Testing Association Vol 1: 11552
International Embryo Transfer Society Vol 1: 11554
International Executive Service Corps Vol 1: 11557
International Exhibition Logistics Associates Vol 2: 6397
International Exhibitors Association Vol 1: 20146
International Facility Management Association Vol 1: 11559
International Family Recreation Association Vol 1: 11573
International Fan Club Organization Vol 1: 11575
International Federation for Housing and Planning Vol 2: 4808
International Federation for Information Processing Vol 2: 737
International Federation for the Roofing Trade Vol 2: 2958
International Federation for Theatre Research Vol 2: 7921
International Federation of Air Line Pilots Associations Vol 2: 7923
International Federation of Air Traffic Controllers' Associations Vol 1: 11577
International Federation of Airworthiness Vol 2: 7927
International Federation of Asian and Western Pacific Contractors' Associations Vol 2: 5262
International Federation of Audit Bureaux of Circulations Vol 2: 5587
International Federation of Automotive Engineering Societies Vol 2: 7931
International Federation of Beekeepers' Associations Vol 2: 3967
International Federation of Biomedical Laboratory Science Vol 1: 11579
International Federation of Bodybuilders Vol 1: 11590
International Federation of Business and Professional Women Vol 2: 7933
International Federation of Catholic Medical Associations Vol 2: 9305
International Federation of Clinical Neurophysiology Vol 2: 7935
International Federation of Consulting Engineers Vol 2: 6399
International Federation of Disabled Working and Civilian Handicaped Vol 2: 2960
International Federation of Essential Oils and Aroma Trades Vol 2: 7938
International Federation of Festival Organizations Vol 1: 11592
International Federation of Hydrographic Societies Vol 2: 7940
International Federation of Interior Architects/Designers Vol 2: 5589
International Federation of Journalists Vol 2: 924
International Federation of Landscape Architects Vol 2: 2467, 2608
International Federation of Leather Guilds Vol 1: 11596
International Federation of Library Associations and Institutions Vol 2: 4811
International Federation of Manufacturers and Converters of Pressure-S - ensitive and Heatseals on Paper and Other Base Materials Vol 2: 4948
International Federation of Netball Associations Vol 2: 7943
International Federation of Operational Research Societies Vol 1: 11598
International Federation of Ophthalmological Societies Vol 1: 11601
International Federation of Oto-Rhino-Laryngological Societies Vol 2: 4819
International Federation of Persons with Physical Disabilities Vol 2: 2960
International Federation of Purchasing and Supply Management Vol 2: 742
International Federation of Shipmasters' Associations Vol 2: 7945
International Federation of Societies for Electroencephalography and Clinical Neurophysiology Vol 2: 7935
International Federation of Societies of Cosmetic Chemists Vol 2: 7947
International Federation of Sound Hunters Vol 2: 6401
International Federation of Sports Medicine Vol 2: 1409
International Federation of Standards Users Vol 2: 6403
International Federation of the Phonographic Industry - Finland Vol 2: 1630
International Federation of the Phonographic Industry - Hong Kong Vol 2: 5228
International Federation of Translators Vol 1: 11605
International Federation of University Women - Switzerland Vol 2: 6405
International Federation of Vexillological Associations Vol 1: 11609
International Fertiliser Society - England Vol 2: 7950
International Festival of Documentary and Short Film - Bilbao Vol 2: 6060
International Festival of Documentary Films on Parks Vol 2: 3969
International Festival of Films for TV Vol 1: 6238
International Festival of Films on Art Vol 1: 11612
International Festival of Maritime and Exploration Films Vol 2: 2469
International Festival of Mountain and Environment Films Vol 2: 6407
International Festival of Red Cross and Health Films Vol 2: 1227

International Film Festival Mannheim - Heidelberg Vol 2: 2962
International Film Festival on Nature, Man and His Environment Vol 2: 3971
International Finn Association Vol 2: 2471
International Fire Buff Associates Vol 1: 11615
International Fire Photographers Association Vol 1: 11618
International Fire Service Training Association Vol 1: 11622
International Fiscal Association Vol 2: 4822
International Flanders Film Festival - Ghent Vol 2: 885
International Flat Earth Research Society Vol 1: 11624
International Flat Earth Research Society Vol 1: 11624
International Flavors and Fragrances, Inc. Vol 1: 19095
International Fluid Power Society Vol 1: 11626
International Foodservice Manufacturer Association Vol 1: 11630
International Formalwear Association Vol 1: 11632
International Formula Council Vol 1: 757
International Foundation Mozarteum Vol 2: 745
International Foundation "St. Cyril and Methodius" Vol 2: 1237
International Franchise Association Vol 1: 11635
International Fritz Kreisler Competition Vol 2: 751
International Furnishings and Design Association Vol 1: 11640
International Game Fish Association Vol 1: 11644
International Gas Turbine Institute Vol 1: 4545
International Gay and Lesbian Human Rights Commission Vol 1: 11646
International Geographic Information Foundation Vol 1: 5219
International Geographical Union Vol 1: 11648
International Geographical Union - Commission on Geographical Education - Commission on Geographical Education Vol 2: 1632
International Glaciological Society Vol 2: 7952
International Golf Federation Vol 1: 11650
International Good Neighbor Council Vol 1: 11653
International Gospel Music Hall of Fame Vol 1: 10102
International Graphoanalysis Society Vol 1: 11655
International Guild of Artists Vol 2: 7956
International Guild of Candle Artisans Vol 1: 11657
International Guild of Hair Removal Specialists Vol 1: 11662
International Handball Federation Vol 2: 6409
International Handgun Metallic Silhouette Association Vol 1: 11669
International Harp Contest in Israel Vol 2: 3737
International Hearing Society Vol 1: 11671
International Henryk Wieniawski Competitions Vol 2: 5309
International Horn Society Vol 1: 11673
International Hot Rod Association Vol 1: 11675
International Hotel and Restaurant Association Vol 2: 2475
International House of Poetry Vol 2: 912
International House - World Trade Center Vol 1: 21961
International Hydrofoil Society Vol 1: 11681
International Hydrographic Bureau Vol 2: 4664
International Ice Hockey Federation Vol 2: 6412
International Institute for Applied Systems Analysis Vol 2: 753
International Institute for Promotion and Prestige Vol 2: 6414
International Institute for the Science of Sintering Vol 2: 5931
International Institute of Fisheries Economics and Trade Vol 1: 11683
International Institute of Flint Vol 1: 11687
International Institute of Human Rights Vol 2: 2479
International Institute of Humanitarian Law Vol 2: 3973
International Institute of Integral Human Sciences Vol 1: 11689
International Institute of Public Finance Vol 2: 2964
International Institute of Refrigeration Vol 2: 2481
International Institute of Space Law Vol 2: 2485
International Institute of Welding Vol 2: 2488
International Institute of Wisconsin Vol 1: 11691
International Isotope Society Vol 1: 11693
International Jazz Federation Vol 2: 3122
International Jeunesses Musicales Competition Vol 2: 5935
International Judges Association Vol 1: 20811
International Judo Federation Vol 2: 5497
International Kart Federation Vol 1: 11696
International Kolping Society Vol 2: 2966
International Korfball Federation Vol 2: 4824
International Labor Communications Association, AFL-CIO/CLC Vol 1: 11698
International Labor History Association Vol 1: 11701
International Labor Press Association Vol 1: 11698
International Labor Rights Fund Vol 1: 11703
International Labour Organization Vol 2: 6416
International Lace Biennial, Contemporary Art Vol 2: 926
International Lacrosse Federation Vol 1: 11705
International Lactation Consultant Association Vol 1: 11707
International Landslide Research Group Vol 1: 11710
International Laser Display Association Vol 1: 11712
International Law Students Association Vol 1: 4464, 11714
International League of Antiquarian Booksellers Vol 1: 11717
International League of Associations for Rheumatology Vol 2: 449
International League of Women Composers Vol 1: 11178
International Legal Fraternity Phi Delta Phi Vol 1: 11719
International Life Sciences Institute - North America Vol 1: 10935
International Life Sciences Institute - North America Vol 1: 11724
International Lightning Class Association Vol 1: 11726
International Lilac Society Vol 1: 11729
International Linear Algebra Society Vol 1: 11734
International Luge Federation Vol 2: 2968
International Magnesium Association Vol 1: 11736
International Map Collectors' Society Vol 2: 7958
International Martial Arts Federation Vol 2: 4133
International Masonry Institute Vol 1: 11741
International Mathematical Union Vol 1: 11743
International Measurement Confederation Vol 2: 3293
International Medical Consultants Vol 1: 9236
International Menopause Society Vol 2: 7961
International Metallographic Society Vol 1: 5186
International Microelectronics and Packaging Society Vol 1: 11746
International Mondiale de la Sante - Centre International de Recherche sur le Cancer Vol 2: 6568
International Motor Press Association Vol 1: 11751
International Motor Sports Association Vol 1: 11753
International Motorcycle Federation Vol 2: 6418
International Motorsports Hall of Fame Vol 1: 11759
International Music and Media Centre Vol 2: 757
International Music Competition of the ARD Vol 2: 2970
International Music Council Vol 2: 2605, 5967
International Musical Contest Dr. Luis Sigall Competition Vol 2: 1261
International Narcotic Enforcement Officers Association Vol 1: 11761
International Naturist Federation Vol 2: 928
International Navigation Association - Belgium Vol 2: 929
International Navigation Association - USA Vol 1: 11768
International Newspaper Marketing Association Vol 1: 9163
International Newspaper Marketing Association Vol 1: 11770
International Newspaper Promotion Association Vol 1: 11770
International Nickel Company of Canada Vol 1: 7836
International Old Lacers, Inc. Vol 1: 11772
International Olympic Committee Vol 2: 6424
International Optometric and Optic League Vol 1: 21884
International Order of E.A.R.S. Vol 1: 11774
International Organ Festival at St. Albans Vol 2: 7963
International Organ Festival Society Vol 2: 7963

International Organisation of Vine and Wine Vol 2: 2498
International Organization for Chemical Sciences in Development Vol 1: 11778
International Organization for Succulent Plant Study Vol 2: 6429
International Organization for the Elimination of All Forms of Racial Discrimination Vol 2: 6431
International Organization for the Study of European Ideas Vol 2: 6062
International Organization of Plant Biosystematists Vol 1: 11780
International Organization of Supreme Audit Institutions Vol 2: 760
International Orienteering Federation Vol 2: 1635
International Ozone Association Vol 1: 11782
International Parking Institute Vol 1: 11787
International Partnership for Service-Learning and Leadership Vol 1: 11789
International Paulo Cello Competition Vol 2: 1637
International Peace Academy Vol 1: 11794
International Peace Bureau Vol 2: 6433
International Pharmaceutical Federation Vol 2: 4827
International Pharmaceutical Students' Federation Vol 2: 4835
International Planned Parenthood Federation, Western Hemisphere Region Vol 1: 11796
International Platform Association Vol 1: 11798
International Police Association Vol 2: 7967
International Polka Association Vol 1: 11817
International Potash Institute Vol 2: 6435
International Precious Metals Institute Vol 1: 11821
International Press Institute Vol 2: 763
International Print Biennale Vol 2: 5313
International Print Triennial Society - Krakow Vol 2: 5313
International Professional Security Association - England Vol 2: 7970
International Professional Surfers Vol 1: 5870
International Psychohistorical Association Vol 1: 11825
International Public Management Association for Human Resources Vol 1: 11831
International Public Relations Association Vol 2: 7972
International Publishing Management Association Vol 1: 11835
International Quorum of Film and Video Producers Vol 2: 6437
International Radiation Protection Association Vol 2: 2500
International Radio and Television Society Vol 1: 11846
International Radio and Television Society Foundation Vol 1: 11846
International Reading Association Vol 1: 11849
International Readings at Harbourfront Centre Vol 1: 11881
International Real Estate Federation - France Vol 2: 2502
International Recording Media Association Vol 1: 11883
International Recreation Association Vol 1: 21931
International Religious Liberty Association Vol 1: 11885
International Rescue Committee - USA Vol 1: 11887
International Research Group on Wood Preservation Vol 2: 6162
International Road Federation Vol 1: 11889
International Road Safety Organization Vol 2: 5399
International Road Transport Union Vol 2: 6439
International Robert Schumann Competition Vol 2: 2972
International Save the Pun Foundation Vol 1: 11891
International Sculpture Center Vol 1: 11893
International Seaweed Association Vol 2: 1189
International Section of the National Council on Family Relations Vol 1: 11898
International Service for Human Rights - Switzerland Vol 2: 6441
International Sheep Dog Society Vol 2: 7975
International Short Film Festival, Oberhausen Vol 2: 2975
International Shuffleboard Association Vol 1: 11900
International Side-Saddle Organization Vol 1: 11902
International Sign Association Vol 1: 11904
International Silo Association Vol 1: 11906
International Skating Union Vol 2: 6443
International Ski Federation Vol 2: 6446
International Slurry Surfacing Association Vol 1: 11909
International Snowmobile Manufacturers Association Vol 1: 11911
International Soap Box Derby Vol 1: 11913
International Social Science Council Vol 2: 2504
International Social Security Association Vol 2: 6448
International Society for Astrological Research Vol 1: 11915
International Society for Augmentative and Alternative Communication Vol 1: 11917
International Society for Burn Injuries Vol 1: 11923
International Society for Clinical Laboratory Technology Vol 1: 1093
International Society for Contemporary Music - Netherlands Vol 2: 4837
International Society for Developmental Psychobiology Vol 1: 11925
International Society for Education through Art Vol 1: 11928
International Society for Engineering Education Vol 2: 6450
International Society for Heart and Lung Transplantation Vol 1: 11932
International Society for Heart Transplantation Vol 1: 11932
International Society for Human and Animal Mycology Vol 2: 1639
International Society for Individual Liberty Vol 1: 11934
International Society for Iranian Studies Vol 1: 11936
International Society for Military Law and Law of War Vol 2: 931
International Society for Neurochemistry Vol 2: 1501
International Society for Performance Improvement Vol 1: 11938
International Society for Pharmaceutical Engineering Vol 1: 11948
International Society for Philosophical Enquiry Vol 1: 11953
International Society for Photogrammetry and Remote Sensing Vol 2: 6635
International Society for Plant Pathology Vol 2: 4998
International Society for Rock Mechanics Vol 2: 5401
International Society for Soil Mechanics and Geotechnical Engineering Vol 2: 7978
International Society for the Arts, Sciences and Technology Vol 1: 11956
International Society for the History of Pharmacy Vol 2: 2978
International Society for the Study of Human Ideas on Ultimate Reality and Meaning - Institute for URAM Vol 1: 11961
International Society for Traumatic Stress Studies Vol 1: 11964
International Society for Trenchless Technology Vol 2: 7980
International Society for Vehicle Preservation Vol 1: 11969
International Society of Aerosols in Medicine Vol 1: 956
International Society of Air Safety Investigators Vol 1: 11971
International Society of Applied Intelligence Vol 1: 11973
International Society of Appraisers Vol 1: 11975
International Society of Biometeorology Vol 1: 11977
International Society of Blood Transfusion Vol 2: 4839
International Society of Certified Electronics Technicians Vol 1: 11981
International Society of Chemical Ecology Vol 1: 11985
International Society of Chemotherapy Vol 2: 7982
International Society of Crime Prevention Practitioners Vol 1: 6583
International Society of Dermatology Vol 1: 11989
International Society of Electrocardiology Vol 2: 7984
International Society of Electrochemistry Vol 2: 6452
International Society of Explosives Engineers Vol 1: 11991
International Society of Logistics Vol 1: 11994
International Society of Meeting Planners Vol 1: 12004
International Society of Paediatric Oncology Vol 2: 7986
International Society of Parametric Analysts Vol 1: 12006
International Society of Phonetic Sciences Vol 1: 12012
International Society of Political Psychology Vol 1: 12016
International Society of Psychiatric Mental Health Nurses Vol 1: 12022
International Society of Psychology of Handwriting Vol 2: 3975
International Society of Psychoneuroendocrinology Vol 2: 2981, 2982
International Society of Reliabilty Engineers Vol 1: 19289
International Society of Sugar Cane Technologists Vol 2: 4457

International Society of Surgery Vol 2: 6462
International Society of Travel and Tourism Educators Vol 1: 12024
International Society of Tropical Dermatology Vol 1: 11989
International Society of Typographic Designers Vol 2: 7989
International Society of Weekly Newspaper Editors Vol 1: 12026
International Society of Weighing and Measurement Vol 1: 12029
International Society on Toxinology Vol 2: 2983
International Sociological Association Vol 2: 6064
International Softball Congress Vol 1: 12036
International Softball League Vol 1: 12036
International Solar Energy Society Vol 2: 2985
International Songwriters' Association - Ireland Vol 2: 3642
International Sport Film Festival of Palermo Vol 2: 3977
International Sport Press Association Vol 2: 3296
International Statistical Institute Vol 2: 4841
International Steel Guitar Convention Vol 1: 12042
International Stoke Mandeville Games Federation Vol 2: 7991
International Stoke Mandeville Wheelchair Sports Federation Vol 2: 7991
International Studies Association Vol 1: 12044
International Sunfish Class Association Vol 1: 12049
International Sunflower Association Vol 2: 2506
International Surfing Association Vol 1: 12051
International Swimming Hall of Fame Vol 1: 12053
International Table Tennis Federation Vol 2: 6466
International Tape/Disc Association Vol 1: 11883
International Tchaikovsky Competition Vol 2: 5896
International Technology Education Association Vol 1: 12062
International Telephone and Telegraph Corporation Vol 1: 10867
International Television Association Vol 2: 8010
International Television Festival of Monte Carlo Vol 2: 1112, 4667
International Tennis Federation Vol 2: 7993
International Tennis Hall of Fame Vol 1: 12073
International THEOS Foundation Vol 1: 12079
International Thermographers Association Vol 1: 12081
International Ticketing Association Vol 1: 12083
International TourFilm Festival Vol 2: 3979
International Track and Field Coaches Association Vol 1: 12088
International Trade Council Vol 1: 12090
International Trade Mart Vol 1: 21961
International Transactional Analysis Association Vol 1: 12092
International Trumpet Guild Vol 1: 12094
International Tube Association Vol 2: 7997
International Unicycling Federation Vol 1: 12100
International Union Against Cancer Vol 2: 6468
International Union for Physical and Engineering Sciences in Medicine Vol 2: 6165
International Union for Quaternary Research Vol 2: 3644
International Union for Vacuum Science, Technique and Applications Vol 2: 7999
International Union of Air Pollution Prevention and Environmental Protection Associations Vol 2: 8001
International Union of Architects Vol 2: 2509, 2607
International Union of Crystallography Vol 2: 8008
International Union of Forest Research Organizations Vol 2: 765
International Union of Microbiological Societies Vol 2: 451
International Union of Pure and Applied Physics - USA Vol 1: 12102
International Union of Radio Science Vol 2: 933
International Union of Shoe Industry Technicians Vol 2: 6066
International Union of Students Vol 2: 1431
International Veteran Boxers Association Vol 1: 12111
International Video Week (Biennial of Moving Images) Vol 2: 6475
International Video Week of Geneva (Semaine Internationale de Video de Geneve) Vol 2: 6475
International Visitors Council - Columbus Vol 1: 12123
International Visual Communication Association Vol 2: 8010
International Water Association Vol 2: 8012
International Water Resources Association Vol 1: 12125
International Weightlifting Federation Vol 2: 3298
International Wheat Gluten Association Vol 1: 12130
International Wild Waterfowl Association Vol 1: 12132
International Wildlife Film Festival and Media Center Vol 1: 12140
International Wine and Food Society Vol 2: 8014
International Wire and Machinery Association Vol 2: 8016
International Wizard of Oz Club Vol 1: 12142
International Women's Film Festival Vol 2: 2515
International Women's Media Foundation Vol 1: 12144
International Wood Products Association Vol 1: 12147
International World Games Association Vol 2: 4843
International Yacht Racing Union Vol 1: 20789
International Youth Hostel Federation Vol 2: 8018
International Youth Library Vol 2: 2989
Internationale Carl Nielsen Musik Konkurrencer Vol 2: 1506
Internationale Filmfestspiele Berlin Vol 2: 2669
Internationale Filmwoche Mannheim Vol 2: 2962
Internationale Foderation des Dachdeckerhandwerks Vol 2: 2958
Internationale Gesellschaft fur die Geschichte der Pharmazie Vol 2: 2978
Internationale Gesellschaft fur Felsmechanik Vol 2: 5401
Internationale Gesellschaft fur Ingenieurpadagogik Vol 2: 6450
Internationale Joseph A. Schumpeter Gesellschaft Vol 2: 3053
Internationale Jugendbibliothek Vol 2: 2989
Internationale Kolpingwerk Vol 2: 2966
Internationale Kurzfilmtage Oberhausen Vol 2: 2975
Internationale Liberale Vol 2: 8056
Internationale Messtechnische Konfoderation Vol 2: 3293
Internationale Organisation fur Sukkulentenforschung Vol 2: 6429
Internationale Orientierungslauf Foderation Vol 2: 1635
Internationale Paneuropa Union Vol 2: 3045
Internationale Robert-Schumann-Wettbewerbe Vol 2: 2972
Internationale Stiftung Mozarteum Vol 2: 745
Internationale Vereinigung fur Bruckenbau und Hochbau Vol 2: 6378
Internationale Vereinigung Sport- und Freizeiteinrichtungen Vol 2: 2933
Internationalen Rat der Christen und Juden Vol 2: 2945
Internationaler Draht- und Maschinenverband Vol 2: 8016
Internationaler Johann-Sebastien-Bach-Wettbewerb Vol 2: 2656
Internationaler Musikwettbeweb - Genf Vol 2: 6309
Internationaler Musikwettbewerb ARD Vol 2: 2970
Internationaler Pianistenwettbewerb Busoni Vol 2: 3874
Internationaler Verband des Erwerbsgartenbaues Vol 2: 4796
Internationaler Verband Forstlicher Forschungsanstalten Vol 2: 765
Internationaler Violinwettbewerb Koln Vol 2: 2694, 2696
Internationales Festival der Filmhochschulen Munchen Vol 2: 2766
Internationales Filmwochenende Wurzburg Vol 2: 2991
Internationales Musikzentrum Wien Vol 2: 757
Internationales Trickfilm Festival Stuttgart Vol 2: 3106
Internet Alliance Vol 1: 12149
Interstate Mining Compact Commission Vol 1: 12155
Interstate Printers and Publishers Vol 1: 16403
Inventors Clubs of America Vol 1: 12158
Inventors Workshop International Education Foundation/Entrepreneurs Workshop Vol 1: 12165
Investigative Reporters and Editors Vol 1: 12169
Investment Dealers Association of Canada Vol 1: 12172
Investment Education Institute Vol 1: 12174
IODE - Municipal Chapter of Toronto Vol 1: 12176

IONS - Institute of Noetic Sciences Vol 1: 12178
Iowa Bankers Association Vol 1: 12180
Iowa Horse Industry Council Vol 1: 12182
Iowa Hospice Organization Vol 1: 12184
Iowa League of Cities Vol 1: 12186
Iowa Poetry Association Vol 1: 15001
Iowa School of Letters Vol 1: 12188
Iqbal Academy Pakistan Vol 2: 5189
Iranian Research Organization for Science and Technology Vol 2: 3609
IREM Foundation Vol 1: 11038
Irino Prize Foundation Vol 2: 4135
Irish Amateur Rowing Union Vol 2: 3646
Irish American Cultural Institute Vol 2: 3695
Irish American Cultural Institute Vol 1: 12193
Irish Arts Council Vol 2: 3625
Irish Astronomical Association Vol 2: 3648
Irish Dairy Board Vol 2: 3694
Irish Defence Forces Vol 2: 3651
Irish Farm Centre Vol 2: 3655
Irish Handball Council Vol 2: 3657
Irish Hotels Federation Vol 2: 3659
Irish Institute of Purchasing and Materials Management Vol 2: 3661
Irish Lawn Tennis Association Vol 2: 3711
Irish Master Farriers Association Vol 2: 3694
Irish Security Industry Association Vol 2: 3663
The Irish Times Vol 2: 3665
Irish United Nations Veterans Association Vol 2: 3667
Irish Youth Foundation Vol 2: 3669
Iron and Steel Institution of Japan Vol 2: 4137
Iron and Steel Society of the American Institute of Mining, Metallurgical and Petroleum Engineers Vol 1: 5401
Irrigation Association Vol 1: 12203
Irwin Company; Richard D. Vol 1: 3025
ISA - Instrumentation, Systems, and Automation Society Vol 1: 12209
Islamic Capitals Organization Vol 2: 5927
Islamic Development Bank Vol 2: 5919
Islamic Organization for Medical Sciences Vol 2: 4375
Islamic Propagation Centre Vol 1: 12227
Islamic Research Foundation International Vol 1: 12229
Island Resources Foundation Vol 1: 12233
Iso and Bizzarrini Owners Club Vol 1: 12235
Israel Association of Electronics and Information Industries Vol 2: 3739
Israel Democracy Institute Vol 2: 3741
Israel Humanitarian Foundation Vol 1: 12237
Israel Museum Vol 2: 3743
Israel Society for Biochemistry and Molecular Biology Vol 2: 3756
Israel Translators Association Vol 2: 3758
Israel Youth Hostels Association Vol 2: 3760
Israeli Society for Theoretical and Mathematical Biology Vol 2: 3762
The Issue Exchange Vol 1: 12239
Issue Management Council Vol 1: 12239
Istanbul Foundation for Culture and Arts Vol 2: 6641
Istanbul Kultur ve Sanat Vakfi Vol 2: 6641
Istel Ltd Vol 2: 8328
Istituto Internazionale delle Comunicazioni Vol 2: 3981
Istituto Italiano della Saldatura Vol 2: 4013
Istituto Italo-Latino Americano Vol 2: 3983
Istituto Nazionale di Studi Romani Vol 2: 3985
Istituto Paolo VI: Centro Internazionale di Studi e Documentazione Vol 2: 3987
Istituto Paolo VI: International Centre for Study and Documentation Vol 2: 3987
Istituto Papirologico Girolamo Vitelli Vol 2: 3989
Istituto per la Cooperazione Universitaria Vol 2: 3954
Italian Association for Cancer Research Vol 2: 7454
Italian Association for Metallurgy Vol 2: 3991
Italian Charities of America Vol 1: 12241
Italian Chemical Society Vol 2: 3999
Italian Cultural Institute of New York Vol 1: 12244
Italian Electrical and Electronics Association Vol 2: 4004
Italian Folk Art Federation of America Vol 1: 12246
Italian Historical Society of America Vol 1: 12248
Italian Institute of Culture for the United Kingdom Vol 2: 8971
Italian Institute of Welding Vol 2: 4013
Italian Mathematical Union Vol 2: 4015
Italian Ministry of Education, University and Research Vol 2: 4019
Italian PEN Club Vol 2: 4021
Italian Society of Ecology Vol 2: 4023
Italian Sons and Daughters of America Vol 1: 12251
Italian Wine and Food Institute Vol 1: 12256
Italic Institute of America Vol 1: 12258
Italic Studies Institute Vol 1: 12258
Italy - Ministry for Tourism and Performing Arts Vol 2: 3929, 3930
Italy - Ministry of Education Vol 2: 3875
Italy - the President of the Council of Ministers Vol 2: 3875
Italy-America Chamber of Commerce Vol 1: 12260
Italy Ministry for Culture and the Environment Vol 2: 4025
ITC-Foundation Vol 2: 6640
Itech Vol 1: 21179
ITI Vol 2: 1238
Itinerances: Ales Film Festival Vol 2: 2517
Ittleson Foundation Vol 1: 3621
ITV Network Limited Vol 2: 8021
IUPAP Commission C2: Sun Amco Vol 1: 12109
Ivy Society; Robert H. Vol 1: 17381
Izaak Walton League of America Vol 1: 12262
J-Lab: The Institute for Interactive Journalism Vol 1: 12272
Jackie Robinson Foundation Vol 1: 12274
Jackson County Literacy Council Vol 1: 12277
Jackson State University - Bureau of Business and Economic Research Vol 1: 12279
Jaen International Piano Competition Vol 2: 6068
Jaffe Family Foundation Vol 1: 615
Jaguar Clubs of North America Vol 1: 12281
Jahnsson Foundation; Yrjo Vol 2: 1641
Jahnssonin Saatio; Yrjo Vol 2: 1641
Jamaica Cancer Society Vol 2: 4078
Jamaica Exporters Association Vol 2: 4080
Jamaica Hotel and Tourist Association Vol 2: 4082
James Beard Foundation Vol 1: 12284
James Cook University of North Queensland Vol 2: 370
James E. Guinn Former Student Alliance Vol 1: 12291
James Fine Arts Committee; Lucile Vol 1: 9703
James Joyce Society of Southern Colorado Vol 1: 12293
Jamnalal Bajaj Foundation Vol 2: 3561
Jane Addams Peace Association Vol 1: 12295
Jane Austen Society of North America Vol 1: 12297
Janssen-Ortho Inc. Vol 1: 17372
Janssen Research Council Vol 1: 8200
Japan Academy Vol 2: 4152
Japan America Society Vol 1: 12299
Japan-America Society of Georgia Vol 1: 12301
Japan Art Academy Vol 2: 4156
Japan Art Association Vol 2: 4158
Japan Association of Cultural Film Producers Vol 2: 4311
Japan Construction Mechanization Association Vol 2: 4160
Japan Craft Beer Association Vol 2: 4162
Japan Design Foundation Vol 2: 4164
Japan External Trade Organisation Vol 2: 8897
Japan Federation of Printing Industries Vol 2: 4167
Japan Foundation Vol 2: 4169
Japan Golf Tour Vol 1: 21923
Japan Industrial Design Promotion Organization Vol 2: 4173
Japan International League of Artists Vol 2: 4175
Japan Ministry of Education, Culture, Sports, Science and Technology Vol 2: 4177
Japan National Committee for UICC Vol 2: 6474
Japan Newspaper Publishers and Editors Association Vol 2: 4183
Japan Office of the Prime Minister Vol 2: 4187
Japan Prize Preparatory Foundation Vol 2: 4293
Japan Science and Technology Agency Vol 2: 4196
Japan Society Vol 1: 12303
Japan Society for Analytical Chemistry Vol 2: 4198
Japan Society for the Promotion of Science Vol 2: 3127, 4200
Japan Society of Mechanical Engineers Vol 2: 4202
Japanese Advertising Agencies' Association Vol 2: 4204
Japanese American Citizens League Vol 1: 12305
Japanese Biochemical Society Vol 2: 4206
Japanese Shipbuilding Industry Vol 2: 4367
Japanese Society of Animal Science Vol 2: 4208
Japanese Society of Applied Entomology and Zoology Vol 2: 4210
Japanese Society of Hematology Vol 2: 4213
Japanese Society of Sericultural Science - National Institute of Sericultural and Entomological Science Vol 2: 4216
Japanese Society of Snow and Ice Vol 2: 4219
Japanese Society of Soil Science and Plant Nutrition Vol 2: 4224
Japanese Society of Tribologists Vol 2: 4228

Japanese Society of Veterinary Science Vol 2: 4230
Japanese Society of Zootechnical Science Vol 2: 4208
Jazz Arts Music Society of Palm Beach Vol 1: 12307
Jazz World Database Vol 1: 12309
Jean Pierre Verlanger Vol 2: 2519
Jeantet de Medecine; Fondation Louis Vol 2: 6477
Jefferson County Historical Commission Vol 1: 12311
Jellinek Memorial Fund Vol 1: 12313
JEMS Communications Vol 1: 14217
Jenemann Foundation; Hans R. Vol 2: 2794
Jeppesen Sanderson, Inc. Vol 1: 13919
Jerome Foundation Vol 1: 17398
Jerusalem International Book Fair Vol 2: 3764
Jerusalem Municipality Vol 2: 3766
Jerwood Charity Vol 2: 8023
Jesuit Secondary Education Association Vol 1: 12315
jet2web Internet Vol 2: 703
Jeunesses Musicales of Austria Vol 2: 705
Jewelers Security Alliance Vol 1: 12317
Jewish Book Council Vol 1: 12320
Jewish Book Council/JWB (Jewish Welfare Board) Vol 1: 12320
Jewish Community Center of Cleveland Vol 1: 10225
Jewish Community Center Theatre - Eugene S. and Blanche R. Halle Theatre Vol 1: 12334
Jewish Community Centers Association Vol 1: 12337
Jewish Deaf Congress Vol 1: 12343
Jewish Educators Assembly Vol 1: 12348
Jewish Family and Children's Services of San Francisco, the Peninsula, Marin and Sonoma Counties Vol 1: 12350
Jewish Federation of Metropolitan Detroit Vol 1: 12352
Jewish Foundation for Christian Resevers/ ADL Vol 1: 4980
Jewish Foundation for the Righteous Vol 1: 12354
Jewish Genealogical Society of Greater Philadelphia Vol 1: 12356
Jewish Historical Society of England Vol 2: 8025
Jewish Institute for National Security Affairs Vol 1: 12358
Jewish Labor Committee Vol 1: 12360
The Jewish Museum Vol 1: 12362
Jewish National Fund Vol 1: 12364
Jewish Peace Fellowship Vol 1: 12369
Jewish Reconstructionist Federation Vol 1: 12371
Jewish Reconstructionist Foundation Vol 1: 12371
Jewish Theological Seminary Vol 1: 12373
Jewish War Veterans of the U.S.A. Vol 1: 12385
Jewish War Veterans of the U.S.A. - National Ladies Auxiliary Vol 1: 12389
Jewish Welfare Federation of Metropolitan Detroit Vol 1: 12352
Jewish Women International Vol 1: 12391
Job Corps Advanced Career Training Program Vol 1: 20519
Jobs for America's Graduates Vol 1: 12393
Jockey Club of Canada Vol 1: 12395
John Deere Vol 1: 4019
John Deere & Co. Vol 1: 4228
John Deere and Company Vol 1: 20677
John F. Kennedy Library Foundation Vol 1: 12397
John Pelham Historical Association Vol 1: 12399
John Templeton Foundation Vol 1: 12401
John Wiley & Sons Vol 1: 5428
John Wiley and Sons Inc. Vol 1: 4104
Johns Hopkins University Vol 1: 12416
Johnson & Johnson Vol 1: 764
Johnson & Johnson Medical Vol 1: 5456
JOHNSON & JOHNSON Professional Division Vol 1: 2127
Johnson County Historical Society Vol 1: 12418
Johnson Family Foundation Vol 1: 9161
Johnson Foundation; Robert Wood Vol 1: 5562, 13856, 13857
Johnson Foundation; Stanley Thomas Vol 2: 6503
Johnson Library and Museum; Lyndon Baines Vol 1: 12420
Johnson Matthey plc, Materials Technology Division Vol 2: 8773
Johnson Publishing Co. Vol 1: 3004
Join Hands Day Vol 1: 12423
Joint Baltic American National Committee Vol 1: 12425
Joint Financial Management Improvement Program Vol 1: 12427
Jordan Ministry of Education Vol 2: 4341
Jose Manuel Lara Foundation Vol 2: 6018
Joseph Foundation Vol 1: 10376
Joshua Slocum Society International Vol 1: 12429
Joshua's Tract Conservation and Historic Trust Vol 1: 12439
Jostens Inc. Vol 1: 12441
Journal *Le Soir* - Rossel & Cie; S. A. Vol 2: 937
Journal of Aesthetics and Art Criticism - Department of Philosophy Vol 1: 12443
Journal of Consumer Research - University of Wisconsin, Madison Vol 1: 12445
Journal of Economic Integration Vol 2: 5496
Journal of the APMA Vol 1: 3563
Journalism Education Association Vol 1: 12447
Jowett Car Club Vol 2: 8027
Joy in Singing Vol 1: 12455
Jozef Pilsudski Institute of America for Research in the Modern History of Poland Vol 1: 12457
Jump Memorial Foundation; William A. Vol 1: 12459
Junior Achievement Vol 1: 12461
Junior Achievement of Canada Vol 1: 12463
Junior Engineering Technical Society Vol 1: 12465
Junior Golf Association of Mobile Vol 1: 12467
Junior Philatelic Society of America Vol 1: 12469
Junior Philatelists of America Vol 1: 12469
Junior Wireless Club Vol 1: 17828
Juselius Foundation; Sigrid Vol 2: 1644
Justus-Liebig-Universitat-Giessen Vol 2: 2995
Juvenile Diabetes Research Foundation International - Central Florida Chapter Vol 1: 12472
Juvenile Diabetes Research Foundation of Greater Chicago Vol 1: 12474
Juvenile Welfare Board of Pinellas County Vol 1: 12476
Juventudes Musicales de Espana Vol 2: 6070
JWB Vol 1: 12337
K. G. Saur Publishing Vol 1: 5618
KA-BAR Knife Collectors Club Vol 1: 12478
Kabushiki Kaisha Dentsu Vol 2: 4112
Kairali Children's Book Trust Vol 2: 3564
Kancelaria Prezydenta Rzeczypospolitej Polskiej Vol 2: 5317
Kankakee River Valley Chamber of Commerce Vol 1: 12480
Kansas Arts Commission Vol 1: 12500
Kansas Association of Chiefs of Police Vol 1: 12483
Kansas City Artist Association Vol 1: 12485
Kansas City Barbeque Society Vol 1: 12487
Kansas Crop Improvement Association Vol 1: 12490
Kansas Dietetic Association Vol 1: 12492
Kansas Hearing Aid Association Vol 1: 12495
Kansas State University - Center for Basic Cancer Research Vol 1: 12497
Kansas Watercolor Society Vol 1: 12499
Kansas Wildflower Society Vol 1: 12501
Kanselarij der Nederlandse Orden Vol 2: 4706
Kappa Alpha Theta Foundation Vol 1: 14876
Kappa Delta Epsilon Vol 1: 12503
Kappa Delta Pi Vol 1: 12508
Kappa Delta Rho Vol 1: 12514
Kappa Mu Epsilon Vol 1: 12516
Kappa Publishing Group, St. Martin's Press, and New York Times Digital. Vol 1: 2081
Kappa Tau Alpha Vol 1: 12518
Karg-Elert Archive Vol 2: 8029
Katalysis Partnership Vol 1: 12520
Katanning Shire Council Vol 2: 455
Kaustinen Folk Music Festival Vol 2: 1646
Kaustisen Kansanmusiikkijuhlat Vol 2: 1646
Kay Jewelers Vol 1: 14670
Keats-Shelley Association of America Vol 1: 12522
Keene Center of Japanese Culture; Donald Vol 1: 12525
Keene State College Vol 1: 12527
Keep America Beautiful Vol 1: 12529
Keep Athens-Clarke County Beautiful Vol 1: 12533
Keithley Instruments, Inc. Vol 1: 3459
Keller Worldwide; Helen Vol 1: 10387
Kennedy Center Alliance for Arts Education Network Vol 1: 12535
Kennedy Center American College Theater Festival Vol 1: 12538
Kennedy Center for the Performing Arts; John F. Vol 1: 12549
Kennedy Center for the Performing Arts; John F. - Partners in Education Program Vol 1: 12553
Kennedy School of Government at Harvard University; John F. Vol 1: 10116
Kennel Club Boliviano Vol 2: 1127
Kenosha History Center Vol 1: 12555
Kent State University - Gerontology Center Vol 1: 12557
Kent State University Alumni Association Vol 1: 12559
Kentucky Arts Council Vol 1: 12561
Kentucky Paralegal Association Vol 1: 12563
Kentucky Psychiatric Association Vol 1: 12565

Kentucky Reading Association Vol 1: 19785
Kentucky Right to Life Association Vol 1: 12567
Kentucky School Media Association Vol 1: 19785
Kentucky Watercolor Society Vol 1: 12569
Kenya Association of Hotelkeepers and Caterers Vol 2: 4351
Kenya Institute of Management Vol 2: 4353
Kenya National Academy of Sciences - Ministry of Research, Science and Technology Vol 2: 4355
Kenyan Publishers Association Vol 2: 4360
Kenyan Section of the International Commission of Jurists Vol 2: 4362
Keramos Vol 1: 12571
Keren-Or, Inc. Vol 1: 12573
Keren Wolf Vol 2: 3782
Kettering - Moraine - Oakwood Chamber of Commerce Vol 1: 12575
Keuka College Alumni Association Vol 1: 12577
Keweenaw County Historical Society Vol 1: 12583
Kidde-Graviner, Ltd. Vol 1: 9583
Kidde-Grininer Vol 2: 8407
Kiel Institute for World Economics Vol 2: 3005
Kihara Memorial Yokohama Foundation for the Advancement of Life Sciences Vol 2: 4118
Kilby International Awards Foundation Vol 1: 12585
Kiln Trust; Robert Vol 2: 6922
Kilvert Society Vol 2: 8031
Kinder-und Jugendfilmzentrum in Deutschland Vol 2: 2687
Kindness Incorporated Vol 1: 12587
King Baudouin Foundation Vol 2: 939
King County Bar Association Vol 1: 12589
King Faisal Foundation Vol 2: 5921
Kings County Farm Bureau Vol 1: 12594
King's School Vol 2: 8033
Kinokuniya Co. Vol 2: 4232
Kinsmen and Kinette Clubs of Canada Vol 1: 12596
Kitplanes Magazine Vol 1: 12598
Kiwanis International Vol 1: 12600
Klasina Smelik Stichting Vol 2: 4801
Klingon Strike Force Vol 1: 12602
KM Fabrics, Inc. Vol 1: 20646
Knight Fellowships; John S. Vol 1: 12604
Knight Foundation Vol 1: 12273
Knoll Pharmaceuticals Vol 2: 8773
Knowles/Knoles/Noles Family Association Vol 1: 12606
Kobe International Flute Competition Vol 2: 4234
Kobe YMCA Cross Cultural Center Vol 2: 4236
Kobenhavns Universitet Vol 2: 1539
Kodak Canada Vol 1: 7094
Kodansha Ltd. Vol 2: 4239
Kohler; Stichting Charlotte Vol 2: 4930
Kokusai Geijutsu Renmei Vol 2: 4175
Kokusai Koryu Kikin Vol 2: 4169
Kokusai Kotsu Anzen Gakkai Vol 2: 4131
Kokusai Kowan Kyokai Vol 2: 4129
Kompass Publishers Vol 2: 7278
Kone Instruments Vol 2: 6772
Kongelige Danske Geografiske Selskab Vol 2: 1526
Koning Boudewijnstichting Vol 2: 939
Koninklijk Belgisch Filmarchief Vol 2: 1092
Koninklijk Nederlands Aardrijkskundig Genootschap Vol 2: 4876
Koninklijk Nederlands Geologisch Mijnbouwkundig Genootschap Vol 2: 4878
Koninklijke Academie voor Geneeskunde van Belgie Vol 2: 969
Koninklijke Academie voor Nederlandse Taal-en Letterkunde Vol 2: 951
Koninklijke Beiaardschool Jef Denijn Vol 2: 1087
Koninklijke Maatschappij tot Bevordering der Bouwkunst - Bond van Nederlandse Architekten Vol 2: 4880
Koninklijke Nederlandse Akademie van Wetenschappen Vol 2: 4882
Koninklijke Nederlandse Toonkunstenaars Vereniging Vol 2: 4896
Konoinklijke Nederlandse Chemische Vereniging Vol 2: 4898
Konrad Adenauer Foundation - Germany Vol 2: 3007
Konrad Adenauer Stiftung Vol 2: 3007
Kordelin Foundation; Alfred Vol 2: 1649
Korea Polio Foundation Vol 2: 5499
Korea Veterans Association of Canada Vol 1: 12608
Korean Aerospace Medical Association Vol 1: 233
Korean Culture and Arts Foundation Vol 2: 5501
Kortfilmfestivalen; Stiftelsen Vol 2: 5161
Kosciuszko Foundation Vol 1: 12610
The Koussevitzky Music Foundations Vol 1: 12615
Kraft General Foods Vol 1: 2109
Krause Publications Vol 1: 12617
Kreditanstalt fur Wiederaufbau Vol 2: 2998
Kryolan Vol 1: 20647
KU Queers and Allies (QandA) Vol 1: 12620
Kulturamt Spittal und Singkreis Porcia Vol 2: 715
Kungl. Vetenskapsakademien Vol 2: 6201
Kungliga Fysiografiska Sallskapet i Lund Vol 2: 6185
Kungnip Kugagwon Vol 2: 5510
Kurt J. Lesker Co. Vol 1: 6150
La Batie - Festival de Geneve Vol 2: 6479
La Crosse Area Development Corporation Vol 1: 12622
La Federation des Societes Canadiennes d'Assistance aux Animaux Vol 1: 7090
La Fondation Emile-Nelligan Vol 1: 20304
La Foundation Yves-Saint-Germain Vol 1: 10819
La Leche League International Vol 1: 12627
La Prevention Routiere Internationale Vol 2: 5399
La Salle College Vol 1: 12633
La Salle University Vol 1: 12633
La Sertoma International Vol 1: 12636
Labologists Society Vol 2: 8035
Labor Education and Research Project Vol 1: 12638
Labor Research Association Vol 1: 12640
Laboratory of Plasma Studies Vol 1: 12643
Ladies Association of British Barbershop Singers Vol 1: 10251
Ladies Auxiliary Veterans of Foreign Wars Vol 1: 12645
Ladies' Golf Union Vol 2: 8037
Ladies Professional Golf Association Vol 1: 12649, 21923
Laerdal Medical Corp. Vol 1: 14215
Lahti Organ Festivals Vol 2: 1651
Lake City Area Chamber of Commerce Vol 1: 12664
Lakeshore Humane Society Vol 1: 12666
Lakeshore Publishing Vol 1: 14988
Lamaze International Vol 1: 12668
Lambda Kappa Sigma Vol 1: 12679
Lambda Literary Foundation Vol 1: 12682
Lamoille County Planning Commission Vol 1: 12684
Lancaster Historical Society Vol 1: 12686
Lancaster Synthesis, Inc. Vol 1: 1706
Land Improvement Contractors of America Vol 1: 12688
Landeshauptstadt Munchen Vol 2: 3010
Landeshauptstadt Stuttgart Vol 2: 3099
Landesstudio Oberosterreich Vol 2: 702
Landscape Research Group Vol 2: 8040
Landschaftsverband Westfalen-Lippe Vol 2: 3016
Landstinget Blekinge Vol 2: 6138
Lane Foundation; Allen Vol 2: 8122
Langlois Encounters; International Henri - Poitiers International Film Schools Festival Vol 2: 2521
Lanka Electricity Company Vol 2: 6120
Lannan Foundation Vol 1: 12690
LaPorte Amateur Radio Club Vol 1: 45
Lappeenrannan Kaupunki Vol 2: 1653
Lappeenranta City Orchestra Vol 2: 1653
LaPrensa Vol 1: 11109
Laser Institute of America Vol 1: 12692
Lasker Foundation; Albert and Mary Vol 1: 12694
Latin American Association of Development Financing Institutions Vol 2: 5241
Latin American Banking Federation Vol 2: 1318
Latin American Phytopathology Association Vol 2: 5243
Latin American Studies Association Vol 1: 12698
Latin and Mediterranean Group for Sport Medicine Vol 2: 2523
Latin Liturgy Association Vol 1: 12703
Latino American Management Association Vol 1: 12705
Latino Gerontological Center Vol 1: 12712
Latrobe Area Chamber of Commerce Vol 1: 12714
Laubach Literacy of Canada Vol 1: 12716
Law and Society Association Vol 1: 12718
Law Enforcement Memorial Association Vol 1: 12723
Law of Polk County Vol 1: 12725
Law Society of Zimbabwe Vol 2: 9350
Lawn Tennis Association Vol 2: 8042
Lawrence Foundation Vol 1: 17512
Lawyers Alliance for World Security Vol 1: 12727
Lay Carmelite Order of the Blessed Virgin Mary of Mount Carmel Vol 1: 12729
Laymen's National Bible Committee Vol 1: 6353
LDA Publishers Vol 1: 12731
Le Conseil des Arts du Canada Vol 1: 6783
Le Croy Corporation Vol 2: 2325
Le Giornate del Cinema Muto Vol 2: 4037
Le Mars Community School District Alumni Association Vol 1: 12733
le parc jean-Drapeau Vol 1: 13600
Leaders' Forum Vol 1: 12735
Leadership Conference on Civil Rights Vol 1: 12737
Leadership Fort Wayne Vol 1: 12739

League Against Cruel Sports Vol 2: 8044
League of American Theatres and Producers Vol 1: 12741
League of Canadian Poets Vol 1: 12743
League of Composers - International Society of Contemporary Music Vol 1: 12746
League of Families Vol 2: 941
League of Minnesota Cities Vol 1: 12748
League of Minnesota Poets Vol 1: 15003
League of New York Theatres and Producers, Inc. Vol 1: 12741
League of Off-Broadway Theatres and Producers Vol 1: 12919
League of Women Voters of Arkansas Vol 1: 12751
League of Women Voters of Oklahoma Vol 1: 12753
Leahy Archives Vol 1: 10851
The Leakey Foundation Vol 1: 12755
Learning Disabilities Association of Arkansas Vol 1: 12757
Learning Disabilities Association of California Vol 1: 12759
Leatherneck Magazine Vol 1: 13096
Leavenworth Area Development Vol 1: 12761
Lederle Laboratories Vol 1: 4159
Lee Bennett Hopkins Vol 1: 11859
Lee Foundation Singapore Vol 2: 5940
Lee Gallery; Rudolph E. Vol 1: 18181
Leeds and Northrup Foundation Vol 1: 10874
Leeds International Pianoforte Competition Vol 2: 8049
Lefthanders International Vol 1: 12763
Legal Aid Society of the Orange County Bar Association Vol 1: 12765
Legal Momentum: Advancing Women's Rights Vol 1: 12767
Legion of Valor of the United States of America Vol 1: 12771
Leica Vol 1: 3967
Leica Canada Inc. Vol 1: 6929
LEICA GEOSYSTEMS Vol 1: 5217
Leipzig College of Graphic Arts and Book Design - Academy of Visual Arts Vol 2: 3019
Lemelson-MIT Program - Massachusetts Institute of Technology Vol 1: 12774
Lentz Peace Research Association Vol 1: 12778
Leominster Historical Society Vol 1: 12780
Leon County Department of Education Vol 1: 9633
Leopoldina Academy of Researchers in Natural Sciences Vol 2: 3075
LEPRA Vol 2: 8051
Les Amis d'Escoffier Society Vol 1: 12782
Les Clubs Kin du Canada Vol 1: 12596
Leukemia & Lymphoma Society Vol 1: 5804
Leukemia and Lymphoma Society Vol 1: 12784
Leukemia and Lymphoma Society of America, Northern Florida Chapter Vol 1: 12797
Leukemia Society of America Vol 1: 12784
Leverhulme Trust Vol 2: 8053
Leverhulme Trust Fund Vol 2: 8700
Lewis and Clark Trail Heritage Foundation Vol 1: 12799
Lexis-Nexis Vol 1: 5611
LexisNexis Vol 1: 19551
Liaison Committee on Medical Education in the United States Vol 1: 1948
Liberal International Vol 2: 8056
Libertarian Alliance Vol 2: 8058
Libertarian Futurist Society Vol 1: 12804
Libertarian International Vol 1: 11934
Libertarian Party of California Vol 1: 12807
Liberty Bell Wanderers Vol 1: 12809
Liberty Seated Collectors Club Vol 1: 12811
Library Administration and Management Association Vol 1: 12813
Library and Information Association of New Zealand Vol 2: 5000
Library and Information Research Group Vol 2: 8060
Library and Information Service of Western Australia Vol 2: 610
Library and Information Technology Association Vol 1: 12822
Library Association Vol 2: 7277
The Library Association Vol 2: 9052
Library Association of Australia Vol 2: 222
Library Directory Associates Publishers Vol 1: 12731
Library of Congress Vol 1: 12831
Library Public Relations Council Vol 1: 12835
Lichfield District Council Vol 2: 8062
Liederkranz Foundation Vol 1: 12838
Life Coalition International Vol 1: 12840
Life Insurance Advertisers Association Vol 1: 11091
Life Office Management Association Vol 1: 12842
Lifespan, Inc. Vol 1: 1185
Lifespan/Tufts/Brown Center for AIDS Research Vol 1: 12846
Liga Argentina Contra la Tuberculosis Vol 2: 40
Light Aircraft Manufacturers Association Vol 1: 12599
Lighter-Than-Air Society Vol 1: 12848
Lighting Association Vol 2: 8064
Lighting Industry Federation Vol 2: 8066
Ligue des Familles Vol 2: 941
Ligue Europeenne de Bridge Vol 2: 3904
Ligue Francaise des Droits de l'Animal Vol 2: 2368
Likion ton Ellinidon Vol 2: 3175
Lilly and Company; Eli Vol 1: 1768, 4174
Lilly and Co.; Eli Vol 1: 19072
Lilly Research Centre Ltd. Vol 2: 8773
Lily and Co.; Eli Vol 1: 3629
Lily Products Co Vol 1: 3625
Lily Research Labs Vol 1: 3626
Limnological Society of America Vol 1: 4488
Lincoln Arc Welding Foundation; James F. Vol 1: 12850
Lincoln Center for the Performing Arts Vol 1: 12852
Lincoln Electric Company Vol 1: 4900
Lincoln Forum Vol 1: 12857
Lincoln Group of New York Vol 1: 12859
Lincoln Lancaster Women's Commission Vol 1: 12861
Lincoln University of Missouri - Department of Communications Vol 1: 12865
Lindapter International Ltd. Vol 2: 7773
Lindbergh Fund; Charles A. Vol 1: 7807
Linguistic Association of Canada and the United States Vol 1: 12867
Link Foundation Vol 1: 12869
Linnean Society of London Vol 2: 8068
Lions Club International Foundation Vol 1: 2139
Lipizzan Association of North America Vol 1: 12871
Lisbon Academy of Sciences Vol 2: 5404
Liszt Competition Foundation - Muziekcentrum Vredenburg Vol 2: 4845
Liszt Ferenc Tarsasag Vol 2: 3242
Liszt Society Vol 2: 8076
Literary Television Vol 1: 15512
Literary Translators Association of Canada Vol 1: 12873
Lithuanian American Roman Catholic Women's Alliance Vol 1: 12875
Little Big Horn Associates Vol 1: 12877
Little, Brown & Co. Vol 2: 7369
Little, Inc.; A. D. Vol 1: 2783
Little Mouse Club Vol 1: 12880
Little People of America Vol 1: 12885
Little Theatre of Alexandria Vol 1: 12887
Litton Data Systems Vol 1: 13075
Live Free Inc. Vol 1: 12889
Live Theatre League of Tarrant County Vol 1: 12891
Liverpool School of Tropical Medicine Vol 2: 8078
Livestock Publications Council Vol 1: 12895
Livingston and Doughty Company Ltd Vol 2: 7612
Livingston County Council on Alcohol and Substance Abuse Vol 1: 12899
Llangollen International Musical Eisteddfod Vol 2: 8080
Lo Scoltenna: Accademia Scientifica, Letteraria e Artistics del Frignano Vol 2: 4027
Lo Scoltenna: Scientific, Literary and Artistic Academy of Frignano Vol 2: 4027
Locarno Internationale Film Festival Vol 2: 6481
Lockheed Corporation Vol 1: 13111
Lockheed Martin Vol 1: 13093
Lockheed Martin Aeronautics Vol 1: 13092
Lockheed Martin Fairchild Systems Vol 1: 13082
Lockheed Martin Science and Engineering Service Vol 1: 238
Lockheed Martin Tactical Defense Systems Vol 1: 13081
Lockwood, Kessler, and Bartlett Vol 1: 5209
Locus Publications Vol 1: 12901
The Loft, A Place for Writing and Literature Vol 1: 12903
The Loft Literary Center Vol 1: 12903
Log Cabin Society of Michigan Vol 1: 12907
Logistics and Transport New Zealand Vol 2: 5005
Logistics Management Magazine Vol 1: 13762
Logos Agvet and Standard Bank Vol 2: 5537
Lomond Poets; Ben Vol 1: 15005
London Club Vol 1: 12909
London International Piano Competition Vol 2: 8082
London International Piano Competition Vol 2: 8082
London Mathematical Society Vol 2: 8084
London School of Hygiene and Tropical Medicine Vol 2: 8845
London Stock Exchange Vol 2: 7661
London String Quartet Competition Vol 2: 8094
London Symphony Orchestra Vol 2: 8096
Long and Jacques Thibaud International Competition; Marguerite Vol 2: 2525
Long Branch Historical Association Vol 1: 12911

Long Island University, Brooklyn Campus Vol 1: 12913
Long - Jacques Thibaud; Concours International Marguerite Vol 2: 2525
LoonWatch Vol 1: 12916
Loral Fairchild Systems Vol 1: 19611
l'Organisation hydrographique internationale Vol 2: 4664
Lortel Theatre; Lucille Vol 1: 12918
Los Alamos National Laboratory - Manuel Lujan, Jr. Neutron Scattering Center Vol 1: 12920
Los Angeles Advertising Agencies Association Vol 1: 12922
Los Angeles Athletic Club Vol 1: 12924
Los Angeles Conservancy Vol 1: 12926
Los Angeles Public Library Vol 1: 12928
Los Angeles Times Book Prizes Vol 1: 12930
Lothian and Edinburgh Enterprise Limited Vol 2: 8890
Louisiana Association of School Librarians Vol 1: 12939, 12944
Louisiana Grain and Feed Association Vol 1: 12932
Louisiana Historical Association Vol 1: 10460
Louisiana Library Association Vol 1: 12934
Louisiana Preservation Alliance Vol 1: 12945
Louisiana Psychiatric Medical Association Vol 1: 12947
Louisiana State Paralegal Association Vol 1: 12949
Louisiana State Poetry Society Vol 1: 15007
Louisiana State University - Herbarium Vol 1: 12951
Louisiana State University - Kresge Hearing Research Laboratory of the South Vol 1: 12953
Louisiana State University - U.S. Civil War Center Vol 1: 12956
Louisiana Turfgrass Association Vol 1: 12958
Love Creek Productions Vol 1: 12961
Loveland Beagle Club Vol 1: 12964
Loyola University Chicago Vol 1: 12966
Ludwig Boltzman Gesellschaft - Osterreichische Vereinigung zur Forderung Vol 2: 768
Ludwig Boltzmann Association - Austrian Society for the Promotion of Scientific Research - Institute for Clinical Neurobiology Vol 2: 768
Lufthansa German Airlines Vol 2: 4309
Lumbermen's Association of Texas Vol 1: 12975
Luovan saveltaiteen edistamissaatio Vol 2: 1617
Lupus Foundation of America Vol 1: 12978
Lupus Foundation of America, Arizona Area Coordinator Vol 1: 12982
Lupus Foundation of America, Arkansas Chapter Vol 1: 12984
Lupus Foundation of Minnesota Vol 1: 12986
Lutheran Education Association Vol 1: 12988
Lutheran Historical Conference Vol 1: 12991
Lutherans Concerned/Great Lakes Vol 1: 12993
Lutherans Concerned/North America Vol 1: 12995
LV of Harrison County Vol 1: 12997
Lyceum Club of Greek Women Vol 2: 3175
Lyme Academy College of Fine Arts Vol 1: 15701
Lynchburg Historical Foundation Vol 1: 12999
The Lyric Theatre Vol 1: 13002
Maatschappij Arti et Amicitiae Vol 2: 4848
Maatschappij der Nederlandse Letterkunde Vol 2: 4910
MacArthur Foundation; John D. and Catherine T. Vol 1: 13005
The MacDowell Colony Vol 1: 13007
MacFarland Vol 1: 18630
Machine Vision Association of the Society of Manufacturing Engineers Vol 1: 13009
Macmillan Vol 1: 942
Macra na Feirme Vol 2: 3655
Macworld Vol 1: 17115
Madeira, Regional Secretary of Tourism and Culture Vol 2: 5419
Madeira, Secretaria Regional do Turismo e Cultura Vol 2: 5419
Madison County Tourism Vol 1: 13011
Madison Square Garden Television Productions Vol 1: 13497
Magazine Publishers Association Vol 1: 13013
Magazine Publishers of America Vol 1: 13013
Magistrat der Landeshauptstadt Salzburg Vol 2: 770
Magistrat der Universitatsstadt Giessen Vol 2: 3021
Magnes Museum; Judah L. Vol 1: 13016
The Magnolia Society Vol 1: 13018
Magsaysay Award Foundation; Ramon Vol 2: 5266
Magyar Geofizikusok Egyesulete Vol 2: 3222
Magyar Ingatlanszovetseg Vol 2: 3274
Magyar Kardiologusok Tarsasaga Vol 2: 3282
Magyar Konyvtarosok Egyesulete Vol 2: 3231
Magyar Orvostudomanyi Tarsasagok es Egyesuletek Szovetsege Vol 2: 3233
Magyar Szakszervezetek Orszagos Tanacsa/SZOT Vol 2: 3302
Magyar Ujsagirok Orszagos Szovetsege Vol 2: 3229
Mahomet Chamber of Commerce Vol 1: 13020
Mail Systems Management Association Vol 1: 13022
Mailing and Fulfillment Service Association Vol 1: 13026
Maine Hospice Council Vol 1: 13034
Maine Journeymen Vol 1: 13036
Maine Oil Dealers Association Vol 1: 13038
Maine Space Grant Consortium Vol 1: 13040
Maison de Chateaubriand Vol 2: 2527
Maison Henri Deschamps Vol 2: 3220
Maisons de la Presse Vol 2: 2529
Majors Scientific Books Inc. Vol 1: 13260
Making Music Vol 2: 8098
Malacological Society of London Vol 2: 8102
Malahat Review Vol 1: 13042
Malayan Banking Berhad Vol 2: 4429
Malaysian Rubber Products Manufacturers Association Vol 2: 4438
Malice Domestic Vol 1: 13045
Malko International Competition for Young Conductors; Nicolai Vol 2: 1504
Mallinckrodt Baker Inc. Vol 1: 1775
Malta Amateur Cine Circle Vol 2: 4449
Maltese-American Benevolent Society Vol 1: 13047
Maltsters' Association of Great Britain Vol 2: 8105
Mananan Festival Trust Vol 2: 9120
Manhattan College Vol 1: 13050
Manifestazioni Internazionali della Ceramica Vol 2: 3965
Manitoba Psychological Society Vol 1: 13053
Mankato Area Environmentalists Vol 1: 13055
Manning, Selvage and Lee Vol 1: 13057
Manomet Bird Observatory Vol 1: 13059
Manomet Center for Conservation Sciences Vol 1: 13059
Manpower Society Vol 2: 7622
Manufacturers Association; Chemical Specialties Vol 1: 8463
Manufacturing Technologies Association Vol 2: 8107
March of Dimes Birth Defects Foundation, Central Texas Area Chapter Vol 1: 13061
Marconi International Fellowship Foundation; Guglielmo Vol 1: 13063
Margaret A. Edwards Trust Vol 1: 22050
Marian Library Vol 1: 21012
Marijuana Anonymous World Services Vol 1: 13065
Marin Self Publishers Association Vol 1: 6273
Marin Small Publishers Association Vol 1: 6273
Marine Biological Association of the United Kingdom Vol 2: 8110
Marine Corps Aviation Association Vol 1: 13068
Marine Corps Heritage Foundation Vol 1: 13095
Marine Corps Mustang Association Vol 1: 13102
Marine Corps Reserve Association Vol 1: 13104
Marine Technology Society Vol 1: 13107
Mariological Society of America Vol 1: 13113
Marion County Bar Association Vol 1: 13115
Marion Laboratories Vol 1: 1598, 1604
The Maritime Trust Vol 2: 8112
Marketing and Advertising Global Network Vol 1: 13117
Marketing Science Institute Vol 1: 13119
Marlowe Society of America Vol 1: 13121
Marquette University - Department of Journalism Vol 1: 13123
Marriott Vol 1: 11529
Marriott Corporation Vol 1: 688
Marschall Products-Rhone-Poulenc, Inc. Vol 1: 2108
Marshall Cavendish Corp. Vol 1: 2971
Martin-Bodmer-Stiftung fur einen Gottfried Keller-Preis Vol 2: 6483
Martin Humanitarian Award; C.F. Vol 1: 7064
Mary Potishman Lard Trust Vol 1: 8108
Maryknoll Fathers and Brothers Vol 1: 13126
Maryknoll Lay Missioners Vol 1: 13128
Maryland Association of Private Career Schools Vol 1: 13130
Maryland Jockey Club Vol 1: 13132
Mason Contractors Association of America Vol 1: 13138
Masonic Lodge No. 246 Vol 1: 13140
The Masquers Vol 1: 13142
Massachusetts Association for Children With Learning Disabilities Vol 1: 13144
Massachusetts Association of School Business Officials Vol 1: 13146

Massachusetts Audubon Society Vol 1: 13148
Massachusetts Conveyancers Association Vol 1: 13151
Massachusetts Council for the Social Studies Vol 1: 13153
Massachusetts Cultural Council Vol 1: 9553
Massachusetts Forestry Association Vol 1: 13158
Massachusetts Lodging Association Vol 1: 13161
Massachusetts Paralegal Association Vol 1: 13163
Massachusetts Science Educators Hall of Fame Vol 1: 13166
Massachusetts Society of Professional Engineers Vol 1: 13168
Massachusetts Sports Commission Vol 1: 13170
Massachusetts State Poetry Society Vol 1: 15008
Massey Foundation Vol 1: 18149
Masson Editores Vol 2: 4606
Master of Professional Writing Program Vol 1: 13172
Master Printers of America Vol 1: 13174
Master's Men Ministry - National Associaton of Free Will Baptists Vol 1: 13176
Mastiff Club of America Vol 1: 13178
Materials Research Society Vol 1: 13180
Mathematical Association of America Vol 1: 13186
Mathematical Association of America Vol 1: 18738
Mathematical Programming Society Vol 1: 13198, 18734
Mathematical Society of Japan Vol 2: 4249
Mathematical Society of the Philippines Vol 2: 5289
Mathematics Research Center Vol 1: 13202
Mattel Sports Vol 1: 21921
Mature Market Resource Center Vol 1: 13206
Max-Eyth-Gesselschaft Agrartechnik im VDI Vol 2: 3023
Max-Eyth Society for Agricultural Engineering of the VDI Vol 2: 3023
Max Schmidheiny Foundation Vol 2: 6485
May and Baker Ltd. Vol 2: 8770
MC Sailing Association Vol 1: 13208
McClelland & Stewart, Ltd. Vol 1: 13210
McCord Museum of Canadian History Vol 1: 13212
McDonnell Douglas Aerospace Vol 1: 13078
McDowell Sonoran Land Trust Vol 1: 13214
McGannon Communication Research Center; Donald Vol 1: 13216
McGill University - Gault Nature Reserve Vol 1: 13218
McGovern Fund for the Behavioral Sciences Vol 1: 1051
McGraw-Hill Vol 1: 942
McGraw-Hill Book Company Vol 1: 4027
The McGraw-Hill Companies, Inc. Vol 1: 13220
McGraw-Hill Companies Inc. Vol 1: 14099
McHenry County Historical Society Vol 1: 13222
McKay Welding Products Vol 1: 4882
McKee (Australia); Davy Vol 2: 378
McKinsey Foundation for Management Research Vol 1: 10273
McKnight Foundation Vol 1: 17399
McKnight Programs in Higher Education Vol 1: 9598
McLaughlin Foundation; R. Samuel Vol 1: 18168
McNally Company; Rand Vol 1: 1993
McNeil Consumer Products Company Vol 1: 776
McNeil Pharmaceuticals Vol 1: 3611
McNeill Street Pumping Station Preservation Society Vol 1: 13224
Mead Johnson and Company Vol 1: 631, 4161
Mead Johnson Nutritionals Vol 1: 18621
Meade Instrument Corporation Vol 1: 6002
Meade Instruments Vol 1: 6003
Meadows Foundation, Inc. Vol 1: 19513
Meadville Area Family YMCA Vol 1: 13226
Mechanical Contractors Association of the Capital District Vol 1: 13228
Mechelen Festival Vol 2: 943
Media Alliance Vol 1: 13230
Media and Methods Magazine Vol 1: 13232
Media, Entertainment and Arts Alliance Vol 2: 457
Media Entertainment and Arts Alliance Vol 2: 458
Media Human Resources Association Vol 1: 13234
The Media Project Vol 1: 13237
Media Tenor South Africa Vol 2: 5548
Median Iris Society Vol 1: 13239
Medical Correctional Society Vol 1: 1271
Medical Dental Hospital Business Associates Vol 1: 13241
Medical Education for South African Blacks Vol 1: 13246
Medical Fitness Association Vol 1: 13248
Medical Library Association Vol 1: 13250
Medical Mycological Society of the Americas Vol 1: 13268
Medical Society of the State of New York Vol 1: 13271
Medical Women's International Association Vol 2: 3025
Medieval Academy of America Vol 1: 13273
Medieval Academy of America Vol 1: 18038
Medikinale International Parma Vol 2: 3935
Mednarodni Graficni Likovni Center Vol 2: 5977
Medsep Corporation Vol 1: 1109
Meeting Professionals International Vol 1: 13277
Meetings and Conventions Vol 1: 13286
Melbourne International Film Festival Vol 2: 459
Mellado Communications Vol 1: 7586
Mellemfolkeligt Samvirke Vol 2: 1447
Melpomene Institute Vol 1: 13288
Melpomene Institute for Women's Health Research Vol 1: 13288
Membership, Education and Training Committee Vol 2: 7860, 7868
Memorial Foundation for Jewish Culture Vol 1: 13290
Memphis State Review Vol 1: 18066
Menlo Park Chamber of Commerce Vol 1: 13293
Mensa International Vol 2: 8114
Mental Handicap of Germany; National Association for Persons with Vol 2: 3037
Mental Health Association of the Piedmont Vol 1: 13296
Merchandise Mart Properties, Inc. Vol 1: 13298
Merck and Company Vol 1: 1126, 1127, 3919
Merck and Co. Vol 1: 4137
Merck & Co., Inc. Vol 1: 3509
Merck & Co. Inc. Vol 1: 4696
Merck Company Foundation Vol 1: 13841
Merck Frosst Centre for Therapeutic Research Vol 1: 7845
Merck Ltd. Vol 2: 8773
Merck Research Laboratories Vol 1: 1761
Merck Sharp & Dohme Research Laboratories Vol 1: 1761
Merck U.S. Human Health Vol 1: 2362
Merck U.S. Human Health Division Vol 1: 4137
Mercury Communications Vol 2: 9101
Mercy Corps Vol 1: 13300
Merial Ltd. Vol 1: 4254
Meridian Energy Vol 2: 4996
Merkaz Zalman Shazar Le'Historia Yehudit/ Ha'Hevra Ha'Historit Ha 'Israelit Vol 2: 3767
Merrill Lynch Vol 1: 16981
Merrimack Valley Chamber of Commerce Vol 1: 13302
Merriman Smith Memorial Fund Vol 1: 21604
Mesa Arts Center Vol 1: 13304
Messe Frankfurt GmbH Vol 2: 3030
Metal Construction Association Vol 1: 13306
Metal Powder Industries Federation Vol 1: 13308
Metallurgical and Engineering Consultants (India) Limited Vol 2: 3458
Metallurgical Society Vol 1: 13439
Meteoritical Society Vol 2: 8116
MetLife Foundation Vol 1: 4636, 20055
Metropolitan Area Planning Council Vol 1: 13315
Metropolitan Botanical Club Vol 1: 20123
Metropolitan Opera Vol 1: 13317
Metropolitan Opera Guild Vol 1: 13320
Metropolitan Owners' Club Vol 2: 8119
Mexican Academy of Dermatology Vol 2: 4552
Mexican Academy of Sciences Vol 2: 4554
Mexican-American Engineering Society Vol 1: 19183
Mexican Electric Research Institute Vol 2: 4560
Mexican Organization for the History of Science and Technology Vol 2: 4562
Mexico Chamber of Deputies Vol 2: 4564
Mexico Ministry of Foreign Affairs Vol 2: 4566
Mexico Ministry of Labor and Social Security Vol 2: 4568
Mexico Ministry of Public Education Vol 2: 4570
Mexico Ministry of the Interior Vol 2: 4582
Meyer-Viol Foundation Vol 2: 5366
Mezinarodni festival filmu a televiznich poradu o zivotnim prostredi Ekofilm Vol 2: 5964
Mezinarodni hudebni festival Prazske jaro Vol 2: 1433
MG Drivers Club of North America Vol 1: 13322
Miami Beach Film Society Vol 1: 13324
Michael E. DeBakey International Surgical Society Vol 1: 13326
Michener Awards Foundation Vol 1: 13328
Michigan Association for Infant Mental Health Vol 1: 13331
Michigan Association for the Education of Young Children Vol 1: 13334

Organization Index

Michigan Association of Metal Finishers Vol 1: 13336
Michigan Competing Band Association Vol 1: 13338
Michigan Concrete Paving Association Vol 1: 13340
Michigan Department of State Police Vol 1: 13342
Michigan Hackney and Shetland Club Vol 1: 13347
Michigan Humane Society Vol 1: 13350
Michigan Mosquito Control Association Vol 1: 13352
Michigan Outdoor Writers Association Vol 1: 13354
Michigan Sea Grant Vol 1: 13356
Michigan Space Grant Consortium Vol 1: 13359
Michigan Towing Association Vol 1: 13361
Michigan United Conservation Clubs Vol 1: 13363
Microelectronic Devices, Circuits, and Systems Vol 1: 13365
Micronet R & D Vol 1: 13365
Mid-America Publishers Association Vol 1: 13367
Mid-America Regional Council Vol 1: 13369
Mid-Atlantic States Association of Avian Veterinarians Vol 1: 13371
Mid-West Truckers Association Vol 1: 13374
Middle East Report - Middle East Research and Information Project Vol 1: 13378
Middle East Studies Association of North America Vol 1: 13380
Middle Georgia Historical Society Vol 1: 13385
Middletown Pee Wee Football League Vol 1: 13387
Midland Bank Vol 2: 8707
Midland-Odessa Symphony & Chorale, Inc. Vol 1: 13389
Midwest Archives Conference Vol 1: 13391
Midwest Center for Nonprofit Leadership - University of Missouri—Kansas City L.P. Cookingham Institute of Public Affairs Vol 1: 13395
Midwest Roofing Contractors Association Vol 1: 13397
Miedzynarodowe Konkursy Im. Henryka Wieniawskiego Vol 2: 5309
Miescher Institute of Novartis, Basel, Switzerland.; Friedrich Vol 2: 6510
Military Audiology Association Vol 1: 13399
Military Chaplains Association of the U.S.A. Vol 1: 13402
Military Operations Research Society Vol 1: 13405
Military Order of Foreign Wars of the United States Vol 1: 13411
Military Order of the World Wars Vol 1: 13417
Milk Industry Foundation Vol 1: 2109
Milkweed Chronicle Vol 1: 13420
Milkweed Editions Vol 1: 13420
Millbrook Society Vol 1: 13423
Miller Fellowship Fund; John William Vol 1: 13425
Miller Lite Vol 1: 15086
Mills County Historical Society Vol 1: 13427
Milton Bradley Co. Vol 1: 15696
MIND - National Association for Mental Health Vol 2: 8121
Mind Science Foundation Vol 1: 13429
Mine Safety and Health Administration Vol 1: 15387
Mine Safety Appliances Company Vol 1: 2621, 4605
Mineralogical Society of America Vol 1: 13431
Minerals Engineering Society Vol 2: 8123
Minerals, Metals, and Materials Society Vol 1: 13439
Miniature Piano Enthusiast Club Vol 1: 13460
Mining and Metallurgical Society of America Vol 1: 13462
Ministarstvo Znanosti Vol 2: 1383
Ministerium Fuer Wissenschaft, Forschung und Kunst Baden-Wuerttemberg Vol 2: 2769
Ministry of Culture Vol 2: 5450
Ministry of Culture of Croatia Vol 2: 1387
Ministry of Culture of Republic Bulgaria Vol 2: 1237
Ministry of International Trade and Industry Vol 2: 4165, 4166
Ministry of Justice, Poland - Institute of Forensic Research Vol 2: 5315
Ministry of Science, Research and the Arts of the State of Baden-Wurttemberg Vol 2: 3032
Minnesota Advocates for Human Rights Vol 1: 13464
Minnesota Association of Townships Vol 1: 13466
Minnesota Concrete Masonry Association Vol 1: 13468
Minnesota Conservation Federation Vol 1: 13470
Minnesota Funeral Directors Association Vol 1: 13472
Minnesota Historical Society Vol 1: 13474
Minnesota Holstein Association Vol 1: 13477
Minnesota Psychological Association Vol 1: 13481
Minnesota Stroke Association, NSA Chapters Vol 1: 13484
Minnewaukan Community Club Vol 1: 13486
Minot State University - Northwest Art Center Vol 1: 13489
Miracle Flights for Kids Vol 1: 13492
Mirror Group Newspapers Vol 2: 8127
Miss America Foundation Vol 1: 13496
Miss America Organization Vol 1: 13494
Miss America Pageant Vol 1: 13494
Miss Universe Vol 1: 13497
Mississippi-Alabama Sea Grant Consortium Vol 1: 13501
Mississippi Association of Public Accountants Vol 1: 13503
Mississippi Ballet International, Inc. Vol 1: 21184
Mississippi Historical Society Vol 1: 13505
Mississippi Poetry Society Vol 1: 15010
Mississippi State Medical Association Vol 1: 13512
Mississippi State University - Cobb Institute of Archaeology Vol 1: 13514
Mississippi; The University of Southern - School of Library and Information Science Vol 1: 13516
Mississippi Urban Forest Council Vol 1: 13518
Mississippi Valley Historical Association Vol 1: 16879
Missouri Archaeological Society Vol 1: 13520
Missouri Arts Council Vol 1: 7771
Missouri Association of Meat Processors Vol 1: 13524
Missouri Association of School Librarians Vol 1: 13526
Missouri Bass Federation Vol 1: 13529
Missouri Botanical Garden Vol 1: 6548
Missouri Dental Association Vol 1: 13531
Missouri Department of Elementary and Secondary Education Vol 1: 13534
Missouri Hotel and Lodging Association Vol 1: 13536
Missouri Rural Foundation Vol 1: 13538
Missouri Sheriffs Association Vol 1: 13540
Missouri Southern International Piano Competition Vol 1: 13542
Mita Society for Library and Information Science Vol 2: 4251
Mita Toshokan Joho Gakkai Vol 2: 4251
Mitsubishi Chemical Company Vol 1: 2764
Mixed Blood Theatre Company Vol 1: 13544
Mladinska Knjiga Vol 2: 5979
Mladinska Knjiga Zalozba Vol 2: 5979
Mobil Chemical Company Vol 1: 1719
Mobil Oil Corporation Vol 1: 7585, 9377
Mobil Sekiyu Kabushiki Kaisha Vol 2: 4253
Mobile Opera Guild Vol 1: 13546
Mobile Post Office Society Vol 1: 13548
The Mobius Awards Vol 1: 13550
Model A Restorers Club Vol 1: 13552
Model Missiles Association Vol 1: 14367
Model "T" Ford Club of America Vol 1: 13556
Modern Language Association of America Vol 1: 13558
The Modern Language Journal Vol 1: 2059, 2062
Modern Plastics Vol 1: 13577, 19308
Mokslu Akademija Vol 2: 4383
Molins plc Vol 2: 7382
Molson Family Foundation Vol 1: 6787
Monaghan Photographic Society Vol 2: 3671
Monash University Vol 2: 407
Monde; Le Vol 2: 2534
Monett Chamber of Commerce Vol 1: 13579
Money for Women/Barbara Deming Memorial Fund Vol 1: 13581
Monk Institute of Jazz; Thelonious Vol 1: 13583
Monsanto Vol 2: 8773
Monsanto Agricultural Products Company Vol 1: 4589
Monsanto Co. Vol 1: 4255
Monsanto Company Vol 1: 4607
Montana Arts Council Vol 1: 13585
Montana Mental Health Association Vol 1: 13587
Montana Society of Certified Public Accountants Vol 1: 13589
Montana Wholesale Distributors Association Vol 1: 13591
Monte Carlo Television Festival Vol 2: 4667
Monthly Labor Review Vol 1: 20517
Monticello Vol 1: 13594
Montreal International Festival of New Cinema Vol 1: 13597
Montreal International Fireworks Competition Vol 1: 13599
Montreal Neurological Institute and Hospital Vol 1: 13601
Montreal Symphony Orchestra Vol 1: 13604
Montreal World Film Festival Vol 1: 13606
Montres Rolex Vol 2: 6498
Montreux Choral Festival Vol 2: 6487

Moore Fund for Writers; Jenny McKean Vol 1: 13609
Moore Medical Corp. Vol 1: 14214
Moosejaw Public Library Vol 1: 7254
Morand; Fondation Paul Vol 2: 2102
Morgan 4/4 Club Vol 2: 8129
Morgan Guaranty Trust Company Vol 1: 8745
Morgan Sports Car Club, Ltd. Vol 2: 8129
Morgan Stanley Vol 1: 16981
Morris Agency; William Vol 1: 12546
Mortar Board Vol 1: 13611
Moss-Thorns Gallery of Art Vol 1: 13615
Mostra Cinematografica Internazionale - La Natura, l'Uomo e il suo Ambiente Vol 2: 3971
Mostra de Valencia, Cinema del Mediterrani Vol 2: 6072
Mostra Internacional de Cinema Em Sao Paulo Vol 2: 1193
Mothers Against Munchausen Syndrome by Proxy Allegations Vol 1: 13617
Motion Picture Theatre Associations of Canada Vol 1: 13621
Motor and Equipment Manufacturer Association Vol 1: 13623
Motor Sports Association Vol 2: 8132
Motor Trend Vol 1: 13625
Motorcycle Safety Foundation Vol 1: 13629
Motorola Vol 1: 11311
Motorola Corporation Vol 1: 11353
Motorola Corp. Vol 1: 19078
Mounds View High School Alumni Association Vol 1: 13631
Mount Desert Island Biological Laboratory Vol 1: 13633
Mount Rogers Planning District Commission Vol 1: 13635
Mount Vernon Genealogical Society Vol 1: 13638
Mountain West Center for Regional Studies Vol 1: 13640
Mountaineering Council of Scotland Vol 2: 8134
Mountaineers Books Vol 1: 13644
Mountainfilm Vol 1: 13646
Mountainview Women's Nine Hole Golf Association Vol 1: 13648
Mouvement Pan Africain du Canada Vol 1: 21944
Movies on a Shoestring Vol 1: 18089
Movimento dei Focolari Vol 2: 3926
Mr. Blackwell Vol 1: 13653
MTM Association for Standards and Research Vol 1: 13656
Mu Phi Epsilon Foundation Vol 1: 13659
Mu Phi Epsilon International Vol 1: 13661
Multi-Level Marketing International Association Vol 1: 13663
Multi-Unit Foodservice Operators Vol 1: 16010, 16014
Multiple Sclerosis International Federation Vol 2: 8136
Multiple Sclerosis Society of Canada Vol 1: 13670
Muncie Obedience Training Club Vol 1: 13672
Municipal Art Society of New York Vol 1: 13674
Municipal Council of Budapest Vol 2: 3285
Municipal Finance Officers and Association of the United States and Canada Vol 1: 10109
Municipal Treasurers Association of the United States and Canada Vol 1: 5829
Municipality of Bolzano Vol 2: 3875
Municipality of Brasov Vol 2: 5806
Municipality of Lisbon Vol 2: 5422
Municipality of Terni Vol 2: 3889
Muscular Dystrophy Association Vol 1: 13682
Muscular Dystrophy Association, Lafayette Vol 1: 13684
Museu de Arte Moderna de Sao Paulo Vol 2: 1191
Museu Villa-Lobos Vol 2: 1195
Museum of Comparative Zoology Vol 1: 13686
Museum of Fine Arts Vol 1: 5069
Museum of Modern Art of Sao Paulo Vol 2: 1191
Museum of New Mexico Vol 1: 13688
Museum of Science, Boston Vol 1: 13691
Museum of the City of New York Vol 1: 13694
Mushroom Growers Association Vol 2: 8143
Music Association of Korea Vol 2: 5503
Music Center of Los Angeles County Vol 1: 13697
Music Centre Slovakia Vol 2: 5966
Music Distributors Association Vol 1: 13699
Music Industries Association - England Vol 2: 8146
Music Operators Association Vol 1: 4942
Music Producers Guild Vol 2: 8148
Music Teachers National Association Vol 1: 13701
Musica Sacra Vol 1: 13709
Musical Arts Society of New Orleans Vol 1: 13711
Musical Club of Hartford Vol 1: 13713
Musicians AFM Local 7 Vol 1: 13715
Musicians Benevolent Fund Vol 2: 8151
Musikkollegium Winterthur Vol 2: 6365
Musikschule der Stadt Ettlingen Vol 2: 3035
Muttart Diabetes Research & Training Centre Vol 1: 13717
Mutual of America Vol 1: 14612
Muzicka Omaladina Srbije Vol 2: 5935
Mycological Society of America Vol 1: 13720
Mystery Readers International Vol 1: 13727
Mystery Writers of America Vol 1: 13729
Mystic Seaport Vol 1: 13733
Mystic Valley Railway Society Vol 1: 13736
Mythic Society Vol 2: 3566
Mythopoeic Society Vol 1: 13738
Naantalin Musiikkijuhlat Vol 2: 1637
Naanteli Music Festival Vol 2: 1637
Nabisco Brands Vol 1: 4157
NACE International: The Corrosion Society Vol 1: 13741
NAHB Research Center Vol 1: 17600
NAHRO International Committee Vol 1: 14264
NAHRO Manufacturers and Suppliers Council Vol 1: 14265
Naismith Memorial Basketball Hall of Fame Vol 1: 13749
The Naito Foundation Vol 2: 4256
NAMI Kansas-The Alliance on Mental Illness Vol 1: 13753
Narishige Scientific Instrument Laboratory Vol 2: 4340
NASCENTE - Cooperative Society with Cultural Purposes Vol 2: 5393
Nasco International, Inc Vol 1: 11227
Nasdaq Educational Foundation Vol 1: 14857
Nasdaq Stock Market Vol 1: 9331
Nash Car Club of America Vol 1: 13755
Nashville Film Festival Vol 1: 13757
Nashville Songwriters Association International Vol 1: 13759
Nasionale Wolkwekersvereniging van Suid-Afrika Vol 2: 5591
NASSTRAC Vol 1: 13761, 13762
Nathan Trust; George Jean Vol 1: 13763
Nation Institute Vol 1: 13765
National Academic Advising Association Vol 1: 13767
The National Academy Vol 1: 13773
National Academy Vol 1: 13773
The National Academy of Design Vol 1: 13773
National Academy of Education Vol 1: 13802
National Academy of Engineering Vol 1: 13804
National Academy of Geography Vol 2: 43
National Academy of Medicine Vol 2: 1320
National Academy of Music, Dance and Drama Vol 2: 3568
National Academy of Neuropsychology Vol 1: 13808
National Academy of Opticianry Vol 1: 13810
National Academy of Popular Music Vol 1: 13815
National Academy of Public Administration Vol 1: 13817
National Academy of Recording Arts and Sciences Vol 1: 13821
National Academy of Sciences Vol 2: 2006
National Academy of Sciences Vol 1: 13824
National Academy of Sciences - Institute of Medicine Vol 1: 13855
National Academy of Sciences of Belarus Vol 2: 829
National Academy of Sciences of Bolivia Vol 2: 1132
National Academy of Sciences of the Republic of Korea Vol 2: 5508
National Academy of Songwriters Vol 1: 19402
National Academy of Sports Vol 1: 13858
National Academy of Television Arts and Sciences Vol 1: 13860
National Academy of Television Arts and Sciences; Hollywood Chapter of the Vol 1: 126
National Accreditation Council for Agencies Serving the Blind and Visually Impaired Vol 1: 13867
National Action Committee on the Status of Women Vol 1: 13871
National Action Council for Minorities in Engineering Vol 1: 13873
National Aeroclub of Russia Vol 2: 6321
National Aeronautic Association Vol 1: 13875
National Aeronautics and Space Administration Vol 1: 13882, 17131, 20844
National Agricultural Aviation Association Vol 1: 13901
National Agricultural Center and Hall of Fame Vol 1: 13912
National Air Transportation Association Vol 1: 13916
National Alliance for Research on Schizophrenia and Depression Vol 1: 13922
National Alliance of Children's Trust and Prevention Funds Vol 1: 775
National Amateur Cycle Speedway Association Vol 2: 6994
National American Legion Press Association Vol 1: 13926

National Amputee Golf Association Vol 1: 13930
National and Provincial Parks Association of Canada Vol 1: 7329
National Animal Control Association Vol 1: 13935
National Anti-Vivisection Society Vol 2: 8046
National Apostolate for Inclusion Ministry Vol 1: 13942
National Arbor Day Foundation Vol 1: 13948
National Archery Association of the United States Vol 1: 13951
National Art Education Association Vol 1: 13955
National Art Materials Trade Association Vol 1: 13977
National Arts Centre Orchestra Vol 1: 13981
National Arts Club Vol 1: 13983
National Arts Council of Zimbabwe Vol 2: 9353
National Asphalt Pavement Association Vol 1: 13996
National Association for Cave Diving Vol 1: 14001
National Association for Environmental Education Vol 1: 16370
National Association for Equal Opportunity in Higher Education Vol 1: 14004
National Association for Ethnic Studies Vol 1: 14008
National Association for Gifted Children Vol 1: 14011
National Association for Girls and Women in Sport Vol 1: 14013
National Association for Hospital Development Vol 1: 5378
National Association for Humane and Environmental Education Vol 1: 14015
National Association for Industry-Education Cooperation Vol 1: 14017
National Association for Interpretation Vol 1: 14020
National Association for Persons with Intellectual Disabilities of Germany Vol 2: 3037
National Association for Persons with Mental Handicap of Germany Vol 2: 3037
National Association for Public Continuing and Adult Education Vol 1: 946
National Association for Pupil Transportation Vol 1: 14025
National Association for Recreational Equality Vol 1: 14027
National Association for Remedial Teaching Vol 1: 11849
National Association for Research in Science Teaching Vol 1: 14029
National Association for Search and Rescue Vol 1: 14036
National Association for Sport and Physical Education Vol 1: 14042
National Association for Stock Car Auto Racing Vol 1: 14044
National Association for the Advancement of Colored People Vol 1: 14046
National Association for the Advancement of Humane Education Vol 1: 14015
National Association for the Advancement of Psychoanalysis Vol 1: 14051
National Association for the Specialty Food Trade Vol 1: 14053
National Association for Vocational Education Special Needs Personnel Vol 1: 14056
National Association of Academic Advisors for Athletics Vol 1: 14060
National Association of Academies of Science Vol 1: 14063
National Association of Accountants Vol 1: 10984
National Association of Advertising Publishers Vol 1: 5695
National Association of African-American Sportswriters and Broadcasters Vol 1: 14065
National Association of Amateur Oarsmen Vol 1: 20745
National Association of American Composers and Conductors Vol 1: 14145
National Association of Animal Breeders Vol 1: 14067
National Association of Anorexia Nervosa and Associated Disorders Vol 1: 14071
National Association of Assessing Officers Vol 1: 11266
National Association of Attorneys General Vol 1: 14075
National Association of Bar Executives Vol 1: 14078
National Association of Basketball Coaches Vol 1: 14080
National Association of Biology Teachers Vol 1: 14089
National Association of Black Journalists Vol 1: 14100
National Association of Boards of Education/NCEA Vol 1: 14617, 14619
National Association of Boards of Pharmacy Vol 1: 14103
National Association of Broadcasters Vol 1: 14105
National Association of Catholic Chaplains Vol 1: 14119
National Association of College and University Business Officers Vol 1: 14123
National Association of College and University Food Services Vol 1: 14127
National Association of College Auxiliary Services Vol 1: 14133
National Association of College Gymnastics Coaches Vol 1: 8157
National Association of Colleges and Teachers of Agriculture Vol 1: 16401
National Association of Colored Graduate Nurses Vol 1: 3281
National Association of Community Health Centers Vol 1: 14137
National Association of Competitive Mounted Orienteering Vol 1: 14139
National Association of Composers, U.S.A. Vol 1: 14145
National Association of Conservation Districts Vol 1: 14148
National Association of Conservation Districts Vol 1: 14154
National Association of Consumer Agency Administrators Vol 1: 14161
National Association of Corrosion Engineers Vol 1: 13741
National Association of Counties Vol 1: 14164
National Association of Counties Vol 1: 14180
National Association of County Agricultural Agents Vol 1: 14169
National Association of County and City Health Officials Vol 1: 14172
National Association of County and Prosecuting Attorneys Vol 1: 14915
National Association of County Engineers Vol 1: 14178
National Association of County Information Officers Vol 1: 14180
National Association of Credit Management Vol 1: 14182
National Association of Criminal Defense Lawyers Vol 1: 14184
National Association of Diaconate Directors Vol 1: 14187
National Association of Diocesan Ecumenical Officers Vol 1: 14193
National Association of Display Industries Vol 1: 14195
National Association of Dramatic and Speech Arts Vol 1: 14199
National Association of Elementary School Principals Vol 1: 14205
National Association of Elementary School Principals Vol 1: 17887, 20489
National Association of Emergency Medical Technicians Vol 1: 14208
National Association of Evangelicals Vol 1: 21947
National Association of Farm Broadcasters Vol 1: 19876
National Association of Federal Credit Unions Vol 1: 14221
National Association of Federal Veterinarians Vol 1: 14225
National Association of Federally Licensed Firearms Dealers Vol 1: 14227
National Association of Fire Investigators Vol 1: 14229
National Association of First Responders Vol 1: 14231
National Association of Fleet Administrators Vol 1: 14233
National Association of Foreign-Trade Zones Vol 1: 14235
National Association of Geoscience Teachers Vol 1: 14237
National Association of Government Communicators Vol 1: 14241
National Association of Greeting Card Publishers Vol 1: 10173
National Association of Health and Welfare Ministries of the United Methodist Church Vol 1: 20347
National Association of Health Underwriters Vol 1: 14245
National Association of Hispanic Journalists Vol 1: 14248
National Association of Hispanic Nurses Vol 1: 14251
National Association of Home and Workshop Writers Vol 1: 14254
National Association of Home Builders Vol 1: 14256, 17598
National Association of Hospital Fire Officers Vol 2: 8153
National Association of Housing and Redevelopment Officials Vol 1: 14262
National Association of Independent Fee Appraisers Vol 1: 14270
National Association of Independent Resurfacers Vol 1: 14273
National Association of Industrial and Office Properties Vol 1: 14275
National Association of Intercollegiate Athletics Vol 1: 14278

National Association of Intercollegiate Athletics Vol 1: 15069, 15076
National Association of Jazz Educators Vol 1: 11248
National Association of Jewelry Appraisers Vol 1: 14294
National Association of Journalism Directors Vol 1: 12447
National Association of Left-Handed Golfers Vol 1: 14297
National Association of Legal Investigators Vol 1: 14301
National Association of Literary Translators Vol 2: 5448
National Association of Metal Finishers Vol 1: 14303
National Association of Musical Merchandise Wholesalers Vol 1: 13699
National Association of Negro Business and Professional Women's Clubs Vol 1: 14310
National Association of Neonatal Nurses Vol 1: 14316
National Association of Norwegian Architects Vol 2: 5129
National Association of Paralegals Vol 2: 8155
National Association of Pastoral Musicians Vol 1: 14319
National Association of Pediatric Nurse Practitioners Vol 1: 14321
National Association of Personal Financial Advisors Vol 1: 14324
National Association of Pet Cemeteries Vol 1: 11374
National Association of Photo Equipment Technicians Vol 1: 14327
National Association of Pipe Coating Applicators Vol 1: 14329
National Association of Printing Ink Manufacturer Vol 1: 14331
National Association of Produce Market Managers Vol 1: 14336
National Association of Professional Baseball Leagues Vol 1: 14338
National Association of Professional Gardeners Vol 1: 17624
National Association of Professional Insurance Agents Vol 1: 14342
National Association of Professional Organizers Vol 1: 14346
National Association of Public Golf Courses Vol 2: 8159
National Association of Purchasing Management Vol 1: 10839
National Association of Quick Printers Vol 1: 17563
National Association of Railroad Passengers Vol 1: 14348
National Association of Real Estate Editors Vol 1: 14351
National Association of Realtors Vol 1: 14353
National Association of Recording Merchandisers Vol 1: 14356
National Association of Rocketry Vol 1: 14367
National Association of Sanitarians Vol 1: 14940
National Association of Scholars Vol 1: 14369
National Association of School Psychologists Vol 1: 3711
National Association of Schools of Public Affairs and Administration Vol 1: 14373
National Association of Science Writers Vol 1: 14379
National Association of Scientific Materials Managers Vol 1: 14381
National Association of Secondary School Principals Vol 1: 14383
National Association of Secondary School Principals Vol 1: 17887, 20489
National Association of Shopfitters Vol 2: 8162
National Association of Social Workers Vol 1: 14387
National Association of Social Workers, Kansas Chapter Vol 1: 14392
National Association of State Chief Information Officers Vol 1: 14394
National Association of State Directors of Vocational Technical Education Vol 1: 15930
National Association of State Information Resource Executives Vol 1: 14394
National Association of State Procurement Officials Vol 1: 14396
National Association of State Purchasing Officials Vol 1: 14396
National Association of State Units on Aging Vol 1: 14398
National Association of Store Fixture Manufacturer Vol 1: 14400
National Association of Student Personnel Administrators Vol 1: 14402
National Association of Summer Sessions Vol 1: 16390
National Association of Swedish Architects Vol 2: 6167
National Association of Swine Test Stations Vol 1: 15830
National Association of Teachers of Singing Vol 1: 14410
National Association of Television Program Executives Vol 1: 14412
National Association of Temporary Staffing Services Vol 1: 4684
National Association of the Bureau of Animal Industry Veterinarians Vol 1: 14225
National Association of the Holy Name Society Vol 1: 14414
National Association of the Physically Handicapped Vol 1: 14424
National Association of the Remodeling Industry Vol 1: 14427
National Association of Theatre Owners Vol 1: 14440
National Association of Towns and Townships Vol 1: 14442
National Association of Towns and Townships - National Center for Small Communities Vol 1: 14444
National Association of Trade and Technical Schools Vol 1: 7582
National Association of Traveling Nurses Vol 1: 14446
National Association of Underwater Instructors Vol 1: 14448
National Association of University Women Vol 1: 14452
National Association of Women and the Law Vol 1: 14454
National Association of Women Artists Vol 1: 14456
National Association of Women Judges Vol 1: 14458
National Association of Youth Orchestras Vol 2: 8164
National Assoiation of Temporary Services Vol 1: 4684
National Athletic Trainers' Association Vol 1: 14460
National Auctioneers Association Vol 1: 14463
National Audio-Visual Association Vol 1: 11497
National Audubon Society Vol 1: 1198
National Audubon Society Vol 1: 14467
National Auricula and Primula Society Vol 2: 8168
National Auto Auction Association Vol 1: 14470
National Automobile Dealers Association Vol 1: 20092
National Automotive Dealers Association Vol 1: 17826
National Autonomous University of Mexico Vol 2: 4586
National Aviation Hall of Fame Vol 1: 14472
National Back Pain Association Vol 2: 6847
National Ballet of Canada Vol 1: 14477
National Band and Choral Directors Hall of Fame Vol 1: 15227
National Band Association Vol 1: 14479
National Bank of Canada Vol 1: 5540
National Bar Association Vol 1: 14489
National Baseball Hall of Fame and Museum Vol 1: 14493
National Basketball Association Vol 1: 14497
National Beep Baseball Association Vol 1: 14510
National Biplane Association Vol 1: 14512
National Bison Association Vol 1: 14517
National Black Lung Association Vol 1: 6429
National Black Police Association Vol 1: 14520
National Black Programming Consortium Vol 1: 14525
National Board for Certification in Hearing Instrument Sciences Vol 1: 14527
National Book Council of Pakistan Vol 2: 5192
National Book Critics Circle Vol 1: 14529
National Book Development Council of Singapore Vol 2: 5939
National Book Foundation Vol 2: 5192
National Book League (England) Vol 2: 6879
National Book Service Vol 1: 7261
National Broadcast Editorial Association Vol 1: 14102
National Broadcasting Society - Alpha Epsilon Rho Vol 1: 14533
National Broiler Council Vol 1: 17498
National Buffalo Association Vol 1: 14517
National Building Museum Vol 1: 14548
National Bureau of Standards Vol 1: 6201, 20474
National Burglar and Fire Alarm Association Vol 1: 14550
National Burglar and Fire Alarm Association - National Training School (NTS) Vol 1: 14558
National Business Aircraft Association Vol 1: 14561
National Business Aviation Association Vol 1: 14561
National Business Education Association Vol 1: 14570
National Cable and Telecommunications Association Vol 1: 14576
National Cancer Institute of Canada Vol 1: 14584

Organization Index

National Carousel Association Vol 1: 14586
National Cartoonists Society Vol 1: 14588
National CASA Association Vol 1: 14874
National Catalog Managers Association Vol 1: 14593
National Catholic Band Association Vol 1: 14595
National Catholic Bandmasters' Association Vol 1: 14595
National Catholic Development Conference Vol 1: 14602
National Catholic Education Association Vol 1: 17887
National Catholic Educational Association Vol 1: 14605
National Catholic Pharmacists Guild of the United States Vol 1: 14626
National Caucus and Center on Black Aged Vol 1: 14632
National Center for Clinical Infant Programs. Vol 1: 22108
National Center for Public Policy Research Vol 1: 14634
National Center for Public Productivity Vol 1: 14636
National Center for State Courts Vol 1: 14639
National Centre for Audiology Vol 1: 14644
National Cervical Cancer Coalition Vol 1: 14646
National Chamber of Commerce and Industry of Malaysia Vol 2: 4440
National Chamber of Commerce for Women Vol 1: 14648
National Child Labor Committee Vol 1: 14651
National Christian College Athletic Association Vol 1: 14653
National Citizens' Coalition Vol 1: 14671
National Civic League Vol 1: 14673
National Classical Music Institute Vol 2: 5510
National Classification Management Society Vol 1: 14675
National Coalition of 100 Black Women Vol 1: 14677
National Coffee Association of U.S.A. Vol 1: 14679
National College of District Attorneys Vol 1: 14681
National Collegiate Athletic Association Vol 1: 14684
National Collegiate Athletic Association Vol 1: 15066, 15071, 15077, 20583
National Collegiate Athletic Association - Division 1 Track Coaches Association Vol 1: 14690
National Commercial Finance Association Vol 1: 8289
National Commission on Correctional Health Care Vol 1: 14697
National Commission on Culture and the Arts Vol 2: 5268
National Commission on Working Women Vol 1: 21617
National Committee for Adoption Vol 1: 14747
National Committee for Bulk Materials Handling Vol 2: 423
National Committee for Recording for the Blind Vol 1: 17903
National Committee for the Observance of Mother's Day Vol 1: 15391
National Committee on American Foreign Policy Vol 1: 14700
National Committee on Bulk Materials Handling Vol 2: 375
National Committee on Coastal and Ocean Engineering Vol 2: 429
National Committee on Water Engineering Vol 2: 366
National Communication Association Vol 1: 14705
National Confectionery Sales Association Vol 1: 14718
National Confederation of Hungarian Trade Unions Vol 2: 3302
National Conference of Editorial Writers Vol 1: 14102
National Conference of Puerto Rican Women Vol 1: 14720
National Conference of Women's Bar Associations Vol 1: 14722
National Conference on Peacemaking and Conflict Resolution Vol 1: 14724
National Constables Association Vol 1: 14726
National Consumers League Vol 1: 14732
National Coordinating Board of Family Planning Vol 2: 3604
National Coordinating Council on Emergency Management Vol 1: 11347
National Corn Growers Association Vol 1: 14735
National Corvette Restorers Society Vol 1: 14737
National Cosmetology Association Vol 1: 14740
National Costumers Association Vol 1: 14744
National Council for Adoption Vol 1: 14747
National Council for Children's Rights Vol 1: 7914
National Council for Community Behavioral Healthcare Vol 1: 14750
National Council for Community Relations Vol 1: 14772
National Council for Continuing Education and Training Vol 1: 14752
National Council for Eurasian and East European Research Vol 1: 14756
National Council for GeoCosmic Research Vol 1: 14758
National Council for Geographic Education Vol 1: 14760
National Council for Interior Design Qualification Vol 1: 14770
National Council for Marketing and Public Relations Vol 1: 14772
National Council for School Sport Vol 2: 8170
National Council for Scientific and Technological Research Vol 2: 9320
National Council for Small Business Management Development Vol 1: 11512
National Council for the Social Studies Vol 1: 14777
National Council of College Publications Advisers Vol 1: 8167
National Council of Commercial Plant Breeders Vol 1: 14792
National Council of Engineering Examiners Vol 1: 14796
National Council of Examiners for Engineering and Surveying Vol 1: 14796
National Council of Farmer Cooperatives Vol 1: 14799
National Council of La Raza Vol 1: 14803
National Council of Less Commonly Taught Languages Vol 1: 14809
National Council of Patent Law Associations Vol 1: 20733
National Council of Physical Distribution Management Vol 1: 8579
National Council of Science and Technology Vol 2: 4563
National Council of Secondary School Athletic Directors Vol 1: 14811
National Council of Senior Citizens Vol 1: 14813
National Council of Social Security Management Associations Vol 1: 14819
National Council of Supervisors of Mathematics Vol 1: 14823
National Council of Teachers of English Vol 1: 8375
National Council of Teachers of English Vol 1: 14825, 14834
National Council of Teachers of English - Assembly on Literature for Adolescents Vol 1: 14845
National Council of Women of Kenya Vol 2: 4364
National Council on Alcoholism Vol 1: 14847
National Council on Alcoholism and Drug Dependence Vol 1: 14847
National Council on Alcoholism and Drug Dependence Greater Detroit Area Vol 1: 14854
National Council on Community Services and Continuing Education Vol 1: 14752
National Council on Community Services for Community and Junior Colleges Vol 1: 14752
National Council on Economic Education Vol 1: 14856
National Council on Family Relations Vol 1: 14858
National Council on Intellectual Disability Vol 2: 461
National Council on Public History Vol 1: 14865
National Council on Schoolhouse Construction Vol 1: 8572
National Council on the Aging Vol 1: 4637
National Council on the Aging Vol 1: 14868
National Council on U.S.-Arab Relations Vol 1: 14871
National Court Appointed Special Advocate Association Vol 1: 14873
National Court Reporters Association Vol 1: 14877
National Court Reporters Foundation Vol 1: 14881
National Cowboy and Western Heritage Museum Vol 1: 14885, 18103, 18104
National Cowboy Hall of Fame and Western Heritage Center Vol 1: 14885
National Cutting Horse Association Vol 1: 14888
National Cyclists Union Vol 2: 6996
National Dairy Shrine Vol 1: 14890
National Dance Association Vol 1: 14894
National Defense Industrial Association Vol 1: 14900
National Defense Transportation Association Vol 1: 14903
National Democratic Institute for International Affairs Vol 1: 14909
National Derby Rallies Vol 1: 14911
National DeSoto Club Vol 1: 14913

National District Attorneys Association Vol 1: 14915
National Duckpin Bowling Congress Vol 1: 14917
National Economic Association Vol 1: 14919
National Education Association Vol 1: 17887
National Eisteddfod of Wales Vol 2: 8172
National Electric Sign Association Vol 1: 11904
National Electrical Manufacturer Association Vol 1: 14921
National Electrical Manufacturer Representatives Association Vol 1: 14923
National Electrical Testing Association Vol 1: 11552
National Electronics Sales and Service Dealers Association Vol 1: 14925
National Electronics Service Dealers Association Vol 1: 14925
National Endowment for Democracy Vol 1: 14927
National Endowment for the Arts Vol 1: 9161, 9553
National Endowment for the Arts Vol 1: 14929
National Endowment for the Arts Vol 1: 20052, 20053, 21571, 21666
National Endowment for the Humanities Vol 1: 14934
National Environmental Health Association Vol 1: 14940
National Environmental Health Association Vol 1: 16584
National Environmental, Safety and Health Training Association Vol 1: 14949
National Ethnic Coalition of Organizations Vol 1: 14954
National Eye Research Foundation Vol 1: 14956
National Family Partnership Vol 1: 14958
National Farm-City Council Vol 1: 14960
National Federation Interscholastic Officials Association Vol 1: 14980
National Federation of Abstracting and Information Services Vol 1: 14962
National Federation of Coffee Growers of Colombia Vol 2: 1327
National Federation of Democratic Women Vol 1: 14965
National Federation of Jewish Men's Clubs Vol 1: 9508
National Federation of Local Cable Programmers Vol 1: 457
National Federation of Music Clubs Vol 1: 8348
National Federation of Music Clubs Vol 1: 14969
National Federation of Music Societies Vol 2: 8098
National Federation of Parents for Drug-Free Youth Vol 1: 14958
National Federation of Plastering Contractors Vol 2: 7514
National Federation of Press Women Vol 1: 14971
National Federation of State High School Associations Vol 1: 14976
National Federation of State High School Associations - National Federation Interscholastic Coaches Association Vol 1: 14980
National Federation of State High School Athletic Associations Vol 1: 14976
National Federation of State Poetry Societies Vol 1: 14986
National Federation of the Blind Vol 1: 15038
National Federation of the Blind of South Dakota Vol 1: 15042
National Federation of Women's Institutes Vol 2: 8175
National Field Archery Association Vol 1: 15044
National Film Board of Canada Vol 1: 6033, 20117
National Fisheries Institute Vol 1: 18387
National Fishing Lure Collectors Club Vol 1: 15046
National Flag Foundation Vol 1: 15048
National Flexible Packaging Association Vol 1: 9571
National Fluid Power Association Vol 1: 15053
National Flute Association Vol 1: 15056
National Football Foundation and College Hall of Fame Vol 1: 15065
National Football Foundation and College Hall of Fame, Valley of the Sun Chapter Vol 1: 15078
National Football Foundation and Hall of Fame Vol 1: 15065
National Football League Vol 1: 15083
National Football League Players Association Vol 1: 15090
National Forensic Association Vol 1: 15094
National Forensic League Vol 1: 15096
National Forest Products Assocation Vol 1: 2290
National Forum for Black Public Administrators Vol 1: 15109
National Forum of Greek Orthodox Church Musicians Vol 1: 15112
National Foundation for Advancement in the Arts Vol 1: 15116
National Foundation for Infectious Diseases Vol 1: 15119
National Foundation for Peroneal Muscular Atrophy Vol 1: 7804
National Friends of Public Broadcasting Vol 1: 15126
National Frozen and Refrigerated Foods Association Vol 1: 15131
National Frozen Food Association Vol 1: 15131
National Funeral Directors Association Vol 1: 15133
National Garden Clubs Vol 1: 15135
National Genealogical Society Vol 1: 15137
National Geographic Society Vol 2: 6973
National Geographic Society Vol 1: 15153
National Glass Association Vol 1: 15163
National Golf Course Owners Association Vol 1: 21923
National Golf Foundation Vol 1: 15166, 21923
National Governors Association Vol 1: 15169
National Grange Vol 1: 15171
National Grocers Association Vol 1: 15173
National Guard Association of the United States Vol 1: 15175
National Guild of Community Schools of the Arts Vol 1: 15178
National Gymnastics Judges Association Vol 1: 15181
National Hacky Sack Footbag Players Association Vol 1: 21920, 21921
National Hairdressers and Cosmetologists Association Vol 1: 14740
National Hardwood Lumber Association Vol 1: 15185
National Head Injury Foundation Vol 1: 6604
National Headache Foundation Vol 1: 15187
National Headliner Awards Vol 1: 15193
National Headliner Club Vol 1: 15193
National Health and Medical Research Council Vol 2: 463
National Hearing Aid Society Vol 1: 11671
National Hearing Conservation Association Vol 1: 15195
National Hemophilia Foundation Vol 1: 15200
National Hereford Hog Record Association Vol 1: 15215
National High School Athletic Coaches Association Vol 1: 15222
National High School Band and Choral Directors Hall of Fame Vol 1: 15224
National High School Band Directors Hall of Fame Vol 1: 15224
National High School Band Directors Hall of Fame - College Division Vol 1: 15227
National High School Rodeo Association Vol 1: 15232
National Highway Traffic Safety Administration Vol 1: 11308
National Highway Traffic Safety Administration (NHTSA) Vol 1: 11307
National Hockey League Players' Association Vol 1: 15234
National Home Fashions League Vol 1: 11640
National Home Furnishings Association Vol 1: 15236
National Home Improvement Council Vol 1: 14427
National Horseshoe Pitchers Association of America Vol 1: 15238
National House-Building Council Vol 2: 8590
National Housing Conference Vol 1: 15245
National Humanities Center Vol 1: 15249
National Hypertension Association Vol 1: 15251
National Independent Automobile Dealers Association Vol 1: 15253
National Indian Health Board Vol 1: 15255
National Industries for the Blind Vol 1: 15257
National Institute for Women of Color Vol 1: 11264
National Institute of American Doll Artists Vol 1: 15260
National Institute of Ceramic Engineers Vol 1: 1679, 1683, 1697
National Institute of Governmental Purchasing Vol 1: 15264
National Institute of Mental Health Vol 1: 1899, 3641
National Institute of Nursing Research Vol 1: 15270
National Institute of Real Estate Brokers Vol 1: 8582
National Institute of Standards and Technology Vol 1: 6202
National Intercollegiate Soccer Officials Association Vol 1: 15274
National Interscholastic Swimming Coaches Association of America Vol 1: 15281
National Intramural-Recreational Sports Association Vol 1: 15285
National Intravenous Therapy Association Vol 1: 10800

Organization Index

National Italian American Bar Association Vol 1: 15293
National Jewish Committee on Scouting Vol 1: 15296
National Jewish Girl Scout Committee Vol 1: 15302
National Junior College Athletic Association Vol 1: 15304
National Kidney Foundation Vol 1: 15318
National Kidney Foundation of Arkansas Vol 1: 15329
National Kidney Foundation of Ohio Vol 1: 15331
National Lawyers Wives Vol 1: 2930
National League of American Pen Women Vol 1: 15333
National Legal Aid and Defender Association Vol 1: 15335
National Legislative Council for the Handicapped Vol 1: 15341
National Lesbian and Gay Journalists Association Vol 1: 15343
National Library of Australia Vol 2: 473
National Library of Medicine Vol 1: 13259
National Library of Mexico Vol 2: 4619
National Lighting Bureau Vol 1: 14921
National LP-Gas Association Vol 1: 15551
National Lubricating Grease Institute Vol 1: 15345
National Magazine Awards Foundation Vol 1: 15354
National Male Nurses Association Vol 1: 933
National Marine Educators Association Vol 1: 15356
National Marine Manufacturers Association Vol 1: 15362
National Marine Manufacturers Association Vol 1: 20773
National Marine Representatives Association Vol 1: 15365
National Medical Fellowships Vol 1: 15367
National Mental Health Association Vol 1: 15371
National Micrographics Association Vol 1: 306
National Migraine Foundation Vol 1: 15187
National Military Fish and Wildlife Association Vol 1: 15380
National Military Intelligence Association Vol 1: 15382
National Milk Producers Federation Vol 1: 2102
National Mining Association Vol 1: 15385
National Minority Supplier Development Council Vol 1: 15388
National Mother's Day Committee Vol 1: 15391
National Multiple Sclerosis Society Vol 1: 15393
National Municipal League Vol 1: 14673
National Museum of Racing and Hall of Fame Vol 1: 15403
National Music Council Vol 1: 15405
National Music Council of The United Kingdom Vol 2: 8178
The National Music Festival Vol 1: 15407
National Newspaper Association Vol 1: 15409
National Newspaper Publishers Association Vol 1: 15413
National Notary Association Vol 1: 15415
National Ocean Industries Association Vol 1: 15418
National Office Paper Recycling Project Vol 1: 15421
National Opera Association Vol 1: 15425
National Operatic and Dramatic Association Vol 2: 8180
National Organization for Human Service Education Vol 1: 15431
National Organization for Men Vol 1: 15437
National Organization for Rare Disorders Vol 1: 15439
National Organization for Victim Assistance Vol 1: 15441
National Organization for Women, East End Chapter Vol 1: 15451
National Organization of Black Law Enforcement Executives, Central Virginia Chapter Vol 1: 15453
National Organization of Human Service Educators Vol 1: 15431
National Organization of Single Mothers Vol 1: 15455
National Organization on Disability Vol 1: 15457
National Organization Taunting Safety and Fairness Everywhere Vol 1: 15459
National Orientation Directors Association Vol 1: 15461
National Outdoor Book Awards Vol 1: 15464
National Paint and Coatings Association Vol 1: 15466
National Paperbox and Packaging Association Vol 1: 15474
National Paperbox Association Vol 1: 15474
National Park Academy of the Arts Vol 1: 15476
National Park Service Vol 1: 15492
National Parkinson Foundation Vol 1: 15485
National Parks Association Vol 1: 15488
National Parks Conservation Association Vol 1: 15488
National Peach Council Vol 1: 15493
National Peanut Council Vol 1: 3366
National Pest Control Association Vol 1: 15496
National Piers Society Vol 2: 8182
National Pig Carvers Association Vol 1: 15499
National Pigeon Association Vol 1: 15501
National Playwrights Conference Vol 1: 15506
National Poetry Association Vol 1: 15511
National Pony Society Vol 2: 8185
National Portrait Gallery Vol 2: 8187
National Portraiture Association Vol 2: 8189
National Post Vol 1: 8541
National Press Club Vol 1: 15513
National Press Foundation Vol 1: 15516, 15525
National Press Photographers Association Vol 1: 15530
National Propane Gas Association Vol 1: 15551
National Property Management Association Vol 1: 15557
National PTA - National Congress of Parents and Teachers Vol 1: 15561
National Quality Institute Vol 1: 15567
National Railroad Construction and Maintenance Association Vol 1: 15569
National Ramah Commission Vol 1: 15572
National Recreation and Park Association Vol 1: 15574
National Recreation and Parks Association Vol 1: 4478
National Recreational Vehicle Owners Club Vol 1: 15586
National Recycling Coalition Vol 1: 15588
National Rehabilitation Association Vol 1: 15590
National Rehabilitation Association - Vocational Evaluation and Work Adjustment Association Vol 1: 15598
National Rehabilitation Counseling Association Vol 1: 15602
National Rehabilitation Hospital Vol 1: 15608
National Religious Broadcasters Vol 1: 15610
National Religious Vocation Conference Vol 1: 15619
National Remodeling Association Vol 1: 14427
National Research Council Vol 1: 15621
National Research Council of Canada Vol 1: 16021
National Research Council of the Philippines Vol 2: 5276
National Research Institute for Earth Science and Disaster Prevention - Nagaoka Institute of Snow and Ice Studies Vol 2: 4258
National Restaurant Association Vol 1: 15624
National Restaurant Association Educational Foundation Vol 1: 15629
National Restaurant Association Foundation Vol 1: 15629
National Retail Federation Vol 1: 15632
National Retail Merchants Association Vol 1: 15632
National Reye's Syndrome Foundation Vol 1: 15641
National Rifle Association Vol 2: 8191
National Rifle Association of America Vol 1: 15644
National Rural Health Association Vol 1: 15648
National Rural Health Care Association Vol 1: 15648
National RV Owners Club Vol 1: 15586
National Safety Council Vol 1: 15655
National Safety Council, Northern Ohio Chapter Vol 1: 15661
National Scale Men's Association Vol 1: 12029
National Scholastic Press Association Vol 1: 15663
National Scholastic Press Association/ Associated Collegiate Press Vol 1: 19811
National School Boards Association Vol 1: 12554
National School Plant Managers Association Vol 1: 3886
National School Public Relations Association Vol 1: 15666
National School Sailing Association Vol 2: 8193
National School Transportation Association Vol 1: 15670
National Schools Committee for Economic Education Vol 1: 15674
National Science Foundation Vol 1: 15676
National Science Foundation Vol 1: 20731
National Science Teachers Association Vol 1: 15682
National Scrabble Association Vol 1: 15695
National Sculpture Society Vol 1: 15697
National Sea Grant College Program Vol 1: 13358
National Security Council Vol 1: 15702

National Security Industrial Association Vol 1: 14900
National Sheep Association Vol 2: 8196
National Shellfisheries Association Vol 1: 15704
National Sheriffs' Association Vol 1: 11307
National Shorthand Reporters Association Vol 1: 14877
National Silo Association Vol 1: 11906
National Skeet Shooting Association Vol 1: 15806
National Small-Bore Rifle Association Vol 2: 8198
National Small Shipments Traffic Conference Vol 1: 13761
National Soccer Coaches Association of America Vol 1: 15706
National Society, Daughters of the American Revolution Vol 1: 15711
National Society for Histotechnology Vol 1: 15714
National Society for Park Resources Vol 1: 15723
National Society for Performance and Instruction Vol 1: 11938
National Society of Artists Vol 1: 15727
National Society of Arts and Letters Vol 1: 15729
National Society of Biomedical Equipment Technicians Vol 1: 15736
National Society of Fingerprint Officers Vol 2: 7522
National Society of Insurance Premium Auditors Vol 1: 15738
National Society of Interior Design Vol 1: 4458
National Society of Newspaper Columnists Vol 1: 15741
National Society of Painters in Casein and Acrylic Vol 1: 15743
National Society of Professional Engineers Vol 1: 15745
National Society of Professional Surveyors Vol 1: 15757
National Society of Tole and Decorative Painters Vol 1: 19096
National Society, Sons of the American Revolution Vol 1: 15763
National Softball Congress Vol 1: 12036
National Sojourners Vol 1: 15786
National Space Club Vol 1: 15788
National Speakers Association Vol 1: 15790
National Speleological Society Vol 1: 15793
National Spinal Cord Injury Association Vol 1: 15804
National Spiritual Assembly of the Baha'is of Vanuatu Vol 2: 9303
National Sporting Clays Association Vol 1: 15806
National Sports Law Institute Vol 1: 15808
National Sportscasters and Sportswriters Association Vol 1: 15811
National Spotted Saddle Horse Association Vol 1: 15814
National Starch & Chemical Company Vol 1: 1762
National Steeplechase Association Vol 1: 15817
National Stereoscopic Association Vol 1: 15819
National Stroke Association Vol 1: 15821
National Student Campaign Against Hunger and Homelessness Vol 1: 15825
National Swimming Pool Institute Vol 1: 5814
National Swine Improvement Federation Vol 1: 15830
National Symphony Orchestra Association Vol 1: 15833
National Tattoo Association Vol 1: 15835
National Tattoo Club of the World Vol 1: 15835
National Taxpayers Union Vol 1: 15856
National Telecommunications Cooperative Association Vol 1: 15858
National Telemedia Council Vol 1: 15867
National Telephone Cooperative Association Vol 1: 15858
National Theatre Conference Vol 1: 15869
National Therapeutic Recreation Society Vol 1: 15871
National Thespian Society Vol 1: 9179
National Threshers Association Vol 1: 15879
National Tractor Pullers Association Vol 1: 15881
National Traditional Country Music Association Vol 1: 15894
National Traditionalist Caucus Vol 1: 15899
National Transportation Week Vol 1: 15902
National Trappers Association Vol 1: 15907
National Trust for Historic Preservation Vol 1: 15916
National Turf Writers Association Vol 1: 15920
National Turf Writers Association Vol 1: 20084, 20085
National University Extension Association Vol 1: 20945
National Urban League Vol 1: 15924
National Vegetable Society Vol 2: 8201
National Vocational Agricultural Teachers' Association Vol 1: 16004
National Vocational Technical Education Foundation Vol 1: 15929
National Water Resources Association Vol 1: 15931
National Water Safety Congress Vol 1: 15934
National Watercolor Society Vol 1: 15939
National Westminster Bank plc Vol 2: 7417
National Wheelchair Athletic Association Vol 1: 21595
National Wheelchair Basketball Association Vol 1: 15942
National Whistleblower Center Vol 1: 15946
National Wild Turkey Federation Vol 1: 15948
National Wildlife Federation Vol 1: 15951
National Wildlife Rehabilitators Association Vol 1: 15953
National Woman's Party Vol 1: 15957
National Women's Hall of Fame Vol 1: 15959
National Women's Political Caucus Vol 1: 15961
National Women's Studies Association Vol 1: 15964
National Wood Flooring Association Vol 1: 15969
National Woodland Owners Association Vol 1: 15975
National Wool Growers' Association of South Africa Vol 2: 5591
National Wrestling Coaches Association Vol 1: 15982
National Wrestling Hall of Fame & Museum Vol 1: 15985
National Writers Association Vol 1: 15991
National Writers Union Vol 1: 15997
National Writers United Service Organization Vol 1: 15998
National Writers Workshop Vol 1: 15999
National Young Farmer Educational Association Vol 1: 16002
National Young Farmer Educational Association Vol 1: 16002
National Youth Bureau Vol 2: 6614
National Youth Bureau. Vol 2: 6615
National Youth Service Council Vol 2: 6126
The Nationalist Movement Vol 1: 16006
Nation's Restaurant News - Lebhar-Friedman Inc. Vol 1: 16008
NationsBank of Texas, N.A. Vol 1: 235, 237
Native American Institute Vol 1: 2603
Native Prairies Association of Texas Vol 1: 16015
The Natural History Museum Vol 2: 8204
Natural Resources Defense Council Vol 1: 16019
Natural Sciences and Engineering Research Council of Canada Vol 1: 16021
Natural World Vol 2: 8207
Nature Canada Vol 1: 16026
Nature Conservancy Vol 1: 16030
Nature Conservancy of Minnesota Vol 1: 16035
Nature Saskatchewan Vol 1: 16037
Nature's Window Art Gallery Vol 1: 7540
Naumburg Foundation; Walter W. Vol 1: 16043
Nautical Institute Vol 2: 8209
Nautical Research Guild Vol 1: 16046
Naval Enlisted Reserve Association Vol 1: 16049
Naval Historical Collectors and Research Association Vol 2: 8211
Naval Submarine League Vol 1: 16051
NCEA Parents Office Vol 1: 14621
NCSJ: Advocates on Behalf of Jews in Russia, Ukraine, the Baltic Vol 1: 16059
NCTE Research Foundation Vol 1: 14842
NDT Italiana Company Vol 2: 4014
Near East/South Asia Council of Overseas Schools Vol 2: 3178
Nebraska Dressage Association Vol 1: 16061
Nebraska Hospice and Palliative Care Association Vol 1: 16063
Nebraska Humanities Council Vol 1: 16065
Nebraska Library Association Vol 1: 16067
Nebraska Poultry Industries Vol 1: 16072
The Nebraska Review Vol 1: 16074
Nebraska State Genealogical Society Vol 1: 16076
Nebraska State Poetry Society Vol 1: 15014
Nebraska Sustainable Agriculture Society Vol 1: 16078
NEC Corp Vol 2: 7973
NEC Corporation Vol 1: 10873
Nederlandse Kankerbestirijding -KWF Vol 2: 4726
Nederlandse Taalunie Vol 2: 4851
Nederlandse Triathlon Bond Vol 2: 4853
Nederlandse Vereniging voor Internationaal Recht Vol 2: 4855
Nederlandse Vereniging voor Psychiatrie Vol 2: 4863
Nederlandse Vereniging voor Weer- en Sterrenkunde Vol 2: 4857
Neighborhood Watch Vol 1: 16081
Nelligan; Fondation Emile- Vol 1: 20303

Nematological Society of Southern Africa Vol 2: 5594
Nematologiese Vereniging van Suidelike Afrika Vol 2: 5594
Nepal Association of Tour and Travel Agents Vol 2: 4676
Nestle Nutrition Institute Vol 1: 3961
Nestle Rowntree Vol 2: 6882
Netherlands Design Institute Vol 2: 4859
Netherlands Film Festival Vol 2: 4861
Netherlands Film Institute Vol 2: 4806
Netherlands Psychiatric Association Vol 2: 4863
Netherlands Society for English Studies Vol 2: 4865
Netherlands Society of Photogrammetry Vol 2: 6638
Network for Continuing Medical Education Vol 1: 10330
Networking Institute; Gazette International Vol 1: 17477
Neue Schweizerische Chemische Gesellschaft Vol 2: 6511
Neural Control and Autonomic Regulation Section Vol 1: 3509
Nevada Association of School Boards Vol 1: 16083
New Baltimore Historical Society Vol 1: 16085
New Brunswick Institute of Agrologists Vol 1: 16088
New Canaan Historical Society Vol 1: 16092
New Delta Review Vol 1: 16094
New Dramatists Vol 1: 16096
New England Council Vol 1: 16098
New England Historic Genealogical Society Vol 1: 16100
New England Mountain Bike Association Vol 1: 16102
New England Pest Management Association Vol 1: 16104
New England Poetry Club Vol 1: 16107
New England Press Association Vol 1: 16118
New England Regional Genetics Group Vol 1: 16120
New England Theatre Conference Vol 1: 16122
New England Water Works Association Vol 1: 16130
New England Wild Flower Society Vol 1: 16143
New England Wildflower Preservation Society Vol 1: 16143
New Hampshire Association of Broadcasters Vol 1: 16150
New Hampshire Golf Association Vol 1: 16152
New Hampshire Nurse Practitioner Association Vol 1: 16154
New Hampshire Pharmacists Association Vol 1: 16156
New Hampshire School Transportation Association Vol 1: 16158
New Hanover - Pender County Medical Society Vol 1: 16160
New Holland Vol 1: 21030
New Jersey Center for Visual Arts Vol 1: 16162
New Jersey City University Vol 1: 9161
New Jersey Forest Stewardship Committee Vol 1: 16166
New Jersey Historical Commission Vol 1: 16168
New Jersey Hospice and Palliative Care Organization Vol 1: 16171
New Jersey Humanist Network Vol 1: 16174
New Jersey Intellectual Property Law Association Vol 1: 16176
New Jersey Jazz Society Vol 1: 10983
New Jersey Library Association Vol 1: 16178
New Jersey Literary Hall of Fame Vol 1: 16183
New Jersey Patent Law Association Vol 1: 16176
New Jersey Poetry Society Vol 1: 15016
New Jersey State Council on the Arts Vol 1: 9161
New Jersey Symphony Orchestra Vol 1: 16185
New Jersey Tenants Organization Vol 1: 16187
New Letters Vol 1: 16189
New Mexico Art League Vol 1: 16191
New Mexico Library Association Vol 1: 16193
New Mexico Museum of Space History Vol 1: 16195
New Mexico State Poetry Society Vol 1: 15019
New Orleans Time-Picayune Vol 1: 21603
New Peace History Society Vol 1: 17126
New Rivers Press - Minnesota State University, Moorhead Vol 1: 16197
New School University Vol 1: 16199
New South Wales Film and Television Office Vol 2: 476
New South Wales Ministry for the Arts Vol 2: 478
New Statesman Vol 2: 8213
New West Symphony Vol 1: 16201
New York Academy of Sciences Vol 1: 16203
New York American Marketing Association Vol 1: 16205
New York Biology Teachers Association Vol 1: 16207
New York Board of Trade Vol 1: 16209
New York Botanical Garden Vol 1: 6547
New York Botanical Garden - Institute of Systematic Botany Vol 1: 16212
New York Civil Liberties Union Vol 1: 16215
New York Community Trust Vol 1: 10384, 16218
New York Festivals Vol 1: 16220
New York Financial Writers' Association Vol 1: 16224
New York Flute Club Vol 1: 16226
New York Foundation for the Arts Vol 1: 16228
New York Genealogical and Biographical Society Vol 1: 16230
New-York Historical Society Vol 1: 16232
New York International Ballet Competition Vol 1: 16234
New York Library Association Vol 1: 16236
New York Oil Heating Association Vol 1: 16238
New York Press Club Vol 1: 16240
New York Public Library Vol 1: 16252, 17231
New York Racing Association Vol 1: 16256
New York Road Runners Vol 1: 16258
New York Section of the Illuminating Engineering Society Vol 1: 10696
New York Shipping Association Vol 1: 16261
New York Society for Ethical Culture Vol 1: 16263
New York Society of Architects Vol 1: 16265
New York State Association for Solid Waste Management Vol 1: 16269
New York State Association of Criminal Defense Lawyers Vol 1: 16271
New York State Association of Foreign Language Teachers Vol 1: 2058
New York State Association of Library Boards Vol 1: 16273
New York State Council on the Arts Vol 1: 16275
New York State Court Reporters Association Vol 1: 16277
New York State Department of Health Wadsworth Center Vol 1: 16279
New York State Fair Old Timers Club Vol 1: 16282
New York State Health Facilities Association Vol 1: 16284
New York State Historical Association Vol 1: 16287
New York State Society of CPAs Vol 1: 16291
New York State Writers Institute Vol 1: 16293
The New York Times Vol 1: 16296
New York University - Office for University Development and Alumni Relations Vol 1: 16298
New York University - Office of Publications Vol 1: 16300
New York University Alumni Association Vol 1: 16305
New York Urban League Vol 1: 16308
New York Women in Communications, Inc. Vol 1: 16311
New York Women in Film and Television Vol 1: 21720
New Zealand Academy of Fine Arts Vol 2: 5011
New Zealand Association of Scientists Vol 2: 5013
New Zealand Book Publishers Association Vol 2: 4956
New Zealand Concrete Society Vol 2: 4981
New Zealand Dental Association Vol 2: 5018
New Zealand Department of Internal Affairs Vol 2: 4969
New Zealand Geographical Society Vol 2: 5020
New Zealand Ice Cream Manufacturers Association Vol 2: 5022
New Zealand Institute of Refrigeration Heating and Air Conditioning Engineers Vol 2: 4978
New Zealand Library Association Vol 2: 5000
New Zealand Maori Arts and Crafts Institute Vol 2: 5024
New Zealand Olympic Committee Vol 2: 5027
New Zealand Society of Authors Vol 2: 5030
New Zealand Society of Designers Vol 2: 4966
New Zealand Society of Industrial Design Vol 2: 4966
New Zealand Theatre Federation Vol 2: 5032
New Zealand Veterinary Association Vol 2: 5035
Newark Black Film Festival Vol 1: 16313
Newberry Library Vol 1: 16315
Newbury House Vol 1: 19952, 19953
Newcomen Society in North America Vol 1: 16317

Newcomen Society of the United States Vol 1: 16317
Newfoundland Club of America Vol 1: 16319
Newhouse Newspapers Vol 1: 21603
Newport International Competition for Young Pianists Vol 2: 8216
Newport International Competition for Young Pianists Committee Vol 2: 8216
Newport Pianoforte Competition Vol 2: 8216
Newsday Vol 1: 16321, 16981
Newsletter and Electronic Publishers Association Vol 1: 16323
Newsletter and Electronic Publishers Foundation Vol 1: 16325
Newsletter Association Vol 1: 16325
Newspaper Association of America Vol 1: 16327
Newspaper Association of America Foundation Vol 1: 16336
Newspaper Fund Vol 1: 9007
The Newspaper Guild-CWA Vol 1: 16342
Newspaper Research Council Vol 1: 16335
Newsweek Vol 1: 16981
Newton Lions Club Vol 1: 16344
NFO Worldwide Vol 2: 4740
NGO Committee on Disarmament, Peace and Security Vol 1: 16346
NHK - Japan Broadcasting Corporation Vol 2: 4261
NHK Symphony Orchestra, Tokyo Vol 2: 4264
NHL Broadcasters' Association Vol 1: 10496
Niagara University Vol 1: 16348
Nicol Scales, Inc. Vol 1: 12030
Nicolai Malko Foundation Vol 2: 1505
Nielsen International Music Competitions; Carl Vol 2: 1506
Nieman Foundation Vol 1: 16354
Nieman Foundation for Journalism at Harvard University Vol 1: 16356
Nigerian Association of Chambers of Commerce, Industry, Mines, and Agriculture Vol 2: 5104
Nihon Bunseki Kagaku-Kai Vol 2: 4198
Nihon Gakujutsu Shinko-kai Vol 2: 4200
Nihon Jui Gakkai Vol 2: 4230
Nihon Kensetsu Kikai-ka Kyokai Vol 2: 4160
Nihon Kikai Gakkai Vol 2: 4202
Nihon Seppyo Gakkai Vol 2: 4219
Nihon Shinbun Kyokai Vol 2: 4183
Nihon Sugakukai Vol 2: 4249
Nihon Tenmon Gakkai Vol 2: 4096
Nikon, Inc. Vol 1: 3966
Nimrod: International Journal of Prose and Poetry Vol 1: 16359
Nine Lives Associates Vol 1: 16362
The Ninety-Nines, Inc. Vol 1: 13881
Ninety-Nines, International Organization of Women Pilots Vol 1: 16364
Nippon Chikusan Gakkai Vol 2: 4208
Nippon Dobutsu Gakkai Vol 2: 4339
Nippon Dojo-Hiryo Gakkai Vol 2: 4224
Nippon Gakushiin Vol 2: 4152
Nippon Hoso Kyokai Vol 2: 4261
Nippon Iden Gakkai Vol 2: 4117
Nippon Junkatsu Gakkai Vol 2: 4228
Nippon Kagakukai Vol 2: 4103
Nippon Kaiji Kyokai Vol 2: 4266
Nippon Ketsueki Gakkai Vol 2: 4213
Nippon Sanshi Gakkai Vol 2: 4216
Nippon Seramikkusu Kyokai Vol 2: 4101
Nippon Shokubutsu-Byori Gakkai Vol 2: 4281
Nippon Yakugakkai Vol 2: 4272
Nissen Vol 1: 8163
Niwano Heiwa Zaidan Vol 2: 4268
Niwano Peace Foundation Vol 2: 4268
NMC-Slovkoncert, Slovak Artist Management Vol 2: 5966
NOAA Vol 1: 13358
Nobel Foundation Vol 2: 6170
Nobelstiftelsen Vol 2: 6170
Noir International Festival Vol 2: 3890
Nordic Council Vol 2: 6177, 6179
Nordiska Radet - Sweden Vol 2: 6177
Nordiska Samarbetsradet for Kriminologi Vol 2: 6230
Nordiska Samfundet Mot Plagsamma Djurforsok Vol 2: 6291
Norfolk Southern Vol 1: 10967
Norges Idrettsforbund og Olympiske Komite Vol 2: 5157
Norges Ingeniororganisasjon Vol 2: 5167
Norsk Kjemisk Selskap Vol 2: 5151
Norsk Komponistforening Vol 2: 5164
Norsk Kulturrad Vol 2: 5153
Norsk Oversetterforening Vol 2: 5146
Norsk Presseforbund Vol 2: 5159
Norske Arkitekters Landsforbund Vol 2: 5129
Norske Filmfestivalen Vol 2: 5155
Norske Finansanalytikeres Forening Vol 2: 5172
Norske Videnskaps-Akademi Vol 2: 5143
North Alabama Tourist Association Vol 1: 16366
North American Academy of Liturgy Vol 1: 16368
North American Association for Environmental Education Vol 1: 16370
North American Association for the Diaconate Vol 1: 16379
North American Association of Christians in Social Work Vol 1: 16381
North American Association of Food Equipment Manufacturers Vol 1: 16384
North American Association of State and Provincial Lotteries Vol 1: 16388
North American Association of Summer Sessions Vol 1: 16390
North American Association of Wardens and Superintendents Vol 1: 16392
North American Bluebird Society Vol 1: 16394
North American Catalysis Society Vol 1: 16396
North American Colleges and Teachers of Agriculture Vol 1: 16401
North American Conference on British Studies Vol 1: 16410
North American Council on Adoptable Children Vol 1: 16416
North American Die Casting Association Vol 1: 16420
North American Fruit Explorers Vol 1: 16433
North American Gladiolus Council Vol 1: 16435
North-American Interfraternity Conference Vol 1: 16438
North American Lily Society Vol 1: 16440
North American Manx Association Vol 1: 16443
North American Model Boat Association Vol 1: 16445
North American Mustang Association and Registry Vol 1: 16447
North American Mycological Association Vol 1: 16449
North American Patristics Society Vol 1: 16451
North American Peruvian Horse Association Vol 1: 16453
North American Snowsports Journalists Association Vol 1: 16460
North American Society for Oceanic History Vol 1: 16468
North American Society for Sport History Vol 1: 16470
North American Society for Sport Management Vol 1: 16472
North American Society for the Psychology of Sport and Physical Activity Vol 1: 16474
North American Trail Ride Conference Vol 1: 16478
North American Travel Journalist Association Vol 1: 16494
North American Vexillological Association Vol 1: 16496
North American Warmblood Association Vol 1: 16498
North Atlantic Treaty Organisation Vol 2: 945
North Carolina Agribusiness Council Vol 1: 16500
North Carolina Arts Council Vol 1: 16502
North Carolina Association of County Commissioners Vol 1: 16504
North Carolina Dept. of Agriculture & Consumer Services Vol 1: 16507
North Carolina Herpetological Society Vol 1: 16509
North Carolina Library Association Vol 1: 16511
North Carolina Literary and Historical Association Vol 1: 16515
North Carolina Utility Contractors Association Vol 1: 16522
North Dakota Long Term Care Association Vol 1: 16524
North Dakota Lutherans for Life Vol 1: 16526
North Dakota Tourism Department Vol 1: 16528
North Penn Beagle Club Vol 1: 16530
North San Antonio Chamber of Commerce Vol 1: 16532
North Wales Arts Association Vol 2: 6763
Northcoast Environmental Center Vol 1: 16534
Northcote Parkinson Fund Vol 1: 16536
Northeast Asia Council Vol 1: 5276
Northeast Catholic Alumni Association Vol 1: 16538
Northeast Louisiana Arts Council Vol 1: 16541
Northeast Modern Language Association Vol 1: 16543
Northeast Nebraska Economic Development District Vol 1: 16545
Northeast Ohio Balloon Pilots Association Vol 1: 6222
Northeastern Bird-Banding Association Vol 1: 5680
Northeastern Loggers Association Vol 1: 16547
Northeastern Lumber Manufacturer Association Vol 1: 16549
Northern Arizona Celtic Heritage Society Vol 1: 16551
Northern Arts Vol 2: 8218
Northern Kentucky University - Department of Theatre and Dance Vol 1: 16553
Northern Mariana Islands Swimming Federation Vol 2: 5112

Northern Plains Botanic Garden Society Vol 1: 16555
Northern Territory Library Vol 2: 481
Northland Insurance Company Vol 1: 13377
Northport/B.J. Spoke Gallery Vol 1: 19622
Northrop Grumman Corporation Vol 1: 13087
Northrop Grumman Corp. Vol 1: 19369
Northrop Grumman Electronic Systems and Integration Division Vol 1: 13084
Northwest Business for Culture and the Arts Vol 1: 16557
Northwest Environmental Advocates Vol 1: 15946
Northwest Film Center Vol 1: 16559
Northwest Film Study Center Vol 1: 16559
Northwest Regional Spinners Association Vol 1: 16563
Northwestern University - Center for International and Comparative Studies Vol 1: 16565
Northwestern University - Office of the Provost Vol 1: 16568
Northwood University Vol 1: 16571
Northwood University, Michigan Campus Vol 1: 16574
Norwalk Grassroots Tennis Vol 1: 16581
Norway Ministry of Foreign Affairs Vol 2: 5137
Norwegian Academy of Science and Letters Vol 2: 5143
The Norwegian Association of Literary Translators Vol 2: 5146
Norwegian Authors' Union Vol 2: 5148
Norwegian Broadcasting Corporation Vol 2: 5160
Norwegian Chemical Society Vol 2: 5151
Norwegian Council for Cultural Affairs Vol 2: 5153
Norwegian International Film Festival Vol 2: 5155
Norwegian Newspaper Publishers Association Vol 2: 5160
Norwegian Nobel Committee Vol 2: 6172
Norwegian Olympic Committee and Confederation of Sports Vol 2: 5157
Norwegian Press Association Vol 2: 5159
The Norwegian Short Film Festival Vol 2: 5161
Norwegian Society of Composers Vol 2: 5164
Norwegian Society of Engineers Vol 2: 5167
Norwegian Society of Financial Analysts Vol 2: 5172
Norwegian Translators' Association Vol 2: 5146
Norwegian Union of Journalists Vol 2: 5160
Nouvelle Societe Suisse de Chimie Vol 2: 6511
NOVA Chemicals Corp. Vol 1: 7843
Nova Petrochemicals, Inc. Vol 1: 1793
Novartis Pharmaceuticals Lic Ltd Vol 2: 6871
Novedades Vol 2: 4621
Novo Nordisk Foundation Vol 2: 1508
NSF International Vol 1: 16583
NSU Club of America Vol 1: 16586
Nuclear Age Peace Foundation Vol 1: 16588
Nuclear Energy Institute Vol 1: 16593
Numismatic Association; Canadian Vol 1: 7321
Numismatic News Vol 1: 12619
Nutrition Foundation of the Philippines Vol 2: 5278
Oak Lawn Soccer Club Vol 1: 16595
Oak Ridge Associated Universities Vol 1: 16597
Oak Ridge National Laboratory Vol 1: 16600
Obec Architektu Vol 2: 1435
Oboe International Vol 1: 16602
Obscherossiyskaya Obschestvennaya Organizatsiya Veteranov Voiny i Voyennoi Sluzhby Vol 2: 5888
Observatoire des Energies Renouvelables Vol 2: 2531
Observ'ER Vol 2: 2531
OC Incorporated Vol 1: 13072
Occidental Petroleum Corporation Vol 1: 1725
Occupational and Environmental Medical Association of Canada Vol 1: 16604
Occupational Therapy Association of South Africa Vol 2: 5597
Ocean Conservancy Vol 1: 16606
Ocean Youth Trust Scotland Vol 2: 8221
Oceania Philatelic Society Vol 1: 19030
Ochsner Clinic Foundation Vol 1: 16608
OCLC/Forest Press, Inc. Vol 1: 2972
OCLC Online Computer Center, Inc. Vol 1: 12824
Odense International Film Festival Vol 2: 1513
Odense International Organ Competition and Festival Vol 2: 1515
O'Dochartaigh Clann Association Vol 2: 3673
O'Dochartaigh Family Research Association Vol 2: 3673
Oesterreichischer Tennisverband Vol 2: 785
Offender Aid and Restoration/USA Vol 1: 16610
Office for Mexico, Belize, Central America, and Cuba Vol 2: 4643
Office for the Coordination of Humanitarian Affairs - Geneva Vol 2: 6489
Office of Naval Research Vol 1: 3457
Office of Strategic Services Society Vol 1: 16613
Office of the Americas Vol 1: 16615
Office of the Mayor of Zurich Vol 2: 6491
Office of the President of the Republic of Poland Vol 2: 5317
The Office of the Prime Minister of Malta Vol 2: 4451
Official Gilligan's Island Fan Club Vol 1: 16617
Oglebay Institute Vol 1: 16619
Ohaus Corp. Vol 1: 15690
Ohio Academy of History Vol 1: 16621
Ohio Arts Council Vol 1: 16627
Ohio Construction Suppliers Association Vol 1: 16629
Ohio Federation of Music Clubs Vol 1: 8348
Ohio Genealogical Society, Fairfield County Chapter Vol 1: 16631
Ohio Genealogical Society, Franklin County Vol 1: 16633
Ohio Genealogical Society, Mahoning County Vol 1: 16635
Ohio Genealogical Society, Seneca County Vol 1: 16637
Ohio Genealogical Society, Williams County Vol 1: 16640
Ohio Hospice and Palliative Care Organization Vol 1: 16642
Ohio Middle School Association Vol 1: 16644
Ohio Recorders Association Vol 1: 16646
Ohio State University Vol 1: 7951
Ohio State University Mershon Center Vol 1: 16648
Ohio State University Press Vol 1: 16650
Ohio University Press Vol 1: 16544
Ohio University Press and Swallow Press Vol 1: 16652
Ohio Women's Programs Vol 1: 16654
Ohioana Library Association Vol 1: 16656
Oil and Colour Chemists' Association Vol 2: 8223
Oil Firing Technical Association for the Petroleum Industry Vol 2: 8227
Oita Sports Association for the Disabled Vol 2: 4270
Oklahoma Archaeological Survey Vol 1: 16666
Oklahoma Association of School Library Media Specialists Vol 1: 16668
Oklahoma Hemophilia Foundation Vol 1: 16672
Oklahoma Library Association Vol 1: 16674
Oklahoma Lupus Association Vol 1: 16677
Oklahoma Religious Coalition for Reproductive Choice Vol 1: 16679
Okomedia Institut for Environmental Media Vol 2: 3039
Old Bottle Club of Great Britain/B.B.R. Publishing Vol 2: 6854
Old Dominion Kennel Club of Northern Virginia Vol 1: 16681
Old Timers Soccer Association of Maryland Vol 1: 16683
Oley Valley Combined Training Association Vol 1: 16686
Olin Fine Arts Center Gallery Vol 1: 16689
Oliver Trucking Vol 1: 20428
Olivetti Society Vol 2: 4029
Omaha Symphony Guild Vol 1: 16691
Omicron Chi Epsilon Vol 1: 16693
Omicron Delta Epsilon Vol 1: 16693
Omicron Delta Gamma Vol 1: 16693
Omicron Delta Kappa Vol 1: 16696
Omicron Kappa Upsilon Vol 1: 16703
Omohundro Institute of Early American History and Culture Vol 1: 16706
OMV Vol 2: 803
Onassis Public Benefit Foundation; Alexander S. Vol 2: 3180
Oncology Nursing Foundation Vol 1: 16719
Oncology Nursing Society Vol 2: 6472
Oncology Nursing Society Vol 1: 16708
Onderstepoort Veterinary Institute - Agricultural Research Council Vol 2: 5600
One Club for Art & Copy Vol 1: 16731
One Reel Vol 1: 16733
O'Neill Memorial Theatre Center; Eugene Vol 1: 15506
Ontario Arts Council/Ontario Arts Council Foundation Vol 1: 16735
Ontario County Historical Society Vol 1: 16749
Ontario Ministry of Citizenship and Immigration Vol 1: 16751
Ontario Ministry of Citizenship and Immigration - Ontario Honours and Awards Secretariat Vol 1: 16753
Ontario Nature Vol 1: 16758
Ontario Psychological Association Vol 1: 16767
Openbare Skakelinstituut van Suidelike Afrika Vol 2: 5608
Operation Clean Government Vol 1: 16769
Operation Kindness Animal Shelter Vol 1: 16771

Operation Oswego County Vol 1: 16773
Operational Research Society of the United Kingdom Vol 2: 8229
Operations Research Society of America Vol 1: 11067
Ophthalmic Photographers' Society Vol 1: 16778
Oppenheim-John Downes Memorial Trust Vol 2: 8233
Optical Research Associates Vol 1: 19605
Optical Society of America Vol 1: 16780
Optical Society of India Vol 2: 3574
Optimist International Vol 1: 16801
Oral and Maxillofacial Surgery Foundation Vol 1: 16803
Oral-B Laboratories Vol 1: 11206
Oral Hearing-Impaired Section Vol 1: 16807
Orange Alumni Association Vol 1: 16809
Orange County Endurance Riders Vol 1: 2183
Oratorio Society of New York Vol 1: 16811
Orbis Books Ltd. Vol 1: 1057
Orchard Lake Schools Vol 1: 16814
Orchestra Sinfonica dell'Emilia-Romagna Arturo Toscanini Vol 2: 3928
Orchestras Canada Vol 1: 16816
Orchestre Symphonique de Montreal Vol 1: 13604
Orchestres Canada Vol 1: 16816
Order of Daedalians Vol 1: 16818
Order of Lafayette Vol 1: 16836
Order of St. Lazarus Vol 1: 16838
Order of the Coif Vol 1: 16840
Order of the Founders and Patriots of America Vol 1: 16842
Order Sons of Italy in America Vol 1: 16846
Ordre de Saint-Lazare au Canada Vol 1: 16838
Ordre des Psychologues du Quebec Vol 1: 16848
Oregon Blueberry Growers Association Vol 1: 16852
Oregon-California Trails Association Vol 1: 16854
Oregon Cattlemen's Association Vol 1: 16856
Oregon Newspaper Publishers Association Vol 1: 16858
Oregon Society of Physician Assistants Vol 1: 16860
Oregon State Poetry Association Vol 1: 15029
Oregon Thoroughbred Breeding Association Vol 1: 16863
Oregon Winegrowers Association Vol 1: 16865
ORF Vol 2: 705
Organ Historical Society Vol 1: 16867
Organic Reactions, Inc. Vol 1: 1724
Organic Syntheses, Inc. Vol 1: 1724
Organisation de l'Aviation Civile Internationale Vol 1: 11482
Organisation des Assurances Africaines Vol 2: 1247
L'Organisation des Musees Militaires du Canada Vol 1: 16898
Organisation des Nations Unies pour l'alimentation et l'agriculture Vol 2: 3946
Organisation du Traite de l'Atlantique Nord - Bruxelles Vol 2: 945
Organisation Europeenne et Mediterraneenne pour la Protection des Plantes Vol 2: 2298
Organisation Internationale de la Francophonie Vol 2: 2533
Organisation Internationale de la Vigne et du Vin Vol 2: 2498
Organisation Internationale des Femmes Sionistes Vol 2: 3784
Organisation Internationale des Institutions Superieures de Control des Finances Publiques Vol 2: 760
Organisation Meteorologique Mondiale Vol 2: 6570
Organisation Mondiale de Gastroenterologie Vol 2: 3142
Organisation Mondiale de la Sante Vol 2: 6561
Organisation Mondiale de Labourage Vol 2: 4942
Organisation Mondiale pour la Systemique et la Cybernetique Vol 2: 2629
Organisation of Pharmaceutical Producers of India Vol 2: 3578
Organisation pour l'Etude Phyto-Taxonomique de la Region Mediterraneenne Vol 2: 6074
Organisation Universitaire Interamericaine Vol 1: 11103
Organisme Europeen de Recherche sur la Carie Vol 2: 4767
Organizacion Internacional de las Ciencias Quimicas para el Desarollo Vol 1: 11778
Organizacion de Paises Arabes Exportadores de Petroleo Vol 2: 4377
Organization Development Institute Vol 1: 16872
Organization for the Phyto-Taxonomic Investigation of the Mediterranean Area Vol 2: 6074
Organization International de Protection Civile Vol 2: 6392
Organization of American Historians Vol 1: 16879
Organization of American Historians Vol 1: 18680
Organization of Arab Petroleum Exporting Countries Vol 2: 4377
Organization of Islamic Capitals and Cities Vol 2: 5927
Organization of Military Museums of Canada Vol 1: 16898
Organization of Professional Employees of the United States Department of Agriculture Vol 1: 16900
Organizing Committee of the Shanghai Television Festival Vol 2: 5231
Organon Inc. Vol 1: 18620
Oriental Ceramic Society Vol 2: 8235
Original Paper Doll Artists Guild Vol 1: 16904
Orion Vol 2: 7366
Orphan Train Heritage Society of America Vol 1: 16906
Orsagos Magyar Banyaszati Es Kohaszati Egyesulet Vol 2: 3253
Ortho Biotech Products LP Vol 1: 16718
Ortho Diagnostic Systems Vol 1: 1112
Ortho Diagnostic Systems, Inc. Vol 1: 3969
Orthodox Christian Association of Medicine, Psychology and Religion Vol 1: 16909
Orthopaedic Research Society Vol 1: 16911
Osaka Chamber of Commerce and Industry Vol 2: 4165, 4166
Osborne Association Vol 1: 16917
Oslo Kommune Vol 2: 5174
Oslo University Vol 2: 5177
Osteopathic Physicians and Surgeons of California Vol 1: 16920
Osterreichische Computer Gesellschaft Vol 2: 706
Osterreichische Gesellschaft fur Klinische Chemie Vol 2: 778
Osterreichische Statistische Gesellschaft Vol 2: 712
Osterreichischer Golf-Verband Vol 2: 708
Osterreichischer Komponistenbund Vol 2: 704
Ostomy Association of Springfield Massachusetts Vol 1: 16922
Oswego Heritage Council Vol 1: 16924
Ottawa Field-Naturalists' Club Vol 1: 16926
Ottawa International Animation Festival Vol 1: 16933
Ottawa Little Theatre Vol 1: 16958
Ouachita Council on Aging Vol 1: 16960
Oulu International Children's Film Festival Vol 2: 1655
Outdoor Advertising Association of America Vol 1: 16962
Outdoor Writers Association of America Vol 1: 16965
Outdoor Writers of Canada Vol 1: 16971
Outer Critics Circle Vol 1: 16974
Outfest Vol 1: 16976
Outokumpu Company Vol 2: 1625
Ovarian Cancer National Alliance Vol 1: 16978
Overseas Press Club of America Vol 1: 16980
Owen M. Kupferschmid Holocaust and Human Rights Project Vol 1: 16982
Owens-Corning Vol 1: 19307
Owsley Family Historical Society Vol 1: 16984
OX5 Aviation Pioneers Vol 1: 16988
Oxford Preservation Trust Vol 2: 8237
Oxford University Press Vol 2: 7451, 7452
Oxoid Ltd. Vol 2: 8923
Oy. Yleisradio Ab. Vol 2: 1596
Ozark Society Vol 1: 16991
Pace University Vol 2: 2948
Pacific Area Newspaper Publishers' Association Vol 2: 486
Pacific Area Travel Association Vol 1: 16995
Pacific Arts Association Vol 1: 16993
Pacific Asia Travel Association Vol 1: 16995
Pacific Bell Foundation Vol 1: 13698
Pacific Center for Human Growth Vol 1: 16997
Pacific Coast Archaeological Society Vol 1: 16999
Pacific Coast Paper Box Manufacturers' Association Vol 1: 17001
Pacific Dermatologic Association Vol 1: 17004
Pacific Northwest Booksellers Association Vol 1: 17006
Pacific Northwest Library Association Vol 1: 17008
Pacific Northwest Writers Association Vol 1: 17010
Pacific Science Association Vol 1: 17012
Pacific Sociological Association Vol 1: 17016
Pacific Telecommunications Council Vol 1: 17021
Packaging Education Forum Vol 1: 17023, 17024
Packer Engineering Associates Vol 1: 4231
Painting and Decorating Contractors Association of the East Bay Counties Vol 1: 17026

Organization Index

Painting and Decorating Contractors of America Vol 1: 17028
Paintmakers Association of Great Britain Limited Vol 2: 6983
Pajacam Friends of the Bella Vista Girls Home Vol 1: 17030
Pakistan Academy of Sciences Vol 2: 5196
Pakistan Advertising Association Vol 2: 5198
Pakistan Ministry of Education Vol 2: 5190, 5200
Pakistan Television Corp. Vol 2: 5203
Palanca Foundation; Carlos Vol 2: 5280
Palaontologische Gesellschaft Vol 2: 3041
Palatine Area Chamber of Commerce Vol 1: 17032
Paleontological Research Institution Vol 1: 17034
Paleontological Society Vol 2: 3041
Paleontological Society Vol 1: 17039
Palm Springs International Festival of Short Films Vol 1: 17043
Palme Memorial Fund for International Understanding and Common Security; Olof Vol 2: 6180
Palomino Horse Breeders of America Vol 1: 17045
Pambansang Sanggunian sa Pananaliksik ng Pilipinas Vol 2: 5276
Pan-American Association of Educational Credit Institutions Vol 2: 1330
Pan-American Association of Ophthalmology Vol 1: 17052
Pan American Development Foundation Vol 1: 17054
Pan American Health and Education Foundation Vol 1: 17056
Pan American Society of the United States Vol 1: 4928
Panafrican Film and Television Festival of Ouagadougou Vol 2: 1241
Paneuropean Union Vol 2: 3045
Pantone Color Institute Vol 1: 17061
Paper Federation of Great Britain Vol 2: 8239
Paperboard Packaging Council Vol 1: 17063
PARADE Vol 1: 11310
Parade Vol 1: 17065
Paralyzed Veterans of America Vol 1: 17067
Parapsychology Institute of America Vol 1: 17075
Parasitological Society of Southern Africa Vol 2: 5603
Parasitologiese Vereniging van Suidelike Afrika Vol 2: 5603
Parent Cooperative Preschools International Vol 1: 17078
Parenteral Society Vol 2: 8241
Parents' Choice Foundation Vol 1: 17083
Parents Without Partners Vol 1: 17085
The Paris Review Vol 1: 17092
Parker Harris Partnership Vol 2: 8243
Parkinson Memorial Trust; Dorothy Vol 2: 7599
Parkinson's Disease Foundation Vol 1: 17096
Parnassos Literary Society Vol 2: 3186
Partitioning and Interiors Association Vol 2: 6826
Partitioning Industry Association Vol 2: 6826
Passaic River Coalition Vol 1: 17098
The Passano Foundation Vol 1: 17100
Pastel Society of America Vol 1: 17102
Patriotic Order Sons of America Vol 1: 17107
Paul Guggenheim Foundation Vol 2: 6493
Paul Lowin Trust Vol 2: 489
Paulo Foundation Vol 2: 1638
Pax Christi Flanders Vol 2: 947
Paz y Cooperacion Vol 2: 6077
PBS Vol 1: 17705
PBS - Public Broadcasting Service Vol 2: 1134
PC World Communications Inc. Vol 1: 17113
PCI Bank Group Vol 2: 5289
PCIA - The Wireless Infrastructure Association Vol 1: 17117
Peabody Conservatory of Music Vol 1: 17123
Peabody Institute of Johns Hopkins University Vol 1: 17122
The Peabody Institute of the City of Baltimore Vol 1: 17122
Peace and Cooperation Vol 2: 6077
Peace and Freedom Party Vol 1: 17124
Peace History Society Vol 1: 17126
Peace Research Laboratory Vol 1: 12778
Pearl S. Buck International Vol 1: 17128
Pecora Award Committee; William T. - U.S. Department of the Interior Vol 1: 17130
Pedal Steel Guitar Association Vol 1: 17132
Peerless Rockville Historic Preservation Vol 1: 17134
Pemiscot County Historical Society Vol 1: 17136
PEN American Center Vol 1: 17138
PEN Center U.S.A. Vol 1: 17151
PEN Club Italiano Vol 2: 4021
PEN Club Liechtenstein Vol 2: 4381
PEN Club - Poland Vol 2: 5329
PEN/Faulkner Foundation Vol 1: 17153
PEN New England Vol 1: 17156
PEN New Zealand, Inc. Vol 2: 5030
Pendleton District Historical, Recreational, and Tourism Commission Vol 1: 17159
Penguin Putnam Young Readers Group Vol 1: 5442
Penn State University Vol 1: 12545
Penney Company; JC Vol 1: 21079
Pennsylvania Academy of Fine Arts Vol 1: 15701
Pennsylvania Association of Community Bankers Vol 1: 17161
Pennsylvania Association of Environmental Professionals Vol 1: 17163
Pennsylvania Association of Private School Administrators Vol 1: 17165
Pennsylvania Council on the Arts Vol 1: 17167
Pennsylvania Cystic Fibrosis Vol 1: 17169
Pennsylvania Education of Children in the Arts Network Vol 1: 17171
Pennsylvania Elks State Association Vol 1: 17174
Pennsylvania Library Association Vol 1: 17176
Pennsylvania Manufacturing Confectioners' Association Vol 1: 17178
Pennsylvania Music Educators Association Vol 1: 17180
Pennsylvania Newspaper Association Vol 1: 17183
Pennsylvania Poetry Society Vol 1: 14997
Pennsylvania School Counselors Association Vol 1: 17189
Pennsylvania School Librarians Association Vol 1: 17191
Pennsylvania Society for the Prevention of Cruelty to Animals Vol 1: 17193
Pennsylvania Society of Anesthesiologists Vol 1: 17195
Pennsylvania Society of Newspaper Editors Vol 1: 17187, 17197
Pennsylvania Society of Physician Assistants Vol 1: 17199
Pennsylvania State Education Association Vol 1: 17201
Pennsylvania State Tax Collectors Association Vol 1: 17203
Pennsylvania State University - College of Communications Vol 1: 17205
Pennsylvania State University - Smeal College of Business Administration - Institute for the Study of Business Markets Vol 1: 17207
Pensacola Historical Society Vol 1: 17209
Pensions Management Institute Vol 2: 8249
Pentax Corp. Vol 1: 15759
People for Animal Rights Vol 1: 17211
People for the Ethical Treatment of Animals Vol 1: 17213
People to People International Vol 1: 17215
People With AIDS Coalition, Houston Chapter Vol 1: 17217
Percussive Arts Society Vol 1: 17219
Perfins Club Vol 1: 17221
Performance Textiles Association Vol 2: 8252
Performers of Connecticut Vol 1: 8407
Performing Right Society Vol 2: 8254, 8652
Pergamon Press Vol 2: 2982
Periodical Writers' Association of Canada Vol 1: 17223
Perkin-Elmer Corporation Vol 1: 1735
Perkin-Elmer Ltd. Vol 2: 8773
Perkumpulan Keluarga Berencana Indonesia Vol 2: 3605
Permanent Court of Arbitration Vol 2: 4868
Permanent International Altaistic Conference Vol 1: 17225
Permanent Way Institution Vol 2: 8256
Perpetual Trustee Company Vol 2: 74
Personal Communications Industry Association Vol 1: 17117
Perten Foundation; Harald Vol 2: 729
Peruvian Association for Conservation of Nature Vol 2: 5245
PETA Vol 1: 17214
Peters Corp.; C. F. Vol 1: 18476
Petersen Publishing Company Vol 1: 13625
Petroleos de Venezuela, SA Vol 1: 10845
Petroleos de Venezuela, S.A. Vol 1: 10846
Pettinos Foundation; Charles E. and Joy C. Vol 1: 1647
Pew Memorial Trust Vol 1: 3613
Pezcoller Foundation Vol 2: 4031
Pfizer Vol 1: 4643, 7442, 7446
Pfizer Agricultural Division Vol 1: 21030
Pfizer Inc Vol 1: 814
Pfizer, Inc. Vol 1: 1780
Pfizer Inc. Vol 1: 1898
Pfizer Inc.; Charles Vol 1: 4256
Pfizer Ltd. Vol 2: 8768
Pfizer Ltd. - UK Headquarters Vol 2: 8260
Pfizer Pharmaceuticals Vol 1: 1237
PGA European Tour Vol 1: 21923
PGA Tour Vol 1: 21923
PGA Tour of Australasia Vol 1: 21923
Pharmaceutical Institute of the University of Bern Vol 2: 2683
Pharmaceutical Institute of the University of Strasburg Vol 2: 2683
Pharmaceutical Manufacturers Association Vol 1: 17227

Pharmaceutical Organization of Nigeria Vol 2: 5106
Pharmaceutical Research and Manufacturers of America Vol 1: 17227
Pharmaceutical Society of Japan Vol 2: 4272
Pharmaceutical Society of Slovenia Vol 2: 5989
Pharmaceutical Society of South Africa Vol 2: 5606
Pharmacia Vol 1: 4253
Pharmacia & Upjohn Vol 1: 16723, 16728
Pharmacy Guild of Australia Vol 2: 492
Pharmasave Vol 1: 7334
Pharmind: Die Pharmazeutische Industrie - Editio Cantor Verlag Vol 2: 3047
Phelps-Stokes Fund Vol 1: 17229
Phi Alpha Theta Vol 1: 17232
Phi Beta Kappa Vol 1: 17239
Phi Chi Pharmacy Fraternity Vol 1: 17246
Phi Delta Chi Vol 1: 17246
Phi Lambda Upsilon Vol 1: 17248
Phi Tau Sigma Vol 1: 10938
Phi Theta Kappa, International Honor Society Vol 1: 17251
Phi Upsilon Omicron Vol 1: 17253
Philadelphia County Medical Society Vol 1: 17259
Philadelphia Home and School Council Vol 1: 17261
Philalethes Society Vol 1: 17263
Philanthropic Service for Institutions Vol 1: 17268
Philatelic Foundation Vol 1: 17270
Philatelic Music Circle Vol 1: 17272
Philatelic Traders' Society Vol 2: 8262
Philippine Association of the Record Industry Vol 2: 5282
Philippine Computer Society Vol 2: 5292
Philippine Department of Science and Technology-Science Education Institute Vol 2: 5292
Philippine Sugar Millers Association Vol 2: 5284
Philippines - Department of Education, Culture, and Sports Vol 2: 5291
Philippines Department of Science and Technology Vol 2: 5286
Philippines' Department of Science and Technology-Science Education Institute Vol 2: 5291
Philips Vol 2: 2325
Philips Electronics N.V. Vol 1: 10875
Phillips 66 National Swimming Championships Vol 1: 21194, 21195
Phillips Petroleum Company Vol 1: 21199, 21200
Phillips Publishing Vol 1: 129
Phoenix Community Works Foundation Vol 1: 17274
Phoenix House Vol 1: 17276
Phoenix House Foundation Vol 1: 17276
Phoenix Theatre Vol 1: 17278
Photo Electronic Imaging Vol 1: 17638
Photo Express Vol 2: 290
Photographic Art and Science Foundation Vol 1: 17280
Photographic Historical Society of New York Vol 1: 3442
Photographic Organization of Japan Vol 2: 4279
Photographic Society of America Vol 2: 3122
Photographic Society of America Vol 1: 17282
PhotoImaging Manufacturers and Distributors Association Vol 1: 17295
Phycological Society of America Vol 1: 17300
Physical Education Association of Ireland Vol 2: 3675
Physical Society Vol 2: 7729
Physician Insurers Association of America Vol 1: 17304
Physiological Society of New Zealand Vol 2: 5041
Phytochemical Society of Europe Vol 2: 5331
Phytopathological Society of Japan Vol 2: 4281
Pi Gamma Mu Vol 1: 17306
Pi Kappa Alpha Vol 1: 17308
Pi Kappa Alpha Memorial Foundation Vol 1: 17308
Pi Kappa Phi Vol 1: 17314
Pi Lambda Theta Vol 1: 17320
Pi Tau Sigma Vol 1: 4526, 4538, 4542
Piano Technicians Guild Vol 1: 17329
PICA Vol 1: 3563
Pica Press Vol 2: 6957
Pickerington Area Chamber of Commerce Vol 1: 17334
Pickle Packers International Vol 1: 17336
Pierce-Arrow Society Vol 1: 17339
Pierre Fauchard Academy Vol 1: 17344
Pijls Foundation; Catharina Vol 2: 1120
Pilipinas Shell Foundation Vol 2: 5288
Pinball Owner's Association Vol 2: 8264
Pioneer Hi-Bred International Vol 1: 2113
Pioneer Hi-Bred International, Inc. Vol 1: 14154
Pipe Collectors Club of America Vol 1: 17354
Pipe Collectors International Vol 1: 17354
Pitch and Putt Union of Ireland Vol 2: 3678
Pitcher Insurance Agency Inc. Vol 1: 17531
Pittaluga Premio Citta' Di Alessandria; Concorso Internazionale di Chitarra Classica Michele Vol 2: 4034
Pittsburgh History and Landmarks Foundation Vol 1: 17356
Pittsburgh New Music Ensemble Vol 1: 17358
Pittstown Historical Society Vol 1: 17360
Plain English Campaign Vol 2: 8266
Plainville Association for Retarded Citizens Vol 1: 17362
Planet Drum Foundation Vol 1: 17364
Planetary Geology Division Vol 1: 9949
The Planetary Society Vol 1: 17366
Planned Parenthood Federation of America Vol 1: 17368
Planned Parenthood Federation of Canada Vol 1: 17371
Plant Growth Regulation Society of America Vol 1: 17373
Plastic Surgery Educational Foundation Vol 1: 17376
Plastic Surgery Research Council Vol 1: 17389
Plastics Academy Vol 1: 17391
Plastics Compounding Vol 1: 19308
Playboy Vol 1: 17393
Playboy Foundation Vol 1: 17395
Player Piano Group Vol 2: 8271
Players Inc. Vol 1: 15091
Playmarket Vol 2: 5044
Playwrights' Center Vol 1: 17397
Please Touch Museum Vol 1: 17401
Plumsock Fund Vol 1: 21368
Plymouth Community Arts Council Vol 1: 17403
Plymouth Owners Club Vol 1: 17405
Plymouth Rock Foundation Vol 1: 17407
PMNETwork Vol 1: 17668
PNC Bank, Delaware Vol 1: 17409
P.O.B. Publishing Co. Vol 1: 15762
Podiatry Management Vol 1: 17411
Poet Lore Vol 1: 17413
Poetry Vol 1: 17417
The Poetry Center Vol 1: 17425
The Poetry Center & American Poetry Archives Vol 1: 17425
Poetry International Foundation Vol 2: 4870
Poetry Society Vol 2: 8273
Poetry Society of America Vol 1: 17427
Poetry Society of Michigan Vol 1: 15021
Poetry Society of Oklahoma Vol 1: 15022
Poetry Society of Tennessee Vol 1: 15023
Poetry Society of Texas Vol 1: 15024
Poetry Society of Texas Vol 1: 15031
Poets' Roundtable of Arkansas Vol 1: 15025
Poets' Study Club of Terre Haute Vol 1: 15000
Point-of-Purchase Advertising International Vol 1: 17440
Points of Light Foundation Vol 1: 17442
Points of Light Volunteer Organization Vol 1: 17442
Polaroid Foundation Vol 1: 16789
Police Federation of England and Wales Vol 2: 8276
Policy Studies Organization Vol 1: 17448
Polish Academy of Sciences Vol 2: 5333, 5351
Polish American Historical Association Vol 1: 17454
Polish Chemical Society Vol 2: 5335
Polish Composers Union Vol 2: 5342
Polish Football Association Vol 2: 5345
Polish Genealogical Society of America Vol 1: 17458
Polish Geological Society Vol 2: 5349
Polish Institute and Sikorski Museum Vol 2: 8278
Polish Librarians Association Vol 2: 5352
Polish Medical Association Vol 2: 5355
Polish Organization for Commodity Science Vol 2: 5357
Polish Phonetic Association Vol 2: 5359
Polish Physical Society Vol 2: 5361
Polish Psychological Association Vol 2: 5370
Polish Society of Hygiene Vol 2: 5373
Polish Society of Veterinary Science Vol 2: 5380
Political Studies Association Vol 2: 8280
Politiken Vol 2: 1517
Politzer Society - International Society for Otological Surgery Vol 2: 6643
Pollock-Krasner Foundation Vol 1: 17460
Polska Akademia Nauk Vol 2: 5333
Polski PEN Vol 2: 5329
Polski Towarzystwo Lekarskie Vol 2: 5355
Polskie Towarzystwo Chemiczne Vol 2: 5335
Polskie Towarzystwo Fizyczne Vol 2: 5361
Polskie Towarzystwo Fonetyczne Vol 2: 5359
Polskie Towarzystwo Geologiczne Vol 2: 5349
Polskie Towarzystwo Higieniczne Vol 2: 5373
Polskie Towarzystwo Nauk Weterynaryjnych Vol 2: 5380

Polskie Towarzystwo Psychologiczne Vol 2: 5370
Polskie Towarzystwo Towaroznawcze Vol 2: 5357
Polycystic Ovarian Syndrome Association Vol 1: 17462
Polymer Alliance Zone of West Virginia Vol 1: 17466
Polynesian Society Inc. Vol 2: 5046
Polysar Rubber Corporation Vol 1: 7835
Polytechnic Institute of New York Vol 1: 2088
Pontifica Academia delle Scienze Vol 2: 9307
Pontifical Academy of Sciences Vol 2: 9307
Pontificia Universidad Javeriana Vol 2: 1334
Pony Club of Great Britain Vol 2: 8282
Population Institute Vol 1: 17468
Pordenone Silent Film Festival Vol 2: 4037
Porter and Zwickel Vol 1: 8163
Portland Art Museum Vol 1: 16559
Portland Opera Vol 1: 17470
Portland State University - Research and Training Center on Family Support and Children's Mental Health Vol 1: 17472
Portugal Ministry of Education and Culture Vol 2: 5442
Portugal State Secretariat of Culture Vol 2: 5444
Portuguesa Multiple Sclerosis Society Vol 2: 5478
Portuguese Academy of History Vol 2: 5480
Portuguese American Police Association Vol 1: 17475
Portuguese Association of Music Education Vol 2: 5487
Portuguese Pen Club Vol 2: 5456
Post-Polio Health International Vol 1: 17477
Postal History Society Vol 1: 17479
Postal History Society of Canada Vol 1: 17483
Postmodern Culture Vol 1: 17486
Postpartum Support, International Vol 1: 17488
Potamkin Foundation Vol 1: 704
Poteet Strawberry Festival Association Vol 1: 17491
Pott National Inland Waterways Library; Herman T. Vol 1: 17493
Poultry Science Association Vol 1: 17495
Pound-American Trial Lawyers Foundation; Roscoe Vol 1: 18119
Pound Foundation; Roscoe Vol 1: 18119
Poynter Institute for Media Studies Vol 1: 17507
PR News Vol 1: 131
Practical Builder Vol 1: 17597
Prague Spring International Music Competition Vol 2: 1433
Prairie Schooner Vol 1: 17510
Prasidialabteilung der Stadt Zurich Vol 2: 6491
Pratt Free Library; Enoch Vol 1: 6230
Pratt Institute Vol 1: 17519
Praxair, Inc. Vol 1: 2779
Precast/Prestressed Concrete Institute Vol 1: 17521
Precision Metalforming Association Vol 1: 17530
Prehistoric Society Vol 2: 8284
Prehistoric Society of East Anglia Vol 2: 8284
Prentice-Hall Publishing Company Vol 1: 1376, 5302
Preservation Maryland Vol 1: 17533
Preservation Pennsylvania Vol 1: 17535
President of the Republic of Bulgaria Vol 2: 1229
President's Commission on White House Fellowships Vol 1: 17538
President's Committee on the Arts and the Humanities Vol 1: 12550
President's Council on Physical Fitness and Sports Vol 1: 17540
President's Council on Youth Fitness Vol 1: 17540
Pressamt der Stadt Nurnberg Vol 2: 3049
Primer Concurso Internacional de Piano Mozart Vol 2: 45
Prince Edward Island Council of the Arts Vol 1: 17542
Prince George's County Genealogical Society Vol 1: 17550
Princess Grace Foundation - USA Vol 1: 17552
Princeton Applied Research; EG&G Vol 1: 1734
Princeton University - MicroFluidic Research and Engineering Laboratory Vol 1: 17556
Princeton University Alumni Council Vol 1: 17558
The Print Center Vol 1: 17561
PrintImage International Vol 1: 17563
Printing Industries of America Vol 1: 17567
Printing Industries of America - Non-Heatset Web Section Vol 1: 17570
Pritsker Corp. Vol 1: 10964
Pritzker Architecture Prize Vol 1: 17572
Private Practice Section/American Physical Therapy Association Vol 1: 17574
Private Sector Organisation of Jamaica Vol 2: 4087
Prix Cazes Vol 2: 2536
Prix de Lausanne Vol 2: 6495
Prix du Jeune Ecrivain Vol 2: 2538
Prix Jeunesse Foundation Vol 2: 3051
Prix Theophraste Renaudot Vol 2: 2541
Prizer Inc. Vol 1: 13843
Pro Familia Hungarian Scientific Society Vol 2: 3304
Pro Femina Theatre Vol 1: 10546
Pro Football Hall of Fame Vol 1: 17576
Pro Musicis Vol 1: 17579
Procter & Gamble Company Vol 1: 1715, 1783, 11218
Procter & Gamble Health Care Vol 1: 3400
Proctor and Gamble Denture Care Vol 1: 11213
Producers and Composers of Applied Music Vol 2: 8287
Professional Association of Nursery Nurses Vol 2: 8289
Professional Association of Teachers - UK - Incorporating Professional Association of Nursery Nurses Vol 2: 8291
Professional Aviation Maintenance Association Vol 1: 17581
Professional Basketball Writers Association Vol 1: 14505
Professional Bowlers Association Vol 1: 11432
Professional Bowlers Association of America Vol 1: 17591
Professional Builder - Reed Business Information Vol 1: 17597
Professional Construction Estimators Association of America Vol 1: 17602
Professional Engineers in Government Vol 1: 15747
Professional Engineers in Industry Vol 1: 15748
Professional Engineers Ontario Vol 1: 17604
Professional Fraternity Association Vol 1: 17609
Professional Golf Tournaments Association Vol 1: 21923
Professional Golfers' Association - England Vol 2: 8293
Professional Golfers' Association of America Vol 1: 17612, 21923
Professional Golfers' Associations of Europe Vol 2: 8305
Professional Grounds Management Society Vol 1: 17624
Professional Hockey Writers' Association Vol 1: 10495
Professional Institute of the Public Service of Canada Vol 1: 17629
Professional Insurance Marketing Association Vol 1: 17632
Professional Insurance Mass-Marketing Association Vol 1: 17632
Professional Interfraternity Conference Vol 1: 17609
Professional Landcare Network Vol 1: 17634
Professional Panhellenic Association Vol 1: 17609
Professional Photographers of America Vol 1: 17637
Professional Photographers of Iowa Vol 1: 17640
Professional Picture Framers Association Vol 1: 17642
Professional Putters Association Vol 1: 17648
Professional Recreation Council Vol 1: 1030, 1032
Professional Rehabilitation Workers With the Adult Deaf Vol 1: 178
Professional Rodeo Cowboys Association Vol 1: 17650
Professional Services Management Association Vol 1: 17657
Professional Skaters Association Vol 1: 17659
Professional Women's Bowling Association Vol 1: 11432
Progeria Research Foundation Vol 1: 17661
Program to Assist Foreign Sinologists to Carry Out Research in the R.O.C. Vol 2: 6591
Programme des Nations Unies pour l'Environnement Vol 2: 4366
Project Censored Vol 1: 17663
Project Management Institute Vol 1: 17665
Projectgroup Cesar Franck Orgel Concours Vol 2: 4775
ProLiteracy Worldwide Vol 1: 17671
ProLiteracy Worldwide - Rochester New York Affiliate Vol 1: 17675
PROMAX Vol 1: 17678
Promoting Enduring Peace Vol 1: 17680
Promotion Marketing Association Vol 1: 17682
Promotional Products Association International Vol 1: 17684
Property Council of Australia Vol 2: 496
Prorodeo Sports News Vol 1: 17652
Prospectors and Developers Association of Canada Vol 1: 17688
Protein Foods and Nutrition Development Association of India Vol 2: 3580

Protex International Vol 2: 2543
Providence Associates, Inc. Vol 1: 2988
Province of Upper Austria Vol 2: 703
Provincia di Trento Vol 2: 4066
Provinzialverband Westfalen Vol 2: 3016
Psi Chi Vol 1: 18916
Psi Chi, National Honor Society in Psychology Vol 1: 17693
Psychological Assessment Resources, Inc. Vol 1: 3662
Psychological Dimensions of Peacework Fund Vol 1: 17702
Psychological Society Ireland Vol 2: 3681
Psychologists for Social Responsibility Vol 1: 17699
Public Broadcasting Service Vol 1: 17704
Public Choice Society Vol 1: 17706
Public Employees Roundtable Vol 1: 17708
Public Health & Hygiene and Society of Public Health; Royal Institute of Vol 2: 8604
Public Library Association Vol 1: 17711
Public Relations Consultants Association Vol 2: 8307
Public Relations Institute of Southern Africa Vol 2: 5608
Public Relations Society of America Vol 1: 17719
Public Relations Society of America - Health Academy Vol 1: 17725
Public Risk Insurance Management Association Vol 1: 17727
Public Risk Management Association Vol 1: 17727
Public Utilities Communicators Association Vol 1: 21264
Publicity Club of London Vol 2: 8309
Publicity Club of New England Vol 1: 17731
Publishers' Association of South Africa Vol 2: 5610
Publishers' Association of Tanzania Vol 2: 9286
Publishers Association of the South Vol 1: 17734
Publishers Association of the West Vol 1: 17736
Publishers Association; Yellow Pages Vol 1: 22020
Publishers Marketing Association Vol 1: 17738
Publishing, Printing and Media Association Vol 2: 5981
Pudding House Publications Vol 1: 17740
Puerto Rico Manufacturers Association Vol 1: 17743
Puffin Foundation Vol 1: 9161
The Pulitzer Prizes - Columbia University Vol 1: 17747
Pulliam Family Vol 1: 6212
Pulmonary Hypertension Association Vol 1: 17750
Pulp and Paper Safety Association Vol 1: 17754
Puppeteers of America Vol 1: 17758
Purchasing Management Association of Boston Vol 1: 17762
Purdue University - African American Studies and Research Center Vol 1: 17764
Purina Mills Vol 1: 4260
Pushcart Press Vol 1: 17768
Pushkov Institute of Terrestrial Magnetism, Ionosphere and Radiowave Propagation - Russian Academy of Sciences Vol 2: 5898
Putnam County Historical Society Vol 1: 17771
PXE International Vol 1: 17773
Pyrotechnics Guild International Vol 1: 17775
Quality Digest Vol 1: 17777
Quality Paperback Book Club Vol 1: 17779
Quarter Century Wireless Association, Southeast Wisconsin Chapter 162 Vol 1: 17782
Quarterly West Vol 1: 17784
Quaternary Geology and Geomorphology Division Vol 1: 9945
Quebec Federation of Historical Societies Vol 1: 17786
Quebec Film Critics Association Vol 1: 13598
Quebec-Labrador Foundation/Atlantic Center for the Environment Vol 1: 17790
Quebec Ministere de la Culture et des Communications Vol 1: 17792
Quebec Writers' Federation Vol 1: 17798
Queen Elisabeth International Music Competition of Belgium Vol 2: 949
The Queen Sonja International Music Competition Vol 2: 5179
Queen's Awards Office Vol 2: 8311
Queen's English Society Vol 2: 8318
Queens Opera Association Vol 1: 17802
Queen's University Vol 1: 17804
Queensland University of Technology Vol 2: 385
Quest Diagnostics, Inc Vol 1: 4394
Quilters Hall of Fame Vol 1: 17811
Quincy Jones/David Salzman Productions Vol 1: 16000
R & D Magazine - Reed Business Information Vol 1: 17813
Racegoers Club Vol 2: 8320
Radgivende Ingeniorers Forening Vol 2: 5119
The Radiance Technique International Association Vol 1: 17819
Radiation Research Society Vol 1: 17822
Radical Libertarian Alliance Vol 2: 8058
Radio Advertising Bureau Vol 1: 17825
Radio Club of America Vol 1: 17828
Radio Creative Fund Vol 1: 17827
Radio Exterior de Espana Vol 2: 6078
Radio Industries Club Vol 2: 9115
Radio Talk Show Hosts Association Vol 1: 19904
Radio Technical Commission for Aeronautics Vol 1: 18178
Radio-Television Correspondents Association Vol 1: 17845
Radio-Television News Directors Association Vol 1: 17847
Radio-Televizija Sarajevo Vol 2: 1134
Radiological Society of North America Vol 1: 1943
Radiological Society of North America Vol 1: 17851
Rafto Foundation for Human Rights; Thorolf Vol 2: 5181
RAI-Radiotelevisione Italiana Vol 2: 4039
Railway Tie Association Vol 1: 17857
Rain Bird, Inc. Vol 1: 4235
Rainbow Resource Centre: Serving Manitoba's Gay, Lesbian, Bisexual, Transgendered, and Two-Spirited Communities Vol 1: 17860
Rainforest Action Network Vol 1: 17862
Rainforest Alliance Vol 1: 17864
Raissa Tselentis Memorial Johann Sebastian Bach International Competitions Vol 1: 17867
Raleigh Outlaw League Vol 1: 17869
Ralston Purina Company Vol 1: 9658
Ralston Purina International Vol 1: 2104
Ramsay Memorial Fellowships Trust Vol 2: 8323
Ramsey County Historical Society Vol 1: 17871
Rand McNally & Company Vol 1: 2000
R&D magazine Vol 1: 18365
Randolph Chamber of Commerce Vol 1: 17873
Rannsoknarrad Islands Vol 2: 3319
Raoul Wallenberg Committee of the United States Vol 1: 17875
Rassegna di Palermo/International Sportfilmfestiva Vol 2: 3977
Rassegna Internazionale del Film di Documentazione Sociale; Festival dei Popoli - Vol 2: 3924
Rat fur Formgebung Vol 2: 2828
Ravenswood Community Council Vol 1: 17879
Rawlings Sporting Goods Co. Vol 1: 17881
Raytheon Electronic Systems Company Vol 1: 13074
Reader's Digest Association Vol 1: 17886
Reader's Digest Foundation Vol 1: 6601
Reading-Berks Democratic Socialists Vol 1: 17888
Real Academia de Farmacia Vol 2: 6084
Real Estate Educators Association Vol 1: 17890
Real Estate Institute of Canada Vol 1: 17899
Real Sociedad Espanola de Fisica Vol 2: 6101
Rebecca Caudill Young Readers' Book Award Committee Vol 1: 17901
Recording for the Blind Vol 1: 17903
Recording for the Blind and Dyslexic Vol 1: 17903
Recording Industry Association of America Vol 1: 17906
Recording Industry Association of Japan Vol 2: 4284
Records and Information Management Liaison Group Vol 2: 611
Recreation Vehicle Industry Association Vol 1: 17912
Recruitment and Employment Confederation Vol 2: 8325
Recycling Council of Alberta Vol 1: 17920
Recycling Council of Ontario Vol 1: 17922
Red Cross; International Committee of the Vol 2: 1228
Red Cross Society of China Vol 2: 5233
Redd Center for Western Studies; Charles Vol 1: 17924
Redditch Music Society Vol 2: 8327
Redshaw Ltd.; James Vol 2: 8063
Reebok Human Rights Foundation Vol 1: 17932
Reference and USER Services Association of American Library Association Vol 1: 17934
Reference Sources Committee Vol 1: 17944
Reflectone, Inc. Vol 1: 13071
REFORMA Vol 1: 5434
REFORMA: National Association to Promote Library Services to the Spanish-Speaking Vol 1: 17949
The Refractories Institute Vol 1: 17952
Regional Business Partnership Vol 1: 17954
Regional Centre for Seismology for South America Vol 2: 5247
Regional Government of Carinthia Vol 2: 716

Regional Government of Emilia-Romagna Vol 2: 3930
Regional Organization for the Protection of the Marine Environment Vol 2: 4379
Regional Plan Association Vol 1: 17957
Regional Studies Association Vol 2: 8329
Regione Lombardia Vol 2: 3869
Regular American Veterans Vol 1: 17959
Regular Veterans Association Vol 1: 17959
Rehabilitation International Vol 1: 17963
Relay and Switch Industry Association Vol 1: 17967
Religion Communicators Council Vol 1: 17970
Religion Newswriters Association Vol 1: 17972
Religious and Military Order of Knights of the Holy Sepulchre of Jerusalem Vol 1: 17978
Religious Communication Association Vol 1: 17980
Religious Freedom Council of Christian Minorities Vol 1: 17982
Remodeling Vol 1: 14261
Remote Sensing and Photogrammetry Society Vol 2: 8331
Renaissance Society of America Vol 1: 17984
Rencontres chorales internationales de Montreux Vol 2: 6487
Rencontres Internationales de Chant Choral de Tours Vol 2: 2343
Rencontres Internationales de la Photographie Vol 2: 2545
Rencontres Internationales Henri Langlois Vol 2: 2521
Renewable Natural Resources Foundation Vol 1: 17987
RenewAmerica Vol 1: 17990
Renshaw-Heilman and Associates Vol 1: 15737
REO Club of America Vol 1: 17992
Replacement Parts Industrie Vol 1: 15737
Republic of China Motion Picture Development Foundation Vol 2: 6598
Republic of Croatia Ministry of Science, Education and Sports Vol 2: 1383
Republic of South Africa Department of Sport and Recreation Vol 2: 5612
Republika Hrvatska Vol 2: 1383
Research and Development Associates for Military Food and Packaging Systems Vol 1: 17995
Research and Information Institute for Geosciences, Mining, Environment, and Nuclear Affairs Vol 2: 1338
Research Centre for Islamic History, Art and Culture Vol 2: 6645
Research Corporation Vol 1: 3472
Research Society for Victorian Periodicals Vol 1: 17998
Reseau canadien de l'environment Vol 1: 7081
Reseau de radios rurales des pays en developpement Vol 1: 8899
Reseau juridique canadien VIH/SIDA Vol 1: 7156
Reserve Officer Training Corps Vol 1: 15787
Residential Meeting of the Child and Adolescent Psychiatry Faculty Vol 2: 8458
Resistance Welder Manufacturers' Association Vol 1: 4898
Resistol Vol 1: 17654
Resort and Commercial Recreation Association Vol 1: 18000
Resource and Information Center for Chinese Studies Vol 2: 6591
Restaurant Hospitality - Penton Media, Inc. Vol 1: 18009
Results Vol 1: 18012
Retail Advertising and Marketing Association Vol 1: 18015
Retail Advertising Conference Vol 1: 18015
Retail Council Vol 1: 16334
Retail Merchants Association of New Hampshire Vol 1: 18019
Reticuloendothelial Society Vol 1: 18784
Retirement Research Foundation Vol 1: 18021
Reuters Foundation Vol 2: 8338
Review of Social Economy Vol 1: 5475
Rheims; Fondation Vol 2: 1982
Rhetoric Society of America Vol 1: 18023
Rhode Island Council of Community Mental Health Centers Vol 1: 18025
Rhode Island Health Center Association Vol 1: 18029
Rhode Island Turfgrass Foundation Vol 1: 18031
Rhodes 19 Class Association Vol 1: 18033
Rhododendron Species Foundation Vol 1: 18035
Ricardo Group, plc. Vol 2: 8376
Riccione per il Teatro Vol 2: 4041
Richard-Allan Scientific Vol 1: 15715
Richard III Society, American Branch Vol 1: 18037
Richard the III Foundation Vol 1: 18039
Richards Free Library Vol 1: 18041
RID - U.S.A. Vol 1: 18043
Rider University Student Government Association Vol 1: 18046
Riders of the Wind, The Field Events Player's Association Vol 1: 18048
Ridgefield Chamber of Commerce Vol 1: 18050
Rielo Foundation; Fernando Vol 2: 6082
Right Livelihood Awards Foundation Vol 2: 6183
Rijksakademie van Beeldende Kunsten Vol 2: 4872
Rijksuniversiteit Limburg Vol 2: 1117
Riminicinema International Film Festival of Independent Cinema Vol 2: 3838
Rin Tin Tin Fan Club Vol 1: 18052
Rio Tinto plc Vol 2: 8342
Riot Relief Fund Vol 1: 18054
Ripon Society Vol 1: 18056
Risk and Insurance Management Society Vol 1: 18059
Risk Management Association Vol 1: 18063
Rittenhouse Book Distrbutors, Inc. Vol 1: 13267
River City Vol 1: 18066
R.J. Reynolds Co. Vol 1: 8769
RMIT University Vol 2: 498
Road Racing Drivers Club Vol 1: 19690
Road Runners Club of America Vol 1: 18068
Road Vehicle Association; European Electric Vol 2: 852
Robert A. Welch Foundation Vol 1: 21511
Robert Bosch Stiftung Vol 2: 2661
Robert E. Lee Memorial Association Vol 1: 18071
Robert F. Kennedy Memorial Vol 1: 18073
Robert Foster Cherry Awards Committee Vol 1: 18077
Roberts Theatre; Forest Vol 1: 18080
Robot Institute of America Vol 1: 18082
Robotic Industries Association Vol 1: 18082
Roche Vol 1: 16724
Roche Laboratories Vol 1: 3637
Roche Products Ltd. Vol 2: 8773
Roche Vitamins, Inc. Vol 1: 4252
Rochester Association for the United Nations Vol 1: 20361
Rochester Institute of Technology Vol 1: 18084
Rochester International Amateur Film Festival Vol 1: 18088
Rochester International Film Festival Vol 1: 18088
Rock and Roll Hall of Fame and Museum Vol 1: 18090
Rockefeller Brothers Fund Vol 1: 18092
Rockefeller Foundation Vol 1: 2471, 3427
Rockford College Vol 1: 18094
Rockwell International Vol 1: 3997, 14368
Rocky Mountain Coal Mining Institute Vol 1: 18096
Rocky Mountain Elk Foundation Vol 1: 18098
Rocky Mountain Masonry Institute Vol 1: 18100
Rodeo Cowboys Association Vol 1: 17650
Rodeo Historical Society Vol 1: 18102
Rohm and Haas Company Vol 1: 1794
Rohrer, Hibler and Replogle Vol 1: 3753
Rolex Awards for Enterprise Vol 2: 6497
Rolex Watch U.S.A. Vol 1: 11147, 12659
Rolex Watch U.S.A. Inc Vol 1: 12660
Roll Call Inc. Vol 1: 18105
Rolling Stone Vol 1: 18108
Rolls-Royce Enthusiasts' Club Vol 2: 8344
Rolls Royce, Inc. Vol 1: 13080
Romance Writers of America Vol 1: 18111
Romanian Academy Vol 2: 5809
Romantic Novelists' Association Vol 2: 8346
Ronald McDonald House Charities Vol 1: 18116
Roosevelt Memorial Association Vol 1: 20065
Rosary College Vol 1: 8986
Roscoe Pound Institute Vol 1: 18119
Rose Brand Vol 1: 20642
Rose d'Or Festival Vol 2: 6499
Rose Hybridizers Association Vol 1: 18123
Rose of Tralee International Festival Vol 2: 3684
Rosenstiel Basic Medical Sciences Research Center Vol 1: 18125
Rosenthal Foundation; Richard and Hinda Vol 1: 1927
Ross Products Division, Abbott Laboratories Vol 1: 3959
Ross Products Division of Abbott Laboratories Vol 1: 16725
Rostropovitch International Competitions Vol 2: 2276
Rotary International Vol 1: 18128
Rotary International District 3810 Vol 2: 5272
Rothko Chapel Vol 1: 18131
Rotorua Maori Arts and Crafts Institute Vol 2: 5024
Rotterdam Arts Council Vol 2: 4874
Rotterdam Arts Foundation Vol 2: 4784
Rotterdamse Kunststichting Vol 2: 4874
Roucoules; Fondation Vol 2: 2098
Rough and Smooth Collie Training Association Vol 2: 8349
Routman; Regie Vol 1: 11874
Royal Academy of Arts Vol 2: 8351
Royal Academy of Dance Vol 2: 8355

Royal Academy of Dutch Language and Literature Vol 2: 951
Royal Academy of Engineering Vol 2: 570, 8365
Royal Academy of Medicine Vol 2: 969
Royal Academy of Medicine in Ireland Vol 2: 3687
Royal Academy of Music Vol 2: 8372
Royal Academy of Pharmacy Vol 2: 6084
Royal Academy of Science, Humanities and Fine Arts of Belgium - Division of Fine Arts Vol 2: 985
Royal Academy of Science, Humanities and Fine Arts of Belgium - Division of Humanities Vol 2: 1005
Royal Academy of Science, Humanities and Fine Arts of Belgium - Division of Sciences Vol 2: 1034
Royal Academy of Sciences, Humanities and Fine Arts of Belgium Vol 2: 1072
Royal Aeronautical Society - United Kingdom Vol 2: 8375
Royal Agricultural Society of England Vol 2: 8408
Royal Air Force Historical Society Vol 1: 376
Royal and Ancient Golf Club of St. Andrews Vol 2: 8419
Royal Anthropological Institute of Great Britain and Ireland Vol 2: 8421
Royal Architectural Institute of Canada Vol 1: 18133
Royal Asiatic Society of Great Britain and Ireland Vol 2: 8426
Royal Association for Disability and Rehabilitation Vol 2: 6667
Royal Astronomical Society Vol 2: 8430
Royal Astronomical Society of Canada Vol 1: 18140
Royal Australasian College of Dental Surgeons Vol 2: 501
Royal Australasian College of Surgeons Vol 2: 504
Royal Australian Chemical Institute Vol 2: 377, 506
Royal Australian College of General Practitioners Vol 2: 522
Royal Australian Institute of Architects Vol 2: 524
Royal Bath and West of England Society Vol 2: 8437
Royal Beiaardschool Jef Denyn Vol 2: 1087
Royal Blind Society Vol 2: 527
Royal Canadian Geographical Society Vol 1: 18147
Royal Canadian Golf Association Vol 1: 21923
Royal Canadian Legion Vol 1: 7313
Royal College of General Practitioners Vol 2: 5955
Royal College of Obstetricians and Gynaecologists - United Kingdom Vol 2: 8440
Royal College of Pathologists of Australasia Vol 2: 529
Royal College of Physicians Vol 2: 8713
Royal College of Physicians and Surgeons of Canada Vol 1: 18150
Royal College of Physicians and Surgeons of Glasgow Vol 2: 8450
Royal College of Psychiatrists Vol 2: 8455
Royal College of Radiologists - United Kingdom Vol 2: 8475
Royal College of Surgeons of Edinburgh Vol 2: 8477
Royal College of Surgeons of England Vol 2: 8482
Royal College of Veterinary Surgeons Vol 2: 8491
Royal Commonwealth Society Vol 2: 8500
The Royal Danish Academy of Fine Arts Vol 2: 1519
Royal Danish Geographical Society Vol 2: 1526
Royal Dublin Society Vol 2: 3693
Royal Dutch Geographical Society Vol 2: 4876
Royal Economic Society Vol 2: 8503
Royal Entomological Society Vol 2: 8507
Royal Entomological Society of Antwerp, Belgium Vol 2: 1090
Royal Film Archive of Belgium Vol 2: 1092
Royal Force Historical Society Vol 2: 6678
Royal Geographic Society Vol 2: 8509
Royal Geographical Society of Queensland Vol 2: 531
Royal Geographical Society with the Institute of British Geographers Vol 2: 8509
Royal Geological and Mining Organization of the Netherlands Vol 2: 4878
Royal Hibernian Academy Vol 2: 3696
Royal Historical Society - United Kingdom Vol 2: 8529
Royal Horticultural Society Vol 2: 8534
Royal Horticultural Society of Ireland Vol 2: 3698
Royal Humane Society Vol 2: 8577
Royal Incorporation of Architects in Scotland Vol 2: 8579
Royal Institute of British Architects Vol 2: 7515, 8588
Royal Institute of Dutch Architects Vol 2: 4880
Royal Institute of Navigation Vol 2: 8593
Royal Institute of Oil Painters Vol 2: 8602
Royal Institute of Public Health Vol 2: 8604
Royal Institute of Public Health & Hygiene and Society of Public Health Vol 2: 8604
Royal Institution of Great Britain Vol 2: 8611
Royal Institution of Naval Architects Vol 2: 7763, 8613
Royal Irish Academy Vol 2: 3700
Royal Life Saving Society Vol 2: 8624
Royal Mail Vol 2: 7189, 7385
Royal Meteorological Society Vol 2: 8627
Royal Musical Association Vol 2: 8631
Royal National Rose Society Vol 2: 8633
Royal Navy Hydrographic Department Vol 2: 7261
Royal Neighbors of America Vol 1: 18156
Royal Netherlands Academy of Arts and Sciences Vol 2: 4882
Royal Netherlands Association of Musicians Vol 2: 4896
Royal Netherlands Chemical Society Vol 2: 4898
Royal New Zealand Aero Club Vol 2: 5049
Royal Northern College of Music Vol 2: 8637
Royal Norwegian Society of Sciences and Letters Vol 2: 5183
Royal N.S. Historical Society - Genealogical Committee Vol 1: 9908
Royal Over-Seas League Vol 2: 8641
Royal Philatelic Society Vol 2: 8644
Royal Philharmonic Society Vol 2: 8649
Royal Philosophical Society of Glasgow Vol 2: 8658
Royal Photographic Society of Great Britain Vol 2: 8661
Royal Physiographic Society in Lund Vol 2: 6185
Royal School of Church Music Vol 2: 8669
Royal Scottish Academy Vol 2: 8671
Royal Scottish Automobile Club Vol 2: 8875
Royal Scottish Forestry Society Vol 2: 8673
Royal Scottish Geographical Society Vol 2: 8678
Royal Society Vol 2: 7763, 8055, 8689
Royal Society for Mentally Handicapped Children and Adults Vol 2: 8706
Royal Society for Nature Conservation Vol 2: 8848
Royal Society for the Encouragement of Arts, Manufactures & Commerce Vol 2: 8708
Royal Society for the Prevention of Accidents Vol 2: 8714
Royal Society for the Promotion of Health Vol 2: 8721
Royal Society for the Protection of Birds Vol 2: 8730, 9213
Royal Society of British Artists Vol 2: 8732
Royal Society of British Sculptors Vol 2: 8735
Royal Society of Canada Vol 1: 18159
Royal Society of Chemistry Vol 2: 8737
Royal Society of Edinburgh Vol 2: 8779
Royal Society of Health Vol 2: 8721
Royal Society of Literature Vol 2: 8793
Royal Society of London Vol 2: 2272
Royal Society of Medicine Vol 2: 8798, 8988
Royal Society of Miniature Painters, Sculptors and Gravers Vol 2: 8839
Royal Society of New South Wales Vol 2: 534
Royal Society of New Zealand Vol 2: 5077
Royal Society of South Africa Vol 2: 5615
Royal Society of South Australia Vol 2: 545
Royal Society of Tropical Medicine and Hygiene Vol 2: 8841
The Royal Society of Victoria Vol 2: 550
Royal Society of Western Australia Vol 2: 552
Royal Society of Wildlife Trusts Vol 2: 8848
Royal Swedish Academy of Engineering Sciences Vol 2: 6197
Royal Swedish Academy of Sciences Vol 2: 6159, 6173, 6175, 6201
Royal Television Society Vol 2: 8850
Royal Town Planning Institute Vol 2: 8590, 8860, 8890
Royal United Services Institute for Defence and Security Studies Vol 2: 8864
Royal Watercolour Society Vol 2: 8868
Royal Welsh Agricultural Society Vol 2: 8870
Royal Western Australian Historical Society Vol 2: 554
Royal Yachting Association Vol 2: 8872
Royal Zoological Society of New South Wales Vol 2: 557
R.R. Bowker LLC Vol 1: 18176
RSAC Motorsport Ltd. Vol 2: 8875
RTCA Vol 1: 18178
RTE (Irish Television) Vol 2: 3625
The RTZ Corporation PLC Vol 2: 8342
Rudder Memorial Fund; William Vol 2: 6470
Rudolph E. Lee Gallery - College of Architecture, Arts, and Humanities Vol 1: 18180
Runyon - Walter Winchell Cancer Fund; Damon Vol 1: 8727
Rural Nurse Organization Vol 1: 18182
Rural Sociological Society Vol 1: 18184
Rural Youth Europe Vol 2: 780

RuralScotland Vol 2: 8877
Russian Academy of Sciences Vol 2: 2275, 5900
Russian Academy of Sciences - Section of Social Science Vol 2: 5903
Russian PEN Club Vol 2: 3088
Russian Society of Sociologists Vol 2: 5907
Rutgers University - John J. Heldrich Center for Workforce Development Vol 1: 18190
Rutland Region Chamber of Commerce Vol 1: 18192
RV Owners Club; National Vol 1: 15586
Ryan Foundation; Irene Vol 1: 12547
SA Holstein Friesland Society Vol 2: 5618
SABAM Vol 2: 912
Sacramento Convention and Visitors Bureau Vol 1: 18194
Sadler's Wells Vol 2: 8879
Safeguarding European Photographic Images for Access - *SEPIA* Vol 2: 4901
Sagebrush Vol 1: 22055
Sagebrush Education Resources Vol 1: 5431
Sahitya Akademi Vol 2: 3550
Sail America Vol 1: 4922
St. Bonaventure University - Russell J. Jandoli School of Journalism and Mass Communication Vol 1: 18196
St. Cecilia Society Vol 1: 18202
St. Cecilia Society of St. Mark's Lutheran Church Vol 1: 6232
St. David's Society of the State of New York Vol 1: 18204
St. George's Society of New York Vol 1: 18206
St. Joan's International Alliance U.S. Section Vol 1: 18208
St. Johns Area Chamber of Commerce Vol 1: 18210
St. John's University Vol 1: 17803
St. Kilda Film Festival Vol 2: 559
St. Louis Black Gay and Lesbian Pride Committee Vol 1: 18212
Saint Louis University Vol 1: 18214
Saint Lucia Tourist Board Vol 2: 5914
St. Nicholas Society of the City of New York Vol 1: 18219
Sakura Europe Vol 2: 5627
Sakura Finetek, USA, Inc. Vol 1: 15715
Sakura Finetek U.S.A. Inc. Vol 1: 15722
Salerno International Film Festival Vol 2: 4045
Sales and Marketing Executives International Vol 1: 18222
Sales Professionals USA Vol 1: 18225
Salina Arts and Humanities Commission Vol 1: 18227
Salmon Unlimited Vol 1: 18229
Salon du Livre de l'Estrie Vol 1: 18231
Salon du Livre de Montreal Vol 1: 18233
Salter Company Vol 2: 8883
Salter Street Films, Ltd. Vol 1: 6033
Salters' Institute Vol 2: 8881
Saltire Society Vol 2: 8887
Salvadoran Demographic Association Vol 2: 1560
Samahang Pisika ng Pilipinas Vol 2: 5290
Samarbetsorganisationen for Emballagefragor i Skandinavien Vol 2: 1533
Samasevaya Vol 2: 6128
Samojedhunde Klubben I Danmark Vol 2: 1463
San Angelo Symphony Vol 1: 18236
San Antonio International Piano Competition Vol 1: 18238
San Antonio Rocks Vol 1: 18240
San Diego County Fair - Exhibits Department Vol 1: 18242
San Francisco Film Festival Vol 1: 18245
The San Francisco Foundation Vol 1: 18247
San Francisco Planning and Urban Research Association Vol 1: 18252
San Jose Astronomical Association Vol 1: 18254
San Jose State University Vol 1: 18256
San Juan 21 Class Association Vol 1: 18258
San Martin Society of United States of America, Washington DC Vol 1: 18260
San Remo Municipality Vol 2: 3885
San Sebastian International Film Festival Vol 2: 6095
Sander's Vol 1: 13093
Sankei Shimbun Vol 2: 4286
Sankei Shinbun-Sha Vol 2: 4286
Sanofi-Synthelabo Inc. Vol 1: 16719
Santa Fe Partners in Education Vol 1: 18263
Santander International Piano Competition Vol 2: 6097
Santander International Piano Competition; Paloma O'Shea Vol 2: 6097
Sao Paulo International Film Festival Vol 2: 1193
Sapporo Sports Promotion Corporation Vol 2: 4288
Sargeson Trust Vol 2: 5088
Sarnoff Corporation; Vol 1: 10880
Sarton Comite van de Rijksuniversiteit Gent Vol 2: 1095
Sarton Committee of the University of Ghent Vol 2: 1095
SAS Institute Inc. Vol 1: 18265
Saskatchewan Library Association Vol 1: 18268
Saskatchewan Lotteries Vol 1: 22048
Saskatchewan Motion Picture Association Vol 1: 22048
Saskatchewan Music Festival Association Vol 1: 18271
Saskatchewan Natural History Society Vol 1: 16037
Sasol Ltd. Vol 2: 5695
Sauve Qui Peut le Court Metrage Vol 2: 2548
Save the Children Canada Vol 1: 18322
SBA Consulting Group Vol 2: 4290
Scale Dealers Association Vol 1: 12031
Scandinavian Collectors Club Vol 1: 18324
Scandinavian Packaging Association Vol 2: 1533
Scandinavian Plant Physiology Society Vol 2: 1535
Scandinavian Research Council for Criminology Vol 2: 6230
Scandinavian Society for the Study of Diabetes Vol 2: 1511
Scandinavian Tobacco Company Vol 2: 1459
Scarab Club Vol 1: 18329
Scarecrow Press, Inc. Vol 1: 2967
Schenectady Museum Association Vol 1: 18332
Schering Oncology/Biotech Vol 1: 16726, 16727
Schering-Plough Corporation Vol 1: 1759
Scheveningen Internationaal Muziek Concours Vol 2: 4903
Scheveningen International Music Competition Vol 2: 4903
Schmidheiny Stiftung; Max Vol 2: 6485
Scholastic Vol 1: 15565
Scholastic, Inc. Vol 1: 14787
Schomburg Center for Research in Black Culture Vol 1: 17231
Schonstedt Instrument Company Vol 1: 2004
School and Community Safety Society of America Vol 1: 18334
School Library Journal Vol 1: 22053
School Library Media Specialists of Southeastern New York Vol 1: 18338
School Nurses Organization of Arizona Vol 1: 18340
School Nutrition Association Vol 1: 18342
School of American Ballet Vol 1: 18351
School of American Research Vol 1: 18353
School of Natural Resources and Environment Vol 1: 21063
School of Oriental and African Studies Vol 2: 8896
Schumpeter Gesellschaft; Internationale Joseph A. Vol 2: 3053
Schumpeter Society; International Joseph A. Vol 2: 3053
Schwartz Foundation; Ruth Vol 1: 16746
Schweizer Musikedition Vol 2: 6532
Schweizerische Akademie der Medizinischen Wissenschaften Vol 2: 6504
Schweizerische Gesellschaft fur Biochemie Vol 2: 6509
Schweizerische Gesellschaft fur Theaterkultur Vol 2: 6507
Schweizerischer Verband fur Weiterbildung Vol 2: 6528
The Science and Technology Foundation of Japan Vol 2: 4293
Science and Technology-Science Education Institute Vol 2: 5290
Science Council of Japan Vol 1: 17014
Science Fiction and Fantasy Writers of America Vol 1: 18355
Science Fiction Foundation Vol 2: 8898
Science Fiction Writers of America Vol 1: 18355
Science Fiction Writers of Earth Vol 1: 18359
Science Service Vol 1: 18361
Scientific and Technical Research Council of Turkey Vol 2: 6647
Scientific Association for Infocommunications Hungary Vol 2: 3306
Scientific Equipment and Furniture Association Vol 1: 18364
Scientific Program Committee Vol 1: 3614
Scientific Research Society of America Vol 1: 18510
Scientific Society of Mechanical Engineering Vol 2: 3309
Scleroderma Foundation Vol 1: 18366
Scotland On Sunday Newspaper Vol 2: 7401
Scott Arboretum of Swarthmore College Vol 1: 18368
Scott Horticultural Foundation Vol 1: 18368
Scott Joplin International Ragtime Foundation Vol 1: 18370
Scottish Bowling Association Vol 2: 8900
Scottish Canoe Association Vol 2: 8902
Scottish Ecological Design Association Vol 2: 8905
Scottish Environmental Protection Agency Vol 2: 8889
Scottish Football Association Vol 2: 8907
Scottish Industrial and Trade Exhibitions Vol 2: 8910
Scottish International Piano Competition Vol 2: 8912

Scottish Motor Neurone Disease Association Vol 2: 8914
Scottish Opera Vol 2: 8916
Scottish Photographic Federation Vol 2: 8918
Scottish Studies Program/Scottish Studies Foundation Vol 1: 18372
Scottish Tartans Society Vol 2: 9111
Scouting Ireland CSI Vol 2: 3704
Scrabble Players Vol 1: 15695
Screen Actors Guild Vol 1: 18374
Scribes Vol 1: 18378
Scripps School of Journalism; E. W. Vol 1: 18382
Sea Grant Association Vol 1: 18385
Seagram & Sons; Joseph E. Vol 1: 11326
Seaplane Pilots Association Vol 1: 18388
Search for Common Ground Vol 1: 18390
Searle Vol 1: 818
Seattle Art Museum Vol 1: 18392
Seattle International Film Festival Vol 1: 18394
Seattle Writers Association Vol 1: 18398
SECO: Technical Control Bureau for Construction Vol 2: 1098
Secondary School Admission Test Board Vol 1: 18400
Secretaria de Comercio y Fomento Industrial Vol 2: 4625
Secretaria de Desarrollo Urbano y Ecologia Vol 2: 4627
Secretaria de Education Publica Vol 2: 4570
Section for Women in Public Administration - Section for Women in Public Administration Vol 1: 18402
Security Equipment Industry Association Vol 1: 18406
Security Industry Association Vol 1: 18406
Selby Scientific Foundation Vol 2: 131
Self-Service Storage Association Vol 1: 18408
Self Storage Association Vol 1: 18408
Semaine Internationale de Video (Biennale de l'Image en Mouvement) Vol 2: 6475
Semana Internacional de Cine de Valladolid Vol 2: 6111
SEMI International Vol 1: 18411
Semiconductor Equipment and Materials Institute Vol 1: 18411
Semiconductor Equipment and Materials International Vol 1: 18411
Seminar on the Acquisition of Latin American Library Materials Vol 1: 18414
Senate of the Republic of Mexico Vol 2: 4629
Senior Citizens Council of Bethlehem Vol 1: 18416
Serbian Academy of Sciences and Arts Vol 2: 5937
Service of Peace and Justice Vol 2: 1263
Servicio Paz y Justicia Vol 2: 1263
Seventh Day Baptist Historical Society Vol 1: 18418
Severn River Association Vol 1: 18422
The Sewanee Review Vol 1: 18424
Seybold Publications Vol 1: 18426
The Shakespeare Theatre Vol 1: 18428
Shakespeare Theatre at the Folger Vol 1: 18428
Shandon Vol 1: 4389
Shark Awards Festival Vol 2: 3709
Sharp Corporation Vol 1: 18770
Shaw Mudge & Co. Vol 1: 19095
Shawnee Council of Camp Fire Vol 1: 18430
Shazar Center for Jewish History; Zalman Vol 2: 3767
Shell Foundation Vol 1: 1328
Shell Global Solutions Inc. Vol 1: 2759
Shell Oil Co. Vol 1: 15692
Shell Research Ltd. Vol 2: 8773
Shell South Africa Vol 2: 5580
Shell UK Ltd. Vol 2: 8097, 8773
Shenan Arts Vol 1: 18432
Shenandoah International Playwrights Retreat Vol 1: 18432
Shenango Valley Chamber of Commerce Vol 1: 18435
Sherwin-Williams Company Vol 1: 1786
Shin-Norinsha Company Limited of Japan Vol 1: 4226
Shiras Institute Vol 1: 18081
Shirika la Utafiti na Maendeleo va Viwanda, Tanzania Vol 2: 9290
Shogakukan Vol 2: 4295
Shorenstein Center on the Press, Politics and Public Policy; Joan - Goldsmith Awards Vol 1: 18437
Shreveport Civic Opera Vol 1: 18441
Shreveport Opera Company Vol 1: 18441
Shurgain Ltd. Vol 1: 7445
S.I.A.T.L Vol 2: 3331
Sibelius International Violin Competition; Jean Vol 2: 1657
Sibelius Society of Finland Vol 2: 1658
SID Award (Store Interior Design Award) Vol 1: 14400
Sidewise Awards for Alternate History Vol 1: 18443
Sidney-Shelby County Young Men's Christian Association Vol 1: 18445
Siemens AG Vol 2: 2325
Siemens A.G. Vol 2: 2730
Siena College - Department of Creative Arts Vol 1: 18447
Sierra Club Vol 1: 18449
Sigma Alpha Iota Foundation Vol 1: 18475
Sigma Alpha Iota Philanthropies, Inc. Vol 1: 18475
Sigma Delta Epsilon - Graduate Women in Science Vol 1: 18478
Sigma Diagnostics Inc. Vol 1: 15722
Sigma Gamma Tau Vol 1: 18482
Sigma Iota Epsilon Vol 1: 18484
Sigma Phi Alpha Vol 1: 18486
Sigma Phi Epsilon Fraternity Vol 1: 18488
Sigma Pi Sigma Trust Fund Vol 1: 2841
Sigma Tau Delta, the International English Honor Society Vol 1: 18490
Sigma Theta Tau International Vol 1: 18492
Sigma Xi Vol 1: 18510
Sigma Xi, The Scientific Research Society Vol 1: 18510
Sigma Zeta Vol 1: 18514
SIGNIS Vol 2: 1101
Sikkens Foundation Vol 2: 4905
Sikorsky Aircraft Vol 1: 10405, 13083
Silver Wings Fraternity Vol 1: 18516
Silverfish Review Press Vol 1: 18518
Silvermine Guild Arts Center Vol 1: 18520
Simba Information Inc. Vol 1: 18524
Simon Fraser University - Office of Vice Preseident and Research Services Vol 1: 18526
Simon Wiesenthal Center Vol 1: 18528
Singapore Association of Convention and Exhibition Organisers and Suppliers Vol 2: 5942
Singapore Exhibition Services Pte. Ltd. Vol 2: 5945
Singapore Industrial Automation Association Vol 2: 5947
Singapore National Committee of the International Water Association Vol 2: 5950
Singapore Press Holding Vol 2: 5940
Singer Museum Vol 2: 4908
Singkreis Porcia-Spittal an der Drau Vol 2: 716
Single Service Institute Vol 1: 9664
Sioux Empire Homeless Coalition Vol 1: 18531
SIPA Footbags and Adidas Footbags Vol 1: 21921
Sir Ernest Lee Steere Vol 2: 555
Sir Henry Royce Memorial Foundation Vol 2: 561
Sir Patrick Geddes Memorial Trust Vol 2: 8890
Sister Cities International Vol 1: 18533
Sister Kenny Rehabilitation Institute Vol 1: 18535
Sitka Historical Society Vol 1: 18537
Sixteenth Century Society and Conference Vol 1: 18539
Ski Racing - Inside Communications Inc. Vol 1: 18547
Skills USA - VICA Vol 1: 18549
SLE Foundation Vol 1: 18553
Slick 50 Vol 1: 11757
Slingofand Drum Co. Vol 1: 13703
Slipstream Vol 1: 18555
Slobodna Dalmacija Vol 2: 1378
Slovak Studies Association Vol 1: 18557
Slovak Television Vol 2: 5968
Slovakia Ministerstvo Kultury Slovenskej Republik Vol 2: 5970
Slovakia Ministry of Culture Vol 2: 5970
Slovene Writers' Association Vol 2: 5986
Slovenian Pharmaceutical Society Vol 2: 5989
Slovenian Writers Organization Vol 2: 5987
Slovenska televizia, Bratislava Vol 2: 5968
Slovkoncert, Czechoslovakia Artists Agency Vol 2: 5966
Small Business Council of America Vol 1: 18559
Small Motor and Motion Association Vol 1: 18563
Small Motor Manufacturers Association Vol 1: 18563
Smith and Son; W. H. Vol 2: 9277
Smith Breeden Associates Vol 1: 2244
Smith Kline Corporation Vol 1: 4172
Smith Performing Arts Center; Clarice Vol 1: 18566
SmithKline Beecham Corporation Vol 1: 1742
SmithKline Beecham Pharmaceuticals Vol 1: 236
Smithson Society; James Vol 1: 18568
Smithsonian Institution Vol 1: 18571
Smithsonian Institution Libraries Vol 1: 5614
Smithsonian Women's Committee Vol 1: 18573
Snipe Class International Racing Association Vol 1: 18575
SNP Corporation Vol 2: 5941
SNS Bank Vol 2: 1121
Soaring Society of America Vol 1: 18577
The SOCAN Foundation Vol 1: 18592
SOCAN Foundation Vol 1: 18593
Soccer Association for Youth Vol 1: 18594

Soccer Industry Council of America Vol 1: 18597
Social Issues Resources Series Vol 1: 1413, 1417, 2987, 11398, 12935, 19972
Social Issues Resources Series, Inc. Vol 1: 1413
Social Research Association Vol 2: 8920
Social Science Research Council Vol 1: 18599
Social Studies School Service Vol 1: 14790
Socialist Party of Rhode Island Vol 1: 18601
Sociedad Argentina de Botanica Vol 2: 23
Sociedad Argentina de Estudios Geograficos Vol 2: 25
Sociedad de Autores y Compositores de Musica Vol 2: 4631
Sociedad Espanola de Quimica Industrial Vol 2: 2749
Sociedad Espanola para el Estudio de la Obesidad Vol 2: 6099
Sociedad Geografica de Lima Vol 2: 5239
Sociedad Interamericana de Cardiologia Vol 2: 4550
Sociedad Interamericana de Prensa Vol 1: 11105
Sociedad Mexicana de Cardiologia Vol 2: 4633
Sociedad Mexicana de Historia de La Ciencia y de La Tecnologia Vol 2: 4562
Sociedad Quimica de Mexico Vol 2: 4468
Sociedade Brasileira para o Progresso da ciencia Vol 2: 1165
Sociedade de Geografia de Lisboa Vol 2: 5489
Sociedade Portuguesa de Autores Vol 2: 5491
Sociedade Portuguesa de Esclerose Multipla Vol 2: 5478
Societa Chimica Italiana Vol 2: 3999
Societa del Quartetto Vol 2: 4047
Societa Geologica Italiana Vol 2: 4049
Societa Internazionale di Psicologia della Scrittura Vol 2: 3975
Societa Italiana di Ecologia Vol 2: 4023
Societa Olivetti Vol 2: 4029
Societas Biochemica, Biophysica Microbiologica Fenniae Vol 2: 1575
Societas Europaea Herpetologica Vol 2: 3906
Societas Internationalis Limnologiae Vol 1: 11405
Societas Physiologiae Plantarum Scandinavica Vol 2: 1535
Societe Africaine de Reassurance Vol 2: 5102
Societe Astronomique de France Vol 2: 2249, 2551
Societe Belge des Auteurs, Compositeurs et Editeurs Vol 2: 1104
Societe Belge des Auteurs Compositeurs et Editeurs Vol 2: 1104
Societe Bibliographique du Canada Vol 1: 6358
Societe canadienne de genie chimique Vol 1: 7405
Societe Canadienne de Genie Civil Vol 1: 7409
Societe Canadienne de Genie Mecanique Vol 1: 7424
Societe Canadienne de Geotechnique Vol 1: 7121
Societe Canadienne de la Sclerose en Plaques Vol 1: 13670
Societe Canadienne de Meteorologie et d'Oceanographique Vol 1: 7274
Societe Canadienne de Pediatrie Vol 1: 7317
Societe Canadienne de Phytopathologie Vol 1: 7335
Societe Canadienne de Psychologie Vol 1: 7344
Societe Canadienne de Sante Internationale Vol 1: 7422
Societe Canadienne de Sociologie et d'Anthropologie Vol 1: 7501
Societe Canadienne de Zoologie Vol 1: 7495
Societe Canadienne de Zootechnie Vol 1: 7438
Societe canadienne des auteurs, compositeurs, et editeurs de musique Vol 1: 18592
Societe Canadienne des Directeurs d'Association Vol 1: 7447
Societe Canadienne des Microbiologistes Vol 1: 7477
Societe Canadienne des pharmaciens d'Hopitaux Vol 1: 7456
Societe Canadienne des Relations Publiques Vol 1: 7359
Societe Canadienne des Sciences de la Nutrition Vol 1: 7434
Societe Canadienne des Sciences du Cerveau, du Comportement et de la Cognition Vol 1: 5380
Societe Canadienne pour les Traditions Musicales Vol 1: 7436
Societe Chimique de Belgique Vol 2: 1106
Societe Civile des Auteurs Multimedia Vol 2: 2566
Societe de Biologie Experimentale Vol 2: 8928
Societe de Chimie Industrielle Vol 2: 2360
Societe de Chimie Therapeutique Vol 2: 2568
Societe de Linguistique Romane Vol 2: 2591
Societe de Musique des Universites Canadiennes Vol 1: 7528
Societe de Pathologie Exotique Vol 2: 2572
Societe des Auteurs, Compositeurs et Editeurs de Musique Vol 2: 2575
Societe des Auteurs et Compositeurs Dramatiques Vol 2: 2588
Societe des Indexateurs Vol 2: 9050
Societe des Ornithologistes du Canada Vol 1: 19079
Societe du Comte Dracula Vol 2: 7390
Societe Europeenne de Chirurgie Cardiovasculaire Vol 2: 3911
Societe Europeenne de Culture Vol 2: 3918
Societe Europeenne pour la Formation des Ingenieurs Vol 2: 870
Societe Francaise d'Acoustique Vol 2: 2582
Societe Francaise de Physique Vol 2: 2725
Societe Genealogique Canadienne-Francaise Vol 1: 9769
Societe Geologique de Belgique Vol 2: 894
Societe Geologique de France Vol 2: 2399
Societe historique du Canada Vol 1: 7148
Societe Internationale de Chimiotherapie Vol 2: 7982
Societe Internationale de Chirurgie Vol 2: 6462
Societe Internationale de Droit Militaire et de Droit de la Guerre Vol 2: 931
Societe Internationale de Mecanique des Roches Vol 2: 5401
Societe Internationale de Mecanique des Sols et de la Geotechnique Vol 2: 7978
Societe Internationale de Mycologie Humaine et Animales Vol 2: 1639
Societe Internationale de Neurochimie Vol 2: 1501
Societe Internationale de Transfusion Sanguine Vol 2: 4839
Societe Internationale d'Oncologie Pediatrique Vol 2: 7986
Societe Internationale pour l'Education Artistique Vol 1: 11928
Societe pour l'etude de l'architecture du Canada Vol 1: 6446
Societe quebecoise pour la promotion de la litterature de langue anglaise Vol 1: 17798
Societe Royale de Chimie Vol 2: 1106
Societe Royale des Sciences de Liege Vol 2: 1109
Societe Royale Du Canada Vol 1: 18159
Societe Saint-Jean-Baptiste de Montreal Vol 1: 18603
Societe Suisse de Radiodiffusion et Television et la Ville de Montreux Vol 2: 6499
Societe Universitaire Europeenne de Recherches Financieres Vol 2: 719
Society for Adolescent Medicine Vol 1: 18616
Society for Advancement of Management Vol 1: 18622
Society for American Baseball Research Vol 1: 18629
Society for Applied Anthropology Vol 1: 912
Society for Applied Microbiology Vol 2: 8922
Society for Applied Spectroscopy Vol 1: 16790
Society for Applied Spectroscopy Vol 1: 18639
Society for Behavioral Pediatrics Vol 1: 18662
Society For Biomaterials Vol 1: 18646
Society for Cinema and Media Studies Vol 1: 18650
Society for Clinical and Experimental Hypnosis Vol 1: 18653
Society for Developmental and Behavioral Pediatrics Vol 1: 18662
Society for Drug Research Vol 2: 8939
Society for Economic Botany Vol 1: 18664
Society for Engineering in Agriculture Vol 2: 580
Society for Environmental Exploration Vol 2: 8925
Society for Environmental Graphic Design Vol 1: 18667
Society for Epidemiologic Research Vol 1: 18669
Society for Ethnomusicology Vol 1: 18671
Society for Experimental Biology Vol 2: 8928
Society for Film Art in Tampere Vol 2: 1659
Society for French Historical Studies Vol 1: 7925
Society for French Historical Studies Vol 1: 18675
Society for General Microbiology Vol 2: 8931
Society for Historians of American Foreign Relations Vol 1: 18677
Society for Historical Archaeology Vol 1: 18682
Society for History in the Federal Government Vol 1: 18687
Society for Human Resource Management Vol 1: 18693
Society for Humanistic Judaism Vol 1: 18707

Society for Imaging Science and Technology Vol 1: 16789
Society for Imaging Science and Technology Vol 1: 18709
Society for In Vitro Biology Vol 1: 18722
Society for Industrial and Applied Mathematics Vol 1: 3041
Society for Industrial and Applied Mathematics Vol 1: 18730
Society for Industrial and Organizational Psychology Vol 1: 18749
Society for Industrial Microbiology Vol 1: 18759
Society for Information Display Vol 1: 18764
Society for Integrative and Comparative Biology Vol 1: 18773
Society for International Hockey Research Vol 1: 18775
Society for Investigative Dermatology Vol 1: 18777
Society for Italian Historical Studies Vol 1: 2479
Society for Italian Historical Studies Vol 1: 18779
Society for Italic Handwriting Vol 2: 8937
Society for Judgement and Decision Making Vol 1: 18782
Society for Leukocyte Biology Vol 1: 18784
Society for Marketing Professional Services Vol 1: 18789
Society for Medical Decision Making Vol 1: 18793
Society for Medicinal Plant Research Vol 2: 3055
Society for Medicines Research Vol 2: 8939
Society for Medieval Archaeology Vol 2: 8941
Society for Military History Vol 1: 18799
Society for Mining, Metallurgy, and Exploration Vol 1: 18804
Society for Nautical Research Vol 2: 8945
Society for Nondestructive Testing Vol 1: 4142
Society for Pediatric Dermatology Vol 1: 18830
Society for Range Management Vol 1: 18833
Society for Research into Higher Education Vol 2: 8947
Society for Research into Hydrocephalus and Spina Bifida Vol 2: 8949
Society for Sedimentary Geology Vol 1: 18839
Society for Sedimentary Geology Vol 1: 18839
Society for Sedimentary Geology, Great Lakes Section Vol 1: 18850
Society for Sex Therapy and Research Vol 1: 18852
Society for Social Studies of Science Vol 1: 18854
Society for Spinal Research Vol 2: 3057
Society for Technical Communication Vol 1: 18859
Society for the Advancement of Anaesthesia in Dentistry Vol 2: 8951
Society for the Advancement of the Arts and Film Vol 1: 21644
Society for the Family of Man Vol 1: 18864
Society for the Historians of the Early American Republic Vol 1: 18866
Society for the History of Alchemy and Chemistry Vol 2: 8954
Society for the History of Technology Vol 1: 18870
Society for the Preservation of American Business History Vol 1: 21408
Society for the Preservation of Bluegrass Music of America Vol 1: 18878
Society for the Preservation of Old Mills Vol 1: 18880
Society for the Promotion of New Music Vol 2: 9104
Society for the Protection of Unborn Children Vol 2: 8956
Society for the Psychological Study of Social Issues Vol 1: 18882
Society for the Scientific Investigation of Para-Sciences Vol 2: 3059
Society for the Scientific Study of Sexuality Vol 1: 18889
Society for the Study of Amphibians and Reptiles Vol 1: 18891
Society for the Study of Evolution - Evolution: International Journal of Organic Evolution Vol 1: 18893
Society for the Study of Inborn Errors of Metabolism Vol 2: 8958
Society for the Study of Lesbian, Gay and Bisexual Concerns (Division 44) Vol 1: 18895
Society for the Study of Midwestern Literature Vol 1: 18921
Society for the Study of Social Problems Vol 1: 18924
Society for the Study of Southern Literature Vol 1: 18927
Society for the Study of Symbolic Interaction Vol 1: 18929
Society for Theatre Research Vol 2: 8960
Society for Utopian Studies Vol 1: 18933
Society for Women in Philosophy Vol 1: 18936
Society of Actuaries Vol 1: 18938
Society of Allied Weight Engineers Vol 1: 18944
Society of American Archivists Vol 1: 18950
Society of American Business Editors and Writers Vol 1: 18963
Society of American Florists Vol 1: 18965
Society of American Foresters Vol 1: 18968
Society of American Graphic Artists Vol 1: 18979
Society of American Military Engineers Vol 1: 18981
Society of American Registered Architects Vol 1: 19002
Society of American Travel Writers Vol 1: 19014
Society of Antiquaries of London Vol 2: 8963
Society of Antiquaries of Scotland Vol 2: 8966
Society of Applied Botany Vol 2: 3061
Society of Architectural and Associated Technicians Vol 2: 7032
Society of Architectural Historians Vol 1: 19017
Society of Army Historical Research Vol 2: 8968
Society of Arts and Crafts Vol 1: 19027
Society of Australasian Specialists Vol 1: 19030
Society of Australasian Specialists/ Oceania Vol 1: 19030
Society of Authors Vol 2: 8971, 8973, 8975
Society of Authors - Translators Association Vol 2: 8970
Society of Authors - England Vol 2: 8978
Society of Authors (ZAiKS) Vol 2: 5382
Society of Automotive Engineers Vol 1: 19032
Society of Automotive Engineers (Australasia) Vol 2: 582
Society of Automotive Historians Vol 1: 19063
Society of Biological Psychiatry Vol 1: 19070
Society of Border Leicester Sheep Breeders Vol 2: 8994
Society of Cable Telecommunications Engineers Vol 1: 19076
Society of Cable Television Engineers Vol 1: 19076
Society of Canadian Ornithologists Vol 1: 19079
Society of Cardiovascular Anesthesiologists Vol 1: 19081
Society of Chemical Industry Vol 2: 8740, 8996
Society of Chemical Industry - American Section Vol 1: 19083
Society of Children's Book Writers Vol 1: 19086
Society of Children's Book Writers and Illustrators Vol 1: 19086
Society of Clinical Ecology Vol 1: 650
Society of Community Medicine Vol 2: 8604
Society of Cosmetic Chemists Vol 1: 19090
Society of Czech Architects Vol 2: 1435
Society of Decorative Painters Vol 1: 19096
Society of Design Administration, Hilton Head Chapter Vol 1: 19100
Society of Designer Craftsmen Vol 2: 9026
Society of Diagnostic Medical Sonography Vol 1: 19102
Society of Die Casting Engineers Vol 1: 16420
Society of Dramatic Authors and Composers Vol 2: 2588
Society of Dyers and Colourists - England Vol 2: 9030
Society of Economic Geologists Vol 1: 19105
Society of Economic Paleontologists and Mineralogists Vol 1: 18839
Society of Engineers Vol 2: 9041
Society of Environmental Graphic Designers Vol 1: 18667
Society of Experimental Test Pilots Vol 1: 19111
Society of Exploration Geo-physicists Vol 1: 19116
Society of Exploration Geophysicists of Japan Vol 2: 4297
Society of Film and Television Arts Vol 2: 6904
Society of Fire Protection Engineers Vol 1: 19126
Society of Flight Test Engineers Vol 1: 19131
Society of Floristry Vol 2: 9047
Society of Forensic Toxicologists Vol 1: 19134
Society of German Cooks Vol 2: 3063
Society of Illinois Bacteriologists Vol 1: 10689
Society of Illustrators Vol 1: 19136
Society of Indexers Vol 2: 9050
Society of Insurance Research Vol 1: 19138
Society of Legal Scholars in the United Kingdom and Ireland Vol 2: 9053
Society of London Theatre Vol 2: 9056

Organization Index

Society of Magazine Writers Vol 1: 4466
Society of Manufacturing Engineers - Composites Manufacturing Association Vol 1: 19141
Society of Medical-Dental Management Consultants Vol 1: 19179
Society of Medical Friends of Wine Vol 1: 19181
Society of Medical Laboratory Technologists of South Africa Vol 2: 5620
Society of Metaphysicians Vol 2: 9058
Society of Mexican American Engineers and Scientists Vol 1: 19183
Society of Midland Authors Vol 1: 19185
Society of Motion Picture and Television Engineers Vol 1: 19187
Society of Municipal Arborists Vol 1: 19201
Society of National Association Publications Vol 1: 19204
Society of Naval Architects and Marine Engineers Vol 1: 19057
Society of Naval Architects and Marine Engineers Vol 1: 19206
Society of Nematologists Vol 1: 19218
Society of Netherlands Literature Vol 2: 4910
Society of Nuclear Medicine Vol 1: 19224
Society of Operations Engineers Vol 2: 9061
Society of Ornamental Turners Vol 2: 9067
Society of Packaging and Handling Engineers Vol 1: 11022
Society of Petroleum Engineers Vol 1: 19233
Society of Petroleum Engineers of the American Institute of Mining, Metallurgical and Petroleum Engineers Vol 1: 19233
Society of Petrophysicists and Well Log Analysts Vol 1: 19251
Society of Physics Students Vol 1: 2837, 2839, 2841
Society of Plastics Engineers Vol 1: 19258
Society of Procurement Officers in Local Government Vol 2: 9075
Society of Professional Investigators Vol 1: 19270
Society of Professional Journalists Vol 1: 8773
Society of Professional Journalists Vol 1: 19273
Society of Publication Designers Vol 1: 19279
Society of Ration Token Collectors Vol 1: 19282
Society of Real Estate Appraisers Vol 1: 5005
Society of Recreation Executives Vol 1: 19287
Society of Reliability Engineers Vol 1: 19289
Society of Research Administrators Vol 1: 19293
Society of Rheology Vol 1: 19298
Society of Romance Linguistics Vol 2: 2591
Society of Romanian Architects Vol 2: 5877
Society of Science for the People Vol 2: 3582
Society of Shoe Fitters Vol 2: 9077
Society of South African Geographers Vol 2: 5637
Society of Southwest Archivists Vol 1: 18957
Society of Surgical Oncology Vol 1: 19300
Society of Systematic Biologists Vol 1: 19304
Society of Systematic Zoology Vol 1: 19304
Society of Technical Writers and Publishers Vol 1: 18859
Society of the Plastics Industry Vol 1: 13578
Society of the Plastics Industry - Moldmakers Division Vol 1: 19306
Society of the Silurians Vol 1: 19326
Society of Toxicology Vol 1: 19329
Society of Tribologists and Lubrication Engineers Vol 1: 19342
Society of United States Air Force Flight Surgeons Vol 1: 19350
Society of USAF Flight Surgeons of the Aerospace Medical Association Vol 1: 243
Society of Vertebrate Paleontology Vol 1: 19353
Society of West End Theatre Vol 2: 9056
Society of Wildlife Artists Vol 2: 9079
Society of Woman Geographers Vol 1: 19359
Society of Women Artists Vol 2: 9085
Society of Women Engineers Vol 1: 19362
Society of Women Writers, Victoria Branch Vol 2: 588
Society of Wood Science and Technology Vol 1: 19370
Sociological Practice Association Vol 1: 19373
Sociologists for Women in Society Vol 1: 19375
Sofia Municipality Vol 2: 1237
Software and Information Industry Association Vol 1: 19382
Software Publishers Association Vol 1: 17114
Soil and Water Conservation Society Vol 1: 19384
Soil Association Vol 2: 9090
Soil Conservation Society of America Vol 1: 19384
Soil Science Society of America Vol 1: 19391
Solothurn Film Festival Vol 2: 6502
Solvent Extractors' Association of India Vol 2: 3584
Somali International Cat Club Vol 1: 19400
Songtalk Vol 1: 19402
Songwriters Guild of America Vol 1: 19405
Songwriters' Resources and Services Vol 1: 19402
Sonia Shankman Orthogenic School Vol 1: 19407
Sonnings Music Foundation; Leonie Vol 2: 1537
Sonnings Musikfond; Leonie Vol 2: 1537
Sonoma County Culinary Guild Vol 1: 19409
Sons and Daughters of Oregon Pioneers Vol 1: 19411
Sons of the Republic of Texas Vol 1: 19413
Sons of the Revolution in the State of New York Vol 1: 19416
Sony Broadcast Vol 2: 9093
Sony Corporation of America Vol 1: 10866
Sony United Kingdom Ltd. Vol 2: 9093
Soroptimist International of the Americas Vol 1: 19418
Soroptimist International of the South West Pacific Vol 2: 594
Soul Train Music Awards Vol 1: 19422
Source Theatre Company Vol 1: 19424
Sousa Foundation; John Philip Vol 1: 19427
South African Academy of Science and Arts Vol 2: 5642
South African Association for Learning and Educational Difficulties Vol 2: 5671
South African Association of Botanists Vol 2: 5673
South African Association of Consulting Engineers Vol 2: 5677
South African Association of Paediatric Surgeons Vol 2: 5679
South African Branch of the Royal Academy of Dancing Vol 2: 8361
South African Broadcasting Corporation Vol 2: 5681
South African Chemical Institute Vol 2: 5688
South African Geographical Society Vol 2: 5637
South African Institute of Architects Vol 2: 5698
South African Institute of Electrical Engineers Vol 2: 5705
South African Institute of Forestry Vol 2: 5707
South African Medical Association Vol 2: 5712
South African National Council for the Blind Vol 2: 5724
South African National Defence Force Vol 2: 5726
South African Society for Plant Pathology Vol 2: 5777
South African Society for Plant Pathology and Microbiology Vol 2: 5777
South African Society of Music Teachers Vol 2: 5761
South African Sugar Technologists' Association Vol 2: 5763
South African Veterinary Association Vol 2: 5765
South Asia Council Vol 1: 5274
South Atlantic Modern Language Association Vol 1: 19437
South Australia Arts and Industry Development Vol 2: 596
South Australian Photographic Federation Vol 2: 599
South Carolina Arts Commission Vol 1: 19440
South Carolina Association of School Librarians Vol 1: 19442
South Carolina Poultry Federation Vol 1: 19444
South Dakota Broadcasters Association Vol 1: 19448
South Dakota Library Association Vol 1: 19451
South Dakota Poetry Society Vol 1: 15030
South Dakota State Historical Society Vol 1: 19453
South East Asia Iron and Steel Institute Vol 2: 4442
South East Chicago Commission Vol 1: 19455
South Haven/Van Buren County Lakeshore Convention and Visitors Bureau Vol 1: 19457
South Metropolitan Planning Council Vol 1: 19459
South Monmouth Board of Realtors Vol 1: 19461
Southam Vol 1: 6878
Southdown Press Vol 2: 627
Southeast Booksellers Association Vol 1: 19463
The Southeast Review - Florida State University Vol 1: 19465
Southeastern American Society for Eighteenth-Century Studies Vol 1: 19467
Southeastern Composers' League Vol 1: 19469

Southeastern Conference Vol 1: 19472
Southeastern Library Association Vol 1: 19474
Southeastern Surgical Congress Vol 1: 19482
Southeastern Theatre Conference Vol 1: 19484
Southern Africa Association for the Advancement of Science Vol 2: 5772
Southern African Institute of Forestry Vol 2: 5707
Southern African Society for Plant Pathology Vol 2: 5777
Southern Appalachian Botanical Society Vol 1: 19492
Southern Baptist Historical Society Vol 1: 6242
Southern California Injury Prevention Research Center Vol 1: 19494
Southern Early Childhood Association Vol 1: 19496
Southern Economic Association Vol 1: 19498
Southern Electricity Board Vol 2: 7824
Southern Historical Association Vol 1: 19500
Southern Humanities Review Vol 1: 19506
Southern Illinois University at Carbondale - School of Journalism Vol 1: 19508
Southern Methodist University - Caruth Institute for Entrepreneurship Vol 1: 19510
Southern Methodist University - Caruth Institute of Owner-Managed Business Vol 1: 19510
Southern Methodist University - Meadows School of the Arts Vol 1: 19512
Southern Poetry Review Vol 1: 19514
Southern Pressure Treaters Association Vol 1: 19516
Southern Psychiatric Association Vol 1: 19518
Southern Regional Council Vol 1: 19520
The Southern Review - Louisiana State University Vol 1: 19522
Southern States Communication Association Vol 1: 19524
Southwest Review Vol 1: 19526
Southwestern Association of Naturalists Vol 1: 19529
Sovinterfest Vol 2: 5894
Space Coast Writers' Guild Vol 1: 19534
Spain-United States Chamber of Commerce Vol 1: 19536
Spain's '92 Foundation Vol 1: 21059
Spanish Institute Vol 1: 19538
Spanish Ministry of Culture Vol 2: 6071
Spanish Mustang Registry Vol 1: 19540
Spanish Royal Society of Physics Vol 2: 6101
Spear & Jackson Vol 2: 6923
Special Interest Group on Knowledge Discovery and Data Mining - Association for Computing Machinery Vol 1: 19543
Special Libraries Association Vol 1: 19546
Special Libraries Association - Museums, Arts and Humanities Division Vol 1: 19558
Special Libraries Association - News Division Vol 1: 19561
Special Libraries Association - Transportation Division Vol 1: 19566
Special Olympics Canada Vol 1: 19568
Special Recreation for Disabled International Vol 1: 19572
Special Recreation, Inc. Vol 1: 19572
Specialized Carriers and Rigging Association Vol 1: 19574
Specialty Equipment Market Association Vol 1: 19587
Specialty Graphic Imaging Association Vol 1: 19589
Species Survival Commission Vol 2: 6559
The Spectator Vol 2: 9095
Spectroscopy Society of Pittsburgh Vol 1: 19602
Spectrum Emergency Care Vol 1: 9238
Speech Association of America Vol 1: 14705
Speech Communication Association Vol 1: 14705
Speed Equipment Market Association Vol 1: 19587
Spencer Foundation Vol 1: 13803
Spero Communications Vol 2: 9098
SPIE: International Society for Optical Engineering Vol 1: 19604
Spill Control Association of America Vol 1: 19612
Spina Bifida Association of Greater St. Louis Vol 1: 19614
Spinks Scale Company Vol 1: 12034
Spiritual Science Fellowship Vol 1: 19616
Spiritualist Yoga Fellowship Vol 1: 19618
Spitball, the Literary Baseball Magazine Vol 1: 19620
SPNM - Promoting New Music Vol 2: 9104
Spoke Gallery; B. J. Vol 1: 19622
Spolak slovenskych spisovatelov Vol 2: 5956
Spolecnost Fryderyka Chopina v CSSR Vol 2: 1414
Sport Australia Hall of Fame Vol 2: 601
Sport Canada Vol 1: 19624
Sport Interuniversitaire Canadien Vol 1: 7207
Sporting Goods Agents Association Vol 1: 19635
Sporting News Vol 1: 18630, 19639
Sports Car Club of America Vol 1: 19680
Sports Federation of Canada Vol 1: 19624
Sports Foundation - National Sporting Goods Association Vol 1: 19725
Sports Illustrated Vol 1: 19728
Sports Information Directors Association Vol 1: 14292
The Sports Network Vol 1: 7217
Sports Philatelists International Vol 1: 19731
Springer-Verlag Vol 1: 5297
Springfield Art Museum Vol 1: 19733
Springfield Association for Retarded Citizens Vol 1: 19735
Springfield Labor Council, AFL-CIO Vol 1: 19737
Sprinkler Irrigation Association Vol 1: 12203
Sri Lanka Association for the Advancement of Science Vol 2: 6130
Sri Lanka Eksath Jatheenge Sangamaya Vol 2: 6136
Srpska Akademij Naukai Umetnosti Vol 2: 5937
Stadt Braunschweig-Kulturamt Vol 2: 2677
Stadt Buxtehude Vol 2: 3065
Stadt Darmstadt Vol 2: 3136
Stadt Dortmund Vol 2: 3067
Stadt Mannheim Vol 2: 3069
Stadt Pforzheim, Kulturamt Vol 2: 3072
Stadt Schweinfurt Vol 2: 3074
Stadt Villach Vol 2: 782
Stamford Community Arts Council Vol 1: 19739
Stand Magazine Vol 2: 9106
Standard Bank Investment Corporation Vol 2: 5572
Standard Electrica Portuguesa Vol 2: 5407
Standards Council of Canada Vol 1: 19742
Standards Engineering Society Vol 1: 5985
Standards Engineering Society Vol 1: 19744
Standing Committee of Correspondents Vol 1: 19751
Stanford University Vol 2: 8341
Stanford University - Center for Integrated Facility Engineering Vol 1: 19754
Stanford University - Stanford Center on Conflict and Negotiation Vol 1: 19756
State Bar of California Vol 1: 19758
State Bar of Michigan Vol 1: 19762
State Capital Global Law Firm Group Vol 1: 19764
State Debt Management Network Vol 1: 19767
State Department and Construction Corporation Vol 2: 6124
State Farm Insurance Vol 1: 19770
State Historical Society of Missouri Vol 1: 19772
State Library of New South Wales Vol 2: 603
State Library of Victoria Vol 2: 607
State Library of Western Australia Vol 2: 610
Statistical Society of Canada Vol 1: 8293
Status of Women Canada Vol 1: 19774
Steacie Memorial Fund; E. W. R. Vol 1: 19776
Stedman Art Gallery Vol 1: 19778
Steel Authority of India, Ltd. Vol 2: 3461
Steel Founders' Society of America Vol 1: 19780
Steely Library Vol 1: 19784
Stein Collectors International Vol 1: 19786
Stephen Leacock Association Vol 1: 19789
Sterm Chemicals Vol 1: 1708
Sternway & Sons Vol 1: 13703
Stgorz; Karl Vol 1: 4797
Stichting Collectieve Propaganda van het Nederlandse Boek Vol 2: 4713
Stichting Conamus Vol 2: 4720
Stichting Dramaastricht Vol 2: 4735
Stichting Gaudeamus Vol 2: 4782
Stichting Internationaal Orgelconcours Vol 2: 4918
Stichting Kijkhuis Vol 2: 4946
Stichting Koningin Wilhelmina Fonds Vol 2: 4726
Stichting Nederlandse Film Festival Vol 2: 4861
Stichting Poetry International Vol 2: 4870
Stichting Praemium Erasmianum Vol 2: 4736
Stichting Sikkensprys Vol 2: 4905
Stichting Wereld Muziek Concours Kerkrade Vol 2: 4934
Stichting Wonen Textel Vol 2: 4920
Stiftelsen Kortfilmfestivalen Vol 2: 5161
Stiftung F.V.S.; Alfred Ttoepfer Vol 2: 3077
Stiftung Global Harmony Vol 2: 6366
Stiftung Internationaler Karlspreis zu Aachen Vol 2: 3097
Stiftung Niedersachsen Vol 2: 2770
Stiftung zur Forderung der DGE Vol 2: 2896
Stowarzysenie Bibliotekarzy Polskich Vol 2: 5352
Stowarzyszenie Miedzynarodowe Triennale Grafiki Vol 2: 5313
Strafford County Wind Symphony Vol 1: 19792
Strategic Account Management Association Vol 1: 19794
Stratton Mountain and Valley Community Benefit Foundation Vol 1: 19796

Street Sled Sports Racers International Vol 2: 9109
Strega Alberti Benevento Vol 2: 4051
Structural Board Association Vol 1: 19798
Structural Chemistry - Kratos Group plc. Vol 2: 8773
Structural Geology and Tectonics Division Vol 1: 9956
Studebaker Driver's Club Vol 1: 19800
Student American Veterinary Medical Association Vol 1: 19805
Student Council for Exceptional Children Vol 1: 8549
Student Film & Video Festival Vol 1: 19807
Student Press Law Center Vol 1: 19809
Studiengesellschaft fur Unterirdische Verkehrsanlagen Vol 2: 3112
Studio Museum in Harlem Vol 1: 19812
Stulberg International String Competition Vol 1: 19815
Stuttgart City Council Vol 2: 3099
Stuttgart International Festival of Animated Film Vol 2: 3106
Suburban Newspapers of America Vol 1: 19817
Successful Meetings Magazine Vol 1: 19820
Sudden Infant Death Syndrome Alliance-Greater Houston Chapter Vol 1: 19825
Sudler Foundation of Chicago; Louis Vol 1: 19433, 19436
Sugar Industry Technologists Vol 1: 19827
Suid-Afrikaanse Chemiese Instituut Vol 2: 5688
Suid-Afrikaanse Vereniging van Kinderchirurge Vol 2: 5679
Suider-Afrika Genootskap vir die Bevordering van die Wetenskap Vol 2: 5772
Sulabh International Social Service Organisation Vol 2: 3586
Sulphur Institute U.S.A. Vol 2: 3369
Sumi-e Society of America Vol 1: 19830
Summer and Casual Furniture Manufacturer Association Vol 1: 19832
Summit Art Center Vol 1: 16162
Sun Chemical Hartmann Vol 2: 7116
Suncoast Waldorf Association Vol 1: 19834
The Sunday Star Times Vol 2: 5045
Sunday Telegraph Vol 2: 8707
Sunday Times Business Times Vol 2: 5781
Sundstrand Corporation Vol 1: 4019
Sunset Center Vol 1: 19836
Sunset Magazine Vol 1: 19838
Sunshine Tour Vol 1: 21923
Suntory Foundation Vol 2: 4299
Suntory Limited of Japan Vol 2: 4114
Suomen Geologinen Seura-Geologiska Sallskapet I Finland Vol 2: 1624
Suomen Historiallinen Seura Vol 2: 1603
Suomen Kirjastoseura Vol 2: 1605
Suomen Kulttuurirahasto Vol 2: 1598
Suomen Museoliitto Vol 2: 1607
Suomen Naytelmakirjailijaliitto Vol 2: 1601
Suomen Sadankomitealiitto Vol 2: 1580
Suomen Taideyhdistys-Finska Konstforeningen Vol 2: 1594
Suomen Taiteilijaseura/Konstnarsgiller i Finland Vol 2: 1573
SUPELCO, Inc. Vol 1: 1714
SuperGen Inc. Vol 1: 16717
Support Systems International Vol 1: 1599
Surface Design Journal - Surface Design Association Vol 1: 19842
Surfrider Foundation Vol 1: 19844
Surgipath Medical Industries Inc. Vol 1: 15718
Susan G. Komen Breast Cancer Foundation Vol 1: 16715, 19846
Susan Smith Blackburn Prize Vol 1: 19853
Svensk Biblioteksforening Vol 2: 6283
Svenska Akademien Vol 2: 6240
Svenska Arkitekters Riksforbund Vol 2: 6167
Svenska Dagbladet Vol 2: 6232
Svenska Filminstitutet Vol 2: 6278
Svenska Forsakringsforeningen Vol 2: 6281
Svenska Matematikersamfundet Vol 2: 6287
Sveriges Dovas Riksforbund Vol 2: 6289
Sveriges Film- och Videofoerbund Vol 2: 6276
Svjetski Festival Animiranih Filmova, Zagreb Vol 2: 1391
Swedish Academy Vol 2: 6240
Swedish Academy of Pharmaceutical Sciences Vol 2: 6274
Swedish-American Chambers of Commerce, USA Vol 1: 19855
Swedish Council of America Vol 1: 19857
Swedish Federation of Film and Video Amateurs Vol 2: 6276
Swedish Film Institute Vol 2: 6278
Swedish Insurance Society Vol 2: 6281
Swedish Library Association Vol 2: 6283
Swedish Mathematical Society Vol 2: 6287
Swedish National Association of the Deaf Vol 2: 6289
Swedish Society Against Painful Experiments on Animals Vol 2: 6291
Swedish Society of Aeronautics and Astronautics Vol 2: 6294
Swedish Society of Crafts and Design Vol 2: 6297
Swinburne College of Technology Vol 2: 374
Swiss Academy of Medical Sciences Vol 2: 6504
Swiss Association for Theatre Studies Vol 2: 6507
Swiss Association of Chemists Vol 2: 6511
Swiss Biochemical Society Vol 2: 6509
Swiss Broadcasting Corporation and the City of Montreux Vol 2: 6499
Swiss Chemical Society Vol 2: 6511
Swiss Cooperative Society Vol 2: 6541
Swiss Federal Institute of Technology Zurich Vol 2: 6516
Swiss Federation for Adult Learning Vol 2: 6528
Swiss Graphic Designers Vol 2: 6530
Swiss Music Edition Vol 2: 6532
Swiss Pharmaceutical Association Vol 2: 2683
Swope Art Museum; Sheldon Vol 1: 19860
Sydney Film Festival Vol 2: 477, 613
Sylva Gelber Foundation Vol 1: 6794
Symphony Australia Vol 2: 618
Symphony of the Mountains Vol 1: 19862
SYMRISE Vol 1: 19095
Synchro Swimming U.S.A. Vol 1: 19864
Syngenta Vol 1: 19223, 19871
Syngenta Corporation Vol 1: 3541
Syracuse University - Newhouse School of Public Communications; S. I. Vol 1: 19878
Syracuse University Press Vol 1: 19881
System Safety Society Vol 1: 19883
Szent-Gyorgyi Albert Orvostudomanyi Egyetem Szeged Vol 2: 3312
Szent-Gyorgyi Medical University; Albert Vol 2: 3312
T. & A.D. Poyser Vol 2: 6957
T-Town Paws Vol 1: 19893
Tacoma-Pierce County Sports Commission Vol 1: 19895
Tafelberg Publishers Ltd. Vol 2: 5785
The Taft Group Vol 1: 19897
Tahtitieteellinen yhdistys Ursa Vol 2: 1661
Taipei Golden Horse Film Festival Vol 2: 6597
Taipei International Film Exhibition Vol 2: 6597
Taiwan Association of Stationery Industries Vol 2: 6599
Taiwan Ministry of Education Vol 2: 6601
Taiwan Pediatric Association Vol 2: 6603
Talbot County Arts Council Vol 1: 19899
Talented Youth Development Vol 1: 19902
Talk Show Hosts.com Vol 1: 19904
Tall Clubs International Vol 1: 19907
Tallahassee Soccer Association Vol 1: 19911
Tampa Bay Business Committee for the Arts Vol 1: 19914
Tampa Builders Exchange Vol 1: 19916
Tampere Film Festival Vol 2: 1659
Tampereen elokuvajuhlat Vol 2: 1659
Tanzania Association of Non Governmental Organizations Vol 2: 9288
Tanzania Industrial Research and Development Organization Vol 2: 9290
Tanzania Scouts Association Vol 2: 9292
Tanzania Teachers' Union Vol 2: 9294
TAPPI - Technical Association of the Pulp and Paper Industry Vol 1: 19918
Tarmac Quarry Products Inc. Vol 2: 6918
Tartans of Scotland Vol 2: 9111
TASH Vol 1: 19925
Tasmanian Canine Association Vol 2: 621
Tatry Housing Organization Vol 1: 19928
Tau Beta Pi Association Vol 1: 19930
Tau Beta Sigma Vol 1: 19935
Tau Sigma Delta Vol 1: 19939
Tax Foundation Vol 1: 19943
Taxpayers Association of Europe Vol 2: 3108
TBS Britannica Company Vol 2: 4302
T.D Financial Group Vol 1: 19791
Te Roopu Whaka Waihanga Iwi O Aotearoa Vol 1: 12840
Tea Council Vol 2: 9113
Teachers Association of Baltimore County Vol 1: 19945
Teachers of English; National Council of Vol 1: 14834
Teachers of English to Speakers of Other Languages Vol 1: 19947
Teatro Municipale Valli Vol 2: 4053
Teatrul Sica Alexandrescu, Brasov Vol 2: 5805
Technical Association for Solid Wastes Management Vol 2: 6104
Technical Association of the Graphic Arts Vol 1: 19955
Technikon Witwatersrand Vol 2: 5789
Technology-Science Education Institute Vol 2: 5289
Technology Student Association Vol 1: 19957
Teen Court of Huerfano County Vol 1: 19961
Teen International Entomology Group Vol 1: 22060
Tel Aviv Museum of Art Vol 2: 3769
Telefilm Canada Vol 1: 6033, 22048
Television and Radio Industries Club Vol 2: 9115

Telly Awards Vol 1: 19963
Temple de la Renommee des Sports du Canada Vol 1: 6841
TENN-SHARE Vol 1: 19971
Tennessee Council of Teachers of English Vol 1: 19965
Tennessee Library Association Vol 1: 19967
Tennis Vol 1: 11147
Tennis Association of Austria Vol 2: 785
Tennis Ireland Vol 2: 3711
Tennis Magazine - Miller Sports Group LLC Vol 1: 19976
Tennis Week Vol 1: 19983
TENOVUS - SCOTLAND Vol 2: 9118
Terrier Klub; Dansk Vol 2: 1465
Tertis International Viola Competition and Workshop; Lionel Vol 2: 9120
Test and County Cricket Board Vol 2: 7416
Texas Association of Bank Counsel Vol 1: 19985
Texas Association of Sports Officials - Baseball, Houston Chapter Vol 1: 19987
Texas Cable and Telecommunications Association Vol 1: 19989
Texas Council for the Social Studies Vol 1: 19992
Texas Daily Newspaper Association Vol 1: 19994
Texas Engineering Experiment Station Vol 1: 20001
Texas Fine Arts Association, The Jones Center for Contemporary Art Vol 1: 20004
Texas Heart Institute Vol 1: 20006
Texas Independent Producers and Royalty Owners Association Vol 1: 20008
Texas Institute of Letters Vol 1: 20010
Texas League for Nursing Vol 1: 20024
Texas Library Association Vol 1: 20027
Texas Medical Association Vol 1: 20029
Texas Nonprofit Theatres Vol 1: 20033
Texas Oral History Association Vol 1: 20035
Texas Sign Association Vol 1: 20039
Texas Society of Architects/ AIA Vol 1: 20041
Texas Tech University - College of Mass Communications Vol 1: 20044
Texas Western Press Vol 1: 20047
Textile Institute Vol 2: 9122
Textile Study Group of New York Vol 1: 20049
Textilipari Muszaki es Tudomanyos Egyesulet Vol 2: 3267
Thai Chamber of Commerce Vol 2: 6618
Thai Youth Hostels Association Vol 2: 6620
Theatre Communications Group Vol 1: 20051
Theatre Historical Society of America Vol 1: 20056
Theatre Library Association Vol 1: 20058
Theatre World Vol 1: 20061
Theodore Roethke Memorial Foundation Vol 1: 20063
Theodore Roosevelt Association Vol 1: 20065
Thermal Syndicate, Ltd Vol 2: 7201
Thermo Electron Corp. Vol 1: 15717, 15722, 19603
Thessaloniki International Film Festival Vol 2: 3189
Theta Alpha Phi Vol 1: 20067
Theta Sigma Phi Vol 1: 5521
Thibaud; Concours International Marguerite Long - Jacques Vol 2: 2525
Thimble Press Vol 2: 9137
Third Reich Study Group Vol 1: 20069
Third Street Music School Settlement Vol 1: 20071
Third World Academy of Sciences Vol 2: 2637, 4056, 4057, 4356, 4357, 4359
Third World Network of Scientific Organizations Vol 2: 4055
Thistle Class Association Vol 1: 20074
Thomas Paine National Historical Association Vol 1: 20077
Thomas Wolfe Society Vol 1: 20079
Thompson Learning Vol 1: 5301
Thomson Financial Vol 1: 17936
Thomson Foundation Vol 2: 9139
Thomson Gale Vol 1: 17940, 17948
Thomson Scientific Vol 1: 5613, 13258, 18855
Thomson Tubes Electroniques Vol 2: 2325
Thoroughbred Racing Associations Vol 1: 20083
Thorpe Smith Vol 1: 2002
Thurber House Vol 1: 20086
ThyssenKrupp Mexinox Vol 2: 4639
Tibetan Youth Congress Vol 2: 3590
Tilburg University Vol 2: 4922
Tile Contractors' Association of America Vol 1: 20088
Time & Life Magazine Vol 1: 16981
Time Inc. Vol 1: 20090
Time Out Communications Ltd. Vol 2: 9141
The Times Vol 2: 9103
Times Educational Supplement Vol 2: 9145
Times Publishing Group Vol 2: 5940
Tioxide Group Plc. Vol 2: 8773
Tissue Culture Association, Inc. Vol 1: 18722
Tmmob Jeoloji Muhendisleri Odasi Vol 2: 6628
TMN: The Move Network Vol 1: 6033
Toastmasters International Vol 1: 20094
Tokens and Medals Society Vol 1: 2880
Tokyo Chigaku Kyokai Vol 2: 4303
Tokyo Geographical Society Vol 2: 4303
Tokyo International Film Festival Vol 2: 4305
Tokyo International Music Competition Vol 2: 4307
Tolkien Society Vol 2: 9148
Tolkien Society of America Vol 1: 13738
Tonga and Tin Can Mail Study Circle - Society of Australasian Specialists/ Oceania Vol 1: 20096
Toni Morrison Society Vol 1: 20099
Top Blacks in Law Enforcement Vol 1: 6441
Topps Chewing Gum Vol 1: 20101
Topps Company, Inc. Vol 1: 20101
Toray Industries Inc., and Kyowa Hakko Kogyo Co. Ltd. Vol 2: 6474
Torello Excursionist Center Vol 2: 6106
Torello International Festival of Mountain and Adventure Films Vol 2: 6106
Toronto Arts Council Foundation Vol 1: 20110
Toronto International Film Festival Group Vol 1: 20113
Toronto International Salon of Photography Vol 1: 20119
Toronto Press Club Vol 1: 20121
Torrey Botanical Club Vol 1: 20123
Torrey Botanical Society Vol 1: 20123
Touchdown Club Charities of Washington, D.C. Vol 1: 20127
Touche, Ross and Company Vol 1: 10985
Tourism, Hotels and Restaurants Association Vol 2: 5991
Tourism Industry Association New Zealand Vol 2: 5090
Towarzystwo imienia Fryderyka Chopina Vol 2: 5304
Tower Publishing Services, Ltd. Vol 2: 7189
Towing and Recovery Association of America Vol 1: 20139
Town and Country Planning Association Vol 2: 9150
Town of New Scotland Historical Association Vol 1: 20142
Townsville Foundation for Australian Literary Studies Vol 2: 347
Towson University - College of Liberal Arts Vol 1: 20144
Trade Show Exhibitors Association Vol 1: 20146
Trading Stamp Institute of America Vol 1: 5832
Traditional Irish Music, Singing and Dancing Society Vol 2: 3713
Traditional Irish Singing and Dancing Society Vol 2: 3713
Trama Visual, AC Vol 2: 4641
Transco Vol 2: 6924
Transcultural Nursing Society Vol 1: 20148
Transparency International Deutschland e.V. Vol 2: 3110
Transparency International - Germany Vol 2: 3110
Transplant Recipients International Organization Vol 1: 20151
Transport Insurance Company Vol 1: 4774
Transportation and Logistics Council Vol 1: 20154
Transportation Lawyers Association Vol 1: 20156
Transportation Research Board Vol 1: 20158
Travel Air Club Vol 1: 20167
Travel and Tourism Research Association Vol 1: 20169
Travel Industry Association of America Vol 1: 20175
Travel Research Association Vol 1: 20169
Treasure Coast Builders Association Vol 1: 20178
Treasury Board of Canada Secretariat Vol 1: 20180
Tree Care Industry Association Vol 1: 20184
Trees for Tomorrow Vol 1: 20186
Trento Filmfestival Internazionale Montagna Esplorazione Vol 2: 4058
Trento International Film Festival of Mountains and Exploration Vol 2: 4058
Tri-City Gang Prevention Task Force Vol 1: 20189
Tri-County Arts Council Gallery Vol 1: 20191
Tri-County Specialty Contractors Association Vol 1: 20193
TRI-M Music Honor Society Vol 1: 20195
Tri-State Bird Rescue and Research Vol 1: 20201
Trial Lawyers for Public Justice Vol 1: 20203
Triathlon Federation Vol 1: 21246
Tribune Entertainment Vol 1: 19422
Trident Insurance Services LLC Vol 1: 17730
Triple Crown Productions, Inc. Vol 1: 20205
Trophy Dealers of America Vol 1: 6165
Trout Unlimited Vol 1: 20208
Trout Unlimited Canada Vol 1: 20212
Trout Unlimited, Naugatuck Valley Vol 1: 20214
Troy Rotary Club Vol 1: 20216

Truck Renting and Leasing Association Vol 1: 20219
Trudeau Institute Vol 1: 20221
True Value Vol 1: 15089
True Value Hardware Stores Vol 1: 20427
Truman Good Neighbor Award Foundation; Harry S. Vol 1: 20224
Trust Co. Vol 2: 624
Trustees Savings Bank Vol 2: 8787
TRW Vol 1: 10878
Tucker Music Foundation; Richard Vol 1: 20228
Tucson Arts Brigade Vol 1: 20232
Tugac Foundation; Husamettin Vol 2: 6651
Tulsa Library Trust Vol 1: 20234, 20235, 20236, 20237
Tunbridge Wells International Young Concert Artists Competition Vol 2: 9152
Turk dil Karumu Vol 2: 6652
Turkish Language Institute Vol 2: 6652
Turkish Studies Association Vol 1: 20238
Turkiye Bilimsel ve Teknik Arastirma Kurumu Vol 2: 6647
Turkiye Radyo Televizyon Kurumu Vol 2: 6658
Tuskegee United Women's League Vol 1: 20244
Tusquets Editores S.A. Vol 2: 6108
TV Week - Pacific Publications Vol 2: 627
TVR Car Club North America Vol 1: 20246
TVR Car Club of England Vol 1: 20246
Tweed Shire Council Vol 2: 629
Twin Cities Musicians Union, Local 30-73 Vol 1: 20248
Two/Ten Foundation Vol 1: 20250
Two/Ten International Footwear Foundation Vol 1: 20250
UCD Photographic Society Vol 2: 3715
UCLA Alumni Association Vol 1: 20253
Ucross Foundation Vol 1: 20264
Ufficio Stampa - Casino de la Vallee E Manifestatzioni Vol 2: 4060
Uglies Unlimited Vol 1: 20266
UICC International Cancer Foundation Vol 2: 6473
UK Committee for the Thouron Awards Vol 2: 9154
UK Council on Deafness Vol 2: 9156
UK Fashion Exports Vol 2: 9158
Ukrainian Congress Committee of America Vol 1: 20268
Ukrainian Institute of America Vol 1: 20270
Ukrainian National Women's League of America Vol 1: 20272
Ukrainian Philatelic and Numismatic Society Vol 1: 20275
Ulster Teachers' Union Vol 2: 9160
Ultimate Players Association Vol 1: 20280
Ultrasonic Industry Association Vol 1: 20283
Unda Association Catholique Internationale pour la Radio et la Television Vol 2: 1111
Unda International Catholic Association for Radio and Television Vol 2: 1111
Unda-USA, the National Catholic Association of Broadcasters and Commun - icators Vol 1: 7632
Underfashion Club Vol 1: 20285
Underground Transportation Research Association Vol 2: 3112
Undersea and Hyperbaric Medical Society Vol 1: 20288
Undersea Medical Society, Inc. Vol 1: 20288
Underwater Society of America Vol 1: 20293
UNESCO Vol 2: 2286, 2446, 2593, 5967
UNESCO International Book Committee Vol 2: 789
Unicam Vol 2: 8773
Unicycling Society of America Vol 1: 20297
UniJapan Film Vol 2: 4310
Unilever Research Vol 2: 8773, 8932
Unilever Research and Engineering Vol 2: 8773
Unilever Research Laboratory Vol 2: 6865
UNIMA-U.S.A., American Center of the Union Internationale de la Marionnette Vol 1: 20299
Union Carbide Corporation Vol 1: 1751, 1781, 4019
Union des Annonceurs Vol 2: 2612
Union des Ecrivaines et Ecrivains Quebecois Vol 1: 20302
Union des Femmes Artistes et Musiciennes Vol 2: 2614
Union des Foires Internationales Vol 2: 2616
Union Europeenne de la Presse Sportive Vol 2: 6146
Union Europeenne de Radio-Television Vol 2: 6314
Union for the International Language Ido Vol 2: 9163
Union Geographique Internationale Vol 1: 11648
Union Internacional de Tecnicos de la Industria del Calzado Vol 2: 6066
Union International des Transports Routiers Vol 2: 6439
Union Internationale Contre le Cancer Vol 2: 6468
Union Internationale de Cristallographie Vol 2: 8008
Union Internationale de Physique Pure et Appliquee Vol 1: 12102
Union Internationale des Architectes Vol 2: 2509
Union Internationale des Etudiants Vol 2: 1431
Union Internationale des Instituts de Recherches Forestieres Vol 2: 765
Union Internationale des Societes de Microbiologie Vol 2: 451
Union Internationale pour la Science, la Technique et les Applications du Vide Vol 2: 7999
Union Internationale pour les livres de jeunesse Vol 2: 6388
Union Internationale pour l'Etude du Quarternaire Vol 2: 3644
Union Mathematique Internationale Vol 1: 11743
Union Mondiale pour la Nature Vol 2: 6555
Union Mundial para la Naturaleza Vol 2: 6555
Union of Architects of Romania Vol 2: 5877
Union of Architects of the SRR Vol 2: 5877
Union of Associations of Slovene Librarians Vol 2: 5993
Union of Bulgarian Actors Vol 2: 1217
Union of Bulgarian Artists Vol 2: 1234, 1237
Union of Bulgarian Filmmakers Vol 2: 1217
Union of Councils for Jews in the Former Soviet Union Vol 1: 20305
Union of Councils for Soviet Jews Vol 1: 20305
Union of Czech Architects Vol 2: 1435
Union of International Fairs Vol 2: 2616
Union of Japanese Scientists and Engineers Vol 2: 4312
Union Postale Universelle Vol 2: 6534
Union Radio Scientifique Internationale Vol 2: 933
Unione Matematica Italiana Vol 2: 4015
Uniono por la Linguo Internaciona Ido Vol 2: 9163
Uniroyal Chemical Company Vol 1: 1772
Unisys Corporation Vol 1: 5300
Unitarian Universalist Association of Congregations Vol 1: 20307
Unitarian Universalist Service Committee Vol 1: 20314
United Airlines Vol 1: 20944
United Cerebral Palsy Association of Central Minnesota Vol 1: 20319
United Cerebral Palsy Association of Metropolitan Detroit Vol 1: 20321
United Church of Christ Coordinating Center for Women in Church and Society Vol 1: 20323
United Citizens and Neighborhoods Vol 1: 20325
United Commercial Travelers of America, Butler Council 465 Vol 1: 20327
United Daughters of the Confederacy Vol 1: 20329
United Engineering Foundation Vol 1: 20331
United Hellenic Voters of America Vol 1: 20333
United HIAS Service Vol 1: 10370
United in Group Harmony Association Vol 1: 20335
United Israel Appeal - Keren Hayesod Vol 2: 3777
United Israel World Union Vol 1: 20337
United Jewish Appeal - Federation of Jewish Philanthropies of New York Vol 1: 20339
United Kennel Club Vol 1: 20344
United Kingdom Department of Trade and Industry Vol 2: 9165
United Methodist Association of Health and Welfare Ministries Vol 1: 20347
United Methodist Church, Board of Global Ministries - Health and Welfare Ministries Division Vol 1: 20356
United Nations Vol 1: 20359
United Nations Association in the Democratic Socialist Republic of Sri Lanka Vol 2: 6136
United Nations Association of Rochester Vol 1: 20361
United Nations Association of the United States of America Vol 1: 20363
United Nations Association of the U.S.A. Vol 1: 20365
United Nations Economic and Social Commission for Asia and the Pacific Vol 2: 6622
United Nations Environment Programme Vol 2: 4366
United Nations High Commission for Refugees - Regional Office Mexico Vol 2: 4643
United Nations Population Fund Vol 1: 20367
United Parcel Service (UPS) Vol 1: 15458
United Press International Vol 1: 20369
United Seamen's Service Vol 1: 20372
United State Aquatic Sports Vol 1: 21201
United States Air Force Vol 1: 15627
United States Air Force Academy Vol 1: 20381
United States Amateur Boxing, Inc. Vol 1: 20383
United States Amateur Confederation of Roller Skating Vol 1: 20390

U.S. Aquatic Sports Vol 1: 20392
United States Arms Control and Disarmament Agency Vol 1: 20401
United States Army Corps of Engineers Vol 1: 20404
U.S. Association for Blind Athletes Vol 1: 20406
United States Association of Former Members of Congress Vol 1: 20411
United States Auto Club Vol 1: 20413
United States Badminton Association Vol 1: 21144
United States BASE Association Vol 1: 20430
U.S. Bicycling Hall of Fame Vol 1: 20432
United States Billiard Association Vol 1: 20434
U.S. Boomerang Association Vol 1: 20436
U.S. Bureau of Mines and Explosives Engineers Vol 1: 15387
U.S. Cancellation Club Vol 1: 20439
U.S. Catholic - Claretians Ministries Vol 1: 20441
U.S. Census Bureau Vol 1: 20443
United States Chess Federation Vol 1: 20445
United States Civil Defense Council Vol 1: 11347
United States Civil Service Commission Vol 1: 20716
U.S. Committee for Scientific Cooperation With Vietnam Vol 1: 20447
United States Committee of the International Council on Monuments and Sites Vol 1: 20451
United States Conference of Mayors Vol 1: 20453
United States Congress - Committee on Banking, Finance, and Urban Affairs Vol 1: 20458
U.S. Council for Energy Awareness Vol 1: 16593
United States Council for International Business Vol 1: 20460
United States Council for IYDP Vol 1: 15457
United States Council of the International Chamber of Commerce Vol 1: 20460
United States Curling Association Vol 1: 20462
United States Department of Army - Civilian Marksmanship Program Vol 1: 20465
United States Department of Commerce Vol 1: 20467
United States Department of Commerce - International Trade Administration Vol 1: 20471
United States Department of Commerce - National Institute of Standards and Technology Vol 1: 20474
United States Department of Defense - Defense Logistics Agency Vol 1: 20484
United States Department of Defense - Office of the Secretary of Defense Vol 1: 20486
U.S. Department of Education Vol 1: 14207
United States Department of Education - Office of Intergovernmental and Interagency Affairs Vol 1: 20488
United States Department of Education - White House Commission on Presidential Scholars Vol 1: 20490
United States Department of Energy Vol 1: 20492, 20731
United States Department of Health and Human Services Vol 1: 20496
United States Department of Health and Human Services - National Institutes of Health Vol 1: 20498
United States Department of Health and Human Services, Public Health Service - Centers for Disease Control and Prevention (CDC) Vol 1: 20500
U.S. Department of Housing and Urban Development Vol 1: 3559
United States Department of Interior Vol 1: 17130
United States Department of Justice - Federal Bureau of Investigation Vol 1: 20503
United States Department of Justice - Office of Justice Programs Vol 1: 20505
United States Department of Labor Vol 1: 20508
United States Department of Labor - Bureau of Labor Statistics Vol 1: 20516
U.S. Department of Labor - Office of Job Corps Vol 1: 20518
United States Department of Navy - U.S. Naval Observatory Vol 1: 20523
United States Department of State Vol 1: 20527
United States Department of the Treasury - Financial Management Service Vol 1: 20556
United States Department of Transportation - Federal Highway Administration Vol 1: 20558
United States Department of Veterans Affairs - Regional Office Vol 1: 20560
United States Dressage Federation Vol 1: 20562
U.S. Energy Association Vol 1: 20572
United States Environmental Protection Agency Vol 1: 20574
U.S. Environmental Protection Agency - Office of Research and Development Vol 1: 20576
United States Executive Office of the President Vol 1: 13884, 20459, 20487, 20506, 20507, 20575, 20718
United States Federation for Culture Collections Vol 1: 4139
U.S. Federation for Culture Collections Vol 1: 20578
United States Fencing Coaches Association Vol 1: 20580
United States Figure Skating Association Vol 1: 20588
United States Fish and Wildlife Service - Federal Duck Stamp Program Vol 1: 20591
U.S. Forest Service - Northeastern Research Station Vol 1: 20593
U.S. Fund for UNICEF - U.S. Committee Vol 1: 20595
United States General Services Administration Vol 1: 20600
United States Golf Association Vol 1: 20602, 21923
United States Handball Association Vol 1: 20609
U.S. Hang Gliding Association Vol 1: 20611
United States Harness Writers' Association Vol 1: 20617
United States Harness Writers' Association, Vernon Chapter Vol 1: 20634
United States Hockey Hall of Fame Vol 1: 20636
U.S. Holocaust Memorial Council Vol 1: 20638
United States Institute for Theatre Technology Vol 1: 20641
U.S. Institute of Peace Vol 1: 20654
United States Intercollegiate Lacrosse Association Vol 1: 20658
U.S. International Film and Video Festival Vol 1: 20674
U.S.-Israel Binational Science Foundation Vol 2: 3779
United States Jaycees Vol 1: 20676
U.S. Junior Chamber of Commerce Vol 1: 20676
U.S. Lacrosse and The Lacrosse Museum and National Hall of Fame Vol 1: 20679
United States Lawn Tennis Association Vol 1: 20852
United States Lighthouse Society Vol 1: 20681
U.S. Maimed Soldiers League Vol 1: 17959
U.S. Marine Corps Combat Correspondents Association Vol 1: 20683
United States Masters Swimming Vol 1: 20689
U.S. Metric Association Vol 1: 20694
U.S.-Mexico Border Health Association Vol 1: 20696
United States-Mexico Chamber of Commerce Vol 1: 20698
United States Military Academy Association of Graduates Vol 1: 20700
U.S. Mirror Class Association Vol 1: 20702
United States Modern Pentathlon Association Vol 1: 20704
United States Naval Academy Vol 1: 11125
United States Naval Institute Vol 1: 16057
United States Naval Institute Vol 1: 20706
United States Navy Vol 1: 2346
United States of America Amateur Boxing Federation Vol 1: 20383
United States of America Rugby Football Union Ltd. Vol 1: 20756
United States Office of Personnel Management Vol 1: 20716
United States Olympic Committee Vol 1: 20719
United States Orienteering Federation Vol 1: 20726
U.S. Pan Asian American Chamber of Commerce Vol 1: 20728
U.S. Particle Accelerator School Vol 1: 20730
United States Patent and Trademark Office Vol 1: 20732
United States Police Canine Association Vol 1: 20734
U.S. Powerlifting Federation Vol 1: 20737
United States Powerlifting Federation of the AAU Vol 1: 20737
United States Professional Tennis Association Vol 1: 20739
United States Professional Tennis Association Vol 1: 20872
United States Rowing Association Vol 1: 20745
United States Rugby Football Union Vol 1: 20756
United States Sailing Association Vol 1: 20769
United States Ski and Snowboard Association Vol 1: 20790
United States Ski Association Vol 1: 20790
United States Ski Writers Association Vol 1: 16460
U.S. Small Business Administration Vol 1: 20828

United States Soccer Federation Vol 1: 20837
United States Space Foundation Vol 1: 20840
U.S. Speedskating Vol 1: 20845
U.S. Sports Acrobatics Vol 1: 20847
United States Stamp Society Vol 1: 20849
United States Synchronized Swimming Vol 1: 19864
U.S. Table Tennis Association Vol 1: 21209
United States Tennis Association Vol 1: 20852
United States Trotting Association Vol 1: 20875
United States Water Polo Vol 1: 20880
United States Women's Curling Association Vol 1: 20887
U.S. Wrestling Foundation Vol 1: 577
U.S. Yacht Racing Union Vol 1: 20769
United States Youth Soccer Association Vol 1: 20890
United Synagogue of Conservative Judaism Vol 1: 20901
United Technologies Corporation Vol 1: 2439
United Technologies Research Center Vol 1: 16782
United Way of America Vol 1: 20903
United Way of Chester County Vol 1: 20906
United Way of Illinois Valley Vol 1: 20909
United Way of Jay County Vol 1: 20911
United Way of South Central Nebraska Vol 1: 20913
United Way of the Berwick Area Vol 1: 20915
United Way of the Valley Area Vol 1: 20917
Unity-and-Diversity World Council Vol 1: 20919, 20920
Uniunea Arhitectilor din Romania Vol 2: 5877
Universal Vol 1: 16000
Universal Esperanto Association Vol 2: 4924
Universal Oil Products Vol 1: 2774
Universal Pantheist Society Vol 1: 20922
Universal Postal Union Vol 2: 6534
Universal Ship Cancellation Society Vol 1: 20924
Universala Esperanto-Asocio Vol 2: 4924
Universidad Autonoma de Ciudad Juarez Vol 2: 4645
Universidad Autonoma Metropolitana Vol 2: 4563
Universidad de Medellin Vol 2: 1340
Universidad del Valle Vol 2: 1343
Universidad Externado de Colombia Vol 2: 1345
Universidad Nacional Autonoma de Mexico Vol 2: 4563, 4586
Universidade de Lisboa Vol 2: 5493
Universita degli Studi di Bologna Vol 2: 4064
Universitat Basel Vol 2: 6539
Universitat Karlsruhe (Technische Hochschule) Vol 2: 3114
Universite de Geneve Vol 2: 6536
Universite de Montreal; Centre de recherches mathematiques, Vol 1: 13202
Universite de technologie de Compiegne Vol 2: 2618
Universite Libre de Bruxelles Vol 2: 2949
Universitetet I Oslo Vol 2: 5177
Universities Federation for Animal Welfare Vol 2: 9168
Universities Research Association Vol 1: 3467
University Aviation Association Vol 1: 20941
University College of Central Queensland Vol 2: 391
University College of Southern Queensland Vol 2: 438
University Continuing Education Association Vol 1: 20945
University Council for Educational Administration Vol 1: 20970
The University Foundation Vol 2: 1114
University Mozarteum, Salzburg Vol 2: 791
The University Museum Vol 1: 21095
University Musical Society Vol 1: 20974
University of Adelaide Vol 2: 416
University of Alabama at Birmingham - Department of Theatre Vol 1: 20976
University of Albany Vol 1: 18333
University of Alberta - Perinatal Research Centre Vol 1: 20978
University of Arizona - Department of Journalism Vol 1: 20980
University of Arizona - Udall Center for Studies in Public Policy Vol 1: 20982
University of Barcelona Vol 2: 6024
University of Basel Vol 2: 6539
University of Bologna Vol 2: 4064
University of British Columbia - Wine Research Centre Vol 1: 20985
University of California, Davis - Davis Arboretum Vol 1: 20987
University of California, Los Angeles - Anderson School of Management Vol 1: 20989
University of Canberra Vol 2: 425
University of Chicago Vol 2: 2931
University of Chicago - Cancer Research Center Vol 1: 20991
University of Chicago - Department of Music Vol 1: 20993
University of Chicago Alumni Association Vol 1: 20995
University of Chicago Medical Alumni Association Vol 1: 21002
University of Chicago Medical and Biological Sciences Alumni Association Vol 1: 21002
University of Chicago Press Vol 1: 21005
University of Colorado - School of Journalism and Mass Communication Vol 1: 21007
University of Colorado at Boulder - Center of the American West Vol 1: 21009
University of Copenhagen Vol 2: 1539
University of Dayton - Office of Provost Vol 1: 21011
University of Denver - Daniels College of Business Vol 1: 21014
University of Edinburgh - Department of English Literature Vol 2: 9171
University of Georgia - Artificial Intelligence Center Vol 1: 21016
University of Georgia - Grady College of Journalism and Mass Communication Vol 1: 21018
University of Georgia - Language Education Office Vol 1: 21021
University of Georgia Press Vol 1: 21024
University of Hawaii Vol 1: 5344
University of Hawaii at Manoa - School of Communications Vol 1: 21027
University of Houston Vol 1: 7586
University of Illinois Vol 1: 21029
University of Illinois - College of Fine & Applied Arts Vol 1: 21031
University of Illinois - Graduate School of Library and Information Science Vol 1: 21033
University of Illinois at Chicago - Center for Urban Economic Development Vol 1: 21035
University of Illinois at Urbana-Champaign - Agricultural Bioprocess Laboratory Vol 1: 21037
University of Kentucky - Lucille Parker Markey Cancer Center Vol 1: 21039
University of Limburg Vol 2: 1117
University of Liverpool Vol 2: 8054, 9173
University of Louisville - College of Education and Human Development Vol 1: 21041
University of Louisville - Labor-Management Center Vol 1: 21043
University of Louisville - Louisville Presbyterian Theological Seminary Vol 1: 21045
University of Louisville - School of Education Vol 1: 21047
University of Louisville - School of Music Vol 1: 21049
University of Manitoba Vol 1: 18135
University of Maryland - College of Library and Information Services Vol 1: 21051
University of Maryland Center for Quality and Productivity Vol 1: 21053
University of Maryland International Music Competitions, Rossborough Festival Vol 1: 18566
University of Massachusetts Press Vol 1: 21056
University of Melbourne Vol 2: 388
University of Melbourne - Assessment Research Centre Vol 2: 631
University of Melbourne - Faculty of Arts Vol 2: 633
University of Melbourne - Faculty of Science Vol 2: 635
University of Miami - School of International Studies Vol 1: 21058
University of Michigan Vol 1: 21060
University of Michigan - Matthaei Botanical Gardens and Nichols Arboretum Vol 1: 21062
University of Michigan - Stephen M. Ross School of Business Vol 1: 21064
University of Michigan Press Vol 1: 21066
University of Minnesota - Center for Advanced Feminist Studies Vol 1: 21068
University of Minnesota - Center for Labor Policy Vol 1: 21070
University of Minnesota - Children's Literature Research Collection Vol 1: 21072
University of Minnesota - Office of the Sencor Vice President for Academic Affairs and Provost Vol 1: 21075
University of Missouri-Columbia - School of Journalism Vol 1: 21077
University of Missouri—St. Louis - Center for International Studies Vol 1: 21082
University of Missouri—St. Louis - Center for Trauma Recovery Vol 1: 21084
University of Music and Dramatic Arts in Graz Vol 2: 793
University of New Orleans Eisenhower Center for American Studies Vol 1: 21086
University of New South Wales Vol 2: 381, 637
University of Newcastle Vol 2: 382
University of Notre Dame - News and Information Vol 1: 21088
University of Oregon - Institute for a Sustainable Environment Vol 1: 21091
University of Otago Vol 2: 5092

University of Oxford - Faculty of Music Vol 2: 9177
University of Padua - P.P. Vergerio European Prize for Children's Literature Vol 2: 4066
University of Pennsylvania - David Mahoney Institute of Neurological Sciences Vol 1: 21093
University of Pennsylvania Museum of Archaeology and Anthropology Vol 1: 21095
University of Peradeniya, Sri Lanka Vol 2: 6122
University of Pittsburgh Press Vol 1: 21098
University of Queensland Vol 2: 415
University of Rochester Vol 1: 21101
University of San Diego - School of Law - Children's Advocacy Institute Vol 1: 21103
University of South Australia Vol 2: 404
University of Sussex Library Vol 2: 9179
University of Sydney Vol 2: 419
University of Tasmania Vol 2: 406
University of Technology of Compiegne Vol 2: 2618
University of Toronto - Faculty of Law Vol 1: 21105
University of Toronto - Pulp and Paper Centre Vol 1: 21107
University of Toronto - University College Vol 1: 21111
University of Toronto Innovations Foundation Vol 1: 21113
University of Toronto Law Alumni Association Vol 1: 21106
University of Virginia - Center for Russian and East European Studies Vol 1: 21115
University of Virginia - Center for South Asian Studies Vol 1: 21118
University of Western Australia Vol 2: 387
University of Wisconsin—Madison - Center for South Asia Vol 1: 21120
University of Wisconsin—Madison - Institute on Aging Vol 1: 21122
University of Wisconsin Press - Department of English Vol 1: 21124
University Photographers Association of America Vol 1: 21126
Upjohn Co. Vol 1: 4253
Upper Austria State Government Vol 2: 795
Upper Cumberland Funeral Directors Association Vol 1: 21130
Uppsala International Short Film Festival Vol 2: 6299
Upsilon Pi Epsilon Association Vol 1: 21132
Uptown Chamber of Commerce Vol 1: 21134
Urban Affairs Association Vol 1: 21136
Urban Land Institute Vol 1: 21139
Urdd Cerddoriaeth Cymru Vol 2: 9208
Ursa Astronomical Association Vol 2: 1661
US Black Engineer Vol 1: 7585
US International Film and Video Festival Vol 1: 21141
USA Badminton Vol 1: 21144
U.S.A. Baseball Vol 1: 21152
USA Cycling Vol 1: 21161
USA Deaf Sports Federation Vol 1: 21163
USA Diving Vol 1: 21166
USA Hockey Vol 1: 21173
USA International Ballet Competition Vol 1: 21183
USA International Harp Competition Vol 1: 21185
USA Swimming Vol 1: 21187
USA Swimming Safety Education Committee Vol 1: 21203
U.S.A. Table Tennis Vol 1: 21209
USA Today Vol 1: 9331
U.S.A. Track and Field Vol 1: 21211
USA Triathlon Vol 1: 21246
USA Water Ski Vol 1: 21251
USC Canada Vol 1: 21253
USF Faculty Association, California Federation of Teachers (AFL-CIO), Local 4269 Vol 1: 21255
USO of Metropolitan New York Vol 1: 21257
USS Nevada Association (BB-36/SSBN-733) Vol 1: 21260
USSA Eastern Alpine Official's Committee Vol 1: 20798
Utah Professional Videographers Association Vol 1: 21262
Utility Communicators International Vol 1: 21264
UWO - Faculty of Applied Health Science Vol 1: 14644
Vaestoliitto Vol 2: 1584
Val de Marne; Festival International de Films de Femmes de Creteil et du Vol 2: 2515
Valladolid International Film Festival Vol 2: 6111
Valley Industrial Development Corp. Vol 1: 21266
Valley Players Vol 1: 21268
Van Alen Institute Vol 1: 21270
Vancouver International Film Festival Vol 1: 21272
Vanderbilt University Press Vol 1: 21274
Vanguard Youth Services Vol 1: 21276
Varian Associates Vol 1: 6157
Varian Medical Systems Vol 1: 16716
Variety International - The Children's Charity Vol 1: 21278
Varna International Ballet Competition Vol 2: 1239
Vatel-Club Luxembourg Vol 2: 4412
The Vatican Vol 2: 9309
Vaughan & Bushnell Manufacturing Co. Vol 1: 14255
Veeco Instruments, Inc Vol 1: 6155
Vegetarian Awareness Network Vol 1: 21282
Vegetarian Resource Group Vol 1: 21284
Vehicle Association; European Electric Road Vol 2: 852
Veitch Historical Society Vol 1: 21286
Velo-Cardio-Facial Syndrome Vol 1: 21288
Venezuelan American Association of the United States Vol 1: 21291
Venezuelan Association of Mining and Metallurgical Industries Vol 2: 9326
Ventura County Symphony Association Vol 1: 16201
Venture Clubs Vol 1: 21293
Venture Scotland Vol 2: 9181
Verband Deutscher Elektrotechniker (VDE) Vol 2: 2642
Verband Deutscher Schulmusiker Vol 2: 2903
Verband Hannoverscher Warmblutzuechter Vol 2: 3116
Verbandder Koche Deutschlands Vol 2: 3063
Verbatim, The Language Quarterly Vol 2: 7460
Verein der Zellstoff-und Papier-Chemiker und-Ingenieure Vol 2: 2644
Verein Deutscher Textilveredlungsfachleute e.V Vol 2: 3118
Verein Ungarischer Chemiker Vol 2: 3248
Vereinigung fur Angewandte Botanik Vol 2: 3061
Vereinigung Osterreichischer Bibliothekarinnen und Bibliothekare Vol 2: 682
Vereniging van Geneeskundige Laboratorium Tegnoloe van Suid-Afrika Vol 2: 5620
Vereniging van Schouwburg en Concertgebouwdirecties Vol 2: 4927
Vereniging van Schrijvers en Vertalers Vol 2: 4929
Vereniging van Suid-Afrikaanse Bourekenaars Vol 2: 5517
Verizon Vol 1: 16981
Vermont Business Round Table Vol 1: 21295
Vermont Chamber of Commerce Vol 1: 21297
Vermont Historical Society Vol 1: 21300
Vermont Parent Teacher Association Vol 1: 21303
Vermont Society of Land Surveyors Vol 1: 21305
Vermont Superintendents Association Vol 1: 21307
Vernacular Architecture Forum Vol 1: 21309
Vernon County Historical Society Vol 1: 21312
Vesterheim Norwegian-American Museum Vol 1: 21315
Veteran Corps of Artillery, State of New York Vol 1: 21319
Veteran Corps of Artillery, State of New York, Constituting the Military Society of the War of 1812 Vol 1: 21321
Veteran Wireless Operators Association Vol 1: 21323
Veterans Bedside Network Vol 1: 21327
Veterans for Peace Vol 1: 21329
Veterans of Foreign Wars of the United States Vol 1: 21331
Veterans of Foreign Wars of the U.S., Department of Alabama Vol 1: 21344
Veterans of Foreign Wars Post 5850 Vol 1: 21346
Veterans of Safety Vol 1: 4606, 21348
Veterans of the Office of Strategic Services in World War II Vol 1: 16613
VHS-Fotogruppe Burghausen Vol 2: 3121
Via Christi Research, Inc. Vol 1: 21350
Victor Company of Japan Vol 2: 4315
Victorian Artists Society Vol 2: 639
Victorian Military Society Vol 2: 9184
Video Data Bank - School of the Art Institute of Chicago Vol 1: 21352
Video Software Dealers Association Vol 1: 21354
Videotex Industry Association Vol 1: 12149
Vieilles Maisons Francaises Vol 2: 2620
Vienna Chamber Opera Vol 2: 802
Vienna University of Music and Dramatic Arts Vol 2: 804
Vietnam Combat Veterans Vol 1: 21357
Vietnam Red Cross Society Vol 2: 9328
Vietnam Veterans of America Vol 1: 21359
Vietnamese Culture and Science Association Vol 1: 21363
Vietnamese Medical Association in the U.S.A. Vol 1: 21365
VIEW Clubs of Australia Vol 2: 642
Viking Society for Northern Research Vol 2: 9186
Villa I Tatti - Harvard University Center for Italian Renaissance Studies Vol 2: 4068
Villa-Lobos Museum Vol 2: 1195

The Village Voice Vol 1: 21367
Vinas International Singing Competition; Francisco Vol 2: 6113
Vinegar Connoisseurs International Vol 1: 21369
Vinifera Wine Growers Association Vol 1: 21371
Vintage Arms Association Vol 2: 9188
Vintage Sailplane Association Vol 1: 21375
Vintage Thunderbird Club International Vol 1: 21379
Vintage Thunderbird Club of America Vol 1: 21379
Vinyl Window and Door Institute Vol 1: 19309
Viola d'Amore Society of Great Britain Vol 2: 9190
Violin Society of America Vol 1: 21381
Virginia Association of Chiefs of Police Vol 1: 21383
Virginia Association of Independent Specialized Education Facilities Vol 1: 21385
Virginia Film Office Vol 1: 21387, 21388
Virginia Interscholastic Athletic Administrators Association Vol 1: 21389
Virginia Library Association Vol 1: 21391
Virginia Peninsula Chamber of Commerce Vol 1: 21393
Virginia Quarterly Review Vol 1: 21395
Virginia Recreation and Park Society Vol 1: 21397
Virginia Volkssport Association Vol 1: 21399
Virginia Waring International Piano Competition Vol 1: 21401
Virginians Opposing Drunk Driving - State Headquarters Vol 1: 21403
Visa USA Vol 1: 2567
Visa USA. Vol 1: 2569
Visa USA Vol 1: 7989
Vision Australia Foundation Vol 2: 645
Visions du Reel International Documentary Film Festival Vol 2: 6542
Visions in Action Vol 1: 21405
Vitae Apoio a Cultura, Educacao e Promocao Social Vol 2: 1198
Vitromex SA de CV Vol 2: 4647
VM & SD Vol 1: 11044
VMI Cadet Investment Group Vol 1: 21407
VMI Research Laboratories Vol 1: 21409
Voestapline Vol 2: 703
Voetslaan Suid-Afrika Vol 2: 5575
Voice of the Listener and Viewer Vol 2: 9192
Voice of Youth Advocates Vol 1: 22054
Volunteer Coordinators Forum Vol 1: 10688
Volunteer Group Khoop Khun Maak Vol 2: 4318
von Humboldt Foundation; Alexander Vol 1: 18160
von Humboldt Foundation of New York; Alexander Vol 1: 12417
von Humboldt-Stiftung Foundation; Alexander Vol 2: 3123
von Siemens Music Foundation; Ernst Vol 2: 6544
Von Siemens-Musikstiftung; Ernst Vol 2: 6544
Vormgevingsinstituut Vol 2: 4859
Vrouwen in de Volkspartij voor Vrijheid en Democratie Vol 2: 4932
VSA Arts Vol 1: 21412
Vserossiiskoe Obschestvo Slepykn Vol 2: 5884
W. V. Publications Vol 2: 9194
Wagner Society of Dallas Vol 1: 21415
Wagner Society of New York Vol 1: 21417
Wahpeton Area Chamber of Commerce and CVB Vol 1: 21420
WAIF Vol 1: 21422
Wales Craft Council Vol 2: 9196
Wales Young Farmers' Clubs Vol 2: 9199
Walkaloosa Horse Association Vol 1: 21425
Walking Horse Trainers Association Vol 1: 21427
Wall Colmonoy Corporation Vol 1: 4891
The Wall Street Journal Vol 1: 9256
Wallace Reader's Digest Fund; Lila Vol 1: 21429
Wallenbergs Stiftelse Vol 2: 6288
Walter Cronkite Endowment for Journalism and Telecommunication Vol 1: 8656
Waltham Worldwide Vol 2: 1544, 1545
WAMSO Young Artist Competition Vol 1: 21431
WAQT Productions Vol 1: 6260
Warman International Vol 2: 435
Warner-Lambert Company Vol 1: 11208, 11210
Warner-Lambert Company Consumer Health Products Group Vol 1: 2128
Warner-Lambert/Parke-Davis Vol 1: 4171
Warringah Council Vol 2: 651
Warsaw Philharmonic Vol 2: 5386
Warszawskie Towarzystwo Higieniczne Vol 2: 5373
Waseda Daigaku Vol 2: 4320
Waseda University Vol 2: 4320
Washington Academy of Sciences Vol 1: 21436
Washington-Baltimore Newspaper Guild Vol 1: 21438
Washington College Vol 1: 21440
Washington County Historical Society Vol 1: 21442
Washington Craft Show Vol 1: 18573
Washington Crossing Foundation Vol 1: 21444
Washington Independent Writers Vol 1: 21446
Washington International Trade Association Vol 1: 21448
The Washington Monthly Vol 1: 21451
Washington National Opera Vol 1: 21454
The Washington Post - Children's Book Guild of Washington, D.C. Vol 1: 21456
The Washington Post Company Educational Foundation Vol 1: 21458
Washington State Bar Association Vol 1: 21460
Washington Theatre Awards Society Vol 1: 21462
Washington University in St. Louis - Diabetes Research and Training Center Vol 1: 21464
Washington Writers' Publishing House Vol 1: 21466
Washingtonian Magazine Vol 1: 21468
Washtenaw Contractors Association Vol 1: 21470
Washtenaw Literacy Vol 1: 21473
Water Environment Federation Vol 1: 21475
Water Environment Research Foundation Vol 1: 21503
Water Institute of Southern Africa Vol 2: 5791
Water Instituut van Suidelike Africa Vol 2: 5791
Wayne State University - Merrill-Palmer Institute Vol 1: 21505
Weatherby Health Care Vol 1: 9235, 9239
Wedding and Portrait Photographers International Vol 1: 21507
Wedding Photographers International Vol 1: 21507
Wedding Photographers of America Vol 1: 21507
Wedgwood Group Vol 2: 6925
Weed Society of Victoria Vol 2: 655
Weekly Reader Corporation Vol 1: 11864
Weiser Chamber of Commerce Vol 1: 21509
The Welch Foundation Vol 1: 21511
Weld Racing Vol 1: 20422
Welding Technology Institute of Australia Vol 2: 658
Wellcome Trust Vol 1: 5789
Welsh Arts Council Vol 2: 9204
Welsh Books Council Vol 2: 9201
Welsh Centre for International Affairs Vol 2: 9206
Welsh Joint Education Committee Vol 2: 9204
Welsh Music Guild Vol 2: 9208
Welsh National Centre for Children's Literature Vol 2: 9201
Welsh Pony and Cob Society of America Vol 1: 21513
Welsh Pony Society of America Vol 1: 21513
Welsh Society of Philadelphia Vol 1: 21515
Welsh Youth Libraries Group Vol 2: 9204
Welt-Tierarztegesellschaft Vol 2: 4672
West African College of Surgeons Vol 2: 5108
West African Examinations Council Vol 2: 3157
West Agro Vol 1: 2114
West Coast Book Prize Society Vol 1: 21517
West Coast Classical Ballet Society Vol 1: 21524
West London Synagogue Vol 2: 8026
West Michigan Tourist Association Vol 1: 21526
West Texas Press Association Vol 1: 21528
West Virginia Children's Book Award Vol 1: 21530
West Virginia Poetry Society Vol 1: 15035
West Virginia University Reading Center Vol 1: 21530
Westchester Library Association Vol 1: 21532
Westerby-fondet; Erik Vol 2: 1541
Westerby Foundation; Erik Vol 2: 1541
Western and English Manufacturers Association Vol 1: 21545
Western Associated Modelers Vol 1: 21534
Western Association of Map Libraries Vol 1: 21536
Western Building Material Association Vol 1: 21539
Western Canada Wilderness Committee Vol 1: 21541
Western Economic Association International Vol 1: 21543
Western Electronic Manufacturers Association - American Electronics Association Vol 1: 224
Western-English Trade Association Vol 1: 21545
Western Forestry and Conservation Association Vol 1: 21548
Western Interpretation Association Vol 1: 14020
Western Kentucky Construction Association Vol 1: 21551

Western North Carolina Historical Association Vol 1: 21553
Western Political Science Association Vol 1: 21556
Western Reserve Historical Society Vol 1: 21558
Western Snow Conference Vol 1: 21563
Western Society of Engineers Vol 1: 21565
Western States Advertising Agencies Association Vol 1: 12922
Western States Arts Federation Vol 1: 21570
Western Women Professional Bowlers Vol 1: 21572
Western Writers of America Vol 1: 21575
Westerners International Vol 1: 21578
Westerners International Association Vol 1: 17238
Westerville Area Chamber of Commerce Vol 1: 21583
Westminster Kennel Club Vol 1: 21585
Westport Historical Society Vol 1: 21590
Wexner Center for the Arts Vol 1: 21592
WFK Cleaning Technology Research Institute Vol 2: 3132
WHAT Video Vol 2: 9195
Whatman Scientific Ltd. Vol 2: 8773
Wheelchair Sports, USA Vol 1: 21595
Whirly-Girls - International Women Helicopter Pilots Vol 1: 21598
White Foundation; William Allen Vol 1: 10813
White House Commission on Presidential Scholars Vol 1: 20490
White House Correspondents' Association Vol 1: 21601
White House News Photographers Association Vol 1: 21605
White Library; William Allen Vol 1: 21607
Whitesides Company; George Vol 1: 11907
Whiting Foundation; Mrs. Giles Vol 1: 21609
Whooping Crane Conservation Association Vol 1: 21611
Wichita Art Museum Vol 1: 12500
Wichita Falls Board of Commerce and Industry Vol 1: 21613
Wichita State University Center for Entrepreneurship Vol 1: 21615
Wider Opportunities for Women Vol 1: 21617
Wiener Kammeroper Vol 2: 802
Wiener Library Vol 2: 9211
Wiesel Foundation for Humanity; Elie Vol 1: 21619
Wiggins Tea Vol 2: 7116
Wilcher Fund; Denny and Ida Vol 1: 18474
Wild Heerbrugg Instruments Vol 1: 2007
Wilderness Medical Society Vol 1: 21622
The Wilderness Society Vol 1: 21624
Wildlife and Environment Society of South Africa Vol 2: 5795
Wildlife and Environment Zimbabwe Vol 2: 9355
Wildlife Clubs of Kenya Association Vol 2: 4369
Wildlife Clubs of Uganda Vol 2: 6660
Wildlife Explorer Vol 2: 9213
The Wildlife Society Vol 1: 21628
Wildlife Society of Southern Africa Vol 2: 5795
Wiley & Sons; John Vol 1: 11530
Wiley & Sons Publishing Company; John Vol 1: 4049
Wilhelm-Lehmbruck-Museum Duisburg Vol 2: 3134
Wilkinson Sword Vol 2: 6995
William F. White Vol 1: 6033
William Hill plc Vol 2: 9215
William Morris Society Vol 2: 9217
William T. Grant Foundation Vol 1: 21632
Williams College Vol 1: 13426
Williams Real Estate Company Vol 1: 13679
Williamson-White Medal Vol 1: 13240
Wilson Company; H. W. Vol 1: 4457, 19557
Wilson Co.; H.W. Vol 1: 21634
Wilson Ornithological Society Vol 1: 21636
Wilson Sporting Goods Company Vol 1: 1543, 11152
Winchell Cancer Fund; Damon Runyon - Walter Vol 1: 8727
Windsor Chamber of Commerce Vol 1: 21641
Wine Country Film Festival Vol 1: 21643
Wine Spectator Vol 1: 21647
Wines of France Vol 1: 21650
Wingfoot Lighter than Air Society Vol 1: 12848
Wings Club Vol 1: 21652
Winston Churchill Foundation Vol 1: 21655
Wire Association International Vol 1: 21657
Wireless Communications Association International Vol 1: 21661
Wisconsin Agri-Service Association Vol 1: 21663
Wisconsin Arts Board Vol 1: 21665
Wisconsin Cheese Makers' Association Vol 1: 21667
Wisconsin Educational Media Association Vol 1: 21669
Wisconsin Farm Bureau Federation Vol 1: 21671
Wisconsin Fertilizer and Chemical Association Vol 1: 21673
Wisconsin Historical Society Vol 1: 21675
Wisconsin Labor History Society Vol 1: 21679
Wisconsin Library Association Vol 1: 21682
Wisconsin Park and Recreation Association Vol 1: 21686
Wisconsin Parkinson Association Vol 1: 21688
Wisconsin State Genealogical Society Vol 1: 21690
Wisconsin State Legislature Vol 1: 21666
Wissenschaftlicher Verein fur Bauwesen Vol 2: 3278
Wissenschaftsstadt Darmstadt Vol 2: 3136
Wizarat-At-Tarbiya Wat Ta'lim Vol 2: 4341
W.K. Kellogg Foundation Vol 1: 21693
WMC Foundation Vol 2: 4934
WMX Technologies, Inc. (Waste Management, Inc.) Vol 1: 20456
Wolf Foundation Vol 2: 3782
Wolfe Pack Vol 1: 21695
Wolfson Foundation Vol 2: 9219
Woman's Building - Slide Archive Vol 1: 21697
Woman's Day Vol 1: 9661
Women for Faith and Family Vol 1: 21699
Women Health Executives Network Vol 1: 21701
Women in Agribusiness Vol 1: 21703
Women in Cable and Telecommunications Vol 1: 21705
Women in Direct Marketing International Vol 1: 21707
Women in Endocrinology Vol 1: 21709
Women in Film Vol 1: 21711
Women in Film and Television-Florida Vol 1: 21721
Women in Film and Video Vol 1: 21724
Women in Film and Video/New England Vol 1: 21733
Women in Government Relations and WGR LEADER Foundation Vol 1: 21735
Women in Government Relations LEADER Foundation Vol 1: 21737
Women in Insurance and Financial Services Vol 1: 21739
Women in Literacy and Life Assembly Vol 1: 14834
Women in Livestock Development Vol 1: 21743
Women in Management Vol 1: 21745
Women in Production Vol 1: 21747
Women in Publishing Vol 2: 9221
Women in Scholarly Publishing Vol 1: 21750
Women in Science and Engineering Vol 1: 21752
Women in Show Business for Children Vol 1: 21756
Women in Technology International Vol 1: 21759
Women in the Wind Vol 1: 21762
Women Marines Association Vol 1: 21764
Women on Stamps Study Unit Vol 1: 21766
Women's Action for New Directions Vol 1: 21768
Women's All-Star Association Vol 1: 21771
Women's Art Association of Canada Vol 1: 21778
Women's Association of Romania Vol 2: 5882
Women's Bar Association of the District of Columbia Vol 1: 21784
Women's Basketball Coaches Association Vol 1: 14014
Women's Business Enterprise National Council Vol 1: 21786
Women's Caucus for Art Vol 1: 21788
Women's Caucus of the Australian Political Studies Association Vol 2: 104
Women's Center of Fayetteville Vol 1: 21790
Women's Economic Club Vol 1: 21792
Women's Electoral Lobby - Australia Vol 2: 663
Women's Engineering Society Vol 2: 9224
Women's Health and Economic Development Association Vol 2: 5110
Women's International Bowling Congress Vol 1: 11432
Women's International League for Peace and Freedom, U.S. Section Vol 1: 21794
Women's International Network of Utility Professionals Vol 1: 21796
Women's International Zionist Organization - Israel Vol 2: 3784
Women's National Book Association Vol 1: 21798
Women's National Book Association - New York Chapter Vol 1: 21801
Women's Services Worldwide Vol 1: 21803
Women's Sports Foundation Vol 1: 21805
Women's Studies Association Vol 2: 5096
Women's Transportation Seminar Vol 1: 21813
Women's Union of Russia Vol 2: 5909
Women's Veterinary Medical Association Vol 1: 5532
Wood County Historical Society Vol 1: 21817
Wood Design and Building Magazine - Janam Publications Inc. Vol 1: 21819
Woodmen of the World/Omaha Woodmen Life Insurance Society Vol 1: 21822

Woodrow Wilson National Fellowship Foundation Vol 1: 21824
Woodson Art Museum; Leigh Yawkey Vol 1: 21827
Woodstock School of Art Vol 1: 21829
Woolknit Associates Vol 1: 21831
The Word Works Vol 1: 21833
Words+ Inc. Vol 1: 11922
Workers' Defense League Vol 1: 21835
Workers' Music Association Vol 2: 9228
Workforce Management - Crain Communications Inc. Vol 1: 21837
The Works Festival Vol 1: 6878
World Academy of Art and Science Vol 2: 453
World Affairs Council of Pittsburgh Vol 1: 21839
World Airlines Clubs Association Vol 1: 21843
World Amateur Golf Council Vol 1: 11650
World Archaeological Society Vol 1: 21847
World Association for Animal Production Vol 2: 4070
World Association for Public Opinion Research Vol 1: 21849
World Association for Small and Medium Enterprises Vol 2: 3594
World Association for the Advancement of Veterinary Parasitology Vol 1: 21852
World Association for the History of Veterinary Medicine Vol 2: 806
World Association of Christian Radio Amateurs and Listeners Vol 2: 9230
World Association of Community Radio Broadcasters Vol 1: 21857
World Association of Detectives Vol 2: 9232
World Association of Girl Guides and Girl Scouts Vol 2: 9237
World Association of Industrial and Technological Research Organizations Vol 2: 4445
World Association of Industrial and Technological Research Organizations Vol 1: 21859
World Association of Newspapers Vol 2: 2622
World Association of Research Professionals Vol 2: 4940
World Association of Societies of Pathology and Laboratory Medicine Vol 2: 4326
World Association of Travel Agencies Vol 2: 6546
World Atlatl Association Vol 1: 21861
World Bank Group Vol 1: 21866
World Beefalo Association Vol 1: 1554
World Book Vol 1: 7656
World Book, Inc. Vol 1: 2984, 3004, 15562
World Bowling Writers Vol 1: 11432, 21868
World Boxing Council Vol 2: 4649
World Chess Federation Vol 2: 3191
World Coin News Vol 1: 12618
World Commission on Protected Areas Vol 2: 6553
World Communication Association Vol 1: 21874
World Confederation for Physical Therapy Vol 2: 9242
World Confederation of Productivity Science Vol 1: 21876
World Conservation Union Vol 2: 6555
World Council for Curriculum and Instruction Vol 1: 21878
World Council of Credit Unions Vol 1: 21882
World Council of Optometry Vol 1: 21884
World Cultural Council Vol 2: 4651
World Curling Federation Vol 2: 9244
World Dance and Dance Sport Council Vol 2: 9246
World Development Federation Vol 1: 21888
World Diving Coaches Association Vol 1: 21890
World Environment Center Vol 1: 21892
World Evangelical Alliance Vol 1: 21894
World Expeditionary Association International Vol 2: 9248
World Federalist Association Vol 1: 21896
World Federalist Association, Minnesota Chapter Vol 1: 21898
World Federalist Association of Pittsburgh Vol 1: 21900
World Federation for Culture Collections Vol 2: 9250
World Federation for Mental Health Vol 1: 21902
World Federation of Catholic Medical Associations Vol 2: 9318
World Federation of Direct Selling Associations Vol 1: 21904
World Federation of Engineering Organisations Vol 2: 2624
World Federation of Estonian Women's Clubs Vol 1: 21906
World Federation of Hemophilia Vol 1: 21908
World Federation of Journalists and Travel Writers Vol 2: 2627
World Federation of Neurology Vol 2: 9252
World Federation of Neurosurgical Societies Vol 1: 21910
World Federation of Personnel Management Associations Vol 1: 21914
World Federation of the Deaf Vol 2: 1663
World Festival of Underwater Pictures Vol 2: 2341
World Folk Music Association Vol 1: 21916
The World Food Prize Foundation Vol 1: 21918
World Footbag Association Vol 1: 21920
World Gastroenterology Organisation Vol 2: 3142
World Golf Championships Vol 1: 21923
World Golf Hall of Fame Vol 1: 21922
World Golf Village Vol 1: 21923
World Health Organization Vol 2: 1228, 6561
World Health Organization - International Agency for Research on Cancer Vol 2: 6568
World Hunger Year Vol 1: 21924
World International Nail and Beauty Association Vol 1: 21927
World Jersey Cattle Bureau Vol 2: 9254
World Learning Vol 1: 21929
World Leisure and Recreation Association Vol 1: 21931
World Literature Today Vol 1: 21933
World Meteorological Organization Vol 2: 2446, 6570
World Methodist Council Vol 1: 21935
World Ocean and Cruise Liner Society Vol 1: 21937
World Organisation of General Systems and Cybernetics Vol 2: 2629
World Organisation of Systems and Cybernetics Vol 2: 2629
World Organization for Human Potential Vol 1: 21939
World Organization of Building Officials Vol 1: 21941
World Organization of Family Doctors Vol 2: 5952
World Organization of the Scout Movement Vol 2: 6575
World Pan African Movement - Canada Vol 1: 21944
World Petroleum Council - The Global Forum for Oil and Gas Science, Technology, Economics and Management Vol 2: 9256
World Phosphate Institute Vol 2: 4670
World Phosphate Rock Institute Vol 2: 4670
World Ploughing Organisation Vol 2: 4942
World Press Photo Vol 2: 4944
World Relief Vol 1: 21946
World Relief Commission Vol 1: 21946
World Research Foundation Vol 1: 21948
World Road Association - France Vol 2: 2631
World Science Fiction Society Vol 1: 21950
World Ship Trust - United Kingdom Vol 2: 9260
World Sidesaddle Federation Vol 1: 21952
World Small Animal Veterinary Association Vol 2: 1543
World Taekwondo Federation Vol 2: 5512
World Teleport Association Vol 1: 21956
World Trade Center for North Carolina Vol 1: 21959
World Trade Center Moscow Vol 2: 5912
World Trade Center of New Orleans Vol 1: 21961
World Veterans Federation Vol 2: 2634
World Veterinary Association Vol 2: 4672
World Veterinary Poultry Association Vol 2: 3146
World Wide Pet Industry Association Vol 1: 21964
World Wide Video Festival Vol 2: 4946
World Wildlife Fund Vol 2: 6579
Worlddidac Foundation Vol 2: 6577
WORLDFEST - Houston International Film and Video Festival Vol 1: 21968
Worldpress.org - All Media Inc. Vol 1: 21970
WorldRadio Vol 1: 21972
World's Poultry Science Association Vol 2: 9262
Worldwide Association of Self-Adhesive Labels and Related Products Vol 2: 4948
Worshipful Company of Armourers & Brasiers' Vol 2: 8690
Worshipful Company of Carmen Vol 2: 572
Worshipful Company of Chartered Architects Vol 2: 7782
Worshipful Company of Constructors Vol 2: 7782
Worshipful Company of Ironmongers Vol 2: 7659
Worshipful Company of Plaisterers Vol 2: 7515
Worshipful Company of Scientific Instrument Makers Vol 2: 9264
Worshipful Company Of Weavers' Vol 2: 9136
Worshipful Society of Apothecaries of London Vol 2: 9266
Worthington Pump, Inc. Vol 1: 4554
WPC Club Vol 1: 21974
Wright; Orville and Wilbur Vol 1: 13880
Wright State University Vol 1: 17702
Wrigley, Jr. Company; William Vol 1: 11214
Writers' Development Trust Vol 1: 21981, 22003
Writer's Digest Vol 1: 21977

Writers' Federation of Nova Scotia Vol 1: 21980
Writers Guild of Alberta Vol 1: 21983
Writers Guild of America, West Vol 1: 21988
Writers' Journal Vol 1: 21995
Writers' Trust of Canada Vol 1: 22003
Writers Workshop Vol 1: 15999
WWF International Vol 2: 6579
Wyeth Ayerst Research Vol 1: 4175
Wyeth Research Vol 1: 3766
Wyeth Vaccines Research Vol 1: 10794
WYOpoets of Wyoming Vol 1: 15037
Xavier University Vol 1: 22005
Xerox Corporation Vol 1: 3468, 4004, 16800
Xerox Corp. Vol 1: 18711
Xirka Vol 2: 4452
Xplor International Vol 1: 22007
XYZ Digital Map Co. Ltd. Vol 2: 8688
Yacht Brokers, Designers and Surveyors Association Vol 2: 9269
Yachting Journalists' Association Vol 2: 9271
Yad Vashem Vol 2: 3786
Yale Series of Younger Poets Vol 1: 22010
Yale University - Beinecke Rare Book and Manuscript Library Vol 1: 22012
Yale University - Yale Center for International and Area Studies Vol 1: 22014
Yamaha Music Corporation of America Vol 1: 13706
Yankee Magazine Vol 1: 22016
Yasme Foundation Vol 1: 22018
YBP, Inc. Vol 1: 5427
Yellow Pages Association Vol 1: 22020
Yellow Pages Publishers Association Vol 1: 22020
Yeshiva University Vol 1: 22022
YMCA of Greater New York Vol 1: 22034
YMCA of the United States of America Vol 1: 22038
Ymgyrch Diogelu Cymru Wledig Vol 2: 7235
Yomiuri Shimbun Vol 2: 4329
York County Astronomical Society Vol 1: 22041
Yorkshire Post Vol 2: 9274
Yorkshire Terrier Club of America Vol 1: 22043
Yorkton International Short Film & Video Festival 1981 Vol 1: 22047
Yorkton Short Film & Video Festival Vol 1: 22047
Young Adult Library Services Association Vol 1: 22049
Young Adult Services Interest Group Vol 1: 7252
Young Archeologists' Club Vol 2: 6926
Young Audiences of Greater Cleveland Vol 1: 22056
Young Australians Best Book Award Council Vol 2: 665
Young Concert Artists Vol 1: 22058
Young Concert Artists Trust Vol 2: 9276
Young Entomologists' Society Vol 1: 22060
Young Israel Youth Vol 1: 22063
Young Menswear Association Vol 1: 22066
Young Menswear Association of the Men's Apparel Industry Vol 1: 22066
Young Ornithologists' Club Vol 2: 9213
Young Playwrights Inc. Vol 1: 22068
Young Republican National Federation Vol 1: 22070
Young Women's Christian Association - Barbados Vol 2: 827
Young Women's Christian Association - Hong Kong Vol 2: 5235
Young Women's Christian Association of Elmira and the Twin Tiers Vol 1: 22075
Young Women's Christian Association of Lubbock Vol 1: 22077
Young Women's Christian Association of San Diego County Vol 1: 22079
Young Women's Christian Association of the United States of America YWCA of the U.S.A. Vol 1: 22081
Youth Assisting Youth Vol 1: 22083
Youth Book Publishing House Vol 2: 5979
Y's Men International Vol 2: 6585
Yuchi Indian Tribe Vol 1: 10842
Yuchi Tribal Organization Vol 1: 10842
Yuki Teikei Haiku Society Vol 1: 22087
YWCA El Paso del Norte Region Vol 1: 22089
YWCA of Houston Vol 1: 22092
YWCA of the City of New York Vol 1: 22095
YWCA of Vermont Vol 1: 22098
Zagreb World Festival of Animated Films Vol 2: 1391
Zeiss Foundation; Carl Vol 2: 2892
Zelienople-Harmony Chamber of Commerce Vol 1: 22100
Zelienople Historical Society Vol 1: 22102
Zen-do Kai Martial Arts Vol 1: 22104
Zeneca Pharmaceuticals Vol 1: 815
ZENECA Pharmaceuticals Group Vol 1: 242
Zero to Three: National Center for Infants, Toddlers and Families Vol 1: 22108
ZESPRI International Vol 2: 5098
Zeta Beta Tau Vol 1: 22110
Zeta Phi Eta A National Arts Fraternity Vol 1: 894
Zijlstra Foundation; Adama Vol 2: 4904
Zimbabwe Institution of Engineers Vol 2: 9358
Zimbabwe National Environment Trust Vol 2: 9368
Zimbabwe Scientific Association Vol 2: 9372
Zimcare Trust Vol 2: 9375
Zionist Organization of America Vol 1: 22113
Zisking-Somerfeld Research Foundation Vol 1: 19075
Zoll Medical Corp. Vol 1: 14209
Zoological Society of Japan Vol 2: 4339
Zoological Society of London Vol 2: 9278
Zoological Society of Southern Africa Vol 2: 5799
Zveza Bibliotekarskih Drustev Slovenije Vol 2: 5993
Zwiazek Kompozytorow Polskich Vol 2: 5342

Award Index

The Award Index provides an alphabetical listing of all awards appearing in both volumes, as well as alternate-language, former, and popular award names. Identically named awards are followed by an indented alphabetical list of the organizations administering an award by that name. Each award name is followed by the volume in which it appears. The numbers following the volume references refer to award book entry numbers, not page numbers.

1st Class International Social Merit Award Vol. 2: 1664
2nd Class International Social Merit Award Vol. 2: 1665
3-A Bronze Plaque Vol. 1: 2
3M Talking Book Award Vol. 2: 528
3M Vehicle Theft Investigators Award Vol. 1: 11194
3rd Marquis of San-Payo Vol. 2: 5481
4H-Genealogy Award Vol. 1: 16632
5 Band WAZ Award Vol. 1: 8628
10Best Cars Vol. 1: 7581
$24 Citizenship Award Vol. 1: 13696
25 Year Award Vol. 1: 15286
50 Books/50 Covers Competition Vol. 1: 2808
50 Greatest U.S. Tennis Resorts Vol. 1: 19977
50 Year Membership Certificates Vol. 2: 507
"54" Founders Award Vol. 1: 12263
100-lecie czasopisma *Zdrowie* Vol. 2: 5377
125th Anniversary Medals Vol. 1: 8028
369th Veterans' Association Service Award Vol. 1: 25
500 Mile Limited Distance Horse Program Vol. 1: 2174
$1000 King of Bridge Award Vol. 1: 2016
1000 Mile Horse Program Vol. 1: 2175
$30,000 Lemelson-MIT Student Prize Vol. 1: 12775
$100,000 Lemelson-MIT Lifetime Achievement Award Vol. 1: 12776
$500,000 Lemelson-MIT Prize Vol. 1: 12777
A. E. Modeen-mitali Vol. 2: 1623
A. J. Shawcross Prize Vol. 2: 7648
A-Level Chemistry Prizes Vol. 2: 8882
A. Lewis Smith Award Vol. 1: 8852
A.A. Michelson Award Vol. 1: 8328
AAAE Outstanding Young Member Award Vol. 1: 960
AAAM Service Award Vol. 1: 5478
AAAS Academy Research Grants Vol. 1: 1044
AAAS Award for Public Understanding of Science and Technology Vol. 1: 1045
AAAS Mass Media Science and Engineering Fellowship Vol. 1: 3506
AAAS Mentor Award Vol. 1: 1046
AAAS Science Journalism Awards Vol. 1: 1047
AAAS Scientific Freedom and Responsibility Award Vol. 1: 1048
AAAS Thousand Dollar Prize Vol. 1: 1052
AAAS Westinghouse Award for Public Understanding of Science and Technology Vol. 1: 1045
AAAS Westinghouse Science Journalism Awards - Whitaker Science Journalism Awards Vol. 1: 1047
AABB Scholarship Awards Vol. 1: 1100
AABE Scholarship Vol. 1: 1098
AACC International Travel Fellowship Award Vol. 1: 971
AACC Lectureship Award Vol. 1: 972
AACC Past President's Award Vol. 1: 973
AACD Distinguished Professional Service Award Vol. 1: 2070
AACP Clinical Research Award Vol. 1: 631
AACT Corporate Award Vol. 1: 1163
AACT Research Award Vol. 1: 633
AADA Alumni Achievement Award Vol. 1: 643
AAEA Founders Award for Painting Vol. 1: 655
AAEA Founders Award for Sculpture Vol. 1: 656
AAEA Museum Directors Award Vol. 1: 657
AAEA Sporting Art Award Vol. 1: 658
AAES-EF Engineering Journalism Awards Vol. 1: 20332
AAF Best in the West Creative Competition Vol. 1: 854
AAFCS Leaders Award Vol. 1: 936
AAFCS New Achievers Awards Vol. 1: 937
AAFP Award of Merit Vol. 1: 672
AAHA Award Vol. 1: 902
AAHE Distinguished Service Award Vol. 1: 1016
AAHE Scholar Award Vol. 1: 1017
AAHS Trophy (American Aviation Historical Society) Vol. 2: 6673
AAIE Hall of Fame Vol. 1: 5483
AALAS Animal Technician Award Vol. 1: 1024
AALAS Technical Notes Award Vol. 1: 1028
AALL Lexis Nexis Call for Papers Awards Program Vol. 1: 1244
AALL Public Access to Government Information Award Vol. 1: 1245
AALL Spectrum Article of the Year Award Vol. 1: 1246
AALL/West Excellence in Marketing Award Vol. 1: 1247
AAMI Annual Meeting Manuscript Awards Vol. 1: 5486
AAMI Foundation Laufman - Greatbatch Prize Vol. 1: 5487
AAMI/GE Healthcare BMET of the Year Award Vol. 1: 5488
AAMO-RMIT MBA (IM) Best Student Award Vol. 2: 4423
AAMR Awards Vol. 1: 1494
AAN Media Award Vol. 1: 708
Aanmoedigingsprijs Vol. 2: 4684
Aanmoedigingsprijzen Vol. 2: 4683
AAP Excellence in Public Service Award Vol. 1: 756
AAP Nutrition Award Vol. 1: 757
AAPA Humanitarian Physician Assistant of the Year Vol. 1: 813
AAPA National and International Humanitarian Physician Assistant of the Year Vol. 1: 813
AAPA Outstanding Physician Assistant of the Year Award Vol. 1: 814
AAPA PA Awareness Achievement Award Vol. 1: 815
AAPA Rural Physician Assistant of the Year Vol. 1: 816
AAPL Outstanding Service Award Vol. 1: 824
AAPOR Award Vol. 1: 1036
Aarestrup Prize; Emil Vol. 2: 1470
Aaron Allan Awards Vol. 1: 7706
AARWBA All-America Auto Racing Teams Vol. 1: 1522
AARWBA Hall of Fame Award (Legends of Racing) Vol. 1: 1523
AAS - American Society for Eighteenth-Century Studies Fellowships Vol. 1: 916
AAS Distinguished Service Medallions Vol. 1: 5100
AAS Flight Achievement Award Vol. 1: 1497
AAS Honorary National Commander Vol. 1: 5101
AAS Individual Awards Vol. 1: 5102
AAS National Commander Awards Vol. 1: 5103
AAS National Medal and Ribbon Vol. 1: 5104
AAS Outstanding Area Advisor Vol. 1: 5105
AAS Outstanding Squadron Advisor Vol. 1: 5106
AAS Space Flight Award Vol. 1: 1498
AAS Squadron Awards Vol. 1: 5107
AASCU Distinguished Alumnus Award Vol. 1: 1428
AASCU Showcase for Excellence Awards Vol. 1: 1429
AASECT Award Vol. 1: 1423
AASL ABC/CLIO Leadership Grant Vol. 1: 1409
AASL Collaborative School Library Media Award Vol. 1: 1410
AASL/EB School Library Media Program of the Year Award - AASL National School Library Media Program of the Year Award Vol. 1: 1418

AASL/Highsmith Research Grant Vol. 1: 1411
AASL Information Plus Continuing Education Scholarship Vol. 1: 1412
AASL President's Award Vol. 1: 1414
AASL/SIRS Intellectual Freedom Award Vol. 1: 1417
AASLH Award Vol. 1: 17872
AATA Animal Welfare Award Vol. 1: 4961
AATE Distinguished Book Award Vol. 1: 883
AATE Research Award Vol. 1: 884
AAU Association Communications Award Vol. 1: 526
AAU James E. Sullivan Memorial Award Vol. 1: 527
AAU Media Award Vol. 1: 528
AAU Outstanding Wrestling Official of the Year Vol. 1: 529
AAU Promotions Award Vol. 1: 530
AAU Volunteer Hall of Fame Vol. 1: 531
AAU Wrestling Person of the Year Vol. 1: 532
AAUA Foundation Award; Dr. Donald A. Gatzke Vol. 1: 14326
AAUA Foundation Award; Dr. Leo and Margaret Goodman-Malamuth Vol. 1: 14326
AAUP Award for Excellence in Coverage of Higher Education Vol. 1: 1464
AAUP Design Show Vol. 1: 5567
AAZPA Bean Award Vol. 1: 1490
A.B. Gregory Award Vol. 1: 18255
ABA Ostwald Band Composition Award Vol. 1: 1527
The Abafazi-Africana Women's Studies Essay Award Vol. 1: 15965
ABB Transformatori and Telettra Vol. 2: 4005
Abbey Fellowships in Painting Vol. 2: 7130
Abbey Scholarship in Painting Vol. 2: 7131
Abbot Award; Charles Greeley Vol. 1: 4656
Abbott Award
Canadian Society of Hospital Pharmacists Vol. 1: 7457
Society of Medical Laboratory Technologists of South Africa Vol 2: 5621
Abbott Award for Innovative Research and Development in Virology Vol. 2: 5622
Abbott Laboratories Award in Clinical and Diagnostic Immunology Vol. 1: 4128
Abbott Laboratories Distinguished Research Award Vol. 1: 3507
Abbott Lowell Cummings Award Vol. 1: 21310
Abbott Prize Vol. 2: 8988
ABBY Award Vol. 1: 1582
ABC Breed Promotion Vol. 1: 1549
ABC Certification Award Vol. 1: 5582
ABC Champion Performance Horse Vol. 1: 1550
ABC Champion Trail Horse Vol. 1: 1551
ABC-CLIO America: History and Life Award Vol. 1: 16880
ABC/CLIO Leadership Grant; AASL Vol. 1: 1409
ABC Concerts and Vocal Competition Vol. 2: 620
ABC Excellence in Construction Awards Vol. 1: 5233
ABC Young Performers' Competition Vol. 2: 620
ABCA Twenty-Five Year Awards Vol. 1: 1539
Abe Issa Award for Excellence Vol. 2: 4083
Abe Prize Vol. 2: 4263
Abel Award; Paul Vol. 1: 17915
Abel Cultural and Creative Arts Program; Alice Vol. 1: 3141
Abele Award; Jack Vol. 1: 21277
Abella; Prix Francoise Vol. 2: 1672
Abelson Prize; AAAS Philip Hauge Vol. 1: 1049
Abendroth Award; Evelyn A. Vol. 1: 1612
Aberconway Medal Vol. 2: 7557
Abercrombie Prize; Sir Patrick Vol. 2: 2510
Aberdeen Memorial Trophy; Stuart W. Vol. 1: 7208
Aberg Post Graduate Award; Ulf Vol. 2: 7441
ABET Honor Roll Vol. 1: 59
ABI/BMA Trophy Vol. 2: 7061
Ability Fund/ March of Dimes Canada Vol. 1: 7372
Able ALDA Award Vol. 1: 5747
ABM Gold Medal Vol. 2: 1161
ABM Silver Medal Vol. 2: 1162
ABOA Foundation - National Scholastic Press Association Pacemaker Awards Vol. 1: 16339
ABOHN Research Award Vol. 1: 1570
Aboriginal Torres Strait Islander Writers' Award; Dymocks Vol. 2: 484
Abragam; Fondation Anatole et Suzanne Vol. 2: 1791
Abrams Award; Eugene Vol. 2: 6304
Abrams Award in Geriatric Clinical Pharmacology; William B. Vol. 1: 3972
Abrams Award; Mark Vol. 2: 8921
Abrams Award; Talbert Vol. 1: 5208
Abrams Medal; General Creighton W. Vol. 1: 5883
ABS Annual Award Vol. 2: 6796
ABS Founders' Memorial Award Vol. 1: 4957
ABTA Gold Award Vol. 2: 6798
ABU Engineering Award Vol. 2: 4419
ABU Prize Competitions for Radio and Television Programs Vol. 2: 4420
Abzug Memorial Award; Martin Vol. 1: 15962
ACA Extended Research Award Vol. 1: 2064
ACA Gold Medal Award Vol. 1: 5589
ACA Honors Award Vol. 1: 1991
ACA Legislative Service Award Vol. 1: 2065
ACA Outstanding Achievement Award Vol. 1: 1992
ACA Professional Development Award Vol. 1: 2066
ACA Public Service Award Vol. 1: 2083
ACA Research Award Vol. 1: 2067
Acacia Leadership Scholarship Vol. 1: 74
Academic Achievement Award Vol. 1: 4837
Academic All-American By Sport Award Vol. 1: 15307
Academic Athletes of the Year (All Academic Team) Vol. 1: 14691
Academic Awards Vol. 2: 7499
Academic Excellence Award Vol. 2: 5530
Academic Excellence Awards - Joint Military Intelligence College Vol. 1: 15383
Academic Excellence for Leadership of Engineering and Technical Management for Undergraduate Programs Vol. 1: 4051
Academic Journal Award Vol. 2: 7873
Academic Librarians' Distinguished Service Award Vol. 1: 6942
Academic Purposes Fund Vol. 2: 9054
Academic/Research Librarian of the Year Award Vol. 1: 5602
Academic Scholarships Vol. 1: 10408
Academic Team-of-the-Year Vol. 1: 15305
Academic Year Grant Program Vol. 1: 11062
Academy & Achievement Awards Vol. 1: 80
The Academy Award Vol. 1: 740
Academy Award for Scholarship Vol. 2: 48
Academy Award of Sports Vol. 1: 13859
Academy Fellow
Academy of Criminal Justice Sciences Vol. 1: 88
Academy of Security Educators and Trainers Vol 1: 125
Academy Honorary Awards Vol. 1: 111
Academy Nikola Obreshkov Prize Vol. 2: 1207
Academy of Athens Medal Vol. 2: 3161
Academy of Athens Prize Vol. 2: 3162
Academy of Authors Vol. 1: 11031
Academy of Country Music Awards Vol. 1: 86
Academy of Distinguished Entrepreneurs Vol. 1: 6178
Academy of Fellows Vol. 1: 12063
Academy of Pharmaceutical Research and Science Fellow Vol. 1: 3376
Academy of Pharmacy Practice and Management Fellow Vol. 1: 3377
Academy of Research Honorary Member Vol. 1: 3290
Academy of Sciences of the Czech Republic Awards Vol. 2: 1413
Accelerator Prize Vol. 2: 2323
Access Award Vol. 1: 8044
Access Awards Vol. 1: 2300
Accessible America Award; Community Partnership Program Vol. 1: 15458
ACCI Thesis/Dissertation Award Vol. 1: 2045
Accolades Award Vol. 1: 21706
Accomplishment Award Vol. 1: 1259
Accord Award Vol. 1: 10243
Accountants, Bankers and Factors Division Award Vol. 1: 2890
ACDS Mentoring Award Vol. 1: 2012
ACE Award Vol. 1: 14589
Ace Award Vol. 1: 19821
ACE Distinguished Service Award for Lifetime Achievement Vol. 1: 2053
ACE Eddie Award Vol. 1: 1804
ACE Education Program Award Vol. 1: 5649
ACE Fellows Program Vol. 1: 2054
Aceves; Premio Maestro Salvador Vol. 2: 4638
ACF Public Service Award Vol. 1: 5645
ACFAS/Caisse de Depot et Placement du Quebec Prize (in Finance) Vol. 1: 5536
ACFOA Human Rights Award Vol. 2: 160
ACHA Article Award Vol. 1: 1867
Acha Award for Veterinary Public Health; Pedro N. Vol. 1: 17057
ACHA World Champion Coonhound Vol. 1: 2020
ACHEMA-Plakette in Titan Vol. 2: 2908
ACHEMA Plaque in Titanium Vol. 2: 2908
Achievement Vol. 1: 7008
Achievement and Hall of Fame Award Vol. 1: 3164
Achievement Award
Alpha Omega International Dental Fraternity Vol. 1: 486
American Academy of Ophthalmology Vol 1: 710
American Association of Managing General Agents Vol 1: 1257
American Association of Meat Processors Vol 1: 1260

American Association of University Women Educational Foundation Vol 1: 1469
American Equilibration Society Vol 1: 2199
American Fuchsia Society Vol 1: 2312
American Meat Science Association Vol 1: 3049
American Scientific Glassblowers Society Vol 1: 3895
American Trucking Associations Vol 1: 4765
British Birds Vol 2: 6954
Creative Studies Alumni Foundation Vol 1: 8645
Deafness Research Foundation Vol 1: 8777
Foundation of American Women in Radio and Television Vol 1: 9715
Historic Chattahoochee Commission Vol 1: 10452
Liberty Bell Wanderers Vol 1: 12810
Lighter-Than-Air Society Vol 1: 12849
National Association of County Agricultural Agents Vol 1: 14170
National Black Police Association Vol 1: 14521
National Junior College Athletic Association Vol 1: 15306
National Peach Council Vol 1: 15494
Resort and Commercial Recreation Association Vol 1: 18001
Society of Toxicology Vol 1: 19330
Society of Women Engineers Vol 1: 19363
Tourism, Hotels and Restaurants Association Vol 2: 5992
U.S.A. Baseball Vol 1: 21153
Achievement Awards
Health Science Communications Association Vol. 1: 10323
National Association of Counties Vol 1: 14165
National Horseshoe Pitchers Association of America Vol 1: 15239
Rough and Smooth Collie Training Association Vol 2: 8350
Royal Society for the Prevention of Accidents Vol 2: 8715
Achievement Awards in Writing Vol. 1: 14826
Achievement in Communication Vol. 1: 11295
Achievement in Consumer Education Awards Vol. 1: 14162
Achievement in Health Care Management Vol. 1: 21702
Achievement in the Arts Award Vol. 1: 16575
Achievement Medal: Air Force Vol. 1: 8797
Achievement Medal: Army Vol. 1: 8798
Achievement Medal: Coast Guard Vol. 1: 8799
Achievement Medal for Innovation in Small Business Vol. 2: 7791
Achievement Medal: Navy - Marine Corps Vol. 1: 8800
Achievement of Excellence Vol. 1: 7014
Achievement of Social Studies Education General Grant Vol. 1: 14780
Achievement of the Year Award Vol. 1: 5708
Achievement Through Action Award Vol. 2: 2986
Achiever Awards Vol. 2: 7374
Achiever of the Year Vol. 1: 10081
Achieving Chapter Excellence (ACE) Vol. 1: 12509
Achieving Excellence Award Vol. 1: 11536
Achieving Professional Excellence in Education Administration Vol. 1: 1158
ACI Annual Awards Vol. 1: 5327
ACI Commemorative Lecture Series Vol. 1: 1957
ACI Construction Award Vol. 1: 1958
ACI Design Award Vol. 1: 1959
ACI Fellows Vol. 1: 1960
ACI Founders Award Vol. 1: 4977
ACIT Award Vol. 2: 2242
Acker; Prix Ernest Vol. 2: 991
Ackerley Prize for Autobiography; J. R. Vol. 2: 7425
Ackermann Medal for Excellence in Water Management; William C. Vol. 1: 4822
ACM Doctoral Dissertation Award Vol. 1: 5297
ACM Eugene Lawler Award for Humanitarian Contributions within Computer Science and Informatics Vol. 1: 5298
ACM Fellows Vol. 1: 5299
ACMS Scientific Achievement Award Vol. 1: 7929
Acorn Award Vol. 1: 1632
Acorn Poetry Award; Milton Vol. 1: 17543
The (ACP) American College of Psychiatrists Bowis Award Vol. 1: 1935
The (ACP) American College of Psychiatrists Dean Award Vol. 1: 1936
ACP-CRM/CAP-CRM Prize in Theoretical and Mathematical Physics Vol. 1: 13203
ACPA Young Scholars Award Vol. 1: 1660
ACS Award for Computers in Chemical and Pharmaceutical Research Vol. 1: 1704
ACS Award for Creative Invention Vol. 1: 1705
ACS Award for Creative Work in Fluorine Chemistry Vol. 1: 1706
ACS Award for Creative Work in Synthetic Organic Chemistry Vol. 1: 1707
ACS Award for Distinguished Service in the Advancement of Inorganic Chemistry Vol. 1: 1708
ACS Award for Nuclear Applications in Chemistry Vol. 1: 1785
ACS Award for Nuclear Chemistry Vol. 1: 1785
ACS Award for Outstanding Performance by Divisions Vol. 1: 1709
ACS Award for Outstanding Performance by Local Sections Vol. 1: 1710
ACS Award for Research at an Undergraduate Institution Vol. 1: 1711
ACS Award in Analytical Chemistry Vol. 1: 1712
ACS Award in Applied Polymer Science Vol. 1: 1713
ACS Award in Chemical Education Vol. 1: 1781
ACS Award in Chromatography Vol. 1: 1714
ACS Award in Colloid and Surface Chemistry Vol. 1: 1715
ACS Award in Industrial Chemistry Vol. 1: 1716
ACS Award in Inorganic Chemistry Vol. 1: 1717
ACS Award in Organometallic Chemistry Vol. 1: 1718
ACS Award in Petroleum Chemistry Vol. 1: 1777
ACS Award in Polymer Chemistry Vol. 1: 1719
ACS Award in Pure Chemistry Vol. 1: 1720
ACS Award in Separations Science and Technology Vol. 1: 1721
ACS Award in the Chemistry of Materials Vol. 1: 1722
ACS Award in Theoretical Chemistry Vol. 1: 1723
ACS Medal of Honor Vol. 1: 1634
ACSA Collaborative Practice Award Vol. 1: 5632
ACSA Creative Achievement Award Vol. 1: 5632
ACSA Distinguished Professor Award Vol. 1: 5632
ACSA Faculty Design Award Vol. 1: 5632
ACSA Honors and Awards Program Vol. 1: 5632
ACSA New Faculty Teaching Award; AIAS/ Vol. 1: 5632
ACSA Topaz Medallion; AIA/ Vol. 1: 5632
ACSA Topaz Medallion for Excellence in Architectural Education; AIA/ Vol. 1: 2707
ACSM Map Design Competition Awards Vol. 1: 1993
ACT-NUCEA Innovations in Continuing Education Awards Vol. 1: 20962
ACTA Special Medallion Award Vol. 1: 380
ACTF Awards for Theatrical Design Excellence Vol. 1: 12539
ACTF Musical Theatre Award Vol. 1: 12540
Action for Birds Award Vol. 2: 9214
Active Duty Literary Prize Vol. 1: 16052
Actonian Prize Vol. 2: 8612
Actor of the Year Award Vol. 2: 7391
Actors' Fund Medal Vol. 1: 170
ACU Development Fellowships Vol. 2: 6808
ACUHO-I Award Vol. 1: 5622
Acupuncture Patient of the Year Vol. 1: 1314
Acupuncturist of the Year Vol. 1: 1315
Ad Astra Decoration Vol. 2: 5727
ADA Career Development Awards Vol. 1: 2134
Ada-EASD Trans-Atlantic Fellowship Award Vol. 1: 2135
ADA Foundation Award for Excellence in the Practice of Clinical Nutrition Vol. 1: 2145
ADA Foundation Awards for Excellence Vol. 1: 2145
ADA Foundation Scholarships Vol. 1: 2146
ADA Research Awards Vol. 1: 2136
ADAM Award Vol. 2: 2764
Adam Hirschfeld Creativity Scholarship Vol. 1: 9847
Adams Article Prize; Percy G. Vol. 1: 19468
Adams Award; Dorothy Garrigus Vol. 1: 18500
Adams Award for Conservation Photography; Ansel Vol. 1: 18450
Adams Award in Organic Chemistry; Roger Vol. 1: 1724
Adams Award; James Luther Vol. 1: 20315
Adams Chapter Heritage Award; Mildred Vol. 1: 18493
Adams Conservation Award; Ansel Vol. 1: 21625
Adams Lecture Award; Comfort A. Vol. 1: 4875
Adams Memorial Membership Award Vol. 1: 4876
Adams Memorial Trophy; Mrs. Charles Francis Vol. 1: 20787
Adams Prize; Henry Vol. 1: 18688
Adams Prize; Herbert Baxter Vol. 1: 2463
Adams Prize; Willi Paul Vol. 1: 16881

Award Index

Adams Short Story Contest; Nick Vol. 1: 5243
Adams Trophy; U.S. Women's Sailing Championship - Mrs. Charles Francis Vol. 1: 20788
Adamson Award for Distinguished Service in the Advancement of Surface Chemistry; Arthur W. Vol. 1: 1725
Adapted Committee Award Vol. 1: 21188
ADARN of the Year Vol. 1: 181
Adaskin Memorial Award; Canadian Music Centre John Vol. 1: 16738
ADC Swiss Award Vol. 2: 6531
Addams Award; Homer Vol. 1: 4417
Addams Children's Book Award; Jane Vol. 1: 12296
Addams Medal; Jane Vol. 1: 18095
Addison Pope, MD Award Vol. 1: 6431
Additional Honours Vol. 1: 6815
ADE Francis Andrew March Award Vol. 1: 5656
A'Deane Coke Medal; Major John Sacheverell Vol. 2: 7558
Adelaide Festival Vol. 2: 597
Adelaide International Exhibition of Photography; Interphot - Vol. 2: 600
Adelskoldska Medaljen Vol. 2: 6202
Adenauer-Forschungspreis; Konrad Vol. 2: 3124
Adenauer Research Award; Konrad
  Royal Society of Canada Vol. 1: 18160
  Alexander von Humboldt-Stiftung Foundation Vol 2: 3124
ADG Award for Outstanding Achievement in Dance Vol. 1: 2119
Adhesion Society Award for Excellence in Adhesion Science Vol. 1: 184
Adhesives Award Vol. 1: 5926
ADIRCAE Prizes Vol. 2: 5997
Adirondack Council Annual Awards Vol. 1: 186
Adirondack Wilderness Award Vol. 1: 5153
Adirondacks National Exhibition of American Watercolors Vol. 1: 5153
Adkins Award; James C. Vol. 1: 6049
Adkins Memorial Instructor Membership Award; Howard E. Vol. 1: 4877
Adler Award Vol. 1: 17202
Adler Lectureship Award in the Field of Materials Physics; David Vol. 1: 3445
Adler Prize; Elmer Vol. 1: 9814
Administrative Committee Prize Vol. 1: 2900
Administrative Division Executive Committee Award Vol. 1: 2317
Administrative Psychiatry Award Vol. 1: 3610
Administrator of the Year
  American Federation of School Administrators Vol. 1: 2231
  Cooperative Council for Oklahoma School Administration Vol 1: 8500
  International Association of Industrial Accident Boards and Commissions Vol 1: 11367
  National Association of Intercollegiate Athletics Vol 1: 14279
  United Methodist Association of Health and Welfare Ministries Vol 1: 20348
Administrator of the Year Award Vol. 1: 1882
Administrators' Award Vol. 1: 9180
Admiral of the Ocean Sea Vol. 1: 20373
ADO National Champions Vol. 1: 2122
ADO Points Champions Vol. 1: 2123
Adolescent Health Award Vol. 1: 776
Adolf-Dietzel-Industriepreis der DGG Vol. 2: 2890
Adopt-Action Service Award Vol. 1: 16417
Adoption Activist Awards Vol. 1: 16417
Adoption Hall of Fame Award Vol. 1: 14748
Adrian Advertising Awards; HSMAI Vol. 1: 10554
Adriaticocinema Awards Vol. 2: 3839
Adult Amateur Award Vol. 1: 20563
Adult Book Award Vol. 2: 3323
Adult Learners Week Vol. 2: 58
Adult Volunteer of the Year Vol. 1: 2393
Advanced Ceramic Award Vol. 1: 5927
Advanced Manufacturing Technology Engineering Certification Vol. 1: 6352
Advanced Member Award Vol. 2: 5234
Advanced Oncology Certified Nurse of the Year Award Vol. 1: 16709
Advanced Person in Smoking Control Award Vol. 2: 5213
Advanced Unit in Smoking Control Award Vol. 2: 5214
Advancement and Preservation of Civilization Award Vol. 1: 15900
Advancement of Literacy Award Vol. 1: 17712
Advertiser of the Year Award Vol. 1: 16329
Advertising Age Awards Vol. 1: 202
Advertising and Marketing Awards
  National Association of Recording Merchandisers Vol. 1: 14357
  Society of National Association Publications Vol 1: 19205
Advertising Awards
  ABA Marketing Network Vol. 1: 55
  National Auctioneers Association Vol 1: 14464
Advertising Campaign of the Year Vol. 1: 9720
Advertising Council Award for Public Service Vol. 1: 208
Advertising Credit Executive of the Year Vol. 1: 210
Advertising Design Club of Canada Awards Vol. 1: 204
Advertising Executive of the Year Vol. 1: 10515
Advertising Hall of Achievement Vol. 1: 855
Advertising Hall of Fame Vol. 1: 856
Advertising Leader of the Year Award Vol. 1: 12923
Advertising/Promotion Awards Vol. 1: 19818
Advertising Woman of the Year Vol. 1: 214
Advisor of the Year
  BACCHUS Network Vol. 1: 6189
  National Broadcasting Society - Alpha Epsilon Rho Vol 1: 14534
Advisory Board Member of the Year Vol. 1: 14535
Advocacy Award
  International Reading Association Vol. 1: 11850
  Rhode Island Council of Community Mental Health Centers Vol 1: 18026
Advocacy for the Disabled Award Vol. 1: 2931
Advocates for Children Award Vol. 1: 15562
Advocates for Justice Award Vol. 1: 1143
AE 50 Company Recognition Program Vol. 1: 4212
Aebersold Award; Paul C. Vol. 1: 19225
AECI Medal Vol. 2: 5689
AECT Annual Achievement Award Vol. 1: 5347
AECT Distinguished Service Award Vol. 1: 5348
AECT Leadership Development Grants Vol. 1: 5349
AECT Memorial Scholarship Award Vol. 1: 5350
AECT National Convention Internship Program Vol. 1: 5351
AECT/SIRS Intellectual Freedom Award Vol. 1: 5352
AECT Special Service Award Vol. 1: 5353
AEG Art and Ecology Prize Vol. 2: 2641
AEG Publication Award Vol. 1: 5672
AEJMC Ethics Prize; Carol Burnett/University of Hawaii/ Vol. 1: 5344
Aelod o Orsedd Beirdd Ynys Prydain Vol. 2: 8173
AERA - American College Testing Program Award Vol. 1: 2162
AERA - PDK Award for Distinguished Contributions Relating Research to Practice Vol. 1: 2160
AERC Hall of Fame Vol. 1: 2176
Aereskalejdoskop Vol. 2: 1490
Aeresmedlem Vol. 2: 1531
AERF Practitioners Award Vol. 1: 18939
Aerial Achievement Medal Vol. 1: 8801
Aero Club of America Trophy Vol. 1: 13877
Aero Engine Services Trophy Vol. 2: 5050
Aeroacoustics Award Vol. 1: 2630
Aerobics Athlete of the Year Vol. 1: 533
Aerobics Contributor of the Year Vol. 1: 534
Aerobics Man and Woman of the Year Vol. 1: 535
Aerobics Official of the Year Vol. 1: 536
Aerodynamic Measurement Technology Award Vol. 1: 2631
Aerodynamics Award Vol. 1: 2632
Aeronautical Program Management; AIAA HAP Arnold Award for Excellence in Vol. 1: 2653
Aerophilatelic Class Award Vol. 2: 8263
Aerosol Package Design Award Vol. 1: 8464
Aerospace Communications Award Vol. 1: 2633
Aerospace Contribution to Society Award Vol. 1: 2634
Aerospace Design Engineering Award Vol. 1: 2635
Aerospace Division/AIAA Educational Achievement Award Vol. 1: 3997
Aerospace Engineering Leadership Award Vol. 1: 19033
Aerospace Maintenance Award Vol. 1: 2636
Aerospace Power Systems Award Vol. 1: 2637
AES Awards of Excellence Vol. 1: 66
AES Man of the Year Award Vol. 1: 67
AES Publications Award Vol. 1: 6051
AESE Award for Outstanding Editorial or Publishing Contributions Vol. 1: 5660
AESF Charles Henry Proctor Leadership Award Vol. 1: 2167
AESF Franklane Industrial Achievement Award Vol. 1: 2168
AESF Gold Medal Vol. 1: 2169
AESF Kergan Wells Service Award Vol. 1: 2170
AESF Scientific Achievement Award Vol. 1: 2171
AESF Silver Medal Vol. 1: 2172
AF ROTC Cadet of the Year Award Vol. 1: 328

AFA Air Force Reserve Troop Carrier Wing Trophy Vol. 1: 352
AFA Newsletter Award Vol. 1: 5691
AFA Perspectives Award Vol. 1: 5691
AFAA Airmanship Award Vol. 1: 2235
AFAA Honorees Vol. 1: 2236
AFAEP Awards Vol. 2: 6837
AFAEP/Kodak Student Competition Vol. 2: 6838
AFAR Award of Distinction Vol. 1: 2223
AFCA Coach of the Year Vol. 1: 2267
AFDCS Distinguished Service Award Vol. 1: 2246
Affair on the Square Art Festival Vol. 1: 7816
Affaire in the Gardens Vol. 1: 8035
AFFHO Award for Meritorious Service Vol. 2: 101
Affiliate Award Vol. 1: 16027
Affiliate Corporation Award Vol. 1: 11560
Affiliate of the Year Award
International Society for Pharmaceutical Engineering Vol. 1: 11949
National Council of La Raza Vol 1: 14804
Affiliated Chapter Awards Vol. 1: 10342
Affiliated Group Award Vol. 1: 1866
Affiliated Societies' Cup Vol. 2: 8535
Affirmative Action and Equal Employment Opportunity Award Vol. 1: 21559
Affirmative Action Award; CMA Vol. 1: 3276
Affordable Food; Award for Technical Innovation in Enhancing Production of Safe Vol. 1: 7439
AFGE Local 3523 Education Award Vol. 1: 10106
AFI Awards - The Australian Film Institute Awards Vol. 2: 175
AFJ Awards Competition Vol. 1: 5686
AFMA Technical Person of the Year; Barney van Niekerk/ Vol. 2: 5516
AFMC Junior Management Award Vol. 1: 329
AFMC Logistics Executive Management Award Vol. 1: 330
AFMC Middle Management Award Vol. 1: 331
AFMS Scholarship Foundation Honorary Award Vol. 1: 2229
AFP Award for Excellence in Fund Raising Vol. 1: 5699
AFRES Outstanding Unit Award Vol. 1: 332
Africa; Environmental Personality of the Year in Vol. 1: 255
Africa Prize for Leadership for the Sustainable End of Hunger Vol. 1: 10614
African-American Culture and Philosophy Award Vol. 1: 17765
African Insurance Organisation Awards Vol. 2: 1248
African Wildlife Leadership Award Vol. 1: 267
AFROSAI Prize Vol. 2: 6625
AFS Award for Excellence in Fisheries Education Vol. 1: 2250
AFS Award of Excellence Vol. 1: 2251
AFS Distinguished Service Award Vol. 1: 2252
AFS Meritorious Service Award Vol. 1: 2253
AFT Foster Scholarship Vol. 1: 196
AFUD Ph.D. Research Scholar Program Vol. 1: 4799
AFUD Research Scholars Vol. 1: 4800
AFUW-SA Inc. Trust Fund Bursary Vol. 2: 164
Aga Khan Award for Architecture Vol. 2: 6302
Aga Khan Trophy Vol. 2: 3694
AGA Student Summer Research Fellowships Vol. 1: 9713
Agan Award; Tessie Vol. 1: 1240
Agassiz Medal; Alexander Vol. 1: 13825
Agatha Awards Vol. 1: 13046
AGC/GVS Fellowship Vol. 2: 8441
AGC/IAATI Award Vol. 1: 11195
The Age Book of the Year Awards Vol. 2: 60
Age Diversity in the Workplace Award Vol. 1: 1396
Age d'Or Prize Vol. 2: 1093
Age Group Diving Coach of the Year Vol. 1: 21167
Agell Award for Excellence in Research; Gladys Vol. 1: 927
Agency of the Year Award Vol. 1: 14163
Agfa - Gevaert Gold Medal Award Vol. 1: 19188
AGGIE Award Vol. 1: 19406
Aggiornamento Award Vol. 1: 7650
Aggrey Medal Vol. 1: 17230
AGHE Award Vol. 1: 5374
AGIR's Prize Vol. 2: 5808
AGLBIC Service Award Vol. 1: 5368
Aglient Technologies Award for Excellence in Laboratory Instruction Vol. 1: 3994
Agnon Gold Medal; S. Y. Vol. 1: 2306
AGO/ECS Publishing Award in Choral Composition Vol. 1: 2368
AGO Examination Prize Vol. 1: 2369
AGO Scholarship Vol. 1: 2377
Agopoff Award; Agop Vol. 1: 13774
Agopoff Memorial Prize; Agop Vol. 1: 15698
AGPAM National Recognition Award Vol. 1: 1213
Agricola Denkmuenze; Georg Vol. 2: 2877
Agricola-Medaille; Georg- Vol. 2: 2717
Agricultural Bioprocess Laboratory Awards Vol. 1: 21038
Agricultural Engineering Award
Institution of Engineers Australia/Engineers Australia Vol. 2: 365
Society for Engineering in Agriculture Vol 2: 581
Agricultural Hall of Fame Vol. 1: 13913
Agricultural Initiative Award Vol. 1: 16089
Agricultural Institute of Canada Fellow Vol. 1: 285
Agricultural Institute of Canada Honorary Member Award Vol. 1: 286
Agricultural Leadership Award Vol. 1: 16090
Agricultural Organization of the Year Public Sector Vol. 1: 16091
Agrinaut Award Vol. 1: 13902
Agronomic Extension Education Award Vol. 1: 4239
Agronomic Industry Award Vol. 1: 4240
Agronomic Resident Education Award Vol. 1: 4241
Agronomic Service Award Vol. 1: 4242
AGS Award for Outstanding Contributions to Gravestone Studies Vol. 1: 5376
Agway Inc. Young Scientist Award Vol. 1: 2099
AHA Hospital Awards for Volunteer Excellence Vol. 1: 2541
AHA National Homebrew Competition Awards Vol. 1: 2522
AH&MA Achievement Awards Vol. 1: 2567
Ahmed Book Publication Award; Dr. Tajuddin Vol. 1: 12230
AHS Best Variegated Hosta in a Tour Garden Award Vol. 1: 2550
AHS Business Partner Award Vol. 1: 2452
AHS Fellows Vol. 1: 2425
AHS/Merck US Human Health Migraine and Women's Health Research Award Vol. 1: 2388
Ahwash Literary Award; Kamal M. Vol. 1: 12812
AIA/ACSA Award for Architectural Education Vol. 1: 2707
AIA/ACSA Topaz Medallion Vol. 1: 5632
AIA/ACSA Topaz Medallion for Excellence in Architectural Education Vol. 1: 2707
AIA/ALA Library Buildings Award Vol. 1: 2708
AIAA Aerospace Software Engineering Award Vol. 1: 2638
AIAA Air Breathing Propulsion Award Vol. 1: 2639
AIAA Aircraft Design Award Vol. 1: 2640
AIAA Career Enhancement Award Vol. 1: 2641
AIAA Certificate of Merit Awards Vol. 1: 2642
AIAA Command, Control, Communication & Intelligence Award Vol. 1: 2643
AIAA Computer-Aided Engineering and Manufacturing Award Vol. 1: 2644
AIAA Digital Avionics Award Vol. 1: 2645
AIAA Distinguished Service Award Vol. 1: 2646
AIAA Energy Systems Award Vol. 1: 2647
AIAA Engineer of the Year Award Vol. 1: 2648
AIAA Fluid Dynamics Award Vol. 1: 2649
AIAA Foundation National Student Conference Awards Vol. 1: 2650
AIAA Ground Testing Award Vol. 1: 2651
AIAA Haley Space Flight Award Vol. 1: 2652
AIAA HAP Arnold Award for Excellence in Aeronautical Program Management Vol. 1: 2653
AIAA History Manuscript Award Vol. 1: 2654
AIAA Information Systems Award Vol. 1: 2655
AIAA International Cooperation Award Vol. 1: 2656
AIAA Losey Atmospheric Science Award Vol. 1: 2657
AIAA Mechanics and Control of Flight Award Vol. 1: 2658
AIAA National Faculty Advisor Award Vol. 1: 2659
AIAA Outstanding Section Awards Vol. 1: 2660
AIAA Pendray Aerospace Literature Award Vol. 1: 2661
AIAA Piper General Aviation Award Vol. 1: 2662
AIAA Pre-College Outreach Award Vol. 1: 2663
AIAA Propellants and Combustion Award Vol. 1: 2664
AIAA Public Service Award Vol. 1: 2665
AIAA Reed Aeronautics Award Vol. 1: 2666
AIAA Section Public Policy Award Vol. 1: 2667
AIAA Space Processing Award Vol. 1: 2668
AIAA Space Science Award Vol. 1: 2669
AIAA Space Systems Award Vol. 1: 2670
AIAA Structures, Structural Dynamics, and Materials Award Vol. 1: 2671
AIAA Support Systems Award Vol. 1: 2672

AIAA System Effectiveness and Safety Award Vol. 1: 2673
AIAA Thermophysics Award Vol. 1: 2674
AIANYS Educator Award Vol. 1: 294
AIANYS Student Award Vol. 1: 295
AIAS/ACSA New Faculty Teaching Award Vol. 1: 5632
AIASA Recognition Awards Vol. 1: 19960
AIASAC Design Award Vol. 1: 2732
AIBD Design Competition Vol. 1: 2743
AIBS Distinguished Service Award Vol. 1: 2740
AIC Ethics Award Vol. 1: 2798
AICP National Historic Planning Landmarks and Pioneers Program Vol. 1: 3545
AICP Student Project and Outstanding Student Awards Vol. 1: 3546
AICPA Accredited in Business Valuation (ABV) Hall of Fame Award Vol. 1: 2745
AICPA Business and Industry Hall of Fame Vol. 1: 2746
AICPA Distinguished Achievement in Accounting Education Award Vol. 1: 2747
AICPA Gold Medal Award for Distinguished Service Vol. 1: 2748
AICPA Medal of Honor Vol. 1: 2749
AICPA Outstanding CPA in Government Award Vol. 1: 2750
AICPA PFP Distinguished Service Award Vol. 1: 2751
AICPA Public Service Award Vol. 1: 2752
AICPA Special Recognition Award Vol. 1: 2753
Aid to Advertising Education Award Vol. 1: 857
Aide a la diffusion de films de qualite en Belgique Vol. 2: 1094
AIDIS Prize Vol. 1: 11099
AIDS and Human Rights; Awards for Action on HIV/ Vol. 1: 7157
AIGA Design Leadership Award Vol. 1: 2811
AIGA Medal Vol. 1: 2809
AIIE Award for Excellence in Productivity Improvement Vol. 1: 10958
AIIM Company of Fellows Vol. 1: 307
Aikat Oration Award; Professor B. K. Vol. 2: 3403
Aikenhead Memorial Choral Scholarship; The Roy Vol. 1: 18272
Aim Quarterly Magazine Short Story Award Vol. 1: 316
AIME Distinguished Service Award Vol. 1: 2815
AIMR Distinguished Service Award Vol. 1: 5391
AIMR Special Service Award Vol. 1: 5392
AIMS Award Vol. 2: 3621
AIP Science Writing Awards Vol. 1: 2831
AIPEA Medal Vol. 2: 902
AIPH and Grand Prix d'Excellence; Grand Prix de l' Vol. 2: 4797
AIQS National President's Award Vol. 2: 219
Air Canada People's Choice Award Vol. 1: 20114
Air Force Academy Award Vol. 1: 369
Air Force Association AFLC Logistics Executive Management Award Vol. 1: 330
Air Force Association AFLC Logistics Junior Management Awards Vol. 1: 329
Air Force Association AFLC Logistics Middle Management Award Vol. 1: 331
Air Force Association AFSC Distinguished Award for Management Vol. 1: 330
Air Force Association AFSC Junior Management Award Vol. 1: 329
Air Force Association AFSC Management Awards Vol. 1: 331
Air Force Association Special Presidential Citations Vol. 1: 5108
Air Force Cross
Central Chancery of the Orders of Knighthood Vol. 2: 7246
South African National Defence Force Vol 2: 5728
Air Force Historical Foundation Award; Joe and Josephine Warth Vol. 1: 377
Air Force Institute of Technology Award Vol. 1: 370
Air Force ROTC Scholarship Vol. 1: 371
Air Force Test Team of the Year Award Vol. 1: 333
Air League Challenge Trophy Vol. 2: 6676
Air League Founders' Medal Vol. 2: 6677
Air League Gold Medal Vol. 2: 6678
Air National Guard Outstanding Unit Award Vol. 1: 334
Air Reserve Forces Meritorious Service Medal - Air Force Vol. 1: 8802
Air Service Training Blind Flying Trophy Vol. 2: 5059
Air Traffic Control Specialist of the Year Award Vol. 1: 381
Air Transport World Awards Vol. 1: 395
Air War College Award for Research and Writing Vol. 1: 372
Airborne Regiment Trophy Vol. 1: 7510
Aircraft Safety Prize Vol. 2: 8628
Airline of the Year Vol. 2: 6547
Airman of the Year Vol. 1: 9640
Airman's Award Vol. 1: 8269
Airone Vol. 2: 3980
Airport Commissioners Roundtable Congressional Leadership Award Vol. 1: 401
Airport Crash/Fire/Rescue/Medical Preparedness Award Vol. 1: 6132
Airport Safety Award Vol. 1: 9576
Airtour Sword Vol. 2: 7604
Airway Facilities Technician of the Year Vol. 1: 382
Airway Transportation Systems Specialist of the Year Vol. 1: 382
Airways Corporation Trophy Vol. 2: 5051
Airwork Cup Vol. 2: 5052
Aisenstadt Prize; Andre Vol. 1: 13204
Aitken Memorial Award; Irene Vol. 2: 5623
Aizstrauts Team Sportsmanship; Arnie Vol. 1: 537
The AJL Scholarship for Library School Students Vol. 1: 5740
Akashvani Annual Awards Vol. 2: 3343
Akashvani Annual Awards for Technical Excellence Vol. 2: 3344
AKC Licensed Field Trail for Championship Points Vol. 1: 16531
Ake Memorial Award; Claude Vol. 1: 259
Akermarks Stipendium; Carl Vol. 2: 6241
Akiva Club Award Vol. 1: 5806
Akiyama Prize Vol. 2: 4130
AL and NL Baseball Player Comeback of the Year Vol. 1: 19640
AL and NL Comeback Players of the Year Vol. 1: 19640
AL and NL Hillerich and Bradsby/*The Sporting News* Silver Slugger Awards Vol. 1: 19641
AL and NL Manager of the Year Vol. 1: 19642
AL and NL Pitchers of the Year Vol. 1: 19643
AL and NL Relief Pitcher of the Year Vol. 1: 19644
AL and NL Rookie Pitchers of the Year Vol. 1: 19645
Al Padur Scholarship Fund Vol. 1: 8116
ALA Equality Award Vol. 1: 2967
ALA/Information Today Library of the Future Award Vol. 1: 2968
ALA Library Buildings Award; AIA/ Vol. 1: 2708
ALA/Mecklermedia Library of the Future Award Vol. 1: 2968
Alabama Authors Award Vol. 1: 405
Alabama Pet Hall of Fame Vol. 1: 19894
Alabama Sheriffs Association Scholarship Vol. 1: 407
Alabama Sportswriters Hall of Fame Vol. 1: 11760
Alabama State Poetry Society Award Vol. 1: 14987
Alain Intellectual Freedom Award; Alex P. Vol. 1: 12935
ALAN Award Vol. 1: 14846
Alaska Cup Award Vol. 1: 20791
Alaux; Fondation Jean-Paul Vol. 2: 1717
Albano Memorial Award; John Vol. 1: 21439
"ALBENA" Vol. 2: 1235
Albena Zlatni Piassatsi Sliven Vol. 2: 1235
Albers Award; William H. Vol. 1: 9660
Albert Award; Henry J. Vol. 1: 11822
Albert Hourani Book Award Competition Vol. 1: 13381
Albert Lectureship; Adrien Vol. 2: 8738
Albert Medal Vol. 2: 8709
Albert; Prix Jos Vol. 2: 995
Alberta Book Awards
Book Publishers Association of Alberta Vol. 1: 6502
Book Publishers Association of Alberta Vol 1: 6503
Book Publishers Association of Alberta Vol 1: 6504
Book Publishers Association of Alberta Vol 1: 6505
Book Publishers Association of Alberta Vol 1: 6506
Book Publishers Association of Alberta Vol 1: 6507
Book Publishers Association of Alberta Vol 1: 6508
Alberta Book Design Awards Vol. 1: 6502
Alberta Children's Book of the Year Vol. 1: 6503
Alberta Educational Book of the Year Vol. 1: 6504
Alberta Emerging Publisher of the Year Vol. 1: 6505
Alberta Film and Television Awards Vol. 1: 422
Alberta Publisher of the Year Award Vol. 1: 6506
Alberta Scholarly Book of the Year Vol. 1: 6507
Alberts Award for Distinguished Contributions to Science Education; ASCB/Bruce Vol. 1: 3940
Albion Book Prize/NACBS Book Prize Vol. 1: 16411
Albrand Award for First Nonfiction; PEN/Martha Vol. 1: 17139
Albrand Award for the Art of the Memoir; PEN/Martha Vol. 1: 17140

Albright Award; Fuller Vol. 1: 3929
Albritton, Jr. Award; Claude C. Vol. 1: 10844
Album of the Year Vol. 1: 11424
ALCA Safety Award Contests Vol. 1: 17635
Alcan Jazz Prize Vol. 1: 9537
Alcan Lecture Award Vol. 1: 7826
Alcuin Book Design Awards Vol. 1: 430
ALDA Angel Award Vol. 1: 5748
Aldeburgh Poetry Festival Prize Vol. 2: 6686
Aldre Linnemadeljen I guld Vol. 2: 6203
Aldrich Award; C. Anderson Vol. 1: 758
Aldrich Service Award; Robert B. Vol. 1: 8939
ALEA International Composition Prize Vol. 1: 6534
Alec and Mora Dickson Scholarship Vol. 1: 11790
Aleph Award Vol. 1: 15297
Ales Film Festival Vol. 2: 2518
Alex Awards Vol. 1: 22050
Alexander Award; J. Allen Vol. 1: 3894
Alexander Award; Mary Vol. 1: 7876
Alexander Medal; G.N. Vol. 2: 366
Alexander Prize Vol. 2: 8530
Alexander, Sr., NAACP State Conference President's Award; Kelly M. Vol. 1: 14047
Alexander Shield Vol. 2: 7428
Alexopoulos Prize; C.J. Vol. 1: 13721
Alfa Laval Agri Dairy Extension Award Vol. 1: 2100
Alfond Scholar-Athlete Award; Harold Vol. 1: 15073
Alfred N. Goldsmith Award Vol. 1: 10664
Alfred Soffer Research Awards Vol. 1: 1843
Algebra and Number Theory; Frank Nelson Cole Prizes in Vol. 1: 3043
Alger Awards; Horatio Vol. 1: 10539
Algren Awards for Short Fiction; Nelson Vol. 1: 7892
Alice Award
National Woman's Party Vol. 1: 15958
Society of Women Writers, Victoria Branch Vol 2: 589
Alice H. Hayden Fellowship Vol. 1: 19926
Alice Hamilton Prize Vol. 1: 4065
Alice Paul Award Vol. 1: 15958
ALISE Award for Professional Contribution to Library and Information Science Education Vol. 1: 5418
ALISE Service Award Vol. 1: 5419
Alison Award; John R. Vol. 1: 335
All-America Awards
National Association of Intercollegiate Athletics Vol. 1: 14280
National Soccer Coaches Association of America Vol 1: 15707
All-America Basketball Team Vol. 1: 19646
All-America City Awards Vol. 1: 14674
All-America Football Team Vol. 1: 19647
All-America Rose Selections Award of Excellence Vol. 1: 438
All-America Rose Selections Certificate of Merit Vol. 1: 439
All-America Scholar-Athlete Awards Vol. 1: 14281
All America Team Vol. 1: 9671
All-American Association Award Vol. 1: 538
All-American Award Vol. 1: 585
All American Awards Vol. 1: 14692
All-American Awards Vol. 1: 15307
All American Dive Team Vol. 1: 20294
All American Hall of Fame Vol. 1: 15664
All American Inter-Collegiate Sailor Vol. 1: 11123
All-American Soap Box Derby Vol. 1: 11914
All American Team Vol. 1: 2268
All-Around Amateur Golden Horse Vol. 1: 17046
All-Around Cowboy Vol. 1: 17656
All-Around Golden Horse Award Vol. 1: 17048
All Around NAMAR Mustang Vol. 1: 16448
All Breed Master Judge Vol. 1: 15504
All-Breeds Awards Vol. 1: 20564
All-Defensive Team Vol. 1: 14498
All India Competition for Radio Playwrights Vol. 2: 3345
All-Ireland Horseshoe Pitching Championship Vol. 2: 3694
All-NBA Team Vol. 1: 14499
All Poets Award Vol. 1: 14988
All-Rookie Team; got milk? Vol. 1: 14503
All Sonatina, All Sonata, All Bach Programs Vol. 1: 1887
All Sport Insurance Marketing Ltd. Volunteer of the Year Award Vol. 1: 19634
All-Star Community Awards Vol. 1: 12187
All-Star Game Most Valuable Player Vol. 1: 8479
All-Tournament Team Vol. 1: 14654
All-Tournament Teams/Outstanding Athlete Award Vol. 1: 14282
Allan Award; William Vol. 1: 4449
Allard Silver Medal; Peter Vol. 2: 8376
Allderdice Award; Charles Vol. 1: 8465
Allee Best Student Paper Award of the Animal Behavior Society; Warder Clyde Vol. 1: 4958
Allegro Award Vol. 1: 17172
Allen Award; Alfred Vol. 1: 5337
Allen Award; Alfred W. Vol. 1: 1666
Allen Award; Arthur A. Vol. 1: 8518
Allen Award for Scholarhip and Service; TESOL Virginia French Vol. 1: 19948
Allen Award; Helen Vol. 1: 191
Allen Award; Ruth Vol. 1: 3533
Allen Awards; The Gracie Vol. 1: 9716
Allen Distinguished Service Award; Harvey Stuart Vol. 1: 1598
Allen Ergen Scholarship Vol. 1: 16525
Allen Leadership and Achievement Award; George Vol. 1: 20132
Allen Memorial Cup; D.M. Vol. 2: 5053
Allen Prize; Cath Vol. 2: 7269
Allen Prize; The David Vol. 2: 91
Allen Prize; Derek Vol. 2: 6894
Allen Scholarship Award; Dr. J. Frances Vol. 1: 2254
Allendoerfer Awards; Carl B. Vol. 1: 13187
Allhands Essay Competition; James L. Vol. 1: 273
Alliance Award Vol. 1: 885
Alliance Group New Products Awards Vol. 2: 6690
Alliance of Independent Retailers Awards Vol. 2: 6691
Allianz Cornhill Musical Insurance Youth Orchestra Award Vol. 2: 8165
Allied Arts Medal Vol. 1: 18134
Allied Corporation Award Vol. 1: 11561
Allied Industry Individual Award Vol. 1: 13903
Allied Member Award Vol. 1: 4624
Allied Professional Award; Morton Bard Vol. 1: 15443
Allied Signal Award for Research on Aging Vol. 1: 10526
Allied-Signal Awards Vol. 1: 2839
AlliedSignal Outstanding Student Branch Award Vol. 1: 19045
Allin Prize; Russell Vol. 2: 7756
Allis Prize for Study of Ionized Gases; Will Vol. 1: 3446
Allison Award; American Center for Children's Television - Fran Vol. 1: 1663
Allison City of Sydney Piano Scholarship; The John Vol. 2: 312
Alliss and Roy Beckett Crystal Rose Bowl; Peter Vol. 2: 8160
Allorge; Prix Octave Mirbeau et Valentine Vol. 2: 2003
Allport Intergroup Relations Prize; Gordon Vol. 1: 18883
Alluisi Award; Earl A. Vol. 1: 3650
Allwork Grants Vol. 1: 2725
Ally Award Vol. 1: 16774
Allyn & Bacon Psychology Awards Vol. 1: 17694
Aloha Aina Award Vol. 1: 10528
The Alouette Award Vol. 1: 6866
Alpar Erem Vol. 2: 3279
Alpar Medal Vol. 2: 3279
Alpenlandischer Volksmusikwettbewerb Vol. 2: 671
Alpha Awards Vol. 1: 1664
Alpha Beta Kappa Award Vol. 1: 8904
Alpha Chi Sigma Pure Chemistry Award Vol. 1: 475
Alpha Chi Sigma Scholarship Award Vol. 1: 476
Alpha Kappa Psi Award Vol. 1: 3036
Alpha Omega Alpha Distinguished Teacher Awards Vol. 1: 482
Alpha Omega Alpha Student Essay Award Vol. 1: 483
Alpha Omega Alpha Student Research Fellowships Vol. 1: 484
Alpha Sigma Nu National Jesuit Book Award Vol. 1: 5736
Alpine Club of Canada Award for Best Film on Climbing Vol. 1: 6236
Alpine Garden Society Award of Honour Vol. 2: 6695
Alpine World Cup Champions Vol. 2: 6447
ALS Service of the Year Award Vol. 1: 14209
ALSA/Econo-Clad Award for Outstanding Young Adult Reading or Literature Program Vol. 1: 22055
ALSC/Book Wholesalers Summer Reading Program Grant Vol. 1: 5430
ALSC/Econo-Clad Literature Program Award Vol. 1: 5431
ALSC/Sagebrush Education Resources Literature Grant Vol. 1: 5431
Alsobrook Industrial Minerals Distinguished Service Award; A. Frank Vol. 1: 18805
Alsop Award Vol. 1: 2941
Alston Award; Ralph E. Vol. 1: 6536
Alston Canine Award; The Alison Vol. 2: 8492
ALTA/Gale Outstanding Trustee Conference Grant Vol. 1: 5446
ALTA Literacy Award Vol. 1: 5447
ALTA Major Benefactor Honor Award Vol. 1: 5448
ALTA Outstanding Translations of the Year Vol. 1: 3009
Altamirano Medal; Ignacio Manuel Vol. 2: 4571
Altamirano Prize for Novel; Ignacio Manuel Vol. 2: 4527

Award Index

Alter Cup; National Multihull Championship - Vol. 1: 20775
Alternative Nobel Prize Vol. 2: 6184
Altman (Figure) Prize; Benjamin Vol. 1: 13775
Altman (Landscape) Prize; Benjamin Vol. 1: 13776
Alumni Achievement Award Vol. 1: 643
Alumni Achievement Awards Vol. 1: 7664
Alumni Career Achievement Award Vol. 1: 8179
Alumni Medal Vol. 1: 20996
Alumni PRN Grant Vol. 1: 491
Alumni Scholarship Vol. 1: 16810
Alumni Service Award Vol. 1: 515
Alumni Service Citations Vol. 1: 20997
Alumni Service Medal Vol. 1: 20998
Alumni Volunteer Leadership Award Vol. 1: 8180
Alumnus-of-the-Decade Vol. 1: 8496
Alumnus of the Year Vol. 1: 8496
Alumnus of the Year Award Vol. 1: 18197
Alvarez Memorial Award; Walter C. Vol. 1: 3081
Alves de Carvalho Fernandes; Premio Antonio Vol. 2: 5407
Alzheimer Obezisk Grant Vol. 2: 769
AMA/Irwin Distinguished Marketing Educator Award Vol. 1: 3025
AMA Marketing Scholar of the Year; George Hay Brown/ Vol. 1: 3026
AMADE-UNESCO; Prix Vol. 2: 4669
Amadeus Prize Vol. 2: 8095
Amado de Encenacao Teatral; Premio Municipal Fernando Vol. 2: 5428
Amanda Award for Cinematographic Merit Vol. 2: 5156
Amanda Film - OG Fjernsynspris Vol. 2: 5156
AMAS Scholarship Vol. 1: 5163
Amateur Achievement Award Vol. 1: 6006
Amateur Astronomers Medal Vol. 1: 521
Amateur Athletic Fund Vol. 1: 19896
Amateur Baseball Hall of Fame Vol. 1: 10161
Amateur Bowler of the Year Vol. 1: 6561
Amateur Golden Horse Vol. 1: 17046
Amateur PSA/VMPD American International Film and Video Festival Vol. 1: 17283
Amateur Radio Award; Barry M. Goldwater Vol. 1: 17835
Amateur Supreme Champion Vol. 1: 17047
Ambassador Award
American Council of the Blind Vol. 1: 2043
Federation of Fly Fishers Vol 1: 9471
Ambassador Award of Hospitality Vol. 1: 15630
Ambassador Book Awards Vol. 1: 9277
Ambassador for Epilepsy Award Vol. 2: 3640
Ambassador of Honor Book Awards Vol. 1: 9277
Ambassador of Hospitality Award Vol. 1: 15630
Ambassador of the Month Vol. 1: 9223
Ambassadors Award Vol. 1: 7288
Ambatielos; Prix Vol. 2: 1760
Ambedkar Centenary Award for Excellence in Biomedical Research; Dr. B. R. Vol. 2: 3404
Ambulance Service Medal Vol. 2: 180
AmCham Annual Award Vol. 2: 3202
AMCSUS President's Medal Vol. 1: 5761
Ameghino; Premio Florentino Vol. 2: 19
Amer Award; Mohamed Vol. 1: 8187
Amerbach-Preis Vol. 2: 6540
America: History and Life Award; ABC-CLIO Vol. 1: 16880
America/Israel Friendship Award Vol. 1: 4934
American Academy Award for Humanistic Studies Vol. 1: 618
American Academy of Periodontology Student Award Vol. 1: 801
American Academy of Psychiatry and the Law Vol. 1: 3619
American Accordionists' Association Contest and Festival Vol. 1: 849
American Advertising Awards Vol. 1: 6023
The American Advertising Awards Vol. 1: 858
American Agri-Women Awards Vol. 1: 864
American and National League Managers of the Year Vol. 1: 19648
American Architecture Awards Vol. 1: 7872
American Association for Geodetic Surveying Graduate Fellowship Award Vol. 1: 1013
American Association of Cat Enthusiasts Annual Awards Vol. 1: 1130
American Association of Collegiate Registrars and Admissions Officers Division of Psychopharmacology and Substance Abuse Vol. 1: 511
American Association of Community Theatre Festival Award Vol. 1: 1164
American Association of University Women Award in Juvenile Literature Vol. 1: 16516
American Ballet Competition Vol. 1: 1525
American Bar Association Medal Vol. 1: 1531
American Beefalo World Registry's National Beefalo Show & Sale Vol. 1: 1555
American Beefalo World Registry's Regional Beefalo Shows Vol. 1: 1556
American Bible Society Award Vol. 1: 1563
American Book Awards Vol. 1: 6302
American Cancer Society Eleanor Roosevelt International Cancer Fellowships Vol. 2: 6469
American Cancer Society International Cancer Research Fellowships Vol. 2: 6469
American Cartographic Association Scholarship Award Vol. 1: 1994
American Center for Children's Television - Fran Allison Award Vol. 1: 1663
American Center for Children's Television - Ollie Awards Vol. 1: 1664
American Children's Television Festival - Fran Allison Award Vol. 1: 1663
American Citizenship Award Vol. 1: 17108
American College of Legal Medicine Foundation Vol. 1: 7725
American College of Physicians Award Vol. 1: 1915
American College of Physicians Distinguished Teacher Award Vol. 1: 1916
The American College of Psychiatrists Award for Creativity in Psychiatric Education Vol. 1: 1937
The American College of Psychiatrists Distinguished Service Award in Psychiatry Vol. 1: 1938
American College of Surgeons Faculty Fellowship Vol. 1: 1945
American Community Leadership Award Vol. 1: 14443
American Concrete Pipe Association Award of Excellence Vol. 1: 1981
American Continental Championship Vol. 1: 19681
American Council of Learned Societies Fellowships Vol. 1: 2037
American Craft Council Fellows Vol. 1: 2076
American Craft Council Honorary Fellow Vol. 1: 2076
American Crossword Puzzle Champion Vol. 1: 2081
American Culinary Classic Vol. 1: 15625
American Cured Meat Championships Vol. 1: 1261
American Dance Guild Award
American Dance Guild Vol. 1: 2119
Congressional Medal of Honor Society Vol 1: 8402
American Eagle Award Vol. 1: 15406
American Education Award Vol. 1: 1403
American Egg Board Research Award Vol. 1: 17496
American Eurocopter Golden Hour Award Vol. 1: 10390
American Exemplar Medal Vol. 1: 9764
American Experiment Award Vol. 1: 7760
American Express America's Best Chef Vol. 1: 12287
American Express Tribute Vol. 1: 21463
American Family Therapy Academy Awards Vol. 1: 2215
American Family Therapy Association Awards Vol. 1: 2215
American Farm Bureau Federation's Award for Distinguished Service Vol. 1: 2220
American Feed Industry Association Award
American Dairy Science Association Vol. 1: 2097
American Society of Animal Science Vol 1: 4251
American Feed Industry Association Award (AFIA) Vol. 1: 4808
American Feed Manufacturers Association Award Vol. 1: 2097
American Friendship Medal Vol. 1: 9764
American Graphic Design Awards Vol. 1: 10139
American Head and Neck Society Vol. 1: 1948
American Heritage Award Vol. 1: 15895
American Hero Award Vol. 1: 12335
American Heroes in Education Awards Vol. 1: 17887
American Hiking Society Award Vol. 1: 2452
American Image Enhancement Award Vol. 1: 14741
American Independent Award Vol. 1: 18396
American Indian Festival of Words Author Award Vol. 1: 20235
American Initiative for Creativity, Invention and Entrepreneurship Vol. 1: 12166
American International Film and Video Festival; Amateur PSA/VMPD Vol. 1: 17283
American International Film/Video Festival Vol. 1: 3147
American Iris Society Gold Medal Vol. 1: 2866
American Iron and Steel Institute Medal Vol. 1: 2873
American Jazz Hall of Fame Vol. 1: 10983
American Jazz Masters Fellowship Awards Vol. 1: 14931
American Kennel Club Career Achievement Award in Canine Research Vol. 1: 4809
American Kennel Club Excellence in Research Awards Vol. 1: 4810

American Laryngological Association Award Vol. 1: 2924
American League All-Star Team Vol. 1: 19649
American League Most Valuable Player Vol. 1: 6266
American League Rookie of the Year Vol. 1: 19650
American Legion Fourth Estate Award Vol. 1: 2946
American Legion Mercury Award Vol. 1: 2946
American Liberties Medallion Vol. 1: 2884
American Library Association Literary Awards; Black Caucus of the Vol. 1: 6413
American Library Association Trustee Citation Vol. 1: 5449
American Machinist Award Vol. 1: 3023
American Mineralogist Undergraduate Award Vol. 1: 13432
American Music Awards Vol. 1: 3160
American National Chopin Piano Competition Vol. 1: 7937
American Needlepoint Guild Book Award Vol. 1: 3190
American Needlepoint Guild Literary Award Vol. 1: 3190
American North Country Cheviot Hall of Fame Vol. 1: 3194
American Numismatic Society Graduate Fellowship Vol. 1: 3271
American Occupational Therapy Foundation Awards Vol. 1: 3303
American ORT Chapter of the Year Vol. 1: 3342
American Patriots Medal Vol. 1: 9764
American Pharmacists Association Fellows Vol. 1: 3378
American Pianists Association Classical Fellowship Awards Vol. 1: 3543
American Poultry Historical Society Award Vol. 1: 17497
American Preparedness Award Vol. 1: 1806
American Revolution Round Table Book Award Vol. 1: 3845
American Romanian Academy Awards Vol. 1: 3869
American School and University Annual Architectural Portfolio Vol. 1: 3883
American Society of Cytology Award for Meritorious Achievement in Cytology Vol. 1: 4398
American Society of Mammalogists Award Vol. 1: 4494
American Society of Pharmacognosy Awards and Grants Vol. 1: 4584
American Society of Safety Engineers Fellow Vol. 1: 4602
American Society of Swedish Engineers Award Vol. 1: 4615
American Spirit Award Vol. 1: 15633
American Stars Awards Vol. 1: 601
American Statesman Award Vol. 1: 2294
American Statesman Medal Vol. 1: 9764
American Therapeutic Recreation Association Awards Vol. 1: 4743
American Veterinary Medical Association Explorer Award Vol. 1: 6573
American Woman of the Year Vol. 1: 18209
American Wood Council Wood Design Award Vol. 1: 21820
Americanism Award
American Legion A.J. Jurek Post 1672 Vol. 1: 2950
American Legion Virginia Vol 1: 2956
Americanism News Media Award Vol. 1: 7671
Americas 2000: All Media Competition Vol. 1: 13490
Americas 2000 Paper Works Competition Vol. 1: 13491
Americas Book Award for Children's and Young Adult Literature Vol. 1: 7733
America's Cup Vol. 1: 4923
America's Democratic Legacy Award Vol. 1: 4979
America's Junior Miss Vol. 1: 4927
America's Old-Time Country Music Hall of Fame Vol. 1: 15896
America's Old-Time Fiddler's Hall of Fame Vol. 1: 15897
America's Ten Outstanding Young Men Vol. 1: 20678
America's Young Woman of the Year Vol. 1: 4927
AmeriStar Package Awards Vol. 1: 11023
Ames Award; Rosemary Vol. 1: 2574
Ames Histology Award Vol. 2: 5627
AMGEN Award Vol. 1: 7458
Amgen Award; ASBMB/ Vol. 1: 3917
Amgen Outstanding Investigator Award Vol. 1: 4118
AMHA Man of the Year Award/AMHA Woman of the Year Award Vol. 1: 3122
AMHA Medal Class Awards Vol. 1: 3123
AMHA Open Competition Awards Vol. 1: 3124
AMHA Trail Ride Award Vol. 1: 3125
AMHA Woman of the Year Award; AMHA Man of the Year Award/ Vol. 1: 3122
AMHA Youth of the Year Award Vol. 1: 3126
AMHA Youth Person of the Year Award Vol. 1: 3127
AMHAY Horsemastership Awards Vol. 1: 3128
AMI Salon Awards Vol. 1: 5756
Amicus Award Vol. 1: 825
Amiens International Film Festival Vol. 2: 2226
Amir Chand Prize; Basanti Devi Vol. 2: 3405
Amir Chand Prizes; Shakuntala Vol. 2: 3406
Amirikian Memorial Maritime Welding Award; Arsham Vol. 1: 4878
Amis d'Escoffier Society Awards Vol. 1: 12783
Amistad Award Vol. 1: 21292
Ammann Research Fellowship in Structural Engineering; O. H. Vol. 1: 4290
AMOA Cigarette Vending Machine Promotion Award Vol. 1: 4943
AMOA Games Awards Vol. 1: 4944
AMOA Jukebox Awards Vol. 1: 4945
Amoroso Award Vol. 2: 7157
Amory Prize; Francis Vol. 1: 619
Amos Award Vol. 1: 15410
AMP W.G. Walkley Awards for Journalism Vol. 2: 458
AMRC P&E Awards Vol. 1: 5793
AMS 50 Dissertation Fellowships; Alvin H. Johnson Vol. 1: 3177
AMS 50 Fellowships Vol. 1: 3177
AMSA International Piano Competition Vol. 1: 3166
Amsterdam Prize for Art Vol. 2: 4886
Amsterdam Prize for History Vol. 2: 4889
Amsterdam Prize for Medicine Vol. 2: 4890
Amsterdam Prize for the Environment Vol. 2: 4888
Amstutz-Williams Award Vol. 1: 1123
AMSUS Award for Excellence in Clinical Pharmacy Practice Vol. 1: 5763
AMSUS Medical Student Award Vol. 1: 5764
Amtmann Fellowship Vol. 1: 6359
AMT's Outstanding Medical Assistant Students Vol. 1: 3068
Amundson Student Presentation Award; Terry Vol. 1: 21631
AMVETS National Awards Program Vol. 1: 4947
AMVETS National Employer of the Year Award Vol. 1: 4948
AMVETS Silver Helmet Awards Vol. 1: 4949
AMWA Medical Book Awards Vol. 1: 3082
AMY Awards Vol. 1: 22067
Amy Writing Awards Vol. 1: 4951
ANA Numismatic Art Award for Excellence in Medallic Sculpture Vol. 1: 3197
ANAD Award Vol. 1: 14072
ANAD Service Awards Vol. 1: 14073
Anand Endowment Lecture; Dr. Nitya Vol. 2: 3468
ANCEC Vol. 2: 5209
Anda Audience Prize; Geza Vol. 2: 6365
Anda International Piano Competition; Geza Vol. 2: 6365
Andeoud; Prix Jules Vol. 2: 2064
Anders Bording Prisen and Kraftproven Vol. 2: 1450
Anderson Award; Arthur R. Vol. 1: 1961
Anderson Award; Elda E. Vol. 1: 10317
Anderson Award; F. Paul Vol. 1: 4418
Anderson Award; H. C. L. Vol. 2: 223
Anderson Award; Harlan J. Vol. 1: 5928
Anderson Award; Inge Vol. 1: 7070
Anderson Award; Jack Vol. 1: 11799
Anderson Award; Mayer Vol. 1: 18237
Anderson Award; Nelson Paul Vol. 1: 17005
Anderson Bank Prize Vol. 2: 7551
Anderson-Berry Medal; David Vol. 2: 8780
Anderson Essay Prize Vol. 2: 8946
Anderson Lectureship on World Food Security; Glenn Vol. 1: 7336
Anderson Lifetime Achievement Award; Eric Vol. 1: 16329
Anderson Memorial Senior Woodwind Scholarship; Mary Vol. 1: 18273
Anderson Merit Award; William G. Vol. 1: 876
Anderson Playwrights Series Prize; Maxwell Vol. 1: 19740
Anderson Prize for Violin; Emily Vol. 2: 8650
Anderson Research Grant; Kathleen S. Vol. 1: 13060
Anderson Sr. Micrographics Awards; Thomas P. Vol. 1: 308
Anderson Silver Medal; Sir Rowand Vol. 2: 8580
Anderson Student Paper Award Vol. 1: 89
Anderson Trophy; Samuel E. Vol. 1: 5107
Anderson Vocal Arts Competition; Marian Vol. 1: 18567
Andes National Award; Ammon S. Vol. 1: 18483
Andreescu Prize; Ion Vol. 2: 5810
Andrew Award Vol. 1: 20124
Andrew Common Grants; Thomas Vol. 2: 7857
Andrew Rutherford Scholarship Vol. 1: 10745
Andrews Bibliographic Award; Joseph L. Vol. 1: 1248
Andrus Award Vol. 1: 1397

Andry Award; Nicolas Vol. 1: 5584
ANDY Awards Vol. 1: 206
ANDY Awards; International Vol. 1: 11184
Angel Award
Lutherans Concerned/Great Lakes Vol. 1: 12994
Zelienople Historical Society Vol 1: 22103
Angel Escobar Prizes; Alejandro Vol. 2: 1310
Angel of the Year Vol. 1: 21757
Angeli Prize; Marguerite de Vol. 1: 8845
Angler Award; Master Vol. 2: 242
Anglian Water Award Vol. 2: 4975
ANGOC Award for Rural Development Vol. 2: 5254
Angus Award Vol. 2: 4976
Angus Medal; Robert W. Vol. 1: 7425
Anhinga Poetry Prize Vol. 1: 8425
Aniara Priset Vol. 2: 6284
Aniara Prize Vol. 2: 6284
Animal Behavior Society Best Student Paper Award Vol. 1: 4958
Animal Behavior Society Film Festival Awards Vol. 1: 4959
Animal Clinical Chemistry Vol. 1: 974
Animal Control Employee of the Year Vol. 1: 13936
Animal Growth and Development Award Vol. 1: 4252
Animal Industry Service Award Vol. 1: 4253
Animal Management Award Vol. 1: 4254
Animal Physiology and Endocrinology Award Vol. 1: 4255
Animal Welfare Award
American Veterinary Medical Association Vol. 1: 4811
Animal Transportation Association - European Office Vol 2: 6731
Anisfield-Wolf Book Award in Race Relations Vol. 1: 8097
Anisfield-Wolf Book Awards Vol. 1: 8097
Ann Arbor Film Co-op Award Vol. 1: 4968
Annaley Naegle Redd Student Award in Women's History Vol. 1: 17925
Annecy Festival Prizes Vol. 2: 2440
Annecy International Animated Film Festival and Market Vol. 2: 2440
Annett Award for Children's Literature; R. Ross Vol. 1: 21987
Annie Award for Best Animated Feature Vol. 1: 11186
Annie Award for Best Animated Television Commercial Vol. 1: 11187
Annie Award for Best Animated Television Production Vol. 1: 11188
Annie Award for Outstanding Individual Achievement in the Field of Animation Vol. 1: 11189
Annie Awards Vol. 1: 11192
Annin Award; Douglas H. Vol. 1: 12210
Anniversary of National Service 1951-1972 Medal Vol. 2: 181
Annual Academy Lecturer Vol. 1: 741
Annual Achievement Award Vol. 1: 62
Annual Achievement Awards Vol. 1: 3899
Annual Art Competition & Exhibition Vol. 1: 19831
Annual Art Show Vol. 1: 16163
Annual Aviation Mechanic Safety Award Vol. 1: 9425
Annual Award for Excellence in Writing on an Information Topic Vol. 1: 10798
Annual Award for Junior Researchers Vol. 2: 1384
Annual Award for Popularization and Promotion of Science Vol. 2: 1385
Annual Award for Psychiatrists in Training Vol. 1: 19519
Annual Award for the Most Environment - Friendly Sugar Hill Vol. 2: 5285
Annual Award of the Dozenal Society of America Vol. 1: 9016
Annual Award to Regular Columnists Vol. 1: 10799
Annual Awards
Asian Football Confederation Vol. 2: 4425
Bulgarian National Television Vol 2: 1215
Guild of Television Cameramen Vol 2: 7595
Annual Awards Competition Vol. 1: 8565
Annual Awards for Chapter Programming Vol. 1: 17086
Annual Awards for Distinction in Financial Management Vol. 1: 20557
Annual Awards in International News Coverage Vol. 1: 16981
Annual Awards Program Vol. 1: 21949
Annual Caribbean Review Award Vol. 1: 7594
Annual Central Prize Award and Certificate of Merit Award Vol. 1: 7764
Annual Central Prize Award, President's Certificate of Merit Award, and Central Poster Award Vol. 1: 7764
Annual Championship Prizes Vol. 1: 9523
Annual Chautauqua National Exhibition of American Art Vol. 1: 7819
Annual Children's Choice Award Vol. 1: 454
Annual Competition - Grand Award Vol. 1: 8134
Annual Competition - Grand Award (One-Frame Competition) Vol. 1: 8134
Annual Conference and EXPO Awards Vol. 1: 19307
Annual Conference Paper Awards Vol. 1: 19308
Annual Contest Vol. 1: 11117
Annual Contests Vol. 1: 14989
Annual Display Award Vol. 1: 14196
Annual Distinction Award Vol. 1: 11243
Annual Essay Contest Award Vol. 1: 9003
Annual Exhibition
Allied Artists of America Vol. 1: 473
Audubon Artists Vol 1: 6061
National Watercolor Society Vol 1: 15940
Royal Scottish Academy Vol 2: 8672
Annual Exhibition Awards
National Association of Women Artists Vol. 1: 14457
National Sculpture Society Vol 1: 15698
Society of Illustrators Vol 1: 19137
Annual Exhibitions Vol. 1: 5115
Annual Gold Leaf Awards Vol. 1: 6846
Annual High Point Awards Vol. 1: 16454
Annual Home and School Council Merit Awards Vol. 1: 17262
Annual International Competition Vol. 1: 17562
Annual Lecturer Award Vol. 1: 13722
The Annual LMP Awards Vol. 1: 18177
Annual Manuscript Award Vol. 1: 6319
Annual Medal Design Award Vol. 1: 2879
Annual Meeting Best Of Show Founders Award Vol. 1: 12236
Annual Meeting Best Paper Award Vol. 1: 21137
Annual Meeting International Visitors Award Vol. 1: 260
Annual Merit (Professional Librarian) Vol. 1: 8528
Annual National Art Exhibition Vol. 1: 3504
Annual National Chief's Challenge Vol. 1: 11307
Annual News Award Vol. 1: 11871
Annual One Act Play Festival Award Vol. 2: 5033
Annual Open Exhibition Vol. 1: 5121
Annual Open Juried Exhibition
Pastel Society of America Vol. 1: 17103
Pastel Society of America Vol 1: 17105
Annual Photography Contest Vol. 1: 20682
Annual Political Book Award Vol. 1: 21452
Annual Prize Vol. 1: 18940
Annual Prize for Best Restoration Program Vol. 2: 2295
Annual Prize for Hearing Research Vol. 1: 12954
Annual Prize for Scientific Works Vol. 2: 9321
Annual Public Medallion Award Vol. 1: 21296
Annual Publication Award Vol. 2: 5381
Annual Recognition Award Vol. 1: 19929
Annual Report Award Vol. 1: 3784
Annual Report Awards Vol. 2: 4972
Annual School and College Publications Contest Vol. 1: 15669
Annual Science Award Vol. 2: 1386
Annual Spring Show Award Vol. 1: 9325
Annual Tour Scholarship Vol. 1: 19018
Annual Vocal Competition Vol. 1: 17803
Annual Writing Competition Vol. 1: 8979
Anonymous Prize Vol. 1: 13777
ANPA Foundation - Associated Collegiate Press Pacemakers Awards Vol. 1: 16337
ANPA Foundation - International Circulation Managers Association C. K. Jefferson Award Vol. 1: 16338
ANPA Foundation - Newspaper in Education Program Excellence Award Vol. 1: 16340
Anslinger Award Vol. 1: 11762
Anson Award; Jack L. Vol. 1: 5692
Antarctica Service Medal Vol. 1: 8803
Anthem Essay Contest Vol. 1: 6173
Anthony Memorial Award; Dennis Vol. 2: 4421
Anthropology in Media Award Vol. 1: 909
Anti-Animalia Awards Vol. 2: 1571
Anti-Priset Vol. 2: 6292
Anti-Prize Vol. 2: 6292
Anti-Slavery Award Vol. 2: 6736
Antipa Prize; Grigore Vol. 2: 5811
Anton Boisen Professional Service Award Vol. 1: 5820
Antonov Aeromodelling Diploma Vol. 2: 6321
Antwerp Diamond Career Award Vol. 2: 835
Antwoorden Prijsvragen, Klasse der Letteren Vol. 2: 1073
Antwoorden Prijsvragen, Klasse der Schone Kunsten Vol. 2: 1074
Antwoorden Prijsvragen, Klasse der Wetenschappen Vol. 2: 1075
Anugerah Sastera Negara Vol. 2: 4427
Anuvrat Award for International Peace Vol. 2: 3351
ANZAAS International Scientific Film Exhibition and Competition; Orbit Award of the Vol. 2: 144
ANZAAS Medal Vol. 2: 142
ANZIAM Medal Vol. 2: 68
AOCS/Supelco Research Award Vol. 1: 3305
AOJT Award Vol. 1: 5806

AOP Open Vol. 2: 6837
AOPA Awards for Achievement & Endeavor in Light Aviation Vol. 2: 6682
AORC Award Vol. 1: 5799
AOS Show Trophy Vol. 1: 3320
AOTA COTA/OTR Partnership Award Vol. 1: 3293
AOTOS Mariner's Plaque Vol. 1: 20374
APA Assembly Warren Williams Awards Vol. 1: 3611
APA Award for Research in Psychiatry Vol. 1: 3612
APA Journalism Awards Vol. 1: 3547
APA/PDC Prize for Excellence and Innovation in Philosophy Programs Vol. 1: 3421
APA/Pennwalt Resident Research Award Vol. 1: 3625
APA Public Policy and Advocacy Award Vol. 1: 591
APA Research Award Vol. 1: 592
APA Teaching Award Vol. 1: 593
APALA Distinguished Service Award Vol. 1: 5171
Apathy Commemorative Medal; Istvan Vol. 2: 3313
Apathy Istvan Emlekerem Vol. 2: 3313
APBA Gold Cup Vol. 1: 3587
APBA Honor Squadron Vol. 1: 3588
APCAC Award Vol. 2: 5250
Apel-les Mestres Prize Vol. 2: 6013
APEX - Awards for Publication Excellence Vol. 1: 4994
Apgar Award; Virginia Vol. 1: 759
APHA - APPM Merit Awards Vol. 1: 3379
APHA Award for Excellence Vol. 1: 3778
APHBA Amateur Register of Merit Vol. 1: 17047
APIC New Investigator Research Award Vol. 1: 5456
Apker Award; Leroy Vol. 1: 3447
Aplan Award Vol. 1: 10424
Aplan Award; Frank F. Vol. 1: 2816
APO Award Vol. 2: 4095
APO National Awards Vol. 2: 4094
APO Regional Award Vol. 2: 4095
APO Special National Award Vol. 2: 4094
Apollo Award
American Optometric Association Vol. 1: 3315
Arnold Air Society Vol 1: 5107
Summer and Casual Furniture Manufacturer Association Vol 1: 19833
Apotex Award Vol. 1: 7459
APPA Awards for Excellence in Community Crime Prevention Vol. 1: 3598
APPA Century Award Vol. 1: 3785
APPA Community Awareness Through Media Award Vol. 1: 3599
APPA Honor Roll Vol. 1: 3786
APPA Member of the Year Award Vol. 1: 3600
APPA Safety Contest Awards Vol. 1: 3787
Appalachian Ohio Peace Prize Vol. 1: 4999
Appeal of Conscience Award Vol. 1: 5004
Appel-Denkmunze; Inhaber de Otto- Vol. 2: 2861
Appert Award; Nicholas Vol. 1: 10934
Applause Award Vol. 1: 21787
Applebaum Award; William Vol. 1: 9653
Applebaum Composers Award; Louis Vol. 1: 16736
Appleseed Award; Johnny Vol. 1: 9882
Application Award Vol. 1: 11737
Application to Practice Award Vol. 1: 13440
Applied Consumer Economics Award Vol. 1: 2046
Applied Meteorology; Dr. Andrew Thomson Prize in Vol. 1: 7282
Applied Research Award Vol. 1: 20475
Applied Research Medal Vol. 2: 508
Applied Social Issues Internship Vol. 1: 18884
Appraiser of the Year Award Vol. 1: 14271
Appreciation Award
Arden Terrace Neighborhood Association Vol. 1: 5043
Lewis and Clark Trail Heritage Foundation Vol 1: 12800
National Intramural-Recreational Sports Association Vol 1: 15287
National Junior College Athletic Association Vol 1: 15308
Pedal Steel Guitar Association Vol 1: 17133
Appreciation Certificates for Service to NATRC Vol. 1: 16479
Apprentice Award Vol. 2: 328
Apprentice of the Year Vol. 2: 7117
Apprenticeship Awards Vol. 1: 20194
APRA/Australian Music Centre Classical Music Awards Vol. 2: 238
APS Fellow Vol. 1: 3534
Apsey Playwriting Award; Ruby Lloyd Vol. 1: 20977
Apt Lecture; Leonard Vol. 1: 760
Apuraha tai Palkinto Vol. 2: 1618
APWA Distinguished Service Award Vol. 1: 3798
Aqua Awards Vol. 1: 11430
Aqueous Show Vol. 1: 12570
Aqueous USA Exhibition Vol. 1: 12570
Aquinas Medal Vol. 1: 1661
ARA Annual Award Vol. 1: 3870
ARA Awards for Contribution to the Cause of Freedom and Human Rights Vol. 1: 3869
ARA Hall of Fame Award Vol. 1: 6166
ARA Pacis Award (Altar of Peace) Vol. 1: 12259
Arafura Short Story Award Vol. 2: 482
Arafura Short Story Award; Dymocks Vol. 2: 484
Arango Design Award Vol. 1: 5023
Aranytoll Vol. 2: 3230
Arata Award; Yoshiaki Vol. 2: 2489
Arbeitsgemeinschaft Schweizer Grafiker Competitions Vol. 2: 6531
Arbor Day Awards Vol. 1: 13949
Arboricultural Association Award Vol. 2: 6738
Arbuse Gold Medals; Gussie and Samuel Vol. 1: 16235
Arbuthnot Award Vol. 1: 11851
ARCA Championship Hall of Fame Vol. 1: 11760
Arce; Premio Julio G. Vol. 2: 4506
Archaeological Book Award Vol. 2: 6915
Archaeological Geology Division Award Vol. 1: 9955
Archambault Prize in Physical Sciences and Mathematics; Urgel Vol. 1: 5537
Archbishop Iakovos' Years of Service Award Vol. 1: 15113
Archer Award; Ellinor Vol. 2: 224
Archer Award; Harry Vol. 1: 1910
Archer-Burton Poetry Competition; Kitty Vol. 2: 590
Archer Pioneer Award; Ellinor Vol. 2: 224
Arches Papers Award Vol. 1: 4840
Archibald Prize Vol. 2: 74
Archie Carr Lifetime Achievement Award Vol. 1: 7590
Architect Magazine Art of CAD Competition; Canadian Vol. 1: 6878
Architect Magazine Awards of Excellence; Canadian Vol. 1: 6879
Architects Rome Scholarship in Architecture; South African Institute of Vol. 2: 7143
Architectural Awards
Arab Towns Organization Vol. 2: 4374
Historic Mobile Preservation Society Vol 1: 10458
Architectural Awards of Excellence Vol. 1: 2848
Architectural Critics and Writers Award Vol. 2: 5699
Architectural Study Tour Scholarship Vol. 1: 19018
Architecture Award Vol. 2: 6588
Architecture Awards Vol. 2: 8589
Architecture Firm Award Vol. 1: 2709
Arctowski Medal Vol. 1: 13826
Arderne Medal and Prize; John Vol. 2: 8799
Ardley Prize; Bimcam Vol. 2: 7714
Area Community Service Awards Vol. 1: 1399
Area/Regional Impact Award Vol. 1: 15256
Arena Memorial Scholarship; John Vol. 1: 12760
Arenth Excellence in Cancer Nursing Management Award; Linda Vol. 1: 16710
Arets pris i svensk forsakring Vol. 2: 6282
Arets Verk Vol. 2: 5165
Arfvedson-Schlenk-Preis Vol. 2: 2802
Argentinean Association of Dermatology Awards Vol. 2: 30
Argyll Postal History Salver Vol. 2: 8263
Ari Medal of Merit; Carina Vol. 2: 6142
Ari Medaljen; Carina Vol. 2: 6142
Arial Anaker Award Vol. 1: 14028
Arid Lands Hydraulic Engineering Award Vol. 1: 4291
Arima Award for Applied Microbiology Vol. 2: 452
Arinos Prize; Afonso Vol. 2: 1152
Arisawa Awards; Hiromi Vol. 1: 5568
Arizona Author Award Vol. 1: 5052
Arizona Authors' Association Annual National Literary Contest Vol. 1: 5048
Arizona Heritage Grant Vol. 1: 13215
Arizona Highways Adult Nonfiction Book Award Vol. 1: 5053
Arizona State Poetry Society Award Vol. 1: 14990
Arizona Young Readers Award Vol. 1: 5054
Arjomaria/Arches/Rivers Award Vol. 1: 4840
Arkitekturprisen Vol. 2: 1492
Arlen Memorial Fund Award; Stephen Vol. 2: 6744
Arlt Award in the Humanities; Gustave O. Vol. 1: 8578
ARM of the Year Vol. 1: 11032
Armada Dish (Biffa Trophy) Vol. 2: 7532
Armand; Fondation Louis Vol. 2: 1924
Armed Forces Expeditionary Medal Vol. 1: 8804
Armed Forces Joint Warfighting Essay Contest Vol. 1: 20707
Armed Forces Reserve Medal Vol. 1: 8805
Armenian Numismatic Memorial Award Vol. 1: 5096
Armourers and Brasier's Award Vol. 2: 8690
Armstrong Award; Anne Vol. 2: 6746
Armstrong Award; Robert H. Vol. 1: 5006

Armstrong Lecture Vol. 2: 8997
Armstrong Medal Vol. 1: 17829
Armstrong Memorial Award for Outstanding Regional Coordinator; Terry Vol. 1: 3198
Armstrong Memorial Research Foundation Awards Vol. 1: 5098
Armwrestler of the Year (Male and Female) Vol. 1: 924
Army Cross Vol. 2: 5729
Army of Occupation Medal - Army-Air Force Vol. 1: 8806
Army Reserve Components Achievement Medal Vol. 1: 8807
Arnbergska Priset Vol. 2: 6204
Arnold Air Letter Trophy Vol. 1: 5102
Arnold Award; H. H. Vol. 1: 336
Arnold Sabre; H. H. Vol. 1: 5102
Arnow Award; Philip Vol. 1: 20509
Arpino Award Vol. 1: 16235
ARRL Herb S. Brier Instructor of the Year Award Vol. 1: 45
ARRL Professional Educator of the Year Award Vol. 1: 46
Arrowhead Biennial Exhibition Vol. 1: 9047
ARS Distinguished Achievement Award Vol. 1: 3820
Arsenault Senior Arts Award; Father Adrien Vol. 1: 17544
Art and Innovation Commission Vol. 2: 9099
Art Award Vol. 1: 16241
Art Award; AAEA Sporting Vol. 1: 658
Art Competition Vol. 1: 5145
Art Directors Awards Vol. 1: 5116
Art Directors Club Hall of Fame Vol. 1: 5117
Art Directors Club of Toronto Awards and Show Presentation Vol. 1: 204
Art in the Park Awards Vol. 1: 9855
Art of Listening Award Vol. 1: 9929
Art of Reporting Award Vol. 1: 9930
Art of the Automobile Competition Vol. 1: 6100
Art of the Northeast Competition Vol. 1: 18521
Art Scholarship
  Artists Guild of the Santa Ynez Valley Vol. 1: 5141
  Royal Bath and West of England Society Vol 2: 8438
Art Song Festival Vol. 1: 8099
ARTBA Award Vol. 1: 3859
Artes Awards Vol. 2: 5682
Artflight - Arts Council/Aer Lingus Award Vol. 2: 3612
Arthroscopy Research Grants Vol. 1: 5131
Arthur A. Hitchcock Award for Distinguished Service Vol. 1: 2070
Arthur Andersen Artist & Business Award for Adviser of the Year Vol. 2: 6749
Arthur, M.D. Award; Capt. Ransom J. Vol. 1: 20690
The Arthur Quern Quality Award Vol. 1: 18060
Arthur Sidney Bedell Award Vol. 1: 21476
Article Award
  Canadian Railroad Historical Association Vol. 1: 7367
  Religious Communication Association Vol 1: 17981
Article of the Year Vol. 1: 10348
Article Prize
  American Philosophical Association Vol. 1: 3422
  Law and Society Association Vol 1: 12719
  Society for the Historians of the Early American Republic Vol 1: 18867
Artist Achievement Award Vol. 1: 6377
Artist Award Vol. 1: 19813
Artist Award for a Distinguished Body of Work, Exhibition, Presentation or Performance Vol. 1: 8142
Artist Awards
  National Association of Teachers of Singing Vol. 1: 14411
  Society of Arts and Crafts Vol 1: 19028
Artist Equipment Access Awards Vol. 1: 6276
Artist of the Month Vol. 2: 640
Artist of the Year
  Billboard - VNU Business Publications USA Vol. 1: 6377
  Indian Arts and Crafts Association Vol 1: 10753
  Victorian Artists Society Vol 2: 641
Artist-Teacher Award Vol. 1: 4700
Artistic Capacity-Building Program Vol. 1: 11083
Artistic Certificate (for Artistic Display of Orchids in Use) Vol. 1: 3321
Artistiche Sculture del noto Maestro Enzo Assenza Rappresentante la X musa Vol. 2: 4046
Artists Association of Finland Award Vol. 2: 1574
Artists' Fellowships Vol. 1: 16229
Artists for Nature Foundation Award Vol. 2: 9080
Artists in Residence Program Vol. 1: 11084
Artists-in-Residence Program Vol. 1: 19814
Artists International New York Debut Award Auditions Vol. 1: 5143
The *Artist's Magazine Annual Painting Competition* Vol. 1: 5146
The Artist's Magazine Art Competition Vol. 1: 5146
The Artist's Magazine Award Vol. 1: 4841
The Artist's Magazine Still Life Painting Competition Vol. 1: 5146
Artists; TCG/MetLife Foundation Extended Collaboration Grants for Vol. 1: 20055
Artot; Prix Paul Vol. 2: 999
Arts Achievement Award Vol. 2: 4178
Arts and Crafts in Architecture Award Vol. 2: 8888
Arts and Letters Award Vol. 1: 7029
Arts and Tourism Grants Program Vol. 1: 10430
Arts Council of England Helen Chadwick Fellowship Vol. 2: 7132
Arts Council of England Schemes Vol. 2: 6753
Arts Council of Northern Ireland Bursaries and Awards Vol. 2: 6761
Arts Council of Northern Ireland Fellowship Vol. 2: 7133
Arts Council of Wales Book of the Year Awards Vol. 2: 9202
Arts Festival Award Vol. 2: 4179
Arts for the Parks Competition Vol. 1: 15477
Arts Management Award for Arts Administrator of the Year Vol. 1: 5155
Arts Management Award for Career Service Vol. 1: 5156
Arts Management Special Award Vol. 1: 5157
Arts Recognition and Talent Search (ARTS) Vol. 1: 15117
Artz Distinguished Service Award; Curtis P. Vol. 1: 1599
Arvon Foundation International Poetry Competition Vol. 2: 6766
Aryabhata Medal Vol. 2: 3469
Arzt Distinguished Rabbinic Service Award; Rabbi Max Vol. 1: 12374
The ASA Award Vol. 1: 4635
ASA-Metlife Foundation MindAlert Awards Vol. 1: 4636
ASA National Championships Vol. 1: 586
ASA Undergraduate Student Award Vol. 1: 4637
ASABE Fellows Vol. 1: 4213
ASABE Paper Awards Vol. 1: 4214
Asada Medal Vol. 2: 4138
ASAE Fellow Vol. 1: 4267
ASAE Past Presidents Award Vol. 1: 4215
ASAE Student Paper Awards Vol. 1: 4216
ASALH/DLAMC African American History Essay Contest Vol. 1: 5509
Asali Scholarship Award; Joe Vol. 1: 13037
ASAP - Gralnick Foundation Research Award Vol. 1: 3903
ASAS Extension Award Vol. 1: 4256
ASAS Fellow Vol. 1: 4257
ASBC - Merck Award Vol. 1: 3919
ASBMB/Amgen Award Vol. 1: 3917
ASBMB/Avanti Award in Lipids Vol. 1: 3918
ASBMB - Merck Award Vol. 1: 3919
ASBMB/Schering Plough Institute Award Vol. 1: 3920
ASC Recognition Award Vol. 1: 3985
ASCA Awards of Excellence Vol. 1: 4719
ASCA Chapter Age Group Coaches of the Year Vol. 1: 4720
ASCA Coaches Hall of Fame Vol. 1: 4721
ASCAP Chamber Music Awards Vol. 1: 4375
ASCAP - Deems Taylor Awards Vol. 1: 4376
ASCAP Foundation College Musical Theatre Award Vol. 1: 12540
ASCAP - Richard Rodgers Award Vol. 1: 4377
ASCAP Triple Play Award Vol. 1: 4378
ASCB/Promega Early Career Life Scientist Award Vol. 1: 3941
ASCE News Correspondent Award Vol. 1: 4292
ASCE Presidents' Award Vol. 1: 4293
ASCE Presidents' Medal Vol. 1: 4294
ASCE State-of-the-Art of Civil Engineering Award Vol. 1: 4295
ASCLA Exceptional Service Award Vol. 1: 5854
ASCLA Leadership Achievement Award Vol. 1: 5855
ASCP Associate Member Lifetime Achievement Award Vol. 1: 3963
ASCP Associate Member Section Distinguished Service Award Vol. 1: 3964
ASCP - CAP Joint Annual Award Vol. 1: 3965
ASCP - CAP Joint Distinguished Service Award Vol. 1: 3965
ASCP Medical Photography Competition Vol. 1: 3966
ASCP Sheard - Sanford Medical Student Award Vol. 1: 3967
ASEA-Brown Boveri-Forschungspreis Vol. 2: 6517
ASEE Minorities in Engineering Award Vol. 1: 3995
ASEE Section Outstanding Teaching Award Vol. 1: 3996

ASEM Fellows Vol. 1: 4052
ASF Awards for Scandinavians Vol. 1: 3878
ASF Translation Prize Vol. 1: 3879
ASFA Web Awards Vol. 1: 5847
ASFD Life-Time Achievement Award Vol. 1: 4410
ASFSA Thelme Fienegan Gold Award Vol. 1: 18347
ASGSB Founder's Award Vol. 1: 4077
ASGSB President's Award Vol. 1: 4078
ASH Scholar Awards Vol. 1: 4443
ASHA Media Awards for Journalists Vol. 1: 4662
Ashe Award; Arthur Vol. 1: 16582
Ashe Award for Courage; Arthur Vol. 1: 9337
Ashe Collegiate Awards for Leadership and Sportsmanship; Tennis Magazine/ Arthur Vol. 1: 11137
Ashford Medal; Bailey K. Vol. 1: 4629
Ashisoma Environmental Award Vol. 2: 4344
Ashley Award; Larry Vol. 1: 6946
Ashok Chakra Vol. 2: 3375
ASHRAE - Alco Medal for Distinguished Public Service Vol. 1: 4419
ASHRAE ASHAE - Homer Addams Award Vol. 1: 4417
ASHRAE Energy Awards Vol. 1: 4441
ASHRAE Fellows Vol. 1: 4420
ASHRAE Journal Paper Award Vol. 1: 4421
ASHRAE Symposium Paper Award Vol. 1: 4422
ASHRAE Technical Paper Award Vol. 1: 4423
ASHS Hall of Fame Vol. 1: 4084
Asia-Pacific Cancer Society Training Grants (APCASOT) Vol. 2: 6470
Asian American Journalists Association National Awards Vol. 1: 5165
Asian American Literary Awards Vol. 1: 5169
Asian/Asian-American Award Vol. 1: 3624
Asian Banking Awards Vol. 2: 5256
ASID Designer of Distinction Award Vol. 1: 4459
ASID Human Environment Award Vol. 1: 4460
ASIFA Special Award Vol. 2: 1382
ASIS Research Award Vol. 1: 4100
ASJA Outstanding Article Award Vol. 1: 4467
ASJA Outstanding Author Award Vol. 1: 4468
ASJMC Distinguished Service Award Vol. 1: 5845
ASJSA Citation of Merit Award Vol. 1: 5845
The ASLA Design Medal Vol. 1: 4472
ASLA Medal Vol. 1: 4473
ASLA President's Medal Vol. 1: 4474
ASM Award in Applied and Environmental and Microbiology Vol. 1: 4138
ASM Founders Distinguished Service Award Vol. 1: 4129
ASM International and The Metallurgical Society Distinguished Lectureship in Materials and Society Vol. 1: 5173
ASM International and The Minerals, Metals and Materials Society Distinguished Lectureship in Materials and Society Vol. 1: 5173
ASME Medal Vol. 1: 4502
ASMR Medal Vol. 2: 264
ASMR Research Award Vol. 2: 265
ASNE Distinguished Writing Awards Vol. 1: 17508
ASNT Fellows Vol. 1: 4143
ASNT Fellowship Award Vol. 1: 4144
ASNT Gold Medal Vol. 1: 4148
ASP World Title Vol. 1: 5871
ASPA/NASPAA Distinguished Research Award Vol. 1: 14374
Aspen Filmfest Vol. 1: 5196
Aspen Gold Award Vol. 1: 10358
Aspen Institute Corporate Award for Excellence in Leadership Vol. 1: 5199
Aspen Institute Public Service Award for Excellence in Leadership Vol. 1: 5200
ASPEN Research Scholar Award Vol. 1: 4165
Aspen Shortsfest Vol. 1: 5197
ASPET Award for Experimental Therapeutics Vol. 1: 4169
Asselin; Prix Olivar- Vol. 1: 18613
Assistant Coach of the Year Award Vol. 1: 11138
Assistant Referee of the Year Vol. 2: 4425
Assistants' Awards Vol. 2: 6835
Associate and Master Awards Vol. 2: 6669
Associate Member of the Year Vol. 1: 8975
Associate of the Royal Academy of Dance Vol. 2: 8356
Associate of the Year Vol. 1: 12976
Associate Remodeler of the Year Award Vol. 1: 14257
Associated American Artists Purchase Award Vol. 1: 18980
Associated Collegiate Press Pacemakers Awards; NAA Foundation - Vol. 1: 16337
Associated Member Distinguished Service Award Vol. 1: 3964
Associates Award Vol. 1: 14578
Associates Premium Vol. 2: 7792
Associateship (APMI) Vol. 2: 8250
Associateship of Honour Vol. 2: 8536
The Associateship of the City and Guilds of London Institute Vol. 2: 7305
Association and Industry Awards Vol. 1: 9610
Association des Musees Canadiens - Americain Foundation de Affaire de Coeur Societe Vol. 1: 511
Association Executive of the Year Vol. 1: 5924
Association Fellowship Award Vol. 1: 15531
Association for Civil Rights in Israel Awards Vol. 2: 3722
Association for Industrial Archaeology Award Vol. 2: 6916
Association for the Protection of Rural Scotland Annual Award Vol. 2: 8878
Association in Scotland to Research Into Astronautics Honorary Member Vol. 2: 6785
Association Internationale de la Presse Sportive Awards Vol. 2: 3297
Association of Clinical Biochemists Foundation Award Vol. 2: 6768
Association of Development Financing Institutions in Asia and the Pacific Honorary Member Vol. 2: 5257
Association of Faculties of Pharmacy of Canada Excellence in Teaching Award Vol. 1: 6624
Association of Irish Choirs Trophy Vol. 2: 3627
Association of Jewish Libraries Reference Book Award Vol. 1: 5741
Association of Orthodox Jewish Teachers Awards Vol. 1: 5806
Association of South African Quantity Surveyors Gold Medal of Honour Vol. 2: 5518
Association of Southeast Asian Institutions of Higher Learning Awards Vol. 2: 5259
Association of Subspecialty Professors Young Investigator Award in Geriatrics Vol. 1: 15125
Association of the United States Army Awards Vol. 1: 5883
Association-of-the-Year Award Vol. 1: 21212
Association of Track and Field Statisticians Honorary Member Vol. 2: 88
Association Silver Pin Awards Vol. 1: 539
Association Wrestling Award Vol. 1: 540
Association Youth Sport Membership Award Vol. 1: 541
Association Youth Sport Programming Award Vol. 1: 542
Astar Award Vol. 1: 18018
Astin Measurement Science Award; Allen V. Vol. 1: 20476
Astin - Polk International Standards Medal Vol. 1: 3181
ASTM Award of Merit Vol. 1: 5929
ASTM Robert J. Painter Memorial Award; SES/ Vol. 1: 19748
Astor Award Vol. 2: 7342
Astor Award; Brooke Russell Vol. 1: 16253
Astor Award for Philanthropy; Brooke Russell Vol. 1: 8013
Astor Memorial Leadership Essay Contest; Vincent Vol. 1: 20708
Astor Presidents Cup; Lady Vol. 2: 7106
Astor Trophy for Occupational Health Management Vol. 2: 8716
ASTRA Trophy Vol. 2: 6786
AstraZeneca Award Vol. 2: 6861
AstraZeneca Traveling Lectureship Award Vol. 1: 19331
Astrobiology Award Vol. 1: 4932
Astrological Association Awards Vol. 2: 6844
Astronautical Literature Award; Eugene M. Emme Vol. 1: 1501
Astronautics Award Vol. 1: 2652
Astronautics Award; John F. Kennedy Vol. 1: 1503
Astronautics Award; Military Vol. 1: 1505
Astronautics Literature Award Vol. 1: 1501
Astronomical League Award Vol. 1: 6001
Astronomical League Observing Awards Vol. 1: 6251
Astronomical Society of France Awards Medals Vol. 2: 2250
Astwood Lecture Award; Edwin B. Vol. 1: 9258
ASU Commander's Cup Vol. 1: 5102
Asundi Memorial Lecture; Prof. R. K. Vol. 2: 3470
At-Large Award Vol. 1: 1602
ATA National Truck Driving Championships Vol. 1: 4769
ATA National Truck Rodeo Vol. 1: 4769
AT&T Foundation Awards Vol. 1: 3996
AT&T Istel Young Musicians Awards Vol. 2: 8328
AT&T National Pro-Am Youth Award Vol. 1: 7797
AT&T Nonfiction Award Vol. 2: 6885
Ataturk International Peace Prize Vol. 2: 6627
Ataturk Uluslararasi Baris Odulu Vol. 2: 6627
ATCA Industrial Award Vol. 1: 383

ATCA Life Cycle Management Award Vol. 1: 384
ATCA Small Business Award Vol. 1: 392
ATEM Fellow Vol. 2: 79
ATHENA Award Vol. 1: 16331
Athena Award
Kankakee River Valley Chamber of Commerce Vol. 1: 12481
North San Antonio Chamber of Commerce Vol 1: 16533
Athena Cup Vol. 1: 20898
Athenaeum Literary Award Vol. 1: 6014
Athlete of the Month Vol. 2: 5113
Athlete of the Year
Special Olympics Canada Vol. 1: 19569
USA Deaf Sports Federation Vol 1: 21164
Athlete of the Year Award Vol. 1: 20393
Athlete Service Award Vol. 1: 21168
Athletes Appreciation Award Vol. 1: 21189
Athletes of the Year Vol. 1: 21596
Athletes United for Peace Award Vol. 1: 6021
Athletic Competition Vol. 1: 1138
Athletic Director of the Year Vol. 1: 15223
Athletic Director of the Year Award Vol. 1: 14812
Athletic Therapy Educator Award; Distinguished Vol. 1: 6949
Ati Vishisht Seva Medal Vol. 2: 3376
Atkins Communications Award; George Vol. 1: 8900
Atkinson Award for Excellence in Arkansas Teaching; J.H. Vol. 1: 5075
Atkinson Memorial Award; Hugh C.
Association of College and Research Libraries Vol. 1: 5603
Illinois Library Association Vol 1: 10673
Atlanta Film and Video Festival Vol. 1: 6025
Atlantic Chrysler Cup Vol. 1: 2501
Atlantic Film Festival Vol. 1: 6033
Atlantic High School Scholarship Vol. 1: 8861
Atlantic Journalism Awards Vol. 1: 6035
Atlantic Lottery Corporation Achievement Award
Atlantic Journalism Awards Vol. 1: 6035
Atlantic Journalism Awards Vol 1: 6036
Atlantic Offshore Fishermen's Association Annual Award Vol. 1: 6041
Atlas Award; Ronald B. Vol. 1: 16188
Atlas Travel Marketing Campaign Awards Vol. 1: 5903
Atlas Travel Marketing Executive Award Vol. 1: 5902
ATME Atlas Awards Vol. 1: 5902
ATME Awards Vol. 1: 5903
The Atomic Energy of Canada Ltd. Award Vol. 1: 7426
Atrium Award Vol. 1: 21019
Atsumi Award; IFAWPCA- Vol. 2: 5264
Attack Squadron of the Year Vol. 1: 13089
Atwood Award; J. Leland Vol. 1: 2675
Atwood Award; John Leland Vol. 1: 3997
Aubry Award; Claude Vol. 2: 6389
Aubuchon Freedom of the Press Award; John Vol. 1: 15514
Auctori Excellenti Scientiarum Veterinariarum Pertinensis Vol. 2: 5381
Audience and Juried Awards Vol. 1: 16977
Audience Awards Vol. 1: 9603
Audience Participation Award Vol. 2: 3716
Audience Prize Vol. 2: 8095
Audience Prizes Vol. 2: 2992
Audio Book of the Year Award Vol. 2: 646
Audio Engineering Society Medal Award Vol. 1: 6052
Audio Music/VID Product Grant; Baker & Taylor Entertainment Vol. 1: 17713
Audio Narrator of the Year Vol. 2: 647
Audiovisual Competition Vol. 1: 18863
Audubon A Award Vol. 1: 13149
Audubon Medal Vol. 1: 14468
Auerbach Award; Isaac L. Vol. 2: 738
Auerbach Trophy; Coach of the Year - Red Vol. 1: 14500
Augier; Prix Emile Vol. 2: 2142
Augur Scholarship Vol. 1: 17363
August Memorial Award; Helen Vol. 1: 3404
Augusta International Helicopter Fellowship Award; Gruppo Vol. 1: 2426
Aujeszky Medal Vol. 2: 3245
Ault Award Vol. 1: 14332
Aurbach Lecture Award; Gerald D. Vol. 1: 9259
Aurelian Prize; Petre S. Vol. 2: 5812
Aurelio Award for Altruism; Santo J. Vol. 1: 14882
Aurora Award Vol. 1: 8981
Austern Memorial Writing Competition; H. Thomas Vol. 1: 9651
The Austin Chronicle Best of Austin Vol. 1: 6093
The Austin Chronicle Hot Sauce Contest Vol. 1: 6094
The Austin Chronicle Readers' Poll Music Awards Vol. 1: 6095
The Austin Chronicle Readers' Restaurant Poll Vol. 1: 6096
Austin MacCormick Award Vol. 1: 16918
Austin Music Awards Vol. 1: 6095
Austin Prize; Lord Vol. 2: 7818
Australasian Corrosion Association Awards Vol. 2: 99
Australia Council Residencies Award Vol. 2: 7134
Australia Day Awards Vol. 2: 652
Australia/New Zealand Chapter Traveling Fellowship Vol. 1: 1946
Australian Active Service Medal Vol. 2: 187
Australian Active Service Medal 1945-1975 Vol. 2: 187
Australian Antarctic Medal Vol. 2: 182
Australian Applied Health Sciences Fellowships Vol. 2: 464
Australian Audio Book of the Year Vol. 2: 474
Australian Bravery Decorations Vol. 2: 183
Australian Cadet Forces Service Medal Vol. 2: 184
Australian Camellia Research Society Trophy Vol. 1: 1613
Australian College of Education Medal Vol. 2: 154
Australian Engineering Excellence Awards Vol. 2: 367
Australian Fire Service Medal Vol. 2: 185
Australian Geography Competition Vol. 1: 11253
Australian Institute of Energy Medal Vol. 2: 209
Australian International Widescreen Festival Vol. 2: 290
Australian Junior Water Prize Vol. 2: 285
Australian Library and Information Association Fellow Vol. 2: 225
Australian Literature Society Gold Medal Vol. 2: 81
Australian Mathematical Society Medal Vol. 2: 235
Australian Music Center Awards Vol. 2: 239
Australian Musical Association Prize Vol. 2: 8643
Australian Natural History Medallion Vol. 2: 344
Australian Nuclear Association Annual Award Vol. 2: 248
Australian Numismatic Society Bronze Medal Vol. 2: 251
Australian Photographic Portrait Prize Vol. 2: 75
Australian Police Medal Vol. 2: 186
Australian Post-Doctoral Fellowships Vol. 2: 465
Australian Service Medals Vol. 2: 187
Australian Society of Archivists Honorary Member Vol. 2: 270
Australian Sports Medal Vol. 2: 188
Australian Teachers of Media Awards Vol. 2: 277
Australian Transport Industry Award Vol. 2: 301
Australian/Vogel Literary Award Vol. 2: 64
Austriaprijs; Maria Vol. 2: 4684
Auszeichnung fur wissenschaftliche Arbeiten zu der Geschichte der Justus-Liebig-Universitat Vol. 2: 2996
Author Award; Arizona Vol. 1: 5052
Author of the Year Award
American Society of Journalists and Authors Vol. 1: 4468
Canadian Booksellers Association Vol 1: 6981
Author's Award Vol. 1: 5709
Authors' Award Vol. 1: 15346
Auto-Alloys Precision Trophy Vol. 2: 7605
Automated Imaging Achievement Award Vol. 1: 6098
Automobilclub von Deutschland Awards Vol. 2: 2655
Automobile Competition; Art of the Vol. 1: 6100
Automotive Achievement Award Vol. 1: 13309
Automotive Aftermarket Education Award Vol. 1: 16576
Automotive Dealer Education Award Vol. 1: 16577
Automotive Hall of Fame; Induction into the Vol. 1: 6110
Automotive Industry Leader of the Year Vol. 1: 6111
Automotive Innovation Award Vol. 1: 13310
Automotive Leader of the Year Vol. 1: 6123
Automotive Man of the Year Vol. 1: 6123
Automotive Replacement Management Award Vol. 1: 16576
Automotive Training Awards Vol. 1: 6121
Autosound Grand Prix Awards Vol. 1: 6057
Auxiliary Excellence Award Vol. 1: 2932
Avanti Award in Lipids; ASBMB/ Vol. 1: 3918
Avatar Award Vol. 1: 6641
Avenir Award Vol. 2: 2243
Aventis Prizes for Science Books Vol. 2: 8691
Avery Award; Oswald Vol. 1: 10790
Aviation Awards Vol. 1: 367
Aviation Education Award Vol. 1: 7704
Aviation Education Certificates of Merit Vol. 1: 6125
Aviation Environment Award Vol. 1: 9426

Aviation Ground Marine of the Year Vol. 1: 13072
Aviation Hall of Fame and Museum of New Jersey Vol. 1: 6128
Aviation Hall of Fame Award Vol. 1: 14475
Aviation Hall of Fame Gold Medal of Honor and Achievement Vol. 1: 14474
Aviation Hall of Fame Silver Medal of Outstanding Service Vol. 1: 14476
Aviation Journalism Award Vol. 1: 13917
Aviation Maintenance Department Safety Award Vol. 1: 14562
Aviation Maintenance Technician of the Year Award Vol. 1: 17582
Aviation Ordnance Marine of the Year Vol. 1: 13077
Aviation Supply Marine of the Year Vol. 1: 13091
Aviation Support Services Safety Award Vol. 1: 14563
Aviation Week & Space Technology Distinguished Service Award Vol. 1: 9577
Avioli Founders Award; Louis Vol. 1: 3930
Avionics Technician Award Vol. 1: 17584
AVMA Award Vol. 1: 4812
AVMA Humane Award Vol. 1: 4813
AVMA Student Chapter Certificates Vol. 1: 19806
Avy Award Vol. 1: 2225
A.W. Farrall Young Educator Award Vol. 1: 4220
AWAPA (Academy of Wind and Percussion Arts) Award Vol. 1: 14480
Award Certificates Vol. 1: 17076
Award Emeritus Vol. 1: 17891
Award for Aboriginal and Torres Strait Islander Writers Vol. 2: 483
Award for Academic Excellence in Global Awareness Vol. 1: 5896
Award for Achievement Vol. 1: 15347
Award for Achievement in Business Growth Vol. 1: 8290
Award for Achievement in Engineering Enterprise Vol. 2: 368
Award for Achievement in Technical Services Vol. 1: 7248
Award for Achievement: Individual Vol. 1: 15138
Award for Achievement: Organization Vol. 1: 15139
Award for Advanced Study in Music Vol. 2: 9203
Award for Application of Science & Technology for Rural Development Vol. 2: 3563
Award for Behavioral Research Relevant to the Prevention of Nuclear War Vol. 1: 13827
Award for Best Exam Vol. 1: 4619
Award for Best Practices in Human Resources and Aging Vol. 1: 4638
Award for Book Review in the Daily Press Vol. 2: 3727
Award for Career Development in Honor of L.P. Cookingham Vol. 1: 11474
Award for Chemical Engineering Research Vol. 1: 477
Award for Community Service Vol. 1: 15164
Award for Comprehensive Services in Education Vol. 1: 1144
Award for Contributions to Amateur Mycology Vol. 1: 16450
Award for Cooperative Research in Polymer Science and Engineering Vol. 1: 1726
Award for Creative Advances in Environmental Science and Technology Vol. 1: 1727
Award for Creative Work in Synthetic Organic Chemistry Vol. 1: 1728
Award for Distinguished Achievement Vol. 1: 8237
Award for Distinguished Achievement in Music Vol. 1: 20072
Award for Distinguished Achievement in the Arts Vol. 1: 20072
Award for Distinguished Contributions in the Application of Psychology Vol. 1: 7345
Award for Distinguished Contributions to Education and Training in Psychology Vol. 1: 7346
Award for Distinguished Contributions to Psychology as a Profession Vol. 1: 7347
Award for Distinguished Contributions to Public or Community Service Vol. 1: 7348
Award for Distinguished Contributions to the International Advancement of Psychology Vol. 1: 7349
Award for Distinguished Public Service
American Mathematical Society Vol. 1: 3040
United States Conference of Mayors Vol 1: 20454
Award for Distinguished Research in the Biomedical Sciences Vol. 1: 5559
Award for Distinguished Service
American Society for Dermatologic Surgery Vol. 1: 3989
Federal Aviation Administration Vol 1: 9427
Mathematical Association of America Vol 1: 13192
Award for Distinguished Service to Children Vol. 1: 14206
Award for Distinguished Service to Historical Recordings Vol. 1: 5460
Award for Distinguished Service to Music Vol. 1: 20073
Award for Distinguished Service to N4A Vol. 1: 14061
Award for Distinguished Service to the Arts Vol. 1: 20073
Award for Distinguished Services to Art Vol. 2: 4321
Award for Distinguished Services to Sports Vol. 2: 4322
Award for Divisional Scientific Contributions Vol. 2: 4273
Award for Drug Discovery Vol. 2: 8940
Award for Encouraging Disadvantaged Students into Careers in the Chemical Sciences Vol. 1: 1729
Award for Encouraging Women into Careers in the Chemical Sciences Vol. 1: 1730
Award for Environmental Achievement Vol. 1: 9572
Award for Excellence
American Liszt Society Vol. 1: 3007
Order of the Founders and Patriots of America Vol 1: 16845
Award for Excellence: Genealogical Methods and Sources Vol. 1: 15140
Award for Excellence: Genealogy and Family History Vol. 1: 15141
Award for Excellence in Association Leadership Vol. 1: 7448
Award for Excellence in Book Publication Vol. 1: 830
Award for Excellence in Clinical Teaching Vol. 1: 3486
Award for Excellence in Corporate Community Service Vol. 1: 17443
Award for Excellence in Corporate Reporting Vol. 1: 5393
Award for Excellence in Encouraging Equity Vol. 1: 14090
Award for Excellence in Environmental Conservation Vol. 1: 15419
Award for Excellence in Environmental Health Vol. 1: 14173
Award for Excellence in Fusion Engineering Vol. 1: 9840
Award for Excellence in Integrated Pest Management Vol. 1: 9281
Award for Excellence in Labor Diplomacy Vol. 1: 20528
Award for Excellence in Multicultural Health Vol. 1: 14174
Award for Excellence in Plasma Physics Research Vol. 1: 3448
Award for Excellence in Poetry for Children Vol. 1: 14827
Award for Excellence in Power Distribution Engineering Vol. 1: 10903
Award for Excellence in Professional Writing Vol. 1: 1153
Award for Excellence in Teaching
American Academy of Religion Vol. 1: 830
American Chemical Society Vol 1: 1731
Award for Excellence in Teaching Geography Vol. 1: 6908
Award for Excellence in Workplace Volunteer Programs Vol. 1: 17443
Award for Excellence: *National Genealogical Society Quarterly* Vol. 1: 15142
Award for Executive Excellence Vol. 1: 8286
Award for Exemplary State/University Collaboration Vol. 1: 3613
Award for Extraordinary Service Vol. 1: 9428
Award for First Published Book Vol. 2: 5982
Award for Geography in the Service of Government or Business Vol. 1: 6909
Award for Heroism Vol. 1: 20529
Award for Historical Works Pertaining to Justus-Liebig University Vol. 2: 2996
Award for Innovation and Excellence in Media Coverage of Plastic Surgery Vol. 1: 17377
Award for Innovative Management Vol. 1: 11028
Award for Journalistic Excellence Vol. 1: 18064
Award for Life Work in Publishing and Bookselling Vol. 2: 5983
Award for Lifetime Service Vol. 1: 5320
Award for Literature Vol. 2: 6656
Award for Local Government Education Vol. 1: 11472
Award for Local Sales Achievement Vol. 1: 6721
Award for Measured Drawing Vol. 2: 8581
Award for Notable Endeavor ("The Jane") Vol. 1: 12298
Award for Original Hebrew Novel Vol. 2: 3728
Award for Original Hebrew Poetry Vol. 2: 3729
Award for Outstanding Achievement
Easter Seals Vol. 1: 9084
Nine Lives Associates Vol 1: 16363
Award for Outstanding Achievement in International Business Vol. 1: 21962
Award for Outstanding Achievement in Management Vol. 1: 10949

Award for Outstanding Candidate Vol. 1: 4619
Award for Outstanding Contribution in the Field of Constructive Work Vol. 2: 3563
Award for Outstanding Contribution to Public Understanding of the Geosciences Vol. 1: 2339
Award for Outstanding Contribution to Uplift the Welfare of Women and Children Vol. 2: 3563
Award for Outstanding Contributions in Research and Education Vol. 1: 1859
Award for Outstanding Creative Achievement in the American Theatre Vol. 1: 16123
Award for Outstanding Doctoral Research Vol. 2: 7120
Award for Outstanding Forestry Legislation Vol. 1: 15976
Award for Outstanding Forestry Magazine of an Affiliated State Woodland Owner Association Vol. 1: 15977
Award for Outstanding International Investigative Reporting Vol. 1: 11508
Award for Outstanding Leadership and Service to NHCA Vol. 1: 15199
Award for Outstanding Paper *The Energy Journal* Vol. 1: 11222
Award for Outstanding Performance in Third World Studies Vol. 1: 5897
Award for Outstanding Portrayal of the American Scene Vol. 1: 18375
Award for Outstanding Publication Vol. 1: 5661
Award for Outstanding Research Vol. 1: 7337
Award for Outstanding Research in the Pathophysiology of Osteoporosis Vol. 1: 3931
Award for Outstanding Research Paper Vol. 1: 4620
Award for Outstanding Scholastic Achievement Vol. 1: 2756
Award for Outstanding Service Vol. 1: 9085
Award for Outstanding Service to Maltreated Children Vol. 1: 761
Award for Outstanding Service to Physics in Australia Vol. 2: 213
Award for Outstanding Service to the Society Vol. 1: 16144
Award for Patient Advocacy Vol. 1: 3614
Award for Person of Cultural Merit Vol. 2: 4180
Award for Private Mint Issues Vol. 1: 3199
Award for Professional Excellence
- Association for Investment Management and Research Vol. 1: 5394
- Society for Human Resource Management Vol 1: 18694

Award for Programs for the Disadvantaged Vol. 1: 11477
Award for Promotion of Physics Vol. 2: 5362
Award for Pure or Applied Inorganic Chemistry Vol. 1: 7827
Award for Quality Printing Vol. 2: 5984
Award for Research on Automotive Lubricants Vol. 1: 19034
Award for Scene Design Vol. 1: 20642
Award for Service Vol. 1: 13247
Award for Service To People Vol. 1: 4296
Award for Service to Society Vol. 1: 2757
Award for Services to the Game Vol. 2: 7994
Award for Skill in Intergovernmental Relations Vol. 1: 11473
Award for Social Accomplishment Vol. 2: 3641
Award for Special Librarianship in Canada Vol. 1: 6939
Award for Special Service to Hospital Dentistry Vol. 1: 1235
Award for Teaching Excellence in the Field of Library and Information Science Education Vol. 1: 5420
Award for Team Innovation Vol. 1: 1732
Award for Technical Excellence
- American Chemical Society Vol. 1: 1772
- British Institute of Architectural Technologists Vol 2: 7033

Award for Technical Innovation in Enhancing Production of Safe Affordable Food Vol. 1: 7439
Award for Technical Innovation in Industrial Engineering Vol. 1: 10950
Award for the Advancement of Surface Irrigation Vol. 1: 4217
Award for the Best Photography Vol. 2: 6096
Award for the Innovative Use of Technology Vol. 1: 1145
Award for the Promotion of International Education Vol. 2: 7464
Award for the Promotion of Polish Entertainment Creativity Vol. 2: 5383
Award for the Public Understanding of Sociology Vol. 1: 4647
Award for Valour Vol. 2: 6965
Award for Young Academics in Medical Ethics Vol. 2: 2639
Award for Young Chemists in Technical Development Vol. 2: 4104
Award for Young Investigators Vol. 1: 636
Award for Young Leadership and Excellence Vol. 1: 6112
Award in Chemical Engineering Practice Vol. 1: 2758
Award in Chemical Instrumentation Vol. 1: 1733
Award in Economics Vol. 2: 1642
Award in Electrochemistry Vol. 1: 1734
Award in Forest Science Vol. 1: 18969
Award in Geriatric Oral Research Vol. 1: 11203
Award in Industrial Practice Vol. 1: 7406
Award in Magnetism Vol. 1: 12103
Award in Science Vol. 1: 17240
Award in Spectrochemical Analysis Vol. 1: 1735
Award in the Chemistry of Plastics and Coatings Vol. 1: 1713
Award of Achievement
- National Transportation Week Vol. 1: 15903
- Passaic River Coalition Vol 1: 17099

Award of Appreciation Vol. 1: 16086
Award of Artistry Vol. 1: 2120
Award of Commendation Vol. 1: 8340
Award of Distinction
- American Association for State and Local History Vol. 1: 1039
- American Orchid Society Vol 1: 3322
- American Phytopathological Society Vol 1: 3535
- International Technology Education Association Vol 1: 12064
- Investment Dealers Association of Canada Vol 1: 12173
- Professional Picture Framers Association Vol 1: 17643

The Award of Distinction Vol. 1: 95
Award of EuroArts Vol. 2: 3107
Award of Excellence
- Academy of Operative Dentistry Vol. 1: 115
- Business Forms Management Association Vol 1: 6706
- Canadian Sport Massage Therapists Association Vol 1: 7506
- Canadian Toy Testing Council Vol 1: 7516
- Colorado Society of Association Executives Vol 1: 8223
- *ENR: Engineering News-Record* - The McGraw-Hill Cos., Inc. Vol 1: 9279
- Equine Guelph Vol 1: 9323
- Film Advisory Board Vol 1: 9541
- Genetics Society of Canada Vol 1: 9935
- Image Industry Council International/Institute for Image Management Vol 1: 10699
- International Reading Association Vol 1: 11852
- National Transportation Week Vol 1: 15904
- Oregon Society of Physician Assistants Vol 1: 16861
- Professional Aviation Maintenance Association Vol 1: 17583

Award of Excellence for Distinguished Educators Vol. 1: 14878
Award of Excellence of the Pipeline Division Vol. 1: 4297
Award of Fellow Vol. 1: 3354
Award of Gratitude Vol. 1: 13493
Award of Honor
- American Association of Homes and Services for the Aging Vol. 1: 1222
- American Dairy Science Association Vol 1: 2098
- American Hospital Association Vol 1: 2542
- California Avocado Society Vol 1: 6735

Award of Honour
- British Canoe Union Vol. 2: 6966
- Canadian Camping Association Vol 1: 7015
- World Association of Industrial and Technological Research Organizations Vol 2: 4446

Award of Hope and Courage Vol. 1: 15822
Award of Merit
- AACE International Vol. 1: 35
- AIIM - The Enterprise Content Management Association Vol 1: 309
- American Association for State and Local History Vol 1: 1040
- American Association of Botanical Gardens and Arboreta Vol 1: 1120
- American College of Dentists Vol 1: 1853
- American Concrete Pipe Association Vol 1: 1978
- American Heart Association Vol 1: 2402
- American Occupational Therapy Association Vol 1: 3291
- American Oil Chemists' Society Vol 1: 3306
- American Orchid Society Vol 1: 3323
- American Otological Society Vol 1: 3359
- American Philological Association Vol 1: 3419
- American Public Works Association Vol 1: 3799
- American Revolution Round Table Vol 1: 3846
- American Society for Information Science and Technology Vol 1: 4101
- American Spaniel Club Vol 1: 4658
- Associated Church Press Vol 1: 5238

Association for Research in Otolaryngology, Inc. Vol 1: 5462
Association for the Advancement of Automotive Medicine Vol 1: 5477
B'nai Brith Canada Vol 1: 6487
British Canoe Union Vol 2: 6967
Canadian Association of Career Educators and Employers Vol 1: 6897
Canadian Dermatology Association Vol 1: 7073
Canadian Motorcycle Association Vol 1: 7289
Canadian Parks and Recreation Association Vol 1: 7323
City of Toronto Vol 1: 8045
Conference of California Historical Societies Vol 1: 8370
Conference of California Historical Societies Vol 1: 8371
Deafness Research Foundation Vol 1: 8777
Door and Hardware Institute Vol 1: 8996
Federation of Genealogical Societies Vol 1: 9494
International Association of Workforce Professionals Vol 1: 11413
International Weightlifting Federation Vol 2: 3299
Jewish Deaf Congress Vol 1: 12344
Kenosha History Center Vol 1: 12556
Lambda Kappa Sigma Vol 1: 12680
Michigan Association of Metal Finishers Vol 1: 13337
Military Order of the World Wars Vol 1: 13418
National Association of Federally Licensed Firearms Dealers Vol 1: 14228
National Association of Metal Finishers Vol 1: 14304
National Commission on Correctional Health Care Vol 1: 14698
National Federation of State High School Associations - National Federation Interscholastic Coaches Association Vol 1: 14981
National Genealogical Society Vol 1: 15143
National Religious Broadcasters Vol 1: 15615
National Religious Broadcasters Vol 1: 15616
National Transportation Week Vol 1: 15904
National Water Safety Congress Vol 1: 15935
New Baltimore Historical Society Vol 1: 16087
New England Water Works Association Vol 1: 16131
North American Association of Food Equipment Manufacturers Vol 1: 16387
Ontario Psychological Association Vol 1: 16768
Pittsburgh History and Landmarks Foundation Vol 1: 17357
Polymer Alliance Zone of West Virginia Vol 1: 17467
Professional Aviation Maintenance Association Vol 1: 17584
Society for Historical Archaeology Vol 1: 18683
Society of Manufacturing Engineers - Composites Manufacturing Association Vol 1: 19142
Swedish Council of America Vol 1: 19858
Tree Care Industry Association Vol 1: 20185
Union for the International Language Ido Vol 2: 9164
Award of Merit Certificate Vol. 1: 14627
Award of Merit - Commercial Vol. 1: 8364
Award of Merit/Distinguished Service Award Vol. 1: 14814
Award of Merit - Earth Shelter and Architecture Vol. 1: 4777
Award of Merit - Governmental Vol. 1: 8365
Award of Merit in Broadcasting Vol. 1: 17971
Award of Merit in Journalism Vol. 1: 17971
Award of Merit - Individual Vol. 1: 8366
Award of Merit - Life Member Vol. 1: 4906
Award of Merit - Planning and Development Vol. 1: 4778
Award of Merit - Preservation Vol. 1: 8367
Award of Merit - Scholastic/Authorship Vol. 1: 8368
Award of Merit - Tunnels and Deep Space Vol. 1: 4779
Award of Meritorious Achievement Vol. 1: 12801
Award of Minarik Vol. 2: 5990
Award of Outstanding Achievement Vol. 1: 7137
Award of Quality Vol. 1: 3324
Award of Recognition
AACE International Vol. 1: 41
Alliance of Cardiovascular Professionals Vol 1: 466
International Conference of Funeral Service Examining Boards Vol 1: 11506
Organization Development Institute Vol 1: 16873
Professional Picture Framers Association Vol 1: 17644
Riot Relief Fund Vol 1: 18055
Ukrainian National Women's League of America Vol 1: 20273
Ultrasonic Industry Association Vol 1: 20284
Veterans of Safety Vol 1: 21349
Women on Stamps Study Unit Vol 1: 21767
Award of Recognition: AACRAO Internships Vol. 1: 1158
Award of Recognition: State/Regional Professional Activity Vol. 1: 1159
Award of Recognition: Workshop Grant Vol. 1: 1160
Award of Safety Excellence Vol. 1: 17755
Award of Special Merit Vol. 1: 17585
Award of Special Recognition
Black Mental Health Alliance Vol. 1: 6432
National Association of Metal Finishers Vol 1: 14305
Award of the Circle of the Greek Children's Book Vol. 2: 3168
Award of the Greek Association of Alzheimer's Disease Vol. 2: 3172
Award of the Order of the Brass Jackass Vol. 1: 8270
Award of Valor
American Association of Airport Executives, Great Lakes Chapter Vol. 1: 1080
National Collegiate Athletic Association Vol 1: 14685
National Transportation Week Vol 1: 15905
Award to Honor Excellence in Newspaper Advertising Vol. 1: 16331
Award to the Most Outstanding Third Year Student in Zoology Vol. 2: 5800
Awards
A.D. Johnson Family Association Vol. 1: 176
Center for Design of Analog-Digital Integrated Circuits Vol 1: 7721
International Association for the Scientific Study of Intellectual Disabilities Vol 2: 7897
Near East/South Asia Council of Overseas Schools Vol 2: 3179
Awards for Achievement in Arc Welded Design, and Engineering and Fabrication Vol. 1: 12851
Awards for Action on HIV/AIDS and Human Rights Vol. 1: 7157
Awards for Bravery of the Chamber of Mines of South Africa Vol. 2: 5528
Awards for Courage Vol. 1: 15947
Awards for Distinguished Service in Environmental Planning Vol. 1: 8513
Awards for Educational Excellence Vol. 1: 18695
Awards for Excellence
Association of Consulting Engineers of Australia Vol. 2: 86
Fork Lift Truck Association Vol 2: 7541
Government Finance Officers Association of United States and Canada Vol 1: 10110
HR Alliance Vol 2: 358
Rural Sociological Society Vol 1: 18185
Society for the Family of Man Vol 1: 18865
Awards for Excellence in Broadcasting Vol. 2: 9193
Awards for Excellence in Cable Marketing and Advertising Vol. 1: 8684
Awards for Excellence in Community Service, Philanthropy, and Media Vol. 1: 19847
Awards for Excellence in Distance Learning Vol. 1: 11090
Awards for Excellence in Teaching of the Classics Vol. 1: 3418
Awards for Outstanding Achievements in Cartographic Design Vol. 1: 1995
Awards for Outstanding Area Research Vol. 1: 8514
Awards for Outstanding Consultancy Practice Vol. 2: 8308
Awards for Outstanding Performance Vol. 1: 19309
Awards for Program Excellence Vol. 1: 11477
Awards for Published Accounts Vol. 2: 7661
Awards for Research and Outstanding Publications in Agricultural Economics Vol. 1: 868
Awards for School Bands Youth Groups Vol. 1: 9357
Awards for Science and Ethics in Transportation Research Vol. 1: 460
Awards for Scientific Achievement Vol. 1: 21437
Awards for Sustainability Reporting Vol. 2: 6804
Awards for Technological Advancement Vol. 2: 4225
Awards for Valor Vol. 1: 12484
Awards for Work Displaying Engineering Excellence Vol. 2: 369
Awards in History Vol. 2: 4969
Awards in Oral History Vol. 2: 4970
Awards in Recognition of Excellence Vol. 2: 4828
Awards of Appreciation Vol. 1: 1291

Awards of Distinction
American Craft Council Vol. 1: 2077
Society of the Plastics Industry - Moldmakers Division Vol 1: 19310
Awards of Distinction in Programs Vol. 1: 15201
Awards of Excellence
Alliance for Children and Television Vol. 1: 453
Association for Communication Excellence in Agriculture, Natural Resources, and Life and Human Sciences Vol 1: 5291
Association of Consulting Engineers New Zealand Vol 2: 4951
Association of Consulting Engineers of Canada Vol 1: 5639
International Magnesium Association Vol 1: 11739
National Association of County Information Officers Vol 1: 14181
National Council for Community Behavioral Healthcare Vol 1: 14751
Treasury Board of Canada Secretariat Vol 1: 20181
Awards of Merit
American Association of Blood Banks Vol. 1: 1101
Historical Society of Michigan Vol 1: 10464
International Federation of Audit Bureaux of Circulations Vol 2: 5588
National Association of Intercollegiate Athletics Vol 1: 14283
National Park Academy of the Arts Vol 1: 15478
Awards of Recognition
Family Mediation Canada Vol. 1: 9410
Marine Corps Reserve Association Vol 1: 13105
Awards of the ESTRO Vol. 2: 873
Awards Program
American Design Drafting Association Vol. 1: 2132
American Hanoverian Society Vol 1: 2386
American Holsteiner Horse Association Vol 1: 2520
Awards to Authors of Books on Natural Sciences, Mathematics and Three Social Sciences Vol. 2: 5193
Awgie Awards Vol. 2: 292
AWIS Educational Foundation Predoctoral Award Vol. 1: 5530
AWIS Educational Foundation Undergraduate Award Vol. 1: 5531
AWIT Awards Vol. 2: 5283
AWP Award Series Vol. 1: 5259
AWRA Board of Directors Service Awards Vol. 1: 4823
AWRA Outstanding State Section Award Vol. 1: 4824
AWS Bronze Medal of Honor Vol. 1: 4842
AWS Gold Medal of Honor Vol. 1: 4843
AWS Silver Medal of Honor Vol. 1: 4844
AXA Dublin International Piano Competition Vol. 2: 3623
Ayers Award; A. Jean Vol. 1: 3303
AYH Pioneer Leader Award Vol. 1: 10559
Aylesworth Foundation Advancement Award Vol. 1: 9617
Ayrton Premium Vol. 2: 7808
Azevedo Prize; Arthur Vol. 2: 1153
AzLA/SIRS Intellectual Freedom Award Vol. 1: 5055
AZO Achievement Medal Vol. 1: 496
AZO Meritorious Award Vol. 1: 497
AZO Undergraduate Award Vol. 1: 498
Azorin Prize Vol. 2: 6014
BAAL Book Prize Vol. 2: 6928
Babb-Stanley; Premio Sor Maria del Roble and Pamela Vol. 2: 4634
Babbidge, Jr. Award; Homer D. Vol. 1: 5511
Babcock and Wilcox Trophy Vol. 2: 7606
Babcock-Hart Award Vol. 1: 10935
Baber Member Booster Award; Al Vol. 1: 3200
Baber Research Grant; Carrol Preston Vol. 1: 2998
Babes Prize; Victor Vol. 2: 5813
Bablik Medal Vol. 2: 7472
BACB Editing for Industry Awards Vol. 2: 6938
BACB National House Journal Competition Vol. 2: 6938
Bach Competitions Vol. 1: 17868
Bachauer International Piano Competition; Gina Vol. 1: 6193
Bachus Gold Medal; Walter O. Vol. 1: 18982
Bacigalupi Program of Distinction Awards; Tadini Vol. 1: 15442
Back Award Vol. 2: 8510
Back Award for Best Canadian Film; Frederick Vol. 1: 16934
Back Pain Association Medal Vol. 2: 6848
Backmans Stipendium; Ida Vol. 2: 6242
Backus Award Vol. 1: 13724
Bacon Award; Lionel and Joyce Vol. 2: 6696
Bacon Award; Paul Vol. 1: 20792
Bacon Person of the Year Award; Clare E. Vol. 1: 19311
Bacteria Section Awards Vol. 2: 4999
Bactlab Systems Gold Award Vol. 2: 5624
Bactlab Systems Premier Award for Best Paper Vol. 2: 5625
Baddams Bursary; Thenie Vol. 2: 165
Baden-Wurttemberg Schiller Memorial Prize Vol. 2: 3034
Bader Award Vol. 2: 8739
Bader Award in Bioinorganic or Bioorganic Chemistry; Alfred Vol. 1: 1736
Bader Award in Organic Chemistry; Alfred Vol. 1: 7828
Bader Prize; A Vol. 2: 1417
Badge of Honour in Gold, Silver and Bronze Vol. 2: 2674
Badge of Merit Vol. 2: 1608
Badminton Hall of Fame Vol. 1: 21145
Baekeland Lecture Vol. 2: 8998
Baekelmans Prize; Lode Vol. 2: 952
Baes; Prix Professeur Louis Vol. 2: 1068
Baethke - Eleanor J. Carlin Award for Excellence in Academic Teaching; Dorothy E. Vol. 1: 3483
Baethke - Eleanor J. Carlin Award for Teaching Excellence; Dorothy E. Vol. 1: 3483
BAGMA Annual Awards Vol. 2: 6908
Bagnoud Award; Francois Xavier Vol. 1: 2427
Baguley Award; R. M. Vol. 2: 8285
Bagutta Prize Vol. 2: 3867
Baier Technical Achievement Award; Edward J. Vol. 1: 2609
Bailey Award; Alton E. Vol. 1: 3307
Bailey Award; E.G. Vol. 1: 12211
Bailey Distinguished Member Award; Marilyn and Sturges W. Vol. 1: 8089
Bailey Medal; Clyde H. Vol. 2: 728
Bailey Medal; Liberty Hyde Vol. 1: 2524
Baillie Award; Andrew D. Vol. 1: 7481
Bailly; Prix Antoine-Nicolas Vol. 2: 1673
Bainton Book Prize; Roland H. Vol. 1: 18540
Bair Endowment Award; Clifford E. Vol. 1: 15430
Baird Gold Ribbon Audience Development Awards; Audrey Vol. 1: 4729
Baird Memorial Competition for Young Composers; Tadeusz Vol. 2: 5343
Baird Oncology Excellence in Writing Award in Clinical Practice; Susan Vol. 1: 16711
Baker and Taylor Conference Grants Vol. 1: 22051
Baker & Taylor Entertainment Audio Music/VID Product Grant Vol. 1: 17713
Baker Award; "Cannonball" Vol. 1: 8764
Baker Award; Florence Vol. 2: 6697
Baker Award for Highway Safety; J. Stannard Vol. 1: 11308
Baker Award; Ron Vol. 1: 19799
Baker Distinguished Research Award; Dr. David F. Vol. 1: 10951
Baker Foundation for the Prevention of Blindness Fellowships; E.A. Vol. 1: 7301
Baker Memorial Award; Eugene Vol. 1: 5636
Baker Memorial Award; Hobey Vol. 1: 10493
Baker Prize Award; W. R. G. Vol. 1: 10855
Baker Research Award; Philip Noel Vol. 2: 2951
Baker-Wilkins Award for Outstanding Deputy Chief of Mission Vol. 1: 20530
Bakjian Award; Andy Vol. 1: 21213
Balakian Citation for Excellence in Reviewing Award; Nona Vol. 1: 14530
Balasaraswati/Joy Ann Dewey Beinecke Chair for Distinguished Teaching Vol. 1: 2116
Balbuena; Medalla Bernardo Vol. 2: 4503
Balcescu Prize; Nicolae Vol. 2: 5814
Balch Prize; Emily Clark Vol. 1: 21396
Balcon Award; Michael Vol. 2: 6906
Bald is Beautiful Vol. 1: 6200
Baldrige Community Award; Malcolm Vol. 1: 10168
Baldrige National Quality Award; Malcolm Vol. 1: 6202
Baldwin Award; F. W. (Casey) Vol. 1: 6867
Baldwin Distinguished Service Award; A. Richard Vol. 1: 3308
Balfour Scholarship Vol. 1: 11720
Balfour Silver and Golden Anniversary Award Vol. 1: 14086
BALI National Landscape Awards Vol. 2: 6942
Balint Memorial Award; Michael J. Vol. 1: 18239
Balint Society Essay Prize Vol. 2: 6853
Ball Memorial Award; Clifford Vol. 1: 16990
Ballantine Medal; Stuart Vol. 1: 9739
Ballantyne Award; Harry M. Vol. 2: 6586
Balleroy; Prix Vol. 2: 2429
Ballew Directing Award; Leighton M. Vol. 1: 19485
Ballogie Cup Vol. 2: 8674
Ballot Medal; Buys Vol. 2: 4883
Ballroom Championship Vol. 2: 7915
Balsdon Fellowship Vol. 2: 7135
Baltic Freedom Award
Baltic American Freedom League Vol. 1: 6228
Joint Baltic American National Committee Vol 1: 12426
Baltimore Independent Film/Video Makers Competition Vol. 1: 6230
Balvenie Medal Vol. 2: 7317
Balzan Prize Vol. 2: 3961

BAMP Award Vol. 2: 817
Banana Club (R) Man/Woman of the Year Vol. 1: 11416
Bananister Award Vol. 1: 11416
Bananistry Medal; Doctorate of Vol. 1: 11417
Bananistry Medal; Master of Vol. 1: 11418
Banbury Award; Fernley H. Vol. 1: 1737
Bancroft Award Vol. 1: 18161
Bancroft History Prize; Caroline Vol. 1: 8887
Bancroft - Mackerras Medal Vol. 2: 267
Bancroft Prizes Vol. 1: 8238
Band Booster Award Vol. 1: 14481
Band Director of the Year; National College Vol. 1: 15229
Band Director of the Year; National High School Vol. 1: 15226
Bandeira Paulista Vol. 2: 1194
Bandeirante Trophy Vol. 2: 1168
Banff Concours International de Quatuor A Cordes Vol. 1: 6234
Banff International String Quartet Competition Vol. 1: 6234
Banff Mountain Book Festival Vol. 1: 6235
Banff Mountain Film Festival Vol. 1: 6236
Banff Mountain Photography Competition Vol. 1: 6237
Banff Rockie Award Vol. 1: 6239
Banff Television Festival Vol. 1: 6239
Bangkok Bank Prize for Thai Traditional Music Competition Vol. 2: 6614
Bank of Sweden Prize in Memory of Alfred Nobel Vol. 2: 6171
Bank Senior Silver Medal; Hermann Vol. 2: 2832
Banki Award; Donat Vol. 2: 3310
Banki Donat Dij Vol. 2: 3310
Banks Music Award; Don Vol. 2: 106
Banksiam Medal Vol. 2: 3699
Banner Award Vol. 1: 20316
Banner Competition Vol. 1: 7773
Banta Awards Vol. 1: 21683
Baoren's Award; Professor Wang Vol. 2: 6596
Bappu Memorial Award; INSA - Vainu Vol. 2: 3471
BAPS Annual Prize Vol. 2: 6944
Baptista Rosa de Video; Premio Municipal Joao Vol. 2: 5429
Barbados National Trust Vol. 2: 821
Barbara Hanrahan Fellowship Vol. 2: 597
Barbara Hollander Award Vol. 1: 9403
Barbara Jordan Youth Debates on Health Vol. 1: 15107
Barbato Award; Lewis Vol. 1: 1822
Barbed Wire Award Vol. 1: 2210
Barbier; Prix Vol. 2: 2400
Barbier Prize; Dr. Karel Vol. 2: 953
Barbirolli Memorial; Sir John Vol. 2: 8651
Barbizon Award for Lighting Design Vol. 1: 20643
Barbosa Earth Fund Award; Joseph Vol. 1: 18451
Barbour Award; Buchanan Vol. 2: 8377
Barbour Award; Laura Taber Vol. 1: 9578
Barchi Prize; Richard H. Vol. 1: 13406
Barclay Bank Prize Vol. 2: 7690
Barco Volunteer of the Year; George Vol. 1: 13227
Bard Allied Professional Award; Morton Vol. 1: 15443
Bard Award Vol. 2: 6946
Bard Award; Al Vol. 1: 10551
Bard Awards for Excellence in Architecture and Urban Design Vol. 1: 8026
Bard Foundation Prize; C. R. Vol. 1: 15368
Bard UTI Research Award Vol. 1: 5457
Bardeen Award; John Vol. 1: 13441
Bardet; Prix Rene Vol. 2: 2206
Bareback Horse of the Year Vol. 1: 17655
Baritiu Prize; Gheorghe Vol. 2: 5815
Barkan Article Prize; Omer Lutfi Vol. 1: 20239
Barkan Memorial Award; Manuel Vol. 1: 13956
Barker Award; Kathleen Vol. 2: 8962
Barker Distinguished Research Contribution Award; Roger Vol. 1: 3708
Barker Silver Medal Vol. 2: 7282
Barlow Award of Honor; Thomas E. Vol. 1: 19781
Barlow International Competition Vol. 1: 6249
Barlow Memorial Award Vol. 1: 7181
Barlow Prize Vol. 1: 6249
Barnard Award; Bernard L. Vol. 1: 11267
Barnard Prize; Henry Vol. 1: 10481
Barnard Short Story Award; Marjorie Vol. 2: 335
Barnato Trophy; Woolf Vol. 1: 19682
Barneby Award; Rupert Vol. 1: 16213
Barner Teacher of the Year Award; John C. Vol. 1: 886
Barnes Award; C.H. Vol. 1: 7343
Barnes Award; CMSAF Thomas N. Vol. 1: 337
Barnes Award for Excellence for Community History Projects; Mary Faye Vol. 1: 20036
Barnes Award for Leadership in Chemical Research Management; Earle B. Vol. 1: 1738
Barnes Award; Minnie Vol. 1: 19801
Barnes Award; Rudolph John Vol. 1: 17603
Barnes Life Membership Award; Charles Reid Vol. 1: 4586
Barnes Student Paper Award; K.K. Vol. 1: 4216
Barnett Award; Henry L. Vol. 1: 762
Barnett Prize; Helen Foster Vol. 1: 13778
Barnouw Award; Erik Vol. 1: 16882
Barnum Industry Award; Harold Vol. 1: 11227
Barnutiu Prize; Simion Vol. 2: 5816
Barometer Star Poll Vol. 1: 6570
Baron Award in Fluid-Particle Systems; Thomas Vol. 1: 2759
Baron de Joest; Prix du Vol. 2: 1767
Baron; Premio Fundacion Rene Vol. 2: 9
Baron Travelling Scholarship; Bernhard Vol. 2: 8442
Barr Award; Andy Vol. 1: 5710
Barr Award; Jere. Hess Vol. 1: 3405
Barr Award; Mel Vol. 1: 15366
Barr Award; Myer Vol. 1: 8905
Barr, Jr. Award; Alfred H. Vol. 1: 8143
Barr Memorial Cup; Peter Vol. 2: 8537
Barrabe; Prix Vol. 2: 2401
Barraza Leadership Award; Maclovio Vol. 1: 14805
Barre; Prix Andre Vol. 2: 2108
Barreda; Gabino Vol. 2: 4496
Barrer Award Vol. 2: 8740
Barrett Award; Roland Vol. 1: 21127
Barrett-Colea Foundry Prize Vol. 1: 15698
Barringer Medal
 American Association of Genito-Urinary Surgeons Vol. 1: 1204
 Meteoritical Society Vol 2: 8117
Barringer Memorial Trophy; Lewin B. Vol. 1: 18578
Barrot; Prix Odilon Vol. 2: 2079
Barrow Award; Dame Nita Vol. 2: 9300
Barry Award Vol. 1: 1658
Barry Award; Gerald Vol. 2: 8022
Barry Award in Human Relations; Lillian and Henry Vol. 1: 17321
Barry Award; Redmond Vol. 2: 226
Barry Moffatt Award Vol. 1: 22084
Barry Ohioana Award for Editorial Excellence; James P. Vol. 1: 16657
Barry Prize; Robertine Vol. 1: 7376
Barsauskas premija; Kazimiero Vol. 2: 4384
Barstow Award for Strings - Coleman Vol. 1: 8130
Bart Feminist Activist Award; Pauline Vol. 1: 19376
Bartels Leadership Recognition Award; Elmer C. Vol. 1: 15805
Bartels Medal; Julius Vol. 2: 2308
Bartelsmeyer Award Vol. 1: 3860
Barter Award; Gwen Vol. 2: 8045
Barth Service Award; Alan Vol. 1: 1811
Barthel Jr. Award; Christopher Vol. 2: 1428
Barthel, Jr. Award; Christopher E. Vol. 2: 8002
Bartholome Award for Ethical Excellence; William G. Vol. 1: 763
Bartholomew Award; Harland Vol. 1: 4298
Bartholomew Award; John Vol. 2: 6970
Bartholomew Award; Marshall Vol. 1: 11133
Bartholomew Globe Vol. 2: 8679
Barthou; Prix Alice Louis Vol. 2: 2106
Barthou; Prix Louis Vol. 2: 2177
Barthou; Prix Max Vol. 2: 2189
Bartlett Award; Charlie Vol. 1: 10077
Bartlett Award; Ford Vol. 1: 5209
Bartlett Award; George S. Vol. 1: 1431
Bartlett Lecture Vol. 2: 7496
Bartlett Medal; Sir Frederic Vol. 2: 7442
Bartley Award; Mel W. Vol. 1: 7182
Bartolozzi; Premio Giuseppe Vol. 2: 4016
Barton Medal; C.N. Vol. 2: 370
Barton Top Debate Speaker Award; Phyllis Flory Vol. 1: 15097
Bartow Award; Edward Vol. 1: 1739
Bartow Memorial Award; Buzz
 Meeting Professionals International Vol. 1: 13282
 Meeting Professionals International Vol 1: 13283
Bartram Memorial Education Award Fund; Walt Vol. 1: 19143
Bartsch Award; Paul Vol. 1: 6063
Bartter Award; Frederic C. Vol. 1: 3932
Baruch Essay Award For Students; Bernard M. Vol. 1: 1983
Baruch University Award; Mrs. Simon Vol. 1: 20330
BASE Award Vol. 1: 20431
Baseball Outstanding Volunteer Award Vol. 1: 543
Baseball Players Scholarship Award Vol. 1: 19988
Baseball Research Awards Vol. 1: 18630
Based on Training Programme Classification Award Vol. 2: 7324
Basic Business Management Vol. 2: 9333
Basic Research Prize Vol. 1: 2403
Basic Subvention to the Arts and Cultural Work Vol. 1: 11085
Bass Arts Award Vol. 2: 6762
Bass Ireland Arts Award Vol. 2: 6762

Award Index

Bassett Memorial Award; Johnny F. Vol. 1: 19625
Bassford Student Award; Forrest Vol. 1: 12896
Bassow Award; Whitman Vol. 1: 16981
Bastian-prisen Vol. 2: 5147
Bastian Prize Vol. 2: 5147
Bastien-Lepage; Prix Vol. 2: 1702
Bastien Memorial Cello Award; Vincent R. Vol. 1: 21432
Bastien Memorial Trophy (Outstanding Goaltender); Aldege Baz Vol. 1: 2498
Bastos e Antonio Silva de Interpretacao Teatral; Premios Municipais Palmira Vol. 2: 5441
Basu Memorial Lecture; Professor Sadhan Vol. 2: 3472
Batchelder Award; Mildred L. Vol. 1: 5432
Batchelor Award; J. E. Vol. 2: 583
Batcher Memorial Award; Ralph Vol. 1: 17830
Batchy, Hickey, and Powers Award Vol. 1: 16389
Bates Medal; Sir David Robert Vol. 2: 2309
Bates Memorial Award; P. H. Vol. 1: 5930
Bath County Historical Society Scholarship Vol. 1: 6272
Baton Twirling Achievement Vol. 1: 544
Batten Awards for Excellence in Civic Journalism Vol. 1: 12273
Batten Awards for Innovations in Journalism Vol. 1: 12273
Batten Memorial Trophy; Jean Vol. 2: 5054
Battisti Award; Eugenio Vol. 1: 18934
Battle Award; Helen I. Vol. 1: 7496
Bauer Founders Award; Louis H. Vol. 1: 230
Bauer Memorial Exhibit Award; George Vol. 1: 3201
Bauer Prize; Alfred Vol. 2: 2670
Bauer Prize; Evelyn Vol. 1: 11826
Baum Award; Albert H. Vol. 1: 6678
Baum Memorial Award; L. Frank Vol. 1: 12143
Bauman Award; Mary K. Vol. 1: 5338
Baumann-Trophy; Hans- Vol. 2: 6410
Baumgardt Memorial Fellowship; David Vol. 1: 3423
Baumgarten Award; Alexander Gottlieb Vol. 2: 2936
Baumont; Prix Fanny et Maurice Vol. 2: 2045
Bavarian Academy of Science Competition Prize Vol. 2: 2664
Bavarian Academy of Science Prize Vol. 2: 2665
Baxter Allegiance Prize Health Services Research Vol. 1: 5912
Baxter American Foundation Prize Vol. 1: 5912
Baxter Award Vol. 1: 7460
Baxter Award for Healthcare Management in Europe Vol. 2: 3632
Baxter Awards; Annette K. Vol. 1: 4705
Baxter Diagnostics MicroScan Young Investigator Award Vol. 1: 4134
Baxter Healthcare, Scientific Products Division Graduate Scholarship Vol. 1: 3951
Baxter Prize; Samuel Vol. 2: 8614
Bayer Award Vol. 2: 6769
Bayer Crop Science Award Vol. 1: 17374
Bayer Diagnostics Academic Achievement Award Vol. 2: 5626
Bayer en Ciencias Veterinarias; Premio Vol. 2: 6
Bayer Inc. Awards for High School Chemistry Teachers Vol. 1: 7841
Bayer-Mills Histology Award Vol. 2: 5627
Bayer/Sakura Histology Achievement Award Vol. 2: 5627
Bayer-Snoeyenbos New Investigator Award Vol. 1: 1085
Bayfield Award; St. Clair Vol. 1: 165
Bayle Prijs; Pierre Vol. 2: 4875
Bayles Award Vol. 1: 16093
Baytown Chamber of Commerce Scholarship Vol. 1: 6285
Bazin; Fondation Henry Vol. 2: 1885
BBA's Award for the Best Edited Book Vol. 2: 1213
BBC Award for Best Play Vol. 2: 9057
BBC Environment Award Vol. 1: 7723
BBC Four Samuel Johnson Prize for Non-Fiction Vol. 2: 6885
BBC Wildlife Magazine Art Award Vol. 2: 9081
BC Prize for Poetry Vol. 1: 21521
BCL Award Lecture Vol. 2: 6771
BCLA/BCLT Translation Competition Vol. 2: 6986
BD Biosciences Investigator Award Vol. 1: 1242
BDA International Design Award Vol. 1: 6296
BDMA/Post Office Direct Marketing Awards Vol. 2: 7385
Beadleston Memorial Award; Sam Vol. 1: 3111
Beal Award; James Hartley Vol. 1: 4177
Beale Medal Vol. 2: 8230
Beale Memorial Award; John A. Vol. 1: 18970
Bealer Award Vol. 1: 5135
Beamish Award; Fred Vol. 1: 7829
Beamish Award; Jim Vol. 1: 7398
Bean Award; Dan Vol. 1: 20793
Bean Award; Edward H. Vol. 1: 4913
Bean Memorial Trophy; Gladys Vol. 1: 7209
Beard Award; J. Howard Vol. 1: 14175
Beard Foundation Book Awards; The James Vol. 1: 12285
Beard Foundation/Cervena Council/ D'Artagnan Who's Who of Food and Beverage in America; The James Vol. 1: 12286
Beard Foundation Restaurant Awards; The James Vol. 1: 12287
Beard Humanitarian Award; James Vol. 1: 12287
Beard Memorial Award; Ralph H. Vol. 1: 9016
Bearns Prizes in Music; Joseph H. Vol. 1: 8239
Beasley Award Vol. 1: 8713
Beatrice Pris Vol. 2: 1444
Beattie Medal; Catherine Vol. 1: 9876
Beaubien Award Vol. 1: 5640
Beaudet Award in Orchestra Conducting; Jean-Marie Vol. 1: 6784
Beaujour; Prix Felix de Vol. 2: 2046
Beauperthuy; Fondation Louis-Daniel Vol. 2: 1925
Bechtel Fellowship; Louise Seaman Vol. 1: 5433
Bechtel, Jr. Energy Award; Stephen D. Vol. 1: 4299
Bechtel Pipeline Engineering Award; Stephen D. Vol. 1: 4300
Beck Award; Carl Vol. 1: 12045
Beck International Award Vol. 1: 20794
Beck Scholarship Fund Vol. 1: 7890
Beckenback Book Prize Vol. 1: 13188
Becker Award; Henry E. and Pauline S. Vol. 1: 17340
Becker Award; Joseph Vol. 1: 5402
Becker Distinguished Service Award; Samuel L. Vol. 1: 14706
Becket Memorial Trophy; DeMarco - Vol. 1: 7100
Beckett Crystal Rose Bowl; Peter Alliss and Roy Vol. 2: 8160
Beckman Award; Aldo Vol. 1: 21602
Beckman Founder Award; Arnold O. Vol. 1: 12212
The Becky Award Vol. 1: 3062
Becquerel; Fondation Henri Vol. 2: 1880
Becton Dickinson and Company Award in Clinical Microbiology Vol. 1: 4130
Becton Dickinson Career Achievement Award Vol. 1: 5494
Bedat Award; Andre
International Pharmaceutical Federation Vol. 2: 4828
International Pharmaceutical Federation Vol 2: 4829
Bedells Bursary; Phyllis Vol. 2: 8357
Bedi-Makky Foundry Prize Vol. 1: 15698
Beebe Award; Frank Huntington Vol. 1: 9733
Beekeeper of the Year Vol. 1: 6763
Beekler Award; Martin V. Vol. 1: 10147
Beer and E. Russell Johnston Jr. Outstanding New Mechanics Educator Award; Ferdinand P. Vol. 1: 3998
Beer Prize; George Louis Vol. 1: 2464
Beernaert Prize; August Vol. 2: 954
Beers Award; Clifford W. Vol. 1: 15372
Beeson Career Development Awards in Aging Research; Paul B. Vol. 1: 2222
Beeson Physician Faculty Scholar in Aging Research Award; Paul Vol. 1: 2222
Beethoven Piano Competition; International Vol. 2: 805
Beethoven Scholarship; The Gordon C. Wallis Intermediate Vol. 1: 18318
Beethoven Scholarship; The Gordon C. Wallis Senior Vol. 1: 18320
Begay Memorial Award; Tony Vol. 1: 10424
Behavior Therapy; Distinguished Friend to Vol. 1: 5266
Behavioral Acoustics; Alexander Graham Bell Student Prize in Speech Communication and Vol. 1: 14645
Behavioral Science and Health Service Research Award Vol. 1: 11204
Behavioral Sciences Librarian Award; Distinguished Education and Vol. 1: 5605
Behnke, Award; Albert R. Vol. 1: 20289
Behrens Award Vol. 1: 9606
Beigel Research Award; Hugo G. Vol. 1: 18890
Beijerinck Virology Medal; M. W. Vol. 2: 4884
Beilby Medal and Prize Vol. 2: 8741
Beilstein-Denkmunze; Gmelin- Vol. 2: 2803
Beisswenger Memorial Award; Robert H. Vol. 1: 14578
Belcher Memorial Lectureship; Ronald Vol. 2: 8742
Belford Award; Elizabeth Russell Vol. 1: 18500
Belgian American Educational Foundation Fellowships Vol. 1: 6304
Belgium Prize Vol. 2: 2633

Belinsky Prize Vol. 2: 5904
Belkin Memorial Award; John N. Vol. 1: 3135
Bell Award Vol. 1: 16667
Bell Award; Alexander Graham Vol. 1: 432
Bell Award; Elliott V. Vol. 1: 16225
Bell Award; Grover E. Vol. 1: 2428
Bell Canada Award in Video Art Vol. 1: 6785
Bell DHHS Youth Achievement Award (Deaf and Hard of Hearing Section); Alexander Graham Vol. 1: 433
Bell Honors; Alexander Graham Vol. 1: 434
Bell, Jr. Visiting Scholars Program; Alfred D. Vol. 1: 9694
Bell Lifetime Achievement Award; Campton Vol. 1: 887
Bell Medal; Alexander Graham Vol. 1: 15154
Bell Memorial Award; Lawrence D. Vol. 1: 10391
Bell Prize for Choral Conducting; Leslie Vol. 1: 16737
Bell Prize; Gordon Vol. 1: 10885
Bell Ringer Awards Vol. 1: 17732
Bell Student Prize in Speech Communication and Behavioral Acoustics; Alexander Graham Vol. 1: 14645
Bell Volta Award; Alexander Graham Vol. 1: 435
Bellarmine Medal Vol. 1: 6306
Belleau Award; Bernard Vol. 1: 7830
Belleek Hall of Fame Award Vol. 1: 6308
Beller Medal; Esther Hoffman Vol. 1: 16781
Bellfasher Award Vol. 1: 179
Bellman/Bellwoman of the Year Vol. 1: 2569
Bellman Control Heritage Award; Richard E. Vol. 1: 2760
Bellmanpriset Vol. 2: 6243
Bello; Prix Andres Vol. 2: 6373
Belloise Award; Steve Vol. 1: 12112
Bellwether Prize for Social Justice Fiction Vol. 1: 15998
Belmont Medal Vol. 1: 13321
Belmont Memorial Cup; August Vol. 1: 16257
Belmont Stakes
New York Racing Association Vol. 1: 16257
Triple Crown Productions, Inc. Vol 1: 20206
Belpre Award; Pura
Association for Library Service to Children Vol. 1: 5434
REFORMA: National Association to Promote Library Services to the Spanish-Speaking Vol 1: 17950
Belt of Orion Award Vol. 1: 6834
Beltran de Historia de La Ciencia y La Tecnologia; Premio Dr. Enrique Vol. 2: 4563
Beltran Prize of the History of Science and Technology; Dr. Enrique Vol. 2: 4563
Belvedere Singing Competition; International Hans Gabor Vol. 2: 803
Bemis President's Trophy; F. Gregg Vol. 1: 11157
Bemis Trophy; F. Gregg Vol. 1: 20784
Bemmers Award; H.H. Vol. 1: 17766
Ben David Award; Mordecai Vol. 1: 22023
The Ben Shuster Memorial Award Vol. 1: 666
Benda Prize; Harry J. Vol. 1: 5273
Bendix Automotive Electronics Engineering Award; Vincent Vol. 1: 19035
Bendix Award; Vincent
American Society for Engineering Education Vol. 1: 3995
American Society for Engineering Education Vol 1: 4020
Bendix Minorities in Education Award; Vincent Vol. 1: 3995
Bene Merenti de Patria; Prix Vol. 1: 18605
Benefactor Award Vol. 1: 15908
Benefactors Prize Vol. 2: 7793
Benemerenti Medals
Bavarian Academy of Sciences and Humanities Vol. 2: 2666
The Vatican Vol 2: 9310
Benet Culinary Scholarship; Jane G. Vol. 1: 19410
Benham Award; Rhoda Vol. 1: 13269
Beni Solow Award Vol. 2: 7476
Benjamin Award; Robert Spiers Vol. 1: 16981
Benjamin Castleman Award Vol. 1: 20375
Benjamin Franklin Medal for Distinguished Achievement in Science Vol. 1: 3433
The Benjamin Franklin Medals Vol. 1: 9740
Benjamin Medal; L. R. Vol. 2: 72
Benjamin Memorial Award; Burton Vol. 1: 8297
Benjamin National Memorial Trophy; Henry Vol. 2: 6706
Benjamin Rush Award Vol. 1: 17260
Benjamin; Special Citation in Honor of Rudy and Hertha Vol. 1: 3443
Bennett Award; Harry Vol. 1: 1324
Bennett Award; Hugh Hammond Vol. 1: 19385
Bennett Award; John Vol. 1: 21214
Bennett County Booster Award Vol. 1: 10424
Bennett Fellowship; Viscount Vol. 1: 6964
Bennett Memorial Award; Walter H. Vol. 1: 10727
Bennett Prize; Mrs. Louis Vol. 1: 15698
Bennett Research Awards; A. E. Vol. 1: 19071
Bennett Travelling Fellowship; W. H. Vol. 2: 7841
Bennick New Leadership Award; Paul Vol. 1: 3343
Benny Vol. 1: 17569
Benoist Prize; Marcel Vol. 2: 6308
Benoit Mid-Career Award; Anthony H. Vol. 1: 12936
Benoit; Prix Pierre Vol. 2: 2201
Benoliel de Fotografia; Premio Municipais Joshua Vol. 2: 5424
Benson and Hedges Awards Vol. 2: 615
Benson and Hedges Media Awards Vol. 2: 7617
Benson Award; Clara Vol. 1: 7831
Benson Medal Vol. 2: 8794
Benson Scholarship Fund; Charles E. and Marian Vol. 1: 16630
Bent Spoon Award Vol. 2: 261
Benveniste; Prix de la Fondation Emile Vol. 2: 1745
Benz Award; Carl Vol. 1: 19064
Berakah Award Vol. 1: 16369
Berber Memorial Award; Naomi Vol. 1: 10132
Berdie Memorial Research Award; Ralph F. Vol. 1: 2068
Berg Award; Patty Vol. 1: 12650
Berger Award; Frederick J. Vol. 1: 3999
Berger Award; Meyer Vol. 1: 8248
Berger; Fondation Jean-Jacques Vol. 2: 1901
Berger Memorial Prize; Fred Vol. 1: 3424
Berger; Prix Jean Jacques Vol. 2: 1674
Berggrens pris; Sven Vol. 2: 6186
Bergh Medal of Honor; Henry Vol. 1: 4195
Bergman Plaquette; Ingmar Vol. 2: 6279
Bergmann Memorial Award; Prof. E. D. Vol. 2: 3780
Bergmann; Prix Anton Vol. 2: 1012
Bergstrom Research Award Vol. 1: 5681
Bering Medaillen; Vitus Vol. 2: 1527
Bering Medal; Vitus Vol. 2: 1527
Berkeley Memorial Award; Maureen Vol. 1: 4403
Berkman Chapter of the Year Award; Frank W. Vol. 1: 10552
Berkner Award; Lloyd V. Vol. 1: 1499
Berkowitz Memorial Award; Edward B. Vol. 1: 15820
Berlanda Preis; Emil Vol. 2: 672
Berlin Children's Jury; Prize of the Vol. 2: 2670
Berlin International Film Festival Vol. 2: 2670
Berlin Memorial Outstanding Dissertation Award; CCCC James Vol. 1: 8377
Berliner Award; Emile Vol. 1: 6055
Berliner Morgenpost, Readers Prizes of the Vol. 2: 2670
Bernabei Honor Award; Dr. Raymond Vol. 1: 15275
Bernabei Prize; Emilio Vol. 1: 11827
Bernal Prize; John Desmond Vol. 1: 18855
Bernard Award; Jessie Vol. 1: 4648
Bernard Foundation Prize; Leon Vol. 2: 6562
Bernard Lecture; Claude Vol. 2: 2737
Bernard Lowy Fund Vol. 1: 12952
Bernard R. Sarchet Award Vol. 1: 4053
Bernard Simons Memorial Award Vol. 2: 7909
Bernath Book Prize; Stuart L. Vol. 1: 18678
Bernath Lecture Prize; Stuart L. Vol. 1: 18679
Bernath Scholarly Article Prize; Stuart L. Vol. 1: 18680
Bernays Award; Edward L. Vol. 1: 10555
Bernays Prize Vol. 2: 9046
Berne Memorial Award; Eric Vol. 1: 12093
Bernhard Gold Medal Award; Dianne B. Vol. 1: 17103
Bernhard-Harms-Medaille Vol. 2: 3006
Bernhardt Distinguished Service Award; Homer I. Vol. 1: 4000
Bernheim European Prizes; Emile Vol. 2: 1115
Bernheimer, Jr. Award; Leo G. Bill Vol. 1: 13027
Bernstein Book Award for Excellence in Journalism; Helen B. Vol. 1: 16254
Bernstein-Crosman Scholarship Vol. 1: 13662
Bernstein Grant Vol. 1: 667
Bernstein, M.D. Award; Albion O. Vol. 1: 13272
Bernt Carlesson Memorial Award Vol. 1: 8606
Berntsen Scholarship in Surveying Vol. 1: 1996
Berry Fellowship; Rosann S. Vol. 1: 19019
Berry Medal; Albert E. Vol. 1: 7410
Berry Prize; David Vol. 2: 8531
Berry Scholar Award for Excellence in Writing; Chester A. Vol. 1: 5629

Award Index

Berryman Award for Editorial Cartoons; Clifford K. and James T. Vol. 1: 15526
Berryman Student Research Award; Doris L. Vol. 1: 15878
Berson-Yalow Award Vol. 1: 19226
Bertelsen Prize; Paul and Margaret Vol. 1: 13779
Bertelson Award; Paul Vol. 2: 6026
Berthault; Prix Claude
Academie des Sciences Morales et Politiques Vol. 2: 2028
Academie des Beaux-Arts Vol 2: 1675
Berthault; Prix de Madame Claude Vol. 2: 1991
Berthe; Fondation Aime Vol. 2: 1782
Berthold-Preis Vol. 2: 2881
Bertholf Award for Chapter Efficiency; Lloyd M. Vol. 1: 6323
Bertholf Award for Chapter Excellence; Lloyd M. Vol. 1: 6323
Berton Award; Pierre Vol. 1: 6836
Bertrand; Fondation Paul Vol. 2: 1945
Bertrand; Prix Leon Vol. 2: 2402
Berwick Prize Vol. 2: 8085
Berwick Prize; Senior Vol. 2: 8086
Berzeliusmedaljen I guld Vol. 2: 6205
Besancon International Competition for Young Conductors Vol. 2: 2337
Beskow Plaketten; Elsa Vol. 2: 6285
Beskow Plaque; Elsa Vol. 2: 6285
Beskowska resestipendiet Vol. 2: 6244
BESLA Award Vol. 1: 6421
Bessant Environmental Management Trophy; Martin Vol. 2: 7874
Bessaraboff Prize; Nicolas Vol. 1: 3170
Bessemer Prize Vol. 2: 9046
Bessey Award; Charles Edwin Vol. 1: 6537
Bessie Awards Vol. 1: 8745
Best Academic Paper Vol. 1: 17892
Best American Mouse Award Vol. 1: 12881
Best Animation Making Use of Unusual Techniques Vol. 1: 16935
Best Animation Short Made for the Internet Vol. 1: 16936
Best Annual Bird Report Vol. 2: 6955
Best Appraiser of the Year Vol. 2: 3275
Best Apprentice Competition Vol. 2: 2267
Best Article Award Vol. 1: 6633
Best Article Awards Vol. 2: 3365
Best Article by an Environmental Journalist Vol. 2: 6116
Best Article - *Journal of Parametrics* Award Vol. 1: 12007
Best Article of Journal Amerikastudien/ American Studies Vol. 2: 2786
Best Artificer Award Vol. 2: 9062
Best Athlete Vol. 2: 1401
Best Bet Awards Vol. 1: 7517
Best Bird Book of the Year Vol. 2: 6956
Best Bird of the Christmas Count Vol. 1: 8511
Best Black/Gray Back Piece Vol. 1: 15836
Best Black/Gray Tattoo Vol. 1: 15837
Best Black/White Design Sheet Vol. 1: 15838
Best Book Awards Vol. 2: 9287
Best Booth Award Vol. 1: 1262
Best Booth in Show Vol. 1: 4806
Best Born in Bolivia Vol. 2: 1128
Best Breeder Vol. 2: 1129
Best Broker of the Year Vol. 2: 3276
Best Builder Award Vol. 1: 5245
Best Canadian Feature Award Vol. 1: 6033
Best Canadian Short Award Vol. 1: 6033
Best Cars Vol. 1: 3107
Best CBD's Award Vol. 2: 4346
Best Chapter Event Award Vol. 1: 4102
Best Christmas Tree Vol. 2: 6982
Best Colored Back Piece Vol. 1: 15839
Best Colored Design Sheet Vol. 1: 15840
Best Conference Program Award Vol. 1: 11800
Best Cover-Up Tattoo Vol. 1: 15841
Best Design Vol. 1: 16937
Best Design Award Vol. 2: 3347
BeST Design Awards Vol. 2: 4967
Best Developer of the Year Vol. 2: 3277
Best Doctoral Dissertation Vol. 1: 9404
Best Doctoral Dissertation of the Year Award Vol. 1: 105
Best Documentary Vol. 2: 2977
Best Documentary Award Vol. 2: 8011
Best Drama Award Vol. 2: 8011
Best-Dressed Women Vol. 1: 13654
Best Ecobusinessman Vol. 2: 3359
Best Ecocompany Vol. 2: 3360
Best Educational Production Vol. 1: 16938
Best Educators Award Vol. 2: 3340
Best Electrical Vehicle Award Vol. 2: 853
Best English Mouse Award Vol. 1: 12882
Best Environment Protection Awards Vol. 2: 4765
Best Feature Film Vol. 2: 3839
Best Feature-Length Mountain Film Award Vol. 1: 6236
Best Film Made for Children Vol. 1: 16939
Best Film on Mountain Culture Award Vol. 1: 6236
Best Film on Mountain Environment Award Vol. 1: 6236
Best Film on Mountain Sports Award Vol. 1: 6236
Best First Article Award Vol. 1: 16452
Best First Book Award Vol. 1: 17233
Best First Book in the History of Religions Vol. 1: 831
Best First Feature Award Vol. 1: 21644
Best First Paper Vol. 2: 7942
Best First Presentation Vol. 2: 3223
Best First-time Direction Award Vol. 1: 6033
Best Food Photography Vol. 1: 12285
Best Foreign Feature; Krzysztof Kieslowski Award for Vol. 1: 8883
Best Foreign Film Award Vol. 2: 176
Best Gesneriad Vol. 1: 2364
Best Graduate Film Vol. 1: 16940
Best Graphic Design - Recorded Project Vol. 1: 11424
Best Hosta in a Tour Garden Award Vol. 1: 2551
Best Hosta Seedling or Sport in a Tour Garden Award Vol. 1: 2552
Best Ideas Contest Vol. 1: 4723
Best Illustrated Children's Books of the Year Vol. 1: 16297
Best in American Living Awards
National Association of Home Builders Vol. 1: 14258
Professional Builder - Reed Business Information Vol 1: 17598
Best in Breed Award Vol. 2: 8995
Best in Business Award Vol. 1: 6342
Best in Business Contest Vol. 1: 18964
Best in Media Awards Vol. 1: 7915
Best in Show
American Physicians Art Association Vol. 1: 3504
Westminster Kennel Club Vol 1: 21586
Best In Show Award Vol. 1: 12883
Best in Topical Awards Vol. 1: 4748
Best Indy 500 Camaro Award Vol. 1: 11444
Best Information Science Book Award Vol. 1: 4103
Best Italian Film Vol. 2: 3839
Best *JASIS* Paper Award Vol. 1: 4104
Best Kids Menu Competition Vol. 1: 18010
Best Large Tatoo/Female Vol. 1: 15842
Best Large Tattoo/Male Vol. 1: 15843
Best Letter Award; Taylor and Francis Vol. 2: 8336
Best Liner Notes - Recorded Project Vol. 1: 11424
Best Manager Award Vol. 2: 5973
Best Memorial Award; Elmer S. Vol. 1: 17345
Best Memorial Medal; Elsdon Vol. 2: 5047
Best Music Video Vol. 1: 16941
Best New Design Vol. 1: 6101
Best New Divisional Road Rally Vol. 1: 19702
Best New National Rally Award Vol. 1: 19683
Best New Product Award Vol. 1: 1249
Best New Products Vol. 2: 9197
Best New Regional Road Rally Program Vol. 1: 19702
Best New Technology Vol. 1: 6102
Best of Breed Vol. 1: 8722
Best of Breed or Best of Variety of Breed Vol. 1: 21587
Best of Category Awards; Intel Vol. 1: 18362
Best of Collegiate Design Vol. 1: 8168
Best of Conference Paper Award Vol. 1: 13578
Best of Europe Award Vol. 2: 883
Best of Europe - International Direct Marketing Awards Vol. 2: 884
The Best of Finnish Graphic Design and Advertising Competition Vol. 2: 1627
Best of *Grist* Awards Vol. 1: 15724
Best of Home Architectural Design Award Vol. 1: 5229
Best of Image Awards Vol. 1: 18494
Best of LRTS Award Vol. 1: 5422
Best of Saskatchewan Award Vol. 1: 22048
Best of Show Vol. 1: 9597
Best of Show Award
KA-BAR Knife Collectors Club Vol. 1: 12479
Minot State University - Northwest Art Center Vol 1: 13490
Retail Advertising and Marketing Association Vol 1: 18016
Smithsonian Women's Committee Vol 1: 18574
Best of Show Awards Vol. 1: 12814
Best of the Online Journal Award Vol. 1: 18495
Best of the Rest Award Vol. 1: 20925
Best One-Year Safety Record Award Vol. 1: 17756
Best Paper Vol. 2: 7942
Best Paper Award
American Association of Petroleum Geologists Vol. 1: 1326
American Society for Engineering Education Vol 1: 4001
European Weed Research Society Vol 2: 4771
Geological Society of America Vol 1: 9956
Indian Dairy Association Vol 2: 3441

International Association for Vehicle System Dynamics Vol 2: 1429
International Cryogenic Materials Conference Vol 1: 11532
International Institute of Public Finance Vol 2: 2965
International Wheat Gluten Association Vol 1: 12131
Society of Petrophysicists and Well Log Analysts Vol 1: 19252
West African College of Surgeons Vol 2: 5109
The Best Paper Award Vol. 1: 12126
Best Paper Awards Vol. 1: 19308
Best Paper in *Geophysics* Award Vol. 1: 19117
Best Paper in the *Journal of Sedimentary Research* Award Vol. 1: 18840
Best Paper of the Year Award Vol. 1: 8287
Best Paper on Medical Deontology Vol. 2: 9319
Best Paper Presentation Award Vol. 1: 19253
Best Paper Presented at the Annual Meeting Award Vol. 1: 19118
Best Paper Published in History of Psychology Vol. 1: 3729
Best Paper Published in the *Canadian Journal of Chemical Engineering* Vol. 1: 7832
Best Paper Student Presentation Vol. 1: 18851
Best Papers of the Year Vol. 2: 3224
Best Performance of a Chamber Work Vol. 1: 8108
Best Performance of a New Work Vol. 1: 8108
Best Pet Mouse Award Vol. 1: 12884
Best Portrait Tattoo Vol. 1: 15844
Best Poster Award Vol. 2: 3763
Best Poster Prize Vol. 2: 7005
Best Practical Report Award Vol. 2: 4952
Best Practice Award for Gender Equality Vol. 1: 1146
Best Practice Award for Global and International Teacher Education Vol. 1: 1147
Best Production Performance Awards Vol. 2: 3366
Best Programme ID Vol. 1: 16942
Best Publication Awards Vol. 1: 13927
Best Published Monographs Vol. 2: 5908
Best Radio Script for "Money Talks" Award Vol. 1: 3202
Best Research Cooperative Work Vol. 2: 830
Best Research Paper Vol. 1: 3759
Best Research Paper Award Vol. 2: 5252
Best Restored Steam Engine; John F. Limmer Award for Vol. 1: 15880
Best Scientific or Technological Journal Prize Vol. 2: 9322
Best Scientific Publication Award Vol. 2: 5557
Best Scientific Work Vol. 2: 831
Best Scientific Work of a Young Scientist Vol. 2: 832
Best Seedling Award Vol. 1: 18124
Best Seller Awards Vol. 1: 14358
Best Short Film
Adriaticocinema Festival Vol. 2: 3839
Atlantic Film Festival Association Vol 1: 6033
Best Short Mountain Film Award Vol. 1: 6236
Best Short Subject; Stan Brakhage Award for Vol. 1: 8881
Best Show of the Year Vol. 2: 5552
Best SIG Publication Award Vol. 1: 4105
Best Single Education Program Vol. 1: 17893
Best Sleeve Vol. 1: 15845
Best Space Operations Crew Award Vol. 1: 338
Best Stand Vol. 2: 9198
Best Stand of the Year Vol. 2: 5553
Best Stock Z28 Award Vol. 1: 11445
Best Student Film Vol. 2: 1392
Best Student Paper Vol. 1: 18774
Best Student Paper Award
American Association of Petroleum Geologists Vol. 1: 1327
American Society for Information Science and Technology Vol 1: 4112
International Institute of Fisheries Economics and Trade Vol 1: 11684
Micronet R & D Vol 1: 13366
Society of Nematologists Vol 1: 19219
Best Student Paper of the Year Award Vol. 1: 106
Best Student Paper/Poster Award Vol. 1: 8674
Best Student Poster Award Vol. 1: 1328
Best Student Presentation Award Vol. 1: 7338
Best Student Scientific Work Vol. 2: 833
Best Student Writer Award Vol. 1: 15355
Best Subscriber Communication Program Vol. 1: 15859
Best Subsequent Book Award Vol. 1: 17234
Best Suppliers Award; CEDA Grand Prix Award and CEDA Vol. 2: 7242
Best Tattooed Female Vol. 1: 15846
Best Tattooed Male Vol. 1: 15847
Best Tattooist Vol. 1: 15848
Best Teacher of the Year Vol. 2: 9295
Best Team Vol. 2: 1402
Best Television Commercial/Advertising Film of the Year Vol. 2: 5204
Best Television Series for Adults Vol. 1: 16943
Best Television Special Vol. 1: 16944
Best Theoretical Paper Award Vol. 1: 3760
Best Theoretical Paper on Hypnosis Award Vol. 1: 18657
Best Trade Show Product and Best Booth Display Vol. 1: 6167
Best Traditional Tattoo Vol. 1: 15849
Best Transaction Paper Vol. 1: 10654
Best Travel Air Vol. 1: 20168
Best UKRAINPEX Show Theme Exhibit Vol. 1: 20276
Best Unionist Vol. 2: 3341
Best Unique Tattoo Vol. 1: 15850
Best Unpublished Research Paper Vol. 1: 9405
Best Use of Music or Sound Vol. 1: 6848
Best Wine Lists in America Awards Vol. 1: 18011
Best Written and Researched Article Vol. 1: 8651
Bet Nahrain National Awards Vol. 1: 6317
Beta Phi Mu Award Vol. 1: 2969
Better Business Bureau Integrity Award Vol. 1: 6340
Better Communications Contest Vol. 1: 21265
Better Life Award Vol. 1: 2394
Better Newspaper Advertising Contest Vol. 1: 15411
Better Newspaper Contest Vol. 1: 15411
Better Newspapers Competition Vol. 1: 7034
Bettineski Child Advocate of the Year Award; G. F. Vol. 1: 14874
Bettis Fellowship Award; John Vol. 1: 19403
Betton Youth Exhibit Award; James L. Vol. 1: 3203
Between the Lines Award Best Gay/Lesbian Film Vol. 1: 4969
Beule; Fondation de Mme. Veuve Vol. 2: 1717
Beule; Prix Karl Vol. 2: 1676
Beveridge Award; Albert J. Vol. 1: 2465
Beverly Buntin Volunteer of the Year Vol. 1: 7695
Beverly Hills Theatre Guild Play Competition for Children's Theatre Vol. 1: 6349
Beville, Jr. Award; Hugh Malcolm Vol. 1: 14106
Beydoun Memorial Award for Best International Poster; Ziad Vol. 1: 1329
Beyer Award; Robert Vol. 1: 10985
BFA President's Award Vol. 1: 6215
BG Wildlife Photographer of the Year Competition Vol. 2: 8205
BGA Tribute Award Vol. 1: 6346
BGRC Silver Jubilee Oration Award Vol. 2: 3407
BGS Prize Vol. 2: 7022
Bhabha Medal; Homi J. Vol. 2: 3473
Bharat Ratna Vol. 2: 3377
Bharati Prize; Vidya Vol. 2: 3445
Bhargava Memorial Medal; Professor K.P. Vol. 2: 3474
Bhasha Samman Vol. 2: 4308
Bhasker Award Vol. 2: 4677
Bhatnagar Award Vol. 2: 3373
Bhatt Young Investigator Award; Pravin N. Vol. 1: 1023
BHCA Award Vol. 2: 7029
Bhoruka Gold Medal Vol. 2: 3446
Bi-Annual Image Awards Vol. 1: 21734
Bialkowski Prize; Grzegorz Vol. 2: 5363
Bianchi Cup Vol. 1: 15646
Biancotto Aerobatics Diploma; Leon Vol. 2: 6322
BIAT Open Award for Technical Excellence in Architectural Technology Vol. 2: 7034
Bibby Cup Vol. 2: 7195
Bible Society Award; American Vol. 1: 1563
Biblioteca Breve Prize Vol. 2: 6015
BIBM Awards Vol. 2: 914
Bicentenary Medal
Linnean Society of London Vol. 2: 8069
Royal Society for the Encouragement of Arts, Manufactures & Commerce Vol 2: 8710
Bicentennial Fiction Award Vol. 2: 619
Bick Award Vol. 1: 12948
Bick Ehrenmedaille; Dr. Josef Vol. 2: 683
Bickel Award; John O. Vol. 1: 4301
Bickersteth Memorial Medal; Julian Vol. 2: 7698
Bicking Award; Lew Vol. 1: 15794
Bidault de l'Isle; Prix G. Vol. 2: 2552
Biedenbach Distinguished Service Award; Joseph M. Vol. 1: 4002
Biedma Award; Dr. Carlos A. Vol. 2: 26
Bienal de Iberoamericana de Arte Vol. 2: 4515
Bienal Internacional de Cine Cientifico Vol. 2: 9297

Bienal Internacional del Cartel en Mexico Vol. 2: 4642
Bienek Preis fur Lyrik; Horst Vol. 2: 2659
Biennale Internationale de Gravure Vol. 2: 5978
Biennale Jonge Nederlandse Architecten Vol. 2: 4921
Biennial AIDIS Prize Vol. 1: 11100
Biennial Award Vol. 1: 141
Biennial Communications Award Vol. 1: 447
Biennial Composers Competition Vol. 1: 847
Biennial Exhibition Awards
Museum of New Mexico Vol. 1: 13689
Museum of New Mexico Vol 1: 13690
Biennial of Young Dutch Architects Vol. 2: 4921
Bier Award; William C. Vol. 1: 3701
Biesbroeck Prize; George Van Vol. 1: 1508
Bietila Award; Paul Vol. 1: 20795
BIFA Freight Services Award Vol. 2: 7051
Big Brother of the Year Vol. 1: 6366
Big Bucks Award Vol. 1: 2553
Big Chief Award Vol. 1: 10097
Big East Conference Academic Awards Vol. 1: 6369
Big Muddy Film Festival Awards Vol. 1: 6372
Big Oscars Vol. 1: 6280
Big Sister of the Year Vol. 1: 6367
Big Stick Award; Rawlings Vol. 1: 17882
Bigelow Trophy Vol. 1: 8079
Biggs Fellowship; E. Power Vol. 1: 16868
Bignami Prize; Paolo Vol. 2: 4042
Bigsby Medal Vol. 2: 7559
Bijnsprijs; Anna Vol. 2: 4703
Bikila Award; Abebe Vol. 1: 16259
Bilac Prize; Olavo Vol. 2: 1154
Bilgrami Memorial Medal; Professor Krishna Sahai Vol. 2: 3475
Bilim Odulu Vol. 2: 6648
Bill Griffiths Memorial Conservation Award Vol. 1: 20213
Bill Napoli Award Vol. 1: 17218
Bill Ogden Memorial Prize Vol. 2: 8330
Bill Rosenberg Award Vol. 1: 9416
Billard Award; Admiral Frederick C. Vol. 1: 15384
Billboard Music Awards Vol. 1: 6377
Billboard Radio Awards Vol. 1: 6378
Billingsley Memorial Scholarship; Dewayne Vol. 1: 20040
Billington Book Award; Ray A. Vol. 1: 21579
Billington Prize; Ray Allen Vol. 1: 16883
Billwiller Award Vol. 1: 7797
Biltris Prize; Doctor Raoul Vol. 2: 970
Binani Gold Medal Vol. 2: 3447
Binder Award; Joseph Vol. 2: 6531
Bindesboll Medal; Thorvald Vol. 2: 1520
Binet-Sangle; Prix Docteur Vol. 2: 2135
Bing Award; Elisabeth Vol. 1: 12669
Bing Prize; Robert Vol. 2: 6505
Bingham Medal Vol. 1: 19299
Bingham Media Award; Barry Vol. 1: 12566
Bingham Poetry Prize Vol. 1: 6521
Bingham Prize; Worth Vol. 1: 6386
Binkhorst Medal Lecture Vol. 1: 4273
Binkley Award; Thomas Vol. 1: 9058
Binkley-Stephenson Award Vol. 1: 16884
Binneweg Trophy; Ed Vol. 1: 20618
Binney Memorial Award Vol. 2: 7573
Bio-Medical Research Vol. 1: 5129
Bio-Mega/Boehringer Ingelheim Award for Organic or Bioorganic Chemistry Vol. 1: 7833
Bio-Serv Award in Experimental Animal Nutrition Vol. 1: 4156
Bio-Tech Award Vol. 2: 4828
Biochemical Society Award Vol. 2: 6862
Biochemical Society Honorary Member Vol. 2: 6863
Biochemical Society Travel Fund Vol. 2: 6864
Biological Mineralization Research Award Vol. 1: 11205
Biological Physics Prize Vol. 1: 3449
Biomedical Engineering Outstanding Educator Award Vol. 1: 4039
Biomedical Instrumentation & Technology Outstanding Paper Awards Vol. 1: 5489
bioMerieux Award Vol. 1: 11580
bioMerieux Sonnenwirth Award for Leadership in Clinical Microbiology Vol. 1: 4131
Biometeorological Research Foundation Award Vol. 1: 11978
Biota Award for Medicinal Chemistry Vol. 2: 509
Biotechnology Research Award Vol. 1: 4132
Biotechnology Teaching Award Vol. 1: 14091
Bir Nycomed Amersham Fellowship Vol. 2: 7043
Birch Award; Carroll L. Vol. 1: 3077
Birch Tree Books Awards Vol. 2: 5033
Bird Dog Award Vol. 1: 8302
Bird Illustrator of the Year Vol. 2: 6957
Bird Photograph of the Year Vol. 2: 6958
Birds in Art Vol. 1: 21828
Birdsall Prize in European Military and Strategic History; Paul Vol. 1: 2466
Birdseye Award; Clarence Vol. 2: 2483
Birkebeinerrennet Ski Race Vol. 2: 5126
Birkenhead International Colour Salon Vol. 2: 6876
Birkhoff Prize; George David Vol. 1: 18731
Birkhoff Prize in Applied Mathematics; George David Vol. 1: 3041
Birla Award; R. D. Vol. 2: 3527
Birla Memorial Gold Medal; G. D. Vol. 2: 3448
Birmingham Medal Vol. 2: 7842
BIS Bibilographic Instruction Publication of the Year Award Vol. 1: 5610
Bischoff Award; Ernst Vol. 1: 992
Bishop Award; Joan Fiss Vol. 1: 18403
Bishop, III Memorial Trophy; Louis F. Vol. 1: 21588
Bisson Award; Edmond E. Vol. 1: 19343
Bittner Extension Award in Horticulture; Carl S. Vol. 1: 4089
Bittner Service Citation for Outstanding Service in UCEA; Walton S. Vol. 1: 20946
Bizet; Prix Georges
Academie des Beaux-Arts Vol. 2: 1677
Institut de France Vol 2: 2422
Bjerknes Medal; Vilhelm Vol. 2: 2310
Blachowski Award; Professor Stefan Vol. 2: 5371
Blachowskiego; Nagroda im. Profesora Stefana Vol. 2: 5371
Black Award; Elliott - Vol. 1: 2202
Black Award for Excellence in Children's Literature; Irma S. and James H. Vol. 1: 6241
Black Award for Excellence in Children's Literature; Irma Simonton Vol. 1: 6241
Black Award for Outstanding Achievement in the Practice of Counseling Psychology; John D. Vol. 1: 3661
Black Award; Mary Vol. 2: 6707
Black Caucus Award for Excellence in Librarianship; DEMCO/ALA Vol. 1: 6417
Black Caucus Certificate of Appreciation Vol. 1: 6412
Black Caucus of the American Library Association Literary Awards Vol. 1: 6413
Black Caucus of the American Library Association Trailblazer's Award Vol. 1: 6414
Black Caucus Special Recognition Plaques Vol. 1: 6415
Black Engineer of the Year Awards Vol. 1: 7585
Black History Month Contest Vol. 1: 12912
Black Lung Association Award Vol. 1: 6429
Black Lyon Vol. 2: 3891
Black Memorial Prizes; James Tait Vol. 2: 9172
Black Prize; Duncan Vol. 1: 17707
Black Tie Award Vol. 1: 11633
Black Travel Fellowship; Malcolm Vol. 2: 8443
Blackall Machine Tool and Gage Award Vol. 1: 4503
Blackburn Prize; Susan Smith Vol. 1: 19854
Blackhorse Scholarship Vol. 1: 6
Blackstone Award; Harry Vol. 1: 11801
Blackwell Medal; Elizabeth Vol. 1: 3079
Blackwell Memorial Lecture; W. H. M. Vol. 2: 4977
Blackwell's Scholarship Award Vol. 1: 5423
The Blade Magazine Manufacturers Awards Vol. 1: 6444
Blagoev Prize; Dimiter Vol. 2: 1207
Blaine Award Vol. 2: 7158
Blair-Bell Medal Vol. 2: 8800
Blair-Bell Memorial Lectureship in Obstetrics and Gynaecology; William Vol. 2: 8444
Blair Biorheology Scholarship; Pergamon Scott Vol. 2: 7191
Blair Eminent Naturalist Award; W. Frank Vol. 1: 19530
Blair Leadership Services Awards; Trish Vol. 1: 1484
Blair Memorial Award; W. Frank Vol. 1: 7895
Blair Service Award; Lucy Vol. 1: 3484
Blair Trophy; Hunter Vol. 2: 8675
Blake Award for Distinguished Graduate Teaching; M. A. Vol. 1: 4090
Blakeley Lifetime Achievement Award; Dr. Phyllis R. Vol. 1: 9516
Blakely Award; S. J. Vol. 1: 9613
Blakeslee Fellowship in Science Writing; Rennie Taylor/Alton Vol. 1: 8563
Blakey Memorial Prize; O. F. Vol. 2: 371
Blanc; Prix Armand Vol. 2: 2944
Blanc Prize; Armand Vol. 2: 2944
Blanche; Prix Robert Vol. 2: 2009
Blaskeslee Awards; Howard W. Vol. 1: 2404
Blasters Leadership Award Vol. 1: 11992
BIAT National Student Award Vol. 2: 7035
Blaylock Medal; Selwyn G. Vol. 1: 7183
Bledisloe Aviation Trophy Vol. 2: 5055
Bledisloe Gold Medal for Landowners Vol. 2: 8409
Bledisloe Veterinary Award Vol. 2: 8416
Bledsoe Award; C. Warren Vol. 1: 5339
Blegen Award; Julius Vol. 1: 20796
Blegen Award; Theodore C.
Forest History Society Vol. 1: 9695
Minnesota Historical Society Vol 1: 13475
Bleininger Award; Albert Victor Vol. 1: 1667
Blekinge County Council Culture Prize Vol. 2: 6139

Blekinge County Council Environment Prize Vol. 2: 6140
Blekinge lans landstings kulturpris Vol. 2: 6139
Blekinge lans landstings Miljo vardspris Vol. 2: 6140
Blenheim Award Vol. 1: 7984
Bleriot Medal; Louis Vol. 2: 6323
Blewett Playwright's Award; Jill Vol. 2: 597
BLG Awards Vol. 1: 7210
Blick Art Materials Award; Dick Vol. 1: 17103
Blick Merchandise Award; Dick Vol. 1: 18980
Blignault Medal; Andries Vol. 2: 5713
Blind Service Association Scholarships Vol. 1: 6453
Bliss Editors' Award; A. Harry Vol. 1: 14941
Bliss Medal Vol. 1: 18983
Bliss Memorial Award; Gordon M. Vol. 1: 4204
Bliss Prize Fellowship in Byzantine Studies Vol. 1: 9049
Blizil Memorial Literature Award; George A. Vol. 1: 9984
Bloch Award; Herbert Vol. 1: 4384
Block Community Lecture Series; I. E. Vol. 1: 18732
Block Prize; Jochen Vol. 2: 2909
Blodger Diversity Award; John D. Vol. 1: 13235
Bloem Distinguished Service Award; Delmar L. Vol. 1: 1962
Blomska stipendiet Vol. 2: 6245
Bloom Memorial Award; A. A. Vol. 1: 20251
Bloom Memorial Scholarship Fund; Amy L. Vol. 1: 20249
Bloomer Award; H. H. Vol. 2: 8070
Bloomfield Award; John J. Vol. 1: 2610
BLS Service of the Year Award Vol. 1: 14219
Blue Angel Vol. 2: 2670
Blue Heron, Green Heron Vol. 1: 18423
Blue Pencil Awards Vol. 1: 14242
Blue Planet Prize Vol. 2: 4090
Blue Ribbon Awards Vol. 1: 6571
Bluebird Research Grants Vol. 1: 16395
Bluegrass Music Awards Vol. 1: 18879
Blues Hall of Fame Vol. 1: 6473
Blues Music Awards (W. C. Handy Awards) Vol. 1: 6474
Blum; Bourse Marcelle Vol. 2: 2010
Blumer Award; Herbert Vol. 1: 18930
Blumlein-Brown-Willans Premium Vol. 2: 7794
Blundell Grants; K. Vol. 2: 8979
Blunk Memorial Award; Jim Vol. 1: 20414
Blutet; Fondation Paul Doistau - Emile Vol. 2: 1946
Bly Cub Reporter Award; Nellie Vol. 1: 16242
BMA Hall of Fame Vol. 1: 6712
BMC Research Paper Prize Vol. 1: 7138
BMEC Donald Maxwell Award Vol. 2: 7706
BMI Student Composer Awards Vol. 1: 6643
BMMA Awards Vol. 1: 6393
BNA - Cube Vol. 2: 4881
BNA - Kubus Vol. 2: 4881
BNES Conference Awards Vol. 2: 7089
BNES International Conference Award Vol. 2: 7090
Board Awards Vol. 1: 5835
Board of Directors' Award
American Gear Manufacturer Association Vol. 1: 2318
Healthcare Financial Management Association Vol 1: 10337
National Religious Broadcasters Vol 1: 15611
Board of Directors Award of Recognition Vol. 1: 5574
Board of Directors Awards Vol. 1: 14606
Board of Directors Distinguished Service Award for Senior ACS Administrators Vol. 1: 1740
Board of Directors Student Paper Awards Vol. 1: 8489
Board of Governors Award Vol. 1: 6053
Board of Governors Service Award—Model State/Regional Society Program Vol. 1: 745
Board of Governors Trophy Vol. 1: 14298
Board of Publications Award for the Best Paper in *Toxicological Sciences* Vol. 1: 19332
Boardman Tasker Award for Mountain Literature Vol. 2: 6878
Boas Medal; Walter Vol. 2: 214
Boase Award of the Reinforced Concrete Research Council; Arthur J. Vol. 1: 4302
Boating Writers International Annual Writing Contest Vol. 1: 6494
Bob Craig Memorial Scholarship Vol. 1: 21529
Bob Gomulinski Community Service Award Vol. 1: 4947
Bob Houston Memorial Award Vol. 1: 20070
Bob McLaughlin Vintage Spirit Award Vol. 1: 8516
Bob Sawyer Award Vol. 1: 8343
Bob Show Golden Age Award Vol. 1: 15851
Bob Stroud Memorial Rookie of the Year Award National Midget Car Div. Vol. 1: 20415
Bob Welby Memorial Recognition of Service Award Vol. 1: 12037
Bobbitt National Prize for Poetry; Rebekah Johnson Vol. 1: 12832
Bobby Chapter of the Year Award; Lloyb Vol. 1: 8429
Bobst Literary Awards; Elmer Holmes Vol. 1: 16301
Bocher Memorial Prize Vol. 1: 3042
Bock Prize; Frederick Vol. 1: 17418
Bocking Award; Douglas Vol. 1: 6625
Bocking Memorial Award; James H. Vol. 1: 6965
Bockus Medal; H. L. Vol. 2: 3143
Bode - Pearson Prize Vol. 1: 4706
Boedecker Jr. Distinguished Service Award; Kenneth J. Vol. 1: 5931
Boehm Graduate Fellowship in the Fisheries Sciences; Andrew J. Vol. 1: 4671
Boehm Medal Vol. 2: 2884
Boehringer Ingelheim Award for Organic or Bioorganic Chemistry Vol. 1: 7833
Boehringer Mannheim Award Vol. 1: 7452
Boehringer Mannheim Prize Vol. 2: 5628
Boehringer Mannheim S.A. Award Vol. 2: 5628
Boehringer Mannheim Student Poster Awards Vol. 1: 7452
Boeing Award Vol. 1: 5210
Boeing Student Research Award Vol. 1: 20170
Boerma Award; A. H. Vol. 2: 3947
Boger Award; Robert F. Vol. 1: 8446
Bogg Memorial Award; Wm. G. Vol. 1: 8357
Boggess Award; William R. Vol. 1: 4825
Boggs Award; Larry Vol. 1: 14577
Boggs Award; Lindy Vol. 1: 3292
Boggs Award; Phil Vol. 1: 21169
Boggs Service Award; Andrew T. Vol. 1: 4424
Bogie Prize; David Vol. 2: 7665
Bogin Memorial Award; George Vol. 1: 17428
Bogomolny National Service Award; Richard J. Vol. 1: 7792
Bohlen Award; Avis Vol. 1: 2278
Bok Award; Priscilla and Bart Vol. 1: 1509
The Bok Prize Vol. 2: 92
Bold Award; Harold C. Vol. 1: 17301
Boldenweck Voice Scholarship; Elizabeth Vol. 1: 13662
Boldrewood Award; Rolf Vol. 2: 324
Boldy Memorial Award; Julian Vol. 1: 7184
Bolivar Award; Simon Vol. 1: 3615
Bolivar Prize; International Simon Vol. 2: 2594
Bolliger Memorial Lecture; Hans R. Vol. 2: 8999
Bolling Cross Vol. 1: 15
Bollingen Prize in Poetry Vol. 1: 22013
Bollinger Humanitarian Award; Glen Vol. 1: 10352
Bolsa de Cereales de Buenos Aires; Premio Vol. 2: 7
Bolster Memorial Award; Harry Vol. 1: 21254
Bolt Award; CAA Carol Vol. 1: 6952
Bolton Award for Professional Excellence Vol. 1: 14079
Bolton Memorial Prize; Herbert Eugene Vol. 1: 8380
Boltzmann Medal Vol. 1: 12104
Bombardier Prize in Technological Innovation; J. Armand Vol. 1: 5538
Bomford Prize; Guy Vol. 2: 1500
Bomm/Presidential Citation Vol. 1: 5578
Bonazinga Award; Marie T. Vol. 1: 18785
Bonchev Prize; Academician George Vol. 2: 1207
Bond Award Vol. 2: 9348
Bond Award; Polly Vol. 1: 9310
Bond Memorial Consumer Award; Ethel Vol. 1: 14138
Bonder Scholarship for Applied Operations Research in Military Applications Vol. 1: 11068
Bonder Scholarship in Health Care Vol. 1: 11069
Bonderman IUPUI Youth Theatre Playwriting Competition and Workshop; Waldo M. and Grace C. Vol. 1: 10777
Bonduelle; Prix Paul Vol. 2: 1000
Bonhoeffer-Eucen-Scheibe Memorial Lecture Vol. 2: 2793
Bonin Award; Wilbrod Vol. 1: 6625
Bonn Mileata Calmachta; An Vol. 2: 3653
Bonn Seirbhise Dearscna; An Vol. 2: 3652
Bonner Prize in Nuclear Physics; Tom Vol. 1: 3450
Bonnet; Fondation Andre C. Vol. 2: 1793
Bonniers donationsford; Stipendium ur Gerard Vol. 2: 6246
Bonniers Pris; Gerard Vol. 2: 6247
Bono Engineering Communications Award; Jack Vol. 1: 19127
Bonsai and Orchid Association Award Vol. 1: 6500
Book Award
British Psychological Society Vol. 2: 7121
Canadian Railroad Historical Association Vol 1: 7368

New York Genealogical and Biographical Society Vol 1: 16231
Please Touch Museum Vol 1: 17402
The Poetry Center & American Poetry Archives Vol 1: 17426
Religious Communication Association Vol 1: 17981
Scribes Vol 1: 18379
Society for Human Resource Management Vol 1: 18696
Wisconsin State Genealogical Society Vol 1: 21691
Book Award; Children's Literature Association Vol. 1: 7909
Book Award; World Vol. 1: 7656
Book Awards
Children's Literature Council of Southern California Vol. 1: 7913
South Carolina Association of School Librarians Vol 1: 19443
Book Awards; Gold Medallion Vol. 1: 9354
Book Awards; Land of Enchantment Vol. 1: 16194
Book Awards of the National Book Development Council of Singapore Vol. 2: 5940
Book Design Awards Vol. 2: 255
Book of Honor Vol. 2: 5033
Book of Spring, Summer, Autumn, Winter in Slovakia; Most Beautiful and the Best Children's Vol. 2: 5960
Book-of-the-Month Club Translation Prize; PEN Vol. 1: 17146
Book of the Year
British Chess Federation Vol. 2: 6977
Healthcare Information and Management Systems Society Vol 1: 10348
Hungarian Publishers and Booksellers Association Vol 2: 3272
Book of the Year Award
Academy of Parish Clergy Vol. 1: 119
MIND - National Association for Mental Health Vol 2: 8122
Book-of-the-Year Award Vol. 1: 12510
Book of the Year Award: Early Childhood Vol. 2: 303
Book of the Year Award; Fiction Vol. 1: 6988
Book of the Year Award; Non-Fiction Vol. 1: 6991
Book of the Year Award: Older Readers Vol. 2: 304
Book of the Year Award; Sanderson Young Adult Vol. 2: 649
Book of the Year Award: Younger Readers Vol. 2: 305
Book of the Year for Children Award Vol. 1: 7259
Book of the Year for Children Award; Canadian Library Association Vol. 1: 7254
Book of the Year for Children Medal Vol. 1: 7254
Book of the Year; Specialty Vol. 1: 6994
Book Prize Vol. 2: 905
Book Prize
American Philosophical Association Vol. 1: 3425
British Association for Applied Linguistics Vol 2: 6929
Canadian Society of Animal Science - Agricultural Institute of Canada Vol 1: 7440
Law and Society Association Vol 1: 12721
Singapore Industrial Automation Association Vol 2: 5948
Society for the Historians of the Early American Republic Vol 1: 18868
Society of Legal Scholars in the United Kingdom and Ireland Vol 2: 9055
Book Prize; Edmonton Vol. 1: 21984
Book Prize; Marshall Shulman Vol. 1: 1058
Book Prize; W.O. Mitchell City of Calgary Vol. 1: 21986
Book Prizes of the Circle of the Greek Children's Book Vol. 2: 3169
Book Publishers of Texas Children's/Young People's Award Vol. 1: 20011
Book Sense Book of the Year Award Vol. 1: 1582
Bookbuilders West Book Show Vol. 1: 6513
Booker McConnell Prize Vol. 2: 6880
Booker Prize Vol. 2: 6880
Booker Russian Novel Prize Vol. 2: 6881
Books Abroad/Neustadt International Prize Vol. 1: 21934
Bookseller of the Year Award Vol. 1: 6982
Bookseller of the Year Award; Campus Vol. 1: 6983
Bookseller of the Year Award; Chain Vol. 1: 6984
Bookseller of the Year Award; Specialty Vol. 1: 6995
Boom Award; Roger W. Vol. 1: 8679
Boone and Crockett Award Vol. 1: 11357
Boone Award; Joel T. Vol. 1: 5765
Boosey and Hawkes Youth Orchestra Award Vol. 2: 8166
Boosey Award; Leslie
Performing Right Society Vol. 2: 8255
Royal Philharmonic Society Vol. 2: 8652
Booster Award Vol. 1: 1979
Booth Award Vol. 1: 19590
Booth Award; Edwin Vol. 1: 8054
Booth Award; Taylor Vol. 1: 10886
Boothby Award; Walter M. Vol. 1: 231
Boothby - Edwards Award Vol. 1: 231
Boothman Bursary; Harry Vol. 1: 7324
Boots Romantic Novel of the Year Vol. 2: 8347
Borciani; Premio Paolo Vol. 2: 4054
Bordalo Pinheiro de Banda Desenhada, Cartoon e Caricaturista; Premio Municipal Rafael Vol. 2: 5435
Borden Award
American Association Family Consumer Sciences Vol. 1: 938
American Dairy Science Association Vol 1: 2105
Association of American Medical Colleges Vol 1: 5559
Borden Award in Nutrition Vol. 1: 7435
Bordin; Prix
Academie des Beaux-Arts Vol. 2: 1703
Academie des Inscriptions et Belles-Lettres Vol 2: 1761
Borduas; Prix Paul-Emile- Vol. 1: 17797
Borgia; Fondazione Premio Dotte Giuseppe Vol. 2: 3822
Boright Hewitt and Maybelle E. Ball Hewitt Award; William Vol. 1: 3536
Borman Award; Alvah K. Vol. 1: 4003
Born Award; Max Vol. 1: 16782
Born Medal and Prize; Max Vol. 2: 7723
Born-Preis; Max- Vol. 2: 2722
Bosch Foundation Fellowship Program; Robert Vol. 1: 7687
Bose Medal; A. K. Vol. 2: 3449
Bose Medal; Satyendranath Vol. 2: 3476
Bose Memorial Award; Anil Kumar Vol. 2: 3477
Boston College Student Paper Competition Vol. 1: 6523
Boston Globe - Horn Book Awards Vol. 1: 6526
Boston Marathon Vol. 1: 6519
Bosustow Award; Grace Vol. 2: 8358
Boswell Award Vol. 2: 5766
Botein Fellowships; Stephen Vol. 1: 916
Botelho da Costa Veiga Prize; Augusto Vol. 2: 5482
Botelho de Pintura; Premio Municipal Carlos Vol. 2: 5427
Bottle Show Champion; National Vol. 2: 6855
Bottorf Award; Jim Vol. 1: 68
Bottorff Award; Lasher- Vol. 1: 1086
Bouchard; Fondations Bellion - Charles Vol. 2: 1977
Bouchard; Prix Charles Vol. 2: 1977
Boucher-OCLC Distinguished Interlibrary Loan Library Award; Virginia Vol. 1: 17935
Bouchet Award; Edward A. Vol. 1: 3451
Bouffault Memorial Award in International Animal Agriculture Vol. 1: 4258
Bouillon Award; Lincoln Vol. 1: 4425
Bouland; Prix Leclerc - Maria Vol. 2: 1678
Boulanger Award; Jean P. Vol. 1: 19003
Bound to Stay Bound Books Scholarship Vol. 1: 5435
Bouquet of the Month Vol. 1: 16535
Bourcart; Fondation Jacques Vol. 2: 1892
Bourcart; Prix Jacques Vol. 2: 2403
Bourgelat Award Vol. 2: 7159
Bourke Lectureship Vol. 2: 8743
Bourne Student Poetry Award; Louise Louis/ Emily F. Vol. 1: 17433
Bourse Vol. 2: 2573
Bourse Bancroft Vol. 1: 18161
Bourse Harry Boothman Vol. 1: 7324
Bourse Marcelle Blum Vol. 2: 2010
Bourses Commemoratives E. W. R. Steacie Vol. 1: 16025
Bourses de quatre mois Vol. 1: 13330
Boury Prize; Karel Vol. 2: 955
Bouscatel; Prix Jean Vol. 2: 2165
Bouwer Prize; Alba Vol. 2: 5643
Bouwhuis Memorial Scholarship; Rev. Andrew L. Vol. 1: 7651
Bovey Award; Edmund C. Vol. 1: 8543
Bow Making Competition; International Violin and Vol. 2: 2281
Bowditch Award Lecture Vol. 1: 3508
Bowen Award; N.L. Vol. 1: 2343
Bowen Medal; R. W. Vol. 2: 5725
Bowen Memorial Award Competition; Betty Vol. 1: 18393
Bowen Public Relations Award; Harold S. Vol. 1: 10728
Bower Award and Prize for Achievement in Science Vol. 1: 9741
Bower Award for Business Leadership Vol. 1: 9742
Bower Memorial Award; Ros Vol. 2: 110
Bowers Scholarship; Bob Vol. 1: 21404
Bowie Medal; William Vol. 1: 2344
Bowie Young Investigator; Lemuel J. Vol. 1: 978
Bowis Award; E.B. Vol. 1: 1938
Bowker/Ulrich's Serials Librarianship Award Vol. 1: 5424
Bowler Award; Eugene C. Vol. 1: 17118
Bowler of the Month Vol. 1: 6562

Bowler of the Year
Bowling Writers Association of America Vol. 1: 6563
Western Women Professional Bowlers Vol 1: 21573
Bowles Cup Vol. 2: 8538
Bowling Hall of Fame and Museum Vol. 1: 11432
Bowling Magazine Writing Competition Vol. 1: 1585
Bowling National Mine Reclamation Awards; Kenes C. Vol. 1: 12156
Bowman Award; Raymond C. Vol. 1: 18710
Bowman Memorial Award for Painting; Jean Vol. 1: 659
Box Office of the Year Award Vol. 1: 12084
Boxer of the Year Vol. 1: 20384
Boxing Hall of Fame Award Vol. 1: 12113
Boyd Award for Housing; Robin Vol. 2: 525
Boyd Hall of Fame Award; John A. Vol. 1: 8169
Boyd Humanitarian Award; Benjamin F. Vol. 1: 17053
Boyd Lectureship; William Vol. 1: 6928
Boyd Literary Award; W.Y. Vol. 1: 2970
Boyd-Orr International Award Vol. 1: 12504
Boyd Trophy; Lennox Vol. 2: 6682
Boyer Lecture on Public Policy; Frances Vol. 1: 2195
Boyer Medal; Marian Angell Godfrey Vol. 1: 21096
Boyle Award; Hal Vol. 1: 16981
Boyle Award; The Sister Vol. 1: 18274
Boyle Medal; Robert Vol. 2: 8744
The Boyle Memorial Senior French Music Scholarship Vol. 1: 18275
The Boyle Memorial Senior Hayden and Mozart Scholarship Vol. 1: 18276
Boyle/Norma Farber Award; Rosalie Vol. 1: 16108
Boynton Award; Melbourne W. Vol. 1: 1500
Boynton Award; Ruth E. Vol. 1: 1823
Boynton's G.A.L.A. Artist Awards Vol. 1: 6594
Boys - A Rahman Lectureship; S. F. Vol. 2: 8745
Boys & Girls Club Medallion Vol. 1: 6596
Boys' Basketball Past Chair Recognition Vol. 1: 545
Boys' Basketball Vision Award Vol. 1: 546
Boys Cup; Sir Francis Vol. 2: 5056
Boys Medal and Prize; Charles Vernon Vol. 2: 7724
Boys State Scholarship Vol. 1: 2954
Bozart Research Grant; Jane Vol. 1: 16678
Bozett Award; Dr. Fred Vol. 1: 14860
BP Conservation Programme Vol. 2: 6874
bp Nichol Chapbook Award Vol. 1: 17275
BP Portrait Award Vol. 2: 8188
BP Prize Lectureship in the Humanities Vol. 2: 8781
BPAA Special Award Vol. 1: 6559
B.P.E. Inter-Federation Award Vol. 2: 8263
Brace Consistency Award; Beagle Vol. 1: 6198
Brachet; Prix Albert Vol. 2: 1043
Brackenbury Award Vol. 2: 7059
Bracket World Finals Team Championship Vol. 1: 11676
Brackett Memorial Award; Dexter Vol. 1: 16132
Braddock Award; CCCC Richard Vol. 1: 14828
Braddock Award; Richard Vol. 1: 8375
Bradley Award Vol. 2: 903
Bradley Award; Barbara Vol. 1: 16109
Bradley Distinguished Service Award; James J. Vol. 1: 19065
Bradways Rogers Information Advancement Award; Frank Vol. 1: 13258
Brady Award; Ken Vol. 1: 13553
Brady Award; Robert Vol. 1: 2737
Brady Memorial Awards; Gerald Vol. 1: 10219
Brady/Schuster Award Vol. 1: 3764
Bragg Gold Medal for Excellence in Physics Vol. 2: 215
Bragg Medal and Prize Vol. 2: 7725
Brahney Grant; James M. Vol. 1: 11836
Braille Book of the Year Award Vol. 2: 648
Brakhage Award for Best Short Subject; Stan Vol. 1: 8881
Bralco Gold Medal Vol. 2: 3450
Branch Leadership Award Vol. 1: 6168
Brand Annual Art Competition Vol. 1: 5261
Brand Building Initiative of the Year Vol. 2: 7186
Branding Hammer Award Vol. 1: 17858
Brandt Volunteer Service Award; Sandy Vol. 1: 15373
Brannon Award; R. A. Vol. 1: 13742
BRASS Primark Student Travel Award Vol. 1: 17936
Brass Scholarship; The Dr. W.C. Murray Senior Vol. 1: 18304
BRASS Thomson Financial Student Travel Award Vol. 1: 17936
Brasted Memorial Lecture Vol. 1: 1741
Brattle Prizes in Corporate Finance Vol. 1: 2243
Brauer Prize; Hamburg Max Vol. 2: 3078
Braun Award; E. Lucy Vol. 1: 9131
Braun Award; Fred Vol. 1: 20797
Braun Prize; Karl Ferdinand Vol. 1: 18765
BraunPrize Vol. 2: 2676
Braunstein Memorial Award; Jules Vol. 1: 1330
Brautigam Award; Frank C. Vol. 1: 5932
Bravo Award
Dominican University Vol. 1: 8987
Horizons Theatre Vol 1: 10547
Bray Accompanist Prize; John Vol. 2: 9153
Bray Award; Robert S. Vol. 1: 2039
Bray National Poetry Award; John Vol. 2: 597
Brazdziunas premija; Povilo Vol. 2: 4385
Brazier Young Investigator Award; M. A. B. Vol. 2: 7936
Brazilian Packaging Design Award Vol. 2: 1164
Brazos Bookstore Short Story Award Vol. 1: 20012
Bread and Roses Award Vol. 1: 8879
Breakfast of Champions Vol. 1: 16558
Breakthrough Director Award Vol. 1: 10720
Breasted Prize; James Henry Vol. 1: 2467
Breaute; Prix Vol. 2: 1704
Brechner Freedom of Information Award; Joseph L. Vol. 1: 6614
Brecht Denkmunze; Walter Vol. 2: 2645
Breed Awards Vol. 1: 16480
Breeden Prizes; Smith Vol. 1: 2244
Breeder Awards Vol. 1: 16864
Breeder of Top Ten Winning Bichon Frises, Owner of Top Ten Winning Bichon Frises Vol. 1: 6363
Bregger Essay Award Vol. 1: 3583
Breir Award; Nabila Vol. 2: 9301
Breithaupt Award; Chef Herman Vol. 1: 11523
Breitkreutz Leadership Award - Volleyball; Emil Vol. 1: 547
Bremner Awards; M. D. K. Vol. 1: 844
Brennan Award for Outstanding Jurist; Hon. William J. Vol. 1: 16272
Brennan Award; Thomas J. Vol. 1: 6007
Brennan Medal Vol. 2: 7743
Brenner Prize Vol. 2: 3736
Bretnall Award; William B. Vol. 1: 18401
Brett Award; Philip Vol. 1: 3174
Breuil; Fondation Jean du Hamel de Vol. 2: 1900
Brewer of the Year Vol. 1: 10535
Brewer Prize; Frank S. and Elizabeth D. Vol. 1: 4284
Brewer Trophy; Frank G. Vol. 1: 13876
Brewster Award for Creative Ingenuity Vol. 1: 6616
Brewster Memorial Award; William Vol. 1: 3339
Brey Award; Karl Vol. 1: 12808
Brice Outstanding Student Leadership Award; Leonard R. Vol. 1: 18697
Brick Awards Vol. 2: 6890
Bridge Awards Vol. 1: 6620
Bridge Book of the Year Vol. 1: 1589
Bridge School International Award Vol. 1: 11918
Bridgeport Prize Vol. 2: 7795
Bridges Memorial Award; Polly Vol. 1: 16481
Bridgman Memorial Award; Laura Vol. 1: 1459
The Bridport Prize Vol. 2: 6892
Brief-Writing Award Vol. 1: 18380
Brier Instructor of the Year Award; ARRL Herb S. Vol. 1: 45
Briggs Award; Charles W.
Association for Iron and Steel Technology Vol. 1: 5403
ASTM International Vol 1: 5933
Briggs Dissertation Award; George E. Vol. 1: 3651
Briggs Folklore Award; Katharine Vol. 2: 7534
Briggs Memorial Scientific Inquiry Award; Dorothy Vol. 1: 3485
Briggs Memorial Technical and Operating Medal; Charles W. Vol. 1: 19782
Brigham Award; Reuben Vol. 1: 5292
Brigham Award; Richard and Grace Vol. 1: 19066
Bright Idea Awards Vol. 1: 19995
Bright Memorial Award; Norman and Marion Vol. 1: 7834
Bright Smiles, Bright Futures Award Vol. 2: 2449
Brill Trophy; John Vol. 1: 13179
Brindley Lecture; George W. Vol. 1: 8090
Brine Awards; W. H. Vol. 1: 20659
Brinell Medal Vol. 2: 6198
Briner Nuclear Pharmacy Practice Award; William H. Vol. 1: 3380
Brink Award for Distinguished Service; Victor Z. Vol. 1: 10969
Brinker Award; Maureen Connolly Vol. 1: 20853
Brinker International Award for Breast Cancer Research Vol. 1: 19848
Brinker Outstanding Junior Girl Award; Maureen Connolly Vol. 1: 20853
Brinkhous Physician of the Year Award; Dr. Kenneth Vol. 1: 15202

Brinkley Award; Rawn Vol. 1: 10986
Brisbane Prize; MakDougall- Vol. 2: 8790
Brissett Award; Belva B. Vol. 1: 14107
Bristol Award
Canadian Society of Hospital Pharmacists Vol. 1: 7461
Infectious Diseases Society of America Vol 1: 10791
Bristol-Myers Squibb Award Vol. 1: 7461
Bristol-Myers Squibb Award for Excellence in Medical Teaching Vol. 1: 6625
Bristol-Myers Squibb Award for Excellence in Pharmaceutical Teaching Vol. 1: 6626
BRIT Awards Vol. 2: 7108
Britain in Bloom Awards Vol. 2: 7413
British Academy Fellow Vol. 2: 6895
British Academy Research Awards Vol. 2: 6896
British Academy Television Awards Vol. 2: 6905
British Aerophilatelic Federation Award Vol. 2: 8263
British Aerospace Prize Vol. 2: 7690
British Amateur Video Awards Vol. 2: 9195
British Appaloosa Society National Champions Vol. 2: 6912
British Archaeological Awards
Association for Industrial Archaeology Vol. 2: 6778
British Universities Film and Video Council Vol 2: 7212
British Association Medal Vol. 2: 5773
British Association of Dermatologists Fellowships Vol. 2: 6940
British Association of Paediatric Surgeons Awards Vol. 2: 6944
British Book Design and Production Awards Vol. 2: 7113
British Bronze Medal Vol. 2: 8378
British Caribbean Philatelic Study Group Award Vol. 2: 8263
British Cartographic Society Design Award Vol. 2: 6971
British Cartographic Society Student Award Vol. 2: 6975
British Championship Vol. 2: 8133
British Chess Federation Player of the Year Vol. 2: 6978
British Computer Society Awards Vol. 2: 6988
British Council Book Prize Vol. 1: 16411
British Deaf Association Medal of Honour Vol. 2: 6999
British Design & Art Direction Award - Yellow Pencils Award Vol. 2: 7001
British Design Awards Vol. 2: 7381
British Ecological Society Grants and Awards Vol. 2: 7006
British Ecological Society President's Medal Vol. 2: 7007
British Empire Medal Vol. 2: 7247
British Federation Crosby Hall Fellowship Vol. 2: 6406
British Film Institute Fellowships Vol. 2: 7019
The British Film Institute Sutherland Trophy Vol. 2: 7020
British Foundry Medal and Prize Vol. 2: 7653
British Gold Medal Vol. 2: 8379
British Grassland Society Award Vol. 2: 7025
British Helicopter Advisory Board Trophy Vol. 2: 7607
British Institute of Architectural Technologists Student Award Vol. 2: 7035
British Lichen Society Awards Vol. 2: 7057
British Medical Association Film and Video Competition Vol. 2: 7060
British Medical Association Medicine in the Media Award Vol. 2: 7061
British Mexican Society Postgraduate Prize Vol. 2: 7085
British Music Society Awards Vol. 2: 7087
British Nautical Awards Vol. 2: 8873
British Open Golf Championship
Professional Golfers' Association - England Vol. 2: 8299
Professional Golfers' Association - England Vol 2: 8301
Professional Golfers' Association - England Vol 2: 8302
British Petroleum Conservation Programme Award Vol. 2: 6874
British Phonographic Industry Certified Awards Vol. 2: 7109
British Psychological Society Honorary Fellow Vol. 2: 7122
British Psychological Society Honorary Life Member Vol. 2: 7123
British Psychological Society Presidents' Award Vol. 2: 7124
British Reserve Insurance Conducting Prize Vol. 2: 8167
British School at Rome Fellowship Vol. 2: 6761
British Show Pony Society Rosettes Vol. 2: 7150
British Silver Medal Vol. 2: 8380
British Society of Magazine Editors Awards Vol. 2: 7186
British Society of Rheology Annual Award Vol. 2: 7192
British Society of Rheology Gold Medal Vol. 2: 7193
British Society of Scientific Glassblowers Literary Prizes Vol. 2: 7196
British Trust for Ornithology Jubilee Medal Vol. 2: 7208
Brito Award; Gene Vol. 1: 20128
Britt Literary Award Vol. 1: 5087
Brittell COTA/OTR Partnership Award; Terry Vol. 1: 3293
Britten Award; John Vol. 2: 4967
Britten International Composers' Competition; Benjamin Vol. 2: 7222
Britten Prize; John Vol. 2: 8381
Brittingham Prize in Poetry and Felix Pollak Prize in Poetry; The Vol. 1: 21125
The Brittingham Prize in Poetry and Felix Pollak Prize in Poetry Vol. 1: 21125
Britton Award for Inquiry within the English Language Arts; CEE James N. Vol. 1: 14829
Brizard; Prix Vol. 2: 1705
Broad Axe Award
Catboat Association Vol. 1: 7629
Railway Tie Association Vol 1: 17859
Broadcast Excellence Award Vol. 1: 6890
Broadcast Media Awards for Radio and Television Vol. 1: 11853
Broadcast Media Awards for Television Vol. 1: 11853
Broadcast Personality of the Year Vol. 1: 11424
Broadcasting Hall of Fame Vol. 1: 14108
Brochure Award Vol. 1: 13997
Brock Awards Vol. 1: 6645
Brock Gold Medal Award Vol. 2: 6636
Brodie Award in Drug Metabolism; Bernard B. Vol. 1: 4170
Brodie Medal; John A. Vol. 2: 372
Brodman Award for the Academic Medical Librarian of the Year; Estelle Vol. 1: 13251
Brody Young Investigator Award; Michael J. Vol. 1: 3509
Broedel Award; Max Vol. 1: 5756
Brohee Medal Vol. 2: 3144
Broida Prize; Herbert P. Vol. 1: 3452
Broiler Research Award Vol. 1: 17498
Brokaw Award; Tom Vol. 1: 19449
Brokaw Memorial Trophy; Irving Vol. 1: 20589
Bronce; Medallion de Vol. 1: 16456
Bronfenbrenner Award; Urie Vol. 1: 3668
Bronfman Award for Excellence in the Crafts; Saidye Vol. 1: 6647
Bronze Anchor Vol. 2: 2470
Bronze Anvil Awards Vol. 1: 17720
The Bronze Baby Vol. 1: 7211
Bronze Elephant Award Vol. 2: 3355
Bronze Figure of the Rainbow Goddess Vol. 2: 5910
Bronze Good Citizenship Medal Vol. 1: 15764
Bronze Irrigation Award Vol. 1: 418
Bronze Key Award Vol. 1: 14848
Bronze Medal
International Federation of Sports Medicine Vol. 2: 1410
National Association of Paralegals Vol 2: 8156
Royal Aeronautical Society - United Kingdom Vol 2: 8382
Royal Institute of Navigation Vol 2: 8594
Tau Sigma Delta Vol 1: 19940
Bronze Medal Award Vol. 1: 15826
Bronze Plaque Awards Vol. 1: 7948
Bronze Wolf Vol. 2: 6576
Brook Lifetime Achievement Award; Elston Vol. 1: 12892
Brooker Collegiate Scholarship for Minorities; George M. Vol. 1: 11033
Brookes Award for Excellence in Journalism; Warren Vol. 1: 2958
Brookhart Memorial Intermediate Pipe Organ Scholarship; The Ray Vol. 1: 18277
Brooklyn School Scholarship Vol. 1: 6651
Brooks Award for Excellence in Student Research; Frank G. Vol. 1: 6324
Brooks Award for Excellence in the Teaching of Culture; ACTFL Nelson Vol. 1: 2056
Brooks Memorial Award; Charles E.
Federation of Fly Fishers Vol. 1: 9472
Federation of Fly Fishers Vol 1: 9484
Brooks' Memorial Award; John Vol. 1: 6072
Brooks Moore Scholarship; Bradley Vol. 1: 13530
Brooks Undergraduate Essay Competition; F. G. Vol. 1: 6324
Broome County Farm Bureau Scholarship Vol. 1: 6653
Brophy AAO Distinguished Service Award; James E. Vol. 1: 1318
Bross Prize Vol. 1: 6655
Brosseau Memorial Award; Robert P. Vol. 1: 8433
Brough Memorial Prize; Frederick Vol. 2: 373
Broun Award; Heywood Vol. 1: 16343
Broun Award; Maurice Vol. 1: 10299
Brouwer Award; Dirk Vol. 1: 1510
Brower Environmental Journalism Award; David R. Vol. 1: 18452

Brown/AMA Marketing Scholar of the Year; George Hay Vol. 1: 3026
Brown Award; Antoinette Vol. 1: 20324
Brown Award for Meritorious Service; Lydia Vol. 2: 6949
Brown Award; Gwilym Vol. 1: 21215
Brown Award; Ham Vol. 1: 16966
Brown Award; Howard Mayer Vol. 1: 9059
Brown Award; James Barrett Vol. 1: 1381
Brown Award; Ray E. Vol. 1: 5766
Brown Award; Roger J. E. Vol. 1: 7122
Brown Award; Rosemary Vol. 1: 5227
Brown Bear Award Vol. 1: 6661
Brown Boettner Award for Outstanding Public Education; Beth Vol. 1: 15589
Brown Boveri-Forschungspreis fur Energietechnik Vol. 2: 6517
Brown Expedition Award; Ralph Vol. 2: 8511
Brown Freedom Medal; Colin M. Vol. 1: 14672
Brown Grant; Amber Vol. 1: 19089
Brown-Hazen Lectureship for Research Excellence in Life Sciences Vol. 1: 16280
Brown IV Annual Award of Excellence for Outstanding Community Service; James Vol. 1: 7883
Brown, Jr. Root Cutter Award; Samuel W. Vol. 1: 10842
Brown Medal; W.P. Vol. 2: 374
Brown Memorial Award; Dr. Charlie Vol. 1: 14449
Brown Memorial Award; J. Hammond Vol. 1: 16966
Brown Memorial Public Service Award; Aaron L. Vol. 1: 14138
Brown Memorial Sportsmanship Award; Cecil J. Vol. 1: 3129
Brown Memorial Training Award in Diabetes; Dr. Gordon D. Vol. 1: 13718
Brown Prize; John Nicholas Vol. 1: 13274
Brown Prize; Sir Vernon Vol. 2: 8383
Brown Public Service Award; the James Wright Vol. 1: 8773
Brown Publication Award; James W. Vol. 1: 5354
Brown Research Recognition Award; Mary Louise Vol. 1: 1305
Brown Shield; The Goodfellow Memorial Award in Voice/The Chief Justice J.T. Vol. 1: 18286
Brown Trophy; Jack Vol. 1: 20770
Brown Voluntarism Award; H. Barksdale Vol. 1: 448
Brown Volunteer/Community Service Award; H. Barksdale Vol. 1: 449
Browne Gold Medal; Denis Vol. 2: 6944
Browne Medal for Original Research Vol. 2: 9185
Browne Memorial Bowl; George H. Vol. 1: 20589
Brownell Media Award; Emery A. Vol. 1: 15336
Brownell Press Award; Emery A. Vol. 1: 15336
Browning Award; Alice C. Vol. 1: 11420
Brownlee Fund; Richard S. Vol. 1: 21313
Brownlow Award; Louis Vol. 1: 4180
Brownlow Book Award; Louis Vol. 1: 13818
Brownlow Publications Award; Cecil Vol. 1: 9579
Brubaker Memorial Award; John Vol. 1: 7652
Bruce Award for Humour; Gordon Vol. 1: 16945
Bruce Medal; Catherine Wolfe Vol. 1: 6008
Bruce Medal; W. S. Vol. 2: 8782
Bruce Memorial Award; James D. Vol. 1: 1917
Bruce-Preller Prize Lectureship Vol. 2: 8783
Bruce Prize; Alexander Ninian Vol. 2: 8784
Bruck Award Vol. 1: 10363
Brudney Award; Ruth P. Vol. 1: 15374
Bruel Noise Control and Acoustics Medal; Per Vol. 1: 4504
Bruemmer Award; Mary A. Vol. 1: 18215
Bruhn Prize; Erik Vol. 1: 14478
Brun; Fondation Edmond Vol. 2: 1854
Brunauer Award; S. Vol. 1: 1668
Brunauer Best Paper Award Vol. 1: 1668
Bruner Award for Urban Excellence; Rudy Vol. 1: 6668
Brunet Memorial Trophy; Jean-Pierre Vol. 1: 20589
Brunet; Prix Vol. 2: 1762
Brunetti Award; Cledo Vol. 1: 10856
Brunner Grant; Arnold W. Vol. 1: 2726
Brunnstrom Award for Excellence in Clinical Teaching; Signe Vol. 1: 3486
Bruno Cagol Press Prize Vol. 2: 4059
Bruno E. Jacob Trophy Vol. 1: 15102
Brussels International Festival of Fantastic Film Vol. 2: 841
Brussels International Festival of Fantasy, Thriller, and Science-Fiction Films Vol. 2: 841
Brussels International Festival of Scientific and Technical Films Vol. 2: 845
Bruton Medal Vol. 2: 7552
Brya Award; Brig Gen Edward N. Vol. 1: 5112
Bryan Aitken Award Vol. 2: 5033
Bryan Award; Kirk Vol. 1: 9945
Bryan, Jr. Scholarships; Joseph M. Vol. 1: 9113
Bryan Scholarship; John K. Vol. 1: 13537
Bryant Gold Medal; Henry Grier Vol. 1: 9941
Bryant Outstanding Service Award; David C. Vol. 1: 1165
Bryson Memorial Senior Speech Arts Scholarship; L.I. Vol. 1: 18278
BSA Merit Awards Vol. 1: 6538
BSAS Science Fair Prize Vol. 1: 6252
BSFA Award Vol. 2: 7146
BSIA/IFSEC Security Industry Awards Vol. 2: 7148
BSS Student Research Award Vol. 1: 9987
BTA Trophy Vol. 2: 7206
BuaLuang Art Competition Prize Vol. 2: 6615
Bublick Hebrew University Awards; Solomon Vol. 1: 2307
Bucchi Prize of Rome Capital City; Valentino Vol. 2: 3945
Buchanan Cup Vol. 1: 18489
Buchanan Medal Vol. 2: 8692
Buchanan Outstanding Chapter Award Vol. 1: 18489
Buchanan Prize in Esperanto; John Vol. 2: 9174
Buchannon Scholarship; Donald A. Vol. 1: 20519
Bucher Medal; Walter H. Vol. 1: 2345
Bucher Prize; Heinrich Hatt- Vol. 2: 6518
Buchner Forschungsstiftung; DECHEMA Preis der Max Vol. 2: 2912
Buchner-Preis; Georg- Vol. 2: 2773
Buck Award; Solon J. Vol. 1: 13476
Buck International Woman of the Year Award; Pearl S. Vol. 1: 17129
Buckendale Lecture; L. Ray Vol. 1: 19036
Buckeye Children's Book Award/Teen Buckeye Vol. 1: 6670
Buckley Prize in Condensed Matter Physics; Oliver E. Vol. 1: 3453
Buckner Medal; Emory Vol. 1: 9441
Buckwell Memorial Scholarship; Arthur Vol. 1: 18135
Budapest International Music Competition Vol. 2: 3285
Budapest Prize Vol. 2: 3273
Buddingh Prize for New Dutch Poetry; C. Vol. 2: 4871
Buddle Findlay Sargeson Fellowship Vol. 2: 5089
BUDDY Award (Bringing Up Daughters Differently) Vol. 1: 12768
Budeanu Prize; Constantin Vol. 2: 5817
Budgen Award Vol. 2: 6817
Budget Service Award Vol. 1: 12651
Budo Koro Sho Vol. 2: 4134
Bueche Award; Arthur M. Vol. 1: 13805
Buell Award; Murray F. Vol. 1: 9132
Buerger Award; Martin J. Vol. 1: 2084
Buffalo Hall of Fame Vol. 1: 14518
Buga premija; Kazimiero Vol. 2: 4386
Bugnet Award for Novel; Georges Vol. 1: 21987
Build a Building Competition Vol. 2: 7782
Build America Beautiful Award Vol. 1: 12532
Builder and Associate of the Year Vol. 1: 20179
Builder of the Year Vol. 1: 17599
Builders' Awards Vol. 2: 5263
Builder's Choice Awards for Excellence in Design and Planning Vol. 1: 6676
Builder's Choice Design and Planning Awards Vol. 1: 6676
Builders of a Better World Prize Vol. 1: 21899
Building Assets Fund Grants Program; Massachusetts Avenue Vol. 1: 941
Building Manager of the Year Awards Vol. 2: 7274
Building with Trees Awards of Excellence Vol. 1: 13950
Building World Citizenship Vol. 2: 9238
Bulbridge Award; ISPA Keith Vol. 1: 12008
Bulgarian Academy of Science Honorary Badge - Marin Drinov Medal Vol. 2: 1206
Bulgarian Academy of Science - Kliment Ohridski University of Sofia Prizes Vol. 2: 1207
Bulk Materials Handling Award Vol. 2: 375
Bulkley Medal Vol. 1: 9876
Bull of the Year Vol. 1: 17655
Bullard Scholarship; Helen Vol. 1: 15261
Bullen Prize; John Vol. 1: 7149
Bulletin Contest Vol. 1: 10244
Bullivant Student Prize; Mary Vol. 2: 5042
Bulpitt Woman of the Year Award; Mildred Vol. 1: 1068
Bulwer-Lytton Fiction Contest Vol. 1: 18257
Bumbershoot, The Seattle Arts Festival Vol. 1: 16734
Bunche Award; Ralph Vol. 1: 21461
Bunche Memorial Award; Ralph Vol. 1: 20254
Bundespreis fur Forderer des Designs Vol. 2: 2830
Bundespreis Gute Form Vol. 2: 2829
Bunge Prize; Paul Vol. 2: 2794
Bunka Korosha Vol. 2: 4180
Bunka-Kunsho Vol. 2: 4181
Bunn Award; John W. Vol. 1: 13750

Award Index

Bunsen-Denkmuenze Vol. 2: 2795
Bunsen Medal Vol. 2: 2795
Bunyan Award; Paul Vol. 1: 70
Buonocore Memorial Lecturer Vol. 1: 116
Burbank Award; Luther Vol. 1: 2525
Burch Memorial Safety Award; Dr. Gary Vol. 1: 14349
Burchfield Award; Laverne Vol. 1: 4181
Burden Research Prize Vol. 2: 8456
Burdett, Jr. Army Aviation Flight Safety Award; Lt. Gen. Allen M. Vol. 1: 16819
Burdgick Award; Gary Vol. 1: 14912
Burdick; ASCP Distinguished Service to Clinical Pathology Award Honoring Ward Vol. 1: 3968
Burdin Scholarship; Edythe G. Vol. 1: 13662
Burdy; Prix Jeanne Vol. 2: 2423
Bureau of International Recycling Gold Medal Vol. 2: 843
Burfitt Prize; Walter Vol. 2: 535
Burgdorf Award Vol. 1: 16208
Burger Award; Eric and Amy Vol. 1: 16981
Burger Award in Medicinal Chemistry; Alfred Vol. 1: 1742
Burger Award; Warren E. Vol. 1: 14640
Burger Healer Awards; Chief Justice Warren E. Vol. 1: 7916
Burger Memorial Award Vol. 2: 5975
Burgess Award; Ernest W. Vol. 1: 14859
Burggraf Award; Fred Vol. 1: 20159
Burgheim Medaille; Hedwig- Vol. 2: 3022
Burka Award Vol. 1: 11011
Burkan Memorial Competition; Nathan Vol. 1: 4379
Burke Essay Contest; Arleigh Vol. 1: 20709
Burke Memorial Award; John "Sonny" Vol. 1: 20735
Burke Memorial Award; Tom Vol. 1: 19684
Burke Memorial Lecture; Donal Vol. 2: 3688
Burke Perpetual Challenge Machinery Trophy; Sir Roland Vol. 2: 8410
Burke Perpetual Challenge Trophy Vol. 2: 8410
Burket Award; Lester Vol. 1: 734
Burkett-Dodge Award Vol. 1: 20798
Burkitt Medal for Biblical Studies Vol. 2: 6897
Burleigh Prize; J. C. Vol. 2: 7666
Burley Prize; Joseph Fraunhofer Award/Robert M. Vol. 1: 16785
Burn Award; Harry T. Vol. 1: 6310
Burn Prevention Award Vol. 1: 1600
Burn Prize; Sir Joseph Vol. 2: 7648
Burnet Lecture Vol. 2: 118
Burnet Memorial Award; Sir John Vol. 2: 8582
Burnett Prizes in Journalism Ethics; UH Journalism Carol Vol. 1: 21028
Burnett/University of Hawaii/AEJMC Ethics Prize; Carol Vol. 1: 5344
Burnham Award; Daniel Vol. 1: 3548
Burnham Manufacturing Management Award; Donald C. Vol. 1: 19144
Burns Award; Bernard J. Vol. 1: 10729
Burns Best of the Festival Award; Ken Vol. 1: 4970
Burr Award; Franklin L. Vol. 1: 15155
Burr/Worzalla Award; Elizabeth Vol. 1: 21684
Burrin Award; Esther V. Vol. 1: 5383
Bursaries Vol. 2: 9225
Bursary Competition Vol. 1: 13982
Burt Award; Karen Vol. 2: 9226
Burton Award; Gale Cotton Vol. 1: 20799
Burton Medal; Sir Richard Vol. 2: 8427
Burwell, Jr., Award; E. B. Vol. 1: 9946
Burwell Lectureship in Catalysis; Robert Vol. 1: 16397
Busch Series Vol. 1: 14045
Bush Artist Fellows Program Vol. 1: 6700
Bush Award; Vannevar Vol. 1: 15677
Bush Foundation Fellowships for Artists Vol. 1: 6700
Bushkin Friend of the Foundation Award; Ellyn Vol. 1: 16712
Bushnell Trophy; Asa S. Vol. 1: 15066
Busignies Memorial Award; Henri Vol. 1: 17831
Business and Aging Awards Vol. 1: 4639
Business and Culture Award Vol. 1: 12261
Business and Economic Reporting Contest Vol. 1: 8170
Business and Industry Award Vol. 1: 461
Business and Industry Awards Vol. 1: 148
Business Aviation Meritorious Award Vol. 1: 9580
Business Award
Council for Exceptional Children Vol. 1: 8546
New York Press Club Vol 1: 16243
Business Conservation Leadership Award Vol. 1: 14149
Business; Dun & Bradstreet Award for Outstanding Service to Minority Vol. 1: 17938
Business/Economic Writing Award Vol. 1: 8170
Business-Education Partnership Award Vol. 1: 21267
Business Energy Award Vol. 2: 7411
Business Enterprise Awards Vol. 2: 8707
Business Ethics Award Vol. 1: 6314
Business Excellence Award Vol. 1: 16775
Business Executive; Future Vol. 1: 9843
Business Executive of the Year Vol. 1: 17874
Business in the Arts Vol. 1: 8209
Business in the Arts Award Vol. 1: 19915
Business in the Arts Awards Vol. 1: 6702
Business Leader of the Year Award Vol. 1: 19537
Business Leadership Award Vol. 1: 21065
Business Management Award Vol. 1: 19259
Business Marketing Doctoral Award Support Completion; ISBM Vol. 1: 17208
Business of the Year
Evergreen Area Chamber of Commerce Vol. 1: 9359
Galt District Chamber of Commerce Vol 1: 9860
South Haven/Van Buren County Lakeshore Convention and Visitors Bureau Vol 1: 19458
Business of the Year Award Vol. 2: 809
Business Recognition Award Vol. 1: 1306
Business Speaks Award Vol. 1: 16210
Business Volunteers for the Arts Awards Vol. 1: 6715
Businessperson of the Year Vol. 1: 12706
Businessperson of the Year Award Vol. 2: 812
Busk Medal Vol. 2: 8512
Busk Prize Vol. 2: 8384
Busoni Prize; F. Vol. 2: 3875
Busse (M.D.) Research Awards; Ewald W. Vol. 2: 1187
Bustad Companion Animal Veterinarian Award Vol. 1: 4814
The Buster Vol. 1: 8724
Bustillo; Premio Jose Maria Vol. 2: 10
Buszek Memorial Award; Buz Vol. 1: 9473
Butch Henley Award Vol. 1: 2453
Butcher Award for Lifetime Achievement; Goler T. Vol. 1: 10051
Butcher Medal; Goler T. Vol. 1: 4462
Butler Award/Most Outstanding Nursery Professional; Wendell E. Vol. 1: 9610
Butler Council No. 465, UCT Scholarship Award Vol. 1: 20328
Butler Faculty Research Awards; John Tropham and Susan Redd Vol. 1: 17926
Butler Literary Award Vol. 1: 12194
Butler Medal Vol. 1: 8240
Butsuri-Tansa Gakkai-sho Vol. 2: 4298
Butt Award in Hepatology or Nutrition; H.R. Vol. 1: 9711
Butterfield Trophy; Jack A. Vol. 1: 2499
Butterley - F. Earle Hooper Award; H. M. Vol. 2: 326
Butterworth Prize Vol. 1: 3325
Buttgenbach; Prix Henri Vol. 2: 1059
Butts - Whiting Award Vol. 1: 5630
Butzel Memorial Award for Distinguished Community Service; Fred M. Vol. 1: 12353
Buxtehuder Bulle Vol. 2: 3066
"Buy Recycled" Campaign Awards Program Vol. 1: 20455
Buyer of the Year Award Vol. 1: 15265
BVA Achievement Award Vol. 1: 6458
BVRLA Awards Vol. 2: 7214
BWI/YALSA Collection Development Grant Vol. 1: 22052
By-Line Award Vol. 1: 13124
Byline Awards Vol. 1: 16244
Byrd Young Artist Competition; William C. Vol. 1: 18203
Byrne Memorial Literary Award; Ray Vol. 1: 3204
The Byzantine-Patristic Medal and Certificate Vol. 1: 2626
C SADF Commendation Medal Vol. 2: 5744
CA Advertising Annual Vol. 1: 8308
CA Design Annual Vol. 1: 8309
CAA Awards for Adult Literature Vol. 1: 6953
CAA Jubilee Award for Short Stories Vol. 1: 6954
CAA Lela Common Award for Canadian History Vol. 1: 6955
CAA MOSAID Technologies, Inc. Award for Fiction Vol. 1: 6956
CAA National Awards Vol. 2: 7320
CAA Trophy Vol. 2: 5057
CAAO Scholarship Vol. 1: 8410
Caballo de Trabajo Award; El Vol. 1: 19542
Cabanne; Premio Prof. Dr. Alejandro Vol. 2: 32
Cabaud Memorial Award Vol. 1: 3350
Cable Book Award; Gerald Vol. 1: 18519
Cabot and Louis Delezenne Prize of the LMGMS; Joachim Vol. 2: 2524
Cabot Prizes; Maria Moors Vol. 1: 8249
Caccioppoli; Premio Renato Vol. 2: 4017
Cacique's Crown of Honor Vol. 2: 3206
Cacique's Crown of Valor Vol. 2: 3207
Cactus d'Or Vol. 2: 6430
CAD Competition; Canadian Architect Magazine Art of Vol. 1: 6878
Cadbury Medal; Christopher Vol. 2: 8849
Cade Memorial Fellowship; Lady Vol. 2: 5524
Cadmus Memorial Award; Bradford Vol. 1: 10970
Cady Award; Gilbert H. Vol. 1: 9947

Cady Award; Harrison Vol. 1: 4845
CAEAL Appreciation Award Vol. 1: 6881
Caernarfon Award Vol. 2: 7741
CAF Unit Letter of Commendation Vol. 1: 8271
Caffey Award for Excellence for Pre-Collegiate Teaching; W. Stewart Vol. 1: 20037
CAG Award for Scholarly Distinction in Geography Vol. 1: 6910
CAG Award for Service to the Profession of Geography Vol. 1: 6911
Cagigal Award in Physical Education; International Jose Maria Vol. 2: 900
Cahn Award; Jean Camper Vol. 1: 14633
Cahn Lifetime Achievement Award; Sammy Vol. 1: 13816
Cahours; Prix Vol. 2: 1813
Caille Memorial Medal; Pierre Francois Vol. 1: 11606
Cain Memorial Award; Bruce F. Vol. 1: 964
Caisse de Depot et Placement du Quebec Prize (in Finance); ACFAS/ Vol. 1: 5536
Caitlin Lynch Memorial Fund Award Vol. 1: 21289
Cajal Medal Vol. 1: 6725
Cake Show Competition Plaques Vol. 1: 7494
Cal Haworth Leadership Award Vol. 1: 8953
Caldecott Medal; Randolph Vol. 1: 5436
Calder Cup (Playoff Champion) Vol. 1: 2500
Calder Prize Vol. 2: 8615
Caldicott Leadership Award; Helen Vol. 1: 21769
Caledonian Research Foundation Prize Lectureship in Biomedical Sciences and Arts and Letters Vol. 2: 8785
Calgary Book Prize; W.O. Mitchell City of Vol. 1: 21986
Calhoun Scholarship; Hermoine Grant Vol. 1: 15039
California Gold Medal Vol. 2: 3695
California History Day Award Vol. 1: 8369
California Young Reader Medal Vol. 1: 6745
Calihan Fellowships Vol. 1: 159
Call for Papers Awards Program; AALL Lexis Nexis Vol. 1: 1244
Callan Memorial Medal; Elizabeth Vol. 1: 4846
Callas Gold Medal; Maria Vol. 2: 3165
Callas Grand Prix for Pianists; Maria Vol. 2: 3165
Callas Grand Prix, Opera, Oratorio-Lied; Maria Vol. 2: 3166
Callas International Music Competitions; Maria
  Athenaeum International Cultural Center Vol. 2: 3165
  Athenaeum International Cultural Center Vol 2: 3166
Callas International Opera, Oratorio-Lied Competition; Maria Vol. 2: 3166
Callas International Piano Competition; Maria Vol. 2: 3165
Callaway Award; Joe A. Vol. 1: 166
Callaway Prize for the Defense of the Right to Privacy; Joe Vol. 1: 16216
Callebaut Prize; Octaaf Vol. 2: 1076
Callendar Medal Vol. 2: 7715
CALLERLAB Milestone Award Vol. 1: 6771
Callimaci Memorial Supporters Award; Fulvio Vol. 1: 7290
Callison Award; Charles H. Vol. 1: 14469
Callow Memorial Award; Russell S. Vol. 1: 9101
Calvin Award; Melvin Vol. 1: 11694
Calvo; Prix Carlos Vol. 2: 6373
Camden Freeholders Award Vol. 1: 11135
CAMEO Award Vol. 1: 16329
Camera d'Or Vol. 2: 2259
Camera Operator of the Year Vol. 2: 8858
Cameron Award; T. W. N. Vol. 1: 7497
Cameron Young Investigator Award; John R. Vol. 1: 1366
Camoes Prize Vol. 2: 5445
Camp Hemlocks Camperships Vol. 1: 9093
Camp Memorial Trophy; Mary C. Vol. 1: 15647
Campana Translation Prize Vol. 1: 12245
Campbell & Company Award for Excellence in Fundraising Vol. 1: 5699
Campbell Award; A. B. Vol. 1: 13743
Campbell Award; Donald Vol. 1: 17449
Campbell Award; Estelle Vol. 1: 15730
Campbell Award for Distinguished Research in Social Psychology; Donald T. Vol. 1: 3726
Campbell Award; Francis Joseph Vol. 1: 5856
Campbell Award; Frank W. Vol. 1: 17484
Campbell Award of Merit; E. K. Vol. 1: 4426
Campbell Award; Roald Vol. 1: 20971
Campbell Award; Robert D Vol. 2: 6732
Campbell; Medal in Memory of Ian Vol. 1: 2340
Campbell Memorial Award; Dr. Robert Vol. 1: 4962
Campbell Memorial Award; John W.
  Center for the Study of Science Fiction Vol. 1: 7752
  World Science Fiction Society Vol 1: 21951
Campbell Memorial Lecture; Edward DeMille Vol. 1: 5174
Campbell Memorial Travel Award; George Vol. 2: 3613
Campbell Memorial Trophy; Sir George Vol. 2: 8676
Campbell Outstanding Public Broadcasting Award; Elizabeth Vol. 1: 15127
Campiello Prize Vol. 2: 3879
Campion Award; Saint Edmund Vol. 1: 7635
Campionato Europeo Baseball Vol. 2: 858
Campos Memorial Award for Best International Student Paper; Carlos Walter M. Vol. 1: 1331
Camps For Kids Vol. 1: 7577
Campus Bookseller of the Year Award Vol. 1: 6983
Camus; Prix Gustave Vol. 2: 992
CAN-AM Amity Award Vol. 1: 7411
Can-AM Civil Engineering Amity Award Vol. 1: 4303
Canada - Australia Literary Prize Vol. 1: 6786
Canada Award; Forest Capital of Vol. 1: 7119
Canada Awards for Business Excellence Vol. 1: 15568
Canada Awards for Excellence Vol. 1: 15568
Canada Council Molson Prizes Vol. 1: 6787
Canada Export Award Vol. 1: 9686
Canada Gold Medal for Science and Engineering; Gerhard Herzberg Vol. 1: 16023
Canada International Award Lecture Vol. 2: 9000
Canada - Japan Literary Awards Vol. 1: 6788
Canada Lecture and Medal Vol. 2: 9001
Canada Memorial Foundation Scholarships Vol. 2: 6809
Canada Packers' Medal Vol. 1: 7445
Canada Post Corporation Journalism Prize Vol. 1: 6035
Canada's Sports Hall of Fame Vol. 1: 6842
Canadian Agricultural Engineering of the Year Award. Vol. 1: 7404
Canadian Architect Magazine Art of CAD Competition Vol. 1: 6878
Canadian Architect Magazine Awards of Excellence Vol. 1: 6879
Canadian Architect Yearbook Vol. 1: 6879
Canadian Authors Association Award for Fiction Vol. 1: 6956
Canadian Authors Association Award for Poetry Vol. 1: 6957
Canadian Award for Financial Reporting
  Government Finance Officers Association of United States and Canada Vol. 1: 10111
  Government Finance Officers Association of United States and Canada Vol 1: 10114
Canadian Basketball Hall of Fame Vol. 1: 8971
Canadian Business Hall of Fame Vol. 1: 12464
Canadian Cardiovascular Society Research Achievement Award Vol. 1: 6627
Canadian Championship Trophies Vol. 1: 7527
Canadian Chrysler Cup Vol. 1: 2501
Canadian Coast Guard Exemplary Service Medal Vol. 1: 6816
Canadian Conservation Achievement Award Vol. 1: 7538
Canadian Country Music Association's Citation Awards Vol. 1: 7064
Canadian Engineers' Award-Gold Medal Award Vol. 1: 7051
Canadian Engineers' Awards Vol. 1: 7058
Canadian Engineers' Awards-Award for the Support of Women in the Engineering Profession Vol. 1: 7052
Canadian Engineers' Awards-Gold Medal Student Award Vol. 1: 7053
Canadian Engineers' Awards-Meritorious Service Award for Community Service Vol. 1: 7054
Canadian Engineers' Awards-Meritorious Service Award for Professional Service Vol. 1: 7055
Canadian Engineers' Awards-National Award for Engineering Achievement Vol. 1: 7056
Canadian Engineers' Awards-Young Engineer Achievement Award Vol. 1: 7057
Canadian Federation of Humane Societies Media Award Vol. 1: 7091
Canadian Football Hall of Fame and Museum Vol. 1: 7101
Canadian Forces Decoration Vol. 1: 6817
Canadian Forestry Achievement Award Vol. 1: 7172
Canadian Forestry Group Achievement Award Vol. 1: 7173
Canadian Forestry Scientific Achievement Award Vol. 1: 7174
Canadian Friends of Yeshiva University Bora Laskin Distinguished Service Award Vol. 1: 22024
Canadian Geotechnical Colloquium Vol. 1: 7123
Canadian Healthcare Association Award for Distinguished Service Vol. 1: 7145

Award Index

Canadian Hospital Librarian of the Year Award Vol. 1: 7139
Canadian Information Productivity Awards Vol. 1: 10796
Canadian Information Technology Innovation Award Vol. 1: 7163
Canadian Institute of Chartered Accountants Prize Vol. 2: 7667
Canadian International Amateur Film Festival Vol. 1: 7206
Canadian International Annual Film/Video Festival Vol. 1: 7206
Canadian International Medal Lecture Vol. 2: 9000
Canadian Library Association Book of the Year for Children Award Vol. 1: 7254
Canadian Mineral Analysts Scholarships Vol. 1: 7286
Canadian Music Centre John Adaskin Memorial Award Vol. 1: 16738
Canadian Music Competitions Vol. 1: 7299
Canadian News Hall of Fame Vol. 1: 20122
Canadian Outdoorsman of the Year Award Vol. 1: 7540
Canadian Pacific Railway Medal Vol. 1: 9269
Canadian Pediatric Society Research Award Vol. 1: 7318
Canadian Prize Vol. 1: 10176
Canadian Rockies Award Vol. 1: 6235
Canadian School Library Association Merit Award Vol. 1: 7262
Canadian Society for Chemical Engineering Award in Industrial Practice Vol. 1: 7835
Canadian Society of Microbiologists Award Vol. 1: 7478
Canadian Software Systems Award Vol. 1: 7164
Canadian Student Film Festival Vol. 1: 13607
Canadian Studies; Donner Medal in Vol. 1: 5282
Cancer Campaign Medals of Merit Vol. 2: 1578
Cancer Control Society Awards Vol. 1: 7551
Cancer Research; AACR-Pezcoller International Award for Vol. 2: 4033
Cancer Research Award Program Vol. 1: 12498
Candace Award Vol. 1: 14678
Cande Memorial Trophy; Donald H. Vol. 1: 3112
Candle Artisan of the Year Vol. 1: 11658
Candler Bursary; Cathy Vol. 2: 166
Candy Hall of Fame Vol. 1: 14719
Candy Salesman of the Year Vol. 1: 13592
Cane Cutters' Competition Vol. 2: 4074
Cane Pace Vol. 1: 20878
Canedo; Premio Gustavo D. Vol. 2: 4506
Canham Graduate Studies Scholarship Vol. 1: 21477
Caniff Spirit of Flight Award; Milton Vol. 1: 14473
CANMET Technology Transfer Award Vol. 1: 7185
Cann Plaque; R. C. Vol. 1: 13928
Cannes International Film Festival Awards Vol. 2: 2259
Canning Trophy; Richard F. Vol. 1: 2502
Cannizzaro; Medaglia Stanislao Vol. 2: 4000
Cannon Award in Astronomy; Annie Jump
  American Association of University Women Educational Foundation Vol. 1: 1470
  American Astronomical Society Vol 1: 1511
Cannon Lecture; Physiology in Perspective: Walter B. Vol. 1: 3510
Cannon Prize Vol. 1: 13780
Canoeist of the Year Vol. 2: 8903
Canon Photo Essay Award Vol. 1: 15544
Cansave Children Award Vol. 1: 18323
The Canticum Dominum Vocal Competition Vol. 1: 6232
CAP Medal for Achievement in Physics Vol. 1: 6932
Capa Gold Medal; Robert Vol. 1: 16981
CAPAM International Innovations Award Vol. 1: 8304
Capanema Prize; Gustavo Vol. 2: 1170
Capar Award; Wes Vol. 1: 20277
Capdeville (De Beziers); Prix Auguste Vol. 2: 2113
Cape Cod Art Association Awards Vol. 1: 7571
Capezio Dance Award Vol. 1: 7575
Capital Clear Trophy Vol. 2: 8267
Capital Leadership Award Vol. 1: 18698
CAPL Public Library Services Award Vol. 1: 7256
Caplet; Prix Andre Vol. 2: 1679
Capote Award for Literary Criticism in Memory of Newton Arvin; Truman Vol. 1: 12189
A Cappella Recording Awards ("CARAs"); Contemporary Vol. 1: 8474
Cappella Recording Awards ("CARAs"); Contemporary A Vol. 1: 8474
Cappon Prize for Essay; Dorothy Churchill Vol. 1: 16190
Cappon Prize for Fiction; Alexander Patterson Vol. 1: 16190
Capra Achievement Award; Frank Vol. 1: 8940
Capranica Foundation Award in Neuroethology Vol. 1: 7579
Captain Joseph H. Linnard Prize Vol. 1: 19212
CAR Coach of the Year Award Vol. 1: 21806
Car of the Year Awards Vol. 1: 6103
Car of the Year (COTY) Vol. 1: 6104
Car Rental Co. of the Year Vol. 2: 6548
Caraccio Purchase Award; Kathleen Vol. 1: 18980
Caragiale Prize; Ion Luca Vol. 2: 5818
Carbohydrate Chemistry Award Vol. 2: 8746
Carbonell; Premi Josep M. Vol. 2: 6001
Carborundum Golden Jubilee Trophy Vol. 2: 6704
Carcinogenesis Young Investigator Award Vol. 2: 7451
Carclew Fellowship Vol. 2: 597
Card Award; George Vol. 1: 2040
Cardiff Singer of the World Competition Vol. 2: 6963
Cardiovascular Section Young Investigator Award Vol. 1: 3511
Cardiovascular Young Investigator Award Vol. 1: 19227
Cardozo School of Law Distinguished Public Service Award; Benjamin N. Vol. 1: 22025
Carducci Prize; Giosue Vol. 2: 4065
Career Achievement Award
  Film Music Society Vol. 1: 9543
  Professional Fraternity Association Vol 1: 17610
  Society for Medical Decision Making Vol 1: 18794
Career Achievement Award in Canine Research; American Kennel Club Vol. 1: 4809
Career Achievement Award - Professional Theatre Vol. 1: 5514
Career Achievement Award - Teacher in Higher Education Vol. 1: 5515
Career Advancement of Visual Artists (CAVA) Vol. 1: 15118
Career Award; EDRA Vol. 1: 9300
Career Awareness Award Vol. 1: 6336
Career Development Award Vol. 1: 20149
Career Development Award in Skin Research Vol. 1: 8891
Career Development Awards
  American Association for Cancer Research Vol. 1: 965
  National Institute of Nursing Research Vol 1: 15271
Career Development Fund Vol. 1: 21751
Career Development Grants Vol. 1: 1471
Career Development Resource Award Vol. 1: 7588
Career Grants Vol. 1: 20229
Career/Lifetime Achievement Award Vol. 1: 5265
Career of Distinguished Scholarship Award Vol. 1: 4649
Caregiver Appreciation Certificate Vol. 1: 506
Carey Award Vol. 2: 9051
Carey Distinguished District Chair Awards; Ralph E. Vol. 1: 15098
Carey, Jr. Distinguished Service Award; W. N. Vol. 1: 20160
Cargill Animal Nutrition Young Scientist Award Vol. 1: 2099
Carhartt National Team Award Vol. 1: 15233
Caribbean Hotel Association Awards Vol. 1: 7592
Caribbean Hotelier of the Year Vol. 1: 7592
Caribbean Prize for Peace Through the Pursuit of Justice Vol. 2: 825
Caribbean Review Award; Annual Vol. 1: 7594
Carillon School Prize Vol. 2: 1089
Caring Award Vol. 1: 7597
Caring for the Earth Vol. 1: 17791
Caring Person; Gilbert and Kathleen Wrenn Award for a Humanitarian and Vol. 1: 2074
Caritas Medal Vol. 1: 16349
Carl E. Darrow Student Wood Design Competition Vol. 1: 2855
Carl I. Brahce Gerontology Award Vol. 1: 12558
Carl XVI Gustavs Medalj Vol. 2: 6206
Carleton Award; Robert H. Vol. 1: 15683
Carlin Service Award; John Vol. 1: 20746
Carlisle Award; JF Vol. 2: 9343
Carll Award; John Franklin Vol. 1: 19234
Carlo Mauri Memorial Trophy Vol. 2: 4059
Carlos Teixeira Prize Vol. 2: 5405
Carlsburg Light People's Choice Award Vol. 1: 20114
Carlsen Award; Emil and Dines Vol. 1: 13781
Carlson Award; Chester F. Vol. 1: 18711
Carlson Award for Innovation in Engineering Education; Chester F. Vol. 1: 4004
Carmel Chamber Music Competition Vol. 1: 7797
Carmichael Members and Fellows Lecture Award; Emmitt B. Vol. 1: 2799
Carmody-Lebo Memorial Award for Outstanding District Delegate; Helen Vol. 1: 3205
Carne Service Award; Herbert O. Vol. 1: 975

Carnegie International Exhibition Vol. 1: 7607
Carnegie Medal Vol. 1: 7603
Carnegie Medal; Andrew Vol. 1: 5437
Carnegie Prize Vol. 1: 7607
Carnegie Prize; Andrew Vol. 1: 13782
Carnot Award in Energy Conservation; Sadi Vol. 1: 20493
Carnot Award; Sadi Vol. 2: 2483
Carnot; Prix Lazare Vol. 2: 1999
Caro and Rufino Jose Cuervo National Order; Miguel Antonio Vol. 2: 1314
Caro y Rufino Jose Cuervo; Orden Nacional de Miguel Antonio Vol. 2: 1314
Carol Ruppe Distinguished Service Award Vol. 1: 18684
Caroline tum Suden/France Hellebrandt Professional Opportunity Awards Vol. 1: 3512
Carothers Medal Vol. 2: 9123
Carpenter Award; Leroy H. Vol. 1: 9203
Carpenter Award; William W. Vol. 1: 16385
Carpenter Prize; Margaret Haley Vol. 1: 13003
Carper Award for Best Entry by a Young Journalist; James D. Vol. 1: 14352
Carr Award; Alice Vol. 1: 2933
Carr Flower Arranging Award; Celia Vol. 1: 8915
Carr Music Award; Celia Vol. 1: 8916
Carr Premium; Robert Alfred Vol. 2: 7757
Carr Scholarship; Alice Vol. 1: 2935
Carrel Award; Alexis Vol. 2: 2483
Carrier Award; ASHRAE - Willis H. Vol. 1: 4427
Carriere Award; Jean P. Vol. 1: 19743
Carriere; Prix Eugene Vol. 2: 2145
Carriker, Jr. Memorial Award; Clyde Vol. 1: 20097
Carringer Mental Health Journalism Award; Helen Vol. 1: 15378
Carroll Advancement of Management Awards; Phil Vol. 1: 18623
Carroll Foundation Award Vol. 2: 7509
Carroll Literary Award; John M. Vol. 1: 12878
Carroll Prize; Mitchell B. Vol. 2: 4823
The Carroll Society Vol. 1: 7613
Carron Award; I. Louis Vol. 1: 20075
Carron Keeper Vol. 1: 20075
Carski Foundation Distinguished Teaching Award Vol. 1: 4133
Carsoel; Prix Pierre Vol. 2: 1001
Carson Award; Rachel Vol. 1: 18856
Carsten Nielsen Prize Vol. 2: 1479
Carstensen Memorial Award; Vernon Vol. 1: 281
Carta de Reconocimiento Vol. 1: 11120
Cartan; Fondation Elie Vol. 2: 1855
Carter Award; Jonathan Vol. 1: 10237
Carter Award; Leona Lyons Vol. 1: 3063
Carter Bronze Medal Vol. 2: 7283
Carter Supply Effectiveness Award; Maj. Gen. Warren R. Vol. 1: 16820
Carter Trophy Vol. 1: 10987
Cartianu Prize; George Vol. 2: 5819
Cartier Diamond Dagger Award Vol. 2: 7362
Cartoon Award Vol. 1: 11106
Cartoon Network Award for Best Animation Vol. 1: 16946
Cartwright Award; L. J. Vol. 1: 6917
Cartwright Prize Vol. 2: 8483
Carty Award for the Advancement of Science; John J. Vol. 1: 13828
Carus Lectures Vol. 1: 3426
Carus-Medaille Vol. 2: 2702
Carus Medal
Deutsche Akademie der Naturforscher Leopoldina Vol. 2: 2702
Stadt Schweinfurt Vol 2: 3075
Carus Preis Vol. 2: 3075
Caruso International Jazz Trumpet Solo Competition; Carmine Vol. 1: 12095
Caruthers Memorial Award; Jimmy Vol. 1: 20416
Caruthers Memorial Championship Rookie Driver of the Year Award; Jimmy Vol. 1: 20416
CAS Award for Accomplishment on Aerophilately Vol. 1: 6874
CASA/SME Industry and University LEAD Awards Vol. 1: 8326
Casadesus International Piano Competition; Robert Vol. 1: 8100
Casagrande International Piano Competition; Alessandro Vol. 2: 3889
Casagrande Professional Development Award; Arthur Vol. 1: 4304
Casals Violoncello Competition; Pablo Vol. 2: 3285
Casati in Discipline Scientifiche; Premio di Laurea Luigi Vol. 2: 3829
Casati in Discipline Uranistiche; Premio di Laurea Luigi Vol. 2: 3830
CASE Award of Excellence Vol. 1: 14878
Case Medal; Cyrus Hall McCormick - Jerome Increase Vol. 1: 4229
CASE Outstanding Administrator Award Vol. 1: 8567
Casey Award Vol. 1: 19621
Casey Minnesota Award; Ralph D. Vol. 1: 10811
Cash Award Vol. 1: 20531
CASH Hall of Fame Award Vol. 2: 5217
Cash-In-A-Flash Award Program Vol. 1: 20468
Casida Award; L. E. Vol. 1: 4259
CASME Award Vol. 2: 7322
Caso; Premio Alfonso Vol. 2: 4534
Cass Correctional Achievement Award; E. R. Vol. 1: 2022
Cassavetes Award; John Vol. 1: 8882
Casselberry Award Vol. 1: 2925
Casselberry Fund Vol. 1: 2925
Cassels Reporter of the Year Award Vol. 1: 17973
Cassin; Prix Rene Vol. 2: 2083
Casteel Memorial Award; Marvin Vol. 1: 12038
Castellani - Reiss Medal and Award Vol. 1: 11990
Castelltort I Ferrer Trophy; Josep Vol. 2: 6011
Castelo Branco Prize; Camilo Vol. 2: 5492
Castex; Prix Louis Vol. 2: 2178
Castiau; Prix Adelson Vol. 2: 1011
Castle of Good Hope Decoration Vol. 2: 5730
Castle Trophy Vol. 1: 15646
Castleman Award for Excellence in Chamber Music Teaching Vol. 1: 7793
CASTME Awards Vol. 2: 7322
Castner Lecture and Medal Vol. 2: 9002
Castro Prize; Ferreira de Vol. 2: 5446
Cat of the Year Awards Vol. 2: 333
CATA Merit Award Vol. 1: 6947
CATA Writing Award Vol. 1: 6948
Catalan; Prix Eugene Vol. 2: 1055
Catalog of the Year Awards Vol. 1: 14594
Catalunya Trophy; Generalitat de Vol. 2: 6011
Catalyst Award Vol. 1: 13236
Catalyst for Change Award; Elizabeth Futas Vol. 1: 2975
Catalyst Grants Vol. 1: 17865
Category Awards Vol. 1: 14590
Catenacci; Prix Vol. 2: 1706
Catenacci; Prix Hercule
Academie Francaise Vol. 2: 2162
Institut de France Vol 2: 2424
Caterer Award Vol. 1: 11324
Caterpillar Scholars Award Fund Vol. 1: 19145
Catholic Book Awards Vol. 1: 7658
Catholic Pharmacist of the Year Vol. 1: 14628
Catholic Secondary Education Award Vol. 1: 14607
Catlin Peace Pipe Award
Continental Confederation of Adopted Indians Vol. 1: 8487
American Indian Lore Association Vol 1: 2604
Cattell Cup Vol. 2: 9068
Cattell Early Career Award for Programmatic Research; Raymond B. Vol. 1: 2159
Cattell Memorial Award; McKeen Vol. 1: 1847
Caty; Prix Charles Vol. 2: 986
Cauble Short Play Award; John Vol. 1: 12541
Caudill Young Readers' Book Award; Rebecca Vol. 1: 17902
Caulfield, Jr. Medal for Exemplary Contributions to National Water Policy; Henry P. Vol. 1: 4826
Cavallaro Medal Vol. 2: 2747
Cavanaugh Award; Catherine A. M. Vol. 1: 15731
Cavanaugh Award for Excellence in Training and Education in Aging; The Gloria Vol. 1: 4640
Cavanaugh Memorial Award; W. T. Vol. 1: 5934
Cavanaugh Memorial Prize; John Vol. 1: 15698
Cavanaugh Student Grant; William M. Vol. 1: 17733
Cavender Award of Service; Maggie Vol. 1: 13760
Cavendish Area Tourist Association Creative Writing Award for Children Vol. 1: 17545
Cavendish Excellence in Library Programming Award; Marshall Vol. 1: 2971
Caveness, M.D. Memorial Award; William Fields Vol. 1: 6605
Caves Award; Philip K. Vol. 1: 11933
Cavett Award Vol. 1: 15791
Cavin Award; Sheri Lynette Vol. 1: 5112
Cavling Prize Vol. 2: 1480
Cavour Prize; Grinzane Vol. 2: 3881
Cawood Award; Harold Vol. 1: 1614
Cawood Japonica Award; Arminta Vol. 1: 1615
Cayeux; Fondation Lucien Vol. 2: 1927
Cayla-Martin; Prix E. du Vol. 2: 987
CBA National Music Award Vol. 1: 6962
CBA President's Award Vol. 1: 6966
CBA University Law School Essay Contest; Department of Justice - Vol. 1: 6967
CBC Honors Program Vol. 1: 7904
CBC Literary Awards Vol. 1: 6789

Award Index

CBC Medal Vol. 1: 8011
CBC Radio National Competition for Amateur Choirs Vol. 1: 6997
CBC Radio National Competition for Young Composers Vol. 1: 6998
CBC Radio National Competition for Young Performers Vol. 1: 6999
CBC Radio Talent Competition Vol. 1: 6999
CBC Young Composers Competition Vol. 1: 6790
CBI International Environmental Award Vol. 1: 2877
CBR Scholar Awards Vol. 1: 7707
C.C. Knight Award Vol. 1: 17027
C.C. Ludwig Award Vol. 1: 12749
CCA Competition Vol. 1: 7025
CCA Member Recognition Vol. 2: 7226
CCCC Exemplar Award Vol. 1: 8376
CCCC James Berlin Memorial Outstanding Dissertation Award Vol. 1: 8377
CCCC Outstanding Book Award Vol. 1: 8378
CCCC Outstanding Dissertation Award Vol. 1: 8377
CCCC Richard Braddock Award Vol. 1: 14828
CCFC Book Prize Vol. 1: 8653
CCFC/CAG Student Research Award Vol. 1: 8654
CCIA Gavel Award Vol. 1: 8455
CCID Faculty Fellowship Award Vol. 1: 8319
CCID Presidents' Award Vol. 1: 8320
CCL Book of the Year Award Vol. 1: 8373
Ccol ASDC Associateship Vol. 2: 9031
Ccol FSDC Fellowship Vol. 2: 9032
CCP Awards for Alternative Film and Video Vol. 2: 5269
CCP Awards for Radio Vol. 2: 5270
CCP Awards for the Arts Vol. 2: 5271
CCPE Faculty Teaching Award Vol. 1: 7058
CD-ROM Underwater Prize Vol. 2: 2342
CDC Medal of Excellence Vol. 1: 20502
The CDS/Honickmand First Book Prize in Photography Vol. 1: 9044
CEA Honorary Life Membership Vol. 1: 8152
CEA Professional Achievement Award Vol. 1: 8153
CEA Whitworth Award for Educational Research Vol. 1: 7080
CEB-Cup Vol. 2: 858
CEB Honour List Vol. 2: 857
CEC Leadership Award Vol. 1: 8547
CEC Outstanding Contributor Award Vol. 1: 8547
CEC Research Award Vol. 1: 8548
Cecil Arthritis Medical Journalism Awards; Russell L. Vol. 1: 5125
Cecil Award; Lawrence K. Vol. 1: 2761
Cecil Kimber Enthusiasts Award Vol. 1: 13323
Cecil Writing Awards; Russell L. Vol. 1: 5125
CEDA Grand Prix Award and CEDA Best Suppliers Award Vol. 2: 7242
CEE James N. Britton Award for Inquiry within the English Language Arts Vol. 1: 14829
CEE Richard A. Meade Award Vol. 1: 14830
CEFIC Environment Award Vol. 2: 861
Celebrate Life Essay and Poster Contest Vol. 1: 8106
Celebrate Literacy Vol. 1: 10809
Celebrating Women Awards Vol. 1: 21791
Celebration Awards Vol. 1: 13949
Celette Prize Vol. 2: 7843
Cell Biology; Women in Vol. 1: 3948
Cellier; Prix Alphonse Vol. 2: 1680
Cello Award; Vincent R. Bastien Memorial Vol. 1: 21432
Cello/Viola/Double Bass Scholarship; CTBI Intermediate Vol. 1: 18282
Cello/Viola/Double Bass Scholarship; Kiwania of Wascana Senior Vol. 1: 18296
Cellular Toxicology Graduate Student Award Vol. 1: 18723
Celtic Cross Award Vol. 1: 7672
Cements Award Vol. 1: 1670
CEN-IP Vol. 1: 7082
Cena Chopinovy klavirni souteze Vol. 2: 1415
Cena Frantisek Kriegel Vol. 2: 6144
Cena Jaroslava Seiferta Vol. 2: 6145
Cena Obce Architektu za Realizaci Roku Vol. 2: 1436
Cena Pavla Orszagha Hviezdoslava Vol. 2: 5957
Cena Vilenica Vol. 2: 5987
Cenafor Prize for a Monograph Vol. 2: 1171
CenE Bankiers Audience Award Vol. 2: 4846
Census Award of Excellence Vol. 1: 20444
Centenarian Award Vol. 1: 17832
Centenary Lectureship Vol. 2: 8747
Centenary Medal
Australian Honours Secretariat Vol. 2: 189
Royal Photographic Society of Great Britain Vol 2: 8662
Royal Scottish Geographical Society Vol 2: 8680
Centennial Medal
Alumni Association of the City College of New York Vol. 1: 516
Society of Designer Craftsmen Vol 2: 9027
Centorino Award; James Vol. 1: 15357
Central Florida Film and Video Awards Vol. 1: 9724
Central Nervous System Section Van Harrevold Memorial Award Vol. 1: 3513
Central Neuropsychiatric Association Resident Award Vol. 1: 3192
Central Poster Award Vol. 1: 7764
Centurion Award Vol. 1: 548
Century Award
American Numismatic Association Vol. 1: 3206
Billboard - VNU Business Publications USA Vol 1: 6377
Century Awards Vol. 1: 18586
Century Club Award Vol. 1: 1540
Century Scholarship Vol. 1: 5857
CEO Recognition Award Vol. 1: 21760
CERES Vol. 1: 21704
Ceresis Award Vol. 2: 5248
CERSS Award Vol. 2: 4102
Certamen Anual Nacional de Tesis de Ingenieria Vol. 2: 4561
Certamen Capitolinum Vol. 2: 3986
Certamen Internacional de Cine Amateur Ciutat d'Igualada Vol. 2: 6011
Certamen Internacional de Guitarra Francisco Tarrega Vol. 2: 5999
Certamen International de Films Cortos, Ciudad de Huesca Vol. 2: 6030
Certamen Nacional de Cortomrtrajes Award Vol. 2: 6028
Certamen Nacional de Literatura *El Porvenir* Vol. 2: 4485
Certamen Nacional de Periodismo Rogelio Cantu Gomez Vol. 2: 4486
Certamen Nacional la Letra Impresa Vol. 2: 4622
Certificado Especial Vol. 1: 11121
Certificate Vol. 2: 3154
Certificate for Outstanding Service Vol. 1: 15675
Certificate of Achievement
American Urological Association Vol. 1: 4786
Chesapeake and Ohio Historical Society Vol 1: 7854
Herb Society of America Vol 1: 10410
Library Administration and Management Association Vol 1: 12815
Certificate of Achievement for Excellence in Financial Reporting
Government Finance Officers Association of United States and Canada Vol. 1: 10112
Government Finance Officers Association of United States and Canada Vol 1: 10114
Certificate of Achievement of Focused Studies Vol. 1: 120
Certificate of Appreciation
Activ Foundation Vol. 2: 52
American Occupational Therapy Association Vol 1: 3294
American Police Hall of Fame Vol 1: 3565
American Psychological Association - Division of Family Psychology (Division 43) Vol 1: 3670
American Society of Artists Vol 1: 4264
Blinded Veterans Association Vol 1: 6455
Canadian Camping Association Vol 1: 7016
Chesapeake and Ohio Historical Society Vol 1: 7855
Construction Specifications Institute Vol 1: 8435
Federal Aviation Administration Vol 1: 9429
Federation of Genealogical Societies Vol 1: 9495
The Gardeners of America/Men's Garden Clubs of America Vol 1: 9883
Herb Society of America Vol 1: 10411
Huntington Society of Canada Vol 1: 10622
International Union of Forest Research Organizations Vol 2: 766
John Pelham Historical Association Vol 1: 12400
Lakeshore Humane Society Vol 1: 12667
National Aeronautics and Space Administration Vol 1: 13883
National Amputee Golf Association Vol 1: 13931
National Carousel Association Vol 1: 14587
National Genealogical Society Vol 1: 15144
National Society, Sons of the American Revolution Vol 1: 15765
National Trappers Association Vol 1: 15909
Owsley Family Historical Society Vol 1: 16985
Rural Sociological Society Vol 1: 18186
Soaring Society of America Vol 1: 18579
Women in Film and Video Vol 1: 21725
Certificate of Appreciation and Recognition Vol. 1: 19562
Certificate of Appreciation Award
Lay Carmelite Order of the Blessed Virgin Mary of Mount Carmel Vol. 1: 12730
Specialty Graphic Imaging Association Vol 1: 19591
Certificate of Appreciation from the Ambassador of Mongolia to Japan Vol. 2: 4319
Certificate of Botanical Recognition Vol. 1: 3326

Certificate of Commendation
American Academy of Family Physicians Vol. 1: 673
American Association for State and Local History Vol 1: 1041
Federal Aviation Administration Vol 1: 9430
International Badminton Federation Vol 2: 4432
Royal Life Saving Society Vol 2: 8625
Certificate of Competence Vol. 2: 9334
Certificate of Completion Vol. 2: 62
Certificate of Craftsmanship Vol. 1: 13175
Certificate of Cultural Merit Vol. 1: 3327
Certificate of Distinguished Service Vol. 1: 15766
Certificate of Excellence in Exhibit Renovation Vol. 1: 1486
Certificate of Good Work in VOS Vol. 2: 5885
Certificate of Honor
American Association for Clinical Chemistry Vol. 1: 976
American Society for Advancement of Anesthesia and Sedation in Dentistry Vol 1: 3908
India Office of the Prime Minister Vol 2: 3378
International Institute of Space Law Vol 2: 2486
Certificate of Honor - HSA Vol. 1: 10510
Certificate of Honour Vol. 2: 4963
Certificate of Literature Vol. 1: 17264
Certificate of Merit
American Association of Teachers of German Vol. 1: 1444
American Red Cross National Headquarters Vol 1: 3822
American Society for Engineering Education Vol 1: 4005
American Society of International Law Vol 1: 4463
Bookbuilders West Vol 1: 6514
Canadian Public Health Association Vol 1: 7355
Canadian Society of Diagnostic Medical Sonographers Vol 1: 7454
Governor Baxter School for the Deaf Vol 1: 10124
Huntington Society of Canada Vol 1: 10623
International Animated Film Society, ASIFA - Hollywood Vol 1: 11190
International Youth Hostel Federation Vol 2: 8019
Mathematical Association of America Vol 1: 13189
Mount Vernon Genealogical Society Vol 1: 13639
National Association of the Physically Handicapped Vol 1: 14425
National Environmental Health Association Vol 1: 14942
National Speleological Society Vol 1: 15795
Pierre Fauchard Academy Vol 1: 17346
Specialty Graphic Imaging Association Vol 1: 19592
United States Fencing Coaches Association Vol 1: 20581
Zoological Society of Southern Africa Vol 2: 5800
Certificate of Merit Award Vol. 1: 17522
Certificate of Merit - Commercial Wool Production in Canada Vol. 1: 7031
Certificate of Merit for Marching Excellence Vol. 1: 14482
Certificate of Merit for Zookeeper Education Vol. 1: 1487
Certificate of Meritorious Arrangement Vol. 1: 3328
Certificate of Outstanding Work in the Field of Voluntary Service Vol. 2: 2287
Certificate of Recognition
Audubon of Florida Vol. 1: 6073
Cajal Club Vol 1: 6726
The Gardeners of America/Men's Garden Clubs of America Vol 1: 9884
Society of Automotive Engineers Vol 1: 19054
Certificate of Satisfaction Vol. 2: 5930
Certificate of Service Vol. 1: 7427
Certificate of String Performance Vol. 2: 9191
Certificate of Thanks Vol. 2: 53
Certificate of Victory Vol. 1: 15176
Certificate; World Association of Christian Radio Amateurs and Listeners Award Vol. 2: 9231
Certificates, Diplomas, and Licentiates in Genealogy and Heraldry Vol. 2: 7699
Certificates for Skills Competency Vol. 2: 7397
Certificates of Appreciation, Citations, and Commendations Vol. 1: 18453
Certificates of Appreciation, Citations, Commendations, First Class Award Vol. 1: 18453
Certificates of Excellence Vol. 1: 10228
Certificates of Honor and Appreciation Vol. 1: 1940
Certificates of Merit
American Association of Petroleum Geologists Vol. 1: 1332
Municipal Art Society of New York Vol 1: 13675
National Academy Vol 1: 13783
Certificates of Merit Awards - Regional History Vol. 1: 7150
Certificates of Merit for Excellence in Writing - *Journal of Allied Health* Vol. 1: 5836
Certificates of Recognition/Appreciation Vol. 1: 3699
Certification Excellence Award Vol. 1: 1214
Certifications of Appreciation Vol. 1: 21844
Certified International Financier Vol. 1: 11685
Certified Kapnismologist Award Vol. 1: 17355
Certified Property Manager (CPM) of the Year Award Vol. 1: 11034
Certified Remodeler (CR) "Superstar" Award Vol. 1: 14428
Certified Residential Specialist Designation Vol. 1: 8583
Cervenka Scholarship Award; Arthur and Gladys Vol. 1: 19146
Cervi Award; Eugene Vol. 1: 12027
Cesar Machado de Jornalismo; Premio Municipal Julio Vol. 2: 5432
Cesery Award Vol. 1: 20089
Cetacean Citation Vol. 1: 7788
Cetus Corporation Biotechnology Research Award Vol. 1: 4132
Cevenini; Premio Angela Vol. 2: 4014
Cevenini Prize; Angela Vol. 2: 4014
Ceylon Development Engineering Award Vol. 2: 6118
CFA Distinguished Service Award Vol. 1: 8462
CFA Totem Vol. 1: 7098
CFDA Fashion Awards Vol. 1: 8575
CFF/NIH Funding Award Vol. 1: 8696
CFIC Book Prize Vol. 1: 8653
CFIC/CAG Student Research Award Vol. 1: 8654
CFL Outstanding Player Awards Vol. 1: 7102
CFM Award Vol. 1: 5645
CFMS Scholarship Vol. 1: 6741
CFS Medal Vol. 1: 4847
CFUW A. Vibert Douglas International Fellowship Vol. 2: 6406
CGS Prize Vol. 1: 7129
Chabas; Prix Paul Vol. 2: 1681
Chabon Award; Irwin Vol. 1: 12670
Chadwick Fellowship; Arts Council of England Helen Vol. 2: 7132
Chai Award Vol. 1: 6483
Chaim and Simcha Tova Mizel Memorial Exhibit Award; Menachem Vol. 1: 3207
Chain Bookseller of the Year Award Vol. 1: 6984
Chainlink Fence Design Award Vol. 1: 7790
Chairman of the Board Awards Vol. 1: 6216
Chairman's Award
Alcoa Inc. Vol. 1: 426
American Academy of Medical Administrators Vol 1: 684
American Association of Engineering Societies Vol 1: 1196
Concrete Society of Southern Africa Vol 2: 5533
Friends of the Pendleton District Vol 1: 9812
Goodwill Industries International Vol 1: 10082
International Society of Certified Electronics Technicians Vol 1: 11982
Machine Vision Association of the Society of Manufacturing Engineers Vol 1: 13010
National Association for the Advancement of Colored People Vol 1: 14049
National Biplane Association Vol 1: 14513
National Kidney Foundation Vol 1: 15319
National Religious Broadcasters Vol 1: 15612
Outdoor Advertising Association of America Vol 1: 16963
Pendleton District Historical, Recreational, and Tourism Commission Vol 1: 17160
ProLiteracy Worldwide Vol 1: 17672
Society of Cable Telecommunications Engineers Vol 1: 19077
Special Olympics Canada Vol 1: 19570
Chairman's Award for Career Achievement Vol. 1: 6289
Chairman's Awards Vol. 1: 17709
Chairman's Citation Vol. 1: 12785
Chairman's Citation of Merit Awards Vol. 1: 385
The Chairman's Cup Vol. 1: 1095
Chairman's Leadership Award Vol. 1: 1702
Chairman's Safety Award Vol. 1: 17953
Chairman's Special Award Vol. 1: 21143
Chairs and Professorships Awards Vol. 1: 20002
Chair's Award Vol. 1: 17463
Chair's Citation
American Association of Homes and Services for the Aging Vol. 1: 1223
Council of Scientific Society Presidents Vol 1: 8587

Chakravarty Awards; Prof. Hira Lal Vol. 2: 3529
Chalice Award Vol. 1: 9656
Challenge for Road Safety Vol. 2: 2454
Challenge Shield Vol. 2: 8130
Challenge Trophies Vol. 1: 2218
Challenger Award Vol. 1: 14583
Chalmers Award for Poetry; CAA Jack Vol. 1: 6957
Chalmers Memorial Medal Vol. 2: 8842
Chamber Music America Commissioning Program Vol. 1: 7794
Chamber Music Competition Vol. 1: 13702
Chamber Music Society of the Monterey Peninsula Competition Vol. 1: 7797
Chamber Music Yellow Springs Competition Vol. 1: 7801
Chamber of Commerce Vol. 1: 13428
Chamber of Commerce Scholarship Award Vol. 1: 7803
Chamber Opera Competition Vol. 1: 15426
Chamber Person of the Year Vol. 1: 18436
Chamber Scholarship Award Vol. 1: 10233
Chamberlain Award; C. K. Vol. 1: 9082
Chambers Award; Frank A. Vol. 1: 318
Chamorro Inter-American Relations Award; Pedro Joaquin Vol. 1: 11107
Champion Cup Holder Vol. 2: 4656
Champion Exporter Vol. 2: 4081
Champion of Champions Vol. 1: 3414
Champion of the Student Press Award Vol. 1: 19810
Champion of the Trail Award Vol. 1: 9637
Champion of the Year Award Vol. 2: 8122
Champion Outstanding Player of the Year Vol. 1: 15316
Champion Shots Medal Vol. 2: 190
Champions for Children Vol. 1: 9705
Champions of Higher Independent Education in Florida (C.H.I.E.F.) Awards Vol. 1: 10715
Championship Award Vol. 1: 20926
Championship Awards
National Derby Rallies Vol. 1: 14912
Spanish Mustang Registry Vol 1: 19541
Championship Banners Vol. 1: 14655
Championship Director Awards, Competition Division Vol. 1: 6217
Championship of Champions Vol. 1: 20770
Championship Silver Challenge Trophy Vol. 2: 8161
Championships, Cups, and Trophies Vol. 2: 2455
The Championships, Wimbledon Vol. 2: 6688
Champlain Award Vol. 1: 7049
Champlin Research Award Vol. 1: 10845
Champney Prize; Philip Vol. 1: 12644
Chancellor's Medal Vol. 1: 8029
Chandra Bose Medal; Jagdish Vol. 2: 3478
Chaney Award Vol. 1: 977
Chang Award for Lipid or Flavor Science; Stephen S. Vol. 1: 10936
Chang Award; Stephen S. Vol. 1: 3309
Change Student Travel Grants; Incubic/Milton Vol. 1: 16788
Channel 4 Archaeological Film Awards Vol. 2: 7212
The Channel Four Awards Vol. 2: 6917
Chant Medal; C. A. Vol. 1: 18141
Chanute Award; Octave Vol. 1: 2676
Chanute Flight Award Vol. 1: 2676
Chanute Medal; Octave Vol. 1: 21566
Chapanis Best Student Paper Award; Alphonse Vol. 1: 10577
Chapbook Competition Vol. 1: 17741
Chapelle Award for Nautical Research; Howard I. Vol. 1: 16047
Chapin Award for Volunteers in the Arts; Elizabeth Vol. 1: 8013
Chapin Award; Harold C. Vol. 1: 1455
Chapin Media Awards; Harry Vol. 1: 21925
Chapin Memorial Humanitarian Award; Harry Vol. 1: 14359
Chapin Self-Reliance Award; Harry Vol. 1: 21926
Chaplain Emeritus Award Vol. 1: 5821
Chaplain of the Year Vol. 1: 20349
Chapline Land Stewardship Award; W. R. Vol. 1: 18834
Chapline Research Award; W. R. Vol. 1: 18835
Chapman Award; Dr. Wilfred Vol. 2: 659
Chapman Medal Vol. 2: 8431
Chapman Medal; R. W. Vol. 2: 376
Chapman Memorial Award; Charles F. Vol. 1: 15363
Chapman Memorial Award for Outstanding Contributions to Technical Services Law Librarianship; Renee D. Vol. 1: 1250
Chapman Memorial Fund Award; Frank M. Vol. 1: 3155
Chapman Prize Essay Vol. 2: 7099
Chapter Achievement Award
Door and Hardware Institute Vol. 1: 8997
Women in Insurance and Financial Services Vol 1: 21740
Chapter Activities Award Vol. 1: 1963
Chapter Activity Award Contest Vol. 1: 9434
Chapter and Regional Director of the Year Vol. 1: 6168
Chapter Award for Excellence in Educational Programming Vol. 1: 11562
Chapter Award for Excellence in Membership Marketing Vol. 1: 11563
Chapter Award for Excellence in Newsletter Publishing Vol. 1: 11564
Chapter Award for Minority Enhancement Vol. 1: 3487
Chapter Awards
International Society of Logistics Vol. 1: 11995
Society of Cosmetic Chemists Vol 1: 19091
Tau Beta Pi Association Vol 1: 19931
Chapter Best Speaker Award Vol. 1: 19091
Chapter Competition Vol. 1: 10988
Chapter Excellence Vol. 1: 1215
Chapter Excellence Award Vol. 1: 16713
Chapter Excellence Awards Vol. 1: 11950
Chapter Excellence Awards and Chapter of the Year Award Vol. 1: 3027
Chapter History Award Vol. 1: 6325
Chapter Hope Chest Award Vol. 1: 15394
Chapter Key Awards Vol. 1: 18496
Chapter Leader of the Year Vol. 1: 13281
Chapter Member-of-The-Year Award Vol. 1: 4106
Chapter Merit Award Vol. 1: 19091
Chapter Merit Awards Vol. 1: 4685
Chapter Merit Awards for Professional Chapters Vol. 1: 18699
Chapter Merit Awards for Students Vol. 1: 18700
Chapter Newsletter Awards Vol. 1: 18497
Chapter Newsletter of the Year Award Vol. 1: 5088
Chapter of Excellence Award Vol. 1: 11939
Chapter of the Year
ARMA International - The Association of Information Management Professionals Vol. 1: 5089
Association for Professionals in Infection Control and Epidemiology Vol 1: 5458
Audubon of Florida Vol 1: 6074
BACCHUS Network Vol 1: 6190
Lamaze International Vol 1: 12671
National Broadcasting Society - Alpha Epsilon Rho Vol 1: 14536
National Property Management Association Vol 1: 15558
Professional Aviation Maintenance Association Vol 1: 17586
System Safety Society Vol 1: 19884
U.S. Hang Gliding Association Vol 1: 20612
Chapter of the Year Award
American Humanist Association Vol. 1: 2583
American Society for Information Science and Technology Vol 1: 4107
American Society of Certified Engineering Technicians Vol 1: 4276
Association for Facilities Engineering Vol 1: 5365
International Facility Management Association Vol 1: 11565
Mail Systems Management Association Vol 1: 13023
National Institute of Governmental Purchasing Vol 1: 15266
Chapter or Unit Anniversary Awards Vol. 1: 1398
Chapter President Award Vol. 1: 18790
Chapter President of the Year Award Vol. 1: 7964
Chapter Presidents Trophy Award Vol. 1: 10801
Chapter Program of the Year Vol. 1: 12672
Chapter Project of the Year Award; Majors/MLA Vol. 1: 13260
Chapter Publication of the Year Award Vol. 1: 4108
Chapter Publications Contest Vol. 1: 10971
Chapter Research Advancement Award Vol. 1: 18498
Chapter Research Award Vol. 1: 10972
Chapter Service Award Vol. 1: 5711
Chapter Volunteer of the Year Vol. 1: 12673
Chapters Council Award Vol. 1: 10904
Chapters of the Year Vol. 1: 13278
Charcot Award; J. B. Vol. 1: 12430
Charcot Award; Jean-Martin Vol. 2: 8137
Chard Decoration; John Vol. 2: 5731
Chard Medal; John Vol. 2: 5732
Chardonnay Challenge Vol. 1: 20986
Charity Accounts Award Vol. 2: 7662
Charles A. Black Award Vol. 1: 8533
Charles Alvin Emerson Medal Vol. 1: 21478
Charles Carroll Award Vol. 1: 10200
Charles Darwin University Essay Award Vol. 2: 484
Charles E. Szper Memorial Fund Vol. 1: 2085
Charles Frankel Prize Vol. 1: 14935
Charles Kreupper Award Vol. 1: 18024
Charles L. Towle Award Vol. 1: 13549
Charles Loring Brace Award Vol. 1: 16907
Charles River Prize Vol. 1: 4815
Charlotte Festival/New Plays in America Vol. 1: 7812
Charlotte Kohlerprijs Vol. 2: 4930

Charlson Award; Jim Vol. 1: 5546
Charlton Lifetime Achievement Award; Thomas L. Vol. 1: 20038
Charmian Medal Vol. 2: 8773
Charnwood Memorial Award; Lord Vol. 2: 6725
Chartered Accountant of the Year Vol. 2: 4973
Chartered Accountants/Beta Alpha Psi Scholarships Vol. 1: 5597
Chartered Institute of Journalists Gold Medal Vol. 2: 7276
Chartered Institute of Transport Annual Innovation Award Vol. 2: 5006
Chartered Society of Designers Honorary Fellow Vol. 2: 7299
Chartered Society of Designers Medal Vol. 2: 7300
Chartered State Association Executive Director of the Year Vol. 1: 14551
Chartered State Association of the Year Vol. 1: 14552
Chartered State Association President of the Year Vol. 1: 14553
Chartier; Prix Vol. 2: 1707
Chase Award for Excellence in Issue Management; W. Howard Vol. 1: 12240
Chase Award for Physician Executive Excellence; John D. Vol. 1: 5767
Chase Award; Joe Vol. 1: 17587
Chase Award; Joe M. Vol. 1: 9581
Chasko Award; Lawrence J. Vol. 1: 1236
Chasman Scholarship for Women; Renate W. Vol. 1: 6649
Chassie Awards Vol. 1: 17826
Chassis Inspectors Award Vol. 1: 10978
Chastain Renal Research Award; J.D. Vol. 1: 15330
Chatt Lectureship; Joseph Vol. 2: 8748
Chattanooga Research Award Vol. 1: 3488
Chatterjee Memorial Award; G. P. Vol. 2: 3530
Chatterjee Memorial Lecture; Dr. Guru Prajad Vol. 2: 3479
Chaudesaigues; Prix Vol. 2: 1708
Chautauqua International Exhibition of American Art Vol. 1: 7819
Chauveau Medal; Pierre Vol. 1: 18162
Chauvenet Prize Vol. 1: 13190
Chavee; Prix Honore Vol. 2: 1771
Chavez; Premio Maestro Ignacio Vol. 2: 4636
Chavez Young Investigator Award; Professor Ignacio Vol. 2: 4551
Chayefsky Laurel Award for Television; Paddy Vol. 1: 21989
Chedanne; Fondation Vol. 2: 1717
Cheek Exemplary Service Award; Willard D. Vol. 1: 4006
Cheese Hunt Chase Vol. 2: 3694
Chef Award Vol. 1: 11325
Chef Ireland
Chefs and Cooks Circle Vol. 2: 7303
National Restaurant Association Vol 1: 15625
Society of German Cooks Vol 2: 3064
Chef of the Year Vol. 1: 7592
Chef of the Year; National Vol. 1: 7066
Cheiron Medal Vol. 2: 807
Chelsea Award Vol. 1: 7821
Chemeca Medal Vol. 2: 377
Chemeca Student Design Prize Vol. 2: 378
Chemical Education Medal Vol. 2: 5690
Chemical Health and Safety Award Vol. 1: 1743
Chemical Industry Medal Vol. 1: 19084
Chemical Institute of Canada Awards for High School Chemistry Teachers Vol. 1: 7841
Chemical Institute of Canada Medal Vol. 1: 7836
Chemical Pioneer Awards Vol. 1: 2800
Chemical Society of Japan Award Vol. 2: 4105
Chemical Society of Japan Award for Chemical Education Vol. 2: 4106
Chemical Society of Japan Award for Distinguished Technical Achievements Vol. 2: 4107
Chemical Society of Japan Award for Technological Development Vol. 2: 4108
Chemical Society of Japan Award for Young Chemists Vol. 2: 4109
Chemical Society of Japan Award of Merit for Chemical Education Vol. 2: 4110
Chemical Technology Award Vol. 2: 4464
Chemistry Teaching Award Vol. 2: 8883
Cheney Award; Frances Neel Vol. 1: 19968
Chennault Award; Lt. General Claire Lee Vol. 1: 339
Chennault Trophy Vol. 1: 5107
Cherokee National Hall of Fame Vol. 1: 7852
Cherry Award for Great Teachers; Robert Foster Vol. 1: 18078
Cherry Chair for Distinguished Teaching; Robert Foster Vol. 1: 18079
Cherry Prize; Professor J. Vol. 2: 7818
Cherry Student Prize; T. M. Vol. 2: 69
Cherry Tree Marathon Vol. 1: 16260
Chesley Awards Vol. 1: 5848
Chesney Gold Medal Vol. 2: 8865
Chess Championship; U.S. Vol. 1: 20446
Chess Journalism Merit Awards Competition Vol. 1: 7862
Chess Olympiad for the Blind Vol. 2: 6156
Chess; President's Award for Services to Vol. 2: 6980
Chess World Champions Vol. 2: 3192
Chester County Community Hero Vol. 1: 20907
Chester County Youth Community Hero Vol. 1: 20908
Chester Paul Siess Award for Excellence in Structural Research Vol. 1: 1964
Chetwynd Award for Entrepreneurial Excellence Vol. 1: 7093
Chevalier; Fondation Auguste Vol. 2: 1803
Chevallier; Prix Jean-Baptiste Vol. 2: 2058
Cheviot Hall of Fame; American North Country Vol. 1: 3194
Chevron - Times Mirror Magazines Conservation Awards Program Vol. 1: 7864
Chevron U.S.A. Marketing Award Vol. 1: 15348
ChevronTexaco Conservation Awards Program Vol. 1: 7864
Chia Hsin Prize Vol. 2: 6594
Chicago Film Critics Awards - Chicago Flame Vol. 1: 7886
Chicago Folklore Prize Vol. 1: 20994
Chicago International Children's Film Festival Vol. 1: 7888
Chicago International Festival of Children's Films Vol. 1: 7888
Chicago International Film Festival Vol. 1: 8001
Chick Trophy (Empire Division Champion); John Vol. 1: 2503
Chicken Council Award; National Vol. 1: 17498
Chief Financial Officers Award for Distinction in Public Finance Vol. 1: 20532
Chief Justice J.T. Brown Shield; The Goodfellow Memorial Award in Voice/ The Vol. 1: 18286
Chief Minister's History Book Vol. 2: 484
Chief of Engineers Award of Excellence Vol. 1: 20405
Chief of Engineers Design and Environmental Awards Program Vol. 1: 20405
Chief of the South African Defense Force Commendation Medal Vol. 2: 5744
Chiiki Koryu Shinko Sho Vol. 2: 4171
Chilcote Young Investigator Award; Max E. Vol. 1: 978
Child Advocate of the Year
Children's Watch International Vol. 1: 7919
North American Council on Adoptable Children Vol 1: 16418
Child Award; Julia Vol. 1: 11326
Child Cookbook Awards; Julia Vol. 1: 11326
Child Health Foundation Prize Vol. 2: 6564
Childers Award for Distinguished Graduate Teaching; Norman F. Vol. 1: 4090
Childers, Jr., Award; Waco F. Vol. 1: 2572
Children Author/Illustrator Award Vol. 1: 5052
Children Award; Canadian Library Association Book of the Year for Vol. 1: 7254
Children's ABBY Award Vol. 1: 1582
Children's Africana Book Awards Vol. 1: 261
Children's Book Award
Association of Jewish Libraries Vol. 1: 5744
Children's Book Committee Vol 1: 7901
Federation of Children's Book Groups Vol 2: 7511
Icelandic Library and Information Science Association Vol 2: 3324
South Carolina Association of School Librarians Vol 1: 19443
Children's Book Council Award Vol. 2: 3608
Children's Book of Spring, Summer, Autumn, Winter in Slovakia; Most Beautiful and the Best Vol. 2: 5960
Children's Book of the Year; Alberta Vol. 1: 6503
Children's Book Prize Vol. 1: 21519
Children's Choice Award
Alliance for Children and Television Vol. 1: 454
Canadian Toy Testing Council Vol 1: 7518
Children's Illustrator of the Year Award Vol. 1: 6985
Children's Literature Association Article Award Vol. 1: 7908
Children's Literature Association Book Award Vol. 1: 7909
Children's Literature Association Research Fellowship Vol. 1: 7910
Children's Literature Festival Award Vol. 1: 12528
Children's Novel Writing Competition Vol. 2: 4428
Children's Story Prize Vol. 2: 4528
Childs Award; Gayke B. Vol. 1: 20947
Childs Award; James Lawton Vol. 1: 12264
Chili Cook-off; International Vol. 1: 4667
Chilton Prize; Ken Vol. 1: 18142
China Service Medal - Navy, Marine Corps, Coast Guard Vol. 1: 8808
Chinard Prize; Gilbert Vol. 1: 18676

Chinard Prize; The Gilbert Vol. 1: 7925
Chinese-American Librarians Association Distinguished Service Award Vol. 1: 7927
Chinese American Medical Society Scientific Achievement Award Vol. 1: 7929
Chinese Chemical Society Awards Vol. 2: 6596
Chinese Martial Arts Leadership Award Vol. 1: 549
Chinese Martial Arts Outstanding Service Award Vol. 1: 550
Chipman Award; John Vol. 1: 5404
Chipp Memorial Award; Rodney D. Vol. 1: 19364
Chiron Therapeutics Award for Excellence of Scholarship and Consistency of Contribution to the Oncology Nursing Literature Vol. 1: 16717
Chiron Therapeutics Chapter Excellence Award Vol. 1: 16713
Chiron Therapeutics Susan Baird Excellence in Writing Awards in Clinical Practice and Nursing Research Vol. 1: 16711
Chiropractor of the Year
Chiropractic Association of South Africa Vol. 2: 5531
International Chiropractors Association Vol 1: 11466
Chisholm Award for Lifetime Achievement; Jack Vol. 1: 7094
Chisholm Intermediate Woodwind Scholarship; The F. W. Vol. 1: 18279
Choice Outstanding Academic Books and Nonprint Materials Vol. 1: 7935
Choice's Outstanding Academic Books Vol. 1: 7935
Choir of the World at Llangollen Vol. 2: 8081
Cholmondeley Award for Poets Vol. 2: 8980
Chon'guk Kugak Kyongyon Tachoe Vol. 2: 5511
Chopin Competition; Warsaw Vol. 2: 2691
Chopin; Grand Prix du Disque Frederic Vol. 2: 5305
Chopin-Klavierwettbewerb; Europaischer Vol. 2: 2691
Chopin Piano Competition Vol. 2: 1415
Chopinovy klavirni souteze; Cena Vol. 2: 1415
Choppin Memorial Award; IEA - Bruce H. Vol. 2: 4795
Chopra Lecture; Bashambar Nath Vol. 2: 3480
Choral Awards Vol. 2: 313
Chorbachi Prizes; Walid Vol. 2: 7668
Choreography and Flamenco Dance Competition Vol. 1: 9227
Chorpenning Playwright Award; Charlotte B. Vol. 1: 888
Chorus America/ASCAP Awards for Adventurous Programming Vol. 1: 7941
Chow Award; Ven Te Vol. 1: 4305
Chow Chow Club Annual Awards Vol. 1: 7945
Chow Memorial Endowed Lecturer Vol. 1: 12127
Chree Medal and Prize; Charles Vol. 2: 7726
CHRIE Industry Recognition Award Vol. 1: 11524
Chris Statuette Vol. 1: 7948
Christensen Memorial Exhibit Award; Henry Vol. 1: 3208
Christensen Memorial Prize; F. G. Vol. 2: 502
Christian Management Award Vol. 1: 7965
Christian Stewardship Award Vol. 1: 11455
Christian Unity Award Vol. 1: 9152
Christie Lectureship; Barnett Vol. 2: 7031
Christman Award; Luther Vol. 1: 934
Christman Scholarship; Irene R. Vol. 1: 17181
Christoff International Competition for Young Opera Singers - Sofia; Boris Vol. 2: 1204
Christopher Awards Vol. 1: 7971
Christopher J. Georges Fellowship Vol. 1: 16355
Christophers Medal; Sir Rickard Vol. 2: 8843
Christopherson Lectureship Award; E. H. Vol. 1: 764
Christus Magister Award Vol. 1: 12989
Christy Award; Teresa E. Vol. 1: 1065
Chromacolour Award for Best Use of Colour Vol. 1: 16947
Chronic Daily Headache; Kaplan Award for Vol. 1: 2389
Chrysler Corporation Cup Vol. 1: 21975
Chrysler Cup Vol. 1: 17406
Chrysler Triple Crown Challenge Vol. 1: 20207
Chuck and Linda Pratt Essay Award of the Lincoln Forum Vol. 1: 12858
Chugai Award for Meritorious Mentoring and Scholarship Vol. 1: 4119
Church Medal; Edwin F. Vol. 1: 4505
Churchill Award; H. V. Vol. 1: 5935
Churchill Award; Harold E. Vol. 1: 19802
Churchill Award; Winston
International Platform Association Vol. 1: 11802
Winston Churchill Foundation Vol 1: 21656
Churchill Bowl Vol. 1: 7239
Churchill Medal Vol. 2: 9042
Churchill Memorial Award; Winston Vol. 1: 14635
Ciapetta Lectureship in Catalysis; F. G. Vol. 1: 16398
Ciardi; Fondazione Professor Giuseppe Vol. 2: 932
CIB Developing Countries Fellowships Vol. 2: 4805
CIBA Crop Protection and Sandoz Agro Vol. 1: 19873
CIBA-GEIGY Corporation Vol. 1: 19873
CIBA-GEIGY Exemplary Middle Level and High School Science Teaching Award Vol. 1: 15684
CIBA Specialty Chemicals Exemplary Middle Level and High School Principal Awards Vol. 1: 15684
CIBA Specialty Chemicals Exemplary Middle Level and High School Science Teaching Awards Vol. 1: 15685
CIBC National Music Festival Vol. 1: 15408
CIC Fellowship Vol. 1: 7837
CICAE Prizes (International Confederation of Art Cinemas) Vol. 2: 2670
Ciccoli Joint Operations Award Vol. 1: 5113
Cichan Award; Michael Vol. 1: 6539
CICS Graduate Research Awards Vol. 1: 16566
CID Hall of Fame Vol. 1: 7992
CID Soldier of the Year Vol. 1: 7993
CIDA Awards for Canadians Vol. 1: 7005
CIDA Awards for Professionals Vol. 1: 7006
Cidermaker of the Year Vol. 1: 2522
Cihon Exhibit Award; Fred Vol. 1: 3209
Cillie Award; Dr. G. G. Vol. 2: 5792
CIM Distinguished Lecturers Vol. 1: 7186
CIM Fellowship Vol. 1: 7187
CIM/NRCan Journalism Awards Vol. 1: 7188
CIM Student Essay Competition Vol. 1: 7189
CINANIMA Vol. 2: 5393
Cincinnati Opera Education Program Vol. 1: 7999
Cinderella Stamp Club Trophy Vol. 2: 8263
CINE Eagle Award Vol. 1: 8608
CINE Golden Eagle Award Vol. 1: 8609
CINE Master's Series Award Vol. 1: 8610
Cin(E)-Poetry Festival Vol. 1: 15512
Cinema Under the Stars Vol. 1: 13607
Cinematography Award Vol. 1: 6033
CINOA Award Vol. 2: 918
Cintas Foundation Fellowships Vol. 1: 10981
Cipariu Prize; Timotei Vol. 2: 5820
CIPPS Distinguished Service Awards Vol. 1: 7159
Circulation Council Awards Vol. 1: 16328
Circulation Federation Awards Vol. 1: 16328
Circulation Hall of Fame Vol. 1: 8005
Circus Fans Association of American Award Vol. 1: 8009
CISAC Prize Vol. 2: 2460
Cisneros Award; Rosa Vol. 1: 11797
CISS Medallions of Honor Vol. 1: 11494
Citation Award
Awana Clubs International Vol. 1: 6162
Institute of Quarrying - England Vol 2: 7741
International Association for Food Protection Vol 1: 11228
USA Hockey Vol 1: 21174
Citation for Career Achievement Vol. 1: 18780
Citation for Distinguished Service Vol. 1: 8080
Citation for Excellence in Community Architecture Vol. 1: 2717
Citation for Outstanding Radio and Television Weather Presentation Vol. 1: 7275
Citation of Appreciation Vol. 1: 6354
Citation of Excellence Vol. 1: 14483
Citation of Excellence in Advertising Vol. 1: 21479
Citation of Honor
Air Force Association Vol. 1: 340
Associated Church Press Vol 1: 5239
Citation of Merit Vol. 1: 11414
Citation of Merit Award Vol. 1: 21726
Citation of Outstanding Achievement Vol. 1: 7325
Citation of Outstanding Service to the Society Vol. 1: 19189
Citations Vol. 1: 14146
Citations for Contributions to Chemistry and the Chemical Profession Vol. 2: 510
Citations of Merit
Football Writers Association of America Vol. 1: 9672
National Arts Club Vol 1: 13984
Citations pour Service Eminent Vol. 1: 7325
Citibank Choral Awards Vol. 2: 313
Citizen Activist Award Vol. 1: 10039
Citizen Diplomat Award Vol. 1: 12124
Citizen Involvement Program Excellence Award Vol. 1: 11477
Citizen of the Year
American Association of Dental Examiners Vol. 1: 1182
Center for Philosophy, Law, Citizenship Vol 1: 7741
Darien Chamber of Commerce Vol 1: 8752
Greater Mount Airy Chamber of Commerce Vol 1: 10151

Greater Quitman Area Chamber of Commerce Vol 1: 10159
Kankakee River Valley Chamber of Commerce Vol 1: 12482
Minnewaukan Community Club Vol 1: 13487
Rutland Region Chamber of Commerce Vol 1: 18193
Vermont Chamber of Commerce Vol 1: 21298
Citizen of the Year Award Vol. 2: 652
Citizen's Award Vol. 1: 10763
Citizens for Alternatives to Chemical Contamination Award Vol. 1: 8015
Citizens Savings Athletic Foundation Gymnastics Hall of Fame Vol. 1: 8159
Citizenship Award Vol. 1: 20140
Citizensip Education Program Excellence Award Vol. 1: 11477
City Achievement Award Vol. 1: 12750
City and Guilds Prizes Vol. 2: 8884
City Livability Awards Program Vol. 1: 20456
City of Alessandria International Competition in Classical Guitar Vol. 2: 4035
City of Antibes Prize Vol. 2: 2342
City of Ottawa Heritage Day Prize Vol. 1: 8041
City of Sondrio Gold Plaque Vol. 2: 3970
City of Springvale Short Story Awards Vol. 2: 310
City of Sydney Eisteddfod Pianoforte Scholarship Vol. 2: 312
City of Sydney Piano Scholarship Vol. 2: 312
City of Toronto Apprenticeship Screen Award Vol. 1: 8046
City of Toronto Awards for Excellence in Fashion Design Vol. 1: 8047
City of Toronto Book Awards Vol. 1: 8048
CITYN Award for Best Canadian First Feature Film Vol. 1: 20115
Ciutat d'Igualada Grand Prize Vol. 2: 6011
Civic Achievement Award Vol. 1: 6347
Civic Award Citation Vol. 1: 12967
Civic Courage Award Vol. 1: 17876
Civic Leadership Award Vol. 1: 8022
Civic Scholarship Vol. 1: 6460
Civic Service Award Vol. 1: 8018
Civic Trust Awards Vol. 2: 7313
Civil Air Patrol Aerospace Education Cadet of the Year Vol. 1: 341
Civil Air Patrol Cadet of the Year Vol. 1: 341
Civil Courage Prize Vol. 1: 16537
Civil Engineering Award Vol. 2: 8889
Civil Engineering History and Heritage Award Vol. 1: 4306
Civil Engineering Manager of the Year Award Vol. 2: 7758
Civil Engineering Students Papers Competition Vol. 2: 7759
Civil Government Award Vol. 1: 4307
Civil Liberties Award
American Civil Liberties Union of Vermont Vol. 1: 1814
American Civil Liberties Union, Ohio Affiliate Vol 1: 1818
Civil Service Secretary of the Year; Foreign Service Office Management Specialist of the Year/ Vol. 1: 20543
Civilian Awards Vol. 1: 342
Civilian of the Year Award Vol. 1: 13343
Civilian Service Medal 1939-1945 Vol. 2: 191
Civilization Award; Advancement and Preservation of Vol. 1: 15900
Civitan International Honor Keys Vol. 1: 8061
CLA Award Scholarship Vol. 1: 8166
CLA/Information Today Award for Innovative Technology Vol. 1: 7249
CLA/Meckler Award for Innovative Technology Vol. 1: 7249
Cladan Award Vol. 2: 317
Clagett Trophy; U.S. Sailing/Rolex Junior Women's Championship - Nancy Leiter Vol. 1: 20771
Clair Jr. Award; John J. Vol. 1: 20800
Clapper Memorial Awards; Raymond Vol. 1: 19752
Clare Flanagan Youth Art Month Grand Award Vol. 1: 8535
Clarence Camp Award Vol. 1: 9628
Clarion Awards Vol. 1: 5522
Clark Award Vol. 1: 9191
Clark Award; Allen W. Vol. 1: 15467
Clark Award; John Vol. 1: 7399
Clark Award; John William Vol. 2: 7062
Clark Award; Justice Tom C. Vol. 1: 9435
Clark Award; Mary Higgins Vol. 1: 13732
Clark Award; Russell Vol. 2: 5001
Clark Elementary Teacher Scholarship; Leta Vol. 1: 13223
Clark, Jr. Trophy; W. Van Alan Vol. 1: 20777
Clark McCoy Service Award; Lois Vol. 1: 14037
Clark Medal; Grahame Vol. 2: 6898
Clark Medal; John Bates Vol. 1: 2154
Clark Memorial Award; F. Ambrose Vol. 1: 15818
Clark Memorial Educational Scholarship; Robert A. Vol. 1: 15715
Clark National Memorial Trophy; G. Melville Vol. 2: 6708
Clark Prize; Matt Vol. 1: 16095
Clark Research Award; Kenneth E. Vol. 1: 7718
Clark Travelling Fellowship Vol. 2: 7844
Clark Trophy; Jim Vol. 2: 8876
Clarke Award; Alan Vol. 2: 6905
Clarke Award; Arthur C. Vol. 2: 8899
Clarke Award; Ethel Palmer Vol. 1: 18500
Clarke Award; The Polly Vol. 1: 16669
Clarke Conservation Award; Doug Vol. 1: 7539
Clarke Cup; Stephenson R. Vol. 2: 8539
Clarke Medal Vol. 2: 536
Clarke Memorial Lecture Vol. 2: 537
Clarke Outstanding Educator Award; Robert B. Vol. 1: 8931
Clarke Prize; Thomas B. Vol. 1: 13784
Clarke Trophy (Western Conference Trophy); Robert W. Vol. 1: 2504
Class Prizes in British Amateur Tape Recording Contest Vol. 2: 7204
Classic Television Hall of Fame Vol. 1: 8112
Classified Advertising Managers Executive Order Award Vol. 1: 16329
Classified Council Awards Vol. 1: 16329
Classified Federation Awards Vol. 1: 16329
Clausse; Fondation Gustave Vol. 2: 1717
Clavijero; Premio Francisco Javier Vol. 2: 4536
Clay Award; Garland W. Vol. 1: 716
Clayman Award; Jacob Vol. 1: 14815
Claypoole, Sr. Memorial Award; Ralph O. Vol. 1: 1918
Clayton Doctoral Dissertation Proposal Award; Alden G. Vol. 1: 13120
Clayton Grants Vol. 2: 7857
Clayton Grants for Postgraduate Studies Vol. 2: 7857
Clear-Com Intercom Systems Sound Achievement Award Vol. 1: 20644
Cleary Award; Edward J. Vol. 1: 645
Cleaver Club Award Vol. 1: 1264
Clemm Denkmunze; Hans Vol. 2: 2646
Clemson Awards Vol. 1: 18647
Clemson National Print and Drawing Exhibition Vol. 1: 18181
Clendenin Award; David L. Vol. 1: 21836
Clercq; Prix de la Fondation Louis de Vol. 2: 1746
Clermont-Ferrand International Short Film Festival Vol. 2: 2549
Clermont-Ferrand National Short Film Festival Vol. 2: 2550
Clermont-Ganneau; Prix Charles Vol. 2: 1747
Cleveland International Piano Competition Vol. 1: 8100
Cleveland State University Poetry Center Prize Vol. 1: 8104
Cliburn International Piano Competition; Van Vol. 1: 8108
Clifford Prize; James L. Vol. 1: 3991
Climatics Award Vol. 1: 10918
Cline Memorial Prize; Howard Francis Vol. 1: 8381
Clinedinst Memorial Medal; Benjamin West Vol. 1: 5138
Clinical Award of the SAVA Vol. 2: 5767
Clinical/Biomedical Engineering Achievement Award Vol. 1: 5490
Clinical Center of Excellence Vol. 1: 21689
Clinical Instructor of the Year Award Vol. 1: 1292
Clinical Investigator Awards Vol. 1: 7560
Clinical Investigator Lecture Award Vol. 1: 9260
Clinical Medicine Person-in-Training Award Vol. 1: 9988
Clinical Medicine Research Award Vol. 1: 9989
Clinical MRI Prize Vol. 2: 7044
Clinical Nursing Excellence Award Vol. 1: 5768
Clinical/Pharmacotherapeutic Practice; Distinguished Achievement Award in Vol. 1: 3381
Clinical Practitioner Award; Alice Magaw Outstanding Vol. 1: 1297
Clinical Research Award Vol. 1: 5634
Clinical Research Award; AACP Vol. 1: 631
Clinical Research Award in Periodontology Vol. 1: 802
Clinical Research Grants Vol. 1: 2137
Clinical Scientist in Nephrology Fellowship Award Vol. 1: 2919
Clinical Systems Award Vol. 1: 10343
Clinician - Scientist Award Vol. 1: 2405
Clinician Scientist Awards Vol. 1: 7549
Clinton S. Lee Market Services and Engineering Award of Excellence Vol. 1: 9210
Clio Awards Vol. 1: 8112
Clore International Award; Gerald R. Vol. 1: 10083
Clowes, Jr., M.D., F.A.C.S. Memorial Research Career Development Award; George H. A. Vol. 1: 1947
Clowes Memorial Award; G. H. A Vol. 1: 966
Clown of the Year Vol. 1: 17651

Award Index

CLTA Achievement in Literacy Award Vol. 1: 7264
CLTA Merit Award Vol. 1: 7265
Club Championship President's Cup Vol. 1: 13649
Club Development Award Vol. 2: 3679
Club of Champions Award Vol. 1: 7678
Club of the Year
British Chess Federation Vol. 2: 6979
Camanachd Association Vol 2: 7230
Club Professional Championship; PGA Vol. 2: 8296
Club Professional Player of the Year Vol. 1: 17613
Clubok Award; Miriam Vol. 1: 15432
CM Yonge Award Vol. 2: 8103
CMA Affirmative Action Award Vol. 1: 3276
CMA/ASCAP Awards for Adventuresome Programming Vol. 1: 7795
CMA Awards for Outstanding Achievement Vol. 1: 7297
Co-Founders Book Award Vol. 1: 21579
Co-op Feeds Young Scientist's Award Vol. 1: 7446
Co-Op Student of the Year Award Vol. 1: 8502
Co-Sponsor Award Vol. 1: 7009
Coach of the Year
American Football Coaches Association Vol. 1: 2269
Asian Football Confederation Vol 2: 4425
Baseball Canada Vol 1: 6262
Canadian Federation of Amateur Baseball Vol 1: 7086
College Gymnastics Association Vol 1: 8158
Continental Basketball Association Vol 1: 8480
England Basketball Vol 2: 7419
Ladies Professional Golf Association Vol 1: 12652
National Association of Basketball Coaches Vol 1: 14081
National Christian College Athletic Association Vol 1: 14656
Special Olympics Canada Vol 1: 19571
United States Amateur Boxing, Inc. Vol 1: 20385
United States Professional Tennis Association Vol 1: 20740
Coach of the Year Award
American Baseball Coaches Association Vol. 1: 1541
American Hockey Coaches Association Vol 1: 2488
American Swimming Coaches Association Vol 1: 4722
Football Writers Association of America Vol 1: 9676
National Association of Intercollegiate Athletics Vol 1: 14284
National Soccer Coaches Association of America Vol 1: 15708
U.S. Aquatic Sports Vol 1: 20394
Coach of the Year Award; Speedo/USMS Vol. 1: 20692
Coach of the Year Awards Vol. 1: 15983
Coach of the Year; Eddie Robinson Vol. 1: 9676
Coach of the Year; Edward Jeremiah Award/College Division Vol. 1: 2490
Coach of the Year - Red Auerbach Trophy Vol. 1: 14500
Coaches Association Awards Vol. 1: 15309
Coaches of the Year Vol. 1: 15223
Coaching Qualifications Awards Vol. 2: 3658
Coal and Energy Division Distinguished Service Award Vol. 1: 18806
Coal Award Vol. 1: 7190
Coalbourn Trust Grants Vol. 2: 7012
Coan, Sr. Award; Carl A.S. Vol. 1: 15246
Coanda Prize; Henri Vol. 2: 5821
Coast Guard Arctic Service Medal Vol. 1: 8809
Coast Guard Essay Contest Vol. 1: 20710
Coast Guard Exemplary Service Medal; Canadian Vol. 1: 6816
Coast Guard Reserve Good Conduct Medal Vol. 1: 8810
Cobalcescu Prize; Grigore Vol. 2: 5822
Cobb, Jr. Award for Initiative and Success in Trade Development; Charles E. Vol. 1: 20533
Cobb Memorial Award; Grover C. Vol. 1: 14109
Cobb Young Investigator Award; W. A. Vol. 2: 7937
Cobbing Travelling Fellowship; Natalie Vol. 2: 8457
Coble Award for Young Scholars; Robert L. Vol. 1: 1669
Coca-Cola Cup Vol. 2: 6361
Cochrane Award; Vice Admiral E. L. Vol. 1: 19207
Cochrane Sr. Scholarship Award; Thomas Vol. 1: 212
Cockayne Memorial Lecture; Leonard Vol. 2: 5078
Cockcroft Award; Ron Vol. 2: 6163
Codazzi Medal; Agustin Vol. 2: 1316
Codd Innovations Award; Edgar F. Vol. 1: 5313
Coddington Award of Merit Vol. 1: 16101
Coder of the Year Award Vol. 1: 820
Codes and Standards Medal Vol. 1: 4513
Codie Awards Vol. 1: 19383
Coelho Prize; P. M. Laranjo Vol. 2: 5483
Coffee Grower of the Year Award Vol. 2: 9341
Cogan Award Vol. 1: 5464
COGEL Award Vol. 1: 8603
Cohen Award for a Distinguished Edition of Letters; Morton N. Vol. 1: 13559
Cohen Award; Harry and Martha Vol. 1: 424
Cohen Award; Herb Vol. 1: 16813
Cohen Award; Nathan Vol. 1: 7514
Cohen Award; Riva Vol. 1: 444
Cohen Award; Seymour R. Vol. 1: 2926
Cohen Gold Medal; Lord Vol. 2: 8722
Cohen Medal; Lord Vol. 2: 7171
Cohen Purchase Award; Joan Vol. 1: 18980
Cohn Hope Award; The Norman Vol. 1: 15394
Coif Book Award Vol. 1: 16841
Coin of the Year Award Vol. 1: 12618
Coker Award; C.F.W. Vol. 1: 18951
Colaco de Azulejaria; Premio Municipal Jorge Vol. 2: 5430
Colaianni Award for Excellence and Achievement in Hospital Librarianship; Lois Ann Vol. 1: 13252
Colas; Prix Eugene Vol. 2: 2146
Colbert Medal Vol. 1: 18984
Colburn Award for Excellence in Publications by a Young Member of the Institute; Allan P. Vol. 1: 2762
Colby Award; William E. Vol. 1: 18454
Colby Memorial Award; Dorothy Vol. 1: 3406
Cole Award; Art Vol. 1: 1166
Cole Award for Automotive Engineering Innovation; Edward N. Vol. 1: 19037
Cole Grants-in-Aid; Arthur H. Vol. 1: 9143
Cole Human Rights Award; Kitty Vol. 1: 2069
Cole Prize; Arthur H. Vol. 1: 9144
Cole Prizes in Algebra and Number Theory; Frank Nelson Vol. 1: 3043
Cole Research Grant; Monica Vol. 2: 8513
Cole Sportsmanship Award; Mark Vol. 1: 14912
Coleman - Barstow Award for Strings Vol. 1: 8130
Coleman Chamber Ensemble Competition Vol. 1: 8130
Colen Memorial Grant; Kimberly Vol. 1: 19089
Coleopterists Society Youth Award Vol. 1: 8132
Coler - Maxwell Medal Vol. 1: 11957
Coley Award; William B. Vol. 1: 7561
Colgate-Palmolive Post-Doctoral Fellowship Award in In Vitro Toxicology Vol. 1: 19333
Colgate-Palmolive Research Scholarship Award Vol. 1: 1482
Colgate-Palmolive/SOT Awards for Student Research Training in Alternative Methods Vol. 1: 19334
The Colibri Diploma Vol. 2: 6324
Colibri Microlight Diploma Vol. 2: 6324
Collaborative Community Award Vol. 1: 16546
Collaborative Research Award Vol. 1: 9071
Collacott Prize Vol. 2: 7789
Collar of the Supreme Order of the Chrysanthemum Vol. 2: 4188
Collection Development Grant; BWI/YALSA Vol. 1: 22052
Collection System Award Vol. 1: 21480
Collectors Club Medal for Best Program Presented to the Collectors Club Vol. 1: 8135
Collectors Club Medal for Devoted Service Vol. 1: 8138
Collectors Club Medal for Outstanding Article in *The Collectors Club Philatelist* Vol. 1: 8136
College Art Association/National Institute for Conservation Award Vol. 1: 8144
College Athletics Top Ten Vol. 1: 14689
College Awards Vol. 1: 2034
College Basketball Coach of the Year Vol. 1: 19651
College Basketball Player of the Year Vol. 1: 19652
College Division Coach of the Year; Edward Jeremiah Award/ Vol. 1: 2490
College Fiction Contest Vol. 1: 17394
College Football Coach of the Year Vol. 1: 19653
College Football Defensive Player of the Year Trophy Vol. 1: 9673
College Football Hall of Fame Vol. 1: 15067
College Football Player of the Year Vol. 1: 19654
College Journalism Competition Vol. 1: 18109
College Medal
Australian College of Educators Vol. 2: 154
Royal College of Surgeons of Edinburgh Vol 2: 8478
College of Diplomats Award Vol. 1: 15631

College of Electrical Engineers Student Prizes Vol. 2: 379
College of Fellows Grants Vol. 1: 2710
College Player of the Year Vol. 1: 21175
College Press Freedom Award Vol. 1: 19811
College Scholar All-America Award Vol. 1: 15707
College/University Distinguished Teaching Achievement Award Vol. 1: 14764
College/University Excellence of Scholarship Award Vol. 1: 14761
Collegiate Advisor Award Vol. 1: 17254
Collegiate Athlete of the Year Vol. 1: 19865
Collegiate Bowlers of the Year Vol. 1: 6564
Collegiate Coach of the Year Vol. 1: 20582
Collegiate or University Teacher of the Year Vol. 1: 14571
Collier Award Vol. 1: 9696
Collier Trophy; Robert J. Vol. 1: 13877
Collin Prijs; Fernand Vol. 2: 1116
Collingwood Prize Vol. 1: 4308
Collins Award; Carr P. Vol. 1: 20013
Collins Award; George R. Vol. 1: 1024
Collins Award; Joseph P. Vol. 1: 14820
Collins Award; Samuel C. Vol. 1: 8677
Collins Award; W. Leighton Vol. 1: 4007
Collins, Jr. Research Promotion Award; William J. Vol. 1: 4428
Collins Memorial Award; Norman Vol. 2: 7197
Collins Poetry Award; Tom Vol. 2: 336
Collip Diabetes Studentship; J.B. Vol. 1: 13719
Colmont; Prix Vol. 2: 1709
Cologne International Pianoforte Competition Vol. 2: 2693
Cologne International Singing Competition Vol. 2: 2697
Cologne International Violin Competition Vol. 2: 2695
Cologne International Vocal Competition Vol. 2: 2697
Colombe D'Oro per la Pace Vol. 2: 3843
Colombe Unda Vol. 2: 1112
Colombian Academy of Exact, Physical and Natural Sciences to the Integral Work of a Scientist Vol. 2: 1267
Colonial Dames of America Scholarship Vol. 1: 18952
Colonna Prize; Antonina Vol. 2: 3953
Color Slide Division Awards Vol. 1: 17284
Colposcopy Recognition Award Vol. 1: 3978
Colt Fund Vol. 2: 8942
Columbia/Embassy Television Playwriting Award Vol. 1: 12542
Columbia Journalism Award Vol. 1: 8241
Columbia Pictures Television Playwriting Award Vol. 1: 12542
Columbine Poets of Colorado Award Vol. 1: 14991
Columbus Award; Christopher Vol. 1: 7947
Columbus International Film and Video Festival Vol. 1: 7951
Columbus International Film and Video Festival Vol. 1: 7948
Columbus Prize Vol. 2: 3982
Column Writing Contest Vol. 1: 15742
Colvin Awards; Ruth J. Vol. 1: 17673
Colwell Cooperative Engineering Medal; Arch T. Vol. 1: 19038
Colwell Merit Award; Arch T. Vol. 1: 19039
Colworth Medal Vol. 2: 6865
Colworth Prize Lecture Vol. 2: 8932
Colyer Gold Medal Vol. 2: 8484
Colyer Prize Vol. 2: 8801
Comas; Premio Juan Vol. 2: 4538
Comas Prize; Juan Vol. 1: 1355
Combat Readiness Medal Vol. 1: 8811
Comeback Player of the Year Vol. 1: 19978
Comer Awards Vol. 1: 625
Comer Minority Research Fellowship for Medical Students; James Vol. 1: 625
Comfort Memorial Award; A. C. Vol. 2: 8802
Comiant; Prix Pol Vol. 2: 2204
Command and Control Unit of the Year Vol. 1: 13074
Commandant's Aviation Trophy Vol. 1: 13069
Commander-in-Chief's Annual Award for Installation Excellence Vol. 1: 20487
Commemorative Arts Awards Vol. 1: 20111
Commemorative Award Vol. 1: 16140
Commemorative Lecture Award Vol. 1: 939
Commendation and Promotion Vol. 1: 12603
Commendation Award Vol. 1: 19386
Commendation Awards Vol. 1: 11763
Commendation by the Minister of State for Science and Technology Vol. 2: 4197
Commendation for Distinguished Service Vol. 2: 194
Commendation for Gallantry Vol. 2: 196
Commendation Medal: Navy Vol. 1: 8812
Commentary/Column Writing Vol. 1: 4576
Commercial Award Vol. 1: 2526
Commercial Award; Paul Ecke Jr. Vol. 1: 2526
Commercial Director Award Vol. 1: 8941
Commercial Horticulture Distinguished Achievement Award Vol. 1: 4085
Commercial Wine Competition Awards Vol. 1: 4907
Commercial Wool Production in Canada; Certificate of Merit - Vol. 1: 7031
Commission for the Defense of Human Rights in Central America Awards Vol. 2: 1349
Commission Matching Grants Vol. 1: 9902
Commission on Geographical Education Awards Vol. 2: 1633
Commissioner's Award
  Canadian Football League Vol. 1: 7103
  Ladies Professional Golf Association Vol 1: 12653
Commissioners' Award Vol. 1: 21618
Commissioner's Trophy Awards Vol. 1: 6370
Commitment to Chicago Award and Big Shoulders Vol. 1: 7886
Committee D-2 Award Vol. 1: 5936
Committee D-12 Award Vol. 1: 5937
Committee D-20 Award of Excellence Vol. 1: 5938
Committee E-8 Fracture Mechanics Medal Vol. 1: 5939
Committee E-8 on Fatigue and Fracture Best Student Paper Award Vol. 1: 5940
Committee Man of the Year Vol. 1: 1309
Committee of the Year Award Vol. 1: 15497
Committee on Multiethnic Concerns J. Eugene Grisby, Jr. Award Vol. 1: 13957
Committee Person of the Year Award Vol. 1: 15498
Commodore Cooper Trust Vol. 2: 4665
Common Ground Award for Journalism in the Middle East Vol. 1: 18391
Common Wealth Awards of Distinguished Service Vol. 1: 17410
Commons Award; Veblen - Vol. 1: 5363
Commonwealth Club of California Book Awards Vol. 1: 8306
Commonwealth Council for Educational Administration and Management Fel Vol. 2: 1398
Commonwealth Essay Competition Vol. 2: 8501
Commonwealth Fund Fellowships Vol. 1: 10239
Commonwealth Games Federation Vol. 2: 7336
Commonwealth Magistrates' Hall of Fame Vol. 2: 7338
Commonwealth Press Union Scholarships Vol. 2: 7343
Commonwealth Scholarship and Fellowship Plan Vol. 2: 6810
Commonwealth Shared Scholarship Scheme Vol. 2: 6811
Commonwealth Short Story Competition Vol. 2: 7330
Commonwealth Writers Prize Vol. 2: 7331
Commonwealth Youth Service Awards Vol. 2: 7345
Communication and Marketing Awards Vol. 1: 11035
Communicator Award Vol. 1: 7714
Communication Policy Research Award Vol. 1: 13217
Communications Award
  American Institute of Aeronautics and Astronautics Vol. 1: 2677
  American Jewish Congress Vol 1: 2891
  American Staffing Association Vol 1: 4689
Communications Award; Marketing Vol. 1: 8448
Communications Awards Vol. 1: 10084
Communications Graphics Vol. 1: 2810
Communications Media Award Vol. 1: 21279
Communications Program Awards Vol. 1: 9658
Communicator of Achievement Award Vol. 1: 14972
Communicator of the Year Vol. 2: 6937
Communicator of the Year Award
  International Association of Business Communicators Vol. 1: 11295
  National Council for Marketing and Public Relations Vol 1: 14773
  Utility Communicators International Vol 1: 21265
Communicators in Business Awards Vol. 2: 6938
Community and Ambulatory Practice; Distinguished Achievement Award in Vol. 1: 3382
Community Association Board Member of the Year Vol. 1: 8315
Community Awards Program (Encore Awards) Vol. 1: 18022
Community College Learning Resources and Library Achievement Awards; EBSCO Vol. 1: 5608
Community College Learning Resources Library Achievement Awards Vol. 1: 5604
Community College Scholarship Award Vol. 1: 19147
Community-Constable Partnership Award Vol. 1: 14727
Community Counselling Service Award for Outstanding Fundraising Professional Vol. 1: 5700
Community Crime Prevention; APPA Awards for Excellence in Vol. 1: 3598
Community Dental Health Award Vol. 2: 819
Community Development Award Vol. 1: 296

Community Education Award Vol. 1: 15823
Community, Environment, Art, and Design (CEAD) Award Vol. 2: 111
Community Event of the Year Vol. 2: 652
Community Hospital Award Vol. 1: 7765
Community Improvement Award Vol. 2: 4365
Community Leadership Award Vol. 1: 10812
Community Leadership Awards Vol. 1: 18248
Community Leadership; Frank Mayborn Award for Vol. 1: 19998
Community of the Year Vol. 1: 8313
Community Outreach Award Vol. 1: 2763
Community Partnership Grant Vol. 1: 1641
Community Partnership Program Accessible America Award Vol. 1: 15458
Community Preventive Dentistry Award Vol. 1: 2127
Community Psychology Dissertation Award Vol. 1: 3714
Community Relations Award (Labor) Vol. 1: 2892
Community Service Award
American Academy of Facial Plastic and Reconstructive Surgery Vol. 1: 668
American Association of Critical-Care Nurses Vol 1: 1171
American Association of Homes and Services for the Aging Vol 1: 1224
American Correctional Association Vol 1: 2023
American Public Power Association Vol 1: 3788
American Society of Landscape Architects Vol 1: 4475
Black Archives of Mid-America Vol 1: 6406
East Mount Airy Neighbors Vol 1: 9076
Essex Community Heritage Organization Vol 1: 9339
Florida State Grange Vol 1: 9631
Helicopter Association International Vol 1: 10392
Inland Press Association Vol 1: 10812
Keuka College Alumni Association Vol 1: 12578
Latrobe Area Chamber of Commerce Vol 1: 12715
Livingston County Council on Alcohol and Substance Abuse Vol 1: 12900
National Association of Black Journalists Vol 1: 14101
National Council of Social Security Management Associations Vol 1: 14821
National Grange Vol 1: 15172
Sierra Club Vol 1: 18455
UCLA Alumni Association Vol 1: 20255
Community Service Award/Certificate of Merit Vol. 1: 14816
Community Service Awards Vol. 1: 17162
Community Service Fellowship Vol. 1: 7884
Community Service Grant Vol. 1: 13062
Community Service Leadership Award Vol. 1: 20326
Compadre Award Vol. 1: 19542
Companion Membership Vol. 2: 9124
Company Appreciation Award Vol. 1: 17588
Company Award of Excellence Vol. 1: 14343
Company of Fellows Vol. 1: 5090
Company of the Year Award Vol. 1: 11951
Company of the Year Awards Vol. 2: 4354
Company of World Traders Silver Salver Vol. 2: 7690
Company Representative of the Year Vol. 1: 14344
Company Safety Awards Vol. 1: 16421
Comparative Physiology Section Scholander Award Vol. 1: 3514
Compass Distinguished Achievement Award Vol. 1: 13108
Compass Industrial Award Vol. 1: 13109
Compass International Award Vol. 1: 13110
The Compassionate Friends Award Vol. 1: 8322
Competitie de Impact van Muziek op Film Vol. 2: 886
Competition and Achievement Awards Vol. 1: 4804
Competition for Children's Theater or Stories Vol. 2: 4502
Competition for Films and Videos on Japan Vol. 2: 4311
Competition for Overseas Study Award Vol. 2: 5504
Competition for Performing Artists Vol. 1: 8476
Competition for Young Researchers Vol. 2: 6436
Competition for Young Statisticians from Developing Countries Vol. 2: 4842
Competition Honors Vol. 1: 20437
Competitions Vol. 2: 342
Competitions and Tournaments Vol. 2: 6149
Competitive Awards Vol. 1: 14970
Competitive Papers Award Vol. 1: 9549
Complete Single Mother Award Vol. 1: 15456
Completion of Service Award Vol. 1: 15288
Composition Competition, Tours Vol. 2: 2344
Composition Competitions Vol. 2: 9105
Composition of the Year Vol. 2: 5165
Composition Prize Vol. 2: 8653
Compton Award; Karl Taylor Vol. 1: 2832
Compton Award; Neil Vol. 1: 16992
Computer Animation Vol. 1: 6849
Computer Educator of the Year Vol. 1: 11201
Computer Entrepreneur Award Vol. 1: 10887
Computer Personality of the Year Award; National Vol. 2: 5545
Computer Pioneer Award Vol. 1: 10888
Computer Science and Engineering Undergraduate Teaching Award Vol. 1: 10889
Computer Sciences Man of the Year Vol. 1: 5731
Computing in Chemical Engineering Award Vol. 1: 2764
Computing Practice Award Vol. 1: 2765
Comstock Prize in Physics Vol. 1: 13829
Comunidad de Madrid Prize Vol. 2: 6028
Conamus Export Prize Vol. 2: 4721
Conamus Golden Harp Vol. 2: 4722
Conant Award in High School Chemistry Teaching; James Bryant Vol. 1: 1744
Conant Award; James Bryant Vol. 1: 9168
Conceicao Silva de Espacos Interiores Abertos ao Publico; Premio Municipal Francisco da Vol. 2: 5423
Concerned Broadcaster of the Year Vol. 1: 14541
Concertino Prague International Radio Competition for Young Musicians Vol. 2: 1420
Concerto Competition Vol. 1: 18280
Concorso Esercitazioni Agrarie Vol. 2: 3801
Concorso Internacional de Violao Villa-Lobos Vol. 2: 1196
Concorso Internazionale della Ceramica d'Arte Vol. 2: 3966
Concorso Internazionale di Chitarra Classica "Michele Pittaluga" Premio Citta' di Alessandria Vol. 2: 4035
Concorso Internazionale di Chitarra Mauro Giuliani Vol. 2: 3877
Concorso Internazionale di Composizione Goffredo Petrassi Vol. 2: 3929
Concorso Internazionale di Direzione d'Orchestra Arturo Toscanini Vol. 2: 3930
Concorso Internazionale di Musica e Danza G. B. Viotti Vol. 2: 4048
Concorso Internazionale di Violino Premio Rodolfo Lipizer Vol. 2: 3893
Concorso Internazionale Luigi Russolo Vol. 2: 3943
Concorso Internazionale per Quartetto d'Archi Vol. 2: 4054
Concorso Internazionale Pianistico Liszt - Premio Mario Zanfi Vol. 2: 3871
Concorso Pianistico Internazionale Alessandro Casagrande Vol. 2: 3889
Concorso Pianistico Internazionale Ettore Pozzoli Vol. 2: 3887
Concorso Pianistico Internazionale Rina Sala Gallo Vol. 2: 3858
Concours Vol. 1: 7973
Concours Annuel de Sauvegarde Vol. 2: 2621
Concours Awards Vol. 1: 21380
Concours Canadien de Journalisme Vol. 1: 7309
Concours Clara Haskil Vol. 2: 6371
Concours de Composition, Tours Vol. 2: 2344
Concours de musique du Canada Vol. 1: 7299
Concours des Antiquites de la France Vol. 2: 1748
Concours et Seminaire International d'alto Vol. 2: 9121
Concours Geza Anda Vol. 2: 6365
Concours International de Ballet, Varna Vol. 2: 1240
Concours International de campagnes de Marketing Direct Vol. 2: 884
Concours International de Chant Choral de Tours Vol. 2: 2345
Concours International de Chant de Paris Vol. 2: 2615
Concours International de Chant Francisco Vinas Vol. 2: 6114
Concours International de Cinema de la Montagne Vila de Torello Vol. 2: 6107
Concours International de Composition Musicale Vol. 2: 2338
Concours International de Composition Vienne Vol. 2: 705
Concours International de Harpe en Israel Vol. 2: 3738
Concours International de Jeunes Chanteurs d'Opera Vol. 2: 1204
Concours International de Jeunes Chefs d'Orchestre Besancon Vol. 2: 2337
Concours International de l'Orgue a Lahti Vol. 2: 1652
Concours international de Violoncelle Paulo Vol. 2: 1638
Concours International de Violoncelle Rostropovitch Vol. 2: 2283
Concours International des Jeunesses Musicales - Belgrade Vol. 2: 5936

Concours International d'Execution Musicale - Geneve Vol. 2: 6310
Concours International Printemps de la Guitare Vol. 2: 916
Concours Max-Pol Fouchet Vol. 2: 2252
Concours OSM Vol. 1: 13605
Concours Promethee Vol. 2: 2253
Concrete Achiever of the Year Vol. 1: 107
Concrete Element Prize Vol. 2: 5130
Concrete Paving Awards Vol. 1: 13341
Concrete Person of the Year Awards Vol. 2: 5534
Concrete Society Award Vol. 2: 7347
Concrete Structure Plaque Vol. 2: 5131
Concurs Internacional de Cant Francesc Vinas Vol. 2: 6114
Concurso Anual Vol. 1: 11117
Concurso Anual de Literatura Premios Franz Tamayo Vol. 2: 1123
Concurso Carmen Lyra Vol. 2: 1358
Concurso de anto Beca Francsco Araiza Vol. 2: 4587
Concurso de Caricatura Periodistica Vol. 2: 4488
Concurso de Cuento de Ciencia Ficcion Vol. 2: 4588
Concurso de cuento y de Teatro Infantil Vol. 2: 4502
Concurso de Jovenes Solistas Vol. 2: 4589
Concurso de Resena Teatral Vol. 2: 4590
Concurso Internacional de Piano de Santander Paloma O'Shea Vol. 2: 6098
Concurso Internacional de Piano Villa-Lobos Vol. 2: 1197
Concurso Internazionale per Direttori d'Orchestra Antonio Pedrotti Vol. 2: 3847
Concurso Joven Creacion Vol. 2: 1359
Concurso la Mejor Tesis sobre la Mujer in la UNAM Vol. 2: 4591
Concurso Nacional Carta a mi Hijo Vol. 2: 4623
Concurso Nacional de Cuartetos de Cuerdas Vol. 2: 4592
Concurso Nacional de Diseno para Uso y aplicacon del Aluminio Vol. 2: 4508
Concurso Nacional de Ensino de Redacao Vol. 2: 1177
Concurso Nacional de Fotografia Vol. 2: 1346
Concurso Nacional de Fotografia Cientifica Vol. 2: 4593
Concurso Nacional de Obras Medicas Vol. 2: 1321
Concurso Nacional de Violin Vol. 2: 4594
Concurso Nacional del Cuento Vol. 2: 1347
Concurso Permanente De Jovenes Interpretes Vol. 2: 6071
Concurso Sobre Banca de Desarrollo Vol. 2: 5242
Concurso Univeritario de Cuento Vol. 2: 4595
Concurso Universitario de Artes Plasticas Vol. 2: 4596
Concurso Universitario de Fotografia Vol. 2: 4597
Condecoracion al Merito Social Vol. 2: 4503
Condecoracion del Merito Universitario Vol. 2: 1341
Condecoracion Servicios Distinguidos en Guerra Exterior Vol. 2: 1280
Condon Award; Edward Uhler Vol. 1: 20477
Conductor of the Year Vol. 1: 9790
Conductor's Award Vol. 1: 16186
Conference Awards for Young Members Vol. 2: 7860
Conference Best Paper Vol. 2: 7796
Conference Chairperson of the Year Vol. 1: 20357
Conference Contribution Award Vol. 1: 10890
Conference Coordinator Award Vol. 1: 11663
Conference Division Chairman Award Vol. 1: 20357
Conference Grant Scheme Vol. 2: 8504
Conference on Latin American History Prize Vol. 1: 8382
Conference Speaker Award and Best Workshop Speaker Awards Vol. 1: 12009
Congress Medal Vol. 2: 6792
Congressional Award Vol. 1: 18560
The Congressional Award Vol. 1: 8396
Congressional Baseball Trophy Vol. 1: 18106
Congressional Gold Medal Vol. 1: 20459
Congressional Leadership Award Vol. 1: 18013
Congressional Research Grant Program Vol. 1: 8951
Congressional Space Medal of Honor Vol. 1: 13884
Congressional Staff Award Vol. 1: 18107
Congressman of the Year Vol. 1: 15395
CONI Prize Vol. 2: 4059
Conkling Memorial Award; Robert J. Vol. 1: 4879
Conley Award; Dean Vol. 1: 1867
Conley Award; Fred O. Vol. 1: 19260
Connare Award for Distinguished Service; Bishop William G. Vol. 1: 11456
Connecticut Association Membership Award Vol. 1: 10730
Connecticut Poetry Society Award Vol. 1: 14992
Connecticut River Watershed Council Conservation Award Vol. 1: 8420
Connell Award; Edward P. Vol. 1: 2319
Connell Award; W.F. Vol. 1: 6625
Connelly Heroism Award; Robert P. Vol. 1: 12601
Conner Memorial Scholarship; Paul W. Vol. 1: 11154
Conners Prize for Poetry; Bernard F. Vol. 1: 17093
Connie Award Vol. 1: 8472
Connor Award; Robert D. W. Vol. 1: 16517
Conover-Porter Award Vol. 1: 262
Conrad Award/Lecturer; Miles Vol. 1: 14963
Conrady Award; A. E. Vol. 1: 19605
Consagracion a la Geografia-Al Merito Geografico Vol. 2: 27
Conscience In Media Award Vol. 1: 4469
Conservation and Heritage Management Award Vol. 1: 5030
Conservation Award
International Wild Waterfowl Association Vol. 1: 12133
Joshua's Tract Conservation and Historic Trust Vol 1: 12440
Nature Saskatchewan Vol 1: 16038
New England Wild Flower Society Vol 1: 16145
Ottawa Field-Naturalists' Club Vol 1: 16927
Conservation Award - Private Citizen Vol. 1: 6064
Conservation Award - Public Official Vol. 1: 6065
Conservation Awards Vol. 1: 4914
Conservation Guest Scholars Vol. 1: 10003
Conservation Medal Vol. 1: 16145
Conservation/Outdoor Recreation Film/Video Award Program Vol. 1: 16967
Conservation Teacher of the Year Vol. 1: 13150
Conservation Tillage Awards Vol. 1: 14150
Conservationist of the Year
Audubon of Florida Vol. 1: 6075
Chesapeake Bay Foundation Vol 1: 7859
Minnesota Conservation Federation Vol 1: 13471
Conservationist of the Year Award Vol. 1: 186
Considine Award; Bob
Overseas Press Club of America Vol. 1: 16981
St. Bonaventure University - Russell J. Jandoli School of Journalism and Mass Communication Vol 1: 18198
Conspicuous Leadership Decoration Vol. 2: 5733
Conspicuous Service Cross Vol. 2: 192
Conspicuous Service Decorations Vol. 2: 192
Conspicuous Service Medal Vol. 2: 192
Constable of the Year Vol. 1: 14728
Constance M. Rourke Prize Vol. 1: 4707
Constantin Prize; Mac Vol. 2: 5878
Constituent Association Award Vol. 1: 1307
Construction Award; Facilities and Vol. 1: 19240
Construction Excellence Award Vol. 1: 7689
Construction Industry Computing Association Awards Vol. 2: 7351
Construction Management Award Vol. 1: 4309
Construction Person of the Year Vol. 1: 21552
Constuction's Man of the Year Vol. 1: 9279
Consular Service Award Vol. 1: 20555
Consumer Conference Awards Vol. 1: 15256
Consumer Education Award Vol. 1: 17894
Consumer Horticulture Distinguished Achievement Award Vol. 1: 4086
Consumer Involvement Award Vol. 1: 7267
Consumer Journalism Award Vol. 1: 15515
Consumer Participation Award Vol. 1: 7267
Consumer Plastics Product Design Award Vol. 1: 19261
Consumer Research Award Vol. 1: 12446
Consumer Sciences Teacher of the Year Award; National Family and - Home Economics Teacher of the Year Award Vol. 1: 942
Conta Prize; Vasile Vol. 2: 5823
Contact Vamp Trophee Vol. 2: 5303
Container Inspectors Award Vol. 1: 10979
Contemporary A Cappella Recording Awards ("CARAs") Vol. 1: 8474
Contemporary Music Award
Embassy of Spain in the United States - Cultural Office Vol. 1: 9228
Jaen International Piano Competition Vol 2: 6069
Contemporary Music; International Oliver Messiaen Competition for Interpertation of Vol. 2: 2279
Contemporary Poetry Series Vol. 1: 21025
Contender's Award Vol. 1: 2035
Continental Casualty Award Vol. 1: 20425
Continental Grain Company Poultry Products Research Award Vol. 1: 17502

Continuare Protessus Articulatus Excellare Vol. 1: 15792
Continuing Education Achievement Awards Vol. 1: 746
Continuing Education Awards Vol. 2: 6529
Continuing Higher Education; International Futures Award for Exceptional and Innovative Leadership in Vol. 1: 20956
Continuing Publication Commendation Vol. 1: 8434
Continuing Service Award Vol. 1: 14451
Continuous Service Award Vol. 1: 71
Continuous Service Excellence Award to the Forestry Industry Vol. 2: 5708
Continuum Women's Studies Award Vol. 1: 8672
Contractor of the Year Vol. 1: 12689
Contractor of the Year Award
American Public Works Association Vol. 1: 3800
Concrete Foundations Association Vol 1: 8344
Contractor of the Year Awards (CotY Awards) Vol. 1: 14429
Contractors' Awards Vol. 2: 6827
Contributions to Public Awareness of the Importance of Animals in Toxicology Research Award Vol. 1: 19335
Control Systems Award Vol. 1: 10857
Convention Performers Competition Vol. 1: 15057
Convention Service Manager of the Year Vol. 1: 19822
Converse Coach of the Year Awards Vol. 1: 15316
Conway Lecture Vol. 2: 3689
Coogler Award; J. Gordon Vol. 1: 4660
Cook - Douglas Medal Vol. 1: 13240
Cook Award; Col. Donald G. Vol. 1: 15384
Cook Medal; James Vol. 2: 538
Cook Memorial Trophy; Jim Vol. 1: 19724
Cook-off; International Chili Vol. 1: 4667
Cook Prize; Gladys Emerson Vol. 1: 13785
Cook Regional Services Award; Glenn J. Vol. 1: 6612
Cook Travel Book Award; Thomas Vol. 2: 7353
Cook Travelling Fellowship; William Vol. 2: 6947
Cookbook Hall of Fame Vol. 1: 12285
Cookbook of the Year Vol. 1: 12285
Cooke Award Vol. 2: 6818
Cooke Memorial Award; Sybil Vol. 1: 16959
Cooking Teacher of the Year Award Vol. 1: 11327
Cookingham; Award for Career Development in Memory of L.P. Vol. 1: 11474
Cookson Paleobotanical Award; Isabel C. Vol. 1: 6540
Cooley Award; Charles Horton Vol. 1: 18931
Cooley Award; George R.
American Society of Plant Taxonomists Vol. 1: 4593
Botanical Society of America Vol 1: 6541
Cooley Leadership Award; Denton A. Vol. 1: 20007
Cooley Memorial Award; Emily
American Association of Blood Banks Vol. 1: 1102
American Association of Blood Banks Vol 1: 1103
Cooley Memorial Lectureship; Emily Vol. 1: 1103
Coolidge Award; Edgar D. Vol. 1: 1191
Coolidge Award; William D. Vol. 1: 1367
Coomaraswamy Book Prize; Anada Kentish Vol. 1: 5274
Coombes Medal; L.P. Vol. 2: 380
Cooney Award; Joe Vol. 1: 14166
Coonley Medal; Howard Vol. 1: 3182
Coons Achievement Award Vol. 1: 8081
Cooper Architecture Award; Shirley Vol. 1: 1404
Cooper Award Vol. 1: 979
Cooper Award; Mario Vol. 1: 4848
Cooper Award; W. S. Vol. 1: 9133
Cooper Lifetime Achievement Award; Jack Vol. 1: 7512
Cooper Medal; Commodore A. H. Vol. 2: 4665
Cooper Memorial Lecturer; Lenna F. Vol. 1: 2147
Cooper Memorial Medal and Prize; E. R. Vol. 2: 5079
Cooper Memorial Meridian Award; Billy H. Vol. 1: 13270
Cooper Memorial Prize; Duff Vol. 2: 7399
Cooper Prize; Duff Vol. 2: 7399
Cooperating Atty Award Vol. 1: 1815
Cooperative Marketing and Sales Council Awards Vol. 1: 16330
Cooperative Month Awards Vol. 1: 14800
Cooperative Prize Vol. 2: 6541
Cooperman-Boque Awards Vol. 1: 12477
Coopers Hill War Memorial Prize Vol. 2: 7760
Coopers Hill War Memorial Prize and Medal Vol. 2: 7797
Coordinator Award Vol. 1: 8520
Coors "Man in the Can" Vol. 1: 17651
Coote-Lake Medal for Folklore Research Vol. 2: 7535
Cope Award; Arthur C. Vol. 1: 1745
Cope Fund Grant; Arthur C. Vol. 1: 1745
Cope Scholar Award; Arthur C. Vol. 1: 1746
Cope Travel Grant; Arthur C. Vol. 1: 1746
Copeland Award Vol. 1: 1670
Copeland Award; Arthur E. Vol. 1: 20407
Copeland Award; Edith Moore Vol. 1: 18500
Copeland Scholarship; Arthur E. Vol. 1: 20408
Copeland Scholarship; Helen Vol. 1: 20409
Coplen Roll of Honor Award; Ron Vol. 1: 19559
Copley Medal Vol. 2: 8693
Copova Diploma Vol. 2: 5994
Copp Award; Nan Vol. 1: 7212
Copp Traveling Fellowship; Dax Vol. 2: 8514
Coppens Prize; J. Vol. 2: 1077
Copper Club Award/Committee B-5 Award Vol. 1: 5941
Copying Assistance Program Vol. 1: 3162
Corbeil; Prix Gilles - Vol. 1: 20304
Corbett Medal; Arthur Vol. 2: 381
Corbetta Concrete Constructor Award; Roger H. Vol. 1: 1965
Corbitt Ultra Runner-of-the-Year Award; Ted Vol. 1: 21216
Corcoran Award; William H. Vol. 1: 4008
Corcoran Craft Awards; William and Mary Vol. 1: 16739
Corday-Morgan Medal and Prize Vol. 2: 8749
Cordoba; Orden del Merito Jose Maria Vol. 2: 1290
Coremans; Premio Paul Vol. 2: 4543
CORESTA Prize Vol. 2: 2285
Coretta Scott King Award Vol. 1: 6416
Corey Award; Albert B. Vol. 1: 1042
Corey Prize in Canadian-American Relations; Albert B.
American Historical Association Vol. 1: 2468
Canadian Historical Association Vol 1: 7151
Cork International Choral and Folk Dance Festival Vol. 2: 3627
Cork International Choral Festival Vol. 2: 3627
Cork International Film Festival Vol. 2: 3625
Corlette Medal; J.M.C. Vol. 2: 382
Cornell Religion Reporter of the Year Award for Mid-Sized Papers; George Vol. 1: 17974
Cornette Prize; Arthur H. Vol. 2: 956
Cornforth Medal Vol. 2: 511
Corning Cup Vol. 2: 7195
COROS Ribbon Vol. 1: 8140
Corpas Prize; Juan N. Vol. 2: 1322
Corporate Achievement Award Vol. 1: 11747
Corporate Advocate Leadership Award Vol. 1: 12707
Corporate and Professional Firm Leadership Award Vol. 1: 7627
Corporate Award
Audubon Naturalist Society of the Central Atlantic States Vol. 1: 6066
Audubon of Florida Vol 1: 6076
Black Entertainment and Sports Lawyers Association Vol 1: 6422
Ecological Society of America Vol 1: 9134
Live Theatre League of Tarrant County Vol 1: 12893
Sport Canada Vol 1: 19626
Corporate/Commercial Business Flying Safety Awards Vol. 1: 14564
Corporate Conscience Award Vol. 1: 8591
Corporate Environmental Achievement Award Vol. 1: 1671
Corporate Excellence Award Vol. 1: 19626
Corporate Health Achievement Award
American College of Occupational and Environmental Medicine Vol. 1: 1904
American College of Occupational and Environmental Medicine Vol 1: 1904
Corporate Leadership Award
American Institute of Graphic Arts Vol. 1: 2811
National Hemophilia Foundation Vol 1: 15203
Western Reserve Historical Society Vol 1: 21560
Corporate Membership Certificate Vol. 2: 4348
Corporate Recognition Award Vol. 1: 11747
Corporate Sponsor Plaque Vol. 2: 5918
Corporate Technical Achievement Award Vol. 1: 1672
Corporation of the Year Vol. 1: 15390
Corps d'Elite Award Vol. 1: 8258
Correctional Officer of the Year Vol. 1: 11318
Corrections Film Festival Vol. 1: 2024
Correspondence Award; Washington Vol. 1: 15524
Correspondence Student of the Year Vol. 2: 6790
Correspondent Membership; Finnish Historical Society Vol. 2: 1604
Corresponding Members
Botanical Society of America Vol. 1: 6542
German Society for Physical Medicine and Rehabilitation Vol 2: 2885

Corstorphine Medal Vol. 2: 5565
Corwin Award; Joseph M. Vol. 1: 5255
Cory Cup Vol. 2: 8540
Cory Memorial Cup; Reginald Vol. 2: 8540
Cory - Wright Cup Vol. 2: 5058
CoSIDA Backbone Award Vol. 1: 8189
Cosio, RN Award; Mary Jo Vol. 1: 15332
COSPAR Space Science Award Vol. 2: 2269
Costa Award; Joseph Vol. 1: 15532
Costa Courtroom Photography Award; Joseph Vol. 1: 6204
Costello Fellowships; Jeanne Timmins Vol. 1: 13602
COTA Award of Excellence Vol. 1: 3295
Cothenius-Medaille Vol. 2: 2703
Cothenius Medal Vol. 2: 2703
Cottle Honor Award; Dr. Maurice H. Vol. 1: 3848
Cotton Foundation Fellowship Awards; Dr. M. Aylwin Vol. 2: 7355
Cotton Foundation Publication Grants; Dr. M. Aylwin Vol. 2: 7356
CotY Awards Vol. 1: 14429
Cotzias Lecture; George Vol. 1: 696
Couch Award Vol. 2: 8476
Coudenhove-Kalergi Award Vol. 2: 3046
Coues Award; Elliott Vol. 1: 3340
Coulee Region Entrepreneurial Award Vol. 1: 12623
Coulter Memorial Lecturer; John Stanley Vol. 1: 1984
Council Award of Excellence Vol. 1: 9474
Council Medal Vol. 2: 7744
Council Meritorious Service Award Vol. 1: 1860
Council of Europe Museum Prize Vol. 2: 2289
Council of Peers Award for Excellence/ Speaker Hall of Fame Vol. 1: 15792
Council of the Year Vol. 1: 15390
Council of the Year Award Vol. 1: 11566
Councilman Creative Coaching Awards Vol. 1: 4723
Council's Distinguished Pathologist Award Vol. 1: 20376
Counselor Educator of the Year Vol. 1: 3087
Counselor of the Year Vol. 1: 3088
Counselor of the Year Award Vol. 1: 15603
Counselors of the Year Award Vol. 2: 4675
Counsilman Coach of the Year Award Vol. 1: 21190
Counterpoise Grand Design Award Vol. 1: 19307
Counting Coup Award Vol. 1: 2599
Country Award Vol. 1: 17469
Country Music Association Awards Vol. 1: 8620
Country Music Hall of Fame Vol. 1: 8621
County Engineer of the Year Awards Vol. 1: 14179
Coupe Olympique Vol. 2: 6426
Coupes Merites Aux Individus Vol. 1: 7780
Courage Award Vol. 1: 1635
Courage in Journalism Award Vol. 1: 12145
Courage to Care Award Vol. 1: 4980
Courrier; Fondation Janine Vol. 2: 1894
Course Rally Rookie of the Year Vol. 1: 19685
Courtois; Prix Gustave Vol. 2: 1682
Cousin; Prix Victor Vol. 2: 2089
Cousins National Chapter Award; Psi Chi/Ruth Hubbard Vol. 1: 17698
Coutinho Prize; Admiral Gago Vol. 2: 5490
Coutts Bank Award for Singers Vol. 2: 8643
Couture Award for Outstanding Volunteer Service to Eastern Surfing; Dr. Colin J. Vol. 1: 9119
Covarrubias; Premio Miguel Vol. 2: 4540
Covenant Awards Vol. 1: 7133
Cover Plaque Award Vol. 1: 47
The Covey Girls' Voice Scholarship Vol. 1: 18281
Cowart Plaque Vol. 1: 18985
Cowen Award for Public Buildings; Sir Zelman Vol. 2: 525
Cowie Prize; James M. Vol. 2: 7669
Cox Award; Morgan Vol. 1: 21990
Cox Award; Norman W. Vol. 1: 6243
Cox Family Rookie of the Year Award Vol. 1: 14912
Cox Memorial Prize; Jennifer Vol. 2: 383
CP Writers Award Vol. 1: 8355
CPB Public Radio Program Awards Vol. 1: 8523
CPB Public Television Local Program Awards Vol. 1: 8524
CPhA Centennial Award Vol. 1: 7334
CPR Institute for Dispute Resolution Awards for Excellence and Innovation in Alternative Dispute Resolution Vol. 1: 8626
CPRS Award of Attainment Vol. 1: 7361
CPRS Awards of Excellence Program Vol. 1: 7360
CPRS Lamp of Service Vol. 1: 7361
CPRS Lectern Vol. 1: 7361
CPRS Major Awards Program Vol. 1: 7361
CPRS Shield of Public Service Vol. 1: 7361
CPRS Societal Award Vol. 1: 7361
CQ DX Awards Vol. 1: 8629
CQ DX Honor Roll Vol. 1: 8630
CQ Press Award Vol. 1: 8404
CRA Award Vol. 2: 384
CRA Distinguished Service Vol. 1: 8333
Crabtree Foundation Award; Harold Vol. 1: 13982
Cracow International Festival of Short Films Vol. 2: 5301
Crafoord Prize Vol. 2: 6207
Craft America Competition Vol. 1: 18522
Craft and Design Awards Vol. 2: 8851
Crafts Council of Ireland Purchase Award Vol. 2: 3695
Crafts National Exhibition Vol. 1: 7774
Craftsman Degree Vol. 1: 15970
Craftsman/NSTA Young Inventors Awards Vol. 1: 15686
Craftsman Truck Series Vol. 1: 14045
Craigie Award; Andrew Vol. 1: 5769
Crain Award; American Business Media G. D. Vol. 1: 1607
Crain Desert Palm Achievement Award; Charles A. Vol. 1: 17044
Crain Jr. Award; G. D. Vol. 1: 6712
Craine Award; Zur Vol. 1: 11907
Cram Scholarships Vol. 1: 14762
Cramer Award; W. E. Vol. 1: 1673
Cramer Zone Flower Arrangement Award; Barbara Spaulding Vol. 1: 9876
Cramphorn Theater Scholarship; Rex Vol. 2: 479
Crampton Prize Vol. 2: 7761
Crane and Rigging Safety/Safety Improvement Awards Vol. 1: 19575
Crane Distinguished Service Award; Fred C. Vol. 1: 10952
Craniofacial Biology Group Distinguished Scientist Award Vol. 1: 11206
Craniofacial Biology Research Award Vol. 1: 11206
Cranko Memorial Award; John Vol. 2: 4978
Crase Bursary; Barbara Vol. 2: 167
Crasilneck Award; Sherry K. and Harold B. Vol. 1: 18654
Crate and Barrel Israeli Product Design Award for the Home and its Surroundings Vol. 2: 3744
Crater Software Award for Best Graduate Film Vol. 1: 16940
Crave the Dave Award Vol. 1: 8760
Craven Award; Avery O. Vol. 1: 16885
Crawford Art Award; Charlotte Vol. 1: 8917
Crawford Award Vol. 1: 9117
Crawford Award; Dorothy Vol. 2: 292
Crawford Award; Hector Vol. 2: 292
Crawford Award; J. G. Vol. 2: 246
Crawford Fantasy Award; William L. Vol. 1: 11259
Crawford Medal
Australian Academy of the Humanities Vol. 2: 135
Royal Philatelic Society Vol 2: 8645
Crawford Young Professional Award; Robert W. Vol. 1: 15575
Crawley Plaque Vol. 2: 6934
Crawshaw Memorial Prize; Philip Vol. 2: 8643
Crawshay Cup Vol. 2: 7393
Crawshay Prize for English Literature; Rose Mary Vol. 2: 6899
CRC for Polymers Prize Vol. 2: 320
CRC Multicultural Award Vol. 2: 614
CRCD Award Vol. 1: 7373
Creanga Prize; Ion Vol. 2: 5824
Creasey Memorial Award; John Vol. 2: 7363
Creative Achievement Award Vol. 1: 14413
Creative and Innovative Awards Vol. 1: 16391
Creative Arts Award Vol. 1: 12159
Creative Arts Emmy Awards Vol. 1: 13862
Creative Caf Sound Completion & Design Grant Vol. 1: 21712
Creative Commercial Production Awards Vol. 1: 6722
Creative Drama Award Vol. 1: 889
Creative Ticket National Schools of Distinction Award Vol. 1: 12536
Creative Video Productions Awards Vol. 1: 21263
Creative Writing Competition Vol. 2: 6892
Creativity Awards Vol. 1: 10612
Credit Executive of the Year; Advertising Vol. 1: 210
Crescendo Award Vol. 1: 17173
Cressey Memorial Award; Donald R. Vol. 1: 5594
Cressman ACE Award Recognizing Commitment to Staff Development; Reginald J. Vol. 1: 5650
Cresta International Advertising Awards Vol. 1: 11171
Cretsos Leadership Award; James M. Vol. 1: 4109
Crew Chief of the Year Award Vol. 1: 337
Crew of the Year Award Vol. 1: 10393
CRFA Fellowship Grants Vol. 1: 7555
Crichlow Trust Prize; Walter J. and Angeline H. Vol. 1: 2678
Crighton Trophy; Hec Vol. 1: 7213
Crikelair, Snyder, Gingras, Hardesty, Shenaq Vol. 1: 17390
Crile Award; George Vol. 1: 11803

Crime Prevention; APPA Awards for Excellence in Community Vol. 1: 3598
Criminal Investigation Award Vol. 1: 3566
Crimson Glory Award; Colonel A. T. Reid Vol. 1: 5112
Crisp Medal Vol. 2: 103
Crisp Television News Photographer of the Year; Ernie Vol. 1: 15533
Cristal du Centre National de la Recherche Scientifique Vol. 2: 2395
The Cristy Award Vol. 1: 18061
Critical Writing Awards Competition Vol. 1: 19843
Critics' and Readers' Pick Vol. 1: 18110
Critics Prize Vol. 2: 5447
Crittenden Award; Eugene Casson Vol. 1: 20478
Crittenden Memorial Award; Christopher Vol. 1: 16518
Crittenden Memorial Award; John and Jessie Vol. 1: 6169
CRM-Fields-PIMS Prize Vol. 1: 13205
Croatian Republic Prizes Vol. 2: 1387
Crocker Award; Allen Vol. 1: 16121
Croes Medal; J. James R. Vol. 1: 4310
Croiset; Prix Alfred Vol. 2: 1749
Croix de Guerre Vol. 2: 2356
Croly/GFWC Print Journalism Award; Jane Cunningham Vol. 1: 9916
Cromer Greek Awards Vol. 2: 6900
Crompton Premium Vol. 2: 7808
Cromwell Essay Competition Vol. 2: 7372
Cronin Award; Joe Vol. 1: 2939
Cronin Club Award Vol. 1: 14397
Cronkite Award for Excellence in Journalism and Mass Communication; Walter Vol. 1: 8657
Crop Science Award Vol. 1: 8659
Crop Science International Activity Award Vol. 1: 8660
Crop Science Teaching Award Vol. 1: 8661
Crosfield Cup Vol. 2: 8541
Crosman Memorial Award Vol. 1: 10674
Cross Country Coach of the Year Vol. 1: 20801
Cross Country Contributor Award Vol. 1: 21217
Cross Country Journal Award Vol. 1: 15316
Cross of Mannerheim Vol. 2: 1588
Cross of Merit Vol. 2: 5318
Cross of Merit for Bravery Vol. 2: 5319
Cross of Merit for Moral and Civic Education Vol. 2: 1172
Cross of Merit with Swords Vol. 2: 5320
Cross of Mourning Vol. 2: 1588
Cross of Valour
- Canada - The Chancellery Vol. 1: 6818
- Office of the President of the Republic of Poland Vol 2: 5321

Crossroads Market/NLGJA Print Awards Vol. 1: 15344
Crouch Fellowship; John Mitchell Vol. 2: 505
Crouch Medal; Herbert Vol. 2: 81
Crow Award; Horace Vol. 1: 21218
Crow Award; Jake White Vol. 1: 15256
Crowe Memorial Exhibit Award; Dr. Charles W. Vol. 1: 3210
Crowley Scholarship; Francis X.
- New England Water Works Association Vol. 1: 16133
- New England Water Works Association Vol 1: 16139

Crown Awards Vol. 1: 8232
Crown Cup Vol. 2: 6729
Crowninshield Award; Louise du Pont Vol. 1: 15917
CRSI Design Awards Program Vol. 1: 8346
Cruce Trophy; Marion C. Vol. 1: 18580
Cruess Award; William V. Vol. 1: 10937
Cruickshank Alumni Leadership Award Vol. 1: 6179
Cruickshank Award; Dr. James W. Vol. 1: 694
Cruickshank Memorial Award; Allan D. Vol. 1: 6077
Cruikshank Award; Nelson Vol. 1: 14817
Cruiseline of the Year Vol. 2: 6549
Crum Distinguished Service Award; Roy W. Vol. 1: 20161
Crumbine Consumer Protection Award; Samuel J.
- Foodservice and Packaging Institute Vol. 1: 9665
- International Association for Food Protection Vol 1: 11229

Crump Trophy; Jack Vol. 2: 6704
Cruz de Boyaca Vol. 2: 1275
Cruz Prize; Oswaldo Vol. 2: 1143
Crymes TESOL Fellowship for Graduate Study; Ryan Vol. 1: 19949
Crystal Apple Award Vol. 1: 18419
Crystal Award
- American Staffing Association Vol. 1: 4689
- National Association of Negro Business and Professional Women's Clubs Vol 1: 14311
- Sugar Industry Technologists Vol 1: 19828

Crystal Awards Vol. 1: 21713
Crystal Clear Day Vol. 2: 8267
Crystal Clear Trophy Vol. 2: 8267
Crystal Drop Award Vol. 1: 12128
Crystal Goblet Award Vol. 2: 9153
Crystal Helmet; Planetary Award/ Vol. 1: 5852
Crystal Prism Award Vol. 1: 215
Crystal Radio Awards Vol. 1: 14110
Crystallographic Research Grant Vol. 1: 13433
CSA Trophy Vol. 1: 8356
CSAE/CSSBI Award Vol. 1: 7403
CSAE Fellow Vol. 1: 7400
CSAE Maple Leaf Award Vol. 1: 7401
Csallany Institutional Award for Exemplary Contributions to Water Resources Management; Sandor C. Vol. 1: 4827
CSAS Fellowship Award Vol. 1: 7441
CSBMCB Merck Frosst Prize Vol. 1: 7452
CSD Medal Vol. 2: 7301
CSIH Lifetime Achievement Award for International Health Vol. 1: 7423
CSL Gold Medal Vol. 1: 7814
CSLA Awards of Excellence Vol. 1: 7476
Csokor Prize; Franz Theodor Vol. 2: 711
Csontos Medal Vol. 2: 3246
CSPA Service Award Vol. 1: 7508
CSPG Graduate Students Thesis Awards Vol. 1: 7482
CSPG Undergraduate Scholarship; Norcen/ Vol. 1: 7488
CSRT Essay Award Vol. 1: 6917
CSSP Educational Research Award Vol. 1: 8586
CT History Day Awards Vol. 1: 10262
CTBI Intermediate Cello/Viola/Double Bass Scholarship Vol. 1: 18282
CTHS Annual Award Vol. 1: 7520
Cubitt Award Vol. 2: 8283
Cudecki International Business Award; ACTFL Edwin Vol. 1: 2057
Cuervo National Order; Miguel Antonio Caro and Rufino Jose Vol. 2: 1314
Cuervo; Orden Nacional de Miguel Antonio Caro y Rufino Jose Vol. 2: 1314
Cuesta National Poetry Prize; Jorge Vol. 2: 4500
Cuesta; Premio Nacional de Poesia Jorge Vol. 2: 4500
Cugnot Award Vol. 1: 19064
Cugnot Award; Nicholas-Joseph Vol. 1: 19067
Culbertson Award; Jack A. Vol. 1: 20972
Culbertson Outstanding Volunteer Service Award; Charles V. Vol. 1: 4603
Culinary Arts Salon
- Chefs and Cooks Circle Vol. 2: 7303
- National Restaurant Association Vol 1: 15625
- Society of German Cooks Vol 2: 3064

Culinary Educator Award Vol. 1: 11327
Culinary Masters
- Chefs and Cooks Circle Vol. 2: 7303
- National Restaurant Association Vol. 1: 15625
- Society of German Cooks Vol 2: 3064

Culinary Olympics
- Chefs and Cooks Circle Vol. 2: 7303
- Society of German Cooks Vol 2: 3064

Culinary World Cup
- Chefs and Cooks Circle Vol. 2: 7303
- National Restaurant Association Vol 1: 15625
- Society of German Cooks Vol 2: 3064
- Vatel-Club Luxembourg Vol 2: 4413

Culley Memorial Award; David Vol. 2: 249
Cullis Grants; Winifred Vol. 2: 6406
Cullum Geographical Medal Vol. 1: 2328
Cultural Achievement Award Vol. 1: 2893
Cultural and Economic Diversity Award Vol. 1: 2216
Cultural Award Vol. 1: 17907
Cultural Cooperation Award Vol. 1: 9229
Cultural Development Fund Vol. 1: 5151
Cultural Diversity Grant; LAMA Vol. 1: 12817
Cultural Diversity Outreach Award Vol. 1: 3823
Cultural Heritage Award Vol. 2: 3716
Cultural Leadership; Keith Kelly Award for Vol. 1: 7037
Cultural Medal Vol. 1: 11086
Cultural Pluralism Award Vol. 1: 5837
Culture Prize Vol. 2: 5154
Culver Award; Byron G. Vol. 1: 18085
Culver Distinguished Service Award; Essae M. Vol. 1: 12937
Cumiskey Hall of Fame; Frank J. Vol. 1: 15182
Cummings Memorial Award; Donald E. Vol. 1: 2611
Cumont; Prix Franz Vol. 2: 1023
Cumulative Mileage Awards Vol. 1: 16482
Cunningham Award; Glenn Vol. 1: 21219
Cunningham Award (Marine Aviator of the Year); Alfred A. Vol. 1: 13070
Cunningham Award (Most Valuable Player); Les Vol. 1: 2505
Cunningham Award; Robinson/ Vol. 1: 626
Cunningham Award; Thomas F. Vol. 1: 21963
Cunningham-Beate Award Vol. 2: 7183
Cunningham Distinguished Citizen Award Vol. 1: 18030
Cunningham Inter-American Award; Thomas F. Vol. 1: 21963

Cunningham Memorial Award; Ann Marie Vol. 1: 14964
Cunningham Memorial Award; Ed Vol. 1: 16981
Cunningham Memorial International Fellowship Vol. 1: 13253
Cup for Historic Grand Touring Cars Vol. 2: 2455
Cup for Thoroughbred Grand Prix Cars Vol. 2: 2455
Cup of Cups Vol. 2: 858
Cups Vol. 2: 1370
Curatorial Research Fellowships Vol. 1: 10004
Cured Meat Awards Vol. 1: 10669
Cured Meat Championships; American Vol. 1: 1261
Cured Meats Hall of Fame Vol. 1: 1263
Curie Award; Marie Vol. 1: 1072
Curl Award; Earl Vol. 1: 12030
Curl Essay Prize Vol. 2: 8422
Curren Award Vol. 1: 20881
Current Topic Award Vol. 1: 3549
Currey Book-Length Publications Award; Cecil B. Vol. 1: 5898
Currey Memorial Fellowship; C. H. Vol. 2: 604
Curti Award; Merle Vol. 1: 16886
Curtin Medal; Bill Vol. 2: 7762
Curtin Plaque Vol. 1: 18986
Curtis Award; Len Vol. 2: 8332
Curtis Cup Vol. 1: 20603
Curtis G. Benjamin Award for Creative Publishing Vol. 1: 5564
Curtis Lecture Award; John A. Vol. 1: 4009
Curtis Medal; J.H. Vol. 2: 385
Cushman Award; Joseph A. Vol. 1: 8690
Customer First League Table Vol. 2: 8268
Customer Service Award Vol. 1: 7165
Customer Service Excellence Award Vol. 1: 1274
Cut Leaf Show Awards Vol. 1: 2554
Cutler Award for Residential Lighting; Aileen Page Vol. 1: 10695
Cutler Award; Lady Vol. 2: 306
Cutlery Hall of Fame Vol. 1: 6445
Cutting Edge Gemstone Competition Vol. 1: 2324
Cutts Scholarships; Donna Vol. 1: 18952
Cutty Sark Medal Vol. 2: 8113
Cuvillier; Fondation Jean Vol. 2: 1897
CVMA Humane Award Vol. 1: 7531
CVMA Plaque Vol. 1: 7532
The CWA Gold Dagger for Nonfiction Vol. 2: 7364
The CWA Silver Dagger for Fiction Vol. 2: 7365
CWI of the Year Award Vol. 1: 4881
CWT Award Vol. 1: 8467
Cycle Award Vol. 1: 904
Cyr Gold Reel Award; Helen Vol. 1: 6230
Cyril and Methodius Prize Vol. 2: 1208
Cystic Fibrosis Foundation Special Research Awards Vol. 1: 8697
CYTECH Vol. 2: 6821
Cytotechnologist Award for Outstanding Achievement Vol. 1: 4389
Cytotechnologist Award of the American Society of Cytology Vol. 1: 4390
Cytotechnologist of the Year Award Vol. 1: 4389
Cytotechnologist Scientific Presentation Award Vol. 1: 4390
Czerny Preis; Adalbert Vol. 2: 2899
D. O'Sullivan Graphic Supplies Ltd. Award Vol. 2: 3697
Da Gama Machado; Fondation Vol. 2: 1832
da Vinci Award; The Leonardo Vol. 1: 11066
Da Vinci Diploma; Leonardo Vol. 2: 6325
Da Vinci Medal; Leonardo Vol. 1: 18871
da Vinci Medal; Leonardo Vol. 2: 871
DAAD Prize for Distinguished Scholarship in German Studies Vol. 1: 2623
d'Abbadie; Fondation Antoine Vol. 2: 1798
DAC Trophy Vol. 1: 10386
Dacco Award; Aldo Vol. 2: 3992
Dach InVEST Award Vol. 1: 10731
Dade Behring Award Vol. 2: 5629
Dade Behring MicroScan Young Investigator Award Vol. 1: 4134
Dade International Award Vol. 1: 11581
Daedalian Award Vol. 1: 16823
Daedalian Civilian Air Safety Award Vol. 1: 16827
Daedalian Distinguished Achievement Award Vol. 1: 16821
Daedalian Foundation Award of Recognition Vol. 1: 8707
Daedalian Scholarship Awards Vol. 1: 16822
Daedalian Supply Effectiveness Award Vol. 1: 16820
Daedalian Trophy
Order of Daedalians Vol. 1: 16819
Order of Daedalians Vol 1: 16820
Order of Daedalians Vol 1: 16824
Order of Daedalians Vol 1: 16825
Order of Daedalians Vol 1: 16826
Order of Daedalians Vol 1: 16827
Order of Daedalians Vol 1: 16828
Order of Daedalians Vol 1: 16829
Order of Daedalians Vol 1: 16830
Order of Daedalians Vol 1: 16831
Order of Daedalians Vol 1: 16833
Order of Daedalians Vol 1: 16834
Daedalian Weapon Systems Award Vol. 1: 16823
Daeyang Prize Vol. 2: 5496
Dag Hammarskjold Award Vol. 1: 11382
Dagenais Award; Camille A. Vol. 1: 7412
Daggs Award; Ray G. Vol. 1: 3515
Dagnan-Bouveret; Fondation Jean Vol. 2: 1898
Dagnan-Bouveret; Prix
Academie des Beaux-Arts Vol. 2: 1710
Academie des Sciences Morales et Politiques Vol 2: 2011
Dahlgrens Pris; Rolf Vol. 2: 6187
Dahlquist Prize; Germund Vol. 1: 18733
D.A.I. Goring Award Vol. 1: 21108
Dailey Award; Janet Vol. 1: 18112
Dain Library History Dissertation Award; Phyllis Vol. 1: 2993
Dairy Progressive Breeder Awards Vol. 1: 3113
Daiwa Scholarships Vol. 2: 7377
Dakin Award Vol. 1: 10651
Dalby Prize Vol. 2: 8803
Dale Award; Edgar
Association for Indiana Media Educators Vol. 1: 5384
The Chris Awards Vol 1: 7949
Dale Medical Products Excellent Clinical Nurse Specialist Award Vol. 1: 1172
Dalinkevicius premija; Juozo Vol. 2: 4387
Dallas 100 Award Vol. 1: 19511
Dallas Opera Young Artist Competition Vol. 1: 21416
Dall'Onda Borghese Prize; Fondazione Contessa Caterina Pasolini Vol. 2: 3815
Dallos Award; Joseph Vol. 1: 8470
d'Alviella; Prix Eugene Goblet Vol. 2: 1021
Daly Award; Sgt. Maj. Dan Vol. 1: 13096
Daly Medal; Charles P. Vol. 1: 2329
d'Alzon Medal; Emmanuel Vol. 1: 6091
Damele Memorial Award; Peter L. Vol. 1: 1552
Damen Award Vol. 1: 12968
Dameshek Award; William Vol. 1: 12786
Dameshek Prize Vol. 1: 4444
Damien - Dutton Award Vol. 1: 8726
D'Amour Award; O'Neil Vol. 1: 14608
Dana Award; John Cotton
Special Libraries Association Vol. 1: 19547
H.W. Wilson Co. Vol 1: 21635
Dana Award; Margaret Vol. 1: 5942
Dana Awards for Pioneering Achievements in Higher Education; Charles A. Vol. 1: 8730
Dana Library Public Relations Awards; John Cotton Vol. 1: 12816
Dana Publicity Award; John Cotton Vol. 1: 12816
Dance Grants Vol. 1: 17553
Dance Magazine Annual Awards Vol. 1: 8736
Dance Screen Award Vol. 2: 758
Dance/USA National Honors Vol. 1: 8747
Dandurand Trophy; Leo Vol. 1: 7104
DANDY Awards Vol. 1: 16331
Danieli Young Professional Award; Chaim Vol. 1: 11965
Danielopolu Prize; Daniel Vol. 2: 5825
Daniels Award; Farrington
American Association of Physicists in Medicine Vol. 1: 1368
International Solar Energy Society Vol 2: 2987
Danielson Award; Philip A. Vol. 1: 21580
Danis Prize; Robert Vol. 2: 6463
Danish Academy Prize for Literature Vol. 2: 1444
Danish Prize for Children's Illustration Vol. 2: 1482
Danish Prize for Children's Literature Vol. 2: 1483
Danish Town Planning Prize Vol. 2: 1488
Dannon Institute Award for Excellence in Medical/Dental Nutrition Education Vol. 1: 3957
Dansk Oversaetterforbunds Aerespris Vol. 2: 1471
Danstrom Award; Charlotte Vol. 1: 21746
Dantas; Premio General Casimiro Vol. 2: 5406
Dantas Prize; General Casimiro Vol. 2: 5406
Dante Prize Vol. 1: 8749
Dantzig Dissertation Award; George B. Vol. 1: 11070
Dantzig Prize Vol. 1: 13199
Dantzig Prize; George B. Vol. 1: 18734
Danzig Award; Sarah Palfrey Vol. 1: 20854
Dapaepe-Willems Award Vol. 2: 930
Darbaker Prize Vol. 1: 6543
Darby Award for Inspirational Leadership and Excellence of Command; Jack N. Vol. 1: 16053
Darlin Arts Award; Elisha Vol. 1: 9031
Darling Foundation Prize Vol. 2: 6563
Darling Medal for Distinguished Achievement in Collection Development in the Health Sciences; Louise Vol. 1: 13254
Darracq; Fondation Alexandre Vol. 2: 1785

Darracq; Fondation Louise Vol. 2: 1926
Darrow Award; Clarence Vol. 1: 11804
Dartmouth Medal Vol. 1: 17937
Darwin Lifetime Achievement Award; Charles R. Vol. 1: 1356
Darwin Medal Vol. 2: 8694
Darwin-Plakette Vol. 2: 2704
Darwin Plaque Vol. 2: 2704
Darwin - Wallace Medals Vol. 2: 8071
Das Jaigopal Memorial Award; Chaturvedi Ghanshyam Vol. 2: 3408
Das Memorial Award; Chaturvedi Kalawati Jagmohan Vol. 2: 3409
DASA Scholarship Vol. 1: 8848
Dasher Best Paper Award; Benjamin J. Vol. 1: 4010
Daskalov Prize; Academician Hristo Vol. 2: 1207
Datascope Excellence in Collaboration Award - Multidisciplinary Teams Vol. 1: 1173
Datascope Excellence in Collaboration Award - Nurse to Family Vol. 1: 1174
Date Able Image Award Vol. 1: 8754
Datta Memorial Oration Award; Dr. Dharamvir Vol. 2: 3410
Dauberville; Prix Henri Vol. 2: 1683
Daubney Research Fellowship in Virology and Helminthology; Robert Vol. 2: 8493
Daughters of Liberty Medal Vol. 1: 15767
Daughters of Union Veterans of the Civil War, 1861-1865 Award Vol. 1: 8756
Daukantas premija; Simono Vol. 2: 4388
Daula (Frigate Bird) Award; Manu Vol. 1: 16994
Daulat Singh Kothari Memorial Lecture Award Vol. 2: 3481
d'Aumale; Prix Vol. 2: 2430
Daumet; Fondation Vol. 2: 1717
Dauphinee Volunteer of the Year; Judy Vol. 1: 17676
Dauzat; Prix Albert Vol. 2: 2592
Davenport Distinguished Service Award Vol. 1: 13297
Davenport Memorial Exhibit Award; John S. Vol. 1: 3211
Davenport Prize; Margaret Vol. 2: 8458
David Film Awards Vol. 2: 3895
David G. Imig Award for Distinguished Achievement in Teacher Education Vol. 1: 1148
David - Gerald Award Vol. 1: 20247
David Library of the American Revolution Award for Playwriting on American Freedom Vol. 1: 12543
David Medal; Edgeworth Vol. 2: 539
David; Prix Athanase- Vol. 1: 17794
David; Prix Maxime Vol. 2: 1684
Davidoff Award; Paul Vol. 1: 3550
Davids Award; Bob Vol. 1: 18631
Davidson ASPRS President's Award for Practical Papers; John I. Vol. 1: 5211
Davidson Award; Murray Vol. 1: 765
Davidson Medal Vol. 1: 19208
Davidson Medal; George Vol. 1: 2330
Davidson Memorial Award for Sportsmanship; Kenneth R. Vol. 1: 21146
Davidson Memorial Trophy; Sam Vol. 1: 7214
Davidson Practice of the Profession Award; Park O. Vol. 1: 6636
Davies Award; Valentine Vol. 1: 21991
Davies Memorial Scholar Award for Scholarly Activities in Humanities and History of Medicine; Nicholas E. Vol. 1: 1919
Davis and Helen Miles Davis Prize; Watson Vol. 1: 10485
Davis Article Award; Donald G. Vol. 1: 2994
Davis Award; Arthur Vining Vol. 1: 427
Davis Award; Donald E. Vol. 1: 13071
Davis Award; Henry B. Vol. 1: 4611
Davis Award; Jefferson Vol. 1: 8351
Davis Award; John P. Vol. 1: 4506
Davis Award; Niles Vol. 1: 14066
Davis Award; W. Allison and Elizabeth Stubbs Vol. 1: 13676
Davis Award; Watson Vol. 1: 4110
Davis Awards of Excellence; Graham L. Vol. 1: 10338
Davis Business of the Year; Diane C. Vol. 1: 21299
Davis Cup Vol. 1: 20855
Davis Cup Award Vol. 1: 10675
Davis Fund Awards; Henry and Lily Vol. 2: 8152
Davis Graduate Scholarship Award; Keith Vol. 1: 18485
Davis, Jr. Award; Sammy Vol. 1: 19423
Davis Lecture Series; Raymond E. Vol. 1: 1957
Davis Medal; George E. Vol. 2: 7745
Davis Memorial Award; Suzanne M. Vol. 1: 19486
Davis Memorial Award; William J. Vol. 1: 20973
Davis Memorial Lecture; E. H. Vol. 2: 386
Davis Prairie Restoration Award; Arnold Vol. 1: 16016
Davis Prize; Philip Vol. 2: 8459
Davis Productivity Awards Program Vol. 1: 9635
Davis Sherry Memorial Trophy; The Goodfellow Memorial Oratorio Scholarship/ The Helen Vol. 1: 18292
Davis Silver Medal Award; A. F. Vol. 1: 4880
Davis Trophy; Margaret Vol. 2: 6709
Davison Chamber of Commerce Service Scholarship Vol. 1: 8758
Davisson-Germer Prize in Atomic or Surface Physics Vol. 1: 3454
Davy Award; Bob Vol. 2: 9063
Davy Medal Vol. 2: 8695
Dawdon Trophy Vol. 2: 6710
Dawson Awards Vol. 1: 5810
Dawson Medal; Sir John William Vol. 1: 18163
Day Cup; Colonel George E. Vol. 1: 5102
Day Medal; Arthur L. Vol. 1: 9948
Day of Tennis Vol. 2: 1404
Day Prize and Lectureship; Arthur L. Vol. 1: 13830
Daytime Emmy Awards Vol. 1: 13861
Dayton Playhouse Future Fest Vol. 1: 8762
Dayton Playhouse National Playwriting Competition Vol. 1: 8762
Daytona 200 Vol. 1: 3150
Daytona 500 NASCAR Winston Cup Series Stock Car Race Vol. 1: 8766
Daytona Gatorade Victory Lane Award Vol. 1: 8765
DCA Scholarship Vol. 1: 8850
De Angelis Award; George Vol. 1: 13554
de Araujo Pereira de Design; Premio Municipal Roberto Vol. 2: 5436
De Backer Prize; Paul Vol. 2: 971
de-Bary-Medaille; Anton- Vol. 2: 2862
de Beaufort-prijs; Henriette Vol. 2: 4911
de Caen; Fondation Vol. 2: 1717
de Caldas; Medalla Militar Francisco Jose Vol. 2: 1282
de Carli Award; Felice Vol. 2: 3993
de Carvalho Fernandes Prize; Antonio Alves Vol. 2: 5407
de Castilho de Olisipografia; Premio Municipal Julio Vol. 2: 5433
de Chenier; Prix Vol. 2: 1763
De Clercq Prize; C. Vol. 2: 1078
de Conway Little Medal of Honor; Helen Vol. 1: 10412
de Dios Batiz; Medalla Juan Vol. 2: 4548
de Donder; Prix Theophile Vol. 2: 1069
de Ferranti Premium; Sebastian Z. Vol. 2: 7808
De Florez Award for Flight Simulation Vol. 1: 2679
De Florez Award for Modeling and Simulation Vol. 1: 2679
de Florez Flight Safety Award; Admiral Luis Vol. 1: 9582
De Francis Award; Vincent Vol. 1: 2573
de Hauteroche; Prix Allier Vol. 2: 1759
De Internationale Carl Nielsen Musik Konkurrencer Vol. 2: 1507
de Jouvenal; Prix Roland Vol. 2: 2209
De Keyn; Prix Joseph Vol. 2: 1026
de Kieffer International Fellowship Award; Robert Vol. 1: 5355
De la Court Prizes Vol. 2: 4885
de la Maza; Premio Francisco Vol. 2: 4535
De La Vaulx Medal Vol. 2: 6326
De Laszlo Medal Vol. 2: 8733
de Laveleye; Prix Emile Vol. 2: 1019
de Martens; Prix Frederic Vol. 2: 6373
De Mellis; Premio Cavolini - Vol. 2: 3836
de Menasce Memorial Trust; George Vol. 2: 8236
de Mendizabal; Premio Miguel Othon Vol. 2: 4541
de Menezes Veiga; Premio Frederico Vol. 2: 1159
de Menezes Veiga Prize; Frederico Vol. 2: 1159
de Meyer; Fondation Jean Vol. 2: 1035
De Mille Award; Cecil B. Vol. 1: 10512
de Monaco; Fondation Albert I Vol. 2: 1784
De Morgan Medal Vol. 2: 8087
de Morogues; Fondation Bigot Vol. 2: 1808
de Morogues; Prix Bigot Vol. 2: 2020
de Neuville et Sanford Saltus; Prix Alphonse Vol. 2: 1701
de Paepe; Prix Polydore Vol. 2: 1030
de Parville; Fondation Henri Vol. 2: 1881
de Poesie; Prix Annuel Vol. 2: 2110
de Pontecoulant; Fondation G. Vol. 2: 1867
De Potter; Prix Agathon Vol. 2: 1042
de Regnier; Prix Pierre Vol. 2: 2202
de Rothschild Cup; Lionel Vol. 2: 8542
de Rufz de La Vison; Fondation Jean Vol. 2: 1899
De Ruyck Prize; Dr. Roland Vol. 2: 972
de Sagarra; Premi Josep Maria Vol. 2: 6002
de Sahagun; Premio Fray Bernardino Vol. 2: 4537
de Saridakis; Fondation Laura Mounier Vol. 2: 1916
de Selys Longchamps; Prix Edmond Vol. 2: 1052
de Sousa Prego Freedom Prize; Visconde Vol. 2: 5443
de Souza Award; Ruth Vol. 2: 1141
de Tiere Prize; Nestor Vol. 2: 957
de Tocqueville Prize; Alexis Vol. 2: 4763

de Varona Award; Donna Vol. 1: 21810
de Vattel; Prix Emer Vol. 2: 6373
de Veres Award Vol. 2: 3697
de Wegmann; Prix Vega et Lods Vol. 2: 2219
De Wet Decoration Vol. 2: 5734
De Wet Medal Vol. 2: 5735
de Wolmar; Prix Valentine Vol. 2: 2218
DEA Award Vol. 1: 8732
DEA Explorer Drug Abuse Prevention Service Award Vol. 1: 6574
Deadline Club Awards Vol. 1: 8773
Deaf/Hard of Hearing Entrepreneur of the Year Vol. 1: 8775
Deafness Research Foundation Otological Research Fellowship for Medical Students Vol. 1: 8778
Deak Award; Francis Vol. 1: 11715
Deak Award; Francis O. Vol. 1: 4464
Deakin Award; Charles Vol. 2: 3150
Dealer and Exhibit Awards Vol. 1: 8357
Dealer and Supplier Volunteer of the Year Award Vol. 1: 6171
Dealer Awards Vol. 1: 6170
Dealer Booster Award Vol. 1: 3212
Dealer Education Award Vol. 1: 16577
Dean John A. Knauss Marine Policy Fellowship Vol. 1: 9618
Dean Memorial Award; H. Trendley Vol. 1: 11207
Deane Award; Hamilton Vol. 2: 7391
Deaver Award; Sally Vol. 1: 20802
Deb Memorial Award for Popularisation of Science; Dr. B. C. Vol. 2: 3531
Deb Memorial Award for Soil/Physical Chemistry; Dr. B. C. Vol. 2: 3532
DeBakey Award; Michael E. Vol. 1: 13327
DeBellis Award; Anthony Vol. 1: 5943
DeBenedetti Prize in Peace History; Charles Vol. 1: 17127
Deborah Award Vol. 1: 2894
Debra Research Grants Vol. 1: 9054
Debreczeni Medal; Marton Vol. 2: 3254
Debs Award; Dorr- Vol. 1: 18602
Debs Award; Eugene V. Vol. 1: 9350
Debut Dagger Vol. 2: 7366
Debye Award in Physical Chemistry; Peter Vol. 1: 1747
Debye Prize; Peter Vol. 2: 1118
Decades of Excellence Crystal Bell Teacher Award Vol. 1: 12734
DeCelle Award; Robert E. Vol. 1: 21220
Dechelle; Fondation Ernest Vol. 2: 1858
DECHEMA Award of the Max-Buchner-Forschungsstiftung Vol. 2: 2699
DECHEMA Ehrenmitgliedschaft Vol. 2: 2910
DECHEMA Honorary Membership Vol. 2: 2910
DECHEMA-Medaille Vol. 2: 2911
DECHEMA Medal Vol. 2: 2911
DECHEMA Preis der Max Buchner Forschungsstiftung Vol. 2: 2912
Decision Maker Award; Outstanding Vol. 1: 5061
Decker Memorial Outreach Award; Bea Vol. 1: 12080
Decoration for Merit in Gold Vol. 2: 5736
Decorations Vol. 2: 2961
Decorative Arts Collection Awards Vol. 1: 19097
Dedicated Service Award
American Society of Mechanical Engineers Vol. 1: 4507
Society of Decorative Painters Vol 1: 19098
South African Institute of Forestry Vol 2: 5709
Dedication Award Vol. 1: 9235
Dedrick, Jr. Award; Dewey R. Vol. 1: 4612
Deen Distinguished Lectureship; Thomas B. Vol. 1: 20162
Deere Awards; NACTA John Vol. 1: 16406
Deere Medal; John Vol. 1: 4218
Defant-Medaille; Albert Vol. 2: 2712
Defence Long Service Medal Vol. 2: 193
Defenders of Justice Vol. 2: 1297
Defense Distinguished Service Medal Vol. 1: 8813
Defense Industry Award Vol. 1: 14901
Defense Meritorious Service Medal Vol. 1: 8814
Defense of Academic Freedom Award Vol. 1: 14778
Defense Superior Service Medal Vol. 1: 8815
Defensive Player of the Year
Continental Basketball Association Vol. 1: 8481
National Association of Basketball Coaches Vol 1: 14082
National Basketball Association Vol 1: 14501
Defensores de la Justicia Vol. 2: 1297
Deflandre et Marthe Deflandre-Rigaud; Fondation Georges Vol. 2: 1872
Deflandre-Rigaud; Fondation Georges Deflandre et Marthe Vol. 2: 1872
DeForest Audion Award Vol. 1: 21324
DeForest Audion Gold Medal Award Vol. 1: 21324
DeForest Award; Lee Vol. 1: 17833
Defresne Prize Vol. 2: 4897
Defries Award; R. D. Vol. 1: 7356
Degelleke Award Vol. 1: 7690
DeGolyer Distinguished Service Medal Vol. 1: 19235
DeGolyer Memorial Fund Award; Clare Hart Vol. 1: 8716
DeGreef; Prix Arthur Vol. 2: 988
Deguchi Prize Vol. 2: 4925
Dehem; Prix Louise Vol. 2: 998
Del Gaudio Award; Matthew W. Vol. 1: 297
del Toro; Premio Carlos Perez Vol. 2: 4473
Delacorte Press Prize for a First Young Adult Novel Vol. 1: 8846
Delacroix; Prix Eve Vol. 2: 2148
Delalande-Guerineau; Prix Vol. 2: 1766
Delano Award; Jane A. Vol. 1: 3824
DeLaval Dairy Extension Award Vol. 1: 2100
DeLaval, Inc. Dairy Extension Award Vol. 1: 2100
Delavan Award Vol. 1: 2279
Delbos; Prix Victor Vol. 2: 2090
Delcros, Houllevigue, Saintour, Jules Mahyer; Fondations Estrade Vol. 2: 1978
Delcros; Prix Estrade Vol. 2: 1978
Delcros; Prix Estrade- Vol. 2: 1770
Delegate Award Vol. 1: 9496
Delius Medal; Christoph Traugott Vol. 2: 3255
Dellinger Gold Medal; John Howard Vol. 2: 934
Delphinium Society Awards Vol. 2: 7379
Delta Air Lines Puffer Award Vol. 1: 13904
Delta Art Exhibition Vol. 1: 5070
Delta; Penelope Vol. 2: 3170
Delta Pi Epsilon Research Award Vol. 1: 8874
Delta Sigma Rho - Tau Kappa Alpha Trophy Vol. 1: 15102
Delwart Foundation Prize; Jean-Marie Vol. 2: 1039
DeMaio Award for Trade Union Activism; Ernest Vol. 1: 12641
DEMCO/ALA Black Caucus Award for Excellence in Librarianship Vol. 1: 6417
Demco New Leaders Travel Grant Vol. 1: 17714
DeMello School Scholarships Vol. 1: 8877
Dement Academic Achievement Award; William C. Vol. 1: 837
Deming Application Prize Vol. 2: 4313
Deming Prize Vol. 2: 4313
Deming Prize for Individual Person Vol. 2: 4313
Demingu Sho Vol. 2: 4313
Demmond Award; Jack W. Vol. 1: 13072
Demolon; Fondation de Madame Albert Vol. 2: 1838
Dempster Travelling Fellowship Vol. 2: 7845
Den Danske Byplanpris Vol. 2: 1488
Den gronne Nal Vol. 2: 1489
Den Store Journalistprisen Vol. 2: 5160
Dendinger Driver of the Year; William Vol. 1: 13362
Dendy Award
Sydney Film Festival Vol. 2: 614
Sydney Film Festival Vol 2: 617
Dendy Awards Vol. 2: 477
Dendy Awards for Australian Short Films Vol. 2: 615
Dengo Memorial Award for Best International Paper; Gabriel Vol. 1: 1333
Denig Distinguished Service Award; Brig. Gen. Robert L. Vol. 1: 20684
Denk Congressional Award; Horst G. Vol. 1: 10713
Denk Scholarship for Violin, Viola, Cello; Alberta Vol. 1: 13662
Denman Cup; Lady Vol. 2: 8177
Denmark National Faculty Advisor Award; Psi Chi/Florence L. Vol. 1: 17697
Denning Award; Anthony Vol. 2: 8962
Dennis Prospector of the Year Award; Bill Vol. 1: 17689
Dennis Scholarship; John Vol. 1: 13541
Denny Gold Medal Vol. 2: 7707
Densmore Prize; Frances Vol. 1: 3171
Dent Medal Vol. 2: 8632
Dental Student Award Vol. 1: 726
Dental Trade and Industry Award of Recognition Vol. 1: 17347
Dentist Citizen of the Year Vol. 1: 1182
Dentist of the Year Vol. 1: 13532
Dentsu Advertising Awards Vol. 2: 4113
Denver International Film Festival; Starz
Denver Film Society Vol. 1: 8881
Denver Film Society Vol 1: 8882
Denver Film Society Vol 1: 8883
Denver Film Society Vol 1: 8884
Denver Film Society Vol 1: 8885
Denyn Prize; Jef Vol. 2: 1089
Department of Defense Distinguished Service Award Vol. 1: 14905
Department of Defense Distinguished Service Award Vol. 1: 14904
Department of Justice - CBA University Law School Essay Contest Vol. 1: 6967
Department of Trade and Industry Prizes Vol. 2: 7690

Department of Transportation Award for Heroism Vol. 1: 9431
Department of Veteran's Affairs Employee of the Year Award Vol. 1: 343
Derazy Violin Award Vol. 1: 21779
Derek Price-Rod Webster Award Vol. 1: 10486
deRoaldes Award Vol. 1: 2927
Deruyts; Prix Francois Vol. 2: 1056
Deruyts; Prix Jacques Vol. 2: 1060
Derwent Award (British); Clarence Vol. 2: 7439
Derwent Award; Clarence Vol. 1: 167
Derwood Award; Oscar Williams and Gene Vol. 1: 16219
des Vosges; Prix Blaise Vol. 2: 2021
Desai Prize Award; Dr. D.K. Vol. 2: 3548
Deschamps Literary Prize; Henri Vol. 2: 3221
Desert Palm Achievement Award Vol. 1: 17044
DESI Awards Vol. 1: 10139
Design Achievement Award; Pinnacle Vol. 1: 4413
Design and Application Award
  International Magnesium Association Vol. 1: 11737
  International Magnesium Association Vol 1: 11738
Design and Craft Innovation Award Vol. 2: 8851
Design and Engineering Exhibition Award Vol. 1: 9211
Design Award
  AIA Pennsylvania Vol. 1: 303
  Dedicated Wooden Money Collectors Vol 1: 8788
  International Magnesium Association Vol 1: 11738
  Internet Alliance Vol 1: 12150
  National Federation of Women's Institutes Vol 2: 8176
  Society of American Registered Architects Vol 1: 19004
  Texas Society of Architects/ AIA Vol 1: 20042
Design Award; Writing and Vol. 1: 5241
Design Awards
  American Institute of Architects, Arizona Chapter Vol. 1: 2730
  Society for Marketing Professional Services Vol 1: 18791
Design Awards Competition Vol. 1: 18668
Design Competitions Vol. 2: 6531
Design Council Awards Vol. 2: 7381
Design Council British Aerospace Engineering Design Prizes Vol. 2: 7382
Design Council Molins Design Prize Vol. 2: 7382
Design for Humanity Award Vol. 1: 4460
Design Management Prize Vol. 2: 6233
Design Medal; The ASLA Vol. 1: 4472
Design Partnership Award Vol. 2: 8163
Design Plus Vol. 2: 3031
Design Prize of the Federal Republic of Germany Vol. 2: 2829
Design Standards Award Vol. 1: 13958
Designpreis der Bundesrepublik Deutschland Vol. 2: 2829
Desjardins President of the Year Award; Carolyn Vol. 1: 1069
Desmond Memorial Award, Competition Division; Albert Vol. 1: 6218
Desnuelle; Prix Pierre Vol. 2: 2005
DeSoto Award; Hernando Vol. 1: 14914
Detwiler Memorial Service Award; The Jack Vol. 1: 8058
Deutsch Award; Karl Vol. 1: 12046
Deutsch Memorial Award; Wilbur Vol. 1: 19344
Deutsch Memorial Trophy Vol. 1: 8082
Deutsche Meteorologische Gesellschaft Ehrenmitgliedschaft Vol. 2: 2713
Deutsche Meteorologische Gesellschaft e.V. Forderpreis Vol. 2: 2714
Deutsche Meteorologische Gesellschaft e.V. Jugendpreis Vol. 2: 2714
Deutscher Jugend-Video-Preis Vol. 2: 2688
Deutz-Allis National Student Design Competition Vol. 1: 4233
Deux Magots Prize Vol. 2: 2257
Developer of the Year Vol. 1: 14276
Developing Country Grants Vol. 1: 11854
Developing Entrepreneur Award Vol. 2: 813
Developing Scientist Awards Vol. 1: 11230
Development Education Grants Vol. 2: 9207
Development Grants Vol. 2: 4830
Developmental Awards Vol. 1: 12847
Developmental Coach of the Year Vol. 1: 21191
Developmental Disabilities Awareness Award Vol. 1: 6337
Developmental Disabilities Scholastic Achievement Scholarship Vol. 1: 6338
Developmental Psychology Awards Vol. 1: 3668
DeVilliers Award Vol. 1: 12787
Devine Memorial Award; Edward A. Vol. 1: 20660
Devlin Memorial Award for Poetry; Denis Vol. 2: 3614
Devonshire Trophy Vol. 2: 8543
Devoted Service Award Vol. 1: 20948
Dew Award; G. Richard Vol. 1: 17184
Dewey Humanist Award; John Vol. 1: 2584
Dewey Medal; Melvil Vol. 1: 2972
Dewhurst Award Vol. 2: 9257
DeWolf Award; L. Harold Vol. 1: 16611
Dexter Award in the History of Chemistry Vol. 1: 1748
Dexter Prize Vol. 1: 18873
Dey Award; Joseph Vol. 1: 20604
DFAP National One-Act Playwriting Contest Vol. 1: 9035
DFISA-ASAE Food Engineering Award Vol. 1: 11362
Dharmaraja - King of Dharma Vol. 1: 11342
Dhere; Fondation Charles Vol. 2: 1819
DHL International (UK) Prize Vol. 2: 7690
Di Castagnola Award; Alice Fay Vol. 1: 17429
Di Guglielmo; Fondazione Giovanni Vol. 2: 3819
di Nola; Premio Mario Vol. 2: 3833
Di Valerio Technician of the Year Award; Lou Vol. 1: 4145
Diabetes Camp Educator Award Vol. 1: 1184
Diabetes Educator of the Year Award Vol. 1: 1185
Diabetes Research Grants Vol. 1: 12473
Diables d'Or Vol. 2: 6408
Dial Award Vol. 1: 20129
Dialogue-Silver Foundation Awards Vol. 1: 8902
Dialogue Writing Awards Vol. 1: 8902
Diamond Anniversary Book Award Vol. 1: 14709
Diamond Clinical Fellowship in Headache Education; Seymour Vol. 1: 15188
Diamond Coach Vol. 1: 15099
Diamond ECHO Award Vol. 1: 8924
Diamond Jubilee Bursary Vol. 2: 168
Diamond Key Award Vol. 1: 15099
Diamond Memorial Prize; A. S. Vol. 2: 8026
Diana Award Vol. 1: 5310
DiBello Memorial Exhibit Award; Gaston Vol. 1: 3213
Dibner Award for Excellence in Museum Exhibits Vol. 1: 18872
Dick Medal of Merit; Charles Vol. 1: 15176
Dickerman Lectureship; Herbert W. Vol. 1: 16281
Dickerson Award; Ben F. Vol. 1: 18807
Dickinson Award; *The Writer* Magazine/ Emily Vol. 1: 17439
Dickinson Career Achievement Award; Becton Vol. 1: 5491
Dickinson College Arts Award Vol. 1: 8911
Dickinson Teacher Award; John Vol. 1: 669
Dickson Alumnus of the Year Achievement Award; Edward A. Vol. 1: 20256
Dickson Award; J. Frank Vol. 1: 4766
Dickson Memorial Award; Donald L. Vol. 1: 20685
Dickson Memorial Award; Dorothy Stredicke Vol. 1: 3593
Dicus Award; Robert G. Vol. 1: 17575
Didactic Instructor of the Year Award Vol. 1: 1293
Didusch Award; William P. Vol. 1: 4787
Die Weissen Raben Vol. 2: 2990
Dieckman Distinguished Educational Award of Honor; The John Vol. 1: 15642
Diederich Award Vol. 1: 10424
Diederich Landscape Award Vol. 1: 10424
Diehl; Prix Charles and Marguerite Vol. 2: 1750
Diener Award; Irving Vol. 1: 6456
Diesel and Gas Engine Power Award Vol. 1: 4521
Dieterichs/Maclay Memorial Prize Vol. 2: 7846
Dieterichs Memorial Prize; William Vol. 2: 7846
Dietrich Trophy Vol. 1: 8083
Dietsch Sculpture Prize; C. Percival Vol. 1: 15698
Dietz Award; August Vol. 1: 8358
Dietz Service Award; Albert A. Vol. 1: 980
DiFiore Parental Choice Advocate Award; Leonard F. Vol. 1: 14606
Digital Apprentice of the Year Vol. 2: 7117
Digital Channel Programme Award Vol. 2: 8855
Dillard Award; Harrison Vol. 1: 21221
Dillman's Creative Arts Scholarship Award Vol. 1: 8922
Dillon Medal for Research in Polymer Physics; John H. Vol. 1: 3455
The Dilys Award Vol. 1: 10743
Dimbleby Award; Richard Vol. 2: 6905
Dimock Award; Hedley S. Vol. 1: 1625
Dimock Award; Marshall E. Vol. 1: 4182
Dine Award; Joe and Laurie Vol. 1: 16981
Dinerman Memorial Prize; Helen S. Vol. 1: 1037
Dingle Prize Vol. 2: 7177
Dingley Memorial Award; Dr. H. B. Vol. 2: 3411
Dingley Oration Award; Smt. Swaran Kanta Vol. 2: 3412

Dining Idea Exchange Contest Vol. 1: 14129
Dinkeloo Fellowship Vol. 1: 21271
Diploma Vol. 2: 5911
Diploma al Merito Universitario Vol. 2: 4598
Diploma Award for Active Participation in Life of Kyrgyz Republic Vol. 2: 4372
Diploma for Outstanding Airmanship Vol. 2: 6327
Diploma in International Employee Benefits Vol. 2: 8251
Diploma of Engineering Management Stage One Prize Vol. 2: 7798
Diploma of Honour and Medal Vol. 2: 7968
Diploma Trade Prize Vol. 2: 7553
Diplomate Award Vol. 1: 14120
Diplomate of the American Board of Psychological Hypnosis Vol. 1: 1580
Diplomatic Security Employee of the Year Award Vol. 1: 20534
Diplome d'honneur Vol. 1: 7036
Diplomes de Medailles Vol. 2: 1668
Dipple Carcinogenesis Award; Anthony Vol. 2: 7452
DiPrima Prize; Richard C. Vol. 1: 18735
Dirac Medal Vol. 2: 3789
Dirac Medal and Prize; Paul Vol. 2: 7727
Direct Marketing International ECHO Awards Vol. 1: 8924
Direct Marketing Woman of the Year Award Vol. 1: 21708
Direct Vocational Special Needs Support Person of the Year Vol. 1: 14057
Director General's Award for Excellence in Human Resource Management Vol. 1: 20535
Director General's Award for Reporting and Analysis Vol. 1: 20536
Director of the Year
International Association of Pet Cemeteries Vol. 1: 11375
National Trappers Association Vol 1: 15910
Director of the Year Award Vol. 1: 18343
Directorate Award Vol. 1: 11519
Director's Award
American Alliance for Theatre and Education Vol. 1: 896
American Helicopter Society Vol 1: 2427
Federation of Genealogical Societies Vol 1: 9497
International Order of E.A.R.S. Vol 1: 11775
La Crosse Area Development Corporation Vol 1: 12624
National Marine Manufacturers Association Vol 1: 15364
Polycystic Ovarian Syndrome Association Vol 1: 17464
Directors Award Vol. 1: 19132
Directors Award of The Friends of Algonquin Park Vol. 1: 9781
Directors' Awards Vol. 1: 6850
Director's Choice Award Vol. 1: 15827
Directors Emeriti Award Vol. 1: 12853
Director's Franklin Award Vol. 1: 9555
Directors Scholarship Fund Vol. 1: 19148
Disability Awareness Award Vol. 1: 17071
Disabled Athletes of the Year Vol. 1: 20410
Disabled People; Institution of Electrical Engineers Prize for Helping Vol. 2: 7811
Disaster Relief Fund Vol. 1: 20005
Discailles; Prix Ernest Vol. 2: 1020
Disciplined Services Medal for Long Service and Good Conduct Vol. 2: 3208
Disciplined Services Medal for Meritorious Service Vol. 2: 3209
Disciplined Services Star for Distinguished Service Vol. 2: 3210
Discover America National Travel Marketing Awards Vol. 1: 20177
Discover Award Vol. 1: 6254
Discoverers Awards Vol. 1: 17228
Discovery Artist Award Vol. 1: 16202
"Discovery" Award Vol. 1: 19
Discovery of New Celestial Bodies Award Vol. 2: 4097
Discovery Prize Vol. 1: 17095
"Discovery"/*The Nation* Contest Vol. 1: 19
Display Contest Vol. 1: 14360
Dissertation Award
American Psychological Association - American Psychology-Law Society (Division 41) Vol. 1: 3647
American Society for Theatre Research Vol 1: 4198
American Society for Training and Development Vol 1: 4205
American Sociological Association Vol 1: 4650
Austrian Statistical Society Vol 2: 713
Ohio Academy of History Vol 1: 16622
Religious Communication Association Vol 1: 17981
Society for Cinema and Media Studies Vol 1: 18651
Dissertation Competition Vol. 1: 15427
Dissertation Honors Vol. 2: 2997
Dissertation in Nuclear Physics Award Vol. 1: 3456
Dissertation of the Year Award Vol. 1: 14012
Dissertation Prize Vol. 2: 8041
Dissertation Prize in Economics Vol. 2: 1643
Dissertation Research Awards Vol. 1: 18896
Dissertation Year Fellowship Vol. 1: 16412
Distance Award and Best-Conditioned & Trail Class Award Vol. 1: 10634
Distance Learning Course Awards Vol. 1: 20949
Distant Accords Awards Vol. 1: 11593
Distincion Universidad Nacional para Jovenes Academicos Vol. 2: 4599
Distinction for Distinguished Services Vol. 2: 1298
Distinction for Time of Service Vol. 2: 1299
Distinghished Member Vol. 1: 21736
Distinguised Service Award Vol. 1: 21883
Distinguish Service to Social Work Vol. 1: 16382
Distinguished 50-Year Member Award Vol. 1: 4429
Distinguished Academic All-American Award Vol. 1: 15307
Distinguished Achievement Award
Alberta Motion Picture Industries Association Vol. 1: 422
AMIT USA Vol 1: 4935
Australian Society of Archivists Vol 2: 271
Foundation for Digestive Health and Nutrition Vol 1: 9707
Society of Exploration Geo-physicists Vol 1: 19119
USA Hockey Vol 1: 21176
Wings Club Vol 1: 21653
Distinguished Achievement Award for Community Service Vol. 1: 10812
Distinguished Achievement Award for Petroleum Engineering Faculty Vol. 1: 19236
Distinguished Achievement Award in Clinical/Pharmacotherapeutic Practice Vol. 1: 3381
Distinguished Achievement Award in Community and Ambulatory Practice Vol. 1: 3382
Distinguished Achievement Award in Hospital and Institutional Practice Vol. 1: 3383
Distinguished Achievement Award in Specialized Pharmaceutical Services Vol. 1: 3384
Distinguished Achievement Award to Fluid Power Educator Vol. 1: 11627
Distinguished Achievement Awards Vol. 1: 3064
Distinguished Achievement Awards for Local Public Affairs Vol. 1: 10815
Distinguished Achievement in Agriculture Award Vol. 1: 9867
Distinguished Achievement in Basic or Applied Fiber Science Vol. 1: 9539
Distinguished Achievement in Occupational Safety and Health Award Vol. 1: 15658
Distinguished Achievement in RV Journalism Award Vol. 1: 17913
Distinguished Achievement in RV Standards Award Vol. 1: 17914
Distinguished Advertising Educator Award Vol. 1: 859
Distinguished Adviser Award Vol. 1: 8171
Distinguished Africanist Award Vol. 1: 263
Distinguished Alumni Award Vol. 1: 13632
Distinguished Alumni Citation of the Year Vol. 1: 14005
Distinguished Alumnus Award
National Association of Intercollegiate Athletics Vol. 1: 14285
Tau Beta Pi Association Vol 1: 19932
University of Maryland - College of Library and Information Services Vol 1: 21052
Distinguished American Award Vol. 1: 15068
Distinguished Arizonan Award Vol. 1: 15079
Distinguished Artist Award Vol. 1: 6759
Distinguished Artist Award for Lifetime Achievement Vol. 1: 8145
Distinguished Assessment Jurisdiction Award Vol. 1: 11268
Distinguished Athletic Therapy Educator Award Vol. 1: 6949
Distinguished Author Award Vol. 1: 11567
Distinguished Awards Vol. 1: 9764
Distinguished Awards for the Contributions to the Science and Professional of Clinical Psychology Vol. 1: 3744
Distinguished Book Award Vol. 1: 18800
Distinguished Budget Presentation Award Vol. 1: 10113
Distinguished Building Award Vol. 1: 19005
Distinguished Career Award
Ambulatory Pediatric Association Vol. 1: 594
American Academy of Pediatrics Vol 1: 766
Real Estate Educators Association Vol 1: 17895
Southeastern Theatre Conference Vol 1: 19487
Distinguished Career Award for the Practice of Sociology Vol. 1: 4651
Distinguished Career Awards Vol. 1: 6142
Distinguished Career Contribution to Education and Training in Psychology Vol. 1: 18897
Distinguished Career in Clinical Sociology Vol. 1: 19374

Award Index

Distinguished Career Service Awards Vol. 1: 20510
Distinguished Ceramist Award Vol. 1: 1674
Distinguished Chapter Award
Association of the Wall and Ceiling Industries - International Vol. 1: 5885
International Society for Performance Improvement Vol 1: 11940
Distinguished Citizen Vol. 1: 21394
Distinguished Citizen Award
Congressional Medal of Honor Society Vol. 1: 8401
National Consumers League Vol 1: 14734
World Federation for Mental Health Vol 1: 21903
Distinguished Citizen's Award Vol. 1: 21443
Distinguished Citizens Awards Vol. 2: 812
Distinguished Communicator Award Vol. 1: 18201
Distinguished Contribution Award
American Planning Association Vol. 1: 3551
American Urological Association Vol 1: 4788
Project Management Institute Vol 1: 17666
Psychologists for Social Responsibility Vol 1: 17700
Distinguished Contribution to Building Cultures of Peace Vol. 1: 17701
Distinguished Contribution to Child Advocacy Award Vol. 1: 3715
Distinguished Contribution to Education and Training in Psychology Vol. 1: 18898
Distinguished Contribution to Ethnic Minority Issues Award Vol. 1: 18899
Distinguished Contribution to Nursing Science Award Vol. 1: 3287
Distinguished Contribution to Practice in Community Psychology Award Vol. 1: 3716
Distinguished Contribution to Psychology and Law Vol. 1: 3648
Distinguished Contribution to Psychology and the Media Vol. 1: 18900
Distinguished Contribution to Psychology in the Public Interest Vol. 1: 18901
Distinguished Contribution to Research Administration Award Vol. 1: 19294
Distinguished Contribution to Scholarship Award Vol. 1: 4653
Distinguished Contribution to Social Justice Award Vol. 1: 2216
Distinguished Contribution to Theory and Research in Community Psychology Award Vol. 1: 3717
Distinguished Contribution to Workplace Learning and Performance Vol. 1: 4206
Distinguished Contributions to Applied Psychology as a Professional Practice Vol. 1: 18902
Distinguished Contributions to Asian Studies Vol. 1: 5275
Distinguished Contributions to Education Research Vol. 1: 2160
Distinguished Contributions to Research in Public Policy Vol. 1: 18903
Distinguished Contributions to Science Education Through Research Award Vol. 1: 14030
Distinguished Contributions to Slavic Studies Award Vol. 1: 1054
Distinguished Contributions to Teaching Vol. 1: 17017
Distinguished Contributions to Teaching Award Vol. 1: 4652
Distinguished Contributions to the International Advancement of Psychology Vol. 1: 18904
Distinguished Creative Contribution to Gerontology Award Vol. 1: 9990
Distinguished Dairy Cattle Breeder Award Vol. 1: 14891
Distinguished Dealer of the Year Vol. 1: 21540
Distinguished Designer Award Vol. 1: 4411
Distinguished Dietitian of the Year Vol. 1: 12493
Distinguished Diplomatic Award Vol. 1: 9445
Distinguished Dissertation Award
Association for Canadian Studies in the United States Vol. 1: 5281
Kappa Delta Pi Vol 1: 12511
Distinguished Dissertation Award in Higher Education Vol. 1: 14012
Distinguished Dissertation in Teacher Education Vol. 1: 5878
Distinguished Drinking Water Public Involvement Award Vol. 1: 16134
Distinguished Eagle Scout Award Vol. 1: 6575
Distinguished Early Career Contributions Award Vol. 1: 18750
Distinguished Economic Botanist Vol. 1: 18665
Distinguished Education and Behavioral Sciences Librarian Award Vol. 1: 5605
Distinguished Educational Contribution Award Vol. 1: 18905
Distinguished Educator and Service Award Vol. 1: 4011
Distinguished Educator Award
American Association of Petroleum Geologists Vol. 1: 1344
American Society for Gastrointestinal Endoscopy Vol 1: 4072
National Rural Health Association Vol 1: 15649
North American Colleges and Teachers of Agriculture Vol 1: 16402
Distinguished EEA - SHIP Member Award Vol. 1: 12065
Distinguished Engineering Educator Award Vol. 1: 19365
Distinguished Extension-Industry Service Award Vol. 1: 3050
Distinguished Extension Programs Vol. 1: 869
Distinguished Faculty Award Vol. 1: 14682
Distinguished Fellow
American College of Cardiology Vol. 1: 1836
American Economic Association Vol 1: 2155
American Park and Recreation Society Vol 1: 3362
Royal College of Pathologists of Australasia Vol 2: 530
Distinguished Fellow Award
American College of Neuropsychiatrists Vol. 1: 1889
History of Economics Society Vol 1: 10477
International Council on Education for Teaching Vol 1: 11521
Distinguished Fellows Award Vol. 1: 2047
Distinguished Fellowship Vol. 1: 96
Distinguished Fellowship Award Vol. 2: 512
Distinguished Flying Medal
Central Chancery of the Orders of Knighthood Vol. 2: 7248
Commemorative Air Force Vol 1: 8272
Distinguished Flying Unit Plaques Vol. 1: 15176
The Distinguished Forestry Award of the Southern African Institute of Forestry Vol. 2: 5710
Distinguished Founders Award Vol. 1: 1334
Distinguished Friend to Behavior Therapy Vol. 1: 5266
Distinguished Friends of Council Award Vol. 2: 3158
Distinguished Geographer Award Vol. 2: 5021
Distinguished Graduate Award in Premium Auditing Vol. 1: 15739
Distinguished Grant Maker Award Vol. 1: 8597
Distinguished Grasslander Award Vol. 1: 2273
Distinguished Honor Award Vol. 1: 20537
Distinguished Humanities Educator Vol. 1: 8317
Distinguished Individual of Foreign Birth Award Vol. 1: 11460
Distinguished Informal Science Education Award Vol. 1: 15687
Distinguished Informal Science Educator Award Vol. 1: 6749
Distinguished Information Sciences Award Vol. 1: 5731
Distinguished International Colleague Award Vol. 1: 10578
Distinguished International Fellow Vol. 2: 447
Distinguished Investigator Award
American College of Clinical Pharmacology Vol. 1: 1848
National Alliance for Research on Schizophrenia and Depression Vol 1: 13923
Distinguished Journalism Award Vol. 1: 9446
Distinguished Leadership Award for a Citizen Planner Vol. 1: 3552
Distinguished Leadership Award for a Professional Planner Vol. 1: 3553
Distinguished Leadership Award for a Student Planner Vol. 1: 3554
Distinguished Leadership Award for an Elected Official Vol. 1: 3555
Distinguished Leadership for Landslide Research Vol. 1: 11711
Distinguished Lecture Award Vol. 1: 910
Distinguished Lecturer Award Vol. 1: 6388
Distinguished Lectureship Vol. 1: 20162
Distinguished Lectureships Vol. 1: 19106
Distinguished Life Member
American Ceramic Society Vol. 1: 1675
ASM International Vol 1: 5175
North American Die Casting Association Vol 1: 16422
Distinguished Local Government Leadership Award Vol. 1: 5712
Distinguished Maintenance Award Vol. 1: 8273
Distinguished Member Vol. 1: 19237
Distinguished Member Award
American Congress of Rehabilitation Medicine Vol. 1: 1985
Association for Iron and Steel Technology Vol 1: 5405
Association of Women Surgeons Vol 1: 5914
International Facility Management Association Vol 1: 11568
Society for Mining, Metallurgy, and Exploration Vol 1: 18808

Women in Government Relations LEADER Foundation Vol 1: 21738
Distinguished Membership Award Vol. 1: 3277
Distinguished Mentor Award Vol. 1: 14763
Distinguished Mentorship in Gerontology Award Vol. 1: 9991
Distinguished Merit Award Vol. 1: 1167
Distinguished Mission Support Plaques Vol. 1: 15176
Distinguished Musician Award Vol. 2: 7631
Distinguished Mycologist Award Vol. 1: 13723
Distinguished Neuropsychologist Award Vol. 1: 13809
Distinguished New Engineer Award Vol. 1: 19366
Distinguished Officer of the Year Vol. 1: 6442
Distinguished Paper in Phychology Award Vol. 1: 6544
Distinguished Patriot Award Vol. 1: 15768
Distinguished Peace Leadership Award Vol. 1: 16589
Distinguished Peacekeeper Award Vol. 1: 11795
Distinguished Performance Award Vol. 1: 20686
Distinguished Physician Award Vol. 1: 1282
Distinguished Pi Lambda Thetan Award Vol. 1: 17322
Distinguished Play Awards Vol. 1: 890
Distinguished Policy Contribution Vol. 1: 870
Distinguished Popular Scientific Publishing of Plant Physiology Vol. 2: 1536
Distinguished Practice Award
International Pharmaceutical Federation Vol. 2: 4828
Pacific Sociological Association Vol 1: 17018
Distinguished Presidential Citation Vol. 1: 19006
Distinguished Principal Awards Vol. 1: 14609
Distinguished Principal Founding Member Vol. 2: 754
Distinguished Professional Achievement in Psychology Vol. 1: 1578
Distinguished Professional Contribution Award Vol. 2: 4356
Distinguished Professional Contributions Award Vol. 1: 18751
Distinguished Professional Contributions to Knowledge Vol. 1: 18906
Distinguished Professional Contributions to Public Service Vol. 1: 18907
Distinguished Programs in Teacher Education Vol. 1: 5879
Distinguished Psychologist Award Vol. 1: 3704
Distinguished Psychologist of the Year Vol. 1: 3768
Distinguished Public Service Vol. 1: 15294
Distinguished Public Service Award
American Psychological Association Division of Independent Practice - Division of Independent Practice Vol. 1: 3769
Center for National Policy Vol 1: 7737
Distinguished Public Service Medal
Mineralogical Society of America Vol. 1: 13434
National Aeronautics and Space Administration Vol 1: 13885
Distinguished Recent Alumnus Award Vol. 1: 6180
Distinguished Recognition Award Vol. 1: 11730
Distinguished Research and Development Award Vol. 1: 11269
Distinguished Research Award
American Meat Science Association Vol. 1: 3051
National Council of Teachers of English Vol 1: 14840
Section for Women in Public Administration - Section for Women in Public Administration Vol 1: 18404
Distinguished Research in Teacher Education Vol. 1: 5880
Distinguished Researcher Award
American Association of Neuromuscular and Electrodiagnostic Medicine Vol. 1: 1283
National Rural Health Association Vol 1: 15650
Oncology Nursing Society Vol 1: 16714
Distinguished Researcher's Award Vol. 2: 6166
Distinguished Rural Sociologist Award Vol. 1: 18187
Distinguished Scholar Award
International Association of Human-Animal Interaction Organizations Vol. 1: 11364
Keats-Shelley Association of America Vol 1: 12523
North American Society for the Psychology of Sport and Physical Activity Vol 1: 16475
Wings Club Vol 1: 21654
Distinguished Scholar Program Vol. 1: 3288
Distinguished Scholarly Publication Award Vol. 1: 4653
Distinguished Scholarship Award Vol. 1: 17019
Distinguished School Administrators Award Vol. 1: 1413
Distinguished Science Award Vol. 2: 4828
Distinguished Scientific Achievement Award Vol. 1: 10318
Distinguished Scientific Award for an Early Career Contribution to Psychology Vol. 1: 18908
Distinguished Scientific Award for the Applications of Psychology Vol. 1: 18909
Distinguished Scientific Contribution Award
American Psychological Association - Society of Clinical Psychology (Division 12) Vol. 1: 3745
Society for the Study of Lesbian, Gay and Bisexual Concerns (Division 44) Vol 1: 18910
Distinguished Scientific Contributions Award Vol. 1: 18752
Distinguished Scientist Vol. 1: 1837
Distinguished Scientist Award
American Psychological Association - Society of Clinical Psychology (Division 12) Vol. 1: 3746
Heart Rhythm Association Vol. 1: 10365
Distinguished Service
American College of Cardiology Vol. 1: 1838
Medical Fitness Association Vol 1: 13249
Missouri Dental Association Vol 1: 13533
Distinguished Service/Achievement Awards Vol. 1: 18456
Distinguished Service Award Vol. 1: 19768
Distinguished Service Award
303rd Bomb Group (H) Association Vol. 1: 23
Alpine Club of Canada Vol 1: 501
Alpine Club of Canada Vol 1: 504
American Academy of Advertising Vol 1: 610
American Academy of Medical Administrators Vol 1: 685
American Academy of Otolaryngology - Head and Neck Surgery Vol 1: 747
American Academy of Pediatrics Vol 1: 767
American Academy of Pediatrics Vol 1: 768
American Arbitration Association Vol 1: 918
American Association for Agricultural Education Vol 1: 961
American Association for Clinical Chemistry Vol 1: 981
American Association of Collegiate Registrars and Admissions Officers Vol 1: 1161
American Association of Diabetes Educators Vol 1: 1186
American Association of Homes and Services for the Aging Vol 1: 1225
American Association of Motor Vehicle Administrators Vol 1: 1275
American Association of Museums Vol 1: 1278
American Association of Oral and Maxillofacial Surgeons Vol 1: 1310
American Association of Public Health Physicians Vol 1: 1394
American Association of School Administrators Vol 1: 1405
American Association of School Librarians Vol 1: 1414
American Association of Teachers of Italian Vol 1: 1450
American Association of Teachers of Spanish and Portuguese Vol 1: 1452
American Association of University Administrators Vol 1: 1461
American Camping Association Vol 1: 1626
American Cancer Society Vol 1: 1636
American Catholic Historical Society Vol 1: 1658
American Chemical Society Vol 1: 1749
American College of Dentists Vol 1: 1854
American College of Neuropsychiatrists Vol 1: 1890
American College of Preventive Medicine Vol 1: 1930
American Dairy Science Association Vol 1: 2101
American Forensic Association Vol 1: 2286
American Hospital Association Vol 1: 2543
American Industrial Hygiene Association Vol 1: 2612
American Institute of Chemical Engineers Vol 1: 2766
American Iris Society Vol 1: 2867
American Liver Foundation Vol 1: 3011
American Moving and Storage Association Vol 1: 3153
American Optometric Association Vol 1: 3316
American Phytopathological Society Vol 1: 3537
American Police Hall of Fame Vol 1: 3567
American Psychological Association - Society of Clinical Psychology (Division 12) Vol 1: 3747
American Public Gas Association Vol 1: 3775

American Public Power Association Vol 1: 3794
American Railway Development Association Vol 1: 3818
American Society for Adolescent Psychiatry Vol 1: 3904
American Society for Bioethics and Humanities Vol 1: 3925
American Society for Engineering Education Vol 1: 4012
American Society for Gastrointestinal Endoscopy Vol 1: 4073
American Society of Abdominal Surgeons Vol 1: 4210
American Society of Heating, Refrigerating and Air-Conditioning Engineers Vol 1: 4430
American Urological Association Vol 1: 4789
AMIT USA Vol 1: 4936
Association for Asian Studies Vol 1: 5275
Association for Library Service to Children Vol 1: 5438
Association for Women Veterinarians Vol 1: 5533
Association of Fraternity Advisors Vol 1: 5693
Association of Free Community Papers Vol 1: 5696
Association of Professional Chaplains Vol 1: 5822
Association of Schools of Allied Health Professions Vol 1: 5838
Association of University Architects Vol 1: 5909
Ayrshire Breeders' Association Vol 1: 6176
Baptist History and Heritage Society Vol 1: 6244
Black Caucus of the American Library Association Vol 1: 6418
Bookbuilders West Vol 1: 6515
California Walnut Commission Vol 1: 6769
Catholic Kolping Society of America Vol 1: 7644
Caucus for Television Producers, Writers and Directors Vol 1: 7683
Chicago Book Clinic Vol 1: 7877
Christian Holiness Partnership Vol 1: 7959
Citizens Union of the City of New York Vol 1: 8022
Commercial Development and Marketing Association Vol 1: 8288
Concordia Historical Institute Vol 1: 8341
Conference on Latin American History Vol 1: 8383
Congress of Neurological Surgeons Vol 1: 8389
Congressional Hispanic Caucus Institute Vol 1: 8398
Construction Specifications Institute Vol 1: 8435
Council of Chief State School Officers Vol 1: 8570
Council of Logistics Management Vol 1: 8580
Cranial Academy Vol 1: 8638
Dance Notation Bureau Vol 1: 8742
Deep Foundations Institute Vol 1: 8792
Defense Credit Union Council Vol 1: 8795
Easter Seals Vol 1: 9086
Electronic Industries Alliance Vol 1: 9212
European Association for Animal Production Vol 2: 3901
Family, Career and Community Leaders of America Vol 1: 9398
Federation of Genealogical Societies Vol 1: 9498
Federation of Jewish Men's Clubs Vol 1: 9509
Financial Planning Association Vol 1: 9551
Florida Association of Colleges and Universities Vol 1: 9591
Flying Physicians Association Vol 1: 9641
Georgia Agricultural Commodity Commission for Peanuts Vol 1: 9962
Golf Course Superintendents Association of America Vol 1: 10066
Health Science Communications Association Vol 1: 10324
Healthcare Convention and Exhibitors Association Vol 1: 10335
Heart Rhythm Association Vol 1: 10366
Illuminating Engineering Society of North America Vol 1: 10692
Independent Free Papers of America Vol 1: 10723
Institute of Nuclear Materials Management Vol 1: 11019
International Association of Cancer Victors and Friends Vol 1: 11301
International Badminton Federation Vol 2: 4433
International Institute of Fisheries Economics and Trade Vol 1: 11686
International Measurement Confederation Vol 2: 3294
International Society of Logistics Vol 1: 11996
Internet Alliance Vol 1: 12151
La Crosse Area Development Corporation Vol 1: 12625
Lamaze International Vol 1: 12669
Lewis and Clark Trail Heritage Foundation Vol 1: 12802
Little People of America Vol 1: 12886
Lutheran Historical Conference Vol 1: 12992
Military Chaplains Association of the U.S.A. Vol 1: 13403
Military Order of the World Wars Vol 1: 13419
Minerals, Metals, and Materials Society Vol 1: 13442
NACE International: The Corrosion Society Vol 1: 13744
National Accreditation Council for Agencies Serving the Blind and Visually Impaired Vol 1: 13868
National Air Transportation Association Vol 1: 13918
National Association of Academies of Science Vol 1: 14064
National Association of Animal Breeders Vol 1: 14068
National Association of Biology Teachers Vol 1: 14092
National Association of Broadcasters Vol 1: 14111
National Association of Catholic Chaplains Vol 1: 14120
National Association of Conservation Districts Vol 1: 14151
National Association of County Agricultural Agents Vol 1: 14171
National Association of Fleet Administrators Vol 1: 14234
National Association of Personal Financial Advisors Vol 1: 14325
National Association of Realtors Vol 1: 14354
National Association of the Holy Name Society Vol 1: 14415
National Business Education Association Vol 1: 14572
National Council of Examiners for Engineering and Surveying Vol 1: 14797
National Council of Teachers of English Vol 1: 14831
National Court Reporters Association Vol 1: 14879
National Genealogical Society Vol 1: 15145
National Kidney Foundation Vol 1: 15320
National Mining Association Vol 1: 15386
National Newspaper Publishers Association Vol 1: 15414
National Parkinson Foundation Vol 1: 15486
National Propane Gas Association Vol 1: 15552
National Religious Broadcasters Vol 1: 15613
National Retail Federation Vol 1: 15634
National School Transportation Association Vol 1: 15671
National Society of Professional Engineers Vol 1: 15746
National Swine Improvement Federation Vol 1: 15831
National Therapeutic Recreation Society Vol 1: 15872
National Water Resources Association Vol 1: 15932
Nevada Association of School Boards Vol 1: 16084
Ohio Academy of History Vol 1: 16623
Optical Society of America Vol 1: 16783
Organ Historical Society Vol 1: 16869
Owsley Family Historical Society Vol 1: 16986
Pennsylvania Society of Anesthesiologists Vol 1: 17196
Plastic Surgery Educational Foundation Vol 1: 17378
Professional Golfers' Association of America Vol 1: 17614
Prospectors and Developers Association of Canada Vol 1: 17690
Public Risk Management Association Vol 1: 17728
Regional Business Partnership Vol 1: 17955
Relay and Switch Industry Association Vol 1: 17968
Rhode Island Council of Community Mental Health Centers Vol 1: 18027
Royal Geographical Society with the Institute of British Geographers Vol 2: 8515
School and Community Safety Society of America Vol 1: 18335
Small Motor and Motion Association Vol 1: 18564
Society for Applied Spectroscopy Vol 1: 18640
Society for Medical Decision Making Vol 1: 18795
Society for Range Management Vol 1: 18836
Society for Sedimentary Geology Vol 1: 18841

Society of American Archivists Vol 1: 18953
Society of Naval Architects and Marine Engineers Vol 1: 19209
Society of Petroleum Engineers Vol 1: 19238
Society of Petrophysicists and Well Log Analysts Vol 1: 19254
Society of Research Administrators Vol 1: 19296
Society of Wood Science and Technology Vol 1: 19371
Specialized Carriers and Rigging Association Vol 1: 19576
Specialty Graphic Imaging Association Vol 1: 19593
Tasmanian Canine Association Vol 2: 622
Tax Foundation Vol 1: 19944
Towing and Recovery Association of America Vol 1: 20141
Transportation Lawyers Association Vol 1: 20157
Trout Unlimited Vol 1: 20209
United Kennel Club Vol 1: 20345
United States Association of Former Members of Congress Vol 1: 20412
Washington International Trade Association Vol 1: 21449
The Wildlife Society Vol 1: 21630
Wine Spectator Vol 1: 21648
World Communication Association Vol 1: 21875
World Development Federation Vol 1: 21889
World Jersey Cattle Bureau Vol 2: 9255
Zelienople-Harmony Chamber of Commerce Vol 1: 22101
Distinguished Service Award by Ortho-McNeil Vol. 1: 7462
Distinguished Service Award (Coaching) Vol. 1: 14982
Distinguished Service Award for an Administrator or Supervisor Vol. 1: 14573
Distinguished Service Award for Elected County Official Vol. 1: 14167
Distinguished Service Award in Investment Education Vol. 1: 12175
Distinguished Service Award (Officiating) Vol. 1: 14982
Distinguished Service Award (Outside the Profession) Vol. 1: 13959
Distinguished Service Award (Within the Profession) Vol. 1: 13960
Distinguished Service Awards
American Association of Petroleum Geologists Vol. 1: 1335
American Catholic Historical Society Vol 1: 1658
American Psychiatric Association Vol 1: 3616
American School Health Association Vol 1: 3888
American Speech Language Hearing Association Vol 1: 4663
National Association of Elementary School Principals Vol 1: 14206
National Center for State Courts Vol 1: 14641
National Federation of State High School Associations Vol 1: 14977
National Federation of State High School Associations - National Federation Interscholastic Coaches Association Vol 1: 14983
National Governors Association Vol 1: 15170
National Institute of Governmental Purchasing Vol 1: 15267
National Small-Bore Rifle Association Vol 2: 8199
Royal Society for the Prevention of Accidents Vol 2: 8717
University of Chicago Medical and Biological Sciences Alumni Association Vol 1: 21003
Distinguished Service Certificate
National Council of Examiners for Engineering and Surveying Vol. 1: 14797
Pharmacy Guild of Australia Vol 2: 493
Distinguished Service Citation
Acoustical Society of America Vol. 1: 137
AIIM - The Enterprise Content Management Association Vol 1: 310
American Association of Physics Teachers Vol 1: 1371
American Society for Engineering Education Vol 1: 4013
Automotive Hall of Fame Vol 1: 6113
Ecological Society of America Vol 1: 9135
International Order of E.A.R.S. Vol 1: 11776
Lambda Kappa Sigma Vol 1: 12681
Pierre Fauchard Academy Vol 1: 17348
Distinguished Service Contributions Award Vol. 1: 18753
Distinguished Service Cross Vol. 2: 194
Distinguished Service Decorations Vol. 2: 194
Distinguished Service in Aging Award Vol. 1: 1226
Distinguished Service in the Cause of Open and Competitive World Trade Award Vol. 1: 8468
Distinguished Service Key
National Forensic League Vol. 1: 15100
Omicron Delta Kappa Vol 1: 16697
Distinguished Service Key and Certificate for Retiring Continuing Educators Vol. 1: 20950
Distinguished Service Medal
American Legion Vol. 1: 2947
Australian Honours Secretariat Vol 2: 194
Commemorative Air Force Vol 1: 8274
Committee on Space Research Vol 2: 2270
Irish Defence Forces Vol 2: 3652
Pharmacy Guild of Australia Vol 2: 494
Distinguished Service Medal Awards Vol. 1: 19879
Distinguished Service Medal (NASA Medal) Vol. 1: 13886
Distinguished Service Medals Vol. 1: 6129
Distinguished Service Order Vol. 2: 7249
Distinguished Service Star Vol. 1: 12609
Distinguished Service to Agriculture Vol. 1: 4405
Distinguished Service to Children Award
National Association of Elementary School Principals Vol. 1: 14206
Parents Without Partners Vol 1: 17087
Distinguished Service to College Award Vol. 1: 6181
Distinguished Service to Education Award Vol. 1: 14206
Distinguished Service to Families Award Vol. 1: 14860
Distinguished Service to Powder Metallurgy Award Vol. 1: 13311
Distinguished Service to Rural Life Award Vol. 1: 18188
Distinguished Service to Safety Education Vol. 1: 18335
Distinguished Service to Science Education Award Vol. 1: 15688
Distinguished Service to Social Welfare Vol. 1: 16383
Distinguished Service to the Cause of Liberal Religion Vol. 1: 20308
Distinguished Service to the Cause of Unitarian Universalism Vol. 1: 20308
Distinguished Service to the RV Industry Award Vol. 1: 17915
Distinguished Society Service Award Vol. 1: 12213
Distinguished Speaker Award Vol. 1: 1676
Distinguished Student Paper Awards Vol. 1: 17020
Distinguished Student Scholar Award Vol. 1: 17323
Distinguished Teacher Award
American Society of Animal Science Vol. 1: 4260
Heart Rhythm Association Vol 1: 10367
North American Colleges and Teachers of Agriculture Vol 1: 16403
Distinguished Teaching Achievement Awards Vol. 1: 14764
Distinguished Teaching Award Vol. 1: 3052
Distinguished Teaching Award Vol. 1: 4014
Distinguished Teaching Award Vol. 1: 15689
Distinguished Teaching Award
Ohio Academy of History Vol. 1: 16624
UCLA Alumni Association Vol 1: 20257
Distinguished Teaching Awards
American Agricultural Economics Association Vol. 1: 871
Kent State University Alumni Association Vol 1: 12560
Distinguished Teaching, Distinguished Research Vol. 1: 21256
Distinguished Teaching in Journalism Award Vol. 1: 19274
Distinguished Teaching of Art Award Vol. 1: 8146
Distinguished Teaching of Art History Award Vol. 1: 8147
Distinguished Technical Achievement Award Vol. 1: 19255
Distinguished Technology Educator Award Vol. 1: 12066
Distinguished Topical Philatelist Award Vol. 1: 4749
Distinguished Unit Citation Vol. 1: 8275
Distinguished Unit Maintenance Award Vol. 1: 8276
Distinguished Vanguard Awards for Leadership Vol. 1: 14577
Distinguished Volunteer Service Award Vol. 1: 445
Distinguished Woman Philosopher Award Vol. 1: 18937
Distinguished Women's Awards Vol. 1: 16572
Distinguished World Citizen Vol. 1: 9801
Distinguished Writing Award Vol. 1: 17185
Distinguished Writing Award in Commentary/Column Writing Vol. 1: 4576
Distinguished Writing Award in Editorial Writing Vol. 1: 4577
Distinguished Writing Award in Local Watchdog Reporting Vol. 1: 4578
Distinguished Writing Award in Non-Deadline Writing Vol. 1: 4579
Distinguished Young Couple Vol. 1: 13478

Distinguished Younger Member Award Vol. 1: 19040
Distintivo de Antiguedad; El Vol. 2: 1299
Distintivo de Servicios Distinguidos; El Vol. 2: 1298
Distribution Executive of the Year Vol. 1: 7161
Distributor of the Year Award
Canadian Booksellers Association Vol. 1: 6986
Multi-Level Marketing International Association Vol 1: 13664
National Association of the Remodeling Industry Vol 1: 14430
District Award Vol. 1: 17079
District Award of Merit Vol. 1: 6576
District Bulletin Award Vol. 1: 8062
District Coach of the Year Vol. 1: 14693
District Distinguished Service Awards Vol. 1: 7191
District Newsletter Contest Vol. 1: 14152
District Proficiency Medals Vol. 1: 7192
District Representatives Award Vol. 1: 11664
District/Section Newsletter Award Vol. 1: 11048
Ditson Conductor's Award; Alice M. Vol. 1: 8242
Dittus Award; Ray Vol. 1: 16436
DivCHAS College Health and Safety Award Vol. 1: 1750
DiVelbiss Award Vol. 1: 9095
Diversity Awards Vol. 1: 17186
Diversity Grant; LAMA Cultural Vol. 1: 12817
Divine Award; Thomas F. Vol. 1: 5473
Diving Award; Glenn McCormick Memorial Vol. 1: 20396
Diving Coach of the Year Award; Moose Moss Age Group Vol. 1: 20397
Division I Player of the Year Vol. 1: 14083
Division II Player of the Year Vol. 1: 14084
Division III Player of the Year Vol. 1: 14085
Division Leadership and Service Award Vol. 1: 19919
Division of the Year Vol. 1: 20741
Division Technical Awards Vol. 1: 19920
Divisional Achievement Award Vol. 1: 19686
Divisional Award of the Chemical Society of Japan Vol. 2: 4111
Divisional Premium; Institution of Electrical Engineers Vol. 2: 7808
Divisional PRO Rally of the Year Vol. 1: 19702
Divisional Pro Rally of the Year Award Vol. 1: 19687
Divisional PRO Rally Program of the Year Vol. 1: 19702
Divisional Pro Rally Program of the Year Award Vol. 1: 19688
Divisional Pro Rally Region of the Year Award Vol. 1: 19689
Divisions' Council Awards Vol. 1: 3556
Divisions Safety Professional of the Year Vol. 1: 4607
Diwang Sining Awards Vol. 2: 5272
Dix Leadership Award; Marion Quin Vol. 1: 13961
Dixon Award; Russell A. Vol. 1: 2048
Dixon, DDS Leadership Award; F. Gene Vol. 1: 8863
Dixon Lecture; W. E. Vol. 2: 8804
Dixon Medal; John W. Vol. 1: 5883
Dixon Trophy Vol. 2: 7532
DMA Annual Award Vol. 1: 8738
DMA Awards, in Association with Royal Mail Vol. 2: 7385
DMA Hall of Fame Vol. 1: 8925
DMA President's Award Vol. 1: 8739
DMA/Royal Mail Direct Marketing Awards Vol. 2: 7385
do Piaui (Brasil) Prize; Alvarenga Vol. 2: 5408
do Piaui; Premio Alvarenga Vol. 2: 5408
do Rego Prize; Abilio Lopes Vol. 2: 5409
Doane Award; D. Howard Vol. 1: 4406
Dobbelsteyn Memorial Trophy; Ernest Vol. 1: 7040
Dobbins Award for Community Service; Bertha Vol. 2: 9304
Dobbs Award; Ella Victoria Vol. 1: 17324
Doberman Pinscher Club of America Awards Program Vol. 1: 8969
Dobie-Paisano Writing Fellowships Vol. 1: 20014
Dobinson Award Vol. 2: 7358
Doblougska priset Vol. 2: 6248
Dobrolyubov Prize; N. A. Vol. 2: 5905
Dobson Lecture Vol. 2: 4979
Dobzhansky Prize; Theodosius Vol. 1: 18894
Dock Award; Lavinia L. Vol. 1: 1066
Dockers Khakis for Women of Independent Vision Grant Vol. 1: 21714
d'Octon; Prix Paul Vigne Vol. 2: 2082
Dr. Eisenhower Medal Vol. 1: 9193
Dr. J. van der Bilt prijs Vol. 2: 4858
Dr. May K. Simon Memorial Scholarship Vol. 1: 5740
Dr. Robert M. Lollar Prize Paper Award Vol. 1: 2942
Doctoral Awards Program Vol. 1: 14326
Doctoral Dissertation Award Vol. 1: 8581
Doctoral Dissertation Competition Vol. 1: 611
Doctoral Dissertation Fellowship Vol. 1: 5606
Doctoral Dissertation Grants in Women's Studies Vol. 1: 21825
Doctoral Fellowship Vol. 1: 8856
Doctoral Prizes Vol. 1: 16022
Doctorate of Bananistry Medal Vol. 1: 11417
Doctorate of Food Service Award Vol. 1: 16386
Documentaries of the World Vol. 1: 13607
Documentary of the Year Vol. 2: 5205
Dodge Award Vol. 1: 22035
Dodge Award; Harold F. Vol. 1: 5944
Doe Lectureship; Janet Vol. 1: 13255
Doehler Award Vol. 1: 16423
Doerfer Engineering Concept of the Year Award
American Society of Agricultural and Biological Engineers Vol. 1: 4214
American Society of Agricultural and Biological Engineers Vol 1: 4235
Dog of the Year
American Brittany Club, Heart of Illinois Vol. 1: 1592
Loveland Beagle Club Vol 1: 12965
Rin Tin Tin Fan Club Vol 1: 18053
Dogramaci Family Health Foundation Fellowship and Prize; Ihsan Vol. 2: 6564
Dohrenwend Lecture in Social and Community Epidemiology; Barbara Vol. 1: 3718
Doistau - Emile Blutet; Fondation Paul Vol. 2: 1946
Dole Award; Gertrude Vol. 1: 10147
Doll Award; Edgar A. Vol. 1: 3691
Dolly Award Vol. 1: 6622
Dolphin Award Vol. 1: 7630
Dolphin Fellowship Vol. 1: 4849
Dolphin Medal Vol. 1: 4849
Domac Medal; Julije Vol. 2: 1380
Domac; Medalja Julije Vol. 2: 1380
Domestic Alpine Coach of the Year Vol. 1: 20803
Dominguez Medal of Honor; Belisario Vol. 2: 4630
Domtar Awards of the Chemical Institute of Canada for High School Chemistry Teachers Vol. 1: 7841
Domus Dei Vol. 1: 12704
Don Banks Composer Fellowship Vol. 2: 106
Don Fox Memorial Scholarship Vol. 1: 414
Don Niccolo D'Ardia Caracciolo RHA Award Vol. 2: 3697
Donal Knight Memorial Grand Master Award Vol. 1: 18356
Donald Award; Diana Vol. 1: 3557
Donald Medal Vol. 2: 7746
Donaldson Award of Merit; Mary Vol. 1: 18269
Donaldson Gold Medal Vol. 2: 8723
Donath Medal Vol. 1: 9958
Donato; Premio Magda Vol. 2: 4460
Donato Prize; Magda Vol. 2: 4460
Donegani; Fondazione Guido Vol. 2: 3820
Donehoo Essay Award Vol. 1: 11270
Donlan Memorial Exhibit Award; William Vol. 1: 3214
Donne Essay Prize on the Anthropology of Art; J. B. Vol. 2: 8423
Donnellan Award; J. Edward Vol. 1: 21658
Donnelley & Sons Co. Awards; R.R. Vol. 1: 1993
Donnelley & Sons Co. Exhibit Award; R.R. Vol. 1: 3215
Donner Medal in Canadian Studies Vol. 1: 5282
Donohue Award; Mark Vol. 1: 19690
Donovan Award; William J. Vol. 1: 16614
Donovan Individual Achievement Award; James D. Vol. 1: 3789
Doolitte Award; Arthur K. Vol. 1: 1751
Doolittle Award; James H. Vol. 1: 19112
Dorcus Award; Roy M. Vol. 1: 18655
Dornstein Memorial Creative Writing Contest for Young Adult Writers; David Vol. 1: 8118
Dorothea Award for Conservation Vol. 2: 6779
Dorothy Shaw Deaf Australian of the Year Award Vol. 2: 146
Dorothy's 60 Award Vol. 1: 12486
Dorros Award; Donna and Sidney Vol. 1: 17097
D'Orta Award; Augustine Vol. 1: 9236
Dorweiler Prize Vol. 1: 7621
Doswell Award; John P. "Jack" Vol. 1: 14565
Dott, Sr., Memorial Award; Robert H. Vol. 1: 1336
Double Bass Scholarship; CTBI Intermediate Cello/Viola/ Vol. 1: 18282
Double Bass Scholarship; Kiwania of Wascana Senior Cello/Viola/ Vol. 1: 18296
Doubleday Lectureship Vol. 2: 8805
Doublemard; Prix Vol. 2: 1714
Doublespeak Award Vol. 1: 14832
Dougherty Award; John L. Vol. 1: 5250
Douglas Award; Marjory Stoneman Vol. 1: 15489
Douglas Award; William O. Vol. 1: 18457
Douglas Gold Medal; James Vol. 1: 2817
Douglas International Fellowship; CFUW A. Vibert Vol. 2: 6406

Douglas Lecture; George Vol. 2: 9033
Douglas Medal - Cook Vol. 1: 13240
Douglas Memorial Medal; R. J. W. Vol. 1: 7483
Douglas Scholarship Award Fund; Roscoe Vol. 1: 19149
Douglass Award; Frederick Vol. 1: 16309
The Douglass Foundation Graduate Business Plan Competition Vol. 1: 6182
Douglass Prize; Jane Dempsey Vol. 1: 4285
Douthit Public Service Award; Richard Vol. 1: 2454
Dove Awards Vol. 1: 10101
Dove Medal Award; Allan B. Vol. 1: 21660
Dow Award for Excellence in Composites Research Vol. 1: 19312
Dow Creativity Center Summer Residency Fellowships; Alden B. Vol. 1: 16578
Dow Outstanding New Faculty Award Vol. 1: 4015
Dower Prize Vol. 2: 7634
Dowling Lecturerships Vol. 2: 8806
Down Award; Vera Vol. 2: 7063
Downes Jr. Memorial Award; William E. Vol. 1: 402
Downes Memorial Trust; Oppenheim John Vol. 2: 8234
Downes Resident Research Award; John J. Vol. 1: 769
Downing Award; Antoinette Forrester Vol. 1: 19020
Downing Award; C. N. Vol. 1: 7428
Downing Award; Glenn Vol. 1: 7402
Downs Intellectual Freedom Award; Robert B. Vol. 1: 21034
Downs Travelling Scholarship Vol. 2: 8807
Downtown Jaycees Teachers Grant Awards Vol. 1: 9014
Doyle Award; William H. Vol. 1: 2767
Dozier Travel Grant; Otis and Velma Davis Vol. 1: 8717
Dracea Prize; Marin Vol. 2: 5826
Dracup Scholarship Award; Joseph F. Vol. 1: 1014
Draddy Trophy Vol. 1: 15073
Draeger Young Investigators Award Vol. 2: 7985
Drake Award; Russell Vol. 1: 5756
Drake Memorial Award; Howard Vol. 2: 7650
Drama Desk Awards Vol. 1: 9018
Drama Development Trust Award Vol. 2: 5033
Drama Festival (Jashan-E-Tamseel) Awards Vol. 2: 5206
Drama League's Delia Austrian Medal for Distinguished Performance Vol. 1: 9020
Drama League's Distinguished Performance Award Vol. 1: 9020
Drama League's Musical Achievement Award Vol. 1: 9021
Drama League's Unique Contribution to the Theatre Award Vol. 1: 9022
Dramatic Arts Creativity Special Encouragement Award Vol. 2: 4178
Draper Medal; Henry Vol. 1: 13831
Draper Memorial Medal Vol. 2: 5566
Draper Prize; Charles Stark Vol. 1: 13806
Drechsel Achievement Award; Helmet Vol. 1: 3895
Dreher Memorial Award; Raymond H. Vol. 1: 11196
Dress Making Levels Vol. 2: 9335
Drew Award; Charles R. Vol. 1: 3825
Drewes Scholarship; Tom C. Vol. 1: 2973
Drewitt Award; Gerald Vol. 2: 7684
Drexel Medal; Lucy Wharton Vol. 1: 21097
Dreyer Award in Applied Economic Geology; Robert M. Vol. 1: 18809
Driller Accreditation Award Vol. 2: 7003
Drilling and Completion Award Vol. 1: 19239
Drilling Engineering Award Vol. 1: 19239
Drinking Water Protection Business Awards Program Vol. 1: 16135
Drinov Medal; Marin Vol. 2: 1206
Driscoll Fellowship; Governor Alfred E. Vol. 1: 16169
Driscoll Prize; Alfred E. Vol. 1: 16169
Driver Award; Captain William Vol. 1: 15049
Driver of the Year
Austin Ten Drivers Club Ltd. Vol. 2: 6846
New Hampshire School Transportation Association Vol 1: 16159
Truck Renting and Leasing Association Vol 1: 20220
Driver of the Year Award
American Trucking Associations - Safety Management Council Vol. 1: 4770
Guild of Motoring Writers Vol 2: 7587
Specialized Carriers and Rigging Association Vol 1: 19577
Drivers World Champions Vol. 1: 2565
Dromkeen Librarian's Award Vol. 2: 351
Dromkeen Medal Vol. 2: 352
Drossos Award; Erani P. Vol. 1: 3407
Droste Hulshoff Preis; Annette von Vol. 2: 3017
Drotman Memorial Award; Jay S. Vol. 1: 3779
Drouin; Prix Edmond Vol. 2: 1751
Drug Abuse Prevention Service Award; DEA Explorer Vol. 1: 6574
Drum Memorial Scholarship Award; Douglas R. Vol. 1: 3109
Drummond-Jackson Prize Vol. 2: 8952
Drury Award; Mike Vol. 2: 9369
Dryburgh Memorial Trophy; Dave Vol. 1: 7105
Dryden Lectureship in Research; AIAA Vol. 1: 2680
Dryerre Prize Lectureship; Henry Vol. 2: 8786
Du Bois-Mandela-Rodney Fellowship Vol. 1: 7699
Du Bois Medal; William Edward Burghardt Vol. 1: 14048
du Breuil; Prix Andre Jullien Vol. 2: 2109
du Fay; Fondation Arthur Vol. 2: 1802
Du Perron-Prijs; E. Vol. 2: 4923
du Pont Crowninshield Award; Louise Vol. 1: 15917
du Pont Trophy; Richard C. Vol. 1: 18581
du Pre Fellowship; Jacqueline Vol. 2: 8138
du Pre Grant; Jacqueline Vol. 2: 8139
du Teil; Prix Joseph Vol. 2: 2060
Duais Bhonn De Hide Vol. 2: 3616
Duais don bhFiliocht i nGaelige; An Vol. 2: 3618
Dublin Award; Louis I. Vol. 1: 1437
Dublin Horse Show Vol. 2: 3694
Dubner Research Prize; Ronald Vol. 1: 11262
Duboff Award; Samuel J. Vol. 1: 9831
Dubois Award; Mark Vol. 1: 9817
DuBois-Johnson-Frazier Award Vol. 1: 4654
Duc de Loubat; Prix du Vol. 2: 1768
Duc; Prix Vol. 2: 1715
Duchalais; Prix Vol. 2: 1769
Duckworth Award; Muriel Vol. 1: 7377
Ductile Iron Society Annual Award Vol. 1: 9037
Duculot; Prix Jules Vol. 2: 1028
Duddell Medal and Prize Vol. 2: 7728
Duddell Premium Vol. 2: 7808
Duden Preis der Stadt Mannheim; Konrad Vol. 2: 3070
Dudley Instruction Librarian Award; Miriam Vol. 1: 5607
Dudley Medal; Charles B. Vol. 1: 5945
Dudrick Research Scholar Award; Stanley J. Vol. 1: 4165
Duer Scholarship Award; A. O. Vol. 1: 14286
Duffy Award Vol. 1: 11697
Dufrenoy; Prix Jean Vol. 2: 1669
Dufresne Award; A.O. Vol. 1: 7193
Dufton Silver Medal Award Vol. 2: 7284
Duggan Medal; G. H. Vol. 1: 7429
Duisberg-Gedachtnispreis; Carl- Vol. 2: 2804
Duisberg-Plakette; Carl- Vol. 2: 2805
Dujarric de la Riviere; Fondation Rene Vol. 2: 1960
Dukaatti Prizes for Young Artists Vol. 2: 1595
Duke and Duchess of York Prize in Photography Vol. 1: 6791
Duke-Elder Award Vol. 1: 11602
Duke Lifeline Earthquake Engineering Award; Charles Martin Vol. 1: 4311
Duke of Buccleuch Memorial Trophy Vol. 2: 8677
The Duke of Edinburgh Conservation Medal Vol. 2: 6580
Duke of Edinburgh Prize Vol. 2: 4153
Duke of Edinburgh Prize for the Japan Academy Vol. 2: 4153
Duke of Edinburgh's Designer's Prize Vol. 2: 7383
Duke of Westminster Medal for Military Literature Vol. 2: 8866
Dulac; Fondation Vol. 2: 1689
Dumas; Fondation Jean-Baptiste Vol. 2: 1896
Dumas Medal; Russell Vol. 2: 387
Dumas-Millier; Prix Vol. 2: 1716
Dumbarton Oaks Fellowships Vol. 1: 9050
Dumesnil; Prix Rene Vol. 2: 1685
Dumfries Octocentenary Trophy Vol. 2: 8919
DuMont Citation; Allen B. Vol. 1: 17834
Dumont Medal; Andre H. Vol. 2: 895
Dun & Bradstreet Award for Outstanding Service to Minority Business Vol. 1: 17938
Dun & Bradstreet Public Librarian Support Award Vol. 1: 17939
Dunbar Award; Dr. Bonnie J. Vol. 1: 5113
Dunbar Medal; William Vol. 2: 2762
Dunbar Memorial Award; Walter Vol. 1: 3601
Duncan Legacy Award; Todd Vol. 1: 15430
Duncan Media Award; Cameron Vol. 1: 18014
Duncan Prize Lectureship; Henry Vol. 2: 8787
Dunham Award for Excellence in Teaching; Meneve Vol. 1: 8077
Dunkin Award Vol. 2: 7160
Dunlap Lecture Award Vol. 1: 7843
Dunleavy Award Vol. 1: 16350
Dunlop Memorial Award; Jerry Vol. 1: 10245
Dunlop Piping Scholarship; William C. Vol. 1: 16552
Dunn Award for Excellence; James Clement Vol. 1: 20538
Dunn Award; Gano Vol. 1: 8497
Dunning Award; H. A. B. Vol. 1: 3385

Award Index

Dunning Award; John and Harriet Vol. 1: 16031
Dunning Prize in United States History; John H. Vol. 1: 2469
Dunsford Memorial Award; Ivor Vol. 1: 1104
Dunton Memorial Award; Loren Vol. 1: 11395
Duntov Mark of Excellence Award Vol. 1: 14738
Dupau; Prix Georges Vol. 2: 2153
Dupin; Prix Charles
Academie des Sciences Morales et Politiques Vol. 2: 2024
Academie des Sciences Vol 2: 1900
DuPont Award; International Confederation for Thermal Analysis Vol. 2: 5585
Dupont; Fondation Octave Vol. 2: 1038
Dupont; Prix Lucien Vol. 2: 2073
Dupont Prize; O. Vol. 2: 1079
Dupree Prize for Research on Central Asia; Louis Vol. 1: 18600
Dupuis; Fondation Eugene et Amelie Vol. 2: 1859
Durand-Claye; Fondation Alfred Vol. 2: 1787
Durand et Edouard Ordonneau; Prix Auguste Vol. 2: 1686
Durand Lectureship for Public Service Vol. 1: 2681
Durand; Prix Jacques Vol. 2: 1687
Durban International Exhibition of Photography Vol. 2: 5541
Durban International Film Festival Awards Vol. 2: 5543
Durenberger Grassroots Government Leadership Award; Dave Vol. 1: 14443
Duseigneur; Prix Raoul Vol. 2: 1773
Dusmet World Championship Cup; Edith Oliver Vol. 1: 11727
Dussich Founder's Award; John J. P. Vol. 1: 15444
Dutch Cancer Society Press Award Vol. 2: 4727
Dutch International Vocal Competition - Hertogenbosch Vol. 2: 4730
Dutens; Fondation Alfred Vol. 2: 1788
Dutens; Prix Alfred Vol. 2: 1752
Dutens; Prix Joseph Vol. 2: 2061
Duthie Booksellers' Choice; Bill Vol. 1: 21518
Dutt Memorial Award; Raj Kristo Vol. 2: 3533
Dutton Award; Damien - Vol. 1: 8726
Duttweiler Prize; Gottlieb Vol. 2: 6369
Duvand; Prix Adrien Vol. 2: 2015
Duvernay; Prix Ludger- Vol. 1: 18611
Duvivier; Prix Charles Vol. 2: 1014
Dwiggins Award; William A. Vol. 1: 6510
Dwyer Scholarships; Peter Vol. 1: 6792
DX Hall of Fame Vol. 1: 8631
DXer of the Year Vol. 1: 5797
Dyckman Award for Service; Herbert P. Vol. 1: 1559
Dyer Award; Edward C. Vol. 1: 13073
Dyer Award; Janice Marie Vol. 1: 6126
Dykes Medal Award Vol. 1: 2868
Dyksterhuis Memorial Award; E.J. Vol. 1: 16017
Dymocks Aboriginal Torres Strait Islander Writers' Award Vol. 2: 484
Dymocks Arafura Short Story Award Vol. 2: 484
Dymocks Red Earth Poetry Award Vol. 2: 484
Dymond Public Service Award; J. R. Vol. 1: 16759
Dystel Prize for Multiple Sclerosis Research; John Vol. 1: 697
Dystel Prize; John Vol. 1: 15396
E. Benjamin Nelson Government Service Award Vol. 1: 10180
E-Cubed Awards Vol. 1: 9370
E. H. Trophy Vol. 2: 8544
E3 Environmental Excellence in Exploration Award Vol. 1: 17691
EAA Research Scholarship Vol. 2: 875
EAAP Annual Meeting Awards Vol. 2: 3902
EAAP Young Scientists Awards Vol. 2: 3902
EACR-MSD Meeting Awards Vol. 2: 7453
Eadie Medal; Thomas W. Vol. 1: 18164
Eagle Award
American College of Forensic Examiners International Vol. 1: 1864
Patriotic Order Sons of America Vol 1: 17109
Eagle Awards for Volunteer Service Vol. 1: 9056
Eagle Scholarship Vol. 1: 9750
Eagle Scout Vol. 1: 6577
Eagle Scout Scholarship; Arthur M. and Berdena King Vol. 1: 15782
Eagle Star Award for Keyboard Vol. 2: 8643
Eagle Star Award for Strings Vol. 2: 8643
Eagle Trophy Vol. 1: 5107
EAI Award Vol. 1: 4016
Earhart Medal; Amelia Vol. 1: 16365
Earl Trophy (Daytona 500); Harley J. Vol. 1: 8766
Earle Award; Wilton R. Vol. 1: 18724
Earle Memorial Award; Clarence E. Vol. 1: 15349
Earle Trophy; Sir George Vol. 2: 8718
Early Advocate of the Year Award; Joseph D. Vol. 1: 15204
Early Career Award Vol. 1: 13943
Early Career Distinguished Scholar Award Vol. 1: 16476
Early Career Life Scientist Award; ASCB/Promega Vol. 1: 3941
Early Career Research Award Vol. 1: 14031
Early Childhood; Book of the Year Award: Vol. 2: 303
Early Music Brings History Alive Award Vol. 1: 9060
Earth Award Vol. 1: 6682
Earth Day Award Vol. 1: 9062
Earth Fund Award; Joseph Barbosa Vol. 1: 18451
Earth Keeper of the Year Vol. 1: 13056
Earthcare Award Vol. 1: 18458
Earthwatch Education Awards Vol. 1: 9064
EARTHWATCH Film Awards Vol. 1: 9065
EASA Exceptional Achievement and Service Award Vol. 1: 9199
East & West Artists International Auditions Vol. 1: 9067
East Anglian Trophy Vol. 2: 8131
East Baton Rouge Parish Medical Society Premedical Scholarship Award Vol. 1: 9069
East Medal; L.R. Vol. 2: 388
East Prize; Ben Vol. 1: 13364
Easter Seals Canada Award Vol. 1: 7374
Eastern Section Annual Achievement Award Vol. 1: 19313
Eastman Award Vol. 1: 14083
Eastman Kodak Award Vol. 1: 21969
Eastman Kodak Gold Medal Award Vol. 1: 19190
Eaton Literary Awards Program Vol. 1: 9125
Eaton Memorial Trophy; Warren E. Vol. 1: 18582
Eavenson Award; Howard N. Vol. 1: 18810
EBEE Award Vol. 1: 9298
Ebenseer Bear Vol. 2: 726
Eberhardt Memorial Awards; Constance Vol. 1: 15430
Ebert Prize Vol. 1: 3386
Ebright Service Award; Harry E. Vol. 1: 1677
EBSCO ALA Conference Sponsorship Vol. 1: 2974
EBSCO Community College Learning Resources and Library Achievement Awards Vol. 1: 5608
Eby Memorial Award for the Art of Teaching; Harvey L. Vol. 1: 20257
ECAC Distinguished Achievement Award Vol. 1: 9108
ECAC Merit Medal Vol. 1: 9109
ECAC - SIDA Media Award Vol. 1: 9110
Eccles Medal Vol. 1: 11997
Echeverria Prize; Aquileo J. Vol. 2: 1351
Ecke Jr. Commercial Award; Paul Vol. 1: 2526
Eckel Student Prize in Noise Control Vol. 1: 6851
Eckersberg Medal Vol. 2: 1521
Eckert - Mauchly Award Vol. 1: 10891
Eckhardt-Gramatte National Competition for the Performance of Canadian Music Vol. 1: 9129
Eckle Clark Citizenship Award; Rhea Vol. 1: 9644
Eckman Education Award; Donald P. Vol. 1: 12214
Eclipse Awards Vol. 1: 20084
Eclipse Awards for Media Vol. 1: 20085
ECMA Awards Vol. 1: 9267
ECO Award Vol. 2: 1139
Ecobusiness Medal Vol. 2: 3361
Ecological Award Vol. 1: 13998
Ecological Section Award Vol. 1: 6545
Ecology Institute Prize Vol. 2: 2956
Economic Award Vol. 1: 11828
Economic Developer Award Vol. 1: 16776
Economic Development Volunteer Vol. 1: 12762
Economic Inquiry Article Award Vol. 1: 21544
Economics and Evaluation Award Vol. 1: 19245
Economics Award; Mineral Vol. 1: 2822
ECRI Medical Technology Media Awards Program Vol. 1: 9150
Ecroyd Award for Outstanding Teaching in Higher Education; Donald H. Vol. 1: 14707
Ecumenical Leadership Award Vol. 1: 7027
Ecumenical Prize Vol. 2: 1102
Eddington Medal Vol. 2: 8432
Edds Memorial Lecture in Developmental Biology; Mac V. Vol. 1: 6665
Edeiken Trophy Vol. 1: 2922
Edelman Award for Achievement in Management Science and Operations Research; Franz Vol. 1: 11071
Edelstein Prize Vol. 1: 18873
Eden Travelling Fellowship in Obstetrics and Gynaecology Vol. 2: 8445
Edenburn Trophy; Eddie Vol. 1: 20417
Edgars Vol. 1: 13732
Edgerton Award; Harold E. Vol. 1: 19606
Edgerton Civil Liberties Award; Henry W. Vol. 1: 1812

Edgerton-Lenker Memorial Youth Exhibit Award Vol. 1: 3216
Edholm Award; Otto Vol. 2: 7443
EDI Award for Corporate Leadership Vol. 1: 9087
Edi Awards Vol. 1: 17660
EDI Awards (Equality/Dignity/ Independence) Vol. 1: 9088
Edib Adivar Scholarship Citation; Halide Vol. 1: 20240
Edilia de Montequin Fellowship in Iberian and Latin American Architecture Vol. 1: 19025
Edinburgh Festival Critics' Awards Vol. 2: 7401
Edinburgh International Film Festival Vol. 2: 7407
Edison Award Vol. 1: 9159
Edison Awards Vol. 1: 3028
Edison Black Maria Film and Video Festival; Thomas A. Vol. 1: 9161
Edison Classical Music Award Vol. 2: 4732
Edison Medal Vol. 1: 10858
Edison Populair - Awards for Popular Music Vol. 2: 4733
Edison Popular Music Award Vol. 2: 4733
Edith Stager Memorial Award Vol. 1: 8075
Edith Stevens Groundwater Hero Award Vol. 1: 10181
Edition International Film Festival Vol. 1: 9230
Editions Barenreiter, Basle & Kassel Prize Vol. 2: 6488
Editor & Publisher/INMA Marketing Awards Vol. 1: 9163
Editor of the Year Award
Canadian Booksellers Association Vol. 1: 6987
National Press Foundation Vol 1: 15527
Editor-Publisher Award Vol. 1: 14302
Editorial and Cartoon Strip Contest Vol. 1: 8172
Editorial and Design Awards Vol. 1: 5572
Editorial and Design Excellence Awards Vol. 1: 4270
Editorial and Graphics Awards Vol. 1: 19205
Editorial Awards
Photographic Society of America Vol. 1: 17285
Suburban Newspapers of America Vol 1: 19819
Editorial Costa Rica Literary Prize Vol. 2: 1360
Editorial Excellence Award Vol. 1: 10813
Editorial Fellowship Program Vol. 2: 3765
Editor's Award Vol. 1: 11237
Editor's Award - *Journal of Allied Health* Vol. 1: 5839
Editors' Book Award Vol. 1: 17769
Editor's Chioce Award Vol. 1: 16048
Editor's Editor of the Year Vol. 2: 7186
Editors of the Year Vol. 2: 7186
Edlundska Priset Vol. 2: 6208
Edmonds Playwriting Award; S. Randolph Vol. 1: 14200
Edmonds Young Scholars Competition; S. Randolph Vol. 1: 6436
Edmonton Book Prize Vol. 1: 21984
Edmund S. Muskie Distinguished Public Service Award Vol. 1: 7737
EdPress Distinguished Achievement Awards for Excellence in Educational Journalism Vol. 1: 5663
EdPress Honor Awards - Best Newsletter Vol. 1: 5664
EdPress Honor Awards - Golden Lamp Award Vol. 1: 5665
EdPress Honor Awards - Golden Shoestring Vol. 1: 5666
EdPress Honor Awards - Most Improved Publication Vol. 1: 5667
EDRA Career Award Vol. 1: 9300
EDRA Student Award Vol. 1: 9301
EDRA Student Design Competition Vol. 1: 9302
Edstrom Medal Vol. 2: 2490
Education Achievement Award
National Academy of Opticiarny Vol. 1: 13811
United States Space Foundation Vol 1: 20841
Education and Behavioral Sciences Librarian Award; Distinguished Vol. 1: 5605
Education and Training Awards Vol. 1: 5713
Education Award
American Association for Clinical Chemistry Vol. 1: 982
American Institute of Chemical Engineers Vol 1: 2787
American Water Works Association Vol 1: 4838
American Zoo and Aquarium Association Vol 1: 4915
Association of Surgical Technologists Vol 1: 5873
Audubon Naturalist Society of the Central Atlantic States Vol 1: 6067
New England Wild Flower Society Vol 1: 16146
Society of Forensic Toxicologists Vol 1: 19135
Society of Manufacturing Engineers - Composites Manufacturing Association Vol 1: 19150
Society of Toxicology Vol 1: 19336
Education Award; Ivan B. Rahn Vol. 1: 18823
Education Award; Mineral Industry Vol. 1: 2823
Education Awards
Escambia Amateur Astronomer's Association Vol. 1: 9335
Charles Redd Center for Western Studies Vol 1: 17927
Education Council/GATF Individual Award Vol. 1: 10133
Education Excellence Award Vol. 1: 15649
Education, Friend of the Trails Award Vol. 1: 16855
Education; International Futures Award for Exceptional and Innovative Leadership in Continuing Higher Vol. 1: 20956
Education Medal Vol. 2: 4342
Education Ministry Award Vol. 2: 6621
Education; Nancy C. A. Roeske Certificate of Recognition for Excellence in Medical Student Vol. 1: 3636
Education Program; Cincinnati Opera Vol. 1: 7999
Education Research Award; School Division Vol. 1: 5565
Education Training Scholarship Vol. 1: 19615
Educational Aids Competition Blue Ribbon Awards Vol. 1: 4219
Educational Assistance Award Vol. 1: 6468
Educational Book of the Year; Alberta Vol. 1: 6504
Educational Exhibit Vol. 1: 3329
Educational Foundation Grant Vol. 2: 923
Educational Foundation Undergraduate Award; AWIS Vol. 1: 5531
Educational Interiors Showcase Vol. 1: 3884
Educational Materials Award Vol. 1: 4087
Educational Research Award Vol. 1: 19135
Educational Scholarships Vol. 1: 15715
Educational Sponsorship Award Vol. 1: 14018
Educational Television Awards Vol. 2: 8852
Educator Award
International Association for Food Protection Vol. 1: 11231
International Facility Management Association Vol 1: 11569
Minerals, Metals, and Materials Society Vol 1: 13443
Educator Award; Edward M. Osetek Vol. 1: 1193
Educator Award; Outstanding Vol. 1: 275
Educator-Industry Award
International Association for Food Protection Vol. 1: 11227
International Association for Food Protection Vol 1: 11231
Educator of the Year Award Vol. 1: 19885
Edwards Award; Boothby - Vol. 1: 231
Edwards Award; Douglas Vol. 1: 18199
Edwards Award; Howard K. Vol. 1: 231
Edwards Award; Margaret A. Vol. 1: 22053
Edwards Industry Advancement Award; Harry H. Vol. 1: 17523
Edwards Memorial Award; Everett Eugene Vol. 1: 282
Edwards Memorial Award; John Vol. 2: 9209
Edwards Prize; Alan Vol. 2: 8808
Eeckhout Prize; Joris Vol. 2: 958
Eells Award for Program Excellence; Eleanor P. Vol. 1: 1627
EEMS Award Vol. 2: 2306
EERA Scholarships Vol. 1: 9201
Effective Use of Retirement Award Vol. 1: 12579
Efficiency Medal Vol. 2: 3211
Efficiency Service Awards for the Public Sector Vol. 2: 4441
Effie Awards Vol. 1: 16206
Efron Research Award; Daniel H. Vol. 1: 1895
Egan Memorial Trophy; Raymond Vol. 2: 3712
Egede Medaillen Vol. 2: 1528
Egede Medal Vol. 2: 1528
Egerton Medal; Sir Alfred Vol. 1: 8264
Egg Commission Promotion and Marketing Award; International Vol. 2: 7920
Eggleston Award for Non-fiction; Wilfrid Vol. 1: 21987
Egleston Medal Vol. 1: 8229
Egoff Children's Prize; Sheila A. Vol. 1: 21519
Egon - Eloed Award Vol. 2: 3119
Egyed Laszlo emlekerem Vol. 2: 3225
Egyed Memorial Award; Laszlo Vol. 2: 3225
Egypt Exploration Society Centenary Studentship Vol. 2: 7409
Egyptian Red Crescent Society Competitions Vol. 2: 1559
Ehlenfeldt Memorial Scholarship Vol. 1: 17033
EHMA Award Vol. 2: 3909
Ehninger Distinguished Rhetorical Scholar Award; Douglas W. Vol. 1: 14708
Ehrenburgerbrief Vol. 2: 771
Ehrenmitglied Vol. 2: 3042

Ehrenmitgliedschaft Vol. 2: 714
Ehrennadel der Deutschen Apotheker Vol. 2: 2682
Ehrenpreis des Osterreichischen Buchhandels Vol. 2: 701
Ehrenring der Stadt Salzburg Vol. 2: 772
Ehrenstein Award Vol. 1: 9980
Ehrentafel Vol. 2: 2969
Ehrenzeichen Vol. 2: 2961
Ehrenzeichen der deutschen Arzteschaft Vol. 2: 2846
Ehrlich; Lecon Paul Vol. 2: 2569
Ehrnrooth Prize; Professor Magnus Vol. 2: 1613
Eifler Award; Col. Carl Vol. 1: 15384
Eikenberry Voice Scholarships; Sara Vol. 1: 13662
Eileen Young Husband Speaker Vol. 2: 7903
Einbond Renku Competition; Bernard Lionel Vol. 1: 10220
Einhorn New Investigator Award Vol. 1: 18783
Einstein Award Vol. 1: 3175
Einstein Award; Albert Vol. 1: 4193
Einstein Award; Hans Albert Vol. 1: 4312
Einstein Commemorative Award; Albert Vol. 1: 22026
Einstein World Award of Science; Albert Vol. 2: 4652
Eisenhower Distinguished Service Award; VFW Dwight David Vol. 1: 21337
Eisenhower Liberation Medal Vol. 1: 20639
Eisenhower Medallion Vol. 1: 17216
Eisenhower Trophy Vol. 1: 11651
Eisenhower Trophy; Dwight D. Vol. 1: 15069
Eisenman Award; William Hunt Vol. 1: 5176
Ekblad-Eldhs pris; Signe Vol. 2: 6249
Ekotopfilm Festival Vol. 2: 5965
El Angel Award - Distinguished Hispanic-American Artist Vol. 1: 6374
El Angel Award - For Corporate Contribution to the Development of Hispanic-American Arts Vol. 1: 6375
El-Bassioury Award; Mahmoud Vol. 1: 11929
El Caballo de Trabajo Award Vol. 1: 19542
Elan Awards Vol. 1: 11450
Elaut Prize; Prof. Leon Vol. 2: 959
Elder Statesman of Aviation Award Vol. 1: 13878
Eldredge Award; Bart Vol. 1: 16105
Eldredge Award; Marie H. Vol. 1: 3617
Eleanor Roosevelt Award for Outstanding Contributions to the Cause of Human Rights Vol. 1: 20539
Eleazar and Rose Tartakow Levinson Prize; Samuel Vol. 1: 18874
Electric Furnace Honorable Mention Vol. 1: 5406
Electro Solar Cup Vol. 2: 2455
Electrochimica Acta Gold Medal Vol. 2: 6453
Electronic Communication Award Vol. 1: 18459
Electronic Imaging Management Award Vol. 1: 311
Electronic Innovation Commendation Vol. 1: 8436
Electronic Media Award Vol. 1: 11328
Electronic Media Awards; Publications and Vol. 1: 15669
Electronic Systems News Premium Vol. 2: 7799
Electronic Warfare Squadron of the Year Vol. 1: 13084
Electronics Division Award Vol. 1: 1684
Electronics Education Premium Vol. 2: 7799
Electronics Letters Premium Awards Vol. 2: 7800
Elementary Departmental Award in Recognition of Commitment to Catholic Elementary Education Vol. 1: 14610
Elementary, Middle, and Secondary School Physical Education Teacher of the Year Vol. 1: 14043
Elementary Teachers of Excellence in Social Studies Vol. 1: 13154
Elf Oil UK Trophy Vol. 2: 7394
Eli Lilly Fellowship in Infectious Diseases Vol. 1: 15124
Eli Lilly Travel Fellowship Award Vol. 1: 19072
Elion Cancer Research Award; Gertrude Vol. 1: 967
Eliot Award; Abigail Vol. 1: 6517
Eliot II Award; Charles Vol. 1: 13316
Elizabeth A. Wood Science Writing Award Vol. 1: 2086
Elizabeth Guild Award Vol. 1: 13400
Elizabeth N. Watrous Gold Medal Vol. 1: 13801
Elkes International Award; Joel Vol. 1: 1896
Elkins Award; Goodhue- Vol. 1: 6083
The Ellery Lectureship Vol. 2: 93
Ellery Memorial Award (Outstanding Media); James H. Vol. 1: 2506
Ellet Award; Charles Vol. 1: 21567
Ellinger-Gardonyi Award Vol. 2: 8224
Elliot-Drake Intermediate Chopin Scholarhip; Janice Vol. 1: 18283
Elliot Medal; Daniel Giraud Vol. 1: 13832
Elliott Distinguished Service Award; Henry W. Vol. 1: 3973
Elliott Memorial Award; Clarence Vol. 2: 6698
Elliott Memorial Award; John Vol. 1: 1105
Elliott Prize; Van Courtlandt Vol. 1: 13275
Ellis Award Vol. 1: 16750
Ellis Award; Arthur Vol. 1: 8649
Ellis Award; Perry Vol. 1: 8575
Ellis Award; Wayne P. Vol. 1: 5946
Ellis Dissertation Award; John Tracy Vol. 1: 1653
Ellis Island Medals of Honor Vol. 1: 14955
Ellison-Cliffe Medal and Lecture Vol. 2: 8809
Ellison Memorial Prize; Ralph W. Vol. 1: 15369
Ellison Postdoctoral Fellowship in International Infectious Diseases Vol. 1: 15124
Elly Africa Environmental Award for Conservation of Wildlife and Environment Vol. 2: 6661
Elmer Award
Harvard Lampoon Vol. 1: 10275
Medical Dental Hospital Business Associates Vol 1: 13242
Elovitz Prize; Rose and Michael David Vol. 1: 11829
Elsdon-Dew Medal Vol. 2: 5604
Elsevier/LIRG Research Award Vol. 2: 8061
Elsevier Research Initiative Award Vol. 1: 9708
Elsey Award for Outstanding Involvement of Youth; George M. Vol. 1: 3826
Elson Award for International Achievement in Physical Therapy; Mildred Vol. 2: 9243
Elvehjem Award for Public Service in Nutrition; Conrad A. Vol. 1: 4157
Elver Mineral Economics Award; Robert Vol. 1: 7194
Ely *Human Factors* Article Award; Jerome H. Vol. 1: 10579
Ely Lecture; Richard T. Vol. 1: 2156
EMA Creative Excellence Awards Vol. 1: 9255
EMA Foundation School/Business Partnership Award Vol. 1: 9256
Emberson Award; Richard M. Vol. 1: 10859
EMBO Medal Vol. 2: 2751
Emden; Fondation Fanny Vol. 2: 1860
Emens Award for Support of a Free Student Press; John R. Vol. 1: 6205
Emera Prize for Journalism Excellence Vol. 1: 6035
Emergency Medical Services Exemplary Service Medal Vol. 1: 6819
Emergency Services Medal Vol. 2: 195
Emergent Entrepreneur Award Vol. 2: 5580
Emerging Artist of the Year Vol. 1: 11424
Emerging Company Award Vol. 1: 5331
Emerging Journalist of the Year Award Vol. 1: 14101
Emerging Scholars Award Vol. 1: 21138
Emeritus Award
Association for the Education of Teachers in Science Vol. 1: 5499
The Wildlife Society Vol 1: 21629
Emeritus Membership Vol. 1: 13392
Emerson Award; Ralph Waldo
International Platform Association Vol. 1: 11805
Phi Beta Kappa Vol 1: 17241
Emil Christian Hansen Foundation for Microbiological Research Award Vol. 2: 1442
Emil Memorial Award; Allan D. Vol. 2: 2452
Eminent Ecologist Vol. 1: 9136
Eminent Service Award Vol. 1: 717
Eminescu Prize; Mihail Vol. 2: 5827
Emirates AFI Awards (The Australian Film Awards) Vol. 2: 175
Emma Muuvi Award Vol. 2: 1631
Emme Astronautical Literature Award; Eugene M. Vol. 1: 1501
Emmett Award in Fundamental Catalysis; Paul H. Vol. 1: 16399
Emmons Award Vol. 1: 5575
Emmy Awards Vol. 1: 13862
Emmy Awards; Daytime Vol. 1: 13861
Emmy Awards for Primetime Programming Vol. 1: 127
Emmy Awards; News and Documentary Vol. 1: 13863
Emmy Awards; Public and Community Service Vol. 1: 13864
Emmy Awards; Sports Vol. 1: 13865
Emperess Elizabeth National Champion Vol. 1: 11903
Employer of the Month Award Vol. 1: 4277
Employer of the Year Award
American Society of Certified Engineering Technicians Vol. 1: 4278
Blinded Veterans Association Vol 1: 6457
Employer Recognition Award Vol. 1: 1571
Employer's Award Vol. 2: 7117
Employers of the Year Vol. 1: 10085
Employment Equity Gold Medals Vol. 1: 10587
Empowerment Award Vol. 1: 20322
EMRA Academic Excellence Award Vol. 1: 9237
EMRA Award for Excellence in Teaching Vol. 1: 9238

EMRA Clinical Excellence Award Vol. 1: 9239
EMRA Leadership Award Vol. 1: 9240
EMS Award Vol. 1: 9304
EMT - Paramedic of the Year Vol. 1: 14232
EMT-Paramedic Emergency Medical Service of the Year Award (ALS Service of the Year Award) Vol. 1: 14209
EMT-Paramedic of the Year Award Vol. 1: 14215
ENA Micromedex Best Original Research Award Vol. 1: 9244
Encore Award Vol. 2: 8981
Encore Awards Vol. 1: 18022
Endeavor Student Writing Award; LITA/ Vol. 1: 12826
Endowment Fund
AACC International Vol. 1: 32
American Schleswing-Holstein Heritage Society Vol 1: 3881
Energy Achievement Award; Environmental and Vol. 1: 2291
Energy amd Environmental Design Award Vol. 1: 10695
Energy Innovator Award Vol. 1: 3790
Enersen Award; Lawrence Vol. 1: 13949
Enescu Prize; George Vol. 2: 5828
Enforcement Officer of the Year Vol. 1: 1141
Engel Award; Marian Vol. 1: 22004
Engelbart Best Paper Award; Douglas Vol. 1: 5325
Engelberger Awards; Joseph F. Vol. 1: 18083
Engelberger Robotics Awards; Joseph F. Vol. 1: 18083
Engestromska medaljen for tillampad naturvetenskap Vol. 2: 6188
Engineer of the Year Vol. 1: 19886
Engineering 2000 Awards Vol. 2: 389
Engineering Achievement Award
American Institute of Mining, Metallurgical, and Petroleum Engineers Vol. 1: 2821
Zimbabwe Institution of Engineers Vol 2: 9359
Engineering Achievement Awards Vol. 1: 14112
Engineering Achievement Awards Program Vol. 1: 4220
Engineering Achievement in Radio Vol. 1: 14112
Engineering Achievement in Television Vol. 1: 14112
Engineering and Construction Contracting Division Award Vol. 1: 2768
Engineering Award Vol. 1: 14112
Engineering Award of Excellence Vol. 1: 9213
Engineering Council Young Engineer for Britain Competition Vol. 2: 562
Engineering Excellence Award Vol. 1: 8453
Engineering Excellence Awards
American Consulting Engineers Council Vol. 1: 2009
Optical Society of America Vol 1: 16784
Engineering Fellowship; AAAS Mass Media Science and Vol. 1: 3506
Engineering Journals Premium Vol. 2: 7801
Engineering Manager of the Year Award Vol. 1: 4054
Engineering Materials Achievement Award Vol. 1: 5177
Engineering Medal Vol. 1: 17605
Engineering Meetings Board Outstanding Oral Presentation Award Vol. 1: 19041
Engineers Members Prize; Institution of Plant Vol. 2: 7883
Engineers Special Awards; Institution of Structural Vol. 2: 7887
Engineers Students of the Year; Institute of Road Transport Vol. 2: 9064
England Intermediate Hayden and Mozart Scholarship; The Frances Vol. 1: 18284
Engle Fellowship; James A. Michener - Paul Vol. 1: 12191
Engleheart Cup Vol. 2: 8545
Engler Gold Medal Vol. 2: 734
English Academy Medal Vol. 2: 5547
English Badminton Award Vol. 2: 6850
English Basket Ball Association Player of the Year (Men and Women) Vol. 2: 7420
English; David H. Russell Award for Distinguished Research in the Teaching of Vol. 1: 14840
English Language Arts; CEE James N. Britton Award for Inquiry within the Vol. 1: 14829
English Speaking Union Prize for an Outstanding Graduate Vol. 2: 8359
Engstrom Award; Victor Vol. 1: 18327
Enhancement of Animal Welfare Award Vol. 1: 19337
Enhancing Production of Safe Affordable Food; Award for Technical Innovation in Vol. 1: 7439
Enlisted Essay Contest Vol. 1: 20711
Enners Award; Lt. Raymond J. Vol. 1: 20661
Ennis Award; Peter Vol. 1: 7215
Ennor Manufacturing Technology Award; William T. Vol. 1: 4508
Ensemble Company of Cincinnati Opera (ECCO) Vol. 1: 7999
Enterprise Computing Award Vol. 1: 18266
Enterprise Spirit Award Vol. 1: 12576
Entertainer of the Year Vol. 1: 11424
Entertainment Audio Music/VID Product Grant; Baker & Taylor Vol. 1: 17713
Entomological Society of Canada Gold Medal Award Vol. 1: 9293
Entomology Writing Competition Award Vol. 1: 22061
Entrepreneur Award Vol. 1: 11329
Entrepreneur of the Year
Ernst & Young Vol. 1: 9331
International Franchise Association Vol 1: 11636
Latino American Management Association Vol 1: 12708
Entrepreneurial Success Award Vol. 1: 20829
Entrepreneurs Workshop International Vol. 1: 12166
Entry Films Competition Vol. 1: 6372
Entwicklungslanderpreises der Justus-Liebig-Universitat Giessen Vol. 2: 2998
Environment and Energy Achievement Awards Program Vol. 1: 2288
Environment Data and Space Weather Forcasts Award Vol. 2: 5899
Environment, Health and Safety Award Vol. 1: 19243
Environment Medal Vol. 2: 9003
Environment; National Award for the Protection of Vol. 2: 1264
Environment Prize Vol. 2: 4380
Environmental Achievement Award
Association of New Jersey Environmental Commissions Vol. 1: 5795
Canadian Construction Association Vol 1: 7041
Environmental and Energy Achievement Award Vol. 1: 2291
Environmental and Exercise Physiology Section Gatorade Young Investigator Award Vol. 1: 3516
Environmental and Safety Distinguished Achievement Award Vol. 1: 19243
Environmental Award
Institute of Packaging Professionals Vol. 1: 11023
Institution of Professional Engineers New Zealand Vol 2: 4980
International Hotel and Restaurant Association Vol 2: 2476
Natural Resources Defense Council Vol 1: 16020
Sri Lanka Association for the Advancement of Science Vol 2: 6131
Environmental Awards Vol. 2: 8238
Environmental Citation Vol. 1: 7276
Environmental Conservation Distinguished Service Award Vol. 1: 2818
Environmental Education Award Vol. 1: 14950
Environmental Educator of the Year Vol. 1: 7860
Environmental Excellence Award Vol. 1: 8412
Environmental Heritage Award Vol. 2: 3716
Environmental Improvement Awards Program Vol. 1: 17636
Environmental Issues Council Corporate Award Vol. 1: 9214
Environmental Personality of the Year in Africa Vol. 1: 255
Environmental Quality Research Award Vol. 1: 4243
Environmental Reporting; Robert L. Kozik Award for Vol. 1: 15519
Environmental Science Award Vol. 1: 235
EOS Poster Award Vol. 2: 7477
EOS Research Grant Vol. 2: 7478
Eotvos Memorial Medal; Lorand Vol. 2: 3226
E.P. Taylor Award of Merit Vol. 1: 12396
Epilepsy Foundation of America Awards Vol. 1: 9308
Epilepsy Research Award for Outstanding Contributions to the Pharmacology of Antiepileptic Drugs Vol. 1: 4171
Epilepsy Research Awards Program Vol. 1: 2197
The Epiphany Prizes Vol. 1: 12402
Episteme Award Vol. 1: 18499
Eppler Memorial Scholarship; Don Vol. 1: 12564
EPSC Award Vol. 2: 7488
Epstein Foundation Awards; Norma Vol. 1: 21112
Equal Employment Opportunity Award
United States Department of Commerce - National Institute of Standards and Technology Vol. 1: 20479
United States Department of State Vol 1: 20540
Equal Employment Opportunity Awards Vol. 1: 20511
Equal Employment Opportunity Medal Vol. 1: 13887
Equal Justice Award Vol. 1: 14490
Equal Opportunities Award Vol. 2: 4766
Equal Opportunity/Affirmative Action Exemplary Practices Award Vol. 1: 4183
Equal Opportunity Award Vol. 1: 12769
Equal Opportunity Day Award Vol. 1: 15925

Award Index

Equity Award Vol. 1: 1476
ERA Awards Vol. 1: 9218
Erasmus Correll Award Vol. 1: 12862
Erasmus Medal Vol. 2: 6663
Erasmus Prijs Vol. 2: 4737
Erasmus Prize Vol. 2: 4737
ERB Life Achievement Award Vol. 1: 6697
Ergonomics Society Honorary Fellow Vol. 2: 7444
Ergonomics Society Lecturer Vol. 2: 7445
Ergonomics Society President's Medal Vol. 2: 7446
Ergonomics Society Special Award Vol. 2: 7447
Ergonomics Society's Meritorious Service Award Vol. 2: 7448
Ericksen Award; Anna Mae Vol. 1: 18183
Erickson Award; Bonnie Vol. 1: 10424
Ericson's Award for Outstanding Doll Sculpture; Rolf Vol. 1: 8982
Ericsson Award in Renewable Energy; John Vol. 1: 20494
Ericsson Medal Award; John Vol. 1: 4616
Erikson Award; Erik H. Vol. 1: 12017
Eriksson Prize; Jakob Vol. 2: 6209
Eriksson Prize Medal; Jakob Vol. 2: 6159
Erikssons Pris; Hilda och Alfred Vol. 2: 6210
Erikssons stipendium; Lydia och Herman Vol. 2: 6250
Ernest Hemingway Foundation Award Vol. 1: 17157
Ernst-Kuntze Prize Vol. 2: 2788
Ernst Mayr Grants Vol. 1: 13687
Errera; Prix Leo Vol. 2: 1063
Erskine Outstanding Achievement Award; Addine Vol. 1: 1091
Erslev Award Vol. 2: 1529
Erslev Prisen Vol. 2: 1529
ERT Scholarship; Christopher J. Hoy/ Vol. 1: 2964
ertzoff Prize; Vladimar A. P Vol. 1: 21116
Erwin Memorial Trophy; Franklin Vol. 1: 20927
ESA Distinguished Achievement Award in Extension Vol. 1: 9287
ESA Distinguished Achievement Award in Regulatory Entomology Vol. 1: 9288
ESA Distinguished Achievement Award in Teaching Vol. 1: 9289
ESA Founder's Memorial Award Vol. 1: 9290
Esau Award; Katherine Vol. 1: 6546
ESB Clinical Biomechanics Award Vol. 2: 3914
ESB Research Award Vol. 2: 3916
ESB Student Award Vol. 2: 3915
Escorts Book Award Vol. 2: 3363
ESCPB Young Scientists Awards Vol. 2: 877
Eseman Award; Eugene (Butch) Vol. 1: 13133
Esguerra Prize; Carlos Vol. 2: 1323
Eskola Medal Vol. 2: 1625
Eskola-Mitali Vol. 2: 1625
ESOMAR Awards Vol. 2: 4739
Espasa Ensayo Prize Vol. 2: 6016
Espenschade Award; Park W. Vol. 1: 10919
Espirito Santo Trophy Vol. 1: 11652
Espiritualidad Prize Vol. 2: 6017
ESPY Awards Vol. 1: 9337
ESRA Award Vol. 1: 9368
ESRI Award for Best Scientific Paper in Geographic Information Systems Vol. 1: 5212
Essar Gold Medal Vol. 2: 3451
Essay Competition
Islamic Research Foundation International Vol. 1: 12231
LEPRA Vol 2: 8052
Essay Contest Vol. 1: 15452
Essay Contest for College Students Vol. 1: 4921
Essay Contest for Professionals in Rehabilitation Vol. 1: 1986
Essay Contest; High School Vol. 1: 6396
Essay Contest in Progress in Religion Through the Sciences Vol. 1: 12403
Essey Award; Shelia Vol. 1: 698
Essig Award; Otto Vol. 1: 21222
Esso Award Vol. 2: 390
Established Investigator Award
American Heart Association Vol. 1: 2406
National Alliance for Research on Schizophrenia and Depression Vol 1: 13923
Esterhazy Prize Vol. 2: 8095
Estes Memorial Pioneer Jujitsu Award; Bud Vol. 1: 551
Estrada; Premio Genaro Vol. 2: 4506
Estrelicia Dourada Vol. 2: 5420
Estridge, Jr. Award; Capt. W. W. Vol. 1: 20942
Etancelin; Fondation Leon-Alexandre Vol. 2: 1919
ETE Erdemerem Vol. 2: 3281
Ete Macskasy Arpad-Diz Medal Vol. 2: 3280
ETE Merit Medal Vol. 2: 3281
ETEBA Scholarship Vol. 1: 9080
Eternal Light Medal Vol. 1: 12375
Ethel Minter Award Vol. 1: 12998
Ethical Culture School Book Award Vol. 1: 9348
Ethical Humanist Award Vol. 1: 16264
Ethicon Foundation Fund Traveling Fellowship Vol. 2: 8451
Ethics Award Vol. 1: 9245
Ethnic Minorities Screenwriting Competition Vol. 1: 16000
Etoile d'Or Vol. 2: 6480
ETR&D Young Scholar Award Vol. 1: 5356
ETS Award for Distinguished Service to Measurement Vol. 1: 9177
Etta Nathan Award Vol. 1: 6283
Etter Student Travel Award Fund; Peggy Vol. 1: 2087
Ettl Grant; Alex J. Vol. 1: 15699
Ettlingen International Competition for Young Pianists Vol. 2: 3036
Etz Chaim (Tree of Life) Award Vol. 1: 15298
Eu Achievement Award; March Fong Vol. 1: 15416
Eubank Morale, Welfare and Recreation Award; Maj. Gen. Eugene L. Vol. 1: 16824
Eubanks Award; Jackie Vol. 1: 3002
Eugene Rogers Award Vol. 1: 21542
Eurail Award Vol. 2: 4742
Eurich Award; Alvin C. Vol. 1: 76
EURO Golden Medal Vol. 1: 11599
EuroBest Awards Vol. 2: 7889
EUROCALL Research Award Vol. 2: 3630
Euromusica Competition Vol. 2: 6079
Europa Award Vol. 1: 9352
Europa Nostra Awards Vol. 2: 4745
Europa Preis fur Denkmalpflege Vol. 2: 3080
Europaischer Chopin-Klavierwettbewerb Vol. 2: 2691
Europe Impresa Award Vol. 2: 3556
Europe Prize Vol. 2: 2290
European 1600 Cup for Autocross Vol. 2: 2455
European Association for Cancer Research Italian Fellowship Program Vol. 2: 7454
European Association for Signal, Speech and Image Processing Awards Vol. 2: 5398
European Athlete of the Year Award; Waterford Crystal Vol. 2: 2745
European Awards Program Vol. 1: 11515
European Baseball Championships Vol. 2: 858
European Baseball Cup Vol. 2: 859
European Bridge Champion Vol. 2: 3905
European Chopin Piano Competition Vol. 2: 2691
European Competitions Vol. 2: 4404
European Coordinating Committee for Artificial Intelligence Awards Vol. 2: 718
European Council of International Schools Awards Vol. 2: 7465
The European Diploma of Protected Areas Vol. 2: 2291
European Disposables and Nonwovens Association Awards Vol. 2: 863
European Drag Racing Championship Vol. 2: 2455
European Engineer Award Vol. 2: 867
European Environmental Mutagen Society Award to Young Scientists Vol. 2: 2305
European Exchange Fellowships Vol. 2: 3701
European Federation of Corrosion Medal Vol. 2: 2748
European Figure Skating Championships Vol. 2: 6445
European Film Academy Short Film Award Vol. 2: 7407
European Film Prize; John Templeton Vol. 2: 6312
European Finn Seniors Championship Vol. 2: 2472
European General Galvanizers Association Honorary Member Vol. 2: 7473
European General Galvanizers Association Pin Vol. 2: 7474
European Historic Rally Trophy Vol. 2: 2455
European Hotel Manager of the Year Vol. 2: 3910
European Human Rights Prize Vol. 2: 2292
European Junior Finn Championship Vol. 2: 2473
European Juvenile Championships Vol. 2: 858
European Music and Poetry Competitions Vol. 2: 855
European Music Prize for Youth Vol. 2: 2760
European Nuclear Society Awards Vol. 2: 869
European Packaging Competition Vol. 2: 2321
European Parliament Sakharov Prize for Freedom of Thought Vol. 2: 7484
European Prize for Statesmanship Vol. 2: 3079
European Prize for the Preservation of Historic Monuments Vol. 2: 3080
European Prizes for Folk Art Vol. 2: 3081
European Rhinologic Society Prizes Vol. 2: 1583
European Speed Skating Championships for Ladies and Men Vol. 2: 6445
European Sportsman and Sportswoman of the Year Vol. 2: 6147

European Surfing Championships - Open Champion Vol. 2: 7492
European Thyroid Association Awards Vol. 2: 1486
European Tour Order of Merit Vol. 2: 8303
European Trophy for Historic Sports Car Vol. 2: 2455
European Truck Racing Cup Vol. 2: 2455
European Union Contest for Young Scientists Vol. 1: 18362
European Union Prize for Cultural Heritage/ Europa Nostra Awards Vol. 2: 4746
European Urban and Regional Planning Awards Vol. 2: 7468
European Young Jazz Artists Vol. 1: 12310
Eurosense Award Vol. 2: 8332
Eurostar Awards for Packaging Vol. 2: 2321
Eurovision for Young Dancers; Grand Prix Vol. 2: 6316
Eurovision for Young Musicians; Grand Prix Vol. 2: 6317
Eurovision Song Contest; Grand Prix of the Vol. 2: 6318
Euverard Innovation Award Vol. 1: 5947
EVA Event Award Vol. 2: 2765
Evans Award; John K. Vol. 1: 11223
Evans Biography Award Vol. 1: 13641
Evans Handcart Award Vol. 1: 13642
Evans Memorial Lecture; Everett Idris Vol. 1: 1601
Evans Nonfiction Prize; Hubert Vol. 1: 21520
Evans Trophy; Edward S. Vol. 1: 18581
Evanshen Trophy; Terry Vol. 1: 7106
Eva's Choice Award Vol. 1: 8983
Evening News Capital Awards Vol. 2: 7402
Events of the Year Vol. 1: 21247
Everard Trophy Vol. 2: 7608
Everest and Jennings Player of the Year Vol. 1: 508
Everett Award; Anderson - Vol. 1: 11238
Everett Award; Woody Vol. 1: 4017
Evergreen Latex Award Vol. 1: 11582
Everychild Conference Honors Program Vol. 1: 7904
Ewald Prize Vol. 2: 8009
Ewald Prize; Johannes Vol. 2: 1472
Ewing Layman Award; James Vol. 1: 19301
Ewing Lecturer; James Vol. 1: 19302
Ewing Medal; James Alfred Vol. 2: 7763
Ewing Medal; Maurice
  American Geophysical Union Vol. 1: 2346
  Society of Exploration Geo-physicists Vol 1: 19120
EXCEL Awards Vol. 1: 19205
Excellence 200 Awards Vol. 1: 20729
Excellence Award
  Society of Research Administrators Vol. 1: 19295
  West African Examinations Council Vol 2: 3159
Excellence Awards
  British Printing Industries Federation Vol. 2: 7115
  Chartered Institute of Public Relations Vol 2: 7280
  Join Hands Day Vol 1: 12424
  World Petroleum Council - The Global Forum for Oil and Gas Science, Technology, Economics and Management Vol 2: 9258
Excellence for Innovation Award Vol. 1: 7326
Excellence in Academic Libraries Award Vol. 1: 5609
Excellence in Administration Award Vol. 1: 20601
Excellence in Advertising Awards Vol. 1: 14431
Excellence in Aerospace Education Vol. 2: 3329
Excellence in Art Direction Award Vol. 1: 6033
Excellence in Baha'i Studies Vol. 1: 5279
Excellence in Breast Cancer Education Award Vol. 1: 16715
Excellence in Caring Practices Award Vol. 1: 1175
Excellence in Collaboration Award - Multidisciplinary Teams; Datascope Vol. 1: 1173
Excellence in Collaboration Award - Nurse to Family; Datascope Vol. 1: 1174
Excellence in Communication Award Vol. 1: 13978
Excellence in Communication Leadership (EXCEL) Vol. 1: 11295
Excellence in Communications Award Vol. 1: 10394
Excellence in Communications Awards Vol. 1: 14153
Excellence in Craft Awards Vol. 1: 16968
Excellence in Craft Contests Vol. 1: 16970
Excellence in Direct Selling Vol. 2: 7387
Excellence in Documentation Award Vol. 1: 12215
Excellence in Editing Award Vol. 1: 6033
Excellence in Education Award
  American Association of Critical-Care Nurses Vol. 1: 1176
  American Society of Cytopathology Vol 1: 4391
  Life Office Management Association Vol 1: 12843
  Pi Lambda Theta Vol 1: 17325
Excellence in Education Awards Vol. 1: 9205
Excellence in EIFS Construction Vol. 1: 9189
Excellence in Environmental Engineering Vol. 1: 646
Excellence in Extension Award
  American Association Family Consumer Sciences Vol. 1: 940
  American Phytopathological Society Vol 1: 3538
Excellence in Financial Journalism Vol. 1: 16292
Excellence in Geophysical Education Award Vol. 1: 2347
Excellence in Government Leadership Award Vol. 1: 5714
Excellence in Highway Design Awards Vol. 1: 20559
Excellence in Hot-Dip Galvanizing Awards Vol. 1: 2315
Excellence in In-Plant Promotion Award Vol. 1: 11837
Excellence in Landscape Vol. 1: 5248
Excellence in Manufacturing Technology Achievement Awards Vol. 1: 3023
Excellence in Marketing Award; AALL/ West Vol. 1: 1247
Excellence in Media Award Vol. 1: 1227
Excellence in Mentorship Awards Vol. 1: 3937
Excellence in Military Scholarship Vol. 1: 15383
Excellence in Music Composition Award Vol. 1: 6033
Excellence in Pilot Training Award Vol. 1: 13919
Excellence in Practical Farming Award Vol. 2: 8411
Excellence in Practice Award Vol. 1: 1228
Excellence in Pre-College Physics Teaching Award Vol. 1: 1372
Excellence in Professional Journalism Vol. 1: 15758
Excellence in Programming Award Vol. 1: 18002
Excellence in PXE Research Vol. 1: 17774
Excellence in Radiation Therapy Nursing Award Vol. 1: 16716
Excellence in Records Management Award Vol. 2: 611
Excellence in Research Vol. 1: 8675
Excellence in Research Awards Vol. 1: 3351
Excellence in Research Awards; American Kennel Club Vol. 1: 4810
Excellence in Science Teaching Awards Vol. 1: 20030
Excellence in Small and/or Rural Public Library Service Award Vol. 1: 17715
Excellence in Software Awards Vol. 1: 19383
Excellence in Sound Design Award Vol. 1: 6033
Excellence in Sports Journalism Award Vol. 1: 7755
Excellence in Swedish Design Prize Vol. 2: 6298
Excellence in Teaching Award
  AACC International Vol. 1: 33
  American Phytopathological Society Vol 1: 3539
  Dominican University Vol 1: 8988
Excellence in Teaching Veterinary Parasitology Vol. 1: 21853
Excellence in the Arts Award Vol. 1: 21360
Excellence in the Media Award Vol. 1: 21361
Excellence in Training Vol. 1: 5825
Excellence in Ultrasound Vol. 1: 7455
Excellence in Undergraduate Physics Teaching Award Vol. 1: 1373
Excellence in Undergraduate Teaching Award Vol. 1: 5031
Excellence in Zookeeping Award; Jean M. Hromadka Vol. 1: 1488
Excellence of Poster Presentation Award Vol. 1: 18842
Excellence of Scholarship and Consistency of Contributions to the Oncology Nursing Literature Award Vol. 1: 16717
Excellent Clinical Nurse Specialist Award; Dale Medical Products Vol. 1: 1172
Excellent Environmental Educator Award Vol. 2: 5891
Excellent Member of VOS Award Vol. 2: 5886
Excellent Nurse Manager Award Vol. 1: 1177
Excellent Swedish Design Prize Vol. 2: 6298
Excelsior Endurance Award Vol. 2: 6857
Exceptional Achievement Award Vol. 1: 18583
Exceptional Achievement Medal Vol. 1: 13888
Exceptional Administrative Achievement Medal (EAAM) Vol. 1: 13889
Exceptional Bravery Medal Vol. 1: 13890
Exceptional Engineering Achievement Medal Vol. 1: 13891
Exceptional Media Merit Award Vol. 1: 15963

Exceptional Merit Awards Vol. 1: 3065
Exceptional Scientific Achievement Medal Vol. 1: 13892
Exceptional Service Vol. 1: 20613
Exceptional Service Award
Cranial Academy Vol. 1: 8638
Soaring Society of America Vol 1: 18584
Exceptional Service Medal Vol. 1: 13893
Exceptional Technology Achievement Medal (ETAM) Vol. 1: 13894
Executive Board Merit of Exhibit Award Vol. 1: 19283
Executive Committee Award
National Council of Teachers of English Vol. 1: 14841
Western Association of Map Libraries Vol 1: 21537
Executive Committee Members Award Vol. 2: 9289
Executive of the Year
Caucus for Television Producers, Writers and Directors Vol. 1: 7684
Federal Executive Institute Alumni Association Vol 1: 9449
National Basketball Association Vol 1: 14502
R & D Magazine - Reed Business Information Vol 1: 17814
Executive of the Year Award Vol. 1: 19795
Executive Scholar and Research Fellow Programs Vol. 1: 6315
Exemplar of Humanics Award Vol. 1: 2580
Exemplary Journalism Award Vol. 1: 15136
Exemplary Offender Program Award Vol. 1: 2025
Exemplary Papers in Humility Theology Vol. 1: 12404
Exemplary Program Award Vol. 1: 20951
Exemplary Research in Social Studies Award Vol. 1: 14779
Exemplary Service Award Vol. 1: 3217
Exemplary State and Local Awards Program Vol. 1: 14637
Exhibit and Poster Award Vol. 1: 748
Exhibit Award
American Zoo and Aquarium Association Vol. 1: 4916
Society of the Plastics Industry - Moldmakers Division Vol 1: 19307
Exhibit Focus Awards Vol. 1: 20147
Exhibition of Photography Vol. 1: 18243
Exhibitor Awards Vol. 1: 14611
Exhibitors' Choice Awards Vol. 1: 18574
Exhibitors Competition Vol. 1: 17645
Expedition Award; Ralph Brown Vol. 2: 8511
Expedition Grant Vol. 2: 8135
Expedition Grants Vol. 2: 7008
Expeditionary Awards Vol. 2: 9249
Experiment Citation Award Vol. 1: 21930
Experimental Analysis of Behavior Dissertation Award Vol. 1: 3654
Experimental Pathologist-in-Training Award Vol. 1: 4120
Experimental Psychology Society Prize Vol. 2: 7497
ExploraVision Awards; Toshiba/NSTA Vol. 1: 15693
Explorer Award Vol. 1: 5688
Explorer Drug Abuse Prevention Service Award; DEA Vol. 1: 6574
Explorer Leadership Award Vol. 1: 6578
Explorers Medal Vol. 1: 9375
EXPO Juried Competition Vol. 1: 19623
Export Promotion and Research and Development Award Vol. 2: 3353
Exporter of the Year Vol. 1: 12091
Expository Writing Award Vol. 1: 11072
Express Ranches the Great American Cowboy Award Vol. 1: 14886
Extended Neuroscience Research Award Vol. 1: 702
Extension 2000 Award Vol. 1: 940
Extra Mile Award
Blue Ridge Literacy Council Vol. 1: 6464
Wahpeton Area Chamber of Commerce and CVB Vol 1: 21421
Extraction and Processing Distinguished Lecture Award Vol. 1: 13444
Extraction and Processing Science Award Vol. 1: 13445
Extraction and Processing Technology Award Vol. 1: 13446
Extractive Metallurgy Division Best Paper Award
Minerals, Metals, and Materials Society Vol. 1: 13445
Minerals, Metals, and Materials Society Vol 1: 13446
Extraordinary Plaque Vol. 1: 11118
Extraordinary Service/Hero Award Vol. 1: 14729
Exxon Supreme GT Vol. 1: 11754
Exxon World Sports Car Championship Vol. 1: 11755
ExxonMobil Solid State Chemistry Faculty Fellowship Vol. 1: 1752
Eyck Memorial Trophy; Jim Ten Vol. 1: 11135
F. K. Mostofi Distinguished Service Award Vol. 1: 20377
Faber Award; John Vol. 1: 16981
Fabregas; Premi Xavier Vol. 2: 6003
Fabri Prize; Ralph Vol. 1: 13786
Fabulous Fashion Independents Vol. 1: 13654
Face in the Crowd Vol. 1: 19729
Facilities and Construction Award Vol. 1: 19240
Facilities Management Excellence Awards (FAME Awards) Vol. 1: 5366
Facility Management Achievement Award Vol. 1: 11570
Facility of the Year Vol. 1: 18409
FACSS Student Award Vol. 1: 9464
Faculty Award of Excellence Vol. 1: 17611
Faculty Career Development Award for Toncology of the Head and Neck Vol. 1: 1948
Faculty Psychiatric Technician of the Year Vol. 1: 1387
Faculty Publication of the Year Vol. 1: 686
Faculty Research Award Vol. 1: 9072
Faculty Service Award
Alumni Association of the City College of New York Vol. 1: 517
University Continuing Education Association Vol 1: 20952
Fagley Awards Competition Vol. 1: 8387
Fagnan; Fondation Edmond Vol. 2: 1006
Faguet; Prix Emile Vol. 2: 2143
FAI Aeromodelling Gold Medal Vol. 2: 6328
FAI Airsport Medal Vol. 2: 6329
FAI Bronze Medal Vol. 2: 6330
FAI Gold Air Medal Vol. 2: 6331
FAI Gold Parachuting Medal Vol. 2: 6332
FAI Gold Space Medal Vol. 2: 6333
FAI Silver Jubilee Award Vol. 2: 3367
Failor Award; Clarence W. Vol. 1: 2066
Fain, Jr. Award; P. Kemp Vol. 1: 9551
Fair Memorial Award; Gordon Maskew Vol. 1: 647
Fair Play Award
England Basketball Vol. 2: 7421
Polish Football Association Vol 2: 5346
Fair Play Trophy; FIM Vol. 2: 6420
Fairall Award; The G. R. Vol. 2: 9344
Fairbank Prize in East Asian History; John K. Vol. 1: 2470
Fairchild Education Achievement Award; Gen. Muir S. Vol. 1: 16825
Fairless Award; Benjamin F. Vol. 1: 2819
Fairless Memorial Award; Benjamin F. Vol. 1: 2874
Fairley Award for Editorial Excellence; Tom Vol. 1: 9166
Fairley Fellowships; Neil Hamilton Vol. 2: 466
Fairplay Award Vol. 2: 4425
Faisal International Prize for Arabic Literature; King Vol. 2: 5922
Faisal International Prize for Islamic Studies; King Vol. 2: 5923
Faisal International Prize for the Service of Islam; King Vol. 2: 5924
Faisal International Prize in Medicine; King Vol. 2: 5925
Faisal International Prize in Science; King Vol. 2: 5926
Faith & Medicine Competitive Grant Award Vol. 1: 12405
Falcon Golden Spike Award; George Vol. 1: 14350
Falder Award; Bob Vol. 2: 6908
Faletti-Nosari; Premio Maria Vol. 2: 4012
Faligatter Distinguished Service Award; Florence Vol. 1: 17255
Fallot-Jeremine; Fondation Paul Vol. 2: 1947
Family Faith & Freedom Vol. 1: 9412
Family History Writing Contest Award of Excellence Vol. 1: 15146
Family International Talent Awards Program Vol. 1: 17088
Family Life Award Vol. 2: 7503
Family Psychologist of the Year Vol. 1: 3671
Famous Grouse Trophy Vol. 2: 7609
FAMY Awards Vol. 1: 12351
Fann Memorial Challenge Trophy; J. W. Vol. 1: 15815
Fanny Award Vol. 1: 9373
Fantus, M.D., Medal; Bernard Vol. 1: 1106
FAO Technical Assistance Fellowship Vol. 2: 3948
FAO-WAGGGS Nutrition Award Vol. 2: 9239
Faraday House Commemorative Prize Vol. 2: 7802
Faraday Lectureship Vol. 2: 8750
Faraday Medal Vol. 2: 7803
Faraday Prize; Michael Vol. 2: 8696
Farber Award; Rosalie Boyle/Norma Vol. 1: 16108
Farber First Book Award; Norma Vol. 1: 17430
Farm and Ranch Management Award Vol. 1: 16003
Farm Buildings Award Scheme Vol. 2: 7360
Farm-City Award Vol. 1: 14961
Farm Management Conservation Award Vol. 1: 14154
Farmer Appreciation Award Vol. 1: 6219
Farmer Award; Paul and Kate Vol. 1: 14833

Farmer International Business Dissertation Award; Richard N. Vol. 1: 102
Farnsworth Senior Player of the Year Award; Ted Vol. 1: 11139
Faro Trophy; R. Vale Vol. 1: 17341
Farquhar Award; Francis P. Vol. 1: 18460
Farquhar Mountaineering Award; Francis P. Vol. 1: 18460
Farr Award; Donald E. Vol. 1: 21840
Farr Medal; Bertrand Vol. 1: 2444
Farradine Award; Jason Vol. 2: 7278
Farrall Young Educator Award; A. W. Vol. 1: 4221
Farrant Award; Arthur Vol. 2: 97
Farrell Distinguished Teacher Award; Miriam Joseph Vol. 1: 14612
Farrer Memorial Medal Vol. 2: 331
Farrer Trophy Vol. 2: 8546
Farriery Competitions Vol. 2: 3694
Farrington Award of Excellence; J. D. Vol. 1: 14210
Farrow Award Vol. 1: 7985
Fasching Antal Emlekplakett Vol. 2: 3289
Fasching Commemorative Plaque; Anthony Vol. 2: 3289
FASEB Excellence in Science Award Vol. 1: 9462
Fashion Export Awards; UK Vol. 2: 9159
Fashion Fiasco of the Year Vol. 1: 13655
Fashion Forward Awards Vol. 1: 2325
Fast 50 Award Vol. 1: 17956
Father of the Year Vol. 1: 9421
Father of the Year Award Vol. 1: 8714
Father Washington Award Vol. 1: 7673
Fatigue Achievement Award Vol. 1: 5948
Fauchard Academy Bronze Service Citation; Pierre Vol. 1: 17349
Fauchard Academy Plaque; Pierre Vol. 1: 17350
Fauchard Gold Medal Vol. 1: 17351
Faucher; Prix Leon Vol. 2: 2069
Faulding Memorial Fellowship; Francis Hardy Vol. 2: 523
Faulding Multimedia Award Vol. 2: 597
Faulkes Award; W. F. Vol. 1: 15591
Faulkner Award for Excellence in Writing; Virginia Vol. 1: 17511
Faulkner Award for Fiction; PEN/ Vol. 1: 17154
Faulstich Grand Award; Edith M. Vol. 1: 17480
Fauna and Flora International 100% Fund Grants Vol. 2: 7507
Fauna and Flora Preservation Society Grants Vol. 2: 7507
Fauria Award; Mrs. Inez M. Vol. 1: 8614
Faustus Poster Awards Vol. 2: 7455
Favorite Book of the Year Award Vol. 1: 18113
Favre; Prix Jules Vol. 2: 2168
Fawcett Award; James Waldo Vol. 1: 3408
FBI Honorary Medals Vol. 1: 20504
FBI Medal for Meritorious Achievement Vol. 1: 20504
FBI Medal of Valor Vol. 1: 20504
FBI Memorial Star Vol. 1: 20504
FBI Shield of Bravery Vol. 1: 20504
FBI Star Vol. 1: 20504
FCCEAM Fellowship Award Vol. 2: 1399
FE Cook Cup and Keliher Vol. 2: 8310
Fearnley's Olympic Prize Vol. 2: 5158
Feasibility Grants Vol. 1: 2136
Feature Article Award Vol. 1: 17546
Feature Photo Award Vol. 1: 16245
Feature Photography Award Vol. 1: 16981
Feature Stories Awards Vol. 1: 16246
Feature Video Photo Award Vol. 1: 16247
Features Award Vol. 1: 11108
Fechner Award; Gustav-Theodor- Vol. 2: 2937
FECS-Pezcoller Recognition for Contribution to Oncology Vol. 2: 4032
Fedden Award; Sir Roy Vol. 2: 8385
Federacion Nacional de Cultivadores de Cereales y de Leguminosas Competitions Vol. 2: 1312
Federal City Club Award for Very Distinguished Public Service Vol. 1: 9447
Federal Credit Union of the Year Vol. 1: 14223
Federal Duck Stamp Contest Vol. 1: 20592
Federal Engineer of the Year Award Vol. 1: 15747
Federal Health Care Executive Special Achievement Award Vol. 1: 2544
Federal Migratory Bird Hunting and Conservation Stamp Contest Vol. 1: 20592
Federal Nursing Service Award Vol. 1: 5770
Federal Property Person of the Year Vol. 1: 15559
Federation Internationale de Canoe Vol. 2: 6056
Federation Internationale de l'Art Photographique Awards Vol. 2: 4406
Federation Internationale de l'Art Photographique Medals Vol. 2: 4407
Federation Internationale de l'Art Photographique Service Awards Vol. 2: 4408
Federation Internationale de l'Art Photographique World Cups Vol. 2: 4409
Federation Leadership Award Vol. 1: 10764
Federation of Afrikaans Cultural Societies Awards Vol. 2: 5555
Federation of British Artists Prizes and Awards Vol. 2: 7509
Federation of Insurance and Corporate Counsel Annual Award Vol. 1: 9469
Federation of Insurance Counsel Award Vol. 1: 9469
Fee Outstanding Young Engineer Award; Walter Vol. 1: 10905
Fehring Award of Merit; William P. "Dutch" Vol. 1: 21154
Fein Prize; Ruth B. Vol. 1: 2901
Feinberg Award; Frederick L. Vol. 1: 2429
Feinbloom Award; William Vol. 1: 718
Feinstein Award; The Martin and Bernice Vol. 1: 21455
Feis Award for Nonacademically-Affiliated Historians; Herbert Vol. 1: 2471
Feis Award; Herbert Vol. 1: 2471
Feitelson Research Award; Dina Vol. 1: 11855
Feldman Award; Dr. Harold Vol. 1: 14860
Feldman Award; Hillel Vol. 1: 3909
Feldman Memorial Exhibit Award; Aaron Vol. 1: 3218
Feline Research; West Scholarship for Vol. 2: 8498
Felix Awards, Artistic Vol. 1: 188
Felix Awards, Industrial Vol. 1: 189
Felix; Fondation Clement Vol. 2: 1828
Felix Memorial Award; John R. Vol. 1: 20882
Fell Pony Society Ridden Championship Vol. 2: 7517
Fell Student Award; Honor B. Vol. 1: 18725
Fellers Award; Carl R. Vol. 1: 10938
Fellini Award; Federico Vol. 2: 3840
Fellow
AACE International Vol. 1: 36
American Academy of Periodontology Vol 1: 803
American Academy of Somnology Vol 1: 842
American Camellia Society Vol 1: 1616
American Ceramic Society Vol 1: 1678
American Geophysical Union Vol 1: 2348
American Meteorological Society Vol 1: 3096
American Osteopathic College of Pathologists Vol 1: 3357
American Society for Adolescent Psychiatry Vol 1: 3905
American Society for Nutritional Sciences Vol 1: 4158
ASM International Vol 1: 5178
ASPRS - The Imaging and Geospatial Information Society Vol 1: 5213
Canadian Phytopathological Society Vol 1: 7339
Canadian Society for Civil Engineering Vol 1: 7413
Center for Advanced Study in the Behavioral Sciences Vol 1: 7697
Engineering Institute of Canada Vol 1: 9270
Garden Writers Association Vol 1: 9878
Hymn Society in the United States and Canada Vol 1: 10625
Institute of Environmental Sciences and Technology Vol 1: 10920
International Society of Logistics Vol 1: 11998
Philalethes Society Vol 1: 17265
Royal Geographical Society of Queensland Vol 2: 532
Society for Advancement of Management Vol 1: 18624
Society for Information Display Vol 1: 18766
Soil and Water Conservation Society Vol 1: 19387
Soil Science Society of America Vol 1: 19392
World Organization of Family Doctors Vol 2: 5953
Fellow Award
Institute of Industrial Engineers Vol. 1: 10953
Minerals, Metals, and Materials Society Vol 1: 13447
MTM Association for Standards and Research Vol 1: 13657
National Association for Interpretation Vol 1: 14021
Precast/Prestressed Concrete Institute Vol 1: 17524
Project Management Institute Vol 1: 17667
Resort and Commercial Recreation Association Vol 1: 18003
Society of Allied Weight Engineers Vol 1: 18945
Standards Engineering Society Vol 1: 19745
Fellow Awards Vol. 1: 10319
Fellow Designation
American Association for Agricultural Education Vol. 1: 962
Illuminating Engineering Society of North America Vol 1: 10693

Fellow for Research in Esoteric Areas of Knowledge Vol. 1: 5025
Fellow Grade Membership Vol. 1: 4018
Fellow Grade of Membership
Air and Waste Management Association Vol. 1: 319
Society of Automotive Engineers Vol 1: 19042
Fellow Member
American Water Resources Association Vol. 1: 4828
Institute of Packaging Professionals Vol 1: 11024
Fellow Membership Vol. 1: 7931
Fellow of ESA Vol. 1: 9291
Fellow of the Academy of Professional Reporters Vol. 1: 14880
Fellow of the American Society of Agronomy Vol. 1: 4244
Fellow of the A.S.S.E. Vol. 1: 4613
Fellow of The Athenaeum Vol. 1: 6015
Fellow of The Cranial Academy Award Vol. 1: 8639
Fellow of the Crop Science Society of America Vol. 1: 8662
Fellow of the CSME Vol. 1: 7430
Fellow of the Metallurgical Society Vol. 1: 13447
Fellow of the National Genealogical Society Vol. 1: 15147
Fellow of the Phytopathological Society of Japan Vol. 2: 4282
Fellow of the Royal Academy of Dance Vol. 2: 8360
Fellow of the Society Vol. 1: 19262
Fellow of the Society
AVS Vol. 1: 6147
International Microelectronics and Packaging Society Vol 1: 11748
National Speleological Society Vol 1: 15796
Society of Nematologists Vol 1: 19220
Fellow of the Special Libraries Association Vol. 1: 19548
Fellow or Foreign Honorary Member Vol. 1: 620
Fellow Recognition Vol. 1: 11641
Fellow; Society of South African Geographers Vol. 2: 5640
Fellows and Honorary Members Vol. 1: 13256
Fellows Award
East Texas Historical Association Vol. 1: 9082
National Lubricating Grease Institute Vol 1: 15350
Nature Saskatchewan Vol 1: 16039
Virginia Recreation and Park Society Vol 1: 21398
Fellows Awards
American Psychological Association - Division of Family Psychology (Division 43) Vol. 1: 3672
International Centre for Heat and Mass Transfer Vol 2: 6633
Society of Women Engineers Vol 1: 19367
Fellows Distinguished Award of Merit Vol. 1: 2010
Fellows Medal Vol. 1: 4476
Fellows' Medal Vol. 1: 6733
Fellows of the American Association of Community Theatre Vol. 1: 1168
Fellows of the American Statistical Association Vol. 1: 4692
Fellows of the Association Vol. 1: 4664
Fellows of the Metallurgical Society of AIME Vol. 1: 13447
Fellows of the SID Vol. 1: 18767
Fellows Program Award Vol. 1: 5840
Fellowship
American Institute of Architects Vol. 1: 2711
Construction Specifications Institute Vol 1: 8437
Creative Glass Center of America Vol 1: 8643
National Humanities Center Vol 1: 15250
Royal Institute of Navigation Vol 2: 8595
Society for Imaging Science and Technology Vol 1: 18712
Society for Industrial Microbiology Vol 1: 18760
Fellowship and Grant Award Program Vol. 1: 8892
Fellowship Award
Architectural Institute of the Republic of China Vol. 2: 6589
Damon Runyon Cancer Research Foundation Vol 1: 8728
Pharmaceutical Organization of Nigeria Vol 2: 5107
University Photographers Association of America Vol 1: 21128
World Atlatl Association Vol 1: 21862
Fellowship Awards of the Jane Coffin Childs Memorial Fund for Medical Research Vol. 1: 7921
Fellowship for Cancer Research Vol. 1: 968
Fellowship for Creative and Performing Arts and Writers Vol. 1: 914
Fellowship in Aviation History Vol. 1: 373
Fellowship in the Association Vol. 1: 2366
Fellowship of the Augustan Society Vol. 1: 6089
Fellowship of the Australian College of Education Vol. 2: 155
Fellowship of the Australian Society of Archivists Vol. 2: 272
Fellowship of the City and Guilds of London Institute Vol. 2: 7306
Fellowship of the Pharmacy Society of South Africa Vol. 2: 5607
Fellowship of the Scottish Tartans Society Vol. 2: 9112
Fellowship Program
American Association of University Women Educational Foundation Vol. 1: 1472
Pennsylvania Council on the Arts Vol 1: 17168
Fellowship Scheme to Promote Commonwealth Understanding Vol. 2: 7332
Fellowships and Scholarships Vol. 2: 479
Fellowships for Playwrights Vol. 1: 18433
Fellowships in Arts and Crafts Vol. 2: 7333
Feltrinelli; Premi Antonio Vol. 2: 3827
Female Athlete of the Year
Sport Canada Vol. 1: 19627
United States Rowing Association Vol 1: 20747
Female Style Maker of the Year Vol. 1: 14742
Female Vocalist of the Year Vol. 1: 11424
Feminist Activist Award Vol. 1: 19376
Feminist Lecturer Award Vol. 1: 19377
Feminist Theory and Gender Studies Graduate Paper Award Vol. 1: 12047
Femmy Vol. 1: 20286
The Femmy Awards Vol. 1: 9531
Femoyer Trophy; Robert E. Vol. 1: 5107
Fencer of the Year (Men and Women) Vol. 1: 20583
Fenderbosch Leadership Award; Henry Vol. 1: 14432
Feneon; Prix Felix Vol. 2: 2349
Fennell Award; Earle J. Vol. 1: 1997
Fennell International Young Conductor Competition; Frederick Vol. 1: 19429
Fenner Medal Vol. 2: 119
Fennia Gold Medal Vol. 2: 1620
Fennia Silver Medal Vol. 2: 1621
Fenno, Jr. Book Prize; Richard F. Vol. 1: 3581
Fenton Medal Vol. 2: 8663
Fentress Memorial Award for Editorial Excellence; H. M. Vol. 1: 19996
Fenwick Medal Vol. 1: 9876
Ferber Award for Consumer Research; Robert Vol. 1: 12446
Ferguson Award; Virginia Vol. 1: 18461
Ferguson Medal; Cedric K. Vol. 1: 19241
Ferguson Memorial Award; Elmer Vol. 1: 10495
Ferguson; Premio Massey Vol. 2: 5
Ferguson Prize; Wallace K. Vol. 1: 7152
Fermi Award; Enrico Vol. 1: 20495
Fern Award; Harold Vol. 2: 6711
Fern National Trophy; Harold Vol. 2: 6712
Fernanda Monti Award Vol. 2: 4941
Fernandez Award; USCU Vol. 1: 20928
Fernandez Madrid; Orden del Merito Sanitario Jose Vol. 2: 1293
Fernandez Trophy; Anthony Vol. 1: 20928
Fernando Lara Prize Vol. 2: 6018
Fernbach Memorial Award; Sidney Vol. 1: 10892
Fernoy Memorial Prize; Ruth Vol. 2: 9121
Fernschopernpreis der Stadt Salzburg Vol. 2: 777
Ferrari Challenge Vol. 1: 11756
Ferraris; Premio AEI Galileo Vol. 2: 4006
Ferrez Photography Award; Marc Vol. 2: 1173
Ferrier; Prix Gabriel Vol. 2: 1688
Ferris Bowl; William Vol. 2: 8263
Ferst Award; Monie A. Vol. 1: 18511
Fertilizer Trainee Awards Vol. 2: 3634
Feser Award; Leo Vol. 1: 10067
FESPP Award Vol. 2: 7513
Fessenden Award; Reginald Vol. 1: 19121
Fessenden Student Prize in Underwater Acoustics Vol. 1: 6852
Festival Awards for Literature Vol. 2: 597
Festival de Cine de Alcala de Henares Vol. 2: 6028
Festival de Cinema de Montagne Vol. 2: 6107
Festival dei Popoli Vol. 2: 3925
Festival du Court-Metrage en Plein Air Vol. 2: 2333
Festival du Film Court de Villeurbanne Vol. 2: 2335
Festival du Film de l'Atlantique Vol. 1: 6033
Festival du Film d'Etudes Cinematographiques Vol. 2: 2522
Festival du Film Sportif Lille Vol. 2: 2263
Festival du Nouveau Cinema de Montreal Vol. 1: 13598
Festival Internacional de Cine de Bilbao Documental y Cortometraje Vol. 2: 6061
Festival Internacional de Cine Iberoamericano Vol. 2: 6044

Festival Internacional de Cine para la Juventud de Gijon Vol. 2: 6037
Festival Internacional de Cinema de Muntanya, Vila de Torello Vol. 2: 6107
Festival Internacional de Cinema do Porto - Fantasporto Vol. 2: 5396
Festival Internacional de Video de Canarias Vol. 2: 6009
Festival International de Diaporamas Vol. 2: 944
Festival International de Films de Femmes de Creteil et du Val de Marne Vol. 2: 2516
Festival International de Television de Monte Carlo Vol. 2: 4669
Festival International de Television Prague d'Or Vol. 2: 1424
Festival International des Programmes Audiovisuels Vol. 2: 2372
Festival International du Cinema d'Animation Annecy Vol. 2: 2440
Festival International du Court Metrage de Clermont-Ferrand Vol. 2: 2549
Festival International du Film Alpin et de l'Environement de Montagne, Les Diablerets, Suisse Vol. 2: 6408
Festival International du Film, Cannes Vol. 2: 2259
Festival International du Film d'Amiens Vol. 2: 2226
Festival International du Film d'Architecture, d'Urbanisme, et d'Environement Urbain de Bordeaux Vol. 2: 2228
Festival International du Film de Berlin Vol. 2: 2670
Festival International du Film de Vol Libre Vol. 2: 2340
Festival International du Film Ethnographique et Sociologique Cinema du Reel Vol. 2: 2261
Festival International du Film Fantastique, de Science-Fiction, et Thriller de Bruxelles Vol. 2: 841
Festival International du film Maritime et d'Exploration Vol. 2: 2470
Festival International du Film Scientifique et Technique, Bruxelles Vol. 2: 845
Festival International du Film sur l'Art Montreal Vol. 1: 11613
Festival Internationl du Film d'Aventure de la Plagne Vol. 2: 2416
Festival Internazionale Cinema Giovani Vol. 2: 3883
Festival Internazionale de Film Locarno Vol. 2: 6482
Festival Internazionale di Danza Modern-Jazz Vol. 2: 3845
Festival Mondial de l'Image Sous-Marine Vol. 2: 2342
Festival National du Court Metrage de Clermont-Ferrand Vol. 2: 2550
Festival of American Community Theatre Vol. 1: 1164
Festival of Community Theatre Vol. 2: 5033
Festival of Contemporary Theatre Vol. 2: 5806
Festival of Emerging American Theatre New Plays Competition Vol. 1: 17279
Festival of Firsts Playwriting Competition Vol. 1: 19837
Festival of New Plays; Year End Series Vol. 1: 16554
Festival of the Americas Vol. 1: 21969
Festival of Underwater Images Vol. 2: 2342
Festival Panafrican du Cinema de Ouagadougou et de la Television de Ouagadougou Vol. 2: 1242
Festivalul de Teatru Contemporan Vol. 2: 5806
Fevre Memorial Prize; R.J.W. Le Vol. 2: 120
FEW Distinguished Service Award Vol. 1: 9453
FFA Award Vol. 1: 9096
FFC Award of Recognition Vol. 1: 9535
FFF Conservation Award Vol. 1: 9475
FGF Awards Vol. 1: 9419
FHA International Salon Culinaire Vol. 2: 5946
FIA F3000 International Champion Vol. 2: 2456
FIA Formula 1 World Champion Vol. 2: 2457
FIA Intercontinental Formula 3 Cup Vol. 2: 2455
FIA Marathon Trophy Vol. 2: 2455
FIA World Cup for Cross Country Rallies Vol. 2: 2455
FIA World Rally Champion Vol. 2: 2458
Fiabci Prix d'Excellence Vol. 2: 2503
FIAP Medals Vol. 1: 10149
FICC Prize Vol. 2: 2977
Fiction Award
Black Caucus of the American Library Association Vol. 1: 6413
River City Vol 1: 18067
Fiction Book of the Year Award Vol. 1: 6988
Fiction Contest Vol. 1: 21996
FIDE Master Vol. 2: 3193
Fidelitas Medal Vol. 1: 16815
Fiducia Award; Freddie Vol. 1: 12114
Field and Joe L. Franklin Award for Outstanding Achievement in Mass Spectrometry; Frank H. Vol. 1: 1753
Field Award; Carolyn W. Vol. 1: 17177
Field Award; Crosby Vol. 1: 4431
Field Awards Vol. 1: 11999
Field Maintenance Award Vol. 1: 1542
Fieldgate Trophy; Norm Vol. 1: 7107
Fields Medal Vol. 1: 11744
Fieldwork Award Vol. 2: 6780
Fienegan Gold Award; ASFSA Thelme Vol. 1: 18347
Fies Award; John Vol. 1: 11502
FIFA Five-a-Side (Indoor Football) World Championship Vol. 2: 6356
FIFA Futsal (Indoor Football) World Championship Vol. 2: 6356
FIFA U-17 World Championship Vol. 2: 6357
FIFA U-17 World Tournament Vol. 2: 6357
FIFA Women's World Cup Vol. 2: 6358
FIFA World Cup Trophy Vol. 2: 6359
Fife Memorial Award; Mary Perry Vol. 1: 15732
FIFI Awards Vol. 1: 9720
Fifth Sense Commendation Vol. 1: 9719
Fifty Books of the Year Vol. 1: 2808
Fifty-Year Award Vol. 1: 9525
Fifty Year Club Vol. 1: 7195
Fifty Year Club Member Certificate Vol. 1: 3219
Fifty Year Membership Medal and Pin Vol. 1: 3220
Figeroa Keeper Scholarship; Raymond Vol. 1: 1492
Fighter Against Drug Abuse Vol. 1: 14730
Fighter/Attack Squadron of the Year Vol. 1: 13078
Fighter of the Year Vol. 1: 12115
Figueroa Nogueron Prize; Gilberto Vol. 2: 4494
Filipovic Awards; Ivan Vol. 2: 1388
Filley Memorial Awards for Excellence in Respiratory Physiology and Medicine; Giles F. Vol. 1: 3517
Film and Video Competition; British Medical Association Vol. 2: 7060
Film Grants Vol. 1: 17554
Film Prize; John Templeton European Vol. 2: 6312
Film Society of the Year Award Vol. 2: 7014
Filmotheque Vol. 2: 2976
Filtration Society Gold Medal Vol. 2: 7519
FIM Environmental Prize Vol. 2: 6419
FIM Fair Play Trophy Vol. 2: 6420
FINA Prize Vol. 2: 6363
FINA Prize Eminence Vol. 2: 6363
Financial Executive of the Year Vol. 1: 11004
Financial Management Improvement Award Vol. 1: 12428
Financial Planner of the Year Vol. 1: 14325
Financial Post Annual Report Awards Vol. 1: 8537
Financial Post Awards for Business in the Arts Vol. 1: 8541
Financial Post Design Effectiveness Awards Vol. 1: 8538
Financial Post Environment Awards for Business Vol. 1: 8539
Financial Post Outstanding CEO of the Year Award Vol. 1: 8540
Financial Security Nest Egg Award Vol. 1: 11092
Finch Law Day U.S.A. Speech Award; Judge Edward R. Vol. 1: 1532
Finders Award Vol. 2: 6918
Findlay Plaque Vol. 1: 10246
Fine Art Award Vol. 1: 15852
Fine Art Show Vol. 1: 18244
Fine Arts Association of Finland Awards Vol. 2: 1595
Fine Arts; Wingate Rome Scholarship in the Vol. 2: 7144
Fine Arts Work Center Fellowships Vol. 1: 9553
Fine Awards; Benjamin Vol. 1: 14384
Fine Dining Hall of Fame Vol. 1: 16009
Fine Printing Awards Vol. 1: 11838
Finegan Standards Medal Vol. 1: 3183
Fink Literary Award; Louis C. Vol. 1: 14416
Fink Prize Award; Donald G. Vol. 1: 10860
Finkelstein Award Vol. 1: 8655
Finlaison Medal Vol. 2: 7645
Finlandia Award Vol. 1: 20804
Finlay Prize; Carlos J. Vol. 2: 2595
Finley Award; John H. Vol. 1: 518
Finn Gold Cup Vol. 2: 2474
Finneburgh Sr. Award of Excellence; M. L. Vol. 1: 14926
Finnish Academy of Technology Craftsman's Award Vol. 2: 1592
Finnish Academy of Technology Medal of Merit Vol. 2: 1593
Finnish Cultural Foundation's Annual Prize Vol. 2: 1599
Finnish Historical Society Correspondent Membership Vol. 2: 1604
Finnish Library Association Awards Vol. 2: 1606
Finnish Museums Association 50th Anniversary Medal Vol. 2: 1609

Award Index

Finnish Museums Association Medal Vol. 2: 1610
Finocchiaro Award for Excellence in the Development of Pedagogical Materials; Mary Vol. 1: 19950
Finot; Prix Jean Vol. 2: 2059
FIP Fellowships Vol. 2: 4831
FIP International Travel Scholarships Vol. 2: 4832
FIPRESCI Diploma Vol. 2: 5301
FIPRESCI Prize Vol. 2: 2670
FIRE Excellence Award Vol. 1: 16718
Fire Explorer Post Award Vol. 1: 11352
Fire Fighter of the Quarter Vol. 1: 6286
Fire Fighter of the Year Vol. 1: 14554
Fire Investigator of the Year Vol. 1: 14230
Fire Management Award Vol. 1: 9556
Fire Protection Man/Woman of the Year Vol. 1: 19128
Fire Safety Award
  Association of Building Engineers Vol. 2: 6800
  Fire Protection Association - England Vol 2: 7525
Fireball International Worlds Trophy Vol. 2: 7527
Fireman of the Year Vol. 1: 11616
Fireman of the Year (Relief Pitcher) Vol. 1: 19644
Firm of the Year Vol. 1: 20043
First Amendment Defender Award Vol. 1: 10823
First Book Prize Vol. 1: 18869
First Breeding Award
  Avicultural Advancement Council of Canada Vol. 1: 6140
  International Wild Waterfowl Association Vol 1: 12134
First Class Certificate Vol. 1: 3330
First Class Order of the Rising Sun Paulownia Flowers Vol. 2: 4189
First Data Corp. Outland Trophy Dinner Award Vol. 1: 10155
First Encounters Award Vol. 1: 10827
First Families Award Vol. 1: 9825
First Families of Seneca County Gold Award Vol. 1: 16638
First Families of Seneca County Silver Award Vol. 1: 16639
First Films World Competition Vol. 1: 13607
First Interstate Athletic Foundation Gymnastics Hall of Fame Award Vol. 1: 8159
First Novel Award
  Mordechai Bernstein Literary Prizes Association Vol. 2: 3730
  Black Caucus of the American Library Association Vol 1: 6413
First Poetry Book Award Vol. 2: 3731
First Professional Work Award Vol. 1: 16948
First Responder Award Vol. 1: 14232
First Step Award Vol. 1: 5428
First-Time Author of the Year Award Vol. 1: 6989
First-Time Exhibitor Award Vol. 1: 18574
First-Year Student Scholarship Vol. 1: 14883
Firth Essay Prize; J. B. Vol. 2: 7539
Fischer Environmental Award; Kermit Vol. 1: 12216
Fischer-Medaille; Emil- Vol. 2: 2806
Fischer-Medaille; Hellmuth Vol. 2: 2913
Fischer Medal; Helen Field Vol. 1: 2445
Fischer Memorial Cup; Donn Vol. 1: 2448
Fischer-Preis; Georg A. Vol. 2: 6519
Fischer Scholarship Vol. 1: 8894
Fischetti Editorial Cartoon Competition; John Vol. 1: 9564
Fischoff National Chamber Music Competition Vol. 1: 9566
Fish Memorial Award; Robert L. Vol. 1: 13730
Fisher Article Award; Irving Vol. 1: 16694
Fisher Award; Elaine R. "Boots" Vol. 1: 9436
Fisher Award; Eunice Vol. 1: 2555
Fisher Award for Media Support of the Arts; John P. Vol. 1: 8544
Fisher Award; Henry Johnson Vol. 1: 13014
Fisher Award; Ming Vol. 1: 5861
Fisher Award; R. A. Vol. 1: 8292
Fisher Career Grants; Avery Vol. 1: 12854
Fisher Children's Book Award; Dorothy Canfield Vol. 1: 21304
Fisher Diagnostics/Fisher Healthcare Educational Scholarship Vol. 1: 15715
Fisher Distinguished Writing Award; M. K. Vol. 1: 12288
Fisher Graduate Student Paper Prize; Sydney N. Vol. 1: 20241
Fisher Memorial Lecture Vol. 1: 11006
Fisher Memorial Lectureship; Jeanne Mannery Vol. 1: 7452
Fisher Memorial Prize; John
  American Society for Aesthetics Vol. 1: 3913
  Journal of Aesthetics and Art Criticism - Department of Philosophy Vol 1: 12444
Fisher Prize; Avery Vol. 1: 12855
Fisher Resident Award; Alexander A. Vol. 1: 2013
Fisher Scientific Company Award for Applied and Environmental Microbiology Vol. 1: 4138
Fisher Scientific Lecture Award Vol. 1: 7829
Fisherman Foundation Awards for Clinical Research; Miles and Shirley Vol. 1: 9711
Fisherman of the Year Vol. 1: 18230
Fishman Memorial Award; Miles D. Vol. 1: 12031
F.I.S.I. Prize Vol. 2: 4059
FISITA Travelling Fellowship Vol. 2: 7932
Fisk Fiction Prize Vol. 1: 6521
FIT C. B. Nathhorst Translation Prize Vol. 1: 11607
FIT - Translation Prize Vol. 1: 11607
Fiterman Foundation Basic Research Awards; Miles and Shirley Vol. 1: 9709
Fitts Education Award; Paul M. Vol. 1: 10580
Fitz Award; Mr. Vol. 1: 15921
Fitzgerald Award; Aidan P. Vol. 2: 3649
Fitzgerald Award for Ecumenism; James Vol. 1: 14194
Fitzgerald Award; James Vol. 1: 14194
Fitzgerald Coke Medal; Major Edward D'Ewes Vol. 2: 7560
Fitzgerald Rookie of the Year; Jim Vol. 1: 19691
FitzPatrick Award for Youth Literature; Percy Vol. 2: 5548
FitzPatrick Prize; Percy Vol. 2: 5548
Five Star Hospitality Awards Vol. 1: 18195
Five State Exhibition Vol. 1: 12500
Five Year Research Support Program Vol. 1: 12979
Fixed Wing Scholarship Vol. 1: 5547
The F.L. "Gus" Cooper Award for Meritorous Service Vol. 1: 11093
Flach; Prix Jacques Vol. 2: 2057
Flach; Prix Marcel Vol. 2: 2076
Flack Memorial Trophy; David Vol. 2: 7198
Flag Certificate Vol. 1: 15769
Flagg Multicultural Award; Ann Vol. 1: 891
Flags of America Award Vol. 1: 15050
Flaherty Documentary Award Vol. 2: 6905
Flaherty Memorial Lectureship; Mara Mogensen Vol. 1: 16719
Flaiano; Premio Internazionale Enno Vol. 2: 3849
Flame Award Vol. 2: 7529
Flame of Courage Award Vol. 1: 7553
Flammarion; Plaquette du Centenaire de Camille Vol. 2: 2561
Flammarion; Prix Gabrielle et Camille Vol. 2: 2553
Flanagan Award; John C. Vol. 1: 18754
Flandrin/Michon Life Achievement Award Vol. 1: 2382
Flat; Prix Paul Vol. 2: 2196
Flattie International Yacht Racing Association Championship Vol. 1: 9905
Flavelle Medal Vol. 1: 18165
Fleck Prize; Ludwik Vol. 1: 18857
Fleet Safety Award
  American Trucking Associations - Safety Management Council Vol. 1: 4775
  Specialized Carriers and Rigging Association Vol 1: 19585
Fleet Safety Improvement Award Vol. 1: 19585
Fleet Safety/Safety Improvement Awards Vol. 1: 19578
Fleischmann International Trophy Competition Vol. 2: 3628
Fleischner Society Memorial Award Vol. 1: 9570
Fleming Award; Alexander Vol. 1: 10791
Fleming Award for Environmental Achievement; Charles Vol. 2: 5080
Fleming Award; John Adam Vol. 1: 2349
Fleming Award; Rodney R. Vol. 1: 3801
Fleming Lecture Vol. 2: 8933
Fleming Premium; Ambrose Vol. 2: 7808
Fleming Prize; Robert Vol. 1: 6793
Flemming Steel Dagger; The Ian Vol. 2: 7367
Fletcher Award; George Vol. 1: 7062
Fletcher Memorial Lecture; Ernest Vol. 2: 8810
Fletcher Research Award; Eric Vol. 2: 8942
Fletcher Scholar Awards Vol. 1: 7557
Fleur-de-Lis Awards Vol. 1: 12980
Fleuroselect Gold Medal Vol. 2: 4773
Fleuroselect Quality Award Vol. 2: 4774
Fleury-Mesplet Literary Prize Vol. 1: 18234
Flexner Award for Distinguished Service to Medical Education; Abraham Vol. 1: 5560
Flight Achievement Award; AAS Vol. 1: 1497
Flight Instructor of the Year Award Program Vol. 1: 9432
Flight Nurse of the Year Award Vol. 1: 234
Flight Simulation Silver Medal Vol. 2: 8386
Flinders Medal and Lecture Vol. 2: 121
Flinn III Award; Edward A. Vol. 1: 2350
Flintoff Medal Vol. 2: 8751
Flipper trophies Vol. 2: 2342
Flisser; Premio Lola e Igo Vol. 2: 4600
FLMI Insurance Education Award Vol. 1: 12844
Floor of the Year Contest Vol. 1: 15971
Florence Roberts Head Memorial Award; Ohioana Award, Vol. 1: 16658
Florey Fellowship; Howard Vol. 2: 6812
Florian Prize; Mircea Vol. 2: 5829
Floricultural Hall of Fame Vol. 1: 18966

Floriculture Award Vol. 1: 9613
Florida Artists Hall of Fame Vol. 1: 9587
Florida Arts Recognition Awards Vol. 1: 9588
Florida Citrus Sports Scholar-Athlete Award Vol. 1: 15073
Florida Folk Heritage Awards Vol. 1: 9626
Florida Space Coast Writers Conference Awards Vol. 1: 19535
Florida State Poets Association, Inc. Award Vol. 1: 14993
Florio Prize; John Vol. 2: 8971
Flormanska Beloningen Vol. 2: 6211
Flory Polymer Education Award; Paul J. Vol. 1: 1754
Fluckiger Medaille Vol. 2: 2683
Flude Memorial Prize Vol. 2: 7045
Fluegelman Award; Andrew Vol. 1: 17114
Fluid and Plasmadynamics Award Vol. 1: 2649
Fluid Dynamics Prize Vol. 1: 3457
Fluid Power Achievement Award Vol. 1: 15054
Fluidized Processes Recognition Award Vol. 1: 2769
Fluids Engineering Award Vol. 1: 4509
Fluke Corporation Award for Excellence in Laboratory Instruction Vol. 1: 3994
Flute Competition; Jean-Pierre Rampal International Vol. 2: 2282
Fluvanna Prize Vol. 1: 13003
Fly Neighborly Award Vol. 1: 10392
Flying Fifteen World Championship Vol. 2: 7532
Flynn Humanitarian Award; Charles H. Vol. 1: 20918
Flynn Initiative for Peace Award; William J. Vol. 1: 14701
FM Foundation Downtown Beautification Grant Vol. 1: 16556
FMCT Playwrights Competition Vol. 1: 9414
FMI - *Woman's Day* Advertising Merit Awards Vol. 1: 9661
FOCAL Award Vol. 1: 12929
Foch; Prix Marechal Vol. 2: 2184
"Focus on Disability" Grant Vol. 1: 21715
"Focus on Discrimination" Grant Vol. 1: 21716
Focus on Education Vol. 1: 8694
Focus on World Cinema Vol. 1: 13607
Foer Memorial Award; Melvin B. Vol. 1: 8906
Foerderpreis der Werner-Sunkel-Stiftung Vol. 2: 2855
Foerderpreis des AULA-Verlags Vol. 2: 2856
Foerster Memorial Lecture; Theodor Vol. 2: 2796
Folger Shakespeare Library Fellowships and National Endowment for the Humanities Senior Fellowships Vol. 1: 9646
Foliage Hall of Fame Vol. 1: 9611
Foliage Writer of the Year Contest Vol. 1: 9612
Folk Heritage Award Vol. 1: 16503
Folk Music Festival - Plaketti Vol. 2: 1647
Folklife Museum of Trentino Prize Vol. 2: 4059
Follereau; Prix Raoul Vol. 2: 2205
Follett Library Resources & Software Companies Excellence in Teaching Award (Graduate School of Library and Information Science) Vol. 1: 8989
Follett School Librarian of the Year Award Vol. 1: 5056
Foltz Award; Clara Shortridge Vol. 1: 15337
FOLUSA/Baker & Taylor Books Award Vol. 1: 9792
Folz Memorial Award Vol. 1: 14739
FON Achievement Award Vol. 1: 16760
FON Achievement Certificates Vol. 1: 16765
FON Conservation Award Vol. 1: 16763
FON Conservation Trophy Vol. 1: 16762
FON Corporate Award Vol. 1: 16761
FON Distinguished Service Award Vol. 1: 16759
Fond; Operasangerinnen Fanny Elstas Vol. 2: 5123
Fondation Aime Berthe Vol. 2: 1782
Fondation Aime Laussedat Vol. 2: 1783
Fondation Albert I de Monaco Vol. 2: 1784
Fondation Alexandre Darracq Vol. 2: 1785
Fondation Alexandre Joannides Vol. 2: 1786
Fondation Alfred Durand-Claye Vol. 2: 1787
Fondation Alfred Dutens Vol. 2: 1788
Fondation Alhumbert Vol. 2: 1789
Fondation Alphonse Laveran Vol. 2: 1790
Fondation Anatole et Suzanne Abragam Vol. 2: 1791
Fondation Ancel Vol. 2: 1792
Fondation Andre C. Bonnet Vol. 2: 1793
Fondation Andre Lallemand Vol. 2: 1794
Fondation Andre Policard-Lacassagne Vol. 2: 1795
Fondation Andre-Romain Prevot Vol. 2: 1796
Fondation Aniuta Winter-Klein Vol. 2: 1797
Fondation Antoine d'Abbadie Vol. 2: 1798
Fondation Antoinette Janssen Vol. 2: 1799
Fondation Arago Vol. 2: 1800
Fondation Argut Vol. 2: 1801
Fondation Arthur du Fay Vol. 2: 1802
Fondation Auguste Chevalier Vol. 2: 1803
Fondation Ayme Poirson Vol. 2: 1804
Fondation Barbier Vol. 2: 1805
Fondation Bariot-Faynot Vol. 2: 1806
Fondation Berthelot Vol. 2: 1807
Fondation Bigot de Morogues Vol. 2: 1808
Fondation Binoux Vol. 2: 1809
Fondation Boileau Vol. 2: 1810
Fondation Bordin Vol. 2: 1811
Fondation Breant Vol. 2: 1812
Fondation Cahours, Houzeau Vol. 2: 1813
Fondation Camere Vol. 2: 1814
Fondation Carre-Bessault Vol. 2: 1815
Fondation Carriere de Mathematiques Vol. 2: 1816
Fondation Carriere de Mineralogie Vol. 2: 1817
Fondation Charles-Adam Girard Vol. 2: 1818
Fondation Charles Dhere Vol. 2: 1819
Fondation Charles Eugene Guye Vol. 2: 1820
Fondation Charles Fremont Vol. 2: 1821
Fondation Charles Jacob Vol. 2: 1822
Fondation Charles-Leopold Mayer Vol. 2: 1823
Fondation Charles-Louis de Saulses de Freycinet Vol. 2: 1824
Fondation Chaussier Vol. 2: 1825
Fondation Chedanne Vol. 2: 1717
Fondation Claude Lallemand Vol. 2: 1826
Fondation Clavel Vol. 2: 1827
Fondation Clement Felix Vol. 2: 1828
Fondation Coron-Thevenet Vol. 2: 1829
Fondation Costantino Gorini Vol. 2: 1830
Fondation Cuvier Vol. 2: 1831
Fondation Da Gama Machado Vol. 2: 1832
Fondation Damoiseau Vol. 2: 1833
Fondation Dandrimont-Benicourt Vol. 2: 1834
Fondation Danton Vol. 2: 1835
Fondation Daumet Vol. 2: 1717
Fondation de Caen Vol. 2: 1717
Fondation de Coincy Vol. 2: 1836
Fondation de la Fons-Melicocq Vol. 2: 1837
Fondation de Madame Albert Demolon Vol. 2: 1838
Fondation de Madame Edmond Hamel Vol. 2: 1839
Fondation de Madame Victor Noury Vol. 2: 1840
Fondation de Mme. Veuve Beule Vol. 2: 1717
Fondation Delalande-Guerineau Vol. 2: 1841
Fondation Delesse Vol. 2: 1842
Fondation Demolombe Vol. 2: 1843
Fondation Deslandres Vol. 2: 1844
Fondation Desmazieres Vol. 2: 1845
Fondation du Baron de Joest Vol. 2: 1846
Fondation du Baron Larrey Vol. 2: 1847
Fondation du Docteur et de Madame Henri Labbe Vol. 2: 1848
Fondation du Docteur et de Madame Peyre Vol. 2: 1849
Fondation du Docteur Jean Toy Vol. 2: 1850
Fondation du General Ferrie Vol. 2: 1851
Fondation du General Muteau Vol. 2: 1852
Fondation Dulac Vol. 2: 1689
Fondation Dusgate Vol. 2: 1853
Fondation Edmond Brun Vol. 2: 1854
Fondation Edmond Fagnan Vol. 2: 1006
Fondation Elie Cartan Vol. 2: 1855
Fondation Emil Picard Vol. 2: 1856
Fondation Emile Jungfleisch Vol. 2: 1857
Fondation Emile Waxweiler Vol. 2: 1007
Fondation Ernest Dechelle Vol. 2: 1858
Fondation Ernest Mahaim Vol. 2: 1008
Fondation Eugene et Amelie Dupuis Vol. 2: 1859
Fondation Fanny Emden Vol. 2: 1860
Fondation Fernand Holweck Vol. 2: 1861
Fondation Fontannes Vol. 2: 1862
Fondation Foulon Vol. 2: 1863
Fondation Fourneyron Vol. 2: 1864
Fondation Francoeur Vol. 2: 1865
Fondation Frederic Forthuny Vol. 2: 1866
Fondation G. de Pontecoulant Vol. 2: 1867
Fondation Gabrielle Sand Vol. 2: 1868
Fondation Gaston Rousseau Vol. 2: 1869
Fondation Gay Vol. 2: 1870
Fondation Gegner Vol. 2: 1871
Fondation General Muteau Vol. 2: 2094
Fondation Georges Deflandre et Marthe Deflandre-Rigaud Vol. 2: 1872
Fondation Georges Millot Vol. 2: 1873
Fondation Godard Vol. 2: 1874
Fondation Grammaticakis-Neuman Vol. 2: 1875
Fondation Gustave Clausse Vol. 2: 1717
Fondation Gustave Germain Vol. 2: 1717
Fondation Gustave Ribaud Vol. 2: 1876
Fondation Gustave Roussy Vol. 2: 1877
Fondation Gustave Roux Vol. 2: 1878
Fondation Helene Helbronner-Fould Vol. 2: 1879
Fondation Henri Becquerel Vol. 2: 1880
Fondation Henri de Parville Vol. 2: 1881
Fondation Henri Mondor Vol. 2: 1882
Fondation Henri Pirenne Vol. 2: 1009
Fondation Henri Poincare Vol. 2: 1883
Fondation Henriette Regnier Vol. 2: 1884
Fondation Henry Bazin Vol. 2: 1885
Fondation Henry Giffard Vol. 2: 1886
Fondation Henry Le Chatelier Vol. 2: 1887
Fondation Henry Wilde Vol. 2: 1888

Award Index

Fondation Hirn Vol. 2: 1889
Fondation Hughes Vol. 2: 1890
Fondation Ivan Peyches Vol. 2: 1891
Fondation Jacques Bourcart Vol. 2: 1892
Fondation Jaffe Vol. 2: 2425
Fondation James Hall Vol. 2: 1893
Fondation Janine Courrier Vol. 2: 1894
Fondation Janssen Vol. 2: 1895
Fondation Jean-Baptiste Dumas Vol. 2: 1896
Fondation Jean Cuvillier Vol. 2: 1897
Fondation Jean Dagnan-Bouveret Vol. 2: 1898
Fondation Jean de Meyer Vol. 2: 1035
Fondation Jean de Rufz de La Vison Vol. 2: 1899
Fondation Jean du Hamel de Breuil Vol. 2: 1900
Fondation Jean-Jacques Berger Vol. 2: 1901
Fondation Jean Lebrun Vol. 2: 1036
Fondation Jean-Marie Le Goff Vol. 2: 1902
Fondation Jean-Paul Alaux Vol. 2: 1717
Fondation Jean Reynaud Vol. 2: 1903
Fondation Jean Thore Vol. 2: 1904
Fondation Jecker Vol. 2: 1905
Fondation Jerome Ponti Vol. 2: 1906
Fondation Joseph Labbe Vol. 2: 1907
Fondation Kastner-Boursault Vol. 2: 1908
Fondation Kodak-Pathe-Landucci Vol. 2: 1909
Fondation L. La Caze Vol. 2: 1910
Fondation La Caille Vol. 2: 1911
Fondation Lamb Vol. 2: 1912
Fondation Langevin Vol. 2: 1913
Fondation Lannelongue Vol. 2: 1914
Fondation Laplace Vol. 2: 1915
Fondation Laura Mounier de Saridakis Vol. 2: 1916
Fondation Lavoisier Vol. 2: 1917
Fondation Le Conte Vol. 2: 1918
Fondation Leon-Alexandre Etancelin Vol. 2: 1919
Fondation Leon Grelaud Vol. 2: 1920
Fondation Leon Lutaud Vol. 2: 1921
Fondation Leon Velluz Vol. 2: 1922
Fondation Lonchampt Vol. 2: 1923
Fondation Louis Armand Vol. 2: 1924
Fondation Louis-Daniel Beauperthuy Vol. 2: 1925
Fondation Louise Darracq Vol. 2: 1926
Fondation Lucien Cayeux Vol. 2: 1927
Fondation Marie Guido Triossi Vol. 2: 1928
Fondation Marie Leon-Houry Vol. 2: 1929
Fondation Marmottan Vol. 2: 1717
Fondation Marquet Vol. 2: 1930
Fondation Martin-Damourette Vol. 2: 1931
Fondation Maujean Vol. 2: 1932
Fondation Max-Fernand Jayle Vol. 2: 1933
Fondation Max Poll Vol. 2: 1037
Fondation Mege Vol. 2: 1934
Fondation Memain-Pelletier Vol. 2: 2426
Fondation Mergier-Bourdeix Vol. 2: 1935
Fondation Millet-Ronssin Vol. 2: 1936
Fondation Montagne Vol. 2: 1937
Fondation Montyon de Medicine et Chirugie Vol. 2: 1938
Fondation Montyon de Physiologie Vol. 2: 1939
Fondation Montyon des Arts Insalubres Vol. 2: 1940
Fondation Montyon des Statistiques Vol. 2: 1941
Fondation Nicolas Zvorikine Vol. 2: 1942
Fondation Octave Dupont Vol. 2: 1038
Fondation Odette Lemenon Vol. 2: 1943
Fondation Parkin Vol. 2: 1944
Fondation Paul Bertrand Vol. 2: 1945
Fondation Paul Doistau - Emile Blutet Vol. 2: 1946
Fondation Paul Fallot-Jeremine Vol. 2: 1947
Fondation Paul Gallet Vol. 2: 1948
Fondation Paul Marguerite de la Charlonie Vol. 2: 1949
Fondation Paul Pascal Vol. 2: 1950
Fondation Petit d'Ormoy Vol. 2: 1951
Fondation Philipeaux Vol. 2: 1952
Fondation Philippe A. Guye Vol. 2: 1953
Fondation Pierre Lafitte Vol. 2: 1954
Fondation Pierson-Perrin Vol. 2: 1955
Fondation Pinette Vol. 2: 1717
Fondation Plumey Vol. 2: 1956
Fondation Poncelet Vol. 2: 1957
Fondation Pouchard Vol. 2: 1958
Fondation Pourat Vol. 2: 1959
Fondation Redon Vol. 2: 1717
Fondation Rene Dujarric de la Riviere Vol. 2: 1960
Fondation Roberge Vol. 2: 1961
Fondation Rochat-Juliard Vol. 2: 1962
Fondation Rogissart-Sarazin-Vandevyere Vol. 2: 1963
Fondation Roy-Vaucouloux Vol. 2: 1964
Fondation Savigny Vol. 2: 1965
Fondation Schutzenberger Vol. 2: 1966
Fondation Serres Vol. 2: 1967
Fondation Servant Vol. 2: 1968
Fondation Tchihatchef Vol. 2: 1969
Fondation Theurlot Vol. 2: 1970
Fondation Thorlet
  Academie des Sciences Vol. 2: 1971
  Academie des Sciences Morales et Politiques Vol 2: 2012
Fondation Tregouboff Vol. 2: 1972
Fondation Tremont Vol. 2: 1973
Fondation Vaillant Vol. 2: 1974
Fondation Victor Raulin Vol. 2: 1975
Fondation Victor Thebault Vol. 2: 1976
Fondations Bellion - Charles Bouchard Vol. 2: 1977
Fondations Estrade Delcros, Houllevigue, Saintour, Jules Mahyer Vol. 2: 1978
Fondations Gaston Plante, Francois Hebert-Paul Jousselin Vol. 2: 1979
Fondations Lalande - Benjamin Valz Vol. 2: 1980
Fondazione Eugenio Morelli Vol. 2: 3816
Fondazione Francesco Sarerio Nitti Prize Vol. 2: 3817
Fondazione Giorgio Maria Sangiorgi Vol. 2: 3818
Fondazione Giovanni Di Guglielmo Vol. 2: 3819
Fondazione Guido Donegani Vol. 2: 3820
Fondazione Guido Lenghi e Flaviano Magrassi Vol. 2: 3821
Fondazione Premio Dotte Giuseppe Borgia Vol. 2: 3822
Fondazione Valeria Vincenzo Landi Vol. 2: 3823
Fondazione Wilhelm Conrad Rontgen Vol. 2: 3824
Fondiller Prize; Woodward - Vol. 1: 7622
Fondo Puertorriqueno para el Financiamiento del Quehacer Cultural Vol. 1: 11087
Fones Award; Alfred C. Vol. 1: 2130
Fontaine Prize; Rene Vol. 2: 7462
Fontaine Trophy; Frank Vol. 1: 2514
Fontannes; Prix Vol. 2: 2407
Food & Hotel Asia Competition
  Chefs and Cooks Circle Vol. 2: 7303
  National Restaurant Association Vol 1: 15625
  Society of German Cooks Vol 2: 3064
Food; Award for Technical Innovation in Enhancing Production of Safe Affordable Vol. 1: 7439
Food Industry Award Vol. 1: 14943
Food, Pharmaceutical and Bioengineering Division Award in Chemical Engineering Vol. 1: 2770
Food Technology Industrial Achievement Award Vol. 1: 10939
Foodservice Operator of the Year Vol. 1: 11631
Foot in Mouth Award Vol. 2: 8270
Football Writer of the Year Vol. 2: 4425
Foote Award; Lucy B. Vol. 1: 12938
Footing of the Year Award Vol. 1: 20565
Footwear Fashion Future Award Vol. 2: 2867
FOP86 Scholarship Fund Vol. 1: 9752
For Budapest Award Vol. 2: 3236
For Church and Profession (of Pharmacy) Award Vol. 1: 14629
For Peace and Friendship International Song Contest Vol. 1: 11594
For Service of the Capital Award Vol. 2: 3237
FORATOM Award Vol. 2: 891
Foray Award; June Vol. 1: 11191
Forbes Award; Harriette Merrifield Vol. 1: 5376
Forbes Award; Malcolm Vol. 1: 16981
Forbes Memorial Award; Carrol Vol. 1: 12039
Ford Award; Betty Vol. 1: 19849
Ford Award; Fred Vol. 1: 19314
Ford Award of Excellence; Henry Vol. 1: 13555
Ford Awards; Lester R. Vol. 1: 13191
Ford Distinguished Fellow Award; Loretta C. Vol. 1: 14322
Ford/Farmer's Journal Riding Club Jumping Chase Vol. 2: 3694
Ford Foundation Postdoctoral Diversity Fellowships Vol. 1: 15622
Ford II Distinguished Award for Excellence in Automotive Engineering; Henry Vol. 1: 19043
Ford Prize for Distinguished Reporting on National Defense; Gerald R. Vol. 1: 9681
Ford Prize for Distinguished Reporting on the Presidency; Gerald R. Vol. 1: 9682
Forder Lectureship Vol. 2: 8088
Forderpreis der ITG Vol. 2: 2928
Forderpreis fur hervorragende Diplomarbeiten auf dem Gebiet der Innenarchitektur Vol. 2: 2841
Forderungspreis der Osterreichische Gesellschaft fur Klinische Chemie Vol. 2: 779
Fordetungspreis fur Wissenschalt Vol. 2: 673
Fordham Award for Cartobibliography; Sir George Vol. 2: 8516
Fordham - Stein Prize Vol. 1: 9684
Foreign Honorary Fellow Vol. 2: 2328
Foreign Honorary Member Vol. 1: 2157
Foreign Language and Area Studies Awards
  Columbia University - Southern Asian Institute Vol. 1: 8256
  University of Wisconsin—Madison - Center for South Asia Vol 1: 21121

The Foreign Press Association British Media Award Vol. 2: 7537
Foreign Service Award Vol. 1: 20541
Foreign Service National of the Year Award Vol. 1: 20542
Foreign Service Office Management Specialist of the Year/Civil Service Secretary of the Year Vol. 1: 20543
Foreman Award; Robert L. Vol. 1: 5007
Foremarke Cup Vol. 2: 8547
Forensic Science Society Awards Vol. 2: 7539
The Forensic Sciences Award Vol. 1: 5949
Forero Prize; Manuel Vol. 2: 1324
Forest Capital of Canada Award Vol. 1: 7119
Forest Landowner Award Vol. 1: 9699
Forest Products Division Award in Chemical Engineering Vol. 1: 2771
Forest Runes Award Vol. 1: 5153
Forest Stewardship State of the Year Vol. 1: 15978
Foresters' Ring Vol. 1: 7178
Forestry Award of the Southern African Institute of Forestry; The Distinguished Vol. 2: 5710
Forestry Department Accreditation Vol. 1: 19202
Forkosch Prize; Morris D. Vol. 1: 2472
Forman Award; Jonathan Vol. 1: 651
Formation Evaluation Award Vol. 1: 19242
Forms and Brochures Contest Awards Vol. 1: 11035
Forrest Medal; James Vol. 2: 7764
Forrestal III, Leadership Award for Professional Ethics and Standards of Investment Practice; Daniel J. Vol. 1: 5395
Forster Award Vol. 1: 10652
Forsyth Award; Charles Vol. 1: 7637
Fort Dodge Animal Health - Bovine Practitioner of the Year Award Vol. 1: 1124
Fortescue Fellowship; Charles LeGeyt Vol. 1: 10861
Forthuny; Fondation Frederic Vol. 2: 1866
Fortuny; Prix Pascal Vol. 2: 2195
Forty Year Membership Pin Vol. 1: 3221
Forty Year Plaque Vol. 1: 8030
Foss Award; Hal Vol. 1: 14038
Foss Award; Joseph J. Vol. 1: 2237
Foster Award; Eugene Vol. 1: 2448
Foster Fellows Visiting Scholars Program; William C. Vol. 1: 20402
FosterGrant Reading Glasses Romantic Novel of the Year Vol. 2: 8347
Fould; Prix Louis Vol. 2: 1772
Fould-Stirbey; Prix Achille Vol. 2: 1699
Foulois Memorial Award; Maj. Gen. Benjamin D. Vol. 1: 16826
Foundation Award Vol. 1: 11847
Foundation Award for Outstanding Achievement Vol. 1: 15355
Foundation Award to the Technician of the Year in the Rolls-Royce Dealer Network Chosen by a Craft Competition Vol. 2: 563
Foundation Clinical Surgery Fellowship Vol. 1: 1311
Foundation for Gifted and Talented Children Vol. 1: 12166
Foundation for Hematological Research Vol. 2: 4214
Foundation for Research Science and Technology Science Communicator Awards Vol. 2: 5014
Foundation for the Promotion of Finnish Music Grant or Prize Vol. 2: 1618
Foundation Grants-in-Aid Vol. 1: 1337
Foundation Prestige Lectures Vol. 2: 564
Foundation Prize Awards Vol. 1: 2379
Foundation Research Award Vol. 1: 1312
Founder and First President Award Vol. 1: 11665
Founder Award Vol. 1: 4756
Founder's Award
Academy of Criminal Justice Sciences Vol. 1: 90
American Academy of Neurology Vol 1: 699
American Academy of Optometry Vol 1: 719
American Alliance for Theatre and Education Vol 1: 896
Civitan International Vol 1: 8063
Military Audiology Association Vol 1: 13401
Polycystic Ovarian Syndrome Association Vol 1: 17465
Pratt Institute Vol 1: 17520
Society of Architectural Historians Vol 1: 19021
Founders Award
American Academy of Pediatrics Vol. 1: 770
American Hockey Coaches Association Vol 1: 2493
American Society for Engineering Management Vol 1: 4055
American Statistical Association Vol 1: 4693
American Truck Historical Society, Arizona Chapter Vol 1: 4759
American Truck Historical Society, Metro Jersey Chapter Vol 1: 4763
Brain Injury Association of America Vol 1: 6606
Business Committee for the Arts Vol 1: 6703
Confederate Memorial Literary Society Vol 1: 8352
Environmental and Conservation Organization Vol 1: 9296
Health Physics Society Vol 1: 10320
Indiana Black Expo Vol 1: 10757
International Council of the National Academy of Television Arts and Sciences Vol 1: 11519
National Academy of Engineering Vol 1: 13807
National Association of Display Industries Vol 1: 14197
National Federation of State Poetry Societies Vol 1: 14994
Niagara University Vol 1: 16351
Scouting Ireland CSI Vol 2: 3705
Society For Biomaterials Vol 1: 18648
Founders' Award
CIIT Centers for Health Research Vol. 1: 7995
Educational Theatre Association Vol 1: 9181
The Founders Award Vol. 1: 6169
Founder's Award for Humane Excellence Vol. 1: 4196
Founders Award for Outstanding Contributions to the Field of Chemical Engineering Vol. 1: 2772
Founders' Award for Public Service Vol. 1: 5701
Founders Award of American Truck Historical Society Vol. 1: 4761
Founders Award Program Vol. 1: 15725
Founders' Awards Vol. 1: 18500
Founder's Day Alumni/Alumnae Citations Vol. 1: 12969
Founder's Favorite Winner Award Vol. 1: 15479
Founder's Lecture Vol. 2: 9004
Founder's Medal
Association of Military Surgeons of the United States Vol. 1: 5771
Royal Geographical Society with the Institute of British Geographers Vol 2: 8520
Founders Medal
Institute of Electrical and Electronics Engineers Vol. 1: 10862
International Society of Logistics Vol 1: 12000
National Academy of Engineering Vol 1: 13807
Founders' Memorial Award Vol. 1: 8998
Founders of Adolescent Health Award Vol. 1: 771
Founders' Prize Vol. 2: 7009
Founder's Trophy Vol. 1: 20772
Founding Chapter Scholarship Award Vol. 1: 19151
Founding Societies' Centenary Award Vol. 2: 7663
Foundrymen Honorary Fellow; Institute of British Vol. 2: 7655
Fountain of Universal Peace Award Vol. 1: 11343
The Fountainhead Essay Contest Vol. 1: 6174
Four Freedoms Medal Vol. 1: 9737
Four Masters Award Vol. 1: 12195
Four Seasons Critics Awards Vol. 1: 20116
Four Wheel Drive Truck Puller of the Year Vol. 1: 15882
Four-Year College Biology Teaching Award Vol. 1: 14093
Fourmarier; Prix Paul Vol. 2: 1066
Fournier Prize; Pierre Vol. 2: 2283
Fowler Award; Raymond D. Vol. 1: 18911
Fox Award; Ruth Berrien Vol. 1: 16110
Fox Communications Award; Muriel Vol. 1: 12770
Fox Founder's Award; A. Roger Vol. 1: 14211
Fox Manuscript Prize; Dixon Ryan Vol. 1: 16288
Fox, M.D. Memorial Lectureship; Everett C. Vol. 1: 637
Fox Medal; E. J. Vol. 2: 7654
Fox Trophy; UFFA Vol. 2: 7532
The Foxy Vol. 1: 12770
FPGA Scholarship Program Vol. 1: 9615
Fracture Mechanics Medal; Committee E-8 Vol. 1: 5939
Fraenkel Prize Vol. 2: 9212
Fraenkel Prize in Contemporary History Vol. 2: 7686
Fragrance Foundation Hall of Fame Vol. 1: 9720
Fragrance Foundation Recognition Awards (FIFI Awards) Vol. 1: 9720
The Fragrance Hall of Fame Award (Men's and Women's) Vol. 1: 9720
Fragrance Packaging Introductions of the Year Vol. 1: 9720
Fraiberg Award; Selma Vol. 1: 13332
Framstaende Popularvetenskaplig Publicering I Vaxtfysiologi Vol. 2: 1536
France Hellebrandt Professional Opportunity Awards; Caroline tum Suden/ Vol. 1: 3512

France Telecom; Prix Vol. 2: 1996
Francia Downes Memorial Shield Vol. 2: 828
Francis New Medal Vol. 2: 7951
Franciscan International Award Vol. 1: 9728
Francisco da Gama Caeiro Vol. 2: 5484
Franck Organ Competition; Cesar Vol. 2: 4776
Franck Orgelconcours; Cesar Vol. 2: 4776
Francke Leadership Mentor Award; Gloria Niemeyer Vol. 1: 3387
Francken-prijs; Dr. Wijnaendts Vol. 2: 4912
Franco-British Landscape Gardening Award Vol. 2: 7543
Franco Prize; Roberto Vol. 2: 1325
Francoeur; Prix Albert-Emile Vol. 1: 6626
Francois Award; Jules Vol. 1: 11603
Francoisprijs Vol. 2: 4856
Francou Legacy; Andre Vol. 1: 18136
Francqui Prize Vol. 2: 893
Frandson Award for Innovative Programming; Phillip E. Vol. 1: 20953
Frandson Award for Sustained Excellence; Phillip E. Vol. 1: 20954
Frank Award; Josette Vol. 1: 7901
Frank Award; Morton Vol. 1: 16981
Frank Memorial Lecturer Award; Sally Vol. 1: 1107
Frank Munro Memorial Trophy Vol. 1: 8073
Frankfurter Guckkastenmaennchen - Lucas Vol. 2: 2689
Frankland Fellowship; Sir Edward Vol. 2: 8752
Frankland Prize Lectureship; Sir Edward Vol. 2: 8753
Franklin Award; Ben Vol. 1: 7950
Franklin Award for Federal Excess Personal Property Vol. 1: 9557
Franklin Award for State Fire Assistance Vol. 1: 9558
Franklin Award for Volunteer Fire Assistance Vol. 1: 9559
Franklin Award; John A. Vol. 1: 7124
Franklin Awards; Benjamin Vol. 1: 17739
Franklin B.W. Woodbury Award for Special Achievement Vol. 1: 4056
Franklin Literary Award; Miles Vol. 2: 625
Franklin Medal; Benjamin Vol. 2: 8711
Franklin Medal for Distinguished Public Service; Benjamin Vol. 1: 3434
Franklin Medal; Ned Vol. 2: 7747
Franklin Mint Exhibit Award Vol. 1: 3199
Franklin Publication Prize; John Hope Vol. 1: 4708
Franklin Service Award; Jack Vol. 1: 20748
Franques Medal; Marti I. Vol. 2: 2749
Franz Schubert and the Music of Modern Times International Competition Vol. 2: 794
Franzmeier Memorial Award; Chapman- Vol. 1: 1108
Frary Award; Francis C. Vol. 1: 428
Fraser Award for Best Book of Translation; Soeurette Diehl Vol. 1: 20015
Fraser Award; Soeurette Diehl Vol. 1: 20015
Fraser Sculpture Award; James Earle Vol. 1: 14886
Fraternal Order of Eagles Education Scholarship Vol. 1: 9748
Fraternalist of the Year Award Vol. 1: 18157
Fraunces Tavern Museum Book Award Vol. 1: 19417
Fraunhofer Award/Robert M. Burley Prize; Joseph Vol. 1: 16785
Fred Graham Award for Innovation in Improving Community Health Vol. 1: 1883
The Fred H. Bossons Award Vol. 1: 18062
Frederic Ives Medal Vol. 1: 16786
Frederic Ives Medal/Jarus W. Quinn Endowment Vol. 1: 16786
Frederick Award for Outstanding Soldier - Major General Robert F. Frederick Award Vol. 1: 9562
Frederick Quality of Life Lecture; Purdue Vol. 1: 16720
Fredericq; Prix Leon et Henri Vol. 2: 1064
Free Enterprise Award Vol. 1: 11637
Free Market Award Vol. 2: 5561
Free Media Pioneer Vol. 2: 764
Free Spirit Award Vol. 1: 9756
Freedley Memorial Award; George Vol. 1: 20059
Freedman Award; Alfred M. Vol. 1: 12018
Freedom Award
 Action for Post-Soviet Jewry Vol. 1: 157
 Carolina's Citizens Freedom Foundation Vol 1: 7609
 Freedom House Vol 1: 9760
 Georgia Public Policy Foundation Vol 1: 9969
 Indiana Black Expo Vol 1: 10758
 International Rescue Committee - USA Vol 1: 11888
 Order of Lafayette Vol 1: 16837
Freedom Forum Playwriting Award Vol. 1: 12544
Freedom Leadership Medal Vol. 1: 9764
Freedom of Expression Award Vol. 1: 12294
Freedom of Information Award Vol. 1: 5251
Freedom of Speech Award Vol. 1: 19905
Freedom of the Human Spirit Award Vol. 1: 10629
Freedom Prize
 Max Schmidheiny Foundation Vol. 2: 6486
 Politiken Vol 2: 1518
Freedom to Read Roll of Honor Vol. 1: 9762
Freedom Torch Vol. 1: 11935
Freeman Award; Joseph T. Vol. 1: 9992
Freeman Award; Ruth Vol. 1: 2738
Freeman Fellowship Vol. 1: 4313
Freeman Lectureship in Geriatrics Vol. 1: 9992
Freeman Memorial Grant-in-Aid; Don Vol. 1: 19089
Freeman Scholar Award Vol. 1: 4510
Freeman Writing Award; Ned E. Vol. 1: 2041
Freese Environmental Engineering Award and Lecture; Simon W. Vol. 1: 4314
Freiburg Ecological Film Festival Vol. 2: 3040
Freiheitspreis Vol. 2: 6486
Freiman Award; Frank Vol. 1: 12010
Fremont; Fondation Charles Vol. 2: 1821
French-American Chamber of Commerce Person of the Year Award Vol. 1: 9768
French Association of Conchology Prize Vol. 2: 2342
French Medal; Sidney Vol. 2: 7094
French Most Valuable Player Award; William Vol. 1: 15316
French Music Scholarship; The Boyle Memorial Senior Vol. 1: 18275
French Tastemaker Awards; R. T. Vol. 1: 12285
French Wine and Spirits Sommelier Competition Vol. 1: 21651
Frend Medal Vol. 2: 8964
Frenkel Prize Vol. 2: 5932
Fresenius-Preis Vol. 2: 2807
Freshley Award; Marylene Vol. 1: 14528
Fresno-Madera Medical Society Scholarship Vol. 1: 9773
Freud Award; Sigmund Vol. 1: 4598
Freud-Preis; Sigmund- Vol. 2: 2774
Freudenthal Medal; Alfred M. Vol. 1: 4315
Freund Award; Clement J. Vol. 1: 4019
Freville; Prix Edmond Vol. 2: 2040
Frew National Leadership Award; Stephen A. Vol. 1: 14212
Freyssinet Award Vol. 2: 4981
Frick Award; Ford C. Vol. 1: 14494
Friedberg Lecture Vol. 1: 1679
Friedenpreis des Deutschen Buchhandels Vol. 2: 2865
Friedenwald Award Vol. 1: 5467
Friedenwald Memorial Award Vol. 1: 5465
Friedenwald Memorial Award; Jonas S. Vol. 1: 5465
Friedlander Award; Sheldon K. Vol. 1: 955
Friedlander/Sunday Times Watercolour competition; Singer Vol. 2: 8244
Friedman Award Medal; Lee Max Vol. 1: 2902
Friedman Essay Contest; Milton Vol. 1: 4921
Friedman Medal; Sue Tyler Vol. 2: 7561
Friedman Memorial Award; Harold Vol. 1: 10371
Friedman Professional Recognition Award; Edmund Vol. 1: 4316
Friedman Young Engineer Award for Professional Achievement; Edmund Vol. 1: 4317
Friel Memorial Lecture; Ernest Sheldon Vol. 2: 7479
Friend of Adoption Vol. 1: 14749
Friend of Automotive History Award Vol. 1: 19068
Friend of Casco Bay Award Vol. 1: 9788
Friend of Children Vol. 1: 19497
Friend of Children Award Vol. 1: 16419
Friend of Consumers Award Vol. 1: 2049
Friend of Education Award Vol. 1: 9387
Friend of History Vol. 1: 10504
Friend of Libraries U.S.A. Award (Friend of the Year) Vol. 1: 9793
Friend of Literacy Award Vol. 1: 17677
Friend of Recreation Vol. 1: 1030
Friend of the American Indian Vol. 1: 2596
Friend of the Florida Trail Award Vol. 1: 9638
Friend of the Homeless Award Vol. 1: 18532
Friend of the Industry Award Vol. 1: 422
Friend of the Legal Profession Award Vol. 1: 12590
Friend of the Maine Hospice Council Vol. 1: 13035
Friend of the Rottweiler Vol. 1: 3874
"Friend of the Satellite Dealer" Award; Pat Porter Memorial Award - Vol. 1: 9220
Friend of the Year Vol. 1: 9793
Friend of Tourism Vol. 1: 9849
Friend to Behavior Therapy; Distinguished Vol. 1: 5266
Friendly Sugar Hill; Annual Award for the Most Environment - Vol. 2: 5285
Friends of Historical Museum Awards Vol. 1: 9808
Friends of Libraries U.S.A. Award Vol. 1: 9792
Friends of Libraries U.S.A. Public Service Award Vol. 1: 9794
Friends of Old-Time Radio Award Vol. 1: 9797

Friends of Patrick Henry Awards Vol. 1: 9799
Friends of SEAISI Award Vol. 2: 4443
Friends of the Dallas Public Library Award Vol. 1: 20016
Friendship Award Vol. 1: 4727
Friendship Cup Vol. 2: 9069
Friendship Trophy Vol. 2: 4943
Frihedspris Vol. 2: 1518
Friman Best in Show; Elmer Vol. 1: 10333
Frink Medal for British Zoologists Vol. 2: 9279
Fris Award (Command and Control Unit of the Year); Edward S. Vol. 1: 13074
Frisch Medal Award Vol. 1: 9141
Frishmuth Memorial Award; Harriet W. Vol. 1: 5121
Friskies Canine Frisbee Disc World Championships Vol. 1: 13058
Frite Award Vol. 1: 1820
Frits Sobels Award Vol. 2: 2306
Fritz Award Vol. 1: 1820
Fritz Medal; John Vol. 1: 4318
Front Page Award Vol. 1: 10814
Front Page Awards Vol. 1: 21439
Front Range Young Farmers Scholarship Vol. 1: 9821
Frontiers of Science and Society - Rustum Roy Lecture Vol. 1: 1680
Frost Award; Dr. Lawrence A. Vol. 1: 12879
The Frost Medal Vol. 1: 17431
Froude Medal; William Vol. 2: 8616
Froude Research Scholarship in Naval Architecture Vol. 2: 8617
Frumkin Memorial Medal Vol. 2: 6454
Fry Award; Margery Vol. 1: 15445
Fry Lecture Award; Glenn A. Vol. 1: 720
Fry Medal Vol. 1: 7498
Fry Memorial Award; Elizabeth Vol. 1: 6903
Fry Memorial Lecture; William J. Vol. 1: 2857
FT/ARTS And Business Awards Vol. 2: 6750
FT/CEREC Award for Sponsorship of the Arts in a European Country Vol. 2: 6751
FTEC Certificate Vol. 2: 8228
Fuels and Petrochemical Division Award Vol. 1: 2773
Fuentes Fiction Award; Carlos Vol. 1: 8225
Fuerison; Prix Irene Vol. 2: 993
Fuertes Award; Louis Agassiz Vol. 1: 21637
Fuji/Association of Photographers Assistants' Awards Vol. 2: 6835
Fuji Gold Medal Award Vol. 1: 19191
Fujihara Award Vol. 2: 4116
Fulbright Awards - American Program Vol. 2: 139
Fulbright Awards - Australian Program Vol. 2: 140
Fulkerson Prize Vol. 1: 13200
Fuller Award; Oliver Torry Vol. 1: 5453
Fuller Award; Solomon Carter Vol. 1: 3618
Fuller Triennial Prostate Award; Eugene Vol. 1: 4790
Fullerton Award; Jim Vol. 1: 2489
Fulling Award; Edmund H. Vol. 1: 18666
Fullum Award; Ernest F. Vol. 1: 9039
Fulrath Award; Richard M. Vol. 1: 1681
Fulton Award Vol. 2: 5535
Fulton Awards Vol. 1: 108
Fulton-Downer Award Vol. 2: 4982
Fulton Toekenning Vol. 1: 108
Fund Dr. en Mevr. Schamelhout-Koettlitz Vol. 2: 973
Fund for New American Plays Vol. 1: 12550
Fund for the Advancement of Social Studies Education (FASSE) Grant Vol. 1: 14780
Furkert Award Vol. 2: 4983
Furlong Grant; Miriam Fay Vol. 1: 492
Furness Consumer Media Service Award; Betty Vol. 1: 8460
Furniss Award; Edgar S. Vol. 1: 16649
Furon; Prix Raymond et Madeleine Vol. 2: 2404
Furrand Award; Richard Vol. 2: 8664
Furuseth Award; Andrew Vol. 1: 20374
Futas Catalyst for Change Award; Elizabeth Vol. 1: 2975
Future Business Executive Vol. 1: 9843
Future Business Leaders Vol. 1: 9844
Future Business Teacher Vol. 1: 9845
Future Leader Award Vol. 2: 4953
Future Leader Awards Vol. 1: 11725
Future Science Teacher Awards Vol. 1: 6750
Futuristic Award
National Federation of State Poetry Societies Vol. 1: 14989
National Federation of State Poetry Societies Vol 1: 14995
Fvan Public Library Research Grant; Loleta D. Vol. 1: 2976
G. Trombetta Teaching Award Vol. 1: 3979
Gabbay Award in Biotechnology and Medicine; Jacob Heskel Vol. 1: 18126
Gabor Award; Dennis Vol. 1: 19607
Gabor Medal Vol. 2: 8697
Gabreski Award; Francis S. Vol. 1: 2238
Gabriel Award Vol. 1: 7633
Gabriel Award for Personal Achievement Vol. 1: 7633
Gabriel Dissertation Prize; Ralph Henry Vol. 1: 4709
Gaede-Langmuir Award Vol. 1: 6148
Gagarin Gold Medal; Yuri A. Vol. 2: 6334
Gagne Instructional Development Research Award; Robert M. Vol. 1: 5357
Gahan Scholarship or Development Grant; Muriel Vol. 2: 3695
Gaige Fund Award Vol. 1: 4451
Gain Program Awards Vol. 1: 3114
Gaines Award Vol. 1: 904
Gaines Medal for Good Sportsmanship Vol. 1: 16320
Gairn E.E.C. Medal Vol. 2: 9043
Gakujutsu-sho Vol. 2: 4221
GALA (Got a Lot Accomplished) Award Vol. 1: 7166
Galantiere Literary Translation Prize; Lewis Vol. 1: 4751
Galathea Medaillen Vol. 2: 1530
Galathea Medal Vol. 2: 1530
Galatti Award for Outstanding Volunteer Service Vol. 1: 271
Galbraith Award Vol. 1: 8390
Gale Award for Excellence in Business Librarianship/BRASS; Thomson Vol. 1: 17940
Gale Award for Excellence in Reference and Adult Services; Thomson Vol. 1: 17948
Gale/EMIERT Multicultural Award Vol. 1: 2962
Gale Financial Development Award Vol. 1: 2977
Gale Outstanding Trustee Conference Grant; ALTA/ Vol. 1: 5446
Galen Medal Vol. 2: 9267
Galerie d'Essai; La Vol. 2: 2546
Galey, Sr. Memorial Public Service Award; John T. Vol. 1: 2843
Galileo Galilei Award Vol. 2: 6058
Galkin Award; Harry Vol. 1: 11271
Gall Jr./CIO Award; HIMSS John E. Vol. 1: 10344
Gallagher Award; Mike Vol. 1: 20805
Gallagher Award; William F. and Catherine T. Vol. 1: 2301
Gallagher Distinguished Service Award; Marian Gould Vol. 1: 1251
Gallant Prize for Non-Fiction; Mavis
Quebec Writers' Federation Vol. 1: 17799
Quebec Writers' Federation Vol 1: 17801
Gallantry Decorations Vol. 2: 196
Gallatin Medal; Albert Vol. 1: 16299
Gallet; Fondation Paul Vol. 2: 1948
Gallo; Concorso Pianistico Internazionale Rina Sala Vol. 2: 3858
Gallo International Piano Competition; Rina Sala Vol. 2: 3858
Galloway Spacemodeling Service Award; H. Vol. 1: 14368
Galton Award; Sir Francis Vol. 2: 2938
Galva Arts Council Scholarship Vol. 1: 9863
Galvani Prize; Luigi Vol. 2: 6007
Galvin Scholarship Vol. 1: 8895
GAMA Excellence in Aviation Education Award Vol. 1: 9911
GAMA Learn to Fly Award for Excellence in Aviation Education Vol. 1: 9911
Gamble Award; Sam G. Vol. 2: 6637
Gamble Research Prize; Norman Vol. 2: 8811
Gamgee Medal Vol. 2: 4673
GAMNI-SMAI; Prix Blaise Pascal du Vol. 2: 1985
Gamzu Prize; Dr. Haim Vol. 2: 3770
Ganassini; Premio Europeo Prof. D. Vol. 2: 3941
Gandhi Prize for Popularization of Science; Indira Vol. 2: 3482
Gang Prevention Scholarship Vol. 1: 20190
Gans Distinguished Overseas Lectureship; Stephen L. Vol. 1: 772
Gantrelle; Prix Joseph Vol. 2: 1027
Gantt Medal; Henry Laurence Vol. 1: 4511
Gar Wood of the Year Award Vol. 1: 9872
Garant Awards; Serge Vol. 1: 18593
Garavito; Orden al Merito Julio Vol. 2: 1304
Garcia Monge Prize; Joaquin Vol. 2: 1352
Garcia-Tunon Memorial Award in Human Dignity; Miguel Vol. 1: 1824
Gard Superior Citizen Volunteer Award; Robert E. Vol. 1: 1169
Gard Superior Volunteer Award; Robert E. Vol. 1: 1169
Garde Nationale Trophy Vol. 1: 15176
Garden Awards Vol. 2: 653
Garden Club of America Medals and Awards Vol. 1: 9876
Garden Club of America Small Flower Show Award Vol. 1: 9876
Garden Machinery Annual Awards Vol. 2: 6908
Garden State Children's Book Awards Vol. 1: 16179
Garden State Teen Book Awards Vol. 1: 16180
Garden Trophy; Oscar Vol. 2: 5059
Gardeners of America/Men's Garden Clubs of America Scholarship Vol. 1: 9885
Gardening From the Heart Award Vol. 1: 9886
Gardner Award; Harry L. Vol. 1: 3021
Gardner Award; Henry A. Vol. 1: 5950

Gardner Leadership Award; John W. Vol. 1: 10747
Gardner Trophy Vol. 1: 20787
Garel Award; Georges Vol. 2: 6404
Garfield Humanitarian Award; President Vol. 1: 13141
Garibay Kintana Prize for Literary Essay; Angel Maria Vol. 2: 4529
Garland Educator Award; Robin F. Vol. 1: 15534
Garland Refrigeration Award; Milton W. Vol. 1: 4432
Garlick Lifetime Achievement Award; Betty Vol. 1: 13335
Garneau Medal; Francois-Xavier Vol. 1: 7153
Garner-Themoin Medal Vol. 2: 743
Garnsey Trainers Award; Glen Vol. 1: 20619
Garrett Memorial Award (Rookie of the Year); Dudley (Red) Vol. 1: 2507
Garrett Turbomachinery Engineering Award; Cliff Vol. 1: 19044
Garrod Medal Vol. 2: 7167
Garrod Prize Vol. 2: 7173
Garrud Fellowship; T. V. Vol. 2: 7847
Garry/Labbe Award Vol. 1: 983
Garulat Award; Bernard J. Vol. 1: 984
Garvan-John M. Olin Medal; Francis P. Vol. 1: 1755
Garvey Award; Joseph J. Vol. 1: 1025
Gary Medal Vol. 1: 2875
Gas Balloon Championships Vol. 1: 6220
Gas Turbine Award
American Society of Mechanical Engineers Vol. 1: 4512
Society of Automotive Engineers (Australasia) Vol 2: 584
Gascoigne Medal; George Bradley Vol. 1: 21481
Gascoigne Prize; Trench Vol. 2: 8867
Gaskell Medal and Prize Vol. 2: 8460
Gaskellprijs; Sonia Vol. 2: 4685
Gassner Award; John Vol. 1: 16975
Gassner Memorial Playwriting Award; John Vol. 1: 16124
Gaster Bronze Medal; Leon Vol. 2: 7285
Gaston-Gouin, Alfred-DesRochers et Alphonse-Desjardins Vol. 1: 5263
Gaston Writing Award Vol. 1: 3168
Gates Memorial Award; Roy Vol. 1: 19284
GATF Awards of Excellence in Education for an Individual in Industry and in Education Vol. 1: 10133
Gatorade Rookie of the Year Vol. 1: 12660
Gatorade Victory Lane Award; Daytona Vol. 1: 8765
Gatorade Young Investigator Award; Environmental and Exercise Physiology Section Vol. 1: 3516
Gatto; Premio Internazionale Paolo Vol. 2: 3831
Gatzke AAUA Foundation Award; Dr. Donald A. Vol. 1: 14326
Gaudeamus Prize Vol. 2: 4785
The Gaudeamus Prize Vol. 2: 4783
Gaudin Award; Antoine M. Vol. 1: 18811
Gaudry; Prix Vol. 2: 2408
Gaul Competition; Harvey Vol. 1: 17359
Gauss Award; Christian Vol. 1: 17242
Gavel Award Vol. 1: 919
Gavel Awards Vol. 1: 1533
Gaver Scholarship; Mary V. Vol. 1: 2978
Gawad AGKATEK (Agham, Kapaligiran at Teknolohiya) Vol. 2: 5287
Gawad CCP Para sa Alternatibong Pelikula at Video Vol. 2: 5269
Gawad CCP Para sa Radyo Vol. 2: 5270
Gawad CCP Para sa Sining Vol. 2: 5271
Gawad Manlilikha Ng Bayan (GAMABA) Vol. 2: 5274
Gawad Panitikan ng Republika Vol. 2: 5275
Gay, Lesbian, Bisexual and Transgender Community Leader Scholarship Vol. 1: 12621
Gay/Lesbian Book Award Vol. 1: 3003
Gay Teddy Bear Vol. 2: 2670
Gaylord Award for Achievement in Library and Information Technology; LITA/ Vol. 1: 12823
Gazzola Prize Vol. 2: 2466
GBPS Hassan Shaida Trophy Vol. 2: 8263
GCN Agency Awards Vol. 1: 10104
GCN Government Executive of the Year Vol. 1: 10104
GCN Industry Executive of the Year Vol. 1: 10104
GEAC Scholarship in Library and Information Technology; LITA/ Vol. 1: 12827
Geach Memorial Award; Portia Vol. 2: 626
Geary 18 International Yacht Racing Association Championship Regatta Vol. 1: 9905
Geddes Planning Award; Patrick Vol. 2: 8890
Geesink Prize; Joop Vol. 2: 4791
Geh Grant; Hans-Peter Vol. 2: 4812
Gehrt Memorial Award; Jack Vol. 1: 8084
GEI Award Vol. 1: 10186
Geiger Award Vol. 1: 13097
Geijsbeek Award; Samuel Vol. 1: 1682
Geijutsu-in Sho Vol. 2: 4157
Geijutsu Sensho Vol. 2: 4178
Geijutsusai Sho Vol. 2: 4179
Geijyutsu Korosha Vol. 2: 4321
Geilfuss Fellowship; John C. Vol. 1: 21676
Geils Memorial Award; G. Ruth Vol. 1: 10247
Geis Memorial Award Vol. 1: 3731
Geisness Outstanding Lawyer or Non-Lawyer Award; Helen M. Vol. 1: 12591
Gelber Foundation Award; Sylva Vol. 1: 6794
Gelin Conference Travel Award; Lars-Erik Vol. 2: 2755
Gelsted pris; Otto Vol. 2: 1444
Gelsthorpe Cup Vol. 2: 7429
GEM Awards Vol. 1: 18812
Gemant Award; Andrew Vol. 1: 2833
Gemeaux Awards Vol. 1: 81
Gemell Cup; David Vol. 2: 7602
Gemenis Award; Maria Vol. 2: 227
Geminis Vol. 1: 82
Gemma Yates Trophy Vol. 2: 6713
Gender Equity Architects Award Vol. 1: 1149
Gender Equity Award Vol. 1: 17469
Genealogical Publishing Company Award Vol. 1: 17941
Genealogical Research Award Vol. 1: 177
Genealogist of the Year Vol. 2: 5563
Genee Award; Adeline Vol. 2: 8361
General Aviation Award Vol. 1: 2662
General Aviation Maintenance Technician Award Vol. 1: 17584
General Aviation Service Technician Award Vol. 1: 13920
General Award Vol. 2: 4759
General Bryce Pow II Award Vol. 1: 370
General Commendation Vol. 1: 3568
General Diagnostics Lectureship in Clinical Chemistry Vol. 1: 972
General Electric Senior Research Award Vol. 1: 4020
General Knowledge Contest on the UN Vol. 2: 6137
General Knowledge Quiz on International Flags, National Emblems, Coats-of-Arms, and National Anthems of UN member States Vol. 2: 6137
General Laubach Award Vol. 1: 9423
General Research Committee Award Vol. 2: 6132
General Service Medal Vol. 2: 5737
General Services Achievement Award Vol. 1: 20544
Generalitat de Catalunya Trophy Vol. 2: 6011
Genetics Society of America Medal Vol. 1: 9932
Geneva-Europe Prizes Vol. 2: 6315
Genie Awards Vol. 1: 8046
Genies Vol. 1: 83
Geno Saccamanno, M.D. New Frontiers in Cytology award Vol. 1: 4392
Genossenschaftspreis Vol. 2: 6541
Gentilli Prize; Edgar Vol. 2: 8446
Geochimie; Prix de Vol. 2: 1873
Geographic Education Dissertation Award Vol. 1: 14765
Geographical Award Vol. 2: 8517
Geographical Merit Prize Vol. 2: 44
Geological Society of South Africa Honorary Member Vol. 2: 5567
Geological Society of South Africa Honours Award Vol. 2: 5568
Geological Society of South Africa Jubilee Medal Vol. 2: 5569
Geological Society President's Awards Vol. 2: 7562
Geologiska Foreningens Medaljfondsstipendium Vol. 2: 6152
Georg Award; Lucille K. Vol. 2: 1640
Georg-Jayme-Denkmunze Vol. 2: 2647
George A. Hall/Harold F. Mayfield Award Vol. 1: 21638
George Civilian Airmanship Award; Lt. Gen. Harold L. Vol. 1: 16827
George Cross Vol. 2: 7250
George J. Schroepfer Medal Vol. 1: 21482
George Medal Vol. 2: 7251
George Perkins Marsh Prize Vol. 1: 4066
George Polya Lectureship Vol. 1: 13196
George R. Mach Distinguished Service Award Vol. 1: 12517
George W. Burke, Jr. Award Vol. 1: 21483
Georges Petitpas Memorial Award Vol. 1: 21915
Georgescu-Roegen Prize in Economics Vol. 1: 19499
Georgia Author of the Year Awards Vol. 1: 9972
Georgia Children's Book Award Vol. 1: 21022
Georgia Children's Picture Storybook Award Vol. 1: 21023
Georgia Media Award Vol. 1: 9963
Georgia No Excuses Awards Vol. 1: 9970
Georgia Peanut Export Award Vol. 1: 9964
Georgia Peanut Research and Education Award Vol. 1: 9965
Georgia Poetry Society Award Vol. 1: 14996
Georgiev Prize; Academician Vladimir Vol. 2: 1207

Geotechnical Research Medal Vol. 2: 7765
Geraldine Colby Zeiler Award Vol. 1: 4393
Gerard; Prix Auguste Vol. 2: 2018
Gerdes Distinguished Service Award; Betty Vol. 1: 15740
Gerhold Award; Clarence (Larry) G. Vol. 1: 2774
Geriatric Oral Health Care Award Vol. 1: 2128
Geriatric Oral Research; Award in Vol. 1: 11203
Geriatrician of the Year Vol. 1: 5050
Gerke Collegiate Artist Scholarships Vol. 1: 13662
Gerke Scholarship; Madge Cathcart Vol. 1: 13662
Germain; Fondation Gustave Vol. 2: 1717
German Educator Award; Outstanding Vol. 1: 1447
German Marshall Fund of the United States Fellowships and Awards Vol. 1: 9974
German Nutrition Foundation Travel Scholarship Vol. 2: 2894
German; Outstanding High School Senior in Vol. 1: 1448
German Prize for Design Promoters Vol. 2: 2830
German Studies; DAAD Prize for Distinguished Scholarship in Vol. 1: 2623
German Summer Study Award Vol. 1: 1445
German Translation Award Vol. 1: 4752
Gerrad Outstanding Service Award; Steve Vol. 1: 14002
Gerrard Award; Louise B. Vol. 1: 14399
Gerrish Trophy; Ebby Vol. 2: 8263
Gerrity Award; Thomas P. Vol. 1: 344
Gerry Fellowships; Eloise Vol. 1: 18479
Gerschenkron Prize; Alexander Vol. 1: 9145
Gershoy Award; Leo Vol. 1: 2473
Gersoni Military Psychology Award; Charles S. Vol. 1: 3722
Gerstacker Trooper of the Year Award; Carl A. Vol. 1: 13344
Gerstaecker-Preis; Friedrich- Vol. 2: 2678
Gervais Award; Arthur J. Vol. 1: 19692
Getchell Award; Charles M. Vol. 1: 19488
Getman Award; G. N. Vol. 1: 8184
Getty Postdoctoral Fellowships in the History of Art and the Humanities; J. Paul Vol. 1: 10005
Getty Scholars Vol. 1: 10006
Getty Wildlife Conservation Prize; J. Paul Vol. 1: 21967
Gevaert Medal; Lieven Vol. 1: 18718
Gezelle Prize; Guido Vol. 2: 960
GFWC Print Journalism Award; Jane Cunningham Croly/ Vol. 1: 9916
GGAS Service Awards Vol. 1: 10059
Ghandi Peace Award Vol. 1: 17681
Ghatage Award; Dr. V. M. Vol. 2: 3330
Ghirshman; Prix Roman et Tania Vol. 2: 1774
Ghost Contest; Horror/ Vol. 1: 21997
GI Joe Fan Award Vol. 1: 10015
GIAA Entertainment Achievement Awards Vol. 1: 10202
Giant of the Year (The Gaines Award) Vol. 1: 10017
Giant Schnauzer of the Year, Dog Vol. 1: 10018
Gibb Award; Jack Vol. 1: 16874
Gibbons Cup; Stanley Vol. 2: 8263
Gibbons Medal; Cardinal Vol. 1: 7665
Gibbs Brothers Medal Vol. 1: 13833
Gibbs, Jr. Memorial Award; Robert H. Vol. 1: 4452
Gibson Award (Marine Air Command and Control Officer of the Year); Robert F. Vol. 1: 13075
Gibson Award; Milo Vol. 1: 16434
Gibson Research Scholarship for Medical Women; William Vol. 2: 8812
Gibson Trophy; Frank M. Vol. 1: 7108
Giegengack Award; Robert Vol. 1: 21223
Gieh ir-Repubblika Honor Society Vol. 1: 4452
Gierows pris for hangiven bildningsverksamhet; Karin Vol. 2: 6251
Gierows pris for kunskapsformedlande framstallningskonst; Karin Vol. 2: 6252
Gies Award; William John Vol. 1: 1855
Gies Foundation Award in Memory of Arthur Hastings Merritt; William J. Vol. 1: 804
Giese Structures and Environment Award; Henry Vol. 1: 4222
Giffard; Fondation Henry Vol. 2: 1886
Giffuni Memorial Award; Andrew Vol. 1: 17103
Gift of Music Best Seller Awards Vol. 1: 14358
Gift of Sight Award Vol. 1: 9381
Gift of Sight Award Vol. 1: 10194
Gifted Teacher Vol. 1: 1839
Gifts and Decorative Accessories Merchandising Achievement Awards Vol. 1: 10011
Giguere Award; John P. Vol. 1: 13076
Gijon International Film Festival for Young People Vol. 2: 6037
Gijutsu-sho Vol. 2: 4223
Gilbert Award; G. K. Vol. 1: 9949
Gilbert Award; Gaines G. Vol. 1: 13077
Gilbert Award; John Vol. 1: 14138
Gilbert Foundation Research Award; Robert O. Vol. 1: 12023
Gilbert Memorial Award; Gerard Vol. 1: 9726
Gilbert Memorial Award; Glen A. Vol. 1: 386
Gilbert Memorial Trustee Award; Gloria F. "Mike" Vol. 1: 3952
Gilbert National Leadership Award; Glenn Vol. 1: 14824
Gilbert Prize; Geoffery Vol. 1: 15059
Gilbreth Industrial Engineering Award; Frank and Lillian Vol. 1: 10954
Gilbreth Medal Vol. 1: 18625
Gilchrist Fieldwork Award Vol. 2: 8518
Giles Award; Annie T. Vol. 1: 2448
Giles; Prix Herbert Allen Vol. 2: 1753
Gill Medal Vol. 2: 5520
Gill Memorial Award Vol. 2: 8519
Gill Memorial Award; Tom Vol. 2: 7326
Gill Prize; Brendan Vol. 1: 13677
Gill Prize; Roma Vol. 1: 13122
Gillet Performance Competition; Fernand Vol. 1: 11544
Gillet Young Artist Performance Competition; Fernand Vol. 1: 11544
Gillette Cup Vol. 2: 7417
Gilliams Prize; Maurice Vol. 2: 961
Gillihan Award Vol. 1: 10424
Gillingham Award; Kent K. Vol. 1: 232
Gillis Prize; J. Vol. 2: 1080
Gilliss Award for Outstanding Service; Captain James M. Vol. 1: 20524
Gilman Award in Drug Receptor Pharmacology; Goodman and Vol. 1: 4172
Gilmanton Historic Essay Competition Vol. 1: 10026
Gilmore Award; Mary Vol. 2: 82
Gilmore Bursary; Jean Vol. 2: 169
Gilmore - Woman Behind the Scenes Award; Diana Fell Vol. 1: 20418
Gilpin County Arts Association Annual Exhibition Vol. 1: 10028
Gilruth Prize Vol. 2: 279
Giltner Memorial Trophy; Joe Vol. 1: 18585
Gina Bachauer First Prize Vol. 1: 6193
Gingles Award; Violet B. Vol. 1: 5076
Gingrich Literary Memorial Award; Arnold Vol. 1: 9484
Gingrich Memorial Award; Arnold Vol. 1: 9476
Ginwala Gold Medal; Sir Padamji Vol. 2: 3452
GIO Australia Ballet Scholarship Vol. 2: 314
Giolitti Steel Medal; Federico Vol. 2: 3994
Girard; Fondation Charles-Adam Vol. 2: 1818
Girard; Prix Antoine Vol. 2: 2111
Girard; Prix Edmond Vol. 2: 2554
Girardeau; Prix Emile Vol. 2: 2041
Girls' 18 National Championships Sportsmanship Award Vol. 1: 20856
Girls' Basketball National Volunteer of the Year Vol. 1: 552
Gitelson Memorial Essay Awards; Moses Leo Vol. 1: 7758
Gitlin Literary Prize; Zelda Vol. 1: 20080
Gitlin Literary Prize; Zelda & Paul Vol. 1: 20080
Givry; Prix Alexandre Vol. 2: 1839
Gladstone History Book Prize Vol. 2: 8532
Glaser Award; John Vol. 1: 9779
Glaser Distinguished Service Award; Jerome Vol. 1: 773
Glasgow Achievement Award; Janet M. Vol. 1: 3078
Glasgow-Rubin Student Achievement Vol. 1: 3079
Glass Dealer of the Year Vol. 1: 15165
Glass Globe Vol. 2: 4877
Glass Prize Vol. 2: 5132
Glass Professional of the Year Vol. 1: 15165
Glassco Translation Prize; John Vol. 1: 12874
Glaxco Award Vol. 1: 7463
Glaxo Prize for Medical Writing Vol. 2: 8988
GlaxoSmithKline Prize and Lecture Vol. 2: 8698
Glazebrook Medal and Prize Vol. 2: 7729
Glazen Globe Vol. 2: 4877
Gleason Award; Henry Vol. 1: 16214
Gleason Award; Henry Allan Vol. 1: 6547
Gleason Book Award; Eliza Atkins Vol. 1: 2995
Gleason Music Book Awards; Ralph J. Vol. 1: 16302
Glen Award; Esther Vol. 2: 5002
Glen Helen Ecology Institute Awards Vol. 1: 4986
Glenayre Award Vol. 1: 21804
Glenfiddich Trophy Vol. 2: 7318
Glenn Award; R. A. Vol. 1: 5951
Glick Award; David Vol. 1: 21841
Global 500 Vol. 2: 5246
Global Citizen Award Vol. 1: 7731
Global Citizenship Award Vol. 1: 21083
Global CONTACT Award Vol. 2: 4760
Global Justice Award Vol. 1: 21406
Global Leaders Award Vol. 1: 17469
Global Leadership Award Vol. 1: 2624

Global Media Awards for Excellence in Population Reporting Vol. 1: 17469
Global Paragon Awards Vol. 1: 13279
Global Service Award; Jerry Mische Vol. 1: 10044
Global Statesman Award Vol. 1: 6782
Globe International Gold Award Vol. 1: 16618
Gloria Medal Vol. 1: 15701
Gloria Medicinae Award Vol. 2: 5356
Gloucester Navigation Trophy Vol. 2: 5060
Glueck Award; Sellin - Vol. 1: 4385
Gluge; Prix Theophile Vol. 2: 1070
Glushien Award; Ann Williams Vol. 1: 4850
Go See Award Vol. 2: 3615
Goal of the Year Vol. 2: 4425
Godbey Award; William D. Vol. 1: 5734
Goddard Astronautics Award Vol. 1: 2682
Goddard Award Vol. 1: 2682
Goddard Award; George W. Vol. 1: 19608
Goddard Medal Vol. 1: 18987
Goddard Scholarship; Dr. Robert H. Vol. 1: 15789
Gode Medal; Alexander Vol. 1: 4753
Godeaux; Prix Lucien Vol. 2: 1110
Godel Prize Vol. 1: 5316
Godfrey Award; Kneeland Vol. 1: 8447
Godin Award; Jean-Cleo Vol. 1: 5285
Godlove Award Vol. 1: 11127
Godman-Salvin Medal Vol. 2: 7096
Goedken Meritorious Service Awards; Ryan White and Loras Vol. 1: 15214
Goethals Medal; George W. Vol. 1: 18988
Goethe Medaille Vol. 2: 2918
Goethe Prize; Hanseatic Vol. 2: 3082
Goetze 21st Century Award; Mandy Vol. 1: 11177
Gold Anchor Vol. 2: 2470
Gold and Platinum Video Awards Vol. 1: 11884
Gold and Silver Medals Vol. 1: 16439
Gold and Silver Shield Awards Vol. 1: 12318
Gold Anvil Award Vol. 1: 17721
Gold Award
  American Healthcare Radiology Administrators Vol. 1: 2400
  Recording Industry Association of America Vol 1: 17908
Gold Awards
  Meetings and Conventions Vol. 1: 13287
  Pacific Asia Travel Association Vol 1: 16996
Gold Badge
  Association of Jewish Ex-Servicemen and Women Vol. 2: 6829
  English Folk Dance and Song Society Vol 2: 7431
Gold Badge of Honour Vol. 2: 6997
Gold Ball Award Vol. 1: 18595
Gold Baton Award Vol. 1: 4730
Gold Book Awards Vol. 1: 5658
Gold Butterfly of Trentino Prize Vol. 2: 4059
Gold Camera Award
  U.S. International Film and Video Festival Vol. 1: 20675
  US International Film and Video Festival Vol 1: 21143
Gold Cane Award Vol. 1: 4791
Gold Certificate Vol. 1: 3331
Gold Circle Awards Vol. 1: 8233
Gold Crown Awards Vol. 1: 8232
Gold Cup of Industry Award Vol. 1: 9078
Gold Cystoscope Award Vol. 1: 4792
Gold Diploma of Honor Vol. 2: 3194
Gold Edelweiss Vol. 2: 6107
Gold Good Citizenship Medal Vol. 1: 15770
Gold Headed Cane Vol. 2: 4327
Gold-Headed Cane Vol. 1: 18420
The Gold-Headed Cane Award Vol. 1: 4121
Gold Heart Award Vol. 1: 2407
Gold Honor Medal Vol. 1: 3872
Gold Irrigation Award Vol. 1: 419
Gold Key Award
  American Congress of Rehabilitation Medicine Vol. 1: 1987
  Columbia Scholastic Press Association Vol 1: 8234
  Incentive Manufacturer and Representatives Alliance Vol 1: 10709
  National Council on Alcoholism and Drug Dependence Vol 1: 14849
Gold Key Awards
  Society of Professional Journalists Vol. 1: 19276
  University of Chicago Medical and Biological Sciences Alumni Association Vol 1: 21004
Gold Key Laureates Vol. 1: 130
Gold Level Achievement Awards Vol. 1: 19958
Gold Lifesaving Medal Vol. 1: 8816
Gold Mailbox Award Vol. 1: 8924
Gold Medal
  Academia Europaea Vol. 2: 6664
  Acoustical Society of America Vol 1: 138
  Acta Materialia, Inc. Vol 1: 154
  American College of Radiology Vol 1: 1941
  American Craft Council Vol 1: 2078
  American Institute of Architects Vol 1: 2712
  American Institute of Chemists Vol 1: 2801
  American Irish Historical Society Vol 1: 2871
  American Petroleum Institute Vol 1: 3374
  American Rhododendron Society Vol 1: 3851
  ASM International Vol 1: 5179
  Australian Council for Educational Leaders Vol 2: 157
  Canadian Institute of Forestry Vol 1: 7175
  European and Mediterranean Plant Protection Organization Vol 2: 2299
  The Gardeners of America/Men's Garden Clubs of America Vol 1: 9887
  Institute of Actuaries - United Kingdom Vol 2: 7646
  Institute of Chartered Accountants of Scotland Vol 2: 7667
  Institution of Civil Engineers Vol 2: 7766
  Inter-American Safety Council Vol 1: 11119
  International Academy of Aviation and Space Medicine Vol 1: 11162
  International Federation of Sports Medicine Vol 2: 1411
  National Association of Paralegals Vol 2: 8157
  National Football Foundation and College Hall of Fame Vol 1: 15070
  National Vegetable Society Vol 2: 8202
  Alexander S. Onassis Public Benefit Foundation Vol 2: 3181
  Professional Institute of the Public Service of Canada Vol 1: 17630
  Radiological Society of North America Vol 1: 17852
  Royal Aeronautical Society - United Kingdom Vol 2: 8387
  Royal Architectural Institute of Canada Vol 1: 18137
  Royal Canadian Geographical Society Vol 1: 18148
  Royal Institute of Navigation Vol 2: 8596
  Royal Philharmonic Society Vol 2: 8654
  Royal Scottish Geographical Society Vol 2: 8687
  Royal Society of Medicine Vol 2: 8813
  Royal Television Society Vol 2: 8853
  Society of American Registered Architects Vol 1: 19007
  Society of Manufacturing Engineers - Composites Manufacturing Association Vol 1: 19152
  State Capital Global Law Firm Group Vol 1: 19765
  Tau Sigma Delta Vol 1: 19941
Gold Medal and Fellowship of the Society Vol. 2: 252
Gold Medal Annual Vol. 1: 18330
Gold Medal Award
  American Academy of Periodontology Vol. 1: 805
  American College of Healthcare Executives Vol 1: 1868
  American Society of Naval Engineers Vol 1: 4566
  Anchor Bay Chamber of Commerce Vol 1: 4953
  Audio Engineering Society Vol 1: 6054
  British Association of Aviation Consultants Vol 2: 6932
  Fertilizer Society of South Africa Vol 2: 5558
  Fundacion Pablo Neruda Vol 2: 1258
  International Radio and Television Society Foundation Vol 1: 11848
  Mining and Metallurgical Society of America Vol 1: 13463
  National Retail Federation Vol 1: 15635
  National Student Campaign Against Hunger and Homelessness Vol 1: 15827
  Professional Grounds Management Society Vol 1: 17625
  The Royal Danish Academy of Fine Arts Vol 2: 1522
  Society of Biological Psychiatry Vol 1: 19073
  Society of Woman Geographers Vol 1: 19360
  Spanish Institute Vol 1: 19539
Gold Medal Award for Distinguished Archaeological Achievement Vol. 1: 5032
Gold Medal Award for Distinguished Lifetime Contributions to Canadian Psychology Vol. 1: 7350
Gold Medal Award for Distinguished Service Vol. 1: 21258
Gold Medal Award for Outstanding Leadership in the Protection of the Environment and the Conservation of Natural Resources Vol. 2: 6611
Gold Medal Award for Technical Achievement Vol. 1: 19256
Gold Medal Awards
  BC Innovation Council Vol. 1: 6290
  North American Gladiolus Council Vol 1: 16437
Gold Medal for Achievement in Science and Technology Vol. 2: 5644
Gold Medal for Development of the Technological Environment Vol. 2: 5168
Gold Medal for Distinguished Achievement Vol. 1: 10506

Gold Medal for Distinguished Merit Vol. 2: 7064
Gold Medal for Distinguished Service Vol. 1: 18982
Gold Medal for Distinguished Services to Agriculture Vol. 2: 8412
Gold Medal for Outstanding Architectural Achievement Vol. 2: 2511
Gold Medal Forum Vol. 1: 19483
Gold Medal of Achievement Vol. 1: 3332
Gold Medal of Excellence for Photography Vol. 1: 13985
Gold Medal of Honor Vol. 1: 21911
Gold Medal of Honor and Achievement Vol. 1: 14474
Gold Medal of Honor for Dance Vol. 1: 13986
Gold Medal of Honor for Design Vol. 1: 13987
Gold Medal of Honor for Education Vol. 1: 13988
Gold Medal of Honor for Film/Video Vol. 1: 13989
Gold Medal of Honor for Theater/Drama Vol. 1: 13990
Gold Medal of Honor for Visual Arts Vol. 1: 13991
Gold Medal of Merit Vol. 1: 12386
Gold Medal of the Academy of Greece Vol. 2: 3174
Gold Medal of the FIM Vol. 2: 6421
Gold Medal of the Society Vol. 1: 19609
Gold Medal to His Majesty, the King of Thailand, King Bhumibol Adulyadej for Outstanding Leadership in Rural Development Vol. 2: 6612
Gold Medallion Vol. 1: 6597
Gold Medallion Award Vol. 1: 15667
Gold Medallion Book Awards Vol. 1: 9354
Gold Medals Vol. 2: 8520
Gold Member Vol. 1: 11164
Gold Memorial Bowl Vol. 2: 8840
Gold Music Video Award Vol. 1: 17909
Gold Nibs Award Vol. 1: 2383
Gold Plate Award Vol. 1: 11631
Gold Quill Award Vol. 1: 4407
Gold Ribbon for Community Service (Radio) Vol. 1: 6891
Gold Ribbon for Community Service (Specialty/Pay/PPV) Vol. 1: 6892
Gold Ribbon for Community Service (Television) Vol. 1: 6893
Gold Ribbon for Distinguished Service Vol. 1: 6890
Gold Ribbon for Outstanding Community Service by an Individual Broadcaster Vol. 1: 6894
Gold Ribbon for Promotion of Canadian Talent (Radio) Vol. 1: 6895
Gold Rotorcraft Medal Vol. 2: 6335
Gold Sales Award Vol. 2: 5229
Gold Screen Awards Vol. 1: 14243
Gold Show Award Vol. 1: 6844
Gold, Silver and Bronze Medals Vol. 2: 8618
Gold, Silver, and Bronze Medals Vol. 1: 8692
Gold Star Award Vol. 1: 15468
Gold Star for Bravery Vol. 2: 5738
Gold Trout Award Vol. 1: 20210
Gold Typewriter Award Vol. 1: 16248
Gold Veitch Memorial Medal Vol. 2: 8548
Gold Vine Award Vol. 1: 6657
Gold Wing Award for Excellence In Journalism Vol. 1: 14566
Goldberg Prize for Manuscripts in American Philosophy; Norman L. and Roselea J. Vol. 1: 21275
Goldberg Young Investigator Award of the ASCPT; Leon I. Vol. 1: 3974
Goldblatt Cytology Award; Maurice Vol. 2: 2931
Golde Award Vol. 1: 12261
Golden Achievement Award
ISA - Instrumentation, Systems, and Automation Society Vol. 1: 12217
National School Public Relations Association Vol 1: 15668
Specialized Carriers and Rigging Association Vol 1: 19579
Golden Acorn Award Vol. 1: 13294
Golden Age Award Vol. 1: 12713
Golden & Silver Penguin Awards Vol. 1: 10145
Golden Anniversary Award Vol. 1: 14086
Golden Anniversary Monograph Awards Vol. 1: 14709
Golden Antenna International Television Festival Vol. 2: 1216
Golden Apple
Slovakia Ministry of Culture Vol. 2: 5971
World Federation of Journalists and Travel Writers Vol 2: 2628
Golden Apple Award Vol. 1: 826
Golden Apple Awards for Service in Health Promotion and Disease Prevention Vol. 1: 20031
Golden ARC Awards Vol. 1: 292
Golden Archer Award Vol. 1: 21670
Golden Arrow of Achievement Vol. 2: 3212
Golden Arrow of Courage Vol. 2: 3213
Golden Award
National Association of College Auxiliary Services Vol. 1: 14134
Tennis Association of Austria Vol 2: 786
Golden Berlin Bear Vol. 2: 2670
Golden Bobbin Vol. 2: 927
Golden Broom Award Vol. 1: 16770
Golden Bug Statuette Vol. 2: 6280
Golden Bull Award Vol. 2: 8270
Golden Cactus Vol. 2: 6430
Golden Chain Award
Nation's Restaurant News - Lebhar-Friedman Inc. Vol. 1: 16010
Nation's Restaurant News - Lebhar-Friedman Inc. Vol 1: 16013
Golden Chest International Television Festival Vol. 2: 1217
Golden Chili Pepper Award Vol. 1: 4667
Golden Circles Award Vol. 1: 11571
Golden Cleaver Award Vol. 1: 1264
Golden Diamond Awards Vol. 1: 21155
Golden Dozen Vol. 1: 12028
Golden Dragon Vol. 2: 5301
Golden Eagle Award
Society of American Military Engineers Vol. 1: 18989
Wireless Communications Association International Vol 1: 21662
Golden Eagle Grant Vol. 1: 9746
Golden Elephant Award Vol. 2: 3355
"Golden Eye" Vol. 2: 4945
Golden Field Award Vol. 1: 21156
Golden Furrows Challenge Trophy Vol. 2: 4943
Golden Gate Awards Vol. 1: 18246
Golden Gavel Award Vol. 1: 20095
Golden Globe Awards Vol. 1: 10513
Golden Hammer Award Vol. 1: 17330
Golden Hammer Awards Vol. 1: 14255
Golden Hammer Scenic Technology Award Vol. 1: 20645
Golden Heart Award Vol. 1: 18114
Golden Honor Medal Vol. 2: 3120
Golden Horse Award Vol. 1: 17048
Golden Horse Awards Vol. 2: 6598
Golden Hysteroscope Award Vol. 1: 1207
Golden Image Award Vol. 1: 19594
Golden Jubilee Commemoration Medal for Biology Vol. 2: 3483
Golden Jubilee Commemoration Medal for Chemistry Vol. 2: 3484
Golden Key Scholar Awards Vol. 1: 10062
Golden Kiss Vol. 2: 4714
Golden Kite Awards Vol. 1: 19087
Golden Knight International Amateur Film and Video Festival Vol. 2: 4450
Golden Knight International Amateur Film Festival Vol. 2: 4450
Golden Laparoscope Award Vol. 1: 1208
Golden Lion Vol. 2: 9337
Golden Lion Award Vol. 1: 6698
Golden Medal Vol. 2: 1221
Golden Medallion Media Awards Vol. 1: 19759
Golden Merit Award Vol. 1: 15672
Golden Mike Awards Vol. 1: 16151
Golden Paintbrush Vol. 2: 4715
Golden Peanut Research and Education Award Vol. 1: 3368
Golden Pen
Association of Hungarian Journalists Vol. 2: 3230
Eastern Coast Breweriana Association Vol 1: 9105
Golden Pen Award Vol. 1: 3489
Golden Pen of Freedom Award Vol. 2: 2623
Golden Pencil Vol. 2: 4716
Golden Penguin Awards Vol. 1: 15132
Golden Pig Award Vol. 1: 9533
Golden Plough Trophy Vol. 2: 4943
Golden Pyramid Competition Vol. 1: 17685
Golden Quill Award Vol. 1: 12028
Golden R Vol. 2: 3841
Golden Ram Award Vol. 2: 5592
Golden Raster Award Vol. 1: 10325
Golden Rat Award Vol. 2: 6293
Golden Reins Award Vol. 1: 3130
Golden Rookie of the Year; Harry Vol. 1: 17592
Golden Rose Award Vol. 1: 16111
Golden Rose of Montreaux Award Vol. 2: 6500
Golden Saddleman Award Vol. 1: 21577
Golden Score Award Vol. 1: 4560
Golden Scorpion Award for Outstanding Service Vol. 1: 57
Golden Screen Award Vol. 1: 8336
Golden Sheaf Awards Vol. 1: 22048
Golden Sheaf Craft Awards Vol. 1: 22048
Golden Shell Vol. 2: 6096
Golden Ship Grand Prix of the President of the Bulgarian Red Cross Vol. 2: 1228
Golden Sower Awards Vol. 1: 16068
Golden Space Needle Audience Awards Vol. 1: 18395
Golden Spike Vol. 2: 6112
Golden Spikes Award Vol. 1: 21157
Golden Spur Awards Vol. 1: 21576
Golden Star Vol. 2: 6480
Golden Toonie Award Vol. 1: 7615

Award Index

Golden Torch Award
Better Business Bureau Serving Upstate South Carolina Vol. 1: 6344
Insurance Marketing Communications Association Vol 1: 11095
Golden Triangle Award Vol. 1: 10560
Golden Trident Vol. 1: 20277
Golden Trowel Award Vol. 1: 11742
Golden Tulip Award Vol. 2: 6642
Golden Unicorn
Amiens International Film Festival Vol. 2: 2226
Filmfestival Alpinale Vol 2: 724
Golden Werner-Medaille Vol. 2: 6515
Golden Wheel Society Awards Vol. 1: 3861
Golden Youth Awards Vol. 1: 6598
Goldene Mozart-Medaille Vol. 2: 746
Goldene Mozart-Nadel Vol. 2: 747
Goldene Vereinsnadel Vol. 2: 2648
Goldener Ehrenring fur Papiergeschichte Vol. 2: 2649
Goldener Gehlhoff-Ring Vol. 2: 2891
Goldhill Award for Sculpture; Jack Vol. 2: 8352
Goldman Environmental Prize Vol. 1: 10064
Goldschmidt-Clermont Prize Vol. 2: 2491
Goldschmidt Medal; V. M. Vol. 1: 9939
Goldschmidt Preis; Viktor-Moritz- Vol. 2: 2718
Goldsmith Award; Emily Vol. 1: 4851
Goldsmith Award; Richard S. Vol. 1: 19757
Goldsmith Book Prize Vol. 1: 18438
Goldsmith Cup; Tony Vol. 2: 7804
Goldsmith Prize for Investigative Reporting Vol. 1: 18439
Goldsmith Research Awards Vol. 1: 18440
Goldstein Award for Washington Regional Reporting; Robin Vol. 1: 15516
Goldstein Distinguished Publication Award; Geron Corporation - Samuel Vol. 1: 9993
Goldstein Foundation Purchase Award; Ben and Beatrice Vol. 1: 18980
Goldstein Public Service Award; Jerome C. Vol. 1: 749
Goldwater Amateur Radio Award; Barry M. Vol. 1: 17835
Golf Award Vol. 2: 709
Golf Digest - LPGA Founders Cup Vol. 1: 12654
Golf Professional of the Year Vol. 1: 17615
Golf Scramble Vol. 2: 9100
Golfer of the Year
Association of Golf Writers Vol. 2: 6825
Austrian Golf Association Vol 2: 709
Golgi Lecture Vol. 2: 2740
Gollancz Prize; Sir Israel Vol. 2: 6901
Golmick Scholarship; Paul Vol. 2: 7295
Golseth Young Investigator Award Vol. 1: 1284
Gomez Award; Lefty Vol. 1: 1543
Gomez Prize; Rodrigo Vol. 2: 4467
Gompers American Red Cross National Labor Award; Samuel Vol. 1: 3827
Gondos Memorial Service Award; Victor Vol. 1: 18801
Gonin Award Vol. 1: 11604
Gonzalez Ochoa Award; Dr. Antonio Vol. 2: 4553
Gonzalez - PUIC; Premio Gea Vol. 2: 4510
Good Citizenship Medal; Bronze Vol. 1: 15764
Good Citizenship Medal; Gold Vol. 1: 15770
Good Citizenship Medal; Silver Vol. 1: 15783
Good Conduct Medal Vol. 1: 8817
Good Design Award Vol. 2: 4174
GOOD DESIGN Competition and Exhibition Vol. 1: 7873
G.O.O.D. for You Award Vol. 1: 9869
G.O.O.D. Friendship Award Vol. 1: 9870
Good Funeral Guide Awards Vol. 2: 6833
Good Government Pharmacist of the Year Award Vol. 1: 3388
Good Grant Award Vol. 1: 8994
Good Memorial Award; Harry M. Vol. 1: 10893
Good Neighbor Award
American Red Cross National Headquarters Vol. 1: 3828
International Good Neighbor Council Vol 1: 11654
United States-Mexico Chamber of Commerce Vol 1: 20699
Good Neighbor Teacher Award Vol. 1: 19771
Good Poster Award Vol. 1: 11583
Good Samaritan Award
American Police Hall of Fame Vol. 1: 3569
National Catholic Development Conference Vol 1: 14603
Good Servant Medal Vol. 1: 7047
Good Sportsmanship Award Vol. 1: 3875
Good Steward Award Vol. 1: 13949
Goodacre Medal and Gift; Walter Vol. 2: 6950
The Goodchild Prize Vol. 2: 8319
Goodeve Medal Vol. 2: 8231
The Goodfellow Memorial Award for Senior Vocal Concert Groups Vol. 1: 18285
The Goodfellow Memorial Award in Voice/The Chief Justice J.T. Brown Shield Vol. 1: 18286
The Goodfellow Memorial Canadian Vocal Music Scholarship Vol. 1: 18287
The Goodfellow Memorial Grade A Female Voce Scholarship Vol. 1: 18288
The Goodfellow Memorial Grade A Male Voice Scholarship Vol. 1: 18289
The Goodfellow Memorial Lieder Scholarship Vol. 1: 18290
The Goodfellow Memorial Operatic Scholarship Vol. 1: 18291
The Goodfellow Memorial Oratorio Scholarship/ The Helen Davis Sherry Memorial Trophy Vol. 1: 18292
Goodfellowship Award Vol. 1: 3222
Goodhue-Elkins Award Vol. 1: 6083
Goodman Award; Arnold Vol. 1: 20366
Goodman Fielder Wattie Book Award Vol. 2: 4957
Goodman-Malamuth AAUA Foundation Award; Dr. Leo and Margaret Vol. 1: 14326
Goodnight Award for Outstanding Performance as a Dean; Scott Vol. 1: 14403
Goodwill Ambassadors for UNICEF Vol. 1: 20596
Goodwill Industries Volunteer Services (GIVS) Volunteer Group of the Year Vol. 1: 10086
Goodwill Industries Volunteer Services (GIVS) Volunteer of the Year Vol. 1: 10087
Goodwin Award of Merit; Charles J. Vol. 1: 3419
Goodyear Award; John and Mary Vol. 2: 4740
Goodyear Conservation Awards Vol. 1: 14155
Goodyear Medal; Charles Vol. 1: 1756
Gooley Humanitarian of the Year Award; Mary M. Vol. 1: 15205
Gordan Book Prize; Phyllis Goodhart Vol. 1: 17985
Gordon Award; Eva L. Vol. 1: 3188
Gordon Award for Children's Science Literature; Eva L. Vol. 1: 3188
Gordon Award; Marjorie Vol. 1: 15430
Gordon Award; Seth Vol. 1: 11358
Gordon Award; Winston Vol. 1: 7302
Gordon Editor of the Year Award; Jim Vol. 1: 15535
Gordon-Lennox Trophy Vol. 2: 8549
Gordon Maskew Fair Medal Vol. 1: 21484
Gordon Memorial Award; Harold R. Vol. 1: 14246
Gore "Remember the Children" Award; Tipper Vol. 1: 15375
Gore Scholarship; Len Vol. 2: 7928
Gorgas Medal Vol. 1: 5772
Gorin Award for Outstanding Achievement in Rural Health Care; Louis Vol. 1: 15651
Gorin Award; Susan Phillips Vol. 1: 8549
Gorini; Fondation Costantino Vol. 2: 1830
Gorman Memorial Award; Tom Vol. 1: 10162
Gorman Trophy; Peter Vol. 1: 7216
Gorterprijs; Herman Vol. 2: 4686
Goslin Award - Man of the Year Vol. 1: 19912
Gospel Music Hall of Fame Vol. 1: 10102
Gospel Recorded Performance of the Year Vol. 1: 11424
Gosselet; Prix Vol. 2: 2409
Gosset Award; George R. Vol. 1: 2547
got milk? All-Rookie Team Vol. 1: 14503
got milk? Rookie of the Year - Eddie Gottlieb Trophy Vol. 1: 14504
Gotham Awards
Independent Feature Project Vol. 1: 10720
Independent Feature Project Vol 1: 10721
Gotlieb Contribution Award; C. C. Vol. 1: 7167
Gotshal World Trade Arbitration Medal; Sylvan Vol. 1: 920
Gottesdiener Foundation; Nathan Vol. 2: 3771
Gottesfeld Award Vol. 1: 19103
Gottheil Award; Richard J. H. Vol. 1: 22111
Gottlieb Prize; Murray Vol. 1: 13257
Gottlieb Trophy; got milk? Rookie of the Year - Eddie Vol. 1: 14504
Gottschalk Medal Vol. 2: 122
Gottschalk Prize; Louis Vol. 1: 3992
Gouden Griffel Vol. 2: 4716
Gouden Penseel Vol. 2: 4715
Gouden Zoen Vol. 2: 4714
Goudy Distinguished Lecture; Frederic W. Vol. 1: 18086
Goueram-Toekenning Vol. 2: 5592
Gould Memorial Fund for Cancer Research; Cecille Vol. 1: 2298
Gould Memorial Literary Award Vol. 1: 3223
Gould; Prix de la Fondation Florence Vol. 2: 1690
Gould Prize; Glenn Vol. 1: 6795
Goulden Memorial Award; Loran L. Vol. 1: 9457
Governing Board's Award for the Best Paper Vol. 1: 21137
Government Achievement Award Vol. 1: 15206
Government Advocate Leadership Award Vol. 1: 12709

Government Affairs Award
American Society of Heating, Refrigerating and Air-Conditioning Engineers Vol. 1: 4433
National Association of the Remodeling Industry Vol 1: 14433
Government Affairs Award of Recognition Vol. 1: 6683
Government Civil Engineer of the Year Award Vol. 1: 4319
Government Communicator of the Year Vol. 1: 14244
Government Computer News Awards Program Vol. 1: 10104
Government Executive Leadership Award Vol. 1: 10108
Government Relations Award; Carl D. Perkins Vol. 1: 2073
Government Technology Leadership Award Vol. 1: 10108
Governor General Art Award Vol. 2: 5012
Governor General's Award Vol. 1: 6837
Governor General's Awards in Commemoration of the Persons Case Vol. 1: 19775
Governor General's Awards in Visual and Media Arts Vol. 1: 6796
Governor General's International Award in International Studies Vol. 1: 11510
Governor General's Literary Awards Vol. 1: 6797
Governor General's Literary Awards for Children's Literature Vol. 1: 6797
Governor General's Literary Awards for Translation Vol. 1: 6797
Governor of the Year Vol. 1: 15397
Governor of the Year Award Vol. 1: 6395
Governor's Arts Awards Vol. 1: 16276
Governor's Award Vol. 1: 11983
Governors Award Vol. 1: 16501
Governor's Award for Distinguished Achievement in Culture the Arts and Humanities Vol. 1: 10294
Governor's Award for Distinguished Achievement in the Arts Vol. 1: 10294
Governor's Awards for History Vol. 1: 19454
Governor's Awards for the Arts Vol. 1: 9588
Governor's National Leadership Award Vol. 1: 14212
Governor's Screenwriting Competition Vol. 1: 21388
Gowdy Media Award; Curt Vol. 1: 13751
Goyau; Prix Georges Vol. 2: 2154
GPA Citation for Service Vol. 1: 9893
GPA Recognition Award Vol. 1: 9894
GRA Annual Awards Vol. 1: 10122
Graber Award of Special Merit; Thomas M. Vol. 1: 1319
Graber Female Student-Athlete-of-the-Year; Betty Jo Vol. 1: 15310
Grace Award; Oliver R. Vol. 1: 7562
Grace Memorial Award; Dorman John Vol. 1: 14997
Grace Memorial Award; Ed Vol. 1: 4988
Gradiva Awards Vol. 1: 14052
Graduate and Students Papers Competition (Local Association) Competition Vol. 2: 7767
Graduate and Undergraduate Essay Awards Vol. 1: 10828
Graduate and Undergraduate Scholarships Vol. 1: 12512
Graduate Assistantships Vol. 1: 21017
Graduate Awards Vol. 1: 14801
Graduate Confectionery Fellowship - Penn State University Vol. 1: 17179
Graduate Fellowships Vol. 1: 10533
Graduate Fellowships in Mycology Vol. 1: 13724
Graduate Internships Vol. 1: 19408
Graduate of the Year Vol. 1: 10088
Graduate Research Award
AVS Vol. 1: 6149
Institute of Industrial Engineers Vol 1: 10955
Graduate Research Awards; CICS Vol. 1: 16566
Graduate Research Prizes Vol. 1: 13725
Graduate Student Vol. 1: 15832
Graduate Student Award
Canadian Society of Microbiologists Vol. 1: 7479
Eastern Apicultural Society of North America Vol 1: 9097
Materials Research Society Vol 1: 13181
Society for Applied Spectroscopy Vol 1: 18641
Southern Appalachian Botanical Society Vol 1: 19493
Graduate Student Awards
American Psychological Association - Psychotherapy Division (Division 29) Vol. 1: 3705
Biomedical Engineering Society Vol 1: 6389
International Association for the Fantastic in the Arts Vol 1: 11260
Graduate Student Fellowship/Novartis Award Vol. 1: 19338
Graduate Student Paper Award
Canadian Geotechnical Society Vol. 1: 7125
Rural Sociological Society Vol 1: 18189
Graduate Student Paper Competition Awards Vol. 1: 7442
Graduate Student Plant Breeding Award Vol. 1: 14793
Graduate Student Research Award Vol. 1: 4641
Graduate Student Research Competition in Population and Environmental Psychology Vol. 1: 3693
Graduate Student Research Grant Vol. 1: 4594
Graduate Student Scholar Award Vol. 1: 17326
Graduate Student Teaching Award Vol. 1: 16404
Graduateship of the City and Guilds of London Institute Vol. 2: 7307
Graduation Awards Vol. 1: 8550
Grady Award for Interpreting Chemistry for the Public; James T. Vol. 1: 1757
Grady - James H. Stack Award for Interpreting Chemistry for the Public; James T. Vol. 1: 1757
Graff Excellence Award; Margarite Ahern Vol. 1: 1572
Graffin Lectureship Award Vol. 1: 1645
Graffis Award; The Vol. 1: 15167
Graffis Award; Herb Vol. 1: 15167
Graffis Award; Joe Vol. 1: 15167
Graham and Dodd Award Vol. 1: 5396
Graham Award; Duncan Vol. 1: 18151
Graham Award; Harry J. Vol. 1: 17763
Graham Award of Merit; James H. Vol. 1: 18152
Graham Foundation Grant Vol. 1: 10126
Graham Gallery Award; Gavin Vol. 2: 9082
Graham Medal Vol. 2: 8659
Graham Trophy for Achievement in Applied Mathematics; Victor W. Vol. 2: 3636
Grain d'Or Vol. 2: 6408
Grainger Medallion; Percy Vol. 1: 12146
Gramatica; Premio Filippo Vol. 2: 3861
Gramatky Memorial Award; Hardie Vol. 1: 4852
Grambs Distinguished Career Research in Social Studies Award; Jean Dresden Vol. 1: 14781
Grammy Awards Vol. 1: 13822
Gran Canaria International Short Film Festival Vol. 2: 6009
Gran Cruz de la Universidad del Valle Vol. 2: 1344
Gran Premio Citta di Trento Vol. 2: 4059
Gran Premio de Cine Espanol Vol. 2: 6061
Gran Premio de Cine Vasco Vol. 2: 6061
Gran Premio del Festival de Bilbao Vol. 2: 6061
Gran Premio Felaban a las Comunicaciones Vol. 2: 1319
Gran Trofeo Golfo di Salerno Vol. 2: 4046
Granberg Award; Mickey Vol. 1: 14361
Grand Award
American First Day Cover Society Vol. 1: 2247
Wine Spectator Vol 1: 21649
Grand Challenge Award Vol. 1: 15422
Grand Champion Vol. 1: 14514
Grand Champion and Reserve Grand Champion Boar and Gilt Vol. 1: 15216
Grand Champion Primitive and Modern Equipment - U.S. and Europe Vol. 1: 21863
Grand Conceptor Award Vol. 1: 2009
Grand Concours Litteraire Vol. 1: 18232
Grand Cordon of the Supreme Order of the Chrysanthemum Vol. 2: 4190
Grand Cross International Social Merit Award Vol. 2: 1666
Grand Effie Vol. 1: 16206
Grand International Trophy for Excellence of Design and Fabric Vol. 1: 14745
Grand Journalism Prize Vol. 2: 5160
Grand Jury Awards Vol. 1: 9604
Grand Marketing Achievement Award Vol. 1: 15554
Grand Master Award Vol. 1: 18356
Grand National Exhibition Vol. 1: 930
Grand National Pulling Circuit Rookie of the Year Vol. 1: 15883
Grand Prix
Association Aeronautique et Astronautique de France Vol. 2: 2230
International Organisation of Vine and Wine Vol 2: 2499
U.S. International Film and Video Festival Vol 1: 20675
Grand Prix Annual Prize of the Society of Czech Architects Vol. 2: 1436
Grand Prix Award Vol. 2: 8011
Grand Prix d'Architecture de l'Academie des Beaux-Arts Vol. 2: 1691
Grand Prix de Chimie Industrielle Vol. 2: 2360
Grand Prix de Jazz General Motors Vol. 1: 9537
Grand Prix de la Chanson Francaise Vol. 2: 2576
Grand Prix de la Fondation de la Maison de la Chimie Vol. 2: 2347

Grand Prix de la Fondation pour la Recherche Medicale Vol. 2: 2364
Grand Prix de la Francophonie Vol. 2: 2095
Grand Prix de la Musique Symphonique Vol. 2: 2577
Grand Prix de la Poesie Vol. 2: 2580
Grand Prix de la Societe de Chimie Vol. 2: 2360
Grand Prix de la Ville de Tours Vol. 2: 2345
Grand Prix de la Ville de Villeurbanne Vol. 2: 2335
Grand Prix de l'Academie des Sciences Morales et Politiques Vol. 2: 2013
Grand Prix de l'AIPH and Grand Prix d'Excellence Vol. 2: 4797
Grand Prix de l'Edition Musicale Vol. 2: 2578
Grand Prix de l'Humour Vol. 2: 2579
Grand Prix de Litterature Vol. 2: 2096
Grand Prix de Philosophie Vol. 2: 2097
Grand Prix de Poesie Vol. 2: 2098
Grand Prix de S. A. S. Le Prince Rainier III Vol. 2: 4658
Grand Prix des Biennales Internationales de Poesie Vol. 2: 912
Grand Prix des Poetes Vol. 2: 2580
Grand Prix des Sciences Chimiques et Naturelles Vol. 2: 1995
Grand Prix des Sciences Mathematiques et Physiques Vol. 2: 1995
Grand Prix d'Histoire Vol. 2: 2528
Grand Prix d'Histoire de la Vallee aux Loups Vol. 2: 2528
Grand Prix d'Honneur Vol. 2: 6440
Grand Prix du Jazz Vol. 2: 2581
Grand Prix du Livre de Montreal Vol. 1: 18235
Grand Prix du Rayonnement de la Langue Francaise Vol. 2: 2099
Grand Prix du Roman Vol. 2: 2100
Grand Prix du Romantisme Vol. 2: 2528
Grand Prix du Souvenir Napoleonien Vol. 2: 2354
Grand Prix Eurovision for Young Dancers Vol. 2: 6316
Grand Prix Eurovision for Young Musicians Vol. 2: 6317
Grand Prix National de la Chanson Vol. 2: 2371
Grand Prix National de la Creation Audiovisuelle Vol. 2: 2372
Grand Prix National de la Creation Industrielle Vol. 2: 2373
Grand Prix National de la Danse Vol. 2: 2374
Grand Prix National de la Museographie Vol. 2: 2375
Grand Prix National de la Musique Vol. 2: 2376
Grand Prix National de la Peinture Vol. 2: 2377
Grand Prix National de la Photographie Vol. 2: 2378
Grand Prix National de la Poesie Vol. 2: 2379
Grand Prix National de la Sculpture Vol. 2: 2380
Grand Prix National de la Traduction Vol. 2: 2381
Grand Prix National de l'Archeologie Vol. 2: 2382
Grand Prix National de l'Architecture Vol. 2: 2383
Grand Prix National de l'Entreprise Culturelle Vol. 2: 2384
Grand Prix National des Arts
French Ministry of Culture and Communication Vol. 2: 2377
French Ministry of Culture and Communication Vol 2: 2380
French Ministry of Culture and Communication Vol 2: 2385
Grand Prix National des Arts Graphique Vol. 2: 2385
Grand Prix National des Lettres Vol. 2: 2386
Grand Prix National des Metiers d'Art Vol. 2: 2387
Grand Prix National d'Histoire Vol. 2: 2388
Grand Prix National du Cinema Vol. 2: 2389
Grand Prix National du Cirque Vol. 2: 2390
Grand Prix National du Patrimoine Vol. 2: 2391
Grand Prix National du Theatre Vol. 2: 2392
Grand Prix of Sofia Vol. 2: 1204
Grand Prix of the Americas Vol. 1: 13607
Grand Prix of the Dutch Film Golden Calf Vol. 2: 4862
Grand Prix of the Eurovision Song Contest Vol. 2: 6318
Grand Prix of the League of Red Cross and Red Crescent Societies Vol. 2: 1228
Grand Prix of the Town of Varna Vol. 2: 1236
Grand Prix Rolex pour la Protection du Monde Sous-Marin Vol. 2: 2470
Grand Prix SACD Vol. 2: 2589
Grand Prix Technique Vol. 2: 2259
Grand Prize Vol. 1: 7601
Grand Prize for Commissioned Animation Vol. 1: 16949
Grand Prize of AIPM/Grand Prize of Excellence Vol. 2: 4797
Grand Prize Winner Award Vol. 1: 15480
Grand Prizes Vol. 1: 16950
Grand Slam of Tennis Vol. 2: 7995
Grande Premio de Traducao Vol. 2: 5448
Grande Premio do romance e novela Vol. 2: 5449
Grandgent Award; Charles Hall Vol. 1: 8750
Grandmaster Vol. 2: 3195
Grandmaster Award Vol. 1: 13731
GRANDY Award Vol. 1: 206
Granjon Prize; Henry Vol. 2: 2492
Grant Award; Eugene L. Vol. 1: 4021
Grant Faculty Scholars; William T. Vol. 1: 21633
Grant for Geographic Literacy Vol. 1: 14782
Grant for Student Research in Mineralogy and Petrology Vol. 1: 13435
Grant Program Vol. 1: 20655
Grant/Stan Getz Award; Felix Vol. 1: 6470
Grants for Arts Projects Vol. 1: 14930
Grants for Astrological Research Vol. 1: 11916
Grants for Girls Vol. 1: 13171
Grants for Otologic and Related Science Research Projects Vol. 1: 8779
Grants-in-Aid of Research Vol. 1: 18512
Grants-in-Aid Program
Lyndon Baines Johnson Library and Museum Vol. 1: 12421
Society for the Psychological Study of Social Issues Vol 1: 18885
Grants in Herpetology Vol. 1: 18892
Grants to Eastern Europeans Vol. 2: 7480
Grants to Young Composers Vol. 1: 4380
Graphic Arts Awards Competition for Non-Heatset Printers Vol. 1: 17571
Graphic Journalism; Anthony Majeri Jr. Award for Innovation and Leadership in Vol. 1: 6210
Grasselli Medal Vol. 1: 19084
Grassland Society of Southern Africa Awards Vol. 2: 5574
Grasslander Award; Distinguished Vol. 1: 2273
Grassroots Award Vol. 1: 5570
Grassroots Government Leadership Award Vol. 1: 14443
Grau Turfgrass Science Award; Fred V. Vol. 1: 8663
Grauls Prize; Noordstarfonds - Dr. Jan Vol. 2: 962
Graves Lecture
Royal Academy of Medicine in Ireland Vol. 2: 3690
Royal Academy of Medicine in Ireland Vol 2: 3692
Gray Award; Asa Vol. 1: 4595
Gray Award; Eva Kenworthy Vol. 1: 1560
Gray Award; Henry Vol. 1: 1082
Gray Award; Stanley Vol. 2: 7708
Gray Citation of Merit; William S. Vol. 1: 11856
Gray Matter Medal Vol. 2: 7169
Gray Medal; ICRU - Vol. 1: 11492
Gray Medal; Stanley Vol. 2: 7709
Gray Papers Awards; Stanley Vol. 2: 7710
Grealis Special Achievement Award; Walt Vol. 1: 6846
Great American Artificer Award Vol. 1: 15051
Great American Main Street Award Vol. 1: 15918
Great Award of the Year Vol. 2: 2567
Great Friend to Kids Award Vol. 1: 5600
Great Gold Medal; Royal Swedish Academy of Engineering Sciences Vol. 2: 6200
Great Heart Award Vol. 1: 21280
Great Idea Contest Vol. 1: 12166
Great Lake Crew Award of Merit; Ocean Crew and Vol. 1: 20379
Great Lakes Commission - Sea Grant Fellowship Vol. 1: 13357
Great Lakes Crew Award of Merit Vol. 1: 3091
Great Lakes Division Foundation Vol. 1: 1643
Great Lakes Skakel Award Vol. 1: 1648
Great Menu Contest Vol. 1: 15626
Great Plains National Exhibition Vol. 1: 13616
Great Plains National Exhibition of Small, Two-Dimensional Works Vol. 1: 13616
Great Prize for Literary Translation Vol. 2: 5448
Great Prize for Romance Novels Vol. 2: 5449
Great Stone Face Book Award Vol. 1: 7906
Great Swedish Heritage Award Vol. 1: 19859
Great Teachers Award Vol. 1: 16306
Greater Dandenong Short Story Competition Vol. 2: 310
Greater Haverhill Arts Association Annual Exhibition Vol. 1: 10147
Greater Lynn International Color Slide Salon Vol. 1: 10149
Greater Midwest International Exhibition Vol. 1: 7771
Greater Union Awards Vol. 2: 615
Greathouse Distinguished Leadership Award; Frank Vol. 1: 5715

Greathouse Medal; Walser S. Vol. 1: 4853
Greaves-Walker Award; Arthur Frederick Vol. 1: 1683
Greaves-Walker Roll of Honor Award Vol. 1: 12572
Grebe Award; Alfred H. Vol. 1: 17836
Greeley Award; Horace Vol. 1: 16119
Greeley Award; Samuel Arnold Vol. 1: 4320
Greeley Local Government Service Award; Samuel A. Vol. 1: 3802
Green and Charles W. Ramsdell Award; Fletcher M. Vol. 1: 19501
Green Apple Award Vol. 2: 7575
Green Apple Awards Vol. 2: 7435
Green-Armytage and Spackman Travelling Scholarship Vol. 2: 8447
Green Award Vol. 1: 9667
Green Award; Brian and Maria Vol. 1: 8357
Green Award; Daniel H. Vol. 1: 5952
Green Award; Fletcher M. Vol. 1: 19501
Green Award for Technology Entrepreneurship; Cecil Vol. 1: 6291
Green Award for Young Concert Artists; Philip and Dorothy Vol. 2: 8099
Green Award for Young Concert Artists; Philip & Dorthy Vol. 2: 8100
Green City Hands-On Activist Award Vol. 1: 17365
Green Codes and Standards Medal; Melvin R. Vol. 1: 4513
Green Free Enterprise Scholarship; Warren Vol. 1: 5085
Green Globe Award for Environmental Achievement Vol. 1: 9572
Green Hotel of the Year Vol. 1: 7592
Green Journalism Awards; Charles E. Vol. 1: 10308
Green Mountain Power Vol. 1: 7749
Green Needle Vol. 2: 1489
Green Outstanding Young Scientist Award; Gordon J. Vol. 1: 7340
Green Prize; Leonard W. Vol. 2: 7648
Green Round Hill Trophy; Colonel Vol. 1: 3589
Green School Educator Award; Elizabeth A.H. Vol. 1: 4701
Green Section Award Vol. 1: 20605
Green Star Awards Vol. 1: 17626
Greenberg Award; Noah Vol. 1: 3176
Greenberg Rabbinic Achievement Award; Rabbi Simon Vol. 1: 12376
Greenblatt Prize; Bob Vol. 2: 7962
Greene Award in Bryology; Stanley Vol. 1: 11290
Greene Homeland Defense Award; Lorne Vol. 1: 1807
Greene, Jr., Award; General Wallace M. Vol. 1: 13098
Greene Medal; Arnold Vol. 2: 7748
Greene Memorial Award; Jerry Vol. 1: 14583
Greene Memorial Awards; Bert Vol. 1: 11330
Greene Memorial United States Numismatics - YN Exhibit Award; Gordon Z. Vol. 1: 3216
Greene Telecommunications Research Fund Award; Paul F. Vol. 1: 6186
Greenfield Award; Sylvia Sorkin Vol. 1: 1369
Greenford Award; Stephen Vol. 1: 6914
Greening of Design Vol. 1: 2812
Greenman Award; Jesse M. Vol. 1: 6548
The Greensboro Review Literary Awards Vol. 1: 10170
Greenstone Diving Safety Award; Leonard Vol. 1: 14450
Greenwich Prize; Royal Naval College, Vol. 2: 7866
Greenwood Publishing Group Award; Louis Shores - Vol. 1: 17947
Greer Cup; Don Vol. 1: 20891
Gregg Award; Dr. Randy Vol. 1: 7217
Gregg Award in Business Education; John Robert Vol. 1: 10042
Gregori Aminoffs Pris Vol. 2: 6212
Gregory Award; Joseph T. Vol. 1: 19354
Gregory Awards; Eric Vol. 2: 8982
Gregory Medal; Herbert E. Vol. 1: 17013
Gregson's Founder Award Vol. 1: 19008
Greim Award; Willard Vol. 1: 553
Grelaud; Fondation Leon Vol. 2: 1920
Grenzebach Awards; John Vol. 1: 43
Gresham Award; D. Todd Vol. 1: 13019
Gretzky Scholarship Foundation; Wayne and Walter Vol. 1: 7303
Greve Memorial Award; Belle Vol. 1: 15592
Grey Cup Vol. 1: 7109
Grice Award; Winthrop W. Vol. 1: 10553
Grierson International Gold Medal Award; John Vol. 1: 19192
Griffin Award; Charles A. Vol. 1: 1026
Griffin Award for Urban Design; Walter Burley Vol. 2: 525
Griffin Poetry Prize Vol. 1: 10176
Griffin Rolex Award; Ellen Vol. 1: 12655
Griffith Award; D. W. Vol. 1: 8942
Griffith Award; Ruby Vol. 1: 9233
Griffith Awards; David Wark Vol. 1: 8944
Griffith Memorial Award; Clark C. Vol. 1: 20130
Griffith Review Lecture; Fred Vol. 2: 8934
Griffiths Property Person of the Year; Jack Vol. 1: 15560
Grimes Award for Excellence in Chemical Engineering; William W. Vol. 1: 2775
Grimley Award; Horace Vol. 2: 8028
Grimm Leadership and Service Award; James C. Vol. 1: 5623
Grimm Prize; Harold J. Vol. 1: 18541
Grimme Preis; Adolf Vol. 2: 2780
Grimwade Medal; John Vol. 2: 7037
Grindley Medal Vol. 1: 287
Griner Award; John Vol. 1: 7449
Grinter Distinguished Service Award; Linton E. Vol. 1: 60
Grisby, Jr. Award; Committee on Multiethnic Concerns J. Eugene Vol. 1: 13957
Griscom Award; Ludlow Vol. 1: 1566
Griswold Award; S. Smith Vol. 1: 320
Griswold Prize in American Law and Society; Littleton - Vol. 1: 2474
Grocers Care Awards Vol. 1: 15174
Grohmann Award; H. Victor Vol. 1: 10554
Grolier Foundation Award Vol. 1: 2979
Grolier National Library Week Grant Vol. 1: 3000
Grolier Poetry Prize Vol. 1: 10178
Grolla D'Oro Vol. 2: 4061
Gross Animation Award; Yoram Vol. 2: 616
Gross Memorial Award; Barry R. Vol. 1: 14370
Gross Restoration Award; Frank Vol. 1: 21376
Grosse Literaturstipendien des Landes Tirol Vol. 2: 674
Grosser Literaturpreis der Bayerischen Akademie der Schonen Kunste Vol. 2: 2660
Grossman Award; Louis I. Vol. 1: 1192
Grossmann Young Author Award; Marcus A. Vol. 1: 5180
Grosvenor Medal Vol. 1: 15156
Grote Prijs van de Nederlandse Film Gouden Kalf Vol. 2: 4862
Grotius; Prix Vol. 2: 6373
Grotthuss premija; Teodor Vol. 2: 4389
Ground Transportation Company of the Year Vol. 2: 4084
Grounds Management Awards Vol. 1: 17626
Group Achievement Award Vol. 1: 13895
Group and Grotto Conservation Award Vol. 1: 15797
Group Trophies Vol. 1: 21588
Group Volunteer of the Year Award Vol. 1: 2395
Grove Prizes; Sir Charles Vol. 2: 8101
Grove-Rasmussen Memorial Award; Morten Vol. 1: 1109
Groves Fund; Donald Vol. 1: 3272
Grow Award; Malcolm C. Vol. 1: 19351
Grower of the Year Award Vol. 1: 9613
Growth and Promotion Award Vol. 1: 20076
Grubenwehrehrenzeichen Vol. 2: 685
Gruber Award and Heidi Castleman Award for Excellence in Chamber Music Vol. 1: 7793
Gruber Fund Award of the AAD; Lila Vol. 1: 640
Gruber Grant; Ada Vol. 1: 7785
Gruber Memorial Cancer Research Award and Lectureship; Lila Vol. 1: 638
Grulee Award; Clifford G. Vol. 1: 774
Grumbacher Gold Medal Vol. 1: 16690
Grumbacher Gold Medallion Award Vol. 1: 10147
Grumbridge Pacific Island Trophy; Jack Vol. 2: 8263
Grunfeld-Preis; Paul Vol. 2: 2878
Grunfeld Prize; Paul Vol. 2: 2878
Grunzweig Human Rights Award; Emil Vol. 2: 3723
Gruver Memorial Scholarship; Sarah Louise Vol. 1: 16073
GSA Distinguished Service Award Vol. 1: 9950
GSBA Scholarships Vol. 1: 10164
GTE Academic All-America Hall of Fame Vol. 1: 8190
GTE Academic All-American of the Year Vol. 1: 8191
Guardia Memorial Trophy; Ed Vol. 1: 20615
Guardian New Director's Award Vol. 2: 7407
Guardian of Liberty Vol. 1: 2295
Guardian of Seniors' Rights Vol. 1: 9
Guardians of the Seas Award Vol. 1: 20929
Guay-Lebrun; Prix Le Vol. 2: 1720
Gude, Jr. Award; Adolph E. Vol. 1: 4587
Guelph Spring Festival Vol. 1: 10190
Guelph Spring Festival Music Competition Vol. 1: 10190
Guenther Award in the Chemistry of Essential Oils and Related Products; Ernest Vol. 1: 1758
Guenther Award in the Chemistry of Natural Products; Ernest Vol. 1: 1758
Guerin; Prix Andre- Vol. 1: 18604
Guerin; Prix Marcelin Vol. 2: 2182
Guerrera Medal Vol. 2: 2493
Guest Lectureship Award on Basic Cell Research in Cytology Vol. 1: 4394
Guest of Honor Vol. 1: 711
Guest of Honor Award Vol. 1: 14892
Guetzkow Prize; Harold Vol. 1: 16567
Guggenheim Memorial Foundation Fellowships; John Simon Vol. 1: 10192
Guggenheim; Prix Paul Vol. 2: 6494

Award Index

Guggenheim Prize; Paul Vol. 2: 6494
Guha Memorial Lecture; B. C. Vol. 2: 3534
Guha Memorial Lecture; Bires Chandra Vol. 2: 3485
Guild of Food Writers Award Vol. 2: 7583
Guild of Professional Toastmasters Best After Dinner Speaker of the Year Vol. 2: 7585
Guild of Taxidermists Acredited Member Vol. 2: 7593
Guilday Prize; Peter Vol. 1: 1654
Guilford Undergraduate Research Awards; J. P. Vol. 1: 17695
Guilhermina Suggia Gift for the Cello Vol. 2: 8152
Guinn Awards; James L. Vol. 1: 12292
Guise Medal; Arthur B. Vol. 1: 19129
Guitar Foundation of America Solo Guitar Competition Vol. 1: 10204
Guiteras Award; Ramon Vol. 1: 4793
Gulbenkian Foundation Grants; Calouste Vol. 2: 7228
Gulbenkian Prizes for History; Calouste Vol. 2: 5485
Gulbenkian Translation Prize; Calouste Vol. 2: 5410
Gulbertian Prize; Calouste Vol. 2: 8972
Guldbaggar Vol. 2: 6280
Guldberg and Waage's Law of Mass Action Memorial Medal Vol. 2: 5152
Gulf of Salerno Grand Trophy Vol. 2: 4046
Gulick Award; Luther Halsey Vol. 1: 877
Gullmedalje for Utvikling av det Teknologiske Miljo Vol. 2: 5168
Gullo and Treiber Award Vol. 1: 16424
Gun och Olof Engqvists stipendium Vol. 2: 6253
Gundhall School Gold Medal Vol. 2: 7597
Gundolf-Preis fur die Vermittlung deutscher Kultur im Ausland; Friedrich- Vol. 2: 2775
Gung and Dr. Charles Y. Hu Award for Distinguished Service to Mathematics; Yueh-Gin Vol. 1: 13192
Gungywamp Society Scholarship Vol. 1: 10208
Gunlogson Countryside Engineering Award; G. B. Vol. 1: 4223
Gunlogson Medal; G. B. Vol. 1: 2527
Gunn Conservation Award; W. W. H. Vol. 1: 16762
Gunnarson Award; Arthur B. Vol. 1: 10989
Gunnells Intellectual Freedom Award; Danny Vol. 1: 10765
Gunnerus Medal; J. E. Vol. 2: 5184
Gunnerusmedaljen Vol. 2: 5184
Gunning Victoria Jubilee Prize Lectureship Vol. 2: 8788
Gunter Russell Prize Vol. 2: 7100
Gunter Scholarship Award Fund; Connie and Robert T. Vol. 1: 19153
Gunther Award; Frank A. Vol. 1: 17837
Gunton Award; T. P. Vol. 2: 7065
Gunzo Fiction Prize Vol. 2: 4240
Gunzo Prize for New Writers Vol. 2: 4240
Gusti Prize; Dimitrie Vol. 2: 5830
Gustin Memorial Intermediate Chopin Scholarship; The Lyell Vol. 1: 18283
Gustin Memorial Senior Chopin Scholarship; The Lyell Vol. 1: 18314
Gutenberg Award Vol. 2: 2920
Gutenberg Medal; Beno Vol. 2: 2311
Gutenberg-Preis Vol. 2: 2920
Gutenberg Prize; Johann Vol. 1: 18768
Guth Memorial Award for Interior Lighting Design; Edwin F. Vol. 1: 10695
Guthrie Award; RSA Vol. 2: 8672
Guthrie Medal and Prize Vol. 2: 7730
Guthrie Medal; Faldt Vol. 2: 391
Guthrie Prize Vol. 2: 7670
Guthrie Prize; Michael Vol. 2: 7648
Guthrie Training Fellowship; Duncan Vol. 2: 6666
Guttentag Award; Marcia Vol. 1: 2204
Guttentag Fellowship; Marcia Vol. 1: 2204
Guttmacher Award; Manfred S. Vol. 1: 3619
Guye; Fondation Charles Eugene Vol. 2: 1820
Guye; Fondation Philippe A. Vol. 2: 1953
Guyot Memorial Award; Arnold Vol. 1: 15157
Guyton Awards for Excellence in Integrative Physiology; Arthur C. Vol. 1: 3518
Guze Award; Henry Vol. 1: 18656
GWAA Hall of Fame Vol. 1: 9879
GWAA Honorary Member Vol. 1: 9880
The GWIC Award Vol. 1: 10055
Gwobr Goffa Alun Llywelyn-Williams Vol. 2: 6764
Gwobr Goffa Sir Bryner Jones Vol. 2: 8871
Gwobrau Tir na n-Og Vol. 2: 9204
GWUP Prize Vol. 2: 3060
Gyldendal Prisen; Soren Vol. 2: 1498
Gyllenbergs pris; Fabian Vol. 2: 6189
Gymnastics National Volunteer of the Year Vol. 1: 554
Gzowski Medal Vol. 1: 7414
H. Browning Ross Long Distance Running Merit Award Vol. 1: 21224
H. W. Nelson Award Vol. 1: 10209
Haas Award; Otto Vol. 1: 17536
Haas Award; Walter H. Vol. 1: 5751
Haber Award; William Vol. 1: 10432
Haber Prize; William Vol. 1: 3344
Habif; Prix Mondial Nessim Vol. 2: 6538
Habif Prize; Nessim Vol. 2: 2596
Habitat Solaire, Habitat d'aujourd'hui Vol. 2: 2532
Hachemeister Prize; Charles A. Vol. 1: 7623
Hacke Scholar-Teacher Award; Robert Vol. 1: 8154
Hacker Memorial Award; William J. Vol. 1: 15716
Hackett Award; James K. Vol. 1: 8031
Hackney Award; L. R. Mike Vol. 1: 18946
Hackney Literary Awards Vol. 1: 6402
Haddings pris; Assar Vol. 2: 6190
Haddon Jr., M.D., Memorial Top Student Paper; William Vol. 1: 19495
Haddonfield Symphony Solo Competition Vol. 1: 10217
Haddonfield Symphony Solo Competition for Young Instrumentalists Vol. 1: 10217
Haddow Lecture; Alexander Vol. 2: 8814
Hadford Professional Achievement Award; Gary Vol. 1: 7168
Hadia Cerpen Malayan Banking - DBP Vol. 2: 4429
Hadiah Cerpen Maybank - DBP Vol. 2: 4429
Hadiah Sastera Perdana Malaysia Vol. 2: 4430
Hadley Memorial Achievement Award; Ross Vol. 1: 20419
Hadow/Donald Stuart Short Story Award; Lyndall Vol. 2: 337
Hafner VTOL Prize Vol. 2: 8388
Hagan Trophy Vol. 1: 5107
Hague Academy of International Law Scholarships Vol. 2: 4789
Hague Award; John L. Vol. 1: 5953
Hahn-Preis fur Chemie und Physik; Otto- Vol. 2: 2723
Haig-Brown Award; Roderick Vol. 1: 9477
Haight Award; Walter Vol. 1: 15922
Haiku Literature Awards; Museum of Vol. 1: 10223
Haiman Award Vol. 1: 14710
Haiman Award for Distinguished Scholarship in Freedom of Expression; Franklyn S. Vol. 1: 14710
Haiman Award; Mieczyslaw Vol. 1: 17455
Haimo Award for Distinguished College or University Teaching of Mathematics; Deborah and Franklin Tepper Vol. 1: 13193
Hair Prize; Paul Vol. 1: 264
Hajek Prize; Louise Vol. 1: 13003
Hakanson Award; R. C. Vol. 1: 9361
Hake Basic/Applied Research Award; Don F. Vol. 1: 3655
Hakluyt Award Vol. 1: 12431
Hal Jackson's Michigan Talented Teens Scholarship Vol. 1: 19903
Hal Rogers Endowment Fund Vol. 1: 12597
Hala-Negri Award Vol. 1: 10603
Halas Trophy; George S. Vol. 1: 15084
Halbouty Human Needs Award; Michel T. Vol. 1: 1338
Halcrow Premium Vol. 2: 7768
Hale Award; Sarah Josepha Vol. 1: 18042
Hale Prize; George Ellery Vol. 1: 1512
Halecki Award; Oscar Vol. 1: 17456
Hales Prize; Stephen Vol. 1: 4588
Haley Memorial Award for Clinical Excellence; Sarah Vol. 1: 11966
Haley Space Flight Award; AIAA Vol. 1: 2652
Hall Award for Library Literature; G. K. Vol. 1: 2980
Hall Award; G. Stanley Vol. 1: 3668
Hall Award; Marilyn Vol. 1: 6349
Hall Book Prize; John Whitney Vol. 1: 5276
Hall Composites Manufacturing Award; J. H. "Jud" Vol. 1: 19154
Hall; Fondation James Vol. 2: 1893
Hall Freedom Cup; George Robert Vol. 1: 5107
Hall/Harold F. Mayfield Award; George A. Vol. 1: 21638
Hall Medal for Research into Animal Diseases; G. Norman Vol. 2: 8494
Hall Memorial Award; Albert H. Vol. 1: 15268
Hall Memorial Award; Lee G. Vol. 1: 20912
Hall Memorial Award; Melody Vol. 1: 14094
Hall of Champions
American Power Boat Association Vol. 1: 3590
World Association of Industrial and Technological Research Organizations Vol 1: 21860
Hall of Distinguished Americans Vol. 1: 15986
Hall of Fame
American Baseball Coaches Association Vol. 1: 1544
American Morgan Horse Association Vol 1: 3131
American Society of Heating, Refrigerating and Air-Conditioning Engineers Vol 1: 4434
American Theatre Organ Society Vol 1: 4737
Billiard Congress of America Vol 1: 6382
Brotherhood of Working Farriers Association Vol 1: 6659

Canadian Hardware and Housewares Manufacturers Association Vol 1: 7135
Cleveland Police Historical Society and Museum Vol 1: 8102
Council for Health and Human Services Ministries, United Church of Christ Vol 1: 8557
Country Music Showcase International Vol 1: 8623
Libertarian Futurist Society Vol 1: 12805
Minnewaukan Community Club Vol 1: 13488
Multi-Level Marketing International Association Vol 1: 13665
National Association of Display Industries Vol 1: 14198
National Association of Left-Handed Golfers Vol 1: 14299
National Auto Auction Association Vol 1: 14471
National Baseball Hall of Fame and Museum Vol 1: 14495
National Christian College Athletic Association Vol 1: 14657
National Forensic League Vol 1: 15101
National Museum of Racing and Hall of Fame Vol 1: 15404
National Pigeon Association Vol 1: 15502
National Sportscasters and Sportswriters Association Vol 1: 15812
National Wheelchair Basketball Association Vol 1: 15943
American Indian Lore Association Vol 1: 2605
O'Dochartaigh Clann Association Vol 2: 3674
OX5 Aviation Pioneers Vol 1: 16989
Palomino Horse Breeders of America Vol 1: 17049
Pastel Society of America Vol 1: 17104
Percussive Arts Society Vol 1: 17220
Pi Kappa Phi Vol 1: 17315
Piano Technicians Guild Vol 1: 17331
Pickle Packers International Vol 1: 17337
Professional Bowlers Association of America Vol 1: 17593
Relay and Switch Industry Association Vol 1: 17969
Retail Advertising and Marketing Association Vol 1: 18017
Special Libraries Association Vol 1: 19549
Specialty Equipment Market Association Vol 1: 19588
United States Curling Association Vol 1: 20463
U.S. Speedskating Vol 1: 20846
United States Water Polo Vol 1: 20883
USA Deaf Sports Federation Vol 1: 21165
Wheelchair Sports, USA Vol 1: 21597
Women's All-Star Association Vol 1: 21772
Zen-do Kai Martial Arts Vol 1: 22105
Hall of Fame and Band of the Year Award Vol. 1: 15225
Hall of Fame and Distinguished Service Vol. 1: 12148
Hall of Fame Award
American Society on Aging Vol. 1: 4642
American Sportscasters Association Vol 1: 4675
Asphalt Emulsion Manufacturer Association Vol 1: 5202
Catholic University of America Alumni Association Vol 1: 7666
Direct Selling Association Vol 1: 8934
International Federation of Leather Guilds Vol 1: 11597
Livestock Publications Council Vol 1: 12897
National Association of Pipe Coating Applicators Vol 1: 14330
National Auctioneers Association Vol 1: 14465
National Aviation Hall of Fame Vol 1: 14475
National Forum for Black Public Administrators Vol 1: 15110
National Intercollegiate Soccer Officials Association Vol 1: 15276
National Interscholastic Swimming Coaches Association of America Vol 1: 15282
National School Transportation Association Vol 1: 15673
Pitch and Putt Union of Ireland Vol 2: 3680
Small Motor and Motion Association Vol 1: 18565
Hall of Fame Awards
Consumer Electronics Association Vol. 1: 8458
National Academy of Recording Arts and Sciences Vol 1: 13823
United in Group Harmony Association Vol 1: 20336
Hall of Fame - Contributor Vol. 1: 19866
Hall of Fame in Philanthropy Vol. 1: 20350
Hall of Fame Meritorious Award Vol. 1: 20838
Hall of Fame Museum Vol. 1: 10780
Hall of Fame of Distinguished Band Conductors Vol. 1: 14484
Hall of Fame Outstanding Service Vol. 1: 13525
Hall of Fame Program Vol. 1: 14287
Hall of Flame Vol. 1: 12488
Hall of Foam Vol. 1: 9106
Hall of Outstanding Americans Vol. 1: 15986
Hall Prize; R. T. Vol. 2: 296
Halle Research Award; Herman L. Vol. 1: 9985
Hallinan Award; Archbishop Paul Vol. 1: 7638
Hallmark Award Vol. 1: 17252
Hallock Card Award Vol. 1: 17222
Hallopeau; Prix Vol. 1: 11783
Halmshaw Award; Ron Vol. 2: 7038
Halmstad Prize Vol. 1: 18941
Halperin Electric Transmission and Distribution Award; Herman Vol. 1: 10863
Halpern Award for Distinguished Professional Contributions; Florence Vol. 1: 3748
Halpern Religious Freedom Award; Judy Vol. 1: 16680
Halsell Prize; Willie D. Vol. 1: 13506
Ham-Wasserman Lecture Vol. 1: 4445
Hamel; Fondation de Madame Edmond Vol. 2: 1839
Hamel; Prix Joseph Vol. 2: 2062
Hamer and Elizabeth Hamer Kegan Award; Philip M. Vol. 1: 18954
Hamilton Award; Alice Vol. 1: 2613
Hamilton Award; Constance E. Vol. 1: 8049
Hamilton Award; James A. Vol. 1: 1869
Hamilton Award; Jimmy Vol. 1: 4567
Hamilton Award; Mary Ellen Vol. 1: 15338
Hamilton Award; Samuel Vol. 1: 3772
Hamilton Award; Scott Vol. 1: 21225
Hamilton Hospital Administrators' Book Award; James A. Vol. 1: 1869
Hamilton Memorial CWI of the Year Award; Dalton E. Vol. 1: 4881
Hamilton Memorial Prize Vol. 2: 5081
Hamilton Memorial Prize; Max Vol. 1: 8199
Hamilton Traveling Fellowship; John Vol. 2: 8461
Hamilton Volunteer of the Year Award; Katherine Vol. 1: 15376
Hammerman Spirit of Education Award; Harold Vol. 1: 14434
Hammett Award; Dashiell Vol. 2: 1394
Hammett Prize Vol. 1: 11322
Hamming Medal; Richard W. Vol. 1: 10864
Hammond Award; Thomas T. Vol. 1: 21117
Hammond Memorial Prize; Sir John Vol. 2: 7181
Hammond Prize; Dr. George P. Vol. 1: 17237
Hampel Award; Leslie A. Vol. 1: 1216
Hancock Brick and Tile Soil and Water Engineering Award Vol. 1: 4224
The Hancock Memorial Award in Piano Vol. 1: 18293
Hancor Soil and Water Engineering Award Vol. 1: 4224
Hand Award for Academic Achievement in Folklore and Mythology Studies; Wayland D. Vol. 1: 8889
Hand Award; Judge Learned Vol. 1: 2885
Hand Medal; Learned Vol. 1: 9442
"Hands Across South Madison" Community Services Initiative Vol. 1: 19460
Handy Awards; W. C. Vol. 1: 6474
Hanes Natural History Award; Anne Vol. 1: 16928
Hanford Sr. Distinguished Faculty Award; Lloyd D. Vol. 1: 11036
Hang Gliding Diploma Vol. 2: 6336
Hank IBA Defensive Player of the Year Vol. 1: 14082
Hanken Gold Medal Vol. 2: 8605
Hanks, Jr., Scholarship in Meteorology; Howard H. Vol. 1: 3097
Hanks Memorial Award for Professional Excellence; Nancy Vol. 1: 1279
Hanlon Award Vol. 1: 9895
Hann Award; Elmer L. Vol. 1: 19210
Hannah Medal; Jason A. Vol. 1: 18166
Hannan Medal Vol. 2: 123
Hanovenian Stallion of the Year Vol. 2: 3117
Hanover International Violin Competition Vol. 2: 2771
Hanover Memorial Recognition Award; Phillip Vol. 1: 12345
Hans Dahs Plakette Award Vol. 2: 2791
Hans Jurgen Engell Prize Vol. 2: 6455
Hans Schneider Prize in Linear Algebra Vol. 1: 11735
Hans Stille Medaille Vol. 2: 2834
Hansberger Leadership in Global Investing Award; Thomas L. Vol. 1: 5397
Hansberry Playwriting Award; Lorraine Vol. 1: 12545
Hansell Publication Award; Dorothy E. Vol. 1: 1121
Hansen Award; Ann Vol. 1: 20806
Hansen Fondets Pris for Mikrobiologisk Forskning; Emil Christian Vol. 2: 1442
Hansen Foundation's Award for Microbiological Research; The Emil Christian Vol. 2: 1442
Hansen Medal; C. F. Vol. 2: 1523
Hansen; Premio Profesor Dr. Ricardo Vol. 2: 41

Award Index

Hansens Bibliotekspris; R. Lysholt Vol. 2: 1461
Hanson Award (Fighter/Attack Squadron of the Year); Robert M. Vol. 1: 13078
Hanson Awards Program; Abel Vol. 1: 5702
Hanson Medal Vol. 2: 7749
Hanson Medal; Carl Vol. 2: 9005
Hanus Medal Vol. 2: 1418
Hanyo Award; George T. Vol. 1: 6150
Happold Brilliant Award Vol. 2: 7286
Harabaszewski Medal; Jan Vol. 2: 5336
Harbourfront Festival Prize Vol. 1: 11882
Hardee Dissertation of the Year Award; Melvene D. Vol. 1: 14404
Hardeman Prize; D. B. Vol. 1: 12422
Harden Medal Vol. 2: 6867
Hardesty Award; Shortridge Vol. 1: 4321
Hardhat Award; Silver Vol. 1: 8450
Harding Award Vol. 2: 6667
Harding Trophy; Olga E. Vol. 2: 5034
Hardinge Award; Hal Williams Vol. 1: 18813
Hardingham Presidential Sword; Sir Robert Vol. 2: 8389
Hardison Award; J. Brown Vol. 1: 17913
Hardison Jr. Poetry Prize; O. B. Vol. 1: 9647
Hardy Award; Samuel Vol. 1: 12074
Hardy Awards; W. J. Vol. 1: 3115
Hardy Keynote Address; R.M. Vol. 1: 7126
Hardy Lectureship Vol. 2: 8089
Hardy Medal Award; Robert Lansing Vol. 1: 13448
Hardy Prize; William Bate Vol. 2: 7233
Haret Prize; Spiru Vol. 2: 5831
Harger Memorial Award; Don
Federation of Fly Fishers Vol. 1: 9478
Federation of Fly Fishers Vol 1: 9484
Hargrove Award; Bill Vol. 1: 21226
Haring Prize; Clarence H. Vol. 1: 2475
Harington-De Visscher Prize Vol. 2: 1486
Harkin Conservation Award; J. B. Vol. 1: 7330
Harkin Medal; J. B. Vol. 1: 7330
Harkness Fellowships Vol. 1: 10239
Harlan D. Mills Award Vol. 1: 10894
Harlequin Award Vol. 2: 7128
Harley Award; Herbert Vol. 1: 2911
Harlow Business-Government Relations Award; Bryce Vol. 1: 10241
Harman Award; Katherine Bishop Vol. 2: 7066
Harman Award; Nathaniel Bishop Vol. 2: 7067
Harmer Award; Bill Vol. 1: 6480
Harmers Diamond Jubilee Trophy Vol. 2: 8263
Harmon Award; Lt. Gens. Millard F. and Hubert R. Vol. 1: 16828
Harmony Queens Vol. 1: 10248
Harms-Preis; Bernhard- Vol. 2: 3006
Harness Horse of the Year Vol. 1: 20876
Harness Track of America's Art Competition/ Auction Vol. 1: 10258
Harold Butner Award Vol. 1: 8789
Harper Lecture; Roland Vol. 2: 9006
Harpers Ferry Memorial Scholarship Vol. 1: 20520
Harrelson Service Award; Major Vol. 1: 14746
Harrevold Memorial Award; Central Nervous System Section Van Vol. 1: 3513
Harriman Award for Distinguished Volunteer Service Vol. 1: 3829
Harriman Award; W. Averell Vol. 1: 2280
Harriman Democracy Award; W. Averell Vol. 1: 14910
Harriman Memorial Trophy Horse of the Year Award; E. Roland Vol. 1: 20620
Harrington Award Vol. 1: 18685
Harrington-Lux Creative Design Award; Holly Vol. 1: 10333
Harris Award; Albert J. Vol. 1: 11857
Harris Award; Charles Vol. 1: 8918
Harris Award; Gilbert Vol. 1: 17035
Harris Award; Hayden- Vol. 1: 845
Harris Award; Paul Vol. 1: 20217
Harris Hybrid Award Vol. 1: 1617
Harris Literature Award; Albert H. Vol. 2: 8263
Harris Medal; Townsend Vol. 1: 519
Harris Playwright Award Competition; Julie Vol. 1: 6350
Harris Ribbon; JPA H. E. Vol. 1: 12470
Harris State Leadership Award; Jeffrey S. Vol. 1: 14213
Harrison Award Vol. 1: 17534
Harrison Award; James Vol. 2: 2483
Harrison Award; John Vol. 2: 8597
Harrison Award of Merit; Bernard P. Vol. 1: 14698
Harrison Awards Vol. 1: 11172
Harrison/Florida Irrigation Society Scholarship; Dalton S. Vol. 1: 9608
Harrison Memorial Award; Bernie Vol. 1: 21439
Harrison Memorial Prize Vol. 2: 8754
Harrison Prescott Eddy Medal Vol. 1: 21485
Harrison Prize (Laryngological Section); W. J. Vol. 2: 8815
Harry E. Schlenz Medal Vol. 1: 21486
Harshbarger Landscape Design Plaque Vol. 1: 2556
Hart Award of Merit for Lifetime Achievement; Kitty Carlisle Vol. 1: 10035
Hart Cup Award Vol. 1: 20807
Hart Memorial Award; Moss Vol. 1: 16125
Hart Public Service Award; Philip Vol. 1: 8461
Hart Service Award; Ray L. Vol. 1: 832
Hart Trophy; Nelson C. Vol. 1: 7218
Hartford-Nicholsen Award Vol. 1: 19296
Hartley Medal; Sir Harold Vol. 2: 7716
Hartman Excellence in Sportswriting Award; Fred Vol. 1: 19997
Hartnett Award Vol. 2: 585
Hartranft Award; Joseph B. Vol. 1: 397
Hartree Premium Vol. 2: 7808
Hartshorne Trophies Vol. 1: 20589
Hartwig Prize; Dr. Vol. 1: 2386
Harvard Alumni Association Award Vol. 1: 10270
Harvard Medal Vol. 1: 10271
Harvard-Newcomen Postdoctoral Fellowship Vol. 1: 16318
Harvest Award Vol. 1: 15620
Harvey Cup Vol. 2: 6704
Harveys Leeds International Pianoforte Competition Vol. 2: 8050
Harwick Lifetime Achievement Award; Harry J. Vol. 1: 1884
Hasdeu Prize; Bogdan Petriceicu Vol. 2: 5832
Haseltine Memorial Fellowship in Science Writing; Nate Vol. 1: 8563
Haskell Awards Vol. 1: 2727
Haskil Competition; Clara Vol. 2: 6371
Haskins Medal Vol. 1: 13276
Haslam Award for Excellence in Bookselling; Charles S. Vol. 1: 19464
Haslam International Scholarship; Charley Vol. 1: 1583
Hasler Award; Maurice F. Vol. 1: 19603
Hasler Medal; Georg Vol. 2: 6444
Hasluck Short Story Competition; Dame Alexandra Vol. 2: 591
Hasse Prize; Merten Vol. 1: 13194
Hastings Award; Sir Charles Vol. 2: 7068
Hatai Medal; Shinkishi Vol. 1: 17014
Hatch Award; James E. Vol. 1: 13079
HateBuster Hero Award Vol. 1: 10290
Hatfield Award; W. Wilbur Vol. 1: 14831
Hatfield Public Policy Award; Mark O. Vol. 1: 838
Hatieganu Prize; Iuliu Vol. 2: 5833
Hatikvah Award Vol. 1: 12365
Hat's Off Award Vol. 1: 20009
Hattaway Award (Marine Aviation Ground Officer of the Year); Earle Vol. 1: 13080
Hatton Awards Competition for Junior Investigators; Edward H. Vol. 1: 11208
Hattori Prize Vol. 2: 4139
Hattori Prize; S. Vol. 1: 11291
Haub Prize for Environmental Diplomacy; Elizabeth Vol. 2: 2948
Haub Prize for Environmental Law; Elizabeth Vol. 2: 2949
Hauer Spelean History Award; Peter M. Vol. 1: 15798
Haueter Award; Paul E. Vol. 1: 2430
Haughton Good Guy Award; Bill Vol. 1: 20621
Hauling Job of the Year Award Vol. 1: 19580
Haumont; Prix Vol. 2: 1718
Haupt Alumni Chapter Project Grants; Helen Vol. 1: 13662
Haupt Piano Scholarship; Helen Vol. 1: 13662
Havenga Prize for Science and Technology Vol. 2: 5645
Haverhill Library Award Vol. 1: 10147
Havez-Planque; Prix Marie Vol. 2: 2186
Haviland Award; P. H. Vol. 2: 9360
Hawaii Award for Literature Vol. 1: 10295
Hawaiian Architectural Arts Award Vol. 1: 10296
Hawaiian Vintage Chocolate Outstanding Pastry Chef Vol. 1: 12287
Hawes NEA National Heritage Award; Bess Lomax Vol. 1: 14932
Hawk Migration Association of North America Research Award Vol. 1: 10300
Hawk Mountain Sanctuary Award Vol. 1: 10304
Hawk Mountain - Student Research Award Vol. 1: 10302
Hawk Trophy; One Ton Championship - Vol. 1: 20778
Hawkins Award; Ann T. Vol. 1: 5112
Hawley Fearless Leader Award; Bob Vol. 1: 5749
Hawley Prize; Ellis W. Vol. 1: 16887
Haworth Memorial Lectureship Vol. 2: 8755
Hawryliuk Memorial Fund; Donald Vol. 1: 7140
Hawryliuk Rural and Remote Opportunities Grant; Donald Vol. 1: 7140
Hawthorne Award; Charles Oliver Vol. 2: 7069
Hay Award; Louise Vol. 1: 5527
Hay Medal; Logan Vol. 1: 63
Hay Memorial Award; Roy Vol. 2: 7549

Hayashi Prize Vol. 2: 4140
Hayden and Mozart Scholarship; The Boyle Memorial Senior Vol. 1: 18276
Hayden and Mozart Scholarship; The Frances England Intermediate Vol. 1: 18284
Hayden Award; Alice H. Vol. 1: 19926
Hayes Award; Sheldon G. Vol. 1: 14000
Hayes Awards; Helen Vol. 1: 21463
Hayes Student Prize Paper Award; T. Burke Vol. 1: 10906
Hayhow Award; Edgar C. Vol. 1: 1870
Hayling Island SC Trophy Vol. 2: 7532
Hayman Award for Distinguished Staff Service; Harry Vol. 1: 10895
Hayman Trophy; Lew Vol. 1: 7110
Haynes Prize for Best Paper Vol. 1: 103
Hays Award Vol. 1: 11012
Hays Award; Hazel Vol. 1: 9371
Haythorntwaite Cup Vol. 2: 9070
Hayward Trophy Vol. 1: 18576
Hazardous Waste Management Award Vol. 1: 21487
Hazell Scholarship; Howard Vol. 2: 7114
Hazen Education Prize; Joseph H. Vol. 1: 10487
Hazzard Voice Scholarship; Brena Vol. 1: 13662
Head and Neck; Faculty Career Development Award for Toncology of the Vol. 1: 1948
Head Arthur Ashe Sportsmanship Award Vol. 1: 11137
Head Bequest; Francis Vol. 2: 8983
Head Memorial Award; Ohioana Award, Florence Roberts Vol. 1: 16658
Head of Public Service Award Vol. 1: 20182
Headache; Kaplan Award for Chronic Daily Vol. 1: 2389
Headliner Award
  Association for Women in Communications Vol. 1: 5523
  Livestock Publications Council Vol 1: 12898
  United States Harness Writers' Association Vol 1: 20622
Headliner Awards Vol. 1: 12866
Heads Up Award Vol. 1: 21581
Healey Award; The Jay Vol. 1: 4486
Health Achievement in Occupational Medicine Award Vol. 1: 1904
Health Advancement Award Vol. 1: 15321
Health Advocate Award Vol. 1: 3296
Health Advocate of the Year Vol. 1: 16979
Health & Human Rights Award; Jonathan Mann Vol. 1: 11384
Health and Safety Award
  American Red Cross National Headquarters Vol. 1: 3837
  British Printing Industries Federation Vol 2: 7115
Health Care Delivery Award Vol. 1: 595
Health Education Professional of the Year Awards Vol. 1: 1018
Health Information Management Scholarship Vol. 1: 2398
Health Journalism Awards Vol. 1: 1802
Health Management Research Award Vol. 1: 1871
Health Research Foundation; PMAC Vol. 1: 6840
Health, Safety, and Environment Award Vol. 1: 19243
Health Science Award Vol. 1: 4794
Healthcare and Aging Awards Vol. 1: 4643
Heaney Memorial Scholarship; Peter F. Vol. 1: 16239
Heaps Prize; Norman Vol. 2: 7270
Hearn Cup; George Vol. 2: 6714
Hearst, Jr. Prize; The William Randolph Vol. 1: 10356
Hearst Memorial Trophy; John Randolph Vol. 1: 10356
Hearst/National PTA Excellence in Education Partnership Award; Phoebe Aperson Vol. 1: 15563
Hearst Newspapers Writing and Photography Contests Vol. 1: 10356
Heart Award; Lawton S. Vol. 1: 9593
Heart of America Vol. 1: 2952
Heart of Humanity Award Vol. 1: 20920
Heart of New York Awards; Rev. Mychal Judge Vol. 1: 16249
Heart of the Program Award Vol. 1: 18344
Heart of the Year Award Vol. 1: 2408
Heartland Arts Fund Vol. 1: 5159
Heartland Prizes Vol. 1: 7893
Heat Transfer & Energy Conversion Division Award Vol. 1: 2776
Heat Transfer Memorial Award Vol. 1: 4514
Heath Award; Edward Vol. 2: 8521
Heath Literary Award Vol. 1: 3224
The Heather Laxdal Memorial Vocal Award/ The Golan E. Hoole Memorial Shield Vol. 1: 2281
Heaviside Premium Vol. 2: 7808
Hebb Award for Distinguished Contributions to Psychology as a Science; Donald O. Vol. 1: 7351
Hebb Distinguished Contribution; Donald O. Vol. 1: 5381
Hebb Distinguished Scientific Contribution Award; D. O. Vol. 1: 3659
Hebel-Preis; Johann-Peter- Vol. 2: 3033
Hebert; Prix Louis-Phillipe- Vol. 1: 18610
Hebrew Play Award Vol. 2: 3732
Hecht Award; Max Vol. 1: 5954
Heck Prize; Mathilda Vol. 1: 21435
Heckel Award; George Baugh Vol. 1: 15469
Hector Memorial Medal and Prize Vol. 2: 5082
Hedberg Award in Energy; Hollis D. Vol. 1: 10846
Hedley Memorial Award; George Vol. 2: 8197
Hedrick Awards; U. P. Vol. 1: 3583
Hedrick Lectureship Vol. 1: 13195
Hedwig Medal Vol. 1: 11292
Heeney Memorial Award; Robert C. Vol. 1: 14185
Hefley Educator of the Year Award; Sue Vol. 1: 12939
Hefner First Amendment Award; Hugh M. Vol. 1: 17396
Hefty Scholarship Vol. 1: 6695
Hegarty Prize Vol. 2: 487
Hegel-Preis der Landeshauptstadt Stuttgart Vol. 2: 3100
Heideman Award Vol. 1: 172
Heidseick Award; RPS Charles Vol. 2: 8657
Heilprin Literary Award Medal; Angelo Vol. 1: 9942
Heiman Impact Award for Excellence in Educational Support; John C. Vol. 1: 2777
Heimann Service Award; Jack Vol. 1: 19787
Heineken Prize for Art; Dr. A.H. Vol. 2: 4886
Heineken Prize for Biochemistry and Biophysics; Dr. H. P. Vol. 2: 4887
Heineken Prize for Environmental Sciences; Dr. A.H. Vol. 2: 4888
Heineken Prize for History; Dr. A.H. Vol. 2: 4889
Heineken Prize for Medicine; Dr. A.H. Vol. 2: 4890
Heineman Prize for Astrophysics; Dannie N. Vol. 1: 2834
Heineman Prize for Mathematical Physics; Dannie N. Vol. 1: 2835
Heineman Trophy Vol. 1: 18018
Heinemann Memorial Trustee Award for Educational Development; Ruth I. Vol. 1: 3953
Heinl, Jr., Memorial Award in Marine Corps History; Colonel Robert D. Vol. 1: 13099
Heinz Award; H. John Vol. 1: 15446
Heinz Award in Public Policy Vol. 1: 10378
Heinz Award in Technology, the Economy and Employment Vol. 1: 10379
Heinz Award in the Arts and Humanities Vol. 1: 10380
Heinz Award in the Environment Vol. 1: 10381
Heinz Award in the Human Condition Vol. 1: 10382
Heinz Literature Prize; Drue Vol. 1: 21099
Heinzerling Trophy Vol. 1: 18576
Heise Award Vol. 1: 9382
Heiser Program for Research in Leprosy and Tuberculosis Vol. 1: 10384
Heiskell Awards; Andrew Vol. 1: 20091
Heisler Prize; The Charlene Vol. 2: 94
Heisman Memorial Trophy Vol. 1: 10386
Heizer Prize; Robert F. Vol. 1: 4070
Helbronner-Fould; Fondation Helene Vol. 2: 1879
Helen Dinerman Award Vol. 1: 21850
Helen Keller Award; Spirit of Vol. 1: 10388
Helfer Award; Ray E.
  Ambulatory Pediatric Association Vol. 1: 596
  American Academy of Pediatrics Vol 1: 775
Helicopter Airframe Technician Award Vol. 1: 10395
Helicopter Avionics Technician Award Vol. 1: 10396
Helicopter Club of Great Britain Championship Trophy Vol. 2: 7610
Helicopter Electrical/Electronics Technician Award Vol. 1: 10397
Helicopter Maintenance Award Vol. 1: 10398
Helicopter Powerplant Technician Award Vol. 1: 10399
Helin International Singing Competition; Mirjam Vol. 2: 1600
Hellebrandt Professional Opportunity Awards; Caroline tum Suden/France Vol. 1: 3512
Heller Award; Florence G. Vol. 1: 12338
Heller Prize; The Dr. Bernard Vol. 1: 10375
Hellinger Award; Mark Vol. 1: 18200
Hellings Award; Susan R. Vol. 1: 14658
Hellman-Hammet Award Vol. 1: 10595
Hellman Research Award; Milo Vol. 1: 1320
Hellrung Award; Robert T. Vol. 1: 13243
Hellthaler International GmbH Award Vol. 2: 3107
Helm Award; McKay - Vol. 1: 4882
Helmerich Distinguished Author Award; Peggy V. Vol. 1: 20236
Helmholtz-Preis Vol. 2: 2922
Helmholtz Prize Vol. 2: 2922

Award Index

Helmholtz-Rayleigh Interdisciplinary Silver Medal Vol. 1: 139
Helms Award for Staff and Graduate Staff; Edgar J. Vol. 1: 10089
Helping Hand Award Vol. 1: 21328
Helping Hands Award Vol. 1: 21947
Helpmann Awards Vol. 2: 162
Helpmann Scholarship; Robert Vol. 2: 479
Helsinki International Ballet Competition Vol. 2: 1629
Helton Manufacturing Scholarship Award Fund; Clinton J. Vol. 1: 19155
Helvetia Trophy; H.L. Katcher Vol. 2: 8263
Helzberg Scholarship; Barnett Vol. 1: 8907
Hemans Prize for Lyrical Poetry; Felicia Vol. 2: 9175
Hemingway Foundation/PEN Award Vol. 1: 17157
Hemisphere Award Vol. 1: 11101
Hemley Memorial Award; Cecil Vol. 1: 17432
Hemphill-Jordan Leadership Award Vol. 1: 1110
Hemphill Memorial Award; Bernice Vol. 1: 1111
Hemschemeyer Award; Hattie Vol. 1: 1902
Hench Award; Philip Vol. 1: 5773
Hendershott Award; Robert Vol. 1: 3225
Henderson Alumni Award; William M. Vol. 1: 8865
Henderson Award; Alexander Vol. 2: 211
Henderson Award; R.A. Vol. 1: 7386
Henderson Memorial Award; Harold G. Vol. 1: 10221
Henderson Memorial Exhibit Award; William C. Vol. 1: 3226
Henderson Memorial Grant for Foreign Experience; Mabel Vol. 1: 13662
Henderson Memorial Prize; Ian Vol. 2: 392
Henderson Memorial Student Award; Edward Vol. 1: 2361
Henderson Service to the Section Award; Julia Vol. 1: 18405
Hendy Memorial Award (Outstanding Executive); James C. Vol. 1: 2508
Henebry Roll of Honor Award; Agnes Vol. 1: 19563
Henk de by Incentive Prize Vol. 2: 4846
Henley Media Award; Vernon Vol. 1: 2042
Henne Award; Frances Vol. 1: 1415
Henne Research Grant; Frances Vol. 1: 22054
Henne YALSA/VOYA (Voice of Youth Advocates) Research Grant; Frances Vol. 1: 22054
Hennessy Awards Vol. 1: 15627
Hennessy Travelers Association Award of Excellence Vol. 1: 15627
Hennessy Trophy; John L. Vol. 1: 15627
Henniker Premium; Harry Vol. 2: 7805
Henning Prize Vol. 2: 1486
Henrich Award; Emo Vol. 1: 19797
Henry Award; Charles D. Vol. 1: 878
Henry Award; Edward C. Vol. 1: 1684
Henry Award; O. Vol. 1: 20017
Henry Award; Patrick Vol. 1: 15176
Henry Chapman Mercer Award Vol. 1: 6672
Henry Fonda Young Playwrights Project Vol. 1: 21413
Henry Hampton Award for Excellence in Film and Digital Media Vol. 1: 8598
Henry J. Kaiser Policy Debate Vol. 1: 15107
Henry Johns Award Vol. 2: 6972
Henry Knowles Beecher Award Vol. 1: 10286
Henry Student Research Award; Ted Vol. 1: 18701
Henry Volunteer of the Year Award; Robert Lee Vol. 1: 15207
Hensel Award; Catherine "Cathy" Vol. 1: 9026
Henshall Award; Dr. James Vol. 1: 9479
Henshel Award; Colonel Harry D. Vol. 1: 555
Hensler Award; Bill and Sue Vol. 1: 10424
Hepburn/Sigma Theta Tau International Award; Audrey Vol. 1: 18501
Hepites Prize; Stefan Vol. 2: 5834
Heraldic Ring Vol. 2: 772
Heraldo Music Prizes; El Vol. 2: 4481
Heraldo Prizes; El Vol. 2: 4482
Heraldo Sport Prizes; El Vol. 2: 4483
Herb S. Brier Instructor of the Year Award Vol. 1: 45
Herb Society of America Grant Vol. 1: 10413
Herbert A. Rothman Award Vol. 1: 12238
Herbert Medal Vol. 1: 11440
Herbert Memorial Scholarships; Richard A. Vol. 1: 4829
Herbert S. Schweitzer Memorial Youth Services Award Vol. 1: 22064
Herbert Youth Exhibit Award; Alan Vol. 1: 3227
Herder Prizes Vol. 2: 3083
Hereford Airport Communication Excellence Award; Peggy Vol. 1: 403
Hereford Excellence in Communications Award; Peggy Vol. 1: 403
Hering Medal; Henry Vol. 1: 15700
Hering Medal; Rudolph Vol. 1: 4322
Heritage APA Service Award Vol. 1: 3732
Heritage Award
  American Psychological Association - Society for the Psychology of Women (Division 35) Vol. 1: 3732
  American Public Works Association Vol 1: 3803
  Canadian Heritage Vol 1: 7147
  Irish American Cultural Institute Vol 1: 12196
  National Dance Association Vol 1: 14895
  North American Manx Association Vol 1: 16444
Heritage Award; Doris Vol. 1: 21227
Heritage Award for Outstanding Career Achievement Vol. 1: 19423
Heritage Canada Achievement Awards Vol. 1: 10420
Heritage in Britain Award Vol. 2: 6919
Heritage Practice Award Vol. 1: 3732
Heritage Public Policy Award Vol. 1: 3732
Heritage Publications Award Vol. 1: 3732
Heritage Research Award Vol. 1: 3732
Heritage Toronto Awards of Merit Vol. 1: 10426
Herlitzka per la Fisiologia; Premio Internazionale Amedeo e Frances Vol. 2: 3805
Herman Memorial Award; M. Justin Vol. 1: 14263
Herman Memorial Award; Robert H. Vol. 1: 3958
Hermann Memorial Award; Fred Vol. 1: 10921
Hermanns International Competition; Heida Vol. 1: 8408
Hermes Award Vol. 2: 865
Herndon National Legislative Award; Maurice G. Vol. 1: 10732
Hero Awards Vol. 1: 5230
A Hero for Our Time Award Vol. 1: 17876
Hero of Baseball Award Vol. 1: 18632
Hero of the Year Vol. 1: 4676
Heroism Award
  Flight Safety Foundation Vol. 1: 9583
  National Telecommunications Cooperative Association Vol 1: 15860
Heroism Medal Vol. 1: 15771
Heroy, Jr. Award for Distinguished Service to AGI; William B. Vol. 1: 2341
Herpetologists' League Award for Graduate Research Vol. 1: 10428
Herpetologists' League Student Prize Vol. 1: 10428
Herrera al Merito en Ecologia y Conservacion; Medalla Alfonso L. Vol. 2: 4523
Herreshoff Trophy; Nathaniel G. Vol. 1: 20773
Herrick Award; C. Judson Vol. 1: 1083
Herrick Award; James B. Vol. 1: 2409
Herring Memorial Prize; Sir Edward Vol. 2: 116
Herriot Award; James Vol. 1: 10597
Herrman Founder's Award; Margaret S. Vol. 1: 14725
Herschel Medal Vol. 2: 8433
Herschel Medal; John F. W. Vol. 2: 5616
Herschfus Memorial Award Vol. 1: 735
Hersey Award; Mayo D. Vol. 1: 4515
Hershberg Award for Important Discoveries in Medicinally Active Substances; E. B. Vol. 1: 1759
Hersholt Humanitarian Award; Jean Vol. 1: 112
Herskovits Award Vol. 1: 265
Herter Award; Christian A. Vol. 1: 2282
Hertert Memorial Award; Lucien Dean Vol. 1: 1092
Herty, Jr., Award; Charles W. Vol. 1: 5407
Hertz Medal; Heinrich Vol. 1: 10865
Hertz Preis; Heinrich Vol. 2: 3115
Hertz-Preis (Physik-Preis); Gustav- Vol. 2: 2724
Hertz; Prix Henri Vol. 2: 2350
Hertzog Prize Vol. 2: 5646
Hervey Broadcasters' Awards George Smallreed Award; John Vol. 1: 20877
Hervey Journalism Award; John Vol. 1: 20877
Hervey - Torrey Botanical Club Award; Annette Vol. 1: 20125
Hervieu; Prix Paul Vol. 2: 2197
Herzberg Canada Gold Medal for Science and Engineering; Gerhard Vol. 1: 16023
Herzberg Medal Vol. 1: 6933
Herzl Award; Theodore Vol. 1: 22114
Herzog; Premio Anual de Investigacion Economica Jesus Silva Vol. 2: 4602
Hesburgh, C.S.C., Award; Rev. Theodore M. Vol. 1: 5591
HeSCA Film Festival Vol. 1: 10326
HeSCA/Gilbert Altschul Film Festival Vol. 1: 10326
HeSCA Interactive Materials Festival Vol. 1: 10327
HeSCA JBC Literary Award Vol. 1: 10328
HeSCA/Marion Laboratories Print Media Festival Vol. 1: 10329
HeSCA/Milton E. Adsjt in Veterinary Medicine Award Vol. 1: 10333
HeSCA/NCME Award Vol. 1: 10330
HeSCA Print Media Festival Vol. 1: 10329
HeSCA Video Festivals Vol. 1: 10330

Heschel Peace Award; Abraham Joshua Vol. 1: 12370
Hess Award; Barbara A. Vol. 1: 5548
Hess Award; Henry Vol. 1: 4516
Hess Medal; Harry H. Vol. 1: 2351
Hessayon New Writers' Award; Joan Vol. 2: 8348
Hesselroth Leadership Award; Frank Vol. 1: 14288
Heston Award for Outstanding Scholarship in Interpretation and Performance Studies; Lilla A. Vol. 1: 14711
Hestrin Prize Vol. 2: 3757
Hetherington Award Vol. 1: 682
Hettinger Memorial Scholarship; Stanley Vol. 1: 19793
Heubner Preis; Otto Vol. 2: 2900
Heuer Timing Road Rally Rookie Vol. 1: 19685
Hevesy Nuclear Pioneer Award; Georg Charles de Vol. 1: 19228
Hewes Design Awards; American Theatre Wing's Henry Vol. 1: 4741
Hewett Prize; Ed A. Vol. 1: 1055
Hewitt Award; Barnard Vol. 1: 4199
Hewitt Award; C. Gordon Vol. 1: 9294
Hewitt Award; Richard Vol. 2: 8816
Hewitt Memorial Award; Foster Vol. 1: 10496
Hewlett Packard Crystal Vision Award Vol. 1: 21969
Hewlett-Packard Europhysics Prize Vol. 2: 2324
Hexagono de Oro Vol. 2: 5238
Hexter Prize; Margaret Vol. 1: 15698
Hexter Prize; Maurice B. Vol. 1: 15698
Heymans; Prijs Jan-Frans Vol. 2: 974
HG Andrewartha Medal Vol. 2: 546
HGA Award Vol. 1: 10229
HHS Distinguished Public Service Award Vol. 1: 20497
Hi-Fi Grand Prix Awards Vol. 1: 6058
Hibiscus of the Year Award Vol. 1: 2450
Hickey Memorial Award; Joseph V. Vol. 1: 14998
Hickinbottom Fellowship Vol. 2: 8756
Hickman Medal; Henry Hill Vol. 2: 8817
Hickman Memorial Research Award; Susan Vol. 1: 17489
Hicks Award for Outstanding Contributions to Academic Law Librarianship; Frederick Charles Vol. 1: 1252
Higdon Distinguished Educator Award; Archie Vol. 1: 4022
Higenbottam Memorial Prize; Frank Vol. 2: 7698
Higgins Award; Colm Vol. 2: 3676
Higgins Award; Justice J.A. Vol. 1: 7020
Higgins Lectureship Award; T. R. Vol. 1: 2849
Higgins Redesign Award Vol. 1: 17532
High Energy and Particle Physics Prize Vol. 2: 2325
High Point Honors Vol. 1: 6449
High Point Horsemenship Award Vol. 1: 16483
High Point Performance Horse Awards Vol. 1: 16455
High School All-American Awards Vol. 1: 21147
High School Award; Temuco Vol. 2: 1260
High School Awards Program Vol. 1: 523
High School Band Director of the Year; National Vol. 1: 15226
High School Essay Contest Vol. 1: 6396
High School Flute Choir Competition Vol. 1: 15058
High School Jazz Student Award Vol. 1: 14485
High School Literary Arts Award Vol. 1: 412
High School Scholar All-America Award Vol. 1: 15707
High School Science Fair National Award Vol. 1: 21488
High School Solo Competition Vol. 1: 11485
High School Soloist Competition Vol. 1: 15059
High School Teachers of Excellence in Social Studies Vol. 1: 13155
High-Score Award Vol. 1: 16687
High Winds Medal Vol. 1: 4854
Higher Education Student Achievement Award Vol. 1: 13962
Higher Education Writers Award Vol. 1: 1464
Highland Park Parliamentarian of the Year Awards; Spectator/ Vol. 2: 9097
Highly Commended Certificate Vol. 1: 3333
The Highsmith Library Innovation Award Vol. 1: 17716
Highsmith Library Innovative Award Vol. 1: 10676
Highsmith Library Literature Award Vol. 1: 2980
Highway Research Board Distinguished Service Award Vol. 1: 20161
Higuchi Research Prize; Takeru Vol. 1: 3389
Hildebrand Award in the Theoretical and Experimental Chemistry of Liquids; Joel Henry Vol. 1: 1760
Hilditch Lecture Vol. 2: 9007
Hildreth Award; Harold M. Vol. 1: 3698
Hilendarski Prize; Paisiy Vol. 2: 1207
Hilgard Award; Ernest and Josephine Vol. 1: 18657
Hilgard Award for Distinguished Contributions to General Psychology; Ernest R. Vol. 1: 3684
Hilgard Best Graduate Level Academic Thesis Award; E. R. Vol. 1: 3761
Hilgard Hydraulic Prize; Karl Emil Vol. 1: 4323
Hill Arbuthnot Honor Lecture Award; May Vol. 1: 5439
Hill Award; Dorothy Vol. 2: 124
Hill Award; Errol Vol. 1: 4200
Hill Award; Jimmie D. Vol. 1: 15384
Hill Award; Reuben Vol. 1: 14861
Hill Community Development Awards; Charlotte Vol. 1: 15129
Hill Memorial Award; Bill Vol. 1: 15553
Hill New Investigator Award; Martha N. Vol. 1: 2410
Hill Sports Book of the Year; William Vol. 2: 9216
Hill Volunteers in Fund-Raising Award; Charlotte Vol. 1: 15128
The Hillenbrand Award Vol. 1: 97
Hillier Award; Doris Vol. 2: 7070
Hillis Achievement Award for Choral Excellence; Margaret Vol. 1: 7942
Hillman Foundation Prize Awards; The Sidney Vol. 1: 10435
Hill's Animal Welfare and Humane Ethics Award Vol. 1: 903
Hilti-Preis fur Innovative Forschung Vol. 2: 6520
Hime Memorial Trophies; Alan Vol. 2: 6715
HIMSS John E. Gall Jr./CIO Award Vol. 1: 10344
Hinchley Medal; John William Vol. 2: 7750
Hincks Award; C. M. Vol. 1: 7268
Hinderstein Award; Jeanette Robinson Vol. 1: 13027
Hinds Award; Julian Vol. 1: 4324
Hindustan Zinc Gold Medal Vol. 2: 3453
Hine Awards; Lewis Vol. 1: 14652
Hines Award; Al Vol. 1: 9595
Hinman Trophy; U.S. Team Race Championship - George R. Vol. 1: 20786
Hinton Medal Vol. 2: 7861
Hinzelin; Prix Emile Vol. 2: 2144
Hippocratic Oath Award Vol. 1: 11302
Hirata Award; Dr. Vol. 2: 4220
Hirata-sho Vol. 2: 4220
Hiroshima International Amateur Film and Video Festival Vol. 2: 4120
Hirsch Award for Excellence in Broadcasting; Harold S. Vol. 1: 16461
Hirsch Award for Excellence in Ski Photography; Harold S. Vol. 1: 16462
Hirsch Award; Harold S. Vol. 1: 16463
Hirsch Director's Award; John Vol. 1: 16740
Hirsch Medaille; Otto Vol. 2: 3101
Hirsch Prize; John Vol. 1: 6798
Hirschfeld Scholar Award Vol. 1: 9465
Hirschmann Award in Peptide Chemistry; Ralph F. Vol. 1: 1761
Hirschs pris; Axel Vol. 2: 6254
Hirsh Award Vol. 1: 1878
Hirst Premium; Lord Vol. 2: 7808
Hirt Prize; Victor Vol. 2: 6787
Hiser Exemplary Publication Award; Paul T. Vol. 1: 9313
Hislop Award for Outstanding Contributions to Professional Literature; Helen J. Vol. 1: 3490
Hispanic Council Scholarship Vol. 1: 10444
Hispanic Engineer National Achievement Awards Vol. 1: 7586
Hispanic Leadership Award Vol. 1: 12710
Historian of the Year
Fulton County Historical Society Vol. 1: 9827
Goshen Historical Society Vol 1: 10099
Historic Harmony Heritage Award Vol. 1: 10454
Historic New York City Business Award Vol. 1: 13695
Historic Plaque Vol. 1: 16925
Historic Preservation Award
Billings Preservation Society Vol. 1: 6384
Fairfield Historical Society Vol 1: 9394
Historic Augusta Vol 1: 10450
Peerless Rockville Historic Preservation Vol 1: 17135
Historic Preservation Awards Vol. 1: 8114
Historical Achievement Award
Ohio Academy of History Vol. 1: 16623
Ohio Academy of History Vol 1: 16625
Historical Dagger; Ellis Peters Vol. 2: 7369
Historical Landmarks Designation Vol. 1: 5181
Historical Metallurgy Society Grants Vol. 2: 7621
History Book Contest Vol. 1: 10249
History; Charles DeBenedetti Prize in Peace Vol. 1: 17127
History of Education Society Award Vol. 1: 10482
History of Geology Award Vol. 1: 9951
History of Macon Award Vol. 1: 13386
History Prize Vol. 1: 12781
Historymaker Award Vol. 1: 16233

Histotechnologist of the Year Award Vol. 1: 15717
Hit of the Season Vol. 2: 1135
Hitchcock Award; Alice Davis Vol. 1: 19022
Hitchcock Award; Edward Vol. 1: 1825
Hitchcock Distinguished Professional Service Award; Arthur A. Vol. 1: 2070
Hitchcock Landscape in Sunlight Prize; George Vol. 1: 13787
HIV/AIDS and Human Rights; Awards for Action on Vol. 1: 7157
Hizmet Odulu Vol. 2: 6649
Hlushko Award to Young Co-operative Educators; The William Vol. 1: 5651
HMS Sultan Prize Vol. 2: 7862
Hnatyshyn Award for Law; Ramon John Vol. 1: 6968
Hoag Scholarship; Jim Vol. 1: 19462
Hoagland Award; Dennis Robert Vol. 1: 4589
Hoar Award Vol. 1: 7499
Hobart Memorial Medal Award; W. H. Vol. 1: 4883
Hobart Seven Hats Award; Larry Vol. 1: 3791
Hobbs Award; Nicholas Vol. 1: 3719
HOC Order Vol. 2: 3266
Hoch Distinguished Award; Paul Vol. 1: 1897
Hockey Hall of Fame and Museum Honored Member Vol. 1: 10497
Hockey Hall of Fame Builder Category Vol. 1: 6859
Hockey Hall of Fame International Friends Vol. 1: 6860
Hockey Hall of Fame John Sergnese Category (Friends of CARHA) Vol. 1: 6861
Hockey Hall of Fame Media Category Vol. 1: 6862
Hockey Hall of Fame Player Category Vol. 1: 6863
Hockey Hall of Fame Team Category Vol. 1: 6864
Hodder Cup Vol. 1: 20788
Hodges International Piano Competition/ Virginia Waring International Piano Competition; Joanna Vol. 1: 21402
Hodgins Award for Outstanding Accomplishment; Agatha Vol. 1: 1294
Hodgkin Fellowships; Dorothy Vol. 2: 8702
Hodgkiss Canadian Outdoorsman Award; Stan Vol. 1: 7540
Hodgson Distinguished Service Award; Kenneth O. Vol. 1: 16136
Hodgson Prize Vol. 2: 8390
Hodsoll Award; Sir John Vol. 2: 7684
Hodson Award; Walter D. Vol. 1: 19345
Hoechst Marion Roussel Postdoctoral Fellowship in Nosocomial Infection Research and Training Vol. 1: 15120
Hoepfner Awards; Theodore Christian Vol. 1: 19507
Hoffman Award; Dorothy M. and Earl S. Vol. 1: 6151
Hoffman Award for the Best Postgraduate Paper; Jerome J. Vol. 1: 1209
Hoffman Award; Paul R. Vol. 1: 15599
Hoffman Award; Phillip R. Vol. 1: 4325
Hoffman LaRoche-American Association of Bovine Practitioners Award for Excellence Vol. 1: 1125
Hoffman-LaRoche Ltd. Award Vol. 1: 7830
Hoffman Memorial Award; Cecile Pollack Vol. 1: 11303
Hoffman Memorial Award; Craig Vol. 1: 20290
Hoffman Prize; Artists Fund Malvina Vol. 1: 13788
Hoffman Prize; Edward Fenno Vol. 1: 15701
Hoffman Prize for Distinguished Publication on Christopher Marlowe; Calvin and Rose G. Vol. 2: 8034
Hoffman Scholarship; Dorothy M. and Earl S. Vol. 1: 6152
Hofheimer Prize Vol. 1: 3612
Hofheimer Prize Award Vol. 1: 3612
Hofmann Award; Adele Dellenbaugh Vol. 1: 776
Hofmann Visiting Professor in Adolescent Medicine and Health Award; SAM/Adele D. Vol. 1: 18617
Hofmeyr Prize; W. A. Vol. 2: 5786
Hofmeyr-prys; W. A. Vol. 2: 5786
Hog Promoter of the Year Vol. 1: 15217
Hogan Award; Ben Vol. 1: 10078
Hogan Distinguished Service Award; John F. Vol. 1: 17848
Hogan Environmental Law Essay Contest; Roscoe Vol. 1: 18120
Hogan Memorial Award; John R. Vol. 1: 17291
Hogentogler Award; C. A. Vol. 1: 5955
Hogg Medal Vol. 2: 8551
Hogg Young Artist Competition; Houston Symphony Ima Vol. 1: 10499
Hoggard Performance Medallion; Lara Vol. 1: 13390
Hogsflesh Trophy; George Vol. 2: 6704
Hohl Service Award; Shirley Vol. 1: 3933
Hoke, Sr. Award; Henry Vol. 1: 13028
Hokin Prize; Bess Vol. 1: 17419
Holberg Medal Vol. 2: 1473
Holbrook Alumni Award; Frances Morton Vol. 1: 17256
Holden Medal Vol. 2: 9125
Holdredge Award; Claire P. Vol. 1: 5673
Hole Medal; Dean Vol. 2: 8634
Holford Medal Vol. 2: 8550
Holgersson Plaketten; Nils Vol. 2: 6286
Holgersson Plaque; Nils Vol. 2: 6286
Holiness Exponent of the Year Vol. 1: 7960
Holladay Distinguished Fellow Award; Louise and Bill Vol. 1: 4435
Hollaender Award; Alexander Vol. 1: 9305
Holland Animation Film Festival Vol. 2: 4791
Holland Award for Outstanding Achievement in Career or Personality Research; John Vol. 1: 3662
Holland Award; Maurice Vol. 1: 10786
Holland Trophy Vol. 2: 6716
Hollenback Memorial Prize Vol. 1: 117
Holley Medal Vol. 1: 4517
Holliday Award; Polly Vol. 1: 19489
Hollister Award; Jean Vol. 1: 9241
Hollomon Award; J. Herbert Vol. 1: 155
Holloway Distinguished Service Award; George T. Vol. 1: 14604
Holloway Medal; Tienie Vol. 2: 5647
Holly Memorial Award; T. Kenyon Vol. 1: 20252
Holman Award; C. Hugh Vol. 1: 18928
Holmenkoll Medal Vol. 2: 5117
Holmenkollen Ski Festival Vol. 2: 5118
Holmenkollmedaljen Vol. 2: 5117
Holmes Award; John Vol. 1: 16112
Holmes Bill of Rights Award; Oliver Wendell Vol. 1: 1812
Holmes Medal; Arthur- Vol. 2: 2329
Holmes Memorial Award (Outstanding Goaltender); Harry (Hap) Vol. 1: 2509
Holmes Pioneer Award; Joseph H. Vol. 1: 2858
Holmes Scholars; William Cartwright Vol. 2: 7855
Holmes Scholarship; Sylvia Vol. 1: 10030
Holmes Travel Award; Oliver Wendell Vol. 1: 18955
Holmes - Weatherly Award Vol. 1: 20309
Holonyak Jr. Award; Nick Vol. 1: 16787
Holst Medal; Gilles Vol. 2: 4891
Holst-prijs; Henriette Roland Vol. 2: 4913
Holt Award; Charlotte Vol. 1: 5756
Holt Award; Geoffrey Vol. 2: 7071
Holtby Memorial Prize; Winifred Vol. 2: 8795
Holte Literary Prize; Clarence L. Vol. 1: 17231
Holter Memorial Prize; Casey Vol. 2: 8950
Holtkamp/AGO Award in Organ Composition Vol. 1: 2370
Holweck; Fondation Fernand Vol. 2: 1861
Holweck Medal and Prize Vol. 2: 7731
Holzman Distinguished Educator Award; Albert G. Vol. 1: 10956
Homage Award Vol. 2: 5479
Home Baking Association Educator Award Vol. 1: 10518
Homebrew Club of the Year Vol. 1: 2522
Homebrew Competition Awards; AHA National Vol. 1: 2522
Homebrewer of the Year Vol. 1: 2522
Homen Prize; Professor Theodor Vol. 2: 1614
Homer D. Babbidge, Jr. Award Vol. 1: 5511
Homer Shoop $5000 Preteen 10-Year Maturity Bond Certificate Vol. 1: 2017
Homeric Award Vol. 1: 7866
Homes of Distinction Awards Vol. 1: 19323
Hometown Video Festival Vol. 1: 458
Homewood Chiropractic Heritage Award; Lee - Vol. 1: 5505
Honda Medal; Soichiro Vol. 1: 4518
Honda Prize Vol. 2: 4124
The Hone Te Kauru Taiapa Memorial Vol. 2: 5025
Honens International Piano Competition; Esther Vol. 1: 10524
Honest Man of the Year Vol. 2: 3587
Honesty and Clarity in Public Language; George Orwell Award for Distinguished Contribution to Vol. 1: 14836
Honeywell International Medal Vol. 2: 7717
Honeywell Prize Vol. 2: 7718
Honeywell SAE Outstanding Student Branch Award Vol. 1: 19045
Hong Kong Awards for Industry - Productivity Category Vol. 2: 5226
Hong Kong Awards for Services - Productivity Category Vol. 2: 5227
Hong Kong Film Awards Vol. 2: 5221
Hong Kong Independent Short Film Competition/Urban Council Short Film Awards Vol. 2: 5222
Hong Kong International Film Festival Vol. 2: 5221
Hong Kong Medical Association Prize Vol. 2: 5224
Honikman Volunteer Award; Jane Vol. 1: 17490
HONOLULU Magazine/Borders Books and Music Fiction Contest Vol. 1: 10531
Honor al Merito Vol. 2: 7934

Honor Award
American Alliance for Health, Physical Education, Recreation and Dance Vol 1: 879
American Association for Leisure and Recreation Vol 1: 1031
American Camping Association Vol 1: 1628
ASPRS - The Imaging and Geospatial Information Society Vol 1: 5214
Association of Indians in America Vol 1: 5726
Black Caucus of the American Library Association Vol 1: 6413
National Building Museum Vol 1: 14549
National Soccer Coaches Association of America Vol 1: 15709
E. W. Scripps School of Journalism Vol 1: 18383
Sigma Zeta Vol 1: 18515
Soil and Water Conservation Society Vol 1: 19388
Tennessee Library Association Vol 1: 19969
Whooping Crane Conservation Association Vol 1: 21612
Honor Awards
American Academy of Otolaryngology - Head and Neck Surgery Vol. 1: 750
American Baseball Coaches Association Vol 1: 1545
Association of University Architects Vol 1: 5910
University Photographers Association of America Vol 1: 21129
Honor Awards for Program Excellence Vol. 1: 6599
Honor Awards Program Vol. 1: 20469
Honor Certificate Vol. 1: 1132
Honor Club of Distinction Vol. 1: 8064
Honor Club of Distinction Award Vol. 1: 8064
Honor Coach Award Vol. 1: 8160
Honor Coach Certificate Vol. 1: 8161
Honor Council Program Vol. 1: 11858
Honor et Veritas Award Vol. 1: 7674
Honor Medal with Crossed Palms Vol. 1: 6585
Honor Roll
International Buckskin Horse Association Vol. 1: 11436
Society of Motion Picture and Television Engineers Vol 1: 19193
Honor Roll Adviser Award Vol. 1: 8173
Honor Roll for Education in a Free Society Vol. 1: 12406
Honor Roll of Excellence in Communication Vol. 1: 5826
Honor Roll of Housing Vol. 1: 15247
Honorable Award Vol. 2: 1223
Honorable Mention Vol. 2: 2846
Honorable Mention Award Vol. 1: 3092
Honorable Mentions Vol. 1: 4971
Honorary Alumnus Award Vol. 1: 20258
Honorary and Life Fellowships Vol. 1: 721
Honorary Award
Association for the History of Chiropractic Vol. 1: 5505
Plastic Surgery Educational Foundation Vol 1: 17379
Honorary Awards to Private Citizens and Organizations Vol. 1: 20485
Honorary Badge War Veteran Vol. 2: 5889
Honorary Beekeeper of the Year Vol. 1: 6764
Honorary Certificate Vol. 2: 5539
Honorary Citation Vol. 1: 17380
Honorary Citations Vol. 1: 11348
Honorary Citizen of the City of Salzburg Vol. 2: 771
"Honorary Citizen" Title Vol. 2: 3238
Honorary Companionship Vol. 2: 8391
Honorary Distinguished Physicians Award Vol. 1: 1891
Honorary Distinguished Service Award Vol. 1: 1892
Honorary Doctor of Hobbit Letters (DhL) Vol. 2: 9149
Honorary Emeritus Membership Vol. 1: 5499
Honorary Fellow
Acoustical Society of America Vol. 1: 140
American Academy of Oral Medicine Vol 1: 736
American College of Cardiology Vol 1: 1840
American College of Physicians Vol 1: 1920
American College of Radiology Vol 1: 1942
American Society of Civil Engineers Vol 1: 4326
Association for Social Anthropology in Oceania Vol 1: 5471
The Chemical Institute of Canada Vol 1: 7838
Geological Society of America Vol 1: 9952
Institute of Environmental Sciences and Technology Vol 1: 10922
Royal Agricultural Society of England Vol 2: 8413
Royal Asiatic Society of Great Britain and Ireland Vol 2: 8428
Royal College of Surgeons of Edinburgh Vol 2: 8479
Royal Institute of Navigation Vol 2: 8598
Royal Society of Tropical Medicine and Hygiene Vol 2: 8844
Society of Experimental Test Pilots Vol 1: 19113
Honorary Fellow Award
American Association of Teachers of Spanish and Portuguese Vol. 1: 1452
American Institute of Chemists Vol 1: 2802
American Institute of Ultrasound in Medicine Vol 1: 2859
Society of Allied Weight Engineers Vol 1: 18947
Honorary Fellow of the College of Human Sciences Vol. 1: 11690
Honorary Fellow of the Genesis Academy Vol. 1: 9924
Honorary Fellow of the Photographic Society Vol. 1: 9925
Honorary Fellow of the Royal Academy of Dance Vol. 2: 8362
Honorary Fellow of the Society of Antiquaries of Scotland Vol. 2: 8967
Honorary Fellows Vol. 1: 2431
Honorary Fellows Award Vol. 2: 8724
Honorary Fellowship
Academy of Dentistry International Vol. 1: 98
American College of Dentists Vol 1: 1856
American College of Healthcare Executives Vol 1: 1872
American College of Preventive Medicine Vol 1: 1933
American Institute of Architects Vol 1: 2713
Institute of Quarrying - England Vol 2: 7741
International Cartographic Association Vol 2: 4803
Royal Aeronautical Society - United Kingdom Vol 2: 8392
Royal Photographic Society of Great Britain Vol 2: 8665
Royal Scottish Geographical Society Vol 2: 8681
Honorary Fellowship Award Vol. 1: 1849
Honorary Fellowships Vol. 1: 687
Honorary Founder of the Guild Vol. 1: 14630
Honorary Gold Pin Vol. 2: 2822
Honorary Group Diploma Vol. 2: 6337
Honorary Human Rights Award Vol. 1: 3278
Honorary Knights of the Golden Fleece Vol. 1: 7032
Honorary Life Direct Member Vol. 2: 5954
Honorary Life Fellow Vol. 1: 17015
Honorary Life Governor Vol. 2: 54
Honorary Life Member
AACE International Vol. 1: 37
Activ Foundation Vol 2: 55
American Art Therapy Association Vol 1: 928
American Helvetia Philatelic Society Vol 1: 2442
Canadian Parks and Recreation Association Vol 1: 7327
Canadian Public Health Association Vol 1: 7357
Canadian Seed Growers' Association Vol 1: 7388
Canadian Society for Traditional Music Vol 1: 7437
Church and Synagogue Library Association Vol 1: 7975
Confederate Stamp Alliance Vol 1: 8359
Cranial Academy Vol 1: 8640
Directors Guild of America Vol 1: 8943
European Herpetological Society Vol 2: 3907
European Union of Jewish Students Vol 2: 881
International Double Reed Society Vol 1: 11545
Northeastern Lumber Manufacturer Association Vol 1: 16550
Society for Leukocyte Biology Vol 1: 18786
Society for the Preservation of Old Mills Vol 1: 18881
Standards Engineering Society Vol 1: 19746
Honorary Life Members
American Wine Society Vol. 1: 4908
European Aquaculture Society Vol 2: 851
Sierra Club Vol 1: 18462
Honorary Life Membership
American Association of State Climatologists Vol. 1: 1425
American Hospital Association Vol 1: 2545
American Hosta Society Vol 1: 2557
American Humanics Vol 1: 2581
Canadian Health Libraries Association Vol 1: 7141
Canadian Society of Animal Science - Agricultural Institute of Canada Vol 1: 7443
International Association of Astacology Vol 1: 11285
New Zealand Veterinary Association Vol 2: 5036
Parent Cooperative Preschools International Vol 1: 17080

Award Index

Honorary Life Membership Award Vol. 1: 11232
Honorary Life Officer Vol. 2: 5105
Honorary Life President Vol. 2: 4439
Honorary Lifetime Member Vol. 1: 17564
Honorary Lifetime Membership
American Adoption Congress Vol. 1: 851
Suncoast Waldorf Association Vol 1: 19835
Western Association of Map Libraries Vol 1: 21538
Honorary Lifetime Membership Award Vol. 1: 10032
Honorary Long Service Award Vol. 2: 8908
Honorary Member
Air and Waste Management Association Vol. 1: 321
American Academy of Environmental Engineers Vol 1: 648
American Academy of Family Physicians Vol 1: 674
American Academy of Periodontology Vol 1: 806
American Association of Neuromuscular and Electrodiagnostic Medicine Vol 1: 1285
American Association of Nurse Anesthetists Vol 1: 1295
American Bridge Teachers' Association Vol 1: 1590
American Bugatti Club Vol 1: 1596
American Ceramic Society Vol 1: 1685
American Concrete Institute Vol 1: 1966
American Congress on Surveying and Mapping Vol 1: 1998
American Industrial Hygiene Association Vol 1: 2614
American Institute of Architects Vol 1: 2714
American Institute of Professional Geologists Vol 1: 2844
American Otological Society Vol 1: 3360
American Pharmacists Association Vol 1: 3390
American Physical Therapy Association Vol 1: 3491
American Public Works Association Vol 1: 3804
American Society for Engineering Education Vol 1: 4023
American Society for Microbiology Vol 1: 4135
American Society of Agronomy Vol 1: 4245
American Society of Artists Vol 1: 4265
American Society of Civil Engineers Vol 1: 4327
American Society of Furniture Designers Vol 1: 4412
American Society of Heating, Refrigerating and Air-Conditioning Engineers Vol 1: 4436
American Society of Landscape Architects Vol 1: 4477
American Society of Mechanical Engineers Vol 1: 4519
American Society of Safety Engineers Vol 1: 4604
American Society of Swedish Engineers Vol 1: 4617
American Theatre Organ Society Vol 1: 4738
American Water Resources Association Vol 1: 4830
American Watercolor Society Vol 1: 4855
Arnold Air Society Vol 1: 5109
ASM International Vol 1: 5182
ASPRS - The Imaging and Geospatial Information Society Vol 1: 5215
Association of Asphalt Paving Technologists Vol 1: 5576
Association of Pulp and Paper Chemists and Engineers in Germany Vol 2: 2650
Austrian Statistical Society Vol 2: 714
AVS Vol 1: 6153
Beta Beta Beta National Biological Honor Society Vol 1: 6326
Canadian Actors' Equity Association Vol 1: 6856
Canadian Phytopathological Society Vol 1: 7341
Canadian Society of Petroleum Geologists Vol 1: 7484
Chesapeake and Ohio Historical Society Vol 1: 7856
Chicago Book Clinic Vol 1: 7878
Churchill Center Vol 1: 7986
Crop Science Society of America Vol 1: 8664
Danish Dental Association Vol 2: 1457
Ecological Society of America Vol 1: 9137
Engineering Institute of Canada Vol 1: 9271
European Geosciences Union Vol 2: 2312
European Perforators Association Vol 2: 4402
Flying Physicians Association Vol 1: 9642
German Bunsen Society for Physical Chemistry Vol 2: 2797
German Dental Association Vol 2: 2823
German Society for Physical Medicine and Rehabilitation Vol 2: 2886
Guild of Carillonneurs in North America Vol 1: 10198
Ibsen Society of America Vol 1: 10627
Incorporated Society of Musicians Vol 2: 7632
Indian Institute of Metals Vol 2: 3454
Institute of Packaging Professionals Vol 1: 11025
International Aluminium Institute Vol 2: 7893
International Association of Hydraulic Engineering and Research Vol 2: 6049
International Flat Earth Research Society Vol 1: 11625
International Pharmaceutical Federation Vol 2: 4828
International Silo Association Vol 1: 11908
International Track and Field Coaches Association Vol 1: 12089
ISA - Instrumentation, Systems, and Automation Society Vol 1: 12218
Latin American Phytopathology Association Vol 2: 5244
Medical Women's International Association Vol 2: 3026
Missouri Archaeological Society Vol 1: 13521
National Association for Interpretation Vol 1: 14022
National Association of Metal Finishers Vol 1: 14306
National Environmental Health Association Vol 1: 14944
National Federation of Press Women Vol 1: 14973
National Marine Educators Association Vol 1: 15358
National Speleological Society Vol 1: 15799
New England Water Works Association Vol 1: 16137
Organ Historical Society Vol 1: 16870
Ottawa Field-Naturalists' Club Vol 1: 16929
Phi Lambda Upsilon Vol 1: 17249
Photographic Society of America Vol 1: 17286
Physical Education Association of Ireland Vol 2: 3677
Piano Technicians Guild Vol 1: 17332
Pierre Fauchard Academy Vol 1: 17352
Royal Astronomical Society of Canada Vol 1: 18143
Royal Danish Geographical Society Vol 2: 1531
Royal Philharmonic Society Vol 2: 8655
Sigma Delta Epsilon - Graduate Women in Science Vol 1: 18480
Sigma Phi Alpha Vol 1: 18487
Singapore National Committee of the International Water Association Vol 2: 5951
Society of American Foresters Vol 1: 18971
Society of Motion Picture and Television Engineers Vol 1: 19193
Society of Nematologists Vol 1: 19221
Society of Nuclear Medicine Vol 1: 19229
Special Libraries Association Vol 1: 19550
Ulster Teachers' Union Vol 2: 9161
United States Harness Writers' Association Vol 1: 20623
U.S. Mirror Class Association Vol 1: 20703
World Federation of Estonian Women's Clubs Vol 1: 21907
Honorary Member and Honorary Associate Vol. 2: 8272
Honorary Member Award
Association for the Protection of Consumers Vol. 2: 5804
Association of Women Surgeons Vol 1: 5915
Institute of Industrial Engineers Vol 1: 10957
Joshua Slocum Society International Vol 1: 12432
Honorary Member (Individual) Vol. 1: 15148
Honorary Member (Institutional) Vol. 1: 15149
Honorary Member of AUA New York State Award Vol. 1: 298
Honorary Member of VOS Award Vol. 2: 5887
Honorary Membership
American Association of Handwriting Analysts Vol. 1: 1211
American Association of Petroleum Geologists Vol 1: 1339
American Fisheries Society Vol 1: 2255
Association of Hungarian Geophysicists Vol 2: 3227
Construction Specifications Institute Vol 1: 8438
European Federation of Clean Air and Environmental Protection Associations Vol 2: 4755
International Association of Sedimentologists Vol 2: 908
International Federation of Shipmasters' Associations Vol 2: 7946
International Glaciological Society Vol 2: 7953
International Society of Psychology of Handwriting Vol 2: 3976

International Union of Air Pollution Prevention and Environmental Protection Associations Vol 2: 8003
National Association of Biology Teachers Vol 1: 14095
National Lubricating Grease Institute Vol 1: 15351
Oncology Nursing Society Vol 1: 16721
Organization of Military Museums of Canada Vol 1: 16899
Polish Chemical Society Vol 2: 5337
Polish Physical Society Vol 2: 5364
Polish Society of Veterinary Science Vol 2: 5381
Royal Academy of Music Vol 2: 8373
Royal Geographical Society with the Institute of British Geographers Vol 2: 8522
Society for Imaging Science and Technology Vol 1: 18713
Society for Sedimentary Geology Vol 1: 18843
Society of Exploration Geo-physicists Vol 1: 19122
Society of Manufacturing Engineers - Composites Manufacturing Association Vol 1: 19156
Society of Petroleum Engineers Vol 1: 19244
Water Environment Federation Vol 1: 21489
Weed Society of Victoria Vol 2: 656
Honorary Membership & Long Service Vol. 2: 9376
Honorary Membership Award
American Nurses Association Vol. 1: 3277
American Welding Society Vol 1: 4884
Hiking South Africa Vol 2: 5576
Karg-Elert Archive Vol 2: 8030
National Athletic Trainers' Association Vol 1: 14461
National Fishing Lure Collectors Club Vol 1: 15047
National Intramural-Recreational Sports Association Vol 1: 15289
Society for Applied Spectroscopy Vol 1: 18642
Southeastern Library Association Vol 1: 19475
Honorary Membership for life Vol. 2: 7220
Honorary Membership of IUCN Vol. 2: 6556
Honorary Membership of the ESM Vol. 2: 2756
Honorary Membership (Outstanding Contributors) Vol. 1: 14694
Honorary memberships Vol. 1: 7378
Honorary Nurse Practitioner Award Vol. 1: 3279
Honorary Nursing Practice Award Vol. 1: 3279
Honorary Plaque Vol. 2: 2824
Honorary President
American Pharmacists Association Vol. 1: 3391
International Pharmaceutical Federation Vol 2: 4828
Honorary President and Honorary Member Vol. 1: 11784
Honorary President of the Guild Vol. 1: 14631
Honorary President's Award Vol. 2: 6154
Honorary Recognition Vol. 1: 11642
Honorary Recognition Award Vol. 1: 3280
Honorary Recognition Awards Vol. 1: 12096
Honorary Research Lecture Vol. 1: 4062
Honorary Ring Vol. 2: 2643
Honorary Rings of the City of Salzburg Vol. 2: 772
Honorary Scholar Vol. 2: 755
Honorary Service Awards Vol. 1: 4955
Honorary Society Membership Vol. 1: 13225
Honorary Title of Inventor Vol. 1: 12160
Honorary Vanguard Degree Vol. 1: 15972
Honorary Vice President
Institute of Food Science and Technology - UK Vol. 2: 7694
Ulster Teachers' Union Vol 2: 9162
Honored Members Awards Vol. 2: 4415
Honored Service Member Award Vol. 1: 19263
Honored Student Award Vol. 1: 3310
Honoree of the Quilters Hall of Fame Vol. 1: 17812
Honoree of the Year Award Vol. 1: 14459
"Honoris Causa" Doctor's Degree (Honorary Doctor) Vol. 2: 3314
Honoris Crux Vol. 2: 5739
Honoris Crux Silver Vol. 2: 5740
Honors and Achievement Award Vol. 1: 11731
Honors of the Association
American Speech Language Hearing Association Vol. 1: 4665
International Society of Phonetic Sciences Vol 1: 12013
Honour Award Vol. 2: 3706
Honour Diploma Vol. 2: 5883
Honour Roll Vol. 2: 2969
Honourably Mentioned in Despatches Vol. 2: 5741
Honourary Membership Vol. 1: 502
Honourary President Vol. 2: 1406
Hood Award; E. I. Vol. 1: 6918
Hood Award for Diplomatic Correspondence; Edwin M. Vol. 1: 15517
Hook Industry Award; Daryl Van Vol. 1: 14128
Hook Memorial Award; Sidney
National Association of Scholars Vol. 1: 14371
Phi Beta Kappa Vol 1: 17243
Hooker of the Year Vol. 1: 15884
Hoole Memorial Shield; The Heather Laxdal Memorial Vocal Award/The Golan E. Vol. 1: 2281
Hoosier Intellectual Freedom Award Vol. 1: 10766
Hooten Plaque; George W. Vol. 1: 13927
Hoover Award; VFW J. Edgar Vol. 1: 21341
Hoover Book Award; Herbert Vol. 1: 10416
Hoover Humanitarian Award; Herbert Vol. 1: 6600
Hoover Medal
American Society of Civil Engineers Vol. 1: 4328
American Society of Mechanical Engineers Vol 1: 4520
Hoover Memorial Award; Herbert Vol. 1: 6600
Hoover Police Service Award; John Edgar Vol. 1: 3570
Hope Award; John Vol. 1: 6662
Hopeinen Fennia-mitali Vol. 2: 1621
Hopkins Lecture Vol. 2: 4984
Hopkins Memorial Lecture; Sir Frederick Gowland Vol. 2: 6866
Hopkins Prize; William Vol. 2: 7234
Hopkins Promising Poet Award; Lee Bennett Vol. 1: 11859
Hopkinson Award Vol. 1: 20850
Hopkinson Premium; John Vol. 2: 7808
Hopper Award; Grace Murray Vol. 1: 5300
Hopps Award; Hope E. Vol. 1: 18726
Hora Memorial Medal; Chandrakala Vol. 2: 3486
Horizon Award
American Association for Health Education Vol. 1: 1019
League of Women Voters of Arkansas Vol 1: 12752
New York State Court Reporters Association Vol 1: 16278
Horizons Grants Program Vol. 1: 18228
Horn Memorial Scholarship; Frank Walton Vol. 1: 15039
Hornaday Bronze and Silver Medals; William T. Vol. 1: 6579
Hornaday Gold Certificate; William T. Vol. 1: 6580
Hornaday Gold Medal; William T. Vol. 1: 6581
Hornaday Unit Award; William T. Vol. 1: 6582
Horne Lecture; Robert Vol. 2: 9008
Horne Memorial Award; John Robert Vol. 1: 13905
Horner Award; B. Elizabeth Vol. 1: 4495
Horner Award; Wesley W. Vol. 1: 4329
Horner Sportsmanship Award; Frederic S. Vol. 1: 12282
Horner Travel Award Vol. 1: 7464
Horning Memorial Award; Harry L. Vol. 1: 19046
Horonjeff Award of the Air Transport Division; Robert Vol. 1: 4330
Horror/Ghost Contest Vol. 1: 21997
Hors Concours Vol. 1: 13607
Horse and Rider Awards Vol. 1: 16062
Horse Awards Vol. 1: 14140
Horse Hall of Fame Vol. 1: 14889
Horse of the Year Vol. 1: 12396
Horse of the Year Award Vol. 1: 20620
Horse of the Year Awards
National Spotted Saddle Horse Association Vol. 1: 15815
United States Dressage Federation Vol 1: 20566
Horseback Hours Award Vol. 1: 2600
Horseback Miles Award Vol. 1: 2601
Horseshoe Hall of Fame Vol. 1: 15240
Horseshoe Tournament; World Vol. 1: 15244
Horst Pracejus-Preis Vol. 2: 2808
Horta; Prix Baron Vol. 2: 989
Horticultural Communication Award Vol. 1: 2528
Horticultural Therapy Award Vol. 1: 2529
Horticultural Writing Citation Vol. 1: 2530
Horton Award; Dutch Vol. 1: 5683
Horton Award; Robert E. Vol. 1: 2353
Horton Dining Awards; Loyal E. Vol. 1: 14129
Horton Medal; Robert E. Vol. 1: 2352
Horwitz Award for Leadership in Inter-American Health; Abraham Vol. 1: 17058
Horwitz Prize; Louisa Gross Vol. 1: 8243
Hosei International Fund Foreign Scholars Fellowship Vol. 2: 4126
Hoso Bunka Foundation Prize Vol. 2: 4263
Hospice Team Awards Vol. 1: 16172
Hospital and Institutional Practice; Distinguished Achievement Award in Vol. 1: 3383

Award Index

Hospital Librarian of the Year Award; Canadian Vol. 1: 7139
Hospitality Award Vol. 1: 21527
Host Awards Vol. 1: 16126
Host-Madsen Medal
International Pharmaceutical Federation Vol. 2: 4828
International Pharmaceutical Federation Vol 2: 4833
Hosto Distinguished Service Award; Lester E. Vol. 1: 14104
Hot Concepts! Awards Vol. 1: 16011
Hot Mix Asphalt Hall of Fame Vol. 1: 13999
Hotel Chain of the Year Vol. 2: 6550
Hotel Manager of the Year; European Vol. 2: 3910
Hotel Worker of the Year Vol. 2: 4085
Hotelier of the Year Vol. 2: 4086
Hotelympia
National Restaurant Association Vol. 1: 15625
Society of German Cooks Vol 2: 3064
Hotelympia Competition Vol. 2: 7303
Houdry Award in Applied Catalysis; Eugene J. Vol. 1: 16400
Hough-Grassby Memorial Award; Alec Vol. 2: 7719
Houghton Award; Firman Vol. 1: 16113
Houghton Award; Lord Vol. 2: 8046
Houghton Lecture Award Vol. 2: 3147
Houle World Award for Literature in Adult Education; Cyril O. Vol. 1: 947
Houllevigue; Prix
Academie des Beaux-Arts Vol. 2: 1719
Academie des Sciences Vol 2: 1978
Houphouet-Boigny Peace Prize; Felix Vol. 2: 2597
House of the Year Vol. 1: 14258
Houseparents Length of Service Awards Vol. 1: 10561
Housing Design Awards
Royal Institute of British Architects Vol. 2: 8590
Saltire Society Vol 2: 8891
Housing Person of the Year Award Vol. 1: 15247
Houston Opera Studio Member Vol. 1: 10569
Houston Research Award Vol. 2: 7477
Houston Research Award; Charles S. Vol. 1: 21623
Houston Research Awards; W. J. B. Vol. 2: 7481
Houston Reserach Scholarship Vol. 2: 7101
Houston Scholarship Award; W. J. B. Vol. 2: 7482
Houston State University Award; Sam Vol. 1: 3602
Houston Symphony League Concerto Competition Vol. 1: 10500
Houston Symphony Student Auditions Vol. 1: 10500
Houzeau; Prix Vol. 2: 1813
Houziaux; Prix Joseph Vol. 2: 1010
Hovey Trophy; Chandler Vol. 1: 20774
The Howard A. Berry Scholarship Vol. 1: 11791
Howard Award; Ernest E. Vol. 1: 4331
Howard Award for Courage; Paul Vol. 1: 2981
Howard Award for Horticulture; Nancy Putnam Vol. 1: 10414
Howard Christensen Award Vol. 1: 21823
Howard Citation of Musical Excellence for Military Concert Bands; Colonel George S. Vol. 1: 19428
Howard Fellows Vol. 1: 10571
Howard-Gibbon Illustrator's Award; Amelia Frances Vol. 1: 7260
Howard Maibach Travel Award Vol. 1: 2014
Howard Memorial Medal; Ebenezer Vol. 2: 9151
Howard Plaque; Mary B. Vol. 1: 13927
Howe Award; C. D. Vol. 1: 6868
Howe Award; William A. Vol. 1: 3889
Howe Cup Vol. 2: 9071
Howe Medal Vol. 1: 3313
Howe Medal; Henry Marion Vol. 1: 5183
Howe Memorial Foundation Engineering Awards Program; C.D. Vol. 1: 5905
Howe Memorial Lecture Vol. 1: 5408
Howe Memorial Trophy; Henry Wainwright Vol. 1: 20589
Howell Award; A. Brazier Vol. 1: 8490
Howell Award; Brazier Vol. 1: 4496
Howells Award; Albert Vol. 2: 7340
Howland Award; John Vol. 1: 3370
Howley, Sr. Prize for Research in Arthritis; Lee C. Vol. 1: 5126
Howlin' Wolf Award Vol. 1: 6475
Hoy/ERT Scholarship; Christopher J. Vol. 1: 2964
Hoyen Medal; N. L. Vol. 2: 1524
Hoyt Award; National Milk Producers Federation - Richard M. Vol. 1: 2102
Hoyt Mid Atlantic Art Show Vol. 1: 10573
Hoyt National Drawing and Painting Show Vol. 1: 10573
HRD Award Vol. 2: 6623
Hrdlicka Prize; Ales Vol. 1: 1357
HRH Princess Michael of Kent Award Vol. 2: 9086
HRLSD Exceptional Service Award Vol. 1: 5854
Hromadka Excellence in Zookeeping Award; Jean M. Vol. 1: 1488
Hrycak Award; The John and Judy Vol. 1: 18294
Hsieh Award; T. K. Vol. 2: 7769
HSMA Advertising Awards Vol. 1: 10554
HSMAI Adrian Advertising Awards Vol. 1: 10554
HSMAI Golden Bell Public Relations Awards Vol. 1: 10555
HSMAI Hall of Fame Vol. 1: 10556
HSMAI Public Relations Competition Vol. 1: 10555
HSSFC Scholarly Book Prizes Vol. 1: 7084
HTA/Hanover Show Farms Caretaker of the Year Award Vol. 1: 10259
HTCNE Service Award Vol. 1: 10310
HTEC Division Award Vol. 1: 2778
Hubbard Award; Prevost Vol. 1: 5956
Hubbard Lemon Award; Harlan Page Vol. 1: 7745
Hubbard Medal Vol. 1: 15158
Hubbard Memorial Prize; John Vol. 2: 5043
Hubbard Race Relations Award; William P. Vol. 1: 8050
Hubbard's Writers of the Future Contest; L. Ron Vol. 1: 6618
Hubbs Award; Carl L. Vol. 1: 8897
Hubele National Graduate Student Award; Glen E. Vol. 1: 2071
Huber Civil Engineering Research Prizes; Walter L. Vol. 1: 4332
Huber Learning Through Listening Awards; Marion Vol. 1: 17904
Huch-Preis; Ricarda- Vol. 2: 3137
Hudgens Memorial Award - Young Healthcare Executive of the Year; Robert S. Vol. 1: 1873
Hudgens Memorial Award - Young Hospital Administrator of the Year; Robert S. Vol. 1: 1873
Hudiburg Award; Everett E. Vol. 1: 11623
Hudson Award in Carbohydrate Chemistry; Claude S. Vol. 1: 1762
Hudson Award; Sir William Vol. 2: 367
Hudson Medal; Manley O. Vol. 1: 4465
Hudson Service Award; Floyd G. Vol. 1: 8559
Hudson Valley Foie Gras Outstanding Wine & Spirits Professional Vol. 1: 12287
Hudson Valley Foie Gras Outstanding Wine Service Award Vol. 1: 12287
Hueck and Norman Walford Career Achievement Awards in the Performing Arts and in Visual Arts; Paul de Vol. 1: 16741
Huetprijs; Busken Vol. 2: 4687
Hug Teacher of the Year Award; Clarissa Vol. 1: 8551
Huggins-Quarles Award Vol. 1: 16888
Hugh Last Fellowship and Hugh Last Prize Vol. 2: 7136
Hughes Award; Howard Vol. 1: 2432
Hughes Award; John T. Vol. 1: 15384
Hughes Award; Langston Vol. 1: 6717
Hughes, Jr., Memorial Award; Daniel C. Vol. 1: 11749
Hughes Law Enforcement Award Vol. 1: 10401
Hughes Medal Vol. 2: 8699
Hughes Scholarship; John Vol. 1: 12181
Hughes Water Award; Peter Vol. 2: 286
Hugo Awards Vol. 1: 21951
The Hugos: The Chicago International Television Awards Vol. 1: 8002
Hulbert Memorial Trophy; Ruth and Jim Vol. 2: 6702
Hull Award; T. J. Vol. 1: 13745
Hull - Kate Warriner Award; Elizabeth Vol. 1: 9024
Hulse Memorial Award; William F. Vol. 1: 5957
Hult Medal; Ragnar Vol. 2: 1622
Hult-mitali; Ragnar Vol. 2: 1622
Hulubei Prize; Horia Vol. 2: 5835
Human Needs Award Vol. 1: 1338
Human Needs Award; Michel T. Halbouty Vol. 1: 1338
Human Relations Award Vol. 1: 18626
Human Rights Award
American Federation of Teachers, AFL-CIO Vol. 1: 2233
American Psychiatric Association Vol 1: 3620
Council on Economic Priorities Vol 1: 8592
Human Rights Campaign Vol 1: 10591
International Association of Official Human Rights Agencies Vol 1: 11371
Jewish Labor Committee Vol 1: 12361
National Committee on American Foreign Policy Vol 1: 14702
Human Rights Award; ACFOA Vol. 2: 160
Human Rights Award; Kitty Cole Vol. 1: 2069
Human Rights Awards Vol. 2: 1244
Human Rights Medal Vol. 2: 2480
Human Rights Prize Vol. 1: 20360

Humana Festival of New American Plays Vol. 1: 172
Humane Award
American Humane Association Vol. 1: 2574
People for Animal Rights Vol 1: 17212
Humane Societies Media Award; Canadian Federation of Vol. 1: 7091
Humanist Arts Award Vol. 1: 2585
Humanist Contributions to Science Award Vol. 1: 2586
Humanist Distinguished Service Award Vol. 1: 2587
Humanist Fellow Award Vol. 1: 2587
Humanist Hero Award Vol. 1: 2588
Humanist Heroine Award Vol. 1: 2589
Humanist Media Award Vol. 1: 2590
Humanist Music Award Vol. 1: 16175
Humanist of the Year Vol. 1: 10606
Humanist of the Year Award Vol. 1: 2591
Humanist Pioneer Award Vol. 1: 2592
Humanitarian and Caring Person; Gilbert and Kathleen Wrenn Award for a Vol. 1: 2074
Humanitarian Award
American Cancer Society Vol. 1: 1637
American College of Oral and Maxillofacial Surgeons Vol 1: 1911
American Sportscasters Association Vol 1: 4677
AMIT USA Vol 1: 4937
B'nai Brith Canada Vol 1: 6488
Brith Sholom Vol 1: 6631
Canadian Psychological Association Vol 1: 7352
Doctors to the World Vol 1: 8973
International Association of Cancer Victors and Friends Vol 1: 11304
International Veteran Boxers Association Vol 1: 12116
Inventors Clubs of America Vol 1: 12161
National Association of Recording Merchandisers Vol 1: 14359
National Association of the Holy Name Society Vol 1: 14417
National Council on Alcoholism and Drug Dependence Vol 1: 14850
National Federation of Democratic Women Vol 1: 14966
National Parkinson Foundation Vol 1: 15487
National Press Photographers Association Vol 1: 15536
People for the Ethical Treatment of Animals Vol 1: 17214
Variety International - The Children's Charity Vol 1: 21281
Elie Wiesel Foundation for Humanity Vol 1: 21620
The Humanitarian Award Vol. 1: 99
Humanitarian Award; Benjamin F. Boyd Vol. 1: 17053
Humanitarian-Brotherhood Award Vol. 1: 20338
Humanitarian Efforts Award Vol. 1: 751
Humanitarian of the Year Vol. 1: 13301
Humanitarian Overseas Service Medal Vol. 2: 197
Humanitarian Service Medal Vol. 1: 8818
Humanitas Prize Vol. 1: 10608
Humanities Award Vol. 1: 17299
Humanity Award Vol. 1: 12390
Humanity Award; Heart of Vol. 1: 20920
Humble Award; Joe Vol. 1: 5136
Humboldt International Film Festival Vol. 1: 10610
Humboldt Research Awards to Foreign Scholars Vol. 2: 3125
Humboldt Research Fellowships Vol. 2: 3126
Hume Memorial Award; David M. Vol. 1: 15322
Hume Memorial Award for Excellence in Political Journalism; Annual National Press Club Sandy Vol. 1: 15518
Hume-Rothery Award; William Vol. 1: 13449
Hummer Award; Glen S. Vol. 1: 21192
Humorous Poetry Award Vol. 1: 14999
Humphrey Award; Hubert H.
American Pharmacists Association Vol. 1: 3392
Policy Studies Organization Vol 1: 17450
Humphrey Award; Touchdown Club Hubert H. Vol. 1: 20134
Humphrey Civil Rights Award; Hubert H. Vol. 1: 12738
Humphrey Doctoral Fellowships in Arms Control and Disarmament; Hubert H. Vol. 1: 20403
Humphrey First Amendment Freedoms Prize; Hubert H. Vol. 1: 4981
Humphrey Freedom Award; John Vol. 1: 11464
Humphrey/OCLC/Forest Press Award; John Ames Vol. 1: 2990
Humphrey Research Grant; Hubert Vol. 1: 18345
Humphry/Forest Press Award; John Ames Vol. 1: 2990
Hun Sen Library Awards Vol. 2: 1246
Hungarian Academy of Sciences Gold Medal Vol. 2: 3247
Hunger Cleanup Rookie of the Year Vol. 1: 15829
Hunkins Award; Ruth E. Vol. 1: 10147
Hunt Award for Administrative Excellence; Leamon R. Vol. 1: 20545
Hunt Award; Robert W. Vol. 1: 5409
Hunt Memorial Award; Captain Alfred E. Vol. 1: 19346
Hunt Memorial Award (Sportsmanship, Determination, and Dedication to Hockey); Fred T. Vol. 1: 2510
Hunt Memorial Medal; Charles Vol. 2: 7848
Hunt Memorial Prize; Renee Redfern Vol. 2: 7770
Hunt Trophy Vol. 2: 7581
Hunt Trophy; Lamar Vol. 1: 15085
Hunt Young Historian Award; Rockwell D. Vol. 1: 8370
Hunter Artists Awards; K. M. Vol. 1: 16742
Hunter Fellowship; Amy Louise Vol. 1: 21677
Hunter, Jr. Award Thesis; Charles A. Vol. 1: 2379
Hunter Medal and Triennial Prize; John Vol. 2: 8485
Hunter Memorial Award in Therapeutics of the ASCPT; Oscar B. Vol. 1: 3975
Hunter Memorial Award; J. Norman Vol. 1: 8439
Hunterdon Museum of Art National Print Exhibition Purchase Awards Vol. 1: 10618
Hunterdon Museum or Art and Johnson & Johnson Purchase Prizes Vol. 1: 10618
Hunterian Medal Vol. 2: 7629
Hunterian Oration Vol. 2: 8486
Hunterian Oration and Festival Vol. 2: 8486
Hunting Art Prizes Vol. 2: 8245
Hunting Group Art Prizes Vol. 2: 8245
Hunting Retriever Champion Vol. 1: 20346
Huntington Medal Award; Archer M. Vol. 1: 3273
Huntington Prize; Everett Curtis Vol. 1: 18942
Hunziker Medal Vol. 2: 3959
Hurd Award; James A. Vol. 1: 5624
Hurdler of the Year Vol. 1: 21244
Hurley Association Officers Award for Outstanding Achievement; The Ira Vol. 1: 556
Hurmuzachi Prize; Eudoxiu Vol. 2: 5836
Hurmuzescu Prize; Dragomir Vol. 2: 5837
Hurowitz Award Vol. 1: 20340
Hurst Prize Vol. 1: 12720
Hurter Lecture Vol. 2: 9009
Husain Prize for Young Scientists; Javed Vol. 2: 2598
Husband/Wife Team Award Vol. 1: 2177
Husodo Award; Wahidin Sudiro Vol. 2: 3600
Hustinx Prize for Science; Edmond Vol. 2: 1119
Hustinxprijs; Edmond Vol. 2: 4735
Hutchins Award; Lee M. Vol. 1: 3540
Hutchinson Award; G. Evelyn Vol. 1: 4489
Hutchison Medal Vol. 2: 7751
Hutton Memorial Award; Brig. Gen. Carl I. Vol. 1: 16829
Hutton Memorial Medal and Prize Vol. 2: 5083
Huxley Award; Thomas Henry Vol. 2: 9280
Huybers Prize; D Vol. 2: 6046
Huygens Award; Descartes Vol. 2: 4780
Huysmans; Prix Quadriennal de Composition Musicale Camille Vol. 2: 839
Huysmans; Vierjaarlijkse prijs voor muziekcompositie Camille Vol. 2: 839
Hvass prisen Vol. 2: 1444
Hvatningarverdlaun Rannsoknarads Vol. 2: 3320
Hviezdoslav Prize; Pavol Orszagh Vol. 2: 5957
HWBTA Service Award Vol. 1: 10522
Hyatt Award; John W. Vol. 1: 19264
Hybridizer's Medal Vol. 1: 2869
Hydar Memorial Award; Eleonora Vol. 1: 7521
Hyde Award; Donald F. Vol. 1: 9815
Hyde Award; Walter Vol. 2: 8106
Hyde Gold Medal; Douglas Vol. 2: 3616
Hyde Graduate Student Research Award Vol. 1: 3733
Hyde Graduate Student Research Grant Vol. 1: 3734
Hyde Memorial Lecture; Samuel Vol. 2: 8818
Hydraulic Structures Medal Vol. 1: 4333
Hydrolab/IAGLR Best Student Paper and Poster Competition Vol. 1: 11239
Hydrology Section Award Vol. 1: 2353
Hyman Award; Women's Sports Foundation Flo Vol. 1: 21807
Hyman Memorial Award; Flo Vol. 1: 21807
IAA Gold Medal Vol. 2: 1225
IAA Honorary Diplomas Vol. 2: 1226
IAAF/Coca World Road Relay Championships Vol. 2: 4662
IAAF Grand Prix Final Vol. 2: 4662
IAAF World Athletic Series Vol. 2: 4662
IAAF World Championships Vol. 2: 4663
IAAF World Cross Country Championships Vol. 2: 4662
IAAF World Cup in Athletics Vol. 2: 4662

Award Index

IAAF World Cup of Race Walking Vol. 2: 4662
IAAF World Half Marathon Championships Vol. 2: 4662
IAAF World Indoor Championships Vol. 2: 4662
IAAF World Junior Championships Vol. 2: 4662
IAAF World Marathon Cup Vol. 2: 4662
IAAO Global Award Vol. 1: 11272
IAAO Journalism Citation Vol. 1: 11273
IAATI Award of Merit Vol. 1: 11197
IAATI Lo-Jack Award Vol. 1: 11198
IABC Chairman's Award Vol. 1: 11296
IABC Fellow Vol. 1: 11297
IABSE Outstanding Structure Award Vol. 2: 6379
IABSE Prize Vol. 2: 6380
IACP Cookbook Awards Vol. 1: 11326
IAE/AIE Best Papers Award Vol. 1: 11974
IAEE Journalism Award Vol. 1: 11223
IAEWP Diploma of Honour Vol. 1: 11344
IAEWP Membership in Good Standing Vol. 1: 11345
IAF Student Paper Award Vol. 2: 7053
IAFF International Media Awards Vol. 1: 11355
IAFF Media Awards Contest Vol. 1: 11355
IAFIS-FPEI Food Engineering Award Vol. 1: 4225
IAGLR Scholarship Vol. 1: 11240
IAHR-APD Award Vol. 2: 6050
IAHR Lecturer Award Vol. 2: 6051
IAIA - Rose Hulman Award Vol. 1: 11247
IAJE Hall of Fame Vol. 1: 11249
IALD International Lighting Design Awards Vol. 1: 11369
IAM Commendation Vol. 2: 7648
IAM Medal Vol. 2: 7648
IAMA Award Vol. 1: 11970
IAMLT Award for Outstanding Services to Medical Laboratory Technology Vol. 1: 11584
IAMLT General Award Vol. 1: 11585
IAMLT Scholarship Vol. 1: 11586
IAPA-Pedro Joaquin Chamorro Inter-American Relations Award Vol. 1: 11109
IAPAC Hero In Medicine Vol. 1: 11383
IASL/SIRS International Commendation Award Vol. 1: 11398
IAWQ-Pergamon Publications Award Vol. 2: 8004
IAWRT Radio and TV Awards Vol. 2: 3560
IBC Award Vol. 2: 7911
IBC John Tucker Award Vol. 2: 7911
Iben Award; Icko Vol. 1: 4831
Iberoamerican Film Festival Vol. 2: 6044
IBF Distinguished Service Award Vol. 1: 21148
IBF Gold Medal Vol. 2: 6150
IBF Meritorious Service Award Vol. 1: 21149
IBM MEng Project Prize Vol. 2: 7818
IBMA Award of Merit Vol. 1: 11423
Ibuka Consumer Electronics Award; Masaru Vol. 1: 10866
ICAAC Young Investigator Awards; Merck Vol. 1: 4137
ICASE Award Vol. 2: 7913
ICCROM Award Vol. 2: 3963
ICCS Certificate of Merit Vol. 1: 11511
ICDO Medal Vol. 2: 6393
Ice Carving Classic Vol. 1: 15628
Ice Cream Awards Vol. 2: 5023
Ice Skating Hall of Fame Vol. 1: 10631
Ice Skating Man and Woman of the Year Vol. 1: 10632
The Icelandic Literature Prizes Vol. 2: 3327
Icelandic Research Council Stimulation Prize Vol. 2: 3320
ICI Award
British Archaeological Awards Vol. 2: 6920
Institution of Engineers Australia/Engineers Australia Vol 2: 393
ICI Prize Vol. 2: 7720
ICIA Distinguished Achievement Award Vol. 1: 11498
ICIA Excellence in the Communications Industry Achievement Awards Vol. 1: 11498
ICMR Prize for Biomedical Research Conducted in Underdeveloped Areas Vol. 2: 3413
ICMR Prize for Biomedical Research for Scientists Belonging to Under-Privileged Communities Vol. 2: 3414
ICO-ICTP Prize Vol. 2: 3790
ICO Prize Vol. 1: 12105
ICON Awards; Technology Marketing Vol. 1: 223
ICPE Medal Vol. 2: 6161
ICPE Medal for Physics Teaching Vol. 1: 12106
ICRU - Gray Medal Vol. 1: 11492
ICSA Award of Excellence Vol. 1: 11534
ICSC Annual Awards Vol. 1: 11516
ICSC International Design and Development Awards Vol. 1: 11516
ICSID/Compiegne Industrial Design Award Vol. 2: 2619
ICSSPE Sport Science Award of the IOC President Vol. 2: 2952
ICTP Prize Vol. 2: 3791
ID Annual Design Review Vol. 1: 10636
IDA Downtown Achievement Awards Vol. 1: 11547
IDA Prizes Vol. 1: 11314
Idaho Quality Award Vol. 1: 10638
Idea Awards Vol. 2: 6836
IDEA Fitness Inspiration Award Vol. 1: 10642
IDEA Fitness Instructor of the Year Vol. 1: 10643
IDEA Personal Trainer of the Year Award Vol. 1: 10644
IDEA Program Director of the Year Vol. 1: 10645
Iditarod Trail International Sled Dog Race Vol. 1: 10649
IDTA Classics Championship Vol. 2: 7916
IEA - Bruce H. Choppin Memorial Award Vol. 2: 4795
IEE Award; MTTA/ Vol. 2: 7821
IEEE Award in International Communication Vol. 1: 10867
IEEE Corporate Innovation Recogniton Award Vol. 1: 10868
IEEE Education Medal Vol. 1: 10869
IEEE Engineering Leadership Recognition Vol. 1: 10870
IEEE Life Members' Prize in Electrical History Vol. 1: 18875
IEEE Medal of Honor Vol. 1: 10871
IEEE Process Improvement Award Vol. 1: 7605
IERE Benefactors Premium Vol. 2: 7806
IES Gold Medal Vol. 1: 10694
IES Medal Vol. 1: 10694
IESL Award Vol. 2: 6119
IFA Award Vol. 2: 6920
IFA Hall of Fame Award Vol. 1: 11638
IFA International Aviation Scholarship Vol. 2: 7928
IFAFA Award Vol. 1: 12247
IFATCA Award of Merit Vol. 1: 11578
IFAWPCA-Atsumi Award Vol. 2: 5264
IFAWPCA-CHOI Construction Fieldman Award Vol. 2: 5265
IFCO Tex Ritter Award Vol. 1: 11576
IFHP International Film/Video Competition Vol. 2: 4809
IFHP International Student Competition Vol. 2: 4810
IFI Award Vol. 2: 5590
IFOS Thanking Award Vol. 2: 4820
IFT Food Science Journalism Awards Vol. 1: 10940
IFT International Award Vol. 1: 10941
IFUW Ida Smedley MacLean International Fellowship Vol. 2: 6406
IGIP Award Vol. 2: 6451
IGIP-Preis Vol. 2: 6451
Iglesias; Premi Ignasi Vol. 2: 6004
Ignatian Educator Vol. 1: 12316
IHIC Scholarship Vol. 1: 12183
IHRA Pro Alcohol Funny Car World Champion Vol. 1: 11677
IHRA Pro Nitro Dragster World Champion Vol. 1: 11679
IHRA Pro Stock World Championship Vol. 1: 11678
IHRA Pro Top Fuel Dragster World Champion Vol. 1: 11679
IIAA Publications Award Vol. 1: 10733
IIE Award for Excellence in Productivity Improvement Vol. 1: 10958
IIE Distinguished Educator Award Vol. 1: 10956
IIE Doctoral Dissertation Award Vol. 1: 10964
IIE Excellence Award for Minority Advancement Vol. 1: 10959
IIE - Joint Publishers Book of the Year Award Vol. 1: 10960
IIE Transactions Award Vol. 1: 10961
IIE Transactions Development and Applications Paper Award Vol. 1: 10962
IIR Science and Technology Medal Vol. 2: 2482
IIR Young Researchers Awards Vol. 2: 2483
IIS Award Vol. 1: 11695
Ilavsky Memorial Scholarship; Jan Vol. 1: 10468
ILCA Film and Broadcast Competition Vol. 1: 11699
ILCA Media Awards Contest Vol. 1: 11700
ILDA Award Vol. 1: 11713
ILHA Book of the Year Vol. 1: 11702
Illges Seedling Japonica Award Vol. 1: 1618
Illinois Academic Librarian of the Year Award Vol. 1: 10677
Illinois - NWSA Graduate Scholarship Award Vol. 1: 15966
Illustration Annual Vol. 1: 8310
Image Award Vol. 1: 9195
Image Awards Vol. 1: 14049
Image Awards Hall of Fame Vol. 1: 14049
Image Consultant of the Year Vol. 1: 10700
Images Competition Vol. 1: 7775
Imagination Fair Great Idea Contest Vol. 1: 12167
Imagine Mutual Fund Industry Corporate Citizenship Award Vol. 1: 10702
Imagineer Awards Vol. 1: 13430

IMCC National Annual Minerals Education Awards Vol. 1: 12157
IMHOF-Koch Award Vol. 2: 8005
Imison Memorial Award; Richard Vol. 2: 8984
Imitate Keeler Contest Vol. 1: 10268
Immroth Memorial Award for Intellectual Freedom; John Phillip Vol. 1: 2986
Impact Award Vol. 1: 12736
Impact of Music on Film Competition Vol. 2: 886
Impact of Workload on Diagnostic Accuracy Award Vol. 1: 4395
Impact Through Applied Photography Vol. 1: 17638
IMPC Award for Excellence in Parking Design Vol. 1: 11788
IMPC Award for Excellence in Parking Design and Program Innovation Vol. 1: 11788
Imperial Oil Prize for Excellence Vol. 1: 6037
Imperial Prize
Japan Academy Vol. 2: 4154
Japan Art Academy Vol 2: 4157
Imperial Service Order Vol. 2: 7252
Imperial Tobacco Awards Vol. 2: 9094
Imperial Tobacco Portrait Award Vol. 2: 8188
Imperial Tobacco Trophy Vol. 2: 7611
IMPHOS-FAI Award Vol. 2: 4671
Implications of Research for Educational Practice Vol. 1: 5500
Impresa Europe Vol. 2: 3357
Improvisation Prize Vol. 2: 7964
In-Depth Reporting Award Vol. 1: 11110
In-House Promotional Excellence Award Vol. 1: 11837
In-Print Award Vol. 1: 11838
In the Tradition of the American Cowboy Award Vol. 1: 21546
In the Tradition of the American West Award Vol. 1: 21546
INATAPROBU Rejection Scroll Vol. 1: 11388
INATAPROBU Spirometric Citation Vol. 1: 11389
Incentive Award Vol. 2: 4370
Incentive for Publications of Articles in International Journals Vol. 2: 5194
Inclan; Premio Valle Vol. 2: 8974
INCO Medal Vol. 1: 7196
Incoming President Award Vol. 1: 3228
Incubic/Milton Change Student Travel Grants Vol. 1: 16788
Independent Accountants Scholarship Award Vol. 1: 10711
Independent Bakers Association Congressional Award Vol. 1: 10713
Independent Distributors Best Seller Awards - Indie Best Sellers Vol. 1: 14362
Independent Investigator Award Vol. 1: 13924
Independent Research and Creative Work Awards Vol. 1: 17928
Independent Research Award Vol. 1: 8875
Independent Retail Organization Awards Vol. 2: 6691
Independent Retailer Information Technology Trophy Vol. 2: 6692
Independent Retailer of the Year Award Vol. 2: 6693
Independent Study Catalog Awards Vol. 1: 20955
INDEX Awards for Advances in Nonwovens Vol. 2: 863
India Study Circle Award Vol. 1: 10749
Indian Books Centre Oriental Studies Award Vol. 2: 3397
Indian Festival of Words Author Award; American Vol. 1: 20235
Indian Horse Hall of Fame Award Vol. 1: 2602
Indian Institute Metals Platinum Medal Vol. 2: 3455
Indian Institute of Metals Rolling Trophy Vol. 2: 3456
Indiana Governor's Arts Awards Vol. 1: 10755
Indiana Journalism Award Vol. 1: 6206
Indiana Scholastic Journalism Award Vol. 1: 6207
Indiana State Federation of Poetry Clubs Award Vol. 1: 15000
Indiana State Senator Carolyn Mosby Above and Beyond Award Vol. 1: 10759
Indiana University Prize for Altaic Studies Vol. 1: 17226
Indianapolis 500 Mile Race Vol. 1: 10779
Indianapolis Motor Speedway Hall of Fame Vol. 1: 10780
Indie Awards Competition Vol. 1: 13118
Indigenisation of Aeronautical Equipment Award Vol. 2: 3331
Indirect Provider of Major Support Services and Contributions to the Field of Vocational Special Needs Education Award Vol. 1: 14058
Individual and Organizational Vol. 1: 7957
Individual Artist Fellowship
Montana Arts Council Vol. 1: 13586
Ohio Arts Council Vol 1: 16628
Individual Artists Fellowship and Merit Awards Vol. 1: 10297
Individual Artists Fellowships Vol. 1: 10297
Individual Award
American Printing History Association Vol. 1: 3595
British Printing Industries Federation Vol 2: 7117
Electronic Industries Alliance Vol 1: 9215
Individual Citation Vol. 1: 15873
Individual Maintenance Award Vol. 1: 8277
Individual of the Year Award Vol. 1: 9459
Industrial Appreciation Award Vol. 1: 38
Industrial Arts Teacher Educator of the Year Vol. 1: 8612
Industrial Automation Award Vol. 2: 5949
Industrial Chemistry Medal Vol. 2: 5691
Industrial Design Excellence Awards (IDEA) Vol. 1: 10782
Industrial Leadership Award Vol. 1: 1502
Industrial Lectureship Vol. 2: 8757
Industrial Minerals Young Scientist Award Vol. 1: 18814
Industrial Plastics Product Design Award Vol. 1: 19265
Industrial Research Institute Achievement Award Vol. 1: 10787
Industrial Research Institute Medal Vol. 1: 10788
Industrial Research Ltd. Science Journalism Award Vol. 2: 5015
Industrial Safety Contest Vol. 1: 4771
Industrial Scientist Award Vol. 1: 10942
Industrial Water Quality Achievement Award Vol. 1: 21490
Industriepreis fur technisch-wissenschaftliche Arbeiten Vol. 2: 2890
Industry Achievement Award
Irrigation Association Vol. 1: 12204
National Paint and Coatings Association Vol 1: 15470
Industry Advancement Award Vol. 1: 3045
Industry Appreciation Award Vol. 1: 14128
Industry Award
Institute of Nuclear Materials Management Vol. 1: 11020
Meeting Professionals International Vol 1: 13280
Industry Award for Effective Communication Vol. 2: 8011
Industry Award of Distinction
Health Industry Distributors Association Vol. 1: 10312
PrintImage International Vol 1: 17565
Industry Awards Program Vol. 1: 17119
Industry Division ASHS President's Corporate Council Award Vol. 1: 4088
Industry Excellence Awards Vol. 1: 22021
Industry/Government Graduate Fellowships Vol. 1: 3098
Industry Hall of Fame Vol. 1: 17686
Industry Information Technology Awards Vol. 1: 10104
Industry Innovation Award Vol. 1: 8935
Industry Leader Hall of Fame Award Vol. 1: 4686
Industry Leadership Award
Canadian Animal Health Institute Vol. 1: 6876
Music Distributors Association Vol 1: 13700
Industry Recycler of the Year Award Vol. 1: 12534
Industry Research Scholar Awards Vol. 1: 9712
Industry Service Award Vol. 1: 6380
Industry Specific Group of the Year Award Vol. 1: 5091
Industry Statesman Awards Vol. 1: 15471
Industry Undergraduate Scholarships Vol. 1: 3099
INEOA Medal of Valor Vol. 1: 11764
Inez C. Peterson Citizenship Award Vol. 1: 20914
Infinity Awards Vol. 1: 11462
Infographics Award Vol. 1: 11111
Information Graphics: Design of Understanding Vol. 1: 2813
Information Processing Public Service Award Vol. 1: 5732
Information Systems Award
Babson College - Center for Information Management Studies Vol. 1: 6187
Healthcare Information and Management Systems Society Vol 1: 10345
Information Technology Hall of Fame Vol. 1: 10104
Information Technology Pathfinder Award Vol. 1: 1416
Information Technology Scholarship Vol. 1: 20521
INFORMS Fellow Award Vol. 1: 11073
INFORMS Prize Vol. 1: 11074
ING New York City Marathon Vol. 1: 16260
Ingbar Distinguished Lectureship Award; Sidney H. Vol. 1: 4745
Ingbar Distinguished Service Award; Sidney H. Vol. 1: 9261
Ingberg Award; S. H. Vol. 1: 5958
Ingersoll Award; E. P. Vol. 1: 19069
Ingle Service Award; Robert Vol. 1: 2205
Inglehart First Amendment Award; Louis E. Vol. 1: 8174
Inglis Award; Rewey Belle Vol. 1: 14834

Ingold-Albert Lectureship Vol. 2: 8758
Ingold Lectureship; Christopher Vol. 2: 8758
Initiative Awards Vol. 1: 17537
Initiative for Peace Award Vol. 1: 14701
Injalbert; Prix Vol. 2: 1717
Inklings Vol. 1: 13739
Inner City Physician Assistant of the Year Vol. 1: 817
Innis Award (Aviation Command and Control Marine of the Year); The Kenneth A. Vol. 1: 13081
Innis-Gerin Medal Vol. 1: 18167
Innovation Award
California School Library Association Vol. 1: 6747
Direct Selling Association Vol 1: 8935
Internet Alliance Vol 1: 12152
Special Interest Group on Knowledge Discovery and Data Mining - Association for Computing Machinery Vol 1: 19544
Innovation in Civil Engineering Award Vol. 1: 4334
Innovation in Higher Education Vol. 1: 9206
Innovation in Instruction Award; Les B. Strickler Vol. 1: 3856
Innovation in Teaching Science Teachers Vol. 1: 5501
Innovation of the Year Vol. 2: 7186
Innovation of the Year Awards Vol. 1: 1229
Innovation; Queen's Award for Enterprise: Vol. 2: 8312
Innovation Showcase Award Vol. 1: 14222
Innovation Writer of the Year Vol. 2: 7187
Innovations Challenge Vol. 1: 21114
Innovations in American Government Awards Program Vol. 1: 10116
Innovations in Technology Award Vol. 1: 19551
Innovative Awards; Creative and Vol. 1: 16391
Innovative Educational Theatre Award Vol. 1: 9182
Innovative Intermodal Solutions for Urban Transportation Award Vol. 1: 11049
Innovative Teaching of Secondary School Physics Award Vol. 1: 1374
Innovative Technology Awards Vol. 1: 21491
Innovative Veterinary Diets Award Vol. 1: 904
Innovator Award Vol. 1: 4274
Innovator of the Year Vol. 1: 17815
Innovator of the Year Award Vol. 1: 22008
INSA Medal for Young Scientists Vol. 2: 3487
INSA Prize for Material Sciences Vol. 2: 3488
Insatsu Bunka Sho Vol. 2: 4168
Inside Write Awards
Plain English Campaign Vol. 2: 8269
Plain English Campaign Vol 2: 8270
Insignia for Mention in Dispatches Vol. 1: 6820
Insole Award Vol. 2: 7072
Institut Francais de Washington Vol. 1: 18676
Institute Award for Excellence in Industrial Gases Technology Vol. 1: 2779
Institute for Latin American Integration Award Vol. 2: 37
Institute for Manufacturing Awards Vol. 2: 7636
Institute for Reading Research Fellowship Vol. 1: 11860
Institute for University Cooperation Awards Vol. 2: 3955
Institute Honor Awards for Architecture Vol. 1: 2715
Institute Honor Awards for Interiors Vol. 1: 2716
Institute Honor Awards for Regional and Urban Design Vol. 1: 2717
Institute Honors for Collaborative Achievements Vol. 1: 2718
Institute Manuscript Award Vol. 1: 16707
Institute Medal Vol. 2: 9126
Institute Medal for Distinguished Service Vol. 1: 7197
Institute of Administrative Accountants Awards Vol. 2: 7692
Institute of Administrative Management Awards Vol. 2: 7648
Institute of British Foundrymen Honorary Fellow Vol. 2: 7655
Institute of Chartered Accountants of Scotland Gold Medal Vol. 2: 7671
Institute of Civil Defence and Disaster Studies Competitions Vol. 2: 7684
Institute of Export Prizes Vol. 2: 7690
Institute of Financial Accountants Awards Vol. 2: 7692
Institute of Food Science and Technology Honorary Fellow Vol. 2: 7695
Institute of Golf Club Management Award Vol. 2: 6823
Institute of Management Gold Medal Vol. 2: 7703
Institute of Marine Engineers Award Vol. 2: 7711
Institute of Marine Engineers Silver Medal Vol. 2: 7712
Institute of Metals Division Award Vol. 1: 13456
Institute of Metals Lecturer and Robert Franklin Mehl Award Vol. 1: 13450
Institute of Practitioners in Advertising Effectiveness Awards Vol. 2: 7739
Institute of Quarrying Awards Vol. 2: 7741
Institute of Road Transport Engineers Students of the Year Vol. 2: 9064
Institute Recognition Award Vol. 1: 288
Institute Service Awards Vol. 1: 17631
Institution First Award Vol. 2: 8257
Institution Medal and Premium (Local Association) Competition Vol. 2: 7767
Institution Medal and Premium (London Universities) Competition Vol. 2: 7759
Institution Medal and Premium (Universities) Competition Vol. 2: 7759
Institution of Electrical Engineers Achievement Medal Vol. 2: 7807
Institution of Electrical Engineers Divisional Premium Vol. 2: 7808
Institution of Electrical Engineers Measurements Prize Vol. 2: 7809
Institution of Electrical Engineers Prize Vol. 2: 7810
Institution of Electrical Engineers Prize for Helping Disabled People Vol. 2: 7811
Institution of Electrical Engineers Scotland North Premium Vol. 2: 7812
Institution of Engineers, Australia Award Vol. 2: 394
Institution of Engineers, Australia Award - LaTrobe University College of Northern Victoria Vol. 2: 395
Institution of Engineers, Australia Award - Monash University - Caulfield Campus Vol. 2: 396
Institution of Engineers, Australia Award - Monash University Gippsland Vol. 2: 397
Institution of Engineers, Australia Award - Royal Melbourne Institute of Technology Vol. 2: 398
Institution of Engineers, Australia Award - University of New South Wales Vol. 2: 399
Institution of Engineers, Australia Award - University of Technology, Sydney Vol. 2: 400
Institution of Engineers, Australia Award - Victoria University of Technology - Footscray Campus Vol. 2: 401
Institution of Engineers Medal Vol. 2: 402
Institution of Gas Engineers Bronze Medal Vol. 2: 7849
Institution of Gas Engineers Gold Medal Vol. 2: 7850
Institution of Gas Engineers Silver Medal Vol. 2: 7851
Institution of Mechanical Engineers Awards Vol. 2: 7857
Institution of Nuclear Engineers Graduate Award Vol. 2: 7863
Institution of Nuclear Engineers Honorary Fellowship Vol. 2: 7864
Institution of Plant Engineers Members Prize Vol. 2: 7883
Institution of Structural Engineers Gold Medal Vol. 2: 7886
Institution of Structural Engineers Special Awards Vol. 2: 7887
Institution of the Year Vol. 1: 20358
Institution Premium Vol. 2: 7813
Institutional Award Vol. 1: 3596
Institutionalist Prize Vol. 1: 5362
Instruction Award; Les B. Strickler Innovation in Vol. 1: 3856
Instruction Publication of the Year Award Vol. 1: 5610
Instruction Section Innovation Award Vol. 1: 5611
Instructional Innovation Award Vol. 1: 8786
Instructor of the Year
National Burglar and Fire Alarm Association - National Training School (NTS) Vol. 1: 14559
Zen-do Kai Martial Arts Vol 1: 22106
Instrumental Album of the Year Vol. 1: 11424
Instrumental and Vocal Competition Vol. 2: 620
Instrumental Group of the Year Vol. 1: 11424
Instrumental Performers of the Year Vol. 1: 11424
Insurance Law Prize Vol. 2: 5494
Integrated Young Playwrights Project Vol. 1: 21413
Integrative Physiology; Arthur C. Guyton Awards for Excellence in Vol. 1: 3518
Intel Achievement Awards Vol. 1: 18362
Intel Best of Category Awards Vol. 1: 18362
Intel Foundation Young Scientist Award Vol. 1: 18362
Intel International Science and Engineering Fair Vol. 1: 18362
Intel Science Talent Search Vol. 1: 18363
Intellectual Freedom Award
American Association of School Librarians Vol. 1: 1417

Illinois Library Association Vol 1: 10678
Louisiana Library Association Vol 1: 12935
Intellectual Freedom Round Table State and Regional Achievement Award Vol. 1: 2987
Intellectual Freedom Round Table State Program Award Vol. 1: 2987
Intelligent Community Awards Vol. 1: 21957
Inter-American Agricultural Award for Young Professionals Vol. 2: 1362
Inter-American Agricultural Medal Vol. 2: 1363
Inter-American Award for the Participation of Women in Rural Development Vol. 2: 1364
Inter-American Awards Vol. 1: 1651
Inter-American Health; Abraham Horwitz Award for Leadership in Vol. 1: 17058
Inter-American Institute of Human Rights Awards Vol. 2: 1366
Inter-American Music Awards Vol. 1: 18476
Inter-Collegiate Sailing Hall of Fame Vol. 1: 11124
Inter-Collegiate Sailor of the Year Vol. 1: 11125
Inter Nations Cup Vol. 2: 2455
InterAd Vol. 1: 11173
Interamerica Prize Vol. 1: 11104
Interbrew-Baillet Latour Health Prize Vol. 2: 889
Intercollege Award Vol. 2: 1408
Intercollegiate All-Star Team Vol. 1: 11147
Intercollegiate Meat Judging Meritorious Service Award Vol. 1: 3053
Intercollegiate Pistol Championships Vol. 1: 15645
INTERCOM: International Communication Film and Video Festival Vol. 1: 8003
Interdisciplinary Award Vol. 1: 9406
Interdisciplinary Awards Vol. 2: 8759
Interior Architecture Awards of Excellence Vol. 1: 2716
Interior Design Awards Vol. 1: 19839
Interlaboratory Testing; W. J. Youden Award in Vol. 1: 4698
Intermediate Certificate in Floristry Vol. 2: 9048
Internal Combustion Engine Award Vol. 1: 4521
Internal Recognition Awards Vol. 1: 21094
Internationaal Vocalisten Concours 's-Hertogenbosch Vol. 2: 4730
International Vol. 2: 6733
International Academy of Astronautics Book Awards Vol. 2: 2435
International Academy of Astronautics Section Awards Vol. 2: 2436
International Achievement Awards Competition Vol. 1: 10784
International Activist Award Vol. 1: 10040
International Activities Award Vol. 1: 4437
International Adult Talent Awards Vol. 1: 17088
International Advertising Festival, Cannes Vol. 2: 7890
International Advertising Festival of Ireland Vol. 2: 3710
International Advertising Festival of New York Vol. 1: 16221
International Advertising Press & Poster Festival Vol. 2: 7891
International Affairs Committee Foreign Scholarship Award Vol. 1: 700
International Affairs Fellowship Program Vol. 1: 8595
International Agency for the Prevention of Blindness Awards Vol. 2: 3558
International Aluminum Extrusion Design Competition Vol. 1: 513
International ANDY Awards Vol. 1: 11184
International Animal Agriculture Award Vol. 2: 4071
International Animation Festival in Japan, Hiroshima Vol. 2: 4122
International Arbiter Vol. 2: 3196
International Art Show by Artists with Disabilities Vol. 1: 18536
International Association for Engineering Geology and the Environment Awards Vol. 2: 4793
International Association for the Exchange of Students for Technical Experience Award Certificate Vol. 2: 3638
International Association of Arts Critics Prize Vol. 2: 5450
International Association of Cancer Registries Honorary Member Vol. 2: 2444
International Association of Penal Law Honorary Member Vol. 2: 2442
International Association of Ports and Harbors Essay Contest Vol. 2: 4130
International Association of Sedimentologists Awards and Grants Vol. 2: 909
International Association of Technological University Libraries Essay Prize Vol. 2: 7906
International Association of Technological University Libraries Poster Prize Vol. 2: 7907
International Association of Traffic and Safety Sciences Award Vol. 2: 4132
International Auctioneers Championship Vol. 1: 14466
International Award Vol. 2: 8855
International Award
Alliance for Transportation Research Institute - University of New Mexico Vol. 1: 462
American Meat Science Association Vol 1: 3054
Animal Transportation Association Vol 1: 4963
Family Firm Institute Vol 1: 9407
Girls' Brigade International Council Vol 2: 7570
International Association of Assessing Officers Vol 1: 11274
North American Die Casting Association Vol 1: 16425
Parent Cooperative Preschools International Vol 1: 17081
Pro Musicis Vol 1: 17580
Society of American Registered Architects Vol 1: 19009
Society of Plastics Engineers Vol 1: 19266
Society of Tribologists and Lubrication Engineers Vol 1: 19347
System Safety Society Vol 1: 19887
Women in Film Vol 1: 21717
International Award for Promoting Gandhian Values Outside India
Jamnalal Bajaj Foundation Vol. 2: 3562
Jamnalal Bajaj Foundation Vol 2: 3563
International Award for the Furtherance of Human Understanding Vol. 2: 6432
International Award of Merit Vol. 1: 11912
International Award of Merit in Structural Engineering Vol. 2: 6381
International Awards Vol. 1: 5670
International Awards of Excellence Vol. 1: 5815
International Badminton Federation Distinguished Service Award Vol. 2: 4434
International Badminton Federation Honorary Life Vice-Presidents Vol. 2: 4435
International Badminton Federation Meritorious Service Award Vol. 2: 4436
International Belvedere Competition for Opera Singers Vol. 2: 803
International Benjamin Franklin Fire Service Award Vol. 1: 11353
International Best Newspaper Online Services Award Vol. 1: 9164
International Biennial of Graphic Art Vol. 2: 5978
International Biennial of Illustrations Bratislava Vol. 2: 5971
International Biennial of the Poster in Mexico Vol. 2: 4642
International Biennial Scientific Films Vol. 2: 9297
International Blindness Prevention Award Vol. 1: 712
International Bluegrass Music Awards Vol. 1: 11424
International Book Award Vol. 2: 790
International Bowling Hall of Fame Vol. 1: 21869
International Braille Chess Association Awards Vol. 2: 6157
International Broadcasting Awards Vol. 1: 10516
International Broadcasting Excellence Award Vol. 1: 14113
International Business Dissertation Award Vol. 1: 102
International Cancer Research Technology Transfer Project Vol. 2: 6471
International Carillon Competition - Queen Fabiola Vol. 2: 1088
International Ceramic Art Competition Vol. 2: 3966
International Certificate of Appreciation Vol. 1: 3830
International Championship Chorus Vol. 1: 10250
International Charlemagne Prize of Aachen Vol. 2: 3098
International Chartered Accountants Education Award Vol. 1: 5598
International Children's Film Festival of India Vol. 2: 3355
International Children's Peace Prize Vol. 1: 7897
International Chili Cook-off Vol. 1: 4667
International Choral Competition, Tours Vol. 2: 2345
International Citation Award Vol. 2: 7741
International Citation of Merit Vol. 1: 11861
International Coastal Engineering Award Vol. 1: 4335
International Commission for Optics Prize Vol. 2: 6059
International Committee for Studies of Bauxites and Aluminum-Oxides-Hydroxides Medal Vol. 2: 3256
International Company Award Vol. 1: 13666
International Competition Vol. 2: 6646
International Competition Cinema in Industry (CINDY) Vol. 1: 11287
International Competition for Choirs Vol. 2: 716

International Competition for Film and Video Vol. 2: 722
International Competition for Musical Performers - Geneva Vol. 2: 6310
International Competition of Music Composition Vol. 2: 2338
International Competitions for New Instruments and Bows Vol. 1: 21382
International Composers Competition Vol. 2: 4136
International Composition Competition for Classical Guitar "Michele Pitaluga" Vol. 2: 4036
International Composition Contest Vol. 2: 4935
International Conductors' Competition Vol. 2: 4936
International Conductors Competition of the Hungarian Television Vol. 2: 3286
International Confederation for Thermal Analysis DuPont Award Vol. 2: 5585
International Confederation for Thermal Analysis Young Scientist Award Vol. 2: 5586
International Conservation Award Vol. 1: 4914
International Contest for Carillon Composition Vol. 2: 1089
International Contest of Short Films, City of Huesca Vol. 2: 6030
International Cooperation Awards Vol. 1: 8859
International Cooperation Medal Vol. 2: 2271
International Council of Christians and Jews International Sternberg Award Vol. 2: 2946
International Council of Graphic Design Associations Excellence Awards Vol. 2: 920
International Council of Graphic Design Associations President's Trophy Vol. 2: 921
International Council of the French Language Competitions Vol. 2: 2464
International Critics Award Vol. 1: 20116
International Cytotechnology Award of the IAC Vol. 2: 2932
International Dairy Foods Association Research Award Vol. 1: 2103
International Dairy Production Award Vol. 1: 2104
International Democracy Award Vol. 2: 2940
International Dentist of the Year Vol. 1: 100
International Design Award, Osaka Vol. 2: 4165
International Design Competition, Osaka Vol. 2: 4166
International Design, Print and Outdoor Advertising Awards Vol. 1: 16221
International Designer Awards Vol. 1: 11314
International Diaporama Festival Vol. 2: 944
International Director's Award Vol. 1: 9185
International DLG Prize Vol. 2: 2784
International Doctoral Scholarship for Studies Specializing in Jewish Fields Vol. 1: 13291
International Documentary and Short Film Festival of Bilbao Vol. 2: 6061
International Documentary Association Achievement Awards Vol. 1: 11541
International Documentary Film Festival Amsterdam Vol. 2: 4807
International Editor of the Year Vol. 1: 21971
International Egg Commission Promotion and Marketing Award Vol. 2: 7920
International Egg Marketing Award Vol. 2: 7920
International Emmy Award Vol. 1: 11519
International Environmental Film Festival Vol. 2: 3040
International Excellence in Masonry Award Vol. 1: 13139
International Exhibition Logistics Associates Awards Vol. 2: 6398
International Exhibition of Professional Photography Vol. 1: 17639
International Federation for the Roofing Trade Pin of Honour Vol. 2: 2959
International Federation of Beekeepers' Associations Medals Vol. 2: 3968
International Federation of Bowlers Awards Vol. 2: 5261
International Federation of Essential Oils and Aroma Trades Distinguished Service Medal Vol. 2: 7939
International Federation of Information-Processing Competitions Vol. 2: 739
International Federation of Landscape Architects Competitions Vol. 2: 2468
International Federation of Library Associations Honorary Fellow Vol. 2: 4813
International Federation of Library Associations Honorary President Vol. 2: 4814
International Federation of Library Associations Medal Vol. 2: 4815
International Federation of Netball Associations Service Awards Vol. 2: 7944
International Federation of Societies of Cosmetic Chemists Award and Honorary Mention Vol. 2: 7948
International Federation of University Women Awards Competition Vol. 2: 6406
International Fellowship of Certified Collectors Vol. 1: 72
International Fellowships in Jewish Studies Vol. 1: 13292
International Ferenc Liszt Piano Competition Vol. 2: 3287
International Festival of Adventure Film Vol. 2: 2416
International Festival of Animated Film Stuttgart Vol. 2: 3107
International Festival of Film and Television in the Celtic Countries Vol. 2: 7244
International Festival of Maritime and Exploration Films Vol. 2: 2470
International Festival of Modern Jazz Dance Vol. 2: 3845
International Festival of Mountain and Adventure Films, Vila de Torello Vol. 2: 6107
International Festival of Mountain Environment and Alpine Films, Les Diablerets, Switzerland Vol. 2: 6408
International Festival of Red Cross and Health Films Vol. 2: 1228
International Festival of Urban Architecture, Town Planning, and Environment Films of Bordeaux Vol. 2: 2228
International Film and Television Festival of New York Vol. 1: 16223
International Film Festival Bludenz Vol. 2: 724
International Film Festival - Nature, Man and His Environment Vol. 2: 3972
International Film Festival of Visual Anthropology and Social Documentation Vol. 2: 2261
International Filmfestival Mannheim/Heidelberg Vol. 2: 2963
International Force East Timor Medal Vol. 2: 198
International Forestry Achievement Award Vol. 1: 7176
International Foundation Award Vol. 2: 4237
International Franz Liszt Piano Competition Vol. 2: 4846
International Franz Liszt Pianoconcours Vol. 2: 4846
International Frederic Chopin Piano Competition Vol. 2: 5306
International Futures Award for Exceptional and Innovative Leadership in Continuing Higher Education Vol. 1: 20956
International Game Fish Association Awards Vol. 1: 11645
International Gas Turbine Institute Scholar Award Vol. 1: 4522
International Gaudeamus Interpreters Competition Vol. 2: 4784
International Gaudeamus Musicweek for Young Composers Award Vol. 2: 4785
International Geological L. A. Spendiarov Prize of the Academy of Sciences Vol. 2: 5901
International Golden Rose Award Vol. 1: 21727
International Good Neighbor Award Vol. 1: 20226
International Graduate Student Paper Contest Vol. 1: 5184
International Grand Prix for Liszt Records Vol. 2: 3243
International Graphoanalyst of the Year Vol. 1: 11656
International Greeting Card Awards (Louie Awards) Vol. 1: 10174
International Guest Scholarships Vol. 1: 1949
International Hall of Fame World Award Vol. 1: 12162
International Harp Contest in Israel Vol. 2: 3738
International Health Advocacy Award Vol. 1: 10046
International Health Service Award for Individuals Vol. 1: 10047
International Health Service Award for Organizations Vol. 1: 10048
International Hemophilia Training Centres Fellowships Vol. 1: 21909
International Henryk Wieniawski Composers Competition Vol. 2: 5310
International Henryk Wieniawski Violin Competition Vol. 2: 5311
International Henryk Wieniawski Violinmakers Competition Vol. 2: 5312
International Honorees Vol. 1: 6331
International Human Rights Law Award Vol. 1: 10052
International Human Rights Partners Award Vol. 1: 10053
International Humanitarian Award
AARL Foundation Vol. 1: 48
American Red Magen David for Israel - American Friends of Magen David Vol 1: 3843
CARE Guatemala Vol 2: 3204
La Sertoma International Vol 1: 12637
International Humanitarian Service Award Vol. 1: 3831
International Hydrology Prize Vol. 2: 2446
International Ice Hockey Federation Championships Vol. 2: 6413

International Illumination Design Awards Program Vol. 1: 10695
International Inn of the Year Vol. 1: 11721
International Institute for Promotion and Prestige Awards Vol. 2: 6415
International Iqbal Award Vol. 2: 5190
International J. S. Bach Competition Vol. 2: 2657
International Jeunesses Musicales Competition - Belgrade Vol. 2: 5936
The International Jose Marti Prize Vol. 2: 2599
International Judo Federation Awards Vol. 2: 5498
International Juried Show Vol. 1: 16164
International Korfball Federation Badge of Honour Vol. 2: 4825
International Korfball Federation Honorary Member Vol. 2: 4826
International Labor Rights Advocate Award Vol. 1: 11704
International Leadership Award
International Association for Food Protection Vol. 1: 11233
Simon Wiesenthal Center Vol 1: 18529
United States Council for International Business Vol 1: 20461
International Leadership Citation Vol. 1: 19047
International Letter-Writing Competition for Young People Vol. 2: 6535
International Literary Award Vilenica Vol. 2: 5988
International Map Collectors' Society Awards Vol. 2: 7959
International Marathon Swimming Hall of Fame Award Vol. 1: 12054
International Marketing Executive of the Year Vol. 1: 18223
International Martial Solal Piano-Jazz Competition Vol. 2: 2277
International Master Vol. 2: 3197
International Maurice Andre Trumpet Competition Vol. 2: 2278
International Medal
National Society, Sons of the American Revolution Vol. 1: 15772
Society of Chemical Industry Vol 2: 9010
International Mediation Medal Vol. 1: 921
International Medical Scientific Film Festival Vol. 2: 3936
International Member of the Year Award Vol. 1: 11839
International Mercedes-Benz Sponsorship Award for the Animated Film Vol. 2: 3107
International Meteorological Organization Prize Vol. 2: 6571
International Motorsports Hall of Fame Vol. 1: 11760
International Mozart Competition Vol. 2: 792
International MS in the Media Award Vol. 2: 8140
International Multimedia Science Film Festival Vol. 2: 3936
International Music Award Vol. 2: 6310
International Music Council Prize Vol. 2: 2605
International Mystery Festival Vol. 2: 3891
International Navies Essay Contest Vol. 1: 20712
International Navies Photo Contest Vol. 1: 20713
International New Music Competition Vol. 1: 16692
International Newspaper Color Quality Club Awards Vol. 2: 2926
International No-Dig Award Vol. 2: 7981
International Old Lacers Contest Vol. 1: 11773
International Oliver Messiaen Competition for Interpertation of Contemporary Music Vol. 2: 2279
International Oncology Nursing Fellowships Vol. 2: 6472
International Online Communication Competition Vol. 1: 18860
International Opera Singers Competition Vol. 1: 7716
International Optometrist of the Year Vol. 1: 21885
International Order of Educational Credit Vol. 2: 1331
International Organ Competition Vol. 2: 2280
International Organ Competition, Odense Vol. 2: 1516
International Organ Festival Vol. 2: 7965
International Organ Improvisation Competition Vol. 2: 4919
International Organization for Chemical Sciences in Development Awards Vol. 1: 11779
International Organization of Plant Biosystematists Life Membership Vol. 1: 11781
International Orienteering Federation Pins of Honour Vol. 2: 1636
International Oxidative Therapists Award Vol. 1: 11251
International Parking Awards Competition Vol. 1: 11788
International Paul VI Prize Vol. 2: 3988
International Paulo Cello Competition Vol. 2: 1638
International Pharmaceutical Students' Federation Honorary Life Member Vol. 2: 4836
International Photography Hall of Fame and Museum Vol. 1: 17281
International Piano Competition Liszt - Mario Zanfi Prize Vol. 2: 3871
International Piano Competition Prize Vol. 1: 9231
International Pin of Merit (Kolping Award) Vol. 2: 2967
International Platform Association Award Vol. 1: 11806
International Playwrights' Competition Vol. 1: 18448
International Polka Festival Vol. 1: 11820
International Poster Award Vol. 1: 1329
International Premium Vol. 2: 7814
International Press Freedom Award Vol. 1: 7245
International Press Freedom Awards Vol. 1: 8298
International Print Biennal - Varna Vol. 2: 1236
International Print Biennale Vol. 2: 5314
International Print Framing Competition Vol. 1: 17646
International Print Triennial Vol. 2: 5314
International Prints Competition Vol. 1: 18523
International Prize Vol. 1: 10176
International Prize for Biology Vol. 2: 4201
International Prize Paladino D'Oro Vol. 2: 3978
International Pro-Comm Awards Competition Vol. 1: 6713
International Property Tax Achievement Award Vol. 1: 11275
International ProSieben Award for Animation Vol. 2: 3107
International Public Relations Association Golden World Awards for Excellence Vol. 2: 7973
International Public Relations Association President's Award Vol. 2: 7974
International Radio Festival of New York Vol. 1: 16222
International Radio Programming and Promotion Awards Vol. 1: 16222
International Rapeseed Award Vol. 2: 2462
International Reading Association Prize Vol. 2: 2606
International Recognition and Scholarship Award Vol. 1: 11410
International Recognition Award Vol. 1: 289
International Retailer of the Year Vol. 1: 15636
International Retired Member of the Year Award Vol. 1: 11840
International Robert Schumann Choir Competition Vol. 2: 2973
International Rostrum of Young Performers/ UNESCO Vol. 2: 5967
International Sales Executive of the Year Vol. 1: 18224
International Scholarship Program Vol. 1: 9114
International Science and Engineering Fair Vol. 1: 2862
International Seaweed Association Awards Vol. 2: 1190
International Service Award
Association for the Advancement of Policy, Research and Development in the Third World Vol. 1: 5497
Epsilon Sigma Phi Vol 1: 9316
International Geographical Union - Commission on Geographical Education - Commission on Geographical Education Vol 2: 1634
International Service in Agronomy Award Vol. 1: 4246
International Short Film Festival Oberhausen Vol. 2: 2977
International Short Film Prize Vol. 2: 2963
International Show and Sale Vol. 1: 3195
International Social Security Association Medal of Merit Vol. 2: 6449
International Society for Contemporary Music Honorary Member Vol. 2: 4838
International Society for Education through Art Awards Vol. 1: 11930
International Society of Aircraft Traders (ISTAT) Scholarship Vol. 2: 7929
International Society of Biometeorology Honorary Member Vol. 1: 11979
International Soil Science Award Vol. 1: 19393
International Songwriters' Association Awards Vol. 2: 3643
International Space Hall of Fame Vol. 1: 16196
International Special Librarians Day/National Library Week Award Vol. 1: 19552
International Sportscasters of The Year Vol. 1: 4678
International Standard Accurracy ATLATL Contest-U.S and Europe Vol. 1: 21864

International Stepping-Stone Scholarships Vol. 1: 7299
International Store Interior Design Competition Vol. 1: 11044
International Student Paper Contest Vol. 1: 5185
International Superintendent of the Year Vol. 1: 5484
International Swimming Hall of Fame Gold Medallion Award Vol. 1: 12055
International Swimming Hall of Fame Honoree Vol. 1: 12056
International Tchaikovsky Competition Vol. 2: 5897
International Technical Art Competition Vol. 1: 18861
International Technical Publications Competition Vol. 1: 18862
International Television Festival Golden Prague Vol. 2: 1424
International Television Festival of Monte Carlo Vol. 2: 4669
International Television Programming and Promotions Awards Vol. 1: 16223
International Tennis Hall of Fame Enshrinement Vol. 1: 12075
International Thermographers Association Product Excellence Contest Vol. 1: 12082
International Thermographers Product Excellence Contest Vol. 1: 12082
International Travel Fellowship Awards Vol. 1: 9710
International Triennial of Contemporary Plastic Arts - Sofia Vol. 2: 1237
International Triennial of Stage Poster - Sofia Vol. 2: 1238
International Trophy Competition Vol. 2: 3627
International Trumpet Guild Composition Contest Vol. 1: 12097
International Union for Quaternary Research Honorary Member Vol. 2: 3645
International Vasco Vilalva Prize Vol. 2: 5411
International Veterinary Congress Prize Vol. 1: 4816
International Video Competition Vol. 1: 18863
International Video Week Vol. 2: 6476
International Video Week of Geneva (Semaine Internationale de Video de Genve) Vol. 2: 6476
International Villa-Lobos Guitar Competition Vol. 2: 1196
International Villa-Lobos Piano Contest Vol. 2: 1197
International Violin and Bow Making Competition Vol. 2: 2281
International Visual Communications Association Awards Vol. 2: 8011
International Week of Scientific Films Vol. 2: 9297
International Weightlifting Federation National Award Vol. 2: 3300
International West German Short Film Festival, Oberhausen Vol. 2: 2977
International Wildlife Film Festival Vol. 1: 12141
International Wind Ensemble Competition Vol. 2: 4937
International Women's Film Festival, Creteil Vol. 2: 2516
International Women's Sports Hall of Fame Vol. 1: 21808
International Youth Exhibit Awards Vol. 1: 17088
Internationale Beiaardwedstrijd Koningin Fabiola Vol. 2: 1088
Internationale Filmfestspiele Berlin Vol. 2: 2670
Internationale Filmwoche Mannheim Vol. 2: 2963
Internationale Kompositiewedstrijd voor Beiaard Vol. 2: 1089
Internationale Kurzfilmtage Oberhausen Vol. 2: 2977
Internationale Tage des Okologischen Films Vol. 2: 3040
Internationalen Karlpreis der Stadt Aachen Vol. 2: 3098
Internationalen Klavierwettbewerb Koln Vol. 2: 2693
Internationaler Beethoven Klavierwettbewerb Vol. 2: 805
Internationaler Belvedere Wettbewerb fur Opernsanger Wien Vol. 2: 803
Internationaler Chorbewerb Vol. 2: 716
Internationaler Direct Marketing Wettbewerb Vol. 2: 884
Internationaler DLG-Preis Vol. 2: 2784
Internationaler Fotosalon Vol. 2: 3122
Internationaler Karlspreis zu Aachen Vol. 2: 3098
Internationaler Kompositionswettbewerb Wien Vol. 2: 705
Internationaler Mercedes-Benz Forderpreis fur Animationsfilm Vol. 2: 3107
Internationaler Mozart Wettbewerb Vol. 2: 792
Internationaler Musikwettbewerb der ARD Vol. 2: 2971
Internationaler Musikwettbewerb Tokyo Vol. 2: 4309
Internationaler Violin-Wettbewerb Hannover Vol. 2: 2771
Internationaler Violinwettbewerb Koln Vol. 2: 2695
Internationaler Wettbewerb Franz Schubert und die Musik des 20 Jahrhunders Vol. 2: 794
Internationaler Wettbewerb fur Junge Pianisten Ettlingen Vol. 2: 3036
Internationaler Wettbewerb und Seminar fur Bratsche Vol. 2: 9121
Internationales Festival der Filmhochschulen Munchen Vol. 2: 2767
Internationales Trickfilm Festival Stuttgart Vol. 2: 3107
Internship Vol. 1: 21818
Interpertation of Contemporary Music; International Oliver Messiaen Competition for Vol. 2: 2279
Interphot - Adelaide International Exhibition of Photography Vol. 2: 600
Interpret America Award Vol. 1: 10562
Interpret Britain and Interpret Ireland Award Vol. 2: 6776
Interpretation Competition Vol. 2: 7965
Interscholastic Member Recognition Award Vol. 1: 15277
InterTech Technology Awards Vol. 1: 10134
Intra-Society Merit Award Vol. 1: 8783
Invent/Lightbulb Magazine Vol. 1: 12166
InVEST Award Vol. 1: 10734
Investigator Award; BD Biosciences Vol. 1: 1242
Investigator of the Year Vol. 2: 9233
IOC/IAKS Award Vol. 2: 2934
ION Navigation Award (California Maritime Academy) Vol. 1: 11013
ION Navigation Award (U.S. Air Force Academy) Vol. 1: 11014
Ionescu de la Brad Prize; Ion Vol. 2: 5838
Ionescu-Sisesti Prize; Gheorge Vol. 2: 5839
IOOL Emeritus Vol. 1: 21886
IOOL Medal Vol. 1: 21887
Iorga Prize; Nicolae Vol. 2: 5840
Iowa Country Music Hall of Fame Vol. 1: 15896
Iowa Poetry Association Award Vol. 1: 15001
Iowa School of Letters Award for Short Fiction Vol. 1: 12190
Iowa Short Fiction Award Vol. 1: 12190
IP TOP Awards Vol. 2: 6375
IPA silver bowl Vol. 1: 11816
IPA Top Discovery in the Field of Humor Vol. 1: 11807
Ipatieff Prize Vol. 1: 1763
IPDC - UNESCO Prize for Rural Communication Vol. 2: 2600
IPENZ Craven Post-Graduate Research Scholarship Vol. 2: 4985
IPENZ Structural Award Vol. 2: 4986
IPMA Award for Excellence Vol. 1: 11832
IPMA Educational Award Vol. 1: 11836
IPMA Fellow Member Vol. 1: 11841
IPMA Honorary Life Membership Vol. 1: 11833
IPMA International Vendor/Associate Member of the Year Award Vol. 1: 11842
IPMI Distinguished Achievement Award Vol. 1: 11823
IPMI Graduate Student Award Vol. 1: 11824
IPMI Student Award Vol. 1: 11824
IPPA's Award Vol. 2: 3606
Ippen Award; Arthur Thomas Vol. 2: 6052
IPS Award Vol. 2: 3957
IR-100 Competition Vol. 1: 17817
IRA Children's Book Award Vol. 1: 11862
IRA Presidential Award for Reading and Technology Vol. 1: 11863
Irby Distinguished Service Award; Charles C. Vol. 1: 14009
IRE Awards Vol. 1: 12170
IREAD Awards Vol. 1: 10679
Ireland Special Award; Philip W. Vol. 1: 7923
Irino Prize Vol. 2: 4136
Irish Advertising Awards Festival Vol. 2: 3710
Irish American Cultural Institute Awards Vol. 1: 12197
Irish American Cultural Institute Poetry Award Vol. 1: 12198
Irish Federation of Musicians & Associated Professions Trophy Vol. 2: 3627
Irish Open Audio-Visual Championship Vol. 2: 3716
Irish Pony Club Mounted Games Vol. 2: 3694
Irish Research Funds Vol. 1: 12199
The Irish Times Literature Prizes Vol. 2: 3666
Irish Trophy Vol. 2: 3694
Irish United Nations Veterans Service Medal Vol. 2: 3668
Irish Way Scholarships Vol. 1: 12200
Irish Youth Foundation Award Vol. 2: 3670
IRLA Award Vol. 1: 11886
Iron and Steel Development Award Vol. 2: 4142

Iron and Steel Institute of Japan Honorary Member Vol. 2: 4141
Iron and Steel Merit Award Vol. 2: 4142
Iron Cloud Family Award Vol. 1: 10424
Iron Eyes Cody Award Vol. 1: 12530
Ironbridge Award Vol. 2: 6778
IRPE Prize International Recognition of Professional Excellence Vol. 2: 2957
Irregular Shillings Vol. 1: 6195
Irrgang Memorial Award; William Vol. 1: 4885
Irvine Memorial Award; Charles H. Vol. 1: 5959
Irving Children's Book Choice Award; Washington Vol. 1: 21533
Irving Medal of Literary Excellence; Washington Vol. 1: 18220
Irwin Award; Robert B. Vol. 1: 15258
Irwin Distinguished Marketing Educator Award; AMA/ Vol. 1: 3025
Irwin Medal; George R. Vol. 1: 5960
Irwin Memorial Cup; Bert Vol. 1: 7291
IS Management Awards Vol. 2: 6989
ISA Fellow Vol. 1: 12219
The ISA Gold Medal Vol. 2: 3546
Isaac Composition Contest; Merle J. Vol. 1: 4703
Isaacs Awards for Outstanding Newsletter; Marx Vol. 1: 2780
Isaacs Lifetime Achievement Award Vol. 1: 6355
Isaacs Scholarship Vol. 1: 6753
Isakson Prize for Optical Effects in Solids; Frank Vol. 1: 3458
ISBM Business Marketing Doctoral Award Support Completion Vol. 1: 17208
Isbrandt Automotive Safety Engineering Award; Ralph H. Vol. 1: 19048
ISC All-World Awards Vol. 1: 12041
ISC Hall of Fame Vol. 1: 12040
ISC World Championship Trophy Vol. 1: 12039
ISC World Tournament Vol. 1: 12039
ISCA Young Scientists' Awards Vol. 2: 3535
ISCC Service Award Vol. 1: 11129
ISCE Silver Medal Vol. 1: 11986
ISCPP National Law Enforcement Explorer Community Crime Prevention Award Vol. 1: 6583
ISDP Dissertation Prize Vol. 1: 11926
ISEM Seed Grants Vol. 1: 10847
ISHOF Service Award Vol. 1: 12057
ISHR Human Rights Award Vol. 2: 6442
ISI Frank Bradway Rogers Information Advancement Award Vol. 1: 13258
ISIA Awards Vol. 2: 3664
Isidor Fankuchen Award Vol. 1: 2088
Isidor Memorial Medal; Joseph S. Vol. 1: 13789
ISIJ Award for Service Vol. 2: 4146
Isker Award; Colonel Rohland A. Vol. 1: 17996
Islamic Capitals and Cities Awards; Organization of Vol. 2: 5928
Islamic Development Bank Prizes in Islamic Economics and Islamic Banking Vol. 2: 5920
ISN Medal Vol. 2: 1502
ISO 9002 Award Vol. 2: 3761
ISP Student Competition Vol. 1: 11043
ISP/*VM & SD* International Design Competition Vol. 1: 11044
ISPE Distinguished Achievement Award Vol. 1: 11952
ISPE Engineer of The Year Vol. 1: 11952
Israel Democracy Institute Democracy Award Vol. 2: 3742
Israel Discount Bank Prize for an Israeli Artist Vol. 2: 3745
Israel Museum Fellowships; The Wolgin Foundation/ Vol. 2: 3755
Israel Museum Honorary Fellow Vol. 2: 3746
Israel's Parliament Speaker's Award on Quality of Life Vol. 2: 3725
Issaccs Trophy Vol. 1: 18576
Isserlis Scholarship; Julius Vol. 2: 8656
Istanbul International Film Festival Vol. 2: 6642
ISTD Typographic Award Vol. 2: 7990
ISWM Woody Woodland Memorial Award Vol. 1: 12032
ITA All America Team Vol. 1: 11140
ITA Golden Videocassette Awards Vol. 1: 11884
ITA/Osuna Sportsmanship Award Vol. 1: 11141
ITA Player of the Year; Tennis Magazine/ Vol. 1: 11150
ITA Rookie Player of the Year Vol. 1: 11142
ITA Scholar-Athlete All-American Vol. 1: 11143
ITA Senior Player of the Year Vol. 1: 11144
Italian Alpine Club Prize Vol. 2: 4059
Italian Association for Metallurgy Awards Vol. 2: 3995
Italian Ministry for Culture and the Environment Prizes Vol. 2: 4026
Italian PEN Prize Vol. 2: 4022
Itek Award Vol. 1: 18714
ITG Student Performance Competitions Vol. 1: 12098
Itschner Plaque Vol. 1: 18990
ITTF Merit Award Vol. 2: 6467
Ittleson Research in Child Psychiatry Award; Blanche F. Vol. 1: 3621
IUAPPA World Clean Air Congress Award Vol. 2: 1430
IUPUI National Children's Theatre Playwriting Competition Vol. 1: 10777
Iuventus Mundi Cantat Competition Vol. 2: 1426
Ivanausko premija; Tado Vol. 2: 4390
Ivens Film Prize; Joris Vol. 2: 4807
Ivens; Prix Joris Vol. 2: 2261
Ives Journal Award (Engineering); Charles E. Vol. 1: 18715
Ives Medal/Jarus W. Quinn Endowment; Frederic Vol. 1: 16786
IVOMEC Award for Effective Sheep Breeding Vol. 2: 5537
Ivy Society Award; Robert H. Vol. 1: 17381
IWEM Award Vol. 1: 16141
IWES Award Vol. 1: 16141
The IWF Order Vol. 2: 3301
IWLA Conservation Award Vol. 1: 12265
IWLA Hall of Fame Award Vol. 1: 12266
IWLA Honor Roll Award Vol. 1: 12267
IWRA Distinguished Lecturer Vol. 1: 12129
Iyengar Memorial Award; Dr. M. O. T. Vol. 2: 3415
Iyer Oration Award; Dr. C. G. S. Vol. 2: 3416
J. B. Firth Essay Prize Vol. 2: 7539
J. I. Hambleton Award Vol. 1: 9098
J. W. Hook Memorial Award Vol. 1: 9225
JA Campbell Research Award Vol. 1: 7022
Jaag-Gewasserschutz-Preis; Otto Vol. 2: 6521
J.A.B. Townsend Prize Vol. 2: 9187
Jack Edward McKee Medal Vol. 1: 21492
Jack Kavanagh Memorial Youth Baseball Research Award Vol. 1: 18633
Jack Quilter Award Vol. 1: 7
The Jackie Award Vol. 1: 5028
Jackling Award; Daniel C. Vol. 1: 18815
Jackson Award; Anna M. Vol. 1: 4497
Jackson Award; Hartley H. T. Vol. 1: 4498
Jackson Award; Lawrence Vol. 1: 17224
Jackson Award; William E. Vol. 1: 18179
Jackson Awards; C. C. Vol. 1: 21228
Jackson Distinguished Service Award; Henry M. Vol. 1: 12359
Jackson-Gwilt Medal Vol. 2: 8434
Jackson Lecture and Medal; Hughlings Vol. 2: 8819
Jackson Literary Award; Joseph Henry Vol. 1: 18249
Jackson Memorial Award; Sara E. Vol. 1: 14555
Jackson Memorial Cup; C. N. Vol. 2: 6704
The Jackson Memorial Intermediate Piano Scholarship Vol. 1: 18295
Jackson Memorial Lecture Award; Edward Vol. 1: 713
Jackson Memorial Music Therapy Scholarship; La Verne Vol. 1: 13662
Jackson Mid-Career Clay Scientist Award; Marion L. and Chrystie M. Vol. 1: 8091
Jackson Prize; John Brinckerhoff Vol. 1: 5556
Jackson Prize; The W. Turrentine Vol. 1: 2484
Jackson Research Fellowship; RITF Noel Vol. 1: 18032
Jackson Social Responsibility Award; Hobart Vol. 1: 1230
Jacksonian Prize Vol. 2: 8487
Jacob Book Prize; Herbert Vol. 1: 12721
Jacob; Fondation Charles Vol. 2: 1822
Jacob Scholarship; Jerry Vol. 1: 13295
Jacob Trophy; Pi Kappa Delta/Bruno E. Vol. 1: 15102
Jacobi Award; Abraham Vol. 1: 777
Jacobs Award; Alvin H. Vol. 1: 778
Jacobsen Award; Earl Grant Vol. 1: 18325
Jacobson Award for Women Working in Health Care Law; Elaine Osborne Vol. 1: 18121
Jacobson Award; Richard S. Vol. 1: 18122
Jacobus Award; Donald Lines Vol. 1: 4415
Jacoby Prize Vol. 1: 12841
Jacoby Prize; Statistics New Zealand/ Vol. 1: 12841
Jacqueline Kennedy Onassis Awards Vol. 1: 2628
Jacquemetton; Prix Marius Vol. 2: 2555
Jacquet Gold Medal and the Francis F. Lucas Award for Excellence in Metallography; Pierre Vol. 1: 5186
Jacquet-Lucas Award for Excellence in Metallography; IMS and ASM Vol. 1: 5186
Jade of Chiefs Vol. 1: 16969
Jaeger Medal Vol. 2: 125
Jaeger Memorial Award; Australian Geomechanics Award - John Vol. 2: 403
Jaeger Prize; Thomas A. Vol. 1: 11257
Jaen Prize Vol. 2: 6069
Jaezat Al Malik Faisal Al Alamiyyah Li Khidmt Al Islam Vol. 2: 5924
Jaezat Al Malik Faisal Al Alamiyyah Lil Adab Al Arabi Vol. 2: 5922
Jaezat Al Malik Faisal Al Alamiyyah Lil Derasat Al Islamiyyah Vol. 2: 5923

Jaezat Al Malik Faisal Al Alamiyyah Lil Tib Vol. 2: 5925
Jaezat Al Malik Faisal Al Alamiyyah Lil Ulum Vol. 2: 5926
Jaffe Family Foundation Food Allergy Research Award Vol. 1: 615
Jaffe; Fondation Vol. 2: 2425
Jahns Distinguished Lecturer in Engineering Geology Award; Richard H. Vol. 1: 5674
Jahre Prize in Medicine; Anders Vol. 2: 5178
Jakob Memorial Award; Max Vol. 1: 4523
JALMA Trust Fund Oration Award in the Field of Leprosy Vol. 2: 3417
James Adam Salesroom Award Vol. 2: 3697
James Award; William Vol. 1: 3702
James B. White JSA Award Vol. 1: 12319
James Beard/Perrier Jouet Restaurant Awards Vol. 1: 12287
James Beard/Seagram Restaurant Awards Vol. 1: 12287
James Beard Who's Who of Food and Beverage in America Vol. 1: 12286
James Book Award; William Vol. 1: 3685
James Fellowship; T. V. Vol. 2: 7073
James International Award; John F. Vol. 1: 4437
James K. Mathews Service Award Vol. 1: 7982
James L. Goodwin Memorial Scholarship Vol. 1: 8416
James Lynah Memorial Award Vol. 1: 9108
James Memorial Trophy; Eddie Vol. 1: 7111
James R. Andrews Award for Excellence in Baseball Sports Medicine Vol. 1: 4673
Jameson Archival Advocacy Award; J. Franklin Vol. 1: 18956
Jameson Fellowship in American History; J. Franklin Vol. 1: 12833
Jameson Prize for Editorial Achievement; J. Franklin Vol. 1: 2476
Jamestown Foundation Award Vol. 1: 16707
Jamestown Prize Vol. 1: 16707
Jamestown Scholars: New Dissertation Fellowships from the National Park Service and OAH Vol. 1: 16889
Jamieson Fellowship; Donald Vol. 1: 7415
Jamieson Prize; Laura Vol. 1: 7379
Jamison Scholarship; Ines Pratt Vol. 1: 13662
Jamnalal Bajaj Foundation Awards Vol. 2: 3563
JAMS Scholarship Vol. 1: 12308
Jancso Commemorative Medal; Miklos Vol. 2: 3315
Jancso Miklos emlekerem es jutalomdij Vol. 2: 3315
Jandoli Award of Excellence Vol. 1: 18201
Jane Addams Children's Book Award Vol. 1: 21795
Jane Honikman Volunteer Award Vol. 1: 17490
Jane Memorial Lecture Award; R. S. Vol. 1: 7839
Jane Memorial Lecture Award; R.S. Vol. 1: 7407
Janeway Medal Vol. 1: 3814
Janin; Prix Jules Vol. 2: 2169
Janssen Award Vol. 1: 7465
Janssen; Fondation Antoinette Vol. 2: 1799
Janssen-Ortho Award Vol. 1: 7358
Janssen; Prix Vol. 2: 2556
Janssen; Prix Paul Vol. 2: 1107
Janssen Research Award Vol. 1: 607
Janssen Schizophrenia Research Award; Dr. Paul Vol. 1: 8200
Janssens; Prix Rene Vol. 2: 1002
Japan Academy Prize Vol. 2: 4155
Japan Art Academy Prize Vol. 2: 4157
Japan Association for Education Broadcasting Prize Vol. 2: 4263
Japan Beer Cup Vol. 2: 4163
Japan Foundation Awards Vol. 2: 4170
Japan Foundation Prizes for the Promotion of Community-Based Cultural Exchange Vol. 2: 4171
Japan Foundation Special Prizes Vol. 2: 4172
Japan Gold Disk Award Vol. 2: 4285
Japan Prize Vol. 2: 4294
Japan Quality Medal Vol. 2: 4314
Japan Society Award Vol. 1: 12304
Japan Society for Analytical Chemistry Award Vol. 2: 4199
Japan Society for the Promotion of Science Research Fellowships Science and Technology Vol. 2: 3127
Japan Society of Mechanical Engineers Medal Vol. 2: 4203
Japan Sports Prize Vol. 2: 4330
Japan-U.S. Friendship Commission Prize for the Translation of Japanese Literature Vol. 1: 12526
Japanese Biochemical Society's Shorei-Sho Awards Vol. 2: 4207
Japanese Government Research Awards Vol. 2: 4260
Japanese Government Research Awards for foreign specialists Vol. 2: 4259
Japanese Society of Animal Science Award Vol. 2: 4209
Japanese Society of Sericultural Science Award Vol. 2: 4217
Japanese Society of Snow and Ice Science Award Vol. 2: 4221
Japanese Society of Snow and Ice Service Award Vol. 2: 4222
Japanese Society of Soil Science and Plant Nutrition Award Vol. 2: 4226
Japanese Society of Veterinary Science Award Vol. 2: 4231
Jarabak Memorial International Teachers and Research Award; Louise Ada Vol. 1: 1321
Javeriana University Order Vol. 2: 1335
Javits Excellence in Public Service Award; Jacob K. Vol. 1: 18057
Javits Public Service Award; Jacob K. Vol. 1: 3622
Jayanti Award; Swarna Vol. 2: 3332
Jayezeye Shoraye Ketabe Koudak Vol. 2: 3608
Jayle; Fondation Max-Fernand Vol. 2: 1933
Jazz Band Director of the Year Vol. 1: 15226
Jazz Competition; International Martial Solal Piano- Vol. 2: 2277
Jazz Contribution Awards Vol. 1: 6471
Jazz Flute Masterclass Vol. 1: 15060
Jazz Masters Fellowships Vol. 1: 14931
Jazz Prize Vol. 1: 9537
Jazz Scholarship Vol. 1: 13662
Jazzpar Prize Vol. 2: 1459
JB Awards Vol. 1: 15091
JCC Biennial Communications Awards Competition Vol. 1: 12339
JCC Program Awards Vol. 1: 12340
JCMA Chairman's Award Vol. 2: 4161
JCPenney - University of Missouri Awards in Lifestyle Journalism Vol. 1: 21079
JCPenney - University of Missouri Television Awards for Community Leadership Vol. 1: 21081
JE Church Award Vol. 1: 21564
JEA Research and Development Fund Award Vol. 1: 12349
Jean Garton Award Vol. 1: 16527
Jean-Marc Boivin Prize Vol. 2: 2416
Jean-Marie Delwart Foundation Prize Vol. 2: 1039
Jeanbernat et Barthelemy de Ferrari Doria; Fondation Jules et Louis Vol. 2: 1981
Jeanbernat et Barthelemy de Ferrari Doria; Prix Jules et Louis
 Academie des Beaux-Arts Vol. 2: 1692
 Academie des Sciences Morales et Politiques Vol 2: 2014
 Academie Francaise Vol 2: 2101
 Institut de France Vol 2: 2427
"Jeanie" Musical Scholarship Winner Vol. 1: 9601
Jeantet Prize for Medicine; Louis- Vol. 2: 6478
Jeevan Raksha Padak Vol. 2: 3379
Jefferson Award Vol. 1: 8016
Jefferson Award; Thomas Vol. 2: 6305
Jefferson Awards Vol. 1: 2628
Jefferson Awards for Public Architecture; Thomas Vol. 1: 2719
Jefferson Cup Award Vol. 1: 21392
Jefferson Freedom Award; Thomas Vol. 1: 2959
Jefferson Grape-wine Loving Cup Trophy Vol. 1: 21373
The Jefferson Lecture Award Vol. 1: 14936
Jefferson Lecture in the Humanities Vol. 1: 14937
Jefferson Medal Vol. 1: 16177
Jefferson Medal for Distinguished Achievement in the Arts, Humanities, or Social Sciences; Thomas Vol. 1: 3435
Jefferson Memorial Foundation Award in Law; Thomas Vol. 1: 13595
Jefferson Memorial Foundation Medal in Architecture; Thomas Vol. 1: 13596
Jefferson Prize; Thomas Vol. 1: 18689
Jeffery Award; Thomas B. Vol. 1: 13756
Jeffords, Jr. Trophy; Walter M. Vol. 1: 21588
Jeffries Aerospace Medicine and Life Sciences Research Award Vol. 1: 2683
Jeffries Award; John Vol. 1: 2683
Jehlinger Award; Charles Vol. 1: 642
Jelavich Prize; Barbara Vol. 1: 1056
Jellinek Memorial Award; E. M. Vol. 1: 12314
Jenkins Award; Samuel H. Vol. 2: 8006
Jenner Medal Vol. 2: 8820
Jennifer Lash Memorial Genealogical Award Vol. 1: 16641
Jennings Education Prize; Margaret Vol. 2: 273
Jennings Medal; Annie Burr Vol. 1: 9876
Jennings Memorial Award; Charles H. Vol. 1: 4886
Jensen Award; Harry T. Vol. 1: 2433
Jensen Award; Paul Vol. 1: 18327
Jeoloji Muhendisleri Odasi Emek Odulu Vol. 2: 6629
Jephcott Lectures Vol. 2: 8821
Jeppson Medal; John Vol. 1: 1686
Jerard Fund Award; PEN/ Vol. 1: 17147
Jeremiah Award/College Division Coach of the Year; Edward Vol. 1: 2490
Jernigan Scholarship; Kenneth Vol. 1: 15039

Jerome Award Vol. 1: 7653
Jerome Award; Harry Vol. 1: 6409
Jerome Fellowships Vol. 1: 17398
Jerome Scholarship; Harry Vol. 1: 6410
Jerusalem Prize for the Freedom of the Individual in Society Vol. 2: 3766
Jerwood Awards Vol. 2: 8024
The Jerwood Painting Prize Vol. 2: 8246
Jerwood Prize Vol. 2: 8885
The Jerwood Sculpture Prize Vol. 2: 8247
Jeske Award Vol. 1: 16371
Jesselson Prize for Contemporary Judaica Design Vol. 2: 3747
Jessie T. MacKnight Award Vol. 1: 6626
Jessies Vol. 1: 10166
Jessup Botanical Trophy; Ann and Phil Vol. 1: 3334
Jeter Award; Frank Vol. 1: 5293
Jetfonden Vol. 2: 6295
Jetfoundation Vol. 2: 6295
JETS National TEAMS Awards Vol. 1: 12466
Jewett Memorial Award; Lew
Federation of Fly Fishers Vol. 1: 9480
Federation of Fly Fishers Vol 1: 9484
Jewish Community Center Theater of Cleveland Playwriting Competition Vol. 1: 10226
Jewish Historical Society of New York Fellowships Vol. 1: 2903
Jewish Humanist Leadership Award Vol. 1: 18708
Jewish Prize Vol. 1: 15967
Jewish Woman of the Year Award Vol. 2: 4965
Jeyes Lectureship; John Vol. 2: 8760
J.H. Hall Composites Manufacturing Award Vol. 1: 8324
Jidou-Syuppan-Bunka-Sho Vol. 2: 4296
Jimmy Rattlesnake Award Vol. 1: 7087
Jindal Gold Medal; O. P. Vol. 2: 3457
Jiro Matsui Award Vol. 1: 21965
J.J. Supniewski Foundation Award Vol. 2: 5308
JNMA Awards for Medical Journalism Vol. 1: 15370
Joachim Distinguished Service Award; TAPPI Herman L. Vol. 1: 19921
Joan Shorenstein Barone Award Vol. 1: 17846
Joannides; Fondation Alexandre Vol. 2: 1786
Joaste Grant; Helena Vol. 2: 5601
Job Corps Hall of Fame Vol. 1: 20522
Jobs Award Vol. 1: 16777
Jobst Foundation Award; Annual Conrad Vol. 1: 1988
Jobst Research Award; Conrad Vol. 1: 19483
Joest; Fondation du Baron de Vol. 2: 1846
Joest; Prix du Baron de Vol. 2: 1693
Jofa All American Hockey Squad (East and West) for Colleges Vol. 1: 2491
Jofa-Titan/USA Hockey Distinguished Achievement Award Vol. 1: 21176
Jofan All-American Hockey Squad (East and West) for Universities Vol. 1: 2492
Johann Friedrich von Cotta-Literary and Translation-Prize of Stuttgart City Vol. 2: 3102
Johinke Medal; K. Vol. 2: 404
John Alexander Media Award Vol. 1: 13671
John Britten Award Vol. 2: 4967
John Charnley Award Vol. 1: 10441
John Guice Award Vol. 1: 13618
John Horrocks Scholarship Vol. 2: 9229
John L. Cotter Award Vol. 1: 18686
John Paul Careet Award Vol. 2: 7238
John Paul II Award Vol. 1: 15620
John Paul II Religious Freedom Award Vol. 1: 7647
John Templeton European Film Prize Vol. 2: 6312
John Templeton Religion Writer of the Year in Europe Vol. 2: 6313
John Tyndall Award Vol. 1: 10658
John W. Cox Award Vol. 1: 18635
John W. Kaufmann Award Vol. 1: 8357
John Wiley & Sons Award for Innovation in Teaching Vol. 1: 11525
John Youngblood Scholarships Vol. 1: 21390
Johnson Achievement Award; Alfred E. Vol. 1: 1432
Johnson AMS 50 Dissertation Fellowships; Alvin H. Vol. 1: 3177
Johnson and Johnson Award Vol. 2: 5630
Johnson Annual Prize; Walter J. Vol. 1: 10235
Johnson Annual Scholarship Winners; Edward Vol. 1: 10190
Johnson Award; Bob Vol. 1: 21177
Johnson Award; Charles A. Vol. 1: 5961
Johnson Award; Eleanor M. Vol. 1: 11864
Johnson Award; G. Wesley Vol. 1: 14866
Johnson Award; John C. Vol. 1: 6327
Johnson Award; Kelly Vol. 1: 19133
Johnson Award; Lady Bird Vol. 1: 13949
Johnson Award; Laurence B. Vol. 1: 5668
Johnson Award; Mrs. Lyndon B. Vol. 1: 12531
Johnson Award; Pyke Vol. 1: 20163
Johnson Award; Robert B. Vol. 1: 10563
Johnson Award; Stanley Thomas Vol. 2: 6503
Johnson Award; Thomas W. Vol. 1: 675
Johnson Exhibition Catalogue Award; Philip Vol. 1: 19023
Johnson Forderpreis/Prix Cinegramm; Stanley Thomas Vol. 2: 6503
Johnson Health Policy Fellowships; Robert Wood Vol. 1: 13856
Johnson Honorary Member Award; Philip D. Vol. 1: 4146
Johnson Image Award; Peter H. Vol. 1: 14435
Johnson, Jr., Award; J. E. Vol. 1: 5410
Johnson Lecture; Axel Axson Vol. 2: 6199
Johnson Medal Vol. 1: 7365
Johnson Memorial Award; Palmer O. Vol. 1: 2161
Johnson Memorial Award; Richard B. Vol. 1: 13152
Johnson Memorial Trophy; Joe Vol. 1: 7219
Johnson Nutritionals New Investigator Award; SAM/Mead Vol. 1: 18621
Johnson Outstanding Achievement Award; A. Ivan Vol. 1: 5962
Johnson Pioneer Citation; Edgar F. Vol. 1: 17838
Johnson President's Trophy; John H. Vol. 1: 14339
Johnson Prize; Alfred Vol. 2: 7287
Johnson Prize; Harry G. Vol. 1: 7078
Johnson Writing Award; Orinne Vol. 1: 17257
Johnston Award; William M. Vol. 1: 20857
Johnston Distinguished Lecture Award Vol. 1: 11922
Johnston Memorial Shield; William Vol. 2: 7648
Johnston Service Award; Floyd T. Vol. 1: 5675
Johnstone Award; Fraser Vol. 1: 1764
Johnstone III Trophy (Singlehanded); Robert L. Vol. 1: 20789
Joint AICPA/AAA Accounting Literature Award Vol. 1: 2754
Joint Service Achievement Medal Vol. 1: 8819
Joint Service Commendation Medal Vol. 1: 8820
Joja Prize; Constantin Vol. 2: 5879
Jomo Kenyatta Prize for Literature Vol. 2: 4361
Jonah E. Kelley Award Vol. 1: 13
Jonathatn Mann Award for Global Health and Human Rights Vol. 1: 10049
Jonckheere; Prix Tobie Vol. 2: 1032
Jones and Bailey K. Howard World Book Encyclopedia - ALA Goal Awards; J. Morris Vol. 1: 2984
Jones & Shipman Prize Vol. 2: 7818
Jones Award; Bob Vol. 1: 20606
Jones Award; Col. James L. Vol. 1: 15384
Jones Award; Dexter Vol. 1: 15701
Jones Award for Best Work of Fiction; Jesse Vol. 1: 20018
Jones Award for Executive Leadership; Roger W. Vol. 1: 4784
Jones Award; Jesse H. Vol. 1: 20018
Jones Award; Mary Vaughan Vol. 2: 9205
Jones Award - Most Miles Stallion Award; Jim Vol. 1: 2178
Jones Award; Tom Vol. 1: 5756
Jones Awards; Mander Vol. 2: 274
Jones-Bateman Cup Vol. 2: 8551
Jones Community Service Award; Edward C. Vol. 1: 3046
Jones Distinguished Service Award; Reginald H. Vol. 1: 13874
Jones Fleet Engineer Award; Claud A. Vol. 1: 4568
Jones; Gwobr Goffa Sir Bryner Vol. 2: 8871
Jones London Medal; H. E. Vol. 2: 7852
Jones, M.D., Award; Anson Vol. 1: 20032
Jones Perpetual Memorial Award; Sir Bryner Vol. 2: 8871
Jones Prize; Alice Hanson Vol. 1: 9146
Jonssons pris; Bengt Vol. 2: 6191
Jordaanprijs; L. J. Vol. 2: 4688
Jordan Award Vol. 2: 8225
Jordan Christian Book of the Year Award Vol. 1: 9355
Jordan Memorial Award; W. Quinn - X Vol. 1: 1110
Jordan Memorial Challenge Trophy; Lynn Vol. 1: 15815
Jorgenson Award; Wally Vol. 1: 14114
Jose Award for General Excellence; Vic Vol. 1: 10724
Josep Pla Prize Vol. 2: 6019
Joseph Award; Stephen Vol. 2: 8962
Joseph Award; Thomas L. Vol. 1: 5411
Joseph F. Boyle Award for Distinguished Public Service Vol. 1: 1921
Joseph Prize
European Academy of Facial Plastic Surgery Vol. 2: 3899
Society of Medical Laboratory Technologists of South Africa Vol 2: 5631
Joseph Prize for Human Rights Vol. 1: 4982
Joseph Prize; Roger E. Vol. 1: 10376
Joseph W. Rosenbluth Memorial Award Vol. 1: 4626

Award Index

Joseph W. Rosenbluth Memorial Travel Agent of the Year Award Vol. 1: 4626
Joseph/Wilson Study Grant Vol. 1: 10153
Josey Scholarship Award; E. J. Vol. 1: 6419
Joshua Trophy Vol. 1: 12433
Josie Tomforde Competition Vol. 1: 10500
Joslin Essay Award Vol. 1: 20143
Jost Memorial Lecture; Wilhelm Vol. 2: 2798
Jostens Most Improved National Midget Championship Series Driver Award Vol. 1: 20420
Joukowsky Distinguished Service Award; Martha and Arlenis Vol. 1: 5033
Joule Award; James Vol. 2: 2483
Joule Medal; James Prescott Vol. 2: 7771
Journal Award
  National Council on Public History Vol. 1: 14866
  Society for Applied Spectroscopy Vol 1: 18643
  Society of Motion Picture and Television Engineers Vol 1: 19194
The Journal Award in Poetry Vol. 1: 16651
Journal Award (Science) Vol. 1: 18716
Journal Certificate Vol. 1: 19194
Journal Contributor Awards Vol. 1: 4909
Journal of Advertising Best Article Award Vol. 1: 612
Journal of Allied Health Award Vol. 1: 5842
Journal of Geography Awards Vol. 1: 14766
Journal of Property Management Article of the Year Awards Vol. 1: 11037
Journal of Research in Science Teaching Award JRST Award Vol. 1: 14032
Journalism Achievement on Aesthetic Surgery Award Vol. 1: 3911
Journalism Alumni Award Vol. 1: 6208
Journalism; Anthony Majeri Jr. Award for Innovation and Leadership in Graphic Vol. 1: 6210
Journalism Award
  American Association of Petroleum Geologists Vol. 1: 1340
  American Podiatric Medical Association Vol 1: 3562
  Audubon Naturalist Society of the Central Atlantic States Vol 1: 6068
  Australian Skeptics - NSW Branch Vol 2: 262
  Catholic Press Association Vol 1: 7659
  Drug Strategies Vol 1: 9029
  Road Runners Club of America Vol 1: 18069
Journalism Awards
  James Beard Foundation Vol. 1: 12288
  Leukemia and Lymphoma Society Vol 1: 12788
  New York Press Club Vol 1: 16243
  Newsletter and Electronic Publishers Foundation Vol 1: 16326
Journalism Awards; MDA Broadcast Vol. 1: 13683
Journalism Awards Program Vol. 1: 10354
Journalism Citation Vol. 1: 11276
Journalism Competition Vol. 2: 513
Journalism Hall of Fame Vol. 1: 6209
Journalist of the Year Vol. 1: 6105
Journalist of the Year Award
  MIND - National Association for Mental Health Vol. 2: 8122
  National Association of Black Journalists Vol 1: 14101
Journalist Prize of the DGE Vol. 2: 2895
Journalistenpreis of the DGE Vol. 2: 2895
Journalistic Achievement Award Vol. 1: 6038
Journalists in Distress Vol. 1: 7246
Journee des Recompenses Vol. 2: 4411
Journey Prize Vol. 1: 13211
Jousselin; Fondations Gaston Plante, Francois Hebert-Paul Vol. 2: 1979
Jousselin; Prix Henri Vol. 2: 2160
Jowett Medal Vol. 2: 9072
Joy In Singing Award Recital Vol. 1: 12456
Jozwiak Memorial Special Achievement Award; Joseph Vol. 1: 11818
JPA Blue Ribbon and Certificate Vol. 1: 12471
JRST Award Vol. 1: 14032
JSID Outstanding Student Paper of the Year Award Vol. 1: 18769
JSLE Best Paper Award Vol. 2: 4229
JTPA Awards for Excellence Vol. 1: 14168
JTTM Award for Excellence in Travel and Tourism Education Vol. 1: 12025
Jubilee Award for an Honours Student in Geography Vol. 2: 5638
Jubilee Lecture and Harden Medal Vol. 2: 6867
Jubilee Trophy Vol. 2: 5061
Jucys premija; Adolfo Vol. 2: 4391
Judd AIC Award Vol. 2: 2942
Judeen Memorial Award; Erik Vol. 1: 20808
Judge Heart of New York Awards; Rev. Mychal Vol. 1: 16249
Judge of the Year Vol. 1: 11453
Judge of the Year Award
  National Association of Women Judges Vol. 1: 14459
  National Court Appointed Special Advocate Association Vol 1: 14875
Judges Appreciation Award Vol. 1: 3229
Judges*]* Award Vol. 2: 8857
Judges Award Vol. 1: 3132
Judges' Award
  Royal Television Society Vol. 2: 8851
  Royal Television Society Vol 2: 8855
Judges Award of Merit Vol. 1: 15481
Judges Choice Award Vol. 1: 11659
Judges' Commendation Vol. 1: 3335
Judith Grove Adoption Activist Award Vol. 1: 192
Judkins Young Clinical Investigator Award; Melvin Vol. 1: 2411
Judson Daland Prize Vol. 1: 3436
Judy Goddard/Libraries Limited Awards Vol. 1: 5057
Jujitsu Outstanding Competitor Vol. 1: 557
Jules Leger Prize for New Chamber Music Vol. 1: 6799
Julia Hull Schilling Award Vol. 1: 9153
Julien; Prix Stanislas Vol. 2: 1775
Julin Trophy; Bengt Vol. 1: 20779
Julius Medal; George Vol. 2: 405
Julius Stulberg Auditions Vol. 1: 19816
Julliard Prize; Jean Vol. 2: 4840
Jump Award; William A. Vol. 1: 12460
Jumper of the Year Vol. 1: 21244
June Moray Award Vol. 1: 6350
Jungfleisch; Fondation Emile Vol. 2: 1857
Junior Achievement National Business Hall of Fame Vol. 1: 12462
Junior Award Vol. 1: 4516
Junior Book Award Vol. 1: 19443
Junior Captain Scott Commemorative Medal Vol. 2: 5648
Junior Director of the Year Award Vol. 1: 18158
Junior Division Award Vol. 1: 2179
Junior Encouragement Award Vol. 2: 241
Junior European Baseball Champion Vol. 2: 858
Junior Faculty Award Vol. 1: 2138
Junior Faculty Scholar Award Vol. 1: 4443
Junior Fellowship Awards Vol. 2: 8505
Junior Female Athlete of the Year Vol. 1: 19628
The Junior Golf Association of Mobile Scholarship Vol. 1: 12468
Junior Golf Grant Vol. 1: 9629
Junior Golf Leader Vol. 1: 17616
Junior Grand Champion Vol. 1: 16484
Junior High Average Horsemanship Vol. 1: 16485
Junior, Intermediate, and Senior Championship Awards Vol. 1: 9197
Junior Inventor of the Year Vol. 2: 6120
Junior Male Athlete of the Year Vol. 1: 19629
Junior Moulton Medal Vol. 2: 7752
Junior National Championship Vol. 1: 16486
Junior National Championships Vol. 1: 21162
Junior Paper Award Vol. 1: 19214
Junior Player of the Year Vol. 1: 21178
Junior Players of the Year Vol. 1: 19979
Junior Research Award in Gerontology Vol. 2: 5893
Junior Research Fellowship Vol. 2: 3371
Junior Scholarship Vol. 1: 13590
Junior Science Award Vol. 2: 6650
Junior Showmanship Vol. 1: 15218
Junior Travelling Fellowship Vol. 2: 9253
Junior Triathletes of the Year Vol. 1: 21249
Junior/Young Rider Awards Vol. 1: 20567
Juniper Prize Vol. 1: 21057
Junner Rose-Bowl Trophy; Mackenzie Vol. 2: 9065
Junner Technical Award; Mackenzie Vol. 2: 9066
Juno Awards Vol. 1: 6846
Jupiter Award Vol. 1: 13600
Jurdant Prize in Environmental Science; Michel Vol. 1: 5539
Juried Crafts Exhibition Vol. 1: 7774
Jurist of the Year Award Vol. 2: 4363
Jury Award
  San Sebastian International Film Festival Vol. 2: 6096
  Stuttgart International Festival of Animated Film Vol 2: 3107
Jury Discretionary Awards Vol. 1: 8108
Jury Prize for the Dance on Camera Festival Vol. 1: 8734
Just Lecture Award; E.E. Vol. 1: 3942
Justica Awards Vol. 1: 6969
Justice Award
  American Judicature Society Vol. 1: 2912
  Canadian Institute for the Administration of Justice Vol 1: 7170
Justice Award/Fund for Religious Liberty Award Vol. 1: 2895
Juvenile Awards Vol. 1: 9783
Juvenile Literature; American Association of University Women Award in Vol. 1: 16516
Juvenile Stake Challenge Trophy Vol. 1: 15815
JVC President Award Vol. 2: 4316
K-9 Dog Award Vol. 1: 3571
K-12 Dance Educator of the Year Vol. 1: 14896
K-12 Distinguished Teaching Achievement Award Vol. 1: 14764
KAB System Awards Vol. 1: 12532

Kable Electrification Award; George W. Vol. 1: 4232
Kadis Memorial Scholarship; Larry Vol. 1: 16345
Kagin Family Paper Money Youth Exhibit Award Vol. 1: 3230
Kagy Education Award of Excellence; Frederick D. Vol. 1: 10135
Kahan Scholars Prize; Gerald Vol. 1: 4201
Kahlil Gibran Spirit of Humanity Award Vol. 1: 5019
Kahn Award; Noah A. Vol. 1: 5963
Kahn Award; Sanders A. Vol. 1: 5008
Kahuna Award Vol. 1: 12052
Kaigler; Fay B. Vol. 1: 13517
Kaiser Educational Award; L. U. "Luke" Vol. 1: 13029
Kaitz Award; Idell Vol. 1: 14577
Kal Kan Award Vol. 1: 906
Kal Kan Volunteer of the Year Vol. 1: 2575
Kala Prapoorna in Dance; Bharta Vol. 2: 3569
Kala Prapoorna in Drama; Nataka Vol. 2: 3570
Kala Prapoorna in Music; Gana Vol. 2: 3571
Kala Praveena Award Vol. 2: 3572
Kalan Fund Award; Pavle Vol. 2: 5995
Kalbache and Zahara Ben Mamou Award; Azar Vol. 1: 11830
Kaleidoscope - A Fair of the Arts Vol. 1: 7816
Kaleidoscope of Honor Vol. 2: 1490
Kaletta Award; Father Paul Vol. 1: 11455
Kalinga Prize Vol. 2: 2601
Kalish Innovative Publication Award; Richard Vol. 1: 9994
Kallebergerstipendiet Vol. 2: 6255
Kallen Award; Horace M. Vol. 1: 2896
Kalmus Gold Medal Award; Technicolor/Herbert T. Vol. 1: 19199
Kalokerinos Foundation Prize for Theatre Vol. 2: 3187
Kalven Prize Vol. 1: 12722
Kamani Gold Medal Vol. 2: 3461
Kameny Award Vol. 1: 9451
Kammer Merit in Authorship Award; Adoph G. Vol. 1: 1905
Kanai Award; Tsutomu Vol. 1: 10896
Kandhari Award; Lala Ram Chand Vol. 2: 3418
Kandutsch Preis; Jorg Vol. 2: 761
Kane Award; Robert J. Vol. 1: 20720
Kane Medal; Elisha Kent Vol. 1: 9943
Kanellakis Theory and Practice Award; Paris Vol. 1: 5301
Kanev Memorial Award; Sydney M. Vol. 1: 1893
Kanin Playwriting Award Program; Michael Vol. 1: 12540
Kanin Playwriting program; Michael Vol. 1: 12548
Kanjilal Traveling Fellowship; Ferdinande Johanna Vol. 2: 8462
Kannisto Fund Award; Vaino Vol. 2: 1585
Kansainvalinen Mirjam Helin laulukilpailu Vol. 2: 1600
Kansainvalinen Paulon Sellokilpailu Vol. 2: 1638
Kansas National Small Painting, Drawing, and Print Exhibition Vol. 1: 13616
Kansas Premier Seed Grower Vol. 1: 12491
Kapell Piano Competition; University of Maryland International Piano Festival and William Vol. 1: 18567
Kapitan Award; Josef S. Vol. 1: 5412
Kapitza Award; Peter Vol. 2: 2483
Kaplan Award; David Vol. 1: 16981
Kaplan Award for Chronic Daily Headache Vol. 1: 2389
Kaplan Award; Gordin Vol. 1: 7089
Kaplan Medal Vol. 1: 12372
Kaplan Sportsmanship Award; Bobby Vol. 1: 20858
Kapp Foundation Engineering Award; Martin S. Vol. 1: 4336
Kappa Alpha Theta Program Director of the Year Award Vol. 1: 14876
Kappa Delta Pi National Student Teacher/Intern of the Year Award Vol. 1: 5881
Kappa Tau Alpha Research Award; Frank Luther Mott- Vol. 1: 21080
Kappe Award; Stanley E. Vol. 1: 649
Karant Award for Excellence in Aviation Journalism; Max Vol. 1: 398
Karibu Vol. 2: 5395
Karlin Grant; Barbara Vol. 1: 19089
Karling Graduate Student Research Award; J. S. Vol. 1: 6549
Karlson Lifetime Achievement Award; Adele Vol. 1: 19736
Karlsson Award for Leadership and Achievement through Collaboration; Hans Vol. 1: 10897
Karlstrom Outstanding Educator Award; Karl V. Vol. 1: 5302
Karmel Award; Marjorie Vol. 1: 12674
Karo Plaque Vol. 1: 18991
Karpinskij Prize; Alexander Petrowitsch Vol. 2: 3084
Kasdan Award Best Narrative Film; Lawrence Vol. 1: 4972
Kastler-Prize; Gentner- Vol. 2: 2725
Katanning Art Prize Vol. 2: 456
Kathern Mathies Grant Vol. 1: 20215
Katz Award; Donald L. Vol. 1: 9896
Katz Award for Excellence in the Coverage of Immigration Vol. 1: 7729
Katz Award; Joseph Vol. 1: 5371
Katz Basic Science Research Prize for Young Investigators; Louis N. Vol. 1: 2412
Kauffman Gold Medal; Virgil Vol. 1: 19123
Kaufman Women's Scholarship Fund; Lucille B. Vol. 1: 19157
Kaufmann Award; Richard Harold Vol. 1: 10872
Kaufmann Memorial Lecture Vol. 2: 2873
Kaufmann Prize; H. P. Vol. 2: 2874
Kautz Merit Award; Sena Vol. 1: 5385
Kavlin Photography Grant; Enrique Vol. 2: 3748
Kavod Award Vol. 1: 7568
Kay Award; Won Chuel Vol. 1: 233
Kay Co-Op Scholarship Award; Wayne Vol. 1: 19158
Kay Elemetrics Award for Research in Phonetics Vol. 1: 12014
Kay Graduate Fellowship; Wayne Vol. 1: 19159
Kay High School Scholarship; Wayne Vol. 1: 19160
Kay Jeweler's/J.B. Robinson Award Vol. 1: 14670
Kay Scholarship Fund; Wayne Vol. 1: 19161
Kazdin Memorial Fund Award; S. Edwin Vol. 1: 5009
KCFB Scholarship Vol. 1: 12595
Kean Medal; Ben Vol. 1: 4630
Keane; Award for Excellence in Honor of Mark E. Vol. 1: 11475
Keane Award for Excellence; Mark E. Vol. 1: 11475
Keane Distinguished Service Award; Charles V. Vol. 1: 39
Kearton Medal and Award; Cherry Vol. 2: 8523
Keating McLoughlin Medal Vol. 2: 3697
Keats/Kerlan Collection Fellowship; Ezra Jack Vol. 1: 21073
Keats Memorial Fellowship; Ezra Jack Vol. 1: 21073
Keats - Shelley Association Annual Prize Vol. 1: 12524
Keefer Medal Vol. 1: 7416
Keeling Dissertation Award; William B. Vol. 1: 20171
Keep America Beautiful National Awards Vol. 1: 12532
Keepers Preservation Education Fund Fellowship Vol. 1: 19024
Keeping the Blues Alive Awards Vol. 1: 6476
Keesiing Fellowship; Nancy Vol. 2: 605
Kegan Award; Philip M. Hamer and Elizabeth Hamer Vol. 1: 18954
Kegans Award for Victim Services in Probation and Parole; Joe Vol. 1: 3603
Kehoe Award of Merit; Robert A. Vol. 1: 1906
Kehoe Memorial Award; Fr. George Vol. 1: 7220
Kehrlein Award; Oliver Vol. 1: 18463
Keilin Memorial Lecture Vol. 2: 6868
Keith Award; Nathaniel S. Vol. 1: 15248
Keith Medal Vol. 2: 8789
Keithley for Advances in Measuresment Sciences; Joseph F. Vol. 1: 3459
Kelleher Award; Judith C. Vol. 1: 9246
Kellendonk-prijs; Frans Vol. 2: 4914
Keller Achievement Awards; Helen Vol. 1: 2302
Keller Award; James Vol. 1: 7971
Keller Award; Spirit of Helen Vol. 1: 10388
Keller Behavioral Education Award; Fred S. Vol. 1: 3656
Keller High Average Award; Jean-Fish-Pearl Vol. 1: 21773
Keller Prize; Gottfried Vol. 2: 6484
Keller Trophy Vol. 1: 10990
Kellett Island Trophy Vol. 2: 7532
Kelley Consumer Leadership Award; Florence Vol. 1: 14733
Kelley - Wyman Award Vol. 1: 14076
Kellgrenpriset Vol. 2: 6256
Kelliher Student of Honour; Sir Henry Vol. 2: 5026
Kellogg Award Vol. 1: 1820
Kellogg National Leadership Program Vol. 1: 21694
Kelly Award for Cultural Leadership; Keith Vol. 1: 7037
Kelly Award; Jack Vol. 1: 20749
Kelly Award; Joe W. Vol. 1: 1967
Kelly Award of Excellence; Billy Vol. 2: 3660
Kelly Award; Stephen E. Vol. 1: 13015
Kelly Fair Play Award; Jack Vol. 1: 20721
Kelly - Founder's Award; John Snooks Vol. 1: 2493
Kelly Memorial Award; John B. Vol. 1: 21193
Kelly Memorial Award; Robert Vol. 1: 14867
Kelly Memorial Prize; Joan Vol. 1: 2477
Kelly Peace Poetry Awards; Barbara Mandigo Vol. 1: 16590

Kelly Trophy; C. Markland Vol. 1: 20662
Kelman Innovator's Lecture; Charles D. Vol. 1: 4274
Kelsey Award; Guy Vol. 1: 3862
Kelvin Medal
Institution of Civil Engineers Vol. 2: 7772
Royal Philosophical Society of Glasgow Vol 2: 8660
Kelvin Medal and Prize Vol. 2: 7732
Kelvin Premium Vol. 2: 7808
Kempe Award for the International Society for the Prevention of Child Abuse and Neglect; Henry Vol. 2: 6617
Kemper Award; Edward C. Vol. 1: 2720
Kempf Fund Award for Research Development in Psychobiological Psychiatry; APA/ Vol. 1: 3623
Kendall and Florence P. Kendall Award for Outstanding Achievement in Clinical Practice; Henry O. Vol. 1: 3492
Kendall Award; Katherine Vol. 2: 7904
Kendall Oration and Medal Vol. 2: 280
Kenna Scholar-Athlete Award; E. Douglas Vol. 1: 15073
Kennan Award for Distinguished Public Service; George F. Vol. 1: 14703
Kennedy Astronautics Award; John F. Vol. 1: 1503
Kennedy Award; Byron Vol. 2: 177
Kennedy Award; Henry L. Vol. 1: 1968
Kennedy Award; William M. Vol. 1: 19211
Kennedy Book Awards; Robert F. Vol. 1: 18074
Kennedy Center Alliance for Arts Education Network/National School Boards Association Award Vol. 1: 12554
Kennedy Center Alliance for the Arts Education Network and National School Board Association Award Vol. 1: 12537
Kennedy Center Friedheim Awards for New Music Vol. 1: 12551
Kennedy Center Honors Vol. 1: 12552
Kennedy Center/National School Boards Association Award Vol. 1: 12554
Kennedy Citizenship Award; J. Walter Vol. 1: 14505
Kennedy-Clerk Maxwell Award; Joe Vol. 1: 17290
Kennedy Human Rights Award; Robert F. Vol. 1: 18075
Kennedy Journalism Awards; Robert F. Vol. 1: 18076
Kennedy Medal; Sir John Vol. 1: 9272
Kennedy Memorial Prize; Byron Vol. 2: 177
Kennedy Profile in Courage Award; John F. Vol. 1: 12398
Kennedy Student Paper Competition; John F. Vol. 2: 6053
Kennedy Trophy; John F. Vol. 1: 15071
Kenneth D. Naden Award Vol. 1: 14801
Kenneth N. Trueblood Awards Vol. 1: 2089
Kenny Award; Dr. John J. Vol. 1: 12789
Kent Award; Donald P. Vol. 1: 9995
Kentucky Artists Fellowships Vol. 1: 12562
Kentucky Bluegrass Awards Vol. 1: 19785
Kentucky Derby
Churchill Downs Inc. Vol. 1: 7989
Triple Crown Productions, Inc. Vol 1: 20206
Kentucky Oaks Vol. 1: 7990
Kentucky State Poetry Society Award Vol. 1: 15002
Kenya National Academy of Sciences General Award Vol. 2: 4357
Kenya National Academy of Sciences Honorary Fellow Vol. 2: 4358
Kenya National Academy of Sciences Scholastic Award Vol. 2: 4359
Kenyon Medal for Classical Studies Vol. 2: 6902
Keogh Award for Distinguished Public Service; Eugene J. Vol. 1: 16307
Kerkrade World Music Contest Vol. 2: 4938
Kerlan Award Vol. 1: 21074
Kern Award; Donald Q. Vol. 1: 2781
Kern Award; Jim Vol. 1: 2455
Kern Lecture Award; Richard A. Vol. 1: 5774
Kerpely Medal; Antal Vol. 2: 3257
Kerr Dissertation Award competition; Malcolm H. Vol. 1: 13382
Kerr History Prize Vol. 1: 16289
Kerr Prize; Sophie Vol. 1: 21441
Kerr Veterinary Student Award; Don Vol. 2: 281
Kershaw Award; John Vol. 2: 8606
Kershner Memorial Chapter Leader Award; Marion Vol. 1: 13281
Kesselring Fund Award; Joseph Vol. 1: 13992
Kesselring Prize Vol. 1: 13992
Kessler Awards; Henry H. Vol. 1: 17964
Kessler Awards in International Rehabilitation; Henry and Estelle Vol. 1: 17964
Kestenberg Medal; Leo Vol. 2: 2904
Kesteven Medal Vol. 2: 282
Ketcham Memorial Award; Albert H. Vol. 1: 1576
Ketchum Award for Outstanding Volunteer Fundraiser Vol. 1: 5703
Ketner Productivity Awards Vol. 1: 16505
Ketsuekigaku Kenkyu-Kikin Vol. 2: 4214
Kettering Award; Charles F.
American Society of Plant Biologists Vol. 1: 4590
Cooperative Education and Internship Association Vol 1: 8503
Kettering Medal; Charles F. Vol. 1: 9920
Keuffel and Esser Awards Vol. 2: 6975
Key Award
American Society of Association Executives Vol. 1: 4268
Specialty Graphic Imaging Association Vol 1: 19595
Key Employee Award Vol. 1: 15861
Key History Award; Whitaker Vol. 1: 17772
Key to the Highway Award Vol. 1: 6477
Keyes Award; Marjorie Hiscott Vol. 1: 7269
Keyes Medal Vol. 1: 1205
Keyhoe Journalism Award; Donald E. Vol. 1: 9836
Keymer Prize; Anne Vol. 2: 7010
Keysa Scholarship; Louise Vol. 1: 12687
Keystone Award Vol. 1: 14418
Keystone Press Awards Vol. 1: 17187
Keytone Press Awards Vol. 1: 17198
KFAS Awards in Islamic Medical Sciences Vol. 2: 4376
Khan Prize for Fiction; Aga Vol. 1: 17094
Kharazmi Prize Vol. 2: 3610
Kheel Award of the Institute for Mediation and Conflict Resolution; Theodore W. Vol. 1: 10825
Kho Liang Ie-prijs Vol. 2: 4689
Kibbee Award for Public Service and Achievement; Robert J. Vol. 1: 8032
Kibble Literary Award; Nita B. Vol. 2: 606
Kibler Memorial Award; Robert J. Vol. 1: 14712
Kidd Award; Bruce Vol. 1: 19630
Kidd Award; J. Roby Vol. 2: 9302
Kidder Award for Eminence in the Field of American Archaeology; Alfred Vincent Vol. 1: 911
Kidder Early Career Award; Louise Vol. 1: 18886
Kideney Gold Medal Award; James William Vol. 1: 299
Kieslowski Award for Best Foreign Feature; Krzysztof Vol. 1: 8883
Kihara Award Vol. 2: 4118
Kihara Sho Vol. 2: 4118
Kilbourne Award; Judith Vol. 1: 7392
Kilby Awards of Excellence; Jack St. Clair Vol. 1: 12586
Kilby International Awards Vol. 1: 12586
Kilby Young Innovator Vol. 1: 12586
Kilgour Award for Research in Library and Information Technology; Frederick G. Vol. 1: 12824
Killam Memorial Prizes; Izaak Walton Vol. 1: 6800
Killam Memorial Scholarship; Elson T.
New England Water Works Association Vol. 1: 16138
New England Water Works Association Vol 1: 16139
Killam Research Fellowships; Izaak Walton Vol. 1: 6800
Kilmer Prize Vol. 1: 3393
Kilpatrick Trophy Vol. 1: 2511
Kilrea Trophy; Wally Vol. 1: 2518
Kimball Award; Justin Ford Vol. 1: 2546
Kimball Medal; George E. Vol. 1: 11075
Kimball Medallion; Miles Vol. 1: 13030
Kimberly Cup Vol. 1: 19693
"Kimble" - Fugitive of the Year Vol. 1: 9823
Kimbrough Fund Award; Anne Giles Vol. 1: 8718
Kimbrough Fund Award; Arch and Anne Giles Vol. 1: 8718
Kincheloe Award; Iven C. Vol. 1: 19114
Kind-Preis der ETG; Herbert- Vol. 2: 2734
Kindness to Animals Award Vol. 1: 16772
King Award; Dr. Lyndon Vol. 1: 8262
King Award; Martin Luther Vol. 1: 12914
King Baudouin Award of EGIAR 2000 Vol. 2: 1368
King Baudouin International Development Prize Vol. 2: 940
King Book Award; Coretta Scott Vol. 1: 3004
King Contest Vol. 1: 15219
King Contribution Award; Billie Jean Vol. 1: 21809
King Eagle Scout Scholarship; Arthur M. and Berdena Vol. 1: 15782
King Faisal International Prize for Arabic Literature Vol. 2: 5922
King Faisal International Prize for Islamic Studies Vol. 2: 5923
King Faisal International Prize for the Service of Islam Vol. 2: 5924
King Faisal International Prize in Medicine Vol. 2: 5925
King Faisal International Prize in Science Vol. 2: 5926
King, Jr. - Abraham Joshua Heschel Award; Martin Luther Vol. 1: 6490
King, Jr. Achievement Award; Martin Luther Vol. 1: 8394
King, Jr. Award; Martin Luther Vol. 1: 9528
King, Jr. Leadership Awards; Martin Luther Vol. 1: 8965

King, Jr. Medal; Martin Luther Vol. 1: 8033
King, Jr. Scholarship Award; Martin Luther Vol. 1: 2026
King Lucille Award; B. B. Vol. 1: 6473
King Management Award; Kenneth K. Vol. 1: 10090
King Medal; Haddon Vol. 2: 126
King Memorial Award; Donald Vol. 1: 19634
King Memorial Award; Robert W. Vol. 1: 5716
King Memorial Certificate; Milton W. Vol. 1: 15834
King Sejong Literacy Prize Vol. 2: 2606
King-Sun Fu Award Vol. 2: 732
Kingery Award; W. David Vol. 1: 1687
King's Cross for Distinguished Service Vol. 2: 5138
King's Medal for Distinguished Service Vol. 2: 5138
King's Prize Vol. 2: 8192
Kingslake Medal and Prize; Rudolf Vol. 1: 19610
Kingsley Medal; Mary Vol. 2: 8079
Kingsolver Award; Barbara Vol. 1: 9795
Kinias Service Award; George A. Vol. 1: 14951
Kinkeldey Award; Otto Vol. 1: 3178
Kinley Memorial Fellowship; Kate Neal Vol. 1: 21032
Kinnard, Jr. Academic Award; Dr. William Vol. 1: 5010
Kinokuniya Theatre Awards Vol. 2: 4233
Kinsale Yacht Club Trophy Vol. 2: 7532
Kinsley Memorial Trophy; Charles A.
Photographic Society of America Vol. 1: 17283
Photographic Society of America Vol 1: 17284
Photographic Society of America Vol 1: 17287
Photographic Society of America Vol 1: 17288
Photographic Society of America Vol 1: 17289
Photographic Society of America Vol 1: 17290
Photographic Society of America Vol 1: 17291
Photographic Society of America Vol 1: 17294
Kintner Award for Distinguished Service; Earl Vol. 1: 9437
Kiphuth Award Vol. 1: 21194
Kiplinger Distinguished Contributions to Journalism Award Vol. 1: 15528
Kipping Award in Silicon Chemistry; Frederic Stanley Vol. 1: 1765
Kirby Memorial Medal for Outstanding Service to Canadian Physics; Peter Vol. 1: 6934
Kirby Scholar-Athlete Award; Jefferson Walker Vol. 1: 15073
Kirjeenvaihtajajasenyys Vol. 2: 1604
Kirk Award; David Vol. 1: 193
Kirk Award for Outstanding Graduate Student Research; Barbara A. Vol. 1: 3663
Kirk Award; Samuel Vol. 1: 13145
Kirklin M.D. Award for Professional Excellence; John W. Vol. 1: 1440
Kirklin MD Award; John W. Vol. 1: 1442
Kirkpatrick Chemical Engineering Achievement Award Vol. 1: 7823
Kirsch Award; Robert Vol. 1: 12931
Kirschner-Lewis Study Grant; Lee Vol. 1: 16564
Kirsner Award in Gastroenterology; J.B. Vol. 1: 9711
Kirti Chakra Vol. 2: 3380
Kishida International Award Vol. 1: 4226
Kittiwake Gallery Award Vol. 2: 9083
Kitz Award; James M. Vol. 1: 7177
Kivalo Egyesuleti Munkaert Erem Vol. 2: 3268
Kivalo Oktatd Vol. 2: 3316
Kiwania of Wascana Senior Cello/Viola/Double Bass Scholarship Vol. 1: 18296
Kiyoshi Tokutomi Memorial Haiku Contest Vol. 1: 22088
Kjeld Abell Pris Vol. 2: 1444
KKI Black Belt Certification Vol. 1: 2917
Klaus Juren Vetter Prize for Electrochemical Kinetics Vol. 2: 6456
Klausmeyer Distinguished Service Award; Otto Vol. 1: 17342
Kleemeier Award; Robert W. Vol. 1: 9996
Klein Award; Eugene Vol. 1: 3409
Klein Award; Lawrence R. Vol. 1: 20517
Klein Award; Morton J. Vol. 1: 11785
Klein Award; Walt Vol. 1: 6481
Klein Prize for Poetry; A. M.
Quebec Writers' Federation Vol. 1: 17799
Quebec Writers' Federation Vol 1: 17801
Kleiner Memorial Awards; Joseph J. Vol. 1: 3954
Kleinhans Fellowships Vol. 1: 17866
Kleitman Distinguished Service Award; Nathaniel Vol. 1: 839
Klemin Award; Dr. Alexander Vol. 1: 2434
Klemm-Preis; Wilhelm- Vol. 2: 2809
Klineberg Intercultural and International Relations Award; Otto Vol. 1: 18887
Klingensmith EMS Administrator of the Year Award; William Vol. 1: 14214
Klinger Memorial Award; William A. Vol. 1: 274
Klinker Award; Mary T. Vol. 1: 234
Klopsteg Memorial Lecture Vol. 1: 1375
Klose Prize; Hans Vol. 2: 3085
Klumpke - Isaac Roberts; Prix Dorothea Vol. 2: 2557
Klumpke-Roberts Award Vol. 1: 6009
The KM Fabrics Technical Production Award Vol. 1: 20646
Knacke Aerodynamic Decelerator Systems Award; Theodor W. Vol. 1: 2684
Knauss Marine Policy Fellowship Vol. 1: 13358
Knauss National Marine Policy Fellowship Vol. 1: 6754
KNCV Gold Medal Vol. 2: 4899
Knebel Best of Show Memorial Award; Clarence Vol. 1: 1265
Knee/Whitman Lifetime Achievement Award Vol. 1: 14388
Knife in North America Award; Sharpest Vol. 1: 1267
Knight-Bagehot Fellowships Vol. 1: 8250
Knight Essay Contest; George S. and Stella M. Vol. 1: 15782
Knight Fellowships; John S. Vol. 1: 12605
Knight Medal; Allen Vol. 2: 406
Knight Memorial Grand Master Award; Damon Vol. 1: 18357
Knight *NACTA Journal* Award; E. B. Vol. 1: 16405
Knight Research Grant; Elva Vol. 1: 11865
Knights of Justice Award Vol. 1: 3572
Knights of the Golden Fleece; Honorary Vol. 1: 7032
Knott Award; Judge R. Vol. 1: 10466
Knouff Line Officer of the Year Award; Scotia Vol. 1: 3604
Knowledge Industry Publications, Inc. Award for Library Literature Vol. 1: 2980
Knowles Award for Outstanding Adult Education Program Leadership; Malcolm Vol. 1: 948
Knowles Kousin Vol. 1: 12607
Knowlton Medal Vol. 1: 13240
Knox Reticulata Award; Charlotte C. Vol. 1: 1619
Knud Lind Larsen Prize Vol. 2: 1446
Knudsen Award Vol. 1: 1907
Knuth Prize; Donald E. Vol. 1: 5317
Knutson Award; Jeanne N. Vol. 1: 12019
Kobayashi Computers and Communications Award; Koji Vol. 1: 10873
Kobe City International Association Vol. 2: 4238
Kobe International Flute Competition Vol. 2: 4235
Koch Award; Erwin T. Vol. 1: 13522
Koch Award; Fred Conrad Vol. 1: 9262
Koch Memorial Medal Award; Carel C. Vol. 1: 722
Kocher Playwrights Award; Eric Vol. 1: 15507
Kodak All-American Team Vol. 1: 15316
Kodak Coach of the Year Vol. 1: 14081
KODAK International Educational Literature Award Vol. 1: 5216
Kodak International Newspaper Snapshot Awards Vol. 1: 9121
Kodak U.K. Film Council Award Vol. 2: 7407
Kodansha Manga Award Vol. 2: 4241
Kodansha Prize Vol. 2: 4242
Kodansha Prize for Cartoon Book Vol. 2: 4241
Kodiat Award; M. Vol. 2: 3601
Koehl Award; Albert E. Vol. 1: 10557
Koenig/Organon/Nourpharma Poster Prize; M. Pierre Vol. 2: 1486
Koenigsberg Award; Nancy and Harry Vol. 1: 20050
Koga Gold Medal; Issac Vol. 2: 935
Kogalniceau Prize; Mihail Vol. 2: 5841
Kohl Memorial Exhibit Award; Melvin and Leona Vol. 1: 3231
Kohler Prize; Charlotte Vol. 2: 4930
Kohlstedt Exhibit Award Vol. 1: 2965
Kohrtz' stipendium; Ilona Vol. 2: 6257
Kokoku Dentus Sho Vol. 2: 4113
Kokusai Koryu Kikin Sho Vol. 2: 4170
Kokusai Koryu Shorei Sho Vol. 2: 4172
Kokusai Seibutsugaku-sho Vol. 2: 4201
Kolb Prize; Eugene Vol. 2: 3772
Kolk Air Transportation Progress Award; Franklin W. Vol. 1: 19049
Kolliner Award for a Young Israeli Artist; Beatrice S. Vol. 2: 3749
Kolovakos Award; Gregory Vol. 1: 17141
Kolping Award Vol. 1: 7645
Kolping Award); International Pin of Merit (Vol. 2: 2967
Kolstad Junior Soaring Awards Vol. 1: 18586
Kolstad Youth Scholarship Vol. 1: 18586
Komarov Diploma; V. M. Vol. 2: 6338
Komen Award of Scientific Distinction Vol. 1: 19850
Kompositionspreis der Landeshauptstadt Stuttgart Vol. 2: 3104
Komura Prize Vol. 2: 4143
Kondic Medal; Voya Vol. 2: 7656

Award Index

Konheim Award; Beatrice G. Vol. 1: 1465
Konig-Gedenkmunze; Joseph- Vol. 2: 2810
Konkurs Mlodych Kompozytorow im. Tadeusza Bairda Vol. 2: 5343
Konnik Order; Madarski Vol. 2: 1230
Konrad-Zuse-Medaille Vol. 2: 2839
Koob Award; C. Albert Vol. 1: 14613
Koob Merit Award; C. Albert Vol. 1: 14606
Koprulu Book Prize; M. Fuat Vol. 1: 20242
Korczak Literary Competition; Janusz Vol. 1: 4983
Kordelin Prize Vol. 2: 1650
Korean Composition Award Vol. 2: 5505
Korean Literature Translation Award Vol. 2: 5502
Korean Service Medal Vol. 1: 8821
Korevaar Outstanding Paper Award; Jan Vol. 2: 448
Korey Award; Saul R. Vol. 1: 702
Korn Award; Martin P. Vol. 1: 17525
Korn Founder's Award; The Michael Vol. 1: 7943
Korolev Diploma Vol. 2: 6339
Korrespondierendes Mitglied Vol. 2: 3043
Koryagin Award; Anatoly Vol. 2: 4787
Kosar Award; William F. Vol. 1: 10508
Kosar Memorial Award Vol. 1: 18717
Kosciuszko Foundation Doctoral Dissertation Award Vol. 1: 12611
Kosciuszko Foundation Exchange Program with Poland Vol. 1: 12612
Koseki-sho Vol. 2: 4222
Koshnitsky Award Vol. 1: 11378
Kosoff Memorial Literary Award; Abe Vol. 1: 3232
Kossler, USCG Award; Captain William J. Vol. 1: 2435
Kostanecki Medal; Stanislaw Vol. 2: 5338
Kostov Prize; Academician Doncho Vol. 2: 1207
Kotler Award for Excellence in Healthcare Marketing; The Philip Vol. 1: 3029
Kotyk Award; Eugene Vol. 1: 20278
Koussevitzky Commissions Vol. 1: 12616
Koutlidios Award Vol. 2: 3176
Kovacs Prize; Katherine Singer Vol. 1: 13560
Kovacs Prize; Richard Vol. 2: 8822
Kovalenko Medal; Jessie Stevenson Vol. 1: 13834
Kovaleskaia Award Vol. 1: 20448
Kozik Award for Environmental Reporting; Robert L. Vol. 1: 15519
KPMG Vol. 1: 11028
KPMG Peat Marwick Award Vol. 1: 21463
Kraft Innovator Award; Jack A. Vol. 1: 10581
Kralik Distinguished Service Award; Gary M. Vol. 1: 5964
Kramer Award of Excellence; William S. Vol. 1: 16704
Kramer - John Preston Personal Service Award; Harold Vol. 1: 3792
Kramer; Murray Vol. 1: 6530
Kramer Scarlet Quill Award; Murray Vol. 1: 6530
Krasner Memorial Award; Jack D. Vol. 1: 3706
Kraus Award; Francis L. (Babe) Vol. 1: 20663
Krebs Memorial Scholarship Vol. 2: 6869
Krebs-Preis; Hans Adolf Vol. 2: 2896
Kreisel Award for Best First Book; Henry Vol. 1: 21987
Kreisher Award; Peter Vol. 1: 19031
Kreisler International Competition Prizes; Fritz Vol. 2: 752
Kretchmer Memorial Award in Nutrition and Development; Norman Vol. 1: 3959
Kreve-Mickevicius premija; Vinco Vol. 2: 4392
Krieg Cortical Kudos Vol. 1: 6727
Kriegel Prize; Dr. Frantisek Vol. 2: 6144
Krieger Award; Richard Vol. 1: 8357
Krieghbaum Under-40 Award Vol. 1: 5345
Kris Prize; Ernst Vol. 1: 4600
Krisciunas premija; Jono Vol. 2: 4393
Krishnan Award for Educational Excellence; Mandayam Chakravarthi Vol. 1: 9926
Krishnan Memorial Lecture; K. S. Vol. 2: 3489
Kriske Memorial Award; George W. Vol. 1: 387
Kristol Lecture on Public Policy; Irving Vol. 1: 2195
Krogh Lecture and Award; August Vol. 2: 1509
Krommert Award Vol. 2: 4928
Krooss Prize Vol. 1: 6710
Krout Memorial; Ohioana Poetry Award, Helen and Laura Vol. 1: 16659
Krout Ohioana Poetry Award; Helen and Laura Vol. 1: 16659
Krueger Paper Money - YN Exhibit Award; Kurt Vol. 1: 3230
Kruszynski Achievement Award; Edward A. Vol. 1: 16426
Krutch Medal; Joseph Wood Vol. 1: 10598
Kruth Award Vol. 2: 6290
Kruyskamp-prijs Vol. 2: 4915
Kryger Prize (DR Radio) Vol. 2: 1452
Krygerprisen Vol. 2: 1452
Kryolon Makeup Design Award Vol. 1: 20647
Kryski Canadian Heritage Award; Antoinette (Nettie) Vol. 1: 22048
Krzyz Narodowego Czynu Zbrojnego Vol. 2: 5324
Krzyz Walecznych Vol. 2: 5321
Krzyz Zaslugi Vol. 2: 5318
Krzyz Zaslugi z Mieczami Vol. 2: 5320
Krzyz Zaslugi za Dzielnosc Vol. 2: 5319
Kshanika Oration Award to a Woman Scientist for Research in the Field of Biomedical Sciences Vol. 2: 3419
KSO Young People's Concerto Competition Award Vol. 1: 19863
Ku Meritorious Award; P. M. Vol. 1: 19348
Kubasik Award; Norman Vol. 1: 985
Kucharski Young Investigator Award for Research in Developmental Psychobiology; David Vol. 1: 11927
Kuchler-Killian Memorial Scholarship Vol. 1: 15039
Kucyna International Composition Prize Vol. 1: 6534
Kuczynski Diploma; G. C. Vol. 2: 5933
Kuder Early Career Scientist/Practitioner Award; Fritz and Linn Vol. 1: 3664
Kuebler Award; John R. Vol. 1: 478
Kuehl Prize for Documentary Editing; Arthur S. Link Prize/Warren F. Vol. 1: 18681
Kuhlmann Award; Frank W. Reinhart and Henry "Butch" Vol. 1: 5978
Kuhmerker Award Vol. 1: 5451
Kuhn Advocate of the Year Award; Dr. L. Michael Vol. 1: 15208
Kuhn-Medaille; Richard- Vol. 2: 2811
Kuhn-Preis; Julius- Vol. 2: 2863
Kuhring Award; Mike Vol. 2: 4799
Kuiper Prize; Gerard P. Vol. 1: 1513
Kukuljevic Charter Vol. 2: 1372
Kukuljeviceva Povelja Vol. 2: 1372
Kulp Memorial Award; Clarence Arthur Vol. 1: 3854
Kulp Wright Award Vol. 1: 3854
Kultainen Fennia-mitali Vol. 2: 1620
Kultureller Ehrenpreis Vol. 2: 3011
Kulturministeriets Bornebogspris Vol. 2: 1483
Kulturpreis der Stadt Villach Vol. 2: 783
Kumar Memorial Award; Prof. L. S. S. Vol. 2: 3490
Kun-Po Soo Award Vol. 1: 3624
Kungliga priset Vol. 2: 6258
Kunitz Poetry Award; Stanley Vol. 1: 8225
Kunst Prize; Jaap Vol. 1: 18672
Kunstpreis der Stadt Darmstadt Vol. 2: 3138
Kunstpreis der Stadt Zurich Vol. 2: 6492
Kunstpreis Oekologie Vol. 2: 2641
Kuntz '07 Award; Frank A. Vol. 1: 7667
Kupfer Award Vol. 1: 5466
Kupferman Award Vol. 1: 6356
Kupferschmid Award; Owen M. Vol. 1: 16983
Kupfmuller-Preis der ITG; Karl- Vol. 2: 2929
Kupfmuller Prize; Karl Vol. 2: 2929
Kurien Award; Dr. Vol. 2: 3442
Kusnetz Award Vol. 1: 2615
Kusworm Award; Sidney G. Vol. 1: 6484
Kutter-Preis; Fritz Vol. 2: 6522
Kuykendall; Rufus C. Vol. 1: 13116
Kwapil Memorial Award; Joseph F. Vol. 1: 19564
Kwazulu Natal Conservationist of the Year Vol. 2: 5796
Kwit Distinguished Service Award; Nathaniel T. Vol. 1: 1850
KWS Great 8 Exhibition Vol. 1: 12500
Kyoto Prizes Vol. 2: 4128
KYU & Dan Grades Award Vol. 2: 6910
L/M Award Vol. 1: 1820
"L. PeRCy" Awards Vol. 1: 12836
La Caze; Fondation L. Vol. 2: 1910
La Croix Award Vol. 1: 14328
La Cumbres Ameteur Outreach Award Vol. 1: 6010
La Fons-Melicocq; Prix de Vol. 2: 1764
La Gorce Medal; John Oliver Vol. 1: 15159
La Grange; Prix de Vol. 2: 1765
La Guardia Award; Fiorello H. Vol. 1: 16200
La Parada Award Vol. 1: 19542
La Pietra Dissertation Travel Fellowship in Transnational History Vol. 1: 16890
La Reine Pittman Memorial Award Vol. 1: 1594
La Salle Collegian Award Vol. 1: 12634
Lab of the Year Award Vol. 1: 18365
Labatt Classic Film Award; John Vol. 1: 20114
Labatt's Award for the Most Popular Film Vol. 1: 20114
Labbe; Fondation du Docteur et de Madame Henri Vol. 2: 1848
Labbe; Fondation Joseph Vol. 2: 1907
Labbe-Vauquelin; Prix Paul Vol. 2: 2198
LABBS Trophy Vol. 1: 10251
Label of the Year Competition Vol. 2: 8036
Labor Affairs Award Vol. 1: 15926
Labor History High School Essay Contest Vol. 1: 21680
Labor-Management Annual Award Vol. 1: 21044
Labor Participation Citation for Services Vol. 1: 3832

Labor Press Journalistic Awards Contest Vol. 1: 11700
Laboratory Analyst Excellence Award Vol. 1: 21493
Laboratory of the Year Vol. 1: 17816
Labotec-Shandon Award for Achievement in the Field of Cytology Vol. 2: 5632
Labrow Grant Vol. 2: 7857
Lackman Jr. Award; William F. Vol. 1: 15384
LaCorbeau Grand Prix Vol. 2: 841
Lacquet; Fund Professor Doctor A. Vol. 2: 975
Lacy Award; Alfred and Norma Vol. 1: 18442
Ladd Award; William E. Vol. 1: 779
Ladies' British Open Amateur Championship Vol. 2: 8038
Lady Canoeist of the Year Vol. 2: 8904
Lady Denman Cup Vol. 2: 8177
Lady Finniston Award Vol. 2: 9227
Lady Illingworth Award Vol. 2: 9119
Lady Members Group Prize Vol. 2: 7678
Lady of the Year Award Vol. 1: 12033
Lady Phillips Scholarship Vol. 2: 4079
Lady Riders Challenge Trophy Vol. 1: 15815
Laerdal Award for Excellence (EMT-Paramedic of the Year Award); Asmund S. Vol. 1: 14215
Laetare Medal Vol. 1: 21089
LaFage Graduate Student Research Award; Jeffery P. Vol. 1: 9282
Lafferty Memorial Trophy; Terry Vol. 1: 7510
Lafitte; Fondation Pierre Vol. 2: 1954
LaGasse Medal; Alfred B. Vol. 1: 4478
LaGrange National Vol. 1: 7817
Lagrange; Prix Charles Vol. 2: 1046
Lahden Kansainvalinen Urkukilpailu Vol. 2: 1652
Lahm Memorial Award for Flight Safety; Brig. Gen. Frank P. Vol. 1: 16830
Lahti International Organ Competition Vol. 2: 1652
Laidler Award Vol. 1: 7840
Laine Memorial Scholarship Program; David Vol. 1: 16427
Laing Prize; Gordon J. Vol. 1: 21006
The Laing Seascape and Landscape Competition Vol. 2: 8248
Lake Placid Education Foundation / NYLA Scholarship Vol. 1: 16237
Lallemand; Fondation Andre Vol. 2: 1794
Lallemand; Fondation Claude Vol. 2: 1826
Lally Distinguished Alumni Merit Award; Jack and Julie Vol. 1: 18216
LAMA Cultural Diversity Grant Vol. 1: 12817
LAMA President's Award Vol. 1: 12818
Lamaze Childbirth Educator Program Scholarship Vol. 1: 12675
Lamb Memorial Trophy; Charles Vol. 1: 15815
Lamb Outstanding Educator Award; Helen Vol. 1: 1296
Lambacher Trophy Vol. 1: 12849
Lambda Literary Awards Vol. 1: 12683
Lambert, Jr. Forest Stewardship Award; John Vol. 1: 13159
Lambert Memorial Award Vol. 2: 3662
Lambert; Prix Charles Vol. 2: 2025
Lamberton Award for Teaching High School Science; Bernice G. Vol. 1: 21437
Lameere; Prix Eugene Vol. 2: 1022
LaMer Award; Victor K. Vol. 1: 1766
Lamme Award; Benjamin Garver Vol. 1: 4024
Lamothe; Prix de Vol. 2: 2405
Lampe-Kunkle Memorial Award Vol. 1: 634
Lampert Memorial Award; Gerald Vol. 1: 12744
Lampert Student Writing Award; Herb Vol. 1: 7382
Lampitt Medal Vol. 2: 9011
Lamplighter of the Year Vol. 1: 14855
Lancaster Award Vol. 1: 1133
Lanchester Prize; Frederick W. Vol. 1: 11076
Land Medal; Edwin H. Vol. 1: 16789
Land of Enchantment Book Awards Vol. 1: 16194
Land O'Lakes, Inc. Vol. 1: 2105
Land O'Lakes/Purina Teaching Award in Dairy Production Vol. 1: 2106
Landa Music Scholarship for Pianists; David Paul Vol. 2: 479
Landberg Award for Excellence in Applied Climatology; Helmut Vol. 1: 1426
Landen ARTBA Annual Highway Safety Award; John C. "Jake" Vol. 1: 3863
Landesgirokasse Stuttgart Award Vol. 2: 3107
Landeskreditbank Baden-Wuerttemberg (L-Bank) Audience Award Vol. 2: 3107
Landeskulturpreis fur Architektur Vol. 2: 801
Landeskulturpreis fur Bildende Kunst Vol. 2: 797
Landeskulturpreis fur Film und Video Vol. 2: 796
Landeskulturpreis fur Literatur Vol. 2: 798
Landeskulturpreis fur Musik Vol. 2: 799
Landeskulturpreis fur Wissenschaft Vol. 2: 800
Landi; Fondazione Valeria Vincenzo Vol. 2: 3823
Landis Award (Most Valuable Player); Kenesaw M. Vol. 1: 6266
Landis Medal; James N. Vol. 1: 4524
The Landmark Award Vol. 1: 4479
Landmarks Vol. 1: 10418
The Landscape Architecture Film Award Vol. 1: 4480
Landscape Architecture Medal of Excellence Vol. 1: 4481
Landscape Awards Vol. 1: 9613
Landscape Design Award Vol. 1: 2531
Landslide Research; Distinguished Leadership for Vol. 1: 11711
Landsteiner Memorial Award; Karl Vol. 1: 1112
Lane Award; Ben B. Vol. 1: 21301
Lane Award; Bishop Loris Vol. 1: 14614
Lane Award; Kenneth S. Vol. 1: 4780
Lane Award; Margaret T. Vol. 1: 12940
Lane Award; Richard Vol. 2: 292
Lane Award; Sister M. Claude Vol. 1: 18957
Lane History Award; Helen H. Vol. 1: 8919
Lane Industrial Award; Frank E. Vol. 1: 2168
Lane Memorial Award; Diane Vol. 1: 13937
Lang Medal Vol. 2: 8828
Lang Prize Paper Award; Warren R.
American Society of Cytopathology Vol. 1: 4396
American Society of Cytopathology Vol 1: 4396
Lang Resident Physician Award; Warren R. Vol. 1: 4396
Lange/CQ Press Award; Marta Vol. 1: 5612
Lange International Award; John D. Vol. 1: 14264
Lange - Paul Taylor Prize; Dorothea Vol. 1: 9045
Langendorff Award; Hans Vol. 1: 17853
Langenhoven Prize; C. J. Vol. 2: 5649
Langer Award; William L. Vol. 1: 10184
Langer Nuclear Codes and Standards Award; Bernard F. Vol. 1: 4525
Langlands Medal; Ian Vol. 2: 407
Langley Award Vol. 2: 6840
Langmuir Award; Gaede- Vol. 1: 6148
Langmuir Award in Chemical Physics; Irving Vol. 1: 1767
Langmuir Prize in Chemical Physics; Irving Vol. 1: 3460
Langmuir Prize in Chemical Physics Langmuir Prize in Chemical Physics Vol. 1: 3461
Language Award (DR Radio and TV) Vol. 2: 1453
Language Proficiency Award Vol. 1: 9978
Lankester Investigatorship; Ray Vol. 2: 8111
Lannan Literary Awards Vol. 1: 12691
Lanxess Inc. Award for High School Chemistry Teachers Vol. 1: 7841
Lapeenranta National Singing Competition Awards Vol. 2: 1654
Lapham Outstanding Service Award; Robert Vol. 1: 9010
Laporte Award for Research in Fluid Dynamics; Otto Vol. 1: 3462
Lappeenrannan Valtakunnalliset Laulukilpailut Vol. 2: 1654
LaQue Memorial Award; Francis L. Vol. 1: 5965
Larragoiti; Premio Vol. 2: 5412
Larragoiti Prize; Antonio Vol. 2: 5412
Larrey; Fondation du Baron Vol. 2: 1847
Larsen-Miller Community Service Award Vol. 1: 13906
Larson Award; Gustus L. Vol. 1: 4526
Laryngological Association Award; American Vol. 1: 2924
Lasas premija; Vlado Vol. 2: 4394
Lascoff Memorial Award; J. Leon Vol. 1: 1833
Laser Institute of America Honored Speaker Award Vol. 1: 12693
Lashley Award; Karl Spencer Vol. 1: 3437
Laskaridios Vol. 2: 3177
Lasker Award; Albert D. Vol. 1: 2418
Lasker Award for Public Service in Behalf of Medical Research; Mary Woodard Vol. 1: 12695
Lasker Award for Special Achievement in Medical Research; Albert Vol. 1: 12696
Lasker Basic Medical Research Award; Albert Vol. 1: 12697
Lasker Civil Liberties Award; Florina Vol. 1: 16217
Lasker Public Service Award; Albert Vol. 1: 12695
Lasky Humanitarian Service Award; Elaine J. Vol. 1: 15643
LASL Educator's Award Vol. 1: 12939
Lasswell Award; Harold D. Vol. 1: 12020
Last Fellowship; Hugh Vol. 2: 7136
LATA Scholarship Award Vol. 1: 5058
Latham Memorial Grants; Barbara Aronofsky Vol. 1: 21353
Latham Sportsman Service Award; Roger M. Vol. 1: 15949
Latin America COPES Training and Education Fellowships (LACTEF) Vol. 2: 6473
Latsis-Preis Vol. 2: 6523
Laubach Literacy of Canada Award Vol. 1: 12717
Lauch Memorial Grant; Robert Vol. 1: 21418
Lauer Safety Award; A. R. Vol. 1: 10582

Laufer PhD Memorial Award for Outstanding Scientific Achievement; Robert S. Vol. 1: 11967
Laufer; Prix Docteur Rene-Joseph Vol. 2: 2034
Laughlin Prize Vol. 2: 8463
Launch of the Year Vol. 2: 7186
Laureat d'Honneur of the International Geographical Union Vol. 1: 11649
Laureate of the Federation Vol. 1: 11610
Laureates Vol. 1: 900
Laureateship of the Australian Society of Archivists Vol. 2: 271
Laurel Award for Screen Vol. 1: 21992
Laurel Crowned Circle Award Vol. 1: 16698
Laurel Leaf Award Vol. 1: 1955
Laurels/Laureates Awards Vol. 1: 6136
Laurendeau Prize in Humanities; Andre Vol. 1: 5541
Laurent; Prix Emile Vol. 2: 1054
Laurent; Prix Marie Vol. 2: 2077
Laurie Prize; James Vol. 1: 4337
Laursen Award; Capt. V. L. Vol. 1: 20943
Laussedat; Fondation Aime Vol. 2: 1783
Lavachery; Prix Henri Vol. 2: 1024
Lavallee; Prix Calixa- Vol. 1: 18606
Laventhol Prize for Deadline News Reporting; Jesse Vol. 1: 17509
Laventhol Prizes for Deadline News Reporting; Jesse Vol. 1: 4580
Laver Award; Keith Vol. 1: 7316
Laveran; Fondation Alphonse Vol. 2: 1790
Law Alumni Association's Distinguished Alumnus Award Vol. 1: 21106
Law Award; Frank G. Vol. 1: 4569
Law Books in Hindu Prize Vol. 2: 3466
Law Day U.S.A. Vol. 1: 2934
Law Day U.S.A. Public Service Awards Vol. 1: 1534
Law Enforcement and Fire Safety Commendation Medal Vol. 1: 15773
Law Enforcement Assistance Explorer Award Vol. 1: 6584
Law Enforcement Award
Association of Former Agents of the U.S. Secret Service Vol. 1: 5689
National Black Police Association Vol 1: 14522
Law Enforcement Commendation Medal Vol. 1: 15774
Law Library Journal Article of the Year Award Vol. 1: 1253
Law Library Publications Award Vol. 1: 1254
Law-Related Education Teacher of the Year Award Vol. 1: 2935
Law-Review Award Vol. 1: 18381
Law Society Prize Vol. 2: 9351
Lawn Tennis Association National Awards Vol. 2: 8043
Lawrence Foundation Award Vol. 1: 17512
Lawrence Medal Vol. 2: 8552
Lawrence Memorial Award Vol. 1: 10616
Lawrence; Prix Alfred-Joseph Vol. 1: 6626
Lawrence Prize; Robert G. Vol. 1: 5286
Lawrie Factor Ltd. Prize; Alex Vol. 2: 7690
Laws of Life Essay Contest - Christian Education Movement/BT Campus World Vol. 1: 12407
Laws of Life Essay Contest - Franklin County, Tennessee Vol. 1: 12408
Laws of Life Essay Contest - Nassau, Bahamas Vol. 1: 12409
Laws of Life Essay Contest - Peale Center for Christian Living Vol. 1: 12410
Lawson Prize; John Vol. 2: 8448
Lawton Distinguished Contribution Award for Applied Gerontology; M. Powell Vol. 1: 3644
The Laxdal Memorial Grade B Female Voice Scholarship Vol. 1: 18297
Laxdal Memorial Vocal Award/The Golan E. Hoole Memorial Shield; The Heather Vol. 1: 2281
Lay Education Project Award Vol. 1: 780
Lay Memorial Award; Herman Vol. 1: 5817
Layman Award; Paul Nash Vol. 1: 20809
Layman of the Year Vol. 1: 13177
Layman Support Award Vol. 1: 15189
Layn Award; Kristine M. Vol. 1: 17557
Lazar Deak Emlekerem Vol. 2: 3290
Lazar Prize; Gheorghe Vol. 2: 5842
Lazarsfeld Award for Evaluation Theory Vol. 1: 2206
Lazarsfeld Award for Research Vol. 1: 2206
Lazarus Commemorative Medal; Diaconus Vol. 2: 3290
Lazarus Memorial Award Vol. 1: 2446
Lazarus Memorial Prize; Henry Vol. 2: 9352
Lazerow Fellowship for Research in Collections and Technical Services in Academic and Research Libraries; Samuel Vol. 1: 5613
LBJ Cup Vol. 1: 5107
LDA Award for Excellence in Library Achievement Vol. 1: 12732
Le Caine Awards; Hugh Vol. 1: 18593
Le Chatelier; Fondation Henry Vol. 2: 1887
Le Goff; Fondation Jean-Marie Vol. 2: 1902
Le Mans 24-hour Grand Prix d'Endurance Vol. 2: 2255
Le Pegase Prize of the Audience Vol. 2: 841
Le Prix D' Excellence Aliant Vol. 1: 6039
Le Prix du Mexique Vol. 2: 2632
Le Sueur Award; Herbert Vol. 2: 8393
Le Sueur Memorial Lecture Vol. 2: 9012
LEA Award Vol. 2: 1602
LEA-palkinto Vol. 2: 1602
Leab and Daniel J. Leab *American Book Prices Current* Exhibition Catalogue Awards; Katharine Kyes Vol. 1: 5614
Leach Award; Victoria Vol. 1: 194
Leach Medal; Digby Vol. 2: 408
Leacock Medal for Humour; Stephen Vol. 1: 19790
Leader of the Year Award Vol. 1: 16699
Leaders Cards Vol. 2: 5298
Leaders Recognition Society Award Vol. 1: 21741
Leadership and Service Awards Vol. 1: 5623
Leadership Award
American Hospital Association Vol. 1: 2547
American Society for Competitiveness Vol 1: 3981
American Society on Aging Vol 1: 4644
Association of Surgical Technologists Vol 1: 5874
Business Committee for the Arts Vol 1: 6704
Camp Fire USA El Dorado Council Vol 1: 6778
Corona Norco United Way Vol 1: 8521
Horace Mann League of the U.S.A. Vol 1: 10537
International Association of Cancer Victors and Friends Vol 1: 11305
Minerals, Metals, and Materials Society Vol 1: 13451
National Apostolate for Inclusion Ministry Vol 1: 13944
National Association for Equal Opportunity in Higher Education Vol 1: 14006
National Trappers Association Vol 1: 15911
Pan American Development Foundation Vol 1: 17055
Society for the Study of Lesbian, Gay and Bisexual Concerns (Division 44) Vol 1: 18912
The Leadership Award Vol. 1: 21109
Leadership Award for Residents Vol. 1: 627
Leadership Awards Vol. 1: 9841
Leadership Citation Vol. 1: 8587
Leadership Development Awards Vol. 1: 12341
Leadership for Learning Award Vol. 1: 1406
Leadership in Human Services Award Vol. 1: 3782
Leadership in Library Acquisitions Award Vol. 1: 5425
Leadership in Oncology Social Work Award Vol. 1: 5803
Leadership in Public Service Award Vol. 1: 15637
Leadership in Sport Award Vol. 1: 19631
Leadership in the Americas Award Vol. 1: 11046
Leading Chapter Award Vol. 1: 15103
Leading Producer Round Table Awards Vol. 1: 14247
League Executive of the Year Awards Vol. 1: 14340
League of Minnesota Poets Award Vol. 1: 15003
League Volunteer Award Vol. 1: 16186
Leahy Award; Emmett Vol. 1: 10851
Leakey Foundation Prize for Multidisciplinary Research on Ape and Human Evolution; L. S. B. Vol. 1: 12756
Lean Award; David Vol. 2: 6906
Lear Award for Achievement in Comedy Playwriting; Norman Vol. 1: 12542
Learning Resources and Library Achievement Awards; EBSCO Community College Vol. 1: 5608
Leary Award; Dick Vol. 1: 10564
Leary Sportsmanship Award; Cissie Vol. 1: 11145
Leaven Award Vol. 1: 865
Leavey Awards for Excellence in Private Enterprise Education Vol. 1: 9765
Lebrun; Fondation Jean Vol. 2: 1036
Leche League International Award of Achievement; La Vol. 1: 12628
Leche League International Award of Appreciation; La Vol. 1: 12629
Leche League International Award of Excellence; La Vol. 1: 12630
Leche League International Award of Recognition; La Vol. 1: 12631
Leche League International Founders' Award; La Vol. 1: 12632
Leclere; Prix Achille Vol. 2: 1700
Leclere; Prix Leon Vol. 2: 1029
Lecturer of Merit Vol. 1: 14683
Lectureship in Developmental and Behavioral Pediatrics Vol. 1: 18663
Lederer Award; Jerome F. Vol. 1: 11972
Lederle Award in Human Nutrition Vol. 1: 4159
Lederman Memorial Lectures; Leah Vol. 2: 8823
Lee Allen Award Vol. 1: 18634

Lee Award; Carlton Vol. 1: 652
Lee Award; Mabel Vol. 1: 880
Lee Award; Walker S. Vol. 1: 6679
Lee Award; Wellington Vol. 1: 17290
Lee B. Lusted Student Prizes Vol. 1: 18796
Lee Consumer Education Award; Stewart M. Vol. 1: 2050
Lee Founders Award Vol. 1: 18925
Lee Grand Prize; Norman H. Vol. 1: 2247
Lee - Homewood Chiropractic Heritage Award Vol. 1: 5505
Lee Integrity Award Vol. 1: 18072
Lee International Award; R.A.G. Vol. 2: 8263
Lee Memorial Award; James W. Vol. 1: 20884
Lee Memorial Trophy; Penny West Vol. 1: 15815
Lee Prize; Jesse Vol. 1: 9913
Lee Scholarship Award; Ed Vol. 1: 20757
Lee Trophy; Mike Vol. 1: 20624
Leeds Award; Morris E. Vol. 1: 10874
Leeds International Pianoforte Competition Vol. 2: 8050
Leet Grants; Dorothy Vol. 2: 6406
Lefcowitz Prize; Rose Vol. 1: 17414
Lefebvre Memorial Award; Jacques Vol. 2: 7490
Lefebvre; Prix de l'adjudant Hubert Vol. 2: 1050
Lefkowitz Award Vol. 1: 16235
Lefort; Prix Jules Vol. 2: 2065
Lefthanders of the Year Awards Vol. 1: 12764
Lefuel; Prix Hector Vol. 2: 1694
Legacy Award Vol. 1: 9903
Legal & General Silver Trowel Award Vol. 2: 6923
Legal Writing Contest Vol. 1: 11333
Legendary Station of the Year Vol. 1: 14115
Legends Award Vol. 1: 6423
Legends of Dance Awards Vol. 1: 21525
Legends of Racing Vol. 1: 1523
Leger Medal; Gabrielle Vol. 1: 10421
Leggatt Memorial Award; Pat Vol. 2: 7218
Legget Award; R.F. Vol. 1: 7127
Legion of Honor Vol. 1: 12366
Legion of Honor Award Vol. 2: 3595
Legion of Merit Vol. 1: 8822
Legion of Valor Bronze Cross for Achievement Vol. 1: 12772
Legion of Valor Silver Cross for Valor Vol. 1: 12773
Legislation Award Vol. 1: 5875
Legislative Excellence Award Vol. 1: 6078
Legislative Service Award Vol. 1: 15596
Legislative Service Award; ACA Vol. 1: 2065
Legislator Award Vol. 1: 10767
Legislator of the Year
  American Association of Oriental Medicine Vol. 1: 1316
  Pennsylvania State Tax Collectors Association Vol 1: 17204
  South Carolina Poultry Federation Vol 1: 19445
  United Hellenic Voters of America Vol 1: 20334
  Vietnam Veterans of America Vol 1: 21362
Legislator of the Year Award
  AeA Vol. 1: 225
  AIA New York State, Inc. Vol 1: 300
  Biotechnology Industry Organization Vol 1: 6397
Lehman Award; Arnold J. Vol. 1: 19339
Lehman Ethics Award; Herbert H. Vol. 1: 12377
Lehman Human Relations Award; Herbert H. Vol. 1: 2886
Lehman Memorial Award; Bill Vol. 1: 13938
Lehmann-Medaille; Lilli- Vol. 2: 748
Lehmann Medal; Inge Vol. 1: 2354
Lehmann; Prix Henri Vol. 2: 1695
Lehmbruck Prize; Wilhelm Vol. 2: 3135
Lehr Ferenc Textilipari Ifjusagi Erem Vol. 2: 3269
Leica Canada Scientific Award Vol. 1: 6929
LEICA Geosystems Award for Best Scientific Paper in Remote Sensing Vol. 1: 5217
Leica Geosystems Internship Vol. 1: 5218
Leica Scientific Award Vol. 1: 6929
Leica Surveying Scholarships Vol. 1: 1999
Leicht-Bowers Bowler of the Year; Barbara Vol. 1: 21774
Leighton Memorial Medal Vol. 2: 514
Leininger Transcultural Nursing Award Vol. 1: 20150
Leipholz Medal Vol. 1: 7417
Leipoldt Memorial Medal; Louis Vol. 2: 5714
Leiter Clagett Trophy; U.S. Junior Women's Sailing Championship - Nancy Vol. 1: 20771
Leiter Lectureship; Joseph Vol. 1: 13259
Leitman Memorial Award; Samuel Vol. 1: 4856
Lejins Research Award; Peter P. Vol. 1: 2027
Leland Award for International Health Service; Mickey Vol. 1: 10047
Leland Award; Waldo Gifford Vol. 1: 18958
Leland Memorial Prize; Waldo Gifford Vol. 1: 18958
Leland Prize; Waldo G. Vol. 1: 2478
Lemaire; Prix Charles Vol. 2: 1047
Lemaitre; Prix Troyon et Edouard Vol. 2: 1696
LeMay Bomber Aircrew Award; General Curtis E. Vol. 1: 345
LeMay Morale, Welfare, and Recreation Award; Gen. Curtis E. Vol. 1: 16831
Lemay-Ohio Award Vol. 1: 5107
LeMay Strategic Aircrew Award; General Curtis E. Vol. 1: 345
Lembright Award; Katharine A. Vol. 1: 2413
Lemburg Award for Distinguished Service; Wayne A. Vol. 1: 3030
Lemelson-MIT Lifetime Achievement Award; $100,000 Vol. 1: 12776
Lemelson-MIT Prize; $500,000 Vol. 1: 12777
Lemelson-MIT Student Prize; $30,000 Vol. 1: 12775
Lemen Award; J. Winton Vol. 1: 15537
Lemenon; Fondation Odette Vol. 2: 1943
Lemieux Award; Fabian Vol. 1: 16743
Lemieux Award for Organic Chemistry; R. U. Vol. 1: 7842
Lemieux Prize; Jacqueline Vol. 1: 6801
Lemkin Medal Vol. 2: 9127
Lemmon Prize Vol. 2: 35
Lemonon; Prix Ernest Vol. 2: 2042
Lemos; Premio Aboim Sande Vol. 2: 5413
Lemos Prize; Aboim Sande
  Lisbon Academy of Sciences Vol. 2: 5413
  Portuguese Academy of History Vol 2: 5486
Lenaerts Prize; R. Vol. 2: 1081
Lendholt-Denkmunze; Eugen- Vol. 2: 2651
Lenehan Log Cabin Photography Competition Vol. 1: 12908
Lenghi e Flaviano Magrassi; Fondazione Guido Vol. 2: 3821
Lenington All-American Award Vol. 1: 2448
LeNoire Award; Rosetta Vol. 1: 162
Lentz International Peace Research Award Vol. 1: 12779
Leo Award
  Independent Curators International Vol. 1: 10718
  National Eye Research Foundation Vol 1: 14957
Leo Award for Technical Innovation Vol. 1: 10206
Leon-Houry; Fondation Marie Vol. 2: 1929
Leon; Premio Nicolas Vol. 2: 4542
Leonard Award; Donald S. Vol. 1: 13345
Leonard Award; Richard M. Vol. 1: 18464
Leonard Medal Vol. 2: 8118
Leonard W. Green Prize Vol. 2: 7648
Leonardo Award for Excellence Vol. 1: 11957
Leonardo da Vinci Award Vol. 1: 12252
Leonardslee Bowl Vol. 2: 8553
Leonor Magro de Radio; Premio Municipal Maria Vol. 2: 5434
Leopold-Hidy Prize Vol. 1: 4067
Leopold Memorial Award; Aldo Vol. 1: 21630
Leopold Prize; Richard W. Vol. 1: 16891
Leopold-von-Buch-Plakette Vol. 2: 2835
Leopoldina Prize for Junior Scientists Vol. 2: 2705
LEOS Distinguished Service Award Vol. 1: 10659
LEOS Engineering Achievement Award Vol. 1: 10660
LEOS William Streifer Award Vol. 1: 10661
LePrince Medal; Joseph Augustin Vol. 1: 4631
Lequeux; Prix Andre
  Academie des Sciences Morales et Politiques Vol. 2: 2016
  Institut de France Vol 2: 2428
Leriche Prize; Rene Vol. 2: 6464
Lerner-Gray Fund for Marine Research Award Vol. 1: 3156
Lerner Memorial Medal; Victor Vol. 1: 6557
Lerner-Scott Dissertation Prize Vol. 1: 16892
Lerner Student Scholarship; Irwin S. Vol. 1: 15722
Leroy-Beaulieu; Prix Paul Vol. 2: 2080
Leroy Fellowship; A. M. Vol. 2: 3903
Leroy J. Ellis Humane Educator of the Year Vol. 1: 17194
Leroy Prize; Andre Vol. 2: 2494
Les Ecrans De L'Aventure Vol. 2: 2416
Lesbian Book Award; Gay/ Vol. 1: 3003
Lesbian Caucus Prize Vol. 1: 15968
Lesinsky Award; Adam P. Vol. 1: 14596
Leskinen Memorial Award; Lauri W. Vol. 1: 12584
Leslie Kirkley Award for Service to the Ageing (Hai-London) Vol. 2: 1126
Lesmuller-Medaille Vol. 2: 2684
Lessing Medal Vol. 2: 8124
Lester Award; Elmer Vol. 1: 9504
Lester Honor Lecture Vol. 1: 4147
Letelier - Moffitt Memorial Human Rights Awards Vol. 1: 10830
Letourneau Award Vol. 1: 1879
Letourneau Student Research Paper of the Year Award; Marriott Corporation Health Care Services Charles U. Vol. 1: 688
Letras de Oro Literary Prizes Vol. 1: 21059

Award Index

Letter from the CCA/ACC President Vol. 1: 7017
Letter of Citizenship of the City of Salzburg Vol. 2: 773
Letter of Commendation
Commemorative Air Force Vol. 1: 8278
National Soccer Coaches Association of America Vol 1: 15710
Letter of Commendation (Non-CAF Member) Vol. 1: 8279
Letter of Distinction Vol. 1: 3162
Letter of Recognition
Australian Library and Information Association Vol. 2: 228
Inter-American Safety Council Vol 1: 11120
Letterstedtska Forfattarpriset Vol. 2: 6213
Letterstedtska Medaljen I guld Vol. 2: 6214
Letterstedtska Priset for Oversattningar Vol. 2: 6215
Leukemia Society of America Journalism Awards Vol. 1: 12791
Leuver Exhibit Award; Robert J. Vol. 1: 3233
Level 3 BTEC Certificate in Expedition Management Vol. 2: 8926
Level 3 BTEC Certificate in Tropical Habitat Conservation Vol. 2: 8927
Leven Prize for Poetry; Grace Vol. 2: 354
Levenson Prizes in Chinese Studies; Joseph Vol. 1: 5277
Leveque; Prix Charles Vol. 2: 2026
Leverett Graduate Student Merit Award for Outstanding Achievement in Dental Public Health Vol. 1: 1392
Leverett, Jr. Environmental Science Award; Sidney D. Vol. 1: 235
Leverhulme Lecture Vol. 2: 9013
Leverhulme Medal Vol. 2: 8700
Leverhulme Memorial Lecture Vol. 2: 8054
Leverhulme Tercentenary Medal Vol. 2: 8055
Levin Prize; Harry Vol. 1: 1952
Levine; ASCP Outstanding Research Award Honoring Philip Vol. 1: 3969
LeVine Award; IFA Bonny Vol. 1: 11639
Levine Award; P.P. Vol. 1: 1087
Levine Memorial Award for Excellence in Public Service; Charles E. Vol. 1: 4184
Levine Young Clinical Investigator Award; Samuel A. Vol. 1: 2414
Levins Festspillfond; Robert Vol. 2: 5122
Levinson Award; Harry and Miriam Vol. 1: 3752
Levinson Prize Vol. 1: 17420
Levinson Prize; Samuel Eleazar and Rose Tartakow Vol. 1: 18874
Levinstein Memorial Lecture; Ivan Vol. 2: 9014
Levis Prize for Poetry; Larry Vol. 1: 17513
Levorsen Memorial Award; A. I. Vol. 1: 1341
Levstik Prize; Fran Vol. 2: 5980
Levy Citizen's Award; Commodore Uriah P. Vol. 1: 12387
Levy Memorial Prize; Leonard Vol. 2: 7046
Levy Prize for a Young Photographer; Gerard Vol. 2: 3750
Lewin Award; Elizabeth Vol. 1: 14649
Lewin Memorial Prize; The Lord Vol. 2: 8212
Lewis Award; Arthur O. Vol. 1: 18935
Lewis Award for Contributions in Chemical Engineering Education; Warren K. Vol. 1: 2782
Lewis Award; H.D. Vol. 1: 19426
Lewis Award; Henry Vol. 1: 16186
Lewis Award; John F. Vol. 1: 3438
Lewis Award; Ralph Vol. 2: 9180
Lewis Book Award; Gordon K. Vol. 1: 7595
Lewis Hine Awards Vol. 1: 14652
Lewis Medal; Bernard Vol. 1: 8265
Lewis Memorial Award; Richard B. Vol. 1: 5358
Lewis Memorial Executive of the Year Award Vol. 1: 17568
Lewis Memorial Lifetime Achievement Award Vol. 1: 17568
Lewkowitsch Memorial Lecture; Julius Vol. 2: 9015
Lexis Nexis Call for Papers Awards Program; AALL Vol. 1: 1244
LGFF Scholarship Award Vol. 1: 12933
Liaison with Industry Committee Novel Disease Model Award Vol. 1: 3519
Liang Memorial Award; Ta Vol. 1: 5219
LIANZA Young People's Non-fiction Award Vol. 2: 5003
Liard; Prix Louis Vol. 2: 2071
Liberty Award Vol. 1: 10372
Liberty Awards Vol. 2: 8059
Liberty Bell Award Vol. 1: 10716
Liberty Legacy Foundation Award Vol. 1: 16893
Liberty Live Wire Grant Vol. 1: 21718
Liberty Medal Vol. 1: 15775
Liberty St. Video Award Vol. 1: 4969
Librarian Award; Distinguished Education and Behavioral Sciences Vol. 1: 5605
Librarian of the Year Vol. 1: 10680
Librarian of the Year Award; Canadian Hospital Vol. 1: 7139
Libraries Prize Vol. 2: 3855
Library Achievement Awards; EBSCO Community College Learning Resources and Vol. 1: 5608
Library Association Book of the Year for Children Award; Canadian Vol. 1: 7254
Library Buildings Award Program Vol. 1: 12819
Library Contest Awards Vol. 2: 3856
Library Hi Tech Award; LITA/ Vol. 1: 12828
Library Leadership Award Vol. 1: 5059
Library Manager of the Year Vol. 2: 229
Library Public Relations Council Award Vol. 1: 12836
Library Research and Development Grants Vol. 1: 6940
Library Research Grants Vol. 1: 10007
Library Service Awards Vol. 1: 16181
Library Technician of the Year Vol. 2: 230
Licentiateship of the City and Guilds of London Institute Vol. 2: 7308
Licette Scholarship; Miriam Vol. 2: 8152
Lichfield Prize Vol. 2: 8063
Lichten Award; Robert L. Vol. 1: 2436
Lichtenfelt Award; Richard Vol. 1: 14130
Lichtenstein Medal; Alfred F. Vol. 1: 8137
Lieber Awards Competition; Eleanor Vol. 1: 17471
Lieber Awards for Young Singers; Eleanor Vol. 1: 17471
Lieber; Prix Francis Vol. 2: 6373
Lieber Purchase Award; Judith Vol. 1: 18980
Lieberman Student Poetry Award; Elias Vol. 1: 17433
Liebig-Denkmunze Vol. 2: 2812
Liebmann Book Award; Fred L. Vol. 1: 16266
Liechtenstein Preis zur Forderung Junger Lyriker Vol. 2: 4382
Liederkranz Scholarship Awards Competitions Vol. 1: 12839
Liegeois; Fondation Camille Vol. 2: 1040
Lienhard Award; Gustav O. Vol. 1: 13857
Lieutenant-Governor's Medal Vol. 1: 10422
Lieutenant-Governor's Medal for Historical Writing Vol. 1: 6634
Lieven Gevaert Medal Vol. 1: 18718
Life Achievement Award
The Christophers Vol. 1: 7971
Republic of Croatia Ministry of Science, Education and Sports Vol 2: 1389
Screen Actors Guild Vol 1: 18376
Zagreb World Festival of Animated Films Vol 2: 1392
Life and Freedom Award Vol. 1: 12890
Life and Work of a Scientist Prize Vol. 2: 1268
Life Fellowship Vol. 2: 7591
Life Member
Canadian Actors' Equity Association Vol. 1: 6857
National Association of Metal Finishers Vol 1: 14307
Life Membership
Australian Secondary Principals Association Vol. 2: 257
Genealogical Association of Nova Scotia Vol 1: 9909
Historical Radio Society of Australia Vol 2: 356
Insolvency Practitioners Association of Australia Vol 2: 360
Monaghan Photographic Society Vol 2: 3672
Society of Exploration Geo-physicists Vol 1: 19124
Tasmanian Canine Association Vol 2: 623
Life Membership Award
American Association of Petroleum Geologists Vol. 1: 1342
American Road and Transportation Builders Association Vol 1: 3864
Canadian Association of Career Educators and Employers Vol 1: 6898
National Intramural-Recreational Sports Association Vol 1: 15290
Life Scientist Award; ASCB/Promega Early Career Vol. 1: 3941
Life-Time Membership Award Vol. 1: 8624
Lifesaving and Meritorious Action Awards of the National Court of Honor Vol. 1: 6585
Lifesaving or Merit Award Vol. 1: 14232
Lifetime Achievement
Adult Video Association Vol. 1: 200
Bay Improvement Group Vol 1: 6281
Canadian Railroad Historical Association Vol 1: 7369
Home Builders Association of Western Massachusetts Vol 1: 10520
Lifetime Achievement Award
ACSM Health Promotion Vol. 1: 149
Alliance for Children and Television Vol 1: 455
American Academy of Ophthalmology Vol 1: 710
American Association of Colleges for Teacher Education Vol 1: 1150
American Association of Zoo Keepers Vol 1: 1489
American Chesterton Society Vol 1: 1799
American Numismatic Association Vol 1: 3234
American-Slovenian Polka Foundation Vol 1: 3900

American Society for Bioethics and Humanities Vol 1: 3926
American Spinal Injury Association Vol 1: 4669
AMIT USA Vol 1: 4938
Asian American Journalists Association Vol 1: 5166
Association of Medical Illustrators Vol 1: 5757
Aviation Week & Space Technology Vol 1: 6137
Before Columbus Foundation Vol 1: 6302
The Blues Foundation Vol 1: 6478
Canadian Film Centre Vol 1: 7096
Council of Fashion Designers of America Vol 1: 8576
Directors Guild of America Vol 1: 8944
Georgia Writers Association and Young Georgia Writers Vol 1: 9972
Glass Art Society Vol 1: 10033
IES, Institute for the International Education of Students Vol 1: 10666
Institution of Occupational Safety and Health Vol 2: 7875
International Association of Diecutting and Diemaking Vol 1: 11336
International Institute of Space Law Vol 2: 2487
International Society for Traumatic Stress Studies Vol 1: 11968
International Ticketing Association Vol 1: 12085
Journalism Education Association Vol 1: 12448
Lupus Foundation of America, Arizona Area Coordinator Vol 1: 12983
Medical Dental Hospital Business Associates Vol 1: 13244
National Association of Black Journalists Vol 1: 14101
National Association of Dramatic and Speech Arts Vol 1: 14201
National Association of Television Program Executives Vol 1: 14413
National Telecommunications Cooperative Association Vol 1: 15862
National Wildlife Rehabilitators Association Vol 1: 15954
New York Society of Architects Vol 1: 16267
Newspaper Association of America Vol 1: 16328
Newspaper Association of America Vol 1: 16332
North American Snowsports Journalists Association Vol 1: 16464
Podiatry Management Vol 1: 17412
Royal Television Society Vol 2: 8851
Royal Television Society Vol 2: 8857
Songtalk Vol 1: 19404
South Carolina Poultry Federation Vol 1: 19446
Washington International Trade Association Vol 1: 21450
Lifetime Achievement Award (Author) Vol. 1: 6990
Lifetime Achievement Award in News Direction Vol. 1: 8945
Lifetime Achievement Award in Paper Doll Art Vol. 1: 16905
Lifetime Achievement Award in Sports Direction Vol. 1: 8946
Lifetime Achievement Awards
Columbus Blues Alliance Vol. 1: 8260
Guild Hall Vol 1: 10196
Lifetime Achievement in Contemporary Sculpture Vol. 1: 11894
Lifetime Achievement in the Pharmaceutical Practice Award Vol. 2: 4828
Lifetime Achievement in the Pharmaceutical Science Award Vol. 2: 4828
Lifetime Golfer Vol. 2: 709
Lifetime Membership Award Vol. 1: 13619
Lifetime Mentor Award Vol. 1: 1050
Lifetime of Service to Aviculture Award Vol. 1: 12135
Lifetime Sales Achievement Award Vol. 1: 19636
Light Metals Award Vol. 1: 13452
Light Metals Distinguished Service Award Vol. 1: 13453
Light Metals Division *JOM* Best Paper Award Vol. 1: 13454
Light Metals Technology Award Vol. 1: 13455
Lighten Your Life Award Vol. 1: 15004
Lilienfeld Student Prize Paper; Abraham Vol. 1: 18670
Lilienthal Medal Vol. 2: 6340
Liljencrantz Award; Eric Vol. 1: 236
Lille Sport Film Festival Vol. 2: 2263
Lillegren Award; Austin T. Vol. 1: 16428
Lillehammer Award Vol. 2: 847
Lillian MacKeller Distinguished Service Award Vol. 1: 20395
Lillian S. 3Fisher Prize in Environmental Law and Public Policy Vol. 1: 20983
Lillie Award; Ralph D. Vol. 1: 10446
Lillie Memorial Award; Howard Vol. 1: 1688
Lilly and Company Research Award; Eli Vol. 1: 4136
Lilly Award in Biological Chemistry; Eli Vol. 1: 1768
Lilly/EASD Research Fellowship in Diabetes and Metabolism; Eli Vol. 2: 2738
Lilly Poetry Fellowship; Ruth Vol. 1: 17421
Lilly Poetry Prize; Ruth Vol. 1: 17422
Lilly Products Resident Research Award; APA/ Vol. 1: 3625
Lilly Psychiatric Research Fellowship; APA/ Vol. 1: 3626
Lilly Traveling Fellowship; Eli Vol. 2: 8464
Lima Award for Excellence in Disaster Psychiatry; Bruno Vol. 1: 3627
Limited Distance Program Vol. 1: 2180
Limmer Award for Best Restored Steam Engine; John F. Vol. 1: 15880
Lin Award; T. Y. Vol. 1: 4338
Lincoln Arc Welding Design and Engineering Awards Program; James F. Vol. 1: 12851
Lincoln Award; Abraham Vol. 1: 2594
Lincoln Financial Group Awards of Excellence Vol. 1: 15104
Lincoln Financial Group Lincoln Douglas Debates Vol. 1: 15107
Lincoln Foodservice Grant for Innovations in School Foodservice Vol. 1: 18346
Lincoln Gold Medal Award; James F. Vol. 1: 4887
Lincoln the Lawyer Award Vol. 1: 64
Lind Award; Erv Vol. 1: 587
Lind Award; Wilbur H. Vol. 1: 6680
Linda D. Barber Award Vol. 1: 4079
Linda Joy Most Promising New Director Award Vol. 1: 6033
Lindapter Award Vol. 2: 7773
Lindau Award; Alfred E. Vol. 1: 1969
Lindberg Award; Robert A. Vol. 1: 1602
Lindbergh Diploma; Charles Vol. 2: 6341
Lindbergh Grants Vol. 1: 7808
Lindbomska Beloningen Vol. 2: 6216
Linde Memorial Award; W. J. van der Vol. 2: 5595
Lindeman Award; R. Vol. 1: 4490
Linderman Award Vol. 1: 17652
Lindgren Award; Waldemar S. Vol. 1: 19107
Lindgren Translation Prize; FIT Astrid Vol. 1: 11608
Lindquist Award; E. F. Vol. 1: 2162
Lindsay Award; Hilarie Vol. 2: 592
Lindsay Award; R. Bruce Vol. 1: 141
Lindsey Award for Distinguished Research in Teacher Education; Margaret B. Vol. 1: 1151
Lindzey Dissertation Award; Gardner Vol. 1: 3686
Linear Algebra Prize Vol. 1: 18736
Lines Award in Astronomy; Richard D. Vol. 1: 11182
Lingeman Award; Marie Hippenstell Vol. 1: 18500
Link Award Vol. 1: 7485
Link Award; Fred M. Vol. 1: 17839
Link Foundation Energy Fellowship Program Vol. 1: 12870
Link House Thematic Trophy Vol. 2: 8263
Link Prize/Warren F. Kuehl Prize for Documentary Editing; Arthur S. Vol. 1: 18681
Linn Chapter Scholarship Vol. 1: 1270
Linnard Prize; American Bureau of Shipping - Captain Joseph H. Vol. 1: 19212
Linnean Medal Vol. 2: 8072
Linnemedaljen for botanik Vol. 2: 6192
Linnepriset Vol. 2: 6193
Linnert Honorary Award; Fritz Vol. 2: 2825
Linsley Award; Betty M. Vol. 1: 5512
Linville's R. H. Wright Award in Olfactory Research; Frank Allison Vol. 1: 18527
Lion Trophy Vol. 1: 8866
Lions Club International Clinical Research Program in Diabetic Eye Disease Vol. 1: 2139
Lions SightFirst Diabetic Retinopathy Research Program Vol. 1: 2139
Lipizer Prize; International Violin Competition Rodolfo Vol. 2: 3893
Lipmann Lectureship; Fritz Vol. 1: 3921
Lippert Memorial Award; George R. Vol. 1: 18407
Lipphard Award for Distinguished Service to Religious Journalism; William B. Vol. 1: 5240
Lippincott Award; Ellis R. Vol. 1: 16790
Lippincott Award; Joseph W. Vol. 1: 2982
Lippman Jr. USA Swimming Combined Team Traveling Trophy; William A. Vol. 1: 21195
Liquid Tide Trans-Am Tour Vol. 1: 19721
Liscombe Trophy; Carl Vol. 1: 2518
Liskin Foundation Award; Joyce and Elliot Vol. 1: 15698
Lissitzky Career Award Vol. 2: 1486
Lissner Award; H. R. Vol. 1: 4527
List Purchase Award; Vera Vol. 1: 18980
Lister Memorial Lecture Vol. 2: 9016
Lister Memorial Medal Vol. 2: 8488
Liston Award; Emil S. Vol. 1: 14289
Liszt - Piano Competition Vol. 2: 3285
Liszt Medal Vol. 1: 3007
Liszt Society Prize Vol. 2: 8077
LITA Award for Achievement in Library and Information Technology Vol. 1: 12823

LITA/Christian Larew Memorial Scholarship in Library and Information Technology Vol. 1: 12825
LITA/Endeavor Student Writing Award Vol. 1: 12826
LITA/GEAC Scholarship in Library and Information Technology Vol. 1: 12827
LITA/Library Hi Tech Award Vol. 1: 12828
LITA-LSSI Minority Scholarship in Library and Information Technology Vol. 1: 12829
LITA/OCLC Minority Scholarship in Library and Information Technology Vol. 1: 12830
Litchfield Award; Jessie Vol. 2: 299
Litehiser Memorial Award; Robert R. Vol. 1: 5966
Literacy Leadership Awards Vol. 1: 17674
Literarischer Marz Vol. 2: 3139
Literary Award
  Association of Medical Illustrators Vol. 1: 5758
  Canadian Paper Money Society Vol 1: 7321
  Dedicated Wooden Money Collectors Vol 1: 8790
Literary Award; American Needlepoint Guild Vol. 1: 3190
Literary Award; Louis C. Fink Vol. 1: 14416
Literary Awards
  Boston Book Review Vol. 1: 6521
  Friends of American Writers Vol 1: 9784
  Germans From Russia Heritage Society Vol 1: 9982
  PEN Center U.S.A. Vol 1: 17152
Literary Awards Program Vol. 1: 8059
Literary Competition Vol. 2: 324
Literary Honorarium Award Vol. 1: 16054
Literary Magazines; Program to Recognize Excellence in Student Vol. 1: 14837
Literary Prize-Concurso Literario Cidade de Moura Vol. 2: 5451
Literary Prize for Translation Vol. 2: 5650
Literary Prize of PLA Vol. 2: 5353
Literary Prize-Premio Antonio Feliciano de Castilho Vol. 2: 5452
Literary Prize-Premio Literario Maria Amalia Vaz de Carvalho Vol. 2: 5453
Literary Prize-Premio Literario Paulo Cid Vol. 2: 5454
Literary Prizes for Fiction, Poetry, Essays, and Theatre-Premios Eca de Queiroz Vol. 2: 5455
Literary Writers Competition Vol. 1: 9467
Literature and Art Awards Vol. 2: 6602
Literature and Video Awards Vol. 1: 14277
Literature Association Article Award; Children's Vol. 1: 7908
Literature Award Vol. 1: 19092
Literature Award; Eugene M. Emme Astronautical Vol. 1: 1501
Literature Awards; Museum of Haiku Vol. 1: 10223
Literature; Neustadt International Prize for Vol. 1: 21934
Literature of the Year Awards Vol. 1: 14277
Literature Paper Prize Vol. 1: 18542
Literature pveis der Stadt Dortmund - Nelly-Sachs-Preis Vol. 2: 3068
Literaturpreis der Bayerische Akademie der Schonen Kunste Vol. 2: 2660
Literaturpreis der ETG Vol. 2: 2735
Literaturpreis der Konrad-Adenauer-Stiftung Vol. 2: 3008
Literaturpreis der Landeshauptstadt Stuttgart Vol. 2: 3102
Literavision Preis Vol. 2: 3012
Lithuanian Catholic Women Vol. 1: 12876
Lithuanian Woman Award; Outstanding Vol. 1: 12876
Litman Memorial Youth Exhibit Award; Charles "Cheech" Vol. 1: 3235
Litt Medal; Mary S. Vol. 1: 4857
Little Award; Bud and Mary Vol. 1: 20810
Little Award for Chemical Engineering Innovation; Arthur Dehon Vol. 1: 2783
Little Brown Jug Vol. 1: 20878
Little General Vol. 1: 5111
Little Theatre of Alexandria National One-Act Playwriting Competition Vol. 1: 12888
Littlewood Memorial Lecture; William
  American Institute of Aeronautics and Astronautics Vol. 1: 2685
  Society of Automotive Engineers Vol 1: 19050
Liversidge Lectureship Vol. 2: 540
Livesay Poetry Prize; Dorothy Vol. 1: 21521
Livi Outstanding Aviation Maintenance Technology Instructor; Ivan D. Vol. 1: 6134
Living Hall of Fame Vol. 1: 20625
Living Legends Award Vol. 1: 15927
Livingood Lectureship; Clarence S. Vol. 1: 639
Livingston and Doughty Trophy Vol. 2: 7612
Livingston Award for Poetry; Myra Cohn Vol. 1: 7913
Livingston Awards for Young Journalists Vol. 1: 21061
Livingstone Centenary Medal; David Vol. 1: 2331
Livingstone Medal Vol. 2: 8682
Llangollen International Musical Eisteddfod Vol. 2: 8081
Llewellyn Award; Allan Vol. 2: 324
Lloyd Conservation Award; Stanley Vol. 1: 9481
Lloyd Prize; David D. Vol. 1: 10266
Llywelyn-Williams; Gwobr Goffa Alun Vol. 2: 6764
Llywelyn-Williams Memorial Award; Alun Vol. 2: 6764
LNBA Lifetime Achievement Award Vol. 1: 6355
Lo Medal; K.Y. Vol. 1: 9273
Lobato Prize; Monteiro Vol. 2: 1155
Local Association Public Relations Contest Vol. 1: 1586
Local Association Publications Contest Vol. 1: 1586
Local Association Service Award Vol. 1: 1587
Local Chapeter of the Year Vol. 1: 821
Local Chapter Community Project Award Vol. 1: 14436
Local Chapter Excellence Award Vol. 1: 14437
Local Chapter President Award Vol. 1: 14438
Local Committee Appreciation Vol. 1: 3236
Local Community College Award Vol. 1: 20222
Local Council Community Service Award Vol. 1: 11866
Local Ecumenical Award for Christian Unity and Mission Vol. 1: 10671
Local Government Engineering Medal Vol. 2: 409
Local History Award Vol. 1: 9327
Local Horticulture Award Vol. 1: 2532
Local Impact Award Vol. 1: 15256
Local News Writing Awards Vol. 1: 10815
Local Society Awards Vol. 1: 21302
Local, State Branch, and Regional Award Vol. 1: 2072
Locarno International Film Festival Vol. 2: 6482
Locher Memorial Award; John Vol. 1: 5554
Lock Award; Ottis Vol. 1: 9082
Lockette Humanitarian Award; Rutherford B. Vol. 1: 12067
Lockhart Prize; George Vol. 2: 7690
Lockheed Award for Ocean Science and Engineering Vol. 1: 13111
Lockheed/Martin Ocean Engineering Award Vol. 1: 13111
Lockwood Award; Admiral Vol. 1: 20930
Locus Awards Vol. 1: 12902
Locy Award; Francis E. Vol. 1: 20931
Loder Cup Vol. 2: 8554
Loder Rhododendron Cup Vol. 2: 8555
Lodge Award for Medical Engineering; J. A. Vol. 2: 7815
Lodge Premium; Oliver Vol. 2: 7808
Loeb Awards; Gerald Vol. 1: 20990
Loeb Fellowship Vol. 1: 10281
Loebner Prize Turing Test Award Vol. 1: 6773
Loew Jr. Crystal Vision Award; Arthur Vol. 1: 5684
Lof-Duffie Award for the Best Paper Vol. 2: 2988
Loft Creative Nonfiction Award Vol. 1: 12904
Loft-McKinght Award Vol. 1: 12906
Loft Mentor Series Award Vol. 1: 12905
Log of Mystic Seaport Prize Article Contest Vol. 1: 13734
Logistics Executive Management Award; AFMC Vol. 1: 330
Logistics Lessons Learned Award Vol. 1: 374
Lohse Information Technology Medal; Edward Vol. 1: 3184
Loiseau; Prix Yvan Vol. 2: 2222
Lojek Award; Jerzy Vol. 1: 12458
Lokaljournalistenpreis des Konrad-Adenauer-Stiftung Vol. 2: 3009
Lomb Medal; Adolph Vol. 1: 16791
Lombardi Trophy; Vince Vol. 1: 15088
Lomond Poets Award; Ben Vol. 1: 15005
Lomonosov Gold Medal Vol. 2: 5902
Loncin Research Prize; Marcel Vol. 1: 10943
London Award Vol. 1: 12107
London Club Award Vol. 1: 12910
London International Piano Competition Vol. 2: 8083
London International String Quartet Competition Vol. 2: 8095
London Memorial Award; Fritz Vol. 1: 9042
Londres; Prix Albert Vol. 2: 2235
Loney Trophy; Don Vol. 1: 7221
Long and Jacques Thibaud International Competition; Marguerite Vol. 2: 2526
Long Employment Award; Wilburn H. Vol. 1: 6457
Long et Jacques Thibaud; Concours International Marguerite Vol. 2: 2526
Long-Form Award Vol. 1: 18444
Long Memorial Award; Amelia Reynolds
  National Federation of State Poetry Societies Vol. 1: 14989
  National Federation of State Poetry Societies Vol 1: 15006
Long Poem Prize
  Malahat Review Vol. 1: 13043

Malahat Review Vol 1: 13044
Long Service Award Vol. 2: 3707
Long Service Awards Vol. 2: 8181
Long Service Decoration Vol. 2: 9338
Long Service Medal Vol. 2: 8556
Longacre Award; Raymond F. Vol. 1: 237
Longevity Award Vol. 1: 2313
Longevity Awards Vol. 1: 19581
Longfellow Award Vol. 1: 1980
Longfellow Award; Richard C. Vol. 1: 1980
Longford Award; Raymond Vol. 2: 178
Longstaff Medal Vol. 2: 8761
Longtime Meritorious Service Vol. 1: 13479
Lonsdale Cup Vol. 2: 5028
Lopes do Rego; Premio Abilio Vol. 2: 5409
Lopes Hang Gliding Medal; Pepe Vol. 2: 6342
Lopes of Ameida Prize; Julia Vol. 2: 1156
Lopez Community Service Award in New York; Diego Vol. 1: 10592
Lopin Nash Award; Ruth Vol. 1: 16812
Lora Romero First Book Publication Prize Vol. 1: 4710
Loraine Award for Nature Conservation Vol. 2: 9091
Lord Prize; Walter Frewen Vol. 2: 8502
Lorentz Medal Vol. 2: 4892
Lorentzen Medal; Gustav Vol. 2: 2484
Lorenz Memorial Medal; Frederick A. Vol. 1: 19783
Lorenz Research Award; Walter Vol. 1: 1912
Lorimer Memorial Award; Sir Robert Vol. 2: 8583
Lortel Award; Lucille Vol. 1: 12919
Lortie; Prix Leon- Vol. 1: 18609
Los Angeles Area Emmy Awards Vol. 1: 13862
Los Angeles Times Book Prizes Vol. 1: 12931
Losana Gold Medal; Luigi Vol. 2: 3996
Loschimidt Prize; Josef Vol. 2: 8762
Losey Atmospheric Science Award; AIAA Vol. 1: 2657
Losey Award; Robert M. Vol. 1: 2657
Lotus Decoration Vol. 2: 3382
Lotz Commemorative Medal; John Vol. 2: 3292
Lotz Janos Emlekerem Vol. 2: 3292
Lou Gordon Humanitarian Award Vol. 1: 13593
Lougheed Memorial Award; Robert Vol. 1: 14886
Louie Awards Vol. 1: 10174
Louis/Emily F. Bourne Student Poetry Award; Louise Vol. 1: 17433
Louisiana Literary Award Vol. 1: 12941
Louisiana State Poetry Society Award Vol. 1: 15007
Louisville Award for Innovation in Financial Management Vol. 1: 10110
Louisville Grawemeyer Award in Religion Vol. 1: 21046
Louisville Slugger Vol. 1: 14659
Lounsbery Award; Richard Vol. 1: 13835
Lounsbery; Prix Richard Vol. 2: 2006
Loup de Bronze Vol. 2: 6576
Louw Gold Medal; J.H. Vol. 2: 5680
Love Creek Mini Festival Vol. 1: 12962
Love Creek Short Play Festival Vol. 1: 12963
Love Prize in History; Walter D. Vol. 1: 16413
Love Token Society Exhibit Award Vol. 1: 3237
Lovejoy Award; Elijah Parish
Colby College Vol. 1: 8126
Southern Illinois University at Carbondale - School of Journalism Vol 1: 19509
Lovejoy Fellowship Loan Award Vol. 2: 3027
Lovelace Award; Augusta Ada Vol. 1: 5525
Lovelace II Award; W. Randolph Vol. 1: 1504
Loveland Memorial Award; Edward R. Vol. 1: 1922
Lovenmedaljen Vol. 2: 6217
Lovett Memorial Award; E. Dean Vol. 1: 1826
Low Award; George M. Vol. 1: 13896
Low Gross Vol. 1: 13650
Low Net Vol. 1: 13651
Low Space Transportation Award; AIAA George M. Vol. 1: 2686
Lowe Memorial Award; Emily Vol. 1: 4858
Lowell Award; Ralph Vol. 1: 8525
Lowell Mallett Award Vol. 1: 17206
Lowell Poetry Traveling Scholarship; Amy Vol. 1: 7933
Lowell Prize; James Russell Vol. 1: 13561
Lowenfeld Award Vol. 1: 13963
Lowenheim Memorial Award; Frederick A. Vol. 1: 5967
Lowery Memorial Award; Louis R. Vol. 1: 20687
Lowi Award and Jeffrey Pressman Award; Theodore Vol. 1: 17451
Lowin Composition Awards; Paul Vol. 2: 479
Lowin Orchestral Prize; Paul Vol. 2: 490
Lowin Song Cycle Prize; Paul Vol. 2: 491
Lowman Award; Edward W. Vol. 1: 1989
Lowrie Leadership Development Grant; Jean Vol. 1: 11399
Lowry Award; SCN Elizabeth Vol. 1: 22048
Lowther Memorial Award; Pat Vol. 1: 12745
Loyalty Award
National Junior College Athletic Association Vol. 1: 15311
Pi Kappa Alpha Vol 1: 17309
Loye and Alden Miller Research Award Vol. 1: 8491
Loyola Camellia Vol. 1: 12970
LPA Honor Awards Vol. 1: 12946
LPGA Hall of Fame Vol. 1: 12656
LRA Labor Award Vol. 1: 12642
LSDC Licentiateship Vol. 2: 9034
Lubalin Award; Herb Vol. 1: 19280
Lubatti Award; Eugenio Vol. 2: 3997
Luby Senior Hall of Fame Award; Mort Vol. 1: 6565
Lucarelli International Competition for Solo Oboe Players Vol. 1: 16603
Lucas Automotive Engineering Award; Oliver Vol. 2: 7816
Lucas Gold Medal; Anthony F. Vol. 1: 2820
Lucas Landscape Award; Homer Vol. 1: 16147
Lucas Memorial Award; Tad Vol. 1: 18103
Lucia Trade Award Vol. 1: 19856
Lucille Award; B. B. King Vol. 1: 6473
Luck and Pluck Award Vol. 1: 10541
Luck Award; James Murray Vol. 1: 13838
Ludington Memorial Award; Jeremiah Vol. 1: 9175
Ludovic-Trarieux International Human Rights Prize Vol. 2: 2418
Ludwig-Seidel Award Vol. 1: 597
Lueshen Harris' Sparrow Endowment; Willetta Vol. 1: 10805
Lueshen Student Membership Award; Willetta Vol. 1: 10806
Luff Awards Vol. 1: 3415
Luikov Medal Vol. 2: 6634
Luke Award; Hugh J. Vol. 1: 17514
Lum Award; Louise and Y. T. Vol. 1: 5011
Lum Award; Louise L. and Y. T. Vol. 1: 11038
Lumberman of the Year Vol. 1: 12977
Lumen Award Program Vol. 1: 10696
Lumen Christi Award Vol. 1: 7640
Luminaire Vol. 1: 21748
Luminosa Award for Unity Vol. 2: 3927
Luna Foreign Travel Scholarship; Lee G. Vol. 1: 15718
Lund Award; A. J. (Jack) Vol. 1: 11503
Lund Public Service Award; Paul M. Vol. 1: 17722
Lundell-Bright Memorial Award Vol. 1: 5968
Lurani Trophy for Formula Junior Class Vol. 2: 2455
Lush Award; J. L. Vol. 1: 2107
Lush Biomedical Postgraduate Scholarships; Dora Vol. 2: 467
Lutaud; Fondation Leon Vol. 2: 1921
Lutheran Educator of the Year Vol. 1: 12989
Luthi Award; Dr. Max Vol. 2: 6512
Lutoslawski International Composers Competition; Witold Vol. 2: 5387
Lutyens Award Vol. 2: 6801
Lybrand Medals Vol. 1: 10991
Lyell Medal Vol. 2: 7563
Lyle Medal Vol. 2: 127
Lyman Award; Robert J. Vol. 1: 17526
Lyman Book Awards; John Vol. 1: 16469
Lynch-Staunton Awards; Victor Martyn Vol. 1: 6802
Lynen Research Fellowships; Feodor Vol. 2: 3128
Lynn Award for Excellence; John Vol. 2: 329
Lyon Book Award; Thomas J. Vol. 1: 13643
Lyon-Caen; Prix Charles Vol. 2: 2027
Lyon Memorial Award; James P. Vol. 1: 9111
Lyons Award; Louis M. Vol. 1: 16357
Lyons Award; Sir William Vol. 2: 7588
Lyons Memorial Award; Ronald D. Vol. 1: 20688
Lyra Literary Prize; Carmen Vol. 2: 1358
The Lyric Annual Awards Vol. 1: 13003
The Lyric Memorial Prize Vol. 1: 13003
Lyric Poetry Award Vol. 1: 17434
Lysakowski Scientific Prize; Adam Vol. 2: 5354
Lyster Award; Theodore C. Vol. 1: 238
Lyttel Lily Cup Vol. 2: 8557
Lyttel Trophy Vol. 2: 6699
M & E Outstanding Young Professional Award Vol. 1: 18816
M. E. R. Prize Vol. 2: 5787
M. E. R.-prys Vol. 2: 5787
The M'4s Brewer Memorial Scholarship Vol. 1: 19826
Maas Achievement Award; Major General Melvin J. Vol. 1: 6458
Maber Award; Arthur Vol. 2: 8258
Maberley Memorial Scholarships; Charles Thomas Astley Vol. 2: 5797
MAC Poster Awards Vol. 1: 3943
"Mac Tools" SCCA Mechanic of the Year Vol. 1: 19707
The Macallan Gold Dagger For Fiction Vol. 2: 7368

Award Index

MacAllister Awards for Opera Singers Vol. 1: 10775
MacArthur Award; Robert H. Vol. 1: 9138
MacArthur Fellows Vol. 1: 13006
MacArthur Fellowship; Charles Vol. 1: 15508
MacArthur Prize Fellows Vol. 1: 13006
MacArthur Trophy Vol. 1: 15072
Macaulay Fellowship Vol. 2: 3617
Macavity Awards Vol. 1: 13728
Macbeth Award Vol. 1: 11128
MacBride Peace Prize; Sean Vol. 2: 6434
Maccabee Award Vol. 1: 15299
Maccoby Book Award; Eleanor Vol. 1: 3668
MacColl Award; Hugh Vol. 2: 7039
Macdonald; Le Prix Sir John Vol. 1: 7154
Macdonald Medal; George Vol. 2: 8845
MacDonald Memorial Award; Thomas H. Vol. 1: 1433
Macdonald Prize; Sir John A. Vol. 1: 7154
Macdougall Medal Vol. 2: 9263
MacDowell Medal; Edward Vol. 1: 13008
MacEachern Award Vol. 1: 17726
Macelwane Annual Awards in Meteorology; Father James B. Vol. 1: 3100
Macelwane Medal; James B. Vol. 1: 2355
MacFarland Award; Douglas Vol. 1: 5340
MacFarlane Award; Brian Vol. 1: 18776
Machado Award; Angie Vol. 1: 7797
Machado de Assis Prize Vol. 2: 1157
Machine Design Award Vol. 1: 4528
Machinery Award Scheme Vol. 2: 8414
MacInnes Award; John Vol. 1: 2494
MacIntosh Award Vol. 1: 10252
Mackay Award; Roland P. Vol. 1: 702
Mackay Medal; Donald Vol. 2: 8846
Mackay Trophy Vol. 1: 13879
MacKeller Distinguished Service Award; Lillian Vol. 1: 19867
MacKenzie Award; Agnes Mure Vol. 2: 8893
MacKenzie Book Prize; W. J. M. Vol. 2: 8281
Mackey Assistance Fund; Agnes K. Vol. 1: 8688
Mackie Awards; Howard Vol. 1: 7210
Maclaren Travelling Fellowship; John Vol. 2: 8584
Maclay Memorial Prize; James Archibald Vol. 2: 7846
MacLean Award; Angus H. Vol. 1: 20310
MacLean Citation Vol. 2: 4987
MacLean International Fellowship; IFUW Ida Smedley Vol. 2: 6406
MacLenan Prize for Fiction; Hugh Vol. 1: 17801
MacLennan Prize for Fiction; Hugh Vol. 1: 17799
Macleod Memorial Award; John Vol. 2: 8915
MacLeod Prijs Vol. 2: 1082
MacMillan Awards; Sir Ernest Vol. 1: 18593
MacMillan Developer's Award; Viola R. Vol. 1: 17692
Macmillan Prize; Ian Vol. 2: 8725
Macnab Medal Vol. 2: 7753
MacNeill New Journalist Award; Jim Vol. 1: 6035
MacPhail Trophy; Larry Vol. 1: 14341
MacPherson New Editor of the Year; Fiona Vol. 2: 7186
Macquarie Award for Conservation; Lachlan Vol. 2: 525
MacRae Award in Creative Leadership; A. E. Vol. 1: 17805
MacRobert Award Vol. 2: 8366
Macromolecular Science and Engineering Lecture Award Vol. 1: 7843
Macworld Editors' Choice Awards Vol. 1: 17115
Maddison Prize Vol. 2: 8607
Madersperger; Tiroler Erfinderpreis Josef Vol. 2: 675
Madgearu Prize; Virgil Vol. 2: 5843
Madison Award; Dolley Vol. 1: 22109
Madison Award for Distinguished Public Service; James Vol. 1: 4902
Madison Medal; James Vol. 1: 17559
Madison Prize; James Vol. 1: 18690
Madrina/Padrino Scholarship Vol. 1: 19184
Madsen Medal; John Vol. 2: 410
Maeda Prize Vol. 2: 4263
Maerskline UK Prize Vol. 2: 7690
Magaw Outstanding Clinical Practitioner Award; Alice Vol. 1: 1297
Magazine Awards; National Vol. 1: 4492
Magazine Merit Awards Vol. 1: 19088
Magazine of the Year Vol. 1: 19281
Magazine of the Year Award Vol. 1: 4271
Magazine Photographer of the Year Vol. 1: 15544
Magazine Website of the Year Vol. 2: 7186
The Magazines - Awards for Editorial and Publishing Excellence Vol. 2: 7188
Magellanic Premium Award Vol. 1: 3439
Magge Award Vol. 1: 8984
Maggie Awards Vol. 1: 17369
Maggio Award; Charles Vol. 1: 18442
Magic Lantern Vol. 1: 16495
Magida Award Vol. 1: 9392
Magill Distinguished Service Award; Arthur Napier Vol. 1: 7304
Magna Charta Day Award Vol. 1: 6258
Magnel Prize Vol. 2: 1099
Magnes Award; Judah L. Vol. 1: 2308
Magnetism; Award in Vol. 1: 12103
Magnolia Prize Vol. 2: 5232
Magnus Award Vol. 1: 19596
Magnus Hirschfeld Award Vol. 2: 2888
Magnussen Award; Ann Vol. 1: 3833
Magnusson Memorial Prize; Bengt Vol. 2: 2450
Magny; Prix Adrien Constantin de Vol. 2: 1982
Magon National Prize of Culture Vol. 2: 1353
Magrassi; Fondazione Guido Lenghi e Flaviano Vol. 2: 3821
Magruder Award for Museology (Museum Displays) Vol. 1: 13100
Magruder Scholarship; Neil Vol. 1: 13504
Magsaysay Award; Ramon Vol. 1: 18093
Magsaysay Awards; Ramon Vol. 2: 5267
MaGuire Award (Exceptional Achievement); James Vol. 1: 13082
Magyar Konyvtarosok Egyesuleteert Emlekerem Vol. 2: 3232
Magyar Televizio Nemzetkozi Karmesterversenye Vol. 2: 3286
Maha Vir Chakra Vol. 2: 3381
Mahaim; Fondation Ernest Vol. 2: 1008
Mahalanobis Medal; P. C. Vol. 2: 3491
Mahan Prize; Acrhie Vol. 1: 16792
Maharam Theatrical Design Awards Vol. 1: 4741
Maheshwari Memorial Lecture; Prof. Panchanan Vol. 2: 3492
Mahnke Film Production Award; Carl F. and Viola V. Vol. 1: 5359
Mahomet Chamber of Commerce Scholarship Vol. 1: 13021
Mahoney Award; Mary Vol. 1: 3281
Mahyer; Prix Jules Vol. 2: 1978
Mai Service Award; Ludwig Vol. 1: 5474
Mail System Management Hall of Fame Vol. 1: 13025
Mailing Industry Ingenuity Award Vol. 1: 13031
Mailloux Award; Noel Vol. 1: 16849
Mailly; Prix Edouard Vol. 2: 1053
Main Awards; Charles T. Vol. 1: 4529
Main Excellence in Clinical Practice Award; Robyn Vol. 1: 14317
Maine Space Grant Consortium Internships Vol. 1: 13041
Maintenance/Avionics Technician Safety Award Vol. 1: 14567
Maisonneuve; Prix Chomedey-de- Vol. 1: 18607
Maisons solaire, maisons, d'aujourd'hui Vol. 2: 2532
Majeri Jr. Award for Innovation and Leadership in Graphic Journalism; Anthony Vol. 1: 6210
Majewska Medal; Pelagia Vol. 2: 6343
Major Awgie Award Vol. 2: 292
Major League All-Star Team Vol. 1: 19649
Major League Baseball Player of the Year Vol. 1: 19655
Major League Executive of the Year Vol. 1: 19656
Majors/MLA Chapter Project of the Year Award Vol. 1: 13260
MakDougall-Brisbane Prize Vol. 2: 8790
Make a Difference Day Awards Vol. 1: 17444
Make-Up Competition Vol. 1: 245
Makeup and Design Award Vol. 1: 10814
Making Democracy Work Award Vol. 1: 12754
Making the Difference Vol. 2: 462
Maksymczuk Award; Julian Vol. 1: 20279
Malacological Society of London Annual Award Vol. 2: 8104
Malamud Memorial Award; PEN/ Vol. 1: 17155
Malan Medal; D. F. Vol. 2: 5651
Malan Prize; Recht Vol. 2: 5788
Malan-prys; Recht Vol. 2: 5788
Malaysian Literary Prize Vol. 2: 4430
Malchow Award - Woman of the Year Vol. 1: 19913
Malcolm H. Stern Award; Rabbi Vol. 1: 12357
Malcuzynski Award; Karol Vol. 2: 5384
Male and Female Bowler of the Year Award Vol. 1: 21870
Male Athlete of the Year
Sport Canada Vol. 1: 19632
United States Rowing Association Vol 1: 20750
Male/Female Most Improved Swimmer Vol. 2: 5114
Male/Female Outstanding Swimmer Vol. 2: 5115
Male Style Maker of the Year Vol. 1: 14743
Male Team of the Year Vol. 1: 19633
Male Thrower of the Year Vol. 1: 21229
Male Vocalist of the Year Vol. 1: 11424
Malheiros; Premio Artur Vol. 2: 5414
Malheiros; Premio Ricardo Vol. 2: 5415
Malheiros Prize; Artur Vol. 2: 5414
Malheiros Prize; Ricardo Vol. 2: 5415
Malina - Leonardo Prize for Lifetime Achievement; Frank J. Vol. 1: 11958

Malkin Prize; Harold Vol. 2: 8449
Malko International Competition for Young Conductors; Nicolai Vol. 2: 1505
Mallett Student Award; Dr. M. Vol. 1: 6919
Mallory Cup; U.S. Men's Sailing Championship - Clifford D. Vol. 1: 20782
Malloy Leadership Award; B. Charles Vol. 1: 5969
Malo Medal Award; Urbain J.H. Vol. 1: 21660
Malone Fellowship in Arab and Islamic Studies; Joseph J. Vol. 1: 14872
Malone Memorial Diving Award; Mike Vol. 1: 21170
Malone Post-Doctoral Fellows Program; Joseph J. Vol. 1: 14872
Malpighi Medal Vol. 2: 2757
Malta Journalism Awards/Gold Award Vol. 2: 4448
Malta Self-Government Re-introduction Seventy-Fifth Anniversary Medal Vol. 2: 4453
Malting Diploma Vol. 2: 8106
Malusardi; Premio F. Vol. 2: 4011
Mambembe Trophy Vol. 2: 1174
Mamoulian Award; Rouben
  New South Wales Film and Television Office Vol. 2: 477
  Sydney Film Festival Vol 2: 617
Man of the Year
  Federation of Fly Fishers Vol. 1: 9482
  International Electrical Testing Association Vol 1: 11553
  International Fire Photographers Association Vol 1: 11619
  International Road Federation Vol 1: 11890
  Italian Charities of America Vol 1: 12242
  National Association of Fire Investigators Vol 1: 14230
  National Association of Jewelry Appraisers Vol 1: 14296
  Society of the Plastics Industry - Moldmakers Division Vol 1: 19315
  Tall Clubs International Vol 1: 19908
  United Hellenic Voters of America Vol 1: 20334
Man of the Year Award
  American ORT Vol. 1: 3345
  Brazilian-American Chamber of Commerce Vol 1: 6610
  Italian Sons and Daughters of America Vol 1: 12253
Man of the Year in Law Enforcement Vol. 1: 19271
Man of the Year in Travel Vol. 1: 20176
Man or Woman of the Year Vol. 1: 10515
Man/Woman of the Year
  African Peoples' Christian Organization Vol. 1: 257
  Juvenile Diabetes Research Foundation of Greater Chicago Vol 1: 12475
Man/Woman of Vision Vol. 1: 9385
Management Accounting Award Vol. 2: 5211
Management Achievement Award
  American College of Medical Practice Executives Vol. 1: 1882
  National Association of College and University Business Officers Vol 1: 14124
  National Telecommunications Cooperative Association Vol 1: 15863
Management Achievement Awards Vol. 1: 17658
Management and Information Award Vol. 1: 19245
Management Award
  Art Directors Club Vol. 1: 5118
  International Publishing Management Association Vol 1: 11843
  Thai Chamber of Commerce Vol 2: 6619
Management Division Award Vol. 1: 2784
Management Effectiveness Awards Vol. 1: 3885
Management Engineering Award Vol. 1: 10346
Management Gold Medal; Institute of Vol. 2: 7703
Management Information Systems Annual Professional Award (MISAPA) Vol. 1: 10118
Management Innovation Award Vol. 1: 11477
Management Innovation Poster Session Award Vol. 1: 1874
Manager of the Year
  Croatian Managers' and Entrepreneurs Association Vol. 2: 1375
  International Veteran Boxers Association Vol 1: 12117
  Self Storage Association Vol 1: 18410
  System Safety Society Vol 1: 19888
Manager of the Year Award
  Baseball Writers Association of America Vol. 1: 6267
  Mail Systems Management Association Vol 1: 13024
  National Institute of Governmental Purchasing Vol 1: 15269
Manamperi (Engineering) Award Vol. 2: 6133
Mancini; Prix Vol. 2: 6373
Manco Award; Jeanne Vol. 1: 7311
Mandatory Award Vol. 2: 1555
Mandel Young Investigator Award; Lazaro J. Vol. 1: 3520
Mandile Award; Julie Vol. 2: 322
Mangled Skyscraper Award Vol. 1: 10057
Mangold Award; Walter S. Vol. 1: 14945
Manhattan College De La Salle Medal Vol. 1: 13051
Manhattan College Pacem in Terris Medal Vol. 1: 13052
Manheim Medal for Translation; PEN/Ralph Vol. 1: 17142
Mankin Award; John E. Vol. 1: 19990
Manly Memorial Medal; Charles M. Vol. 1: 19051
Mann Citation; Margaret Vol. 1: 5426
Mann Founder's Award; Marty Vol. 1: 14851
Mann Guardian Award; Horace Vol. 1: 10537
Mann Health & Human Rights Award; Jonathan Vol. 1: 11384
Mann Plaque; Emerson O. Vol. 1: 13927
Mann Plaque; R. C. Vol. 1: 13927
Mann Prize; John Vol. 2: 7672
Mannersfelt Medal Vol. 2: 6400
Mannheim Award; Herman Vol. 1: 11458
Mannheim International Filmweek Vol. 2: 2963
Manning Award; Robert E. Vol. 1: 9333
Manning Awards Vol. 1: 9329
Manpower Society Essay Competition Vol. 2: 7623
Mansel-Pleydell and Cecil Trusts Vol. 2: 7389
Mansfield Award; Mike Vol. 1: 12302
Manson Medal Vol. 2: 8847
Manton Award; Irene Vol. 2: 8929
Manton Prize; Irene Vol. 2: 8073
Mantz Best of Show Student Award; Jean Vol. 1: 10306
Manufacturer Member of the Year Vol. 1: 8975
Manufacturers Appreciation Award Vol. 1: 19637
Manufacturing Engineering Student Prize Vol. 2: 7817
Manufacturing Manager of the Year/Service Sector Manager of the Year Vol. 1: 17744
Manufacturing Prize Vol. 2: 7818
Manus Scholarship; Mark E. Vol. 1: 18020
Manuscript Award
  International Lactation Consultant Association Vol. 1: 11708
  Phi Alpha Theta Vol 1: 17235
Manzie Youth Literary Award; Kath Vol. 2: 484
Manzullo; Premio Fundacion Alfredo Vol. 2: 8
Map Collectors' Society Awards; International Vol. 2: 7959
MAPCS Scholarship Program Vol. 1: 13131
Maple Leaf Award Vol. 2: 744
Maple/Longman Memorial Travel Grant; Robert Vol. 1: 19954
Mara Memorial CYO Sportsman of the Year Award; John V. Vol. 1: 7679
Marais Prize; Eugene Vol. 2: 5652
Maravich Memorial Award; Pete Vol. 1: 14660
Marceneiro de Fado; Premio Municipal Alfredo Vol. 2: 5425
March Fong Eu Achievement Award Vol. 1: 15416
Marchal; Prix Joseph-Edmond Vol. 2: 996
Marchesan Award; Dr. Marco Vol. 1: 10835
Marchetti Award; Roberto Vol. 2: 4024
Marcia and Bobby French Van Cliburn Competition Silver Medal Vol. 1: 8108
Marckwardt Travel Grants; Albert H. Vol. 1: 19951
Marconi Award; Guglielmo Vol. 1: 16847
Marconi International Fellowship Vol. 1: 13064
Marconi Memorial Gold Medal of Service Vol. 1: 21325
Marconi Memorial Scroll of Honor Vol. 1: 21326
Marconi; Premio AEI Guglielmo Vol. 2: 4007
Marconi Premium Vol. 2: 7808
The Marconi Prize Vol. 1: 13064
Marconi Radio Awards Vol. 1: 14115
Marcorelles; Prix Louis Vol. 2: 2261
Marcus Award; Colonel Mickey Vol. 1: 12388
Marcus Award for Book Design; Stanley Vol. 1: 20019
Marcus Young Investigator Awards in Cardiovascular Sciences; Melvin L. Vol. 1: 2415
Mardon Prize; Jasper Vol. 2: 72
Mares; Premio Nacional de Literatura Jose Fuentes Vol. 2: 4646
Margaret C. Etter Early Career Award Vol. 1: 2090
Margaret W. Rossiter History of Women in Science Prize Vol. 1: 10488
Margolin Prize for Distinguished Business Reporting; Morton Vol. 1: 21015
Margreet Kamp Award Vol. 2: 4933
Marguerite de la Charlonie; Fondation Paul Vol. 2: 1949
Mari; Premio Maria Teresa Messori Roncaglia and Eugenio Vol. 2: 3832
Maria Sklodowska-Curie Medal Vol. 2: 5339
Marian Award for Priests Vol. 1: 13114

Marian Library Award Vol. 1: 21012
Marian Prize; Simion Florea Vol. 2: 5844
Marianist Award Vol. 1: 21013
Marie du Toit Award Vol. 2: 5598
Marie-Paule Nolin Award Vol. 1: 13213
Marimo; Prix Zerilli Vol. 2: 2092
Marine Aerial Refueler Squadron of the Year Vol. 1: 13094
Marine Aviation Logistics Squadron of the Year Vol. 1: 13071
Marine Aviator of the Year Vol. 1: 13070
Marine Corps Essay Contest Vol. 1: 20714
Marine Corps Expeditionary Medal Vol. 1: 8823
Marine Education Award Vol. 1: 15359
Marine Light/Attack Helicopter Squadron of the Year Vol. 1: 13076
Marine Medium Helicopter Squadron of the Year Vol. 1: 13073
Marine Naval Flight Officer of the Year Vol. 1: 13087
Marine Wing Support Squadron of the Year Vol. 1: 13079
Mariner's Rosette Vol. 1: 20378
Marinescu Prize; Gheorghe Vol. 2: 5845
Mariological Award Vol. 1: 13114
Marion; Prix Seraphin- Vol. 1: 18614
Maritime Heritage Award Vol. 1: 10647
Maritime Heritage Award Medal Vol. 2: 9261
Mariucci Award; John Vol. 1: 2495
Marjolin Award Vol. 2: 720
Mark Division of Polymer Chemistry Award; Herman F. Vol. 1: 1769
Mark Memorial Award; Peter Vol. 1: 6154
Mark Twain Award
By Word of Mouth Storytelling Guild Vol. 1: 6718
Society for the Study of Midwestern Literature Vol 1: 18922
Market Development and Promotion Council Awards Vol. 1: 16332
Market Development and Promotion Federation Awards Vol. 1: 16332
Market Manager of the Year Vol. 1: 14337
Marketer of the Year Vol. 1: 3031
Marketing Achievement Vol. 1: 15864
Marketing Achievement Award Vol. 1: 18792
Marketing Achievement Awards Vol. 1: 15554
Marketing and Publications Awards Vol. 1: 20957
Marketing Award Vol. 1: 14579
Marketing Award; AALL/West Excellence in Vol. 1: 1247
Marketing Award; International Egg Commission Promotion and Vol. 2: 7920
Marketing Awards Vol. 1: 17120
Marketing Awards Program Vol. 1: 17121
Marketing Communications Award Vol. 1: 8448
Marketing Computers ICON Awards Vol. 1: 223
Marketing Genius Awards Vol. 2: 7530
Marketing Man of the Year Vol. 1: 19795
Marketing Man/Woman of the Year Award Vol. 2: 5581
Marketing Master Award Vol. 1: 16332
Marketing Methods Competition Vol. 1: 17633
Marketing Person of the Year and Marketing Firm of the Year Vol. 1: 3032
Marketing Practitioner of the Year Award Vol. 1: 109
Marketing Publicist Award Vol. 1: 11331
Marklund Scholarship; Anna Vol. 1: 15043
Markowe Public Education Prize; Morris Vol. 2: 8465
Marks Award; Louis B. Vol. 1: 10697
Marks of Excellence Award Vol. 1: 15111
Marksmanship Vol. 1: 21320
Marksmanship Award Vol. 1: 21322
Markwardt Award; L. J. Vol. 1: 5970
Marlow Medal and Prize Vol. 2: 8763
Marlowe Award Vol. 2: 9028
Marlowe Award; Donald E. Vol. 1: 4025
Marmier; Prix Xavier Vol. 2: 2221
Marmottan; Fondation Vol. 2: 1717
Marmottan; Prix Paul Vol. 2: 1697
Marotta; Medaglia d'oro Domenico Vol. 2: 4001
Marquee Award Vol. 1: 20057
The Marquette Excellence Award Vol. 1: 15826
Marquez, Santiago Perez, and Antonio Ricaurte Prizes; Jose Ignacio de Vol. 2: 1300
Marquis Memorial Award; John E. Vol. 1: 1689
Marra Award; George Vol. 1: 19372
Marraro Prize; Helen and Howard R. Vol. 1: 18781
Marraro Prize; Howard R.
American Catholic Historical Association Vol. 1: 1655
Modern Language Association of America Vol 1: 13562
Marraro Prizes in Italian History; Howard R. Vol. 1: 2479
Marriott-Carlson Award Vol. 1: 5549
Marriott President's Award; Phyllis B. Vol. 1: 3142
Marrs Plaques; Lieutenant Theodore C. Vol. 1: 5110
Marsalis Scholarship; Wynton Vol. 1: 9115
Marschall Rhodia Award Vol. 1: 2108
Marschall - Rhone - Poulenc International Dairy Science Award Vol. 1: 2108
Marsden Award Vol. 1: 19108
Marsden Medal for Outstanding Service to Science; Sir Ernest Vol. 2: 5016
Marsh and Henning Awards Vol. 1: 21351
Marsh Award; Alan Vol. 2: 8394
Marsh Award for Conservation Biology Vol. 2: 9281
Marsh Award for Ecology Vol. 2: 7011
Marsh Distinguished Service Award; Burton W. Vol. 1: 11050
Marsh Graduate Fellowship; Burton W. Vol. 1: 11051
Marsh Medal; Alan Vol. 2: 8395
Marsh Medal for Exemplary Contributions to the Protection and Wise Use of the Nation's Water Resources; Mary H. Vol. 1: 4832
Marsh Memorial Prize; James R. Vol. 1: 10618
Marsh Safety Award; William O. Vol. 1: 13907
Marshall Award; Louis Vol. 1: 12378
Marshall Award; Robert Vol. 1: 21626
Marshall Education Award; Richard Vol. 1: 986
Marshall Medal; George Catlett Vol. 1: 5883
Marshall Scholarships Vol. 2: 6813
Marshall Travel Fellowship; Thomas F. Vol. 1: 4202
Marshall Urist Award Vol. 1: 16912
Marti Prize; The International Jose Vol. 2: 2599
Martial Solal Piano-Jazz Competition; International Vol. 2: 2277
Martin Award; Allie Beth Vol. 1: 17717
Martin Award; G. Harold Vol. 1: 12058
Martin Award; J. J. Vol. 1: 4026
Martin Fellowships; C. J. Vol. 2: 468
Martin Medallion; E. O. Vol. 1: 1363
Martin Memorial Award; Eric W. Vol. 1: 3083
Martin Memorial Scholarship; George C. Vol. 2: 5596
Martin Outstanding Younger Member Award; John Vol. 1: 10923
Martin Overseas Biomedical Fellowship; C. J. Vol. 2: 468
Martin; Prix Marie-Eugene Simon Henri Vol. 2: 2185
Martin Trophy; Dr. Beattie Vol. 1: 7112
Martin Willcocks Prize Vol. 2: 7505
Martinez-Marquez Journalism Award; Guillermo Vol. 1: 14249
Martino Award; John O. Vol. 1: 6566
Marty Public Understanding of Religion Award; Martin E. Vol. 1: 833
Marulic's Days Vol. 2: 1377
Marvel Creative Polymer Chemistry Award; Carl S. Vol. 1: 1770
Marvin Award; C. Raymond Vol. 1: 14077
Marvin Award; Jim Vol. 1: 12685
Marvin Grant; Walter Rumsey Vol. 1: 16660
Marwah Award; Prof. Surindar Mohan Vol. 2: 3420
Marx Memorial Scholarship; Ellie Vol. 2: 5762
Mary Bancroft Memorial Scholarship Vol. 1: 12502
Mary C. Turpie Award Vol. 1: 4711
Mary Louise Brown Research Award Vol. 1: 1305
Maryknoll Mission Award Vol. 1: 13127
Maryknoll Student Essay Contest Vol. 1: 13129
Maryland Cup Vol. 1: 5107
Maryland Performance Excellence Award Vol. 1: 21054
Maryland Quality Awards Vol. 1: 21054
Marzocco d'Ora Vol. 2: 3925
MASA President's Plaque Vol. 1: 13032
Masako Shoji Scholarship Vol. 1: 21879
Masefield Memorial Trust; John Vol. 2: 8985
Mashman Safety Award; Joe Vol. 1: 10400
Masliansky Award; Zvi Hirsch Vol. 1: 10373
Mason Anderson Williams Award; Mary Vol. 1: 5507
Mason Award; Jack Vol. 1: 6274
Mason Award; Karl Vol. 1: 17164
Mason Award; Peter Vol. 2: 8183
Mason Playwrights' Award; *The Sunday Star Times* Bruce Vol. 2: 5045
Mason Prize; Michael Vol. 2: 7174
Mason Reference Award; Harold Vol. 1: 5741
Masonry Prize Vol. 2: 5133
Masotto Cup; Patricia L. Vol. 1: 20892
Maspero; Prix Gaston Vol. 2: 1754
Masri Singarimbun Research Awards for Indonesian Scholars. Vol. 2: 3598
Mass Communications Hall of Fame Vol. 1: 20045
Mass Communications Outstanding Alumni Awards Vol. 1: 20046
Mass Media Science and Engineering Fellowship; AAAS Vol. 1: 3506
Massachusetts Avenue Building Assets Fund Grants Program Vol. 1: 941

Massachusetts Bay Trophy Vol. 1: 20784
Massachusetts State Poetry Society Award Vol. 1: 15008
Massachusetts Tree Farmer of the Year Vol. 1: 13160
Massey Award Vol. 2: 2272
Massey-Ferguson Educational Award Vol. 1: 4227
Massey Medal Vol. 1: 18149
Massie Medal and Prize; Harrie Vol. 2: 216
Massine Prize for the Art of the Dance; Leonida Vol. 2: 3865
Masson Memorial Scholarship Prize Vol. 2: 515
Master Angler Award Vol. 2: 242
Master Breeder Award Vol. 1: 15503
Master Cartoonist Vol. 2: 7240
Master Clinician Award Vol. 1: 807
Master Craftsman Degree Vol. 1: 15973
Master Endoscopist Award Vol. 1: 4074
Master Fire Photographer Vol. 1: 11620
Master Judge Award Vol. 1: 15504
Master Musician Award Vol. 1: 20196
Master of Bananistry Medal Vol. 1: 11418
Master of Ceremonies - ANA Banquet Vol. 1: 3238
Master of the Game Award Vol. 1: 15809
Master Pastelist Vol. 1: 17105
Master Steinologist Vol. 1: 19788
Master Triathletes of the Year Vol. 1: 21249
Master Wildlife Artist Vol. 1: 21828
Masterclass Performers Competition Vol. 1: 15061
Masterix Vol. 2: 2743
Mastermind Award Vol. 2: 6961
Masters Vol. 1: 1923
Masters Administrator of the Year Vol. 1: 21230
Masters and Johnson Award Vol. 1: 18853
Masters Athlete of the Year Vol. 1: 19868
Masters Award Vol. 1: 19868
Masters Golf Tournament Vol. 1: 6087
Masters Long Distance Running Awards (Age Group) Vol. 1: 21231
Masters Race Walking Award Vol. 1: 21232
Master's Thesis Award Vol. 1: 10832
Masters Transportation Engineering Award; Frank M. Vol. 1: 4339
Masterson Award & Outstanding Women's Awards; Carroll Sterling Vol. 1: 22093
Masterson Memorial Trophy; Glenn R. Vol. 1: 7509
Masterworks in Masonry Awards Vol. 1: 18101
Masubuchi Award; Professor Koichi Vol. 1: 4888
Masursky Award for Meritorious Service; Harold Vol. 1: 1514
Materials Handling Award Vol. 1: 18627
Mathematical Contest in Modeling Vol. 1: 18737
Mathematics Excellence Award Vol. 1: 3038
Mather Award; Frank Jewett Vol. 1: 8148
Mather Award; Katharine and Bryant Vol. 1: 5971
Mather Award; Stephen Tyng Vol. 1: 15490
Mather Premium Vol. 2: 7808
Mathers Trophy; Frank Vol. 1: 2512
Mathewson Award; Champion H. Vol. 1: 13456
Mathiasen Award; Geneva Vol. 1: 14869
Mathilde Award Vol. 2: 1468
Mathy and Opera Awards Vol. 2: 259
Mathy Scholarship; Marianne Vol. 2: 259
Matrix Award Vol. 1: 16312
Matson Memorial Award; George C. Vol. 1: 1343
Matson Memorial Award; Theodore M. Vol. 1: 11052
Matt Weyuker Scholarship Vol. 1: 16921
Matthew Award; Robert Vol. 2: 7320
Matthew Prize; Sir Robert Vol. 2: 2512
Matthews Award; Austin- Vol. 1: 7222
Matthews Memorial Fair Play Award; Billy Vol. 1: 7292
Matthews Outstanding Chapter Award; R.C. Vol. 1: 19931
Mattin Award; Harry Vol. 1: 9123
Matulis premija; Juozo Vol. 2: 4395
Mature Women Scholarship Grant Vol. 1: 15334
Mauchly Award; Eckert -
Association for Computing Machinery Vol. 1: 5303
Institute of Electrical and Electronics Engineers - Computer Society Vol 1: 10891
Maud Montgomery Children's Literature Award; Lucy Vol. 1: 17547
Maugham Awards; Somerset Vol. 2: 8986
Mauguin; Prix Georges Vol. 2: 2051
Mauldin Award; R.C. Vol. 1: 16018
Maurer-Stump Award Vol. 1: 17889
Maurice Berman Prize Vol. 2: 7102
Maurice Rookie of the Year; Lisa Vol. 1: 21775
Maury and Hinman research awards Vol. 1: 21410
Mauss; Premio Marcos y Celia Vol. 2: 4612
Mauthner Memorial Fellowship; Robert Vol. 2: 8339
Mawson Lecture Vol. 2: 128
Max-Buchner-Forschungsstiftung; DECHEMA Award of the Vol. 2: 2699
Max-Eyth-Gedenkmunze Vol. 2: 3024
Max-Pruss Medal Vol. 2: 2789
MAXI Awards Program Vol. 1: 11517
Maxie T. Collier, MD Award Vol. 1: 6433
Maxillofacial Radiology Award; Howard R. Raper Oral and Vol. 1: 729
Maxim Gold Medal; Hiram Percy Vol. 1: 49
Maxim Memorial Award; Hiram Percy Vol. 1: 49
Maximum Export Award Vol. 2: 3348
Maxwell Award; BMEC Donald Vol. 2: 7706
Maxwell Award; Joe Kennedy-Clerk Vol. 1: 17290
Maxwell Medal and Prize Vol. 2: 7733
Maxwell Premium Vol. 2: 7808
Maxwell Prize for Plasma Physics; James Clerk Vol. 1: 3463
Maxwell Prizes Vol. 2: 6063
May and Baker Lectureship Vol. 2: 8770
May and Baker Pharmaceuticals Prizes Vol. 2: 8824
May Award; Arthur A. Vol. 1: 5012
May Award; Douglas Vol. 2: 7966
May Foundation Scholarship; New South Wales Government and Frederick Vol. 2: 479
Mayborn Award for Community Leadership; Frank Vol. 1: 19998
Mayer Award for Educational Leadership; Edward N. Vol. 1: 8932
Mayer; Fondation Charles-Leopold Vol. 2: 1823
Mayer Memorial Trophy; Lady Dorothy Vol. 2: 3627
Mayer Research Award; Cecile Lehman Vol. 1: 1844
Mayfield Award Vol. 1: 8391
Mayfield Award; George A. Hall/Harold F. Vol. 1: 21638
Mayfield Cotton Engineering Award Vol. 1: 4228
Mayiyham Award for Public Service Vol. 1: 8013
Maynard Award; Harold H. Vol. 1: 3033
Maynard Book of the Year Award; H. B. Vol. 1: 10960
Maynard Cup Vol. 2: 7395
Maynard Jensen Award Vol. 1: 10288
Maynard Memorial Medal; Hamilton Vol. 2: 5715
Maynard Prize; Isaac N. Vol. 1: 13790
Mayo/Rubin Jones Scholarship; Billy Vol. 1: 9649
Mayor's Arts Awards Vol. 1: 8771
Mayor's Awards for Excellence in Science and Technology Vol. 1: 8039
Mayor's Lifetime Achievement Award Vol. 1: 8884
Mayr Award in Systematic Biology; Ernst Vol. 1: 19305
Mays Award; Captain "Willie" Vol. 1: 5107
Mays Award; Robin Vol. 1: 17735
Mazzetti Scholarship Award; Guilliano Vol. 1: 19162
MBC Paper of the Year Award Vol. 1: 3944
MBE Coordinator of the Year Vol. 1: 15390
MBFS Vol. 1: 13325
MC National Championship Regatta Vol. 1: 13209
MCA Annual Merit Awards Program Vol. 1: 13307
McAllister Editorial Fellowship Award Vol. 1: 10012
McAlpin, Jr. Mental Health Research Achievement Award; William R. Vol. 1: 15377
McAnsh Award; James Vol. 1: 7564
McArthur Prize; Robert Vol. 2: 7673
McAulay Award; John H. Vol. 1: 5341
McAuliffe Memorial Award; Christa Vol. 1: 228
McAuliffe Reach for the Stars Award; Christa Vol. 1: 14783
McAuslan First Book Prize
Quebec Writers' Federation Vol. 1: 17799
Quebec Writers' Federation Vol 1: 17801
MCBA Scholarship Vol. 1: 13339
McBryde Medal; W. A. E. Vol. 1: 7844
McCaffree Award; Charles Vol. 1: 8195
McCaffrey Trophy; James P. Vol. 1: 7113
McCall Life Pattern Fund (Training Award) Vol. 1: 19421
McCallam Award; James A. Vol. 1: 5775
McCallum Scholarship; Heather Vol. 1: 5287
McCampbell Award; David Vol. 1: 2239
McCandless Award; Boyd R. Vol. 1: 3668
McCanse Award; Jessie Vol. 1: 15868
McCarren Award Vol. 1: 11277
McCarthy Bursary; Doreen Vol. 2: 170
McCarthy Good Guy Award; Clem Vol. 1: 20621
McCay Award; Windsor Vol. 1: 11192
McClarren Legislative Development Award; Robert R. Vol. 1: 10681
McCloskey Award; Mike Vol. 1: 18465
McCloy Memorial Award; John J. Vol. 1: 9832
McClung Award Vol. 1: 6328

McClure Award for Outstanding Environmental and Community Leadership; Tim Vol. 1: 15589
McCluskey Award of Excellence; Roger Vol. 1: 20421
McClusky Research Award; Dean and Sybil Vol. 1: 5360
McColl Family Fellowship Vol. 1: 2332
The McCollum Award Vol. 1: 3960
McCollum International Lectureship in Nutrition; E. V. Vol. 1: 4160
McCommon Memorial Trophy; May Vol. 1: 13673
McConnell Award; Robert Earll Vol. 1: 2821
McConnell Distinguished Service Award; Douglas Rand Vol. 1: 2816
MCConnell Scholar-Athlete Award; John M. Vol. 1: 15073
McCord Education Award; L. P. Vol. 1: 10735
McCormack Award Vol. 1: 5865
McCormick Award for Distinguished Early Career Contributions; Earnest J. Vol. 1: 18750
McCormick - Jerome Increase Case Medal; Cyrus Hall Vol. 1: 4229
McCormick, M.D. Award; J. B. Vol. 1: 15719
McCormick Medal; Cyrus Hall Vol. 1: 4229
McCormick Memorial Diving Award; Glenn Vol. 1: 20396
McCormick Prize; Richard P. Vol. 1: 16170
McCoy Award; Walter R. Vol. 1: 3410
McCrae Cup Vol. 1: 7223
McCredie; Kenneth B. Vol. 1: 12790
McCree, Jr. Awards for the Advancement of Justice; Wade H. Vol. 1: 19763
McCulloch Award; Warren Sturgis Vol. 1: 3986
McCulloch Prizes for Public Speaking; Andrina Vol. 1: 17806
McCullough Award; Constance M. Vol. 1: 11867
McCurdy Award Vol. 1: 6869
McCutcheon Award (Marine Heavy Helicopter Squadron of the Year); Keith B. Vol. 1: 13083
McDaniel Ambassador Award; Durward K. Vol. 1: 2043
McDonald Achievement Award; Touchdown Club Arch Vol. 1: 20133
McDonald Award; Gerald Vol. 2: 8097
McDonald House Charities Awards of Excellence; Ronald Vol. 1: 18117
McDonald House Charities Grants Program; Ronald Vol. 1: 18118
McDonald's Ballet Scholarship Vol. 2: 314
McDonald's City of Sydney Performing Arts Challenge Vol. 2: 314
McDonald's Operatic Aria Vol. 2: 315
McDonald's Performing Arts Challenge Vol. 2: 313
McDonnell Award; James A. Vol. 1: 5113
McDonnell Douglas Law Enforcement Award Vol. 1: 10401
McDowell Award; W. Wallace Vol. 1: 10898
McEwan Memorial Award (Masters Athlete of the Year); May Vol. 1: 19868
McFaden Cartography Award; Bill Vol. 1: 14003
McFarland Award; Forest R. Vol. 1: 19052
McFarlane Environmental Award; Euan P. Vol. 1: 12234
McGan Silver Antenna Award; Philip J. Vol. 1: 50
McGavin Award; Agnes Purcell Vol. 1: 3628
McGee Service Award; George Vol. 1: 16930
McGee Trophy; Francis J. Vol. 1: 15647
McGee Trophy; W. P. Vol. 1: 7224
McGibbon Award; Pauline Vol. 1: 16744
McGill Award; John Vol. 1: 19694
McGillen Award; Pete Vol. 1: 16972
McGinnis Memorial Award; John H. Vol. 1: 19527
McGinnis-Ritchie Award Vol. 1: 19527
McGivern Challenge Bowl Vol. 1: 21588
McGovern Award Vol. 1: 16333
McGovern Award; James M. Vol. 1: 16329
McGovern Award; John P. Vol. 1: 3084
McGovern Award Lecture in the Behavioral Sciences; John P. Vol. 1: 1051
McGovern Award Lectureship; John P. Vol. 1: 13261
McGovern Umpires' Award; John T. Vol. 1: 20859
McGraw Award; James H. Vol. 1: 4027
McGraw, Jr. Prize in Education; Harold W. Vol. 1: 13221
McGraw Research Award; Curtis W. Vol. 1: 4028
McGroddy Prize in New Materials; James C. Vol. 1: 3464
McGuire Cup; James P. Vol. 1: 20893
McGuire Memorial Intermediate Piano Scholarship; The Maude Vol. 1: 18298
McGuire Memorial Senior Piano Scholarship; The Maude Vol. 1: 18299
McHenry Award; Lawrence C. Vol. 1: 701
McHugh Award; Walter P. Vol. 1: 5776
McIntyre Award Vol. 2: 5521
McIver Public Health Nurse Award; Pearl Vol. 1: 3282
MCJROTC Awards Vol. 1: 13106
McKean Award; Arch Vol. 1: 11732
McKean Award; Tom Vol. 1: 19695
McKee Award; Harley J. Vol. 1: 5454
McKenna Award; Father Vol. 1: 14419
McKenzie Award; Dorothy C. Vol. 1: 7913
McKenzie Award (Outstanding Executive - PR and Marketing); Ken Vol. 1: 2513
McKenzie Award; R. Tait Vol. 1: 881
McKenzie Cup Vol. 1: 9483
McKenzie Plaque Vol. 1: 9483
McKinney Award Vol. 1: 15412
McKinney Award; George Vol. 1: 9585
McKinney Award; William M. Vol. 1: 4573
McKinnon Award; Marthe T. Vol. 1: 4859
McKinsey Awards Vol. 1: 10273
McKitterick Prize Vol. 2: 8987
McKnight Advancement Grants Vol. 1: 17399
McKnight Artist Fellowships for Writers Vol. 1: 12906
McKnight Black Doctoral Fellowship Program Vol. 1: 9599
McKnight Doctoral Fellowship Program in Arts and Sciences, Mathematics, Business and Engineering Vol. 1: 9599
McKune Memorial Award; Frank B. Vol. 1: 5413
McLaren Award Vol. 2: 7407
McLaren Cup Vol. 2: 8558
McLaren Heritage Award; Norman Vol. 1: 16951
McLaughlin Award of Merit; Kenneth P. Vol. 1: 15538
McLaughlin, Jr. Memorial Award; Lt. Donald Vol. 1: 20664
McLaughlin Medal Vol. 1: 18168
McLaughry Award; Tuss Vol. 1: 2270
McLemore Prize Vol. 1: 13507
McLeod Literary Prize; Enid Vol. 2: 7544
McLeod Society Trophy; Stuart Cameron Vol. 1: 10992
McLintock Prize; Sir William Vol. 2: 7674
McMaster Award; Albert Vol. 2: 7074
McMaster Gold Medal; Robert C. Vol. 1: 4148
McMillan Lecture Award; Mary Vol. 1: 3493
McMullen Weapon System Maintenance Award; Maj. Gen. Clements Vol. 1: 16832
McNally Award; Andrew Vol. 1: 2000
McNally Awards; Rand Vol. 1: 1993
McNamara Fellowships Program; Robert S. Vol. 1: 21867
McNamee Award; Graham Vol. 1: 4679
McNamee CSJ Award; Catherine T. Vol. 1: 14606
McNaughton Exemplary Communication Award; Shirley Vol. 1: 11919
McNeer Award; Lenore Vol. 1: 15433
McNeil Medal for the Public Awareness of Science Vol. 1: 18169
McNichol Prize; J. N. Vol. 2: 499
McNulty Award; J. D. Vol. 1: 5886
McParland Memorial Award Vol. 1: 7198
McPherson Memorial Lecture Vol. 2: 7741
McPherson Memorial Piano Award; The Mildred Spence Vol. 1: 18300
McQuade Memorial Fund Award; Gerard Vol. 1: 12136
McRae Russell Award; Walter Vol. 2: 83
McWhorter Scholar-Athlete Award; H. Boyd Vol. 1: 19473
MDA Broadcast Journalism Awards Vol. 1: 13683
Meacham Award; Monte Vol. 1: 892
Mead Award; George Herbert Vol. 1: 18932
Mead Award; Margaret
American Anthropological Association Vol. 1: 912
International Community Corrections Association Vol 1: 11500
Mead Johnson Award Vol. 1: 4161
Mead Johnson Pediatric Research Award Vol. 2: 6604
Mead Johnson Research Award in Endocrinology and Metabolism Vol. 1: 3521
Mead Prize; Sidney E. Vol. 1: 4286
Mead Prizes; Daniel W. Vol. 1: 4340
Meade Award; CEE Richard A. Vol. 1: 14830
Meade Award; George and Eleanore Vol. 1: 19829
Meadmaker of the Year Vol. 1: 2522
Meadows Award for Excellence in the Arts; Algur H. Vol. 1: 19513
Meadows Memorial Award; C. F. "Buzz" Vol. 1: 14265
Measuresment Sciences; Joseph F. Keithley for Advances in Vol. 1: 3459
Meat Processing Award Vol. 1: 3055
Meats Hall of Fame; Cured Vol. 1: 1263
Meats Research Award Vol. 1: 4261
MEC Art Prizes Vol. 2: 1181
Mechaelis Memorial Prize Vol. 2: 5093
Mechanic of the Year Award
Professional Aviation Maintenance Association Vol. 1: 17582
United States Auto Club Vol 1: 20422
Mechanical Engineering Prize Vol. 2: 405
Mechelen Prize; Stad Vol. 2: 1089
MECON Award Vol. 2: 3458

Medaglia d'Acciaio Federico Giolitti Vol. 2: 3994
Medaglia d'Oro AIM Vol. 2: 3998
Medaglia d'Oro Icilio Guareschi Vol. 2: 3923
Medaglia d'oro Luigi Losana Vol. 2: 3996
Medaille Boris Rajewsky Vol. 2: 2303
Medaille d'Argent du Centre National de la Recherche Scientifique Vol. 2: 2396
Medaille de Bronze du Centre National de la Recherche Scientifique Vol. 2: 2397
Medaille de l'ACP pour Contribution Exceptionnelle a la Physique Vol. 1: 6932
Medaille de l'AISS Vol. 2: 6449
Medaille der Mozartstadt Salzburg Vol. 2: 774
Medaille des Anciens Presidents Vol. 2: 2558
Medaille des Soixante Ans et Fondation Manley-Bendall Vol. 2: 2559
Medaille d'Or Vol. 2: 2299
Medaille d'Or du Centre National de la Recherche Scientifique Vol. 2: 2398
Medaille d'Or Laveran Vol. 2: 2574
Medaille du Lieutenant-Gouverneur Vol. 1: 10422
Medaille Flavelle Vol. 1: 18165
Medaille fur Naturwissenschaftliche Publizistik Vol. 2: 2726
Medaille Gabrielle Leger Vol. 1: 10421
Medaille Henry Marshall Tory Vol. 1: 18174
Medaille Innis - Gerin Vol. 1: 18167
Medaille Jason A. Hannah Vol. 1: 18166
Medaille Jean Thevenot Vol. 2: 6402
Medaille Lorne Pierce Vol. 1: 18171
Medaille McLaughlin Vol. 1: 18168
Medaille Militaire Vol. 2: 2357
Medaille Pierre Chauveau Vol. 1: 18162
Medaille Pierre Francois Caille Vol. 1: 11606
Medaille Thomas W. Eadie Vol. 1: 18164
Medaille Tisserand Vol. 2: 1668
Medaille Willet G. Miller Vol. 1: 18170
Medailles de la SFA Vol. 2: 2583
Medailles et Diplomes Olympique Vol. 2: 6427
Medal Vol. 2: 9329
Medal: 80 lat PTH Vol. 2: 5374
Medal: 80 Years of the Polish Society of Hygiene Vol. 2: 5374
Medal Award Vol. 1: 19121
Medal Awards Vol. 1: 1568
Medal Federacion Espanola de Montanismo Vol. 2: 6107
Medal for Armed Forces in the Service of the Fatherland Vol. 2: 5294
Medal for Brave Performance in Mining Vol. 2: 685
Medal for Bravery Vol. 2: 1301
Medal for Civic Virtue Vol. 2: 5139
Medal for Courage Vol. 2: 4454
Medal for Distinction in Engineering Education Vol. 1: 7058
Medal for Distinguished Conduct and Loyal Service Vol. 2: 5742
Medal for Distinguished Philanthropy Vol. 1: 1280
Medal for Excellence in Craft Award Vol. 1: 19029
Medal for Excellence in Teaching Vol. 1: 6935
Medal for Gallantry Vol. 2: 196
Medal for Long Marital Life Vol. 2: 5322
Medal for Outstanding Achievement in Industrial and Applied Physics Vol. 1: 6936
Medal for Participation in the Battle for Berlin Vol. 2: 5295
Medal for Peace and Friendship through Music and Arts Vol. 1: 11595
Medal for Scientific Achievement Vol. 2: 1133
Medal for Self-Sacrifice and Courage Vol. 2: 5323
Medal for Service to the Republic Vol. 2: 4455
Medal for Services to Bibliography Vol. 2: 6859
Medal for Serving the Association of Hungarian Librarians Vol. 2: 3232
Medal for the Advancement of Research Vol. 1: 5187
Medal in Medicine Vol. 1: 18153
Medal in Surgery Vol. 1: 18154
Medal Jubilee: One Hundred Years of the PSH Vol. 2: 5375
Medal Jubileuszowy: 90 Lat PTH Vol. 2: 5376
Medal Jubileuszowy: 100 lat PTH Vol. 2: 5375
Medal Mariana Smoluchowskiego Vol. 2: 5367
Medal of Achievement Vol. 1: 226
Medal of Agricultural Science Vol. 2: 207
Medal of Appreciation Vol. 1: 15776
Medal of Bravery Vol. 1: 6821
Medal of Courage Vol. 1: 15987
Medal of Freedom Vol. 1: 9364
Medal of Honor
- American Institute of Architects, Tampa Bay Vol. 1: 2734
- Electronic Industries Alliance Vol 1: 9216
- Federation of Danish Architects Vol 2: 1491
- Fragrance Foundation Vol 1: 9721
- Herb Society of America Vol 1: 10412
- International Association of Professional Numismatists Vol 2: 906
- Niagara University Vol 1: 16352
- St. George's Society of New York Vol 1: 18207
- Society of Automotive Engineers Vol 1: 19053

Medal of Honor Award
- American Mosquito Control Association Vol. 1: 3136
- Precast/Prestressed Concrete Institute Vol 1: 17527

Medal of Honor for Career Service Vol. 1: 19257
Medal of Honor for Literature Vol. 1: 13993
Medal of Honor for Music Vol. 1: 13994
Medal of Honor for Promotion of a Scientific Field Vol. 2: 5653
Medal of Honor of the Great Promoters of Education Vol. 2: 1332
Medal of Honor of the Physical Sciences and Technique Vol. 2: 5654
Medal of Honour
- Canada's Research-Based Pharmaceutical Companies Vol. 1: 6839
- National Pony Society Vol 2: 8186

Medal of Honour for Afrikaans Television and Radio Vol. 2: 5655
Medal of Liberty
- American Civil Liberties Union Vol. 1: 1809
- American Civil Liberties Union Vol 1: 1809

Medal of Merit
- American Numismatic Association Vol. 1: 3239
- Canadian Society of Petroleum Geologists Vol 1: 7486
- Deutsche Akademie der Naturforscher Leopoldina Vol 2: 2706
- Journalism Education Association Vol 1: 12449
- National Federation of Coffee Growers of Colombia Vol 2: 1328
- St. Nicholas Society of the City of New York Vol 1: 18221

Medal of Merit; Finnish Academy of Technology Vol. 2: 1593
Medal of Military Valour Vol. 1: 6822
Medal of Service Vol. 2: 3214
Medal of the Endocrine Society Vol. 1: 9262
Medal of the Estonian Academy of Sciences Vol. 2: 1563
Medal of the Mozart City of Salzburg Vol. 2: 774
Medal of the President of Union of Romanian Architects Vol. 2: 5880
Medal of the Tokyo Geographical Society Vol. 2: 4304
Medal of Union of Romanian Architects Vol. 2: 5881
Medal of Valor Vol. 1: 17962
Medal of Valor Award Vol. 1: 2028
Medal Za Dlugoletnie Pozycie Malzenskie Vol. 2: 5322
Medal Za Ofiarnosc i Odwage Vol. 2: 5323
Medal Za Udzial w Walkach o Berlin Vol. 2: 5295
Medalha de Merito Turistico Vol. 2: 5421
Medalja Julije Domac Vol. 2: 1380
Medalje til minne om Guldberg og Waages Massevirkningslov Vol. 2: 5152
Medalla Agricola Interamericano Vol. 2: 1363
Medalla Agustin Ramirez Vol. 2: 4503
Medalla al Merito Cafetero Manuel Mejia Vol. 2: 1329
Medalla al Merito Logisgtico y Administrativo Contralmirante Rafael Tono Vol. 2: 1281
Medalla al Valor Vol. 2: 1301
Medalla Alfonso L. Herrera al Merito en Ecologia y Conservacion Vol. 2: 4523
Medalla Antonio Rosales Vol. 2: 4503
Medalla Bernardo Balbuena Vol. 2: 4503
Medalla Carmen y Aguiles Serdan Vol. 2: 4497
Medalla de Honor Belisario Dominguez Vol. 2: 4630
Medalla de Oro
- Inter-American Safety Council Vol. 1: 11119
- Society of Mexican American Engineers and Scientists Vol 1: 19184

Medalla de Plata Vol. 1: 19184
Medalla Eduardo Neri Vol. 2: 4565
Medalla Gabin Barreda Vol. 2: 4496
Medalla Ignacio Manuel Altamirano Vol. 2: 4571
Medalla Ing. Salvador Toscano Vol. 2: 4471
Medalla Juan de Dios Batiz Vol. 2: 4548
Medalla Militar Francisco Jose de Caldas Vol. 2: 1282
Medalla Militar Soldado Juan Bautista Solarte Obando Vol. 2: 1283
Medalla Rafael Ramirez Vol. 2: 4580
Medalla R.S.E.F. Vol. 2: 6102
Medalla Servicios Distinguidos a la Aviacion Naval Vol. 2: 1284
Medalla Servicios Distinguidos en Orden Publico Vol. 2: 1285

Award Index

Medalla Servicios Distinguidos Infanteria de Marinia Vol. 2: 1286
Medalla Servicios Distinguidos la Fuerza de Superficie Vol. 2: 1287
Medalla Tiempo de Servicio Vol. 2: 1288
Medallas de Geografia Fisica, Humana, Economica Vol. 2: 5240
Medallion Award
American Forage and Grassland Council Vol. 1: 2274
Council of Residential Specialists Vol 1: 8584
National Safety Council, Northern Ohio Chapter Vol 1: 15662
Medallion Circle Award Vol. 1: 14420
Medallion de Bronce Vol. 1: 16456
Medallion de Oro Vol. 1: 16457
Medallion de Plata Vol. 1: 16458
Medallion for Entrepreneurship Vol. 1: 6332
Medallion of Excellence for Distinguished Service Vol. 1: 8398
Medallion of Excellence for Role Model Vol. 1: 8399
Medallion of Honor
All-America Selections Vol. 1: 442
Theta Alpha Phi Vol 1: 20068
Medallion of Merit Vol. 1: 3066
Medals and Certificates Vol. 2: 9293
Medals for Excellence Vol. 2: 7309
Medals of Honour Vol. 2: 4747
Medals of the Society of Dyers and Colourists Vol. 2: 9035
Medbery Nature Landscape/Seascape Award; Lorena Vol. 1: 17287
Medellin University Prize Vol. 2: 1342
Media and Methods Magazine Awards Portfolio Competition Vol. 1: 13233
Media and Methods Maxi Awards Vol. 1: 13233
Media Award
American Association of Critical-Care Nurses Vol. 1: 1178
Canadian Motorcycle Association Vol 1: 7293
Canadian Nurses Foundation Vol 1: 7312
Emergency Nurses Association Vol 1: 9247
International Society of Appraisers Vol 1: 11976
National Hearing Conservation Association Vol 1: 15196
Society for the Study of Lesbian, Gay and Bisexual Concerns (Division 44) Vol 1: 18914
Special Libraries Association Vol 1: 19553
United Nations Association of Rochester Vol 1: 20362
U.S.A. Baseball Vol 1: 21158
Media Award; British Medical Association Medicine in the Vol. 2: 7061
Media Awards
American Institute of Biological Sciences Vol. 1: 2741
American Society on Aging Vol 1: 4645
International Association of Emergency Managers Vol 1: 11349
Leukemia and Lymphoma Society Vol 1: 12791
Plain English Campaign Vol 2: 8270
Sigma Theta Tau International Vol 1: 18502
Media Awards Competition Vol. 1: 14862
Media Awards for Excellence Vol. 1: 4941
Media Awards; Publications and Electronic Vol. 1: 15669
Media Citation Vol. 1: 12450
Media Excellence Awards
St. Bonaventure University - Russell J. Jandoli School of Journalism and Mass Communication Vol. 1: 18197
St. Bonaventure University - Russell J. Jandoli School of Journalism and Mass Communication Vol 1: 18198
St. Bonaventure University - Russell J. Jandoli School of Journalism and Mass Communication Vol 1: 18199
St. Bonaventure University - Russell J. Jandoli School of Journalism and Mass Communication Vol 1: 18200
Media-Field Award Vol. 1: 5291
Media Medal Vol. 1: 12699
Media Psychology Graduate Student Research Award Vol. 1: 18913
Media Save Art Award Vol. 2: 3964
Media Support Award Vol. 1: 15190
Median Iris Awards Vol. 1: 13240
Mediaweek's Media All-Stars Vol. 1: 221
Mediaweek's Media Plan of the Year Vol. 1: 222
Medical and Dental Postgraduate Research Scholarships Vol. 2: 469
Medical Association of South Africa Awards for Excellence in Medical Reporting (Press, Radio, Television) Vol. 2: 5716
Medical Association of South Africa Branch Award for Meritorious Service Vol. 2: 5717
Medical Association of South Africa Bronze Medal Award Vol. 2: 5718
Medical Association of South Africa Gold Medal Award Vol. 2: 5719
Medical Association of South Africa Group Award for Meritorious Service Vol. 2: 5720
Medical Association of South Africa Pro Meritis Award Vol. 2: 5721
Medical Association of South Africa Silver Medal Award Vol. 2: 5722
Medical Book Prizes Vol. 2: 8988
Medical Crew/Crew Member of the Year Award Vol. 1: 5550
Medical Education Awards Vol. 1: 781
Medical Education Lifetime Achievement Awards Vol. 1: 782
Medical Electives Bursaries Vol. 2: 7334
Medical Executive Award Vol. 1: 1885
Medical Research Grants
Sigrid Juselius Foundation Vol. 2: 1645
SLE Foundation Vol 1: 18554
Medical Services Cross Vol. 2: 5743
Medical Student and Resident Travel Stipend Vol. 1: 608
Medical Student Diabetes Research Fellowship Program Vol. 1: 2140
Medical Student Education; Nancy C. A. Roeske Certificate of Recognition for Excellence in Vol. 1: 3636
Medical Student Essay Awards Vol. 1: 702
Medical Students' Prize Vol. 2: 5723
Medical Technologist of the Year Vol. 1: 3963
Medicinal Chemistry Award Vol. 1: 1771
Medicine in the Media Award; British Medical Association Vol. 2: 7061
Medicine Pipe Bearer's Award Vol. 1: 21576
Medien-Preis Vol. 2: 3038
Medienpreis fur Sprachkultur Vol. 2: 2843
Medieval Archaeology Research Grant Vol. 2: 8943
Medina Award; Jose Toribio Vol. 1: 18415
Mediterranean Games Vol. 2: 2524
Mediterranean Trophy Vol. 2: 3921
Medlar Award Vol. 1: 17641
Medlicott Medal; Norton Vol. 2: 7619
Medwick Memorial Award; Lucille Vol. 1: 17435
Medzinarodna tribuna mladych interpretov/ UNESCO Vol. 2: 5967
Meek Award; Howard B. Vol. 1: 11526
Meeker Award Vol. 1: 20811
Meeking Award for Poetry; Charles Vol. 2: 593
Meering Award Vol. 2: 8290
Meering Award (PANN) Vol. 2: 8292
Mees Medal; C. E .K. Vol. 1: 16793
Meesterschap; Prijs voor Vol. 2: 4916
Meeting Facility of the Year Vol. 1: 12005
Meeting Planner of the Year Vol. 1: 5329
Megaw Memorial Prize; Eric Vol. 2: 7819
Meggers Award; William F.
Optical Society of America Vol. 1: 16794
Society for Applied Spectroscopy Vol 1: 18643
Meggers Project Award; William F. and Edith R. Vol. 1: 2836
Meghnad Saha Medal Vol. 2: 3493
Mehedinti Prize; Simion Vol. 2: 5846
Mehl Award; Institute of Metals Lecturer and Robert Franklin Vol. 1: 13450
Mehl Award; Robert Franklin Vol. 1: 13450
Mehl Honor Lecture Vol. 1: 4149
Mehr Award; Robert I Vol. 1: 3855
Meiklejohn Award; Alexander Vol. 1: 1466
Meillet; Prix Antoine Vol. 2: 1755
Meinzer Award; O. E. Vol. 1: 9953
Meiselman Memorial Award for Painting; Leonard J. Vol. 1: 660
Meiselman Memorial Award for Sculpture; Leonard J. Vol. 1: 661
Meiselman Prize; Leonard J. Vol. 1: 15698
Meisner Foundry Award; Joel Vol. 1: 15698
Meissner Prize; Leo Vol. 1: 13791
Mejia Medal of Merit in the Coffee Industry; Manuel Vol. 2: 1329
Melbourne International Film Festival Shorts Awards Vol. 2: 460
Melcher Book Award; Frederic G. Vol. 1: 20311
Melcher Scholarship; Frederic G. Vol. 1: 5440
Melchers Memorial Medal; Gari Vol. 1: 5139
Meldola Medal and Prize Vol. 2: 8764
Mellon Award; Richard Beatty Vol. 1: 322
Mellon Centre Rome Fellowship; Paul Vol. 2: 7137
Mellon Post-Dissertation Fellowship Vol. 1: 915
Mellor Award; Sam Vol. 1: 15539
Melpomene Outstanding Achievement Award Vol. 1: 13289
Melton Award Vol. 2: 7161
Melville Award; Stanley Vol. 2: 7047
Melville Medal Vol. 1: 4530
Member Association Safety Awards Vol. 1: 21494
Member Awards Vol. 1: 16465
Member Director Award Vol. 1: 14069
Member of Honour Vol. 2: 3028
Member of Note Vol. 1: 17333
Member of the United Way Vol. 1: 7769
Member of the Year
Automotive Oil Change Association Vol. 1: 6119
Caucus for Television Producers, Writers and Directors Vol 1: 7685

Document Management Industries Association Vol 1: 8976
Institute of Packaging Professionals Vol 1: 11026
National Broadcasting Society - Alpha Epsilon Rho Vol 1: 14537
National Railroad Construction and Maintenance Association Vol 1: 15570
National Therapeutic Recreation Society Vol 1: 15874
Ottawa Field-Naturalists' Club Vol 1: 16931
Society of Cable Telecommunications Engineers Vol 1: 19078
World Sidesaddle Federation Vol 1: 21953
Young Women's Christian Association - Barbados Vol 2: 828
Member of the Year Award
American Society of Certified Engineering Technicians Vol. 1: 4279
Dance Masters of America Vol 1: 8740
Infusion Nurses Society Vol 1: 10802
International Association of Assessing Officers Vol 1: 11278
International Camaro Club Vol 1: 11446
International Family Recreation Association Vol 1: 11574
Maltese-American Benevolent Society Vol 1: 13048
National Pig Carvers Association Vol 1: 15500
National Recreational Vehicle Owners Club Vol 1: 15587
Society of Recreation Executives Vol 1: 19288
Member of the Year - Regional Vol. 1: 6707
Member or Fellow Awards Vol. 2: 9078
Member Organization of the Year Vol. 1: 20860
Member Recognition for Excellence in Public Relations Vol. 1: 19555
Member Scholarship Vol. 1: 21674
Member Service Award Vol. 1: 17589
Members and Fellows Lecture Award Vol. 1: 2799
Member's Award Vol. 2: 8666
Members Award Vol. 1: 7199
Members Choice Award Vol. 1: 11660
Members Prize; Institution of Plant Engineers Vol. 2: 7883
Membership Achievement Award Vol. 1: 7361
Membership Award
American Association for Adult and Continuing Education Vol. 1: 949
American Institute of Aeronautics and Astronautics Vol 1: 2687
Membership Awards Vol. 1: 15564
Membership Bursary Vol. 2: 8736
Membership Enrichment Award Vol. 1: 16429
Membership in Omicron Kappa Upsilon Vol. 1: 16705
Membership in the Gorsedd of Bards Vol. 2: 8173
Membership of the City and Guilds of London Institute Vol. 2: 7310
Membership Service Award Vol. 1: 10736
Membre d'honneur Vol. 2: 2239
Membres Honoraires a Vie Vol. 1: 7327
Memorial Award; Bruce F. Cain Vol. 1: 964
Memorial Awards Vol. 1: 20958
Memorial Fellowships Vol. 1: 2882
Memorial Grants Vol. 1: 9103
Memorial Hall of Fame Award Vol. 1: 2860
Memorial Lecturer Award and Honoree(s) Vol. 1: 3137
Memorial Life Membership Awards Vol. 1: 9484
Memorial NAMA Fellowship Vol. 1: 13724
Memorial Plaques Vol. 1: 4
Memorial Scholarship Vol. 1: 21600
Memphis Chapter High School Incentive Scholarship Vol. 1: 19163
Menapace Fellowship in Urban Land Use Law; Ralph C. Vol. 1: 13678
Mendal Memorial Award in Strings and Trophy; The Fred S. Vol. 1: 18301
Mendal Memorial Senior Violin Scholarship and Trophy; Mrs. Clare K. Vol. 1: 18302
Mendel Award; Osborne and Vol. 1: 4162
Mendel-Medaille Vol. 2: 2707
Mendel Medal Vol. 2: 2707
Mendel; Prix Gustave Vol. 2: 1756
Mendelson Memorial Awards; Robin H. Vol. 1: 3955
Mendelssohn Award Vol. 2: 2954
Mendes Award; Chico Vol. 1: 18466
Mendes Prize; Odorico Vol. 2: 1175
Mendoza; Premio Vicente T. Vol. 2: 4544
Menefee Memorial Award; Jim Vol. 1: 16487
Menniger Award; William C. Vol. 1: 3192
Menninger Memorial Award; William C. Vol. 1: 1924
Menon Medical Research Award; Dr. Kamala Vol. 2: 3421
Men's and Women's 18-Under Combined Team Champion Vol. 1: 21205
Men's and Women's Combined Team Vol. 1: 21205
Men's and Women's Combined Team Champion Vol. 1: 21205
Men's and Women's Combined Team Runner-up Champion Vol. 1: 21205
Men's and Women's Combined Team Top Ten Vol. 1: 21205
Men's Garden Clubs of America Scholarship; Gardeners of America/ Vol. 1: 9885
Men's National Championship Cup Finals Vol. 2: 7422
Men's Team Champion Vol. 1: 21205
Men's Team Runner-up Vol. 1: 21205
Men's Team Top Ten Vol. 1: 21205
Mensa International Competitions Vol. 2: 8115
Mensforth International Gold Medal; Sir Eric Vol. 2: 7820
Mental Health in the Workplace Award Vol. 1: 7270
Mental Health Media Awards Vol. 1: 15378
Mentor Vol. 1: 11954
Mentor Award
Association for the Education of Teachers in Science Vol. 1: 5502
Specialty Graphic Imaging Association Vol 1: 19597
Mentor Award in Developmental Psychology Vol. 1: 3668
Mentor-Based Minority Fellowship Vol. 1: 2141
Mentor-Based Postdoctoral Fellowships Vol. 1: 2142
Mentoring Award
American Association of Critical-Care Nurses Vol. 1: 1179
Middle East Studies Association of North America Vol 1: 13383
Mentorship Award Vol. 1: 19378
Mentzer des Rencontres de Chimie Therapeutique; Prix Charles Vol. 2: 2570
Menu Idea Exchange Award Vol. 1: 15626
Menuhin Prize Vol. 2: 8095
Menzel Award; Margaret Vol. 1: 6550
Mercer Award; George Vol. 1: 9139
Mercer Award; Johnny Vol. 1: 13816
Mercer Awards for Innovation; Brian Vol. 2: 8702
Mercer Joint Prize; Thomas T. Vol. 1: 956
Merchandise Mart Hall of Fame Vol. 1: 13299
Merchandiser of the Year Award
National Association of Recording Merchandisers Vol. 1: 14365
Newspaper Association of America Vol 1: 16328
Merchandisers of the Year Vol. 1: 17617
Merchant Manufacturing Medal; M. Eugene Vol. 1: 4531
Merck Award Vol. 2: 5633
Merck Award for Achievement in Poultry Science Vol. 1: 17499
Merck Ehrung; Johann-Heinrich- Vol. 2: 3140
Merck European Thyroid Von-Basedow-Research Prize Vol. 2: 2850
Merck Frosst Award Vol. 1: 7466
Merck Frosst Centre for Therapeutic Research Lecture Award Vol. 1: 7845
Merck Frosst-CSBMCB Travel Awards Vol. 1: 7452
Merck ICAAC Young Investigator Awards Vol. 1: 4137
Merck KGaA Prize Vol. 2: 1486
Merck Preis; Johann-Heinrich- Vol. 2: 2776
Merck Sharp & Dohme Lecture Award Vol. 1: 7845
Merck US Human Health Migraine and Women's Health Research Award; AHS/ Vol. 1: 2388
Mercure Awards; Pierre Vol. 1: 18593
Mercury Communications Award for the Prince's Trust Vol. 2: 9101
Mercury Gold Award Vol. 1: 17827
Mercury Silver Award Vol. 1: 17827
Merghelynck Prize; Arthur Vol. 2: 963
Merit and Participation Certificates Vol. 2: 5186
Merit Award
ACSM Health Promotion Vol. 1: 150
Afro-Asian Book Council Vol 2: 3338
American Baptist Homes and Hospitals Association Vol 1: 1529
American Forage and Grassland Council Vol 1: 2275
American Society for Enology and Viticulture Vol 1: 4063
ASM International Vol 1: 5188
Association for Indiana Media Educators Vol 1: 5385
Association of Consulting Engineers of Canada Vol 1: 5641
Association of European Toxicologists and European Societies of Toxicology Vol 2: 1438
Association of Official Seed Analysts Vol 1: 5801
Decalogue Society of Lawyers Vol 1: 8784
Fur Commission U.S.A. Vol 1: 9838
German Dental Association Vol 2: 2826
Gift from the Heart Foundation Vol 1: 10022
Institute of Landscape Architects of South Africa Vol 2: 5578

International Confederation of Accordionists Vol 2: 736
Lynchburg Historical Foundation Vol 1: 13000
National Association of Hospital Fire Officers Vol 2: 8154
National Junior College Athletic Association Vol 1: 15312
North American Die Casting Association Vol 1: 16430
Scouting Ireland CSI Vol 2: 3708
Society of Cosmetic Chemists Vol 1: 19093
Society of Toxicology Vol 1: 19340
Soil and Water Conservation Society Vol 1: 19389
South African Institute of Forestry Vol 2: 5711
Merit Award for Breeders and Yorkshire Terrier Vol. 1: 22044
Merit Award for Excellent Arrest Vol. 1: 3573
Merit Award for Somali Vol. 1: 19401
Merit Awards Vol. 2: 2246
Merit awards Vol. 1: 17473
Merit Book Awards Vol. 1: 10222
Merit Citation Vol. 1: 17316
MERIT Competition Vol. 2: 7774
MERIT Game Vol. 2: 7774
Merit of Breeding Award Vol. 1: 2149
Merit of Exhibits Vol. 1: 3240
Merit Shop Award of Excellence in Construction Vol. 1: 5236
Meritorious Accountant of the Americas Vol. 1: 11131
Meritorious Achievement Award
American Association of Zoo Keepers Vol. 1: 1490
American Industrial Hygiene Association Vol 1: 2616
Meritorious Awards Vol. 1: 16839
Meritorious Contributions to Psychology on the Part of Nonpsychologists Vol. 1: 18914
Meritorious Honor Award Vol. 1: 20546
Meritorious Service Vol. 1: 19619
Meritorious Service Award
Alpha Omega International Dental Fraternity Vol. 1: 487
American Association for Leisure and Recreation Vol 1: 1032
American Association of Homes and Services for the Aging Vol 1: 1231
American Baseball Coaches Association Vol 1: 1546
American College of Occupational and Environmental Medicine Vol 1: 1908
American Horticultural Society Vol 1: 2533
American Mosquito Control Association Vol 1: 3138
American National Standards Institute Vol 1: 3185
American Park and Recreation Society Vol 1: 3363
American Philatelic Congress Vol 1: 3411
American Public Works Association Vol 1: 3805
Australian Veterinary Association Vol 2: 283
Cranial Academy Vol 1: 8640
Institute of Electrical and Electronics Engineers - Power Engineering Society Vol 1: 10907
Institute of Nuclear Materials Management Vol 1: 11021
International Technology Education Association Vol 1: 12068
National Association for Interpretation Vol 1: 14023
National Christian College Athletic Association Vol 1: 14661
National Council of Examiners for Engineering and Surveying Vol 1: 14798
National Therapeutic Recreation Society Vol 1: 15875
Nebraska Library Association Vol 1: 16069
Occupational and Environmental Medical Association of Canada Vol 1: 16605
Society of Nematologists Vol 1: 19222
Spiritual Science Fellowship Vol 1: 19617
Meritorious Service Cross - Civil Division Vol. 1: 6823
Meritorious Service Cross - Military Division Vol. 1: 6824
Meritorious Service in Communications Award Vol. 1: 4408
Meritorious Service Medal
Defense Logistics Agency - United States Air Force Vol. 1: 8824
National Society, Sons of the American Revolution Vol 1: 15777
Meritorious Service Medal - Civil Division Vol. 1: 6825
Meritorious Service Medal - Military Division Vol. 1: 6826
Meritorious Service to Aviation Award Vol. 1: 14568
Meritorious Service Trophy Vol. 1: 15352
Meritorious Services Medal Vol. 2: 7657
Meritorious Trophy Vol. 1: 6163
Meritorious Unit Citation Vol. 2: 204
Merkelbachprijs Vol. 2: 4690
Merl Baker Best Conference Paper Award Vol. 1: 4057
Merlin Medal and Gift Vol. 2: 6951
Merriam Award; C. Hart Vol. 1: 4499
Merrill Nordic Award; Al Vol. 1: 20812
Merrill-Palmer Citation Award Vol. 1: 21506
Merrit Williamson Best Student Paper Award Vol. 1: 4058
Merryfield Design Award; Fred Vol. 1: 4029
The Merton Bernfield Memorial Award Vol. 1: 3945
Mertz Trophy; Allegra Knapp Vol. 1: 20787
Merwe Award; Marina Van Der Vol. 1: 7225
Merwe Prize; Koos van der Vol. 2: 5515
Merwin Award for Distinguished Service; Richard E. Vol. 1: 10899
Mesa Contemporary Arts Vol. 1: 13305
Meshorer Prize; The Ya'akov Vol. 2: 3751
Messel Medal and Lecture Vol. 2: 9017
Messenger Stake Vol. 1: 20878
Messier Observing Certificate Vol. 1: 22042
Mestaripelimanni, Mestarikansanlaulaja Vol. 2: 1648
Mesucora; Prix Vol. 2: 2000
Metal Bene Merenti Award Vol. 2: 3873
Metal Mining Division Award Vol. 1: 7200
Metallized Package/Label of the Year Vol. 1: 5728
The Metallurgical Society Vol. 1: 13459
Metallurgist of the Year Award Vol. 2: 3459
Metcalf Exemplary Dissertation Award; Larry Vol. 1: 14784
Metcalfe Award Vol. 2: 231
Metcalfe Medallion Vol. 2: 231
Meteorology; Dr. Andrew Thomson Prize in Applied Vol. 1: 7282
Meteorology Prize Vol. 2: 8629
Metiro pro Societate Vol. 2: 5381
MetLife Foundation Extended Collaboration Grants for Artists; TCG/ Vol. 1: 20055
Metlife Foundation MindAlert Awards; ASA- Vol. 1: 4636
Metras Trophy; J. P. Vol. 1: 7226
Metro Awards Vol. 1: 21616
Metropolitan Award Vol. 1: 14087
Metropolitan Opera National Council Auditions Vol. 1: 13318
Meucci Award Vol. 1: 12249
Meurand; Prix Vol. 2: 1722
Mewaldt-King Student Research Award Vol. 1: 8492
Mexican Order of the Aztec Eagle Vol. 2: 4567
Mexican Prize Vol. 2: 2632
Mexinox Prize Vol. 2: 4640
Meyer Lectureship; Adolf Vol. 1: 3629
Meyer Medaille; Hans Vol. 2: 2685
Meyer Memorial Award; Irving Vol. 1: 3116
Meyer Memorial Medal; Frank N. Vol. 1: 8665
Meyer Outstanding Teacher Awards; Agnes Vol. 1: 21459
Meyer Prize; Carl S. Vol. 1: 18543
Meyer Prize; Ernst Vol. 2: 6384
Meyer-Whitworth Award Vol. 2: 6754
Meyerhof Award; Geofrey G. Vol. 1: 7128
Meyers Award; John F.
National Catholic Educational Association Vol. 1: 14606
National Catholic Educational Association Vol 1: 14615
Meyerson Award; Dean Vol. 1: 4782
Meyerson Award; Stanley C. Vol. 1: 16813
Mezinarodni hudebni soutez Prazske jaro Vol. 2: 1434
Mezinarodni rozhlasova soutez Mladych hudebniku Concertino Praga Vol. 2: 1420
Mezinarodni Televizni Festival Zlata Praha Vol. 2: 1424
MGCA Beautification Certificate Vol. 1: 9888
MGCA Golden Quill Award Vol. 1: 9889
MIA Music Awards Vol. 2: 8147
The Michael Vol. 1: 16184
Michael Guthrie Prize Vol. 2: 7648
Michael Shaara Award Vol. 1: 12957
Michaelangelo Award Vol. 1: 12254
Michaels Memorial Film Award; John Vol. 1: 6372
Michal Award for Outstanding Emerging Director; Ray Vol. 1: 10166
Michaut; Prix Narcisse Vol. 2: 2193
Michel Award; Dr. Vol. 1: 11666
Michelbacher Prize Vol. 1: 7624
Michell Medal; A. G. M. Vol. 2: 411
Michell Medal; J.H. Vol. 2: 70
Michels New Investigator Award; Eugene Vol. 1: 3494
Michelson Award; Albert A. Vol. 1: 7619
Michelson - Morley Award Vol. 1: 7619
Michener Award Vol. 1: 13329
Michener Conservation Award; Roland Vol. 1: 7541
Michener de Journalism; Prix Vol. 1: 13329
Michener-Deacon Fellowship Vol. 1: 13329
Michener Four-Month Fellowships Vol. 1: 13330
Michener - Paul Engle Fellowship; James A. Vol. 1: 12191
Michener Prize in Writing Award; James Vol. 1: 14785
Michigan Hall of Fame Vol. 1: 13348

Michigan Industrial Hygiene Society Award for Authorship Vol. 1: 2617
Mick Aston Presentation Award Vol. 2: 6921
Mickle Award; D. Grant Vol. 1: 20164
Microcomputer in the Media Center Award Vol. 1: 1416
Micromedex/ENA Emergency Nursing Research Award Vol. 1: 9244
Miculescu Prize; Constantin Vol. 2: 5847
Mid-America Publishers Association (MAPA) Awards Program Vol. 1: 13368
Mid American Award Vol. 1: 18923
Mid Career Award Vol. 1: 2051
Midalja ghall-Qadi tar-Repubblika Vol. 2: 4455
Midalja ghall-Qlubija Vol. 2: 4454
Middle School Teachers of Excellence in Social Studies Vol. 1: 13156
Middle School Teaching Award Vol. 1: 14096
Middlebrooks Award; Thomas A. Vol. 1: 4341
Middlemore Award Vol. 2: 7075
Middleton Award; William S. Vol. 1: 20561
Middletown Pee Wee Football Scholarship Award Vol. 1: 13388
Midland Assurance Trophy Vol. 2: 8720
Midwest Bank Excellence in Teaching Award (School of Education) Vol. 1: 8990
Midwest Section Founder's Award Vol. 1: 19316
Miedzynarodowe Triennale Grafiki Krakow Vol. 2: 5314
Miedzynarodowy Konkurs Kompozytorski im-Witolda Lutoslawskiego Vol. 2: 5387
Miescher Prize; Friedrich Vol. 2: 6510
Migel Medal for Outstanding Service to Blind Persons Vol. 1: 2303
Mignet Diploma; Henry Vol. 2: 6344
Mignott Scholarship; T.G. Vol. 2: 4073
Mignott Trophy; T.G. Vol. 2: 4074
Migraine and Women's Health Research Award; AHS/Merck US Human Health Vol. 1: 2388
Mike Gribble Peel of Laughter Award Vol. 1: 16952
Mikeldi de Oro Vol. 2: 6061
Mikeldi Plata Vol. 2: 6061
Mikoviny Medal; Samuel Vol. 2: 3258
Milankovitch Medal; Milutin Vol. 2: 2313
Milburn Award; C. H. Vol. 2: 7076
Mildenberger Outstanding NESDA Officer Award; Richard Vol. 1: 14926
Mildenberger Prize; Kenneth W. Vol. 1: 13563
Mildon Award; James R. Vol. 1: 10924
Miles and Shirley Fisherman Foundation Awards for Clinical Research Vol. 1: 9711
Miles - Marschall International Award Vol. 1: 2108
Milestone Award Vol. 1: 15614
Militaire Willems-Orde Vol. 2: 4707
Military Astronautics Award Vol. 1: 1505
Military Cross Vol. 2: 7253
Military Medal for Gallantry Vol. 2: 3653
Military Merit Medal Vol. 2: 5744
Military Order of William Vol. 2: 4707
Military Photographer of the Year Vol. 1: 15540
Military Psychology Student Paper Award Vol. 1: 3723
Military Service Medal Vol. 2: 3215
Military Service Star Vol. 2: 3216
The Military Star Vol. 2: 3654
Miljovernpris Vol. 2: 5171
Milk Industry Foundation and Kraft General Foods Teaching Award in Dairy Science Vol. 1: 2109
Milkweed National Fiction Prize Vol. 1: 13421
Milkweed Prize for Children's Literature Vol. 1: 13422
Millar Award Vol. 2: 7293
Millar Award for Innovative Approaches to Adolescent Health Care; Hilary E. C. Vol. 1: 18618
Millbrook-Proctor and Gamble Student Service Vol. 1: 13424
Millennium Residencies in Production Animal Medicine Vol. 2: 8495
Millennium Volunteer Award Vol. 2: 9182
Miller Award; Carroll R. Vol. 1: 15495
Miller Award/Chapter Service Awards; Susan E. Vol. 1: 18467
Miller Award; Douglas Vol. 1: 6970
Miller Award; Elizabeth McWilliams Vol. 1: 18500
Miller Award for Excellence in Cold Planning; John A. Vol. 1: 5206
Miller Award; Frances Hubbs Vol. 1: 8898
Miller Award; George A. Vol. 1: 3687
Miller Award; Merl K. Vol. 1: 4030
Miller Award; Muriel McLatchie Vol. 1: 5756
Miller Cartographic Medal; O. M. Vol. 1: 2333
Miller Distinguished Service Award; George J. Vol. 1: 14767
Miller Essay Prizes and Research Fellowships; John William Vol. 1: 13426
Miller International Award; S. Ray Vol. 1: 11337
Miller Legal Services Award; Loren Vol. 1: 19760
Miller Lite Women's Sports Journalism Awards Vol. 1: 21812
Miller Medal; Willet G. Vol. 1: 18170
Miller Memorial Award; Barse Vol. 1: 4860
Miller Memorial Award; Monte Vol. 2: 292
Miller Memorial Lecture Award; Samuel Charles Vol. 1: 737
Miller Memorial Medal Award; Samuel Wylie Vol. 1: 4889
Miller Memorial Prize; Robert A. Vol. 1: 8155
Miller Memoriam; Jane Vol. 1: 8216
Miller Outstanding Doctoral Dissertation Award; Gerald R. Vol. 1: 14713
Miller; Prix Louis P. Vol. 2: 2179
Miller Prizes Vol. 2: 7775
Miller Scholarship; Cheryl Allyn Vol. 1: 19379
Miller Service Award; Isabel Vol. 1: 18538
Miller Story Teller Award; Ron Vol. 1: 16973
Milli Award Vol. 2: 152
Millie Award Vol. 1: 8985
Millier; Prix Marcelle Vol. 2: 2183
Millikan Medal; Robert A. Vol. 1: 1376
Million Mile Club Award Vol. 1: 15656
Million Miler Award for Safety Excellence
Specialized Carriers and Rigging Association Vol. 1: 19582
Specialized Carriers and Rigging Association Vol 1: 19585
Millot; Fondation Georges Vol. 2: 1873
Millot; Prix Georges Vol. 2: 2406
Mills Award; C. Wright Vol. 1: 18926
Mills Award for Meritorious Service Vol. 1: 1861
Mills Award; Miriam Vol. 1: 17452
Mills Outstanding Contribution to Emergency Medicine; James D. Vol. 1: 1861
Millson Award for Invention; Henry E. Vol. 1: 1456
Milne Memorial Award; Jack Vol. 1: 558
Milner Award Vol. 1: 9804
Milton E. Adsjt in Veterinary Medicine Award; HeSCA/ Vol. 1: 10333
Mimografieprijs Amsterdam Vol. 2: 4691
Minah Distinguished Service Award; Theodore W. Vol. 1: 14131
Minarikovo Odlicje Vol. 2: 5990
Minasian Award; George T. Vol. 1: 323
Mine Safety Appliance Company Student Section Scholarship Award Vol. 1: 4605
Miner Award; Neil A. Vol. 1: 14238
Mineral Economics Award Vol. 1: 2822
Mineral Industry Education Award Vol. 1: 2823
Mineralogical Society of America Award Vol. 1: 13436
Minerva Awards Vol. 1: 16255
Mini Rod Puller of the Year Vol. 1: 15885
Mini Sled of the Year Vol. 1: 15886
Mining and Exploration Division Distinguished Service Award Vol. 1: 18817
Minister for International Trade Challenge Cup Vol. 1: 9687
Minister of National Defense Prize Vol. 2: 5296
Minister of Transport's Award in Transport Vol. 2: 5007
Ministere des Affaires etrangeres et du Commerce international Vol. 1: 9686
Minister's Award for Consular Excellence Vol. 1: 9688
Minister's Award for Foreign Policy Excellence Vol. 1: 9689
Ministry of Defence Medal Vol. 2: 565
Ministry of Urban Development, Culture and Sports of North Rhine-Westphalia Award Vol. 2: 2977
Ministry Support Award Vol. 1: 6270
Mink Award; Walter D. Vol. 1: 13482
Minkowski Prize Vol. 2: 2739
Minks Award; Nancy Vol. 1: 2551
Minneapolis Foundation Vol. 1: 13588
Minnesmedaljen i guld Vol. 2: 6194
Minnesota Award Vol. 1: 21071
Minnesota Awards for Human Rights Vol. 1: 13465
Minnesota Blue Award Vol. 1: 2558
Minnesota Gold Award Vol. 1: 2559
Minnesota International Human Rights Award Vol. 1: 13465
Minnesota Masonry Project Awards Vol. 1: 13469
Minnesota Voices Project Vol. 1: 16198
Minor League Executive of the Year Vol. 1: 19657
Minor League Manager of the Year Vol. 1: 19658
Minor League Player of the Year Vol. 1: 19659
Minority Achievement Award Vol. 1: 3495
Minority Business; Dun & Bradstreet Award for Outstanding Service to Vol. 1: 17938
Minority Business Leadership Awards Vol. 1: 15389
Minority Initiatives Award Vol. 1: 3496
Minority Issues Award Vol. 1: 8773
Minority Scholarship Vol. 1: 19380
Minority Scientist Development Award Vol. 1: 2416

Minority Summer Fellowship Award; Pfizer Vol. 1: 1898
Minority Travel Fellowship Awards Vol. 1: 3522
Minshall Award; Lewis Vol. 2: 7523
Minter Award; Jerry B. Vol. 1: 17840
Mintz Award; Morton Vol. 1: 21439
Minute Award Vol. 1: 15009
Minuteman Medal Vol. 1: 15778
Minville; Prix Esdras- Vol. 1: 18608
Miriam Dudley Award for Bibliographic Instruction Vol. 1: 5607
Mirkin Service Award; A. J. Vol. 1: 5478
Mirlo Poetry Prize; Josue Vol. 2: 4530
Mische Global Service Award; Jerry Vol. 1: 10044
Misener Award; Chandler - Vol. 1: 11241
Mishima Medal Vol. 2: 4144
Miss America Vol. 1: 13495
Miss America Women's Achievement Award Vol. 1: 13496
Miss Dance of Great Britain Vol. 2: 7917
"Miss Dorothy" Heart Vol. 1: 5586
Miss Exotic World Contest Vol. 1: 9373
Miss Galaxy Vol. 1: 9853
Miss Indian World Vol. 1: 9900
Miss Pioneer Oregon Scholarship Vol. 1: 19412
Miss Tall International Vol. 1: 19909
Miss Teen USA Vol. 1: 13498
Miss Teen USA Pageant Vol. 1: 13498
Miss Universe Vol. 1: 13499
Miss Universe Pageant Vol. 1: 13499
Miss USA Vol. 1: 13500
Miss USA Pageant Vol. 1: 13500
Missarel; Prix Nicolas Vol. 2: 2194
Missile Systems Award Vol. 1: 2688
Mission Accomplished Creative Commercial Production Awards Vol. 1: 6722
Mission Award Vol. 1: 8280
Mission Support Trophy Vol. 1: 15176
Mississippi-Alabama Sea Gran Consortium Grants Vol. 1: 13502
Mississippi Poetry Society Award Vol. 1: 15010
Missouri Honor Awards Vol. 1: 21078
Missouri Lifestyle Journalism Award Vol. 1: 21079
Missouri Rural Foundation Awards Vol. 1: 13539
Missouri Southern International Piano Competition Vol. 1: 13543
Missouri State Poetry Society Award Vol. 1: 15011
Missouri Teacher of the Year Program Vol. 1: 13535
Mita Society for Library and Information Science Prize Vol. 2: 4252
Mita Toshokan Joho Gakkai-Sho Vol. 2: 4252
Mitch Trubitt Community Asthma Champion Award Vol. 1: 7870
Mitchell Award for C4 Excellence; General Billy Vol. 1: 346
Mitchell Award; Gen. Billy Vol. 1: 346
Mitchell Award; H. L. Vol. 1: 19502
Mitchell Award; James G. Vol. 1: 15800
Mitchell Award; S. Weir Vol. 1: 703
Mitchell Bowl
Canadian Interuniversity Sport Vol. 1: 7221
Canadian Interuniversity Sport Vol 1: 7233
Mitchell City of Calgary Book Prize; W.O. Vol. 1: 21986
Mitchell Community Development Award; Jan Vol. 1: 15129
Mitchell Convention Travel Grant; Ronald W. Vol. 1: 11868
Mitchell Memorial Intermediate Violin Scholarship and Trophy; Robert C. Vol. 1: 18303
Mitchell National Debate Trophy; Harland B. Vol. 1: 15105
Mitchell Prize; Lillias Vol. 2: 3695
Mitchell Young Extension Worker Award; Nolan Vol. 1: 4220
Mitchell Young Extension Worker Award; Nolan Vol. 1: 4230
Mitford Memorial Scholarship Vol. 1: 13231
Mitra Memorial Lecture; Sisir Kumar Vol. 2: 3494
Mitry Award; Jean Vol. 2: 4038
Mitscherlich-Denkmunze; Alexander- Vol. 2: 2652
Mittasch-Medaille; Alwin Vol. 2: 2914
Mittelstadt Ski Jumping Officials Award Vol. 1: 20813
Mittlemann Achievement Award Vol. 1: 10656
Mixed Blood versus America Vol. 1: 13545
Mizel Memorial Exhibit Award; Menachem Chaim and Simcha Tova Vol. 1: 3207
MLA Award for Distinguished Public Service Vol. 1: 13262
MLA Research, Development and Demonstration Projects Awards Vol. 1: 13263
MLA Scholarship for Minority Students Vol. 1: 13264
MLA Scholarships and Fellowships Vol. 1: 13264
MLM Company of the Year Vol. 1: 13667
MMCA Annual Scholarship Vol. 1: 13353
Mobil Children's Culture Award Vol. 2: 4254
Mobil Five-Star Award Vol. 1: 9378
Mobil Music Award Vol. 2: 4255
Mobius Advertising Awards
The Mobius Awards Vol. 1: 13551
US International Film and Video Festival Vol 1: 21142
Mobius Broadcasting Awards Vol. 1: 21142
Mobral Journalism Prize Vol. 2: 1144
MOC Cup Vol. 2: 8120
Modeen Medal; A. E. Vol. 2: 1623
Modisette Award Vol. 1: 12942
Mody-Unichem Prize for Research in Cardiology, Neurology and Gastroenterology; Amrut Vol. 2: 3422
Mody-Unichem Prize for Research in Maternal and Child Health and Chest Diseases; Amrut Vol. 2: 3423
Moe Prize for Catalogs of Distinction in the Arts; Henry Allen Vol. 1: 16290
Moe Prize in the Humanities; Henry Allen Vol. 1: 3440
Moffat - Frank E. Nichol Harbor and Coastal Engineering Award; John G. Vol. 1: 4342
Moffat Larry Lillo Award; John Vol. 1: 10166
Moffitt Memorial Human Rights Awards; Letelier - Vol. 1: 10830
Mohawk-Hudson Regional Art Exhibition Award Vol. 1: 18333
Mohr Medal; William Vol. 1: 5045
Moir Medal; James Vol. 2: 5692
Moisseiff Award Vol. 1: 4343
Molesworth Award; Jack Vol. 1: 8357
Molfenter-Preis der Landeshauptstadt Stuttgart/Galerie; Hans- Vol. 2: 3103
Molins Award; Desmond Vol. 2: 7382
Moll Memorial Quality Management Award; Dale C. Vol. 1: 8440
Mollenhoff Award for Excellence in Investigative Reporting; Clark Vol. 1: 9829
Moller/AGO Award in Choral Competition Vol. 1: 2368
Molly Award Vol. 1: 10359
Molodovsky Award; Nicholas Vol. 1: 5398
Mols Award; Herbert Joseph Vol. 1: 559
Molteno Medal Awards of Excellence and Merit Vol. 2: 5526
Monash Medal; John Vol. 2: 412
Monbinne; Prix Vol. 2: 1723
Moncado Prizes for Best Article Vol. 1: 18802
Moncrieff Prize; Scott Vol. 2: 8973
Mond Lectureship; Ludwig Vol. 2: 8765
Mondor; Fondation Henri Vol. 2: 1882
Mondor; Prix Henri Vol. 2: 2161
Mondriaan Lecture; Piet Vol. 2: 4906
Monell Medal and the Ambrose Monell Prize for Distinguished Service in Mineral Technology; Ambrose Vol. 1: 8244
Monetary Gifts Vol. 2: 7016
Money for Women/Barbara Deming Memorial Fund Grants Vol. 1: 13582
Monica Browning Award Vol. 1: 5112
Monk International Jazz Competition; Thelonious Vol. 1: 13584
Monk International Jazz Instrumental Competition; Thelonious Vol. 1: 13584
Monk International Jazz Piano Competition; Thelonious Vol. 1: 13584
Monod; Prix Gabriel Vol. 2: 2047
Monpetit; Prix Michel Vol. 2: 2001
Monro Memorial Cup; George Vol. 2: 8559
Monroe Library Adult Services Award; Margaret E. Vol. 1: 17942
Monsanto Crop Science Distinguished Career Award Vol. 1: 8666
Montagu Human Nurturance Award; Ashley Vol. 1: 10604
Montague Distinguished Resident Award in Radiation Oncology; Eleanor Vol. 1: 1073
Montaigne Prize Vol. 2: 3086
Montald; Prix Constant Vol. 2: 990
Montana Memorial Prize; Pietro and Alfrieda Vol. 1: 15698
Montana New Zealand Book Awards Vol. 2: 4957
Montana New Zealand Book Awards Vol. 2: 4959
Monte Carlo International Forum for New Images Imagina Vol. 2: 4668
Monte Carlo International Prize of Contemporary Art Vol. 2: 4658
Montefiore Foundation Prize; George Vol. 2: 898
Montefiore; Prix de la Fondation George Vol. 2: 898
Monteiro; Premio Manuel Alves Vol. 2: 5416
Monteiro Prize; Manuel Alves Vol. 2: 5416
Montequin Fellowship; Edilia and Francois-Auguste de Vol. 1: 19025
Montgolfier Diploma Vol. 2: 6345
Montgolfier Trophy Vol. 1: 12849
Montgomery Award; Morley/ Vol. 1: 6196
Montgomery Distinguished Service Award; Reid H. Vol. 1: 8175
Montgomery Doctoral Grant; Merle Vol. 1: 13662
Montgomery Medal Vol. 1: 15176
Montgomery Memorial Award Vol. 1: 7042

Monthly Most Valuable Player Award Vol. 1: 6438
Montreal International Festival of Films on Art Vol. 1: 11613
Montreal International Festival of New Cinema and Video Vol. 1: 13598
Montreal International Fireworks Competition Vol. 1: 13600
Montreal Medal Vol. 1: 7846
Montreal World Film Festival Vol. 1: 13607
Montreux International Choral Festival Vol. 2: 6488
Mookerjee Memorial Award; Asutosh Vol. 2: 3536
Moon Award; A. Ramsay Vol. 2: 660
Mooney Distinguished Technology Award; Melvin Vol. 1: 1772
Moore Alumni Award; Mary Vol. 1: 5113
Moore Award Vol. 1: 1287
Moore Award for Outstanding New Academic Faculty Member; Margaret L. Vol. 1: 3497
Moore Award for Voluntary Service; Clarence H. Vol. 1: 17059
Moore Award; Harry T. Vol. 1: 8702
Moore Award; Royal N. Vol. 1: 13084
Moore Award; Velma Vol. 1: 16274
Moore Award; Virginia P. Vol. 1: 6804
Moore Distinguished Service Award; Dr. Richard L. Vol. 1: 3348
Moore Medal for Paleontology; Raymond C. Vol. 1: 18844
Moore Medal; George Vol. 2: 8560
Moore Medal; Leo B. Vol. 1: 19747
Moore Medal; Patrick Vol. 2: 7054
Moore Memorial Award; Barrington Vol. 1: 18972
Moore Memorial Award; Lucy B. Vol. 1: 4861
Moore Memorial Award; Robert P. Vol. 1: 14515
Moore Prize; Glover Vol. 1: 13508
Moore Writer-in-Washington; Jenny McKean Vol. 1: 13610
Moose Moss Age Group Diving Coach of the Year Award Vol. 1: 20397
Moragas; Premi Ricard Vol. 2: 6005
Moral Leadership Award Vol. 1: 15317
Moran Medal for Statistical Science Vol. 2: 129
Moran National Portrait Prize; Doug Vol. 2: 630
Moran Portraiture Prize; Douglas J. Vol. 2: 630
Morand; Grand Prix de Litterature Paul Vol. 2: 2102
Morando Lifetime Achievement Award; Rocco V. Vol. 1: 14216
Mordica Memorial Award Vol. 1: 21659
More Medal for Book Collecting; Sir Thomas Vol. 1: 10037
Morelli; Fondazione Eugenio Vol. 2: 3816
Moreno Award; Perito Francisco P. Vol. 2: 28
Morey Award; George W. Vol. 1: 1690
Morey Book Award; Charles Rufus Vol. 1: 8149
Morgan Award; Frederick C. Vol. 1: 10339
Morgan Award; Joseph F. Vol. 1: 18727
Morgan Individual Achievement Award; Frederick C. Vol. 1: 10339
Morgan Medal; Thomas Hunt Vol. 1: 9933
Morgan Prize for Outstanding Research in Mathematics by an Undergraduate Student; Frank and Brennie Vol. 1: 18738
Morgan Scholarship; Hazel B. Vol. 1: 13662
Morgenthau Award; Hans J. Vol. 1: 14704
Morgenthau Memorial Award; Hans J. Vol. 1: 14704
Morgotch Memorial Award; Larry Vol. 1: 16040
Morguard Literary Award Vol. 1: 17900
Morin; Prix Victor- Vol. 1: 18615
Morison Prize; Samuel Eliot Vol. 1: 18803
Morisset; Prix Gerard- Vol. 1: 17796
Morlan Faculty Secretary Award; Robert L. Vol. 1: 16700
Morley Award; Colonel Bill Vol. 1: 5113
Morley Award; Elise Vol. 1: 5112
Morley/Montgomery Award Vol. 1: 6196
Morneau Distinguished Service Award; Robert F. Vol. 1: 14604
Morrell Memorial Award; David Vol. 1: 19696
Morrill Volunteer Award; Lisa Vol. 1: 6465
Morris Award; Arthur J. Vol. 1: 8456
Morris Award; Old Tom Vol. 1: 10068
Morris Award; Robert Vol. 1: 21516
Morris Humanitarian Award; AAMI Foundation/ ACCE Robert L. Vol. 1: 5495
Morris Memorial Prize; Lindsay Vol. 1: 15698
Morris Memorial Trophy; Ted Vol. 1: 7227
Morris Prize Article Contest; Gerald E. Vol. 1: 13734
Morris Scholarship; Ruth Dean Vol. 1: 13662
Morris Student Research Award; Charles R. Vol. 1: 728
Morris Sustaining Member of the Year Award; J. W. Vol. 1: 18992
Morrison Award Vol. 1: 4262
Morrison Award; Francis Vol. 1: 18270
Morrison Book Prize Vol. 1: 20100
Morrison Communicator Award; Thomas Vol. 1: 20547
Morrison Information Management Award; Thomas Vol. 1: 20547
Morrison Jr. Award; Major Gen. John E. Vol. 1: 15384
Morrison Trophy; W. A. Vol. 2: 5062
Morrow Award; Elizabeth Cutter Vol. 1: 22096
Morrow Public Outreach Award; Douglas S. Vol. 1: 20842
MORS Prize Vol. 1: 13407
Morse Lectureship Award; Philip McCord Vol. 1: 11077
Morse Medal; Samuel Finley Breese Vol. 1: 2334
Morse Writer's Award; Robert T. Vol. 1: 3630
Morsey Award; David Vol. 1: 11469
Mortar Board Chapter Citation Award Vol. 1: 13612
Mortar Board Honorary Member Vol. 1: 13613
Mortimer Memorial Silver Plated Trophy; James Vol. 1: 21589
Morton Award; J. Sterling Vol. 1: 13949
Morton Lecture Vol. 2: 6870
Mosaic Foundation Best of the Festival Award Vol. 1: 4970
Mosby Award; Henry S. Vol. 1: 15950
Moscow International Film Festival Vol. 2: 5895
Moseley Award; Harry G. Vol. 1: 239
Moser Memorial Trophy; Mike Vol. 1: 7228
Mosher and Frederick C. Mosher Award; William E. Vol. 1: 4185
Most Active Woman Award Vol. 1: 13908
Most Ancient and Most Noble Order of the Thistle Vol. 2: 7254
Most Beautiful and the Best Children's Book of Spring, Summer, Autumn, Winter in Slovakia Vol. 2: 5960
Most Beautiful Book in Slovenia Vol. 2: 5985
Most Beautiful House in America Competition Vol. 1: 7874
Most Beautiful House in the World Competition Vol. 1: 7874
Most Colorful Walkaloosa Vol. 1: 21426
Most Distinguished Greek American Vol. 1: 20334
Most Distinguished Order of St. Michael and St. George Vol. 2: 7255
Most Distinguished Project Award Vol. 1: 2315
Most Excellent Order of the British Empire Vol. 2: 7256
Most Honourable Order of the Bath Vol. 2: 7257
Most Improved Award Vol. 1: 17757
Most Improved Bowler Vol. 1: 17870
Most Improved Championship Driver Award Vol. 1: 20423
Most Improved Chapter of the Year Vol. 1: 14538
Most Improved Driver Vol. 1: 11755
Most Improved Driver Award Vol. 1: 20424
Most Improved Golfer Vol. 1: 13932
Most Improved Golfer Men/Women Pros Vol. 1: 10071
Most Improved Player Vol. 1: 14506
Most Improved Pros Vol. 1: 19980
Most Improved Sprint Car Driver Award Vol. 1: 20424
Most Interesting Surveying Project of the Year Award Vol. 1: 15759
Most Meritorious Capture Award Vol. 2: 243
Most Noble Order of the Garter Vol. 2: 7258
Most Outstanding Abstract Award Vol. 1: 3934
Most Outstanding Catholic War Veteran Vol. 1: 7675
Most Outstanding Educational Program Vol. 1: 17896
Most Outstanding Post of the Year Award Vol. 1: 7676
Most Outstanding Wrestler Vol. 1: 15984
Most Participants Award Vol. 1: 15828
Most Popular Convention Award Vol. 1: 3105
Most Realistic Tattoo Vol. 1: 15853
Most Registrations Vol. 1: 15220
Most Valuable Member Award Vol. 1: 11279
Most Valuable Player
Continental Basketball Association Vol. 1: 8482
National Wheelchair Basketball Association Vol 1: 15944
Most Valuable Player Award Vol. 1: 6439
Most Valuable Player Award - Maurice Podoloff Trophy Vol. 1: 14507
Most Valuable Player in the Rose Bowl Vol. 1: 524
Most Versatile Horse Award Vol. 1: 8217
Mostra Cinematografica Internazionale - La Natura, l'Uomo e il suo Ambiente Vol. 2: 3972
Mostra de Valencia, Palmero de Oro Vol. 2: 6073
Moten Award; Ollie B. Vol. 1: 1827
MOTESZ-Dij Vol. 2: 3234
MOTESZ Prize Vol. 2: 3234
Mother/Father of the Year Award Vol. 1: 15398

Mother of All Vinegar Contest Vol. 1: 21370
Mother of the Humanitarian Scholarship Vol. 1: 17031
Mother of the Year Vol. 1: 3143
Motion Picture Academy Awards/Television Emmy Awards: Black Tie Award Vol. 1: 11634
Motley EMT of the Year Award; Robert E. Vol. 1: 14217
Motor Carrier Officer of the Year Vol. 1: 13346
Motor Trend Car of the Year Vol. 1: 13626
Motor Trend Import Car of the Year Vol. 1: 13627
Motor Trend Truck of the Year Vol. 1: 13628
Motorcycle Safety Foundation Awards Program Vol. 1: 13630
Motru prize; Constantin Radulescu Vol. 2: 5848
Mott, Jr. Awards Program; William Penn Vol. 1: 15725
Mott Jr. Park Leadership Award; William Penn Vol. 1: 15491
Mott-Kappa Tau Alpha Research Award; Frank Luther Vol. 1: 21080
Mott - Kappa Tau Alpha Research/Book Award; Frank Luther Vol. 1: 12519
Mott Macdonald Award Vol. 2: 7876
Mott Medal; Charles S. Vol. 1: 9921
Mott Scholarship; Gerald O. Vol. 1: 8667
Mounfield Award Vol. 2: 7696
Mountainfilm in Telluride Vol. 1: 13647
Mountbatten Medal Vol. 2: 8626
Mountbatten Premium Vol. 2: 7808
Mounte Carlo Television Festival Vol. 2: 4669
Movie Worsts Awards Vol. 1: 10276
Moye; Prix Marcel Vol. 2: 2560
Moyer Resident Award; Carl A. Vol. 1: 1603
Moynihan Cup; Laura Vol. 1: 20894
Mozart International Piano Competition Vol. 2: 46
Mozart Medal Vol. 2: 4516
Mozart Opera Prize Vol. 2: 803
Mozart-Prize Vol. 2: 6365
Mozart Scholarship; The Boyle Memorial Senior Hayden and Vol. 1: 18276
Mozart Scholarship; The Frances England Intermediate Hayden and Vol. 1: 18284
MPA Kelly Awards Vol. 1: 13015
MPD Outstanding Young Engineer Award Vol. 1: 18818
MPEC Award Vol. 1: 13461
MPI Planner of the Year Vol. 1: 13282
MPI Supplier of the Year Vol. 1: 13283
MPT Benchmark Award Vol. 1: 2386
Mr. Blackwell's Hall of Fame Vol. 1: 13655
Mr. H.G. Van der Vies Prize Vol. 2: 4931
Mr. OX5 Vol. 1: 16990
Mr. Pi Kappa Phi Vol. 1: 17317
Mrazec Prize; Ludovic Vol. 2: 5849
Mrazik-Cleaver Canadian Picture Book Award; Elizabeth Vol. 2: 6390
MRCA Foundation Scholarship Grants Vol. 1: 13398
Mrost Prize; Mischa Vol. 2: 5693
Mrozowski Award; Stanislaw W. Vol. 1: 1646
MRS Medalist Program Vol. 1: 13182
MS Achievement Award Vol. 1: 15399
MS Patient Achievement Award Vol. 1: 15399
MS-Prize Vol. 2: 1448
MS Public Education Awards Vol. 1: 15400
MSD AGVET AABP Award for Excellence in Preventive Veterinary Medicine Beef Cattle Vol. 1: 1126
MSD AGVET AABP Award for Excellence in Preventive Veterinary Medicine Dairy Cattle Vol. 1: 1127
MSD-EACR Research Awards Vol. 2: 7456
MSI Annual Doctoral Dissertation Proposal Award Vol. 1: 13120
MSMA Community Service Award Vol. 1: 13513
MSMA Distinguished Service Award Vol. 1: 13025
MTNA Collegiate Artist Competition Vol. 1: 13703
MTNA Junior High School Piano Competition Vol. 1: 13704
MTNA Junior Performance Competitions Vol. 1: 13705
MTNA National Student Composition Contest Vol. 1: 13708
MTNA Senior Performance Competition Vol. 1: 13706
MTNA-Shepherd Distinguished Composer of the Year Award Vol. 1: 13707
MTNA Student Composition Competition Vol. 1: 13708
MTS Special Commendation Vol. 1: 13112
MTTA Award Vol. 2: 8108
MTTA/IEE Award Vol. 2: 7821
Mu Phi Epsilon Annual Grants and Scholarships Vol. 1: 13662
Mu Phi Epsilon International Competition Vol. 1: 13660
Mudd Award for Studies in Basic Microbiology; Stuart Vol. 2: 453
Mudge Citation; Isadore Gilbert Vol. 1: 17943
Mudge - R. R. Bowker Award; Isadore Gilbert Vol. 1: 17943
Muellen Whirly-Girls Scholarship; Doris Vol. 1: 21599
Mueller Human Services Award; Sister Mary Lea Vol. 1: 8181
Mueller Lecture Award; James I. Vol. 1: 1691
Mueller Medal Vol. 2: 143
MUFSO Innovator Award Vol. 1: 16012
Muhlmann Prize; Maria and Eric Vol. 1: 6011
Muir Award; John
Sierra Club Vol. 1: 18468
Venture Scotland Vol 2: 9183
Mullard Award Vol. 2: 8701
Mullen National Arts and Humanities Award; Dorothy Vol. 1: 15576
Muller Award Vol. 2: 5402
Muller Jr. Undergraduate Business Plan Competition; John H. Vol. 1: 6183
Muller Lectureship; Hugo Vol. 2: 8766
Muller Prize; Dr. Erich Vol. 2: 2827
Mullins Award; Nicholas C. Vol. 1: 18858
Multatuliprijs Vol. 2: 4692
Multi-Event Outstanding Women Award Vol. 1: 21243
Multidisciplinary Design Optimization Award Vol. 1: 2689
Multimedia Award Vol. 2: 8854
Multinational Force and Observers Medal Vol. 1: 8825
Mumford Prize; Erika Vol. 1: 16114
Mumm International Award; Norbert Gerbier- Vol. 2: 6572
Mumpton Memorial Award; Dick Vol. 1: 20635
Munasinghe Memorial Award; T. P. de S. Vol. 2: 6121
Mundt Trophy; Senator Karl E. Vol. 1: 15106
Mungo Park Medal Vol. 2: 8683
Munich International Filmschool Festival Vol. 2: 2767
Munich International Music Competition of the Broadcasting Stations of the Federal Republic of Germany (ARD) Vol. 2: 2971
Municipal Chapter of Toronto IODE Children's Book Award Vol. 1: 12177
Munro Oration; C. H. Vol. 2: 413
Munson Aquatic Conservation Exhibitory Award Vol. 1: 4917
Munson Award; Ida Vol. 1: 2448
Munson Memorial Student Awards; Emily Vol. 1: 19010
Muntendamprijs; Prof. Dr. P. Vol. 2: 4728
Murchison Award Vol. 2: 8524
Murchison Medal Vol. 2: 7564
Murdoch Award; Connie Vol. 1: 18561
Murgoci Prize; Gheorghe Vol. 2: 5850
Murgulescu Award; I.G. Vol. 2: 5851
Murie Award; Olaus and Margaret Vol. 1: 21627
Murillo Annual Salon of Visual Arts Prizes; Pedro Domingo Vol. 2: 1124
Murofushi Research Award; Takeshi Vol. 1: 11400
Murphree Award in Industrial and Engineering Chemistry; E. V. Vol. 1: 1773
Murphy Award for Excellence in Copy Editing; John Vol. 1: 19999
Murphy Award; Glenn Vol. 1: 4031
Murphy Award; John Killam Vol. 1: 7631
Murphy Excellence in Teaching Award; Mother Evelyn Vol. 1: 8991
Murphy Medal; R. K. Vol. 2: 516
Murphy Memorial Award; Jack Vol. 1: 15012
Murphy Prize; Forbes Vol. 2: 7675
Murphy Scholarship; Joseph Vol. 1: 16139
Murray Award for Outstanding Philanthropist; Paschal Vol. 1: 5704
Murray Award; Henry A. Vol. 1: 3727
Murray Award; John Courtney Vol. 1: 7662
Murray Award; Robert J. Vol. 1: 18442
Murray Distinguished Educator Award; Grover E. Vol. 1: 1344
Murray - Green Award Vol. 1: 2227
Murray-Green-Meany-Kirkland Award for Community Service Vol. 1: 2227
Murray Senior Brass Scholarship; The Dr. W.C. Vol. 1: 18304
Murrell Award; Hywel Vol. 2: 7449
Murrow Award; Edward R.
Corporation for Public Broadcasting Vol. 1: 8526
Overseas Press Club of America Vol 1: 16981
Murrow Awards; Edward R. Vol. 1: 17849
Murtagh Memorial Prize; Lillian Vol. 1: 2372
Museum Acquisition Award Vol. 1: 18574
Museum Directors Award; AAEA Vol. 1: 657
Museum of Art National Print Exhibition Purchase Awards; Hunterdon Vol. 1: 10618
Museum of Haiku Literature Awards Vol. 1: 10223
Museum Publication of the Year/Museum Poster of the Year Vol. 2: 1611
Musgrave Medal Vol. 2: 4077
Music Arts and Flowers History Award Vol. 1: 8920
Music Award Vol. 1: 15013
Music Award; PCAM Vol. 2: 8288

Music Awards Vol. 2: 8657
Music Campers Citation Vol. 1: 14486
Music Center Spotlight Awards Vol. 1: 13698
Music Educator of the Year Award Vol. 1: 14363
MUSICA SACRA Bach Vocal Competition Vol. 1: 13710
Musical Freestyle Awards Vol. 1: 20568
Musician of the Year
Incorporated Society of Musicians Vol. 2: 7631
Norwegian Society of Composers Vol 2: 5166
Musician of the Year Award Vol. 2: 5506
Musicians Benevolent Fund Awards Vol. 2: 8152
Muskett Award; Nevva Vol. 2: 8348
Musselman Award; Dawn Vol. 1: 20691
Mustang Spirit Award Vol. 1: 13103
Mustard Seed Awards Vol. 1: 14616
MUTA Safety Certificate Vol. 2: 8253
Muteau; Prix General Vol. 2: 2050
MVP of Year Vol. 1: 5647
MVSA Goue Medalje Vol. 2: 5558
MVSA Silwer Medalje vir Navorsing Vol. 2: 5559
MWSP Meritorious Award Vol. 1: 5414
Mycology Postdoctoral Fellowship/John P. Utz Award; Pfizer Vol. 1: 15121
Myer Award; Haydn Vol. 1: 8360
Myers Award for Applied Research in the Workplace; M. Scott Vol. 1: 18755
Myers Award; Paul W. Vol. 1: 347
Myers Man of the Year Award; Howdy Vol. 1: 20665
Myers Nelson Achievement Awards; Beverly Vol. 1: 13812
Myers Nelson Student Awards; Beverly Vol. 1: 13813
Myers Writers Award; Cordelia Vol. 1: 3297
Myhre Awards; Paul Vol. 1: 21079
Myrdal Award for Government Service Vol. 1: 2207
Myrdal Award for Science Vol. 1: 2206
Myrdal Human Service Delivery Award; Gunnar Vol. 1: 2208
Myrdal Practice Award; Alva and Gunnar Vol. 1: 2208
Myrtle Butts Fleming Award Vol. 1: 6496
Mythic Society Scholar Vol. 2: 3567
Mythopoeic Fantasy Awards Vol. 1: 13739
Mythopoeic Scholarship Awards Vol. 1: 13740
N4A National Academic Achievement Award Vol. 1: 14062
NAA Foundation - Associated Collegiate Press Pacemakers Awards Vol. 1: 16337
NAA Foundation - International Circulation Managers Association C. K. Jefferson Award Vol. 1: 16338
NAA Foundation - National Scholastic Press Association Pacemaker Awards Vol. 1: 16339
NAA Foundation - Newspaper in Education Program Excellence Award Vol. 1: 16340
NAAA Falcon Club Vol. 1: 13909
NAAB Research Award Vol. 1: 14070
NAAFI Rosebowl Award Vol. 2: 6747
NABE Board Member of the Year Vol. 1: 14617
NABE Executive Officer of the Year Vol. 1: 14618
NABE Honor Roll of Outstanding Members Vol. 1: 14619
NABS Research Grants Vol. 1: 16395
NAC Award Vol. 1: 13869
NAC Orchestra Association Award Vol. 1: 13982
NACADA Student Research Award Vol. 1: 13768
NACBS Book Prize; Albion Book Prize/ Vol. 1: 16411
NACBS-Huntington Library Fellowship Vol. 1: 16414
NACD - Allis Chalmers Conservation Teacher Awards Vol. 1: 14157
NACD Deutz/Allis Chalmers Conservation District Awards Vol. 1: 14156
NACD - ICI Americas Conservation District Awards Vol. 1: 14156
NACD - ICI Americas Conservation Teacher Awards Vol. 1: 14157
Nachison Award; Judith Vol. 1: 16186
NACHO Achievement Award Vol. 1: 14175
Nachtsheim; John Vol. 1: 5972
Nacional de Metalurgica y Mineria Vol. 2: 9327
NACTA John Deere Awards Vol. 1: 16406
Nadai Medal Vol. 1: 4532
Nadal Prize Vol. 2: 6020
NADD Award Vol. 1: 14188
Nadebaum Distinguished Service Award; Oertel Vol. 2: 72
NADEO Annual Award for Ecumenism Vol. 1: 14194
Nadi Prize; Yunus Vol. 2: 6631
Nadi Yarismasi; Yunus Vol. 2: 6631
Nadine Williams Scholarship Vol. 1: 13662
NADSA Outstanding Service Award Vol. 1: 14202
NADSA Research Award Vol. 1: 14203
NADSA Scholar Award Vol. 1: 14204
NADSA Special Recognition Vol. 1: 14201
Nadzhakov Prize; Academician Georgi Vol. 2: 1207
NAE/Spencer Postdoctoral Fellowship Program Vol. 1: 13803
NAEA Art Educator of the Year Vol. 1: 13964
NAEA State/Province Newsletter Editor Award Vol. 1: 13974
Naegelin Dramatic Interpretation Contest; Lanny D. Vol. 1: 15107
NAFCU Awards Program Vol. 1: 14223
Nagel Most Improved Chapter Award; R.H. Vol. 1: 19931
Nagroda im. Bohdana Zawadzkiego Vol. 2: 5372
Nagroda im. Henryka Swidzinskiego Vol. 2: 5350
Nagroda im. Ludwika Zejsznera Vol. 2: 5351
Nagroda im. Profesora Stefana Blachowskiego Vol. 2: 5371
Nagroda imienia Karola Malcuzynskiego Vol. 2: 5384
Nagroda Literacka SBP Vol. 2: 5353
Nagroda Ministra Obrony Narodowej Vol. 2: 5296
Nagroda Naukowa im. Adama Lysakowskiego Vol. 2: 5354
Nagroda Polskiego Towarzystwa Fonetycznego Vol. 2: 5360
Nagroda Sekretarza Naukowego Polskiej Akademii Nauk Vol. 2: 5334
Nagroda za popularyzacje polskiej tworczosci rozrywkowej Vol. 2: 5383
Nagroda Zwiazku Kompozytorow Polskich Vol. 2: 5344
Naguib Memorial Prize; Moshen Vol. 2: 8466
Nagurski Award; Bronko Vol. 1: 9673
Naha Memorial Medal; Professor K. Vol. 2: 3495
NAHRO Agency Awards of Excellence in Housing and Community Development Vol. 1: 14266
NAHRO Agency Awards of Merit in Housing and Community Development Vol. 1: 14267
NAHWW/Stanley Awards (Stanleys) Vol. 1: 14255
NAIA Academic All-America Awards Vol. 1: 14281
NAIA - SIDA All-Sports Championship Awards Vol. 1: 14290
NAIA-SIDA Top Web Sites of the Year Vol. 1: 14291
NAIOP Man of the Year Award Vol. 1: 14276
Naipaul Memorial Prize; Shiva Vol. 2: 9096
Naismith Award; Frances Pomeroy Vol. 1: 13752
Naismith College Coach of the Year Vol. 1: 6027
Naismith College Officials of the Year Vol. 1: 6028
Naismith College Player of the Year Vol. 1: 6029
Naismith Collegiate Awards (Naismith Trophy) Vol. 1: 6029
Naismith High School Awards Vol. 1: 6030
Naismith Outstanding Contribution to Basketball Award Vol. 1: 6031
Naismith Prep Player of the Year Vol. 1: 6030
Naismith Trophy Vol. 1: 6029
Naito Foundation Research Prize Vol. 2: 4257
Naito Kinen Kagaku Shinko Sho Vol. 2: 4257
Naiwu Osahon Award Vol. 1: 21945
Najkrajsia a najlepsia detska kniha jari, leta, jesene a zimy na Slovensku Vol. 2: 5960
Nakanishi Prize Vol. 1: 1774
Nakkula Award for Police Reporting; Al Vol. 1: 21008
NALPA Past President Award Vol. 1: 13929
NAMBA Hall of Fame Vol. 1: 16446
NAMI Kansas Award of Appreciation Vol. 1: 13754
NAMIC Engineering Safety Award Vol. 1: 4231
NAMO Marketing Award Vol. 1: 16508
NAMTA Hall of Fame Award Vol. 1: 13979
Nancy Lee and Perry R. Bass Gold Medal Vol. 1: 8108
Nanette LaCross Memorial Prize Vol. 1: 21063
Nansen Award; Fridtjof Vol. 2: 5144
Nansen Medal Vol. 2: 4644
Nansen Medal; Fridtjof Vol. 2: 2314
Napapijri Award Vol. 2: 3891
NAPH Medallion Vol. 1: 14426
Napier Sailing Club Trophy Vol. 2: 7532
Napier - Shaw Bronze Medal Vol. 2: 7288
Naples Prize for Literature Vol. 2: 3938
Napoleon; Grands Prix de la Fondation Vol. 2: 2354
Napolitano Award; Luigi Vol. 2: 2437
NAPT Distinguished Service Award Vol. 1: 14026
Nardini Award; Dr. John Vol. 1: 2211
Narino; Orden del Merito Militar Antonio Vol. 2: 1291
Narlikar Memorial Lecture; Professor Vishnu Vasudeva Vol. 2: 3496

Narrative Poetry Prize Vol. 1: 17415
Narrative Screenwriting Award Vol. 1: 7953
NAS Award for Chemistry in Service to Society Vol. 1: 13836
NAS Award for Initiatives in Research Vol. 1: 13837
NAS Award for Scientific Reviewing Vol. 1: 13838
NAS Award for the Industrial Application of Science Vol. 1: 13839
NAS Award in Aeronautical Engineering Vol. 1: 13840
NAS Award in Chemical Sciences Vol. 1: 13841
NAS Award in Mathematics Vol. 1: 13842
NAS Award in Molecular Biology Vol. 1: 13843
NAS Award in the Neurosciences Vol. 1: 13844
NASA Medal Vol. 1: 13886
NASAR Service Award Vol. 1: 14037
NASCAR Championships Vol. 1: 14045
NASCAR Grand National Championship Vol. 1: 8769
NASCAR Mechanics Hall of Fame; Western Auto Vol. 1: 11760
NASCAR Winston Cup Series Stock Car Race; Daytona 500 Vol. 1: 8766
Nasdaq National Teaching Awards; NCEE/ Vol. 1: 14857
Nash Award; Ruth Lopin Vol. 1: 16813
Nash Gold Medal; Kevin Vol. 2: 7979
Nash Patterson Grants; Alfred Vol. 1: 7939
Nash Student History Journal Prize Vol. 1: 17236
Nashville Film Festival Vol. 1: 13758
Nashville Songwriters Association International Awards Vol. 1: 13760
NASIRE Recognition Awards for Outstanding Achievement in the Field of Information Technology Vol. 1: 14395
NASPAA Annual Dissertation Award Vol. 1: 14375
NASPAA/ASPA Distinguished Research Award Vol. 1: 4186
NASPAA Public Courage Award Vol. 1: 14378
NASSH Book Award Vol. 1: 16471
NASSTRAC Awards Program Vol. 1: 13762
Natali Prize for Journalists; Lorenzo Vol. 2: 925
Natelson Senior Investigation Award; Samuel Vol. 1: 987
Nath Memorial Lecture; Professor Vishwa Vol. 2: 3497
Nathan Award for Dramatic Criticism; George Jean Vol. 1: 13764
Nathaniel Dwings Award Vol. 1: 6767
National 100 Mile Award Vol. 1: 2181
The National Academy Hall of Fame Award Program Vol. 1: 13814
National Academy of Sciences Award Vol. 2: 5509
National Academy of Sciences Award in Microbiology Vol. 1: 13851
National Academy of Western Art Exhibition Vol. 1: 14886
National Access Awareness Week Student Awards Program Vol. 1: 5906
National Achievement Award Vol. 1: 14312
National ADDY Campaign Awards Vol. 1: 858
National Advisor of the Year Award Vol. 1: 493
National Aeronautical Prize Vol. 2: 3333
National Affairs Award Vol. 1: 4207
National Agricultural Award Vol. 2: 8415
National Amateur Wine Competition Awards Vol. 1: 4910
National Amputee Golf Champion (Men and Women) Vol. 1: 13933
National and International High Points Competition Vol. 1: 4904
National and Regional Continuing Education Award Vol. 1: 18155
National Annual Exhibition of Fine Arts Vol. 2: 1176
National Appreciation Award Vol. 1: 14313
National Aquatic Service, Inc. - Annual Service Recognition Award Vol. 1: 15316
National Architecture Awards Vol. 2: 525
National Armed Act Cross Vol. 2: 5324
National Art Educator Award Vol. 1: 13964
National Art Honor Society Sponsor Award Vol. 1: 13965
National Artist Award Vol. 2: 5273
National Artist Award/International Artist Award Vol. 2: 5273
National Arts Merit Awards Vol. 2: 9354
National Assessment Awards Vol. 2: 632
National Association of Community Health Centers Awards Vol. 1: 14138
National Association of First Responders Awards Vol. 1: 14232
National Association of Shopfitters Design Vol. 2: 8163
National Association of University Women National Fellowship Vol. 1: 14453
National Athletic Director of the Year Vol. 1: 14812
National Audio Book of the Year Award Vol. 2: 474
National Award
  Alliance for Transportation Research Institute - University of New Mexico Vol. 1: 463
  American Cancer Society Vol 1: 1634
  Kennedy Center American College Theater Festival Vol 1: 12546
  National Water Safety Congress Vol 1: 15936
National Award for Best Organization Vol. 2: 6600
National Award for Demonstrated Leadership Vol. 1: 17082
National Award for Media Excellence Vol. 1: 15577
National Award for Painting and Graphics Vol. 2: 5201
National Award for the Protection of Environment Vol. 2: 1264
National Award of Achievement Vol. 1: 12860
National Award of Merit Vol. 1: 8430
National Awards Vol. 2: 9193
National Awards
  Academy of Scientific Research and Technology Vol. 2: 1551
  National Forensic League Vol 1: 15107
National Awards Contest Vol. 1: 5522
National Awards for Education Reporting Vol. 1: 9170
National Awards for Environmental Sustainability - Searching for Success Program Vol. 1: 17991
National Awards for Teaching Economics Vol. 1: 14857
National Awards Program
  Freedoms Foundation at Valley Forge Vol. 1: 9766
  OX5 Aviation Pioneers Vol 1: 16990
National Awards; State Awards and Vol. 1: 14144
National Back Pain Association Medal Vol. 2: 6848
National Ballet of Canada School Scholarship Vol. 1: 21780
National Banking Commission Prize Vol. 2: 4475
National Best Condition Award Vol. 1: 2182
National Book Awards Vol. 1: 14532
National Book Critics Circle Awards Vol. 1: 14530
National Book Service Teacher-Librarian of the Year Award Vol. 1: 7261
National Bottle Show Champion Vol. 2: 6855
National Bowling Hall of Fame and Museum Vol. 1: 11432
National Boy of the Year Vol. 1: 6601
National Breeders Trophy Vol. 1: 20626
National Business Calendar Awards Vol. 2: 7116
National Cadet Bisley Grand Champion Medal Vol. 2: 5745
National Camellia Hall of Fame Vol. 1: 1620
National Champion
  Accordion Society of Australia Vol. 2: 50
  U.S. Sports Acrobatics Vol 1: 20848
National Champion Bronze Statue Vol. 1: 11903
National Champion Challenge Cup Vol. 2: 6913
National Champion Donkey, National Champion Mule Vol. 1: 2150
National Champions Vol. 1: 18259
National Championship
  American Baseball Coaches Association Vol. 1: 1547
  American Motorcyclist Association Vol 1: 3150
  Rhodes 19 Class Association Vol 1: 18034
National Championship Awards Vol. 1: 925
National Championship Cup Finals Vol. 2: 7422
National Championship Regatta Vol. 1: 11135
National Championships
  Canadian Sport Parachuting Association Vol. 1: 7510
  National Rifle Association of America Vol 1: 15646
  Scottish Bowling Association Vol 2: 8901
  United States Curling Association Vol 1: 20464
  USA Badminton Vol 1: 21150
  USA Cycling Vol 1: 21162
National Chapter of the Year Vol. 1: 20197
National Chef of the Year Vol. 1: 7066
National Chicken Council Award Vol. 1: 17498
National Chief of Protocol Vol. 1: 5111
National Chopin Piano Competition Vol. 1: 12613
National Citation Vol. 1: 13614
National Citation Awards Vol. 1: 15604
National Citizen of the Year Vol. 1: 13404
National, City and Regional Magazine Editorial and Design Awards Vol. 1: 8024
National City Challenge to Stop Drunk Driving Vol. 1: 20457

National Classical Music Contest Vol. 2: 5511
National Club Achievement Competition Vol. 1: 860
National Club Championship Award (Men) Vol. 1: 20758
National Club Championship Award (Women) Vol. 1: 20759
National Club Sevens Championship Award (Men) Vol. 1: 20760
National Coach of the Year Vol. 1: 14695
National Coin Week Vol. 1: 3241
National College Band and Choral Directors Hall of Fame Band of the Year Vol. 1: 15228
National College Band Director of the Year Vol. 1: 15229
National College Championship Award Vol. 1: 20761
National College Championship Award (Women) Vol. 1: 20762
National College Choral Director of the Year Vol. 1: 15230
National College Choral Directors Hall of Fame Choir of the Year Vol. 1: 15231
National College Football Champions Vol. 1: 14686
National Collegiate All Conference Championships Award Vol. 1: 20763
National Collegiate and Scholastic Swimming Trophy Vol. 1: 15283
National Collegiate and Scholastic Swimming Trophy Vol. 1: 8196
National Commander's Public Relations Award Vol. 1: 2948
National Community Service Award
  Jewish Theological Seminary Vol. 1: 12379
  National Association of Negro Business and Professional Women's Clubs Vol 1: 14314
National Community Service Awards Vol. 1: 1399
National Competition Vol. 1: 1139
National Competition for Composers Recording Vol. 1: 8477
National Competition in Organ Improvisation Vol. 1: 2371
National Competition in Teaching of Journalism Prize Vol. 2: 1177
National Composers' Competition Vol. 1: 12747
National Computer Personality of the Year Award Vol. 2: 5545
National Conference of Puerto Rican Women Award Vol. 1: 14721
National Congressional Award Vol. 1: 15578
National Conservation Award Vol. 2: 6831
National Contest for Opera Singers Vol. 2: 1178
National Contest of Medical Research Works Vol. 2: 1321
National Convention Awards Program Vol. 1: 3812
National Corn Yield Contest Vol. 1: 14736
National Corporate Humanitarian Award Vol. 1: 15579
National Council Awards Vol. 1: 16334
National Course Rally Manufacturer Champion Vol. 1: 19702
National Court Reporters Foundation Scholarships Vol. 1: 14883
National Credit Executive of the Year Vol. 1: 14183
National Cultural Awards Vol. 2: 1145
National Cup Boys Under 18 (Boys National Championship) Vol. 1: 20895
National Cup Girls Under 17 Cup Vol. 1: 20894
National Cup Girls Under 18 (Girls National Championship) Vol. 1: 20896
National Defense Service Medal Vol. 1: 8826
National Design Competition for the Use of Aluminum Vol. 2: 4508
National Diploma of the Society of Floristry Vol. 2: 9049
National Distinction of the Environment Vol. 2: 1272
National Distinguished Principal Award Vol. 1: 14207
National Distinguished Professional Award Vol. 1: 15580
National Distinguished Service Award Vol. 1: 15605
National Distinguished Service Awards Vol. 1: 7271
National Distinguished Service Ruby Award Vol. 1: 9317
National Division Art Educator Award Vol. 1: 13966
National Division Art Educator of the Year Vol. 1: 13966
National Drama Contest Vol. 2: 1184
National Editors Award Vol. 1: 1217
National Endowment for the Arts Programs Vol. 1: 14930
National Endowment for the Humanities Fellowships Vol. 1: 916
National Endowment for the Humanities Grant Programs Vol. 1: 14938
National Engineering Award Vol. 1: 1197
National Environmental Achievement Award - Searching for Success Program Vol. 1: 17991
National Equal Employment/Affirmative Action Exemplary Practices Award Vol. 1: 4183
National Essay Contest on Public Health as Social Justice Vol. 1: 8870
National Essay Contest on "The Role of Public Health in Healthcare Reform" Vol. 1: 8870
National Excellence Awards for Engineering Journalism Vol. 2: 414
National Exhibition of Rosemaling in the Norwegian Tradition Vol. 1: 21316
National Exhibition of Weaving in the Norwegian Tradition Vol. 1: 21317
National Exhibition of Woodworking in the Norwegian Tradition Vol. 1: 21318
National Family and Consumer Sciences Teacher of the Year Award - Home Economics Teacher of the Year Award Vol. 1: 942
National Federation Citations Vol. 1: 14978
National Federation Interscholastic Coaches Association Annual Awards Vol. 1: 14984
National Federation Interscholastic Officials Association Vol. 1: 14984
National Federation of Music Clubs Awards and Scholarships Vol. 1: 14970
National Federation of the Blind Educator of Tomorrow Award Vol. 1: 15039
National Federation of the Blind Humanities Scholarship Vol. 1: 15039
National Federation of the Blind Scholarship Program Vol. 1: 15039
National Field Archery Championship Vol. 1: 15045
National Film Board Award for Best Short Film Vol. 1: 20117
National Film Board Kathleen Shannon Award Vol. 1: 22048
National Film Board of Canada Prize for Creativity Vol. 1: 11613
National Film Board of Canada Public Prize Vol. 1: 16953
National Fleet Safety Contests Vol. 1: 15657
National Food and Energy Council Electric Technology Award Vol. 1: 4232
National Footbag Championships Vol. 1: 21921
National Football League Scholar-Athlete Award Vol. 1: 15073
National Forensic Association Awards Vol. 1: 15095
National Fresenius Award Vol. 1: 17250
National Friend of Extension Award Vol. 1: 9318
National Genealogy Hall of Fame Vol. 1: 15150
National Geographic Society Award
  American Congress on Surveying and Mapping Vol. 1: 2001
  British Cartographic Society Vol 2: 6973
National Geographic Society Centennial Award Vol. 1: 15160
National Gold Medal Awards Vol. 1: 19726
National Gold Pin Awards Vol. 1: 560
National Golden Target Award Vol. 1: 13066
National Goodwill Worker of the Year Vol. 1: 10081
National Graphic Design Awards Vol. 2: 4967
National Guard Association of the United States Awards Program Vol. 1: 15176
National Headache Foundation Lectureship Award Vol. 1: 15191
National Headliner Awards Vol. 1: 15194
National Health Information Awards Vol. 1: 10315
National Health Law Moot Court Competition Vol. 1: 7725
National Heritage Fellowships Vol. 1: 14932
National High Point Awards Vol. 1: 14141
National High School Band Director of the Year Vol. 1: 15226
National High School Championships Award Vol. 1: 20764
National High School Finals Rodeo Vol. 1: 15233
National High School Hall of Fame Vol. 1: 14984
National High School Journalism Teacher of the Year Vol. 1: 9008
National High School Journalist of the Year Vol. 1: 12451
National High School Sports Hall of Fame Awards Vol. 1: 14979
National High Score Awards Vol. 1: 21514
National Honor Society Scholarship Program Vol. 1: 14385
National Housing Hall of Fame Vol. 1: 14259
National Housing Quality Award Vol. 1: 17600
National Human Relations Award Vol. 1: 2887
National Humanitarian Award
  National Recreation and Park Association Vol. 1: 15581
  RID - U.S.A. Vol 1: 18044
  WAIF Vol 1: 21423
National Humanities Medal Vol. 1: 14939

Award Index

National Hunt Champion Award Vol. 2: 8321
National Hypertension Association Recognition Award Vol. 1: 15252
National Impact Award Vol. 1: 15256
National Institute of Insurance International Prizes Vol. 2: 3825
National Inventor of the Year Vol. 1: 11097
National Inventor's Hall of Fame Vol. 1: 20733
National Iqbal Award Vol. 2: 5191
National Iway Awards Vol. 1: 7547
National Jewish Book Award - Autobiography/ Memoir Vol. 1: 12321
National Jewish Book Award - Children's Literature Vol. 1: 12322
National Jewish Book Award - Children's Picture Book Vol. 1: 12323
National Jewish Book Award - Contemporary Jewish Life Vol. 1: 12324
National Jewish Book Award - Fiction Vol. 1: 12325
National Jewish Book Award - Holocaust Vol. 1: 12326
National Jewish Book Award - Israel Vol. 1: 12327
National Jewish Book Award - Jewish History Vol. 1: 12328
National Jewish Book Award - Jewish Thought Vol. 1: 12329
National Jewish Book Award - Scholarship Vol. 1: 12330
National Jewish Book Award - Sephardic Studies Vol. 1: 12331
National Jewish Book Award - Visual Arts Vol. 1: 12332
National Jewish Book Award - Yiddish Literature Vol. 1: 12333
National Jockeys Hall of Fame Vol. 1: 13134
National Journal Award Vol. 1: 1218
National Journalism Award Vol. 1: 6212
National Junior Art Honor Society Sponsor Award Vol. 1: 13967
National Junior Tennis League Chapter of the Year Award Vol. 1: 20871
National Kind Teacher Award Vol. 1: 14016
National Labor Prize Vol. 2: 4569
National Lacrosse Hall of Fame Vol. 1: 20680
National Law Enforcement Saved by the Belt/ Air Bag Awards Program Vol. 1: 11309
National Leader's Award - Moe Dollinger Award Vol. 1: 9027
National Leadership
Jobs for America's Graduates Vol. 1: 12394
Simon Wiesenthal Center Vol 1: 18529
National Leadership Award
Irish Farm Centre Vol. 2: 3656
Leukemia and Lymphoma Society Vol 1: 12792
National Council for Continuing Education and Training Vol 1: 14753
National Leadership Awards
AIDS Action Council Vol. 1: 305
National Office Paper Recycling Project Vol 1: 15423
National League All-Star Team Vol. 1: 19660
National League Most Valuable Player Vol. 1: 6266
National League Player of the Year
England Basketball Vol. 2: 7423
Sporting News Vol 1: 19661
National League Rookie of the Year Vol. 1: 19662
National Legislative Award Vol. 1: 17916
National Lifesaving Leadership Award Vol. 1: 18045
National Lighting Awards Program Vol. 1: 14922
National Lighting Design Awards Vol. 2: 8067
National Limited Distance Mileage Award Vol. 1: 2183
National Literary Award Vol. 1: 15582
National Living Treasures Award Vol. 2: 5274
National Looking Glass Poetry Competition for a Single Poem Vol. 1: 17741
National Lupus Hall of Fame Vol. 1: 12981
National Magazine Awards Vol. 1: 4492
National Magazine Awards Vol. 1: 15355
National Man/Woman of the Year Vol. 1: 18517
National Marine Science Prize Vol. 2: 1308
National Mass Media Award Vol. 1: 2888
National Materials Advancement Award Vol. 1: 9514
National Mature Media Awards Program Vol. 1: 13207
National Medal Vol. 2: 199
National Medal of Arts Vol. 1: 14933
National Medal of Technology Vol. 1: 15678
National Media Award Vol. 1: 7272
National Media Awards
American College of Allergy, Asthma and Immunology Vol. 1: 1829
American Society of Colon and Rectal Surgeons Vol 1: 4373
National Member of the Year Award Vol. 1: 494
National Merit Award Vol. 1: 15278
National Merit of Exhibit Award Vol. 1: 19285
National Meritorious Award Vol. 1: 4890
National Mileage Championship Vol. 1: 2184
National Military Championships Award Vol. 1: 20765
National Military Intelligence Association Annual Awards Vol. 1: 15384
National Milk Producers Federation Graduate Student Paper Presentation Contest Vol. 1: 2110
National Minority Supplier Development Council Awards Vol. 1: 15390
National Minority Supplier Development Council Conference Vol. 1: 15390
National Model Car Racing Champion Vol. 2: 7155
National Most Colorful Contest Vol. 1: 21426
National Multihull Championship - Alter Cup Vol. 1: 20775
National Music Award Vol. 2: 1179
National Music Council Award to Local Authorities and Local Education Authorities Vol. 2: 8179
National Music Festival Vol. 1: 18305
The National Music Festival Vol. 1: 15408
National Newspaper Association - Quill and Scroll Award Vol. 1: 16341
National Newspaper Awards Vol. 1: 7309
National Officials Outstanding Service Award Vol. 1: 21213
National Offshore Championship - Lloyd Phoenix Trophy Vol. 1: 20776
National One-Act Play Contest Vol. 1: 172
National Optometrist of the Year Award Vol. 1: 3317
National Order of Education Vol. 2: 1146
National Order of Merit Vol. 2: 4456
National Order of the Southern Cross Vol. 2: 1147
National Organization for Rare Disorders Awards Vol. 1: 15440
National Organization on Disability Award Vol. 1: 1232
National Outdoor Book Awards Vol. 1: 15465
National Outstanding Advisor Award Vol. 1: 19933
National Paper Writing Competition Award Vol. 1: 18065
National Paperboard Packaging Competition Vol. 1: 17064
National Peace Essay Contest Vol. 1: 20656
National Person of the Year Award Vol. 1: 14753
National Philatelic Society Queen Elizabeth II Silver Jubilee Trophy Vol. 2: 8263
National Philharmonic Award Vol. 2: 5306
National Photography Award Vol. 2: 1180
National Photography Competition Vol. 2: 1346
National Playwrights Conference and New Drama for Media Project Vol. 1: 15508
National Playwrights Conference and New Drama for Television Project Vol. 1: 15508
National Playwriting Competition Vol. 1: 16959
National Poetry Competition Vol. 2: 8274
National Point Leader Award, Competition Division Vol. 1: 6221
National Police Award for Traffic Safety Vol. 1: 6813
National Police Shooting Championships Vol. 1: 15647
National Post Awards for Business in the Arts Vol. 1: 8541
National Postal Museum Medal Vol. 2: 8263
National Poster Challenge Award Vol. 1: 7120
National Preservation Honor Awards Vol. 1: 15919
National President's Award Vol. 1: 1219
National President's Awards Vol. 1: 5717
National President's Trophy - Man of the Year Vol. 1: 22112
National Print and Drawing Exhibition Vol. 1: 13491
National Print Exhibition Vol. 1: 18980
National Prize for Advertising Vol. 2: 686
National Prize for Advertising Films Vol. 2: 687
National Prize for Approved Quality Vol. 2: 688
National Prize for Chemistry Vol. 2: 1339
National Prize for Civic Merit Vol. 2: 4583
National Prize for Commercial and Industrial Buildings Vol. 2: 689
National Prize for Consulting Vol. 2: 690
National Prize for Design Vol. 2: 691
National Prize for Financial Research Vol. 2: 4521
National Prize for Good Building Vol. 2: 5134
National Prize for Handicraft Vol. 2: 692
National Prize for History, Social Sciences and Philosophy Vol. 2: 4572
National Prize for Innovation Vol. 2: 693
National Prize for Jewelry Vol. 2: 694
National Prize for Journalism and Information Vol. 2: 4584
National Prize for Linguistics and Literature Vol. 2: 4573
National Prize for Model Packaging Vol. 2: 695

National Prize for Physics, Mathematics and Natural Sciences Vol. 2: 4574
National Prize for Public Relations Vol. 2: 696
National Prize for Quality Vol. 2: 4626
National Prize for Radio Advertising Vol. 2: 697
National Prize for Sports Vol. 2: 4575
National Prize for Technical Development/ Colombia Vol. 2: 9323
National Prize for Technology and Design Vol. 2: 4576
National Prize for the Most Beautiful Book Vol. 2: 698
National Prize for Timber Marketing Vol. 2: 699
National Prize in Science and Art Vol. 2: 4577
National Prize of the President of the Republic Vol. 2: 3826
National Pro-Am Championship Vol. 2: 8294
National PRO Rally of the Year Vol. 1: 19702
National Pro Rally of the Year Award Vol. 1: 19697
National Psychiatric Technician of the Year Vol. 1: 1388
National Psychology Awards for Excellence in the Media Vol. 1: 18915
National Public Citizen of the Year Vol. 1: 14389
National Public Relations Achievement Award Vol. 1: 6211
National Public Service Awards Vol. 1: 13819
National Putting Championship Vol. 1: 17649
National Quality Dealer Award Vol. 1: 15254
National Radio Award Vol. 1: 14116
National Rally Award; Best New Vol. 1: 19683
National Ranking Award Vol. 1: 14918
National Recognition Award
America the Beautiful Fund Vol. 1: 601
National Family Partnership Vol 1: 14959
National Recognition Medal Vol. 1: 9764
National Record Award Vol. 2: 1148
National Recreational Fisheries Awards Vol. 1: 9568
National Recycling Coalition Annual Awards Vol. 1: 15589
National Research Awards Vol. 1: 5127
National Research Council Canada, Division of Mechanical Engineering Award Vol. 1: 7431
National Research Service Awards Vol. 1: 15272
National Rifle and Pistol Championship Trophy Match Vol. 1: 20466
National Scholar-Athlete Awards Vol. 1: 15073
National Scholastic Award Vol. 1: 17917
National Scholastic Press Association Pacemaker Awards; NAA Foundation - Vol. 1: 16339
National School Library Media Program of the Year Award Vol. 1: 1418
National School Plant Manager of the Year Award Vol. 1: 3886
National Science, Literature and Art Prize Vol. 2: 3163
National Science Prize Vol. 2: 9324
National Scrabble Championship Vol. 1: 15696
National Sculpture Competition Vol. 1: 15701
National Security Medal Vol. 1: 15703
National Series Championship Vol. 1: 2185
National Service Award
Chamber Music America Vol. 1: 7792
Recreation Vehicle Industry Association Vol 1: 17918
National Service Medal Vol. 1: 9764
National Short Story Competition Vol. 2: 1347
National Ski and Snowboard Week Best Event Vol. 1: 7393
National Ski Hall of Fame Vol. 1: 20814
National Ski Safety Award Vol. 1: 7394
National Small Business Person of the Year Vol. 1: 20830
National Small Painting Exhibition Vol. 1: 16192
National Small Works Exhibition Vol. 1: 20192
National SMLTSA Virology Prize Vol. 2: 5621
National Smokey Bear Awards Vol. 1: 9560
National Snow Industries Association Recognition Award Vol. 1: 7395
National Soaring Hall of Fame Vol. 1: 9735
National Soccer Hall of Fame Award Vol. 1: 20839
National Social Worker of the Year Vol. 1: 14390
National Society of Artists Awards Vol. 1: 15728
National Society of Arts and Letters First Place Award Vol. 1: 15733
National Softball Hall of Fame Vol. 1: 588
National Sportscaster and Sportswriter of Year Vol. 1: 15813
National Sportscaster of the Year Vol. 1: 4680
National Sportscaster of the Year/Play by Play/Studio Host/Color Analyst/Reporter Award Vol. 1: 4680
National Sportsmanship Award Vol. 1: 20777
National Student Advertising Competition (NSAC) Vol. 1: 861
National Student Award for Excellence Vol. 1: 15726
National Student Competition Vol. 1: 4482
National Student Design Competition Vol. 1: 4233
National Student Playwriting Award Vol. 1: 12546
National Student Production Awards Competition Vol. 1: 14539
National Student Teacher/Intern of the Year Award; Kappa Delta Pi Vol. 1: 5881
National Student Teacher of the Year Vol. 1: 12513
National Superintendent of the Year Award Vol. 1: 1407
National Sweepstakes Champion Vol. 1: 16491
National Tagging Excellence Award Vol. 2: 244
National Target Championships Vol. 1: 13952
National Teacher of the Year Vol. 1: 8571
National Temporary Employee of the Year Award Vol. 1: 4687
National Ten-Minute Play Contest Vol. 1: 172
National Territorial Union Championship Award Vol. 1: 20766
National Testing and Awards Program for Secondary Students Vol. 1: 1446
National Theatre Awards Vol. 2: 5202
National Torchbearer Award Vol. 1: 2920
National Touring Rally Manufacturer Champion Vol. 1: 19702
National Touring Rally of the Year Vol. 1: 19702
National Track and Field Hall of Fame Vol. 1: 21233
National Traditional Music Performer Award Vol. 1: 15898
National Training and Development Awards Vol. 2: 7117
National Translation Award Vol. 1: 3009
National Transportation Award Vol. 1: 14906
National Travel Marketing Awards Vol. 1: 20177
National Treasure Award Vol. 1: 22039
National Trophy Vol. 1: 14918
National Turkey Federation Research Award Vol. 1: 17500
National Unicycle Meet Top Point Winners Vol. 1: 20298
National Voluntary Service Award Vol. 1: 15583
National Volunteer Disaster Services Award Vol. 1: 3834
National Volunteer Leadership Award Vol. 1: 1638
National Water and Energy Conservation Award Vol. 1: 12205
National Watercolor Society Arts and Humanities Award Vol. 1: 15941
National Westminster Bank Prize Vol. 2: 7690
National Westminster Bank Trophy Vol. 2: 7417
National Wildlife Photo Contest Vol. 1: 15952
National Wildlife Week Awards Vol. 1: 7542
National Wohelo Order Award Vol. 1: 6776
National Women's Hall of Fame Vol. 1: 15960
National Woodland Owners Award of Merit Vol. 1: 15979
National Works on Paper Exhibition Vol. 1: 13491
National Wrestling Hall of Fame Distinguished Member Vol. 1: 15988
National Yearbook Adviser of the Year Vol. 1: 12452
National Young Artist Competition Vol. 1: 13390
National Young Artists Competition in Organ Performance Vol. 1: 2372
National Young Astronomer Award Vol. 1: 6002
National Young Performers Competition Vol. 1: 6803
National Younger Members' Premiums Awards Vol. 2: 7822
National Youth Award Vol. 1: 14315
National Youth Cup Boys Vol. 1: 20897
National Youth of the Year Award Vol. 1: 6601
National Youth Prize Vol. 2: 4578
The Nations Cup Vol. 2: 6447
Nationwide Medalist of the Year Vol. 2: 7918
NATJA Awards Competition Vol. 1: 16495
NATO Awards Vol. 1: 14441
NATRC Honorary Lifetime Membership Vol. 1: 16488
NATRC National Champions Vol. 1: 16489
NATRC Ride Awards Vol. 1: 16490
Natta; Medaglia d'oro Giulio Vol. 2: 4002

Award Index

NATTS Hall of Fame Vol. 1: 7583
Natural History Award Vol. 1: 6069
Natural World Book Prize Vol. 2: 8208
Naturalistes de l'Annee Vol. 1: 7781
Nature Division Awards Vol. 1: 17287
Nature Photographer of the Year Vol. 2: 9356
Naturskyddsmedaljen Vol. 2: 6218
NatWest Bank Engineering Marketing Award Vol. 2: 7415
Naude Medal; Meiring Vol. 2: 5617
Naumann - August Thienemann Medal; Einar Vol. 1: 11406
Naumburg Chamber Music Award Vol. 1: 16044
Naumburg International Competition Vol. 1: 16045
Nautica/U.S. SAILING Youth Championship Vol. 1: 20789
Nautical Institute Competitions Vol. 2: 8210
Nautical Research; Howard I. Chapelle Award for Vol. 1: 16047
Naval and Maritime Photo Contest Vol. 1: 20715
Naval Reserve Award Vol. 1: 15384
Naval Reserve Medal Vol. 1: 8827
Navarre Medal Award; Maison G. de Vol. 1: 19094
Navigation Distinction Vol. 2: 1553
Navy Cross Vol. 2: 5746
Navy Expeditionary Medal Vol. 1: 8828
Navy Occupation Service Medal - Navy-Marine Corps-Coast Guard Vol. 1: 8829
NAWL Trust for Research & Education - Essay Competition Vol. 1: 14455
Nax Trophy Vol. 1: 3334
Nayacakalou Medal Vol. 2: 5048
Naylor Prize and Lectureship Vol. 2: 8090
Naylor Working Writer Fellowship; PEN/Phyllis Vol. 1: 17143
Nayudamma Memorial Award; Professor Vol. 2: 3583
Nazar Grant for Latino Projects and/or Latina Filmmakers; Jose L. Vol. 1: 21719
NBA All-Rookie Team Vol. 1: 14503
NBA All-Star Team Vol. 1: 19663
NBA Coach of the Year Vol. 1: 19664
NBA Executive of the Year Vol. 1: 19665
NBA Player of the Year Vol. 1: 19666
NBA Rookie of the Year Vol. 1: 19667
NCAA National Championships Vol. 1: 14687
NCBA Service Award Vol. 1: 14597
NCCC Focus Award Vol. 1: 14647
NCCPB Genetics and Plant Breeding Award for Industry Vol. 1: 8668
NCEA Merit Award Vol. 1: 14613
NCEA Presidential Award Vol. 1: 14620
NCEE/Nasdaq National Teaching Awards Vol. 1: 14857
NCHS Grants in Herpetology Vol. 1: 16510
NCIC Awards for Excellence in Cancer Research Vol. 1: 14585
NCLA Distinguished Library Service Award Vol. 1: 16512
NCLA/SIRS Intellectual Freedom Award Vol. 1: 16513
NCMR Prize Vol. 2: 7823
NDTA Distinguished Service Award Vol. 1: 14907
NEA/TCG Career Development Program for Designers Vol. 1: 20052
NEA/TCG Career Development Program for Directors Vol. 1: 20053
Neal National Business Journalism Awards; Jesse H. Vol. 1: 1608
Neatby en Histoire des Femmes; Le Prix Hilda Vol. 1: 7155
Neatby Prize; Hilda Vol. 1: 7155
Neave Research Fellowship; Airey Vol. 2: 6684
Neave Scholarship; Airey Vol. 2: 6684
Nebraska Hospice Volunteer of the Year Vol. 1: 16064
Nebraska State Poetry Society Award Vol. 1: 15014
Nebula Awards Vol. 1: 18357
NECCC Medal Vol. 1: 10149
Necho Award Vol. 2: 8599
Neck; Faculty Career Development Award for Toncology of the Head and Vol. 1: 1948
NED Democracy Award Vol. 1: 14928
Nederlandse Grafiekprijs Vol. 2: 4909
Nee; Prix Alfred Vol. 2: 2104
Neech Prize Vol. 2: 8608
Needlepoint Guild Literary Award; American Vol. 1: 3190
Neel Medal; Louis Vol. 2: 2315
Neff Distinguished Service Award; Thelma J. Vol. 1: 470
Nehru Award for International Understanding; Jawaharlal Vol. 2: 3399
Nehru Birth Centenary Award; Jawaharlal Vol. 2: 3537
Nehru Birth Centenary Lectures; Jawaharlal Vol. 2: 3498
Nehru Birth Centenary Medal; Jawaharlal Vol. 2: 3499
Nehru Birth Centenary Visiting Fellowship; Jawaharlal Vol. 2: 3500
Nehru Literacy Award Vol. 2: 3394
Neighborhood Greening Project Vol. 1: 9898
Neiland Award Vol. 1: 279
Neill Medal Vol. 2: 8791
Neill Memorial Prize in Music; Philip Vol. 2: 5094
Neilson-Bell Comeback Award Vol. 1: 21196
Neinken Medal; Mortimer L. Vol. 1: 17271
Neitz Junior Medal/Senior Medal; W.O. Vol. 2: 5605
Nelissenprijs; Jan Vol. 2: 4693
Nelligan; Prix Emile- Vol. 1: 20303
Nelson Award; Byron Vol. 1: 10072
Nelson Award for Diagnosis of Yield Limiting Factors; Werner L. Vol. 1: 4247
Nelson Award; Ruth and Bill Vol. 1: 10565
Nelson Engineering Award; Carl E. Vol. 1: 312
Nelson Fly Tying Teaching Award; Dick Vol. 1: 9485
Nelson Prize; William Vol. 1: 17986
Nelson Scholarship; Jason Vol. 1: 16673
Nelson Service Award; Harold E. Vol. 1: 19130
Nelvana Grand Prize for Independent Short Animation Vol. 1: 16954
NEMBA Trail Grant Vol. 1: 16103
Nemet Award Vol. 2: 7040
NEMLA Book Prize Vol. 1: 16544
Nemmers Prize in Economics; Erwin Plein Vol. 1: 16569
Nemmers Prize in Mathematics; Frederic Esser Vol. 1: 16570
NEMRA Manufacturer of the Year Vol. 1: 14924
Nemzetkoezi Liszt Hanglemez Nagydij Vol. 2: 3243
Nene Award Vol. 1: 10292
Nenitescu Prize; C. D. Vol. 2: 5852
Neometaphysical Merit Award Vol. 2: 9059
Neonatal Education Award Vol. 1: 783
Neri; Medalla Eduardo Vol. 2: 4565
Nerken Award; Albert Vol. 1: 6155
Nernst - Haber - Bodenstein-Preis Vol. 2: 2799
Nernst Medal Vol. 2: 2800
Nero Award Vol. 1: 21696
Neruda; Premio Pablo Vol. 2: 1259
Neruda Prize for Poetry; Pablo Vol. 1: 16360
Nesburn Award; Dr. Henry and Lilian Vol. 1: 6350
NESDA Awards Vol. 1: 14926
Ness Award Vol. 2: 8525
Ness Book Award; Frederic W. Vol. 1: 5552
NESS Communications Award Vol. 1: 9088
Ness Memorial Seminary Award; John Harrison Vol. 1: 9914
Nestle Smarties Book Prize Vol. 2: 6882
NETA Special Service Award Vol. 1: 14951
Netherlands Fund for Chemistry Prize Vol. 2: 4893
Netherlands Graphic Art Prize Vol. 2: 4909
Netherthorpe Award Vol. 2: 7577
Network Affiliate Sales Achievement Award Vol. 1: 6723
Network/Syndicated Personality of the Year Vol. 1: 14115
Networker of the Year Award Vol. 1: 822
Neue Stimmen - International Singing Contest Vol. 2: 2672
Neue Stimmen - Internationaler Gesangswettbewerb Vol. 2: 2672
Neufeld Memorial Research Grant; Prof. Henry Vol. 2: 3781
Neuharth Free Spirit of the Year Award; A.I Vol. 1: 9756
Neuman Award; William F. Vol. 1: 3935
Neumann Prize; Bernhard H. Vol. 2: 236
Neumueller Award in Optics; Julius F. Vol. 1: 723
Neustadt International Prize for Literature Vol. 1: 21934
Nevada Poetry Society Award Vol. 1: 15015
Nevanlinna Prize; Rolf Vol. 1: 11745
Neves Memorial Scholarship; Sgt. Edward Vol. 1: 17476
Nevins Physiology and Human Environment Award; Ralph G. Vol. 1: 4438
Nevins Prize; Allan Vol. 1: 9147
New American Cinema Award Vol. 1: 18396
New American Talent Show Vol. 1: 5123
New and Creative Framing Competition Vol. 1: 17647
New and Creative Ideas Framing Competition Vol. 1: 17647
New Constellation Award Vol. 1: 15052
New Directors Prize Vol. 2: 6096
New Directors Showcase Vol. 1: 18397
New England Book Show Juried Selection Vol. 1: 6511
New England Prize Vol. 1: 13003
New Englander of the Year Awards Vol. 1: 16099
New Focus Student Travel Grants Vol. 1: 16788
New Frontiers in Cytology Award Vol. 1: 4397
New Generations Award Vol. 1: 12380
New Hanover-Pender Co. Medical Society Premedical Scholarship Vol. 1: 16161
New Holland Young Researcher Award Vol. 1: 4220

New Holland Young Researcher Award Vol. 1: 4234
New Horizons Award for Innovation Vol. 1: 11959
New Investigator Award; Bayer-Snoeyenbos Vol. 1: 1085
New Investigator Awards
American Geriatrics Society Vol. 1: 2362
University of Wisconsin—Madison - Institute on Aging Vol 1: 21123
New Investigator Recognition Awards Vol. 1: 16913
New Jersey Exemplary State and Local Awards Vol. 1: 14638
New Jersey Poetry Society Award Vol. 1: 15016
New Leaders Travel Grant Vol. 1: 17714
New Leaders Travel Grant; Demco Vol. 1: 17714
New Letters Writing Awards Vol. 1: 16190
New Member Sponsor Award Vol. 1: 1220
New Mexico Fine Arts Competition Vol. 1: 13689
New Mexico Juried Exhibition Vol. 1: 13689
New Orleans International Piano Competition Vol. 1: 13712
New Play Project Vol. 1: 19488
New Product Award
Inventors Clubs of America Vol. 1: 12163
National Society of Professional Engineers Vol 1: 15748
New Product Showcase Award Vol. 1: 3372
New Professional Reporter Grant Vol. 1: 14884
New Scholar Award Vol. 1: 8703
New Scholar's Prize Vol. 2: 7922
New South Wales Premier's Literary Awards Vol. 2: 480
New Spirit of Community Partnership Awards Program Vol. 1: 10703
New Talent Award Vol. 1: 3005
New Venture Award Vol. 2: 9222
New Vision Award; New Voices Award/ Vol. 1: 17780
New Visions Award; QPB Vol. 1: 17781
New Voices Award/New Vision Award Vol. 1: 17780
New Writers Awards Vol. 1: 10141
New York Awards; New Yorker for Vol. 1: 8013
New York Chapter History of Military Medicine Essay Award Vol. 1: 5777
New York City Marathon; ING Vol. 1: 16260
New York Dance and Performance Awards (Bessie Awards) Vol. 1: 8745
New York Fellowship Vol. 2: 6761
New York International Ballet Competition Vol. 1: 16235
New York International Competition for Solo Oboists Vol. 1: 16603
New York Poetry Forum Award Vol. 1: 15017
New York Preservation Awards Vol. 1: 13679
New York Press Club/AT&T Award Vol. 1: 16243
New York Women in Film and Television Post Production Completion Grants Vol. 1: 21720
New Yorker for New York Awards Vol. 1: 8013
New Zealand Academy of Fine Arts Academy Awards Vol. 2: 5012
New Zealand Association of Scientists Research Medal Vol. 2: 5017
New Zealand Book Awards; Montana Vol. 2: 4959
New Zealand Chapter Traveling Fellowship; Australia/ Vol. 1: 1946
New Zealand Dental Association Awards Vol. 2: 5019
New Zealand Herald Challenge Trophy Vol. 2: 5063
New Zealand Science and Technology Medals Vol. 2: 5084
New Zealand Science, Mathematics and Technology Teacher Fellowship Vol. 2: 5085
New Zealand Tourism Awards Vol. 2: 5091
"New Zealand Wings" Trophy Vol. 2: 5064
New Zealand Young Engineer of the Year Award Vol. 2: 4988
Newark Black Film Festival Vol. 1: 16314
Newbery Medal; John Vol. 1: 5441
Newbigin Prize Vol. 2: 8684
Newbold V/STOL Award; AIAA F. E. Vol. 1: 2690
Newcastle Award; Lena Vol. 1: 4862
Newcomb Award for Research Achievement; Simon Vol. 1: 20525
Newcomb Award; James E. Vol. 1: 2928
Newcomb Award; Simon Vol. 1: 18144
Newcomb Cleveland Prize Vol. 1: 1052
Newcombe Doctoral Dissertation Fellowship; Charlotte W. Vol. 1: 21826
Newcomer Award Vol. 1: 18004
Newcomer Health Care Executive of the Year Award; William Vol. 1: 689
Newcomer of the Year Vol. 1: 8483
Newell Award; Allen Vol. 1: 5304
Newell Prize; W. W. Vol. 1: 2264
Newhouse Citation Vol. 1: 19880
Newington Prize Vol. 1: 930
Newkirk Award; Burt L. Vol. 1: 4533
Newman Award; Clark - Vol. 1: 7389
Newman Award; Ewell L. Vol. 1: 2486
Newman Award for Excellence in Research; Edwin B. Vol. 1: 18916
Newman Cup Vol. 2: 5065
Newman Graduate Research Award; Psi Chi/ APA Edwin B. Vol. 1: 17696
Newman International Memorial Award; Tom Vol. 2: 7111
Newman Iron Ore Award; Mt. Vol. 2: 4444
Newmark Medal; Nathan M. Vol. 1: 4344
Newnham Memorial Lecture; W. L. Vol. 2: 4989
Newport International Competition for Young Pianists Vol. 2: 8217
News and Documentary Emmy Awards Vol. 1: 13863
News Coverage Award Vol. 1: 11112
News Media Award for Community Service Vol. 1: 3574
News Picture Contest Vol. 1: 10816
Newsboy Award Vol. 1: 10542
Newsfilm Cameramen of the Year Vol. 1: 15533
Newsletter Association Journalism Awards Vol. 1: 16326
Newsletter Award Vol. 1: 10925
Newsletter Awards Vol. 1: 5718
Newsletter Competition
Institute of Management Accountants Vol. 1: 10993
National Genealogical Society Vol 1: 15151
Newsletter Contest Vol. 1: 9505
Newsletter Journalism Award Vol. 1: 15520
Newsletter Journalism Awards Vol. 1: 16324
Newsletter of the Year
U.S. Hang Gliding Association Vol. 1: 20614
United States Professional Tennis Association Vol 1: 20742
Newsletter of the Year Award Vol. 1: 15720
Newson Award; John Vol. 2: 8880
Newspaper Advertising Prize Vol. 2: 4184
Newspaper Award Vol. 1: 499
Newspaper Carrier of the Year Award Vol. 1: 16328
Newspaper Cartoon Competition Vol. 2: 4488
Newspaper Culture Award Vol. 2: 4185
Newspaper in Education Award Vol. 1: 11113
Newspaper in Education Program Excellence Award; NAA Foundation - Vol. 1: 16340
Newspaper Language Prize Vol. 2: 6653
Newspaper Leader of the Year; Pat Taggart Award for Texas Vol. 1: 20000
Newspaper of the Year Award Vol. 2: 488
Newspaper of the Year Contest Vol. 1: 17188
Newspaper Photographer of the Year Vol. 1: 15544
Newspapers Competition; Better Vol. 1: 7034
Newth Memorial Prize; Arthur Vol. 2: 8609
Newton Award; Winsor Vol. 2: 9087
Newton Medal; The Isaac Vol. 2: 8435
Newton Memorial Award for Outstanding Achievement in Human Lactation; Niles Vol. 1: 11709
NEWWA Scholarships Vol. 1: 16139
Nex Prize; Martin Andersen Vol. 2: 1474
Nextel Cup Vol. 1: 14045
Neyman Lecture Vol. 1: 11007
NFICA Certificates for Each State Vol. 1: 14985
NFICA Contributor Awards Vol. 1: 14985
NFID - Actra USA, Inc. Postdoctoral Fellowship in Infectious Disease Training and Herpes Virus Research Vol. 1: 15123
NFID - Burroughs Welcome Fund Young Investigator Awards Vol. 1: 15125
NFID - Marion Murrell Dow, Inc. Postdoctoral Fellowship in Nosocomial/Gram Positive Infection Research and Training Vol. 1: 15120
NFL All-Star Team Vol. 1: 19668
NFL Coach of the Year Vol. 1: 19669
NFL Executive of the Year Vol. 1: 19670
NFL Player of the Year; *The Sporting News* Vol. 1: 19677
NFWT Service Award Vol. 1: 509
Nganakarrawa Award Vol. 2: 158
NHK Broadcast Cultural Award Vol. 2: 4262
NHK Broadcasting Culture Prize Vol. 2: 4262
NHK Japan Prize Vol. 2: 4263
NHL All-Star Team Vol. 1: 19671
NHL Coach of the Year Vol. 1: 19672
NHL Executive of the Year Vol. 1: 19673
NHL Player of the Year Vol. 1: 19674
NHL Rookie of the Year Vol. 1: 19675
NHPA Scholarship Trust Fund Vol. 1: 16157
NHTSA Vol. 1: 21384
Nicest Studio Award Vol. 1: 15854
Nichol Chapbook Award; bp Vol. 1: 17275
Nicholas Outerside Medallion Vol. 2: 221
Nicholls Award; Percy Vol. 1: 4534
Nicholls Award; Percy W. Vol. 1: 18819
Nichols Award; Charles Walter Vol. 1: 3806

Nichols Award; Christopher D. Vol. 1: 5102
Nichols Fellowship Vol. 2: 8825
Nichols Innovation Award; Albert L. Vol. 1: 988
Nicholson Award Vol. 2: 8141
Nicholson Award; J. Lee Vol. 1: 10994
Nicholson Award; Lt. Col. Arthur D. Vol. 1: 15384
Nicholson Award (Marine Non-Commissioned Officer Leadership Award); James E. Vol. 1: 13085
Nicholson Award; Mollie Davis Vol. 1: 15734
Nicholson Distinguished Service Award; Margaret Vol. 1: 6751
Nicholson Gold Medal Award; Gunnar Vol. 1: 19922
Nicholson Student Paper Competition; George Vol. 1: 11078
Nickerson-ISCC Award; Dorothy Vol. 1: 11129
Nicklaus Family Award; Jack Vol. 1: 15168
Nicklaus Golf Family of the Year Award; Jack Vol. 1: 15168
Nicklin Memorial Trophy; Jeff Vol. 1: 7114
Nico Haberman Vol. 1: 8334
Nicol Trophy; William A. Vol. 2: 8720
Nicolau Prize; Stefan S. Vol. 2: 5853
Nicolo; Prix Vol. 2: 1724
NIDRR Scholar Vol. 1: 17474
Niederman Award; Allan and Joyce Vol. 1: 10424
Niekerk/AFMA Technical Person of the Year; Barney van Vol. 2: 5516
Niels Nielsen Prisen Vol. 2: 1532
Nielsen Award; Niels Vol. 2: 1532
Nielsen International Music Competitions; Carl Vol. 2: 1507
Nieman Fellowships for Journalists Vol. 1: 16358
Nightingale; Medaille Florence Vol. 2: 6395
Nightingale Medal; Florence Vol. 2: 6395
NIGP Fellow Award Vol. 1: 15268
Nihon Ketsueki Gakkai Shorei Sho Vol. 2: 4215
Nihon Shinbun Kyokai Awards Vol. 2: 4186
Nihon Sugakukai Iyanaga Sho Vol. 2: 4250
Nihon Tenmon Gakki Kenkyu Shoreisho Vol. 2: 4098
Nihon Yakugakkai Gakujutsukokensho Vol. 2: 4273
Nihon Yakugakkai Gijutsusho Vol. 2: 4276
Nihon Yakugakkai Korosho Vol. 2: 4275
Nihon Yakugakkai Kyoikusho Vol. 2: 4277
Nihon Yakugakkai sho Vol. 2: 4274
Nihon Yakugakkai Shoreisho Vol. 2: 4278
NII Amaa Ollennu Award Vol. 2: 3152
Nijhoff International West European Specialist Study Grant; WESS Coutts Vol. 1: 5615
Nikolsky Honorary Lectureship; Alexander A. Vol. 1: 2437
Nile Gold Medal Vol. 2: 6346
Niles Award; Colonel Elliott A. Vol. 1: 6485
Nimmo Medal; W.H.R. Vol. 2: 415
Nimmo Premium; Henry Vol. 2: 7824
NINDS Javits Neuroscience Investigator Award Vol. 1: 20499
Ninety-Nines NIFA Awards Vol. 1: 16365
Nininger Meteorite Award Vol. 1: 7735
Ninkasi Award Vol. 1: 2522
Niotis Cup; D. J. Vol. 1: 20897
Nippon Chikusan Gakkai Sho Vol. 2: 4209
Nippon Dojohiryo Gakkai Gijyutsu Sho Vol. 2: 4225
Nippon Dojohiryo Gakkai Sho Vol. 2: 4226
Nippon Dojohiryo Gakkai Shorei Sho Vol. 2: 4227
Nippon Gakushiin Ejinbara-ko Sho Vol. 2: 4153
Nippon Gakushiin Sho Vol. 2: 4155
Nippon Kaiji Kyokai Prize Vol. 2: 4267
Nippon Oyo Dobutsu Konchu Gakkai Sho Vol. 2: 4211
Nippon Oyo Dobutsu Konchu Gakkai Shoreisho Vol. 2: 4212
Nishiyama Medal Vol. 2: 4145
Nissan - Fitzgerald Vol. 1: 19691
Nissen Award Vol. 1: 8162
Nissen-Emery Award Vol. 1: 8162
Nissim Award; Rudolf Vol. 1: 4381
Nitti Prize; Fondazione Francesco Sarerio Vol. 2: 3817
Nivaud Award; Francois L. Vol. 1: 13162
Niwano Peace Prize Vol. 2: 4269
NJACI Merit Award Vol. 1: 1976
NJCAA All-American Baseball Team Vol. 1: 15316
Nkruma Prize in African Studies; Kwame Vol. 2: 3156
NLAG Regrant Program Vol. 1: 16542
NMRT Mid-Career Award Vol. 1: 12936
No Small Change Award Vol. 1: 12588
Noah Bee Award Vol. 1: 2908
Nobel Laureate Signature Award for a Graduate Student in Chemistry Vol. 1: 1775
Nobel Laureate Signature Award for Graduate Education in Chemistry Vol. 1: 1775
Nobel Peace Prize Vol. 2: 6172
Nobel Prize for Chemistry Vol. 2: 6173
Nobel Prize for Literature Vol. 2: 6174
Nobel Prize for Physics Vol. 2: 6175
Nobel Prize for Physiology or Medicine Vol. 2: 6176
Nobel Prizes Vol. 2: 6219
Noble Award; John Vol. 2: 8917
NOBLE Central Virginia Chapter Vol. 1: 15454
Noble Educational Scholarship; Leonard Vol. 1: 15715
Noble Prize; Alfred Vol. 1: 4345
NODA Scholarship Vol. 1: 15463
Noel-des-Vergers; Prix Adolphe Vol. 2: 1758
Nofflet William Up-and-Coming Leadership Award Vol. 1: 20959
NOGI Awards Vol. 1: 20295
Nolan Service Award; William G. Vol. 1: 11621
Nolte Award for Extraordinary Leadership; Julius M. Vol. 1: 20960
Nolting; International Award in Honor of Orin F. Vol. 1: 11476
Noma Award for the Translation of Japanese Literature Vol. 2: 4243
Noma Concours for Picture Book Illustrations
Asia/Pacific Cultural Centre for UNESCO Vol. 2: 4092
Kodansha Ltd. Vol 2: 4244
Noma Illustation Prizes Vol. 2: 4244
Noma Prize Vol. 2: 2606
Noma Prize for Juvenile Literature Vol. 2: 4245
Noma Prize for Literature Vol. 2: 4246
Non-Clinical Bursary Vol. 2: 7175
Non-Deadline Writing Vol. 1: 4579
Non-Fiction Book of the Year Award Vol. 1: 6991
Non-Heatset Web Printing Awards Competition Vol. 1: 17571
Nonfiction Award Vol. 1: 6413
Nonfiction Contest Vol. 1: 15992
Nonnenmacher Industry Service Award; Tom Vol. 1: 14274
Noranda Lecture Award Vol. 1: 7840
Norcen/CSPG Undergraduate Scholarship Vol. 1: 7488
Nordberg Medal; William Vol. 2: 2273
Nordberg Traveling Scholarship Vol. 2: 7741
Nordic Award
International Federation of Biomedical Laboratory Science Vol. 1: 11587
United States Ski and Snowboard Association Vol 1: 20815
Nordic Combined World Cup Leaders Vol. 2: 6447
Nordic Council Literature Prize Vol. 2: 6178
Nordic Council Music Prize Vol. 2: 6179
Nordic World Cup Leaders Vol. 2: 6447
Nordisk Insulinfonds H.C. Jacobaeus Lectures and Award Vol. 2: 1510
Nordisk Rads Musikpris Vol. 2: 6179
Nordiska Radets Litteraturpris Vol. 2: 6178
Norkool Award; Diane Vol. 1: 6256
Norman Cousins Award Vol. 1: 21901
Norman Cousins Global Governance Award Vol. 1: 21897
Norman Medal Vol. 1: 4346
Norman Scholarship Vol. 1: 12758
Normann Medal; W. Vol. 2: 2875
Noro Prize Vol. 2: 4146
Norris Award in Physical Organic Chemistry; James Flack Vol. 1: 1776
Norsk Varekrigsforsikringsfonds Prisbelonning for Yngre Forskere Vol. 2: 5145
Norske Sivilingeniorers Forenings Teknologipris Vol. 2: 5171
North America Award; Sharpest Knife in Vol. 1: 1267
North American Championship Trophy Vol. 1: 11728
North American Conservation Award
American Zoo and Aquarium Association Vol. 1: 4914
American Zoo and Aquarium Association Vol 1: 4918
North American Hairstyling Awards Vol. 1: 6298
North American Mixing Forum Award Vol. 1: 2785
North American Sculpture Exhibition Awards Vol. 1: 9678
North American Shortwave Broadcast DXer of the Year Vol. 1: 5797
North American Warmblood Association Awards Vol. 1: 16499
North Country Cheviot Hall of Fame; American Vol. 1: 3194
North of Scotland Sub Centre Premium Vol. 2: 7812
North Shore Trophy Vol. 2: 5066
Northcroft Memorial Lecture Vol. 2: 7103
Northeastern Loggers' Association Awards Program Vol. 1: 16548
Northern Arts Literary Fellowship Vol. 2: 8219
Northern Arts Writers' Awards Vol. 2: 8220
Northern Light Award Vol. 1: 12434
Northern New England Playwrights Award Vol. 1: 21269
Northern Rockies Sustainable Agriculture Award Vol. 1: 511
Northern Science Award Vol. 1: 10751
Northern Telecom Arts Europe Vol. 2: 9102

Northern Territory Literary Awards Vol. 2: 484
Northrop Distinguished Service Award; Cynthia Vol. 1: 1302
Northup Lecturer Award; Thomas L. Vol. 1: 741
Northwest Film and Video Festival Vol. 1: 16560
Northwest Flower & Garden Show Garden Award Vol. 1: 18036
Norton Award; Andre Vol. 1: 18357
Norton Award; Joseph Vol. 1: 5369
Norton Award; Margaret Cross Vol. 1: 13393
Norton Distinguished Ceramist Award; F. H. Vol. 1: 1692
Norton Memorial Scholarship Award for Women; Mary R. Vol. 1: 5973
Norwich Union Risk Services Award Vol. 2: 7877
Norwood Cultural Council Vol. 1: 9810
Nostra Aetate Award Vol. 1: 7712
Notable Achievements Vol. 1: 5334
Notable Wisconsin Authors Vol. 1: 21685
Notary of the Year Award Vol. 1: 15417
Notre Dame Award Vol. 1: 21090
Nourse Award; Edwin G. Vol. 1: 14801
Noury; Fondation de Madame Victor Vol. 2: 1840
NOVA Award Vol. 1: 8427
Nova Awards Vol. 1: 10260
NOVA Program of Distinction Awards Vol. 1: 15442
Novak Award Vol. 1: 160
Novartis Award; Graduate Student Fellowship/ Vol. 1: 19338
Novartis Corp Protection American Phytopathological Society Award Vol. 1: 19872
Novartis Crop Protection Agricultural Writing Award Vol. 1: 19873
Novartis Crop Protection Award in Agronomy Vol. 1: 19874
Novartis Crop Protection Entomological Society of America Award Vol. 1: 19875
Novartis Crop Protection NAFB Farm Broadcasting Award Vol. 1: 19876
Novartis Crop Protection Weed Science Society of America Award Vol. 1: 19877
NOVARTIS-ILAR Prize Vol. 2: 450
Novartis Medal and Prize Vol. 2: 6871
Novartis Nematology Award Vol. 1: 19223
Novel Disease Model Award; Liaison with Industry Committee Vol. 1: 3519
Novel Manuscript Award Vol. 1: 15993
Novella Award Vol. 1: 17785
Novella Prize Vol. 1: 13044
November 17th Medal Vol. 2: 1432
Nover Memorial Awards; Barnet Vol. 1: 19753
Novice Award Vol. 1: 20932
Novice Team Award Vol. 1: 19698
Novikoff Memorial Award; Philip A. Vol. 1: 7362
Novo Nordisk Foundation Lecture and Award Vol. 2: 1511
Novo Nordisk Prize Vol. 2: 1512
NovoPharm Award Vol. 1: 7467
Novotel Conference Organizer Award Vol. 2: 6774
Noyes Award; Marcia C. Vol. 1: 13265
NPI National Heritage Awards Vol. 2: 9103
NPM Scholarships Vol. 1: 14320
NPPA Citations Vol. 1: 15541
NRA Club Achievement Award Vol. 1: 10264
NRCA Fellow Vol. 1: 15606
NRCP Achievement Award Vol. 2: 5277
NROTC Essay Contest Vol. 1: 16055
NSES Award Vol. 2: 4866
NSES Graduation Prize Vol. 2: 4867
NSF-Funded Paid Internships Vol. 1: 7727
NSF-REV Vol. 1: 13634
NSPCA Annual Exhibition Vol. 1: 15744
NSPE Award Vol. 1: 15749
NSPS Scholarship Vol. 1: 15760
NSRA Heritage Foundation Scholarships Fund Vol. 1: 14883
NSSA Awards Vol. 2: 8194
NSTA ExploraVision Awards; Toshiba/ Vol. 1: 15693
NSTA Young Inventors Awards; Craftsman/ Vol. 1: 15686
NTC Citation Vol. 1: 15870
Nuclear Ships Trophy Vol. 1: 20933
Nuffield Lecture Vol. 2: 8826
Nuffield Silver Medal; Viscount Vol. 2: 7825
Number Theory; Frank Nelson Cole Prizes in Algebra and Vol. 1: 3043
Numerous Award Vol. 2: 8169
Numismatic Ambassador Award Vol. 1: 12619
Numismatic Error Collectors Exhibit Award Vol. 1: 3242
Nunn Award; Camp Scholarships Carl Vol. 1: 16763
Nuremberg International Human Rights Award Vol. 2: 3050
Nurse Manager Award Vol. 1: 9248
Nurse of the Year
  National Association of Traveling Nurses Vol. 1: 14447
  New York State Health Facilities Association Vol 1: 16285
Nurse of the Year Award Vol. 1: 15209
Nurse Practitioner of the Year Vol. 1: 16155
Nursery Extension Award for Distinguished Service to the Nursery Industry Vol. 1: 4089
Nursey Prize Vol. 2: 9046
Nursing Education Award Vol. 1: 9249
Nursing Practice Award Vol. 1: 9250
Nursing Professionalism Award Vol. 1: 9251
Nursing Research Award
  Emergency Nurses Association Vol. 1: 9252
  Texas League for Nursing Vol 1: 20025
Nursing Scholarship Vol. 1: 8418
Nursing Service Cross Vol. 2: 200
Nutrition Education Award Vol. 1: 1187
Nutrition Professionals, Inc. Applied Dairy Nutrition Award Vol. 1: 2111
Nutritional Research Award Vol. 1: 17170
NWAA Athletes of the Year Vol. 1: 21596
NWAA Hall of Fame Vol. 1: 21597
NWC Nonfiction Contest Vol. 1: 15992
NWC Novel Manuscript Award Vol. 1: 15993
NWC Poetry Award Vol. 1: 15994
NWC Short Story Award Vol. 1: 15996
NWRA Grants Vol. 1: 15955
NWRA Woman of the Year Vol. 1: 20755
Nycomed Prize Vol. 2: 7988
Nyholm Lectureship; Sir Ronald Vol. 2: 8767
Nymph Awards Vol. 2: 4669
Nypels Prijs; Charles Vol. 2: 4712
Nyselius Award Vol. 1: 16431
Nystrom Award; J. Warren Vol. 1: 5557
Nystrom's Prize; Professor E. J. Vol. 2: 1615
Nystroms Prize; Professor E. J. Vol. 2: 1615
NZNFFA Trophy Vol. 2: 7532
NZVA Award for Leading Second Year Student in Biology Vol. 2: 5037
NZVA Clinical Studies Award Vol. 2: 5038
OA Medal Vol. 1: 16919
Oaboos Prize for Environmental Preservation; Sultan Vol. 2: 2602
Oak Leaf Award Vol. 1: 16032
Oakley Certificate of Merit Vol. 1: 5377
OAPEC Award for Scientific Research Vol. 2: 4378
Obando; Medalla Militar Soldado Juan Bautista Solarte Vol. 2: 1283
Obee Small Player Award; V. C. "Bub" Vol. 1: 15316
Oberle Award for Outstanding Teaching in Grades K-12; Marcella E. Vol. 1: 14714
Oberly Award for Bibliography in the Agricultural Sciences Vol. 1: 5616
Oberly Memorial Award; Eunice Rockwell Vol. 1: 5616
Oberman and Rich Award Vol. 1: 10682
Oberst Award; Byron B. Vol. 1: 784
OBIE Awards; The Village Voice Vol. 1: 21368
Object Animation Vol. 1: 16955
Oboler Memorial Award; Eli M. Vol. 1: 2988
Obreshkov Prize; Academy Nikola Vol. 2: 1207
O'Brien Award; Jane Vol. 1: 10683
O'Brien Award; Robert F. Vol. 1: 14598
O'Brien Prize; Patrick Vol. 2: 7676
O'Brien Project Grants; Ruth Vol. 1: 943
O'Brien Trophy; World Championship - Larry Vol. 1: 14509
Obrig Prize; Adolph and Clara Vol. 1: 13792
Obrig Prize for Painting in Oil; Adolph and Clara Vol. 1: 13793
O'Byrne Award; Father Patrick Vol. 1: 21226
OC Award Vol. 1: 16817
Occupational Safety/Health Award Program Vol. 1: 15658
Occupational Safety/Health Contests Vol. 1: 15659
Ocean Crew and Great Lake Crew Award of Merit Vol. 1: 20379
Ocean Crew and Great Lakes Awards of Merit Vol. 1: 3093
Ocean Crew Award of Merit Vol. 1: 3094
Ocean Sciences Award Vol. 1: 2356
Oceaneering International Award Vol. 1: 20291
Ochal Award for Distinguished Service to the Profession; Bethany J. Vol. 1: 1255
Ochsner Award Relating Smoking and Health; Alton Vol. 1: 16609
OCIC-Prize Vol. 2: 1103
O'Connor Award for Short Fiction; Flannery Vol. 1: 21026
O'Connor Essay Award; Richard Vol. 1: 5132
OCTM Prize Vol. 2: 6488
ODAS Youth Achievement Award Vol. 1: 433
O'Day Trophy; U.S. Singlehanded Sailing Championship - George D. Vol. 1: 20785
O'Dell Award; William Vol. 1: 3034
Odense International Film Festival Vol. 2: 1514
Odesser Judaic Literary Award; Ben and Sylvia Vol. 1: 2880
Odlum Award; Doris Vol. 2: 7077
O'Donoghue Sports Injury Research Award Vol. 1: 3352

Odontological Commemorative Lecture Vol. 2: 8827
Odyssey Diploma Vol. 2: 6347
Oehlenschlager Prize; Adam Vol. 2: 1475
Oehmler Award; George C. Vol. 1: 21842
Oelke Memorial Award for Painting; Kimbel E. Vol. 1: 662
Oenslager Scholastic Achievement Awards; Mary P. Vol. 1: 17905
Oersted Medal Vol. 1: 1377
Offensive and Defensive Linemen of the Year Vol. 1: 15086
The Office Building of the Year (TOBY) Vol. 1: 6685
Office of Civilian Radioactive Waste Management Graduate Fellowship Program Vol. 1: 16598
Office of Civilian Radioactive Waste Management Historically Black Colleges and Universities Undergraduate Scholarship Program Vol. 1: 16599
Office of the Americas Peace & Justice Award Vol. 1: 16616
Office of the Prime Minister Medals of Honor Vol. 2: 4191
Office of the Status of Women Award Vol. 2: 664
Officer of the Year Awards Vol. 1: 11411
Officers Medallion Vol. 1: 11667
Official of the Year Vol. 1: 20386
Official of the Year Award Vol. 1: 21248
Official UNESCO Award for Distinguished Services to Physical Education and Sport Vol. 2: 2603
O'Flaherty Service Award; Fred Vol. 1: 2943
Ofsthun Award; SRE Stan Vol. 1: 19292
Ogden Award; H. R. "Russ" Vol. 1: 5974
O'Hagan Award for Short Fiction; Howard Vol. 1: 21987
O'Hair Memorial Award; Robert C. Vol. 1: 12268
O'Hana Prize; Jacques and Eugenie Vol. 2: 3773
Ohaus Award for Innovations in Science Teaching; Gustav Vol. 1: 15690
O'Henry Awards Vol. 1: 9006
Ohio Award Vol. 1: 15018
Ohioana Award for Editorial Excellence Vol. 1: 16657
Ohioana Book Awards Vol. 1: 16661
Ohioana Career Award Vol. 1: 16662
Ohioana Citation for Distinguished Service to Ohio Vol. 1: 16663
Ohioana Pegasus Award Vol. 1: 16664
OHIS Youth Achievement Vol. 1: 16808
Oils and Fats Group International Lecture Vol. 2: 9018
Oita International Wheelchair Marathon Vol. 2: 4271
Oke Trophy (New England Division Champion); F. G. (Teddy) Vol. 1: 2514
Oken Medaille; Lorenz Vol. 2: 2906
Okes Award; Imogene Vol. 1: 950
Oklahoma School Administrator Award Vol. 1: 16670
OKOMEDIA International Ecological Film Festival Vol. 2: 3040
Okuma Academic Commemorative Prize Vol. 2: 4323
Okuma Academic Encouragement Prize Vol. 2: 4324
Okuma Gakujutsu Kinensho Vol. 2: 4323
Okuma Gakujutsu Shoreisho Vol. 2: 4324
Olah Award in Hydrocarbon or Petroleum Chemistry; George A. Vol. 1: 1777
O'Laoghaire Memorial Trophy; Pilib Vol. 2: 3627
Olave Award Vol. 2: 9240
Old Forge Hardware Prize Vol. 1: 5153
Old Guard Prizes Vol. 1: 4535
Old Hilltop Award Vol. 1: 13135
Old Masters Award Vol. 2: 7957
Old Tackle Makers Vol. 1: 15047
Old Timers Vol. 1: 16283
Oldenburger Medal; Rufus Vol. 1: 4536
Oldendorf Award; William H. Vol. 1: 4574
Oldfield Cup (Premier Award); Lucy Vol. 2: 7199
Oldman Prize; C. B. Vol. 2: 7901
Ole Dyrhauge Commemorative Award Vol. 2: 5943
O'Leary Award; Bart Vol. 1: 14189
O'Leary Award; Vincent Vol. 1: 5808
Olfactory Research Fund Sense of Smell Award Vol. 1: 9722
Olin Fellowships Vol. 1: 6043
Olin Fox (Memorial) Award Vol. 1: 17783
Olin Medal; Francis P. Garvan-John M. Vol. 1: 1755
Olivarez La Raza Award; Graciela Vol. 1: 14806
Oliver Memorial Award; Leslie Vol. 2: 9270
Oliver Prize; Brian Vol. 2: 8467
Olivier Awards; Laurence Vol. 2: 9057
Olle Prize; Archibald D. Vol. 2: 541
Ollie Awards; American Center for Children's Television - Vol. 1: 1664
Olman Publishers Award; Abe Vol. 1: 13816
Olmsted Award; Frederick Law Vol. 1: 13949
Olmsted Award; George Vol. 1: 2289
Olmsted Liberal Education Award for Innovation Vol. 1: 4032
Olmsted Medal; Frederick Law Vol. 1: 4483
Olney Medal Vol. 1: 1457
OLSC Youth Grant Vol. 1: 16596
Olson Award; Harris Vol. 1: 2448
Olson Common Loon Research Award; Sigurd T. Vol. 1: 12917
Olympiart Vol. 2: 6425
Olympic Cup Vol. 2: 6426
Olympic Football Tournaments (Men and Women) Vol. 2: 6360
Olympic Medals and Diplomas Vol. 2: 6427
Olympic Order Vol. 2: 6428
Olympic Spirit Award Vol. 1: 20722
Olympique; Ordre Vol. 2: 6428
O'Mahony Bursary; Eoin Vol. 2: 3702
O'Malley Art Award Vol. 1: 12201
O'Malley Award; Diane Vol. 1: 5112
O'Malley Award; General Jerome F. Vol. 1: 348
Omicron Delta Kappa Scholarships Vol. 1: 16701
OMSA Recognition and Component Awards Vol. 1: 16645
On Behalf of Youth Award Vol. 1: 6775
On-the-Spot Awards Vol. 1: 20470
Onassis International Cultural Competition Prizes Vol. 2: 3182
Onassis International Prize for Culture, Arts and Humanities Vol. 2: 3183
Onassis International Prize for International Understanding and for Social Achievement Vol. 2: 3184
Onassis International Prize for the Environment Vol. 2: 3185
Onassis Medal; Jacqueline Kennedy Vol. 1: 13680
Onassis Prize for Man and Culture - Olympia Vol. 2: 3183
Onassis Prize for Man and His Environment - Delphi Vol. 2: 3185
Onciul Prize; Dimitrie Vol. 2: 5854
Oncology Social Worker of the Year Vol. 1: 5804
Ondaatje Vol. 2: 7509
Ondaatje Prize Vol. 2: 8795
One Club Award Vol. 1: 18469
One Hundred Years of the Periodical *Health* Medal Vol. 2: 5377
One Show Awards Vol. 1: 16732
One Ton Championship - Hawk Trophy Vol. 1: 20778
One World Award
International Quorum of Film and Video Producers Vol. 2: 6438
U.S. International Film and Video Festival Vol 1: 20675
O'Neal Safety Award; Jack Vol. 1: 20425
O'Neill Award; Joseph E. Vol. 1: 15810
O'Neill Awards Vol. 1: 15509
Ong Memorial Award; William A. "Bill" Vol. 1: 13921
Online Journalism Award Vol. 1: 15521
Ono Memorial Awards; Azusa Vol. 2: 4325
Ono Memorial Awards for Art; Azusa Vol. 2: 4325
Ono Memorial Awards for Sports; Azusa Vol. 2: 4325
ONS/AMGEN Inc. Award for Excellence in Patient/Public Education Vol. 1: 16722
ONS/Pharmacia & Upjohn Excellence in Oncology Nursing Private Practice Award Vol. 1: 16723
ONS/Roche Distinguished Service Award Vol. 1: 16724
ONS/Ross Products Division of Abbott Laboratories Award for Excellence in Cancer Nursing Education Vol. 1: 16725
ONS/Schering Excellence in Biotherapy Nursing Award Vol. 1: 16726
ONS/Schering Excellence in Cancer Nursing Research Award Vol. 1: 16727
ONS/Upjohn Quality of Life Award Vol. 1: 16728
Onsager Prize; Lars Vol. 1: 3465
Onshi Sho Vol. 2: 4154
Ontario College of Art & Design Scholarship Vol. 1: 21781
Ontario Medal for Firefighter Bravery Vol. 1: 16754
Ontario Medal for Good Citizenship Vol. 1: 16755
Ontario Medal for Police Bravery Vol. 1: 16756
Ontario Waste Minimization Awards Vol. 1: 17923
Open Art Exhibition Prize Vol. 2: 8642
Open Bible Award Vol. 1: 17110
Open Book Awards Vol. 1: 4470
Open Championship Vol. 2: 8420
Open Division Overall Vol. 1: 21252
Open Door Award Vol. 1: 10566
Open Dutch Championships for Concert Division Vol. 2: 4939
Open Palm Award Vol. 1: 10720
Open Water Swimmer of the Year Vol. 1: 21197
Opera Prize Vol. 2: 6234
Opera Production Competition Vol. 1: 15428

Opera Screen Award Vol. 2: 759
Operasangerinnen Fanny Elstas Fond Vol. 2: 5123
Operational Research Development Prize Vol. 1: 11600
Operations-Services Awards Vol. 1: 10091
Operator of the Year Vol. 1: 16013
Opernwelt Prize Vol. 2: 803
Ophthalmology Fund Prizes and Lectures Vol. 2: 8828
Opie Prize; Peter and Iona Vol. 1: 2265
Opik Award Vol. 2: 3650
Opinion Award Vol. 1: 11114
Oporto International Film Festival - Fantasporto Vol. 2: 5396
Oppenheim John Downes Memorial Trust Vol. 2: 8234
Oppenheimer Award Vol. 1: 4033
Oppenheimer Memorial Award; Ernst Vol. 1: 9263
Oppenheimer/*Newsday* Playwriting Award; George Vol. 1: 16322
OPPI Best Vendor Award Vol. 2: 3579
Oppy Award Vol. 1: 16322
Oprescu Prize; George Vol. 2: 5855
The Opthalmological Gold Medal Vol. 2: 1557
Optical Society of India Award Vol. 2: 3575
Optical Special Citation Award Vol. 2: 3891
OPTIMA Gold Medal Vol. 2: 6075
OPTIMA Silver Medal Vol. 2: 6076
Optimas Awards Vol. 1: 21838
Optimist International Awards Vol. 1: 16802
Optometry Outstanding Service and Recognition Award Vol. 1: 5786
Ora Award Vol. 1: 15303
Oral and Maxillofacial Radiology Award; Howard R. Raper Vol. 1: 729
Oral Science Research Award Vol. 1: 11218
The Orange British Academy Film Awards Vol. 2: 6906
Orators Hall of Fame Vol. 1: 11808
Orban Prize; Balint Vol. 1: 808
Orbis Books Prize for Polish Studies Vol. 1: 1057
Orbis Pictus Nonfiction Award Vol. 1: 14835
Orbit Award of the ANZAAS International Scientific Film Exhibition and Competition Vol. 2: 144
ORCA Rolex Prize Vol. 2: 4768
ORCA Zsolnay Prize Vol. 2: 4769
Orchard-Hays Prize Vol. 1: 13201
Orchestral Audition and Masterclass Competition Vol. 1: 15062
Orde van Oranje-Nassau Vol. 2: 4708
Orden al Merito Julio Garavito Vol. 2: 1304
Orden del Merito Aeronautico Antonio Ricaurte Vol. 2: 1289
Orden del Merito Agricola Vol. 2: 1273
Orden del Merito Jose Maria Cordoba Vol. 2: 1290
Orden del Merito Militar Antonio Narino Vol. 2: 1291
Orden del Merito Naval Almirante Padilla Vol. 2: 1292
Orden del Merito Penitenciario Vol. 2: 1302
Orden del Merito Sanitario Jose Fernandez Madrid Vol. 2: 1293
Orden Mexicana del Aguila Azteca Vol. 2: 4567
Orden Militar San Mateo Vol. 2: 1294
Orden Nacional al Merito Vol. 2: 1276
Orden Universidad Javeriana Vol. 2: 1335
Order Ingenio et Arti Vol. 2: 1484
Order Odrodzenia Polski Vol. 2: 5326
Order of Australia Vol. 2: 201
Order of Canada Vol. 1: 6827
Order of Cultural Vol. 2: 4181
Order of Culture Vol. 2: 4192
Order of Excellence of Guyana Vol. 2: 3217
Order of Honour Service Awards Vol. 1: 17606
Order of Hospitality Vol. 2: 5913
Order of Magellan Vol. 1: 8007
Order of Mariposa Vol. 1: 19791
Order of Merit
Central Chancery of the Orders of Knighthood Vol. 2: 7259
International Basketball Federation Vol 2: 6386
National Wrestling Hall of Fame & Museum Vol 1: 15989
Religious and Military Order of Knights of the Holy Sepulchre of Jerusalem Vol 1: 17979
Order of Merit in Agriculture Vol. 2: 1273
Order of Merit of the Police Forces Vol. 1: 6815
Order of Merit of the Republic of Poland Vol. 2: 5325
The Order of NSU Vol. 1: 16587
Order of Ontario Vol. 1: 16757
Order of Orange-Nassau Vol. 2: 4708
Order of Pius IX Vol. 2: 9311
Order of Red Triangle Vol. 1: 22036
Order of Rio Branco Vol. 2: 1149
Order of Roraima of Guyana Vol. 2: 3218
Order of St. Gregory the Great Vol. 2: 9312
Order of St. John of Jerusalem Vol. 1: 6815
Order of St. Sylvester Vol. 2: 9313
Order of San Carlos Vol. 2: 1277
Order of Sancta Barbara Vol. 1: 7201
Order of the Academic Palms Vol. 2: 2393
Order of the Bird Vol. 1: 11390
Order of the Companions of Honour Vol. 2: 7260
Order of the Compassionate Heart Vol. 1: 17960
Order of the Cross of Liberty Vol. 2: 1588
Order of the Eagle Vol. 1: 16
Order of the Egg Vol. 1: 11391
Order of the Golden Ark Vol. 2: 4709
Order of the Golden Eagle Vol. 1: 17961
Order of the Golden Lion Vol. 1: 21
Order of the Golden Microscope Vol. 1: 3067
Order of the Golden Rose Vol. 2: 3685
Order of the Golden Spur (Golden Militia) Vol. 2: 9314
Order of the Lapis Lazuli Vol. 1: 9486
Order of the Lion of Finland Vol. 2: 1589
Order of the Netherlands Lion Vol. 2: 4710
Order of the Rebirth of Poland Vol. 2: 5326
Order of the Rose Vol. 2: 1231
The Order of the Royal Huntsman Award Vol. 2: 7315
Order of the White Rose of Finland Vol. 2: 1590
Order of West Range Vol. 1: 17310
Order of White Eagle Vol. 2: 5327
Order Wojenny Virtuti Militari Vol. 2: 5328
Order Zaslugi Rzeczypospolitej Polskiej Vol. 2: 5325
Orders of the Precious Crown Vol. 2: 4193
Orders of the Rising Sun Vol. 2: 4194
Orders of the Sacred Treasure Vol. 2: 4195
Orders of the U.S. Air Force Vol. 1: 8830
Orders of the U.S. Army Vol. 1: 8831
Orders of the U.S. Coast Guard Vol. 1: 8832
Orders of the U.S. Marine Corps Vol. 1: 8833
Orders of the U.S. Navy Vol. 1: 8834
Ordnance Survey Award Vol. 2: 6974
Ordo Honorium Award Vol. 1: 12515
Ordre du Conseil de la Vie Francaise en Amerique Vol. 1: 8422
Ordre Olympique Vol. 2: 6428
Ordway Stewardship Award; Katherine Vol. 1: 16036
Orenstein Memorial Fund; Doris Vol. 1: 5742
Orford String Quartet Scholarship Vol. 1: 16745
Organ Competition; International Vol. 2: 2280
Organ Historical Society Archival Fellowship Vol. 1: 16871
Organic Food Awards Vol. 2: 9092
Organic or Bioorganic Chemistry; Boehringer Ingelheim Award for Vol. 1: 7833
Organization and Institution Citations Vol. 1: 15876
Organization of Islamic Capitals and Cities Awards Vol. 2: 5928
Organization of the Year Vol. 1: 20351
Organizational Award Vol. 1: 15593
Organizational Certificate of Appreciation Vol. 1: 8441
Organizing Excellence Award Vol. 1: 14347
Organon Award Vol. 1: 7468
Orientation Profession Award; Outstanding Contributions to the Vol. 1: 15462
Orlando Award; Babe Vol. 1: 12118
Orme Prize; Margaret Vol. 2: 9187
Ormes Trophy; Sam Vol. 1: 20131
Ormond Medal; Francis Vol. 2: 500
Ornish Award; Natalie Vol. 1: 20020
Ornithologen-Preis Vol. 2: 2857
Oro; Medallion de Vol. 1: 16457
Oronzio De Nora Foundation Prize of ISE on Electrochemical Energy Conversion Vol. 2: 6457
Oronzio De Nora Foundation Prize of ISE on Electrochemical Technology and Engineering Vol. 2: 6458
Oronzio De Nora Foundation Young Author Prize Vol. 2: 6459
Orpherians Vol. 1: 21591
Orr Award; Joan Vol. 1: 349
Orr Award; Paul G. Vol. 2: 1549
Orr Award; Verne Vol. 1: 350
Orr E. Reynolds Distinguished Service Award Vol. 1: 4080
ORSA Prize Vol. 1: 11074
Ortega y Gasset Award for Journalism Vol. 2: 6039
Ortho Pharmaceutical Corporation and McNeil Pharmaceutical Young Investigator Award in Infectious Diseases Vol. 1: 10792
Orthopedic Allied Professional of the Year Vol. 1: 4582
Orton Award; Samuel T. Vol. 1: 11549
Orton, Jr., Memorial Lecturer; Edward Vol. 1: 1693
Orville Scholarship in Meteorology; Howard T. Vol. 1: 3101
Orwell Award for Distinguished Contribution to Honesty and Clarity in Public Language; George Vol. 1: 14836
OSA Leadership Award/New Focus Bookham Prize Vol. 1: 16795
OSA Leadership Award/New Focus Prize Vol. 1: 16795

Osas Festspillfond; Sigbjorn Bernhoft Vol. 2: 5124
Osborne Award; Ernest Vol. 1: 14863
Oscar Howe Memorial Award Vol. 1: 10424
Oscars in Agriculture Vol. 1: 21030
Osetek Educator Award; Edward M. Vol. 1: 1193
Osgood Prize Vol. 1: 17036
O'Shannessy Award Vol. 2: 586
Osiris Award Vol. 2: 3949
Osiris; Prix Vol. 2: 2431
Osler Award Vol. 1: 6625
Osler Medal; William Vol. 1: 1061
Oslo Bys Kulturpris Vol. 2: 5176
Oslo Kommune Artist Prizes Vol. 2: 5175
Oslo Kommune Culture Prize Vol. 2: 5176
Ostermeier Memorial Award; Rosemary and Donald Vol. 1: 15721
Osterreichischer Graphikwettbewerb Vol. 2: 676
Osterweil Award for Poetry; PEN/Joyce Vol. 1: 17144
OSU Photography and Cinema Alumni Society Award Vol. 1: 7951
Osuna Sportsmanship Award Vol. 1: 11141
Otaka Prize Vol. 2: 4265
Otology Politzer Society Award Vol. 2: 4821
O'Toole Agency Award Vol. 1: 1076
O'Toole Multicultural Advertising Award Vol. 1: 1077
O'Toole Public Service Award Vol. 1: 1078
OTR Partnership Award; Terry Brittell COTA/ Vol. 1: 3293
Otremba Memorial Award; Elke Vol. 1: 7522
Ott Award for Outstanding Contribution to Children's Literature; Helen Keating Vol. 1: 7976
Ott Prize; Theodore Vol. 2: 6506
Ottawa Architectural Conservation Awards Vol. 1: 8042
Otto A. Rothert Award Vol. 1: 9547
Otto Aufranc Award Vol. 1: 10442
Our American Indian Heritage Award
- National Federation of State Poetry Societies Vol. 1: 14989
- National Federation of State Poetry Societies Vol 1: 15019

Our Native American Heritage Award Vol. 1: 15019
Ousley Special Service Award; Robert Vol. 1: 4724
Outdoor Classic Award Vol. 1: 15465
Outdoor Communications Awards Vol. 1: 16973
Outdoor Ethics Awards Vol. 1: 12269
Outdoor Writing Awards Vol. 1: 16973
Outgoing Governor Award Vol. 1: 3243
Outgoing Officer Award Vol. 1: 11668
Outgoing President Award Vol. 1: 3244
Outland Trophy Vol. 1: 9674
Outler Prize in Ecumenical Church History; Albert C. Vol. 1: 4287
Outline of Sanity Award Vol. 1: 1800
Outreach Services Award Vol. 1: 5060
Outstanding Academic Librarian Award Vol. 1: 12943
Outstanding Accountant of the Year Award Vol. 1: 6320
Outstanding Achievement Award
- Alliance for Children and Television Vol. 1: 456
- American Association of Blood Banks Vol 1: 1113
- American Historic Inns Vol 1: 2461
- Armenian Behavioral Science Association Vol 1: 5094
- Automotive Industry Action Group Vol 1: 6115
- Canadian Association of Career Educators and Employers Vol 1: 6899
- Internet Alliance Vol 1: 12153
- National Association of Metal Finishers Vol 1: 14308
- Northeast Catholic Alumni Association Vol 1: 16539
- Renewable Natural Resources Foundation Vol 1: 17988
- Society for the Study of Lesbian, Gay and Bisexual Concerns (Division 44) Vol 1: 18917
- Society of Woman Geographers Vol 1: 19361
- Treasury Board of Canada Secretariat Vol 1: 20183

Outstanding Achievement Award-Group Vol. 1: 2804
Outstanding Achievement Award-Individual Vol. 1: 2805
Outstanding Achievement Awards
- International Wild Waterfowl Association Vol. 1: 12137
- Texas Engineering Experiment Station Vol 1: 20003

Outstanding Achievement in Adolescent Medicine Award Vol. 1: 18619
Outstanding Achievement in Water Quality Improvement Award Vol. 1: 21495
Outstanding Administrator Award Vol. 1: 1111
Outstanding Adult Advisor Award Vol. 1: 3245
Outstanding Adult Learner Vol. 1: 951
Outstanding Advising Awards Vol. 1: 13769
Outstanding Advising Program Awards Vol. 1: 13770
Outstanding Advocate Award
- American Association of Nurse Attorneys Vol. 1: 1303
- Easter Seals Vol 1: 9089

Outstanding Affiliate Award Vol. 1: 16372
Outstanding Alumni Achievement Award Vol. 1: 16579
Outstanding Alumnus Award Vol. 1: 16540
Outstanding American Films of the Year Awards Vol. 1: 2241
Outstanding American Indian Awards Vol. 1: 2597
Outstanding Animal Control Agency of the Year Vol. 1: 13939
Outstanding Article Award Vol. 1: 180
Outstanding Article in *American Journal of Agricultural Economics* Award Vol. 1: 872
Outstanding Arts Educator Award Vol. 1: 19900
Outstanding Associate Business Member of the Year Vol. 1: 13375
Outstanding Association Executive Award Vol. 1: 5887
Outstanding Band Musician Award Vol. 1: 14487
Outstanding Biology Teacher Award Vol. 1: 14097
Outstanding Book Award
- Academy of Criminal Justice Sciences Vol. 1: 91
- American Educational Research Association Vol 1: 2163
- History of Education Society Vol 1: 10483

Outstanding Booth Awards Vol. 1: 13980
Outstanding Business, Industry, Organization, or Individual Contribution Award Vol. 1: 15930
Outstanding Business Leader Awards Vol. 1: 16573
Outstanding Business Person of the Year Vol. 1: 21584
Outstanding Certified Flight Instructor Award Vol. 1: 10402
Outstanding Chapter Advisor Award Vol. 1: 3394
Outstanding Chapter Award
- Arnold Air Society Vol. 1: 5113
- Eta Kappa Nu Vol 1: 9342
- International Association of Assessing Officers Vol 1: 11280
- International Fluid Power Society Vol 1: 11628
- Kappa Delta Epsilon Vol 1: 12505

Outstanding Chapter Awards
- American Academy of Pediatrics Vol. 1: 785
- Institute of Electrical and Electronics Engineers - Power Engineering Society Vol 1: 10908

Outstanding Chapter Communication Products Award Vol. 1: 11941
Outstanding Chapter Leadership Award Vol. 1: 15210
Outstanding Chapter Newsletter Award Vol. 1: 15211
Outstanding Chapter of the Year Award Vol. 1: 1188
Outstanding Citizen Award Vol. 1: 8509
Outstanding Citizenship Award Vol. 1: 15779
Outstanding Civil Engineering Achievement Vol. 1: 4347
Outstanding Civitan Awareness Project Vol. 1: 8065
Outstanding Club Bulletin Vol. 1: 8066
Outstanding Club Publication Award Vol. 1: 3246
Outstanding Club Representative Award Vol. 1: 3247
Outstanding Coach's Award Vol. 1: 15080
Outstanding Colleague Award Vol. 1: 14121
Outstanding Committee Chairman Award Vol. 1: 5888
Outstanding Community College Educator Award Vol. 1: 4034
Outstanding Community Service Award Vol. 1: 5561
Outstanding Community Service Awards Vol. 2: 654
Outstanding Community Service Project Vol. 1: 8067
Outstanding Competition Management Awards Vol. 1: 20569
Outstanding Competitor Award Vol. 1: 16466
Outstanding Congregational Librarian Vol. 1: 7977
Outstanding Congregational Library Vol. 1: 7978
Outstanding Continuing Education Student Awards Vol. 1: 20961
Outstanding Contribution Award
- Canadian Sociology and Anthropology Association Vol. 1: 7502
- National Association of Jewelry Appraisers Vol 1: 14295

Outstanding Contribution by an Individual for Educational/Training Activities Vol. 1: 5267

Outstanding Contribution by an Organization Vol. 1: 15434
Outstanding Contribution in the Field of Tibetan Literature Vol. 2: 3591
Outstanding Contribution to ACE by an Organization Vol. 1: 5652
Outstanding Contribution to ACM Award Vol. 1: 5305
Outstanding Contribution to Amateur Football Award Vol. 1: 15074
Outstanding Contribution to Campus Ministry Award Vol. 1: 5850
Outstanding Contribution to Co-operative Education and Training Vol. 1: 5653
Outstanding Contribution to Congregational Libraries Vol. 1: 7979
Outstanding Contribution to Forest Industry Education Vol. 1: 16548
Outstanding Contribution to Higher Education Award Vol. 1: 14405
Outstanding Contribution to Literature or Research Award Vol. 1: 14406
Outstanding Contribution to Ophthalmic Photography Vol. 1: 16779
Outstanding Contribution to Publishing Award Vol. 1: 6413
Outstanding Contribution to Rehabilitation Award Vol. 1: 3709
Outstanding Contribution to Research Award Vol. 1: 613
Outstanding Contribution to Rural Life Award Vol. 1: 18188
Outstanding Contribution to Safety Vol. 1: 16548
Outstanding Contribution to the Adoption Community Vol. 1: 9396
Outstanding Contributions for a Publication in the *Journal of Clinical Chemistry* Award Vol. 1: 989
Outstanding Contributions in Education Vol. 1: 990
Outstanding Contributions Through Service to the Profession of Clinical Chemistry Vol. 1: 991
Outstanding Contributions to Clinical Chemistry Vol. 1: 992
Outstanding Contributions to Clinical Chemistry in a Selected Area of Research Vol. 1: 993
Outstanding Contributions to Clinical Chemistry Through Science or Technology Vol. 1: 994
Outstanding Contributions to Education Vol. 1: 995
Outstanding Contributions to Health Psychology Vol. 1: 3689
Outstanding Contributions to Research in Veterinary Parasitology Vol. 1: 21854
Outstanding Contributions to the IAEE Vol. 1: 11224
Outstanding Contributions to the Orientation Profession Award Vol. 1: 15462
Outstanding Contributions to the Profession Award Vol. 1: 11225
Outstanding Contributor Awards Vol. 1: 10973
Outstanding Corporate Growth Award Vol. 1: 5332
Outstanding Corporation Award Vol. 1: 5705
Outstanding Council Award Vol. 1: 1033
Outstanding County Program Awards Vol. 1: 16506
Outstanding Decision Maker Award Vol. 1: 5061
Outstanding Directorial Achievement Award for Feature Films Vol. 1: 8947
Outstanding Directorial Achievement Award for Television Vol. 1: 8948
Outstanding Disabled Athlete of the Year Vol. 1: 21234
Outstanding Disabled Veteran of the Year Vol. 1: 8955
Outstanding Disabled Veteran Outreach Coordinator Vol. 1: 8956
Outstanding Dissertation Award
American Association of Colleges for Teacher Education Vol. 1: 1152
American Psychological Association - Exercise and Sport Psychology Division (Division 47) Vol 1: 3682
American Psychological Association - Society of Clinical Psychology (Division 12) Vol 1: 3749
American Psychological Association (Division 28) Vol 1: 3765
National Association for Research in Science Teaching Vol 1: 14033
Outstanding Dissertation of the Year Award Vol. 1: 11869
Outstanding Division Award Vol. 1: 12220
Outstanding Doctoral Thesis Award Vol. 1: 873
Outstanding Doctoral Thesis Research in Atomic, Molecular, or Optical Physics Award Vol. 1: 3466
Outstanding Doctoral Thesis Research in Beam Physics Award Vol. 1: 3467
Outstanding Donor Recruiter Award Vol. 1: 1108
Outstanding Earth Science Teacher Award Vol. 1: 14239
Outstanding Educator Award Vol. 1: 275
Outstanding Educator Award
American Ceramic Society Vol. 1: 1694
American Society for Engineering Education Vol 1: 4035
Association for Women Geoscientists Vol 1: 5520
Public Relations Society of America Vol 1: 17723
Radiological Society of North America Vol 1: 17854
Outstanding Elected Democratic Woman Holding Public Office Vol. 1: 14967
Outstanding Electrical Engineering Junior Award Vol. 1: 9343
Outstanding Electrical Engineering Student Award Vol. 1: 9344
Outstanding Elementary, Middle Level and Secondary Teachers Vol. 1: 19993
Outstanding Elementary Social Studies Teacher of the Year Award Vol. 1: 14786
Outstanding Engineer Award Vol. 1: 10909
Outstanding Environmental and Engineering Geologic Project Award Vol. 1: 5676
Outstanding Executive Director of a State, Provincial, and Territorial Association (SPTA) Award Vol. 1: 3675
Outstanding Exhibit Award Vol. 1: 9517
Outstanding Explorer Award Vol. 1: 1345
Outstanding Extension Educator Award Vol. 1: 4089
Outstanding Faculty Adviser Vol. 1: 17327
Outstanding Faculty Development Award Vol. 1: 6321
Outstanding Federal Services Health Administrator Award Vol. 1: 5778
Outstanding Field Chapter Vol. 1: 17326
Outstanding Financial Manager Vol. 1: 5102
Outstanding Fluid Power Educator Vol. 1: 11627
Outstanding Football Official Award Vol. 1: 15075
Outstanding Forest Steward of the Year Vol. 1: 16167
Outstanding Forestry Extension Publication Award Vol. 1: 15980
Outstanding Forestry Extension Video Award Vol. 1: 15981
Outstanding Forestry Journalism Award Vol. 1: 18973
Outstanding Foundation Award Vol. 1: 5706
Outstanding Fund Raising Executive Award Vol. 1: 5700
Outstanding Genealogists Vol. 1: 16077
Outstanding General Manager Vol. 1: 2568
Outstanding German Educator Award Vol. 1: 1447
Outstanding Giant Schnauzer Award Vol. 1: 10019
Outstanding Government Service Award
American Bar Association Vol. 1: 1535
American Numismatic Association Vol 1: 3248
Outstanding Graduate Educator Award Vol. 1: 4090
Outstanding Graduate Student Award Vol. 1: 20259
Outstanding Graduate Student Member of the Year Award Vol. 1: 8552
Outstanding Grassland Farmer or Rancher Award Vol. 1: 2276
Outstanding Health Worker Vol. 1: 20697
Outstanding Hearing Conservationist Award Vol. 1: 15197
Outstanding High School Player Vol. 1: 16684
Outstanding High School Senior in German Vol. 1: 1448
Outstanding Human Performance Intervention Award Vol. 1: 11942
Outstanding Human Service Student Vol. 1: 15435
Outstanding Humanitarian Service Award Vol. 1: 714
Outstanding IIE Publication Award Vol. 1: 10962
Outstanding Individual at the Local Level Vol. 1: 16373
Outstanding Individual at the National/International Level Vol. 1: 16374
Outstanding Individual Volunteer Award Vol. 1: 2936
Outstanding Industry Activist Vol. 1: 16548
Outstanding Industry Leader Vol. 1: 11629
Outstanding Industry Scientist Award Vol. 1: 4091
Outstanding Information Science Teacher Award Vol. 1: 4111
Outstanding Instructional Communication Award Vol. 1: 11943
Outstanding Instructional Product Vol. 1: 11944
Outstanding Instructional Product or Intervention Award Vol. 1: 11944
Outstanding Instructor Vol. 2: 3316
Outstanding International Horticulturist ASHS Career Awards Vol. 1: 4092
Outstanding International Service Award Vol. 1: 10092
Outstanding Jazz Educator Award Vol. 1: 14488

Award Index

Outstanding Journalism Award Vol. 1: 2029
Outstanding Journalist Award Vol. 1: 6079
Outstanding Judge Award Vol. 1: 12592
Outstanding Junior Member Contest Vol. 1: 15712
Outstanding Junior Shorthorn Breeder Award Vol. 1: 2915
Outstanding Large and Small Employer Award Vol. 1: 8957
Outstanding Large Chapter Award Vol. 1: 10908
Outstanding Law Enforcement Achievement Award Vol. 1: 11359
Outstanding Lawyer Award Vol. 1: 12593
Outstanding Leader in Oregon Blueberry Industry Vol. 1: 16853
Outstanding Leadership and Research in Physical Activity and Aging Award Vol. 1: 7747
Outstanding Leadership Award
Africa Travel Association Vol. 1: 249
American Defense Institute Vol 1: 2125
Outstanding Leadership in the Industry Vol. 1: 16548
Outstanding Leadership Medal Vol. 1: 13897
Outstanding Lecture Award Vol. 1: 15198
Outstanding Librarian Award Vol. 1: 10768
Outstanding Library Award Vol. 1: 10769
Outstanding Library Board Award Vol. 1: 5062
Outstanding Library Service Award Vol. 1: 5063
Outstanding Lithuanian Woman Award Vol. 1: 12876
Outstanding Local Chapter Vol. 1: 22071
Outstanding Local Leadership Award Vol. 1: 5823
Outstanding Local Section Member Award Vol. 1: 19923
Outstanding Local Veterans' Employment Representative Vol. 1: 8958
Outstanding Lodging Employee of the Year Vol. 1: 2569
Outstanding Lodging Manager Vol. 1: 2570
Outstanding Logging Operator Vol. 1: 16548
Outstanding Male and Female Athlete of the Year Vol. 1: 14696
Outstanding Management Innovator Award Vol. 1: 11475
Outstanding Management of Resources Vol. 1: 16548
Outstanding Master's Thesis Award Vol. 1: 874
Outstanding Masters Thesis Award Vol. 1: 14034
Outstanding Media Arts Productions Award Vol. 2: 4178
Outstanding Media Coverage of Child Maltreatment Award Vol. 1: 3608
Outstanding Medical Information Management Executive Award Vol. 1: 5779
Outstanding Member Vol. 1: 4911
Outstanding Member Award Vol. 1: 5841
Outstanding Member of the Year Vol. 1: 13376
Outstanding Member of the Year Award Vol. 2: 810
Outstanding Mentor Award Vol. 1: 489
Outstanding Merchandising Achievement Awards Competition Vol. 1: 17441
Outstanding Middle Level Social Studies Teacher of the Year Vol. 1: 14787
Outstanding Mother Award Vol. 1: 15392
Outstanding National Guard Unit Award Vol. 1: 16843
Outstanding National Touring Rally of the Year Award Vol. 1: 19699
Outstanding New Biology Teacher Achievement Award Vol. 1: 14098
Outstanding New Librarian Award Vol. 1: 10770
Outstanding New Systematic Application Award Vol. 1: 11946
Outstanding Newsletter Award
Amateur Athletic Union Vol. 1: 561
National Press Photographers Association Vol 1: 15542
Outstanding NFDW Member of the Year Vol. 1: 14968
Outstanding Offensive and Defensive Linemen of the Year Awards Vol. 1: 15092
Outstanding Organization at the Local Level Vol. 1: 16375
Outstanding Organization at the National/ International Level Vol. 1: 16376
Outstanding Organization Development Article of the Year Award Vol. 1: 16875
Outstanding Organization Development Consultant of the Year Award Vol. 1: 16876
Outstanding Organization Development Project of the Year Award Vol. 1: 16877
Outstanding OTC Geophysical Paper Award Vol. 1: 19125
Outstanding Paper Award
American Society for Engineering Education Vol. 1: 4036
International Association for Bridge and Structural Engineering Vol 2: 6382
National Association for Research in Science Teaching Vol 1: 14035
Outstanding Paper Award in *Palaios* Vol. 1: 18845
Outstanding Paper Awards
American Society for Nondestructive Testing Vol. 1: 4150
International Council on Hotel, Restaurant and Institutional Education Vol 1: 11527
Outstanding Paper in Surveying Vol. 1: 2002
Outstanding Paper Presented at Convention Vol. 1: 18842
Outstanding Paralegal Award
Central Pennsylvania Paralegal Association Vol. 1: 7778
Massachusetts Paralegal Association Vol 1: 13164
Outstanding Pennsylvania Author or Illustrator Vol. 1: 17192
Outstanding Performance Aid Award Vol. 1: 11945
Outstanding Performance Award Vol. 1: 10803
Outstanding Performance Awards Vol. 1: 18377
Outstanding Performance by an Actor Award Vol. 1: 6033
Outstanding Philanthropist Award Vol. 1: 5704
Outstanding Physician Award Vol. 1: 17751
Outstanding Planning Awards Vol. 1: 3558
Outstanding Plant Engineering Program Awards Vol. 1: 5366
Outstanding Player Vol. 1: 14662
Outstanding Playwright for Year Vol. 1: 9907
Outstanding Post Service Officer Award Vol. 1: 21332
Outstanding Power Engineering Educator Award Vol. 1: 10910
Outstanding Presentation Award Vol. 1: 16878
Outstanding Professional Designee Vol. 1: 11281
Outstanding Professional Service Award Vol. 1: 5753
Outstanding Program Vol. 1: 6191
Outstanding Program Awards Vol. 1: 20962
Outstanding Program Awards for Credit and Non-Credit Programs Vol. 1: 20963
Outstanding Progress Award Vol. 1: 20387
Outstanding Project Award Vol. 1: 8793
Outstanding Project Award for Biomedical Research in Aging Vol. 1: 10526
Outstanding Promoter Award Vol. 1: 15816
Outstanding Promotion Award Vol. 1: 9518
Outstanding Promotional Service Award Vol. 1: 250
Outstanding Psychologist Award Vol. 1: 3676
Outstanding Public Affairs Award Vol. 1: 5107
Outstanding Public Service Announcement Vol. 1: 13864
Outstanding Public Service Award
Archaeological Institute of America Vol. 1: 5034
Council for Exceptional Children Vol 1: 8553
Outstanding Publication Award
National Press Photographers Association Vol. 1: 15542
Ohio Academy of History Vol 1: 16625
Outstanding Reference Sources Vol. 1: 17944
Outstanding Region Advisor Vol. 1: 5112
Outstanding Region Executive Officer Award Vol. 1: 5112
Outstanding Regional Chairman Award Vol. 1: 5889
Outstanding Regional Director Vol. 1: 8999
Outstanding Research Award
International Society for Performance Improvement Vol. 1: 11946
National Hardwood Lumber Association Vol 1: 15186
Outstanding Researcher Vol. 2: 4350
Outstanding Researcher Award
American Society for Horticultural Science Vol. 1: 4093
Council for Learning Disabilities Vol 1: 8560
Radiological Society of North America Vol 1: 17855
Outstanding ROTC Cadet Award Vol. 1: 16844
Outstanding ROTC Unit Award Vol. 1: 16845
Outstanding Rural Health Practice Vol. 1: 15652
Outstanding Rural Health Program Vol. 1: 15653
Outstanding Rural PA Award Vol. 1: 9011
Outstanding Sate Association Award Vol. 1: 13940
Outstanding Sawmill Operator Vol. 1: 16548
Outstanding School Award Vol. 1: 9183
Outstanding School Health Educator Award Vol. 1: 3890
Outstanding School Nurse of the Year Award Vol. 1: 3891
Outstanding School Psychological Services in Public Schools Award Vol. 1: 3711
Outstanding Science Educator of the Year Vol. 1: 5503

Outstanding Scientific Achievements by a Young Investigator Vol. 1: 996
Outstanding Scientific Materials Managers Award Vol. 1: 14382
Outstanding Sculpture Educator Vol. 1: 11895
Outstanding Secondary Social Studies Teacher of the Year Vol. 1: 14788
Outstanding Section and Region Award Vol. 1: 40
Outstanding Section Campus Representative Award Vol. 1: 4037
Outstanding Section/Student Chapter Partnership Award Vol. 1: 19054
Outstanding Senior Award Vol. 1: 20260
Outstanding Service Vol. 1: 11670
Outstanding Service Award
Africa Travel Association Vol. 1: 251
American Association of Meat Processors Vol 1: 1266
American Concrete Pipe Association Vol 1: 1981
ASPRS - The Imaging and Geospatial Information Society Vol 1: 5220
Association of Building Engineers Vol 2: 6801
Association of Medical Illustrators Vol 1: 5759
California Engineering Foundation Vol 1: 6739
Canadian Sociology and Anthropology Association Vol 1: 7503
Chicago Book Clinic Vol 1: 7876
Colorado River Watch Network Vol 1: 8221
Council on Governmental Ethics Laws Vol 1: 8604
Great Lakes Commission Vol 1: 10143
International Federation for Information Processing Vol 2: 740
National Association of College Auxiliary Services Vol 1: 14135
National Association of Underwater Instructors Vol 1: 14451
National Pigeon Association Vol 1: 15505
Private Practice Section/American Physical Therapy Association Vol 1: 17575
Soil and Water Conservation Society Vol 1: 19390
South Carolina Poultry Federation Vol 1: 19447
Specialty Graphic Imaging Association Vol 1: 19598
WAIF Vol 1: 21424
World Federation of Direct Selling Associations Vol 1: 21905
Outstanding Service Award for Military Pediatrics Vol. 1: 786
Outstanding Service Award - Karate Vol. 1: 562
Outstanding Service Awards
National Agricultural Aviation Association Vol. 1: 13910
National Interscholastic Swimming Coaches Association of America Vol 1: 15284
Outstanding Service in Fire Management Award Vol. 1: 9556
Outstanding Service Medallion Vol. 1: 952
Outstanding Service to Environmental Education Award Vol. 1: 16377
Outstanding Service to Librarianship Award Vol. 1: 7250
Outstanding Service to the Constable System by a Non-Constable Award Vol. 1: 14731
Outstanding Service to the Forest Industry Vol. 1: 16548
Outstanding Service to the Mentally and/or Physically Handicapped Vol. 1: 8068
Outstanding Service to the Public Health Award Vol. 1: 15440
Outstanding Short Course Vol. 1: 18797
Outstanding Small Chapter Award Vol. 1: 10908
Outstanding Society Awards Vol. 1: 12845
Outstanding Southeastern Author Award Vol. 1: 19476
Outstanding Southeastern Library Program Award Vol. 1: 19477
Outstanding Sponsor Award Vol. 1: 6905
Outstanding SPS Chapter Advisor Award Vol. 1: 2837
Outstanding State Leader Award Vol. 1: 5823
Outstanding Statistical Application Awards Vol. 1: 4694
Outstanding Student Achievement in Contemporary Sculpture Vol. 1: 11896
Outstanding Student Award
American Medical Technologists Vol. 1: 3068
Resort and Commercial Recreation Association Vol 1: 18005
Outstanding Student CEC Undergraduate Member of the Year Award Vol. 1: 8554
Outstanding Student Chapter Award
American Water Resources Association Vol. 1: 4833
Society for Mining, Metallurgy, and Exploration Vol 1: 18820
Outstanding Student Recognition Awards Vol. 1: 14897
Outstanding Student Research Award Vol. 1: 11947
Outstanding Support Staff Award Vol. 1: 10771
Outstanding Teacher Award
Council for Learning Disabilities Vol. 1: 8561
Eta Kappa Nu Vol 1: 9345
National Marine Educators Association Vol 1: 15360
North American Colleges and Teachers of Agriculture Vol 1: 16407
Pennsylvania Association of Private School Administrators Vol 1: 17166
Outstanding Teacher Educator in Reading Award Vol. 1: 11870
Outstanding Teacher of American History Vol. 1: 15713
Outstanding Teacher of the Year Awards Vol. 1: 1453
Outstanding Teacher of Theatre in Higher Education Award Vol. 1: 5516
Outstanding Technical Paper Award Vol. 1: 13312
Outstanding Technologist Award Vol. 1: 19230
Outstanding Theatre Education Vol. 1: 9184
Outstanding Total Service to the Mentally and/or Physically Handicapped Vol. 1: 8069
Outstanding Total Youth Vol. 1: 8070
Outstanding Trailblazer Award Vol. 1: 11
Outstanding Training Programs Vol. 1: 5268
Outstanding Transportation & Logistics Executive in North America Vol. 1: 4621
Outstanding Trustee Award Vol. 1: 10772
Outstanding Undergraduate Educator Award Vol. 1: 4094
Outstanding Use of Wood Vol. 1: 16548
Outstanding Vocational Educators Vol. 1: 18550
Outstanding Vocational Special Needs Teacher of the Year Vol. 1: 14059
Outstanding Volunteer Award Vol. 1: 17752
Outstanding Volunteer Clinical Teacher Award Vol. 1: 1925
Outstanding Volunteer Fund Raiser Award Vol. 1: 5703
Outstanding Volunteer Service Award Vol. 1: 15401
Outstanding Woman Veterinarian Award Vol. 1: 5534
Outstanding Women in Music Award Vol. 1: 19936
Outstanding Women in Swimming Award Vol. 1: 20398
Outstanding Women of Color Vol. 1: 11265
Outstanding Writer's Award Vol. 1: 6033
Outstanding Writing Award Vol. 1: 1153
Outstanding Young Agents Committee Award Vol. 1: 10737
Outstanding Young Agrologist Award Vol. 1: 290
Outstanding Young Alumnus Vol. 1: 9857
Outstanding Young Dentist Award Vol. 2: 5019
Outstanding Young Electrical Engineer Award Vol. 1: 9346
Outstanding Young Farmer Advisor Vol. 1: 16004
Outstanding Young Farmer Awards Vol. 1: 20677
Outstanding Young Industrial Engineer Award Vol. 1: 10963
Outstanding Young Investigator Award Vol. 1: 13183
Outstanding Young Manufacturing Engineer Award Vol. 1: 19164
Outstanding Young Numismatist of the Year Vol. 1: 3249
Outstanding Young Range Professional Award Vol. 1: 18837
Outstanding Young Scientist Award Vol. 2: 2330
The Outstanding Young Scientists (TOYS) Vol. 2: 5288
Outstanding Young Volunteer of the Year Award Vol. 1: 12646
Outstanding Young Woman Volunteers Award Vol. 2: 5236
Outstanding Younger Member Award Vol. 1: 19055
Outstanding Youth Project Vol. 1: 8071
Outstanding Youth Science Researchers Vol. 2: 5288
Outstanding YR State Chapter Vol. 1: 22072
Outstanding Zone Campus Activity Coordinator Award Vol. 1: 4038
Outstanding Zone Campus Representative Award Vol. 1: 4038
Overall Control Line Flyers Champion Vol. 1: 21535
Overall Triathletes of the Year Vol. 1: 21249
Overly Scholarship; Helene Vol. 1: 21814
Oversaetterprisen Vol. 2: 1444
Overseas Premium Vol. 2: 7776
Overseas Prize Vol. 2: 8643
Overseas Student Medallion Vol. 2: 7832
Overseas Study Bursaries and Flatman Grants Vol. 2: 7857
OWA Founders Award/President's Award Vol. 1: 16866

Owen Award; Wilfred Vol. 2: 7701
Owen Book Prize; Walter Vol. 1: 6971
Owen Medal; Morgan Vol. 2: 7296
Owen Memorial Scholarship; Charles and Melva T. Vol. 1: 15039
Owen Memorial Trophy Vol. 1: 20589
Owen National Prize for Literature; Gilbert Vol. 2: 4504
Owen Poetry Prize; Guy Vol. 1: 19515
Owen; Premio Nacional de Literatura Gilberto Vol. 2: 4504
Owens Award; Jesse Vol. 1: 21235
Owens Scholarly Achievement Award; William A. Vol. 1: 18756
Owe's Prisbelonningsfond; Generaldirektor Aage W. Vol. 2: 5169
Owlglass Prize Vol. 2: 2977
Owsley Award; Frank L. and Harriet C. Vol. 1: 19503
OX5; Mr. Vol. 1: 16990
Oxford Turville-Petre Prize Vol. 2: 9187
Oxford University Fellowship Vol. 2: 8340
P1-prisen Vol. 2: 1454
P1-Prize (DR Radio) Vol. 2: 1454
PA Service to the Underserved Award Vol. 1: 817
PAA Excellence Awards Vol. 2: 5199
Paatsama Award; WSAVA Vol. 2: 1547
Pablos Editorial Merit Prize; Juan Vol. 2: 4579
PACC Scholarship Vol. 1: 17335
PACCAR Scholarship Award Fund Vol. 1: 19165
Pace Award Vol. 1: 563
Pace Award; Frank Vol. 1: 11558
Pacemaker Award Vol. 1: 15665
Pacesetter Award Vol. 1: 13771
Pacesetter of the Year Award Vol. 1: 14774
Pacing Triple Crown Vol. 1: 20878
Package Printing and Converting's Diecutter/Diemaker of the Year Award Vol. 1: 11338
Packaging Competition Awards Vol. 1: 15475
Packaging Hall of Fame Vol. 1: 17024
Packaging Leader of the Year Vol. 1: 17025
Packaging Man of the Year Vol. 1: 17025
Packard International Parks Merit Award; Fred M. Vol. 2: 6554
Packard International Parks Merit Award/World Commission on Protected Areas; Fred M. Vol. 2: 6557
Packard Outstanding Educator Award; Robert L. Vol. 1: 19531
Packer Engineering Safety Award Vol. 1: 4231
PACS Technology Award Vol. 1: 6920
Padilla; Orden del Merito Naval Almirante Vol. 2: 1292
Padma Bhushan Vol. 2: 3382
Padma Shri Vol. 2: 3383
Padma Vibhushan Vol. 2: 3384
Padnendadlu Graduate Bursary Vol. 2: 171
Page Award for Young Investigators; Irvine H. Vol. 1: 2417
Page Award; Handley Vol. 2: 8396
The Page Medal Vol. 2: 95
Page Outstanding Service Award; John A. Vol. 1: 10347
Page Prize; Gillian Vol. 2: 8468
Pagels Human Rights of Scientists Award; Heinz R. Vol. 1: 16204
Pahlsons pris; Margit Vol. 2: 6259
Paid Internships Vol. 1: 16607
Paid Research Appointments Vol. 1: 21085
Paine Award; Thomas Vol. 2: 6306
Paine Journalism Award; Thomas Vol. 1: 20078
Paine Memorial Award; Thomas O. Vol. 1: 17367
Paine Prize; Robert Troup Vol. 1: 10283
Painter Memorial Award; SES/ASTM Robert J. Vol. 1: 19748
Painton Award; Harry R. Vol. 1: 8493
PAJLO Award Vol. 1: 6972
Pake Prize; George E. Vol. 1: 3468
Pakistan Institute of Engineers Gold Medal Vol. 2: 5188
Pakistan Institute of Sciences Gold Medal Vol. 2: 5197
Pal Memorial Award; George Vol. 1: 123
Palanca Memorial Awards for Literature; Don Carlos Vol. 2: 5281
Palazzo Community Service Award; A. Eric Vol. 1: 18028
Paleontological Society Medal Vol. 1: 17040
Paletou Award; J. Wallace Vol. 1: 11039
Palladium Medal Vol. 1: 1198
Palmai-Tenser Scholarship; Rose Vol. 1: 13547
Palme d'Or
Cannes International Film Festival Vol. 2: 2259
International Advertising Festival Vol 2: 7890
Shark Awards Festival Vol 2: 3710
Palme Memorial Fund Scholarships; Olof Vol. 2: 6181
Palme Prize; Olof Vol. 2: 6182
Palmer Award; Joe Vol. 1: 15923
Palmer Award; Katherine Vol. 1: 17037
Palmer Memorial Prize; Edwin Vol. 1: 13794
Palmer Memorial Trophy; Eugene Vol. 1: 13349
Palmer Prize; Frederick Vol. 2: 7777
Palmes Academiques Vol. 2: 2393
Paloma O'Shea Santander International Piano Competition Vol. 2: 6098
PAMA/ATP Award Vol. 1: 17590
Pamplin Distinguished Awards Vol. 1: 9764
Pan American Gold Insigne of the Americas Society Vol. 1: 4929
Pan American Gold Medal of the Americas Society Vol. 1: 4930
Panafrican Film and Television Festival of Ouagadougou Vol. 2: 1242
Panchaud Medallions; John Vol. 2: 7375
Pandora Award Vol. 2: 9223
Panetti e Professor Carlo Ferrari; Premio Internazionale e Medaglia d'oro, Professor Modesto Vol. 2: 3806
Panetti International Prize with Gold Medal; Professor Modesto Vol. 2: 3806
Pani; Premio de Composicion Arquitectonica Alberto J. Vol. 2: 4607
Pannell Award; Lucile Micheels Vol. 1: 21799
Panofsky Prize in Experimental Particle Physics; W. K. H. Vol. 1: 3469
Panorama Brasilian Art Vol. 2: 1192
Panorama de Arte Brasileira Vol. 2: 1192
Panowski Playwriting Award; Mildred and Albert Vol. 1: 18081
Pantalla Abierta Award Vol. 2: 6028
Pantone Color Award Vol. 1: 17062
Papalia Award for Excellence in Teacher Education; ACTFL Anthony Vol. 1: 2058
Papanicolaou Award of the American Society of Cytology Vol. 1: 4398
Paper Industry Gold Medal Vol. 2: 8240
Paper Prize Awards Vol. 1: 17237
Papers and Publications Committee Prizes Vol. 2: 8125
Papers Award Vol. 2: 7998
Papinger Endowment Award; Henry and Anna Vol. 1: 12346
Pappas Research Award; Doug Vol. 1: 18635
Paracelsus Medaille Vol. 2: 2847
Paracelsus-Preis Vol. 2: 6513
Paracelsus Ring Vol. 2: 772
Paracelsusring der Stadt Villach Vol. 2: 784
Parade - IACP Police Service Award Vol. 1: 11310
Parade/Kodak Photography Contest Vol. 1: 17066
Paragon Awards Vol. 1: 14775
Paralegal of the Year Vol. 1: 8711
Param Vir Chakra Vol. 2: 3385
Param Vishisht Seva Medal Vol. 2: 3386
Parametrician of the Year Vol. 1: 12011
Parandowski Prize; Jan Vol. 2: 5330
Paraprofessional of the Year Award Vol. 1: 5066
Parapsychology Hall of Fame Vol. 1: 17077
Parbo Medal; Sir Arvi Vol. 2: 416
Parcel - Leif J. Sverdrup Civil Engineering Management Award; John I. Vol. 1: 4348
Pard'ners Award Vol. 1: 2186
Pardoe Space Award Vol. 2: 8397
Parent Organization Recognition Awards Vol. 1: 14621
Parent Partnership Awards Vol. 1: 14622
Parent-Patient Leadership Award Vol. 1: 8094
Parenteau Memorial Award; William A. Vol. 1: 388
Parenting Awards Vol. 1: 7917
Parents' Choice Awards Vol. 1: 17084
Parents' Choice Classic Award Vol. 1: 17084
Parents' Choice FunStuff Award Vol. 1: 17084
Parham Memorial Award; Ethel Vol. 1: 3144
Parhon; Constantin I. Vol. 2: 5856
Parish Pastor of the Year Vol. 1: 121
Parish Volunteer Award Vol. 1: 7680
Parisot Foundation Fellowship; Jacques Vol. 2: 6565
Parizeau Prize in Biology; Leo Vol. 1: 5540
Park Award in Critical Writing; Betty Vol. 1: 19843
Park Communicator Award Vol. 1: 186
Park Educator Award Vol. 1: 186
Park Heritage Award Vol. 1: 186
Park Stewardship Award Vol. 1: 186
Parke-Davis Award
American Society for Investigative Pathology Vol. 1: 4118
Canadian Society of Hospital Pharmacists Vol 1: 7469
Parker Award; Ely ("Eli") S. Vol. 1: 2607
Parker Award; Virginia Vol. 1: 6804
Parker Awards for Spoken Business Japanese; Sir Peter Vol. 2: 8897
Parker Education Gold Ribbon Awards; Sally Vol. 1: 4731
Parker Memorial Award; Jim Vol. 1: 14176
Parker Memorial Award; R. Hunt Vol. 1: 16519
Parker Memorial Medal; Ben H. Vol. 1: 2845
Parker Romantic Novel of the Year Vol. 2: 8347
Parker Trophy; Jackie Vol. 1: 7115

Parkinson Award for Young British Musicians; Dorothy Vol. 2: 7599
Parkman Medal Vol. 2: 7778
Parks Award; Orville Vol. 1: 5756
Parks Commemorative Photography Competition; Gordon Vol. 1: 9703
Parlin Award Vol. 1: 3035
Parmalee Scholarship Vol. 1: 11688
Parmele Award Vol. 1: 19599
Parnassos Foundation Prize for Prose and Poetry Vol. 2: 3188
Parole; Joe Kegans Award for Victim Services in Probation and Vol. 1: 3603
Parran Award; Thomas Vol. 1: 7899
Parry Award; Evan Vol. 2: 4990
Parsons Award; Charles Lathrop Vol. 1: 1778
Parsons Award; Frank Vol. 2: 292
Parsons Memorial Prize; R. W. Vol. 2: 417
Parsons Prize for Social Science; Talcott Vol. 1: 621
Participation Awards Vol. 1: 21954
Partington Prize Vol. 2: 8955
Partner of the Year Vol. 1: 12206
Partnership Award
  American Red Cross National Headquarters Vol. 1: 3835
  Direct Selling Association Vol 1: 8936
  Indiana Library Federation Vol 1: 10773
The Partnership Award Vol. 1: 4622
Parvan Prize; Vasile Vol. 2: 5857
Pascal du GAMNI-SMAI; Prix Blaise Vol. 2: 1985
Pascal; Fondation Paul Vol. 2: 1950
Pascatti Rotary Prize; Antonio Vol. 2: 4059
Paschal Award; James Frederick Vol. 1: 8235
Passano Foundation Award Vol. 1: 17101
Past President Scholarship Vol. 1: 10231
Past President's Award
  Bristol-Myers Squibb Canada Co. Vol. 1: 6628
  International Federation of Biomedical Laboratory Science Vol 1: 11588
Past Presidents' Award
  American Association of Petroleum Geologists Vol. 1: 1346
  National Environmental Health Association Vol 1: 14946
  New England Water Works Association Vol 1: 16140
Past Presidents' Award for Merit in Transportation Vol. 1: 11053
Past President's Best Practices Award Vol. 1: 15600
Past Presidents' Canadian Legislator Award Vol. 1: 7543
Past-President's Certificate Vol. 1: 7444
Past Presidents' Memorial Medal Vol. 1: 7202
Pasteur Award Vol. 1: 10690
Pasteur Medal; Louis Vol. 2: 1796
Patch Awards; Dan Vol. 1: 20627
Pate Award; Tom Vol. 1: 7116
Pate Memorial Award; Maurice Vol. 1: 20597
Paterno; Medaglia Emanuele Vol. 2: 4003
Paterno Scholar-Athlete Award; William Pearce/Joseph V. Vol. 1: 15073
Paterson Award; Donald G. Vol. 1: 13483
Paterson Medal and Prize Vol. 2: 7734
Pathfinder Award
  Automotive Occupant Restraints Council Vol. 1: 6117
  Institute for Public Relations Vol 1: 10833
Pathfinder Award; Information Technology Vol. 1: 1416
Patient Aid Vol. 1: 12798
Paton Award Vol. 1: 9383
Paton Prize; Evgenij Vol. 2: 2495
Paton Prize; William A. Vol. 1: 13795
Patria; Prix Bene Merenti de Vol. 1: 18605
Patriach Athenagoras Diocesan Service Award Vol. 1: 15114
Patrick Award; Dan Vol. 1: 11438
Patrick Henry Memorial Oratorical Contest Vol. 1: 15107
Patriot Award
  Congressional Medal of Honor Society Vol. 1: 8402
  Paralyzed Veterans of America Vol 1: 17068
Patriot Medal Vol. 1: 15780
Patriot of the Nation Vol. 1: 16007
Patriot's Award Vol. 1: 17111
Patriots Award Vol. 1: 3575
Patron Honor Award Vol. 1: 15262
Patron/Matrons Award Vol. 2: 5111
Patron of Architecture Award Vol. 2: 5700
Patron of the American Community Theatre Association Vol. 1: 1168
Patron of the Arts Award Vol. 1: 10166
Patron of the Year Award Vol. 1: 12894
Patrons' Additional Award Vol. 2: 7289
Patrons and Fellows Vol. 2: 3443
Patron's Medal Vol. 2: 8520
Patron's Prize Vol. 2: 7290
Patron's Recognition Award Vol. 1: 11897
Pattantyus Abraham Geza Dij Vol. 2: 3311
Pattantyus Award; Abraham Geza Vol. 2: 3311
Patterson Award; A. Lindo Vol. 1: 2091
Patterson Memorial Grant; Bryan Vol. 1: 19355
Patton, Jr. Memorial Trophy; General George S. Vol. 1: 20705
Patwardhan Prize in Nutritional Sciences; Dr. V. N. Vol. 2: 3424
Paul Award; Alice Vol. 1: 12863
Paul Buchanan Award Vol. 1: 21311
Paul E. Tsongas Economic Patriot Award Vol. 1: 8338
Paul L. Busch Award Vol. 1: 21504
Paul Prize; Barbara Vol. 1: 17807
Paul VI Prize; International Vol. 2: 3988
Paul Ylvisaker Award for Public Policy Engagement Vol. 1: 8599
Pauling Prize Vol. 1: 2092
Paumgartner-Medaille; Bernhard- Vol. 2: 749
Pavarotti Trophy Vol. 2: 8081
Pavement Awards Vol. 1: 14000
Pawsey Medal Vol. 2: 130
Payen Award; Anselme Vol. 1: 1779
Payne Award; Ed Vol. 1: 18948
Paz; Premio Ramos Vol. 2: 5417
Paz Prize; Ramos Vol. 2: 5417
P.B. Dews Award Vol. 1: 4173
PBS Advertising and Promotion Awards Vol. 1: 17705
The PC World Award Vol. 2: 9345
PC World World Class Awards Vol. 1: 17116
PCA Financial Assistance Fund Vol. 2: 4869
PCAM Music Award Vol. 2: 8288
Peabody Awards Collection Vol. 1: 21020
Peabody Awards; George Foster Vol. 1: 21020
Peabody Medal; George Vol. 1: 17123
Peace Award Vol. 2: 948
Peace Award of Committee of 100 Vol. 2: 1581
Peace Education Awards Vol. 1: 17820
Peace History; Charles DeBenedetti Prize in Vol. 1: 17127
Peace Play Contest Vol. 1: 10095
Peace Prize of the German Book Trade Vol. 2: 2865
Peace Profiles Vol. 1: 17821
Peace Quilt Awards Vol. 1: 6498
PEACE Trophy Vol. 2: 3627
Peak Award Vol. 1: 16367
Peanut Hall of Fame
  American Peanut Council Vol. 1: 3367
  Georgia Agricultural Commodity Commission for Peanuts Vol 1: 9966
Peanut Research and Education Award Vol. 1: 3368
Pearce Award; William T. Vol. 1: 5975
Pearce/Joseph V. Paterno Scholar-Athlete Award; William Vol. 1: 15073
Pearl Soil Hunger Fighter of the Year Vol. 1: 7868
Pearson Award; Drew Vol. 1: 11800
Pearson Award; Ike Vol. 1: 14292
Pearson Award; L. B. "Mike" Vol. 1: 7229
Pearson Award; Lester B. Vol. 1: 15235
Pease Award; Theodore Calvin Vol. 1: 18959
Peaslee Brazing Award; Robert L. Vol. 1: 4891
Peat Marwick Award; KPMG Vol. 1: 21463
Peccei; Premio Aurelio Vol. 2: 3897
Peccei Prize; Aurelio Vol. 2: 3897
Peccei Scholarship Vol. 2: 756
Pech Medal; Antal Vol. 2: 3259
Peck Award; Walter D. Vol. 1: 17914
Peckham Memorial Fund; Joyce Vol. 1: 17361
Pecora Award; William T. Vol. 1: 17131
Pedersens Biblioteksfonds Forfatterpris; Edvard Vol. 2: 1462
Pederson, CTC Award; Melva C. Vol. 1: 4625
Pediatric Dermatology Fellows/Residents Research Award Vol. 1: 18831
Pediatric Dermatology Research Grant Vol. 1: 18832
Pediatric Division Award for Outstanding Contributions to Pediatric Clinical Chemestry Vol. 1: 997
Pediatric Resident Research Award Vol. 1: 787
Pediatric Urology Medal Vol. 1: 788
Pedler Lectureship Vol. 2: 8768
Pedro Joaquin Chamorro Inter-American Relations Award; IAPA- Vol. 1: 11109
Pedroli Prize; Castelli Vol. 2: 2740
Pedrotti; Concurso Internazionale per Direttori d'Orchestra Antonio Vol. 2: 3847
Pedrotti International Competition for Orchestra Conductors; Antonio Vol. 2: 3847
Peek Award; Cuthbert Vol. 2: 8526
Peek into the Future Award Vol. 2: 1586
Peele Memorial Award; Robert Vol. 1: 18821
Peer Sasanqua Award Vol. 1: 1621
Peet Travelling Prize; Thomas Eric Vol. 2: 9176
Pegasus Award Vol. 1: 18049
Pegasus Prize for Literature Vol. 1: 9379
Pegasus Trophy
  Mobil Sekiyu Kabushiki Kaisha Vol. 2: 4254
  Mobil Sekiyu Kabushiki Kaisha Vol 2: 4255

PEI Distinguished Service Award Vol. 1: 15750
Peirce Essay Contest Award; C. S. Vol. 1: 7810
Pekar Memorial Scholarship; Anne Vol. 1: 15039
Pelander Award; Carl E. Vol. 1: 18326
Pelletier; Prix Denise- Vol. 1: 17795
Pels Foundation Awards for Drama; PEN/Laura Vol. 1: 17145
Peltier Award; Leslie C. Vol. 1: 6003
Peltier Plaque Vol. 1: 18993
Pelton Award; Jeanette Siron Vol. 1: 6551
Pelzer Memorial Award; Louis Vol. 1: 16894
Pemberton Trophy Vol. 2: 7589
PEN Book-of-the-Month Club Translation Prize Vol. 1: 17146
PEN/Faulkner Award for Fiction Vol. 1: 17154
PEN/Jerard Fund Award Vol. 1: 17147
PEN/Malamud Memorial Award Vol. 1: 17155
PEN/Martha Albrand Award for First Nonfiction Vol. 1: 17140
PEN New England Award; Laurence L. Winship Vol. 1: 17158
PEN Prison Writing Awards Vol. 1: 17148
PEN Publisher Award Vol. 1: 17149
PEN/Voelcker Award for Poetry Vol. 1: 17150
Penaud Diploma; Alphonse Vol. 2: 6348
Pendleton Award; S. Alden Vol. 1: 10995
Pendray Award; G. Edward Vol. 1: 2661
Penguin Putnam Books for Young Readers Group Award Vol. 1: 5442
Penick Award for Excellence in the Game of Life; Harvey Vol. 1: 7599
Penitentiary Order of Merit Vol. 2: 1302
Penn/ITA Player to Watch Vol. 1: 11146
Penner Prize; Donald W. Vol. 1: 6930
Penney - University of Missouri Newspaper Awards; JC Vol. 1: 21079
Penning Award Excellence in Low-Temperature Plasma Physics Vol. 1: 12108
Pennsylvania Diving Association Award Vol. 1: 21167
Penrose Award/University Division Coach of the Year; Spencer Vol. 1: 2496
Penrose Medal Vol. 1: 19109
Penrose Medal Award Vol. 1: 9954
Pensacola Heritage Award Vol. 1: 17210
People Online Awards Vol. 2: 8214
People's Choice Award
American Numismatic Association Vol. 1: 3250
American Physicians Art Association Vol 1: 3504
The People's Choice Award Vol. 1: 6033
People's Choice Award; Starz Vol. 1: 8885
Peplau Award; Hildegard Vol. 1: 3283
Pepler International Award; George Vol. 2: 8861
PEPP Chairman's Award Vol. 1: 15751
PEPP Merit Award Vol. 1: 15752
Peppe Award; Mike
U.S. Aquatic Sports Vol. 1: 20399
USA Diving Vol 1: 21171
Pepper Award; Claude Vol. 1: 14818
Pepper Trophy; W. J. Vol. 2: 6704
Pepsi 400 Trophy Vol. 1: 8767
Pepsi-Cola Award Vol. 2: 6704
Pepys Medal; Samuel Vol. 2: 7437
Pereira Award; Professor E. O. E. Vol. 2: 6122
Perera Memorial; Aylet Lilly Vol. 2: 6123
Pereyra Prize; Carlos Vol. 2: 4492
Perfect Ten (Equine Only) Award Vol. 1: 2187
Performance Awards Vol. 1: 16975
Performance Citation Award Vol. 1: 7642
Performance Scholarships Vol. 1: 11674
Performance Test Codes Medal Vol. 1: 4537
Periwinkle Award Vol. 1: 8120
Perkin Medal
Society of Chemical Industry - American Section Vol. 1: 19085
Society of Dyers and Colourists - England Vol 2: 9036
Perkins Award; Dud Vol. 1: 3151
Perkins Award for Professional Excellence; R. Marlin Vol. 1: 4919
Perkins Award; Marlin Vol. 1: 1488
Perkins Government Relations Award; Carl D. Vol. 1: 2073
Perkins, Jr. Memorial Award; John F. Vol. 1: 3523
Perlemuter Piano Scholarship; Vlado Vol. 2: 7545
Perlman Award for Human Advancement Vol. 1: 12392
Perlman Award; Itzhak Vol. 1: 21414
Perlman Gallery Cash Award; Miriam Vol. 1: 18980
Perloff President's Prize Vol. 1: 2204
Permanent Force Good Service Medal Vol. 2: 5754
Permio Nacional Vol. 2: 1256
Perpetual World Championship Trophies Vol. 2: 7532
Perren Research Award; S. M. Vol. 2: 3916
Perret; Prix Paul-Michel Vol. 2: 2081
Perret Prize; Auguste Vol. 2: 2513
Perrier Award Vol. 2: 7403
Perrier-Jouet Rising Star Chef of the Year Vol. 1: 12287
Perrier Outstanding Restaurant Vol. 1: 12287
Perrier Pick of the Fringe Season Vol. 2: 7403
Perron Award; E. du Vol. 2: 4923
Perrot; Medaille Georges Vol. 2: 1757
Perry Award; Newel Vol. 1: 15040
Perry Awards (Tony Awards); Antoinette Vol. 1: 12742
Perry Distinguished Authors Award; J. Warren Vol. 1: 5842
Perry Research Scholarship; John Lord Vol. 2: 8496
Perseverance Award Vol. 1: 13934
Pershing Memorial Membership Award; Everett Vol. 1: 14926
Pershing Plaque Vol. 1: 15176
Person of the Year
Minnesota Holstein Association Vol. 1: 13480
National Association of Foreign-Trade Zones Vol 1: 14236
PhotoImaging Manufacturers and Distributors Association Vol 1: 17296
Person of the Year Award
Brazilian-American Chamber of Commerce Vol. 1: 6610
Irrigation Association Vol 1: 12207
National Association of Jewelry Appraisers Vol 1: 14296
Person of the Year Award; Linn Stuckenbruck Vol. 1: 17669
Person of the Year in Education Vol. 1: 9172
Personal Achievement Award Vol. 1: 13685
Personal Achievement in Chemical Engineering Awards Vol. 1: 7824
Personal Contribution Award Vol. 1: 6906
Personal Narratives Award Vol. 1: 21069
Personal or Academic Achievement Award Vol. 1: 6407
Personal Recognition Awards in Education Vol. 2: 4020
Personal Service Award Vol. 1: 3776
Personal Trainer of the Year Award; IDEA Vol. 1: 10644
Personality of the Year Award Vol. 2: 6888
Persons Awards Vol. 1: 19775
Persoon Medal; Christiaan Hendrik Vol. 2: 5778
Perten Award; The Harold Vol. 2: 729
Peryam Award; David R. Vol. 1: 5976
Pessimist of the Year Vol. 1: 6312
Peter Floud Award Vol. 2: 9218
Peter Nancen Award for Young Scientists Vol. 1: 21855
Peter Wayne Award Vol. 2: 7899
Peters Historical Dagger; Ellis Vol. 2: 7369
Peterson Agricultural Scholarship Award; John W. Vol. 1: 16901
Peterson Christian Sportsmanship Award; Ben Vol. 1: 14663
Peterson Consumer Service Award; Esther
Consumer Federation of America Vol. 1: 8462
Food Marketing Institute Vol 1: 9662
Peterson Distinguished Service Award; Elaine Vol. 1: 15130
Peterson Fellows; Charles E. Vol. 1: 6016
Peterson Fellowships/Internships; Charles E. Vol. 1: 6016
Peterson Fellowships; Kate B. and Hall J. Vol. 1: 916
Peterson Foundation Awards; William F. Vol. 1: 11980
Petiet; Prix Rene Vol. 2: 2207
Petinos Foundation Award Vol. 1: 1647
Petitpas Memorial Award; Georges Vol. 1: 21915
Petrassi; Concorso Internazionale di Composizione Goffredo Vol. 2: 3929
Petrassi International Competition for Composers; Goffredo Vol. 2: 3929
Petrie Memorial Award; Dr. Vol. 1: 6921
Petrizzo Award for Career Achievement; D. Richard Vol. 1: 14776
Petro-Canada Award in New Media Vol. 1: 6805
Petrovici Prize; Ion Vol. 2: 5858
Pets in Cities Award Vol. 1: 11365
Petsavers Award Vol. 2: 7162
Pettigrew Award; Kenneth J. Vol. 1: 21198
Pettijohn Medal; Francis J. Vol. 1: 18846
Peurifoy Construction Research Award Vol. 1: 4349
Peyches; Fondation Ivan Vol. 2: 1891
Peyre; Fondation du Docteur et de Madame Vol. 2: 1849
Peyton Award for Cold Regions Engineering; Harold R. Vol. 1: 4350
Pezcoller International Award for Cancer Research; AACR- Vol. 2: 4033
Pezcoller Recognition for Contribution to Oncology; FECS- Vol. 2: 4032
Pfeffer Peace Prize Vol. 1: 9529
Pfeifer Medal; Ignac Vol. 2: 3249
Pfeiffer Service Award; Peggy Leach Vol. 1: 5386
Pfeil Prize; Wilhelm Leopold Vol. 2: 3087

Pfister Award; Oskar Vol. 1: 3631
Pfizer Academic Awards Vol. 2: 8261
Pfizer Animal Health-AABP Distinguished Service Award Vol. 1: 1128
Pfizer Animal Health Physiology Award Vol. 1: 2112
Pfizer Award Vol. 1: 10489
Pfizer Award in Enzyme Chemistry Vol. 1: 1780
Pfizer Extension Award Vol. 1: 17501
Pfizer Minority Summer Fellowship Award Vol. 1: 1898
Pfizer Mycology Postdoctoral Fellowship Vol. 1: 15124
Pfizer Mycology Postdoctoral Fellowship/John P. Utz Award Vol. 1: 15121
Pfizer Outstanding Investigator Award Vol. 1: 4118
Pfizer Predoctoral Excellence in Renal Research Award; Renal Section Vol. 1: 3527
PGA Assistants Professional Championship Vol. 2: 8295
PGA Championship Vol. 1: 17618
PGA Club Professional Championship Vol. 2: 8296
PGA Cup Vol. 2: 8297
PGA Trainee of the Year Vol. 2: 8304
Pham bieu Tam MD Award Vol. 1: 21366
Pharmacia-ASPET Vol. 1: 4174
Pharmacy Guild of Australia Honorary Life Member Vol. 2: 495
Pharmingen Investigator Award Vol. 1: 1242
PHAUP Vol. 2: 9349
PHBA Amateur Superior Award Vol. 1: 17047
PHBA National Youth Congress Horse Show High Point Youth Vol. 1: 17051
Phelan Art Awards; James D. Vol. 1: 18250
Phelan Literary Award; James D. Vol. 1: 18251
Phelan Memorial Award; Paul F. Vol. 1: 3865
Phenix - U.D.A. Vol. 2: 2613
Phi Alpha Theta/Westerners International Award Vol. 1: 17238
Phibro Animal Health Excellence in Poultry Research Award Vol. 1: 1088
Philadelphia International Film Festival (Philafilm Awards) Vol. 1: 468
Philadelphia Liberty Medal Vol. 1: 10157
Philadelphia Section Award Vol. 1: 1796
Philadelphia Section Awards for Excellence in Science Teaching Vol. 1: 1797
Philafilm Awards Vol. 1: 468
Philalethes Lecture Vol. 1: 17266
Philatelic Foundation Medal Vol. 1: 17271
Philatelic Hall of Fame Vol. 1: 3416
Philatelic Traders Vol. 2: 8263
Philbin Award Vol. 1: 14190
Philbro Extension Award Vol. 1: 17501
Philia Award Vol. 2: 150
Philip Crosby Award Vol. 1: 3982
Philip F. Morgan Medal Vol. 1: 21496
Philip Morris International Prize Vol. 2: 2285
Philippine Mathematical Olympiad Vol. 2: 5289
Philippine Physics Olympiad Vol. 2: 5290
Philips Award; Frederik Vol. 1: 10875
Philips Prize in Jurisprudence; Henry M. Vol. 1: 3441
Philips Rose Bowl Vol. 1: 6922
Philips Trophy Vol. 2: 6704
Phillips Award; A.T. Vol. 1: 11199
Phillips Award; Dr. Jackson R. E. Vol. 1: 5830
Phillips Award; Mary Vol. 1: 10166
Phillips Award; Melba Newell Vol. 1: 1378
Phillips Award; Rutherford T. Vol. 1: 2576
Phillips Leadership Award; Sarah Thorniley Vol. 1: 17258
Phillips Memorial Award; John Vol. 1: 1926
Phillips Memorial Medal; John C. Vol. 2: 6558
Phillips Performance Award
USA Diving Vol. 1: 21172
USA Swimming Vol 1: 21199
Phillips Performance of the Meet Award Vol. 1: 21200
Phillips Petroleum Company ISC All-World Awards Vol. 1: 12041
Phillips Petroleum Performance Award Vol. 1: 15104
Phillips Prize; A.A. Vol. 2: 84
Phillips Trophy, P.T.S. Trophy Vol. 2: 8263
Philos Award - Philanthropist of the Year Vol. 1: 3836
Phoenix Award
Children's Literature Association Vol. 1: 7911
Society of American Travel Writers Vol 1: 19015
Phoenix Award for Outstanding Contributions to Disaster Recovery Vol. 1: 20831
Phoenix Award for Small Business Disaster Recovery Vol. 1: 20832
Phoenix Diploma Vol. 2: 6349
Phoenix House Award for Public Service Vol. 1: 17277
Phoenix Trophy; National Offshore Championship - Lloyd Vol. 1: 20776
Photo Challenge Vol. 1: 17577
Photo Contest Vol. 1: 21998
Photo Travel Division Awards Vol. 1: 17288
Photogrammetric (Fairchild) Award Vol. 1: 5221
Photographers' Awards Vol. 2: 6837
Photographers Fellowship Fund Vol. 1: 7743
Photographic Society of Japan Awards Vol. 2: 4280
Photography Annual Vol. 1: 8311
Photography Award
Inter American Press Association Vol. 1: 11115
VIEW Clubs of Australia Vol 2: 643
Photography Awards
American Hemerocallis Society Vol. 1: 2446
Outdoor Writers Association of America Vol 1: 16970
Photojournalism Award Vol. 1: 14250
Photojournalism Division Awards Vol. 1: 17289
Physical Education School Recognition Award Vol. 1: 6883
Physical Science Award Vol. 2: 6134
Physician Assistant Award Vol. 1: 5780
Physician Assistant Educator of the Year Award Vol. 1: 818
Physician Assistant of the Year Vol. 1: 16862
Physician Award; Distinguished Vol. 1: 1282
Physician Executive Award Vol. 1: 1885
Physician of the Year
American Association of Physician Specialists Vol. 1: 1364
United States Amateur Boxing, Inc. Vol 1: 20389
Physician Scientist Training Award Vol. 1: 2143
Physicians Award; American College of Vol. 1: 1915
Physicians Distinguished Teacher Award; American College of Vol. 1: 1916
Physiological Section Award Vol. 1: 6552
Phytochemical Society of Europe Medal Vol. 2: 5332
Pi Gamma Mu Scholarships Vol. 1: 17307
Pi Kapp Scholar Vol. 1: 17318
Pi Kappa Alpha Chapter and Alumni Awards Vol. 1: 17311
Pi-Prijs; Professor Vol. 2: 4694
Pi Tau Sigma Gold Medal Vol. 1: 4538
Piafsky Award of the Canadian Society for Clinical Pharmacology; K.M. Vol. 1: 6629
Piafsky Young Investigator Award of the Canadian Society for Clinical Pharmacology; K. M. Vol. 1: 6629
Piano Award; The Mildred Spence McPherson Memorial Vol. 1: 18300
Piano; The Hancock Memorial Award in Vol. 1: 18293
Piano-Jazz Competition; International Martial Solal Vol. 2: 2277
Piano Scholarship; The Jackson Memorial Intermediate Vol. 1: 18295
Piano Scholarship; The Maude McGuire Memorial Intermediate Vol. 1: 18298
Piano Scholarship; The Maude McGuire Memorial Senior Vol. 1: 18299
Picard; Fondation Emil Vol. 2: 1856
Piccard; Prix Eugene Vol. 2: 2147
Piccolo Prix Vol. 1: 13982
Pickell Award; Mark Vol. 1: 12034
Pickering Award for Playwriting Excellence; Robert J. Vol. 1: 8128
Picot; Prix Georges Vol. 2: 2052
Pictorial Print Color Division Awards Vol. 1: 17290
Pictorial Print Monochrome Division Awards Vol. 1: 17291
Picture Book Award Vol. 1: 19443
Picture Book of the Year Award Vol. 2: 307
Picture Editor of the Year Vol. 1: 15543
"Picture It Painted Professionally" Awards Vol. 1: 17029
Pictures of the Year Competition Vol. 1: 15544
Pied Piper Award Vol. 1: 4382
Piekara Prize; Arkadiiusz Vol. 2: 5365
Piepenbrink Award for Outstanding Service to the Field of Mental Health Administration; Harold C. Vol. 1: 5580
Pier of they Year Award Vol. 2: 8184
Pierce Award; Jack A. Vol. 1: 11769
Pierce Award; Janette Vol. 1: 9311
Pierce Medal; Lorne Vol. 1: 18171
Pierce Memorial Prize; W. H. Vol. 2: 8923
Pierce Prize in Astronomy; Newton Lacy Vol. 1: 1515
Piercy Award; Esther J. Vol. 1: 5427
Pieri Memorial Award (Coach of the Year); Louis A. R. Vol. 1: 2515
Pierre Fournier Prize Vol. 2: 2283
Pietsch Preis; Erich Vol. 2: 2871
Pijls Prize; Catharine Vol. 2: 1120
Pijlsprijs; Catharina Vol. 2: 1120
Pike Prize for Service to People with Disabilities Vol. 1: 6532
Pike Prize for the Handicapped Vol. 1: 6532
Pilgrim of the Year Vol. 1: 17408

Pilkington Outstanding Educator Award; Theo C. Vol. 1: 4039
The Pillar Award Vol. 1: 3069
Pillsbury Bake-Off (R) Contest Vol. 1: 9918
Pilot and Feasibility Awards
Cystic Fibrosis Foundation Vol. 1: 8698
Washington University in St. Louis - Diabetes Research and Training Center Vol 1: 21465
Pilot of the Year Vol. 1: 18389
Pilot of the Year Award Vol. 1: 10403
Pilot Project Research Awards Vol. 1: 21040
Pilot Research Award for Junior Faculty and Child Psychiatry Fellows Vol. 1: 628
Pilot Safety Award
Helicopter Association International Vol. 1: 10404
National Business Aviation Association Vol 1: 14569
PIME Communications Award Vol. 2: 869
Pimentel Award in Chemical Education; George C. Vol. 1: 1781
Pimlott Conservation Award; Douglas H. Vol. 1: 16028
Pimsleur Award for Research in Foreign Language Education; ACTFL - MLJ Paul Vol. 1: 2059
Pinball Wizard Award Vol. 2: 8265
Pinchot Medal; Gifford Vol. 1: 18974
Pinckney Award; Robert L. Vol. 1: 2438
Pinet; Prix Vol. 2: 1725
Pinette; Fondation Vol. 2: 1717
Pinkard Leader in Federal Equity Award; Mary D. Vol. 1: 9455
Pinkerton Award Vol. 2: 7865
Pinkerton Prize Vol. 1: 20988
Pinkett Minority Student Award; Harold T. Vol. 1: 18960
Pinnacle Award
Association of the Wall and Ceiling Industries - International Vol. 1: 5890
Canadian Society of Association Executives Vol 1: 7450
Medical Dental Hospital Business Associates Vol 1: 13245
Specialized Carriers and Rigging Association Vol 1: 19583
Pinnacle Awards
Society for Human Resource Management Vol. 1: 18702
Society of National Association Publications Vol 1: 19205
Pinnacle Awards for Convention and Visitor Bureaus Vol. 1: 19823
Pinnacle Awards for Hotels/Resorts Vol. 1: 19824
Pinnacle Design Achievement Award Vol. 1: 4413
Pinsker Merit Award; Leon J. Vol. 1: 11373
Pinto Prize; Roquette Vol. 2: 1150
Pintrich Outstanding Dissertation Award; Paul R. Vol. 1: 3678
Pioneer Award
AIIM - The Enterprise Content Management Association Vol. 1: 313
American Association of Petroleum Geologists Vol 1: 1347
American Endurance Ride Conference Vol 1: 2188
American Institute of Ultrasound in Medicine Vol 1: 2858
Assisted Living Federation of America Vol 1: 5231
Association for Communication Excellence in Agriculture, Natural Resources, and Life and Human Sciences Vol 1: 5293
Council on Economic Priorities Vol 1: 8593
Heart Rhythm Association Vol 1: 10368
International Society for Traumatic Stress Studies Vol 1: 11968
Kansas Hearing Aid Association Vol 1: 12496
National Dairy Shrine Vol 1: 14893
Pioneer Award for Milestones Vol. 1: 11555
Pioneer Certificate Vol. 1: 9033
Pioneer Citation Vol. 1: 17838
Pioneer Families of Franklin Co. Vol. 1: 16634
Pioneer Families of Mahoning County Award Vol. 1: 16636
Pioneer Family Certificates and Century Family Certificates Vol. 1: 21692
Pioneer Heritage Award Vol. 1: 17137
Pioneer Hi-Bred Forage Award Vol. 1: 2113
Pioneer in Clay Science Lecture Vol. 1: 8092
Pioneer Man-of-the-Year Chinese Martial Arts Award Vol. 1: 564
Pioneer of the Year Vol. 1: 16014
Pioneer Trophy Vol. 1: 15353
Pioneer Woman Award Vol. 1: 6528
Pioneer Women of the Podium Vol. 1: 21728
Pioneers of Discovery Vol. 1: 15160
Pioneers of Underwater Acoustics Medal Vol. 1: 142
Piore Award; Emanuel R. Vol. 1: 10876
Piot; Prix Eugene Vol. 2: 1698
Pipe Organ Scholarship; The Blanche Squires Memorial Senior Vol. 1: 18315
Pipe Organ Scholarship; The Ray Brookhart Memorial Intermediate Vol. 1: 18277
Pipe Smoker of the Year Vol. 1: 11386
Piper Prize; C. S. Vol. 2: 517
Pirenne; Fondation Henri Vol. 2: 1009
Pires Prize; Dr. Antonio Vol. 2: 2
Pirouette Award; Poetry Society of Tennessee Vol. 1: 15023
Pisk Prize; Paul A. Vol. 1: 3179
Pitcher Insurance Agency Safety Award Vol. 1: 17531
Piteau Outstanding Young Member Award; Douglas R. Vol. 1: 5677
Pitirre Award; El Vol. 1: 17745
Piton Awards Vol. 2: 5915
Pitt Rivers Award Vol. 2: 6922
Pittman, Sr. Memorial Exhibit Award; John Jay Vol. 1: 3251
Pittman Wildlife Art Award; Major General and Mrs. Don D. Vol. 1: 14886
Pius IX; Order of Vol. 2: 9311
Pius XI Medal Vol. 2: 9308
PJC Award for Individual Merit Vol. 2: 6957
Placa Extraordinaria Vol. 1: 11118
Plain English Awards Vol. 2: 8270
Plain English Campaign Awards Vol. 2: 8270
Plain English Web Award Vol. 2: 8270
Plains Poets Award Vol. 1: 15020
Plaisterers Trophy Vol. 2: 7515
Planck-Medaille; Max- Vol. 2: 2727
Planck Research Awards for International Cooperation; Max Vol. 2: 3129
Planeta Prize Vol. 2: 6021
Planetary Award/Crystal Helmet Vol. 1: 5852
Planner of the Year Vol. 1: 8573
Planning Consultancy of the Year Award Vol. 2: 8862
Plant Award; Richard Vol. 1: 5288
Plant Engineer of the Year Award Vol. 2: 7884
Plant Engineers Members Prize; Institution of Vol. 2: 7883
Plante, Francois Hebert-Paul Jousselin; Fondations Gaston Vol. 2: 1979
Plants Award for Special Events; Helen L. Vol. 1: 4040
Plaquette du Centenaire de Camille Flammarion Vol. 2: 2561
Plarski Award; Lea Vol. 1: 15313
Plaskett Medal Vol. 1: 18145
Plasmadynamics and Lasers Award Vol. 1: 2691
Plass Award; William T. Vol. 1: 4556
Plastics Hall of Fame Vol. 1: 17392
Plata; Medalla de Vol. 1: 19184
Plata; Medallion de Vol. 1: 16458
Plateau Audience Award; Joseph Vol. 2: 887
Plateau Life Achievement Award; Joseph Vol. 2: 887
Plateau Music Award; Joseph Vol. 2: 887
Plateau Prize; Joseph Vol. 2: 887
Plateauprijzen; Joseph Vol. 2: 887
Platinum Award Vol. 1: 17910
Platinum Jubilee Lectures Vol. 2: 3538
Platinum Music Video Award Vol. 1: 17911
Platinum Sales Award Vol. 2: 5230
Platinum Wing Award Vol. 1: 14566
Platt Corning Medal; Elizabeth Vol. 1: 9876
Plaut Community Leadership Award; Johanna Cooke Vol. 1: 9090
Player of the Year
Asian Football Confederation Vol. 2: 4425
Camanachd Association Vol 2: 7231
Professional Golfers' Association of America Vol 1: 17619
United States Professional Tennis Association Vol 1: 20743
Player of the Year Award Vol. 1: 6440
Player of the Year; Chris Schenkel Vol. 1: 17594
Player of Year Vol. 1: 16153
Player Portrait Award; John Vol. 2: 8188
Players Appreciation Award Vol. 1: 21151
Players Appreciation Cup Vol. 1: 21151
PlayLabs Festival Vol. 1: 17400
Playoff Most Valuable Player Vol. 1: 8484
Playthings Merchandising Achievement Awards Vol. 1: 10013
Playwright Award Competition Vol. 1: 6350
Playwriting Competition Prize; Dorothy Silver Vol. 1: 12336
Pleissner Memorial Award; Mary Vol. 1: 4863
Pleissner Memorial Award; Ogden Vol. 1: 4864
Pless International Graduate of the Year; J. Will Vol. 1: 11722
Plimpton Prize Vol. 1: 17095
Pluma de Oro Vol. 1: 21059
Plummer Memorial Educational Lecture Award Vol. 1: 4892
Plyler Prize for Molecular Spectroscopy; Earle K. Vol. 1: 3470
PMAC Health Research Foundation Vol. 1: 6840
PMC Electronic Test Award Vol. 1: 17487
PMDA Celebrity Photographer Award Vol. 1: 17297
PNBA Book Awards Vol. 1: 17007
PNWA Literary Contest Vol. 1: 17011
Podoloff Trophy; Most Valuable Player Award - Maurice Vol. 1: 14507

Poe Award; Edgar A. Vol. 1: 21603
Poe Awards (Edgars); Edgar Allan Vol. 1: 13732
Poehlman Award; William J. Vol. 1: 18644
Poel Memorial Festival; William Vol. 2: 8961
Poet Laureate, Consultant in Poetry Vol. 1: 12834
Poetker Award; Frances Jones Vol. 1: 2534
Poetry and Poster Contest Vol. 1: 14699
Poetry Award
National Writers Association Vol. 1: 15994
River City Vol 1: 18067
VIEW Clubs of Australia Vol 2: 644
Poetry Books Award Vol. 1: 21467
Poetry Chapbook Competition, Artist Residency Program Vol. 1: 7710
Poetry Contest Vol. 1: 21999
Poetry, Fiction and Essay Prizes Vol. 2: 5456
Poetry, Fiction and Nonfiction Contest Vol. 1: 8225
Poetry Film Festival Vol. 1: 15512
Poetry International Festival Vol. 2: 4871
Poetry Prize-Premio de Poesia Polibio Gomes dos Santos Vol. 2: 5457
Poetry Society of Michigan Award Vol. 1: 15021
Poetry Society of Oklahoma Award Vol. 1: 15022
Poetry Society of Tennessee Pirouette Award Vol. 1: 15023
Poetry Society of Texas Award
National Federation of State Poetry Societies Vol. 1: 14989
National Federation of State Poetry Societies Vol 1: 15024
Poets Greatest Hits National Archive Vol. 1: 17742
Poets' Roundtable of Arkansas Award Vol. 1: 15025
Poggendorf Lecture; Walter Vol. 2: 542
Pohl-Preis; Robert-Wichard- Vol. 2: 2728
Poincare; Fondation Henri Vol. 2: 1883
Poincare; Prix Henri Vol. 2: 1820
Points and Awards Program Vol. 1: 19542
Poirson; Fondation Ayme Vol. 2: 1804
Pol Gold Medal; Balthasar van der Vol. 2: 936
Polakoff Award; Joseph Vol. 1: 2907
Polanyi Lecture Award; John C. Vol. 1: 7847
Polar Medal Vol. 2: 7261
Polaris Award Vol. 2: 7924
Policard-Lacassagne; Fondation Andre Vol. 2: 1795
Police Bravery Award Vol. 2: 8277
Police Exemplary Service Medal Vol. 1: 6828
Police Medal of Honor Vol. 1: 3576
Police Officer of the Year
American Police Hall of Fame Vol. 1: 3577
National Burglar and Fire Alarm Association Vol 1: 14556
Police Officer of the Year Award Vol. 1: 11310
Police Overseas Service Medal Vol. 2: 202
Police Posthumous Medal of Honor Vol. 1: 3578
Police Reporting; Al Nakkula Award for Vol. 1: 21008
Policymaker of the Year Vol. 1: 11551
Polish Chemical Society Medal Vol. 2: 5339
Polish Composers Union Prize Vol. 2: 5344
Polish Cup Vol. 2: 5347
Polish-German Marian Smoluchowski-Emil Warburg Physics Prize Vol. 2: 5366
Polish Institute and Sikorski Museum Awards Vol. 2: 8279
Polish PEN Centre Prizes Vol. 2: 5330
Polish Phonetic Association Award Vol. 2: 5360
Polish Radio Award Vol. 2: 5306
Polish Society for Commodity Science Honorary Member Vol. 2: 5358
Polish Society of Hygiene Honorary Member Vol. 2: 5378
Polish Society of Hygiene Plaques Vol. 2: 5379
Polish Society of Veterinary Science Awards Vol. 2: 5381
Political Journalism Award Vol. 1: 15518
Politis Composition Prize Vol. 1: 6534
Politzer Prize Vol. 2: 6644
Politzer Society Award; Otology Vol. 2: 4821
Polk Awards; George Vol. 1: 12915
Polk Memorial Awards; George Vol. 1: 12915
Polka Music Awards Vol. 1: 11819
Polka Music Hall of Fame Vol. 1: 11820
Poll; Fondation Max Vol. 2: 1037
Pollack Distinguished Achievement Award; Seymour Vol. 1: 827
Pollak Prize in Poetry; The Brittingham Prize in Poetry and Felix Vol. 1: 21125
Pollak-Virag Award Vol. 2: 3307
Pollie Awards Vol. 1: 1385
Pollock Award; Herbert C. Vol. 1: 9040
Pollock Award; R. C. Vol. 1: 3056
Pollock-Krasner Foundation Grants Vol. 1: 17461
Pollock Memorial Lecture Vol. 2: 543
Pollock Trophy; Sam Vol. 1: 2516
Pollution Prevention Award Vol. 1: 15472
Polya Award; George Vol. 1: 13196
Polya Prize Vol. 2: 8091
Polya Prize; George Vol. 1: 18739
Polymer Physics Prize Vol. 1: 3471
Polyurethane Division Awards Vol. 1: 19317
Polyurethane Division Hall of Fame Awards Vol. 1: 19318
Pomer Award; Vic Vol. 1: 13982
Pomerance Award Vol. 1: 16347
Pomerance Award for Scientific Contributions to Archaeology Vol. 1: 5035
Pomeroy Award; Edward C. Vol. 1: 1154
Pon Memorial Award; Ernest M. Vol. 1: 14010
PONCHO Special Recognition Awards Vol. 1: 18393
Poniatoff Gold Medal Award; Alexander M. Vol. 1: 19195
Ponti; Fondation Jerome Vol. 2: 1906
Poodles, Sr. Award; Joe Vol. 1: 12119
Pool Postgraduate Research Fellowships in Hemophilia; Judith Graham Vol. 1: 15212
Poort-Prize Vol. 2: 5657
Pop Award Vol. 2: 4723
Pope Award; E. P. Vol. 1: 1480
Pope John XIII Peace Prize Vol. 2: 9315
Pope John XXI Prize Vol. 2: 9306
Popescu Prize for European Poetry Translation; Corneliu M. Vol. 2: 8275
Poppe Prize Vol. 2: 6235
Poppele Broadcast Award; Jack Vol. 1: 17841
Popper Memorial Prize; Jan Vol. 2: 89
Pops Medal Award; Horace Vol. 1: 21660
Popular Annual Financial Reporting Award Program Vol. 1: 10114
Popular Choice Award Vol. 1: 663
Popular Science Book Prize Vol. 2: 1564
Population-Specific Research Project Award Vol. 1: 19851
Poque Prize; Forrest C. Vol. 1: 21087
Porcellati Award Vol. 2: 3241
Poretsky Prize in Photography; Rita Vol. 2: 3774
Porges; Prix Helene Vol. 2: 2159
Porraz International Coastal Engineering Award; Mauricio Vol. 1: 4335
Porter Award; Charles Vol. 1: 18761
Porter Award; J. Roger Vol. 1: 20579
Porter Award; USFCC/J. Roger Vol. 1: 4139
Porter Grant for Graduate Work in Composition; Ellen Jane Lorenz Vol. 1: 13662
Porter Lecture Award; William C. Vol. 1: 5781
Porter Memorial Award; Frank C. Vol. 1: 21439
Porter Memorial Award - "Friend of the Satellite Dealer" Award; Pat Vol. 1: 9220
Porter Memorial Book Prize; John Vol. 1: 7504
Porter Physiology Fellowships for Minorities Vol. 1: 3524
Porter Prize; Arthur Kingsley Vol. 1: 8150
Porter Prize for Fiction; Katherine Anne Vol. 1: 16361
Porter Prize; Marion Vol. 1: 7380
Porter Tradition of Excellence Book Award; John Vol. 1: 7504
Porterfield Award; Robert Vol. 1: 19490
Portland International Film Festival Vol. 1: 16561
Portland Opera Lieber Awards Vol. 1: 17471
Portrait Award; BP Vol. 2: 8188
Porumbescu Prize; Ciprian Vol. 2: 5859
Poseidon Trophy Vol. 1: 14450
Positiva Priset Vol. 2: 6293
Positive Images Award Vol. 1: 19927
Positive Prize Vol. 2: 6293
Posner Prize; Fellows' Ernst Vol. 1: 18961
Post-Doctoral Fellowship Award in In Vitro Toxicology; Colgate-Palmolive Vol. 1: 19333
Post-Secondary Scholarship Vol. 1: 20320
Postal History Award Vol. 2: 8263
Postal History Journal Awards Vol. 1: 17481
Postal History Society Medal Vol. 1: 17482
Postdoctoral Fellowship Awards for Minorities Vol. 1: 1899
Postdoctoral Fellowship in Emerging Infectious Diseases Vol. 1: 15122
Postdoctoral Fellowship in Infectious Disease Training and Herpes Virus Research Vol. 1: 15123
Postdoctoral Fellowship in Physiological Genomics Vol. 1: 3525
Postdoctoral Fellowship Program Vol. 1: 3157
Postdoctoral Fellowships in Infectious Diseases Vol. 1: 15124
Poster Award Vol. 2: 3917
Poster Contest Vol. 1: 9777
Poster Paper Prize Vol. 2: 8333
Poster Prize
Challenger Society for Marine Science Vol. 2: 7269
International Federation of Societies of Cosmetic Chemists Vol 2: 7949

Poster Session Awards Vol. 1: 2618
Postgraduate Best Paper Award Vol. 1: 3395
Postgraduate Scholarship
British Association for Applied Linguistics Vol. 2: 6930
Canadian Meteorological and Oceanographic Society Vol 1: 7277
Postgraduate Student Prize Vol. 2: 547
Postlethwait Award; Samuel Noel Vol. 1: 6553
Postsecondary Teacher of the Year Vol. 1: 14574
Potamkin Prize for Research in Pick's, Alzheimer's, and Related Diseases Vol. 1: 704
Potier-Boes; Prix Diane Vol. 2: 2134
Potorff Professional Designee of the Year Award; Verne W. Vol. 1: 11281
Pott Memorial Award; Anthony Vol. 2: 6740
Potter Award; Dennis Vol. 2: 6905
Potter Award of Special Recognition; Helen Vol. 1: 5475
Potter Award; Stuart G. Vol. 1: 6126
Potter Gold Medal; James Harry Vol. 1: 4539
Potts Memorial Award; John H. Vol. 1: 6054
Potts Memorial Fellowship Award; Ralph H. Vol. 1: 3311
Poultry Products Research Award Vol. 1: 17502
Poultry Science Association Fellows Vol. 1: 17503
Poultry Science Association Research Award Vol. 1: 17504
Poultry Welfare Research Award Vol. 1: 17505
Poverello Medal Vol. 1: 9730
P.O.W. of the Year Vol. 1: 2213
Powder Metallurgy Design Competition Vol. 1: 13313
Powder Metallurgy Pioneer Award Vol. 1: 13314
Powell Award; Cedric Vol. 1: 5977
Powell Award; Elizabeth Vol. 1: 20964
Powell Award; Michael Vol. 2: 7407
Powell Award; William and Mousie Vol. 1: 12657
Powell Joint Warfighting Essay Contest; Colin L. Vol. 1: 20707
Powell Minority Postdoctoral Fellowship in Tropical Disease Research; Colin L. Vol. 1: 15124
Powell Prize; John Wesley Vol. 1: 18691
Power Award; Sask Vol. 1: 18306
Power-Life Award Vol. 1: 10911
Power Missile Crew Award; General Thomas S. Vol. 1: 351
Power of Woman Award Vol. 1: 15026
Power of Women Award Vol. 1: 14989
Power Point Rankings Award Vol. 1: 15291
Power Strategic Combat Missle Crew Award; General Thomas S. Vol. 1: 351
Powerlifting National Hall of Fame Vol. 1: 20738
Powers Award Vol. 1: 10424
Powers Memorial Award; Sidney Vol. 1: 1348
Powers Research Achievement Award in Pharmaceutical Analysis; Justin L. Vol. 1: 3397
Pownall Award for Information Books; Eve Vol. 2: 308
Pozzetta Dissertation Research Award; George E. Vol. 1: 10705
Pozzoli International Piano Competition; Ettore Vol. 2: 3887
PPFA Hall of Fame
Professional Picture Framers Association Vol. 1: 17646
Professional Picture Framers Association Vol 1: 17647
PPIC-FAI Award Vol. 2: 3368
PR Professional of the Year Vol. 1: 131
Practical Project Award Vol. 2: 7878
Practice Excellence Award Vol. 1: 3399
Practicing Urologist Research Awards Vol. 1: 4801
Practitioner Excellence Award Vol. 1: 752
Practitioner of the Year Vol. 1: 14773
Practitioner of the Year Award Vol. 1: 905
Practitioner Research Award
American Academy of Pediatrics Vol. 1: 789
American Veterinary Medical Association Vol 1: 4817
Praemium Erasmianum Vol. 2: 4737
Praemium Imperiale Vol. 2: 4159
Prague Spring International Music Competition Vol. 2: 1434
Prairie Pasque Children's Book Award Vol. 1: 19452
Prakash Memorial Medal; Professor Brahm Vol. 2: 3501
Prakken Professional Cooperation Award Vol. 1: 12069
Pramie fur die Beantwortung einer literarischen oder philologischen Frage Vol. 2: 2777
Prangey Award Vol. 2: 8013
Pras Hestrin Vol. 2: 3757
Pras l'Bikoret Sifrutit Vol. 2: 3727
Pras Leib Yaffe Vol. 2: 3778
Pras l'Roman Ivri Mekori Vol. 2: 3728
Pras l'Sefer Shira Ivri Mekori Vol. 2: 3729
Pras Zalman Shazar Le'heker Toldot Am Israel Vol. 2: 3768
Prasad Award; Dr. Rajendra Vol. 2: 3401
Prasad Memorial Lecture; Prof. M. R. N. Vol. 2: 3502
Prasad Memorial Oration Award; Dr. D. N. Vol. 2: 3425
Prather Award; Victor A. Vol. 1: 1506
Pratley Award; P. L. Vol. 1: 7418
Pratt & Whitney Canada Grand Prix Vol. 1: 11614
Pratt and Whitney Canada Grand Prize Vol. 1: 11613
Pratt Award; Haraden Vol. 1: 10877
Pratt International Library Travel Fund; Bogle/ Vol. 1: 2991
Pratt Memorial Award; Burtram J. Vol. 1: 8124
Pratt Memorial Award; Wallace E. Vol. 1: 1349
Pratt-Severn Best Student Research Paper Award Vol. 1: 4112
Pratte Scholarship Vol. 1: 19845
Pre-College Award Vol. 1: 1372
Preakness Stakes
Maryland Jockey Club Vol. 1: 13136
Triple Crown Productions, Inc. Vol 1: 20206
Precision Timing Trophy Vol. 2: 7613
Preedy Post-Graduate Bursary; Winifred E. Vol. 2: 172
Prego; Premio Ing. Agr. Antonio J. Vol. 2: 3
Prego Prize; Antonio J. Vol. 2: 3
Preis der Deutschen Physikalische Gesellschaft Vol. 2: 2724
Preis der Gesellschaft Deutcher Chemiker fur Schriftsteller Vol. 2: 2813
Preis der Gesellschaft Deutscher Chemiker fur Journalistein und Schriftsteller Vol. 2: 2813
Preis der Justus-Liebig-Universitat Giessen Vol. 2: 2999
Preis der Landes Baden-Wuerttemberg Vol. 2: 3107
Preis der Landeshauptstadt Stuttgart Vol. 2: 3107
Preis der Neuen Darmstadter Sezession fur Junge Kunstler Vol. 2: 3141
Preis der Stiftung Kunststoff-Technik Vol. 2: 6524
Preis des Suddeutschen Rundfunks Vol. 2: 3107
Preis fur Pharma-Technik Vol. 2: 3048
Preise fur herausragende wissenschaftliche Leistungen Vol. 2: 2782
Preisich Prize; Miklos Vol. 2: 3250
Preliminary Trade Prize Vol. 2: 7554
Preller Prize; Gustav Vol. 2: 5656
Premi
Accademia di Medicina di Torino Vol. 2: 3809
Accademia di Studi Storici Aldo Moro Vol 2: 3811
Associazione Napoletana Amici di Malta Vol 2: 3860
Premi Antonio Feltrinelli Vol. 2: 3827
Premi culturali Vol. 2: 3813
Premi David di Donatello per la Cinematografia Internazionale Vol. 2: 3895
Premi del Ministro per i Beni Culturali e Ambientali Vol. 2: 3828
Premi Giosue Carducci Vol. 2: 4065
Premier Breeder at the North American International Livestock Exposition Vol. 1: 2031
Premier Print Awards Vol. 1: 17569
Premier Property Award Vol. 1: 18006
Premier Recreation Operation Award Vol. 1: 18006
Premier Technology Shandon Award Vol. 2: 5632
Premier's Literary Award Vol. 2: 598
Premies voor de verspreiding van de betere film in Belgie Vol. 2: 1094
Premio a Investigadores Noveles Vol. 2: 6103
Premio A. J. Merito Paleontologico Vol. 2: 20
Premio a la Mejor Revista Cientifica o Tecnologica Vol. 2: 9322
Premio a la Obra Integral de un Cientifico Vol. 2: 1268
Premio ABB Vol. 2: 4005
Premio Abilio Lopes do Rego Vol. 2: 5409
Premio Aboim Sande Lemos Vol. 2: 5413
Premio Academia Argentina de Letras Vol. 2: 16
Premio Academia Argentina de Letras e Egresados de la carrera de Letras de universidades estates o privadas Vol. 2: 17
Premio Academia Nacional de Agronomia y Veterinaria Vol. 2: 4
Premio Academia Nacional de la Historia Vol. 2: 12
Premio AEI Galileo Ferraris Vol. 2: 4006
Premio AEI Guglielmo Marconi Vol. 2: 4007
Premio AEI - Milano Section Vol. 2: 4008
Premio AEI Ricerche Vol. 2: 4007

Premio Agricola Interamericano para Profesionales Jovenes Vol. 2: 1362
Premio AICA Vol. 2: 5450
Premio al Deportista Universitario Vol. 2: 4601
Premio al Desarrollo Agropecuario Vol. 2: 5
Premio al Egresado con Mejor Promedio en las Carreras de Historia Vol. 2: 13
Premio Al Merito Cientifico Vol. 2: 1306
Premio Alejandro Zazuete Vol. 2: 4506
Premio Alfonso Caso Vol. 2: 4534
Premio Alvarenga do Piaui Vol. 2: 5408
Premio Ama Vol. 2: 6085
Premio Angela Cevenini Vol. 2: 4014
Premio Antonio Alves de Carvalho Fernandes Vol. 2: 5407
Premio Anual de Investigacion Economica Jesus Silva Herzog Vol. 2: 4602
Premio Anual de Investigacion en Epilpsia Vol. 2: 4546
Premio Anual de Servicio Social Gustavo Baz Prada Vol. 2: 4603
Premio Aquilino Ribeiro Vol. 2: 5418
Premio Argentino de Paleobotanica Vol. 2: 21
Premio Artur Malheiros Vol. 2: 5414
Premio Aurelio Peccei Vol. 2: 3897
Premio Balzan Vol. 2: 3961
Premio Banco de la Republica Vol. 2: 1270
Premio Bayer en Ciencias Veterinarias Vol. 2: 6
Premio Beca Nacional de Diseno Industrial Clara Porset Vol. 2: 4604
Premio Bolsa de Cereales de Buenos Aires Vol. 2: 7
Premio Bonazzi Vol. 2: 4009
Premio Bottani Vol. 2: 4010
Premio Cacho Pallero Vol. 2: 6030
Premio Campiello Vol. 2: 3879
Premio Carlos del Castillo Leiva Vol. 2: 6086
Premio Carlos Mateo Sanchez Vol. 2: 4506
Premio Carlos Perez del Toro Vol. 2: 4473
Premio Carlos Teixeira Vol. 2: 5405
Premio Cavolini - De Mellis Vol. 2: 3836
Premio Cenafor de Monografica Vol. 2: 1171
Premio Ceresis Vol. 2: 5248
Premio Cinema d'Essai - Targa AIACE Vol. 2: 3853
Premio Comillas de Biografia, Autobiografia y Memorias Vol. 2: 6109
Premio Comision Nacional Bancaria Vol. 2: 4475
Premio Compasso d'oro ADI Vol. 2: 3863
Premio Condumex Vol. 2: 4605
Premio Corazon de Oro Vol. 2: 4632
Premio da critica Vol. 2: 5447
Premio da traducao cientifica e tecnica Vol. 2: 5474
Premio David Martin Castilla Vol. 2: 6087
Premio de Ciencas Morfologicas Dr. Enrique Acosta Vidrio Vol. 2: 4606
Premio de Composicion Arquitectonica Alberto J. Pani Vol. 2: 4607
Premio de Cuento para Ninos Vol. 2: 4528
Premio de Ecologia Vol. 2: 4628
Premio de Ensayo Literario Angel Maria Garibay Kintana Vol. 2: 4529
Premio de la Real Academia de Farmacia Vol. 2: 6088
Premio de Novela Ignacio Manuel Altamirano Vol. 2: 4527
Premio de Pesquisa Estudantil Instituto Nacional do Livro Vol. 2: 1182
Premio de Poesia Josue Mirlo Vol. 2: 4530
Premio de Tecnologia Quimica Vol. 2: 4464
Premio de Tecnologia Textil Vol. 2: 4465
Premio de Traducao Calouste Gulbenkian Vol. 2: 5410
Premio Deguci Vol. 2: 4925
Premio del Colegio Oficial de Farmaceuticos Vol. 2: 6089
Premio del Grisejo General de Glegics Officiales de Farmaveutics Vol. 2: 6090
Premio del Instituto Nacional de Administracion Publica Vol. 2: 4532
Premio del Rey Prize Vol. 1: 2480
Premio del Seminario de Economia Agricola del Tercer Mundo Vol. 2: 4608
Premio Derechos Humanos Vol. 2: 4609
Premio di Laurea Luigi Casati in Discipline Scientifiche Vol. 2: 3829
Premio di Laurea Luigi Casati in Discipline Uranistiche Vol. 2: 3830
Premio Direito dos Seguros Vol. 2: 5494
Premio Dr. Antonio Pires Vol. 2: 2
Premio Dr. Enrique Beltran de Historia de La Ciencia y La Tecnologia Vol. 2: 4563
Premio dos Culturas en Origen Vol. 2: 4479
Premio Editiorial Costa Rica Vol. 2: 1360
Premio el Professor Distinguido Vol. 2: 4518
Premio Elvire Moragas Vol. 2: 6091
Premio Enrique Pena Vol. 2: 14
Premio Europeo di Letteratura Giovanile "Pier Paolo Vergerio" Vol. 2: 4067
Premio Europeo Prof. D. Ganassini Vol. 2: 3941
Premio F. Busoni Vol. 2: 3875
Premio F. Malusardi Vol. 2: 4011
Premio Facultad de Derecho a la Mejor Tesis Vol. 2: 4610
Premio Faes Espanola de Productos Quimicos y Farmaceuticos Vol. 2: 6092
Premio Felipe Tena Ramirez Vol. 2: 4611
Premio Ferreira de Castro Vol. 2: 5446
Premio Filippo Gramatica Vol. 2: 3861
Premio Francisco de la Maza Vol. 2: 4535
Premio Francisco Javier Clavijero Vol. 2: 4536
Premio Fray Bernardino de Sahagun Vol. 2: 4537
Premio Frederico de Menezes Veiga Vol. 2: 1159
Premio Fundacion Alfredo Manzullo Vol. 2: 8
Premio Fundacion Rene Baron Vol. 2: 9
Premio G. Vitelli Vol. 2: 3990
Premio Gea Gonzalez - PUIC Vol. 2: 4510
Premio Genaro Estrada Vol. 2: 4506
Premio General Casimiro Dantas Vol. 2: 5406
Premio Gilberto Figueroa Nogueron Vol. 2: 4494
Premio Giorgio Dal Piaz Vol. 2: 4050
Premio Grinzane Cavour Vol. 2: 3881
Premio Gustavo D. Canedo Vol. 2: 4506
Premio Iberoamericano Book Award Vol. 1: 12700
Premio Interamericano a la Participacion de la Mujer en el Desarrollo Rural Vol. 2: 1364
Premio Internacional Almirante Gago Coutinho Vol. 2: 5490
Premio Internacional de Educacion Fisica Jose Maria Cagigal Vol. 2: 900
Premio Internacional Vasco Vilvalva Vol. 2: 5411
Premio Internazionale Accademia Musicale Chigiana Siena Vol. 2: 3793
Premio Internazionale Amedeo e Frances Herlitzka per la Fisiologia Vol. 2: 3805
Premio Internazionale di Meridionalistica Guido Dorso Vol. 2: 3851
Premio Internazionale e Medaglia d'oro, Professor Modesto Panetti e Professor Carlo Ferrari Vol. 2: 3806
Premio Internazionale Enno Flaiano Vol. 2: 3849
Premio Internazionale Maria Luisa Ferrari Soave e Dott. Luigi Soave Vol. 2: 3807
Premio Internazionale Paladino D'Oro Vol. 2: 3978
Premio Internazionale Paolo Gatto Vol. 2: 3831
Premio Internazionali dell' Instituto Nazionale delle Assicurazioni Vol. 2: 3825
Premio Istituto Italo-Latino Americano Vol. 2: 3984
Premio Jean Mitry Vol. 2: 4038
Premio Jinete Iberico Vol. 2: 6030
Premio Jose Cayetano Valdez Vol. 2: 4506
Premio Jose Maria Bustillo Vol. 2: 10
Premio Joven Investigador Profesor Ignacio Chavez Vol. 2: 4551
Premio Juan Comas Vol. 2: 4538
Premio Juan Pablos al Merito Editorial Vol. 2: 4579
Premio Julio G. Arce Vol. 2: 4506
Premio La Ceramica n la Arquitectura Vol. 2: 4648
Premio La Sonrisa Vertical Vol. 2: 6110
Premio Laboratories CEPA Schwart Pharma SL Vol. 2: 6093
Premio Larragoiti Vol. 2: 5412
Premio Letterario del Frignano Riccio d'Oro Vol. 2: 4028
Premio Linceo Vol. 2: 3834
Premio Literario Internacional *Novedades* y Diana Vol. 2: 4624
Premio Literario Ramon Llull Vol. 2: 6022
Premio Liverdade-Visconde de Sousa Prego Vol. 2: 5443
Premio Lorenzo R. Parodi Vol. 2: 24
Premio Luis de Camoes Vol. 2: 5445
Premio Luis Zambrano a la Inventiva Tecnologica Nacional Vol. 2: 9325
Premio Maestro Arturo Rosenblueth Vol. 2: 4635
Premio Maestro Ignacio Chavez Vol. 2: 4636
Premio Maestro Manuel Vaquero Vol. 2: 4637
Premio Maestro Salvador Aceves Vol. 2: 4638
Premio Magda Donato Vol. 2: 4460
Premio Manuel Alves Monteiro Vol. 2: 5416
Premio Manuel Toussaint Vol. 2: 4539
Premio Marcos y Celia Mauss Vol. 2: 4612
Premio Maria Faletti-Nosari Vol. 2: 4012
Premio Maria Teresa Messori Roncaglia and Eugenio Mari Vol. 2: 3832
Premio Mario di Nola Vol. 2: 3833
Premio MEC de Arte Vol. 2: 1181
Premio Mesquite Vol. 1: 10188
Premio Mexinox Vol. 2: 4640
Premio Miguel Covarrubias Vol. 2: 4540
Premio Miguel Hidalgo Vol. 2: 4585
Premio Miguel Othon de Mendizabal Vol. 2: 4541
Premio Municipais Joshua Benoliel de Fotografia Vol. 2: 5424
Premio Municipal Alfredo Marceneiro de Fado Vol. 2: 5425
Premio Municipal Augusto Vieira da Silva de Investigacao Vol. 2: 5426

Award Index

Premio Municipal Carlos Botelho de Pintura Vol. 2: 5427
Premio Municipal Fernando Amado de Encenacao Teatral Vol. 2: 5428
Premio Municipal Joao Baptista Rosa de Video Vol. 2: 5429
Premio Municipal Jorge Colaco de Azulejaria Vol. 2: 5430
Premio Municipal Jose Simoes de Almeida de Escultura Vol. 2: 5431
Premio Municipal Julio Cesar Machado de Jornalismo Vol. 2: 5432
Premio Municipal Julio de Castilho de Olisipografia Vol. 2: 5433
Premio Municipal Maria Leonor Magro de Radio Vol. 2: 5434
Premio Municipal Rafael Bordalo Pinheiro de Banda Desenhada, Cartoon e Caricaturista Vol. 2: 5435
Premio Municipal Roberto de Araujo Pereira de Design Vol. 2: 5436
Premio Municipal Trabalho e Estudo Vol. 2: 5437
Premio Nacional a Desarollo Tecnologico Vol. 2: 9323
Premio Nacional de Arte Vol. 2: 1250
Premio Nacional de Calidad Vol. 2: 4626
Premio Nacional de Ciencia Vol. 2: 9324
Premio Nacional de Ciencia y Tecnologia de Alimentos Vol. 2: 4477
Premio Nacional de Ciencias Vol. 2: 1251
Premio Nacional de Ciencias del Mar Vol. 2: 1308
Premio Nacional de Ciencias Fisico - Matematicas y Naturales Vol. 2: 4574
Premio nacional de Ciencias y Artes Vol. 2: 4577
Premio Nacional de Ciencias y Tecnologia Clodomiro Picado Twight Vol. 2: 1354
Premio Nacional de Deportes Vol. 2: 4575
Premio Nacional de Historia Vol. 2: 1252
Premio Nacional de Historia, Ciencias Sociales y Filosofia Vol. 2: 4572
Premio Nacional de Investigacion Financiera IMEF Vol. 2: 4521
Premio Nacional de la Contaduria Publica Vol. 2: 4519
Premio Nacional de la Juventud Vol. 2: 4578
Premio Nacional de Linguistica y Literatura Vol. 2: 4573
Premio Nacional de Literatura Vol. 2: 1253
Premio Nacional de Literatura Gilberto Owen Vol. 2: 4504
Premio Nacional de Literatura Jose Fuentes Mares Vol. 2: 4646
Premio Nacional de Merito Civico Vol. 2: 4583
Premio Nacional de Periodismo Vol. 2: 1254
Premio Nacional de Periodismo Pio Viquez Vol. 2: 1355
Premio Nacional de Periodismo y de Informacion Vol. 2: 4584
Premio Nacional de Poesia Jorge Cuesta Vol. 2: 4500
Premio Nacional de Quimica Vol. 2: 1339
Premio Nacional de Teatro Vol. 2: 1356
Premio Nacional de Tecnologia y Diseno Vol. 2: 4576
Premio Nacional de Trabajo Vol. 2: 4569
Premio Nacional Teponaxtli de Malinalco Vol. 2: 4462
Premio Napoli di Narrativa Vol. 2: 3938
Premio Nazionale Composizione Vol. 2: 3934
Premio Nazionale del Presidente della Repubblica Vol. 2: 3826
Premio Nicolas Leon Vol. 2: 4542
Premio Norman Sverdlin Vol. 2: 4613
Premio Omeyocan Vol. 2: 4614
Premio Pablo Villavicencio Vol. 2: 4506
Premio Paolo Borciani Vol. 2: 4054
"Premio Paolo Borciani" - International String Quartet Competition Vol. 2: 4054
Premio Paul Coremans Vol. 2: 4543
Premio Planeta de Novela Vol. 2: 6021
Premio Positano Leonida Massine per l'Arte della Danza Vol. 2: 3865
Premio Prof. Dr. Alejandro Cabanne Vol. 2: 32
Premio Puma Vol. 2: 4615
Premio Rafael Heliodoro Valle Vol. 2: 4620
Premio Ramos Paz Vol. 2: 5417
Premio Reina Sofia de Investigacion sobre prevencion de las deficiencias Vol. 2: 6033
Premio Reuniao Anual de SBPC Vol. 2: 1166
Premio Revista Punto de Partida Vol. 2: 4616
Premio Ricardo Malheiros Vol. 2: 5415
Premio Riccione Ater Vol. 2: 4042
Premio Riccione per il Teatro Vol. 2: 4042
Premio Romulo Garza para Investigacion Vol. 2: 4512
Premio Romulo Garza para Publicaciones Vol. 2: 4513
Premio Saint-Vincent per il Cinema Italiano Vol. 2: 4061
Premio Saint-Vincent per il Giornalismo Vol. 2: 4062
Premio Saint-Vincent per l'economia Vol. 2: 4063
Premio Sinaloa de Ciencias y Artes Vol. 2: 4505
Premio Sinaloa de Periodismo Vol. 2: 4506
Premio Tenco Vol. 2: 3885
Premio Tenore Vol. 2: 3837
Premio Trienal Instituto Torcuato di Tella Mozarteum Argentina Vol. 2: 39
Premio Triennale per la Fisica Francesco Somaini Vol. 2: 3932
Premio TWAS (Third World Academy of Sciences) Vol. 2: 4555
Premio TWNSO (Third World Network of Scientific Organizations) Vol. 2: 4556
Premio Universidad Nacional Vol. 2: 4617
Premio Valentino Bucchi di Roma Capitale Vol. 2: 3945
Premio Valle Inclan Vol. 2: 8974
Premio Valmor e Municipal de Arquitectura Vol. 2: 5438
Premio Varese Vol. 2: 3980
Premio Vicente T. Mendoza Vol. 2: 4544
Premio Zamenhof por Internacia Komprenigo Vol. 2: 4926
Premios a la Investigacion Medica Vol. 2: 4525
Premios ADIRCAE Vol. 2: 5997
Premios Anuales a los Mejores Trabajos Cientificos Vol. 2: 9321
Premios de Beneficencia Alejandro Angel Escobar Vol. 2: 1310
Premios de Investigacion Cientifica Vol. 2: 4557
Premios de poesia, ficcao e ensaio Vol. 2: 5456
Premios Municipais Eca de Queiroz de Literatura Vol. 2: 5439
Premios Municipais Joly Braga Santos de Musica Vol. 2: 5440
Premios Municipais Palmira Bastos e Antonio Silva de Interpretacao Teatral Vol. 2: 5441
Premios Principe de Asturias Vol. 2: 6035
Premios Revelacao Vol. 2: 5471
Premios Vitalicios Vol. 2: 6032
Premios Weizmann de la Academia Mexicana de Ciencias Vol. 2: 4559
Prentice Medal; Charles F. Vol. 1: 724
Prescott Award; Gerald W. Vol. 1: 17302
Prescott Award; Samuel Cate Vol. 1: 10944
Presea Carlos Vallejo Marquez Vol. 2: 4549
Presea Ignacio Zaragosa Vol. 2: 4498
Presea La Familia Vol. 2: 1561
Presenter of the Year Vol. 2: 8858
Preservation Award
- Birmingham Historical Society Vol. 1: 6400
- Canadian Railroad Historical Association Vol 1: 7370
- Historical Society of Frederick County Vol 1: 10462
- Los Angeles Conservancy Vol 1: 12927

Preservation Awards
- Essex Community Heritage Organization Vol. 1: 9340
- Historical Society of Princeton Vol 1: 10470

Preservation Merit Awards Vol. 1: 10448
Preservation of Civilization Award; Advancement and Vol. 1: 15900
Preservation Publication Award Vol. 1: 18962
Preservationist of the Year Vol. 1: 13001
President & Vice President's Choice Award Vol. 2: 9088
President Award
- Association of European Chambers of Commerce and Industry Vol. 2: 837
- Paralyzed Veterans of America Vol 1: 17069

President of Chamber Award Vol. 1: 9861
President Prize Vol. 2: 7272
Presidental Award Vol. 1: 4059
Presidential Academic Fitness Awards Vol. 1: 20489
Presidential Active Lifestyle Award Vol. 1: 17541
Presidential Award
- American Academy of Periodontology Vol. 1: 809
- American Association of Blood Banks Vol 1: 1113
- American Association of Mental Health Professionals in Corrections Vol 1: 1272
- Federation of Jewish Men's Clubs Vol 1: 9510
- Food Distribution Research Society Vol 1: 9654
- International Association of Diecutting and Diemaking Vol 1: 11339
- International Camaro Club Vol 1: 11447
- National Association of Recording Merchandisers Vol 1: 14364
- National Association of the Holy Name Society Vol 1: 14421
- Plastic Surgery Educational Foundation Vol 1: 17382

Presidential Award for Outstanding Contribution to Peace Psychology Vol. 1: 3740
Presidential Award for Outstanding Contributions to the Promotion of Scholarship in the Third World Vol. 1: 5899

Presidential Award of the RES - Annie R. Beasley Memorial Award Vol. 1: 18787
Presidential Award (Presidential Citation) Vol. 1: 17383
Presidential Awards Vol. 2: 1188
Presidential Champions Bronze Award Vol. 1: 17541
Presidential Champions Gold Award Vol. 1: 17541
Presidential Champions Silver Award Vol. 1: 17541
Presidential Citation
American Academy of Otolaryngology - Head and Neck Surgery Vol. 1: 753
American Association for Health Education Vol 1: 1020
American College of Cardiology Vol 1: 1841
American Mosquito Control Association Vol 1: 3139
Genetics Society of Canada Vol 1: 9936
International Association of Emergency Managers Vol 1: 11350
National Environmental Health Association Vol 1: 14947
Society of American Registered Architects Vol 1: 19011
U.S. Hang Gliding Association Vol 1: 20615
Presidential Citation Award Vol. 1: 13968
Presidential Citation; Bomm/ Vol. 1: 5578
Presidential Citations Vol. 1: 4795
Presidential Citations and Awards Vol. 1: 15877
Presidential Citations for Exceptional Service Vol. 1: 2003
Presidential Citations for Meritorious Service Vol. 1: 5222
Presidential Citizens Medal Vol. 1: 9363
Presidential Commendation
British Canoe Union Vol. 2: 6968
Executive Office of the President Vol 1: 9366
National Association of Criminal Defense Lawyers Vol 1: 14186
Presidential Commendations Vol. 1: 3632
Presidential Distinguished Service Award Vol. 1: 19231
Presidential Honor Award Vol. 1: 12059
Presidential Leadership Award Vol. 1: 14218
Presidential Medal of Freedom Vol. 1: 9364
Presidential Proclamation Vol. 1: 19196
Presidential Public Safety Communication Award Vol. 1: 9366
Presidential Rank Awards Vol. 1: 20717
Presidential Scholar Award Vol. 1: 629
Presidential Scholars in the Arts Vol. 1: 15117
Presidential Service Awards Vol. 2: 6607
Presidential Sports Award (Gold) Vol. 2: 5613
Presidential Sports Award (Silver) Vol. 2: 5614
Presidential Student/Post-Doctoral Award Vol. 1: 18787
President's 1st and 2nd Awards Vol. 2: 8259
President's Achievement Award Vol. 1: 9460
Presidents Achievement Award Vol. 1: 19889
President's Appreciative Award Vol. 1: 3355
President's Award
Accreditation Association for Ambulatory Health Care Vol. 1: 135
Advertising Women of New York Vol 1: 216
AIA New York State, Inc. Vol 1: 301
American Association of Petroleum Geologists Vol 1: 1336
American Association of Petroleum Geologists Vol 1: 1349
American Handwriting Analysis Foundation Vol 1: 2383
American Humane Association Vol 1: 2577
American Lung Association Vol 1: 3013
American Medical Technologists Vol 1: 3070
American Probation and Parole Association Vol 1: 3605
American Society for Nondestructive Testing Vol 1: 4151
American Society for Pharmacy Law Vol 1: 4178
American Society of Cytopathology Vol 1: 4399
American Society of Naturalists Vol 1: 4562
American Veterinary Medical Association Vol 1: 4818
Asphalt Recycling and Reclaiming Association Vol 1: 5205
Association for Counselors and Educators in Government Vol 1: 5335
Association for Industrial Archaeology Vol 2: 6781
Association of Conservation Engineers Vol 1: 5637
Association of Consulting Engineers New Zealand Vol 2: 4954
Association of Psychologists of Nova Scotia Vol 1: 5828
Association of Schools of Allied Health Professions Vol 1: 5843
Barbados Union of Teachers Vol 2: 823
Canadian Association of Home and Property Inspectors Vol 1: 6915
Canadian Culinary Federation Vol 1: 7067
Canadian Society of Petroleum Geologists Vol 1: 7487
Canadian Veterinary Medical Association Vol 1: 7533
The Chris Awards Vol 1: 7952
Document Management Industries Association Vol 1: 8977
Educational Theatre Association Vol 1: 9185
Flexible Packaging Association Vol 1: 9573
Institute of Environmental Sciences and Technology Vol 1: 10926
Institution for Operations Research and the Management Sciences Vol 1: 11079
Institution of Professional Engineers New Zealand Vol 2: 4991
International Association of Business Communicators Vol 1: 11296
International Association of Industrial Accident Boards and Commissions Vol 1: 11367
International Association of Pet Cemeteries Vol 1: 11376
International Association of Registered Financial Consultants Vol 1: 11396
International Board of Environmental Medicine Vol 1: 11426
International Fluid Power Society Vol 1: 11628
International Lilac Society Vol 1: 11733
International Slurry Surfacing Association Vol 1: 11910
International Society of Explosives Engineers Vol 1: 11993
Kitplanes Magazine Vol 1: 12599
La Crosse Area Development Corporation Vol 1: 12626
Lamaze International Vol 1: 12676
Machine Vision Association of the Society of Manufacturing Engineers Vol 1: 13010
Massachusetts Association of School Business Officials Vol 1: 13147
Medical Library Association Vol 1: 13266
Meeting Professionals International Vol 1: 13284
Midwest Archives Conference Vol 1: 13394
MTM Association for Standards and Research Vol 1: 13658
National Association for the Advancement of Colored People Vol 1: 14049
National Association of Social Workers Vol 1: 14391
National Catholic Band Association Vol 1: 14599
National Council of La Raza Vol 1: 14807
National Defense Transportation Association Vol 1: 14908
National District Attorneys Association Vol 1: 14916
National Federation of Press Women Vol 1: 14974
National Guild of Community Schools of the Arts Vol 1: 15179
National Kidney Foundation Vol 1: 15323
National Marine Educators Association Vol 1: 15361
National Organization for Human Service Education Vol 1: 15436
National Press Photographers Association Vol 1: 15545
National Rehabilitation Association Vol 1: 15594
National School Sailing Association Vol 2: 8195
National Trappers Association Vol 1: 15912
National Water Safety Congress Vol 1: 15937
New Zealand Veterinary Association Vol 2: 5039
North American Association for Environmental Education Vol 1: 16378
North American Association of Food Equipment Manufacturers Vol 1: 16387
North American Society for the Psychology of Sport and Physical Activity Vol 1: 16477
Ottawa Little Theatre Vol 1: 16959
Professional Grounds Management Society Vol 1: 17627
ProLiteracy Worldwide Vol 1: 17672
Puppeteers of America Vol 1: 17759
Radio Club of America Vol 1: 17842
Royal Academy of Dance Vol 2: 8363
Royal Scottish Geographical Society Vol 2: 8685
Small Motor and Motion Association Vol 1: 18564
Society of Cable Telecommunications Engineers Vol 1: 19077
Society of Insurance Research Vol 1: 19139
Society of Medical-Dental Management Consultants Vol 1: 19180

Award Index

Society of Naval Architects and Marine Engineers Vol 1: 19207
South African Veterinary Association Vol 2: 5768
Southeastern Library Association Vol 1: 19478
U.S. Boomerang Association Vol 1: 20438
United States Rugby Football Union Vol 1: 20767
U.S.A. Track and Field Vol 1: 21236
Women's Sports Foundation Vol 1: 21810
World Atlatl Association Vol 1: 21865
WPC Club Vol 1: 21976
Presidents Award Vol. 1: 4487
Presidents' Award
Committee of Presidents of Statistical Societies Vol. 1: 8293
Institute of Management Accountants Vol 1: 10996
President's Award for Distinguished Federal Civilian Service Vol. 1: 20718
President's Award for Educational Excellence Vol. 1: 20489
President's Award for Educational Improvement Vol. 1: 20489
President's Award for Environmental Stewardship Vol. 1: 10069
President's Award for Exceptional and Innovative Leadership in Adult and Continuing Education Vol. 1: 953
President's Award for Merit Vol. 1: 12001
President's Award for Outstanding Service Vol. 1: 4834
President's Award for Services to Chess Vol. 2: 6980
Presidents' Award for the AFRES Vol. 1: 352
President's Award for the Outstanding Conference Paper Vol. 1: 14952
President's Award; LAMA Vol. 1: 12818
President's Award of Excellence, Honor and Merit Vol. 1: 4484
Presidents Award of Merit Vol. 1: 5868
President's Awards
Chesapeake and Ohio Historical Society Vol. 1: 7857
Federation of Nova Scotian Heritage Vol 1: 9519
Horatio Alger Society Vol 1: 10543
School Nutrition Association Vol 1: 18347
President's Book Award Vol. 1: 3936
President's Certificate of Merit Award Vol. 1: 7764
President's Challenge Physical Fitness Awards Program Vol. 1: 17541
President's Chris Award Vol. 1: 7952
President's Citation
American Association of Homes and Services for the Aging Vol 1: 1223
Federation of Genealogical Societies Vol 1: 9499
Society for Imaging Science and Technology Vol 1: 18719
Society for Mining, Metallurgy, and Exploration Vol 1: 18822
Presidents Citation Vol. 1: 10210
President's Citation for Outstanding Section/ Chapter Partnership Vol. 1: 19054
President's Club Vol. 1: 21568
President's Commendation Vol. 2: 9361
President's Commendation for Brave Conduct Vol. 2: 3219
President's Community Volunteer Award Vol. 1: 17445
President's Conservation Achievement Award Vol. 1: 16033
President's Continuing Education Grant Vol. 1: 1604
President's Corporate Council Award; Industry Division ASHS Vol. 1: 4088
President's Cup
Canadian Dermatology Association Vol. 1: 7074
Society of Plastics Engineers Vol 1: 19267
Sports Car Club of America Vol 1: 19700
Presidents Cup Vol. 1: 16491
President's Cup; Society of Ornamental Turners Vol. 2: 9073
Presidents' Distinguished Service Award Vol. 1: 5592
President's "E" Award for Exports Program Vol. 1: 20472
President's "E Star" Award Vol. 1: 20473
President's Eagle Award Vol. 1: 18051
The President's Education Award Program Vol. 1: 20489
President's Environment and Conservation Challenge Awards Vol. 1: 9365
President's Environmental Merit Awards Program Vol. 1: 20575
President's Environmental Youth Awards (PEYA) Vol. 1: 20575
President's Excellence in Presentation Award Vol. 1: 1358
President's Exhibit Award Vol. 1: 19286
President's Exhibitor Trophy Vol. 1: 2560
President's Fishery Conservation Award Vol. 1: 2256
President's Gold Medal
India Office of the Prime Minister Vol. 2: 3387
Royal College of Surgeons of Edinburgh Vol 2: 8480
President's International Gold Medal Vol. 2: 8635
President's International Trophy Vol. 2: 8636
President's Leadership Award Vol. 1: 14754
President's Medal
Bowling Proprietors' Association of America Vol. 1: 6558
Municipal Art Society of New York Vol 1: 13680
National Magazine Awards Foundation Vol 1: 15355
Niagara University Vol 1: 16353
Operational Research Society of the United Kingdom Vol 2: 8232
Royal Academy of Engineering Vol 2: 8367
Society of American Military Engineers Vol 1: 18994
Society of Chemical Industry Vol 2: 9019
President's Medal for Merit Vol. 1: 8138
President's Medallion Vol. 1: 12971
President's Medallist Vol. 2: 8930
President's Modal Awards Vol. 1: 1434
President's National Leadership Vol. 1: 565
President's National Medal of Science Vol. 1: 15679
President's New Researcher Awards Vol. 1: 7353
President's New Researcher's Award Vol. 1: 5269
Presidents Paper Trophy Award Vol. 2: 8017
President's Pin Award Vol. 1: 9487
President's Plaques Vol. 1: 8442
President's Points Award Vol. 1: 4151
President's Prize
Australian Acoustical Society Vol. 2: 137
Canadian Meteorological and Oceanographic Society Vol 1: 7278
Chartered Institution of Building Services Engineers - England Vol 2: 7291
Institution of Engineers Australia/Engineers Australia Vol 2: 418
International Federation of Hydrographic Societies Vol 2: 7941
Ottawa Field-Naturalists' Club Vol 1: 16932
Presidents' Prize Vol. 1: 12868
President's Prizes for Outstanding Achievement in Primary and Secondary Education Vol. 1: 9283
President's Pro Bono Service Award Vol. 1: 19761
President's Public Service Award Vol. 1: 16033
President's Service Awards Vol. 1: 17445
President's Shield Vol. 1: 19626
President's Stewardship Award Vol. 1: 16034
President's Trophy
American Trucking Associations - Safety Management Council Vol. 1: 4772
Confederate Stamp Alliance Vol 1: 8361
International 210 Association Vol 1: 11157
President's Trophy (Football) Vol. 1: 7230
Presidents's Award Vol. 1: 16987
Presidio La Bahia Award Vol. 1: 19414
Press Award; John Aubuchon Freedom of the Vol. 1: 15514
Press; John R. Emens Award for Support of a Free Student Vol. 1: 6205
Press Language Prize Vol. 2: 6653
Press Prize for Broadcasters and Producers Vol. 2: 6501
Pressure Vessel and Piping Award Vol. 1: 4540
Prestigious Award Vol. 1: 14122
Preston Manufacturer of the Year Award; Thomas F. Vol. 1: 14924
Preston Personal Service Award; Harold Kramer - John Vol. 1: 3792
Prestwich Medal Vol. 2: 7565
Prestwich; Prix Vol. 2: 2410
Prevention of Blindness Fellowships; E.A. Baker Foundation for the Vol. 1: 7301
Prevot; Fondation Andre-Romain Vol. 2: 1796
PRI Service Medal Vol. 2: 5400
Price Chapter Award; John M. Vol. 1: 17070
Price for Literature About Sea Biology and Oceanography-Premio do Mar Rei D. Carlos Vol. 2: 5458
Price Journalist and Scholar of the Year Awards Vol. 1: 21104
Price Medal Vol. 2: 8436
Price Oration; Joseph Vol. 1: 2380
Priddle Medal; R.A. Vol. 2: 419
Pride and Progress Vol. 1: 13580
Pride and Recognition Vol. 1: 17808
Pride of the 20th Century Award Vol. 1: 6639
Priestley Award; Joseph Vol. 1: 8912
Priestley Medal Vol. 1: 1782
Priestley Memorial Medal; H. T. Vol. 2: 348
Prijs der Nederlandse Letteren Vol. 2: 4852
Prijs van de Jonge Jury Vol. 2: 4717
Prijs van de Nederlandse Kinderjury Vol. 2: 4718
Prijs voor Meesterschap Vol. 2: 4916
Primary Care Award Vol. 1: 14177
PRIMA's Risk Management Achievement Awards Vol. 1: 17729
Primavera Prize Vol. 2: 6023

Prime Contractor of the Year Vol. 1: 20833
Prime Movers Committee Award Vol. 1: 4541
Primo Scolastico di Raccordo Vol. 2: 3803
Prince Albert I Medal Vol. 2: 4666
Prince Award; Morton Vol. 1: 18658
Prince, M.D. Award; Morton Vol. 1: 10836
Prince Meritorious Service Award; Max T. Vol. 1: 15595
Prince of Asturias Award for Communications and Humanities Vol. 2: 6035
Prince of Asturias Award for International Co-operation Vol. 2: 6035
Prince of Asturias Award for Letters Vol. 2: 6035
Prince of Asturias Award for Social Sciences Vol. 2: 6035
Prince of Asturias Award for Sports Vol. 2: 6035
Prince of Asturias Award for Technical and Scientific Research Vol. 2: 6035
Prince of Asturias Award for the Arts Vol. 2: 6035
Prince of Asturias Prizes Vol. 2: 6035
Prince of Wales Bowl; U.S. Match Racing Championship - Vol. 1: 20781
Prince of Wales Prizes Vol. 1: 17809
Prince Philip Medal
City and Guilds of London Institute Vol. 2: 7311
Royal Academy of Engineering Vol 2: 8368
Prince Philip Prize Vol. 2: 9282
Prince Philip Prize for the Designer of the Year Vol. 2: 7383
Prince Rainier III; Grand Prix de S. A. S. Le Vol. 2: 4658
Princesse Grace; Prix Fondation Vol. 2: 4658
Principal's Leadership Award Vol. 1: 14386
Pringle Award; Thomas Vol. 2: 5549
Print Media Award Vol. 1: 11871
Print Media Personality of the Year Vol. 1: 11424
Print on Demand Applications Award Vol. 1: 11844
Print on Demand Award Vol. 1: 11845
Printer of the Year Vol. 1: 17566
Printing Culture Prize Vol. 2: 4168
Printing Ink Pioneer Award Vol. 1: 14333
Prints, Drawings and Photographs Exhibition Vol. 1: 5071
Prinz Wilhelm Obedience Award (The Willie Award) Vol. 1: 10020
Prisbelonning - Eydes Pris Vol. 2: 5170
Prism Awards Vol. 2: 5609
Prison Writing Awards; PEN Vol. 1: 17148
Prisoner of War Medal Vol. 1: 8835
Pritchard-Higgins Award for Design; R. D. Vol. 1: 17532
Pritchett Memorial Prize; V.S. Vol. 2: 8796
Pritsker Doctoral Dissertation Award Vol. 1: 10964
Pritzker Architecture Prize Vol. 1: 17573
Private Enterprise Exemplar Medal Vol. 1: 9764
Private Plant Breeding Award Vol. 1: 14794
Private Practice Professional Development Award Vol. 1: 15753
Private Sector Financial Excellence Award Vol. 1: 5719
Private Sector Hall of Fame Vol. 2: 4088
Prix Achille Fould-Stirbey Vol. 2: 1699
Prix Achille Leclere Vol. 2: 1700
Prix Adelson Castiau Vol. 2: 1011
Prix Adolphe Crevecoeur Vol. 2: 1091
Prix Adolphe Noel-des-Vergers Vol. 2: 1758
Prix Adolphe Wetrems Vol. 2: 1041
Prix Adrien Constantin de Magny Vol. 2: 1982
Prix Adrien Duvand Vol. 2: 2015
Prix Agathon De Potter Vol. 2: 1042
Prix Alberic Rocheron Vol. 2: 2103
Prix Albert Brachet Vol. 2: 1043
Prix Albert-Emile Francoeur Vol. 1: 6626
Prix Albert-Tessier Vol. 1: 17793
Prix Alfred-Joseph Lawrence Vol. 1: 6626
Prix Alfred Kastler Vol. 2: 2369
Prix Alfred Nee Vol. 2: 2104
Prix Alfred Verdaguer
Academie des Sciences Vol. 2: 1983
Academie Francaise Vol 2: 2105
Prix Alice Louis Barthou Vol. 2: 2106
Prix Allier de Hauteroche Vol. 2: 1759
Prix Alphonse de Neuville et Sanford Saltus Vol. 2: 1701
Prix Alvine-Belisle Vol. 1: 5920
Prix AMADE-UNESCO Vol. 2: 4669
Prix Ambatielos Vol. 2: 1760
Prix Ampere d'Electricite de France Vol. 2: 1984
Prix Anais Segalas Vol. 2: 2107
Prix Andre Barre Vol. 2: 2108
Prix Andre-Guerin Vol. 1: 18604
Prix Andre Jullien du Breuil Vol. 2: 2109
Prix Andre Lequeux Vol. 2: 2016
Prix Andres Bello Vol. 2: 6373
Prix Annuel de Poesie Vol. 2: 2110
Prix Antoine Girard Vol. 2: 2111
Prix Antoine Grandmaison Vol. 2: 4400
Prix Anton Bergmann Vol. 2: 1012
Prix Antony Valabregue Vol. 2: 2112
Prix Archange-Godbout Vol. 1: 9770
Prix Armand Blanc Vol. 2: 2944
Prix Ars Electronica - International Competition for Cyberarts Vol. 2: 703
Prix Athanase-David Vol. 1: 17794
Prix Audiffred Vol. 2: 2017
Prix Auguste Capdeville (De Beziers) Vol. 2: 2113
Prix Auguste Gerard Vol. 2: 2018
Prix Auguste Sacre Vol. 2: 1044
Prix Auguste Teirlinck Vol. 2: 1013
Prix Balleroy Vol. 2: 2114
Prix Balleroy Vol. 2: 2429
Prix Baron Van Ertborn Vol. 2: 1045
Prix Bastien-Lepage Vol. 2: 1702
Prix Bellion Vol. 2: 1977
Prix Bene Merenti de Patria Vol. 1: 18605
Prix Benjamin Valz Vol. 2: 1980
Prix Berriat Saint-Prix Vol. 2: 2019
Prix Bigot de Morogues Vol. 2: 2020
Prix Biguet Vol. 2: 2115
Prix Blaise des Vosges Vol. 2: 2021
Prix Blaise Pascal du GAMNI-SMAI Vol. 2: 1985
Prix Bordin
Academie des Beaux-Arts Vol. 2: 1703
Academie des Inscriptions et Belles-Lettres Vol 2: 1761
Prix Bordin
Academie des Sciences Morales et Politiques Vol. 2: 2022
Academie Francaise Vol 2: 2116
Prix Botta Vol. 2: 2117
Prix Boudenoot Vol. 2: 2118
Prix Breaute Vol. 2: 1704
Prix Brieux Vol. 2: 2119
Prix Brizard Vol. 2: 1705
Prix Broquette-Gonin Vol. 2: 2120
Prix Brunet Vol. 2: 1762
Prix Calixa-Lavallee Vol. 1: 18606
Prix Calmann-Levy Vol. 2: 2121
Prix Canada pour l'excellence Vol. 1: 15568
Prix Capuran Vol. 2: 2122
Prix Cardinal Grente Vol. 2: 2123
Prix Carlier Vol. 2: 2023
Prix Carlos Calvo Vol. 2: 6373
Prix Catenacci Vol. 2: 1706
Prix Cazes-Brasserie Lipp Vol. 2: 2537
Prix CCRH Vol. 1: 7373
Prix Champlain Vol. 1: 8423
Prix Charles Blanc Vol. 2: 2124
Prix Charles Bouchard Vol. 2: 1977
Prix Charles Dupin Vol. 2: 2024
Prix Charles Duvivier Vol. 2: 1014
Prix Charles Lagrange Vol. 2: 1046
Prix Charles Lambert Vol. 2: 2025
Prix Charles Lemaire Vol. 2: 1047
Prix Charles Leveque Vol. 2: 2026
Prix Charles Lyon-Caen Vol. 2: 2027
Prix Charles Mentzer des Rencontres de Chimie Therapeutique Vol. 2: 2570
Prix Chartier Vol. 2: 1707
Prix Chaudesaigues Vol. 2: 1708
Prix Chavasse de la SFA Vol. 2: 2584
Prix Chavasse - GALF Vol. 2: 2584
Prix Chomedey-de-Maisonneuve Vol. 1: 18607
Prix Cinema du Reel Vol. 2: 2261
Prix CINOA Vol. 2: 918
Prix Ciudad de Huesca Vol. 2: 6030
Prix Claire Virenque Vol. 2: 2125
Prix Claude Aubry Vol. 2: 6389
Prix Claude Berthault Vol. 2: 2028
Prix COGEDIM Vol. 2: 2265
Prix Colmont Vol. 2: 1709
Prix Constant Dauguet Vol. 2: 2126
Prix Corail du Livre Vol. 2: 2342
Prix Corbay Vol. 2: 2029
Prix CORESTA Vol. 2: 2285
Prix Crouzet Vol. 2: 2030
Prix d'Aeronautique Vol. 2: 2231
Prix Dagnan-Bouveret Vol. 2: 1710
Prix Danube Festival, Bratislava Vol. 2: 5969
Prix d'Astronautique Vol. 2: 2232
Prix d'Aumale
Academie des Sciences Vol. 2: 1986
Academie des Sciences Morales et Politiques Vol 2: 2031
Prix d'Aumale Vol. 2: 2430
Prix de Biologie Alfred Kastler Vol. 2: 2369
Prix de Boelpaepe Vol. 2: 1048
Prix de Chenier Vol. 2: 1763
Prix de Composition Musicale Vol. 2: 4659
Prix de Gnseil Regional Vol. 2: 2335
Prix de Joest
Academie des Sciences Morales et Politiques Vol. 2: 2032
Academie Francaise Vol 2: 2127
Prix de Journalisme Science et Societe Vol. 1: 7384
Prix de Jouy Vol. 2: 2128
Prix de la Belgica Vol. 2: 1049
Prix de la Belgique Vol. 2: 2633
Prix de la Biographie Vol. 2: 2129
Prix de la Confederation Mondiale des Activites Subaquatiques Vol. 2: 2470
Prix de la Critique Vol. 2: 2130
Prix de la Critique Internationale Vol. 1: 5922
Prix de la Federation Francaise d'Etudes et Sports Sous-Marins Vol. 2: 2470

Prix de la Fonction Publique du Canada pour Services Insignes Vol. 1: 20183
Prix de la Fondation Athena Vol. 2: 1987
Prix de la Fondation du 150e anniversaire de la Societe royale des Sciences de Liege Vol. 2: 1110
Prix de la Fondation George Montefiore Vol. 2: 898
Prix de la Fondation pour la Recherche Medicale Vol. 2: 2365
Prix de la Fondation Xavier - Bernard Vol. 2: 1670
Prix de La Fons-Melicocq Vol. 2: 1764
Prix de La Grange Vol. 2: 1765
Prix de la Marine Nationale Vol. 2: 2470
Prix de la Meilleure Nouvelle Francophone Vol. 2: 2534
Prix de la Memoire Vol. 2: 2352
Prix de la Nouvelle Vol. 2: 2131
Prix de la Presse Vol. 2: 2470
Prix de la Sante et du Bien-Etre Psychologique Vol. 1: 16850
Prix de la Scam Vol. 2: 2261
Prix de la Societe Francaise de Gravure Vol. 2: 1711
Prix de la ville de Toulon Vol. 2: 2470
Prix de l'Academie des Sciences du Tiers Monde Vol. 2: 2637
Prix de l'adjudant Hubert Lefebvre Vol. 2: 1050
Prix de l'Age d'Or Vol. 2: 1093
Prix de l'Association des Musiciens de Geneve Vol. 2: 6310
Prix de Lausanne Vol. 2: 6496
Prix de l'Ecole Centrale Vol. 2: 1988
Prix de l'Essai Vol. 2: 2132
Prix de l'Information Scientifique Vol. 2: 1989
Prix de l'Institut Francais du Petrole Vol. 2: 1990
Prix de Madame Claude Berthault Vol. 2: 1991
Prix de Merite Vol. 1: 7323
Prix de Poesie *SEPIA* Vol. 2: 4902
Prix de Psychologie Vol. 2: 1015
Prix de Rome Fine Art Vol. 2: 4873
Prix de Rome in Architecture Vol. 1: 6806
Prix de Saint-Genois Vol. 2: 1016
Prix de Sciences Humaines Esdras-Minville Vol. 1: 18608
Prix de Soussay Vol. 2: 2133
Prix de Stassart Vol. 2: 1017
Prix de Stassart pour Histoire Nationale Vol. 2: 1018
Prix de West Invitational Exhibition Vol. 1: 14886
Prix de West Purchase Award Vol. 1: 14886
Prix Delahautemaison Vol. 2: 2366
Prix Delalande-Guerineau Vol. 2: 1766
Prix Demolombe Vol. 2: 2033
Prix d'Encouragement a la recherche en Chimie Therapeutique Vol. 2: 2571
Prix Denise-Pelletier Vol. 1: 17795
Prix des Ambassadeurs Vol. 2: 4781
Prix des Bibliotheques Vol. 2: 2261
Prix des Cathedrales Vol. 2: 1712
Prix des Dames Vol. 2: 2562
Prix des Deux-Magots Vol. 2: 2257
Prix des Jeunes Vol. 2: 2233
Prix des Maisons de la Presse Prize Vol. 2: 2530
Prix des Montreal Vol. 1: 13608
Prix des Sciences de la Mer Vol. 2: 1992
Prix des Timbres de Paques Vol. 1: 7374
Prix Desprez Vol. 2: 1713
Prix d'Excellence Aliant Vol. 1: 6035
Prix d'Excellence d'Heritage Vol. 1: 10420
Prix d'Excellence; Fiabci Vol. 2: 2503
Prix d'Histoire de la Vallee aux Loups Vol. 2: 2528
Prix Diane Potier-Boes Vol. 2: 2134
Prix Docteur Binet-Sangle Vol. 2: 2135
Prix Docteur Rene-Joseph Laufer Vol. 2: 2034
Prix Dr. Max-Luthi Vol. 2: 6512
Prix Dodo Vol. 2: 2136
Prix Doublemard Vol. 2: 1714
Prix Drouyn de Lhuys Vol. 2: 2035
Prix du Baron de Courcel Vol. 2: 2137
Prix du Baron de Joest Vol. 2: 1767
Prix du Budget Vol. 2: 2036
Prix du Chanoine Delpeuch Vol. 2: 2037
Prix du Cinema - Prix Jean Leduc Vol. 2: 2138
Prix du Commisariat a l'Energie Atomique Vol. 2: 1993
Prix du Court Metrage Vol. 2: 2261
Prix du Duc de Loubat Vol. 2: 1768
Prix du Gaz de France Vol. 2: 1994
Prix du Jeune Ecrivain avec Pa Fondahon BNP Pari Bas Vol. 2: 2539
Prix du Jeune Ecrivain Francophone Vol. 2: 2540
Prix du Jury Vol. 2: 2259
Prix du Jury de l'Universite Paris Vol. 2: 2516
Prix du Livre de Photographie/Arles Book Award Vol. 2: 2547
Prix du Merite Motocycliste Vol. 2: 6422
Prix du Patrimoine Vol. 2: 2261
Prix du Public
Festival du Film Court de Villeurbanne Vol. 2: 2335
Florilege Vocal de Tours Vol 2: 2345
International Festival of Maritime and Exploration Films Vol 2: 2470
Prix du Public du Meilleur Court-Metrage Europeen Vol. 2: 841
Prix du Quebec
Center for the Study of Canada Vol. 1: 7750
Quebec Ministere de la Culture et des Communications Vol 1:
Quebec Ministere de la Culture et des Communications Vol 1:
Quebec Ministere de la Culture et des Communications Vol 1: 17794
Quebec Ministere de la Culture et des Communications Vol 1: 17795
Quebec Ministere de la Culture et des Communications Vol 1: 17797
Prix du Theatre Vol. 2: 2139
Prix du Troisieme Cycle Vol. 2: 2240
Prix Dubois - Debauque Vol. 2: 1051
Prix Duc Vol. 2: 1715
Prix Duchalais Vol. 2: 1769
Prix Dulac Vol. 2: 2038
Prix Dumas-Millier Vol. 2: 1716
Prix Dumas-Millier Vol. 2: 2140
Prix Dupin Aine Vol. 2: 2039
Prix Durchon-Louvet Vol. 2: 2141
Prix Edmond de Selys Longchamps Vol. 2: 1052
Prix Edmond Freville Vol. 2: 2040
Prix Edouard Mailly Vol. 2: 1053
Prix Elizabeth Mrazik Cleaver pour le meilleur livre d'images canadien Vol. 2: 6390
Prix Emer de Vattel Vol. 2: 6373
Prix Emile Augier Vol. 2: 2142
Prix Emile de Laveleye Vol. 2: 1019
Prix Emile Faguet Vol. 2: 2143
Prix Emile Girardeau Vol. 2: 2041
Prix Emile Hinzelin Vol. 2: 2144
Prix Emile Laurent Vol. 2: 1054
Prix Emile-Nelligan Vol. 1: 20303
Prix Enzymologia Vol. 2: 1830
Prix Ernest Acker Vol. 2: 991
Prix Ernest Discailles Vol. 2: 1020
Prix Ernest Lemonon Vol. 2: 2042
Prix Ernest Thorel Vol. 2: 2043
Prix Ernst Meyer Vol. 2: 6384
Prix Esdras-Minville Vol. 1: 18608
Prix Estrade Delcros Vol. 2: 1978
Prix Estrade-Delcros Vol. 2: 1770
Prix et Fondations Concernant l'Academie de France a Rome Vol. 2: 1717
Prix Eugene Carriere Vol. 2: 2145
Prix Eugene Catalan Vol. 2: 1055
Prix Eugene Colas Vol. 2: 2146
Prix Eugene Goblet d'Alviella Vol. 2: 1021
Prix Eugene Lameere Vol. 2: 1022
Prix Eugene Piccard Vol. 2: 2147
Prix Eugene Salvan Vol. 2: 2044
Prix Europa for Television Programs Vol. 2: 2293
Prix Europeens Emile Bernheim Vol. 2: 1115
Prix Eve Delacroix Vol. 2: 2148
Prix Ex Aequo - International Children's and Youth Radio Drama Festival Vol. 2: 6319
Prix Fabien Vol. 2: 2149
Prix Fanny et Maurice Baumont Vol. 2: 2045
Prix Felix de Beaujour Vol. 2: 2046
Prix Feydau de Brou Vol. 2: 2150
Prix FIT - de la Traduction Vol. 1: 11607
Prix FIT de la Traduction Astrid Lindgren Vol. 1: 11608
Prix Fondation Princesse Grace Vol. 2: 4658
Prix Fonde par l'Etat Vol. 2: 1995
Prix Fontannes Vol. 2: 2407
Prix France Telecom Vol. 2: 1996
Prix Frances E. Russell Vol. 2: 6391
Prix Francis Lieber Vol. 2: 6373
Prix Franco-Britannique de l'Academie des Sciences Vol. 2: 1997
Prix Francois Coppee Vol. 2: 2151
Prix Francois Deruyts Vol. 2: 1056
Prix Francqui Vol. 2: 893
Prix Franz Cumont Vol. 2: 1023
Prix Frederic de Martens Vol. 2: 6373
Prix Frederic Swarts Vol. 2: 1057
Prix Fuji Vol. 2: 2335
Prix Furtado (de Bayonne) Vol. 2: 2152
Prix G. Rolin-Jaequemyns Vol. 2: 6373
Prix Gabriel Monod Vol. 2: 2047
Prix Galeano d'excellence Pedagogique Vol. 1: 6625
Prix Gallet Vol. 2: 2048
Prix Gaudry Vol. 2: 2408
Prix Gazzola Vol. 2: 2466
Prix Gegner Vol. 2: 2049
Prix Gemeaux
Academy of Canadian Cinema and Television Vol. 1: 81
Academy of Canadian Cinema and Television Vol 1: 84
Prix General Muteau Vol. 2: 2050
Prix Georges Dupau Vol. 2: 2153
Prix Georges Goyau Vol. 2: 2154
Prix Georges Mauguin Vol. 2: 2051
Prix Georges Picot Vol. 2: 2052
Prix Georges Vanderlinden Vol. 2: 1058
Prix Gerard-Morisset Vol. 1: 17796
Prix Gilles - Corbeil Vol. 1: 20304

Prix Gobert Vol. 2: 2155
Prix Gosselet Vol. 2: 2409
Prix Grammaticakis-Neuman Vol. 2: 2053
Prix Grotius Vol. 2: 6373
Prix Guizot Vol. 2: 2156
Prix Gustave Camus Vol. 2: 992
Prix Gustave Chaix d'Est Ange Vol. 2: 2054
Prix Gustave Le Metais Lariviere Fils (Prix d'Academie) Vol. 2: 2157
Prix Guy-Fregault Vol. 1: 10818
Prix Halphen Vol. 2: 2158
Prix Haumont Vol. 2: 1718
Prix Helene Porges Vol. 2: 2159
Prix Henri Buttgenbach Vol. 2: 1059
Prix Henri Jousselin Vol. 2: 2160
Prix Henri Lavachery Vol. 2: 1024
Prix Henri Mondor Vol. 2: 2161
Prix Henri Texier Vol. 2: 2055
Prix Henri Texier II Vol. 2: 2056
Prix Henri Wheaton Vol. 2: 6373
Prix Hercule Catenacci Vol. 2: 2162
Prix Heredia Vol. 2: 2163
Prix Herman Schoolmeesters Vol. 2: 1025
Prix Honore Chavee Vol. 2: 1771
Prix Honorius Provost Vol. 1: 17787
Prix Houllevigue
Academie des Beaux-Arts Vol. 2: 1719
Academie des Sciences Vol 2: 1978
Prix Injalbert Vol. 2: 1717
Prix International de la Societe Europeenne de Culture Vol. 2: 3919
Prix Irene Fuerison Vol. 2: 993
Prix Italia Vol. 2: 4040
Prix J. J. Weiss Vol. 2: 2164
Prix Jacques Deruyts Vol. 2: 1060
Prix Jacques Flach Vol. 2: 2057
Prix Jacques Lavalleye-Coppens Vol. 2: 994
Prix Jacques Lefebvre Vol. 2: 7490
Prix Jacques Tacussel Vol. 2: 6460
Prix Japon - Concours International de Programmes Educatifs Vol. 2: 4263
Prix Jean-Baptiste Chevallier Vol. 2: 2058
Prix Jean Bouscatel Vol. 2: 2165
Prix Jean Finot Vol. 2: 2059
Prix Jean Reynaud Vol. 2: 2166
Prix Jeanne Scialtel Vol. 2: 2167
Prix Jeune Chercheur Vol. 2: 2586
Prix Jeunesse International Munchen Vol. 2: 3052
Prix Joachim Cabot et Louis Delezenne/Prix du GLMMS Vol. 2: 2524
Prix John L. Synge Vol. 1: 18173
Prix John Westlake Vol. 2: 6373
Prix Jos Albert Vol. 2: 995
Prix Joseph De Keyn Vol. 2: 1026
Prix Joseph du Teil Vol. 2: 2060
Prix Joseph Dutens Vol. 2: 2061
Prix Joseph-Edmond Marchal Vol. 2: 996
Prix Joseph Gantrelle Vol. 2: 1027
Prix Joseph Hamel Vol. 2: 2062
Prix Joseph Saillet Vol. 2: 2063
Prix Joseph Schepkens Vol. 2: 1061
Prix Jules Andeoud Vol. 2: 2064
Prix Jules Duculot Vol. 2: 1028
Prix Jules Favre Vol. 2: 2168
Prix Jules Janin Vol. 2: 2169
Prix Jules Lefort Vol. 2: 2065
Prix Jules Mahyer Vol. 2: 1978
Prix Jules Raeymaekers Vol. 2: 997
Prix Juteau-Duvigneaux Vol. 2: 2170
Prix Kastner-Boursault Vol. 2: 2171
Prix Koenigswarter Vol. 2: 2066
Prix L. E. Rivot Vol. 2: 1998
Prix Lac Vol. 2: 1830
Prix Lafontaine Vol. 2: 2172
Prix Lalande Vol. 2: 1980
Prix Lamarck Vol. 2: 1062
Prix Lambert Vol. 2: 2173
Prix Lange Vol. 2: 2174
Prix Langlois Vol. 2: 2175
Prix Latsis Vol. 2: 6537
Prix Lazare Carnot Vol. 2: 1999
Prix Le Bel Vol. 2: 2361
Prix Le Dissez de Penanrun Vol. 2: 2067
Prix Le Fevre-Deumier (de Pons) Vol. 2: 2176
Prix Le Guay-Lebrun Vol. 2: 1720
Prix Lefevre-Deumier de Pons Vol. 2: 2068
Prix Leo Errera Vol. 2: 1063
Prix Leon et Henri Fredericq Vol. 2: 1064
Prix Leon Faucher Vol. 2: 2069
Prix Leon Leclere Vol. 2: 1029
Prix Leon-Lortie Vol. 1: 18609
Prix Leonardo Vol. 2: 3936
Prix Leonidas-Belanger Vol. 1: 17788
Prix Lespiau Vol. 2: 1827
Prix Limantour Vol. 2: 2070
Prix Lionel-Groulx-Foundation Yves-Saint-Germain Vol. 1: 10819
Prix Lionel - Groulx - les Cooperants Vol. 1: 10819
Prix Litteraire Henri Deschamps Vol. 2: 3221
Prix Litteraire International Charles-Helou Vol. 2: 2535
Prix Litteraire Prince Pierre-de-Monaco Vol. 2: 4660
Prix Louis Barthou Vol. 2: 2177
Prix Louis Castex Vol. 2: 2178
Prix Louis d'Or Vol. 2: 1110
Prix Louis Fould Vol. 2: 1772
Prix Louis-Jeantet de medecine Vol. 2: 6478
Prix Louis Liard Vol. 2: 2071
Prix Louis P. Miller Vol. 2: 2179
Prix Louis-Phillipe-Hebert Vol. 1: 18610
Prix Louis Renault Vol. 2: 6373
Prix Louise Dehem Vol. 2: 998
Prix Lucien de Reinach Vol. 2: 2072
Prix Lucien Dupont Vol. 2: 2073
Prix Lucien Tisserand Vol. 2: 2180
Prix Ludger-Duvernay Vol. 1: 18611
Prix Maille-Latour-Landry Vol. 2: 2181
Prix Maisondieu Vol. 2: 2074
Prix Malouet Vol. 2: 2075
Prix Mancini Vol. 2: 6373
Prix Marcel Flach Vol. 2: 2076
Prix Marcelin Guerin Vol. 2: 2182
Prix Marcelle Millier Vol. 2: 2183
Prix Marechal Foch Vol. 2: 2184
Prix Marie-Eugene Simon Henri Martin Vol. 2: 2185
Prix Marie Havez-Planque Vol. 2: 2186
Prix Marie Laurent Vol. 2: 2077
Prix Maujean Vol. 2: 2187
Prix Maurice R.D. Vol. 2: 1721
Prix Maurice-Richard Vol. 1: 18612
Prix Maurice Travers Vol. 2: 2078
Prix Maurice Trubert Vol. 2: 2188
Prix Max Barthou Vol. 2: 2189
Prix Maxime-Raymond Vol. 1: 10820
Prix Mesucora Vol. 2: 2000
Prix Meurand Vol. 2: 1722
Prix Michel-Brunet Vol. 1: 10821
Prix Michel Monpetit Vol. 2: 2001
Prix Michener de Journalism Vol. 1: 13329
Prix Monbinne Vol. 2: 1723
Prix Mondial Nessim Habif Vol. 2: 6538
Prix Monseigneur Marcel Vol. 2: 2190
Prix Montyon Vol. 2: 2191
Prix Montyon de Mecanique Vol. 2: 2002
Prix Mottart Vol. 2: 2192
Prix Narcisse Michaut Vol. 2: 2193
Prix Nicolas Missarel Vol. 2: 2194
Prix Nicolo Vol. 2: 1724
Prix Nine Choucroun Vol. 2: 2420
Prix Noel-Mailloux Vol. 1: 16849
Prix Octave Mirbeau et Valentine Allorge Vol. 2: 2003
Prix Odilon Barrot Vol. 2: 2079
Prix Olivar-Asselin Vol. 1: 18613
Prix Osiris Vol. 2: 2431
Prix Pascal Fortuny Vol. 2: 2195
Prix Paul and Marie Stroobant Vol. 2: 1065
Prix Paul Artot Vol. 2: 999
Prix Paul Bonduelle Vol. 2: 1000
Prix Paul-Emile-Borduas Vol. 1: 17797
Prix Paul Flat Vol. 2: 2196
Prix Paul Fourmarier Vol. 2: 1066
Prix Paul Guggenheim Vol. 2: 6494
Prix Paul Hervieu Vol. 2: 2197
Prix Paul Labbe-Vauquelin Vol. 2: 2198
Prix Paul Leroy-Beaulieu Vol. 2: 2080
Prix Paul-Michel Perret Vol. 2: 2081
Prix Paul Streit Vol. 2: 6310
Prix Paul Teissonniere Vol. 2: 2199
Prix Paul Verlaine Vol. 2: 2200
Prix Paul Vigne d'Octon Vol. 2: 2082
Prix Pechiney Vol. 2: 2004
Prix Percy-W.-Foy Vol. 1: 9771
Prix Philips Vol. 2: 2585
Prix Philips - France Vol. 2: 2585
Prix Pierre Benoit Vol. 2: 2201
Prix Pierre Carsoel Vol. 2: 1001
Prix Pierre de Regnier Vol. 2: 2202
Prix Pierre Desnuelle Vol. 2: 2005
Prix Pierre Sue Vol. 2: 2362
Prix Pierre Villey Vol. 2: 2203
Prix Pinet Vol. 2: 1725
Prix Pol and Christiane Swings Vol. 2: 1067
Prix Pol Comiant Vol. 2: 2204
Prix Polydore de Paepe Vol. 2: 1030
Prix pour jeunes diplomes Vol. 2: 2483
Prix pour le Meilleur Film d'Exploration Vol. 2: 2470
Prix pour les Droits de l'Homme Vol. 1: 20360
Prix Prestwich Vol. 2: 2410
Prix Professeur Louis Baes Vol. 2: 1068
Prix Professionel Vol. 1: 16851
Prix Protex Vol. 2: 2544
Prix Pyral Vol. 2: 2335
Prix quadrennial de Bibliographie Vol. 1: 11718
Prix Quadriennal de Composition Musicale Camille Huysmans Vol. 2: 839
Prix Raoul Duseigneur Vol. 2: 1773
Prix Raoul Follereau Vol. 2: 2205
Prix Renaudot Vol. 2: 2542
Prix Rene Bardet Vol. 2: 2206
Prix Rene Cassin Vol. 2: 2083
Prix Rene Janssens Vol. 2: 1002
Prix Rene Petiet Vol. 2: 2207
Prix Richard Lounsbery Vol. 2: 2006
Prix Richtenberger Vol. 2: 1726
Prix Roberge Vol. 2: 2208
Prix Rodolphe-Fournier Vol. 1: 17789
Prix Roland de Jouvenal Vol. 2: 2209
Prix Roman et Tania Ghirshman Vol. 2: 1774
Prix Rosen de Cancerologie Vol. 2: 2367
Prix Rossi Vol. 2: 2084
Prix Rossini Vol. 2: 1727
Prix Rouyer Vol. 2: 1728

Award Index

Prix Ruhlman Vol. 2: 1729
Prix Saint-Cricq-Theis Vol. 2: 2210
Prix Saintour Vol. 2: 1978
Prix Saintour Vol. 2: 2085
Prix Samuel Pufendorf Vol. 2: 6373
Prix Sandmeyer Vol. 2: 6514
Prix Science et Defense Vol. 2: 2358
Prix Scientifique IBM France Vol. 2: 4847
Prix Seraphin-Marion Vol. 1: 18614
Prix Sir John William Dawson Vol. 1: 18163
Prix Sivet Vol. 2: 2211
Prix Sobrier-Arnould Vol. 2: 2212
Prix Special ASIFA Vol. 2: 1382
Prix Stanislas Julien Vol. 2: 1775
Prix Stassart Vol. 2: 2086
Prix Steacie Vol. 1: 19777
Prix Suisse Vol. 2: 6310
Prix Susse Freres Vol. 2: 1730
Prix Suzanne Tassier Vol. 2: 1031
Prix Talents Nouveau Vol. 2: 2590
Prix Tanesse Vol. 2: 2087
Prix Theodore Ott Vol. 2: 6506
Prix Theophile de Donder Vol. 2: 1069
Prix Theophile Gluge Vol. 2: 1070
Prix Therouanne Vol. 2: 2213
Prix Thiers Vol. 2: 2214
Prix Thorlet Vol. 2: 1731
Prix Tobie Jonckheere Vol. 2: 1032
Prix Toirac Vol. 2: 2215
Prix Toutain Vol. 2: 2216
Prix Toutain-Blanchet Vol. 2: 1776
Prix TPS Vol. 2: 2335
Prix Triennal de la Societe Royale de Chimie Vol. 2: 1108
Prix Trillium Vol. 1: 16752
Prix Ugo Papi - Gaston Leduc Vol. 2: 2088
Prix UNESCO d'Architecture Vol. 2: 2607
Prix Universalis Vol. 2: 2297
Prix Valentine Abraham Verlain Vol. 2: 2217
Prix Valentine de Wolmar Vol. 2: 2218
Prix Vega et Lods de Wegmann Vol. 2: 2219
Prix Victor Cousin Vol. 2: 2089
Prix Victor Delbos Vol. 2: 2090
Prix Victor-Morin Vol. 1: 18615
Prix Victor Tourneur Vol. 2: 1033
Prix Viquesnel Vol. 2: 2411
Prix Vitet Vol. 2: 2220
Prix Vitoria Vol. 2: 6373
Prix Volney Vol. 2: 2432
Prix Wegmann Vol. 2: 2412
Prix Wolowski Vol. 2: 2091
Prix Xavier Marmier Vol. 2: 2221
Prix Yvan Loiseau Vol. 2: 2222
Prix Zerilli Marimo Vol. 2: 2092
Prixa UNDA Vol. 2: 6500
Priz UIP Vol. 2: 7407
Prize Bridge Award Vol. 1: 2850
Prize De Schaepdryver-Caenepeel Vol. 2: 976
Prize for a Distinguished Bibliography Vol. 1: 13564
Prize for a Distinguished Scholarly Edition Vol. 1: 13565
Prize for a First Book Vol. 1: 13566
Prize for A-Level Psychology Vol. 2: 7125
Prize for Achievement in Accelerator Physics and Technology Vol. 1: 20731
Prize for Artistic Creation-Premio Carlos Bonvalot Vol. 2: 5459
Prize for Best Work in Cultural Anthropology-Premio Dr. Careira da Costa Vol. 2: 5460
Prize for Children's Film Vol. 2: 2993
Prize for Comics-Premio Rafael Bordalo Pinheiro Vol. 2: 5461
Prize for Composers and Performers of Afrikaans Folk Musik Vol. 2: 5683
Prize for Distinguished Service to the Profession Vol. 1: 18740
Prize for Essay-Premio Dasvid Mourao-Ferreira Vol. 2: 5462
Prize for Fiction-Premio Literario Ferreira de Castro Vol. 2: 5463
Prize for Freedom Vol. 2: 8057
Prize for Helping Disabled People; Institution of Electrical Engineers Vol. 2: 7811
Prize for Independent Scholars Vol. 1: 13567
Prize for Industrial Applications of Physics Vol. 1: 2838
Prize for Innovative Applied Physics of the Division of Industrial and Applied Physics Vol. 1: 6936
Prize for Journalists Vol. 2: 1209
Prize for Literature for Children-Premio Literario Adolfo Simoes Muller Vol. 2: 5464
Prize for Literature for Children-Premio Matilde Rosa Araujo Vol. 2: 5465
Prize for Meritorious Achievement Vol. 1: 20731
Prize for Outstanding Books in Theology and the Natural Sciences Vol. 1: 12411
Prize for Performers of Classical Music Vol. 2: 5684
Prize for Poetry in Irish Vol. 2: 3618
Prize for Poetry-Premio Literario Alfonso Lopes Vieira Vol. 2: 5466
Prize for Published Poetic Work-Premio Literario Ruy Belo Vol. 2: 5467
Prize for Research in Education of the National Institute of the Book Vol. 2: 1182
Prize for Short Stories-Premio Literario Damiano de Odemira Vol. 2: 5468
Prize for Television and Radio Vol. 2: 5655
Prize for Terror Short Stories-Premio Branquinho da Fonseca Vol. 2: 5469
Prize for the Best German Short Film Vol. 2: 2977
Prize for the Promotion and Dissemination of International Humanitarian Law Vol. 2: 3974
Prize for the Teaching of OR/MS Practice Vol. 1: 11080
Prize for Travel Literature Vol. 2: 5470
Prize in Applied Oceanography Vol. 1: 7279
Prize in Economic Sciences in Memory of Alfred Nobel Vol. 2: 6219
Prize in Humanities Vol. 1: 5541
Prize in Theoretical and Mathematical Physics Vol. 1: 6937
Prize Mission Special Japan Vol. 2: 4291
Prize Naples Foreign Press Vol. 2: 3939
Prize Objective Japan Vol. 2: 4292
Prize Objective Japan - Students Vol. 2: 4292
Prize of Architecture Vol. 2: 1492
Prize of EOS Vol. 2: 2753
Prize of Excellence Vol. 2: 5128
Prize of INTERFILM Vol. 2: 2977
Prize of Janko Hrasko Vol. 2: 5969
Prize of the AOSS Vol. 2: 5958
Prize of the Berlin Children's Jury Vol. 2: 2670
Prize of the Capital of Slovak Republic Bratislava Vol. 2: 5962
Prize of the Catholic Film Association Vol. 2: 2977
Prize of the Children's Cinema Vol. 2: 2977
Prize of the Churches Vol. 2: 2670
Prize of the FIPRESCI Vol. 2: 2977
Prize of the German Art Film Theatre Association Vol. 2: 2670
Prize of the Mayor of the Bratislava City Vol. 2: 5969
Prize of the Mayor of the Capital of the Slovak Republic of Bratislava Vol. 2: 5963
Prize of the Photo Book Vol. 2: 2547
Prize of the Societe Internationale de Chirurgie Vol. 2: 6465
Prize of UNICEF Vol. 2: 2670
Prize of USTT and Literary Fund Vol. 2: 5969
Prize Paper Award Vol. 1: 10912
Prize Paper Awards; Technical Committee Vol. 1: 10913
Prize to a Faculty Member for Research in an Undergraduate Institution Vol. 1: 3472
Prize to Outstanding Students of Translation Vol. 2: 3759
"Prized Pieces" International Film and Video Festival Vol. 1: 14526
Prizes for Answering a Literary or Philogical Question Vol. 2: 2777
Prizes for Short Films Vol. 2: 2994
Prizes for the Distribution of Quality Films in Belgium Vol. 2: 1094
Pro-Animal Awards Vol. 2: 1572
Pro Bono Award
 Massachusetts Paralegal Association Vol. 1: 13165
 National Italian American Bar Association Vol 1: 15295
Pro Bono Publico Awards Vol. 1: 1536
Pro Bono Service Awards Vol. 1: 12766
Pro Ecclesia et Pontifice Medal Vol. 2: 9316
Pro Ecclesia et Professione (Pharmaciae) Vol. 1: 14629
Pro Football Hall of Fame Vol. 1: 17578
PRO LABORE SECURO Statuette Vol. 2: 5299
Pro Lingua Award Vol. 1: 9691
Pro Merito Decoration Vol. 2: 5747
Pro Merito Medal Vol. 2: 5748
Pro Modified World Champion Vol. 1: 11680
Pro Patria Medal Vol. 2: 5749
PRO Rally Region of the Year Vol. 1: 19702
Pro Rodeo Hall of Fame Vol. 1: 17653
Pro Scientia Veterinaria Plona Vol. 2: 5381
Pro Stock Puller of the Year Vol. 1: 15887
Pro Universitate Emlekerem Vol. 2: 3318
Pro Urbe Budapest Award Vol. 2: 3239
Pro Virtute Decoration Vol. 2: 5750
Pro Virtute Medal Vol. 2: 5751
Probation and Parole; Joe Kegans Award for Victim Services in Vol. 1: 3603
Process Award Vol. 1: 11739
Process Improvement Award Vol. 1: 14125
Procopiu Prize; Stefan Vol. 2: 5860
Procter & Gamble Award in Applied and Environmental Microbiology Vol. 1: 4138
Procter & Gamble Award in Physical Chemistry Vol. 1: 1783
Procter & Gamble Professional Opportunity Awards Vol. 1: 3526
Procter Prize for Scientific Achievement; William Vol. 1: 18513
Proctor Medal
 Association for Research in Vision and Ophthalmology Vol. 1: 5465
 Association for Research in Vision and Ophthalmology Vol 1: 5467
Proctor Memorial Leadership Award; Charles Henry Vol. 1: 2167
Proctor Prize; George Vol. 1: 7529

Proctor Prize; Thomas R. Vol. 1: 13796
Proctor Research Medal Award; Francis I. Vol. 1: 5467
Procurement Awards Vol. 1: 20833
Producer of the Year; Radio Program Vol. 1: 15615
Producer of the Year; Television Program Vol. 1: 15618
Producers Guild Fellowship Award Vol. 2: 8149
Product and Service Awards Vol. 1: 12154
Product Division Executive Committee Award Vol. 1: 2317
Product of the Year Vol. 2: 9116
Production and Operations Award Vol. 1: 19246
Production Award Vol. 1: 7002
Production Engineering Award Vol. 1: 19246
Production Technology Award Vol. 2: 3334
Professional Achievement Vol. 1: 12580
Professional Achievement Award
- Association of Specialized and Cooperative Library Agencies Vol. 1: 5858
- Institute of Real Estate Management Vol 1: 11040
- Special Libraries Association - Transportation Division Vol 1: 19567

Professional Achievement Awards
- *Professional Builder* - Reed Business Information Vol. 1: 17601
- UCLA Alumni Association Vol 1: 20261

Professional Achievement Citations Vol. 1: 20999
Professional Agent of the Year Vol. 1: 14345
Professional Alarm Technician of the Year Vol. 1: 14560
Professional Assistance Awards Vol. 1: 12562
Professional Associateship Vol. 2: 8686
Professional Award
- American Horticultural Society Vol. 1: 2535
- Association for Communication Excellence in Agriculture, Natural Resources, and Life and Human Sciences Vol 1: 5294
- Ordre des Psychologues du Quebec Vol 1: 16851
- Special Libraries Association Vol 1: 19554

Professional Awards Program Vol. 1: 4484
Professional Commitment Award Vol. 2: 4992
Professional Contribution by an ACE Member Vol. 1: 5654
Professional Development Vol. 1: 21797
Professional Development Award
- IES, Institute for the International Education of Students Vol. 1: 10667
- System Safety Society Vol 1: 19890

Professional Development Awards
- National Society of Professional Engineers Vol. 1: 15754
- School Nutrition Association Vol 1: 18348

Professional Development Coordinator of the Year Vol. 1: 14540
Professional Development Program Awards Vol. 1: 18551
Professional Education Project Award Vol. 1: 790
Professional Engineer of the Year
- Institution of Engineers Australia/Engineers Australia Vol. 2: 420
- Institution of Engineers Australia/Engineers Australia Vol 2: 440

Professional Engineers Citizenship Award Vol. 1: 17607
Professional Engineers Gold Medal Vol. 1: 17608
Professional Excellence in Religious Communication Award Vol. 1: 13125
Professional Flute Choir Competition Vol. 1: 15063
Professional Instructor of the Year Award Vol. 1: 51
Professional Member of the Year Vol. 1: 14541
Professional of the Year
- Association of Jewish Center Professionals Vol. 1: 5738
- Ladies Professional Golf Association Vol 1: 12658
- Organization of Professional Employees of the United States Department of Agriculture Vol 1: 16902
- United States Professional Tennis Association Vol 1: 20744

Professional of the Year Award
- Association of Jewish Center Professionals Vol. 1: 5738
- Professional Golfers' Associations of Europe Vol 2: 8306

Professional Organization Awards Vol. 1: 9073
Professional Photographer Award Vol. 1: 17297
Professional Preparation Award Vol. 1: 151
Professional Progress Award for Outstanding Progress in Chemical Engineering Vol. 1: 2786
Professional Recognition Award Vol. 1: 5918
Professional Recruitment Award Vol. 1: 18007
Professional Research Award Vol. 1: 15878
Professional Risk Management Services Inc Vol. 1: 3619
Professional Safety Paper Awards Vol. 1: 4606
Professional Service Award Vol. 1: 14158
Professional Service to Health Education Award Vol. 1: 1021
Professional Service to Safety Education Vol. 1: 18337
Professional Support Award Vol. 1: 15192
Professional Teacher of the Year Award Vol. 1: 46
Professionalism Award
- National Association of the Remodeling Industry Vol. 1: 14439
- Teen Court of Huerfano County Vol 1: 19962

Professor Ira James Cunningham Prize in Animal Nutrition Vol. 2: 5040
Professor Shambu Nath De Memorial Lecture Vol. 2: 3503
Professors' Prize Vol. 2: 6770
Prognosticator of the Year Vol. 1: 20131
Program Award Vol. 1: 13945
Program Director of the Year Award Vol. 1: 1298
Program Director of the Year; IDEA Vol. 1: 10645
Program Directors' Award Vol. 1: 8431
Program Excellence Award Vol. 1: 12070
Program Excellence Award for Innovations in Local Government Management Vol. 1: 11477
Program Excellence Awards Vol. 1: 11477
Program Standards Award Vol. 1: 13969
Program to Recognize Excellence in Student Literary Magazines Vol. 1: 14837
Programme Awards Vol. 2: 8855
Programming; Phillip E. Frandson Award for Innovative Vol. 1: 20953
Programming Systems and Languages Paper Award Vol. 1: 5307
Progress Award
- Amateur Athletic Union Vol. 1: 566
- Photographic Society of America Vol 1: 17292

Progress Award of Japanese Society of Soil Science and Plant Nutrition Vol. 2: 4227
Progress Medal Vol. 2: 8667
Progress Medal Award Vol. 1: 19197
Project Community Award Vol. 1: 19991
Project Funding Program Vol. 1: 5161
Project of the Year Award Vol. 1: 17668
PROMAX Awards Vol. 1: 17679
Promega Early Career Life Scientist Award; ASCB/ Vol. 1: 3941
Prometheus Award Vol. 1: 12806
Promise to the Earth Award Vol. 1: 13949
Promising Personality Vol. 1: 20062
Promising Playwright Award Vol. 1: 8205
Promising Researcher Award Vol. 1: 14838
Promising Young Writers Program Vol. 1: 14839
Promoter of the Year Vol. 1: 20426
Promotion and Marketing Award; International Egg Commission Vol. 2: 7920
Promotion of Children's Literature Vol. 2: 5195
Promotion Retailer of the Year Award Vol. 1: 5833
Promotional Achievement Awards Vol. 1: 6108
Promotional Prizes Vol. 2: 3013
Property Council Rider Hunt Award Vol. 2: 497
Property Person of the Year; Jack Griffiths Vol. 1: 15560
Prosceniumprijs Vol. 2: 4928
Proskauer Prize; Edith H. and Richmond Vol. 1: 15698
Prospector of the Year Award; Bill Dennis Vol. 1: 17689
Prost; Prix Gabriel-Auguste Vol. 2: 1777
Protege Awards Vol. 1: 20111
Protein Awards Vol. 1: 3117
Prouty and Elsie S. Prouty Memorial Award; Morton D. Vol. 1: 15027
Provasoli Award; Luigi Vol. 1: 17303
Province of Nova Scotia Scholarship Vol. 1: 6035
Provincial Police Award Vol. 2: 6806
Proximity Achievement Award Vol. 1: 20628
Pruszynski Prize; Ksawery Vol. 2: 5330
Pruvost; Prix Fondation Pierre Vol. 2: 2413
Pruzansky Memorial Fund for Maternal and Child Health Nursing; Donna Vol. 1: 8095
Pryne Memorial Award, Competition Division; Annie Vol. 1: 6222
Pryor Award; Susy Vol. 1: 5083
Pryor Memorial Award; Bill Vol. 1: 21439
Prys vir Televisie en Radio Vol. 2: 5655
PSA Contemporary Medal Vol. 1: 10149
PSA International Exhibition
- Photographic Society of America Vol. 1: 17284
- Photographic Society of America Vol 1: 17287
- Photographic Society of America Vol 1: 17288
- Photographic Society of America Vol 1: 17289

Photographic Society of America Vol 1: 17293
Photographic Society of America Vol 1: 17294
PSA Medal Vol. 1: 10149
PSA Yankee Medal Vol. 1: 10149
PSCA Graduate Student Scholarship Vol. 1: 17190
PSFA Scholarship Program Vol. 1: 17492
Psi Chi/APA Edwin B. Newman Graduate Research Award Vol. 1: 17696
Psi Chi/Florence L. Denmark National Faculty Advisor Award Vol. 1: 17697
Psi Chi/Ruth Hubbard Cousins National Chapter Award Vol. 1: 17698
PSI Gold Medals Vol. 2: 3717
PSI Medals Vol. 2: 3718
PSJ Award Vol. 2: 4274
PSJ Award for Distinguished Service Vol. 2: 4275
PSJ Award for Drug Research and Development Vol. 2: 4276
PSJ Award for Educational Services Vol. 2: 4277
PSJ Award for Young Scientists Vol. 2: 4278
PSO Book Award Vol. 1: 17453
PSPA Student Scholarship Vol. 1: 17200
Psychoanalysis Doctoral Award Vol. 1: 3695
Psychoanalysis Post-Doctoral Award Vol. 1: 3696
Psychological Dimensions of Peacework Award Vol. 1: 17702
Psychology Association Award Vol. 1: 5194
Psychotherapy Prize Vol. 2: 8469
PTC Essay Prize Vol. 1: 17022
PTV Annual Award Vol. 2: 5207
Public Access to Government Information Award; AALL Vol. 1: 1245
Public Affairs Competition Vol. 1: 1276
Public Affairs Network Awards Vol. 1: 3633
Public and Community Service Emmy Awards Vol. 1: 13864
Public Communications Award Vol. 1: 19341
Public Education Award Vol. 1: 21497
Public Education Award for Excellence in Plastic Surgery Journalism Vol. 1: 17384
Public Education Prize Vol. 2: 1326
Public Health Award Vol. 2: 8610
Public Health Travelling Fellowships Vol. 2: 470
Public History Award Vol. 1: 16626
Public Information Program Award Vol. 1: 11282
Public Language; George Orwell Award for Distinguished Contribution to Honesty and Clarity in Vol. 1: 14836
Public Person Vol. 1: 8529
Public Plant Breeding Award Vol. 1: 14795
Public Policy Award Vol. 1: 4207
Public Policy; Donald E. Santarelli Award for Vol. 1: 15447
Public Programming Awards Vol. 1: 17929
Public Promotion of Engineering Medal Vol. 2: 8369
Public Recreation Department of the Year Vol. 1: 567
Public Recreation Man and Woman of the Year Vol. 1: 568
Public Recreation Volunteer of the Year Award Vol. 1: 569
Public Relations Achievement Vol. 1: 15865
Public Relations Award
Amateur Athletic Union Vol. 1: 570
Association of Surgical Technologists Vol 1: 5876
National Association of Independent Fee Appraisers Vol 1: 14272
United Methodist Association of Health and Welfare Ministries Vol 1: 20352
Public Relations Awards Vol. 1: 17089
Public Relations Competition Vol. 1: 10997
Public Relations Coordinator of the Year Vol. 1: 14542
Public Relations/Development/Marketing/ Director of the Year Award Vol. 1: 20352
Public Relations Flim/Video Competition Vol. 1: 17720
Public Relations' Hall of Fame Vol. 1: 131
Public Relations Member Achievement Award Vol. 1: 19555
Public Relations Recognition Award Vol. 1: 1299
Public Relations Regional Achievement Award Vol. 1: 19701
Public Risk Manager of the Year Award Vol. 1: 17730
Public Rose Garden Achievement Award Vol. 1: 440
Public Safety Program Excellence Award Vol. 1: 11477
Public Safety Recognition Vol. 1: 6287
Public Service Achievement Awards Vol. 1: 8300
Public Service Award
The Adirondack Council Vol. 1: 186
Alliance for Transportation Research Institute - University of New Mexico Vol 1: 464
American Crystallographic Association Vol 1: 2093
American Institute of Professional Geologists Vol 1: 2843
American Public Power Association Vol 1: 3793
American Society for Cell Biology Vol 1: 3946
American Veterinary Medical Association Vol 1: 4819
Animal Transportation Association Vol 1: 4964
Animal Transportation Association - European Office Vol 2: 6734
Associated Press Managing Editors - Managing Editors Association Vol 1: 5252
Association of Consulting Engineers of Canada Vol 1: 5642
National Conference of Women's Bar Associations Vol 1: 14723
National Kidney Foundation Vol 1: 15324
National Legislative Council for the Handicapped Vol 1: 15342
National Rehabilitation Association Vol 1: 15596
National Science Foundation Vol 1: 15680
Oncology Nursing Society Vol 1: 16729
Sigma Theta Tau International Vol 1: 18503
Society of Petroleum Engineers Vol 1: 19247
UCLA Alumni Association Vol 1: 20262
Public Service Award; Leadership in Vol. 1: 15637
Public Service Awards
American Association of Petroleum Geologists Vol. 1: 1350
Fund for the City of New York Vol 1: 9834
Public Service Citations Vol. 1: 21000
Public Service Excellence Awards Vol. 1: 17710
Public Service Group Achievement Award Vol. 1: 13898
Public Service Medal
Australian Honours Secretariat Vol. 2: 203
National Aeronautics and Space Administration Vol 1: 13899
Public Service National Leadership Award Vol. 1: 2456
Public Utility Vol. 2: 5488
Public Welfare Medal Vol. 1: 13845
Publication Award Vol. 1: 14768
Publication Awards Vol. 1: 17981
Publication Design Awards Vol. 1: 19281
The Publication Medal Vol. 2: 548
Publications and Electronic Media Awards Vol. 1: 15669
Publications Award
AACE International Vol. 1: 40
Association for Industrial Archaeology Vol 2: 6782
Flight Safety Foundation Vol 1: 9579
Publications Awards Vol. 1: 10348
Publications Board's Newsletter Competition Vol. 1: 9438
Publisher of the Year Vol. 1: 5697
Publisher of the Year Award Vol. 1: 6992
Publishers Award Vol. 1: 9785
Publisher's Prizes Vol. 2: 4834
Publishing Division Honor Roll Vol. 1: 19559
Publishing Division Roll of Honor Award Vol. 1: 19559
Publishing Hall of Fame Vol. 1: 18525
Puckett Creativity Award; Harriet Dewaele Vol. 1: 9876
Puckey Prize; Sir Walter Vol. 2: 7818
Pufendorf; Prix Samuel Vol. 2: 6373
Puffer Award; Delta Air Lines Vol. 1: 13904
Puhlev Prize; Academician Aleksi Vol. 2: 1207
PUK-Councilers Prize Vol. 2: 5657
Pulitzer Fellowships Vol. 1: 17748
Pulitzer Prizes Vol. 1: 17749
Pull of the Year Vol. 1: 15888
Pullara Award Vol. 1: 2735
Puller of the Year Vol. 1: 15893
Pulliam Fellowship for Editorial Writing; Eugene C. Vol. 1: 19275
Pulliam National Journalism Writing Award; Eugene S Vol. 1: 6212
Pulling Family of the Year Vol. 1: 15889
Pulling Hall of Fame Vol. 1: 15890
Pulp Biology Research Award Vol. 1: 11209
Pulp Press International Three-Day Novel Competition Vol. 1: 4990
Pundik Fund; Mendel Vol. 2: 3775
Punster of the Year Vol. 1: 11892
Pupin Medal Vol. 1: 8230
Puppeteers of America Award Vol. 1: 17760
Purchasing Manager of the Year Award Vol. 1: 15269
Purdy Award Vol. 1: 11379
Purdy Award; Ken W. Vol. 1: 11752
Purdy Award; Ross Coffin Vol. 1: 1695
Purina Mills, Inc. Teaching Award Vol. 1: 2106
Purina Mills Teaching Award Vol. 1: 17506
Purkey, Jr. Memorial Outstanding Pitcher Award; Robert Vol. 1: 15316
Purse Doctoral Fellowship; Ross C. Vol. 1: 7305
Pursuit of Excellence Award Vol. 1: 15134
Pursuit Trophy Vol. 2: 7992

Purvis Memorial Award Vol. 2: 9020
Puschkin Prize; Alexander Vol. 2: 3088
Pushcart Prize: Best of the Small Presses Vol. 1: 17770
Pushkin Prize; Alexander Sergeovich Vol. 2: 5906
Puskas Tivadar Award Vol. 2: 3308
Pustovoit Award Vol. 2: 2507
- Putnam & Grosset Group Award Vol. 1: 5442
Putnam Publishing Group Award Vol. 1: 5442
Putnam Service Award; Allan Ray Vol. 1: 5189
PVA Donor Recognition Award Vol. 1: 17068
Pyramid Award Vol. 1: 4835
Pyramid Awards Vol. 1: 21471
Pyrotechnics Guild International Competition Vol. 1: 17776
Q107 Homegrown Contest Vol. 1: 7997
QBS Award Vol. 1: 15755
QPB New Visions Award Vol. 1: 17781
QSF Awards Vol. 1: 17799
QSPELL Awards Vol. 1: 17801
QSPELL Book Awards Vol. 1: 17799
QSPELL Community Award Vol. 1: 17800
Quadrennial Prize for Bibliography Vol. 1: 11718
Qualey Article Award; Carlton C. Vol. 1: 10706
Quality Award
American Society for Competitiveness Vol. 1: 3983
California Canning Peach Association Vol 1: 6737
Indian Institute of Metals Vol 2: 3460
Israel Association of Electronics and Information Industries Vol 2: 3740
Quality Digest Award Vol. 1: 17778
Quality Graduate Education Vol. 2: 6041
Quality in Construction Award Vol. 1: 14000
Quality Management Award Vol. 1: 10349
Quality of Life; Israel's Parliament Speaker's Award on Vol. 2: 3725
Quantum Electronics Award Vol. 1: 10662
Quantum Electronics Prize Vol. 2: 2326
Quarter-Century Honor Roll Vol. 1: 14224
Quarter Century Life Member Vol. 2: 1137
Quarter Midgets of America Hall of Fame Vol. 1: 11760
Quarterly Awards Vol. 1: 13004
Queen Award; Ellery Vol. 1: 13732
Queen Contest Vol. 1: 15221
Queen Elisabeth International Music Competition of Belgium Prizes Vol. 2: 950
Queen Elizabeth II Coronation Award Vol. 2: 8364
Queen Elizabeth Silver Jubilee Endowment Fund for Study in a Second Official Language Award Program Vol. 1: 5907
The Queen Elizabeth The Queen Mother Bursary RHS Vegetable Cup Vol. 2: 8561
Queen Fabiola; International Carillon Competition - Vol. 2: 1088
Queen Fabiola Prize Vol. 2: 927
Queen Sofia Award for Research into Mental Retardation Vol. 2: 6033
The Queen Sonja International Music Competition Vol. 2: 5180
Queen's Award Vol. 2: 7571
Queen's Award for Enterprise: Innovation Vol. 2: 8312
Queen's Award for Environmental Achievement Vol. 2: 8313
Queen's Award for Export Achievement Vol. 2: 8315
Queen's Award for Forestry Vol. 2: 7327
Queen's Award for Technological Achievement Vol. 2: 8314
Queen's Awards for Enterprise Vol. 2: 8313
Queen's Awards for Enterprise in Innovation Vol. 2: 8314
Queen's Awards for Enterprise in International Trade Vol. 2: 8315
Queen's Awards for Enterprise: International Trade Vol. 2: 8316
Queen's Awards for Enterprise: Sustainable Development Vol. 2: 8317
Queen's Commendation for Excellence Vol. 2: 8374
Queen's Fire Service Medal Vol. 2: 7262
Queen's Gallantry Medal Vol. 2: 7263
Queen's Medal for Champion Shot Vol. 1: 6829
Queen's Medals Vol. 2: 8703
Queen's Police Medal for Distinguished Service Vol. 2: 7264
Queen's Prize Vol. 2: 8192
Queen's Silver Jubilee Competition Vol. 2: 566
Queensland Division Chemical Branch Award Vol. 2: 421
Queeny Safety Professional of the Year Award; Edgar Monsanto Vol. 1: 4607
Queneau Palladium Medal; Joan Hodges Vol. 1: 1199
Quesada Award; General E. R. Vol. 1: 389
Quesada Memorial Award; General E. R. Vol. 1: 389
Quigley Award; R.M. Vol. 1: 7129
Quill and Scroll Award; National Newspaper Association - Vol. 1: 16341
Quill Medal; Jeffrey Vol. 2: 6679
Quilt National Awards Vol. 1: 8709
Quilts Japan Prize Vol. 1: 8709
Quimby Regional Competitions for Young Organists Vol. 1: 2373
Quinn Award; Jim Vol. 1: 14511
Quinn, Class of '50 Distinguished Service Award; George J. Vol. 1: 7668
Quinn Endowment; Frederic Ives Medal/Jarus W. Vol. 1: 16786
Quran Recitation Vol. 1: 12228
QWF Awards Vol. 1: 17801
QWF Translation Prize Vol. 1: 17799
R & D 100 Awards Vol. 1: 17817
R D'Oro Vol. 2: 3841
The R. Tait McKenzie Award of Honour Vol. 1: 6884
R38 Memorial Prize Vol. 2: 8398
Rabb Award; Sidney R. Vol. 1: 9663
Rabbinical Service Award of Appreciation Vol. 1: 12381
Rabi Prize in Atomic, Molecular and Optical Physics; I. I. Vol. 1: 3473
Rabone Award Vol. 2: 4993
RAC Awards
Retail Advertising and Marketing Association Vol. 1: 18017
Retail Advertising and Marketing Association Vol 1: 18018
Race Organizer of the Year Vol. 1: 20426
Race Relations Gold Medal Vol. 1: 10588
Race Relations Trophy Vol. 1: 10589
Racehorse of the Year Award Vol. 2: 8322
Rachel Carson Prize Vol. 1: 4068
Rachelle White Memorial Award; Donette Vol. 1: 6608
Rackoff Humanitarian Award; Bella Vol. 1: 21758
Racovita Prize; Emil Vol. 2: 5861
RAD Magazine Award Vol. 2: 8476
RAD Magazine Best Poster Prize Vol. 2: 7048
Radcliffe Awards; Mrs. Ann Vol. 1: 8615
Radcliffe Travelling Fellowship in Reliability and Quality Assurance; Frank Vol. 2: 8399
Raddall Atlantic Fiction Award; Thomas Vol. 1: 21981
Radde - Educator of the Year Award; Leon R. Vol. 1: 10974
Radin Distinguished Service Award; Alex Vol. 1: 3794
Radio and Television Language Prize Vol. 2: 6654
Radio Bantu Prize for Works Written for the Radio Vol. 2: 5685
Radio Broadcasting Hall of Fame Vol. 1: 14108
Radio Exterior de Espana Prize Vol. 2: 6080
Radio Mercury Awards Vol. 1: 17827
Radio Mercury Gold Award Vol. 1: 17827
Radio Mercury Public Service Award Vol. 1: 17827
Radio Program Producer of the Year Vol. 1: 15615
Radio Station of the Year Vol. 1: 15616
Radio Technical Commission for Aeronatics Vol. 1: 18179
Radiology News Awards Competition Vol. 1: 1943
Radish Award (Marine Enlisted Aircrew of the Year); Danny Vol. 1: 13086
Radix Pin; Harry E. Vol. 1: 20589
Radix Trophy Vol. 1: 20589
Radix Trophy; Henry E. Vol. 1: 17623
Radomir Shaper Prize Vol. 2: 6387
Radulescu Award; Andrei Vol. 2: 5862
Raeymaekers; Prix Jules Vol. 2: 997
RAF Apprentice Engineering Technician Prize Vol. 2: 7826
Rafaelsen Fellowship Award Vol. 1: 8201
Raffles Award; Stamford Vol. 2: 9283
Rafto Memorial Prize; Professor Thorolf Vol. 2: 5182
Ragazzini Award; John R. Vol. 1: 2787
Raginsky Award; Bernard B. Vol. 1: 18659
Rahman Prize for Computational Physics; Aneesur Vol. 1: 3474
Rahn Education Award; Ivan B. Vol. 1: 18823
RAI Prize Vol. 2: 4059
RAIA Gold Medal Vol. 2: 526
Raikes Medal Vol. 2: 5694
Railroad Calendar Color Slide Contest Vol. 1: 13737
Railsplitter of the Year Vol. 1: 17
Railway Engineering Award Vol. 2: 422
Rain Bird Engineering Concept of the Year Award Vol. 1: 4235
Raine Award; Noel Vol. 2: 8959
Rainsford Memorial Scholarship; Joanne T. Vol. 1: 9157
Raise Your Sites Award Vol. 1: 10392
Rajchman Prize; Jan Vol. 1: 18770
Rajiv Gandhi Award for Ecology and Sanitation Vol. 2: 3588
Raju Oration Award; Dr. P. N. Vol. 2: 3426
Raleigh Award for Fiction; Sir Walter Vol. 1: 16520
Rally Awards Vol. 1: 19702
Ralph W. Westcott Award Vol. 1: 20874

Ralston Purina Company Teaching Award in Dairy Science Vol. 1: 2106
The Ram Award Vol. 1: 5754
Ramachandran 60th Birthday Commemoration Medal; Prof. G. N. Vol. 2: 3504
Ramaermedaille Vol. 2: 4864
Ramage Grant for Graduate Study in Composition; Lillian Harlan Vol. 1: 13662
Ramah Leadership Award Vol. 1: 15573
Raman Birth Centenary Award; C. V. Vol. 2: 3539
Raman Medal; Chandrasekhara Venkata Vol. 2: 3505
Ramanathan Medal; K. R. Vol. 2: 3506
Ramanujan Birth Centenary Award; Srinivasa Vol. 2: 3540
Ramdohr Prize; Paul Vol. 2: 2719
Ramirez Medal; Rafael Vol. 2: 4580
Ramirez; Medalla Agustin Vol. 2: 4503
Ramirez; Premio Felipe Tena Vol. 2: 4611
Ramo Medal; Simon Vol. 1: 10878
Ramos Awards; Elise Vol. 1: 5270
Ramp Safety Award Vol. 1: 9576
Rampal International Flute Competition; Jean-Pierre Vol. 2: 2282
Ramsay Medal; Erskine Vol. 1: 2824
Ramsay Memorial Fellowships for Postdoctoral Chemical Research Vol. 2: 8324
Ramsdell Award; Charles Vol. 1: 19501
Ramsdell Award; Fletcher M. Green and Charles W. Vol. 1: 19501
Ramsden Awards; John Vol. 2: 8962
Rand Memorial Gold Medal; Charles F. Vol. 1: 2825
Rand Trophy; Remington Vol. 1: 10998
Randall Award; Ollie A. Vol. 1: 14870
Randolph Achievement Award; A. Philip Vol. 1: 27
Randolph/Bayard Rustin Freedom Award; A. Philip Vol. 1: 28
Randolph Freedom Award; A. Philip Vol. 1: 28
Randolph Program for International Peace; Jennings Vol. 1: 20657
Raney Fund Award Vol. 1: 4453
Ranki Prize in Economic History Vol. 1: 9148
Ranking Winner Vol. 2: 1130
Ransom Memorial Medals; James Vol. 2: 7853
Rao Award; Dr. T. Ramachandra Vol. 2: 3427
Rao Award; Tilak Venkoba Vol. 2: 3428
Rao Forestry Research Award; Dr. Y.S. Vol. 2: 4417
Rao Memorial Lecture; Prof. K. Rangadhama Vol. 2: 3507
Rao Oration Award in Microbiology; Dr. Y. S. Narayana Vol. 2: 3429
Raper Oral and Maxillofacial Radiology Award; Howard R. Vol. 1: 729
Raphel Memorial Award; Arnold L. Vol. 1: 20548
Rare Books and Manuscripts Librarianship Award Vol. 1: 5617
Raster Award Vol. 1: 10325
Ratcliff Trophy; Tom Vol. 2: 7532
Rating; Standard and Poor's 'BBB Vol. 2: 5103
Ratner Award; Bret Vol. 1: 791
Rattlesnake Award; Jimmy
  Baseball Canada Vol. 1: 6263
  Canadian Federation of Amateur Baseball Vol 1: 7087
Raulin; Fondation Victor Vol. 2: 1975
Rauriser Literaturpreis Vol. 2: 668
Raven Award
  Mystery Writers of America Vol. 1: 13732
  Ravenswood Community Council Vol 1: 17880
Raven Award; Peter Vol. 1: 4596
Raven Lecturer Vol. 2: 1502
Rawley Prize; James A. Vol. 1: 16895
Rawlings Award for Energy Conservation (Manager and Technician); General Edwin W. Vol. 1: 353
Rawlings Award for Environmental Achievement (Manager and Technician); General Edwin W. Vol. 1: 353
Rawlings Big Stick Award Vol. 1: 15316
Rawlings Big Stick Award Vol. 1: 17882
Rawlings Bronze Glove Award Vol. 1: 17883
Rawlings Gold Glove Award Vol. 1: 17884
Rawlings Silver Glove Award Vol. 1: 17885
Rawlings Sporting Goods Company ISC All-World Awards Vol. 1: 12041
Rawlinson Award; Peter Vol. 2: 66
Rawls-Palmer Progress in Medicine Lecture and Award Vol. 1: 3976
Rawnsley Traveling Fellowship; Kenneth Vol. 2: 8470
Ray Award in Memory of Margaret Sutermeister; Isaac Vol. 1: 3634
Ray Moore Award Vol. 1: 16514
Ray of Light Vol. 1: 12574
Rayleigh Book Award Vol. 2: 7827
Rayleigh Medal Vol. 2: 7640
Raymond Award; W. Vol. 1: 2826
Raymond Literary Award; Wayte and Olga Vol. 1: 3252
RBMS Exhibition Catalogue Awards Vol. 1: 5614
RBS Talking Book Award Vol. 2: 528
Rea Award for the Short Story Vol. 1: 9052
Rea Non-Fiction Prize Vol. 1: 6521
REACH Award Vol. 1: 5813
Reach for the Stars Award Vol. 1: 15901
REACH Racial Justice Corporate Award Vol. 1: 22090
Reaching Out Award - Diving Hall of Fame Vol. 1: 8967
Read Award; Sir Herbert Vol. 1: 11931
Reader Prize; Ralph Vol. 2: 297
Readers' and Critics' Poll Vol. 1: 18110
Readers' Choice Awards Vol. 1: 17515
Readers Digest Student Award Vol. 2: 6975
Readers Prizes of the *Berliner Morgenpost* Vol. 2: 2670
Reading and Technology; IRA Presidential Award for Vol. 1: 11863
Reading/Literacy Award Vol. 1: 15565
Reading/Literacy Research Fellowship Vol. 1: 11872
Reagan Award; John H. Vol. 1: 8357
Real Estate Educator of the Year Vol. 1: 17897
Real Estate Journalism Competition Vol. 1: 14352
Real Estate Regulator of the Year Vol. 1: 17898
Reale Memorial Award; Nicholas Vol. 1: 4865
Realia Honors Vol. 1: 10849
An Realt Mileata Vol. 2: 3654
Realtor of the Year Vol. 1: 14355
Realtor of the Year (ROTY) Vol. 1: 10529
Reardon Award; Paul C. Vol. 1: 14642
Reason Memorial Cup; George Vol. 1: 6923
Rebbot Award; Olivier Vol. 1: 16981
Recent Graduate Award Vol. 1: 12581
Reckord Trophy; Major Gen. Milton A. Vol. 1: 15176
Reclamation Researcher of the Year Vol. 1: 4557
Reclamationist of the Year Vol. 1: 4558
Recognition Award
  American Association of School Personnel Administrators Vol. 1: 1421
  Asian Confederation of Credit Unions Vol 2: 6609
  Association for the Education of Teachers in Science Vol 1: 5502
  International Association of Campus Law Enforcement Administrators Vol 1: 11299
  Lupus Foundation of America Vol 1: 12981
  National Association of Diaconate Directors Vol 1: 14191
  National Intercollegiate Soccer Officials Association Vol 1: 15279
Recognition Award for Young Scholars Vol. 1: 1473
Recognition Awards Vol. 1: 1383
Recognition for Legal Achievement Vol. 1: 8414
Recognition of achievement Vol. 1: 9976
Recognition of Achievement Award Vol. 1: 5203
Recognition of Goodness Award Vol. 1: 12355
Recognition of Group Achievement Award Vol. 1: 12820
Recognition of Long Service to the Society Vol. 2: 5522
Recognition of Professional Service Award Vol. 1: 5820
Recognition of Service Vol. 1: 8051
Recognition of Service and Involvement Vol. 1: 9000
REcognized ACHievement-REACH Awards for Women Vol. 1: 22091
Recognizes outstanding performance in the field of productivity. New chapters and academy fellows are eligible. Vol. 1: 21877
Record Houses of the Year Vol. 1: 5040
Record Interiors of the Year Vol. 1: 5041
Record of the Year Prize Vol. 2: 1597
Recorded Event of the Year Vol. 1: 11424
Recorder of the Year Vol. 1: 16647
Recording and Fieldwork Award Vol. 2: 6783
Recruitment Industry Awards Vol. 2: 8326
Rector's Medal Vol. 2: 5790
Recycler of the Year Vol. 1: 15589
Recycler of the Year Award Vol. 1: 15424
Red Apple Award Vol. 1: 828
Red Award for ANG Aerospace Maintenance; Chief Master Sergeant Dick Vol. 1: 354
Red Cloud Indian Art Show Vol. 1: 10424
Red Earth Poetry Award Vol. 2: 485
Red Earth Poetry Award; Dymocks Vol. 2: 484
Red Ochre Award Vol. 2: 112
Red Rose-White Rose Award Vol. 1: 12568
Redd Center Publication Grants; Charles Vol. 1: 17930
Reddick Memorial Scholarship Award; Dr. Lawrence Dunbar Vol. 1: 5900
Reden Plakette Vol. 2: 2879
Redford Memorial Award; Polly Vol. 1: 6080
Redhouse Student Prize; James W. Vol. 1: 20243
Redi Award Vol. 2: 2984

Redmond Award for Nursing; Juanita Vol. 1: 355
Redon; Fondation Vol. 2: 1717
Redon; Prix Gustave-Francois Vol. 2: 1732
Redwood Lectureship; Theophilus Vol. 2: 8769
Reebok Human Rights Award Vol. 1: 17933
Reed and Mallik Medal Vol. 2: 7779
Reed Award; President Dr. Donald A. Vol. 1: 8616
Reed Award; Sylvanus Albert Vol. 1: 2666
Reed Medal; Walter Vol. 1: 4632
Reed Memorial Award; Dave Vol. 1: 15913
Reed Technology Medal; Robert F. Vol. 1: 10136
Reese Research Prize; Raymond C. Vol. 1: 4351
Reese Structural Research Award; Raymond C. Vol. 1: 1964
Reeve Memorial Award; John Peter Vol. 1: 21110
Reeves Award; Roberta Wright Vol. 1: 2574
Reeves Premium; A. H. Vol. 2: 7828
Referee of the Year Vol. 2: 4425
Reference Service Press Award Vol. 1: 17945
Reference Services Award Vol. 1: 10684
REFORMA Scholarship Vol. 1: 17951
The Regan Grant Memorial Musical Theatre Scholarship Vol. 1: 18307
Regeneration of Scotland Design Award Vol. 2: 8585
Regennitter AAU Jujitsu Service Award; Professor Vol. 1: 571
Reger Memorial Award; Harley B. Vol. 1: 15607
Reggie Awards Vol. 1: 17683
Regifting Grants Program Vol. 1: 8686
Regina Medal Vol. 1: 7654
Region Newsletter of the Year Award Vol. 1: 5223
Region of the Year Vol. 1: 14543
Region of the Year Award Vol. 1: 5224
Regional Achievement Award Vol. 1: 19703
Regional and Major Sports Grants Vol. 1: 9624
Regional Awards
National Association of Student Personnel Administrators Vol. 1: 14407
National Park Academy of the Arts Vol 1: 15482
National Water Safety Congress Vol 1: 15938
New England Theatre Conference Vol 1: 16127
Service of Peace and Justice Vol 2: 1265
Regional Best Conditions Award Vol. 1: 2189
Regional Chapter Research Advancement Award Vol. 1: 18498
Regional Clubs of the Year Vol. 1: 21845
Regional Coach of the Year Vol. 1: 20584
Regional Cultural Merits Award Vol. 2: 4182
Regional Director of the Year Vol. 1: 15241
Regional Director of the Year Award Vol. 1: 690
Regional Directors Award Vol. 1: 6223
Regional Distinguished Service Award Vol. 1: 9319
Regional Diver of the Year Award Vol. 1: 20296
Regional Division Art Educator Award Vol. 1: 13970
Regional Division Art Educator of the Year Vol. 1: 13970
Regional Ecumenism Award Vol. 2: 826
Regional Graduate Scholarships Vol. 1: 7488
Regional Horse Awards Vol. 1: 16492
Regional Information Technology Award Vol. 1: 18504
Regional Innovative Chapter Award Vol. 1: 18505
Regional Judge of the Year Award Vol. 1: 15183
Regional Leadership Award
Mid-America Regional Council Vol. 1: 13370
National Council for Continuing Education and Training Vol 1: 14755
Regional Medallions Vol. 1: 16459
Regional Mid-Career Award Vol. 1: 9320
Regional Multimedia Award Vol. 1: 18506
Regional Person of the Year Award Vol. 1: 14755
Regional Plan Association Award Vol. 1: 17958
Regional Presidents Award Vol. 1: 14132
Regional Psychiatric Technician of the Year Vol. 1: 1389
Regional Publication Awards Vol. 1: 19704
Regional Recognition Award Vol. 1: 6900
Regional Representative of the Year Vol. 1: 14544
Regional Retired Member of the Year Vol. 1: 11840
Regional Safety Professional of the Year Vol. 1: 4607
Regional Service Award Vol. 1: 13636
Regional Service Award for the Disabled Vol. 1: 13637
Regional Team Award Vol. 1: 9321
Regional Television Photographer of the Year Vol. 1: 15546
Register of Merit Award Vol. 1: 6364
Registrar's Prize Vol. 2: 8824
Regnier; Fondation Henriette Vol. 2: 1884
Regnone Service Award; Debbie Vol. 1: 18008
The Rehabilitation International Presidential Award Vol. 1: 17965
Rehabilitation Prize; WVF Vol. 2: 2635
Rehnquist Award for Judicial Excellence; William H. Vol. 1: 14643
Reichart Award; Stuart Vol. 1: 356
Reid Memorial Award; Crawford Vol. 1: 12208
Reid Memorial Fellowship; J.H. Stewart Vol. 1: 6943
Reid Prize in Mathematics; W. T. and Idalia Vol. 1: 18741
Reiner Award; Miriam Vol. 1: 998
Reiner Diamond Pin Award; Abraham Vol. 1: 738
Reinhart and Henry "Butch" Kuhlmann Award; Frank W. Vol. 1: 5978
Reinhart Award; Frank W. Vol. 1: 5979
Reinhart Ring; Hans Vol. 2: 6508
Reinhold Award for Innovation in Teaching; Van Nostrand Vol. 1: 11525
Reinhold Research Award; Van Nostrand Vol. 1: 11528
Reinman, Jr. Award; Alfred E. Vol. 1: 5013
Reiss Memorial Judaica Library Awards; Joseph Vol. 1: 20341
Reitman Memorial Award; Stanley S. Vol. 1: 1093
Related Industry Award Vol. 1: 13911
Relating Research to Practice Awards Vol. 1: 2164
Reliability Test and Evaluation Award Vol. 1: 10927
Relief Pitcher Vol. 1: 19644
Religion Reporter of the Year Award Vol. 1: 12412
Religion Writer of the Year in Europe; John Templeton Vol. 2: 6313
Religious Broadcasting Hall of Fame Award Vol. 1: 15617
Religious Education Excellence Awards Vol. 1: 14623
Religious Freedom Award Vol. 1: 2296
Religious Liberty Award
Institute on Religion and Democracy Vol. 1: 11064
Religious Freedom Council of Christian Minorities Vol 1: 17983
World Evangelical Alliance Vol 1: 21895
Remington Honor Medal Vol. 1: 3396
Remington Painting Award; Frederic Vol. 1: 14886
Remmey AWS Memorial Award; Paul B. Vol. 1: 4866
Remodeler of the Month/Year Awards Vol. 1: 14260
Remote Sensing and Photogrammetry Society Award Vol. 2: 8334
Remote Sensing Society Medal Vol. 2: 8334
Remote Sensing Society President's Prize Vol. 2: 8337
Renaissance Award Vol. 1: 12255
Renaissance Awards Vol. 1: 14261
Renal Research Award; Renal Section Pfizer Predoctoral Excellence in Vol. 1: 3527
Renal Section Pfizer Predoctoral Excellence in Renal Research Award Vol. 1: 3527
Renault; Prix Louis Vol. 2: 6373
Renchard Prize Vol. 1: 10472
Rencontres chorales internationales de Montreux Vol. 2: 6488
Render Awards Vol. 2: 6993
Renie; Prix Henriette Vol. 2: 1733
Renner Crime Reporting Award; Thomas Vol. 1: 12171
Renner Memorial Award; J. Vol. 2: 3228
Rennie Memorial Award for Excellence in Government Public Relations; Don Vol. 1: 7363
Rennie Memorial Medal Vol. 2: 518
Renold Fellowship; Albert Vol. 2: 2741
Renovated Laboratory of the Year Vol. 1: 17816
Repligen Corporation Award in Chemistry of Biological Processes Vol. 1: 1784
Replogle Award for Management Improvement; Luther I. Vol. 1: 20549
Reporter of the Year Award Vol. 1: 1980
Reporting; Robin Goldstein Award for Washington Regional Vol. 1: 15516
Repro International Recording Award Vol. 2: 8150
Republic Literary Award Vol. 2: 5275
Republic of Vietnam Campaign Medal Vol. 1: 8836
Republican of the Year Vol. 1: 18058
Research Achievement Award
American Heart Association Vol. 1: 2418
National Association for Equal Opportunity in Higher Education Vol 1: 14007
Research Achievement Award in Economic, Social and Administrative Sciences Vol. 1: 3397

Research Achievement Award in Natural Products Vol. 1: 3397
Research Achievement Award in Pharmaceutical and Medicinal Chemistry Vol. 1: 3397
Research Achievement Award in Pharmacodynamics Vol. 1: 3397
Research Achievement Awards Vol. 1: 5720
Research Achievement Awards in the Pharmaceutical Services Vol. 1: 3397
Research and Audit Fund Vol. 2: 7104
Research and Development Award
- American Diabetes Association Vol. 1: 2134
- Institute of Food Technologists Vol 1: 10945

Research and Development Team Award Vol. 2: 8857
Research and Education Award Vol. 1: 16079
Research and Special Libraries Award Vol. 1: 5741
Research and Travel Grants Vol. 2: 6231
Research Appointments/Fellowships Vol. 2: 8702
Research Assistantships Vol. 1: 21036
Research Associateship Programs Vol. 1: 15623
Research Award
- American Institute of Aeronautics and Astronautics Vol. 1: 2680
- Astronomical Society of Japan Vol 2: 4098
- Charcot-Marie-Tooth Association Vol 1: 7805
- College Gymnastics Association Vol 1: 8163
- Fellows of the American Bar Foundation Vol 1: 9526
- Lamaze International Vol 1: 12677
- Lupus Foundation of Minnesota Vol 1: 12987
- Society of Insurance Research Vol 1: 19140
- Society of Plastics Engineers Vol 1: 19268
- Tanzania Industrial Research and Development Organization Vol 2: 9291
- World Association for the Advancement of Veterinary Parasitology Vol 1: 21856
- World Organization of Building Officials Vol 1: 21942

Research Award Competition Vol. 1: 2045
Research Award for Amateurs Vol. 2: 4099
Research Award for Junior Astronomers Vol. 2: 4100
Research Award for Outstanding Booklength Study Vol. 1: 5517
Research Award for Outstanding Journal Article Vol. 1: 5518
Research Award in Teacher Education Vol. 1: 5880
Research Award of Merit Vol. 1: 16335
Research Award of the SAVA Vol. 2: 5769
Research Award on Psychotherapy with Women Vol. 1: 3735
Research Awards
- American Heart Association, Talbot County Branch Vol. 1: 2423
- Fraternal Order of Eagles, Havre No. 166 Vol 1: 9744
- Jackson State University - Bureau of Business and Economic Research Vol 1: 12280
- National Institute of Nursing Research Vol 1: 15273
- National Therapeutic Recreation Society Vol 1: 15878
- Post-Polio Health International Vol 1: 17478
- Society for Theatre Research Vol 2: 8962

Research Awards in Otolaryngology Vol. 1: 754
Research Contracts Vol. 1: 14757
Research Council Award Vol. 1: 3892
Research Council Awards Vol. 1: 16335
Research Dissemination Award Vol. 1: 18507
Research Dissertation Award Vol. 1: 18508
Research Excellence Award Vol. 1: 15650
Research Fellowship Award in Cerebrovascular Disease Vol. 1: 15824
Research Fellowship Grants Vol. 1: 17385
Research Fellowships
- Pulmonary Hypertension Association Vol. 1: 17753
- Susan G. Komen Breast Cancer Foundation Vol 1: 19852

Research Gallery Vol. 2: 2546
Research Grant
- American Association of Feline Practitioners Vol. 1: 1202
- Galpin Society Vol 2: 7547
- National Speleological Society Vol 1: 15801
- Special Libraries Association Vol 1: 19556

Research Grant of the Lupus Foundation of America Vol. 1: 12979
Research Grant Program to Assist Foreign Scholars in Chinese Studies Vol. 2: 6592
Research Grants
- American Lung Association of Eastern Missouri Vol. 1: 3017
- Plastic Surgery Educational Foundation Vol 1: 17386

Research in Action Award Vol. 1: 1300
Research in Dental Caries Award Vol. 1: 11210
Research in Oral Biology Award Vol. 1: 11211
Research in Periodontal Disease Award Vol. 1: 11212
Research in Prosthodontics and Implants Award Vol. 1: 11213
Research in Prosthodontics Award Vol. 1: 11213
Research Medal
- Royal Agricultural Society of England Vol. 2: 8416
- Royal Scottish Geographical Society Vol 2: 8680

Research Paper Award Vol. 2: 6590
Research Performance Awards Vol. 1: 21411
Research Presentation Award Vol. 1: 11393
Research Prize and Bronze Medal Vol. 2: 8471
Research Program Grants Vol. 2: 471
Research Project Grants Vol. 2: 472
Research Recognition Award Vol. 1: 16804
Research Scholar Award Vol. 1: 9712
Research Scholarships Vol. 1: 6329
Research Seed Grant Program Vol. 1: 13360
Research Starter Grant Vol. 1: 19082
Research Training Fellowships Vol. 2: 6569
Research Utilization Award Vol. 1: 18509
Research Visiting Professor Award Vol. 1: 18620
Researcher of the Year Vol. 1: 3089
Reserve Grand Award Vol. 1: 20934
Reserve Grand Champion Vol. 1: 14516
Reservoir Description and Dynamics Award Vol. 1: 19248
Reservoir Engineering Award Vol. 1: 19248
Resident and Fellow Achievement Awards Vol. 1: 792
Resident Award
- American College of Preventive Medicine Vol. 1: 1931
- Congress of Neurological Surgeons Vol 1: 8392
- Society of Surgical Oncology Vol 1: 19303

Resident Case of the Year Award Vol. 1: 3849
Resident Dramatist Attachment Award Vol. 2: 6755
Resident Essay Award Vol. 1: 3815
Resident/Fellow Essay Award Vol. 1: 5133
Resident/Fellow Travel Award Program - Annual Scientific Meeting Vol. 1: 2390
Resident Physician's Prize Paper Award Vol. 1: 4396
Resident Research Award
- American Rhinologic Society Vol. 1: 3849
- California Society of Anesthesiologists Vol 1: 6757
- Oral and Maxillofacial Surgery Foundation Vol 1: 16805

Resident Research Competition Vol. 1: 19082
Resident Research Grants Vol. 1: 670
Resident Research Scholarship Vol. 1: 1950
Resident/Trainee Award Vol. 1: 3915
Residential Fellowships Vol. 1: 9758
Resident's Award Vol. 1: 4191
Resistol Rookie of the Year Vol. 1: 17654
Resnik Award; Judith A. Vol. 1: 10879
Resnik Challenger Medal Vol. 1: 19368
Resolutio pro Laude Vol. 2: 5381
Resort Condominiums International (RCI) Festival of Emerging American Theatre Competition Vol. 1: 17279
Resource Enhancement Award Vol. 1: 14126
Respiratory Diseases Research Award Vol. 1: 616
Restaurant Award of Excellence Vol. 1: 14519
Restaurant Design and Graphics Awards Vol. 1: 12289
Restaurateur of the Year Vol. 1: 8854
Restoration Fund Vol. 2: 4748
Restrepo; Distincion Felix Vol. 2: 1336
Restrepo Medal; Felix Vol. 2: 1336
Retail Design Awards Vol. 1: 14401
Retail Nurseryman Award - Jack F. Schneider Award Vol. 1: 9874
Retailer of the Year Vol. 1: 10640
Retailer of the Year Award Vol. 1: 14365
Retailer of the Year Awards Vol. 1: 6170
Retired Art Educator Award Vol. 1: 13971
Retreat Alumni Fellowship Vol. 1: 18434
Return of the Child Award Vol. 1: 12793
Reuben Award Vol. 1: 14591
Reuchlinpreis der Stadt Pforzheim Vol. 2: 3073
Reuter Foundation Stanford Fellowship Vol. 2: 8341
Reuter Prize; Fritz Vol. 2: 3089
Reuter Prize; Paul Vol. 2: 6396
Revelation Prize Vol. 2: 5471
Revelation Prize for Poetry-Premio Revelacao de Poesia Ary dos Santos Vol. 2: 5472

Revelation Prize-Premio Manuel Teixeira Gomes Vol. 2: 5473
Revelle Medal; Roger Vol. 1: 2357
Revenue Society of G.B. Award Vol. 2: 8263
Reves Award; Emery Vol. 1: 7987
Review of Research Award Vol. 1: 2165
Rex Ide Award Vol. 2: 7184
Rex Tasker Award for Best Documentary Vol. 1: 6033
Rey; Prix Henri Vol. 2: 2563
Reyes Prize; Alfonso Vol. 2: 4581
Reynaud; Fondation Jean Vol. 2: 1903
Reynaud; Prix Jean
Academie des Beaux-Arts Vol. 2: 1734
Academie Francaise Vol 2: 2166
Reynolds Award; Orr E. Vol. 1: 3528
Reynolds Medal; Osborne Vol. 2: 7748
Reynolds Media Awards; Nancy Susan Vol. 1: 13238
Rhatigan Award; Frank M. Vol. 1: 10313
Rhoads Lecture; Jonathan E. Vol. 1: 4166
Rhomberg Preis; Alexander Vol. 2: 2844
Rhondda Award; Margaret Vol. 2: 8989
Rhone-Poulenc Lectureship Vol. 2: 8770
Rhone Poulenc Rorer Clinical Investigator Lecture Award Vol. 1: 9260
RHR International Award for Excellence in Consultation Vol. 1: 3753
Rhys Memorial Prize; John Llewellyn Vol. 2: 6883
Rhys Prize; *The Mail on Sunday* - John Llewellyn Vol. 2: 6883
Rhythm and Blues Award Show Vol. 1: 6260
Riada Memorial Trophy; Sean O. Vol. 2: 3627
RIAS/Acanthus Award for Measured Drawing Vol. 2: 8581
RIAS/Alastair Hunter Award for Architectural Photography Vol. 2: 8587
RIAS/Dunedin Award for Architectural Photography Vol. 2: 8587
RIBA Client of the Year Award Vol. 2: 8591
Ribalow Prize; Harold U. Vol. 1: 10213
Ribaud; Fondation Gustave Vol. 2: 1876
Ribeiro Literary Prize; Aquilino Vol. 2: 5418
Ribeiro; Premio Aquilino Vol. 2: 5418
Ricaurte; Orden del Merito Aeronautico Antonio Vol. 2: 1289
Riccione TTV - Teatro Televisione Video Vol. 2: 4043
Rice - Drama Desk Awards; Vernon Vol. 1: 9018
Rice Innovative Program Award; Robert Vol. 1: 450
Rice National Championship Trophy; Grantland Vol. 1: 9675
Rich Award; Oberman and Vol. 1: 10682
Rich Awards for Excellence in Communications; Wilmer Shields Vol. 1: 8600
Rich Memorial Award; Margaret Elden Vol. 1: 451
Rich Moot Court Competition; Giles Sutherland Vol. 1: 2863
Richard-Allan Educational Scholarship Vol. 1: 15715
Richard Beckhard Practice Award Vol. 1: 9408
Richard III Scholarship for Medieval Studies Vol. 1: 18040
Richard Memorial Prize; Therese and Edwin H. Vol. 1: 15698
Richard; Prix Maurice- Vol. 1: 18612
Richard S. Brownlee Fund Vol. 1: 19773
Richard S. Engelbrecht International Activities Service Award Vol. 1: 21498
Richard S. Kennedy Student Essay Prize Vol. 1: 20081
Richards Award for Media Criticism; Bart Vol. 1: 17206
Richards Award; Robert H.
American Institute of Mining, Metallurgical, and Petroleum Engineers Vol. 1: 2827
Society for Mining, Metallurgy, and Exploration Vol 1: 18824
Richards Award; Tudor Vol. 1: 6084
Richards Distinguished Alumni Award; Loretta Vol. 1: 8182
Richards Education and Medical Award Vol. 1: 16764
Richards Graduate Student Research Grant; Albert G. Vol. 1: 730
Richards Memorial Award; Charles Russ Vol. 1: 4542
Richards Prize; Audrey Vol. 2: 6671
Richardson Award Lecture Vol. 2: 9021
Richardson Award; Richard Vol. 2: 6957
Richardson Award; Violet Vol. 1: 19419
Richardson Award; William D. Vol. 1: 10079
Richardson Gold Medal; Benjamin Ward Vol. 2: 8726
Richardson Medal Vol. 2: 7954
Richardson Medal; David Vol. 1: 16796
Richardson Memorial Literary Trust; Evelyn Vol. 1: 21982
Richardson Research Grant; Henry and Sylvia Vol. 1: 9284
Richardson Theatre Awards (Jessies); Jessie Vol. 1: 10166
Richardson Trophy Vol. 2: 8562
Richart Award; Frank E. Vol. 1: 5980
Richmond Cerebral Palsy Center Award Vol. 1: 603
Richmond Lectureship; Dale Vol. 1: 793
Richner, Jr. Scholarship Award; Cedric A. Vol. 1: 4688
Richtenberger; Prix Vol. 2: 1726
Richter Award; Jed Vol. 1: 18327
Richter Awards for Art Critics Vol. 2: 1595
Richter Prize; Curt P. Vol. 2: 2982
Richtmyer Memorial Lecture Vol. 1: 1379
Rickard Scholarship; Howard Brown Vol. 1: 15039
Ricker Resource Conservation Award; William E. Vol. 1: 2257
Rickey Medal Vol. 1: 4352
Rickham Prize; Peter Paul Vol. 2: 6944
Ricks Award; Earl T. Vol. 1: 357
Ricky's Red Rose Challenge Trophy Vol. 1: 15815
Riddell Trophy for Vegetables Vol. 2: 8563
Ride Managers Vol. 1: 14142
Rider Award Program Vol. 1: 20570
Rider Awards Vol. 1: 14143
Rider Hunt Award; Property Council Vol. 2: 497
Rider Mileage Championship Vol. 1: 2190
Rider Mileage Program Vol. 1: 2191
Ridges Memorial Award; Robert V. Vol. 1: 19705
Ridgway Student Chapter Award; Robert Vol. 1: 4353
Riding Hours and Riding Miles Awards Vol. 1: 2151
Ridley; In-Service Training Award in Memory of Clarence E. Vol. 1: 11478
Ridout Awards; Godfrey Vol. 1: 18593
Riegelman Research Achievement Award in Pharmaceutics; Sidney Vol. 1: 3397
Rietz Lecture Vol. 1: 11008
Rifbjerg; Klaus Vol. 2: 1444
Rigging Job of the Year Award Vol. 1: 19584
Right Livelihood Award Vol. 2: 6184
Righteous Among the Nations Vol. 2: 3787
Rigo Award; Joseph T. Vol. 1: 5311
Riley Prize; Franklin L. Vol. 1: 13509
Rimet Cup; Jules Vol. 2: 6359
Rimka premija; Albino Vol. 2: 4396
Ring Award for Investigative Reporting; Selden Vol. 1: 4974
Ring Award; Nancy McNeir Vol. 1: 18217
Ringwood Award for Drama; Gwen Pharis Vol. 1: 21987
Rink Medaillen Vol. 2: 1496
Rink Medal Vol. 2: 1496
Rinkel Award; Herbert J. Vol. 1: 653
Rio de La Loza Prize; Dr. Vol. 1: 17662
Rio National Prize in Chemistry; Andres Manuel del Vol. 2: 4469
Rio; Premio Nacional de Quimica Andres Manuel del Vol. 2: 4469
Rip Rapp Archaeological Geology Award Vol. 1: 9955
Ripperton Award; Lyman A. Vol. 1: 324
Rising Moon Outstanding Youth Services Librarian Award Vol. 1: 5064
Rising Star Award
American College of Preventive Medicine Vol. 1: 1932
United States Harness Writers' Association Vol 1: 20629
Rising Star Leadership Award Vol. 1: 12711
Rispens Award; Bart Vol. 2: 3148
Rist Prize; David Vol. 1: 13407
RITA Award Vol. 1: 18115
Rittenhouse Award Vol. 1: 13267
Ritter Award; R. Max Vol. 1: 21201
Rittle, Sr. Memorial Scholarship Award; Paul H. Vol. 1: 11041
Rivenes Award - Taekwondo; David G. Vol. 1: 572
Rivis Prize; Mrs. F. E. Vol. 2: 8564
Rivkin Award; William R. Vol. 1: 2283
Rivot; Prix L. E. Vol. 2: 1998
RMA of the Year Vol. 1: 3071
RNR Chapter Community Service Award Vol. 1: 9620
Roadrunners of the Year Award Vol. 1: 18070
Roanoke-Chowan Award for Poetry Vol. 1: 16521
Roark Jr. Meritorious Service Certificate; Eldridge W. Vol. 1: 16702
Roback Scholarship; Herbert Vol. 1: 13820
Robb Fellowship; Preston Vol. 1: 13603
Robbins Award; Harold Vol. 1: 4660
Robbins Award; William J. Vol. 1: 20126
Robe of Achievement Vol. 1: 18421
Robel Award Vol. 2: 5316
Robert A. Mooney Distinguished Service Award Vol. 1: 9208
Robert C. Slater Vol. 1: 13473
Robert E. Graham Development Entrepreneur of the Year Award Vol. 1: 12521
Roberts Award; A.W. Vol. 2: 423
Roberts Award for Young Filmmakers; Bill Vol. 1: 6236
Roberts Award; Frances Vol. 1: 8494
Roberts Award; Phil Vol. 1: 11504
Roberts Award; Summerfield G. Vol. 1: 19415

Roberts Lecture; Lloyds Vol. 2: 8829
Roberts Memorial Prize Vol. 1: 13003
Roberts Playwriting Award; Forest A. Vol. 1: 18081
Roberts Vocal Scholarship; W. Towyn Vol. 2: 8174
Robertson Associate Vol. 1: 7390
Robertson Continuing Professional Educator Award; Adelle F. Vol. 1: 20965
Robertson Memorial Lecture Vol. 1: 13846
Robertson Memorial Prize; James Alexander Vol. 1: 8384
Robertson Memorial Trophy; Heaton R. Vol. 1: 20589
Robertson Most Outstanding Undergraduate Award Vol. 1: 17312
Robeson Award; Paul Vol. 1: 163
Robeson Awards; Paul Vol. 1: 16314
Robeson Citation Award; Paul Vol. 1: 168
Robichaux Award; Joseph Vol. 1: 21237
Robie Award for Achievement in Industry Vol. 1: 12275
Robie Humanitarianism Award Vol. 1: 12276
Robin Memorial Award; Andrew E. Vol. 1: 10277
Robinson Award; Charlie Vol. 1: 17718
Robinson Award; J. Franklin Vol. 1: 626
Robinson Award (Marine Naval Flight Officer of the Year); Robert Guy Vol. 1: 13087
Robinson Award; Renault Vol. 1: 14523
Robinson Award; Starkey Vol. 1: 6912
Robinson Awards; Robert L. Vol. 1: 3635
Robinson Coach of the Year; Eddie Vol. 1: 9676
Robinson Distinguished Service Award; Stanley C. Vol. 1: 20966
Robinson Grant; Helen M. Vol. 1: 11873
Robinson Lectureship; Robert Vol. 2: 8771
Robinson Memorial Lectureship; R. A. Vol. 2: 8772
Robinson Memorial Medal for Begonia Hybrid; Alfred D. Vol. 1: 1561
Robinson Periodontal Regeneration Award; R. Earl Vol. 1: 810
Robinson Prize; James Harvey Vol. 1: 2481
Robinson Prize; Joan Cahalin Vol. 1: 18876
Robinson Scholar-Athlete Award; Coach Eddie Vol. 1: 15073
Robinson Scholarship/Award in Conducting; Thelma A. Vol. 1: 8348
Robson Award; Clifford J. Vol. 1: 13054
Rocard; Prix Yves Vol. 2: 2586
Rocha Medal; Manuel Vol. 2: 5403
Roche Award Vol. 1: 7470
Roche Diagnostics Award Vol. 2: 6771
Roche Distinguished Service Award; ONS/ Vol. 1: 16724
Rochelle Scholarship Vol. 1: 12950
Rocheron; Prix Alberic Vol. 2: 2103
Rochester International Film Festival Vol. 1: 18089
Rock and Roll Hall of Fame Vol. 1: 18091
Rock Mechanics Award Vol. 1: 18825
Rockefeller Prize Vol. 1: 3427
Rockefeller Trophy; William A. Vol. 1: 21588
Rockower Awards for Excellence in Jewish Journalism; Simon Vol. 1: 2908
Rockwell Award; Martha Vol. 1: 20816
Rocky Mountain National Watermedia Exhibition Awards Vol. 1: 9679
Rodan Excellence in Mentorship Award; Gideon A. Vol. 1: 3937
Rodas de Prata - Silver Cup Vol. 2: 5389
Rodda Award Vol. 2: 587
Rode Memorial Lecture; Professor K. P. Vol. 2: 3541
Rodeo Hall of Fame Vol. 1: 18104
Roderick Award; Colin Vol. 2: 348
Roderick Haig-Brown Regional Prize Vol. 1: 21522
Roderick Lectures; Colin Vol. 2: 349
Roderick Prize; Colin Vol. 2: 348
Rodermund Service Award; Matthew Vol. 1: 7625
Rodgers Achievement Award; Samuel U. Vol. 1: 14138
Roe Award Vol. 1: 999
Roe Award; Kenneth Andrew Vol. 1: 1200
Roe Award; Ralph Coats Vol. 1: 4041
Roe Medal; Ralph Coats Vol. 1: 4543
Roebling Award Vol. 1: 4354
Roebling Medal Vol. 1: 13437
Roebuck Cup Vol. 2: 7014
Roelen Medal; Otto Vol. 2: 2915
Roelker Award; James E. Vol. 1: 4767
Roelker Prize; Nancy Lyman Vol. 1: 18544
Roemer Conservation Awards; Elsie Vol. 1: 10060
Roentgen-Preis Vol. 2: 3000
Roentgen Resident/Fellow Research Award Vol. 1: 17856
Roerig Fellow in Hospital Dental Practice Vol. 1: 1237
Roeske Certificate of Recognition for Excellence in Medical Student Education; Nancy C. A. Vol. 1: 3636
Roesler Scholarship; Eldon Vol. 1: 21664
Roethke Memorial Foundation Poetry Prize; Theodore Vol. 1: 20064
Roger A. Morse Teaching/Extension/ Regulatory Award Vol. 1: 9099
Rogers Award; David E. Vol. 1: 5562
Rogers Award; John Vol. 1: 7701
Rogers Award; William Vol. 1: 6663
Rogers Communications Inc. Media Award for Coverage of the Arts Vol. 1: 7038
Rogers Memorial Award; Russell Hill Vol. 1: 18239
Rogers Memorial Exhibit Award; Lelan G. Vol. 1: 3253
Rogers Prize Vol. 2: 9268
Rohrer Consulting Psychology Practice Award; Perry L. Vol. 1: 3753
Rokkan Prize in Comparative Social Science Research; Stein Vol. 2: 2505
Roland Grant; Johnny Vol. 1: 7786
Role Model Award Vol. 1: 8399
Role of Law Award Vol. 1: 7566
Rolex Awards for Enterprise Vol. 2: 6498
Rolex Collegiate All-Star Team Vol. 1: 11147
Rolex International Women's Keelboat Championship Vol. 1: 20779
Rolex Junior Championships; U.S. Sailing/ Vol. 1: 20784
Rolex Player of the Year Vol. 1: 12659
Rolex Player to Watch Vol. 1: 11146
Rolex Rookie of the Year Vol. 1: 12660
Rolex Rookie of the Year Men/Women Pros Vol. 1: 10073
Rolex/Tennis Magazine College Player of the Year Vol. 1: 11148
Rolex Trophy Vol. 1: 8768
Rolex Watch/*Tennis* Magazine Rookies of the Year Vol. 1: 19981
Rolf Kjenzel Ring Vol. 2: 787
Rolin-Jaequemyns; Prix G. Vol. 2: 6373
The Roll of Distinguished Philatelist Vol. 2: 6793
Roll of Honor
European Association for Distance Learning Vol. 2: 4750
International Professional Security Association - England Vol 2: 7971
Roll of Honour Vol. 2: 8020
Rollins Graduate Student Research Grant; William H. Vol. 1: 731
Rolls-Royce Enthusiasts Awards Vol. 2: 8345
Rolls Royce Jubilee Award Vol. 2: 7829
Romance Contest Vol. 1: 22000
Romanell Lecture; Patrick Vol. 1: 3428
Romanell - Phi Beta Kappa Professorship in Philosophy Vol. 1: 17244
Romanowski Medal; Miroslaw Vol. 1: 18172
Romantic Novel of the Year Vol. 2: 8347
Romantic Novel of the Year; FosterGrant Reading Glasses Vol. 2: 8347
Rombaux; Prix Egide Vol. 2: 1003
Rome Awards Vol. 2: 7138
Rome Memorial Award; Sidney R. Vol. 1: 499
Rome Memorial Award; Stuart Vol. 1: 6230
Rome Prize Fellowships Vol. 1: 605
Rome Scholarship in Architecture Vol. 2: 7139
Rome Scholarship in Fine Arts Vol. 2: 7140
Romer - G. G. Simpson Medal; A. S. Vol. 1: 19356
Romer Prize; Alfred Sherwood Vol. 1: 19357
Romero Award; Rothko Chapel Oscar Vol. 1: 18132
Romero Folklore Prize; Silvio Vol. 2: 1183
Rominger Plaque; William E. Vol. 1: 13927
Romney Citizen Volunteer Award; Lenore and George W. Vol. 1: 17446
Romney Prize; Hans Vol. 2: 9153
Romney Volunteer Center Excellence Award Vol. 1: 17447
Roms Guldmedalje; N. C. Vol. 2: 1477
Ronald J. Thom Award for Early Design Achievement Vol. 1: 6807
Roncaglia and Eugenio Mari; Premio Maria Teresa Messori Vol. 2: 3832
Rontgen; Fondazione Wilhelm Conrad Vol. 2: 3824
Rood Award; Roy S. Vol. 1: 9613
Rookie Businessperson of the Year Vol. 2: 813
Rookie Chapter of the Year Vol. 1: 14545
Rookie Member of the Year Vol. 1: 14546
Rookie Newsletter Award Vol. 1: 573
Rookie of the Year
Balloon Federation of America Vol. 1: 6224
Continental Basketball Association Vol 1: 8485
Mountainview Women's Nine Hole Golf Association Vol 1: 13652
National Student Campaign Against Hunger and Homelessness Vol 1: 15828
Western Women Professional Bowlers Vol 1: 21574
Rookie of the Year Award National Sprint Care Div. Vol. 1: 20427
Rookie of the Year Award Silver Crown Div. Vol. 1: 20428
Rookie of the Year - Eddie Gottlieb Trophy; got milk? Vol. 1: 14504
Rookie of the Year; Harry Golden Vol. 1: 17592
Rookie of the Year; Lisa Maurice Vol. 1: 21775
Rookie of the Year; Resistol Vol. 1: 17654

Rookies of the Meet Award Vol. 1: 21202
Roosevelt Award; Eleanor Vol. 1: 11809
Roosevelt Award for Excellence in Recreation and Park Research; Theodore and Franklin Vol. 1: 15584
Roosevelt Award; Franklin Delano Vol. 1: 18692
Roosevelt Award; Theodore
International Platform Association Vol. 1: 11810
National Collegiate Athletic Association Vol 1: 14688
Roosevelt Distinguished Service Medal; Theodore Vol. 1: 20066
Roosevelt Four Freedoms Awards; Franklin D. Vol. 1: 9737
Roosevelt Fund Award; Eleanor Vol. 1: 1474
Roosevelt Memorial Fund Award; Theodore Vol. 1: 3158
Roosevelt Trophy; Theodore Vol. 1: 15076
Root Award; H. Paul Vol. 1: 3036
Root Award; Lt. Charles S. Vol. 1: 15384
Root Memorial Award; Charles D. Vol. 1: 20440
Roozeboom Medal; Bakhuis Vol. 2: 4894
Roquemore Memorial Award; A. D. Vol. 1: 2446
Roraback Award; Catherine Vol. 1: 8682
Rosa Award; Edward Bennett Vol. 1: 20480
Rosa Camuna Vol. 2: 3869
Rosa Sabater Prize Vol. 2: 6069
Rosales; Medalla Antonio Vol. 2: 4503
Roscoe Fellowship; H. C. Vol. 2: 7078
Rose Award for Press Criticism; Annual Arthur Vol. 1: 15522
Rose Award; Rod Vol. 1: 19297
Rose Award; William C. Vol. 1: 3922
Rose Bowl Player in the Game Vol. 1: 524
Rose-Bowl Trophy; Mackenzie Junner Vol. 2: 9065
Rose Brand Award for Scenic Lighting Vol. 1: 20648
Rose-Higgins Design Award; A.J. Vol. 1: 17532
Rose International Cello Competition and Festival; Leonard Vol. 1: 18567
The Rose of Sharon Award Vol. 1: 9927
Rose of Tralee Vol. 2: 3686
Rosemaling in the Norwegian Tradition; National Exhibition of Vol. 1: 21316
RoseMary Seymour Award Vol. 2: 5097
Rosen Memorial Award; Harvey M. Vol. 1: 11786
Rosen Prize Vol. 1: 12921
Rosenau Silver Medallion; Ruth Vol. 1: 5153
Rosenbaum Memorial Award; Colonel Samuel Vol. 1: 15180
Rosenberg Award for Poems on the Jewish Experience; Anna Davidson Vol. 1: 13017
Rosenberg Memorial Award; Adeline Vol. 1: 9701
Rosenblueth; Premio Maestro Arturo Vol. 2: 4635
Rosenblum Dissertation Award; Barbara Vol. 1: 19381
Rosenkjaer Prize (DR Radio) Vol. 2: 1455
Rosenkjaerprisen Vol. 2: 1455
Rosenstiel Award for Distinguished Work in Basic Medical Research; Lewis S. Vol. 1: 18127
Rosenthal Award; Walter Vol. 1: 13557
Rosenthal Foundation Awards; Richard and Hinda Vol. 1: 1927
Rosenzweig Biennial Competition; Irene Vol. 1: 5149
Rosenzweig Distinguished Service Award Vol. 1: 5065
Rosewater Indiana High School Book Award; Eliot Vol. 1: 5387
Rosica, Jr. Memorial Award; Albert E. Vol. 1: 1834
Rosie Award Vol. 1: 5387
Rosie Awards Vol. 1: 422
Rosner/Johnson Memorial Scholarships Vol. 1: 9004
Ross Award
Canadian Paediatric Society Vol. 1: 7319
Royal College of Radiologists - United Kingdom Vol 2: 8476
Ross Award for Best New Magazine Writer; Alexander Vol. 1: 15355
Ross Award; Harland Vol. 1: 21377
Ross Award; Madeline Dane Vol. 1: 16981
Ross Award; Thomas Vol. 2: 8586
Ross Awards; Arthur Vol. 1: 10853
Ross Dissertation Award; Jacqueline A. Vol. 1: 9178
Ross Education Awards Vol. 1: 781
Ross Medal; Will Vol. 1: 3014
Ross Prize; John Munn Vol. 2: 7677
Ross Products Division of Abbott Laboratories Award for Excellence in Cancer Nursing Education; ONS/ Vol. 1: 16725
Ross Safety Award; Pete Vol. 1: 13088
Ross Student Paper Award; Carl A. Vol. 1: 5001
Rosse Cup Vol. 2: 8565
Rossel; Prix Victor Vol. 2: 938
Rossi Prize; Bruno Vol. 1: 1516
Rossini; Prix Vol. 2: 1727
Roster of Fellows Vol. 1: 3298
Roster of Honor Vol. 1: 3299
Rostkowski Award; Nicolaus Vol. 1: 10424
Rostropovitch; Concours International de Violoncelle Vol. 2: 2283
Rostropovitch International Cello Competition Vol. 2: 2283
Rotary Award for World Understanding and Peace Vol. 1: 18129
Rotary Scholarship Vol. 1: 10130
ROTC Award Vol. 1: 14902
ROTC Awards; Sojourners Vol. 1: 15787
ROTC (Junior) Scholarship Vol. 1: 21347
ROTC Medals Vol. 1: 15781
Roth Award for a Translation of a Literary Work; Lois Vol. 1: 13568
Roth Manufacturing Engineering Scholarship; Edward S. Vol. 1: 19166
Rotheim Medal; Erik Vol. 2: 849
Rothko Chapel Oscar Romero Award Vol. 1: 18132
Rothman Memorial Award; Stephen Vol. 1: 18778
Rothmans Foundation Ballet Scholarship Vol. 2: 314
Rothrock Award Vol. 1: 19479
Rothschild Challenge Cup Vol. 2: 8566
Rotorua Trophy Vol. 2: 5067
Rottimans World Film International Critics' Award as Selected by Fipresci Vol. 1: 20116
Roubaix; Prix Francois de Vol. 2: 2470
Round Table Award Vol. 1: 10975
Rous-Whipple Award Vol. 1: 4122
Rousch McCafferty C.G. Award; Jane Vol. 1: 17551
Rouse Gold Medallion Vol. 1: 5153
Rouse Hydraulic Engineering Lecture; Hunter Vol. 1: 4355
Rousseau; Fondation Gaston Vol. 2: 1869
Rousseau; Prix Samuel Vol. 2: 1735
Roussy; Fondation Gustave Vol. 2: 1877
Routh Student Research Grant Vol. 1: 3755
Routman Teacher Recognition Award; Regie Vol. 1: 11874
Roux; Fondation Gustave Vol. 2: 1878
Rouyer; Prix Vol. 2: 1728
Rover Midlander Open Design Award Vol. 2: 567
Rowan-Legg Award; Edward K. Vol. 1: 6973
Rowe & John O. Rowe Citizen of the Year Award; Lillian B. Wood Vol. 1: 3118
Rowe Marketing Award Vol. 1: 7257
Rowe Medals; N. E. Vol. 2: 8400
Rowing Awards Vol. 2: 3647
Rowing Hall of Fame Vol. 1: 20751
Rowland Award; Dunbar Vol. 1: 13510
Rowland Prevention Award; Lela Vol. 1: 15379
Rowland Prize; Thomas Fitch Vol. 1: 4356
Rowlands Male Student-Athlete-Of-The-Year; David Vol. 1: 15314
Roxane Laboratories Linda Arenth Excellence in Cancer Nursing Management Award Vol. 1: 16710
Roy Award; Thomas Vol. 1: 7130
Roy Memorial Lecture; Dr. Biren Vol. 2: 3508
Roy Space Science and Design Award; Dr. Biren Vol. 2: 3335
Roy Trust Award; Dr. Biren Vol. 2: 3336
Royal Academy Summer Exhibition Vol. 2: 8353
Royal Asiatic Society Award Vol. 2: 8429
Royal Bath and West Scholarship Awards (World and European) Vol. 2: 8439
Royal Canadian Legion Fellowships in Gerontological Nursing Vol. 1: 7313
Royal Canadian Mounted Police Long Service Medal Vol. 1: 6830
Royal Canin Award
American Animal Hospital Association Vol. 1: 906
American Veterinary Medical Association Vol 1: 4820
Royal College of Radiologists Award Vol. 2: 8476
Royal College of Surgeons of England Honorary Medal Vol. 2: 8489
Royal Companies Award Vol. 2: 5782
Royal Conservatory of Music Scholarship Vol. 1: 21782
Royal Designer for Industry Award Vol. 2: 8712
Royal Dublin Society Crafts Competition Vol. 2: 3695
Royal Economic Society Prize Vol. 2: 8506
Royal Gold Medal Vol. 2: 8592
Royal Hibernian Academy of Arts Awards Vol. 2: 3697
Royal Historical Society Today Prize Vol. 2: 608
Royal Horticultural Society Honorary Fellow Vol. 2: 8567
Royal Horticultural Society of Ireland Flower Show Vol. 2: 3694
Royal Humane Society Awards Vol. 2: 8578
Royal Mail Trophy Vol. 2: 8263
Royal Medals Vol. 2: 8703
Royal Naval College, Greenwich Prize Vol. 2: 7866

Award Index

Royal Northern College of Music Companion Vol. 2: 8638
Royal Northern College of Music Fellow Vol. 2: 8639
Royal Northern College of Music Honorary Member Vol. 2: 8640
Royal Norwegian Order of Merit Vol. 2: 5140
Royal Norwegian Order of St. Olav Vol. 2: 5141
Royal Over-Seas League Music Competition Vol. 2: 8643
Royal Philatelic Society London Medal Vol. 2: 8646
Royal Red Cross Vol. 2: 7265
Royal Society for the Protection of Birds Medal Vol. 2: 8731
Royal Society of Chemistry Sponsored Awards Vol. 2: 8773
Royal Society of Literature Ondaatji Prize Vol. 2: 8797
Royal Society of Victoria Medal Vol. 2: 551
Royal Society of Western Australia Medal Vol. 2: 553
Royal Swedish Academy of Engineering Sciences Great Gold Medal Vol. 2: 6200
Royal Victorian Order
  Canada - The Chancellery Vol. 1: 6815
  Central Chancery of the Orders of Knighthood Vol 2: 7266
Royal Watercolour Society Award Vol. 2: 8869
Royal Yachting Association Award Vol. 2: 8874
Royal Yachting Association Cruising Award Vol. 2: 8222
Royce Award for Achievement; IIE Sir Henry Vol. 2: 568
Royce Award in Mechanical Engineering; Sir Henry Vol. 2: 569
Royce Award; Sir Henry Vol. 2: 7830
Royce Bursaries - Panasonic Trust; Sir Henry Vol. 2: 570
Royce Initiative Award; Sir Henry Vol. 2: 571
Royce, Jr. Award; Steven Vol. 1: 3060
Royce Lectures in the Philosophy of the Mind Vol. 1: 3429
Royce Memorial Award; Sir Henry Vol. 2: 572
Royce Memorial Lecture; Sir Henry Vol. 2: 573
Royce Prestige Lecture on the Institution of Incorporated Engineers; Sir Henry Vol. 2: 574
Royce Prize for Young Engineers; Sir Henry Vol. 2: 575
Royce Pupil Prize; Sir Henry Vol. 2: 576
Royce Trophy for the Pursuit of Excellence; Sir Henry Vol. 2: 577
Rozelle Trophy; Pete Vol. 1: 15087
RRS Research Award Vol. 1: 17823
RRS Young Investigator Travel Award Vol. 1: 17824
Rs of Excellence Vol. 1: 17921
RSA Benno Schotz Prize Vol. 2: 8672
RSA Guthrie Award Vol. 2: 8672
RSA Medal for Architecture Vol. 2: 8672
RSPB Fine Art Award Vol. 2: 9084
The RTZ David Watt Memorial Prize Vol. 2: 8343
Rube Goldberg Award Vol. 1: 14591
Rube Hornstein Prize in Operational Meteorology Vol. 1: 7280
Rubens-Alcais Challenge Vol. 1: 11495
Rubincam Youth Award Vol. 1: 15152
Rubinstein Award Vol. 1: 1288
Rubinstein International Piano Master Competition in Conjuction with the Israel Philharmonic Orchestra; Arthur Vol. 2: 3720
Rubinstein Memorial Prize; The Artur Vol. 2: 9121
Rubner-Preis; Max Vol. 2: 2897
Ruby Honorarium; Mike Vol. 1: 8218
Ruckert Preis; Friedrich Vol. 2: 3076
Rudd Award; Steele Vol. 2: 294
Rudolphi-Medaille; Carl-Asmund- Vol. 2: 2710
Rudolphi Medal; Carl Asmund Vol. 2: 2710
Rudyard Boulton Award Vol. 2: 9370
Ruger World Team Trophy; William B. Vol. 1: 15647
Ruggles Travel Awards; Nancy Vol. 1: 11255
Ruhlman; Prix Vol. 2: 1729
Ruiz; Premio Santos Vol. 2: 6094
Rumbaugh Historical Oration Contest; Joseph S. Vol. 1: 15782
Rumford Medal Vol. 2: 8704
Rumford Prize Vol. 1: 622
Rumsey Buyers' Choice Award; Nona Jean Hulsey Vol. 1: 14886
Runcorn-Florensky Medal Vol. 2: 2316
Runcorn Travel Award; Keith Vol. 2: 2316
Runermark Award; Jan Vol. 2: 869
Runner of the Year
  U.S.A. Track and Field Vol. 1: 21238
  U.S.A. Track and Field Vol 1: 21244
Runyon - Walter Winchell Cancer Fund Fellowships; Damon Vol. 1: 8728
Rural County Engineer of the Year Award Vol. 1: 14179
Rural Health Practitioner of the Year Vol. 1: 15654
Rural Life Project Awards Vol. 2: 9200
Rural Wales Award Vol. 2: 7236
Rural Youth Europe Awards Vol. 2: 781
Rush Award; Benjamin Vol. 1: 8913
Rush Award; Gertrude E. Vol. 1: 14491
Rush Lectureship Award; Benjamin Vol. 1: 3637
Rusk Award; Dean Vol. 1: 11716
Russell and Burch Award Vol. 1: 10599
Russell Award Vol. 1: 8130
Russell Award for Distinguished Research in the Teaching of English; David H. Vol. 1: 14840
Russell Award; Frances E. Vol. 2: 6391
Russell Award; T. Randolph Vol. 1: 8449
Russell, Jr. Award; Emmett Vol. 1: 5724
Russell, Jr., Memorial Award; Louis B. Vol. 1: 2419
Russell Lectureship; Henry Norris Vol. 1: 1517
Russell Memorial Medal; Peter Nicol Vol. 2: 424
Russell Naval Aviation Flight Safety Award; Adm. James S. Vol. 1: 16833
Russell Scholarship; Norman K. Vol. 1: 15463
Russolo; Concorso Internazionale Luigi Vol. 2: 3943
Rustin Freedom Award; A. Philip Randolph/ Bayard Vol. 1: 28
Rustin Humanitarian Award; Bayard Vol. 1: 29
Rutgers National/Works on and of Paper Competition Vol. 1: 19779
Rutherford Medal and Prize Vol. 2: 7735
Rutherford Memorial Lecture Vol. 2: 7735
Rutman Award; Irwin R. Vol. 1: 19272
Rutter Gold Medal and Prize Vol. 2: 7297
Ruzicka-Preis Vol. 2: 6525
Ruzicka-Prize Vol. 2: 6525
RV Automotive Achievement Award Vol. 1: 17919
RVL Walker Award Vol. 1: 7534
Ryan Award; Cornelius Vol. 1: 16981
Ryan Memorial Award; Robert G. Vol. 1: 9001
Ryan Trophies; John T. Vol. 1: 7203
Ryan Winners Circle Acting Awards; Irene Vol. 1: 12547
Ryan Winners Circle Evening of Scenes; Irene Vol. 1: 12547
Ryder Cup Vol. 2: 8298
Ryle Award for Excellence in Writing on the Problems of Geriatrics; Annual National Press Club Joseph D. Vol. 1: 15523
Ryle Memorial Medal Vol. 2: 8299
RYOC Vol. 1: 2375
Ryser SGI Vol. 2: 6972
S-B Power Tool Scholarship Award Fund Vol. 1: 19167
S. Lewis Elmer Award Vol. 1: 2369
S2A3 Bronze Medal Vol. 2: 5774
SA Holstein Friesland Society Gold Medal Vol. 2: 5619
SA Scientific Award Vol. 2: 5634
SAACE Excellence Awards Vol. 2: 5678
SAAD Dental Student Prize Vol. 2: 8953
SAALED Bursary Vol. 2: 5672
Saban Scholar-Athlete Award; Coach Lou Vol. 1: 15073
Sabbatical Exchange Program Vol. 1: 14948
Sabex Award Vol. 1: 7471
Sabina Fund Vol. 1: 9417
Sabine Medal; Wallace Clement Vol. 1: 143
The SABR Salute Vol. 1: 18636
SABR Special Achievement Award Vol. 1: 18637
Sacher Student Award; George Vol. 1: 9997
Sachs Award; Curt Vol. 1: 3172
Sack Award; Ernest Vol. 2: 2244
Sacre; Prix Auguste Vol. 2: 1044
Sacre; Prix Emile Vol. 2: 1004
Sadasivan Lecture; Prof. T. S. Vol. 2: 3509
Saddle Bronc of the Year Vol. 1: 17655
Saddlemyer Award; Ann Vol. 1: 5289
Sadek Award Vol. 2: 8600
SAE Lloyd L. Withrow Distinguished Speaker Award Vol. 1: 19041
SAE Section/Chapter Partnerships of Distinction Awards Vol. 1: 19054
Safe Affordable Food; Award for Technical Innovation in Enhancing Production of Vol. 1: 7439
Safe and Courteous Driver of the Year Vol. 1: 13377
Safe Contractor of the Year Awards Vol. 1: 15571
Safe Driver Award Program Vol. 1: 15660
Safe Driving Award Vol. 1: 20550
Safe Mileage Award Vol. 1: 21763
Safe Worker Award Vol. 1: 4773
Safety Achievement Vol. 1: 409
Safety and Health Award Vol. 1: 4893
Safety and Health Awards Vol. 1: 20512
Safety and Occupational Health Awards Vol. 1: 17746
Safety and Service Vol. 1: 19517
Safety Award
  International Association of Diecutting and Diemaking Vol. 1: 11340

International Association of Wildland Fire Vol 1: 11408
National Propane Gas Association Vol 1: 15555
North Carolina Utility Contractors Association Vol 1: 16523
Pacific Coast Paper Box Manufacturers' Association Vol 1: 17002
Safety award Vol. 1: 6693
Safety Award for Superior Accomplishment Vol. 1: 20481
Safety Award Program Vol. 1: 19319
Safety Awards
Canadian Association of Oilwell Drilling Contractors Vol. 1: 6926
National Paint and Coatings Association Vol 1: 15473
New York Shipping Association Vol 1: 16262
Safety Awards of Commendation Vol. 1: 15473
Safety Awards of Excellence Vol. 1: 15473
Safety Awards of Honor Vol. 1: 15473
Safety Awards of Merit Vol. 1: 15473
Safety Codes and Standards Medal Vol. 1: 4544
Safety Commendation Award Vol. 1: 21203
Safety Director of the Year Award Vol. 1: 4774
Safety Engineer of the Year Vol. 1: 19886
Safety Excellence; Award of Vol. 1: 17755
Safety in Construction Medal Vol. 2: 7780
Safety in Seas Award Vol. 1: 15420
Safety Manager of the Year Vol. 1: 19888
Safety Professionals of the Year Vol. 1: 4609
Safety Recognition Award Vol. 1: 19600
Safety Society Presidential Citation Vol. 1: 18336
Sagan Award for Public Understanding of Science Vol. 1: 8588
Sagar Award; Dr. Vidya Vol. 2: 3430
Sagarmatha Award Vol. 2: 4678
Sagebrush Award; YALSA Vol. 1: 22055
Sagebrush Education Resources Literature Grant; ALSC/ Vol. 1: 5431
Sagendorph Memorial Prize for Art; Robb Vol. 1: 22017
Saget; Prix Julien Vol. 2: 2564
Sagittarius Prize Vol. 2: 8990
Sagrave Award Vol. 2: 578
Sahitya Akademi Awards Vol. 2: 3551
Sahitya Akademi Bhasha Samman Award Vol. 2: 3552
Sahitya Akademi Fellowship Vol. 2: 3553
Sahitya Akademi Translation Prize Vol. 2: 3554
Sahitya Award; Bala Vol. 2: 3565
Saidi-Sirjani Memorial Book Prize Vol. 1: 11937
Saidye Bronfman Award Vol. 1: 6808
Sail Gold Medal Vol. 2: 3461
Saillet; Prix Joseph Vol. 2: 2063
Sailors of the Year on SSBN-733 Vol. 1: 21261
Sainsbury Scholarship in Painting and Sculpture Vol. 2: 7141
St. Cuthberts Mill Award for Works on Paper Vol. 2: 8734
St. David's Society Scholarship Vol. 1: 18205
St. Francis de Sales Award Vol. 1: 7660
St. Francis International Masters Regatta Vol. 1: 20772
St. Gaudens Medal; Augustus Vol. 1: 8498
St. George National Award Vol. 1: 1639
St. Gregory the Great; Order of Vol. 2: 9312
St. Hubert's Giralda Trophy Vol. 1: 21588
St. Johns Area Chamber of Commerce/Mint Festival Scholarship Vol. 1: 18211
St. Katharine Drexel Award Vol. 1: 7655
St. Kilda Film Festival Vol. 2: 560
Saint La Salle Medal Vol. 1: 13051
St. Louis Black Pride Scholarship Vol. 1: 18213
St. Louis Chapter 17 Scholarship Fund Vol. 1: 19168
St. Louis Refractories Award Vol. 1: 1696
Saint Luke's Lecture Vol. 2: 3691
St. Luke}s Lecture Vol. 2: 3692
St. Michael Religious Freedom Award Vol. 1: 7648
St. Olav Medal Vol. 2: 5142
St. Paul Federal Bank for Savings Excellence in Teaching Award (Graduate School of Business) Vol. 1: 8992
St. Petersburg Yacht Club Trophy Vol. 1: 20780
Saint-Prix; Prix Berriat Vol. 2: 2019
St. Romanos the Melodist Medallion Vol. 1: 15115
St. Stephen Recognition of Diaconal Ministry Vol. 1: 16380
St. Sylvester; Order of Vol. 2: 9313
Saintour; Prix Vol. 2: 1978
Sajous Achievement Award; Edward T. Vol. 1: 14054
Sakharov Prize for Freedom of Thought; European Parliament Vol. 2: 7484
Saksena Memorial Medal; Professor Shyam Bahadur Vol. 2: 3510
Sakura Finetek Student Scholarship Vol. 1: 15722
Sakurai Prize for Theoretical Particle Physics; J. J. Vol. 1: 3475
Salao Nacional de Artes Plasticas Vol. 2: 1176
Salazar Award for Communications; Ruben Vol. 1: 14808
Salcedo, Jr. Memorial Lecture; Dr. Juan Vol. 2: 5279
Salcedo Jr. Science Education Award; Dr. Juan S. Vol. 2: 5291
Salem Conference Grant; Dr. Shawky Vol. 2: 4816
Sales Executive of the Year Award Vol. 1: 16328
Sales Representative of the Year Award Vol. 1: 6993
Saligny Prize; Anghel Vol. 2: 5863
Salin Prize; Kasper Vol. 2: 6168
Salinger Award; Ronald Vol. 2: 442
Salinpriset; Kasper Vol. 2: 6168
Salivary Research Award Vol. 1: 11214
Salmon Award - Blind Worker of the Year; Peter J. Vol. 1: 15259
Salmon Award; Dr. Daniel E. Vol. 1: 14226
Salon Anual de Artes Plasticas Premios Pedro Domingo Murillo Vol. 2: 1124
Salon Culinaire Mondial
Chefs and Cooks Circle Vol. 2: 7303
National Restaurant Association Vol 1: 15625
Society of German Cooks Vol 2: 3064
Saloutos Memorial Book Award in Immigration History; Theodore Vol. 1: 10707
Saloutos Memorial Book Award; Theodore Vol. 1: 283
Salter Award; Janet & Maxwell Vol. 1: 6350
Salters' Graduate Prizes Vol. 2: 8886
Saltire Society and The Royal Bank of Scotland - Scottish Science Award Vol. 2: 8894
Saltire Society Award Vol. 2: 7407
Saltire Society Scottish Literary Awards Vol. 2: 8892
Saltus Medal Award; J. Sanford Vol. 1: 3274
Saltus Medal; Sanford Vol. 2: 7092
Saltus; Prix Alphonse de Neuville et Sanford Vol. 2: 1701
Salute; The SABR Vol. 1: 18636
Salute to Excellence Awards
National Association of Black Journalists Vol. 1: 14101
National Restaurant Association Educational Foundation Vol 1: 15631
Salvan; Prix Eugene Vol. 2: 2044
Salvatori Teaching Award Vol. 1: 10437
Salzberg Mentorship Award; Arnold M. Vol. 1: 794
Salzburg Heraldic Medal Vol. 2: 775
Salzburg Prize for the Promotion of the Arts, Science and Literature Vol. 2: 776
Salzman Award for Excellence in International Economic Performance; Herbert Vol. 1: 20551
Sam-Ae Award Vol. 2: 5500
SAM/Mead Johnson Nutritionals New Investigator Award Vol. 1: 18621
SAM/Organon Visiting Professor in Adolescent Research Award Vol. 1: 18620
Samaritan Award Vol. 1: 12661
Sammy Lee Award Vol. 1: 21891
Samoyed of the Year: Male, Female, Veteran, Senior, & Danish champion in Sledge Racing Vol. 2: 1464
Sample Student Excellence Award; W. Frederick Vol. 1: 19104
Sampson Excellence in Teaching Award; Donald K. Vol. 1: 6637
Samsonov Prize Vol. 2: 5934
San Antonio Chapter of Rocks Inc. Scholarship Vol. 1: 18241
San Antonio Cine Festival Vol. 1: 10188
San Antonio International Piano Competition Vol. 1: 18239
San Martin Bicentennial Medal Vol. 1: 18261
San Martin Palms Vol. 1: 18262
San Sebastian International Film Festival Awards Vol. 2: 6096
Sanchez Memorial Award; George I. Vol. 1: 17951
Sanchez; Premio Carlos Mateo Vol. 2: 4506
Sand Dollar Vol. 1: 8203
Sand; Fondation Gabrielle Vol. 2: 1868
Sand Volunteer of the Year Award; Rebecca Vol. 1: 7806
Sandberg Grant for Research and/or Development Vol. 2: 3752
Sandberg Prize for Israeli Art Vol. 2: 3753
Sandbergprijs Vol. 2: 4695
Sandburg Award; Carl Vol. 1: 11811
Sandburg Literary Arts Award; Carl Vol. 1: 9806
Sanderson Award; A. B. Vol. 1: 7419
Sanderson Award (Attack Squadron of the Year); Lawson H. M. Vol. 1: 13089
Sanderson Award; Sandy Vol. 1: 7068
Sanderson Young Adult Book of the Year Award Vol. 2: 649
Sanderson Young Adult Narrator of the Year Award Vol. 2: 650

The Sandlot Kid Vol. 1: 19655
Sandmeyer Prize Vol. 2: 6514
Sandoz Award Vol. 1: 7472
Sandoz Award; Mari Vol. 1: 16070
Sandoz Oration Award for Research in Cancer Vol. 2: 3431
Sandrof Lifetime Achievement Award; Ivan Vol. 1: 14530
Sanford Award; Nevitt Vol. 1: 12021
Sanford-Springvale Rotary Club Scholarship Fund Vol. 1: 13039
Sanger Award; Margaret Vol. 1: 17370
Sangiorgi; Fondazione Giorgio Maria Vol. 2: 3818
Sangster Memorial Award; Allan Vol. 1: 6958
Sanitarian's Award Vol. 1: 11234
Sanitation Award; Sulabh Global Vol. 2: 3589
Sankei Jidoh Bunka Shuppan Shoh Vol. 2: 4287
Sanshigaku Shinpo Sho Vol. 2: 4218
Sanshigaku Sho Vol. 2: 4217
Sansome President's Trophy; Hugh Vol. 2: 7998
Sansone Award; Michael Vol. 1: 8052
Sansum Medal; W.E. Vol. 2: 425
Santarelli Award for Public Policy; Donald E. Vol. 1: 15447
Santos-Dumont Gold Airship Medal Vol. 2: 6350
Santos Prize; Reynaldo Dos Vol. 2: 3912
Santos Ruiz; Premio Vol. 2: 6094
Sao Paulo International Film Festival Vol. 2: 1194
Saouma Award; Edouard Vol. 2: 3950
Sapop Memorial Award; Arnold Vol. 1: 19470
Sapporo International Ski Marathon Vol. 2: 4289
Sarabhai Medal; Vikram Vol. 2: 2274
Sarah Sikes Sequence Award Vol. 1: 2446
Sarbadhikari Gold Medal Vol. 2: 3527
Sarby Trophy; Richard Vol. 2: 2472
Sargant Fellowship Vol. 2: 7142
Sargeet Natak Akademi Fellowships Vol. 2: 3573
Sargent Award Vol. 1: 643
Sargent, Jr. Award; Lowrie B. Vol. 1: 5981
Sargent Medal Vol. 1: 18995
Sargent Medal; M. A. Vol. 2: 426
Sargent Progress Award; Albert M. Vol. 1: 19169
Sargeson Fellowship; Buddle Findlay Vol. 2: 5089
Sarli Memorial Scholarship; Frank Vol. 1: 14883
Sarnat Award in Craniofacial Biology; Bernard G. Vol. 1: 11215
Sarnat Prize; Bernard G. Vol. 1: 11220
Sarnoff Award; David Vol. 1: 10880
Sarnoff Citation Vol. 1: 17843
Sarnoff Medal Award; David Vol. 1: 19198
SARs planpris Vol. 2: 6169
Sarton Award; May Vol. 1: 16115
Sarton Chair Vol. 2: 1096
Sarton Leersoel Vol. 2: 1096
Sarton Medaille Vol. 2: 1097
Sarton Medal
History of Science Society Vol. 1: 10490
Sarton Committee of the University of Ghent Vol 2: 1097
Sarvotten Jeevan Raksha Padak Vol. 2: 3388
Sasakawa - DHA Disaster Prevention Award Vol. 2: 6490
Sasakawa Health Prize Vol. 2: 6566
The Saskatchewan Choral Federation Choral Scholarship Vol. 1: 18308
Sasol Post-Graduate Medal Vol. 2: 5695
Sass Medal; Hans and Jacob Vol. 1: 13240
Satbir Award; Smt. Kamal Vol. 2: 3432
Satgur Prasad-Prag Parmeshwari Devi Memorial Awards Vol. 2: 3576
Satomi Prize Vol. 2: 4147
Saturn Awards Vol. 1: 123
Saulses de Freycinet; Fondation Charles-Louis de Vol. 2: 1824
Saunders Award; Harold E. Vol. 1: 4570
Saunders Gold Medal; William Lawrence Vol. 1: 2828
Saunders Memorial Award; Robert G. Vol. 1: 7043
Saunders Natural History Award; W. E. Vol. 1: 16765
Saunders Sr. Award; Harris Vol. 1: 4757
Saunderson Award Vol. 1: 8130
Saur Award for Best Article in *College and Research Libraries*; K. G. Vol. 1: 5618
Sauveur Achievement Award; Albert Vol. 1: 5190
Savage Memorial Award; Warren F Vol. 1: 4894
Savage "Miles From Nowhere" Memorial Award; Barbara Vol. 1: 13645
Savago New Voice Award; Joe Vol. 1: 17780
Save Our Earth Award Vol. 1: 15028
Save Our Streams Award Vol. 1: 12270
Save the Children - Canada Award Vol. 1: 18323
Savory Award for Science Communication; Eve Vol. 1: 6292
Savory Shield Award Vol. 1: 2552
Savulescu Prize; Traian Vol. 2: 5864
Sawtelle Scholarship; B. Douglas Vol. 1: 13716
Sawyer Award; R. Tom Vol. 1: 4545
Saxen Medal; Erkki Vol. 2: 1579
Saxton Memorial Exhibit Award; Burton Vol. 1: 3254
Sayen Award; Clarence N. Vol. 2: 7925
SBET/Renshaw-Heilman BMET of the Year Award Vol. 1: 15737
SBET/Replacement Parts Industries BMET of the Year Award Vol. 1: 5488
SBPC Annual Meeting Award Vol. 2: 1166
SCA Distinguished Service Award Vol. 1: 14706
SCA Golden Anniversary Fund Awards Vol. 1: 14709
Scaglione Prize for a Translation of a Literary Work; Aldo and Jeanne Vol. 1: 13569
Scaglione Prize for a Translation of a Scholarly Study of Literature; Aldo and Jeanne Vol. 1: 13570
Scaglione Prize for Comparative Literary Studies; Aldo and Jeanne Vol. 1: 13571
Scaglione Prize for French and Francophone Studies; Aldo and Jeanne Vol. 1: 13572
Scaglione Prize for Italian Literary Studies; Aldo and Jeanne Vol. 1: 13573
Scaglione Prize for Studies in Germanic Languages and Literatures; Aldo and Jeanne Vol. 1: 13574
Scaglione Prize for Studies in Slavic Languages and Literatures; Aldo and Jeanne Vol. 1: 13575
Scanstar Packaging Competiton Vol. 2: 1534
Scantlebury Memorial Award; Donald L. Vol. 1: 12428
Scarpette d'Argente Vol. 2: 3865
Scattergood System Achievement Award; E. F. Vol. 1: 3795
SCC Award Medals Vol. 1: 18327
SCCA/CASCT North American Rally Cup Vol. 1: 19706
SCCA Mechanic of the Year Vol. 1: 19707
SCCA Pro Rally Cup Vol. 1: 19708
SCCA Pro Rally Manufacturer's Award Vol. 1: 19709
SCCA Road Rally Rookie of the Year Vol. 1: 19685
Scenic Technology Award Vol. 1: 20649
Schaar Biennium Playwright Award; Ruby Yoshino Vol. 1: 12306
Schachern Memorial Award Award; Harold J. Vol. 1: 17975
Schaefer Award; Hugo H. Vol. 1: 3398
Schaeffer Environmental Award; William D. Vol. 1: 10137
Schaeffler Award; Willy Vol. 1: 20817
Schafer Award; George E. Vol. 1: 19352
Schafer Prize; Alice T. Vol. 1: 5528
Schaff Prize; Philip Vol. 1: 4288
Schaffer Young Investigator Award; Rita Vol. 1: 6390
Schaffner Achievement Award; Franklin J. Vol. 1: 8949
Schallek Memorial Graduate Fellowship Awards; William B. and Maryloo Spooner Vol. 1: 18038
Schamelhout-Koettlitz; Fund Dr. en Mevr. Vol. 2: 973
Scharansky Freedom Award; Anatoly Vol. 1: 20306
Schary Awards; Dore Vol. 1: 4984
Schatz Award; Jack Vol. 1: 574
Schauer Memorial Scholarship; Lee E. Vol. 1: 18446
Schawlow Award; Arthur L. Vol. 1: 12693
Schawlow Prize in Laser Science; Arthur L. Vol. 1: 3476
Schechter Medal; Solomon Vol. 1: 12382
Scheel-Preis; Karl- Vol. 2: 2729
Scheele Award Vol. 2: 6275
Scheele Medal; Herbert Vol. 2: 6851
Scheele Plakette Vol. 2: 2686
Scheele-priset Vol. 2: 6275
Scheele Trophy; Herbert Vol. 2: 4437
Scheepers Prize Vol. 2: 5658
Scheffer; Prix Ary Vol. 2: 1736
Schelenz Plaque Vol. 2: 2979
Schell Memorial Intermediate Piano Scholarship; The Minnie Vol. 1: 18309
Schenck Award; Carl Alwin Vol. 1: 18975
Schenkel Player of the Year; Chris Vol. 1: 17594
Schenley Award - Most Outstanding Player Vol. 1: 7102
Schepkens; Prix Joseph Vol. 2: 1061
Schering Award Vol. 1: 7473
Schering Clinical Lecture Vol. 1: 16730
Schering Excellence in Biotherapy Nursing Award; ONS/ Vol. 1: 16726
Schering Excellence in Cancer Nursing Research Award; ONS/ Vol. 1: 16727
Schering Plough Institute Award; ASBMB/ Vol. 1: 3920
Schering Veterinary Award Vol. 1: 7535
Schermerhorn Award Vol. 2: 6638

Scheveningen International Music Competition Vol. 2: 4904
Schiebold-Gedenkmunze Vol. 2: 2882
Schiefer "Old Timer's" Memorial Award; Paul Vol. 1: 19588
Schiller-Gedachtnispreis des Land Baden-Wurttemberg Vol. 2: 3034
Schiller Preis der Stadt Mannheim Vol. 2: 3071
Schimmel Award for Distinguished Contribution to Archaelogy in Israel; Percia Vol. 2: 3754
Schindler Award Vol. 1: 4075
Schlack Award; Carl A. Vol. 1: 5782
Schlafman Award; Sophie Vol. 1: 10147
Schlegel - Tieck Prize Vol. 2: 8975
Schleiden-Medaille Vol. 2: 2708
Schleiden Medal Vol. 2: 2708
Schlich Memorial Award; Sir William Vol. 1: 18976
Schlich Memorial Trust Award Vol. 2: 7328
Schlueter Stroke Awards National Winners Vol. 1: 4725
Schlumberger Award; Conrad Vol. 2: 4752
Schlumberger; Prix Gustave Vol. 2: 1778
Schlumpf Award; Mildred Vol. 1: 2446
Schmeisser Award; William Vol. 1: 20666
Schmeisser Memorial Trophy; William Vol. 1: 20666
Schmid Service Award; John A. Vol. 1: 16685
Schmidheiny Prize for Free Enterprise and Political Liberty; Max Vol. 2: 6486
Schmidt Prize; Annie M. G. Vol. 2: 4724
Schmitt Award for Outstanding Corporate Leadership; Fred Vol. 1: 15589
Schmitt; Prix Florent Vol. 2: 1737
Schmitthoff Prize; Clive and Twinkie Vol. 2: 7690
Schmitz Award for Outstanding Contributions to the Frontiers in Education Conference; Ronald J. Vol. 1: 4042
Schmitz Silver Spoon Award; Ronald C. Vol. 1: 14055
Schmocker Memorial Award; Hanna Vol. 1: 7523
Schmorl-Preis; Georg- Vol. 2: 3058
Schmutz Award; George L. Vol. 1: 5014
Schneck Award; Shirley R. Vol. 1: 18660
Schneider Achievement Award; Dean Herman Vol. 1: 8504
Schneider Award; Jack F. Vol. 1: 9874
Schneider Director Award; Alan Vol. 1: 20054
Schneidermeyer Regional Leadership Award; Melvin J. Vol. 1: 7767
Schoeller-Junkmann-Preis Vol. 2: 2851
Schoemaker Award; Harold Jan Vol. 2: 6054
Schoenberg International Award in Neuroepidemiology; Bruce S. Vol. 1: 705
Schoenbrun Award; Michael Vol. 1: 12794
Schoenfield Media Award; Al Vol. 1: 12060
Scholander Award; Comparative Physiology Section Vol. 1: 3514
Scholar/Artist Award Vol. 1: 14898
Scholar-Athlete Vol. 1: 14664
Scholar-Athlete Awards Vol. 1: 15081
Scholar Award Vol. 1: 21474
Scholar Award; AAHE Vol. 1: 1017
Scholarly Paper Competition Vol. 1: 15429
Scholarly Studies Prize Vol. 2: 6655
Scholarship Award
American Bible Society Vol. 1: 1564
Cooperstown Art Association Vol 1: 8507
Indiana Holstein Association Vol 1: 10761
Scholarship Award; Alpha Chi Sigma Vol. 1: 476
Scholarship Contest Vol. 1: 17387
Scholarship Contests Vol. 1: 15782
Scholarship for Enterostomal Therapy Education Vol. 1: 16923
Scholarship Fund CBMC Area Local Vol. 1: 7881
Scholarship/Grant Program of SAI Philanthropies Inc. Vol. 1: 18477
Scholarship Loan Fund Vol. 2: 3029
Scholarship Program
Rocky Mountain Coal Mining Institute Vol. 1: 18097
Wisconsin Farm Bureau Federation Vol 1: 21672
Scholarship to VPI-Veterinary College Vol. 1: 16682
Scholarships Vol. 1: 20225
Scholarships and Research Grants, Behavioral Studies Vol. 1: 14650
Scholarships of the City of Munich Vol. 2: 3014
Scholarships, Writing Awards, Internships Vol. 1: 18491
Scholastic Achievement Awards Vol. 1: 17905
Scholastic Press Freedom Award Vol. 1: 19811
Scholdstroms pris; Birger Vol. 2: 6260
Scholl-Preis; Geschwister- Vol. 2: 3015
Schonfeld Award (Honorary Members); William A. Vol. 1: 3906
Schonstedt Scholarship in Surveying Vol. 1: 2004
School Administrators Distinguished Library Service Award Vol. 1: 1413
School & Community Award for Youth in Health & Safety Vol. 1: 3837
School Division Education Research Award Vol. 1: 5565
School Librarian's Workshop Scholarshp Vol. 1: 1419
School Library Media Specialist Award Vol. 1: 12944
School Nurse of the Year Vol. 1: 18341
School of Advanced Airpower Studies Thesis Award Vol. 1: 375
School of Medicine Award Vol. 1: 6625
School Superintendents of the Year Vol. 1: 17182
Schoolboy Motorcross Award Vol. 1: 7294
Schooley World Team Trophy; John M. Vol. 1: 15647
Schoolmeesters; Prix Herman Vol. 2: 1025
Schott Denkmunze; Otto Vol. 2: 2892
Schottky-Preis fur Festkorperforschung; Walter- Vol. 2: 2730
Schotz Prize; RSA Benno Vol. 2: 8672
Schoutedenprijs; H. Vol. 2: 1083
Schreder 15-Meter Class Trophy Vol. 1: 18587
Schreiber Award; Frederick C. Vol. 1: 181
Schreiner Prize; Olive Vol. 2: 5550
Schreyer Award Vol. 1: 5643
Schroeder Distinguished Service Award; Bill Vol. 1: 11404
Schubert and the Music of Modern Times International Competition; Franz Vol. 2: 794
Schubert Award for Teaching College Science; Leo Vol. 1: 21437
Schuchert Award; Charles Vol. 1: 17041
Schuckska priset Vol. 2: 6261
Schultz High School Excellence Award; Dave Vol. 1: 15990
Schultz Perpetual Memorial Trophy; Jack Vol. 1: 20630
Schumacher Memorial Award; Max Vol. 1: 10392
Schumacher Prize; Fritz Vol. 2: 3090
Schuman Award; William Vol. 1: 8254
Schuman Prize; Henry and Ida Vol. 1: 10491
Schumann and Piano and Song Competition; International Robert Vol. 2: 2974
Schumann Choir Competition; International Robert Vol. 2: 2973
Schumpeter-Preis Vol. 2: 3054
Schumpeter Prize Vol. 2: 3054
Schunk-Preis fur Medizin; Ludwig Vol. 2: 3002
Schunk-Preis fur Veterinarmedizin; Ludwig Vol. 2: 3003
Schunk-Preis fur Wirtschaftswissenschaften Vol. 2: 3001
Schunk Prize for Medicine; Ludwig Vol. 2: 3002
Schunk Prize for Veterinary Medicine; Ludwig Vol. 2: 3003
Schuster Award; Brady/ Vol. 1: 3764
Schutt Silver Cup Vol. 1: 2561
Schutz Lecture Vol. 1: 3430
Schutz Perpetual Trophy Vol. 2: 3627
Schwab Award; Fred E. Vol. 1: 19269
Schwartz Award Vol. 1: 1880
Schwartz Award for Best Story; Zack Vol. 1: 16956
Schwartz Children's Book Awards; Ruth and Sylvia Vol. 1: 16746
Schwartz Emergency Medical Service of the Year Award (BLS Service of the Year Award); Leo R. Vol. 1: 14219
Schwartz Memorial Award; Paul Vol. 1: 4867
Schwartz Memorial Poetry Award; Delmore Vol. 1: 16303
Schwartzwalder - PACE Award Vol. 1: 1697
Schwarzenberger Prize in International Law; Georg Vol. 2: 7651
Schweikert, Jr. Disability Awareness Award; Harry A. Vol. 1: 17071
Schweisguth Prize Vol. 2: 7987
Schweitzer Award; Albert Vol. 2: 7895
Schweitzer Medal; Albert Vol. 1: 4966
Schweitzer Medal; Friedrich Vol. 2: 730
Schweitzer Prize for Humanitarianism; Albert Vol. 1: 12417
Schweitzer Prizes; William P. and Gertrude Vol. 1: 13797
Schweizer Musikedition Vol. 2: 6533
Schwidefsky Medal Vol. 2: 6639
Schwiglhofer Trophy; Oscar Vol. 2: 6788
Scialtel; Prix Jeanne Vol. 2: 2167
Science and Engineering Fellowship; AAAS Mass Media Vol. 1: 3506
Science and Religion Course Program Vol. 1: 12413
Science Award
Scientific and Technical Research Council of Turkey Vol. 2: 6648
Trudeau Institute Vol 1: 20223
Science Award; Health Vol. 1: 4794
Science Award; Northern Vol. 1: 10751
Science Award; Women in Vol. 1: 20450
Science Books; Aventis Prizes for Vol. 2: 8691
Science Education; ASCB/Bruce Alberts Award for Distinguished Contributions to Vol. 1: 3940

Science Educator's Hall of Fame Vol. 1: 13167
Science Fair Vol. 1: 3103
Science Fair Award Vol. 1: 20695
Science Fiction/Fantasy Short Story Contest Vol. 1: 18360
Science in Society Book Awards Vol. 1: 7383
Science in Society Journalism Awards Vol. 1: 7384
Science-in-Society Journalism Awards Vol. 1: 14380
Science Journalism Awards; AAAS Vol. 1: 1047
Science Popularization Awards Vol. 2: 6135
Science Prize Vol. 2: 3834
Science Recognition Award for New Investigators Vol. 1: 8110
Science Screen Report Award Vol. 1: 15691
Science Teaching Award Vol. 1: 15692
Scientific Achievement Award
International Union of Forest Research Organizations Vol. 2: 767
System Safety Society Vol 1: 19891
Scientific Achievement Meritorious Award Vol. 2: 4148
Scientific and Technical Translation Prize Vol. 2: 5474
Scientific Award
American Association of Hospital Dentists Vol. 1: 1238
American Horticultural Society Vol 1: 2536
Hildegard Doerenkamp and Gerhard Zbinden Foundation for Realistic Animal Protection in Bio-Medical Research Vol 2: 2924
Society of Medical Laboratory Technologists of South Africa Vol 2: 5635
Scientific Communication Vol. 2: 6042
Scientific Communication Award; Technical and Vol. 1: 14843
Scientific Exhibit Awards Vol. 1: 19232
Scientific Freedom and Responsibility Award; AAAS Vol. 1: 1048
Scientific Investigation and Research Award Vol. 1: 2200
Scientific Medal; Zoological Society of London Vol. 2: 9284
Scientific Merit Award Vol. 2: 1306
Scientific or Technical Achievement Award Vol. 1: 17298
Scientific Poster Awards Vol. 1: 1913
Scientific Prize; Wojciech Rubinowicz Vol. 2: 5369
Scientific Research and Development Award Vol. 1: 19891
Scientific Research Prizes Vol. 2: 4557
Scientific Researcher of the Year Vol. 1: 11467
Scientific Secretary of the Polish Academy of Sciences Award Vol. 2: 5334
Scientist of the Year Award Vol. 1: 17818
SCN Elizabeth Lowry Award Vol. 1: 22048
Scobee Lecturer Vol. 1: 1134
Scobie Memorial Award for Preliminary Ph.D. Research; James R. Vol. 1: 8385
Scopus Award Vol. 1: 2309
Scotlan Award for Distinguished Service; Priscilla A. Vol. 1: 1011
Scotland North Premium; Institution of Electrical Engineers Vol. 2: 7812
Scotsman Fringe First Awards Vol. 2: 7404
Scott Award; Arnold H. Vol. 1: 5982
Scott Award; Elizabeth L. Vol. 1: 8294
Scott Award; Jessie M. Vol. 1: 3284
Scott Award; John Vol. 1: 6492
Scott Award of Merit; Margaret B. Vol. 1: 7262
Scott-Farnie Medal Vol. 2: 6680
Scott Joplin Foundation of Sedalia Lifetime Achievement Award
Scott Joplin International Ragtime Foundation Vol. 1: 18371
Singapore Association of Convention and Exhibition Organisers and Suppliers Vol 2: 5944
Scott Medal Award Vol. 1: 18369
Scott Medal for Conservation Merit; Peter Vol. 2: 6559
Scott Memorial Trophy (Doublehanded); Manton D. Vol. 1: 20789
Scott Prize Lectureship; James Vol. 2: 8792
Scott Prize; Primrose Vol. 2: 7678
Scott Prizes; James Brown Vol. 2: 6373
Scott Quartette Service Award; Chris Vol. 1: 10253
Scott Student Research Fellowship; David B. Vol. 1: 11216
Scotti Prize; Alexander S. Vol. 2: 2977
Scottish Book of the Year Awards Vol. 2: 8892
Scottish First Book of the Year Vol. 2: 8892
Scottish Geographical Medal Vol. 2: 8687
Scottish Historical Book Award Vol. 2: 8893
Scottish International Piano Competition Vol. 2: 8913
Scottish Marketing Awards Vol. 2: 8911
Scottish Salon of Photography Vol. 2: 8919
Scottish Science Award Vol. 2: 8894
Scottish Song Competition Vol. 2: 8895
Scottish Tartans Society; Fellowship of the Vol. 2: 9112
Scourby Narrator of the Year Award; Alexander Vol. 1: 2304
Scoville Award Vol. 1: 21912
Scrabble Championship; National Vol. 1: 15696
Scrapbook Award Vol. 1: 12506
Screen Awards Vol. 1: 21993
Screener's Choice Award for Narrative Integrity Vol. 1: 4972
Screenplay Contest Vol. 1: 15995
Screenwriter's Contest Award and Promotion Vol. 1: 16001
Scribner Award; B.F. Vol. 1: 5983
Scripps/American Dance Festival Award; Samuel H. Vol. 1: 2117
Scrivner Award for Creative Grantmaking; Robert W. Vol. 1: 8601
Scroggie, M.D. Memorial Award; Val D. Vol. 1: 19710
Scroll of Excellence Vol. 1: 21729
Scroll of Honor Vol. 1: 19937
Scroll of Merit Vol. 2: 7926
SD Broadcaster of the Year Vol. 1: 19450
SDA Scholarship Award Vol. 1: 19101
SDC Concours Awards Vol. 1: 19803
SDC Publication Committee Awards Vol. 1: 19804
SDE Fellowships Vol. 1: 18481
SEA Awards Vol. 2: 3585
Sea Grant Association Award Vol. 1: 18386
Sea Grant State Fellowship Vol. 1: 6755
Seaborg Award for Nuclear Chemistry; Glenn T. Vol. 1: 1785
Seaborg Award; Glenn Vol. 1: 11812
Seaborg Award; Glenn T. Vol. 1: 2457
Seaborg SIYSS Award Vol. 1: 18362
Seal Memorial Trophy Award; George H. Vol. 1: 8959
Sealants Hall of Fame Award Vol. 1: 5984
Seaman Awards for Oustanding Operational Support; Lewis L. Vol. 1: 5783
Seaman Memorial Scholarship; Anne Vol. 1: 17628
Search for New Music Vol. 1: 11179
Search for Outstanding Contributions to Science Education Vol. 2: 5291
Searching for Success Program Vol. 1: 17991
Searle Award Vol. 1: 9996
Sears Cup Vol. 1: 20784
SEASECS Article Prize Vol. 1: 19468
Seastrom Safety Award Vol. 1: 17531
Seavey Quality in Law Enforcement Award Program; Webber Vol. 1: 11311
Second Century Award Vol. 1: 12383
Second Intellectual List of Leaders Yearbook Vol. 1: 5026
Secondary Art Achievement Award Vol. 1: 13972
Secondary Students; National Testing and Awards Program for Vol. 1: 1446
Secondary Teacher of the Year Vol. 1: 14575
Secretary of State's Distinguished Service Award Vol. 1: 20552
Secretary of the Year, Executive of the Year Vol. 1: 11169
Secretary's Award Vol. 1: 20553
Secretary's Exceptional Achievement Awards Vol. 1: 20513
Secretary's Opportunity and Empowerment Award Vol. 1: 3559
Section Achievement Award Vol. 1: 1857
Section Activities Award Vol. 1: 11054
Section on the Psychology of Black Women Award Vol. 1: 3736
Section Performance Award Vol. 1: 12221
Section Technical Award Vol. 1: 11054
Sector Awards Vol. 2: 8719
Security Officer of the Year Award Vol. 1: 20534
Security Professional of the Year Vol. 2: 9234
Seddon Award; Richard Vol. 1: 10544
Sedgwick Memorial Medal Vol. 1: 3780
Seed and Pilot Programs Vol. 1: 9074
Seed Research Awards Vol. 1: 19755
Seed Science Award Vol. 1: 8669
Seedsman of the Year, Honorary Member Vol. 1: 6045
Seeger Prize; Charles Vol. 1: 18673
Seeker of the Truth Vol. 1: 11625
Seemen Preis; Hans von Vol. 2: 2902
Sefika Awards Vol. 2: 5611
Segal Award; Martin E. Vol. 1: 12856
Segalas; Prix Anais Vol. 2: 2107
Seidel Award; Harris F. Vol. 1: 5582
Seidenbaum Award; Art Vol. 1: 12931
Seifert Prize; Jaroslav Vol. 2: 6145
Sejong Literacy Prize; King Vol. 2: 2606
Selby Fellowship Vol. 2: 131
Seldin Award; Donald W. Vol. 1: 15325
Seldin Award; Joel R. Vol. 1: 17703
Selecon Design Award Vol. 2: 5033
Selected Marine Corps Reserve Medal Vol. 1: 8837
Selenick - CASE Distinguished Service Award; Harrie M. Vol. 1: 8568
Self-Adhesive Labelling Awards Vol. 2: 4949
Selfe Medal; Norman Vol. 2: 427

Seligman Award; Monroe Vol. 1: 10928
Seligman Crystal Vol. 2: 7955
Seligman Lecture; Richard Vol. 2: 9022
Seligson/Golden Award Vol. 1: 1000
Selskabets pris Vol. 2: 1444
Seltzer Distinguished Service Recognition; Mildred M. Vol. 1: 5373
Selwyn Award Vol. 2: 8668
Selye Award; Hans Vol. 1: 2853
Semaine Internationale de Video Vol. 2: 6476
Sembrich Scholarship in Voice; Marcella Vol. 1: 12614
SEMI Award for North America Vol. 1: 18412
Seminary Award Vol. 1: 9914
Sen Award; B. R. Vol. 2: 3951
Sen Oration Award for Practice of Medicine; M. N. Vol. 2: 3433
Sen Prize; Dr. S. R. Vol. 2: 3549
Senart; Prix de la Fondation Emile Vol. 2: 1779
Senior Achievement Award Vol. 1: 710
Senior Bowler of the Year
Bowling Writers Association of America Vol. 1: 6567
Women's All-Star Association Vol 1: 21776
Senior Captain Scott Commemoration Medal Vol. 2: 5659
Senior Collaborative Research Grants Vol. 1: 10008
Senior High Youth Voluntarism Award Vol. 1: 20916
Senior Ladies Bonspiel Vol. 1: 20888
Senior Membership Vol. 1: 18720
Senior Moulton Medal Vol. 2: 7754
Senior PGA Championship Vol. 2: 8300
Senior Player of the Year Vol. 1: 17595
Senior Recognition Award for Distinguished Contributors to the Division of Counseling Psychology Vol. 1: 3665
Senior Rookie of the Year Vol. 1: 17596
Senior Scholarships Vol. 1: 5068
Senior Team Canada Junior MVP Vol. 1: 6264
Senior Visiting Fellowship Vol. 2: 3703
Senior Whitehead Prize Vol. 2: 8092
Seniors Division - Highest Point Car over 900 Points Vol. 1: 7973
Seniors' Service Award Vol. 1: 20861
Senn Lectureship and Award; Milton J. E. Vol. 1: 795
Senne; Prix Emile Le Vol. 2: 1780
Sense of Smell Award Vol. 1: 9722
Sensenbaugh Environmental Technology Award; J. Deane Vol. 1: 325
Sent Lisi Par Excellence Vol. 2: 5916
Sent Sovi Prize Vol. 2: 6024
Sentinels of Safety Vol. 1: 15387
Sentner Short Story Award; Carl Vol. 1: 17548
Seoul Music Festival Award Vol. 2: 5507
Separation Science Lecture Vol. 2: 9023
Sequoyah Children's Book Award Vol. 1: 16675
Sequoyah Young Adult Book Award Vol. 1: 16676
Serbian Academy of Sciences and Arts Awards Vol. 2: 5938
Serdan Prize; Carmen and Aguiles Vol. 2: 4497
Serena Medal for Italian Studies Vol. 2: 6903
Sericultural Science Advancement Award Vol. 2: 4218
Servaas Award Vol. 1: 10456
Service and Performance Award Vol. 1: 12442
Service Award
ACSM Health Promotion Vol. 1: 152
American Camping Association Vol 1: 1629
American Occupational Therapy Association Vol 1: 3300
Association for Communication Excellence in Agriculture, Natural Resources, and Life and Human Sciences Vol 1: 5295
Association for Indiana Media Educators Vol 1: 5386
Association of Specialized and Cooperative Library Agencies Vol 1: 5859
Foodservice Consultants Society International Vol 1: 9668
History of Economics Society Vol 1: 10478
Middle East Studies Association of North America Vol 1: 13384
National Accreditation Council for Agencies Serving the Blind and Visually Impaired Vol 1: 13870
National Apostolate for Inclusion Ministry Vol 1: 13946
National Gymnastics Judges Association Vol 1: 15184
National Junior College Athletic Association Vol 1: 15315
Royal Astronomical Society of Canada Vol 1: 18146
Scientific and Technical Research Council of Turkey Vol 2: 6649
Society for Imaging Science and Technology Vol 1: 18721
Special Interest Group on Knowledge Discovery and Data Mining - Association for Computing Machinery Vol 1: 19545
World Organization of Building Officials Vol 1: 21943
Service Award for the Promotion and Teaching of Football Vol. 2: 8909
Service Award; Mel Allen Vol. 1: 4681
Service Award (Non-CAF Member) Vol. 1: 8281
Service Award of Chamber of Geological Engineers Vol. 2: 6629
Service Awards
American Crystallographic Association Vol. 1: 2094
Association of Public Treasurers of the United States and Canada Vol 1: 5831
Canadian Society of Petroleum Geologists Vol 1: 7489
Health Science Communications Association Vol 1: 10331
National Association of Underwater Instructors Vol 1: 14451
U.S.A. Baseball Vol 1: 21159
USA Hockey Vol 1: 21179
Western Society of Engineers Vol 1: 21569
Service Badge Vol. 1: 501
Service Bowl Award Vol. 1: 20862
Service - Life Member Vol. 2: 815
Service Medal in Gold Vol. 2: 5752
Service Medal; Textile Institute Vol. 2: 9134
Service Pin Award Vol. 1: 6247
Service Sector Manager of the Year; Manufacturing Manager of the Year/ Vol. 1: 17744
Service to Children Television Awards Vol. 1: 14117
Service to Democracy Award Vol. 1: 932
Service to Keuka Vol. 1: 12582
Service to NACADA Award Vol. 1: 13772
Service to Others Vol. 1: 9858
Service to Youth Award
Boys and Girls Clubs of America Vol. 1: 6602
YMCA of Greater New York Vol 1: 22037
Servicios Distinguidos a la Fuerza Submarina Vol. 2: 1295
Serviscope Trophy Vol. 2: 9116
SES - ASTM Robert J. Painter Memorial Award Vol. 1: 5985
Seshadri Prize in the Field of Practice of Community Medicine; Dr. M. K. Vol. 2: 3434
Seshadri Seventieth Birthday Commemoration Medal; Professor T. R. Vol. 2: 3511
Sesher Sportsmanship Award; Charles Vol. 1: 15316
Sessions Memorial Award; John Vol. 1: 17946
Seton Award; Elizabeth Ann Vol. 1: 14624
Seton Award; Ernest Thompson Vol. 1: 11360
Seton Award; Saint Elizabeth Ann Vol. 1: 14625
Seton Distinguished Volunteer Award; Fenmore R. Vol. 1: 17966
Setterfield Memorial Scholarship; Ellen Vol. 1: 15039
Seva Keerthi Vol. 2: 6129
Seven State Exhibition Vol. 1: 12500
Seventeen Seventy-Six Award ("1776 Award") Vol. 1: 16050
Seventy-Five Year Club Member Certificate Vol. 1: 3255
Sevigne Award; Frank Vol. 1: 21239
Sewell Medal Vol. 2: 8568
Sewell Mutant Award Vol. 1: 1622
Sexual Orientation and Gender Identity Conference Awards Vol. 1: 6974
Seybold Vision Award Vol. 1: 18427
Seyffert Memorial Award; Richard Vol. 1: 13995
Seymour Award Vol. 1: 5379
Seymour Award; Whitney North Vol. 1: 9443
Seymour Cray Computer Science and Engineering Award Vol. 1: 10479
The Seymour Eskow Scholarship Vol. 1: 11792
Seymour Medal Vol. 1: 18638
Seymour, Sr. Award; Whitney North Vol. 1: 922
Seymour Vestermark Award Vol. 1: 3641
SFORZA Medal Vol. 1: 5619
SGA Service Award Vol. 1: 18047
Sgambati Award; Fred Vol. 1: 7231
SGL Carbon Award Vol. 1: 1648
Shaara Outstanding Writer Award; Michael Vol. 1: 19535
Shacklock Trophy Vol. 2: 6717
Shadle Fellowship; Albert R. and Alma Vol. 1: 4500
Shafer Award; Stephen Vol. 1: 15448
Shaffer Award for Academic Excellence as a Graduate Faculty Member; Robert H. Vol. 1: 14408
Shaffer Award; Robert H. Vol. 1: 5694
Shaffer Award; Thomas E. Vol. 1: 796
Shah Memorial Lecture; Professor R. C. Vol. 2: 3542
Shaine Memorial Award; The Elsa Vol. 1: 10278
Shakespeare Award for Classical Theatre (Will Award); William Vol. 1: 18429

Award Index

Shakespeare Library Fellowships and National Endowment for the Humanities Senior Fellowships; Folger Vol. 1: 9646
Shakespeare Prize Vol. 2: 3091
Shaler Company's Rislone Most Improved Championship Driver Award Vol. 1: 20423
Shalom Peace Award Vol. 1: 12367
Shands Award Vol. 1: 16914
Shanghai Television Festival Vol. 2: 5232
Shankar Memorial Lecture; Dr. Jagdish Vol. 2: 3512
Shannon Award; National Film Board Kathleen Vol. 1: 22048
Shanti Swarup Bhatnagar Medal Vol. 2: 3513
Shantz Award; Stan Vol. 1: 17485
Shapira Prize; Francois Vol. 2: 3776
Shapiro Award; Arthur Vol. 1: 18661
Shapiro Prize; Alec Vol. 2: 8472
Share the Wealth Packets Vol. 1: 12837
Shared Vision Award Vol. 1: 16082
Sharman Award Vol. 2: 275
Sharp Award; A.J. Vol. 1: 6554
Sharp Memorial Prize; Frank Chapman Vol. 1: 3431
Sharpe Award; Norma Vol. 1: 6888
Sharpe Prize; Roy Vol. 2: 7041
Sharpest Knife in North America Award Vol. 1: 1267
Sharples Perpetual Award; Laurence P. Vol. 1: 399
Shatalov Award; Mikhail and Ekateryna Vol. 1: 13798
Shattuck Award; Charles B. Vol. 1: 5015
Shattuck Public Service Awards; Henry L. Vol. 1: 6524
Shaughnessy Prize; Mina P. Vol. 1: 13576
Shaurya Chakra Vol. 2: 3389
Shaw Award; Cliff Vol. 1: 16041
Shaw Memorial Award; Peter Vol. 1: 14372
Shaw Postdoctoral Prize in Acoustics; Edgar and Millicent Vol. 1: 6853
Shaw Prize; Bernard Vol. 2: 8976
Shaw-Worth Memorial Scholarship Vol. 1: 10601
Shawcross Prize; A. J. Vol. 2: 7648
Shawn Barnett Memorial Award Vol. 1: 22085
Shazar Award for Research in Jewish History; Zalman Vol. 2: 3768
Shea Award; James H. Vol. 1: 14240
Shea Prize; John Gilmary Vol. 1: 1656
Sheahan Award; John Drury Vol. 1: 8580
Shedden Uhde Medal and Prize Vol. 2: 428
Sheehan Award for U.S. Paper Money Studies; Catherine Vol. 1: 3256
Sheehan Memorial Educational Scholarship; Dezna C. Vol. 1: 15715
Sheeline Award for Excellence in Public Relations; Randall D. Vol. 1: 2788
Shehadi New Writers Award; Philip Vol. 1: 13379
Shelburne Award; Tilton E. Vol. 1: 5986
Sheldon Audio-Visual Award; M. Vernon Vol. 1: 3257
Shell - LSO Music Scholarship Vol. 2: 8097
Shell Playwriting Award Vol. 2: 5034
Shelley Memorial Award Vol. 1: 17436
Shelton Award; Robert M. Vol. 1: 10340
Shenk Award Vol. 1: 13953
Shepard Award; Glenn Vol. 1: 15880
Shepard Award; Paul Vol. 1: 3584
Shepard Medal for Excellence in Marine Geology; Francis P. Vol. 1: 18847
Shepard Medal for Marine Geology; Francis P. Vol. 1: 18847
Shepard Science Award; Charles C. Vol. 1: 20501
Shephard Award; Will Vol. 1: 5756
Shepherd Distinguished Composer of the Year Award; MTNA- Vol. 1: 13707
Shepherd Teaching Award; Margaret Vol. 1: 21386
Sheppard Award; C. Stewart Vol. 1: 5399
Sheppard Award; Eugenia Vol. 1: 8575
Shercliff Prize; University of Cambridge Arthur Vol. 2: 7869
Sherif Award; Carolyn Wood Vol. 1: 3737
Shering Award Vol. 1: 7474
Sherlock Meritorious Service Award; Charles N. Vol. 1: 4152
Sherman Leadership Award; Simon Vol. 1: 18598
Sherrard Awards; J. M. Vol. 2: 4961
Sherrington Memorial Lecture Vol. 2: 8830
Sherwin Award; Raymond J. Vol. 1: 18470
Sherwin-Williams Student Award in Applied Polymer Science Vol. 1: 1786
Shetland People Hall of Fame Vol. 1: 3897
Shevchenko Freedom Award Vol. 1: 20269
Shiebler Award; George L. Vol. 1: 9111
Shield Award Vol. 1: 17112
Shield of Blessed Gregory X Crusader Vol. 1: 14422
Shields Medal Vol. 1: 18996
Shields-Trauger Award Vol. 1: 6225
Shigeka Talumura Scholarship Vol. 1: 21880
Shilling Award; Charles W. Vol. 1: 20292
Shilling Award; David C. Vol. 1: 358
Shimbun Bunka Sho Vol. 2: 4185
Shimbun Kokoku Sho Vol. 2: 4184
Shin Award Vol. 1: 12384
Shinbum Kyokai Sho Vol. 2: 4186
SHINE (Sexual Health in Entertainment) Awards Vol. 1: 13238
SHIP Citation Vol. 1: 9173
Ship of the Year Vol. 1: 21938
Shipley Award; Robert M. Vol. 1: 2322
Shipman Gold Medal Award; J. Vol. 1: 10840
Shiras Institute/Mildred & Albert Panowski Playwriting Award Vol. 1: 18081
Shiu-Ying Hu Award Vol. 1: 10509
Shneidman Award; Edwin Vol. 1: 1438
Shock Compression Science Award Vol. 1: 3477
Shock New Investigator Award; Nathan Vol. 1: 9998
Shockley Memorial Award; Woodland G. Vol. 1: 5987
Shoemaker Award of Merit; Ralph J. Vol. 1: 19565
Shofar Award Vol. 1: 22065
Shofar Award (Ram's Horn) Vol. 1: 15300
Shogren Award Vol. 1: 11235
Shore Plaque (Outstanding Defenseman); Eddie Vol. 1: 2517
Shores - Greenwood Publishing Group Award; Louis Vol. 1: 17947
Short Film Award Vol. 1: 21645
Short Film Festival Prize Vol. 2: 5162
Short-Form Award Vol. 1: 18444
Short Papers Evening Vol. 2: 7831
Short Play Awards Program Vol. 1: 12541
Short Stories-Concurso Literario Dr. Joao Isabel Vol. 2: 5475
Short Story Award Vol. 1: 15996
Short Story Contest
Affaire de Coeur Magazine Vol. 1: 247
Writers' Journal Vol 1: 22001
Short Story Dagger Vol. 2: 7370
Short Story of the Year Award Vol. 2: 338
Short Story Prize-Grande Premio da Cronica Vol. 2: 5476
Short Term Scientific Missions Vol. 2: 6164
Shorten Award; Sarah Vol. 1: 6944
Shotwell Memorial Award; Ambrose M. Vol. 1: 5342
Shousha Foundation Prize and Fellowship; Dr. A. T. Vol. 2: 6567
Show a Little Heart Vol. 1: 13351
Show Award Vol. 1: 7003
Show Awards Vol. 1: 10361
Show Canada Showmanship Awards Vol. 1: 13622
Show Flyer/Poster Contest Vol. 1: 9506
Show Hunter Ponies Awards Vol. 2: 7151
Show Me Award Vol. 1: 13527
Show Ponies Awards Vol. 2: 7152
Showcase for Excellence Awards Vol. 1: 1429
Shows Titles Vol. 2: 1131
Shri Dhanwantari Prize Vol. 2: 3514
SHRM Foundation Award for Graduate Student Research Vol. 1: 18703
SHRM Foundation Outstanding Graduate Student Award Vol. 1: 18704
Shrobehn Internship Program; AECT National Convention - Earl F. Vol. 1: 5351
Shryock Medal; Richard H. Vol. 1: 1062
Shubitz Award Vol. 1: 20992
Shull Award; Charles Albert Vol. 1: 4591
Shulman Book Prize; Marshall Vol. 1: 1058
Shulman Challenge Award; Neville Vol. 2: 8527
Shumavon Award; Leo Vol. 1: 14926
Shurgain Award for Excellence in Nutrition and MeatScience Vol. 1: 7445
Shy Award; G. Milton Vol. 1: 702
SIA Service Award Vol. 1: 18407
SIAD Medal Vol. 2: 7300
SIAM Activity Group on Optimization Prize Vol. 1: 18742
SIAM Prize in Numerical Analysis and Scientific Computing Vol. 1: 18748
Sibelius Violin Competition; International Jean Vol. 2: 1658
Sibert Informational Book Award; Robert F. Vol. 1: 5443
Sibley Fellowship; Mary Isabel Vol. 1: 17245
Sicher First Research Essay Award; Harry Vol. 1: 1322
SID Award (Store Interior Design Award) Vol. 1: 14401
Sidewalk Sale and Exhibition Vol. 1: 7776
Sidewise Awards for Alternate History Vol. 1: 18444
Sidey Medal and Prize; T. K. Vol. 2: 5086
Sidley Memorial Award; Dorothy Vol. 2: 7627
Sidmar Prize Vol. 2: 977
Sidney Griller Award Vol. 2: 8095
Sidney Poitier Fellowship Vol. 1: 6425
Siebold Award; Philipp Franz von Vol. 2: 3130
Siedenburg Award Vol. 1: 12972
Siefkes Justice Maker Award; Jim Vol. 1: 12996
Siegel Award; Robt. Vol. 1: 8357
Siegel Memorial Award; Joseph A. Vol. 1: 19170

Siegel Service Award; Joseph A. Vol. 1: 19170
Siemens Investigators Award Vol. 2: 7985
Siesel Award for Community Service; E. Hank Vol. 1: 15164
Sievers Trophy; Art Vol. 1: 15646
Sievert Award Vol. 2: 2501
SIG Excellence in Advanced Practice Award Vol. 1: 14318
SIG Leadership Award Vol. 1: 14318
SIG Member-of-The-Year Award Vol. 1: 4113
SIG-of-the-Year Award Vol. 1: 4114
SIGACT Distinguished Service Prize Vol. 1: 5318
Sigal Peace and Justice Scholarship; Dr. Phillip Vol. 1: 9187
Sigall Competition; International Musical Contest Dr. Luis Vol. 2: 1262
SIGCOMM Award Vol. 1: 5323
SIGCSE Award Vol. 1: 5321
Sight Award; Gift of Vol. 1: 9381
Sigma Delta Chi Awards Vol. 1: 19276
Sigma Diagnostics Student Scholarship Vol. 1: 15722
Sigma Iota Epsilon Scholarship Awards Vol. 1: 18485
Sigma Pi Sigma Undergraduate Research Award Vol. 1: 2839
SIGMOD Contributions Award Vol. 1: 5314
SIGMOD Innovations Award Vol. 1: 5313
Sigmund's Price Vol. 2: 1422
Sign Design Competition Vol. 1: 11905
Signal Poetry Award Vol. 2: 9138
Signal Service Award Vol. 1: 3057
Signature Membership Vol. 1: 17106
Signature of Excellence Award Vol. 1: 20967
Significant Achievement Award
  National Wildlife Rehabilitators Association Vol. 1: 15956
  Rotary International Vol 1: 18130
Signum Fidei Medal Vol. 1: 12635
Signy Foreign Fellowship; Gordon Vol. 2: 4328
SIGPLAN Distinguished Service Award Vol. 1: 5306
Sikkens Prize Vol. 2: 4907
Sikorsky Award for Humanitarian Service; Igor I. Vol. 1: 10405
Sikorsky International Trophy; Igor I. Vol. 1: 2439
Silas prisen Vol. 2: 1444
Silky Award; Fran Vol. 1: 17993
Silurian Excellence in Journalism Awards Vol. 1: 19327
Silva de Interpretacao Teatral; Premios Municipais Palmira Bastos e Antonio Vol. 2: 5441
Silva Service Award Vol. 1: 20727
Silver Anchor Vol. 2: 2470
Silver Anchor Award Vol. 1: 9819
Silver & Golden Brooms Vol. 2: 6105
Silver Anniversary Award Vol. 1: 14689
Silver Antelope Vol. 1: 6586
Silver Anvil Awards Vol. 1: 17724
Silver Apple Vol. 1: 8929
Silver Award
  National Association of Paralegals Vol. 2: 8158
  Tennis Association of Austria Vol 2: 788
Silver Ball Award Vol. 1: 18596
Silver Baton Award Vol. 1: 21730
Silver Beaver Vol. 1: 6587
Silver Berlin Bear Vol. 2: 2670
Silver Buffalo Award Vol. 1: 6588
Silver Combustion Medal Vol. 1: 8266
Silver Core Award Vol. 2: 741
Silver Crown Awards Vol. 1: 8232
Silver Dart Aviation History Award Vol. 1: 6960
The Silver Dirac Medal Vol. 2: 638
Silver Eagle Vol. 2: 9339
Silver Edelweiss Vol. 2: 6107
Silver Elephant Award Vol. 2: 3355
Silver-gilt Medal for Bibliography Vol. 2: 6859
Silver Good Citizenship Medal Vol. 1: 15783
Silver Hardhat Award Vol. 1: 8450
Silver Harp Vol. 2: 4725
Silver Hawk Award Vol. 1: 13090
Silver Helmet Award Vol. 1: 17962
Silver Irrigation Award Vol. 1: 420
Silver Jubilee Commemoration Medal Vol. 2: 3515
Silver Key Award Vol. 1: 14852
Silver Kisses Vol. 2: 4714
Silver Lifesaving Medal Vol. 1: 8838
Silver Magnolia Blossom Award Vol. 1: 8282
Silver Mailcoach Vol. 2: 8263
Silver Medal
  Acoustical Society of America Vol. 1: 144
  American Rhododendron Society Vol 1: 3852
  British Coatings Federation Vol 2: 6984
  The Gardeners of America/Men's Garden Clubs of America Vol 1: 9890
  Institute of Actuaries - United Kingdom Vol 2: 7645
  Institute of Materials Engineering Australasia Vol 2: 362
  National Vegetable Society Vol 2: 8203
  Royal Academy of Engineering Vol 2: 8370
  Royal Academy of Medicine in Ireland Vol 2: 3692
  Royal Aeronautical Society - United Kingdom Vol 2: 8401
  Royal Institute of Navigation Vol 2: 8601
  Scarab Club Vol 1: 18331
  Society of Economic Geologists Vol 1: 19110
  State Capital Global Law Firm Group Vol 1: 19766
  Tau Sigma Delta Vol 1: 19942
Silver Medal and Associate Fellowship of the Society Vol. 2: 253
Silver Medal Award
  Advertising Women of New York Vol. 1: 217
  American Advertising Federation Vol 1: 862
  Audio Engineering Society Vol 1: 6055
  Fertilizer Society of South Africa Vol 2: 5559
  National Student Campaign Against Hunger and Homelessness Vol 1: 15829
Silver Medal of Merit Vol. 1: 3336
Silver Medal of Outstanding Service Vol. 1: 14476
Silver Medallion Vol. 1: 6603
Silver Medallion Award Vol. 1: 4939
Silver Member Medal Vol. 1: 11165
Silver Memorial Award; Henry K. Vol. 1: 14323
Silver Otter Award Vol. 2: 7027
Silver Page Award Vol. 1: 4407
Silver Palette Award Vol. 1: 19099
Silver Pen Award Vol. 2: 7426
Silver Plaque Award Vol. 1: 15638
Silver Playwriting Competition; Dorothy Vol. 1: 10226
Silver Playwriting Competition Prize; Dorothy Vol. 1: 12336
Silver Quill Editorial Achievement Award Vol. 1: 4895
Silver Ram Award Vol. 2: 5593
Silver Ribbon Award to Outstanding Volunteer Vol. 1: 10001
Silver Ring Vol. 1: 7178
Silver Rope Award for Leadership Vol. 1: 503
Silver Rose Bowl Vol. 2: 4943
Silver Satellite Award Vol. 1: 9717
Silver Screen Award
  U.S. International Film and Video Festival Vol. 1: 20675
  US International Film and Video Festival Vol 1: 21143
The Silver Service Award Vol. 1: 3072
Silver Service/Silver Cup Awards Vol. 1: 14680
Silver Shadow Award Vol. 1: 17338
Silver Shell Awards Vol. 2: 6096
Silver Shovel Award Vol. 1: 11771
Silver Slugger Team Vol. 1: 19676
Silver Spike Vol. 2: 6112
Silver SPUR Awards Vol. 1: 18253
Silver Star for Bravery Vol. 1: 3579
Silver Star: Navy Vol. 1: 8839
Silver T-Square Vol. 1: 14592
Silver Torch Award Vol. 1: 14136
Silver Trowel Award Vol. 2: 6923
Silver Turnbuckle Award Vol. 2: 8402
Silver Wings Individual Awards Vol. 1: 5112
Silver Wings Unit Award Vol. 1: 5113
Silver World Award Vol. 1: 6589
Silverfish Review Poetry Chapbook Award Vol. 1: 18519
Silverman Award; Irving Vol. 1: 12120
Silverstein-Simeone Award Lecture Vol. 1: 11987
Silvert Award; Kalman Vol. 1: 12701
Sily Zbrojne w Sluzbie Ojczyzny Vol. 2: 5294
Sim Awards Vol. 2: 9265
Simionescu Award; Nicolae Vol. 2: 5865
Simkins Award; Francis B. Vol. 1: 19504
Simmonds Medal Vol. 2: 8569
Simmons First National Bank Grand Purchase Award Vol. 1: 5149
Simmons Short Fiction Award; John Vol. 1: 12192
Simms Medal Vol. 2: 9044
Simms Prize Vol. 2: 8403
Simms Scholar-Athlete Award; Robert A. Vol. 1: 15073
Simoes de Almeida de Escultura; Premio Municipal Jose Vol. 2: 5431
Simon/Anderson Publishing Outstanding Paper Award; William L. Vol. 1: 92
Simon Award Vol. 2: 7163
Simon Award; Fannie Vol. 1: 19560
Simon Award; George Vol. 1: 9570
Simon Award; Norma P. Vol. 1: 5862
Simon Children's Book Award; Charlie May Vol. 1: 5073
Simon Medal; Andre Vol. 2: 8015
Simon Memorial Prize Vol. 2: 7736
Simon Sherman Industry Service Award Vol. 1: 18598
Simonaviciaus premija; Kazimiero Vol. 2: 4397
Simons Prize; Harden- Vol. 1: 4043
Simonsen Lectureship Vol. 2: 8774

Simpers Award; Lucille Vol. 1: 2562
Simpson Medal; A. S. Romer - G. G. Vol. 1: 19356
Simpson Memorial Award; W. Arthur Vol. 1: 3119
Simpson Technical Editor's Award; Maurice Vol. 1: 10929
Sims Award Vol. 2: 6819
Sims Encouragement Fund Award for Work in the Comedic Arts; Tim Vol. 1: 16747
Simulation and Ground Testing Award Vol. 1: 2651
Sinclair Award; David Vol. 1: 957
Sinclaire Award; Matilda W. Vol. 1: 2284
Sinden Award Vol. 2: 8144
Singapore Literature Prize Vol. 2: 5941
Singer Award; Colonel Merton Vol. 1: 17997
Singer of the Year Vol. 1: 18442
Singer Prize Vol. 2: 7178
Singh Memorial Award; Harvans Vol. 2: 3577
Singh of Kalsia Memorial Cancer Research Award; Raja Ravi Sher Vol. 2: 3435
Single Parent of the Year Award Vol. 1: 17090
Sinha Memorial Award; Professor Umakant Vol. 2: 3543
Sinking Creek Film Celebration Vol. 1: 13758
Sintra; Prix Thomson Vol. 2: 2587
SIOP Awards Vol. 2: 7988
Sir Antony Fisher International Memorial Award Vol. 1: 6047
Sir Eric Rideal Lecture Vol. 2: 9024
Sir Joseph Burn Prize Vol. 2: 7648
Sir Lance Cross Vol. 2: 5029
Sisco Excellence in Teaching Award; John I. Vol. 1: 19525
Sise Outstanding Alpine Masters Award; Al Vol. 1: 20818
Sister Cities Expressions of Peace Youth Art Contest Vol. 1: 18534
Sister Irene Award Vol. 1: 16908
Sister Kenny Institute International Art Show for Artists with Disabilities Vol. 1: 13485
Sister Mary Arthur "Sharing the Light" Award Vol. 1: 6924
Sisyphus Award Vol. 1: 14759
SITPRO Prize Vol. 2: 7690
Sivickis premija; Pranciskaus Vol. 2: 4398
Sixteen One Frame Exhibit Vol. 1: 20935
Sixteenth Century Journal Literature Prize Vol. 1: 18545
Sixteenth Century Society and Conference Medal Vol. 1: 18546
Sixth Man Award Vol. 1: 14508
Sixty Year Membership Medal Vol. 1: 3258
Skanderbeg Medal Vol. 1: 416
Skeffington Award; A. M. Vol. 1: 8185
Skellerup Award Vol. 2: 4994
Skelnar Award; Joe Vol. 1: 10725
Skempton Medal Vol. 2: 7023
SKF Award Vol. 2: 9362
Ski Jumping/Nordic Combined Coach of the Year Vol. 1: 20819
Ski Magazine Cup Vol. 1: 20820
Skier of the Year
International Ski Federation Vol. 2: 6447
Ski Racing - Inside Communications Inc. Vol 1: 18548
Skier/Snowboarding Development Recognition Award Vol. 1: 7396
Skiing Magazine Development Cup Vol. 1: 20821
SkillsUSA Championships Vol. 1: 18552
Skinner Award; Clarence R. Vol. 1: 20312
Skinner Award; Constance Lindsay Vol. 1: 21800
Skinner Award; Morris F. Vol. 1: 19358
Skinner Memorial Fund Award Vol. 1: 2258
Skinner New Researcher Award; B. F. Vol. 1: 3657
Skinner Sermon Award Vol. 1: 20312
Skolnik Award; Herman Vol. 1: 1787
Skolnok Award; Tillmanns- Vol. 1: 1788
Skrzypek Award; Alexander J. Vol. 1: 10685
SLA Meckler Award for Innovations in Technology Vol. 1: 19551
Slack Award for Excellence; Pamela Vol. 1: 13372
Slade Prize; Ivan Vol. 2: 7179
Slager sezone Vol. 2: 1135
Slagle Lectureship; Eleanor Clarke Vol. 1: 3301
Slate - MacDaniels Award Vol. 1: 16441
Slates Memorial Award; Philip Vol. 1: 19471
Slatter Memorial Volunteer of the Year Award Vol. 1: 18417
Slattery Marketing Awards; J. Desmond Vol. 1: 20172
Slavescu Award; Victor Vol. 2: 5866
Sledz - Lou Wener Community Service Award in Washington, DC; Carroll Vol. 1: 10593
Sleeks Prize; Ary Vol. 2: 964
Slessor Prize; Kenneth Vol. 2: 480
Slichter Award; William P. Vol. 1: 20482
Slick 50 Pro Series Vol. 1: 11757
Sliffe Awards for Distinguished Junior High and High School Mathematics Teaching; Edyth May Vol. 1: 13197
Slipper Gold Medal; Stanley Vol. 1: 7490
Slipstream's Annual Poetry Chapbook Contest Vol. 1: 18556
Sloam Memorial Award; Norman J. Vol. 2: 9235
Sloan, Jr. Medal; Alfred P. Vol. 1: 9922
Sloan Public Service Awards of the Fund for the City of New York Vol. 1: 9834
Slocum Award Vol. 1: 12435
Slote Award; Bernice Vol. 1: 17516
Slovak Studies Association Prize Vol. 1: 18558
Smail Memorial Piano Award; Mary Winston Vol. 1: 21433
Small and Commercial Print Division Awards Vol. 1: 17293
Small and Disadvantaged Business Award Vol. 1: 390
Small Animal Practitioner Award Vol. 1: 7536
Small Business Advocates of the Year Vol. 1: 20834
Small Business Exporter of the Year Vol. 1: 20835
Small Business Person of the Year Vol. 1: 18562
Small Business Person of Year Vol. 1: 21614
Small Craft Group Medal Vol. 2: 8619
Small Ecological Project Grants Vol. 2: 7012
Small Firms Merit Awards for Research and Technology Vol. 2: 9166
Small Memorial Award; Ben John Vol. 1: 8443
Small Project Grants Vol. 2: 9169
Small Research Grants Program Vol. 1: 10585
Small Retailer of the Year Award Vol. 1: 15639
Small Town America Hall of Fame Vol. 1: 14445
Smallreed Award; John Hervey Broadcasters' Awards; George Vol. 1: 20877
SMART Vol. 2: 9167
SMART Awards Vol. 2: 9166
Smart Competition; Harold Vol. 2: 8670
Smarties Prize for Children's Books Vol. 2: 6882
SME Education Foundation Family Scholarship Award Vol. 1: 19171
SME Fellow Vol. 1: 19172
SME Progress Award Vol. 1: 19169
SME Research Medal Vol. 1: 19173
Smedley Memorial Award; Glenn Vol. 1: 3259
Smelik/IBBY Prize; Jenny Vol. 2: 4801
Smelik-Kiggenprijs; Jenny Vol. 2: 4801
SMFA Brass Award Vol. 1: 18312
The SMFA Intermediate Brass Scholarship Vol. 1: 18310
The SMFA Intermediate Percussion Scholarship Vol. 1: 18311
SMFA Past President's Brass Scholarship Vol. 1: 18312
The SMFA Senior Percussion Scholarship Vol. 1: 18313
The SMFA Senior Speech Arts Scholarship Vol. 1: 18278
The SMFA Senior Woodwind Scholarship Vol. 1: 18273
Smiley Memorial Award; Gordon Vol. 1: 19711
Smissman-Bristol-Myers-Squibb Award Vol. 1: 1789
Smith; ASCP Distinguished Pathology Educator Award Honoring H. P. Vol. 1: 3970
Smith Award; Adam Vol. 1: 5818
Smith Award; Arthur Vol. 2: 2496
Smith Award; Daniel B. Vol. 1: 3399
Smith Award for Submarine Support Achievement; Levering Vol. 1: 16056
Smith Award; Georgina Vol. 1: 1467
Smith Award; Horton Vol. 1: 17620
Smith Award; I. W. Vol. 1: 7432
Smith Award; Isabel and Monroe Vol. 1: 10567
Smith Award; Job Lewis Vol. 1: 797
Smith Award; Mary Jacobs Vol. 1: 18442
Smith Award; Merriam Vol. 1: 21604
Smith Award; Nila Banton Vol. 1: 11875
Smith Award; NZSA Lilian Ida Vol. 2: 5031
Smith Award; Reginald Heber Vol. 1: 15339
Smith Award; Robert M. Vol. 1: 798
Smith Award; Roger C. Vol. 1: 5863
Smith Award; Wilbur S. Vol. 1: 4357
Smith Awards; Edward A. Vol. 1: 13396
Smith Awards for Science Promotion; Michael Vol. 1: 16024
Smith Book Awards; Lillian Vol. 1: 19521
Smith Breeden Prizes Vol. 1: 2244
Smith Distinguished Transportation Educator Award; Wilbur S. Vol. 1: 11055
Smith Fellowship; Alice E. Vol. 1: 21678
Smith Fellowships; Al Vol. 1: 12562
Smith Free Enterprise Award; Adam Vol. 1: 2960
Smith Hydraulic Fellowship; J. Waldo Vol. 1: 4358
Smith Medal; Blakely Vol. 1: 19213
Smith Medal; Gilbert Morgan Vol. 1: 13847
Smith Medal; H. G. Vol. 2: 519

Smith Medal in Anthropology; Percy Vol. 2: 5095
Smith Medal; J. Lawrence Vol. 1: 13848
Smith Medal; Julian C. Vol. 1: 9274
Smith Medal; Waldo E. Vol. 1: 2358
Smith Medal; William Vol. 2: 7566
Smith Memorial Vol. 1: 12015
Smith Memorial Award; Dale Vol. 1: 1114
Smith Memorial Award; H. G. Vol. 2: 519
Smith Memorial Award; Howard DeWitt Vol. 1: 5988
Smith Memorial Exhibit Award; Sidney W. Vol. 1: 3260
Smith Memorial Medal; S. G. Vol. 2: 9128
Smith National Award; Sidney O. Vol. 1: 10738
Smith Playwriting Award; Jean Kennedy Vol. 1: 12548
Smith Practice Excellence Award; Daniel B. Vol. 1: 3399
Smith Prize; Rufus Z. Vol. 1: 5283
Smith Research Award; Bob Vol. 2: 8286
Smith Research Fellowships; Sir Frederick Vol. 2: 8497
Smith Sr. Award; Bruce Vol. 1: 93
Smith Solo Performance Competition; Ellsworth Vol. 1: 12099
Smith - U.S. Water Polo Award; James R. "Jimmy" Vol. 1: 20885
Smithers Award; R. Brinkley Vol. 1: 14853
Smithson Society Founder Medal; James Vol. 1: 18569
Smithson Society Grants; James Vol. 1: 18570
Smithsonian Craft Show Vol. 1: 18574
Smithsonian Institution Fellowship Program Vol. 1: 18572
Smokies of the Seas Award Vol. 1: 20929
Smolar Award for Excellence in North American Jewish Journalism; Boris Vol. 1: 2909
Smoluchowski Medal; Marian Vol. 2: 5367
Smoot Organizational Meritorious Award; Willie Vol. 1: 14524
Smyth Salver Vol. 2: 8039
Smyth Statesman Award; Henry DeWolf Vol. 1: 16594
Smythe International Service Citation; Hugh H. and Mable M. Vol. 1: 11155
Smythe Trophy; D. Verner Vol. 1: 20784
Smythies Award; Jill Vol. 2: 8074
SNC-Lavalin Plant Design Competition Vol. 1: 7848
Snedecor Award; George W.
American Statistical Association Vol. 1: 4695
Committee of Presidents of Statistical Societies Vol 1: 8295
Snell Premium Vol. 2: 7808
Snelling Economic Development Award; Richard A. Vol. 1: 5246
Sniadecki Medal; Jedrzej Vol. 2: 5340
Snively Memorial Award; Dr. George G. Vol. 1: 19712
Snodgrass Memorial Research Award Vol. 1: 9285
Snow Academic Travel Scholarship Vol. 2: 6605
Snow Award; Roland B. Vol. 1: 1698
Snow Early Career Award in Educational Psychology; Richard E. Vol. 1: 3679
Snow Foundation Prize; John Ben Vol. 1: 16415
Snow Prize; John Ben Vol. 1: 19882
Snowmobile Excellence Award Vol. 1: 7060
SNS-Limburg Prize Vol. 2: 1121
Snyder Award; Anne D. Vol. 1: 8056
Snyder Award; Walter F. Vol. 1: 16584
Soaring Hall of Fame Vol. 1: 18588
Sober Award; Herbert Vol. 1: 3923
SOCAN Awards for Young Composers Vol. 1: 18593
Soccer Coach of the Year Vol. 1: 7232
Soccer Outstanding Service Award Vol. 1: 575
Social Action Leadership Award Vol. 1: 20317
Social Activist of the Year Award Vol. 1: 253
Social & Technical Awards Vol. 2: 9259
Social Inventions Prizes Vol. 2: 7638
Social Issues Dissertation Award Vol. 1: 18888
Social Justice Award Vol. 1: 21561
Social Research, Policy & Practice Student Research Award Vol. 1: 9999
Social Science Prize Vol. 2: 4558
Social Science Prize of the American Academy Vol. 1: 621
Social Service Award Vol. 2: 3592
Social Studies Programs of Excellence Vol. 1: 14789
Social Worker of the Year; Public Citizen of the Year Vol. 1: 14393
Society Awards for Journal Articles Vol. 2: 7942
Society Citation Vol. 1: 10793
Society Diplomas Vol. 2: 7539
Society for Analytical Chemistry Silver Medal Vol. 2: 8775
Society for In Vitro Biology Student Travel Awards Vol. 1: 18724
Society for Italic Handwriting Award Vol. 2: 8938
Society for Research into Higher Education Awards Vol. 2: 8948
Society for the Psychological Study of Lesbian and Gay Issues Distinguished Student Award Vol. 1: 18918
Society for the Study of Inborn Errors of Metabolism Award Vol. 2: 8959
Society of Analytical Chemistry Gold Medal Vol. 2: 8776
Society of Antiquaries of London Gold Medal Vol. 2: 8965
Society of Applied Botany Honorary Member Vol. 2: 3062
Society of Australasian Specialists/Oceania Medals Vol. 1: 19031
Society of Authors Travelling Scholarships Vol. 2: 8991
Society of Children's Book Writers and Illustrators Grants Vol. 1: 19089
Society of Cosmetic Chemists Awards Vol. 1: 19095
Society of Designer Craftsmen Award Vol. 2: 9028
Society of Dyers and Colourists Honorary Fellow Vol. 2: 9037
Society of Dyers and Colourists Honorary Member Vol. 2: 9038
Society of Engineers President's Medal Vol. 2: 9045
Society of Engineers Prizes Vol. 2: 9046
Society of Exploration Geophysicists of Japan Award Vol. 2: 4298
Society of Midland Authors Awards Vol. 1: 19186
Society of Municipal Arborists Awards Vol. 1: 19203
Society of Ornamental Turners President's Cup Vol. 2: 9073
Society of Petroleum Engineers of AIME Distinguished Service Award Vol. 1: 19238
Society of Shipping Executives Education Trust Prize Vol. 2: 7690
Society of South African Geographers Bronze Medal Vol. 2: 5639
Society of South African Geographers Fellow Vol. 2: 5640
Society of South African Geographers Gold Medal Vol. 2: 5641
Society of West End Theatre Vol. 2: 9057
Society of Women Musicians Prize Vol. 2: 8643
Society's Medal Vol. 2: 544
Society's Medal and Lecture Vol. 2: 9025
Socio Colabrador Vol. 2: 33
Soderberg Scholarship Vol. 1: 17000
Soderbergs Pris Vol. 2: 6220
Soderstrom Gold Medal Vol. 2: 6221
Soderstromska Medaljen I guld Vol. 2: 6221
Soest Preis; Konrad von Vol. 2: 3018
Soffer Research Awards; Alfred Vol. 1: 1843
Sofia de Investigacion sobre prevencion de las deficiencias; Premio Reina Vol. 2: 6033
Software and Micromouse Competition Vol. 2: 5292
Software Process Achievement Award Vol. 1: 10900
Software System Award Vol. 1: 5307
Soil Science Applied Research Award Vol. 1: 19394
Soil Science Distinguished Service Award Vol. 1: 19395
Soil Science Education Award Vol. 1: 19396
Soil Science Professional Service Award Vol. 1: 19397
Soil Science Research Award Vol. 1: 19398
Sojourners ROTC Awards Vol. 1: 15787
Sokhey Award; Maj. Gen. Saheb Singh Vol. 2: 3436
Solberg Award Vol. 1: 4571
Soldier; Frederick Award for Outstanding - Major General Robert F. Frederick Award Vol. 1: 9562
Solid-State Circuits Award Vol. 1: 10881
Solid Waste Manager of the Year Vol. 1: 16270
Solidarity Award for Lifetime Contribution to the Labor Movement Vol. 1: 21681
Solidarity of Educational Credit Order Vol. 2: 1333
Solidarity Prize Vol. 1: 21858
Sollenberger Trophy (Leading Scorer - Regular Season); John B. Vol. 1: 2518
Sollmann Award in Pharmacology; Torald Vol. 1: 4175
Solo Competition Vol. 1: 16813
Solo Driver of Eminence Award Vol. 1: 19713
Solo I Event of the Year Award Vol. 1: 19714
Solo II Cup Vol. 1: 19715
Solo II Divisional of the Year Award Vol. 1: 19716
Solo II Driver of Eminence Award Vol. 1: 19717
Solo II Driver of the Year Vol. 1: 19717
Solo II Rookie of the Year Vol. 1: 19718
Solomon Award; King Vol. 1: 599
Solomon Memorial Award; Joel Vol. 1: 1115

Solomon Prize Vol. 2: 3734
Solomon Schechter Award Vol. 1: 20902
Soloviev Medal; Sergey Vol. 2: 2317
Solti International Young Conductors Competition; George Vol. 1: 19429
Soltz Medal; Vilmos Vol. 2: 3260
Somaini; Premio Triennale per la Fisica Francesco Vol. 2: 3932
Sommer Award; Ralph F. Vol. 1: 1194
Sommerfeld Preis; Arnold Vol. 2: 2667
Sommers Award; Ben Vol. 1: 8743
Sommerville Prize; Helen Vol. 2: 7679
Somogyi-Sendroy Award Vol. 1: 1001
Son Diabetes Educator Award; Allene Von Vol. 1: 1189
Song Award; John S. Vol. 1: 18728
Song Foundation Award for Plant Tissue Culture; John S. Vol. 1: 18728
Song of the Year Vol. 1: 11424
Songwriter of the Year
  Dallas Songwriters Association Vol. 1: 8720
  Nashville Songwriters Association International Vol 1: 13760
Songwriters Hall of Fame Vol. 1: 13816
Songwriting Award Vol. 2: 8152
Sonnenwirth Award for Leadership in Clinical Microbiology; bioMerieux Vol. 1: 4131
Sonnenwirth Memorial Award Vol. 1: 4131
Sonnichsen Book Award; C. L. Vol. 1: 20048
Sonning Music Award; Leonie Vol. 2: 1538
Sonning Prize Vol. 2: 1540
Sonnings Musikpris; Leonie Vol. 2: 1538
Sonntag Award; Al Vol. 1: 19349
Sons of Martha Medal Vol. 1: 17606
Sons of Norway Jumping Award Vol. 1: 20822
Sontheime Award Vol. 1: 4769
Sony Radio Awards Vol. 2: 9094
Soper Award for Excellence in Health Literature; Fred L. Vol. 1: 17060
Soper Award; Lord Vol. 2: 8047
Soper Lecture; Fred L. Vol. 1: 4633
SOPO Award for Outstanding Achievement in Procurement Vol. 2: 9076
Sorantin Award for Young Artists; Hemphill-Wells Vol. 1: 18237
Sorantin Young Artist Award Vol. 1: 18237
Sorby Medal Vol. 2: 910
Soria; Premio Miguel F. Vol. 2: 22
Sorokin Lecture Vol. 1: 4653
Soroptimist International of the South West Pacific Awards Vol. 2: 595
Sorum Awards; Assembly William Vol. 1: 3638
Sosman Memorial Lecture Award Vol. 1: 1699
Souder Award; Wilmer Vol. 1: 11217
Soul Train Music Awards Vol. 1: 19423
Source Awards Vol. 1: 19425
Sousa Prize in Conducting Vol. 1: 19429
South African Academy of Science and Arts Literary Prize Vol. 2: 5657
South African Academy of Science and Arts Medal of Honor Vol. 2: 5660
South African Association for the Advancement of Science Certificate of Merit Vol. 2: 5775
South African Association of Botanists Junior Medal for Botany Vol. 2: 5674
South African Association of Botanists Senior Medal for Botany Vol. 2: 5675
South African Broadcasting Corporation Prize Vol. 2: 5686
South African Chemical Institute Gold Medal Vol. 2: 5696
South African Defence Force Champion Shot Medal Vol. 2: 5753
South African Defence Force Good Service Medal Vol. 2: 5754
South African Institute of Architects Award for Excellence Vol. 2: 5701
South African Institute of Architects Award of Merit Vol. 2: 5702
South African Institute of Architects Gold Medal for Architecture Vol. 2: 5703
South African Institute of Architects Medal of Distinction Vol. 2: 5704
South African Institute of Architects Rome Scholarship in Architecture Vol. 2: 7143
South African Institute of Electrical Engineers Awards Vol. 2: 5706
South African Medal Vol. 2: 5776
South African Medal for Botany Vol. 2: 5676
South African Sports Merit Award Vol. 2: 5614
South African Sugar Technologists' Association Gold Medal Vol. 2: 5764
South African Veterinary Association Gold Medal Vol. 2: 5770
South Asia Foreign Language and Area Studies Fellowships Vol. 1: 21119
South Atlantic Review Essay Prize Vol. 1: 19438
South California Educator of the Year Award Vol. 1: 7955
Southcomb Award; Kenneth W. Vol. 1: 13091
Southeastern Librarian Wilson Award Vol. 1: 19480
Southern Africa Medal Vol. 2: 5755
Southern African Society for Plant Pathology Fellow Vol. 2: 5779
Southern African Society for Plant Pathology Honorary Member Vol. 2: 5780
Southern Books Competition Vol. 1: 19481
Southern Cross Decoration Vol. 2: 5756
Southern Cross Medal Vol. 2: 5757
Southern Journalism Award Vol. 1: 10838
Southgate Award Vol. 1: 20851
Southwest Asia Service Medal Vol. 1: 8840
Southwest Fine Arts Competition Vol. 1: 13690
Southwest Juried Exhibition Vol. 1: 13690
Southwest Regional Beefalo Show Vol. 1: 1557
Southwick Memorial Award in Aviculture; Justin A. Vol. 1: 12138
Souza Award; Felipa da Vol. 1: 11647
Sovereign Award Vol. 1: 12396
Soviet Jewry Freedom Awards Vol. 1: 16060
Sower Award Vol. 1: 16066
SP USA Award Vol. 1: 18226
Spaatz Trophy Vol. 1: 15176
Space Achievement Award Vol. 1: 20843
Space Achievement Medal Vol. 2: 7055
Space Coast Writers Guild Conference Awards Vol. 1: 19535
Space Flight Award; AAS Vol. 1: 1498
Space Flight Medal Vol. 1: 13900
Space Grant Fellowship Program Vol. 1: 9622
Space Imaging Award for Application of High Resolution Digital Satellite Imagery Vol. 1: 5225
Space Operations and Support Award Vol. 1: 2692
Space Simulation Award Vol. 1: 10930
Space Technology Hall of Fame Vol. 1: 20844
Spacecraft Design Award Vol. 1: 2670
Spacelabs/AAMI Annual Meeting Research-Manuscript Award Vol. 1: 5486
Spacu Prize; Gheorghe Vol. 2: 5867
Spalding Player of the Year Vol. 1: 14084
Spanos Best Graduate Student Paper Award; Nicholas P. Vol. 1: 3762
Sparks Medal; Ben C. Vol. 1: 4546
Sparks-Thomas Award Vol. 1: 1790
Sparks Tutoring Award; G'anne Vol. 1: 6466
Sparlin Award; Ezra M Vol. 1: 10739
Sparreska Priset Vol. 2: 6222
Speaker Hall of Fame; Council of Peers Award for Excellence/ Vol. 1: 15792
Spearman Medal Vol. 2: 7126
Speas Airport Award; AIAA Jay Hollingsworth Vol. 1: 2693
Special Achievement Award
  Association of Government Accountants Vol. 1: 5721
  Aviation Week & Space Technology Vol 1: 6138
  Health Science Communications Association Vol 1: 10332
  National Council of Social Security Management Associations Vol 1: 14822
  National Telecommunications Cooperative Association Vol 1: 15866
  Philalethes Society Vol 1: 17267
  Plastic Surgery Educational Foundation Vol 1: 17388
Special Achievement Awards
  Academy of Motion Picture Arts and Sciences Vol. 1: 113
  American Psychological Association - Psychologists in Public Service Division (Division 18) Vol 1: 3699
Special Achievement - Man/Woman of the Year Vol. 1: 12257
Special Act Award Vol. 1: 15381
Special Ad Hoc Awards Vol. 1: 12955
Special Agency Awards Vol. 1: 11765
Special Award
  AIIM - The Enterprise Content Management Association Vol. 1: 314
  American Psychological Association - Society for Community Research and Action: Division of Community Psychology (Division 27) Vol 1: 3720
  American Society for Information Science and Technology Vol 1: 4115
  International Magnesium Association Vol 1: 11740
  International Veteran Boxers Association Vol 1: 12121
  National Association for Interpretation Vol 1: 14024
  National Association of Diaconate Directors Vol 1: 14192
  National Legal Aid and Defender Association Vol 1: 15338
  PhotoImaging Manufacturers and Distributors Association Vol 1: 17299
  Polish Physical Society Vol 2: 5368
  Psychological Society Ireland Vol 2: 3682
Special Award for Dedicated Service Vol. 1: 13772
Special Award of Stelvio National Park Vol. 2: 3970
Special Award or Citation to Institutions and Individuals Vol. 1: 20968

Special Awards
American Association of Petroleum Geologists Vol. 1: 1351
Association of Engineering Geologists Vol 1: 5678
Avon Books - HarperCollins Publishers Inc. Vol 1: 6143
Georgia Agricultural Commodity Commission for Peanuts Vol 1: 9967
Health Science Communications Association Vol 1: 10333
Journalism Education Association Vol 1: 12453
New England Theatre Conference Vol 1: 16128
United States Harness Writers' Association Vol 1: 20631
Special Awards Established by the President Vol. 1: 9366
Special Awards of Honor Vol. 1: 11766
Special Board Recognition Award Vol. 1: 9253
Special Breed Master Judge Vol. 1: 15504
Special Certificate Vol. 1: 11121
Special Certificate of Appreciation Vol. 1: 4796
Special Christopher Awards Vol. 1: 7971
Special Citation Award Vol. 1: 2851
Special Citation in Honor of Rudy and Hertha Benjamin Vol. 1: 3443
Special Citation in Journalism Vol. 1: 6213
Special Citations
American Academy of Periodontology Vol. 1: 811
National Press Photographers Association Vol 1: 15547
Special Commendation Award Vol. 1: 6081
Special Contributor Award Vol. 1: 1180
Special Distinguished & Outstanding Service Award Vol. 1: 4081
Special Educational Merit Award for Women Vol. 1: 12078
Special Focus Awards Vol. 1: 6676
Special Gold Medal Vol. 1: 15159
Special Grand Prix of the Jury Vol. 1: 13607
Special Honor Award Vol. 2: 3596
Special Innovation Award Vol. 1: 10999
Special Jubilee Awards Vol. 2: 9354
Special Jury Award Vol. 2: 6096
Special Jury Prize Vol. 1: 16957
Special Legend Awards Vol. 1: 15927
Special Medals for Fitness Achievement Vol. 1: 11591
Special Merit Citation Vol. 1: 2913
Special National Geographic Society Award Vol. 1: 15161
Special NJCAA Awards Vol. 1: 15316
Special President's Award of Merit Vol. 1: 1435
Special Prize Vol. 2: 4059
Special Prize in Memoriam of Rainer Werner Fassbinder Vol. 2: 2963
Special Recognition Vol. 2: 56
Special Recognition and Presidential Awards Vol. 1: 15242
Special Recognition Award
American Camping Association Vol. 1: 1630
American College of Preventive Medicine Vol 1: 1933
American Meat Science Association Vol 1: 3058
Asian American Journalists Association Vol 1: 5167
Asphalt Recycling and Reclaiming Association Vol 1: 5206
Association for Research in Vision and Ophthalmology Vol 1: 5468
Canadian Athletic Therapists Association Vol 1: 6950
Canadian Mental Health Association Vol 1: 7273
Christians Concerned for Racial Equality Vol 1: 7969
Inventors Clubs of America Vol 1: 12164
Lamaze International Vol 1: 12678
Leukemia and Lymphoma Society Vol 1: 12795
National Association of Conservation Districts Vol 1: 14159
Western-English Trade Association Vol 1: 21547
Special Recognition Awards
National Agricultural Center and Hall of Fame Vol. 1: 13914
Society for Information Display Vol 1: 18771
Special Recognition Citation Vol. 1: 12071
Special Recognition for Excellence in Public Relations Vol. 1: 19552
Special Recreation Awards Vol. 1: 19573
Special Recreation for Disabled Awards Vol. 1: 19573
Special Recreation for People with Disabilities Awards Vol. 1: 19573
Special Service/Achievement Awards Vol. 1: 18471
Special Service Award
American Association of Avian Pathologists Vol. 1: 1089
College Gymnastics Association Vol 1: 8164
International Reading Association Vol 1: 11876
National Association of Conservation Districts Vol 1: 14160
National Intramural-Recreational Sports Association Vol 1: 15292
North American Die Casting Association Vol 1: 16432
Special Service Awards
National Small-Bore Rifle Association Vol. 2: 8200
South East Chicago Commission Vol 1: 19456
Special Service Awards (Citations) Vol. 1: 19012
Special Service Citation Vol. 1: 2694
Special Services Award Vol. 1: 17844
Special Student Awards Vol. 1: 1495
Specialist Award Vol. 2: 9060
Specialist Awards Vol. 2: 7615
Specialists in Blood Banking Scholarship Awards Vol. 1: 1116
Specialized Pharmaceutical Services; Distinguished Achievement Award in Vol. 1: 3384
Specialty Book of the Year Vol. 1: 6994
Specialty Bookseller of the Year Award Vol. 1: 6995
Spectator/Highland Park Parliamentarian of the Year Awards Vol. 2: 9097
Spector Award; Beryl Vol. 1: 17705
Spectrum Award Vol. 1: 21940
Spectrum Awards Design Competition Vol. 1: 2326
Spectrum of Aviation Vol. 2: 7579
Spedding Award; Frank H. Vol. 1: 16601
Speed and Figure Skating Championships Vol. 2: 6445
Speedo/USMS Coach of the Year Award Vol. 1: 20692
Speedy Award Vol. 1: 17072
Speirs Award; Doris Huestis Vol. 1: 19080
Speiss Award; Ray H. Vol. 1: 4044
Speller Award; Frank Newman Vol. 1: 13746
Speller Award; Thomas H. Vol. 1: 19056
Spellman Award; Cardinal Vol. 1: 7662
Spellman Jazz Masters Award; A. B. Vol. 1: 14931
Spelvin Award; George Vol. 1: 13143
Spence Trophy; G. M. Vol. 2: 5068
Spencer Artistic Achievement Award; Sara Vol. 1: 893
Spencer Award; Beulah K. Vol. 1: 471
Spencer Award; William I. Vol. 1: 22097
Spencer Best After Dinner Speaker of the Year; Ivor Vol. 2: 7585
Spencer Memorial Award; The Norman Vol. 2: 5008
Spencer Postdoctoral Fellowship Program; NAE/ Vol. 1: 13803
Speropolus Sportsmanship Award; Nick Vol. 1: 21510
Sperry Award; AIAA Lawrence Vol. 1: 2695
Sperry Award; Elmer A. Vol. 1: 19057
Sperry Founder Award; Albert F. Vol. 1: 12222
Sperry Young Achievement Award; Lawrence Vol. 1: 2695
Spes Hominum Award Vol. 1: 16585
Speyer Memorial Prize; Ellin P. Vol. 1: 13799
SPFD, MO Labor Council, AFL-CIO Endowment Fund Vol. 1: 19738
SPHE International Packaging and Handling Design Competition Vol. 1: 11023
SPHE Packaging Competition Vol. 1: 11023
SPI Structural Foam Division Annual Recognition Award Vol. 1: 19320
SPIE Technology Achievement Award Vol. 1: 19611
Spielvogel Award; Carl Vol. 1: 16981
Spiers Memorial Lecture and Prize Vol. 2: 8777
Spingarn Medal Vol. 1: 14050
Spink Award; J. G. Taylor Vol. 1: 14496
Spinoza Award Vol. 1: 20923
Spiral of Life Award Vol. 1: 12796
Spirit Award
Amateur Athletic Union Vol. 1: 576
International Ticketing Association Vol 1: 12086
Spirit of America Award
National Council for the Social Studies Vol. 1: 14790
United Way of America Vol 1: 20904
The Spirit of America Award Vol. 1: 4925
Spirit of Broadcasting Award Vol. 1: 14118
Spirit of Caring Award Vol. 1: 7762
Spirit of Education Award; Harold Hammerman Vol. 1: 14434
Spirit of Fighting Awards Vol. 2: 4134
Spirit of Flight Award Vol. 1: 14473
Spirit of Hospice Award Vol. 1: 12185
Spirit of Hospice Awards Vol. 1: 16173
Spirit of Saint Louis Award Vol. 1: 18218
Spirit of St. Louis Medal Vol. 1: 4547
Spiritus Awards Vol. 1: 11451
Spitler Memorial Award; Gary Vol. 1: 14293
Spivack Volunteer Service Award; Martin Vol. 1: 6606

Split Summer Festival Vol. 2: 1378
Splitsko ljeto Vol. 2: 1378
Spokesperson for Agriculture Vol. 1: 16005
Sport Australia Hall of Fame Vol. 2: 602
Sport in Society Hall of Fame Vol. 1: 7756
Sporting Art Award; AAEA Vol. 1: 658
Sporting Goods Agents Hall of Fame Vol. 1: 19638
The Sporting News Man of the Year Vol. 1: 19679
The Sporting News NFL Player of the Year Vol. 1: 19677
The Sporting News/NFL Rookie of the Year Vol. 1: 19678
The Sporting News Sportsman of the Year Vol. 1: 19679
Sportive et Sportif Europeen de l'Annee Vol. 2: 6147
Sports and Recreation Award Vol. 1: 17073
Sports Emmy Awards Vol. 1: 13865
Sports Illustrated Sportsman/Sportswoman of the Year Vol. 1: 19730
Sports Korosha Vol. 2: 4322
Sports Legend of the Year Award Vol. 1: 4682
Sports Lifetime Achievement Award Vol. 1: 13865
Sports Ministries Award Vol. 1: 14665
Sports Personality of the Year Award Vol. 1: 4683
Sports Philatelists International Awards Vol. 1: 19732
SportsCar Awards Vol. 1: 19719
SportsMan and SportsWoman of the Year Vol. 1: 20723
Sportsman/Sportswoman of the Year Vol. 1: 11496
Sportswoman of the Year Award Vol. 1: 21777
Sportswomen of the Year Awards Vol. 1: 21811
Spot News Photo Award Vol. 1: 16250
Spot News Video Award Vol. 1: 16251
Spotton Award for Best Canadian Short Film; NFB - John Vol. 1: 20117
Spowers Marketing Award; Gale M. Vol. 1: 17528
Sprague Memorial Award; Joseph A. Vol. 1: 15548
Spraragen Memorial Membership Award; William Vol. 1: 4896
Spray Trophy Vol. 1: 12436
Sprengel Agronomic Research Award; Carl Vol. 1: 4248
Sprent Prize; John Frederick Adrian Vol. 2: 268
Spriestersbach Award for Excellence in Teaching; The Barbara Vol. 1: 16671
Spring Art Founder Award; John Vol. 1: 15698
Spring Conference Scholarships Vol. 1: 8211
Springbok Radio Sarie Awards Vol. 2: 5687
Springer Award; Bonnie J. Vol. 1: 5113
Springer Award; Fred Vol. 1: 3365
Springer Award; LT GEN. Robert D. Vol. 1: 5112
Springer Award; Russell S. Vol. 1: 19058
SPRINT UK Street Luge Championship Vol. 2: 9110
Sprinter of the Year Vol. 1: 21244
SPRITE undergraduate summer research Vol. 1: 7708
Sprogprisen Vol. 2: 1453
Sproule Award (Aviation Maintenance Marine of the Year); Willie D. Vol. 1: 13092
Sproule Memorial Award; J. C. "CAM" Vol. 1: 1352
Sproule Memorial Plaque; J.C. Vol. 1: 7204
Sprout Award; Harold and Margaret Vol. 1: 12048
Spruance Safety Award; William W. Vol. 1: 15176
Spruce Award; Richard Vol. 1: 11293
Spruiell Medical Field Training Excersize Planner Award; Colonel Thomas L. Vol. 1: 5784
SPUR Vol. 2: 9167
Spur Awards Vol. 1: 21576
Spurgeon III Award; William H. Vol. 1: 6590
Squibb Award Vol. 1: 10790
Squibb Pan American Award; Doctor Vol. 1: 6628
Squire Award; James R. Vol. 1: 14841
Squire Distinguished Resident Award in Diagnostic Radiology; Lucy Frank Vol. 1: 1074
Squires Memorial Senior Chopin Scholarhip; Blanche Vol. 1: 18314
Squires Memorial Senior Pipe Organ Scholarship; The Blanche Vol. 1: 18315
Squires Memorial Woodwind Award; The Blanche Vol. 1: 18316
SRE Certificate of Excellence Vol. 1: 19290
SRE Certificate of Recognition Vol. 1: 19291
SRE Stan Ofsthun Award Vol. 1: 19292
Srinivasa Ramanujan Medal Vol. 2: 3516
Srivastav Award in the Field of Virology; Dr. J. B. Vol. 2: 3437
Srivastava Foundation Award; Prof. B. C. Vol. 2: 3438
S.S. Kosmos and Damian Award Vol. 1: 16910
St-Laurent Award of Excellence; Louis Vol. 1: 6975
STA Fellowship Vol. 2: 4260
Staatpreis fur Holzmarketing Vol. 2: 699
Staatpreis fur Vorbildliche Verpackung Vol. 2: 695
Staats Award; Elmer Vol. 1: 5722
Staats Award; Elmer B. Vol. 2: 762
Staats International Journal Award; Elmer B. Vol. 2: 762
Staats Public Service Career Awards; Elmer B. Vol. 1: 14376
Staatspreis fur Consulting Vol. 2: 690
Staatspreis fur das Schonste Buch Vol. 2: 698
Staatspreis fur Design Vol. 2: 691
Staatspreis fur geprufte Qualitat Vol. 2: 688
Staatspreis fur gestaltendes Handwerk Vol. 2: 692
Staatspreis fur Gute Form Vol. 2: 691
Staatspreis fur Innovation Vol. 2: 693
Staatspreis fur Public Relations Vol. 2: 696
Staatspreis fur Radiowerbung Vol. 2: 697
Staatspreis fur Schmuck aus Edelmetall Vol. 2: 694
Staatspreis fur Werbefilm Vol. 2: 687
Staatspreis fur Wirtschaftsbauten Vol. 2: 689
Staatspreise fur Werbung Vol. 2: 686
Stachiewicz Medal; Jules
Canadian Society for Mechanical Engineering Vol. 1: 7433
The Chemical Institute of Canada Vol 1: 7849
Staf Nees Prize Vol. 2: 1089
Staffing Industry Communications Awards Vol. 1: 4689
Stafford Memorial Award; William Vol. 1: 15029
Stage Awards Vol. 2: 7405
Stage Management Award Vol. 1: 20650
Stagg Award; Amos Alonzo Vol. 1: 2271
Stagg Trophy; Amos Alonzo Vol. 1: 15077
Stahl Award; Egon Vol. 2: 3056
Stahl Preis; Egon Vol. 2: 3056
Stahr Award; Jack Vol. 1: 20863
Stainer Preis; Jakob Vol. 2: 677
Staley Prize; J. I. Vol. 1: 18354
Stalker Award; John Vol. 1: 18349
Stall Memorial Award; Pat Vol. 1: 15263
Stals Prize for the Humanities Vol. 2: 5661
Stamford Radio Theater Competition Vol. 1: 19741
Stamp Memorial Fund; Dudley Vol. 2: 8702
Stampar Medal Vol. 2: 2248
Stampex Exhibition Awards Vol. 2: 8263
Stamprijs; Mart Vol. 2: 4696
Stand International Short Story Competition Vol. 2: 9107
Stand Poetry Competition Vol. 2: 9108
Standard and Poor's 'BBB Rating Vol. 2: 5103
Standard Bank Young Artist Awards Vol. 2: 5572
Standard Class Trophy Vol. 1: 18589
Standard Life Audience Award Vol. 2: 7407
Standards Achievement Award Vol. 1: 4439
Standards and Practices Award Vol. 1: 12223
Standards Development Awards Vol. 1: 15055
Standards Medal Vol. 1: 3183
Standish Award; Myles Vol. 1: 16963
Standish-Barry Prize Vol. 2: 8473
Stanfield Distinguished Service Award; Howard E. Vol. 1: 19613
Stanfield Trophy; Robert L. Vol. 1: 7233
Stanford Poetry Prize; Ann Vol. 1: 13173
Stanhope Gold Medal Vol. 2: 8578
Stanley Award; Edward Vol. 1: 17517
Stanley Award; Robert Vol. 1: 21378
Stanleys Vol. 1: 14255
Stanton Scholarships; Mary Vol. 1: 3502
Stapp Award; John Paul Vol. 1: 240
STAR Awards Vol. 1: 9401
Star Boy Award Vol. 2: 1656
STAR Events - Students Taking Action with Recognition Vol. 1: 9399
Star for Bravery in Gold Vol. 2: 5758
Star for Bravery in Silver Vol. 2: 5759
Star of Courage Vol. 1: 6831
Star of Gallantry Vol. 2: 196
Star of Military Valour Vol. 1: 6832
STAR Program Vol. 1: 20577
Stara Planina Order Vol. 2: 1232
Stark Memorial Award; Kevin Vol. 2: 429
Starkey Award; J. W. Vol. 2: 8727
Starr Award; Bart Vol. 1: 6019
Starr Award; Walter A. Vol. 1: 18472
Starr Clinical Day Lectureship Prize; Paul Vol. 1: 4746
Starrett Poetry Prize Competition; Agnes Lynch Vol. 1: 21100
Stars of the Year Vol. 1: 14441
Starz Denver International Film Festival
Denver Film Society Vol. 1: 8881
Denver Film Society Vol 1: 8882
Denver Film Society Vol 1: 8883
Denver Film Society Vol 1: 8884

Denver Film Society Vol 1: 8885
Starz People's Choice Award Vol. 1: 8885
State Allocated Scholarship Award Vol. 1: 17175
State Award for Excellence Vol. 1: 13067
State Awards Vol. 1: 16148
State Awards and National Awards Vol. 1: 14144
State/Canadian Province SAR Award Vol. 1: 14039
State Capital Stuttgart Award Vol. 2: 3107
State Chapter of the Year Award Vol. 1: 20198
State Coordinator Vol. 1: 14547
State Development and Construction Corporation Award Vol. 2: 6124
State Director of the Year Award
American Academy of Medical Administrators Vol. 1: 691
National Propane Gas Association Vol 1: 15556
State History Society of Missouri Vol. 1: 21314
State of Baden-Wuerttemberg Award Vol. 2: 3107
State of Florida Fellowship Vol. 1: 9589
State of Hawaii Order of Distinction for Cultural Leadership Vol. 1: 10294
State of the Art Award Vol. 1: 17529
State Park Awards Vol. 1: 19727
State President's Sport Award Vol. 2: 5613
State/Province Art Educator Award Vol. 1: 13973
State/Province Art Educator of the Year Vol. 1: 13973
State/Province Association Newsletter Award Vol. 1: 13974
State Psychiatric Technician of the Year Vol. 1: 1390
State Public Official Award for Significant Legislative Achievement Vol. 1: 1400
State Society Publications Awards Vol. 1: 3073
States Award; John D. Vol. 1: 5479
Statesman of the Year Vol. 1: 692
Statistician of the Year Award Vol. 2: 6815
Statistics in Chemistry Award Vol. 1: 4696
Statistics New Zealand/Jacoby Prize Vol. 1: 12841
Statton Lecture; Henry M Vol. 1: 4446
The Statuette with Pedestal Vol. 1: 11160
Staudinger-Preis; Hermann- Vol. 2: 2814
Stauffer Prizes; Joseph S. Vol. 1: 6809
Steacie Memorial Fellowships Vol. 1: 16025
Steacie Prize Vol. 1: 19777
Stead Prize; Christina Vol. 2: 480
Steadfast Service Award Vol. 1: 20034
Steadman Award; Richard Vol. 1: 8197
Steavenson Memorial Award Vol. 2: 6952
Stebbins, Jr. Distinguished Service Award; H. Grady Vol. 1: 5016
Stebbins Trophy; James F. Vol. 1: 21588
Steck - Vaughn Award Vol. 1: 20011
Steel and Tube Travelling Scholarship Vol. 2: 4995
Steel Distributor of the Year Award Vol. 1: 5869
Steel Eighties Award Vol. 2: 3462
Steel Guitar Hall of Fame Vol. 1: 12043
Steel Oleander Award Vol. 1: 9865
Steele-Bodger Memorial Scholarship; Harry Vol. 2: 7216
Steelmaking Conference Award Vol. 1: 5415
Steen Award; Ralph W. Vol. 1: 9082
Steere History Essay Competition; Lee Vol. 2: 555
Stefanko Best Paper Award Vol. 1: 18826
Steffens Award; Lincoln Vol. 1: 11799
Steffens Prize; Henrik Vol. 2: 3092
Stegner Award; Wallace Vol. 1: 21010
Stegner Fellowships in Creative Writing; Wallace E. Vol. 1: 8647
Steiger Award; William Vol. 1: 2619
Stein Award Vol. 1: 16643
Stein Make-up Award; Jack Vol. 1: 16129
Stein Memorial Arts Person of the Year Award; Ann G. Vol. 1: 16165
Stein Prize; Fordham - Vol. 1: 9684
Steinberg Award; S. S. Vol. 1: 3866
Steinberg Prize; Harold and Mimi Vol. 1: 15510
Steindler Award; Arthur Vol. 1: 16915
Steiner Award Vol. 1: 11380
Steiner Award for Leadership in Foreign Language Education, K-12; ACTFL Florence Vol. 1: 2060
Steiner Award for Leadership in Foreign Language Education, Postsecondary; ACTFL Florence Vol. 1: 2061
Steiner Award for Leadership in Foreign Language Research in Foreign Language Education; ACTFL - MLJ Emma Marie Vol. 1: 2062
Steiner Trophy Vol. 1: 8085
Steinmetz Award; Charles Proteus Vol. 1: 10882
Stella Arcti Award Vol. 2: 1662
Stenersen Prize; Rolf Vol. 2: 5149
Stengel Memorial Award; Alfred Vol. 1: 1928
Stennis Student Congress Awards; John C. Vol. 1: 15108
Steno Medal Vol. 2: 1494
Steno Medaljen Vol. 2: 1494
Stephansson Award for Poetry; Stephan G. Vol. 1: 21987
Stephens Lecture Vol. 2: 7641
Stephens Memorial Award; George Findlay Vol. 1: 7145
Stephenson Award for Outstanding Service; William J. Vol. 1: 15802
Stephenson Medal; George Vol. 2: 7781
Stephenson Memorial Lecture; Marjory Vol. 2: 8935
Stephenson Prize Lecture; Marjory Vol. 2: 8935
Steptoe Memorial Award; Patrick Vol. 2: 7017
Stereo Division Awards Vol. 1: 17294
Sterling Staff Competition Vol. 1: 13660
Stern Award Vol. 2: 8226
Stern Award; Philip M. Vol. 1: 21447
Stern Humanitarian Award; Rabbi Malcolm H. Vol. 1: 9500
Stern Silver Pen Award for Non-Fiction; The James Vol. 2: 7426
Steven Edeiken Memorial Kiteflier of the Year Award Vol. 1: 2922
Stevens Award; J. C. Vol. 1: 4359
Stevens Award; K. G. Vol. 2: 9363
Stevens Family History Award; Edythe Vol. 1: 9155
Stevens Memorial Award; Barbara Vol. 1: 15030
Stevens Memorial Award; Don C. Vol. 1: 2448
Stevenson Cup; Roza Vol. 2: 8570
Stevenson Fletcher Achievement Award Vol. 1: 11529
Stevenson - Hamilton Award Vol. 2: 5801
Stevenson Trophy Vol. 1: 11000
Stewardship Award Vol. 1: 16080
Stewart Award; Claude A. Vol. 2: 363
Stewart Award; Jack Vol. 1: 15082
Stewart Award; James E. Vol. 1: 1096
Stewart Awards; Ada Mayo Vol. 1: 1573
Stewart Awards; Paul A. Vol. 1: 21639
Stewart Cup; Ross Vol. 1: 20898
Stewart Endowment; Paul Vol. 1: 10807
Stewart Engineering-Humanities Award; Robert E. Vol. 1: 4236
Stewart Prize; Douglas Vol. 2: 480
Steyn Prize for Achievement in Science and Technology; M. T. Vol. 2: 5662
Stichting Internationaal Orgelconcours Vol. 2: 4919
Stichting Sikkensprijs Vol. 2: 4907
Stickel Awards; William J. Vol. 1: 3563
Stier Award; Elizabeth Fleming Vol. 1: 10946
Stiftelsen Kortfilmfestivalen Vol. 2: 5162
Stiftelsen Natur och Kulturs oversattarpris Vol. 2: 6262
Stiles Memorial Award; William C. Vol. 1: 20667
Still Medallion of Honor; Andrew Taylor Vol. 1: 742
Stillman Award; William O. Vol. 1: 2578
Stimulation of Research Award Vol. 1: 3402
Stimulus Drama Prize Vol. 2: 1184
Stinchcomb Memorial Lecture and Award; Wayne W. Vol. 1: 5989
Stine Award in Materials Engineering and Science; Charles M. A. Vol. 1: 2789
Stipendium ur Lena Vendelfelts minnesfond Vol. 2: 6263
Stir-the-Pot Award Vol. 1: 15460
Stirling Medal; John B. Vol. 1: 9275
Stitt Award Vol. 1: 5785
Stitt Lecture Award; Edward Rhodes Vol. 1: 5785
STLE National Award Vol. 1: 19347
Stock-Gedachtnispreis; Alfred- Vol. 2: 2815
Stock of the Year Vol. 1: 17655
Stockberger Achievement Award; Warner W. Vol. 1: 11834
Stockholm Prize Vol. 2: 6236
Stockman Award Vol. 2: 5173
Stodghill Award; Don R. Vol. 1: 15031
Stoeger Composer's Chair; Elise L. Vol. 1: 7799
Stoeger Prize; Elise L. Vol. 1: 7799
Stohr Medal; A.E. Vol. 2: 430
Stoilov Prize; Simon Vol. 2: 5868
Stokdyk Award; E. A. Vol. 1: 14801
Stoker Awards; Bram Vol. 1: 10549
Stokes Memorial Award Vol. 1: 15243
Stokinger Award; Herbert E. Vol. 1: 2620
Stokinger Award Lecture Vol. 1: 2620
Stokstad Award; E.L.R. Vol. 1: 4163
Stollery Award; Robert Vol. 1: 7044
Stolz Trophy for Music Philately; Robert Vol. 1: 17273
Stone Award Vol. 1: 21135
Stone Award; Donald C.
American Public Works Association Vol. 1: 3807
American Society for Public Administration Vol 1: 4187
Stone Award; I. F. Vol. 1: 13766
Stone Award; Peter Vol. 2: 6802
Stone Graduate Fellowship; Ralph W. Vol. 1: 15803
Stone Memorial Award; Walter Vol. 2: 339

Stone Prize Vol. 2: 5135
Stora Linnemedaljen I guld Vol. 2: 6223
Stora priset Vol. 2: 6264
Storch Award in Fuel Chemistry; Henry H. Vol. 1: 1791
Storer Award Vol. 1: 4454
Storey International Award; Robert G. Vol. 1: 7702
Stork Fellow; Charles Wharton Vol. 1: 6017
Storm Award; Paul Vol. 1: 8908
Storrs Memorial Piano Scholarships; Evelyn Bonar Vol. 1: 13714
StoryTeller of the Year Award Vol. 1: 6719
Storywriting and Art Project Vol. 2: 116
Stouffer Award Vol. 1: 4649
Stoughton Award for Young Teachers; Bradley Vol. 1: 5191
Stoughton Award for Young Teachers of Metallurgy; Bradley Vol. 1: 5191
Stout Medal Vol. 1: 2448
Stover Memorial Award; Elizabeth Matchett Vol. 1: 19528
Stowe Award; Allen B. Vol. 1: 20864
Stowe Sportsmanship Award; Dr. Allen B. Vol. 1: 20864
Stowell-Orbison Awards for Pathologists-in-Training Vol. 1: 20380
Stoye Awards Vol. 1: 4455
STP Most Improved Championship Driver Award Vol. 1: 20423
Strachauer Medal; Ehrma Vol. 1: 21435
Strader Memorial Award; Noel Ross Vol. 1: 8176
Stradford Award; C. Francis Vol. 1: 14492
Straelen; Prix van Vol. 2: 2414
Stranahan Award; Jason G. (Stranny) Vol. 1: 20668
Strategic Communications Award Vol. 1: 17705
Strathglass Trophy Vol. 1: 21588
Strating Prize; Albert Vol. 2: 5663
Stratton Award; Samuel Wesley Vol. 1: 20483
Stratton Medal; Henry M. Vol. 1: 4446
Straus Award; Flora Stieglitz Vol. 1: 7902
Straus Award; Ralph I. Vol. 1: 15402
Strausbaugh Club Relations Award; Bill Vol. 1: 17621
Strauss Award; Sidney L. Vol. 1: 16268
Street Stock Endurance Championship Vol. 1: 11758
Strega Prize Vol. 2: 4052
Stresemann-Foerderung; Erwin- Vol. 2: 2858
Strickler Innovation in Instruction Award; Les B. Vol. 1: 3856
Striker Junior Paper Award; Gyorgy Vol. 2: 3295
Strimple Award Vol. 1: 17042
String Teacher of the Year Award Vol. 1: 4701
Stritch Medal Vol. 1: 12973
Strive and Succeed Award Vol. 1: 10545
Strock Award; Lester W. Vol. 1: 18645
Stromer-Ferrnerska Beloningen Vol. 2: 6224
Strong Award; Dorothy and Bruce Vol. 1: 15735
Stroobant; Prix Paul and Marie Vol. 2: 1065
Stroud Memorial Award; Clara Vol. 1: 4868
Stroud Memorial Award; Ida Wells Vol. 1: 4869
Stroukoff Memorial Trophy; Larissa Vol. 1: 18590
Strousse Award Vol. 1: 17518
Structural Engineers Special Awards; Institution of Vol. 2: 7887
Structural Foam Division Awards Vol. 1: 19321
Structural Geology and Tectonics Division Career Contribution Award Vol. 1: 9956
Structural Materials Distinguished Materials Scientist/Engineer Award Vol. 1: 13457
Structural Materials Distinguished Service Award Vol. 1: 13458
Structural Plastics Division Annual Recognition Vol. 1: 19320
Structural Plastics Division Awards Vol. 1: 19321
Struggle for Liberation of Bulgaria Award Vol. 1: 6689
Strzelecki Prize; Jan Vol. 2: 5330
Stuart Memorial Lectureship; Charles A. Vol. 1: 6666
Stuart Prize; Akroyd Vol. 2: 8404
Stubbs Medal; Oliver Vol. 2: 7658
Stubbs Research Grant; E. L. Vol. 1: 13373
Stuckenbruck Person of the Year Award; Linn Vol. 1: 17669
Stuckey Award; Bill Vol. 1: 2192
Student Achievement Award
American Animal Hospital Association Vol. 1: 907
Califon Historical Society Vol 1: 6731
Student Advocacy Award Vol. 1: 11167
Student Aid Award Vol. 1: 21294
Student and New Investigator Travel Awards Vol. 1: 9306
Student and Young Professional Grant Vol. 1: 21419
Student Architect Award Vol. 2: 8906
Student Article Contest Vol. 1: 7251
Student-Athlete of the Week Vol. 1: 14666
Student Award
American Academy of Oral and Maxillofacial Radiology Vol. 1: 732
American Society of Heating, Refrigerating and Air-Conditioning Engineers Vol 1: 4440
Association of Consulting Engineers New Zealand Vol 2: 4955
Canadian Association for Health, Physical Education, Recreation and Dance Vol 1: 6885
Canadian Dam Association Vol 1: 7071
Canadian Society of Microbiologists Vol 1: 7479
Dechema - Society for Chemical Engineering and Biotechnology Vol 2: 2700
Gesellschaft fur Chemische Technik und Biotechnologie Vol 2: 2916
National Council on Family Relations Vol 1: 14864
National Federation of State Poetry Societies Vol 1: 15032
Society of Allied Weight Engineers Vol 1: 18949
Student Award for Excellence Vol. 1: 10965
Student Award for International Understanding Vol. 2: 7466
Student Award for Scholarly Writing Vol. 1: 18652
Student Award Medallion Vol. 2: 7832
Student Award - Postgraduate Division Vol. 2: 7441
Student Award - Undergraduate Division Vol. 2: 7449
Student Awards
American Association of Veterinary Immunologists Vol. 1: 1478
American Institute of Chemical Engineers Vol 1: 2790
Association of Photographers Vol 2: 6838
Czechoslovak Society of Arts and Sciences Vol 1: 8700
Health Physics Society Vol 1: 10321
Remote Sensing and Photogrammetry Society Vol 2: 8335
Sea Grant Association Vol 1: 18387
The Wildlife Society Vol 1: 21631
Student Awards for Outstanding Research Vol. 1: 18649
Student Business Initiative Award Vol. 1: 6184
Student Chapter Award Vol. 1: 11056
Student Chapter Awards Vol. 1: 1875
Student Chapter of the Year Award
American Society for Information Science and Technology Vol. 1: 4116
American Society of Certified Engineering Technicians Vol 1: 4280
International Facility Management Association Vol 1: 11572
Student Chapter Sponsor Award of Excellence Vol. 1: 13975
Student CHEMECA Awards Vol. 2: 520
Student Competition Vol. 1: 11556
Student Design Competition
Institution of Professional Engineers New Zealand Vol. 2: 4996
Southeastern Theatre Conference Vol 1: 19491
Student Design Project Competition Vol. 1: 4440
Student Design-School Competition Vol. 1: 17003
Student Dissertation Award Vol. 1: 5271
Student Essay Competition in Healthcare Management Vol. 1: 1876
Student Fellowship Award Vol. 1: 8329
Student Impact Award Vol. 1: 12453
Student Intern Scholarship Award Vol. 1: 13012
Student Involvement Award Vol. 1: 15566
Student Leadership Awards Vol. 1: 3400
Student Liaison Award Vol. 1: 8444
Student Lighting Design Awards Vol. 2: 8065
Student Literary Award Vol. 1: 14899
Student Loan Vol. 1: 8963
Student Medal Vol. 1: 18138
Student of the Year Vol. 1: 17319
Student Paper Award
American Society for Bioethics and Humanities Vol. 1: 3927
Institute of Transportation Engineers Vol 1: 11057
Religious Communication Association Vol 1: 17981
Student Paper Award; Carl A. Ross Vol. 1: 5001
Student Paper Award for Four and Five Year Students Vol. 1: 12224
Student Paper Award for Two and Three Year Students Vol. 1: 12225
Student Paper Awards Vol. 1: 19214
Student Paper Competition Vol. 1: 1037
Student Paper of the Year Awards Vol. 1: 17670
Student Paper Prize Vol. 1: 18743
Student Papers Award Vol. 2: 9364
Student Planner Award Vol. 1: 3560

Student Presentation Award Vol. 1: 6854
Student Press; John R. Emens Award for Support of a Free Vol. 1: 6205
Student Prize Essay/Project Vol. 1: 13620
Student Prize of Excellence Vol. 1: 6035
Student Prize Paper Award Vol. 1: 1359
Student Professional Paper Vol. 1: 5679
Student Project of the Year Award Vol. 1: 15761
Student Research Award
- American Psychological Association - Division of Family Psychology (Division 43) Vol. 1: 3673
- Gerontological Society of America Vol 1: 9999

Student Research Award Competition Vol. 1: 3756
Student Research Award for Clinical Child Psychology Vol. 1: 3750
Student Research Awards
- American Association for Clinical Chemistry Vol 1: 1002
- American Psychological Association - Adult Development and Aging Division (Division 20) Vol 1: 3645

Student Research Awards in Systematic Paleontology Vol. 1: 17038
Student Research Fellowships Vol. 1: 9713
Student Research Prize Vol. 2: 1565
Student Research Training Award Vol. 1: 16806
Student Research Training in Alternative Methods; Colgate-Palmolive/SOT Awards for Vol. 1: 19334
Student/Resident Award Vol. 1: 1284
Student Scholarship Vol. 1: 17404
Student Scholarships
- Japan America Society Vol. 1: 12300
- National Society for Histotechnology Vol 1: 15722

Student Science Project Contest Vol. 1: 6398
Student Section Advisor Award Vol. 1: 4548
Student Television Awards Vol. 2: 8856
Student Translation Award Vol. 1: 4754
Student Travel Awards
- International Society of Chemical Ecology Vol. 1: 11988
- Society for Industrial and Applied Mathematics Vol 1: 18744
- Society for the Study of Lesbian, Gay and Bisexual Concerns (Division 44) Vol 1: 18919

Student/Tutor Recognition Certificates Vol. 1: 6300
Student with a Disability Scholarship Vol. 1: 14883
Student Writing and Development Award Vol. 1: 12821
Student Writing Contest Vol. 1: 2259
Students Aid Fund Vol. 2: 7857
Student's Articles Competition Vol. 2: 9365
Students Taking Action with Recognition; STAR Events - Vol. 1: 9399
Studer Preis; Willi Vol. 2: 6526
Studies Book Award Vol. 1: 19439
Study Abroad Award Vol. 1: 17767
Study Awards Program Vol. 1: 7314
Study Grant Awards Vol. 2: 232
Stukus Trophy - Coach of the Year; Annis Vol. 1: 7117
Stulberg International String Competition Vol. 1: 19816
Stuparich "Heart of Gold" Award; The Geri Vol. 1: 2384
Sturdy Oaks Award Vol. 1: 5079
Sture Centerwalls Pris Vol. 2: 6225
Sturgeon Memorial Award; Theodore Vol. 1: 7753
Sturgis Medal Vol. 1: 18997
Stuttgart City Prize for Young Composers Vol. 2: 3104
Stuttgart Literary Prize Vol. 2: 3102
STUVA-Prize Vol. 2: 3113
Stzanski Award; Professor Iwan Vol. 2: 1211
SubbaRow Memorial Lecture; Dr. Yellapragada Vol. 2: 3517
Subcontractor of the Year Vol. 1: 20833
Sublette Award of Excellence; Louise Vol. 1: 18350
Submarine/ASW Writing Award Vol. 1: 16057
Subscription Awards Vol. 2: 7189
Suburban Journalist of the Year Vol. 1: 19819
Suddeutscher Rundfunk Award Vol. 2: 3107
Sudjono Djuned Poesponegoro Award Vol. 2: 3602
Sudler Cup Vol. 1: 19430
Sudler Flag of Honor Vol. 1: 19431
Sudler International High School Marching Band Championship Video Competition Vol. 1: 19434
Sudler International Wind Band Composition Competition; Louis Vol. 1: 19432
Sudler Order of Merit Vol. 1: 19433
Sudler Shield Vol. 1: 19434
Sudler Silver Scroll Vol. 1: 19435
Sudler Trophy Vol. 1: 19436
Sudreys Fund Vol. 2: 8944
Sugg Heritage Award Vol. 2: 7854
Sulabh Global Sanitation Award Vol. 2: 3589
Sulkin Prize; Sidney Vol. 1: 17416
Sullins Award for Outstanding Service in Optometry; W. David Vol. 1: 5786
Sullivan Fishery Conservation Award; Carl R. Vol. 1: 2260
Sullivan Memorial Award; AAU James E. Vol. 1: 527
Sullivan Memorial Membership Award; Carl R. Vol. 1: 2261
Sullivan Trophy; Senator Joseph A. Vol. 1: 7234
Sulman Prize Vol. 2: 76
Sulphur Institute Award Vol. 2: 3369
Sultan Prize; HMS Vol. 2: 7862
Sulzberger Award; Mayer Vol. 1: 12363
Sulzberger Memorial Award and Lectureship; Marion B. Vol. 1: 640
Summer Awards for Upper Division and Graduate Students Vol. 1: 17931
Summer Fellowship Vol. 1: 6674
Summer Music Centers Awards Vol. 1: 14970
Summer Paid Internships Vol. 1: 20594
Summer Scholarship Vol. 2: 2477
Summer Stipends Vol. 1: 13219
Summer Student Fellowships Vol. 1: 4802
Summer Study Grants Vol. 1: 20202
Summers Distinguished Merit Award; Alex J. Vol. 1: 2563
Summers Memorial Award; Rev. Dr. Montague Vol. 1: 8617
Summers Poetry Prize; Hollis Vol. 1: 16653
Summit Award Vol. 1: 19186
The Summit Award Vol. 1: 11245
Summit Awards Vol. 1: 20905
Sumpter Excellence in Teaching Award; Robert Vol. 1: 15280
SunAmco Medal Vol. 1: 12109
Sunday People Tattersall Trophy Vol. 2: 8128
Sunday Times Watercolour competition; Singer Friedlander/ Vol. 2: 8244
Sunder Lal Hora Medal Vol. 2: 3518
Sungurlu Memorial Award for Best International Student Poster; Ozan Vol. 1: 1353
Sunkist Young Designer Award Vol. 1: 4220
Sunkist Young Designer Award Vol. 1: 4237
Sunshine Award
- Society of Professional Journalists Vol. 1: 19277
- Young Audiences of Greater Cleveland Vol 1: 22057

Suntory Awards for Mystery Fiction Vol. 2: 4114
Suntory Prize for Community Cultural Activities Vol. 2: 4300
Suntory Prize for Social Sciences and Humanities Vol. 2: 4301
Suomen museoliiton 50-vuotisjuhlamitali Vol. 2: 1609
Suomen Taiteilijaseuran tunnustusapuaraha Vol. 2: 1574
Super Bowl Vol. 1: 15088
Super Bowl Most Valuable Player Vol. 1: 15087
Super Cup Vol. 2: 5348
Super Senior Service Award Vol. 1: 20865
Super Stock Puller of the Year Vol. 1: 15891
Superchannel Award Vol. 1: 22048
Superintendent of the Year Award Vol. 1: 7691
Superintendent's Award for Distinguished Service Vol. 1: 20526
Superior Achievement Award Vol. 1: 11015
Superior Honor Award Vol. 1: 20554
Superior Scientist Award Vol. 2: 2508
Supervisor of Excellence in Social Studies Vol. 1: 13157
Supple Religion Writer of the Year Award Vol. 1: 17976
Supplier Development Council Awards; National Minority Vol. 1: 15390
Supplier Excellence Award Vol. 1: 2440
Supplier Member of the Year Award Vol. 1: 5891
Supplier of the Year Vol. 1: 13668
Supplier of the Year Award
- American Meat Institute Vol. 1: 3047
- Awards and Recognition Association Vol 1: 6171
- National Minority Supplier Development Council Vol 1: 15390

Suppliers Golden Achievement Award Vol. 1: 17687
Support Company of the Year Vol. 1: 13669
Support of Diversity Award Vol. 1: 1155
Support of Science Award Vol. 1: 8589
Support of Teacher Education Accreditation Award Vol. 1: 1156
Supreme Champion
- International Sheep Dog Society Vol. 2: 7976
- Palomino Horse Breeders of America Vol 1: 17050

Supreme Order of Christ (Militia of Our Lord Jesus Christ) Vol. 2: 9317
Surgan Award; Edith Vol. 1: 15449
Surrency Prize; Erwin C. Vol. 1: 4125

Award Index

Survey and General Instrument Company Award Vol. 2: 6972
Surveying and Mapping Award Vol. 1: 4360
Surveying Excellence Award Vol. 1: 15762
Survivability Award Vol. 1: 2696
Survivors' Club Vol. 1: 11312
Susan B. Anthony Award Vol. 1: 22099
Susse Freres; Prix Vol. 2: 1730
Sustainable Business Award Vol. 1: 21092
Sustainable Development Award of Excellence Vol. 1: 10120
Sustainable Development; Queen's Awards for Enterprise: Vol. 2: 8317
Sustained Achievement Award Vol. 1: 17989
Sustained Excellence; Phillip E. Frandson Award for Vol. 1: 20954
Sustained Lifetime Achievement Award Vol. 1: 18838
Sustained Superior Performance Award Vol. 1: 577
Sustaining Member Recognition Award Vol. 1: 22062
Sustaining Members Twenty-Year Awards Vol. 1: 2005
Sustaining Membership Award Vol. 1: 5787
Sustaining Membership Lecture Award Vol. 1: 5787
Sutermeister; Isaac Ray Award in Memory of Margaret Vol. 1: 3634
Sutherland Award; Edwin H. Vol. 1: 4386
Sutherland Memorial Lecture Vol. 1: 8641
Sutherland Prize; Donald M. Vol. 1: 4126
Sutherland Prize; Kenneth J. G. Vol. 2: 503
Sutherland Trophy Vol. 2: 7020
Suttle Award; H. K. Vol. 2: 7520
Svante Arrhenius Medaljen Vol. 2: 6226
The Sven Groennings Scholarship Vol. 1: 11793
Svenska Akademiens Finlandspris Vol. 2: 6265
Svenska Akademiens Nordiska Pris Vol. 2: 6266
Svenska Akademiens Oversattarpris Vol. 2: 6267
Svenska Akademiens pris for introduktion av svensk kultur utomlands Vol. 2: 6268
Svenska Akademiens Sprakvardspris Vol. 2: 6269
Svenska Akademiens Svensklararpris Vol. 2: 6270
Svenska Akademiens Teaterpris Vol. 2: 6271
Svenska Akademiens Tolkningspris Vol. 2: 6272
Svenska Dagbladet Gold Medal Vol. 2: 6237
Svenska Dagbladet Literary Award Vol. 2: 6238
Sverdlin; Premio Norman Vol. 2: 4613
Sverdrup Medal Vol. 1: 18998
Svjetski Festival Animiranih Filmova Vol. 2: 1392
Swackhamer Peace Essay Contest Vol. 1: 16591
Swaminathan 60th Birthday Commemoration Lecture; Professor S. Vol. 2: 3519
Swan Premium Vol. 2: 7808
Swanberg Distinguished Service Award; Harold Vol. 1: 3085
Swanson Wilson Memorial Scholarship; Cristine Vol. 1: 12726
Swarts; Prix Frederic Vol. 2: 1057
Swarup Memorial Lecture; Professor Har Vol. 2: 3520
Swastek Award; Rev. Joseph V. Vol. 1: 17457
Swearingen Award; Harry S. Vol. 1: 3808
Swearingen Award; Noble G. Vol. 1: 5866
Swecker Award; Herbert N. Vol. 1: 8219
Swedish Mathematical Society Fellowship Vol. 2: 6288
Sweeney; Academic Award in Memory of Stephen B. Vol. 1: 11479
Sweeney Award; Catherine H. Vol. 1: 2537
Sweeney Award; Craig Vol. 1: 20768
Sweeney Medal; Edward C. Vol. 1: 9376
Sweepstakes Trophy Vol. 1: 15104
Sweepstakes Winner Vol. 1: 14975
Sweet Award; Ralph Vol. 1: 5756
Sweet Fellowship; Georgina Vol. 2: 173
Sweetland Award of Excellence; Peter Vol. 1: 17305
Swenson Leadership Award; Reed K. Vol. 1: 15317
SWFA Author Emeritus Award Vol. 1: 18358
Swidzinski Award; Henryk Vol. 2: 5350
Swidzinskiego; Nagroda im. Henryka Vol. 2: 5350
Swimmer of the Year Award Vol. 1: 21204
Swimming Coach of the Year Vol. 1: 7235
Swimming Enterprises Trophy for Synchronised Swimmer of the Year Vol. 2: 6718
The Swimming Times Water Polo Award Vol. 2: 6719
Swiney Prize for a Work on Jurisprudence Vol. 2: 8713
Swings; Prix Pol Vol. 2: 1110
Swings; Prix Pol and Christiane Vol. 2: 1067
Swiss Music - Edition Vol. 2: 6533
Swiss Poster Award Vol. 2: 6531
Swissair/Crossair Special Prize Vol. 2: 6482
Sword of Ignatius Loyola Award Vol. 1: 18218
Sword of Loyola Vol. 1: 12974
Swormstedt Award Vol. 1: 19601
Sydney International Piano Competition of Australia Vol. 2: 318
Sydney *Sun* Aria Contest Vol. 2: 315
Sydnor Award; Charles S. Vol. 1: 19505
Sykes Memorial Award; George Vol. 2: 8242
Sylvester Medal Vol. 2: 8705
Sylvia Cup Design Competition Vol. 1: 18967
Syme Professorship Vol. 2: 8481
Syme Research Prize; David Vol. 2: 636
Symington Award; W. Stuart Vol. 1: 359
Symmes Community Award; Lee Vol. 1: 16766
Symons Memorial Medal Vol. 2: 8630
Syncrude Canada Innovation Award Vol. 1: 7408
Synder Excellence Award; Mayrose Vol. 1: 1574
Synergy Award Vol. 1: 19013
Synge Award; John L. Vol. 1: 18173
Syngenta Award Vol. 1: 3541
Syngenta Crop Protection Recognition Award Vol. 1: 4249
Syngenta Nematology Award Vol. 1: 19223
Syntex Award in Physical Organic Chemistry Vol. 1: 7830
Sysmex Award Vol. 1: 11589
System Safety Technology Innovation Award Vol. 1: 19892
Systems Modeling Student Competition - Student Vol. 1: 10966
Szakszervezeti Muveszeti Kulturalis Dij Vol. 2: 3303
Szczesny Prize; Commander Kazimierz Vol. 2: 5330
Szent-Gyorgyi Albert Emlekerem Vol. 2: 3317
Szent-Gyorgyi Commemorative Medal; Albert Vol. 2: 3317
Szentkiralyi Medal; Zsigmond Vol. 2: 3261
Szepski Award; Richard E. Vol. 1: 8283
Szigeti Violin Competition; Jozsef Vol. 2: 3285
Szilard Lectureship Award; Leo Vol. 1: 3478
Szold Award; Henrietta Vol. 1: 10215
SZOT Prize Vol. 2: 3303
Szymanski Award; Walter A. Vol. 1: 19307
T & R (Insurance Services) Limited Prize Vol. 2: 7690
TABCO Recognition Award Vol. 1: 19946
Tableau d'honneur Vol. 2: 2969
Tableman Award; Betty Vol. 1: 13333
Tabler Memorial Award; Pat Vol. 1: 7980
TAC Heptathlon Award Vol. 1: 21243
Tachau Teach of the Year Award; Mary K. Bonsteel Vol. 1: 16896
Taft Awards Program for Non-Profit Resource Centers Vol. 1: 19898
TAGA Honors Award Vol. 1: 19956
Taggart Award; Arthur F. Vol. 1: 18827
Taggart Award for Texas Newspaper Leader of the Year; Pat Vol. 1: 20000
Tagore Literacy Award Vol. 2: 3395
Taguchi Award Vol. 1: 4717
Taishoff Award for Excellence in Broadcast Journalism; Sol Vol. 1: 15529
Tait Award of Excellence; John Vol. 1: 6976
Tait Trophy Vol. 1: 10254
Tajima Prize Vol. 2: 6461
Talbert Junior Sportsmanship Award; Bill Vol. 1: 12076
Talbert Junior Sportsmanship Awards; Bill Vol. 1: 20866
Talbot-Ponsonby Prize for Agricultural Valuation Vol. 2: 8417
Talbot Prize for African Anthropology; Amaury Vol. 2: 8424
Talk Show Host of the Year Vol. 1: 19906
Talking Book of the Year Vol. 1: 7306
Tall Man Water Freezer Award Vol. 1: 10279
Talley EMS Instructor/Coordinator of the Year Award; Mary Ann Vol. 1: 14220
Tallix Foundry Prize Vol. 1: 15698
Tallmadge Award for Contributions to Coating Technology; John A. Vol. 1: 2791
Tamayo Annual Competition for Literature Prizes; Franz Vol. 2: 1123
Tamid Award; Ner Vol. 1: 15301
Tamisiea Award; John A. Vol. 1: 241
Tammsaare Medal Vol. 2: 1569
Tampere International Short Film Festival Vol. 2: 1660
Tampereen Kansainvaliset lyhytelokuvajuhlat Grand Prix Vol. 2: 1660
Tanabe Young Investigator Award Vol. 1: 1851
Tanaka Memorial Dissertation Award in Psychology; Jeffrey S. Vol. 1: 18920
Tanasescu Prize; Tudor Vol. 2: 5869
Tanner Award; Martin W. Vol. 1: 19720
Tanner-Vandeput-Boswick Prize for Burn Research Vol. 1: 11442
Tanner-Vandeput Prize for Burn Research
International Burn Foundation Vol. 1: 11442
International Society for Burn Injuries Vol 1: 11924

Tanneyhill Award; Ann Vol. 1: 15928
Tantramar Trophy Vol. 1: 7236
Tanya Gritz Award for Excellence in Public Finance Vol. 1: 19769
Taormina Memorial Award; Silvio C. Vol. 1: 14309
Tapling Medal Vol. 2: 8647
TAPPI Fellow Award Vol. 1: 19924
TAPPI Gold Medal Vol. 1: 19922
Targa D'Oro Citta Di Sondrio Vol. 2: 3970
Target Award Vol. 1: 8927
Targhe d'Oro per l'Ecologia Vol. 2: 3972
Tarjan Award; George Vol. 1: 3639
Tarnopol Trophy Vol. 1: 8086
Tarnopolsky Human Rights Award; The Honourable Walter S. Vol. 1: 6977
Tarnopolsky Medal; Hon. Walter S. Vol. 1: 11490
Tarrega; Certamen Internacional de Guitarra Francisco Vol. 2: 5999
Tarrega International Guitar Competition; Francisco Vol. 2: 5999
Tasmania Division Award of Merit Vol. 2: 431
Tassier; Prix Suzanne Vol. 2: 1031
Tata Gold Medal Vol. 2: 3463
Tate Award; Barbara Vol. 2: 9089
Tate Award for Undergraduate Academic Advising; John Vol. 1: 21076
Tate International Award; John T. Vol. 1: 2840
Tattersall Trophy Vol. 2: 8128
Tau Beta Pi Laureate Vol. 1: 19934
Tauber Prize; Richard Vol. 2: 6727
Tauffer Medallion Vol. 2: 3305
Taurman Voice Scholarship; Mikanna Clark Vol. 1: 13662
Tausk-Preis; Marius- Vol. 2: 2852
Taussig Article Award; Frank W. Vol. 1: 16695
Tawara Gold Medal Vol. 2: 4149
Taxpayers Award Vol. 2: 3109
Taxpayer's Friend Award Vol. 1: 15857
Taylor/Alton Blakeslee Fellowship in Science Writing; Rennie Vol. 1: 8563
Taylor and Francis Best Letter Award Vol. 2: 8336
Taylor Award; Alan Vol. 2: 6990
Taylor Award; Florence Vol. 2: 661
Taylor Award for Private Gardens; Kathryn S. Vol. 1: 16149
Taylor Award for Voluntary Service; Dwain Vol. 1: 17074
Taylor Award; Franklin V. Vol. 1: 3652
Taylor Award in Modern American Poetry; Aiken Vol. 1: 18425
Taylor Award; M. N. "Mully" Vol. 1: 20187
Taylor Award; Vice Admiral Rufus L. Vol. 1: 15384
Taylor Body of Work Award; Sydney Vol. 1: 5743
Taylor Children's Book Awards; Sydney Vol. 1: 5744
Taylor Distinguished Service Award; Fannie Vol. 1: 5811
Taylor Key Award Vol. 1: 18628
Taylor Manuscript Competition; Sydney Vol. 1: 5745
Taylor Medal; David W. Vol. 1: 19215
Taylor Medal; J. Hall Vol. 1: 4549
Taylor Memorial Bowl; Joanna Vol. 1: 18328
Taylor Memorial Medal; Braid Vol. 2: 8301
Taylor (of Australia) Prize; George Vol. 2: 8405
Taylor Prize; Lilian Coleman Vol. 1: 17810
Taylor Research Medal; Frederick W. Vol. 1: 19173
Taylor Spink Minor League Player-of-the-Year; Topps - J. G. Vol. 1: 20102
TBE Scholarship Fund Vol. 1: 19917
TBS Britanicas Award Vol. 2: 4302
TBS, INC. Technical Services Award Vol. 1: 10686
TCAC Grants Vol. 1: 19901
TCG/MetLife Foundation Extended Collaboration Grants for Artists Vol. 1: 20055
TCG/NEA Designer Fellows Vol. 1: 20052
Tchaikovsky Competition; International Vol. 2: 5897
T.D Financial Group Vol. 1: 19790
TDMA Hall of Fame Vol. 1: 6166
Te Kura Pounamu Award Vol. 2: 5004
Teacher as Researcher Grant Vol. 1: 11877
Teacher Award Vol. 1: 8214
Teacher Award; Artist- Vol. 1: 4700
Teacher Educational Mini-Grant Vol. 1: 7693
Teacher Fellow Award Vol. 1: 16408
Teacher of the Year
Correctional Education Association - Region III Vol. 1: 8531
Ladies Professional Golf Association Vol 1: 12662
Teacher of the Year Award
American Association Family Consumer Sciences Vol. 1: 944
Estonian Education Personnel Union Vol 2: 1567
Fairbanks Education Association Vol 1: 9388
Professional Golfers' Association of America Vol 1: 17622
Teacher of the Year Awards Vol. 1: 14043
Teacher Recognition Awards Vol. 1: 12072
Teacher-Researcher Grants Vol. 1: 14842
Teacher's Award Vol. 2: 8171
Teachers Quest Awards Vol. 1: 9633
Teachers Scramble Vol. 2: 9100
Teachers Who Inspire Vol. 1: 18264
Teaching Award Vol. 1: 2538
Teaching Award; Distinguished
American Meat Science Association Vol. 1: 3052
National Science Teachers Association Vol 1: 15689
Teaching Award; Science Vol. 1: 15692
Teaching Awards Program Vol. 1: 3742
Teaching Career Enhancement Awards Vol. 1: 3529
Teaching Excellence Award Vol. 1: 20026
Teaching Excellence Awards Vol. 1: 2705
Teaching; J.H. Atkinson Award for Excellence in Arkansas Vol. 1: 5075
Teaching of English; David H. Russell Award for Distinguished Research in the Vol. 1: 14840
Teague Space Award; Olin E. Vol. 1: 1503
Team Awards
International Shuffleboard Association Vol. 1: 11901
USA Swimming Vol 1: 21205
Team Canada Junior MVP; Senior Vol. 1: 6264
Team of the Year
Asian Football Confederation Vol. 2: 4425
Kansas City Barbeque Society Vol 1: 12489
Teambuild Vol. 2: 7782
Tech-Savvy Hotels Award Vol. 1: 8406
Technical Achievement Award
Institute of Electrical and Electronics Engineers - Computer Society Vol. 1: 10901
International Microelectronics and Packaging Society Vol 1: 11750
NACE International: The Corrosion Society Vol 1: 13747
National Association of Printing Ink Manufacturer Vol 1: 14334
Technical Achievement Award; Edward J. Baier Vol. 1: 2609
Technical and Feature Writing Awards Vol. 1: 3074
Technical and Scientific Communication Award Vol. 1: 14843
Technical Associate Member Service Award Vol. 1: 14335
Technical Association of the Australian and New Zealand Pulp and Paper Industry Awards Vol. 2: 72
Technical Committee Prize Paper Awards Vol. 1: 10913
Technical Council Distinguished Individual Service Award Vol. 1: 10914
Technical Division Executive Committee Award Vol. 1: 2320
Technical Engineering Achievement Awards Vol. 1: 13866
Technical Excellence Award
AARL Foundation Vol. 1: 52
International Society of Weighing and Measurement Vol 1: 12035
Technical Innovation in Enhancing Production of Safe Affordable Food; Award for Vol. 1: 7439
Technical Paper Awards
Institute of Quarrying - England Vol. 2: 7741
Wire Association International Vol 1: 21660
Technical Standards Board Certificate of Appreciation Vol. 1: 19059
Technical Standards Board Outstanding Contribution Award Vol. 1: 19059
Technical Writing Awards Vol. 1: 391
Technician of the Month Award Vol. 1: 4281
Technician of the Year
Electronics Technicians Association, International Vol. 1: 9221
International Motor Sports Association Vol 1: 11755
Technician of the Year Award
American Association for Laboratory Animal Science Vol. 1: 1027
International Society of Certified Electronics Technicians Vol 1: 11984
Professional Aviation Maintenance Association Vol 1: 17582
Technician Publication Award Vol. 1: 1028
Technician Recognition Award Vol. 1: 1027
Technician Safety Practitioner Scholarship Vol. 2: 7879
Technician/Technologist of the Year Award Vol. 1: 4282
Technicians Paper Award Vol. 2: 9366
Technicolor/Herbert T. Kalmus Gold Medal Award Vol. 1: 19199
Technologist of the Year
American Medical Technologists Vol. 1: 3075
American Society for Clinical Pathology Vol 1: 3963

Society of Medical Laboratory Technologists of South Africa Vol 2: 5634
Technologists Awards Vol. 2: 5583
Technology Award
European Federation of the Contact Lens Industry Vol. 2: 4761
Japanese Society of Snow and Ice Vol 2: 4223
Royal Agricultural Society of England Vol 2: 8418
Technology Award/Award of Engineering Excellence Vol. 1: 4441
Technology Awards Vol. 2: 8857
Technology Honor Society Vol. 1: 19959
Technology; IRA Presidential Award for Reading and Vol. 1: 11863
Technology Marketing ICON Awards Vol. 1: 223
Technology of the Year Vol. 1: 5729
Technology Prize Vol. 2: 5171
Technology Teacher Educator of the Year Vol. 1: 8612
Technology Transfer Award
Arkansas Technology Transfer Society Vol. 1: 5081
Society of American Foresters Vol 1: 18977
Teclu Prize; Nicolae Vol. 2: 5870
Ted Eschenbach Best EMJ Journal Paper Award Vol. 1: 4060
Teddy Award Vol. 1: 14688
Teen Health Leadership Award Vol. 1: 219
Teen Scholarship Vol. 1: 7962
Teen Volunteer of the Year Vol. 1: 2396
Teenage Festival of Life Award Vol. 2: 5101
Teenage Youth Award Vol. 1: 7681
Teer, Jr. Award; Nello L. Vol. 1: 3867
Teetor Educational Award; Ralph R. Vol. 1: 19060
Teichmueller Price and Hermann Ciedner Prize Vol. 2: 2836
Teichmueller Stipendium and Hermann Credner Stipendium Vol. 2: 2837
Teirlinck; Prix Auguste Vol. 2: 1013
Teissonniere; Prix Paul Vol. 2: 2199
Teixeira; Premio Carlos Vol. 2: 5405
Teixeira Prize; Carlos Vol. 2: 5405
Tekakwitha Award Vol. 1: 6451
Telecommunications Award Vol. 1: 10350
Teleport Awards for Excellence Vol. 1: 21958
Televised Opera Prize of the City of Salzburg Vol. 2: 777
Televisio de Catalunya (TV3) Award Vol. 2: 6011
Television and Radio Industries Club Annual Celebrity Awards Vol. 2: 9117
Television Journalism Awards Vol. 2: 8858
Television Journalist of the Year Vol. 2: 8858
Television Newsfilm Awards Vol. 1: 15549
Television Program Producer of the Year Vol. 1: 15618
Television Programming and Promotions Awards; International Vol. 1: 16223
Television Quarterly Clip Contest Vol. 1: 15546
Television-Radio Awards Vol. 1: 21994
Television Sports Awards Vol. 2: 8859
Telford Medal Vol. 2: 7783
Telford Prize; Sir Robert Vol. 2: 7818
Telly Awards Vol. 1: 19964
TELO Award Vol. 1: 4735
Temple Award for Creative Altruism Vol. 1: 12179
Templer Medal Vol. 2: 8969
Templeton European Film Prize; John Vol. 2: 6312
Templeton Prize for Progress toward Research or Discoveries about Spiritual Realities Vol. 1: 12414
Templeton Prizes for Inspiring Movies and TV Vol. 1: 12402
Templeton Religion Reporter of the Year Award Vol. 1: 17977
Templeton Religion Writer of the Year in Europe; John Vol. 2: 6313
Templeton United Kingdom Project Trust Award Vol. 1: 12415
Templin Award; Richard L. Vol. 1: 5990
Temuco High School Award Vol. 2: 1260
Ten Best Amateur Films Vol. 1: 17283
Ten Best of the West Film Festival Vol. 1: 3148
Ten Outstanding Young Americans Vol. 1: 20678
TenBroek Award; Jacobus Vol. 1: 15041
Tenenbaum Award; Michael Vol. 1: 5416
Tenhoff Award; Ray E. Vol. 1: 19115
Tenneco Student Section Scholarship Award Vol. 1: 4605
Tennessee Big "I" Advertising Award Vol. 1: 10740
Tennessee Children's Choice Book Award Vol. 1: 19974
Tennessee History Book Award Vol. 1: 19970
Tennessee Resource Sharing Award Vol. 1: 19971
Tennessee Teacher of Excellence Vol. 1: 19966
Tennis Educational Merit Award Vol. 1: 12077
Tennis Educational Merit Award for Men Vol. 1: 12077
Tennis Educational Merit Award for Women Vol. 1: 12078
Tennis Facility Awards Vol. 1: 20867
Tennis Magazine Collegiate Journalism Award Vol. 1: 11149
Tennis Magazine /ITA College Players of the Year Vol. 1: 19982
Tennis Magazine/ITA Player of the Year Vol. 1: 11150
Tennis Week Great American Tennis Writing Awards Vol. 1: 19984
Tennis World Champions Vol. 2: 7996
Tentai Hakkensho Vol. 2: 4097
Tenth Anniversary Commemorative Award Vol. 1: 7142
Teodorescu Prize; Emanoil Vol. 2: 5871
Teodorov-Balan Prize; Academician Aleksandar Vol. 2: 1207
Terman Award; Frederick Emmons Vol. 1: 4045
Terrier of the Year Award Vol. 2: 1466
Terry Preservation Awards; Lucille Vol. 1: 9082
Tertia M.C. Hughes Memorial Prize Vol. 1: 7281
Tertis Award; The Lillian Vol. 2: 9121
Tertis International Viola Competition and Workshop; Lionel Vol. 2: 9121
Terzaghi Lecture; Karl Vol. 1: 4361
Tesla Award; Nikola Vol. 1: 10883
Tesla Awards; Nikola Vol. 2: 1390
TESOL Fellowship for Graduate Study Vol. 1: 19949
TESOL/Newbury House Award for Excellence in Teaching Vol. 1: 19953
TESOL/Regents Publishing Company Fellowship Vol. 1: 19949
TESOL Research Interest Section/Newbury House Distinguished Research Award Vol. 1: 19952
TESOL Research Interest Section/Thomson Heinle Distinguished Research Award Vol. 1: 19952
TESOL Thomson Heinle Award for Excellence in Teaching Vol. 1: 19953
TESOL Travel Grant Vol. 1: 19954
Tess Award in Coatings; Roy W. Vol. 1: 1792
Tessenow Gold Medal; Heinrich Vol. 2: 3093
Tessier; Prix Albert- Vol. 1: 17793
Tesvik Odulu Vol. 2: 6650
TETYC Best Article of the Year Award Vol. 1: 14844
Texas Bluebonnet Award Vol. 1: 20028
Texas Collector's Institute Award Vol. 1: 20019
Texas Newspaper Leader of the Year; Pat Taggart Award for Vol. 1: 20000
Texas Service Award for Outstanding Contributions to Clinical Chemistry Vol. 1: 1003
Texas Star Award Vol. 1: 22094
Texas Tech Law School Foundation Vol. 1: 19986
Texier II; Prix Henri Vol. 2: 2056
Texier; Prix Henri Vol. 2: 2055
Text Prize Vol. 1: 264
Textile Citizen of the Year Vol. 1: 410
Textile Institute Design Medal Vol. 2: 9129
Textile Institute Development Award Vol. 2: 9130
Textile Institute Honorary Fellow Vol. 2: 9131
Textile Institute Honorary Life Member Vol. 2: 9132
Textile Institute Jubilee Award Vol. 2: 9133
Textile Institute Service Medal Vol. 2: 9134
Textile Section Award Vol. 1: 16211
Textile Technology Award Vol. 2: 4465
A Textilipar Fejleszteseert Erem Vol. 2: 3270
Thalia Prize Vol. 2: 6239
Thames Television Award Vol. 2: 6925
Thames Valley Award Vol. 2: 7200
Than Medal; Karoly Vol. 2: 3251
Thant Peace Award; U Vol. 1: 20364
Thayer Award; Sylvanus Vol. 1: 20701
The Dominion Sunday Times Bruce Mason Playwrights Award Vol. 2: 5045
Thea Sybesma Award Vol. 2: 4854
Theater P.E.I. Playwriting Awards Vol. 1: 17549
Theatre for Young Audiences Juried Awards Vol. 1: 10166
Theatre Grants Vol. 1: 17555
Theatre Library Association Award Vol. 1: 20060
Theatre Organist of the Year Vol. 1: 4739
Theatre Translations Schemes Vol. 2: 6756
Theatre World Awards Vol. 1: 20062
Theatre Writing Bursaries Vol. 2: 6757
Theatrical Plays for Children-Premio "As Palavras do Amor" Vol. 2: 5477
Thebault; Fondation Victor Vol. 2: 1976
Theiler Memorial Trust Award Vol. 2: 5602
Thelin Researcher of the Year Award; Dr. Murray Vol. 1: 15213
Theo Limperg Prize Vol. 2: 4860

Theoretical and Mathematical Physics; ACP-CRM/CAP-CRM Prize in Vol. 1: 13203
Therapist of the Year Vol. 1: 11320
Therapy Horse of the Year Award Vol. 1: 3133
Thermo Electron Clinical Chemistry and Automation Systems Award Vol. 2: 6772
Thermoforming Institute National Awards Vol. 1: 19322
Thessaloniki Film Festival Vol. 2: 3190
Thevenot Medal; Jean Vol. 2: 6402
Thew Fund Awards; H.A. Vol. 2: 8152
Thibaud; Concours International Marguerite Long et Jacques Vol. 2: 2526
Thibaud International Competition; Marguerite Long and Jacques Vol. 2: 2526
Thiele-Denkmunze; Dr. Edmund- Vol. 2: 2653
Thienpont Prize; Denis Vol. 2: 978
Third World Academy of Science Prize Vol. 2: 2637
Thirteen Centuries of Bulgaria Order Vol. 2: 1233
Thistle Student Award Vol. 2: 5636
Thom Award; Charles Vol. 1: 18762
Thomas Award; Clayton J. Vol. 1: 13408
Thomas Award; Isaiah Vol. 1: 18087
Thomas Award; Lowell
International Platform Association Vol. 1: 11813
Overseas Press Club of America Vol 1: 16981
Thomas Award; Major General Jack E. Vol. 1: 15384
Thomas Award; Moyer D. Vol. 1: 5991
Thomas Award; Theodore Vol. 1: 8349
Thomas CEA Distinguished Service Award; Joe D. Vol. 1: 8156
Thomas Lecture and Prize; E. Donnall Vol. 1: 4447
Thomas Medal Vol. 2: 2497
Thomas Memorial Award; Jesse Burgess Vol. 1: 20936
Thomas Memorial Award; R. D. Vol. 1: 4897
Thomas Nast Award Vol. 1: 16981
Thomas National Memorial Trophy; Norma Vol. 2: 6720
Thomas R. Camp Medal Vol. 1: 21499
Thomas Reed Memorial Scholarship Vol. 1: 20245
Thomas Sportsmanship Award; Homa S. Vol. 1: 15316
Thomas Starzl Humanitarian Award Vol. 1: 20152
Thomas Travel Journalism Awards; Lowell Vol. 1: 19016
Thomas Unipresser Award; Helen Vol. 1: 20370
Thomason, Jr. Award; Colonel John W. Vol. 1: 13101
Thompson Award Vol. 1: 13954
Thompson Award; E. H. Vol. 2: 8337
Thompson Award for Distinguished Service; George N. Vol. 1: 19074
Thompson Award; Helen M. Vol. 1: 4732
Thompson Award; Mary Anee Vol. 1: 5112
Thompson Award; S. Earl Vol. 1: 5625
Thompson Award; Sanford E. Vol. 1: 5992
Thompson Award; W. F. Vol. 1: 2806
Thompson Foundation Gold Medal; J. P. Vol. 2: 533
Thompson Medal; Mary Clark Vol. 1: 13849
Thompson Memorial Award; Arthur R. Vol. 1: 12271
Thompson Memorial Award; Robert D. Vol. 1: 5993
Thompson Memorial Public Service Award; Locksin Vol. 1: 6761
Thompson Premium; J. Langham Vol. 2: 7833
The Thoms Hatton Memorial Grade B. Male Voice Scholarship Vol. 1: 18317
Thomson Foundation Fellowships Vol. 2: 9140
Thomson Gale Award for Excellence in Reference and Adult Services Vol. 1: 17948
Thomson Gold Medal; Sir George Vol. 2: 7721
Thomson Medal Vol. 2: 5087
Thomson Medal; J. J. Vol. 2: 7834
Thomson Medal; J. P. Vol. 2: 533
Thomson Premium; J. J. Vol. 2: 7808
Thomson Prize in Applied Meteorology; Dr. Andrew Vol. 1: 7282
Thomson Resistance Welding Award; Elihu Vol. 1: 4898
Thora W. Halstead Young Investigator's Award Vol. 1: 4082
Thorarinsson Medal Vol. 2: 444
Thore; Fondation Jean Vol. 2: 1904
Thoreau Award Vol. 1: 7573
Thoreau Medal; Emerson - Vol. 1: 623
Thorel; Prix Ernest Vol. 2: 2043
Thorlet; Prix Vol. 2: 1731
Thornburgh Family Award; Bill Vol. 1: 2193
Thorndike Award for Career Achievement in Educational Psychology; Edward L. Vol. 1: 3680
Thornton Award; John Vol. 2: 6704
Thornton Gold Challenge Award; Mark Vol. 1: 11682
Thornton Memorial Award and Lecture; John A. Vol. 1: 6156
Thorpe Award; Jim Vol. 1: 21240
Thorvaldsen Medal Vol. 2: 1525
Thouron Fellowship Vol. 2: 9155
Threadgill Award; Michael Beall Vol. 1: 15199
Three-Day Novel Contest Vol. 1: 4990
The Thrity-One Award Vol. 2: 8957
Thrower of the Year Vol. 1: 21244
Thulinmedaljen Vol. 2: 6296
Thunbergmedaljen Vol. 2: 6195
Thurber Prize for American Humor Vol. 1: 20087
Thurgood Marshall Journalism Award Vol. 1: 8781
Thurlow Award Vol. 1: 11016
Thurlow Trophy; Philip Vol. 2: 7880
Thurston Award; John B. Vol. 1: 10976
Thurston Grand President's Award; Emory W. Vol. 1: 17247
Thygesen Membership Award; Jake Vol. 1: 7045
TI Integrity Awards Vol. 2: 3111
Tibbitts Award; Clark Vol. 1: 5374
Tibbitts Grand Champion Horse Award; Bev Vol. 1: 16493
Tibetan Freedom Fighter Vol. 2: 3593
Tibor Greenwalt Scientific Lectureship Vol. 1: 1117
Tice Friend of the AphA-ASP Award; Linwood F. Vol. 1: 3401
Ticketing Professional of the Year Award Vol. 1: 12087
Tickey Award; Bertha Vol. 1: 589
Tiemann Award; Walter Vol. 2: 3020
Tiffany Awards for Employee Excellence Vol. 1: 3838
Tilak Lecture; Prof. B. D. Vol. 2: 3521
Tilden Award; Freeman Vol. 1: 15492
Tilden Canadian Literary Awards Vol. 1: 7000
Tilden Lectureship Vol. 2: 8778
Tilleard Medal Vol. 2: 8648
Tillyer Award; Edgar D. Vol. 1: 16797
Tilton Memorial Award; Randy Vol. 1: 3591
Time Life Silver Pen Award for Non-Fiction Vol. 2: 7426
Time Magazine Award for Outstanding Map Design on Current Events Vol. 1: 2006
Time Magazine Quality Dealer Award Vol. 1: 20092
Time Man of the Year Vol. 1: 20093
Time Out/01 - for London Awards Vol. 2: 9143
Time Out Eating and Drinking Awards Vol. 2: 9142
Time Out Live Awards Vol. 2: 9143
Time Out Student Awards Vol. 2: 9144
The Times Educational Supplement Information Book Awards Vol. 2: 9146
The Times Educational Supplement Schoolbook Award Vol. 2: 9147
The Times Higher Educational Supplement Award Vol. 2: 7382
Timmie Awards Vol. 1: 20132
Timoshenko Medal Vol. 1: 4550
Timothy Trophy Vol. 1: 6164
Tinbergen Awards for Young Statisticians from Developing Countries; Jan Vol. 2: 4842
Tindall Trophy; Frank Vol. 1: 7237
Tinkle Award; Lon Vol. 1: 20021
Tinkle Research Excellence Award; Donald W. Vol. 1: 19532
Tinsley Prize; Beatrice M. Vol. 1: 1518
Tipton Award; Royce J. Vol. 1: 4362
Tir na n-Og Awards Vol. 2: 9204
Tiroler Landespreis fur Kunst Vol. 2: 678
Tiroler Landespreis fur Wissenschaft Vol. 2: 679
Tirumurti Memorial Lecture; Dr. T.S. Vol. 2: 3522
Tison Award Vol. 2: 2447
Tissandier Diploma; Paul Vol. 2: 6351
Tisserand; Prix Lucien Vol. 2: 2180
Titan All America Hockey Squad (East and West) for Colleges Vol. 1: 2491
Titan All-America Hockey Squad (East and West) for Universities Vol. 1: 2492
Titeica Prize; Gheorghe Vol. 2: 5872
Titulescu Prize; Nicholae Vol. 2: 5873
Titus Award; Cedric Vol. 2: 4075
Titus Award; Shirley Vol. 1: 3285
Titus Memorial Trophy Award; Jerry Vol. 1: 1522
Tjokronegoro Award; Sutomo Vol. 2: 3603
TLA/SIRS Freedom of Information Award Vol. 1: 19972
Tlwas y Cerddor (Composers Medal) Vol. 2: 9210
TMS/ASM Joint Distinguished Lectureship in Materials and Society Award Vol. 1: 13459
TNR Awards in Fiction and Poetry Vol. 1: 16075
Tobacco-Free Schools Award Vol. 2: 5215
Tobin Award; Mrs. Edgar Vol. 1: 13318
Tocze Memorial Trophy; Emile Vol. 1: 21846
Today's Workplace of Tomorrow Vol. 1: 21793
TOEFL Award Vol. 1: 9178

Award Index

Toison d'Or Vol. 2: 2416
Toit Award; Marie du Vol. 2: 5599
Toit Malherbe Prize for Genealogical Research; D. F. du Vol. 2: 5664
Toit Medal; Frans du Vol. 2: 5665
Toit Memorial Lecturer; Alex L. du Vol. 2: 5570
Tokle Award; Torger Vol. 1: 20823
Tokyo International Competition for Chamber Music Composition Vol. 2: 4176
Tokyo International Competition for Guitar Compositions Vol. 2: 4176
Tokyo International Film Festival Vol. 2: 4306
Tokyo International Music Competition Vol. 2: 4309
Tokyo Video Festival Vol. 2: 4316
Toll Innovation Awards Vol. 1: 11434
Tollefsen Award; Lois Vol. 1: 11661
Tolstoi Award; Alexei Vol. 2: 1395
Tom-Gallon Award Vol. 2: 8992
Tom Tyrell Trophy and Award Vol. 2: 4352
Tomes Award; Gilbert Vol. 2: 7867
Tomkinson Award; Helen Vol. 2: 7079
Tomorrow's Leaders of MPI Award Vol. 1: 13285
Tompkins Fellowship; Sally Kress Vol. 1: 19026
Tondelli; Premio Piervittorio Vol. 2: 4044
Toner, Jr. Memorial Award; Arthur Carling Vol. 1: 578
Tony Awards Vol. 1: 12742
Tony Lipson Memorial Fund Award Vol. 1: 21290
Tooley Award Vol. 2: 7960
Toonder Award; Marten Vol. 2: 3619
Tooting Bec Cup Vol. 2: 8302
Top 10 Orienteers Vol. 2: 1219
Top 25 Censored Stories of the Year Vol. 1: 17664
Top 100 Companies Award Vol. 2: 5783
Top Archite Vol. 1: 3876
Top Businessman of the Year Award Vol. 2: 5784
Top Case of the Year Vol. 1: 20736
Top Female Pilot Vol. 1: 16365
Top Honor Books, Chicago Book Clinic Annual Exhibit Vol. 1: 7879
Top Packaging Awards Vol. 1: 9574
Top Performance Awards Vol. 1: 5253
Top-Producing Dogs Vol. 1: 22045
Top Ranking Cotswold Breeder's Young Flock at the Illinois State Fair Vol. 1: 2032
Top Tea Place of the Year Vol. 2: 9114
Top Ten Business Women of ABWA Vol. 1: 1610
Top Ten Female Style Makers of the Year Vol. 1: 14742
Top Ten Public Works Leaders of the Year Vol. 1: 3809
Top-Winning Yorkshire Terrier in the United States Award Vol. 1: 22046
Topical Awards; Best in Vol. 1: 4748
Toppers in Food Technology Vol. 2: 3581
Topps All-Star Scout Award Vol. 1: 20103
Topps Major League Rookie All-Star Team Vol. 1: 20104
Topps Minor League Player-of-the-Month Vol. 1: 20105
Topps National Association All-Star Teams Vol. 1: 20106
Topps Organization Trophy Vol. 1: 20107
Topps Scout-of-the-Month Awards Vol. 1: 20108
Torch Award
American Society for Training and Development Vol. 1: 4208
Federation of Jewish Men's Clubs Vol 1: 9511
Torch of Learning Award Vol. 1: 2310
Torga - Cidade de Coimbra; Premio Literario Miguel Vol. 2: 5391
Torgi Talking Book of the Year Vol. 1: 7306
Tornov-Loeffler; Prix Ch. M. Vol. 2: 1738
Toronto Arts Awards Vol. 1: 20112
Toronto-City Award for Best Canadian Feature Film Vol. 1: 20118
Toronto City Award for Excellence in Canadian Production Vol. 1: 20118
Toronto International Salon of Photography Vol. 1: 20120
Toronto Press Club National Newspaper Awards Vol. 1: 7309
Torrens Award; Richard R. Vol. 1: 4363
Tory; Medaille Henry Marshall Vol. 1: 18174
Tory Medal; Henry Marshall Vol. 1: 18174
Toscanini; Concorso Internazionale di Direzione d'Orchestra Arturo Vol. 2: 3930
Toscanini International Competition for Conductors; Arturo Vol. 2: 3930
Toscano Medal; Salvador Vol. 2: 4471
Toscano; Medalla Ing. Salvador Vol. 2: 4471
Toshiba/NSTA ExploraVision Awards Vol. 1: 15693
Tosney AAUA Award for Excellence in the Practice of Higher Education Administration; Eileen M. Vol. 1: 1462
Totius Prize for Theology and the Original Languages of the Bible Vol. 2: 5666
Touch of Knowledge Award Vol. 1: 4690
Touchdown Club Arch McDonald Achievement Award Vol. 1: 20133
Touchdown Club Hubert H. Humphrey Award Vol. 1: 20134
Touchdown Club Local Personality Makes Good Award Vol. 1: 20135
Touchdown Club Mr. Sam Award Vol. 1: 20136
Touchdown Club's Board of Governors Award Vol. 1: 20137
Touchstone Award Vol. 1: 6978
Touchstone Award; F. Morris Vol. 1: 20669
Toulmin Medal Vol. 1: 18999
Tour Award; Sam Vol. 1: 5994
Tour de France Vol. 2: 2224
Touring Car World Cup Vol. 2: 2455
Tourism Award Vol. 1: 16529
Tourism Employee Excellence Award Vol. 1: 10128
Tourism Promotion Grant Vol. 1: 10620
Tourneur; Prix Victor Vol. 2: 1033
Toussaint; Premio Manuel Vol. 2: 4539
Toutain-Blanchet; Prix Vol. 2: 1776
Tovey Memorial Prize; Donald Vol. 2: 9178
Tower and Carillon Prize Vol. 2: 1089
Tower Trophy Vol. 1: 20589
Towers Flight Safety Award; Adm. John H. Vol. 1: 16834
Towley Award; Carl Vol. 1: 12454
Townes Award; Charles Hard Vol. 1: 16798
Towngate Theatre National Playwriting Contest Vol. 1: 16620
Townshend Award; B. W. O. Vol. 2: 8406
Township Leader of the Year Vol. 1: 13467
Townsville Foundation for Australian Literary Studies Award Vol. 2: 348
Towson University Prize for Literature Vol. 1: 20145
Toy and Game Inventors of America Vol. 1: 12166
Toy; Fondation du Docteur Jean Vol. 2: 1850
Toynbee Memorial Lectureship; Joseph Vol. 2: 8831
Toyota Tapestry Grant Vol. 1: 15694
Trabajador del Ano en Salud Vol. 1: 20697
Tracey Memorial Award; Anna Vol. 1: 17328
Track & Field News Award Vol. 1: 21241
Tracks Award Vol. 1: 7491
Trade Book of the Year Vol. 1: 6508
Trade NZ Major Exporter of the Year Vol. 2: 5099
Trade Union's Art and Cultural Prize Vol. 2: 3303
Traditional Irish Music, Singing and Dancing Awards Vol. 2: 3714
Trail - Crisp Award Vol. 2: 8075
Trail Development Award Vol. 1: 2458
Trailblazer Award Vol. 1: 11643
Trailblazer in Philanthropy Award Vol. 1: 17269
Trainee of the Year; PGA Vol. 2: 8304
Trainee Travel Awards Vol. 1: 4123
Trainer of the Year
International Veteran Boxers Association Vol. 1: 12122
Walking Horse Trainers Association Vol 1: 21428
Trainer of the Year Award Vol. 1: 14953
Training Trophy Vol. 2: 8720
Trakl Preis fur Lyrik; Georg Vol. 2: 669
Trakl Prize for Poetry; Georg Vol. 2: 669
Trampoline and Tumbling National Leadership Award Vol. 1: 579
Trans-Am Tour Vol. 1: 19721
Trans-American Sedan Championship Vol. 1: 19721
Trans Atlantic Reciprocal Award Vol. 1: 16141
Trans-Canada (McKee) Trophy Vol. 1: 6870
Transco Press Award Vol. 2: 6924
Transfusion Medicine Fellowship Awards Vol. 1: 1118
Translation Prize Vol. 1: 17801
Translators Association Unger Award Vol. 1: 4752
Transplant Recipients International Organization Scholarship Vol. 1: 20153
Transport Award Vol. 2: 5009
Transport Engineering Medal Vol. 2: 432
Transport Research and Educational Trust Board Scholarship Vol. 2: 5010
Transportation Achievement Award Vol. 1: 11058
Transportation Administrator of the Year Vol. 1: 14026
Transportation Man of the Year Vol. 1: 8868
Transportation Person of the Year Vol. 1: 15906
Transportation Professional of the Year Vol. 1: 20155
Transportation Research Board Distinguished Service Award Vol. 1: 20160
Transportation Safety Awards Vol. 1: 19585
Trapper/Conservationist Award Vol. 1: 15914
Trapper of the Year Vol. 1: 15915
Trask Prize and Awards; Betty Vol. 2: 8993
Trautman Minor League Player-of-the-Year; Topps - George M. Vol. 1: 20109
Travel Agent of the Year Award Vol. 1: 4626
Travel and Study Abroad Vol. 2: 7521

Travel Award
Alpine Garden Society Vol. 2: 6700
European Wound Management Association Vol 2: 7494
Minerals Engineering Society Vol 2: 8126
Travel Awards Vol. 1: 20979
Travel Bursaries Vol. 2: 7049
Travel Fellowships Vol. 2: 7457
Travel Grant
American Association for Clinical Chemistry Vol. 1: 1004
American Society for Microbiology, Arizona Chapter Vol 1: 4141
Travel Grants
American Association for Cancer Research Vol. 1: 969
American Institute of Architects - New York Chapter Vol 1: 2728
Travel Grants for Educators Vol. 1: 11878
Travel Grants to Students Coming to USA from Developing Countries Vol. 1: 12232
Travel Hall of Fame Vol. 1: 4627
Travel Industry Awards for Excellence Vol. 1: 20177
Travel Industry Hall of Leaders Vol. 1: 20176
Travel Industry Odyssey Awards Vol. 1: 20177
Travel Journalist of the Year Vol. 1: 19016
Travel Research Contest Vol. 1: 20170
Travel Scholarships Vol. 2: 2301
Travel to Artists Grant Vol. 1: 11088
Travel Writing Award Vol. 1: 22002
Traveling Fellowship Award Vol. 1: 1605
Traveling Show Appreciation Award Vol. 1: 4870
Travelling Fellowships Vol. 2: 8452
Travers; Prix Maurice Vol. 2: 2078
Tree of Learning Award Vol. 2: 6560
Tree of Life Award
Canadian Institute of Forestry Vol. 1: 7179
Jewish National Fund Vol 1: 12368
Trees for Tomorrow Award Vol. 1: 20188
Tregre Award; Louis S. Vol. 1: 14771
Tremaine Fellowship Vol. 1: 6360
Tremaine Medal; Marie Vol. 1: 6361
Trendsetter Award Vol. 1: 9669
Trent - Crede Medal Vol. 1: 145
Trento Filmfestival Internazionale Montagna Esplorazione Vol. 2: 4059
Trento International Film Festival of Mountain and Exploration Vol. 2: 4059
Tressler - VNR/AVI Teacher Award Vol. 1: 16409
Trevethan Award; P. J. Vol. 1: 10093
Trevithick Premium Vol. 2: 7784
Trevor Award Vol. 1: 20247
Tri-Color Trophy Vol. 1: 2447
Tri-M Leadership Award Vol. 1: 20199
Tri-M Service Award Vol. 1: 20200
Trial and Show Trophies Vol. 1: 8705
Trial Lawyer of the Year Award Vol. 1: 20204
Triangle Award Vol. 1: 13624
Trianti Grand Prix; Alexandra Vol. 2: 3166
Triathletes of the Year Vol. 1: 21249
Triathlon Federation USA Appreciation Award Vol. 1: 21250
Tributary Awards Vol. 1: 9127
Tribute of the Film Society of Lincoln Center Vol. 1: 9545
Tribute to Women Award Vol. 1: 22076
Tribute to Women in Industry Award Vol. 1: 22082
Tricerri; Premio Vol. 2: 4018
Tricks for Kids Vol. 2: 3107
Triennial Challenge Cup Vol. 2: 4458
Triennial Composition Competition Vol. 1: 8872
Triennial Prize Vol. 1: 18943
Trieschman Award; Albert E. Vol. 1: 1136
Trillium Book Award Vol. 1: 16752
Trillium Book Award for Poetry Vol. 1: 16752
Trimble History Award; Maude C. Vol. 1: 6691
Trimble Memorial Award; Robert E. Vol. 1: 10406
Trimmer Merit Shop Teaching Award of Excellence; John Vol. 1: 5234
Triossi; Fondation Marie Guido Vol. 2: 1928
Triple Crown Vol. 1: 7990
Triple Crown Champion
Churchill Downs Inc. Vol. 1: 7989
New York Racing Association Vol 1: 16257
Triple Crown Trophy Vol. 1: 20206
Troland Research Awards Vol. 1: 13850
Troll-Preis; Thaddaeus- Vol. 2: 2769
Trollope Medal; D. H. Vol. 2: 433
Trophee du Fairplay FIM Vol. 2: 6420
Trophee Environment Vol. 1: 7782
Trophee International de la Reliure d'Art Vol. 2: 4400
Trophees Desjardins Vol. 1: 7783
Trost Award; Jan Vol. 1: 11899
Trotter Prize; Mildred Vol. 1: 1360
Trotting Triple Crown Vol. 1: 20879
Troubadour de la SABAM Vol. 2: 1105
Troublemaker Awards Vol. 1: 12639
Trout Conservationist of the Year Vol. 1: 20211
Trouw Publieksprijs voor het Nederlandse Boek Vol. 2: 4719
Troy Rotary Scholarship Awards Vol. 1: 20218
Trubert; Prix Maurice Vol. 2: 2188
Truck Driver of the Year Vol. 1: 19577
Truck of the Year Vol. 1: 6106
Truck Puller of the Year Vol. 1: 15882
Truck Safety Contest Vol. 1: 4775
Trudeau Award Vol. 1: 3015
True Value Man of the Year Vol. 1: 15089
Truman Award; Harry S.
National Guard Association of the United States Vol. 1: 15176
National Guard Association of the United States Vol 1: 15177
Truman Book Award; Harry S Vol. 1: 10266
Truman Good Neighbor Award; Harry S. Vol. 1: 20226
Truman Prize; S. J. Wallace Vol. 1: 13800
Truman Public Service Award; Harry S. Vol. 1: 8037
Truman Silver Veteran's Medal Vol. 1: 20227
Trumpet Competition; International Maurice Andre Vol. 2: 2278
Trumpeter Award Vol. 1: 14734
Trumpler Award; Robert J. Vol. 1: 6012
Truog Soil Science Award; Emil Vol. 1: 19399
Truran, Jr., Medical Materiel and Logistics Management Award; Paul F. Vol. 1: 5788
Trusler Prize Vol. 2: 8620
Trust Fund Vol. 2: 6841
Trustee Award Vol. 1: 19973
Trustee Citation Vol. 1: 10687
Trustee Citation Award Vol. 1: 16071
Trustee of the Year Vol. 1: 20353
Trustee of the Year Award
American Association for Women in Community Colleges Vol. 1: 1070
American Association of Homes and Services for the Aging Vol 1: 1233
Trustee Recognition Award Vol. 1: 16182
Trustee's Award Vol. 1: 17761
Trustees Award
American Hospital Association Vol. 1: 2548
Gungywamp Society Vol 1: 10211
Trustees' Award Vol. 1: 15326
Trustees' Honor Roll Vol. 1: 3901
Trustees Trophy Vol. 1: 8362
Truth in Action Award Vol. 2: 9236
TSA Star Recognition Program Vol. 1: 19960
Tsao Leonardo Award; Makepeace Vol. 1: 11960
TSB Award Vol. 2: 9029
Tschumi Prize; Jean Vol. 2: 2514
TSL Trophy Vol. 2: 7201
Tsuboi Prize Vol. 2: 6047
TTRA Achievement Award Vol. 1: 20173
TTRA Travel Research Award Vol. 1: 20174
TUBITAK Husamettin Tugac Award Vol. 2: 6651
Tucker Architectural Awards Competition Vol. 1: 6687
Tucker Award; Gabriel F. Vol. 1: 2929
Tucker Award; Richard Vol. 1: 20230
Tucker Award; Rosina Vol. 1: 30
Tucker Medal Vol. 2: 7209
Tucker Medal; Bernard Vol. 2: 7210
Tucker Study Grants; Sarah Vol. 1: 20231
Tuckerman Memorial Award for Painting; Else Vol. 1: 664
Tudor Medal Vol. 1: 19000
Tully Medal Vol. 2: 7555
Tully Medal in Oceanography; J.P. Vol. 1: 7283
Tulsa Library Trust Award for Young Readers' Literature Vol. 1: 20237
Tunbridge Wells International Young Concert Artists Competition Vol. 2: 9153
Tunner Aircrew Award; Lt. General William H. Vol. 1: 360
Tuntland Memorial Award; Paul E. Vol. 1: 18591
Tupolev Diploma; Andrei Vol. 2: 6352
Tupolev Medal; Andrei Vol. 2: 6353
Turbayne International Berkeley Essay Prize Competition; Colin and Ailsa Vol. 1: 21102
Turcotte Memorial Award; Robert Vol. 1: 10255
Turf Research Vol. 1: 12959
Turf Scholarship Vol. 1: 12960
Turin International Film Festival Vol. 2: 3883
Turing Award; A. M. Vol. 1: 5308
Turing Test Award; Loebner Prize Vol. 1: 6773
Turkish Language Institute Literature Prize Vol. 2: 6656
Turkish Language Prize Vol. 2: 6657
Turkish Radio and Television Culture, Art and Science Prizes Vol. 2: 6659
Turnbill Trophy Vol. 1: 11706
Turnbull Award; John Vol. 1: 7403
Turnbull Award; Lt. Col. J.L. (Jack) Vol. 1: 20670
Turnbull Award; W. Rupert Vol. 1: 6871
Turnbull Lectureship; The David Vol. 1: 13184
Turnbull Trophy; Jack Vol. 1: 20670
Turner Award; Alfred H. Vol. 2: 6721
Turner Award; Bob Vol. 1: 14912

Turner Award for Outstanding Service to NASPA; Fred Vol. 1: 14409
Turner Award; Frederick Jackson Vol. 1: 16897
Turner Award; Wava Banes Vol. 1: 19938
Turner Entrepreneur Award; Arthur E. Vol. 1: 16580
Turner Lecture Vol. 2: 4997
Turner Lecture; Francis C. Vol. 1: 4364
Turner Medal; Henry C. Vol. 1: 1970
Turner Prize; Dr. Lynn W. Vol. 1: 17237
Turner Prize; Ethel Vol. 2: 480
Turner - Scholefield Award Vol. 2: 9039
Turner Trophy; Joe Vol. 2: 6704
Turnquist Trophy Vol. 1: 8087
Tutor Appreciation Awards Vol. 1: 12278
Tutorial Citation Award Vol. 1: 4153
Tutt Award; Wm. Thayer Vol. 1: 21180
Tuttle Award; Arnold D. Vol. 1: 242
Tuttle Award; Frederick H. Vol. 1: 21308
Tuttle Distinguished Achievement Award; Judge Elbert P. Vol. 1: 17313
TV Hall of Fame Vol. 1: 128
TV Week Logie Awards Vol. 2: 628
Twain Award; Mark
  International Platform Association Vol. 1: 11814
  Missouri Association of School Librarians Vol 1: 13528
  By Word of Mouth Storytelling Guild Vol 1: 6718
  Society for the Study of Midwestern Literature Vol 1: 18922
TWAS Award in Basic Medical Sciences Vol. 2: 3795
TWAS Award in Biology Vol. 2: 3796
TWAS Award in Chemistry Vol. 2: 3797
TWAS Award in Mathematics Vol. 2: 3798
TWAS Award in Physics Vol. 2: 3799
Tweddle Medal Vol. 2: 9074
Tweed Award; Harrison Vol. 1: 1537
Twenhofel Medal Vol. 1: 18848
Twentieth Anniversary Professional Development Award Vol. 1: 7143
Twenty-Five Year Award
  American Institute of Architects Vol. 1: 2721
  National Athletic Trainers' Association Vol 1: 14462
Twenty-Five Year Club Member Certificate Vol. 1: 3261
Twenty-Five Year Membership Medals Vol. 1: 3262
Twenty-Five Year News Achievement Award Vol. 1: 19328
Twenty-Four Dollar Award Vol. 1: 13696
Twin Cities Musicians Union AFM Award Vol. 1: 21434
Twin Tribute to Women and Industry Vol. 1: 22080
Twinkie Vol. 1: 17861
TWNSO Award in Agriculture Vol. 2: 4056
TWNSO Award in Technology Vol. 2: 4057
Two Air Forces Award USAF/RAF Vol. 1: 376
Two Ladies from Texas Award Vol. 1: 15033
Two Wheel Drive Puller of the Year Vol. 1: 15892
Two-Year College Biology Teaching Award Vol. 1: 14099
Tyler Award; Leona Vol. 1: 3666
Tyler Ecology Award Vol. 1: 4975
Tyler, Jr. Miniature Award; John A. Vol. 1: 1623
Tyler Prize for Environmental Achievement Vol. 1: 4975
Tyler Prize for Stimulation of Research Vol. 1: 3402
Tyler Research Award; Dr. Ralph W. Vol. 1: 8505
Tylman Research Grant Program; Stanley D. Vol. 1: 678
Tylman Student Essay Award; Stanley D. Vol. 1: 678
Tyndall Award; John Vol. 1: 16799
Tyndall Medal Vol. 2: 7642
Tyneside Trophy Vol. 2: 6935
Tyrrell Historical Medal; J. B. Vol. 1: 18175
Tyrrell IABA Award for Young Achievement in Beef Industry Vol. 2: 148
Tzedakah Award Vol. 1: 20342
Tzvi & Mara Propes Prize; Aharon Vol. 2: 3738
U S Open Three Cushion Billiard Championships Vol. 1: 20435
U.C.F.D.A. Scholarship Vol. 1: 21131
Ucross Foundation Artists-in-Residence Program Vol. 1: 20265
Udall Center Prize in American Indian Public Policy Vol. 1: 20984
Udupg Ratna Award Vol. 2: 3349
Ueberroth - U.S. Water Polo Award; Peter V. Vol. 1: 20885
Ugly Stick Vol. 1: 20267
UHVA Awards Vol. 1: 20334
U.I.A.A. Prize Vol. 2: 4059
UITIC Awards Vol. 2: 6067
UJA - Federation Distinguished Communal Service Award Vol. 1: 20343
UK Company of the Year Vol. 2: 7118
UK Fashion Export Awards Vol. 2: 9159
Ukrainian of the Year Award Vol. 1: 20271
ULI Awards for Excellence Vol. 1: 21140
Ullman Award; Edwin F. Vol. 1: 1005
Ulmer, Jr. Applied Research Award; Walter F. Vol. 1: 7719
Ulrich's Serials Librarianship Award; Bowker/ Vol. 1: 5424
Ultra Distance Athlete-of-the-Year Vol. 1: 21242
Uluslararasi Istanbul Film Festivali Vol. 2: 6642
Umezawa Memorial Award for Chemotherapy (Cancer and Antimicrobial); Hamao Vol. 2: 7983
Umgeni Award Vol. 2: 5793
UMI/Data Courier Award Vol. 1: 10798
Umpire Award Vol. 1: 21160
UMS Distinguished Artist Award Vol. 1: 20975
Umweltpreis der Landeshauptstadt Stuttgart Vol. 2: 3105
UN/INEOA Law Enforcement Medal Vol. 1: 11767
UNA Study Circles Challenge Trophies Vol. 2: 6137
Unda Dove Vol. 2: 1112
Unda Rose Vol. 2: 1113
Underfashion Club Scholarship Program Vol. 1: 20287
Undergraduate Award Vol. 1: 18483
Undergraduate Award for Outstanding Students in Mineralogy Vol. 1: 13438
Undergraduate Awards Vol. 1: 14802
Undergraduate Certificate of Merit Vol. 1: 17353
Undergraduate Research Assistantships Vol. 1: 13515
Undergraduate Research Paper Awards Vol. 1: 6334
Undergraduate Scholarships Vol. 1: 7284
Undergraduate Student Awards for an Outstanding Horticulture Student Vol. 1: 4095
Undergraduate Student Paper Competition
  Alpha Kappa Delta Vol. 1: 480
  Institute of Industrial Engineers Vol 1: 10967
Undergraduate Student Thesis and Report Awards Vol. 1: 7131
Undergraduate Studentships in Nuclear Engineering Vol. 2: 7868
Undergraduate Water Prize Vol. 2: 287
Underwater Athletes of the Year Vol. 1: 20294
UNEP Sasakawa Environment Prize Vol. 2: 4367
UNESCO Crafts Prize Vol. 2: 2604
UNESCO - International Music Council Music Prize Vol. 2: 2605
UNESCO Literacy Prizes Vol. 2: 2606
UNESCO Prize for Architecture Vol. 2: 2607
UNESCO Prize for Landscape Architecture Vol. 2: 2608
UNESCO Prize for Peace Education Vol. 2: 2609
UNESCO Prize for the Teaching of Human Rights Vol. 2: 2610
UNESCO Science Prize Vol. 2: 2611
Unger Award; Heinz Vol. 1: 16748
UNICA Medal Vol. 2: 6277
UNICA-medaljen Vol. 2: 6277
UNICEF Award for Distinguished Service Vol. 1: 20598
UNICEF Award for Films Vol. 1: 20599
UNICEF Prize Vol. 2: 4263
UNICEF; Prize of Vol. 2: 2670
UNIMA Citation for Excellence in the Art of Puppetry Vol. 1: 20300
UNIMA-USA Scholarships Vol. 1: 20301
Union Carbide Award for Chemical Education Vol. 1: 7850
Union Carbide Lectureship Award Vol. 1: 4046
Union League Civic and Arts Foundation Poetry Prize Vol. 1: 17423
Union Medal Vol. 2: 7097
Union of Architects of the SRR Prize Vol. 2: 5881
Union of International Fairs Awards Vol. 2: 2617
Unit Citation for Gallantry Vol. 2: 204
Unit Citations Vol. 2: 204
Unitas Medal Vol. 2: 5760
United Methodist Association Award of Distinguished Service Vol. 1: 20354
United Nations Environment Program Awards Vol. 2: 4368
United Nations Medal Vol. 1: 8841
United Nations Medals Vol. 1: 6815
United Nations Population Award Vol. 1: 20368
United Nations Prize in the Field of Human Rights Vol. 1: 20360
United Nations Service Medal (Korea) Vol. 1: 8842
U.S. Air Force Academy Physics Award Vol. 1: 13412
United States Air Force Twelve Outstanding Airmen of the Year Vol. 1: 361
U.S. Art Magazine Award of Merit Vol. 1: 15483

U.S. Bicycling Hall of Fame Vol. 1: 20433
United States Boxing Hall of Fame Vol. 1: 20388
U.S. Catholic Award Vol. 1: 20442
U.S. Chess Championship Vol. 1: 20446
U.S. Coast Guard Academy Most Proficient Cadet in Handling a Sailing Vessel Vol. 1: 13413
United States Dressage Federation All Breed Award Vol. 1: 12872
U.S. Energy Award Vol. 1: 20573
United States Figure Skating Champions Vol. 1: 20589
United States Hang Gliding Association Commendation Vol. 1: 20616
U.S. History Award Vol. 1: 10439
United States Hockey Hall of Fame Vol. 1: 20637
U.S. Independence Cup Vol. 1: 20774
U.S. Industrial Film and Video Festival Vol. 1: 21143
U.S. International Film and Video Festival
 U.S. International Film and Video Festival Vol. 1: 20675
 US International Film and Video Festival Vol 1: 21143
U.S. Junior Sailing Championships Vol. 1: 20784
U.S. Match Racing Championship - Prince of Wales Bowl Vol. 1: 20781
U.S. Medal of Remembrance Vol. 1: 20640
U.S. Men's Sailing Championship - Clifford D. Mallory Cup Vol. 1: 20782
U.S. Military Academy General Management Award Vol. 1: 13414
U.S. Military Male and Female Athletes Vol. 1: 20138
U.S. National Hot Air Balloon Champion Vol. 1: 6226
United States National Roller Skating Championships Vol. 1: 20391
U.S. Naval Academy Mathematics Award Vol. 1: 13415
United States of America Counties Award Vol. 1: 8632
U.S. Olympic Hall of Fame Vol. 1: 20724
United States Open Tennis Championships Vol. 1: 20868
U.S. Outdoor Travel Film Festival Vol. 1: 13355
United States Presidential Scholars Program Vol. 1: 20491
U.S. Sailing One-Design Awards Vol. 1: 20783
U.S. Sailing/Rolex Junior Championships Vol. 1: 20784
U.S. Senate Productivity Award for Maryland Vol. 1: 21055
U.S. Singlehanded Sailing Championship - George D. O'Day Trophy Vol. 1: 20785
United States Skill Olympics Vol. 1: 18552
United States Steel Foundation Award in Molecular Biology Vol. 1: 13843
United States Swimming Award Vol. 1: 21206
United States Swimming Life Members Vol. 1: 21207
U.S. Team Race Championship - George R. Hinman Trophy Vol. 1: 20786
U.S. Television & Radio Commercials Festival Vol. 1: 21142
United States Water Polo Award Vol. 1: 20886
U.S. Women's Open Championships Vol. 1: 20787
U.S. Women's Sailing Championship - Mrs. Charles Francis Adams Trophy Vol. 1: 20788
U.S. Youth Sailing Championship Vol. 1: 20789
United States Youth Soccer Association Coach of the Year for Boys and Girls Vol. 1: 20899
United States Youth Soccer Association Youth Referee of the Year Vol. 1: 20900
Unity-and-Diversity Service Award Vol. 1: 20921
Unity Awards in Media Vol. 1: 12866
University Commemorative Medal Vol. 2: 3318
University Cup Vol. 1: 7238
University Division Coach of the Year; Spencer Penrose Award/ Vol. 1: 2496
University Founders Award Vol. 1: 9731
University Law School Essay Contest; Department of Justice - CBA Vol. 1: 6967
University Medal
 Case Western Reserve University Vol. 1: 7617
 New York University - Office of Publications Vol 1: 16304
University Medal for Excellence Vol. 1: 8245
University of Cambridge Arthur Shercliff Prize Vol. 2: 7869
University of Cincinnati Award Vol. 1: 3606
University of Louisville Grawemeyer Award for Ideas Improving World Order Vol. 1: 21042
University of Louisville Grawemeyer Award for Music Composition Vol. 1: 21050
University of Louisville Grawemeyer Award in Education Vol. 1: 21048
University of Manchester Prize Vol. 2: 7870
University of Maryland International Music Competitions Vol. 1: 18567
University of Michigan Press Book Award Vol. 1: 21067
University of Missouri Television Awards for Community Leadership Vol. 1: 21081
University of Southern Mississippi Medallion Vol. 1: 13517
University of Tasmania - Launceston Award Vol. 2: 434
University of Toronto Faculty of Music Scholarship Vol. 1: 21783
University Prizes Vol. 2: 579
University Service Awards Vol. 1: 20263
University Women's Association-Schaible-Strohmaier Vol. 1: 9390
Unlimited Modified Puller of the Year Vol. 1: 15893
Uno Lamm High Voltage Direct Current Award Vol. 1: 10915
Unsung Hero Award
 Association of the Wall and Ceiling Industries - International Vol. 1: 5892
 Organization of Professional Employees of the United States Department of Agriculture Vol 1: 16903
Unsung Unitarian Universalist Award Vol. 1: 20313
UNWL Scholarship Vol. 1: 20274
UOP Technology Award Vol. 1: 12226
UPA National Championships Vol. 1: 20281
UPA Spirit of the Game Awards Vol. 1: 20282
Upchurch Award; Avery Vol. 1: 21960
UPE Scholarship Awards Vol. 1: 21133
UPI National Broadcast Awards Vol. 1: 20371
Upjohn Award Vol. 2: 6842
Upjohn Quality of Life Award; ONS/ Vol. 1: 16728
Upper Austria Culture Prize for Film Vol. 2: 796
Upper Austria Culture Prize for Fine Arts Vol. 2: 797
Upper Austria Culture Prize for Literature Vol. 2: 798
Upper Austria Culture Prize for Music Vol. 2: 799
Upper Austria Culture Prize for Science Vol. 2: 800
Upper Austria Prize for Architecture Vol. 2: 801
Upper Secondary School Teachers Prizes Vol. 2: 1616
Uppsala Short Film Festival Vol. 2: 6300
Upson-Loren B. Miller Fellowship; The Lent D. Vol. 1: 8020
The Upstarts Awards Vol. 2: 8215
Upward Mobility Award Vol. 1: 19369
URAM Award for Excellence in Creative Endeavors for Research and Scholarship Vol. 1: 11962
URAM Award for Excellence in Creative Scholarly Writing Vol. 1: 11963
Urbahn Medal Vol. 1: 19001
Urban and Community Forestry Award Vol. 1: 13519
Urban Beautification Award Vol. 1: 2539
Urban Council Short Film Awards Vol. 2: 5222
Urban County Engineer of the Year Award Vol. 1: 14179
Urban Design Awards for Excellence Vol. 1: 2717
Urban Traffic Engineering Achievement Awards Vol. 1: 11059
Urbanek Memorial Award; Karel Vol. 1: 18413
Ure Award for Sportsmanship; Captain James S. Vol. 1: 15945
Uren Award; Lester C. Vol. 1: 19249
Urey Prize; Harold C. Vol. 1: 1519
US/ICOMOS Fellows Vol. 1: 20452
US Merchant Marine Academy Award Vol. 1: 13416
USA/British Isles Visiting Fellowship Vol. 2: 8441
USA-CA Award Vol. 1: 8632
USA International Ballet Competition Vol. 1: 21184
USA International Harp Competition Vol. 1: 21186
USA Swimming Combined Team Traveling Trophy; William A. Lippman Jr. Vol. 1: 21195
USA Table Tennis National Championships Vol. 1: 21210
USA Today Sports Weekly Award Vol. 1: 18635
USA Triathlon Appreciation Award Vol. 1: 21250
USAC Special Recognition Awards Vol. 1: 20429
USAF Personnel Manager of the Year Vol. 1: 362
USAT Girls' Sportsmanship Trophy Award Vol. 1: 20752
USATF Heptathlon Award Vol. 1: 21243

USCG Award; Captain William J. Kossler, Vol. 1: 2435
User Feedback Award Vol. 1: 18267
USF Grant Awards Vol. 1: 18367
USFCA All-America Certificates (Men) Vol. 1: 20585
USFCA All-America Certificates (Women) Vol. 1: 20586
USFCA Honorable Mention Vol. 1: 20587
USFCC/J. Roger Porter Award Vol. 1: 4139
USGA Championships Vol. 1: 20607
USHA National Championships Vol. 1: 20610
Usher Award; Barney Vol. 1: 7075
Usher Prize; Abbott Payson Vol. 1: 18877
Ushkow Community Service Award; Martin C. Vol. 1: 799
USHWAn-of-the-Year Vol. 1: 20632
USILA Awards Vol. 1: 20671
USILA Trophy Vol. 1: 20672
USITT Architecture Design Award Vol. 1: 20651
USITT/Edward Kook Endowment Fund Vol. 1: 20652
USO Woman of the Year Vol. 1: 21259
USOC Sports Equipment Student Design Contest Vol. 1: 20725
USRowing Medal Vol. 1: 20753
USSA Outstanding Alpine Masters Award Vol. 1: 20818
USSS Athlete of the Year Vol. 1: 19869
USSS Coach of the Year Vol. 1: 19870
USTA Community Service Award Vol. 1: 20869
USTA Girls' Sportsmanship Award Vol. 1: 20870
USTA Junior and Boys' Sportsmanship Award Vol. 1: 20864
USTA Tennis NJTL Chapter of the Year Award Vol. 1: 20871
USTA/USPTA Public Service Award Vol. 1: 20872
Ustinov Award; Peter Vol. 2: 6367
USWCA Senior Ladies Trophy Vol. 1: 20888
USX Foundation Award in Molecular Biology Vol. 1: 13843
Utah State Poetry Society Award Vol. 1: 15034
Uteck Bowl
Canadian Interuniversity Sport Vol. 1: 7239
Canadian Interuniversity Sport Vol 1: 7240
Utility Design Awards Vol. 1: 3790
Utilization Award Vol. 1: 14019
Utmarkt Svensk Form Vol. 2: 6298
Uttam Jeevan Raksha Padak Vol. 2: 3390
Utz Award; John P.
National Foundation for Infectious Diseases Vol. 1: 15121
National Foundation for Infectious Diseases Vol 1: 15124
VA Wapensky Award Vol. 1: 6559
Vaccarezza; Premio Consagracion Rodolfo A. Vol. 2: 42
Vachon Award; Romeo Vol. 1: 6872
Vahue Memorial Award; L. Ray Vol. 1: 16964
Vaisala Award; Prof. Dr. Vilho Vol. 2: 6573
Valabregue; Prix Antony Vol. 2: 2112
Valdes; Premio Miguel Aleman Vol. 2: 4490
Valdez; Premio Jose Cayetano Vol. 2: 4506
Valencia Film Festival, Golden Palm Award Vol. 2: 6073
Valencia Prize for Hispanic Culture; Guillermo Vol. 2: 1278
Valent Biosciences- Best Paper Awards Vol. 1: 17375
Valladolid International Film Festival Vol. 2: 6112
Valle Inclan; Premio Vol. 2: 8974
Valley Forge Certificate Vol. 1: 15176
Valley Forge Cross for Heroism Vol. 1: 15176
Valley Prize; George E. Vol. 1: 3479
Vallis Agri Prize Vol. 2: 4059
Valor Award
National Association for Search and Rescue Vol. 1: 14040
World Conservation Union Vol 2: 6557
Valor Awards Vol. 1: 20514
Valz; Fondations Lalande - Benjamin Vol. 2: 1980
Valz; Prix Benjamin Vol. 2: 1980
van Ameringen Award in Psychiatric Rehabilitation; Arnold L. Vol. 1: 3640
Van Anda Award; Carr Vol. 1: 18384
Van Antwerpen Award for Service to the Institute; F. J. & Dorothy Vol. 1: 2792
Van Beneden; Prix Edouard Vol. 2: 1110
Van Beneden; Prix P. J. et Edouard Vol. 2: 1071
Van Bercken Award; Lode Vol. 1: 8909
van Buren Structural Engineering Award; Maurice P. Vol. 1: 1959
Van Cleef Memorial Medal Vol. 1: 2335
Van Cliburn Competition Bronze Medal Vol. 1: 8108
Van Collen Prize; Willink Vol. 2: 4849
Van Couvering Memorial Award; Martin C. Vol. 1: 2846
Van Dalsumprijs; Albert Vol. 2: 4697
Van de Vate Prize for Orchestral Music Vol. 1: 11180
van de Woestijne Prize; Karel Vol. 2: 965
Van Den Heever Prize for Jurisprudence; Toon Vol. 2: 5667
van der Gracht-Penning; Van Waterschoot Vol. 2: 4879
van der Gracht Plaque; Van Waterschoot Vol. 2: 4879
Van der Hoogt-prijs; Lucy B. and C. W. Vol. 2: 4917
van der Mueren Prize; Floris Vol. 2: 1084
van Drimmelen Medal; Rev. Pieter Vol. 2: 5668
Van Dyck; Prijs Albert Vol. 2: 979
Van Eck Medal; Hendrik Vol. 2: 5697
Van Elven Fund Prize; Paul Tetar Vol. 2: 4850
Van Ertborn; Prix Baron Vol. 2: 1045
Van Ginderachter Prize; Jozef Vol. 2: 966
Van Goidsenhoven; Prijs Franz Vol. 2: 980
Van Grover Youth Exhibit Award; Melissa Vol. 1: 3263
Van Helmont; Prijs J. B. Vol. 2: 981
Van Leersumprijs; Emmy Vol. 2: 4698
Van Leeuwenhoek Distinctive Travel Award Vol. 2: 2758
Van Leeuwenhoek Medal Vol. 2: 4895
van Looyprijs; Jacobus Vol. 2: 4778
Van Marum Medaille Vol. 2: 4900
Van Marum Medal Vol. 2: 4900
Van Niel International Prize for Studies in Bacterial Systematics Vol. 2: 454
Van Nostrand Memorial Award; John Vol. 1: 11151
Van Orman Trophy Vol. 1: 12849
van Oyeprijs; Paul Vol. 2: 1085
Van Remortel Service Award; Harold Vol. 1: 1006
Van Sant Memorial Award; Gene and Mary Vol. 1: 15241
Van Slyke Award Vol. 1: 1007
Van Vliet Trophy; M. L. Vol. 1: 7240
van Vught Award; The Jean Vol. 2: 9346
van Wesemael Literary Prize; Guust Vol. 2: 4817
Van Winkle Award; Rip Vol. 1: 6568
van Wyk Louw Medal; N. P. Vol. 2: 5669
Van Zandt Citizenship Award; VFW James E. Vol. 1: 21342
VanArsdel Prize Vol. 1: 17999
Vance Award; James A. Vol. 1: 7420
Vance Award; John C. Vol. 1: 20165
Vance Award; Robert W. Vol. 1: 8680
Vancouver International Film Festival Vol. 1: 21273
Vancouver Professional Theatre Alliance Career Achievement Award Vol. 1: 10166
Vandenberg Award; Hoyt S. Vol. 1: 363
VanderHyden Award; Nelson Vol. 1: 21472
Vanderlinden; Prix Georges Vol. 2: 1058
Vanderlinden Prize; H. L. Vol. 2: 1086
Vanderlinde Public Official Award; Spence Vol. 1: 3796
Vandiver Award; Willard T. (Billy) Vol. 1: 580
Vanguard Award for Associates and Affiliates Vol. 1: 14578
Vanguard Award for Marketing Vol. 1: 14579
Vanguard Award for Programmers Vol. 1: 14580
Vanguard Award for Public Relations Vol. 1: 14581
Vanguard Award for Public Relations/ Vanguard Award for State/Regional Association Leadership Vol. 1: 14581
Vanguard Award for Science and Technology Vol. 1: 14582
Vanguard Award for State/Regional Association Leadership Vol. 1: 14581
Vanguard Award for Young Leadership Vol. 1: 14583
Vanguard Degree Vol. 1: 15974
Vanier Cup Vol. 1: 7227
Vanier Cup Trophy Vol. 1: 7241
Vanier Medal Vol. 1: 11029
VanMeter Humanitarian Award for International Relations; Harriet Vol. 1: 11428
Vannprisen Vol. 2: 5120
Vaquero; Premio Maestro Manuel Vol. 2: 4637
Vardon Trophy Vol. 1: 17623
Vardon Trophy; Harry Vol. 2: 8303
Vare Trophy Vol. 1: 12663
Vargo Memorial; Alan J. Vol. 1: 12724
Varian Fellowship; Russell and Sigurd Vol. 1: 6157
Varietal Awards Vol. 1: 2448
Varna International Ballet Competition Vol. 2: 1240
Varnell Memorial Award for Small Business; Charles E. Vol. 1: 392
Varoujan Award; Daniel Vol. 1: 16116
Varrazano Award Vol. 1: 12250
Vars Award; Harry M. Vol. 1: 4167
Vasconcelos World Award of Education; Jose Vol. 2: 4653
Vaughan and Bushnell Awards (Golden Hammer Awards) Vol. 1: 14255
Vaughan Scholarship Fund; M. C. Vol. 1: 4715

Vaughn Concerto Competition; Elizabeth Harper Vol. 1: 19863
Veale Prize; Sir Alan Vol. 2: 7818
Veblen - Commons Award Vol. 1: 5363
Veforda Vol. 2: 3325
Vegetable Breeding Working Group Award of Excellence; Working Group Vol. 1: 4096
Vegetarian Awareness Month Awards Vol. 1: 21283
Vegetarian Essay Contest Vol. 1: 21285
Vehicle Theft Investigators Award; 3M Vol. 1: 11194
Veitch Historical Society Scholarship Vol. 1: 21287
Veitch Memorial Medal; Gold Vol. 2: 8548
Velluz; Fondation Leon Vol. 2: 1922
Vender Heide Award Vol. 1: 6404
Ventris Memorial Award; Michael Vol. 2: 6741
Venture Grants Vol. 1: 20910
The Venture Student Aid Awards Vol. 1: 19420
Venzie Award; E. F. Vol. 1: 5890
Verband Ehrenring Vol. 2: 2643
Verbatim Award Vol. 2: 7460
Vercelli Medal Vol. 1: 14423
Verco Medal Vol. 2: 549
Verco Medal; Sir Joseph Vol. 2: 549
Vercoullie Prize; Jozef Vol. 2: 967
Verdaguer; Prix Alfred
Institut de France Vol. 2: 2433
Academie des Sciences Vol 2: 1983
Academie Francaise Vol 2: 2105
Verdeyen Prize for Soil Mechanics Vol. 2: 1100
Verdi Medal of Achievement Vol. 1: 13319
Verdienstmedaille Vol. 2: 2706
Verdonk; Fund Professor Doctor G. Vol. 2: 982
Vergerio European Prize for Children's Literature; Pier Paolo Vol. 2: 4067
Verissimo Prize; Jose Vol. 2: 1185
Veritas Award Vol. 1: 866
Verlain; Prix Valentine Abraham Vol. 2: 2217
Verlaine; Prix Paul Vol. 2: 2200
Verlanger; Prix Julia Vol. 2: 2520
Verleysen Prize; Dr. Karel Vol. 2: 983
Verlot; Prix de la Fondation Jean-Bernard Vol. 2: 2237
Vermeulenprijs; Matthijs Vol. 2: 4699
Vermont Playwrights Award Vol. 1: 21269
Vern Haverstick Groundwater Hero Award Vol. 1: 10182
Verner Awards; Elizabeth O'Neill Vol. 1: 19441
Vernon Memorial Lecture Award; Dr. Robert O. Vol. 1: 11538
Vernon; Prix Frederic et Jean de Vol. 2: 1739
Verona Award; Nagrada Eva Vol. 2: 1373
Versatility Hall of Fame Vol. 1: 2152
Versele; Prix Bernard Vol. 2: 942
Verstraete Fund; Prof. Dr. Marc Vol. 2: 984
Vertical Smile Vol. 2: 6110
Vertin Award; James R. Vol. 1: 5400
Verulam Medal Vol. 2: 7704
Very Special Arts Playwright Discovery Program Vol. 1: 21413
Very Special Arts Young Playwrights Program Vol. 1: 21413
Vesaas Debutant Prize; Tarjei Vol. 2: 5150
Vesper Cup Vol. 1: 20754
Vess Award (Avionics Marine of the Year); Paul G. Vol. 1: 13093
Vesta Award Vol. 1: 21698
Vestermark Award for Psychiatric Education; Seymour D. Vol. 1: 3641
Veteran's Administration Employee of the Year Award Vol. 1: 343
Veterans Award Vol. 1: 581
Veteran's Community Service Award Vol. 1: 21358
Veterans Employment Awards Vol. 1: 20515
Veterinarian Award; Outstanding Woman Vol. 1: 5534
Veterinarian of the Year Award; Young Vol. 2: 5771
Veterinary Association Gold Medal; South African Vol. 2: 5770
Vetlesen Prize Vol. 1: 8246
VEWAA Service Award Vol. 1: 15601
Vexillon Vol. 1: 11611
VFP Medal Vol. 1: 21330
VFW Americanism Award Vol. 1: 21333
VFW Armed Forces Award Vol. 1: 21334
VFW Aviation and Space Award Vol. 1: 21335
VFW Congressional Award Vol. 1: 21336
VFW Dwight David Eisenhower Distinguished Service Award Vol. 1: 21337
VFW Emergency Medical Technician Award Vol. 1: 21338
VFW Emergency Services Award Vol. 1: 21338
VFW Firefighter Award Vol. 1: 21339
VFW Hall of Fame Award Vol. 1: 21340
VFW J. Edgar Hoover Award Vol. 1: 21341
VFW James E. Van Zandt Citizenship Award Vol. 1: 21342
VFW News Media Award Vol. 1: 21343
VGP Award Vol. 1: 2343
Viareggio Prize Vol. 2: 4030
Vice Admiral "Jerry" Land Medal Vol. 1: 19216
Vice President Life Membership Vol. 2: 8032
Vice Presidents' Award Vol. 1: 11001
Vice Presidents Emiriti Award Vol. 2: 8728
Vice-President's Trophy Vol. 1: 11158
Vick Outstanding Province President Award; A. Frank Vol. 1: 11723
Vickrey Award; James "Tick" Vol. 1: 5544
Victim Services in Probation and Parole; Joe Kegans Award for Vol. 1: 3603
Victor Memorial Prize; Mildred Vol. 1: 15698
Victoria Cross Vol. 2: 7267
Victoria Cross for Australia Vol. 2: 196
Victoria Medal Vol. 2: 8528
Victoria Medal of Honour Vol. 2: 8571
Victorian Premier's Literary Awards Vol. 2: 609
Victory Awards Vol. 1: 15609
VID Product Grant; Baker & Taylor Entertainment Audio Music/ Vol. 1: 17713
Video Competition; British Medical Association Film and Vol. 2: 7060
Video Competition Unicaja Vol. 2: 9298
Video Grand Prix Vol. 2: 4316
Video Grand Prix Awards Vol. 1: 6059
Video Opera Prize Vol. 2: 759
Videotex Design Award Vol. 1: 12150
Videotex Innovation Award Vol. 1: 12152
Vidrio; Premio de Ciencas Morfologicas Dr. Enrique Acosta Vol. 2: 4606
Vieira da Silva de Investigacao; Premio Municipal Augusto Vol. 2: 5426
Viener Prize; Saul Vol. 1: 2904
Vienna International Composition Contest Vol. 2: 705
Viennet-Damien; Prix Vol. 2: 2565
Vierjaarlijkse prijs voor muziekcompositie Camille Huysmans Vol. 2: 839
Vietnam Educational Exchange Program Vol. 1: 20449
Vietnam Logistic and Support Medal Vol. 2: 205
Vietnam Medal Vol. 2: 205
Vietnam Service Medal Vol. 1: 8843
Vietnamese Youth Excellence Award Vol. 1: 21364
Vietor Maritime Research Award; A.G Vol. 1: 13735
Vigen-Prisen; Terje Vol. 2: 5163
Vigen Prize; Terje Vol. 2: 5163
Vigness Memorial Award; Dr. Irwin Vol. 1: 10931
Viking Range Awards for Broadcast Media Vol. 1: 12290
Viking Society for Northern Research Awards Vol. 2: 9187
Vilalva Prize; International Vasco Vol. 2: 5411
Vilardi Humanitarian Award; Emma May Vol. 1: 852
Vilas Literary Award; Carl H. Vol. 1: 12437
Vilella Award; Joseph R. Vol. 1: 5995
Vilis Vitols Award Vol. 1: 5481
Viljoen Medal for Journalism; Markus Vol. 2: 5670
Villa I Tatti Fellowships Vol. 2: 4069
Villaescusa Community Service Award; Henrietta Vol. 1: 14252
Village Award Vol. 1: 10172
The Village Voice OBIE Awards Vol. 1: 21368
Villavicencio; Premio Pablo Vol. 2: 4506
Villey; Prix Pierre Vol. 2: 2203
Vilvalva; Premio Internacional Vasco Vol. 2: 5411
Vinas; Concours International de Chant Francisco Vol. 2: 6114
Vinas; Concurs Internacional de Cant Francesc Vol. 2: 6114
Vinas International Singing Contest; Francisco Vol. 2: 6114
Vincent Memorial Scholarship; Susan Vol. 1: 9012
Vincent Prize in Human Sciences; Marcel Vol. 1: 5542
Vinci World Award of Arts; Leonardo da Vol. 2: 4654
Vinifera Perpetual Monteith Trophy Award Vol. 1: 21372
Vinifera Perpetual Wine-Grape Productivity Trophy Vol. 1: 21374
Vinsant Flight Nurse of the Year Award; Dolly Vol. 1: 8284
Vinson Award; H. B. Vol. 1: 9027
Vintage Arms Award Vol. 2: 9189
Vintage Cup Awards Vol. 1: 20571
Vinyl Siding Institute Awards of Distinction Vol. 1: 19323
Vinyl Window and Door Institute Awards for Outstanding Performance Vol. 1: 19324
Viola/Double Bass Scholarship; CTBI Intermediate Cello/ Vol. 1: 18282
Viola/Double Bass Scholarship; Kiwania of Wascana Senior Cello/ Vol. 1: 18296
Violin and Bow Making Competition; International Vol. 2: 2281
Viotti; Concorso Internazionale di Musica e Danza G. B. Vol. 2: 4048

Viotti International Music and Dance Competition; G. B. Vol. 2: 4048
Viquesnel; Prix Vol. 2: 2411
Vir Chakra Vol. 2: 3391
Virgilio Memorial Haiku Competition; Nicholas A. Vol. 1: 10224
Virgin Group Award Vol. 2: 6921
Virginia Film Festival Vol. 1: 21388
Virginia Literacy Foundation Vol. 1: 6462
Virginia Prize Vol. 1: 13003
Virginia Waring International Piano Competition; Joanna Hodges International Piano Competition/ Vol. 1: 21402
Virginia Wine Competition Vol. 1: 21373
Virginius Dabney Award Vol. 1: 8353
Virtanen Award; A. I. Vol. 2: 1576
VISA Triple Crown Challenge Vol. 1: 20207
Vishisht Seva Medal Vol. 2: 3392
Vishwakarma Medal Vol. 2: 3523
Vision Award Vol. 1: 5119
Vision Award; Boys' Basketball Vol. 1: 546
Vision for Tomorrow Award Vol. 1: 8937
Vision of Justice Sermon Award Vol. 1: 20318
Visionary Art Show Awards Vol. 1: 10502
Visionary Award Vol. 1: 6743
Visions du Reel International Documentary Film Festival Vol. 2: 6543
Visiting Fellowship in Irish Studies at University College Galway Vol. 1: 12202
Visiting Professor in Adolescent Medicine Award Vol. 1: 18617
Visiting Research Fellowships Vol. 1: 916
Visiting Scholars Vol. 1: 10009
Visser-Nederlandia Dramaprijzen Vol. 2: 4680
Visser-Neerlandiaprijs Vol. 2: 4681
Visual Arts Emeritus Award Vol. 2: 113
Visual Arts Emeritus Medal Vol. 2: 114
Visual Communicators Department of the Year Awards Vol. 1: 11288
Vitae's Fellowships in the Arts Vol. 2: 1199
Vitae's Program of Support to Brazilian Museums Vol. 2: 1200
Vitae's Program to Improve Secondary-Level Industrial and AgriculturalVocational Schools Vol. 2: 1201
Vitae's Scholarships for Training and Upgrading of Musicians Vol. 2: 1202
Vitarius Memorial Scholarship; Alec Vol. 1: 9754
Vitelli Prize; G. Vol. 2: 3990
Vitoria; Prix Vol. 2: 6373
Vlaicu Prize; Aurel Vol. 2: 5874
VMI (Virginia Military Institute) Future Captain of Industry Award Vol. 1: 21408
VMPD American International Film and Video Festival; Amateur PSA/ Vol. 1: 17283
Vocal Competition Vol. 1: 15430
Vocal Group of the Year Vol. 1: 11424
Vocational Initiative and Club Achievement Program Awards Vol. 1: 18551
Voelcker Award for Poetry; PEN/ Vol. 1: 17150
Vogels, Jr. Award; David S. Vol. 1: 9501
Vogelsang Memorial Manuscript Award; Frederic M. Vol. 1: 14268
Vogt Prize; Franz Vol. 2: 3004
Vohra Award; Pran Vol. 2: 3544
Voice of Democracy Scholarship Vol. 1: 21345
Voice of Democracy Scholarship Program Vol. 1: 12647
Voice of the Dispora, Founders Achievement Award, UCLA Extension Scholarships Vol. 1: 11421
Voice of the Industry Vol. 1: 16857
Volleyball Coach of the Year Vol. 1: 7242
Vollmer Award; August Vol. 1: 4387
Volney; Prix Vol. 2: 2432
Volume Sales Achievement Award Vol. 2: 7433
Volunteer Achievement Award Vol. 1: 19634
Volunteer Award
  Audubon Naturalist Society of the Central Atlantic States Vol. 1: 6070
  Canadian Camping Association Vol 1: 7018
  Nature Canada Vol 1: 16029
Volunteer Award; Jane Honikman Vol. 1: 17490
Volunteer Awards
  Canadian Payroll Association Vol. 1: 7332
  Canadian Society of Petroleum Geologists Vol 1: 7492
Volunteer Center Excellence Award; Romney Vol. 1: 17447
Volunteer Council Fundraising Gold Ribbon Awards Vol. 1: 4733
Volunteer Fund Raiser of the Year Vol. 1: 3839
Volunteer Leader Vol. 1: 4401
Volunteer of the Year
  American Civil Liberties Union of Vermont Vol. 1: 1816
  American Health Care Association Vol 1: 2393
  BC Innovation Council Vol 1: 6293
  Black Mental Health Alliance Vol 1: 6434
  International Order of E.A.R.S. Vol 1: 11777
  Lupus Foundation of America, Arkansas Chapter Vol 1: 12985
  Pacific Center for Human Growth Vol 1: 16998
Volunteer of the Year Award
  Audubon Society of New Hampshire Vol. 1: 6085
  Easter Seals Vol 1: 9091
  National Agricultural Center and Hall of Fame Vol 1: 13915
  National Hemophilia Foundation Vol 1: 15207
  National Multiple Sclerosis Society Vol 1: 15401
  National Organization for Victim Assistance Vol 1: 15450
  Nature Saskatchewan Vol 1: 16042
  Ouachita Council on Aging Vol 1: 16961
  Planned Parenthood Federation of Canada Vol 1: 17372
Volunteer of the Year/Volunteer Group of the Year Vol. 1: 20355
Volunteer of Year Award Vol. 1: 7010
Volunteer Recognition Award Vol. 1: 6901
Volunteer Service Award
  American Lawyers Auxiliary Vol. 1: 2937
  National Kidney Foundation Vol 1: 15327
  United States Tennis Association Vol 1: 20873
Volunteer Service Award for Law Enforcement Explorers Vol. 1: 6591
Volunteer State Book Award Vol. 1: 19974
Volunteerism Award
  Illinois Library Association Vol. 1: 10688
  YMCA of the United States of America Vol 1: 22040
Volunteers in Fund Raising Awards Vol. 1: 15128
Volunteers of the Year Vol. 1: 16286
Volvo College Players of the Year Vol. 1: 19982
Volvo Tennis/All-America Vol. 1: 11140
Volvo Tennis/Rookie Player of the Year Vol. 1: 11142
Volvo Tennis Scholar Athletes Vol. 1: 11143
Volvo Tennis/Senior Player of the Year Vol. 1: 11144
Volvo Tennis/Tennis College Player of the Year Vol. 1: 11148
Von-Arnim Prize; Bettina Vol. 2: 2680
von-Baeyer-Denkmunze; Adolf- Vol. 2: 2816
von Bekesy Medal Vol. 1: 146
von-Bergmann-Plakette; Ernst- Vol. 2: 2848
von Braun Award for Excellence in Space Program Management Vol. 1: 2697
von Briesen Award; Arthur Vol. 1: 15340
von-Chamisso-Preis der Robert Bosch Stiftung; Adelbert- Vol. 2: 2661
von Gruber Award; Otto Vol. 2: 6640
von Heidenstams Guldmedalj; Verner Vol. 2: 6227
Von Hippel Award Vol. 1: 13185
von-Hofmann-Denkmunze; August-Wilhelm- Vol. 2: 2817
von Humboldt Award for Scientific Cooperation; Alexander Vol. 2: 3131
Von Karman Award Vol. 2: 2438
von Karman Award; Theodore Vol. 1: 364
Von karman Lecture Vol. 1: 2698
von Karman Lectureship in Astronautics Vol. 1: 2698
von Karman Medal; Theodore Vol. 1: 4365
von Karman Prize; Theodore Vol. 1: 18745
Von Liebig Prize; Justus Vol. 2: 3094
von Linde Award; Carl Vol. 2: 2483
von Neumann Lecture; John Vol. 1: 18746
von Neumann Theory Prize; John Vol. 1: 11081
Von-Recklinghausen-Preis Vol. 2: 2853
von Sckell-Ehrenring; Friedrich Ludwig Vol. 2: 2662
von Siemens Music Prize; Ernst Vol. 2: 6545
von Siemens-Musikpreis; Ernst Vol. 2: 6545
von Spee Chapter Award; Graf Vol. 1: 20937
Von Stein Prize; Freiherr Vol. 2: 3095
Vondel Prize; Joost van den Vol. 2: 3096
Vondel Translation Prize Vol. 2: 8977
Vontobel-Fonds; Hans Vol. 2: 6527
Voorhies Award; Amos E. Vol. 1: 16859
Voss Award Vol. 1: 12438
Voss Award; Walter C. Vol. 1: 5996
Voss-Preis fur Uebersetzung; Johann-Heinrich- Vol. 2: 2778
Vossen Memorial Award; John L. Vol. 1: 6158
Vost Celebration of Leadership; Jeanne Vol. 1: 133
Vouras Medal; Paul P. Vol. 1: 2336
Vravio tou Kyklou tou Ellinikou Paidikou Vivliou Vol. 2: 3168
Vrenios Memorial Award; Nick Vol. 1: 15430
VSDA Home Entertainment Awards Vol. 1: 21355
VSDA Presidential Award Vol. 1: 21356
VSLS Education Foundation Scholarships Vol. 1: 21306
Vucinich Prize; Wayne S. Vol. 1: 1059
Vuia Prize; Traian Vol. 2: 5875
VVA Achievement Award Vol. 1: 21400
W & J National Painting Show Vol. 1: 16690

W. Averell Harriman Award Vol. 1: 12728
WA Special Librarian of the Year Award Vol. 2: 233
Wabash Valley Juried Exhibition Vol. 1: 19861
Wachsmann Prize for Advanced and Critical Essays in Organology; Klaus P. Vol. 1: 18674
Waddell Award; Tom Vol. 1: 9492
Waddingham/Doctor Award Vol. 1: 8371
"Waddy" Young Award; Walter R. Vol. 1: 5113
Wade Memorial Award and Honorary Membership; Jake Vol. 1: 8192
Wade Trophy Vol. 1: 14014
Wadia Medal; D. N. Vol. 2: 3524
Wadlin Distinguished Service Award; George K. Vol. 1: 4047
Wadsworth Award; Milton E. Vol. 1: 18828
Wadsworth Prize for Business History Vol. 2: 7224
Waeckerle Founder's Award; Joseph F. Vol. 1: 9242
WAFFA Salver Vol. 2: 7532
Wager Medal Vol. 2: 445
Wager Prize Vol. 2: 445
Wagner Award; C. Corwith Vol. 1: 3412
Wagner Award; Percy and Betty Vol. 1: 5017
Wagner Memorial Award; Martin Vol. 1: 15328
Wagner Memorial Award; SES/CSA Lorne K. Vol. 1: 19749
Wagner Narrative Screenwriting Award; Robert W. Vol. 1: 7953
Wagner Sanitarian Award; Davis Calvin Vol. 1: 835
Wahi Award for Cytology and Preventive Oncology; Dr. Prem Nath Vol. 2: 3439
Wahlbergska Minnesmedaljen I guld Vol. 2: 6228
Wahlner Medal; Aladar Vol. 2: 3262
Wailes Award; B. L. C. Vol. 1: 13511
Waitemata Aero Club Cup Vol. 2: 5069
Wakefield Gold Medal Vol. 2: 8407
Wakenham Prize Vol. 2: 8621
Waksman Award in Microbiology; Selman A. Vol. 1: 13851
Waksman; Fondation Salman A. Vol. 2: 2007
Waksman Outstanding Teaching Award Vol. 1: 18763
Walcott Medal; Charles Doolittle Vol. 1: 13852
Wald Award; Nina Starr Braun Vol. 1: 5916
Wald Memorial Lecture Vol. 1: 11009
Waldo Award; Dwight Vol. 1: 4188
Waldschmidt Award; Ellen Vol. 1: 12990
Wales One-Act Playwriting Competition
Drama Association of Wales Vol. 2: 7393
Drama Association of Wales Vol 2: 7394
Waley Medal; A. J. Vol. 2: 8572
Walford Career Achievement Awards in the Performing Arts and in Visual Arts; Paul de Hueck and Norman Vol. 1: 16741
Walker Award for Excellence in Contributions to Chemical Engineering Literature; William H. Vol. 1: 2793
Walker Award; Jack Vol. 1: 3498
Walker Award; Stanley Vol. 1: 20022
Walker Cup Vol. 1: 20608
Walker Humanitarian Award; Bishop John T. Vol. 1: 269
Walker, Jr. Award; John K. Vol. 1: 13409
Walker Jr. Award; Philip L. Vol. 1: 1649
Walker Memorial Award; Lawrence A. Vol. 1: 19174
Walker Memorial Award; Morris R. Vol. 1: 5595
Walker Memorial Grant; Ronald W. Vol. 1: 8212
Walker Most Valuable Player Award; Preston Vol. 1: 15316
Walker Prize
Museum of Science, Boston Vol. 1: 13692
Royal College of Surgeons of England Vol 2: 8490
Walker Scholarship Fund; Myrtle and Earl Vol. 1: 19175
Walkley Awards for Journalism; AMP W.G. Vol. 2: 458
Wall Young Investigator Award; Patrick D. Vol. 1: 11263
Wallace Award; David Vol. 1: 15705
Wallace Competitor of the Year Award; Bill Vol. 1: 22107
Wallace Dissertation Award; S. Rains Vol. 1: 18757
Wallace Essay Prize; Hugh Vol. 2: 8832
Wallace Memorial Award; Karl R. Vol. 1: 14715
Wallace-Reader's Digest Writers' Awards; Lila Vol. 1: 21430
Wallace's Registrars' Prize; Hugh Vol. 2: 8833
Wallach-Plakette; Otto- Vol. 2: 2818
Wallder Award; Vic and Jessie Vol. 1: 19722
Wallenberg Awards; Raoul Vol. 1: 17876
Wallenberg Civic Courage Award; Raoul Vol. 1: 17877
Wallenberg Hero for Our Time Award; Raoul Vol. 1: 17878
Wallenberg World of Heroes Award; Raoul Vol. 1: 17878
Wallenbergstipendiet Vol. 2: 6288
Wallin Education of Handicapped Children Award; J. E. Wallace Vol. 1: 8555
Wallin Lifetime Achievement Award; J. E. Wallace Vol. 1: 8555
Wallis Intermediate Beethoven Scholarship; The Gordon C. Vol. 1: 18318
Wallis Lecture; C. E. Vol. 2: 8834
The Wallis Memorial Scholarship Vol. 1: 18319
Wallis Senior Beethoven Scholarship; The Gordon C. Vol. 1: 18320
Wallmarkska Priset Vol. 2: 6229
Wallston Award; Barbara Strudler Vol. 1: 3738
Walpole Gold Medal; Horace Vol. 1: 8618
Walsh Award; Edith Vol. 2: 7080
Walsh Award; John G. Vol. 1: 676
Walsh Medal for Service to Industry; Alan Vol. 2: 217
Walsh Scholarship; Richard P. Vol. 1: 13229
Walsh - Weston Bronze Award Vol. 2: 7292
Walter Cronkite Award for Excellence in Journalism and Telecommunication Vol. 1: 8657
Walters Award; Lt. General Vernon A. Vol. 1: 15384
Waltham International Prize for Scientific Achievement Vol. 2: 1544
Waltham International Prize for Service to the Profession Vol. 2: 1545
Walther-Nernst-Denkmuenze Vol. 2: 2800
Waltke Trophy Vol. 1: 14300
Walton Award; A. Ronald Vol. 1: 14810
Walton/Russell L. Miller Award; Norton H. Vol. 1: 2794
WAMSO Young Artist Competition Vol. 1: 21435
WAND Family Award Vol. 1: 21770
Wander Lecture; Albert Vol. 2: 8835
Wang Young Investigator Award; Shih-Chun Vol. 1: 3530
Wanganui Trophy Vol. 2: 5070
Wanner Award; Vance R. Vol. 1: 13410
Wanzer, FPSA, Award; Douglas H. Vol. 1: 17284
Wappenmedaille Vol. 2: 775
War Order Virtuti Militari Vol. 2: 5328
War Service Medal Vol. 1: 15784
Warburg-Medaille; Otto- Vol. 2: 2869
Ward & Award for Outstanding New Children's Theatre & Company; Winifred Vol. 1: 894
Ward, Jr. Memorial Award; Philip H. Vol. 1: 2248
Ward Library Instruction Award; James E. Vol. 1: 19975
Ward Memorial Award; Arch Vol. 1: 8193
Ward Memorial Award; Earl F. Vol. 1: 393
Ward Memorial Award; Julian E. Vol. 1: 243
Ward Memorial Film Award; Jack Vol. 1: 4959
Ward Memorial Posthumous Award; R.D. 'Bob' Vol. 1: 13941
Ward Prize for Outstanding New Children's Theatre Company; Zeta Phi Eta Winifred Vol. 1: 895
Ward Prize for Playwriting; Theodore Vol. 1: 8227
Ward Prize; Lynd Vol. 1: 10618
Ward Prize; Zeta Phi Eta - Winifred Vol. 1: 895
Warden of the Year Vol. 1: 16393
Warder Award for Outstanding Achievement; Frederick B. Vol. 1: 16058
Wardle Award; R. A. Vol. 1: 7500
Ware Award for Distinguished (Undergraduate) Teaching; L. M. Vol. 1: 4094
Wark Medal and Lecture; Ian Vol. 2: 132
Warman International Students Design Award Competition Vol. 2: 435
Warmington Trophy; Ivon Vol. 2: 5071
Warmwater Management Award Vol. 1: 9488
Warner Award; Edward Vol. 1: 11483
Warner Award; Jo Vol. 1: 6708
Warner Awards Program; William E. Vol. 1: 9314
Warner Medal; Worcester Reed Vol. 1: 4551
Warner Memorial Medal Vol. 2: 9135
Warner Memorial Medal Award; Samuel L. Vol. 1: 19200
Warner Prize for Astronomy; Helen B. Vol. 1: 1520
Warner Trophy Vol. 1: 11002
Warrants at Appointment Vol. 2: 7083
Warren Award; Gretchen Vol. 1: 16117
Warren Award; Hugh T. Vol. 1: 19325
Warren Diffraction Physics Award; Bertram E. Vol. 1: 2095
Warren Medal; W. H. Vol. 2: 436
Warren Prize; G. K. Vol. 1: 13853
Warriner Award; Elizabeth Hull - Kate Vol. 1: 9024
Warsaw Chopin Competition Vol. 2: 2691
Warshawsky Award; Celia Vol. 1: 12347
Wartenberg Lecture; Robert Vol. 1: 706
Warth Air Force Historical Foundation Award; Joe and Josephine Vol. 1: 377

Award Index

Wartha Medal; Vince Vol. 2: 3252
Warwick Memorial Award; Irvin Vol. 1: 11175
WAS Special Commendations Vol. 1: 21848
Washburn Award; Bradford Vol. 1: 13693
Washburn Award; Frank M. Vol. 1: 11316
Washburn Award; Sherwood L. Vol. 1: 1361
Washington Award Vol. 1: 4366
Washington Correspondence Award Vol. 1: 15524
Washington Craft Show Vol. 1: 18574
Washington Crossing Foundation Scholarship Vol. 1: 21445
Washington Honor Medal; George Vol. 1: 9766
Washington International Competition Vol. 1: 9775
Washington Medal; Martha Vol. 1: 15785
The Washington Monthly Journalism Award Vol. 1: 21453
The Washington Post Award for Distinguished Community Service Vol. 1: 21463
The Washington Post Award for Excellence in Nonprofit Management Vol. 1: 7739
The Washington Post/Children's Book Guild Award for Nonfiction Vol. 1: 21457
Washington Prize Vol. 1: 21834
Washington State Reserve Police Association Trophy Vol. 1: 15647
Washington Theatre Festival Awards Vol. 1: 19426
Washingtonians of the Year Vol. 1: 21469
Wasito Award; R. Vol. 2: 3604
Wason Medal for Materials Research Vol. 1: 1971
Wason Medal for the Most Meritorious Paper Vol. 1: 1972
Wasserman Foundation Prizes; Leo Vol. 1: 2905
Wasserman Memorial Award; Prof. Dr. Rene D. Vol. 1: 4899
Wassermann Prize Vol. 2: 6100
Waste Management Award Vol. 1: 326
Waste Management Graduate Fellowship Program; Office of Civilian Radioactive Vol. 1: 16598
WATA Hall of Fame Vol. 2: 6551
WATA Travel Agency of the Year Vol. 2: 6552
Watanabe Medal; G. Vol. 2: 4150
Wateler Peace Prize Vol. 2: 4705
Wateler-Vredesprijs Vol. 2: 4705
Water Environment Merit Award Vol. 2: 288
Water Quality Improvement Man of the Year Award Vol. 1: 11539
Water Ski Days Queen Vol. 1: 12665
Water Solutions Unlimited Most Improved Sprint Car Driver Vol. 1: 20424
Water Statesman of the Year Vol. 1: 15933
Water Widget Medal Vol. 1: 10279
Water Works State Leadership Award Vol. 1: 16142
Waterbury Award for Outdoor Lighting; Paul Vol. 1: 10695
Watercolor U.S.A. Vol. 1: 19734
Waterfall Award; Wallace Vol. 1: 5997
Waterford Crystal Award Vol. 2: 7688
Waterford Crystal European Athlete of the Year Award Vol. 2: 2745
Waterfowl Breeders Hall of Fame Vol. 1: 12139
Waterman Award; Alan T. Vol. 1: 15681
Watermedia Exhibition Awards; Rocky Mountain National Vol. 1: 9679
Waters Distinguished Service Award; Gordon M. Vol. 1: 7611
Watkins Award; J. B. C. Vol. 1: 6810
Watrous Award; Harry Vol. 1: 13801
Watson Award; C. W. Vol. 1: 2262
Watson Award for Consular Excellence; Barbara M. Vol. 1: 20555
Watson Award; Leland A. Vol. 1: 11672
Watson Award; Robert C. Vol. 1: 2864
Watson Grants; Neil Vol. 2: 7857
Watson, Jr.; Assistant Excellence in Leadership Award in Memory of Buford M. Vol. 1: 11480
Watson, Jr. Medal of Excellence; William C. Vol. 1: 20502
Watson Medal; Garth Vol. 2: 7785
Watson Medal; James Craig Vol. 1: 13854
Watson Prize; Albert J. Vol. 2: 7680
Watson Prize; Frank Vol. 1: 18373
Watt Award; Gladys Cameron Vol. 1: 16959
Watt International Medal; James Vol. 2: 7858
Watt Medal; James Vol. 2: 7786
Watt Memorial Prize; David Vol. 2: 8343
Watters Memorial Scholarship; George E. Vol. 1: 16139
Watts Prize Vol. 2: 8622
Wauwatosa Event Vol. 1: 20889
Wauwatosa Trophy Vol. 1: 20889
Waxweiler; Fondation Emile Vol. 2: 1007
Wayburn Award; Edgar Vol. 1: 18473
Wayne Award; John Vol. 1: 11815
WBDNA Achievement Award Vol. 1: 21731
WBDNA Performing Artists Award Vol. 1: 21732
WBW Bowlers of the Year Vol. 1: 21871
WBW Distinguished Service Award Vol. 1: 21872
WBW Gosta Zellen Golden Quill Award Vol. 1: 21873
The WCA Award for Excellence in Non-Profit Management Vol. 1: 7739
WCA Honors Vol. 1: 21789
WCO Emeritus Vol. 1: 21886
WCO Medal Vol. 1: 21887
WE Mentor Award Vol. 1: 21710
Weatherford Award Competition; W. D. Vol. 1: 4996
Weatherly Award; Earl Vol. 1: 8357
Weatherly; Sir Alfred Herbert Vol. 2: 8109
Weaver Service Award; Warren Vol. 1: 7967
Weaver's Company Medal and Prize Vol. 2: 9136
Weaving in the Norwegian Tradition; National Exhibition of Vol. 1: 21317
Webb Award; Aileen Osborn Vol. 1: 2079
Webb Award; James E. Vol. 1: 4189
Webb Medal; William H. Vol. 1: 19217
Webb Memorial Award in Woodwind; The Carla Ruth Vol. 1: 18321
Webb Memorial Trophy; Francis Vol. 2: 8263
Webb Prize Vol. 2: 7787
Webb Service Award; Aileen Osborn Vol. 1: 2079
Webb Studentship; Bernard Vol. 2: 6742
Weber Award; Irving Vol. 1: 12419
Weber Preis; Max Vol. 2: 2668
Weber Scholarship; William E. Vol. 1: 14883
Website Award Vol. 1: 8451
Webster Award; Daniel Vol. 1: 11816
WEC Gold Medal for International Corporate Achievement in Sustainable Development Vol. 1: 21893
WEC Gold Medal for International Corporate Environmental Achievement Vol. 1: 21893
Wedding Professional of the Year Vol. 1: 5587
Wedel Award; Cynthia Vol. 1: 3840
Wedemeyer Award; Charles A. Vol. 1: 20969
Wedgwood Sponsorship Award Vol. 2: 6925
Weed Book Prize Vol. 2: 657
Weelden Award; Arie van Vol. 2: 4753
Weems Award Vol. 1: 11017
Weetabix Trophy Vol. 2: 8039
Weetabix Women's British Open Championship Vol. 2: 8039
Wegener-Medaille; Alfred Vol. 2: 2715
Wegener Medal; Alfred- Vol. 2: 2331
Wegmann; Prix Vol. 2: 2412
Wehran Aviation Achievement Award; Fred L. Vol. 1: 6130
Weil Award Vol. 1: 1289
Weil Awards; Frank L. Vol. 1: 12342
Weil Prize; Martin Eli Vol. 1: 6447
Weiler and Mildred B. Frame Piano Scholarship Fund; Eleanor B. Vol. 1: 13662
Weill; Prix de Dessin Pierre David Vol. 2: 1740
Weiller; Prix de Portrait Paul-Louis Vol. 2: 1741
Weiller; Prix Paul-Louis Vol. 2: 1742
Weinberg Memorial Award for Geriatric Psychiatry; Jack Vol. 1: 3642
Weinberg Plaque; Al Vol. 1: 13927
Weindling Prize; Rosalind G. Vol. 2: 3738
Weinstock Award; Morris F. Vol. 1: 14557
Weintal Prize for Diplomatic Reporting; Edward Vol. 1: 9960
Weintraub Scholarship; Mark Vol. 1: 16106
Weinzirl Award; Elizabeth Vol. 1: 15855
Weir Prize; C. J. Vol. 2: 7681
Weis Trophy; Bernard J. Vol. 1: 17343
Weisbrod One-Act Competition Vol. 1: 12888
Weisenfeld Award for Excellence in Ophthalmology; Mildred Vol. 1: 5469
Weisinger Award; Mort Vol. 1: 4467
Weiss Award; Rosalee G. Vol. 1: 3770
Weiss/Brown Publication Subvention Award Vol. 1: 16316
Weiss; Premio Aida Vol. 2: 4618
Weiss; Prix J. J. Vol. 2: 2164
Weissberger Playwriting Award; L. Arnold Vol. 1: 16097
Weissen Raben; Die Vol. 2: 2990
Weitzman Award; Richard E. Vol. 1: 9264
Weizmann Prizes of the Academy of Scientific Research (Premios Weizmann de la Academia de la Investigacion Cientifica) Vol. 2: 4559
Weizmann Prizes of the Mexican Academy of Sciences Vol. 2: 4559
Welch Award in Chemistry Vol. 1: 21512
Welch Award in Vacuum Science; Medard W. Vol. 1: 6159
Welch Foundation Scholarship Vol. 2: 8000
Welch Medal; William H. Vol. 1: 1063
Wellcome Diagnostics Student Award Vol. 2: 5636
Wellcome Medal and Prize; Sir Henry Vol. 1: 5789
Wellcome Medal for Anthropology as Applied to Medical Problems Vol. 2: 8425
Wellcome Prize Vol. 2: 8698
Wellcome Trust Award for Research in Biochemistry Related to Medicine Vol. 2: 6872
Wellek Prize; Rene Vol. 1: 1953

Wellington Prize; Arthur M. Vol. 1: 4367
Wells Appreciation Award; Cliff Vol. 1: 14088
Wells Award; Ida B.
National Association of Black Journalists Vol. 1: 14101
National Association of Black Journalists Vol 1: 14102
Wells Memorial Award; Elizabeth Vol. 1: 14269
Wells Memorial Key Vol. 1: 19278
Welsh Arts Council Prizes Vol. 2: 9202
Welsh M.D. Memorial Research Fund; Edward J. Vol. 1: 3019
Welsh Society Medallion Vol. 1: 21516
Weltmeister im Pflugen Vol. 2: 4943
Welty Prize in Fiction; Eudora Vol. 1: 19523
Wereld Muziek Concours Kerkrade Vol. 2: 4938
Werkmanprijs; H. N. Vol. 2: 4700
Werner Award; Wallace "Buddy" Vol. 1: 20824
Werner Host Club Award; Louis S. Vol. 1: 3264
Werner Medaille; Abraham-Gottlob- Vol. 2: 2720
Werner-Medaille; Golden Vol. 2: 6515
Werner-Preis Vol. 2: 6515
Wesley-Logan Prize Vol. 1: 2482
Wesson Memorial Physician of the Year Award; Dr. Ray Vol. 1: 20389
West Agro, Inc. Award Vol. 1: 2114
West Award; Constance Vol. 2: 9029
West Scholarship for Feline Research Vol. 2: 8498
West Virginia Children's Book Award Vol. 1: 21531
West Virginia Poetry Society Award Vol. 1: 15035
Westbrook Local History Award; Lucille Vol. 1: 5077
Westcott USTA Family of the Year Award; Ralph W. Vol. 1: 20874
Westerby-prisen; Erik Vol. 2: 1542
Westerby Prize; Erik Vol. 2: 1542
Westerfield Award; Samuel Z. Vol. 1: 14920
Western Australia Film and Video Festival Vol. 2: 346
Western Australia Week Literary Awards Vol. 2: 612
Western Australian Premier's Book Awards Vol. 2: 612
Western Australian School of Mines Award Vol. 2: 437
Western Auto NASCAR Mechanics Hall of Fame Vol. 1: 11760
Western Conference Trophy Vol. 1: 7107
Western Electric Fund Award Vol. 1: 3996
Western Forestry Award for Current Achievement Vol. 1: 21549
Western Forestry Award for Lifetime Service Vol. 1: 21550
Western Garden Design Awards Vol. 1: 19840
Western Heritage Awards (Wrangler Award) Vol. 1: 14887
Western Home Awards Vol. 1: 19841
Western North Carolina Historical Association Achievement Award Vol. 1: 21554
Western Political Science Association Awards Vol. 1: 21557
Western States Book Awards Vol. 1: 21571
Western US Design & Production Awards Competition Vol. 1: 17737
Westerners International Award; Phi Alpha Theta/ Vol. 1: 17238
Westfaelischer Kunstpreis Vol. 2: 3018
Westfaelischer Literaturpreis Vol. 2: 3017
Westinghouse Award; George Vol. 1: 4048
Westinghouse Medals; George Vol. 1: 4552
Westinghouse Science Talent Search Vol. 1: 18363
Westlake; Prix John Vol. 2: 6373
Westminster Medal for Military Literature; Duke of Vol. 2: 8866
Weston Award for Teaching Excellence; William H. Vol. 1: 13726
Weston Grant; Martha Vol. 1: 19089
Westonbirt Orchid Medal Vol. 2: 8573
Westrups beloning; Wilhelm Vol. 2: 6196
Wetrems; Prix Adolphe Vol. 2: 1041
Wettbewerb "Musik der Jugend" Vol. 2: 680
Wexner Graduate Fellows Vol. 1: 21593
Wexner Prize Vol. 1: 21594
Weyent Lifetime Achievement Award; J. Thomas Vol. 1: 15640
Weyerhaeuser Award; Charles A. Vol. 1: 9697
Weyhe Gallery Purchase Award; E. Vol. 1: 18980
WFCC Skerman Award for Taxonomy Vol. 2: 9251
WFEO Award for Engineering Excellence Vol. 2: 2625
WFEO Medal of Excellence in Engineering Education Vol. 2: 2626
WFK Award Vol. 2: 3133
Wham Leadership Medal; George S. Vol. 1: 3186
Wharton Citation of Merit for State Author; Edith Vol. 1: 16294
What the Papers Say Award Vol. 2: 8022
Wheatley Award; John Vol. 1: 3480
Wheatley Award; William A. Vol. 1: 20944
Wheatley Medal Vol. 2: 9052
Wheaton; Prix Henri Vol. 2: 6373
Wheeler Awards; Sir Charles Vol. 2: 8190
Wheeler Cross Country Award Vol. 1: 14667
Wheeler Legacy Award; A. O. Vol. 1: 504
Wheeler Prize; Charles B. Vol. 1: 16651
Wheeler Track and Field Awards Vol. 1: 14668
Wheldon Award; Huw Vol. 2: 6905
Wherry Award; Edgar T. Vol. 1: 6555
Wherry Award; Elizabeth Vol. 2: 7081
Wherry Award; Robert J. Vol. 1: 18758
Whetnall Lectureship; Edith Vol. 2: 8836
Whetten Award; Nellie Yeoh Vol. 1: 6160
Whipper Gold Award; Leigh Vol. 1: 468
Whipple Professional Development Grant; Gertrude Vol. 1: 11879
Whirly-Girls Helicopter Flight Training Scholarship Vol. 1: 21600
Whitaker Distinguished Lectureship Vol. 1: 6388
Whitaker Graduate Student Awards Vol. 1: 6389
Whitaker Senior Student Bioengineering Design Awards Vol. 1: 6391
Whitaker Young Investigator Award Vol. 1: 6390
Whitbread Book of the Year Vol. 2: 6886
Whitbread Literary Awards Vol. 2: 6886
Whitby Award for Distinguished Teaching and Research; George Stafford Vol. 1: 1793
Whitby Award; Kenneth T. Vol. 1: 958
Whitcombe Cox Trophy Vol. 2: 8304
White and Loras Goedken Meritorious Service Awards; Ryan Vol. 1: 15214
White Award; Dorothy Vol. 1: 16959
White Award; Marsh W. Vol. 1: 2841
White Award Master List Vol. 1: 21608
White Award; Paul Vol. 1: 17850
White Award; Paul Dudley Vol. 1: 5790
White Awards Vol. 1: 8024
White Children's Book Award; William Allen Vol. 1: 21608
White Distinguished Teacher Award; Albert Easton Vol. 1: 5192
White Fellow; Wilford L. Vol. 1: 11513
White Fellowship; Harold Vol. 2: 475
White Golden Quill Award; The Carson Vol. 1: 16467
White House Fellows Vol. 1: 17539
White House News Photographers' Association Awards Vol. 1: 21606
White Humanitarian Award; Byron "Whizzer" Vol. 1: 15093
White Medal; Clarence G. Vol. 1: 5046
White Membership Award; Sandi Vol. 1: 10256
White Memorial Award for Electronic Journalism; Paul Vol. 1: 17850
White Memorial Award; Philip R. Vol. 1: 18729
White National Defense Award; Thomas D. Vol. 1: 20382
White National Memorial Trophy; Belle Vol. 2: 6722
White Prize; Frederick Vol. 2: 133
White Prize Lecture; T. C. Vol. 2: 8453
White Ravens Vol. 2: 2990
White Scholarship; Sir William Vol. 2: 8623
White Space Trophy Vol. 1: 15162
White Stag Award Vol. 1: 20793
White Travelling Fellowship; T. C. Vol. 2: 8454
White Trophy Vol. 1: 7295
White Visiting Scholarship; T. C. Vol. 2: 8454
Whitehead Award; Fred Vol. 1: 20023
Whitehead Prize Vol. 2: 8093
Whitehill Prize; Walter Muir Vol. 1: 8207
Whitehouse Studio Award for Architectural Photography Vol. 2: 8587
Whitfield Award; Willis J. Vol. 1: 10932
Whitfield Prize Vol. 2: 8533
Whiting Award; Butts - Vol. 1: 5630
Whiting Award; John Vol. 2: 6758
Whiting Memorial Fund Award Vol. 1: 11955
Whiting Writers' Award Vol. 1: 21610
Whitley Awards Vol. 2: 558
Whitley Travel Scholarship; Don Vol. 2: 8924
Whitlock Award; Marvin Vol. 1: 19061
Whitman Award; Walt Vol. 1: 78
Whitman Citation of Merit Award for State Poet; Walt Vol. 1: 16295
Whitney Award Vol. 1: 16497
Whitney Award; Edgar A. Vol. 1: 4871
Whitney Award; Willis Rodney Vol. 1: 13748
Whitney Medal; Charles S. Vol. 1: 1973
Whitney Memorial Award; Eli Vol. 1: 19176
Whitney Productivity Award; Eli Vol. 1: 19176
Whitten Medal; Charles A. Vol. 1: 2359
Whitten Silver Medallion Award; E. B. Vol. 1: 15597
Whittingham Jazz Award; Peter Vol. 2: 8152
Whittington Excellence in Teaching Award; Leslie A. Vol. 1: 14377
Whittle Medal; Sir Frank Vol. 2: 8371

Award Index

Whittle Safety Award Vol. 2: 7930
Wholesaler of the Year Award Vol. 1: 14366
Whyte Award; Andrew Vol. 1: 12283
Whyte Memorial Essay Prize; Jon Vol. 1: 21985
Wibautprijs Vol. 2: 4701
Wichelns Freedom of Speech Award; Herbert A. Vol. 1: 14710
Wichelns Memorial Award for Distinguished Scholarship in Rhetoric and Public Address; James A. Winans/Herbert A. Vol. 1: 14716
Wickard Award; Albert O. Vol. 1: 20938
Wickens Award; Peter Vol. 2: 7881
Widowed Persons Service Award Vol. 1: 1401
Wiebrecht Award Vol. 1: 680
Wiegenstein Award for Meritorious Service Vol. 1: 1862
Wiegenstein Leadership Award; John G. Vol. 1: 1862
Wiehe-Stiftung; Preis der Horst Vol. 2: 2859
Wien Awards; Mae L. Vol. 1: 18352
Wien Prize for Social Responsibility; Lawrence A. Vol. 1: 8252
Wiener Award for Social and Professional Responsibility; Norbert Vol. 1: 8331
Wiener Medal; Norbert Vol. 1: 3987
Wiener Memorial Gold Medal; Norbert Vol. 2: 2630
Wiener Prize; Norbert Vol. 1: 18747
Wiesel Award for Jewish Art and Culture; Elie Vol. 1: 10433
Wiesel Prize in Ethics; Elie Vol. 1: 21621
Wiesenthal Center Humanitarian Award; Simon Vol. 1: 18530
Wiesenthal Center National Leadership Award; Simon Vol. 1: 18529
Wigan Cup Vol. 2: 8574
Wigglesworth Lecture and Medal Award Vol. 2: 8508
Wight MemorialAward; J.A. Vol. 2: 7164
Wightman Special Achievement Award Vol. 1: 9851
Wigilia Medal Vol. 1: 17459
Wigram Cup Vol. 2: 5072
Wigram Cup (Sub-Competition) - Instrument Flying Vol. 2: 5073
Wigram Cup (Sub-Competition) - Junior Landing Vol. 2: 5074
Wigram Cup (Sub-Competition) - Non-instrument Circuits Vol. 2: 5075
Wigram Cup (Sub-Competition) - Senior Landing Vol. 2: 5076
Wijnstroom Fund; Margaret Vol. 2: 4818
Wilborn Foreign Language Teacher of the Year in North Dakota; Graciela Vol. 1: 9692
Wilbur Awards Vol. 1: 17971
Wilby Memorial Scholarship; Ernest Vol. 1: 18139
Wilcher Award; Denny and Ida Vol. 1: 18474
Wilches Award; Belisario Ruiz Vol. 2: 1317
Wilcox Award; Bill Vol. 1: 2459
Wild Award Vol. 1: 21744
Wild Heerbrugg Geodetic Fellowship Vol. 1: 2007
Wild Heerbrugg Surveying Scholarships Vol. 1: 1999
Wild Leitz Photogrammetric Fellowship Award Vol. 1: 5218
Wild-Leitz Scientific Award Vol. 1: 6929
Wild-Leitz Surveying Scholarships Vol. 1: 1999
Wilde; Fondation Henry Vol. 2: 1888
Wildenstein; Prix Georges Vol. 2: 1743
Wilder Award; Laura Ingalls Vol. 1: 5444
Wilder Award; Russell Vol. 1: 20825
Wilder Medal Vol. 1: 3585
Wildfang Award; Henry Vol. 1: 13094
Wildlife Action Award Vol. 2: 9214
Wildlife and Environment Society of South Africa Gold Medal Vol. 2: 5798
Wildlife and Environment Zimbabwe Competitions Vol. 2: 9357
Wildlife Category Award of Merit Vol. 1: 15484
Wildlife Leadership Awards Vol. 1: 18099
Wildman Medal Vol. 1: 8857
Wildy Prize for Microbiology Education; Peter Vol. 2: 8936
Wiley & Sons Award; John Vol. 1: 11530
Wiley Award for Excellence in Engineering Technology Education Vol. 1: 3999
Wiley Award; Harvey W. Vol. 1: 4992
Wiley-Berger Award for Volunteer Service Vol. 1: 945
Wiley Distinguished Author Award; Meriam/ Vol. 1: 4049
Wiley Professional Development Grant; First Step Award - Vol. 1: 5428
Wilhelm Award in Chemical Reaction Engineering; R. H. Vol. 1: 2795
Wilhelmi-Haskell Stewardship Award Vol. 1: 14669
Wilke Memorial Award; Louis G. Vol. 1: 582
Wilkes Award Vol. 2: 6991
Wilkins Award for Outstanding Deputy Chief of Mission; Baker- Vol. 1: 20530
Wilkinson Award Vol. 1: 13303
Wilkinson Outstanding Young Electrical Engineer Award; Roger I. Vol. 1: 9346
Wilkinson Prize in Numerical Analysis and Scientific Computing; James H. Vol. 1: 18748
Wilkinson Sword Award of Merit Vol. 2: 6995
Wilks Award Vol. 1: 19533
Wilks Memorial Award Vol. 1: 4697
Will Award Vol. 1: 18429
Willan Grand Prize; Canada Council Healey Vol. 1: 6997
Willan Prize; Healey Vol. 1: 6811
Willans Premium Vol. 2: 7835
Willauer Cup Award Vol. 1: 20826
Willem Rudolfs Medal Vol. 1: 21500
Willems-Orde; Militaire Vol. 2: 4707
Willems Prize; Gustave Vol. 2: 930
Willems Prize; Leonard Vol. 2: 968
Willensky Fund; Elliot Vol. 1: 13681
Willey Distinguished Service Award; Calvert L. Vol. 1: 10947
William D. Hatfield Award Vol. 1: 21501
William E. Weisel Scholarship Fund Vol. 1: 19177
William Harris Award Vol. 1: 16916
William J. Orchard Medal Vol. 1: 21502
William Johnston Memorial Shield Vol. 2: 7648
William Kapell International Piano Competition and Festival Vol. 1: 18567
Williams and Gene Derwood Award; Oscar Vol. 1: 16219
Williams Award; Amstutz- Vol. 1: 1123
Williams Award; Boyce R. Vol. 1: 182
Williams Award; Burt Vol. 1: 15550
Williams Award for Research in Physical Therapy; Marian Vol. 1: 3499
Williams Award; George E. Vol. 1: 9502
Williams Award; Rohan Vol. 2: 8476
Williams Award; William Carlos Vol. 1: 17437
Williams Awards; APA Assembly Warren Vol. 1: 3611
Williams Community Publishing Prize; Raymond Vol. 2: 6759
Williams Distinguished Leadership Award; Robert H. Vol. 1: 9265
Williams Hardinge Award; Hal Vol. 1: 2829
Williams History Prize; A. E. Vol. 2: 556
Williams/James S. Brown Service Award; Cratis D. Vol. 1: 5002
Williams, Jr., Design Award; Alexander C. Vol. 1: 10583
Williams Jr. International Adaptive Aquatic Award; John K. Vol. 1: 12061
Williams Lecture; Michael Vol. 2: 8837
Williams Memorial Award; Edwin Vol. 2: 7501
Williams Memorial Medal
Royal Horticultural Society Vol. 2: 8564
Royal Horticultural Society Vol 2: 8575
Williams Premium; F. C. Vol. 2: 7808
Williams Prize in Louisiana History; Kemper and Leila Vol. 1: 10460
Williams Prize; Roger T. Vol. 1: 15701
Williams Prizes in Louisiana History; General L. Kemper Vol. 1: 10460
Williams Space Logistics Medal; Jack L. Vol. 1: 12002
Williams Trophy; George Vol. 2: 7422
Williamson Neometaphysical Award Vol. 2: 9059
Williamson Prize; The Ronald Vol. 2: 7682
Willie Award Vol. 1: 10020
Willis Award; Evelyn Vol. 1: 18431
Willis Award; George E. Vol. 1: 4900
Willis Award of Merit Vol. 1: 15237
Willis H. Carrier Award Vol. 2: 2483
Williston Medal; Arthur L. Vol. 1: 4553
Williston Medal Contest; Arthur L. Vol. 1: 4529
Willson Award; Cedric Vol. 1: 1974
Wilmoth Medal; G.R. Vol. 2: 438
Wilson Award Vol. 2: 5794
Wilson Award; E. H. Vol. 1: 16442
Wilson Award for Young Musicians; Clive Vol. 2: 7600
Wilson Award; Gill Robb Vol. 1: 365
Wilson Award in Nuclear Chemical Engineering; Robert E. Vol. 1: 2796
Wilson Award in Spectroscopy; E. Bright Vol. 1: 1794
Wilson Award; Peter Vol. 2: 8048
Wilson Award; Ralph C. Vol. 1: 15585
Wilson Award; *Southeastern Librarian* Vol. 1: 19480
Wilson Award; Thomas J. Vol. 1: 10284
Wilson Award; Tommy Vol. 1: 1034
Wilson Award; Woodrow
American Red Cross National Headquarters Vol. 1: 3841
Princeton University Alumni Council Vol 1: 17560
Wilson Awards; Kenneth Vol. 1: 7012
Wilson Coach of the Year Award Vol. 1: 11152
Wilson Company Award; H. W. Vol. 1: 19557
Wilson Company Indexing Award; H. W. Vol. 1: 4457
Wilson Cypridedioideae Award; W. W. Vol. 1: 3337
Wilson Fiction Prize; Ethel Vol. 1: 21523

Wilson Leadership Award; Janie Menchaca Vol. 1: 14253
Wilson Library Staff Development Grant; H. W. Vol. 1: 2983
Wilson Medal; E. B. Vol. 1: 3947
Wilson Medal; James Lee Vol. 1: 18849
Wilson Memorial Award; Hewitt Vol. 1: 1700
Wilson Memorial Lecture Award; John Arthur Vol. 1: 2944
Wilson Memorial Vase; Guy Vol. 2: 8576
Wilson National High School Coaches - AD of the Year Vol. 1: 15223
Wilson Prize; Alexander Vol. 1: 21640
Wilson Prize for Achievement in the Physics of Particle Accelerators; Robert R. Vol. 1: 3481
Wilson - Toekenning Vol. 2: 5794
Wilwers Fire Buff of the Year; Henry N. Vol. 1: 11617
Wimalasurendra Memorial Award; D. J. Vol. 2: 6125
Wimberly Cup Vol. 1: 19723
Wimps, Grumblers, and Grousers Award Vol. 1: 15438
Winans/Herbert A. Wichelns Memorial Award for Distinguished Scholarship in Rhetoric and Public Address; James A. Vol. 1: 14716
WINBA Championship Title Vol. 1: 21928
Windsor Chamber/Harvest Festival Scholarship Award Vol. 1: 21642
Wine Research Award Vol. 1: 19182
Winegrape Productivity Trophy Vol. 1: 21374
Wingate Rome Scholarship in the Fine Arts Vol. 2: 7144
Wingate Trophy; Wilson Vol. 1: 20673
Wingquist Award Vol. 2: 9362
Wings of Gold Award Vol. 1: 20939
Winking Award; Charles R. Vol. 1: 14600
Winkle Award; Rip Van Vol. 1: 18339
Winkler Plaque; Ludwig Vol. 2: 2980
Winner Award; Lewis and Beatrice Vol. 1: 18772
Winner Memorial Award; Robert H. Vol. 1: 17438
Winners' Circle Award
National Federation of State Poetry Societies Vol. 1: 14989
National Federation of State Poetry Societies Vol 1: 15036
Winner's Circle National Winners Vol. 1: 13555
Winning Spirit Award Vol. 1: 5893
Winsbury-White Lecture Vol. 2: 8838
Winship PEN New England Award; Laurence L. Vol. 1: 17158
Winship Secondary School Theatre Award; F. Loren Vol. 1: 896
Winsor and Newton Award Vol. 1: 4872
Winsor & Newton Young Artists Award Vol. 2: 8603
Winsor Prize Essay; Justin Vol. 1: 2996
Winston Cup (Winston Cup Series) Vol. 1: 8769
Winter Award; George Vol. 1: 4368
Winter-Klein; Fondation Aniuta Vol. 2: 1797
WinterFest Spotlight Award Vol. 1: 13698
Winzen Lifetime Achievement Award; Otto C. Vol. 1: 2699
Wisam Al-Muallim (Al-Tarbiya) Vol. 2: 4342
Wischmeyer Memorial Scholarship Award; Albert E. Vol. 1: 19178
Wisconsin Arts Board Fellowships Vol. 1: 21666
Wisdom Grant in Aid of Research; William B. Vol. 1: 20082
WISE Award for Engineering Achievement Vol. 1: 21753
WISE Award for Scientific Achievement Vol. 1: 21754
Wise Award; Louise Waterman Vol. 1: 2897
Wise Award; Stephen S. Vol. 1: 2898
WISE Lifetime Achievement Award Vol. 1: 21755
Wise - Warren Susman Prize; Gene Vol. 1: 4712
Wisely American Civil Engineer Award; William H. Vol. 1: 4369
Wiseman Book Award; James R. Vol. 1: 5036
Wiskirchen Jazz Award; Reverend George C. Vol. 1: 14601
Wister Award; Owen Vol. 1: 21577
Witherspoon Memorial Chaplain's Award Vol. 1: 6357
WITI Hall of Fame Vol. 1: 21761
Witmer Award; Lightner Vol. 1: 3712
Witt Award Vol. 1: 3857
Witt Supplier of the Year Award; F. W. Vol. 1: 1268
Wittkamper Peace Award; Will Vol. 1: 8961
Wittnauer NCCAA Player of the Year Vol. 1: 14670
Witty Short Story Award; Paul A. Vol. 1: 11880
WMA National Service Award Vol. 1: 21765
WMO Research Award for Young Scientists Vol. 2: 6574
WNBA Award Vol. 1: 21802
W.O. Mitchell City of Calgary Book Prize Vol. 1: 21986
Wohelo Order Vol. 1: 6776
Wohler-Preis "Ressourcenschonende Prozesse" Vol. 2: 2819
Wojciech Rubinowicz Scientific Prize Vol. 2: 5369
Wolf Award; C. R. Vol. 1: 10510
Wolf Chamber Music Award; Andrew Vol. 1: 6278
Wolf-Fenton Award Vol. 1: 10510
Wolf Memorial Award for Best Portrait or Figure Study; Paul J. Vol. 1: 17294
Wolf Memorial Award; Kate Vol. 1: 21917
Wolf Officiating Award; Julian Vol. 1: 20752
The Wolf Prizes Vol. 2: 3783
Wolfe Literary Award; Thomas Vol. 1: 21555
Wolfe Medal of Honor; Catharine Lorillard Vol. 1: 5121
Wolfe Memorial Trophy; Colonel Franklin C. Vol. 1: 16823
Wolfe Sr. Youth Best of Show Exhibit Award; Charles H. Vol. 1: 3265
Wolfe Sr. Youth Exhibit Award; Charles H. Vol. 1: 3266
Wolfe Society Literary Prize; Thomas Vol. 1: 20081
Wolfensohn Award; James D. Vol. 2: 8142
Wolff Lecture Award; Harold G. Vol. 1: 2391
Wolfson Foundation Literary Awards for History Vol. 2: 9220
Wolfson Laboratory Refurbishment Grants Vol. 2: 8702
The Wolgin Foundation/Israel Museum Fellowships Vol. 2: 3755
Wollaston Award; Charles Vol. 2: 8354
Wollaston Medal Vol. 2: 7567
Wolman Award; Abel
American Public Works Association Vol. 1: 3810
Inter-American Association of Sanitary and Environmental Engineering Vol 1: 11102
Wolper Best Documentary Award; David L. Vol. 1: 21646
Wolper Student Documentary Achievement Award; David L. Vol. 1: 11542
Wolskel Industrial Chemistry Essay Award Vol. 2: 521
Womack Outstanding Library Technician Award; The Sharon G. Vol. 1: 5066
Woman FIDE Master Vol. 2: 3198
Woman Grandmaster Vol. 2: 3199
Woman International Master Vol. 2: 3200
Woman Lawyer of the Year Vol. 1: 21785
Woman of Courage Vol. 1: 13872
Woman of the Year
Federation of Fly Fishers Vol. 1: 9489
National Chamber of Commerce for Women Vol 1: 14650
Tall Clubs International Vol 1: 19910
Woman of the Year Award
Society for Women in Philosophy Vol. 1: 18937
Women in Insurance and Financial Services Vol 1: 21742
Woman of the Year in Travel Vol. 1: 20176
Woman Veterinarian Award; Outstanding Vol. 1: 5534
Women and Politics Prize Vol. 2: 104
Women at Work Awards Vol. 1: 21618
Women for Faith and Family Award Vol. 1: 21700
Women Helping Women Awards Vol. 1: 14074
Women in Cell Biology Vol. 1: 3948
Women in Film and Television Florida Independent Filmmaker Grant Vol. 1: 21721
Women in Film Foundation Cash Grant Vol. 1: 21722
Women in Geography Education Scholarship Vol. 1: 14769
Women in Production Scholarship Vol. 1: 21749
Women in Science Award Vol. 1: 20450
Women in the Engineering Profession; Canadian Engineers' Awards-Award for the Support of Vol. 1: 7052
Women Making History-Essay Contest Vol. 1: 16655
Women of Color Recognition Award Vol. 1: 6427
Women of Enterprise Awards Vol. 1: 6145
Women of Excellence Vol. 1: 22078
Women of Outstanding Achievement Vol. 2: 9241
Women of the Year
Italian Charities of America Vol. 1: 12243
United States Rowing Association Vol 1: 20755
Women's Action for Nuclear Disarmament Education Fund Vol. 1: 21769
Women's Advocate Award Vol. 1: 9521
Women's Artist Award Vol. 1: 12864
Women's Development Athletes-of-the-Year Vol. 1: 21244
Women's International Zionist Organization Awards Vol. 2: 3785
Women's Leadership Development and Gender Equity Award Vol. 1: 1146
Women's National Book Association Award Vol. 1: 21800

Award Index

Women's National Championship Cup Finals Vol. 2: 7422
Women's Opportunity Awards Vol. 1: 19421
Women's Player of the Year Vol. 1: 21181
Women's Sports Journalism Awards Vol. 1: 21812
Women's Studies Librarianship Awards; WSS Achievement in - Career Achievement Award Vol. 1: 5620
Women's Team Champion Vol. 1: 21205
Women's Team of the Year Vol. 2: 4425
Women's Team Runner-up Vol. 1: 21205
Women's Top Ten Vol. 1: 21205
WONCA Foundation Award Vol. 2: 5955
Wood Award; Coke Vol. 1: 21582
Wood Award; Raymond M. Vol. 1: 17994
Wood Book Award; Bryce Vol. 1: 12702
Wood Council Wood Design Award; American Vol. 1: 21820
Wood Cup; A. D. Vol. 2: 7202
Wood Design Award Vol. 1: 2292
Wood Design Award; American Wood Council Vol. 1: 21820
Wood Design Awards
Canadian Wood Council Vol. 1: 7545
Wood Design and Building Magazine - Janam Publications Inc. Vol 1: 21821
Wood Medal and Prize; A. B. Vol. 2: 7643
Wood Memorial Award for Best of Show Exhibit; Howland Vol. 1: 3267
Wood Memorial Ohioana Award for Children's Literature; Alice Louise Vol. 1: 16665
Wood Memorial Trophy; W. C. Vol. 1: 3120
Wood Prize Vol. 2: 5136
Wood Prize; J. Howard and Barbara M.J. Vol. 1: 17424
Wood Prize; R. W. Vol. 1: 16800
Woodall, and McMillan Writing Awards; Calvert, Vol. 1: 5627
Woodall and William Cartwright Holmes Postgraduate Award; Corbet & Henry Vol. 2: 7855
Woodall Scholarship; Corbet and Henry Vol. 2: 7855
Woodard Award; M. L. Vol. 1: 10424
Woodbridge Award; Donald B. Vol. 1: 14676
Wooden Award; John R. Vol. 1: 12925
Wooden Horse Award Vol. 2: 340
Wooden Most Valuable High School Player Award; John R. Vol. 1: 12925
Woodford-Williams Prize Vol. 2: 8474
Woodrow Award Vol. 2: 7165
Woods Award; K. B. Vol. 1: 20166
Woods Memorial Award; David F. Vol. 1: 13137
Woodson Award; Carter G. Vol. 1: 4997
Woodson Book Award; Carter G. Vol. 1: 14791
Woodstock National Exhibition Vol. 1: 21830
Woodward Award; Julian Vol. 1: 1036
Woodwind Award; The Blanche Squires Memorial Vol. 1: 18316
Woodwind; The Carla Ruth Webb Memorial Award in Vol. 1: 18321
Woodwind Scholarship; The F. W. Chisholm Intermediate Vol. 1: 18279
Woodworking in the Norwegian Tradition; National Exhibition of Vol. 1: 21318
Woodworth Memorial Award Vol. 1: 10741
Wool Production in Canada; Certificate of Merit - Commercial Vol. 1: 7031
Woolbert Research Award; Charles H. Vol. 1: 14717
Woolfe Award; Clifford G. Vol. 1: 174
Woolknit Design Awards Vol. 1: 21832
Woollard Award; George P. Vol. 1: 9957
Woolley Award; Davis C. Vol. 1: 6245
Woomer Award; J. W. Vol. 1: 18829
Worcester, Nelson and Turner Prizes Vol. 1: 21851
WORDS/ISAAC AAC Consumer User Scholarship Vol. 1: 11920
WORDS/ISAAC Outstanding Consumer User Lecture Award Vol. 1: 11921
Words+ Outstanding Consumer Lecture Award Vol. 1: 11922
Work-in-Progress Grants Vol. 1: 19089
Worked 100 Nations Award Vol. 1: 21973
Worked All Zones Award Vol. 1: 8633
Worker Equity Business Partnerships Award Vol. 1: 1396
Workers' Education Fellowships Vol. 2: 6417
Workforce Innovation Awards Program Vol. 1: 18191
Workhorses of the Fleet Award Vol. 1: 20940
Working Group Recognition Award Vol. 1: 10916
Working Group Vegetable Breeding Working Group Award of Excellence Vol. 1: 4096
Working Groups Distinguished Achievement Award for Nursery Crops Vol. 1: 4097
Working Groups Outstanding Fruit Cultivar Award Vol. 1: 4098
Working Hunter Ponies Awards Vol. 2: 7153
Workplace Diversity Professional Development Award Vol. 1: 11481
World and National Calendar Awards Vol. 1: 6729
World Association of Christian Radio Amateurs and Listeners Award Certificate Vol. 2: 9231
World Book - ALA Goal Grant Vol. 1: 2984
World Book Award Vol. 1: 7656
World Book Prize of Underwater Pictures Vol. 2: 2342
World Boxing Council Awards Vol. 2: 4650
World Challenge Vol. 1: 19724
World Chamion Vol. 2: 6377
World Champion Award Vol. 1: 12050
World Champion Cheesemaker Vol. 1: 21668
World Champions Vol. 1: 17656
World Championship Vol. 2: 2474
World Championship - Larry O'Brien Trophy Vol. 1: 14509
World Championships - World Cup for Club Teams Vol. 2: 6411
World Championships in Ballroom and Latin Dancing Vol. 2: 9247
World Citizen Vol. 1: 11692
World Citizen Humanitarian Vol. 1: 9802
World Citizenship Award Vol. 1: 16592
World Class Awards; PC World Vol. 1: 17116
World Clean Air Congress Award Vol. 2: 8007
World Cup Jumping Leaders Vol. 2: 6447
World Curling Freytag Award Vol. 2: 9245
World Development Awards for Business Vol. 2: 7270
World Evangelical Fellowship Vol. 1: 21895
World Festival of Animated Films Vol. 2: 1392
World Figure Skating Championships Vol. 2: 6445
World Figure Skating Hall of Fame Vol. 1: 20590
World Film Festival of ORL Scientific Films and Videotapes Vol. 2: 4821
World Food Policy Award Vol. 1: 277
The World Food Prize Vol. 1: 21919
World Footbag Championships Vol. 1: 21921
World Games Competitions Vol. 2: 4844
World Golf Hall of Fame Vol. 1: 21923
World Horseshoe Tournament Vol. 1: 15244
World Hunger Media Awards Vol. 1: 21925
World Junior Figure Skating Championships Vol. 2: 6445
World Junior Short Track Speed Skating Championships for Ladies and Men Vol. 2: 6445
World Junior Speed Skating Championships for Ladies and Men Vol. 2: 6445
World Karting Hall of Fame Vol. 1: 11760
World Leisure International Scholarship Vol. 1: 21932
World Marathon Cup Vol. 2: 4663
World Methodist Peace Award Vol. 1: 21936
World Motorcycle Championships Vol. 2: 6423
World Mystical Poetry Prize Vol. 2: 6083
World of Wedding Photography and Portrait Of Excellence Vol. 1: 21508
World Peace Academy Diploma Vol. 1: 11346
World Phosphate Institute Awards Vol. 2: 4671
World Piano Competition Vol. 1: 3166
World Player of the Year Vol. 1: 10074
World Ploughing Championship Awards Vol. 2: 4943
World Police Prize Vol. 2: 7969
World Press Photo Children's Award Vol. 2: 4945
World Press Photo Contest Vol. 2: 4945
World Press Photo of the Year Vol. 2: 4945
World Rainforest Awards Vol. 1: 17863
World Record for Game Fish Award Vol. 1: 11645
World Short Track Speed Skating Team Championships Vol. 2: 6445
World Single Distance Championships for Ladies and Men Vol. 2: 6445
World Skeet Shooting Championships Vol. 1: 15807
World Speed Skating Championship for Ladies and Men Vol. 2: 6445
World Sprint Speed Skating Championships for Ladies and Men Vol. 2: 6445
World Standards Day Paper Awards Vol. 1: 19750
World Taekwondo Federation Competitions Vol. 2: 5513
World Unicycling Championships Vol. 1: 12101
World Wide Video Festival Vol. 2: 4947
World Youth Championship for the FIFA/Coca-Cola Cup Vol. 2: 6361
World Youth Sailing Championship Vol. 1: 20789
Worlddidac Award Vol. 2: 6578
WORLDFEST - Houston International Film and Video Festival Vol. 1: 21969
World's Best Short Short Story Contest Vol. 1: 19466
World's Paper Trade Review Medal Vol. 2: 8240
Worldwide Awards Competition Vol. 1: 8924
Worldwide Competition for Young Sociologists Vol. 2: 6065

Worner Essay Award; Junior NATO Manfred Vol. 2: 946
Worner Essay Award; Senior NATO Manfred Vol. 2: 946
Worner Essay Awards; Manfred Vol. 2: 946
Worner Fellowship; Manfred Vol. 2: 946
Worrall Public Official Award; Jay Vol. 1: 16612
Worshipful Company of Dyers Awards for Woodwind/Brass Vol. 2: 8643
Worshipful Company of Dyers Research Medal Vol. 2: 9040
Worshipful Company of Ironmongers Jubilee Award Vol. 2: 7659
Worst-Dressed Women Vol. 1: 13655
Wortelmann-Preis der Stadt Bochum fur das Amateur-Figurentheater; Fritz Vol. 2: 2732
Wortelmann Preis of the City of Bochum for Amateur Puppetry; Fritz Vol. 2: 2732
Worth Prize; R. H. Vol. 2: 7568
Worth Silver Medal; John Edward Vol. 2: 8729
Worthingham Fellows of APTA; Catherine Vol. 1: 3500
Worthington Medal; Henry R. Vol. 1: 4554
Worts Staff Service Award; Grace Vol. 1: 7307
WPRA Foundation Vol. 1: 21687
WPX Award Vol. 1: 8634
WPX Award of Excellence Vol. 1: 8635
WPX Honor Roll Vol. 1: 8636
Wrangler Award Vol. 1: 14887
Wrangler Jeans World Champion Bullfighter Vol. 1: 17651
Wren Prize; Dr. Peter Vol. 2: 7698
Wrench Scholarship; Jesse Vol. 1: 13523
Wrenn Award for a Humanitarian and Caring Person; Gilbert and Kathleen Vol. 1: 2074
Wrestling Coach of the Year Vol. 1: 7243
Wright Achievement Award; Orville Vol. 1: 16835
Wright AI Service Award; Bob Vol. 1: 6004
Wright Award; Bob Vol. 1: 14041
Wright Award; Captain Donald T. Vol. 1: 17494
Wright Award; E. Whitman Vol. 1: 7421
Wright Award in Olfactory Research; Frank Allison Linville's R. H. Vol. 1: 18527
Wright Award in Olfactory Research; R. H. Vol. 1: 18527
Wright Award; Kulp Vol. 1: 3854
Wright Award; Mackercar Michael Vol. 2: 8499
Wright Award; Mary Tolle Vol. 1: 18500
Wright Award; Mickey Vol. 1: 10075
Wright Award of Distinction; Irving S. Vol. 1: 2223
Wright Award; Sewall Vol. 1: 4563
Wright Brothers Lecture Vol. 1: 2700
Wright Brothers Lectureship in Aeronautics Vol. 1: 2700
Wright Brothers Medal Vol. 1: 19062
Wright Brothers Memorial Trophy Vol. 1: 13880
Wright Cup; John Howie Vol. 1: 13033
Wright Distinguished Service Award; Logan Vol. 1: 3757
Wright Honorary Award; Asa Vol. 2: 3321
Wright Mariological Award; Cardinal John J. Vol. 1: 13114
Wright Memorial Award; Katharine Vol. 1: 13881
Wright Memorial Exhibit Award; B. P. Vol. 1: 3268
Wright Memorial Trophy; Lee O. Vol. 1: 15646
Wright Prize for Poetry; Wesley Michel Vol. 2: 634
Wright Special Recognition Award; AATE Lin Vol. 1: 897
Wrigley-Fairchild Prize Vol. 1: 2337
Writer Fellowship; PEN/Phyllis Naylor Working Vol. 1: 17143
The Writer Magazine/Emily Dickinson Award Vol. 1: 17439
Writer of the Year in Europe; John Templeton Religion Vol. 2: 6313
Writer of the Year; Innovation Vol. 2: 7187
Writers' Award Contest Vol. 1: 12312
Writers Contest
  Federation of Historical Bottle Collectors Vol. 1: 9507
  Tonga and Tin Can Mail Study Circle - Society of Australasian Specialists/ Oceania Vol 1: 20098
Writers Corner Hall of Fame Vol. 1: 20633
Writers Digest Annual Writing Competition Vol. 1: 5147
Writers Digest Short Story Competition Vol. 1: 21978
Writer's Digest Writing Competition Vol. 1: 21979
Writers' Emeritus Award Vol. 2: 108
Writers Guild of Alberta Awards for Excellence Vol. 1: 21987
Writers in Performance Literary Competition Vol. 1: 18399
Writers Program; Promising Young Vol. 1: 14839
Writer's Trophy Vol. 2: 6674
Writing and Design Award Vol. 1: 5241
Writing and Development Award; Student Vol. 1: 12821
Writing Award Vol. 1: 12507
Writing Award; LITA/Endeavor Student Vol. 1: 12826
Writing Awards
  Air Force Historical Foundation Vol. 1: 378
  River City Vol 1: 18067
Writing Awards; Amy Vol. 1: 4951
Writing Awards; *Tennis Week* Great American Tennis Vol. 1: 19984
Writing Contest; Student Vol. 1: 2259
W.S. Gwynn Williams Award Vol. 1: 11402
WSAVA Hills Excellence in Veterinary Healthcare Award Vol. 2: 1546
WSAVA Paatsama Award Vol. 2: 1547
WSS Achievement in Women's Studies Librarianship Awards - Career Achievement Award Vol. 1: 5620
WTIA/Linde National Tradesperson Award Vol. 2: 662
WTS National Member of the Year Vol. 1: 21815
WTS National Woman of the Year Vol. 1: 21816
Wulff Award; Lee Vol. 1: 9490
Wulff Memorial Award; Hans Vol. 1: 7524
Wurdigungspreis des Landes Tirol fur Literatur, Musik etc. Vol. 2: 678
Wurdigungspreis fur Erwadisenenbieolung des Landes Tirol Vol. 2: 681
Wurzweiler School of Social Work Community Service Award Vol. 1: 22027
Wurzweiler School of Social Work Distinguished Professor Award Vol. 1: 22028
WVF Rehabilitation Prize Vol. 2: 2635
WWF Award for Conservation Merit Vol. 2: 6581
WWF Gold Panda Award Vol. 2: 6582
WWF Members of Honour Vol. 2: 6583
WWF Roll of Honour Vol. 2: 6584
Wyeth Award in Clinical Microbiology Vol. 1: 4130
Wyeth-Ayerst Outstanding Chapter Awards Vol. 1: 785
Wyeth Young Investigator Award in Vaccine Development Vol. 1: 10794
Wyeth Young Investigator Award in Vaccine Development Vol. 1: 15125
Wyeth Young Psychopharmacologist Award Vol. 1: 3766
Wyld Propulsion Award Vol. 1: 2701
Wyld Propulsion Award; James H. Vol. 1: 2701
Wyman Award; Kelley - Vol. 1: 14076
Wyman Memorial Award Vol. 1: 14076
Wyman Memorial Award; L. L. Vol. 1: 5998
The Wynne Prize Vol. 2: 77
WYOpoets Award Vol. 1: 15037
Xavier Cross; Saint Francis Vol. 2: 1337
Xavier Medal; St. Francis Vol. 1: 22006
Xenopol Prize; Alexandru Vol. 2: 5876
Xirgu Radio Drama Prize; Margarita Vol. 2: 6081
XL Anniversary Prize Vol. 2: 6069
Xplorer of the Year Award Vol. 1: 22009
XYZ Digital Award Vol. 2: 8688
Y2Y Prize Vol. 1: 6237
Ya B. Zeldovich Gold Medal Vol. 1: 8267
Yachtsman of the Year Award Vol. 2: 9272
Yaciuk Award; Walter Vol. 1: 21182
Yaffe; Pras Leib Vol. 2: 3778
Yaffe Prize; Leib Vol. 2: 3778
Yale Center for International and Area Studies Awards Vol. 1: 22015
Yale Series of Younger Poets Vol. 1: 22011
YALSA Sagebrush Award Vol. 1: 22055
Yamagiwa-Yoshida Memorial International Cancer Study Grants Vol. 2: 6474
Yamaoka Prize Vol. 2: 4151
Yancey Memorial Award Vol. 1: 11334
Yankee Awards Vol. 1: 22017
Yant Award; William B. Vol. 1: 2621
YASD/*School Library Journal* Author Achievement Award Vol. 1: 22053
YASD/*School Library Journal* Young Adult Author Award Vol. 1: 22053
Yasme Award Vol. 1: 22019
Yasuo Sakakibara Prize Vol. 1: 4713
Yeadon Memorial Trophy; T. M. Vol. 2: 6723
Year-End Achievement Award Vol. 1: 8122
Year-end Achievement Award Vol. 1: 16688
Year End Awards Vol. 1: 5021
Year-End High Point Awards Vol. 1: 21955
Year End High Score Awards Vol. 1: 10575
Year End Series Festival of New Plays Vol. 1: 16554
Yearbook Dedication Award Vol. 1: 743
Yearbook Marketing Award Vol. 1: 8177
Yearly Award for Young ICU Investigators Vol. 2: 879
Yenko Memorial Award; Don Vol. 1: 11448
Yennenga Stallion Trophy Vol. 2: 1242
Yerkes Award; Robert M. Vol. 1: 3724
Yeshiva University Award Vol. 1: 22029
Yeshiva University Citation Vol. 1: 22030
Yeshiva University Distinguished Service Award Vol. 1: 22031
Yeshiva University Heritage Award Vol. 1: 22032

Yeshiva University Sephardic Heritage Award Vol. 1: 22033
Yitzah Rabin Award Vol. 1: 3346
YMCA Men, Women and Youth of the Year Vol. 1: 22037
Yoder-Heneman Human Resource Management Creative Application Awards Vol. 1: 18705
Yoder-Heneman Human Resource Management Research Award Vol. 1: 18706
Yoder-Heneman Personnel Creative Application Awards Vol. 1: 18705
Yoder-Heneman Personnel Research Award Vol. 1: 18706
Yokelson Medal Award; Marshall V. Vol. 1: 21660
Yomiuri Bungaku Sho Vol. 2: 4335
Yomiuri Drama Prize Vol. 2: 4331
Yomiuri Education Prize Vol. 2: 4332
Yomiuri Engeki Taisho Vol. 2: 4331
Yomiuri Human Document Prize Vol. 2: 4333
Yomiuri Human Document Taisho Vol. 2: 4333
Yomiuri International Cartoon Contest Vol. 2: 4334
Yomiuri International Cooperation Prize Vol. 2: 4317
Yomiuri Kokusai Kyoryoku Sho Vol. 2: 4317
Yomiuri Kokusai Manga Taisho Vol. 2: 4334
Yomiuri Literature Prize Vol. 2: 4335
Yomiuri Photography Prize Vol. 2: 4336
Yomiuri Prize for the Year's Best Arts and Science Critic Vol. 2: 4337
Yomiuri Prize for the Year's Best Young Arts and Science Critic Vol. 2: 4338
Yomiuri Rondan Sho
  Yomiuri Shimbun Vol. 2: 4337
  Yomiuri Shimbun Vol 2: 4338
Yoneji Ebitani Scholarship Vol. 1: 21881
Yorkdale Memorial Award; Alan H. Vol. 1: 5999
Yorkshire & Humberside Arts Young Composers Awards Vol. 2: 7625
Yorkshire Arts Young Composers Competition Vol. 2: 7625
Yorkshire Post Book of the Year Award Vol. 2: 9275
Yorzyk Memorial Award; David
  U.S. Aquatic Sports Vol. 1: 20400
  United States Masters Swimming Vol 1: 20693
Yoshida Hideo Memorial Award Vol. 2: 4205
Yoshikawa Eiji Bungaku Sho Vol. 2: 4247
Yoshikawa Eiji Prize for Literature Vol. 2: 4247
Yoshikawa Elji Cultural Prize Vol. 2: 4248
Yost Distinguished Services Award; Max Vol. 1: 5257
Yost Professional Service Award; Charles Peter Vol. 1: 18337
Youden Award in Interlaboratory Testing; W. J. Vol. 1: 4698
Young Adult Author Award Vol. 1: 5052
Young Adult Book Award Vol. 1: 19443
Young Adult Book of the Year Award; Sanderson Vol. 2: 649
Young Adult Canadian Book Award Vol. 1: 7252
Young Adult Narrator of the Year Award; Sanderson Vol. 2: 650
Young Agricultural Engineer of the Year Award Vol. 1: 7404
Young Alumni Merit Award Vol. 1: 7669
Young Alumni Service Citations Vol. 1: 21001
Young America Photography Contest Vol. 1: 17066
Young American Awards Vol. 1: 6592
Young American Creative Patriotic Art Competition Vol. 1: 12648
Young American Medal for Bravery Vol. 1: 20506
Young American Medal for Service Vol. 1: 20507
Young Archeologist of the Year Award Vol. 2: 6926
Young Architects Award Vol. 1: 2722
Young Architects Forum Vol. 1: 5038
Young Artist Award Vol. 1: 16202
Young Artist Competition
  Fort Collins Symphony Association Vol. 1: 9701
  National Flute Association Vol 1: 15064
  New York Flute Club Vol 1: 16227
Young Artists and Distinguished Artists Award Auditions Vol. 1: 5143
Young Artists Auditions Competition Vol. 1: 16186
Young Artists Competition
  Connecticut Alliance for Music Vol. 1: 8408
  International Clarinet Association Vol 1: 11486
  Sister Cities International Vol 1: 18534
Young Australians Best Book Award Vol. 2: 666
Young Author Best Paper Award Vol. 1: 12110
Young Award; Cy Vol. 1: 6268
Young Award; Hugh Hampton Vol. 1: 4797
Young Beekeeper of the Year Vol. 1: 6765
Young Canadian Filmmakers Vol. 1: 19808
Young Cancer Researcher Award Vol. 2: 7458
Young Chemists Award Vol. 2: 6596
Young Cinema Festival Vol. 2: 4306
Young Citizen of the Year Award Vol. 2: 652
Young Clinical Chemist Award Vol. 1: 1008
Young Competitor Award Vol. 1: 7525
Young Composers' Competition Vol. 1: 14147
Young Concert Artists International Auditions Vol. 1: 22059
Young Concert Artists; Philip & Dorthy Green Award for Vol. 2: 8100
Young Concert Artists Trust Award Vol. 2: 9277
Young Conservationist of the Year Award Vol. 2: 9371
Young Consultants Award Vol. 1: 11060
Young Contributor's Award Vol. 1: 1438
Young Creators Literary Prize Vol. 2: 1359
Young Crop Scientist Award Vol. 1: 8670
Young Deaf Achiever Vol. 2: 9157
Young Dermatologists' Volunteer Award Vol. 1: 7076
Young Designer Award; Sunkist Vol. 1: 4237
Young Dietitian of the Year Vol. 1: 12494
Young Eco Inventors Contest With Eco Expo Vol. 1: 12168
Young Educator Award; A. W. Farrall Vol. 1: 4221
Young Emerging Scholars Award; Alma H. Vol. 1: 21138
Young Engineer Award Vol. 1: 18829
Young Engineer of the Year Vol. 2: 7836
Young Engineer of the Year Award Vol. 1: 15756
Young Engineers of the Year Vol. 1: 13169
Young Engineers Speaking Competition Vol. 2: 439
Young Enterprise Award Vol. 2: 7837
Young Entrepreneur Award Vol. 1: 20836
Young Extension Worker Award; Nolan Mitchell Vol. 1: 4230
Young FAI Artists Contest Vol. 2: 6354
Young Federal Healthcare Administrator Award Vol. 1: 5791
Young Filmmakers Festival Vol. 1: 16562
Young Forester Leadership Award Vol. 1: 18978
Young Geologist's Prize Vol. 2: 896
Young Government Civil Engineer of the Year Award Vol. 1: 4370
Young Handler Award Vol. 2: 7977
Young Hoosier Book Award Vol. 1: 5388
Young Hoosier Picture Book Award Vol. 1: 5389
Young Hotelier and Restaurateur of the World Award Vol. 2: 2478
Young - Hunter Memorial Award; John Vol. 1: 4873
Young Industrialist Awards of Hong Kong Vol. 2: 5219
Young Innovator Award Vol. 1: 6294
Young Inventors Awards; Craftsman/NSTA Vol. 1: 15686
Young Investigator Award
  American College of Clinical Pharmacology Vol. 1: 1851
  Association for the Advancement of Medical Instrumentation Vol 1: 5492
  Bristol-Myers Squibb Canada Co. Vol 1: 6629
  International College of Angiology Vol 1: 11488
  Japanese Society of Hematology Vol 2: 4215
  National Alliance for Research on Schizophrenia and Depression Vol 1: 13925
  Society for Leukocyte Biology Vol 1: 18788
  Society for Medical Decision Making Vol 1: 18798
  World Gastroenterology Organisation Vol 2: 3145
Young Investigator Award Competition Vol. 1: 3961
Young Investigator Award in Regulatory and Integrative Physiology Vol. 1: 3531
Young Investigator Award in Vaccine Development; Wyeth Vol. 1: 10794
Young Investigator Awards
  American College of Chest Physicians Vol. 1: 1845
  American Society for Bone and Mineral Research Vol 1: 3938
  Cancer Research Foundation Vol 1: 7558
  National Foundation for Infectious Diseases Vol 1: 15125
Young Investigator Memorial Travel Awards Vol. 1: 1900
Young Investigator Prize; Cournand and Comroe Vol. 1: 2420
Young Investigator Prizes in Thrombosis Vol. 1: 2421
Young Investigator's Award Vol. 1: 840
Young Investigators Award
  American College of Angiology Vol. 1: 1831
  Canadian Celiac Association Vol 1: 7023

European Federation of Societies for Ultrasound in Medicine and Biology Vol 2: 7470
International Association for Dental Research Vol 1: 11218
Young Investigators Awards Vol. 1: 10369
Young Investigators' Prizes Vol. 1: 4564
Young Journalist of the Year Vol. 2: 8858
Young Jumper Award Vol. 1: 2386
Young, Jr., Award; Whitney M. Vol. 1: 2723
Young, Jr. Memorial Scholarship; Whitney M. Vol. 1: 16310
Young Lawyers' Pro Bono Award Vol. 1: 6979
Young Lighters of the Year Vol. 2: 7293
Young Logistician Award Vol. 1: 12003
Young Medal and Prize; Thomas Vol. 2: 7737
Young Member Achievement Award Vol. 1: 5894
Young Member Outstanding Service Award Vol. 1: 19250
Young Metallurgist of the Year Award Vol. 2: 3464
Young Mother Representative Vol. 1: 3145
Young Musician Scholarship Vol. 1: 10024
Young Musicians and Distinguished Artists Award Auditions Vol. 1: 5143
Young Musicians Awards; AT&T Istel Vol. 2: 8328
Young NDT Professional Award Vol. 1: 4154
Young Neurosurgeons Award Vol. 1: 21913
Young Oncologist Essay Awards Vol. 1: 3815
Young Oncologist Travel Grants Vol. 1: 3816
Young Optometrist of the Year Vol. 1: 3318
Young Oration; Thomas Vol. 2: 7737
Young Ornithologists of the Year Vol. 2: 6959
Young People's Film and Video Festival Vol. 1: 16562
Young People's Literature Awards Vol. 1: 9786
Young Performers Awards Vol. 2: 620
Young Philately Vol. 2: 6794
Young Pianists Yearly Award Vol. 2: 7486
Young Planner of the Year Award Vol. 2: 8863
Young Player of the Year Vol. 2: 4425
Young Playwrights Festival Vol. 1: 22069
Young Professional Activity Award Vol. 1: 2702
Young Professional Award
Canadian Association for Health, Physical Education, Recreation and Dance Vol. 1: 6886
Canadian Parks and Recreation Association Vol 1: 7328
Young Professional Engineer of the Year Vol. 2: 440
Young Promising Musicians Award Vol. 2: 4255
Young Psychologist of the Year Vol. 2: 3683
Young Readers' Choice Award Vol. 1: 17009
Young Republican Man of the Year Vol. 1: 22073
Young Republican Woman of the Year Vol. 1: 22074
Young Researcher Award; New Holland Vol. 1: 4234
Young Sailor of the Year Award Vol. 2: 9273
Young Scholars Competition Vol. 1: 6436
Young Scientist Award
European Federation of Food Science and Technology Vol. 2: 4757
Genetics Society of Canada Vol 1: 9937
International Society for Neurochemistry Vol 2: 1503
Phytopathological Society of Japan Vol 2: 4283
Young Scientist Award (Donath Medal) Vol. 1: 9958
Young Scientist Award in Noninvasive Cardiovascular Dynamics Vol. 2: 5976
Young Scientist Award; Intel Foundation Vol. 1: 18362
Young Scientist Award; International Confederation for Thermal Analysis Vol. 2: 5586
Young Scientist or Grower of the Year Award Vol. 2: 8145
Young Scientist's Award Vol. 1: 7446
Young Scientists for Rainforests Vol. 2: 7349
Young Scientist's Poster Award Vol. 2: 1439
Young Scientists Publication Awards Vol. 2: 2318
Young Scientists Travel Awards Vol. 2: 2319
Young Sculptor Awards Vol. 1: 15701
Young Soloists Award Vol. 1: 21414
Young Soloists' Competition Vol. 1: 15834
Young Technologist Award Vol. 2: 8857
Young UK Cell Biologist of the Year Award Vol. 1: 3949
Young Veterinarian of the Year Award Vol. 2: 5771
Young Wildlife Photographer of the Year Competition Vol. 2: 8206
Young Writers Program; Promising Vol. 1: 14839
Younger Federal Lawyer Award Vol. 1: 9439
Younger Member Group Award Vol. 1: 4371
Younger Members Award for Achievement Vol. 2: 7838
Younger Members' Premiums Awards; National Vol. 2: 7822
Youngman Award; Bruce Vol. 2: 7871
Youskevitch Award; Igor Vol. 1: 16235
Youth Achievement Award Vol. 1: 12803
Youth Achievement Awards Vol. 1: 436
Youth Art Month Award Vol. 1: 13976
Youth Art Month State Report Awards Vol. 1: 8535
Youth Arts Awards Vol. 1: 20233
Youth as Resources Vol. 1: 12740
Youth Athletics Outstanding Association Award Vol. 1: 21226
Youth Athletics Outstanding Individual Award Vol. 1: 21239
Youth Award
American Bashkir Curly Registry Vol. 1: 1553
National Apostolate for Inclusion Ministry Vol 1: 13947
Youth Awards Vol. 2: 6127
Youth Flight Vol. 1: 2018
Youth Gardening Award Vol. 1: 9891
Youth Leadership Award Vol. 1: 21562
Youth Leadership Awards Vol. 1: 6780
Youth Medallion Vol. 1: 9512
Youth of the Year
Adult Friends for Youth Vol. 1: 198
Parents Without Partners Vol 1: 17091
Youth Recognition Award Vol. 1: 22086
Youth Softball Volunteer of the Year Vol. 1: 583
Youth Theatre Director of the Year Award Vol. 1: 898
Youth World Championship Horse Show Golden Horse Vol. 1: 17051
You've Got a Friend in Pennsylvania Award Vol. 1: 53
Ysgoloriaeth W. Towyn Roberts Vol. 2: 8174
Yugoslav Documentary and Short Films Festival Awards Vol. 2: 9331
Yunus Nadi Gift Vol. 2: 6631
Yuval Award Vol. 1: 7569
Zaheer Medal; S. H. Vol. 2: 3525
ZAiKS Awards for Translators Vol. 2: 5385
ZAiKS Literary Award for Translation's Output Vol. 2: 5385
Zak Award Vol. 1: 1009
Zakon Lectureship; Samuel J. Vol. 1: 10474
Zakon Prize; Samuel J. Vol. 1: 10475
Zambrano National Prize for Inventive Technology; Luis Vol. 2: 9325
Zamenhof Award for International Understanding Vol. 2: 4926
Zammit Award; George Vol. 1: 13049
Zangerle Award Vol. 1: 11283
Zanotti Award for Excellence in Non-Serial Publications; Christine Vol. 1: 5092
Zaragosa Jewel; Ignacio Vol. 2: 4498
Zaragosa; Presea Ignacio Vol. 2: 4498
Zarday Award Vol. 2: 3283
Zarem Award for Distinguished Achievement; Abe M. Vol. 1: 2703
Zarky Humanitarian Award; Norma Vol. 1: 21723
Zarrow Award for Young Readers' Literature; Anne V. Vol. 1: 20237
Zarwell Award; Gerald Vol. 1: 16335
Zauberfloten-Medaille Vol. 2: 750
Zawadzki Award; Prof. Bohdan Vol. 2: 5372
Zawadzkiego; Nagroda im. Bohdana Vol. 2: 5372
Zawidzki Medal; Jan Vol. 2: 5341
Zazuete; Premio Alejandro Vol. 2: 4506
Zbinden Memorial Lecture Award; Gerhard Vol. 2: 1440
Zeigler Lecture Award; Earle F. Vol. 1: 16473
Zeitlin-Ver Brugge Prize Vol. 1: 10486
Zejszner Prize; Ludwik Vol. 2: 5351
Zejsznera; Nagroda im. Ludwika Vol. 2: 5351
Zeldovich Medals Vol. 2: 2275
Zellen Golden Quill Award; WBW Gosta Vol. 1: 21873
Zelma H. Weisfeld Costume Design & Technology Award Vol. 1: 20653
Zemanek Award; Heinz Vol. 2: 707
Zeneca Pharmaceuticals/Komen Foundation Excellence in Breast Cancer Education Award Vol. 1: 16715
ZENECA Research Scholarship Vol. 2: 875
Zenger for Freedom of the Press and the Peoples Right to Know; John Peter and Anna Catherine Vol. 1: 20981
Zerbe Award; Farran Vol. 1: 3269
Zero Accident Award Vol. 1: 19585
Zero Accident Awards Vol. 1: 19586
Zibetska Priset Vol. 2: 6273
Ziegler-Preis; Karl- Vol. 2: 2820
Zimbabwe Institution of Engineers Prizes Vol. 2: 9367
Zimbabwe Scientific Association Fellow Vol. 2: 9373
Zimbabwe Scientific Association Gold Medal Vol. 2: 9374

Zimmerman Founder's Award; O. T. Vol. 1: 41
Zimmerman-Rand Valor Award Vol. 1: 14040
Zinam Award; Oleg Vol. 1: 11470
Zinn Memorial Awards; Captain Ron Vol. 1: 21245
Ziskind-Somerfeld Research Award Vol. 1: 19075
Zittel Medaille; Karl Alfred von Vol. 2: 3044
Zlatarov Prize; Professor Dr. Asen Vol. 2: 1207
Zlatarski Prize; Professor Vasil Vol. 2: 1207
Zlatko Grgic Award Vol. 2: 1392
Zlatnata Antena Vol. 2: 1216
Zlatnata Rakla Vol. 2: 1217
Zola Award Vol. 1: 17011
Zola Award for Journalism; Emile Vol. 1: 17125
Zollman Award; Charles C. Vol. 1: 17529
Zoo Animal Welfare Award Vol. 2: 9170
Zookeeping Award; Jean M. Hromadka Excellence in Vol. 1: 1488
Zoological Science Award Vol. 2: 4340
Zoological Society of London Scientific Medal Vol. 2: 9284
Zoological Society of London Silver Medal Vol. 2: 9285
Zoological Society of Southern Africa Gold Medal Vol. 2: 5802
Zorkoczy Medal; Samu Z. Vol. 2: 3263
Zorn Award; Trish L Vol. 1: 21208
Zsigmondy Medal; Vilmos Vol. 2: 3264
Zubin Award; Joseph Vol. 1: 3773
Zuck Public Courage Award; Alfred M. Vol. 1: 14378
Zue Award; Dick Vol. 1: 20827
Zvorikine; Fondation Nicolas Vol. 2: 1942
Zworykin Premium; Dr. V. K. Vol. 2: 7839